AF819976

NTA CSIR UGC NET/SET

JRF & LECTURERSHIP

Chemical Sciences

NTA CSIR UGC NET/SET

JRF & LECTURERSHIP

Chemical Sciences

Preeti Gupta (JRF)
Dr. Aditya Tomar
Dr. Naveen Sharma

arihant
SUCCESS AND NOTHING LESS

arihant
SUCCESS AND NOTHING LESS

ARIHANT PUBLICATIONS (INDIA) LIMITED

Administrative & Production Offices

Regd. Office

'Ramchhaya' 4577/15, Agarwal Road, Darya Ganj, New Delhi -110002
Tele: 011- 47630600, 43518550

Head Office

Kalindi, TP Nagar, Meerut (UP) - 250002
Tel: 0121-7156203, 7156204

Sales & Support Offices

Agra, Ahmedabad, Bengaluru, Bareilly, Chennai, Delhi, Guwahati, Hyderabad, Jaipur, Jhansi, Kolkata, Lucknow, Nagpur & Pune.

PRICE ₹995.00

PO No : TXT-XX-XXXXXXX-X-XX

Published by Arihant Publications (India) Ltd.

For further information about the books published by Arihant, log on to www.arihantbooks.com or e-mail at info@arihantbooks.com

Follow us on

Preface

NET (National Eligibility Test) determines eligibility for lectureship and for award of Junior Research Fellowship (JRF) for Indian nationals in order to ensure minimum standards for the entrants in the teaching profession and research. The Council of Scientific and Industrial Research (CSIR) conducts the UGC-CSIR NET for other Science subjects, namely, Life Sciences, Physical Sciences, Chemical Sciences, Mathematical Sciences and Earth Sciences jointly with the UGC.

UGC-CSIR NET Tutor for Chemical Sciences has been designed to help the students get away with their initial qualms & hiccups about the UGC-CSIR NET. In the course of preparation of this book we have followed the pattern & syllabus of the examination for the maximum benefit of the aspirants, difficulty level of the questions has also been kept in mind.

Salient Features of the Book

- Only book in the market which has complete & exhaustive theory exactly on the UGC-CSIR NET pattern & difficulty level.
- For complete understanding all units have been divided into individual chapters with sufficient number of Multiple Choice Questions.
- As per the Pattern of Examination separate Exercises have been given for Part 'B' & 'C'.
- Only Book with Previous Years' Solved Papers & solutions to sample questions provided on CSIR Website.

We are thankful to Arihant Publications (India) Limited for giving us this opportunity to make such a book which will help the students to get 100% success. We would like to thank Sorabh Chaudhary (Project Coordinator) for giving us their full support during this project.
Any suggestion for the enhancement of the quality of this book is most welcome.

Preeti Gupta (JRF)
Dr. Aditya Tomar
Dr. Naveen Sharma

Contents

1. **Chemical Periodicity and Chemistry of Main Group Elements** 1-36

Periodicity • Periodic Properties like Atomic and Ionic Radii, Ionization Energy, Electronegativity, Electron Affinity, Atomic Volume, Metallic Character etc • Polarizing Power and Polarizability • Melting and Boiling Points • Oxidising and Reducing Nature, Oxidation State • Compounds like Oxides, Hydrides, Halides, Oxoacids etc • Diagonal Relationship

2. **Chemical Bonding and Structure of Molecules** 37-78

Structure and Bonding in Homo and Heteronuclear Molecules, Ionic Bond, Covalent Bond, Valence Bond Theory, LCAO Theory, Resonance Hybridization, Fluxionality TBP Molecules, Dipole-moment, Bond Angles, Bond Distance and Bond Energies Including Shapes of Molecules, VSEPR Theory

3. **Acid-Base Chemistry** 79-103

Concepts of Acids and Bases • Hard-Soft Acid Base Concept • Non-Aqueous Solvents

4. ***s*-Block Elements** 104-140

Main Group Elements and their Compounds like Oxides, Peroxides, Superoxides, Carbonates, Hydroxides, etc • Diagonal Relationship, Coordination Chemistry of *s*-Block Elements • Metallic Crystal • Bonding in Metals

5. ***p*-Block Elements-I (Group-13)** 141-165

Boranes, Carboranes, Borazine, Boron Nitride, Halides, Boric Acid, Borax, Aluminium Chloride • Synthesis, Structure, Bonding, Properties and Uses • Industrial Importance of the Compounds

6. **The *p*-Block Elements-II** 166-218

Main Groups Elements and their Compounds • Allotropy, Synthesis, Structure and Bonding • Industrial Importance of the Compounds

7. **Noble Gases** 219-240

Elements and their Compounds Occurrence Synthesis, Properties, Structure and Bonding • Industrial Importance of the Noble Gases • Clathrates

8. ***d*-Block Elements or Transition Elements** 241-266

Transition Elements and their Compounds : Structure, Bonding Theories, Spectral and Magnetic Properties

9. **Coordination Chemistry** 267-331

Coordination Compounds : Structure, Bonding Theories, Spectral and Magnetic Properties, Reaction Mechanism

10. Inner Transition Elements 332-366

Introduction, Lanthanides and Actinides, General Characteristics, Spectral and Magnetic Properties, Redox Chemistry, Applications

11. Organometallic Compounds 367-401

Types of Organometallic Compounds • Classification of Ligands and their Uses • 18 Electron Rule and Its Applications, EAN • Synthesis, Bonding Structure and Reactivity • Organometallics in Homogeneous Catalysis

12. Analytical Chemistry 402-442

Separation, Solvent Extraction • Various Spectroscopic Techniques • Chromatography • Thermoanalytical Methods • Electron Analytical Methods

13. Bioinorganic Chemistry 443-462

Porphyrins • Metalloenzymes • Metal Complexes in Medicine • Oxygen Transport • Electron Transfer Reaction • Photosynthesis • Nitrogen Fixation

14. Coordination Compounds, Part-II 463-485

Term Symbols, Electronic Spectra of Transition Metal Complexes, Ligand Field Theory

15. Nuclear Chemistry 486-535

Discovery of Radioactivity, Types, Properties • Nuclear Reactions, Radioactive Disintegration, Nuclear Fission and Fusion • Radioactive Equilibria • Radioactive Series, Radio analytical Techniques and Activation Analysis • Magnetic Confinement • Application of Radioisotopes

16. Quantum Mechanics or Wave Mechanics 536-593

Basic Principles of Quantum Mechanics : Postulates, Operator Algebra; Exactly Solvable Systems-Particle-in-a- Box, Harmonic Oscillator and the Hydrogen Atom • Approximate Methods of Quantum Mechanics; Variational Principle; Perturbation Theory up to Second Order in Energy Application

17. Atomic Structure and Quantum Theory 594-628

Basics of Atomic Structure • Shape of Orbitals • Hydrogen Atom Spectra

18. Chemical Bonding and Diatomics 629-660

Wave Mechanical Model, Variation Principle • Elementary Concepts of MO and VB Theories; Huckel Theory for Conjugated -electron Systems • Dipole Moment, Hydrogen Bonding

19. Molecular Symmetry and Group Theory 661-682

Symmetry Elements and Symmetry Operations • Point Group : Multiplication and Application • Grand Orthogonality Theorem • Character Table and Selection Rules

20. Molecular Spectroscopy 683-735

Basic Principles and Applications of Spectroscopy • Rotational and Vibrational Spectra of Diatomic Molecules, Electronic Spectra • IR and Raman Activities, Selection Rules • Basic UV-Visible, Principles of Magnetic Resonance (NMR, ESR, NQR Mossbauer) MS PES

21. Thermodynamics 736-774

Relativistic Quantum Mechanics : Klein-Gordon and Dirac Equations • Spin Angular Momentum • Semi-classical Theory of Radiation • Selection Rules

22. Statistical Thermodynamics 775-813

Microstates and Macrostates, Thermodynamic Probability • Partition Function and their Relation to Thermodynamic Quantities Calculation for Model System • Classical and Quantum Statistics • Ideal Bose and Fermi Gases • Maxwell Velocity Distribution

23. Electrochemistry 814-845

Electrolytic Conductance- Kohlrausch's Law and its Applictations • Debye-Huckel Theory • Electrochemical Cell, Nernst Equation, Redox Systems • Ionic Equilibria; Conductometric and Potentiometric Titrations

24. Chemical Kinetics 846-887

Empirical Rate Laws • Arrhenius Equations • Theories of Reaction Rates • Determination of Reaction Mechanism • Experimental Techniques for Fast Reactions

25. Surface Chemistry 888-908

Colloids : Classification, Preparation and Properties • Coagulation and Hardy-Schulze Rule • Protective Colloids Sol and Gold Number • Stability of Sols • Adsorption : Types and Various Theories of Isotherm • Structure of Solid Surface

26. Solid State 909-955

Classification of Solids • Symmetry in Crystals • Crystallography and its Law • Miller Indices and Bravais Lattices • Close Packed Structures • Density, Radius Ratio and Coordination Number • Bragg's Equation and its Applications • Electron and Neutron Diffraction • Imperfection in Solids • Band Model of Bonding in Metals • Semiconductors : Their Types and Applications • Electrical, Thermal, Magnetic and Dielectric Properties • Superconductors : Properties and Applications

27. Data Analysis 956-963

Types of Errors • Accuracy • Mean and Standard Deviation • Distribution of Random Errors • Correlation and Regression

28. **IUPAC Nomenclature of Organic Compounds** **964-984**
IUPAC Nomenclature of Organic Molecules Including Regioisomers and Stereoisomers

29. **Stereochemistry** **985-1013**
Principles of Stereochemistry • Configurational and Conformational Isomerism in Acyclic and Cyclic Compounds • Stereogenicity, Stereoselectivity, Enantioselectivity, Diastereoselectivity and Asymmetric Induction

30. **Aromaticity** **1014-1032**
Aromaticity : Benzenoid and Non-benzenoid Compounds • Generation and Reactions

31. **Organic Reaction Mechanism and Reactive Intermediates** **1033-1101**
Organic Reaction Mechanism Involving Addition, Elimination and Substitution Reactions with Electrophilic, Nucleophilic or Radial Species • Determination of Reaction Pathways

32. **Common Named Reactions and Rearrangements** **1102-1144**
Common Named Reactions and Rearrangements • Applications in Organic Synthesis

33. **Organic Transformations and Reagents** **1145-1190**
Functional Group Interconversion Including Oxidations and Reductions • Common Catalysts and Reagents (Organic, Inorganic, Organometallic and Enzymatic) • Chemo, Regio and Stereoselective Transformations

34. **Concept in Organic Synthesis and Asymmetric Synthesis** **1191-1212**
Retrosynthesis, Disconnection, Synthons, Linear and Convergent Synthesis, Umpolung of Reactivity and Protecting Groups • Asymmetric Synthesis Chiral Auxiliaries, Methods of Asymmetric Induction- Substrate, Reagent and Catalyst Controlled Reactions; Determination of Enantiomeric and Diastereomeric Excess; Enantio-Discrimination • Resolution-Optical and Kinetic

35. **Pericyclic Reactions** **1213-1233**
Electrocyclisation, Cycloaddition, Sigmatropic Rearrangements and Other Related Concerted Reactions • Principles and Applications of Photochemical Reactions in Organic Chemistry

36. Photochemistry 1234-1254

Principles and Applications of Photochemical • Reactions in Organic Chemistry

37. Heterocyclic Compounds 1255-1286

Synthesis and Reactivity of Common Heterocyclic Compounds Containing One or Two Heteroatoms (O, N, S)

38. Chemistry of Natural Products 1287-1324

Chemistry of Natural Products • Carbohydrates, Proteins and Peptides • Fatty Acids, Nucleic Acids, Terpenes • Steroids and Alkaloids • Bigenesis of Terpenoids and Alkaloids

39. Interdisciplinary Topics 1325-1346

Chemistry of Nanoscience and Technology • Catalysis and Green Chemistry • Medicinal Chemistry • Supramolecular Chemistry • Environmental Chemistry

- **Sample Questions Provided on CSIR website** 1347-1364
- **Solved Paper 2024** 1-12

NET What, Why, When

The National Educational Testing Bureau of University Grants Commission (UGC) conducts National Eligibility Test (NET) to determine eligibility for lecturership and for award of Junior Research Fellowship (JRF) for Indian nationals in order to ensure minimum standards for the entrants in the teaching profession and research. This test is conducted in Humanities (including languages), Social Sciences, Forensic Science, Environmental Sciences, Computer Science and Applications and Electronic Science.

The Council of Scientific and Industrial Research (CSIR) conducts the UGC-CSIR NET for other Science subjects, namely Life Sciences, Physical Sciences, Chemical Sciences, Mathematical Sciences and Earth Atmospheric Ocean & Planetary Sciences jointly with the UGC. The tests are conducted twice in a year generally in the months of June and December. For candidates, who desire to pursue research, the Junior Research Fellowship (JRF) is available for 5 years subject to fulfillment of certain conditions. UGC has allocated a number of fellowships to the universities for the candidates who qualify the test for JRF. The JRFs are awarded to the meritorious candidates from among the candidates qualifying for eligibility for lecturership in the NET. JRFs are available only to the candidates who opt for it in their application forms.

The test for Junior Research Fellowship is being conducted since 1984. The Government of India, through its notification dated 22nd July, 1988 entrusted the task of conducting the eligibility test for lecturership to UGC. Consequently, UGC conducted the first National Eligibility Test, common to both eligibility for Lecturership and Junior Research Fellowship in two parts, that is, in December 1989 and in March 1990.

NET Schedule

UGC conducts NET twice a year, i.e., in the months of June and December. The notifications announcing the June and December examinations are published in the months of March and September respectively in the weekly journal of nation-wide circulation, *viz*, 'Employment News'.

NET Results Declaration Schedule

The result of June, UGC NET is declared generally in the month of October. Similarly December, UGC NET result is usually declared in the month of April. The UGC NET results published in the 'Employment News' are also available on UGC website.

NET for Science Subject

The NET in major Science subjects, viz., Chemical Sciences, Earth Atmospheric Ocean and Planetary Sciences, Life Sciences, Mathematical Sciences and Physical Sciences is conducted jointly with the Council of Scientific and Industrial Research (CSIR), New Delhi. The concerned notifications are issued separately by CSIR.

Syllabus

CHEMICAL SCIENCES

Inorganic Chemistry

1. Chemical periodicity
2. Structure and bonding in homo- and heteronuclear molecules, including shapes of molecules (VSEPR Theory).
3. Concepts of acids and bases, Hard-Soft acid base concept, Non-aqueous solvents.
4. Main group elements and their compounds: Allotropy, synthesis, structure and bonding, industrial importance of the compounds.
5. Transition elements and coordination compounds: structure, bonding theories, spectral and magnetic properties, reaction mechanisms.
6. Inner transition elements: spectral and magnetic properties, redox chemistry, analytical applications.
7. Organometallic compounds: synthesis, bonding and structure, and reactivity. Organometallics in homogeneous catalysis.
8. Cages and metal clusters.
9. Analytical chemistry- separation, spectroscopic, electro- and thermoanalytical methods.
10. Bioinorganic chemistry: photosystems, porphyrins, metalloenzymes, oxygen transport, electron- transfer reactions; nitrogen fixation, metal complexes in medicine.
11. Characterisation of inorganic compounds by IR, Raman, NMR, EPR, Mössbauer, UV-vis, NQR, MS, electron spectroscopy and microscopic techniques.
12. Nuclear chemistry: nuclear reactions, fission and fusion, radio-analytical techniques and activation analysis.

Physical Chemistry:

1. Basic principles of quantum mechanics: Postulates; operator algebra; exactly- solvable systems: particle-in-a-box, harmonic oscillator and the hydrogen atom, including shapes of atomic orbitals; orbital and spin angular momenta; tunneling.
2. Approximate methods of quantum mechanics: Variational principle; perturbation theory up to second order in energy; applications.
3. Atomic structure and spectroscopy; term symbols; many-electron systems and antisymmetry principle.
4. Chemical bonding in diatomics; elementary concepts of MO and VB theories; Huckel theory for conjugated π-electron systems.
5. Chemical applications of group theory; symmetry elements; point groups; character tables; selection rules.
6. Molecular spectroscopy: Rotational and vibrational spectra of diatomic molecules; electronic spectra; IR and Raman activities – selection rules; basic principles of magnetic resonance.
7. Chemical thermodynamics: Laws, state and path functions and their applications; thermodynamic description of various types of processes; Maxwell's relations; spontaneity and equilibria; temperature and pressure dependence of thermodynamic quantities; Le Chatelier principle; elementary description of phase transitions; phase equilibria and phase rule; thermodynamics of ideal and non-ideal gases, and solutions.
8. Statistical thermodynamics: Boltzmann distribution; kinetic theory of gases; partition functions and their relation to thermodynamic quantities – calculations for model systems.

9. Electrochemistry: Nernst equation, redox systems, electrochemical cells; Debye-Huckel theory; electrolytic conductance – Kohlrausch's law and its applications; ionic equilibria; conductometric and potentiometric titrations.
10. Chemical kinetics: Empirical rate laws and temperature dependence; complex reactions; steady state approximation; determination of reaction mechanisms; collision and transition state theories of rate constants; unimolecular reactions; enzyme kinetics; salt effects; homogeneous catalysis; photochemical reactions.
11. Colloids and surfaces: Stability and properties of colloids; isotherms and surface area; heterogeneous catalysis.
12. Solid state: Crystal structures; Bragg's law and applications; band structure of solids.
13. Polymer chemistry: Molar masses; kinetics of polymerization.
14. Data analysis: Mean and standard deviation; absolute and relative errors; linear regression; covariance and correlation coefficient.

Organic Chemistry

1. IUPAC nomenclature of organic molecules including regio- and stereoisomers.
2. Principles of stereochemistry: Configurational and conformational isomerism in acyclic and cyclic compounds; stereogenicity, stereoselectivity, enantioselectivity, diastereoselectivity and asymmetric induction.
3. Aromaticity: Benzenoid and non-benzenoid compounds – generation and reactions.
4. Organic reactive intermediates: Generation, stability and reactivity of carbocations, carbanions, free radicals, carbenes, benzynes and nitrenes.
5. Organic reaction mechanisms involving addition, elimination and substitution reactions with electrophilic, nucleophilic or radical species. Determination of reaction pathways.
6. Common named reactions and rearrangements – applications in organic synthesis.
7. Organic transformations and reagents: Functional group interconversion including oxidations and reductions; common catalysts and reagents (organic, inorganic, organometallic and enzymatic). Chemo, regio and stereoselective transformations.
8. Concepts in organic synthesis: Retrosynthesis, disconnection, synthons, linear and convergent synthesis, umpolung of reactivity and protecting groups.
9. Asymmetric synthesis: Chiral auxiliaries, methods of asymmetric induction – substrate, reagent and catalyst controlled reactions; determination of enantiomeric and diastereomeric excess; enantio-discrimination. Resolution – optical and kinetic.
10. Pericyclic reactions – electrocyclisation, cycloaddition, sigmatropic rearrangements and other related concerted reactions. Principles and applications of photochemical reactions in organic chemistry.
11. Synthesis and reactivity of common heterocyclic compounds containing one or two heteroatoms (O, N, S).
12. Chemistry of natural products: Carbohydrates, proteins and peptides, fatty acids, nucleic acids, terpenes, steroids and alkaloids. Biogenesis of terpenoids and alkaloids.
13. Structure determination of organic compounds by IR, UV-Vis, 1H & 13C NMR and Mass spectroscopic techniques.

Interdisciplinary topics

1. Chemistry in nanoscience and technology.
2. Catalysis and green chemistry.
3. Medicinal chemistry.
4. Supramolecular chemistry.
5. Environmental chemistry.

1 Chemical Periodicity and Chemistry of Main Group Elements

Periodicity of Properties and Magic Numbers

The term periodicity of properties indicates that the elements with similar properties reappear at certain regular intervals of atomic number in the Periodic Table. In order to understand the concept of periodicity of properties we may consider the properties of the elements of group I A (Alkali metals), zero (Inert gases) and VII A (Halogens) given below :

Periodic number	Group IA	Group zero	Group VIIA
1	H (1)	He (2)	F (9)
2	Li (3)	Ne (10)	Cl (17)
3	Na (11)	Ar (18)	Br (35)
4	K (19)	Kr (36)	I (53)
5	Rb (37)	Xe (54)	At (85)
6	Cs (55)	Rn (86)	
7	Fr (87)		

The examination of the properties of these elements will show that the elements belonging to the same group have similar properties. In other words we can say that the atomic number intervals at which the elements with similar properties reappear are 2, 8, 8, 18, 18, 32 and 32, *i.e.*, we have to pass 2, 8, 8, 18, 18, 32 and 32 elements before we come across an element with similar properties. The repetition of the elements with similar properties in the order of increasing atomic number as in the Periodic Table is called **periodicity of properties** and the numbers 2, 8, 18 and 32 are called **magic numbers.**

Cause of Periodicity of Properties

What is the cause of periodicity of properties, *i.e.*, why do the elements placed in the same group have similar properties?

In order to answer this question we may consider the valence-shell electronic configurations, for example, of the elements of groups IA, zero and VIIA as given below :

Syllabus

- Periodicity
- Periodic Properties like Atomic and Ionic Radii, Ionization Energy, Electronegativity, Electron Affinity, Atomic Volume, Metallic Character etc.
- Polarizing Power and Polarizability
- Melting and Boiling Points
- Oxidising and Reducing Nature, Oxidation State
- Compounds like Oxides, Hydrides, Halides, Oxoacids etc.
- Diagonal Relationship

Group IA	Group zero	Group VIIA
H (1) $1s^1$	He (2) $1s^2$	
Li (3) $2s^1$	Ne (10) $2s^2 p^6$	F (9) $2s^2 p^5$
Na (11) $3s^1$	Ar (18) $3s^2 p^6$	Cl (17) $3s^2 p^5$
K (19) $4s^1$	Kr (36) $4s^2 p^6$	Br (35) $4s^2 p^5$
Rb (37) $5s^1$	Xe (54) $5s^2 p^6$	I (53) $5s^2 p^5$
Cs (55) $6s^1$	Rn (86) $6s^2 p^6$	At (85) $6s^2 p^5$
Fr (87) $7s^1$		

An examination of the valence-shell electronic configurations of the elements given above shows that the elements showing periodicity of properties *i.e*, the elements belonging to the same group, have the same valence-shell electronic configuration. Thus, we see that in any group similar valence-shell electronic configurations of the elements reoccur after certain regular intervals of atomic number and it is this reoccurrence of similar valence-shell electronic configurations of the elements at certain regular intervals of atomic number which becomes the cause of periodicity of properties.

According to modern periodic law, the properties of the elements (*i.e.,* atomic properties) like atomic volume, atomic and ionic radii, ionisation potential, electron affinity, electronegativity, bond energy, polarisation of ions etc., are periodic functions of their atomic number. Here, the word **periodic** means that with the rise of atomic number of the elements in the same period or group, there is a gradual variation (*i.e.,* increase or decrease) in a particular property of the element.

Some Important Concepts

Before discussing the periodic properties we shall discuss some important concepts which are very useful in having a clear understanding of periodic properties. These concepts are :

1. Shielding or screening effect of the inner-shell electrons on the valence shell electron and
2. Effective nuclear charge.

1. Shielding or Screening Effect of Inner-shell Electrons on the Valence Shell Electron

In a multi-electron atom, the valence-shell electrons are attracted by the nucleus and also at the same time repelled by the electrons present between the nucleus and the valence-shell electrons (*i.e.,* inner shell electrons) (See Fig. 1.1).

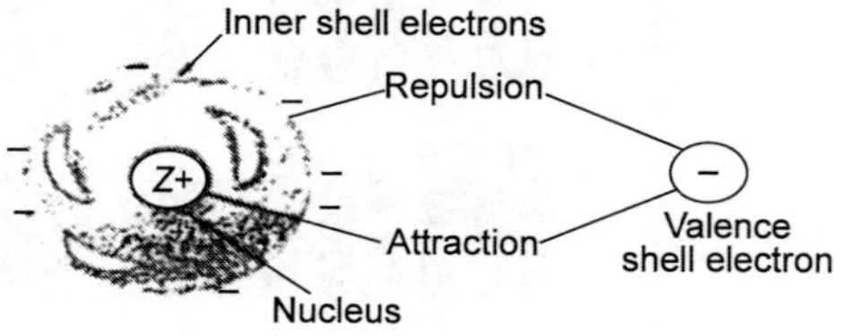

Fig. 1.1 The valence-shell electron experience less attraction from the nucleus due to the presence of inner-shell electrons—called shielding or screening effect of inner shell electrons.

Thus, the nucleus exerts an attractive force on the valence-shell electrons while the inner-shell electrons exert a repulsive force on the valence-shell electron. The combined effect of these two forces is that the actual force exerted by the nucleus on the valence-shell electron is partially decreased or weakened by the presence of repulsive force exerted by the inner-shell electrons on the valence shell electrons. Thus, the valence-shell electrons experience less attraction or pull towards the nucleus. The decrease in the attractive force exerted by the nucleus on the valence-shell electron, which is obviously due to the presence of the electrons lying between the nucleus and valence-shell electrons, (called intervening electrons) is called **shielding effect** or **screening effect.** In other words, the intervening electrons screen or shield the valence-shell electrons from the nucleus.

Following are the important factors on which the magnitude of shielding effect caused by the inner-shell electrons on the valence-shell electron depends.

(a) Number of inner-shell electrons or inner shells

Greater is the number of inner-shell electrons or inner shells, greater is the magnitude of shielding effect caused by the inner electrons on the valence-shell electron. Thus, as we move down a group, the number of inner-shells or inner shells electrons increases and hence the shielding effect also increases. For example, in the elements of group IA, with the increase of the number of inner shells and electrons in them, the shielding effect caused by these electrons on the valence-shell electron also increases from Li to Cs as shown below :

Elements of group IA	Electronic configuration	No. of electrons in the inner shells	No. of inner shells	Order of shielding effect
Li	2, 1	2	1	Increasing ↓
Na	2, 8, 1	2 + 8 = 10	2	
K	2, 8, 8, 1	2 + 8 + 8 = 18	3	
Rb	2, 8, 18, 8, 1	2 + 8 + 18 + 8 = 36	4	
Cs	2, 8, 18, 18, 8, 1	2 + 8 + 18 + 18 + 8 = 54	5	

(b) Type of the orbital occupied by the electrons

From the shapes of electron charge clouds of orbitals, we find that *s*-electrons spend most of their time nearer the nucleus while *p*-electrons belonging to the same shell spend most of their time farther away from the nucleus. This, in other words means that an electron in an *s*-orbital of a given shell penetrates the nucleus more strongly than that in a *p*-orbital of the same shell. Thus, for a given shell the penetration power (or penetration effect) of an *ns* electron is greater than that of an *np* electron ($ns > np$). The penetration power of an *np* electron is greater than that of an *nd* electron ($np > nd$) which has higher penetration power than an *nf* electron ($nd > nf$). Thus, the penetration power of an electron in *ns*, *np*, *nd* and *nf* orbitals of a given *n*th shell is in the following order : (The values of *l* for all the orbitals are also given)

—Penetration power decreasing ⟶

$$ns > np > nd > nf$$

Value of *n* : —same—

Value of *l* : 0 1 2 3

–Increasing⟶

Thus, we see that the **penetration power of *s*, *p*, *d* and *f* orbitals belonging to the same shell (*i.e.*, all the orbitals having the same value of *n*) decreases, as the value of *l* increases.** This order gives an idea of the extent of binding the electrons of various orbitals to the nucleus. The above order indicates that *s*-electrons are more tightly bound with the nucleus than *p*-electrons which, in turn, are bound more tightly than *d*-electrons and so on. Due to greater penetration power of *s*-electron, it screens the nucleus more effectively than a *p*-electron and a *p*-electron screens the nucleus more effectively than a *d*-electron and so on. Thus, the order in which an electron in the intervening *ns*, *np*, *nd* and *nf* orbitals screens the nucleus (*i.e., nuclear charge*) is as :

–Screening power decreasing⟶

$$ns > np > nd > nf$$

This order shows, that **for the same shell, the *s*-electrons are more effective in shielding the nuclear charge than *p*-electrons, the *p*-electrons are more effective than *d*-electrons and *d*-electrons are more effective than *f*-electrons.** This order also means that the electrons present in *d* or *f*-orbitals are more effectively shielded than those in *s* or *p*-orbitals by the inner shell electrons. Thus, an electron in *np* orbital is more effectively screened than the *ns* electron by the inner-shell electrons. This becomes evident when we consider Be and B atoms. 2*p* electron of B atom ($1s^2, 2s^2, 2p^1$) is more effectively shielded by 1*s* and 2*s* electrons while the 2*s* electron of Be atom ($1s^2, 2s^2$) is not effectively shielded by the 1*s* electrons and the second 2*s* electron.

An electron present in *n*th orbital is more effectively screened by the electrons in the (*n* – 1)th orbital while the same electron is not effectively shielded by the other electrons present in the same orbital. For example in Li atom ($1s^2, 2s^1$) $2s^1$ electron is more effectively screened by the two electrons present is 1*s* orbital while in He atom ($1s^2$) one of the two electrons in 1*s*-orbital in not effectively screened by the other electron present in the same orbital *i.e.*, 1*s* orbital.

Applications of shielding effect

(a) The concept of shielding effect has been used to explain why the ionisation potential values of the elements of a given group decrease on descending the group.

(b) This concept has also been used to explain that when we proceed from an inert gas to an alkali metal, a large decrease in the value of ionisation potential is observed.

2. Effective Nuclear Charge-Consequence of Shielding Effect

It is due to the shielding effect of the inner electrons on the outer-electrons that the valence electron experiences less attractive pull from the nucleus. The decrease in the attractive force reduces the nuclear charge, *Z* represented by the atomic number of the element. This decreased nuclear charge is called

effective nuclear charge and is represented by Z^*. It is given by the relation :

$$Z^* = Z - \sigma \qquad ...(1)$$

Here, σ is a constant which is called **screening constant.** This constant is a measure of the extent to which the other electrons in an atom are able to screen the nucleus from the chosen electron. Thus,

Effective nuclear charge, Z^* is defined as the actual nuclear charge, Z minus the screening effect caused by the electrons intervening between the nucleus and the outer electrons.

Greater is the number of electrons intervening between the nucleus and the outer electrons, more will be the magnitude of σ and hence the magnitude of effective nuclear charge, Z^* will decrease.

By putting the value of σ in relation (*i*) the value of Z^* for an element can be calculated. The **value of σ can be calculated from Slater's rules**. Thus, we see that as a result of shielding effect, the effective nuclear charge Z^* that a valence shell electron experiences is not exactly the nuclear charge, Z.

Calculation of σ and Z^* by Slater's rules

The value of σ and hence that of Z^* can be calculated by using Slater's rules. According to these rules the value of σ for a given electron is estimated as follows :

1. Write down the complete electronic configuration of the element and divide the electrons into the following orbitals groups starting from the inside of the atom. $(1s)$; $(2s, 2p)$; $(3s, 3p)$; $(3d)$; $(4s, 4p)$; $(4d)$; $(4f)$; $(5s, 5p)$; $(6s, 6p)$ etc.
2. Now, select the electron for which the value of σ is to be calculated. For this calculation add up the contribution to σ for the other electrons according to the following rules :

	Type of electron	Contribution to σ for each electron of this type
(a)	All electrons in groups outside the electron chosen.	0
(b)	All other electrons in the same group as chosen one.	0.35 (or 0.30 for 1*s*-electron)
(c)	All electrons in shell immediately inside.	0.85
(d)	All electrons further inside.	1.00

In order to understand the above rules let us consider the following examples.

Example 1. *Calculate the effective nuclear charge experienced by the 4s electron in potassium atom.*

Sol. The electronic configuration of K atom ($Z = 19$) is $1s^2, 2s^2p^6, 3s^2p^6, 4s^1$ and this atom has 4 shells in all. Evidently the magnitude of Z^* experienced by 4*s* electron is given by

$$\begin{aligned} Z^* &= Z - \sigma \\ &= 19 - [(0.85 \times \text{No. of electrons in } (n-1)\text{th shell}) \\ &\quad + (1.00 \times \text{Total number of electrons in the inner shells})] \\ &= 19 - [0.85 \times 8 + 1.00 \times 10] \end{aligned}$$

or $Z^* = 2.20$

This is the effective nuclear charge experienced by 4*s* electron in the potassium atom.

Example 2. *Calculate the effective nuclear charge of the last electron in an atom whose configuration is $1s^2, 2s^2p^6, 3s^2p^5$.*

Sol. Evidently the atomic number, Z of the element having this configuration is 17 and it has three shells in all.

$$\begin{aligned} \therefore \quad Z^* &= Z - \sigma \\ &= 17 - [(0.35 \times \text{No. of electrons left in } n\text{th shell}) \\ &\quad + (0.85 \times \text{No. of electrons in } (n-1)\text{th shell}) \\ &\quad + (1.00 \times \text{Total number of electrons in the inner shells})] \\ &= 17 - [(0.35 \times 6) + (0.85 \times 8) + (1 \times 2) \\ &= 17 - 10.9 = 6.1 \end{aligned}$$

Variation of Screening Effect or σ in the Periodic Table

The magnitude of screening constant is a measure of the extent to which the electrons intervening between the nucleus and the valence-shell shield valence-shell electron from the nucleus. Thus, greater is the magnitude of σ, greater is the amount of shielding effect caused by the intervening electrons on the valence-shell electron.

Since, σ increases on descending a group and on proceeding from left to right in a period of the Periodic Table, the magnitude of screening effect also increases in the same direction on proceeding from top to bottom of a group and from left to right in a period. This has been shown for the elements of group IA and 2nd period (Z = atomic number).

Elements of group IA	Li	Na	K	Rb	Cs			
Value of Z	3	11	19	37	55			
Value of σ	1.7	8.8	16.80	34.80	52.80			
Elements of 2nd period	Li	Be	B	C	N	O	F	Ne
Value of Z	3	4	5	6	7	8	9	10
Value of σ	1.70	2.05	2.40	2.75	3.10	3.45	3.80	4.15

Thus, the variation of screening effect or σ in a period and a group can be shown as depicted in Fig. 1.2.

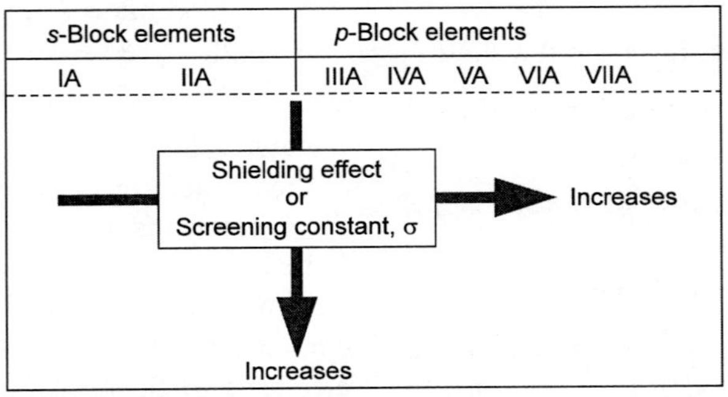

Fig. 1.2 Variation of shielding effect or screening constant, σ in the Periodic Table.

Variation of Effective Nuclear Charge in the Periodic Table

The values of effective nuclear charge of different elements, as calculated by Slater's rules, show that they increase when we proceed from left to right in a period of the Periodic Table.

When we proceed from left to right across a period, the atomic number (*i.e.,* nuclear charge) increases by one at each next element and the next element has one more valence electron with its effective repulsion equal to 0.35 and therefore the effective nuclear charge increases by $1 - 0.35 = 0.65$ from member to member. Consequently the effective nuclear charge of each next atom is greater by 0.65 than the previous atom. For example :

Elements of 2nd period :	Li	Be	B	C	N	O	F	Ne
Effective nuclear charge :	1.30	1.95	2.60	3.25	3.90	4.55	5.20	5.85
Elements of 3rd period :	Na	Mg	Al	Si	P	S	Cl	Ar
Effective nuclear charge :	2.20	2.85	3.50	4.15	4.80	5.45	6.10	6.75

When we descend a group, the values of effective nuclear charge remain almost the same as is evident from these values for the elements of group IA and IIA. Li = 1.30, Na = 2.20, K = 2.20, Rb = 2.20, Cs = 2.20, Fr = 2.20 (Group IA-Li is a typical case); Be = 1.95, Mg = 2.85, Ca = 2.85 and so on (Group IIA).

The variation of effective nuclear charge in the Periodic Table has been shown in Fig. 1.3.

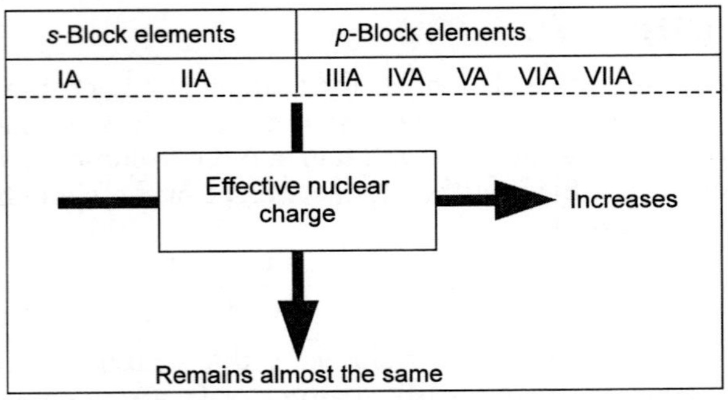

Fig. 1.3 Variation of the effective nuclear charge in a group and a period of *s* and *p*-block elements of the Periodic Table.

Applications of Effective Nuclear Charge

A number of facts can be explained on the basis of the concept of effective nuclear charge. Some examples are given below :

1. 4*s* orbital is filled before 3*d* orbitals

We know that the configuration of argon (atomic number, $Z = 18$) is $1s^2, 2s^2p^6, 3s^2p^6$ while the configuration of potassium ($Z = 19$) is obtained by adding the extra electron to 4*s* orbital and not to 3*d* orbitals, giving $1s^2, 2s^2p^6, 3s^2p^6, 4s^1$ configuration to this atom. Why 4*s* orbital is filled before 3*d* orbitals can be explained as follows on the basis of the concept of effective nuclear charge :

Suppose potassium can have any of the following two configurations :

(a) $1s^2, 2s^2p^6, 3s^2p^6d^0, 4s^1$ (4*s*-orbital is filled before 3*d*-orbitals)

(b) $1s^2, 2s^2p^6, 3s^2p^6d^1, 4s^0$ (3*d*-orbitals are filled before 4*s*-orbital)

Now, let us calculate the effective nuclear charge acting on 4*s* electron [configuration (i)]

$$Z^*_{4s} = 19 - [(0.85\times \text{No. of electrons in } (n-1) \text{ the shell})$$
$$+ (1.00 \times \text{total number of electrons in the inner shells})]$$
$$= 19 - [(0.85 \times 8) + (1.00 \times 10)] = 2.20$$

Now, let us calculate the effective nuclear charge acting on 3*d* electron [configuration (ii)]

$$Z^*_{3d} = 19 - 1.00 \times \text{total number of inner electrons}$$
$$(i.e.,\ 1s^2, 2s^2p^6, 3s^2p^6 \text{ electrons})$$
$$= 19 - 1 \times 18 = 1$$

Lower value of effective nuclear charge acting on 3*d* electron as compared to that acting on 4*s* electron makes it evident that in potassium atom 3*d* electron is less tightly bound to the nucleus than the 4*s* electron. Consequently the additional electron in potassium atom prefers to enter 4*s* orbital than 3*d* orbital.

2. **4*s* electrons are removed before 3*d* electrons in the conversion of 3*d* transition elements into cations**

Let us consider the configuration of vanadium atom (atomic number = 23) which is $1s^2, 2s^2p^6, 3s^2p^6d^3, 4s^2$. Suppose this atom is to be converted into V^{2+} cation. Quite obviously this cation is formed by the removal of two electrons from 4*s* orbitals and not from 3*d* orbital. Thus,

$$V(1s^2, 2s^2p^6, 3s^2p^6d^3, 4s^2) - 2e^- \longrightarrow V^{2+}(1s^2, 2s^2p^6, 3s^2p^6d^3)$$

Why 4*s* electrons prefer to be removed than 3*d* electrons can be explained by calculating the value of effective nuclear charge acting on one of the 4*s* or 3*d* electrons :

Effective nuclear charge acting on one of the 4*s*-electrons is given by

$$Z^*_{4s} = Z - \sigma$$
$$= 23 - [(0.35\times \text{no. of electrons left in } n\text{th shell})$$
$$+ (0.85 \times \text{no. of electrons in } (n-1)\text{th shell})$$
$$+ (1.00 \times \text{no. of electrons in the inner shells})]$$
$$= 23 - [0.35\times 1 + 0.85 \times 11 + 1 \times 10]$$
$$= 23 - 19.70 = 3.30$$

Effective nuclear charge acting on one of the 3*d* electrons is given by

$$Z^*_{3d} = Z - \sigma$$
$$= 23 - [(0.35 \times \text{no. of electrons left in } 3d \text{ orbitals})$$
$$+ (1.00 \times \text{total number of electrons in the inner orbitals } i.e., \text{ in } 1s, 2s, 2p, 3s \text{ and } 3p \text{ orbitals})]$$
$$= 23 - (0.35 \times 2 + 1 \times 18)$$
$$= 23 - 18.70 = 4.30$$

Greater value of effective nuclear charge acting on one of the 3*d* electrons as compared to that acting on one of the 4*s* electrons in vanadium atom makes it evident that in this atom 3*d* electrons are more tightly bound to the nucleus than the 4*s* electrons. Consequently in the conversion of vanadium atom into V^{2+} cation, the electrons to be removed are 4*s* electrons and not 3*d* electrons.

3. **The successive ionisation potentials I_1, I_2, I_3, etc., of an atom are in the following order**

$$I_1 < I_2 < I_3 < \ldots\ldots$$

This order can well be explained on the basis of effective nuclear charge concept.

4. **In going from left to right in a period of *s*-and *p*-block elements, atomic and ionic radii decrease with the increase of atomic number**

This can be explained on the basis of effective nuclear charge.

5. **A cation is smaller in size than its parent atom**

It can be explained on the basis of the concept of effective nuclear charge.

6. **An anion is bigger in size than its parent atom**

It can also be explained on the basis of concept of effective nuclear charge.

Atomic Volume

Atomic volume is defined as the volume in cc occupied by one gram atom of the element in the solid state and hence is commonly called gram atomic volume. It is obtained by dividing the atomic weight of the element by its density; *i.e.,*

$$\text{Atomic volume} = \frac{\text{Atomic weight}}{\text{Density}}$$

In other words atomic volume is the volume in cc occupied by 6.023×10^{23} atoms of an element (Avogadro's number). Thus, the atomic volumes of the elements should be the volumes occupied by the same number of the atoms. The volume occupied by a single atom may be obtained by dividing gram atomic volume with Avogadro's number of atoms. However, this conclusion is not very accurate due to certain variable factors which, in turn, depend on the manner in which the atoms are packed in various elements. It is a common practice to use the term gram atomic volume for volume per atom for assignment of sizes of atoms.

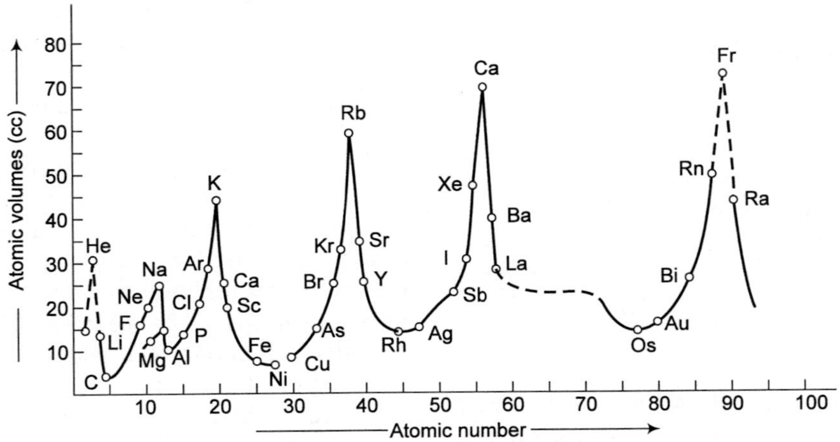

Fig. 1.4 Atomic volume *versus* atomic number curve.

Table 1.1 **Atomic Volumes (in cc) of *s*- and *p*-block Elements. The Numbers Given in Parentheses Indicate the Atomic Numbers**

Group → / Period ↓	*s*-block elements		*p*-block elements					
	IA	IIA	IIIA	IVA	VA	VIA	VIIA	Zero
1	(1) H 14.1							(2) He 31.8
2	(3) Li 13.1	(4) Be 5.0	(5) B 4.6	(6) C 5.3	(7) N 17.3	(8) O 14.0	(9) F 17.1	(10) Ne 16.8
3	(11) Na 23.7	(12) Mg 14.0	(13) Al 10.0	(14) Si 12.1	(15) P 17.0	(16) S 15.5	(17) Cl 18.7	(18) Ar 24.4
4	(19) K 45.3	(20) Ca 29.9	(31) Ga 11.8	(32) Ge 13.6	(33) As 13.1	(34) Se 16.5	(35) Br 23.5	(36) Kr 32.2
5	(37) Rb 55.9	(38) Sr 33.7	(49) In 15.7	(50) Sn 16.3	(51) Sb 18.4	(52) Te 20.5	(53) I 25.7	(54) Xe 42.9
6	(55) Cs 70.0	(56) Ba 39.0	(81) Tl 17.2	(82) Pb 18.3	(83) Bi 21.3	(84) Po –	(85) At –	(86) Rn –

Lother Meyer plotted the atomic volumes (in cc) of different elements against their atomic numbers and obtained a graph shown in Fig. 1.4. An inspection of this graph shows that the curve has five complete well-defined loops and a fraction of the sixth. It may be seen that the maxima of the curve are occupied by the alkali metals (most electropositive elements) while the minima are occupied by C (At. number, $Z = 6$), Al ($Z = 13$), Ni ($Z = 28$), Rh ($Z = 45$) and Os ($Z = 76$). It may also be seen that when we proceed further from alkali metals, the atomic volumes on each occasion first decrease and then increase again till a sharp maximum is reached at the next alkali metal. Not only alkali metals but all the elements belonging to the same group lie at corresponding positions on the curve.

The position of lanthanides [Ce ($Z = 58$) to Lu ($Z = 78$)] is to be noted. The expected increase in their atomic volumes is not observed in the curve because as the atomic number increases, the additional electrons enter into the inner $(n-2)$th shell. This causes a contraction in the atomic volumes of lanthanides. The decrease in atomic volumes on proceeding from Ce to Lu is called **lanthanide contraction.**

Variation of Atomic Volume in a Period and a Group

(a) In a group

Atomic volume increases more or less regularly in going down a group (See Table 1.1). The increase in atomic volume in going down a group is due to the increase in the number of shells. The larger the number of shells, the bigger is the volume of atom.

(b) In a period

In going from left to right in a period, it varies cyclically, *i.e.,* it decreases at first for some elements, becomes minimum in the middle and then increases (See Table 1.1). The variation of atomic volume in going from left to right in a period is influenced by the following two factors :

(i) **Nuclear charge** We know that the nuclear charge (*i.e.*, atomic number) increases by one, as we move from left to right in a period. The increased nuclear charge attracts each electron more strongly towards the nucleus, resulting in a decrease in the volume of the atom.

(ii) **Number of valence electrons** Towards the close of a period, due to an increase in the number of valence-electrons (*i.e.,* electrons in the valence shell) the volume of the atom increases, so that it may accommodate all the electrons.

These two factors, one causing an increase and the other causing a decrease, combine to result that in a period atomic volume decreases at first for some elements, becomes minimum in the middle and then increases.

Size Effects

Among the various physical properties of atoms, the atomic and ionic sizes are the most important. The importance of size effects will become even more obvious during our discussion of some other physical properties, such as ionization energy, electron affinity, metallic behaviour, etc.

1. Atomic Radii

The absolute size of an atom is difficult to define as the electronic probability distribution is never zero even at far away distances from the nucleus. Generally, the radius of an atom or ion is defined as the distance from the centre of the nucleus to the outermost shell of atom or ion. It is impossible to isolate an individual atom and determine its radius. It is assumed that atoms behave as perfect hard spheres and in a homonuclear diatomic molecule two such spheres are just in contact with each other. The distance between the centres of two atoms, *i.e.,* internuclear distances (bond lengths) in molecules can be measured by X-ray and spectral studies of molecules. So the radius of an atom is one-half of the distance between the centres of two atoms. If we consider a homonuclear diatomic molecule say F—F which has 128 pm as the internuclear distance, then we can assign $\frac{1}{2}$ the F—F distance, *i.e.,* 64 pm as the atomic (or covalent) radius of fluorine.

Similarly, atomic radius of 77 pm is assigned to carbon on the basis of C—C single bond length of 154 pm which has been observed in diamond. The atomic radii of the elements which do not form diatomic molecules with single bonds are computed by an indirect method. The atomic radius of nitrogen is obtained by subtracting the atomic radius of carbon from C—N internuclear distance in CH_3NH_2 $(147 - 77 = 70 \text{ pm})$.

The hybridization of atoms should be considered before comparing atomic radii since hybridization of an atom affects atomic radius. It has been shown that the radius of carbon atom in different states of hybridization is different. If carbon atom is sp^3 hybridized, as in CH_4, then its atomic radius is 77 pm, sp^2 hybridized carbon atom is 74 pm in size and sp hybridized carbon atom is only 70 pm. This decrease may be attributed to the increasing s-character in the different hybridization schemes in going from sp^3 to sp. This is because the 2*s* orbital has smaller radius than 2*p* orbital.

It may also be realized that our assessment of atomic radius is dependent on many other factors such as bond order, bond type, oxidation number of atoms concerned and crystal structure. Therefore, while observing atomic radii of various elements we must remember that these are meaningful only for comparison purposes because of the many variables involved in their measurements. The atomic radii of *s*-and *p*-block elements are given in Table 1.2.

Table 1.2 **Atomic Radii of *s*-and *p*-Block Elements** (pm)

Li 152	Be 111	B 88	C 77	N 70	O 66	F 64	Ne –
Na 186	Mg 160	Al 143	Si 117	P 110	S 104	Cl 99	Ar –
K 231	Ca 197	Ga 122	Ge 122	As 121	Se 117	Br 114	Kr 111
Rb 244	Sr 215	In 162	Sn 140	Sb 141	Te 135	I 133	Xe 130
Cs 267	Ba 222	Tl 170	Pb 154	Bi 152	Po 153	At –	Rn –

From the values of atomic radii given in Table 1.2 the following observations may be made :

(i) The atomic radius decreases from left to right across a period in the Periodic Table. In a given period, the alkali metal atom is the largest and the halogen atom the smallest.

(ii) The atomic radius increases on descending in a group of the Periodic Table.

(iii) The column for the atomic radii of zero group elements in Table 1.2 has been left blank. It may be recalled here that these elements are monoatomic in nature, and so the measurement of their atomic radius is impossible. The only values which are known for these elements are the van der Waals' radii. Since van der Waals' radii are much larger than the atomic radii, their mention over here would not be useful.

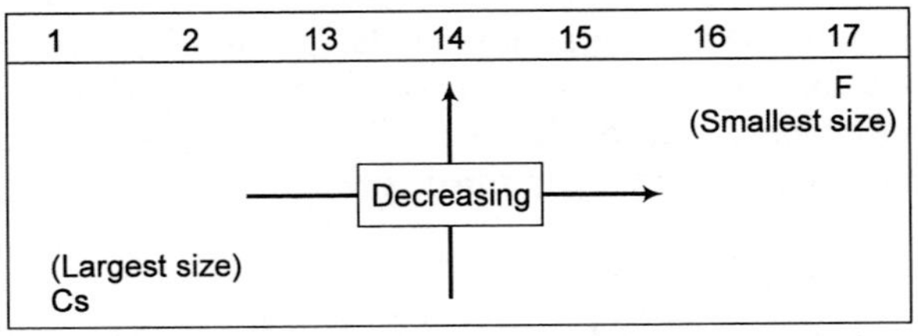

Fig. 1.5 Periodic trends of atomic radii among *s*- and *p*-block elements.

Periodic trends in main group elements are shown in Fig. 1.5.

Variation in a Period

The size of atoms decreases from left to right across the Periodic Table. For example, change in size on moving from Li to F through Be, B, C, N and O is shown below :

Elements	Li	Be	B	C	N	O	F
Atomic radius (pm)	152	111	88	77	70	66	64
Nuclear charge (*Z*)	(+ 3)	(+ 4)	(+ 5)	(+ 6)	(+ 7)	(+ 8)	(+ 9)
Effective nuclear charge (*Z*)	1.3	1.95	2.60	3.25	3.90	4.55	5.20
Electronic configuration	$1s^2 2s^1$	$1s^2 2s^2$	$1s^2 2s^2 2p^1$	$1s^2 2s^2 2p^2$	$1s^2 2s^2 2p^3$	$1s^2 2s^2 2p^4$	$1s^2 2s^2 2p^5$

This decrease in size may be explained by considering these two effects which are operating at the same time when we move across say from Li$\rightarrow$ F.

(a) Electrons are being pulled in by the increasing value of *Z* as we move from Li $\longrightarrow$ F, greater the value of *Z* greater in the contraction in size.

(b) However, as we move across the row (Li $\longrightarrow$ F), the increase in the number of electrons across the row tends to expand the atom because of

(i) mutual repulsion, and

(ii) increased screening from the nuclear charge due to intervening electrons.

Both effects act in opposite directions. We do know from experimental facts that size decreases from Li to F as we move across the period. This fact suggests that effect (*a*) predominates over (*b*). It is clear from the table above that *Z* increases at every step by $\simeq 0.65$ while screening of an electron by others is only about 35%. Thus, resulting in an overall contraction in size as we move across a row of elements in the Periodic Table.

Variation in a group

The size of elements increases on descending in a group. This is attributed to the addition of new shells of electrons at each step while the effective nuclear charge almost remains constant.

Elements of group I	Atomic radius (pm)	Nuclear charge (Z)	Effective nuclear charge (Z^*)	Electronic configuration
Li	152	3	1.3	$1s^2, 2s^1$
Na	186	11	2.2	$1s^2, 2s^2 2p^6, 3s^1$
K	231	19	2.2	$1s^2, 2s^2 2p^6, 3s^2 3p^6, 4s^1$
Rb	244	37	2.2	$1s^2, 2s^2 2p^6, 3s^2 3p^6, 4s^2 3d^{10}, 4p^6 5s^1$
Cs	267	55	2.2	$1s^2, 2s^2 2p^6, 3s^2 3p^6, 4s^2 3d^{10} 4p^6 5s^2 4d^{10} 5p^6 6s^1$

This increase in size is not regular as we go down the group but becomes irregular once the filling of d- and f-series of electrons begins. This expansion in size becomes gentle after the third row.

2. Ionic Radii

When neutral atoms gain or lose electrons, they are converted into ions and the radii are changed. When an atom loses an electron, positive ion (cation) is formed. The size of a cation is always smaller than the neutral atom. This can be attributed to a decrease in the number of electrons whereas the magnitude of the nuclear charge remains the same. The nuclear charge now acts on a fewer number of electrons, attracts them more tightly and hence the electron cloud shrinks in size.

Table 1.3 **Radii of Ions** (pm) **with Inert Gas Configuration**

	H^+ 154	Li^+ 24	Be^{2+} 27	B^{3+} 20	C^{4+} 15	N^{5+} 11	O^{6+} 9	F^{7+} 7
O^{2-} 140	F^- 133	Na^+ 95	Mg^{2+} 65	Al^{3+} 50	Si^{4+} 40	P^{5+} 38	S^{6+} 29	Cl^{7+} 26
S^{2-} 184	Cl^- 181	K^+ 138	Ca^{2+} 100	Ga^{3+} 62	Ge^{4+} 53	As^{5+} 46	Se^{6+} 50	
Se^{2-} 198	Br^- 195	Rb^+ 149	Sr^{2+} 126	In^{3+} 81	Sn^{4+} 69	Sb^{5+} 60	Te^{6+} 97	
Te^{2-} 121	I^- 216	Cs^+ 170	Ba^{2+} 136	Tl^{3+} 95	Pb^{4+} 78	Bi^{5+} 76	–	

When a neutral atom gains an electron, a negative ion (anion) is formed. The size of an anion is always larger than its neutral atom. In this case the same nuclear charge acts over greater number of electrons than were present in the neutral atom. The electron cloud is now less tightly held which causes an expansion in its size.

The evaluation of ionic radius is dependent on several factors such as crystal structure, cation to anion radius ratio, charge on the ions etc. The ionic radii of s-and p-block elements are summarized in Table 1.3.

Periodic Trends

For an isoelectronic series (*i.e.,* ions which have the same number of electrons), the ionic radius decreases very significantly as the nuclear charge increases. This is to be expected because the increased nuclear charge is acting on the same number of electrons.

Ion	C^{4-}	N^{3-}	O^{2-}	F^-	Na^+	Mg^{2+}	Al^{3+}	Si^{4+}
Radii (pm)	260	171	140	133	95	65	50	40
Nuclear charge	+ 6	+ 7	+ 8	+ 9	+ 11	+ 12	+ 13	+ 14
Electronic configuration	(All the ions have neon gas configuration)							

In a column, the ionic radius increases as the atomic number increases. It may simply be remembered here that members of a group do not show any marked change in the radii whenever there is an intervening transitition series. For example, in going from Ca to Sr the first transition series intervenes. This is even more significant when we move down from In (150 pm) to Tl (155 pm) because of the intervening $4f$ block elements.

Ionization Energy

It is possible to remove one or more electrons from an atom, ion or molecule provided sufficient energy is given to the system. The ionization energy (IE) of an element is defined as the amount of energy required to remove the most loosely bound electron from an atom of the element in the gas phase.

$$M(g) + \text{Ionization energy} \longrightarrow M^+(g) + e^-$$

One of the methods employed for measuring ionization energies is the electron impact (EI) method. Atoms of an element are bombarded with fast moving electrons which have sufficient energy to knock out an electron of the atom with which they collide. The bombarding electrons may be given the appropriate amount of energy by accelerating them through an electric potential which can be suitably varied. For example, hydrogen atom can lose an electron if the bombarding electron has a minimum energy of 2.18×10^{-18} J.

$$\text{H}(g) + e^- \longrightarrow \text{H}^+(g) + 2e^-$$

or $$\text{H}(g) + 2.18 \times 10^{-18}\,\text{J} \longrightarrow \text{H}^+(g) + e^-$$

Thus, 2.18×10^{-18} J is the ionization energy of one hydrogen atom. It is convenient to quote the total energy needed to remove an electron from each of the hydrogen atom in 1 mole of hydrogen atoms. That is,

$$\frac{2.18 \times 10^{-18}\,\text{J}}{1\ \text{atom}} \times \frac{6.022 \times 10^{23}\ \text{atoms}}{1\ \text{mol}}$$

$$= 1.31 \times 10^{6}\ \text{J mol}^{-1}$$

$$= 1310\ \text{kJ mol}^{-1}$$

Ionization energies are thus quoted in this form. The value of 1310 kJ mol^{-1} is the IE of hydrogen. Sometimes IE values are quoted in electron volts, eV (1 eV = 23.06 kcal or 96.48 kJ).

Example 3. *How much energy is needed to convert 1.00 g of sodium atoms to gaseous* Na^+ *ions?* *(IE of* Na = 506 kJ mol^{-1}*)*

Sol. Ionization energy of Na = 506 kJ mol^{-1}

Ionization energy of 1 g atoms of Na $= \frac{506}{23} = 22$ kJ

The magnitude of ionization energy is dependent on

(i) the size of atom, and

(ii) magnitude of its nuclear charge.

Some other factors which are also significant and need to be considered are :

(iii) the screening effect of inner shell electrons, and

(iv) the degree of penetration of electron charge cloud.

Variation of Ionization Energy in a Period

Within each period, for example, Li to Ne as atomic size decreases and nuclear charge increases, the ionization energies rise steeply in going from an alkali metal to the following noble gas. It reaches a maximum value at neon which has noble gas configuration ($ns^2\ np^6$), the stable octet. It is very difficult to pull out an electron from a system with an eight electron configuration and that is why the **IE values are the highest for noble gases**. These facts can be explained in terms of the shielding of one electron by others. As we move from, say lithium to neon, the eight electrons are added in the same principal shell. The extent to which these electrons shield one another from the increasing nuclear charge is very small. As a result, the effective nuclear charge shows a steady increase resulting in the tighter binding of the electrons.

Exceptions

The irregularities in the ionization energy values can be explained on the basis of empty, half-filled and completely- filled configurations having extra-stability. Thus, the ionization energies of Be (which has a filled $2s$ sublevel) and nitrogen (which has a half-filled $2p$ sublevel) have higher values than that might be expected normally.

Element	Li	Be	B	C	N	O	F	Ne
Radius (pm)	123	89	80	77	74	74	72	–
Nuclear charge	+ 3	+ 4	+ 5	+ 6	+ 7	+ 8	+ 9	+ 10
Ionization energy (kJ mol^{-1})	520	900	800	1090	1400	1310	1680	2080

Ionization energy of boron is less than that of beryllium This is just the opposite of what may be normally expected. This anomaly can be explained in terms of the greater penetration of s-electrons than p-electrons. In other words, we may say that an s-electron screens the nuclear charge more effectively than a p-electron.

The decrease in the ionization energy in going from nitrogen to oxygen can be explained in terms of their electronic configurations. At nitrogen, each *p*-orbital is singly occupied, the system acquires extra stability due to this half-filled configuration. At oxygen two electrons share the same orbital, the interelectronic repulsion increases and the system is less stable than that in nitrogen. As a consequence, the ionization energy shows a decrease in moving from nitrogen to oxygen.

Example 4. *Why is the ionization energy of* Li, 520 *kJ mol^{-1} lower than that of* H (1310 *kJ mol^{-1}*)?

Sol. 1. The average radius of a 2*s* electron is greater than that of a 1*s* electron.

2. The 2*s* electron in lithium is repelled by the inner core (screening of the nucleus by the inner core) $1s^2$ electron.

Variation of Ionization Energy in a Group

On descending in a group the ionization energy decreases. This can be easily explained in terms of size alone. The size of the first element helium is the smallest and so it is very difficult to pull out an electron whereas the size of Rn is the largest and its electrons are less tightly held by the nucleus and therefore little energy is required to ionize its atom. The effect of increased nuclear charge is not so significant as any increase in nuclear charge is cancelled out the increased screening effect of the inner electrons.

Element	He	Ne	Ar	Kr	Xe	Rn
IE (kJ mol^{-1})	2370	2080	1520	1351	1170	1036

Example 5. *Which element in each of the following pairs would be expected to have higher ionization energy?*

(i) Be, B *(ii)* Na, Mg

(iii) O, O^- *(iv)* He, Ne

Sol. (i) Be (ii) Mg (iii) O (iv) He

Electron Affinity

It is possible to add an electron to any atom, ion or molecule. The electron affinity of an atom is defined as the amount of energy released when an electron is added to neutral gaseous atom, *i.e.*,

$$X(g) + e^- \longrightarrow X^-(g) + \text{Energy}$$

For example, the electron affinity of a H atom is – 72.8 kJ mol^{-1}, *i.e.,* 72.8 kJ energy is released when 1 mole of H atoms combine with 1 mole of electrons to give 1 mole of H^- ions. **The greater the electron affinity, the more negative is the ΔE value and greater is the energy released.** Halogens form very stable halide (X^-) ions, so large amount of energy is released and ΔE values are negative. **Electron affinity values are more difficult to determine directly but are calculated indirectly using Born-Haber cycle.** The electron affinities of only a few elements are known with certainty and are given in Table 1.4.

Table 1.4 **Electron Affinities of Some Gaseous Atoms** (kJ mol^{-1})

H – 72.8						
Li – 52.1	Be –	B – 28.9	C – 109.0	N – 19.3	O – 142.8	F – 328
Na – 71.4	Mg –	Al – 38.6	Si – 183.3	P – 77.2	S – 199.7	Cl – 349
						Br – 325

Electron affinity of an atom depends upon :

(i) the size of the atom, and

(ii) its effective nuclear charge.

If the size of an atom is small, the force of attraction for the additional electron will be large. Similarly, greater the nuclear charge, greater will be the attraction for the additional electron. We may say that **atoms with small size and high nuclear charge shall have high electron affinities.**

Periodic Trends

On moving across a period the size of the atoms decreases and their nuclear charge increases and both these factors favour increase in electron affinity. **Group 17 elements have the highest values for electron affinity** due to their tendency to acquire an additional electron to form a stable octet. In general, elements on the right side of the Periodic Table always have a tendency to acquire more electrons to complete their octet and so they have high electron affinities. **The low**

value for the electron affinity of fluorine relative to that of chlorine is due to the strong interelectronic repulsions in the relatively small and compact 2*p* subshell on the addition of another electron. As a consequence, the electron affinity for chlorine is greater than that of fluorine where the electron is added in the relatively bigger sized 3*p* orbitals which can easily accommodate the additional electron. In general, **electron affinities for members of the third period (from Na to Cl) are greater than the second period member, *i.e.*, Li to F**. This is attributed to the smaller size of the atoms of the second period elements which would produce large electron repulsions for the additional electron when a negative ion is formed.

On moving down a group, size of the atoms increases significantly which leads to a decrease in their electron affinity values. This is obvious from the electron affinity values for chlorine, bromine and iodine.

As we may expect, the values of second electron affinities.

i.e., $$O^- + e^- \longrightarrow O^{2-}$$

are all positive, *i.e.*, energy is required instead of being released. This may be attributed to the electrostatic repulsion of the second electron by the negative charge on the ion.

Electronegativity

Electronegativity is defined as a measure of the ability of an atom in a molecule to attract the shared electron pair towards itself. For example, in a homonuclear diatomic molecule such as H_2 and Cl_2, the shared electron pair is attracted equally by both the bonding atoms and so there is no net polarity in the molecule. This is because the electronegativity of both the atoms is the same. However, in a heteronuclear molecule such as HCl, the shared electron pair is not equally attracted by the bonding atoms, *i.e.*, hydrogen and chlorine. The electron pair is shifted more towards chlorine than hydrogen and the molecule acquires **polarity** ($H^{\delta+}—Cl^{\delta-}$). These charges are of equal magnitude but opposite sign, and the overall charge is zero. Such small charges are denoted by the symbol δ (delta). This implies that chlorine is more electronegative than hydrogen.

Electronegativity is a qualitative concept. There is no direct way of measuring this ability experimentally though a number of indirect methods have been suggested. Pauling was the first to give a general method of computing electronegativities of elements. He proposed that if two atoms *A* and *B* have the same electronegativity value, then the bond energy of the *A*—*B* bond would simply be the geometric mean of the *A*—*a*, and *B*—*B* bond energies, because all the three molecules (*A*—*B*, *A*—*A* and *B*—*B*) are bonded by pure covalent bonds. However, if the two atoms *A* and *B* have different electronegativities, then the energy of the *A*—*B* bond would be greater than the geometric means of the energies of *A*—*A* and *B*—*B* bonds. This excess energy is due to the contribution of ionic structure in addition to the covalent structure.

$A—B$, $A^+ B^-$ (say *B* is more electronegative than *A*)

Pauling, therefore, suggested that this excess bond energy in molecules (containing atoms of different electronegativities) can be used as a measure of the electronegativity differences. The electronegativity values (as given by Pauling) of *s*- and *p*-block elements are listed in Table 1.5.

Table 1.5 **Electronegativities of the Main Group Elements on Pauling Scale**

H 2.2							He
Li 1.6	Be 1.5	B 2.0	C 2.5	N 3.1	O 3.5	F 4.1	Ne –
Na 1.0	Mg 1.2	Al 1.3	Si 1.7	P 2.1	S 2.4	Cl 2.8	Ar –
K 0.9	Ca 1.0	Ga 1.8	Ge 2.0	As 2.2	Se 2.5	Br 2.7	Kr 3.1
Rb 0.9	Sr 1.0	In 1.5	Sn 1.7	Sb 1.8	Te 2.0	I 2.2	Xe 2.4
Cs 0.7	Ba 0.9	Tl 1.8	Pb 1.8	Bi 1.7	Po 1.8	At 2.0	Rn –

According to Coulomb's law, the force of attraction exerted by the positively charged core of an atom on an electron in the valence shell is given by

$$F = k\frac{Q_1Q_2}{r^2} = k\frac{(Ze)(-e)}{r^2}$$

Q_1 = core charge (Ze)

Q_2 = the charge on an electron ($-e$)

r = distance of the electron from the core.

As we would expect from this expression two important trends occur within the Periodic Table.

1. Electronegativity increases across a period as the core charge increases.
2. Electronegativity generally decreases from top to bottom in a group as atomic size increases and the bonding electrons are farther from the nucleus.

Periodic Trends

Electronegativity is a periodic function of atomic number of elements. In moving from left of right across a period (see Table 1.5) the magnitude of electronegativity increases. On the other hand, while moving down a column of elements we observe a steady decrease in their electronegativity value (see Fig. 1.6). It may be noted that the first element of each family is far more electronegative than other members of the group. The most electronegative element occurs on top right hand corner and the most electropositive (least electronegative) element occurs at the bottom of left hand corner of the Periodic Table. Electronegativity depends upon the valence state of an atom. The ability of an atom to attract electrons depends on the environment of that atom. Two main factors which determine the attraction of atoms for electrons are :

(i) the charge on the atom; and

(ii) hybridization of the atom.

(i) Charge on the atom

An atom with a positive charge will attract electrons more readily than a neutral atom. In turn, a negatively charged atom will attract electrons less readily than a neutral atom.

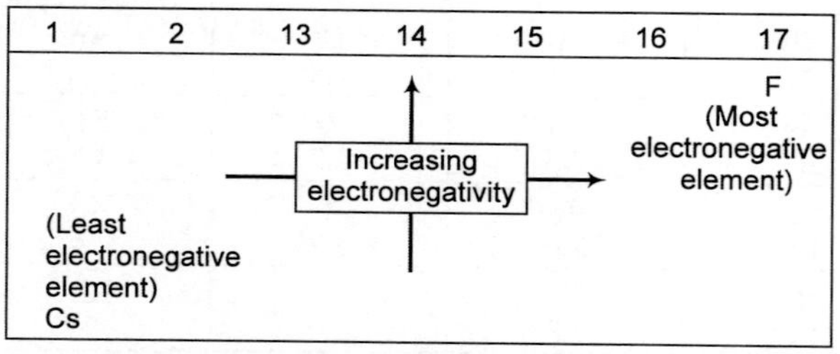

Fig. 1.6 Periodic trends in electronegativity among main-group elements.

(ii) Hybridization of the atom

Electronegativity of an atom varies with hybridization. Those orbitals which have more *s*-character are more electronegative. Methane with sp^3 hybridization (containing 25% *s*-character) is unreactive. In ethylene, the carbon atom is sp^2 hybridized (33% *s*-character) is more reactive, showing increased electronegativity of carbon. Finally, acetylene in which carbon in *sp* hybridized (50% *s*-character) has highly acidic hydrogen atoms. Carbon atom in acetylene is the most electronegative.

Application of Electronegativity

Electronegativity is a useful concept which indicates the electron distribution between two atoms in a molecule. If two atoms have very similar electronegativities, that is, they have same tendency to attract electrons, the bond is said to be a non-polar bond, as found in a homonuclear diatomic molecules such as H_2, F_2, Cl_2. The greater the difference in the electronegativities of the two atoms forming a bond, the more polar is the bond.

Example 6. *Which of the following molecules have polar bonds and which have non-polar bonds? For the polar bonds indicate the charge on the atoms.*

H_2, FCl, ICl, OF, F_2

Sol.

H_2	Non-polar	
FCl	Polar	$\overset{\delta^-}{F} - \overset{\delta^+}{Cl}$
ICl	Polar	$\overset{\delta^+}{I} - \overset{\delta^-}{Cl}$
OF	Polar	$\overset{\delta^+}{O} - \overset{\delta^-}{F}$
F_2	Non-polar	

Predicting the nature of bonds

Electronegativity values can be used to predict if a bond is non-polar (covalent), polar (covalent) or ionic. Unfortunately, the electronegativity values are only approximate in nature, therefore such predictions cannot be made with absolute surety. If the

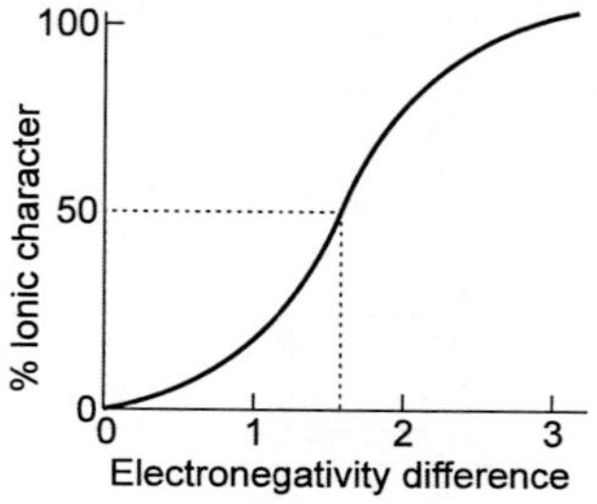

Fig. 1.7 Electronegativity difference *vs* ionic character.

electronegativity difference between two atoms is zero, we can definitely say that the bond is non-polar covalent.

Pauling derived an empirical relationship between electronegativity difference and percentage ionic character. This relationship is based on the ionic characters of HX acids; HF = 45%; HCl = 19%; HBr = 11% and HI = 4%; which have been estimated from dipole moment measurements. From the above relationship **Pauling suggested that a bond is 50% ionic if the electronegativity difference between its atoms is about 1.7. If the difference is more than 1.7 the bond has more than 50% ionic character while if the difference is less than 1.7, the bond is more covalent than ionic.**

Table 1.6 **Partial Ionic Character of Some Substances**

Compound	Formula	Electronegativity difference	Partial ionic character (%)
Cesium fluoride	CsF	3.3	94
Sodium chloride	NaCl	2.1	67
Hydrogen chloride	HCl	0.9	19
Hydrogen bromide	HBr	0.7	11
Hydrogen iodide	HI	0.4	4
Hydrogen	H_2	0.0	0

Polarizing Power and Polarizability

In our discussion on the electrostatic model of bonding in ionic substances, we only considered the coulombic attraction between two oppositely charged ions. Such a model was useful in explaining the behaviour of completely ionic solids such as NaCl or CsCl etc. However, in other compounds such as LiCl or AgCl, the ions not only exert coulombic attraction, but are also polarized due to mutual polarization and their behaviour is modified. For example, LiCl is soluble in non-polar organic solvents whereas NaCl or CsCl is insoluble in these solvents. The polarizing effect introduces a varying degree of non-polar character (*i.e.*, covalence) in these ionic substances. The degree of non-polar character (or covalence) in compounds helps us in predicting certain properties such as melting point, boiling point, etc., (because covalent substances have low melting and boiling points).

Anions are larger in size than cations and therefore their electron clouds are less tightly held. A small highly charged cation shall, therefore, distort the electron cloud of the large anions in a manner that it increases the electron density between the nuclei. For example, the large iodide ion by itself is perfectly symmetrical. However, when a small positively charged lithium ion comes close to the iodide ion, the anion is pulled towards the positive lithium ion. The iodide ion is said to be polarized. The polarization effect introduces covalence in LiI molecule. **The power of an ion to distort the other ion is known as its polarizing power and the tendency of the ion to distortion is known as its polarizability.** The polarizing power of a cation is proportional to its charge/radius ratio. In a compound consisting of large negative ions and small positive ions, the polarization may be so marked that the bond becomes covalent. Examples of such ionic covalent compounds include $AlCl_3$, $FeCl_3$, SnI_4 etc.

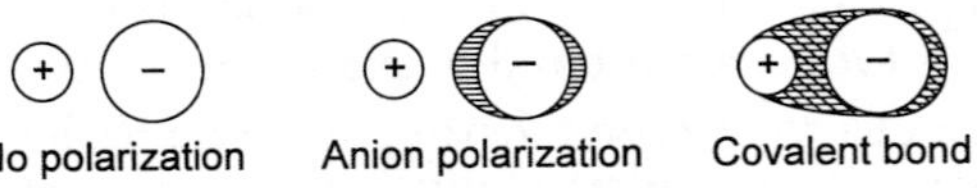

Polarization Effect

Fajan discussed the variation in non-polar character of ionic compounds in terms of polarization effects. He considered that covalent bonding was an extreme example of polarization between two atoms where maximumelectron density is between the two nuclei.

Fajan's Rules : Covalent Character in Ionic Compound

Fajan proposed the following rules for the prediction of non-polar character between two ions.

(i) High charge of the cation or anion.
(ii) Small size of positive ion.
(iii) Large size of negative ion.

(i) High charge of cation or anion

The highly charged cation will exert more polarization on the electron density of the anion and will introduce more covalence in its compounds. On the other hand, the highly charged anion will get more readily polarized. Therefore, the polarizing power of a cation and polarizability of an anion will increase with increase in the charge of the ions.

(ii) Small size of cation

The small sized cation will have high charge density and therefore it will be able to distort (polarize) the electron cloud of the anion more effectively.

(iii) Large size of anion

The polarizability (to be able to get distorted) of an anion increases with increase in its size because its electron charge cloud is not firmly held by its own nuclear charge and can be thus readily polarized by incoming cations.

Periodic Trends

Among the main group elements, the size of the cations increases in moving down a group, therefore, tendency of covalent bond formation decreases. For example Li^+ is more polarizing than other members (Na^+, K^+ etc) of group 1. Therefore, compounds of lithium are covalent in nature while similar compounds of sodium and potassium are ionic. Thus, LiCl is covalent in nature while NaCl or KCl are ionic and that's why LiCl is soluble in organic solvents while NaCl or KCl are insoluble in these solvents.

In moving along a period, the size of the cations decreases and, therefore, degree of covalence increases in their compounds. For example, in moving from lithium to carbon, through beryllium and boron in the second period, the size of the cation decreases and tendency for covalent bond formation increases.

However, as we descend a group, the size of the anions increases, their polarizability increases and their compounds become more covalent. For example, in the series F^-, Cl^-, Br^- and I^-, bromides and iodides are more covalent than the corresponding chlorides and fluorides.

Example 7. *Which of the following ions has larger tendency for polarization?*

(i) Li^+, Na^+ *(ii)* Mg^{2+}, Al^{3+}

(iii) K^+, Ag^+ *(iv)* Cl^-, I^-

Sol. (i) Li^+ (ii) Al^{3+} (iii) Ag^+ (iv) I^-.

Metallic Character

A useful generalization in chemistry is the division of elements into metals and non-metals. This classification of elements is based on certain physical and chemical properties. A substance is termed metallic if it has a silvery lustre and is a good conductor of heat and electricity. Metals are electropositive in character and have a high tendency to lose electrons :

$$M \longrightarrow M^+ + e^-$$

Since this reaction is closely related to the ionization energy of an element, therefore, we may say that the two properties are closely interlinked. The lower the ionization energy of an element, greater is its tendency to undergo this reaction and so more electropositive and metallic that element would be.

Periodic Trends in Metallic Behaviour

1. Variation in a period

Metallic character decreases while non-metallic character increases as we move along a period (from left to right). As we move in a period the size decreases, IE increases and thus, metallic character decreases.

Elements of 3rd Period	Na	Mg	Al	Si	P	S	Cl
	Metals		Semi-metals (Metalloids)		Non-metals		

2. Variation in a group

Metallic character increases in a group as we move from top to bottom. On moving down a group, size of the atom increases, ionization energy decreases and therefore, metallic character increases. For example, in group 14, carbon is a non-metal, silicon and germanium are metalloids (show both metallic and non-metallic behaviour) while tin and lead are distinctly metallic. Similarly, in group 15, nitrogen and phosphorus are non-metals, arsenic and antimony show many metallic properties and bismuth is a typical metal.

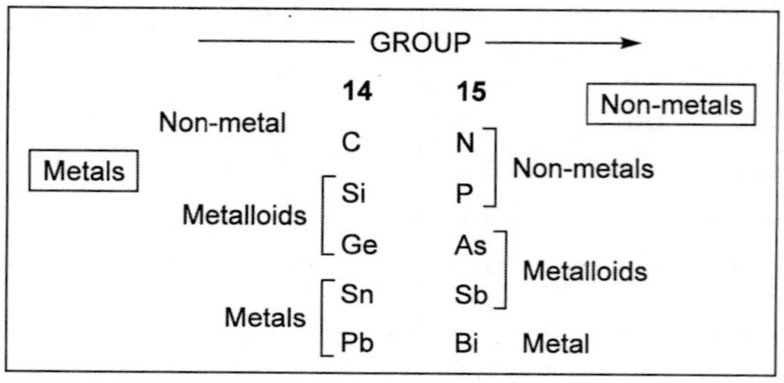

Elements in group 1 are strongly electropositive elements (metallic) while elements of group 17 are strongly electronegative (non-metal). It means that along a period (as the size of the atoms decreases and their ionization energy increases) there is a change from metallic to non-metallic character. Somewhere between these two extremes, we come across **elements which show characteristic properties of both metals and non-metals. These elements are called metalloids**. A classification of main group elements in these categories is shown on next page.

Cause of Metallic and the Non-Metallic Character

The elements on the left hand side of the Periodic Table contain very few electrons than are required to attain the stable octet and they achieve this configuration by losing their extra valence electrons. These elements crystallize out in one of the close packed arrangements with the valence electrons grouped together to make up a sea of negative charges which binds the entire lattice of M^+ ions.

On moving along a period, this tendency to acquire closed shell configuration by losing valence electrons diminishes, whereas tendency to share its electrons with neighbours increases. The arrangement of atoms in space is determined by the number of covalent bonds and this is turn will determine the shape of the crystal. The elements form giant molecules, *e.g.*, the tetrahedral structure of diamond or the network type structure of silicates. Further on, we observe that the number of electrons required to form a stable octet are few and these elements do so by sharing electrons and forming diatomic molecules such as N_2, F_2, Cl_2, I_2, etc. Since, there are no unpaired electrons left over to form covalent bonds with other similar atoms or molecules, the forces which hold these solids together are the weak van der Waals' forces. These elements, therefore, form molecular crystals. Because of their complete shell, the noble gases do not form molecules. However, on cooling they form molecular crystalline solids because even the weak van der Waals' forces of attraction which exist between the atoms are strong enough to bind them into crystal lattice.

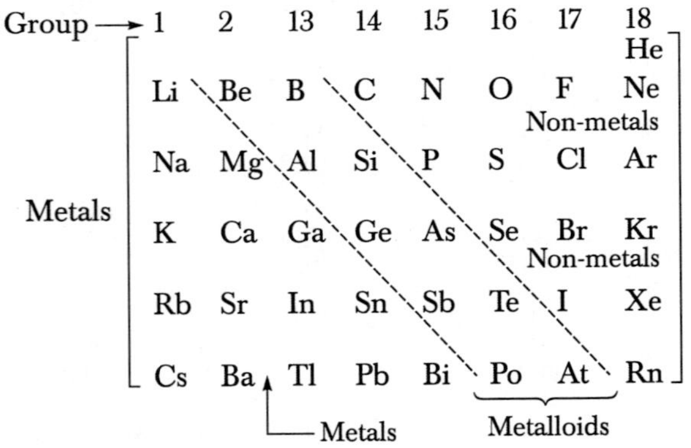

Although it is common amongst chemists to talk in terms of electronegativity of an element, yet it is useful to retain the concept of electropositivity (which is exactly the converse of electronegativity) while describing metals. Some useful generalizations are :

(i) oxides of electropositive metals are basic in character and from ionic compounds.

(ii) electropositive elements from salts which are generally hydrated.

(iii) salts of electropositive metals do not form oxy salts.

Example 8. *(i) Given are the following atoms :*

Na, Al, O, S, Te, Rb, H, Cs

Arrange these atoms in the order of (a) increasing atomic radius; (b) atom with maximum ionization energy; (c) atom with maximum electron affinity; (d) atom with most metallic character.

(ii) Which is the least electronegative element?

Sol. (i) (a) H < O < S < Al < Te < Na < Rb < Cs

(b) H (c) S (d) Cs

(ii) Cs

Density

The density of an element is determined by its four atomic properties, namely atomic weight, atomic volume, packing of atoms and oxidation state. The densities of main group elements are given in Table 1.7.

The alkali metals and the halogens positioned on two extreme sides of the Periodic Table have low values, whereas elements in the middle of each period have high values. The change in the value of density between any two elements is an indication of the empty space between the packing of atoms or molecules in their crystals. For example, in the second period density increases in going from Li to B indicating a decrease in the empty space in their structures. At carbon, the empty space between the atoms decreases indicating a change in type of packing. The elements nitrogen, oxygen, and fluorine form molecular crystals with very wide gaps in the packing of molecules and a steady decrease in the density of these elements.

Table 1.7 **Densities** (g/mL) **of Some Main-Group Elements**

H 0.071						
Li 0.53	Be 1.89	B 2.34	C 2.26	N 0.81	O 1.14	F 1.11
Na 0.97	Mg 1.74	Al 2.70	Si 2.35	P 0.82	S 2.07	Cl 1.56
K 0.86	Ca 1.55	Ga 5.91	Ge 5.36	As 5.70	Se 4.70	Br 3.12
Rb 1.53	Sr 2.60	In 7.30	Sn 6.00	Sb 6.00	Te 6.10	I 4.93
Cs 1.90	Ba 3.50	Tl 11.85	Pb 11.34	Bi 9.80	Po –	At –

Melting and Boiling Points

Melting and boiling points of main group elements are given in Table 1.8. These values are dependent upon the nature of the binding forces operating in the crystalline elements. The magnitude of binding forces varies with the number of valency electrons which take part in bonding. On moving along a period, the number of valency electrons increases progressively from one per atom for first group elements to a maximum of four for the fourteenth group elements, and consequently the melting points show a corresponding increase. Sudden decrease in the melting point in moving from carbon to nitrogen is due to a change in their crystal structures, *i.e.,* from the giant structure of carbon to the soft molecular crystals of nitrogen. Molecular crystals have low melting points because of the weak van der Waals' forces operating between the molecules. Generally speaking, the melting point of a molecular crystal depends on its molecular weight. Substances with high molecular weights exhibit high melting points.

Table 1.8 **Melting and Boiling Point** (°C) **of Some Main-Group Elements***

– 259.2 H – 252.8						
186 Li 1336	1280 Be 2477	2180 B – 3650	≈ 4100 C 4830	– 210.1 N – 195.8	– 218.8 O – 183.0	– 219.6 F – 187.8
98 Na 880	650 Mg 1120	660 Al 2467	1420 Si 3280	44.2 P 280	114.5 S 444.6	– 101 Cl – 34
62.3 K 759	850 Ca 1492	29.78 Ga 2403	945 Ge 2850	817 (36mm) As 613	217.4 Se 684.8	– 72 Br 59.5
38.5 Rb 700	770 Sr 1370	156.6 In 2080	231.9 Sn 2623	630.5 Sb 1587	452 Te 990	113.6 I 184.5
28.5 Cs 670	710 Ba 1638	303.6 Tl 1457	327.4 Pb 1751	271.3 Bi 1564	254 Po 962	(–) At (380)

The variation of melting points in a group does not show any regular behaviour. The interval between the melting and boiling point of elements which form molecular crystals is quite small. This is because the forces operating in molecular crystals are the weak van der Waals' forces. Only a small amount of energy is required to separate the particles (evaporation) after these have undergone melting. Elements which form gaint molecules (element in the middle of the Periodic Table) have their atoms held by strong covalent forces and are operative in the molecule even after the substance has undergone fusion. Therefore, they have high boiling points and the difference between their boiling points and melting points is very large.

Oxidising and Reducing Nature

In general, oxidation is the lose of electron or electrons from an atom, ion or molecule and reduction is the gain of electron or electrons, by an atom, ion or molecule. The two processes occur simultaneously. We may note that in a reaction the more electronegative atom pulls electrons from the less electronegative atom, a process which is very close to oxidation-reduction reaction. Oxidising and reducing power is measured in terms of $E°$, the standard electrode potential ($M^+ + e^- \rightleftharpoons M. E°$). When different electrode reactions are arranged in the order of their standard electrode potentials, we obtain what is known as electro-chemical series or in other words oxidation-reduction series. Metals at the top of the series have a ready tendency to lose electrons, have large negative $E°$ values and are powerful reducing agents. On the other hand, elements with positive $E°$ values are strong oxidising agents. A partial list of standard electrode potentials of main group elements is given in Table 1.9.

Table 1.9 **Standard Electrode Potentials** ($E°$, in volts) **at 25°C**

H^+/H 0.00						
Li^+/Li – 3.045	Be^{2+}/Be – 1.84	B^{3+}/B – 0.87				$\frac{1}{2}F/F^-$ + 2.80
Na^+/Na – 2.714	Mg^{2+}/Mg – 2.37	Al^{3+}/Al – 1.66			S/S^{2-} + 0.51	$\frac{1}{2}Cl_2/Cl^-$ + 1.36
K^+/K – 2.92	Ca^{2+}/Ca – 2.87	Ga^{3+}/Ga – 0.52		As^{3+}/As + 0.25		$\frac{1}{2}Br_2/Br^-$ + 1.08
Rb^+/Rb – 2.99	Sr^{2+}/Sr – 2.89	In^{3+}/In – 0.34	Sn^{2+}/Sn – 0.14	Sb^{2+}/Sb + 0.21		$\frac{1}{2}I_2/I^-$ + 0.54
Cs^+/Cs – 3.02	Ba^{2+}/Ba – 2.90	Ti^{3+}/Ti – 0.34	Pb^{2+}/Pb – 0.18	Bi^{3+}/Bi + 0.23		

Thus, lithium is the strongest reducing agent whereas fluorine is the strongest oxidising agent As mentioned earlier, the trends in electrode potentials show broad similarities with the trends in electronegativities (see Table 1.9). In moving along a period, the reducing character decreases and oxidising power increases, whereas on descending in a group of non-metals reducing power increases and oxidising power decreases.

Oxidation States

The common oxidation state of an element can be readily predicted from the electronic configuration of its atom. Oxidation states of different elements correspond to the gain or loss of electrons by their atoms so that they acquire a closed shell configuration of eight electrons ($ns^2 np^6$). This tendency is particularly predominant in groups 1, 2 and 13 where the elements acquire noble gas configuration by losing electrons and thus show a single positive oxidation state equal to their group number. On the other hand, elements on the right side of the Periodic Table (Groups 15, 16 and 17) show negative oxidation states varying from – 3 to 1. In the fourteenth group, the tendency is to form covalent compounds instead of gaining or losing electrons. In short, we may say that as one moves along a period, *e.g.*, the third period, the positive oxidation state increases and reaches a maximum value at aluminium. The negative oxidation state decreases from – 3 to – 1 as we move from phosphorus to chlorine.

Inert Pair Effect

In a group, the maximum oxidation state shown by a *p*-block element is equal to the total number of its valency electrons, *i.e.*, the sum of its *s*- and *p*-electrons which is the same as the old group numbers. In addition to the usual oxidation state, some *p*-block elements also show another oxidation state, which differs from the group oxidation state by a step of two. A list of elements which show this behaviour is given below.

13	14	15	16
Ga	Ge	–	–
In	Sn	Sb	Te
Tl	Pb	Bi	–

These elements occur in the form of following cations : In^+, Tl^+, Sn^{2+} and Te^{2+}. The greater stability of lower oxidation states (than the group oxidation state) of the heavier *p*-block elements is explained in terms of inert pair effect. The formation of these ions involves the removal of only *p*-electrons. The two *s*-electrons remain a part of the inner core of the electrons and are termed as inert pair.

Causes of Inert Pair Effect

(i) Penetration of *ns* e^- in the 18-electron shell

One of the explanations offered for the inert pair effect refers to the penetration of the outer electrons in the 18 electron shell which is immediately preceding them. They are, therefore, nearer the nucleus and are more strongly held by the atom. Consequently, the energy required to ionize these *s*-electrons is very high and it cannot be compensated by the energy which may be released when two additional bonds are formed. Therefore, this pair of *s*-electrons in heavier *p*-block elements does not take part in bond formation and acts as a part of the inner core.

(ii) Decreasing covalent character

Another explanation which has been offered for this effect refers to the decrease in the covalent bond forming ability of heavy elements due to a decrease in the strength of their covalent bonds. Thus, as the size of the atom increases, its valence electrons get farther away from the nucleus and so their effective overlap and hence the strength of their bonds decreases.

(iii) Relativistic effects

For heavier elements, there is an additional influence on atomic size, namely relativistic contraction. The speed of an electron in heavier atoms (when Z is large) must increase, in order for it to stay in the orbit, otherwise it may fall in the nucleus due to increased attraction. This increase in the speed of an electron in heavier atoms leads to its increase in mass [theory of relativity, $m = m_0 \Big/ \sqrt{1-\left(\frac{v}{c}\right)^2}$] and consequent decrease in its radius (*i.e.*, electrons in heavier atoms come closer to their nuclei). This raises their binding energies. This increased stability of the 6*s* electrons in heavier post-transition elements (Tl, Pb, Bi,...) reduces their availability for bonding and is responsible for these elements to exhibit valencies two less than the group valence as in Tl(I), Pb (II) and Bi(III).

Example 9. *Which compound is more stable toward oxidation :* $SnCl_2$ *or* $PbCl_2$*?*

Sol. $PbCl_2$. Because the effect of the inert pair in the 6th period is more than that in the 5th period.

Nature of Different Compounds

1. Oxides

These compounds may be classified into three types : (a) basic oxides : (b) acidic oxides : (c) amphoteric oxides, depending on their behaviour towards water, acids and alkalies.

(a) Basic oxides

They are formed by the combination of oxygen with highly electropositive metals. For example, alkali and alkaline earth metals form basis oxides. They are soluble in water and react vigorously to give alkaline solutions. They react with acids to form salts. They are ionic in nature with high melting and boiling points. A few of their examples include Li_2O and MgO.

$$Na_2O + H_2O \longrightarrow 2NaOH$$

$$MgO + 2HCl \longrightarrow MgCl_2 + H_2O$$

(b) Acidic oxides

They are formed by the combination of oxygen with non-metals. They react with alkalies to form salts. They dissolve in water to give acidic solutions. These compounds are covalent in nature and are usually gaseous or volatile liquids or solids. Some examples include B_2O_3, CO_2, SiO_2, SO_2, SO_3, N_2O_5 and P_2O_5.

$$N_2O_5 + H_2O \longrightarrow 2HNO_3$$

$$CO_2 + H_2O \longrightarrow H_2CO_3$$

Basic and acidic oxides often combine to give salts.

$$\underset{\text{(Acid)}}{CO_2} + \underset{\text{(Base)}}{2KOH} \longrightarrow \underset{\text{(Salt)}}{K_2CO_3} + H_2O$$

$$\underset{\text{(Acid)}}{SiO_2} + \underset{\text{(Base)}}{Na_2O} \xrightarrow{\text{Fusion}} Na_2SiO_3$$

(c) Amphoteric oxides

They are formed by weakly electropositive elements such as Be, Al, Ga, Sn etc. They show basic as well as acidic behaviour depending on reaction conditions, *i.e.,* they react with bases as acidic oxides and with acids as basic oxides. Amphoteric oxides are mainly ionic in nature and have high melting and boiling points.

For example,

Acidic behaviour

$$\underset{\text{(Acid)}}{Al_2O_3} + \underset{\text{(Base)}}{2NaOH} \longrightarrow \underset{\text{Sod. metaaluminate}}{2NaAlO_2} + H_2O$$

Basic behaviour

$$\underset{\text{(Base)}}{Al_2O_3} + \underset{\text{(Acid)}}{6HCl} \longrightarrow 2AlCl_3 + 3H_2O$$

Table 1.10 **Parameters of the Oxides of Third Period**

Element	Na	Mg	Al	Si	P	S	Cl
Electronegativity	1.0	1.2	1.3	1.7	2.1	2.4	2.8
Electronegativity difference between element and O	2.5	2.3	2.2	1.8	1.4	1.1	0.7
(Electronegativity of oxygen is 3.5)							
Oxide	Na_2O	MgO	Al_2O_3	SiO_2	P_2O_5	SO_2	Cl_2O_7
Behaviour	Strongly basic	Basic	Amphoteric	Weakly acidic	Acidic	Strongly acidic	Very strongly acidic

The change from basis to acidic character takes place because of the increasing electronegativity of the element as we move along a period. The electronegativity difference between an element on the left side of the Periodic Table and oxygen is very large and therefore these oxides are ionic. The electronegativity difference between oxygen and element on the right side of the Periodic Table is small and therefore their oxides are covalent. For example, oxides of elements of the third period are given in Table 1.10 to illustrate their behaviour.

It has been observed that acidic, amphoteric or basic character of the oxides is also governed by the size of the cation.

Size of the cation	Behaviour
Less than 50 pm	Acidic
Between 50 to 90 pm	Amphoteric
Greater than 90 pm	Basic

Other oxides

There are some other oxides, when are inert, and do not dissolve in acids or bases. For example, N_2O or CO.

Example 10. *Which is the most acidic oxide :* Al_2O_3, Tl_2O_3, Tl_2O?

Sol. Al_2O_3. Acidity decreases as we move down the group and with lowering in oxidation state. Tl_2O is most basic.

2. Hydrides

Hydrogen may accept an electron to form hydride ion.

$$H(g) + e^- \longrightarrow H^-(g)$$

This tendency of the hydrogen to form the negative ion is much lower than halogens. For example,

$$\frac{1}{2}H_2(g) \longrightarrow H(g); \qquad \Delta H = 218 \text{ kJ mol}^{-1}$$

$$H(g) + e^- \longrightarrow H^-(g); \qquad \Delta H = -67 \text{ kJ mol}^{-1}$$

The overall reaction is

$$\frac{1}{2}H_2(g) + e^- \longrightarrow H^-(g); \ \Delta H = +151 \text{ kJ mol}^{-1}$$

$$\frac{1}{2}Br_2(g) + e^- \longrightarrow Br^-(g);$$
$$\Delta H = -232 \text{ kJ mol}^{-1}]$$

Therefore, owing to the endothermic character of the H^- ion, only the most electropositive metals form ionic hydrides. Other elements of the main group generally from covalent hydrides. Classification of main group hydrides is given in Table 1.11.

(i) Ionic hydrides

These hydrides are formed by the most electropositive (Groups I and II) elements with the exception of Be and Mg. They are also known as **saline** or **salt-like hydrides**. The ionic nature of these compounds is shown by their high conductance at their melting points and also by the observation that on electrolysis of their melts, hydrogen is liberated at the anode.

Ionic hydrides are prepared by direct reaction between metal and H_2 at 300° to 700°C. The rates are in the order Li > Cs > K > Na.

Ionic hydrides are crystalline solids, while when pure they react spontaneously with water and acids according to the reaction.

$$MH + H^+ \longrightarrow M^+ + H_2$$

The standard potential for H_2/H^- couple is about – 2.25 V, showing that H^- is a powerful reducing agent.

	LiH		
NaCl type Structure	NaH	MgH_2	Rutile structure
	KH	CaH_2	
	RbH	SrH_2	Slightly distorted hcp
	CsH	BaH_2	

BeH_2 and MgH_2 can be prepared by the thermal decomposition of $Be(CMe_3)_2$ and $MgEt_2$, respectively. BeH_2 has a polymeric structure with bridging hydrogen atoms (as in boranes).

Table 1.11 **Some Hydrides of Main Group Elements**

1	2	13	14	15	16	17
		Covalent hydrides				
LiH	$(BeH_2)_n$	B_2H_6	CH_4	NH_3	H_2O	HF
NaH	MgH_2	$(AlH_3)_4$	SiH_4	PH_3	H_2S	HCl
KH	CaH_2	Ga_2H_6	GeH_4	AsH_3	H_2Se	HBr
RbH	SrH_2	*In	SnH_4	SbH_3	H_2Te	HI
CsH	BaH_2	*Tl	PbH_4	BiH_3	H_2Po	–

Ionic hydrides — Change from basic to acidic character — Increasing acidity (down the groups)

Ionic hydrides are strongly basic in nature and along a given period the hydrides becomes increasingly acidic as the atomic number increases. The acid strength of the hydrides increases from left to right and from top to bottom. Two factors may be important in determining the acid strength of non-metal hydrides :

(i) the electronegativity of the non-metal, *i.e.*, the polarity of the *X*–H bond. (where, *X* = non-metal)

(ii) strength of the *X*–H bond (say its bond energy).

In the series CH_4, NH_3, H_2O, HF, the *X*–H bond becomes more polar because of the increasing electronegativity of *X* in moving from C to F. This means that the hydrogen atom acquires an increasing partial positive charge and therefore it becomes easier to ionise as a proton (H^+). We can similarly explain the increase in acidity in moving from SiH_4 to HCl (via PH_3 and H_2S) due to increasing electronegativity of *X*. Both CH_4 and SiH_4 do not behave as acids in water because the C—H and Si—H bonds have very little polarity.

In going down a group, the acidity of the hydrides increases. This can be explained in terms of the decreasing bond energies of the *X*—H bonds. As the size of *X* increases, the bond electron density is at a greater distance from the nuclei that it is holding and so the bond becomes weaker. Thus, it becomes easier to break the *X*—H bond and the acid strength increases. Thus, **HI is the strongest acid among the HF, HCl and HBr compounds.**

The base strengths of the hydrides vary in just the opposite manner. Their basicity decreases from left to right. Basicity depends on the availability of an unshared electron pair to which a proton can be added. Both CH_4 and SiH_4 do not have an unshared electron pair so they do not behave as bases. From NH_3 to HF, the electronegativity of *X* increases which causes the unshared electron pair to be held more strongly and thus makes them less available for sharing with a proton. Therefore, the base strength decreases; NH_3 is a base water is a much weaker base and HF does not behave as a base. With increased size of the atom *X*, the unshared pair becomes larger and less localized. It, therefore, attracts a proton less strongly than a smaller and more concentrated unshared pair. Thus, PH_3 is a much weaker base than NH_3. Similarly, water is a much weaker base and H_2S has no basic properties in water.

Example 11. *Oxygen atom in H_2O has two lone pairs whereas nitrogen in NH_3 has only one unshared electron pair but still NH_3 is a stronger base than H_2O. Explain.*

Sol. Base strength does not depend on the number of unshared pairs but depends on the availability of the unshared pair for sharing with a proton. Although H_2O contains two unshared pairs of electrons, it accepts only one proton to give the H_3O^+ ion. The positive charge thus created attracts the remaining unshared pair and makes it much less available for sharing with another proton. Thus, the H_4O^{2+} ion has never been observed.

3. Halides

Most of the elements (except He, Ne and Ar) react with halogens to form halides. The order of reactivity of the halogens decreases as we descend from fluorine to iodine. The nature of bonding in halides depends on :

(a) nature of the halogen atom, and

(b) nature of the second element.

(a) Nature of the halogen

Many metals exhibit their highest oxidation state in the fluorides. They are generally ionic compounds. The corresponding chlorides are covalent in nature. The degree of covalence increases further in compounds of bromine and iodine (the same conclusions can be predicted by Fajan's rules).

(b) Nature of the second element

The choice of the second element plays an important role in determining the nature of bonding in halides.

(i) Ionic lattices containing X^- ions are formed by electropositive metals such as *s*-block elements. In case of ionic halides, the solubility decreases in the order.

iodide > bromide > chloride > fluoride

Solubility is governed by lattice energy which also increases in the same order (as the ionic radii of X^- decreases).

(ii) Covalent lattices or complex ions are readily formed by electropositive metals of *p*-block elements. Amongst the covalent halides, the order of solubility varies as :

chloride > bromide > iodide

This may be explained in terms of increasing covalent character due to increased polarization as size of the X^- ion increases.

(iii) Molecular halides are formed by non-metallic elements including hydrogen. They are usually volatile. They do not volatilize if present in polymeric form. For example, Teflon $(—CF_2—)_n$ is non-volatile. Similarly, $AlCl_3$ and SnF_4 which are molecular in the gas phase but due to the tendency of the metal atom to have a higher coordination number (4 and 6, respectively for Al and Sn in these examples), the solids acquire extended structures.

Because of the high electronegativity of fluorine, most molecular fluorides are polar in nature. **Because of the low dissociation energy of F_2 and the relatively high energy of bonds with fluorine (C–F 486 kJ mol^{-1}), molecular fluorides are formed exothermally.** The high electronegativity of fluorine has strong influence on the properties of molecules containing fluorine. For example,

$CH_3COOH \longrightarrow$ Weak acid

$(CH_3)_3N \longrightarrow$ Basic and pyramidal

$CF_3COOH \longrightarrow$ strong acid

$(CF_3)_3N \longrightarrow$ Non-basic and planar

NH_3 Basic

NF_3 Non-basic

Reactivity

Properties of a molecular halide depend on the elements involved. However, one general property is their easy hydrolysis.

For example,

$$BCl_3 + 3H_2O \longrightarrow B(OH)_3 + 3HCl$$

$$PCl_3 + 3H_2O \longrightarrow H_3PO_3 + 3HCl$$

$$SiCl_4 + 4H_2O \longrightarrow Si(OH)_4 + 4HCl$$

When the central atom has its maximum stable coordination number, as in CCl_4 or SF_6, the compound is unreactive and is not hydrolysed by water.

The oxidation state of metal ion also influences the bonding in metal halides. For example, higher the oxidation state of the metal ion, smaller will be its radius and this in turn will favour covalent bonding. By similar analogy, lower oxidation state shall favour ionic bonding. Thus, $PbCl_4$ is covalent while $PbCl_2$ is ionic.

From this discussion it may be concluded that along a period ionic character of the halides decreases while covalent character increases. However, as we move down a group the degree of ionic character in halides increases.

Example 12. *Which is more reducing :* $SnCl_2$, $PbCl_2$?

Sol. $SnCl_2$, because $PbCl_2$ is more stable and is thus a weaker reducing agent.

4. Oxo-acids

Phosphorous acid, phosphoric acid, sulphuric acid, perchloric acid are members of an important class of compounds called oxo-acids. Oxo-acids contain one or more OH groups attached to an electronegative atom, *X*. They have the general formula $XO_m(OH)_n$, where

GROUPS						
1	2	13	14	15	16	17
NaOH	$Mg(OH)_2$	$Al(OH)_3$	$Si(OH)_4$	$P(OH)_5$ $-H_2O$	$S(OH)_6$ $-2H_2O$	$Cl(OH)_7$ $-3H_2O$
Na^+OH^-	$Mg^{2+}(OH)_2^-$	$Al(OH)_3$	$Si(OH)_4$	O=P(OH)$_3$	O=S(OH)$_2$ ‖ O	O ‖ O=Cl—OH ‖ O
Strong base	Strong base	Amphoteric ←	Weak acid	Weak acid	Strong acid →	Strong acid
					Acid strength increases	

$m = 0, 1, 2 \ldots$ and $n = 1, 2, 3 \ldots$ For example, H_2SO_4 may be written as $SO_2(OH)_2$, $m = 2$ and $n = 2$ and phosphoric acid, H_3PO_4 can be written as $PO(OH)_3$, where $m = 1$ and $n = 3$, nitric acid, HNO_3 or $NO_2(OH)$, where $m = 2$ and $n = 1$.

Compounds of elements of groups 1 and 2 containing OH groups are ionic hydroxides, Na^+OH^-, $Mg^{2+}(OH^-)_2$ and are therefore strong bases.

How do we know then that a compound containing OH groups is going to behave as an acid or a base?

If the atom X in XOH has a low electronegativity, the X—O bond is polar with the oxygen atom having a negative charge and X a positive charge :

$$\overset{\delta+}{X}—\overset{\delta-}{O}—H$$

When this is the case as in NaOH or $Mg(OH)_2$, X—O—H ionizes to give X^+ and OH^-.

When X has a high electronegativity, X—O bond is less polar and so XOH has a decreased tendency to ionize as X^+ and OH^-. The O–H bond becomes polar.

$$X—\overset{\delta-}{O}—\overset{\delta+}{H}$$

There is an increased tendency for the hydrogen to be donated as a proton to give XO^- and H^+. Therefore, acid strength increases with increasing electronegativity of X (and base strength decreases).

The oxo-acids often do not carry the same number of hydroxyl groups that would be expected from their valencies. Instead pairs of OH groups are replaced by doubly bonded oxygen (=O). For example,

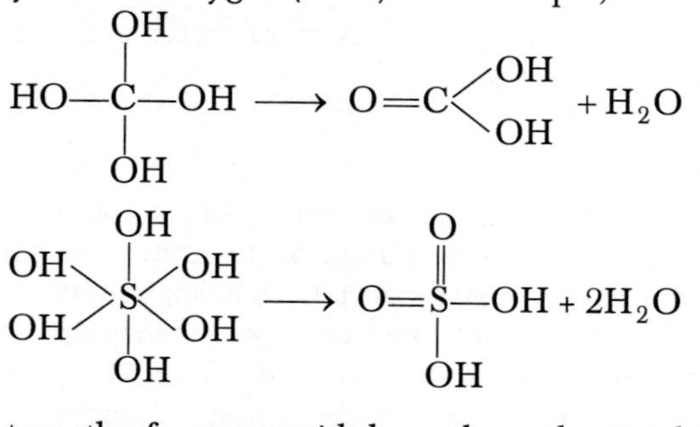

The strength of an oxo-acid depends on the number of double bonded oxygen atoms, *i.e.,* on the value of m. **The larger the value of m or the number of doubly bonded oxygen atoms, the stronger is the acid.** Each oxygen atom attracts electrons away from the central atom X which in turn attracts electrons away from the O—H groups. This increases the polarity of the O—H bonds and thus increasing the strength of the acid. In general if $m = 0$ or 1, we observe that the acid is weak and if $m = 2$ or 3, the acid is strong.

This correlation of acid strength with number of doubly bonded oxygen atoms further suggests that acid strength increases with increasing oxidation state of the central atom, X. Sulphurous acid, H_2SO_3 (S = + 4) is a weak acid, while sulphuric acid H_2SO_4 (S = + 6) is a strong acid.

Example 13. *Classify the following oxo-acids as either weak or strong :*

H_2SO_3, H_5IO_6, H_2SeO_4, HOCl, $HClO_3$

Sol. H_2SO_3 (weak), H_5IO_6 (weak), H_2SeO_4 (strong), HOCl (weak), $HClO_3$ (strong).

Some Special Characteristics of *p*-Block (Main-Group) Elements

Among the *p*-block elements, the first element in each group differs from the other members in two major respects :

(a) small size and (b) lack of *d*-orbitals.

Size of Atoms

Distinctive properties of second row elements are their small atomic size and high electronegativity values. Both these properties can be attributed to the small number of inner shell electrons, only two ($1s^2$), so that the second row valence electrons are strongly bound. Their small size favours covalent character in their compounds, more so as we move towards the right with increase in Z. **From carbon onwards the small atomic size favours strong single and multiple bonding because of good orbital overlap at close approach between the bonding atoms.** Later in the row, beginning with nitrogen and onwards, although multiple bonding is still favoured (because of good $p\pi$ overlap), single bonds are greatly weakened when lone pairs are present because of the strong repulsion at close approach (*e.g.,* weakly bonded nature of H_2O_2 and F_2 in contrast to the strongly bonded nature of elemental boron and diamond).

A unique property of the second row elements (say C, N, O, F) is their strong tendency to form double and triple bonds. This may be attributed to :

1. high electronegativities of these elements; and
2. strong repulsion between the electron pairs in their valence shells.

These elements can hold two or more electron pairs in the bonding region. A double bond occupies less space than two single bonds. Therefore, these elements can minimize electron pair repulsions in their valency shells by forming multiple bonds.

For example, carbonic acid is $(OH)_2$ C═O but silicic acid is $Si(OH)_4$; carbon dioxide (O═C═O) is a volatile monomeric gas while silica (SiO_2) is a polymeric solid containing single bonds between silicon and oxygen. We may further note that oxygen (O═O) and nitrogen (N≡N) gases exist as diatomic molecules whereas heavier members in their groups, form S_8 and P_4 molecules. **In the third row, *pπ*-bonding is less favourable, because of poorer *pπ* overlap for the larger atoms**. Single bond formation is favoured relative to multiple bonding, as in comparison of N_2 or NO with P_4 or P_4O_{10}.

Absence or Presence of *d*-Orbital

First row elements of the *p*-block lack *d*-orbital in their valence shell while heavier elements in each group have *d*-orbitals. The presence of these orbitals affects the chemistry of the heavier elements in a number of ways :

(i) Coordination number

The valence shell configuration of the first row elements of *p*-block elements is $2s^2 2p^n$ and the next available orbital is 3*s* which is separated from 2*p* energy level by a very large energy gap and is therefore not available for bonding. This means that the maximum number of electron pairs is four. The first row elements can thus have a maximum coordination number of four (by using one 2*s* and three 2*p* orbitals). By contrast the elements of the next period (configuration $3s^2 3p^n$) can make 3*d* orbitals available which are only slightly higher in energy than the 3*p* orbitals*. These elements can use empty *d*-orbitals to increase their coordination number. The expenditure of energy in promoting one of the valence electrons to the easily available *d*-orbitals is so modest that the energy released on the formation of two additional bonds will more than that compensate for it. For example, boron forms BF_4^- while aluminium can form AlF_6^{3-} ion.

(ii) Reactivity differences

Due to the availability of *d*-orbitals, elements of the third period are more reactive than those of the second period. For example, CCl_4 does not interact with water while $SiCl_4$ is highly susceptible to attack by water.

(iii) Strength of the homonuclear single bonds

The bond energies of diatomic molecules of first row elements are distinctly low as compared to diatomic molecules of second row elements. For example, bond dissociation energy of F_2 is 155 kJ mol^{-1} and that of Cl_2 is 243 kJ mol^{-1}. The low values of F—F, O—O and N—N may be due to the greater repulsion among the non-bonding electrons of these small molecules. The repulsion term for molecules of second and subsequent rows is not very significant due to their large size. These elements make use of available *d*-orbitals in bonding and reduce any repulsion due to non-bonding electrons.

dπ-*pπ* Bonding

The heavier members among the *p*-block elements exhibit multiple bonding by involving *d*-orbitals. For example, 3*d* orbitals are involved in *dπ*-*pπ* multiple bonding between sulphur and oxygen in SO_2 and SO_3.

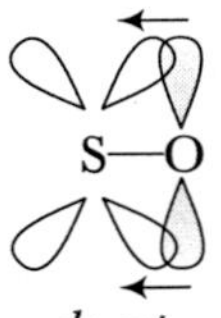

dπ–*πp*

Similarly, we can explain the formation of double bond in Cl_2S═O and Cl_2Se═O in terms of *dπ*-*pπ* bonding. Participation of *d*-orbitals in bonding among compounds of the second period elements leads to the delocalization of the lone pair of N or O in their compounds. For example, delocalization of lone pair into a back-bonding *π* orbital of the silicon atom makes trisilylamine planar and silyl isothoicyanate linear. This also leads to lowered basicity among silyl compounds.

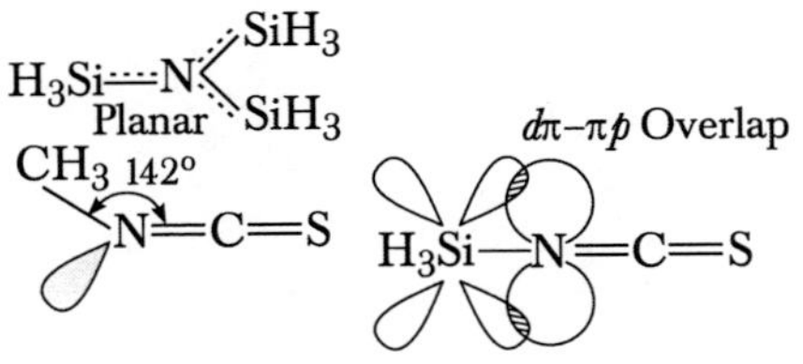

Diagonal Relationship

One of the important features of the elements of the second period of the Periodic Table is that they resemble with the element to their lower right in the third period (*i.e.,* diagonally opposite element) more than their own congeners. The diagonal relationship is best illustrated by the following pairs of elements of the Periodic Table

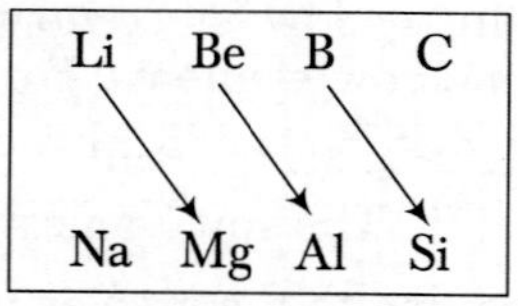

The reasons for similarity between the diagonally opposite members are :

(a) The electropositive nature of the elements increases on descending a group but decreases as we move from left to right. Consequently, the electropositive nature of two diagonally opposite elements will be very similar.

(b) On moving from left to right, charge on the ions increases but their size decreases which causes an increase in the polarizing power of the ions. On moving down a group, size increases and polarizing power decreases. However, on moving diagonally these two effects partly cancel each other and there are a few similarities in the bahaviour of the elements.

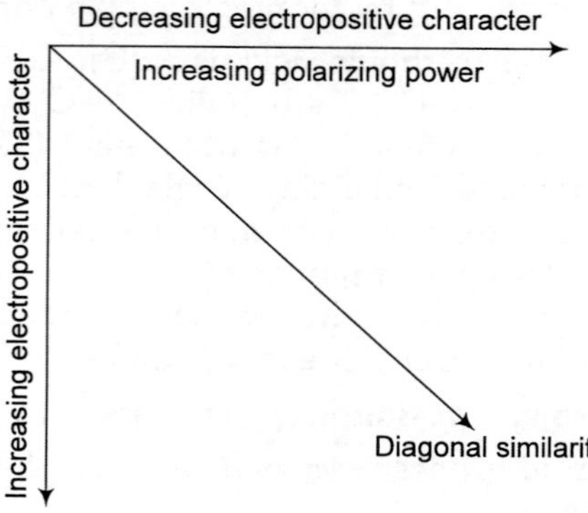

It is interesting to note that inspite of different valencies of the elements, the type and strength of the bond formed and the properties of their compounds are often very similar.

Among *p*-block elements striking diagonal similarity is only observed between boron and silicon. Other elements of the *p*-block show very feeble diagonal similarity and therefore are excluded from our discussion.

Exercise 1
(For Part 'B')

1. Higher values of ionization energies of the $5d$ transition elements are consistent with the
(a) relatively smaller penetration
(b) relatively smaller size of their atoms
(c) relatively smaller effective nuclear charge
(d) All the above are correct

2. Select the correct statement.
(a) $(IE)_1$ of the corresponding elements of $3d$ and $4d$-series are almost similar
(b) $(IE)_1$ of $5d$-series elements are smaller than that of $3d$ and $4d$-series elements
(c) Both (a) and (b) are correct
(d) Both (a) and (b) are incorrect

3. The dominant factor in determining the IE of the elements on moving down the groups is its
(a) atomic radius
(b) effective nuclear charge
(c) Both (a) and (b)
(d) None of the above

4. IE of an element does not depend on
(a) its nuclear charge (b) penetration effect
(c) the shielding effect (d) electron neutrality

5. Which element has the highest first IE?
(a) H (b) He
(c) N (d) Ne

6. Which represents alkali metals based on $(IE)_1$ and $(IE)_2$ values?

		$(IE)_1$	$(IE)_2$
(a)	X	100	110
(b)	Y	95	120
(c)	Z	195	500
(d)	M	200	250

7. Which pair represents incorrect first (IE)?
(a) $Li > Na$ (b) $Be > B$
(c) $N > O$ (d) $He > He^+$

8. Which has maximum IE?
(a) Mg (b) Mg^+
(c) Mg^{2+} (d) Equal

9. SI unit of IE is
(a) J mol^{-1} (b) kJ mol^{-1}
(c) kcal mol^{-1} (d) eV $atom^{-1}$

10. The second ionization energy is always higher than the first ionization energy because the
(a) electron is attracted more by the core electrons
(b) electron is more tightly bound to the nucleous in an ion
(c) ion becomes more stable attaining an octet or duplet configurations
(d) None of the above is the correct explanation

11. Select the incorrect order of size of ions/atoms.
(a) Fe=Co=Ni (b) $I^+ < I < I^-$
(c) Ni < Cu < Zn (d) None is incorrect

12. Select the correct statement(s).
(a) Across a transition series, there is only a small decrease in atomic radius from one element to another due to very small increase in effective nuclear charge.
(b) The rate of decrease in the size across the lanthanide series is less than the across the first transition series.
(c) Both (a) and (b) are correct statements
(d) None of the above statement is correct

13. Select the correct statement about radius of an atom.
(a) The metallic radii are smaller than the van der Waals' radii, since the bonding forces inthe metallic crystal lattice are much stronger than the van der Waals' forces
(b) Values of van der Waals' radii are larger than those of covalent radii because the van der Waals' forces are much weaker than the forces operating between atoms in covalently bonding molecule
(c) Both (a) and (b) are correct
(d) None of the above is correct

14. In which case bond length is shortened?
(a) When electronegativities are different
(b) When multiplicity occurs between atoms
(c) In both cases
(d) In none of the cases

15. Covalent radius of nitrogen is 70 pm. Hence, covalent radius of boron is about
(a) 40 pm (b) 50 pm
(c) 60 pm (d) 110 pm

16. Which one of the following has the smallest atomic radius?
(a) F (b) Cl
(c) Mg (d) Cs

17. State, which one of the following has the largest atomic radius?
(a) Ba (b) Mg
(c) Cr (d) Cs

18. For Cu, effective nuclear charge felt by a $4s$-electron is
(a) 1.0 (b) 1.65
(c) 2.2 (d) 2.95

19. Element unq has atomic number
(a) 102 (b) 103
(c) 104 (d) 112

20. In which case effective nuclear charge is minimum?
(a) Be (b) Be^{2+}
(c) Be^{3+} (d) In all cases

21. Screening effect is not observed in
(a) He^+ (b) Li^{2+}
(c) Be^{3+} (d) In all cases

22. The relative extent to which the various orbitals penetrate the electron clouds of other orbitals is
(a) $s > p > d > f$ (b) $s < p < d < f$
(c) $s > p > f > d$ (d) $d < s < f < p$

23. Element with atomic number 113 has been reported in August 2003. Its electronic configuration is similar to that of
(a) Si (b) Bi (c) Ga (d) At

24. The atoms of the elements belonging to the same group of the Periodic Table will have
(a) the same number of electrons in the valence-shell
(b) the same number of electrons
(c) the same number of protons
(d) the same number of neutrons

25. Recently discovered element with atomic number 115 is
(a) Uub (b) Uun
(c) Uup (d) Uus

26. Which group of elements is analogous to the lanthanides?
(a) Actinides (b) Halides
(c) Borides (d) Chalcogenides

27. Which of the following has the electronic configuration [Ar] $3d^5$?
(a) Mn (b) Cr
(c) V (d) Fe^{3+}

28. Of the following pairs, the one containing examples of metalloid elements in the Periodic Table is
(a) Na and K (b) B and Si
(c) F and Cl (d) Cu and Ag

29. M^{3+} has electronic configuration as [Ar] $3d^{10}$, hence it lies in
(a) *s*-block (b) *p*-block
(c) *d*-block (d) *f*-block

30. Recently discovered elements (August 2003) with atomic number 113 and 115 have valence electrons in
(a) *s*-orbital (b) *p*-orbital
(c) *d*-orbital (d) *f*-orbital

31. Main group elements constitute
(a) *s*-and *p*-block (b) *p*- and *d*-block
(c) *s*-and *d*-block (d) *d*-and *f*-block

32. Element with atomic number 115 has configuration as .... and with most stable cation as ....
(a) [Rn] $7s^2\ 5d^{10}\ 4f^{14}\ 7p^3\ M^{3+}$
(b) [Rn] $7s^2\ 5d^{10}\ 4f^{14}\ 7p^3\ M^{+}$
(c) [Rn] $7s^2\ 5d^{10}\ 4f^{14}\ 7p^3\ M^{5+}$
(d) [Rn] $5d^{10}\ 4f^{14}\ 7p^5\ M^{5+}$

33. Most stable cation of element 113 will be
(a) M^+ (b) M^{2+}
(c) M^{3+} (d) M^{5+}

34. Numbering of groups as 1, 2, ... 18 was adopted by IUPAC in
(a) 1906 (b) 1908 (c) 1986 (d) 1988

35. Element 113 is produced *via*
(a) α-decay of element-115
(b) α-decay of element-111
(c) β-decay of element-112
(d) β-decay of element-114

36. Recently (in August 2003) two new elements have been discovered with atomic numbers
(a) 113, 114 (b) 113, 115
(c) 114, 115 (d) 115, 116

37. Recently (in 2003) element with atomic number 110 has been named by IUPAC as
(a) Mt (b) Sg (c) Hs (d) Ds

38. First long period contains .... elements.
(a) 2 (b) 8 (c) 18 (d) 32

39. The correct decreasing order of ionic radius is
(a) $F^- > O^{2-} > N^{3-} > C^{4-}$ (b) $N^{3-} > O^{2-} > F^- > C^{4-}$
(c) $C^{4-} > N^{3-} > O^{2-} > F^-$ (d) $O^{2-} > F^- > C^{4-} > N^{3-}$

40. Sodium forms Na^+ ion but it does not form Na^{2+} because
(a) low value of $(IE)_1$ and high value of $(IE)_2$
(b) low value of $(IE)_1$ and low value of $(IE)_2$
(c) very low value of $(IE)_1$ and $(IE)_2$
(d) very high value of (IE_1) and $(IE)_2$

41. Ionic radii are
(a) inversely proportional to effective nuclear charge
(b) directly proportional to effective nuclear charge
(c) inversely proportional to square of effective nuclear charge
(d) directly proportional to square of effective nuclear charge

42. The ions $O^{2-}, F^-, Na^+, Mg^{2+}$ and Al^{3+} are isoelectronic. Their ionic radii show
(a) a significant decrease from O^{2-} to Al^{3+}
(b) a significant increase from O^{2-} to Al^{3+}
(c) a decrease from O^{2-} to F^- and then increase from Na^+ to Al^{3+}
(d) an increase from O^{2-} to F^- and then decrease from Na^+ to Al^{3+}

43. Which of the following order is wrong?
(a) $Li^{2+} < Na^{+} < K^{+} < Cs^{+}$–Ionic radius
(b) $NH_3 < PH_3 < AsH_3$–Acidic
(c) $Al_2O_3 < MgO < Na_2O < K_2O$–Basic
(d) $Li < Be < B < C$–$(IE)_1$

44. Which of the following does not represent the correct order of the properties indicated?
(a) $Sc > Ti > Cr > Mn$ (size)
(b) $Ni^{2+} > Cr^{2+} > Fe^{2+} > Mn^{2+}$ (size)
(c) $Ni^{2+} < Co^{2+} < Fe^{2+} < Mn^{2+}$ (unpaired electrons)
(d) $Fe^{2+} > Co^{2+} > Ni^{2+} > Cu^{2+}$ (unpaired electrons)

45. The heat of hydration of Ca^{2+}, Sr^{2+} and Ba^{2+} in the decreasing order is
(a) $Sr^{2+} > Ba^{2+} > Ca^{2+}$
(b) $Ba^{2+} > Sr^{2+} > Ca^{2+}$
(c) $Ca^{2+} > Ba^{2+} > Sr^{2+}$
(d) $Ca^{2+} > Sr^{2+} > Ba^{2+}$

46. The highest first ionization energy of the following elements is that of
(a) Li
(b) Cl
(c) I
(d) Cs

47. The most electron affinity of the following elements is that of
(a) Li
(b) Ba
(c) Br
(d) Sn

48. The most metallic of the following element is
(a) Li
(b) Mg
(c) K
(d) Ca

49. Which of the following properties shows a clear periodic variation?
(a) First ionization energy
(b) Molar mass of the element
(c) Number of isotopes of the atom
(d) All of the above

50. The non-metallic cation is in
(a) PCl_3
(b) VOCl
(c) NH_4Cl
(d) CrO_2Cl_2

51. The first ionization potential of Al is smaller than that of Mg because
(a) the atomic size of Al < Mg
(b) the atomic size of Al > Mg
(c) the atomic number of Al > Mg
(d) Al has one unpaired electron in *p*-orbital

52. Consider the isoelectronic ions

$$K^{+}, S^{2-}, Cl^{-} \text{ and } Ca^{2+}$$

The radii of these ionic species follow the order
(a) $Cl^{-} > S^{2-} > K^{-} > Ca^{2+}$
(b) $K^{+} > Ca^{2+} > S^{2-} > Cl^{-}$
(c) $S^{2-} > Cl^{-} > K^{+} > Ca^{2+}$
(d) $Ca^{2+} > K^{+} > Cl^{-} > S^{2-}$

53. Which set has all the coloured ions?
(a) Na^{+}, Mg^{2+}, Al^{3+}
(b) Cu^{+}, Cu^{2+}, Ni^{2+}
(c) $Cu^{2+}, Fe^{2+}, Co^{2+}$
(d) $Cu^{2+}, Co^{2+}, Sc^{3+}$

54. The metal which gives no amphoteric oxide is
(a) Al
(b) Cu
(c) Zn
(d) Sn

55. Stability order of group IIIA (boron family) element is
(a) $Ga^{3+} > Ga^{+}$
(b) $Ga^{+} < In^{+} < Tl^{+}$
(c) Both (a) and (b)
(d) None of these

56. EN of the element (A) is E_1 and IP is E_2. Hence, EA will be
(a) $2E_1 - E_2$
(b) $E_1 - 2E_2$
(c) $E_1 - E_2$
(d) $\frac{E_1 - E_2}{2}$

57. AB is predominantly ionic as $A^{+}B^{-}$ if
(a) $(IP)_A < (IP)_B$
(b) $(IP)_B < (IP)_A$
(c) $(EN)_A < (EN)_B$
(d) $(EA)_A < (EA)_B$

58. Following graph shows variation of ionization potential (IP) with atomic number in second period (Li–Ne). Value of ionization potential (IP) of Na(11) will be

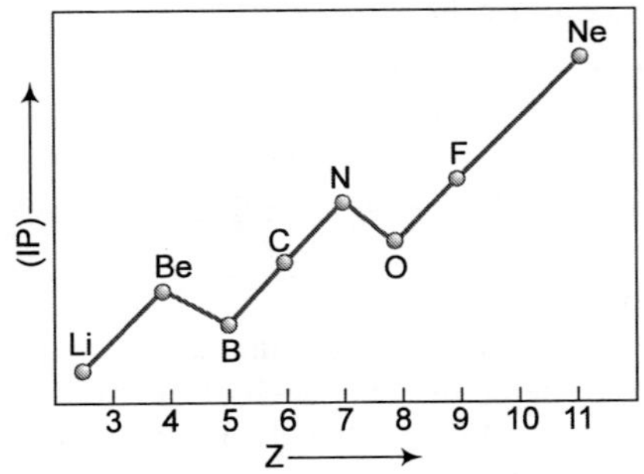

(a) below Li
(b) above Ne
(c) between N and O
(d) below Ne and above O

59. Which of the following statement is false?
(a) Elements of IA and IIA groups are normal elements
(b) Elements of IB and IIB groups are transition elements
(c) Elements of VB group do not contain metalloid
(d) Elements of IVB group are neither strongly electronegative nor strongly electropositive

60. The statement is not true for the long form of the Periodic Table.
(a) It helps to predict the stable valency state of the elements
(b) It reflects trends in physical and chemical properties of the elements
(c) It reflects the sequence of filling the electrons in the order of the sub-energy shells *s*, *p*, *d* and *f*
(d) It helps to predict the relative ionicity of the bond between any two elements

61. The statement that is not correct for the periodic classification of elements is
(a) the first ionization energies of elements along a period do not vary in a regular manner with increase in atomic number
(b) the properties of elements are the periodic functions of their atomic numbers
(c) for transition elements the d-sub-shells are filled with electrons monotonically with increase in atomic number
(d) non-metallic elements are lesser in number than metallic elements

62. The element which does not exist in liquid state at room temperature are
(a) Na (b) Ga
(c) Br (d) Hg

63. The factors that influence the ionization energies are
(a) the size of the atom
(b) the charge on the nucleus
(c) how effectively the inner electron shell screen the nuclear charge
(d) All of the above

64. The sizes of the second and third row transition elements being almost the same. This is due to
(a) d- and f-orbitals do not shield the nuclear charge very effectively
(b) lanthanide contraction
(c) Both (a) and (b) are true
(d) None of the above is true

65. Size of cation is smaller than that of the atom because of
(a) gain of electrons
(b) effective nuclear charge increases
(c) the whole of the outer shell of electrons is removed
(d) statement, that cation is smaller than atom, is wrong

66. Going down in a group from F to I, which of the following properties decreases?
(a) Ionic radius (b) Electronegativity
(c) Ionization energy (d) Oxidising power

67. (A), (B), (C) are elements in the third short period. Oxide of (A) is ionic, that of (B) is amphoteric and of (C) a giant molecule. (A), (B) and (C) will have atomic number in the order
(a) $(A) < (B) < (C)$ (b) $(C) < (B) < (A)$
(c) $(B) < (C) < (A)$ (d) $(C) < (A) < (B)$

68. Fluorine has the highest electronegativity among the $ns^2 np^5$ group on the Pauling scale, but the electron affinity of fluorine is less than that of chlorine because
(a) fluorine being the first member of the family behaves in an unusual manner
(b) the atomic number of fluorine is less than that of chlorine
(c) chlorine can accommodate an electron better than fluorine by utilising its vacant $3d$-orbital
(d) small size, high electron density and an increased electron repulsion makes addition of an electron to fluorine less favourable than that in the case of chlorine

69. The electronegativities of N, C, Si and P are such that
(a) Si < P < C < N (b) N < C < P < Si
(c) C < N < P < Si (d) P < N < Si < C

70. Which is correct order of size of O^-, O^{2-}, F^- and F?
(a) $O^{2-} > O^- > F^- > F$ (b) $F > F^- > O^- > O^{2-}$
(c) $O^- > O^{2-} > F > F^-$ (d) $F^- > F > O^- > O^{2-}$

71. Which is/are amphoteric oxides?
(a) BeO (b) ZnO
(c) SnO (d) All of these

72. Melting points of NaCl, NaBr, NaI and NaF will be in order
(a) NaCl < NaI < NaF < NaBr
(b) NaBr < NaF < NaCl < NaI
(c) NaI < NaBr < NaCl < NaF
(d) NaF < NaCl < NaBr < NaI

73. Catenation properties of C, Si, Ge, Sn and Pb are in order
(a) C > Si > Ge ≈ Sn > Pb
(b) C > Si > Sn > Ge > Pb
(c) C < Si < Ge < Sn < Pb
(d) None of the above

74. The first element of a group in many ways differ from the other heavier members of the group. This is due to
(a) the small size
(b) the unavailability of d-orbitals
(c) the high electronegativity and high ionization potential
(d) All of the above

75. Which is incorrect statement?
(a) Ga^+ salts are better reducing agents
(b) Tl^{3+} salts are better oxidising agents
(c) Pb^{4+} salts are better oxidising agents
(d) As^{5+} salts are better oxidising agents

76. Stability of ions of Ge, Sn and Pb will be in order
(a) $Sn^{4+} > Sn^{2+}$ (b) $Ge^{2+} < Sn^{2+} < Pb^{2+}$
(c) $Ge^{4+} > Sn^{4+} > Pb^{4+}$ (d) All are correct

77. Inert pair effect is shown by
(a) s-block (b) p-block
(c) d-block (d) f-block

78. Which pair is different from the others?
(a) Li–Na (b) Li–Mg
(c) B–Si (d) Be–Al

79. Which pair is different from the others?
(a) Li–Mg (b) Na–K (c) B–Al (d) Ca–Mg

80. Which of the following anions is most easily polarized?
(a) Cl^- (b) Br^- (c) Se^{2-} (d) Te^{2-}

81. Which of the following ions has the largest heat of hydration?
(a) F^- (b) Na^+ (c) Al^{3+} (d) Sr^{2+}

82. For which of the following crystals would you expect the assumption of anion-anion contact to be valid?
(a) KCl (b) NaF (c) NaI (d) CsBr

83. When the following five anions are arranged in order of decreasing ionic radius, the correct sequence is
(a) $I^-, Se^{2-}, O^{2-}, Br^-, F^-$ (b) $I^-, Se^{2-}, Br^-, O^{2-}, F^-$
(c) $Se^{2-}, I^-, Br^-, F^-, O^{2-}$ (d) $Se^{2-}, I^-, Br^-, O^{2-}, F^-$

84. Which of the following ions has the smallest radius?
(a) Ni^{2+} (b) Ti^{2+}
(c) Pt^{2+} (d) Zr^{2+}

85. Following triads have approximately equal size
(a) F^-, Ne, O^{2-} (iso-electronic)
(b) Fe, Co, Ni
(c) Na^+, Mg^{2+}, Al^{3+} (iso-electronic)
(d) Mn^+, Fe^{2+}, Cr (iso-electronic)

86. Electron affinity is positive when
(a) O^+ is formed from O
(b) O^- is formed from O
(c) O^{2-} is formed from O^-
(d) electron affinity is always a negative value

87. Which has maximum polarising power in action?
(a) Li^+ (b) Mg^{2+}
(c) Al^{3+} (d) O^{2-}

Exercise 2
(For Part 'C')

1. For the process,

$$X(g) + e^- \longrightarrow X^-(g), \qquad \Delta H = x$$

and $$X^-(g) \longrightarrow X(g) + e^-, \qquad \Delta H = y$$

Select the correct alternate,
(a) Electron affinity of $X(g)$ is x
(b) Electron affinity of $X(g)$ is $-y$
(c) Ionization energy of $X^-(g)$ is y
(d) All of the above are correct statements

2. Ionization energy of the element $X(g)$ is I and the electron affinity of $X^+(g)$ is E then
(a) $I = E$ (b) $I = -E$
(c) $I = \frac{E}{2}$ (d) $I = -\frac{E}{2}$

3. Gd(64) has .... unpaired electrons with sum of spin ....
(a) 6, 3 (b) 8, 3
(c) 8, 4 (d) 7, 5

4. Which set shows inert pair effect?
(a) B, Al, Ga (b) Ge, Sn, Pb
(c) Fe, Co, Ni (d) He, Ne, Ar

5. For the element (X), student A measured its radius as 102 nm, student B as 103 nm and C as 100 nm using same apparatus. Their teacher explained that measurements were correct by saying that recorded values by (A), (B) and (C) are
(a) crystal, van der Waals' and covalent radii
(b) van der Waals', crystal and covalent radii
(c) covalent, van der Waals' and crystal radii
(d) None of the above is correct

6. Match Column I (atomic number of the elements)with Column II (position in the Periodic Table) and select the correct answer using the codes given below the columns.

	Column I		Column II
A.	52	1.	s-block
B.	56	2.	p-block
C.	57	3.	d-block
D.	60	4.	f-block

Codes

	A	B	C	D
(a)	1	2	3	4
(b)	4	3	2	1
(c)	2	4	1	3
(d)	2	1	3	4

7. Consider the following statements.
1. Cs^+ is more highly hydrated than the other alkali metal ions.
2. Among the alkali metals Li, Na, K and Rb, lithium has the highest melting point.

3. Among the alkali metals only lithium forms a stable nitride by direct combination of these statements.
(a) 1 and 2 are correct (b) 2 and 3 are correct
(c) 1 and 3 are correct (d) 1, 2 and 3 are correct

8. Atomic radii of F and Ne in Å are given by
(a) 0.72, 1.6 (b) 0.72, 0.72
(c) 1.6, 1.6 (d) None of these

9. The first ionization potential (in eV) of N, O atoms are
(a) 14.6, 13.6 (b) 13.6, 13.6
(c) 13.6, 14.6 (d) 14.6, 14.6

10. The ionic radii of O^{2-}, F^-, Na^+ and Mg^{2+} are 1.35, 1.34, 0.95 and 0.66 Å respectively. The radius of the Ne atom is
(a) 0.50 Å (b) 0.85 Å
(c) 1.12 Å (d) 1.39 Å

11. Following are the value of the electron-affinities of (in kJ mol^{-1}) the formation of O^- and O^{2-} from O
(a) 142, 702 (b) −142, −702
(c) −142, 702 (d) −142, −142

12. Which of the following will have maximum electron affinity?
(a) $1s^2\ 2s^2\ 2p^6\ 3s^2\ 3p^6$
(b) $1s^2\ 2s^2\ 2p^6\ 3s^2\ 3p^5$
(c) $1s^1\ 2s^2\ 2p^6$
(d) $1s^2\ 2s^2\ 2p^5$

13. The electron affinity of N, O, S and Cl are such that
(a) N < O < S < Cl (b) Cl < S < O < N
(c) O < N < Cl < S (d) O ≈ Cl < N ≈ S

14. The correct order of increasing ionic character is
(a) $BeCl_2 < MgCl_2 < CaCl_2 < BaCl_2$
(b) $BaCl_2 < CaCl_2 < MgCl_2 < BeCl_2$
(c) $MgCl_2 < BeCl_2 < BaCl_2 < CaCl_2$
(d) $BaCl_2 < CaCl_2 < BeCl_2 < MgCl_2$

15. Melting point is maximum for
(a) LiCl (b) NaCl
(c) KCl (d) RbCl

16. Ionic radii of
(a) $K^+ > Cl^-$ (b) $P^{3+} > P^{5+}$
(c) $^{35}Cl^- < {}^{37}Cl^-$ (d) $Ti^{4+} < Mn^{7+}$

17. Which is maximum hydrated?
(a) $SiCl_4$ (b) $AlCl_3$
(c) $MgCl_2$ (d) NaCl

18. Which has maximum ionization potential?
(a) N (b) O (c) Na (d) O^+

19. For Be Z_{eff} = 1.95, for B^{x+}, Z_{eff} = 2.30, hence ion is
(a) Be (b) Be^+
(c) Be^{2+} (d) Be^{3+}

20. Stability of ions of Ge, Sn and Pb will be in order
(a) $Sn^{2+} < Sn^{4+}$ (b) $Pb^{4+} < Pb^{2+}$
(c) $Pb^{4+} < Sn^{4+} < Ge^{4+}$ (d) $Ge^{2+} < Sn^{2+} < Pb^{2+}$

21. Which is/are correct order of ionic mobility?
(a) $Li^+ < Na^+ < K^+$ (b) $Al^{3+} < Mg^{2+} < Na^+$
(c) $Na^+ < Mg^{2+} < Al^{3+}$ (d) $K^+ < Na^+ < Li^+$

22. Consider the following ionization steps

$$M(g) \longrightarrow M^+(g) + e^-; \quad \Delta H = 100\text{ eV}$$
$$M(g) \longrightarrow M^{2+}(g) + 2e^-; \quad \Delta H = 250\text{ eV}$$

Select the correct statement(s).
(a) $(IE)_1$ of $M(g)$ is 100 eV
(b) $(IE)_1$ of $M^+(g)$ is 150 eV
(c) $(IE)_2$ of $M(g)$ is 150 eV
(d) $(IE)_2$ of $M(g)$ is 250 eV

Assertion & Reason

Codes
(a) Both A and R are true and R is the correct explanation of A.
(b) Both A and R are true but R is not the correct explanation of A.
(c) A is true but R is false.
(d) A is false but R is true.

23. Assertion (A) Tin exhibits +2 and +4 oxidation states only and not +3 oxidation state.
Reason (R) Inert pair effect of electrons in the *s*-orbital is responsible.

24. Assertion (A) Na^+ and Al^{3+} are isoelectronic but the magnitude of ionic radius of Al^{3+} is less than that of Na^+.
Reason (R) The magnitude of effective nuclear charge of the outershell electrons in Al^{3+} is greater than that in Na^+.

25. Assertion (A) The atomic radii of the elements of the oxygen family are smaller than the atomic radii of the corresponding elements of the nitrogen family.
Reason (R) The members of the oxygen family are more electronegative and thus have lower values of nuclear charge than those of the nitrogen family.

26. Assertion (A) The mobility of sodium ion is lower than that of potassium ion.
Reason (R) The ionic mobilities depend upon the effective radius of the ion.

27. Assertion (A) Ionization energy decreases on moving down the group.
Reason (R) Force of attraction between electrons and nucleus decreases on moving down the group.

28. Assertion (A) Li and Mg show diagonal relationship.
Reason (R) Li and Mg are diagonal to each other in the Periodic Table.

29. **Assertion (A)** Fluorine has a less negative electron affinity than chlorine.
Reason (R) There is relatively greater effectiveness of $2p$-electrons in the small F-atom to repel the additional electron entering the atom than to $3p$-electrons in the larger Cl atom.

Directions (Q. Nos. 30 to 33)

Following rule in general, classifies p-block elements into metals, non-metals and metalloids (where P is the period and N the valence electrons)
$(P+1) > N$, the element would be metal
$(P+1) < N$, the element would be non-metal
$(P+1) = N$, the elements would be metalloid
Answer the following questions.

30. Metalloid will be out of elements with atomic number 13, 14, 15, 16
(a) 13 (b) 14
(c) 15 (d) 16

31. Metals will be out of 13, 31, 35, 54
(a) 13, 31, (b) 31, 35 (c) 35, 54 (d) 13, 54

32. Non-metals will be out of 13, 31, 35, 54
(a) 13, 31 (b) 31, 35 (c) 35, 54 (d) 13, 54

33. Which will find use in semi-conductors?
(a) 5, 13 (b) 5, 14 (c) 13, 14 (d) 14, 16

Directions (Q. Nos. 34 to 36)

In the following table I_1, I_2 and I_3 of the main group elements in 2nd period have been given.

	Li	Be	B	C	N	O	F	Ne
I_1	513	899	801	1086	1402	1314	1681	2080
I_2	7298	1757	2427	2352	2856	3388	3374	3952
I_3	11815	14848	3660	4620	4578	5300	6050	6122

Answer the following question based on the above table.

34. There is increase in ionization energy along a period going Li to Ne, but I_1 of B is less than that of Be. This is due to
(a) valence electron in B is in $2p$-orbital of higher energy than that of Be in $2s$-orbital of lower energy.
(b) removal of paired electron in Be requires higher energy than that of removal of unpaired electron in B.
(c) Both (a) and (b)
(d) None of the above

35. We observe that I_1 of Be $> I_1$ of B but I_2 of Be $< I_2$ of B.
Select the correct explanation(s).
(a) Electron in Be are paired while in B, electron is unpaired, hence I_1 of Be $> I_1$ of B.
(b) Electron in Be^+ is unpaired while in B^+, electron is paired, hence I_2 of Be $< I_2$ of B.
(c) Both (a) and (b)
(d) None of the above

36. There occurs a fall while going from N to O. It is due to
(a) stable configuration of N | ↿ | ↿ | ↿ |
(b) higher atomic number of O
(c) stable configuration of O | ↿ | ↿ | |
(d) lone pairs of O.

Directions (Q. Nos. 37 to 39)

The sums of first and second ionization energies and those of third and fourth ionization energies (in kJ mol^{-1}) of nickel and platinum are

	$(IE)_1 + (IE)_2$	$(IE)_3 + (IE)_4$
Ni	2.49	8.80
Pt	2.66	6.70

Based on this information, answer the following questions.

37. Most common oxidation states of Ni and Pt are respectively
(a) + 2, + 2 (b) + 4, + 2
(c) + 2, + 4 (d) + 4, + 4

38. Which is most stable complex of Ni?
(a) $[Ni(CN)_4]^{2-}$ (b) $[Ni(CN)_6]^{2-}$
(c) $[Ni(CN)_3]^-$ (d) $[Ni(CO)_6]$

39. Which is least stable complex of Pt?
(a) $K_2[PtCl_6]$ (b) $[Pt(en)_3]Cl_4$
(c) $K_2[PtCl_4]$ (d) $K_2[Pt(C_2O_4)_3]$

Directions (Q. Nos. 40 to 43)

The $(IE)_1$ and the $(IE)_2$ in kJ mol^{-1} of a few elements are shown below :

Element	$(IE)_1$	$(IE)_2$
A	2372	5251
B	520	7300
C	900	1760
D	1680	3380

Based on the above information, answer the following questions.

40. Which of the above elements is likely to be a reactive metal?
(a) *A* (b) *B* (c) *C* (d) *D*

41. Which of the above elements is likely to be a reactive non-metal?
(a) *A* (b) *B* (c) *C* (d) *D*

42. Which represents a noble gas?
(a) *A* (b) *B* (c) *C* (d) *D*

43. Which of the above elements forms a stable binary halide of the formula MX_2?
(a) *A* (b) *B* (c) *C* (d) *D*

Directions (Q. Nos. 44 to 46)

The heats of formation ($\Delta_f H°$) of the oxides of the third period, sodium to chlorine, are in kJ mol^{-1}.

Na_2O	MgO	Al_2O_3	SiO_2	P_2O_{10}	SO_3	Cl_2O_7
– 416	– 602	– 1676	– 911	– 2984	– 395	+250

Based on these data, answer the following questions.

44. Which oxide has maximum negative heat of formation per oxygen atom?

(a) P_4O_{10} (b) Al_2O_3
(c) Na_2O (d) MgO

45. Most stable and least stable oxides are

(a) P_4O_{10}, Cl_2O_7 (b) Na_2O, Cl_2O_7
(c) MgO, Cl_2O_7 (d) Cl_2O_7, MgO

46. Stability order of the above oxides is

(a) $Cl_2O_7 < SO_3 < P_4O_{10} < SiO_2 < Al_2O_3 < MgO < Na_2O$
(b) $Cl_2O_7 < SO_3 < P_4O_{10} < Na_2O < SiO_2 < Al_2O_3 < MgO$
(c) $Cl_2O_7 < SO_3 < Na_2O < MgO < SiO_2 < Al_2O_3 < P_4O_{10}$
(d) $P_4O_{10} < Al_2O_3 < SiO_2 < MgO < Na_2O < SO_3 < Cl_2O_7$

Directions (Q. Nos. 47 to 50)

The singly-bonded metallic radius of Na is 157 pm. Assume that the increment between radii of different magnitudes is 60 pm. Answer the following questions.

47. The covalent radius of Na is

(a) 157 pm (b) 97 pm (c) 217 pm (d) 267 pm

48. Ionic radius of Na^+ is

(a) 157 pm (b) 97 pm (c) 217 pm (d) 267 pm

49. Ionic radius of Na^- is

(a) 157 pm (b) 97 pm (c) 217 pm (d) 267 pm

50. van der Waals' radius of Na is

(a) 157 pm (b) 97 pm (c) 217 pm (d) 267 pm

Matching Type

51. Match the type of elements (in Column I) with the corresponding electronic configuration (in Column II).

Column I	Column I
A. Inert gas elements	1. ns^1 to ns^2np^5
B. Main group elements	2. $1s^2$ to ns^2np^6
C. Transition elements	3. $(n-2)f^{1-14}$ $(n-1)s^2p^6d^{10}ns^2$
D. Inner transition elements	4. $(n-1)d^{1-9}ns^2$
	5. $(n-1)d^{10}ns^2$

Codes

	A	B	C	D
(a)	5	2	1	1
(b)	2	1	4	3
(c)	1	2	3	4
(d)	4	3	2	1

52. Match the classification (in Column I) with the element (in Column II).

Column I	Column I
A. Alkaline earth metal	1. Rb
B. Radioactive element	2. As
C. Alkali metal	3. Mg
D. Metalloid	4. Fr

Codes

	A	B	C	D
(a)	3	4	2	1
(b)	3	4	1	2
(c)	4	3	2	1
(d)	1	2	3	4

53. Match the element (in Column I) with its unique properties (in Column II).

Column I		Column I
A.	F	1. Maximum ionization energy
B.	Cl	2. Maximum electronegativity
C.	Fe	3. Maximum electron-affinity
D.	He	4. Recently named by IUPAC
E.	Ds	5. Variable valency

Codes

	A	B	C	D	E
(a)	5	2	3	1	4
(b)	5	2	1	4	3
(c)	4	2	3	1	5
(d)	2	3	5	1	4

54. Match the atomic number (in Column I) with its IUPAC nomenclature (in Column II).

Column I		Column I
A.	105	1. Uuh
B.	107	2. Uun
C.	109	3. Uns
D.	110	4. Unp
E.	116	5. Une

Codes

	A	B	C	D	E
(a)	4	3	5	2	1
(b)	3	4	5	2	1
(c)	4	3	2	5	1
(d)	4	3	5	1	2

Answers

Exercise 1

1. (b)	**2.** (a)	**3.** (a)	**4.** (d)	**5.** (b)	**6.** (c)	**7.** (d)	**8.** (c)	**9.** (b)	**10.** (b)
11. (d)	**12.** (c)	**13.** (c)	**14.** (c)	**15.** (d)	**16.** (a)	**17.** (d)	**18.** (c)	**19.** (c)	**20.** (a)
21. (d)	**22.** (a)	**23.** (c)	**24.** (a)	**25.** (c)	**26.** (a)	**27.** (d)	**28.** (b)	**29.** (b)	**30.** (b)
31. (a)	**32.** (a)	**33.** (a)	**34.** (d)	**35.** (a)	**36.** (b)	**37.** (d)	**38.** (c)	**39.** (c)	**40.** (a)
41. (a)	**42.** (a)	**43.** (d)	**44.** (b)	**45.** (c)	**46.** (d)	**47.** (b)	**48.** (c)	**49.** (a)	**50.** (c)
51. (d)	**52.** (c)	**53.** (c)	**54.** (b)	**55.** (c)	**56.** (a)	**57.** (c)	**58.** (a)	**59.** (d)	**60.** (d)
61. (c)	**62.** (a)	**63.** (d)	**64.** (c)	**65.** (b)	**66.** (a)	**67.** (a)	**68.** (d)	**69.** (a)	**70.** (a)
71. (d)	**72.** (c)	**73.** (a)	**74.** (d)	**75.** (d)	**76.** (d)	**77.** (b)	**78.** (a)	**79.** (a)	**80.** (d)
81. (c)	**82.** (c)	**83.** (b)	**84.** (a)	**85.** (b)	**86.** (c)	**87.** (c)			

Exercise 2

1. (d)	**2.** (b)	**3.** (c)	**4.** (b)	**5.** (a)	**6.** (d)	**7.** (b)	**8.** (a)	**9.** (a)	**10.** (d)
11. (c)	**12.** (b)	**13.** (a)	**14.** (a)	**15.** (b)	**16.** (b)	**17.** (a)	**18.** (d)	**19.** (b)	**20.** (a,b,c,d)
21. (a,b)	**22.** (a,b,c)	**23.** (b)	**24.** (a)	**25.** (c)	**26.** (b)	**27.** (b)	**28.** (b)	**29.** (a)	**30.** (b)
31. (a)	**32.** (c)	**33.** (b)	**34.** (c)	**35.** (c)	**36.** (a)	**37.** (c)	**38.** (a)	**39.** (c)	**40.** (b)
41. (d)	**42.** (a)	**43.** (c)	**44.** (d)	**45.** (c)	**46.** (b)	**47.** (a)	**48.** (b)	**49.** (c)	**50.** (c)
51. (b)	**52.** (b)	**53.** (d)	**54.** (a)						

Hints & Solutions

Exercise 1

5. A stable nuclei has the highest ionization energy. The electronic configuration of the given atoms is

$$_1H = 1s^1$$

$$_2He = 1s^2$$

$$_7N = 1s^2, 2s^2, 2p^3$$

$$_{10}Ne = 1s^2, 2s^2, 2p^6$$

Thus, first IE is highest for the He due to its small size and presence of completely filled orbitals.

6. The general electronic configuration of alkali metals is ns^1, *i.e.*, the $(n-1)$ shell is completely filled. Hence, there found a large difference between IE_1 and IE_2 in case of alkali metals.

11. Transition element are almost equal in size. An anion is always larger than its parent atom (because of the presence of extra electron) and a cation is always smaller than its parent atom (as cation contains less number of electrons).

15. Covalent radii decreases as we move left to right in a period. So, the radii of B is larger than N, *i.e.*, 110 pm.

18. The electronic configuration of Cu is

$$_{29}Cu = 1s^2, 2s^2 2p^6, 3s^2 3p^6 3d^{10}, 4s^1$$

$$\sigma = [0.85 \times (n-1)e^-] + 1.00 \times (\text{other inner shell electrons})$$

$$= 8.5 + 18 = 26.5$$

$$Z^* = Z - \sigma = 29 - 26.5 = 2.5$$

19. Unq (Un nil quadium)

1 0 4

Thus, its atomic number is 104.

20. As the positive charge increases, effective nuclear charge increases. Thus, it is minimum in case of Be.

23. Electronic configuration of element having atomic number 113

$$= [Rn]_{86}\ 5f^{14} 6d^{10} 7s^2 7p^1$$

Since, the outer shell (7) contains 3 electrons, it is an element of group 13 (III A) of the Periodic Table. Thus, it resembles with Ga, an element of group 13.

25. Root word for the digit 1 is un and for 5 is pent, so the IUPAC name of element having atomic numer 115 is **Unpentium** and it is symbolised as Uup.

29. Electronic configuration of $M^{3+} = [Ar]3d^{10}$

$\therefore$ EC of $M = [Ar]\ 3d^{10} 4s^2 4p^1$

Since its last electron enters in p-orbital, it is a p-block element.

33. From the outer electronic configuration of element 113, $(7s^2, 7p^1)$ it is evident that its most stable cation is M^+ due to inert pair effect.

39. Ionic radii $\propto$ charge on anion.

40. In case of isoelectronic species, ionic radii decrease with increase in atomic number.

56. Electronegativity (EN) $= \dfrac{\text{EA} + \text{IP}}{2}$

$$\therefore \quad E_1 = \frac{\text{EA} + E_2}{2}$$

$$2E_1 = \text{EA} + E_2$$
$$\text{EA} = 2E_1 - E_2$$

80. A larger anion is polarised more readily.

81. Smaller the size, higher is the heat of hydration. Thus, Al^{3+} has the largest heat of hydration.

Exercise 2

3. $Gd_{64} = [Xe]\, 4f^7 5d^1 6s^2$

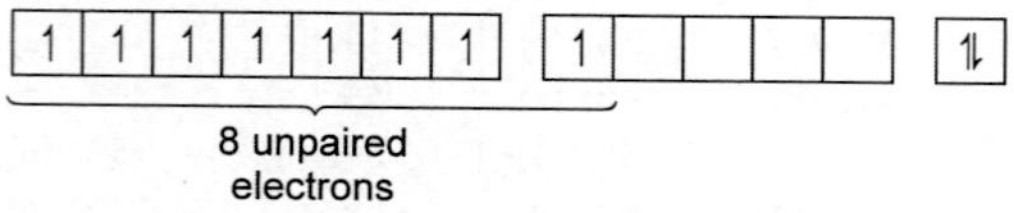

Sum of spins, $S = \dfrac{1}{2} \times 8$

or $\quad S = \dfrac{1}{2} + \dfrac{1}{2} + \dfrac{1}{2} \times \dfrac{1}{2} \times \dfrac{1}{2} + \dfrac{1}{2} + \dfrac{1}{2} + \dfrac{1}{2}$

$$= \frac{8}{2} = 4$$

11. Conversion of O into O^- is an exothermic process (EA – ve) but further conversion of O^- into O^{2-} is an endothermic process (EA + ve) because of interelectronic repulsions (as size of O atom is very small).

12. Electron affinity is maximum for halogens. Electronic configuration $1s^2, 2s^2 2p^6 3s^2 3p^5$ and $1s^2, 2s^2 2p^5$ are of Cl and F respectively and electron affinity of Cl is higher than fluorine due to its small size and hence, interelectronic repulsions.

14. According to Fajan's rule, if anion is same,

ionic character $\propto$ size of cation.

19. ${}_4Be = 1s^2, 2s^2$

For outer $2s$ electron,

$$\sigma = 0.35 \times n \text{ shell } e^- + 0.85 \times (n-1) \text{ shell } e^-$$
$$= 0.35 \times 1 + 0.85 \times 2 = 2.05$$
$$Z_{eff} = 4 - 2.05 = 1.95$$

For Be^{x+} ion, $\quad Z_{eff} = 2.30 \quad$ (given)

$$Z_{eff} = Z - \sigma$$
$$2.30 = 4 - \sigma$$

i.e., $\quad \sigma = 1.7$

$$\sigma = 0.85 \times (n-1)e^- + 0.35 \times n \text{ shell } e^-$$
$$1.7 = 0.85 \times 2 + 0.35 \times 0$$
$$1.7 = 1.7$$

Thus, one of the $2s$ electron is lost, *i.e.*, the ion is Be^+.

30. Elements having atomic number 13, 14, 15, 16 belong to 3rd period and have 3, 4, 5 and 6 valence electrons respectively. For an element to be metalloid,

$$(P + 1) \text{ i.e., } (3 + 1) = 4$$

which is the case of element having atomic number 14.

31. $13 = [Ne]\, 3s^2 3p^1$

[3 period and 3 valence e^-, so $3 + 1 > 3$, it is a metal]

$31 = [Ar]\, 3d^{10}, 4s^2, 4p^1$

[4 period and 3 valence e^-, so $4 + 1 > 3$, *i.e.*, metal]

$35 = [Ar]\, 3d^{10} 4s^2 4p^5$

[4 period and 7 valence e^-, so $4 + 1 < 7$, *i.e.*, non-metal]

$54 = [Kr]_{36}\, 4d^{10} 5s^2, 5p^6 = [Xe]_{54}$

[5 period and 8 valence e^-, so $5 + 1 < 8$, *i.e.*, non-metal]

32. Elements with atomic number 35 and 54 are non-metals.

33. Metalloids are used as semiconductors.

37. Ni^{2+} is more stable because there is a large difference between IE_2 and IE_3 in case of Ni.

But this difference is not so large in case of Pt, so stable oxidation state of Pt is Pt^{4+}.

40. In metals there is generally large difference between, IE_1 and IE_2 values, so B.

41. In non-metals, the difference in IE_1 and IE_2 is not so high, so *D*.

42. For noble gases, IE_1 and IE_2 both are very high as they have stable (completely filled) configuration.

43. *C* forms MX_2 as it is a bivalent metal. This is because its IE_1 is low and the difference between IE_1 and IE_2 is also low.

2

Chemical Bonding and Structure of Molecules

Syllabus

- Structure and Bonding in Homo and Heteronuclear Molecules Ionic Bond, Covalent Bond, Valence Bond Theory, LCAO Theory, Resonance Hybridization, Fluxionality TBP Molecules, Dipole-moment, Bond Angles, Bond Distance and Bond Energies Including Shapes of Molecules, VSEPR Theory

Chemical Bond

Every system in this universe has a tendency to acquire a state of minimum energy. Since, isolated atoms generally have higher energy as compared to combined atoms, therefore, isolated atoms have a natural tendency to form aggregates (element or compound) which have lower energy than individual atoms.

In the formation of aggregates, the extent of lowering of energy varies from system to system but generally if the lowering exceeds 40 kJ/mol of atoms, we can say that chemical bonds are formed to provide species (molecules) which can exist independently and have distinct physical and chemical properties.

A chemical bond may be defined as "the force which holds atoms or ions together".

"The phenomenon of union of two or more atoms involving redistribution of electrons, so that each atom involved in bonding acquires stable configuration in order to gain stability is known as chemical bonding."

Ionic Bond

Bond formed by the complete transference of an electron (or electrons) from one atom to another atom is known as electrovalent or ionic bond.

For example. When sodium reacts with chlorine, ions with opposite electric charges are formed during the chemical reaction.

$$2Na(s) + Cl_2(g) \longrightarrow 2Na^+Cl^-(s)$$

The oppositely charged ions are held together by Coulombic forces. The system will be at a lower potential energy when the two oppositely charged ions are close to each other than when they are far apart.

General Characteristics of Ionic Compounds

1. Melting point

Ionic compounds have high melting points. The electrostatic force of attraction (ionic bond) between cations and anions is strong. It takes a lot of energy to overcome this attraction in order to allow the ions to move more freely and form a liquid.

Factors affecting the melting point of an ionic compound are :

(i) **The charge on the ions** In general, the greater the charge, the greater the electrostatic attraction (cation-anion interaction), the stronger the ionic bond, the higher the melting point. For example :

Ionic compound	Melting point (°C)	Cation charge	Anion charge
NaCl	801	+1	−1
MgO	2800	+2	−2

(ii) **The size of the ions** Smaller ions can pack closer together than larger ions so the electrostatic attraction is greater, the ionic bond is stronger, the melting point is higher. For example :

Ionic compound	Melting point (°C)	Cation radius (pm)
NaF	1270	$Na^+ = 99$
KF	857	$K^+ = 136$
RbF	775	$Rb^+ = 148$
CsF	683	$Cs^+ = 169$

As the radius of the cations increases down group I from Na^+ to Cs^+, the melting points of the fluorides decrease. Similarly,

Ionic compound	Melting point (°C)	Cation radius (pm)
NaF	1270	$F^- = 99$
NaI	925	$I^- = 206$

2. Hardness

Ionic compounds are hard and brittle. The strong ionic bonds between the cations and the anions hold the ions in a very rigid lattice so smaller ions can pack closer together than larger ions and hence are hard. Hardness depends upon.

(i) **Charge of ions** Hardness increases with increase in charge on the ion for crystals of similar interionic distances for ionic compounds having similar structure. For example :

Ionic compound	Interionic distance (Å)	Charge	Hardness (Mohs)
LiCl	2.57	Li = +1, Cl = −1	Less hard (3.0)
SrO	2.57	Li = +2, Cl = −2	More hard (3.5)

LiCl and SrO both have similar structure of NaCl type.

(ii) **Ionic radii** For a given charge hardness increases with decrease in interionic distance for crystals with similar structure.

Ionic compound	Interionic distance (Å)	Charge	Hardness (Mohs)
CaO	2.40	Ca = +2, O = −2	Max hardness (4.5)
SrO	2.57	Sr = +2, O = −2	More hard than BaO (3.5)
BaO	2.77	Ba = +2, O = −2	Least hard (3.3)

On Mohs scale hardness of diamond is 10.

- Noble gas type cation configuration (ns^2, np^6) are harder than cations with pseudo noble gas type or non-noble gas type or other configuration. For example :

Ionic compound	Electronic configuration of cation	Hardness (Mohs)
CaF_2	$Ca^{2+} = 3s^2, 3p^6$	Max hardness(6.0)
CdF_2	$Cd^{2+} = 4s^2, 4p^6, 4d^{10}$	More hard than BaO(4.0)

3. Brittleness

Ionic solids are brittle. When a stress is applied to the ionic lattice, the layers shift slightly. The layers are arranged so that each cation is surrounded by anions in the lattice. If the layers shift then ions of the same charge will be brought closer together. Ions of the same charge will repel each other, so the lattice structure breaks down into smaller pieces.

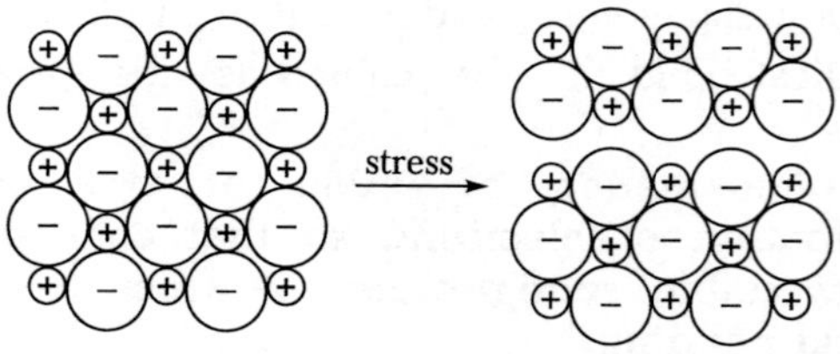

Fig. 2.1 Crystal lattice and effect of stress.

4. Solubility

As "Like dissolves like", ionic compounds dissolve in polar solvents, especially those that ionize, such as water and ionic liquids. They are usually appreciably soluble in other polar solvents such as alcohols, acetone and dimethyl sulphoxide as well. Ionic compounds tend not to dissolve in non-polar solvents such as diethyl ether or petrol.

When the oppositely charged ions in the solid ionic lattice are surrounded by the opposite pole of polar molecule, the solid ions are pulled out of the lattice and into the liquid. When this force is more than the electrostatic attraction of the lattice, the ions become dissolved in the liquid.

5. Conductivity

In order for a substance to conduct electricity it must contain mobile particles capable of carrying charge.

	Ionic solid	Ionic liquid	Aqueous solution
Mobility of ions	very poor	good	good
Electrical conductivity	very poor	good	good

Solid ionic compounds do not conduct electricity because the ions (charged particles) are locked into a rigid lattice or array. The ions cannot move out of the lattice, so the solid cannot conduct electricity.

When molten, the ions are free to move out of the lattice structure.

- Cations (positive ions) move towards the negative electrode (cathode) $M^+ + e^- \longrightarrow M$.
- Anions (negative ions) move towards the positive electrode (anode) $X^- \longrightarrow X + e^-$.

When an ionic solid is dissolved in water to form an aqueous solution, the ions are released from the lattice structure and are free to move so the solution conducts electricity just like the molten (liquid) ionic compound.

Covalent Bond

A type of chemical bond in which there is mutual sharing of electrons between two atoms is called covalent bond.

It is further classified into single, double, and triple covalent bond with respect to mutual sharing of one, two and three bonds respectively. Their symbols are single (–), double (=), and triple (≡) lines between two atoms according to their type of covalent bond like one for single, two for double and so on (*e.g.*, Cl—Cl).

Valence Bond Theory

According to this theory, a covalent bond is formed by the overlapping of two atomic orbitals of proper energy and proper symmetry. This theory was given by Hietler and London and extended by Pauling and Slater.

Hietler and London Concept :

(i) For a covalent bond to form, two atoms must come closer to each other so that orbital of one atom overlaps with the other.

(ii) Overlapping orbitals must have :

(a) half-filled nature, *i.e.*, must have unpaired electron.

(b) antispin electrons.

(iii) As a result of overlapping, **a new localized bond orbital** is formed, in which probability of finding electron pair is maximum.

(iv) Covalent bond energy arises due to

(a) electrostatic attraction between nuclei and the accumulated electron cloud.

(b) concellation or attraction between spins of antispin electrons.

(v) Greater is the overlapping, lesser will be the bond length, more will be the attraction and more will be bond energy and the stability of bond.

Pauling and Slater Extension

(i) The extent of overlapping depends upon :

(a) nature of orbitals involved in overlapping.

(b) nature of overlapping.

(ii) More closer the valence shells are to the nucleus, more will be the overlapping and the bond energy will also be high. Bond energy of $1-1 > 1-2 > 2-2 > 2-3$ shells.

(iii) Between two subshells of same energy level, the subshells more directionally concentrated shows more overlapping.

Bond energy : $2s\text{-}2s < 2s\text{-}2p < 2p\text{-}2p$.

(iv) *s*-orbitals are spherically symmetrical and thus show only head on overlapping. On the other hand, *p*-orbitals are directionally concentrated and thus, show either head on overlapping or lateral overlapping.

Formation of σ-bond (σ-Bond is formed by the axial overlapping of atomic orbitals)

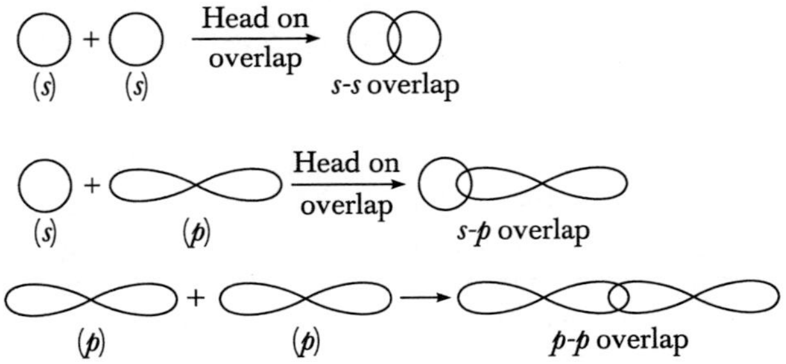

Formation of π-bond (π-bond is formed by the sideways overlapping of atomic orbitals)

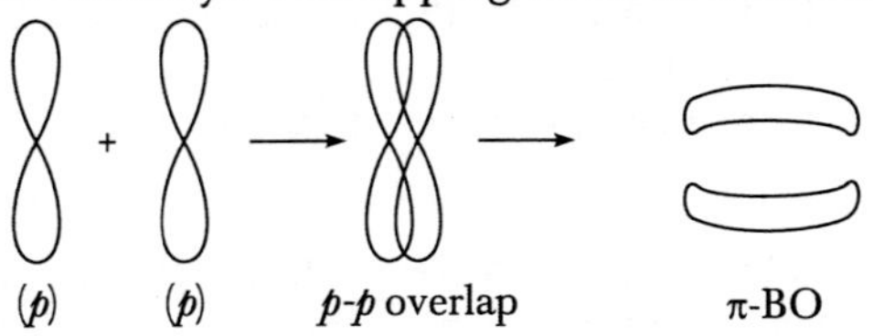

(v) Head on overlapping is stronger than lateral or sideways overlapping.

∴ B.E. $\underbrace{p - p}_{\text{Lateral overlapping}} < \underbrace{s - s < s - p < p - p}_{\text{Head on overlapping}}$

Valence Bond Theory Treatment of π-bonding : The bonding in ClNO

:$\ddot{\text{Cl}}$—$\ddot{\text{N}}$=$\ddot{\text{O}}$:

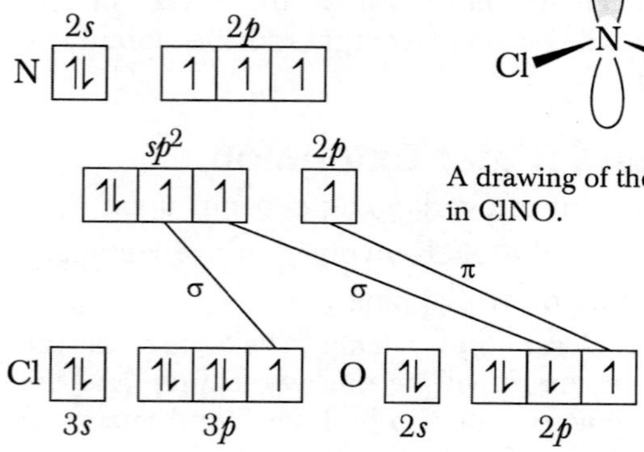

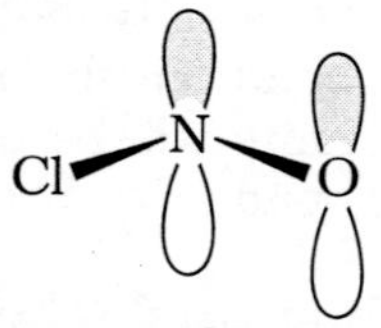

A drawing of the VBT π-bond in ClNO.

The overlap of the sp^2 hybrid orbitals of N with the $3p$-orbital of Cl and the $2p$-orbital of O give the two σ-bonds and it is overlap of the "left over" p orbital on N with the appropriate orbital on O that forms the ($2p$-$2p$) π-bond between the two atoms.

Wave Mechanical Treatment to VBT

VBT utilises the following wave mechanical principles:

1. If ψ_A and ψ_B are the wave functions for any two completely independent (non-interacting) systems A and B, then the total wave function ψ for these independent systems, taken together, would be given by :

$$\psi = \psi_A \psi_B \qquad \ldots(1)$$

2. If the wave function for a many-electrons system has characteristics of several wave functions $\psi_1, \psi_2, \psi_3, \ldots \psi_n$, then according to the Ritz principle of lnear combination, the wave function ψ closest to the true wave function of the system is given by

$$\psi = c_1\psi_1 + c_2\psi_2 + c_2\psi_3 + \ldots + c_n\psi_n \ldots \qquad \ldots(2)$$

where $c_1, c_2 \ldots c_n$ are the various coefficients. These coefficients are so adjusted as to give a state of lowest energy, *i.e., a state of maximum stability.* The function ψ should be *normalised* so that

$$c_1^2 + c_2^2 + c_3^2 + \ldots = 1 \qquad \ldots(3)$$

We will elucidate the Valence Bond theory by taking into consideration the formation of H_2 molecule.

Formation of Hydrogen Molecule

Consider two hydrogen atoms lying far apart from each other so that no interaction between them is possible. Let A and B represent the nuclei and e_1 and e_2 the two electrons. The two atoms of hydrogen may thus be represented as $H_A(e_1)$ and $H_B(e_2)$.

Let the wave functions for the electrons in the separated atoms be represented by $\psi_A(1)$ and $\psi_B(2)$. The wave function $\psi_A(1)$ is also called the wave function of the atomic orbital containing electron (1) and the wave function $\psi_B(2)$ is called the wave fuction of the atomic orbital containing electron (2). According to Eq. (1), the combined wave function ψ for the two separated atoms of hydrogen can be written as

$$\psi = \psi_A(1)\,\psi_B(2) \qquad \ldots(4)$$

When the two atoms are brought close together, their energy changes and consequently, the energy operator $\hat{H}$ also changes. Assuming that the combined wave function ψ, as represented by Eq. (4), still describes the wave function for H_2 molecule, the energy of the hydrogen molecule, would be given by

$$E = \frac{\int_{-\infty}^{+\infty} \psi_A(1)\,\psi_B(2)\,\hat{H}\,\psi_A(1)\,\psi_B(2)\,d\tau}{\int_{-\infty}^{+\infty} [\psi_A(1)\,\psi_B(2)]^2\,d\tau}$$

The energy changes that take place as the two H atoms are gradually brought closer to each other are shown graphically in the following figure.

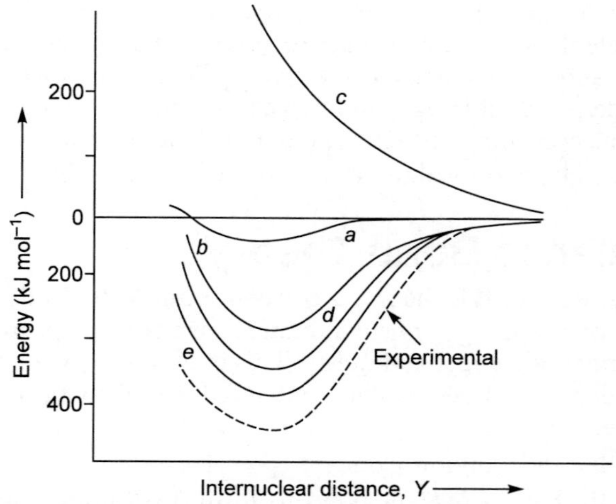

Fig. 2.2 Energy changes as the distance between two H atoms decreases.

In state I, nucleus A is associated with electron 1 and nucleus B is associated with electron 2. In state II, nucleus A is associated with electron 2 and nucleus B is associated with electron 1.

If ψ_I and ψ_{II} are the wave functions representing states I and II, respectively,then, according to Eq. (1), we can write

$$\psi_I = \psi_A(1)\psi_B(2) \text{ and } \psi_{II} = \psi_A(2)\psi_B(1)$$

A linear combination of ψ_I and ψ_{II} (and not ψ_I or ψ_{II} alone) should be employed for calculating the energy of H_2 molecule).

$$\psi_+ = \psi_I + \psi_{II} = \psi_A(1)\,\psi_B(2) + \psi_A(2)\,\psi_B(1) \quad ...(5)$$

and $\psi_- = \psi_I - \psi_{II} = \psi_A(1)\,\psi_B(2) - \psi_A(2)\psi_B(1) \quad ...(6)$

The energy of the system, calculated by using ψ_+ in the wave equation is shown by the curve *b* while that calculated from ψ_- is shwon by the curve c in Fig. It is evident that ψ_-leads to increase of energy. Thus, bonding is not possible in ψ_-. We may, therefore, regard ψ_- as repulsive state. The wave function ψ_+, however, leads to fall of energy. Thus, bonding is possible in this state. We may, therefore, regard ψ_+ as bonding state. The wave function ψ_+ (Eq. 5) which represents the bonding state is also referred to as covalent wave function. Therefore, it may be written as $\psi_{covalent}$. The reason for this terminology is that in state I as well as in state II, there is equal distribution of charge on both the nuclei *A* and *B*.

Since, the calculated value of bond energy is smaller than the experimental value, it is necessary to provide in our model of H_2 molecule an additional factor which will tend to enhance the binding force between the two hydrogen atoms because increase in such a force will lead to increase in the bond energy. The additional factor that has been suggested is the possibility that momentarily both the electrons may simultaneously be present close to one nucleus or the other. This give rise to ionic configurations represented by states III and IV :

(III)	(IV)
(e_2) $(e_1)\,H_AB_B$	(e_2) $H_AH_B(e_1)$

The states III and IV are, amongst themselves, equally probable and the wave functions corresponding to state III (ψ_{III}) and state IV (ψ_{IV}) may be expressed as

$$\psi_{III} = \psi_A(1)\,\psi_A(2) \quad ...(7)$$

and $$\psi_{IV} = \psi_B(1)\,\psi_B(2) \quad ...(8)$$

The total ionic wave function ψ_{ionic} may be expressed as a linear combination of ψ_{III} and ψ_{IV}, as

$$\psi_{ionic} = \psi_A(1)\,\psi_A(2) + \psi_B(1)\,\psi_B(2) \quad ...(9)$$

Considering the possibilites of a covalent as well as ionic structures, the combined wave function for H_2 molecule is written as

$$\psi = \psi_{covalent} + \lambda\psi_{ionic}$$
$$= [\psi_A(1)\psi_B(2) + \psi_A(2)\psi_B(1)] + \lambda\,[\psi_A(1)\,\psi_A(2) + \psi_B(1)\,\psi_B(2)] \quad ...(10)$$

where, λ gives the extent to which the ionic structures contribute to the bonding. For H_2, λ is calculated to be 0.17 Knowing λ, we can find out the extent of the contribution of the ionic structures. The fraction λ is called the mixing coefficient.

Limitations of Valence Bond Theory

This theory could not explain the following facts :

1. It fails to explain the paramagnetic behaviour of O_2 molecules.
2. It fails to explain the bonding in electron deficient compounds as well as in metals and intermetallic compounds.
3. It lacks in mathematical explanation of most chemical species, as the valence bond concept is very close to the classical chemical picture. In classical chemical picture, a bond is denoted by a line whereas in valence bond theory, the electron pair plays the same role.
4. It fails to encounter many molecules where the bonding electrons are not localised, although it involves the concept of resonance where in it is not possible to write a definite structure for a molecule or ion.

Linear Combination of Atomic Orbitals (LCAO Theory)

(i) In wave mechanics, atomic orbitals are expressed in terms of wave functions (ψ's).

(ii) These wave functions are the solutions of Schrodinger wave equation.

(iii) It is not easy to solve Schrodinger wave equation for molecules because of the complex nature of the equation.

(iv) To obtain wave function for molecular orbitals, LCAO theory has been adopted.

(v) Consider ψ_A and ψ_B are the wave functions of atoms *A* and *B* respectively, then according to LCAO method, molecular orbitals wave functions in molecules can be given as :

$$\psi_{MO} = \psi_A \pm \psi_B$$

The two MO's are therefore,

1. $\psi_b = \psi_A + \psi_B$ (where, ψ_b represents bonding MO)
2. $\psi_a = \psi_A - \psi_B$ (ψ_a, represents anti-bonding MO)

1. Bonding Molecular Orbital

'When two waves of combining atomic orbitals are in same phase, then **addition combination of atomic orbitals wave functions** takes place and resulting orbitals are known as bonding molecular orbital.'

In bonding molecular orbital, the concentration of electron density lie between the two nuclei and strongly attracted to both nuclei, it is more stable (lower energy) than it was in the combining atomic orbital.

The charge density for bonding molecular orbitals, ψ^2 can be given as :

$$\psi_b^2 = (\psi_A + \psi_B)^2 = \psi_A^2 + \psi_B^2 + 2\psi_A\psi_B$$

It is thus clear that ψ_b^2 is greater than the sum of the charge density of two isolated atoms $(\psi_A^2 + \psi_B^2)$ by an amount $2\psi_A\psi_B$.

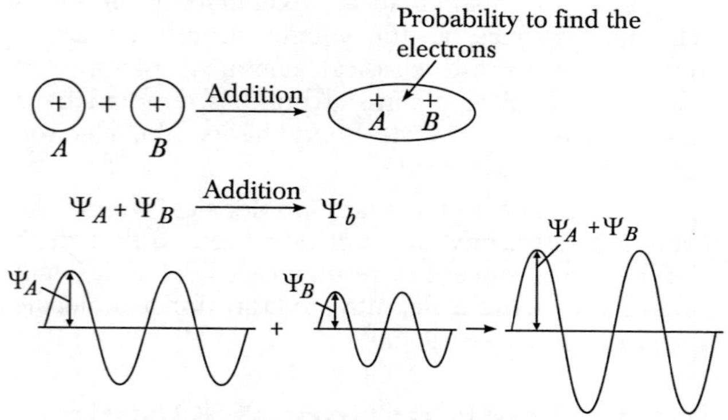

Fig. 2.3 The constructive interference leads to bonding orbitals.

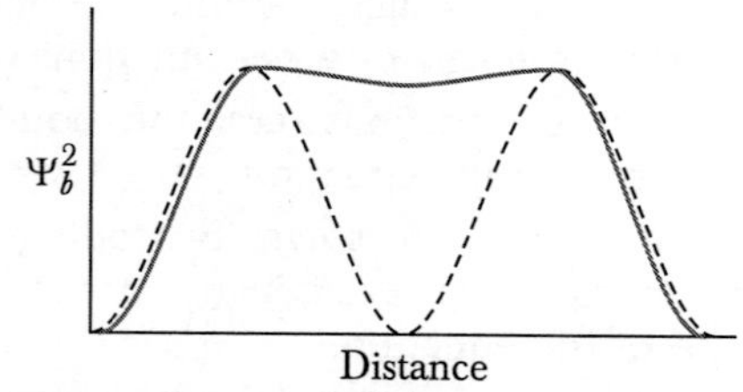

Fig. 2.4 The variation of electron density (probability) for the individual atomic orbitals (dotted line) and for, bonding molecular orbital (solid line).

Important characteristics of bonding orbitals

1. A bonding MO is formed by the addition overlap of atomic orbitals or by constructive interference of waves which have lower energy than parent atomic orbitals.
2. It has high electron density in the region between the two nuclei which is responsible for more stability of bond.
3. Each electron in the bonding orbital contributes to attraction between the two atoms.
4. It may or may not have nodes (node in bonding MO of σ - $2p$ are seen).

2. Anti-bonding Molecular Orbitals

When two waves of combining atomic orbitals are in opposing phase than substraction combination of atomic orbitals or wave functions takes place and molecular orbitals so formed are known as anti-bonding molecular orbitals.

In anti-bonding MO, there is a very little electron density between the two nuclei. There is a node between nuclei, at which the electron density is zero. Infact, the greatest electron density is on opposite side of nuclei. This type of MO arising due to destructive interference (the one in which the amplitude cancel to give zero and a node is formed) and an electron is actually repelled from the bonding region, it is less stable (higher energy) than it was in the combining atomic orbital.

The charge density for anti-bonding MO ψ^2 can be given as

$$\psi_a^2 = (\psi_A - \psi_B)^2 = \psi_A^2 + \psi_B^2 - 2\psi_A\psi_B$$

It is evident that ψ_a^2 for anti-bonding MO is lesser than the sum of the charge density of two isolated atoms $(\psi_A^2 + \psi_B^2)$ by an amount $2\psi_A\psi_B$.

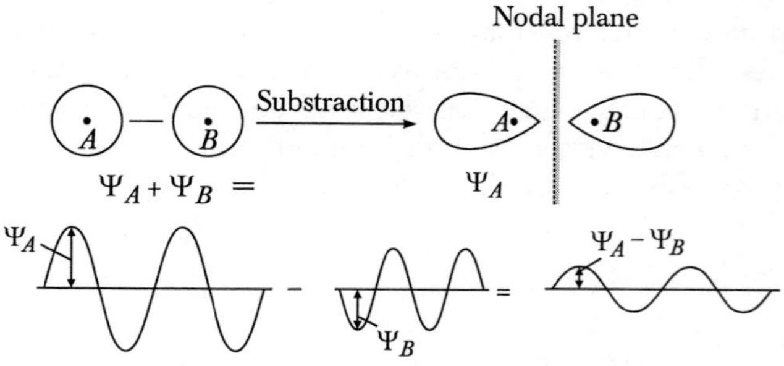

Fig. 2.5 The destructive interference leads to anti-bonding orbitals.

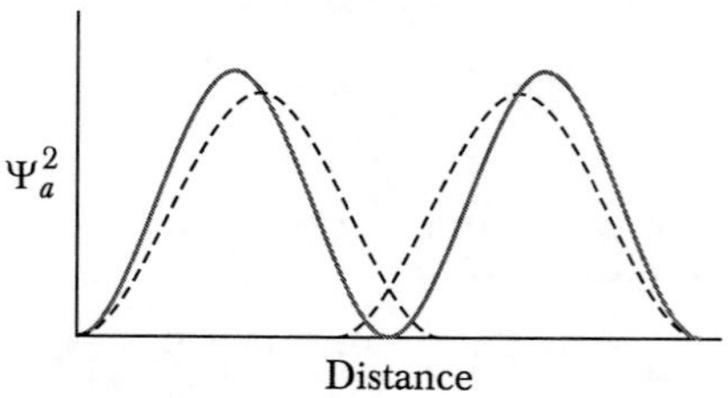

Fig. 2.6 The variation of electron density (probability) for the individual atomic orbitals (dotted line) and for, anti-bonding molecular orbital (solid line).

Important characteristics of anti-bonding orbitals

(i) An anti-bonding orbital is formed by the substraction overlap of atomic orbitals or wave functions having higher energy than parent atomic orbitals.

(ii) It has zero electron density in between two nuclei and the concentration of electron density is on opposite side.

(iii) Each electron in an anti-bonding molecular orbital contributes to repulsion between two atoms.

(iv) It possesses a node in between two nuclei of parent atomic orbitals.

Energy Orbital Diagram for the Molecules up to N_2 (*i.e.,* having Z (No. of Electrons) ≤ 14)

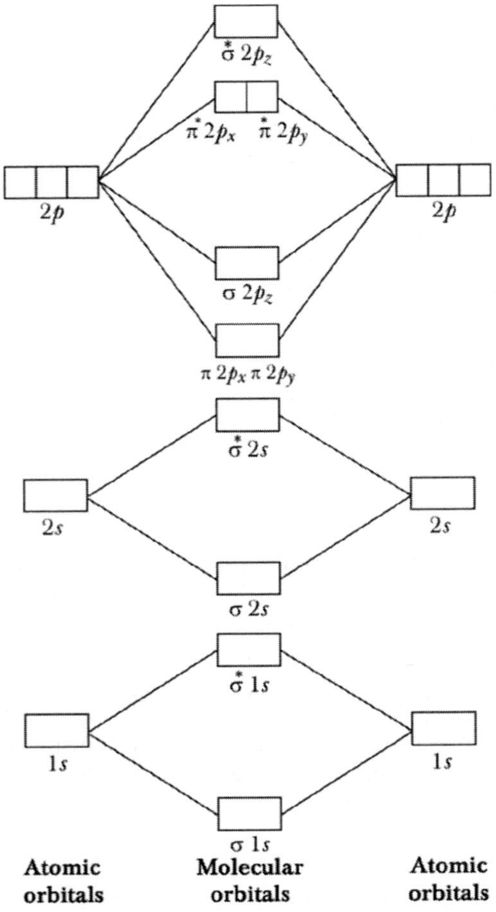

Thus, different molecular orbitals are filled in the following order of increasing energy (according to aufbau's principle)

$$\sigma 1s, \overset{*}{\sigma}1s, \sigma 2s, \overset{*}{\sigma}2s, \quad \pi 2p_x \approx \pi 2p_y, \sigma 2p_z,$$
$$\overset{*}{\pi}2p_x \approx \overset{*}{\pi}2p_y, \overset{*}{\sigma}2p_z$$

Energy Orbital Diagram of the Molecules Beyond N_2, *i.e.,* O_2 and Onwards

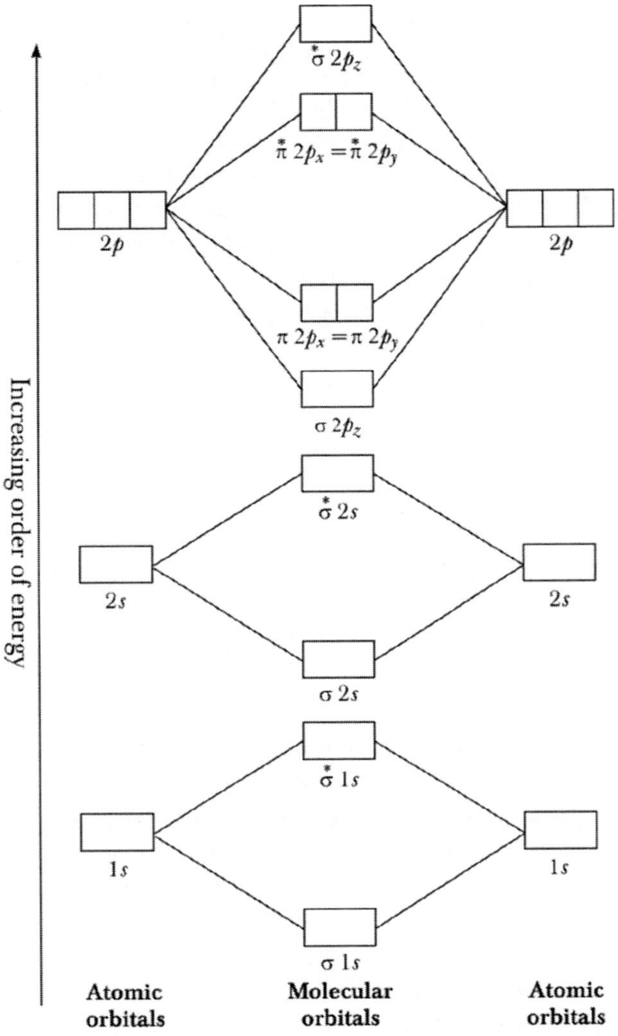

Different molecular orbitals are filled with increase in energy (according to aufbau principle) in the following way :

$$\sigma 1s < \overset{*}{\sigma}1s < \sigma 2s < \overset{*}{\sigma}2s < \sigma 2p_z < \pi 2p_x$$
$$= \pi 2p_y < \overset{*}{\pi}2p_x = \overset{*}{\pi}2p_y < \overset{*}{\sigma}2p_z$$

Bond order

It is half of the difference of bonding electrons (BE) and anti-bonding electrons (AE). Mathematically

$$\text{Bond order} = \frac{1}{2}$$

(Bonding electrons-Anti-bonding electrons)

i.e., $BO = \frac{1}{2}(BE - AE)$

Note Electrons present in bonding molecular orbitals are called bonding electrons while the electrons present in anti-bonding molecular orbitals are called anti-bonding electrons.

Applications Bond order is a measure of the strength of the bond between two atoms. Bond order can be applicable to make a comparison of some characteristics between (among) the molecules as

(i) Bond order ∝ Stability

(ii) Bond order ∝ Dissociation energy (or Bond energy)

(iii) Bond order ∝ Bond strength

(iv) Bond order $\propto \frac{1}{\text{Reactivity}}$

(v) Bond order $\propto \frac{1}{\text{Bond - length}}$

Note (i) If, bond order is zero, the molecule is unstable, *i.e.,* does not exist.

(ii) A positive value of bond-order reveals that the molecule exists and is stable.

Magnetic character

It can be explained on the basis of Molecular Orbital Theory (MOT) as given below.

(i) Molecules having unpaired electrons are paramagnetic in nature and paramagnetic nature of the molecules increases on increasing the number of unpaired electrons.

(ii) Molecules having no unpaired electrons are diamagnetic in nature.

Note (i) The magnetic moment shown by any atom, molecule, or ion is calculated by the formula :

$$\mu = \sqrt{n(n+2)}$$

where, μ = magnetic moment

n = number of unpaired electrons

(ii) Paramagnetic species attract towards magnetic field white diamagnetic species are repelled by magnetic-field.

H_2 (Hydrogen Molecule)

Molecular Orbital Diagram

E.C. of H-atom : $H_1 = 1s^1$

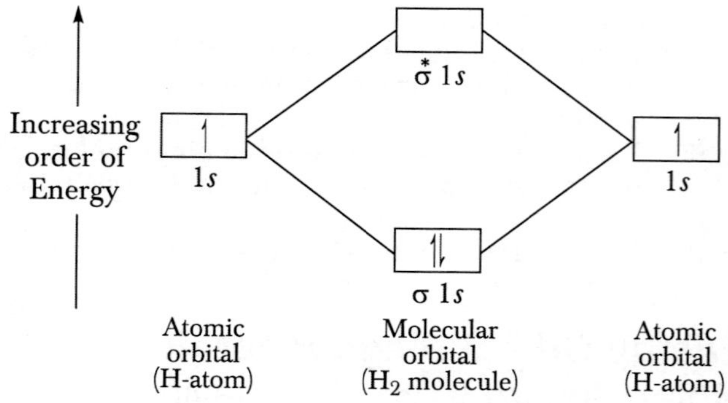

Electronic configuration

$$H_{2(2)} : \sigma\, 1s^2, \overset{*}{\sigma}\, 1s^0$$

Bond order

Bond order

$$= \frac{\text{Bonding electrons} - \text{anti-bonding electron}}{2}$$

$$= \frac{2-0}{2} = 1$$

Magnetic character Diamagnetic (due to the absence of unpaired electrons).

Hydrogen Fluoride molecule (HF)

The electronic configuration of hydrogen and fluorine atoms are,

$${}_1H = 1s^1$$

$${}_9F = 1s^2\, 2s^2\, 2p_x^2\, 2p_y^2\, 2p_z^1$$

In the formation of HF molecule, $2p_z$ orbital of fluorine atom effectively overlaps with 1s atomic orbital of hydrogen resulting in the formation of only one $\sigma(sp_z)$ bonding molecular orbital and corresponding $\overset{*}{\sigma}(sp_z)$ anti-bonding molecular orbital. Spectroscopic studies explain that 1s and 2s orbitals of fluorine do not take part in bonding because of their very low energies and $2p_x$ and $2p_y$ orbitals are unable to combine with s-orbital of hydrogen because of symmetry considerations. Thus, in the formation HF molecule, the bonding results from H (1s) electron and $2p_z^1$ electron of F and the other electrons of fluorine remain in atomic orbitals.

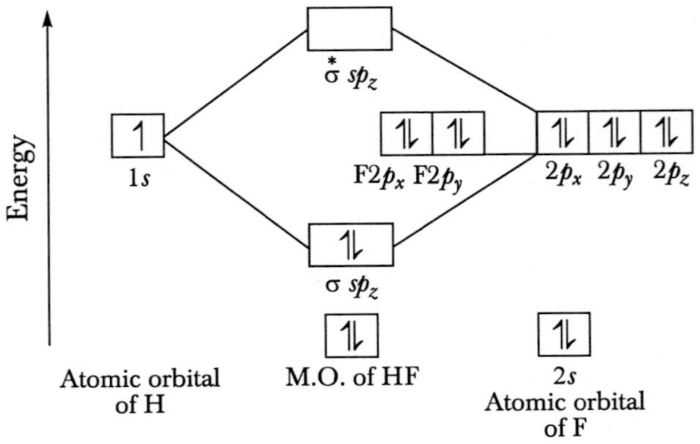

Fig. 2.7 M.O. energy level diagram of hydrogen fluoride molecule (HF).

Molecular orbital configuration of HF is,

$$(1s)^2\ (2s)^2\ ((\sigma sp_z)^2\ (2p_x)^2\ (2p_y^2)$$

$$\text{Bond order} = \frac{N_b - N_a}{2} = \frac{2-0}{2} = 1$$

Table 2.1 **Molecular Orbital Configuration and Characteristics of Some Other Molecules**

Atomic electronic configuration	Molecule	Total number of electrons	Molecular orbital configuration	Bond order	Number of unpaired electrons	Magnetic character
$_3Li: 1s^2\ 2s^1$	Li_2	6	$\sigma 1s^2 < \overset{*}{\sigma} 1s^2 < \sigma 2s^2 < \overset{*}{\sigma} 2s^0$	$\frac{4-2}{2}=1$	Zero	Diamagnetic
$_4Be: 1s^2\ 2s^2$	Be_2	8	$\sigma 1s^2 < \overset{*}{\sigma} 1s^2 < \sigma 2s^2 < \overset{*}{\sigma} 2s^2$	$\frac{4-4}{2}=0$	Zero	Diamagnetic
$_5B: 1s^2\ 2s^2\ 2p_x^1$	B_2	10	$\sigma 1s^2 < \overset{*}{\sigma} 1s^2 < \sigma 2s^2 < \overset{*}{\sigma} 2s^2 < \pi 2p_x^1 \approx \pi 2p_y^1$	$\frac{6-4}{2}=1$	Two	Paramagnetic
$_6C: 1s^2\ 2s^2\ 2p_x^1 2p_y^1$	C_2	12	$\sigma 1s^2 < \overset{*}{\sigma} 1s^2 < \sigma 2s^2 < \overset{*}{\sigma} 2s^2 < \pi 2p_x^2 \simeq 2p_y^2$	$\frac{8-4}{2}=2$	Zero	Diamagnetic

Shapes of Molecular Orbitals formed by Combination of Various Atomic Orbitals

1. Two *s*-orbitals (*i.e., s-s* combination of orbitals)

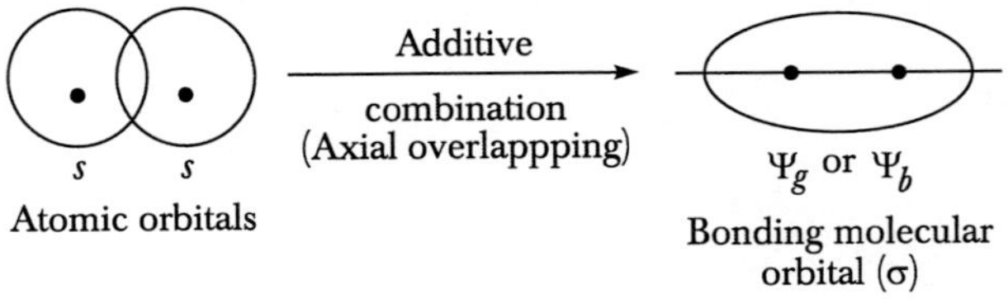

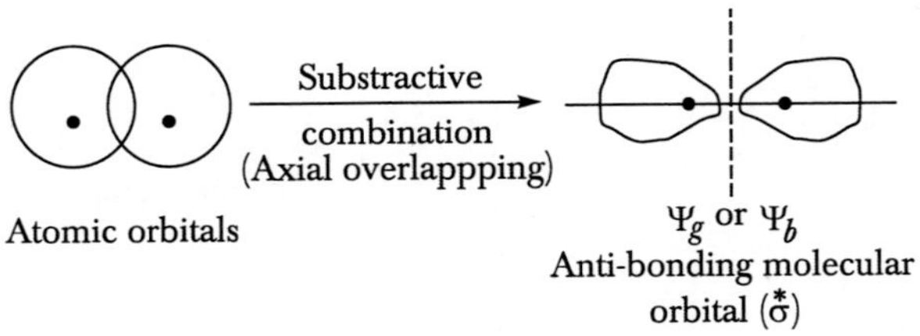

2. **Two *p*-orbitals** (*i.e.*, *p*-*p*-combinations of orbitals)

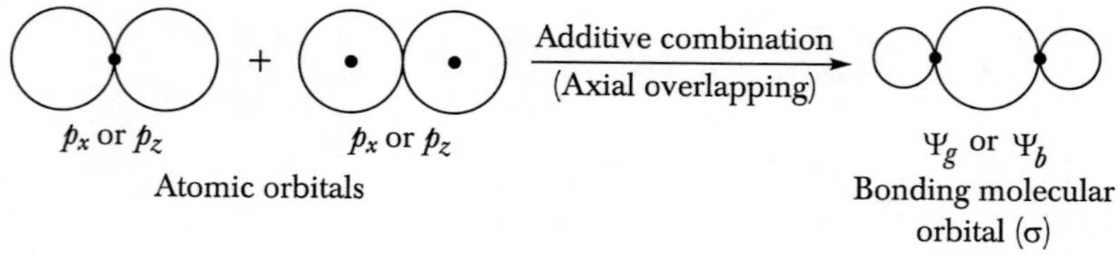

(a)

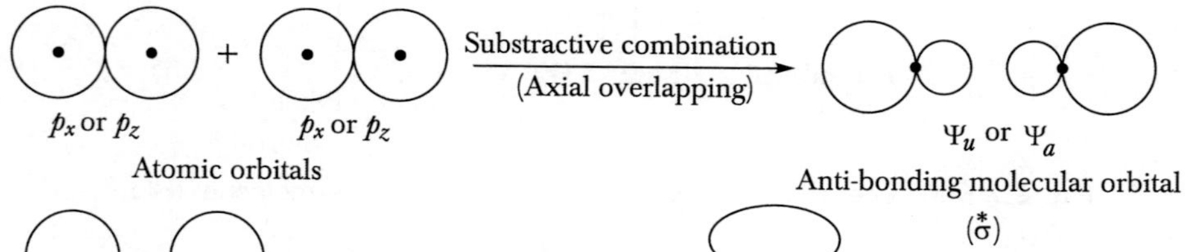

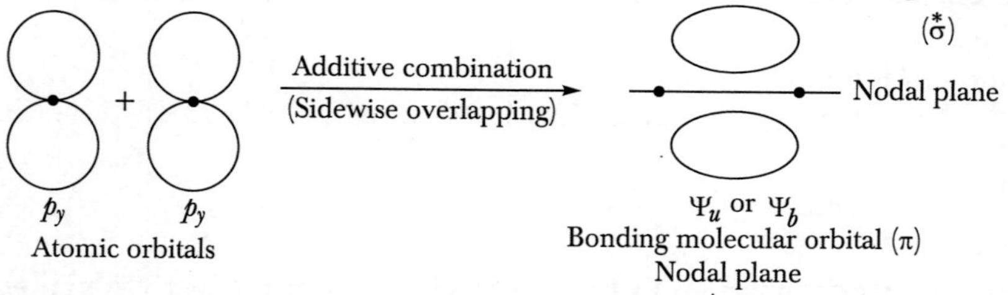

(b)

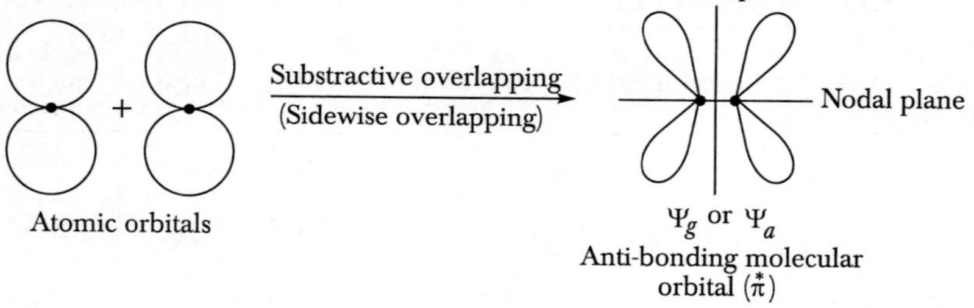

(i) '*g*' in $\psi_{(g)}$ stands for gerade (even) and '*u*' in $\psi_{(u)}$ stands for ungerade (odd), while '*b*' in ψ_b stands for bonding and '*a*' in ψ_a stands for anti-bonding.

(ii) '*g*' and '*u*' refer to the symmetry of the orbital about its centre.

3. **One *s*-and one *p*-atomic orbitals** (*i.e.*, *s*-*p* combination of orbitals)

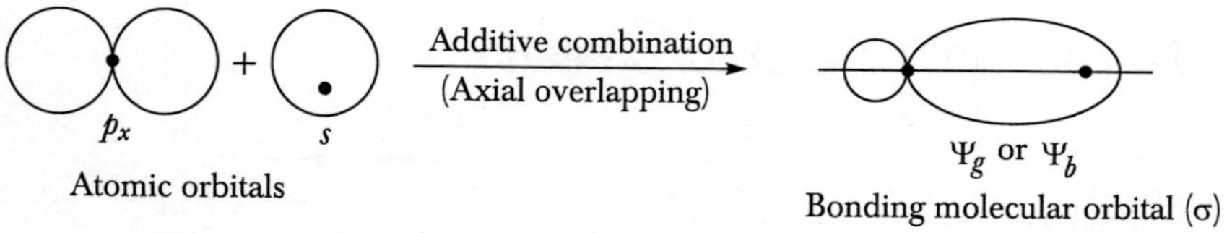

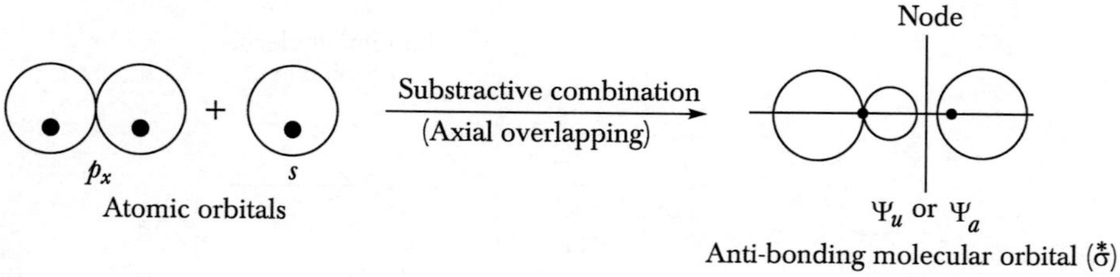

4. **One *p*-and one *d*-atomic orbitals** (*i.e., p-d* combination of orbitals)

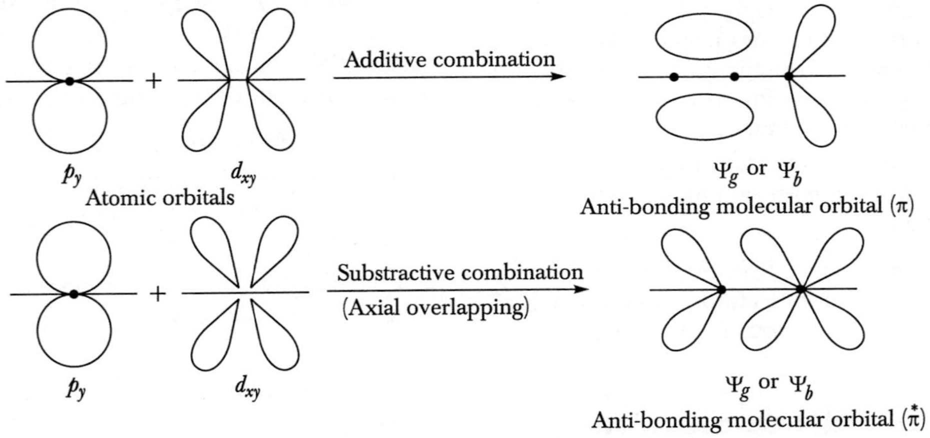

Note This type of bonding is responsible for the short bonds. Such bonding usually found in the oxides and oxoacids of phosphorus and sulphur. It also occurs in transition metal complexes such as the carbonyls and cyanides.

5. **Two *d*-orbitals** (*i.e., d-d* combination of orbitals)

Combination of two *d*-atomic orbitals produces two molecular orbitals, *i.e.*, bonding and anti-bonding molecular orbitals which are called S and S* respectively.

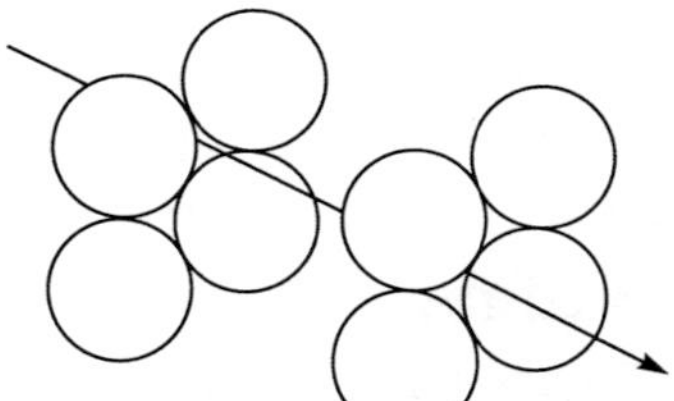

S-bonding molecular orbitals
(Sidewise overlapping of two $d_{x^2-y^2}$ orbitals)

Note On rotating these orbitals about the internuclear axis, the sign of the lobes changes four times compared with two changes with π-overlap and no change for σ-overlap.

6. **Two non-bonding orbitals**
i.e., (Non-bonding combination of orbitals)

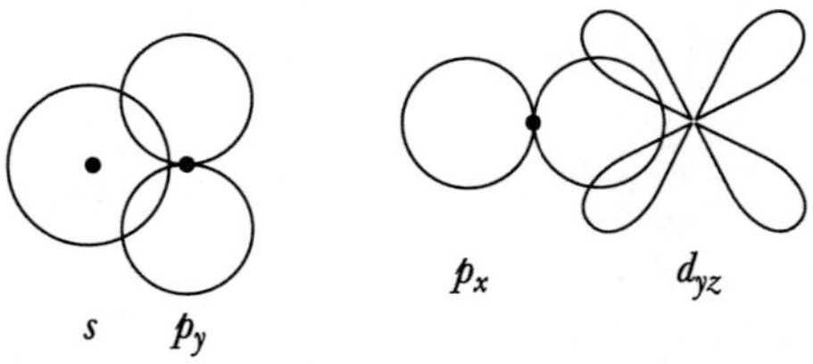

In such bonding there is no overall change in energy. The symmetry of the two atomic orbitals is not different, *i.e.*, rotation about the axis changes the sign of one.

Rules for Drawing Lewis Structure

The Lewis dot structure consists of the electron distribution in a compound and the formal charge on the atom. The following is the brief review of the rules for the Lewis structure.

1. Draw a Skeleton Structure

A skeleton structure is a rough map showing the arrangement of atoms within the molecule. In general, you need to determine the skeleton experimentally, but here are a few guidelines for predicting skeleton structures from molecular formulas.

- Central atoms are usually the atoms with highest valence, or the largest atoms, or the least electronegative atom.
- H and the halogens are usually outside atoms.
- Do not put more than four atoms around a central atom unless the central atom is of third period or lower.

2. Count Total Valence Electrons

- Add the number of electrons in the valence shells of all atoms in the molecule.
- If the molecule is charged, add an electron for each negative charge and subtract an electron for each positive charge.

3. Connect the Structure

- Draw a bond between the central atom and each outside atom.
- Each bond uses two valence electrons.

4. Place Electrons on Outside Atoms

- Use remaining electrons to satisfy the octets for each of the outside atoms.
- If you run out of electrons at this point, the skeleton structure was wrong. Go back to step 1.

5. Place all Remaining Electrons on the Central Atom

- If there are more than eight electrons on the central atom, and the central atom is not of third period or lower, you probably counted the number of valence electrons incorrectly.
- If the octet on the central atom is not complete, try sharing lone pairs of outside atoms to form double or triple bonds. Write one multiply bound structure for each outside atom with a lone pair to share; there are resonance structures.
- If you cannot get an octet on the central atom, at this point, check to see whether the total number of valence electrons for this molecule is odd. It's possible to give octets to all atoms in odd electron molecules. Get as close to an octet as possible by forming multiple bonds.

It is to be remembered that the structure be drawn in such a way that **for most atoms there will be a maximum of eight electrons in the valence shell (octet rule).** For elements with available *d*-orbitals, the valence shell can be expanded beyond an octet.

Example 1. Methane (CH_4)

1. This compound is covalent.
2. Determine the total number of valence electrons available :

   One carbon has 4 valence electrons.

   Four hydrogen, each with one valence electron, total 4.

   This means there are 8 valence electrons, making 4 pairs, available.
3. Organize the atoms so there is a central atom (usually the least electronegative) surrounded by ligand (outer) atoms. Hydrogen is never the central atom.

```
   H
H  C  H
   H
```

4. Determine a provisional electron distribution by arranging the electron pairs (E.P.) until all available pairs have been distributed.

```
  H
  ••
H:C:H
  ••
  H
```

Example 2. SF_4

1. This compound is covalent.
2. Determine the total number of valence electrons available :

   One sulphur has 6 valence electrons.

   Four fluorine, each with 7 valence electrons, total 28.

   This means there are 34 valence electrons, making 17 pairs, available.
3. Organize the atoms so there is a central atom (usually the least electronegative) surrounded by ligand (outer) atoms.

```
F
   F
S
   F
F
```

Fluorines are placed like this as one needs open space for the unbounded pair on the sulphur.

4. Determine the provisional electron distribution by arranging the electron pairs (E.P.) until all available pairs have been distributed :

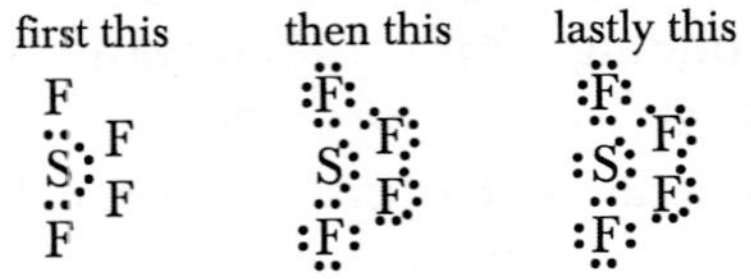

Example 3. I_3^-

1. This compound is covalent.
2. Determine the total number of valence electrons available :

   Three iodine, each with 7 valence electrons, has 21 valence electrons.

   One additional negative charge gives 1.

   This means there are 22 valence electrons, making 11 pairs, available.
3. Organize the atoms so there is a central atom (usually the least electronegative) surrounded by ligand (outer) atoms.

   I
   I
   I
4. Determine a provisional electron distribution by arranging the electron pairs (E.P.) until all available pairs have been distributed :

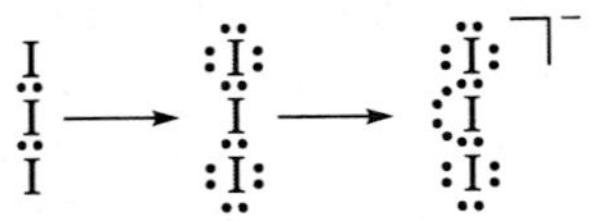

Please note that the iodines are in a straight line. If you placed them at 90 degrees, then this is incorrect. There is a reason for this and it is discussed in the VSEPR section.

Example 4. CO_2

1. The number of valence electrons is **16.** (Carbon has four electrons, and each of the oxygens have six, for a total of $4 + 12 = 16$ electrons).
2. The number of octet electrons is equal to **24.** (Carbon wants eight electrons, and each of the oxygens want eight electrons, for a total of $8 + 16 = 24$ electrons).
3. The number of bonding electrons is equal to the octet electrons minus the valence electrons, or **8.**
4. The number of bonds is equal to the number of bonding electrons divided by two, because there are two electrons per bond. As a result, in CO_2, the number of bonds is equal to **4.** (Because 8/2 is 4).
5. If we arrange the molecule so that the atoms are held together by four bonds, we find that the only way to do it so that we get the following pattern : O=C=O, where carbon is double-bonded to both oxygen atoms.
6. The number of non-bonding electrons is equal to the number of valence electrons (from 1) minus the number of bonding electrons (from 3), which in our case equal 16–8, or **8.** Looking at our structure, we see that carbon already has eight electrons around it. Each oxygen, though, only has four electrons around it. To complete the picture, each oxygen needs to have two sets of non-bonding electrons, as in this Lewis structure.

Failures of the Lewis Octet Model

From the above discussions you may have found that Lewis model is not versatile enough to describe the structures of many molecules. So, we need a new model. Before moving further, here are some of the failures of the Lewis model.

1. A number of molecules with odd numbers of electrons exist *e.g.*, NO.
2. An atom may not have enough electrons to complete octet without having ridiculous formal charges *e.g.*, BF_3.
3. A central atom may clearly have more than 8 electrons *e.g.*, SF_6.
4. O_2 is paramagnetic.

Valence Shell Electron Pair Repulsion (VSEPR) Theory

The **VSEPR** model is an extension of the Lewis's ideas and is quite successful in predicting the shapes of polyatomic molecules. It allows one to predict the shape of molecules from knowledge of their Lewis dot structure. In this model the position of atoms and electrons relative to a central atom are described. Once the position of the atoms and the lone-pairs are placed, the positions of the atoms determine the shape of the molecule. Note that the electron pairs are excluded while describing the shape of the molecules. Below are the rules for determining VSPER geometries.

- Draw a reasonable Lewis structure. Place lone pairs and atoms directly attached to the central atom (N). Remember that atoms in a molecule are bound by electron pairs (bonding pairs or *bp*). Some atoms in molecule may also possess pairs of electrons not involved in bonding, called lone pairs (*lp*).

- **The basic shape** The geometry of a molecule depends only on the valence electron pair repulsions that surrounded a central atom. The followings are the most symmetrical structures.
Linear or planar arrangements (N = 2 or 3)

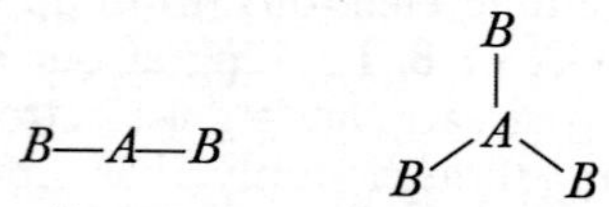

Linear   Trigonal planar

Non-planar arrangements (N = 4, 5, 6, 7, 8)

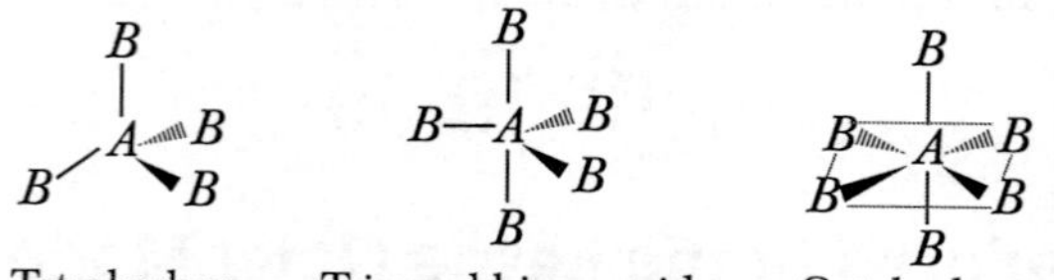

Tetrahedron   Trigonal bipyramid   Octahedron

Pentagonal bipyramid   Tetragonal anti-prism

- The primary assumption of the VSEPR model is that the bonding pairs and lone pairs around any particular atom in a molecule adopt positions in which their mutual interactions are minimized by being **as far apart from each other as possible.**

Consider Distortions

Distortions of an initially more symmetrical shape are due to the following facts :

- Lone pairs occupy more volume on the surface of the central atom than bond pairs. The gradation of repulsion qualitatively may be summarized as : *lp-lp* > *lp-bp* > *bp-bp*.
- Repulsions occurring at angles greater than 90° are insignificant.
- Multiple bonds need more space than single bonds. The triple bond volume is larger than the double bond volume, which in turn is larger than the single bond volume.
- Bonding pairs to electronegative substituents occupy less space than those to more electropositive substituents.
- Smaller "objects" will tend to occupy axial positions in trigonal bipyramids and equatorial positions in pentagonal bipyramids.

Applications of VSEPR Theory

- **Compounds containing lone pairs are assumed to be derived from the corresponding fully bond-pair containing analogues.** Thus, a AX_4 molecule (A = central atom, X = atom attached to A through a *bp*) will have a tetrahedral structure, as this is the most favourable way of minimizing the repulsions between the four bond pairs surrounding A. The molecules of the type AX_3E (E = *lp*) (NH_3) and AX_2E_2 (H_2O) are assumed to be derived from AX_4 and the E will occupy the vertex(vertices) of the tetrahedron. However, since E cannot be seen, the structures of ammonia and water are **pyramidal** and **bent** shaped respectively. Secondly, because *lp*'s occupy more volume, the H-N-H and O-H-O angles are less than the ideal tetrahedral values.
- In AB_5 type of molecules (AB_4E, AB_3E_2, AB_2E_3) the E's always occupy the equatorial position as this causes the least repulsion.
- In geometries where all sites are equal, E's will be *trans* to each other. Similarly, if there is a multiple bond and an E in a molecule, these will be *trans* to each other.
- ***AB*₇ type molecules** Two of the common possibilities of geometries for the AB_7 type of molecules are (a) pentagonal bipyramidal and (b) capped octahedron. VSEPR theory does not distinguish between the two. Thus, XeF_6 (AB_6E) has a structure based upon distorted octahedron, probably the capped octahedron, XeF_5 (AB_5E_2) has a pentagonal planar structure (lone pairs in the apical position of the pentagonal bipyramid) and IF_7 (AB_7) has a pentagonal bipyramid structure.

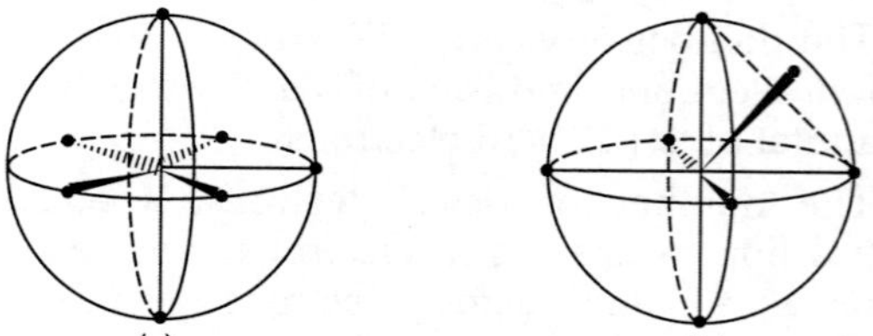

(a)   (b)

Fig. 2.7(a) Pentagonal bipyramid **(b)** Capped octahedron

Shapes of Some Common Molecules

One should be able to deduce the structures following the rules described above.

Table 2.2 **Geometry of Molecules**

Formula	Lone pairs	Example	Geometry
AB_2	0	BeH_2	Linear
	1	CH_2	Bent
	2	H_2O	Bent
	3	XeF_2	Linear
AB_3	0	BF_3	Trigonal planar
	1	NH_3	Trigonal pyramid
	2	IF_3	T-shaped
AB_4	0	BH_4^-	Tetrahedral
	1	SF_4	Butterfly
	2	XeF_4	Square planar
AB_5	0	PF_5	Trigonal bipyramid
	1	IF_5	Tetragonal pyramid
AB_6	0	WF_6	Octahedral
	1	XeF_6	Distorted octahedral
AB_7	0	IF_7	Pentagonal bipyramid
AB_8	0	ZrF_8^{4-}	Tetragonal antiprism
	1	$Mo(CN)_8^{4-}$	Trigonal dodecahedron
AB_9	0	ReH_9^{2-}	Tricapped trigonal prism

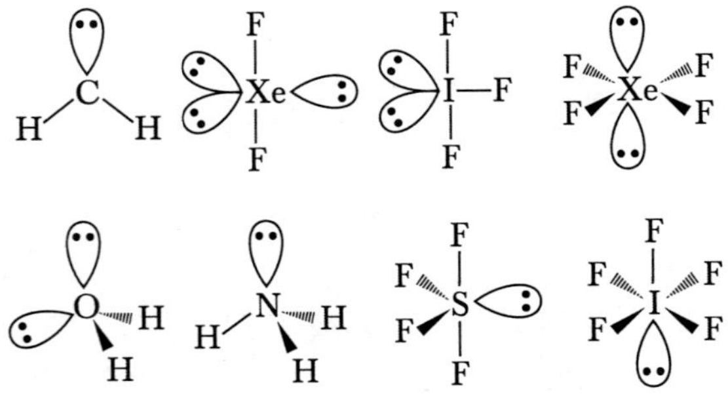

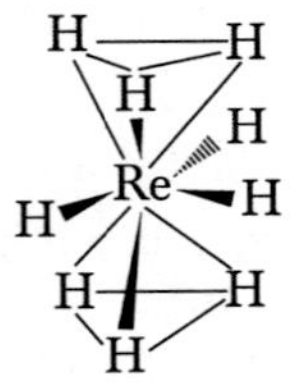

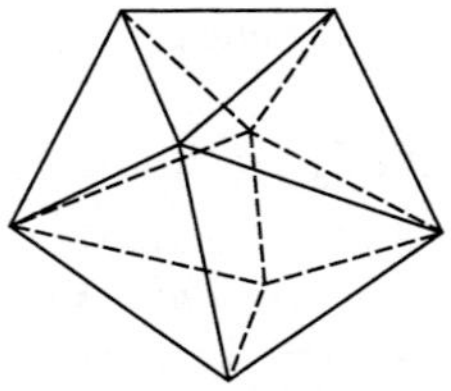

Trigonal dodecahedron

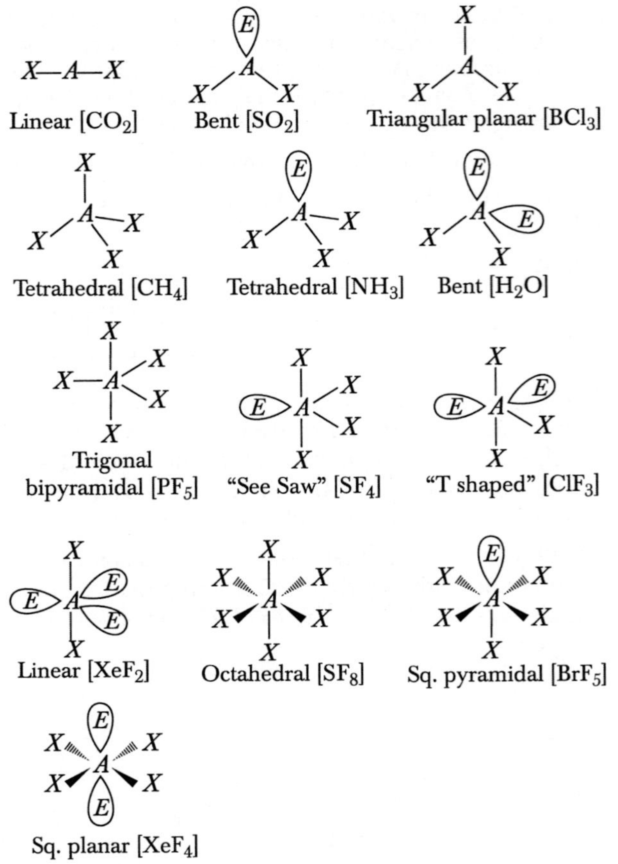

Table 2.3 **Geometry of Molecules or Ions Involving Hybridization with Lone pair of Electrons**

Hybridization	No. of lone pair of electron	Bond angle	Shape	Examples
sp^2	1	< 120°	Angular V-shape	$SnCl_2$, SO_2, NO_2^-
sp^3	1	< 109°28′	Pyramidal	NH_3, PH_3, PCl_3, AsH_3
sp^3	2	< 109°28′	V-shaped	H_2O, H_2S
sp^3d	3	180°	Linear	XeF_2
sp^3d	2	180°, 90°	T-shape	ICl_3, F_3Cl
sp^3d	1	186°, 116°	See-saw	SF_4
sp^3d^2	2	90°	Square planar	XeF_4
sp^3d^2	1	90°, 180°	Square pyramidal	IF_5
sp^3d^3	1	72° and 90°	Pentagonal pyramidal	XeF_6

Note VSEPR works very well for main group compounds but is less useful for transition metal compounds. The problem is that we are assuming that the core of the atom is spherical and has no effect on the arrangement of the valence shell electron pairs.

Examples Shape of NH_3 is pyramidal in place of tetrahedral and shape of H_2O is V-shaped in place of tetrahedral.

1. NH_3

E.C. of N in G.S. = $1s^2, 2s^2, 2p^3$

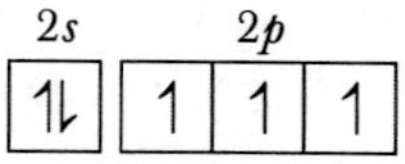

(a) Since, 'N' has three unpaired electrons, it can form three sigma bonds. Also, excitation of electrons in higher *d*-subshell is not possible since second shell does not have *d*-orbitals. That is why N does not form NH_5 or NCl_5 like other members (P, As, etc.)

(b) If all the three *p*-orbitals are involved in sigma bond formation with 1*s*-orbital of hydrogen, the bond angle will be 109°28′ whereas NH_3 has bond angle of 106°51′.

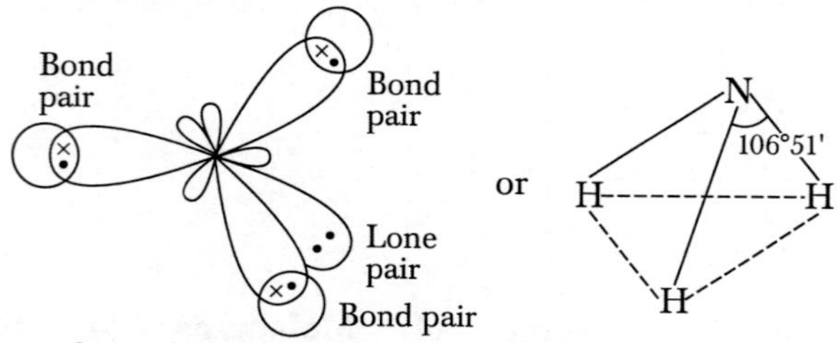

(sp^3-hybridization with one lone pair of electron)

(c) Thus, it is proposed that N-atom in NH_3 is sp^3-hybridized to show pyramidal geometry or tetrahedral nature with one position occupied by lone pair of electrons. The presence of this lone pair of electrons on N-atom contracts the bond angle from 109°28′ to 106°51′.

2. Xenon Fluorides

The bonding in these compounds is covalent and the structure is decided on the basis of hybridization as follows :

(i) **XeF_2** It involves sp^3d hybridization of xenon atoms which gives the molecule a trigonal bipyramidal structure with three positions occupied by lone pair. So, **XeF_2 is linear.**

E.C. of $_{54}$Xe in G.S.
$= 1s^2, 2s^2, 2p^6, 3s^2, 3p^6, 4s^2, 3d^{10}, 4p^6, 5s^2, 4d^{10}, 5p^6$.

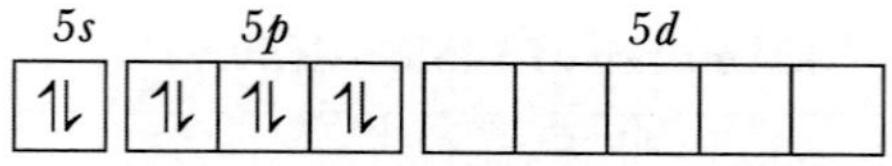

E.C. of Xe in first E.S. = $5s^2, 5p^5, 5d^1$

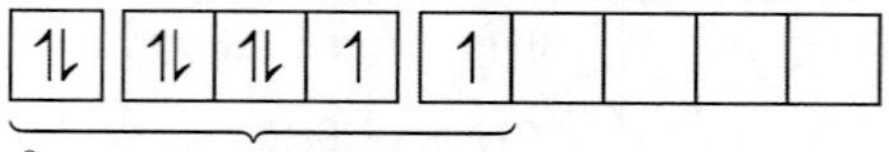

sp^3d hybridization with three lone pair of electrons

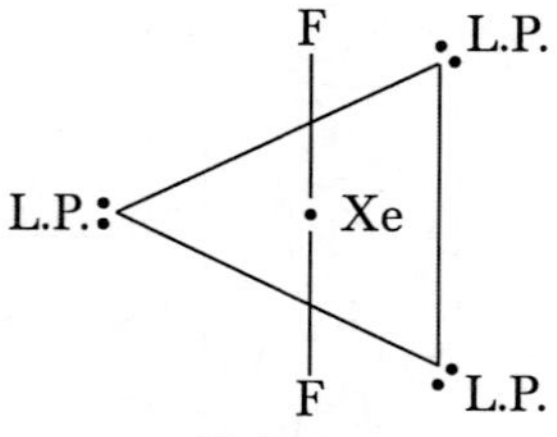

XeF_2 Linear

(ii) **XeF_4** This molecule involves sp^3d^2 hybridization of Xe atom which gives the molecule an octahedral shape with two positions occupied by lone pairs. So, **XeF_4 is square planar.**

E.C. of $_{54}$Xe in G.S.
$= 1s^2, 2s^2, 2p^6, 3s^2, 3p^6, 4s^2, 3d^{10}, 4p^6, 5s^2, 4d^{10}, 5p^6$.

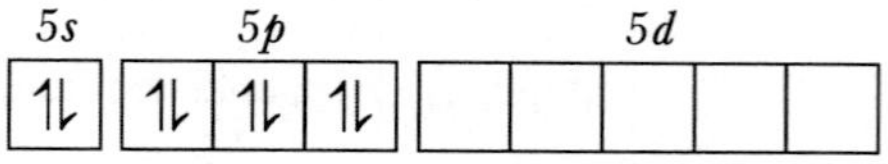

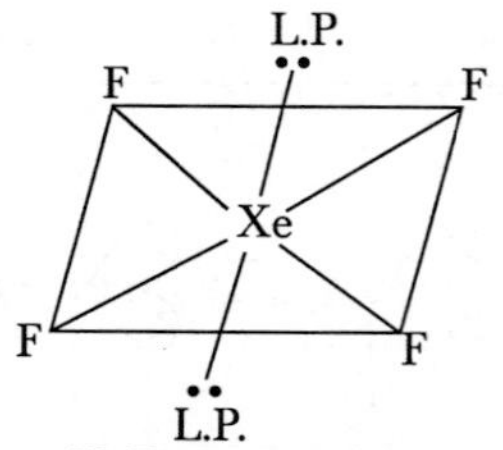

XeF_4 square planar

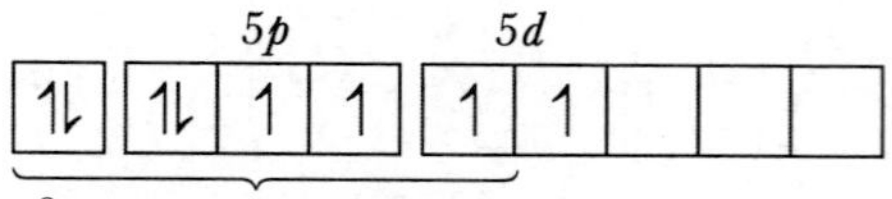

sp^3d hybridization with two lone pair of electrons

(iii) **XeF_6** It involves sp^3d^3 hybridization of Xe atom which gives the molecule a pentagonal bipyramidal structure with one position occupied by lone pair of electrons. Thus, **XeF_6 is pentagonal pyramidal.**

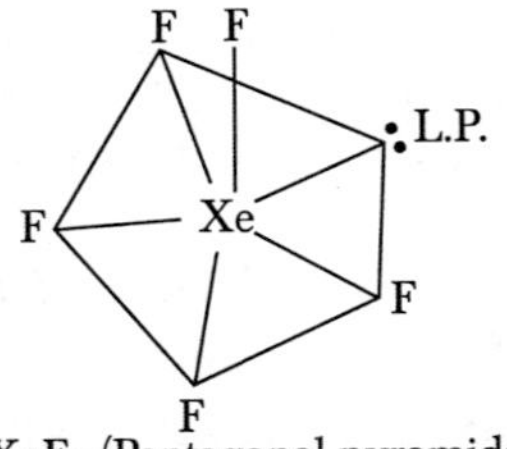

XeF_6 (Pentagonal pyramidal)

Resonance

The structures of some compounds and ions cannot be represented by a single formula. For example, sulphur dioxide (SO_2) and nitric acid (HNO_3) may each be described by two equivalent formulas. If only one formula for sulphur dioxide was correct and accurate, then the double bond to oxygen would be shorter and stronger than the single bond. Since, experimental evidence indicates that this molecule is bent (bond angle 120°) and has equal length of S–O bonds (1.432 Å), a single formula is inadequate, and the actual structure resembles an average of the two formulas. **This averaging of electron distribution over two ore more hypothetical contributing structures (canonical forms) to produce a hybrid electronic structure is called resonance.** Likewise, the structure of nitric acid is best described as a **resonance hybrid** of two structures, the double headed arrow being the unique symbol for resonance.

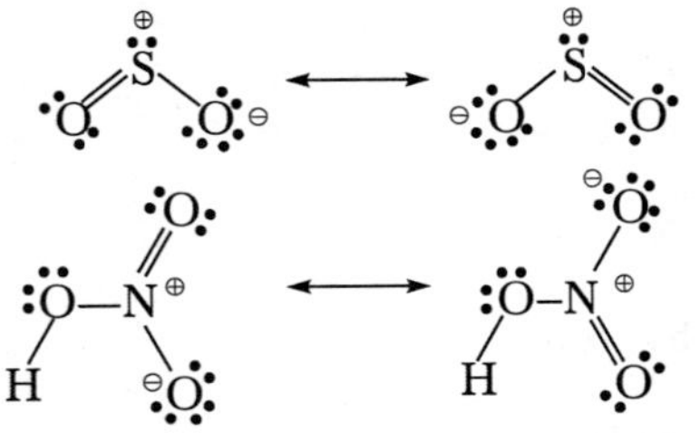

In cases such as these, the electron delocalization described by resonance enchances the stability of the molecules, and compounds or ions composed of such molecules often show exceptional stability. There are examples where one canonical form has a much greater stability than all others. If one canonical form has a much greater stability than all others, the hybrid will closely resemble it electronically and energetically.

Factors Affecting Stability of Canonical Structures

The following factors are important in evaluating the contribution each of these canonical structures makes to the actual molecule.

1. The number of covalent bonds in a structure

The greater the bonding, the more important and the stable contributing structure.

2. Formal charge separation

Other factors aside, charge separation decreases the stability and importance of the contributing structure.

3. Electronegativity of charge bearing atoms and charge density

High charge density is destabilizing. Positive charge is best accommodated on atoms of low electronegativity, and negative charge on high electronegative atoms.

Rules for Writing Resonating Structures

Following rules should be followed for writing resonating structures

(i) **Each structure should have the same number of unpaired electrons**

For example

$$:\dot{N}=\ddot{O}: \longleftrightarrow :\ddot{N}=\dot{O}:$$

(1 unpaired electron) (1 unpaired electron)

(ii) **Nuclei of the atoms in each structure must remain in fixed positions** Thus, only the arrangement of electrons may change. Bond length and bond angles should be closer to the real structure. Various resonating forms should have similar energy.

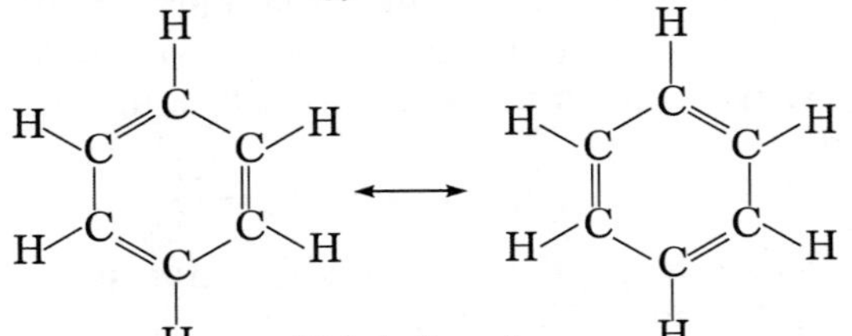

(Kekule forms)

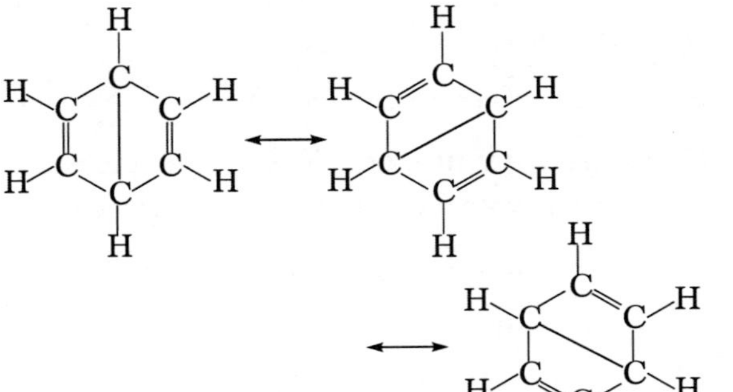

(Dewar form)

(Nuclei of atoms are in fixed position only arrangement of atoms differ)

(iii) **Structures in which negative charge resides on most electronegative atom and positive charge on most electropositive atom is closest to the true structure.**

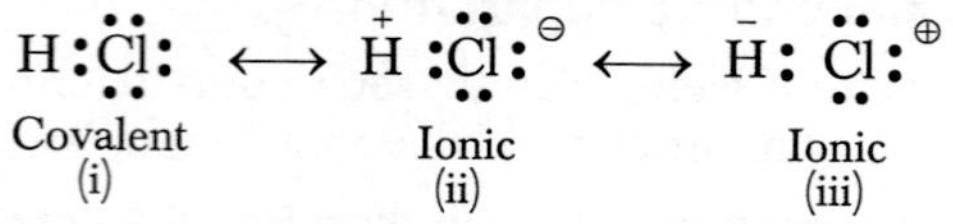

Structure (iii) is not possible.

(iv) **Contributing structures should be so written that unlike charges reside on neighbouring atoms.**

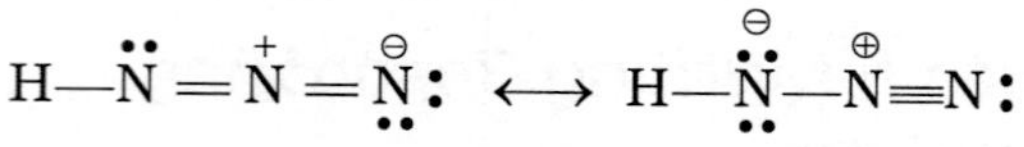

while 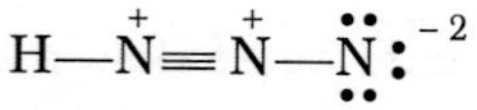

(insignificant structure)

(v) **Greater the number of covalent bonds, greater the contribution of that resonating structure** *e.g.,* the double bonded structures of BF_3 are important because of the formation of an additional covalent bond.

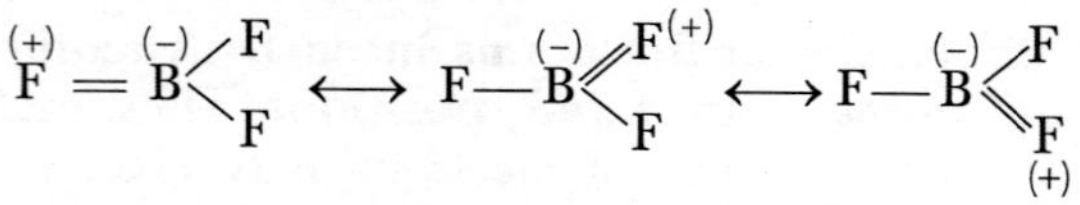

Examples 1. The left hand C═O structure has much greater total bonding than the other canonical form. In the right hand side structure, the numbers of covalent bonds are less and the Lewis octet is not fulfilled for the C. Hence, the structure on the left is the most stable one.

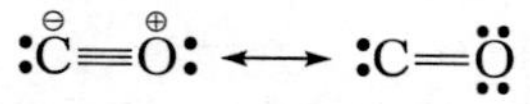

2. Similarly, for the azide ion, the structure on the left is the most stable one.

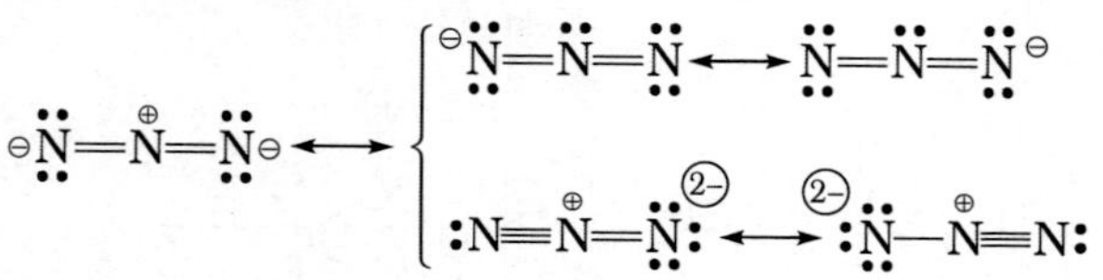

3. **Dinitrogen monoxide** (N_2O) The molecule is isoelectronic with CO_2 and has linear structure.

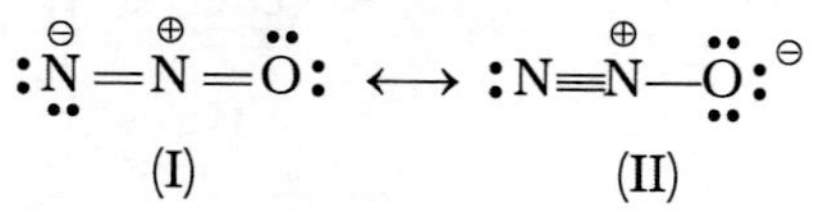

Hybridization

The mixing up of atomic orbitals of nearly same energy, giving rise to the formation of entirely new orbitals, equal in number of mixing orbitals, having identical shape and energy is called hybridization. The newly formed orbitals are called **hybrid orbitals.**

Characteristics of Hybridization

(i) Orbitals of nearly same energy hybridize.

(ii) Number of hybridized orbitals formed = number of orbitals mixed.

(iii) Hybridized orbitals have identical shape and energy.

(iv) Hybridized orbitals are dumb-bell type, one loop larger and one smaller and can, therefore, be directed towards the other atom more effectively than atomic orbitals. Hence, they can overlap more strongly with orbitals of other atoms than atomic orbitals. This leads to stronger bond formation.

(v) Hybridized orbitals have different orientation in space.

sp-hybridization = 2 hybridized orbitals at 180°

sp^2-hybridization = 3 hybridized orbitals at 120°

sp^3-hybridization = 4 hybridized orbitals at 109°28′.

The angle of hybridized orbitals is derived by :

$\cos\alpha = -\left(\frac{1}{m}\right)$, where, m = No. of *p*-orbitals involved in hybridization.

sp-hybridization, $\cos\alpha = -1$, $\therefore \alpha = 180°$

sp^2-hybridization, $\cos\alpha = -\frac{1}{2}$ $\therefore \alpha = 120°$

sp^3-hybridization, $\cos\alpha = -\frac{1}{3}$, $\therefore \alpha = 109°28'$

(vi) Hybridized orbitals show only head on overlapping and thus, form only sigma bond. They never form π-bond.

(vii) Orbitals but not electrons undergo hybridization. That is half-filled or completely filled orbitals may hybridized. However, the presence of lone pair of electron on hybridized orbitals results in distorted geometry of molecules.

(viii) As the *s*-character increases in hybridized orbitals, electronegativity of atom involved in hybridization increases, and the size of the hybridized orbitals becomes smaller leading to greater overlapping and thereby giving rise to smaller bond length and higher bond energy.

Hybridization	s-character	Example	C–C Bond length	C–H Bond length
sp	50% or $\frac{1}{2}$	$HC \equiv CH$	C≡C, 1.20 Å	C—H, 1.03 Å
sp^2	33% or $\frac{1}{3}$	$H_2C{=}CH_2$	C=C, 1.34 Å	C—H, 1.108 Å
sp^3	25% or $\frac{1}{4}$	$H_3C{-}CH_3$	C—C, 1.54 Å	C—H, 1.112 Å

(ix) It is the geometry which suggests the type of hybridization in a molecule.

Types of Hybridization

1. *sp*-hybridization

One *s*-orbital + One *p*-orbital = Two hybridized orbitals.

Shape = Linear, Bond angle = 180°.

Examples BeF_2, $BeCl_2$, CO_2, CS_2, $HgCl_2$, $MgCl_2$, C_2H_2.

$Be = 1s^2, 2s^2$ (ground state)

$Be = 1s^2, 2s^1, 2p^1$ (excited state).

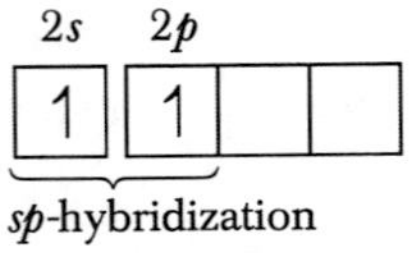

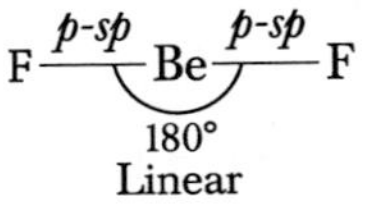

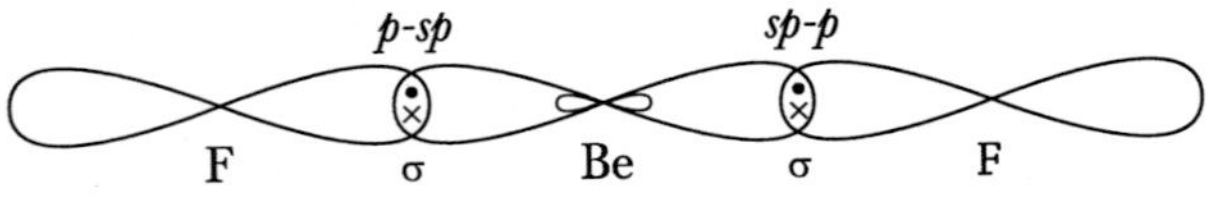

2. *sp*^{2}-hybridization

One $s + 2p$-orbitals = Three hybridized orbitals at 120°

Shape = Trigonal planar, bond angle = 120°

Examples BF_3, BCl_3, BH_3, $AlCl_3$, SO_3, C_2H_4, NO_3^-, CO_3^{2-}.

$B = 1s^2, 2s^2, 2p^1$ (ground state)

$B = 1s^2, 2s^1, 2p^2$ (excited state)

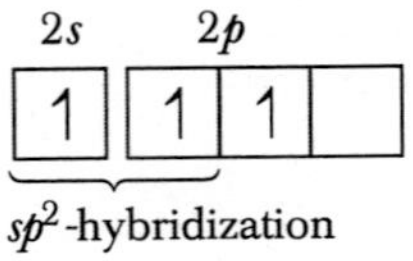

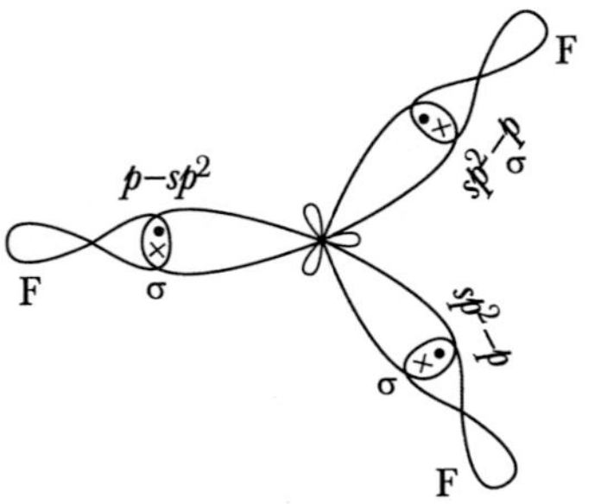

or

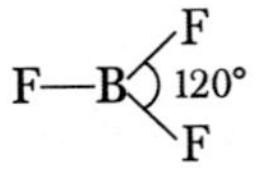

3. *sp*^{3}-hybridization

One *s*-orbital + three *p*-orbitals = Four hybridized orbitals

Shape = Tetrahedral, Bond angle = 109°28′.

Examples $SiCl_4$, CH_4, $SnCl_4$, SO_4^{2-}, ClO_4^-

$C = 1s^2, 2s^2, 2p^2$ (ground state)

$C = 1s^2, 2s^1, 2p^3$ (excited state)

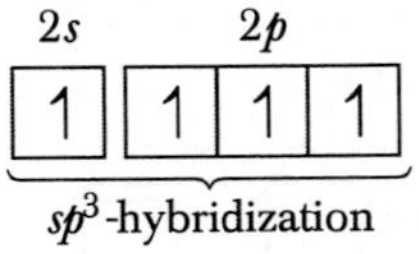

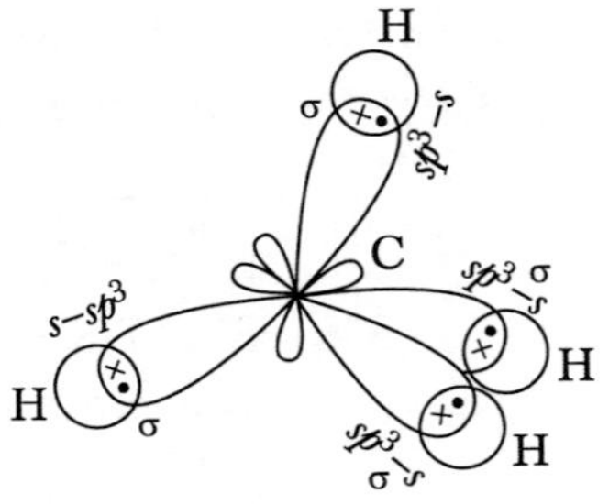

or

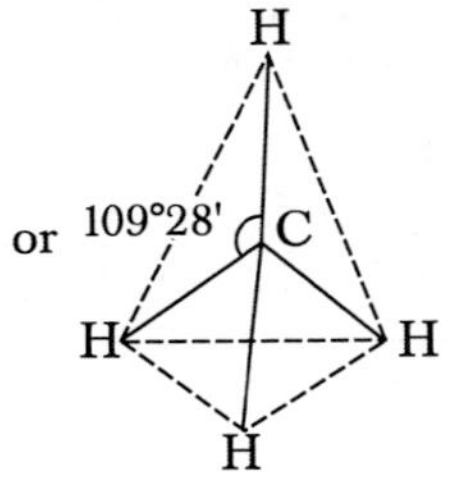

Tetrahedral

4. *sp*^{3}*d*-hybridization

One *s*-orbital + three *p*-orbitals + one *d*-orbital = Five hybridized orbitals (Three coplanar and two perpendicular to this plane).

Shape = Trigonal bipyramidal,

bond angle = 120°, 90°.

Examples PCl_5, PF_5

$P = 1s^2, 2s^2, 2p^6, 3s^2, 3p^3$ (ground state)

$P = 1s^2, 2s^2, 2p^6, 3s^1, 3p^3, 3d^1$ (excited state)

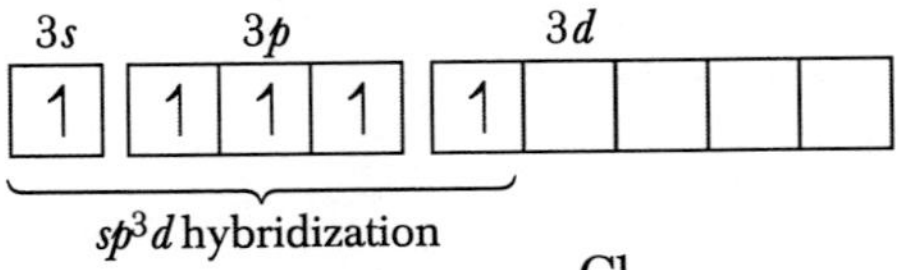

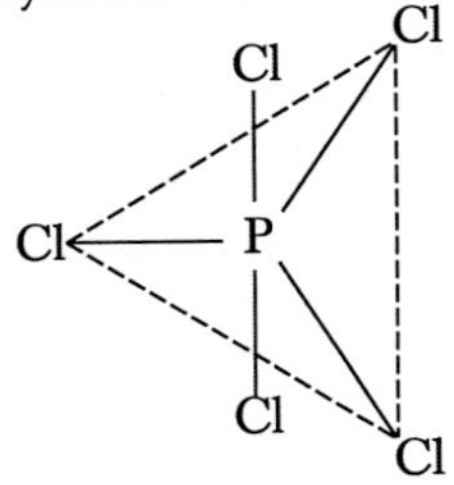

(PCl_5) Trigonal bipyramidal

5. sp^3d^2-hybridization

One *s*-orbital + three *p*-orbitals + two *d*-orbitals = Six hybridized orbitals (Four coplanar and two perpendicular to this plane)

Shape = Octahedral, Bond angle = 90°

Examples SF_6, $SnCl_6^{2-}$, SeF_6

E.C. of S in G.S. = $1s^2, 2s^2, 2p^6, 3s^2, 3p^4$ (S shows two covalency *e.g.*, H_2S)

3s	3p		
↑↓	↑↓	↑	↑

E.C. of S in E.S. = $1s^2, 2s^2, 2p^6, 3s^2, 3p^3, 3d^1$ (S shows four covalence *e.g.*, SO_2)

3s	3p			3d				
↑↓	↑	↑	↑	↑				

E.C. of S in second E.S. = $1s^2, 2s^2, 2p^6, 3s^1, 3p^3, 3d^2$ (S shows six covalence *e.g.*, SF_6)

3s	3p			3d				
↑	↑	↑	↑	↑	↑			

sp^3d^2 hybridization

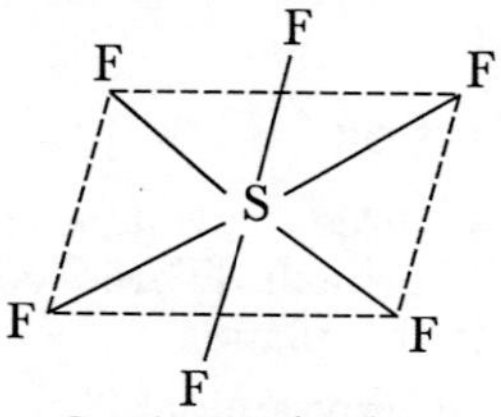

Octahedral (SF_6)

6. sp^3d^3-hybridization

One *s*-orbital + three *p*-orbitals + three *d*-orbitals = Seven hybridized orbitals (five coplanar and two perpendicular to this plane).

Shape = Pentagonal bipyramidal,

Bond angle = 90°, 72°.

Examples IF_7

I (G.S.) : ns^2, np^5

ns	np			nd				
↑↓	↑↓	↑↓	↑					

(where, n = outermost shell) (showing 1 covalence *e.g.*, HF.)

I (E.S.) : ns^2, np^4, nd^1

↑↓	↑	↑	↑	↑	↑			

(showing 3 covalence, *e.g.*, IF_3)

I (2nd E.S.) : ns^2, np^3, nd^2

↑↓	↑	↑	↑	↑	↑			

(showing 5 covalence, *e.g.*, IF_5)

I (3rd E.S.) : ns^1, np^3, nd^3

↑	↑	↑	↑	↑	↑	↑		

sp^3d^3 hybridization

(showing 7 covalence, *e.g.*, IF_7)

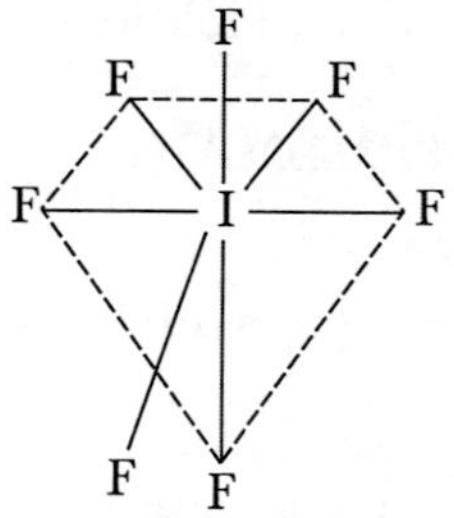

Pentagonal bipyramidal (IF_7)

7. dsp^2-hybridization

One *s*-orbital + two *p*-orbitals + one *d*-orbital = Four hybridized orbitals.

Shape = Square planar, bond angle = 90°

Examples $[Ni(CN)_4]^{2-}$, $[PtCl_4]^{2-}$, $[Cu(NH_3)_4]^{2+}$

E.C. of Ni in G.S.

$= 1s^2, 2s^2, 2p^6, 3s^2, 3p^6, 4s^2, 3d^8$

3d					4s	4p		
↑↓	↑↓	↑↓	↑	↑	↑↓			

E.C. of Ni^{2+} in G.S.

$= 1s^2, 2s^2, 2p^6, 3s^2, 3p^6, 4s^0, 3d^8$

3d					4s	4p		
↑↓	↑↓	↑↓	↑	↑				

E.C. of Ni^{2+} in $[Ni(CN)_4]^{2-}$

3d					4s	4p		
↑↓	↑↓	↑↓	↑↓	××	××	××	××	
				CN	CN	CN	CN	

dsp^2 hybridization

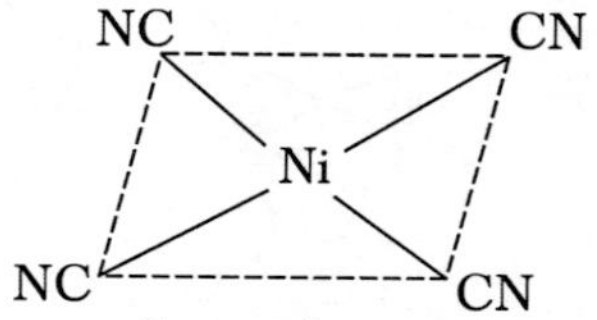

Square planar

Fluxionality

Most molecules have a single, well-defined nuclear configuration. The atoms execute approximately harmonic vibrations about their equilibrium positions, but in other respects the structures may be considered rigid. There are, however, many cases in which molecular vibrations or intramolecular rearrangements carry a molecule from one nuclear configuration into another. **When such processes occur at a rate permitting detection by some physical or chemical means, the molecules are designated as stereochemically non-rigid.** In some cases, the two or more configurations are not chemically equivalent. In these cases, the process of inter-conversion is called isomerization or tautomerization. **In other cases, the two or more configurations are chemically equivalent and they are called fluxional molecules.** The existence of stereochemical non-rigidity can be reveabled by NMR spectroscopy, since its time-scale is typically in the range 10^{-2} to 10^{-5} s. The rearrangements take place at rate processes with activation energies. When the activation energy is in the range of 25 to 100 kJ mol^{-1}, the rates of rearrangements can be brought into the range of 10^2 to 10^5 s^{-1} at temperatures between +150 and −150°C.

Examples A common type of fluxional behaviour is the inversion of pyramidal molecules. In NH_3, the inversion has a very low activation barrier of – 25 kJ mol^{-1} For PH_3, AsH_3 the activation barrier is higher. The 4-coordinate Ni(II) complexes, $Ni(R_3P)_2X_2$ undergo square planar ⟷ tetrahedral rearrangements with an activation barrier of – 45 kJ mol^{-1} and rates of 10^5 s^{-1} at room temperature.

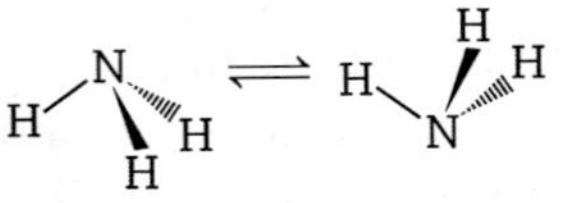

Stereochemical Non-Rigidity in TBP Molecules

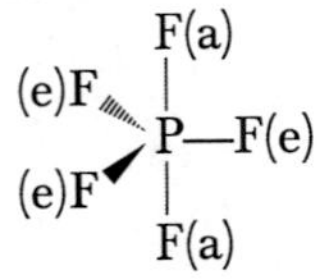

The Case of PF_5

The structure of PF_5 has been found to be trigonal bipyramidal. As stated before the trigonal bipyramidal polyhedron has two distinct sites, the axial site and the equatorial site. The ^{19}F NMR spectrum of this compound shows a doublet with the separation between the lines corresponding to the coupling constant J(P-F). However, for a trigonal bipyramidal structure we anticipate a more complex pattern as the axial fluorine atoms belong to one chemically equivalent set and the equatorial fluorines belong to another chemically equivalent set. Therefore, the spectrum should have been more complicated as shown below.

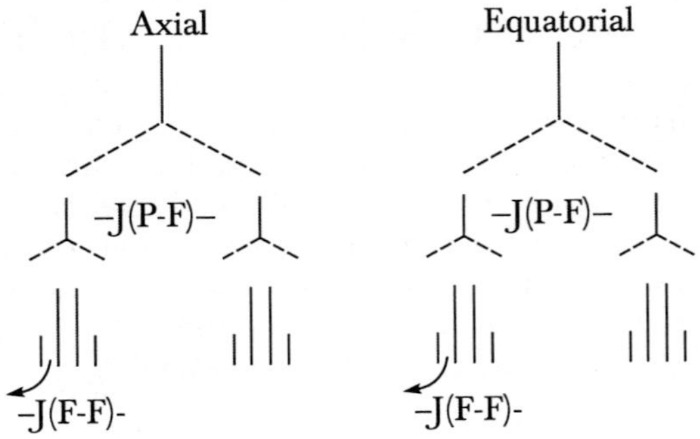

Why is only a doublet seen then?

The answer lies in the fact that the molecule is stereochemically non-rigid and is continuously changing its structure. This is known as fluxional behaviour. The mechanism that accounts for the behaviour of PF_5 is known as Berry Pseudo Rotation and is shown below :

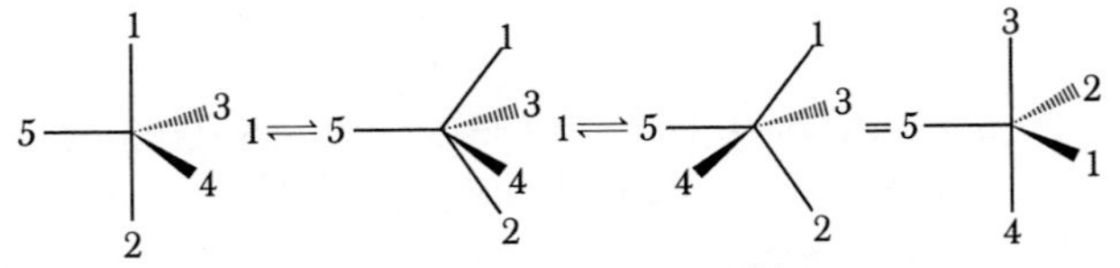

1(a) 2 1(b)

In structure **1a** the angle F1-P-F2 is 180° and the F3-P-F4 angle is 120°. Imagine that the former is shrinking and the latter is expanding so that both the angles become nearly equal and structure **2**, a square pyramid, is obtained. If this process is continued further such that the former F1-P-F2 angle now becomes 120° and the former F3-P-F4 angle becomes 180° we get the second trigonal bipyramidal structure **1b**. Thus, in reaching **1b** from **1a** through **2,** we have essentially exchanged a pair of axial fluorine atoms with a set of equatorial fluorine atoms without breaking any bonds. In this whole process one P-F5 does not change. If this process takes place faster than the NMR time scale in the NMR experiment only one set of fluorines is seen.

For the majority of five-coordinate main-group and transition metal compounds the energy difference between the trigonal bipyramid (**1**) and tetragonal pyramid (**2**) structures is sufficiently low, so that Berry pseudorotation represents a widespread mechanism of **stereochemical nonrigidity.** No angular momentum is generated by this motion; this is the reason for the term.

Keep in mind that we single out one interchange path here, while in reality all atoms will rapidly occupy all possible positions in a very dynamic way.

Having bulky substituents such as chlorine or substitutents that do not prefer to occupy axial positions can slow this process down. Accordingly in PCl_2F_3, although at room temperature all the fluorine atoms are still equivalent and only a doublet is seen in the fluorine NMR spectrum, at – 143°C that exchange is stopped and one sees two sets of peaks (a doublet of doublet for the two axial fluorine atoms and a doublet of triplets for the equatorial fluorine atom).

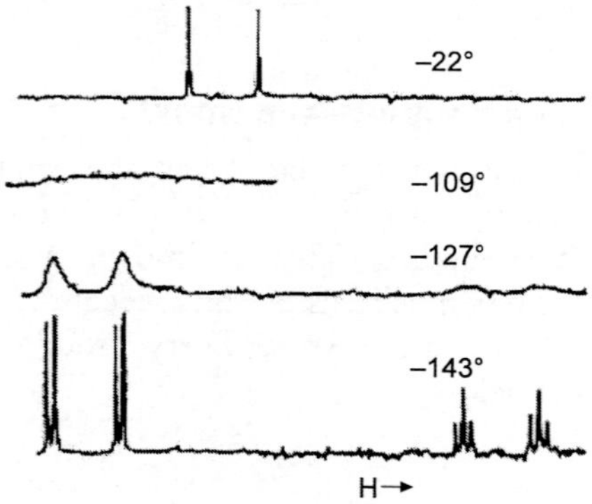

At temperature of – 22°C and above, the resonance of F is observed as a single doublet (^{31}P-^{19}F coupling, 1048 Hz). However, as the temperature is lowered to – 143°C, a downfield doublet (δ-67.4) for the axial F atoms and an upfield doublet (δ 41.5) for the equatorial F atom is observed. The single equatorial F atom further spilt by the two axial F atoms into two triplets. The two axial F atoms is split into doublet by the single equatorial F atom ($2nI + 1$; $n = 2$; $J_{F-F} = 124$ Hz).

Also the weighted avarage of the chemical shifts at – 143°C {2*x* (– 67.4 ppm) + 1*x* (41.5 ppm)} is the same as that at – 22°C {3 × (– 31.1 ppm)} indicating that the structure does not change on warming even though the F atoms exchanges positions.

Dipole Moment

Dipole moment is the property of molecules in which the distribution of charge is unsymmetrical. For non-polar molecules, its value is zero, but for polar molecules, it has certain value. It is given by the product of charge (q) on one atom and the bond-length (l). Therefore,

$$\boxed{\mu = q \times l}$$

The unit of dipole moment is esu-cm or debye (d).

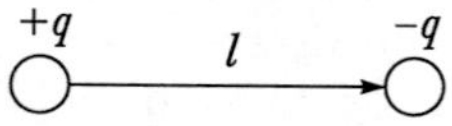

In other words dipole moment is the degree of polarity of a polar covalent bond of a polar molecule. It is equal to the product of the magnitude of electric charge (q) in esu and distance (l) in Å between the positive and negative centres (*i.e.*, bond-length).

Thus, $\mu = q \times l.$

As 'q' is of the order of 10^{-10} esu and 'l' of the order of 10^{-8} cm, μ is known as Debye (D). Thus,

$1D = 10^{-18}$ esu cm $= 3.33 \times 10^{-28}$ C cm.

μ is the vector quantity.

Magnitude of dipole moment of a polar molecule depends on the difference in electronegativities of the bonded atoms. **The greater the difference in electronegativities, the greater is the dipole moment.**

Determination of Dipole Moment

A number of methods are available for determining the dipole moment. One of them is as follows :

Temperature Method

We know that, $P_t = a + \dfrac{b}{T}$

where, a and b are the constants and are given as

$$a = \frac{4}{3}\pi N \text{ and } b = \frac{4}{9}\frac{\pi N}{k}\mu^2$$

where, N = Avogadro's Number,
k = Boltzmann's constant,

μ = Dipole moment, a = degree of polarisability.

If total polarization P_1 and P_2 are determined at two temperatures T_1 and T_2, respectively then

$$P_1 = a + \frac{b}{T_1} \text{ and } P_2 = a + \frac{b}{T_2}$$

$$\therefore \quad b = (P_1 + P_2)\left(\frac{T_1 T_2}{T_1 - T_2}\right) \quad \text{...(i)}$$

The value of dipole moment, μ is easily calculated from the value of 'b', *i.e.*,

$$b = \frac{4\pi N}{9k}\mu^2 \text{ or } \mu = \sqrt{\left(\frac{9k}{4\pi N}\right) b}$$

As $k = 1.3805 \times 10^{-16}$ erg. deg^{-1}, $\pi = 3.14$, $N = 6.023 \times 10^{23}$, we get

$$\mu = \sqrt{\frac{9 \times 1.3805 \times 10^{-16} \times b}{4 \times 3.14 \times 6.023 \times 10^{23}}}$$
$$= 0.0128 \times 10^{-18} \sqrt{b} \text{ esu-cm}$$

So, knowing '*b*' from Eq. (i), we can calculate the dipole moment easily.

Applications of Dipole Moment

1. Determination of the molecular structure of substance

Monoatomic molecules, like those of rare gases, have no dipole moment and are non-polar.

Diatomic molecules, may be either polar or non-polar, molecules of gases like O_2, N_2 etc., have $\mu = 0$, which indicates that the electron pairs binding the constituent atoms exist at the same distance from the two atoms. But diatomic molecules of the compounds have some dipole moment and so their structures are asymmetrical.

Triatomic molecules, may also be either polar or non-polar. The dipole moment of CO_2 is zero. So, it is a non-polar molecule, even though the C—O bonds are polar, as the shared electrons *i.e.,* closer to the oxygen atom than to the C-atom. This shows that CO_2 molecule is linear, as only in this way the dipole moment on one side of the molecule is cancelled by that on the other side and net dipole moment is zero. So, it has the structure.

O=C=O

Water on the other hand, has an appreciable dipole moment ($\mu = 1.85$D). Thus, water molecule cannot be linear. The two H-atoms in a water molecule do not lie linearly on the two sides of the oxygen atoms like H—O—H. Therefore, it should have an unsymmetrical or bent structure as represented by the following figure.

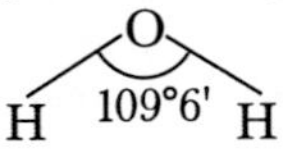

The dipole moment of each O—H bond is 1.60D and the angle between these two bonds should be 109°6′ to have the dipole moment of the molecules as 1.85D.

Note The dipole moment '*M*' of the molecule is given by $\mu = 2m\cos\frac{\theta}{2}$, where, '*m*' is the bond moment and θ is the angle between the two bonds.

The dipole moment for a single H–S bond is nearly 0.8D and so the angle between the two bonds in the molecule of H_2S may be found to be 93° and its structure is represented by the following figure.

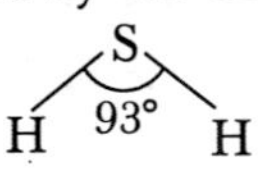

Tetratomic molecules of the type BA_3 may be polar or non-polar. If it is non-polar then all the atoms will lie in one plane and the angles between the different bonds are equal to one another as shown below.

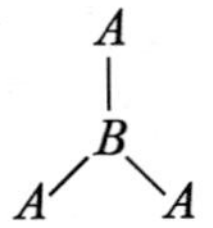

Ammonia molecule has $\mu = 1.26$D and its structure is as

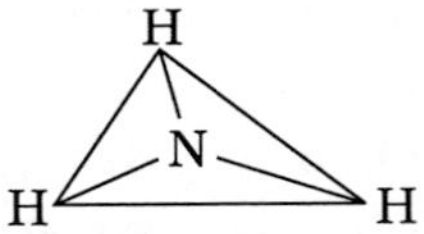

It is assigned as triangular pyramidal structure in which nitrogen atom lies at the apex of the pyramid and the H–atoms lie at the three corners of the triangle, which forms the base of the pyramid.

Molecules of PCl_3 or $AsCl_3$ also have triangular pyramidal structures, with P and As atoms at the apex.

2. Distinguish between *cis*-and-*trans* isomers

The *cis* form will have a dipole moment but in the *trans* form the effect produced in one half of the molecule is generally cancelled by that in the other half of the molecule.

Maleic acid (*cis* form) Fumeric acid (*trans* form)

3. To calculate the ionic character of a bond

Dipole moment give the information about the ionic character of a covalent bond. It has been seen that the H—Cl bond is 17% ionic in nature.

4. In determining the polarity of a bond

It gives us an indication of the polar character of a bond. The dipole moments of HF, HCl, HBr and HI are 1.92, 1.03, 0.87 and 0.38D, respectively. This shows that the polarity of the H–*X* bond decreases gradually as we move from F to I (where, *X* = F, Cl, Br, I).

5. In finding substituted aromatic product

If both the substituents are the same, the dipole moment of *para* derivative should be zero. Its value will be maximum for the *ortho* derivative, while the dipole moment value for the *meta* derivative will lie between that of *para* derivative and *ortho* derivative.

Bond Angles

It might be expected that the bond angles of sp^3 carbon would always be the tetrahedral angle 109°28′, but this is so only where the four groups are identical, as in methane, *neo*-pentane or CCl_4. In most cases the angles deviate a little from the pure tetrahedral value. For example, the C—C—Br angle in 2-bromopropane is 114.2°. Similarly, slight variations are generally found from ideal value of 120° and 180° for sp^2 and *sp* carbon respectively.

For oxygen and nitrogen, angles of 90° are predicted from p^2 bonding. However, as we have seen, **the angles of water and ammonia are much larger than this, as are the angles of other oxygen and nitrogen compound (Table), in fact, they are much closer to the tetrhedral angles of 109°28′ than to 90°. These facts have led to the suggestion that in these compounds oxygen and nitrogen use sp^3-bonding,** *i.e.*, instead of forming bonds by the overlap of two (or three *p*-orbitals with one '*s*'-orbitals of the hydrogen atoms, they hybridize their 2*s* and 2*p* orbitals to form four sp^3 orbitals and then use only two (or three) of these for bonding with hydrogen, the others remaining occupied by unshared pairs (also called lone pairs). If this description is valid, and it is generally accepted by most chemists today, it becomes necessary to explain why the angles of these two compounds are in fact not 109°28′ but a few degrees smaller.

One explanation that has been offered is that **the unshared pair actually has a greater steric requirement than a pair of bond, since there** is no second nucleus to draw away some of the electron density and the bonds are thus crowded together. However, most evidence is that unshared pairs have smaller steric requirements than bonds and the explanation most commonly accepted is that the hybridization is not pure sp^3. As we have seen above, an atom supplies more *p*-character when it is bonded to more electronegative atoms. An unshared pair may be considered to be an 'atom' of the lowest possible electronegativity, since there is no attracting power at all. Consequently, the unshared pairs have more '*s*' and the bonds more *p*-character than pure sp^3 orbitals, making the bonds somewhat more like p^2 bonds and reducing the angle. As seen in the following table, oxygen, nitrogen and sulphur angles generally increase with decreasing electronegativity of the substituents. Note that the explanation given above cannot explain why some of these angles are greater than the tetrahedral angle.

Table 2.4 **Bond Angle for Different Molecules**

Angle	Value	Compound
H—O—H	104°27′	Water
C—O—H	107-109°	Methanol
C—O—C	111°43′	Dimethyl ether
C—O—C	124 ± 5°	Diphenyl ether
H—S—H	92.1°	H_2S
C—S—H	99.4°	Methyl mercaptan
C—S—C	99.1°	Dimethyl sulphide
H—N—H	106°46′	Ammonia
H—N—H	106°	Methyl amine
C—N—H	112°	Methyl amine
C—N—C	108.7°	Trimethyl amine

Bond Distances

The bond distances between atoms in a molecule are characteristic properties of the molecule and can give us information if we compare the same bond in different molecules. The chief methods of determining bond distances and angles are X-rays diffractions (only for solid), electron diffraction (only for gases), and spectroscopic methods.

Measurements vary in accuracy, but indications are that similar bonds have fairly constant lengths from one molecule to the next. The variation is generally less than 1%. Thus, for a bond between two sp^3 carbons the following results have been found.

C—C bond in	Bond length Å	C—C bond in	Bond-length, Å
Diamond	1.544	Cyclohexane	1.540 ± 0.015
C_2H_6	1.5324 ± 0.0011	*t*-butyl chloride	1.532
C_2H_5Cl	1.5495 ± 0.0005	*n*-butane to *n*-heptane	1.531 – 1.34
C_3H_8	1.532 ± 0.003	Isobutane	1.535 ± 0.001

Bond distances for some important bond types are given in the following table. As can be seen in this table, carbon bonds are shortened by increasing '*s*' character. This is most often explained by the fact that, as the percentage of '*s*' character in a hybrid orbital increases, the orbital becomes more like an '*s*' orbital and hence is held more tightly by the nucleus than an orbital with less '*s*' character.

Indications are that a C—D bond is slightly shorter than a corresponding C—H bond. Thus, electron diffraction measurements of C_2H_6 and C_2D_6 showed a C—H bond distance of 1.1122 ± 0.0012 Å and a C—D distance of 1.1071 ± 0.0012 Å.

Bond Energies

There are two kinds of energy. The energy necessary to cleave a bond to give the constituent radicals is called the dissociation energy. *D*, for example, *D* for $H_2O \rightarrow OH + H$ is 118 kcal/mol. However, this is not taken as the energy of the O—H bond in water, since *D* for H—O → H + O is 100 kcal/mol. The average of these two values, 109 kcal/mol, is taken as the bond energy '*E*'. In diatomic molecules, of course, *D* = *E*.

The more usual practice, though, is not to measure the heat of atomization (*i.e.*, the energy necessary to convert a compound to its atom) directly but to calculate it from the heat of combustion.

Heats of combustion are very accurately known for hydrocarbons. For methane the value is 212.8 kcal/mol (at 25°C), which leads to a heat of atomization of 398.0 kcal/mol (at 25°C) or a value of *E* for the C—H bond of 99.5 kcal/mol at 25°C. This method is fine for molecules like methane in which all the bonds are equivalent, but for more complicated molecules assumptions must be made. Thus, for ethane, the heat of atomization of 25°C is 676.1 kcal/mol and we must decide how much of this energy is due to the C—C bond and how much to the six C—H bonds.

If we make the assumption that *E* for each of the C—H bonds is the same as *E* for the C—H bond in methane (99.5 kcal/mol), then $6 \times 99.5 = 594.0$, leaving 79.1 kcal/mol for the C—C bond. However, a similar calculation for propane gives a value of 80.3 for the C—C bond, and for isobutane, the value is 81.6. A consideration of heats of atomization of isomers also illustrates the difficulty.

$$C_2H_6(g) + 3\tfrac{1}{2}\,O_2(g) = 2CO_2(g) + 3H_2O(l) + 372.9 \text{ kcal}$$

$$2CO_2(g) = 2C(\text{graphite}) + 2O_2(g) - 188.2 \text{ kcal}$$

$$3H_2O(l) = 3H_2(g) + 1\tfrac{1}{2}O_2(g) - 204.9 \text{ kcal}$$

$$3H_2(g) = 6H(g) - 312.5 \text{ kcal}$$

$$2C\ (\text{graphite}) = 2C(g) - 343.4 \text{ kcal}$$

$$C_2H_6(g) = 6H(g) + 2C(g) - 676.1 \text{ kcal}$$

Certain generalizations can be derived from the data in the following table :

1. There is a correlation of bond strengths with bond distances. In general shorter bonds are strong bonds. Since, we have already seen that increasing 's' character shortens bonds, it follows that **bond strengths increase with increasing 's' character.**
2. **Bonds become weaker as we move down the Periodic Table.** Compare C—O and C—S or the four C-halogen bonds. This is a consequence of the first generalization, since **bond distances must increase as we go down the Periodic Table because the number of inner electrons increases.**
3. **Double bonds are both shorter and stronger than the corresponding single bonds**, but not twice as strong, because π overlap is less than σ-overlap. This means that a σ-bond is stronger than a π-bond, The difference in energy between a single bond, say C—C, and the corresponding double bond is the amount of energy necessary to cause rotation around the double bond.

Bond energy *E* values for some important bond types *E* values are arranged within each group in order of decreasing strength. The mean values are averaged over a large series of compounds. The calculated values are computed for one compound using values for other bonds from earlier values in table.

Table 2.5 **Mean Value of *E* for Different Bonds**

Bond	Mean value of *E* at 25°C (kcal/mol)	Value	Calculated form
O—H	110-111	110.6	H_2O
C—H	96-99	99.5	CH_4
N—H	93	93.4	NH_3
S—H	82	83	H_2S
C—F	...	116	CF_4
C—H	96-99	99.5	CH_4
C—O	85-91	76.8 84.2	CH_3OH C_2H_5OH
C—C	83-85	79.1	C_2H_6
C—Cl	79	78.3	CCl_4
C—N	69-75	66.5	CH_3NH_2
C—Br	66	69 65	CBr_4 $CHBr_3$
C—S	66	64	C_2H_5CH
C—I	52	50.1	CH_3I
C≡C	199-200	194.4	C_2H_2
C=C	146-151	141.3	C_2H_4
C—C	83-85	79.1	HCN
C≡N	204	206.1	HCHO
C=O	173-181	164	CO_2
C=N	143	192	

Exercise 1
(For Part 'B')

1. The highest occupied molecular orbital in HF is
(a) bonding (b) anti-bonding
(c) non-bonding (d) ionic

2. On the basis of LCAO-MO theory, the magnetic characteristics of N_2 and N_2^+ are
(a) N_2 is paramagnetic and N_2^+ is diamagnetic
(b) N_2 is diamagnetic and N_2^+ is paramagnetic
(c) Both are paramagnetic
(d) Both are diamagnetic

3. Which of the following molecule is planar?
(a) PCl_3 (b) ClO_4^-
(c) CO_3^{2-} (d) NH_3

4. The shape of IF_5 is
(a) pentagon
(b) square pyramid
(c) trigonal bipyramidal
(d) pentagonal bipyramidal

5. The hybridization of sulphur in SF_6 is
(a) sp^3 (b) sp^3d^2
(c) sp^3d^3 (d) sp^2d

6. Double bond between two atoms consists of
(a) two π-bonds
(b) two σ-bonds
(c) one σ-and one π-bond
(d) one σ-bond and one delta bond

7. Which molecule/ion has planar configuration?
(a) BF_4^- (b) XeF_4
(c) SF_4 (d) CCl_4

8. Mark the incorrect statement.
(a) H_2O molecule is angular
(b) BF_3 molecule is planar
(c) CH_4 is tetrahedral
(d) SF_4 is square planar

9. Which of the following molecule is linear?
(a) CO_2 (b) H_2O
(c) SF_2 (d) N_2O

10. Which of the following statement on resonance is false?
(a) The actual structure a hybrid of the various extreme possibilities
(b) Resonance hybrid is more stable than any one of the constituting structures
(c) Resonance leads to extra stability
(d) Any number of resonance hybrid can be proposed

11. Find out the false statement on rules of writing resonance structure.
(a) Resonating structures suffer change in position of atoms
(b) Each structure keeps the same number of unpaired electrons
(c) Contributing structures have bond lengths and bond angles closer to real structure
(d) Unlike charges stay on neighbouring atoms

12. Which of the following statements on hybridization is false?
(a) Hybridization is not a process but a concept
(b) Orbitals involved in hybridization may have different energies but similar symmetry
(c) Hybrid orbitals form stronger bonds than pure atomic orbitals
(d) XeF_2 is sp^3d hybridized

13. Which one of the following statements on the formation of molecular orbitals is false?
(a) The number of molecular orbitals is equal to the number of combining atomic orbitals
(b) They are formed only if symmetry and relative energies of combining atomic orbitals are close to each other
(c) Atomic orbitals or opposite sign overlap
(d) The extent of overlap of atomic orbitals should be large

14. Which one of the following statements on bonding molecular orbitals is false?
(a) Possess lower energy than the atomic orbitals from which they are formed
(b) Every electron in it contributes to attraction
(c) Atomic orbitals of same sign overlap
(d) Have lower electron density in the internuclear region

15. The bond angle in CH_4 is
(a) 90° (b) 104°27′ (c) 120° (d) 109°28′

16. Which of the following is not isoelectronic?
(a) NO^+ (b) CO (c) CN^- (d) O_2^-

17. The shape of $TeCl_4$ molecule is
(a) tetrahedral (b) square pyramidal
(c) trigonal pyramid (d) square planar

18. According to MO theory, for the species 'C_2'
(a) bond order is zero and it is diamagnetic
(b) bond order is two and it is diamagnetic
(c) bond order is two and it is paramagnetic
(d) bond order is zero and it is paramagnetic

19. Among the following, the paramagnetic species is
(a) B_2 (b) C_2 (c) O_2 (d) CO

20. The bond order in O_2^+ is
(a) 1.5 (b) 2 (c) 2.5 (d) 3.5

21. Which statement regarding stable heteronuclear diatomic molecule is not correct?
(a) Bond orders are greater than zero
(b) The bonding molecular orbitals have more of the character of the more electropositive element than of the more electronegative element
(c) The greater the difference in energy between two overlapping atomic orbitals, the more polar is the resulting bond
(d) Their molecular orbitals are less symmetrical than those of homonuclear diatomic molecules

22. The number of electrons in the $\sigma 2p$ molecular orbital in N_2^+ is
(a) 0 (b) 1 (c) 2 (d) 3

23. The correct electronic configuration for the molecular ion, C_2^- is
(a) $\sigma 1s^2, \overset{*}{\sigma} 1s^2, \sigma 2s^2, \overset{*}{\sigma} 2s^2, \pi 2p_y^2, \pi 2p_z^2, \sigma 2p_x^1$
(b) $\sigma 1s^2, \overset{*}{\sigma} 1s^2, \sigma 2s^2, \overset{*}{\sigma} 2s^2, \pi 2p_y^2, \pi 2p_z^2, \sigma 2p_x^2$
(c) $\sigma 1s^2, \overset{*}{\sigma} 1s^2, \sigma 2s^2, \overset{*}{\sigma} 2s^2, \pi 2p_y^2, \pi 2p_z^2$
(d) $\sigma 1s^2, \overset{*}{\sigma} 1s^2, \sigma 2s^2, \overset{*}{\sigma} 2s^2, \pi 2p_y^2, \pi 2p_z^1$

24. What is the bond order in NO_2^+?
(a) 1 (b) 1.5 (c) 2 (d) 2.5

25. Molecular orbital theory predicts the F_2^{2+} ion has a bond order of
(a) 0.5 (b) 1 (c) 1.5 (d) 2

26. In a diatomic molecule, the nuclei are on the z-axis. The bonding MO formed by the overlap of two $2p_y$ orbitals contains
(a) zero nodal plane
(b) one nodal plane between the nuclei
(c) one nodal plane along the internuclear axis
(d) two nodal planes on either side of nuclei

27. The bond order and magnetic behaviour of He_2^{2+} are respectively
(a) zero and diamagnetic (b) one and diamagnetic
(c) two and diamagnetic (d) one and paramagnetic

28. Which of the MO diagram showing, best describes combination of $1s$ (H) and $2p_z$ (F) orbitals of HF^+?

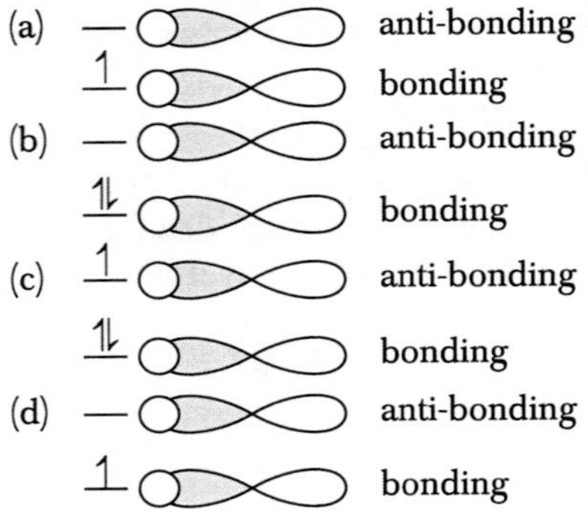

29. The correct one among the following statements about N_2 is
(a) The bond order is 2
(b) It has two unpaired electrons
(c) The highest occupied molecular orbital is $3\sigma_g$
(d) The lowest unoccupied molecule orbital is $1\overset{*}{\pi}_u$

30. Which of the following pairs of orbitals on adjacent atoms are orthogonal?

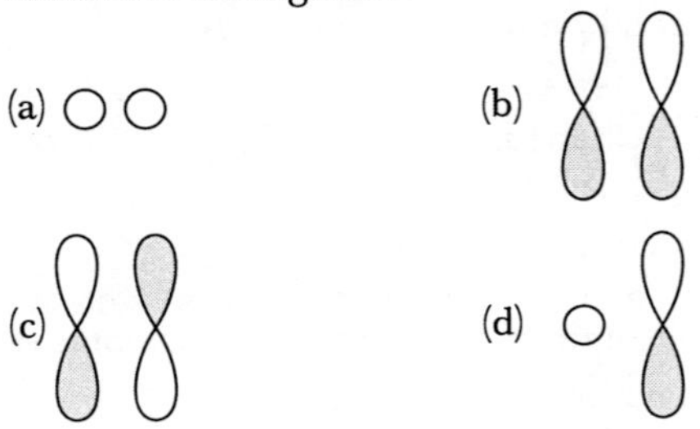

31. The shape of BrF_3 is
(a) T-shaped (b) trigonal planar
(c) trigonal pyramidal (d) trigonal bipyramidal

32. The bond angle of Cl_2O is
(a) smaller than that of F_2O
(b) smaller than that of H_2O
(c) greater than that of H_2O
(d) same as that F_2O

33. The hybridization in SF_6 molecule is
(a) sp^3 (b) sp^3d
(c) sp^3d^2 (d) sp^3d^3

34. Which of the following statements is correct for XeO_2F_2?
(a) It has a square planar structure
(b) It is isostructural with XeF_4
(c) It has a tetrahedral structure
(d) It has a trigonal bipyramidal

35. The square pyramidal molecular shape is adopted by
(a) SOF_4 (b) PF_5
(c) $XeOF_4$ (d) $ScOCl_4$

36. The structure of XeO_2F_2 based on VSEPR theory is best described as
(a) a square planar structure with the fluorines *trans* to each other
(b) a perfect tetrahedral arrangement of substituents around Xe
(c) see-saw structure with F—Xe—F bond angle close to 120°
(d) see-saw structure with O—Xe—O bond angle close to 120°

37. The B–F bond distance in $H_3N \rightarrow BF_3$ is .... than in BF_3.
(a) shorter (b) equal (c) longer (d) double

38. The number of non-bonded electron pairs in ClF_3 is
(a) 0 (b) 1 (c) 2 (d) 3

39. Which of the following is true about the planar structure of $N(SiH_3)_3$?
(a) It is due to π-back bonding from nitrogen to silicon
(b) It is due to π-back bonding from silicon to nitrogen
(c) It is due to σ-back bonding from nitrogen to silicon
(d) It is due to σ-back bonding from silicon to nitrogen

40. The minimum number of electrons needed to form a chemical bond between two atoms is
(a) 1 (b) 2 (c) 3 (d) 4

41. $[XeO_6]^{4-}$ is octahedral whereas XeF_6 is a disordered one, because
(a) Xe-F bond has more ionic character
(b) fluorine is more electronegative than oxygen
(c) XeF_6 is neutral whereas $[XeO_6]^{4-}$ is an ionic species
(d) Xe has no lone pair in XeF_6

42. The structure of SF_4 is
(a) tetrahedral (b) square planar
(c) trigonal bipyramidal (d) octahedral

43. Among the following isostructural compounds, identify the compound which has the highest lattice energy?
(a) LiF (b) LiCl (c) NaCl (d) MgO

44. Which of the following species/molecules has a planar geometry?
(a) SF_4 (b) $Ni(CO)_4$ (c) $CoCl_4^{2-}$ (d) XeF_4

45. Which of the following will have the molecular shape of a trigonal bipyramidal?
(a) PF_3Cl_2 (b) BrF_5 (c) IF_5 (d) SbF_5^{2-}

46. Which statement best describes the polarity of SF_4Cl_2?
(a) Always polar
(b) Always non-polar
(c) Depending on the arrangement of outer atoms, this molecule could be polar or non-polar
(d) None of the above

47. The hybrid orbitals used by bromine atom in BrF_3 are
(a) sp^2 (b) sp^3 (c) sp^3d (d) sp^3d^3

48. Which of the following species has two non-bonded electron pairs on the central atom?
(a) ClF_3 (b) ICl_2^- (c) PCl_3 (d) $TeCl_4$

49. The species which has a square planar structure is
(a) SF_4 (b) BF_4^- (c) $FeCl_4^-$ (d) XeF_4

50. In allene, hybridization of the central and terminal carbons, respectively, are
(a) sp and sp^2 (b) sp^2 and sp^2
(c) sp and sp^3 (d) sp^2 and sp^3

51. The structure of O_3 and N_3^- are
(a) linear and bent respectively
(b) bent and linear respectively
(c) both are linear
(d) both are bent

52. Among the following molecules, the shortest bond length is to be found in
(a) C_2 (b) N_2 (c) O_2 (d) F_2

53. Which ionic solid is expected to have the highest melting point?
(a) NaCl (b) KBr (c) CaF_2 (d) CaO

54. Which example below exhibits the largest bond angle?
(a) Angle H—O—H in H_2O
(b) Angle F—Be—F in BeF_2
(c) Angle F—B—F in BF_3
(d) Angle Cl—C—Cl in $CHCl_3$

55. sp^3d^2 hybridization is observed in
(a) BrF (b) $BrCl_3$ (c) ClF_3 (d) ICl_5

56. The incorrect combination among the following is
(a) ICl–sp^3-Linear
(b) $BrCl_3$–sp^3d-T-shaped
(c) IF_5–sp^3d^2-square pyramidal
(d) None of the above

57. The shape of ICl_4^- is
(a) square planar (b) tetrahedral
(c) see-saw (d) octahedral

58. The electron-domain geometry and molecular geometry of iodine trichloride are .... and .... respectively.
(a) T-shaped, trigonal planar
(b) octahedral, trigonal planar
(c) trigonal bipyramidal, T-shaped
(d) trigonal planar, trigonal planar

59. Of the following, only .... has sp^2 hybridization of the central atom.
(a) CO_3^{2-} (b) PF_5 (c) ICl_3 (d) I_3^-

60. Which of the following is non-linear according to VSEPR theory?
(a) CO_2 (b) $[N_3]^-$ (c) $[I_3]^-$ (d) $[ClF_2]^+$

61. How does the strength of the charge-charge interaction between two ions depend on the separation, r, in the absence of any other ions?
(a) $\propto \frac{1}{r}$ (b) $\propto \frac{1}{r^2}$
(c) $\propto \frac{1}{r^3}$ (d) $\propto \frac{1}{r^6}$

62. The structure of $XeOF_5^-$ ion is
(a) octahedral
(b) distorted octahedral
(c) pentagonal pyramidal
(d) pentagonal bipyramidal

63. Which one of the following compounds contains a cation having non-inert gas outermost configuration?
(a) NaCl (b) KCl
(c) $CaCl_2$ (d) $CuCl_2$

64. Which of the following is the molecule with the lowest bond order?
(a) CO (b) CO_2
(c) NO_3^- (d) CN^-

65. The number of σ and π-bonds between two carbon atoms in CaC_2 is
(a) three σ bonds and no π bond
(b) two π bonds and one σ bond
(c) two σ bonds and one π bond
(d) one π bond and one σ bond

66. The bonds found in the structural formula of carbon dioxide are
(a) $O \underset{\sigma}{\overset{\sigma}{=}} C \underset{\sigma}{\overset{\sigma}{=}} O$ (b) $O \underset{\pi}{\overset{\sigma}{=}} C \underset{\pi}{\overset{\sigma}{=}} O$
(c) $O \underset{\pi}{\overset{\pi}{=}} C \underset{\pi}{\overset{\pi}{=}} O$ (d) $O \underset{\sigma}{\overset{\sigma}{=}} C \underset{\pi}{\overset{\pi}{=}} O$

67. Amongst of the following species, the one having the highest bond strength is
(a) O_2 (b) O_2^+
(c) O_2^{2+} (d) O_2^{2-}

68. Elements X has an outer electronic configuration of $3s^2$. Elements Y is directly below element X in the Periodic Table. The type of bond present in the compound XY is
(a) covalent (b) ionic
(c) coordinate (d) metallic

69. XeF_3^+ belongs to which one of the following AX_nE_m nomenclatures (A central atom, X singly bonded ligand and E an unshared electron pair)?
(a) AX_3E_0 (b) AX_3E_1
(c) AX_3E_2 (d) AX_3E_3

70. Consider the following statements about bonding :
1. When atomic orbitals are combined to give molecular orbitals. The number of molecular orbitals formed equals the number of atomic orbitals used.
2. The interaction of two atomic orbitals of the same phases results in the formation of a bonding molecular orbital.
3. Molecular orbitals, like atomic orbitals can hold only two electrons of the same spin.
4. The energy of the bonding molecular orbital is lower than the energy of the two separate atomic orbitals.

Which of the above statements are correct?
(a) 1, 2 and 4 (b) 2, 3 and 4
(c) 2 and 3 (d) 1 and 4

71. A nodal plane containing the internuclear axis exists in
(a) π-bonds (b) σ-bonds
(c) δ-bonds (d) anti-bonding π-orbitals

72. Considered the given figure showing that possible levels of the energy of H_2^+ ion depending on inter nuclear distance *versus* potential energy of the system.

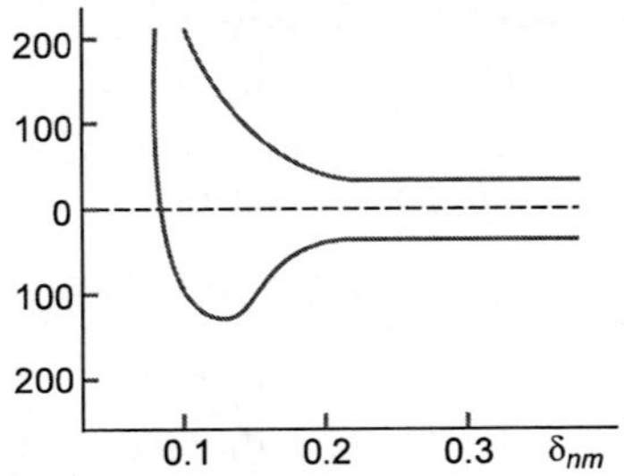

It may be easily assumed that the ground state of the molecular hydrogen ion, H_2^+ corresponds to the lowest level which means that
(a) curve 1 represents the most stable state of the system for H_2^+ ion
(b) curve 2 represents the most stable of the system for H_2^+
(c) curve 1 indicates that the molecular hydrogen ion is formed
(d) curve 2 represents the energy level of the antibonding region

73. The MO configuration of N_2 molecule is
(a) $KK\,(\sigma 2s)^2\,(\overset{*}{\sigma} 2s)^2\,(\sigma 2p_x)^2\,(\pi 2p)^4$
(b) $KK\,(\sigma 2s)^2\,(\overset{*}{\sigma} 2s)^2\,(\pi 2p_x)^2\,(\pi 2p_z)^2\,(\sigma 2p)^2$
(c) $KK\,(\sigma 2p)^2\,(\overset{*}{\sigma} 2s)^2\,(\sigma 2p)^2\,(\pi 2p)^2\,(\overset{*}{\pi} 2p)^2$
(d) $KK\,(\sigma 2s)^2\,(\overset{*}{\sigma} 2s)^2\,(\sigma 2p)^2\,(\pi 2p_y)^2\,(\overset{*}{\pi} 2p)^2$

74. The hybrid bond orbitals used by chlorine in forming ClF are of the type
(a) sp^3 (b) sp^2 (c) sp^2d (d) sp^3d

75. The hybridisation in both CH_4 and NH_3 is sp^3. Yet CH_4 is tetrahedral and NH_3 is of pyramidal shape because
(a) it contains three single bonds and no lone pair
(b) it contains three single bonds and one lone pair
(c) the number of surrounding atoms is 3
(d) nitrogen is more electronegative than carbon

76. The paramagnetism of O_2 molecule is believed to be due to the presence of two electrons with parallel spin in
(a) bonding π-orbitals (b) anti-bonding π-orbitals
(c) bonding σ-orbitals (d) anti-bonding σ-orbitals

77. If one assumes linear structure instead of bent structure of water, then which of the following properties cannot be explained?
(a) The formation of intermolecular hydrogen bond in water
(b) The high boiling point of water
(c) Solubility of polar compounds in water
(d) Ability of water to form coordinates covalent bonds

78. Based on molecular orbital predictions, the net bonds in linear CO_2 molecules are
(a) 1σ, 3π (b) 2σ (c) 2σ, 2π (d) 2π

79. Which of the following have identical bond-order?
(a) O_2^- (b) CN^- (c) O_2^+ (d) NO^+

80. Among the following molecules, the dipole molement is the highest for
(a) NF_3 (b) NH_3
(c) BF_3 (d) *trans*-$[PtCl_2(NH_3)_2]$

81. The dipole moment of a hydrogen halide H—*X* is 1.8D and the bond length is 1.5 Å. The per cent ionic character of H—*X* will be
(a) 25% (b) 50% (c) 75% (d) 80%

82. In a non-polar AX_2, the bond moment of *AX* is 0.56D. The bond angle is
(a) 30° (b) 45° (c) 90° (d) 180°

83. The molecule that does not possess a permanent dipole moment is
(a) NO_2 (b) NF_3 (c) BF_3 (d) CH_2Cl_2

84. Find out the correct increasing order of hardness of the following compounds.
LiCl, SrO, BaO, CaO, CaF_2
(a) LiCl < SrO < BaO < CaO < CaF_2
(b) LiCl < BaO < SrO < CaO < CaF_2
(c) CaF_2 < CaO < BaO < SrO < LiCl
(d) CaF_2 < BaO < CaO < SrO < LiCl

85. Consider ψ_A and ψ_B are the wave-function of atoms *A* and *B* respectively, then the charge density for anti-bonding molecular orbital can be given as
(a) $\psi_a^2 = \psi_A^2 + \psi_B^2$
(b) $\psi_b^2 = \psi_A^2 - \psi_B^2$
(c) $\psi_b^2 = \psi_A^2 + \psi_B^2 + 2\psi_A\psi_B$
(d) $\psi_b^2 = \psi_A^2 + \psi_B^2 - 2\psi_A\psi_B$

86. Number of unpaired electrons in CO molecule is
(a) zero (b) one (c) two (d) three

87. Number of anti-bonding electrons is CO molecule is
(a) zero (b) two (c) four (d) six

88. Number of bonding electrons in HF molecule is
(a) zero (b) two (c) four (d) six

89. Which of the following compound show T-shaped geometry?
(a) BF_3 (b) NH_3 (c) IF_3 (d) PF_5

90. Which of the following compound will show square pyramidal structure?
(a) XeF_4 (b) IF_5 (c) IF_7 (d) XeF_6

91. Two or more configurations which are chemically equivalent, are called
(a) isomers (b) conformers
(c) fluxionals (d) enantiomers

92. The following is an example of

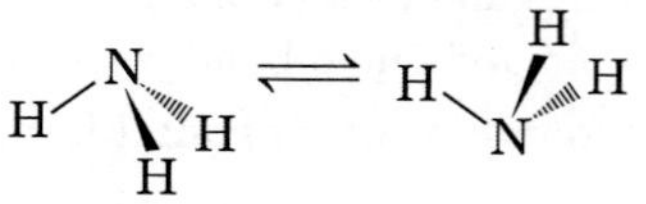

(a) tautomerism (b) metamerism
(c) *R–S*-configuration (d) fluxional

93. Which of the following aromatic substitution have zero dipole moment?
(a) *Ortho*-derivative (b) *Meta*-derivative
(c) *Para*-derivative (d) None of these

94. Which of the following is the correct order of dipole moment value?
(a) *o*-derivative < *m*-derivative < *p*-derivative
(b) *m*-derivative < *o*-derivative < *p*-derivative
(c) *m*-derivative < *p*-derivative < *o*-derivative
(d) *p*-derivative < *m*-derivative < *o*-derivative

95. Which of the following is the correct order of C—C bond length?
(a) $sp^3 - sp^3 < sp^3 - sp^2 < sp^3 - sp < sp^2 - sp^2$
(b) $sp^2 - sp^2 < sp^3 - sp < sp^3 - sp^2 < sp^3 - sp^3$
(c) $sp^3 - sp < sp^2 - sp^2 < sp^3 - sp^2 < sp^3 - sp^3$
(d) $sp^2 - sp^2 < sp^3 - sp^3 < sp^3 - sp^2 < sp^3 - sp$

96. Which of the following is the correct order of C=C bond length?
(a) $sp - sp < sp^2 - sp < sp^2 - sp^2$
(b) $sp^2 - sp^2 < sp^2 - sp < sp - sp$
(c) $sp^2 - sp < sp^2 - sp^2 < sp - sp$
(d) $sp - sp < sp^2 - sp^2 < sp^2 - sp$

Exercise 2

(For Part 'C')

1. Among the following species, the order of first ionization energy is
   (a) $O_2 < O_2^+ < O_2^-$ (b) $O_2^+ < O_2^- < O_2$
   (c) $O_2^- < O_2 < O_2^+$ (d) $O_2 < O_2^- < O_2^+$
2. For a homonuclear diatomic molecule, the bonding orbital is
   (a) σ_g of lowest energy
   (b) σ_u of second lowest energy
   (c) π_g of lowest energy
   (d) π_u of lowest energy
3. From molecular orbital configuration of CO and NO^+, we would predict
   (a) both have a bond order of 3
   (b) both are paramagnetic
   (c) both will readily lose an electron to form CO^+ or NO^{2+}
   (d) both CO and NO^+ should not exist
4. In which set of diatomic molecules is the bond order three?
   (a) NO^+, N_2 and CN^- (b) N_2, O_2 and CO
   (c) NO, N_2 and CN^- (d) CN, N_2 and CO
5. Which of the following diatomic molecules would be stabilized by the removal of an electron?
   (a) C_2 (b) CN (c) N_2 (d) O_2
6. The bond order for N_2, O_2, N_2^-, O_2^- varies as
   (a) $N_2 > N_2^- > O_2 > O_2^-$ (b) $O_2 > N_2 > O_2^- > N_2^-$
   (c) $N_2 > O_2 > N_2^- > O_2^-$ (d) $N_2^- > N_2 > O_2^- > O_2$
7. The species containing paired electrons in anti-bonding molecular orbitals is
   (a) C_2 (b) N_2
   (c) O_2 (d) Both C_2 and N_2
8. Which of the following statement is false?
   (a) LUMO for F_2 molecule is an anti-bonding π-orbital
   (b) a π-molecular orbital is cylindrical symmetric around the internuclear axis
   (c) The bond order of Cl_2^+ is equal to 2
   (d) All of the above
9. The parity labels (u and g) are not given to the MOs of the methane molecule, because
   (a) methane is square planar
   (b) methane is non-centrosymmetric
   (c) parity labels are not used for MOs of centrosymmetric molecules
   (d) parity labels are used only for atomic orbitals
10. Which one of the following statements is not true?
    (a) O_2 has a smaller bond dissociation energy than O_2^+
    (b) The bond length of O_2^+ is greater than that of O_2
    (c) The vibration frequency of O_2^+ is greater than that of O_2
    (d) The bond order of O_2^- is lesser than that of O_2
11. In which one of the following pairs the species have similar geometry?
    (a) CO_2 and SO_2 (b) CO_3^{2-} and SO_3^{2-}
    (c) NH_3 and BH_3 (d) SO_4^{2-} and ClO_4^-
12. BrO_3^- is isostructural with a noble gas species
    (a) XeO_3 (b) XeF_3 (c) XeF_4 (d) XeO_2
13. Using VSEPR theory, the number of lone pairs in PCl_5, IF_5, SOF_4 and $XeOF_4$ are
    (a) 0, 1, 0 and 1 (b) 0, 0, 1 and 1
    (c) 1, 1, 0 and 0 (d) 1, 0, 1 and 0
14. Which among the following pairs is square pyramidal in shape?
    (a) BrF_5, $XeOF_4$ (b) PCl_5, XeO_2F_2
    (c) AsF_5, BrF_5 (d) IF_7, XeF_6
15. Which of the pair is linear in shape and with three lone pairs?
    (a) CO_2, SO_2 (b) XeF_2, SCl_2
    (c) $HgCl_2$, BeF_2 (d) XeF_2, I_3^-
16. The pair of compounds having the same hybridization for the central atom is
    (a) XeF_4 and $[SF_4]^{2-}$
    (b) $Ni(CO)_4$ and XeO_2F_2
    (c) $[NiCl_4]^{2-}$ and $[PtCl_4]^{2-}$
    (d) $[Co(NH_3)_6]^{3+}$ and $[Co(H_2O)_6]^{3+}$
17. The structure of $N(CH_3)_3$ and $N(SiH_3)_3$ are respectively
    (a) trigonal planar and pyramidal
    (b) pyramidal and trigonal planar
    (c) both pyramidal
    (d) both trigonal planar
18. The xenon compounds that are isostructural with IBr_2^- and BrO_3^- respectively are
    (a) linear XeF_2 and pyramidal XeO_3
    (b) linear XeF_2 and tetrahedral XeO_3
    (c) bent XeF_2 and pyramidal XeO_3
    (d) bent XeF_2 and planar XeO_3

19. The compound $(SiH_3)_3N$ is expected to be
(a) planar and more basic than $(CH_3)_3N$
(b) pyramidal and less basic than $(CH_3)_3N$
(c) planar and less basic than $(CH_3)_3N$
(d) pyramidal and more basic than $(CH_3)_3N$

20. The nature of π-bond present in perchlorate ion is
(a) $O(p\pi)$—$Cl(p\pi)$ (b) $O(p\pi)$—$Cl(d\pi)$
(c) $O(d\pi)$—$Cl(d\pi)$ (d) $O(d\pi)$—$Cl(p\pi)$

21. Match up the correct formula and shape of the central atom. Which pair is correct?
(a) CS_2, bent
(b) CO_3^{2-}, trigonal pyramidal
(c) SiH_3^-, trigonal planar
(d) CMe_3^+, trigonal planar

22. In which one of the following pairs, molecules/irons have similar shape?
(a) CO_2 and H_2O
(b) BF_3 and *t*-butyl carbonium ion
(c) CCl_4 and $PtCl_4$
(d) NH_3 and BF_3

23. Where is an electron added during to the change of NO^+ to NO?
(a) σ-orbital (b) π-orbital
(c) σ^*-orbital (d) π^*-orbital

24. Match Column I (compound) with Column II (molecular shape) and select the correct answer using the codes given below the lists.

	Column I	Column II
A.	XeF_4	1. Tetrahedral
B.	SeF_4	2. Square planar
C.	XeO_3	3. Pyramidal
D.	XeO_4	4. Triangular planar
		5. Distorted tetrahedral

Codes

	A	B	C	D
(a)	3	1	4	5
(b)	2	5	3	1
(c)	3	5	4	1
(d)	2	1	3	5

25. Which are the species in which sulphur undergoes sp^3 hybridisation?
1. SF_4 2. SCl_2
3. SO_4^{2-} 4. H_2S
(a) 1 and 3 (b) 2, 3 and 4
(c) 1, 2 and 4 (d) 3 and 4

26.

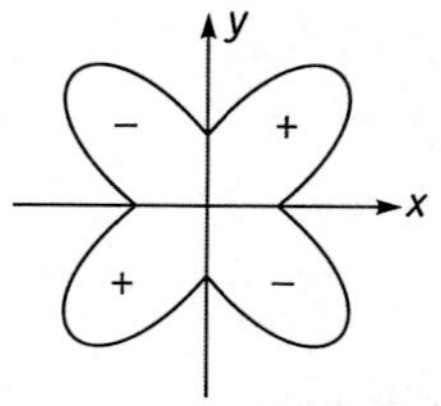

The shape of which one of the follownig orbitals correspond to the angular wave functions shown in the figure given above?
(a) $d_{x^2-y^2}$ (b) d_{xy}
(c) p_y (d) p_x

27. Match Column I (Name of the compound) with Column II (structure/geometry of the molecule) and select the correct answer.

	Column I	Column II
A.	Chlorine trifluoride	1. Triangular planar
B.	Boron trifluoride	2. Triangular pyramidal
C.	Nitrogen trifluoride	3. T-shaped
D.	Sulphur hexafluoride	4. Regular octahedral

Codes

	A	B	C	D
(a)	2	1	3	4
(b)	3	4	2	1
(c)	2	4	3	1
(d)	3	1	2	4

28. Match Column I (Molecule or Ion) with Column II (Hybridisation of the central atom in the molecule) and select the correct answer.

	Column I		Column II
A.	XeF_4	1.	dsp^2
B.	H_2O	2.	sp^3
C.	PCl_5	3.	sp^3d^2
D.	$[Pt(NH_3)_4]^{2+}$	4.	sp^3d

Codes

	A	B	C	D
(a)	3	2	4	1
(b)	1	4	2	3
(c)	3	4	2	1
(d)	1	2	4	3

29. Match Column I and Column II and select the correct answer.

	Column I	List II
A.	XeF_5^+	1. Tetrahedral
B.	SiF_5^-	2. Square planar
C.	AsF_4^+	3. Trigonal bipyramidal
D.	ICl_4^-	4. Square pyramidal
		5. Octahedral

Codes

	A	B	C	D
(a)	1	2	5	3
(b)	4	3	1	2
(c)	1	3	5	2
(d)	4	2	1	3

30. Which of the following compounds has the electron-pair geometry as trigonal bipyramid with three equatorial positions occupied by lone pairs of electrons?

(a) Aluminium chloride
(b) Xenon difluoride
(c) Dichloro-diamino-platinum
(d) Alkyl magnesium bromide

31. I_3 reacts with IO_3 in presence of H_2SO_4 to form a blue coloured solution. The blue colour of the solution is due to

(a) I^+ (b) I_2 (c) IO_4^- (d) I_3^-

32. Azide ion (N_3^-) exhibits an N–N bond order of 2 and may be represented by resonance structures I, II and III given below

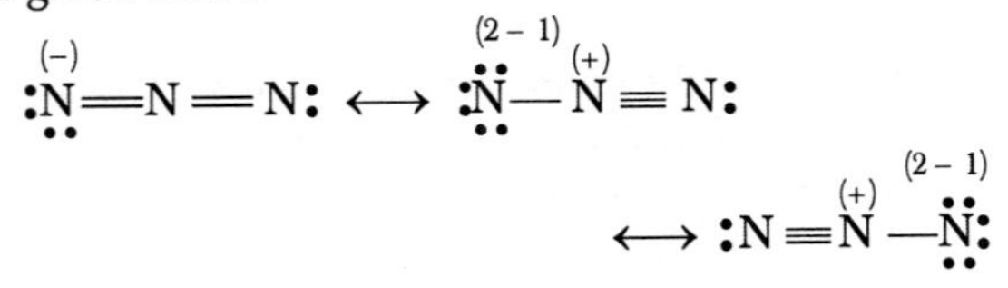

In this context, the statements which will best represent the structure of azide ion is

(a) structure (I) and (II) make greater contribution than structure (III)
(b) all the three structures make equal contribution
(c) structure (II) and (III) make greater contribution than structure (I)
(d) structure (I) and (III) make greater contribution than structure (II)

33. Which of the following electronic configurations represents a molecule *AB* with a bond order of 3?

(a) $\sigma^2\ \pi^4\ \delta^2$ (b) $\sigma^2\ \pi^4\ \delta^2\ \delta^{*2}$
(c) $\sigma^2\ \pi^4\ \delta^2\ \delta^{*2}\ \pi^{*2}$ (d) $\sigma^2\ \pi^4\ \delta^2\ \delta^{*1}\ \pi^{*2}$

34. The correct sequence in which bond order decreases in O_2, O_2^+, O_2^- and O_2^{2-} is such that

(a) $O_2^+ > O_2 > O_2^- > O_2^{2-}$
(b) $O_2^{2-} > O_2^+ > O_2^- > O_2$
(c) $O_2 > O_2^{2-} > O_2^- > O_2$
(d) $O_2 > O_2^- > O_2^{2-} > O_2^+$

35. Which of the following species have bond order of 3?

1. N_2 2. NO 3. NO^- 4. C_2^{2-}

Select the correct answer using the codes given below.

(a) 1 and 2 (b) 1, 2 and 3
(c) 1, 2 and 4 (d) 1, 3 and 4

36. Match Column I with Column II and select the correct answer

	Column I (Ions)		Column II (Shapes)
A.	ICl_2^-	1.	Linear
B.	BrF_2^+	2.	Pyramidal
C.	ClF_4^-	3.	Tetrahedral
D.	$AlCl_4^-$	4.	Square planar
		5.	Angular

Codes

	A	B	C	D
(a)	1	2	4	5
(b)	4	5	2	3
(c)	1	5	4	3
(d)	5	1	3	4

37. Match Column I (Hybrid bond orbitals) with Column II (species) and select the correct answer.

	Column I (Hybrid bond orbitals)		Column II (Species)
A.	d^3s	1.	ICl_4
B.	dsp^2	2.	$TeCl_4$
C.	sp^3d	3.	MnO_4^-
D.	sp^3d^2	4.	$Ni(CN)_4^{2-}$

Codes

	A	B	C	D
(a)	4	3	1	2
(b)	4	3	2	1
(c)	3	4	1	2
(d)	3	4	2	1

38. Match Column I with Column II and select the correct answer.

	Column I (Species)		Column II (Bond order)
A.	N_2	1.	1.0
B.	O_2	2.	2.0
C.	F_2	3.	2.5
D.	O_2^+	4.	3.0

Codes

	A	B	C	D
(a)	4	2	1	3
(b)	1	3	4	2
(c)	1	2	4	3
(d)	4	3	1	2

39. Which one of the following shows paramagnetic behaviour?

(a) H_2O (b) CO_2 (c) SO_2 (d) NO

40. Which one of the following would require the largest amount of energy to cause dissociation?

(a) C≡H in CH_4 (b) C≡C in C_2H_2
(c) N≡N in N_2H_4 (d) N≡N in N_2

41. The bond order of $[He_2]^{4-}$ is

(a) 1 (b) 0.5 (c) 1.5 (d) 0.75

42. Match the following Column I (Hybridization) with Column II (structure) and select the correct answer using the codes given below the Columns.

	Column I		Column II
A.	sp^2	1.	Octahedral
B.	sp^3	2.	Trigonal
C.	sp^2	3.	Square planar
D.	d^2sp^3	4.	Tetrahedral

Codes

	A	B	C	D
(a)	2	4	1	3
(b)	4	2	3	1
(c)	2	4	3	1
(d)	4	2	1	3

43. Which of the following compound(s) has/have linear structure?

1. $BeCl_2$ 2. H_2O 3. SO_2

Select the correct answer using the codes given below.

(a) 1 and 2 (b) 2 and 3 (c) 3 alone (d) 1 alone

44. Dipole moment is shown by

(a) 1, 4-dichlorobenzene
(b) *cis*-1, 2-dichloroethene
(c) *trans*-1, 2-dichloro-2-pentene
(d) *trans*-1, 2-dichloroethene

45. The molecules that will have dipole moment are

(a) *cis*-3-hexene
(b) 2, 2, 3, 3-tetramethyl butane
(c) *trans*-2-pentene
(d) 2, 2-dimethyl propane

46. CO_2 is isostructural with

(a) NO_2 (b) $SnCl_2$ (c) C_2H_2 (d) $HgCl_2$

47. The linear structure assumed by

(a) CS_2 (b) NCO^- (c) NO_2^+ (d) SO_2

48. Match the following Column I and Column I.

	Column I Compound (Melting point) (°C)		Column I Radius of cation (pm)
A.	NaF (1270)	1.	136
B.	KF (857)	2.	148
C.	RbF (775)	3.	99
D.	CsF (683)	4.	169

Codes

	A	B	C	D
(a)	1	2	3	4
(b)	4	3	2	1
(c)	2	3	4	1
(d)	3	1	2	4

49. Which of the following statement (s) is/are correct?

(a) Melting point of ionic compounds is directly proportional to the charge of ions.
(b) Melting point of ionic compounds is directly proportional to the size of ions.
(c) Ionic compounds are hard and brittle.
(d) Hardness of ionic compounds increases with increase in charge on the ions for crystal of similar interionic distances.

50. Match the following Column I and Column II.

	Column I Compounds (Interionic distance Å)		Column I (Hardness Mohs)
A.	CaO (2.40)	1.	3.3
B.	SrO (2.57)	2.	3.5
C.	BaO (2.77)	3.	4.5

Codes

	A	B	C
(a)	1	2	3
(b)	3	2	1
(c)	2	1	3
(d)	1	3	2

51. Which of the following statements (s) is/are correct according to valence bond theory?

(a) Overlapping orbitals must have antispin electrons
(b) Overlapping orbitals must have paired electrons
(c) Overlapping orbitals must have unpaired electrons
(d) Greater is the overlapping, higher will be the bond length

52. Which of the following statement (s) is/are correct about valence bond theory?

(a) This theory provides an adequate relationship for many aspects of molecular structure and bonding.
(b) This theory is used to explain the paramagnetic behaviour of O_2 molecule.
(c) This theory fails to explain the bonding in electron deficient compounds.
(d) This theory is very close to the classical chemical picture.

53. Consider ψ_A and ψ_B are the wave-function of atoms A and B respectively, then the charge density for anti-bonding molecular orbital can be given as :

(a) $\psi_a^2 = \psi_A^2 + \psi_B^2$ (b) $\psi_a^2 = (\psi_A - \psi_B)^2$
(c) $\psi_a^2 = \psi_A^2 - \psi_B^2$ (d) $\psi_a^2 = \psi_A^2 + \psi_B^2 - 2\psi_A\psi_B$

54. Match the following Column I and Column II.

	Column I (Molecules)		Column II (Bond order)
A.	Li_2	1.	0
B.	Be_2	2.	1
C.	C_2	3.	2
D.	N_2	4.	3

Codes

	A	B	C	D
(a)	1	2	3	4
(b)	4	3	2	1
(c)	1	2	4	3
(d)	2	1	3	4

55. Which of the following species is diamagnetic?
(a) B_2 (b) N_2^+ (c) N_2^- (d) N_2^{2+}

56. Which of the following is the correct order of their stability?
(a) $N_2^+ > N_2^- > N_2^{2+}$ (b) $N_2^{2+} > N_2^- > N_2^+$
(c) $N_2^- > N_2^{2+} > N_2^+$ (d) $N_2^+ > N_2^{2+} > N_2^-$

57. Which of the following statement (s) is/are correct?
(a) Bond-length of CO^+ is shorter than CO
(b) Bond-length of CO^+ is longer than CO
(c) Both CO^+ and CO has equal bond-length
(d) Bond order of CO^+ is greater than CO

58. Which of the following is the correct order of their stability?
(a) $CN < NO^+ < NO^-$ (b) $NO^- < CN < NO^+$
(c) $NO^+ < CN < NO^-$ (d) $CN < NO^- < NO^+$

59. Which of the following compounds (s) show linear geometry?
(a) BeH_2 (b) CH_2 (c) XeF_2 (d) H_2O

60. Which of the following compound (s) show bent structure?
(a) BeH_2 (b) CH_2 (c) XeF_2 (d) H_2O

61. Which of the following compound show tetragonal antiprism geometry?
(a) ZrF_8^{4-} (b) $Mo(CN)_8^{4-}$
(c) WF_6 (d) ReH_9^{2-}

62. Match the following Column I and Column II.

	Column I (Compounds)	Column II (Geometry)
A.	ReH_9^{2-}	1. Distorted octahedral
B.	$Mo(CN)_8^{4-}$	2. Tetragonal anti-prism
C.	ZrF_8^{4-}	3. Trigonal dodecahedron
D.	XeF_6	4. Tricapped trigonal prism

Codes

	A	B	C	D
(a)	1	2	3	4
(b)	4	3	2	1
(c)	4	1	2	3
(d)	2	1	3	4

63. Which of the following compound show octahedral geometry?
(a) WF_6 (b) ZrF_8^{4-} (c) XeF_4 (d) SF_4

64. Match the following Column I and Column II.

	Column I	Column II
A.	BF_3	1. T-shaped
B.	IF_3	2. Trigonal planar
C.	BH_4^-	3. Square planar
D.	XeF_4	4. Tetrahedral
E.	SF_4	5. Pentagonal bipyramid
F.	IF_7	6. Butterfly

Codes

	A	B	C	D	E	F
(a)	2	1	4	3	6	5
(b)	1	2	3	4	5	6
(c)	6	5	3	4	5	2
(d)	2	1	3	4	6	5

65. Which of the following compound show tricapped trigonal prism geometry?
(a) ReH_9^{2-} (b) $Mo(CN)_8^{4-}$
(c) ZrF_8^{4-} (d) IF_7

66. Match the following Column I and Column II.

	Column I (Compound)	Column II (Bond angle)
A.	NH_3	1. 98.0
B.	NF_3	2. 102.0
C.	SF_2	3. 102.3
D.	SCl_2	4. 107.2

Codes

	A	B	C	D
(a)	1	2	3	4
(b)	4	3	2	1
(c)	2	1	4	3
(d)	4	3	1	2

67. Which of the following compound (s) show pyramidal shape?
(a) NH_3 (b) PH_3 (c) ICl_3 (d) PCl_3

68. Match the following Column I and Column II.

	Column I (Compound)	Column II (Hybridization)
A.	NO_2^-	1. sp^3
B.	AsH_3	2. sp^3d^2
C.	XeF_2	3. sp^3d
D.	XeF_6	4. sp^2
E.	XeF_4	5. sp^3d^3

Codes

	A	B	C	D	E
(a)	4	1	3	5	2
(b)	1	2	3	4	5
(c)	2	1	4	3	5
(d)	4	1	5	3	2

69. Which of the following statement (s) is/are correct about hybrdization?
(a) Orbitals of different energy may hybridize
(b) Hybridized orbitals have identical shape and energy
(c) Hybridized orbitals show head on and lateral overlapping
(d) Hybridized orbitals never form π-bond.

70. Match the following Column I and Column II.

	Column I (Hybridization)		Column II (C–H Bond length)
A.	sp	1.	1.112 Å
B.	sp^2	2.	1.108 Å
C.	sp^3	3.	1.03 Å

Codes

	A	B	C
(a)	1	2	3
(b)	3	2	1
(c)	2	1	3
(d)	3	1	2

71. If m is the bond moment and θ is the bond angle between two bonds then the dipole moment μ is given by
(a) $\mu = m \cos \theta$
(b) $\mu = m \cos \frac{\theta}{2}$
(c) $\mu = 2m \cos \frac{\theta}{2}$
(d) $\mu = m^2 \cos \frac{\theta}{2}$

72. Which of the following is/are the correct order of bond angle?
(a) H_2S (H—S—H) < Methyl mercaptan (C—S—H) < Methyl amine (H—N—H) < Methyl amine (C—N—H)
(b) H_2S (H—S—H) < Water (H—O—H) < Methanol (C—O—H) < Trimethyl amine (C—N—C)
(c) Water (H—O—H) < Ammonia (H—N—H) < H_2S (H—S—H) < Methanol (C—O—H)
(d) Methanol (C—O—H) < Dimethyl ether (C—O—C) < Ammonia (H—N—H) < Dimethyl sulphide (C—S—C)

Assertion & Reason

(a) Both A and R are true and R is the correct explanation of A.
(b) Both A and R are true but R is not the correct explanation of A.
(c) A is true but R is false.
(d) A is false but R is true.

73. Assertion (A) O_2 is paramagnetic in nature.
Reason (R) Bond-order of oxygen is two.

74. Assertion (A) KO_2 is paramagnetic.
Reason (A) K^+ ion has unpaired electron.

75. Assertion (A) Dipole moment of *o*-dichloro benzene is larger than the theoretical value.
Reason (R) Due to dipole-dipole repulsion of two Cl-atoms in *ortho* position bond angle is greater than 60°.

76. Assertion (A) N-atom in NH_3 is sp^3 hybridised and bond angle is 107°.
Reason (R) *lp-bp* repulsion (VSEPR) decreases bond angle to 107°.

Directions (Q. Nos. 77 to 79)
Assume following structure of N_2O and answer the following questions.

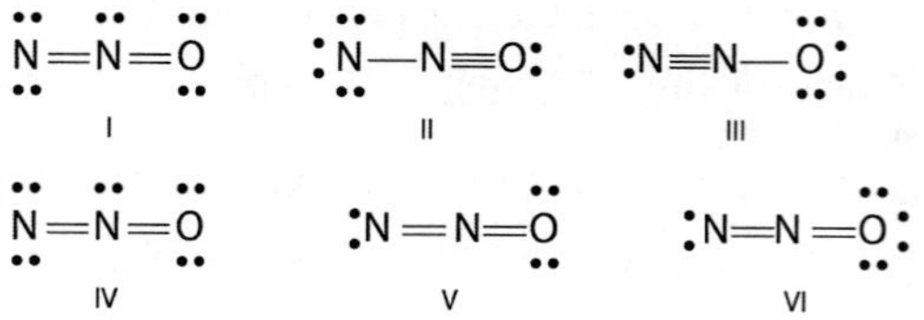

77. Which is the most favourable structure?
(a) I (b) III (c) V (d) VI

78. Select the correct statement (s).
(a) Structure I is not acceptable as there are 10 electron on N atom and 18 electrons total
(b) Structure IV is not acceptable as there are only three bonds
(c) Structure VI is not acceptable as there are 10 electrons on oxygen atom
(d) All the above are correct statements

79. Structure III is represented as
(a) 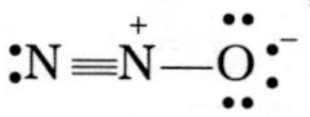
(b) 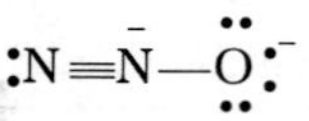
(c) 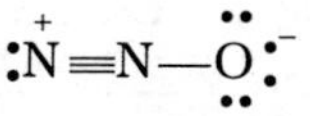
(d) 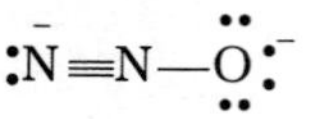

Directions (Q. Nos. 80 to 82)
We consider dissociation energy of different species.

Species	Dissociation energy (kJ mol^{-1})
O_2^+	642.9
O_2	493.6
O_2^-	395.0
N_2^+	840.7
N_2	941.7
N_2^-	765.0
NO^+	1046.9
NO	826.9
NO^-	487.8

Answer the following questions :

80. In which case bond-order increases?
(a) O_2 changes to O_2^+ (b) N_2 changes to N_2^+
(c) NO changes to NO^- (d) In all cases

81. In which case electron from anti-bonding MO (HOMO) is removed? (HOMO : Highest Occupied Molecular Orbital)
(a) O_2 to O_2^+
(b) N_2 to N_2^+
(c) N_2 to N_2^-
(d) In all cases

82. In which case electron from bonding MO is removed?
(a) O_2 to O_2^+ (b) N_2 to N_2^+
(c) NO to NO^+ (d) O_2 to O_2^-

Directions (Q. Nos. 83 and 84)
Consider the following molecules and answer the questions given.

I : H_2O; II : CO_2; III : NH_3
IV : CCl_4; V : ClF

83. In which compound are the bonds most polar?
(a) H_2O (b) CO_2
(c) CCl_4 (d) ClF

84. Which atoms in H_2O and ClF are negatively charged?
(a) O in H_2O and Cl in ClF
(b) H in H_2O and F in ClF
(c) O in H_2O and F in ClF
(d) None of the above is correct

Directions (Q. Nos. 85 to 87)
By the following method you can predict the geometrical shape of species with only one central atom, without first drawing the Lewis structure.

1. Total number of electron pairs = (number of valence electrons ± electrons (for ionic charge)/2
2. Number of bond electron pairs = number of atoms – 1
3. Number of electron pairs around central atom = total number of electron pairs – 3 [number terminal atoms (except H)]
4. Number of lone pair = (number of central electron pairs – number bond pairs)

Read the above method and answer the following questions.

85. If A is the central element of the molecule containing A and X element and E the number of electron pairs round it then VSEPR notation AX_3E will be for the molecules
(a) PCl_5, ICl_4^- (b) NH_3, H_2O
(c) NH_3, ClO_3^- (d) ICl_4^-, ClO_3^-

86. VSEPR notation of PCl_5, H_2O and ICl_4^- are

	PCl_5	H_2O	ICl_4^-
(a)	AX_5	AX_2E_2	AX_4E_2
(b)	AX_5	AX_2E	AX_4E
(c)	AX_5	AX_2	AX_4E
(d)	AX_5	AX_2E_2	AX_4E

87. Based on the above method, structure of the some of the molecules have been matched. Which is the incorrect matching?
(a) PCl_5–trigonal bipyramidal
(b) ClO_3^-–square planar
(c) ICl_4^-–square planar
(d) PCl_4^+–tetrahedral

Answers

Exercise 1

1. (c)	**2.** (b)	**3.** (c)	**4.** (b)	**5.** (b)	**6.** (c)	**7.** (b)	**8.** (d)	**9.** (a)	**10.** (d)
11. (a)	**12.** (b)	**13.** (c)	**14.** (d)	**15.** (d)	**16.** (d)	**17.** (c)	**18.** (b)	**19.** (c)	**20.** (c)
21. (b)	**22.** (b)	**23.** (a)	**24.** (c)	**25.** (d)	**26.** (c)	**27.** (b)	**28.** (a)	**29.** (d)	**30.** (d)
31. (a)	**32.** (c)	**33.** (c)	**34.** (d)	**35.** (c)	**36.** (d)	**37.** (c)	**38.** (c)	**39.** (a)	**40.** (b)
41. (c)	**42.** (c)	**43.** (d)	**44.** (d)	**45.** (a)	**46.** (c)	**47.** (c)	**48.** (a)	**49.** (d)	**50.** (a)
51. (b)	**52.** (b)	**53.** (d)	**54.** (b)	**55.** (d)	**56.** (d)	**57.** (a)	**58.** (c)	**59.** (a)	**60.** (d)
61. (a)	**62.** (c)	**63.** (b)	**64.** (c)	**65.** (b)	**66.** (b)	**67.** (b)	**68.** (d)	**69.** (c)	**70.** (a)
71. (a)	**72.** (b)	**73.** (b)	**74.** (d)	**75.** (b)	**76.** (b)	**77.** (c)	**78.** (c)	**79.** (b)	**80.** (b)
81. (a)	**82.** (d)	**83.** (a)	**84.** (b)	**85.** (c)	**86.** (a)	**87.** (c)	**88.** (b)	**89.** (c)	**90.** (b)
91. (c)	**92.** (d)	**93.** (c)	**94.** (d)	**95.** (c)	**96.** (a)				

Exercise 2

1. (c)	2. (a)	3. (a)	4. (a)	5. (d)	6. (a)	7. (d)	8. (d)	9. (b)	10. (b)
11. (d)	12. (a)	13. (a)	14. (a)	15. (d)	16. (a)	17. (b)	18. (a)	19. (c)	20. (b)
21. (d)	22. (b)	23. (d)	24. (b)	25. (b)	26. (d)	27. (d)	28. (a)	29. (b)	30. (b)
31. (a)	32. (c)	33. (b)	34. (a)	35. (c)	36. (c)	37. (d)	38. (a)	39. (b)	40. (d)
41. (b)	42. (c)	43. (d)	44. (b,c)	45. (a,c)	46. (c,d)	47. (a,b,c)	48. (d)	49. (a,c,d)	50. (b)
51. (a,c)	52. (a,c,d)	53. (b,d)	54. (d)	55. (d)	56. (a)	57. (a,d)	58. (b)	59. (a,c)	60. (b,d)
61. (a)	62. (b)	63. (a)	64. (a)	65. (a)	66. (d)	67. (a)	68. (a)	69. (b,d)	70. (b)
71. (c)	72. (a,b)	73. (b)	74. (c)	75. (d)	76. (a)	77. (b)	78. (d)	79. (a)	80. (a)
81. (a)	82. (b)	83. (a)	84. (c)	85. (c)	86. (a)	87. (b)			

Hints & Solutions

Exercise 1

1. M.O. diagram of HF

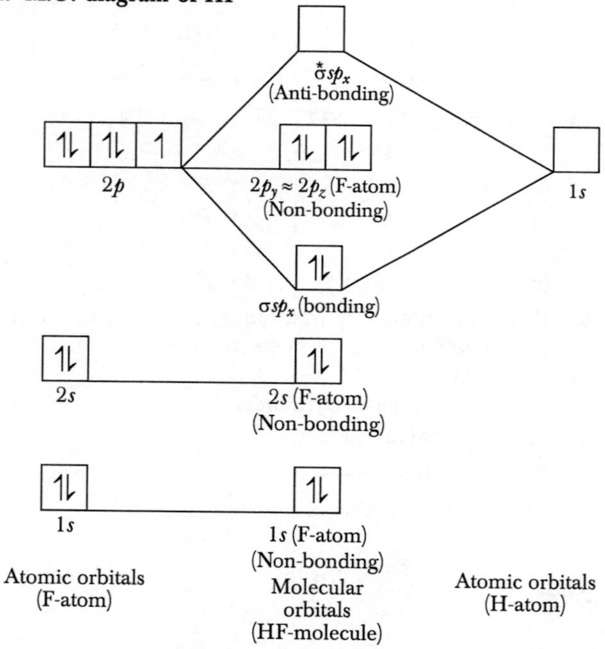

2. Electronic configuration of $N_2 = \sigma 1s^2, \overset{*}{\sigma} 1s^2, \sigma 2s^2, \overset{*}{\sigma} 2s^2,$ $\pi 2p_y^2 \approx \pi 2p_z^2, \sigma 2p_x^2,$

(No unpaired electron so diamagnetic)

Electronic configuration of $N_2^+ = \sigma 1s^2, \overset{*}{\sigma} 1s^2, \sigma 2s^2, \overset{*}{\sigma} 2s^2,$ $\pi 2p_y^2 \approx \pi 2p_z^2 \ \sigma 2p_x^1$

(One unpaired electron so paramagnetic)

21. The bonding orbitals have more of the character of more electronegative element, whereas the character of anti-bonding orbital resembles more of electropositive element.

24. It can be deduced from its Lewis dot formula

$$:\ddot{O}=\overset{+}{N}=\ddot{O}:$$

30. Orthogonal orbitals will not overlap all at all. The overall 'integral of overlapping' is zero for orthogonal orbitals.

31. BrF_3 is a T-shaped molecule. The central 'Br' atom undergoes sp^3d hybridization in first excited state. It is an AX_3 type of interhalogen compound. Other examples are ClF_3, $BrCl_3$ etc.

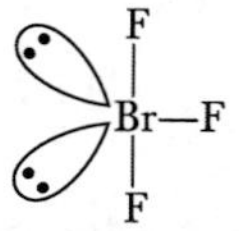

32. The central atom (oxygen) in Cl_2O, F_2O and H_2O undergo sp^3-hybridization. But there are two lone pairs on it.

In case of H_2O, the bond angle is decreased to 104.5° due to repulsion from lone pair.

In case of F_2O, the bond angle is decreased to 103°. (Here, the lone pair repulsion is predominant factor).

In case of Cl_2O, the bond angle is increased to 117.6° due to repulsion between bulky Cl atoms.

Note Cl_2O is a paramagnetic molecule. But it does not dimerize as the unpaired electron (odd electron) is localized over the whole molecule (especially on 'O' atoms).

36. F—Xe—F bond angle close to 90°.

41. Shape of perxenate ion $[XeO_6]^{4-}$.

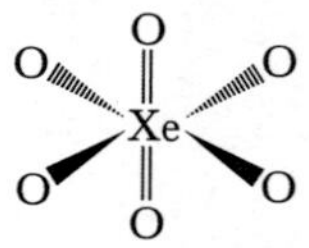

43. Lattice energy is proportional to the product of charges on either ions and inversely related to the distance between them. Greater the charge and smaller the size, greater is the lattice energy.

52.

Species	Bond-length (Å)
C_2	1.24
N_2	1.10
O_2	1.21
F_2	1.42

61. In the absence of any other ion, relation between the various types of interactions and the distance of separation are given below.

$\propto \frac{1}{r}$ for charge-charge interactions.

$\propto \frac{1}{r^2}$ for ion dipole interactions.

$\propto \frac{1}{r^3}$ for dipole-dipole interaction.

$\propto \frac{1}{r^6}$ for dispersion interactions.

63. $NaCl \longrightarrow Na^+ + Cl^-$, $KCl \longrightarrow K^+ + Cl^-$

Na^+ = (10 electrons) $= 1s^2, 2s^2, 2p^6$

K^+ = (18 electrons) $= 1s^2, 2s^2, 2p^6, 3s^2, 3p^6$

$CaCl_2 \longrightarrow Ca^{2+} + 2Cl^-$, $CuCl_2 \longrightarrow Cu^{2+} + 2Cl^-$

Ca^{2+} = (18 electrons) $= 1s^2, 2s^2, 2p^6, 3s^2, 3p^6$

Cu^{2+} = (27 electrons) $= 1s^2, 2s^2, 2p^6, 3s^2, 3p^6, 3d^9$

65. Ca^{2+} $[C{\equiv}C]^{2-}$, *i.e.*, two π-bonds and σ-bond.

66. CO_2 molecules $(O \overset{\sigma}{\underset{\pi}{=}} C \overset{\sigma}{\underset{\pi}{=}} O)$ contains two σ and two π-bonds.

67. M.O. configuration of :

$\underset{(16e^-)}{O_2} = \sigma 1s^2, \overset{*}{\sigma} 1s^2, \sigma 2s^2, \overset{*}{\sigma} 2s^2, \sigma 2p_x^2, \pi 2p_y^2$

$\approx \pi 2p_z^2\ \overset{*}{\pi}\ 2p_y^1 \approx \overset{*}{\pi} 2p_z^1$

$\underset{(17e^-)}{O_2^-} = \sigma 1s^2, \overset{*}{\sigma} 1s^2, \sigma 2s^2, \overset{*}{\sigma} 2s^2, \sigma 2p_x^2, \pi 2p_y^2$

$\approx \pi\ 2p_z^2\ \overset{*}{\pi}\ 2p_y^2 \approx \overset{*}{\pi}\ 2p_z^1$

$\underset{(15e^-)}{O_2^+} = \sigma 1s^2, \overset{*}{\sigma} 1s^2, \sigma 2s^2, \overset{*}{\sigma} 2s^2, \sigma 2p_x^2, \pi\ 2p_y^2 \approx \pi\ 2p_z^2$

$\overset{*}{\pi}\ 2p_y^1$

$\underset{(18e^-)}{O_2^{2-}} = \sigma 1s^2, \overset{*}{\sigma} 1s^2, \sigma 2s^2, \overset{*}{\sigma} 2s^2, \sigma 2p_x^2, \pi\ 2p_y^2 \approx \pi\ 2p_z^2$

$\overset{*}{\pi}\ 2p_y^2 \approx \overset{*}{\pi}\ 2p_z^2$.

Bond order $= \frac{1}{2}$ (bonding electrons − anti-bonding electrons)

Thus, bond order of $O_2 = \frac{1}{2}(10 - 6) = 2$

$O_2^- = \frac{1}{2}(10 - 7) = 1.5$

$O_2^+ = \frac{1}{2}(10 - 5) = 2.5$

$O_2^{2-} = \frac{1}{2}(10 - 8) = 1$

∵ Bond strength ∝ bond order.

$O_2^+ > O_2 > O_2^- > O_2^{2-}$ (order of bond-strength)

69. XeF_3^+

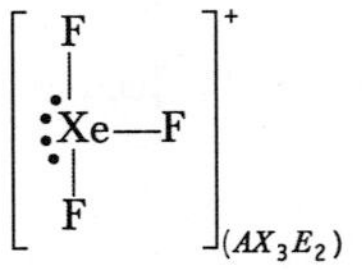

70. Molecular orbitals like atomic orbitals can hold only two electrons of the opposite spins [⇅] (Pauli's exclusion principle).

71. 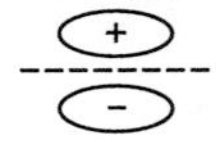

nodal plane

π-overlap bonding orbital contains only one nodal plane along internuclear axis.

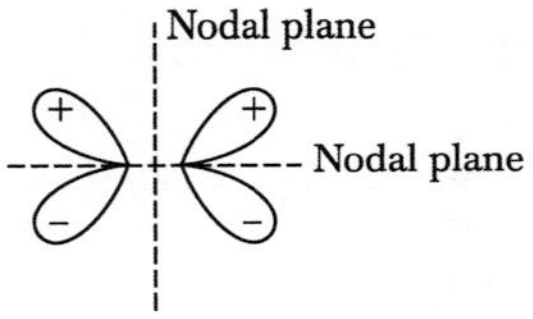

While $\overset{*}{\pi}$ overlap anti-bonding orbital contains two nodal planes, one along internuclear axis and other is perpendicular to internuclear axis.

74. Electronic configuration of Cl-atom in ClF_3.

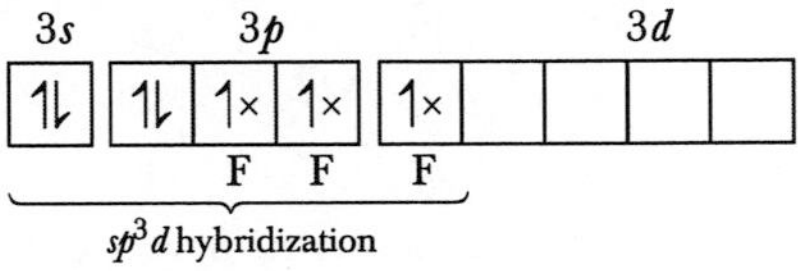

76. M.O. configuration of

$O_2 = \sigma 1s^2, \overset{*}{\sigma} 1s^2, \sigma 2s^2, \overset{*}{\sigma} 2s^2, \sigma 2p_x^2, \pi\ 2p_y^2 \approx \pi\ 2p_z^2,$

$\underbrace{\overset{*}{\pi}\ 2p_y^1 \approx \overset{*}{\pi}\ 2p_z^1}_{\text{Unpaired electrons (paramagnetic)}}$

78. $O \overset{\sigma}{\underset{\pi}{=}} C \overset{\sigma}{\underset{\pi}{=}} O$

79. CN^- and NO^+ are isoelectronic, have the same bond-order 3.

Exercise 2

1. Greater the positive charge, greater is the ionization energy.

2. (i) σ-bonded molecular orbital (σ_g and σ_u) has lower energy than π-bonded (π_g and π_u) molecular orbital.

(ii) Bonding molecular orbital (σ_g) has lower energy than anti-bonding (σ_u) molecular orbital.

3. CO (6 + 8 = 14) $= \sigma 1s^2, \overset{*}{\sigma} 1s^2, \sigma 2s^2, \overset{*}{\sigma} 2s^2, \overset{*}{\sigma} 2p_z^2,$ $\pi 2p_x^2 \approx 2p_y^2$

NO^+ (7 + 8 − 1 = 14) = same

Bond order $= \frac{N_b - N_a}{2}$

$= \frac{10 - 4}{2} = 3$

Isoelectronic species have the same bond order. Since, all the electrons are paired, both the species are diamagnetic.

4. Isoelectronic species have the same bond order.

5. In O_2, the electron is removed from the anti-bonding π-orbital, so it provides stability to the molecule.

6. $N_2 (7 + 7 = 14) = \sigma 1s^2, \overset{*}{\sigma} 1s^2, \sigma 2s^2, \overset{*}{\sigma} 2s^2, \sigma 2p_z^2,$

$$\pi 2p_x^2 \approx \pi 2p_y^2, \overset{*}{\pi} 2p_x \approx \overset{*}{\pi} 2p_y$$

$$BO = \frac{10-4}{2} = 3.$$

$N_2^- \ (14 + 1 = 15)$ (The 15th electron enters in $\overset{*}{\pi} 2p_x$ orbital.)

$$BO = \frac{10-5}{2} = 2.5$$

$O_2 \ (8 + 8 = 16)$ (The 15th and 16 electron enter in $\overset{*}{\pi} 2p_x$ and $\overset{*}{\pi} 2p_y$ orbitals respectively.)

$$BO = \frac{10-6}{2} = 2$$

$O_2^- \ (16 + 1 = 17)$

$$BO = \frac{10-7}{2} = 1.5$$

So, the order of bond order is

$$N_2 > N_2^- > O_2 > O_2^-$$

11. (a) CO_2 is linear whereas SO_2 is angular with a lone pair.

(b) CO_3^{2-} is trigonal planar whereas SO_3^{2-} is pyramidal with a lone pair.

(c) NH_3 is pyramidal with a lone pair whereas BH_3 is trigonal planar.

(d) SO_4^{2-} and ClO_4^- are tetrahedral.

12. BrO_3^- is trigonal pyramidal. It is isostructural with XeO_3. In both the cases, the central atom undergoes sp^3-hybridization.

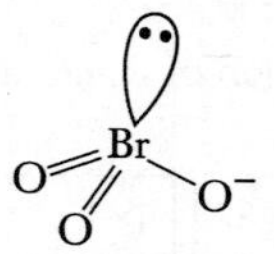

Note There are $2d\pi$ - $p\pi$ bond.

13. Number of lone pairs in the central atom can be calculated by using the following logic.

Number of electrons that are not participating in the bonding = Valence electrons in the central atom – Number of bonds (σ and π) formed by it.

Hence, the formula is

$$\text{Number of lone pairs} = \frac{v-b}{2}$$

where, v = No. of valence electrons in the central atom.

b = Number of (σ and π) bonds formed by central atom.

Note The structure or hybridization is decided by number of lone pairs and number of atoms around the central atom.

For PCl_5,

$$\text{Number of lone pairs} = \frac{v-b}{2} = \frac{5-5}{2} = 0$$

For SOF_4,

$$\text{Number of lone pairs} = \frac{v-b}{2} = \frac{6-6}{2} = 0$$

For $XeOF_4$,

$$\text{Number of lone pairs} = \frac{v-b}{2} = \frac{8-6}{2} = 1$$

For IF_5,

$$\text{Number of lone pairs} = \frac{v-b}{2} = \frac{7-5}{2} = 1$$

14. $BrF_5 = 5bp + 1\,lp \Rightarrow$ may have octahedral shape.

But its actual geometry is square pyramidal because of the presence of one lone pair of electrons.

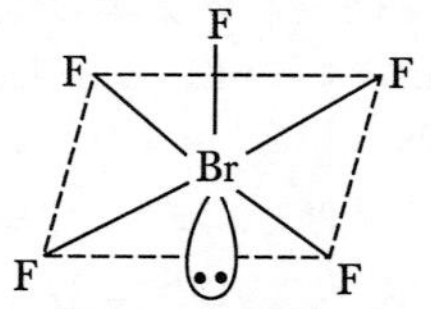

Square pyramidal

$XeOF_4 = 5bp + 1\,lp$ so it also have square pyramidal shape.

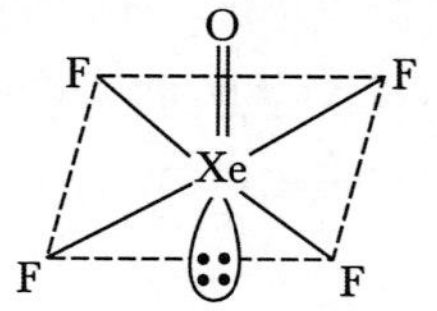

15. O=C=O
Linear
(No lone pair of electron)

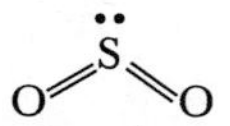

Angular

F—Xe—F (with three lone pairs on Xe)
Linear

Angular

Cl—Hg—Cl

F—Be—F

F—Xe—F (with three lone pairs on Xe)

[I—I—I]$^-$ (with three lone pairs on central I)

Thus, only XeF_2 and I_3^- are the linear species having three lone pairs of electrons.

16. (a) $XeF_4 = \underbrace{4\,bp + 2\,lp}_{\text{6 hybrid orbital}} = \underbrace{sp^3d^2}_{\text{6 hybrid orbital}}$

$[SF_4]^{2-} = 4\,bp + 2\,lp = sp^3d^2$

(b) $Ni(CO)_4 = sp^3$

$XeO_2F_2 \quad \Rightarrow \quad 4\,bp + 1\,lp = sp^3d$

(c) $[NiCl_4]^{2-} = sp^3$

$[PtCl_4]^{2-} = dsp^2$

(d) $[Co(NH_3)_6]^{3+} = d^2sp^3$

$[Co(H_2O)_6]^{3+} = sp^3d^2$

17. Trisilyl amine, $N(SiH_3)_3$ is trigonal planar due to sp^2 hybridization of central nitrogen atom. There is a $p\pi$-$d\pi$ bond formed due to overlapping of p-orbital with lone pair on nitrogen with empty d-orbital on silicon. Hence, not only it is planar and also less basic. Its Lewis basicity is decreased due to involvement of lone pair on nitrogen in π-bonding.

This kind of π-bonding is not possible with carbon as there is no available d-orbital.

18. $IBr_2^- = 2bp + 3\,lp =$ linear geometry (XeF_2)

$BrO_3^- = 3bp + 1\,lp =$ pyramidal (XeO_3)

20. Perchlorate ion

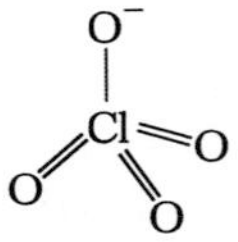

22. Both BF_3 and *t*-butylcarbonium ion have trigonal planar structure.

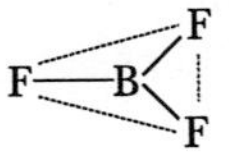

(B is sp^2-hybridized)

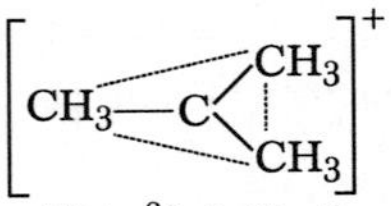

(C is sp^2-hybridized)

CO_2 (linear), H_2O (bent)
CCl_4 (tetrahedral), $PtCl_4$ (square planar)
NH_3 (pyramidal), BF_3 (trigonal planar)

23. NO^+ has (7 + 8 – 1) = 14 electrons while NO has (7 + 8) = 15 electrons. Molecular orbital configuration of NO^+ is :
$\sigma 1s^2, \overset{*}{\sigma} 1s^2, \sigma 2s^2, \overset{*}{\sigma} 2s^2, \sigma 2p_z^2, \pi 2p_x^2 \approx \pi 2p_y^2, \quad \overset{*}{\pi} 2p_x^0 \approx \overset{*}{\pi} 2p_y^0, \overset{*}{\sigma} 2p_z^0.$

Therefore, in NO, an extra electron is added to $\overset{*}{\pi}$ orbital.

24. $XeF_4 = 4\ bp + 2\ lp$ ⇒ square planar
$SeF_4 = 4\ bp + 1\ lp$ ⇒ distorted tetrahedral
$XeO_3 = 3\ bp + 1\ lp$ ⇒ pyramidal
$XeO_4 = 4\ bp + 0\ lp$ ⇒ tetrahedral

25. SCl_2; S is sp^3-hybridized
H_2S; S is sp^3-hybridized
SO_4^{2-}; S is sp^3-hybridized
SF_4; S is sp^3d-hybridized.

27.

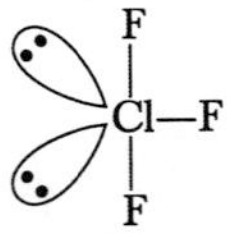

T-shaped

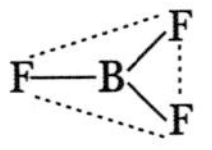

Trigonal planar

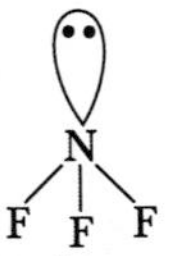

Trigonal pyramidal

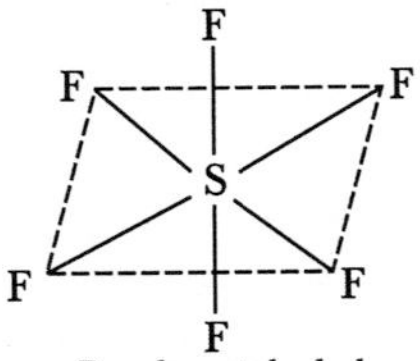

Regular octahedral

28. $XeF_4 = 4\ bp + 2\ lp = sp^3d^2$ (6 hybrid orbitals)
$H_2O = 2\ bp + 2\ lp = sp^3$ (4 hybrid orbitals)
$PCl_5 = 5\ bp + 0\ lp = sp^3d$ (5 hybrid orbitals)
$[Pt(NH_3)_4]^{2+} = dsp^2$

29. $[XeF_5]^+$ $[SiF_5]^-$

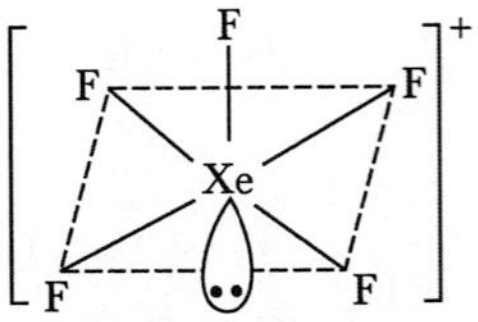

Square pyramidal

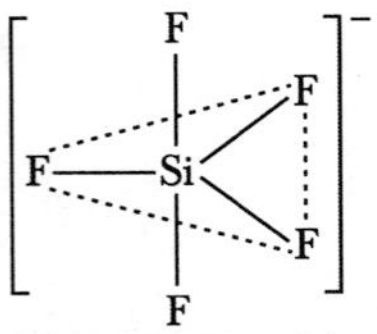

Trigonal bipyramidal

$[AsF_4]^+$ $[ICl_4]^-$

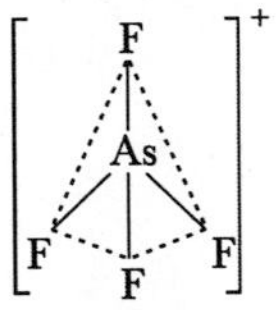

Tetrahedral

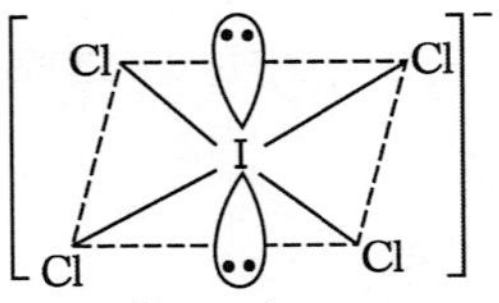

Square planar

30.

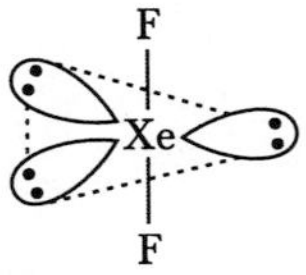

33. $\sigma^2\ \pi^4\ \delta^2\ \overset{*}{\delta}{}^2$

Bond order $= \frac{1}{2}(N_b - N_a)$
$= \frac{1}{2}(8 - 2) = 3.$

34. M.O. configuration of :
$O_2 = \sigma 1s^2, \overset{*}{\sigma} 1s^2, \sigma 2s^2, \overset{*}{\sigma} 2s^2, \sigma 2p_z^2, \pi 2p_x^2 \approx \pi 2p_y^2, \overset{*}{\pi} 2p_x^1 \approx \overset{*}{\pi} 2p_y^1$

Bond order of $O_2 = \frac{1}{2}(10 - 6) = 2$

Bond order of $O_2^+ = \frac{1}{2}(10 - 5) = 2.5$

Bond order of $O_2^- = \frac{1}{2}(10 - 7) = 1.5$

Bond order of $O_2^{2-} = \frac{1}{2}(10 - 8) = 1$

Thus, the order of bond order is
$O_2^+ > O_2 > O_2^- > O_2^{2-}$.

40. N≡N molecule has highest bond energy.

43. $BeCl_2$ H_2O SO_2

Cl—Be—Cl
Linear

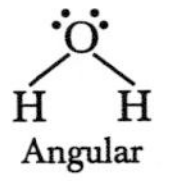

Angular

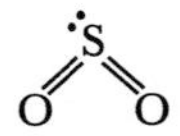

Bent

44. 1, 4-dichlorobenzene is non-polar, individual dipole vectors cancel each other.

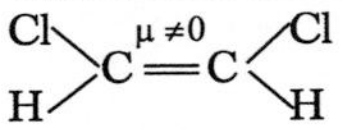

Polar

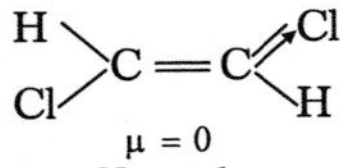

Non-polar

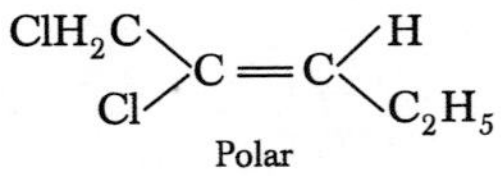

Polar

45. 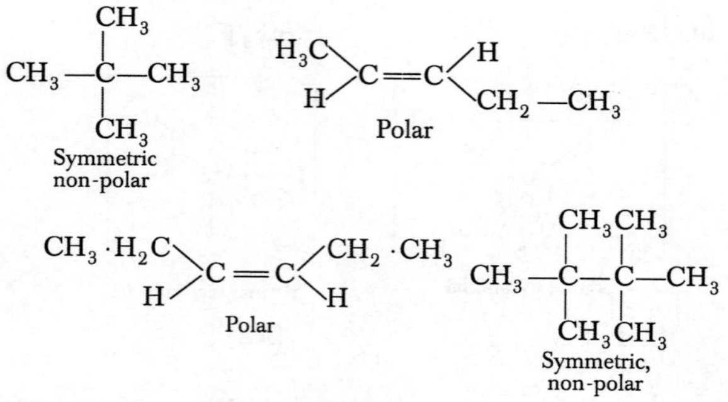

46. CO_2, $HgCl_2$, C_2H_2 are all linear.

47. 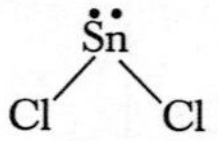

S=C=S (Linear)   O=$\overset{+}{N}$=O (Linear) $\bar{O}$—C≡N (Linear)

48. Ionic character $\propto \frac{1}{\text{size of cation}}$

$\propto$ M.P.

	NaF	KF	RbF	CsF
Thus,	(1270)	(857)	(775)	(683)
Radius	99	136	148	169

50. Hardness increases with increase in charge on the ion for crystal of similar interionic distances having similar structure.

55. $N_2^{2+} (7 + 7 - 2 = 12) = \sigma 1s^2, \overset{*}{\sigma} 1s^2, \sigma 2s^2, \overset{*}{\sigma} 2s^2,$

$\sigma 2p_z^2, \pi 2p_x^1 \approx \pi 2p_y^1$

B_2 $(5+5=10) = \sigma 1s^2, \overset{*}{\sigma} 1s^2, \sigma 2s^2, \overset{*}{\sigma} 2s^2, \sigma 2p_z^2$

Since all the electron are paired, it is a diamagnetic species.

56. Higher the bond order, more will be the stability.

59. H—Be—H (Linear)

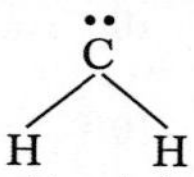

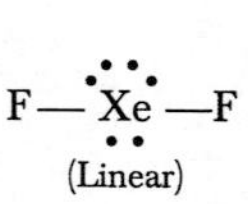

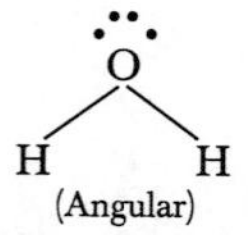

62. ReH_9^{2-}	Tricapped trigonal prism
$[Mo(CN)_8]^{4-}$	Trigonal dodcahedron
ZrF_8^{4-}	Tetragonal antiprism
XeF_6	Distorted octahedral

66. As the number of lone pair increases,bond angle generally decreases.

Moreover,

$$\text{Bond angle} \propto \frac{1}{\text{electronegativity of ligand}}$$

Thus, the order of bond angle is

$$\ddot{N}H_3 > \ddot{N}F_3 > :\ddot{S}Cl_2 > :\ddot{S}F_2$$

73. O_2 $(16) = \sigma 1s^2, \overset{*}{\sigma} 1s^2, \sigma 2s^2, \overset{*}{\sigma} 2s^2, \sigma 2p_z^2, \pi 2p_x^2 \approx \pi 2p_y^2,$

$\overset{*}{\pi} 2p_x^1 \approx \overset{*}{\pi} 2p_y^1$

$$BO = \frac{10-6}{2} = 2$$

Because of the presence of two unpaired electrons, O_2 is paramagnetic.

74. KO_2 is paramagnetic because of the presence of O_2^- ion. K^+has no unpaired electron.

80. Bond order $\propto$ bond energy

Bond energy

$O_2 < O_2^+$; $N_2 > N_2^+$; $NO > NO^-$

So the order of bond order

$O_2^+ > O_2$; $N_2 < N_2^+$; $NO^- > NO$

81. In case of $O_2 \rightarrow O_2^+$, electron is to be removed from antibonding HOMO.

84. F is the most electronegative atom.

3

Acid-Base Chemistry

Several definitions of acids and bases have been proposed from time to time and this has confused the concept of acids and bases. Each definition is correct within its own framework and we should apply the one which is the most suited under the given circumstances.

Modern definitions of acids and bases started with the Arrhenius approach between 1880–1890.

Syllabus

- Concepts of Acids and Bases
- Hard-Soft Acid Base Concept
- Non-Aqueous Solvents

Arrhenius Concept

According to Arrhenius :

Acids Substances which give hydrogen ions (H^+) in aqueous solution are called acids.

e.g.,

$$HCl \rightleftharpoons \mathbf{H^+} + Cl^-$$

Bases Substances which give hydroxyl ions (OH^-) in aqueous solution are called bases. *e.g.,*

$$NaOH \rightleftharpoons Na^+ + \mathbf{OH^-}$$

The process of neutralization of an acid by a base can be represented by the reaction.

$$H^+ + OH^- \rightleftharpoons H_2O$$

Bronsted-Lowry Concept (1923)

Acids Proton donor species are called acids.

Bases Proton acceptor species are called bases.

e.g.,

$$\underset{\text{(As solvent)}}{H_2O + H_2O} \rightleftharpoons \underset{\text{Acid}}{H_3O^+} + \underset{\text{Base}}{OH^-}$$

$$\underset{\text{(As solvent)}}{2NH_3} \rightleftharpoons \underset{\text{Acid}}{NH_4^+} + \underset{\text{Base}}{NH_2^-}$$

$$\underset{\text{(As solvent)}}{2HF} \rightleftharpoons \underset{\text{Acid}}{H_2F^+} + \underset{\text{Base}}{F^-}$$

Conjugate Acid-Base

Species that differ from each other only in terms of a transferred proton are termed as conjugates, *e.g.*,

$$\underset{\text{Acid}}{HCl} + \underset{\text{Base}}{NH_3} \longrightarrow \underset{\substack{\text{Conjugate}\\\text{acid}}}{NH_4^+} + \underset{\substack{\text{Conjugate}\\\text{base}}}{Cl^-}$$

- Strong acid has a weak conjugate base.
- A weak acid has a strong conjugate base.

Acid Base Concept in Non-Aqueous Media

The behaviour of solutes in non-aqueous solvents is often-interpreted in terms of solvent system concept. This definition depends on the mode of self-ionization of the solvent. Each solvent is considered as a parent of acidic and basic species. Each solvent self ionizes into cationic and anionic spcies as does water.

Acid

It is defined as a solute which directly or indirectly increases the concentration of cations characteristic of the solvent.

Base

It is defined as a solute which increases the concentration of the anions characteristic of the solvent.

$$2H_2O \rightleftharpoons \underset{\text{Acid}}{H_3O^+} + \underset{\text{Base}}{OH^-}$$

$$2NH_3 \rightleftharpoons \underset{\text{Acid}}{NH_4^+} + \underset{\text{Base}}{NH_2^-}$$

$$2SO_2 \rightleftharpoons \underset{\text{Acid}}{SO^{2+}} + \underset{\text{Base}}{SO_3^{2-}}$$

$$HF + HF \rightleftharpoons \underset{\text{Acid}}{H_2F^+} + \underset{\text{Base}}{F^-}$$

- Ammonium chloride (NH_4Cl) behaves as an acid in ammonia (NH_3) because it furnishes NH_4^+ ions which are cations characteristics of solvent and KNH_2 behaves as a base in ammonia (NH_3) because it gives NH_2^- ions which are anion characteristics of solvent.

$$\underset{\text{Acid}}{NH_4Cl} \overset{NH_3}{\rightleftharpoons} \mathbf{NH_4^+} + Cl^-$$

$$(2NH_3 \rightleftharpoons \mathbf{NH_4^+} + NH_2^-)$$
Self ionization of NH_3

$$\underset{\text{Base}}{KNH_2} \overset{NH_3}{\rightleftharpoons} K^+ + \mathbf{NH_2^-}$$

$$(2NH_3 \rightleftharpoons NH_4^+ + \mathbf{NH_2^-})$$
Self ionization of NH_3

Neutralization is the reverse of the self ionization reaction.

$$\underset{\text{Acid}}{NH_4Cl} + \underset{\text{Base}}{KNH_2} \overset{NH_3}{\rightleftharpoons} \underset{\text{Salt}}{KCl} + \underset{\text{Solvent}}{2NH_3}$$

Lewis Concept (1923)

This theory is based on electron-pair donation and acceptance. According to this theory,

Acid

Species having a tendency to gain electron pair(s) (electron pair acceptor) are called acids.

Such species has vacant orbitals to accommodate one or more electron pairs.

Base

Species having a tendency to donate electron pair(s) (electron pair donor) are called bases.

Such species has unshared pair of electrons. Therefore, acid-base or neutralization reactions may be termed as donor acceptor reaction or coordinate covalent bond formation reactions as given below :

$$\underset{\text{(Acid)}}{\text{Acceptor}} + \underset{\text{(Base)}}{\text{donor}} \longrightarrow \underset{\text{(Neutralization product)}}{\text{Donor acceptor compound}}$$

$$BF_3 + NH_3 \longrightarrow H_3N{-}BF_3$$

$$SnCl_4 + 2R_2O \longrightarrow (R_2O)_2SnCl_4$$

$$H^+ + NH_3 \longrightarrow NH_4^+$$

$$FeCl_3 + Cl^- \longrightarrow FeCl_4^-$$

$$SO_3 + O_2^{2-} \longrightarrow SO_4^{2-}$$

Classification of Lewis Acids

These can be classified into following categories

(a) **All the cations which have a tendency to accept electron pair(s) are Lewis acids.**

- Smaller cations like H^+, Li^+, Be^{2+}, etc., are likely to act as stronger Lewis acids due to their tendency to accept electrons from stronger bonds.
- Larger cations of alkali and alkaline earth metals behaves as relatively weaker Lewis acids due to their lesser tendency to accept electrons.
- Higher charged cations have a higher tendency to accept electrons relative to the lower charged cation of a given metal, *e.g.*,
  (i) Fe^{3+} behaves as a stronger Lewis acid as compared to Fe^{2+}.
  (ii) Similarly, Sn^{4+} is a stronger Lewis acid than Sn^{2+}.

Some cation acting examples of Lewis acids are :

Lewis acid		Lewis base		Complex	Geometry
Ag^+	+	$2NH_3$	$\longrightarrow$	$[Ag(NH_3)_2]^+$	Linear
Cu^{2+}	+	$4Cl^-$	$\longrightarrow$	$[CuCl_4]^{2-}$	Tetrahedral
Mn^{2+}	+	$6H_2O$	$\longrightarrow$	$[Mn(H_2O)_6]^{2+}$	Octahedral
Ni^{2+}	+	$4CN^-$	$\longrightarrow$	$[Ni(CN)_4]^{2-}$	Square planar

(b) **Electron deficient compound or compounds in which the central atom can expand its valence shell can behave as Lewis acids.**

- BF_3, $AlCl_3$, $GaBr_3$, $GeCl_2$ are electron deficient compounds and have a tendency to accept electron pair to complete their octet.

$$BF_3 + F^- \longrightarrow [BF_4]^-$$

- Compounds like SiF_4, $SnCl_4$, $SbCl_3$, $SbCl_5$, $TeBr_4$, SO_3, etc., where central atom can expand its valence shell, represents Lewis acids.

$$SnCl_4 + 2Cl^- \longrightarrow [SnCl_6]^{2-}$$
$$SiF_4 + 2F^- \longrightarrow [SiF_6]^{2-}$$
$$SO_3 + R_2O \longrightarrow [(R_2O)(SO_3)]$$

Classification of Lewis Bases

These can be classified into following classes

(a) **All the anions which have a tendency to donate electron pair can act as Lewis bases,** *e.g.*, oxides (O^{2-}), hydroxides (OH^-), halides (X^-), amides (NH_2^-) etc.

Note The greater the charge density on the anion, the stronger the base.

(b) **Species having lone pair of electrons act as Lewis bases**

e.g., $H_2\ddot{O}:$, $\ddot{N}H_3$, $R—\ddot{\underset{\cdot\cdot}{O}}—R'$, $R—C\ddot{\underset{\cdot\cdot}{O}}—R'$, etc.

Extended Lewis Concept

The extended Lewis acids include coordinatively unsaturated species like CO_2 and CS_2, where the central atom is bonded to atoms of different electronegativities by one or more multiple bonds. Although both the molecules are devoid of acceptor character of the central atom because carbon atom cannot extend its octet yet these have been indirectly treated as Lewis acids. This is attributed to the polarization of the π-electron cloud on approach of a Lewis base towards carbon atom of CO_2 or CS_2. The polarization leads to a partial positive charge on carbon and a partial negative charge on the more electronegative atom like O. The positively charged carbon then acts as an electron acceptor as shown in the reactions of CO_2 with Lewis bases.

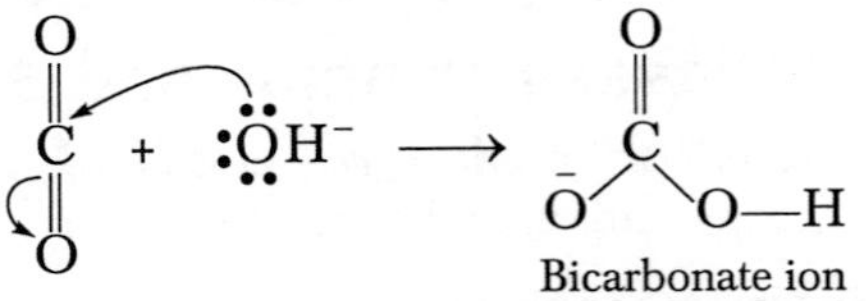

Bicarbonate ion

The extended Lewis bases include species like carbon monoxide (CO) and unsaturated hydrocarbons like alkenes, alkynes, benzene, etc. These may be treated as Lewis bases because of the donation of lone pair of $\ddot{C}O$ or of above said hydrocarbons to form π-complexes with metals in low oxidation states. Both, metal as well as Lewis base show dual characters of donors and acceptors.

$$Ni + 4CO \longrightarrow Ni(CO)_4$$
$$Fe + 5CO \longrightarrow Fe(CO)_5$$
$$Cr + 2C_6H_6 \longrightarrow Cr(C_6H_6)_2$$

Applications of Lewis Concept

(a) The Lewis approach describes an acid-base behaviour as independent of presence or absence of any particular element, group or ion.

(b) It does not involve the presence or absence of a solvent in acid-base behaviour. This makes the Lewis definition highly advantageous and widely applicable.

Limitations of Lewis Concept

(i) It does not give us any uniform scale of acid or base strength.

(ii) It does not tell us whether salt formation is related to acid-base behaviour or not.

(iii) Normal acid-base reactions are fast but complex formation in terms of donor-acceptor bond formation is a slow process.

(iv) It is very general and includes formation of $Ni(CO)_4$ and $Cr(C_6H_6)_2$ as Lewis acid-base reactions. However, bonding in these compounds is more complex and beyond the scope of Lewis concept.

Hard and Soft Acids and Bases

Formation of a stable complex between the vacant orbital of an acid (metal ions) and filled unshared orbitals of a base (ligand) depends upon the nature of metal ion and the ligands. So, Pearson suggested a simple rule for predicting the stability of coordination compound formed between acids and bases and termed it as HSAB principle. He classified acids and bases as hard acid, soft acids, hard base and soft base.

Different Classes of Acids and Bases

(a) **Metal ions or acids are classified** as class (a) metal ions and class (b) metal ions.

(i) Class (a) metal ions

These include alkali and alkaline earth metal ions, lighter transition elements (first row 3*d* metal ions Ti^{4+}, Cr^{3+}, Fe^{3+}, Co^{2+}, etc.) and H^+.

(ii) Class (b) metal ions

These include heavy transition metal ions (2nd and 3rd row transition elements 4*d* and 5*d* metal ions) as Hg^{2+}, Pd^{2+}, Pt^{2+}, Cd^{2+}, etc. and lower oxidation state ions as Cu^+, Ag^+, Hg^+, etc.

(b) Ligands or bases are classified as class (a) ligands include those molecules or ions where donor atom is N, O, F, Cl, *i.e.,* donor atoms is of high electronegativity. Class (b) ligands includes those molecules or ions where donor atom is P, As, S, Se, I, etc. *i.e.,* donor atoms is of lower electronegativity.

In 1963, Pearson used the term hard for class (a) and soft for class (b) acids and bases.

In other words

(i) Class (a) acids as hard acids

(Li^+, Be^{2+}, Al^{3+}, Cr^{3+}, Fe^{3+}, etc.)

- Cations of smaller size and lighter elements.
- Cations of higher charge.
- Not easily polarizable and
- Molecules or ions with lesser number of valence electrons.

(ii) Class (b) acids as soft acid

(Ag^+, Pd^{2+}, Pt^{2+}, Hg^{2+}, etc.)

- Cations of larger size or heavier elements.
- Cations of lower charge.
- Easily polarizable.
- Molecules or ions with larger number of valence electrons.

(iii) Class (a) bases as hard bases

($H_2\ddot{O}\!:$, $\ddot{N}H_3$, F^-, $R\ddot{O}H$, etc.)

- Donor atoms of high electronegativity.
- Donor atoms with low polarizability.

(iv) Class (b) bases as soft bases

(R_3P, R_2S, I^-, SCN^-, etc.)

- Donor atoms of lower electronegativity.
- Donor atoms of higher polarizability.

Table 3.1 **Classification of Acids**

Hard	Soft	Border line
H^+, Li^+, Na^+, K^+, Be^{2+}, Mg^{2+}, Ca^{2+}, Al^{3+}, Ga^{3+}, In^{3+}, Ti^{4+}, Zr^{4+}, SO_3, CO_2, BF_3, $B(OR)_3$, $AlCl_3$, AlH_3, $Al(CH_3)_3$, HX	Cl, Br, I, I_2, Br_2, I^+, Br^+, O, HO^+, RO^+, RS^+, N, BH_3, $GaCl_3$, GaI_3, $InCl_3$, Tl^+, $(CH_3)_3Te$, Cd^{2+}, Hg^{2+}, Hg_2^{2+}, **Cu^+, Ag^+, Au^+, Pd^{2+}, metals**	SO_2, NO^+, Sb^{3+}, Bi^{3+}, Sn^{2+}, Pb^{2+}, $B(CH_3)_3$, GaH_3, Zn^{2+}, **Cu^{2+}**

Table 3.2 **Classification of Bases**

Hard	Soft	Border line
$\ddot{N}H_3$, N_2H_4, $R\ddot{N}H_2$, R—$\ddot{O}H$, $R_2\ddot{O}\!:$, $R_2C\!=\!\ddot{O}\!:$, $H_2\ddot{O}\!:$, $\overset{\ominus}{O}H$, O_2^{2-}, F^-, Cl^-, NO_3^-, SO_4^{2-}, PO_4^{3-}, CH_3COO^- here R = alkyl group	RNC, CO, C_2H_4, C_6H_6, RSH, R_2S, $\overset{\ominus}{S}R$, $\overset{\ominus}{C}N$, $S\overset{\ominus}{C}N$, $S_2O_3^{2-}$, I^-, H^-, R^-, R_3P, $(RO)_3P$, R_3As, where, R = alkyl group	$C_6H_5NH_2$, C_6H_5N, N_2, NO_2^-, SO_3^{2-}, Br^-

HSAB Principle

According to this hard acids prefer to bond to hard bases and soft acids prefer to combine with soft bases. **Hard acids and hard bases are not easily polarizable** and their interaction are predominant ionic and **soft acids and soft bases are usually polarizable** and hence, their interactions are predominant covalent.

Hard bases $\ddot{N}H_3$, $H_2\ddot{O}\!:$, $F^\ominus$, prefer to combine with Fe^{3+}, Al^{3+}, Mg^{2+}.

Soft bases R_3P, R_2S, $I^\ominus$ prefer Pt^{2+}, Pd^{2+}, Hg^{2+}, Ag^+ to combine and form complexes.

Thus, hard acids will show the following order of preference for binding the donor atoms or ions within the group :

$$F^- >> Cl^- > Br^- > I^-$$

$$R_2O > R_2S$$

$$R_3N >> R_3P$$

Soft acids will show the opposite trend to hard acids for binding the donor atoms or ions within a group.

$$I^- > Br^- > Cl^- > F^-$$
$$R_2S >> R_2O$$
$$R_3P >> R_3N$$

Applications of HSAB Principle

HSAB principle is helpful in explaining :

1. Stability of complexes

The complexes formed with hard-hard and soft-soft preference are more stable than with hard-soft interaction.

Examples Complex between soft acid Ag^+ and soft base I^- is quite stable.

(a) $\underset{\text{(Soft acid)}}{Ag^+} + \underset{\text{(Soft base)}}{2I^-} \longrightarrow \underset{\text{(Stable)}}{AgI_2^-}$

(b) $\underset{\text{(Soft acid)}}{Ag^+} + \underset{\text{(Hard base)}}{2F^-} \longrightarrow \underset{\substack{\text{(Unstable)} \\ \text{(Soft-hard interaction)}}}{AgF_2^-}$

2. Course of reaction

Reaction between LiI and CsF always proceeds to give LiF and CsI, *i.e.*, there is more stability of product due to hard-hard soft-soft combinations. **Examples**

(a) $\underset{\text{(Hard-soft)}}{LiI} + \underset{\text{(Soft-hard)}}{CsF} \longrightarrow \underset{\text{(Hard-hard)}}{LiF} + \underset{\text{(Soft-Soft)}}{CsI}$

(b) $\underset{\text{(Hard-soft)}}{CaS} + \underset{\text{(Hard)}}{H_2O} \longrightarrow \underset{\text{(Hard-hard)}}{CaO} + \underset{\text{(Soft)}}{H_2S}$

(c) $\underset{\substack{\text{(Hard-soft)} \\ \text{Cupric iodide}}}{CuI_2} + \underset{\substack{\text{(Soft-hard)} \\ \text{Cuprous fluoride}}}{2CuF} \longrightarrow \underset{\text{(Hard-hard)}}{CuF_2} + \underset{\substack{\text{(Soft-soft)} \\ \text{Cuprous iodide}}}{2CuI}$

Above reactions will proceed in forward direction.

3. Classification of acids and bases

Acids and bases can be classified as hard or soft depending on their behaviour in the following equilibrium. **Examples**

(a) **If base is a soft base** then the reaction with soft acid will be in forward direction as in

$$\underset{\substack{(H^+ = \text{hard acid}) \\ B \rightarrow \text{Base (soft)} \\ \text{like } R_2SH^+}}{B^-H^+} + \underset{\text{(Soft acid)}}{CH_3Hg^+} \longrightarrow CH_3\overset{+}{Hg}B^- + H^+$$

If base is hard like $\ddot{N}H_3$—left hand side reaction will be favoured.

$$B = \ddot{N}H_3, H_3\ddot{N}H^+ \text{ or } \overset{+}{N}H_4$$

$$H_3\ddot{N}H^+ + CH_3Hg^+ \longleftarrow CH_3\overset{+}{Hg}\ddot{N}H_3 + H^+$$

(b) Similarly,

$$AF^- + \underset{\text{(Soft base)}}{SCN^-} \longrightarrow \overset{+}{A}S\overset{-}{C}N + F^-$$

F^- = hard base

A^+ = soft acid like Ag^+ forward reaction favoured.

A^+ = hard acid like Na^+ backward reaction is favoured.

4. Occurrence of ores and minerals

Hard-hard and soft-soft interactions over hard-soft interaction influences the occurrence and formation of important ores and minerals in earth crust. Like Na^+, K^+, Mg^{2+}, Ca^{2+}, Mn^{2+}, Cu^{2+}, Al^{3+}, Fe^{3+}, Cr^{3+}, etc., (hard acids) occur as their oxides, carbonates and halides (O^{2-}, CO_3^{2-}, Cl^-, F^-—hard bases)

While Cu^+, Ag^+, Cs^+, Hg^{2+}, Cd^{2+}, Pd^{2+}, etc., (Soft acids) occur as sulphides or iodides (S^{2-} or I^-—Soft bases).

While border line acids like Fe^{2+}, Ni^{2+}, Zn^{2+}, Pb^{2+}, Co^{2+} can occur both as sulphides (soft bases) as well as oxides and carbonate (hard bases) due to their intermediate nature.

5. Catalytic poisoning

Catalyst get poisoned with conversion of metal into its complex. All soft bases which can complex with metals in atomic state (soft acids) will act as poison towards metal catalysts.

All metal atoms (M^0) are soft acids and Ni, Pt, Cd, V, Cr, Mo, etc., are metal catalyst. These are poisoned by substances like CO, unsaturated hydrocarbons, (alkenes, alkynes, dienes, arenes) organophosphines R_3P, organoarsines R_3As, etc., due to soft-soft interaction.

Normal hard bases (N, O, F) do not act as poison to metal atoms being hard-soft interaction.

Limitations of HSAB Principle

The hard-hard and soft-soft factors according to HSAB principle are independent of acidic or basic character of compounds. However, sometimes this rule is violated by inherent acid or base strengths leading to more stable hard soft systems.

According to HSAB principle following reaction is not feasible

$$\underset{\text{(Soft base)}}{SO_3^{2-}} + \underset{\text{(Hard acid)}}{H—F} \longrightarrow \underset{\text{(Hard-soft)}}{HSO_3^-} + \underset{\text{(Hard)}}{F^-}$$

But, this reaction occurs because, **stronger** soft base SO_3^{2-} displaces **weaker,** hard base (F^-) from hard acid (H^+).

Similarly, OH^- (strong hard base) displaces SO_3^{2-} (less strong soft base)

$$\underset{\text{(Soft-soft)}}{CH_3\overset{+}{Hg}SO_3^-} + \underset{\text{(Hard)}}{OH^-} \longrightarrow \underset{\text{(Soft-hard)}}{CH_3\overset{+}{Hg}\overset{-}{O}H} + \underset{\text{(Soft)}}{SO_3^{2-}}$$

Relative Strength of Acids

The strength of protonic acids like HCl, HNO_3, H_2SO_4, HCN, HF can be compared by their tendencies to give protons.

- Acids like HCl, HNO_3 or H_2SO_4 are strong acids while CH_3COOH, HF, HCN are weak acids.
- Ionization of an acid in water measures the relative strength of the acid.

For instance ionization of an acid HA may be represented as :

$$\underset{C}{HA} \rightleftharpoons \underset{0}{H^+} + \underset{0}{A^-} \quad \text{initially}$$

$$C - \alpha C \qquad \alpha C \quad \alpha C \quad \text{at equilibrium}$$

The equilibrium constant for the reaction is written as :

$$K_a = \frac{[H^+][A^-]}{[HA]} = \frac{\alpha^2 C^2}{C(1-\alpha)} = \frac{\alpha^2 C}{(1-\alpha)}$$

If $\alpha <<< 1, (1-\alpha) \approx 1$

$$K_a = \alpha^2 / C$$

where, K_a is known as dissociation constant or ionization constant of an acid and measures the relative strength of an acid. **The stronger the acid, the larger will be its K_a.**

$$pH = -\log [H^+]$$
$$= -\log [\alpha C]$$

The term pK_a that is, $-\log K_a$ is commonly used to express the dissociation of an acid.

$$pK_a = -\log K_a = \frac{1}{\log K_a}$$

Thus, **higher the value of pK_a, the weaker is the acid.**

Table 3.3 pK_a **Values of Some Acids in Water**

Acid	HF	CH_3COOH	H_2CO_3	HCN
pK_a	3.45	4.76	6.37	9.31

Acidity of an acid depends upon the nature of the compound, its structure or its position in the Periodic Table. The acids are normally classified into three categories :

1. **Hydro acids** *e.g.,* HCl, H_2S, PH_3, H_2Te, etc.
2. **Oxo acids** *e.g.,* $HClO_4$, H_3PO_4, HSO_4^-, etc.
3. **Solvated cations** *e.g.,* $[Al(H_2O)_6]^{3+}$, NH_4^+, etc.

Factors Affecting Strength of Hydro Acids

(a) Electronegativity

There is a general increase in hydro acid strength in going from left to right along a period.

For example, the following trend of acids strength is observed along the second period.

$$\xrightarrow[\text{Increasing order of acid strength}]{CH_4 < NH_3 < H_2O < HF}$$

The trend is explained on the basis of increase in electronegativity as we move from left to right along a period.

$$C < N < O < F$$

With the increase in electronegativity of the central atom, the tendency, to pull the electron pair from H increases, and dissociation of H becomes easier and acidic character increases.

- The above trend based on electronegativity holds true along a period. It does not hold good as we move down a group. In fact, acidity in a group increases with decrease in electronegativity as we move down the group.

For example in the hydro acids of group VII, HI is the strongest acid and HF is the weakest acid, which is opposite to the trend along a period.

$$HF < HCl < HBr < HI$$

Similarly, in group VI the acid strength increases as we move down the group with H_2O as the weakest acid and H_2Te as the strongest acid inspite of H_2O being the most polar on the basis of electronegativity.

$$H_2O < H_2S < H_2Se < H_2Te$$

This shows that electronegativity difference (or bond polarity) is not the only factor that governs acidity.

(b) Size of central atom

Besides electronegativity another factor that governs acid strength qualitatively is the size of the central atom. As we move down a group, the electronegativity decreases but the size increases as given below.

Atom	F	Cl	Br	I
Electronegativity (χ)	4.0	3.0	2.8	2.5
Size (Å)	0.64	0.99	1.14	1.33

The effect of increase in size appears to be more pronounced than the decrease in electronegativity of the central atom. With decrease in electronegativity, the dissociation of H decreases and acidic character decreases but this is more than compensated by the increase in dissociation with increase in size, thereby, leading to increased acidity down a group.

(c) Enthalpy of ionization

The acidic strength of hydro acids also depends on many factors. The factors which influence the degree of electrolytic dissociation of hydro acids HX in aqueous solution can be best under stood by Born-Fajan-Haber cycle. The acidic strength of an acid HX (X = F, Cl, Br, I) may be given by the reaction :

$$HX \overset{\Delta H}{\rightleftharpoons} H^+(aq) + X^-(aq)$$

The value of ΔH is the summation of the following factors as given below.

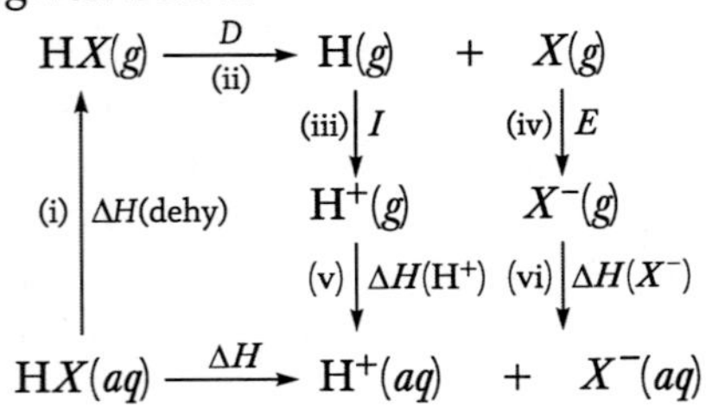

Fig. 3.1 Born-Fajan-Haber cycle for dissociation of HX in queous medium.

(i) Enthalpy of dehydration $(\Delta H)_{(dehy)}$ of the molecule $HX(aq)$ to $HX(g)$. Its value is positive ($\because$ energy is absorbed).

(ii) Dissociation energy (D) of breaking the molecule $HX\ (g)$ into its gaseous atoms H (g) and $X(g)$. It is also positive (+ve).

(iii) Ionization energy (I) of the hydrogen atom into $H^+(g)$. It is positive.

(iv) Electron affinity (E) of the halogen atom $X(g)$ is a negative (–ve) quantity ($\because$ energy is released).

(v) Enthalpy of hydration $\Delta H_{(H^+)}$ of $H^+(g)$ ion has a negative value.

(vi) Enthalpy of hydration $\Delta H_{(X^-)}$ of x^- ion is also negative.

The value of ΔH is the sum of factors (i) to (iv).

$$\Delta H = \Delta H_{(dehy)} + D + I + E + \Delta H_{(H^+)} + \Delta H_{(X^-)}$$

Endothermic changes (i) to (iii) are positive and exothermic changes (iv) to (vi) are –ve.

- For comparison purposes these values are given in table below. The factors (iii) and (v) are common for all the hydrogen halides.

Table 3.4 **Enthalpy Data of H*X* (*aq*)** (kJ/mol)

	Enthalpy symbol	HF	HCl	HBr	HI
(i)	$\Delta H_{(dehy)}$	49	18	21	23
(ii)	D	568	431	366	298
(iii)	I	1312	1312	1312	1312
(iv)	E	–333	–348	–323	–297
(v)	$\Delta H_{(H^+)}$	–1090	–1090	–1090	–1090
(vi)	$\Delta H_{(X)}$	–510	–366	–333	–291
	ΔH	–4	–43	–47	–45

The value of ΔH (given in the above table) give a tantative idea of relative acidities of halogen acids. The larger the negative values of ΔH, the greater is the acidity. For a complete analysis of acid strengths, entropy term ΔS must also be considered to get values of ΔG. This is beyond our scope.

The values of ΔH in the above table indicate a small enthalpy change (4 kJ/mol) for the ionization of HF(aq). This explains the relatively weaker acidic strength of HF compared to other halogen acids.The halo acids HCl, HBr and HI appear to have similar large negative values of ΔH which indicate their higher acidity with relative acidic strength HCl < HI < HBr. This anomaly is taken care of if entropy term is considered to get complete analysis of acid strength which shows the following order.

$$HF < HCl < HBr < HI$$

The relative weakness of acidity of HF compared to other halo acids is attributable mainly to its high heat of dehydration $\Delta H_{(dehy)}$ and higher bond dissociation energy (D).

Similarly, it can be shown that the ΔH values decrease in the order :

$$H_2O > H_2S > H_2Se > H_2Te$$

For group VI hydrides to indicate the following sequence of relative acidity.

$$H_2O < H_2S < H_2Se < H_2Te$$

Along the period, the ΔH values decrease in the sequence

$$CH_4 > NH_3 > H_2O > HF$$

This agrees with relative acidities :

$$CH_4 < NH_3 < H_2O < HF$$

If we consider the energetics involved in the Born-Fajan-Haber cycle for these molecules then it can be inferred that the most important factor which makes HF the strongest acid in the period is the high electron affinity of the fluorine atom relative to low electron affinities of OH, NH_2 and CH_3. This trend in the electron affinities can be accounted for by fluorine's higher effective nuclear charge.

(d) Basic strength of conjugate base

The relative strengths of halo acids can also be explained in terms of relative basic strength of their conjugate bases. For example, for halo hydroacids HF, HCl, HBr, HI, their conjugate bases are F^-, Cl^-, Br^-, I^-, respectively.

As we move from F^- to I^-, the size of the ion increases and hence, electron density decreases. As electron density decreases, the tendency to attract a proton decreases with the consequence basic character decreases from F^- to I^-. That is basic character decreases as :

$$F^- > Cl^- > Br^- > I^-$$

Ion	F^-	Cl^-	Br^-	I^-
Ionic size (Å)	1.36	1.81	1.95	2.16

We know, stronger the conjugate base, weaker the acid and *vice-versa*. Hence, acid strength increases as

$$HF < HCl < HBr < HI$$

Similarly, we can explain the acidity of group VI hydrides :

$$H_2O < H_2S < H_2Se < H_2Te$$

(e) Bond dissociation energy

The relative strengths of hydroacids may also be explained in terms of bond dissociation energy. Bond dissociation energy decreases from HF to HI or from H_2O to H_2Te.

Hydroacids	HF,	HCl,	HBr,	HI	H_2O,	H_2S,	H_2Se,	H_2Te
Bond dissociation energy (kJ mol^{-1})	568,	431,	366,	298	464,	339,	276,	247
pK_a	3,	–7,	–9,	–11	14,	7,	4,	3

Hence, acidic strength increases as :

$$HF < HCl < HBr < HI$$

$$H_2O < H_2S < H_2Se < H_2Te$$

Factors Affecting the Strength of Oxo Acids

The strength of oxo acids depends upon the following factors :

(i) Size of the central atom.

(ii) Electronegativity of the central atom in the molecule.

(iii) Inductive effects of substituents on central atom.

(a) Electronegativity and size of central atom

Consider an oxo acid

$$E—O—H$$

where, E is the central atom. A small and highly electronegative atom E will tend to attract the shared pair of electrons more towards itself. This will create a high polarity in O—H bond thereby allowing the proton to dissociate and make the compound acidic. Thus, higher the electronegativity of E more easily the proton is lost and more is the acidity of oxo acid.

As we move down a group, the electronegativity decreases as the size increases and acidic character decreases.

For example, the acidic character of oxo acids of halogens decreases in the given order as it is clear from pK_a values.

$$\begin{array}{lccc} & HClO > & HBrO > & HIO \\ pK_a = & 7.4 & 8.7 & 11.0 \end{array}$$

It has been observed that the compound EOH behaves as an acid only if E has electronegativity value greater than 1.8. **Example**, ClOH is an acid, while LiOH is a base because electronegativity of Cl is 3.0 which that of Li is 1.0.

(b) Presence of additional groups

Presence of additional groups of E in $(R)_n$ E—OH where, 'R' is the additional group (such as oxygen) increases the acidity. The relative acidity increases with increase in number of oxygen atoms. For example, in the series of oxo acids of chlorine, the acid strength increases in the order.

$$\begin{array}{lcccc} & HClO < & HClO_2 < & HClO_3 < & HClO_4 \\ \text{Oxidation no. of Cl} = & 1 & 3 & 5 & 7 \\ pK_a \text{ values} = & 7.52 & 1.94 & -3 & -10 \end{array}$$

In these compounds, the acidity increases with increasing oxidation numbers of the atom (E). All these four acids have only one protonated, oxygen, *i.e.,* OH group. The rest of the oxygen atoms are surrounding the central atom. With increase in the number of oxygen atoms on the central atom (E = Cl), the extent of electron withdrawl from the O—H bond increases. As a result, the polarity of the O—H bond or tendency for the proton to dissociate increases.

$$\text{Cl—OH} < \text{OCl—OH} < \text{O}_2\text{Cl—OH} < \text{O}_3\text{Cl—OH}$$

(c) Stability of conjugate base

The above increase in acidic strength is also explained in terms of the stability of conjugate base formed by the loss of H^+ ion from the acid.

The anions ClO^-, ClO_2^-, ClO_3^- and ClO_4^- formed by the loss of proton are stabilized by the charge distribution of π or double bonded 'O' atoms. The charge stabilization is minimum in ClO^- and maximum in ClO_4^-. This means that ClO^- will have minimum stability and therefore maximum attraction for H^+ thus making it the weakest acid and ClO_4^- will have maximum stability thus minimum attraction for H^+ therefore making it the strongest acid amongst the four.

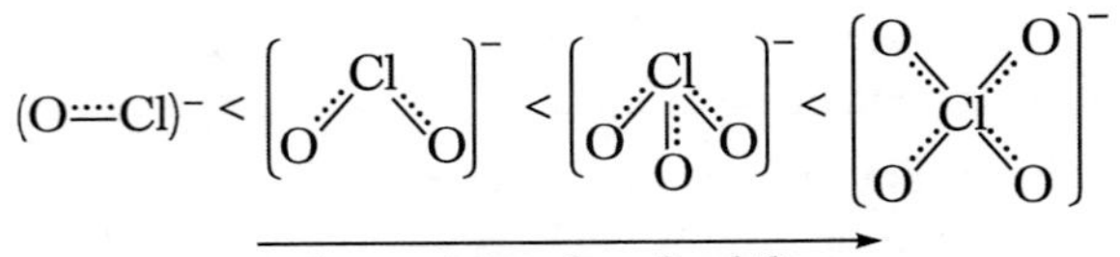

Increasing order of stability

Similarly, OMn(OH) is amphoteric but acidity increases with increase in n (where, n = number of substituent on central atom such as 'O') and $O_3Mn(OH)$ (permanganic acid) is strongly acidic. Likewise, nitrous acid, ON(OH) (pK_a = 3.3) is a weak acid but $O_2N(OH)$ (nitric acid) is a strong (pK_a = −1.4) acid.

(d) Inductive effect

Among carboxylic acids, the inductive effect of substituents is highly pronounced. Acetic acid (CH_3COOH) is a weak acid but replacement of methyl hydrogen by a more electronegative chloro group increases the acidity of the acid as shown by their pK_a values. As the number of electronegative substituents increases, the acidity of the acid increases further.

Acid	CH_3COOH,	$ClCH_2COOH$,	Cl_2CH COOH,	$Cl_3C{\cdot}COOH$
pK_a	4.8,	2.9,	1.3,	0.7

Linus Pauling rationalized the strength of oxo acid in aqueous solutions by a set of two empirical rules :

(i) For a given polybasic acid, the successive pK_{a_1}, pK_{a_2}, pK_{a_3} values approximate to a ratio 1 : 4 : 8 as given below :

Acid	pK_{a_1}	pK_{a_2}	pK_{a_3}
H_3PO_4	2.1	7.2	12.0
H_3AsO_4	2.3	7.0	13.0
$H_4P_2O_7$	0.8	2.2	6.7

(ii) The magnitude of pK_a is given by the formulation :

$$O_m\,E(OH)_n$$

for $m = 0$, p$K_a \geq 7$; very weak acids, *e.g.,* $B(OH)_3$

$m = 1$, p$K_a \simeq 2$; weak acids, *e.g.,* OCl(OH)

$m = 2$, p$K_a \simeq -3$; strong acids, *e.g.,* $O_2Cl(OH)$

$m = 3$, p$K_a \simeq -8$; very strong acids, *e.g.,* $O_3Cl(OH)$

This rule is in close agreement with another generalization by Ricci which state

$$pK_a = 8.0 - 9.0\,m + 4.0\,n$$

where, m = formal charge on central atom E

n = number of non-hydroxyl oxygen atoms in the acid

Formal charge is calculated as

m = number of valence shell electrons on the central atom $-\frac{1}{2}$ (Number of electrons shared with other atoms) $-\frac{1}{2}$ (Number of unshared valence shell electrons)

Thus, formal charge :

$$:\ddot{\underset{..}{Cl}}\text{—OH} = 7 - \frac{1}{2}(2) - 6 = 0$$

$$\text{O—}\ddot{\underset{..}{Cl}}\text{—OH} = 7 - \frac{1}{2}(4) - 4 = +1$$

$$\text{O}_2\ddot{\text{Cl}}\text{—OH} = 7 - \frac{1}{2}(6) - 2 = +2$$

$$\text{O}_3\text{Cl—OH} = 7 - \frac{1}{2}(8) - 0 = +3$$

Examples in $HClO_4$: $m = +3$, $n = 3$

Substituting these values in the above equation, we can calculate pK_a.

$$pK_a = 8.0 - 9(+3) + 4.0(3) = -7$$

Similarly, for $HClO_3$

$$m = +2,\ n = 2$$

$$pK_a = 8.0 - 18 + 8 = -2$$

For H_3PO_4 or $OP(OH)_3$

$$m = 5 - 4 - 0 = 1, n = 1$$

$$pK_a = 8 - 9 + 4 = +3$$

The empirical values calculated according to above given equation are quite close to the reported pK_a values. Thus, knowing the values of formal charge on the central atom in the oxo acid, the number of non-hydroxyl oxygen atoms on the acid, it is possible to get an idea of acid strength.

Factors Affecting Acid Strength of Hydrated Cations

Small and highly charged cations, that is, large charge-to-size ratio, can lead to the rupture of O—H bonds in the hydrated cation to yield hydrolysed species and the hydrated proton as shown :

$$[M(H_2O)_n]^{m+}(aq) + H_2O \rightleftharpoons [M(H_2O)_{n-1}OH]^{(m-1)^+}(aq) + H_3O^+$$

The larger the charge-to-size (acidity) of the cation, the more polar the O—H bond in the coordinated H_2O and the more easily a proton is released as H_3O^+. On the basis of charge-to-size ratio, the relative acid strength decreases as :

$$[Fe(H_3O)_6]^{3+} > [V(H_2O)_6]^{3+} > Cr[(H_2O)_6]^{3+} > [Sc(H_2O)_6]^{3+} > [Al(H_2O)_6]^{3+} > [La(H_2O)_6]^{3+}$$

Among divalent hydrated cations, the acid strength decreases in the order :

$$[Be(H_2O)_n]^{2+} > [Cu(H_2O)_n]^{2+} > [Mg(H_2O)_6]^{2+} > [Ca(H_2O)_n]^{2+} > [Ba(H_2O)_n]^{2+}$$

Relative Strength of Bases

The ionisation equilibria of bases can also be studied like acids. Consider the ionisation of base BOH.

$$BOH \rightleftharpoons B^+ + OH^-$$

The equilibrium constant may be expressed as :

$$K_b = \frac{[B^+][OH^-]}{[BOH]}$$

where, K_b is known as ionization or dissociation constant of the base. It measures the relative strength of the base. **The higher the value of K_b, the stronger is the base.**

K_b may be expressed as

$$pK_b = -\log K_b = \frac{1}{\log K_b}$$

Thus, **larger the value of pK_b, lesser is the dissociation and weaker is the base.**

Table 3.5 **pK_b Values of Some Bases in Water**

Base	NH_4OH	$C_2H_5NH_2$	AgOH	$Ca(OH)_2$
pK_b	4.75	10.80	3.96	2.43

1. Basicity in Amines

$\ddot{N}H_3$ is a weak base in aqueous medium while $CH_3\ddot{N}H_2$ (methylamine), is stronger than $\ddot{N}H_3$ whereas NF_3 (nitrogen trifluoride) is not at all basic.

$$H_3\ddot{N} > H_2\ddot{N}—\ddot{N}H_2 > \ddot{N}H_2—OH > \ddot{N}F_3$$

Decreasing basic strength →

$$(CH_3)_2—\ddot{N}H > CH_3—\ddot{N}H_2 > \ddot{N}H_3$$

Decreasing basicity of amines →

Reason for basicity of amines This order of basicity can be explained on the basis of inductive effects of the substituents on nitrogen atom.

- The replacement of —H in NH_3 by electron withdrawing groups such as $—NH_2$, —OH, —F, etc., decreases the basicity as these groups withdraws the electron density from nitrogen atom making it slightly positive and hence reduces basicity.

  e^- density ↓ $\ddot{N}H_2 \rightarrow —\ddot{O}—H$

- The replacement of —H in $\ddot{N}H_3$ by electron releasing group like alkyl group increases the electron density of nitrogen thus increasing basicity.

  $$CH_3 \rightarrow —\ddot{N}H_2$$

- Basicity increases with increase in alkyl groups as

  $$CH_3 \rightarrow —\ddot{N}(\leftarrow CH_3)— H > CH_3 \rightarrow —\ddot{N}(H)—H$$

But, **tertiary amines are weaker bases than primary amines.**

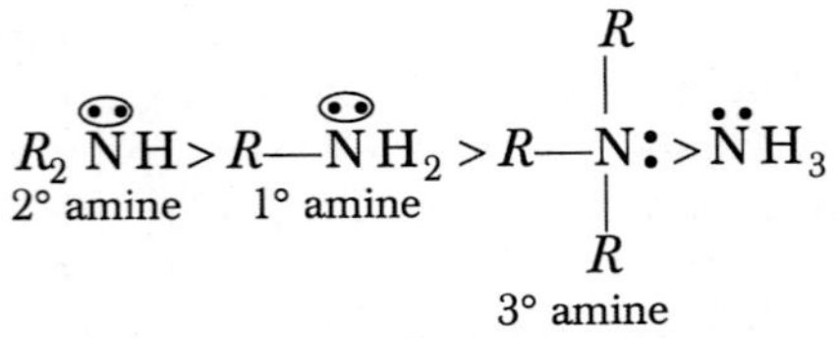

This is due to the increased steric effect of three alkyl groups on a small nitrogen atom and lower energy of solvation of tertiary amines as compared to others.

2. Basicity of Metal Oxides

Metal oxides can be classified as

Acidic oxides Those oxides that **increases** H^+ concentration when dissolved in water. For example

$$N_2O_5 + H_2O \rightleftharpoons 2H^+ + \underset{\text{(Nitrate ion)}}{2NO_3^-}$$

Basic oxide Those oxides that **decreases** H^+ concentration when dissolved in water. For example

$$CaO + H_2O \rightleftharpoons Ca^{2+} + 2OH^-$$

Amphoteric oxides Those oxides which behave as acids as well as bases when dissolved in water. For example

$$Al_2O_3 + \underset{\text{(Decreasing H}^+\text{ ion conc., so basic)}}{6H^+} \rightleftharpoons 2Al^{3+} + 3H_2O \text{ (basic)}$$

$$Al_2O_3 + \underset{\text{(Decreasing OH}^-\text{ ion conc., so acidic)}}{2OH^-} \rightleftharpoons 2AlO_2^- + H_2O \text{ (acid)}$$

Basic character **increases** with **increase in atomic weight along a group in Periodic Table.**

Example

Group 13 oxides	B_2O_3	–	Acidic
	Al_2O_3, Ga_2O_3	–	Amphoteric
	In_2O_3, Tl_2O	–	Basic
Group 2 oxides	BeO	–	Amphoteric
	MgO	–	Weakly basic
	CaO, SrO, BaO	–	Basic (Basicity increases ↓)

Reason for basicity of metal oxides Charge remains same on the metal atom in the group but **size** increases as atomic weight increases. Thus,

Charge-to-size ratio decreases and basicity increases.

However, due to very small size of B^{3+} (high polarizing power) its charge to size ratio is exceptionally large relative to others. So, it is acidic in nature.

Similarly, Be^{2+} has high charge to size ratio so basicity of BeO is significantly lower than the next members of the group.

Factors Affecting the Strength of Acids and Bases

Relative strengths of acids depends upon the following factors :

1. Inductive effects of substituents
2. Resonance
3. Steric effects of substituents

1. Inductive Effect

Electron withdrawing substituent will make a Lewis acid stronger while electron releasing substituent will decrease the acid strength. *e.g.*,

$$\underset{\text{(—CH}_3\text{ group electron releasing)}}{(CH_3)_3B} < BH_3 < \underset{\text{(F-electron withdrawing inductive effect)}}{BF_3} \longrightarrow$$

2. Resonance

According to inductive effect among the boron trihalides BF_3, BCl_3 and BBr_3, BF_3 should have been the strongest acid and BBr_3 weakest but the observed relative strength is

$$BBr_3 > BCl_3 > BF_3$$

Thus, inductive effect cannot explain the acidic strength of boron halides.

This anamoly can be explained by phenomenon of resonance.

Halogen atoms have a tendency to contribute electron density towards boron atom. This is known as **back donation** from halogen to boron.

$$B_5 = 1s^2, 2s^2 2p_x^1, 2p_y^1, \underset{\uparrow \text{ Vacant boron orbital}}{2p_z^0}$$

$$F_9 = 1s^2, \underbrace{2s^2\ 2p_x^2\ 2p_y^2}_{\text{Filled orbitals of F}} 2p_z^1$$

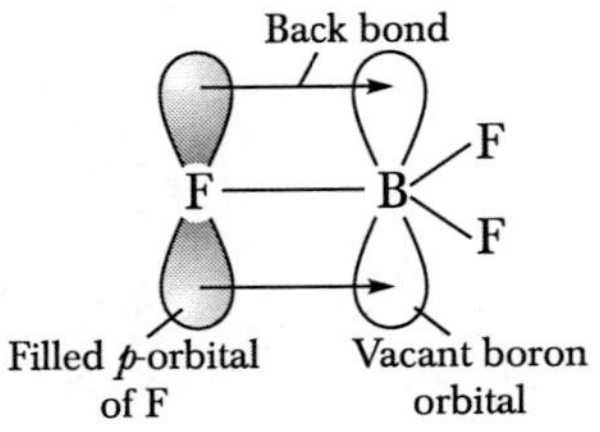

Back donation is more effective in case of BF_3 due to easier overlap of filled $2p$-orbitals of F with empty $2p$-orbitals of boron, as both overlapping orbitals belong to same energy level, thus overlap is more effective and additional bond known as $p\pi$- $p\pi$ **backbond** is formed. This type of back bonding can oscillate among three B–F bonds in BF_3 as shown :

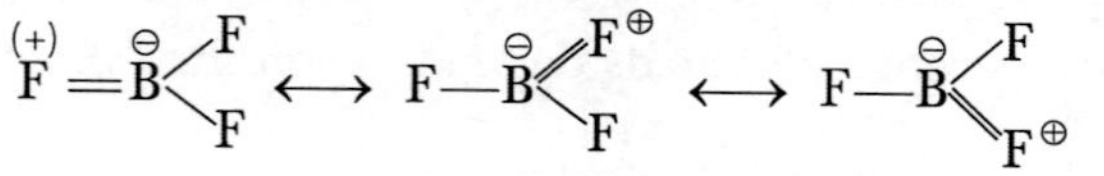

This resonance hybrid and resonance stabilised molecule is

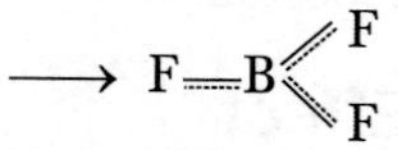

Due to back donation from F to B, now B is no longer so electron deficient so acidic character reduces.

While in case of BBr_3 this back donation from Br to B is not so effective due to difference in energies of the overlapping orbitals, from $4p$-orbital of Br to $2p$-orbital of F. So, B in BBr_3 is still electron deficient and so stronger Lewis acid than BCl_3 which in turn is stronger acid than BF_3.

$$BBr_3 > BCl_3 > BF_3 \xrightarrow{\hspace{3cm}} \text{Acidic strength decreases}$$

Similarly, $B(OR)_3$ is weaker than BR_3 due to resonance stabilization of the former.

3. Steric Effect of Substituents

In the above discussion combined factors like

- Electronegativity
- Size
- Charge, were responsible for relative strength of acidity and basicity.

Here, according to the ability of acids and bases to coordinate with each other and factors that tend to contribute to relative adduct stabilities we can classify acids and bases as :

(i) F-strain or front strain

In reaction between Lewis acids and bases such as pyridine, 2-picoline and 4-picoline with the same acid trimethyl borane $B(CH_3)_3$ the adduct bond energies are 71, 42 and 76 kJ/mol respectively.

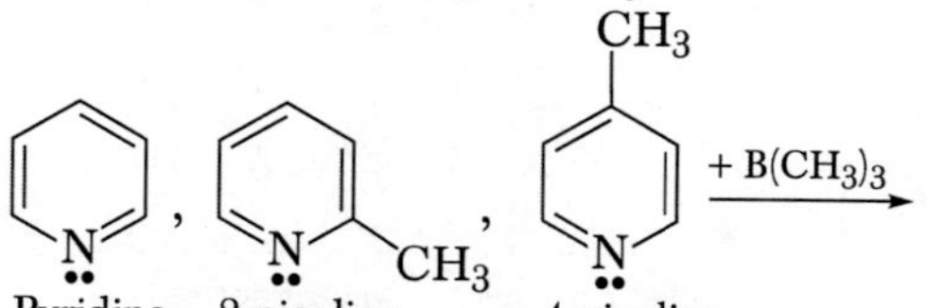

Pyridine 2-picoline 4-picoline

On the basis of inductive effect of methyl group 2-picoline should have acted as a stronger donor than pyridine as already observed towards a proton but it is much weaker donor towards $B(CH_3)_3$. This may be attributed towards the steric hinderance between the CH_3 group of 2-picoline and CH_3 group on boron in $B(CH_3)_3$.

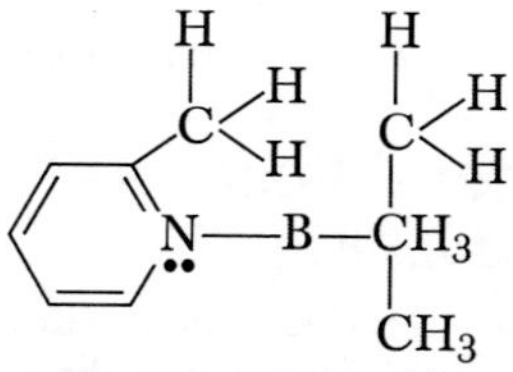

Steric hinderance

(2-picoline . $B(CH_3)_3$)

Such an effect is called F-strain or front strain. It has a significant influence on stability of adduct formed because of alkyl group operate in large volumes as they rotate randomly.

(ii) B-strain or back strain

The large substituents on Lewis acids or bases are forced to fold back behind the acceptor or donor atom due to changed hybridisation on complexation.

Example

Boron is sp^2 hydridised in BR_3 where $R \rightarrow$ alkyl group, but changes to sp^3 hybridisation in its complex with amines $R_3B{:}NR_3$. However, if alkyl group is large it can branch off to reduce its acidic strength.

As a result–A large molecule like trimesityl borane is almost inert towards trialkyl-amines because its plane triangular (sp^2-hybridisation bond angle $= 120°$) geometry is forced to take tetrahedral configuration (sp^3 hybridisation, bond angle 109.5°) on complexation. This causes too much crowding or a considerable steric congestion due to forced fold back mesityl group behind boron atom in going from 120° to tetrahedral 109.5° configuration as shown below :

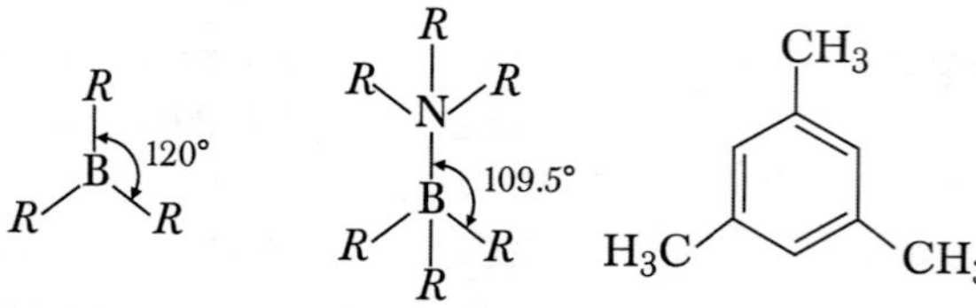

sp^2 -hybridisation sp^3 -hybridisation Mesitylene

In amines B-strain results from structural necessity at the nitrogen atom carrying very large substituents.

Normally amines $R_3N{:}$ are sp^3 hybridised-tetrahedral.

But, if substituents are very large they force the bond angle to open up and in extreme cases the molecule may flatten up to give a plane triangular sp^2 hybridised molecule with a lone pair of electron in pure *p*-orbital.

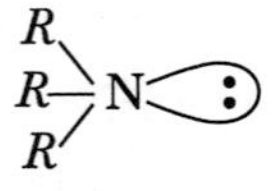

$R = CH_3$–small substituent
- no strain
- good donor
- sp^3 hybridisation
- *e.g.*, $(CH_3)_3N$:

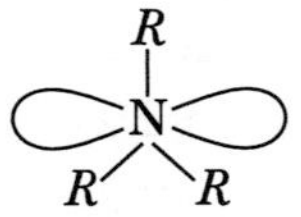

R = large substituent
- B-strain
- weak donor
- sp^2 hybridisation
- *e.g.*, $(SiH_3)_3N$:

Other examples Triethyl amine $(C_2H_5)_3N$: and quinuelidine are expected to have similar basicity and exhibit the same proton affinities. Models show no extra strain on quinolidine relative to triethyl amine.

However, quinuelidine complex with Me_3B shows a large adduct bond energy of 84 kJ/mol (**higher stability**) than Et_3N complex 42 kJ/mol (**lower stability**).

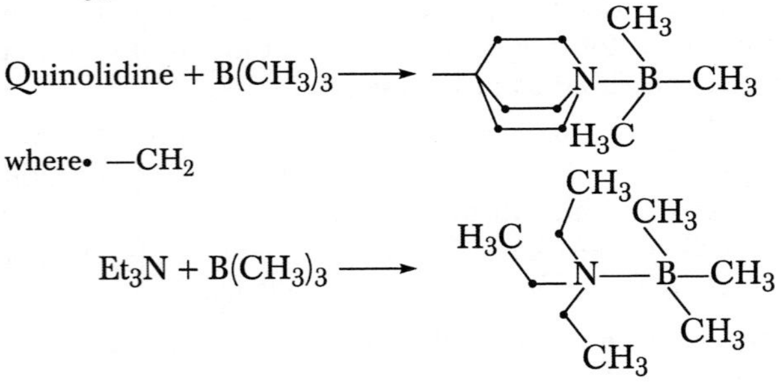

$Et_3N{\cdot}B(CH_3)_3$

Lower stability of $Et_3N \cdot B(CH_3)_3$ is attributed to B-strain in Et_3N because in the process of formation of complex with $B(CH_3)_3$ the ethyl groups in Et_3N have to fold back (to avoid F-strain of methyl groups of $B(CH_3)_3$) which causes steric congestion between terminal methyles of ethyl groups (B-strain).

While, alkyl group in quinuilidine are already structured in back position in the molecule with the result there is no B-strain on complexation.

Effect of Solvents on Acid-Base Strength

Solvents play an important role in altering strength of acid or a base.

For example "Solvation of amines in water"

$$R_2NH > RNH_2 > R_3N$$

$\longleftarrow$ Increasing order of basicity

While in gaseous state amines show the following order

$$H_3N < CH_3 \cdot NH_2 < (CH_3)_2NH < (CH_3)_3\ddot{N}$$

$\longleftarrow$ Decreasing basic strength

Here no steric effect is observed in tertiary amines in gaseous state.

Thus, we can say that lower basicity of tertiary amines lies only in effect of solvent.

When amines are dissolved in water, $\overset{+}{N}H_4$ ions are formed which undergoes hydration through H-bonding. The greater the number of H-bonds formed by ammonium ions of the base amine, the larger would be the heat of hydration.

Greater the number of H-bonds formed $\longrightarrow$ Greater is the heat of hydration.

The energy of hydration of $\overset{+}{N}H_4$ ions decreases in the order

$$R\overset{+}{N}H_3 > R_2\overset{+}{N}H_2 > R_3\overset{+}{N}H$$

$$R\ddot{N}H_2 + H_2O \longrightarrow R\overset{+}{N}H_3 + \bar{O}H$$

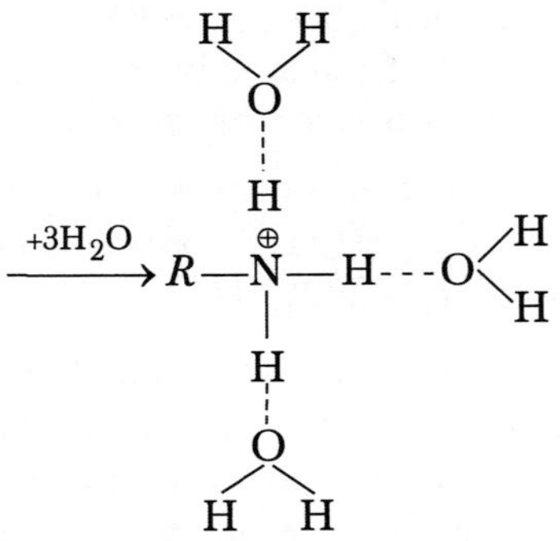

$$R_2\ddot{N}H + H_2O \longrightarrow R_2\overset{+}{N}H_2 + OH^-$$

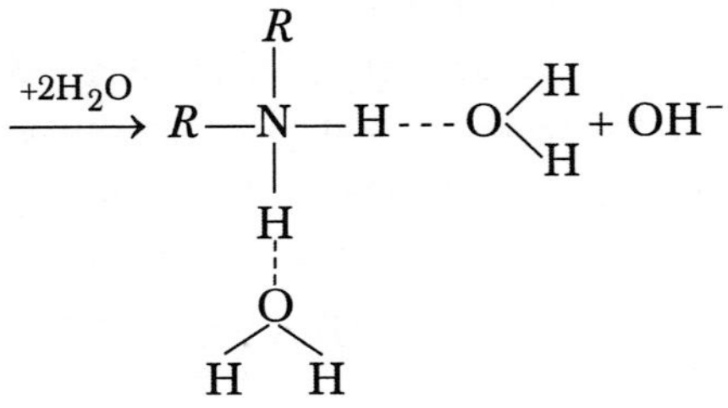

$$R_3\ddot{N} + H_2O \longrightarrow R_3\overset{+}{N}H + OH^- \xrightarrow{+H_2O}$$

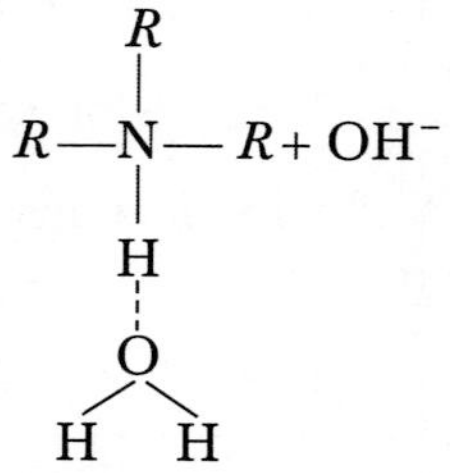

This order of basicity due to solvation is entirely opposite to basicity due to inductive effects.

Thus, basicity of amines in solution is combined effect of inductive effect of substituents and extent of solvation of conjugate acid of the base so, dialkyl amines are strongest base among amines and *tert.* amines are weaker than secondary amines and sometimes weaker than primary also.

Non-aqueous solvents like $\ddot{N}H_3$, $RCONH_2$ (amides), hydrazine, etc., plays an important role, in altering strength of acid or a base.

Non-aqueous solvents are good proton acceptors and thus help acids to ionise in them. Consequently in a basic solvent all acids tend to become strong.

Such solvents are said to exert **a levelling effect on strength of acids.**

Similarly, in solvents like CH_3COOH, HCOOH, hydrogen halides all bases tends to become strong but most acids become relatively weak or even ionise as a base. Such acid solvents tend to exert **differentiating effect on strength of acids.**

H_2O (water) behaves as levelling solvents for acids like $HClO_4$, HI, HBr, HNO_3, HCl and bases like NaH, $NaNH_2$, $NaOC_2H_3^-$.

So, in aqueous medium strength is similar due to levelling effect of water. Therefore, to compare the relative strengths of strong acids and bases such solvent should be selected that ionizes the strong acids and bases to different extent. Such solvent is called **differentiating solvent.**

For example CH_3COOH acts as a differentiating solvent towards halogen acids as their ionization increases with increase in atomic number of halogen.

That is acidic strength decreases as

$$HI > HBr > HCl$$

Thus, acetic acid is used extensively to determine the relative strengths of strong acids like $HClO_4$, H_2SO_4, HNO_3, halogen acids, etc., and it has been observed that

$$HClO_4 > HI > HBr > HCl > H_2SO_4 > HNO_3$$

However, acetic acid exerts a levelling effect on strength of bases. Consequently the relative strength of $\ddot{N}H_3$, $R\ddot{N}H_2$, $R_2\ddot{N}H$, $R_3\ddot{N}$, etc., cannot be distinguished and their basic strength get enhanced and levelled.

∴ **Acidic solvents – Differentiate between acids**

– Level off bases

Basic solvent – Differentiate between bases

– Levels off acids

Usanovich Concept (1939)

M. Usanovich (1939), Russian chemist, proposed a very wide definition of acids and bases. The merits of this concept are : (i) It is the most general of all the different definitions. (ii) It includes all acids and bases, defined by Lewis. (iii) It states that the donation or acceptance of electrons need not take place as shared pairs.Thus, according to this concept, oxidation-reduction reactions are also classified as acid-base reactions.

According to this concept, an acid is any chemical species which (i) reacts with a base, (ii) accepts anions or electrons, (iii) furnishes cations. A base is any chemical species that (i) reacts with an acid, (ii) accepts cations, (iii) furnishes anions or electrons.

Some examples of acid-base reactions in terms of Usanovich concept are given below :

(i) SO_3 (Acid) + Na_2O (Base) $\longrightarrow$ Na_2SO_4 (Salt)

This reaction takes place through the following stages :

$$Na_2O \text{ (Base)} \longrightarrow 2Na^+ + O^{2-}$$

Na_2O gives O^{2-} anion and hence acts as a base.

$$SO_3 \text{ (Acid)} + O^{2-} \longrightarrow SO_4^{2-},$$

SO_3 accepts O^{2-} anion and hence behaves as an acid.

$$Na_2O \text{(Base)} + SO_3 \text{ (Acid)} \longrightarrow 2Na^+ + SO_4^{2-}$$

or Na_2SO_4 (Salt)

(ii) SO_2 (Acid) + Na_2O(Base) $\longrightarrow$ Na_2SO_3 (Salt)

The formation of Na_2SO_3 (salt) by the combination of SO_2 (acid) and Na_2O (base) can also be explained as we have explained the formation of Na_2SO_4 by the combination of SO_3 and Na_2O.

(iii) Cl_2 (Acid) + 2Na (Base) $\longrightarrow$ 2NaCl (Salt)

$$2Na\ (Base) \xrightarrow{-2e^-} 2Na^+$$

Since Na furnishes electrons, it act as a base.

$$2Cl \xrightarrow{+2e^-} 2Cl^-$$

Cl accepts electron and is therefore an acid.

2Na (Base) + 2Cl (Acid) $\longrightarrow$ $2Na^+ + 2Cl^-$

or 2NaCl (Salt)

(iv) $Fe(CN)_2$ (Acid) + 4KCN (Base) $\longrightarrow$ $K_4[Fe(CN)_6]$ (Salt)

$$4KCN\ (Base) \longrightarrow 4K^+ + 4CN^-,$$

KCN acts as a base, since it gives CN^- anions.

$$Fe(CN)_2\ (Acid) + 4CN^- \longrightarrow [Fe(CN)_6]^{4-},$$

$Fe(CN)_2$ behaves as an acid because it adds CN^- anions.

4KCN (Base) + $Fe(CN)_2$ (Acid) $\longrightarrow$ $4K^+[Fe(CN)_6]^{4-}$

or $K_4[Fe(CN)_6]$ (Salt)

Limitation of the Concept

The only point that has been raised against this definition is that it is an extremely general concept, so general that almost all chemical reactions are considered as acid-base reactions in this concept.

Exercise 1

For (Part 'B')

1. If a 0.1 M solution of HCN is 0.01% ionised, the ionisation constant for HCN is
(a) 10^{-6} (b) 10^{-2} (c) 10^{-9} (d) 10^{-8}

2. A 0.1 N solution of sodium bicarbonate has a pH value of
(a) 8.4 (b) 4.8 (c) 4.0 (d) 13

3. Which of the following is not a Lewis acid?
(a) $AlCl_3$ (b) CO_2 (c) SO_2 (d) CN^-

4. The hydrogen ion concentration of a slightly acidic water solution can be represented by
(a) 10^{-pOH} (b) 14–pOH
(c) $\frac{K_w}{pOH}$ (d) $10^{-(14-pOH)}$

5. According to the protonic concept of acids and bases, which one of the following is a substance classified as weak acid?
(a) NH_4^+ (b) NO_3^- (c) ClO_4^- (d) SO_4^{2-}

6. The conjugate base of NH_4^+ is
(a) NH_4OH (b) NH_3 (c) OH^- (d) NH_2

7. According to Bronsted definition of acids and bases
(a) a base may be an electrically neutral substance
(b) the same substance cannot function both as acid and base
(c) any acid can yield a base by gaining a proton
(d) a base cannot be a cation

8. Of the following ions the one which is an ampholyte is
(a) SO_4^{2-} (b) NO_3^- (c) PO_4^{3-} (d) HPO_4^{2-}

9. Which one of the following species may be Lewis base?
(a) Negative ions
(b) Positive ions
(c) Inorganic molecules with double bond
(d) Organic molecules with sigma bond

10. The conjugate base of H_3O^+ is
(a) OH^- (b) H_2O (c) H_2O_2 (d) H^+

11. The most basic species among the following
(a) CH_3^- (b) H_2O (c) F^- (d) OH^-

12. According to Pearson, a hard base is one whose donor atom has
(a) high electronegativity, high polarisability and easy to oxidise
(b) low electronegativity, low polarisability and which is difficult to oxidise
(c) high electronegativity, low polarisability and which is difficult to oxidise
(d) low electronegativity, high polarisability and difficult to oxidise

13. The salt of which one of the following five weak acids will be the most hydrolysed?
(a) $HD: K_a = 4 \times 10^{-10}$ (b) $HC: K_a = 3 \times 10^{-8}$
(c) $HB: K_a = 2 \times 10^{-6}$ (d) $HA: K_a = 1 \times 10^{-8}$

14. Two hypothetical acids HA and HB have the dissociation constant 1×10^{-3} and 1×10^{-5} respectively in water. How many times HA is stronger than HB?
(a) 1000 times (b) 100 times
(c) 10 times (d) Not definite

15. Which of the following is a hard acid?
(a) Ag^+ (b) Au^+ (c) Li^+ (d) Cu^+

16. Which of the following is a soft base?
(a) H^- (b) CO_3^{2-}
(c) NO_3^- (d) CH_3COO^-

17. Which is the correct order of decreasing basicity of halide ion?
(a) $F^- > Cl^- > Br^- > I^-$ (b) $Cl^- > Br^- > I^- > F^-$
(c) $F^- > I^- > Br^- > Cl^-$ (d) $I^- > Br^- > Cl^- > F^-$

18. Which of the following is the most acidic in water?
(a) HF (b) NH_3 (c) CH_4 (d) H_2O

19. Which of the following cationic species can act as Bronsted-Lowry base?
(a) $[Al(H_2O)_6]^{3+}$ (b) $[Fe(H_2O)_5(OH)]^{2+}$
(c) NH_4^+ (d) $[Fe(H_2O)_6]^{3+}$

20. Which of the following is not a Lewis acid?
(a) SbF_5 (b) SO_2 (c) $AlCl_3$ (d) CN^-

21. Which of the following statement is true?
(a) Hard acids are non-polarizable
(b) Pyridine, SO_3 and H_2O are Lewis bases
(c) According to HSAB principle, hard acid prefer to coordinate with soft base
(d) According to solvent system concept of acids and bases, NH_4Cl behaves as a base in liquid ammonia

22. Which of the following will act as an acid in SO_2 according to solvent system concept?
(a) $SOCl_2$ (b) Na_2SO_3
(c) K_2SO_3 (d) HCl

23. Which of the following is not a hard base according to Pearson's concept of hard and soft bases?
(a) O^{2-} (b) NO_3^-
(c) I^- (d) F^-

24. Which of the following is a soft acid, according to Pearson's concept of hard and soft acids?
(a) Ag^+ (b) Sr^{2+}
(c) Al^{3+} (d) I^{7+}

25. Which of the following species is the strongest Bronsted-Lowry base in water?
(a) NH_2^- (b) NH_3
(c) CO_3^{2-} (d) F^-

26. Which of the following compounds possesses Lewis acid character?
I. BF_3 II. SiF_4 III. PF_5
Select the correct answer using the codes given below.
(a) I alone (b) I and III
(c) II and III (d) I, II and III

27. $HClO_4$, HNO_3 and HCl are all very strong acids in aqueous solution. In glacial acetic acid medium their acid strength is such that
(a) $HCl > HClO_4 > HNO_3$ (b) $HNO_3 > HClO_4 > HCl$
(c) $HClO_4 > HCl > HNO_3$ (d) $HCl > HClO_4 \sim HNO_3$

28. For Co^{2+} the stability sequence for its complexes with halides follows the order $Cl^- > Br^- > I^-$, but for Pt^{2+} the order is reversed *viz.*, $I^- > Br^- > Cl$. This can be explained by the
(a) larger size of Pt^{2+} compared to that of Co^{2+}
(b) relative strengths of Co^{2+} and Pt^{2+} as Lewis acids
(c) HSAB principle
(d) higher electron affinity of Pt^{2+} compared to that of Co^{2+}

29. Which one of the following species is capable of functioning both as a Bronsted acid and Bronsted base?
(a) S^{2-} (b) CO_3^{2-}
(c) F^- (d) HS^-

30. Consider the following boron halides.
I. BF_3 II. BCl_3
III. BBr_3 IV. BI_3
The Lewis acid characters of these halides are such that
(a) IV < III < II < I (b) I < II < III < IV
(c) III < IV < I < II (d) II < III < IV < I

31. Which of the following is the weakest base as per the Bronsted concept?
(a) $[ClO]^-$ (b) $[ClO_2]^-$
(c) $[ClO_3]^-$ (d) $[ClO_4]^-$

32. The strength of an oxo acid (*E*–O–H), where *E* is the central atom, depends upon the
(a) atomic size of *E*
(b) electronegativity of *E*
(c) ability of *E* to share electron pair with O
(d) atomic size and electronegativity of *E*

33. Which of the following is the weakest Lewis base?
(a) F^- (b) NH_2^- (c) CH_3^- (d) OH^-

34. H_3PO_2 and $H_4P_2O_7$ are respectively
(a) monobasic and tetrabasic acid
(b) monobasic and dibasic acid
(c) dibasic and tribasic acid
(d) tribasic and tetrabasic acid

35. Which of the following species can act both as Bronsted acid and base?
I. NH_2^- II. HCO_3^- III. NH_4^+ IV. HSO_4^-
(a) I, II (b) II, III
(c) II, IV (d) III, IV

36. Which of the following represents a set of hard acid and soft base respectively?
(a) Mg^{2+}, O_2^{2-} (b) Mg^{2+}, $SR^{\ominus}$
(c) BF_3, F^- (d) BF_3, H_2O

37. Of the following mixtures of two pure acids the strongest acid will be
(a) $HNO_3 + H_2SO_4$ (b) $H_3BO_3 + H_2SO_4$
(c) $HClO_4 + H_2SO_4$ (d) $KHSO_4 + H_2SO_4$

38. The correct arrangement of NH_3, N_2H_4, NH_2OH and CH_3NH_2 in the order of increasing base strength is
(a) $NH_2OH < N_2H_4 < NH_3 < CH_3NH_2$
(b) $CH_3NH_2 < NH_3 < N_2H_4 < NH_2OH$
(c) $NH_3 < N_2H_4 < NH_2OH < CH_3NH_2$
(d) $N_2H_4 < NH_2OH < CH_3NH_2 < NH_3$

39. The correct arrangement of Cr_2O_3, CrO_3, MgO and MnO in increasing order of their base strength is
(a) $MnO < MgO < CrO_3 < Cr_2O_3$
(b) $CrO_3 < Cr_2O_3 < MnO < MgO$
(c) $Cr_2O_3 < CrO_3 < MnO < MgO$
(d) $MnO < Cr_2O_3 < CrO_3 < MgO$

40. Which of the following combination can be regarded as soft acids?
(a) BF_3, CO_2 (b) Cu^{2+}, Cd^{2+}
(c) Li^+, AlH_3 (d) K^+, Ag^+

41. Match List I (molecules/ions) and List II (acid/base) and select the correct answer.

	List I		List II
A.	Mg^{2+}	1.	Hard acid
B.	R_2O	2.	Soft acid
C.	R_3P	3.	Hard acid
D.	Ag^+	4.	Soft acid

Codes

	A	B	C	D
(a)	1	2	3	4
(b)	4	3	2	1
(c)	1	3	4	2
(d)	2	4	3	1

42. Which of the following represents a set of soft acid and soft base?
(a) Cu^+, H_2O (b) Au^{2+}, CO
(c) Ag^+, R_2O (d) Pd^{2+}, F^-

43. Which one of the statements on Lewis acid-base definition is false?
(a) It describes acids as donors and bases as acceptors of electrons.
(b) Neutralization complex can also be called donor-acceptor complex.
(c) It describes acid-base behaviour as independent of presence or absence of any particular group, ion or element.
(d) It does not involve the presence or absence of a solvent in acid-base reaction.

44. Acidic character of oxoacids of halogens
(a) increases as size increases
(b) decreases as electronegativity decreases
(c) increases as electronegativity decreases
(d) None of the above

45. Which one of these order on acidity is false?
(a) HIO > HBrO > HClO
(b) HI > HBr > HCl
(c) $HClO_4 > HClO_3 > HClO_2$
(d) $CCl_3\cdot COOH > CHCl_2COOH > CH_2Cl\cdot COOH$

46. Acidity of oxoacids increases with
(a) decreases in electronegativity
(b) increase in oxidation number
(c) Both (a) and (b)
(d) follow the order HClO < HBrO < HIO

47. Which of the following statements is false?
(a) Ammonia is a hard base
(b) K^+ is a hard base
(c) Acid function is determined by presence of coordinately saturated species
(d) Redox reactions are acid-base reactions

48. Which one of the following statements is false?
(a) Liquid ammonia has a levelling effect on strength of HF and HCl
(b) H_2O has levelling effect on strength of HF and HCl
(c) CH_3COOH has a levelling effect on strength of HF, HCl, HBr, HI
(d) Water is a differentiating solvent for HF and HCl

49. Which one of the following statements is false?
(a) Relative strength of acids follow the order HI > HBr > HCl > HF.
(b) Relative strength of acids follow the order $H_2S > H_2Se > H_2Te$.
(c) Bond dissociation energy plays a significant role in determining relative strengths of acid.
(d) Relative strengths of protonic acids in aqueous solution can be attributed to their pK_a values.

50. According to Ricci generalisation the pK_a values of H_3PO_4 is
(a) 3 (b) 1
(c) –3 (d) –7

51. High basicity of $(CH_3)_2NH$ relative to $(CH_3)_3\ddot{N}$ is attributed to
(a) F-strain of amine
(b) effect of solvent
(c) B-strain of amine
(d) inductive effect of —CH_3

52. Which of the following statement is false?
(a) Relative trends of acidity or basicity depend upon combined effects of electronegativity, size and charge.
(b) Strengths of acids can also be ranked on the basis of their ability to coordinate.
(c) Acids and bases cannot be ranked on the basis of their adduct stability.
(d) Strength of acids is also affected by resonance.

Assertion & Reason

Codes
(a) Both A and R are true and R is the correct explanation of A.
(b) Both A and R are true and R is not the correct explanation of A.
(c) A is true and R is false.
(d) A is false and R is true.

53. **Assertion (A)** Hydrofluoric acid is weaker acid than boric acid.
Reason (R) Higher the ionisation constant of acid, stronger is the acid.

54. **Assertion(A)** BF_3 is a weaker Lewis acid than BCl_3.
Reason (R) The planar BF_3 molecule is stabilised to a greater extent than BCl_3 by B–X π-bonding.

Exercise 2
(For Part 'C')

1. Which of the following is a soft base?
   (i) CH_3COO^- (ii) NO_3^-
   (iii) CO_3^{2-} (iv) H^+
   (v) CN^- (iv) $SCN^{\ominus}$
   (a) (ii), (iv), (v) (b) (i), (ii), (iv)
   (c) (iv), (v), (vi) (d) All of these
2. Which of the following is a soft acid, according to Pearson's concept of hard and soft acids?
   (i) Ag^+ (ii) I^{7+}
   (iii) $N\overset{+}{O}$ (iv) $R\overset{+}{O}$
   (v) Hg^{2+} (vi) Hg_2^{2+}
   (a) All except (i) (b) (i), (iii) and (iv)
   (c) (iv), (v) and (vi) (d) (i), (iv) (v) (vi)
3. Match the following.

	Column I		Column II
1.	$(CH_3)_3Tl$	(i)	Soft acid
2.	*R*SH	(ii)	Soft base
3.	R_2CO	(iii)	Hard acid
4.	CO_2	(iv)	Hard base
5.	CO	(v)	Borderline acid

   (a) 1-(iii), 2-(iv), 3-(iv), 4-(ii), 5-(v)
   (b) 1-(ii), 2-(i), 3-(v), 4-(iv), 5-(iii)
   (c) 1-(i), 2-(ii), 3-(iv), 4-(iii), 5-(ii)
   (d) 1-(ii), 2-(ii), 3-(iii), 4-(iv), 5-(v)
4. Which of the following statements is true?
   (a) Pyridine, SO_3, H_2O are Lewis bases
   (b) Hydrazine, sulphate, H_2O are Lewis bases
   (c) Hard acids are non-polarisable
   (d) Soft bases are polarisable
5. According to Pearson, a hard base is one whose donor atom has
   (a) high electronegativity, low polarisability and which is difficult to oxidise
   (b) high electronegativity, high polarisability, ease to oxidise
   (c) $\ddot{N}H_3$, CN^-, NC^-, NO_3^- are all hard bases
   (d) RNH_2, NO_3^-, OH^-, H_2O are all hard bases.
6. The hard acids bond to bases in the order
   (a) $R_2O < R_3N < R_3P$ (b) $R_2O < R_3P < R_3N$
   (c) $R_3P < R_3N < R_2O$ (d) $R_3P < R_2O < R_3N$
7. Me_3B, BH_3 and BF_3 are three Lewis acids. Which one of the following is the correct sequence of these acids in order of their increasing acid strength?
   (a) $Me_3B < BH_3 < BF_3$ (b) $Me_3B < BF_3 < BH_3$
   (c) $BF_3 < BH_3 < Me_3B$ (d) $BF_3 < Me_3B < BH_3$
8. Which of the statement is false?
   (a) Formation of $Ni(CO)_4$ from Ni and CO is a Lewis acid-base reaction
   (b) Interaction of $CuSO_4$ with ammonia to form $[Cu(NH_3)_4]SO_4$ is a Lewis acid-base reaction
   (c) Interaction of $FeCl_3$ with NH_4Cl to form $[NH_4]^+[FeCl_4]^-$ is a Lewis acid-base reaction.
   (d) Formation of pyridine-N-oxide from pyridine and oxygen is redox reaction and cannot be considered as Lewis acid-base reaction.
9. Which one of these orders of acidic strength of hydrated cations is false?
   (a) $[Fe(H_2O)_6]^{3+} > [Al(H_2O)_6]^{3+}$
   (b) $[V(H_2O)_6]^{3+} > [La(H_2O)_6]^{3+}$
   (c) $[Ba(H_2O)_n]^{2+} > [Be(H_2O)_n]^{2+}$
   (d) $[Cu(H_2O)_n]^{2+} > [Ca(H_2O)_n]^{2+}$
10. Which one of the following statements is false?
    (a) Formation of HCO_3^- by reaction of CO_2 with OH^- cannot be considered as a Usanovich acid-base reaction
    (b) Formation of R_3NO from R_3N and O_2 is also considered as Lewis acid-base reaction
    (c) Formation of R_3NO from R_3N and O_2 is also considered as redox reaction
    (d) Oxidation of Mg with F_2 to form MgF_2 is an acid-base reaction.
11. Which one of the following reactions will not proceed to right hand side?
    (a) $CuI_2 + 2CuF \longrightarrow CuF_2 + 2CuI$
    (b) $BF_4^- + BH_4^- \longrightarrow BF_3H^- + BH_3F^-$
    (c) $R_2S\cdot BF_3 + R_2O \longrightarrow R_2O\cdot BF_3 + R_2S$
    (d) $LiI + CsF \longrightarrow LiF + CsI$
12. Which of the following statements is false?
    (a) Et_3N complex with $B(CH_3)_3$ has lower adduct bond energy due to B-strain in Et_3N.
    (b) Quinolidine complex with $(CH_3)_3B$ has lower adduct energy due to B-strain in quinolidine
    (c) $(SiH_3)_3N$ is sp^2 hybridised and planar molecule due to large substituents
    (d) B-strain in amines result from large substituents at N
13. Which of the following statement (s) are correct?
    (a) No steric effect is observed in tertiary amines
    (b) Lower basicity of tertiary amines lies in effect of solvent
    (c) Greater the number of H-bonds, greater is the heat of hydration
    (d) In gaseous state, the tertiary amines show least basicity

14. Which of the following statements (s) is/are correct?

(a) Solvation of amines in water has following order of basicity

$$R_2NH > RNH_2 > R_3N$$

(b) Solvation of amines in water has following order of basicity

$$R_3N > R_2NH > RNH_2$$

(c) In gaseous state, solvation of amines follow the following order of basicity

$$H_3N < CH_3—NH_2 < (CH_3)_2NH < (CH_3)_3\ddot{N}$$

(d) In gaseous state solvation of amines follow the following order of basicity

$$\ddot{N}H_3 < (CH_3)_3\ddot{N} < CH_3{\cdot}\ddot{N}H_2 < (CH_3)_2\ddot{N}H$$

Assertion & Reason

Codes

(a) Both A and R are true and R is the correct explanation of A.

(b) Both A and R are true but R is not the correct explanation of A.

(c) A is true but R is false.

(d) A is false but R is true.

15. Assertion (A) The energy of hydration of $\overset{+}{N}H_4$ ions decreases in the order

$$R\overset{+}{N}H_3 > R_2\overset{+}{N}H_2 > R_3\overset{+}{N}H$$

Reason (R) Greater the number of H-bonds formed by ammonium ions of base amine, smaller is the heat of hydration.

16. Assertion (A) Solvation of amines in water follows the following order

$$R_2NH > RNH_2 > R_3N$$

Reason (R) Basicity of amines in solution is combined effect of inductive effect of substituents and extent of solvation of conjugate acid of the base.

17. Assertion (A) Lewis acids include unsaturated species like CO_2, CS_2.

Reason (R) Polarisation of π-electron cloud leads to partial positive charge on carbon.

18. Assertion (A) Extended Lewis bases are CO, alkenes and alkynes.

Reason (R) They form π-complexes with metals in low oxidation state.

19. Assertion (A) Extended Lewis bases are CO_2 and CS_2.

Reason (R) Lewis bases form π-complexes with metals in low oxidation state and donates a lone pair of electron.

20. Assertion (A) pK_a values for HCN, CH_3COOH, HF, H_2CO_3 are 9.31, 4.76, 3.45, 6.37 respectively. H_2CO_3 is weaker than HCN.

Reason (R) Higher the value of pK_a stronger the acid.

21. Match the following.

	Column I		Column II
A	ClOH	1.	$pK_a = 7.52$
B.	LiOH	2.	$pK_a = -10.0$
C.	HClO	3.	Acid
D.	$HClO_4$	4.	Base
		5.	$pK_a = -3.0$

Codes

	A	B	C	D
(a)	3	4	2	1
(b)	3	4	1	2
(c)	4	3	2	5
(d)	4	3	1	5

22. Match the following based on reaction with $B(CH_3)_3$.

	Column I		Column II
A.	4-picoline	1.	F-strain and bond energy 42 kJ/mol
B.	Pyridine	2.	Bond energy 76 kJ/mol
C.	2-picoline	3.	Bond energy 71 kJ/mol
		4.	B-strain and bond energy 42 kJ/mol

Codes

	A	B	C
(a)	3	2	4
(b)	3	1	2
(c)	2	4	3
(d)	2	3	1

23. Which of the following statements (*s*) are correct?

(a) Relative strength of hydroacids can be explained on the basis of bond dissociation energy.

(b) Relative strengths of haloacids cannot be explained on the relative basic strength of conjugate base

(c) Larger the negative value of ΔH, greater the acidity

(d) Smaller the negative value of ΔH, greater the acidity

24. Match the following based on the given order of relative acidic strength of haloacids as

$$HF < HCl < HI < HBr$$

	Column I (Haloacids)		Column II (ΔH) values
A.	HF	1.	– 43
B.	HCl	2.	– 45
C.	HBr	3.	– 47
D.	HI	5.	– 4

Codes

	A	B	C	D
(a)	3	2	1	4
(b)	1	4	3	2
(c)	4	1	3	2
(d)	4	1	2	3

25. Which of the following statement is true?
(a) HF is least acidic
(b) HF is most acidic
(c) HF has high heat of dehydration ΔH(dehy)
(d) HF has least bond disociation energy.

26. Match the following for VI group hydrides.

Column I (pK_a values)		Column II (Hydrides)	
A.	14	1.	H_2Te
B.	7	2.	H_2Po
C.	4	3.	H_2S
D.	3	4.	H_2O
		5.	H_2Se

Codes

	A	B	C	D
(a)	2	1	5	3
(b)	4	3	5	1
(c)	1	5	3	4
(d)	3	5	1	2

27. Which of the following statement (s) is/are correct?
(a) ΔH value decreases for VI group hydrides in
$H_2O > H_2S > H_2Se > H_2Te$
(b) Relative acidity of VI group hydrides are
$H_2S < H_2O < H_2Te < H_2Se$
(c) ΔH value increases for VI group hydrides
$H_2O < H_2S < H_2Se < H_2Te$
(d) Relative acidity of VI group hydrides is
$H_2O < H_2S < H_2Se < H_2Te$

28. Which of the following statements are correct?
(a) Stronger the conjugate base, weaker the acid
(b) Stronger the conjugate base, stronger the acid
(c) Weaker the conjugate base, weaker the acid
(d) Weaker the conjugate base, stronger the acid

29. Which of the following statements are right. Relative acidity increases as
(a) $H_2O < H_2S < H_2Se < H_2Te$
(b) $H_2O < H_2S < H_2Se < H_2Te$
(c) $CH_4 > NH_3 > H_2O > HF$
(d) $CH_4 < NH_3 < H_2O < HF$

30. Match the following.

Column I		Column II	
A.	Higher pK_a	1.	Stronger acid
B.	Higher pK_b	2.	Stronger base
C.	Higher K_b	3.	Weak acid
D.	Higher K_a	4.	Weak base, lesser dissociation
		5.	Weak base, large dissociation

Codes

	A	B	C	D
(a)	1	2	4	3
(b)	1	2	5	3
(c)	3	5	2	1
(d)	3	4	2	1

31. Match the following based on decreasing basic strength as

$$Ca(OH)_2 > AgOH > NH_4OH > C_2H_5\ddot{N}H_2$$

Column I (Compounds)		Column II (pK_b)	
A.	$Ca(OH)_2$	1.	4.75
B.	Ag(OH)	2.	10.80
C.	NH_4OH	3.	3.96
D.	$C_2H_5NH_2$	4.	2.43

Codes

	A	B	C	D
(a)	3	4	2	1
(b)	4	3	1	2
(c)	1	2	3	4
(d)	4	3	2	1

32. Which of the following statements are correct?
1. All metal atoms are soft acids
2. All metal atoms are hard acids
3. Soft bases can complex with metals in atomic state

(a) 1, 2 (b) 2, 3
(c) 1, 3 (d) All of these

33. Triethyl amine $(C_2H_5)_3\ddot{N}$ and quinolidine complex with Me_3B. Which of the following statement is correct?
(a) Higher stability of $Et_3N \cdot B(CH_3)_3$ is attributed to B-strain
(b) Lower stability of $Et_3 \cdot B(CH_3)_3$ is attributed to F-strain
(c) Lower stability of $Et_3N \cdot B(CH_3)_3$ is attributed to B-strain
(d) Lower stability of quinolidine is attributed to B-strain

34. Which of the following is true?
(a) $HMnO_4$ is amphoteric
(b) $HMnO_2$ is acidic
(c) $HMnO_2$ is amphoteric and $HMnO_4$ is highly acidic
(d) $O_3Mn(OH)$ is basic

35. If magnitude of pK_a is given by $O_mE(OH)_n$, which of the following statement is correct?
1. For $m = 0$ p$K_a \geq 7$, very weak acid like $B(OH)_3$
2. For $m = 1$ p$K_a \approx 8$, very strong acid, OCl(OH)
3. For $m = 2$ p$K_a \approx 3$, strong acid $O_2Cl(OH)$

(a) 1, 2, 3 (b) 1, 3
(c) 1, 2 (d) 2, 3

36. The correct order of relative acid strength is
(a) $[V(H_2O)_6]^{3+} > [Cr(H_2O)_6]^{3+} > [Fe(H_2O)_6]^{3+} > [Sc(H_2O)_6]^{3+}$
(b) $[Sc(H_2O)_6]^{3+} > [V(H_2O)_6]^{3+} > [Cr(H_2O)_6]^{3+} > [Fe(H_2O)_6]^{3+}$
(c) $[Fe(H_2O)_6]^{3+} > [V(H_2O)_6]^{3+} > [Cr(H_2O)_6]^{3+} > [Sc(H_2O)_6]^{3+}$
(d) $[Cr(H_2O)_6]^{3+} > [Fe(H_2O)_6]^{3+} > [Sc(H_2O)_6]^{3+} > [V(H_2O)_6]^{2+}$

37. Acid strength decreases in the following order.
(a) $[Mg(H_2O)_6]^{2+} > [Ca(H_2O)_n]^{2+} > [Ba(H_2O)_n]^{2+} > [Be(H_2O)_n]^{2+}$
(b) $[Cu(H_2O)_n]^{2+} > [Be(H_2O)_n]^{2+} > [Mg(H_2O)_6]^{2+} > [Ca(H_2O)_6]^{2+}$
(c) $[Ba(H_2O)_n]^{2+} > [Ca(H_2O)_n]^{2+} > [Mg(H_2O)_6]^{2+} > [Be(H_2O)_n]^{2+}$
(d) $[Be(H_2O)_n]^{2+} > [Cu(H_2O)_n]^{2+} > [Mg(H_2O)_6]^{2+} > [Ca(H_2O)_n]^{2+}$

38. Which of the following statement is true?
I. Lower stability of $Et_3N \cdot B(CH_3)_3$ is attributed to B-strain.
II. Alkyl group in quinolidine are structured in back position so no B-strain.
III. Lower stability of $Et_3N \cdot B(CH_3)_3$ is attributed to F-strain.
IV. Alkyl group in quinolidine are structured in front position so no F-strain.
(a) I, II
(b) II, III
(c) III, IV
(d) I, IV

Directions (Q. Nos. 39 and 40)
Reaction between Lewis acids and bases like $B(CH_3)_3$ and pyridine, 2-picoline, 4-picoline, the adduct bond energies are 71, 42, 76 kJ/mol respectively.

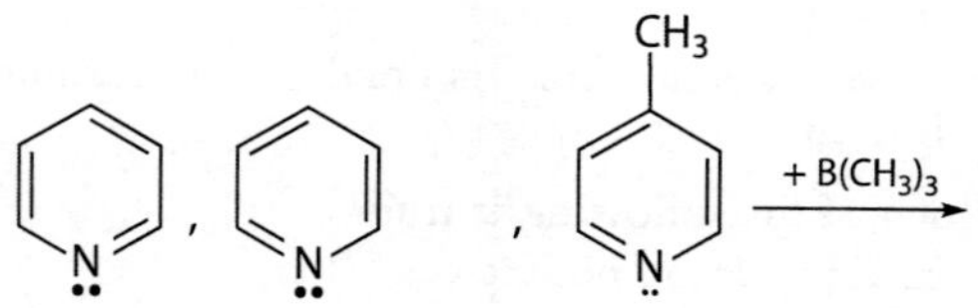

2-picoline should have acted as a stronger donor than pyridine towards a proton.

Answer the following questions.

39. 2-picoline is
(a) as much strong donor towards $B(CH_3)_3$ as towards proton due to $+I$ effect.
(b) much weaker donor towards $B(CH_3)_3$ due to steric hinderance
(c) much stronger donor towards $B(CH_3)_3$ due to steric effect
(d) None of the above

40. Reactivity of 2-picoline with $B(CH_3)_3$ can be explained on the basis of
(a) B-strain or back strain
(b) F-strain or front strain
(c) I effect
(d) E effect

Directions (Q. Nos. 41 to 43)
Catalyst get poisoned with conversion of metal into its complex. Bases like N, O, F do not act as poison to metal atoms. Metal atoms are poisoned with alkynes, arenes etc.

41. Which of the statement is true?
(a) All soft bases are poison for metal catalyst
(b) All hard bases are poison for metal catalyst
(c) Both (a) and (b) are correct
(d) None of the above is correct

42. Which of the following are true?
I. All metal atoms are soft acids.
II. All soft bases are poisons.
III. All metal atoms are hard acids.
IV. All hard bases are poisons.
(a) I, IV are correct
(b) Only I and II are correct
(c) Only I is correct
(d) II and III are correct

43. Substance like CO, alkenes, organophos phines, R_3As are
(a) soft bases
(b) Both (a) and (b)
(c) poisons for metal catalyst
(d) None of the above

Answers

Exercise 1

1. (c)	**2.** (d)	**3.** (b)	**4.** (d)	**5.** (a)	**6.** (b)	**7.** (a)	**8.** (d)	**9.** (a)	**10.** (b)
11. (a)	**12.** (c)	**13.** (a)	**14.** (c)	**15.** (c)	**16.** (a)	**17.** (d)	**18.** (a)	**19.** (b)	**20.** (b)
21. (a)	**22.** (a)	**23.** (c)	**24.** (a)	**25.** (a)	**26.** (a)	**27.** (c)	**28.** (c)	**29.** (d)	**30.** (b)
31. (d)	**32.** (b)	**33.** (a)	**34.** (a)	**35.** (c)	**36.** (b)	**37.** (c)	**38.** (a)	**39.** (b)	**40.** (b)
41. (c)	**42.** (b)	**43.** (a)	**44.** (b)	**45.** (a)	**46.** (c)	**47.** (c)	**48.** (c)	**49.** (b)	**50.** (d)
51. (c)	**52.** (c)	**53.** (b)	**54.** (a)						

Exercise 2

1. (c)	**2.** (c,d)	**3.** (c)	**4.** (b,c,d)	**5.** (a,d)	**6.** (c)	**7.** (b)	**8.** (d)	**9.** (c)	**10.** (c)
11. (b)	**12.** (b)	**13.** (a,b,c)	**14.** (a,c)	**15.** (c)	**16.** (a)	**17.** (a)	**18.** (b)	**19.** (d)	**20.** (e)
21. (b)	**22.** (d)	**23.** (a,c)	**24.** (c)	**25.** (a,c)	**26.** (b)	**27.** (a,d)	**28.** (a,d)	**29.** (b,d)	**30.** (d)
31. (b)	**32.** (c)	**33.** (c)	**34.** (c)	**35.** (c)	**36.** (c)	**37.** (d)	**38.** (a)	**39.** (b)	**40.** (b)
41. (a)	**42.** (c)	**43.** (c)							

Hints & Solutions

Exercise 1

4. $pH = -\log [H^+]$

or, $[H^+] = 10^{-pH}$

$\because$ $pH + pOH = 14$

$\therefore$ $pH = 14 - pOH$

Thus, $[H^+] = 10^{-(14-pOH)}$

6. $NH_4^+ \longrightarrow NH_3 + H^+$

8. HPO_4^- **is an ampholyte,** *i.e.,* an amphoteric electrolyte acting as either a base or an acid.

11. The most basic species would hold most tightly on to a proton. Thus, protonation of a strong base, yields a weak acid and *vice-versa.* Among HF, H_2O, NH_3, CH_4 and H_3O^+, CH_4 is the least acidic. This is due to the fact that carbon is not electronegative enough to polarize the C—H bond and produce a proton. Therefore, among the original alternatives, CH_3^- is the most basic species.

14. $$\frac{\text{Strength of acid 1}}{\text{Strength of acid 2}} = \sqrt{\frac{K_1}{K_2}}$$

$$\frac{\text{Strength of } HA}{\text{Strength of } HB} = \sqrt{\frac{1 \times 10^{-3}}{1 \times 10^{-5}}} = 10$$

Thus, *HA* is 10 times stronger than *HB*.

27. $HClO_4$ is the strongest acid.

28. **HSAB principle** Co^{2+} is hard acid prefers to combine with hard base F^-. Thus, the stability of complexes of Co^{2+} with halides decreases as the softness increases in the order : $F^- < Cl^- < Br^- < I^-$. Pt^{2+} is soft acid prefers to combine with soft base I^-.

29. $$\underset{\text{Bronsted acid}}{HS^-} \longrightarrow S^{2-} + H^+$$

$$\underset{\text{Bronsted base}}{HS^-} + H^+ \longrightarrow H_2S$$

30. Relative Lewis acid strength of the boron trihalides is $BF_3 < BCl_3 < BBr_3 < BI_3$. Lewis acid is an electron pair acceptor. According to electronegativity the order should be $BF_3 > BCl_3 > BBr_3 > BI_3$. The Lewis acid character of boron trihalides depends on the tendency of halogen atoms to back donate its lone pair to the empty *p*-orbital of B-atom through $p\pi$-$p\pi$ bonding. In BF_3, the overlapping of *p*-orbitals of B and F atoms is effective which decreases as the size of the halogen atom increases.

Thus, $BI_3 > BBr_3 > BCl_3 > BF_3$

IV > III > II > I

31. $HClO_4$ is the strongest acid due to the presence of large number of oxygen atoms and high oxidation state of Cl thus its conjugate base $[ClO_4]^-$ is weakest.

33. Acidic strength decreases in the order :

$$HF > H_2O > NH_3 > CH_4$$

HF is a strongest acid so its conjugate base F^- is the weakest base.

34. The basicity of an acid depends upon the number of ionisable hydrogen atoms means the hydrogen atom attached to oxygen atom (–OH). In H_3PO_2, there is only one —OH group, thus it is monobasic acid while $H_4P_2O_7$ contains four —OH groups, thus it is tetrabasic acid.

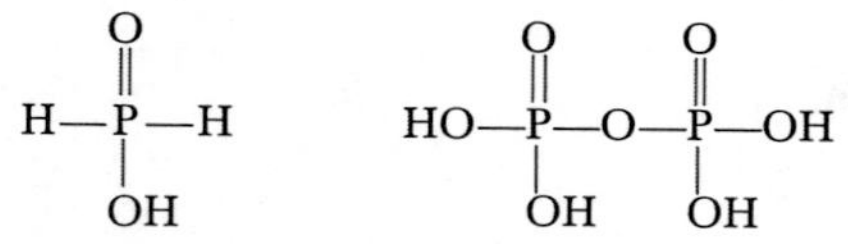

H_3PO_2 Hypophosphorous acid; $H_4P_2O_7$ Pyrophosphoric acid

35.
$$\underset{\text{Bronsted acid}}{HCO_3^-} \longrightarrow H^+ + CO_3^{2-}$$
$$\underset{\text{Bronsted base}}{HCO_3^-} + H^+ \longrightarrow H_2CO_3$$
$$\underset{\text{Bronsted acid}}{HSO_4^-} \longrightarrow H^+ + SO_4^{2-}$$
$$\underset{\text{Bronsted base}}{HSO_4^-} + H^+ \longrightarrow H_2SO_4$$

38. Lewis base is an electron pair donor. Tendency of the N-atom to donate its lone pair of electrons depends upon the group attached to N-atom. Electron releasing group increases the basic strength while electron withdrawing group decreases the basic strength.

NH_3,	$H_2\ddot{N}—H$
CH_3NH_2,	$H_2\ddot{N}—CH_3$
N_2H_4,	$H_2\ddot{N}—NH_2$
NH_2OH,	$H_2\ddot{N}—OH$

CH_3 is electron releasing group but N and O are electron withdrawing groups.

$$CH_3NH_2 > NH_3 > N_2H_4 > NH_2OH$$

39. The oxides of alkali and alkaline earth metals are more basic than transition metals oxides because basic character of the oxides decreases across the period. Among transition metal oxides, the acidic character increases with increase in oxidation state of the transition metal. The order of increasing basic character of the oxides is :

$$\underset{+6}{CrO_3} < \underset{+3}{Cr_2O_3} < \underset{+2}{MnO} < \underset{+2}{MgO}$$

43. **According to Lewis concept** acids are electron acceptors and bases are electron rich species and can donate electrons.

45. As we go down the group, the electronegativity decreases as the size increases. Higher the electronegativity, more easily proton is lost as more polarity in O—H bond allowing the proton to disssociate

	HClO	> HBrO	> HIO
pK_a	7.4	8.7	11

48. CH_3COOH tend to exert differentiating effect on the strength of acids.

Ammonia is good proton acceptor and hence will help acids to ionise in it

49. Bond dissociation energy decreases from H_2O to H_2Te.

50. According to Ricci generalisation

$$pK_a = 8.0 - 8.0m + 4.0n$$

where,

m = formal charge on the central atom

n = the number of non-hydroxyl oxygen atoms in the acid

For, $H_3PO_4 = OP(OH)_3$

$$m = 5 - 4 - 0 = 1$$
$$n = 1$$
$$\therefore \quad pK_a = 8 - 9 + 4 = +3$$

51. $(CH_3)_3\ddot{N}$ is weaker base than $(CH_3)_2NH$. The reason for this anomaly is the increased steric effect of three (CH_3) groups on a small nitrogen atom and lower energy of solvation of tertiary amines as compared to others.

Exercise 2

6. Hard acids prefer to bond with hard bases and higher the electronegativity of the donor atom, harder is the acid.

Order of electronegativity

$$P < N < O$$

Thus, the order of bonding to the hard acid is

$$R_3P < R_3N < R_2O$$

7. Lewis acids are electron deficient species. A species with more deficient central atom, will be a strong Lewis acid.

F^- being an electron withdrawing group, makes B more deficient but on the other hand, it decreases the deficiency by back bonding. H is unable to do such a back bonding due to absence of lone pair. Me is a electron releasing group, thus makes the boron least electron deficient.

9. Higher is charge to size ratio, more will be acidic strength. Thus, the order of acidic strength is

$$[Be(H_2O)_n]^{2+} > [Ba(H_2O)_n]^{2+}$$

11.
$$\underset{\text{(Hard-hard)}}{BF_4^-} + \underset{\text{(Soft-soft)}}{BH_4^-} \longrightarrow \underset{\text{(Hard-soft)}}{BF_3H^-} + \underset{\text{(Soft-hard)}}{BF_3F^-}$$

A hard acid prefer to combine with a hard base and a soft acid prefer a soft base. Hence, BF_4^- and BH_4^- are more stable and the reaction goes in backward direction.

13. An electron donating group makes the lone pair of nitrogen more available for donation. Thus, in gaseous state, 3° amines are most basic.

In aqueous solution, however, the other factors like solvation, H-bonding etc., matters and makes the 3° amine less basic.

More the number of H-bonds, higher is the heat of hydration.

19. CO_2 and CS_2 are Lewis acids due to polarisation of the π-electron cloud.

20. Higher the pK_a value weaker is the acid. Thus, HCN is the weakest acid among the given.

22.

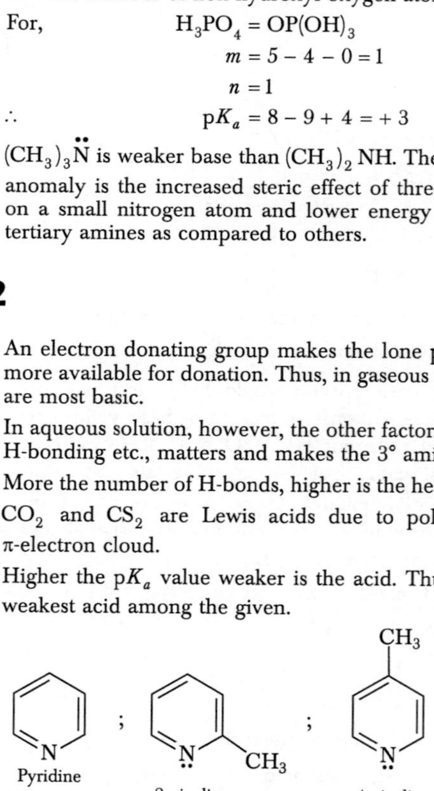

Pyridine ; 2-picoline ; 4-picoline

Among these, only 2-picoline experience F-strain, so the bond energy of adduct formed by it is lowest. Between pyridine and 4-picoline, lone pair of 4-picoline are more available for donation and no hindrance is seen when it form adduct with $B(CH_3)_3$. So the bond energy of adduct formed by it is highest.

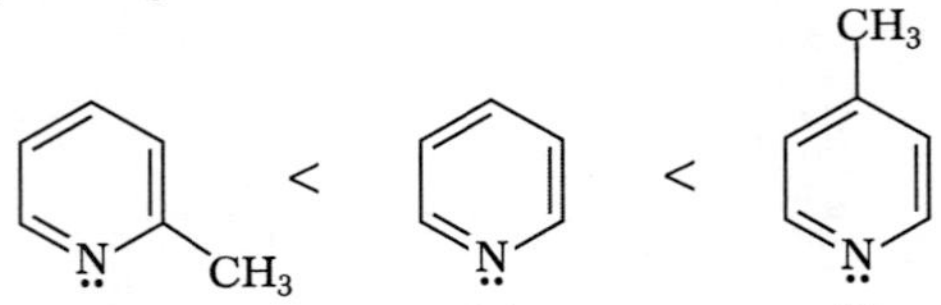

(42) (71) (76)

(Energy of product kJ/mol)

24. ΔH value $\propto$ acidity.

26. $pK_a \propto \frac{1}{\text{acidity}}$

and as the size of 16 group elements increases, H—*A*—H (where $A = 16$ group element) bond length increases and hence acidity increases.

Thus, the order of acidity is

$$H_2O < H_2S < H_2Se < H_2Te < H_2Po$$

and order of pK_a value is

$$\underset{(14)}{H_2O} > \underset{(7)}{H_2S} > \underset{(4)}{H_2Se} > \underset{(3)}{H_2Te} > H_2Po$$

31. Basic strength $\propto \frac{1}{pK_b}$.

33. The complex formed by quinolidine with Me_3B, is more stable than that formed by $(C_2H_5)_3\ddot{N}$ and Me_3B. It is due to B-strain in $Et_3N\cdot(CH_3)_3$, as ethyl group of Et_3N fold back to avoid F-strain of methyl group of $B(CH_3)_3$.

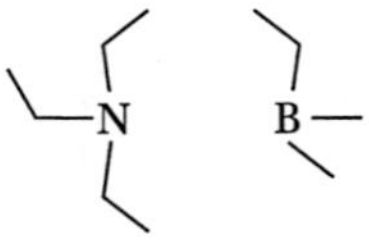

34. In $HMnO_4$, the oxidation state of Mn is +7 which is the maximum oxidation state of Mn. So, $HMnO_4$ is highly acidic. In $HMnO_2$, Mn is in +3 oxidation state, an intermediate oxidation state, so it is an amphoteric substance.

36. Higher the charge to size value, more polar is the O—H bond and higher is the acidity.

All the given complexes and thus the metals present (because of the presence of neutral ligands), have + 3 charge but the order of size is

$$Sc^{3+} > Cr^{3+} > V^{3+} > Fe^{3+}$$

Thus, the order of acidic strength is

$$[Fe(H_2O)_6]^{3+} > [V(H_2O)_6]^{3+} > [Cr(H_2O)_6]^{3+} > [Sc(H_2O)_6]^{3+}$$

38. In quinoline, the alkyl group are already structured in back position so there is no strain on complexation with $B(CH_3)_3$. Lower stability of $Et_3N\cdot B(CH_3)_3$ is due to B-strain.

4

s-Block Elements

The term *s*-block refers to those groups of elements in which *s*-orbitals are being filled. It consists of group 1 (alkali metals) and group 2 (alkaline earth metals). The electronic configuration of group 1 elements is (noble gas) ns^1 while that of group 2 elements is (noble gas) ns^2.

s-Block Elements

Group 1 (Alkali metals)	Group 2 (Alkaline earth metals)
Lithium (Li)	Beryllium (Be)
Sodium (Na)	Magnesium (Mg)
Potassium (K)	Calcium (Ca)
Rubidium (Rb)	Strontium (Sr)
Cesium (Cs)	Barium (Ba)
*Francium (Fr)	*Radium (Ra)

*Being radioactive elements with very short half-life, their chemistry is generally not discussed along with alkali metals or alkaline earth metals.

Syllabus

- Main Group Elements and their Compounds like Oxides, Peroxides, Superoxides, Carbonates, Hydroxides, etc.
- Diagonal Relationship, Coordination Chemistry of *s*-Block elements
- Metallic Crystal
- Bonding in Metals

Chemistry of Alkali Metals

Occurrence

Since, all these elements are extremely reactive so they do not occur in free state. Being most electropositive elements, they are found in nature as cations combined with the most electronegative anions such as chloride ions.Thus, the main source of sodium is sodium chloride present in sea water and as large deposits on earth while that of potassium is carnallite, $KCl \cdot MgCl_2 \cdot 6H_2O$. Lithium, rubidium and cesium are present in minute quantities in some alumino silicates. Francium is radioactive with very short half-life, therefore, it does not occur in nature. Sodium (2.6%) and potassium (2.4%) are high in abundance in the earth's crust (lithosphere).

Extraction of Alkali Metals

The extraction of group 1 metals cannot be carried out by usual procedures due to the following difficulties :

(i) These metals cannot be prepared by the reduction of their oxides as elements of these groups are themselves the strongest reducing agents.

(ii) These elements react with water, therefore, the method of displacing them from their solutions by using elements in the electrochemical series is not possible.

(iii) These elements can be prepared by the electrolysis of their aqueous solutions using mercury cathode only wherein they form amalgams but the recovery of the metal from the amalgam is quite difficult. Moreover, during electrolysis of aqueous solutions the liberated metal at the cathode starts reacting with water to form metal hydroxide.

Keeping in view the above difficulties, alkali metals are usually isolated by the electrolysis of their fused metal halides containing another metal halide (in order to lower the melting point).

Electronic Configuration

The atoms of alkali metals in the ground state consists of one electron in *s*-orbital outside a noble gas core. This similarity in the electronic configuration of all these elements is reflected in the similarities of their physical and chemical properties as discussed below.

Physical Properties

Important physical properties of alkali metals are set out in Table 4.1. We shall confine our discussion to only first five members of the family of alkali metals as very little is known about the last member, namely, francium which is a radioactive element.

A correlation between atomic structure and physical properties is discussed below. Attempt has been made to explain the physical properties of alkali metals on the basis of two facts, namely,

(a) loose binding of *s*-electrons; and

(b) size of the alkali metal atoms and ions.

(a) Loose Binding of *s*-electrons

In alkali metals the noble gas core shields the *s*-electrons from the direct attraction of the charge of the atomic nucleus. Therefore, the *s*-electron is very loosely held. The consequences of loose binding of *s*-electrons are :

(i) Ionisation energy

The first ionization energy of all these elements is low. This is the main factor which enables these metals to form positive ions readily and thus behave as electropositive elements.

$$M(g) \longrightarrow M(g)^+ + e^-$$

Table 4.1 **Physical Properties of Alkali Metals**

Property		Lithium Li	Sodium Na	Potassium K	Rubidium Rb	Cesium Cs
Atomic number		3	11	19	37	55
Electronic configuration		[He] $2s^1$	[Ne] $3s^1$	[Ar] $4s^1$	[Kr] $5s^1$	[Xe] $6s^1$
Atomic radius, pm		123	157	203	216	235
Ionic radius, M^+, pm		68	97	133	148	169
Ionisation energies	1st	527	502	427	410	381
kJ/g atom	2nd	7303	4570	3076	2662	2427
$E°$, M^+/M (V)		−3.04	−2.71	−2.92	−2.99	−3.02
Electronegativity		1.0	0.9	0.8	0.8	0.7
Heat of atomisation (at 25°C, 1 atm), kcal mol^{-1}		38	26	21	19.5	18.7
Atomic volume		12.97	23.68	45.39	55.80	69.95
Atomic weight		6.94	22.99	39.10	85.47	132.91
Density, g/cc		0.53	0.97	0.86	1.53	1.90
Melting point, °C		180	98	63.5	39	28.5
Boiling point, °C		1336	883	759	700	670
Colour of the flame		Carmine red	Yellow	Violet	Reddish violet	Blue
Ionic conductances of M ions Ω^{-1}		33.5	43.5	64.6	67.5	68.0

The second ionisation energy is fairly high which implies that the loss of the second electron is quite difficult. This is due to the fact that the second electron has to be pulled out from the noble gas core. Hence, it can be concluded that the chemistry of these elements is essentially of unipositive ions.

Trend in the group On moving down the group, the ionization energy decreases because the *s*-electrons are getting away from the nucleus due to the addition of new shells. Therefore, their attraction for the nucleus decreases and the electrons can be removed by expending less energy. Hence, their electropositive character (*i.e.,* the ability to lose an electron) increases.

(ii) Reducing property

The tendency of alkali metals to act as strong reducing agents is obvious from the fact that these metals liberate H_2 from water and acids.

$$2M + H_2O \longrightarrow 2MOH + H_2 \uparrow$$

$$2M + 2HCl \longrightarrow 2MCl + H_2 \uparrow$$

This property may be attributed to their strong tendency to lose their outermost (ns^1) electron. Reducing power is measured in terms of the standard electrode reduction potentials $(M^+ + e^- \rightleftharpoons M, E°)$.

These elements show very high negative $E°$ values (See Table 4.1), which suggests that they are extremely powerful reducing agents and since, lithium metal has the highest value $(E° = -3.04 \text{ V})$ therefore, it is the strongest reducing agent among the alkali metals.

However, we have earlier observed that lithium atom loses its ns^1 electron with difficulty (it has the highest IE value) relative to other alkali metals (Cs atom has the lowest IE value). Consequently lithium should have minimum reducing power because of its maximum IE value. As a matter of fact lithium has the maximum reducing power. **Then how to explain this discrepancy?** This can be explained as follows :

The IE values obviously do not reveal the complete picture. The reducing action of an alkali metal in aqueous solution is represented as :

$$M(s) \longrightarrow M^+(aq) + e^-(aq) \quad \ldots(1)$$

The process of reduction may be visualized to take place through the following three steps :

Step I In this step the metal in the solid state, $M(s)$ is evaporated to the gaseous state, $M(g)$. Energy is required for this step and is called the sublimation energy.

$$M(s) + \text{Sublimation energy} \longrightarrow M(g) \quad \ldots(2)$$

For alkali metals sublimation energies are almost the same with only a little variation.

Step II In this step, the outermost (ns^1) electron is removed to form $M^+(g)$ cation.

$$M(g) + \text{IE} \longrightarrow M^+(g) + e^- \quad \ldots(3)$$

In this process also energy is required. As already discussed the IE value for Li atom is the maximum among the alkali metal atoms.

Step III In this step the gaseous cation, $M^+(g)$ obtained in the Step II gets hydrated to form $M^+(aq)$ ion. In this step energy is liberated in the form of hydration energy.

$$M^+(g) + H_2O \longrightarrow M^+(aq) + \text{Hydration energy} \quad \ldots(4)$$

$Li^+(g)$ ion, being the smallest atom in size, gets hydrated to the maximum, *i.e.,* it can attach the maximum number of water molecules around it (because of its very high charge density). Hence, Li^+ has the maximum value of hydratoin energy. This value decreases rapidly from Li$\rightarrow$Na and then there is a gradual decrease to Cs.

The standard reduction potential, $E°$, is the summation of three terms (2) + (3) + (4)

$$E° = (2) + (3) + (4)$$

Thus, when we compare with each other the values of sublimation energy, ionization energy and hydration energy, we observe that the $E°$ value has the maximum negative value for lithium. Although IE of Li is maximum in the 2nd step, this high value is more than compensated by the large value of hydration energy (of $Li^+(aq)$) released in the 3rd step.

Trend in the group Except lithium, the negative value of $E°$ for the elements down the group increases indicating greater reducing character.

(iii) Photoelectric effect

The low energy photons (*i.e.,* light) can eject the loosely held *s*-electron from the surface of these metals. Therefore, these metals especially cesium are used in photoelectric cells which are sensitive to blue light.

(iv) Electronegativity

The values of electronegativity for the alkali metals are very low. This is because these elements have a tendency to lose rather than gain an electron.

Trend in the group The value of electronegativity decreases from lithium to cesium indicating decreasing tendency of the elements to hold their *s*-electron.

(v) Colouration to the flame

These elements give characteristic colouration to the flame. Their salts, particularly chlorides, when heated in a Bunsen burner flame on platinum wire, dissociate into atoms (and not ions). The outermost electron is excited to higher energy states. An electron which is in a higher energy state must lose its excess energy to the surroundings and revert back to original energy level. This excess energy is emitted as light. This emitted light will correspond to a definite energy jump in the atom and is characteristic of the atom in question. The emitted light for each alkali metal will correspond to definite energy jumps corresponding to some definite frequency of the visible part of the spectrum. For this reason, alkali metal compounds impart characteristic colour to the flames, see Table 4.1.

(vi) Electrical conductivity

It has been established that in metals, it is the valence electrons that hold the individual atoms together in the crystal. In fact, metals are often described as "islands" of shielded nuclei in a "sea" of valence electrons. Among the alkali metals, this "sea" is very diffuse and the binding in the solid is relatively weak. Therefore, the valence electrons move freely from one metal ion to another without much difficulty with the result that these metals have high electrical conductivity.

(vii) Ionic compound formation

Since, these elements are highly electropositive, they react readily with highly electronegative elements by the transfer of their *s*-electron. Therefore, the atoms in their compounds so formed have large electronegativity differences resulting in the formation of ionic bonds.

However, these elements also show covalent bonding in certain cases. For example, the vapours of alkali metals contain some diatomic molecules such a Na_2, Cs_2 which are covalently bonded. The strength of the covalent bond in diatomic molecules decreases down the group. Another proof of their ability to form covalent compounds is furnished by the formation of organo-metallic compounds such as CH_3Li, C_2H_5Li, $C_6H_5CH_2Na$.

(b) Sizes of Atoms and Ions

The atoms of the alkali metals have the largest size which is evident from the values of atomic volume and atomic radii listed in Table 4.1. Even after the loss of *s*-electron, the ions of the alkali metals have comparatively large values.

The large size along with only one valence electron per metal atom results in the loosely packed metal lattices of alkali metals. As a consequence of this :

(i) They are soft metals and are malleable and ductile.
(ii) They have high lustre.
(iii) They have low melting and boiling points.
(iv) They have low heats of atomisation which are indicative of weak interatomic bonds in alkali metals.
(v) They have low density because of their large atomic volume.

All of these properties can be accounted for in terms of their structure. The alkali metals crystallize with a body centred cubic lattice in which the lattice points are occupied by M^+ ions. The valence electrons (one from each atom) make up a sea of electron charge cloud which is spread all over the lattice. Since, these electrons are not fixed in positions, they can move freely throughout the metal and thus are responsible for the high electrical conductivity.

The silvery lustre of these metals can also be attributed to the presence of highly mobile electrons of the metallic lattice. The softness, malleability and ductility which are exhibited by alkali metals can also be explained in terms of the binding forces operating in these metals. The force of attraction holding the metal lattices together is principally electrostatic attraction betweem metal ions (M^+) and the valence electron cloud. Since, these forces are uniform in all directions (non-directional), there are no preferred positions or orientations of metal ions. Therefore, metal ions can be easily moved from one lattice position (or layer) to another.

Trend in the group As we move down the group, atomic volume, atomic radii and ionic radii increases. Down the group, the large atoms exert weaker attraction on one another because electrostatic forces decrease with increasing internuclear distance. Therefore, as we go down the group, the metals become soft, their melting and boiling point as well as heats of atomisation decrease.

Example 1. *Which of the following alkali metals has the lowest m.p. (°C)?*

Li, K, Cs

Sol. Cs

Example 2. *Which of the following has the maximum $E°(M^+/M)$ value?*

Li, K, Cs

Sol. Li

Example 3. *Which of the following is a better reducing agent?*

Na or Cs

Sol. Cs

Example 4. *Which of the following alkali metals is the most electropositive?*

Li, Na, K, Rb and Cs

Sol. Cs

Example 5. *Both* Na *and* K *are present in equal abundance in the earth's crust, but* Na *is about* 30 *times as abundant as* K *in the oceans. Why?*

Sol. Because K is bigger in size than Na, therefore, potassium salts with larger anions are less soluble and are thus retained behind while more soluble Na salts are carried to the sea. Also K is more tightly bound with the complex silicates and alumino silicates in the soil and are thus retained. Potassium ions are preferentially absorbed by plants whereas Na ions proceed to the sea.

Chemical Properties

The first ionisation energies and electronegativities of alkali metals are the lowest of all the elements. Moreover, the heats of atomisation of these elements are relatively low. These properties contribute to the high chemical reactivity of these elements especially towards electronegative elements such as chlorine and oxygen. Their important chemical properties are discussed below :

I. Oxides, Peroxides and Superoxides

When alkali metals are burnt in a free supply of air, the main product depends on the metal : Li forms mainly the **oxide, Li_2O**, Na forms the **peroxide, Na_2O_2** and the heavier elements K, Rb, Cs form the **superoxide, MO_2**. However, under the appropriate conditions pure compounds M_2O, M_2O_2 and MO_2 can be prepared for all the alkali metals.

A. Oxides

(i) Pure Li_2O is prepared by thermal decomposition of Li_2O_2

$$Li_2O_2 \xrightarrow{450°C} Li_2O + \frac{1}{2}O_2$$

(ii) Sodium oxide (Na_2O) can be prepared by any one of the following reactions

$$Na_2O_2 + 2Na \longrightarrow 2Na_2O$$

$$NaOH + Na \longrightarrow Na_2O + \frac{1}{2}H_2$$

$$NaNO_2 + 3Na \longrightarrow 2Na_2O + \frac{1}{2}N_2$$

(iii) The normal oxides of other alkali metals (K, Rb and Cs) can be prepared by similar reactions.

Li_2O and Na_2O are white, K_2O yellowish white, Rb_2O bright yellow and Cs_2O orange in colour. The compounds are stable towards heat and decompose only slightly below 500°C.

The oxides M_2O (Li, Na, K, Rb) have the antifluorite structure. The structure is related to CaF_2 (fluorite) structure but with the sites occupied by cations and anions are interchanged.

B. Peroxides

The peroxides contain O_2^{2-} (isoelectronic to F_2)

(i) Li_2O_2 is prepared by the reaction of $LiOH \cdot H_2O$ with H_2O_2 and dehydration of the subsequent hyperperoxide by gentle heating under reduced pressure.

$$LiOH \cdot H_2O + H_2O_2 \longrightarrow LiOOH \cdot H_2O + H_2O$$

$$2LiOOH \cdot H_2O \xrightarrow{\Delta} \underset{\text{(White solid)}}{Li_2O_2} + H_2O_2 + H_2O$$

(ii) Na_2O_2 is prepared by oxidizing Na to Na_2O in a limited supply of air and then allowing it to react with more O_2 to give a pale-yellow powder of Na_2O_2.

$$2Na + \frac{1}{2}O_2 \xrightarrow{\Delta} Na_2O \xrightarrow{1/2\ O_2} \underset{\text{(Pale-yellow)}}{Na_2O_2}$$

(iii) The heavier alkali metal peroxides cannot be prepared by the above method because of their further oxidation to superoxides, MO_2. They are best prepared by the quantitative oxidation of the metals in liquid NH_3.

$$O_2 \xrightarrow{e^-_{am}} O_2^- \xrightarrow{e^-_{am}} O_2^{2-}$$

(e^-_{am} = electrons in ammonia)

Sodium peroxide (Na_2O_2) finds use in industry as a bleaching agent for fabrics, paper, pulp, wood, etc. It is also used as a powerful oxidizing agent. Its reactions with CO and CO_2 gives Na_2CO_3.

$$Na_2O_2 + CO \longrightarrow Na_2CO_3$$

$$Na_2O_2 + CO_2 \longrightarrow Na_2CO_3 + \frac{1}{2}O_2$$

Example 6. *Why sodium metal forms peroxide in preference to its oxide?*

Sol. The positive charge density around Na (relative to small Li) is small and so it is unable to provide stability to a high electron density oxide ion (O^{2-}). However, it can easily hold on to relatively large peroxide ion ($(O—O)^{2-}$). The positive charge density of Na^+ is strong enough to prevent further oxidation of peroxide to superoxide (O_2^-) ion.

C. Superoxides

The superoxides contain the paramagnetic O_2^- ion.

(i) LiO_2 is prepared by matrix isolation experiments at 15 K.

(ii) NaO_2 is prepared by reacting Na with O_2 at 450°C and 150 atm pressure.

(iii) Heavier alkali metals form KO_2 (orange), RbO_2 (brown) and CsO_2 (orange) as normal products when these elements are burnt in air. The heavier peroxides show the tetragonal CaC_2 structure.

Example 7. *Account for the increasing stability of the peroxide and superoxides as the size of the alkali metal ions increases.*

Sol. It may be explained in terms of the stabilization of the larger anions [$O_2^{2-} > O_2^-$] by larger cations. This may be attributed to increasing lattice energy effects.

Distinctive reactions between the various oxides

The various oxides are readily hydrolysed by water

$$M_2O + H_2O \longrightarrow 2M^+ + 2OH^-$$

$$M_2O_2 + 2H_2O \longrightarrow 2M^+ + 2OH^- + H_2O_2$$

$$2MO_2 + 2H_2O \longrightarrow 2M^+ + 2OH^- + H_2O_2 + O_2$$

The different types of oxides can be identified by these reactions.

II. Hydroxides

The normal oxides contain the oxide ion, O^{2-} which is an extremely strong base. Hence, they react with water to form hydroxide by proton exchange as :

Gains proton

$$O^{2-} + H_2O \rightleftharpoons OH^- + OH^-$$

Loses proton

The alkali metal hydroxides are the strongest bases known. The strength of a base depends on the separation of hydroxide ion from the cation. Two factors are mainly responsible for the separation of hydroxide ion from cation as :

(a) Polarity of bond

The greater the polarity of the bond, the greater is the ease of ionisation. The alkali metal hydroxides do not greatly differ in polarity and this factor is not of much significance here.

(b) The internuclear distance between the oxygen of the hydroxide and the metal atom

Since, the cation size increases from lithium to cesium, hence, inter-nuclear distance increases with increasing atomic number of the metal. This results in greater separation of hydroxide ion from the metal ion. Consequently, the separation between the metal ion and OH^- ion becomes easier, Therefore, the strength of the bases increase from LiOH to CsOH.

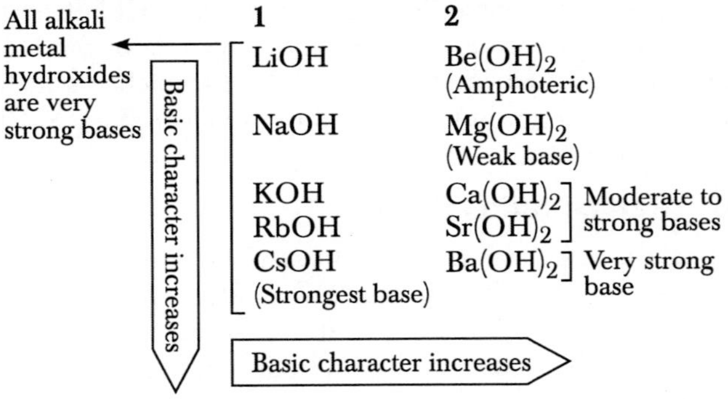

III. Halides

Alkali metals react vigorously with halogens to form metal halides of the general formula MX where M is an alkali metal ion and X is the halide ion. Alkali metal halides are "ideal" ionic compounds, *i.e.,* their physical and chemical properties can be interpreted with reasonable accuracy on the assumption that ions are present in solid state.

The heats of formation (ΔH_f) decrease in magnitude through the series MF, MCl, MBr and MI (M = alkali metal ion). This may be attributed to the increase in repulsion of anions and the coulombic force of attraction decreases due to increase in interionic distance.

Example 8. *The reaction*

$$2MX + X'_2 \longrightarrow 2MX' + X_2$$

proceeds only, if X'_2 is lighter than X_2. Why?

Sol. This is true because only in this situation ΔH will be negative.

Example 9. *The reaction*

$$MBr(s) + M'(s) \longrightarrow M'Br(s) + M(s)$$

proceeds only if M′ is heavier than M. Why?

Sol. This is true because ΔH will be negative when a heavier metal atom replaces M. Heat of formation is more negative for a heavier metal bromide.

The structure and stability of alkali metal halides are determined in part by the lattice energies and radius ratio effects as discussed below :

(a) Lattice energy effect

It is observed that lithium fluoride is insoluble in water whereas fluorides of other alkali metals are soluble. This is because the small lithium cation is in combination with small fluoride anion. This results in a high value for the lattice energy of LiF and thus it does not dissolve in water.

LiCl has exceptionally low melting point. LiCl lattice is very unstable because of the very small size of the Li^+ ion. The Li^+ / Cl^- radius ratio is 0.33, which is much below the minimum (0.414) required for adopting NaCl type structure.

(b) Radius-ratio effects

Alkali metal halides furnish a beautiful example of how coordination number increases with an increase in the size of the cation. The radius ratio in CsCl ($Cs^+/Cl^- = 0.93$) allows a coordination number 8 while radius ratio for NaCl ($Na^+ / Cl^- = 0.52$) allows a coordination number of 6. Lithium, potassium and rubidium also exhibit coordination number 6 in their chlorides, though theoretically lithium should show coordination number 4 only. This anomalous behaviour of lithium is thought to be due to more favourable lattice energy acquired by achieving a higher coordination number.

IV. Carbonates

All alkali metals form carbonates of the formula, M_2CO_3. The stability of alkali metal carbonates increases as we move down the group. Lithium carbonate, Li_2CO_3 is unstable and decomposes on heating.

$$Li_2CO_3 \xrightarrow{\Delta} Li_2O + CO_2$$

The instability of lithium carbonate is due to small size of Li^+ ion which cannot stabilize large sized carbonate ion. On the other hand, Li^+ ion forms stable compound with small O^{2-} ion.

V. Hydration of Alkali Metal Ions

Alkali metal salts are ionic and are highly soluble in water. The alkali metal ions are highly hydrated :

$$M^+(g) + H_2O \longrightarrow [M(aq)]^+ + \text{Hydration energy}$$

The smaller the cation, the greater is the degree of its hydration. As a consequence, the ionic radii of M^+ ions in water (hydrated radii) decreases from $Li^+(aq)$ to $Cs^+(aq)$

Hydration radii (pm)

$$\underset{(Li^+aq)}{340} > \underset{(Na^+aq)}{276} > \underset{(K^+aq)}{232} > \underset{(Rb^+aq)}{228} > \underset{(Cs^+aq)}{227}$$

Hydration of ions is an exothermic process. The energy released when one gram mole of gaseous ion is dissolved in water is called the **hydration energy.** Since, the degree of hydration of $M^+(g)$ ions decreases from Li to Cs, the hydration energy of these ions also decreases in the same order :

$M^+(aq)$	$Li^+(aq)$	$Na^+(aq)$	$K^+(aq)$	$Rb^+(aq)$	$Cs^+(aq)$
Hydration energy; kcal mol	–121	–95	–76	–69	–62

Alkali metal ions in general show low heats of hydration (as compared to other metal ions) because they possess low charge density, *i.e.,* low charge to radius ratio.

The ability to conduct electric current depends upon the size of the hydrated ions. Since, lithium is the most heavily hydrated, it moves slowly under the effect of electric current and thus exhibits the lowest conductivity of all alkali metal ions. On the other hand, Cs atom though the largest atom, is the least hydrated and conducts current most efficiently. Their conductivity power varies in the order :

$$Cs^+(aq) > Rb^+(aq) > K^+(aq) > Na^+(aq) > Li^+(aq)$$

Example 10. *Among alkali metal halides the lattice energy (U_0) is greatest for* LiF *and smallest for* CsI. *Explain.*

Sol. In the expression for lattice energy, r_0 (the internuclear distance) plays a predominant role. Since, r_0 has the smallest value for LiF and the largest value for CsI and so this accounts for the variation in the values.

Example 11. *$\Delta H°_f$ values are much smaller for the hydrides of alkali metals than for the corresponding alkali metal halides. Explain.*

Sol. The lower $\Delta H°_f$ values for MH may be attributed to the much higher heat of dissociation of H_2 compared to X_2.

VI. Solutions of Alkali Metals in Liquid Ammonia

If a small piece of an alkali metal is dissolved in liquefied ammonia, the latter becomes blue in colour. If more alkali metal is added in the ammonia, a point is reached when a bronze coloured phase separates out and floats on the blue solution. Further addition of alkali metal results in the disappearance of blue solution and its complete conversion to bronze solution. Evaporation of ammonia from the bronze solution allows one to recover unchanged alkali metal. This unusual behaviour has fascinated chemists since its discovery in 1864. The interpretation is as follows.

Properties of blue solution

The blue solution exhibits the following characteristics :

(i) Its colour, which is independent of the metal.
(ii) Its density, which is very similar to that of pure ammonia.
(iii) Its conductivity, which is in the same range as those of other electrolytes in ammonia.
(iv) Its paramagnetism, indicating unpaired electrons.
(v) Its reversible nature.
(vi) Its strongly reducing nature.

This has been interpreted in terms of ionisation of alkali metal to form alkali metal cations and electrons which are solvated by ammonia.

$$M \xrightarrow[\text{NH}_3]{\text{Dissolve in}} M^+(\text{amm.}) + [e(\text{NH}_3)_x]^-$$

The dissociation into cation and electron accounts for the electrical conductivity. The presence of a large number of unpaired electrons is responsible for the paramagnetism. The blue colour results due to an absorption band that has a maximum at 5000 Å. The absorption results due to the absorption of photons by the electrons as they are excited to a higher energy level. The dilute solutions thus consist of **free electrons** (thus showing reducing behaviour); such solutions are metastable and when catalysed give hydrogen and amide.

$$[e(\text{NH}_3)_x]^- \xrightarrow[\text{(catalyst)}]{\text{Fe}_2\text{O}_3} \underset{\text{Amide}}{\text{NH}_2^-} + \text{H}_2 + (x-1)\,\text{NH}_3$$

Properties of bronze solution

The bronze solutions show the following characteristics:

(i) bronze colour with a metallic lustre;
(ii) very low densities;
(iii) conductivities in the range of metals;
(iv) magnetic susceptibilities similar to those of pure metals.

All these properties are consistent with a model describing the solution consisting of aggregates of metal atoms (M_2, M_3, etc.) which are moved apart by interspersed molecules of ammonia. The electrons behave essentially in a manner as they would in metals.

Reducing properties of solution of alkali metals in liquid ammonia

These metal solutions are extremely strong reducing agents, much stronger than could exist in water because the oxidizing power of water is greater than that of ammonia. Some important examples of their reducing action are :

(a) Reduce metal halides to free metal.
(b) Reduce sodium nitrite to sodium hydronitrite.
(c) Remove halogen atom from organic molecule.

$$\text{C}_2\text{H}_5\text{Cl} + 2e^- \longrightarrow \text{C}_2\text{H}_5^- + \text{Cl}^-$$

(d) Remove hydrogen atom from acetylenic hydrocarbons.

$$\text{CH}_3\text{C}{\equiv}\text{CH} + e^- \longrightarrow \text{CH}_3\text{C}{\equiv}\text{C}^- + \text{H}$$

(e) Solutions of alkali metals in liquid NH_3 form alkali metal superoxides and peroxide,

$$\text{O}_2 \xrightarrow{e^-_{\text{am}}} \text{O}_2^- \xrightarrow{e^-_{\text{am}}} \text{O}_2^{2-}$$

(f) Transition metals are reduced to unusually low oxidation states, *i.e.,*

$$\text{K}_2[\text{Ni(CN)}_4] + 2\text{K} \xrightarrow[240\ \text{K}]{\text{NH}_3} \text{K}_4[\text{Ni(CN)}_4]$$

$$[\text{Pt(NH}_3)_4\text{Br}_2] + 2\text{K} \xrightarrow[240\ \text{K}]{\text{NH}_3} [\text{Pt(NH}_3)_4] + 2\text{KBr}$$

Ni^{II} and Pt^{II} are reduced to Ni(0) and Pt(0), respectively.

(g) Salts of several main-group elements are reduced to form polyanions such as $Na_4[Sn_4]$, $Na_3[Sb_9]$, $Na_3(Sb_7)$, etc.
(h) Species containing hydrogen react with liberation of hydrogen gas

$$\text{GeH}_4 + e^-_{\text{am}} \longrightarrow \text{GeH}_3^- + \frac{1}{2}\text{H}_2$$

$$\text{AsH}_3 + e^-_{\text{am}} \longrightarrow \text{AsH}_2^- + \frac{1}{2}\text{H}_2$$

$$\text{EtOH} + e^-_{\text{am}} \longrightarrow \text{EtO}^- + \frac{1}{2}\text{H}_2$$

These reactions have great synthetic utility. These solutions have been developed as versatile reducing agents for organic compounds that are otherwise difficult or impossible to reduce.

VII. Solutions of Alkali Metals in other Solvents

The alkali metals are also soluble in aliphatic amines and hexa-methylphosphoramide, $P(NMe_2)_3$ and give coloured solutions which are also strong reducing agents. However, these solutions are less stable and easily decompose into amide and H_2. Larger alkali metals K, Rb and Cs give solutions in THF, ethylene glycol, dimethyl ether and act as reducing agents.

Lithium in Relation to its Congeners

It is observed from the above discussion of the properties of alkali metals that lithium differs from its congeners far more than the congeners differ amongst themselves. The main reasons for the different properties of lithium as compared to other alkali metals are :

(a) The extremely small size of lithium atom and its ion.

(b) The polarizing power of lithium ion is the greatest of all the alkali metal ions which results in its tendency towards solvation and covalent bond formaton. The increased covalent character of its compound makes them more soluble in organic (non-polar) solvents. However, other alkali metal salts are insoluble in organic solvents.

(c) Lithium has the highest ionisation energy and electronegativity when compared to other alkali metals.

Difference between Lithium and its Congeners

Main points of difference between lithium and its congeners are given below :

(i) Lithium is harder and lighter than other alkali metals.

(ii) Its melting and boiling points are high and it can be melted in dry air without losing its brilliance.

(iii) Due to its high ionization energy it does not react with oxygen below 373 K. It reacts slowly with water or with liquid bromine.

(iv) Due to its small size, it readily combines with small anions such as hydrides, carbides and nitrides to form stable compounds. The combination of two elements both with small ions confers a high lattice energy on the crystal. These reactions of lithium are highly exothermic. Lithium hydride is far more stable to heat than other alkali metal hydrides.

(v) Due to its small size lithium combines with oxygen to form lithium oxide while other alkali metals form peroxides and superoxides.

(vi) Lithium oxide dissolves in water quietly while others do it more energetically.

(vii) Lithium hydroxide is sparingly soluble in water and is a weak base.

(viii) Lithium hydroxide decomposes at red heat forming Li_2O whereas other alkali metal hydroxides sublime unchanged as $(MOH)_2$.

(ix) Lithium chloride is deliquescent and is soluble in alcohol as well as pyridine.

(x) Lithium carbonate decomposes on heating to form Li_2O and CO_2. The size of Li^+ makes Li_2O lattice more stable as compared to Li_2CO_3 lattice. However, the bigger size of the other alkali metal ions make the M_2O lattices less stable as compared to the M_2CO_3 lattice and hence they do not decompose.

(xi) Lithium nitrate on heating forms Li_2O, NO_2 and O_2 while other alkali metal nitrates form nitrites and oxygen.

$$4LiNO_3 \longrightarrow 2Li_2O + 4NO_2 + O_2$$

$$2NaNO_3 \longrightarrow 2NaNO_2 + O_2$$

The explanation for the decomposition of lithium nitrate into lithium oxide and not lithium nitrite is the same as given for the decomposition of lithium carbonate.

(xii) When acetylene gas is passed over heated lithium metal, it does not form lithium acetylide while other alkali metals form metal acetylides on reaction with acetylene.

(xiii) Lithium hydrosulphide, LiSH is thermally unstable while the hydrosulphides of other alkali metals are stable and can be fused without extensive decomposition.

(xiv) Some of the lithium salts such as Li_2CO_3, Li_3PO_4 and LiF are insoluble in water while the corresponding compounds of other alkali metals are soluble.

(xv) Lithium is the only alkali metal which combines with silicon when the two are heated together to form lithium silicide. Li_6Si_2-dark violet, hygroscopic crystals.

(xvi) Lithium when heated in ammonia forms imide, Li_2NH while other alkali metals form amides, MNH_2.

(xvii) $LiClO_4$ is remarkably soluble in alcohol, acetone, and ethyl acetate due to the strong solvation of Li^+ ion whereas perchlorates of other alkali metals are almost insoluble in alcohol, acetone and ethyl acetate.

(xviii) Li_2SO_4 is the only alkali metal sulphate which does not form double salts such as alums.

(xix) Lithium ion shows a tendency to form complexes with ammonia, water (to form hydrates) and forms a large number of organo lithium compounds.

Diagional Relationship of Lithium with Magnesium

One of the important features of elements of second period of Periodic Table is that they resemble with the element at their lower right in the third period (*i.e.,* diagonally opposite element) more than their own congeners. The diagonal relationship is best illustrated by the following pairs of elements of the Periodic Table.

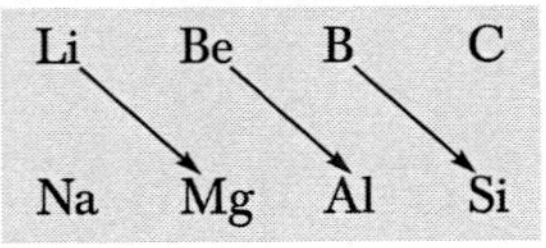

The reasons for similarities between the diagonally opposite members are :

(a) The elements become more electropositive down a group but less electropositive from left to right. This results in the similarity in the electropositive character of the diagonally opposite elements.

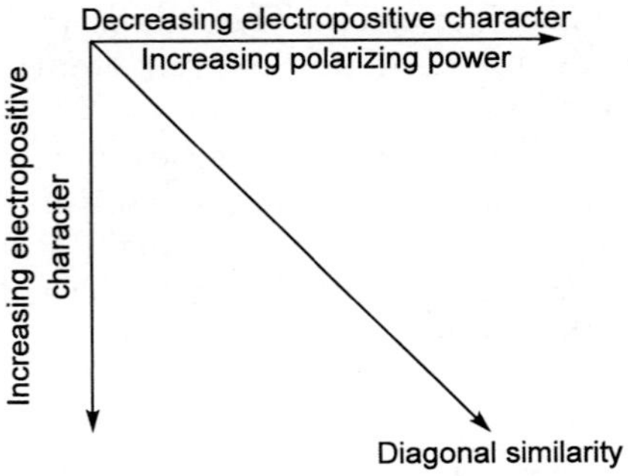

(b) Similarly, on moving from left to right, charge on the ions increases but their size decreases which causes an increase in the polarizing power of the ions. However, on moving down a group the size increases and polarizing power decreases. On moving diagonally these two effects partly cancel each other so that the behaviour of these elements is quite similar. It is interesting to note that in spite of their different valencies, the type and strength of the bonds formed and the properties of their compounds are often very similar.

Lithium resembles more with its diagonally opposite element magnesium than with the other members of the alkali metals as is evident from the following points :

(i) The radii of Li^+ (60 pm) and Mg^{2+} (65 pm) are almost equal.

(ii) The atomic radii of Li (122 pm) and Mg (136 pm) are comparable.

(iii) The atomic volumes of solid Li (12.97 cc) and Mg (14.00 cc) are quite similar.

(iv) Electronegativity of Li (1.00) and Mg (1.20) are quite comparable.

(v) Polarizing power $\dfrac{\text{Ionic charge}}{(\text{Ionic radius})^2}$ of both the elements is similar.

(vi) ΔH, (enthalpies of vaporization) of both these elements are comparable.

(vii) Lithium has a high boiling point (1609 K) which is comparable with that of magnesium (1373 K).

(viii) Lithium is the hardest of all the alkali metals but is comparable to that of magnesium.

(ix) Lithium is the only alkali metal which on burning in an atmosphere of oxygen forms a normal oxide, Li_2O and not a peroxide or superoxide. Magnesium ribbon when burnt in oxygen also forms magnesium oxide, MgO.

(x) Out of all the alkali metal carbonates and nitrates, only Li_2CO_3 and $LiNO_3$ are unstable and decompose on heating forming its oxide. Similarly, $MgCO_3$ and $Mg(NO_3)_2$ on heating form MgO.

(xi) Among the alkali metals only lithium when heated in an atmosphere of nitrogen forms an ionic nitride, Li_3N. Magnesium when heated in nitrogen also forms an ionic nitride, Mg_3N_2.

(xii) Of all the alkali metal hydroxides, only lithium hydroxide is less soluble in water, less basic and decomposes on heating to form Li_2O. Magnesium hydroxide is also sparingly soluble, less basic and decomposes on heating to form MgO.

(xiii) The lithium ion and its compounds are more heavily hydrated than those of the other alkali metal ions. Most of the magnesium compounds are also hydrated, *e.g.,* $MgCl_2 \cdot 6H_2O$; $MgSO_4 \cdot 7H_2O$.

(xiv) Li_2CO_3, LiF, Li_3PO_4 are the only alkali metal salts which are insoluble in water. The corresponding magnesium compounds are also insoluble in water.

(xv) Both the elements directly combine with carbon to form carbides.

(xvi) Of all alkali metal chlorides, only LiCl is soluble in organic solvents such as pyridine and alcohol. Magnesium chloride is also soluble in alcohol.

(xvii) Lithium perchlorate and magnesium perchlorate are extremely soluble in alcohol.

(xviii) Due to their covalent nature, the complex hydrides of lithium and magnesium are soluble in organic solvents, *e.g.*, $LiAlH_4$, $RMgX$ are soluble in ether.

Coordination Chemistry of Alkali Metal Ions

Coordination chemistry as known for transition metals with conventional ligands (say NH_3) is lacking for both alkali metals (M^+) and alkaline earth metals (M^{2+}) due to their very weak coordinating (or complexing) ability. These metals ions were thought to be inadequate for complexation due to their small charge to size ratio. The lack of physico-chemical properties such as UV visible and magnetic properties which help to detect even weak metal-ligand interactions, was a significant reason for this delayed exploration of complexation ability of groups I and II metal cations.

Application of X-ray crystallography to the study of biologically important molecules, such as **antibiotics,** showed that some of these molecules are involved in the complexation of M^+ (Na^+, K^+) or M^{2+} (Ca^{2+}, Mg^{2+}) ions. For example, the antibiotic nonactin functions by transporting potassium ions out of cells. This molecule prefers to bind K^+ ions over Na^+ ions, *i.e.*, it is not only capable of binding a weakly coordinating K^+ but is also highly selective.

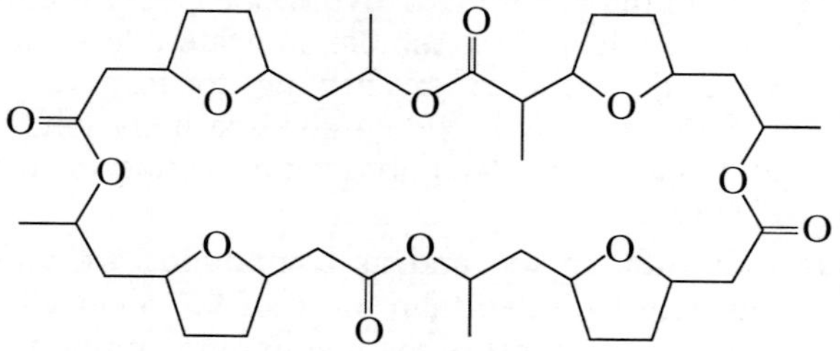

Nonactin

These studies revealed insight into the underlying parameters of **complexation and selectivity.** The stability of these natural complexes is attributed to a large number of donor sites present in a single molecule which can act (donate) simultaneously, *i.e.*, wrap around the cation. The selectivity or preference of a ligand for a particular cation is determined by the size of the **'cavity'** generated by each ligand when it wraps around the metal cation.

Several such studies on natural systems gave chemists an insight into the design of synthetic donor molecules which may be able to form complexes with M^+ and M^{2+} ions, *i.e.*, which may be able to mimic the natural systems.

Synthetic Molecules (Macrocycles) that can Bind Alkali/Alkaline Metal Cations

Recent developments led to the synthesis of large-ring crown ethers. These compounds are cyclic polymers of the simple molecule ethylene glycol, $(OCH_2CH_2)_n$ and are given the name *x*-crown-*y*, where *x* is the total number of atoms in the ring and *y* is the number of oxygens. For example, the cyclic hexamer of ethylene glycol is 18-crown-6.

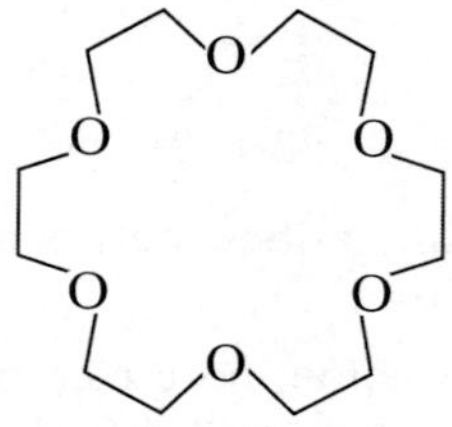

18-crown-6

The crown ethers have the ability to bind cations strongly and selectively. The crown ether, 18-crown-6 can solvate potassium cation. The interior of the crown ether is made up of donor oxygen atoms, but the exterior (boundary wall) is made of $—CH_2—CH_2—$ units, *i.e.*,it has hydrocarbon properties. As a result, the complexed ion is soluble in non-polar organic solvents. For example, $KMnO_4$ which is normally insoluble in benzene, dissolves readily in this solvent in the presence of 18-crown-6.

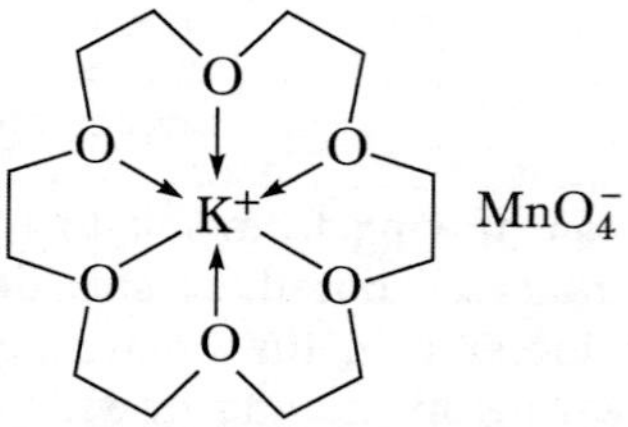

18-crown-6-$KMnO_4$ complex
(soluble in benzene)

In the last 20 years or so, a large number of synthetic crown ethers have been synthesized. A relationship between the structure of crown ether and its ability to solvate a particular cation has been observed. For example, 18-crown-6 shows high affinity for K^+, 15-crown-5 for Na^+, and 12-crown-4 for Li^+. Measurement of molecular models of these molecules shows that the 'cavity size' for each molecule matches the ionic size of the cation which is strongly bonded by

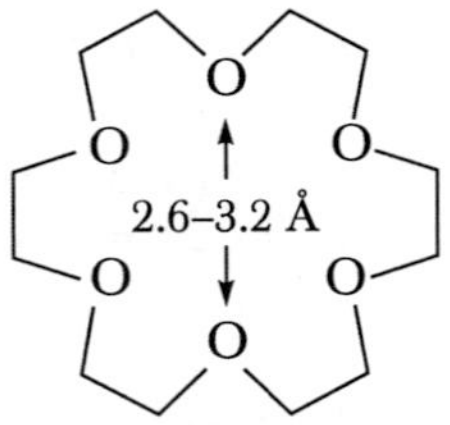

18-crown-6

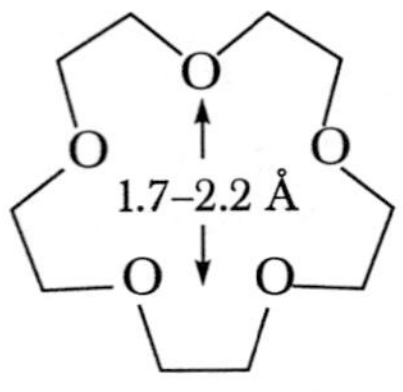

15-crown-5

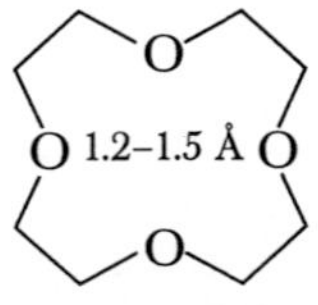

12-crown-4

Ionic diameter	Å
K^+	2.66
Na^+	1.80
Li^+	1.20

the molecule. The molecules are said to "recognize" its host and this phenomenon is called **"molecular recognition".** More recent researches have yielded better preorganized ligands, like the diamino tetraether, commonly called **cryptands** (macrobicyclic polyethers), which are even more selective than crown ethers. Since, then hundreds of modifications of crown ethers (such as changing the ring size, kind of substituents, and the types of donor atom) and macropolycyclic (cage) compounds with unusual shapes have been prepared and their complexation properties have been investigated.

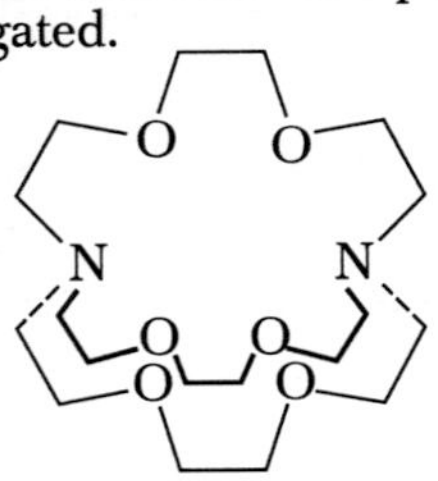

Cryptand

The reaction,

$$2Na(g) \longrightarrow Na^+(g) + Na^-(g) \qquad \ldots(5)$$

is endothermic ($\Delta H = +4.38$ kJ mol^{-1}). However, in the presence of a crypt ligand, in ethylenediamine (en) solution, the compound

$$[Na(2,2,2\text{-crypt})]^+Na^-$$

is obtained which is stable at 263 K. The lattice energy and complexation of the Na^+ by the crypt ligand compensates for the loss in energy in reaction (5) above.

Naturally occurring cyclic polypeptides can also complex alkali and alkaline earth metal ions and thus help in their transport in the living system.

The ability to complex and stabilize alkali metal cations has been helpful in the isolation of several new compounds which otherwise could not be synthesized. For example, the isolation of the compound Cs^+Au^-. This compound is unique as it is formed between two metals and not between a metal and a non-metal. Normally, we would expect that on mixing two metals, an alloy may be formed. The experimental technique involves stabilizing and isolating the alkali metal cation with macrocyclic polyether before reacting it with gold to give [Ma(macrocycle)]$^+$ Au$^-$, etc.

Some Typical Reactions of Group 1 Elements

S.No.	Reaction	General remarks
1.	$M + H_2O \rightarrow MOH + \frac{1}{2}H_2$	Li is slowly attacked by water at 25°C. Na reacts vigorously and K, Rb and Cs react explosively.
2.	$2M + X_2 \rightarrow 2MX$	With liquid Br_2, Li and Na hardly react. K, Rb, and Cs react violently.
3.	$2M + H_2 \rightarrow 2MH$	Ionic saltlike hydrides are formed by all alkali metals on heating between 300 to 700°C.
4.	$6Li + N_2 \rightarrow 2Li_3N$	Li is the only alkali metal to react with N_2 to give Li_3N. The reaction is slow at 25°C but rapid at 400°C.
5.	$4Li + O_2 \rightarrow 2Li_2O$ $2Na + O_2 \rightarrow Na_2O_2$ $M + O_2 \rightarrow MO_2$ (K, Rb, Cs)	Lithium reacts with O_2 to give oxide, Na forms the peroxide while the heavier elements give superoxide when these metals are burnt in a free supply of air. Under suitable conditions pure compounds M_2O, M_2O_2 and MO_2 can be prepared for all metals.
6.	$2M + 2C \rightarrow M_2C_2$ (Li, Na)	Both Li and Na react to form acetylides; K, Rb, Cs react with carbon to give non-stoichiometric compounds.

Chemistry of Alkaline Earth Metals

The elements of this group are also known as **alkaline earth metals** because of the following two reasons

(i) Their oxides are similar to those of alkali metal oxides, *i.e.,* their oxides with water will give hydroxides which are alkalies.

(ii) The name "earth" was given by chemists to substances like alumina which remained unchanged even on heating. Calcium and barium oxides could stand very high temperatures, they were also called "earths". Thus, the metals calcium, barium and strontium came to be known as alkaline earth metals. The name is now applied to all the elements of group 2.

Occurrence

These elements do not occur in free state because of their highly reactive nature. Beryllium does not occur in abundance and is difficult to extract, therefore, it is an unfamiliar element. Magnesium and calcium occur in considerable amounts in the earth's crust. Strontium and barium do not occur as concentrated ores but are easy to extract and are familiar elements. Radium is extremely scarce and was first isolated by Madame Curie in 1910. Because of its radioactive nature, little is known about the chemistry of radium.

Extraction of Elements

Alkaline earth metals are quite reactive like the alkali metals. Therefore, the same difficulties arise during their isolation as were mentioned under 'extraction of alkali metals'. These metals are usually isolated by the electrolysis of their fused metal halides containing sodium chloride (which lowers the melting point and increases the electrical conductivity of alkaline earth metal halides).

Extraction of Beryllium

Fichter method

Beryllium chloride is mixed with sodium chloride in the molar ratio 2 : 1. The mixture is fused in a nickel crucible which serves as a cathode and a carbon anode is dipped into it. On electrolysis, the metal is collected at the cathode. Since, at high temperatures beryllium forms an alloy with nickel, therefore, nickel crucible is kept cooled by water.

The metal (when required for use in nuclear reactors) is purified by distillation in vacuum and is cast into rods under argon.

Physical Properties of Group 2 Elements

The atoms of the alkaline earth metals in the ground state contain two electrons in *s*-orbital outside a noble gas core. This similarity in the electronic structure of all these elements are reflected and they are having similar physical and chemical properties.

Important physical properties of alkaline earth metals are depicted in Table 4.2. A correlation betweeen atomic structure and physical properties of these elements are discussed below :

(a) Loose Binding of *s*-electrons

Just as in alkali metals, the noble gas core shields the *s*-electrons from direct attraction of the nuclear charge of alkaline earth metals. Therefore, the *s*-electrons are very loosely held. The consequences of loose binding of *s*-electrons are :

(i) Formation of dipositive (M^{2+}) ions

The formation of predominantly M^{2+} ions of the alkaline earth metals can be explained in terms of their :

Table 4.2 **Physical Properties of Alkaline Earth Metals**

Property		Beryllium Be	Magnesium Mg	Calcium Ca	Strontium Sr	Barium Ba	Radium Ra
Atomic number		4	12	20	38	56	88
Electronic configuration		[He] $2s^2$	[Xe] $3s^2$	[Ar] $4s^2$	[Kr] $5s^2$	[Xe] $6s^2$	[Rn] $7s^2$
Atomic radii, pm		105	162	197	213	217	–
Ionic radii, M^{2+},pm		31	65	99	113	135	150
Ionisation energies, kJ g, atom	1st	894	734	587	547	500	508
	2nd	1748	1443	1140	1059	960	962
	3rd	14784	7691	4909	4130	3423	–
$E°$, M^{2+}/M(V)		–1.85	–2.34	–2.87	–1.89	–2.90	–2.92
Electronegativity		1.50	1.2	1.1	1.0	0.9	0.9
Heat of atomisation (at 298 K and 1 atm) kcal/mol		78.2	35.1	42.3	39.0	42.0	–
Atomic weight		9.0	24.3	40.0	87.6	137.4	226
Density of solid at 293 K, g/cc		1.86	1.75	1.55	2.6	3.39	5
Melting point, K		3043	1380	1710	1639	1790	1413
Colour of the flame		–	–	Brick red	Crimson	Apple green	–
Enthalpy of hydration, kcal/mol^{-1}		570	460	395	355	305	–

(i) electronic configuration;
(ii) ionisation energies; and
(iii) size.

Further ionisation to give M^{3+} ions is ruled out because values for the third stage ionization energies are extremely high (See Table 4.2) and cannot be recovered by the formation of an additional bond in hypothetical MX_3 molecules.

Why group 2 metals do not form '*MX*' type compounds?

The non-existence of MgCl (s) or MX may be attributed to the much higher standard enthalpy of formation of $MgCl_2$ (s) or MX_2,

$$Mg(s) + Cl_2(g) \longrightarrow MgCl_2(s)$$

$$\Delta H^\circ_f = -642 \text{ kJ mol}^{-1}$$

This suggests that $MgCl_2$ (s) is far more stable than the hypothetical MgCl (s) and it undergoes complete and rapid disproportionation.

$$2MgCl(s) \longrightarrow Mg(s) + MgCl_2(s)$$

$$\Delta H^\circ_{\text{disprop.}} = \frac{-392}{2} = -196 \text{ kJ mol}^{-1}$$

These values also suggests that if some clever experiment can be thought which would hinder disproportionation of MgCl(s), then MgCl(s) may be isolated.

Trend in the group The first and second ionisation energies decrease from beryllium to barium because of increasing size of the atoms down the group. The higher values of the ionisation energies of radium indicate that it is slightly less reactive than barium. The reduced reactivity of radium is due to the fact that it comes after the lanthanide series of elements in the Periodic Table which exhibit **lanthanide contraction.** Therefore, size of the radium atom also decreases resulting in an increase of the ionisation energy.

(ii) Reducing agents

The high negative values of standard electrode reduction potentials (E°) listed in Table 4.2 indicate that in aqueous solutions these elements are good reducing agents quite comparable to alkali metals and this is due to their large hydration energies. The high negative E° values of these elements mean that they all react vigorously with dilute acid, $H^+(aq)$. Those with very high negative values react vigorously with water also.

Trend in the group There is a gradual increase in the E° values of these elements indicating stronger tendency to act as reducing agents as we move down the group.

(iii) Colouration to the flame

Except beryllium and magnesium, the chlorides of these elements produce characteristic colour in flame due to easy excitation of electrons to higher energy levels. In case of Be and Mg, the excitation energy is very high (because of their high ionization energies) and therefore their salts do not impart any colour to the flame.

(b) Sizes of Atoms and Ions

The atoms and ions of alkaline earth metals are smaller than those of the preceding alkali metals because of the increased nuclear charge. This contraction in size results in higher ionization energies of these metals as compared to alkali metals.

In moving down, the group the sizes of atoms and ions increases as new shells are added.

(c) Electronegativity

From beryllium to radium, electronegativity values decrease indicating greater tendency for ionic compound formation down the group. However, the electronegativity values of alkaline earth metals are very close to those of alkali metals. The high electronegativity of beryllium is suggestive of its tendency to form covalent compounds.

(d) Nature of Metallic Bonding in Alkaline Earth Metals

In contrast to the single electron per atom contributed to metallic bonding in alkali metals; two electrons per atom are involved in the metallic bonding in alkaline earth metals. The stronger bonding results in closer packing in the metallic structures. Moreover, the sizes of atoms are smaller than the alkali metal atoms. As a result of these two factors, alkaline earth metals are (i) harder, (ii) denser, (iii) have higher melting and boiling points, and (iv) higher heats of atomisation than the alkali metals.

The metal bond strength (as is evident from their heats of atomisation) decreases with increasing atomic number in the group as the size of the atoms increases.

(e) Conductors of Heat and Electricity

In the metallic state, the two s-electrons resonate and thus form covalent bonds between each atom and its nearest neighbours (roughly 12 in number) in the crystal lattice. These electrons can move through the crystal lattice under the influence of an electrical potential. Consequently, these elements are good conductors of heat and electricity.

Due to the above reason, these elements reflect light and have a silvery shine.

(f) Enthalpies of Hydration of M^{2+}

The enthalpies of hydration for alkaline earth metal ions have two notable features :

(i) The enthalpy of hydration decreases as the size of the ion increases.

(ii) More heat is evolved upon hydration (*i.e.*, high enthalpy of hydration) of alkaline earth metal ions than the preceding alkali metal ions. This difference can be attributed to the increased charge on the alkaline earth metal ions. Even though Na^+ and Ca^{2+} have nearly the same radii, the enthalpy of hydration of Ca^{2+} is nearly four times that of Na^+. This suggests that, in general, the hydration enthalpy is proportional to the square of the charge on the ion and this relation is obeyed in fact to a fair approximation.

It is the increase in hydration enthalpy with ionic charge that is responsible for the existence of the alkaline earth metal ions in the + 2 oxidation state in aqueous solutions.

Example 12. *Although the energies required to (i) vaporize and (ii) ionize alkaline earth metal atom to the M^{2+} ions are much greater than those required to produce the M^{2+} ions of the group 2 elements, yet they form divalent salts.*

Sol. The exceptionally high lattice energies in the solid salts (due to small dipositive ions) and the high hydration energies of the $M^+(aq)$ ions compensate for the increased energies in steps (i) and (ii) above.

Chemical Properties

The combined effect of decreased size and increased charge make the alkaline earth metal ions far better polarizers or 'distorters' than the alkali metal ions. Their oxides are thus more covalent and their hydroxides are less basic than those of the alkali metals. The oxides of beryllium and magnesium are so tightly held together in the solid state that they are insoluble in water.

Due to its extremely small size, beryllium has a unique chemical behaviour. It tends to be covalent in its compounds while magnesium tends to be partly ionic and in some compounds it is covalent. However, calcium, strontium, barium and radium form a closely allied series with the following systematic group trends in physical and chemical properties.

(i) Rates of reaction of the metals with hydrogen increases.

(ii) The tendency of the crystalline salts to form hydrates increases.

(iii) Solubilities of halides (except fluorides), sulphates and nitrates decreases.

(iv) Solubilities of halides in ethanol decreases.

(v) Thermal stability of peroxides, carbonates and nitrates increases.

Compounds of alkaline earth metals are, in most instances, less soluble in water than the corresponding alkali metal compounds. This is mainly due to the following two reasons.

(i) The alkaline earth metal ions are doubly charged.

(ii) The sizes of alkaline earth metal ions are smaller than the alkali metal ions.

As a result of the above factors the lattice energies of the alkaline earth metal compounds are larger than those of the corresponding alkali metal compounds which lead to the decreased solubility of the compounds of alkaline earth metals in water.

(Lattice energy may be defined as the energy required to convert one mole of the ionic lattice into the gaseous ions. Lattices with smaller ions have higher lattice energies. Ionic compounds with higher lattices energies have low solubility because for dissolution, at first, energy equivalent to that of lattice energy has to be supplied to break the lattice into separate ions which then get solvated.)

Some important compounds of alkaline earth metals are discussed below.

I. Oxides

Lattice energies of alkaline earth metal oxides are sensitive to the size of the M^{2+} ion because the sizes of O^{2-} ion and M^{2+} ions are quite comparable. Therefore, oxides of smaller alkaline earth metal cations are more stable than those of larger M^{2+} ions. It may thus be concluded that with decreasing size of the cation, the alkaline earth metal oxides are stabilized which favours the decomposition of their carbonates into oxides.

Preparation

(i) The oxides of alkaline earth metals are produced when these elements are burnt in air.

$$2M(s) + O_2(g) \longrightarrow 2MO(s)$$

However, when magnesium is burnt in air, oxide formation is accompanied by the formation of the nitride :

$$2Mg(s) + O_2(g) \longrightarrow 2MgO(s)$$
$$3Mg(s) + N_2(g) \longrightarrow Mg_3N_2(s)$$

Both these reactions are highly exothermic and energy is released as both heat and light.

When barium is heated in air or oxygen at 600°C, the peroxide, BaO_2 is obtained.

(ii) The oxides are also prepared by decomposing the carbonates by heat :

$$MgCO_3(s) \longrightarrow MgO(s) + CO_2(g)$$
$$\underset{\text{(Limestone)}}{CaCO_3(s)} \longrightarrow \underset{\text{(Lime or Quicklime)}}{CaO(s)} + CO_2(g)$$

Properties

(i) All the oxides are white crystalline solids. BeO shows excellent refractory properties.

(ii) The oxides of Mg, Ca, Sr and Ba, all have the sodium chloride structure (6 : 6) except BeO which has a Wurtzite (4 : 4) structure.

(iii) They are extremely stable. MgO has a very high melting point and it is insoluble in water. This may be attributed to the very high strength of the interionic forces. The electrostatic force of attraction between an M^{2+} ion and an X^{2-} ion is **four** times the force between an M^{2+} ion and an X^- ion at the same distance apart. Their melting points and lattice energies decrease with increasing size of the cation, as we go down in the group.

(iv) The alkaline earth metal oxides are basic. They react with acids to give salts. For example,

$$MgO + 2HCl \longrightarrow MgCl_2 + H_2O$$

(v) BeO and MgO are very tightly held in the solid state. BeO is very hard and has a very high melting point. It is amphoteric in nature. It reacts with strong acids to give $[Be(OH_2)_4]^{2+}$ ions. It reacts with strong bases to give $[Be(OH)_4]^{2-}$ ions. This behaviour may be attributed to the small size and doubly positive charge on the beryllium ion. BeO is insoluble in water. MgO reacts very slowly with water to give insoluble hydroxide :

$$MgO + H_2O \longrightarrow Mg(OH)_2$$

II. Hydroxides

Calcium oxide reacts exothermally with water to give calcium hydroxide, $Ca(OH)_2$ or **slaked lime.** It has a low solubility in water.

$$CaO(s) + H_2O(l) \longrightarrow Ca(OH)_2(s); \quad \Delta H° = -65 \text{ kJ mol}^{-1}$$

A saturated solution of $Ca(OH)_2$ is called **limewater** and it is often used as a test for CO_2. When CO_2 is bubbled through limewater, the solution turns cloudy, because of the formation of insoluble $CaCO_3$:

$$Ca(OH)_2(aq) + CO_2(aq) \longrightarrow CaCO_3(s) + H_2O(l)$$

If the passage of CO_2 is continued further, the precipitate dissolves due to the formation of soluble $Ca(HCO_3)_2$.

$$CaCO_3(s) + CO_2(g) + H_2O(l) \longrightarrow Ca(HCO_3)_2(aq)$$

Calcium hydroxide is a strong base. It is completely dissociated into its ions :

$$Ca(OH)_2(s) \rightleftharpoons Ca^{2+}(aq) + 2OH^-(aq)$$

Lime (CaO) and slaked lime ($Ca(OH)_2$) are very important commercial bases because they are cheap and are easily available. Lime is used in making glass and cement. It is also used in removing SiO_2 and other acidic oxides in various metallurgical processes. For example, in the smelting of iron, it forms a slag such as $CaSiO_3$. Magnesium hydroxide, $Mg(OH)_2$, is only slightly soluble in water. A suspension of magnesium hydroxide in water is called **milk of magnesia.** It is used as an **antacid,** as a medicine to cure excess acidity in the stomach.

The solubility of hydroxides of alkaline earth metals in water increases as we go down the group. This may be attributed to a decrease in lattice energy.

The basicity of the oxides and hydroxides of the alkaline earth metals increases as we go down the group from Be to Ba. This may be attributed to the increasing electropositive character of the metal atom.

The hydroxides of alkaline earth metals are less basic than alkali metal hydroxides. This may be attributed to the former having higher ionisation energies, smaller ionic sizes and bipositive charge on the ions.

$Be(OH)_2$	Amphoteric
$Mg(OH)_2$	Mildly basic
$Ca(OH)_2$, $Sr(OH)_2$	Moderate to strong bases
$Ba(OH)_2$	Strong base; as strong as alkali metal hydroxides

III. Hydrides

All the elements of this group form hydrides of the type MH_2.

Preparation

(i) BeH_2 cannot be prepared by the direct combination of Be and H_2. It is prepared by reducing $BeCl_2$ by LiH or $LiAlH_4$.

$$BeCl_2 + 2LiH \xrightarrow{\text{Ether}} BeH_2 + 2LiCl$$

or $$2BeCl_2 + LiAlH_4 \xrightarrow{\text{Ether}} 2BeH_2 + LiCl + AlCl_3$$

(ii) BeH_2 and MgH_2 are also obtained by thermal decomposition of $Be(CMe_3)_2$ and $MgEt_2$, respectively.

(iii) The saline hydrides (CaH_2, SrH_2 and BaH_2) are prepared by direct reactions between the metals and H_2 between 150–250°C.

(iv) The hydrides of Ca, Sr or Ba can also be prepared by reduction of their oxides or halides with hydrogen.

Properties

(i) BeH_2 is difficult to obtain pure. It is a covalent polymeric compound, $(BeH_2)_n \cdot MgH_2$ is partly ionic while the other hydrides are ionic solids.

(ii) They react with water, releasing H_2. They are thus used as reducing agents.

$$MH_2 + 2H_2O \longrightarrow M(OH)_2 + H_2$$

Calcium hydride is a strong reducing agent but not as powerful as the hydrides of alkali metals. It reacts with water, but the reaction is not vigorous. For its moderate reactivity towards water, CaH_2 is often used in the laboratories as a drying agent (particularly ethers) and is a portable source of hydrogen gas.

Structure

Beryllium hydride is a three-dimensional polymeric solid. It is quite ionic in nature and may be thought of as formally made up of ionic Be^{2+} and H^- ions.

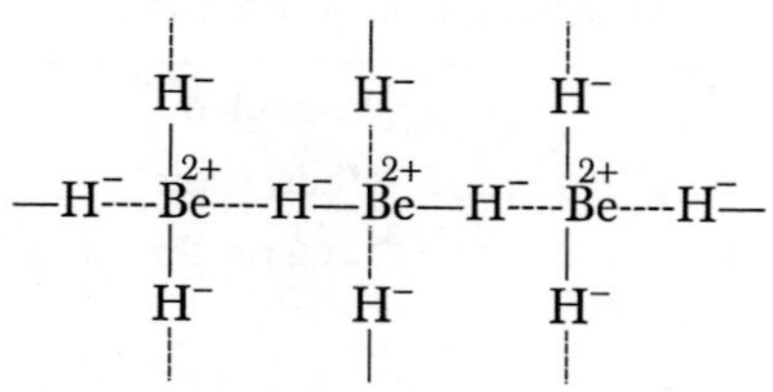

Alternatively, it may be considered to be an electron-deficient molecule, polymerized by means of BeHBe 3-centre bonds (as in diborane) and its structure is probably similar to that of $BeCl_2$ or $BeMe_2$.

IV. Halides

Preparation

Alkaline earth metals combine directly with halogens at appropriate temperatures to form metal halides of the general formula MX_2. Beryllium chloride is prepared by the action of Cl_2 or HCl on the metal. Anhydrous $BeCl_2$ is obtained by the action of Cl_2 at high temperatures on a mixture of BeO and carbon.

$$BeO + C + Cl_2 \xrightarrow{800\,°C} BeCl_2 + CO$$

Properties

Alkaline earth metal halides show a variety of structures depending upon the relative sizes of the ions. For example, beryllium ion having the **smallest size** (along with a high positive charge) exhibits covalent character in its halides. Beryllium chloride has lower melting and boiling points as well as much lower conductivity in the fused state than the other alkaline earth metal chlorides.

Beryllium chloride dissolves in water in an exothermic reaction to form $[Be(H_2O)_4]Cl_2$. Anhydrous $BeCl_2$ is insoluble in chloroform, carbon tetrachloride, CS_2 and benzene but readily soluble in diethylether, acetone, nitromethane, ammonia and amines. This is because the oxygen and nitrogen donor solvents form complexes with $BeCl_2$ of composition $BeCl_2 \cdot L_2$ (L = donor molecule).

Structure

Beryllium chloride, $BeCl_2$ has an unusual chain structure in the solid state. The chain arises because of free electron pairs on chlorine atoms which form intermolecular coordinative covalent bonds as shown in Fig. 4.1.

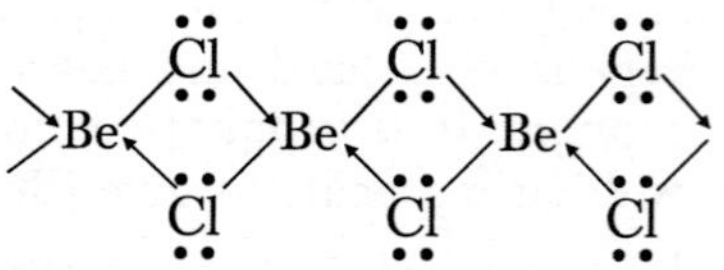

Fig. 4.1 Structure of solid $BeCl_2$.

In this, Be is considered to be sp^3 hybridized with ClBeCl bond angle considerably lower than the tetrahedral angle (of 109.5°C) due to lesser repulsive interactions between Be atoms. Coordination number of Be is 4.

In vapour phase, beryllium chloride exists as a dimer with sp^2 hybridisation (Fig. 4.2). **Beryllium atom is 3-coordinated.**

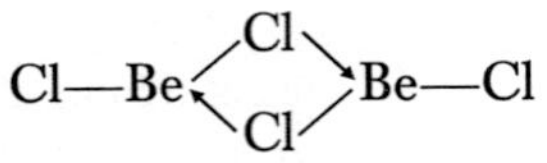

Fig. 4.2 Structure of solid $(BeCl_2)_2$.

The dissociation of dimer into monomer is complete at temperatures higher than 750°C. At 560°C, the vapours contain 20% dimeric molecules and 80% monomer. In monomeric form $BeCl_2$ vapour is linear with *sp* hybridization (Fig. 4.3). Beryllium has C.N. = 2

$$Cl \xrightarrow{177\ pm} Be—Cl$$

Fig. 4.3 Structure of $BeCl_2$ vapour.

Beryllium chloride chain structure is broken by (i) weak ligands (*L*) like Et_2O, $(CH_3)_2C{=}O$, CH_3NO_2, etc., to form 4 coordinated molecular complexes $BeCl_2 \cdot L_2$ and by (ii) strong ligands (*L*) like H_2O, NH_3, py etc., to form ionic complexes $[BeL_4]^{2+}, [Cl_2]^-$. In both cases, beryllium is sp^3 hybridization with tetrahedral arrangement of ligands.

The fluorides of alkaline earth metals (except BeF_2) are insoluble because of the large values of their lattice energies. The chlorides, bromides and iodides of alkaline earth metals (except beryllium) are fairly ionic and the ionic character increases as the atomic number of the cation increases in the group.

Most of the anhydrous alkaline earth metal halides crystallize in the fluorite type structure.

V. Carbides

Preparation

Alkaline earth metals from calcium to barium (or their oxides) when heated in an electric arc furnace with carbon form carbides of the general formula MC_2.

$$CaO + 3C \longrightarrow CaC_2 + CO$$

Properties

(i) These carbides are ionic acetylides.

(ii) They have sodium choride type structure with M^{2+} replacing Na^+ and $[C{\equiv}C]^{2-}$ replacing Cl^-.

(iii) On reaction with water, they liberate C_2H_2 gas.

VI. Carbonates

Calcium and magnesium carbonates are minerals and are the most important preparative sources of these metals.

(i) Thermal stability

Unlike the alkali metal carbonates (except Li_2CO_3), they decompose when heated.

$$CaCO_3 \xrightarrow{Heat} CaO + CO_2$$

The stability of the carbonates of these metals increases on moving down the group. This is indicated by the values of the decomposition temperatures of these carbonates as given below :

$$BeCO_3 = 25°C, MgCO_3 = 540°C, CaCO_3 = 900°C,$$
$$SrCO_3 = 1290°C, BaCO_3 = 1360°C$$

The instability of $BeCO_3$ may be attributed to strong polarizing effect of small Be^{2+} cation on the large polarizable CO_3^{2-} ion.

(ii) Solubility

Solubility of carbonates decreases as the size of the metal ion increases (this trend is opposite to that observed for fluorides and hydroxides). This may be attributed to decrease in hydration energy of the M^{2+} ions as size increases. Since, the size of the carbonate ion is quite large (say 300 pm) variation in the size of the cation has little effect on lattice energy. Thus, for carbonates the term hydration energy is crucial than lattice energy in determining their solubility in water.

VII. Sulphates

Magnesium sulphate is soluble in water and crystallizes out as $MgSO_4 \cdot 7H_2O$ **(Epsom salt).** In medicine, it is used as a purgative.

Calcium sulphate occurs in nature as the mineral gypsum, $CaSO_4 \cdot 2H_2O$. When gypsum is heated to a little above 100°C, it loses three quarters of its water of crystallization, giving a white powder, $CaSO_4 \cdot \frac{1}{2} H_2O$, which is called **plaster of Paris.**

$$CaSO_4 \cdot 2H_2O \xrightarrow{Heat} CaSO_4 \cdot \frac{1}{2} H_2O + \frac{3}{2} H_2O$$

A paste of plaster of Paris and a little water quickly sets to a hard mass. The formation of the dihydrate is accompanied by an increase in volume which is very valuable in making plaster casts.

Solubility of alkaline earth metal sulphates

It decreases regularly from $BeSO_4$ and $MgSO_4$ which are very soluble in water to $CaSO_4$, which is only slightly soluble, to $SrSO_4$ and $BaSO_4$, which are insoluble.

Uses Like all heavy elements barium absorbs X-rays strongly. If a suspension of $BaSO_4$ is swallowed, it coats the alimentary canal. The X-ray photographs of the alimentary canal can be recorded, which is otherwise transparent to X-rays. Barium is poisonous, but the solubility of $BaSO_4$ is extremely small that it passes through the body without causing any ill effects.

VIII. Limestone Caves, Stalactites, and Stalagmites

Natural water is slightly acidic as it contains dissolved CO_2.

$$2H_2O + CO_2 \rightleftharpoons H_3O^+ + HCO_3^-$$

This acidity is enough to dissolve insoluble $CaCO_3$ rocks into soluble $Ca(HCO_3)_2$.

$$CaCO_3 + CO_2 + H_2O \rightleftharpoons Ca^{2+} + 2HCO_3^-$$

In an underground stream, the soluble $CaHCO_3$ is continually washed away. The above equilibrium is never achieved and so $CaCO_3$ continues to dissolve, and thus over a very long time underground caves are formed.

The most impressive and beautiful features of these caves is the formation of **stalactites,** and **stalagmites.** They are formed by the reverse reactions by which the caves are first formed. Water passing through limestone cave is saturated with $Ca(HCO_3)_2$. It seeps through to the roof of a cave and forms a drop hanging from the roof. The water slowly evaporates, some CO_2 is lost, the equilibrium shifts to the left (as per Le-Chatelier's principle) and Ca^{2+} ions are redeposited as $CaCO_3$. This slow process over a long period results in the formation of conical shaped stalactites. The same drop of water may fall from the roof to the floor, where it evaporates slowly again depositing a small amount of $CaCO_3$. If drops keep falling at the same spot, over a period of time, a stalagmite is built up. Sometimes, it may grow sufficiently to join a stalactite to form a column.

Table 4.3 **Some Typical Reactions of Group 2 Elements**

Reaction	General remarks
$M + 2H_2O \rightarrow M(OH)_2 + H_2$	Be reacts with steam; Mg with hot water and Ca, Sr and Ba react rapidly with cold water.
$M + 2HX \rightarrow MX_2 + H_2$	All the metals react with acids, liberating hydrogen.
$Be + 2NaOH \xrightarrow{2H_2O} Na_2[Be(OH)_4] + H_2$	Be is amphoteric.
$2M + O_2 \rightarrow 2MO$	Normal oxide is formed by all group members with excess oxygen.
$Ba + O_2 \rightarrow BaO_2$	Ba also forms the peroxide.
$M + H_2 \rightarrow MH_2$	Ionic 'salt-like' hydrides are formed at high temperatures by Ca, Sr, and Ba.
$3M + N_2 \rightarrow M_3N_2$	All the metals form nitrides at high temperatures.
$3M + 2P \rightarrow M_3P_2$	All the metals form phosphides at high temperatures.
$M + S \rightarrow MS$	All the metals form sulphides.
$M + F_2 \rightarrow MF_2$	All the metals form fluorides.
$M + Cl_2 \rightarrow MCl_2$	All the metals form chlorides.
$M + Br_2 \rightarrow MBr_2$	All the metals form bromides.
$M + I_2 \rightarrow MI_2$	All the metals form iodides.
$M + 2NH_3 \rightarrow M(NH_2)_2 + H_2$	All the metals form amides at high temperatures.

Example 13. *When Mg is burnt in air it forms a white product which when dissolved in water smells of ammonia. Explain.*

Sol.

$$3Mg + N_2 \longrightarrow Mg_3N_2$$

$$Mg_3N_2 + 6H_2O \longrightarrow 3Mg(OH)_2 + 2NH_3$$

Uses of Alkaline Earth Metals

(a) **Beryllium** It is used in X-ray windows as scavenger in alloys, as moderator in fission reactions.

(b) **Magnesium** It is used in the manufacture of alloys; as reducing agent, *e.g.,* extraction of uranium; in Grignard's reagent and in containers for nuclear fuels.

(c) **Calcium** It is used as scavenger, *e.g.,* removal of water from ethanol; air from radio valves.

(d) **Strontium and Barium** They are used as scavengers.

Diagonal Relationship of Beryllium with Aluminium

It has already been mentioned that one of the distinguishing features of the elements of the second period of the Periodic Table is that they resemble more with their diagonally opposite members than their own congeners. The anomalous behaviour of beryllium is mainly due to its tiny size (size of beryllium ion is 1/8th that of magnesium ion and 1/64th that of barium ion). Therefore, it does not resemble with its congeners but there is a great similarity in the physical and chemical properties of beryllium and aluminium. In fact, the resemblance between beryllium and aluminium is so striking that they are considered to be ideal diagonal partners in the Periodic Table. Some of the important points of similarities are discussed below :

(i) Though the ionic radius of beryllium (31 pm) is considerably lesser than that of aluminium (50 pm) the charge/radius ratio for the two ions are quite close.

	Be	Al
Charge on the ion	+2	+3
Ionic radius (pm)	31	50
Charge/radius ratio	6.4	6.0

Since, charge/radius ratio is a measure of the deforming power of the ions, therefore, it can be conclude that both Be^{2+} and Al^{3+} have similar deforming powers.

(ii) Electronegativities of both the elements are 1.5.

(iii) Enthalpy of vaporization for both is 293 kJ.

(iv) The standard electrode reduction potentials of both are of the same order [Be^{2+}/Be, –1.70; Al^{3+}/Al, –1.67 V].

(v) In nature, both occur together in beryl $3BeO \cdot Al_2O_3 \cdot 6SiO_2$.

(vi) The chemistry of beryllium is expected to be dominated by its tendency to form covalent compounds because of its tiny size and high charge. Thus, compounds of beryllium have lower melting points, are soluble in organic solvents and get hydrolysed by water. In this respect, they resemble closely with compounds of aluminium.

Magnesium does show some tendency to form covalent compounds but other alkaline earth metals do not form covalent compounds.

(vii) Out of the alkaline earth metals, only beryllium is resistant to the attack of conc. HNO_3 owing to the formation of an inert and imprevious oxide film on its surface. Aluminium is also resistant to the attack of conc. HNO_3 due to a similar oxide film formation on its surface.

(viii) Among the alkaline earth metals, only beryllium forms beryllate on reaction with caustic alkalies with the evolution of hydrogen. Similarly, aluminium forms aluminate ions.

(ix) Out of the oxides of alkaline earth metals, only beryllium oxide is extremely hard, non-volatile, has very high melting point and is amphoteric. Aluminium oxide shares all these properties.

(x) Like anhydrous aluminium chloride, anhydrous beryllium chloride is soluble in organic solvents; catalyses Friedel-Crafts reaction and behaves as a Lewis acid.

(xi) Out of the alkaline earth metal carbides, only beryllium carbide yields methane on hydrolysis. Similarly, aluminium carbide gives methane on hydrolysis.

$$Be_2C + 4H_2O \longrightarrow 2Be(OH)_2 + CH_4$$

$$Al_4C_3 + 12H_2O \longrightarrow 4Al(OH)_3 + 3CH_4$$

(xii) Among the alkaline earth metals, only beryllium forms many chelate type complexes specially with oxygen donors. Aluminium also forms metal chelates with oxygen donors.

Structures of Metallic Crystals

Before we discuss the structures of metallic crystals, it would be useful to discuss the close-packing of identical spheres in space. We shall soon appreciate that metals adopt structures which closely resemble the arrangement acquired by hard spheres in three-dimensional space. It is assumed that atoms in metals behave like hard spheres.

The Close-packing of Spheres

In most of the structures encountered in inorganic chemistry, it is observed that the structures assumed are simply a consequence of the most efficient packing of the units involved. Since, these units may be either atoms, ions or molecules of **approximately spherical shape,** it may be of interest to study the most efficient ways of packing of hard spheres of equal size in three dimensions.

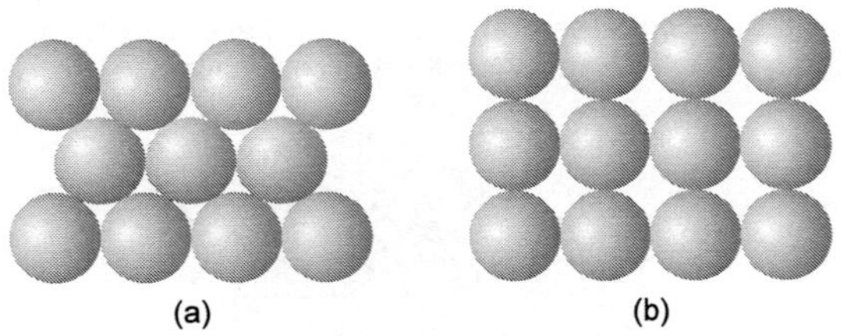

Fig. 4.4 Close-packing of sphere in one plane.

If a large number of spheres of equal size are put in a container and shaken, they will arrange themselves in a manner so as to occupy minimum volume. The arrangement of such spheres in one plane is shown in Fig. 4.4. The arrangements shown in Fig. 4.4 (a) is more economical than that shown in Fig. 4.4 (b). The packing is closest when the spheres arrange themselves so that their centres are at the corners of an equilateral triangle

(Fig. 4.5). Each sphere in the closest packed arrangement is in contact with six other spheres as shown in Fig. 4.5. The centres of each of these six spheres are arranged hexagonally. **The number of spheres which are actually in contact with a particular sphere is called the coordination number of that sphere.** The coordination number is six when spheres are arranged in a close packed arrangement in one plane.

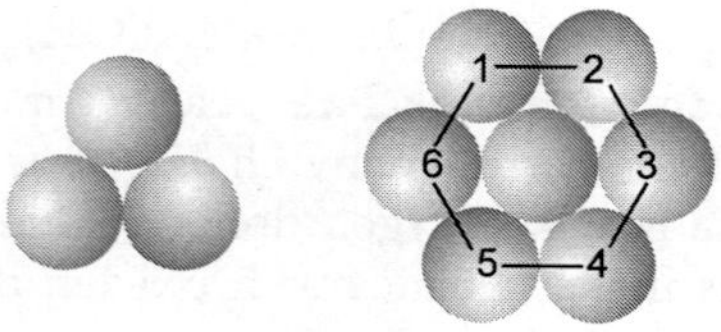

Fig. 4.5

Three-dimensional close packing

Now, if we start building successive layers on top of the first layer, spheres marked *A* (Fig. 4.6), we soon realize that spheres of second layer may be placed either on the hollows which are marked *B* or the other set of hollows which are marked as *C*. It may be noted that while building the second layer, we cannot place spheres both on hollows *B* and *C*. As shown in Fig. 4.6, we may build the second layer on hollows marked *B*.

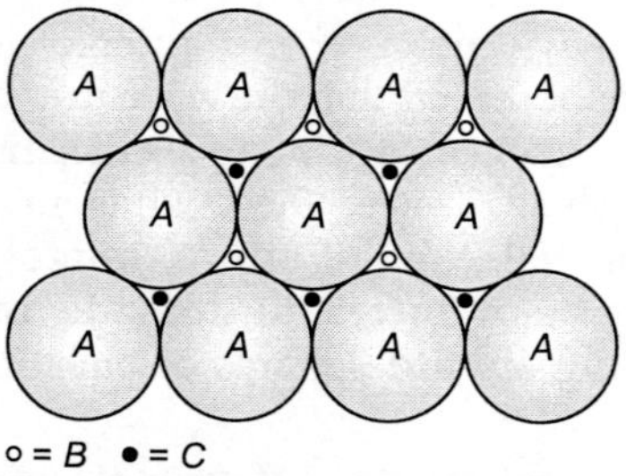

Fig. 4.6 (a) Site created by layer 1 and available to accept atoms in layer 2 either on the hollows called '*B*' or '*C*'.

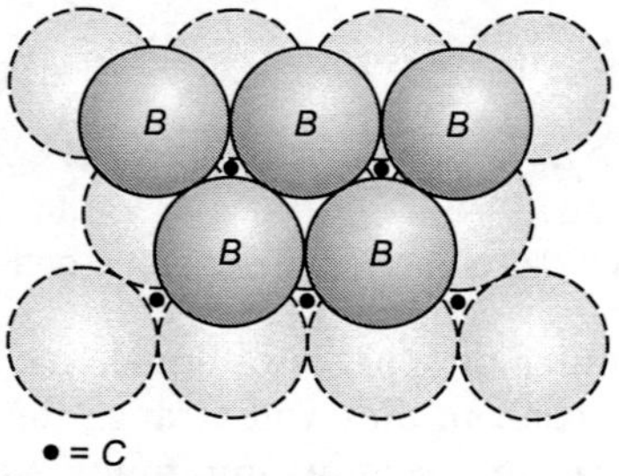

Fig. 4.6 (b) Covering of all '*B*' sites by atoms in the second layer making the '*C*' sites unavailable for occupancy by close-packed atoms.

However, for building the third layer we again have a choice of arranging spheres in two different ways :

(i) The third layer of spheres may be placed on the hollows of the second layer, so that each sphere of the third layer lies strictly above a sphere of the first layer. In such an arrangement the first and the third layers are exactly identical. This arrangement of close packing of spheres is referred to as *ABA* arrangement of packing of spheres.

(ii) Alternatively, the third layer of spheres may be placed on the second set of hollows which were marked *C* in the first layer. These hollows were left uncovered while arranging the second layer of spheres. This arrangement of packing is denoted as *ABC* type packing.

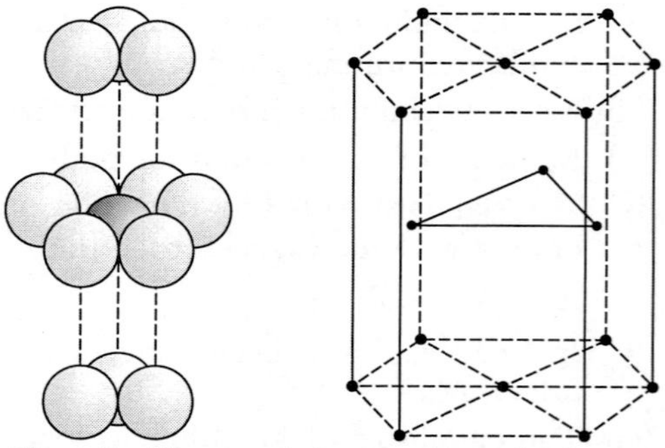
Fig. 4.7 Hexagonal close-packing of spheres.

When the *ABABABA...* arrangement of packing is continued indefinitely, the system possesses hexagonal symmetry. This would imply that the structure possesses a six-fold axis of symmetry which is perpendicular to the planes of the close-packed spheres. Such an arrangement of three dimensional packing of spheres is shown in Fig. 4.7. **Because of its hexagonal symmetry, this arrangement is referred to as hexagonal close packing of spheres often abbreviated as hcp.**

When the *ABCABC...* arrangement of packing is continued (*i.e.,* every fourth layer is situated directly above the first layer) the system then possesses cubic symmetry. The arrangement is shown in Fig. 4.8. The structure now has three 4-fold axes of symmetry. **The arrangement is called cubic close packing of spheres and is often abbreviated as ccp.** It is also clear from this diagram that in this arrangement we have a sphere at the centre of each face of the unit cube. **This arrangement of spheres is also known as face centred cubic (fcc).**

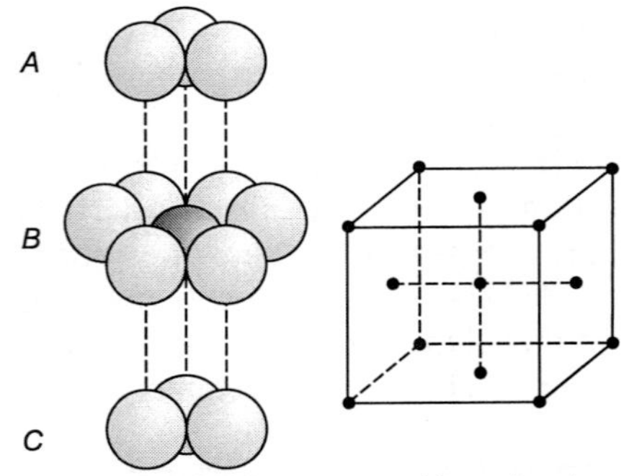

Fig. 4.8 (a) Cubic close packing of sphere.

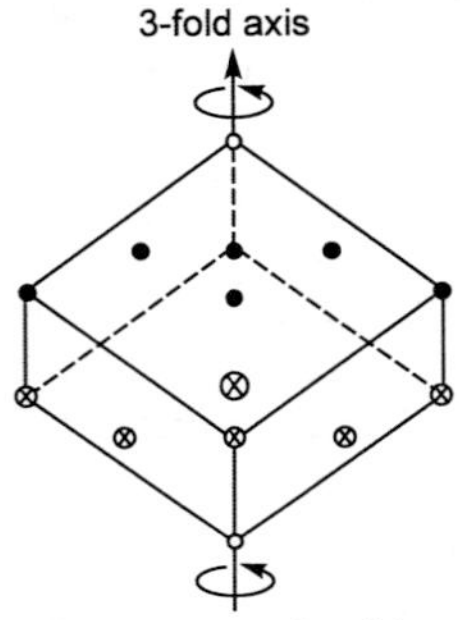

Fig. 4.8 (b) Face centred cubic arrangement (as seen along a 3-fold axis).

In both these arrangements, *i.e.,* hcp and ccp, it is obvious that each sphere is surrounded by twelve equidistant spheres. There are six spheres which are in contact in the same plane and three each in adjacent layers, one just above, and the other just below. The coordination number of each sphere in both these close packed arrangement is twelve. This is shown in Fig. 4.9. For illustration the spheres of top and bottom layers are shown apart.

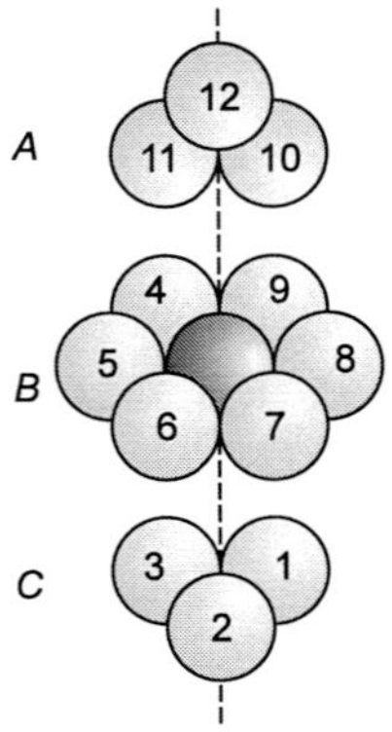

Fig. 4.9

In both these type of close packed arrangements, maximum volume of space, *i.e.,* 74% is actually occupied by the spheres. It may also be understood here that any irregular arrangement like *ABABC-ABABC,* etc., possesses neither cubic nor hexagonal symmetry.

Structures Adopted by Metals

The structures of most of the metals (from *s*- and *d*-blocks of the periodic chart) belong either to one or more of the three simple types of structures.

(i) Cubic close packed (face-centred cubic)
(ii) Hexagonal close packed
(iii) Body centred cubic

The distribution of these structures among the *s*- and *d*-block metals is shown below.

Structures of some metals

c = cubic close packed,
h = hexagonal close packed
b = body centred cubic

Li b	Be h										
Na b	Mg h	Al c									
K b	Ca ch	Sc ch	Ti hb	V b	Cr b	Mn –	Fe cb	Co ch	Ni ch	Cu c	Zn h
Rb b	Sr c	Y h	Zr hb	Nb b	Mo bh	Tc h	Ru ch	Rh c	Pd c	Ag c	Cd h
Cs b	Ba b	La ch	Hf hb	Ta b	W b	Re h	Os ch	Ir c	Pt c	Au c	Hg –

Cubic Close-packed (Face-centred cubic)

In this structure atoms are arranged at the corners and at the centres of all the six faces of a cube. This type of close packing of atoms belongs to *ABCABC*... type of arrangement which has been discussed in detail in the last section. In this structure each atom has 12 nearest neighbours as shown in Fig. 4.10(a).

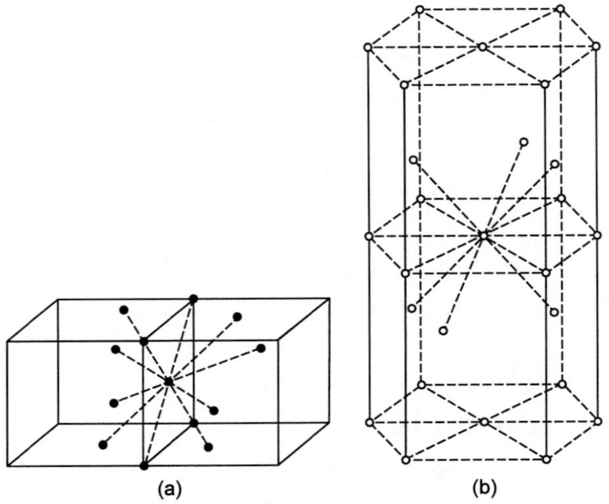

Fig. 4.10 (a) and (b)

Hexagonal Close-packed

In this arrangement, atoms are located at the corners and centre of two hexagons which are placed parallel to each other and three more atoms in a parallel plane midway between these two planes. This arrangement is obtained when we have *ABABA*... type of close packing of atoms discussed in the previous section. Each atom in this arrangements has also 12 nearest neighbours as shown in Fig. 4.10 (b).

Body-centred Cubic

This arrangement of spheres (or atoms) is not exactly close packed. This structure can be obtained if spheres in the first layer (marked *A*) of close packing are slightly opened up. As a result none of these spheres are in contact with each other. Such an arrangement is shown in Fig. 4.11(a). The second layer of spheres (marked *B*) may be placed on top of the first layer, so that each sphere of the second layer is in contact with four spheres of the layer below it. Successive building of the third layer will be exactly like the first layer (*i.e.,* on top of *A*). If this pattern of building layers is repeated infinitely we get an arrangement as shown in Fig. 4.11(b). In a body centred cubic arrangement, the

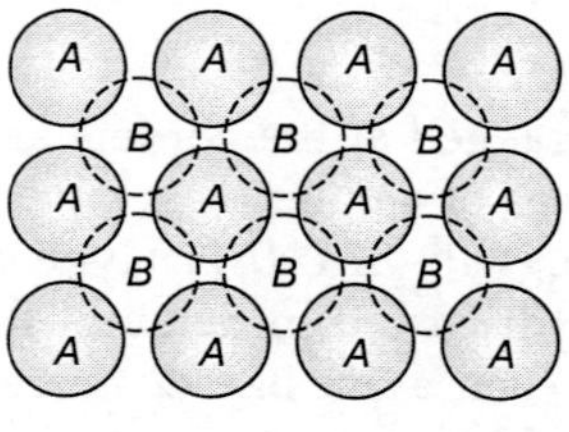

Fig. 4.11 (a) Body-centred cubic packing of spheres.

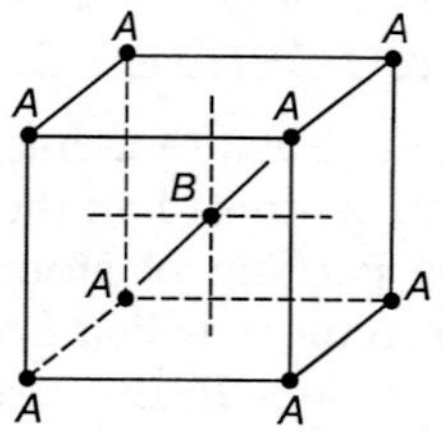

Fig. 4.11 (b) Body-centred cubic arrangement.

atoms occupy corners of a cube with an atom at its centre. In this arrangement each sphere is in contact with eight other spheres (for spheres in the layer just above and four spheres in the layer just below) and so the coordination number in this type of arrangement is only eight. The structure is known as body-centred cubic (bcc). As has already been mentioned, this arrangement of packing is not exactly close packed, and only 68% of the total volume is actually occupied.

Some Other Characteristics

It has been observed that those metals which crystallize in cubic form are more malleable and ductile than those which crystallize in the hexagonal system. Since, malleability (*i.e.,* beating into sheets) and ductility (drawing metal into wires) are related to deformation in crystals, it may be said that crystals with cubic symmetry are easily deformed. Deformation in crystals may mean sliding of one plane of atoms over other planes. Since, the cubic close packed structure contains four sets of parallel close-packed layers, therefore, metals with this structure will have more opportunities for slipping of one layer over the other. Examples of metals with cubic structure which are easily deformed are copper, silver, gold, ion, nickel, platinum, etc. On the other hand, hexagonal close-packed structure contains only one set of parallel close-packed layers. Therefore, the chances of slipping of planes in hexagonal close-packed structures are very little. Metals which show this structure, *e.g.,* chromium, molybdenum, magnesium, zinc, etc., are less malleable, harder and more brittle. Since, iron can adopt both these types of arrangements depending upon temperature, therefore, this is the reason why iron can exhibit a wide variety of properties.

Table 4.4 **Summary on Structures of Metals**

S. No.	Property ↓ Structure →	Cubic close packed (ccp)	Hexagonal close packed (hcp)	Body centred cubic (bcc)
1.	Arrangement of packing	Close packed	Close packed	Not close packed
2.	Volume occupied	74%	74%	68%
3.	Type of packing	*ABCABC*...	*ABABABA*...	–
4.	Coordination number	12	12	8
5.	Other characteristics	Malleable and ductile	Less malleable, hard and brittle	Malleable and ductile
6.	Examples	Cu, Ag, Au, Pt	Cr, Mo, V, Zn	Alkali metals, Fe

Bonding in Metals

Metals exhibit very distinct properties. Any theory of bonding in metals must be able to explain particularly two characteristic properties of metals.

(i) Their high electrical and thermal conductivity.

(ii) Each atom in a metallic crystal has a very high coordination number (8 or 12), *i.e.,* each atom is surrounded by a large number of other atoms.

The first property suggests that electrons in metals are relatively free to move under the influence of an applied potential. The second property suggests that bonding between one atom in metal and its neighbours cannot be normal electron-pair links (like in a normal covalent bond) with metals exhibiting high coordination numbers. There is no simple way in which an atom can form **eight** or **twelve** simultaneous electron-pair bonds.

Molecular Orbital Theory of Metals (Band Theory)

A procedure analogous to our earlier discussion of molecular orbital theory of bonding in molecules, was developed by Helix Block in 1928 to formulate a theory of metallic bond. In this model, the entire metal is considered as a big molecule and molecular orbitals are obtained which cover the entire metal.

In our earlier discussion on MO theory, we had observed that combination of two atomic orbitals (each contributed by one atom) combine to give two molecular orbitals (MOs), one bonding MO and the other anti-bonding MO. If we have three atoms contributing one AO each, the three AOs combine to give three MOs one bonding MO, one non-bonding MO and the third on anti-bonding MO. On similar lines, it can be shown that combination of four AOs from four atoms gives rise to four MOs, two bonding MOs and two antibonding MOs. Similarly, if we have N atoms, each atom contributing one atomic orbital [N is Avogadro's number, 6.023×10^{23} atoms], combining to form N MOs. Since, the number of MOs is very large, the energy levels of MOs are very close together that they form a continuous energy band. Such a close group of energy levels is called an **energy band.**

The molecular orbitals can no longer be treated as discrete energy levels, but are treated as an energy band. The formation of an energy band depends on :

(i) The close proximity of a large number of atoms, and

(ii) The energy difference between pure atomic orbitals.

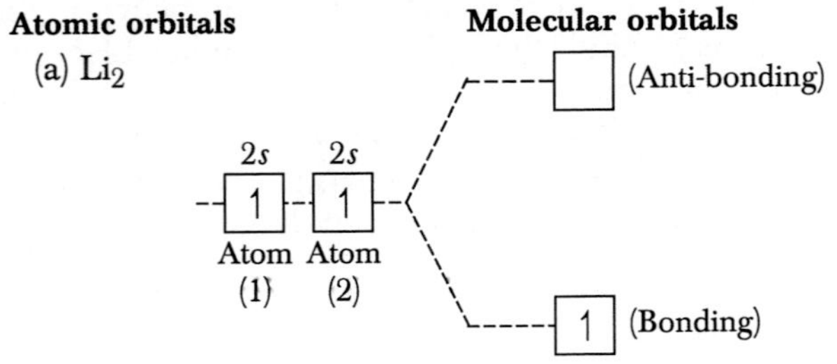

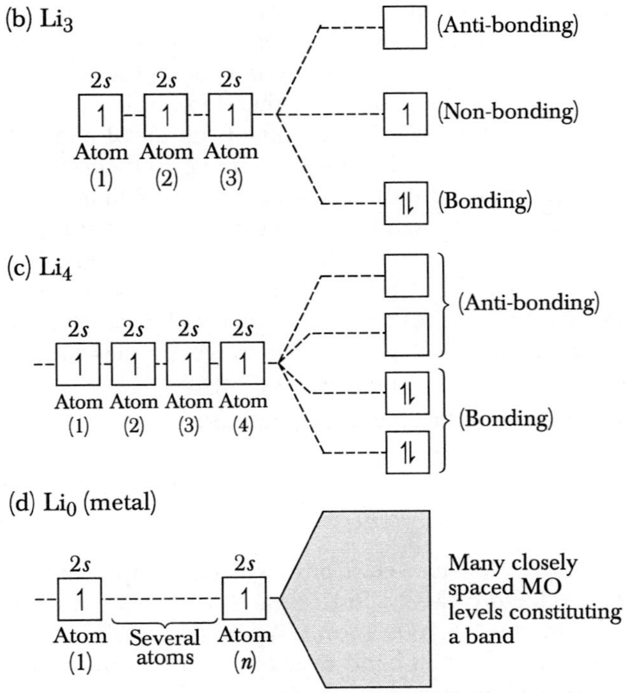

Fig. 4.12 Formation of molecular orbitals into band in metals (Lithium).

The entire process can be demonstrated by showing the formation of these energy bands for the formation of lithium [Fig. 4.12 and 4.13(a)] and beryllium [Fig. 4.13(b)]. The electronic configuration of lithium.

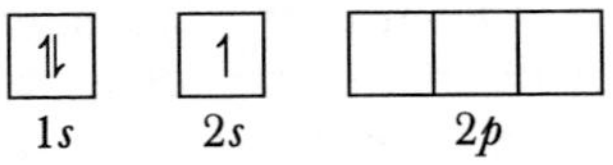

Since, lithium has only one valence electron per atom and two electrons can be accommodated in an MO, it is, therefore, obvious that for lithium only half the MOs in the 2s valence band are filled.

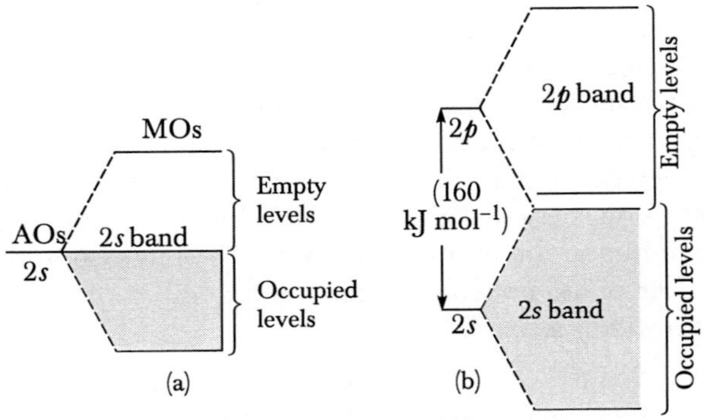

Fig. 4.13 (a) Half-filled 2s band of lithium metal (b) Overlapping 2s and 2p band of Be.

If a small amount of energy is supplied to the system an electron can easily move from an occupied band to an unoccupied part. The MOs extend over all the atoms in the metal. The electrons are, therefore, able to move throughout the three dimensions of the metal and this fact accounts for the high thermal and electrical conductivity of metals. For example, in lithium only half of the 2*s* band is filled with electrons and there is no energy gap between the filled and the unfilled MOs (Fig. 4.13 a). The lithium 2*s* electrons with little disturbance can move into the unoccupied part of the valence band, so that they can move throughout the crystal. Lithium thus behaves as a metal.

Beryllium atom has the configurations,

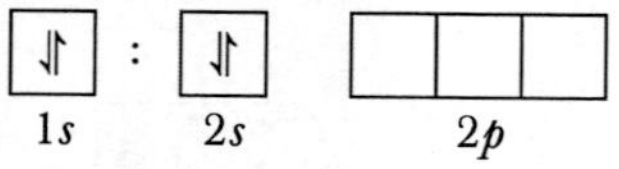

Therefore, valence electrons would occupy the 2*s* valence band of MOs. Just as the 2*s* AOs from a band of MOs, the 2*p* AOs form a 2*p* band of MOs. The upper part of the 2*s* band overlaps with the lower part of the 2*p* band (Fig. 4.13 b). Because of this overlap of the bands, some part of 2*p* band gets occupied while some part of the 2*s* band remains unoccupied. The electrons can be easily perturbed to an unoccupied level in the conduction band, where they can move throughout the crystal. Thus, Be behaves as a metal.

In the **vapour state** (say sodium metal), the atoms are free and far away from each other and therefore the electrons occupy distinct energy levels. But as the atoms come close to each other, the energy gap between the levels is also **reduced** and as the atoms condense to form a metal, an energy band is formed and the bands overlap. This situation for the overlapping of 3*s* and 3*p* valence orbitals is shown diagrammatically in Fig. 4.14. The inner electrons occupy localized orbitals, but the valence orbitals merge into energy bands which represents delocalisation of electrons resulting in free movement of electrons in the energy band over the entire crystal. It may be remembered that the width of any given band depends upon the amount of interaction between the atomic orbitals. It does not depend upon the number of atoms. The increase in the number of atoms only increases the number of energy levels within a band.

The arrangement of electrons in the energy levels determines the characteristics of a metal.

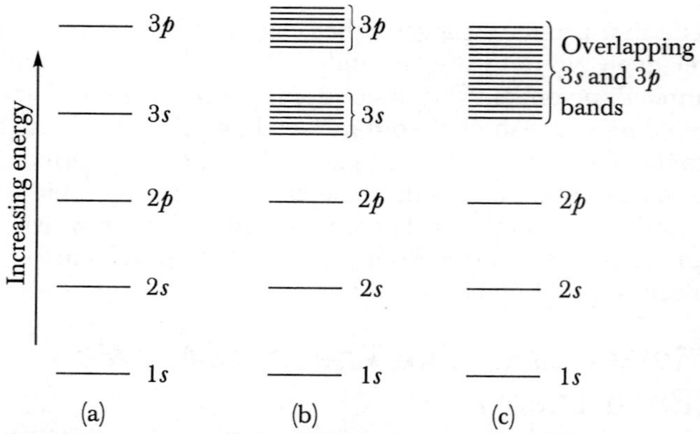

(a) Free gaseous atoms of Na with discrete energy levels.

(b) Atoms of Na approaching each other for metal formation.

(c) Metal formation leads to an overlap of valence band and conduction band.

Fig. 4.14

Conductors, Semiconductors and Insulators

Conductors

In metals or electrical conductors, either the valence band is only partly filled or the valence and conduction bands overlap. There is no gap between filled and unoccupied levels. Only a slight perturbation can cause movement of electrons.

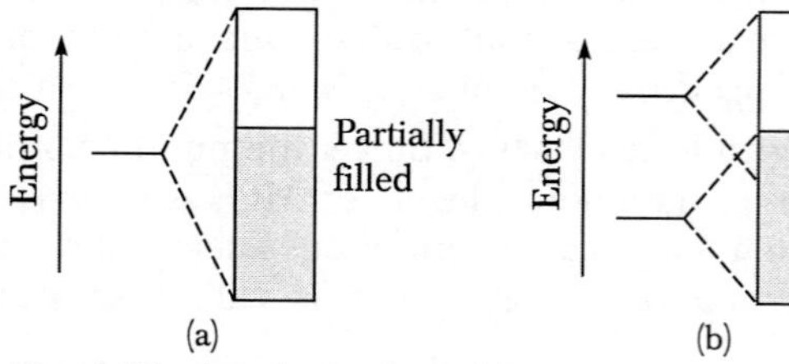

Fig. 4.15 Conductor (metals)
(a) Partly filled valence band
(b) Valence and conduction bands overlap.

Insulators

In insulators (generally non-metals), the valence band is full (no movement of electrons is possible within this band) and there is a wide energy gap between the valence band and the next empty band. Electrons cannot be promoted to the higher energy band and therefore there is no movement of current. Examples are boron and carbon. The energy gap in carbon is about 120 kcal mol^{-1}, which is very large.

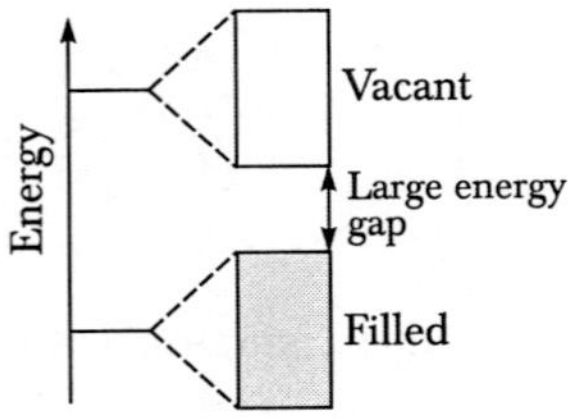

Fig. 4.16 Insulators.

Semiconductors

Semiconductors are practically insulators. However, the energy gap between the valence band and conduction band is **quite small.** For example, the energy gap in silicon is only 2.5 kcal mol^{-1} and in germanium is 14 kcal mol^{-1}. Thermal energy is able to promote some electrons from the fully filled valence band into the empty conduction band. The unpaired electron in the valence band and the promoted electron in the conduction band can conduct current. The **conductivity** of **semiconductors increases with temperature** since the number of electrons which get promoted from the valence band to the conduction band increases with temperature.

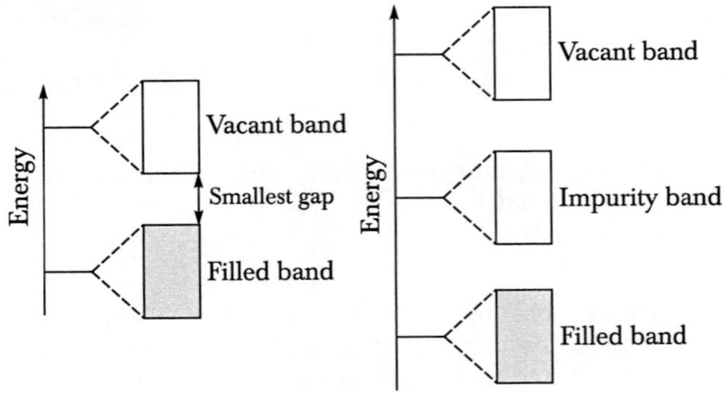

(a) (b)

Fig. 4.17 (a) Semiconductor
(b) Semiconductor with impurity.

Both *n*-type or *p*-type semiconductors are prepared by doping an insulator with a suitable impurity. The band created by the impurity (atoms of another element) lies in between the conduction and the valence bands in the insulator, *i.e.,* it acts as a bridge so that electrons are easily excited from the insulator bands to the impurity bands or *vice-versa.*

Exercise 1

(For Part 'B')

1. Calcium cyanamide reacts with steam to form ammonia and......
   (a) $Ca(OH)_2$ (b) CaO
   (c) $Ca(HCO_3)_2$ (d) $CaCO_3$
2. Lithium has much higher ionisation energy than caesium but in aqueous solution, Li is a more powerful reducing agent because
   (a) the outermost shell e^- is more easily lost by Li
   (b) the outermost e^- is more easily lost by Cs
   (c) the hydration energy of Li^+ is high
   (d) the hydration energy of Cs^+ is high
3. Amongst the following hydroxides,the one which has the lowest value of K_{sp} at ordinary temperature is
   (a) $Mg(OH)_2$ (b) $Ca(OH)_2$
   (c) $Ba(OH)_2$ (d) $Be(OH)_2$
4. Electric cookers have a coating that protects them against fire. The coating is made of
   (a) heavy lead (b) magnesium oxide
   (c) zinc oxide (d) sodium sulphate
5. Microcosmic salt when heated strongly, a transparent bead is formed which is used in identification of
   (a) ZnO (b) Al_2O_3 (c) Fe_2O_3 (d) SiO_2
6. The products of the electrolysis of concentrated common salt solution are
   (a) $Na + Cl_2$ (b) $H_2 + O_2$
   (c) $NaOH + H_2 + Cl_2$ (d) $NaOH + Cl_2 + O_2$
7. The principal products obtained on heating iodine with concentrated caustic soda solution are
   (a) NaOI + NaI (b) $NaIO_3 + NaI$
   (c) $NaOI + NaIO_3 + NaI$ (d) $NaIO_4 + NaI$
8. The chloride that can be extracted with ether is
   (a) NaCl (b) LiCl
   (c) $BaCl_2$ (d) $CaCl_2$
9. Which of the following hydride is most stable?
   (a) CsH (b) NaH
   (c) KH (d) LiH
10. Sulphates of which of the following does not form alum?
    (a) Cs (b) K (c) Na (d) Li
11. K_2CS_3 can be called potassium
    (a) sulphocyanide (b) thiocarbide
    (c) thiocarbonate (d) thiocyanate
12. The setting of plaster of Paris takes place with
    (a) loss of CO_2 (b) hydrolysis
    (c) hydration (d) dehydration
13. Alkali metals in liquid ammonia are blue in colour because
    (a) an ion pair is formed
    (b) an amide ion is formed
    (c) they contain alkali metal cations
    (d) the free electron is trapped in solvent cage
14. Which reagent would enable you to remove SO_4^{2-} ions from solution containing both SO_4^{2-} and Cl^- ions?
    (a) NaOH (b) Pb^{2+}
    (c) $Ba(OH)_2$ (d) $BaSO_4$
15. When HCl gas is passed through saturated solution of $BaCl_2$ a white ppt. is obtained. This is due to
    (a) impurities in $BaCl_2$
    (b) impurities in HCl
    (c) precipitation of $BaCl_2$
    (d) formation of complex
16. Complete the following reaction using following option (s).
    $$KNO_3(s) + K_{(excess)} \longrightarrow$$
    (a) $K_2O_3 + NO_2$ (b) $K_2O_3 + NO$
    (c) $K_2O + NO_2$ (d) $K_2O + N_2$
17. Identify the products of the reaction
    $$NaNH_2 + C \longrightarrow$$
    (a) $NaCN + H_2\uparrow$ (b) $Na_2CN_2 + H_2\uparrow$
    (c) $Na_2(CN)_2 + H_2\uparrow$ (d) $Na_2CN_2 + C_2H_6\uparrow$
18. Identify the products and complete the reaction
    $$NaNH_2 + N_2O \longrightarrow$$
    (a) $Na_2O + N_2 + H_2O$
    (b) $NaN_3 + H_2O$
    (c) $Na_2O + NaN_3 + H_2O$
    (d) $N_2 + NaN_3 + H_2O$
19. In the following reaction identify the products
    $$KNO_3 + C \longrightarrow$$
    (a) $K_2CO_3 + NO_2$ (b) $K_2CO_3 + N_2$
    (c) $K_2CO_3 + CO_2$ (d) $K_2CO_3 + CO_2 + N_2$
20. Identify the products in the following reaction
    $$KNO_3 + KNH_2 \longrightarrow$$
    (a) $KN_3 + H_2O$ (b) $KN_3 + KOH$
    (c) $KOH + NH_3$ (d) $KN_3 + KOH + NH_3$
21. Which of the following elements are called bridge elements?
    (a) Li and Na (b) Be and Mg
    (c) Na and Mg (d) Li and Be

22. Which of the following is the correct order of increasing second ionization energy?
(a) Be < C < B < N < O < F < Ne < He < Li
(b) Li < He < Ne < F < O < N < B < C < Be
(c) O < N < B < C < Be < F < Ne < He < Li
(d) He < Ne < Li < O < N < B < C < Be < F

23. What is the nature of CO when it reacts with NaOH?
(a) Acidic (b) Basic
(c) Amphoteric (d) None of these

24. Which is/are not correct configuration of *s*-block elements?
(a) $[Ar]\,3d^{10}\,4s^2$ (b) $[Ar]\,3d^{10}\,4s^1$
(c) Both (a) and (b) (d) None of these

25. Select the correct statement(s).
(a) Li_3N is stable
(b) LiCl is predominantly covalent
(c) Li_2CO_3 decomposes into oxides while other alkali carbonates are thermally stable
(d) All of the above

26. Alkali metals resemble IB (copper family) in the following respects
(a) +1 valency
(b) sulphates are water soluble
(c) oxides are strong base
(d) oxides are strong acids

27. Which of the following is preferentially formed on reaction of oxygen and potassium?
(a) K_2O (b) KO_2 (c) K_2O_2 (d) K_2O_3

28. CO_2 gas along with solid (*Y*) is obtained when sodium salt (*X*) is heated. (*X*) is again obtained when CO_2 gas is passed into aqueous solution (*Y*). (*X*) and (*Y*) are
(a) Na_2CO_3, Na_2O (b) $NaHCO_3$, Na_2CO_3
(c) Na_2CO_3, NaOH (d) Na_2CO_3, $NaHCO_3$

29. CO_2 cannot be obtained by heating
(a) Na_2CO_3 (b) Li_2CO_3
(c) $CaCO_3$ (d) $Ca(HCO_3)_2$

30. Some of alkali metal salts are coloured. Na_2CrO_4-Yellow, $KMnO_4$-Pink, K_2MnO_4-Green. It is due to
(a) cations are coloured ions
(b) anions are coloured ions
(c) both (a) and (b) are correct
(d) both of the above are incorrect

31. Molten sodium chloride conducts electricity due to the presence of
(a) Na-atom (b) Cl-atom
(c) ions (d) free electrons

32. All alkali metals form following compound except
(a) amide, MNH_2
(b) basic oxides
(c) superoxide like KO_2
(d) ionic 'salt-like' hydride *M*H

33. Which is not the *s*-block element?
(a) $1s^2, 2s^2, 2p^1$ (b) $1s^2, 2s^1, 2p^1$
(c) $[Ar]\,4s^1\,4p^1$ (d) $[Ar]\,4s^2\,3d^{10}\,4p^6\,5s^1$

34. Nitrate can be converted into metal oxide on heating in case of
(a) Li (b) Mg
(c) Both (a) and (b) (d) None of these

35. Which is the incorrect statement?
(a) The heats of hydration of the dipositive alkaline earth metal ions decrease with an increase in their ionic size.
(b) $NaNO_3$ forms Na_2O on heating.
(c) Hydration of alkali metal ion is less than that of IIA.
(d) Alkaline earth metal ions, because of their much larger charge to size ratio, exert a much stronger electrostatic attraction on the oxygen of water molecule surrounding them.

36. Which has the least molar solubility in H_2O?
(a) LiCl (b) NaCl
(c) KCl (d) CsCl

37. Which of the following mixtures cannot be formed?
(a) $NaHCO_3 + Na_2CO_3$ (b) $NaOH + Na_2CO_3$
(c) $NaHCO_3 + H_2CO_3$ (d) $NaHCO_3 + NaOH$

38. Which are involved in various physiological functions in animals?
(a) Na^+ (b) K^+
(c) Both (a) and (b) (d) None of these

39. Select the correct statement(s).
(a) $CaCO_3$ is more soluble in a solution of CO_2 than in H_2O.
(b) Na_2CO_3 is converted to Na_2O and CO_2 on heating.
(c) Li_2CO_3 is thermally stable.
(d) Presence of $CaCl_2$ or $CaSO_4$ in water causes temporary hardness.

40. The alkalide ion is
(a) paramagnetic (b) diamagnetic
(c) represented as CH_3^+ (d) represented as CH_3^-

41. Select the correct statement(s).
(a) operation of $Na^+ - K^+$ pumbs in biological system.
(b) Mg is present in chlorophyll used in photosynthesis in green plants.
(c) Mg^{2+} ions are necessary for the activation of phosphate transfer enzymes.
(d) All of the above

42. The alkali metals dissolve in liquid ammonia (NH_3), it is found that
(a) the dilute solutions are blue but the colour changes to bronze with increasing concentration
(b) the blue solutions are paramagnetic but the bronze coloured solutions are diamagnetic

(c) the blue colour is due to the presence of solvated electrons
(d) all the facts given above are found

43. Which one of the following is the correct sequence followed by molar ionic conductance of the ions?
(a) $Li^+ < Na^+ < K^+ < Rb^+$ (b) $Rb^+ < K^+ < Na^+ < Li^+$
(c) $Na^+ < K^+ < Rb^+ < Li^+$ (d) $Li^+ < Rb^+ < K^+ < Na^+$

44. M_2O_3 (sesquoxides) is paramagnetic in nature. It is due to the presence of
(a) oxide ion (b) peroxide ion
(c) superoxide ion (d) All of these

45. Which is/are coloured and paramagnetic?
(a) KO_2 (b) K_2O_3
(c) Both (a) and (b) (d) None of these

46. Suboxide of Rb has the formula
(a) RbO_2 (b) RbO_3 (c) Rb_6O (d) Rb_2O_2

47. MO_3 on hydrolysis forms
(a) MOH and H_2 (b) MOH and O_2
(c) MOH and M_2O_2 (d) MOH and H_2O_2

48. Which salt has maximum heat of hydration?
(a) LiCl (b) NaCl
(c) KCl (d) LiCl and KCl equally

49. Maximum heat is absorbed in the dissolution of one mole of
(a) LiCl (b) NaCl
(c) KCl (d) equally

50. Which salt can be used to control humidity?
(a) LiCl (b) NaCl
(c) KCl (d) None of these

51. Sesquoxides is said to be double oxide of
(a) oxide, peroxide (b) oxide, superoxide
(c) peroxide, superoxide (d) peroxide, disuperoxide

52. Which is the best reducing agent?
(a) Li (b) Na
(c) Rb (d) Cs

53. Which is the poorest reducing agent?
(a) Li (b) Na
(c) Rb (d) Cs

54. Mg and Zn does not resemble in the following properties
(a) oxides are amphoteric
(b) carbonates on heating form metal oxides
(c) widely used as electrodes
(d) used to prevent corrosion

55. IIA (alkaline earth metals) and IIB (zinc family) resemble
(a) $MgSO_4 \cdot 7H_2O$ is isomorphous with $ZnSO_4 \cdot 7H_2O$
(b) IIA and IIB cations not precipitated by H_2S in acidic medium
(c) Both (a) and (b)
(d) None of the above

56. Be and Al show diagonal relationship hence, both have
(a) same degree of electronegativity
(b) approximately same charge/radius ratio
(c) amphoteric nature of oxides
(d) All of the above

57. Going down to IIA group, following properties increase except
(a) hydration energy
(b) ionic radius
(c) solubility of hydroxide in H_2O
(d) thermal stability of carbonates

58. Lattice energy of IIA group compounds (oxides, carbonates, fluorides)
(a) decreases as size of the ion increases
(b) increases as size of the ion increases
(c) constant for a given type of anion
(d) All the above are incorrect

59. Which of the following statements are true about IIA group elements?
(a) Be is amphoteric
(b) MH_2 is ionic 'salt-like' hydride
(c) All form nitrides in air
(d) All the above are correct statements

60. Which are true statements about *s*-block elements?
(a) Oxides are basic except BeO
(b) Metals are obtained by the electrolysis of fused chlorides
(c) Only one type of valency, +1 for IA and +2 for IIA is shown
(d) All of the above

61. Which is the incorrect statement?
(a) The heats of hydration of the dipositive alkaline earth metal ions decrease with an increase in their ionic size
(b) Hydration of alkali metal ion is less than that of IIA
(c) Alkaline earth metal ions, because of their much larger charge to size ratio, exert a much stronger electrostatic attraction on the oxygen of water molecule surrounding them
(d) $NaNO_3$ forms Na_2O on heating

62. Which of the following is/are correct statement(s)?
(a) Ca^{2+} ions are important in blood clotting
(b) $Ca_3(PO_4)_2$ is part of bones
(c) $3Ca_3(PO)_2 \cdot CaF_2$ is part of enamel on teeth
(d) All of the above are correct

63. $BaC_2 + N_2 \xrightarrow{\Delta} A$; $CaC_2 + N_2 \xrightarrow{\Delta} B$
(A) and (B) are
(a) $BaCN_2$, $CaCN_2$ (b) $Ba(CN)_2$, $CaCN_2$
(c) $Ba(CN)_2$, $Ca(CN)_2$ (d) None of these

64. Which is used to treat acid indigestion?
(a) $Be(OH)_2$ (b) $Mg(OH)_2$
(c) $Ca(OH)_2$ (d) KOH

65. Select the correct statement(s).
(a) BeH_2 contains three-centre two-electron bond
(b) CaH_2, SrH_2 and BaH_2 are ionic
(c) Beryllium and magnesium hydride are covalent and polyatomic
(d) All of the above

66. Select the corrects statement(s).
(a) $CaCO_3$ is more soluble in a solution of CO_2 than in H_2O
(b) Li_2CO_3 is thermally stable
(c) Na_2CO_3 is converted into N_2O and CO_2 on heating
(d) Presence of $CaCl_2$ or $CaSO_4$ in water causes temporary hardness

67. A metal *M* readily forms water soluble MSO_4. It also forms oxide *MO* which becomes inert on heating. Hydroxide $M(OH)_2$ is insoluble in water but soluble in NaOH solution. What is *M*?
(a) Be (b) Mg
(c) Ca (d) Ba

68. Which one of the following has magnesium?
(a) Vitamin B_{12} (b) Chlorophyll
(c) Haemocyanin (d) Carbonic anhydrase

69. In which of the following the hydration energy is higher than the lattice energy?
(a) $MgSO_4$ (b) $BaSO_4$
(c) $SrSO_4$ (d) $RaSO_4$

70. A covalent chloride is
(a) $BeCl_2$ (b) $MgCl_2$
(c) $CaCl_2$ (d) NaCl

71. Which of the following halide of calcium insoluble in water?
(a) CaF_2 (b) $CaCl_2$
(c) $CaBr_2$ (d) CaI_2

72. Lightest alkaline earth metal is
(a) Be (b) Mg
(c) Ca (d) Sr

73. The activity of alkaline earth metals as reducing agent
(a) increases from Be to Ba
(b) decreases from Be to Ba
(c) increases from Be to Ca and decreases from Ca to Ba
(d) decreases from Be to Ca and increases from Ca to Ba

74. Bleaching powder loses its power on keeping for a long time because
(a) it absorbs moisture
(b) it changes into calcium hypochlorate
(c) it changes into calcium chloride and calcium hydroxide
(d) it changes into calcium chloride

75. Ripening of fruits can be carried out in presence of
(a) NaCl (b) CaC_2
(c) $CaCl_2$ (d) Na_2SO_4

76. The right order of the solubility of sulphates of alkaline earth metals in water
(a) Be > Ca > Mg > Ba > Sr
(b) Sr > Ba > Mg > Ca > Be
(c) Mg > Ca > Be > Ba > Sr
(d) Be > Mg > Ca > Ba > Sr

77. Burning of Mg is extinguished by
(a) throwing ice (b) throwing water
(c) throwing sand (d) throwing N_2 liquid

78. The solubility of carbonates decreases down the magnesium group due to a decrease in
(a) interionic attraction
(b) hydration energy of cations
(c) lattice energies of solids
(d) entropy of solution formation

79. The charge/size ratio of a cation determines its polarising power. Which one of the following sequences represents the increasing order of the polarising power of cationic species : K^+, Ca^{2+}, Mg^{2+}, Be^{2+}?
(a) $Be^{2+} < Mg^{2+} < Ca^{2+} < K^+$
(b) $Ca^{2+} < Be^{2+} < Mg^{2+} < K^+$
(c) $K^+ < Ca^{2+} < Mg^{2+} < Be^{2+}$
(d) $Mg^{2+} < Ca^{2+} < Be^{2+} < K^+$

80. Solution of Na metal in liquid NH_3 is a strong reductant due to the presence of
(a) sodium atoms (b) solvated electrons
(c) sodium amide (d) sodium hydride

Exercise 2
(For Part 'C')

1. Which of the following is the correct order of increasing lattice energy?

(i) $NaI < NaBr < NaCl < NaF$
(ii) $LiI < LiBr < LiCl < LiF$
(iii) $CsCl < RbCl < KCl < NaCl < LiCl$

(a) (i) only (b) (ii) only
(c) (i) and (ii) (d) (i), (ii) and (iii)

2. Select the incorrect statement.
(a) Ag^+ forms complexes, Na^+ does not
(b) NaCl is water soluble, AgCl is insoluble
(c) Na_2CO_3 is thermally stable while Ag_2CO_3 decomposes into Ag, CO_2 and O_2
(d) NaCl and AgCl both give colour in flame when ignited

3. Na and Li are placed in dry air, we get
(a) Na_2O, Li_3N, Li_2O
(b) Na_2O, Li_2O
(c) $NaOH, Na_2O, Li_2O$
(d) $Na_2O, Li_2O, Li_3N, Li_2O$

4. The stability of K_2O, K_2O_2 and KO_2 is in order $K_2O < K_2O_2 < KO_2$. This increasing stability at the size of metal ion increases is due to stabilization of
(a) smaller cations by smaller anions through melting point
(b) smaller cations by larger anions through melting point
(c) larger cation by smaller anions through lattice energy effects
(d) larger cation by larger anions through lattice energy effects

5. Selct the correct statement(s).
(a) MO_2 contains the paramagnetic ion O_2^-.
(b) O_2^- is stable only in the presence of large cations as K, Rb and Cs.
(c) KO_2 is paramagnetic and has orange colour.
(d) K_2O has antifluorite structure.

6. Sesquoxide (M_2O_3) of alkali metals
(a) are coloured diamagnetic substance
(b) are colourless diamagnetic substance
(c) are dark-coloured paramagnetic substances
(d) have been prepared by careful thermal decomposition of MO_2

7. Select the correct statement(s).
(a) Alkali metals ozonides are colourless and diamagnetic.
(b) Alkali metals ozonides are coloured and paramagnetic.
(c) Sesquoxide of alkali metals are peroxides disuperoxides $(M^+)_4(O_2^{2-})(O_2^-)_2$.
(d) Sesquoxides are paramagnetic due to the presence of superoxide ion O_2^-.

8. Select the correct statement(s).
(a) All alkali metals form solid bicarbonates.
(b) Except $LiHCO_3$, all alkali metals bicarbonates are solid.
(c) Li_2CO_3 decomposes into CO_2 and Li_2O.
(d) Na_2CO_3 decomposes into CO_2 and Na_2O.

9. Select the correct statement(s).
(a) Ionic mobility of hydrated Li^+ ion is smaller than that of hydrated Cs^+ ion
(b) Hydrated Cs^+ is more conducting that hydrated Na^+ ion
(c) Ionic mobility of hydrated $Cs^+ > Rb^+ > K^+ > Na^+ > Li^+$
(d) Radius of hydrated Li^+ ion is smaller than that of hydrated Cs^+ ion

10. Which is/are true statement(s)?
(a) Hydration of alkali metal ion is less than that of IIA
(b) The heats of hydration of the dipositive alkaline earth metal ions decrease with an increase in their ionic size
(c) Alkaline earth metal ions, because of their much larger charge to size ratio exert a much stronger electrostatic attraction on the oxygen of water molecule surrounding them
(d) None of the above statements is correct

11. Which are true statements about *s*-block elements?
(a) Metals are obtained by the electrolysis of fused chlorides
(b) Oxides are basic except BeO
(c) $+1$ valency by alkali metals and $+2$ valency by alkaline earth metals is shown
(d) Carbonates are thermally stable

Assertion & Reason

Codes
(a) Both A and R are true and R is the correct explanation of A.
(b) Both A and R are true but R is not the correct explanation of A.
(c) A is true but R is false.
(d) A is false but R is true.

12. **Assertion (A)** Lithium does not form alums.
Reason (R) Small $[Li(H_2O)_6]^+$ is too small to form a stable lattice required for alum formation.

13. **Assertion (A)** The superoxide MO_2 contains the paramagnetic ion O_2^-.

Reason (R) O_2^- is stable in the presence of large cations as K, Rb, Cs.

14. **Assertion (A)** The mobility of sodium ion is lower than that of potassium ion.
Reason (R) The ionic mobilities depend on the effective radius of the ion.

15. **Assertion (A)** Among the alkali metals, lithium salts exhibit the least electrical conductance in aqueous solution.
Reason (R) Smaller the radius of the hydrated cation, lower is the electrical conductance in aqueous solutions.

16. **Assertion (A)** Group 2 metals have higher melting points when compared to the group 1 metals.
Reason (R) +2 charge on the cations in the metallic lattice causes them to be more strongly attracted to the 'sea of electrons' and making it difficult to pull them apart.

17. **Assertion (A)** The metals of group 2 (except Be) form ionic compounds.
Reason (R) Electropositive character and the reducing property increase on moving down the group.

18. **Assertion (A)** Divalent compounds of alkaline earth metals are diamagnetic.
Reason (R) M^{2+} ions of group 2 have noble gas configuration.

19. Be and Al do not resemble in
(a) both become passive on reaction with HNO_3 due to the formation of oxide layer
(b) their chlorides are Lewis bases
(c) chlorides exist in polymeric form
(d) hydroxides are soluble in alkali as well as in acid

20. Which is most stable out of the following?
(a) $[Be(H_2O)_4]^{2+}$ (b) $[Mg(H_2O)_4]^{2+}$
(c) $[Ca(H_2O)_4]^{2+}$ (d) $[Sr(H_2O)_4]^{2+}$

21. Be and Al resemble in the following but not in
(a) both are rendered passive by HNO_3
(b) both form amphoteric oxides
(c) both form electron deficient hydrides
(d) both have *sp*-hybridization in their compounds

22. Select the correct statement(s).
(a) Al forms AlF_6^{3-}, an octahedral complex
(b) Be and Al show diagonal relationship
(c) Be forms tetrahedral complexes $[Be(C_2O_4)_2]^{2-}$
(d) All of the above are correct

23. Amongst the following metals, which form peroxide on heating in excess oxygen?
1. Lithium 2. Sodium
3. Barium 4. Aluminim
(a) 1 and 2 (b) 1 and 3
(c) 2 and 3 (d) 3 and 4

24. K, KO_2, Ca, CaH_2, Na, Na_2O_2, Li and Li_2O react with water. Which of the following substances yield the same gaseous product?
(a) K and KO_2
(b) Na and Na_2O_2
(c) Ca and CaH_2
(d) Li and Li_2O

25. Consider the following compounds
1. K_2CO_3 2. $MgCO_3$
3. $CaCO_3$ 4. $BeCO_3$
Which one of the following arrangement in the increasing order of their thermal stabilities is correct?
(a) 1 < 2 < 3 < 4 (b) 4 < 3 < 2 < 1
(c) 4 < 2 < 3 < 1 (d) 2 < 4 < 1 < 3

26. Which of the following properties of alkaline earth metals increase with the increase in atomic number?
1. Ionisation potential
2. Solubility of hydroxide
3. Solubility of sulphates
4. Decomposition temperature of carbonates
Select the correct answer using the codes give below.
(a) 1 and 2 (b) 1 and 3
(c) 2 and 3 (d) 2 and 4

27. Match Column I with Column II and select the correct answer.

	Column I (Compounds)		Column II (Associated uses)
A.	Magnesium chloride	1.	As a purgative
B.	Barium sulphate	2.	As a fertilizer
C.	Magnesium sulphate	3.	As a constituent of sorrel cement
D.	Calcium cyanamide	4.	In the preparation of lithopone
		5.	In the manufacture of plaster of Paris

	A	B	C	D
(a)	1	2	3	4
(b)	5	4	3	2
(c)	3	1	5	2
(d)	3	4	1	2

28. The oxides which are soluble in sodium hydroxide are
1. As_2O_3 2. Sb_2O_3
3. SnO
The correct options are
(a) 1 and 2 only (b) 1, 2 and 3
(c) 1 and 3 (d) 1, 2, 3

29. Chile salt petre contains
1. iodine 2. sodium
3. bromine 4. nitrate

The correct options are
(a) 1 and 2 only (b) 1, 2 and 3 only
(c) 1 only (d) 1, 2 and 4 only

30. Electrometallurgical process (electrolysis of fused electrolyte) is employed to extract
1. iron 2. aluminium
3. sodium
The correct answer is
(a) 1 and 2 (b) 2 and 3
(c) 1 and 3 (d) 1, 2 and 3

31. Highly pure dilute solution of sodium in liquid NH_3
(a) shows blue colour
(b) exhibits electrical conductivity
(c) produces sodium amide
(d) produces hydrogen gas

32. Sodium nitrate decomposes above ~ 800°C to give
(a) N_2 (b) O_2
(c) NO_2 (d) Na_2O

33. The alkaline earth metal which does not give flame colour is
(a) Mg (b) Ca
(c) Sr (d) Be

34. Consider the following statements.
1. Calcium fluoride is soluble in water.
2. Barium sulphate is soluble in water.
3. Barium hydroxide is insoluble in water.
4. Magnesium sulphate is soluble in water.
The correct statements are
(a) 1, 2 only (b) 2, 3 only
(c) 1, 2, 3 only (d) 1, 2, 3 and 4

35. Which salt on heating gives a mixture of two gases?
(a) $RbNO_3$ (b) $LiNO_3$
(c) $Ca(NO_3)_2$ (d) $Mg(NO_3)_2$

36. The carbonate which on heating gives CO_2 is
(a) Li_2CO_3 (b) $SrCO_3$
(c) K_2CO_3 (d) $BeCO_3$

37. Magnesium burns in air to give
(a) MgO (b) Mg_3N_2
(c) $MgCO_3$ (d) None of these

38. Mg is used in
(a) flash light photography (b) signal fires
(c) pyrotechniques (d) None of these

39. Which of the following are amphoteric?
(a) MgO (b) BeO
(c) ZnO (d) As_2O_3

40. $Ba(OH)_2$ is used to estimate the amount of
(a) N_2 (b) CO_2
(c) CO (d) SO_3

41. Cavity size of each molecule of crown ether matches the ionic size of cation. Match Column I with Column II.

Column I		Column II	
A.	18 crown 6	1.	2.90 Å
B.	15 crown 5	2.	1.20 Å
C.	12 crown 4	3.	2.66-3.2 Å
		4.	1.7-2.2 Å

Codes

	A	B	C
(a)	2	1	4
(b)	1	4	3
(c)	3	4	2
(d)	2	3	1

42. Interior of crown ether is made up of
(a) hydrocarbon atoms (b) glycol molecules
(c) oxygen atoms (d) cations or anions

43. Crown ether exterior (boundary wall) is made up of
(a) alternate carbon and oxygen atoms
(b) hydrocarbon atoms only
(c) oxygen atoms only
(d) semipermeable membrane

44. Cryptands are
(a) ethers
(b) crown ethers
(c) bicyclic ethers
(d) macrobicyclic polyethers

45. Nonactin antibiotic is
(a) synthetic antibiotic binding with Na^+ions
(b) synthetic crown ether
(c) natural complex binding with K^+ions
(d) tighting against dengue fever

Assertion & Reason

Codes
(a) Both A and R are true and R is the correct explanation of A.
(b) Both A and R are true but R is not the correct explanation of A.
(c) A is true but R is false.
(d) A is false but R is true.

46. **Assertion (A)** $NaHCO_3$ and $KHCO_3$ exist in solid state.
Reason (R) Alkali metal ions are basic in nature.

47. **Assertion (A)** K_2CO_3 cannot be prepared by Solvay process.
Reason (R) $KHCO_3$ being fairly soluble in water does not precipitate in carbonation tower.

48. **Assertion (A)** FrCl has CsCl structure with coordination number 8.
Reason (R) CN 8 is favoured by the large cation size.

49. **Assertion (A)** $CrClO_4$ and Fr_2PtCl_6 are the salts of low solubility.

Reason (R) All alkali metal ions form insoluble salts.

50. **Assertion (A)** Li is used in photocells.

Reason (R) Cs have lower ionisation energy than Li.

51. **Assertion (A)** Ether can extract LiCl from the aqueous solution of a mixture of LiCl, NaCl and KCl.

Reason (R) Hydration of Li^+ ion is greater than that of Na^+ and K^+ ions.

52. **Assertion (A)** NaOH cannot be stored in a vessel made of Al or Zn.

Reason (R) A protective layer of oxide is formed on the surface of the metal.

Directions (Q. Nos. 53 to 57)
Large ring crown ethers are cyclic polymers and given the name *x* crown *y*. They have the ability to bind cations strongly and selectively crown ethers are more soluble in non-polar organic solvents. A relationship between the structure of crown ether and its ability to solvate a particular cation has been observed.

53. Crown ethers are cyclic polymers of
(a) glycerol (b) ethylene glycol
(c) 1,3-propanediol (d) 1, 4-butandiol

54. In *x* crown *y*
(a) *x* is total number of methylene atoms in the ring and *y* is number of total atoms.
(b) *x* is total number of oxygen atoms in the ring and *y* is the total number of methylene atoms.
(c) *x* is total number of atoms in the ring and *y* is number of oxygens.
(d) *x* is total number of oxygen atoms in the ring and *y* is total number of atoms in the ring.

55. 18 crown 6 shows high affinity for
(a) Na^+ (b) Li^+
(c) K^+ (d) Mg^{2+}

56. 15 crown 5 shows high affinity for
(a) Na^+ (b) Li^+ (c) K^+ (d) Mg^{2+}

57. 12 crown 4 shows high affinity for
(a) Li^+ (b) K^+
(c) Na^+ (d) Rb^+

Directions (Q. Nos. 58 and 59)
Dilute solutions of alkali metals in liquid NH_3 are blue. It is the ammoniated electron which is responsible for the blue colour of the solution and the electrical conductivity is due to the ammoniated cation, $[M(NH_3)_x]^+$ as well as the ammoniated electron, $[e(NH_3)_y]^-$, values of *x* and *y* depend on the extent of solvation (by NH_3). Dilute solutions are paramagnetic due to free electrons.

58. What happens if alkali metal is allowed to react with concentrated ammonia solution?
(a) Paramagnetic character of solvated electrons is retained.
(b) Solvated electrons associate to form electron-pairs and paramagnetic character decreases.
(c) Reducing character is increased.
(d) Reducing character is not affected.

59. Ammoniated solutions of alkali metals are reducing agents due to the presence of free or solvated electrons and can reduce
(a) O_2 to O_2^{2-}
(b) $K_2[Ni(CN)_4]$ to $K_4[Ni(CN)_4]$
(c) Both (a) and (b)
(d) None of the above

Directions (Q. NOs. 60 and 61)
$NaHCO_3$ can be used on its own to make cakes or bread "rise". Baking powder is more commonly used and contains $NaHCO_3$, $Ca(H_2PO_4)_2$ and starch. An improved combination baking powder contains about 40% starch, 30% $NaHCO_3$, 20% $NaAl(SO_4)_2$ and 10% $Ca(H_2PO_4)_2$.

60. $Ca(H_2PO_4)_2$ in baking powder
(a) behaves as an acid in moist condition and decomposes $NaHCO_3$ to give CO_2
(b) behaves as a base in moist condition and gives H_3PO_4
(c) behaves as a binder
(d) behaves as a filler

61. In improved baking powder, $NaAl(SO_4)_2$
(a) makes the decomposition of $NaHCO_3$ faster
(b) slows the decomposition of $NaHCO_3$
(c) acts as filler
(d) makes the bread rise

Directions (Q. Nos. 62 and 63)
The crystal structures of $NaHCO_3$ and $KHCO_3$ both show hydrogen bonding, but are different. Answer the following questions based on this

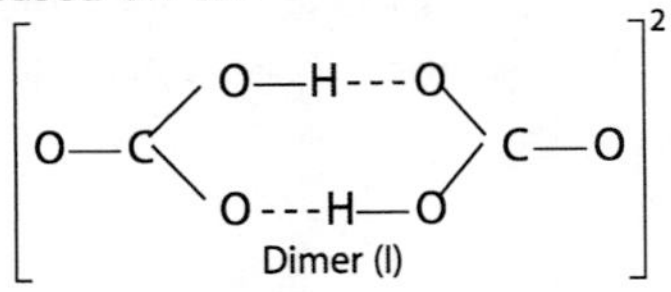

Dimer (I)

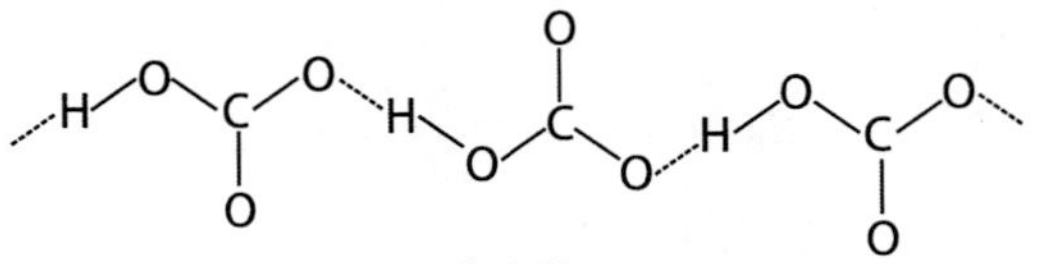

Chain II

62. Which structure is adopted by $NaHCO_3$?
(a) I (b) II
(c) Both (a) and (b) (d) None of these

63. Which structure is adopted by $KHCO_3$?
(a) I (b) II
(c) Both (a) and (b) (d) None of these

Answers

Exercise 1

1. (d)	**2.** (c)	**3.** (d)	**4.** (b)	**5.** (d)	**6.** (c)	**7.** (b)	**8.** (b)	**9.** (d)	**10.** (d)
11. (c)	**12.** (c)	**13.** (d)	**14.** (c)	**15.** (c)	**16.** (d)	**17.** (a)	**18.** (b)	**19.** (d)	**20.** (d)
21. (c)	**22.** (a)	**23.** (a)	**24.** (c)	**25.** (d)	**26.** (a)	**27.** (b)	**28.** (c)	**29.** (a)	**30.** (b)
31. (c)	**32.** (c)	**33.** (a)	**34.** (c)	**35.** (b)	**36.** (c)	**37.** (d)	**38.** (c)	**39.** (a)	**40.** (b)
41. (d)	**42.** (d)	**43.** (a)	**44.** (c)	**45.** (c)	**46.** (c)	**47.** (b)	**48.** (a)	**49.** (c)	**50.** (a)
51. (d)	**52.** (a)	**53.** (b)	**54.** (a)	**55.** (c)	**56.** (d)	**57.** (a)	**58.** (a)	**59.** (d)	**60.** (d)
61. (d)	**62.** (d)	**63.** (b)	**64.** (b)	**65.** (d)	**66.** (b)	**67.** (a)	**68.** (b)	**69.** (a)	**70.** (c)
71. (a)	**72.** (c)	**73.** (a)	**74.** (d)	**75.** (b)	**76.** (a)	**77.** (a)	**78.** (c)	**79.** (c)	**80.** (b)

Exercise 2

1. (d)	**2.** (d)	**3.** (a)	**4.** (d)	**5.** (a,b,c,d)	**6.** (c,d)	**7.** (c,d)	**8.** (b,c)	**9.** (a,b,c)	**10.** (a,b,c)
11. (a,b,c)	**12.** (a)	**13.** (b)	**14.** (a)	**15.** (c)	**16.** (a)	**17.** (a)	**18.** (b)	**19.** (b)	**20.** (a)
21. (d)	**22.** (d)	**23.** (c)	**24.** (c)	**25.** (c)	**26.** (d)	**27.** (d)	**28.** (d)	**29.** (d)	**30.** (b)
31. (a,b)	**32.** (a,b,d)	**33.** (a,d)	**34.** (c)	**35.** (b,c,d)	**36.** (a,b,d)	**37.** (a,b)	**38.** (a,b,c)	**39.** (b,c,d)	**40.** (b,d)
41. (b)	**42.** (c)	**43.** (b)	**44.** (d)	**45.** (c)	**46.** (a)	**47.** (a)	**48.** (a)	**49.** (c)	**50.** (d)
51. (b)	**52.** (c)	**53.** (b)	**54.** (c)	**55.** (c)	**56.** (a)	**57.** (a)	**58.** (b)	**59.** (c)	**60.** (a)
61. (b)	**62.** (b)	**63.** (a)							

Hints & Solutions

Exercise 1

1. $$\underset{\text{Calcium cyanamide}}{CaCN_2} + H_2O + CO_2 \longrightarrow CaCO_3 + \underset{\text{Cyanamide}}{H_2N\cdot CN}$$

3. Solubility of alkaline earth metal hydroxides increases on moving down the group due to decrease in lattice energy and

$$K_{sp} \propto \text{solubility}$$

Thus, $Be(OH)_2$ has the lowest K_{sp} at ordinary temperature.

6. $NaCl \rightleftharpoons Na^+ + Cl^-$

At anode

$$2Cl^- + 2e^- \longrightarrow Cl_2$$

At anode

$$Na^+ \longrightarrow + e^- \xrightarrow[Na]{H_2O} NaOH$$

$$2H^+ \longrightarrow H_2 + 2e^-$$

7. With hot and concentrated solution of NaOH, halogens form halate and halide ions.

$$OH^- + X_2 \longrightarrow X\overline{O}_3 + X^-$$

$$NaOH + I_2 \longrightarrow NaIO_3 + NaI$$

9. Li being smaller in size, forms most stable compound with small hydride ion.

12. When water is added to plaster of Paris, it takes 2/3 moles of water of crystallisation and sets into a hard mass, called gypsum.

$$CaSO_4\cdot\frac{1}{2}H_2O + \frac{3}{2}H_2O \longrightarrow \underset{\text{Gypsum}}{CaSO_4\cdot 2H_2O}$$

16. $2KNO_3 + 10K(\text{excess}) \longrightarrow 6K_2O + N_2$

17. $NaNH_2 + C \longrightarrow NaCN + H_2\uparrow$

21. Na is called bridge element since it links group IA and group IB

$$Li_3 - Na_{11} \begin{cases} K_{19} - Rb_{37} - Cs_{55} - Fr_{87} \\ Cu_{29} - Ag_{47} - Au_{79} \end{cases}$$

Similarly, Mg links IIA and IIB

$$Be_4 - Mg_{12} \begin{cases} Ca_{20} - Sr_{38} - Ba_{56} - Ra_{88} \\ Zn_{30} - Cd_{48} - Hg_{80} \end{cases}$$

23. $$\underset{\text{Acid}}{CO} + \underset{\text{Base}}{NaOH} \longrightarrow HCOONa$$

Thus CO is acidic in this reaction.

27. KO_2 is stable due to larger anion O_2^- which polarises K^+.

28. $\underset{(X)}{NaHCO_3} \longrightarrow \underset{(Y)}{Na_2CO_3} + H_2O + CO_2$

$Na_2CO_3 \xrightarrow{CO_2} NaHCO_3$

31. In molten state

$$NaCl(l) \rightleftharpoons Na^+ + Cl^-$$

Because of the presence of free ions, it is a conductor of electricity in molten state.

34. $2LiNO_3 \longrightarrow Li_2O + 2NO_2 + \frac{1}{2}O_2$

$Mg(NO_3)_2 \longrightarrow MgO + 2NO_2 + \frac{1}{2}O_2$

35. $2NaNO_3 \longrightarrow 2NaNO_2 + O_2$

36. Molar solubility is in mol L^{-1}

$LiCl = 19.6$

$NaCl = 6.2$

$KCl = 4.8$

$RbCl = 7.5$

$CsCl = 11.0$

37. $NaHCO_3$ is acidic and decomposes by NaOH forming Na_2CO_3.

$$\underset{\text{Acid}}{NaHCO_3} + \underset{\text{Base}}{NaOH} \longrightarrow Na_2CO_3 + H_2O$$

43. Smaller the cation, larger is the ease of hydration and thus smaller is the molar ionic conductance.

Ionic size $Li^+ < Na^+ < K^+ < Rb^+$

Ease of hydration $Li^+ > Na^+ > K^+ > Rb^+$

Size of hydration ion $Li^+ > Na^+ > K^+ > Rb^+$

Molar ionic conductance $Li^+ < Na^+ < K^+ < Rb^+$

44. M_2O_3 actually exists as M_4O_6 $[M_4(O_2^{2-})(O_2^-)_2]$

O_2^- is paramagnetic.

45. KO_2 is paramagnetic due to O_2^-.

K_2O_3 is actually K_4O_6

$$K_4\underset{\text{Peroxide}}{(O_2^{2-})} \quad \underset{\text{Superoxide}}{(O_2^-)_2}$$

Thus, it is also paramagnetic.

48. $\Delta H_{(Hydration)} = \Delta H_{hydration}(\text{cation}) + \Delta H_{hydration}(\text{anion})$

49. $\Delta H_{solution} = \Delta H_{hydration} - \Delta H_4$

$\Delta H_{solution}(LiCl) = -499 - 382 + 840$

$= -41 \text{ kJ mol}^{-1}$

$NaCl = -4 \text{ kJ mol}^{-1}$

$KCl = +16 \text{ kJ mol}^{-1}$

54. MgO is basic whereas ZnO is amphoteric.

57. Hydration energy varies inversely with size.

58. Lattice energy $\propto \frac{1}{\text{size of ions}} \propto$ charge of ion.

63. $BaC_2 + N_2 \xrightarrow{\Delta} \underset{\substack{\text{Barium cyanide} \\ \text{'A'}}}{Ba(CN)_2}$

$CaC_2 + N_2 \xrightarrow{\Delta} \underset{\text{Calcium cyanamide}}{CaCN_2}$

69. Due to large SO_4^{2-} ion, the lattice energy of alkaline earth metal sulphates remains the constant but hydration energy decreases on moving downwards. Thus, in case of $MgSO_4$, hydration energy is higher than the lattice energy.

73. As the size increases, tendency to lose outer e^- increases and hence, reducing tendency increases.

Exercise 2

1. Lattice energy $\propto \frac{1}{\text{size of ions}} \propto$ charge of ions.

The order of size are

$F^- < Cl^- < Br^- < I^-$

$Li^+ < Na^+ < K^+ < Rb^+ < Cs^+$

2. AgCl does not impart any colouration to the flame.

3. $2Na + O_2 \longrightarrow Na_2O$

$2Li + O_2 \longrightarrow Li_2O$

$6Li + 3N_2 \longrightarrow 2Li_3N$

15. Li salts exhibit the least electrical conductance in aqueous solution due to largest size of hydrated Li ion.

19. $BeCl_2$ and $AlCl_3$ being electron deficient behave as Lewis acids.

20. A small ion has the high tendency to get hydrate.

23. Sodium and barium have large size, so they form stable compound with larger peroxide ion.

24. $Ca + 2H_2O \longrightarrow Ca(OH)_2 + H_2$

$CaH_2 + 2H_2O \longrightarrow Ca(OH)_2 + 2H_2$

26. On moving downwards in IIA group, ionisation potential and solubility of sulphates decreases while solubility of hydroxide and thermal stability increases.

30. Electrometallurgical process is used to extract highly reactive metals like aluminium, sodium, potassium etc.

32. $2NaNO_3 \longrightarrow 2NaNO_2 + O_2$

$\xrightarrow{\sim 800°C} Na_2O + O_2 + N_2$

33. Be and Mg because of their small size and high ionisation energy do not impart any colouration to flame.

34. Solubility of alkaline earth metal sulphates decreases while that of hydroxides increases on moving down the group.

35.

$$LiNO_3 \longrightarrow Li_2O + NO_2 + O_2$$
$$Ca(NO_3)_2 \longrightarrow CaO + NO_2 + O_2$$
$$Mg(NO_3)_2 \longrightarrow MgO + NO_2 + O_2$$
$$2RbNO_3 \longrightarrow 2RbNO_2 + O_2$$

36. All alkaline earth metal carbonates and lithium carbonate when heated, give CO_2 gas.

37. In air oxygen and nitrogen both are present.

$$2Mg + O_2 \longrightarrow 2MgO$$
$$3Mg + N_2 \longrightarrow Mg_3N_2$$

40. $Ba(OH)_2$ gives $BaCO_3$ and $BaSO_4$ with CO_2 and SO_3 respectively, the amount of which can be calculated.

47. $KHCO_3$ is highly soluble in water, so K_2CO_3 cannot be prepared by Solvay process.

49. Mostly alkali metal salts are soluble.

50. Cs has very low IE, that why it is used in photocells.

52. Al and Zn both dissolve in NaOH.

53. Crown ethers has the following structure,

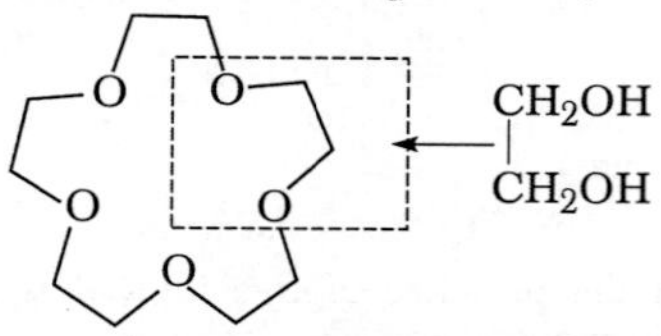

Thus, these are the cyclic polymers of glycol.

54. *x* crown *y* mean *x* atoms are in the ring and *y* oxygen atoms are there.

55-57. A metal with large size fits into a large crown ether.

18 crown 6	K^+
15 crown 5	Na^+
12 crown 4	Li^+

62. $NaHCO_3$ exists as monomer.

63. $KHCO_3$ exists as dimer.

5

p-Block Elements-I (Group-13)

Syllabus

- Boranes, Carboranes, Borazine, Boron Nitride, Halides, Boric Acid, Borax, Aluminium Chloride
- Synthesis, Structure, Bonding, Properties and Uses
- Industrial Importance of the Compounds

The elements having $ns^2 np^6$ configuration are called *p*-block elements. It includes group 13 to 18 of the Periodic Table, placed at the extreme right side of the table. Group 13 is the first group of this block and contains the elements having three electrons in their valence shell, *i.e.*, the outermost shell.

This group constitutes the following elements :

Name	Symbol	Valence electronic configuration
Boron	B	$2s^2\ 2p^1$
Aluminium	Al	$3s^2\ 3p^1$
Gallium	Ga	$4s^2\ 4p^1$
Indium	In	$5s^2\ 5p^1$
Thallium	Tl	$6s^2\ 6p^1$

The general valence electronic configuration is $ns^2\ np^1$. Atoms of elements in this group have fewer valence electrons than the atomic orbitals available for occupation *i.e.*, they are electron deficient elements.

(ns^2) (np^1)

Atoms of these elements can easily make available these orbitals in their chemical reactions with other atoms. In other words, we may say that compounds of elements of this group will show strong tendency to act as Lewis acids, *i.e.*, because of their desire to complete their octet. This property of Lewis acidic nature or electron deficiency will be greatly manifested in their compounds.

Boron Hydrides (BORANES) (Preparation, Properties, Structure and Bonding of Diborane)

Boron hydrides differ from carbon hydrides (*i.e.*, hydrocarbons) that they do not occur in nature because of their great affinity for water and oxygen. The compound BH_3 which would be analogous to BF_3 does not exist because hydrogen atoms lacks the electrons that would be needed to participate in $B \leftarrow H$ π-back bonding and compensate for the incomplete octet of boron. BH_3 can exist only in complex formation with donors such as $H_3B \cdot CO, H_3B \cdot N(CH_3)_3$ and $H_3B \cdot PF_3$. Molecules of BH_3 apparently dimerise spontaneously when they come in contact with each other to form diborane, B_2H_6.

Preparation of Diborane, B_2H_6

Diborane cannot be synthesised directly from its elements as it has a positive enthalpy and a positive free energy of formation, ΔG_f°. This may be attributed to very strong bonds in elemental boron and H_2 which will have to be overcome before forming boron hydrides.

1. Diborane can be easily prepared in small quantities on a laboratory scale by the reaction of iodine on sodium borohydride ($Na\,BH_4$) in diglyme a high boiling ether $[(CH_2OCH_2CH_2)_2O]$.

$$2NaBH_4 + I_2 \xrightarrow{\text{Diglyme}} \underset{\text{(98\% yield)}}{B_2H_6} + 2NaI + H_2$$

2. By the action of phosphoric acid on magnesium boride.

$$Mg_3B_2 + H_3PO_4 \longrightarrow \text{(Mixture of boranes)} \xrightarrow{\text{(Heat)}} B_2H_6$$

3. It can be prepared by the reduction of boron halides by any one of the following methods :

(i) Reduction of boron trifluoride with lithium hydride.

$$8BF_3 + 6LiH \xrightarrow{\text{Ether}} 6LiBF_4 + B_2H_6$$

(ii) Reduction of boron trichloride with lithium aluminium-hydride. This reaction gives quantitative yield.

$$4BCl_3 + 3LiAlH_4 \longrightarrow 2B_2H_6 + 3LiCl + 3AlCl_3$$

(iii) Reduction of boron trichloride vapours with molecular hydrogen by passing a silent electric discharge at low pressure.

$$2BCl_3 + 6H_2 \longrightarrow B_2H_6 + 6HCl$$

(iv) It is quantitatively obtained by the reaction of sodium borohydride with boron trifluoride.

$$4BF_3 + 3NaBH_4 \longrightarrow 3NaBF_4 + 2B_2H_6$$

Properties of Diborane

1. Physical state

It is a colourless gas (b.p., – 92.6° and m.p. – 164.9°C) with a foul smell and is extremely toxic.

2. Thermal stability

It is stable only at low temperatures. On heating at temperatures above 100°C in sealed vessels, it decomposes to form a number of higher hydrides.

$$B_2H_6 \xrightarrow{\text{Heat}} B_4H_{10}, B_5H_9, B_5H_{11}, B_6H_{10} \text{ etc.}$$

3. Reaction with oxygen

It burns in oxygen liberating a lot of energy. It is spontaneously flammable.

$$B_2H_6 + 3O_2 \longrightarrow B_2O_3 + 3H_2O; \quad \Delta H = -2165 \text{ kJ mol}^{-1}$$

Therefore, B_2H_6 is used as a rocket fuel.

4. Hydrolysis

It is immediately hydrolysed by water to give hydrogen and therefore acts as a reducing agent.

$$B_2H_6 + 6H_2O \longrightarrow 2B(OH)_3 + 6H_2\uparrow$$

It reacts with methanol in a similar reaction.

$$B_2H_6 + 6MeOH \longrightarrow 2B(OMe)_3 + 6H_2\uparrow$$

5. Reaction with halogens

It reacts with halogens under different conditions.

$$B_2H_6 + Cl_2 \xrightarrow[\text{at 25°C}]{\text{Explosive}} \underset{\text{Chlorodiborane}}{B_2H_5Cl} + HCl$$

$$B_2H_6 + Br \xrightarrow[\text{100°C}]{\text{Only rapid at}} \underset{\text{Bromodiborane}}{B_2H_5Br} + HBr$$

6. Reaction with halogen acids (H*X*)

Diborane reacts with halogen acids to yield halodiborane.

$$B_2H_6 + HCl \longrightarrow B_2H_5Cl + H_2$$

$$B_2H_6 + HI \longrightarrow \underset{\text{Iododiborane}}{B_2H_5I} + H_2$$

7. Reaction with ammonia

It reacts with ammonia to give different products under different reaction conditions.

(a) $$B_2H_6 \xrightarrow[\text{(low temp.)}]{\text{Excess } NH_3} \underset{\text{Diammoniate of diborane}}{B_2H_6 \cdot 2NH_3}$$

or $[(NH_3)_2BH_2]^+[BH_4]^-$

(b) $B_2H_6 \xrightarrow[\text{(high temp.)}]{\text{Excess } NH_3} \underset{\text{Boron nitride}}{(BN)_x}$

Boron nitride, BN is a white crystalline solid. It is a giant molecule with a graphite-like structure in which boron and nitrogen atoms alternate in the rings giving structure with B N bond length of 145 pm. The bonds are formed by sp^2 hybrid orbitals on boron and nitrogen atoms; the remaining electrons are used for π-bond formation. The layers are arranged in a manner so that boron atoms in one layer are immediately over the nitrogen atoms in an adjacent layer.

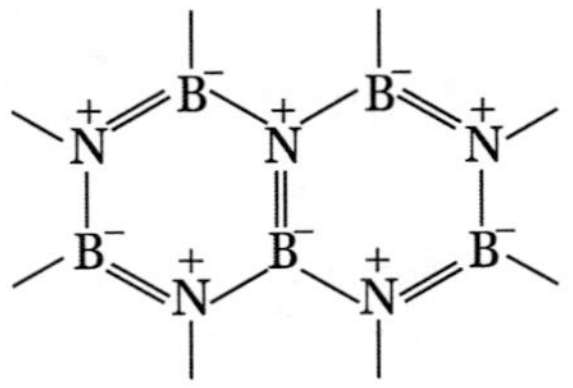

(c) $3B_2H_6 + 6NH_3 \xrightarrow[250°C]{} \underset{\substack{\text{Borazole or borazine} \\ \text{('inorganic benzene')}}}{B_3N_3H_6} + 12H_2$

8. **Reaction with alkalies**

Diborane dissolves in strong alkaline solutions (KOH) giving metaborates and H_2 gas is evolved.

$$B_2H_6 + 2KOH + 2H_2O \longrightarrow \underset{\substack{\text{Potassium} \\ \text{metaborate}}}{2KBO_2} + 6H_2$$

9. **Reaction with metals**

Diborane reacts slowly (over a few days) with electro positive metals such as Na, K, Ca or their amalgams. The reaction becomes fast in ethers (used as solvent).

$$2B_2H_6 + 2Na \longrightarrow NaBH_4 + NaB_3H_8$$

$B_3H_8^-$ was the first polyborate anion prepared by this reaction. This anion is now prepared by the following reaction :

$$B_2H_6 + NaBH_4 \xrightarrow[100°C]{\text{Diglyme}} NaB_3H_8 + 2H_2$$

10. **Reaction with amines**

$$B_2H_6(g) + 2R_3N(g) \longrightarrow 2BH_3—NR_3(l)$$

These complexes can serve as a source of diborane in chemical reactions since they can be stored or shipped safely.

11. **Reaction with hydrides**

It reacts with sodium hydride to form a complex hydride.

$$2NaH + B_2H_6 \longrightarrow \underset{\text{Sodium borohydride}}{2Na^+[BH_4]^-}$$

12. **Reaction with CO**

It combines with carbon monoxide at 100°C and 20 atm pressure to form borine carbonyl, BH_3CO. This is the only example known where CO forms a complex with a non-transition element.

$$B_2H_6 + 2CO \longrightarrow 2BH_3CO$$

13. **Reaction with boron halides**

It reacts with BCl_3 or BBr_3 to give B_2H_5Cl or B_2H_5Br.

$$BCl_3 + B_2H_6 \longrightarrow B_2H_5Cl + BHCl_2$$
$$BBr_3 + B_2H_6 \longrightarrow B_2H_5Br + BHBr_2$$

14. **Reaction with ethers and thioethers**

It combines with ether or thioether to form addition compounds.

$$B_2H_6 + 2(CH_3)_2O \longrightarrow 2BH_3 \leftarrow O(CH_3)_2$$
$$B_2H_6 + 2(C_2H_5)_2S \longrightarrow 2BH_3 \leftarrow S(C_2H_5)_2$$

15. **Reaction with pyridine**

In combines with pyridine to form a salt.

$$B_2H_6 + \underset{\text{Pyridine}}{2C_5H_5N} \longrightarrow 2H_3\overset{-}{B}—\overset{+}{N}C_2H_5$$

16. **Reaction with trimethylaluminium**

It reacts with trimethylaluminium to form aluminium borohydride.

$$Al(CH_3)_3 + 2B_2H_6 \longrightarrow B(CH_3)_3 + Al(BH_4)_3$$

17. **Reaction with alcohols**

Diborane reacts with alcohols to form alkoxides.

$$B_2H_6 + 6CH_3OH \longrightarrow 2B(OCH_3)_3 + 6H_2$$
$$B_2H_6 + 4CH_3OH \longrightarrow 2BH(OCH_3)_2 + 4H_2$$

18. **Reaction with tetraalkyllead**

$$B_2H_6 + (CH_3)_4Pb \longrightarrow B_2H_5(CH_3) + (CH_3)_3PbH$$

19. **Reaction with dialkylphosphines**

$$B_2H_6 + 4Me_2PH \longrightarrow \underset{\text{Tetramer}}{\text{Cyclo}\cdot(Me_2PBH_2)_4} + 4H_2$$

$$1.5B_2H_6 + 3Me_2PH \longrightarrow \underset{\text{Trimer}}{\text{Cyclo}\cdot(Me_2PBH_2)_3} + 3H_2$$

20. **Addition to alkenes** (Hydroboration reaction)

Diborane adds to alkenes and alkynes in ether solvents at room temperature to form alkylboranes. This reaction is known as hydroboration. This reaction leads to the formation of organoboranes which yield to a variety of synthetic organic chemistry. Hydroboration is **regiospecific**, the boron showing preferential attachment to the least substituted carbon atom (anti-Markownikoff).

$$3RCH{=}CH_2 + \frac{1}{2}B_2H_6 \longrightarrow B(CH_2CH_2R)_3$$

(i) On refluxing with anhydrous carboxylic acid, it yields the alkane corresponding to the initial alkene.

$$B(CH_2CH_2R)_3 \xrightarrow{RCOOH} \underset{\text{Alkane}}{3RCH_2CH_3}$$

(ii) Oxidative hydrolysis with alkaline hydrogen peroxide gives the corresponding primary alcohol.

$$B(CH_2CH_2R) \xrightarrow{NaOH/H_2O_2} \underset{\text{Primary alcohol}}{3RCH_2CH_2OH}$$

21. **Reducing property**

Diborane is an electrophilic reducing agent and preferentially attacks a molecule at a position of high electron density (borohydrides, BH_4^-, which is a nucleophilic reagent). Reduction can occur with or without bond breaking. For example, $>C{=}O$ is reduced to $>CH_2$ and nitrites are reduced to amines. For example,

$$RCHO \longrightarrow RCH_2OH$$

and $$RC{\equiv}N \longrightarrow RCH_2NH_2$$

The above reactions from (10) to (17) clearly demonstrate that diborane is an electron deficient molecule.

Structure and Bonding of Diborane

Boron hydrides are quite interesting from the point of view of their structures. The determination of structure of boron hydrides was such an intricate problem that William Lipscomb was awarded a Nobel Prize in 1976 for elucidation of their structures.

The simplest boron hydride is quite interesting as there are not enough valence electrons to form the expected number of covalent bonds. There are twelve valence electrons in B_2H_6 (three per boron atoms and one for each H atom) and for the molecule to have an ethane type structure a minimum of fourteen electrons are required as one electron pair required to form each covalent bond.

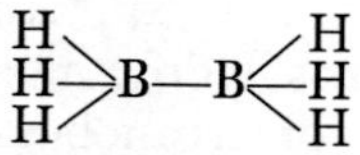

(This structure requires 14 valence electrons but only 12 valence electrons are available)

Therefore, we may conclude that diborane cannot have ethane type structure. Hence, hydrogen bridged structure for diborane was proposed based on the following evidence.

(i) Based on electron diffraction studies, it was concluded that diborane has hydrogen bridged structure as shown in Fig. 5.1.

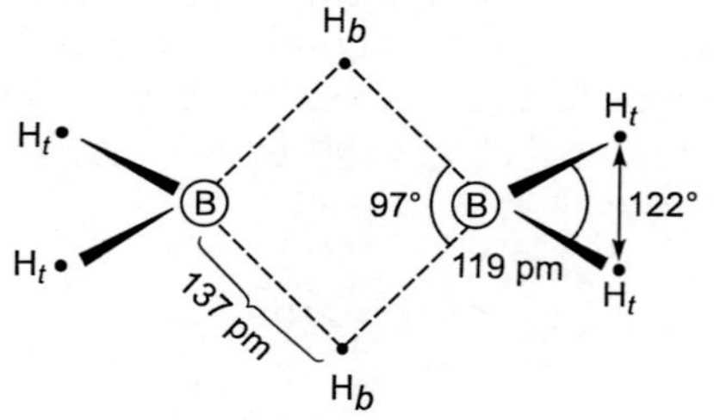

H_t = terminal hydrogen
H_b = bridging hydrogen

Fig. 5.1 Structure of diborane.

Note pm stands for picometer and it reprerents 10^{-12} m. The above structure depicts that there are two types of hydrogen atoms in diborane, namely, H_t type which form normal covalent bonds with boron and H_b type which form bridge between the two boron atoms. The two-bridge hydrogen atoms are in a plane at right angle to the rest of the molecule. Therefore, there is no free rotation between the two boron atoms.

(ii) Specific heat measurements also confirmed that there is no free rotation between the two boron atoms.

(iii) Raman and proton nuclear magnetic resonance (NMR) spectra confirmed that four hydrogen atoms in diborane are different than the other two hydrogen atoms.

(iv) Methylation of diborane also confirmed that four hydrogen atoms in diborane are different than the other two hydrogen atoms as not more than four hydrogen atoms can be methylated to give $(CH_3)_4B_2H_2$.

The nature of the bonds involving bridging hydrogen atoms is now well established. They are different bonds than the conventional two electron bonds. These bridge bonds involve one electron from each boron atom and one from each hydrogen atom. This arrangement involves three atoms with only two electrons.

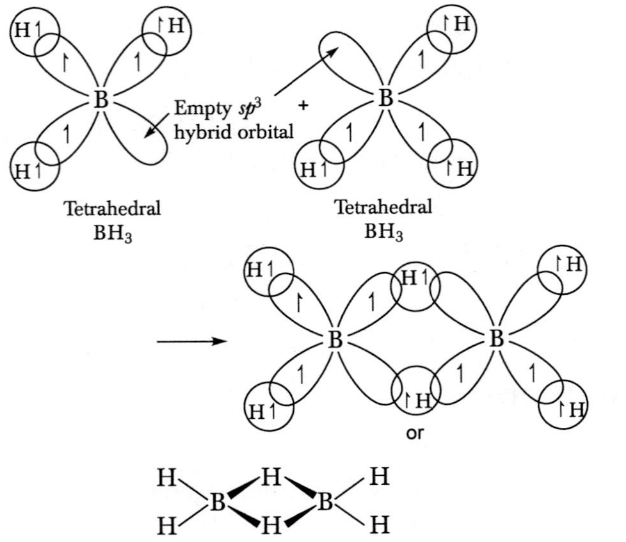

Each boron atom has four sp^3 hybrid orbitals, two of which are used to form bonds to two terminal hydrogen atoms and the other two overlap with 1*s* orbital of hydrogen atoms giving delocalised orbitals covering all three nuclei.

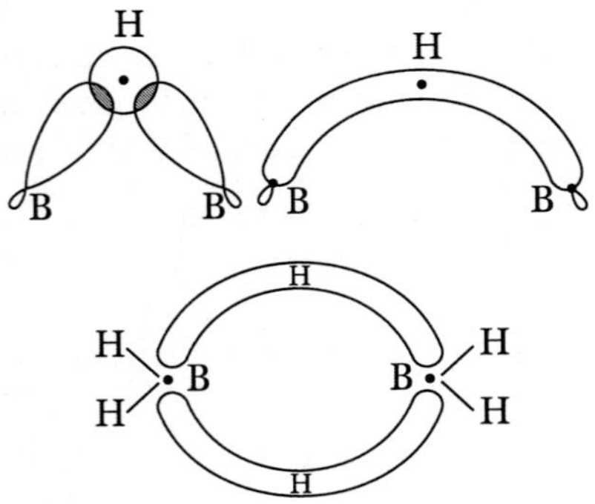

Fig. 5.2 Three centre bond in diborane.

Diborane is thus described as having four two centre B–H bonds and two three centre $B...H_b...B$ bonds. All are sigma covalent bonds having two electrons and therefore account for all the 12 valency electrons. Therefore, terminal B H bonds are commonly referred to as 2*c*—2*e* bonds. The delocalized orbital covering all the three nuclei and containing a pair of electrons is commonly known as three centre electron pair bond (3*c*—2*e*) or banana bond. Such type of 3*c*–2*e* bonds are a common feature of all electron deficient compounds.

We have just discussed that diborane, B_2H_6 has four 2*c* – 2*e* B H bonds and two 3*c*–2*e* B H B bonds.

In terms of M.O. theory, a three centre B H B linkage may be represented as a combination of three orbitals (two sp^3-hybrid orbitals from B and an *s*-orbital of H) resulting in three molecular orbitals.

Note Each bridging BHB bond contains two electrons in the ψ_b bonding M.O.

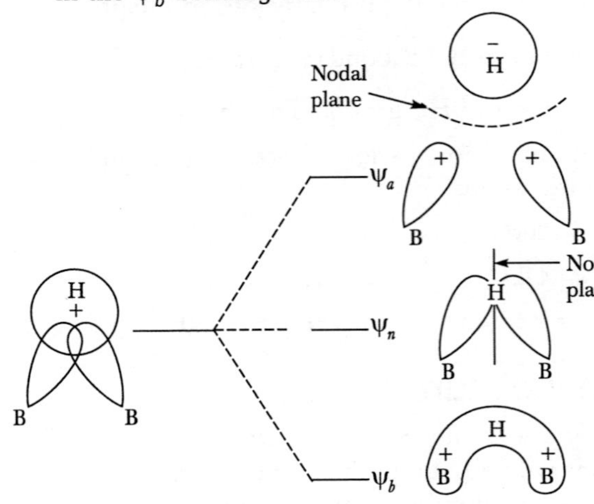

Higher Boranes

Boron forms a large number of hydrides (in addition to diborane). More than 25 neutral boranes and a large number of borane anions have been prepared and characterized. We are only dealing with some very simple higher neutral boranes. These are B_4H_{10}, B_5H_9, B_5H_{11}, B_6H_{10} and $B_{10}H_{14}$.

Classification of Boranes

These can be classified into following categories based on their stoichiometry and structure.

(a) Closo boranes ($B_nH_n^{2-}$)

$B_6H_6^{2-}$

They have completely closed triangulated polyhedral structure.

(b) Nido boranes (B_nH_{n+4})

B_2H_6, B_5H_9, B_6H_{10} and $B_{10}H_{14}$

The word **nido** is derived from the Latin word meaning 'nest'. So they have a nest like open structure.

Arachno-boranes (B_nH_{n+6})

B_4H_{10}, B_5H_{11}

The word **arachno** means spider's web. Their structure is open from both ends. In these compounds, boron atoms occupy *n* contiguous corners of an (*n* + 2) cornered polyhedron.

Styx Number

It is the code system, which represent the overall valence bonding in boranes by four digit number. In this

s = Number of B—H—B bonds (First digit)

t = Number of B B B bonds (Second digit)

y = Number of B B bonds (Third digit)

x = Number of BH_2 groups (Fourth digit)

Styx number for various boranes (on the basis of structures) are as :

$B_2H_6 = 2002$; $B_4H_{10} = 4012$

$B_5H_9 = 4120$; $B_5H_{11} = 3203$

$B_6H_{10} = 4220$; $B_{10}H_{14} = 4620$

Nomenclature

Boranes are usually named by indicating the number of B atoms with a Latin prefix and the number of H atoms by an Arabic number in parentheses.

B_2H_6	diborane (6)
B_4H_{10}	tetraborane (10)
B_5H_9	pentaborane (9)
B_5H_{11}	pentaborane (11)
B_6H_{10}	hexaborane (10)
$B_{10}H_{14}$	decaborane (14)

Preparation

1. Tetraborane (10) (B_4H_{10}) is best prepared by keeping B_2H_6 under pressure at 25° for 10 days.

$$2B_2H_6 \longrightarrow B_4H_{10} + H_2$$

2. (i) Pentaborane-9 (B_5H_9) is prepared by passing a 1 : 5 mixture of B_2H_6 and H_2 at below 1 atm pressure through a furnace maintained at 250°C for 3 s.

   (ii) Alternatively B_5H_9 can be prepared by pyrolysing B_2H_6 for 2.5 days in a hot/cold reactor at 180°/– 80°.

3. Pentaborane-11 (B_5H_{11}) can be prepared in 70% yield by the reaction of B_2H_6 and B_4H_{10} in a hot/cold reactor maintained at + 120°/ – 30°C.

4. Decaborane-14 ($B_{10}H_{14}$) is prepared by pyrolysis of B_2H_6 at 100 – 200°C in the presence of catalytic amounts of Lewis bases such as dimethylether.

5. Synthesis of broron hydrides *via* hydride ion abstraction reactions

   (i) B_2H_6 from BH_4^-

$$M[BH_4] + BX_3 \xrightarrow[\text{r.t.}]{CH_2Cl_2} \frac{1}{2} B_2H_6 + M[HBX_3]$$

$$M = (n\text{-}C_4H_9)_4^+, BX_3 = BCl_3 \text{ or } BBr_3$$

   (ii) B_4H_{10} from $B_3H_8^-$

$$M[B_3H_8] + BX_3 \longrightarrow B_4H_{10} + M[HBX_3] + BH_{\text{residue}}$$

$$M = (n\text{-}C_4H_9)_4^+, BX_3 = BF_3, BCl_3, BBr_3$$

   (iii) B_5H_{11} from $B_4H_9^-$

$$K[B_4H_9] + BX_3 \longrightarrow B_5H_{11} + K[HBX_3] + BH_{\text{residue}}$$

$$(X = F, Cl, Br)$$

Properties

(a) Physical properties

Boranes are colourless, diamagnetic, molecular compounds of low thermal stability.

(b) Reactivity

They are extremely reactive and many boranes are spontaneously flammable in air. All boranes are highly toxic.

The lower hydrides are gases at room temperature but higher hydrides are volatile liquids and solids. The higher molecular weight boranes are much less reactive. For example, decaborane is stable in air.

Compound	Melting point (°C)	Boiling point (°C)	Properties
Diborane (6) B_2H_6	– 165	– 93	Colourless, air sensitive
Tetraborane (10) B_4H_{10}	– 120	18	Colourless, air sensitive
Pentaborane (9) B_5H_9	– 47	60	Colourless, air sensitive
Pentaborane (11) B_5H_{11}	– 122	65	Colourless, air sensitive
Hexaborane (10) B_6H_{10}	– 62	108	Colourless, air sensitive
Decaborane (14) $B_{10}H_{14}$	100	213	Solid, air stable.

(c) Acidic behaviour

B_5H_9 behaves as a weak Bronsted acid. Acidic behaviour increases with increasing size of the borane cluster and arachno-boranes are more acidic than nido boranes.

$$B_5H_9 < B_6H_{10} < B_{10}H_{14} \text{ (nido)}$$

$$B_4H_{10} < B_5H_{11} \text{ (arachano)}$$

Therefore, B_5H_9 can be deprotonated at low temperature by loss of bridging H atom to give $B_5H_8^-$ by using strong MH (M = alkali metal) base.

$$B_5H_9 + NaH \longrightarrow NaB_5H_8 + H_2\uparrow$$

$B_{10}H_{14}$ can be titrated in aqueous media as a monobasic acid

$$B_{10}H_{14} + OH^- \longrightarrow B_{10}H_{13}^- + H_2O$$

(d) Adducts with Lewis bases

Tetraborane undergoes both symmetric and unsymmetric cleavage.

(i) Larger Lewis bases tend to split off BH_3 moieties.

$$B_4H_{10} + 2(CH_3)_3N \longrightarrow (CH_3)_3NB_3H_7 + (CH_3)_3\ NBH_3$$

$$2B_4H_{10} + 2(C_2H_5)_2O \longrightarrow 2(C_2H_5)_2OB_3H_7 + B_2H_6$$

$$2B_4H_{10} + 2(CH_3)_2S \longrightarrow 2(CH_3)_2S\,B_3H_7 + B_2H_6$$

(ii) Small, hard Lewis bases such as OH^- or NH_3 result in unsymmetrical cleavage.

$$B_4H_{10} + 2NH_3 \longrightarrow [H_2B(NH_3)_2]^+ + [B_3H_8]^-$$

$$2B_4H_{10} + 4OH^- \longrightarrow [B(OH)_4]^- + BH_4^- + 2[B_3H_8]^-$$

(iii) B_5H_9 reacts with Lewis bases to form adducts.

$$B_5H_9 + 2P(CH_3)_3 \longrightarrow [B_5H_9\{P(CH_3)_3\}_2]$$

(iv) With NH_3, unsymmetrical cleavage takes place.

$$B_5H_9 + 2NH_3 \xrightarrow{-78^\circ C} [(NH_3)_2BH_2]^+ [B_4H_7]^-$$

Electron addition to $B_{10}H_{14}$ can be carried out by reaction with alkali metals in liquid NH_3 or ethers.

$$B_{10}H_{14} + 2Na \longrightarrow Na_2B_{10}H_{14}$$

Adducts can be prepared by direct reaction.

$$B_{10}H_{14} + 2CH_3CN \longrightarrow B_{10}H_{12}(CH_3CN)_2 + H_2$$

(e) Substitution reactions

The apex-substituted derivatives of B_5H_9 to give 1–X B_5H_8 can be prepared by electrophilic substitution (halogenation or Friedel-Crafts alkylation with RX). Base substituted 2–X B_5H_8 products are obtained when nucleophilic substitution is induced by amines or ethers.

$$B_5H_9 \xrightarrow{I_2/AlX_3} 1\text{-}IB_5H_8 \xrightarrow{\text{Base}} 2\text{-}IB_5H_8$$

1-derivatives can be isomerised into 2-derivatives in the presence of a base. These compounds give the following type reactions

$$2\text{-}ClB_5H_8 + NaMn(CO)_5 \longrightarrow 2\{(CO)_5Mn\}\,B_5H_8$$

(f) Cluster expansion or degradation reaction

Polyhedral boranes undergo both cluster (i) expansion or (ii) degradation reactions :

(i) $$LiB_5H_8 + \frac{1}{2}B_2H_6 \xrightarrow[-78^\circ C]{Et_2O} LiB_6H_{11} \xrightarrow{HCl} B_6H_{12}$$

$$LiB_5H_8 + B_2H_6 \xrightarrow[-78^\circ C]{Me_2O} \{LiB_7H_{14}\} \longrightarrow B_6H_{10} + LiBH_4$$

(This reaction is used for the preparation of B_6H_{10})

(ii) $$[Me_4N][B_5H_8] + 6Pr^1OH \longrightarrow [Me_4N]\,B_3H_8 + 2B(OPr^1)_3 + 3H_2$$

Structures of Higher Boranes

Structures of boranes are shown in Fig. 5.3.

B_4H_{10} It contains 22 valence electrons ($4 \times 3 = 12$ from boron atoms and 10 from 10H atoms). It consists of six 2*c*—2*e* B H bonds, four 3*c*–2*e* B H B bonds and one 2*c*–2*c* B B bonds.

B_5H_9 It contains 24 valence electrons (5×3 from boron atoms and 9 from H atoms). Its structures contains five 2*c*—2*e* B H bonds, four 3*e*–2*e* B H B bonds and one B B B 3*e*–2*e* bond and two 2*c*–2*e* B B bonds.

B_5H_{11} It contains 26 valence electrons. It consists of eight 2*c*–2*e* B H bonds, three 3*c*–2*e* B H B bonds and two B B B 3*c*—2*e* bonds.

B_4H_{10}

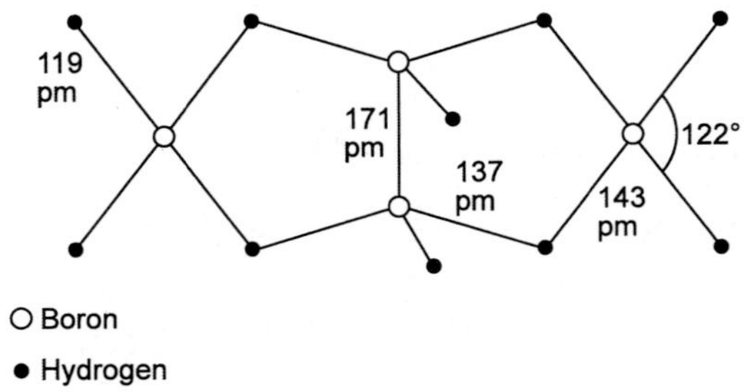

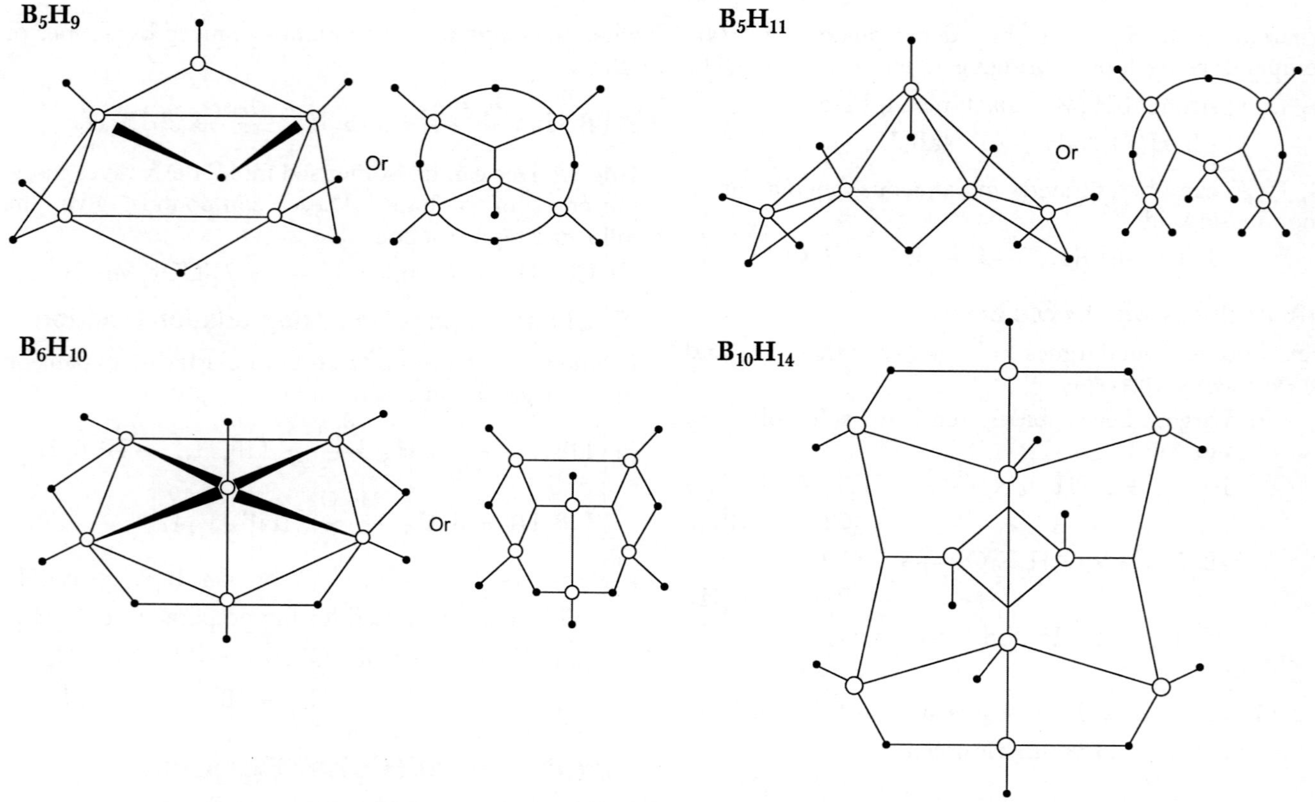

Fig. 5.3 Structure of some higher neutral boranes.

B_6H_{10} It contains 28 valence electrons. It consists of six $2c—2e$ B H bonds, four $3c-2e$ B H B bonds, two $2c—2e$ B B bonds and two B B B $3c—2e$ bonds.

$B_{10}H_{14}$ It contains 44 valence electrons. It consists of ten $2c—2e$ B H bonds, four $3c—2e$ B H B bonds, two $2c—2e$ B B bonds, and four B B B $3c—2e$ bonds and two B B B $3c—2e$ bonds.

Example 1. *Give products of the following reactions :*

(i) $B_2H_6 + NaBH_4 \longrightarrow$

(ii) $B_2H_6 + CH_3OH \longrightarrow$

(iii) $B_2H_6 + KOH \xrightarrow{H_2O}$

(iv) $B_2H_6 + \text{Excess } NH_3 \xrightarrow{\Delta}$

Sol. (i) $B_2H_6 + NaBH_4 \xrightarrow[\text{Diglyme}]{100°} NaB_3H_8 + 2H_2$

(ii) $B_2H_6 + 6CH_3OH \longrightarrow 2B(OCH_3)_3 + 6H_2$

(iii) $B_2H_6 + 2KOH \xrightarrow{2H_2O} 2KBO_2 + 6H_2$

(iv) $B_2H_6 + \text{Excess } NH_3 \xrightarrow{\Delta} (BN)_x$

Carboranes or Carbaboranes

Carboranes or carbaboranes are compounds of carbon, boron and hydrogen in which carbon and boron atoms occupy the vertices of a triangulated polyhedron. These compounds may be considered to have been derived from boranes by the replacement of BH^- units by CH units. The carboranes and the boranes having the same number of electrons in their bonding, frame work have similar skeletal structures. Three structurally different types of carboranes, namely, closo, nido and arachno are known at present.

Dicarbacloso dodecacarborane ($C_2B_{10}H_{12}$) has a closed icosahedral structure. It occurs in three isomeric forms, *viz.*, *ortho*, *meta* and *para*. All the three isomers are quite stable in air.

Preparation

These can be prepared as follows :

Tetraborane (14),

$$B_{10}H_{14} + 2Et_2S \longrightarrow B_{10}H_{12}(SEt_2)_2 + H_2$$

$$\downarrow C_2H_2$$

$$\text{Closo } 1,7\text{-}C_2B_{10}H_{12} \xleftarrow{470°C} \text{Closo } 1,2\text{-}C_2B_{10}H_{12}$$

(*meta* isomer) (*ortho* isomer)

$$\downarrow 700°C$$

$$\text{Closo } 1,12\text{-}C_2B_{10}H_{12}$$

(*para* isomer)

Wade's Rule

Wade's rule are used for finding out the number of electrons present in the multicentred bonding orbitals of the skeletal structure of framework of a given borane or carborane.

1. Each BH unit is assumed to contribute two electrons to the skeletal bonding in borane or carborane.
2. The negative charge on a borane or carborane anion is assumed to be used up in skeletal bonding.
3. Each additional H in borane or carborane is assumed to contribute one electron to the skeletal bonding.
4. Each CH unit in a carborane is assumed to contribute three electrons to the skeletal bonding.

The number of electrons available for framework bonds (H) are also determined by the following equation

$$H = 3b + 4c + h + x - 2n \qquad \ldots(1)$$

where,

b = the number of boron atoms

c = the number of carbon atoms

h = the number of hydrogen atoms

x = the amount of the negative charge on the ion.

n = the number of vertices, that is $b + c$

x is defined so as to be a positive quantity for anions, H is the number that remains after providing for neno-framework $(2c - 2e)$ terminal B—H or C—H bonds.

Rule 1. When the value of H is equal to the quantity $(2n + 2)$, the substance should have a closo structure.

Rule 2. When the value of H is equal to the quantity $(2n + 4)$, the substance should have the nido structure.

Rule 3. When the value of H is equal to the quantity $(2n + 6)$, the compound falls into the arachno category, and the preferred structure is that of the $(n + 2)$ vertex polyhedron, with two vertices missing.

Closo Boranes and Closo Carboranes

There are $(m + 1)$ electron pairs present in the multicentre bonding orbitals of skeletal structure (or 'cage' or 'framework') of closo boranes and closo carboranes (m is the total number of B and C atoms).

In $B_6H_6^{2-}$ anion, $m = 6$. There are six BH units which according to Wade's rules, contribute 6×2 electrons to the bonding molecular orbitals of the skeletal structure. The charge of -2 contributes two more electrons to such bonding orbitals. Thus, the total number of electron pairs present in the multicentre bonding orbitals is $6 + 1 = 7$ $(m + 1 = 7)$.

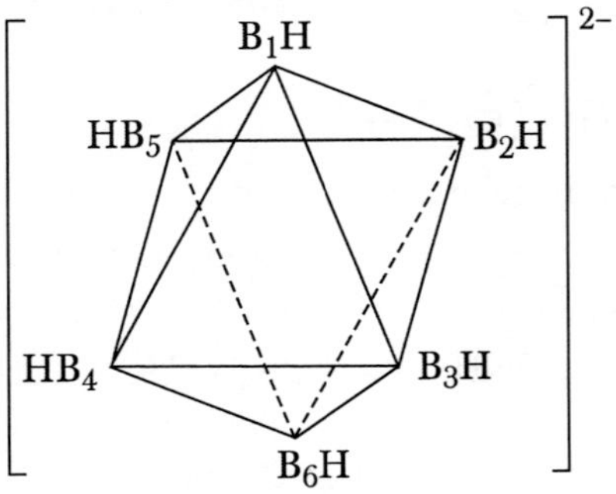

Similarly, in $(CH_2)B_{10}H_{10}$, m is $2 + 10 = 12$. The two CH units, according to Wade's rules contribute 2×3 electrons and the ten BH units contribute 10×2 electrons to the bonding molecular orbitals of the skeletal structure. Thus, there are 13 electron pairs $(m + 1 = 13)$ present in the multicentre bonding orbitals of $(CH)_2B_{10}H_{10}$ or $C_2B_{10}H_{12}$.

Nido Boranes and Nido Carboranes

The nido or nestlike skeletal structure has $(m + 2)$ electron pairs in its multicentre bonding orbitals. The examples are nido B_5H_9 and nido $C_2B_4H_8$, whose structure are given below :

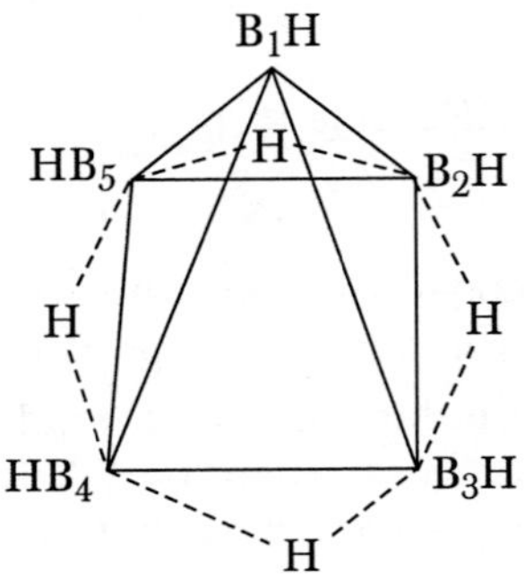

Nido B_5H_9

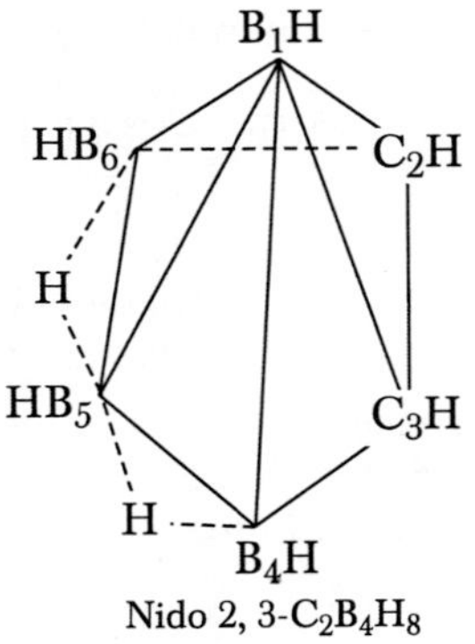

Nido 2, 3-$C_2B_4H_8$

In nido B_5H_9 ($m = 5$) 5 BH units ($= 5 \times 2$ electrons), 4H ($= 4 \times 1$ electrons) contribute to the bonding orbitals of skeletal structure. There are thus $5 + 2 = 7$ elecron pairs in multicentred bonding orbitals of nido B_5H_9. In nido 2, 3-$C_2B_4H_8$ ($m = 2 + 4 = 6$), 2 CH units $= 2 \times 3$ electrons, 4 BH $= 4 \times 2$ electrons, 2H $= 2$ electrons contribute to the bonding orbital of skeletal structure and $m = 6 + 2 = 8$ electrons in the multicentre bonding orbitals of skeletal structure.

Arachno Boranes and Arachno Carboranes

There are $(m + 3)$ electron pairs in the multicentre bonding orbitals of boranes and carboranes *e.g.*, arachno B_5H_{11} and arachno $C_2B_7H_{13}$.

Borazine ($B_3N_3H_6$)

It is commonly called borazole.

(i) It was first prepared by A. Stock in 1926 by reacting B_2H_6 and NH_3 in the ratio (1 : 2) at 250 - 300°C.

$$3B_2H_6 + 6NH_3 \longrightarrow \underset{\text{Borazine}}{2B_3N_3H_6} + 12H_2$$

It is also known as **inorganic benzene** because its physical properties closely resemble those of benzene with which it is isoelectronic.

(ii) It is also prepared by the reduction of boron trichloride which is first converted into trichloroderivative of borazine and then reduced with $NaBH_4$.

$$3BCl_3 + 3NH_4Cl \xrightarrow[-9HCl]{150°C,\ C_6H_5Cl} B_3N_3H_3Cl_3$$

$$B_3N_3H_3Cl_3 + 3NaBH_4 \xrightarrow[-3NaCl]{(C_4H_9)_2O} B_3N_3H_6 + 1.5B_2H_6$$

(iii) It is also prepared by the direct reaction of $NaBH_4$ with ammonium chloride.

$$3NaBH_4 + 3NH_4Cl \xrightarrow{\text{Triglyme}} B_3N_3H_6 + 3NaCl + 9H_2$$

Borazine has a planar hexagonal ring structure in which B and N atoms are sp^2 hybridized. An important difference from benzene is that in borazine the π-bond is a dative bond, formed by the overlap of filled $2p$-orbitals of nitrogen with empty $2p$-orbitals of boron.

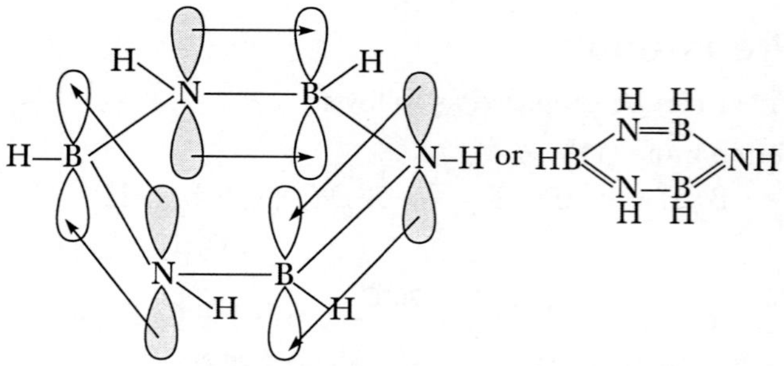

However, there is a little chemical evidence which may suggest that borazine has aromatic character.

Addition reactions

It reacts with water, alcohols and HX to yield 1 : 3 addition products. On heating to 100°C, they lose hydrogen.

$$B_3N_3H_6 + 3H_2O \xrightarrow{0°C} [BH(OH)NH_2]_3 \xrightarrow{100°C} [B(OH)NH]_3 + 3H_2$$

$$B_3N_3H_6 + 6ROH \xrightarrow{0°C} [BH(OR)NH_2]_3 \xrightarrow{100°C} [B(OR)NH]_3 + 3H_2$$

N-or B-substituted borazines can be prepared by suitably choosing amine or borane as starting materials.

Action of heat

On heating, borazines give polymeric substances analogous to naphthalene, biphenyl etc.

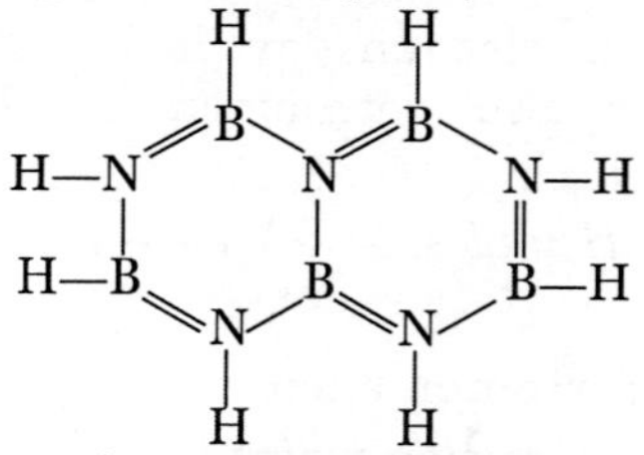

(Inorganic naphthalene)

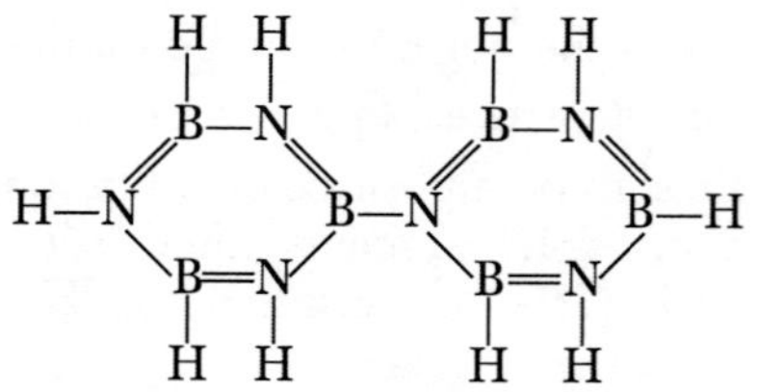

Inorganic diphenyl

'Inorganic cyclohexane' has also been prepared

$$B_3N_3H_6 + 3HCl \longrightarrow B_3N_3H_9Cl \xrightarrow{NaBH_4} \underset{\text{Inorganic cyclohexane}}{B_3N_3H_{12}}$$

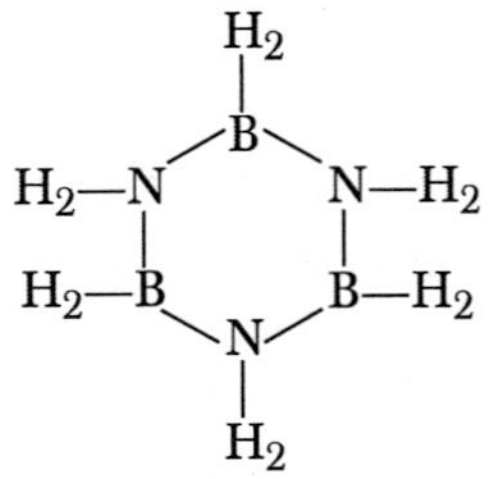

Boron Nitride $(BN)_x$

Boron nitride is a polymeric white solid. It is isoelectronic with graphite. It has been prepared in four allotropic forms. The most common is the hexagonal form which has graphite like structure consisting of layers of fused six membered $(BN)_3$ rings.

Preparation

1. Highly pure hexagonal boron nitride can be prepared by the reaction of ammonia with BCl_3 or BF_3.

$$2BCl_3 + 6NH_3 \xrightarrow[-\ 6HCl]{} 2B(NH_2)_3 \xrightarrow[750°C]{\text{Pyrolysis}} 2(BN)_3$$

2. It is also prepared by the reaction of diboron trioxide (B_2O_3) with NH_3 at 1200°C.

$$B_2O_3 + 2NH_3 \longrightarrow 2(BN)_x + 3H_2O$$

3. In laboratory, it can be prepared by fusion of borax with NH_4Cl or by fusion of urea and boric acid.

Structure

The polymeric solid has a graphite-like structure containing alternate boron and nitrogen atoms. The B N bond distance is 145 pm. The bonds are formed by sp^2 hybrid orbitals on boron and nitrogen atoms. The remaining two electrons on nitrogen are used for forming π-bonds by donation from N to B (vacant $2p$ orbital on boron). As in graphite, there are alternative single and double bonds between B and N atoms. Alternate sheets are located such that boron atoms are directly over nitrogen atoms. This structure gives rise to easily sliding of planes relative to each other lending boron nitride lubricant properties, comparable to those of graphite. Unlike graphite, it is a colourless electrical insulator, as there is a large energy gap between filled and vacant π-bonds.

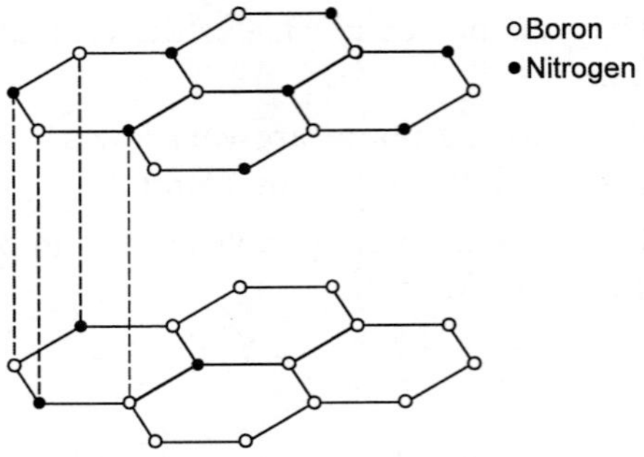

(a) Layer structure of boron nitride.

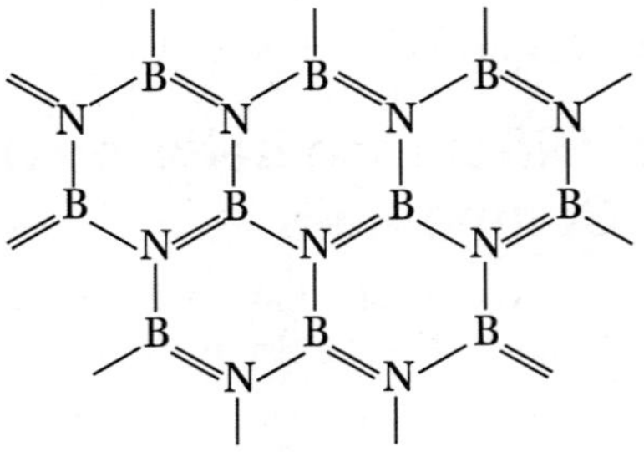

(b) One layer structure of boron nitride.

Fig. 5.4

Halides of Boron

Preparation

Boron forms BF_3, BCl_3, BBr_3 and BI_3 under specific conditions.

1. BF_3 is prepared by the action of HF on boron trioxide as :

$$B_2O_3 + 6HF \longrightarrow 2BF_3 + 3H_2O$$

2. The other boron halides are prepared by the action of halogen with a mixture of boron trioxide and carbon at high temperatures.

$$B_2O_3 + 3C + 3Cl_2 \longrightarrow 2BCl_3 + 3CO$$
$$B_2O_3 + 3C + 3Br_2 \longrightarrow 2BBr_3 + 3CO$$
$$B_2O_3 + 3C + 3I_2 \longrightarrow 2BI_3 + 3CO$$

Properties

(a) BF_3 and BCl_3 are gases, BBr_3 is a liquid while BI_3 is a solid at room temperature.

(b) Melting and boiling points of boron halides are in the order

$$BI_3 > BBr_3 > BCl_3 > BF_3$$

(c) Boron trihalides have covalent character due to small size and high ionisation energy of boron atom. The following facts support the covalent character of boron trihalides.

(i) They do not conduct electricity in the liquid state.

(ii) Their boiling points are very low as compared to the halides of groups 1 and 2.

(iii) They exist as discrete molecules in all phases as shown in Fig. 5.4.

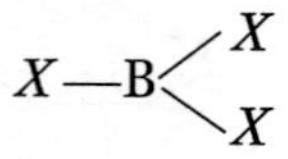

(X = F, Cl, Br, I)

Fig. 5.5 Structure of boron halides.

Structural Difference between BX_3 and AlX_3 Compounds

Boron trihalides exist as monomers while aluminium trihalides ($AlCl_3$ and $AlBr_3$) exist as dimers.

The explanation for this difference in their behaviour can be attributed to the difference in sizes between boron and aluminium atoms. The boron atom is extremely small and is unable to coordinate to four large sized halide ions. However, the explanation applies only to its compounds with Cl^- and Br^- ions. But F^- is a small ion and it should not be difficult for boron atom to hold on four F^- ions. This is also evident from the stability of BF_4^- ion. A possible explanation which can be offered is that the energy released by the formation of an additional bond to another boron atom (as required for the formation of a dimer) is not enough so as to compensate for the loss in energy to the system in overcoming the B F *pπ-pπ* (or π bonding) in the monomer itself.

Acidic Nature of Boron Trihalides

Boron trihalides are planar triangular molecules. Boron atom is sp^2 hybridized. Each sp^2 hybrid orbital containing boron electron overlaps with $2p_z$ electron of F atoms to form planar BF_3 molecule. This leaves one $2p$-orbital vacant on boron. Boron atom in BX_3 contains only six electron in the valence sheell (*i.e.*, 2 electrons short of closed shell configuration, an octet). Thus, BX_3 molecules act as Lewis acids, *i.e.,* electron acceptors.

The boron halides make use of this empty p-orbital by forming tetrahedral complexes of the type $BX_3 \cdot L$ where, L is a neutral or anionic donor, *e.g.,* $L = NH_3$ or F^- to form $BF_3 \cdot NH_3$ or BF_4^-.

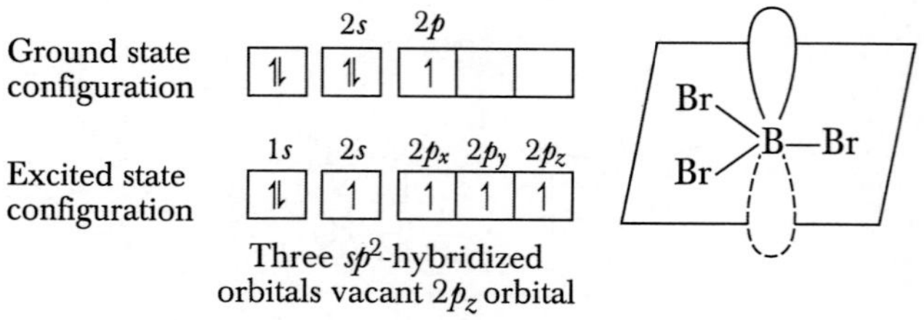

Thus, BF_3 and other trihalides of boron act as strong Lewis acids (*i.e.,* acceptors of electron pair).

Example 2. *Can the molecule* BF_3CO *which is formed between* BF_3 *and* CO *be termed as a complex?*

Sol. BF_3 in the complex $BF_3 \cdot CO$ retains its planar geometry. The adduct exhibits only weak van der Waals' forces.

Relative Lewis acid strengths of BX_3 compounds

The relative acceptor strengths of BF_3, BCl_3 and BBr_3 have been found by measuring the heats of formation and dipole moments of their adducts with pyridine. The results indicate that the electron acceptor power increases in the order

$$BBr_3 \geq BCl_3 > BF_3$$

The order is just the opposite of what may normally be expected on the basis of the electronegativity of X and also on steric grounds. This anomalous behaviour can be explained in terms of boron-halogen π-bonding.

***pπ-pπ* back bonding in BX_3 compounds** In BF_3, flourine has filled $2p$ orbitals whereas boron has a vacant $2p$ orbital. Since, both these orbitals are of same energy they can overlap effectively and as a consequence fluorine electrons are transferred into the vacant $2p$ orbital of boron resulting in the formation of

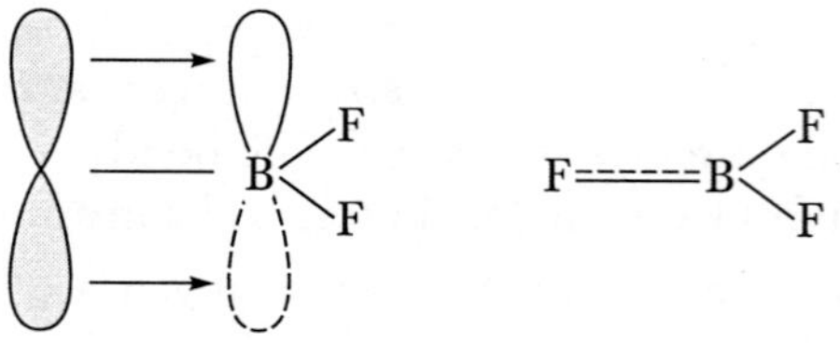

πp-pπ overlap

pπ-pπ bond. The B F bond has some double bond character. This type of bond formation is known as **dative** or **back bonding**. We can write similar structures for the other two B–F bonds which are also equally probable.

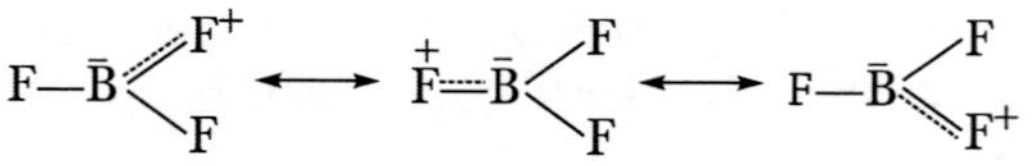

As a consequence of back donation of electrons from fluorine to boron its electron deficiency is conpensated and therefore its Lewis acidity is decreased. The tendency for the formation of $p\pi$-$p\pi$ double bond is maximum in BF_3 and decreases rapidly on moving to BCl_3 and BBr_3 because the overlap between vacant $2p$ orbital of boron with higher energy filled $3p$ and $4p$ orbitals of chlorine and bromine cannot take place effectively.

Example 3. *For a given ligand 'L', stability of the adduct X_3B—L increases in the sequence* $BF_3 < BCl_3 < BBr_3 < BI_3$. *Explain :*

Sol. This may probably be attributed to the loss in π-bonding when the molecule BX_3 changes from planar to tetrahedral geometry in X_3B—L adduct. Since, π-bonding decreases in the sequence $BF_3 > BCl_3 > BBr_3 > BI_3$, therefore stability of the adducts increases in the given order.

Example 4. *Why* BF_3 *forms stable adduct with water* ($BF_3 \cdot OH_2$) *while* BCl_3 *or* BBr_3 *are spontaneously hydrolysed to give* $B(OH)_3$ *and* HX *?*

Sol. The great strength of the B—F bond (due to additional π-bonding) in BF_3 gives extra stability to its adducts than other boron halides. In other words B—Cl or B—Br bond is relatively weak and is easily cleaved by water thus forming strong B—OH bonds.

Uses of Boron Halides

BF_3 is used as a catalyst in Friedel-Crafts reaction, and in polymerisation reactions while other boron halides have limited use in chemical reactions.

Boric Acid, $B(OH)_3$ or H_3BO_3

It is also known as orthoboric acid.

Preparation

It is obtained by adding calculated quantity of hydrochloric acid to a hot concentrated solution of borax ($Na_2B_4O_7 \cdot 10H_2O$). The resulting solution is allowed to cool when crystals of boric acid are obtained.

$$Na_2B_4O_7 + 2HCl + 5H_2O \longrightarrow 2NaCl + 4H_3BO_3$$

Properties

(i) It is a flaky, white crystalline substance in which BO_3 units are joined by unsymmetrical H bonds as shown in Fig. 5.6. There is only weak interaction between the different layers which accounts for its low density, 1.48 g cm^{-3} and easy cleavage.

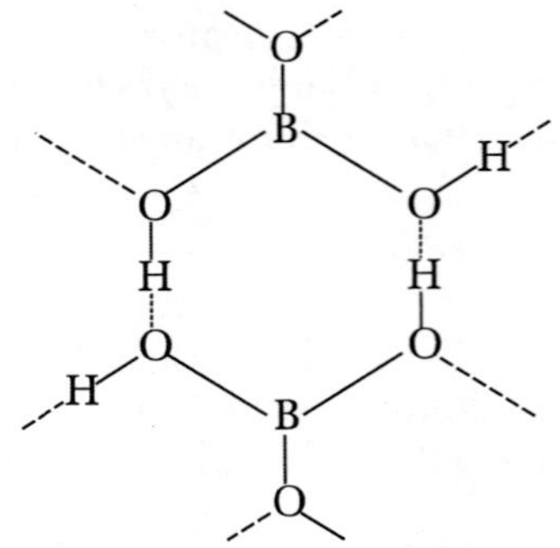

Fig. 5.6 Layer structure of $B(OH)_3$.

(ii) It is a weak monobasic acid and its acidic roperties are manifested in terms of OH^- ion acceptance (as a Lewis acid) rather than H^+ (proton) donation, *i.e.,* it does not act as a Bronsted acid.

$$B(OH)_3 + 2H_2O \rightleftharpoons H_3O^+ + B(OH)_4^-; \quad pK_a = 9.25$$

(iii) Partial dehydration of boric acid yields metaboric acid, HBO_3 which exists in different crystalline forms.

$$\underset{\text{Cubic}}{3HBO_2} \xrightarrow{170°C} B(OH)_3 \xrightarrow{140°C} \underset{\text{Monoclinic}}{HBO_2}$$

$$\xrightarrow[\text{quenching}]{\text{Rapid}} \underset{\text{Orthorhombic}}{HBO_2}$$

Boric acid on heating to red heat gives B_2O_3.

$$2H_3BO_3 \xrightarrow{\text{Red hot}} B_2O_3 + 3H_2O$$

(iv) Being a weak acid, it is difficult to titrate boric acid against sodium hydroxide as the end-point cannot be located correctly. However, it can be successfully titrated in the presence of polyhydroxy alcohols (*e.g.,* glycerol, mannitol, catechol or sugar) which greatly enhance the acidity of boric acid. Boron is complexed by these compounds. These complex ions cannot interact with H^+ as boron atom has already acquired its maximum covalency of four. Consequently, boric acid in the presence of polyhydroxy alcohols can be titrated against strong bases like NaOH to a definite end point.

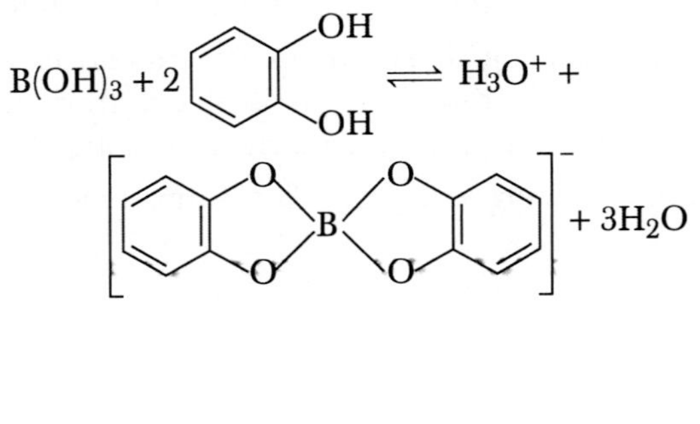

(v) When boric acid is heated with C_2H_5OH and conc. H_2SO_4, volatile triethylborate is obtained. This ester burns with a green flame.

$$H_3BO_3 + 3C_2H_5OH \xrightarrow{\text{Conc. } H_2SO_4} (C_2H_5)_3BO_3 + 3H_2O$$

(vi) When boric acid is reacted with KHF_2 (KF · HF), KBF_4 salt is produced.

$$2KHF_2 + H_3BO_3 \longrightarrow \underset{\text{Potassium fluoroborate}}{KBF_4} + KOH + 2H_2O$$

(vii) When H_3BO_3 is heated with CaF_2 and conc. H_2SO_4, boron trifluoride is formed.

$$3CaF_2 + 3H_2SO_4 + 2H_3BO_3 \xrightarrow{\Delta} 3CaSO_4 + 2BF_3 + 6H_2O$$

Uses

Boric acid is used in the manufacture of enamels and glazes for pottery; its solution acts as an eye-wash; and as a preservative for milk and other food articles, in tanning industry, in candle industry to stiffen wicks and in the manufacture of pigments and borax.

Borax, Sodium Tetraborate Decahydrate, $Na_2B_4O_7 \cdot 10H_2O$

It occurs as borax or tincal in dried up lakes of India, Tibet, Ceylon and California.

Preparation

The native salts is dissolved in boiling water, filtered to remove insoluble impurities of sand, clay etc. The resulting solution is evaporated until crystals separate out.

Properties

(i) It is a white crystalline solid which is sparingly soluble in cold water but is readily soluble in hot water. The solution in water is alkaline in nature.

(ii) On heating, it swells up due to the escape of water of crystallisation as steam from it. The anhydrous product then melts at about 1000 K.

(iii) On heating with NH_4Cl, it forms boron nitride, $(BN)_x$.

Uses

It is used as a flux for soldering and welding, in making enamels and glazes, stiffening of candle wicks; in borosilicate glass (or Pyrex glass); in fire retardants; and in qualitative analysis for borax bead test to detect metallic radicals of coloured salts as described below :

Hot platinum wire loop is dipped in borax and then introduced into the flame. Borax first swells up and then melts to form a transparent glassy bead due to sodium metaborate and boron oxide as :

$$Na_2B_4O_7 \cdot 10H_2O \xrightarrow{\text{Heat}} \underset{\text{Sod. metaborate}}{2NaBO_2} + \underset{\text{Boron oxide}}{B_2O_3} + 10H_2O$$

The transparent bead is then touched with a speck of the coloured salt and again introduced into the flame. The characteristic colour imparted to the bead gives an indication of the metallic radical due to coloured metaborate formation as :

$$CoO + B_2O_3 \longrightarrow \underset{\text{Cobalt metaborate (blue)}}{Co(BO_2)_2}$$

$$NiO + B_2O_3 \longrightarrow \underset{\text{Nickel metaborate (brown)}}{Ni(BO_2)_2}$$

$$Cr_2O_3 + 3B_2O_3 \longrightarrow \underset{\text{Chromium metaborate (green)}}{2Cr(BO_2)_3}$$

Structures of Borates

It is very difficult to predict the structures of the borate anions from the stoichiometry of the complex borates. Anhydrous borates are prepared by fusing boric acid and metal oxides. The hydrated borates may be crystallized from aqueous solutions. The general composition of borates : $KB_5O_8 \cdot 4H_2O$, CaB_2O_4, $Na_2B_4O_7 \cdot 10H_2O$ gives very little information about the structures of the borate anions. They are generally cyclic or linear polymers formed by linking together of BO_3 and/or BO_4 units through shared oxygen atoms. Borates containing one or more than one boron atom (up to 5 B atoms) or polydimensional networks (glasses) are known to exist. They mainly consist of :

(i) Boron atom linked either to three oxygen atoms (BO_3 unit) or four oxygen atoms (BO_4 tetrahedron).

(ii) Polynuclear anions are formed by corner sharing of boron-oxygen triangles or tetrahedrons.

(iii) These units can be protonated to various extents.

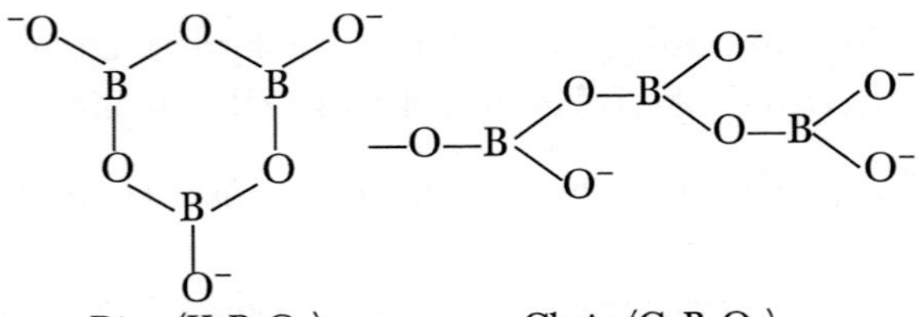

Ring ($K_3B_2O_4$) Chain (CaB_3O_6)

Fig. 5.7 Structure of ring and chain borates.

It may be noted that in contrast to borates, the carbonate ion does not form polymeric structures. This may probably be attributed to the formation of strong C—O π-bonds.

Borax, which is normally written as $Na_2B_4O_7 \cdot 10H_2O$ contains tetranuclear units $[B_4O_5(OH)_4]^{2-}$ comprising of BO_4 and BO_3 units (Fig. 5.7). Borax should therefore be formulated as $Na_2[B_4O_5(OH)_4]5H_2O$.

Aluminium Chloride ($AlCl_3$ or Al_2Cl_6)

It behaves as a strong Lewis acid and forms a number of addition compounds or complexes with bases. Their compositions vary depending upon the stability of the complex.

(i) Ammonia combines with $AlCl_3$ to form $AlCl_3 \cdot 6NH_3$.

(ii) On the other hand, trimethylamine, Me_3N forms complexes of compositions $AlCl_3 \cdot NMe_3$ and $AlCl_3 \cdot 2NMe_3$. The former has four coordinated tetrahedral Al, whereas the latter has five coordinated trigonal bipyramid structure.

(iii) Phosphoryl chloride, $POCl_3$ forms crystalline compounds of three different compositions.

$$AlCl_3 \cdot POCl_3 : AlCl_3 \cdot 2POCl_3 : AlCl_3 \cdot 6POCl_3$$

(iv) It forms non-chelate complex anions of the type $AlCl_4^-$ and $AlCl_6^{3-}$ when heated with alkali metal chlorides.

$$NaCl + AlCl_3 \longrightarrow Na[AlCl_4]$$

$$3NaCl + AlCl_3 \longrightarrow Na_3[AlCl_6]$$

(v) $AlCl_3$ is used for the synthesis of non-metal chlorides from their fluorides. As for example :

$$AlCl_3 + BF_3 \longrightarrow BCl_3 + AlF_3$$

This transhalogenation reaction occurs due to higher stability of the product (AlF_3) with higher electronegativity (of F) and higher electropositive character (of Al).

(vi) $AlCl_3$ finds extensive use as a catalyst in "Friedel-Craft reaction" as for example :

$$C_6H_6 + CH_3AlCl_4 \longrightarrow C_6H_5CH_3 + HCl + AlCl_3$$

(vii) The affinity of $AlCl_3$ for water is so great that on treatment with water, the chloride ions go out of the coordination sphere to form $[Al(H_2O)_6]Cl_3$ (solution enthalpy = 330 kJ/mol). Because of strong aluminium-oxygen linkage, the hydrate cannot be dehydrated toanhydrous $AlCl_3$ by heating.

$$2Al(H_2O)_6Cl_3 \xrightarrow{\Delta} Al_2O_3 + 6HCl + 9H_2O$$

(viii) Aluminium chloride reacts with Na*OR* to form $Al(OR)_3$ and $NaAl(OR)_4$; where, *R*═H or alkyl group.

$$AlCl_3 \xrightarrow[-3NaCl]{3NaOR} Al(OR)_3 \xrightarrow{+NaOR} Na[Al(OR)_4]$$

Structure of $AlCl_3$

In crystalline state, anhydrous aluminium chloride $(AlCl_3)_x$ possesses a closely packed layer structure with six coordinated Al having octahedral arrangement as shown in Fig. 5.8. The rectangles enclosed in dotted lines show how these layers release Al_2Cl_6 molecules on heating.

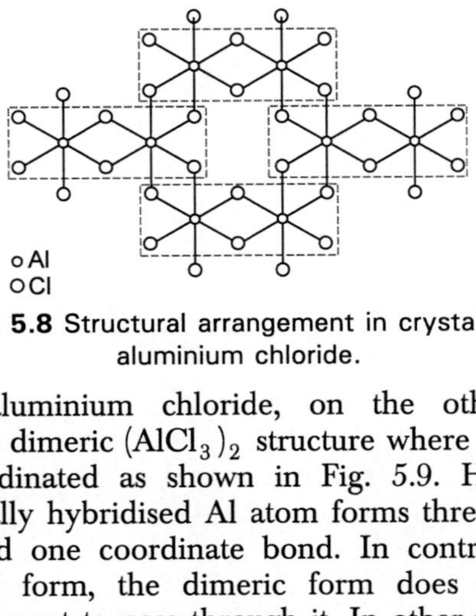

Fig. 5.8 Structural arrangement in crystalline aluminium chloride.

Molten aluminium chloride, on the other hand, acquires a dimeric $(AlCl_3)_2$ structure where each Al is four coordinated as shown in Fig. 5.9. Here, each tetrahedrally hybridised Al atom forms three covalent bonds and one coordinate bond. In contrast to the crystalline form, the dimeric form does not allow electric current to pass through it. In other words, the electrical conductivity of aluminium chloride vanishes at its melting point and reappears on solidification. This also explains transition from closely packed layer structure to loosely held covalently bonded molecular melt. This is also supported by dramatic increase in volume (by almost 85%) on melting.

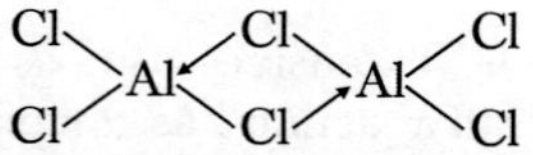

Fig. 5.9 Structure of Al_2Cl_6 (molten state).

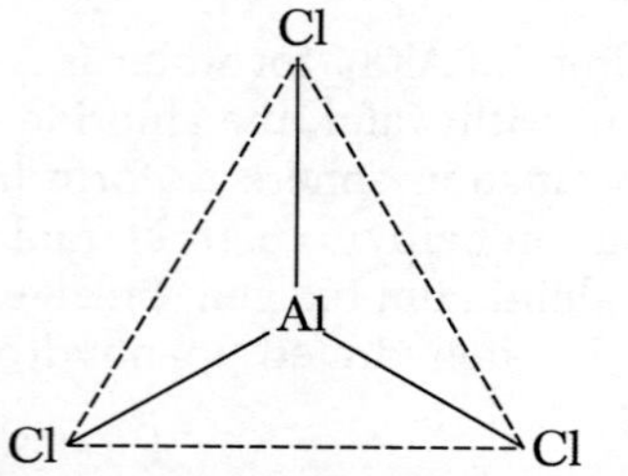

Fig. 5.10 Plane triangular 3-coordinated Al (vapour state).

In gaseous phase at higher temperatures the dimer dissociates into plane triangular molecule $AlCl_3$ isostructural with BCl_3.

$AlBr_3$ and AlI_3 form dimeric molecular compounds (Al_2Br_6 and Al_2I_6) in the solid as well as liquid phases.

Example 5. *Why do aluminium halides preferably acquire dimeric structure over monomeric formulation?*

Sol. The formation of dimers is attributed to the tendency of the Al atoms to complete their octets. The dimeric structure is easily broken down by reaction with donor molecules.

$$Al_2Cl_6 + 2R_3N: \longrightarrow 2AlCl_3 \cdot NR_3$$

Uses

(i) Aluminium fluoride is used in the metallurgy of aluminium.

(ii) Aluminium chloride is used as a catalyst in Friedel-Crafts reaction, cracking of mineral oils and in the manufacture of dyes and perfumes.

Exercise 1

(For Part 'B')

1. The borax bead is
(a) B_2O_3 (b) $Na_2B_4O_2$
(c) Na_3BO_3 (d) $B_2O_3 + NaBO_2$

2. Alum is found to contain hydrated monovalent cation $[M(H_2O)_6^+]$, trivalent cation $[M'(H_2O)_6]^{3+}$ and SO_4^{2-} in the ratio of
(a) 1 : 1 : 1 (b) 1 : 1 : 2
(c) 1 : 2 : 3 (d) 3 : 2 : 1

3. Alums are used as mordant in dyeing because
(a) dye is adsorbed on $Al(OH)_3$ which is deposited on fibre in the hydrolysis process
(b) dye is adsorbed on KOH formed due to hydrolysis
(c) Both (a) and (b)
(d) None of the above

4. Colemanite is a mineral of
(a) Ca (b) Ba
(c) Al (d) Mg

5. Dimer formation can take place with
(a) BH_3 (b) NO_2
(c) $AlCl_3$ (d) All of these

6. Which of the following is not correct in case of boron nitride?
(a) It is also called borazon
(b) It is chemically unreactive
(c) It is hard because of its diamond like structure
(d) It has magnetic properties

7. On passing CO_2 into aqueous solution containing Al^{3+}
(a) $Al(OH)_3$ is precipitated
(b) $Al_2(CO_3)_2$ is formed
(c) $[Al(OH)_4]^-$ is formed
(d) colloidal $Al(OH)_3$ is formed

8. The solubility of $Al(OH)_3$ in strong NaOH solution is best explanation by the formation of
(a) double salt
(b) AlO_3^- ion
(c) a precipitated colloidal salt
(d) a complex hydroxyl aluminate ion

9. Covalency of B in BF_4^- is
(a) 5 (b) 4 (c) 3 (d) 2

10. Which of the following is the false statement?
(a) B_2H_6 reduces alkene to primary alcohol
(b) Reducing action of $NaBH_4$ and $LiAlH_4$ are specific
(c) Both (a) and (b) are the false statements
(d) None of the above is false statement

11. Boron nitride has the structure of the type
(a) graphite (b) diamond
(c) NaCl (d) Both (a) and (b)

12. From B_2H_6 all the following can be prepared except
(a) H_3BO_3 (b) B_2O_3
(c) $NaBH_4$ (d) $B_2(CH_3)_6$

13. In B_2H_6
(a) the B—H bonds are ionic
(b) there is direct boron-boron bond
(c) it is isostructural to C_2H_6
(d) boron atoms are linked through hydrogen bridges

14. Which of the following is false statement?
(a) BH_3 is Lewis acid
(b) Boranes are easily hydrolysed
(c) $LiAlH_4$ reduces BCl_3 to boranes
(d) All the B—H distance in diborane (B_2H_6) are equal

15. BF_3 on hydrolysis forms
(a) H_3BO_3 (b) HBF_4
(c) Both (a) and (b) (d) None of these

16. B_2Cl_4
(a) decomposes at low temperature
(b) can exist on non-eclipsed and planar structure
(c) can be formed by passing BCl_3 over Hg at low pressure in an electric discharge
(d) can show all the facts given above

17. BF_3 behaves as a
(a) Lewis acid and lone pair from the Lewis base is filled into empty $2p_z$ orbital
(b) Lewis base and lone pair on B is donated to empty orbital of the Lewis acid
(c) polymeric substance
(d) amphoteric species due to interaction with acid and base both

18. In BF_3
(a) bond energy and bond length of B F bond indicate its single bond character
(b) all the B F bonds are single covalents in nature
(c) boron-fluorine bond has same double bond character and this bond is delocalised
(d) All the bonds are ionic

19. The structure of BF_3 is
(a) tetrahedral (b) T-shaped
(c) pyramidal (d) planar trigonal

20. Boron sesquoxide is
(a) B_2O_3 (b) BO_3
(c) BO_2^- (d) BO_3^{3-}

21. Select the correct statement(s) about H_3BO_3.
(a) In solid state, molecules are hydrogen bonded
(b) It has trigonal BO_3^{3-} units
(c) Both (a) and (b) are correct
(d) None of the above

22. Orthoboric acid H_3BO_3 behaves as weak monobasic acid giving H_3O^+ and
(a) $H_2BO_2^-$ (b) $H_2BO_2^+$
(c) $[B(OH)_4]^+$ (d) $[B(OH)_4]^-$

23. When orthoboric acid is heated to red heat the residue is
(a) boron (b) boron oxide
(c) pyroboric acid (d) metaboric acid

24. Which of the following statements regarding orthoboric acid (H_3BO_3) is false?
(a) It acts as a tribasic acid
(b) It has a planar structure
(c) It is soluble in hot water
(d) It acts as a monobasic acid

25. B can be obtained from halide by van-Arkel method. This involves reaction
(a) $2BI_3 \xrightarrow{\text{Red hot W or Ta}} 2B + 3I_2$
(b) $2BCl_3 + 3H_2 \xrightarrow[\text{filament}]{\text{Red hot W or Ta}} 2B + 6HCl$
(c) Both (a) and (b)
(d) None of the above

26. $Na_2B_4O_7 \cdot 10H_2O$ is correctly represented as
(a) $Na_2[B_4O_5(OH)_4] \cdot 8H_2O$
(b) $Na_2[B_4(H_2O)_4O_7] \cdot 6H_2O$
(c) $2NaBO_2 \cdot Na_2B_2O_3 \cdot 10H_2O$
(d) All of the above

27. Which of the following is false in case of BF_3?
(a) It is solid at room temperature
(b) It is Lewis acid
(c) It has planar geometry
(d) It forms adduct with NH_3

28. The borax bead test can be used to detect the presence of
(a) Na^+ (b) Mg^{2+} (c) Al^{3+} (d) Fe^{3+}

29. Pure boron is best prepared by
(a) heating B_2O_3 with Na or K.
(b) heating B_2O_3 with H_2.
(c) heating KBF_4 with Na or K.
(d) heating BBr_3 with H_2 in presence of a catalyst.

30. Alzheimer's disease is caused due to Al interaction with internal organs of the body if food is contaminated with Al. This disease
(a) causes memory loss
(b) induces senility in young persons
(c) Both (a) and (b) are correct
(d) None of the above

31. Anodising can be done by electrolysing dilute H_2SO_4 with Al as anode. This results in
(a) the formation of protective oxide layer (Al_2O_3).
(b) the formation of $Al(HSO_4)_3$ and H_2 gas.
(c) the formation of AlH_3 and SO_2 gas.
(d) the formation of $Al_2(SO_4)_3$ and SO_2 gas.

32. N_2 gas is passed or heated Mg and B. Products formed are
(a) MgN, BN (b) Mg_3N_2, BN
(c) Mg_3N_2, BN and Mg_3B_2 (d) No reaction

33. In the reaction, $M + N_2 \xrightarrow{\Delta} \xrightarrow{H_2O} NH_3$
Element M can be
(a) B or Al (b) Ga or Al
(c) Mg or Al or B (d) Mg or B

34. Boric acid is a weak Lewis acid. The proton comes
(a) when it forms borate esters with alcohol
(b) when it forms complex with H_2O
(c) by its ionisation
(d) All of the above

35. Boron does not form B^{3+} cation easily. It is due to
(a) boron is non-metal
(b) boron is semiconductor
(c) energy required to form B^{3+} ion is for more than that which would be compensated by lattice energies or hydration energies of such ion
(d) None of the above

36. In aqueous solution GaCl disproportionates to
(a) Ga and $GaCl_3$ (b) $GaCl_3$ and $GaCl_5$
(c) $GaCl_2$ and $GaCl_3$ (d) $GaCl_2$ and Ga

37. AlO_2^- is known as
(a) meta aluminate ion (b) aluminium dioxo ion
(c) dioxi aluminium ion (d) aluminium oxide ion

38. Select the correct statement(s) about group 13 (IIIA) elements.
(a) $[Al(H_2O)_6]^{3+}$ exists in aqueous solution
(b) MX_3 is a strong Lewis acid
(c) Stability of hydrides (MH_3) decreases as we move down the group
(d) All the above are correct statements

39. The decrease stability of higher oxidation state in p-block with increasing atomic number is due to
(a) energy required to unpair ns^2 electrons is not compensated by the energy released in forming the two additional bonds
(b) decrease in bond energy as going down the group
(c) Both (a) and (b) are correct
(d) None of the above

40. Boric acid is a weak acid. Thus, it behaves as
(a) an electron acceptor as in
$$B(OH)_3 + H_2O \rightleftharpoons [B(OH)_4]^- + H^+$$

(b) proton donor as in
$$H_3BO_3 + H_2O \rightleftharpoons H_3O^+ + H_2BO_3^-$$
(c) an electron donor as in
$$H_3BO_3 \rightleftharpoons H_3BO_3^+ + e^-$$
(d) proton acceptor as in
$$H_3BO_3 + H_2O \rightleftharpoons H_4BO_3^+ + OH^-$$

41. Actual source of the proton in boric acid is based on the following
(a) $B(OH)_3\,(aq) + 2H_2O(l) \rightleftharpoons H_3O^+(aq) + [B(OH)_4]^-(aq)$
(b) $B(OH)_3 \rightleftharpoons H_2BO_2^- + H^+$
(c) $3B(OH)_3\,(aq) \rightleftharpoons [B_3O_3(OH)_4^-](aq) + H^+(aq) + 2H_2O\,(l)$
(d) All of the above

42. Stabilities of adducts formed with boron-halides is in order
(a) $BF_3 < BBr_3 < BCl_3$ (b) $BBr_3 > BCl_3 < BF_3$
(c) $BCl_3 < BBr_3 < BF_3$ (d) $BF_3 < BCl_3 < BBr_3$

43. Light elements B, Al, C and Si are
(a) fluorophiles (high affinity for fluorine)
(b) oxiphiles (high affinity for oxygen)
(c) Both (a) and (b)
(d) None of the above

44. Which is spontaneous in forward side?
(a) $Tl^{3+} + 2e^- \longrightarrow Tl^+$ (b) $Ga^{3+} + 2e^- \longrightarrow Ga^+$
(c) $In^{3+} + 2e^- \longrightarrow In^+$ (d) $Al^{3+} + 2e^- \longrightarrow Al^+$

45. The correct structural representation of diborane is
(a) $[BH_2]^+\,[BH_4]^-$ (b) 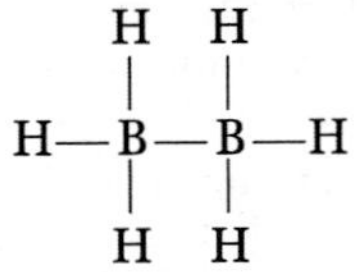
(c) 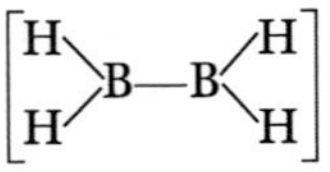 (d) 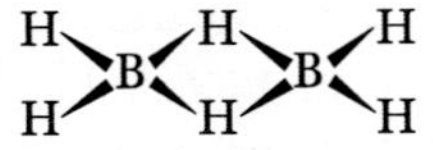

46. Which of the following statement(s) about H_3BO_3 is not correct?
(a) It is strong tribasic acid
(b) It does not acts as a Lewis acid by accepting hydroxyl ion
(c) It has a layer structure in which planar BO_3 units are joined by hydrogen bonds
(d) It is prepared by acidifying an aqueous solution of borax

47. The relative stability of the different oxidation state
$$Tl^+ > Tl^{3+} > Ga^{3+} > Ga^+ > Tl^+ > In^+ > Ga^+$$
is an example of
(a) electron affinity (b) inert pair effect
(c) redox potential (d) disproportionation

48. The composition of mica is
(a) $NaAlSiO_4 \cdot 3H_2O$
(b) $K_2O \cdot 3Al_2O_3 \cdot 6SiO_2 \cdot 2H_2O$
(c) $K_2HAl(SiO_4)_3$
(d) $Na \cdot K \cdot SiO_4 \cdot 10H_2O$

49. Select the correct statement(s).
(a) Aluminium dissolves in dilute mineral acids but is made passive by concentrated nitric acid
(b) Aluminium vessel can be used as storage of NaOH
(c) Both (a) and (b)
(d) None of the above

50. The type of hybridization of boron in diborane is
(a) sp (b) sp^2
(c) sp^3 (d) sp^3d^2

51. Diamagnetic species can be
(a) GaS (b) $GaCl_2$
(c) B_2Cl_4 (d) All of these

52. Which of the following compound(s) is/are possible?
(a) GaS, $GaCl_2$ (b) $Ga(GaCl_4) \cdot Ga_2S_2$
(c) B_2Cl_4, BCl_2, Cl_2B (d) All of these

53. In the reaction, $B_2O_3 + C + Cl_2 \longrightarrow A + CO$, A is
(a) CCl_2 (b) BCl_2
(c) BCl_3 (d) B_2Cl_2

54. Radius of Ga is less than Al because of
(a) inert pair effect (b) greater screening effect
(c) lanthanide contraction (d) None of these

55. Fusion of borane with NaOH produce
(a) $Na_3BO_3 + H_2O$ (b) $NaBO_2 + H_2O$
(c) $B_2O_3 + H_2O$ (d) $Na_2B_4O_7 + H_2O$

56. Which of the following has the highest first ionization energy?
(a) Boron (b) Lithium
(c) Beryllium (d) Carbon

57. B H B bridge in B_2H_6 is formed by sharing of
(a) 2 electrons (b) 4 electrons
(c) 1 electron (d) 3 electrons

58. The solution of sodium meta aluminate on boiling with ammonium chloride gives a white precipitate of
(a) Al_2O_3 (b) $AlCl_3$
(c) $Al(OH)_3$ (d) $(NH_4)_2SO_4 \cdot Al_2(SO_4)_3$

59. $AlCl_3$ fumes in moist air because it
(a) is covalent (b) is hygroscopic
(c) is volatile (d) forms HCl in moist air

60. H_3BO_3 is
(a) monobasic acid and weak Lewis acid
(b) monobasic and strong Lewis acid
(c) monobasic and Bronsted acid
(d) tribasic and weak Bronsted acid

61. $B(OH)_3 + NaOH \rightleftharpoons NaBO_2 + Na[B(OH)_4] + H_2O$
How can this reaction is made to proceed in foward direction?
(a) Addition of borax
(b) Addition of *cis*-1, 2 diol.
(c) Addition of Na_2HPO_4
(d) Addition of *trans*-1, 2-diol

62. Which metal is powdered, suspended in oil and used as paint?
(a) Fe (b) Sn (c) Ag (d) Al

63. Reactivity of borazole is greater than that of benzene because
(a) of localised electrons in it
(b) borazole is polar compound
(c) borazole is non-polar compound
(d) borazole is electron deficient compound

64. Borax $Na_2B_4O_7 \cdot 10H_2O$ is actually
(a) $Na_2[B_4O_5(OH)_4]\cdot 8H_2O$
(b) $Na_2[B_4O_2(OH)_{10}]\cdot 5H_2O$
(c) $Na_2[B_4O_4(OH)_6]\cdot 7H_2O$
(d) $Na_2[B_4O_4(OH)_6]\cdot 6H_2O$

65. Chemical formula of red liquor is
(a) $(CH_3COO)_3Al$ (b) $Al(OH)_3$
(c) $Al_2(CO_3)_3$ (d) $Al_2(SO_4)_3$

66. Which metal is protected by a layer of its own oxide?
(a) Al (b) Ag (c) Au (d) Fe

67. Alumina on heating with carbon in nitrogen atmosphere gives
(a) $Al + CO$ (b) $Al + CO_2$
(c) $AlN + CO$ (d) $Al + CO + N_2$

68. Borax on heating with cobalt oxide forms a bead of
(a) $Co(BO_2)_2$ (b) $CoBO_2$
(c) $Co_3(BO_3)_2$ (d) $Na_3Co(BO_3)_2$

69. BF_3 is used as a catalyst in several industrial processes due to its
(a) stronge reducing nature
(b) weak reducing nature
(c) strong Lewis acid character
(d) weak Lewis acid character

70. General formula B_nH_{n+6} represents a
(a) closoborane (b) nidoborane
(c) arachnoborane (d) hypnoborane

71. In H_2O, Ga^+ changes to
(a) Ga (b) Ga^{3+}
(c) Ga and Ga^{3+} (d) Ga^{2+} and Ga^{3+}

72. Boric acid is the trivial name for
(a) orthoboric acid (b) pyroboric acid
(c) metaboric acid (d) None of these

73. Na_3AlF_6 is added to Al_2O_3 to
(a) improve the electrical conductivity of the cell
(b) decrease the electrical conductivity
(c) increase the melting point
(d) increase rate of production

74. Boron carbide is used
(a) as an abrasive
(b) in nuclear reactor to absorb neutrons
(c) Both (a) and (b)
(d) None of the above

75. Borax is converted into B by steps

$$\text{Borax} \xrightarrow{\text{I}} H_3BO_3 \xrightarrow{\Delta} B_2O_3 \xrightarrow{\text{II}} B$$

I and II are
(a) acid, Al (b) acid, Fe
(c) acid, Mg (d) acid, C

76. While testing BO_3^{3-}, there is green-edged flame on heating the salt with conc. H_2SO_4 and CH_3OH. Green colour is of
(a) B_2O_3 (b) H_3BO_3 (c) $(CH_3)_3B$ (d) $(CH_3O)_3B$

77. Borax is used as a buffer since
(a) its aqueous solution contains equal amount of weak acid and its salt
(b) statement that borax is a buffer, is wrong
(c) its aqueous solution contains equal amount of strong acid and its salt
(d) it is easily available

78. General formula of aluminium alums is (M' is monovalent cation)
(a) $[M'(H_2O)_6][Al(H_2O)_6](SO_4)_4$
(b) $[M'(H_2O)_4][Al(H_2O)_4](SO_4)_4$
(c) $[M'(H_2O)_6][Al(H_2O)_6](SO_4)_2$
(d) $[M'(H_2O)_4][Al(H_2O)_6](SO_4)_2$

79. Diborane is a Lewis acid forming addition compounds $B_2H_6\cdot 2NH_3$ with NH_3, a Lewis base. This
(a) on heating, is converted into borazine, $B_3N_3H_6$ (called inorganic benzene)
(b) is ionic and exists as $[BH_2(NH_3)_2]^+$ and $[BH_4]^-$ ions
(c) Both (a) and (b)
(d) None of the above

80. Thermite welding uses Al because of
(a) its lightness
(b) its low melting point
(c) its greater affinity for oxygen
(d) All of the above

81. Indium is used
(a) in thermistors
(b) in low melting point solder
(c) to drop crystals to make *p-n-p* transistors
(d) All of the above

82. Light-emitting diodes (LED), laser diodes and memory chips of computers are made of
(a) aluminium (b) gallium
(c) arsenic (d) gallium-arsenide

Exercise 2

(For Part 'C')

1. H_3BO_3 and HBO_2 do not differ in
(a) structure (b) basicity
(c) melting point (d) oxidation number

2. Which of the following has the regular tetrahedral structure?
(a) SF_4 (b) BF_4^-
(c) XeF_4 (d) $[Ni(CN)_4]^{2-}$

3. Molecule(s) possessing three-centre-two electron bonds and three-centre-four electron bonds would include
(a) B_2H_6 alone (b) B_2H_6 and SiF_4
(c) B_2H_6 and XeF_6 (d) XeF_6 and BF_6

4. Consider the following statements for diborane.
1. Boron is approximately sp^3-hybridized.
2. B–H–B angle is 180°.
3. There are two terminal B H bonds for each boron atom.
4. There are two terminal B H bonds for each boron atom.

Of these statements
(a) 1, 2 and 3 are correct (b) 2, 3 and 4 are correct
(c) 1, 3 and 4 are correct (d) 1, 2 and 4 are correct

5. The dipole moments of the given molecules are such that
(a) $NH_3 > NF_3 > BF_3$ (b) $BF_3 > NF_3 > NH_3$
(c) $NF_3 > NH_3 > BF_3$ (d) $NH_3 > BF_3 > NF_3$

6. Select the correct statement(s).
(a) Borates and silicates have tetrahedral BO_4 and SiO_4 structural units
(b) Oxides of B and Si (B_2O_3 and SiO_2) are acidic in nature
(c) Hydrides of B and Si are volatile and catches fire on exposure to air
(d) All of the above are correct

7. Select the incorrect statement(s).
(a) B_2H_6 has all B H bond equal
(b) $LiAlH_4$ is ionic compound
(c) AlH_3 is colourless solid and is polymeric containing Al H Al bridge
(d) AlX_3 (X = Cl, Br, I) have low melting point, are covalent and have the halogen-bridged dimeric structure

8. The Styx code for diborane is
(a) 2020 (b) 2200
(c) 2002 (d) 0220

9. Using the Wade rules, the structure of $B_{10}C_2H_{12}$ can be predicted. The structure and the number of isomers of $B_{10}C_2H_{12}$ respectively are
(a) nido and two (b) closo and three
(c) nido and one (d) closo and two

10. Which of the following is an arachno borane?
(a) $[B_6H_6]^{2-}$ (b) $[B_5H_9]$
(c) $[B_2H_6]$ (d) $[B_6H_{12}]$

11. An alloy of boron and aluminium is allowed to react with NH_3. Products formed are
(a) BN, AlN, H_2 (b) $B(NH_2)_3$, AlN, H_2
(c) BN, $Al(NH_2)_3$, H_2 (d) $B(NH_2)_3$, $Al(NH_2)_3$, H_2

12. The thermal disproportionation of B_2Cl_2 gives
(a) B_8Cl_8 (b) B_4Cl_4
(c) BCl_3 (d) All of these

13. Anion containing both three and four coordinated boron is
(a) $B_3O_6^{2-}$ (b) $[B(OH)_4]^-$
(c) $BO_3BO_4^-$ (d) $[B_4O_5(OH)_4]^{2-}$

14. Thermal stability of boron compounds is in the order
(a) $B_2Cl_4 < B_2F_4 < B_2(OR)_4 < B_4(NR_2)_4$
(b) $B_2(NR_2)_4 < B_2(OR)_4 < B_2F_4 < B_2Cl_4$
(c) $B_2F_4 < B_2Cl_4 < B_2(NR_2)_4 < B_2(OR)_4$
(d) $B_2(OR)_4 < B_2(NR_2)_4 < BF_4 < BCl_4$

15. Which of the following are used as transition materials and light emitting devices (LED)?
1. Gallium-arsentes 2. Gallium-phosphides
3. Indium-arsenides 4. Indium-phosphides
(a) Only 4 (b) Except 1, 2, All
(c) Except 1, all (d) All of these

16. Which reactions can be used to prepare diborane?
1. $NaBH_4 + BF_3$ (in ether) $\longrightarrow$
2. $NaBH_4 + I_2 \longrightarrow$
3. $BF_3 + NaH \longrightarrow$
(a) 1, 2 (b) 2, 3
(c) 1, 3 (d) 1, 2 and 3

17. $Na_2B_4O_7 \cdot 10H_2O \xrightarrow{\Delta} NaBO_2 + A + H_2O$

$$A + MnO \xrightarrow{\Delta} B$$

A and B are
(a) $Na_2(BO_2)_2$ and $Mn(BO_2)_2$
(b) Na_3BO_3 and $Mn_3(BO_3)_2$
(c) B_2O_3 and $Mn(BO_2)_2$
(d) None of the above

18. Aqueous solution of borax reacts with 2 moles of acids. This is because of
(a) formation of 2 moles each of $[B(OH)_4]^-$ and $B(OH)_3$ of which only $[B(OH)_4]^-$ reacts with acid.
(b) formation of 1 mole each of $B(OH)_3$ and $[B(OH)_4]^-$
(c) formation of 2 moles of $[B(OH)_4]^-$ only
(d) formation of 2 moles of $B(OH)_3$ only.

19. Select the correct statement(s).
(a) BF_3 fumes strongly in moist air and is partially hydrolysed by excess of water
(b) BF_3 is converted into the adducts $BF_3 \cdot H_2O$ and $BF_3 \cdot 2H_2O$ with small amounts of water at low temperature
(c) H_3BO_3 is a weak acid but HBF_4 is a very strong acid
(d) KBF_4 is sparingly soluble in water

20. Select the correct statement(s).
(a) BCl_3 form adducts with NH_3, H_2O and RNH_2.
(b) BF_3 forms adducts with NH_3, ROH and RNH_2.
(c) BCl_3 reacts with liquid NH_3 and ethanol forming $B(NH_2)_3$ and $B(OEt)_3$.
(d) $[BCl_4]^-$, $[BBr_4]^-$ and $[BI_4]^-$ ions can be made only in non-aqueous media.

21. Select the correct statement(s).
(a) Boron trimethyl is a weaker Lewis acid than the boron trihalides or monoborane.
(b) Lewis acid property when Me_3N is a donor in order :
$$BBr_3 > BCl_3 > BF_3 \sim BH_3 > BMe_3.$$
(c) Lewis acid property when Me_3P is a donor in order :
$$BBr_3 > BCl_3 \sim BH_3 > BF_3 > BMe_3.$$
(d) Lewis acid property when CO is a donor. No adduct is formed with halides and Lewis acid property of
$$BH_3 > BF_3 > BMe_3.$$

22. Select the correct statement(s).
(a) A saturated solution of boric acid in water is neutral to the indicator bromocresol green
(b) Aqueous solution of boric acid and potassium hydrogen difluoride is alkaline to bromocresol indicator
(c) AlF_3 is insoluble in anhydrous HF
(d) Aqueous solution of KHF_2 is basic to the indicator bromocresol green

23. Select the correct statement(s).
(a) Diborane is an electron-deficient compound.
(b) Diborane is stoichiometrically analogous to ethane (C_2H_6).
(c) Total electrons involved in bonding are 12 in diborane and 14 in ethane.
(d) Total electrons involved in bonding are 12 in diborane and ethane.

Assertion & Reason

Codes
(a) Both A and R are true and R is the correct explanation of A.
(b) Both A and R are true and R is not the correct explanation of A.
(c) A is true but R is false.
(d) A is false but R is true

24. Assertion (A) Boron forms BF_4^-.
Reason (R) BF_3 is an electron deficient species.

25. Assertion (A) B_2Cl_4, $GaCl_2$, GaS are diamagnetic.
Reason (R) They show + 2 oxidation state.

26. Assertion (A) $AlCl_3$ exists an $[Al(H_2O)_6]Cl_3$ in dilute aqueous solution.
Reason (R) When water is dropped to a solid $AlCl_3$, vigrous hydrolysis ensues.

27. Assertion (A) $B(OH)_3$ is a good libricant and slippery.
Reason (R) $B(OH)_3$ has a layer structure.

28. Assertion (A) Boric acid does not act as a proton donor but an electron-acceptor.
$$B(OH)_3 + H_2O \rightleftharpoons [B(OH)_4]^- + H^+$$
Reason (R) Boric acid is a very weak acid.

29. Assertion (A) The group BN is isoelectronic with C_2.
Reason (R) No species containing of $B{\equiv}N$ group has yet been discovered.

30. Assertion (A) $B_3N_3H_{12}$ (similar to cyclohexane) exists as chair conformation.
Reason (R) Borazine ($B_3N_3H_6$) is much more reactive than benzene.

31. Assertion (A) Aluminium trimethyl is a dimer having structure like that of $AlCl_3$.
Reason (R) There is three-centre two-electron bonding in Al—C—Al bridge.

32. Assertion (A) Borazine is called inorganic benzene.
Reason (R) Borazine undergoes addition and substitution reactions with HCl and Br_2 etc.

33. Assertion (A) The bond-lengths in BF_3 are 1.30 Å and are shorter than the sum of the covalent radii.
Reason (R) $p\pi$-$p\pi$ interaction exists and all B—F bonds are equivalents are based on modern explanation, the double bond is delocalised.

34. Assertion (A) $AlCl_3$ forms dimer Al_2Cl_6 but is dissolves in H_2O forming $[Al(H_2O)_6]^{3+}$ and Cl^- ions.
Reason (R) Aqueous solution of $AlCl_3$ is acidic due to hydrolysis.

35. Assertion (A) In aqueous solution $AlCl_3$ forms dimer Al_2Cl_6.

Reason (R) The high enthalpy of hydration is sufficient to break the covalent dimer into $[M(H_2O)_6]^{3+}$ and Cl^- ions.

36. Assertion (A) In water, orthoboric acid behaves as a weak monobasic acid.
Reason (R) In water, orthoboric acid acts as a proton donor.

37. Assetion (A) Boron always forms covalent form.
Reason (R) The small size of B^{3+} favours formation of covalent bond.

38. Arrange the following in the decreasing order of their Lewis acidity.

$B(CH_3)_3$, BF_3, BF_3, BCl_3, BBr_3

(a) $BBr_3 > BCl_3 = BH_3 \geq BF_3 > B(CH_3)_3$
(b) $B(CH_3)_3 > BCl_3 > BBr_3 > BF_3 > BH_3$
(c) $BF_3 > BCl_3 > BBr_3 > BH_3 > B(CH_3)_3$
(d) $BH_3 > B(CH_3)_3 > BBr_3 > BCl_3 > BF_3$

39. Match the following.

	Compounds		No. of valence electrons
A.	B_4H_{10}	1.	24
B.	B_5H_9	2.	22
C.	B_5H_{11}	3.	26
D.	B_6H_{10}	4.	38

	A	B	C	D
(a)	1	2	3	4
(b)	3	2	1	4
(c)	2	1	3	4
(d)	1	3	2	4

40. Match the following.

	Reactants		Products
A.	$B_2H_6 + NaBH_4 \rightarrow$	1.	$(BN)_x$
B.	$B_2H_6 + CH_3OH \rightarrow$	2.	$KBO_2 + H_2$
C.	$B_2H_6 + KOH(aq) \rightarrow$	3.	$B(OCH_3)_3 + H_2$
D.	$B_2H_6 + NH_3$ (excess) $\rightarrow$	4.	$NaB_3H_8 + H_2$

	A	B	C	D
(a)	1	2	3	4
(b)	4	3	2	1
(c)	2	4	1	3
(d)	3	2	4	1

41. Which statements about anhydrous aluminium chloride is correct?
(a) It exists an Al_2Cl_6 molecules in solid state
(b) It is easily hydrolysed
(c) It sublimes at 180°C
(d) It reacts with air

42. Which is used in glazing?
(a) Borax (b) Orthoboric acid
(c) Metaboric acid (d) None of these

Directions (Q. Nos. 43 and 44)
The tetrafluoroborate anion, BF_4^-, is a Lewis base. The other tetrahaloborate anions, BBr_4^-, can be prepared in non-aqueous solvents.

43. BF_4^- is
(a) F^- donor
(b) a lone-pair acceptor
(c) a lone-pair donor
(d) solvated in aqeous solution

44. BCl_4^- and BBr_4^- are stable in
(a) H_2O (b) alcohol
(c) Both (a) and (b) (d) None of these

Directions (Q. Nos. 45 to 48) Certain aspects of the aqueous chemistry of aluminium compounds derive from the nature of the hydrated aluminium ion-$[Al(H_2O)_6]^{3+}$.

$$[Al(H_2O)_6]^{3+} + H_2O \rightleftharpoons [Al(H_2O)_5(OH^-)]^{2+} + H_3O^+$$

45. Above equilibrium indicates that
(a) H_2O is a Lowry-Bronsted acid
(b) H_2O is a Lowry-Bronsted base
(c) H_2O is a Lowry-Bronsted acid as well as a base
(d) H_2O is neither acid or base

46. Above equilibrium is represented in
(a) strongly acidic solution
(b) alkaline solution
(c) aqueous solution
(d) Any of the above

47. Ionisation of the above equilibrium is favoured in
(a) strongly acidic solution (b) alkaline solution
(c) aqueous solution (d) Any of the these

48. Aluminate ion can be written as
(a) AlO_2^- (b) $Al(OH)_4^-$
(c) $[Al(H_2O)(OH)_4]^-$ (d) All of these

Directions (Q. Nos. 49 to 52) Diborane is an electron deficient compound. Stoichiometrically, it is analogous to ethane, C_2H_6. However, the total number of electrons involved in bonding are less in diborane.

49. Bonding electrons involved
(a) in B_2H_6 is 14 and in C_2H_6 16
(b) in B_2H_6 is 12 and in C_2H_6 14
(c) in B_2H_6 is 10 and in C_2H_6 12
(d) in B_2H_6 is 16 and in C_2H_6 18

50. Octet is complete in
(a) boron in diborane
(b) carbon in ethane
(c) boron in diborane and carbon in ethane
(d) None of the above

51. In diborane there is
(a) two-electron-three-centre bonds
(b) three-electron-three-centre bonds
(c) two-electron-two-centre bonds
(d) three-electron-two-centre bonds

52. Consider the following statements for diborane

1. Boron is approximately sp^3 hybrised
2. B—H—B angle is 180°
3. There are two terminal B—H bonds for each boron atom
4. Three are only 12 bonding electron available

Of these statements

(a) 1, 3 and 4 are correct (b) 1, 2 and 3 are correct
(c) 2, 3 and 4 are correct (d) 1, 2 and 4 are correct

Directions (Q. Nos. 53 to 56) Study the following sequence of reactions :

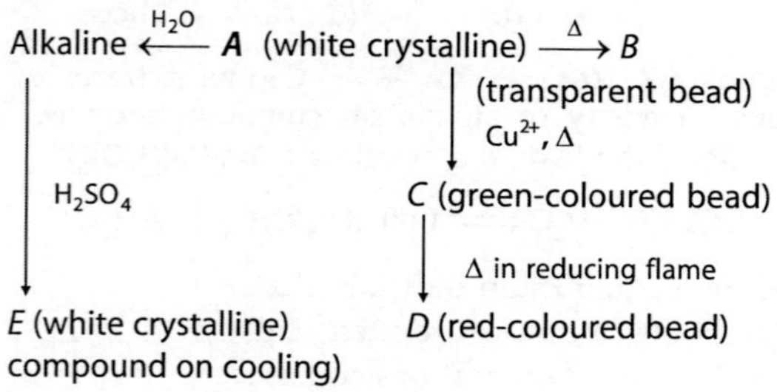

53. *A* is

(a) $NaBO_2$ (b) $Na_2B_4O_7$
(c) H_3BO_3 (d) HBO_3

54. *B* is

(a) $NaBO_2$ (b) B_2O_3
(c) Na_3BO_3 (d) H_3BO_3

55. *C* and *D* respectively are

(a) Cu_2BO_2, CuO
(b) $Cu(BO_2)_2$, $CuBO_2$
(c) $Cu_2B_2O_4$, CuO
(d) $Cu(BO_2)_2$, $Cu_2B_2O_4$

56. Select the correct statement(s) about *E*.

(a) *E* is a weak acid (H_3BO_3)
(b) It is not a protonic acid but electron-pair acceptor
(c) *E* shows following equilibrium

$$B(OH)_3 + H_2O \rightleftharpoons [B(OH)_4]^- + H_3O^-$$

(d) All the above are correct statements

Answers

Exercise 1

1. (d)	2. (b)	3. (a)	4. (b)	5. (d)	6. (d)	7. (a)	8. (d)	9. (b)	10. (d)
11. (a)	12. (d)	13. (d)	14. (d)	15. (c)	16. (d)	17. (a)	18. (c)	19. (d)	20. (a)
21. (c)	22. (d)	23. (b)	24. (a)	25. (a)	26. (a)	27. (a)	28. (d)	29. (a)	30. (c)
31. (a)	32. (c)	33. (a)	34. (b)	35. (a)	36. (a)	37. (a)	38. (d)	39. (c)	40. (a)
41. (a)	42. (c)	43. (d)	44. (c)	45. (d)	46. (a)	47. (b)	48. (b)	49. (a)	50. (c)
51. (d)	52. (d)	53. (c)	54. (b)	55. (a)	56. (d)	57. (a)	58. (c)	59. (b)	60. (a)
61. (b)	62. (d)	63. (a)	64. (a)	65. (a)	66. (a)	67. (c)	68. (a)	69. (d)	70. (c)
71. (c)	72. (a)	73. (a)	74. (c)	75. (c)	76. (d)	77. (a)	78. (c)	79. (c)	80. (c)
81. (d)	82. (d)								

Exercise 2

1. (d)	2. (b)	3. (b,,c,d)	4. (c)	5. (a)	6. (d)	7. (a)	8. (c)	9. (b)	10. (d)
11. (c)	12. (d)	13. (a)	14. (a)	15. (d)	16. (d)	17. (c)	18. (a)	19. (a,b,c,d)	20. (b,c,d)
21. (a,b,c,d)	22. (a,b,c)	23. (a,b,c)	24. (a)	25. (b)	26. (b)	27. (a)	28. (b)	29. (b)	30. (b)
31. (b)	32. (a)	33. (a)	34. (b)	35. (c)	36. (c)	37. (a)	38. (a)	39. (c)	40. (b)
41. (a,b,c)	42. (a,b,c)	43. (c)	44. (d)	45. (c)	46. (a)	47. (b)	48. (d)	49. (b)	50. (b)
51. (a)	52. (a)	53. (b)	54. (b)	55. (b)	56. (d)				

Hints & Solutions

Exercise 1

1. $Na_2B_4O_7 \cdot 10H_2O \xrightarrow{\Delta} \underbrace{2NaBO_2 + B_2O_3}_{\text{Borax bead}} + 10H_2O$

12. From B_2H_6, $B_2(CH_3)_6$ cannot be prepared.

19. $BF_3 \Rightarrow$ 3 bond pair + 0 lone pair

$\Rightarrow sp^2$ hybridisation $\Rightarrow$ planar trigonal geometry

22. $H_3BO_3 + H_2O \rightleftharpoons [B(OH)_4]^- + H_3O^+$

25. In van-Arkel method, impure metal is first converted into its iodide which on heating at high temperature dissociates into pure metal and I_2.

28. Borax bead test is used to detect the presence of transition elements.

36. + 3 oxidation state of Ga is more stable than + 1.

42. All boron halides are Lewis acids and thus form adduct with Lewis bases. Since, BBr_3 is more acidic than BCl_3 and BF_3 so adduct given by it is more stable, than that given by BCl_3 or BF_3.

44. Due to inert pair effect, stability of lower oxidation state increases on moving down the group.

45.

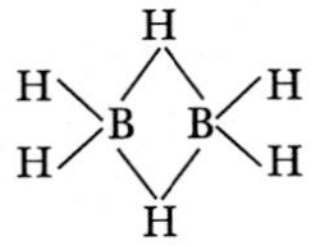

3*c*-2*e*-bond

75. $Na_2B_4O_7 \cdot 10H_2O \xrightarrow[\text{HCl}]{\text{(I)}} H_3BO_3 \xrightarrow{\Delta} B_2O_3 \xrightarrow[\text{Mg}]{\text{(II)}} B + MgO$

76. $H_3BO_3 + CH_3OH \xrightarrow{\text{Conc. } H_2SO_4} (CH_3O)_3B + 3H_2O$

Burns with green flame

Exercise 2

1. H_3BO_3 O.S of B = + 3

HBO_2 O.S. of B = + 3

2. BF_4^- has regular tetrahedral structure because of the presence of four σ-bonds.

SF_4 has distorted tetrahedral structure and $[Ni(CN)_4]^{2-}$ has square planar geometry.

5.

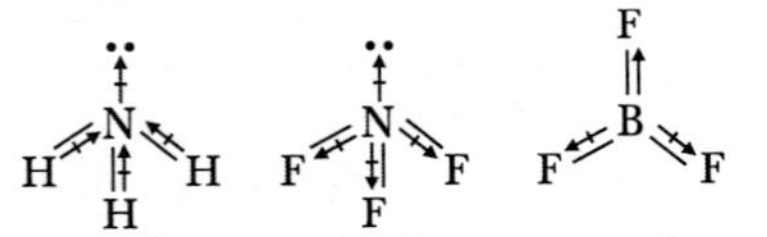

$\mu \neq 0$ $\mu \neq 0$ $\mu = 0$

μ of NH_3 in greater than NF_3. It is due the same direction of N–H bond diple and dipole due to the lone pair.

8. B_2H_6 has the following structure.

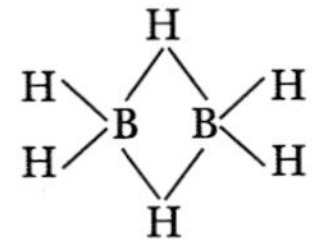

$S = 2$ (no. of B—H—B bonds)

$t = 0$ (no. of B—B—B bonds)

$y = 0$ (no. of B—B bonds)

$x = 2$ (no. of terminal BH_2 units)

So, styx of diborane is 2002.

11. $BAl \xrightarrow{NH_3} BN + Al(NH_2)_3 + H_2$

39. (A) B_4H_{10} $(4 \times 3 + 10 = 22)$

(B) B_5H_9 $(5 \times 3 + 9 = 24)$

(C) B_5H_{11} $(5 \times 3 + 11 = 26)$

(D) B_6H_{10} $(6 \times 3 + 10 = 28)$

40. $B_2H_6 + NaBH_4 \longrightarrow NaB_3H_8 + H_2$

$B_2H_6 + CH_3OH \longrightarrow B(OCH_3)_3 + H_2$

$B_2H_6 + KOH \longrightarrow KBO_2 + H_2$

$B_2H_6 + NH_3 \longrightarrow (BN)_x$

6

The *p*-Block Elements-II

Introduction

Groups 14, 15, 16 and 17 contain the following elements :

Groups

14		15		16		17	
Carbon	C	Nitrogen	N	Oxygen	O	Fluorine	F
Silicon	Si	Phosphorus	P	Sulphur	S	Chlorine	Cl
Germanium	Ge	Arsenic	As	Selenium	Se	Bromine	Br
Tin	Sn	Antimony	Sb	Tellurium	Te	Iodine	I
Lead	Pb	Bismuth	Bi	Polonium	Po	Astatine	At

These elements show the general trend of periodic properties *i.e.*, their atomic radii, ionic radii, basic character of oxides, metallic character etc., decrease in a period and increase on moving down a group. Electronegativity, electron affinity, ionisation potential, acidic character of oxides, non-metallic character etc., are the properties that increases along a period (from C to F) and decrease on moving down a group.

Catenation

Catenation is the property of the atoms of an element to form chains and rings through the formation of covalent bonds with each other. This property is best exhibited by carbon followed by sulphur and silicon.

Conditions for catenation

The conditions necessary for catenation are as follows :

(i) The valency of the element must be greater than or equal to two.

(ii) The element must form strong element– element bonds of strength equal to or greater than those with other elements, especially oxygen.

Syllabus

- Main Groups Elements and their Compounds
- Allotropy, Synthesis, Structure and Bonding
- Industrial Importance of the Compounds

The catenated compounds of carbon owe their stability to the uniquely strong bonds which carbon forms with itself. Some related values of bond energies (kJ mol^{-1}) are given below :

C—C	355.30
Si—Si	225.72
Ge—Ge	167.20
Sn—Sn	158.36
C—O	336
Si—O	368
C—H	425

From the above data, it is evident that the strength of C—C bonds is very high, and thus carbon exhibits catenation to a maximum extent. As we go down the group, the strength of element-element bond decreases sharply and as a result tendency for catenation decreases in the order.

$$C > Si > Ge > Sn$$

The Si—Si bond is weaker than C—C bond because the larger size of silicon atom causes Si—Si bond length to increase. Consequently, the forces holding Si—Si decreases.

In this chapter, we shall be discussing the chemistry of some important compounds of these elements.

Chemistry of Group

Comparison of Carbon with Silicon

Since, carbon and silicon belong to the same group 14 of the Periodic Table and have similar electronic configuration, therefore, they are expected to have similar chemical behaviour. In fact, both do form similar hydrides (CH_4, C_2H_6; SiH_4, Si_2H_6); oxides (CO_2, SiO_2); acids (H_2CO_3, H_2SiO_3) and halides (CCl_4, $SiCl_4$). Inspite of the similarity of the formulae of their compounds, the chemistry of carbon and silicon differs in many ways, these differences are attributed to the following reasons :

(a) Smaller size of carbon as compared to silicon.

(b) Non-availability of *d*-orbitals in carbon.

(c) High catenation capacity of carbon.

Silicon does not form *pπ-pπ* multiple bonds either to itself or to other elements, whereas carbon exhibits great tendency for *pπ* multiple bonding. Because of this simple reason analogs like CO_2 and SiO_2, $(CH_3)_2CO$ and $(CH_3)_2SiO$ have totally different structures. For example, dehydration of $R_2Si(OH)_2$ does not give $R_2Si{=}O$ but a silicone $(R_2SiO)_n$.

Silicon, however, has the ability to form *dπ-pπ* double bonds with elements like oxygen and nitrogen. It may be mentioned here that trisilylamine, $N(SiH_3)_3$ is planar and a very weak base in contrast to trimethylamine, $(CH_3)_3N$ which is pyramidal and a strong base. This is attributed to the existence of *dπ-pπ* bonding in the N–Si linkage. The lone pair of nitrogen is delocalized into the vacant 3*d* orbitals of silicon. Since, carbon has 3*d* orbitals of very high energy and cannot take part in bond formation, such a situation cannot exist in trimethlylamine.

Empty 3*d* orbital of Si   Filled $2p_z$ orbital of N   Overlap (*dπ-pπ* bond)

Example 1. *Explain why* H_3SiNCS *has a linear* SiNCS *group whereas in* H_3C NCS *the* NCS *linkage is angular?*

Sol. This can be attributed to *dπ-pπ* bonding involving empty 3*d* orbitals of silicon overlapping with filled $2p_z$ orbitals of nitrogen or oxygen.

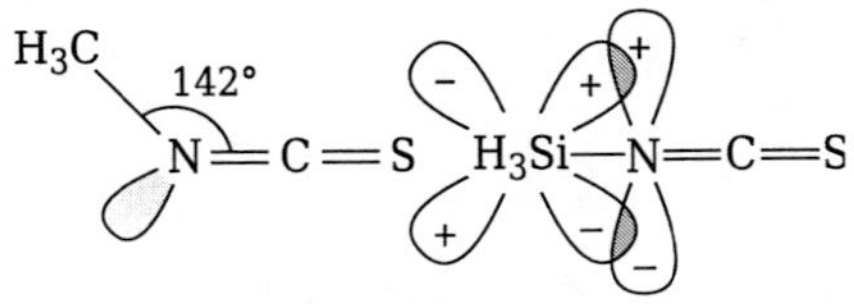

Example 2. *Write equations of reactions of* CS_2 *with* C_2H_5ONa *in ethanol and with* $(C_2H_5)_2NH$ *in the presence of aqueous* NaOH.

Sol. $C_2H_5ONa + CS_2 \xrightarrow{C_2H_5OH} \underset{\text{Sodium ethylxanthate}}{C_2H_5\,OCS_2Na}$

$$(C_2H_5)_2NH + CS_2 \xrightarrow{NaOH} \underset{\text{Sodium dialkyldithiocarbmate}}{(C_2H_5)_2\,NCS_2Na}$$

Cement

Cement "is essentially a finely ground mixture of calcium aluminates and silicates which sets to a hard mass when treated with water". It is also called **Portland cement** because of its resemblance to a famous variety of building stone quarried near Portland (in England).

Raw Materials

Portland cement is made by fusing together two types of materials :

(a) *Calcareous* (or rich in lime) such as limestone, chalk, alkali waste, shells or marine animals.

(b) *Argillaceous* (or rich in alumina and silica) such as clay, shale, slate, blast furnace, slag. The composition of clay is $Al_2O_3 \cdot 2SiO_2 \cdot Fe_2O_3 \cdot 2H_2O$. Clay supplies silica ($SiO_2$) and alumina ($Al_2O_3$) to the cement. Some clays do not contain Fe_2O_3. Cement obtained from the use of these clays is white and hard to burn.

Although (a) and (b) are the main raw materials which are used in the manufacture of cement, another raw material, **gypsum ($CaSO_4 \cdot 2H_2O$) is also required. It helps to reduce the setting time of cement.**

Composition

The relative percentage of the raw materials naturally depends upon the type of the cement desired. The following table indicates the range of composition of raw materials.

Table 6.1 **Composition of Raw Materials**

Constituent	Per cent
CaO	60–65
SiO_2	20–24
Al_2O_3	5–9
Fe_2O_3	2–4
MgO	1–5
SO_3	1–2
Na_2O	0.5–1

Composition of Portland Cement

Microscopic investigations reveal the complex nature of cement. The average composition of Portland cement is as given below :

1.	Tricalcium silicate	$3CaO \cdot SiO_2$	46%
2.	Dicalcium silicate	$2CaO \cdot SiO_2$	26%
3.	Tricalcium aluminate	$3CaO \cdot Al_2O_3$	10%
4.	Tetracalcium alumino ferrite	$4CaO \cdot Al_2O_3 \cdot Fe_2O_4$	9%
5.	Pentacalcium trialuminate	$5CaO \cdot 3Al_2O_3$	3%
6.	Gypsum	$CaSO_4 \cdot 2H_2O$	2%
7.	Other impurities		4%

Impurities Present in Raw Materials and Their Effect on the Product

(i) Limestone often contains $MgCO_3$ and this on calcination gives MgO. The MgO produced at high temperature has the property of hydrating very slowly. If it is present in large amount in cement it will cause delayed expansion giving rise to cracks. Hence, the MgO content in the raw materials should not go beyond 3%.

(ii) Sulphur is also injurious and its amount should not exceed $\frac{4}{3}$%.

(iii) Iron oxide is also associated with most of the raw materials. It should not be in excess, otherwise too much fluxing action would take place.

Role of Water During Setting of Cement

During the setting of cement, water plays an important role because hydration as well as hydrolysis involve reaction with water. Water is essential for the formation of gels since hydration is an exothermic reaction. Therefore, cement structures have to be cooled during setting either by spraying water or circulating cold water through pipes embedded in the heavy structure such as big dams.

Role of Gypsum During Setting of Cement

The addition of gypsum to powdered clinkers helps in the removal of fast setting tricalcium aluminate forming calcium sulphoaluminate.

$$3CaO \cdot Al_2O_3 + 3CaSO_4 + 2H_2O \longrightarrow 3CaO \cdot Al_2O_3 \cdot 3CaSO_4 \cdot 2H_2O$$

Consequently, the process of setting of cement gets retarded and this results in better strength of the mass which sets.

Silicate Minerals

Next to oxygen, silicon is the most abundant element in the Earth's crust (26 per cent). As SiO_2, it accounts for sand, flint and quartz, as complex silicates of aluminium, iron, magnesium and other metals, *i.e.,* it accounts for practically all rocks, clays and soils. Experimental facts have revealed that all silicates have —Si—O—Si linkage and the coordination number of silicon with respect to oxygen is always four *i.e.,* all silicates are built of $(SiO_4)^{4-}$ tetrahedra.

Various silicates are classified according to the linking of $(SiO_4)^{4-}$ tetrahedral units as dicussed below :

1. Ortho Silicates

These contain discrete $(SiO_4)^{4-}$ tetrahedra. This anion is formed in zircon, $ZrSiO_4$ and in garnets, $M_3^a M_2^b (SiO_4)_3$ where M^a can be Ca^{2+}, Mg^{2+}, Mn^{2+} or Fe^{2+}, M^b is Fe^{3+}, Cr^{3+} or Al^{3+}. These garnets are very hard and find extensive use as industrial abrasives.

2. Pyrosilicates

These contain discrete disilicate ion, $(Si_2O_7)^{6-}$ formed by joining two SiO_4 tetrahedra through an oxygen atom. Examples of pyrosilicates are rare and the only well established structure is that of scandium silicate or thorteveitite, $Sc_2(Si_2O_7)$.

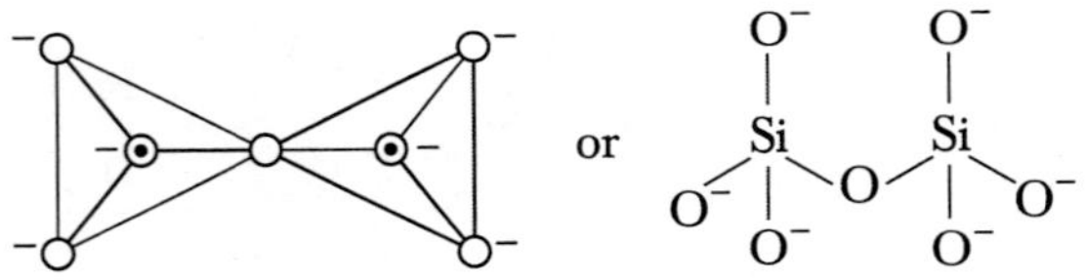

Fig. 6.3 Structure of $(Si_2O_7)^{6-}$ ion.

3. Cyclic Silicates

If each SiO_4 tetrahedron shares an oxygen atom with two of its neighbouring tetrahedra, ring anions are formed. Two different ring sizes are known.

The small size ring contains three SiO_4 tetrahedra linked together as $[Si_3O_9]^{6-}$ ion and is present in Wollasionite, $Ca_3(Si_3O_9)$.

The large sized ring containing six SiO_4 tetrahedra yields the ion $[Si_6O_{18}]^{12-}$ and such an anion is present in beryl, $Be_3Al_2Si_6O_{18}$.

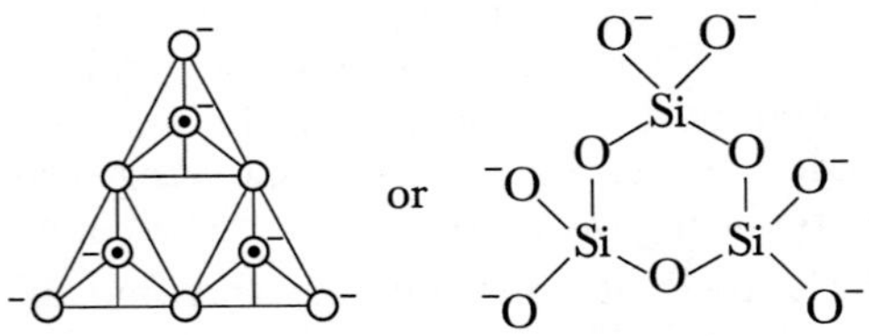

Fig. 6.4 Structure of $[Si_3O_9]^{6-}$ ion.

Minerals such as beryl, quartz and alumina are colourless, but a variety of colours exist in these minerals due to the presence of small amounts of transition metal ions. For example, beyl crystals contain Cr^{3+} in emerald, alumina crystals contain Cr^{3+} in ruby and Fe plus Ti in sapphire. Amethyst is quartz and contains some Fe in place of silicon in SiO_4 tetrahedral.

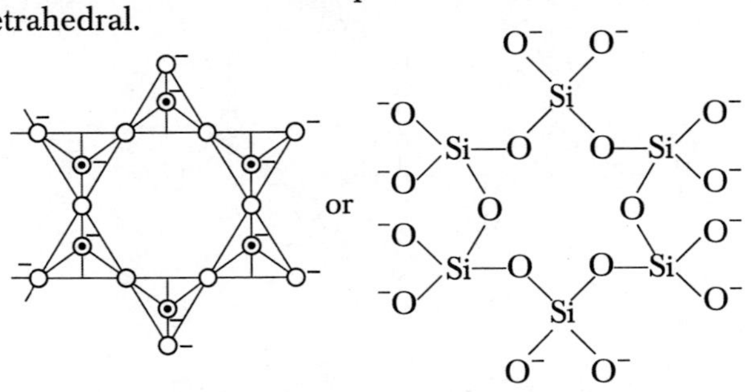

Fig. 6.5 Structure of $[Si_6O_{18}]^{12-}$ ion.

4. Chain Silicates

These are formed by sharing of two oxygens by each tetrahedron. The chain structure is found in many minerals and these are known as **pyroxenes** and contain single-strand chain of composition $(SiO_3)_n^{2n-}$. Examples are $MgSiO_3$ (enstatite) and $CaMg(SiO_3)_2$ (diopiside). In these compounds, the silicate chains lie parallel to each other and the cations lie between the chains and bind them together.

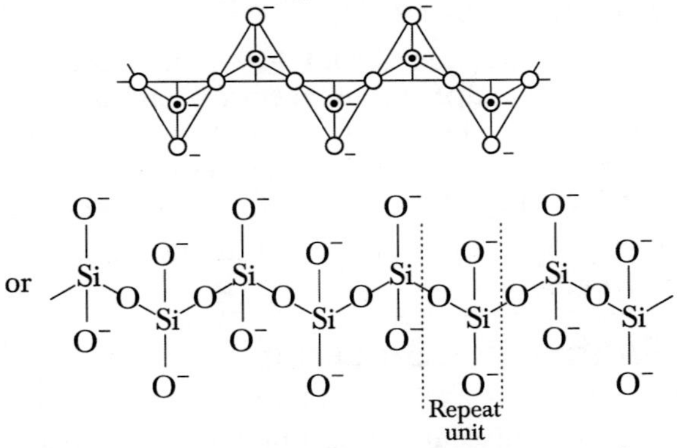

Fig. 6.6 Single strand chain silicate ion, $(SiO_3)_n^{2n-}$.

Two chains may be linked together to form double chains which correspond to the formula $(Si_4O_{11})^{6-}$.

These double chain structures are also common and represented by the class of minerals called amphiboles which include most asbestos minerals. A typical **amphibole is tremolite,** $Ca_2Mg_5(Si_4O_{11})_2(OH)_2$.

Structurally they are similar to pyroxenes though they contain some hydroxyl groups which are attached to the cations. This class of minerals also exhibit a fibrous texture, and the term used for such minerals is asbestos, $CaMg_3O$ (Si_4O_{11}). Asbestos was widely used as insulation, partitions and ceilings and for filtration devices in the laboratory. Now, its use has been greatly reduced because of the hazard of lung cancer due to the inhalation of the fibres.

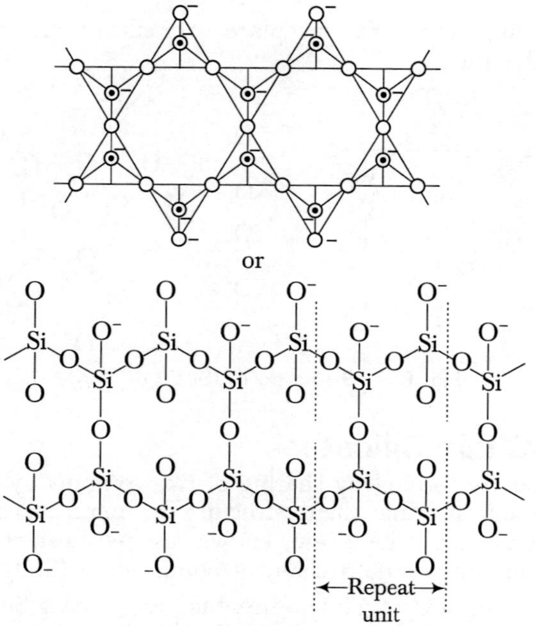

Fig. 6.7 Double chain silicate ion $[Si_4O_{11}]_n^{6n-}$.

5. Sheet Silicates

In case the SiO_4 tetrahedra have three corners in common with adjacent tetrahedra then an infinite two-dimensional sheet structure results (Fig. 6.18). A wide variety of sheet silicate minerals are known, *e.g.,* **talc,** $Mg_3(OH)_2(Si_4O_{10})$ and **kaolin,** $Al_2(OH)_4(Si_2O_5)$. These minerals usually contain hydroxyl groups.

6. Framework Silicates

If all the four oxygen atoms of a SiO_4 tetrahedron are shared with adjacent tetrahedra and the process is repeated, then an infinite three-dimensional structure is formed. The empirical formula for such a substance would correspond to $(SiO_2)_n$. In framework silicates, the SiO_4 units along with randomly present AlO_4 units are linked by the sharing of all four oxygens. The partial replacement of Si by Al requires another cation in the framework silicates. There are three types of framework silicates; the **feldspars, the ultramarines** and the **zeolites.**

The **feldspars** make up for about two-thirds of the igneous rocks and are the most important of the rock-forming minerals. The general formula of the feldspars are $M(Al, Si)_4O_8$ where M can be Na, K, Ca or Ba and the ratio of Si to Al varies from 3 : 1 to 2 : 2. An example is orthoclase, $K[AlSi_3O_8]$.

The **ultramarines** (have basket like framework) are commonly coloured and are used as pigments. They contain negative ions, such as Cl^-, SO_4^{2-} or S^{2-} that are not the part of the framework. **Sodalite,** $Na_8Al_6Si_6O_{24}\cdot Cl_2$ is an ultramarine.

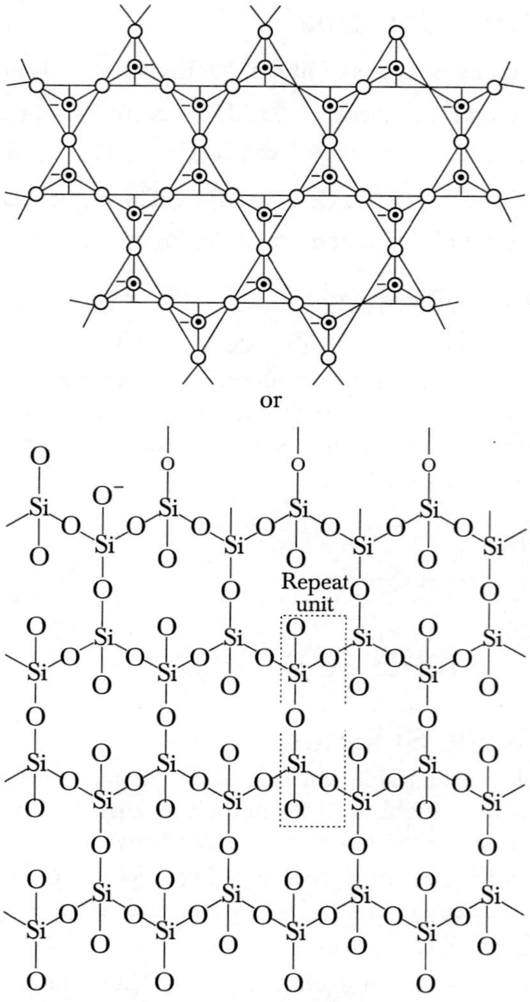

Fig. 6.8 Structure of sheet silicates.

The **zeolites** have very open structures formed by joining silicate chains or cages. There are structures which contain large cavities and channels running through them in three dimensions. The open structures have made zeolites useful as ion-exchanges-softening water by replacing Mg^{2+} or by Na^+. Synthetic zeolites provide channels of optimum size and find extensive use in industry. The size of the channels are of molecular size and function as molecular sieves or as catalysts. Molecular sieves can separate gases based on molecular size, as in gas chromatography.

Example 3. *The melting points of quartz* (SiO_2) *is* 1600°C, *and the sublimation point of* CO_2 *is* −78°C. *Account these facts in terms of these two substances.*

Sol. Difference in melting points suggests a difference in their crystal structures. The intermolecular forces in solid CO_2 (molecular lattice which is held by weak van der Waals' forces between discrete CO_2 molecules) are very low and can overcome at a low temperature. SiO_2 on the other hand is a covalent lattice with a three-dimensional network of bonds. Each silicon is bonded tetrahedrally to 4 oxygens, and each oxygen is bonded to 2 silicon atoms.

Silanes

Saturated hydrides of silicon are called **silanes**. These have the general formula Si_nH_{2n+2}, where n has the maximum value of 6. SiH_4 is called **monosilane**; Si_2H_6 is called disilane and so on.

Preparation

Silanes are prepared by the following methods :

1. By the action of HCl, H_2SO_4 or H_3PO_4 on magnesium silicide, Mg_2Si.

$$Mg_2Si + 4HCl \longrightarrow SiH_4 + 2MgCl_2$$

In addition to SiH_4, other silanes such as Si_2H_6, Si_3H_8 etc., are also formed which are separated by low temperature fractional distillation or by gas-liquid chromatography.

2. By the action of $LiAlH_4$ on $SiCl_4$ in ether at 273 K.

$$LiAlH_4 + SiCl_4 \longrightarrow LiCl + AlCl_3 + SiH_4$$

On the other hand, $LiAlH_4$ reacts with Si_2Cl_6 in ether to form disilane as

$$3LiAlH_4 + 2Si_2Cl_6 \longrightarrow 3LiCl + 3AlCl_3 + 2Si_2H_6$$

Properties

1. They are colourless, volatile covalent gaseous compounds.
2. Their melting and boiling points increase with increase in the number of silicon atoms in the silane.

Table 6.2 **Melting and Boiling Points of Silanes**

Hydride	Monosilane SiH_4	Disilane Si_2H_6	Trisilane Si_3H_8	Tetrasilane Si_4H_{10}	Pentasilane Si_5H_{12}	Hexasilane Si_6H_{14}
Melting point (K)	88.3	140.5	156	179.5	–	–
Boiling point (K)	161	258	326	358	373	373

3. They have characteristic odour and are poisonous.
4. They are not soluble in water but are soluble in benzene as well as carbon disulphide.
5. They are extremely reactive and are spontaneously inflammable in air. The inflammability increases as the number of silicon atom increases in the silane.

$$SiH_4 + 2O_2 \longrightarrow SiO_2 + 2H_2O$$

6. They are rapidly hydrolysed by water (containing traces of alkali) forming silicates and liberating hydrogen.

$$Si_2H_6 + 4KOH + 2H_2O \longrightarrow 2K_2SiO_3 + 7H_2$$

7. They decompose into their elements, on heating above 725 K in absence of air.

$$SiH_4 \longrightarrow Si + 2H_2$$

The thermal stability of silanes decreases with increasing molecular mass.

8. Silanes are strong reducing agents. They reduce silver nitrate to silver.

$$4AgNO_3 + SiH_4 \longrightarrow 4Ag + Si + 4HNO_3$$

9. They react with Cl_2 or Br_2 to form substituted silanes. This reaction is quite vigorous and is controlled by maintaining low temperatures :

$$SiH_4 + Cl_2 \longrightarrow SiH_3Cl + HCl$$
$$SiH_3Cl + Cl_2 \longrightarrow SiH_2Cl_2 + HCl$$
$$SiH_2Cl_2 + Cl_2 \longrightarrow SiHCl_3 + HCl$$
$$SiHCl_3 + Cl_2 \longrightarrow SiCl_4 + HCl$$

10. They react with hydrogen halides in the presence of aluminium halide as a catalyst at 373 K to produce substituted halogenated silanes.

$$SiH_4 + HX \longrightarrow SiH_3X + H_2$$
$$SiH_3X + HX \longrightarrow SiH_2X_2 + H_2$$
$$SiH_2X_2 + HX \longrightarrow SiX_3H + H_2$$
$$SiX_3H + HX \longrightarrow SiX_4 + H_2$$

11. Compounds containing Si—H bonds such as $SiHCl_3$ or Me_3SiH react with alkenes in the presence of chloroplatinic acid as a catalyst to form addition products.

$$RCH{=}CH_2 + SiHCl_3 \longrightarrow RCH_2CH_2SiCl_3$$

The above reaction is known as **Speier reaction** or **hydrosilation reaction** as it involves the hydrosilation of alkenes.

12. Higher silanes such as Si_6H_{14} react with chloroform or carbon tetrachloride forming silicon tetrachloride.

$$Si_2H_6 + 3CHCl_3 \longrightarrow 2SiCl_4 + HCl + 4H_2 + 3C$$
$$Si_2H_6 + 2CCl_4 \longrightarrow 2SiCl_4 + 3H_2 + 2C$$

The above reactions are quite vigorous.

Silicon Polymers [Poly (Organosiloxanes)]

Pure organic polymers such as elastomers, greases, lubricants and heat transfer fluids cannot withstand high temperatures. To find new high temperature polymers, chemists have turned to inorganic chemistry particularly to the field of silicon chemistry because of the high thermal stability of Si—O—Si chains. Recently, chemists have achieved success in the production of high temperature polymers known as **Silicones** which are polymeric organosilicon compounds containing Si—O—Si linkages. These compounds have the general formula $(R_2SiO)_n$ (R = Me, Et or Ph). They may be linear cyclic or cross-linked polymers.

Preparation

Silicones are prepared by the hydrolysis of alkyl or aryl substituted silicon halides. These compounds are initially prepared by passing an alkyl or aryl halide over a Cu/Si catalyst at about 300°C.

$$2MeCl(g) + Si/Cu(s) \longrightarrow Me_2SiCl_2(l) + Cu(s)$$
$$(CH_3)_2SiCl_2 + 2H_2O \longrightarrow \underset{\text{Dimethyldithydroxy silane}}{(CH_3)_2Si(OH)_2} + HCl$$

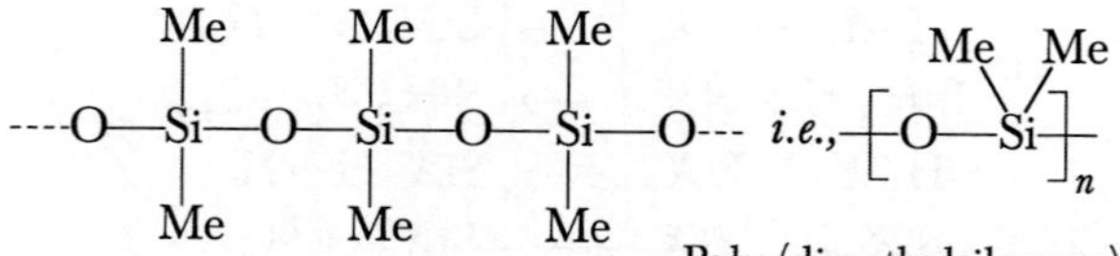

Poly (dimethylsiloxane)

Linear silicones

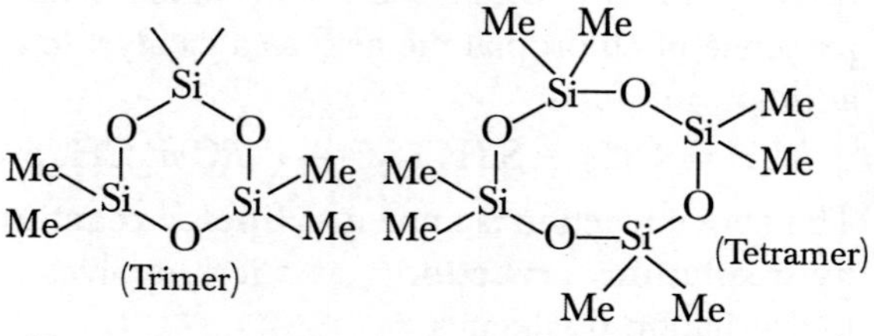

[Cyclo-(Me$_2$SiO)$_3$] [Cyclo-(Me$_2$SiO)$_4$]

Cyclic silicones

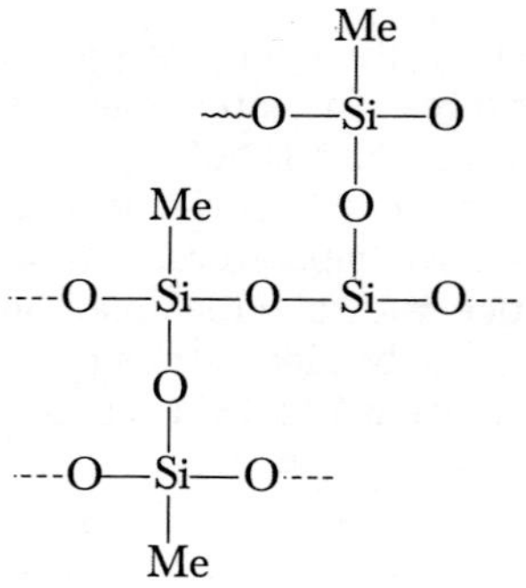

Cross linked silicones

The hydrolysis of dimethyldichlorosilane yields octamethylcyclotetrasiloxane. The cyclic tetramer is a colourless, oily material. When heated above 100°C with a trace of acid or base, it polymerizes to form a highly viscous liquid or gum. The molecular weight of the polymer may be as high as 2×10^6.

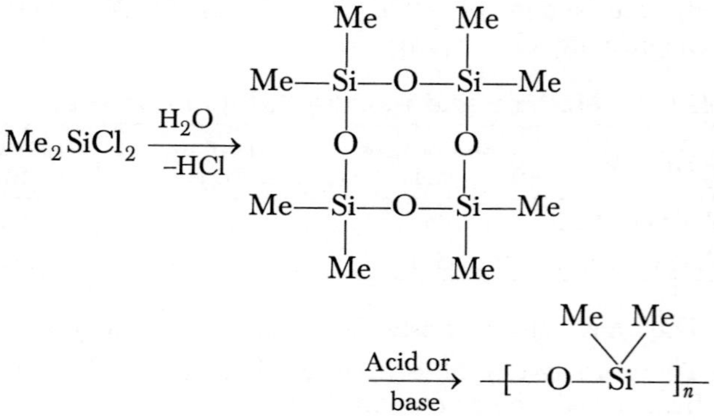

CHEMISTRY OF GROUP 15

Allotropy of Phosphorus

Element phosphorus exists in three main allotropic forms known as white, red and black phosphorus.

1. White Phosphorus

Molecular weight determination suggests that white phosphorus exist as P_4 molecules. Electron diffraction data show that P_4 molecule is tetrahedral (Fig. 6.9).

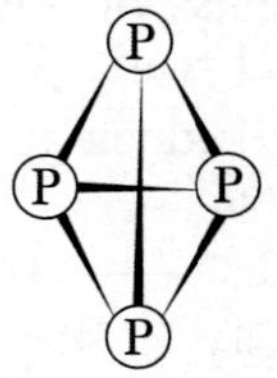

Fig. 6.9 Structure of white phosphorus (P_4)

These molecules are attracted to each other by van der Waals' forces to form the solid. The P—P—P bond angles are only 60° (theoretically required angle is 90° if pure 3*p* orbitals are involved). This suggests that the structure is under strain and unstable. The strained nature of P_4 is confirmed by the high chemical reactivity of white phosphorus. It is highly toxic. It inflames in air (due to its high chemical reactivity) and thus has to be stored under water (insoluble in water) to protect it from air. It is soluble in organic solvents such as benzene, carbon disulphide, liquid SO_2 and liquid NH_3. Some reactions of white (or red P) are given below :

$$P_4 + \xrightarrow{O_2} P_4O_6, P_4O_{10} \xrightarrow{H_2O} \text{Oxo acids}$$
$$P_4 + \xrightarrow{X_2} PX_3, PX_5$$
$$P_4 + \xrightarrow[\text{boil}]{OH^-} PH_3$$
$$P_4 + \xrightarrow{S} P_4S_3, P_4S_5, P_4S_7, P_4S_{10}$$
$$P_4 + \xrightarrow{\text{Metals}} Na_3P$$

2. Red Phosphorus

It is prepared by heating white phosphorus in a sealed vessel at – 400°C. It is dense than white P_4 and has a much higher melting point (~ 600°C). It is much less reactive. It is non-toxic and therefore easier to handle. It is used commercially. It exists as long chains of phosphorus atoms which are covalently bonded to give giant molecular crystal.

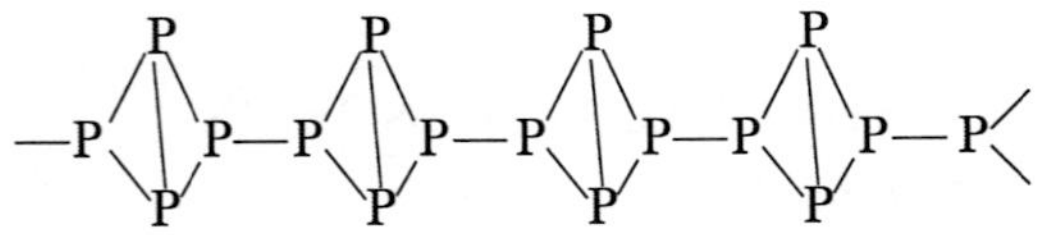

Fig. 6.10 Structure of red phosphorus.

3. Black Phosphorus

It is thermodynamically the most stable form of phosphorus. White phsophorus when subject to very high pressure at 200°C changes into "black phosphorus". It has metallic lustre and conducts heat and electricity moderately well. The crystal lattice consists of double layers, each layer made of adjacent *zig-zig* chains with P—P—P angles of 99°. Each phosphorus atom in a particular layer being 218 pm from its nearest neighbouring phosphorus atoms, two in the same chain and one in a chain in the layers above or below. Distance between two adjacent layers is 368 pm. Binding between the layers is thus weaker than within a particular layer. Similarities between this structure and the graphite structure are striking.

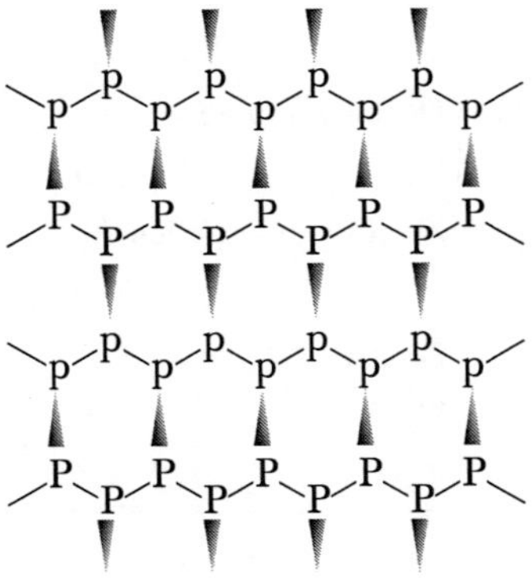

P = Above the plane of the paper
p = Below the plane of the paper

Fig. 6.11 Structure of black phosphorus.

Comparison of allotropic forms of phosphorus

The white phosphorus is the most reactive while black phosphorus is the least reactive. Therefore, the white phosphorus is stored under water to protect it from air, while red and black are stable in air.

Oxides of Nitrogen

Oxides of nitrogen have been known for over 200 years. They have played an important role in verifying Dalton's law of multiple proportions which helped in the formulation of his famous atomic theory. Some important oxides of nitrogen are summarized in Table 6.3.

1. Nitrous Oxide, N_2O

Preparation

$$NH_4NO_3 \xrightarrow{\Delta} N_2O + 2H_2O$$

The gas is collected over hot water, since the gas is soluble in cold water.

Table 6.3 **Oxides of Nitrogen**

Oxidation state of the element	Formula	Name	Structure
+1	N_2O	Dinitrogen monoxide (nitrous oxide)	N—N—O
+2	NO	Nitrogen monoxide	N—O
+3	N_2O_3	Dinitrogen trioxide	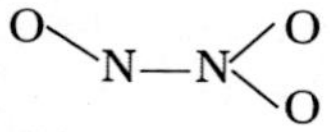
+4	NO_2	Nitrogen dioxide	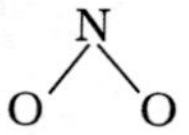
+4	N_2O_4	Dinitrogen tetroxide	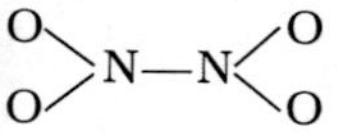
+5	N_2O_5	Dinitrogen pentoxide	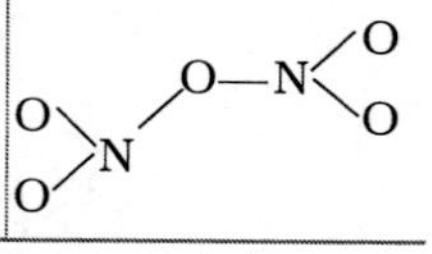

Properties

1. It is a colourless gas (m.p. = −90.8, b.p. = − 88.5°C), with pleasant odour producing mild hysterical and so it used as an anaesthetic in minor operations. It is highly soluble in cold water but insoluble in hot water. When inhaled in small quantities, it causes hysterical laughter and therefore it is also called **laughing gas**.
2. It decomposes into N_2 and O_2.

$$2N_2O \longrightarrow 2N_2 + O_2$$

Therefore, it readily supports combustion acting as a source of oxygen. *e.g.*,

$$Cu + N_2O \xrightarrow{\text{Red hot}} CuO + N_2$$

$$S + 2N_2O \longrightarrow SO_2 + 2N_2$$

3. A mixture of hydrogen and nitrous oxide (equal volumes) explodes violently.

$$N_2O + H_2 \longrightarrow N_2 + H_2O$$

4. Ammonia and nitrous oxide explode violently.

$$3N_2O + 2NH_3 \longrightarrow 4N_2 + 3H_2O$$

Uses

(i) It was formerly used as a mild anaesthetic.

(ii) It is used as a propellent and aerating agent in whipped ice-cream due to its solubility in vegetable fats and because of its non-toxicity in small concentrations.

Structure

It contains linear NNO group in which two nitrogen atoms are bonded to each other. It may be considered as a resonance hybrid of the following structures :

$$:\overset{-}{\ddot{N}}=\overset{+}{N}=\ddot{O}: \longleftrightarrow :N\equiv\overset{+}{N}-\overset{-}{\ddot{\underset{..}{O}}}:$$

2. Nitric Oxide, NO

Preparation

On an industrial scale it is prepared by the catalytic oxidation of NH_3 with O_2 at 500°C in the presence of Pt gauze (**Ostwald's process**).

$$4NH_3 + 5O_2 \longrightarrow 4NO + 6H_2O$$

On the laboratory scale, it may be prepared

(i) By the reduction of acidified nitrates with iodides or ferrocyanides

$$KNO_2 + KI + H_2SO_4 \longrightarrow NO + K_2SO_4 + H_2O + \frac{1}{2}I_2$$

$$KNO_2 + K_4[Fe(CN)_6] + 2CH_3COOH \longrightarrow NO + K_3[Fe(CN)_6] + H_2O + 2CH_3COOK$$

(ii) By the disproportionation of nitrous acid in the presence of dilute sulphuric acid :

$$6KNO_2 + 3H_2SO_4 \longrightarrow 4NO + 2HNO_3 + 2H_2O + 3K_2SO_4$$

Properties

1. It is colourless, monomeric, paramagnetic gas with low m.p. (− 163.6° and b.p. − 151.8°C). It is a thermodynamically unstable molecule and decomposes at 1100°C into its elements (N_2 and O_2).
2. Action with XeF_2

$$XeF_2 + 2NO \longrightarrow 2NOF + Xe$$

3. Action with I_2O_5

$$2I_2O_5 + 10NO \longrightarrow 5N_2O_4 + 2I_2$$

4. Action with nitrogen trichloride

$$NCl_3 + 2NO \longrightarrow NOCl + N_2O + Cl_2$$

5. Action with alkali metal hydroxides

$$2KOH + 4NO \longrightarrow 2KNO_2 + N_2O + H_2O$$

$$4KOH + 6NO \longrightarrow 4KNO_2 + N_2 + 2H_2O$$

6. It reacts with iron(II) salts to form a complex cation $[Fe^{I}(H_2O)_5NO]^{2+}$ which is responsible for the brown ring. **This is used as a test for the confirmation of nitrate ion.**

Structure

In valence bond method, the electronic structure of NO is interesting because the molecule has eleven valency electrons. It is impossible for all of them to be paired. Thus, the molecule contains an odd electron which makes gaseous nitric oxide paramagnetic.

In valence bond theory, the electronic structure of NO can be explained in terms of Pauling's special hypothesis of a three electron bond which is half as strong as a two electron bond.

$$:\overset{\bullet\bullet\bullet}{N=O}:$$

Nitric oxide is a resonance hybrid of the following two structures :

$$:\dot{N}:\ :\ddot{O}: \longleftrightarrow :\overset{-}{\ddot{N}}:\ :\overset{+}{\dot{O}}:$$

The NO molecule has the electronic configuration

$$\text{NO }[\text{KK }(\sigma^b_{2s})^2\ (\overset{*}{\sigma}_{2s})^2, (\sigma^b_z)^2\ (\pi^b_x, \pi^b_y)^4\ (\overset{*}{\pi}_x)^1]$$

The unpaired $\overset{*}{\pi}_x$ electron makes the molecule paramagnetic. The bond order is 2.5 in agreement with the interatomic $N—\overset{x}{O}$ distance of 115 pm which is intermediate between the triple bond distance in NO^+ (106 pm) and N—O double bond distance of about 120 pm. The NO^+ ion is isoelectronic with CO. Like carbon-monoxide, it forms compounds with transition metals.

NO is an odd electron molecule. It dimerizes in the liquid (b.p. – 152°C) and solid state (m.p. – 164°) to NO_2 ($\Delta H \simeq 4$ kcal mol^{-1}). The dimer is colourless and has planar and cyclic structure with long (218 pm), weak bonds between the nitrogens.

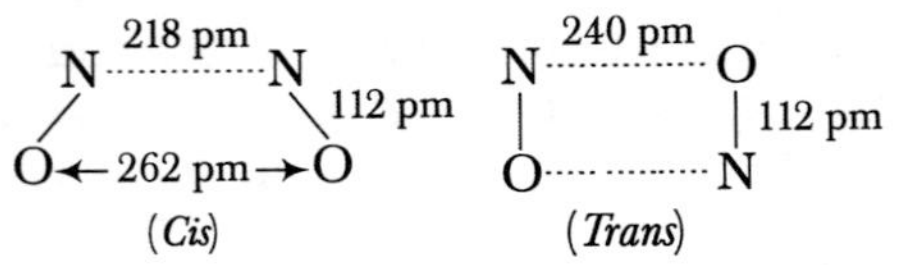

(*Cis*) (*Trans*)

The *cis* structure with very weak N–N bond can be easily rationalized in terms of the half occupied HOMO of NO. The overlap of both the nitrogen *p* and oxygen *p* atomic orbitals of $\overset{*}{\pi}$ HOMO (the M.O. configuration of NO is given above) gives both N......N and O......O bonding.

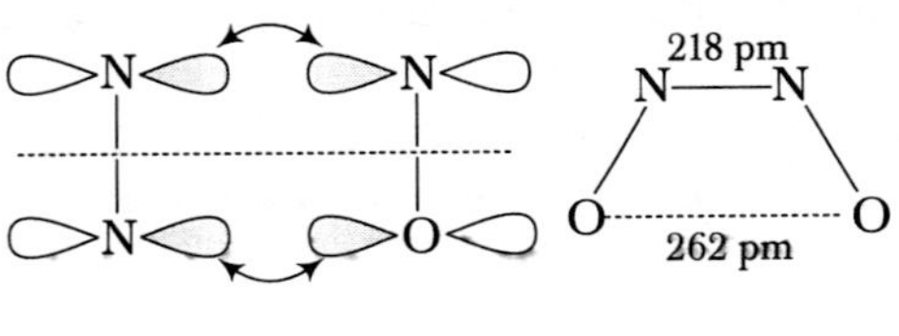

Crystalline nitric oxide also exists in dimeric units and X-ray diffraction data suggests *cis* structure.

3. Dinitrogen Trioxide, N_2O_3

Preparation

It is obtained as a blue liquid when equimolar quantities of nitric oxide and nitrogen dioxide are cooled at about – 20°C.

$$\underbrace{NO + NO_2}_{\text{Brown}} \underset{\text{Room temp.}}{\overset{253\text{ K}}{\rightleftharpoons}} \underbrace{N_2O_3}_{\text{Blue}}$$

On warming to room temperature, it forms a brown equilibrium mixture of NO and NO_2.

It reacts with bases to produce nitrites.

$$N_2O_3 + 2KOH \longrightarrow 2KNO_2 + H_2O$$

It may formally be considered as the anhydride of nitrous acid.

$$2NHO_2 \xrightarrow{-H_2O} N_2O_3$$

Structure

Based on spectroscopic and thermochemical evidences and coupled with molecular orbital concept of bonding, N_2O_3 has been assigned a planar structure containing long and weak N to N bond.

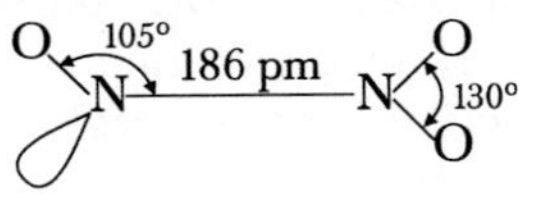

4. Nitrogen Dioxide and Dinitrogen Tetroxide

Both nitrogen dioxide (NO_2) and dinitrogen tetroxide (N_2O_4), exist in equilibrium with each other at ordinary temperatures. The monomer, NO_2 contains one unpaired electron and is paramagnetic. It has brown colour. In dimeric form, N_2O_4 is diamagnetic and colourless. At room temperature, the equilibrium mixture contains 28.5% of NO_2 and at 135°C the mixture is 99% NO_2.

Preparation

NO_2 is prepared in the laboratory by heating dry lead nitrate in a steel vessel.

$$2Pb(NO_3)_2 \longrightarrow 2PbO + 4NO_2 + O_2$$

or by action of conc. HNO_3 on copper.

$$Cu + 4HNO_3 \longrightarrow Cu(NO_3)_2 + 2H_2O + 2NO_2$$

On an industrial scale, it is prepared by the oxidation of NO

$$2NO + O_2 \longrightarrow 2NO_2$$

Properties

1. **Action with water** It reacts with water to give a mixture of nitrous and nitric acids.

$$2NO_2 + H_2O \longrightarrow HNO_2 + HNO_3$$

2. **Action as an oxidising agent** Nitrogen dioxide behaves as an oxidising agent. For example,

$$NO_2 + H_2S \longrightarrow NO + S + H_2O$$
$$2NO_2 + 4HCl \longrightarrow 2NOCl + 2H_2O + Cl_2$$

3. **Action with alkalies** Nitrogen dioxide reacts with alkalies to give nitrites and nitrates.

$$2KOH + 2NO_2 \longrightarrow KNO_2 + KNO_3 + H_2O$$

4. **Action with conc. sulphuric acid** Nitrogen dioxide reacts with conc. sulphuric acid to give nitrosyl hydrogen sulphate and nitric acid.

$$2NO_2 + H_2SO_4 \longrightarrow \underset{\text{Nitrosyl hydrogen sulphate}}{NOHSO_4} + HNO_3$$

Structure of NO_2

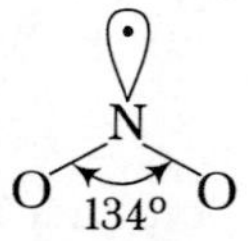

Electron diffraction studies have revealed that nitrogen dioxide is angular while O—N—O angle of 134°. An unshared electron resides on nitrogen which is responsible for its tendency to dimerise (unlike NO). In fact, its constitution is best represented a resonance hybrid of the following structures :

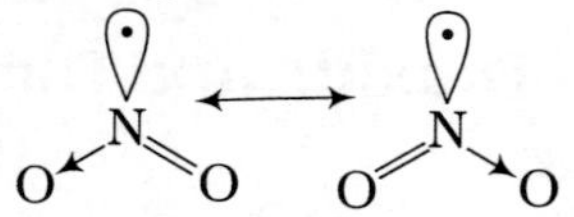

Just like NO, nitrogen dioxide has a great tendency to lose its odd electron and thus form nitronium ion NO_2^+ which is thought to be the precursor for nitration of aromatic compounds.

Structure of N_2O_4

The dimer is known to exist in planar $O_2N—NO_2$ form.

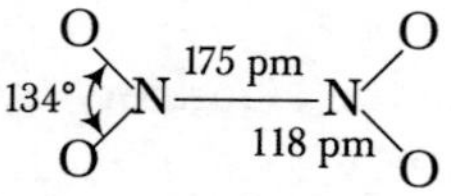

The structure of N_2O_4 is unusual in the sense that

(i) Its planar configuration is more stable than twisted one although oxygen to oxygen repulsions is maximum in this configuration.

(ii) The N—N both length of 175 pm is longer than the single N—N bond distance of 147 pm observed in $H_2N—NH_2$. So far no satisfactory explanation has been given for these observations.

5. Dinitrogen Pentoxide, N_2O_5

Preparation

$$4HNO_3 + P_4O_{10} \longrightarrow 2N_2O_5 + 4HPO_3$$

Thus, N_2O_5 is anhydride of nitric acid

$$N_2O_5 + H_2O \longrightarrow 2HNO_3$$

Properties

1. It is a white crystalline solid which decomposes above 30°C.

$$2N_2O_5 \longrightarrow 4NO_2 + O_2$$

2. It is an excellent oxidising agent *e.g.,* converts I_2 to I_2O_5.

$$5N_2O_5 + I_2 \longrightarrow 10NO_2 + I_2O_5$$

Structure

X-ray studies show that the solid consists of nitronium nitrate, $NO_2^+ \ NO_3^-$.

In gas phase, it exists as N_2O_5 molecules. Electron diffraction and Raman spectral studies indicate that the molecular structure of the compound is

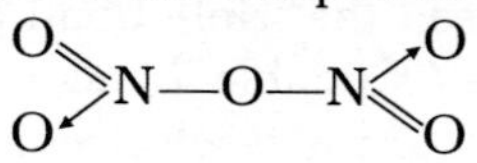

Oxides of Phosphorus

Phosphorus forms several oxides, three of which are well defined. Their formulae are P_4O_6, P_4O_8 and P_4O_{10}. Only these oxides will be discussed here :

1. Phosphorus(III) Oxide, P_4O_6

This oxide is often formulated as P_2O_3 and is called phosphorus trioxide but vapour density measurements have shown that its formula is actually P_4O_6.

Preparation

It is prepared by controlled oxidation of P_4 in an atmosphere of 75% O_2 and 25% N_2 at 50° and at 90 mm Hg. Pure compound is obtained on distillation of the reaction mixture.

Properties

1. It is a soft, white crystalline compound with garlic odour.
2. When P_4O_6 is heated to 200-400°C in a sealed, evacuated tube, it disproportionates into red

phosphorus and solid solution of composition P_4O_n, the value of n depends on conditions.

3. It takes up oxygen from air forming P_4O_{10}.

$$P_4O_6 + 2O_2 \longrightarrow P_4O_{10}$$

4. It reacts with water to give different products depending upon the temperature

$$P_4O_6 + 6H_2O(\text{cold}) \longrightarrow 4H_3PO_3$$
$$P_4O_6 + 6H_2O(\text{hot}) \longrightarrow 3H_3PO_4 + PH_3$$

Structure

Out of the five valence electrons three electrons from each phosphorus are used to form three bonds to oxygen atoms. A lone pair of electrons is present on each phosphorus. Each atom of phosporus is situated at the corners of a tetrahedron (just like P_4 units in elemental phosphorus) and the oxygen atoms are outside the edges. The structure indicates that P–P bonds are absent in P_4O_6 (Fig. 6.12).

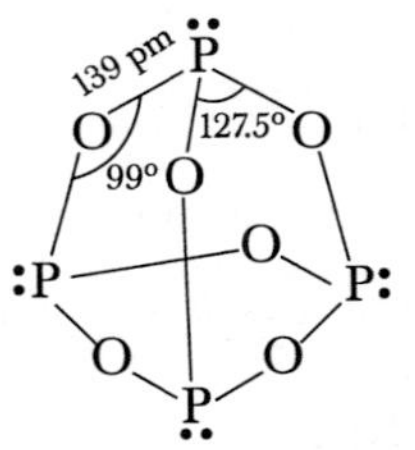

Fig. 6.12 Structure of P_4O_6.

2. Phosphorus(IV) Oxide

P_4O_8 containing phosphorus in + 4 oxidation state is prepared by heating the vapours of P_4O_6 above 210°C.

$$4P_4O_6 \longrightarrow 3P_4O_8 + P_4$$

It dissolves in water forming a mixture of phosphorus and phosphoric acids.

$$P_2O_4 + 3H_2O \longrightarrow H_3PO_3 + H_3PO_4$$

Structure

Its structure is similar to that of P_4O_6. However, two phosphorus atoms form two coordinate bonds with their lone pair of electrons to two oxygen atoms as shown in Fig. 6.13.

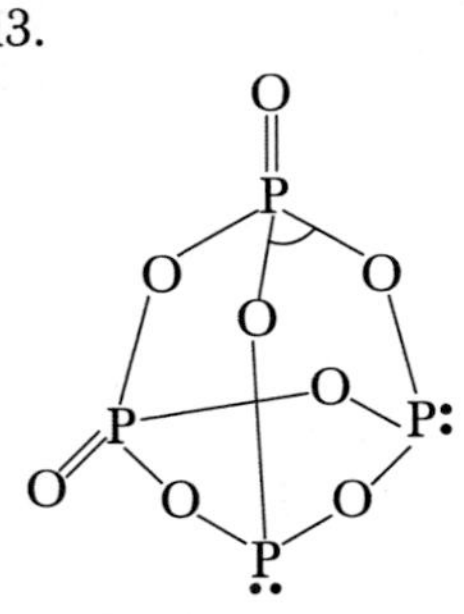

Fig. 6.13 Structure of P_4O_8 of molecule.

3. Phosphorus(V) Oxide, P_4O_{10}

It is the commonest and the most important oxide of phosphorus. This oxide is often formulated as P_2O_5 and is called **phosphorus pentoxide** but its molecular weight corresponds to the formula P_4O_{10}. It is prepared by burning phosphorus in excess of air.

$$P_4 + 5O_2 \longrightarrow P_4O_{10}$$

Properties

Its heat of formation is very high and for this reason it is quite stable and is a very poor oxidising agent. When it is dropped into water, it reacts with hissing sound, and at the same time much heat is liberated. Because of its great affinity for water it is one of the most effective dehydrating agents available. Thus, it is extensively used for drying gases and for removing water from many compounds. For example, it converts nitric acid into N_2O_5 and H_2SO_4 into SO_3. It also dehydrates many organic compounds *i.e.,* converts amides into nitriles. Its largest use is in the industrial production of ortho and polyphosphoric acids. It reacts with ether to form triethyl-phosphate.

$$P_4O_{10} + 6Et_2O \xrightarrow{\text{Heat}} 4PO(OEt)_3$$

1. With limited amount of water, it forms metaphosphoric acid, HPO_3.

$$P_4O_{10} + 2H_2O \longrightarrow 4HPO_3$$

Metaphosphoric acid changes into orthophosphoric acid, H_3PO_4 on reacting with more water.

$$HPO_3 + H_2O \longrightarrow H_3PO_4$$

2. P_4O_{10} reacts with PCl_5 to give phosphorus oxychloride.

$$P_4O_{10} + 6PCl_5 \longrightarrow 10POCl_3$$

3. P_2O_5 on fusion with basic oxides gives solid phosphates.

$$6CaO + 2P_2O_5 \longrightarrow 2Ca_3(PO_4)_2$$

Uses

P_2O_5 is used as a drying and a dehydrating agent in the laboratory.

Structure

Its structure is similar to that of P_4O_6 but in addition each phosphorous atom forms a coordinate bond to an oxygen atom, Fig. 6.14.

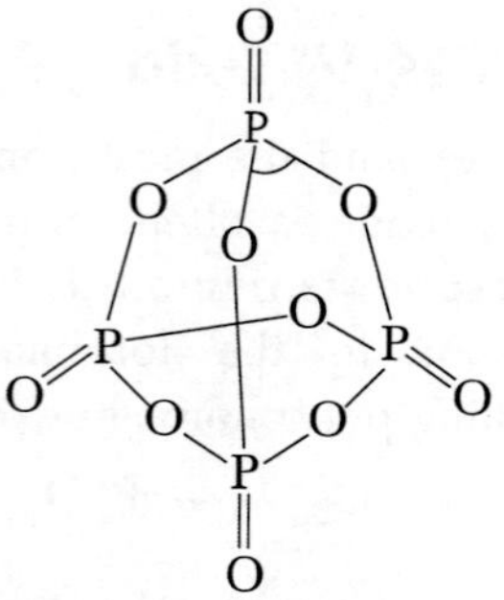

Fig. 6.14 Structure of P_4O_{10} molecule.

Oxo-Acids of Nitrogen

Nitrogen forms several oxo-acids, though some are unstable in the free state and are known only in aqueous solutions or as their salts. They are summarized in Table 6.4.

Table 6.4 **Oxo-Acids of Nitrogen**

Formula	Name	Oxidation state of nitrogen	Comments
$H_2N_2O_2$	Hyponitrous acid	+1	Weak acid, have *trans* configuration, gives NO in aqueous solution.
$H_4N_2O_4$	Nitroxylic acid	+2	Explosive
HNO_2	Nitrous acid	+3	Unstable, weak acid
HNO_3	Nitric acid	+5	Stable, strong acid
HNO_4	Peroxy nitric acid	+5	Unstable, explosive

Nitrous Acid, HNO_2

It is produced as an aqueous solution by dissolving a mixture of NO and NO_2 in ice-cold water. Alternatively, it can be prepared by the acidification of solutions of nitrites.

Properties

1. It is a weak acid ($K_a = 6.0 \times 10^{-6}$) and is known only in aqueous solution. Even its aqueous solution is unstable and decomposes when heated, according to the equation :

$$3HNO_2 \longrightarrow HNO_3 + 2NO + H_2O$$

2. It is a moderate oxidising agent towards many substances such as HI and H_2SO_3.

$$2HNO_2 + 2HI \longrightarrow 2H_2O + 2NO + I_2$$

$$2HNO_2 + H_2SO_3 \longrightarrow H_2O + 2NO + H_2SO_4$$

3. It is oxidised by strong oxidising agents such as Cl_2 or $KMnO_4$.

$$KMnO_4 + 3H_2SO_4 + 5HNO_2 \longrightarrow K_2SO_4 + 2MnSO_4 + 3H_2O + 5HNO_3$$

4. Organic derivatives containing NO_2 group are of two types : nitrites, *R*–ONO and nitro compounds, *R*–NO_2.
5. With aliphatic primary amines, it forms alcohols while with aromatic amino compounds in ice-cold solution, it forms diazonium salts.

$$C_2H_5NH_2 + HNO_2 \longrightarrow C_2H_5OH + N_2 + H_2O$$

$$C_2H_5NH_2 + HNO_2 + HCl \longrightarrow C_2H_5N{=}NCl + 2H_2O$$

Structure

Since, it is not possible to isolate the pure liquid acid, therefore, evidence regarding its structure has been accumulated from its salts. X-ray and Raman spectral data indicate an angular structure for nitrite ion (Fig. 6.15).

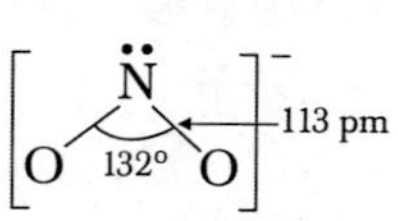

Fig. 6.15 Structure of NO_2^-.

It may be represented as a resonance hybrid of the following structures :

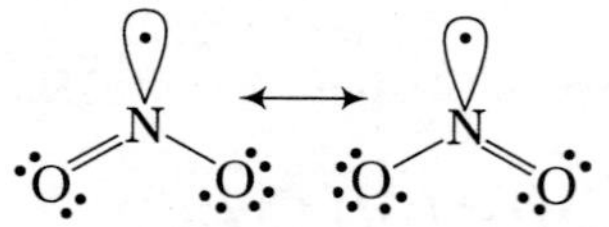

Nitric Acid, HNO_3

Preparation

1. It is prepared in the laboratory by heating a mixture of sodium nitrate and concentrated sulphuric acid.

$$NaNO_3 + H_2SO_4 \longrightarrow NaHSO_4 + HNO_3 \uparrow$$

Nitric acid is readily removed from the reaction mixture by gentle heating because nitric acid boils at 84°C while sulphuric acid boils above 330°C.

2. On an industrial scale, it is prepared by the oxidation of ammonia with air at about 1000°C in the presence of platinum gauge (**Ostwald's process**).

$$4NH_3 + 5O_2 \longrightarrow 4NO + 6H_2O; \quad \Delta H = -903.7 \text{ kJ mol}^{-1}$$

Nitric oxide so formed is oxidised to nitrogen dioxide with excess of air and then reacted with water to form nitric acid.

$$2NO + O_2 \longrightarrow 2NO_2 + 112.8 \text{ kJ}$$

$$3NO_2 + H_2O \longrightarrow 2HNO_3 + NO$$

NO is recycled for conversion into nitric acid.

3. Atmospheric nitrogen and oxygen combine to form nitric oxide in an electric arc (at a temperature of 3000-3500°). This is known as **Birkland and Eyde process.**

$$N_2 + O_2 \rightleftharpoons 2NO; \quad \Delta H = 180 \text{ kJ mol}^{-1}$$

Nitric oxide is oxidised to nitrogen peroxide and then dissolved in water to give nitric acid.

$$2NO + O_2 \longrightarrow 2NO_2$$

$$4NO_2 + 2H_2O + O_2 \longrightarrow 4HNO_3$$

Properties

It is a colourless liquid which boils at 84°C and freezes to a white solid at – 42°C. The acid often turns yellow in colour due to its photochemical decomposition to give NO_2.

$$2HNO_3 \xrightarrow{h\nu} 2NO_2 + H_2O + \frac{1}{2}O_2$$

The yellow colour may be removed by bubbling dry air through it.

It is soluble in water and forms a constant boiling mixture (composition = 68% , boiling point 120.5°C). In moist air, it fumes since its vapours form a mist of very small droplets of aqueous nitric acid. Nitric acid containing dissolved nitrogen dioxide is known as fuming nitric acid.

Fuming nitric acid is a highly corrosive liquid and is a far more powerful oxidising agent and nitrating reagent than concentrated nitric acid.

1. **Acidic properties** It is one of the very strong acids and its aqueous solutions are fully ionized.

$$HNO_3 \xrightarrow{H_2O} H_3O^+ + NO_3^-$$

It reacts with hydroxides, oxides, carbonates and bicarbonates to give corresponding nitrates, *e.g.*,

$$NaOH + HNO_3 \longrightarrow NaNO_3 + H_2O$$

$$Na_2CO_3 + 2HNO_3 \longrightarrow 2NaNO_3 + H_2O + CO_2$$

2. **Thermal stability** Pure acid is unstable and decomposes on heating as

$$4HNO_3 \xrightarrow{\Delta} 4NO_2 + 2H_2O + O_2$$

3. **Oxidising agent** Nitric acid behaves as a strong oxidising agent as it has a tendency to give nascent oxygen.

$$\underset{\text{(Concentrated)}}{2HNO_3} \longrightarrow 2NO_2 + H_2O + [O]$$

$$\underset{\text{(Dilute)}}{2HNO_3} \longrightarrow 2NO + H_2O + 3[O]$$

The nature of the reaction product formed as governed by the following conditions ;

(i) nature of the metal
(ii) concentration of the acid
(iii) reaction temperature

The nature of the metal, *i.e.,* its electropositive character determines the course of the reaction.

(i) **Metals that are more electropositive than hydrogen** (Mg, Al, Mn, Zn, Fe, Pb) In their reaction with nitric acid, nascent hydrogen is first liberated which then reduces nitric acid to further products.

$$M + 2HNO_3 \longrightarrow M(NO_3)_2 + 2H$$

$$HNO_3 + 2H \longrightarrow H_2O + NO_2$$

Reaction on magnesium

Of concentrated nitric acid (forms nitrogen dioxide)

$$[Mg + 2HNO_3 \longrightarrow Mg(NO_3)_2 + 2H] \times 4$$

$$2HNO_3 + 2H \longrightarrow 2NO_2 + 2H_2O$$

$$Mg + 4HNO_3 \longrightarrow Mg(NO_3)_2 + 2H_2O + 2NO_2$$

Of dilute nitric acid (forms nitrous oxide)

$$[Mg + 2HNO_3 \longrightarrow Mg(NO_3)_2 + 2H] \times 4$$

$$2HNO_3 + 8H \longrightarrow 5H_2O + N_2O$$

$$4Mg + 10HNO_3 \longrightarrow 4Mg(NO_3)_2 + N_2O + 5H_2O$$

Of very dilute nitric acid (forms ammonium nitrate)

$$[Mg + 2HNO_3 \longrightarrow Mg(NO_3)_2 + 2H] \times 4$$

$$HNO_3 + 8H \longrightarrow NH_3 + 3H_2O$$

$$HNO_3 + NH_3 \longrightarrow NH_4NO_3$$

$$4Mg + 10HNO_3 \longrightarrow 4Mg(NO_3)_2 + NH_4NO_3 + 5H_2O$$

Extremely dilute nitric acid may react with magnesium to liberate hydrogen gas.

$$Mg + 2HNO_3 \longrightarrow Mg(NO_3)_2 + H_2$$

Manganese also shows similar reactions. **Zn** also reacts in a similar manner.

Reaction to tin Of concentrated nitric acid (forms nitrogen dioxide)

$$Sn + 4HNO_3 \longrightarrow \underset{\text{Metastannic acid}}{H_2SnO_3} + H_2O + 4NO_2$$

Of dilute nitric acid (forms ammonium nitrate)

$$4Sn + 10HNO_3 \longrightarrow 4Sn(NO_3)_2 + NH_4NO_3 + 3H_2O$$

Reaction on lead Of concentrated nitric acid (forms nitrogen dioxide)

$$Pb + 4HNO_3 \longrightarrow Pb(NO_3)_2 + H_2O + 2NO_2$$

Of dilute nitric acid (forms nitric oxide)

$$3Pb + 8HNO_3 \longrightarrow 3Pb(NO_3)_2 + 4H_2O + 2NO$$

Reaction on iron Of moderately concentrated nitric acid (forms nitrogen dioxide)

$$Fe + 6HNO_3 \longrightarrow Fe(NO_3)_3 + 3H_2O + 3NO_2$$

Of concentrated nitric acid.

Pure concentrated nitric acid makes iron passive. Although the exact nature of this passivity is not known, but the formation of hard oxide film is considered important. The oxides FeO, Fe_2O_3 on the metal surface prevent any further action of the acid.

Other metals like aluminium, chromium, cobalt and nickel are also rendered passive when dipped in pure concentrated nitric acid.

Of very dilute nitric acid

Iron reacts with very dilute nitric acid to form ammonium nitrate.

$$4Fe + 10HNO_3 \longrightarrow 4Fe(NO_3)_2 + NH_4NO_3 + 3H_2O$$

(ii) **Metals which are less electropositive than hydrogen** (Cu, Bi, Hg, Ag) In their reactions with nitric acid, nascent hydrogen is not liberated.

$$HNO_3 \longrightarrow \text{Reduced product} + H_2O + [O]$$
$$\text{Metal} + HNO_3 + [O] \longrightarrow \text{Metal nitrate} + H_2O$$

Reaction of copper On concentrated nitric acid (nitrogen dioxide is formed)

$$2HNO_3 \longrightarrow 2NO_2 + H_2O + [O]$$
$$Cu + 2HNO_3 + [O] \longrightarrow Cu(NO_3)_2 + H_2O$$

$$Cu + 4HNO_3 \longrightarrow Cu(NO_3)_2 + 2NO_2 + 2H_2O$$

On very dilute nitric acid (nitric oxide is formed)

$$2HNO_3 \longrightarrow 2NO + H_2O + 3[O]$$
$$Cu + 2HNO_3 + [O] \longrightarrow Cu(NO_3)_2 + H_2O] \times 3$$

$$3Cu + 8HNO_3 \longrightarrow 3Cu(NO_3)_2 + 2NO + 4H_2O$$

Mercury and silver also react with nitric acid to give similar products.

(iii) **Reaction of bismuth** Both concentrated and dilute nitric acid react with bismuth to give the same product.

$$Bi + 6HNO_3 \longrightarrow Bi(NO_3)_2 + 3H_2O + 3NO_2$$

(iv) **Reaction with noble metals** Concentrated nitric acid has no action on metals such as gold and platinum. However, aqua-regia (3 parts of conc. HCl and 1 part of conc. HNO_3 by volume) can dissolve metals like platinum and gold by forming their chlorides.

$$HNO_3 + 3HCl \longrightarrow NOCl + 2H_2O + 2Cl \quad] \times 3$$
$$Au + 3Cl \longrightarrow AuCl_3 \quad] \times 2$$

$$2Au + 3HNO_3 + 9HCl \longrightarrow 2AuCl_3 + 3NOCl + 6H_2O$$

(v) **Reaction on non-metals** Dilute nitric acid has no action on non-metallic elements such as carbon, phosphorus, sulphur and iodine. However, these elements are oxidised by concentrated nitric acid to their oxoacids as :

$$2HNO_3 \longrightarrow H_2O + NO_2 + O] \times 3$$
$$S + 3[O] + H_2O \longrightarrow H_2SO_4$$

(a) $S + 6HNO_3 \longrightarrow H_2SO_4 + 6NO_2\uparrow + 2H_2O$

(b) Carbon is oxidised to carbonic acid

$$C + 4HNO_3 \longrightarrow H_2CO_3 + 4NO_2 + H_2O$$

(c) Iodine is oxidised to iodic acid.

$$I_2 + 10HNO_3 \longrightarrow 2HIO_3 + 10NO_2 + 4H_2O$$

(d) Phosphorus is oxidised to orthophosphoric acid.

$$P + 5HNO_3 \longrightarrow H_3PO_4 + 5NO_2 + H_2O$$

(vi) **Reaction on metalloids** Metalloids like arsenic and antimony are oxidised by nitric acid to the corresponding oxy-acids.

$$As + 5HNO_3 \longrightarrow \underset{\text{Orthoarsenic acid}}{H_3AsO_4} + 5NO_2 + H_2O$$

(vii) **Reaction of inorganic reducing agents** Dilute nitric acid oxidises reducing agents such as H_2S to S, SO_2 to H_2SO_4.

$$2HNO_3 \longrightarrow H_2O + 2NO + 3[O]$$
$$H_2S + O \longrightarrow H_2O + S \quad] \times 3$$

(a) $3H_2S + 2HNO_3 \longrightarrow 4H_2O + 3S + 2NO\uparrow$

(b) SO_2 is oxidised to sulphuric acid.

$$SO_2 + 2HNO_3 \longrightarrow H_2SO_4 + 2NO_2$$

(c) Dilute nitric acid also oxidises ferrous salts to ferric salts as :

$$2HNO_3 \longrightarrow H_2O + 2NO + 3[O]$$
$$2FeSO_4 + H_2SO_4 + O \longrightarrow Fe_2(SO_4)_3 + 4H_2O \quad] \times 3$$

$$6FeSO_4 + 3H_2SO_4 + 2HNO_3 \longrightarrow 2Fe_2(SO_4)_3 + 4H_2O + 2NO$$

The nitric oxide formed gives a dark-brown ring (Ring test for nitrates).

(viii) **Reaction on organic compounds**

(i) Concentrated nitric acid oxidises cane sugar to oxalic acid.

$$[2HNO_3 \longrightarrow H_2O + 2NO_2 + (O)] \times 18$$

$$C_{12}H_{22}O_{11} + 18[O] \longrightarrow 6 \begin{array}{c} COOH \\ | \\ COOH \end{array} + 5H_2O$$

$$C_{12}H_{22}O_{11} + 36HNO_3 \longrightarrow 6 \begin{array}{c} COOH \\ | \\ COOH \end{array} + 36NO_2 + 23H_2O$$

4. Nitrating property Nitric acid in the presence of conc. sulphuric acid acts as a nitrating agent and reacts with organic compounds to form their nitro derivatives. The basic reaction is,

$$HNO_3 + 2H_2SO_4 \longrightarrow NO_2^+ + H_3O^+ + 2HSO_4^-$$

where NO_2^+ (nitronium ion) replaces H^+ in the organic compound, nitration takes place.

$$C_6H_6 + HNO_3 \xrightarrow{H_2SO_4} \underset{\text{Nitrobenzene}}{C_6H_5NO_2} + H_2O$$

A mixture of nitric acid and concentrated sulphuric acid reacts with glycerine to form nitroglycerine, an explosive substance.

$$C_3H_5(OH)_3 + 3HNO_3 \longrightarrow \underset{\text{Nitroglycerine}}{C_3H_5(NO_3)_3} + 3H_2O$$

Cotton when reacted with concentrated nitric acid in the presence of sulphuric acid forms cellulose nitrate, known as gun cotton. Toluene when reacted with concentrated nitric acid and concentrated sulphuric acid forms trinitrotoluene (TNT)–a valuable explosive.

$$CH_3{-}C_6H_5 + 3HNO_3 \xrightarrow{\text{Conc. } H_2SO_4} \underset{\text{TNT}}{CH_3C_6H_2(NO_2)_3} + 3H_2O$$

Structure of nitric acid

Spectroscopic evidence along with electron diffraction data suggests that the gaseous molecules of nitric acid are planar with the following dimensions :

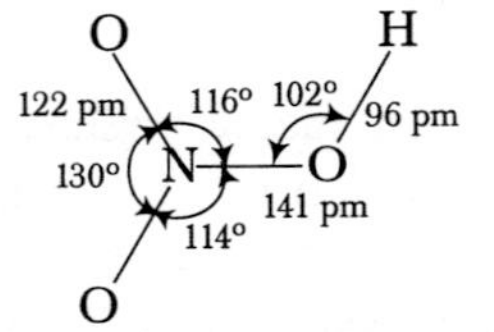

Fig. 6.15 Structure of HNO_3 molecule.

The above structure can be best explained by assuming that nitric acid is a resonance hybrid of the following two structures :

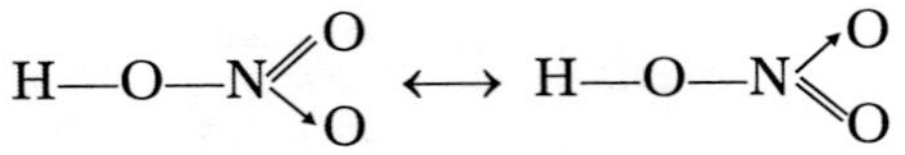

The Raman spectrum of anhydrous nitric acid is characterised by faint lines at 1050 and 1400 cm^{-1} due to the existence of small concentrations of nitrate and nitronium ions, respectively in it as :

$$3HNO_3 \rightleftharpoons NO_3^- + NO_2^+ + HNO_3 + H_2O$$

The peak at 1400 cm^{-1} is due to NO_2^+ and it disappears when the concentration falls below 94 to 95% of HNO_3.

Uses

Nitric acid is used

1. To manufacture different nitrate salts : Basic calcium nitrate is used as a fertilizer. Silver nitrate finds application in photography and sodium nitrate is used in the preparation of gunpowder.
2. In the manufacture of explosives like trinitroglycerine (TNT) and picric acid etc.
3. In the manufacture of artificial silk, dyes and medicines.

Oxo-Acids of Phosphorus

Phosphorus forms two types of oxo-acids, namely, the **phosphorus** and **phosphoric** series. In all these acids, the phosphorus atom forms four sp^3 bonds and there is some lateral overlap between filled p orbitals of oxygen with empty d orbitals of phosphorus resulting in $p\pi$-$d\pi$ back bonding. These acids contain both P–OH and P–H groups. The hydrogen atoms in P–OH groups are ionizable and are therefore acidic. However, hydrogen atoms in P–H groups are not ionizable. The presence of this group gives reducing properties to these acids. A summary on oxo-acids of phosphorus is given in Table 6.5.

Table 6.5 **Oxo-Acids of Phosphorus**

Formula	Name	Oxidation state of phosphorus	Comments
H_3PO_2	Hypophosphorous acid	+1	Weak, monobasic, strong reducing agent
H_3PO_3	Phosphorous acid	+3	Dibasic acid, strong reducing agent
$H_4P_2O_6$	Hypophosphoric acid	+4	Tetrabasic acid

Formula	Name	Oxidation state of phosphorus	Comments
H_3PO_4	Orthophosphoric acid	+ 5	Tribasic acid
$H_4P_2O_7$	Pyrophosphoric acid	+ 5	Tetrabasic acid
HPO_3	Metaphosphoric acid	+ 5	Monobasic acid

1. Phosphorous Acid, H_3PO_3 [HPO(OH)$_2$]

Preparation

By the hydrolysis of phosphorus trichloride in cold CCl_4 solution

$$PCl_3 + 3H_2O \longrightarrow H_3PO_3 + 3HCl\uparrow$$

Properties

1. It is a white deliquescent crystalline solid, m.p. 70.1°C, have garlic odour. It is highly soluble in water and is dibasic, *i.e.,* it forms two series of salts such as $M^1H_2PO_3$ and $M_2{}^1HPO_3$ but none of the type $M^1{}_3PO_3$. Thus, it ionises as :

$$H_3PO_3 \rightleftharpoons H^+ + H_2PO_3^- \ \ldots\ldots \quad K_1 = 1\times 10^{-2}$$

$$H_2PO_3^- \rightleftharpoons H^+ + HPO_3^{2-} \ \ldots\ldots \quad K_2 = 2\times 10^{-7}$$

2. On heating, it gives phosphine according to equation

$$4H_3PO_3 \longrightarrow 3H_3PO_4 + PH_3$$

3. It also acts as a strong reducing agent though its reducing power is less than that of H_3PO_2.
   (a) It reduces mercuric chloride to mercurous chloride.
   $$2HgCl_2 + H_3PO_3 + H_2O \longrightarrow Hg_2Cl_2 + 2HCl + H_3PO_4$$
   (b) Silver nitrate is reduced to metallic silver.
   $$2AgNO_3 + H_3PO_3 + H_2O \longrightarrow 2Ag + 2HNO_3 + H_3PO_4$$
   (c) Copper sulphate is reduced to metallic copper.
   $$CuSO_4 + H_3PO_3 + H_2O \longrightarrow H_3PO_4 + Cu + H_2SO_4$$
   (d) It reduces acidified $KMnO_4$ to Mn^{2+}
   $$2KMnO_4 + 3H_2SO_4 + 5H_3PO_3 \longrightarrow K_2SO_4 + 2MnSO_4 + 5H_3PO_4 + 3H_2O$$
   (e) It reduces iodine to HI.
   $$I_2 + H_3PO_3 + H_2O \longrightarrow H_3PO_4 + 3HI$$
   (f) It reduces sulphur dioxide to sulphur.
   $$2H_3PO_3 + SO_2 \longrightarrow 2H_3PO_4 + S\downarrow$$

Structure

H_3PO_3 has been assigned the following structure :

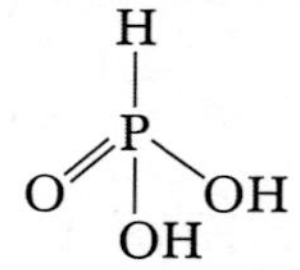

2. Orthophosphoric Acid or Phosphoric Acid, H_3PO_4

Preparation

It is prepared industrially from bone ash.

1. Bone ash (obtained from the destructive distillation of bones) is treated with concentrated H_2SO_4 and heated.

$$\underset{\text{(Bone ash)}}{Ca_3(PO_4)_2} + 3H_2SO_4 \longrightarrow 3CaSO_4\downarrow + 2H_3PO_4$$

2. Bone ash is oxidized with concentrated nitric acid. The entire phosphorus content is oxidized to phophoric acid. This liquid is treated with lead acetate which precipitates lead phosphate. Phosphoric acid is then recovered by treating with H_2S gas :

$$\underset{\text{(Bone ash)}}{P} + \underset{(30\text{-}35\%)}{5HNO_3} \longrightarrow H_3PO_4 + 5NO_2 + H_2O$$

$$\underset{\text{(Impure)}}{2H_3PO_4} + 3(CH_3COO)_2Pb \longrightarrow Pb_3(PO_4)_2\downarrow + 6CH_3COOH$$

$$Pb_3(PO_4)_2 + 3H_2S \longrightarrow 3PbS\downarrow + \underset{\text{(Pure)}}{2H_3PO_4}$$

Properties

1. It forms colourless glassy prisms. The crystals are deliquescent and form a syrupy liquid. The commercial acid is ≃ 83%. It is concentrated by crystallizing it in vacuum which yields anhydrous acid. Phosphoric acid also forms a hemi hydrate $H_3PO_4\cdot H_2O$. It can only be obtained pure in crystalline state, m.p. 42.35°.

2. **Reaction with alkalies** This acid forms three types of salts : NaH_2PO_4, Na_2HPO_4 and Na_3PO_4. Neutralization curve for aqueous H_3PO_4 with $\frac{N}{10}$ NaOH is shown below :

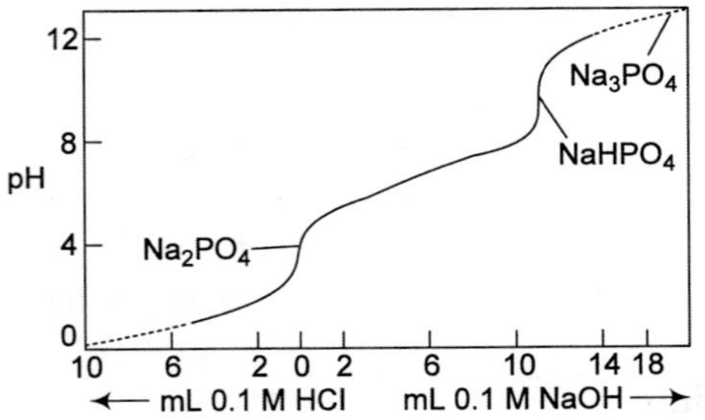

The first inflexion, indicating the formation of NaH_2PO_4 can be detected by methyl orange indicator, the second inflexion corresponding to Na_2HPO_4 is indicated by phenolphthalein. The third equivalence point cannot be detected by an indicator. The pH changes very slowly with the addition of NaOH and this is due to buffer action. Equimolar mixture of Na_2HPO_4 and KH_2PO_4 is an important buffer solution used in chemistry laboratories.

$$H_3PO_4 + NaOH \longrightarrow \underset{\text{(Primary salt)}}{NaH_2PO_4} + H_2O$$

$$H_3PO_4 + 2NaOH \longrightarrow \underset{\text{(Secondary salt)}}{Na_2HPO_4} + 2H_2O$$

$$H_3PO_4 + 3NaOH \longrightarrow \underset{\text{(Tertiary salt)}}{Na_3PO_4} + 3H_2O$$

3. On heating to 250°C, it gives pyrophosphoric acid, $H_4P_2O_7$.

$$2H_3PO_4 \xrightarrow{250°C} H_4P_2O_7 + H_2O$$

On further heating to 320°C, it loses one more molecule of water to give metaphosphoric acid, HPO_3.

$$H_4P_2O_7 \xrightarrow{320°C} 2HPO_3 + H_2O$$

When heated to red heat, it gives phosphorus pentoxide, P_2O_5.

$$2HPO_3 \xrightarrow{600–700°} P_2O_5 + H_2O$$

4. Phosphoric acid reacts with bromides and iodides to give hydrobromic and hydroiodic acids, respectively.

$$H_3PO_4 + 3NaBr \longrightarrow Na_3PO_4 + 3HBr$$
$$H_3PO_4 + 3NaI \longrightarrow Na_3PO_4 + 3HI$$

5. Phosphoric acid does not act as an oxidizing agent below 350°C. At higher temperatures, it is reactive towards metals and is reduced.
6. When phosphoric acid or phosphates are treated with ammonium molybdate in the presence of concentrated nitric acid, a yellow precipitate of ammonium phosphomolybdate is obtained.

$$H_3PO_4 + 12(NH_4)_2MoO_4 + 21HNO_3 \longrightarrow$$
$$(NH_4)_3PO_4 \cdot 12MoO_3 + 21NH_4NO_3 + 12H_2O$$

7. It is a tribasic acid, the first hydrogen is ionized readily, second with difficulty and the third only in the presence of excess of strong alkalies.

$$H_3PO_4 \rightleftharpoons H^+ + [H_2PO_4]^-; K_1 = 7.5 \times 10^{-3}$$
$$[H_2PO_4]^- \rightleftharpoons H^+ + [HPO_4]^{2-}; K_2 = 6.2 \times 10^{-8}$$
$$[HPO_4]^{2-} \rightleftharpoons H^+ + [PO_4]^{3-}; \quad K_3 = 1.1 \times 10^{-12}$$

Structure

Keeping in view the tribasic nature of the acid, it has been assigned the following tetrahedral structure.

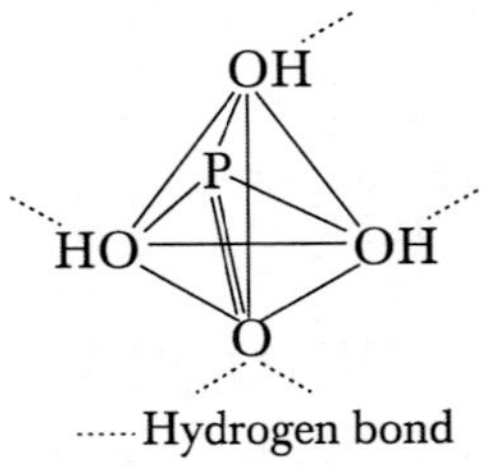

3. Metaphosphoric Acid, HPO_3

Preparation

(i) It is prepared by heating orthophosphoric acid above 400°C.

$$H_3PO_4 \longrightarrow HPO_3 + H_2O$$

(ii) It is prepared by treating P_2O_5 with a small amount of water.

$$P_4O_{10} + 2H_2O \longrightarrow 4HPO_3$$

Properties

1. It is a glassy semi-transparent solid and is commonly known as glacial phosphoric acid. It is hygroscopic and dissolves in water forming orthophosphoric acid.

$$HPO_3 + H_2O \longrightarrow H_3PO_4$$

2. This acid gives **ammonium molybdate test.**
3. This is the only phosphoric acid which coagulates egg albumin (the white of an egg).

Structure

In metaphosphoric acid, oxygen bridges are formed between adjacent phosphorus atoms to build up rings and chains in which there are four oxygen atoms linked to every phosphorus atom. By combining with each other , HPO_3 monomers polymerize into multiple units which may be represented by the formula $(HPO_3)_x$.

Structure of metaphosphate ions

Metaphosphate ion, PO_3^- does not exist as a discrete unit but in the polymerised form as linear chain (Fig. 6.17) or as cyclic trimetaphosphate (Fig. 6.18).

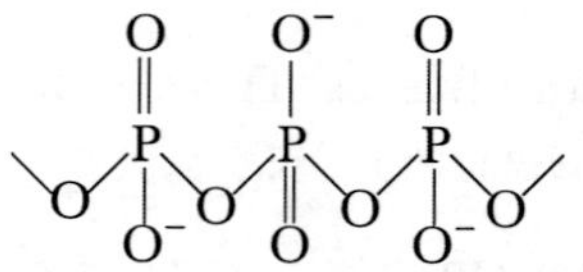

Fig. 6.17 Structure of linear metaphosphate ion.

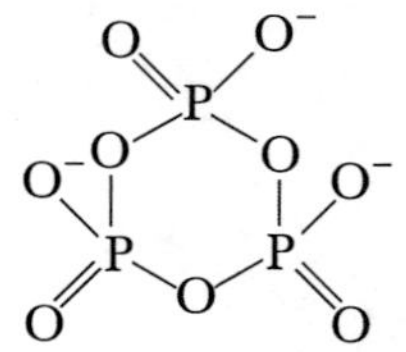

Fig. 6.18 Structure of cyclic trimetaphosphate ion.

Table 6.6 **Distinction between Different Oxo-Acids of Phosphorus**

S. No.	Reaction	Hypo-phosphorous acid (H_3PO_3)	Ortho-phosphoric acid (H_3PO_4)	Pyro-phosphoric acid ($H_4P_2O_7$)	Meta-phosphoric acid (HPO_3)
1.	Silver nitrate	Reduced to metallic silver (ppt.)	Yellow ppt. of Ag_3PO_4	White ppt. of $Ag_4P_2O_7$	White gelatinous ppt. of $AgPO_3$
2.	Barium chloride	No action	White ppt. soluble in acetic acid	White ppt. insoluble in acetic acid	White ppt. insoluble in acetic acid
3.	Copper sulphate solution in acid	Reduced to metallic copper (ppt.)	No action	No action	No action
4.	Acidified $KMnO_4$	Decolourises	No action	No action	No action
5.	Magnesia mixture ($MgCl_2 + NH_4OH$)	No ppt.	White ppt.	White ppt. soluble in excess reagent	No ppt.

Hydrides of Nitrogen

The important hydrides of nitrogen are

1. Ammonia, NH_3
2. Hydrazine, N_2H_4
3. Hydroxylamine, NH_2OH
4. Hydrazoic acid, HN_3

1. Ammonia, NH_3

The most common hydride of nitrogen is ammonia.

Preparation

It is manufactured, on an industrial scale, by **Haber's process** which involves the direct combination of nitrogen (1 vol) and hydrogen (3 vol) at about 425°C under 200 atm pressure in the presence of iron oxide along with small amounts of K_2O and Al_2O_3 (as a catalyst).

$$N_2 + 3H_2 \rightleftharpoons 2NH_3 + 93.6 \text{ kJ mol}^{-1}$$

The reaction is exothermic and is accompanied by decrease in volume.

Properties

It is a colourless gas (b.p. – 33.35° and a freezing point of – 77.8°C) with strong pungent smell and is highly soluble in water. It is lighter than air and causes tears in the eyes. Liquid ammonia on evaporation produces intense cooling and this property forms the basis of referigeration plants.

Due to high electronegativity of nitrogen, ammonia is a polar molecule. The presence of nitrogen-hydrogen bond leads to the formation of hydrogen bridges. As a result, ammonia is highly associated in the liquid state as

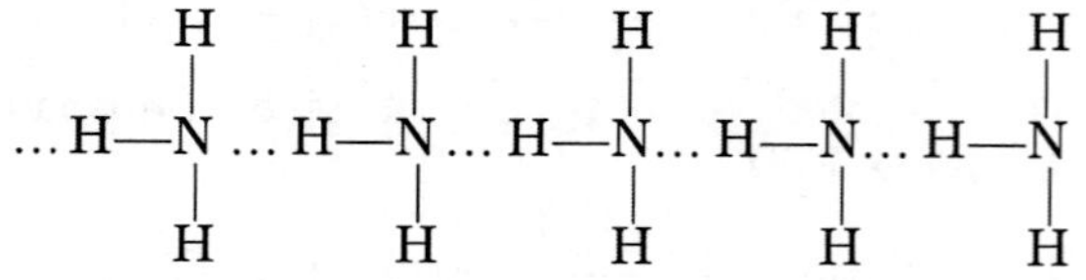

Consequently, ammonia has relatively **high boiling point and high heat of vaporisation.**

1. Ammonia is quite basic and its aqueous solution turns red litmus blue. Its basic character in water is due to the formation of OH^- ions.

$$NH_3 + H_2O \rightleftharpoons [NH_4^+] + OH^-$$

Due to the presence of a lone pair of electrons on nitrogen, ammonia acts as a **Lewis base**. As a Lewis base, ammonia forms complexes with many metal ions as

$$Ag^+ + 2NH_3 \rightleftharpoons [Ag(NH_3)_2]^+$$

On passing ammonia through copper sulphate solution, at first a bluish green precipitate of copper hydroxide is formed which dissolves in excess of ammonia to form a blue solution due to the formation of $(Cu(NH_3)_4]SO_4$.

$$CuSO_4 + 2NH_4OH \longrightarrow \underset{\text{Blue ppt.}}{Cu(OH)_2} + (NH_4)_2SO_4$$

$$Cu(OH)_2 + 2NH_4OH + (NH_4)_2SO_4 \longrightarrow \underset{\substack{\text{Blue complex} \\ \text{tetraamminecopper(II) sulphate}}}{[Cu(NH_3)_4]SO_4} + 4H_2O$$

2. Ammonia burns in air according to the reaction

$$4NH_3 + 3O_2 \longrightarrow 2N_2 + 6H_2O$$

However, ammonia is oxidised by excess of air at about 800°C in presence of platinum gauze or platinum rhodium catalyst to form nitric oxide.

$$4NH_3 + 5O_2 \xrightarrow[\text{Pt catalyst}]{\text{About } 800°C} 4NO + 6H_2O$$

This reaction is very important industrially in the manufacture of nitric acid by **Ostwalt's process.**

3. **Reaction with halogens**

(i) $4NH_3 + 3F_2 \xrightarrow{Cu} NF_3 + 3NH_4F$

(ii) $NH_3 + \underset{\text{Excess}}{3Cl_2} \longrightarrow NCl_3 + 3HCl$

(iii) $\underset{\text{Excess}}{8NH_3} + 3Cl_2 \longrightarrow 6NH_4Cl + N_2$

(iv) $3Br_2 + 8NH_3 \longrightarrow 6NH_4Br + N_2$

Caution! (v)

$$3I_2 + 2NH_3 \longrightarrow \underset{\substack{\text{Nitrogen triodide} \\ \text{ammoniate}}}{NH_3 \cdot NI_3} + 3HI$$

Pure NI_3 has not been obtained. This is a highly shock-sensitive compound and readily explodes. Only the ammonia adduct is obtained.

$$8NH_3 \cdot NI_3 \longrightarrow 5N_2 + 9I_2 + 6NH_4I$$

4. **Reaction with methane (Andrussow process)** The reaction of NH_3 with methane is used for **industrial production of HCN** by the Andrussow process.

$$CH_4 + NH_3 + 1.5\,O_2 \xrightarrow[\text{2 atm/1000–1200°C}]{\text{Pt/Rh}} HCN + 3H_2O$$

The other process involving methane and ammonia is known as the Degussa process.

$$CH_4 + NH_3 \xrightarrow[1200-1300°C]{Pt} HCN + 3H_2$$

5. **Reactions with other non-metals or their halides or oxides**

(i) $C + 2NH_3 \xrightarrow{\text{Red heat}} NH_4CN + H_2$

(ii) $P_4 + 4NH_3 \longrightarrow 4PH_3 + 2N_2$

(iii) $10S + 4NH_3 \longrightarrow S_4N_4 + 6H_2S$

(H_2S further reacts with NH_3 to form ammonium sulphide.)

(iv) Metals react with ammonia to give nitrides.

$$3Mg + 2NH_3 \xrightarrow{900°} Mg_3N_2 + 3H_2$$

(v) Corrosion of Cu and brass by moist NH_3/air precludes its use in pipes and values for handling liquid or gaseous NH_3.

(vi) $PCl_3 + 6NH_3 \longrightarrow P(NH_2)_3 + 3NH_4Cl$

(vii) P_4O_{10} reacts vigorously both with wet and dry NH_3 to form a range of amorphous polymeric products which are used in industry for water softening because of their ability to withdraw Ca^{2+} ions.

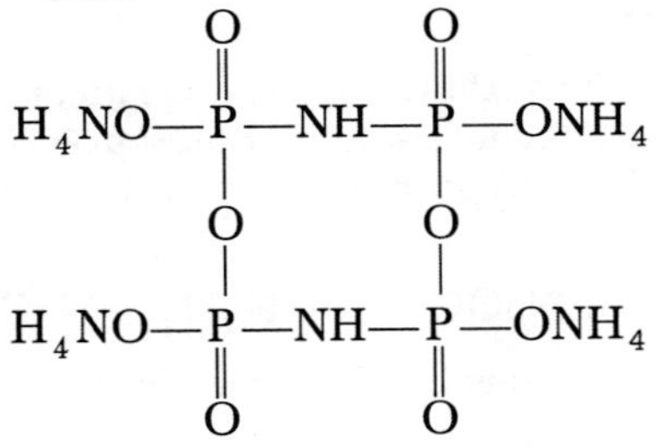

(viii) $2PCl_5 + 16NH_3(\text{liq.}) \longrightarrow [(H_2N)_3P{=}N{-}P(NH_2)_3]^+Cl^- + 9NH_4Cl$

(ix) $6S_2Cl_2 + 16NH_3 \xrightarrow{50°} S_4N_4 + 8S + 12NH_4Cl$

$$6SCl_2 + 16NH_3 \longrightarrow S_4N_4 + 2S + 14NH_4Cl$$

6. **Liquid ammonia as a solvent** Pure ammonia is used as a non-aqueous solvent to carry out several types of inorganic reactions, which otherwise cannot be studied in aqueous solutions. Detailed discussion on the use of liquid NH_3 as a solvent has been given in Chapter 2. Its most important property is its ability to dissolve alkali metals to form blue coloured, paramagnetic, and electrically conducting solutions containing solvated electrons.

Structure

The structure of ammonia molecule is described as pyramidal or tetrahedral with one position occupied by a lone pair.

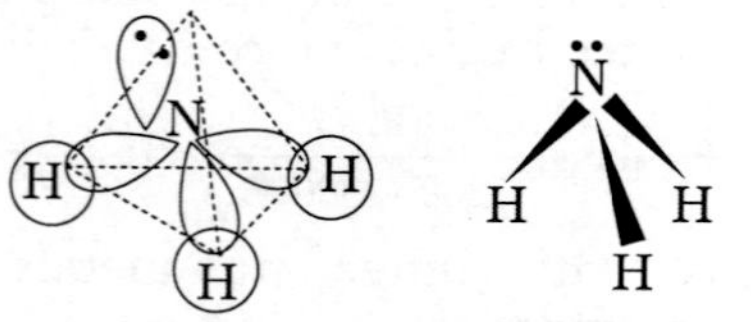

Fig. 6.19 Structure of ammonia molecule.

The H—N—H angle (107.3°) in ammonia is slightly less than the tetrahedral value. This is due to the greater repulsion of the lone pair of electrons while pushes the bond pairs closer to each other. The bond angle is reduced below the tetrahedral angle of 109.5°.

Uses of Ammonia

1. Ammonia is used in the manufacture of nitric acid and HCN.
2. It is used for the synthesis of S_4N_4 and as a refrigerant.

2. Hydrazine, N_2H_4

Hydrazine, N_2H_4 may be considered to be derived from ammonia by replacement of a hydrogen atom by NH_2 group. It is, therefore, expected to act as a base, which it does, but is a weaker base than NH_3.

Preparation

1. **Rasching's method** It is manufactured by oxidising aqueous ammonia present in large excess with sodium hypochlorite, NaOCl in the presence of glue or gelatine.

$$2NH_3 + NaOCl \longrightarrow N_2H_4 + NaCl + H_2O$$

Actually, the reaction proceeds in two steps :

$$NH_3 + NaOCl \longrightarrow NaOH + \underset{\text{Chloramine}}{NH_2Cl}$$

(Fast reaction)

$$NH_3 + NH_2Cl + NaOH \longrightarrow N_2H_4 + \underset{\text{(Slow reaction)}}{NaCl} + H_2O$$

There is another rapid but unwanted reaction in which hydrazine is destroyed.

$$N_2H_4 + 2NH_2Cl \xrightarrow{\text{Fast}} 2NH_4Cl + N_2$$

This reaction is catalysed by traces of heavy metal ions such as Cu^{II}, and the purpose of gelatin is to suppress the above reaction by removing the metal ions.

The resulting solution contains 63-70% of hydrazine which on distillation yields about 85% concentrated solution of hydrazine. Such a solution is distilled over NaOH or KOH when pure hydrazine is obtained as distillate.

Properties

1. Anhydrous hydrazine is a fuming colourless liquid with a high dielectric constant.
2. At room temperature pure hydrazine or its aqueous solutions are kinetically stable with respect to decomposition despite the **endothermic** nature of the compound and its positive free energy of formation.

$$N_2(g) + 2H_2(g) \longrightarrow N_2H_4(l);$$

$$\Delta H_f^\circ = 50.6 \text{ kJ mol}^{-1}$$

$$\Delta G_f^\circ = 149.2 \text{ kJ mol}^{-1}$$

3. When ignited, hydrazine burns rapidly and completely in air with the evolution of large amount of heat

$$N_2H_4(l) + O_2(g) \longrightarrow N_2(g) + 2H_2O;$$

$$\Delta H = -621.5 \text{ kJ mol}^{-1}$$

One of the major uses of hydrazine and its methyl derivatives $(CH_3)NHNH_2$ and $(CH_3)_2NNH_2$ is as a rocket fuel, in missiles, space shuttles etc.

Ozone, nitrous acid (HNO_2) and hydrogen peroxide oxidise hydrazine to hydrazoic acid, HN_3.

$$3N_2H_4 + 5O_3 \longrightarrow 2HN_3 + 5H_2O + 5O_2$$

$$3N_2H_4 + 5H_2O_2 \longrightarrow 2HN_3 + 10H_2O$$

4. Hydrazine decomposes on heating into ammonia and nitrogen.

$$3NH_2 \cdot NH_2 \longrightarrow N_2 + 4NH_3$$

5. **It is a powerful reducing agent.**

(i) It reduces gold chloride to gold; silver nitrate to silver and platinic chloride to platinum :

$$4AuCl_3 + 3N_2H_4 \longrightarrow 4Au + 3N_2 + 12HCl$$

(ii) It reduces halogens to corresponding halogen acids.

$$2Cl_2 + N_2H_4 \longrightarrow N_2 + 4HCl$$

$$2Br_2 + N_2H_4 \longrightarrow N_2 + 4HBr$$

It reduces I_2 to HI quantitatively in the presence of $NaHCO_3$.

$$N_2H_4 + 2I_2 \longrightarrow N_2 + 4HI$$

(iii) It reduces ferric salts to ferrous salts and iodates (IO_3^-) to iodides (I^-).

$$4FeCl_3 + N_2H_4 \longrightarrow 4FeCl_2 + 4HCl + N_2$$

$$2NaIO_3 + 3N_2H_4 \longrightarrow 2NaI + 6H_2O + 3N_2$$

(iv) It reduces $KMnO_4$ in the presence of dilute H_2SO_4.

$$4KMnO_4 + 6H_2SO_4 + 5N_2H_4 \longrightarrow 2K_2SO_4 + 4MnSO_4 + 16H_2O + 5N_2$$

The above reaction is used for the estimation of hydrazine and its salts.

(v) It is readily oxidised by H_2O_2 to free nitrogen and water.

$$N_2H_4(l) + 2H_2O_2(l) \longrightarrow N_2(g) + 4H_2O(g) + \text{heat}$$

Because the products of reaction between these two liquids are both gases at the temperature of the reaction and the reaction is highly exothermic, therefore, there is a tremendous increase in the volume of the products. Hence, hydrazine and hydrogen peroxide have been used in the propulsion of rockets.

Structure

Its structure resembles that of hydrogen proxide. Since, hydrazine possesses dipole moment (1.85 D) the *trans* configuration can be ruled out.

The NH_2 groups in hydrazine molecule are expected to rotate along the N—N single bond (inner rotation) but it has been observed that the inner rotation in N_2H_4 is hindered due to two energetically favoured rotational positions acting against each other. Consequently, molecular rotation of NH_2 groups is possible only over energy barriers as shown in Fig. 6.20.

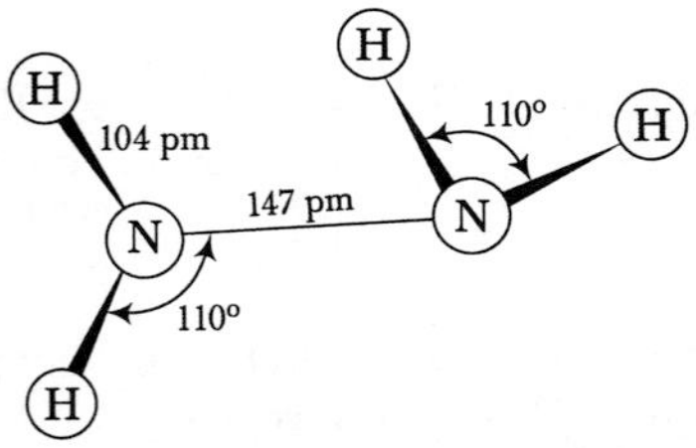

Fig. 6.20 Structure of N_2H_5.

3. Hydrazoic Acid, N_3H (Hydrogen Azide)

It may be considered as a hydride of nitrogen, but it bears no relationship to the other hydrides of nitrogen, namely, NH_3 and N_2H_4. It acts as a weak acid in its aqueous solutions, comparable in strength to acetic acid.

Preparation

It is prepared by the oxidation of aqueous hydrazine with nitrous acid.

$$N_2H_5^+ + HNO_2 \longrightarrow HN_3 + H^+ + 2H_2O$$

Properties

1. It is a colourless volatile liquid; b.p. = 37°C, m.p. $\simeq -80$°C. Even its dilute solutions are potential explosives and should be handled with care. It is a highly poisonous gas.
2. It decomposes into N_2 and H_2 with the evolution of large amount of heat.

$$2HN_3 \longrightarrow 3N_2 + H_2 \qquad \Delta H = -51.5$$

3. It is a weak acid, its strength is comparable to that of acetic acid.

$$HN_3(aq) \rightleftharpoons H^+(aq) + N_3^-(aq); \qquad K_a = 1.8 \times 10^{-5}$$

4. It forms salts with alkali metal hydroxides and active metals like Zn, Mg etc.

$$HN_3(aq) + NaOH \longrightarrow NaN_3 + H_2O$$
$$Mg + 2HN_3(aq) \longrightarrow Mg(N_3)_2 + H_2$$
$$HN_3 + NH_3 \longrightarrow \underset{\text{(Ammonium azide)}}{NH_4^+N_3^-}$$

Azides of heavy metals are highly explosive. Therefore, barium azide or lead azide are used in detonation caps. They explode on being struck by an object.

Alkali metals azides are not explosive but decompose on heating to release nitrogen gas.

$$2NaN_3 \longrightarrow 2Na + 3N_2\uparrow$$

5. Hydrazoic acid is reduced to NH_3 or N_2H_4 by sodium amalgam or finely divided platinum.

$$HN_3 + 4H_2 \longrightarrow 2NH_3$$
$$2HN_3 + 5H_2 \longrightarrow 3NH_2 \cdot NH_2$$

In acid solution, Ti(III), Cr(II) and Sn(II) readily reduce the acid.

$$Sn^{2+} + 3H^+ + HN_3 \longrightarrow Sn^{4+} + NH_4^+ + N_2$$

6. Nitrous acid, Ce^{4+} and acidified $KMnO_4$ oxidise the acid to N_2 and these reactions can be used for the volumetric analysis.

$$HN_3 + HNO_2 \longrightarrow N_2 + N_2O + H_2O$$
$$2HN_3 + \underset{\text{(From acidified } KMnO_4)}{O} \longrightarrow 3N_2 + H_2O$$

7. HN_3 is decomposed by HCl, HI etc., giving N_2.

$$HN_3 + 2HCl \longrightarrow NH_3 + N_2 + Cl_2$$

Structure

The three nitrogen atoms in HN_3 gas are colinear.

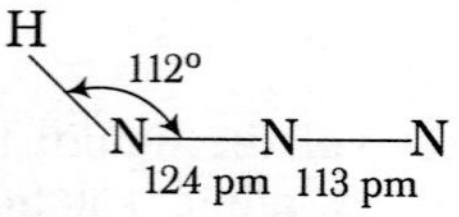

The azide ion, N_3^- is symmetrical and linear (both N—N distances being 116 pm). Its electronic structure may be represented in terms of valence bond theory as resonance hybrid of the following three structures :

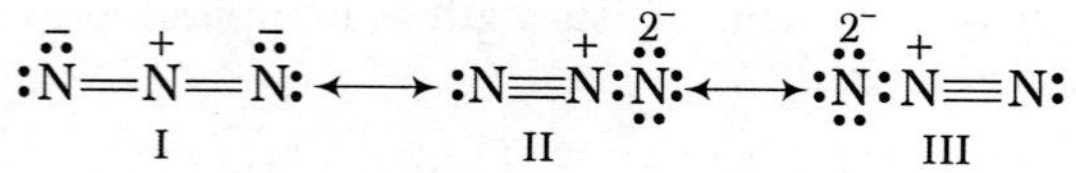

It is isoelectronic with CO_2 and NO_2^+.

The three nitrogen atoms in structure (I) use *sp* hybrid orbitals to form σ-bonds.

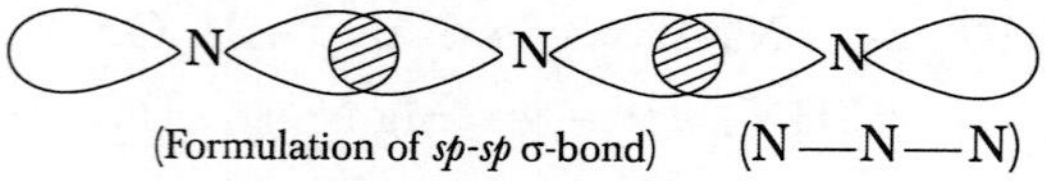

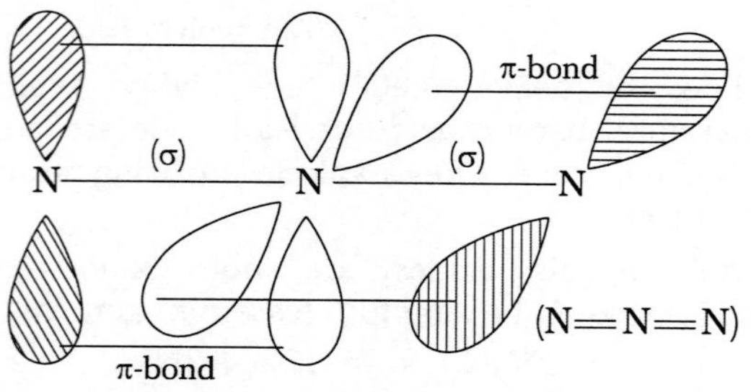

Fig. 6.21 Formation of two π-bonds in N_3^-, each terminal N atom has a lone pair of electrons.

Hydrides of Phosphorus

Phosphorus forms a number of hydrides, out of which two are well known. These are phosphine (PH_3) and dihosphine (P_2H_4).

1. Phosphine, PH_3

Preparation

(i) In the laboratory, it is prepared by heating white phosphorus with 40% sodium hydroxide solution.

$$4P + 3NaOH + 3H_2O \longrightarrow \underset{\text{Sodium hypophosphate}}{3NaH_2PO_2} + PH_3$$

Since, the gas catches fire in air, a current of hydrogen or coal gas is passed through the flask to displace air. Pure phosphine is not inflammable while impure phosphine containing diphosphine (P_2H_4) as impurity is spontaneously inflammable.

(ii) It can also be prepared more conveniently by the action of water on calcium phosphide, Ca_3P_2 or aluminium phosphide, AlP.

$$Ca_3P_2 + 6H_2O \longrightarrow 3Ca(OH)_2 + 2PH_3$$

$$AlP + 3H_2O \longrightarrow Al(OH)_3 + PH_3$$

Properties

(i) It is a colourless, poisonous gas having smell of rotten fish.

(ii) It is heavier than air and is slightly soluble in water.

(iii) It burns in air or oxygen at about 100°C forming metaphosphoric acid as

$$PH_3 + 2O_2 \longrightarrow \underset{\text{Metaphosphoric acid}}{HPO_3} + H_2O$$

(iv) It reduces oxides of nitrogen such as N_2O and NO to nitrogen.

$$PH_3 + 4N_2O \longrightarrow H_3PO_4 + 4N_2$$

$$PH_3 + 4NO \longrightarrow H_3PO_4 + 2N_2$$

(v) On passing phosphine gas through the solutions of certain metallic salts, metals get precipitated as

$$3CuSO_4 + 2PH_3 \longrightarrow \underset{\substack{\text{Cupric phosphide}\\\text{(Black ppt.)}}}{Cu_3P_2} + 3H_2SO_4$$

$$3AgNO_3 + PH_3 \longrightarrow \underset{\substack{\text{Silver phosphide}\\\text{(Black ppt.)}}}{Ag_3P} + 3HNO_3$$

(vi) It combines with halogen acids forming respective phosphonium salts.

$$PH_3 + HI \longrightarrow \underset{\text{Phosphonium iodide}}{PH_4I}$$

Uses

It is used

(i) In preparing Holmes' signals which guide the ships at night regarding the location of rocks in the sea.

(ii) In preparing smoke screens in warfare.

(iii) In making organophosphorus compounds.

Structure

Like ammonia, phosphine molecule has a pyramidal structure. However. H—P—H bond angle in phosphine is only 93°. The P—H bond distance is 124 pm. Unlike

NH_3, phosphine is not associated in the liquid state. Also the barrier to inversion for PH_3 is high as compared with that in NH_3.

Phosphonitrilic Halides (Compounds of Nitrogen with Phosphorus)

Phosphonitrilic halides, commonly called phosphazenes, consists of chains and rings containing X_2PN units. The grouping $\left(-N{=}\overset{X}{\underset{X}{P}}-\right)$ is analogous to the siloxanes $\left(-\overset{R}{\underset{R}{O}}-Si-\right)$ (PN is isoelectronic with SiO).

Polyphosphazenes consist of an alternating sequence of phosphorus and nitrogen atoms, with two substituent groups (halogen or alkyl/aryl groups) attached to each phosphorus.

$$-\!\!\left[-N{=}\overset{X\;\;X}{P}-\right]_n\!\!-$$

(X = F, Cl, Br, R, Ar)

Preparation

1. Reaction of phosphorus pentachloride and ammonium chloride in the chlorocarbon solvent and temperature near 140°C yields a series of inorganic compounds of formula $(NPCl_2)_n$ (n = 3, 4, 5 ...)

$$n\,PCl_5 + n\,NH_4Cl \xrightarrow[\substack{CHCl_2\\|\\CHCl_2}]{\text{Reflux}} (NPCl)_n + 4nHCl$$

The principal product is the cyclic trimer (hexachlorocyclotriphosphazene).

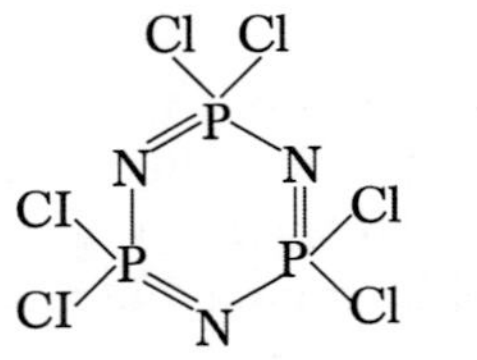

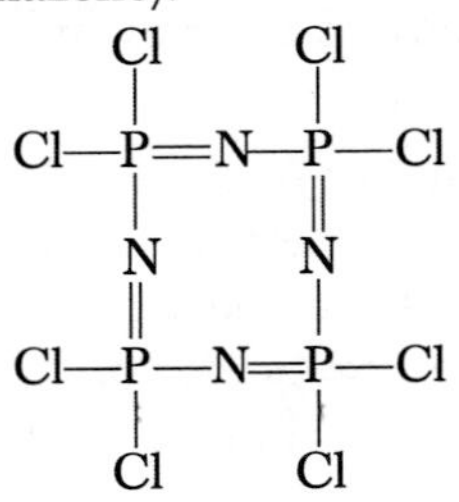

Small amounts of cyclic tetramer and some linear polymers are also formed. The mixture is separated by distilling off the solvent. The residue is treated with petroleum ether (hydrocarbon solvents). The cyclic compounds are soluble in this solvent and are easily separated from the insoluble linear polymers. The cyclic products are separated from each other by distillation. $(PNCl_2)_3$ distills at 124°C at a partial pressure of 10 mm Hg and the tetramer, $(PNCl_2)_4$ distills over at 185°C at the same pressure.

2. Phosphonitrilic fluorides cannot be obtained by the reaction between PCl_5 and NH_4F.

$$nPCl_5 + NH_4F \not\longrightarrow (PNF_2)_n$$

This is because NH_4F acts as a fluorinating agents and forms the product NH_4PF_6. The fluoro derivatives are obtained by fluorination of the chloro compounds with KF in SO_2 solvent.

$$(PNCl_2)_3 + \underset{\text{Potassium fluorosulphite}}{6KSO_2F} \longrightarrow (PNF_2)_3 + 6KCl + 6SO_2$$

$$(PNCl_2)_4 + 8KSO_2F \longrightarrow (PNF_2)_4 + 8KCl + 8SO_2$$

3. Phosphonitrilic bromides are prepared by reacting PBr_5 with NH_4Br, similar to the chloro compounds. Bromine is added to suppress the decomposition of PBr_5.

$$PBr_5 \xrightarrow[\text{excess } Br_2]{NH_4Br} [PNBr_2]_3$$

4. The phosphonitrilic iodides have not been prepared as yet.

Highly polymeric $(PNCl_2)_4$ can be made by heating cyclo $(NPCl_2)_3$ to 150-300°C. However, heating to 350° induces depolymerization.

If the trimer is heated at 230 to 300°C in an evacuated glass tube, it polymerizes to a transparent rubber-like polymer (3). 3 is called poly (dichlorophosphazene). It is also known as **"inorganic rubber"**. The mechanism of this polymerization is still not fully understood.

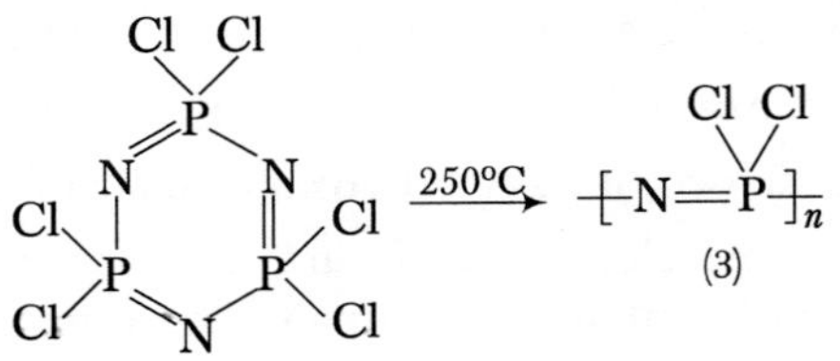

Properties

Physical properties

1. Phosphonitrilic chloride, $(PNCl_2)_3$, has m.p. = 114° and b.p. = 256°C at 1 atm pressure. It is readily soluble in ether, benzene and carbon tetrachloride. $(PNCl_2)_4$ has melting point = 123.5° and b.p. = 328.5°C. It has lower solubility in organic solvents than the trimeric compounds.
2. **Displacement reactions** The reactive chlorine atoms are highly susceptible to nucleophilic attack and replaced by other groups such as F^-, Br^-, OH^-, OR^-, SH^-, SCN^-, NR_2^- etc.

   (i) $[PNCl_2]_n + 2nNaF \longrightarrow [PNF_2]_n + 2nNaF$

   (ii) $[PNCl_2]_n + 2nCH_3MgI \longrightarrow [PN(CH_3)_2]_n + 2nMgI_2$

It has been recently shown that one of the PCl_2 groups in $(PNCl_2)_3$ can be replaced by a C—Cl group. The polymer now has carbon in its backbone. On heating at 120°C, it polymerizes to form poly(carbophosphazene).

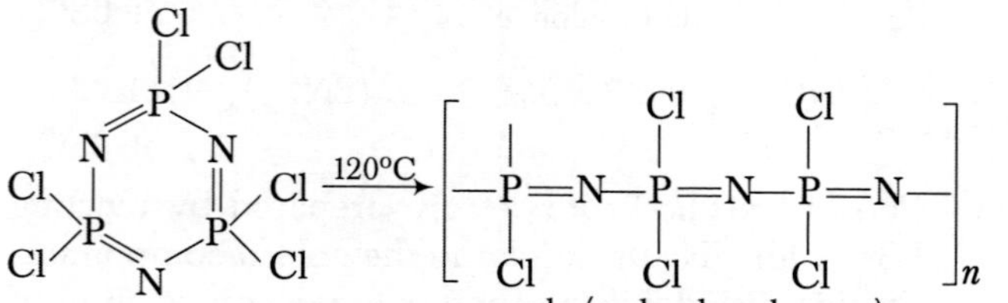

poly (carbophosphazene)

Structure

The cyclic halide trimers $(NPX_2)_3$ consist of planar 6-membered rings in which all the 6 P–N distances are equal.

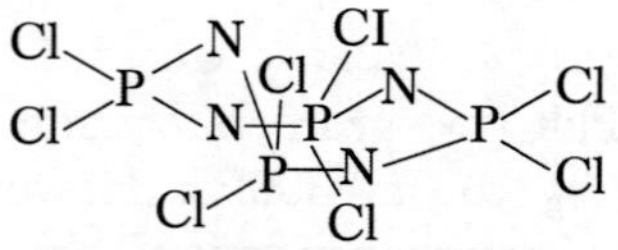
(Metastable boat form)

P–N = 158 pm
P–Cl = 197
∠NPN = 118.4°
∠PNP = 121.4°

P—N bond distance is shorter than the phosphorus-nitrogen single bond length of ≃ 175 pm. This shortening of the P—N bond distance may be attributed to the existence of P ⇇ N π-bonding ($d\pi$-$p\pi$).

The nature of π-bonding is still not well understood. The bond angles are consistent with sp^2 hybridization of the nitrogen and sp^3 hybridization of the phosphorus. Two of the sp^2 hybrid orbitals of nitrogen, containing one electron each, are used for σ-bonding and the third contains a lone pair. The third *p* orbital (p_z) of nitrogen which is unhybridized contains one electron.

The tetramer $(NPCl_2)_4$ exists in the stable chair configuration as shown below. The other form is the metastable tub conformation.

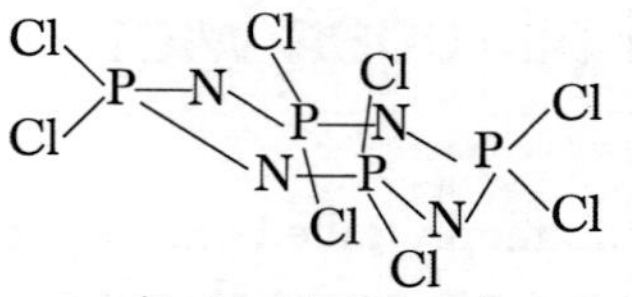
(Stable chair form)

$P_4N_4Cl_8$ (Chair)

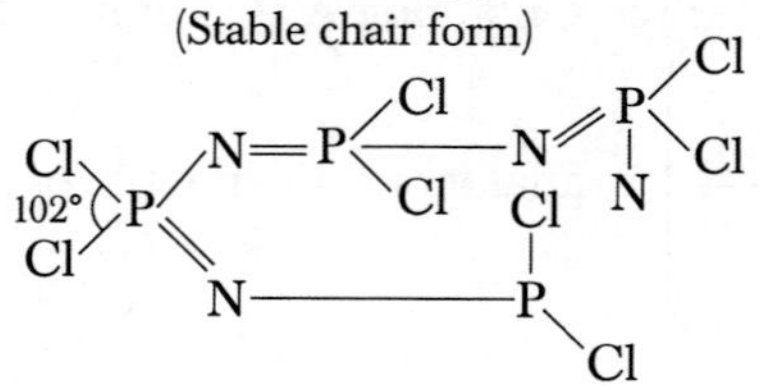

$P_4N_4Cl_8$ (Tub)

Sulphides of Nitrogen Family

Except N, all the elements of group 15 form sulphides. P combines directly with S at a temperature greater than 100°. Some of the important sulphides of P are P_4S_3, P_4S_5, P_4S_7 and P_4S_{10}. The structures of all the four sulphides are well known.

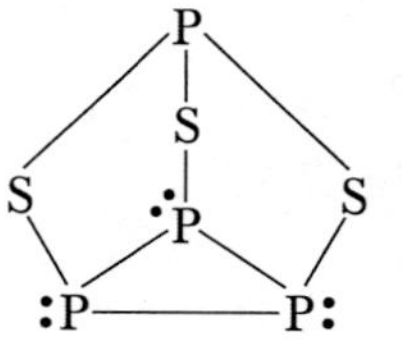
P_4S_3

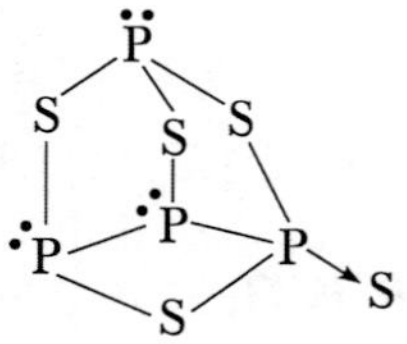
P_4S_5

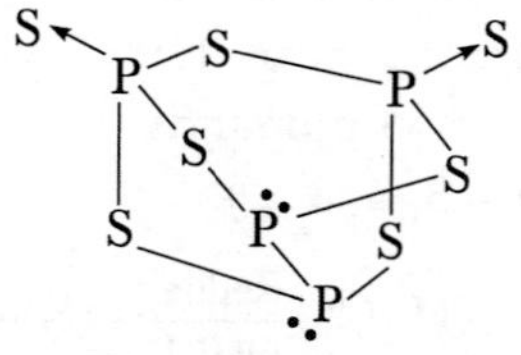
P_4S_7

P_4S_3 is used commercially in match industry.

As forms As_4S_3, As_4S_4, As_2S_3 and As_2S_5.

Antimony (Sb) forms only Sb_2S_3 and Sb_2S_5. Bi form only Bi_2S_3.

The stability of these sulphides increases with increase in atomic mass of the element. The acidic character decreases as the size of the element of group 15 increases. Sulphides of As and Sb are soluble in yellow ammonium sulphide while that of Bi is not.

Sulphur-Nitrogen Compounds

Nitrogen and sulphur form a large number of cyclic and acyclic compounds. These compounds exhibit unusual structures. The recent discovery that a simple binary compound $(SN)_x$, a polymer between two non-metals sulphur and nitrogen, behaves like a metal whose conductivity increases with decrease in temperature and becomes, a superconductor below 0.33 K.

Some of the most important binary neutral sulphur nitrogen compounds are S_4N_4 and $(SN)_x$ which we shall deals in this section.

1. Tetrasulphur Tetranitride, S_4N_4

This is one of the earliest known S—N compounds and is a starting material for many other compounds containing S—N bonds.

Preparation

It is prepared by passing NH_3 gas into a warm solution of S_2Cl_2 (sulphur monochloride) in CCl_4.

$$6S_2Cl_2 + 16NH_3 \xrightarrow{50^\circ} S_4N_4 + S_8\downarrow + 12NH_4Cl$$

Alternatively, it can also be prepared by heating S_2Cl_2 and NH_4Cl at 160°C.

$$6S_2Cl_2 + 4NH_4Cl \longrightarrow S_4N_4 + 8\,S\downarrow + 16HCl$$

Properties

1. It is an orange-yellow crystalline solid, m.p. 178°C.
2. It explodes when struck or if heated. The formation of S_4N_4 is endothermic. This is due to the very high stability of decomposition products *i.e.,* elemental sulphur, S_8 and N_2 ($N{\equiv}N$), and that's why S_4N_4 cannot be prepared by the direct reaction between S_8 and N_2.
3. S_4N_4 is insoluble in water, but undergoes base hydrolysis.
$$2S_4N_4 + 6NaOH + 9H_2O \longrightarrow Na_2S_2O_3 + 2Na_2S_3O_6 + 8NH_3$$
4. S_4N_4 is used as an intermediate for the preparation of several other sulphur-nitrogen compounds.

(a) $S_4N_4 \xrightarrow[\text{Ag wool, 300°C}]{\text{Heating under vacuum}} S_2N_2, (SN)_x$

(b) $S_4N_4 \xrightarrow{Cl_2} S_3N_3Cl_3 \underset{25°C}{\overset{110°C}{\rightleftharpoons}} NSCl$

$\quad\quad \xrightarrow{S_2Cl_2} [S_3N_2Cl^+]\,Cl^-$

(c) $S_4N_4 \xrightarrow{AsF_5} S_3N_2^+\,AsF_6^-$

(d) $S_4N_4 \xrightarrow{AlCl_3} S_3N_2^+ + AlCl_4^-$

(e) $S_4N_4 \xrightarrow{SbCl_5} S_4N_4^{2+}\,(SbCl_6^-)_2$

(f) $S_4N_4 \xrightarrow[100°C]{S_8} S_4N_2$

(g) $S_4N_4 \xrightarrow{NaN_3} S_3N_3^-$

(h) $S_4N_4 \xrightarrow[CCl_4]{\text{AgF in}} S_4N_4H_4 \xrightarrow{300°C} NSF$

Structure

S_4N_4 has an eight-membered cradle-shaped heterocycle structure as shown below :

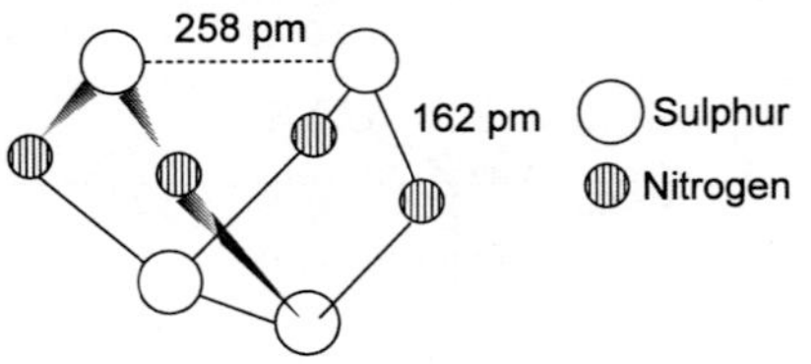

The S—N distance of 162 pm is short as compared to the sum of the covalent radii of sulphur and nitrogen of 178 pm. All S—N distances are equal and suggest some electron delocalization. The *trans*-annular S…S distance of 258 pm is in between S—S covalent distance (208 pm) and non-bonding van der Waals' distance (330 pm) between the two sulphur atoms. This indicates the presence of a weak bond between the two sulphur atoms.

In term of the valence bond theory, several resonance structures can be drawn for S_4N_4.

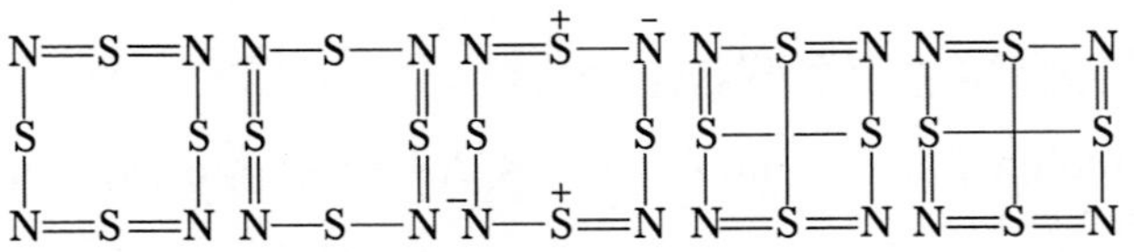

2. Polythiazyl, $(SN)_x$

An extremely remarkable inorganic compound is poly (sulphur nitride), $(SN)_x$. It is prepared by a series of reactions using S_4N_4 as the starting material.

$$S_4N_4 \xrightarrow[\text{0.01 torr}]{\text{Ag wool. (200-300°C)}} S_2N_2 \xrightarrow{25°C} \left(\!-S{=}N-\!\right)_x$$

During polymerization the crystals change from colourless (diamagnetic), to blue-black (paramagnetic), and then to bronze metallic (diamagnetic).

Properties

It is quite stable at 25°C in air and water, but on long exposure to air or water, it breaks down to a white grey powder containing sulphur, nitrogen and other products.

$(SN)_x$ has metallic appearance and exhibits metallic type conductivity. The conductivity increases with decrease in temperature and at 0.3K undergoes a change to a superconductor, at which point it offers no resistance to electric current. The conductivity is anisotropic (*i.e.*, in three dimensions).

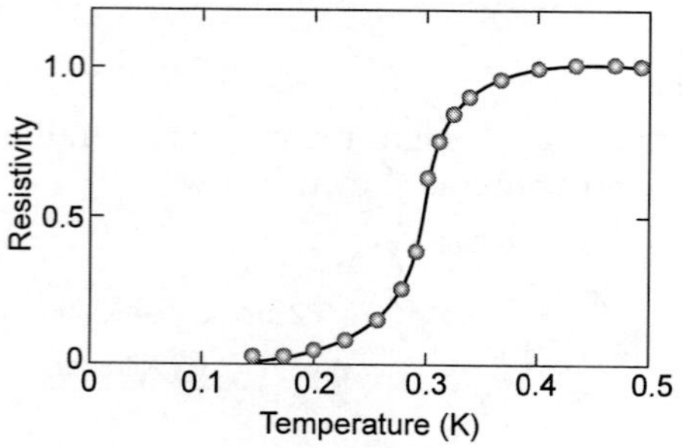

Structure

Crystals of $(SN)_x$ have a parallel fibrous structure. Individual chains occupy a *cis-trans*-planar conformation, the S—N bond lengths are intermediate between those of single and double bonds.

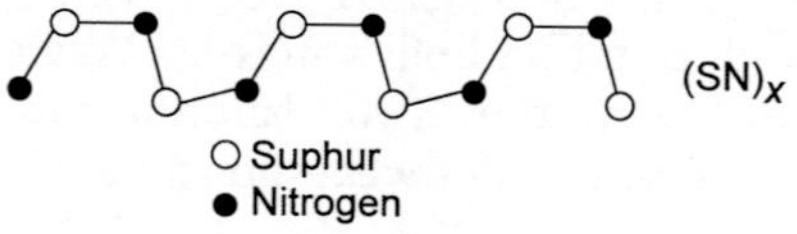

CHEMISTRY OF GROUP 16

Oxides of Sulphur

Sulphur forms a number of oxides which are listed in Table 6.7.

Table 6.7 **Oxides of Sulphur**

Formula	Name	Oxidation state of sulphur
SO	Sulphur monoxide	+ 2
SO_2	Sulphur dioxide	+ 4
SO_3	Sulphur trioxide	+ 6
S_2O_7	Sulphur heptoxide	+ 7

2. Sulphur Dioxide, SO_2

Preparation

It is prepared by burning sulphur in air.

$$S + O_2 \longrightarrow SO_2$$

It is also prepared by burning sulphides in air.

$$4FeS_2 + 11O_2 \longrightarrow 2Fe_2O_3 + 8SO_2$$

Properties

1. It is a colourless gas having suffocating smell and is readily soluble in water. Its aqueous solution has acidic character as it produces H_2SO_3 on dissolution in water.

$$SO_2 + H_2O \longrightarrow H_2SO_3$$

2. It is a good reducing agent and reduces acidified dichromate to Cr^{3+}; $KMnO_4$ to Mn^{2+} and KIO_3 to I_2.
3. In presence of water, it bleaches colouring matter to colourless matter by reduction.

$$SO_2 + 2H_2O \longrightarrow H_2SO_4 + 2(H)$$

$$\text{Colouring matter} + 2(H) \longrightarrow \text{colourless matter} + H_2O$$

Structure

Sulphur dioxide is a triatomic molecule. Electron diffraction experiments on sulphur dioxide give the distance S—O = 143 pm and angle OSO = 120° (Fig. 6.22). Moreover, the molecule has a dipole moment which confirms its V-shaped structure. The OSO angle of 120° suggests that sulphur atom is sp^2 hybridized in which two hybrid orbitals are used to form bonds with oxygen atoms and the third orbital is occupied by a lone pair.

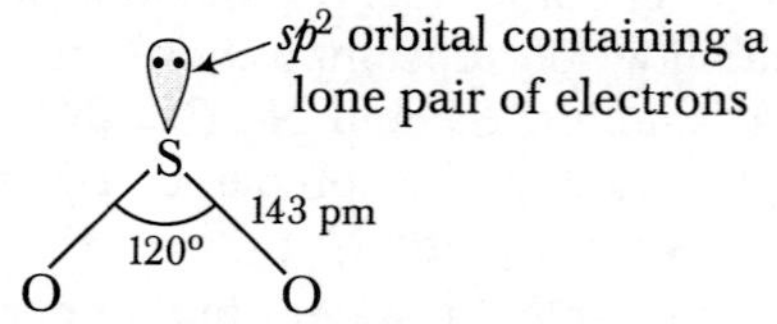

Fig. 6.22 Structure of SO_4 molecules.

Experiments show that two S—O bond lengths in SO_2 are identical and considerably shorter than the expected S—O single bond which is suggestive of multiple bonding. There is presumably *pπ-pπ* bonding

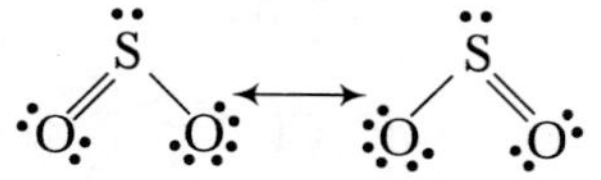

(as indicated in the resonance structures shown below) as well as *pπ-dπ* bonding due to the overlap of filled *pπ* orbitals of oxygen with vacant 3*d* orbitals of sulphur as shown in Fig. 6.23.

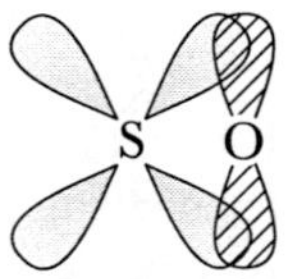

Fig. 6.23 Dative $d\pi$-$p\pi$ bonding.

3. Sulphur Trioxide, SO_3

It is prepared by the direct oxidation of sulphur dioxide with atmospheric oxygen in presence of finely divided platinum or divanadium pentoxide at a pressure of 2 atm and temperature 700 K.

$$2SO_2(g) + O_2(g) \rightleftharpoons 2SO_3(g)$$

Properties

1. It is a white crystalline solid.
2. It reacts with water to give sulphuric acid and this reaction is exothermic.

$$SO_3 + H_2O \longrightarrow H_2SO_4 + \text{heat}$$

3. It acts as a strong Lewis acid towards a number of inorganic and organic compounds. For example :

$$(C_6H_5)_3P + SO_3 \longrightarrow (C_6H_5)_3P \cdot SO_3$$
$$(C_6H_5)_3AsO + SO_3 \longrightarrow (C_6H_5)_3AsO \cdot SO_3$$

Structure

In the gas phase, sulphur trioxide is a planar triangular molecule (sp^2 hybridization of the sulphur atom) with three equivalent S–O bonds as shown in Fig. 6.24.

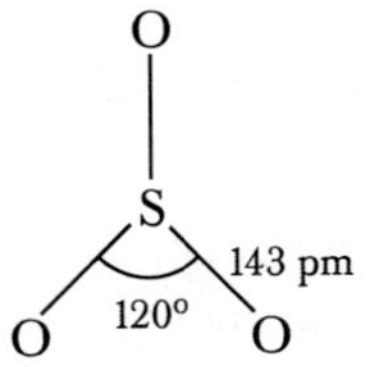

Fig. 6.24 Structure of a gaseous SO_2 molecule.

In order to account for the equivalency of all the S—O bonds and short S—O distance of 143 pm, sulphur trioxide may be considered as a resonance hybrid involving $p\pi$-$p\pi$ S—O bonding along with additional $p\pi$-$d\pi$ bonding as has been shown in SO_2.

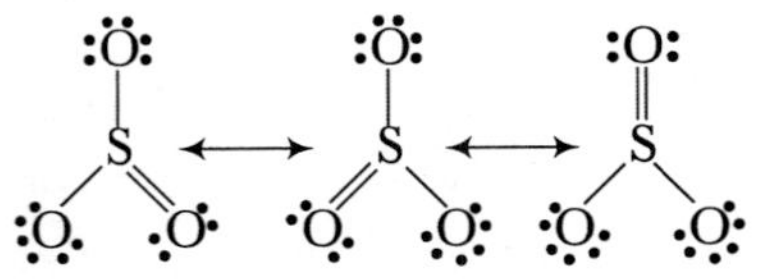

In the solid phase, it polymerizes to puckered rings or to the more stable layer structure (Fig. 6.24).

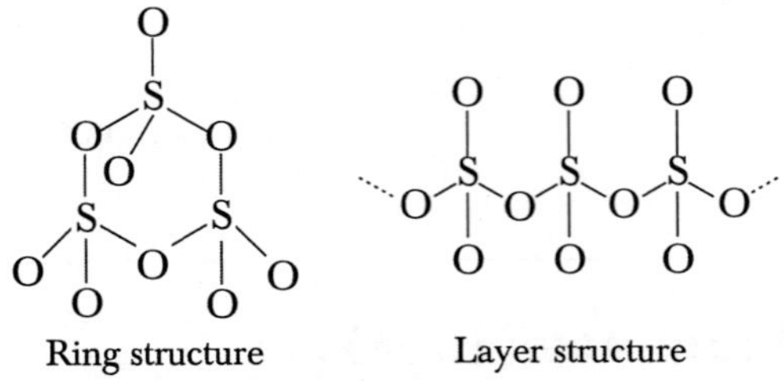

Fig. 6.24 Structure of solid SO_3.

Oxo-Acids of Sulphur

Sulphur forms a number of oxo-acids. However, only a few can be isolated as free acids and a number of them are found only as their aqueous solutions or as salts of their anions. Important oxo-acids of sulphur are listed in Table 6.8. Sulphuric acid is the most important and is prepared industrially on a very large scale. Other acids or their salts, for example, thiosulphates, sulphites, dithionates, are very useful reducing agents.

Table 6.8 **Some Oxo-Acids of Sulphur**

Name	Formula	Structure
Sulphurous* acid	H_2SO_3	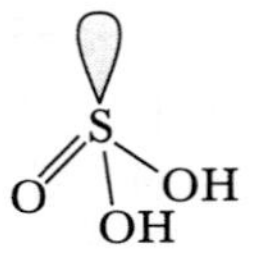
Sulphuric acid	H_2SO_4	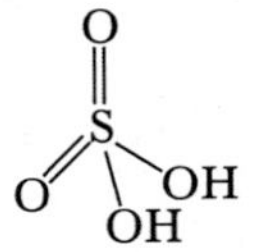
Peroxomonosulphuric acid	H_2SO_5	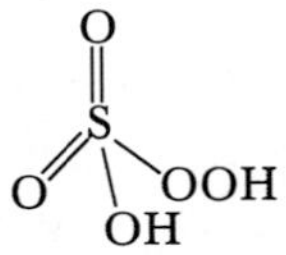
Thiosulphuric acid	$H_2S_2O_3$	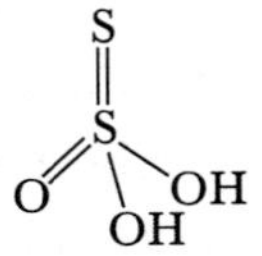
Dithionic acid	$H_2S_2O_6$	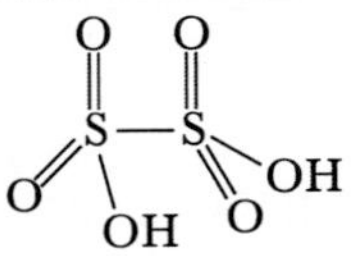
Disulphuric acid	$H_2S_2O_7$	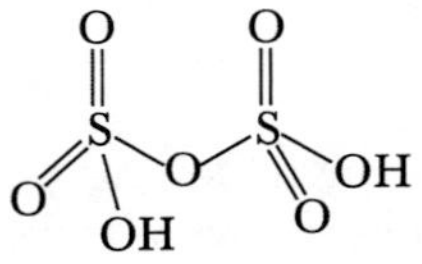

Peroxodisulphuric acid	$H_2S_2O_8$	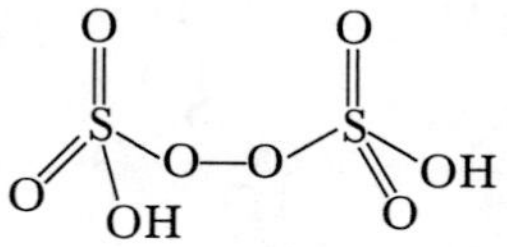

Sulphuric Acid, H_2SO_4

It is manufactured by the catalytic oxidation of sulphur dioxide by the lead chamber and contact processes. It is a strong diprotic acid and ionises as :

$$H_2SO_4 \rightleftharpoons H^+ + HSO_4^-$$

$$HSO_4^- \rightleftharpoons H^+ + SO_4^{2-}$$

It exhibits oxidising properties and is a strong dehydrating agent.

(i) **Reaction with metal oxides**

$$CaO + H_2SO_4 \longrightarrow CaSO_4 + H_2O$$

(ii) **Reaction with carbonates**

$$Na_2CO_3 + H_2SO_4 \longrightarrow Na_2SO_4 + H_2O + CO_2$$

(iii) **Dehydrating properties** When concentrated sulphuric acid is dropped on wood, sugar or paper, it absorbs moisture and brings about charring.

$$\underset{\text{Sugar}}{C_{12}H_{22}O_{11}} \xrightarrow[H_2SO_4]{\text{Conc.}} 12C + \underset{\text{(Absorbed by acid)}}{11H_2O}$$

(iv) **Reaction with formic acid**

$$HCOOH \xrightarrow[H_2SO_4]{\text{Conc.}} CO + \underset{\text{(Absorbed by acid)}}{H_2O}$$

(v) **Oxidising properties** Sulphuric acid acts as an oxidising agent since, it undergoes dissociation to give nascent oxygen.

$$H_2SO_4 \longrightarrow H_2O + SO_2 + [O]$$

It oxidises carbon to carbon dioxide.

$$C + 2H_2SO_4 \longrightarrow CO_2 + 2SO_2 + 2H_2O$$

It oxidises phosphorus to phosphoric acid.

$$P_4 + 10H_2SO_4 \longrightarrow 4H_3PO_4 + 10SO_2 + 4H_2O$$

Structure

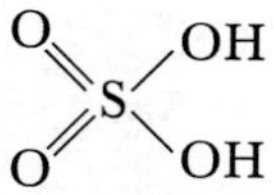

The high boiling point and viscosity of concentrated sulphuric acid indicate association of molecules *via* hydrogen bonding as shown in Fig. 6.25.

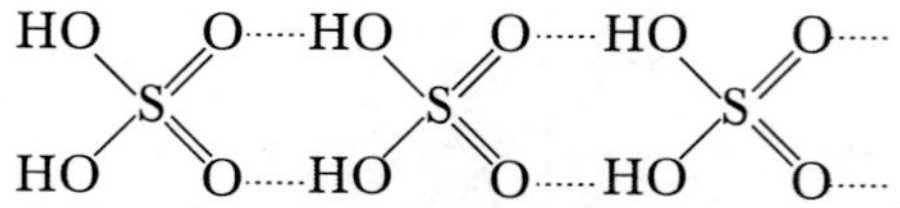

Fig. 6.25 Hydrogen bonded sulphuric acid molecules.

X-ray analysis shows that the SO_4^{2-} ion is tetrahedral and the S—O bond lengths are all equal (149 pm) and have considerable doule bond character. The bonding can be explained as follows :

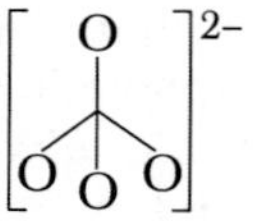

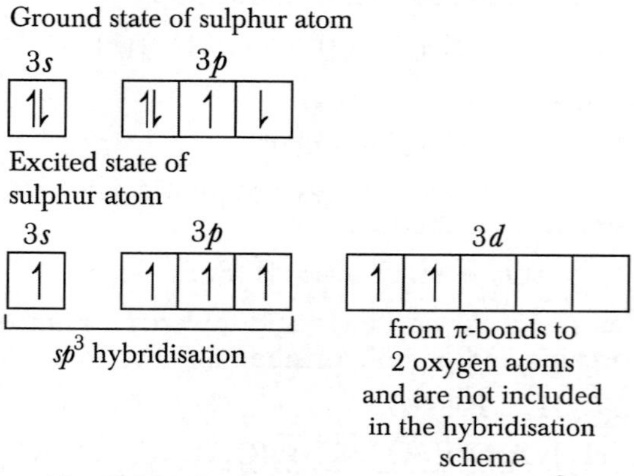

Fig. 6.33 Bonding and structure of SO_4^{2-}.

2. Permonosulphuric Acid, H_2SO_5

It is also known as **Caro's acid**. It is prepared by reacting equimolar proportion of hydrogen peroxide and sulphuric acid.

$$HO—SO_2—O—H + H—O—OH \longrightarrow HOOSO_2OH + H_2O$$

It is crystalline solid which is quite stable. It is a powerful oxidising agent; it oxidises aniline to nitrobenzene. The above method of its perparation clearly brings out its constitution.

3. Thiosulphuric Acid, $H_2S_2O_4$

The structure of sodium thiosulphate can be proved from its method of preparation as :

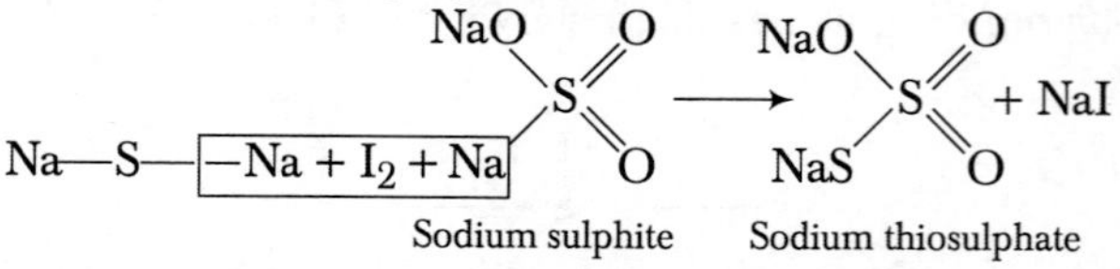

Therefore, thiosulphate ion is structurally similar to the sulphate ion except that one of the positions of the tetrahedron is occupied by sulphur atom as shown in Fig. 6.27.

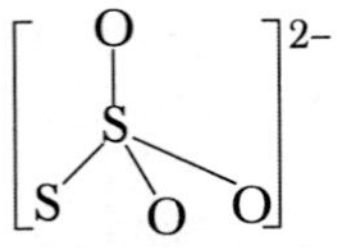

Fig. 6.27 Structure of $S_2O_3^{2-}$ ion.

The alkali thiosulphates are used mainly in photography to dissolve unreacted silver bromide from the emulsion on the photographic paper.

4. Perdisulphuric Acid, $H_2S_2O_8$

It is prepared by reacting one mole of hydrogen peroxide with two moles of chlorosulphonic acid as :

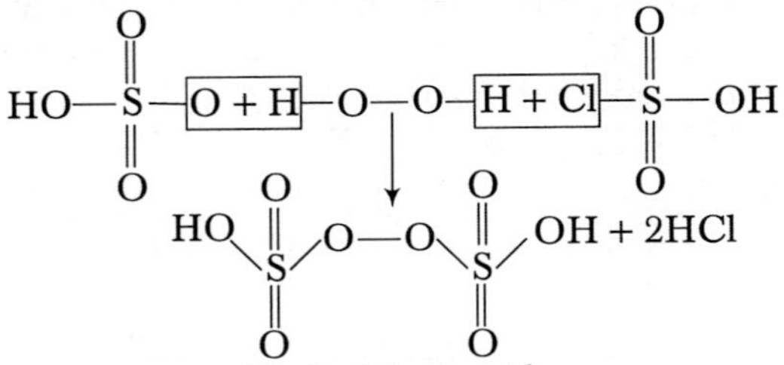

Perdisulphuric acid

By virtue of the peroxy group, it is a strong oxidising agent. It is known as **Marshall's acid**.

Hydrides of Sulphur

Sulphur forms a common hydride known as hydrogen sulphide, H_2S in which sulphur has +2 oxidation state. Sulphur also forms polysulphides known as **sulphanes** which contain —S—S to —SSSSSS— chains. Therefore, formulae of some sulphanes are H_2S_2, H_2S_3, H_2S_4, H_2S_5 and H_2S_6.

1. Hydrogen Sulphide, H_2S

Preparation

It is prepared by the action of dilute sulphuric acid on ferrous sulphide.

$$FeS + H_2SO_4 \longrightarrow FeSO_4 + H_2S$$

Properties

It is a colourless gas having foul smell of rotten eggs. This gas is quite poisonous in nature and if inhaled even in small quantity causes headache.

1. **Acidic behaviour** Aqueous solution of H_2S behaves as a weak diprotic acid.

$$H_2S \rightleftharpoons H^+ + HS^-$$

$$HS^- \rightleftharpoons H^+ + S^{2-}$$

2. **Reaction with SO_2** It reacts with SO_2 in the presence of moisture to produce sulphur.

$$SO_2 + 2H_2S \longrightarrow 2H_2O + 3S$$

3. **Reaction with oxygen** It burns in oxygen of air with a blue flame.

$$2H_2S + 3O_2 \longrightarrow 2H_2O + 2SO_2$$

4. **Reducing character** Hydrogen sulphide is a very active reducing agent because it can release nascent hydrogen.

$$H_2S \longrightarrow 2H + S\downarrow$$

It can also take up oxygen and thus act as a reducing agent.

$$H_2S + O \longrightarrow H_2O + S\downarrow$$

(i) Halogens are reduced by H_2S to halogen acids.

$$H_2S + Cl_2 \longrightarrow 2HCl + S\downarrow$$

(ii) It reduces ferric salts to ferrous salts.

$$2FeCl_3 + H_2S \longrightarrow 2FeCl_2 + 2HCl + S\downarrow$$

$$Fe_2(SO_4)_3 + H_2S \longrightarrow 2FeSO_4 + H_2SO_4 + S\downarrow$$

(iii) Sulphuric acid is reduced to sulphur dioxide.

$$H_2S + 2H_2SO_4 \longrightarrow 2H_2O + 2SO_2 + S\downarrow$$

(iv) Nitric acid is reduced to nitrogen dioxide.

$$H_2S + 2HNO_3 \longrightarrow 2H_2O + 2NO_2 + S\downarrow$$

(v) Sulphur dioxide is reduced to sulphur.

$$2H_2S + SO_2 \longrightarrow 2H_2O + 3S\downarrow$$

(vi) Hydrogen peroxide is reduced to water.

$$H_2S + H_2O_2 \longrightarrow 2H_2O + S\downarrow$$

(vii) Acidified $KMnO_4$ is reduced to Mn^{II}.

$$2KMnO_4 + 3H_2SO_4 + 5H_2S \longrightarrow K_2SO_4 + 2MnSO_4 + 8H_2O + 5S\downarrow$$

(viii) Acidified $K_2Cr_2O_7$ is reduced to chromium(III) sulphate.

$$\underset{\text{(Orange)}}{K_2Cr_2O_7} + 4H_2SO_4 + 3H_2S \longrightarrow K_2SO_4 + \underset{\text{(Green)}}{Cr_2(SO_4)_3} + 7H_2O + 3S\downarrow$$

Hydrogen sulphide is used in qualitative analysis of cations as it causes precipitation of coloured metallic sulphides under controlled hydrogen ion concentration. For example, in acidic medium, H_2S forms sulphides of Hg^{2+}, Pb^{2+}, Cu^{2+}, Cd^{2+}, As^{3+}, Sb^{3+} and Sn^{2+} while in alkaline medium H_2S forms sulphides of Ni^{2+}, Co^{2+}, Mn^{2+} and Zn^{2+}.

Structure

Since, its formula (H_2S) is similar to that of water (H_2O), and oxygen as well as sulphur belong to the same group, it has angular (bent) structure (Fig. 6.28) similar to that of water.

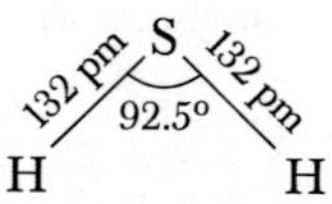

Fig. 6.28 Structure of H_2S molecule.

2. Hydrogen Polysulphides (Sulphanes)

Sulphur forms only a few hydrogen polysulphides because sulphur has much less tendency for catenation due to weak S—S bond. Some of the hydrogen polysulphides are as follows :

Formula	Name	Structure
H_2S_2	Hydrogen disulphide	H—S—S—H
H_2S_3	Hydrogen trisulphide	H—S—S—S—H
H_2S_5	Hydrogen pentasulphide	H—S—S—S—S—S—H

Halides of Sulphur

Sulphur forms a number of binary halides which are listed in Table 6.9.

Table 6.9 **Halides of Sulphur**

Fluorides	Chlorides	Bromide
S_2F_2, SF_4, S_2F_{10}, SF_6	S_2Cl_2, SCl_2, SCl_4	S_2Br_2

It may be pointed out that no compound of sulphur with iodine is known. This is due to the fact that sulphur and iodine have almost equal electronegativities and hence much less tendency to combine.

Moreover, only fluorine forms hexacoordinated compound namely, SF_6. This is because of the small size and high electronegativity of fluorine, it forms hexacoordinated compound.

The thermal stability of sulphur halides decreases in the order.

Sulphur fluorides > sulphur chlorides > sulphur bromides

1. Sulphur Monohalides

Sulphur forms three monohalides, namely, sulphur monofluoride (S_2F_2), sulphur monochloride (S_2Cl_2) and sulphur monobromide (S_2Br_2).

All these halides are formed by direct union of the elements.

Disulphur difluoride S_2F_2, is prepared by the fluorination of sulphur with AgF in a very dried apparatus at 125°C.

S_2F_2 readily isomerizes to thiothionyl fluoride, SSF_2, in the presence of alkali metal fluoride. SSF_2 can also be prepared by the fluorination of S_2Cl_2 using KF in SO_2.

$$S_2Cl_2 + 2KSO_2F \longrightarrow SSF_2 + 2KCl + 2SO_2$$

Disulphur dichloride, S_2Cl_2, is prepared by the direct chlorination of molten sulphur. Pure S_2Cl_2 is obtained by fractional distillation.

Disulphur dibromide, S_2Br_2 can be prepared by the direct reaction of the elements at 100°C. Analogous disulphur diodide, S_2I_2, is not known. Important physical properties are given below :

Formula	Colour and State	Melting point (°C)	Boiling point (°C)
S_2F_2	Colourless gas	−133	+15
S_2Cl_2	Golden yellow liquid	−76	138
S_2Br_2	Red oily liquid	−46	54 (0.18 mm Hg)

Properties

1. Both S_2F_2 and SF_2 are rapidly hydrolysed by water to give sulphur, HF and a mixture of polythionic acids.

$$5S_2F_2 + 6H_2O \longrightarrow \frac{3}{4}S_8 + 10HF + H_2S_4O_6$$

2. S_2Cl_2 reacts with atomic nitrogen to give NSCl.
3. Solution of S_2Cl_2 in CCl_4 reacts with NH_3 gas to give S_4N_4.

$$6S_2Cl_2 + 16NH_3 \xrightarrow{50^\circ} S_4N_4 + 8S + 12NH_4Cl$$

Similar product is obtained by heating S_2Cl_2 with NH_4Cl at 160°.

$$6S_2Cl_2 + 4NH_4Cl \longrightarrow S_4N_4 + 8S + 16HCl$$

4. Reaction between S_4N_4 and S_2Cl_2 in CCl_4 gives $S_4N_3^+Cl^-$.

$$3S_4N_4 + 2S_2Cl_2 \xrightarrow{CCl_4/\Delta} 4[S_4N_3^+]Cl^-$$

Structure

All S_2X_2 compounds resemble H_2O_2, O_2F_2 in their structure.

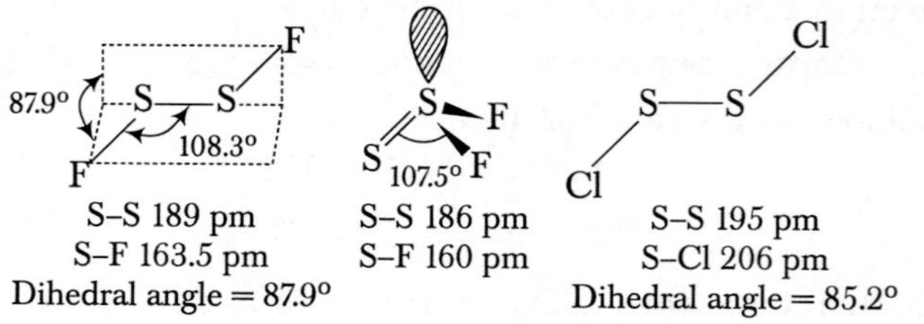

Fig. 6.29 Molecular structures of sulphur monofluoride and chloride.

Uses

S_2Cl_2 is an industrial chemical. It is mainly used in the vapour phase vulcanization of rubber. It is also used in chlorinating and preparation of mono and dichlorohydrins.

2. Sulphur Dihalides

SF_2 is known but is highly unstable. The compound can exist only as a dilute gas at very low temperatures. Sulphur dichoride, SCl_2 is the only stable dihalide of sulphur.

SBr_2 does not exist at room temperature and has been poorly characterized. SI_2 does not exist.

Preparation

SF_2 is prepared by fluorinating gaseous SCl_2 with HgF_2 at 150°C followed by complicated fractionation procedure.

SCl_2 is prepared by the direct chlorination of molten sulphur.

$$\underset{\text{(Molten)}}{2S} + Cl_2 \longrightarrow \underset{\substack{\text{Golden yellow}\\\text{liquid}}}{S_2Cl_2} \xrightarrow[\text{(trace)}]{Cl_2,\ FeCl_3} \underset{\substack{\text{Cherry-red}\\\text{liquid}}}{SCl_2}$$

Properties

1. SCl_2 is a volatile, toxic, cherry-red liquid. Its m.p. = −122° and b.p. = 59°C. SCl_2 resembles S_2Cl_2 in being foul smelling.
2. The pure liquid is unstable due to the existence of an equilibrium.
$$2SCl_2 \rightleftharpoons S_2Cl_2 + Cl_2$$
SCl_2 can be stabilized by adding a small fraction of PCl_5.
3. SCl_2 (like S_2Cl_2) is hydrolysed by water to give a number of products : H_2S, SO_2, H_2SO_3, H_2SO_4 and $H_2S_xO_6$ (polythionic acids).
4. Oxidation of SCl_2 gives thionyl chloride, $SOCl_2$ and sulphuryl chloride, SO_2Cl_2.
5. Reaction with F_2 yields SF_4 and SF_6.
6. Reaction with NaF gives SF_4 and disproportionation products like S_2Cl_2.
$$3SCl_2 + 5NaF \longrightarrow SF_4 + S_2Cl_2 + 4NaCl$$
7. SCl_2 reacts with atomic nitrogen to give NSCl.
8. SCl_2 adds across olefinic double bonds.
$$SCl_2 + 2CH_2{=}CH_2 \longrightarrow \underset{\substack{\text{Mustard gas}\\\text{(war gas)}}}{S(CH_3CH_2Cl)_2}$$

Structure

Sulphur dichloride is angular in shape. The central atom is sp^3 hybridized but the tetrahedral angle of 109° 28′ is distorted by the presence of two lone pairs of electrons. The bond angle is about 103° in SCl_2.

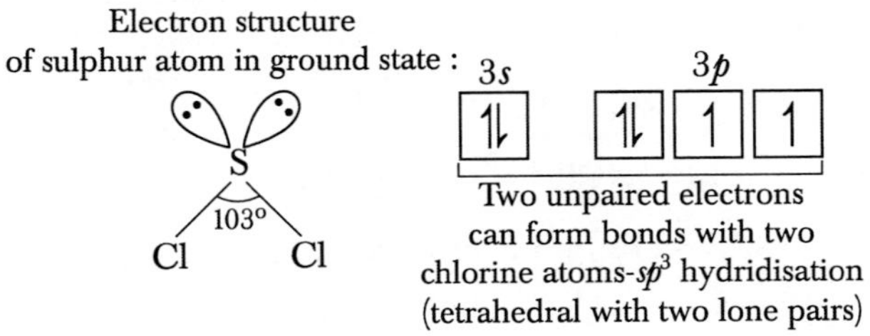

Fig. 6.30 Bonding and structure of SCl_2.

3. Sulphur Tetrahalides

Sulphur forms only two sulphur tetrahalides, namely, sulphur tetrafluoride (SF_4) and sulphur tetrachloride (SCl_4).

(a) Sulphur tetrafluoride, SF_4

It is an extremely reactive fluorinating agent but it is more stable than the lower fluorides S_2F_2 and SF_2. It is prepared by the action of cobalt(III) fluoride on sulphur as

$$S + 4CoF_3 \longrightarrow SF_4 + 4CoF_2$$

Its important properties are :

1. It is a colourless gas; melting point = −121° and b.p. = − 38°C.
2. It is thermally quite stable and is used as a fluorinating agent.
3. It can act both as an electron pair acceptor (Lewis acid) and an electron pair donor (Lewis base). It thus forms stable 1 : 1 adducts with pyridine ($C_5H_5NSF_4$) which has square pyramidal geometry. It also acts as a donor towards many Lewis acids to give 1 : 1 adducts. It forms 1 : 1 compound with BF_3 (SF_4, BF_3), AsF_5 (SF_4, AsF_5) and SbF_5 (SF_4, SbF_5). In these compounds it actually acts as a fluoride ion donor. For example, the adducts may be represented as : $SF_3^+ BF_4^-$, $SF_3^+ AsF_6^-$ and $SF_3^+ SbF_6^-$.
4. It is readily hydrolysed by moisture to give HF and SO_2.
5. It fluorinates aldehydic and ketonic groups, $>C{=}O$ to $>CF_2$ groups and carboxylic acid groups, –COOH to —CF_3.

6. SF_4 reacts with I_2O_5

$$I_2O_5 + 5SF_4 \longrightarrow 2IF_5 + 5SOF_2$$

7. SF_4 reacts with BCl_3

$$4BCl_3 + 3SF_4 \longrightarrow 4BF_3 + 3SCl_2 + 3Cl_2$$

8. It undergoes oxidative addition reactions to give S^{VI} compounds.

$$SF_4 + F_2 \longrightarrow SF_6$$

$$SF_4 + ClF \xrightarrow{380°C} SClF_5$$

$$SF_4 + O_2 \text{ (presence of } NO_2 \text{ as catalyst)} \longrightarrow SOF_4$$

9. $H_2C{=}SF_4$ is obtained by reacting $SF_3{-}CH_2Br$ with ^nBuLi at –110°C.

Some important structures of the compounds mentioned in these reactions are given below :

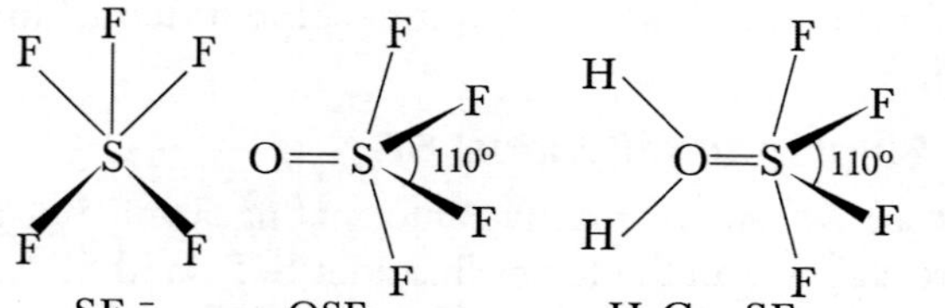

SF_5^- OSF_4 $H_2C = SF_4$

(The CH_2 group is coplanar with the axial SF_2 group.)

Structure of SF_4

It has **see saw** structure which is derived from trigonal bipyramid geometry in which an equatorial position is occupied by a lone pair as shown in Fig. 6.31.

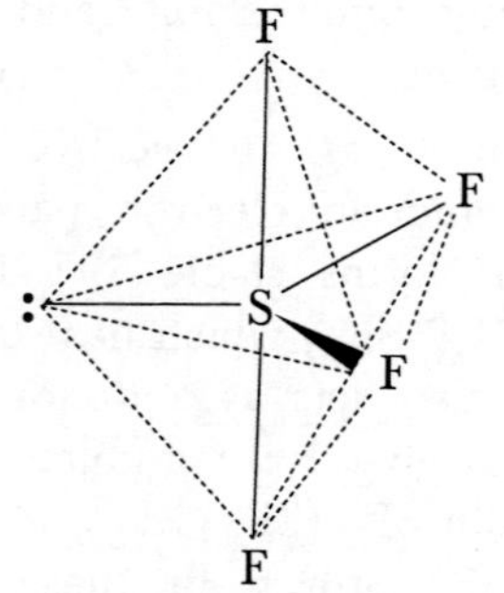

Fig. 6.31 Structure of SF_4.

(b) Sulphur Tetrachloride, SCl_4

Unlike the fluorides, the higher chlorides of sulphur are unstable and poorly characterized.

Preparation

Chlorination of SCl_2 by liquid Cl_2 at –78° yields SCl_4. It is formulated as $SCl_3^+Cl^-$.

Properties

1. It is an off-white solid. It begins to decompose on warming above –30°C.
2. Reactions of SCl_4 with Lewis acids such as $AlCl_3$ yields $SCl_4 \cdot AlCl_3$. It has been characterized as $SCl_3^+AlCl_4^-$.
3. It is hydrolysed on exposure to air forming sulphurous acid.

$$SCl_4 + 3H_2O \longrightarrow H_2SO_3 + 4HCl$$

Structure

Its structure is not reliably known. It is assumed that its structure is similar to that of SF_4.

4. Sulphur pentahalides

Sulphur forms only one pentahalide, namely, sulphur pentafluoride, S_2F_{10}.

Preparation

1. It is formed by the fluorination of sulphur as a by product during the formation of SF_6.
2. It is also prepared by the photolytic reduction of $SClF_5$.

$$2SClF_5 + H_2 \xrightarrow{h\nu} S_2F_{10} + 2HCl$$

Properties

1. It is a liquid having m.p. –92°C and b.p. 29°C. It is quite stable though less stable than SF_6. Like SF_6, it is an inert compound as it neither gets hydrolysed by water nor by alkalies.
2. On heating to about 150°C, it undergoes disproportionation.

$$S_2F_{10} \xrightarrow{150°C} SF_4 + SF_6$$

3. It reacts with halogens (Cl_2 or Br_2) as

$$S_2F_{10} + Cl_2 \longrightarrow 2SClF_5$$

$$S_2F_{10} + Br_2 \longrightarrow 2SBrF_5$$

Structure

It is believed that it consists of two SF_5 groups which are linked through sulphur atoms having octahedral geometry as shown in Fig. 6.32.

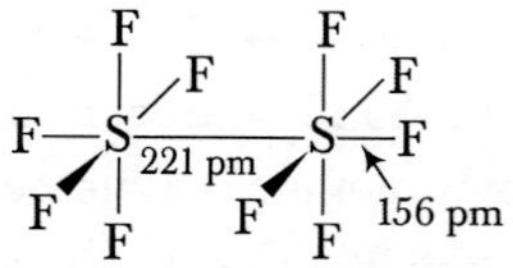

Fig. 6.32 Structure of S_2F_{10} molecule.

5. Sulphur Hexahalides

Sulphur forms only one hexahalide, namely sulphur hexafluoride, SF_6. It is formed when sulphur is burnt in fluorine.

$$S + 3F_2 \longrightarrow SF_6$$

It is a colourless, odourless and tasteless gas which is quite stable. It is inert both thermally and chemically. It is not hydrolysed due to the following reasons :

(i) high bond strength of S–F bond,
(ii) sulphur atom in SF_6 is coordinately saturated
(iii) lack of polarity in SF_6.

However, SF_6 is attacked by boiling sodium

$$SF_6 + 8Na \longrightarrow Na_2S + 6NaF$$

In stability and reactivity, it resembles carbon tetrachloride.

Structure

It has octahedral structure with the central atom (sulphur) acquiring sp^3d^2 hybridisation.

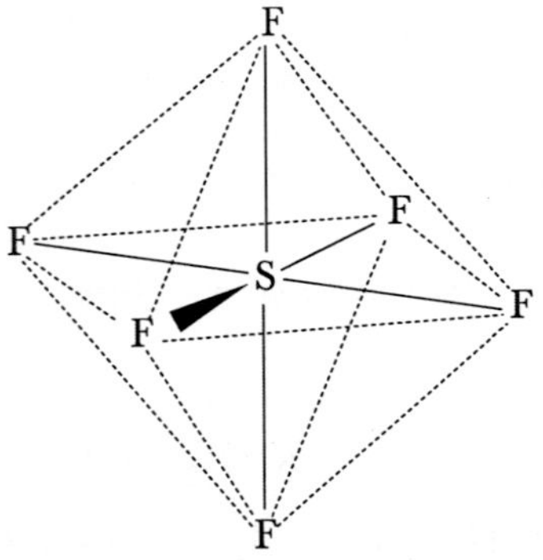

Fig. 6.33 Bonding and structure of SF_6.

CHEMISTRY OF GROUP 17

Oxides of Halogens

Halogens do not combine directly with oxygen. However, binary halogen-oxygen compounds can be prepared by indirect methods and a number of such compounds have been reported although many of them are quite unstable because they (except OF_2) have positive free energies of formation. The known binary halogen oxygen compounds are listed in Table 6.10. The oxides are powerful oxidising agents. These compounds are characteristically reactive and unstable towards heat. The stability of oxides is the greatest for iodine while bromine oxides are the least stable. The higher oxides are more stable than the lower ones.

Table 6.10 **Binary Halogen-Oxygen Compounds**

Fluorine	Chlorine	Bromine	Iodine
OF_2	Cl_2O	Br_2O	I_2O_4
O_2F_2	ClO_2	BrO_2	I_2O_5
	Cl_2O_6	BrO_3	I_4O_9
	Cl_2O_7		

1. Oxygen Difluoride

Oxygen difluoride, OF_2 is prepared by passing F_2 through dilute NaOH solution.

$$2F_2 + 2NaOH \longrightarrow 2NaF + H_2O + OF_2$$

It is a pale-yellow poisonous gas which slowly disolves in water.

$$OF_2 + H_2O \longrightarrow O_2 + 2HF$$

It is thermally stable at 25°C. It is non-explosive because of its negative free energy of formation. It has been used as a rocket fuel.

Structure

It has V-shaped structure with bond angle of 103° 18′.

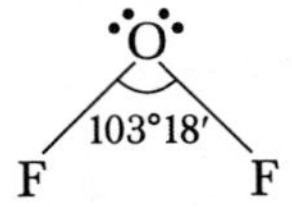

Fig. 6.34 Structure of OF_2.

The bond angle in OF_2 is distorted because of lone pairs.

2. Dioxygen Difluoride

Dioxygen difluoride, O_2F_2 is prepared by passing an electric discharge through fluorine and oxygen cooled at about −185°C. It is a yellow-orange solid. It is highly unstable and decomposes into its elements at −50°C.

It is an extremely strong fluorinating and oxidising agent.

Structure

It has the same structure as that of H_2O_2. The O—O distance is much shorter than in H_2O_2 and is about the same size as in oxygen.

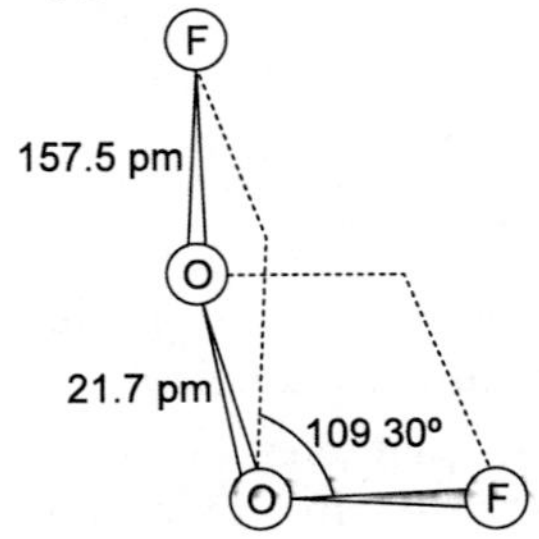

3. Chlorine Monoxide

Chlorine monoxide, Cl_2O is prepared by the action of chlorine on freshly prepared yellow mercuric oxide at 0°C.

$$HgO + 2Cl_2 \longrightarrow HgCl_2 + Cl_2O$$

It is a yellowish-red gas which decomposes explosively. It is an active oxidising agent and dissolves in water forming hypochlorous acid, HClO.

$$Cl_2O + H_2O \longrightarrow 2HClO$$

Gaseous mixture of Cl_2O and NH_3 explode violently.

$$3Cl_2O + 10NH_3 \longrightarrow 2N_2 + 6NH_4Cl + 3H_2O$$

Industrially, Cl_2O is manufactured to prepare calcium hypochlorite, $Ca(OCl)_2$. Therefore, it can be regarded as an anhydride of hypochlorous acid. It is an effective bleach for wood-pulp and textiles.

It has an angular structure as shown below :

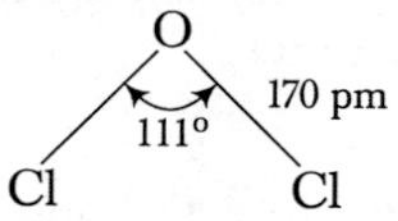

4. Chlorine Dioxide

Chlorine dioxide, ClO_2 is prepared by the reaction of sodium chlorite and chlorine diluted with air.

$$2NaClO_2 + Cl_2 \xrightarrow{Air} 2NaCl + 2ClO_2 \uparrow$$

It is a yellow gas which explodes violently. Because of its explosive nature as a liquid or concentrated gas, it is always prepared at low concentrations.

It is also prepared by reducing $NaClO_3$ with NaCl, HCl, SO_2 in strongly acidic solutions :

$$ClO_3^- + Cl^- + 2H^+ \longrightarrow ClO_2 + \frac{1}{2}Cl_2 + H_2O$$

It is a powerful oxidising and chlorinating agent. Its bleaching power is about 30 times that of chlorine. It reacts with water and alkalies to form chlorites and chlorates :

$$2ClO_2 + 2NaOH \longrightarrow \underset{\text{Sodium chloride}}{NaClO_2} + \underset{\text{Sodium chlorate}}{NaClO_3} + H_2O$$

Therefore, it is a mixed anhydride.

Its molecule is thought to contain a three-electron bond coupled with an electron pair bond. Its structure is considered to be a resonance hybrid of the following two structures :

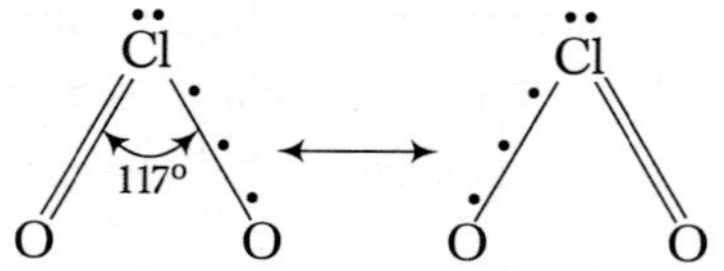

The large bond angle may be attributed to the existence of Cl-Oπ bonding which causes considerable delocalization of the odd electron.

The three-electron bond accounts for the shorter bond length and its paramagnetic nature. Although ClO_2 is an odd molecule yet it shows no tendency to dimerize probably because the odd electron is not fully localized on the central atom unlike in other odd molecules such as NO_2.

It is used for the bleaching of wood-pulp and for water treatment.

Oxo-Acids of Halogens

The oxo acids of halogens with their generalized names and those of the corresponding salts are listed in Table 6.11. Fluorine does not form any oxoacid because of its highly oxidising nature.

Table 6.11 **Oxo-Acids of Halogens**

Oxidation state of halogen	Chlorine	Bromine	Iodine	Name of acid	Name of salt	Thermal stability and acid strength
+1	HClO	HBrO	HIO	Hypohalous	Hypo-halite	Increases
+3	$HClO_2$	–	–	Halous	Halite	Increases
+5	$HClO_3$	$HBrO_3$	HIO_3	Halic	Halate	Increases
+7	$HClO_4$	$HBrO_4$	HIO_4, H_5IO_6	Perhalic	Perhalate	Increases

A few general trends in the properties of the oxoacids and their salts are discussed below :

(i) The acidic character of an oxo-acid increases with increase in oxidation number. For example, the order of increasing strength of the acids of chlorine is

$$HClO_4 > HClO_3 > HClO_2 > HClO$$

Explanation It is a well-known fact that the strength of an acid is intimately related to the strength of its conjugate base, *i.e.,* stronger the acid, the weaker will be its conjugate base and *vice-versa*. The conjugate bases of the above oxoacids of chlorine are $[ClO_4]^-$, $[ClO_3]^-$, $[ClO_2]^-$ and $[ClO]^-$, respectively. The chlorine oxyanions in which the central atom has the highest oxidation number will have a maximum number of oxygen atoms for participation in extension of the π-bond. Thereby, the charge on the ion is delocalised which greatly stabilizes the ion and thus decreases its tendency to accept a proton, *i.e.,* causes the ion to be a very weak base with the result that strength of the acid increases.

It may be pointed out that in this series of anions delocalization of charge is produced by extended $p\pi$ - $d\pi$ bonding.

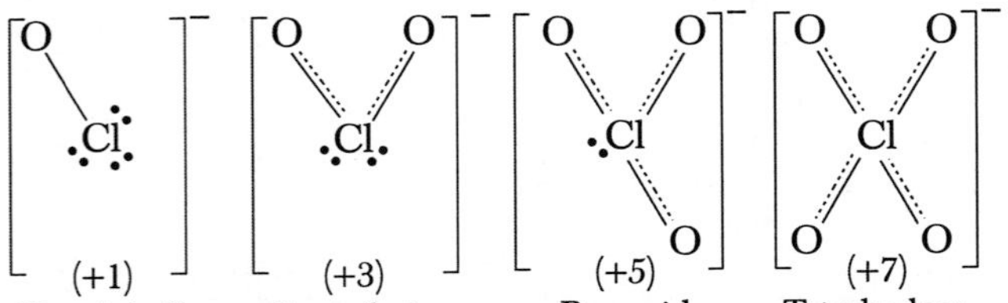

(+1) Dumb-bell | (+3) Bent-chain | (+5) Pyramid | (+7) Tetrahedron

Increasing charge delocalisation →
Decreasing basicity

(ii) The acidity of oxo-acids of different halogens having the same oxidation number decreases with increase in atomic number of the halogen. Thus, oxo-acids of chlorine are more acidic than the corresponding oxo-acids of bromine, and those of bromine are in turn more acidic than the corresponding ones of iodine.

Explanation As the atomic number of the halogen increases, its electronegativity decreases but size increases. This makes the acid a weaker acid.

(iii) All the halogen oxo-acids and their salts are powerful oxidising agents. Their oxidising ability, particularly the rates at which they react depend on the reaction conditions. Their oxidising strengths do not increase with increasing number of oxygen atoms.

Hydrides of Halogens

Halogens react with hydrogen to form volatile hydrides. HX. The reaction of fluorine with hydrogen is quite violent and takes place even in the dark; chlorine reacts with hydrogen in diffused sunlight; bromine reacts with hydrogen only on heating above 500°C while iodine reacts with hydrogen only on heating and in presence of platinum which acts as a catalyst. This clearly illustrates the decreasing reactivity of the halogens with increasing atomic number. Some important characteristics of the hydrides of the halogens are discussed below :

(a) Physical Properties

They are all colourless gases when pure with a sharp choking odour and show no acidic character when perfectly dry. Except hydrogen fluoride, their melting and boiling points increase with increase in atomic mass of the halogen (Table 6.12). The anomalous behaviour of hydrogen fluoride as compared to other hydrogen halides stems from the fact that HF is a highly associated species with a high degree of hydrogen bonding as shown below :

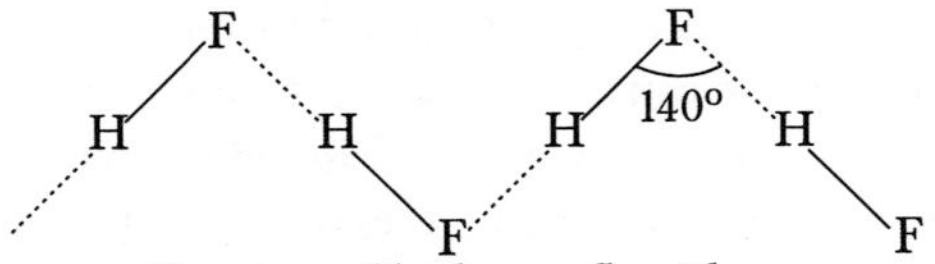

Structure of hydrogen fluoride.

Table 6.12. **Some Properties of Hydrogen Halides**

Property	HF	HCl	HBr	HI
Boiling point, K	293.4	188	206	237
Melting point, K	190	159	187	222
Ionisation constant in water	7×10^{-7}	10^7	10^9	10^{11}
Heat of formation (ΔH_f), kJ mol^{-1}	–271.1	–92.3	–36.4	+26.5
Bond energy, kJ mol^{-1}	574	428	362	295

(b) Reducing Properties

As is evident from the heat of formation data, the stability of hydrogen halides decreases as we move down the group. Thus, HF and HCl are stable upto 1200°C while HBr dissociates slightly (1%) and HI dissociates at 440°C to 20%. This also implies that the reducing character of the hydrogen halides increases as we go down the group.

HI HBr HCl HF →
Diminishing reducing action

Hydrofluoric acid, of course, has no appreciable reducing properties. At the other end, **HI is a strong reducing agent**, it is so easily oxidized that even a dilute solution on exposure to air acquires brown colour due to iodine which is liberated by the action of atmospheric oxygen :

$$4HI + O_2 \longrightarrow 2H_2O + 2I_2$$

From the above discussion, it is evident that during reduction, oxidation of halides ion takes place as :

$$2X^- \longrightarrow X_2 + 2e^-$$

The ease of oxidation of the halide ion is expected to increase in the order of increasing size of the halide ions F^-, Cl^-, Br^- and I^-. The electron which is to be removed during oxidation is closest to the nucleus in F^- and so should be the most difficult to remove. Therefore, HF is a poor reducing agent. It is easy to remove an electron from the large I atom and so HI should be a strong reducing agent.

(c) Acidic strength

Hydrogen halides are soluble in water and their aqueous solutions are acidic. As is evident from their dissociation constants, hydrogen fluoride even in fairly dilute solution is only a weak acid whereas the other three halides are strong acids. **The strength of acids increases in the order HI > HBr > HCl > HF**. This order may seen strange in view of the order of decreasing polarity of H—X bonds. Although the positive charge on H atom in HF molecule is greater than in HCl, HBr and HI molecules, the tendency for HF to release protons to water is less than that of HCl, HBr or HI. This apparent anomaly becomes less surprising if the ionisation of hydrogen halide molecules in aqueous solution is analysed in terms of the following cycle :

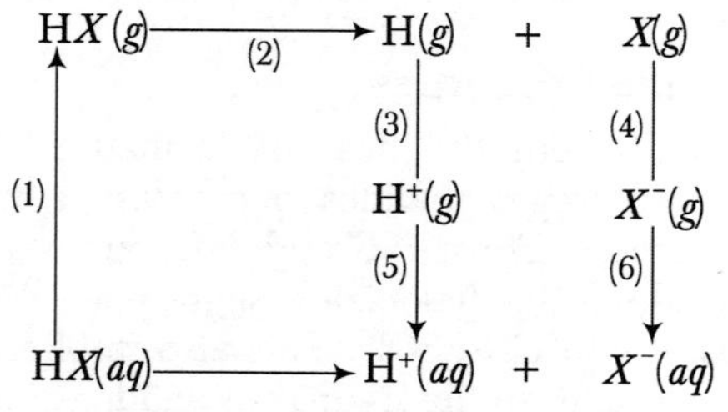

It is clear from this cycle that such ionisation is related to a number of atomic and molecular parameters; energy of dehydration of HX molecules (Step I), energy of dissociation of gaseous HX into atoms (Step 2), ionization energy of H atom (Step 3), electron affinity of the X atom (Step 4), energies of hydration of H^+ and X^- (Step 5 and 6). **A major factor in contribution to the lower acidity of HF is its high bond dissociation energy.**

Inter-Halogen Compounds

They are a unique class of compounds and are of interest as examples of failure of the octet rule. They may be defined as compounds formed by the union of two different halogens under suitable conditions of temperature and pressure. Some important inter-halogen compounds are listed in Table. 6.13.

Table. 6.13 **Inter-halogen Compounds**

(Type) AX (Shape) Linear	AX_3 T-shaped	AX_5 Square pyramid	AX_7 Pentagonal
Chlorine fluoride, ClF	Chlorine trifluoride, ClF_3	Chlorine pentafluoride, ClF_5*	–
Bromide fluoride, BrF	Bromide trifluoride, BrF_3	Bromine pentafluoride, BrF_5	–
Iodine fluoride, IF*	Iodine trifluoride, IF_3*	Iodine pentafluoride, IF_5	Iodine heptafluoride, IF_7
Bromine chloride, BrCl	–	–	–
Iodine chloride, ICl	Iodine trichloride, ICl_3	–	–
Iodine bromide, IBr	–	–	–

*These inter-halogen compounds are unstable.

These are prepared by direct combinations of two different halogens in various compositions.

Inter-halogen compounds are of two types :

(a) Neutral molecules such as ICl, ICl_3 and IF_7.

(b) Polyhalide anions such as I_3^- and polyhalogen cations such as ICl_2^+.

The main reasons for the formation of these compounds is the large electronegativity and size difference among the halogens-ΔG values of these compounds are negative indicating considerable thermodynamic stability. **Why only IF_7 is formed in the series of the type AX_7 can probably be explained in terms of the large size of iodine and the very small size of fluorine atoms.** This is why seven fluorine atoms can be accommodated around the central iodine atom.

General Properties

Some of the important general properties are :

1. Their reactions are similar to those of component halogens but are on the whole more reactive than

halogens due to the weakness of the covalent bond between two dissimilar electronegative elements.

2. They are strong oxidising agents.
3. All neutral inter-halogen molecules and uninegative inter-halogen ions are diamagnetic which is indicative of the fact that their valence electrons are present either as shared or unshared pairs.
4. All inter-halogen compounds undergo hydrolysis to some extent. In the process, the heavier and less electronegative halogen usually behaves as if it were in a positive oxidation state whereas the lighter and more electronegative halogen acts in the opposite manner.

   For example,

$$IF_7 + 6HOH \longrightarrow H_5IO_6 + 7HF$$

$$ICl + HOH \longrightarrow HOI + HCl$$

5. The major differences exhibited by these compounds are due to polarity (since, the halogens differ from one another in electronegativity) and due to atomic radius. Thermal stability is diminished by size differences but increased by polarity. Thus, ClF is thermally more stable as compared to IBr.
6. Halogen fluorides are all very reactive and act as strong fluorinating agents. ClF_3 is as strong a fluorinating agent as is element fluorine. BrF_3 and IF_5 are particularly useful as fluorinating agents for the production of fluorides of elements in intermediate oxidation states.

Structures of Inter-halogen Compounds

All neutral inter-halogen compounds are binary in nature, *i.e.,* they are composed of only two different halogen atoms. Ternary inter-halogen compounds are not known. This is, perhaps, due to the fact that ternary interhalogen compounds are very unstable so that their molecules readily redistribute to form a mixture of more stable binary compounds and elemental halogen.

The general formula of all inter halogen compounds can be written as AX_n, where, n is always an odd number such as 1, 3, 5 or 7. This can be explained on the basis of the concept of hybridisation.

(i) For compounds of the type AX_n, where, $n = 1$, such as IF, ICl, IBr, ClF, BrF and BrCl.

Electronic structure of iodine-ground state :

Iodine atom with one unpaired electron forms a covalent bond with the second halogen atom and therefore the resulting molecule is linear. This case is similar to the formation of iodine molecule from iodine atoms.

(ii) For compounds of the type AX_3, where, $n = 3$ such as IF_3, ICl_3, ClF_3, BrF_3; the only way in which additional covalent bonds could possibly be created is by promoting one of the electron pairs to a higher energy *d*-orbitals. This results in the essential condition of three covalent bonds because of three unpaired electrons each in its separate orbital.

Electronic structure of chlorine atom :

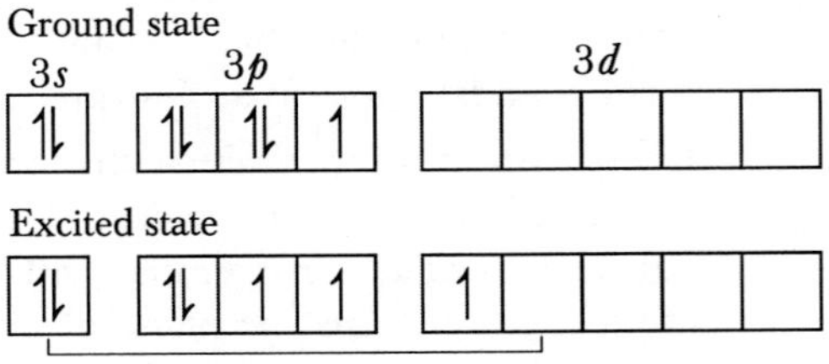

sp^3d hybridisation; trigonal bipyramid with two positions occupied by lone pairs

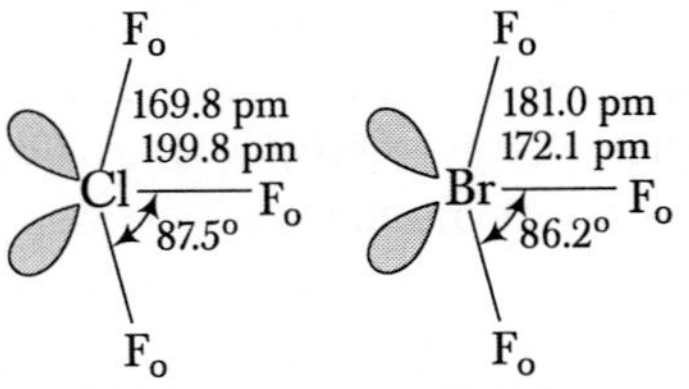

(ClF_3) (BrF_3)

The three unpaired electrons of chlorine atom in the excited state form bonds with three F atoms, it is assumed to undergo sp^3d hybridisation, *i.e.,* trigonal bipyramid geometry with two positions occupied by lone pairs as shown in the diagram above.

The structure of ICl_3 is different, it exists as demeric units 'I_2Cl_6' in the crystalline state. It is a planar molecule.

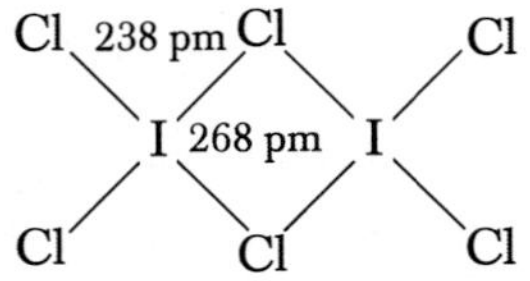

Planar I_2Cl_6 molecule

(iii) For compounds of the type AX_5, where, $n = 5$ such as ClF_5, BrF_5, and IF_5, it is essential that one more electron pair from 5*p*-orbitals of iodine is promoted to the higher energy *d*-orbital and as a result of this we have 5 orbitals each containing one electron.

Electronic structure of iodine atom-excited state :

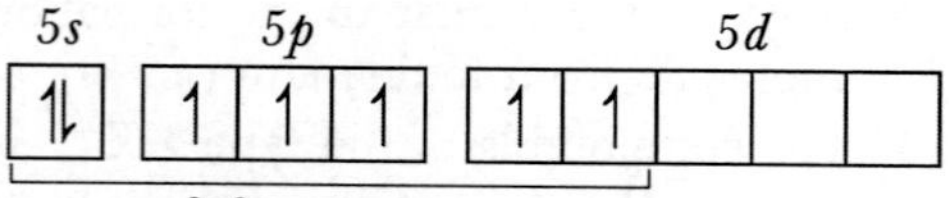

sp^3d^2 hybridisation

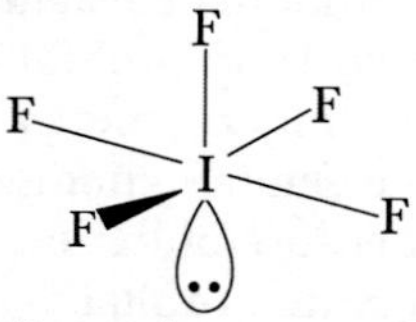

Bonding and structure of IF_5.

Five unpaired electrons in the excited state form bonds with five fluorine atoms-sp^3d^2 hybridization-octahedral with one position occupied by a lone pair. The molecular structure is square pyramidal with the central atom slightly below the plane of the four basal fluorine atoms.

(iv) For compounds of the type AX_7, where, $n = 7$ such as IF_7, it is essential that one more electron pair from 5*s*-orbital of iodine is promoted to the higher energy *d*-orbital as a result of which we have seven orbitals each containing.

Electronic structure of iodine-excited state :

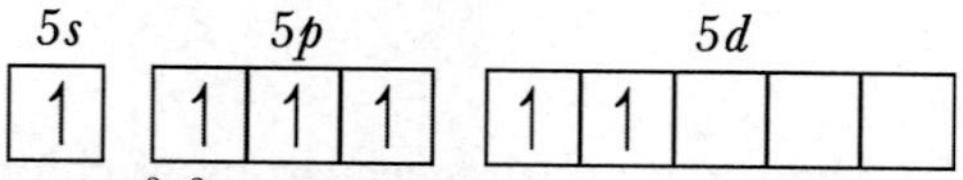

sp^3d^3 hybridisation

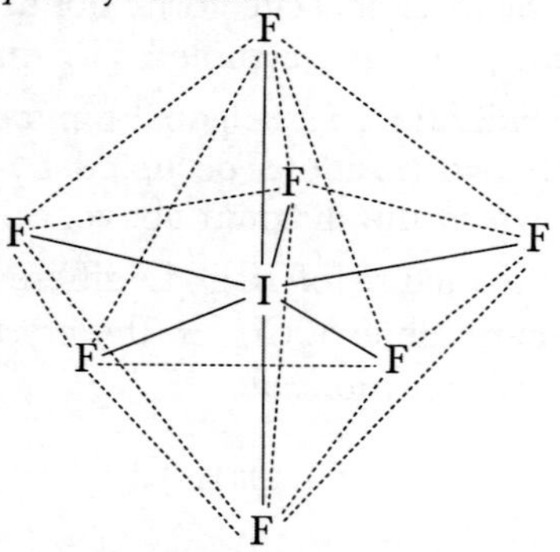

Bonding and structure of IF_7.

One electron from each orbital is thus capable of forming seven covalent bonds with seven fluorine atoms–sp^3d^3 hybridisation. Thus, IF_7 has pentagonal bipyramidal structure.

Polyhalide Ions

In addition to neutral inter-halogen compounds, polyhalide ions containing more than two halogen atoms have been prepared by reacting halogens or inter-halogen compounds with halide ions. The most common example of such polyhalide ion formation is the dissolution of iodine in KI resulting in the formation of I_3^-.

$$KI + I_2 \longrightarrow K^+ + I_3^-$$

A list of important polyhalide ions is given in Table 6.14.

Table 6.14 **Some Important Polyhalide Ions**

Cl_3^-, Br_3^-, I_3^-, ICl_2^-, IBr_2^-
ICl_4^-, BrF_4^-, I_5^-
IF_6^-, I_7^-

The reason for the formation of polyhalide ions can be well explained by taking the example of I_3^-. When the negative iodide ion comes close to a large iodine molecule (whose outer electrons are far from the positive nucleus), it disturbs the electronic arrangement in a way so as to induce a dipole within the molecule. An attraction then exists between the negative iodide ion and the positive end of the polar iodine molecule leading to the formation of I_3^-.

$$I_2 + I^- \longrightarrow I_3^-$$

Structure of polyhalide ions

(i) X-ray data show that the structure of Br_3^-, I_3^- or ICl_2^- is linear and can be explained as follows :

ICl_2^-, the number of electrons involved are $7 + 1 + 2 = 10$ suggestive of dsp^3 hybridisation, *i.e.*, trigonal bipyramidal structure with three pairs of non-bonded electrons around the iodine atom in one plane as shown in the diagram.

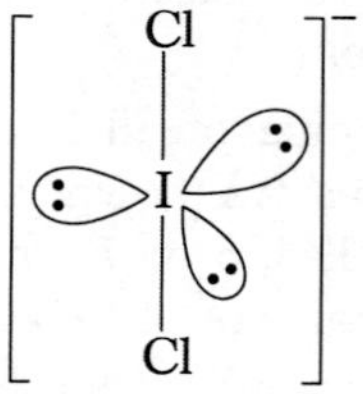

Structure of ICl_2^-.

(ii) In ICl_4^-, the number of electrons involved are $7+1+4=12$ suggestive of d^2sp^3 hybridisation and the six electron pairs around the iodine atom can be regarded as directed towards the corners of an octahedron. Iodine atom is at the centre of a square formed by four chlorine atoms and the two pairs of non-bonded electrons around iodine atom are directed perpendicular to the plane of the ion. Its structure is shown below. Thus, ICl_4^- ion has a planar structure which has been confirmed from X-ray data of $KICl_4$.

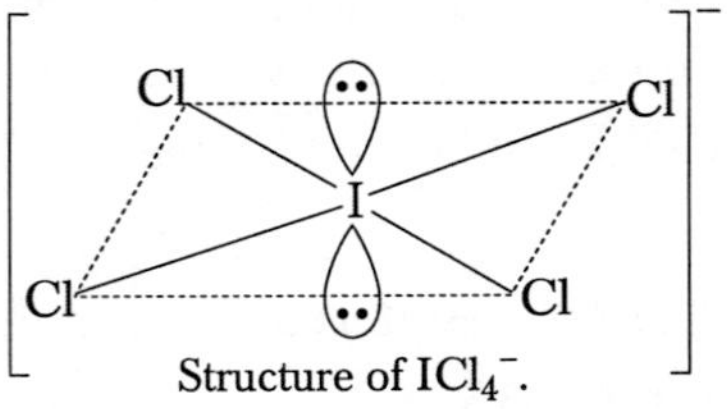

Structure of ICl_4^-.

Electropositive Nature of Iodine

Since, ionisation energy decreases in moving down a group, therefore, tendency to lose electron and form cationic species increases down the group. Although halogens are highly electronegative yet the last member of the family, *i.e.,* iodine has a low ionisation energy of 1008 kJ mol^{-1} which is comparable with metals such as mercury (ionisation energy 1004 kJ mol^{-1}). Consequently, iodine does exhibit some electropositive character resulting in the formation of **cationic compounds.** Evidence for the existence of cationic compounds of iodine is given below :

Compounds of Iodine (I)

(i) Molten ICl is a good conductor of electricity indicating its ability to form I^+ ions.

(ii) Conductivity measurements have revealed that ICl ionises in nitrobenzene or acetic anhydride as

$$2ICl \longrightarrow I^+ + ICl_2^-$$

similar behaviour is also exhibited by IBr.

(iii) Molten ICl_3 is a good conductor of electricity and ionises as :

$$2ICl_3 \longrightarrow ICl_2^+ + ICl_4^-$$

(iv) A large number of compounds have been characterised which contain I^+ ion stabilized by coordination such as

$$[py\text{—}I\text{—}py]^+X^-$$

where, py = pyridine and $X = NO_3^-, ClO_4^-$. Electrolysis of these compounds in anhydrous chloroform yields iodine at the cathode.

(v) Hypoiodous acid is amphoteric. It mainly acts as a base and may be considered as iodine hydroxide; compounds like ICl may be considered as salts of this base.

(vi) Compounds such as $[py\text{—}I\text{—}ONO_2]$ have been isolated which contain iodine having coordination number two.

Compounds of Iodine (III)

(vii) A large number of compounds containing I^{3+} have been isolated which are ionic. They contain oxoanions and do not require stabilization by complexing agents. They are prepared by reacting iodine with an oxidising agent and the anhydrous acid whose compound is to be prepared. Some important examples of compounds containing iodine (III) are :

$$I_2 \xrightarrow[CH_3COOH]{ClO_3\ (\text{Oxidising agent})} \underset{\text{Iodine triacetate}}{I(OOCCH_3)_3}$$

$$I_2 \xrightarrow[HClO_4]{O_3\ (\text{Oxidising agent})} \underset{\text{Iodine triperchlorate}}{I(ClO_4)_3}$$

$$I_2 \xrightarrow[H_3PO_4]{\text{Fuming } HNO_3\ (\text{Oxidising agent})} \underset{\text{Iodine phosphate}}{IPO_4}$$

It can be easily proved that these compounds contain the I^{3+} cations. It electricity is passed through a saturated solution of iodine triacetate in acetic anhydride using silver cathode, iodine is liberated at the cathode and forms silver iodide.

$$I^{3+} + 3e^- + Ag \longrightarrow AgI$$

Iodine Cations

There is good evidence now available for the existence of a number of cationic species of iodine such as I_2^+, I_4^{2+}, I_3^+ and I_5^+ under special conditions. Since, these ions are strong electrophiles, they can exist (or stabilized) only in solvents with low nucleophilic properties (*i.e.,* which are very weakly basic). These species have been isolated either in solvents which are highly acidic, *e.g.,* sulphuric acid, oleum, fluorosulphuric acid or in melts like $KCl/AlCl_3$ which are very weakly basic. Stable compounds of these species have been isolated and their structures elucidated by X-ray crystallography.

Pseudohalogens and Pseudohalides

A pseudohalogen is made up of two electronegative atoms and in its molecular form resembles the halogens. Pseudohalogens form anions which resemble the halide ions in their behaviour. Some common pseudohalide ions and covalent pseudohalogen dimeric species are listed in Table 6.15.

Table 6.15 **Common Pseudohalide Ions and Covalent Pseudohalogen Dimeric Species**

Pseudohalide	Formula	Pseudohalogen	Formula
Cyanide	CN^-	Cyanogen	$(CN)_2$
Cyanate	OCN^-	Oxocyanogen	$(OCN)_2$
Thiocyanate	SCN^-	Thiocyanogen	$(SCN)_2$
Selenocyanate	$SeCN^-$	Selenocyanogen	$(SeCN)_2$
Tellurocyanate	$TeCN^-$	–	–
Azide	N_3^-	–	–
Azidothiocarbonate	$SCSN_3^-$	Azidocarbondisulphide	$(SCSN_3)_2$
Ioscyanate	ONC^-	–	–

Some characteristic reactions of pseudohalogens and pseudohalides are summarized below :

(i) The parent pseudohalogens are volatile molecular compounds and are formed by symmetrical combination of two radicals *X–X*. They react with alkalies in an analogous manner

$$(CN)_2 + 2OH^- \rightleftharpoons CN^- + OCN^- + H_2O$$

$$[Cl_2 + 2OH^- \rightleftharpoons Cl^- + OCl^- + H_2O]$$

(ii) Inter-pseudohalogen and pseudohalogen-halogen compounds are known.

Cyanogen bromide, reacts with sodium azide to give cyanogenazide.

$$CNBr + NaN_3 \rightleftharpoons CNN_3 + NaBr$$

Cyanogen chloride and bromide, CNCl and CNBr, have been obtained from the action of Cl_2 and Br_2 on HCN, respectively.

(iii) The pseudohalogens react with various metals to give salts containing X^- anions. Silver (I), mercury (I) and lead (II) salts are like the corresponding halides (AgCl, Hg_2Cl_2 and $PbCl_2$) is being sparingly soluble in water.

(iv) Pseudohalides (X^-) react with hydrogen to give acids, H*X* which are however weak compared to halogen acids.

HN_3 $pK_a = 4.4$

HCN $pK_a = 8.9$

HCl $pK_a = -7.4$

(v) The pseudohalides form ions analogous to polyhalide ions

$$NH_4(SCN)_3 \text{ and } K(SeCN)_3[KCl_3]$$

(vi) Like the halide ions, a pseudohalide ion is oxidized to the parent pseudohalogen by suitable oxidizing agents.

$$2Fe^{3+} + 2SCN^- \longrightarrow 2Fe^{2+} + (SCN)_2$$

Preparation of various Pseudohalogens

1. Cyanogen $(CN)_2$, is made by heating AgCN or $Hg(CN)_2$ with $HgCl_2$.

$$2AgCN \longrightarrow 2Ag + (CN)_2$$

$$Hg(CN)_2 + HgCl_2 \longrightarrow Hg_2Cl_2 + (CN)_2$$

2. Thiocyanogen, $(SCN)_2$, is obtained by the action of bromine on AgSCN.

$$2AgSCN + Br_2 \longrightarrow 2AgBr + (SCN)_2$$

3. Selenocyanogen, $(SeCN)_2$, is displaced by iodine from AgSeCN.

$$2AgSeCN + I_2 \longrightarrow 2AgI + (SeCN)_2$$

4. Azidocarbondisulphide, $(SCSN_3)_2$, is obtained when $KSCSN_3$ is oxidized with H_2O_2.

$$CS_2 + KN_3 \longrightarrow KSCSN_3 \xrightarrow{H_2O_2} (SCSN_3)_2$$

Special Features of Fluorine Chemistry

It is a common feature among *p*-block elements that the first element differs from heavier members of the same group. Most of the peculiarities of fluorine stem form its :

(a) smallest size,

(b) extreme electronegativity,

(c) absence of low lying *d*-orbitals, and

(d) low dissociation energy of F–F bond in F_2.

Some consequences of the above peculiarities of fluorine are

(i) **Solubility of fluorides is always quite abnormal** The alkaline earth metal halides are all soluble in water except the fluorides which are insoluble; conversely silver fluoride is the only soluble silver halide.

(ii) **Fluorine compounds are always more stable than the corresponding chlorine compounds**. Thus, UF_6 is more stable than UCl_6 : NF_3 is non-explosive while NCl_3 is violently explosive.

(iii) Fluorine is invariably unicovalent whereas other halogens show covalencies such as 3, 5 and 7.

(iv) Reaction of fluorine with oxygen containing compounds such as water or sodium hydroxide are different from those with other halogens.

Reaction with water

$$2H_2O + 2F_2 \longrightarrow 4HF + O_2$$

Contrast

$$H_2O + Cl_2 \longrightarrow HCl + HOCl$$

Reaction with cold sodium hydroxide

$$2F_2 + 2NaOH \longrightarrow 2NaF + OF_2 + H_2O$$

Contrast

$$Cl_2 + 2NaOH \longrightarrow NaCl + NaClO + H_2O$$

Reaction with hot sodium hydroxide

$$2F_2 + 4NaOH \longrightarrow 4NaF + O_2 + 2H_2O$$

Contrast

$$Cl_2 + 6NaOH \longrightarrow 5NaCl + NaClO_3 + 3H_2O$$

(v) Fluorine does not form polyhalide ions (X_n^{-1}) (where $n = 3, 5$ or 7) because of the non-availability of low energy *d*-orbitals in its valency shell.

(vi) Trifluoroacetic acid is a strong acid and the substituted amine $(CF_3)_3N$ is not basic.

Exercise 1

(For Part 'B')

1. Which silicon compound is used as lubricant?
(a) Asbestos (b) Silicones
(c) Zeolite (d) Mica

2. Amphoteric oxides are
(a) SnO, SnO_2 (b) GeO, GeO_2
(c) Both (a) and (b) (d) None of these

3. The minerals having silicate chains are collectively called
(a) olivine (b) zircon
(c) pyroxenes (d) hatrolite

4. Formula of the following silicate anion is

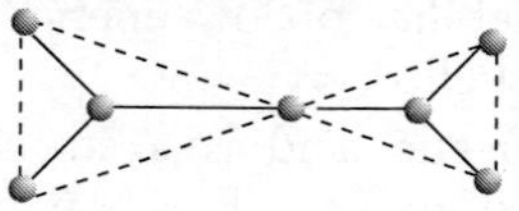

(a) SiO_4^{4-} (b) $Si_2O_7^{6-}$
(c) $Si_2O_8^{6-}$ (d) $Si_3O_9^{6-}$

5. Silicones are
(a) synthetic polymers containing repeated R_2SiO unit
(b) silicates with common SiO_4 unit
(c) ketones with silyl group (SiH_3) similar to alkyl $(SiH_3)_2CO$
(d) zircon (heso silicates)

6. CO_2 in water behaves as
(a) weak dibasic acid H_2CO_3
(b) weak monobasic acid $HO—CO_2H$
(c) weak diacid base $CO(OH)_2$
(d) weak monoacid base $HO—CO_2H$

7. CO behaves as
(a) Lewis acid (b) Lewis base
(c) CO, CO_2 (d) C_2O, C_3O_2

8. When a mixture of carbon monoxide and chlorine is exposed to sunlight, the product formed is
(a) thionyl chloride (b) phosgene
(c) phosphine (d) carbon tetrachloride

9. Silicon reacts with hot solution of NaOH forming
(a) $Si(OH)_4$ (b) $Si(OH)_2$
(c) SiO_2 (d) Na_4SiO_4

10. Hot conc. HNO_3 converts graphite into
(a) graphite oxide
(b) benzene hexacarboxylic acid
(c) Both (a) and (b)
(d) None of the above

11. $p\pi$-$p\pi$ multiple bonds occur between
(a) C and C (b) C and O
(c) C and N (d) In all cases

12. Select the correct statement about stability of cations.
(a) $Ge^{4+} > Sn^{4+} > Pb^{4+}$
(b) $Ge^{2+} < Sn^{2+} < Pb^{2+}$
(c) $Pb^{2+} > Pb^{4+}, Sn^{4+} > Sn^{2+}$
(d) All the above are correct statements

13. Elements of group 14 used in semiconductors are
(a) C, Si, Ge (b) Si, Ge, Sn
(c) Si, Ge (d) B, Si, Ge

14. The variation in element-element bond energy follows the order
(a) C–C > Si–Si > Ge–Ge > Sn–Sn > Pb–Pb
(b) Si–Si > C–C > Pb–Pb > Sn–Sn > Ge–Ge
(c) C–C > Ge–Ge > Sn–Sn > Pb–Pb > Si–Si
(d) C–C > Sn–Sn > Pb–Pb > Ge–Ge > Si–Si

15. Graphite is a soft solid lubricant extremely difficult to melt. The reason for this anomalous behaviour, is that graphite
(a) is a non-crystalline substance
(b) is an allotropic form of diamond
(c) has molecules of variable molecular masses like polymers
(d) has carbon atoms arranged in large plates of rings of strongly bound carbon atoms with weak interplate bonds

16. Silicon is an important constituent of
(a) rocks (b) amalgams
(c) chlorophyll (d) haemoglobin

17. Which of the following is not an acid anhydride?
(a) CO_2 (b) CO
(c) SO_2 (d) SO_3

18. In which of the following the angle between the two covalent bond is maximum?
(a) H_2O (b) CO_2
(c) CH_4 (d) NH_3

19. Which gas is used in aerated water?
(a) CO_2 (b) SO_2
(c) CO (d) Water vapours

20. $(Me_2)_2SiCl_2$ on hydrolysis will produce
(a) $(Me)_2Si(OH)_2$
(b) $(Me)_2Si{=}O$
(c) $[—O—(Me)_2Si—O—]_n$
(d) $Me_2SiCl(OH)$

21. The gas evolved by heating potassium ferrocyanide crystals with conc. H_2SO_4 is
(a) CO (b) CO_2
(c) SO_2 (d) SO_3

22. Name of the structure of silicates in which three oxygen atoms of $[SiO_4]^{4-}$ are shared is
(a) pyrosilicate
(b) sheet silicate
(c) linear chain silicate
(d) three dimensional silicate

23. NO_2 is not obtained when following is heated
(a) $Pb(NO_3)_2$ (b) $AgNO_3$ (c) $LiNO_3$ (d) KNO_3

24. Carborundum is
(a) CaC_2 (b) Fe_3C (c) $CaCO_3$ (d) SiC

25. Which one of the following bonds has the highest bond energy?
(a) C—C (b) Si—Si (c) Ge—Ge (d) Sn—Sn

26. Select the correct statements.
(a) Oxides of carbon family (MO_2) are all network solid with octahedral coordination
(b) Silicon dioxide (silica) is a network solid with tetrahedral coordination and is against molecule
(c) GeO_2, SnO_2 and PbO_2 are all acidic oxides
(d) None of the above appears correct

27. Which forms $p\pi$-$p\pi$ multiple bonds with itself and with C and O?
(a) N (b) N, P (c) N, As (d) P, As

28. In P_4 (tetrahedral)
(a) each P is joined to three P
(b) each P is joined to four P
(c) each P is joined to two P
(d) P_4 does not exist

29. For the hydrides of nitrogen family going down the group
(a) stability decreases
(b) bond angle H*M*H decreases
(c) reducing activity increases
(d) All of the above

30. The dipole moments of the given molecules are such that
(a) $NH_3 > NF_3 > BF_3$ (b) $BF_3 > NF_3 > NH_3$
(c) $NF_3 > BF_3 > NH_3$ (d) $BF_3 > NH_3 > NF_3$

31. Glacial phosphoric acid is
(a) HPO_3 (b) H_3PO_3 (c) H_3PO_4 (d) $H_4P_2O_7$

32. Which are acidic salts?
(a) Na_2HPO_3, Na_2HPO_4 (b) NaH_2PO_2, Na_2HPO_3
(c) $NaHCO_3$, Na_2HPO_4 (d) All of these

33. Which is least basic?
(a) NI_3 (b) NBr_3 (c) NCl_3 (d) NF_3

34. Which is used as a rocket fuel?
(a) Polybutadiene (b) N_2H_4
(c) Both (a) and (b) (d) None of these

35. Red and white phosphorus will differ but not in
(a) smell
(b) reaction with HNO_3
(c) solubility in CH_3
(d) exhibiting phosphorescence

36. N_2O (laughing gas) finds use in the following except
(a) as fuel for rockets
(b) as an anaesthetic
(c) for the preparation of N_3H
(d) as a propellant for whipped ice-cream

37. N_2O is formed when
(a) cold dil HNO_3 reacts with Cu and Zn
(b) Sn^{2+} reacts with conc. HNO_3 in the presence of HCl
(c) moist Fe reacts with NO
(d) All of the above

38. Which of the following compound has the greatest ionic character?
(a) BCl_3 (b) CCl_4 (c) PCl_5 (d) $SiCl_4$

39. All of the following are bases except
(a) NH_3 (b) N_3H (c) N_2H_4 (d) NH_2OH

40. An example of an "ortho" acid is
(a) $H_4As_2O_7$ (b) H_3AsO_4
(c) $HAsO_2$ (d) $(HPO_3)_n$

41. Compound used in safety matches is
(a) P_4 (b) PCl_3 (c) P_2O_5 (d) P_4S_3

42. Cold solution of barium nitrite on mixing with sulphuric acid produces
(a) $BaSO_4 + NO_2$ (b) $BaSO_4 + N_2 + O_2$
(c) $BaSO_4 + HNO_2$ (d) $BaSO_4 + HNO_3$

43. Which of the following oxides of nitrogen is paramagnetic?
(a) N_2O (b) NO_2 (c) N_2O_3 (d) N_2O_5

44. The structural formula of hypophosphorous acid is

(a) 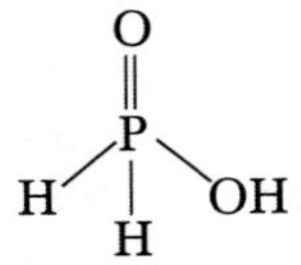

(b) 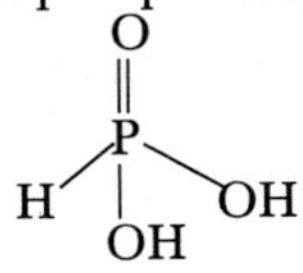

(c) 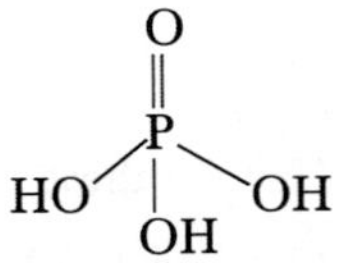

(d) 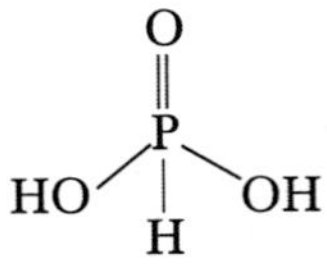

45. Which of the following is most acidic?
(a) N_2O_5 (b) P_2O_5
(c) As_2O_5 (d) Sb_2O_5

46. The percentage of *p*-character in the orbitals forming P–P bonds in P_4 is
(a) 75 (b) 65 (c) 55 (d) 25

47. Which one of the following acid possesses oxidising, reducing and complex forming properties?
(a) HNO_3 (b) HCl (c) H_2SO_4 (d) HNO_2

48. On hydrolysis, PCl_3 gives
(a) H_3PO_3 (b) H_3PO_4
(c) $POCl_3$ (d) HPO_3

49. On photochemical decomposition of HNO_3, the products formed are
(a) NO and O_2 (b) NO_2 and O_2
(c) N_2O_4 and NO_2 (d) N_2O_5 and NO_2

50. Nitric oxide is formed by the reaction of
(a) $C + N_2O$ (b) $Cu + HNO_3$
(c) $Cu + N_2O$ (d) $Cu + NO_2$

51. One heating lead nitrate, the products formed is
(a) NO (b) NO_2 (c) N_2O (d) N_2O_5

52. Polyphosphates are used as water softening agents because they
(a) form soluble complexes with anionic species
(b) precipitate anionic species
(c) form soluble complexes with cationic species
(d) precipitate cationic species

53. Solid crystalline PCl_5 has structure which of the following?
(a) Bipyramidal moieties
(b) Octahedral and tetrahedral ions
(c) Square-pyramidal moieties
(d) Pentagonal moieties

54. Hydrazine is not
(a) a reducing agent (b) an oxidising agent
(c) an acid (d) a base

55. Which of the following oxides of nitrogen is solid?
(a) NO_2 (b) N_2O (c) N_2O_3 (d) N_2O_5

56. The statement true for N_3^- is
(a) it has non-linear structure
(b) it is called pseudohalogen
(c) the formal oxidation state of nitrogen in this anion is +1
(d) it is isoelectronic with N_2O

57. Metallic tin and conc. HNO_3 reacts to form
(a) metastannic acid (b) stannic nitrate
(c) stannous nitrite (d) stannous nitrate

58. The bond angle in AsH_3 is greater than that is
(a) NH_3 (b) H_2O
(c) BCl_3 (d) None of these

59. When PCl_3 reacts with sulphuric acid, sulphuryl chloride is formed as the final products. This shows that sulphuric acid
(a) has two hydroxyl groups in its structure
(b) is a derivative of sulphur dioxide
(c) is a dibasic acid
(d) has greater affinity for water

60. Pentavalency is phosphorus is more stable when compared to that of nitrogen even though they belong to same group. This is due to the
(a) reactivity of phosphorus
(b) inert nature of nitrogen
(c) presence of *d*-orbital
(d) large size of phosphorus atom

61. Bond angle of 109° 28′ is found in
(a) NH_3 (b) $\overset{\oplus}{H_2O}$ (c) CH_5^+ (d) $\overset{\oplus}{NH_4}$

62. Both NF_3 and NCl_3 are covalent but they differ in the extent of hydrolysis because
(a) NF_3 is more stable than NCl_3 and hydrolysis products of NH_3, HOF, does not exist
(b) dipole moment of NH_3 is greater than that of NCl_3
(c) electronegativity of F is greater than that of Cl
(d) Cl can expand its octet by using *d*-orbital

63. Nitrogen differs form P, As, Sb and Bi in the following properties
(a) It forms diatomic molecule
(b) It is not able to extend its coordination number beyond four
(c) Nitrogen does not function as a Lewis acid whereas P, As, Sb and Bi do so
(d) In all the properties given above

64. Substances burn more readily in N_2O than in air because N_2O
(a) is reactive at high temperature
(b) dissociates to give O_2 that supports combustion
(c) the activation energy is increased on increasing temperature
(d) acts as a catalyst

65. Nitric oxide is paramagnetic in
(a) gaseous state (b) liquid state
(c) solid state (d) polymeric state

66. Nitrosonium ion (NO^+) is isoelectronic with
(a) CO_2 (b) CO (c) NO_2 (d) NO

67. With excess Cl_2, ammonia forms
(a) NH_4Cl (b) nitrogen trichloride
(c) NOCl (d) nitrogen

68. $NH_4Cl(s)$ is heated in a test tube. Vapours are brought in contact with red litmus paper, which changes to blue and then to red. It is because of
(a) formation of NH_4OH and HCl
(b) formation of NH_3 and HCl
(c) greater diffusion of NH_3 than HCl
(d) greater diffusion of HCl than NH_3

69. $p\pi$-$p\pi$ multiple bonding between nitrogen atoms is present in
(a) hyponitrous acid (b) nitrous acid
(c) nitric acid (d) All of these

70. A colourless salt gives a white ppt. (soluble in ammonium acetate) and a brown coloured pungent gas on reaction with conc. H_2SO_4. Salt is
(a) $Ba(NO_3)_2$ (b) $Pb(NO_3)_2$
(c) $NaNO_3$ (d) NH_4NO_3

71. One of the acid listed below is formed only from P_2O_3, the rest are formed from P_2O_5. Acid formed from P_2O_3 is
(a) HPO_3 (b) $H_4P_2O_7$ (c) H_3PO_4 (d) H_3PO_3

72. Consider the reaction :

$$(NH_4)_2HAsO_3 + CuSO_4 \longrightarrow \underbrace{CuHAsO_3}_{\text{Green ppt.}} + (NH_4)_2SO_4$$

The green precipitate is also known as
(a) Scheele's green (b) Rinmann's green
(c) Pair's green (d) Verdigris green

73. PCl_3 undergoes hydrolysis to produce an oxoacid. It has the formula
(a) HPO_3 (b) H_3PO_2 (c) H_3PO_3 (d) H_3PO_4

74. The solid PCl_5 exists as
(a) PCl_3 (b) PCl_4^+
(c) PCl_6^- (d) PCl_4^+ and PCl_6^-

75. The high reactivity and low volatility of white phosphorus is due to
(a) increased steric (strain) factor
(b) bond angle of 60°
(c) tetrahedrally arranged P_4 units
(d) weak van der Waals' force of attraction

76. Which of the following has peroxy linkage?
(a) H_2SO_5 (b) $H_2S_2O_3$
(c) $H_2S_4O_6$ (d) $H_2S_2O_7$

77. The thermal stability of hydrides of oxygen family is in the order
(a) $H_2O > H_2S > H_2Se > H_2Te > H_2Po$
(b) $H_2Po > H_2Te > H_2Se > H_2S > H_2O$
(c) $H_2S > H_2O > H_2Po > H_2Te > H_2Se$
(d) $H_2Se > H_2Te > H_2Po > H_2S > H_2O$

78. Which does not have (S–S) bond?
(a) S_3O_9 (b) $H_2S_2O_3$ (c) H_2SO_4 (d) $H_2S_2O_5$

79. Cold solution of barium nitrite on mixing with sulphuric acid produces
(a) $BaSO_4 + NO_2$ (b) $BaSO_4 + HNO_3$
(c) $BaSO_4 + HNO_2$ (d) $BaSO_4 + N_2 + O_2$

80. Which of the following bonds has the least energy?
(a) O—O (b) S—S (c) Se—Se (d) Te—Te

81. Oxalic acid on heating with conc. H_2SO_4 produces
(a) CO and CO_2 (b) CO_2 and H_2S
(c) H_2O and CO_2 (d) CO, CO_2 and H_2O

82. Consider the following compounds.
I. $Na_2S_2O_3$ II. $N_2S_4O_6$ III. $CaOCl_2$
Among these compounds identify those that have different oxidation states for same type of atoms.
(a) I and II (b) I and III
(c) II and III (d) I, II and III

83. When molten sulphur is suddenly cooled by pouring into water, it takes the form of
(a) milk of sulphur (b) flower of sulphur
(c) plastic sulphur (d) colloidal sulphur

84. $HClO_4$, HNO_3 and HCl are all very strong acids in aqueous solution. In glacial acetic acid medium, their acid strength is such that
(a) $HCl < HNO_3 < HClO_4$ (b) $HClO_4 < HNO_3 < HCl$
(c) $HNO_3 < HCl < HClO_4$ (d) $HClO_4 < HCl < HNO_3$

85. Which of the underlined atoms in oxyacids have sp^3-hybridised atoms?
(a) $H\underline{Cl}O_4$, $H\underline{N}O_3$, $H\underline{Cl}O_3$ (b) $H\underline{Cl}O_4$, $H_2\underline{S}O_4$, $H\underline{N}O_2$
(c) $H\underline{Cl}O_4$, $H_2\underline{S}O_4$, $H_2\underline{S}O_5$ (d) $H_2\underline{S}O_4$, $H_3\underline{P}O_4$, $H\underline{N}O_3$

86. Which one of the following oxo-acids of chlorine is the least oxidising in nature?
(a) HClO (b) $HClO_2$ (c) $HClO_3$ (d) $HClO_4$

87. Least stable oxide of chlorine is
(a) ClO_2 (b) Cl_2O_4 (c) Cl_2O_6 (d) Cl_2O_7

88. Which reaction is not feasible?
(a) $2KI + Br_2 \longrightarrow 2KBr + I_2$
(b) $2KBr + Cl_2 \longrightarrow 2KCl + Br_2$
(c) $2KBr + I_2 \longrightarrow 2KI + Br_2$
(d) $2H_2O + 2F_2 \longrightarrow 4HF + O_2$

89. Which one is the strongest bond?
(a) F—F (b) Cl—F (c) Br—F (d) Br—Cl

90. The interhalogen compound not obtained is
(a) ICl (b) IF_5 (c) BrF_5 (d) $BrCl_7$

91. Acid strength of oxo-acids of chlorine is in order
(a) $HClO < HClO_2 < HClO_3 < HClO_4$
(b) $HClO_4 < HClO_3 < HClO_2 < HClO$
(c) $HClO_2 < HClO < HClO_3 < HClO_4$
(d) $HClO_3 < HClO_4 < HClO < HClO_2$

92. Acid strength of oxo-acids of halogen is in order
(a) HOI > HOBr > HOCl > HOF
(b) HOF > HOCl > HOBr > HOI
(c) HOCl > HOBr > HOI > HOF
(d) HOI > HOF > HOBr > HOCl

93. Select the correct statement(s).
(a) I_2O_5 is used in the quantitative estimation of CO
(b) Cl_2O and ClO_2 are used as bleaching agents and as germicides
(c) Bond angle *XOX* varies in the order :
FOF < ClOCl < BrOBr
(d) All of the above are correct

94. ClO_2 is the anhydride of
(a) HOCl (b) $HClO_2$
(c) $HClO_3$ (d) $HClO_2$ and $HClO_3$

95. ClO_3 is the mixed anhydride of
(a) HClO and $HClO_2$ (b) $HClO_2$ and $HClO_3$
(c) $HClO_3$ and $HClO_4$ (d) HClO and $HClO_4$

96. Which of the following will give two acids when subjected to hydrolysis?
I. NCl_3, II. PCl_3 III. $AsCl_3$
(a) I and II only (b) II and III only
(c) I and III only (d) I, II and III

97. The structure of P_4S_3 is

(a) 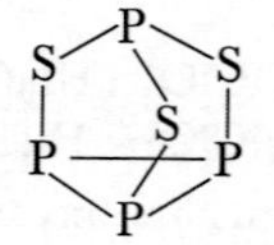

(b) 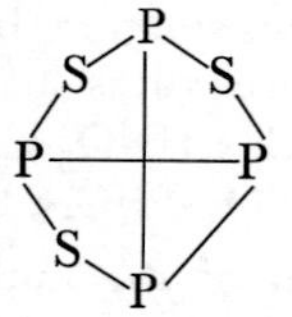

(c) 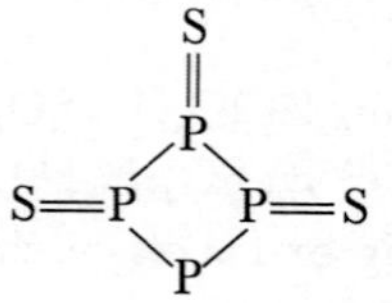

(d) 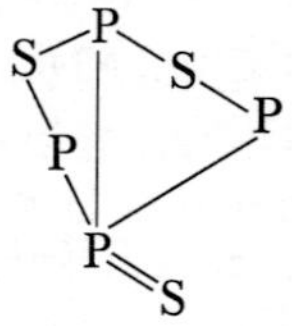

98. The order of strength of E—O bond of a $d\pi$-$p\pi$ bond where E = Si, P, S, Cl) is

(a) P—O > Si—O > S—O > Cl—O
(b) Si—O > P—O > S—O > Cl—O
(c) Cl—O > S—O > P—O > Si—O
(d) Cl—O > S—O > Si—O > P—O

Exercise 2

(For Part 'C')

1. A certain compound on burning in air forms three oxides. One of the oxides turned lime water milky, the other turned anhydrous $CuSO_4$ blue and third formed a solution of pH = 9. Compound formed of

(a) S, N and H
(b) S, N and C
(c) S, C and H
(d) S, H and Na

2. Stable oxides of carbon are

(a) CO, CO_2, C_3O_2
(b) CO_2, C_3O_2, C_2O
(c) CO, CO_2
(d) C_2O, C_3O_2

3. The silicate anion in the mineral kinoite is a chain of three SiO_4 tetrahedra that share corners with adjacent tetrahedra. The mineral also contains Ca^{2+} ions, Cu^{2+} ions, and water molecules in a 1 : 1 : 1 ratio. The mineral is

(a) $Ca_2Cu_2 \cdot Si_3O_{10} \cdot 2H_2O$
(b) $CaCu \cdot Si_3O_{10} \cdot H_2O$
(c) $Ca_2Cu_2 \cdot Si_3O_8 \cdot 2H_2O$
(d) $Ca_2Cu_2 \cdot Si_3O_6 \cdot 2H_2O$

4. In which case hydrolysis is faster?

(a) 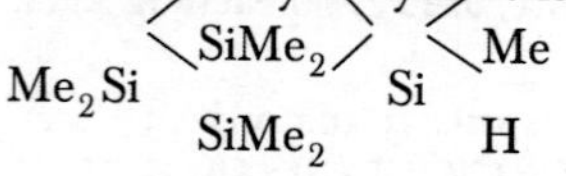

(b) 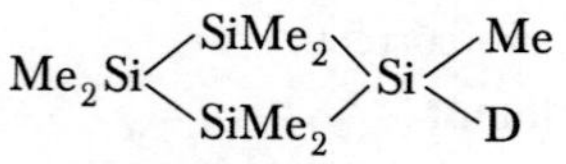

(c) At equal rate
(d) No hydrolysis

5. Which of the following species have undistorted octahedral structures?

I. SF_6 II. PF_6^- III. SiF_6^{2-} IV. SeF_6

Select the correct answer using the codes given below.

(a) II, III and IV
(b) I, III and IV
(c) I, II and III
(d) I, II and IV

6. Which is incorrect statement about silicones?

(a) They are repeating units (SiO_4) in silicates
(b) They are synthetic polymers containing repeated R_2SiO_2 units
(c) They are formed by hydrolysis of R_2SiCl_2
(d) All the above are incorrect statements

7. The great thermal and chemical stability of silicones is attributed to high strength of

(a) silicon-carbon bond
(b) silicon-oxygen bond
(c) silicon-silicon bond
(d) carbon-carbon bond

8. Of the following acids

I. hypophosphorous acid
II. hydrofluoric acid
III. oxalic acid
IV. glycine

(a) I monobasic, II, III dibasic, IV amphoteric
(b) II monobasic, I, III dibasic acid, IV amphoteric
(c) I, II are monobasic, III dibasic, IV amphoteric
(d) I, II, III dibasic, IV amphoteric

9. Which of the following compounds do not exist?

$N_4, P_4, PCl_5, NCl_5, NCl_3, P_2O_5, NO_2, PO_2$

(a) NO_2, N_4, PCl_5
(b) PCl_5, NCl_5, PO_2
(c) N_4, NCl_5, PO_2
(d) All of the above

10. Which of the following is/are paramagnetic?

$NO_2, NO, N_2O_4, N_2O_2, N_2O_5$

(a) Only NO_2
(b) NO_2 and NO
(c) NO, NO_2 and N_2O_5
(d) All the above are paramagnetic

11. Which is/are correct statements about P_4O_6 and P_4O_{10}?
(a) Both forms oxyacids H_3PO_3 and H_3PO_4 respectively
(b) In P_4O_6 each P is joined to four O and in P_4O_{10} each P is joined to six O atoms
(c) Both (a) and (b)
(d) None of the above

12. 1 mole each of H_3PO_2, H_3PO_3 and H_3PO_4 will neutralise *x* moles of NaOH, *y* moles of $Ca(OH)_2$ and *z* moles of $Al(OH)_3$ (assuming all as strong electrolytes). *x, y, z* are in the ratio of
(a) 1 : 1 : 1 (b) 1 : 2 : 3
(c) 3 : 2 : 1 (d) 3 : 1.5 : 1

13. Select the incorrect statement about N_2O_4.
(a) NO_2 dimerises to N_2O_4 with disappearance in paramagnetism
(b) N_2O_4 is paramagnetic
(c) Substance containing NO^+ is said to be acid and that containing NO_3^- is said to be base
(d) It itself ionises as NO^+, NO_3^-

14. The true statement for the acids of phosphorous. H_3PO_2, H_3PO_3 and H_3PO_4 is
(a) the geometry of phosphorus is tetrahedral in all the three of the following
(b) there acidic nature is : $H_3PO_2 > H_3PO_3 > H_3PO_4$
(c) all of them are tribasic acids
(d) all of them are reducing in nature

15. Which blue-liquid is obtained on reacting equimolar amounts of two gases at –30°C?
(a) N_2O (b) N_2O_3
(c) N_2O_4 (d) N_2O_5

16. The number of P—O—P bonds in cyclic metaphosphoric acid is
(a) zero (b) two
(c) three (d) four

17. PI_3 upon hydrolysis give
(a) monobasic acid and dibasic acid
(b) monobasic acid and tribasic acid
(c) monobasic acid and a salt
(d) dibasic acid and tribasic acid

18. *dπ-pπ* bonding is shown in
(a) NO_3^-, NO_2^-, N^{3-}, CN^- (b) P_2O_3, P_2O_5, PO_4^{3-}
(c) NH_3, PH_3, BiH_3 (d) CO, NO, CO_2, NO_2

19. Pure N_2 is prepared in the laboratory by heating a mixture of
(a) NH_4Cl and NaOH (b) NH_4OH and NaCl
(c) NH_4Cl and $NaNO_2$ (d) NH_4Cl and $NaNO_3$

20. *pπ-pπ* multiple bonding is present in
(a) oxides of nitrogen (b) oxides of phosphorus
(c) halides of nitrogen (d) halides of phosphorus

21. Paramagnetic species are
(a) NO, NO_2, O_2 (b) N_2O_2, N_2O_4, O_3
(c) $\overset{+}{N}O$, $\overset{+}{N}O_2$, O_2^+ (d) O_2, CO, CO_2

22. In liquid NH_3
(a) NH_4Cl is an acid
(b) $NaNH_2$ is a base
(c) CH_3COOH behaves as strong acid
(d) All of the above facts

23. A gaseous substance dissolves in water giving a pale blue solution which decolourises $KMnO_4$ and oxidises KI to I_2. Gaseous substances is
(a) N_2O_5 (b) NH_3
(c) N_2O_3 (d) HNO_3

24. $\underset{x}{PCl_5} + \underset{y}{CH_3}\underset{z}{CH_2OH} \longrightarrow$

In the above reaction Cl replaces one of the H-atoms in CH_3CH_2OH, This H is of
(a) C (in *x*) (b) C (in *y*)
(c) O (in *z*) (d) any of *x, y* and *z*

25. Which has maximum pK_a value?
(a) H_2O (b) H_2S
(c) H_2Se (d) H_2Te

26. Consider the following compounds
1. SO_2 2. H_2O_2 3. O_3
Among these compounds, those which can act as bleaching agent(s) would include
(a) 1 only (b) 2 only (c) 1 and 2 (d) 1, 2 and 3

27. Hypervalent ion is/are
(a) SO_3^{2-} (b) SO_4^{2-} (c) PO_4^{3-} (d) ClO_4^-

28. Which is thermochromic?
(a) S_8 (b) S_4N_4
(c) $B_3N_3H_6$ (d) None of these

29. The correct order of O–O bond length in O_2, H_2O_2 and O_3 is
(a) $O_2 > O_3 > H_2O_2$ (b) $H_2O_2 > O_3 > O_2$
(c) $O_3 > O_2 > H_2O_2$ (d) $O_3 > H_2O_2 > O_2$

30. Among CH_4, NH_3 and H_2O, acidity of H_2O is maximum because
(a) H_2O is an associated liquid
(b) oxygen is more electronegative than 'C' and 'N'
(c) oxygen contains two lone pairs of electrons
(d) bond angle in H_2O is less than 109° 28′ due to VSEPR

31. There is *pπ-dπ* multiple bonding in
(a) NO (b) CO_2 (c) NO_2 (d) CS_2

32. S—S bond is present in
(a) $H_2S_2O_3$ (b) $H_2S_2O_8$
(c) α-$(SO_3)_n$ (d) γ-(S_3O_9)

33. Which one of the following is not a true "per acid"?
(a) $HClO_4$ (b) H_2SO_5 (c) $H_2S_2O_8$ (d) H_3PO_5

34. Which of the following compounds possesses Lewis acid character?

I. BF_3 II. SiF_4 III. PF_5

Select the correct answer using the codes given below.

(a) I alone (b) I and III
(c) II and III (d) I, II and II

35. Shape of O_2F_2 is similar to that of

(a) H_2O_2 (b) H_2F_2 (c) C_2H_2 (d) C_2F_2

36. Dissociation of HI into H_2 and I_2 is

(a) kinetically controlled
(b) thermodynamically controlled
(c) kinetically as well as thermodynamically controlled
(d) neither kinetically nor thermodynamically controlled

37. Which has peroxy linkage?

(a) Hypochloro acid (b) Perchloric acid
(c) Para perchloric acid (d) None of these

38. Cl_2O, Br_2O, I_2O have positive value of ΔG (free-energy) indicating that

(a) these oxides can form interhalogen compounds
(b) these disproportionate into X^- and XO^-
(c) these oxides are unstable and changes to X_2 and O_2
(d) these oxides are stable

39. In the structure of

(a) IF_2^+, bond angle is smaller than the tetrahedral angle because of lone pair-lone pair repulsion
(b) IF_4^+, two F-atoms one at equatorial positions and two are inclined at an angle less than 120° due to lone pair-bond pair repulsion
(c) IF_4^+, there is sp^3 hybridization with bond angle of 109° 28′
(d) IF_6^+, there are six bonding electrons and no lone pairs

40. Select the correct statement(s).

(a) Halogen forms clatharates by freezing solution in water
(b) High H—F bond strength makes H—F a weak acid in dilute aqueous solution
(c) K_a values of HX is in order HF < HCl < HBr < HI
(d) pK_a values of HI (strongest halogen acid) is most negative

41. In which case geometry of the molecule is pyramidal?

(a) $N(CH_3)_3$ (b) $N(SiH_3)_3$
(c) Both (a) and (b) (d) None of these

42. Correct statement(s) out of the following is

(a) $N(CH_3)_3$ has pyramidal structure
(b) $N(SiH_3)_3$ shows planar arrangement
(c) SiC is highly volatile
(d) SiO_2 is called silane

43. Which of the following statements are true?

(a) Cold and more concentrated HNO_3 forms NO_2 with Cu
(b) Cold and very dilute HNO_3 forms NH_4NO_3 with Zn or Sn
(c) Concentrated HNO_3 forms H_2SnO_3 with Sn
(d) None of the above

44. N_2H_4 and H_2O_2 show similarity in

(a) molar mass
(b) reducing nature
(c) oxidising nature
(d) hybridisation of central atoms

45. In acidic medium N_2H_4

(a) has equivalent mass 8 (b) loses four electrons
(c) is oxidised to N_2 (d) reduces $AuCl_3$ to AuCl

46. N_2H_4 reduces IO_3^-/H^+

(a) to I^+
(b) indicated by blue colour with starch
(c) with I_2 as an intermediate indicated by violet colour in CCl_4 layer
(d) to I^-

47. Thermodynamic tendency of $PH_3(g)$ to react with $HX(g)$ would favoured by

(a) low H–X bond energy
(b) high lattice energy of $PH_4X(s)$
(c) high electron affinity of X
(d) high electronegativity of P

48. The following side reaction in the production of N_2H_4

$$N_2H_4 + 2NH_2Cl \longrightarrow N_2 + 2NH_4Cl$$

(a) is suppressed by addition of gelatin or glue
(b) is catalysed by traces of heavy metals as Cu^{2+}
(c) is made reversible by adding NaOH
(d) is made reversible by removing N_2

49. Select the correct statement(s).

(a) NCl_5 and PCl_5 are stable compounds
(b) PCl_5 can change to PCl_6^- and PCl_4^+ with no change in hybridisation of P
(c) $SbCl_3$ is hydrolysed to orange SbOCl soluble in dil HCl
(d) $BiCl_3$ is hydrolysed to white BiOCl soluble in dil HCl

Directions (Q. Nos. 50 and 51)

Silicones are synthetic polymers containing repeated R_2SiO units. Since, the empirical formula is that of a ketone (R_2CO), the name silicone has been given to these materials. Silicones can be made into oils, rubbery elastomer and resins. They find a variety of applications because of their chemical inertness, water repelling nature, heat-resistance and good electrical insulating property.

Commercial silicon polymers are usually methyl derivatives and to a lesser extent phenyl derivatives and are synthesised by the hydrolysis of R_2SiCl_2 [R_2 = methyl (Me) or phenyl (ϕ)]

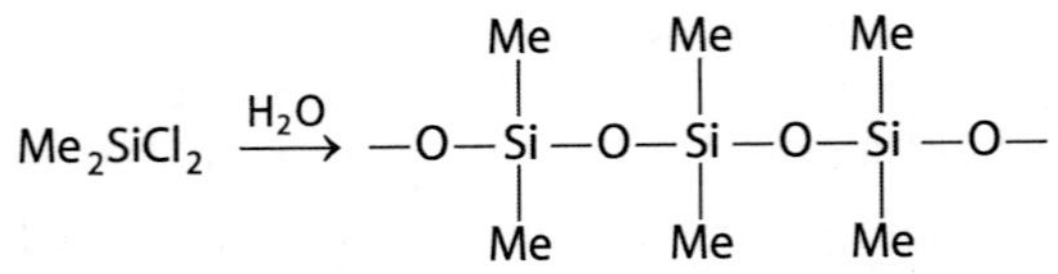

50. If we mix $SiMe_3Cl$ with $SiMe_2Cl_2$, we get silicones of the type

(a) 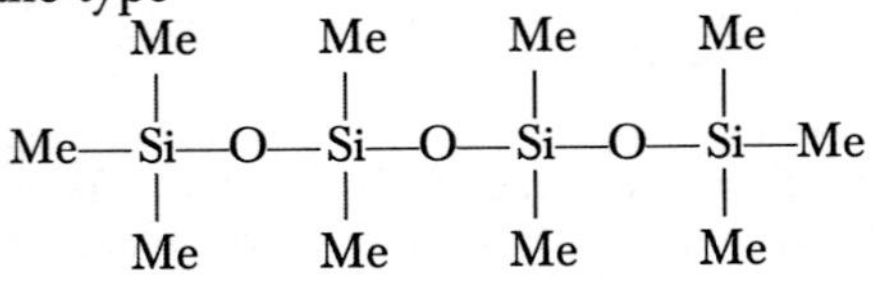

(b) 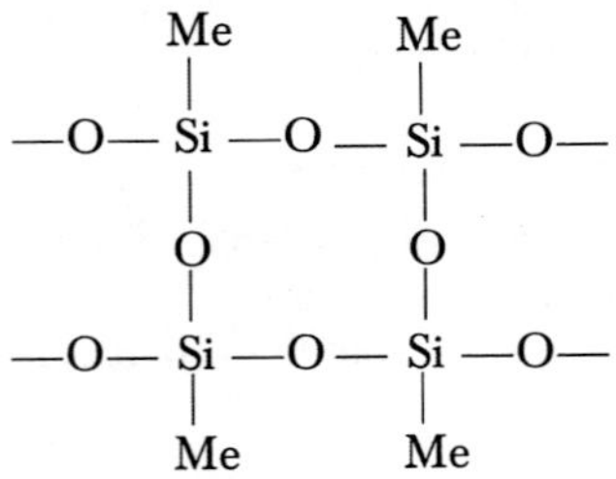

(c) Both (a) and (b)

(d) None of the above

51. If we start with $SiMeCl_3$ as the starting material, silicones formed is

(a) 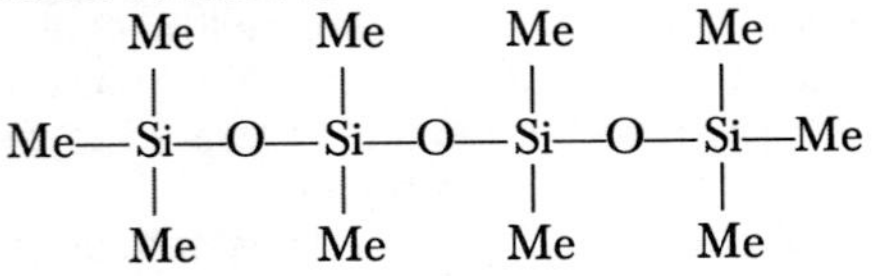

(b) 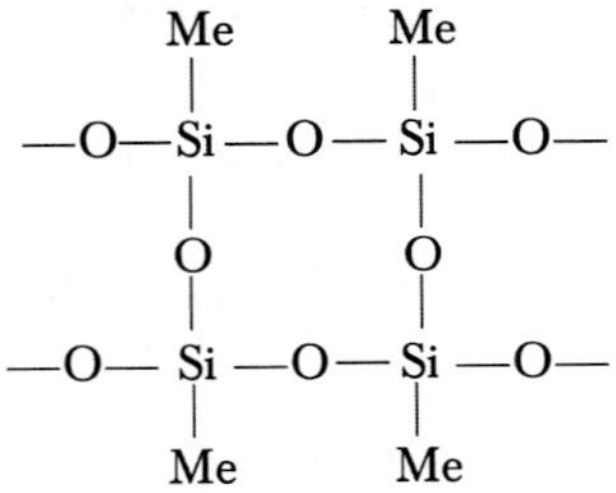

(c) Both (a) and (b)

(d) None of the above

Directions (Q. Nos. 52 to 54)
Consider the six second and third-row elements in group 15-17 of the Periodic Table. Possible molecular structures for common allotropes of these elements are shown below :

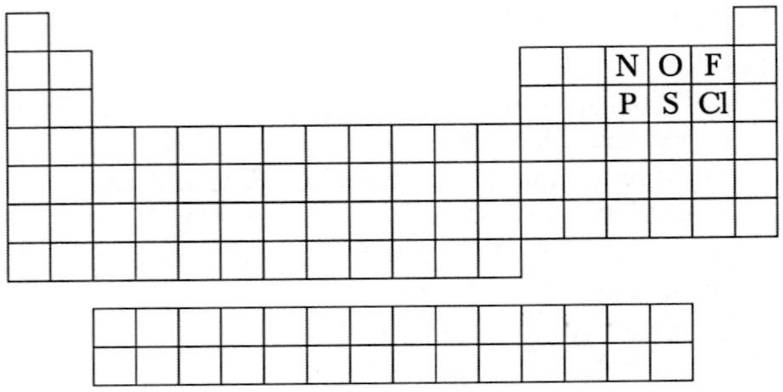

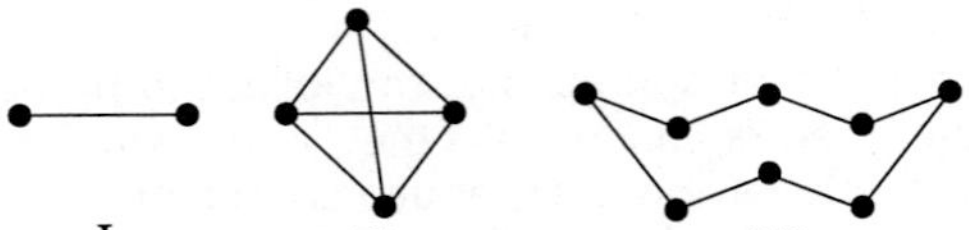

I II III

52. Following is the matching of the structure of molecular form. Which is not the correct matching?

(a) Nitrogen I (b) Phosphorus II
(c) Sulphur III (d) Ozone I

53. Bond energy of

$$(N \equiv N) = 946 \text{ kJ mol}^{-1}$$
$$(P \equiv P) = 481 \text{ kJ mol}^{-1}$$
$$(N - N) = 160 \text{ kJ mol}^{-1}$$
$$(P - P) = 215 \text{ kJ mol}^{-1}$$

which molecules do not exist?

(a) P_4 (b) N_4
(c) N_2 (d) P_2

54. Following table compares properties of red phosphorus and white phosphorus. Which is incorrect comparions?

	Red	White
(a)	Nontoxic and has polymeric structure.	Toxic, waxy discrete tetrahedral P_4 molecule.
(b)	Discrete tetrahedral P_4 molecule.	Polymeric structure.
(c)	High m.p., less reactive.	Low m.p., more reactive.
(d)	Shows no phosphorescence in air.	Shows phosphorescence in air.

Directions (Q. Nos. 55 and 56)
Consider the following scheme involving oxides and oxy-acids of nitrogen. Based on this answer the questions given at the end.

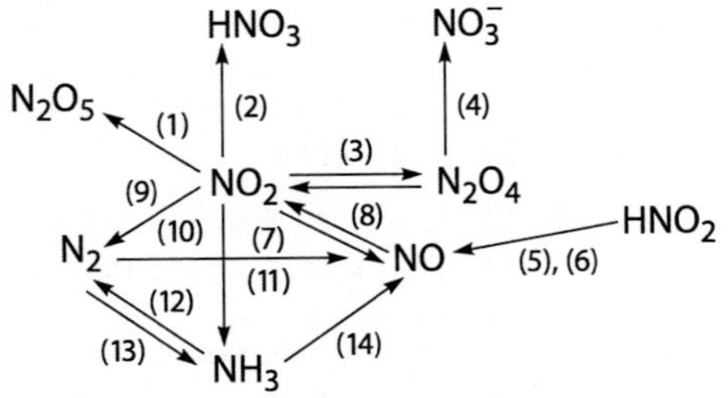

55. Out of the following which reactions are disproportionations?

(a) 2, 10 (b) 2, 3
(c) 1, 11 (d) 13, 14

56. In which case change in oxidation number is maximum?

(a) 1 (b) 10
(c) 5 (d) 11

Directions (Q. Nos. 57 to 59)
An oxy-acid of phosphorus has the following properities. Complete neutralisation of the acid with sodium hydroxide solution gives an aqueous solution of sodium ions and oxy-acid anions in the ratio 2:1. When a solution of the acid is warmed with silver nitrate solution, metallic silver is deposited.

57. What is the structure of the oxy-acid?

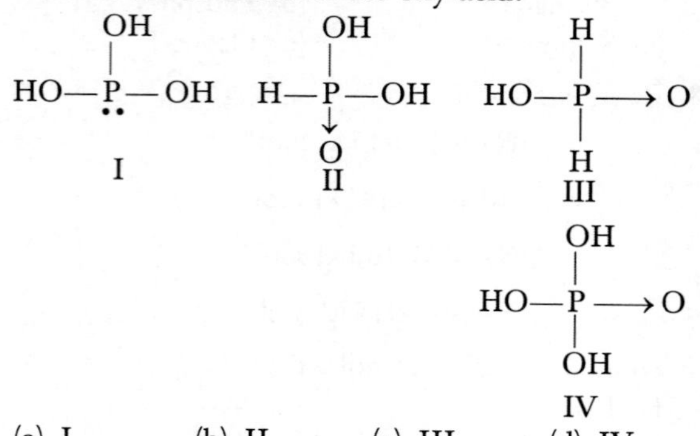

(a) I (b) II (c) III (d) IV

58. This oxy-acid is converted into .... on reaction with acetic anhydride.
(a) $(CH_3CO)_2HPO_4$ (b) $(CH_3CO)_2HPO_3$
(c) P_2O_3 (d) P_2O_5

59. pH of 0.01 M solution of the sodium salt of this acid formed (assume $pK_{\alpha_1} = 2x$) is
(a) $6 + 2x$ (b) $6 - 2x$ (c) $6 - x$ (d) $6 + x$

Directions (Q. Nos. 60 and 61) The following flow diagram represents the industrial preparation of nitric acid from ammonia :

$$NH_3 + O_2 \underset{\text{(excess air)}}{} \xrightarrow[900°C]{(A)} NO \xrightarrow[\text{air}]{(B)} (C) \xrightarrow[\text{water}]{} HNO_3 + NO$$

(NO recycled)

60. Which line of entry describes the undefined reagents, products and reaction conditions?

	A	*B*	*C*
(a)	Catalyst	Cool (– 25°C)	NO_2
(b)	Catalyst	Cool (– 25°C)	N_2O
(b)	Catalyst	High pressure	NO_2
(b)	High pressure	Catalyst	N_2O_3

61. Formation of HNO_3 when (*C*) is dissolved in H_2O takes place through various reactions. Select the reaction not observed in this step.
(a) $NO_2 + H_2O \longrightarrow HNO_3 + HNO_2$
(b) $HNO_2 \longrightarrow H_2O + NO + NO_2$
(c) $NO_2 + H_2O \longrightarrow HNO_3 + NO$
(d) None of the above

Directions (Q. Nos. 62 to 64)
Trimethylamine oxide and trimethyl phosphine oxide can be represented as

$$\underset{\text{(I)}}{(CH_3)_3\overset{+}{N}—O^-} \quad \underset{\text{(II)}}{(CH_3)_3\overset{+}{P}—O^-}$$

62. Select the correct structure.
(a) $(CH_3)_3N{=}O$ (b) $(CH_3)_3P{=}O$
(c) Both (a) and (b) (d) None of these

63. Trimethyl phosphine oxide can be represented by two canonical forms but trimethylamine oxide can't be

$$(CH_3)_3\overset{+}{P}—\overset{-}{O} \longleftrightarrow (CH_3)_3P{=}O$$

It is due to
(a) phosphorus accepts charge density from oxygen and accommodates it in its vacant *d*-orbitals
(b) nitrogen does not possess *d*-orbitals and thus can't form the π-bonded structure
(c) Both (a) and (b)
(d) None forms canonical forms

64. Trimethyl phosphine oxide is stable because
(a) it has two resonating structure
(b) phosphorus-oxygen double bond has high dissociation energy
(c) Both (a) and (b)
(d) None of the above

Directions (Q. Nos. 65 to 67)
This question concerns the elements of group 17-fluorine chlorine, bromine and iodine.
When sodium chloride is treated with concentrated sulphuric acid, a colourless gas, *X*, which fumes in moist air, is formed. When sodium iodide is treated in the same way, a coloured vapour, *Y*, is product.
If 90% phosphoric (*V*) acid is used instead of sulphuric acid, a colourless gas is produced in each reaction.

65. Gases *X* and *Y* are respectively
(a) Cl_2, I_2 (b) HCl, I_2
(c) HCl, HI (d) $HClO, I_2$

66. With 90% phosphoric acid (H_3PO_4), colourless gases formed are
(a) HCl, HI (b) Cl_2, I_2
(c) HCl, I_2 (d) Cl_2, HI

67. Behaviour of H_2SO_4 and H_3PO_4 is different towards NaI because
(a) H_2SO_4 is a stronger acid than H_3PO_4
(b) H_2SO_4 is a strong oxidising agent and oxidises colourless gas to coloured vapour *Y*
(c) H_3PO_4 is tribasic acid
(d) H_2SO_4 is a disbasic acid

Assertion & Reason

Codes
(a) Both A and R are true and R is the correct explanation of A.
(b) Both A and R are true but R is not the correct explanation of A.
(c) A is true but R is false.
(d) A is false but R is true.
(e) A and R both are false.

68. **Assertion (A)** Of all the elements of the group-16, sulphur has the largest tendency to catenation.

Reason (R) Sulphur-sulphur bond energy is very high.

69. **Assertion (A)** $S_3O_6^{2-}$ (trithionate) has S—S bond.

Reason (R) It is a conjugate base of $HS_3O_6^-$.

70. **Assertion (A)** SO_2 turns acidified $K_2Cr_2O_7$ green.

Reason (R) $K_2Cr_2O_7$ is reduced to Cr^{3+} (green) salt by SO_2.

71. **Assertion (A)** SO_2 is a bleaching agent.

Reason (R) Nascent oxygen causes bleaching.

72. **Assertion (A)** One mole of SO_2Cl_2 in aqueous solution is neutralised by 3 moles of NaOH.

Reason (R) 3 moles of H^+ are formed due to reaction with water.

73. **Assertion (A)** Anhydrous sulphuric acid has very high viscosity.

Reason (R) H-bonding makes it viscous.

74. **Assertion (A)** Structure of SO_4^{2-} is identical to $S_2O_3^{2-}$.

Reason (R) Sulphur atoms in $S_2O_3^{2-}$ are in different oxidation states.

75. **Assertion (A)** On cooling, the brown colour of NO_2 disappears.

Reason (R) On cooling NO_2 forms dimer (N_2O_4) resulting in the pairing of the odd electrons in NO_2.

76. **Assertion (A)** Both H_3PO_3 and H_3PO_4 have the same number of hydrogen atoms but H_3PO_4 is a tribasic acid and H_3PO_3 is a dibasic acid.

Reason (R) 1 mole of H_3PO_3 is neutralised by 2 moles of NaOH while 1 mole of H_3PO_4 is neutralised by 3 moles of NaOH.

77. **Assertion (A)** N_2H_4 is kinetically stable compound.

Reason (R) Two N-atoms are bonded by triple bonds.

78. **Assertion (A)** N_3H explodes violently on slight heating.

Reason (R) N_3^- has linear structure and is stable due to resonance.

79. **Assertion (A)** IO_3^- is reduced to I^+ but intermediate gives violet colour in CCl_4 (taken as medium).

Reason (R) I_2 is formed as the intermediate.

80. **Assertion (A)** Each N-atom is sp^3-hybridised in N_2H_4.

Reason (R) It has *gauche* conformation.

81. **Assertion (A)** H_2O_2 and N_2H_4 have oxidant and reductant nature.

Reason (R) Both have equivalent mass of 8.

82. **Assertion (A)** Cl_2 or Br_2 changes KI into I_2 (violet in CCl_4 layer), Cl_2 changes KBr into Br_2 (orange-yellow in CCl_4 layer). Thus, Cl_2 would change mixture of KI and KBr into violet layer in CCl_4.

Reason (R) Oxidising power is in order $I_2 < Br_2 < Cl_2 < F_2$.

83. **Assertion (A)** Hydrofluoric acid forms two series of salts KHF_2, K_2F_2.

Reason (R) It is a dibasic acid due to hydrogen bonding.

84. **Assertion (A)** Aqueous solution of $NaOX$ is alkaline.

Reason (R) It is a salt of weak acid (HOX) and strong base (NaOH).

Matching Type

85. Match the acids (in Column I) with number of acid salts formed by them (in Column II).

	Column I		Column II
A.	Hypophosphorous acid	1.	Two
B.	Orthophosphorous acid	2.	Zero
C.	Orthophosphoric acid	3.	One
D.	Mellitic acid	4.	Five

	A	B	C	D
(a)	2	3	4	1
(b)	1	2	3	4
(c)	2	3	1	4
(d)	4	3	2	1

86. Match the reactions of metals with dilute HNO_3 (in Column I) with the nitrogen compounds (obtained by oxidation/reduction (in Column II).

	Column I		Column II
A.	Mg + dil HNO_3	1.	NO
B.	Zn + dil HNO_3	2.	H_2
C.	Sn + dil HNO_3	3.	N_2O
D.	Pb + dil HNO_3	4.	NH_4NO_3

	A	B	C	D
(a)	1	2	3	4
(b)	2	3	4	1
(c)	2	4	3	1
(d)	4	3	2	1

Answers

Exercise 1

1. (a)	**2.** (c)	**3.** (c)	**4.** (b)	**5.** (a)	**6.** (a)	**7.** (b)	**8.** (b)	**9.** (d)	**10.** (b)
11. (d)	**12.** (d)	**13.** (c)	**14.** (a)	**15.** (b)	**16.** (a)	**17.** (b)	**18.** (b)	**19.** (a)	**20.** (b)
21. (a)	**22.** (b)	**23.** (d)	**24.** (d)	**25.** (a)	**26.** (b)	**27.** (a)	**28.** (a)	**29.** (d)	**30.** (a)
31. (c)	**32.** (c)	**33.** (d)	**34.** (c)	**35.** (b)	**36.** (a)	**37.** (d)	**38.** (d)	**39.** (b)	**40.** (b)
41. (d)	**42.** (c)	**43.** (b)	**44.** (a)	**45.** (a)	**46.** (a)	**47.** (d)	**48.** (a)	**49.** (b)	**50.** (b)
51. (b)	**52.** (c)	**53.** (b)	**54.** (c)	**55.** (c)	**56.** (d)	**57.** (a)	**58.** (d)	**59.** (a)	**60.** (c)
61. (d)	**62.** (a)	**63.** (a)	**64.** (b)	**65.** (a)	**66.** (b)	**67.** (b)	**68.** (c)	**69.** (a)	**70.** (b)
71. (d)	**72.** (a)	**73.** (c)	**74.** (d)	**75.** (a)	**76.** (a)	**77.** (a)	**78.** (a)	**79.** (c)	**80.** (d)
81. (d)	**82.** (d)	**83.** (c)	**84.** (a)	**85.** (c)	**86.** (d)	**87.** (b)	**88.** (c)	**89.** (b)	**90.** (d)
91. (a)	**92.** (a)	**93.** (d)	**94.** (d)	**95.** (c)	**96.** (d)	**97.** (a)	**98.** (c)		

Exercise 2

1. (d)	**2.** (c)	**3.** (a)	**4.** (c)	**5.** (d)	**6.** (a)	**7.** (a,b)	**8.** (a)	**9.** (c)	**10.** (b)
11. (c)	**12.** (a)	**13.** (d)	**14.** (a)	**15.** (b)	**16.** (c)	**17.** (a)	**18.** (b)	**19.** (c)	**20.** (a)
21. (a)	**22.** (d)	**23.** (b)	**24.** (c)	**25.** (a)	**26.** (c)	**27.** (d)	**28.** (b)	**29.** (b)	**30.** (b)
31. (d)	**32.** (a)	**33.** (a)	**34.** (a)	**35.** (a)	**36.** (a)	**37.** (d)	**38.** (c)	**39.** (a,b,d)	**40.** (a,b,c,d)
41. (a)	**42.** (a,b)	**43.** (a,b,c)	**44.** (b,c,d)	**45.** (a,b,c)	**46.** (a,b,c)	**47.** (a,b,c)	**48.** (a,b)	**49.** (c,d)	**50.** (a)
51. (b)	**52.** (d)	**53.** (b,d)	**54.** (b)	**55.** (a,c)	**56.** (d)	**57.** (b)	**58.** (c)	**59.** (d)	**60.** (a)
61. (d)	**62.** (b)	**63.** (a)	**64.** (c)	**65.** (b)	**66.** (a)	**67.** (b)	**68.** (a)	**69.** (b)	**70.** (a)
71. (c)	**72.** (e)	**73.** (a)	**74.** (b)	**75.** (b)	**76.** (b)	**77.** (c)	**78.** (b)	**79.** (a)	**80.** (b)
81. (c)	**82.** (a)	**83.** (a)	**84.** (b)	**85.** (c)	**86.** (b)				

7

Noble Gases

Syllabus

- Elements and their Compounds Occurrence Synthesis, Properties, Structure and Bonding
- Industrial Importance of the Noble Gases
- Clathrates

Introduction

The following elements are collectively known as noble gases and constitute group 18 of the Periodic Table.

Table 7.1 **Outer Configuration and Symbol of Noble Gases**

Name of the element	Symbol	Atomic number
Helium	He	2 $(1s^2)$
Neon	Ne	10 $(2s^2 2p^6)$
Argon	Ar	18 $(3s^2 3p^6)$
Krypton	Kr	36 $(4s^2 4p^6)$
Xenon	Xe	54 $(5s^2 5p^6)$
Radon	Rn	86 $(6s^2 6p^6)$

They are called noble gases because they show very little chemical reactivity (as compared to other elements) and are gases at ordinary temperatures. Due to their chemical inertness, they were also earlier called **inert gases.** The lack of chemical reactivity was attributed to these elements having a **stable octet** in their outermost shell $(ns^2 np^6)$ except helium $(1s^2)$. Due to their inertness towards chemical reactivity, these elements were assigned **zero valency,** and in some earlier periodic classification, group 18 was also referred to as **group zero.**

Occurrence

The noble gases occur only as minor constituents in the atmosphere. **Agron is the most abundant noble gas in air.**

Other sources of helium are natural gas, minerals like pitch blende, monazite etc.

General Properties of Noble Gases

Physical Properties

Their melting and boiling points are very low, due to very weak van der Waals' forces of attraction. As the size increases, van der Waals' forces increases and hence, melting and boiling point is lowest for He.

Atomic Size

On moving down the group atomic size increases, due to increase in the number of shells.

Liquefaction

Noble gases are liquified with great difficulty as their critical temperatures are very low because of weak inter molecular forces existing in these gases. The ease of liquification increases with increase in atomic number as van der Waals' forces or critical temperature increases.

Solubility in Water

These are only slightly soluble in water (8 to 40 mL per litre at 25°C). Solubility increases with increase in the atomic number.

Atomicity

All noble gases are monoatomic. Their monoatomic nature is also confirmed by the value of $\gamma (= C_p/C_V)$ being close to 1.66.

Ionisation Enthalpy and Electron Affinities

Due to stable closed shell configuration, their first ionisation energy is highest in the respective periods. On moving down the group, ionisation energy decreases. The electron affinity of noble gas is close to zero.

Characteristic Spectra

These gases gives characteristic spectra by which these can be identified. He gives a characteristic spectrum containing conspicuous green and yellow lines while neon gives a characteristic spectrum with orange and red lines.

Diffusing Property

Helium has a unusual property of diffusing through most commonly used laboratory materials such as rubber, glass or plastics.

Isolation of Noble Gases from the Atmosphere

The first step involves the removal of oxygen and nitrogen of the atmosphere as NO_2. Then, the noble gases are separated by using Dewar's method, which is based on differential adsorption of these gases by charcoal. In this method, the mixture is kept into a bulb containing coconut charcoal and placed in a cold bath (−100°C) in a Dewar flask. It is allowed to remain there for about an hour. Different gases are separated at different temperatures.

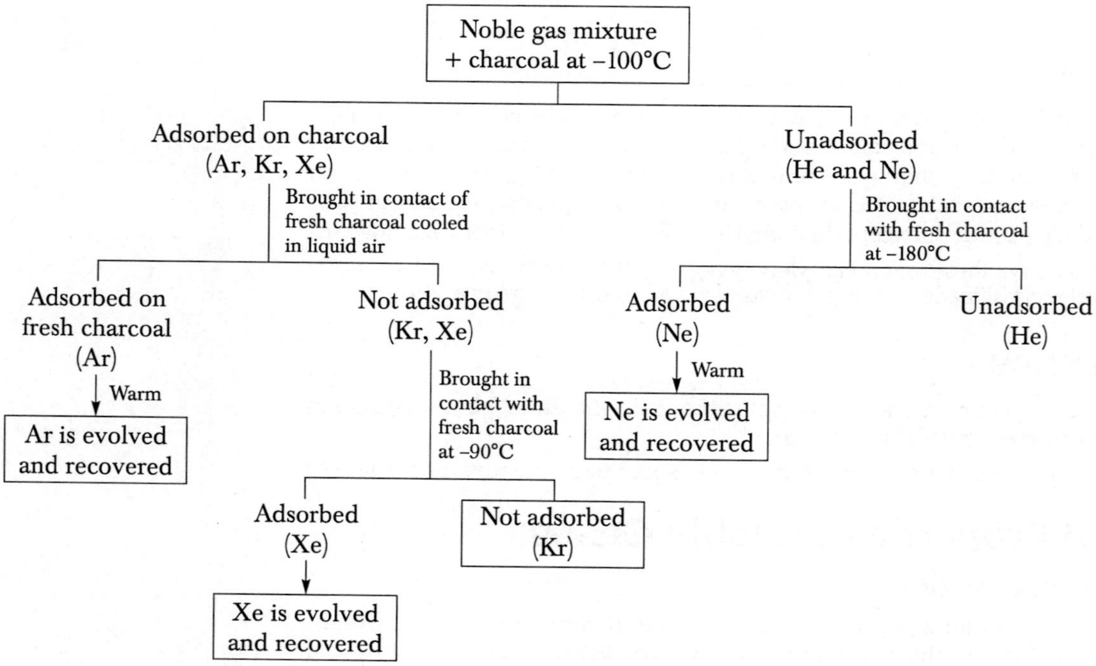

The Chemistry of Noble Gases

Why noble gases are not considered to be chemically reactive?

This may be attributed to the following reasons :

(a) They have high ionisation energies.

(b) Their electron affinities are almost zero.

Both these factors can be explained on the basis of their electronic configuration. In each noble gas the electronic sub-level is just complete ($ns^2 np^6$) and the next available sub-level is of much higher energy. The electron distribution is spherically symmetrical and this particular electronic configuration resists change or disturbance of any kind. Therefore, all noble gases are extremely unreactive as compared to other elements. However, in recent years a fairly good number of compounds of some of these gases have been reported which are discussed now.

The first chemical compound of the noble gases was reported by N. Bartlett in 1962. The preparation of this compound, $XePtF_6$ was based on the chance discovery of another compound formed by the reaction between oxygen gas and platinum hexafluoride. (deep red vapours)

$$O_2(g) + PtF_6(g) \longrightarrow \underset{\text{Dioxygenyl hexa-fluoroplatinate (V)}}{O_2PtF_6(s)}$$

The above compound is formulated as $O_2^+[PtF_6]^-$. This would imply that platinum hexafluoride is a very strong oxidising material, and could even attract electron from molecular oxygen. **Since, the ionization energy of oxygen gas (1165.6 kJ mol^{-1}) is comparable to that of xenon gas (1170 kJ mol^{-1}) and as their molecular diameters are also similar (Xe ≃ 4 Å; O_2 ≃ 4 Å), Bartlett had every reason to believe that xenon would also be susceptible to oxidation with platinum hexafluoride.** Therefore, he proceeded to mix xenon and platinum hexafluoride (both gases) at room temperature and obtained on his first attempt an orange yellow crystalline compound of composition $XePtF_6$, as he had predicted.

$$Xe(g) + PtF_6(g) \longrightarrow Xe^+[PtF_6]^-(s)$$

Since, this discovery, a large number of other noble gas compounds have been prepared. A summary of these compounds are reported in Table 7.3.

Example 1. *Is it likely that a compound $N_2^+PtF_6^-$ (cf. $O_2^+PtF_6^-$) will form?*

Sol. No, I.E. of N_2 (15.576 eV) is more than that of O_2 (12.063 eV). This is due to the fact that the electron in N_2 is to be removed from a bonding M.O. while in O_2 an electron is removed from an anti-bonding π M.O. It appears unlikely that PtF_6 can oxidize N_2 to give N_2^+.

Which Elements of This Family are Expected to be More Reactive and Why?

We may expect only the heavier noble gases which have low ionisation energy values can show some reactivity as a result of electron loss. Ionisation energies of noble gases along with some other reactive elements are given in Table 7.2.

Table 7.2 **Comparison of Ionisation Energy Values of Noble Gases with Other Reactive Elements**

Element	Ionisation energy value, kJ mol^{-1}	Element	Ionisation energy value, kJ mol^{-1}
Helium	2372.3	Carbon	1086.4
Neon	2080.7	Nitrogen	1402.3
Argon	1520.5	Oxygen	1314.0
Krypton	1350.7	Fluorine	1681.0
Xenon	1170.4	Chlorine	1255.7
Radon	1037.0	Bromine	1139.9

From the above ionisation energy values, it is obvious that we may expect radon to go into chemical combination with the greatest ease. Since, radon is radioactive with isotopes having short half-life, therefore, we know very little about its ability to form chemical compounds. **Xenon forms the largest number of compounds as compared to any other noble gas.** Krypton tends to form compounds but with difficulty as compared to xenon. **The lighter noble gases, helium, neon and argon which have very high ionisation energies are expected to show very little reactivity.** So far experimental evidence also suggests that no chemical compounds of these gases have been reported.

Why Most of These Compounds Involve Only Fluorine and Oxygen?

Any chemical reactivity shown by these gases may be attributed to their tendency to lose electrons. For this reason, the combining atom must be highly electronegative.

Xenon forms stable compounds only with the most electronegative elements; fluorine (X = 4.0) and oxygen (X = 3.5) or with highly electronegative groups such as $OSeF_5$ and $OTeF_5$ that contain both oxygen and fluorine. Relatively uncommon bonds of xenon are known with chlorine ($X = 3.0$) and nitrogen ($X = 3.0$).

A list of noble gas compounds which have been prepared till date is given in Table 7.3.

Table 7.3 **Known Compounds of Noble Gases**

Xenon	Krypton	Radon
$Xe[PtF_6]$		RnF_x (where, x is not known)
XeF_2, $XeF_2 \cdot 2SbF_5$, $XeF_2 \cdot TaF_5$	KrF_2	
XeF, $XeOF_2$	KrF_4	
XeF_6, $XeOF_4$, XeO_2F_2, XeO_3		
$XeF_6 \cdot 2SbF_5$		
XeF_8, XeO_4, $M^+XeF_7^-$ (where, M = Na, K, Rb, Cs)		
M_2XeF_8 (where, M = Rb or Cs)		

Compounds of Xenon

Xenon in its compounds exhibits every even valency from two to eight, $+2(XeF_2) + 4(XeF_4)$, $+6(XeF_6)$ and $+8(XeO_4)$. The compounds of xenon involve only fluorine or oxygen. The only other compound, xenon dichloride ($XeCl_2$) is stable at low temperatures. The fluorides of this element can be prepared by the direct method.

Compounds of xenon with oxygen cannot be prepared by their direct combination. The (+8) oxidation state is well established only in XeO_4.

The chemistry of Xe (VI) involves the study of XeF_6, $XeOF_4$, XeO_2F_2 and XeO_3 compounds. Xenon trioxide is thermally unstable and is highly explosive.

Xenon Difluoride, XeF_2

(a) Preparation

1. It is best prepared in the laboratory in high yields and purity by heating xenon and fluorine in the molar ratio of 2 : 1 (excess of xenon is taken to avoid the formation of any xenon tetrafluoride). The reaction is carried out in a nickel vessel at 400°C. The reaction products are quenched to room temperature and XeF_2 is isolated by vacuum sublimation.

$$Xe + F_2 \xrightarrow[1\ \text{atm}]{400^\circ\text{C}} XeF_2 \quad (\text{Xe in excess})$$

2. It may be prepared by simple exposure to sunlight of a mixture of xenon and fluorine contained in a dry pyrex glass vessel at room temperature.
3. It can be prepared quantitatively by photosynthesis, on exposing to sunlight mixtures of xenon and oxygen difluoride (OF_2) or xenon and excess of oxygen monofluoride (O_2F_2) at −118°C.

(b) Properties

1. It is a while, crystalline solid. It can be sublimed.
2. It melts at 140°C.
3. The Xe—F bond in XeF_2 has almost the lowest bond energy among the known fluorides. Due to this reason XeF_2 is an **oxidizing** and **fluorinating** agent. Both these properties have been extensively investigated. XeF_2 is a mild fluorinating agent. The aqueous solutions are powerful oxidising agent. It oxidizes HCl to Cl_2, Ce^{III} to Ce^{IV}, Cr^{III} to Cr^{VI}, Ag^{I} to Ag^{II} and BrO_3^- to BrO_4^-.

$$2HCl + XeF_2 \longrightarrow Xe + Cl_2 + 2HF$$

4. The fluorine ligand of XeF_2 may be substituted by highly electronegative ligands of protonic acids.

$$XeF_2 + HX \longrightarrow FXeX + HF$$
$$FXeX + HX \longrightarrow XeX_2 + HF$$

The formation of HF is highly exothermic step which makes the reactions go in the forward direction. Solid compounds have been obtained for $X = SO_3F(HSO_3F)$, $ClO_4(HClO_4)$, $OTeF_5(HOTeF_5)$ and $OCOCF_3(CF_3COOH)$. However, similar reactions with HCl (or BCl_3) have **failed** to yield FXeCl or $XeCl_2$ but instead xenon gas is evolved.

5. It oxidizes iodine in the presence of fluoride ion acceptor to give IF.

$$I_2 + XeF_2 \xrightarrow{BF_3} 2IF + Xe\uparrow$$
$$IF + XeF_2 \xrightarrow{BF_3} IF_3 + Xe\uparrow$$

6. It reacts with sulphur trioxide to give Xe.

$$XeF_2 + 2SO_3 \longrightarrow Xe\uparrow + S_2O_6F_2$$

7. It is reduced by hydrogen to xenon.

$$XeF_2 + H_2 \longrightarrow Xe\uparrow + 2HF$$

8. It reacts with NO to give nitrosyl fluoride.

$$2NO + XeF_2 \longrightarrow 2NOF + Xe\uparrow$$

It appears that in all of the above fluorination and oxidation reactions the first step involves

the ionization of XeF_2 to XeF^+ followed by electron transfer to give XeF. The XeF species is very weakly bound and is potential source of fluorine atoms.

9. It reacts with SbF_5 or AsF_5 to give solid compounds in which it reacts as a fluoride ion donor.

$$XeF_2 + SbF_5 \longrightarrow XeF_2 \cdot SbF_5$$
$$XeF_2 + AsF_5 \longrightarrow XeF_2 \cdot AsF_5$$

It has now been established that the compounds contain ionic species, XeF^+, AsF_6^- and $XeF^+SbF_6^-$.

$$XeF_2 + 2SbF_5 \longrightarrow XeF_2 \cdot 2SbF_5$$

The compound $XeF_2 \cdot 2SbF_5$ has been shown to contain XeF^+ and $Sb_2F_{11}^-$. The XeF^+ ion is strongly bonded to the $Sb_2F_{11}^-$ by a fluorine bridge.

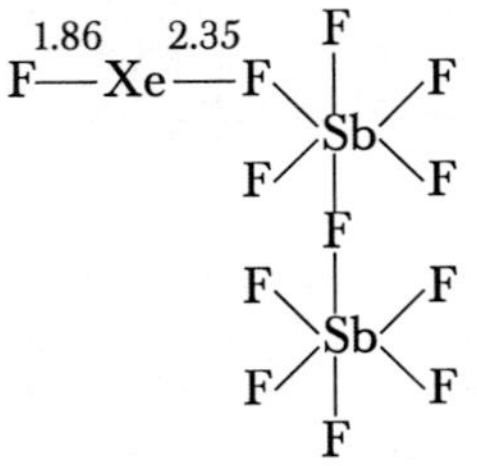

XeF_2 also reacts with AsF_5 in a different stoichiometry :

$$2\,XeF_2 + AsF_5 \longrightarrow 2\,XeF_2 \cdot AsF_5 \longrightarrow [Xe_2F_3]^+[AsF_6]^-$$

The ion $Xe_2F_3^+$ has the expected linear geometry around xenon and an angular geometry at the central fluorine.

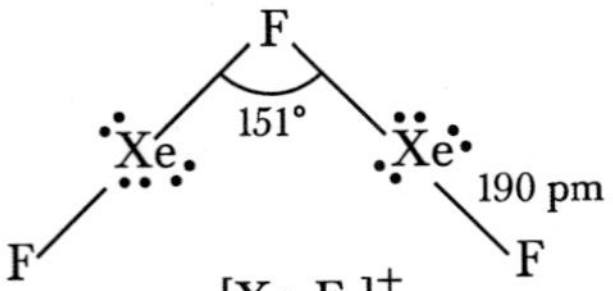

$[Xe_2F_3]^+$

10. It dissolves in HF (hydrofluoric acid) without any reaction. The solution does not show any change in conductivity.

(c) Structure

1. Infrared and Raman spectra show that XeF_2 is a linear molecule in the vapour state.

$$F—Xe—F$$

2. Crystal structure of solid XeF_2 again shows that XeF_2 consists of linear units.

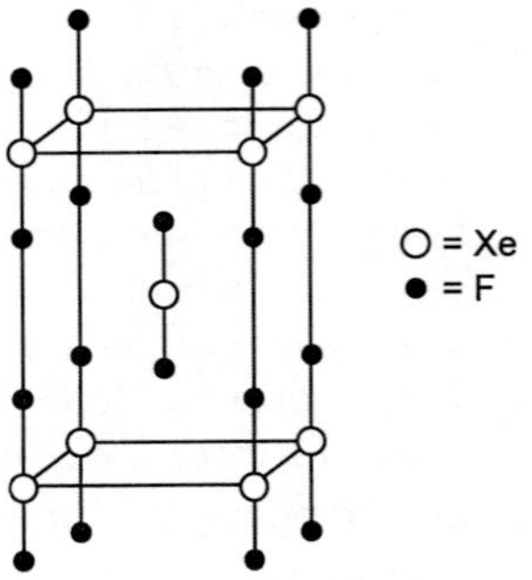

Fig. 7.1 Unit cell diagram of XeF_2.

(d) Bonding

Xenon difluoride may be represented in terms of Lewis electron dot representation as

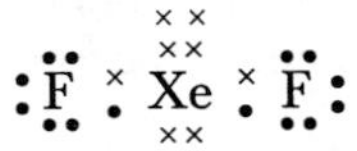

The real structure may be represented as a resonance hybrid of the following two structures :

Valence bond treatment In the valence bond approach, the valence shell of xenon is expanded by promotion of an electron into the higher energy vacant 5*d*-orbitals :

Ground state of Xe : [Kr] $5s^2\ 4d^{10}\ 5p^6$

Valence state of Xe : [Kr] $5s^2\ 4d^{10}\ 5p^5\ 5d^1$

For XeF_2, two $2c$—$2e$ bonds are formed by overlap with 2F $2p_z$ orbitals (one electron each). By using VSEPR theory, we may predict linear geometry for XeF_2 with three non-bonding pairs pointing towards the corners of an equilateral triangle (Fig. 7.2).

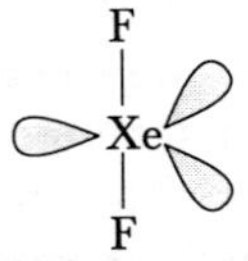

Fig. 7.2 Structure of XeF_2.

However, the most serious objection to this model of bonding is the promotion of a $5p$ electron into high energy $5d$ orbitals. The objection is from where would this energy be compensated? Also valence bond theory predicts the formation of two strong covalent bonds for F—Xe—F and so do not reflect the overall instability of XeF_2. An alternative approach to overcome these objections was offered by Rundle, who offered a simple molecular orbital model.

Molecular orbital approach This model explains the formation of F—Xe—F suggesting the existence of three centre, four electron ($3c$—$4e$) bonds. This model does not require participation of $5d$ atomic orbitals and so the objection of large promotion energy is avoided. In the linear F—Xe—F molecule, interaction of three p-atomic orbitals, a completely filled xenon $5p_z$ atomic orbital and two F $2p_z$ orbitals (one electron each) results in the formation of three three-centred orbitals as shown below; one bonding (σ^b), one non-bonding (σ^{nb}) and one anti-bonding (σ^a). A total of four electrons, two from the central xenon atom and one from each fluorine atom are filled in the bonding and non-bonding orbitals so that overall we have a bonding situation. A single bond is spread over the F—Xe—F system which gives a bond order of 0.5 for each Xe—F bond. This also accounts for the existence of weak Xe—F bonds in XeF_2.

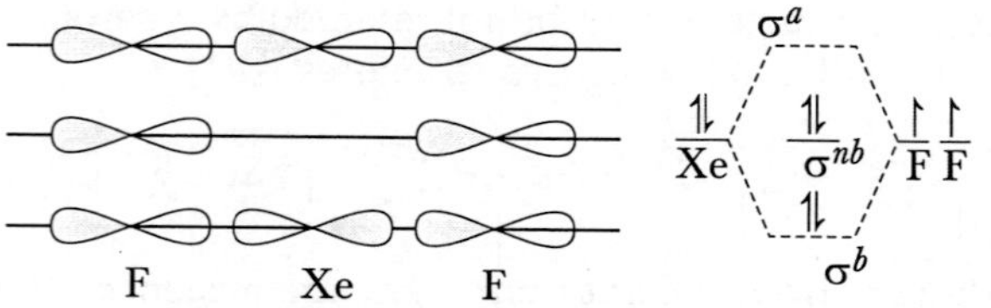

Fig. 7.3 Molecular orbital diagram for XeF_2 three centre four-electron bonds

Xenon Tetrafluoride, XeF_4

(a) Preparation

1. It is prepared in high yield by heating a mixture of xenon and fluorine in a molar ratio 1 : 5 at 400° and 5–6 atm in an enclosed nickel vessel. The sample is purified by fractionation.

$$Xe + 2F_2 \xrightarrow[6\ atm]{600°C} XeF_4 \quad (Xe : F_2 = 1 : 5)$$

2. It is also prepared by passing an electric discharge in a reaction vessel maintained at –80°C containing xenon and fluorine in the molar ratio 1 : 2. The pressure is maintained between 2–15 mm of Hg.
   It would be most appropriate if we take up a problem relating to the preparation to xenon compounds.

Example 2. *A reaction mixture was prepared at 25°C by filling a 1.0 L nickel container with F_2 gas at 8 atm. and Xe gas at 1.7 atm. The reaction mixture was maintained at 400°C for 1 h. Then it was cooled to 25°C and the contents of the nickel container were analysed. All the xenon gas had reacted to form a solid xenon fluorine compound, but some of the fluorine gas had not reacted. The pressure of the F_2 gas was 4.6 atm. What formula would you propose for the xenon fluorine compound?*

Sol. Since, all pressures were measured at the same temperature while the volume of the container was unchanged, *i.e.*, T and V are constant in the equation $pV = nRT$ $\left(\text{or } p = \dfrac{nRT}{V}\right)$. Therefore, we can say that $p \propto n$, *i.e.*, pressure can be taken as a measure of the number of moles of reactants present.

Pressure of F_2 gas before reaction = 8 atm

Pressure of F_2 gas after reaction = 4.6 atm

∴ Pressure difference = 8 – 4.6 = 3.4 atm.

The pressure difference is proportional to the number of moles of F_2 consumed in the reaction. Similarly pressure difference of Xe gas = 1.7 – 0 = 1.7 atm.

$$\text{So that ratio of moles used} = \frac{\text{Moles of } F_2 \text{ used}}{\text{Moles of Xe used}} = \frac{3.4}{1.7} = 2$$

One mole of fluorine gas contains 2 g atoms, whereas one mole of xenon gas contains 1 g atom (∵ It is monoatomic). The formula which satisfies these conditions is XeF_4.

(b) Properties

1. It is a colourless crystalline solid.
2. It melts at 117.1°C and can be readily sublimed.
3. It is reduced by hydrogen gas at 130°C.

$$XeF_4 + 2H_2 \longrightarrow Xe + 4HF$$

4. XeF_4 is a stronger fluorinating agent than XeF_2.

$$Pt + XeF_4 \longrightarrow Xe + PtF_4$$

$$2SF_4 + XeF_4 \longrightarrow Xe + 2SF_6$$

5. It is also reduced by mercury.

$$XeF_4 + 2Hg \longrightarrow Xe + 2HgF_2$$

6. It reacts with boron trichloride to give boron trifluoride.

$$3XeF_4 + 4BCl_3 \longrightarrow 4BF_3 + 3Xe + 6Cl_2$$

7. It forms an addition compound with antimony pentafluoride.

$$XeF_4 + SbF_5 \longrightarrow XeF_4 \cdot SbF_5 \longrightarrow [XeF_3]^+[SbF_6]^-$$

$$XeF_4 + 2SbF_5 \longrightarrow XeF_4 \cdot 2SbF_5 \longrightarrow [XeF_3]^+[Sb_2F_{11}]^-$$

The XeF_3^+ ions have the expected T-shaped structure.

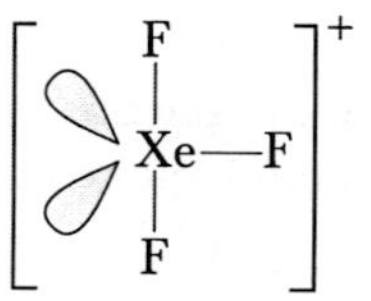

8. It is readily hydrolysed by water. The reaction can be controlled to yield different products.

$$XeF_4 + H_2O \xrightarrow{-80°C} \underset{\text{Xenon oxyfluoride}}{XeOF_2} + 2HF$$

$$XeF_4 + H_2O \longrightarrow \underset{\text{Xenon trioxide}}{XeO_3}$$

9. It forms stable 1 : 1 adducts with strong Lewis bases, such as $Me_4N^+F^-$ (tetramethyl ammonium fluoride) and alkali metal fluorides, *MF* (NaF, KF, RbF, CsF). All these compounds are ionic salts containing pentagonal planar XeF_5^- anions.

$$XeF_4 + M^+F^- \longrightarrow M^+(XeF_5^-)$$

$$(M^+ = Na^+, K^+, Rb^+, Cs^+, Me_4N^+)$$

The XeF_5^- anion (AX_5E_2 species) shows the most unusual pentagonal planar structure in which two axial positions are occupied by two lone pairs (*e.g.*, IF_7).

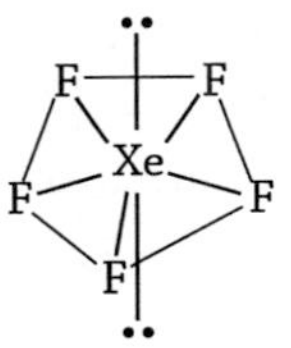

(c) Structure and bonding

1. Vibrational spectroscopy and electron diffraction data have established that XeF_4 is a planar molecule :

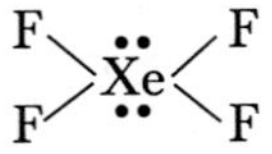

2. The valence bond representation of XeF_4 can be explained that two electrons from the $5p$ sublevel are promoted to high energy $5d$-orbitals.

Ground state configuration of Xe :

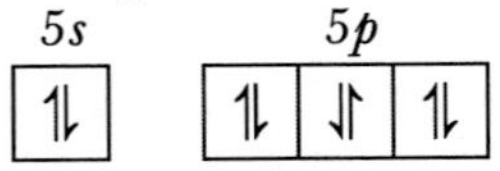

Excited state configuration of Xe :

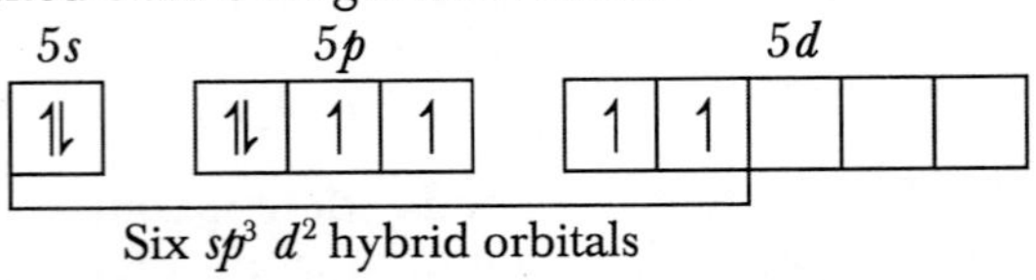

The 5*s*, three $5p$ and two $5d$ atomic orbitals of xenon hybridize to produce six sp^3d^2 hybridized orbitals. The four singly occupied hybridized orbitals are used by fluorine for bond formation to xenon. The other two orbitals contain lone pairs. The molecule has octahedral geometry with two *trans* positions occupied by lone pairs.

Molecular orbital approach Just as for XeF_2, wherein interaction of three *p*-atomic orbitals, (a full xenon $5p_z$ atomic orbital and two $F2p_z$ orbitals, one electron each) results in the formation of three centred orbitals. A total of four electrons are filled in the (σ^b) and σ^{nb} MOs. This gives F—Xe—F a single bond, yielding a bond order of 0.5 for each Xe—F bond. A second $5p$ orbital of xenon at right angle to the first can form another set of similar three-centre four electron F—Xe—F bond forming XeF_4.

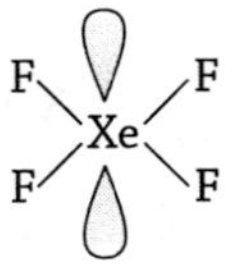

2. Xenon Oxide Difluoride, $XeOF_2$

(a) Preparation

It is prepared by the hydrolysis of XeF_4 at – 80°C.

$$XeF_4 + H_2O \xrightarrow{-80°} XeOF_2 + 2HF$$

(b) Structure

1. It has T-shaped structure.

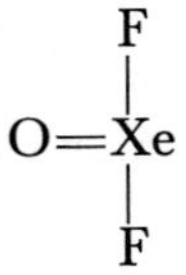

2. The valence bond structure of $XeOF_2$ may be explained if we assume that two electrons from $5p$ sublevel of xenon are promoted to $5d$ sublevel.

Ground state configuration of Xe :

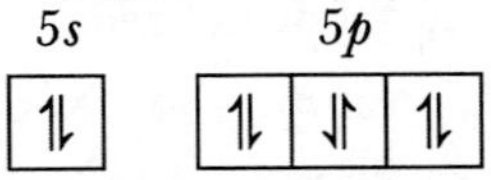

Excited state configuration of Xe

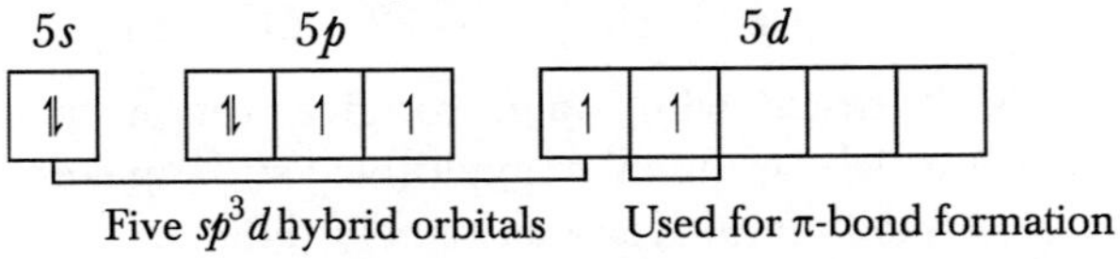

The 5*s*, three $5p$ and $5d$ orbitals of xenon hybridize to form five sp^3d hybridized orbitals. The three singly occupied orbitals are used for σ-bond formation to two fluorine atoms and one oxygen atom. The two positions of trigonal bipyramidal structure are occupied by lone pairs. One of the electrons in the $5d$ orbital which is not used in the hybridization scheme is used for π-bond formation to oxygen atom.

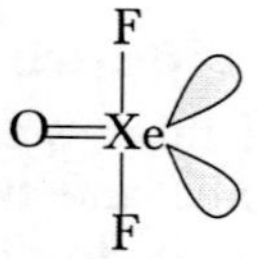

1. Xenon Hexafluoride, XeF_6

(a) Preparation

1. It is best prepared by reacting xenon and fluorine in the ratio 1 : 20 in a nickel vessel. The reaction is carried out at 300°C and at 60 atm pressure.

$$Xe + 3F_2 \xrightarrow[60\ \text{atm}]{300^\circ C} XeF_6 \quad (Xe : F_2 = 1:20)$$

2. XeF_6 may also be prepared by the oxidation of XeF_4 with O_2F_2 at temperatures below –80°C.
3. By the electric discharge of a mixture of fluorine (3 parts) and xenon (1 part) at low temperatures.

(b) Properties

1. It is a colourless solid but its vapours have greenish-yellow colour.
2. It melts at 49.5°C. It is very rapidly hydrolysed.
3. It is a stronger oxidising and fluorinating agent than both XeF_2 and XeF_4.
4. It is reduced to xenon by the action of H_2, HCl and NH_3.

$$XeF_6 + 3H_2 \longrightarrow Xe + 6HF$$
$$XeF_6 + 6HCl \longrightarrow Xe + 3Cl_2 + 6HF$$
$$XeF_6 + 8NH_3 \longrightarrow Xe + 6NH_4F + N_2$$

5. It cannot be stored in glass or quartz vessels owing to the following reactions

$$2XeF_6 + SiO_2 \longrightarrow 2XeOF_4 + SiF_4$$
$$2XeOF_4 + SiO_2 \longrightarrow 2XeO_2F_2 + SiF_4$$
$$2XeO_2F_2 + SiO_2 \longrightarrow 2XeO_3 + SiF_4$$

6. It reacts with water to give xenon trioxide which is highly explosive and makes the handling of XeF_6 extremely difficult.

$$XeF_6 + 3H_2O \longrightarrow XeO_3 + 6HF$$

7. It reacts with fluoride ion acceptors to produce $[XeF_5]^+$ species as

$$XeF_6 + PtF_5 \longrightarrow XeF_6 \cdot PtF_5 \longrightarrow [XeF_5]^+[PtF_6]^-$$
$$XeF_6 + AsF_5 \longrightarrow XeF_6 \cdot AsF_5 \longrightarrow [XeF_5]^+[AsF_6]^-$$
$$XeF_6 + SbF_5 \longrightarrow XeF_6 \cdot SbF_5 \longrightarrow [XeF_5]^+[SbF_6]^-$$
$$XeF_6 + BF_3 \longrightarrow XeF_6 \cdot BF_3 \longrightarrow [XeF_5]^+[BF_4]^-$$

The XeF_5^+ in compound $XeF_5^+PtF_6^-$ has been shown to have the expected square pyramid structure (AX_5E molecule).

8. It reacts with fluoride ion donors to produce $[XeF_8]^{2-}$ species as :

$$CsF + XeF_6 \longrightarrow CsF \cdot XeF_6 \xrightarrow{+CsF} Cs_2XeF_8 \text{ or } 2Cs^+[XeF_8]^{2-}$$
$$2NOF + XeF_6 \longrightarrow [NO]_2^+[XeF_8]^{2-}$$

(c) Structure and bonding

1. The crystal structure of XeF_6 indicates that it is generally present as $[XeF_5^+]F^-$ in the solid state. The pyramidal XeF_5^+ cations are bridged by free fluoride ions. The determination of exact structure of gaseous XeF_6 molecule has proved difficult. It is now well established that it is not a regular octahedral molecule but the arrangement of the fluorines is distorted from the regular octahedral arrangement in such a way as to suggest that the non-bonding electron pair occupies a position in the centre of one face of an octahedron so that the fluorines at the corners of this face are forced apart.

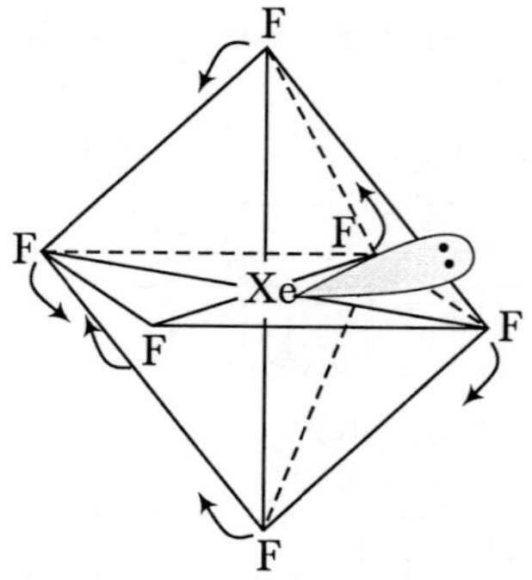

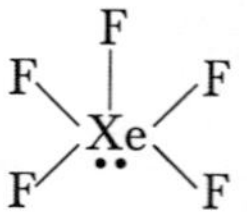

2. The valence bond description predicts pentagonal bipyramid structure of XeF_6 with one *trans* position occupied by a lone pair. It may be assumed that three electrons from the $5p$ sublevel are promoted to $5d$ sublevel as :

Ground state configuration of Xe :

5s	5p		
⇅	⇅	⇅	⇅

Excited state configuration of Xe :

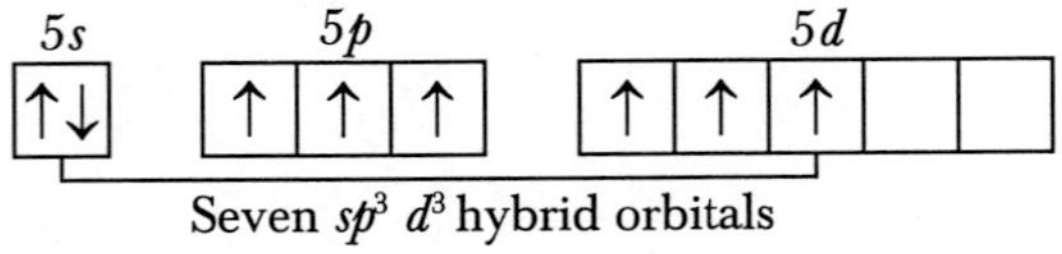

The 5*s*, three 5*p* and three 5*d*-orbitals hybridize to produce seven sp^3d^3 hybrid orbitals. The singly occupied orbitals are used for bond formation to six fluorine atoms. The seventh orbital contains a lone pair.

Molecular orbital approach In continuation of our build up of XeF_2 and XeF_4, if we use the third 5*p* atomic orbital of xenon (at 90° to the other two 5*p* orbitals of xenon), it may form a third set of three-centre bonds forming XeF_6. The observed structure of XeF_6 is quite complex; a distorted octahedron with a lone pair moving from one face to another and distorting the F—Xe—F angle of each face.

Strictly speaking both valence bond and molecular orbital approaches fail to predict the true structure of XeF_6. However, the VSEPR model gives better description than the 3c-4*e* molecular orbital approach.

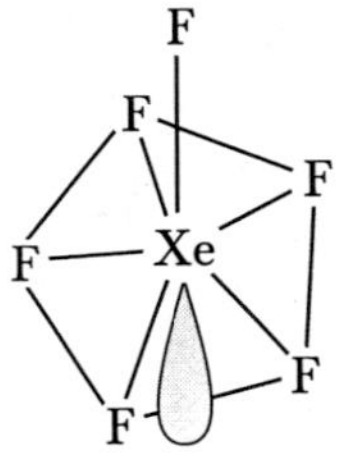

Xenon Oxide Tetrafluoride, $XeOF_4$

(a) Preparation

1. It may be prepared by the partial hydrolysis of XeF_6.

$$XeF_6 + H_2O \longrightarrow XeOF_4 + 2HF$$

2. It can be prepared by the reaction of SiO_2 with XeF_6.

$$2XeF_6 + SiO_2 \longrightarrow 2XeOF_4 + SiF_4$$

3. It can also be prepared by heating a mixture of xenon (1 part) and fluorine (4 parts) with large excess of oxygen around 230°C. The product $XeOF_4$ is purified by vacuum distillation.

(b) Properties

1. It is a colourless substance which melts at –46°C.
2. It reacts with water or SiO_2 to give XeO_2F_2 and XeO_3.

$$XeOF_4 + H_2O \longrightarrow XeO_2F_2 + 2HF$$
$$XeO_2F_2 + H_2O \longrightarrow XeO_3 + 2HF$$
$$2XeOF_4 + SiO_2 \longrightarrow 2XeO_2F_2 + SiF_4$$
$$2XeO_2F_2 + SiO_2 \longrightarrow 2XeO_3 + SiF_4$$

3. It is reduced by hydrogen gas to xenon.

$$XeOF_4 + 3H_2 \longrightarrow Xe + H_2O + 4HF$$

4. It reacts with F^- ion acceptors to form $XeOF_3^+$ cation.

$$\underset{\text{(Excess)}}{XeOF_4} + SbF_5 \longrightarrow XeOF_3^+SbF_6^-$$
$$XeOF_4 + 2SbF_5 \longrightarrow XeOF_3^+Sb_2F_{11}^-$$

The $XeOF_3^+$ cation exhibits an AX_4E type structure as shown below in which the lone pair, the oxygen atom and a fluorine atom occupy the equatorial positions of a trigonal bipyramid and two fluorine atoms occupy the axial positions, consistent with the VSEPR theory.

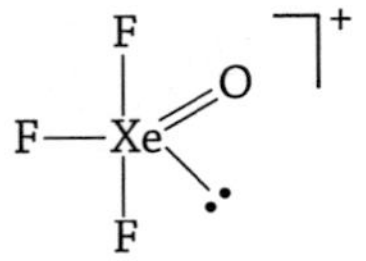

5. It reacts with NOF (nitrosyl fluoride) to yield a crystalline compound $NO^+(XeOF_5^-)$.

The $XeOF_5^-$ ion has a pentagonal-pyramidal structure with the oxygen atom in the apical position.

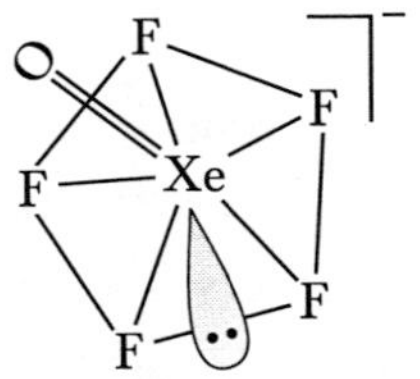

The xenon atom is slightly above the plane of the five fluorine atoms.

(c) Structure and bonding

1. The structure of molecular $XeOF_4$ is square pyramid.

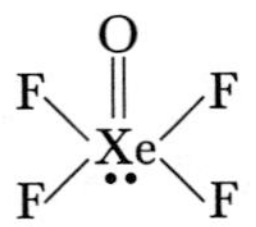

2. The valence bond description of $XeOF_4$ may be explained if we assume that three *p* electrons are promoted to the 5*d* sublevel.

Ground state configuration of Xe

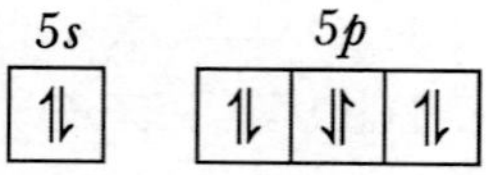

Excited state configuration of Xe

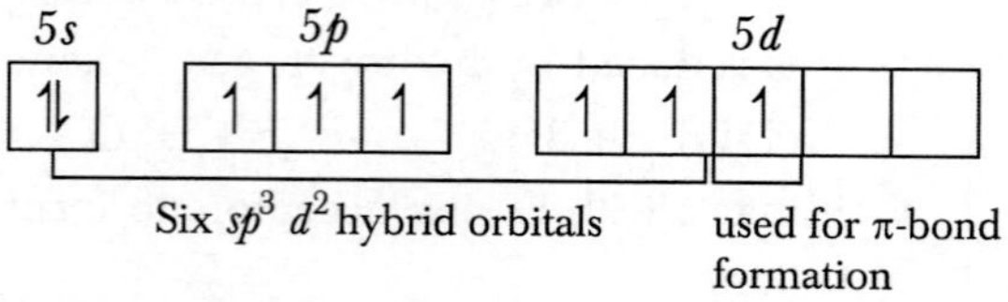

The 5s, three 5p and two 5d atomic orbitals hybridize to give six sp^3d^2 hybrid orbitals. The five singly occupied orbitals are used for σ-bond formation to four fluorine and one oxygen atom. The sixth hybrid orbital is occupied by the lone pair. The single electron in a d-orbital is used for π-bond formation to oxygen atom. This explains the required geometry of $XeOF_4$.

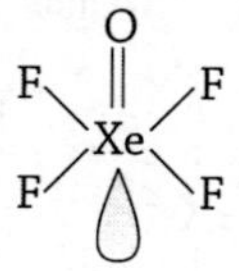

3. Xenon Dioxide Difluoride, XeO_2F_2

(a) Preparation

It is prepared by mixing XeO_3 and $XeOF_4$ at low temperatures (–78°C). The product is purified by fractional distillation.

(b) Properties

1. It is a colourless solid which melts at 30°C.
2. It is easily hydrolysed to give XeO_3.

$$XeO_2F_2 + H_2O \longrightarrow XeO_3 + 2HF$$

3. It slowly decomposes to give XeF_2 and O_2, *i.e.,* it is thermodynamically unstable.

$$XeO_2F_2 \longrightarrow XeF_2 + O_2$$

4. Reaction of XeO_2F_2 with SbF_5 in HF yields a white solid on evacuation which corresponds to $XeO_2F^+Sb_2F_{11}^-$.

$$XeO_2F_2 + 2SbF_5 \longrightarrow XeO_2F^+Sb_2F_{11}^-$$

This compound is unstable at room temperature and slowly decomposes to give $XeF^+\ Sb_2F_{11}^-$ and oxygen.

The XeO_2F^+ cation, according to VSEPR theory shows tetrahedral structure with one position occupied by a lone pair.

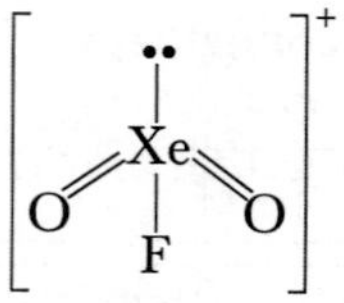

(c) Structure and bonding

1. XeO_2F_2 has a see-saw structure.
2. The valence bond structure suggests trigonal bipyramid geometry with one equatorial position occupied by a lone pair.

Ground state configuration of Xe

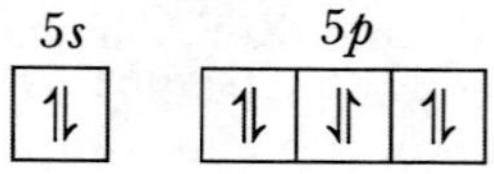

Excited state configuration of Xe

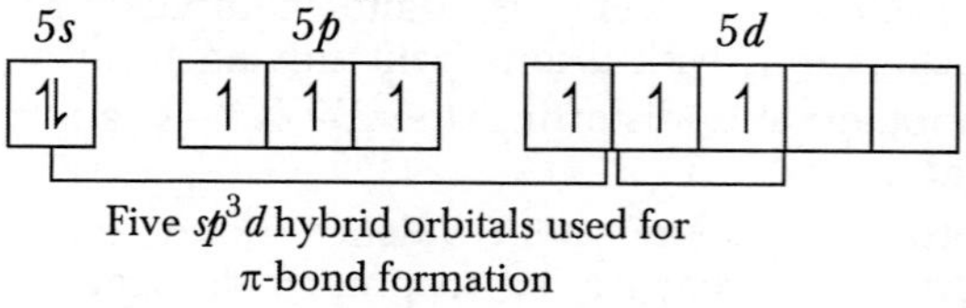

The three 5p electrons are promoted to higher energy 5d sublevel. The 5s, three 5p and one 5d orbitals hybridize to give five sp^3d hybrid orbitals. The four singly occupied orbitals are used for bond formation to two fluorine and two oxygen atoms. The fifth hybrid orbital contains the lone pair. The other two 5d-electrons of xenon which do not take part in the hybridization scheme are involved in π-bond formation to two oxygen atoms. The structure is as shown.

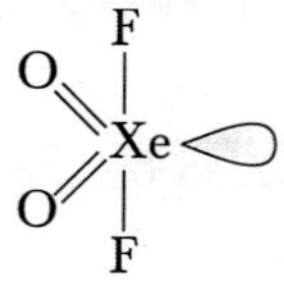

4. Xenon Trioxide, XeO_3

(a) Preparation

It is prepared by the hydrolysis of XeF_6 and XeF_4. Great care is to be taken during its preparation as it is highly explosive.

$$XeF_6 + 3H_2O \longrightarrow XeO_3 + 6HF$$

$$3XeF_4 + 6H_2O \longrightarrow 2\,XeO_3 + 12HF + Xe$$

(b) Properties

1. It is a colourless solid.
2. It is a highly explosive substance.

$$XeO_3(s) \longrightarrow Xe + \frac{3}{2}O_2 + 402\ \text{kJ}$$

(c) Structure

1. The molecule is pyramidal.
2. The valence bond description suggests xenon to acquire sp^3 hybridization and one of the hybrid orbital contains a lone pair.

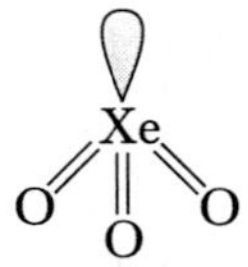

Example 3. *What are the geometries and hybridization of central atom in the following compounds?*
(i) XeF_2, *(ii)* XeF_4, *(iii)* XeF_6, *(iv)* $XeOF_2$,
(v) $XeOF_4$, *(iv)* XeO_3, *(vii)* XeO_2F_2.

Sol. (i) Linear (sp^3d), (ii) Square planar (sp^3d^2), (iii) Distorted octahedron (sp^3d^3), (iv) T-shaped (sp^3d), (v) Square pyramid (sp^3d^2), (vi) Pyramidal (sp^3), (vii) See-saw (sp^3d).

Table 7.4 **Molecular Shapes of Some Noble Gas Compounds in Terms of VSEPR Theory**

Molecule	Shape	Description
1. XeF_2	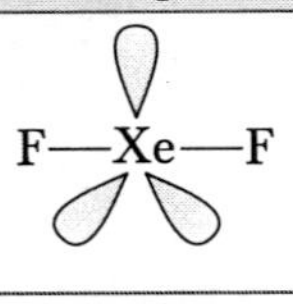	**Linear;** three non-bonding electron pairs at the points of an equilateral triangle.
2. XeF_4	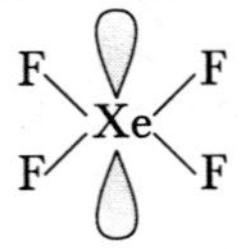	**Square planar;** two non-bonding electron pairs one above and one below the plane of the molecule.
3. XeF_6	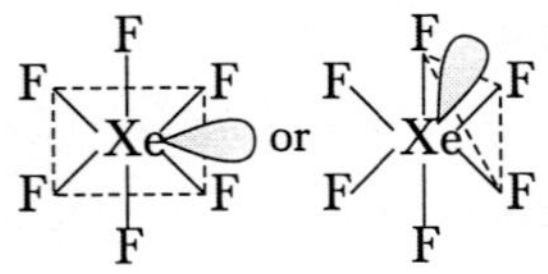	**Distorted octahedron;** one non-bonding electron pair either at the centre of a face or the midpoint of an edge.
4. $XeOF_4$	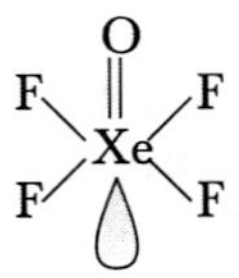	**Square pyramidal;** one non-bonding electron pair coming out from the base of the pyramid.
5. $XeOF_2$	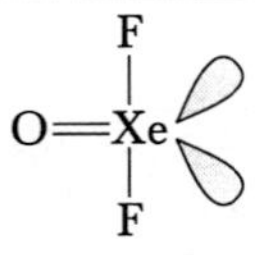	**T-shaped;** two non-bonding electron pairs pointing towards the corners of an equilateral triangle.
6. XeO_2F_2	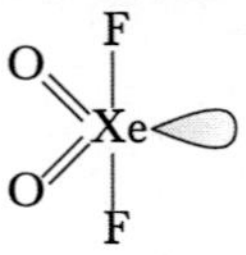	**See-saw;** one non-bonding electron pair pointing towards the corner of an equilateral triangle.
7. XeO_3	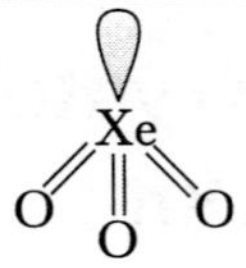	**Trigonal pyramidal;** one non-bonding electron pair pointing out from the apex of the pyramid.
8. XeO_4	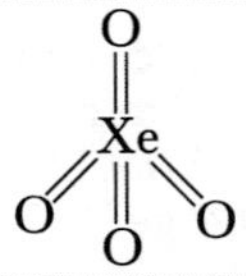	**Tetrahedron**
9. XeF_5^-	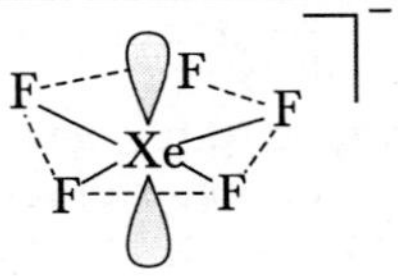	**Pentagonal planar;** two non-bonding electron pairs one above the plane and the other below the plane.

Xenon Octafluoride, XeF_8

Although there have been some reports about the existence of XeF_8, yet these have not been confirmed by more recent work. Coulson has suggested that XeF_8 may have the following shape in which two fluorine atoms in XeF_6 are replaced by fluorine molecules.

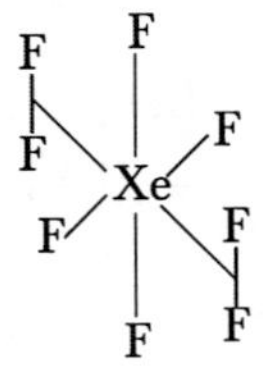

Xenon Tetroxide, XeO_4

(a) Preparation

It is prepared by the action of conc. H_2SO_4 on sodium or barium xenate (Na_4XeO_6, Ba_2XeO_6) at room temperature. It may be purified by vacuum sublimation at –78°C.

$$XeO_6^{4-} + 4H^+ \longrightarrow H_4XeO_6 \xrightarrow{-2H_2O} XeO_4$$

(b) Properties

It is quite unstable and decomposes to xenon and oxygen. It is very explosive and explodes even at –40°C as

$$XeO_2(g) \longrightarrow Xe + 2O_2 + 643 \text{ kJ}$$

(c) **Structure**

The molecule is tetrahedral.

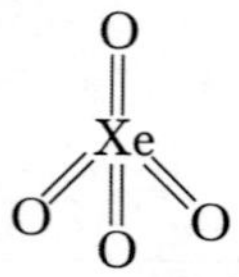

Compounds of Krypton

Krypton Difluoride, KrF_2

(a) **Preparation**

It is prepared by irradiating a mixture of krypton and fluorine at low temperature (–193°C). Irradiation may be carried out by γ-rays, ultra-violet light, or by electric discharge.

$$Kr + F_2 \xrightarrow[-193°C]{UV} KrF_2$$

In the above reaction, krypton acts as a reducing agent because the oxidation number of krypton increases from zero (in krypton) to +2 (in KrF_2).

(b) **Properties**

1. It is a colourless solid.
2. It is a powerful oxidizing and fluorinating agent.
3. It is decomposed by water.
$$KrF_2 + H_2O \longrightarrow Kr + \tfrac{1}{2}O_2 + 2HF$$
4. It forms addition compounds with antimony pentafluoride.
$$KrF_2 + SbF_5 \longrightarrow KrF_2 \cdot SbF_5 \longrightarrow KrF^+ \cdot SbF_6^-$$
$$KrF_2 + 2SbF_5 \longrightarrow KrF_2 \cdot 2SbF_5 \longrightarrow KrF^+ \cdot Sb_2F_{11}^-$$
$$2KrF_2 + SbF_5 \longrightarrow 2KrF_2 \cdot SbF_5 \longrightarrow Kr_2F_3^+ \cdot SbF_6^-$$
Structure of these compounds are similar to those of analogous xenon compounds discussed earlier.
5. It has not been possible to isolate any krypton-oxygen compound. Krypton difluoride, KrF_2 has also proved to be an extremely powerful fluorinating agent. It is used to prepare metal fluorides in extremely (unusually) high oxidation states.
$$2Au + 7KrF_2 \longrightarrow 2KrF^+ AuF_6^- + 5Kr + F_2$$
$$KrF^+ AuF_6^- \xrightarrow{60°} AuF_5 + Kr + F_2$$

(c) **Structure**

Just like XeF_2, the molecule of KrF_2 is linear in shape.

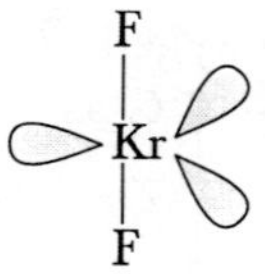

Example 4. *Write equations for the following reactions :*

(i) Action of water on XeO_2F_2
(ii) Action of NaF on XeF_6
(iii) Action of AsF_5 *on* KrF_2
(iv) Action of water on XeF_4
(v) Action of SiO_2 *on* XeO_2F_2

Sol. (i) $XeO_2F_2 + H_2O \longrightarrow XeO_3 + 2HF$

(ii) $XeF_6 + 2NaF \longrightarrow Na_2XeF_8$

(iii) $KrF_2 + 2AsF_5 \longrightarrow KrF^+ + As_2F_{11}^-$

(iv) $XeF_4 + H_2O \xrightarrow{-80°C} XeOF_2 + 2HF$

(v) $2XeO_2F_2 + SiO_2 \longrightarrow 2XeO_3 + SiF_4$

Uses of Nobel Gases

The noble gases are put to a variety of uses which are described below :

Uses of Helium

1. Helium being lighter and inflammable is used for filling air ships, weather balloons etc.
2. Liquid He is used as cryogenic fluid to provide low temperature for studying a number of phenomenon.
3. A mixture of He and O_2 is used by deep sea divers for respiration.

Uses of Neon

1. It is used in neon glow lamps (neon tubes) used for advertising purpose. If Hg vapours are mixed with neon, a blue or green glow is obtained.
2. It has a remarkable property of carrying exceedingly high electric currents even under high voltage. So it is used in safety devices for protecting electrical instruments such as volatmeters, relays etc., from high voltages.

Uses of Argon

1. It is used for filling incandescent metal filament electric bulbs. Its action there is to prevent the volatilisation of the tungsten filament at the high temperature of the lamp.
2. It is used in welding and other operations which require absence of nitrogen as well as a non-oxidising atmosphere.

Clathrates

According to Powell, clathrate compounds consist of atoms or molecules of one substance called the 'guest' held in the crystalline cages formed by the molecules of a second substance called the 'host'.

The only type of interaction in these "cage compounds" is the relatively weak van der Waals' forces and there is no chemical bonding. A simple clathrate may be designated by a maximum composition formula *n*H*m*G where, H and G are host and guest components, respectively; *n* is the number of host molecules per unit cage cell and *m* is the maximum number of guest molecules that can be held in a single cage. It is not necessary that all the cavities in the host structure are filled. As a result, the clathrates are normally non-stoichiometric compounds.

Essential Conditions for Clathrate Formation

(a) Presence of cavities of appropriate size in the crystal lattice of the 'host'.

(b) Size of the 'guest' particle should be such as to fit in the cavities of the 'host' without bringing any atoms closer together than which correspond to the van der Waals' radii of the atoms.

Stability of Clathrate Compounds

Clathrate compounds once formed are quite stable due to the following reasons :

(a) The 'guest' molecules tightly fit in the cavities of the 'host' molecules.

(b) The 'guest' molecules within the cages are at a minimum potential energy.

The 'guest' can escape from the 'host' only when the forces holding the molecular cages together are overcome. This can be achieved by the following two methods :

(i) By heating the crystals.

(ii) By dissolving them in a suitable solvent such as alcohol.

Preparation of Clathrates

Clathrate compounds of argon, krypton and xenon have been isolated by locking up these gases in the cages of water, phenol or quinol.

However, clathrate compounds of helium and neon have not yet been prepared because helium atoms are thought to be too small and difficult to deform or polarize as required by van der Waals' bonding to be imprisoned in the cages. The neon is border-line and its clathrate could possibly be formed at pressures in excess of 160 atm. It is predicted that the clathrate of neon, if formed, the neon atoms (being so small) will diffuse through the crystal from one cavity to another.

Types of Clathrates

(i) Gas hydrates

Clathrates of argon, krypton and xenon in which water forms the cage, are known as "gas hydrates". These gas hydrates have been prepared by solidifying water in presence of these noble gases. The general formula of the gas hydrates is **$5.75\ H_2O \cdot G$ where, G = Ar, Kr or Xe.**

The stability of 'gas hydrates' increases as the atomic number of the 'guest' atom increases. In noble gas hydrates the water molecules are linked to one another by hydrogen bonds leaving roughly spherical voids which are occupied by gas atoms.

(ii) Quinol clathrates

Clathrates of argon, krypton and xenon have been isolated by dissolving any one of these in aqueous saturated solution of quinol, under pressure of 19-40 atm followed by slow cooling.

These clathrates are stable and can be stored for years together. It may be pointed out that quinol molecules which form the cavities are held amongst themselves by hydrogen bonds.

(iii) Phenol and β-hydroquinone clathrates

Clathrates of phenol as well as β-hydroquinone with argon, krypton and xenon have been prepared by dissolving any one of these gases in phenol or β-hydroquinone followed by slow crystallization. These clathrates are also quite stable. The usual composition of the β-hydroquinone clathrates is $G \cdot 3\beta\ C_6H_4(OH)_2$ where, G is Ar, Kr or Xe.

Uses of Clathrates

(i) In the separation of noble gases. For example, neon can be separated from argon, krypton and xenon because neon is the only gas that does not form clathrates with quinol.

(ii) Krypton-85 clathrate provides a safe and useful source of beta radiations which are useful for measuring thickness of gauges.

(iii) Xenon-133 clathrate provides a compact source for gamma radiations.

(iv) The clathrates are a convenient form of handling, processing and shipping of rare gas isotopes.

(v) Clathrates play an important role in some physiological actions, *e.g.*, it is thought that the anaesthetic action of xenon and many other anaesthetics is due to aqueous clathrate formation in physiologically strategic spots. When the anaesthetic is no longer administered, the clathrate equilibrium is destroyed, the clathrates decompose and the consciousness returns.

Exercise 1
(For Part 'B')

1. XeF_2 forms .... with AsF_5.
(a) XeF^+ cation and AsF_4^+
(b) XeF_2^- anion and AsF_4^+
(c) AsF_4^+ cation and AsF_4^-
(d) XeF^+ cation and AsF_6^- anion

2. Which is the best fluorinating agent?
(a) XeF_2 (b) XeF_4
(c) XeF_6 (d) XeO_2F_2

3. XeF_6 is conducting in the presence of
(a) HF (b) BF_3
(c) RbF (d) All of these

4. Xenon fluorides act as fluoride acceptor with
(a) CsF (b) RbF
(c) Both (a) and (b) (d) None of these

5. Xenon fluorides act as fluoride donor with
(a) HF (b) BF_3
(c) AsF_5 (d) All of these

6. Inert atmosphere for welding of metals is obtained by
(a) O_2, N_2 (b) N_2, He
(c) Ar, He (d) Ar, N_2

7. Most abundant noble gas in air is
(a) He (b) Ne
(c) Rn (d) Ar

8. Helium accumulates in the earth's crust through
(a) thermonuclear reactions
(b) α-decay of radioactive element
(c) β-decay of radioactive element
(d) γ-decay of radioactive element

9. Second most abundant element in the universe (after hydrogen) is
(a) He (b) Ne
(c) Al (d) Fe

10. Thermal stability of hydrates of group 18 elements
(a) increases down the group
(b) decreases down the group
(c) remains unchanged
(d) first increase up to Ar than decreases

11. Hydrates of helium and neon have not been prepared because of
(a) small size (b) low boiling point
(c) low polarisability (d) All of these

12. For advertisement the coloured discharged tubes contain
(a) He (b) Ne
(c) Ar (d) Kr

13. Which one of the following is square planar?
(a) XeF_4 (b) XeO_4
(c) XeO_3F (d) XeO_3F_2

14. The gas not absorbed by coconut charcoal is
(a) He (b) Ne
(c) Ar (d) Kr

15. Which of the following gas mixture is used by the divers inside the sea?
(a) $O_2 + N_2$ (b) $O_2 + He$
(c) $O_2 + Ar$ (d) $O_2 + Xe$

16. Neon lamps are used in botanical gardens and in green houses as they
(a) provide better light
(b) provides oxygen
(c) stimulate growth of plants
(d) None of the above

17. Select the correct statement(s).
(a) Ar, Kr and Xe form clathrate
(b) Helium can diffuse through rubber, PVC and even glass
(c) Helium has the lowest melting point and boiling point
(d) All of the above are correct

18. End-product of the hydrolysis of XeF_6 is
(a) XeO_3 (b) XeO_3^- (c) XeF_4O (d) XeF_2O_2

19. Which of the following is not known?
(a) XeF_4 (b) XeF_6
(c) KrF_6 (d) Cs_2XeF_6

20. A rare gas that was detected in the sun before its discovery on earth is
(a) He (b) Ne
(c) Ar (d) Kr

21. Which practical is/are supposed to be correct?
(a) Storing of NaOH in Al vessel
(b) Storing of HNO_3 in Al vessel
(c) Storing of HF in glass or quartz apparatus
(d) Preparation of XeF_6 in glass of quartz apparatus

22. Which of the statements on noble gases is false?
(a) They are monoatomic in nature
(b) They are completely insoluble in H_2O
(c) Their electron affinity are almost zero
(d) Very weak forces are involved in the liquefaction

23. Which one of the statements regarding discovery of noble gases is false?
(a) Rayleigh discovered a new element krypton in 1898
(b) In 1785, Henry Cavendish nearly missed the discovery of argon

(c) In 1868, helium was first discovered in the solar spectrum
(d) Argon was discovered simultaneously by Rayleigh and Ramsay and presented their work in a joint paper in 1895

24. The main constituents of the sun are
(a) H_2 and He (b) H_2 and Xe
(c) H_2 and Ar (d) Ar and Xe

25. Which one of the statements on clathrate compounds is false?
(a) Clathrates are normally stoichiometric compounds
(b) Guest molecule should be a bit smaller than the host cavity
(c) They are formed only when a cavity of appropriate size is available in the host
(d) They are cage compounds with weak van der Waals' interactions operating in them

26. Which noble gas is not well known to form clathrate compound?
(a) Ne (b) Ar (c) Kr (d) Xe

27. Shape of XeF_2 is
(a) linear (b) triangular
(c) tetrahedral (d) octahedral

28. Which one of the molecules is sp^3d hybridized?
(a) XeO_3 (b) $XeOF_2$ (c) $XeOF_4$ (d) XeF_4

29. $XeOF_4$ cannot be prepared by
(a) partial hydrolysis of XeF_6
(b) reaction of XeO_2F_2 in excess of F_2
(c) reaction of XeF_6 with SiO_2
(d) reaction of Xe and F_2 (1 : 4) in excess of O_2

30. Which of the following is the first chemical compound of the noble gases?
(a) $Xe[PtF_6]$ (b) $Rn[PtF_6]$
(c) $Ar[PtF_6]$ (d) $Kr[PtF_6]$

31. The first chemical compound of the noble gases was reported by
(a) Moissan (b) Ramsay
(c) N. Bartlett (d) None of these

32. Which of the following inert gas is most reactive?
(a) Ar (b) Kr (c) Xe (d) Rn

33. Which of the following nobel gases forms the largest number of compounds?
(a) Rn (b) Xe (c) Kr (d) Ar

34. Xenon forms the compounds with the following elements/groups
(a) F, O (b) $OSeF_5$
(c) $OTeF_5$ (d) All of these

35. Xenon exhibit +8 oxidation state in the following compound(s)
(a) XeF_8 (b) XeO_4
(c) Both (a) and (b) (d) None of these

36. XeF_2 is prepared quantitatively by phososynthesis on exposing to sunlight mixtures of xenon with the following at −118°C
(a) OF_2 (b) excess of O_2F_2
(c) Both (a) and (b) (d) None of these

37. Which of the following xenon-fluoride has almost the lowest bond energy of Xe–F bond?
(a) XeF_2 (b) XeF_4
(c) XeF_6 (d) None of these

38. XeF_2 is an
(a) oxidising agent only
(b) fluorinating agent only
(c) both oxidising and fluorinating agent
(d) None of the above

39. Structure of XeF_2 is represented as
(a) Xe^{2+}, F^{2-}
(b) $Xe^{+}, \frac{1}{2}F_2^{-}$
(c) $[XeF]^{+}F^{-}$
(d) It has 2 non-bonding pair of electron

40. XeF_2 according to VSEPR theory has
(a) linear geometry with 3 non-bonding pair of electrons
(b) linear geometry with 2 non-bonding pair of electrons
(c) distorted trigonal planar geometry with 2 non-bonding pair of electrons
(d) distorted trigonal planar geometry with 3 non-bonding pair of electrons

41. According to MOT XeF_2 is a
(a) $2c-2e$ bond (b) $3c-4e$ bond
(c) $2c-3e$ bond (d) $3c-2e$ bond

42. XeF_4 is prepared by
(a) heating Xe and F_2 in 1:4 ratio at 5-6 atm. pressure
(b) heating Xe and F_2 in 1:1 ratio at 5-6 atm. pressure
(c) heating Xe and F_2 in 1:5 ratio at 5-6 atm. pressure
(d) heating Xe and F_2 in 1:20 ratio at 5-6 atm. pressure

43. XeF_4 is prepared by passing electric discharge at −80°C containing
(a) Xe and F_2 in 1:1 ratio
(b) Xe and F_2 in 1:5 ratio
(c) Xe and F_2 in 1:2 ratio
(d) Xe and F_2 in 1:4 ratio

44. XeF_4 reacts with $(CH_3)_4N^+F^-$ to form
(a) $[XeF_3]^+$ (b) $[XeF_2]^+$ (c) $[XeF_5]^-$ (d) $[XeF_7]^-$

45. Shape of $[XeF_5]^-$ is
(a) pentagonal planar with 2 axial positions occupied by lone pair
(b) trigonal pyramidal with no lone pair
(c) pentagonal bipyramidal with 2 axial poisitions occupied by lone pair
(d) square pyramidal with no lone pair

46. XeF_6 is prepared by reacting Xe and F_2 in
(a) 1 : 5 ratio (b) 1 : 10 ratio
(c) 1 : 20 ratio (d) 1 : 200 ratio

47. XeF_6 reacts with glass to form
(a) $XeOF_4$ (b) XeO_3
(c) XeO_2F_2 (d) All of these

48. Partial hydrolysis of XeF_6 (with two moles water) yields
(a) XeO_3 (b) $XeOF_4$ (c) XeO_2F_2 (d) $XeOF_2$

49. $XeOF_4$ has
(a) octahedral geometry (b) square pyramidal
(c) trigonal bipyramidal (d) capped octahedron

50. The geometry of $XeOF_5^-$ ion is
(a) trigonal pyramidal (b) tetrahedral
(c) pentagonal pyramidal (d) trigonal bipyramidal

51. Hybridization of Xe in $XeOF_4$ is
(a) sp^3d (b) sp^3d^2 (c) sp^3d^3 (d) sp^3

52. Melting point of XeO_2F_2 is
(a) 15°C (b) 30°C (c) 45° (d) 60°C

53. XeO_3 and $XeOF_4$ mixes at low temperature to form
(a) $XeOF_2$ (b) XeF_2
(c) XeO_2F_2 (d) XeF_4

54. XeO_2F_2 is hydrolysed to give
(a) $XeOF_2 + HF$ (b) $XeO_2F^+ + HF$
(c) $XeO_3 + HF$ (d) $XeO_3 + XeF_2 + HF$

55. XeO_2F_2 reacts with SbF_5 in HF to yield
(a) $[XeF_5]^+ [SbF_6]^-$ (b) $[XeOF_3]^+ [SbF_6]^-$
(c) $[XeOF_3^+][Sb_2F_{11}]^-$ (d) $[XeO_2F]^+ [Sb_2F_{11}]^-$

56. $[XeO_2F]^+$ cation is having a
(a) trigonal planar geometry
(b) tetrahedral geometry
(c) pyramidal geometry
(d) square planar geometry

57. XeO_2F_2 has
(a) sp^3d^3 hybridisation (b) sp^3d^2 hybridisation
(c) sp^3d hybridisation (d) d^2sp^3 hybridisation

58. Irradiation of mixture of krypton and F_2 at low temperature (– 193°C) with γ rays, UV lights results in
(a) KrF_6 (b) KrF_4
(c) $Kr + \frac{1}{2}O_2 + HF$ (d) KrF_2

59. Clathrates of argon, krypton and xenon in which water forms the cage, are known as
(a) gas hydrates (b) liquid hydrates
(c) solid hydrates (d) coordinate hydrates

60. The general formula of the gas hydrates is (where, G = Ar, Kr or Xe)
(a) $7.55\ H_2O \cdot G$ (b) $5.05\ H_2O \cdot G$
(c) $5.75\ H_2O \cdot G$ (d) $7.57\ H_2O \cdot G$

61. The stability of 'gas hydrates' increases as the atomic number of the 'guest' atom
(a) increases (b) decreases
(c) Both (a) and (b) (d) None of these

62. The usual composition of the β-hydroquinone clathrates is
(where G = Ar, Kr or Xe)
(a) $G \cdot 3\beta\ C_6H_4(OH)_2$ (b) $G \cdot 5\beta\ C_6H_4(OH)_2$
(c) $G \cdot 7C_6H_4(OH)_2$ (d) $G \cdot 3\beta\ C_6H_5OH$

Exercise 2
(For Part 'C')

1. Basic character of fluorides increases in the order
(a) $XeF_2 < XeF_4 < XeF_6$ (b) $XeF_6 < XeF_4 < XeF_2$
(c) $XeF_4 < XeF_2 < XeF_6$ (d) $XeF_2 = XeF_4 = XeF_6$

2. Which is the most basic fluoride?
(a) XeF_2
(b) XeF_4
(c) XeF_6
(d) None is basic, all are acids

3. Which have distorted geometry based on VSEPR model?
(a) NH_3, SO_2, H_2O (b) XeF_2, XeF_4, XeO_3
(c) $XeOF_2, XeO_3, XeF_2$ (d) All of these

4. The $[XeF]^+$ ions are attached to anion $[AsF_6]^-$
(a) with a linear F-bridge
(b) with H-bond
(c) with an angular F-bridge
(d) with tetrahedral F-bridge

5. Match Column I with Column II and select the correct answer using the codes given below the list.

	Column I		Column II
A.	XeF_4	1.	Distorted octahedral
B.	XeF_6	2.	Tetrahedral
C.	XeO_3	3.	Square planar
D.	XeO_4	4.	Pyramidal

Codes

	A	B	C	D
(a)	1	2	3	4
(b)	4	1	2	3
(c)	3	1	4	2
(d)	2	3	1	4

6. Consider the following transformations :

I. $XeF_6 + NaF \longrightarrow Na^+[XeF_7]^-$
II. $2PCl_5(s) \longrightarrow [PCl_4]^+ [PCl_6]^-$
III. $[Al(H_2O)_6]^{3+} + H_2O \longrightarrow [Al(H_2O)_5OH]^{2+} + H_3O^+$

Possible transformations are

(a) I, II (b) II, III
(c) I, III (d) I, II, III

7. When water is allowed to freeze in the presence of Ar, Kr or Xe under pressure then

(a) these are called noble gas hydrates
(b) atoms of noble gas (G) trapped in the crystal lattice of ice giving clathrates corresponding to the composition $8G \cdot 26H_2O$
(c) Both (a) and (b)
(d) None of the above

8. Consider the following properties of the noble gases :

I. They readily form compounds which are colourless.
II. They generally do not form ionic compounds.
III. They have variable oxidation states in their compounds.
IV. They generally do not form covalent compounds.

Select the correct properties.

(a) I (b) I, III
(c) II, III (d) I, II, III

9. According to the Lux-Flood definition XeF_6 behaves as

(a) a base
(b) an oxidising agent
(c) an acid (oxide ion acceptor)
(d) a reducing agent

10. Oxidising agent(s) is/are

(a) XeF_2 (b) XeF_4 (c) XeF_6 (d) $XeOF_4$

11. Which is/are Lewis acid as well as Lewis base (amphoteric)?

(a) XeF_2 (b) XeF_4 (c) XeF_6 (d) XeF_6^{2-}

12. Select the correct statement(s) about XeF_4.

(a) They are thermodynamically stable.
(b) They are exothermic compounds.
(c) Xe—F bond energy is very high.
(d) They are endothermic compounds.

13. Helium is used

(a) as a substituent for nitrogen in the breathing gas for deep sea divers
(b) as a refrigerant (in liquid form) in low-temperature physics
(c) in fluorescent tubes
(d) in radiation therapy

14. Select the correct statement(s).

(a) The noble gases are present to the extent of about 1% in the earth's atmosphere, the chief component being argon.
(b) Helium is the second most abundant element in the universe after hydrogen.
(c) There are two stable isotopes of helium ${}^3_2He$, ${}^4_2He$.
(d) ${}^4_2He$ is formed by thermonuclear fusion reaction in stars.

15. Which of the following statements (s) is/are true about noble gases?

(i) They have high ionisation energies.
(ii) Their electron affinities are almost zero.
(iii) They have zero valency.

(a) (i) and (ii) only (b) (ii) and (iii) only
(c) (i) and (iii) only (d) All of these are correct

16. Xenon forms various compounds with the following elements/groups.

(i) F (ii) O (iii) $OTeF_5$ (iv) Br

(a) (i), (ii) and (iii) (b) (iii) (iv) and (v)
(c) (i), (ii) and (iv) (d) (i), (iii) and (v)

17. Match the following.

	Column A (Compounds)		Column B (Valency of xenon)
A.	XeF_2	(i)	+ 2
B.	XeF_4	(ii)	+ 6
C.	XeF_6	(iii)	+ 4
D.	XeF_8	(iv)	+ 8

Codes

	A	B	C	D
(a)	(i)	(ii)	(iii)	(iv)
(b)	(i)	(iii)	(ii)	(iv)
(c)	(ii)	(iii)	(iv)	(i)
(d)	(iv)	(iii)	(ii)	(i)

18. The simplest generalisation seems to be that any process which exposes xenon to fluorine atoms will result in the production of xenon fluorides. The atomic fluorine may be generated by the following method (s).

(i) Heating F_2 gas
(ii) Electric discharge
(iii) Ionisation radiation

(a) (i) and (ii) only (b) (i) and (iii) only
(c) (ii) and (iii) only (d) (i), (ii) and (iii)

19. Which of the following reaction (s) is/are correct?

(i) $XeF_2 + 2HCl \longrightarrow Xe\uparrow + Cl_2 + 2HF$
(ii) $XeF_2 + HSO_3F \longrightarrow FSO_3F + HF$
(iii) $XeF_2 + 2SO_3 \longrightarrow Xe\uparrow + S_2O_6F_2$
(iv) $XeF_2 + 2SO_3 \longrightarrow Xe\uparrow + S_2O_4F_2 + O_2\uparrow$

(a) (i), (ii) and (iii) (b) (ii), (iii) and (iv)
(c) (i), (ii) and (iv) (d) (i), (iii) and (iv)

20. XeF_2 reacts with iodine in the presence of fluoride ion acceptor (like BF_3) to form the following compound.

(a) IF (b) IF_3
(c) Both (a) and (b) (d) None of these

21. The compound $XeF_2 \cdot 2SbF_5$ contains the following species

(i) XeF^+ (ii) $Sb_2F_{11}^-$
(iii) Xe^+ (iv) SbF_{12}^-

(a) only (i) (b) only (ii)
(c) both (i) and (ii) (d) both (iii) and (iv)

22. The compound $2XeF_2 \cdot AsF_5$ contain the following species

(i) XeF^+ (ii) $As_2F_{11}^-$
(iii) $[Xe_2F_3]^+$ (iv) $[AsF_6]^-$
(v) $[Xe_2F_4]^+$ (vi) $[AsF_5]^-$

(a) (i), (iii) and (iv) (b) (iii) and (iv) only
(c) (i) and (ii) only (d) (ii), (iv) and (v) only

23. Which of the following is true about XeF_4?

(i) It is reduced by H_2 gas to form Xe
(ii) It is reduced by H_2 to form XeF_2
(iii) It is less strong fluorinating agent than XeF_2
(iv) It is hydrolysed by water to form $XeOF_2$

(a) Only (iv) is correct
(b) (i) and (iii) are correct
(c) (i) and (iv) are correct
(d) Only (iii) is correct

24. XeF_4 reacts with SbF_5 to form

(i) $[XeF_3]^+ [SbF_6]^-$ (ii) $[XeF_3]^+ [Sb_2F_{11}]^-$

Which of the statement is true?

(a) XeF_3^+ has trigonal planar structure
(b) XeF_3^+ has pyramidal structure
(c) XeF_3^+ has a T-shape structure
(d) XeF_3^+ has square pyramidal structure

25. $XeOF_2$ and $[XeF_3]^+$ have

(a) T-shaped structure
(b) T-shaped structure and trigonal planar respectively
(c) trigonal planar and T-shaped geometry respectively
(d) trigonal planar geometry

26. Which of the following statement is true?

I. XeF_6 reacts with glass or quartz only.
II. XeF_6 reacts with glass and water to form XeO_3.
III. XeO_3 is highly explosive.
IV. XeF_6 reacts with SiO_2 to form $XeOF_2$.

(a) I, II are correct (b) I, II, III are correct
(c) I and III are correct (d) All are correct

27. $XeOF_4$ reacts with water to form the following compound (s).

(i) XeO_2F_2 (ii) XeO_3
(iii) HF (iv) XeO_2F_6

The set of compounds formed is

(a) (i), (ii) and (iii) (b) (ii), (iii) and (iv)
(c) (i), (ii) and (iv) (d) (i), (iii) and (iv)

28. $XeOF_4$ reacts with hydrogen gas to give the following compound (s).

(i) Xe (ii) HF
(iii) XeO_2 (iv) XeO_2F_2
(v) H_2O

The correct set is

(a) (i), (ii) and (iii) (b) (ii), (iii) and (iv)
(c) (i), (ii) and (v) (d) (i), (ii) and (v)

29. XeO_2F_2 is

(a) red (b) blue
(c) yellow (d) colourless

30. Match the following in Column I with Column II.

	Column I		Column II
I.	XeF_2	(i)	Tetrahedral
II.	XeF_4	(ii)	See-saw
III.	XeF_6	(iii)	Square pyramidal
IV.	$XeOF_4$	(iv)	Linear
V.	$XeOF_4^{\bullet}$	(v)	Square planar
		(vi)	Distorted octahedron

Codes

(a) I-iii, II-ii, III-i, IV-vi, V-iv
(b) I-vi, II-v, III-vi, IV-i, V-iii
(c) I-iv, II-v, III-vi, IV-iii, V-i
(d) I-iii, II-ii, III-i, IV-iv, V-vi

31. Reaction of concentrated H_2SO_4 on barium xenate (Ba_2XeO_6) at room temperature forms

(a) XeO_2F_2 (b) XeO_4
(c) Xe (d) XeO_3

32. Which of the statements are correct about clathrate?

I. Clathrate are normally non-stoichiometric compounds.
II. Clathrate compounds of He and Ne cannot be prepared.
III. He and Ne being small diffuses through crystals.
IV. He and Ne difficult to deform or polarize.
V. Clathrate compounds of Ne and Ar are not known.

(a) I, II, III, IV are correct
(b) I, III, IV, V are correct
(c) Only I is correct
(d) I, III, V is correct
(e) All the above are correct

33. Which of the following statements (s) is/are true about clathrates?

(i) They are used in the separation of noble gases.

(ii) Krypton (Kr-85) clathrate provide a safe and useful source of β-radiations which are useful for measuring thickness of gauges.

(iii) Xe-133 clathrate provides a compact source for gamma (γ)-radiations.

(iv) Xe-13 clathrate provides a compact source for alpha (α)-radiations.

(a) (i), (ii) and (iii) (b) (ii), (iii) and (iv)
(c) (i), (iii) and (iv) (d) (i), (ii), (iii) and (iv)

34. Which of the following compoud(s) is/are known?
(a) $O_2^+[PtF_6]^-$ (b) $Xe^+[PtF_6]^-$
(c) $N_2^+[PtF_6]^-$ (d) None of these

35. Which reacts with fluorine?
(a) Ar (b) Kr (c) Xe (d) He

36. Claude's apparatus is used for the isolation .... from liquid air.
(a) He which has the lowest boiling point
(b) He which has the highest boiling point
(c) He which is monoatomic
(d) Liquid He which has almost zero viscosity

37. Which statement(s) concerning argon in solid state is/are corret?
(a) Its molecules are monoatomic
(b) It is very poor conductor of electricity
(c) The forces between its molecules are weak van der Waals' forces.
(d) Its atoms form a covalent network solid.

38. Which are formed when an electric discharge is passed through helium?
(a) He^+ (b) He_2 (c) He_2^+ (d) He_2^{2+}

39. Which of the following statement(s) is/are correct?
(a) Ramsay has maximum contribution in discovery of rare gases
(b) Ne is used as illuminating advertisement
(c) All the noble gases are present in atmosphere in very minute quantity
(d) Radon,thoron and actinon are the three isotopes of the same element.

40. Which of the following statement(s) is/are correct?
(a) XeO_3 is an explosive compound
(b) XeF_4 shows sp^3d^2 hybridisation of Xe.
(c) XeF_6 is pentagonal bipyramidal
(d) XeF_2 is linear molecule

41. Which of the following statement(s) is/are correct?
(a) Claude's apparatus can be used for the isolation of He and Ar.
(b) On passing air over Mg, N_2 and O_2 can be removed from air.
(c) CaC_2 can remove both N_2 and O_2 from air.
(d) Helium is the lightest gas.

42. Which of the following statement(s) is/are correct?
(a) Noble gases are paramagnetic in nature.
(b) He cannot be adsorbed by coconut charcoal.
(c) The Poisson's ratio for noble gas is 1:4.
(d) Helium is the lightest gas.

Directions (Q. Nos. 43 to 45)

A reaction mixture was prepared at 25°C by filling a 1.0 L nickel container with F_2 gas at 9 atm and Xe gas at 1.7 atm. The reaction mixture was maintained at 400°C for 1 hour. All the Xe gas reacted to form solid xenon fluoride compound and some of F_2 gas remains unreacted. The pressure of F_2 gas was 3.9 atom.

43. What is the ratio of moles of F_2 used to moles of Xe used?
(a) 4 (b) 2
(c) 3 (d) 6

44. Xenon fluoride compound so formed is
(a) XeF_4 (b) XeF_2
(c) $[XeF_3]^+$ (d) XeF_6

45. XeF_4 forms adduct with strong Lewis bases. Which of the following statements are true?

I. XeF_4 forms 1 : 1 adduct with Lewis bases

II. Ionic salts are formed on reaction

III. Covalent salts are formed on reaction

IV. Square planar product is formed

(a) I, II, IV are correct (b) I and II are correct
(c) III and IV are correct (d) I and III are correct

Directions (Q. Nos. 46 and 47)

Xenon in its compounds exhibits every even valency from two to eight, + 2 (XeF_2), + 4 (XeF_4), + 6 (XeF_6) and + 8 (XeO_4). The compounds of xenon involve only fluorine or oxygen. The only other compound, xenon dichloride ($XeCl_2$) is stable at low temperatures. The fluorides of this element can be prepared by the direct method. The simplest generalization seems to be that any process which exposes xenon to fluorine atoms will result in the production of xenon fluorides. The atomic fluorine may be generated by any one of these methods : (i) heating F_2 gas (ii) electric discharge (iii) Ionising radiation (iv) from some fluorine compound.

Compounds of xenon with oxygen cannot be prepared by their direct combination. The (+8) oxidation state is well established only in XeO_4.

46. The compounds of xenon involve the following element(s).
(a) fluorine (b) chlorine
(c) nitrogen (d) oxygen

47. Compounds of xenon can be prepared by the direct combination of the following.
(a) fluorine only
(b) oxygen only
(c) both fluorine and oxygen
(d) None of the above

Directions (Q. Nos. 48 to 50)
The valence bond representation of XeF_4 can be explained that two electron from the $5p$ sub-level are promoted to high energy $5d$-orbitals.
Ground state configuration of Xe

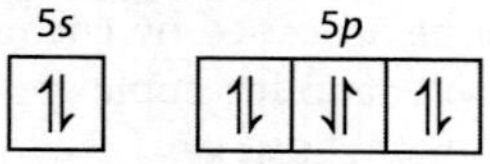

Excited state configuration of Xe

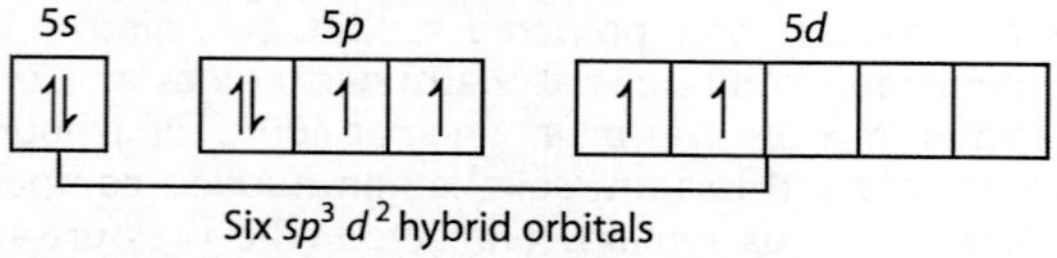

The $5s$, three $5p$ and two $5d$ atomic orbitals of xenon hybridize to produce six sp^3d^2 hybridized orbitals. The four singly occupied hybridized orbitals are used by fluorine for bond formation to xenon. The other two orbitals contain lone pairs. The molecule has octahedral geometry with two *trans* positions occupied by lone pairs.

48. XeF_4 molecule has the following geometry
(a) tetrahedral (b) square pyramidal
(c) octahedral (d) pentagonal pyramidal

49. Xe in XeF_4 contain the following number of unpaired electrons
(a) 2 (b) 4 (c) 6 (d) 5

50. Xe in XeF_4 contain the following number of lone pair(s)
(a) 1 (b) 2 (c) 3 (d) 4

Assertion & Reason

Codes
(a) Both A and R are true and R is the correct explanation of A.
(b) Both A and R are true but R is not the correct explanation of A.
(c) A is true but R is false.
(d) A is false but R is true.

51. Assertion (A) XeF_6 cannot be handled in glass or quartz apparatus.
Reason (R) Reaction between XeF_6 and SiO_2 of glass form explosive XeO_3.

52. Assertion (A) He and Ne do not clathrates.
Reason (R) They are difficult to polarise due to smaller size.

53. Assertion (A) Fluorides of Xe are thermodynamically stable.
Reason (R) They are endothermic compounds.

54. Assertion (A) XeF_4 may be estimated by titrating the I_2 by reaction with KI.
Reason (R) Equivalent weight of $Na_2S_2O_3$ can be determined by iodimetric titration.

55. Assertion (A) XeF_6 can be used as an oxidizing agent.
Reason (R) Oxidation state of Xe in XeF_6 is 6.

Answers

Exercise 1

1. (d)	**2.** (c)	**3.** (d)	**4.** (c)	**5.** (d)	**6.** (c)	**7.** (d)	**8.** (b)	**9.** (a)	**10.** (a)
11. (d)	**12.** (b)	**13.** (a)	**14.** (a)	**15.** (b)	**16.** (c)	**17.** (d)	**18.** (a)	**19.** (c)	**20.** (a)
21. (b)	**22.** (b)	**23.** (a)	**24.** (a)	**25.** (a)	**26.** (a)	**27.** (a)	**28.** (b)	**29.** (b)	**30.** (a)
31. (c)	**32.** (c)	**33.** (b)	**34.** (d)	**35.** (b)	**36.** (c)	**37.** (a)	**38.** (c)	**39.** (c)	**40.** (a)
41. (b)	**42.** (c)	**43.** (c)	**44.** (b)	**45.** (a)	**46.** (c)	**47.** (d)	**48.** (c)	**49.** (b)	**50.** (c)
51. (b)	**52.** (b)	**53.** (c)	**54.** (c)	**55.** (d)	**56.** (c)	**57.** (c)	**58.** (d)	**59.** (a)	**60.** (c)
61. (a)	**62.** (a)								

Exercise 2

1. (b)	**2.** (a)	**3.** (d)	**4.** (a)	**5.** (c)	**6.** (d)	**7.** (c)	**8.** (c)	**9.** (c)	**10.** (a,b,c,d)
11. (c)	**12.** (a,b,c)	**13.** (a,b)	**14.** (a,b,c,d)	**15.** (d)	**16.** (a)	**17.** (b)	**18.** (d)	**19.** (a)	**20.** (c)
21. (c)	**22.** (b)	**23.** (c)	**24.** (c)	**25.** (a)	**26.** (b)	**27.** (a)	**28.** (d)	**29.** (d)	**30.** (c)
31. (b)	**32.** (a)	**33.** (a)	**34.** (a)	**35.** (c)	**36.** (a,c,d)	**37.** (a,b,c)	**38.** (a,c,d)	**39.** (a,b,d)	**40.** (a,b,d)
41. (a,b,c)	**42.** (b,d)	**43.** (c)	**44.** (d)	**45.** (b)	**46.** (a,d)	**47.** (a)	**48.** (c)	**49.** (b)	**50.** (b)
51. (a)	**52.** (a)	**53.** (c)	**54.** (b)	**55.** (b)					

Hints & Solutions

Exercise 1

1. $XeF_2 + AsF_5 \longrightarrow XeF_2 \cdot AsF_5$ or $XeF^+AsF_6^-$
3. XeF_6 generates ions with all the given reagent, so becomes conducting.
10. As the size and polarisability increases, thermal stability of hydrates increases.
13. $XeF_4 = 4bp + 2lp \Rightarrow sp^3d^2$ hybridisation and square planar geometry because of the presence of two lone pairs.

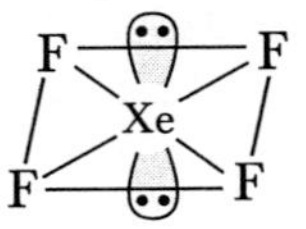

18. $XeF_6 + 3H_2O \longrightarrow XeO_3 + 6HF$
27. $XeF_2 = 2bp + 3lp$.

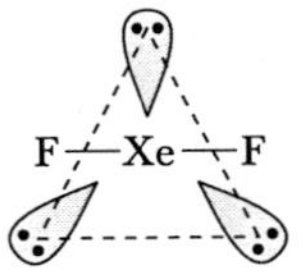

Linear geometry

28. $XeO_3 = 3bp + 1\,lp \qquad \Rightarrow sp^3$ hybridisation

$XeOF_2 = 3bp + 2lp \qquad \Rightarrow sp^3d$ hybridisation

$XeOF_4 = 5bp + 1\,lp \qquad \Rightarrow sp^3d^2$ hybridisation

$XeF_4 = 4\,bp + 2\,lp \qquad \Rightarrow sp^3d^2$ hybridisation

34. Xenon forms compounds with fluorine, oxygen and their compounds.
35. XeF_8

$$x + (-1)\,8 = 0$$
$$x = +\,8$$

XeO_4

$$x + (-2)\,4 = 0$$
$$x - 8 = 0$$
$$x = +\,8$$

40.

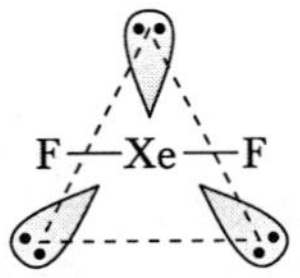

45. $[XeF_5]^- = 5\,bp + 2\,lp = sp^3d^3$ hybridisation.

= pentagonal bypyramidal structure

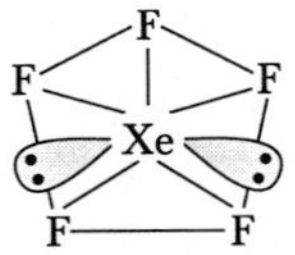

Pentagonal planar geometry (because of the presence of lone pairs)

53. $XeO_3 + XeOF_4 \longrightarrow 2XeO_2F_2$
54. $XeO_2F_2 + H_2O \longrightarrow XeO_3 + 2HF$
56. $[XeO_2F]^+ = 3\,bp + 1\,lp = sp^3$ hybridisation

$\Rightarrow$ pyramidal geometry

Exercise 2

1. $XeF_6 < XeF_4 < XeF_2$

(Basicity decreases as the number of lone pair of electrons decreases)

3. When lone pair is present (in odd number) the geometry is distorted.

(a) $NH_3 \Rightarrow 3bp + 1\,lp$;l SO_2 $(2bp + 1\,lp)$; H_2O $(2bp + 2\,lp)$

(b) XeF_2 $(2bp + 3\,lp)$; XeF_4 $(4\,bp + 2\,lp)$; XeO_3 $(3\,bp + 1\,lp)$

(c) $XeOF_2$ $(3\,bp + 2\,lp)$; XeO_3 $(3\,bp + 1\,lp)$; XeF_2 $(2\,bp + 3\,lp)$

5. $XeF_4 = 4\,bp + 2\,lp \Rightarrow$ square planar geometry

$XeF_6 = 6\,bp + 1\,lp \Rightarrow$ distorted octahedral

$XeO_3 = 3\,bp + 1\,lp \Rightarrow$ pyramidal

$XeO_4 = 4\,bp + 0\,lp \Rightarrow$ tetrahedral

9. According to Lux Flood definition, XeF_6 is an acid as it can accept oxide ion.
10. All xenon fluorides and oxyfluorides behave as oxidising agents.
17. Let the oxidation state of Xe in its compounds is x.

XeF_2 $\qquad x + (-1)2 = 0$, $\quad x = +\,2$

XeF_4 $\qquad x + (-1)4 = 0$, $\quad x = +\,4$

XeF_6 $\qquad x + (-1)6 = 0$, $\quad x = +\,6$

XeF_8 $\qquad x + (-1)\,8 = 0$, $\quad x = +\,8$

18. Atomic fluorine is generated by heating F_2 gas, by passing electric discharge or by ionisation reduction of F_2.
20.

$$XeF_2 + I_2 \xrightarrow{BF_3} 2IF + Xe\uparrow$$
$$IF + XeF_2 \xrightarrow{BF_3} IF_3 + Xe\uparrow$$

21. $XeF_2 \cdot 2SbF_5$ can also be represented as $[XeF]^+\,[Sb_2F_{11}]^-$

$$[XeF]^+[Sb_2F_{11}]^- \longrightarrow [XeF]^+ + [Sb_2F_{11}]^-$$

22. $2XeF_2 \cdot AsF_5 \longrightarrow [Xe_2F_3]^+[AsF_6]^-$

23. XeF_4 gives Xe with H_2 gas. It is a stronger fluorinating agent than XeF_2.

24. $[XeF_3]^+ = 3\,bp + 2\,lp$

The lone pairs occupy equatorial position, so the structure of $[XeF_3]^+$ is T-shape.

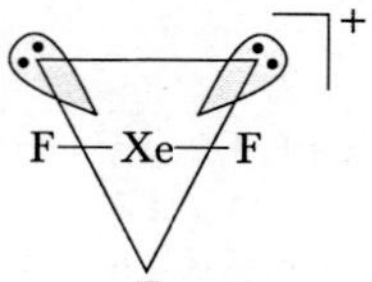

26. XeF_6 reacts with glass (SiO_2) and the final product of the reaction is XeO_3.

$$2XeF_6 + 3SiO_2 \longrightarrow \underset{\text{(Explosive)}}{2XeO_3} + 3SiF_4$$

with water, it also gives XeO_3

$$XeF_6 + 3H_2O \longrightarrow XeO_3 + 6HF$$

27. $2XeOF_4 + 3H_2O \longrightarrow XeO_2F_2 + XeO_3 + 3HF$

28. $XeOF_4 + 3H_2 \longrightarrow Xe + 4HF + H_2O$

31. $Ba_2XeO_6 + H_2SO_4 \longrightarrow H_4XeO_6 \xrightarrow{-2H_2O} XeO_4$

34. $N_2^+[PtF_6]^-$ does not exist due to high ionisation energy of N atom.

35. Xe and Kr react with fluorine as they are reactive due to their low ionisation energy.

40. XeF_6 has pentagonal pyramidal geometry.

42. All noble gases are diamagnetic (as all the electrons are paired). These are monoatomic, so the poisson's ratio is 1.66.

43. Since all pressures were measured at the same temperature while the volume of the container was unchanged, *i.e.*, T and V = constant,

So, $p \propto n$

Thus,

Initial pressure of F_2 gas = 9 atm

Final pressure of F_2 gas = 3.9 atm

Number of moles of F_2 used = 9 – 3.9

= 5.1 moles

$$\frac{\text{Moles of } F_2 \text{ used}}{\text{Moles of Xe used}} = \frac{5.1}{1.7} = 3$$

44. One mole of fluorine contains 2 g atoms so 3 moles contain 6 g-atoms. One mole of Xe contain 1 g-atom. Hence, the formula of xenon fluoride is XeF_6.

45.

$$\underset{1\ :\ 1}{XeF_4 + SbF_5} \longrightarrow \underset{\text{Adduct (ionic)}}{[XeF_3]^+[SbF_6]^-}$$

$$XeF_4 + 2SbF_5 \longrightarrow \underset{\text{(Ionic)}}{[XeF_3]^+[Sb_2F_{11}]^-}$$

The $[XeF_3]^+$ ions have a T-shaped structure.

46. Xenon forms compoundwith highlyelectronegative F and O atom.

47. Xenon fluorides are prepared by direct combination of elements while xenon oxides are prepared by their hydrolysis of xenon halides. (indirect method)

48-50.

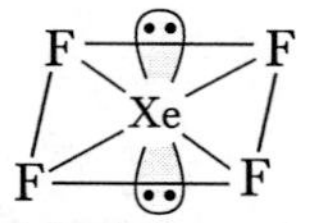

Octahedral geometry

2 lone pairs (*i.e.,* 4 unpaired electrons)

8

d-Block Elements or Transition Elements

Those elements in which last electron or valence electron enters in *d*-shell are called ***d*-block elements.** They are also called **'transition elements'** because they are found between the *s*- and *p*-block elements, in the Periodic Table. Broadly transition elements are those, which have partly filled *d*- or *f*-shells.

Typically the transition elements have an incompletely filled *d* level. The zinc group has a d^{10} configuration and since the *d*-shell is complete, the compounds of this group are not typical and show some differences from the others.

Group / Period	IIIB	IVB	VB	VIB	VIIB		VIII	IB		IIB
4	Sc_{21}	Ti_{22}	V_{23}	Cr_{24}	Mn_{25}	Fe_{26}	Co_{27}	Ni_{28}	Cu_{29}	Zn_{30}
5	Y_{39}	Zr_{40}	Nb_{41}	Mo_{42}	Te_{43}	Ru_{44}	Rh_{45}	Pd_{46}	Ag_{47}	Cd_{48}
6	La_{57}	Hf_{72}	Ta_{73}	W_{74}	Re_{75}	Os_{76}	Ir_{77}	Pt_{78}	Au_{79}	Hg_{80}
7	Ac_{89}	Rf_{104}	Db_{105}	Sg_{106}	Bh_{107}	Hs_{108}	Mt_{109}			

All these transition elements have certain general properties in common :

1. They are all metals.
2. They are practically all hard, strong metals having high melting and boiling point.
3. They are good conductor of heat and electricity.
4. They form alloys with one another and with other metallic elements.
5. Many of them are sufficiently electropositive, hence, dissolve in mineral acids.

   Although a few are 'noble' means, they have such low electrode potentials that they are unaffected by simple acids.
6. They exhibit variable valency, and their ions and compounds are coloured in at least one of the oxidation states, except few exceptions.
7. Because of partially filled shells, they form at least some paramagnetic compounds.

Syllabus

- Transition Elements and their Compounds : Structure, Bonding Theories, Spectral and Magnetic Properties

Transition Series

The elements of *d*-block make up three complete rows of ten elements which are called 3*d*, 4*d* and 5*d* transition series. These are also known as first transition series, second transition series and third transition series respectively. Moreover they makeup an incomplete fourth row, which is called 6*d* transition series (Actinium to Roentgenium).

1. 3*d* or First Transition Series

This series of elements is formed by filling the 3*d* sub-shell of electrons. This series contains the following ten elements : SC_{21}, Ti_{22}, V_{23}, Cr_{24}, Mn_{25}, Fe_{26}, Co_{27}, Ni_{28}, Cu_{29}, Zn_{30}.

Except Cu and Zn, all the elements have partially filled 3*d* sub-shell either in their ground state of the free atom or in one or more of their ions (except Sc). Elements of this series have the outer electronic configuration $4s^{1-2}\ 3d^{1-10}$.

Last element of this series, zinc, which have outer electronic configuration $4s^{2},\ 3d^{10}$, does not form any compound in which the 3*d* shell is ionised.

2. 4*d* or Second Transition Series

This series of elements is formed by filling the 4*d*-subshell of electrons and contains the following elements.

Y_{39}, Zr_{40}, Nb_{41}, Mo_{42}, Te_{43}, Ru_{44}, Rh_{45}, Pd_{46}, Ag_{47}, Cd_{48}

The outer electronic configuration of the elements of this series is $5s^{0-2}\ 4d^{1-10}$. All the elements of this have partly filled 4*d*-shell either in the free element (except Pd, Ag and Cd) or in one or more of their ions (except Y).

3. 5*d* or Third Transition Series

This series of elements is formed by filling the 5*d* shell of electrons and contains the following elements.

La_{57}, Hf_{72}, Ta_{73}, W_{74}, Re_{75}, Os_{76}, Ir_{77}, Pt_{78}, Au_{79}, Hg_{80}

The outer electronic configuration of the elements of this series is $6s^{1-2}\ 5d^{1-10}$. All the elements of this series have partially filled 5*d*-shell in one or more chemically important oxidation states as well as in the neutral atom (except Au and Hg).

Electronic Configuration

In the atoms of transition elements, the outermost energy level has ns^1 or ns^2 configuration while the penultimate shell (*i.e.,* last but one shell) has the configuration $(n-1)\ d^{1-10}$. Hence, the general electronic configuration of transition elements is

$$[\text{Noble gas}]\ (n-1)\ d^{1-10}\ ns^{1-2}$$

where, *n* is the number of outermost shell and $(n-1)$ is the number of penultimate shell.

In the second, third and fourth transition series, the prediction of electronic configuration of a particular atom is difficult. Some of the following interactions play an important role in determining these electronic configurations :

(i) Electron-electron repulsions
(ii) Nucleus-electron attraction
(iii) Shielding of one electron by other electrons
(iv) Exchange forces

(a) First Transition Series or 3*d*-series

The general electronic configuration of the atoms of first transition series is

$$[\text{Ar}]\ 3d^{1-10}\ ns^{1-2}$$

In this series, as we move from scandium $(Z = 21)$ to zinc $(Z = 30)$, electron enters in 3*d*-orbitals as shown in following Table 8.1.

Table 8.1 **Electronic Configuration of First Transition Series Elements**

Element	Symbol	Atomic number	Electronic configuration
Scandium	Sc	21	$[Ar]\ 3d^1 4s^2$
Titanium	Ti	22	$[Ar]\ 3d^2 4s^2$
Vanadium	V	23	$[Ar]\ 3d^3 4s^2$
Chromium	Cr	24	$[Ar]\ 3d^5 4s^1$
Manganese	Mn	25	$[Ar]\ 3d^5 4s^2$
Iron	Fe	26	$[Ar]\ 3d^6 4s^2$
Cobalt	Co	27	$[Ar]\ 3d^7 4s^2$
Nickel	Ni	28	$[Ar]\ 3d^8 4s^2$
Copper	Cu	29	$[Ar]\ 3d^{10} 4s^1$
Zinc	Zn	30	$[Ar]\ 3d^{10} 4s^2$

It is evident from the above table that the electronic configuration of **chromium** $(Z = 24)$ and **copper**

($Z = 29$) do not follow the general trend and thus, show anomalous behaviour. This can be explained on the basis of an important generalization that either exactly half-filled or completely filled subshells have extra stability. Chromium gains extra stability when an electron shifts from the $4s$ subshell to $3d$-subshell so that both $3d$ and $4s$ subshells acquire half-filled configuration. Thus, chromium has the configuration [Ar] $3d^5 4s^1$. Similarly, in the case of copper, an electron moves from $4s$ subshell to $3d$-subshell so that $3d$-subshell becomes fully filled while $4s$ acquires half-filled configuration. This results in extra stability for the electronic configuration of copper as [Ar] $3d^{10} 4s^1$.

(b) Second Transition Series or 4*d*-series

The general electronic configuration of the atoms of this series is :

$$[\text{Kr}]\ 4d^{1-10} 5s^{0-2}$$

On increasing the atomic number of this series, *i.e.,* from Yttrium ($Z = 39$) to Cadmium ($Z = 48$), electrons enter in $4d$-orbitals as shown in the Table 8.2

Table 8.2 **Electronic Configuration of Second Transition Series Elements**

Element	Symbol	Atomic number	Electronic configuration
Yttrium	Y	39	[Kr] $4d^1 5s^2$
Zirconium	Zr	40	[Kr] $4d^2 5s^2$
Niobium	Nb	41	[Kr] $4d^4 5s^1$
Molybdenum	Mo	42	[Kr] $4d^5 5s^1$
Technetium	Tc	43	[Kr] $4d^5 5s^2$
Ruthenium	Ru	44	[Kr] $4d^7 5s^1$
Rhodium	Rh	45	[Kr] $4d^8 5s^1$
Palladium	Pd	46	[Kr] $4d^{10} 5s^0$
Silver	Ag	47	[Kr] $4d^{10} 5s^1$
Cadmium	Cd	48	[Kr] $4d^{10} 5s^2$

It is evident from the above Table that there are many irregularities, *e.g.,* at niobium ($Z = 41$) where electronic configuration should have been [Kr] $4d^3 5s^2$ but actual electronic configuration is [Kr] $4d^4 5s^1$; at ruthenium ($Z = 44$) when electronic configuration should have been [Kr] $4d^6 5s^2$ but actual electronic configuration is [Kr] $4d^7 5s^1$; at rhodium ($Z = 45$) electronic configuration should have been [Kr] $4d^7 5s^2$ but actual electronic configuration is [Kr] $4d^8 5s^1$. Similarly, palladium ($Z = 46$) should have electronic configuration [Kr] $4d^8 5s^2$ but its actual electronic configuration is [Kr] $4d^{10} 5s^0$. The reasons for these irregularities may be attributed to different factors mentioned earlier.

(c) Third Transition Series or 4*d*-series

The general electronic configuration of the atoms of this series is :

$$[\text{Xe}]\ 4f^{0 \text{ or } 14}\ 5d^{1-10}\ 6s^{1-2}$$

On increasing the atomic number of this series, *i.e.,* from lanthanum ($Z = 57$) to mercury ($Z = 80$), electrons enter in $5d$-orbitals as in the Table 8.3.

Table 8.3 **Electronic Configuration of Third Transition Series Elements**

Element	Symbol	Atomic number	Electronic configuration
Lanthanum	La	57	[Xe] $4f^0 5d^1 6s^2$
Hafnium	Hf	72	[Xe] $4f^{14} 5d^2 6s^2$
Tantalum	Ta	73	[Xe] $4f^{14} 5d^3 6s^2$
Tungsten	W	74	[Xe] $4f^{14} 5d^4 6s^2$
Rhenium	Re	75	[Xe] $4f^{14} 5d^5 6s^2$
Osmium	Os	76	[Xe] $4f^{14} 5d^6 6s^2$
Iridium	Ir	77	[Xe] $4f^{14} 5d^7 6s^2$
Platinum	Pt	78	[Xe] $4f^{14} 5d^9 6s^1$
Gold	Au	79	[Xe] $4f^{14} 5d^{10} 6s^1$
Mercury	Hg	80	[Xe] $4f^{14} 5d^{10} 6s^2$

It is evident from Table 8.3 that there are some irregularities in the electronic configuration of this series. For example, tungsten ($Z = 74$) should have electronic configuration [Xe] $4f^{14} 5d^5 6s^1$ but its actual electronic configuration is [Xe] $4f^{14} 5d^4 6s^2$. Similarly, platinum ($Z = 78$) should have electronic configuration [Xe] $4f^{14} 5d^8 6s^2$ but its actual electronic configuration is [Xe] $4f^{14} 5d^9 6s^1$.

(d) Fourth Transition Series or 6*d*-series

It is not possible to write a general electronic configuration for the elements of the fourth transition series, because it is not completed till now yet. Some six elements which have been approved by the IUPAC are as follows.

Table 8.4 **Electronic Configuration of Fourth Transition Series Elements**

Element	Symbol	Atomic number	Electronic configuration
Actinium	Ac	89	[Rn] $6d^1 7s^2$
Rutherfordium	Rf	104	[Rn] $5f^{14} 6d^2 7s^2$
Dubnium	Db	105	[Rn] $5f^{14} 6d^3 7s^2$
Seaborgium	Sg	106	[Rn] $5f^{14} 6d^4 7s^2$
Bohrium	Bh	107	[Rn] $5f^{14} 6d^5 7s^2$
Hassium	Hs	108	[Rn] $5f^{14} 6d^6 7s^2$
Meitnerium	Mt	109	[Rn] $5f^{14} 6d^7 7s^2$

Electronic Configuration of Ions of the Transition Elements

In case of transition elements, electrons can be lost either from *ns* orbital or $(n-1)$ *d*-orbitals. However, which orbital will lose the electrons depends on :

(i) Interelectronic repulsions

(ii) Variation in effective nuclear charge

For example, in the first transition series, 4*s*-orbital is filled first and then 3*d*-orbitals are filled. This means 4*s*-orbital is more stable than 3*d*-orbitals. Hence, in the first transition series, ions should be formed by the loss of 3*d*-electrons rather than 4*s*-electrons. Actually this is not true. In fact, atoms of first transition series lose 4*s* electrons before they lose electrons from 3*d*-orbitals. The reason for this behaviour is that after the electrons have entered 3*d* orbitals, the energy of 3*d*-orbitals becomes less than that of 4*s* orbital. In other words, 3*d*-orbitals become more stable than 4*s* orbital. Hence, in the first transition series, it is the 4*s* orbital (which has higher energy and unstable) which lose electrons first as compared to 3*d*-orbitals. Once both the electrons from 4*s* orbitals are lost, thereafter, electrons are lost from 3*d* orbitals. For example, electronic configuration of titanium $(Z = 22)$ will be as

$$\text{Ti : [Ar] } 3d^2\,4s^2$$

Therefore, electronic configuration of Ti^{2+} will be as

$$Ti^{2+} : \text{[Ar] } 3d^2$$

Similarly, electronic configuration of Ti^{3+} will be as

$$Ti^{3+} : \text{[Ar] } 3d^1$$

Note It may be mentioned that electrons are not lost from *d*-orbitals if *d*-subshell is full, *i.e.*, it has d^{10} system.

For example, in case of Zn $(3d^{10}, 4s^2)$, Cd $(4d^{10}, 5s^2)$ and Hg $(5d^{10}, 6s^2)$ which have d^{10} system, electrons from *d*-subshell do not participate in bonding.

Table 8.5 **Electronic Configuration of Elements and Ions of First Transition Series**

Atom	Electronic configuration	Ion	Electronic configuration
Sc	[Ar] $3d^1 4s^2$	Sc^{3+}	[Ar] $3d^0$
Ti	[Ar] $3d^2 4s^2$	Ti^{2+}	[Ar] $3d^2$
		Ti^{3+}	[Ar] $3d^1$
V	[Ar] $3d^3 4s^2$	V^{2+}	[Ar] $3d^3$
		V^{3+}	[Ar] $3d^2$
		V^{4+}	[Ar] $3d^1$
Cr	[Ar] $3d^5 4s^1$	Cr^{2+}	[Ar] $3d^4$
		Cr^{3+}	[Ar] $3d^3$
Mn	[Ar] $3d^5 4s^2$	Mn^{2+}	[Ar] $3d^5$
Fe	[Ar] $3d^6 4s^2$	Fe^{2+}	[Ar] $3d^6$
		Fe^{3+}	[Ar] $3d^5$
Co	[Ar] $3d^7 4s^2$	Co^{2+}	[Ar] $3d^7$
Ni	[Ar] $3d^8 4s^2$	Ni^{2+}	[Ar] $3d^8$
Cu	[Ar] $3d^{10} 4s^1$	Cu^{+}	[Ar] $3d^{10}$
		Cu^{2+}	[Ar] $3d^9$
Zn	[Ar] $3d^{10} 4s^2$	Zn^{2+}	[Ar] $3d^{10}$

Variable Oxidation State or Variable Valency

From Sc to Mn the maximum oxidation state is determined by the total number of 3*d* and 4*s* electrons. After Mn the maximum oxidation state tends to fall down to +2 for zinc after +3 for Fe and Co (there are some higher oxidation state species, but not that common and not that stable in aqueous media).

- The **relative ease of oxidation state change** for Ti to Cu and the **maximum oxidation state** formed by Sc to Mn, is partly **explained by considering the ionisation energies** involved.

Some Important Points to Remember

(i) For the transition metals, the successive ionisation energies rise relatively gradually, due to the 3*d*/4*s* electron levels being of similar energy. When all the outer *s* and *d* electrons are removed to leave an [Ar] core, there is, as with Groups 1-3 etc., a dramatic rise as an electron must be removed from the inner very stable noble gas (argon) core. Therefore Ti has a maximum oxidation state of +4, but +2 and +3 species are also formed, but not +5 compounds.

(ii) Similarly maximum oxidation state for vanadium would be +5 and chromium +6.

(iii) After manganese, there is a decrease in oxidation state from Mn (+7) to Zn (+2). Zn has a maximum of +2 oxidation states, and many higher oxidation state compounds of Fe, Co, Ni and Cu are unstable and uncommon.

(iv) Due to closeness of the energies of the 3*d* subshell electrons and the stabilising influence of ligand molecules like water or ammonia or ligand ions like chloride or cyanide, vacant 3*d* orbitals (and 4*s*/4*p* orbitals too) can accept pairs of electrons to form stable dative covalent bonds.

(v) All except scandium (Sc^{3+}) form an M^{2+} ion.

(vi) All except zinc form compounds with (III) oxidation state.

(vii) Only copper has important compounds of oxidation state +1.

Table 8.6 **Different Oxidation States Exhibited by Transition Metals**

IIIB	IVB	VB	VIB	VIIB	VIII			IB	IIB
Elements of 3*d*-series (Period 4)									
Sc_{21}	Ti_{22}	V_{23}	Cr_{24}	Mn_{25}	Fe_{26}	Co_{27}	Ni_{28}	Cu_{29}	Zn_{30}
			+1					+1	
+2	+2	+2	+2	(+2)	(+2)	(+2)	(+2)	(+2)	(+2)
(+3)	+3	+3	(+3)	+3	(+3)	(+3)	+3		
	(+4)	+4	+4	(+4)	+4		+4		
		(+5)	+5						
			(+6)	+6	(+6)				
				(+7)					
Elements of 4*d*-series (Period 5)									
Y_{39}	Zr_{40}	Nb_{41}	Mo_{42}	Tc_{43}	Ru_{44}	Rh_{45}	Pd_{46}	Ag_{47}	Cd_{48}
								(+1)	
		+2(?)	+2(?)		(+2)	+2	(+2)	+2(?)	(+2)
(+3)	+3	+3(?)	+3(?)		(+3)	(+3)	+3(?)	(+3)	
	(+4)	+4(?)	+4	(+4)	(+4)	(+4)	+4		
		(+5)	+5		+5	+5	+5		
			(+6)	+6	+6	+6	+6		
				(+7)	+7				
Elements of 5*d*-series (Period 6)									
La_{57}	Hf_{72}	Ta_{73}	W_{74}	Re_{75}	Os_{76}	Ir_{77}	Pt_{78}	Au_{79}	Hg_{80}
								+1	+1
		+2(?)	+2(?)	+2(?)	+2	+2	(+2)		(+2)
(+3)	+3(?)	+3(?)	+3(?)	+3(?)	+3	(+3)		(+3)	
	(+4)	+4(?)	+4	+4(?)	(+4)	(+4)	(+4)		
		(+5)	+5	+5(?)		+5(?)	+5		
			(+6)	(+6)	(+6)	+6	+6		
				(+7)	+8				

Most stable oxidation state is given in brackets. (?) shows the unstable or less common oxidation states.

Formation of Hydrated Salts, Metal-aqua Complex Ions

All metal ions in solution are 'associated' with water. The water molecules can also be weakly bonded or more strongly as a **ligand** to form a complex ion, and these can also present in solid **hydrated** salts on crystallization, *e.g.,*

I. Iron(II) sulphate heptahydrate $FeSO_4 \cdot 7H_2O(s)$,

II. Cobalt(II) chloride hexahydrate $CoCl_2 \cdot 6H_2O(s)$,

III. Copper(II) sulphate pentahydrate $CuSO_4 \cdot 5H_2O(s)$, etc.

The above crystals contain 7, 6 and 5 molecules of **water of crystallisation** respectively.

A hexa-aqua ion is present in the first two, $[M(H_2O_6)]^{2+}$ (M = Fe, Co)

In the case of copper(II) sulphate, 4 water molecules are covalently bonded to form a square planar complex ion, $[Cu(H_2O)_4]^{2+}$ and the 5th water molecule is hydrogen bonded to this ion and a neighbouring sulphate on helping to hold the crystal lattice together.

However, this blue crystal lattice is readily broken down on heating, It is a reversible reacton, since, the white **anhydrous** solid turns blue on adding water (a simple test for water).

$$\underset{\text{Blue}}{CuSO_4 \cdot 5H_2O(s)} \rightleftharpoons \underset{\text{White anhydrous solid}}{CuSO_4(s)} + 5H_2O(g/l)$$

Relative Acidity of Hydrated Salts

According to Lewis-base theory a base is an electron pair donor and an **acid is an electron pair acceptor.** Ligands like water, can donate a pair of non-bonding electrons (lone pair) into a vacant orbital of a central metal ion and so **dative covalent (coordinate) bonds hold a complex** together. The central metal ion with vacant bonding orbitals can act as a Lewis acid. Ligands act as Lewis bases by electron pair donation to form the metal-ligand bond.

According to Bronsted-Lowry acid-base theory a base is a proton acceptor. This is *via* an electron lone pair on the base (a Lewis base is a lone pair donor), *e.g.,* NH_3, HCO_3^-, OH^-, etc. **An acid is proton donor.** This involves a heterolytic breakage of an X–H bond (a Lewis acid is an electron pair acceptor), *e.g.,* HCl, HCO_3^-, H_2SO_4, CH_3COOH, etc.

How Hydrated Salts or Metal-aqua Complex Ions Hydrolysed?

Many hexa-aqua complex ions can undergo acid-base reactions with water to produce solutions of pH less than 7 (Usually group 2, 3 and transition metal ions). The positive central metal ion polarises a water molecule, releasing a proton, H^+. In the deprotonation reaction the proton transfers to water and the overall charge on the complex falls by 1 unit since the $H_2O - H^+ = OH^-$, *i.e.,* one of the ligands is now a hydroxide ion.

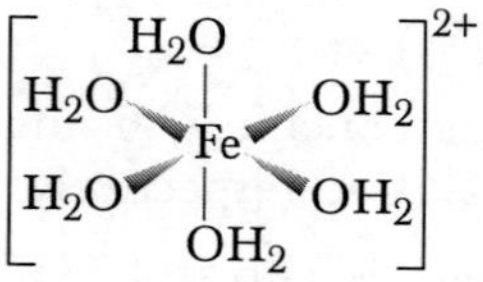

- In these reactions, the **hydrated ions act as Bronsted-Lowry acids** and **water acts as a Bronsted-Lowry base.**
- These reactions are examples of what is termed **salt hydrolysis** because the metal ion (of usually a salt) reacts with water to give, in this case, two products. For example

(a) Hexaaquametal(II) ions

$$\underset{\text{Bronsted-Lowry acid}}{[M(H_2O)_6]^{2+}(aq)} + \underset{\text{Bronsted-Lowry base}}{H_2O(l)} \rightleftharpoons [M(H_2O)_5(OH)]^{+}(aq) + H_3O^{+}(aq)$$

When M = **Mn, Fe, Co, Ni, Cu, Mg**, etc., they gives a very weak acid solutions with pH's just less than 7. Ti(II), V(II) and Cr(II) M^{2+} ions are redox unstable in the presence of air, but theoretically their salts give very weakly acid solutions. They are usually prepared by zinc-acid reduction from higher oxidation states.

(b) Hexaaquametal(III) ions

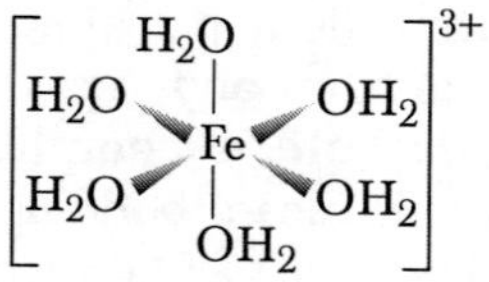

$$[M(H_2O)_6]^{3+}(aq) + H_2O(l) \rightleftharpoons [M(H_2O)_5(OH)]^{2+}(aq) + H_3O^{+}(aq)$$

When M = **Ti, V, Cr, Fe, Al**, etc., give very weak acids solutions (but generally stronger than for M^{2+}) of pH's in the 3-5 region.

Note These are acid-base reactions, not redox reactions, even if they involve transition metal ions-there is no change in oxidation state of the metal.

In the presence of alkali, OH^-, removing H_3O^+ ions, the equilibrium moves more to the right and more protons are lost from the complex in stages until the **hydroxide precipitate** is formed *e.g.,* for iron(III), chromium(III) or aluminium.

$$[M(H_2O)_6]^{3+}(aq) + 3OH^-(aq) \rightleftharpoons [M(H_2O)_3(OH)_3]^{+}(aq) + 3H_2O(l)$$

Some of the M^{3+} hydroxides are **amphoteric** and **dissolve in excess alkali or acid**

$$2[M(H_2O)_3(OH)_3]^{0}(aq) + 3OH^-(aq) \rightleftharpoons \underset{\text{Soluble hexahydroxo complex ion}}{[M(OH)_6]^{3-}(aq)} + 3H_2O(l)$$

$$[M(H_2O)_3(OH)_3]^{0}(aq) + 3H_3O^+(aq) \rightleftharpoons \underset{\text{Original hexa aqua ion}}{[M(H_2O)_6]^{3+}(aq)} + 3H_2O(l)$$

As a general **rule the greater the polarizing power (Polarizing power is a function of ionic charge/ionic radius ratio) of the central metal ion, the lower the pH of the resulting aqueous solution,** *i.e.,* the acid-base equilibrium is shifted more to the right causing an increase in acidity of the solution. This effect and process facilitated by the central metal ion on one water ligand molecule can be envisaged as

$$[M—O—H_2]^{n^+} \longrightarrow [M—O—H]^{n^+-1} + H^+$$

(proton transferred to a water molecule)

One of the O–H bond pairs is 'attracted' onto the oxygen atom by the electric field effect of the central metal ion of charge n^+, allowing proton transfer to the base water.

Consequences of hydrolysis of hexaaqua ions

1. The acidity of the hexaaqua ions $M^{3+}(aq)$ due to the polarizing influence of the central highly charged M^{3+} ion accounts for the **lack of stability/existence** of $M^{3+}(aq)$ then the less polarizing M^{2+} on exist.

   So, aluminium carbonate, iron(III) carbonate or chromium(III) carbonate, are unstable whereas $MgCO_3$, $ZnCO_3$ and $FeCO_3$, etc. with the less polarizing M^{2+} ion exist.
2. It also accounts for why you see bubbles of carbon dioxide when carbonates/hydrogen carbonates are mixed with aluminium chloride, iron(III) chloride or chromium(III) chloride solutions, *e.g.,*

$$2[Fe(H_2O)_6]^{3+}(aq) + CO_3^{2-}(aq) \rightleftharpoons 2[Fe(H_2O)_5(OH)]^{2+}(aq) + H_2O(l) + CO_2(g)$$

or $[M(H_2O)_6]^{3+}(aq) + HCO_3^-(aq) \rightleftharpoons$

$$[M(H_2O)_5(OH)]^{2+}(aq) + H_2O(l) + CO_2(g)$$

Amphoteric nature of ion such as Fe^{3+}

As soon as one proton has been lost the resulting complex ion can then act as a base.

e.g., in solutions of the weakly acidic Fe^{3+} species with excess strong acid the hexa-aqua ion would predominate,

$$\underset{\text{Weakly acidic } Fe^{3+} \text{ species}}{[M(H_2O)_4(OH)_2]^+(aq)} + 2H^+(aq) \rightleftharpoons [M(H_2O)_6]^{3+}(aq)$$

and hydroxide precipitates will readily dissolve on adding an acid which is stronger than the hexa-aqua ion

e.g., $\underset{\text{Hydroxide precipitates}}{Fe(OH)_3(s)} + 3H_3O^+(aq) \longrightarrow [Fe(H_2O)_6]^{3+}(aq)$

Colour of Transition Metal Complexes

The variety of colour among transition metal complexes has long fascinated the chemists. For example, aqueous solutions of $[Fe(H_2O)_6]^{3+}$ are red, $[Co(H_2O)_6]^{2+}$ are pink, $[Ni(H_2O)_6]^{2+}$ are green, $[Cu(H_2O)_6]^{2+}$ are blue and $[Zn(H_2O)_6]^{2+}$ are colourless. Although the octahedral $[Co(H_2O)_6]^{2+}$ are pink, those of tetrahedral $[CoCl_4]^{2-}$ are blue. The green colour of $[Ni(H_2O)_6]^{2+}$ turns blue when ammonia is added to give $[Ni(NH_3)_6]^{2+}$. Many of these facts can be rationalized from CFT.

Why do We See Colour?

When a sample absorbs light, what we see is the sum of the remaining colours that strikes our eyes. If a sample absorbs all wavelength of visible light, none reaches our eyes from that sample, and then the sample appears black. If the sample absorbs no visible light, it is white or colourless. When the sample absorbs a photon of visible light, it is its complementary colour we actually see. For example, if the sample absorbed orange colour, it would appear blue; blue and orange are said to be complementary colours.

The Colour Wheel

The visible part of the electromagnetic spectrum contains light of wavelength 380–750 nm. The colour wheel below gives information on the wavelength of different colour and also the complementary colour. For example : If red light is absorbed, the complex appears green; If purple light is absorbed, the complex appear yellow.

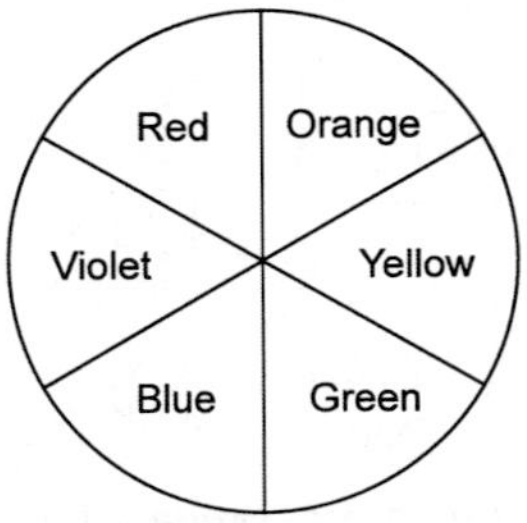

Colour of light absorbed	Approx. λ ranges/nm	Colour of light transmitted
Red	700-620	Green
Orange	620-580	Blue
Yellow	580-560	Violet
Green	560-490	Red
Blue	490-430	Orange
Violet	430-380	Yellow

Colour of Coordination Complexes

The colour of coordination complexes arises from electronic transitions between levels whose spacing corresponds to the wavelengths available in the visible light. In complexes, these transitions are frequently referred to as *d-d* transitions because they involve the orbitals that are mainly *d* in character (for examples : t_{2g} and e_g for the octahedral complexes and e and t_2 for the tetrahedral complexes). Obviously, the colours exhibited are intimately related to the magnitude of the spacing between these levels. Since, this spacing depends on factors such as the geometry of the complex, the nature of the ligands, and the oxidation state of the central metal atom, variation of colours can often be explained by looking carefully at the complexes concerned. Below are a few examples to illustrate this point.

$[V(H_2O)_6]^{3+}$
V(III) = d^2 ion
Violet light absorbed, complex appears yellow

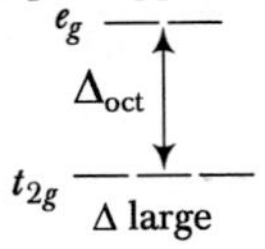

$[V(H_2O)_6]^{2+}$
V(II) = d^3 ion
Yellow light absorbed, complex appears violet

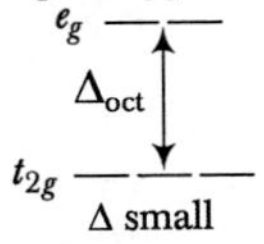

- The variation in the colour of the Cr(III) complexes can be explained following similar argument.

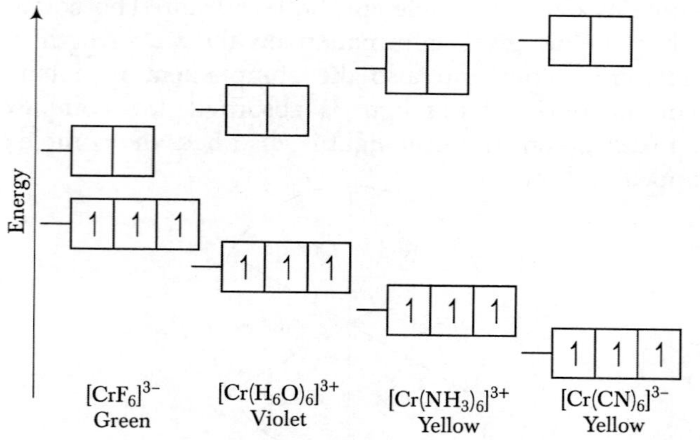

- We observe the appearance of a shoulder in the case of $[Ti(H_2O)_6]^{3+}$. Perfectly octahedral $[Ti(H_2O)_6]^{3+}$ should give only one *d-d* transition. However, distortion occurs to eliminate the degeneracy of the system. If a complex distorts from regular octahedral geometry, the t_{2g} and e_g levels are split, the consequence of which is the appearance of a shoulder as shown in the figure below.

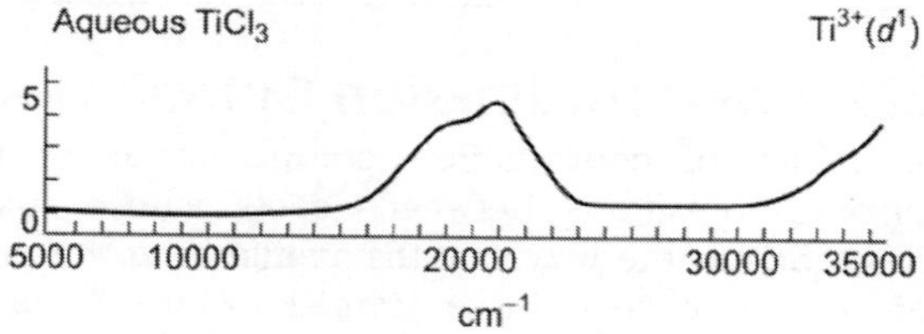

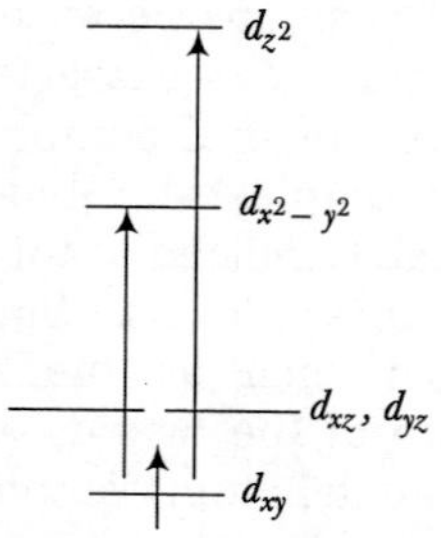

- Complexes that contain metal ions of d^{10} electronic configuration are usually colourless. Examples are $[Cu(PPh_3)_4]^+$ and $[Zn(H_2O)_6]^{2+}$. One would expect a metal complex with no *d*-electron to be colourless as well. However, a few of such complexes are strongly coloured, for example, MnO_4^- or $[Cr_2O_7]^{2-}$. The origin of the colour in these complexes is not the *d-d* transitions, rather it is due to 'charge transfer' that we will briefly discuss later.

- Multi-electron systems exhibit multiple transitions and the assignment of absorption bands is not straightforward. The complexity arises due to inter-electron repulsions that we will not discuss in this course but will take a simpler approach to understand the colour of coordination complexes.

Selection Rules for Electrostatic Transitions

The Beer-Lambert Law

$$A = \log_{10}\left(\frac{I_0}{I}\right) = \varepsilon Cl$$

where, ε is the molar extinction coefficient (in L cm^{-1} mol^{-1}), *C* is concentration in mol L^{-1} and *l* is the path length in cm. *A* is known as 'Absorbance' and it is dimensionless.

To explain the absorption spectra of coordination complexes, it is necessary to know the selection rules that govern electronic transitions. Any transition in violation of selection rule is said to be 'forbidden', but we will see how some rules are 'more forbidden than others'. We shall not pursue the theoretical basis of the rules but merely outline simple tests for their application.

The Laporte rule

In a molecule or ion possessing a centre of symmetry, transitions are not allowed between orbitals of the same parity, for example *d* to *d*. In other words, there must be change in parity ($\Delta l = \pm 1$), *i.e.,* the orbital quantum number should differ by 1. The forbidden transitions are $s \rightarrow s, d \rightarrow d, p \rightarrow f$, etc. The geometries affected by this rule include octahedral and square-planar complexes. The rule is not applicable to tetrahedral complexes as it does not contain any centre of symmetry.

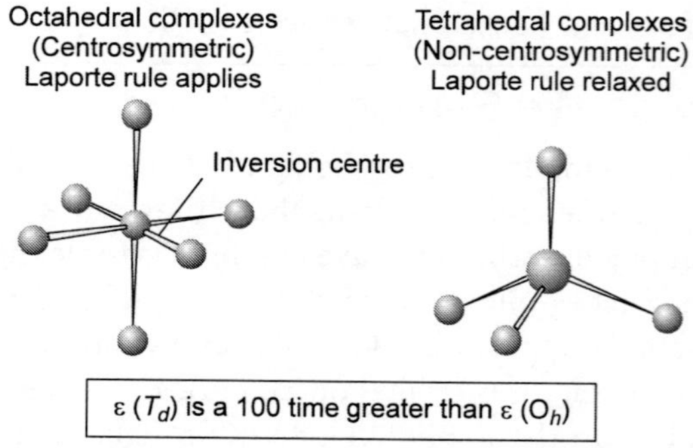

The key element here is that there are mechanisms by which selection rules can be relaxed so that transitions can occur, even if only at low intensities. Unsymmetrical vibrations of an octahedral complex can transiently destroy its centre of symmetry and allow transitions that would otherwise be Laporte forbidden. In cases where the rule applies, the colours of the complexes are usually relatively pale. As examples, consider $[Cu(H_2O)_6]^{2+}$ which is a rather pale blue colour *vs* $[Cu(NH_3)_4]^{2+}$ which is an intense dark blue.

Molecular vibrations : Vibronic coupling

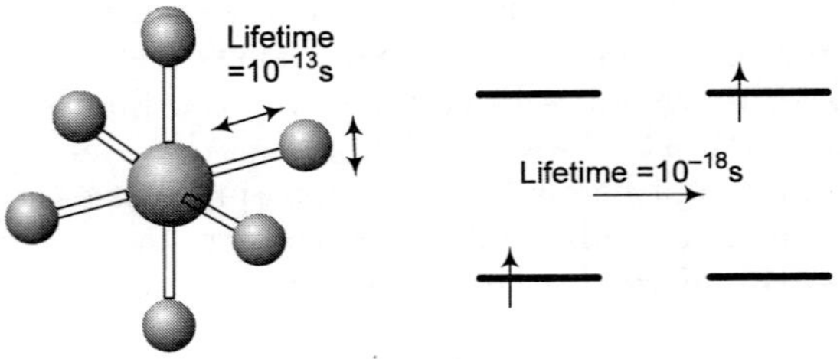

Vibronic coupling removes symmetry, thus allowing *d–d* transition to occur

Spin allowed-spin forbidden

Any transition for which is *strongly* forbidden; that is, in order to be allowed, a transition must involve no change in spin state. Consider the case of the high spin d^5 complex $[Mn(H_2O)_6]^{2+}$. Electronic transition is not only Laporte forbidden but also spin forbidden. When the absorptions are doubly forbidden, transitions are extremely weak. It is understandable, then, that dilute solutions of Mn(II) are colourless.

Promotion of an electron can only proceed if the spin orientation is conserved, *i.e.*, $\Delta S = 0$

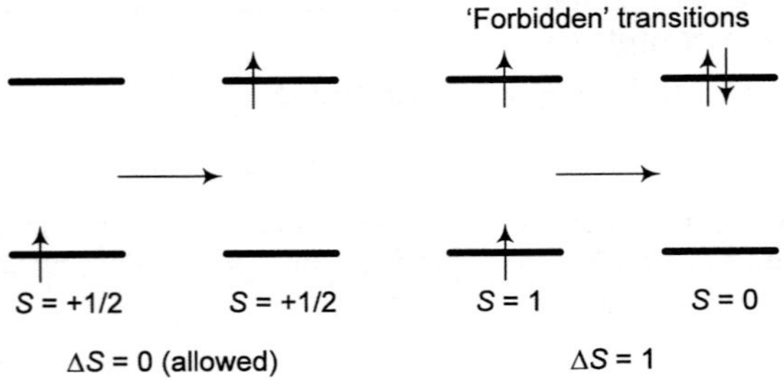

Charge-Transfer (CT) Bands

Similar to *d-d* transitions, charge-transfer (CT) transitions also involve the metal *d*-orbitals. CT bands are observed if the energies of empty and filled ligand- and metal-centred orbitals are similar. The direction of the electron transfer is determined by the relative energy levels of these orbitals : (i) Ligand-to-Metal charge transfer (LMCT) like in MnO_4^-, CrO_4^{2-}, etc. For MnO_4^-, the *d*-electron count on Mn(VII) is d^0. The origin of the colour in this species is not due to *d-d* transition, rather, charge transfer from O^{2-} to Mn(VII), described as LMCT band. (ii) Metal-to-Ligand charge transfer (MLCT) like in $[Fe(bpy)_3]^{2+}$. In this complex the charge transfer occurs from Fe(II) to the empty π^* orbitals of bpy ligand.

Charge-Transfer Absorptions

- Movement of electrons between metal and ligand.
- Often 1000 times stronger than *d-d* transition bands.

Ligand-to-metal charge transfer (LMCT)	**Metal-to-ligand charge transfer** (MLCT)
e.g., transfer of an electron from *p*-orbital on a chloride (*u* symmetry) to a metal's *d*-orbital (*g* symmetry).	*e.g.*, transfer of electron from metal's *d*-orbital to π^* orbital of CO ligand.
Favourable when metal centre is in a high oxidation state.	Favoured electron rich metal centres and those ligated by π-acceptors.
Common for π-donor ligands (like) F^-, O^{2-}, N^{3-}, OH^-)	Often higher in energy (in the UV region)
e.g., colour of $KMnO_4$ (d^0 complex)	

Below is a table that shows typical ε values for different types of transitions.

Expected Intensities of Electronic Transitions

Type of transition	Typical ε /dm³ mol⁻¹ cm⁻¹	Example
Spin-forbidden '*d-d*'	< 1	$[Mn(OH_2)_6]^{2+}$ (high spin d^5)
Laporte-forbidden, spin-allowed '*d-d*'	1–10	Centrosymmetric complexes, *e.g.*, $[Ti(OH_2)_6]^{3+}$ (d^1)
	150–1000	Non-centrosymm. $[NiCl_4]^{2-}$
Charge transfer (fully allowed)	1000–50000	$[MnO_4]^{2-}$

Formation of Coloured Complexes and Colorimetry

Colorimetry is a method of determining the concentration of a substance by measuring the relative absorption of light (usually visible) with respect to a known concentration of the substance.

The instrument by which these measurements are made is called a **colorimeter**

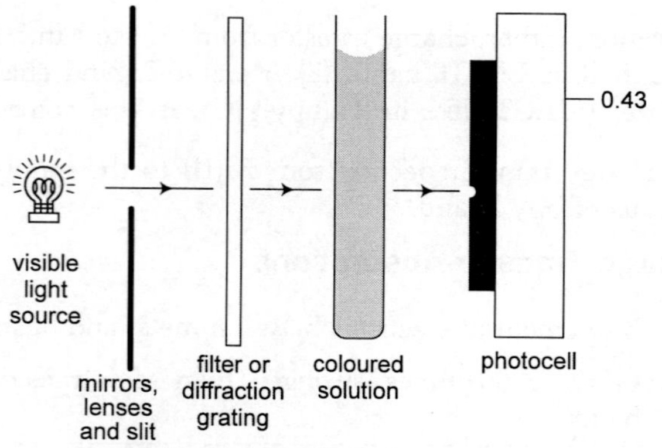

A simplified diagram of a colorimeter.

Light from a suitable source is passed through a light **filter** to select the most appropriate wavelength of light, some of which is then absorbed by the solution held in a special **glass cuvet** (a sort of 'test tube').

The amount of light absorbed is called, and measured as, the **absorbance** which is a function of the coloured solute concentration.

Most expensive instruments use a double beam system of two cuvets, one is a **black** of water and one the actual coloured solution under test, two photocells and sophisticated optics of lenses and mirrors which need not concern as at all.

Cheaper colorimeters (*i.e.,* in school and illustrated above) allow you to put in a cuvet of 'colourless' water, zero the instrument *i.e.,* set it to read zero absorbance, replace with a cuvet of the coloured solution and simply read of the 'absorbance'. The 'zeroing' is necessary because even the apparently 'colourless blank' of glass cuvet and water can absorbed a tiny amount of light. This procedure eliminates this error.

How do we use colorimetry to measure the concentration of a transition metal ion?

If an aqueous transition metal ion is intensely coloured, its concentration can be measured directly, *e.g.,* manganese concentration can be measured if it is oxidised to the deep purple manganate(VII) ion, MnO_4^-.

However, many ions are not as intense as the MnO_4^- ion, but if a suitable ligand or complexing agent is added, then a more intensely coloured complex may be formed, from which accurate measurements of concentration can be made, *e.g.,* the blue hexaaquacopper(II) ion forms a deeper violet-blue ammine complex with ammonia. Yellow-brown iron(III) ions form a deep blood-red complex with the thiocyanate ion (SCN^-) by mixing it with ammonium/potassium cyanate.

Once the method of producing a more intense colour is established, you then need to derive a **calibration curve.**

This is done by **by measuring the absorbance of solutions of known concentrations** of the coloured complex and plotting the calibration curve/graph.

The known concentration range should include any likely absorbance measured from the solutions under test, *i.e.,* those whose concentration is being determined. Generally **at low concentrations the calibration curve is linear,** *i.e.,* it obeys **Beer's Law (Beer-Lambert Law).** Without going into the mathematics of Beer's Law and absorption, it basically states that **a solution's absorbance is directly proportional to the concentration of the coloured solute.**

For various reasons the calibration may curve upwards (positive deviation from Beer's Law) or curve over (negative deviation from Beer's Law). However, a linear or otherwise calibration curve still shows increasing absorption with increasing concentration and curved calibration graphs are acceptable, if not advisable, if your methodology is accurate.

How can we use colorimetry to deduce the formula of a complex?

The method depends on measuring the absorbancies of solutions containing different ratios of transition metal ion to complexing agent. Just for the sake of argument, imagine that one mole of transition metal ion (M^{3+}) reacts with two moles of a monodentate ligand (X^-). The reaction equation for the ligand displacement to form the complex would be :

(i) $[M(H_2O)_6]^{3+}(aq) + 2X^-(aq) \rightleftharpoons [M(H_2O)_4X_2]^+(aq) + 2H_2O(l)$

There are two basic approaches as to how you vary the transiton metal ion-ligand ratio and the results illustrated in the diagram below.

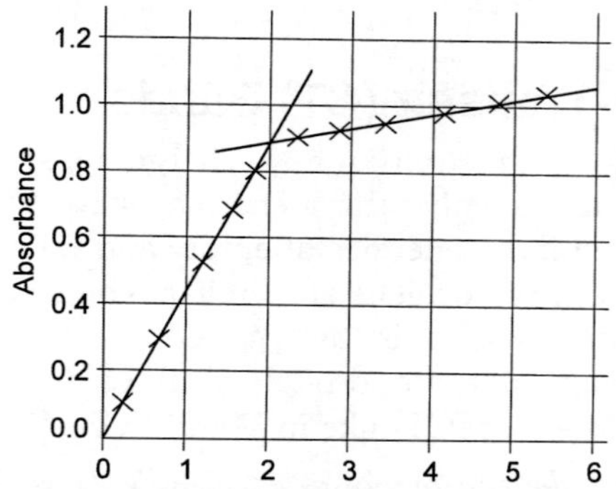

Moles of complexing agent per mole of transition metal ion mol X^- per mol M^{3+} [1] mole ratio method

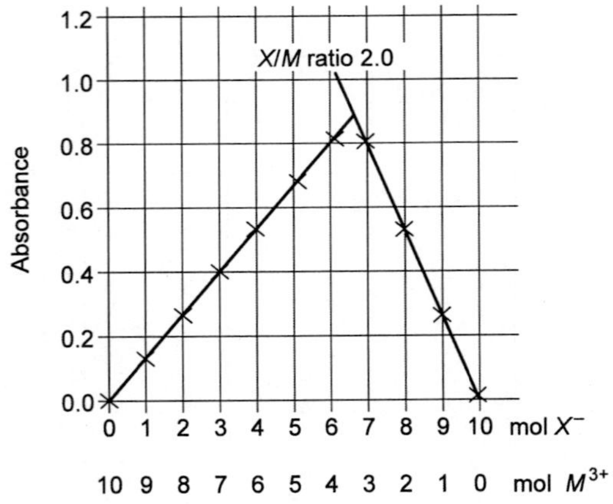

[2] continuous variation method

Method (1) The mole ratio method Keeping M^{n+} constant and gradually increasing the number of moles of ligand X from zero to a large molar excess.

From 0.0 to 2.0 moles of X^- added per 1.0 moles of M^{3+} there is a steady rise in absorbance as more and more of the complex is formed. From over 2.0 of X^- per mole M^{3+} there is a more gradual rise in absorbance.

The point of intersection of the two linear portions of the graph gives you the X^-/M^{3+} ratio in the complex, *i.e.,* 2.0.

Note that ligand exchange reactions are equilibrium reactions so you do not go to the maximum absorbance at 2.0 but the change in the 'rate of change' of absorbance does give the ratio *e.g.,*

1. If you do this for the reaction between iron(III) ions and thiocyanate ions which gives a blood-red complex, you obtain the change in graph gradient at 1.0 mol of CNS^- to 1.0 mol of Fe^{3+} for the reaction

$$[Fe(H_2O)_6]^{3+}(aq) + CNS^-(aq) \rightleftharpoons [Fe(H_2O)_5CNS]^{2+}(aq) + H_2O\ (l)$$

2. For dilute solutions of copper(II) ions and ammonia the graph gradient change occurs at 4.0 moles of NH_3 per mol of Cu^{2+} for the reaction.

$$[Cu\ (H_2O)_6]^{3+}(aq) + 4\ NH_3(aq) \rightleftharpoons [Cu(H_2O)_2(NH_3)_4]^{2+}(aq) + 4H_2O(l)$$

Method (2) The continuous variations method in which you start with zero moles of M^{n+} and an excess of the ligand X. In each successive mixture you then increase the amount of M^{n+} and decrease the amount of X^- and keep the total moles of M^{n+} and X^- constant.

For the sake of argument, if you **assume both stock solutions are the same molarity,** then the ratio of the volumes automatically gives you the *X/M* ratio in the mixture.

For the fictitious M^{3+} and F^- complex, the peak will occur between the $6X^- : 4M^{3+}$ mixture (ratio 1.5) and the $7X^- : 3M^{3+}$ mixture (ratio 2.33). Theoretically the peak should occur at a ratio of 2.0 for X^-/M^{3+}, *i.e.,* theoretically, in terms of a total volume of 10 units, it means a $6.6X^- : 3.3M^{3+}$ mixture by volume.

For the iron(III)-thiocyanate complex in reaction (ii) the peak will occur at $5CNS^- : 5Fe^{3+}$. A CNS^-/Fe^{3+} ratio of 1.0 for the complex $[Fe(H_2O)_5CNS]^{2+}$. For the copper (II) ammonia complex in reaction (III) the peak will occur at $8NH_3 : 2Cu^{2+}$ *i.e.,* an NH_3 / Cu^{2+} ratio of 4.0 for the complex $[Cu(NH_3)_4]^{2+}$ or $[Cu(H_2O)_2(NH_3)_4]^{2+}$.

In both cases, you work out the mole ratios present in the mixtures from the known concentrations and volumes of the stock solutions of M^{n+} and X^- used in each experiment.

Compounds of Transition Metals

Transition metals form complexes due to (i) small size of cation (ii) high effective nuclear charge (iii) availability of *d*-orbitals of appropriate energy for bonding to the ligand. The increased stabilities of complexes within each family occurs with :

Ox. State	Sc	Ti	V	Cr	Mn	Fe	Co	Ni	Cu	Zn
+1, (I)	—	—	—	—	—	—	—	—	CuI white(*s*) $[CuCl_3]^{2-}$	—
+2, (II)		$[Ti(H_2O)_6]^{2+}$ violet(*aq*)	$[V(H_2O)_6]^{2+}$ violet(*aq*)		MnO (*s*) $[Mn(H_2O)_6]^{2+}$ very pale pink(*aq*)	$[Fe(H_2O)_6]^{2+}$ pale green(*aq*)	CoO(*s*) $[Co(H_2O)_6]^{2+}$ pink(*aq*) [Less stable]	$NiCl_2$ (*s*) $[Ni(H_2O)_6]^{2+}$ green(*aq*) $[Ni(CN)_4]^{2-}$	$[Cu(H_2O)_6]^{2+}$ blue green(*aq*)	ZnO, $ZnCO_3$ white(*s*) $[Zn(H_2O)_4]^{2+}$ colourless (*aq*)

+3, (III)	Sc_2O_3 $Sc(OH)_3$ white(*s*) $[Sc(H_2O)_6]^{3+}$ colourless (*aq*)	$[Ti(H_2O)_6]^{3+}$ purple (*aq*)	$[V(H_2O)_6]^{2+}$ violet (*aq*)	Cr_2O_3 (*s*) $[Cr(H_2O)_6]^{3+}$ green (*aq*)	Mn_2O_3 brown (*s*)	Fe_2O_3 brown (*s*) $[Fe(H_2O)_6]^{3+}$ yellowish brown (*aq*)	$[Co(NH_3)_6]^{3+}$ (*aq*) more stable			—
+4, (IV)	—	TiO_2 white(*s*) $[TiO]^{2+}$ colourless (*aq*) $TiCl_4$ colourless (*l*)	$[VO]^{2+}$ blue (*aq*)	—	MnO_2 black (*s*)	—	—	—	—	—
+5, (V)	—	—	V_2O_5 white (*s*) $[VO_4]^{3-}$ $[VO_2]^+$ yellow (*aq*)	—	—	—	—	—	—	—
+6, (VI)	—	—	—	CrO_3 (*s*) $Cr_2O_7^{2-}$ orange (*aq*) CrO_4^{2-} yellow (*aq*)	MnO_4^{2-} green (*aq*)	FeO_4^{2-} (in s)				
+7, (VII)	—	—	—	—	$KMnO_4$ dark purple (*s*) MnO_4^- purple (*aq*)	—	—	—	—	—

(i) **Increase in atomic number of the element** and in a **particular oxidation state with decreasing size of the atom.**

(ii) When a transition metal atom exhibits more than one oxidation state, the ion with the **highest charge forms complexes** of greater stability.

Magnetic Behaviour and Magnetic Susceptibility

If a body is placed in a homogeneous field, H_0, the field within the body varies from the free space value. Chemists often prefer to measure mass rather than volume, and to use moles rather than grams. Hence, molar magnetic susceptibility χ_M is usually reported.

magnetic induction → $B = H_0 + 4\pi M$ ← magnetisation

↑ applied homogeneous field

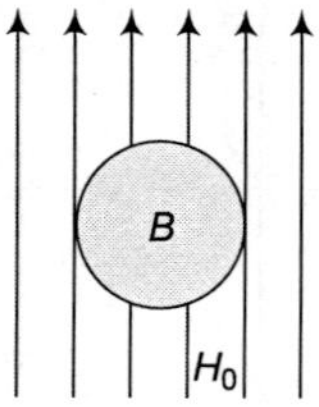

$$\frac{B}{H_0} = 1 + \frac{4\pi M}{H_0}$$

$\kappa = M/H_0$ = volume magnetic susceptibility

$\chi_M + \kappa M_r/\rho$ = molar magnetic susceptibility ($cm^2 mol^{-1}$)

The sign of the induced magnetization (M) defines two basic types of magnetic behaviour. If M (or χ) is negative, it is diamagnetism; if M (or χ) is positive, it is paramagnetism. In a field gradient, diamagnet moves out of field to lower energy ($\chi < 0$) and paramagnet moves in to field to lower energy. Compounds with only paired electrons are diamagnetic and compounds with unpaired electrons are paramagnetic. The ferromagnetism, anti-ferromagnetism and ferrimagnetism are special forms of paramagnetism that are outside the scope of this course.

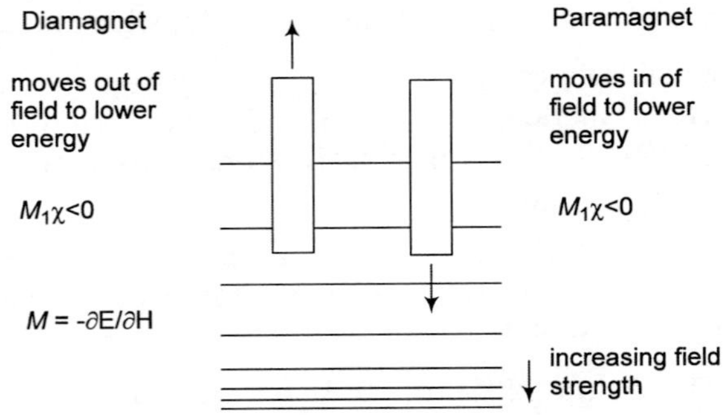

Typically χ_{para} values are higher than χ_{dia}. The χ_M values of diamagnetic N_2 and paramagnetic O_2 illustrate this fact. All substances have a diamagnetic component to the susceptibility. The observed χ_{obs} includes the contribution from both χ_{para} and χ_{dia}.

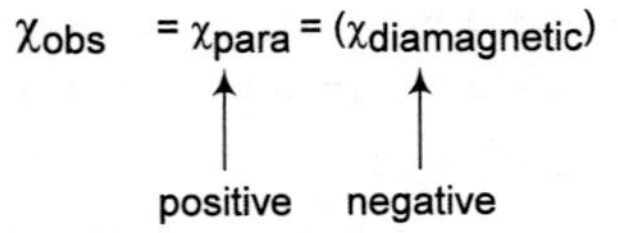

$|\chi_{para}| >> |\chi_{dia}|$

N_2 $\chi_M = 12 \times 10^{-6}$ cm^{3}mol^{-1} diamagnetic

O_2 $\chi_M = 3450 \times 10^{-6}$ cm^{3}mol^{-1} paramagnetic

Paramagnetism

It arises from the interaction between H_0 and the magnetic field of the unpaired electron associated with their spin and orbital angular momenta. In a hypothetical free ion or atom, both the orbital and spin angular momenta give rise to a magnetic moment and contribute to paramagnetism. When the atom or the ion is part of a complex, orbital angular momentum may be eliminated (or quenched). We shall discuss the quenching of the orbital contribution later. However, the spin angular momentum survives and gives rise to **spin-only paramagnetism** which is characteristic of many *d*-block metal complexes.

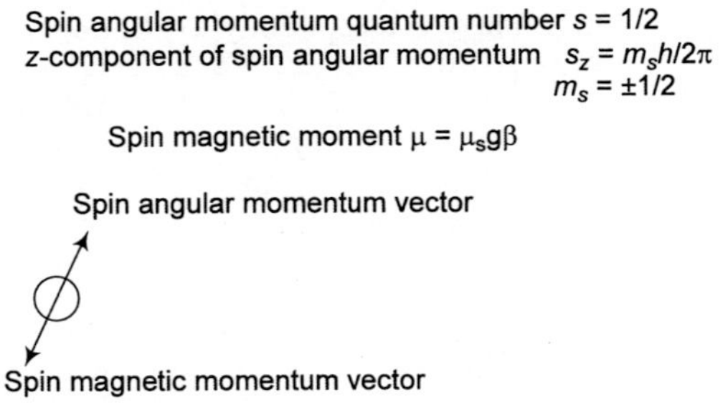

Curie Law

The Curie law relates the molar magnetic susceptibility χ_M as a function of temperature. In Curie equation, N is Avogadro's number, k is Boltzmann constant, g is the gyromagnetic ratio, and β is Bohr magneton. A simplified form of Curie Law : $\chi_M = C/T$ which describe the inverse dependence of χ_M with temperature T. Here, C is a constant that is characteristic of the substance and known as Curie constant.

Curie Law The values of C for different 'S' values can be calculated from the Curie equation. For $S = 1/2$, 1, 3/2, 2 and 5/2, the calculated values of C are 0.375, 1.0, 1.88, 3.0 and 4.375 emu K/mol. Experimentally, if we measure χ_M of a substance at different temperature and plot $\chi_M T$ values against T, we shall obtain a straight line that would intersect the y-axis at the value C. The experimental C value would provide information on the number of unpaired electrons in the system.

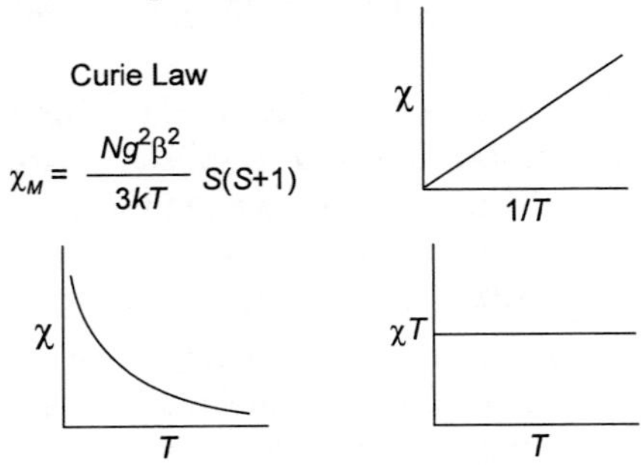

Constant to remember $\frac{N\beta^2}{k} = 0.375$ emu K/mol.

Unpaired electrons	S value	Susceptibility	Curie constant
1	1/2	$\chi_M = \frac{Ng^2\beta^2}{4kT}$	$C = \frac{Ng^2\beta^2}{4k}$
2	1	$\chi_M = \frac{2Ng^2\beta^2}{3kT}$	$C = \frac{2Ng^2\beta^2}{3k}$
3	3/2	$\chi_M = \frac{5Ng^2\beta^2}{4kT}$	$C = \frac{5Ng^2\beta^2}{4k}$

Unpaired electrons	S value	Susceptibility	Curie constant
4	2	$\chi_M = \dfrac{2Ng^2\beta^2}{kT}$	$C = \dfrac{2Ng^2\beta^2}{k}$
5	5/2	$\chi_M = \dfrac{35Ng^2\beta^2}{12kT}$	$C = \dfrac{35Ng^2\beta^2}{12k}$

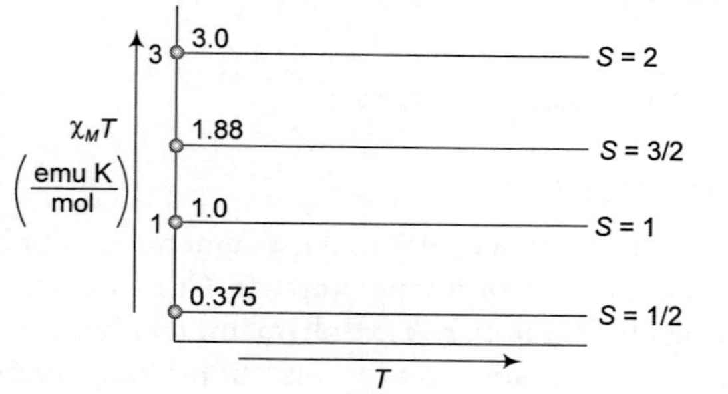

Effective Magnetic Moment

It is a convenient paramater (μ_{eff}) (hugely popular among inorganic chemists) that is related to χ_M. The 'μ_{eff}' is defined as :

$$(\mu_{eff})^2 = g^2 S(S+1)\beta^2$$

If $g = 2$, $\mu_{eff} = 2\sqrt{S(S+1)}$ in units of β or BM

It can also be expressed in terms of number of unpaired electrons :

$$\mu_{eff} = 2\sqrt{S(S+1)} = \sqrt{n(n+2)} \text{ BM}$$

The μ_{eff} is related to the $\chi_M T$ values :

$$\mu_{eff} = \left(\frac{3k}{N\beta^2}\right)^{1/2} (\chi_M T)^{1/2} = \sqrt{8\chi_M T} = 2.83\sqrt{\chi_M T}$$

To recapitulate, one first makes a direct measurement of the volume susceptibility of a substance from which χ_M is calculated, and the above equation allows one to deduce the magnetic moment of the ion, atom or molecule responsible for the paramagnetism.

The μ_{eff}, however, can be calculated very easily if we know the number of unpaired electrons in the system.

Ion	No. of unpaired electrons (n)	S	Predicted μ_{eff} values
Ti^{3+}	1	1/2	$\sqrt{3} = 1.73$
V^{3+}	2	1	$\sqrt{8} = 2.83$
Cr^{3+}	3	3/2	$\sqrt{15} = 3.87$
Mn^{3+}	4	2	$\sqrt{24} = 4.90$
Fe^{3+}	5	5/2	$\sqrt{35} = 5.92$

Inferring Electron Configuration from Magnetic Moment

1. **The magnetic moment of an octahedral Co(II) complex is 4.0 BM. What is its electronic configuration?**

   Co(II) complex is d^7 system. The two possible configurations are $t_{2g}^5 e_g^2$ (high-spin) with three unpaired electrons or $t_{2g}^6 e_g^1$ (low-spin) with one unpaired electron. The spin-only values would be 3.87 and 1.73 BM. Therefore, the only consistent assignment is the configuration $t_{2g}^5 e_g^2$, which means a high-spin complex.

2. **The magnetic moment of the complex $[Mn(NCS)_6]^{4-}$ is 6.06 BM. What is its electron configuration?**

   A Mn(II) complex is d^5 system. The magnetic moment value suggests an electron configuration $t_{2g}^3 e_g^2$, that means it is a high-spin complex.

3. **The anion $[Ni(SPh)_4]^{2-}$ is tetrahedral. Explain why it is paramagnetic?**

   The Ni(II) is d^8 system. In a tetrahedral environment the electron configuration should be $e^4 t_2^4$ containing two unpaired electrons. Hence, it is paramagnetic. On contrary, $[Ni(CN)_4]^{2-}$ is diamagnetic as it adopts a square planar geometry and all eight d-electrons are paired up.

4. **The complexes $NiCl_2(PPh_3)_2$ and $PdCl_2(PPh_3)_2$ are paramagnetic and diamagnetic respectively.**

   The structure of these two complexes can be assigned from the magnetic data. Both the Ni(II) and Pd(II) are d^8 ions. The $PdCl_2(PPh_3)_2$ should have a square-planar geometry and $NiCl_2(PPh_3)_2$ have a tetrahedral structure with two unpaired electrons.

5. **Take two examples of $K_3[CoF_6]$ and $[Co(NH_3)_6]Cl_3$. The first one is a high-spin complex with ground state electron configuration $t_{2g}^4 e_g^2$ and the complex is paramagnetic.**

   The second complex is diamagnetic indicating it as a low-spin complex with electron configuration $t_{2g}^6 e_g^0$.

Orbital Contribution to Magnetic Moments

From a quantum mechanical point of view magnetic moment is dependent on both spin and orbital angular momentum contributions. The spin-only formula used is given as : $\mu_{s.o.} = \sqrt{\{4S(S+1)\}}$ and this can be modified to include the orbital angular momentum as follows :

$$\mu_{eff} = \sqrt{L(L+1) + 4S(S+1)}$$

For orbital angular momentum to contribute, and hence for the paramagnetism to differ significantly from the spin-only value, the orbital in which electron resides must be able to transform the orbital it occupies into an equivalent and degenerate orbital by a simple rotation (it is the rotation of the electrons which induces the orbital contribution).In a free ion, the five *d*-orbitals are degenerate and some orbitals can be transformed into others by rotations. The figure illustrates that a 90° or 45° rotation about *z*-axis transform $d_{xz} \leftrightarrow d_{yz}$ and $d_{xy} \leftrightarrow d_{x^2-y^2}$ orbitals respectively. In an octahedral complex, due to crystal field splitting, the degeneracy between the d_{xy} and $d_{x^2-y^2}$ orbitals is lifted. It causes the partial quenching of the orbital contribution. There is a further factor that needs to be taken into consideration : if all the t_{2g} orbitals are singly occupied, an electron in, say d_{xz} orbital, cannot be transferred into d_{yz} orbital because it already contains an electron having the same spin quantum number as the incoming electron; if all the t_{2g} orbitals are doubly occupied the transfer is not possible. Thus, **only configurations which have t_{2g} electron other than**

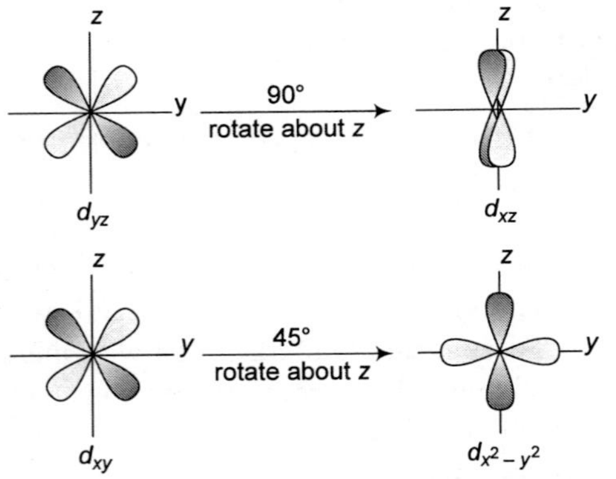

three or six electrons make orbital contributions to the magnetic moments of octahedral complexes : for high-spin complexes, only the configurations t_{2g}^1, t_{2g}^2, $t_{2g}^4 e_g^2$ and $t_{2g}^5 e_g^2$. **Note that e_g electrons do not contribute to orbital moment**. For tetrahedral geometry it is easily shown that the configurations giving rise to an orbital contribution are $e^2t_2^1$, $e^2t_2^2$, $e^4t_2^4$ and $e^4t_2^5$.

It is evident from this discussion that in most cases the orbital moments are quenched in metal complexes and magnetic moments are close to the spin-only value. The tables below give a list of spin-only and spin-orbital magnetic moments with experimental data for d^1 to d^9 configurations.

Configuration $3d^n$, n =	$\mu_{s+o} = [L(L+1) + 4S(S+1)]^{1/2}$ BM	$\mu_s = [4S(S+1)]^{1/2}$ BM	μ_{eff} obs at 300 K
1	3.00	1.73	1.7 – 1.8
2	4.47	2.83	2.8 – 2.9
3	5.20	3.87	3.7 – 3.9
4	5.48	4.90	4.8 – 5.0
5	5.92	5.92	5.8 – 6.0
6	5.48	4.90	5.1 – 5.7
7	5.20	3.87	4.3 – 5.2
8	4.47	2.83	2.9 – 3.9
9	3.00	1.73	1.7 – 2.2
10	0.00	0.00	0

An example helps to understand the quenching of orbital moment in different metal complexes. Lets consider Ni(II) (d^8) complex. As a free ion, the total magnetic moment μ_{s+o} is calculated to be 4.47. In octahedral d^8 complex, the orbital contribution is zero. On the contrary, d^8 tetrahedral complex will have contribution from the orbital magnetic moment. Hence, although both complexes have two unpaired electrons, the $[Ni(H_2O)_6]^{2+}$ has magnetic moment close to the spin-only value but the magnetic moment in $[NiCl_4]^{2-}$ is higher than the spin-only value.

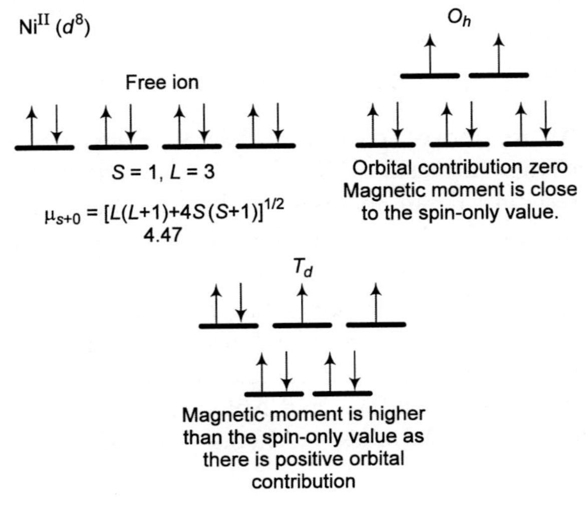

Thus, magnetic property of first transition series elements can be interpreted by using spin only formula and hence the geometry of the complex.

The magnetic behaviour of the heavier transition elements is more complex, as in these filling of electrons in IInd and IIIrd transition series involves *4d* and *5d*-subshells. These *4d* and *5d* orbitals are too much spread out in space and as a result the interelectronic repulsions in these are much less as compared to *3d*-orbitals. These orbitals so can accommodate two electrons without much loss in stability relative to *3d*-orbitals which are much smaller in size.

A given set of ligands produces very large crystal field splitting energies in *4d* and *5d*-orbitals than in the *3d* orbitals. The heavier elements thus tend to show low-spin complexes.

Ist transition series–mainly forms high spin complex

IInd and IIIrd Transition series–form low-spin complex.

Atomic Radii

The variation in atomic radii across each transition series is not as simple as that observed in the *s*- and *p*-block elements. For a quick glance, atomic radii of *d*-block elements are given in Table 8.7. Some overall trends are given below :

Table 8.7 **Atomic Radii Å of *d*-block Elements**

Sc	Ti	V	Cr	Mn	Fe	Co	Ni	Cu	Zn
1.60	1.46	1.31	1.25	1.29	1.26	1.25	1.24	1.28	1.33
Y	Zr	Nb	Mo	Tc	Ru	Rh	Pd	Ag	Cd
1.80	1.57	1.41	1.36	1.30	1.33	1.34	1.38	1.44	1.49
La	Hf	Ta	W	Re	Os	Ir	Pt	Au	Hg
1.88	1.57	1.43	1.37	1.36	1.34	1.35	1.38	1.44	1.55

(i) As we move across a transition series, nuclear charge increases with increasing atomic number resulting in an increase in the attraction of the nucleus for the outermost electron. Consequently, atomic radii decreases across each row.

(ii) However, the decrease in the radii across a period is not uniform. Furthermore, this decrease in radii is not large enough when compared to the decrease in the same period for *s*- and *p*-block elements. This is because in *d*-block elements the addition of electrons takes place in an inner $(n - 1)$ d subshell which thereby adds to the primary screening effect. The additional electrons effectively screen the outer *ns* electrons from the added nuclear charge. Consequently, as the atomic number increases so does the screening effect and as a result the effective nuclear charge increases only slightly. Therefore, there is only a little change in the radii.

(iii) It can be seen from Table 8.7 that atomic size of elements in transition series reaches a minimum amongst the groups 8, 9 and 10 elements and towards the end of the series an increase in the radii takes place. Normally, we expect the radii to decrease continuously. This normally can be attributed to the increased forces of repulsion between the added electrons which exceed the attractive forces due to increased nuclear charge and thereby the electron cloud expands.

(iv) There is an increase in atomic radii with increase in atomic number in a given group. However, this increase is not as significant as in *s*- and *p*-block elements. The very close radii of the elements of second and third transition series is a consequence of the filling of the $4f$ subshell (called lanthanide contraction).

Ionic Radii

Ionic radii of a transition element depends upon the oxidation state of the transition element. For example, Fe^{2+} = 0.76 Å and Fe^{3+} = 0.64 Å; Mn^{2+} = 0.80 Å and Mn^{3+} = 0.66 Å. Therefore, for the sake of comparison, the radii of bivalent ions of the first transition series are given below :

Ion	Ti^{2+}	V^{2+}	Cr^{2+}	Mn^{2+}	Fe^{2+}	Co^{2+}	Ni^{2+}	Cu^{2+}
Radius (Å)	0.90	0.88	0.84	0.80	0.76	0.74	0.72	0.69

(i) From the above data, it is evident that as the nuclear charge increases, the ionic radii decreases. This decrease is due to the fact that with increase of nuclear charge, the incoming electrons enter the inner $(n - 1)$ *d*-orbitals. As a result, there is a gradual decrease in ionic radii.

(ii) The ionic radii of the transition elements are smaller than those of the representative elements of the same period. This is again due to the reason that electrons enter in diffused *d*-orbitals in case of transition elements while they enter *s*- or *p*-orbitals (which are not diffused) in case of representative elements. Hence, transition metal ions experience greater effective nuclear charge than the ions of representative elements which results in a greater decrease in ionic radii of transition metal ions.

Density

The densities of transition elements are very high as compared to the metals of groups 1 and 2. The densities of the electrons in a given transition series increases while moving across a period and reaches a maximum value at groups 8, 9 or 10. This trend can be explained in terms of the small radii and close packed structures of these elements.

There is a substantial increase in density in moving down a group. The atomic sizes of the elements of second and third transition series remain the same but their atomic masses increase two fold. As a result of this, the densities of the elements of third transition series are generally twice those of the corresponding elements of the second transition series as shown in Table 8.8.

Table 8.8 **Comparison of Densities of Some Elements of Second and Third Transition Series**

	Element	Atomic radius	Atomic mass	Density (g. mL)	Element	Atomic radius	Atomic mass	Density (g/mL)
2nd T. series	Nb	1.41	93	8.6	Mo	1.36	96	10.2
3rd T. series	Ta	1.43	181	16.6	W	1.37	186	19.3
2ndT. series	Tc	1.30	99	11.5	Ag	1.44	108	10.5
3rd T. series	Re	1.36	186	20.5	Au	1.44	197	19.3

Melting Point and Boiling Point

The *d*-block elements have very high melting and boiling points. Melting point of a crystalline element is determined by the nature of the binding forces between its constituents. It is obvious that the *d*-block elements are held by strong forces. The melting and boiling points reach a maxima near groups 5 or 6. This can be explained in terms of the number of unpaired *d*-electrons in each atom. They determine the magnitude of binding forces by forming covalent bonds with unpaired electrons of neighbouring atoms. In general, the greater the number of unpaired electrons in the valence shell, the stronger is the metallic bond and hence higher are the melting and boiling points. In moving across a transition series from left to right, the number of unpaired *d*-electrons rises to a maximum of five in group 6 when melting points tends to become very high beyond which electron pairing begins, so that melting point starts decreasing. The only exception are the elements of group 12 (Zn, Cd and Hg) which have low melting and boiling points. The different behaviour of these elements can also be explained in terms of their completely filled *d* subshells with no electrons available for covalent bonding amongst the atoms of these elements. All transition metal groups show an increase in their melting and boiling points.

Ionisation Energies

The ionization energies of *d*-block elements increase as we move across each series though not quite regularly. The increase in the value is not as pronounced as compared to the increase in the same period for the *s*- and *p*-block elements. **The effect of increasing nuclear charge which would tend to increase the ionisation energy seems to be almost offset by the extra screening of the nucleus provided by the inner *d*-electrons. Consequently, ionisation energy increases quite slowly along a transition series. The ionisation energy values of *d*-block elements indicate that the outer-electron of each atom is more strongly bound as compared with that of *s*-block metals whereas it is loosely bound as compared with that of *p*-block elements. This would suggest that the transition metals are less electropositive than the *s*-block elements.**

In the third transition series, the first ionisation energy is generally higher than the elements of first or second transition series. This is due to presence of $4f$ orbitals in the third transition series which cause poor shielding effect and thus cause increased effective nuclear charge on the outer valence electrons. Hence, their first ionisation energy increases.

Standard Oxidation Potentials and Reducing Properties

The values of standard oxidation potentials of 3*d*-series elements for the reactions M/M^{2+} and M/M^{3+} excepting Cu, is higher than that of standard hydrogen electrode (taken as zero). It is, therefore, expected that these metals, excepting Cu, would evolve H_2 gas from acid solutions according to the equation

$$M + 2H^+ \text{ (from acid)} \longrightarrow M^{2+} + H_2 \text{(gas)}$$

In actual practice the rate with which most of the metals react with acid is very slow. Some of the metals get protected from further attack of the acids due to the formation of a thin protective layer of their oxide which prevents the acid to come in further contact with the metals, *e.g.,* although electrode potential of Cr is high, it gets coated with its non-reactive, Cr_2O_3 which makes the chromium metal so unreactive that it can be used as a protective non-oxidising metal.

Reducing Properties

In spite of the fact that the metals of first transition series, excepting Cu, have high values of standard electrode potentials, these are not as good reducing agents as the metals of IA, IIA and IIIA groups, although some of the metals of these groups (*e.g.,* Al) have smaller oxidation potentials. The poor reducing capacity of the transition metals is due to high heats of vaporisation, high ionisation potentials and low heats of hydration of their ions.

The tendency of Cu to change into Cu^{2+} ions is extremely low due to its negative electrode potential. The metal is also not able to displace H^+ ions from acid solutions Cu is, therefore, particularly poor reducing agent, *i.e.,* oxidation of copper metal by H^+ to Cu^{2+} does not occur readily and consequently Cu metal will not dissolve in acids.

Exercise 1
(For Part 'B')

1. The correct ground state electronic configuration of chromium atom is
(a) $[Ar]\,3d^5 4s^1$ (b) $[Ar]\,3d^4 4s^2$
(c) $[Ar]\,3d^6 4s^0$ (d) $[Ar]\,3d^4 4s^1 4p^1$

2. Which oxides will not give metal on heating?
(a) ZnO (b) Ag_2O
(c) HgO (d) All of these

3. In $Na_2[Fe(CN)_5NO]$, sodium nitroprusside
(a) oxidation state of Fe is +2
(b) this has NO^+ as ligand
(c) Both (a) and (b) are correct
(d) None of the above is correct

4. Paramagnetism is given by the relation, $\mu = \sqrt{s(s+1)}$ magnetons where, 's' is the total spin. On the basis, the paramagnetism of Cu^+ ion is
(a) 1.41 magnetons (b) 2.83 magnetons
(c) 3.88 magnetons (d) Zero

5. Ti^{2+} is purple while Ti^{4+} is colourless because
(a) Ti^{2+} has $3d^2$ configuration
(b) Ti^{4+} has $3d^2$ configuration
(c) Ti^{4+} is a very small cation when compared to Ti^{2+} hence, does not absorb any radiation
(d) Ti^{2+} has one unpaired electron

6. Silver ornaments turn black by atmospheric
(a) O_2 (b) Cl_2 (c) H_2S (d) N_2

7. Maximum magnetic moment is shown by
(a) d^5 (b) d^6 (c) d^7 (d) d^8

8. Magnetic moment of Cr $(Z = 24)$, $Mn^+(Z = 25)$ and $Fe^{2+}(Z = 26)$ are x, y, z. They are in the order
(a) $x < y < z$ (b) $z < x = y$
(c) $x = y = z$ (d) $x = y < z$

9. Interstitial compound is formed by
(a) Fe, Ni (b) Fe, Co
(c) Co, Ni (d) All of these

10. A jeweller is selling 22-carat gold articles with 95% purity, it is approximately
(a) 3.5% higher (b) 3.5% lower
(c) 4.5% exact (d) 5% lower

11. Which of the following statements is not true?
(a) Cu^{2+} is colourless ion
(b) Ions of d-block elements are coloured due to d–d transition
(c) Ions of f-block elements are coloured due to f-f transition
(d) $[Sc(H_2O)_6]^{3+}$, $[Ti(H_2O)_6]^{3+}$ are coloured complexes

12. Maximum oxidation state is shown by
(a) Mn (b) Cr (c) Co (d) Os

13. Following elements do not show the characteristics of d-block elements
(a) Sc, Ti, V (b) Fe, Co, Ni
(c) Cu, Ag, Au (d) Zn, Cd, Hg

14. The ability of d-block elements to form complexes is due to
(a) small and highly charged ions
(b) vacant low energy orbitals to accept lone pair of electrons from ligands
(c) Both (a) and (b) are correct
(d) None of the above

15. AgCl and NaCl are colourless. NaBr and NaI are also colourless but AgBr and AgI are coloured. This is due to
(a) Ag^+ polarises Br^- and I^-
(b) Ag^+ has unpaired d-orbital
(c) Ag^+ depolarises Br^- and I^-
(d) None of the above

16. Only +2, +3, +4 oxidation states are shown by
(a) Sc, Ti (b) Ti, Ni
(c) Fe, Ni (d) Zn, Ni

17. Maximum oxidation state of Os is
(a) +5 (b) +6 (c) +7 (d) +8

18. Which forms interstitial compound?
(a) Fe (b) Co
(c) Ni (d) All of these

19. Which shows maximum magnetic moment among the bivalent ions of the first transition series?
(a) Mn^{2+} (b) Fe^{2+}
(c) Co^{2+} (d) Ni^{2+}

20. Which of the following metals has more than one oxidation state?
(a) Ca (b) Sr (c) Mn (d) Zn

21. The element Ds lies in
(a) s-block (b) p-block
(c) d-block (d) f-block

22. The mercury is the only metal which is liquid at 0°C. This is due to its
(a) weak metallic bond (b) high vapour pressure
(c) high ionisation energy (d) Both (a) and (c)

23. A transition element 'X' has a configuration $[Ar]\,3d^4$, in its +3 oxidation state. Its atomic number is
(a) 19 (b) 22 (c) 25 (d) 26

24. Which one of the following ionic species will impart colour to an aqueous solution?
(a) Ti^{4+} (b) Cr^{3+}
(c) Cu^{+} (d) Zn^{2+}

25. Which one of the following characteristics of the transition metals is associated with their catalytic activity?
(a) Paramagnetic behaviour
(b) Colour of hydrated ions
(c) Variable oxidation states
(d) High enthalpy of atomization

26. The reactivity of transition elements decreases with
(a) low heat of hydration
(b) the decrease in the atomic number
(c) the increase in the atomic number
(d) None of the above

27. The incorrect statement for *d*-block element is
(a) it shows magnetic property
(b) it has complete *d*-orbitals
(c) it has variable valency
(d) it has tendency of formation of coloured ions

28. Which of the following transition element shows the highest oxidation state?
(a) V (b) Cr (c) Mn (d) Fe

29. The pair of compounds having metals in their highest oxidation state is
(a) MnO_2, $FeCl_3$ (b) $[NiCl_4]^{2-}$, $[CoCl_4]^-$
(c) $[MnO_4]^-$ CrO_2Cl_2 (d) $[Fe(CN)_6]^{3-}$, $[Co(CN)_3]$

30. Amongst the following, identify the species with an atom in +6 oxidation state
(a) MnO_4^- (b) CrO_2Cl_2
(c) $Cr(CN)_6^{3-}$ (d) NiF_6^{2-}

31. Different (variable) oxidation state is shown by transition elements. It is due to the fact
(a) *ns* electrons may be excited to $(n-1)$ *d*-orbitals
(b) $(n-1)$ *d*-electrons may be excited to *ns*-orbital
(c) $(n-1)$ *d*-electron may get involved along with *ns*-electrons in binding
(d) None of the above facts is correct

32. Select the correct statement for the lesser number of oxidation states, in 3*d*-series
(a) In the beginning of the series, it can be due to the presence of too few electrons to loose or share
(b) Towards the end of the series, it can be ascribed to the presence of too many electrons and thus fewer empty orbitals to share electrons with the ligands
(c) Both (a) and (b) are correct
(d) None of the above

33. First ionisation energy of 5*d*-elements are higher than those of 3*d* and 4*d* elements. This is due to
(a) greater effective nuclear charge acting on outer valence electrons
(b) greater effective nuclear charge is experienced because of weak shielding of the nucleus by 4*f*-electrons
(c) Both (a) and (b)
(d) None of the above

34. Atoms of the transition elements are smaller than those of the *s*-block elements. This is because of
(a) orbital electrons added to the penultimate *d*-shell rather than to the outer shell of the atom
(b) usual contraction in size across a horizontal period
(c) Both (a) and (b)
(d) None of the above

35. The radii of the elements from chromium $(Z = 24)$ to copper $(Z = 29)$ are very close to one another. This is due to
(a) lanthanide contraction
(b) atomic radii do not remain constant but decrease in a normal gradation
(c) the fact that successive addition of *d*-electrons screen the outer electrons (4*s*) from the inward pull of the nucleus
(d) increase in radii due to increase in '*n*' is compensated by decrease in radii due to increase in '*Z*'

36. Which of the following is paramagnetic as well as coloured ion?
(a) Cu^{+} (b) Cu^{2+} (c) Ti^{4+} (d) Sc^{3+}

37. Select the correct statement(s).
(a) Colour we observe is the complimentary colour absorbed by the compound
(b) Colour of the ion arises due to *d*-*d** transition
(c) Both (a) and (b) are correct
(d) None of the above

38. Non-stoichiometry is shown
(a) due to defects in solid structures
(b) due to variable valency of transition elements
(c) Both (a) and (b)
(d) None of the above

39. The outer electronic configuration of transition elements is
(a) $(n+1)\,s^2, nd^{1-5}$
(b) $(n-1)\,s^2\,nd^{1-5}$
(c) $(n-1)\,s^2p^6\,(n-1)\,d^{-10}\,ns^2p^6$
(d) $(n-1)\,s^2p^6d^{1-10}\,ns^2$

40. The highest magnetic moment will be shown by
(a) Sc (b) Fe
(c) Co (d) Ni

41. Which of the following is not a member of 3*d*-transition series?
(a) Fe (b) Co (c) Cu (d) Au

42. The stability of ferric ion is due to
(a) half-filled *d*-orbitals
(b) half-filled *f*-orbitals
(c) completely filled *d*-orbitals
(d) completely filled *f*-orbitals

43. In which one of the following is metal-metal bond present?
(a) Stannous chloride (b) Cupric chloride
(c) Mercurous chloride (d) Mercuric chloride

44. Atomic numbers of a few elements are given below. Which of these belong to *d*-block elements?
(a) 28 (b) 29 (c) 43 (d) 53

45. Among transition metals in a period, the ionisation potential
(a) increase gradually with increase in atomic number
(b) decreases with increase in atomic number
(c) increases abruptly with increase in atomic number
(d) remains reasonably constant with increase in atomic number

46. The nature of electronic spectra of *d*-block elements is mainly due to
(a) incomplete *d*-orbitals
(b) hydrated ions
(c) removal of degeneracy of *d*-orbitals
(d) term splitting in different crystal field geometry and transitions

47. The number of unpaired electrons present in Cr^{2+}, Fe^{2+}, Co^{2+} and Ni^{2+} are respectively
(a) 2, 3, 4 and 4 (b) 4, 4, 3 and 2
(c) 4,4, 2 and 3 (d) 1, 4, 2 and 3

48. The number of unpaired electrons present in Ni^{2+} (atomic number of Ni = 28) is
(a) one (b) two (c) zero (d) four

49. The aqueous solution of the following salts will be coloured in case of
(a) $Zn(NO_3)_2$ (b) $LiNO_3$
(c) $Co(NO_3)_2$ (d) $CrCl_3$

50. Which transition metal is present in carbonic anhydrase?
(a) Cobalt (b) Nickel
(c) Zinc (d) Manganese

51. For $[Ti(H_2O)_5]^{3+}$ the absorption maximum due to *d-d* transition is found at 20000 cm^{-1}. Therefore, the crystal field stabilization energy is
(a) $-20000\ cm^{-1}$ (b) $8000\ cm^{-1}$
(c) $\frac{4}{9}\times 20000\ cm^{-1}$ (d) $-8000\ cm^{-1}$

52. A transition metal complex shows a magnetic moment of 5.20 BM at room temperature. The number of unpaired electrons on the metal is
(a) 3 (b) 4 (c) 5 (d) 2

53. When Na_2CO_3 is added to an aqueous solution of $CuSO_4$, which one of the following is precipitated?
(a) $Cu(CO_3)_2$ (b) $Cu(OH)(CO_3)$
(c) $Cu(HCO_3)_2$ (d) $Cu(OH)_2$

Exercise 2
(For Part 'C')

1. MnO_4^- is of intense pink colour,though Mn is in (+7) oxidation state. It is due to
(a) charge transfer when oxygen gives its electron to Mn making it Mn (+VI) hence, coloured
(b) charge transfer when Mn gives its electron to oxygen
(c) oxygen gives colour to it
(d) None of the above

2. Select the incorrect statement(s).
(a) Cu(I) is diamagnetic while Cu(II) is paramagnetic.
(b) $[Ti(H_2O)_6]^{3+}$ is coloured while $[Sc(H_2O)_6]^{3+}$ is colourless.
(c) Ionisation energies of 5*d*-elements are greater than those of 3*d* and 4*d* elements.
(d) Transition elements cannot form complexes.

3. Spin only magnetic moment of the compound $Hg[Co(SCN)_4]$ is
(a) $\sqrt{3}$ (b) $\sqrt{8}$ (c) $\sqrt{15}$ (d) $\sqrt{24}$

4. In which case(s) there is change in oxidation number?
(a) SO_2 gas is passed into $Cr_2O_7^{2-}/H^+$
(b) $Cr_2O_7^{2-}$ is made alkaline
(c) CrO_2Cl_2 is dissolved in NaOH
(d) Aqueous solution of CrO_4^{2-} is acidified

5. Most transition metals
I. form sets of compounds which display different oxidation states of the metal.
II. form coloured ions in the solution.

III. burn vigorously in oxygen
IV. replaces H_2 from dil. acids of these
(a) I, II, III are correct
(b) II, III, IV are correct
(c) I and II are correct
(d) All of the above are correct

6. There are three electrons unpaired in $[Co(H_2O)_6]^{2+}$ and calculated value of magnetic moment is 3.87 BM which is quite different from the experimental value of 4.40 BM. This is because of
(a) *d–d** transition
(b) change in orbital spin of the electrons
(c) increase in number of unpaired electrons
(d) some contribution of the orbital motion of the electron to the magnetic moment

7. Why does aqueous Fe(III) ion develop intense red colour when it reacts with SCN^- ion while Fe(III) ion does not?
(a) Fe(II) ion forms a charge transfer complex with SCN^- ions
(b) SCN^- ion is oxidised to CN^- which forms red coloured complex with Fe(III) ion
(c) Fe(III) is reduced to Fe(I) which is deep red in colour
(d) SCN^- does not form any complex with Fe(III) ion

8. Select the correct statement(s).
(a) Fe^{2+} is stable and Fe^{3+} is unstable is aerated water
(b) Stabilities of variable oxidation states can be explained by standard electrode potential
(c) Cr^{2+} is unstable and Cr^{3+} is stable in aqueous solution
(d) All of the above are correct statements

9. Select the correct statement(s).
(a) When $FeCl_3$ solution is added to $K_4[Fe(CN)_6]$ solution, in addition to Fe^{III} $[Fe(CN)_6]^-$, Fe^{II} $[Fe^{III}(CN)_6]^-$ is also formed due to side redox reaction
(b) When $FeCl_2$ solution is added to $K_3[Fe(CN)_6]$ solution, in addition to Fe^{II} $[Fe^{II}(CN)_6]^-$, Fe^{III} $[Fe^{II}(CN)_6]^-$ is also formed due to side redox reaction
(c) Fe^{III} $[Fe^{II}(CN)_6]^-$ is diamagnetic, while Fe^{II} $[Fe^{III}(CN)_6]^-$ is paramagnetic
(d) Fe^{III} $[Fe^{II}(CN)_6]^-$ is paramagnetic while Fe^{II} $[Fe^{III}(CN)_6]^-$ is diamagnetic

Assertion & Reason

Codes

(a) Both A and R are true and R is correct explanation of A.
(b) Both A and R are individually true but R is not correct explanation of A.
(c) A is true, R is false.
(d) A is false, R is true.

10. **Assertion (A)** Cr(VI) is much more toxic than Cr(III).
Reason (R) The toxicity of Cr(VI) is due to its strong oxidising property.

11. **Assertion (A)** $KMnO_4$ and $K_2Cr_2O_7$ are intensely coloured compounds.
Reason (R) Transition metal compounds having electrons in *d*-orbitals are coloured due to *d–d* transition.

12. **Assertion (A)** Most of the compounds of the transition elements are coloured in the solid and solution state.
Reason (R) During *d–d* transition, the *d*-electrons absorb certain radiation from the visible region of the spectrum.

13. **Assertion (A)** Polarising power is a function of ionic charge/ionic radius ratio.
Reason (R) The smaller radius and greater the charge on the central metal atom, the lower is pH of solution.

14. Which of the following type of bonds are present in $CuSO_4 \cdot 5H_2O$?
1. Electrovalent 2. Covalent 3. Coordinate
(a) 1 and 2 only (b) 1 and 3 only
(c) 2 and 3 only (d) 1, 2 and 3

15. Which of the following is paramagnetic?
(a) $Cr(CO)_6$ (b) $Fe(CO)_5$
(c) $Ni(CO)_4$ (d) $V(CO)_6$

16. Consider the following pairs of ions :
1. Sc^{3+} and Ti^{4+} 2. Mn^{2+} and Fe^{2+}
3. Fe^{2+} and Co^{3+} 4. Cu^+ and Zn^{2+}
Among these pairs of ions, isoelectronic pairs would include
(a) 1, 2 and 4 (b) 1, 2 and 3
(c) 1, 3 and 4 (d) 2, 3 and 4

17. The atomic number of potassium is 19 and that of manganese is 25. Although $[MnO_4]^-$ has a dark violet colour, that K^+ is colourless. This is due to the fact that

(a) Mn is a transition element, while K^+ is not
(b) the Mn is a high positive oxidation state allows charge transfer transition
(c) the effective atomic number of Mn in $[MnO_4]^-$ is 26 while for K^+, the effective atomic number is 18
(d) $[MnO_4]^-$ is negatively charged species while K^+ has a positive charge

18. Which of the following statement(s) is/are correct?
(a) The electronic configuration of Cr is $[Ar]\,3d^5 4s^1$ (atomic number of Cr = 24).
(b) The magnetic quantum number may have negative value.
(c) In silver atom, 23 electrons have a spin of one type and 24 of the opposite type (Atomic number of Ag = 47).
(d) The oxidation state of nitrogen in HN_3 is −3.

19. Aqueous titanium(IV) solution develops intense orange colour on addition of H_2O_2. The colour is due to
(a) *d-d* transitions
(b) $n \rightarrow \pi$ transitions of peroxo group
(c) reduction of Ti(IV) to Ti(III)
(d) CT transitions

20. Which of the following complex is most easily reduced?
(a) $V(CO)_6$ (b) $Cr(CO)_6$
(c) $Fe(CO)_5$ (d) $Ni(CO)_4$

21. Among the following species, the one possessing CT transition in the visible region is
(a) $Th(C_2O_4)_2$ (b) $[Cr(NCS)_6]^{3-}$
(c) ZnS (d) HgI_2

22. The orange colour of $Cr_2O_7^{2-}$ is due to
(a) metal to ligand charge transfer transition
(b) ligand to metal charge transfer transition
(c) crystal field transition
(d) charge transfer complex formation

23. Stabilization of highest oxidation states of transition metals by strong electronegative ligands is due to
(a) $d\pi(M) \rightarrow d\pi(L)$ bonding
(b) $d\pi(M) \rightarrow p\pi(L)$ bonding
(c) $p\pi(L) \rightarrow d\pi(M)$ bonding
(d) $d\pi(L) \rightarrow d\pi(M)$ bonding

24. Which of the following does not form isopoly acid in acidification?
(a) Na_2MoO_4 (b) Na_2WO_4
(c) Na_2CrO_4 (d) Na_3VO_4

25. The asymmetric nature of visible absorption band of $[Ti(H_2O)_6]^{3+}$ is due to
(a) Laporte's allowed transition
(b) Laporte's forbidden transition
(c) Dynamic John-Teller effect
(d) Intensity stealing transition

26. Which one of the following ligands can bring out the highest oxidation state in a transition metal?
(a) F^- (b) Cl^-
(c) Br^- (d) I^-

27. Which one of the following is least covalent or least acidic?
(a) VCl_2 (b) VCl_3
(c) VCl_4 (d) $VOCl_3$

28. The number of manganese ions in tetrahedral and octahedral sites respectively in Mn_3O_4 are
(a) one Mn^{2+} and two Mn^{3+}
(b) one Mn^{3+} and two Mn^{2+}
(c) two Mn^{3+} and one Mn^{2+}
(d) two Mn^{2+} and one Mn^{3+}

29. The metal ion which is most likely to show the low spin–high spin equilbria in its complexes has the electronic configuration
(a) d^3 (b) d^4
(c) d^6 (d) d^8

30. The magnetic moment of an octahedral Co(II) complex is 4.0 μ_B. The *d*-electron configuration of Co(II) is
(a) $t_{2g}^4 e_g^3$ (b) $t_{2g}^5 e_g^2$
(c) $t_{2g}^6 e_g^1$ (d) $t_{2g}^3 e_g^4$

Directions (Q. Nos. 31 and 32)

Acidity of hexaaqua ions (M^{3+} *aq*) accounts for less stability/existence of M^{2+} (*aq*) then less polarizing M^{2+}. Many hexaaqua- complex ions can undergo acid-base reactions with water to produce solutions of pH less than 7. The positive central metal ion polarizes a water molecule and releases a H^+.

31. Which of the following are unstable?
(a) Aluminium carbonate (b) $MgCO_3$
(c) $ZnCO_3$ (d) $FeCO_3$

32. Which statement is right about $[Fe(H_2O)_6]^{3+}$ ion?
(a) It reacts with carbonates to form $[Fe(H_2O)_5(OH)]^{2+}$
(b) It reacts with carbonates and liberates CO_2
(c) Bubbles comes out on reaction with hydrogen carbonates
(d) All of the above

Directions (Q. Nos. 33 to 35)

The colour of a compound is due to absorption of visible light and if the sample absorbs all the wavelength of light it appears black and if it reflects all the light, it appears white. Colour of transition metals is due to *d-d* transitions.

33. Which of the following statements is not true?
(a) $[V(H_2O)_6]^{3+}$ is yellow in colour
(b) $[V(H_2O)_6]^{2+}$ absorbs yellow light
(c) $[V(H_2O)_6]^{3+}$ is violet in colour
(d) $[V(H_2O)_6]^{2+}$ is violet in colour

34. Match the following.

	Complex		Colour
p	$[Fe(H_2O)_6]^{3+}$	I	Green
q	$[Zn(H_2O)_6]^{2+}$	II	Blue
r	$[CoCl_4]^{2-}$	III	Red
s	$[Ni(H_2O)_6]^{2+}$	IV	Colourless

(a) p-III, q-IV, r-I, s-II (b) p-II, q-IV, r-III, s-I
(c) p-III, q-IV, r-II, s-I (d) p-II, q-IV, r-I, s-III

35. Which of the pairs are coloured due to *d-d* transitions?
(a) $[Fe(bpy)_3]^{2+}$, $[Cu(NH_3)_4]^{2+}$
(b) MnO_4^-, CrO_4^{2-}
(c) $[Cu(H_2O)_6]^{2+}$, $[Cu(PPh_3)_4]^+$
(d) None of the above

Directions (Q. Nos. 36 to 41)
In a molecule or ion possessing centre of symmetry transitions are not allowed between orbitals of same parity for example *d* to *d*. There must be change in parity, *i.e.*, $\Delta l = \pm 1$, orbital quantum number should differ by 1.

36. Forbidden transition are
(a) $s \to s, p \to p$ (b) $s \to p, p \to d$
(c) $p \to p, p \to d$ (d) $p \to f, d \to f$

37. The above passage is a
(a) John-Taller theorem
(b) HOMO-LUMO concept
(c) Laporte rule
(d) Vibronic selection rule

38. Laporte-selection rule is not affecting
(a) octahedral geometry
(b) square-planar geometry
(c) tetrahedral geometry
(d) All of the above

39. Which of the following statement(s) is true?
(a) Unsymmetrical vibrations of an octahedral complex can transiently destroy centre of symmetry
(b) Octahedral complexes are centrosymmetric
(c) $[Cu(H_2O)_6]^{2+}$ is pale blue in colour
(d) $[Cu(NH_3)_4]^{2+}$ is intense blue in colour

40. Laporte forbidden complexes are
(a) colourless always (b) deeply coloured
(c) centrosymmetric (d) None of these

41. $[Mn(H_2O)_6]^{+2}$ ion is
(a) high spin complex (b) laporte forbidden
(c) spin forbidden (d) All of these

Directions (Q. Nos. 42 to 46)
Charge transfer transitions involve metal *d*-orbitals. If energies of filled ligand and metal centred orbitals are similar, charge transfer transitions occur. Charge transfer also involves *d*-orbitals of the metal. The direction of electron transfer is determined by relative energy levels of these orbitals.

42. Metal to ligand charge transfer occurs in
(a) MnO_4^- (b) CrO_4^{2-}
(c) $Cr_2O_7^{2-}$ (d) $[Fe(bpy)_3]^{2+}$

43. MnO_4^- is coloured due to
(a) LMCT
(b) MLCT
(c) *d-d* transitions
(d) *d-d* transitions and LMCT both

44. Ligand-metal CT is favoured when
(a) electron-rich metal centres are there
(b) often in UV region
(c) metal centres is in high oxidation state
(d) All of the above

45. Common ligands for LMCT is
(a) F^- (b) O^{2-}
(c) N^{3-} (d) All of these

46. In complex $[Fe(bpy)_3]^{2+}$ colour arises due to
(a) *d-d* transitions
(b) due to charge transfer from ligand bpy to Fe^{2+} orbitals
(c) due to charge transfer from Fe^{2+} to π^* orbitals of bpy ligand
(d) due to charge transfer from π^* orbitals of bpy to e_g orbitals of Fe^{2+}

Answers

Exercise 1

1. (a)	**2.** (a)	**3.** (c)	**4.** (d)	**5.** (a)	**6.** (c)	**7.** (a)	**8.** (b)	**9.** (d)	**10.** (a)
11. (d)	**12.** (d)	**13.** (d)	**14.** (c)	**15.** (a)	**16.** (b)	**17.** (d)	**18.** (a)	**19.** (c)	**20.** (c)
21. (c)	**22.** (a)	**23.** (c)	**24.** (b)	**25.** (c)	**26.** (c)	**27.** (b)	**28.** (c)	**29.** (c)	**30.** (b)
31. (c)	**32.** (c)	**33.** (b)	**34.** (c)	**35.** (c)	**36.** (b)	**37.** (c)	**38.** (c)	**39.** (d)	**40.** (b)
41. (d)	**42.** (a)	**43.** (c)	**44.** (a)	**45.** (a)	**46.** (a)	**47.** (b)	**48.** (b)	**49.** (c)	**50.** (b)
51. (a)	**52.** (c)	**53.** (c)							

Exercise 2

1. (a)	**2.** (d)	**3.** (c)	**4.** (a)	**5.** (c)	**6.** (d)	**7.** (a)	**8.** (b,c)	**9.** (a,b,c)	**10.** (a)
11. (d)	**12.** (b)	**13.** (d)	**14.** (c)	**15.** (a)	**16.** (b)	**17.** (a,b,c)	**18.** (c)	**19.** (a)	**20.** (b)
21. (b)	**22.** (c)	**23.** (d)	**24.** (b)	**25.** (a)	**26.** (a)	**27.** (a)	**28.** (c)	**29.** (b)	**30.** (a)
31. (a)	**32.** (d)	**33.** (c)	**34.** (c)	**35.** (d)	**36.** (a)	**37.** (c)	**38.** (c)	**39.** (a,b,c,d)	**40.** (c)
41. (d)	**42.** (d)	**43.** (a)	**44.** (c)	**45.** (d)	**46.** (c)				

Hints & Solutions

Exercise 1

2. Metals lying above H in electrochemical series are not obtained from their oxides by heating

$$HgO \longrightarrow Hg + O_2$$
$$ZnO \longrightarrow Zn + O_2$$
$$Ag_2O \longrightarrow Ag + O_2$$

3. $NO \longrightarrow NO^+ + e^-$

$Fe^{3+} + e^- \longrightarrow Fe^{2+}$

Oxidation state of Fe is +2 and NO^+ is ligand.

4. $Cu^+ : [Ar]\, 3d^{10}$

No unpaired electron, thus, $s = 0$

5. Ti(22) : $[Ar]\, 4s^2\, 3d^2$ [↑ | ↑ | | |]

$Ti^{2+} : [Ar]\, 3d^2$

$Ti^{4+} : [Ar]\, 3d^0$

Ti^{2+} has two unpaired electrons in $3d$ and thus d-d^* transition is possible due to absorption of light in visible region.

6. $2Ag^+ + H_2S \longrightarrow \underset{\text{Black}}{Ag_2S}$

7. Maximum unpaired electrons d^5 [↑ | ↑ | ↑ | ↑ | ↑]

8. Magnetic moment, $\mu = \sqrt{N(N+2)}$ BM.

where, N = unpaired electrons

Cr (24) : $[Ar]\, 3d^5\, 4s^1$ $(n = 6)$

$$\mu = \sqrt{6(6+2)} = \sqrt{48}\ \text{BM} = x$$

Mn^+ : $[Ar]\, 3d^5\, 4s^1$ $(N = 6)$

$$\mu = \sqrt{6(6+2)} = \sqrt{48}\ \text{BM} = y$$

Fe^{2+} : $[Ar]\, 3d^6$ $(N = 4)$

$$\mu = \sqrt{4(4+2)} = \sqrt{24}\ \text{BM} = z$$

Thus, $z < x = y$

10. 24 carat gold is 100%

Thus, 22 carat gold is 91.67%

Thus, 3.5% higher.

13. Generally salts are colourless due to d^{10}-configuration.

19. $Mn^{2+}\,(d^5)$ [↑ | ↑ | ↑ | ↑ | ↑]

40. Fe has 4 unpaired electrons.

43. Mercurous chloride (Hg_2Cl_2) : Cl—Hg—Hg—Cl.

47. Cr^{2+} 3d [↑ | ↑ | ↑ | ↑ |], No. of unpaired electrons = 4

Fe^{2+} 3d [↑↓ | ↑ | ↑ | ↑ | ↑], No. of unpaired electrons = 4

Co^{2+} 3d [↑↓ | ↑↓ | ↑ | ↑ | ↑], No. of unpaired electrons = 3

Ni^{2+} 3d [↑↓ | ↑↓ | ↑↓ | ↑ | ↑], No. of unpaired electrons = 2

Exercise 2

3. $[Co(SCN)_4]^{2-}$, cobalt is +2 with three unpaired electrons in 3*d*. Thus, $\mu = \sqrt{15}$ BM.

4. $\underset{+6}{Cr_2O_7^{2-}} + \underset{+4}{SO_4} \longrightarrow \underset{+6}{SO_4^{2-}} + \underset{+3}{Cr^{3+}}$

11. Both A and R are correct but R is not the correct explanation of A. The colour of these compounds is due to charge transfer transition from oxide ion to highly charged metal ions.

13. When radius is small and charge is high, polarising power is high. Larger the polarising power, higher is the acidity or lower is the pH.

14. $CuSO_4 \cdot 5H_2O$ can be written as $Cu^{2+}SO_4^{2-}$. Hence, electrovalent (ionic) bond is present, coordinate bond is formed between Cu^{2+} and SO_4^{2-} and covalent bond is present in SO_4^{2-}.

15. In carbonyl compounds, central metal atom is in neutral state.

[Cr (CO)$_6$] : ($3d^5 4s^1$)

3d					3s	3p		
⇅	⇅	⇅	××	××	××	××	××	××

[Fe (CO)$_5$] : ($3d^6 4s^2$)

3d					4s	4p		
⇅	⇅	⇅	⇅	××	××	××	××	××

[Ni (CO)$_4$] : ($3d^8 4s^2$)

3d					4s	4p		
⇅	⇅	⇅	⇅	⇅	××	××	××	××

[V(CO)$_6$] : ($3d^3 4s^2$)

3d					4s	4p		
⇅	⇅	1	××	××	××	××	××	××

Since, $V(CO)_6$ contains one unpaired electron, it is paramagnetic in nature.

16. (i) Sc (21) : $d^1 s^2$; Ti (22) : $d^2 s^2$

$Sc^{3+} : d^0$; $Ti^{4+} : d^0$

(ii) Mn (25) : $d^5 s^2$; Fe (26) : $d^6 s^2$

$Mn^{2+} : d^5$; $Fe^{2+} : d^6$

(not isoelectronic)

(iii) Cu (29) : $d^{10} s^1$; Zn (30) : $d^{10} s^2$

$Cu^+ : d^{10}$; $Zn^{2+} : d^{10}$

(iv) Fe (26) : $d^6 s^2$; Co (27) : $d^7 s^2$

$Fe^{2+} : d^6$; $Co^{3+} : d^6$

22. In $Cr_2O_7^{2-}$, the oxidation state of Cr is + 6, *i.e.*, in it no electron is present in *d* orbitals. But the oxide ion transfers its one electron to the non-bonding and antibonding MO of the metal atom and makes the $Cr_2O_7^{2-}$ coloured.

23. When the ligand is strongly electronegative, there found $p\pi(L) \rightarrow d\pi(M)$ bonding in the complex, which makes the compound stable.

25. Ti^{3+} = [Ar] $3d^1$

$[Ti(H_2O)_6]^{3+}$ = [Ar]d^1

Since the above complex is centrosymmetric, it is Laporte forbidden.

26. A smaller and more electronegative ligand brings out the highest oxidation state in a transition metal.

27. Covalent character ∝ charge on the ion

$$V^{2+} < V^{3+} < V^{4+} < V^{5+}$$

So VCl_2 is least covalent or least acidic.

29. High spin complex is associated with $\Delta_o < P$ and low spin complexes with $\Delta_o > P$. For complexes in which energy difference between Δ_o and *P* is relatively small, it is possible for two spin states to coexist in equilibrium with each other, *e.g.*, Fe^{2+} (d^6 system).

30. The possible configuration of Co(II) d^7 is $t_{2g}^6 e_g^1$ and $t_{2g}^5 e_g^2$.

When $n = 1$

$$\mu_B = \sqrt{n(n+2)} = \sqrt{3} = 1.73$$

When $n = 3$

$$\mu_B = \sqrt{3(3+2)} = \sqrt{15} = 3.87 \approx 4.0$$

So, the *d*-electron configuration of Co(II) is $t_{2g}^5 e_g^2$.

33. V^{3+} absorbs violet light so the colour of its complex ion is yellow. V^{2+} however absorbs yellow colour, so appears violet.

34. p. $[Fe(H_2O)_6]^{3+}$ = [Ar] $3d^5$ (five unpaired electrons)

q. $[Zn(H_2O)_6]^{2+}$ = [Ar] $3d^{10}$ (0 unpaired electron)

r. $[CoCl_4]^{2-}$ = [Ar] $3d^7$ (3 unpaired electron)

s. $[Ni(H_2O)_6]^{2+}$ = [Ar] $3d^8$ (2 unpaired electrons)

Higher the number of unpaired electrons, higher is the intensity of colour. Zn because of the absence of unpaired electrons, is colourless.

9 Coordination Chemistry

Coordination compounds are addition compounds, formed when two or more salts are crystallised together. In these compounds, the individual ions of the salt lost their identity. Generally these are the compounds of metals coordinated with the ligands. Several theories have been given to explain bonding in them. One of the such theory is Werner theory.

Syllabus

- Coordination Compounds : Structure, Bonding Theories, Spectral and Magnetic Properties, Reaction Mechanism

Werner's Theory

Around the end of the last century the valence bonding and geometry in metal-amine complexes such as $[Co(NH_3)_6]Cl_3$ was a subject of immense interest among chemists. The suggestion from Werner was that these complexes were based on an octahedral array of ligands coordinated to a central metal ion. Consider, for example, the three formulae 1-3 shown below, each with 6 ligands arranged around a central metal ion. In the case of $[MB_2A_4]$ (M = Metal) with the geometry of 1 or 2 there would be three possible isomers, but only two if the correct structure was 3. The available experimental evidence had never revealed the existence of more than two such isomers.

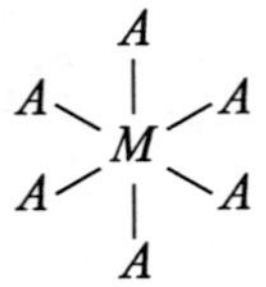

1 Planar

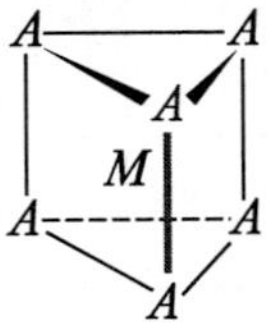

2 Prismatic

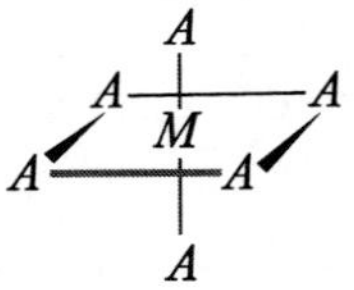

3 Octahedral

The most powerful evidence in favour of this 'octahedral' geometry came from stereochemical studies. Werner isolated *cis*- and *trans*-isomers of the salts 4 and 5, which had been predicted to occur, but had not previously been discovered.

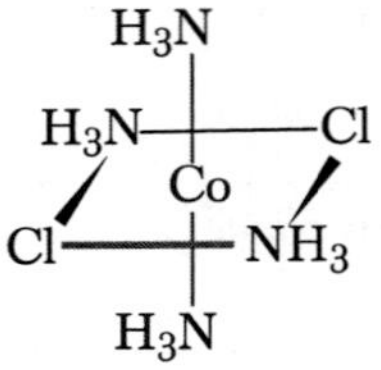

4

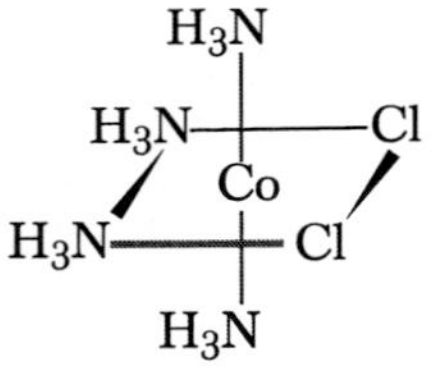

5

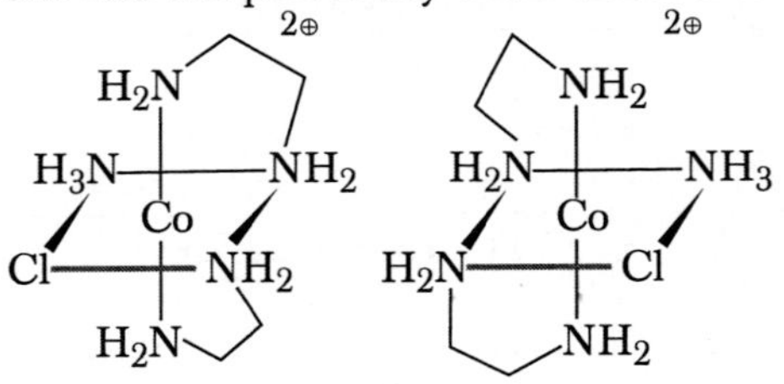

6

The separation and isolation of the two predicted enantiomers of $[Co(NH_2CH_2CH_2NH_2)_2ClNH_3]^{2+}\ 2X^-$ (6) suggest the octahedral geometry.

The basic postulate of Werner's theory is that there are two different types of bonding present in inorganic coordination compounds :

1. The first type of bonding or valences are called the **primary valences**. These are ionisable and essentially represent the oxidation number on the metal; they are non-directional and not affected by secondary valences (see below).
2. The second type of bonding or valences are called the **secondary valences.** Secondary valences are fixed in number by the nature of the central metal atom (usually 4 or 6); they are directional; and are not affected by primary valences.

Metal Complexes

Historically the name complex has been applied to those compounds in which some of the ions were 'not simple' such as $[Co(NH_3)_6]^{3+}$ (in the sense that the cation here is not a mono-atomic species such as Na^+ but the complex multi-atomic assembly). In today's literature the terms 'complex' and 'coordination compound' are used almost interchangeably.

Transition Metal Complexes

A transition metal complex contains a **transition metal ion** surrounded by certain neutral or anionic **ligands.** All of the ligands that we will be considering in this section are typical Lewis bases. Later, when dealing with organometallic compounds we will focus on ligands many of which in the ordinary sense are not Lewis bases. The number of ligand atoms surrounding a metal ion defines its **coordination number.** The oxidation state of the metal ion is determined by looking at the overall charge on the complex and the nature of the ligands that surround the metal ion. The following scheme will help to clarify this.

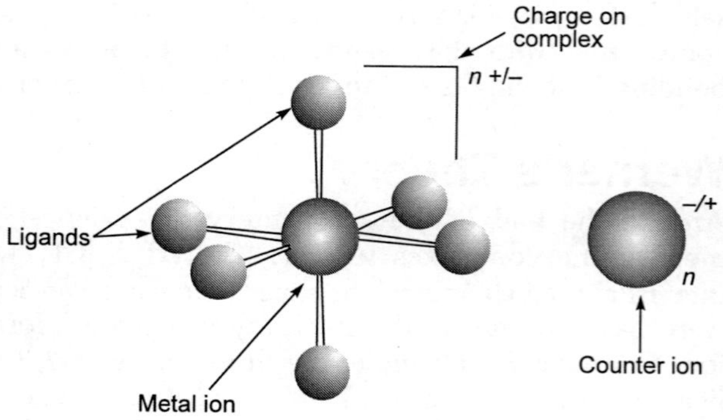

Table 9.1 **Introducing the Ligands**

Ligands	Name	Donor atom	Example
CO	Carbon monoxide	C	$Mo(CO)_6$
H_2O	Water	O	$[Mn(H_2O)_6]^{2+}$
NH_3	Ammonia	N	$[Co(NH_3)_6]^{3+}$
H^-	Hydride	H	$[ReH_9]^{2-}$
Cl^-	Chloride	Cl	$[CuCl_2]^-$
O^{2-}	Oxide	O	$[MnO_4]^-$
CN^-	Cyanide	C/N	$[Au(CN)_2]^-$
SCN^-	Thiocyanate	S/N	$[Fe(SCN)_6]^{3-}$
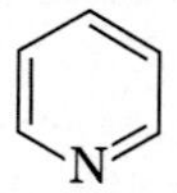	Pyridine	N	$[Ni(py)_6]^{2+}$
	Ethylene diamine(en)	N	$[Co(en)]^{3+}$

Ligands	Name	Donor atom	Example
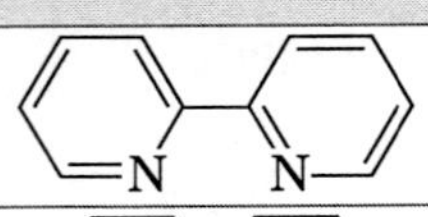	Bipyridine(bpy)	N	$[Ru(bpy)_3]^{2+}$
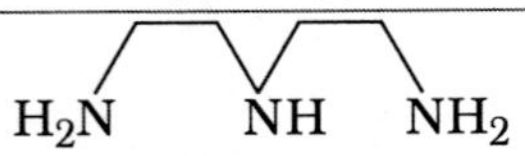	Diethylenetriamine(dien)	N	$[(dien)AuCl]^{2+}$
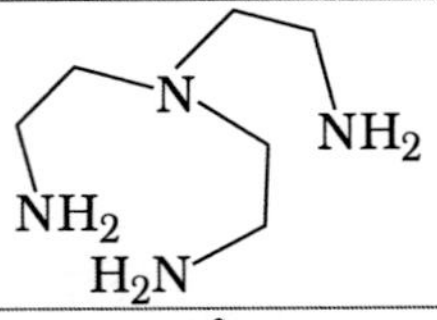	*Tris* (2-aminoethyl) amine (tren)	N	$[(tren)Co(N_3)_2]^+$
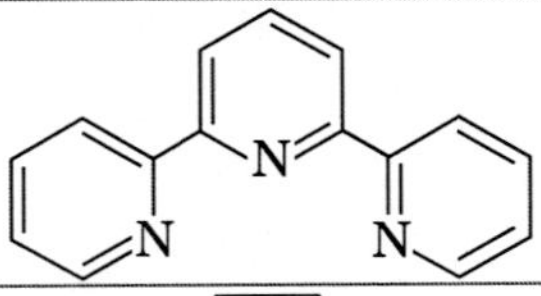	2,2′, 6′, 2′′-terpyridine (tpy)	N	$[(tpy)MnF_3]$
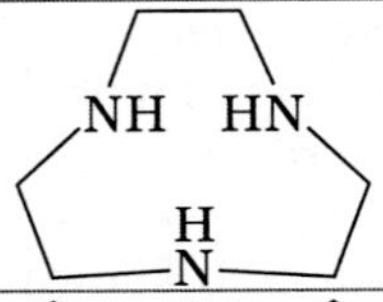	1,4,7-triazacyclononane (tacn)	N	$[(tacn)Mo(CO)_3]$
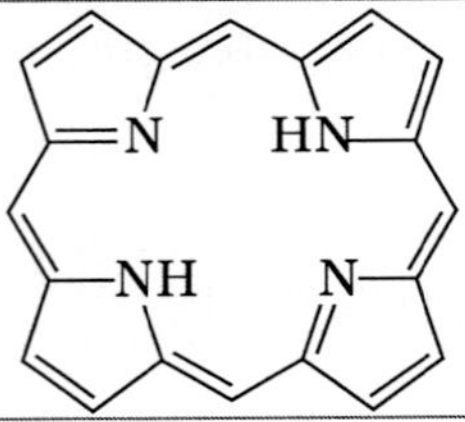	Porphyrin	N	haemoglobin
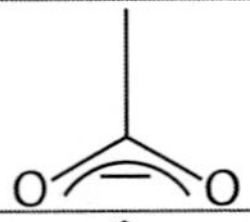	Acetate (OAc)	O	$[Cu_2(OAc)_4]$
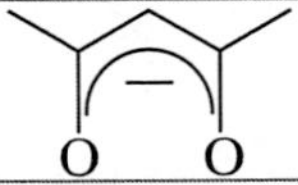	Acetylacetonato (acac)	O	$[(Ru(acac)_3]$
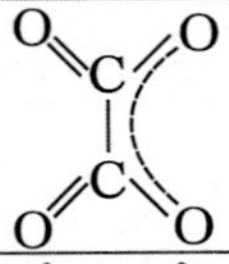	Oxalate (ox)	O	$[Nb(ox)_4]^{4-}$
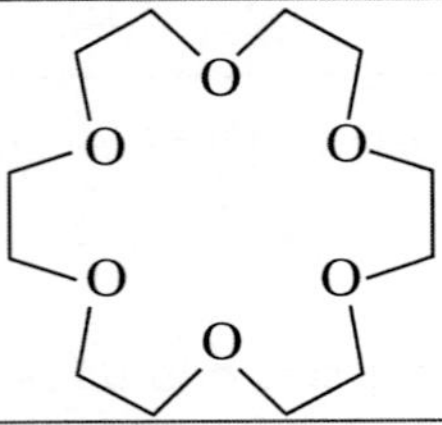	18-crown-6	O	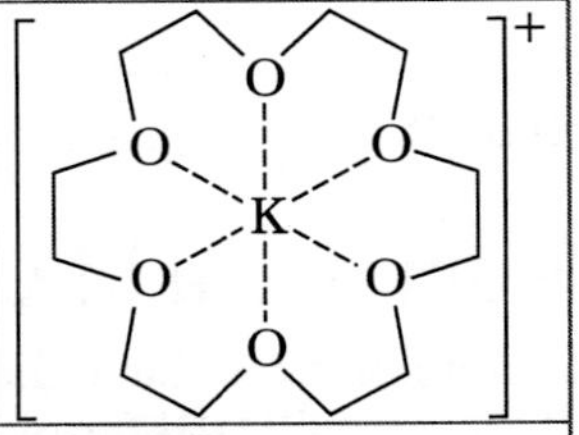
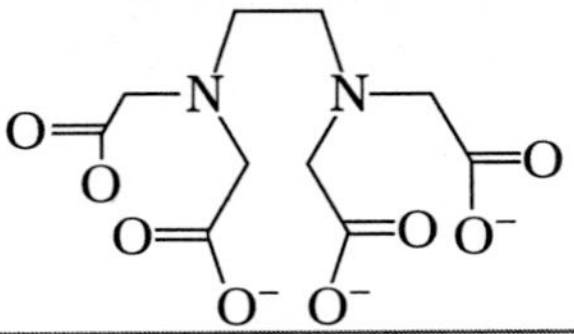	Ethylenediaminetetra acetic acid (EDTA)	N, O	[Ni(EDTA)]

Ligands	Name	Donor atom	Example
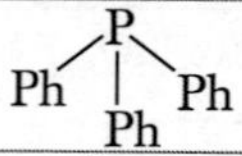	Triphenyl phosphine	P	$[Pd(PPh_3)_4]$
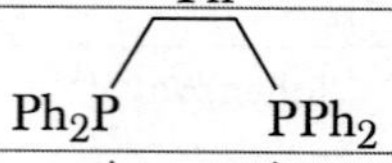	1,2-(*bis*- diphenylphosphino) ethane	P	$[Cu(dppe)_2]^+$
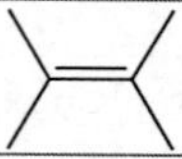	Ethylene	C	$[PtCl_3(C_2H_4)]^-$
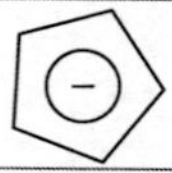	Cyclopentadienyl anion (Cp)	C	$[FeCp_2]$
NO	Nitrosyl	N/O	$[Fe(CN)_5(NO)]^{2-}$
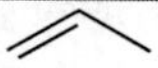	Allyl	C	$Ni(C_3H_5)_2$

Coordination Number and Geometry of the Complexes

Coordination number determines the coordination geometry. Coordination geometry refers to the spatial arrangement of donor atoms around a metal ion in the first coordination sphere. Coordination number, nature of metal ion, ligand size (steric effects) and nature of ligand (electronic properties) control coordination geometry. For *d*-block elements, the *d*-electron configuration/oxidation state also determines the geometry adapted by a complex. We will look into each of these factors separately with examples. Before that, it is important to know the various geometry that are possible for a given coordination number. The following table lists the probable geometries that a metal ion can adapt for a given coordination number.

Table 9.2 **Coordination Numbers**

Coordination numbers	Common geometry	Less common geometry
2	Linear	
3	Trigonal planar	Trigonal pyramidal
4	Tetrahedral, square planar	
5	Trigonal bipyramidal square based pyramidal	
6	Octahedral	Trigonal prismatic
7	Pentagonal pyramidal	Monocapped trigonal prismatic, monocapped octahedral
8	Dodecahedral square antiprismatic hexagonal bipyramidal	Cube, bicapped trigonal
9	Tricapped trigonal prismatic	Prismatic

Note If the energy difference between different structure is small, fluxional behaviour in solution may occur.

Isomerism in Coordination Complexes

Compounds that have the same chemical formula but different structural arrangements are called isomers. Because of the complicated formula of many coordination compounds, the variety of bond types and the number of shapes possible, many different types of isomerism occur. Werner's classification as depicted below is still generally accepted.

Isomerism in coordination complexes

Structural isomerism
(a) Ionisation isomerism
(b) Hydration isomerism
(c) Linkage isomerism
(d) Coordination isomerism
(e) Coordination position

Stereo isomerism
(a) Geometric isomerism
(b) Optical isomerism

Structural Isomerism

(a) Ionisation Isomers

They result from the interchange of an anionic ligand within the first coordination sphere with an anion outside the coordination sphere *e.g.*, $[Co(NH_3)_5Br][SO_4]$ (violet), and $[Co(NH_3)_5(SO_4)]Br$ They (red). Additional examples : $[Pt(NH_3)_4Cl_2]Br_2$ and $[Pt(NH_3)_4Br_2]Cl_2$; $[Co(en)_2(NO_2)Cl]SCN$, $[Co(en)_2(NO_2)SCN]Cl$, $[Co(en)_2(SCN)Cl]NO_2$.

(b) Hydration Isomers

They result from interchange of H_2O and another ligand between the first coordination sphere and the ligands outside it: *e.g.*, $CrCl_3 \cdot 6H_2O$: $[Cr(H_2O)_4Cl_2]Cl \cdot 2H_2O$ (green), $[Cr(H_2O)_5Cl]Cl_2 \cdot H_2O$ (green), $[Cr(H_2O)_6]Cl_3$ (violet).

(c) Linkage Isomers

They arise when one or more of the ligands can coordinate to the metal in more than one way, *e.g.*, $[SCN]^-$; $[Co(NH_3)_5(NCS-N)]^{2+}$ and $[Co(NH_3)_5(SCN-S)]^{2+}$. Additional example : $Co(NH_3)_5(ONO\text{-}O)$ and $Co(NH_3)_5(NO_2\text{-}N)$.

(d) Coordination Isomers

It is only possible for salts in which both cation and anion are complex ions, the isomers arise from interchange of ligands between the two metal centres : $[Co(NH_3)_6][Cr(CN)_6]$ and $[Cr(NH_3)_6][Co(CN)_6]$.

In some of the polynuclear complexes to interchange the ligands between the metal nuclei which are present as part of the complex, is possible. The type of interchange of ligands gives rise to **coordination position isomerism,** *e.g.*,

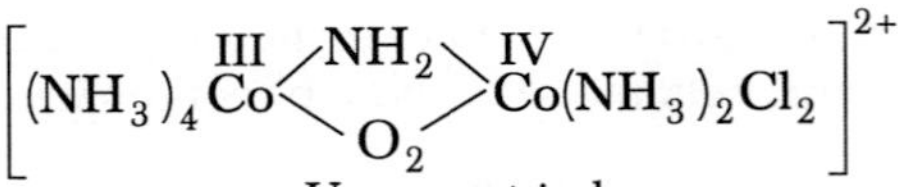

Unsymmetrical

and

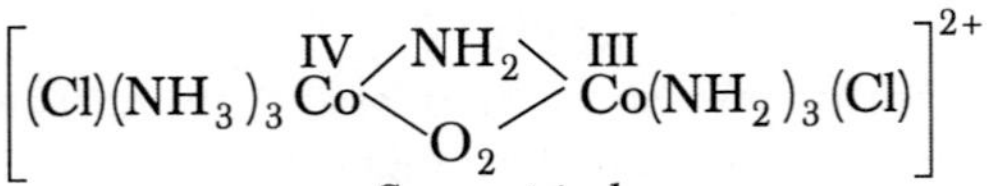

Symmetrical

are coordination position isomers.

Stereoisomerism or Space Isomerism

When two compounds contain the same ligands coordinated to the same central ion, but the arrangement of ligands in space is different, the two compounds are said to be stereoisomers and the type of isomerism is called **stereoisomerism**. It is also called **space isomerism.** Stereoisomers are quite similar, *e.g.*, optical isomers (which are stereoisomers) differ only in their optical activity. On the other hand structural isomers differ from each other in various ways.

Stereoisomerism is of two types : (i) Geometrical or *cis-trans* isomerism, and (ii) Optical or mirror-image isomerism.

1. Geometrical Isomerism in four and six Coordinated Compounds

Geometrical isomers have identical empirical formula but differ in chemical and physical properties because of the different arrangement of ligands. They are usually easily separated by chemical or physical means. Some (not all) of the geometrical isomers may develop optical activity due to distinct mirror-image forms. Thus, geometrical isomer which is capable of existing in non-superimposable mirror-image forms can be used to isolate optical isomers.

In a *cis*-isomer two identical (*i.e.*, similar) groups are adjacent to each other (Latin, *cis*- → same) while in a *trans*-isomer the two identical groups are diametrically (*i.e.*, diagonally) opposite to each other (Latin, *trans*-across), (*i.e.*, a straight line connecting the two groups *trans* to each other passes through the centre at which the metal ion is placed.)

Geometrical isomerism cannot arise in a tetrahedral complex (C.N.= 4) **because this geometry contains all the ligands in *cis*** (*i.e.*, adjacent) **position with respect to each other** *i.e.*, each ligand is equidistant from the other three ligands and all bond angles are the same (=109°). This isomerism is, however, found in many square planar (C.N. = 4) and octahedral (C.N. = 6) complexes.

Square planar complexes

$[Ma_4]^{n\pm}$, $[Ma_3b]^{n\pm}$, $[Mab_3]^{n\pm}$ type square planar complexes do not show geometrical isomerism, since every conceivable spatial arrangement of ligands round the metal ion is exactly equivalent. The following types of square planar complexes usually show *cis-trans* isomerism.

(i) **$[Ma_2b_2]^{n\pm}$ type complexes** Here, M = metal ion and a and b are monodentate ligands. Complexes of this type can exist in *cis-* and *trans-*isomers as shown below in Fig. 9.1.

Examples Examples of this type of complexes are $[Pt^{II}(NH_3)_2Cl_2]^0$ and $[Pd^{II}(NH_3)_2(NO_2)_2]^0$.

(ii) $[Ma_2bc]^{n+}$ type complexes The complexes of this type also exist in *cis-* and *trans-*isomers, *e.g*, $[Pta_2bc]$ type complexes show *cis-trans* isomerism. Here, a is a neutral ligand such as NH_3, py, H_2O and b and c are the anionic ligands like Cl^-, Br^-, NO_2^-, SCN^- etc.

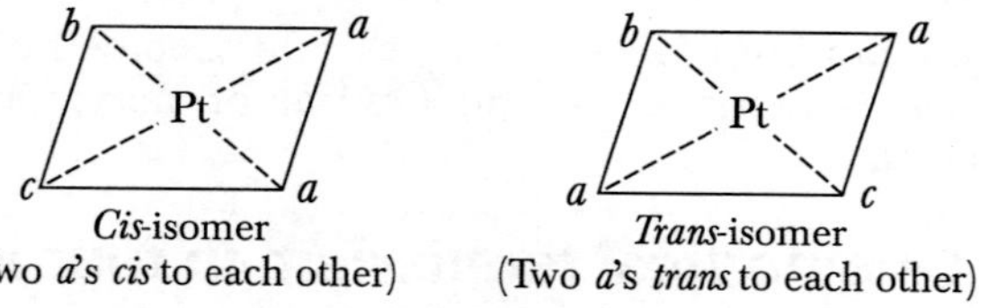

Fig. 9.1 *Cis* and *trans*-isomers of $[Pta_2bc]$ type complex.

(iii) **$[Mabcd]^{n\pm}$ type complexes** Pt^{II} forms a number of complexes of this type. Complexes of this type exist in three isomeric forms as shown in Fig. 9.2.

Fixing any two groups in *trans* positions also fixes the other two positions. The fourth structure shown, in which a is *trans* to d, is identical to the third structure. Either of these structures can be obtained by rotation of the other through 180° about the axis through a-Pt-d. All possible isomers can easily be obtained by selecting one group, say a, and seeing how many different groups can be placed *trans* to a.

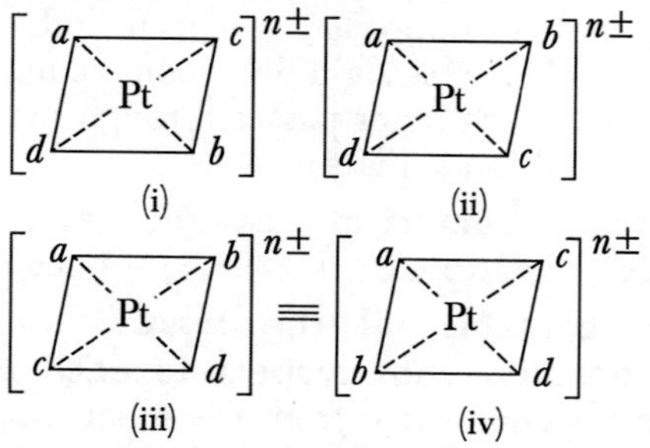

Fig. 9.2 Three isomeric forms of $[Pt^{II}abcd]^{n\pm}$ complex ion (square planar complex ion).

Examples (a) Three isomers have been reported for $[Pt^{II}(NO_2)(py)(NH_3)(NH_2OH)]^+$ ion.

(iv) **Square planar complexes having unsymmetrical bidentate chelating ligands : $[M(AB)_2]^{n\pm}$ type complexes** Here, M is the central metal ion and (AB) represents an unsymmetrical bidentate ligand. A and B are the two ends (*i.e.,* coordinating atoms) of the bidentate chelating ligand, (AB). Such type of complexes also show *cis-* and *trans-*isomerism as shown in Fig. 9.3.

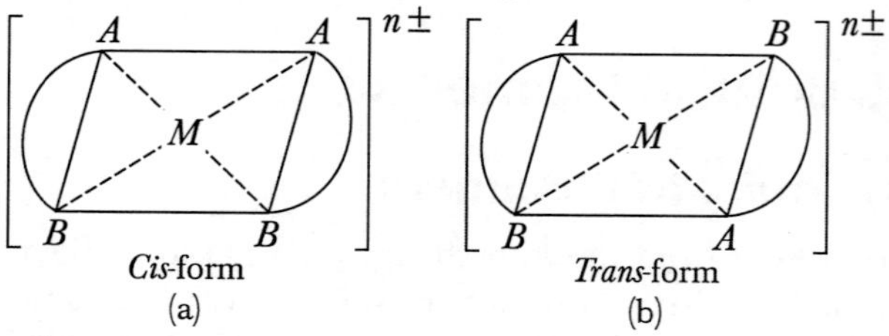

Fig. 9.3 *Cis* and *trans*-isomers of $[M(AB)_2]^{n\pm}$ type square planar complex having two unsymmetrical bidentate chelating ligands.

Example $[Pt^{II}(gly)_2]^0$ where, gly is H_2—CH_2COO- (glycine ion), is an important example of this type of complex. It exists in *cis-* and *trans-*isomers as shown below in Fig. 9.4.

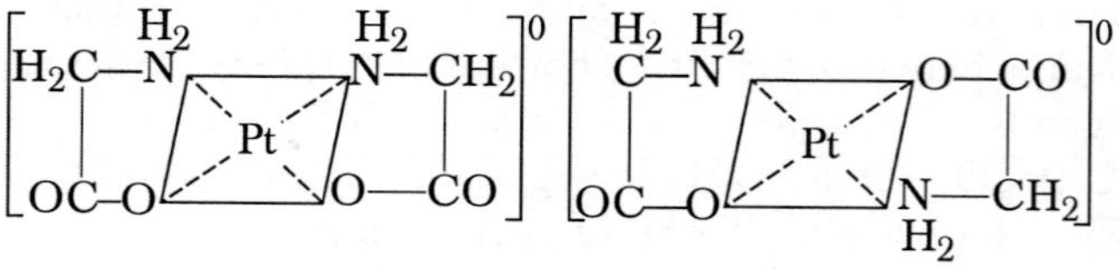

Fig. 9.4 *Cis* and *trans*-isomers of $[Pt^{II}(gly)_2]^0$ where gly is NH_2—CH_2COO^- (glycine ion).

(v) **Square planar complexes having symmetrical bidentate chelating ligands : $[M(AA)_2]^{n+}$ type complexes** Such type of complexes also have *cis-* and *trans-*isomers.

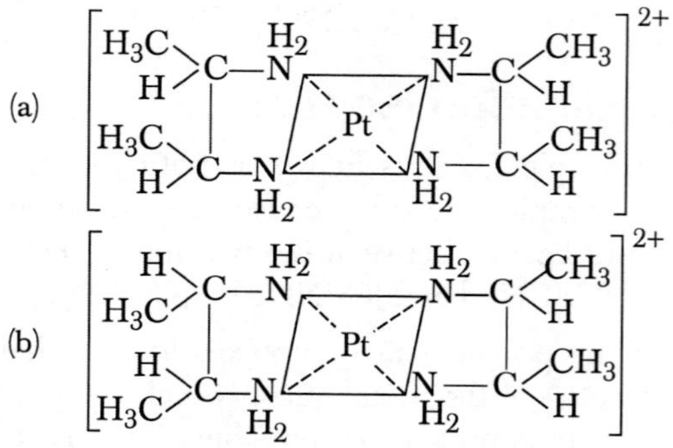

Fig. 9.5 *Cis* and *trans*-isomers of $[Pt^{II}(NH_2CH(CH_3)\cdot CH(CH_3)\cdot NH_2)_2]^{2+}$ (a) *cis*-form; (b) *trans*-form

Example $[Pt^{II}(NH_2CH(CH_3)\cdot CH(CH_3)\cdot NH_2)_2]^{2+}$ is an important example of this type of complexes. It has *cis*- and *trans*- isomers as shown in Fig. 9.5.

(vi) **Bridged binuclear planar complexes of $M_2a_2b_4$ type** In bridged binuclear square planar complexes *cis-trans* isomers as well as unsymmetrical isomers, are possible, although in the example $[Pt(PEt_3)Cl_2]_2$ cited below, and in all other cases, only the first two (*i.e.*, *cis*- and *trans*-forms) have been found.

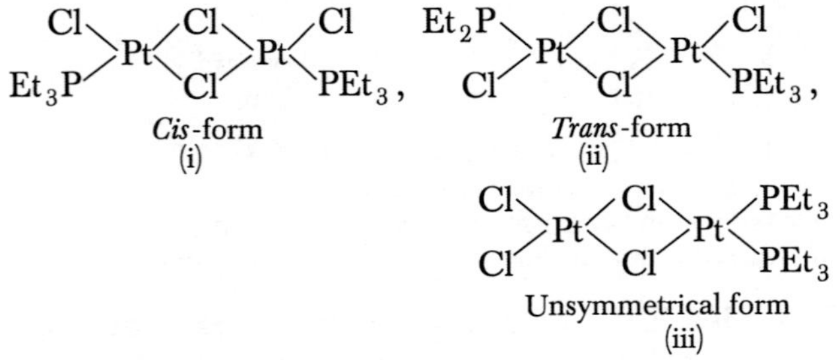

Octahedral complexes

The arrangement of six ligands in a regular octahedral complex round the central metal ion, M can be represented as shown in Fig. 9.6.

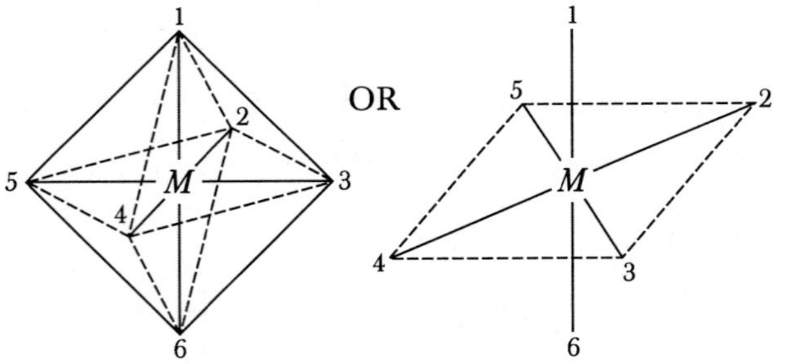

Fig. 9.6 Arrangement of six ligands in a regular octahedral complex round the metall ion, *M*.

Here, we shall discuss the *cis-trans*-isomerism in different types of octahedral complexes containing monodentate ligands such as a and b, symmetrical bidentate chelating ligands, (AA) or unsymmetrical bidentate chelating ligands, (AB). In (AA) the two letters A and A indicate the two ends (*i.e.*, donor atoms-similar atoms) of the chelating ligand which get coordinated with the central metal ion, M. (AA) ligand may be a neutral molecule (*e.g.*, ethylene diammine, $H_2N—CH_2—CH_2—NH_2$, en) or a negative ion (*e.g.*, $C_2O_4^{2-}$ ion). In (AB), A and B are two different coordinating atoms.

It may be seen that octahedral complexes of $[Ma_5b]^{n\pm}$ and $[Ma_6]^{n\pm}$ type will give only single isomer. Thus, these complexes will show no isomerism.

The following types of octahedral complexes show *cis-trans*-isomerism.

(a) **Octahedral complexes containing only monodentate ligands** Such complexes are those which have any of the following general formulae :

(i) **$[Ma_4b_2]^{n+}$ type complexes** In case of this complex, two isomers are possible : *cis*-isomer in which the two b's occupy 1 and 2 positions while in *trans*-isomer two b's are at 1 and 6 positions as shown below in Fig. 9.7.

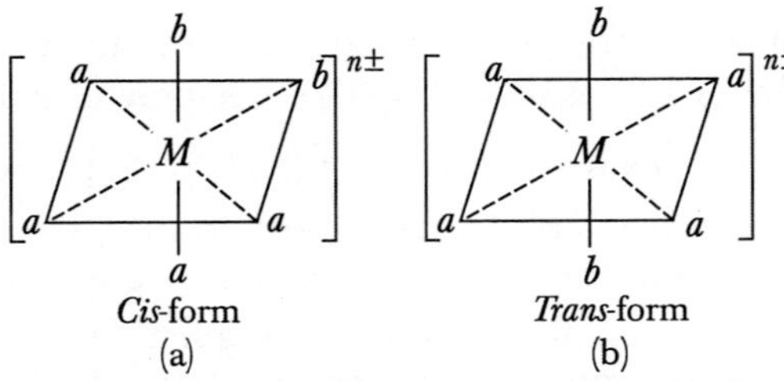

Fig. 9.7 *Cis*- and *trans*-isomers of $[Ma_4b_2]^{n\pm}$ type octahedral complex. In *cis*-isomer two b's have adjacent positions while in *trans*-isomer two b's are diagonally opposite to each other. Numbers indicate positions of b groups.

Examples Dichlorotetraammine cobalt (III) ion, $[Co^{III}(NH_3)_4Cl_2]^+$ is an important example of $[Ma_4b_2]^{n\pm}$ type complex ion. It has *cis*- and *trans*-isomers as shown in Fig. 9.8.

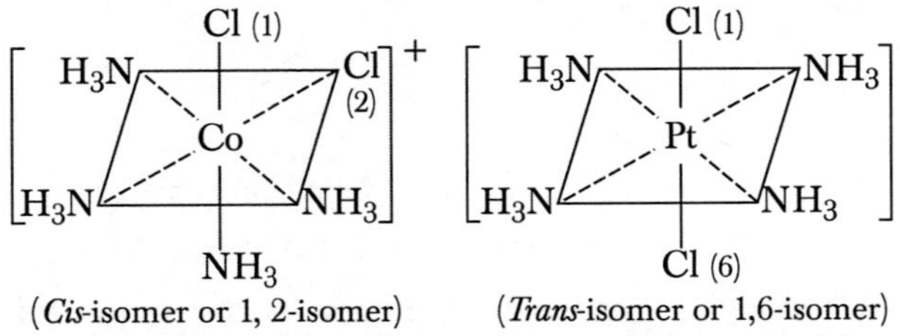

Fig. 9.8 *Cis*- and *trans*-isomers of $[Co^{III}(NH_3)_4Cl_2]^+$ion. In *cis*-isomer two Cl^- ions are in (any) two adjacent positions while in *trans*-isomer these are in (any) two opposite positions.

In *cis*-isomer, the two Cl^- ions are in (any) two adjacent positions. *Cis*-isomer is designated as 1, 2-isomer. In *trans*-isomer the two Cl^- ions are in (any) two opposite positions. *Trans*-isomer is designated as 1, 6-isomer. *Cis*-isomer has a beautiful blue-violet colour while *trans*-isomer has bright green colour.

(ii) **$[Ma_3b_3]^{n\pm}$ type complexes** Complexes of this type also exist in *cis*- and *trans*-isomers. In *cis*-isomer three a's occupy 1, 2 and 3 positions and in *trans*-isomer these are at 1, 2 and 6 positions as shown in Fig. 9.9.

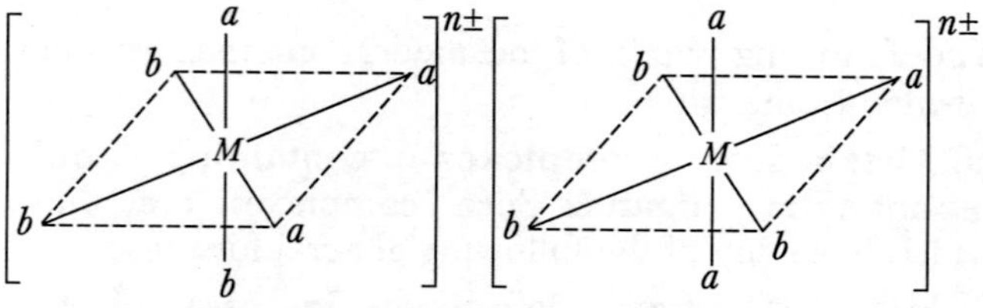

Cis-isomer (1, 2, 3) isomer — *Trans*-isomer (1, 2, 6) isomer

Fig. 9.9 *cis*-and *trans*-forms of $[Ma_3b_3]^{n\pm}$ type octahedral complex ion. Numbers indicate the positions of *a*'s ligands.

Examples (a) Trichloro tripyridine rhodium (III), $[Rh^{III}(py)_3Cl_3]^0$ is an example of this type of ion.

(b) Another example is $[Cr^{III}(NH_3)_3Cl_3]^0$ which exists in two isomeric forms. In one isomer, the three Cl^- ions are on one triangular face and the three NH_3 molecules are on the opposite triangular face of the regular octahedron. This isomer is called 1, 2, 3 or **facial isomer.** In the other isomer the Cl^- ion are around an edge of the octahedron and the NH_3 molecules are around the opposite edge. This isomer is called 1, 2, 6 or **peripheral isomer** or meridional isomers.

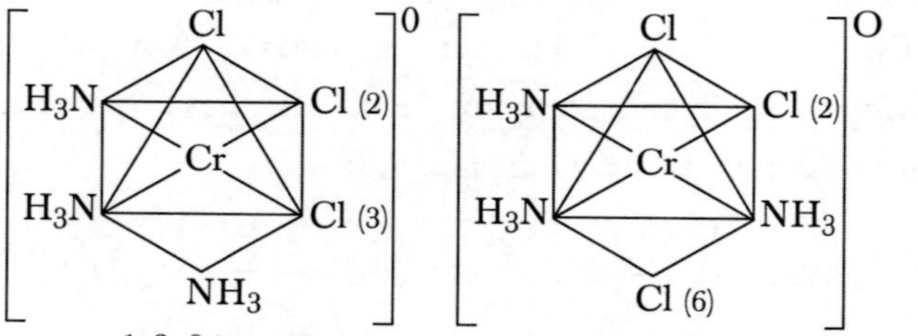

1, 2, 3-isomer (Facial isomer) — 1, 2, 6-isomer (Peripheral isomer)

Fig. 9.10 Two isomeric forms of $[Cr^{III}(NH_3)_3Cl_3]^0$.

(iii) ***[Mabcdef]* type complexes** This type of octahedral complex can exist in 15 different geometrical isomers each of which would also have an optical isomer. The only compound of this type is $[Pt^{IV}(py)(NH_3)(NO_2)(Cl)(Br)(I)]$. It has been obtained in three different forms but no attempt has been made to isolate all the 15 isomers.

(b) **Octahedral complexes containing monodentate and symmetrical bidentate chelating ligands** Now, let us discuss the *cis-trans*-isomerism among octahdral complexes containing monodentate and symmetrical bidentate chelating ligands. These complexes may be those which have any of the following formulae :

(i) $[M(AA)_2a_2]^{n\pm}$ **type complexes** Here, (*AA*) is a symmetrical bindentate chelating ligand in which the two letters *A* and *A* indicate the two similar corrdinating atoms. *a* is a monodentate ligand. Complexes having this general formula exist in *cis*- and *trans*-isomers as shown in Fig. 9.11.

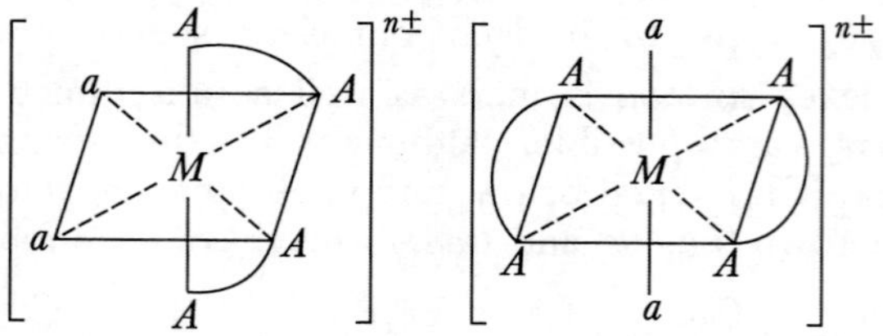

(*a*'s *cis*) (a) — (*a*'s *trans*) (b)

Fig. 9.11 *Cis*- and *trans*-isomers of $[M(AA)_2a_2]^{n\pm}$ type octahedral complex ion;
(a) *Cis*-form in which *a*'s are *cis* to each other.
(b) *Trans*-form in which *a*'s are *cis*- to each other.

Examples The following complex ion are the examples of $[M(AA)_2a_2]^{n\pm}$ type ion :

$[Co^{III}(en)_2Cl_2]^+$, $[Co^{III}(en)_2(NO_3)_2]^+$, $[Ir^{IV}(C_2O_4)_2Cl_2]^{2-}$

$[Ir^{III}(C_2O_4)_2Cl_2]^{3-}$, $[Rh^{IV}(C_2O_4)_2Cl_2]^{2-}$, $[Cr^{III}(C_2O_4)_2(H_2O)_2]^-$

Cis- and *trans*-isomers of $[Co^{III}(en)_2Cl_2]^+$ ion can be represented as given in Fig. 9.12.

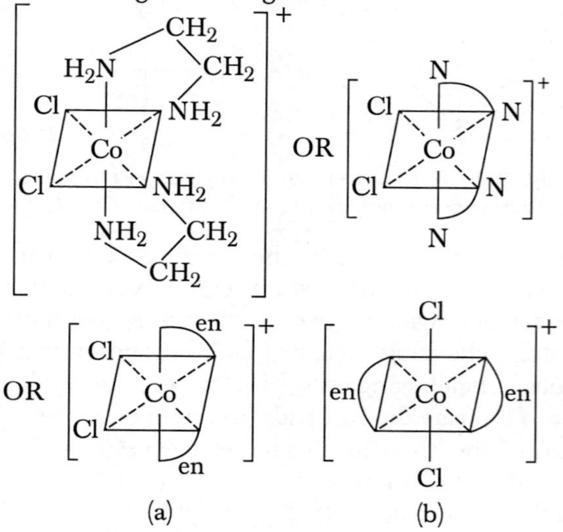

Fig. 9.12 *Cis*- and *trans*-isomers of $[Co^{III}(en)_2Cl_2]^+$ ion. (a) *Cis*-isomer (b) *Trans*-isomer.

(ii) $[M(AA)_2ab]^{n\pm}$ **type complexes** The complexes exist in *cis*- and *trans*- isomers as shown below in Fig. 9.13.

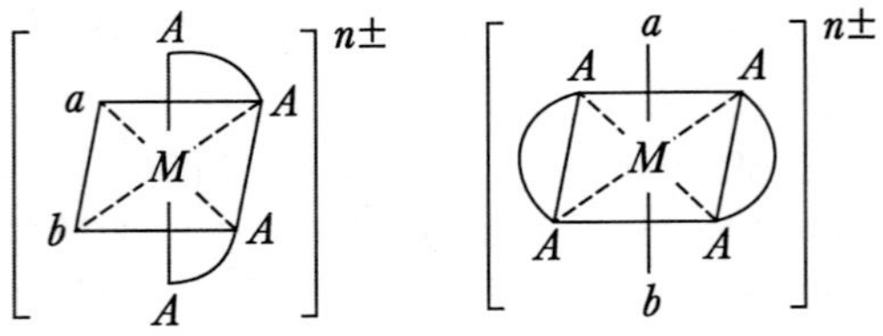

(a) (b)

Fig. 9.13 *Cis-* and *trans*-isomers of $[M(AA)_2 ab]^{n\pm}$ type octahedral complex ion.
(a) *Cis*-form (b) *Trans*-isomer

Examples $[Co^{III}(en)_2(NH_3)(Cl)]^{2+}$ and $[Ru^{III}(py)(C_2O_4)(NO)]^-$. *cis-* and *trans*-isomers of $[Co^{III}(en)_2(NH_3)(Cl)]^{2+}$ ion are given below in Fig. 9.14.

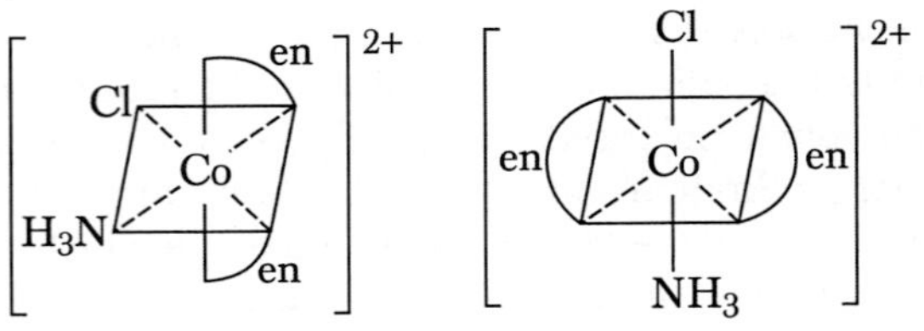

(a) (b)

Fig. 9.14 *Cis-* and *trans*-isomers of $[Co^{III}(en)_2(NH_3)(Cl)]^{2+}$ ion.

(iii) $[M(AA)a_2b_2]^{n\pm}$ **type complexes** Complexes of this type also exist in *cis-* and *trans*-isomers as shown below in Fig. 9.15.

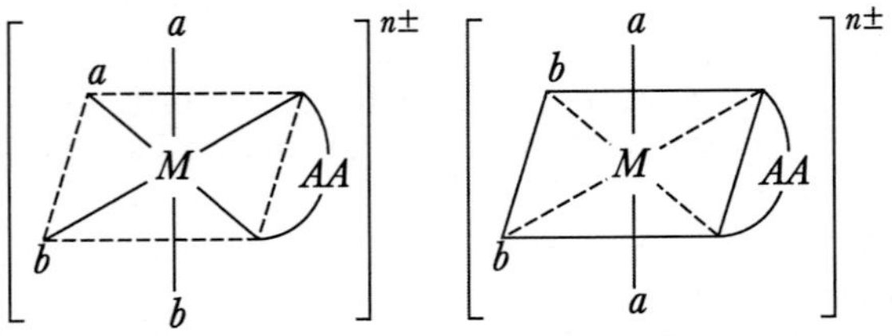

Cis-isomer *Trans*-isomer

Fig. 9.15 *Cis-* and *trans*-isomers of $[M(AA)a_2b_2]^{n\pm}$ type complexes.

Examples $[Co^{III}(en)(NH_3)_2(Cl)_2]^+$ is an important example whose *cis-* and *trans*-isomers are shown below in Fig. 9.16.

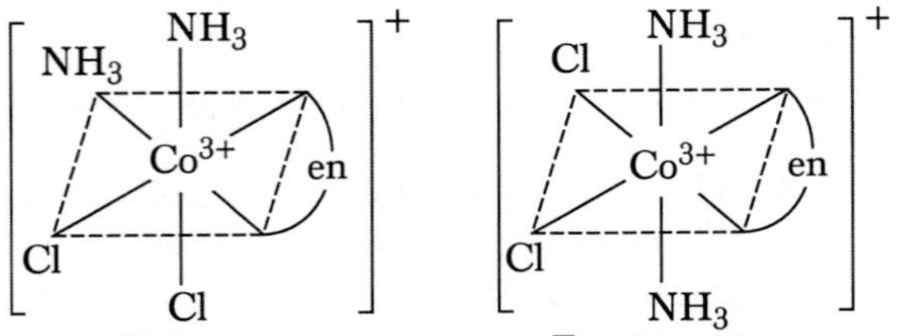

Cis-isomer *Trans*-isomer

Fig. 9.16 *Cis-* and *trans*-isomers of $[Co^{III}(en)(NH_3)_2Cl_2]^+$.

(c) **Octahedral complexes containing unsymmetrical bidentate chelating ligands** $[M(AB)_2]^{n\pm}$ type complex is an important example of octahedral complexes containing unsymmetrical bidentate chelating ligands. Here, (AB) is an unsymmetrical bidentate chelating ligand in which the letters A and B represent the two ends (*i.e.*, coordinating atoms) of the ligand. Complex ion of $[M(AB)_3]^{n\pm}$ type exists as *cis*-and *trans*-isomers as shown below in Fig. 9.17. Both *cis-* and *trans*-isomers have each a pair of optical isomers.

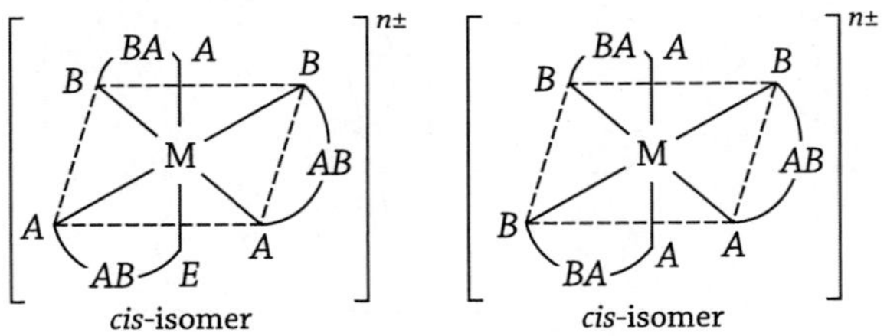

cis-isomer *cis*-isomer

Fig. 9.17 *Cis*-and *trans*-isomers of $[M(AB)_3]^{n\pm}$ complex ion.

Examples *Cis*-and *trans*-isomers of triglycinato chromium (III), $[Cr^{III}(gly)_3]^0$ has the structures as shown in Fig. 9.18. Each of these form is optically active.

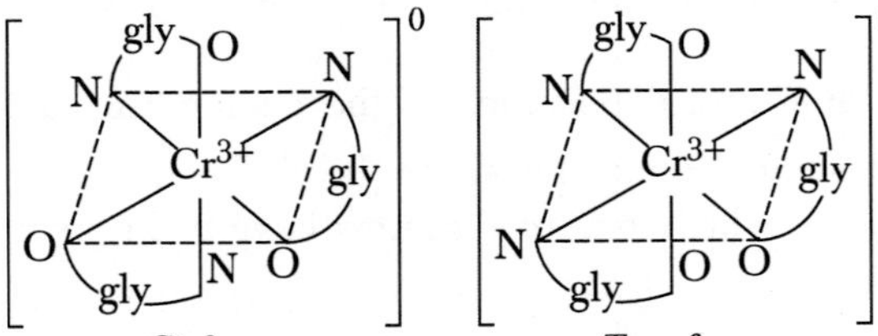

Cis-form *Trans*-form

Fig. 9.18 *Cis*-and *trans*-isomers of $[Co^{III}(gly_3)]^0$.

(d) **Octahedral complexes containing optically active bidentate ligands** $[Co^{III}(en)(pn)(NO_2)_2]^+$ is an important examples of such type of octahedral complexes. Here, 'en' and 'pn' are ethylene diamine and 1,2-diamino propane and have the following formulae :

$$\text{en} \longrightarrow \begin{array}{l} CH_2—NH_2 \\ | \\ CH_2—NH_2 \end{array}, \quad \text{pn} \longrightarrow \begin{array}{lll} \overset{1}{C}H_2 — & \overset{2}{C}H — & \overset{3}{C}H_3 \\ | & | & \\ \underset{*}{N}H_2 & \underset{**}{N}H_2 & \end{array}$$

From their formulae it is evident that both the ligands are bidentate with two neutral donors *viz.* N-atoms and that en is symmetrical and hence optically inactive while pn is unsymmetrical and hence optically active. To differentiate the two donor atoms *viz.*

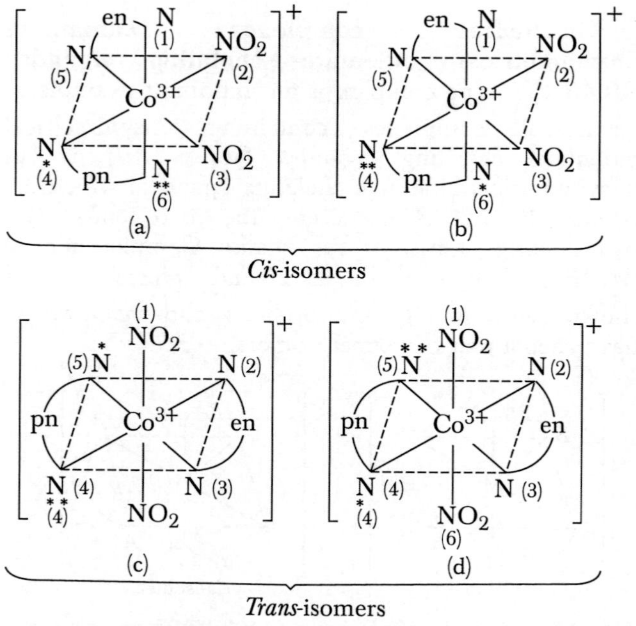

Fig. 9.19 *Cis*-and *trans*-isomers of $[Co^{III}(en)(pn)(NO_2)_2]$.

N-atoms of pn have been shown with one end two asterisks. $[Co^{III}(en)(pn)(NO_2)_2]^+$ ion exists in four geometrical forms : two are *cis* and two are *trans.*

(a) *cis*-isomer has been obtained by placing $\overset{*}{N}H_2$ and $\overset{**}{N}H_2$ at 4 and 6 positions of the octahedron and in (b) *cis*-isomer their positions have been reversed. (c) and (d) which are *trans*-isomers have been obtained similarly.

(e) **Polynuclear complexes** The geometric isomers of a polynuclear hydroxy-bridged complex, $[Fe_2(OH)_4(H_2O)_6]^{2+}$, can be shown as follows (Fig. 9.20).

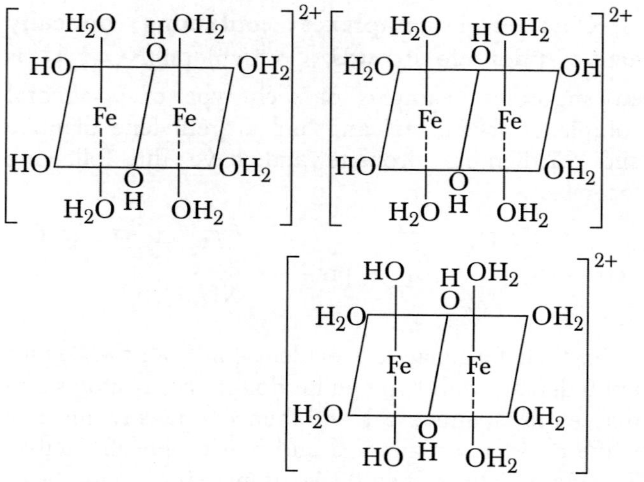

Fig. 9.20 Geometrical isomers of $[Fe_2(OH)_4(H_2O)_6]^{2+}$ion.

Such type of isomerism is called bridge-isomerism which interprets the linkage of two complexed species by ligands that are common to the coordination spheres of both, and which, consequently, must be mutually shared. In $[Fe_2(OH)_4(H_2O)_6]^{2+}$ ion the two OH^- groups act as bridges and connect the respective octahedral components of the overall structure.

2. Optical or Mirror-Image Isomerism

Before discussing the optical isomerism shown by various types of complexes we will define some important terms related to this isomerism.

When the solution of certain complex compounds are placed in the path of a plane-polarised light (the waves of the plane-polarised light vibrate only in one direction; vibrations in other directions are cut-off), they rotate its plane through a certain angle which may be either to the left or to the right. **This property of a complex of rotating the plane of polarised light is called its optical activity and the complex possessing this property is said to be optically active.**

Optically active complexes are said to exist in the following forms :

(a) One which rotates the plane of polarised light towards right (*i.e.*., in clockwise direction) is said to be **dextrorotatory** or ***d*-form.** *d*-form is also represented by placing (+) sign before its name or formula.

(b) One which rotates the plane of polarised light towards left (*i.e.,* in anti-clockwise direction) is called **laevorotatory** or ***l*-form.** *l*-forms is also represented by putting (–) sign before its name of formula.

(+), dextro, and (–), laevo, refer to the sign of rotation of the optical isomer at the sodium *D* line wavelength.

The *d*- and *l*-forms have the following characteristics :

(i) Since, *d*- and *l*-forms are capable of rotating the plane of polarised light, these are said to be **optically active forms** or **optical isomers** and this phenomena is called **optical activity** or **optical isomerism.** These two forms have exactly identical physical and chemical properties, although they differ in their action on polarised light.

(ii) *d*-and *l*-forms are mirror images to each other just as left hand is the mirror image of the right hand. Thus, *d*-and *l*-forms can not be superimposed on each other. Since, these forms are related to each other as mirror-images, they are commonly called **enantiomorphs** (Latin : *enantio* = opposite, *morphs* = forms) or **enantiomers.** Thus, optical isomerism is now often referred to as **enantiomerism.**

(c) One which is not capable of rotating the plane of polarised light is called optically inactive. Such an isomer is called **racemic-*dl*-or (±)-form.** A racemic substance is composed of 50% *d*- and 50% *l*-form. The solution of a racemic (*dl*-mixture) form in a solvent which contains equimolecular amounts of *d*-and *l*-forms is inactive, because the rotation (of the plane of polarised light) produced by one isomer, say *d*-isomer, is balanced or compensated by equal but opposite rotation produced by the other (*i.e.*, *l*-isomer). Optical inactivity produced in *dl*-mixture is said to be due to **external compensation.**

Conditions for a molecule to show optical isomerism

A molecule in which the grouping of the atoms in the molecule in asymmetric is called an **asymmetric or dissymmetric molecule.**

An asymmetric molecule has the following features :

(i) An asymmetric molecule never has a plane of symmetry (also called mirror-image plane) which is defined as an imaginary plane which divides the molecule in such a way that the part of it on one side of the plane is the mirror image of that on the other side of the plane. The molecules possessing such a plane of symmetry are always inactive while those having no plane of symmetry are optically active and hence show optical isomerism.

(ii) An asymmetric molecule cannot be superimposed on its mirror image.

Thus, the most necessary and sufficient condition for a molecule to show optical isomerism (*i.e.,* to exist in *d*-and *l*-forms) is that (a) the molecule should be asymmetric, *i.e.*, it should have no plane of symmetry, and (b) the molecule should not be superimposable on its mirror image.

Optical Isomerism in four and six coordinated compounds

No mirror image isomers are possible with tetrahedral and square planar complexes of the type : $[Ma_4]$, $[Ma_3b]$ and $[Mab_3]$ because all the possible arrangements of the ligands round the central metal ion, M are exactly equivalent.

(A) **Square planar complexes** Optical isomerism rarely occurs in square planar complexes, since they have all the four ligands and the central metal ion in the same plane and hence contain a plane or axis of symmetry. Thus, these complexes are optically inactive, *i.e.,* they cannot show optical isomerism even if all the four ligands are different.

Although, as mentioned above, square planar complexes seldom show optical isomerism, yet a four-coordinate complex of Pt(II) *viz, iso*-butylenediamine-*meso* stilbenediamine platinum (II) cation, $[Pt^{II}(NH_2 \cdot CH(C_6H_5) \cdot CH(C_6H_5) \cdot NH_2)(NH_2 \cdot CH_2C(CH_3)_2 \cdot NH_2)]^{2+}$ which has square-planar shape has been resolved into two forms by Mills and Quibell is 1935.

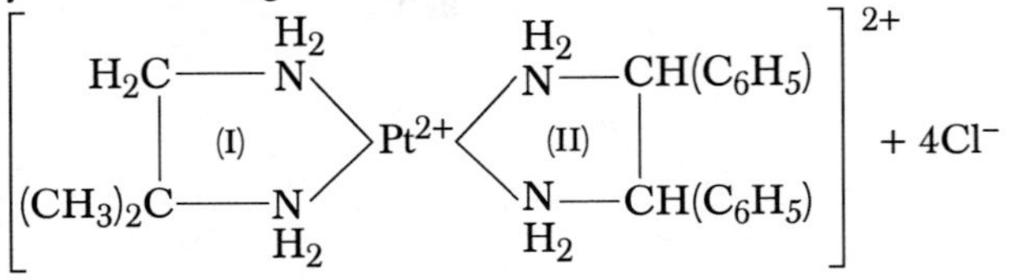

Iso-butylene diamine *meso* stilbenediamine platinum (II) cation

(B) **Tetrahedral complexes** (i) A tetrahedral complex of [*Mabcd*] type occurs in two optical isomers as shown in Fig. 9.21.

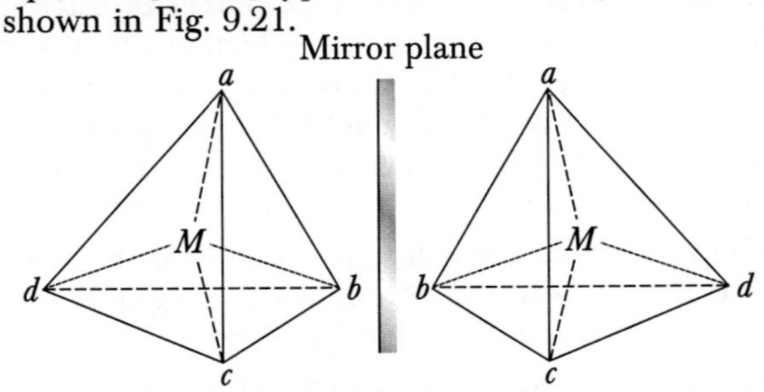

Fig. 9.21 Two optical isomers (mirror image isomers) of a tetrahedral complex of [*Mabcd*] type.

Examples (i) Mirror image isomers of As^{3+} ion complex, $[As^{III}(CH_3)(C_2H_5)(S)(C_6H_4COO)]^{2+}$, with tetrahedral structure are shown below in Fig. 9.22

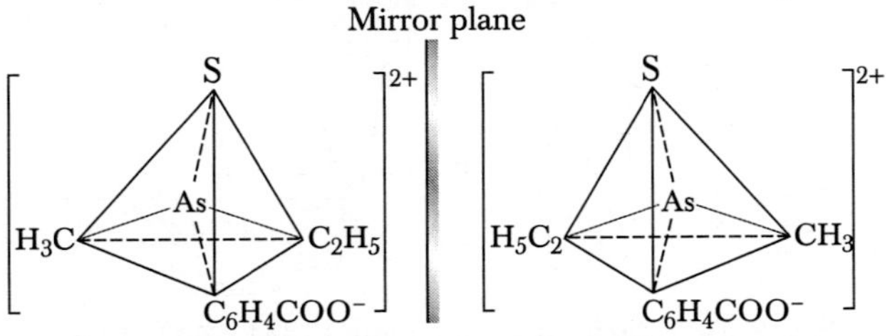

Fig. 9.22 Mirror image isomers of $[As^{III}(CH_3)(C_2H_5)(S)(C_6H_4COO)]^{2+}$ ion having tetrahedral structure.

Here, it may be noted that four different groups round the central metal ion are not the only requirement to make the complex to show mirror-image isomerism. All that is required is that the molecule should be asymmetric (*i.e.*, unsymmetrical), *i.e.*, it should have no plane of symmetry so that, it can exist in two mirror image forms.

(c) **Octahedral complexes** Optical isomerism is very common in the following types of octahedral complexes :

(a) **Octahedral complexes containing only monodentate ligands** The following types of octahedral complexes have optical isomers :

$[Ma_2b_2c_2]$, $[Ma_2b_2cd]$, $[Ma_2bcde]$ and $[Mabcdef]$

(i) **$[Ma_2b_2c_2]n^{\pm}$ type complex** It has two optical isomers as shown below in Fig. 9.23.

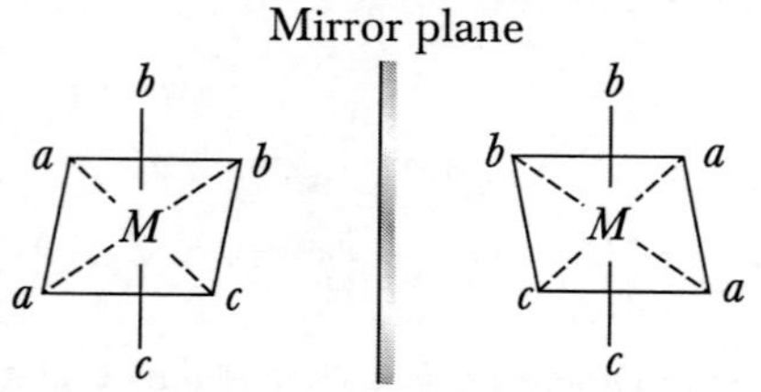

Fig. 9.23 Two optical isomers of an octahedral complex of $[Ma_2b_2c_2]$ type.

(ii) **[*Mabcdef*] type complex** Complexes of this type having six different monodentate ligands have been prepared only for Pt(IV). Only a few isomers have been isolated, but there could be 15 geometrical isomers, each of which could exist in *d*- and *l*-forms to given a total of 30 isomers.

(b) **Octahedral complexes containing only symmetrical bidentate chelating ligands** Such complexes may be of the following types :

(i) **$[M(AA)]_3^{n\pm}$ type complexes** Here, (*AA*) is a symmetrical bidentate chelating ligand which may be a neutral molecule or a negative ion. The optical isomers of this type of complexes are shown below in Fig. 9.24.

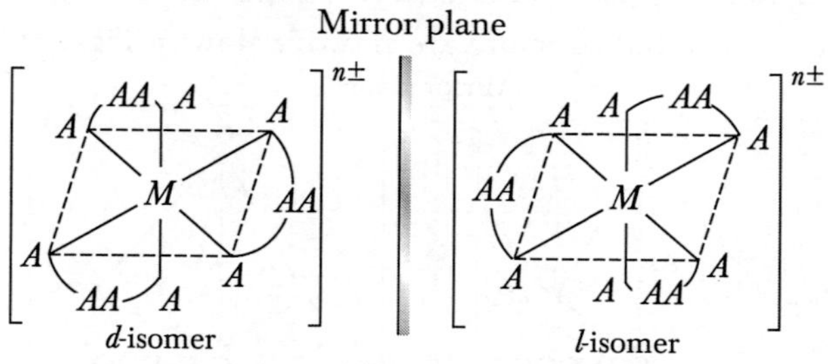

Fig. 9.24 Mirror image isomers of $[M(AA)_3]^{n\pm}$ type octahedral complex ion.

Examples $[Co^{III}(en)_3]^{3+}$, $[Co^{III}(pn)_3]^{3+}$, $[Pt^{IV}(en)_3]^{4+}$, $[Pt^{IV}(pn)_3]^{4+}$, $[Cd^{II}(pn)_3]^{2+}$, $[Fe^{II}(diph)_3]^{2+}$, $[Fe^{III}(diph)_3]^{3+}$, $[Rh^{IV}(en)_3]^{4+}$, $[Ir^{IV}(pn)_3]^{4+}$, $[Zn^{II}(en)_3]^{2+}$, $[M^{III}(C_2O_4)_3]^{2-}$ where, $M^{III} = Al^{3+}, Co^{3+}, Fe^{3+}, Rh^{3+}, Cr^{3+}$ and Ir^{3+}.

The two optical isomers of $[Co^{III}(en)_3]^{3+}$ ion are shown in Fig. 9.25.

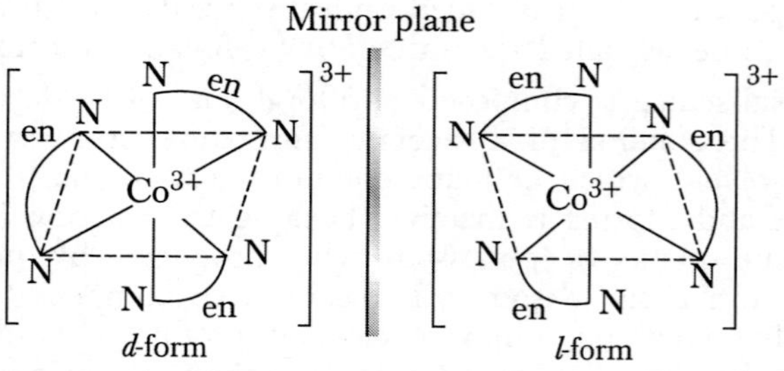

Fig. 9.25 Optical isomers of $[Co^{III}(en)_3]^{3+}$ion. These cannot be superimposed on each other.

The fact that the complexes of $[M(AA)_3]^{n\pm}$ type can be resolved into optical isomers confirms that these complexes have octahedral shape. Neither hexagonal nor trigonal prismatic geometry of 6-coordinate complex can give rise to optical activity.

(ii) **$[M(AA)_2(BB)]^{n\pm}$ type complexes** Here, (*AA*) and (*BB*) are two different symmetrical bidentate chelating ligands. Note that (*AA*) is a neutral ligand while (*BB*) is an anionic ligand. The two enantiomers (or enantiomorphs) of $[M(AA)_2(BB)]^{n\pm}$ type complexes are shown below in Fig. 9.26.

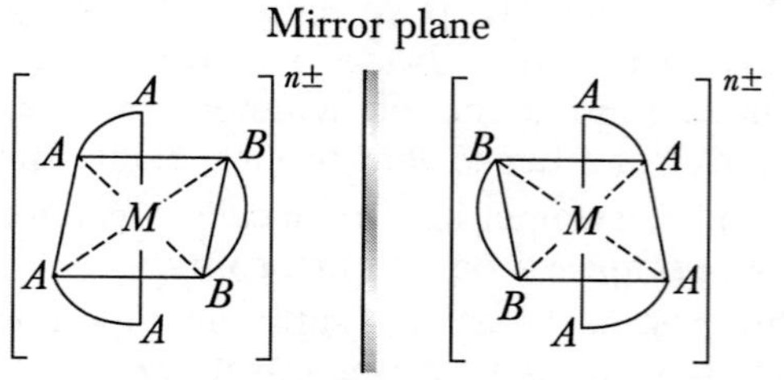

Fig. 9.26 The two enantiomers (or enantiomorphs) of $[M(AA)_2(BB)]^{n\pm}$ type complex ion.

Examples The ions namely $[Co^{III}(en)_2(CO_3)]^+$ and $[Co^{III}(en)_2(C_2O_4)]^+$ belong to this class of complexes.

(c) **Octahedral complexes containing monodentate and symmetrical bidentate chelating ligands.** Such complexes may be of the following types :

(i) $[M(AA)_2a_2]^{n\pm}$ **type complexes** Here, (AA) is a bidentate chelating ligand and a is a unidentate (*i.e.*, monodentate) ligand.

Examples The ions namely $[Co^{III}(en)_2Cl_2]^+$, $[Co^{III}(en)_2(NO_3)_2]^+$, $[Ir^{IV}(C_2O_4)_2Cl]^{2-}$, $[Rh^{IV}(C_2O_4)_2Cl_2]^{2-}$, $[Cr^{III}(C_2O_4)_2(H_2O)_2]^-$, $[Ir^{III}(C_2O_4)_2Cl_2]^{3-}$ etc., belong to this type of complexes.

Optical isomerism in $[Co^{III}(en)_2Cl_2]^+$ ion Now, let us discuss the optical isomerism in $[Co(en)_2Cl_2]^+$ ion in detail. We have already seen that this ion has geometrical isomers namely *cis-* and *trans*-isomers.

The *cis*-isomer of $[Co(en)_2Cl_2]^+$ ion shown in Fig. 9.30(a) can be resolved into two optically active isomers, since it has no plane of symmetry. Its *trans*-isomer shown at (b) cannot be resolved into two forms, since no mirror-image of this ion is possible *i.e.*, it has a plane of symmetry. Thus, *trans*-isomer is an optically inactive form (*meso*-form). Consequently $[Co(en)_2Cl_2]^+$ ion has the following three optical isomers :

(a) Two optically active isomers corresponding to *cis*-configuration (*i.e., d-* and *l*-forms). One form is the mirror image of the other.

(b) One optically inactive form corresponding to *trans*-form (*meso*-form).

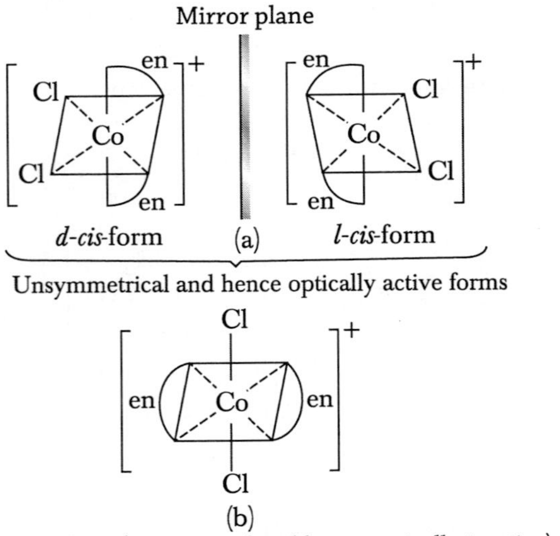

Trans-meso-form (symmetrical and hence optically inactive)

Fig. 9.27 Optical isomers of $[Co(en)_2Cl_2]^+$ ion.

(ii) $[M(AA)_2ab]^{n\pm}$ **type complexes** These complexes exist in three forms : two are optically active (*d-* and *l*-forms) and the third one is inactive (*meso*-form) as shown below in Fig. 9.28.

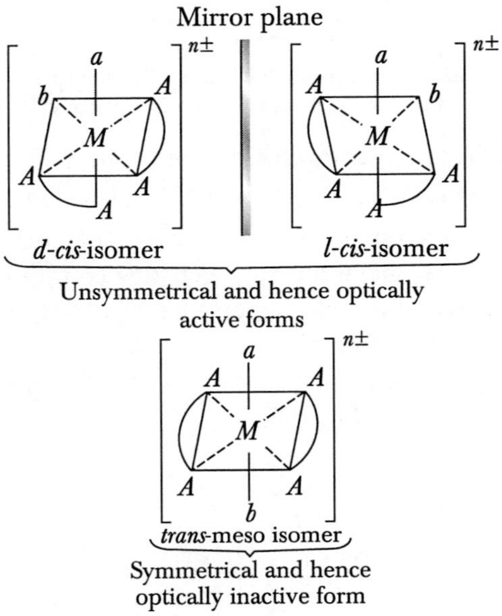

Fig. 9.28 Optical isomers of $M(AA)_2ab]^{n\pm}$ type complex.

Examples Important examples of this type of complexes are :

$[Co^{III}(en)_2(NH_3)Cl)]^{2+}$ and $[Ru^{III}(py)(C_2O_4)_2(NO)]^-$

(iii) $[M(AA)a_2b_2]^{n\pm}$ **type complexes** These also exist in three forms : two are optically active and the third is inactive or symmetrical.

Examples $[Co^{III}(en)(NH_3)_2Cl_2]^+$, $[Co^{III}(C_2O_4)(NH_3)_2(NO_2)_2]^-$ etc. Three forms of $[Co^{III}(C_2O_4)(NH_3)_2(NO_2)_2]^-$ are shown in Fig. 9.29 and 9.30.

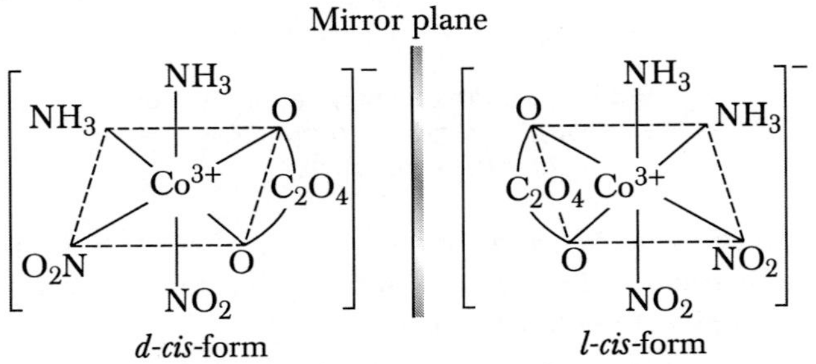

Fig. 9.29 *d* and *l*-forms of *cis*-isomers of $[Co^{III}(C_2O_4)(NH_3)_2(NO_2)_2]^-$. These are unsymmetrical forms and hence are optically active.

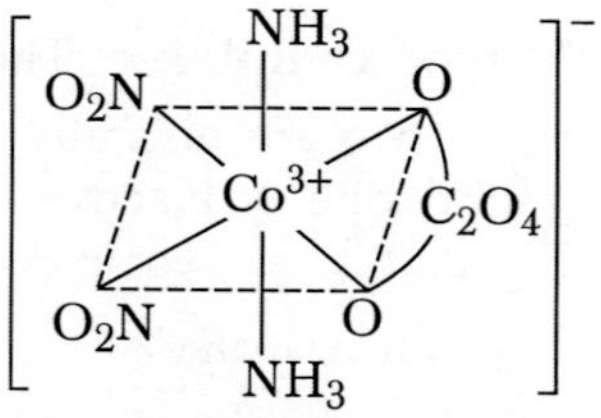

Fig. 9.30 *Trans*-isomer of $[Co^{III}(C_2O_4)(NH_3)_2(NO_2)_2]^-$. It is a symmetrical form and hence is optically inactive.

(d) **Octahedral complexes containing optically active ligands** $[Co^{III}(en)(pn)(NO_2)_2]^+$ ion is an important example of such type of octahedral complexes. We have already seen this complex exists in two *cis* and two *trans*-isomers (see Fig. 9.22). Each of the two *cis*-forms namely (a) and (b) shown below gives its corresponding optical isomer (e) and (f) respectively as shown below in Fig. 9.34.

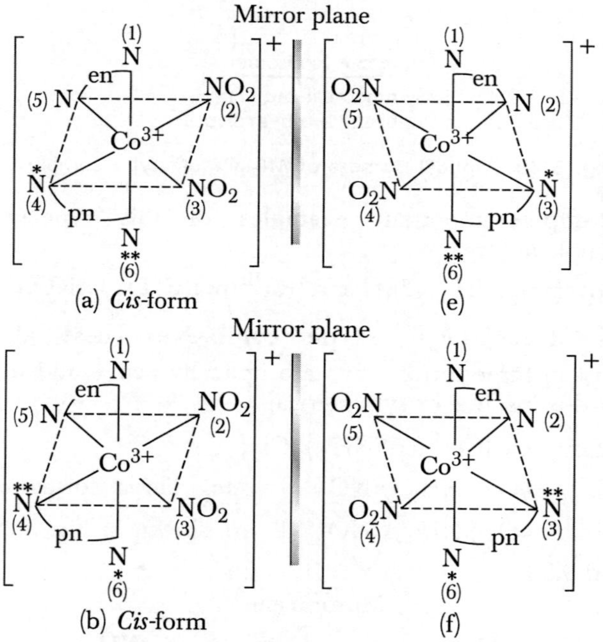

Fig. 9.31 *Cis*-forms namely (a) and (b) of $[Co^{III}(en)(pn)(NO_2)_2]^+$ ion give two optical isomers, (e) and (f) respectively.

Trans-isomers (c) and (d) shown in Fig. 9.19 are symmetrical and hence are optically inactive *i.e.,* they do not give any optical isomers.

If we consider the complex of $M(AA)_3$ type where AA is a symmetric bidentate optically active (*i.e.,* asymmetric) ligand, it would be expected to give the following eight isomers :

D-$[M(d\text{-}AA)_3]$	L-$[M(l\text{-}AA)_2]$
D-$[M(d\text{-}AA)_2(l\text{-}AA)]$	L-$[M(l\text{-}AA)_2(d\text{-}AA)]$
D-$[M(d\text{-}AA)(d\text{-}AA)_2]$	L-$[M(l\text{-}AA)(d\text{-}AA)_2]$
D-$[M(l\text{-}AA)_3]$	L-$[M(d\text{-}AA)_3]$

In these isomers D and L refer to the optical rotation of the complex and d and l refer to the optical rotation of the asymmetric ligand. However, generally only two isomers are obtained, *e.g.,* only two isomers of $[Co(chxn)_3]^{2+}$ where, *chxn* is *trans* 1, 2-cyclohexane diamine have been obtained and these are : D-$[Co(l\text{-}chxn)_3]^{3+}$ and L-$[Co((d\text{-}chxn)_3]^{3+}$.

(e) **Octahedral complexes containing polydentate ligands** Complexes containing hexadentate ligand like ethylene diamine tetra-acetate ion *viz.*

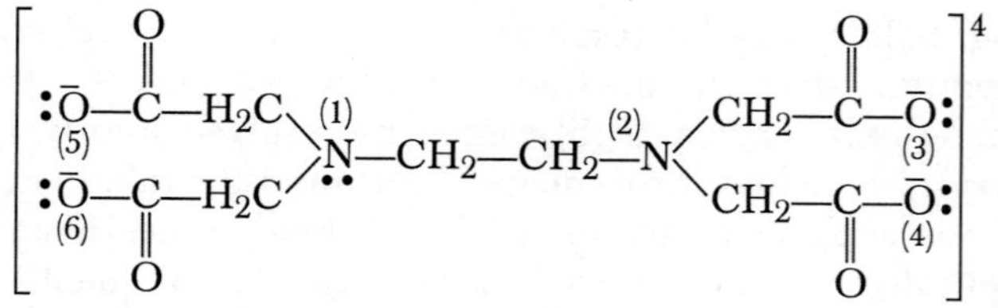

(abbreviated as $EDTA^{4-}$) which is a polydentate ligand also shows optical isomerism, *e.g.,* the complex anion, $[Co^{III}(EDTA)]^-$ exists in two optical isomers : *d*- and *l*-forms (Fig. 9.32).

$[EDTA]^{4-}$ has four donor oxygen atoms (numbered as 3, 4, 5 and 6) and two donor nitrogen atoms (numbered as 1 and 2). Thus, it has six coordinating sites and four negative charges. In $[Co(EDTA)]^-$ ion, Co^{3+} is attached with four oxygens of CH_2COO^- component and with two nitrogen atoms.

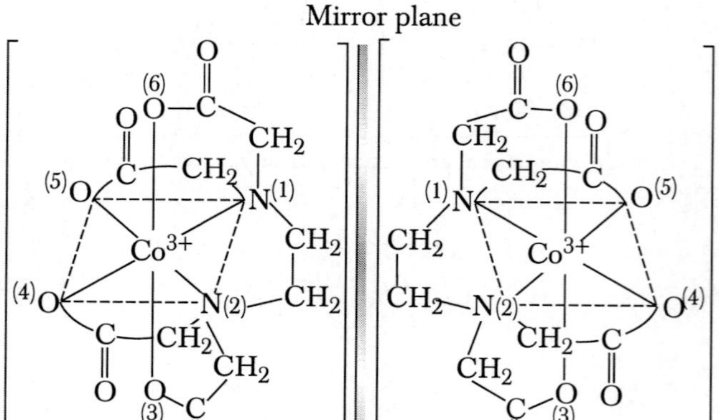

Fig. 9.32 Optical isomers of $[Co^{III}(EDTA)]^-$ ion.

Two optical forms shown in Fig. 9.32 can also be shown in a simpler way as given in Fig. 9.33.

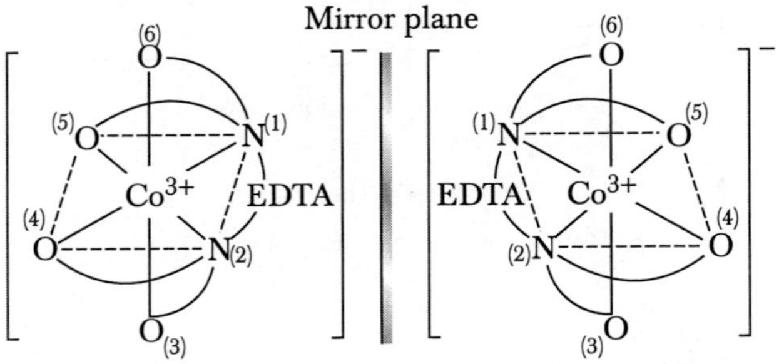

Fig. 9.33 *d*- and *l*-forms of $[Co^{III}(EDTA]^-$ ion shown in simpler way.

(f) **Polynuclear complexes** Optical activity is not limited to mononuclear complexes only. Optical isomerism is also found in polynuclear ions. Werner in 1913 isolated the polynuclear ion,

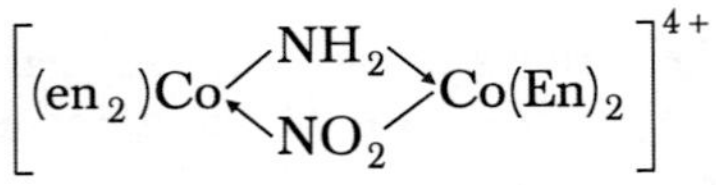

into three forms : (i) *d*- form (ii) *l*-form and (iii) *meso*-form which is optically inactive and is an internally compensated form. *d*- and *l*-forms are mirror images to each other and are optically active. It has been observed that both *d*- and *l*-forms revert to the *meso*-form when their solutions are heated. Optical isomers of this ion are shown in Fig. 34.

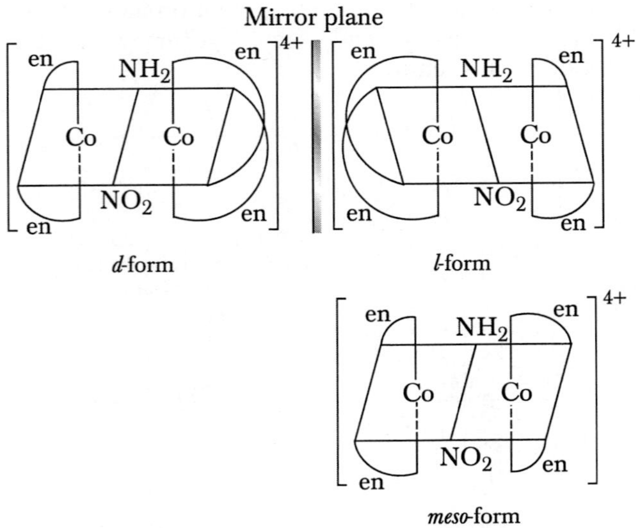

Fig. 9.34 Optical isomers of $[(Co(en)_2)_2(NH_2)(NO_2)]^{4+}$ ion. *d*- and *l*-forms are optically active while *meso*-form is optically inactive.

Bonding in Metal Complexes

Valence Bond Theory

This theory was developed by Pauling. The model utilizes hybridization of metal valence orbitals to account for the observed structures and magnetic properties of complexes. Pauling suggested that $(n-1)\ d$, ns and np orbitals undergo hybridization to give hybridized orbitals. An empty hybrid orbital on the metal centre can accept a pair of electrons from a ligand to form a σ-bond.

Example Octahedral complex of Co(III)

- The atomic orbitals required for an octahedral complex are the $3d_{z^2}$, $3d_{x^2-y^2}$, $4s$, $4p_x$, $4p_y$ and $4p_z$.
- These orbitals must be unoccupied so as to be available to accept six pairs of electrons from the ligands.

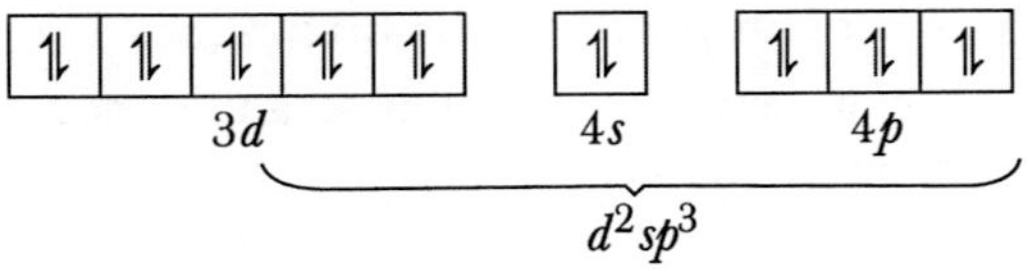

Table 9.3 **Common Geometries and Corresponding Hybridisation Schemes**

C.N.	Geometry	Orbitals	Description	Examples
2	Linear	s, p_z	sp	$[Ag(NH_3)_2]^+$
3	Trigonal planar	s, p_x, p_y	sp^2	$[HgI_3]^-$
4	Tetrahedral	s, p_x, p_y, p_z	sp^3	$[FeBr_4]^{2-}$
5	Square planar	$s, p_x, p_y, d_{x^2-y^2}$	sp^2d	$[Ni(CN)_4]^{2-}$
4	Trigonal bipyramidal	s, p_x, p_y p_z, d_{z^2}	sp^3d	$[CuCl_5]^{3-}$
5	Square-based pyramidal	$s, p_x, p_y, p_z, d_{x^2-y^2}$	sp^3d	$[Ni(CN)_5]^{3-}$
6	Octahedral	$s, p_x, p_y, p_z, d_{z^2}, d_{x^2-y^2}$	sp^3d^2	$[Co(NH_3)_6]^{3+}$
6	Trigonal prismatic	$s, d_{xy}, d_{yz}, d_{xz}, d_{z^2}, d_{x^2-y^2}$	sd^5	$[Mo(S_2C_2Ph_2)_3]$

Example The complex $[PtCl_4]^{2-}$ is diamagnetic, whereas $[NiCl_4]^{2-}$ is paramagnetic with two unpaired electrons. VBT proposes the use of dsp^2 hybridization for Pt (to afford a square-planar geometry around it) and the use sp^3 hybridization for Ni^{2+} (to afford a tetrahedral geometry).

$[PtCl_4]^{2-}$

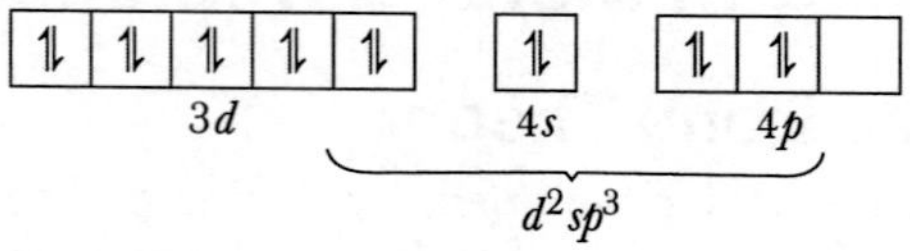

$[NiCl_4]^{2-}$

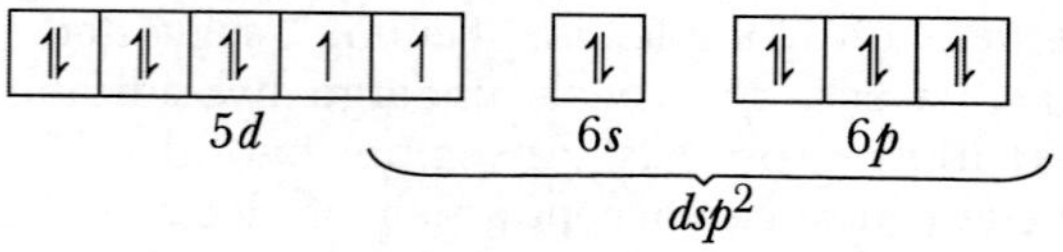

Limitations

- Most transition metal complexes are coloured, but the theory does not provide any explanation.
- The VBT does account for the observed magnetic moment in complexes. However, orbitals of higher energy have to be utilized (quite arbitrarily) for cases as in $[CoF_6]^{3-}$ where, 4s, 4p and 4d orbitals are utilized in the $3p^3d^2$ hybridization. The VBT does not explain the temperature dependent magnetic properties.

Crystal Field Theory

In view of the above weaknesses, an alternative bonding model was applied to transition metal complexes. This is known as **crystal field theory (CFT)**. It has been originally proposed by Hans Bethe and van Vleck in 1929. The assumptions of the crystal field theory are as follows :

1. The interaction between the metal ion and the ligand is assumed to be purely electrostatic (ionic) in nature.
2. The ligands are treated as point charges. Consequent to this assumption, the CFT does not allow for any overlap between the metal orbitals and the ligand orbitals.

In spite of the above unrealistic premise, the CFT has been remarkably successful in explaining many properties of the transition metal complexes. This is mainly due to the fact that the symmetry considerations involved in the crystal field approach are identical to the more sophisticated molecular orbital theory that we will consider later.

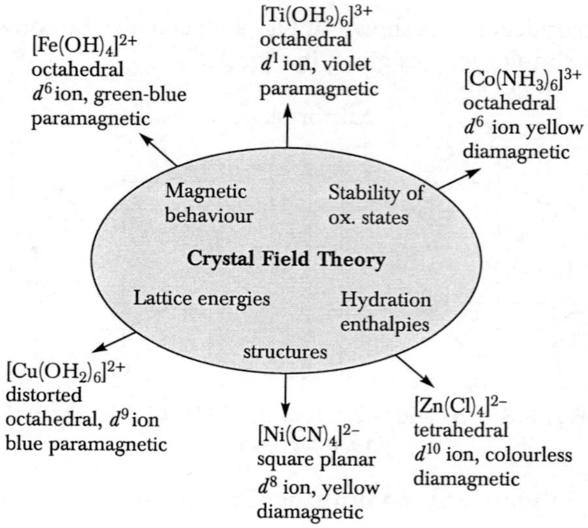

Consequences of the Metal Ion Interaction with Ligands

- The five d-orbitals in an isolated, gaseous metal ion are degenerate (are of the same energy and symmetry).
- If a spherically symmetric field of negative charges is placed around the metal ion, the orbitals will remain degenerate, but all of them will be raised in energy as a result of repulsion between the negative field and the metal electrons in the orbitals.
- If the field results produced by the ligands is not spherically symmetric but of a particular symmetry (octahedral, tetrahedral etc.), the d-orbitals are not affected equally and the degeneracy of the d-orbitals is removed.

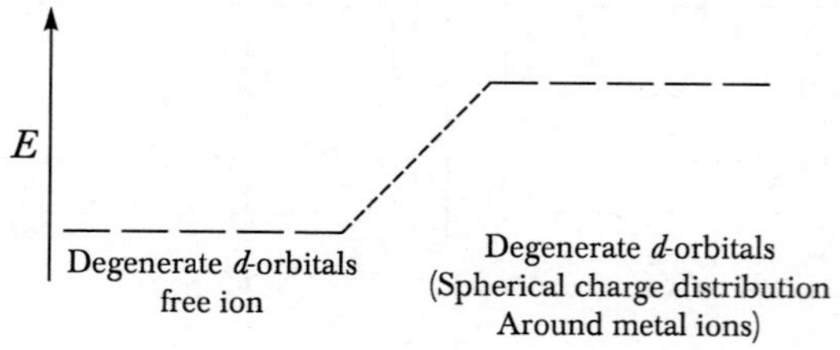

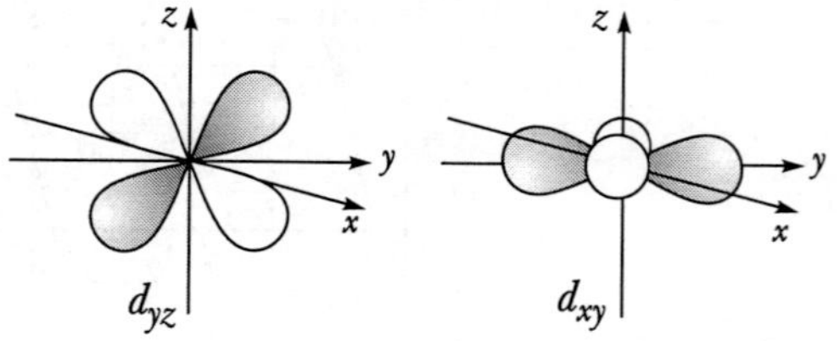

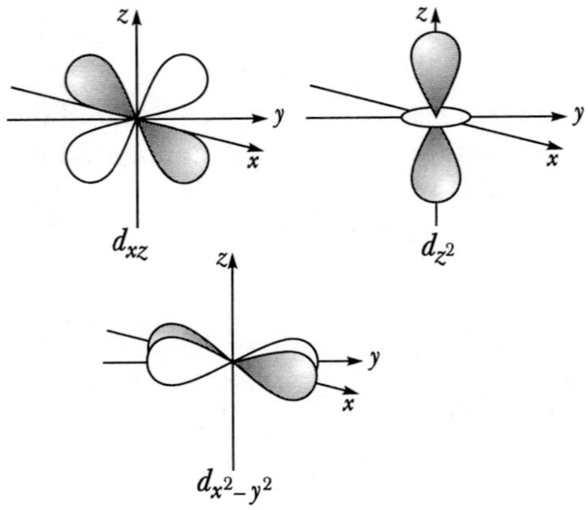

Note There are six wave functions that can be written for these orbitals. The d_{z^2} orbital is regarded as a linear combination of the $d_{z^2-y^2}$ and $d_{z^2-x^2}$. The d_{z^2} and $d_{x^2-y^2}$ orbitals are along the axes, d_{xy}, d_{xz}, d_{yz} orbitals are in-between the axis.

Octahedral Field

An octahedral field is described by six ligands at the six corners of an octahedron and the metal is at the centre.

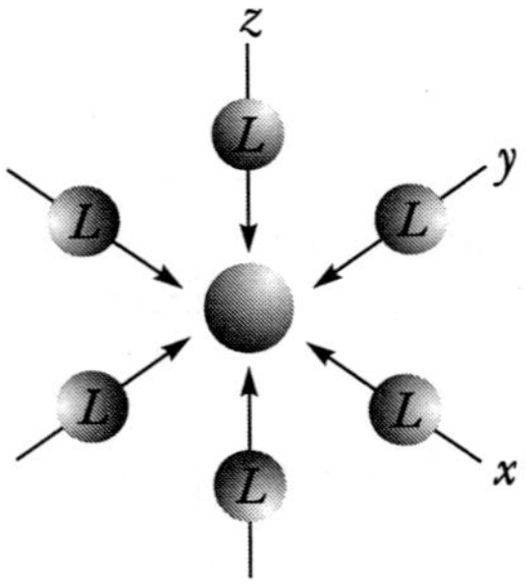

Hence, the orbitals lying along the axes (d_{z^2} and $d_{x^2-y^2}$) will be more strongly repelled than those whose orbitals are lying in between the axes (d_{xz}, d_{yz}, d_{xy}). Thus, the overall consequence is that the degenerate set of five orbitals is now split into two sets, one at a higher energy and one at a lower energy. The higher energy set of orbitals (d_{z^2} and $d_{x^2-y^2}$) are labelled as e_g and the lower energy set is labelled as t_{2g}. The energy separation between the two levels is denoted by Δ_o or 10 Dq. Note that moving from a hypothetical spherical field to an octahedral field does not alter the average energy of the five *d*-orbitals. The weighted mean of these two sets of perturbed orbitals is taken as zero; this is also known as 'barycenter'. To maintain the average energy, the e_g orbitals need to be repelled by an amount of 0.6 Δ_o and the t_{2g} orbitals to be stabilized to the extent of 0.4 Δ_o with respect to the barycentre.

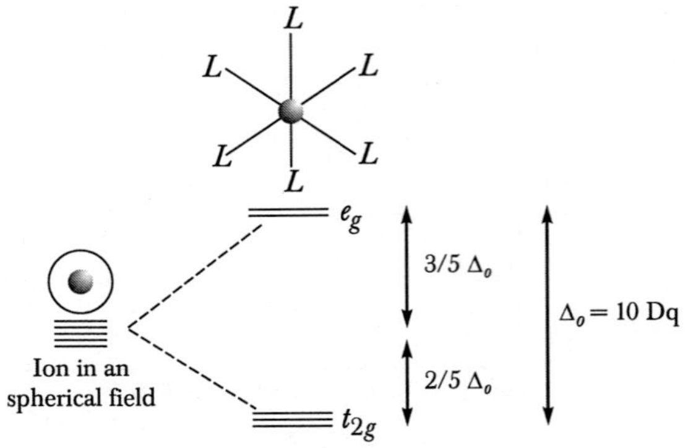

Ion in an octahedral ligand field.

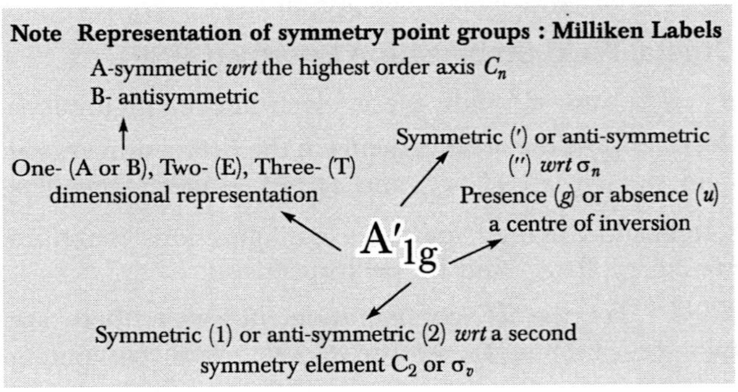

The splitting energy Δ_o can be determined from spectroscopic data. Let us consider the case of $[Ti(H_2O)_6]^{3+}$. This compound is purple in colour. Unlike valence bond theory, the crystal field treatment explains the colour. The lone *d* electron (Ti^{3+} is a d^1 species) in an octahedral crystal field enters the lower energy orbitals to have a ground state electronic configuration, $t_{2g}^1 e_g^0$. The purple colour is the result of the absorption of light and the excitation of the electron to the higher energy e_g level ($t_{2g}^1 e_g^0 \rightarrow t_{2g}^0 e_g^1$). This excitation corresponds to 20300 cm^{-1} corresponding to an energy of absorption of 243 kJ mol^{-1}. This corresponds to Δ_o in this molecule. It should be mentioned here that the d^1 is the simplest case in that the transition from $t_{2g}^1 e_g^0 \rightarrow t_{2g}^0 e_g^1$ reflects the actual energy difference between the t_{2g} and e_g levels. For multielectron system such as (d^2, d^3 etc), electron-electron interactions make the calculations more complicated.

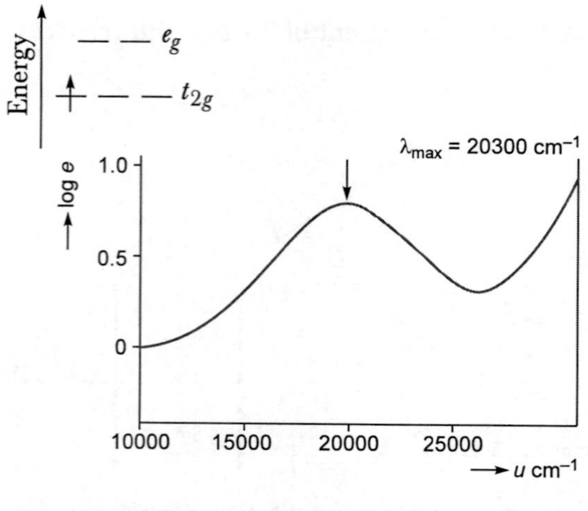

Note The absorption spectrum of $[Ti(H_2O)_6]^{3+}$ appears broad with a shoulder present.

Crystal Field Stabilization Energy (CFSE)

d^1, d^2 and d^3 For these electronic configurations the only possible arrangements in the octahedral crystal field are $t_{2g}^1\ e_g^0$, $t_{2g}^2\ e_g^0$ and $t_{2g}^3\ e_g^0$ respectively. The stabilization energy for these configurations therefore are $0.4\Delta_o$, $0.8\Delta_o$ and $1.2\Delta_o$ respectively.

d^4-d^7 For the d^4 configuration, however, there are two possibilities $t_{2g}^4\ e_g^0$ or $t_{2g}^3\ e_g^1$. Two competing factors determine which configuration is preferred. In order to force an electron to pair with another, an energy called **Pairing energy** (P), has to be invested. This is made up of two terms. One : the **Coulombic repulsion** arising out of forcing two electrons to occupying the same orbital; two : the loss of **exchange energy** that occurs as electrons with parallel spins are forced to have anti-parallel spins. If $P > \Delta_o$, the configuration $t_{2g}^3\ e_g^1$ is preferred. This is known as weak field or high spin situation. If $\Delta_o > P$, the configuration $t_2g^4\ e_g^o$ is adopted. This leads to strong field or low spin situation. **The reason for the nomenclature high and low spin arises from the magnetic moment differences between the two configurations.** Thus, $t_{2g}^4\ e_g^o$, has only two unpaired electrons and therefore would have a magnetic moment of 2.83 BM. In contrast the configuration $t_{2g}^3\ e_g^1$ would have four unpaired electrons with a magnetic moment of 4.90 BM.

d^8-d^{10} For these electronic configurations, the only possible arrangements in the octahedral crystal field are $t_{2g}^6\ e_g^2$, $t_{2g}^6\ e_g^3$ and $t_{2g}^6\ e_g^4$ respectively. The stabilization energy for these configurations therefore are $1.2\Delta_o$, $0.6\Delta_o$ and $0.0\Delta_o$ respectively.

A simplified table showing the CFSE's and the number of unpaired electrons for various configurations under both strong and weak field situations is shown below. This stable neglects the pairing energy contribution.

Table 9.4

	Weak field			Strong field		
d^n	Configu-ration	Unpaired electrons	CFSE	Configur-ation	Unpaired electrons	CFSE
d^1	t_{2g}^1	1	$0.4\Delta_o$	t_{2g}^1	1	$0.4\Delta_o$
d^2	t_{2g}^2	2	$0.8\Delta_o$	t_{2g}^2	2	$0.8\Delta_o$
d^3	t_{2g}^3	3	$1.2\Delta_o$	t_{2g}^3	3	$1.2\Delta_o$
d^4	$t_{2g}^3\ e_g^1$	4	$0.6\Delta_o$	t_{2g}^4	2	$1.6\Delta_o$
d^5	$t_{2g}^3 e_g^2$	5	$0.0\Delta_o$	t_{2g}^5	1	$2.0\Delta_o$
d^6	$t_{2g}^4 e_g^2$	4	$0.4\Delta_o$	t_{2g}^6	0	$2.4\Delta_o$
d^7	$t_{2g}^5 e_g^2$	3	$0.8\Delta_o$	$t_{2g}^6 e_g^1$	1	$1.8\Delta_o$
d^8	$t_{2g}^6 e_g^2$	2	$1.2\Delta_o$	$t_{2g}^6 e_g^2$	2	$1.2\Delta_o$
d^9	$t_{2g}^6 e_g^3$	1	$0.6\Delta_o$	$t_{2g}^6 e_g^3$	1	$0.6\Delta_o$
d^{10}	$t_{2g}^6 e_g^4$	0	$0.0\Delta_o$	$t_{2g}^6 e_g^4$	0	$0.0\Delta_o$

This table is somewhat simplified because pairing energies and electron-electron effects have been neglected.

Tetrahedral Symmetry

Consider the metal ion along with its d-orbitals in the centre of the cube. Arrange the ligands alternately in four corners of the cube. This arrangement would keep two ligands in the top face of the cube and two in the bottom face. Notice that in this arrangement none of the ligands approach the metal along the Cartesian coordinate axes. Consequently the orbitals lying along the axes (d_{z^2} and $d_{x^2-y^2}$) will be less strongly repelled than those whose orbitals are lying in between the axes (d_{xz}, d_{yz}, d_{xy}). Thus, the overall consequence is that the previously degenerate set of five orbitals is now split into two sets, one at a higher energy and one at a lower energy. The higher energy set of orbitals (d_{xy}, d_{yz}, d_{xy}) is labelled as t_2 and the lower energy set (d_{z^2} and $d_{x^2-y^2}$) is labelled as e. [The subscripts 'g' disappear here, since the tetrahedron lacks a centre of inversion]. The energy separation between the two levels is denoted by Δ_t or 10 Dq.

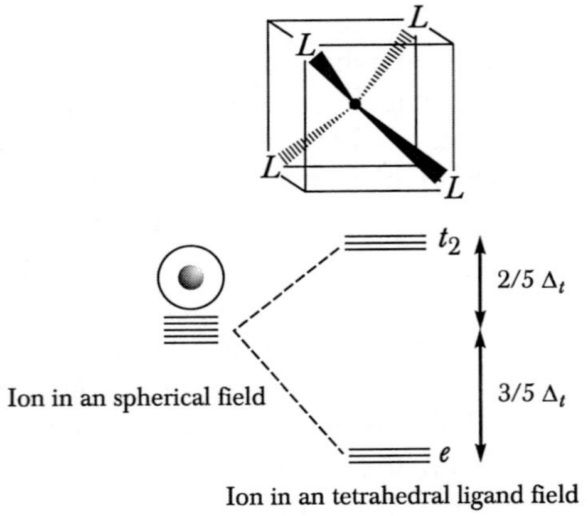

The crystal field splitting in the tetrahedral field is intrinsically smaller than in the octahedral field because (a) there are only four ligands surrounding the metal ion and (b) none of them have a direct effect on the *d*-orbitals. For most purposes the relationship between the two crystal field separation energies may be represented as $\Delta_t = 4/9\Delta_o$.

When to expect tetrahedral geometry

- Ligands are large, less ligand-ligand repulsion.
- Metal ion with zero CFSE (d^0, d^5, d^{10}) or small CFSE (d^2 andd^7) .

Examples MnO_4^- (d^0), $FeCl_4^-$ (d^5, high spin.), $CoCl_4^{2-}$ (d^7, high spin), $ZnCl_4^{2-}$(d^{10}).

Note Having fewer number of ligands (four) and they are not aligned along the orbital axis, the CFSE in most cases are too small to overcome the spin pairing energy, therefore, tetrahedral low-spin complexes are rare. A rare example is $Cr[N(SiMe_3)_2]_3[NO]$.

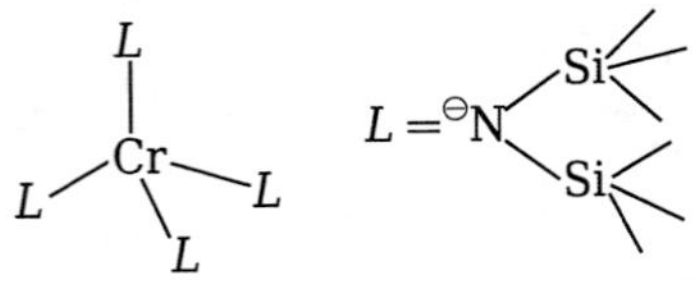

Tetragonal Symmetry : Square Planar Complexes

If two *trans* ligands in an octahedral ML_6 complex (consider those along the *z*-axis) are moved either towards or away from the metal ion, the resulting is said to be tetragonally distorted. Ordinarily such distortions are not favoured since they result in a net loss of bonding energy. In certain situations, however, such a distortion is favoured because of a John-Teller effect (we will study this later in details). A complex of general formula *trans*-MA_2B_4 also will have tetragonal symmetry. For now, we will consider the limiting case of tetragonal elongation, a square planar ML_4 complex, for the purpose of deriving its *d*-orbital splitting pattern.

The crystal field diagram for the tetragonally distorted complex and the square-planar complexes is shown below. Removal of ligands from *z*-direction completely leads to the square-planar geometry. This geometry is favoured by metal ions having a d^8 configuration in the presence of a strong field. This combination gives low-spin complexes where the first four orbitals are occupied and the high energy $d_{x^2-y^2}$ orbital is unoccupied.

When to expect square planar geometry?

- In the case of Ni^{2+} (a first row transition metal ion with a d^8 electronic configuration), a strong field ligand such as CN^- is required to effect a square planar complex formation. **Example** $[Ni(CN)_4]^{2-}$.
- With a second row d^8 metal ion such as Pd^{2+} (which already generates a strong field) even a weak field ligand such as Cl^- leads the formation of a square-planar complex. **Example** $[PdCl_4]^{2-}$.

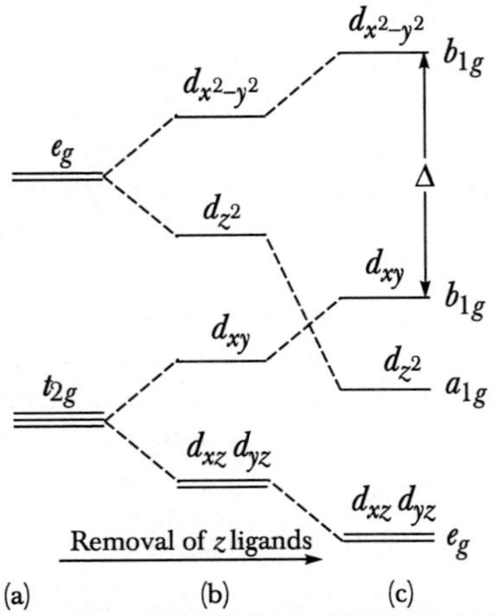

Factors Affecting the Magnitude of Δ

1. Higher oxidation states of the metal atom correspond to larger Δ :

   $\Delta = 10200\ cm^{-1}$ for $[Co^{II}(NH_3)_6]^{2+}$ and $22870\ cm^{-1}$ for $[Co^{III}(NH_3)_6]^{3+}$

   $\Delta = 32200\ cm^{-1}$ for $[Fe^{II}(CN)_6]^{4-}$ and $35000\ cm^{-1}$ for $[Fe^{III}(CN)_6]^{3-}$

2. In groups heavier analogues have larger Δ. For hexaammine complexes $[M^{III}(NH_3)_6]^{3+}$:

   $\Delta = 22870\ cm^{-1}$(Co); $34100\ cm^{-1}$ (Rh);

   $41200\ cm^{-1}$ (Ir)
3. Geometry of the metal coordination unit affects Δ greatly. For example, tetrahedral complexes ML_4 have smaller Δ than octahedral ones ML_6 :

   $\Delta = 10200\ cm^{-1}$ for $[Co^{II}(NH_3)_6]^{2+}$

   $5900\ cm^{-1}$ for $[Co^{II}(NH_3)_4]^{2+}$
4. Ligand can be arranged in a spectrochemical series according to their ability to increase Δ at a given metal centre :

   $$I^- < Br^- < Cl^- < F^-, OH^- < H_2O$$
   $$< NH_3 < NO_2^- < Me^- < CN^- < CO$$

   For $[Co^{II}L_6]$ we have Δ, cm^{-1} : 13100 (F^-), 20760 (H_2O), 22870 (NH_3)

   For $[Co^{III}L_6]$ we have Δ, cm^{-1} : 15060 (F^-), 17400 (H_2O), 26600 (CN^-)

Note $H_2O > HO^-$; this cannot be explained based on electrostatic model of CFT. We shall discuss it in M.O. theory later.

Distortions in Octahedral Geometry

The John-Teller theorem was published in 1937 and states : For a non-linear molecule in an electronically degenerate state, **distortion must occur to lower the symmetry, remove the degeneracy and lower the energy.** Before moving further, the term 'electronically degenerate state' require further elaboration. Consider Ti^{3+} present in an octahedral environment. It is a d^1 system and the lone electron has the possibility of occupying any of the three d-orbitals. Three electronic configurations are possible depending on which orbital is occupied $(d_{xz}^1, d_{xy}^0, d_{yz}^0)$, $(d_{xz}^0, d_{xy}^1, d_{yz}^0)$ and $(d_{xz}^0, d_{xy}^0, d_{yz}^1)$. Such a situation is called an **electronically degenerate state.** Similarly, for Cr^{3+}, that is d^3 system, there is only one way to fill the t_{2g} orbitals $(d_{xz}^1, d_{xy}^1, d_{yz}^1)$ and hence it is an example of electronically non-degenerate state. The John-Teller theorem predicts that a non-linear molecule that has an electronically degenerate state, distortion occurs so that the degeneracy is removed, the consequence is that the symmetry of the molecule is lowered and the system becomes more stable by loosing energy. We will consider two types of distortions to be operating, z-in and z-out.

In the case of octahedral complexes the tetragonal distortion reduces octahedral (O_h) symmetry of the complex to tetragonal (D_{4h}) structures producing either elongated (2-long, 4-short) or compressed (4-long, 2-short) **tetragonal bipyramid** structures. Consider a **case of** $[(Ti(OH_2)_6]^{3+}$**, a** d^1 **system**. To remove the electronic degeneracy, the t_{2g} orbital split and the d_{xz} and d_{yz} orbitals are raised in energy while the d_{xy} orbital is lowered. The separation lets say δ_2. In the e_g set the d_{z^2} orbital is raised in energy in comparison to the $d_{x^2-y^2}$ and the separation is δ_1. In this way,the lone electron is on the d_{xy} orbital and the electronic degeneracy has been removed. The repulsion experienced in the orbitals containing the x, y component is more than the orbitals contain the z-component. The consequence of this is that four long (along x, y axis) and one short (along z-axis) bonds. This is known as z-in case.

Consider the case of Cu(II), the d^9 system. The t_{2g} set split, the d_{xz} and the d_{yz} orbitals are lowered in energy while the d_{xy} orbital is raised. In the e_g set, the d_{z^2} orbital is lowered in energy in comparison to the $d_{x^2-y^2}$. The odd electron resides in $d_{x^2-y^2}$ and the degeneracy in the system is removed. The consequence is that the four short (along x, y-axis) and one long (along z-axis) bonds. This is known as z-out case. The Jahn-Teller effect is more pronounced when the former e_g level is not completely filled $(d_1 > d_2)$ that is for configurations d^4 (high spin), d^7 (low spin) and d^9. In these cases a static John-Teller effect can be observed and the species of D_4h symmetry can exist in a solid phase.

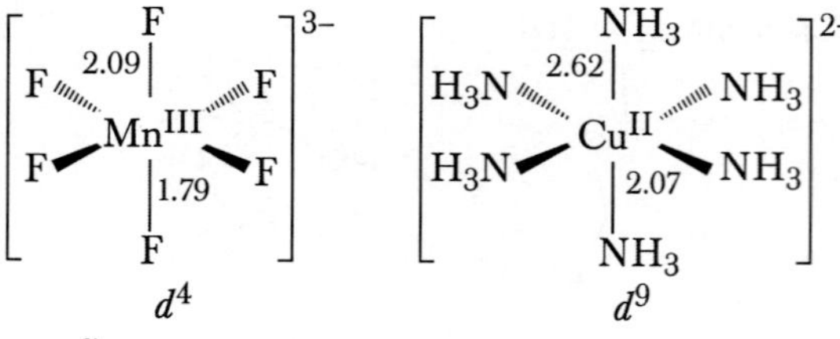

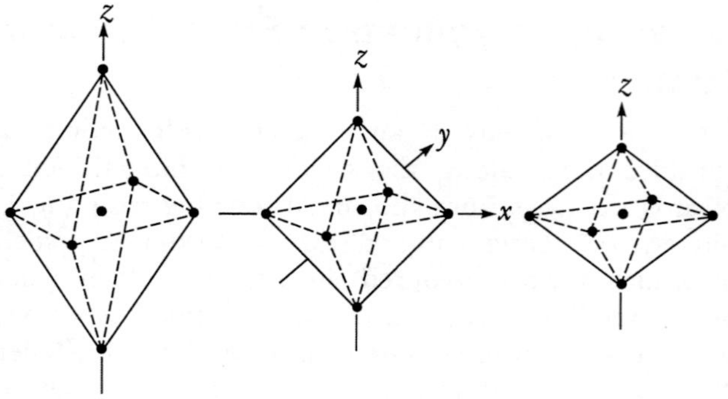

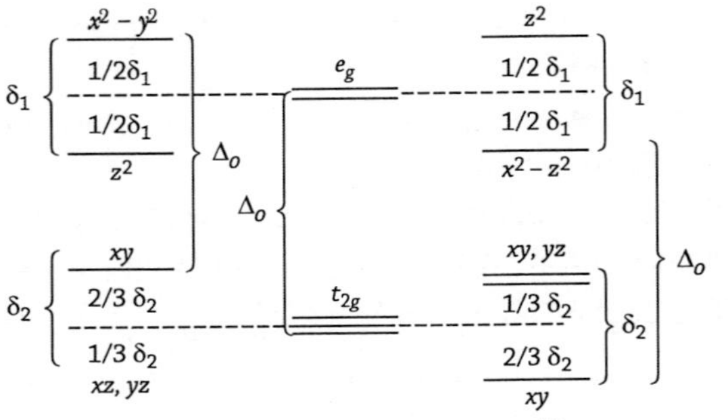

(a) (b)

We can now clearly see that Ti^{3+} with one *d*-electron would prefer *z*-in as here the electronic degeneracy is removed and the energy is lowered ($2/3\ \delta_2$). In contrast V^{3+} with a d^2 configuration would prefer a *z*-out configuration. The Cr^{3+} has a d^3 configuration and in an octahedral crystal field it is not electronically degenerate. Therefore, the question of distortion does not arise. Two further points need to be emphasized. One, the energy separations caused as a result of the distortion are much smaller in comparison to the original separation between t_{2g} and e_g levels and also naturally in comparison with pairing energies. Two, the distortions are better manifested when the electronically degenerate state occurs in the e_g levels rather than in the t_{2g} levels (because the effect of distortion is more *directly* felt). However, it is not possible to predict the type of distortion when the electronic degeneracy occurs in the e_g levels. Consequently a number of Cu^{2+} complexes in an octahedral environment show John-Teller distortion. Although theoretically one is unable to predict the type of distortion that would occur in this molecules, experimentally it is found that elongation (*z*-out)is preferred.

$$\Delta_o >> \delta_1 > \delta_2$$

Limitations of Crystal Field Theory

- Although crystal field theory accounts for many features of complexes including their colour it still leaves some facts unexplained. The colour of compounds like $KMnO_4$ (Mn^{7+} has no *d*-electrons) cannot be explained.
- One of the important experimental facts is the spectrochemical series where many anionic ligands turn out to be quite weak field ligands ($H_2O > OH^-$).
- Also quite strangely neutral ligands and very weak or even poor Lewis bases (for example CO) turn out to be extremely strong field ligands.
- The above is quite contrary to the crystal field theory assumption of an electrostatic interaction between the metal ion and the ligand.

Molecular Orbital Theory of Coordination Complexes

Complexes in Which Metal-Ligand σ-Bonding is Involved

As an example for the above type of situation let us choose the complex $[Co(NH_3)_6]^{3+}$. This complex contains NH_3 as the ligand which can only participate as a σ-donor to the metal ion (The nitrogen atom does not have any low lying orbitals to participate in any additional type of bonding). How do we construct the molecular orbital diagram for this complex? We can use simple symmetry arguments to come out with a picture that would be understandable. Let us first consider the metal orbitals. The valence orbitals available are 3*d*, 4*s* and 4*p*. So a total of 9 orbitals are available. Which of these orbitals are suitable to be used in **σ-bonding**? Remember that we are constructing a molecular orbital diagram for an octahedral complex. This means that the orbitals that we can use should have their lobes pointed along the axes (In order to have a **positive an head-on** overlap with the ligand orbitals). Obviously the 4*s* orbital is quite suitable. This is labelled a_{1g}. All the 4*p* orbitals are also suitable (p_x, p_y, p_z are along the *x*, *y* and *z* directions). These are labelled as t_{1u}. Now, let us inspect the 3*d* orbitals. Only two of them are suitable. The orbitals $d_{x^2-y^2}$ and d_{z^2} are suitable since they have the lobes along the axes. These are labelled e_g; we have seen them before !!!) However, the orbitals d_{xz}, d_{yz} and d_{xy} are not suitable since ligand orbitals cannot overlap with them to give a positive overlap. These cannot be, therefore, utilized by the metal for σ-bonding. These remain non-bonding and are labelled as t_{2g}.

Thus, we conclude that, of 9 valence orbitals of the metal **six** are suitable for forming σ-bonding (a_{1g}, t_{1u}, e_g) and three are non-bonding orbitals (t_{2g}). Let us assume that by a linear combination of the ligand orbitals (one from each ligand) we are able to generate six orbitals of similar symmetry, called ligand

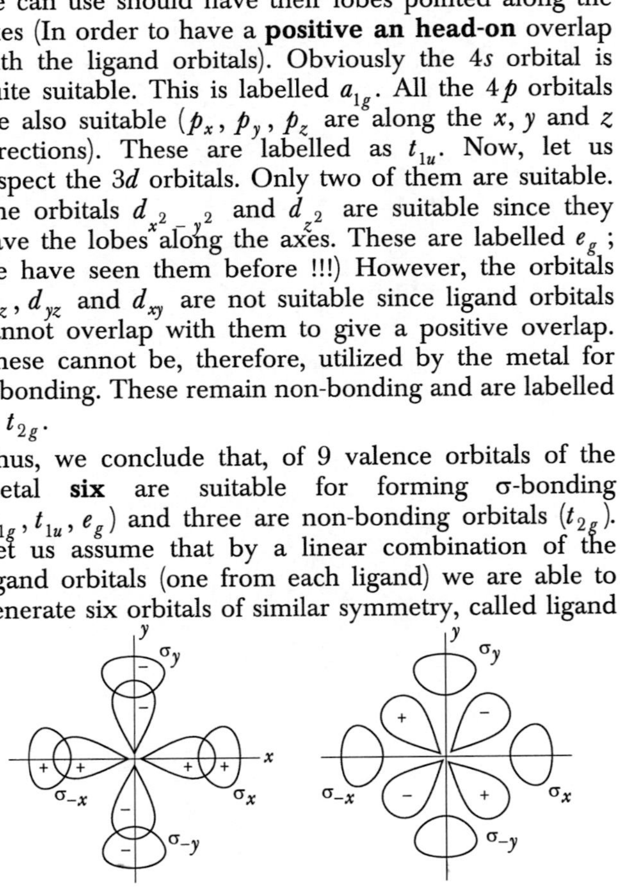

(a) (b)

group orbitals (LGO's) as that of the six metal bonding orbitals. These orbitals on the metal and the ligand now can combine to afford the MO diagram as shown below.

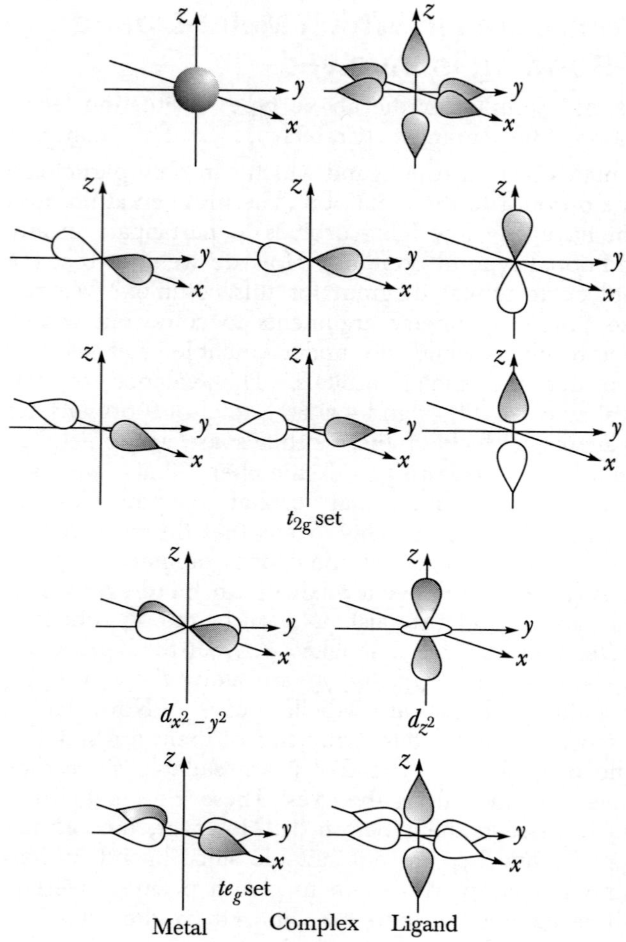

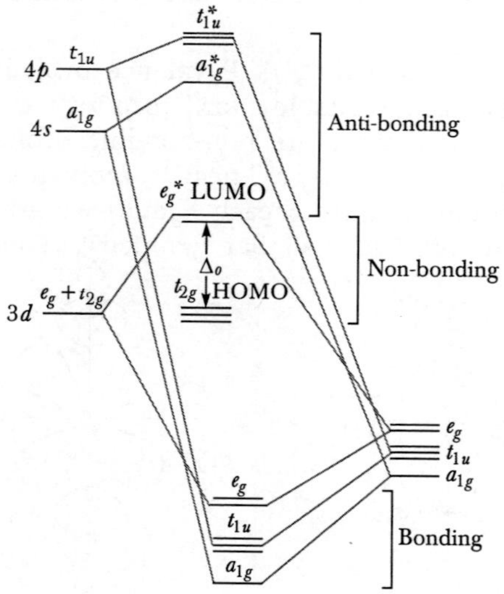

The salient features of the above MO diagram can be summarized as follows :

- The lowest energy orbitals a_{1g}, t_{1u}, e_g are closer in energy to the ligand orbitals.
- The t_{2g} orbitals remain non-bonding and their energy is not changed after forming the MO's.
- The higher energy orbitals $a_{1g}^*, a_{1u}^*, a_g^*$ are closer in energy to the metal orbitals.
- The energy separation between the non-bonding t_{2g} and the a_g^* orbitals represents the Δ_o of the crystal field diagram. As before, if this separation is large, low-spin complexes are formed. If the separation is small, high spin complexes are formed. Thus, $[Co(NH_3)_6]^{3+}$ (Co^{3+} has six electrons; six ammonia ligands contribute twelve electrons) has the electronic configuration, $a_{1g}^2, t_{1u}^6, e_g^4, t_{2g}^6$. In contrast $[CoF_6]^{3-}$ has the configuration $a_{1g}^2, t_{1u}^6, e_g^4, t_{2g}^4, e_g^{*2}$. Notice that the filling of the lower energy orbitals $a_{1g}^2, t_{1u}^6, e_g^4$ is reminiscent of the valence bond treatment and the filling of the higher energy orbitals t_{2g}^6 (for the cobalt hexammine complex) or $t_{2g}^4\ e_g^{*2}$ (for the cobalt hexafluoride) is reminiscent of the crystal field treatment.

π-bonding Involving π-donor Ligands

Ligands like halides or hydroxide, in spite of being ionic, are found in the lower end of the spectrochemical series. The MO theory has a more satisfactory answer to their position. Consider, F^-. In addition to acting as a σ-donor this ligand can be also act as a π-donor. We have already seen the σ-bonding picture. If we have to utilize the metal orbitals for π-bonding we have seen that only the t_{2g} orbitals are available. This can be utilized for π-bonding by forming LGO's of the same symmetry. However, note that the t_{2g} set of LGO's will be lower in energy in comparison with the metal orbitals, because of the greater electronegativity of F^- ligands. Consequently, the π-overlap between the metal and ligand orbitals will give rise to an energy diagram where the metal t_{2g} orbitals will be raised in energy (now they will be called a_{2g}^*). As a result the gap between these orbitals and the a_g^* orbitals is decreased compared to the pre π-bonding situation. Because of this, high spin complexes result.

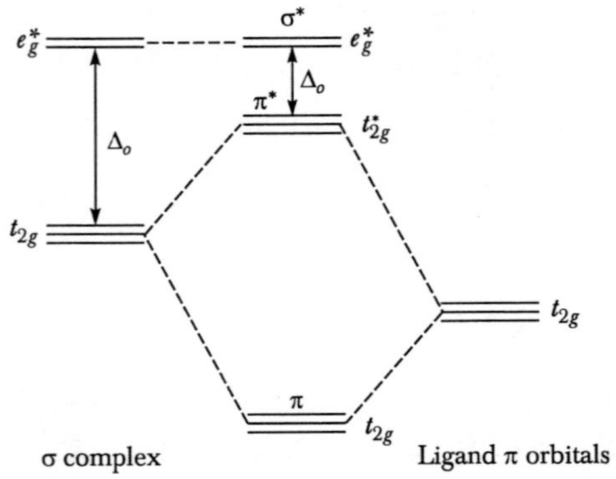

π-bonding Involving π-acceptor Ligands

Ligands such as CO, PR_3 etc., can form σ-bonds with metals similar to ammonia. Unlike ammonia, which does not have any vacant orbitals to receive electron density, CO and PR_3, however have vacant orbitals of the suitable symmetry to form π-**bonds** with the metal. However, since these orbitals are empty, they will be higher in energy in comparison to the metal t_{2g} orbitals with which they have to overlap to form the π-bonds. Consequently the metal t_{2g} orbitals are lowered in energy after formation of the π-bonds. The result is that the energy separation between the t_{2g} and the $e_g{}^*$ orbitals is **increased** after π-bond formation. Note that although the t_{2g} orbitals (LGO's) of the ligand are raised after the π-bond formation it does not matter as these remain empty. Thus, the formation of the π-bond explains quite readily the fact that neutral and weakly Lewis Basic ligands sush as CO and PR_3 are found in the higher end of the spectrochemical series.

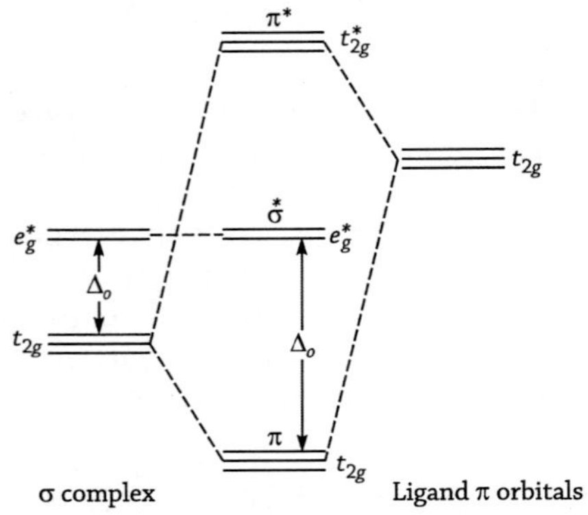

A single scheme below illustrate the effect of both the π-donor and π-acceptor ligands.

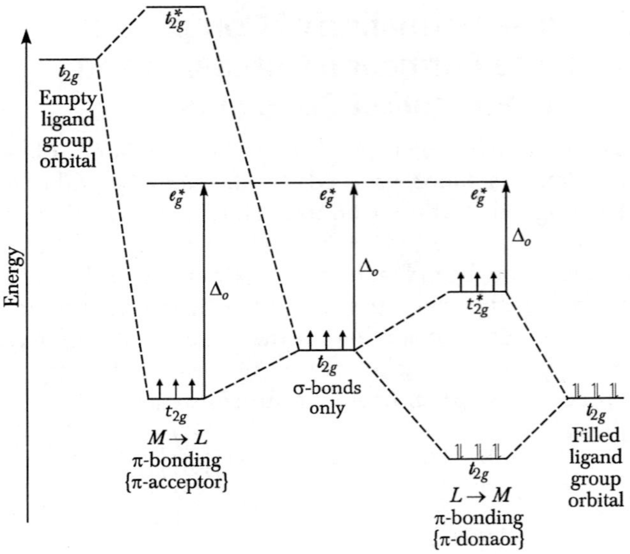

Stability of Complex in Aqueous Solution

In studying the formation of complexes in solution, two kinds of stability of complexes come in question. These are

(i) Thermodynamic stability

This is a measure of the extent to which the complex will form or will be transformed into another species (under certain conditions), when the system has reached equilibrium. When we are concerned with this type of stability, we deal with **metal-ligand** bond energies, stability constants, etc.

(ii) Kinetic stability

This refers to the **speed** with which transformations leading to the attainment of equilibrium will occur. When we are interested in kinetic stability, and this is primarily for complex ions in solutions, we deal with rates and mechanisms of chemical reactions such as substitution, isomerisation, racemisation and electron or group transfer reactions, as well as with the thermodynamic variables involved in the formation of intermediate species or activated complexes. In the kinetic sense it is more proper to call the complexes inert or labile complexes rather than stable or unstable complexes. The complexes in which the ligands are rapidly replaced by others are called **labile** or **non-inert complexes** while those in which substitution occurs slowly are termed as **inert complexes.**

Stepwise Formation of Complexes, Stepwise Formation Constants and Overall Formation Constants

According to J Bjerrum (1941) the formation of a complex in solution proceeds by the stepwise addition of the ligands to the metal ion. Thus, the formation of the complex ML_n (M = central metal cation, L = monodentate ligand and n = maximum coordination number of the metal ion M for the ligand L. n varies from one ligand to another for the same metal ion) may be supposed to take place by the following n consecutive steps and equilibrium constants :

$$M + L \overset{K_1}{\rightleftharpoons} ML, \; K_1 = \frac{[ML]}{[M][L]}$$

$$ML + L \overset{K_2}{\rightleftharpoons} ML_2, \; K_2 = \frac{[ML_2]}{[ML]\,[L]}$$

$$\vdots \quad \vdots \quad \vdots \quad \vdots$$

$$ML_{n-1} + L \overset{K_n}{\rightleftharpoons} ML_n, \; K_n = \frac{[ML_n]}{[ML_{n-1}]\,[L]}$$

The equilibrium constants K_1, K_2,......K_n are called **stepwise formation constants** or **stepwise stability constants.**

The formation of the complex ML_n may also be expressed by the following steps and equilibrium constants

$$M + L \overset{\beta_1}{\rightleftharpoons} ML, \; \beta_1 = \frac{[ML]}{[M][L]}$$

$$M + 2L \overset{\beta_2}{\rightleftharpoons} ML_2, \; \beta_2 = \frac{[ML_2]}{[M]\,[L]^2}$$

$$\vdots \quad \vdots$$

$$M + nL \overset{\beta_n}{\rightleftharpoons} ML_n, \; \beta_n = \frac{[ML_n]}{[M]\,[L]^n}$$

The equilibrium constants β_1, β_2.......β_n are called **overall (or cumulative) formation constants** or **overall** (or **cumulative**) **stability constants. β_n is termed as *n*th overall** (or **cumulative**) **formation constant** or **overall** (or **cumulative**) **stability constant.**

With a few exceptions the values of successive stability constants decrease regularly from K_1 to K_n, *i.e.*, $K_1 > K_2 > K_3 .... K_{n-1} > K_n$. This is illustrated by the data for the Cd^{II}—NH_3 system where the ligands are neutral molecules and by Cd^{II}—CN^- system where the ligands are charged.

$$Cd^{2+} + NH_3 \longrightarrow [Cd(NH_3)]^{2+} \quad K_1 = 10^{2.65}$$

$$[Cd(NH_3)]^{2+} + NH_3 \longrightarrow [Cd(NH_3)_2]^{2+} \quad K_2 = 10^{2.10}$$

$$[Cd(NH_3)_2]^{2+} + NH_3 \longrightarrow [Cd(NH_3)_3]^{2+} \quad K_3 = 10^{1.44}$$

$$[Cd(NH_3)_3]^{2+} + NH_3 \longrightarrow [Cd(NH_3)_4]^{2+} \quad K_4 = 10^{0.98}$$

$$\beta_4 = 10^{7.12}$$

$$Cd^{2+} + CN^- \longrightarrow [Cd(CN)]^+ \quad K_1 = 10^{5.48}$$

$$[Cd(CN)]^+ + CN^- \longrightarrow [Cd(CN)_2] \quad K_2 = 10^{5.12}$$

$$[Cd(CN)_2] + CN^- \longrightarrow [Cd(CN)_3]^- \quad K_3 = 10^{4.63}$$

$$[Cd(CN)_3]^- + CN^- \longrightarrow [Cd(CN)_4]^{2-} \quad K_4 = 10^{3.65}$$

$$\beta_4 = 10^{18.8}$$

The steady decrease in the value of K_1, K_2,...K_n with increasing number of ligands is due to the fact that as more and more ligands move into the coordination zone, less and less aqua-molecules are available to fresh ligands for replacement. With progressive intake of ligands the metal ion becomes less electron greedy. In case of the complexes of the charged ligands the more important factors responsible for the steady decrease are **statistical, steric hindrance** and **coulombic factors.**

The higher the value of stability constant for a complex ion, the greater will be its stability. Alternatively 1/K values sometimes called **instability constant,** give a measure of the extent to which the equilibrium representing the formation of a complex lies to the right. **A high value of $1/\beta_n$ (or $1/\beta$) means an unstable complex ion.**

Stepwise and cummulative stability constants are also expressed as $\log_{10} K_1 .... \log_{10} K_n$ and $\log_{10} \beta_n$ respectively.

In all the above equilibria we have not specified the charge of metal ion and degree of solvation. The former omission is of no importance, since the equilibria may be expressed as above whatever the charges. Omission of water is a matter of convention, since it is usually convenient and harmless. This omission should not be allowed whenever necessary. Square brackets indicate the concentrations of the enclosed species.

Relationship between β_n and K_1, K_2....... K_n

K's and β's are related to one another. Consider, for example, the expression for β_3 *viz.*

$$\beta_3 = \frac{[ML_3]}{[M][L]^3}$$

On multiplying both numerator and denominator by $[ML][ML_2]$ and on rearranging, we get

$$\beta_3 = \frac{[ML_3]}{[M][L]^3} \cdot \frac{[ML][ML_2]}{[ML][ML_2]}$$

$$= \frac{[ML]}{[M][L]} \cdot \frac{[ML_2]}{[ML][L]} \cdot \frac{[ML_3]}{[ML_2][L]}$$

$$= K_1 \cdot K_2 \cdot K_3$$

Thus $$\beta_n = \frac{[ML]}{[M][L]} \cdot \frac{[ML_2]}{[ML][L]} \cdots\cdots \frac{[ML_n]}{[ML_{n-1}][L]}$$

$$= K_1 \cdot K_2 \ldots . K_n \qquad \ldots \text{(i)}$$

or $$\beta_n = \sum_{n=1}^{n=n}, K_n$$

From relation (i) it is evident that the overall stability constant, β_n (or simply β), is equal to the product of the successive (*i.e.*, stepwise) stability constants $K_1, K_2, \ldots . K_{n-1}, K_n$. This in other words means that the value of stability constant for a given complex is actually made up of a number of step wise stability constants as is evident from Table 9.6 in which the value of overall stability constant as β_n and $\log_{10} \beta_n$ for $[Ni^{II}(NH_3)_6]^{2+}$ ion and those of stepwise stability constants as K_1, $K_2, \ldots, K_5, K_6$ and $\log_{10} K_1, \log_{10} K_2, \ldots, \log_{10} K_6$ corresponding to the six equilibria given in the first column through which $[Ni^{II}(NH_3)_6]^{2+}$ ion can be regarded as being formed, are given. This table shows that

$$\beta_n = K_1 \times K_2 \times \ldots \times K_5 \times K_6$$

and $\log_{10} \beta_n = \log_{10} K_1 + \log_{10} K_2 + \ldots + \log_{10} K_6$

In Table 9.6 we also see that $\log K_6$ is negative ($= -0.10$). This negative value shows that the pentammine complex, $[Ni(H_2O)(NH_3)_5]^{2+}$ is thermodynamically favoured with respect to the hexammine complex, $[Ni(NH_3)_6]^{2+}$ [see equilibrium No. (vi)].

Kinetics *vs* Thermodynamic Stability

Since the terms labile and inert show the speed or rates at which the substitution of one ligand by other occurs, these terms represent the kinetic stability of complexes. These terms should, there fore, not be confused with or used for thermodynamic stability terms *viz.* unstable and stable respectively. Although thermodynamically stable complexes may be labile or inert and unstable complexes which are usually labile may also be inert, there is no correlation between thermodynamic and kinetic stability terms, *e.g.*, $[Hg(CN)_4]^{2-}$ which is thermodynamically very stable (formation constant $= 10^{42}$) is labile, since in solution it exchanges CN^- ligands with labelled cyanide ions, $^{14}CN^-$ at a very fast rate.

$$[Hg(CN)_4]^{2-} + 4\,^{14}CN^- \rightleftharpoons [Hg(^{14}CN)_4]^{2-} + 4CN^-$$

Thus, the stability of this complex does not ensure its inertness.

Table 9.5 **Stability Constant Value (*i.e.*, $\log_{10} K$ value) of $[Ni^{II}(NH_3)_6]^{2+}$ Ion**

	Six equilibria	Values of $K_1, K_2, \ldots K_6$ and β_6	Values of $\log_{10}, K_1, \log_{10} K_2, \ldots \log_{10} K_6$ and $\log_{10} \beta_6$
(i)	$[Ni(H_2O)_6]^{2+} + NH_3 \overset{K_1}{\rightleftharpoons} [Ni(H_2O)_5(NH_3)]^{2+} + H_2O$	$K_1 = 5 \times 10^2$	$\log_{10} K_1 = 2.70$
(ii)	$[Ni(H_2O)_5NH_3]^{2+} + NH_3 \overset{K_2}{\rightleftharpoons} [Ni(H_2O)_4(NH_3)_2]^{2+} + H_2O$	$K_2 = 1.3 \times 10^2$	$\log_{10} K_2 = 2.11$
(iii)	$[Ni(H_2O)_4(NH_3)_2]^{2+} + NH_3 \overset{K_3}{\rightleftharpoons} [Ni(H_2O)_3(NH_3)_3]^{2+} + H_2O$	$K_3 = 40$	$\log_{10} K_3 = 1.60$
(iv)	$[Ni(H_2O)_3(NH_3)_3]^{2+} + NH_3 \overset{K_4}{\rightleftharpoons} [Ni(H_2O)_2(NH_3)_4]^{2+} + H_2O$	$K_4 = 12$	$\log_{10} K_4 = 1.08$
(v)	$[Ni(H_2O)_2(NH_3)_4]^{2+} + NH_3 \overset{K_5}{\rightleftharpoons} [Ni(H_2O)(NH_3)_5]^{2+} + H_2O$	$K_5 = 4$	$\log_{10} K_5 = 0.60$
(vi)	$[Ni(H_2O)(NH_3)_5]^{2+} + NH_3 \overset{K_6}{\rightleftharpoons} [Ni(NH_3)_6]^{2+} + H_2O$	$K_6 = 0.8$	$\log_{10} K_6 = -0.10$
On adding (i) to (vi)	$[Ni(H_2O)_6]^{2+} + 6NH_3 \overset{\beta_6}{\rightleftharpoons} [Ni(NH_3)_6]^{2+} + 6H_2O$	$\beta_6 = K_1 \cdot K_2 \ldots K_5 \cdot K_6 = 9.98 \times 10^7$	$\log_{10} \beta_6 = \log_{10} K_1 + \log_{10} K_2 + \ldots + \log_{10} K_6 = 7.99$

On the other hand the complex, $[Co(NH_3)_6]^{3+}$ which is thermodynamically unstable can remain unchanged in acid solution for weeks. Thus, this complex is unstable but inert in acid solution.

It may be concluded from this description that the inert complexes are not necessarily thermodynamically stable and that labile complexes are not necessarily thermodynamically unstable.

The stability of complex depends on the reaction energy while the lability of a compound depends on the activation energy. Larger the activation energy, lower will be the lability of the compound, *i.e.*, the compound with larger activation energy will react slowly.

Labile and Inert Octahedral Complexes According to VBT

We have seen that according to VBT octahedral complexes are of two types (i) outer orbital complexes which involve sp^3d^2 hybridisation and (ii) inner-orbital complexes which result from d^2sp^3 hybridisation. Note that the two *d*-orbitals involved in sp^3d^2 and d^2sp^3 hybridization are $d_{x^2-y^2}$ and d_{z^2} orbitals (e_g set).

With the help of VBT it is possible to predict which octahedral complex is labile and which is inert as shown below :

(i) Outer-orbital octahedral complexes

Outer-orbital octahedral complexes (sp^3d^2 hybridization) are generally labile, *e.g.*, the octahedral complexes of Mn^{2+} ($3d^5$), Fe^{2+} ($3d^6$), Fe^{3+} ($3d^5$), Co^{2+} ($3d^7$), Ni^{2+} ($3d^8$), Cu^{2+} ($3d^9$) and Cr^{2+} ($3d^4$) exchange ligands rapidly and hence are labile. In terms of valence-bond theory this observation can be correlated with the weakness of the bonds of sp^3d^2 type as compared with d^2sp^3 bonds.

(ii) Inner-orbital octahedral complexes

Since, the six d^2sp^3 hybrid orbitals are filled with the six electron pairs donated by the six ligands, d^n electrons of the central metal will occupy d_{xy}, d_{yz} and d_{zx} orbitals. This distribution for labile and inert inner-orbital octahedral complexes is shown in Table 9.7 from which the following points are obvious.

(a) In the labile inner orbital octahedral complexes there is atleast one *d*-orbital of t_{2g} set empty so that this empty *d*-orbital may be used to accept the electron pair from the incoming ligand in forming the transition state (unstable intermediate) with coordination number of seven. The formation of transition state can be shown as :

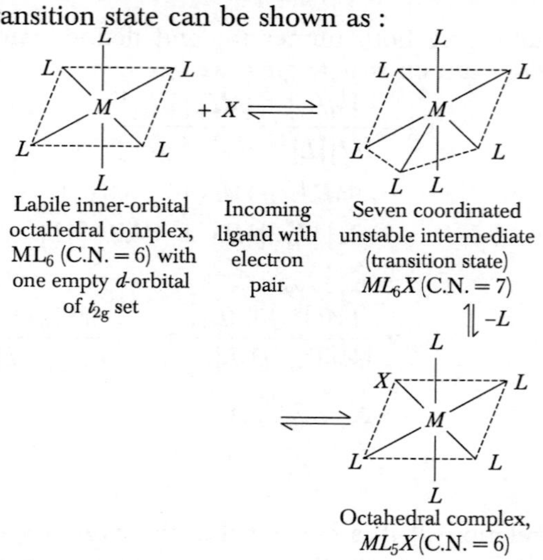

Due to the extremely fast reactions of these complexes it has not been possible to determine whether the intermediate exists in these reactions.

(b) In the inert inner-orbital octahedral complexes every *d*-orbital of t_{2g} set (*i.e.*, d_{xy}, d_{yz} and d_{zx}) contains at least-one electron.

Labile and Inert Octahedral Complexes According to CFT

Whether an octahedral complex reacts by an S_N1 dissociation or S_N2 association mechanism, the symmetry is lowered and a decrease in CFSE usually occurs in going from octahedral to 5-coordinated square pyramidal activated intermediate or from octahedral to 7-coordinated pentagonal bipyramidal transition state.The change in CFSE in going from octaheral to pentagonal bipyramidal (S_N2 mechanism) structure is called **activation energy** and is denoted by E_a. The values of E_a have been calculated by Basolo and Pearson and are given in Tables 9.8 and 9.9. the values of CFSE mentioned are in the units of Dq and have been given for both the fields *viz* strong field (spin paired or low spin complex) and weak field (spin free or high spin complex) and for both the mechanisms. In these tables negative values of E_a denote a loss of CFSE when octahedral complex is changed into an activated complex which may be square pyramidal or pentagonal bipyramidal. In cases where the CFSE of the activated complex is greater than that of octahedral complex, E_a has been given zero value. Thus in case of these complexes it has been assumed that there is no loss in CFSE when they are changed into activated complexes.

The octahedral complexes formed by the ions for which there is **large loss in** CFSE are **least labile,** *i.e.,* such **complexes** are **inert.** On the other hand octahedral complexes given by ions for which there is **little** or **no loss** in CFSE are **labile,** *i.e.,* such complexes react rapidly. Following examples make these facts evident :

(i) Both high spin and low spin octahedral complexes of d^0, d^1 and d^2ions will react rapidly, *i.e.,* **these are labile complexes,** since there is no loss in CFSE for these ions by either mechanisms.

(ii) We have seen that according to VBT inner-orbital octahedral complexes of d^3, d^4, d^5 and d^6ions are inert (see Table 9.7). These inner-orbital complexes are called low-spin or spin-paired complexes by CFT. CFT also predicts that low-spin complexes of these ions are also inert whether the mechanism is assumed to be S_N1 or S_N2, since there is a loss in CFSe values (as indicated by the negative values).

The ion with maximum loss of CFSE will form the most inert (*i.e.,* least labile) complex. Thus, the order of inertness of low-spin complexes formed by d^3, d^4, d^5 and d^6 ions is :

Order of inertness :	d^6	d^3	d^4	d^5
Loss in CFSE for S_N1 mechanism :	−4.00	−2.00	−1.43	−0.86
Loss in CFSE for S_N2 mechanism :	−8.52	−4.26	−2.98	−1.70

Consequently the order of lability or the reactivity (*i.e.,* rate of reaction) will be reverse of that shown above, *i.e.,*

Order of lability ; $d^6 < d^3 < d^4 < d^5$

Experiments have also supported the above order.

(iii) High-spin octahedral complexes of d^3ion will react slowly, *i.e.,* these are inert complexes, because for this ion there is substantial loss in CFSE whether the substitution mechanism is assumed S_N1 or S_N2.

(iv) High-spin octahedral complexes of d^5ion react rapidly, *i.e.,* these are labile complexes, since thee is no loss in CFSF.

(v) Both high-spin and low-spin octahedral complexes of d^8ion (*e.g.,* Ni^{2+}) are inert, since

Table 9.6 **Distribution of d^n-electrons in Various t_{2g} Orbital for Labile and Inert Inner-orbital Octahedral Complexes According to VBT**

Type of the complex	d^n configuration	Distribution of d^n electrons (shown by arrows) in t_{2g} orbitals. Electrons shown by crosses in e_g orbitals have been donated by six ligands to enter d^2sp^3 hybrids and are in opposite spins									Examples of central metal ions
		d					*s*	*p*			
		t_{2g}			e_g						
		xy	*yz*	*zx*	x^2-y^2	z^2		p_x	p_y	p_z	
Inner-orbital labile octahedral complexes	d^0				××	××	××	××	××	××	Sc (+3), Y (+3), rare earth (+3), Te (+4), Zr (+4), Hf (+4), Ce (+4), Th (+4), Nb (+5), Ta (+5), Mo (+6), W (+6)
	d^1	↑			××	××	××	××	××	××	Ti (+3), V (+4), Mo (+5), W (+5), Re (+6)
	d^2	↑	↑		××	××		××	××	××	Ti (+2), V(+3), Nb (+3); Ta (+3), W (+4), Re (+5). Ru (+6)
Inner-orbital inert octahedral complexes	d^3	↑	↑	↑	××	××	××	××	××	××	V (+2), Cr (+3), Mo (+3), W (+3), Mn (+4), Re (+4)
	d^4	↑↓	↑	↑	××	××	××	××	××	××	$[Cr[(CN)_6]^{4-}$, $Mn(CN)_6]^{3-}$Re (+3), Ru (+4), Os (+4)
	d^5	↑↓	↑↓	↑	××	××	××	××	××	××	$[Mn(CN)_6]^{4-}$, Re (+2), $[Fe(CN)_6]^{3-}$, Ru (+3), Os (+3), Ir (+4)
	d^6	↑↓	↑↓	↑↓	××	××	××	××	××	××	$[Fe(CN)_6]^{4-}$, Ru (+2), Os (+2), Co (+3) (except $CoFe_6^{3-}$), Rh (+3), Ir (+3)

for any mechanism there is significant loss of CFSE. Note that, according to VBT, d^8 ion ($3d_{xy}{}^2$, $3d_{yz}{}^2$, $3d_{zx}{}^2$, $3d_{x^2-y^2}{}^2$, $3d_{z^2}$) will form outer orbital complexes which will be labile. Thus we see that in case of d^8 ion VBT and CFT give different predictions.

(vi) Both high-spin and low-spin octahedral complexes of d^{10} ion are labile. The reasons are the same as for other labile complexes.

Other Factors Affecting the Lability of a Complex

In the preceeding pages we have seen that how the electronic configuration of the central metal ion forming the complex affects the lability of the complex. In addition to this the following factors also influence the lability.

(i) Charge of the central ion

Highly charged ions form complexes that react slowly, *i.e.,* with the increase of the charge of the central metal ion for the isoelectronic complexes there is a decreases in lability, *e.g.,*

(a) The lability of the complexes, $[AlF_6]^{3-}$, $[SiF_6]^{2-}$, $[PF_6]^-$ and $[SF_6]^0$ is in the order :

Lability order :

$$[AlF_6]^{3-} > [SiF_6]^{2-} > [PF_6]^- > [SF_6]^0$$

Cationic charge : + 3 < + 4 < + 5 < + 6

(b) The rate of water exchange, represented by

$$[M(H_2O)_6]^{n+} + 6H_2O^* \rightleftharpoons [M(H_2O^*)_6]^{n+} + 6H_2O$$

decreases with the increase of cationic charge in the series : $[Na(H_2O)_n]^+$, $[Mg, (H_2O)_n]^{2+}$, $[Al(H_2O)_6]^{3+}$ in the order :

Rate of water exchange,

$$[Na(H_2O)_n]^+ > [Mg(H_2O)_n]^{2+} > [Al(H_2O)_6]^{3+}$$

Cationic charge : + 1 < + 2 < + 3

(ii) Radii of the central ion

Complexes having central atoms with small ionic radii react more slowly than those having larger central ions, *i.e.,* the lability increases with the increase of ionic radius, *e.g.,*

Order of lability :

$$[Mg(H_2O)_6]^{2+} < [Ca(H_2O)_6]^{2} + < [Sr(H_2O)_6]^{2+}$$

Cationic Size (Å) : 0.65 < 0.99 < 1.13

(iii) Charge-to-radius ratio values

For a series of octahedral complexes containing the same ligands, the complexes having the central metal ions with the largest charge-to-radius ratio will react slowest. The validity of this rule is evident from Fig. 9.10 which contains half-lives for the exchange of water by some hydrated metal ions.

$$[M(H_2O)_x]^{n+} + xH_2O \longrightarrow [M(H_2O)_x]^{n+} + xH_2O$$

From this figure the following points may be noted :

(a) Of the first-row transition elements, $[Ni(H_2O)_6]^{2+}$ (a d^8 system) has the largest value of half life, *i.e.,* it reacts slowest. The same conclusion has been drawn from CFT. The hydrated M^{2+} ions, $[M(H_2O)_x]^{2+}$ of the first-row transition elements are all high-spin complexes.

(b) $[Cu(H_2O)_6]^{2+}$ reacts most rapidly. This may be due to the fact that the two water molecules above and below the square plane of the tetragonally distorted octahedral shape of $[Cu(H_2O)_6]^{2+}$ are exchanged.

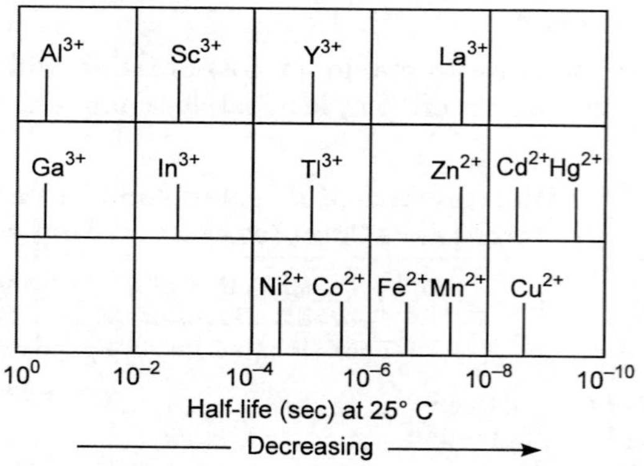

Fig. 9.35 Half-lives (in sec) at 25°C for the exchange of water by some hydrated metal ions.

The remaining four water molecules lying in the square plane react slowly.

For square planar complexes charge-to-radius ratio does not work.

(iv) Geometry of the complex

In general 4-coordinated complexes (both tetrahedral and square planar) react more rapidly than analogous 6-coordinated complexes, *e.g.,* the very stable $[Ni(CN)_4]^{2-}$ undergoes rapid exchange with $^{14}CN^-$

$$[Ni(CN)_4]^{2-} + 4\,^{14}CN^- \rightleftharpoons [Ni(^{14}CN)_4]^{2-} + 4CN^-$$

while 6-coordinated complexes like $[Mn(CN)_6]^{4-}$ and $[Co(CN)_6]^{3-}$ which have almost about the same stability as $[Ni(CN)_4]^{2-}$ undergo slow exchange. The greater reactivity of 4-coordinated complexes may be due to the fact that there is enough room round the central ion for the entry of a fifth group into the coordination sphere to form on activated complex. Presence of this additional group helps in the release of one of the original four ligands already present in the 4-coordinated complexes.

Factors Affecting the Stability of Complexes

A number of factors affect the stability of complexes. Some of these factors depend on the nature of the central ion, while others depend on the nature of the ligand.

(a) Properties of the Central Metal Ion

With reference to the properties of the central metal ion the following factors may be mentioned.

(i) Charge and size

In general the metal ion with larger charge and smaller size form more stable complexes. A smaller but more highly charged cation permits a more closer approach of the ligands and larger electrostatic attraction resulting from large charge on the cation, gives a more stable complex. These points are illustrated in the following examples :

(a) The stability of the hydroxide complexes of the alkaline earth metals in which the central metal cation contains the same.
charge increases with the decrease of the size of the central metal ion as shown by their stability constant values.

(b) The stability of the complexes having the central metal cations with almost equal size but with different charges increases with the increase of the charge on the central metal ion.

The stability of the complexes of non-transition metals of the same group has been found in the following order provided that the ligand is not changed from one ion to the next.

$$Li^+ > Na^+ > K^+ > Rb^+ > Cs^+$$

$$Be^{2+} > Mg^{2+} > Ca^{2+} > Sr^{2+} > Ba^{2+} > Ra^{2+}$$

$$Al^{3+} > Sc^{3+} > Y^{3+} > La^{3+}$$

There are also some exceptions to the above order, *e.g.,* EDTA complex of Mg^{2+} is less stable than that of Ca^{2+}.

For the metal ions of approximately constant ionic radius, the stability constants are in the order :

$$Th^{4+} (= 0.95 \text{ Å}) > Y^{3+} (= 0.93) > Ca^{2+} (= 0.99) > Na^+ (= 0.95)$$

and La^{3+} (= 1.15 Å) > Sr^{2+} (= 1.13) > K^+ (= 1.33)

(ii) Crystal field effects and natural order (or Irving-William order of stability)

Stabilities of high spin complexes of the ions between Mn^{2+} and Zn^{2+} with a given ligand frequently vary in the order :

$$Mn^{2+} < Fe^{2+} < Co^{2+} < Ni^{2+} < Cu^{2+} > Zn^{2+}$$

This order which is called **natural order** (sometimes called the **Irving-William order) of stability** is consistent with charge-to-radius ratio concept, since the radii of these ions are in the order :

$$Mn^{2+} (= 0.91 \text{ Å}) > Fe^{2+} (= 0.83) > Co^{2+} (= 0.82)$$

$$Ni^{2+} (= 0.78) > Cu^{2+} (= 0.69) < Zn^{2+} (= 0.74)$$

The high spin complexes of these ions are primarily octahedral with the exception of those of Cu^{2+} which forms tetragonally distorted octahedral complexes.

The relative stability of high spin octahedral $[M^{II}L_6]^{2+}$ complexes of the first-row transition elements as predicted by crystal field theory is shown in Fig. 9.2.

$$M^{2+} + 6L \rightleftharpoons [ML_6]^{2+}, \beta = \frac{[ML_6^{2+}]}{[M^{2+}][L]^6}$$

It is obvious from this figure that the octahedral complexes of V^{2+} (d^3 ion) and Ni^{2+} (d^8 ion) ions are the most stable with respect to their neighbours. This is because of the fact that the high spin (weak ligand) octahedral complexes of these ions have the greatest crystal field stabilisation energy values (CFSE's values) as given below :

$$d^1 = 0.4\,\Delta_o,\ d^2 = 0.8\,\Delta_o,\ d^3(V^{2+}) = 1.2\Delta_o,$$

$$d^4 = 0.6\Delta_o,\ d^5 = 0.0,\ d^6 = 0.4\Delta_o,\ d^7 = 0.8\Delta_o,$$

$$d^8(Ni^{2+}) = 1.2\,\Delta_o,\ d^9 = 0.6\,\Delta_o,\ d^{10} = 0.0.$$

The order of stability as predicted by crystal field theory and shown in fig. 9.36 is the same as natural order of stability for complexes of these metals except for Cu^{2+}. The discrepancy for Cu^{2+} is not completely, understood but is certainly related to the fact that Cu^{2+} complex assumes a distorted octahedral structure in order to assume maximum CFSE.

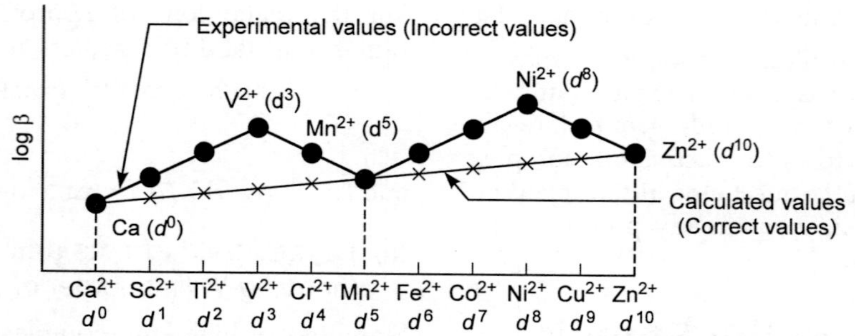

Fig. 9.36 The logrithms of stability constants for a series of $[M^{II}L_6]^{2+}$ complexes as predicted by crystal field theory.

If the experimental values shown by dots are corrected for CFSE for each ion (the correction is done by substracting the calculated CFSE values given as above from the experimental values), we get a smooth curve which has **corrected values** (shown by crosses), since it indicates the expected regular increase in values. The ions *viz.*, Ca^{2+} (d^0), Mn^{2+} (d^5) and Zn^{2+} (d^{10}) which do not have CFSE have experimental values on the smooth curve.

(iii) Class *a* and class *b* metals

Chatt and Ahrland have classified the metals into three categories; *a*, *b* and **borderline,** on the basis of their electron acceptor properties. This classification is shown below (normal valence states are assumed).

Class *a* metals H, the alkali and alkaline earth metals, the elements Sc ⟶ Cr, Al ⟶ Cl, Zn ⟶ Br, In, Sn, Sb and I, the lanthanides and actinides.

Class *b* metals Rh, Pd, Ag, Ir, Pt, Au, Hg.

Borderline metals : The elements Mn ⟶ Cu, Tl ⟶ Po, Mo, Te, Ru, W, Re, Os, cd.

Class *a* metals form more stable complexes with ligands having the coordinating atoms from the second period elements (*e.g.,* N, O, F) than those of an analogous ligand in which the donor atom is from third or later period (*e.g.,* P, S, Cl). Class *b* metals have the relative stabilities reversed. If the ligand contains the heavier donor atoms, class *a* and *b* metals are characterised by the stability order :

$$\left.\begin{array}{l} F^- > Cl^- > Br^- > I^- \\ O >> S > Se > Te \\ N >> P > As > Sb > Bi \end{array}\right\} \text{Class } a \text{ metals}$$

and

$$\left.\begin{array}{l} F^- < Cl^- < Br^- < I^- \\ O << S \simeq Se \simeq Te \\ N << P < As < Sb < Bi \end{array}\right\} \text{Class } b \text{ metals}$$

Class *b* metals are characterised by the presence of a number of *d*-electrons beyond an inert-gas core. These *d*-electrons are used to form π-bond with ligand atoms. It is believed that the stability of the complexes of class *b* metals results from covalent contribution to metal-ligand bonds and from the transfer of electron density from the metal to the ligand *via* π-bonding. The most stable complexes of class *b* metals are formed with ligands like PMe_3, S^{2-} and I^- which have vacant *d*-orbitals or like $COCN^-$ which have vacant molecular orbitals of low energy.

For borderline metals the stability constants do not display either class *a* or class *b* behaviour uniquely.

(iv) Electronegativity of the central ion

The bonding between a central ion and a ligand is, to some extent, due to the donation of electrons by the ligand to the central ion. Thus, it might be concluded that a central ion with higher electronegativity (*i.e.,* a central ion with a strong electron-attracting tendency) would give the most stable complexes.

(b) Properties of the Ligand

With reference to the role of the ligands in determining the stability of the metal complexes, the following factors are important :

(i) Size and charge of ligand

For charged ligands, the higher the charge carried by them and the smaller their size,the more stable are the complexes formed; *e.g.,* the F^-ions, which are smaller, form stable complexes than the Cl^-ions which are larger ions. This fact is evident from the stability constant values of $[Fe^{III}F]^{2+}$ and $[Fe^{III}Cl]^{2+}$ions which are 10^6 and 20 respectively. Thus for class *a* metals the order of stability of the halide complexes is $F^- > Cl^- > Br^- > I^-$, but this order is reversed for class *b* metals (Pt^{II}, Cu^{I}, Ag^{I}, Hg^{II} etc).

For monodentate neutral ligands, the higher the dipole moment and smaller the size, the more stable are the complexes formed.

(ii) Basic character of ligands

The more basic is the ligand, more easily it can donate electron pairs to the central ion and hence more easily it can form complexes of greater stability. The ligands that bind H^+ firmly form stable complexes with metal ions. Thus F^- should form stable complexes than Cl^-, Br^- or I^- and NH_3 should be better ligand than H_2O which in turn should be better than HF. This behaviour is observed for alkali, alkaline earth and other electropositive metals like first-row transition elements, lanthanides and actinides.

(iii) Chelate effect

Complexes containing chelate rings are usually more stable than similar complexes containing no rings. *i.e.*, multidenate ligands (chelating ligands) in general form more stable complexes than the monodentate ligands. This is termed as **chelate effect**. This effect is obvious from the values of stability constants of Ni^{2+}—NH_3 and Ni^{2+}—*en* systems :

$$Ni^{2+}(aq) + 6NH_3(aq) \rightleftharpoons [Ni(NH_3)_6]^{2+}(aq), \quad \log \beta = 8.6$$

$$Ni^{2+}(aq) + 3en(aq) \rightleftharpoons [Ni(en)_3]^{2+}(aq), \quad \log \beta = 18.28$$

Note that NH_3 is a monodentate ligand while ethylene diamine, $NH_2—CH_2—CH_2—NH_2$ (*en*) is a bidentate ligand. Obviously the complex $[Ni(en)_3]^{2+}$ is much more stable than $[Ni(NH_3)_6]^{2+}$, since the former complex contains chelate rings while the latter one has no chelate ring.

(iv) Chelate ring size

The larger the number of the chelate rings in complex, the greater is its stability. This is illustrated in Table 9.7.

Table 9.7 **Overall Stability Constant Values (*i.e.*, $\log_{10}\beta$ values) for Some Ammonia and Polyamine Complexes Illustrating the Effect of Chelate Ring Size on the Stability of the Complexes.**

Metal Complexes	No. of chelate rings	Values of stability constants ($\log_{10}\beta$ values)						
		Mn^{2+}	Fe^{2+}	Co^{2+}	Ni^{2+}	Cu^{2+}	Zn^{2+}	Cd^{2+}
$M(NH_3)_4$	0	–	23.7	5.31	7.79	12.59	9.06	6.92
$M(en)_2$	2	4.9	7.7	10.9	14.5	20.2	11.2	10.3
M(trien)	3	4.9	7.8	11.0	14.1	20.5	12.1	10.0
M(tren)	3	5.8	8.8	12.8	14.0	18.8	14.6	12.3
$M(dien)_2$	4	7.0	10.4	14.1	18.9	21.3	14.4	13.8
M(penten)	5	9.4	11.2	15.8	19.3	22.4	16.2	16.2

Table 9.7 clearly shows that **the greater the number of chelate rings in the complex, the greater is the stability of the complex.**

The stability of the complexes also depends on the number of the atoms present in the ring. The chelates containing 3-membered ring including the metal are very unstable and hence are unknown. 4-membered chelate rings are rare and occur in carbonate (I), nitrate (II) and sulphate (III) chelates.

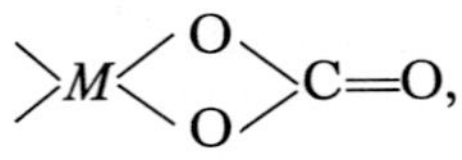

(I)

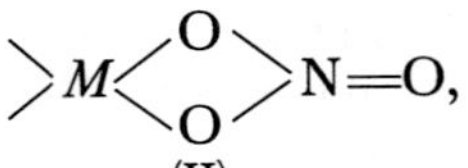

(II)

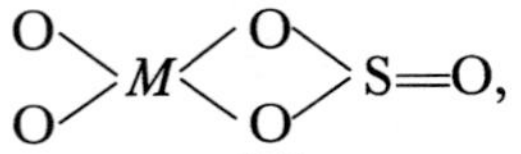

(III)

The most common and the most stable chelates are 5- and 6-membered chelates. 5-membered chelates are frequently more stable than the 6-membered chelates when the atoms in the ring are joined by single bonds only. On the other hand 6-membered chelates are more stable than 5-membered chelates of heterocyclic ligands or of ligands involving conjugation in the chelate ring.

(v) Steric effects

When a bulky group is either attached to or present near the donor atom of a ligand, mutual repulsion among the ligands occurs and consequently the metal-ligand bond is weakened. Thus large bulky ligands form less stable complexes than do the analogous smaller ligands. This effect is commonly referred to as **steric hindrance** (**steric effect** or **steric strain**). This effect can be illustrated by the following examples :

(a) ethylene diamine, $NH_2—(CH_2)_2—NH_2$ complexes are more stable than those of tetramethyl ethylene diamine, $(CH_3)_2N—(CH_2)_2—N(CH_3)_2$ which is the tetramethyl substituted derivative of $NH_2—(CH_2)_2—NH_2$. Thus :

$$[M(NH_2—CH_2—CH_2—NH_2)_3]^{2+} > [M(N(CH_3)_2—CH_2—CH_2—N(CH_3)_2)_3]^{2+}$$

(b) Complex of Ni^{2+} with 8-hydroxy quinoline is more stable than that of 2-methyl-8-hydroxy quinoline. Thus :

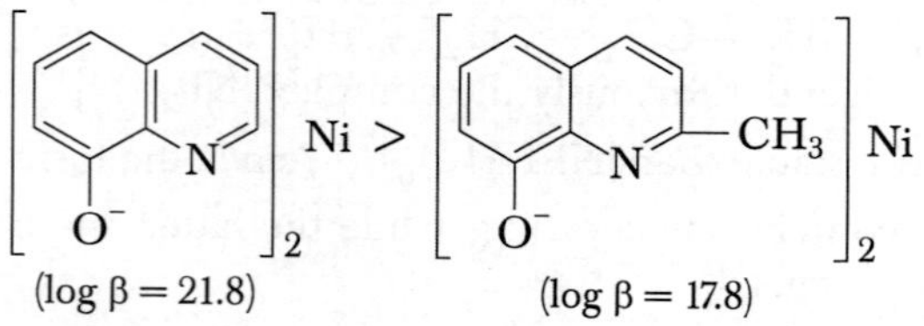

The strain effect is sometimes due to the geometry of ligand coupled with the stereo-chemistry of the metal complex. For example triethylene tetramine, $NH_2—(CH_2)_2—NH(CH_2)_2—NH—(CH_2)_2—NH_2$ (*trien*) can coordinate its all the four nitrogens at the corners of a square but triethyltriamine, $(NH_2—CH_2—CH_2)_3N$ (*tren*) cannot do so. Thus straight-chain in *trien* forms more stable complexes with Cu^{2+} ion than does the branched-chain in *tren* because *tren* is unable to assume the preferred square planar geometry.

Other Factors

The amount of metal-ligand covalent character also influences the stability of the complexes of relatively electronegative metals like those in copper and zinc families and Sn and Pb. For example the order of stability of the complexes, $[AgX_2]^-$ and $[AgX_3]^-$ is as :

$$AgI_2^- > AgBr_2^- > AgCl_2^- \gg AgF_2^-$$

$$AgI_3^- > AgBr_3^- > AgCl_3^- \gg AgF_3^-$$

This order is attributed to the increase in covalent character in Ag—X bond from Ag—F to Ag—I.

Experimental Determination of Stability Constant and Composition of a Complex

1. Spectrophotometric Method

Most of the complexes absorb light differently than the metal ions from which they are formed. The relationship between the absorbance or optical density (A) at a particular wavelength concentration is expressed by **Beer's law** which is given as :

$$A = \epsilon \cdot l \cdot c$$

where ϵ = mole extinction coefficient

l = length of the absorption cell

c = concentration of the complex (in moles/litre)

If we measure the abosrbance (A) with a spectrophotometer, know the extinction coefficient (ϵ) at that wave length and the cell length (l), the concentration (c) can be calculated from the Beer's law equation given above.

How the spectrum of a metal ion, M^{2+}, changes on coordination with ligand, L, has been shown in Fig. 9.37 which contains representative spectra of a metal ion, M^{2+} (shown by broken lines) and its complex ion, ML^{2+} (shown by solid lines). It will be seen that the absorption by the complex takes place over the entire region of the metal ion absorption, while at 550 mμ only the complex absorbs.

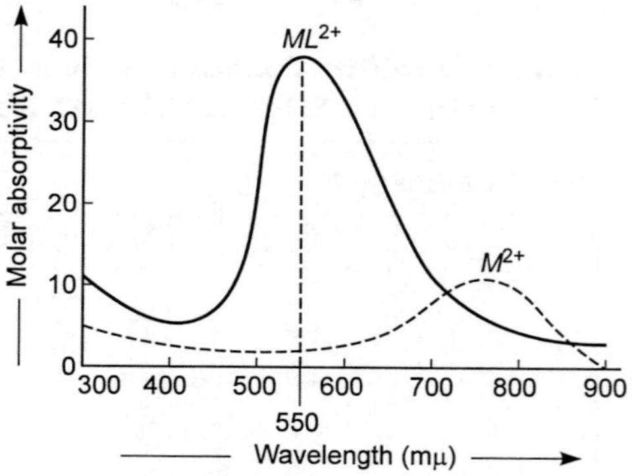

Fig. 9.37 Spectrum of a metal ion, M^{2+} and its complex, ML^{2+}.

Clearly, the value of K_f (formation constant) for the reaction :

$$M^{2+} + L \overset{K_f}{\rightleftharpoons} ML^{2+},$$

will be given by

$$K_f = \frac{[ML^{2+}]}{[M^{2+}][L]} \quad ...(1)$$

In order to obtain the value of formation constant, K_f, solutions containing known amounts of total M^{2+} and total L are equiliberated. The absorption of these solutions at 550 mμ is measured and the value of K_f is evaluated as follows :

We know that :

$$C_M = [M^{2+}] | [ML^{2+}] \quad ...(2)$$

$$C_L = [L] | [ML^{2+}] \quad ...(3)$$

and $$A = \in_{(ML^{2+})} \cdot l \cdot [ML^{2+}]$$

(From Beer's Law)

or $$[ML^{2+}] = \frac{A}{\in_{(ML^{2+})} \cdot l} \quad \ldots(4)$$

where, C_M = total concentration of the metal ion

C_L = total concentration of the ligand.

Put the value of $[ML^{2+}]$ obtained from equation (5) in equation (6) and (7) to get the values of $[M^{2+}]$ and $[L]$. Thus :

$$[M^{2+}] = C_M - \frac{A}{\in_{(ML^{2+})} \cdot l} \quad \ldots(5)$$

$$[L] = C_L - \frac{A}{\in_{(ML^{2+})} \cdot l} \quad \ldots(6)$$

Thus, if we put the values of $[ML^{2+}]$, $[M^{2+}]$ and $[L]$ as obtained from equations (4), (5) and (6) respectively in equation (1), we shall get the value of K_f. For the evaluation of the value of K_f, the values of A, $\in_{(ML^{2+})}$, l, C_M and C_L must be known. The constancy of K_f is checked by repeating the measurements at different C_M and C_L values.

2. Potentiometric Method (Bjerrum Method)

When the ligand is a weak base or acid, competition between hydrogen ions and metal ions for the ligand can be used for the determination of the formation constant.

Let us consider the equilibria in which an acid and metal ions are added to a basic ligand in solution. Thus the following equations hold good :

$$\underset{\text{Basic ligand}}{L} + \underset{\text{Acid}}{H^+} \overset{K_F}{\rightleftharpoons} HL^+, \; K_a = \frac{[HL^+]}{[L][H^+]}$$

$$\underset{\text{Basic ligand}}{L} + \underset{\text{Metal ion}}{M^+} \overset{K_F}{\rightleftharpoons} ML^+, \; K_F = \frac{[ML^+]}{[L][M^+]}$$

Here K_a and K_F are the acid association constant of the ligand and formation constant respectively.

Now if C_H, C_M and C_L are the total amounts in moles/L of acid (H^+), metal (M^+) and basic ligand (L), we have

$$C_H = [H^+] + [HL^+]$$
$$C_L = [L] + [ML^+] + [HL^+]$$
$$C_M = [M^+] + [ML^+]$$

Solving the last three equations given above and using the acid association constant of the ligand, K_a, we get :

$$[ML^+] = C_L - C_H + [H^+] - \frac{C_H - [H^+]}{K_a [H^+]}$$

$$[M^+] = C_M - [ML^+]$$

$$[L] = \frac{C_H - [H^+]}{K_a [H^+]}$$

Electron-Transfer (or oxidation reduction) Reaction in Coordination Compounds

These are the reactions in which the transfer of an electron from one atom to the other occurs, and hence the oxidation state of some atoms change. These reactions may be divided into the following two classes :

(i) Those in which the electron transfer results in no net chemical change. These are called electron-exchange processes and are examplified by $[Fe(CN)_6]^{3-}$—$[Fe(CN)_6]^{4-}$, —$[Co(en)_3]^{3+}$—$[Co(en)_3]^{2+}$, $[Fe(dipy)_3]^{3+}$—$[Fe(dipy)_3]^{2+}$, $[Co(NH_3)_6]^{3+}$—$[Co(NH_3)_6]^{2+}$ etc. These can be followed only indirectly, for example, by isotopic labelling or by NMR.

(ii) Those in which there is net chemical change. These are examplified by $[Cr(NH_3)_5X]^{2+}$—$[Cr(H_2O)_6]^{2+}$, $[Cr(H_2O)_5Cl]^{2+}$—$[Cr(H_2O)_6]^{2+}$ etc, where X = F^-, Cl^-, Br^-, I^-, SO_4^{2-}, NCS^- etc. and can be followed by many standard chemical and physical methods.

Mechanism of One Electron-Transfer Reactions

Most of such reactions are believed to occur by the following two mechanisms : (i) Bridge or inner-sphere mechanism, and (ii) Electron-transfer or outer-sphere mechanism.

1. Atom (or Group)-transfer or inner-sphere mechanism

These are electron-transfer reactions in which concomitant electron transfer and ligand transfer occur. In such reactions an initiamate contact between oxidant and reductant is required. This requirement is fulfilled when a bridged activated complex is formed as a result of an intimate attachment between the oxidant and reductant, and this activated complex has at least one ligand which is common to the coordinate sphere of both the reacting complexes and this forms a bridge between them. Hence, the name inner-sphere mechanism is given. For obvious reasons this mechanism is also called **ligand-bridged, atom (or group) transfer or bridged activated complex mechanism.** It is the bridging group through which the electron can pass.

Taube and his coworkers have shown (1959) that oxidation of aqueous Cr(II), $[Cr(H_2O)_6]^{2+}$ by pentammine cobalt (III) chloride, $[Co(NH_3]_5Cl]^{3+}$ in acidic medium represented by the equation :

$$[Co^{3+}(NH_3)_5Cl] + [Cr^{2+}(H_2O)_6]^{2+} + 5H_3O^+ \longrightarrow$$

Oxidant $Co^{3+} \rightarrow 3d^6$ Low-spin and inert; Reductant $Cr^{2+} \rightarrow 3d^4$ High-spin and labile

$$[Co^{2+}(H_2O)_6]^{2+} + [Cr^{3+}(H_2O)_5Cl]^{2+} + 5NH_4^+$$

Reduced product $Co^{2+} \rightarrow 3d^7$ High-spin and labile; Oxidised product $Cr^{3+} \rightarrow 3d^3$ Low-spin and inert

can be explained by this mechanism as follows :

$$[Co^{3+}(NH_3)_5Cl]^{2+} + [Cr^{2+}(H_2O)_6]^{2+} \xrightarrow{-H_2O}$$

Oxidant (Low-spin and inert) (Co = +3); Reductant (High-spin and labile) (Cr = +2)

$$\left[(NH_3)_5Co^{3+}\text{–}Cl\text{–}Cr^{2+}(H_2O)_5\right]^{4+}$$

(e^- transferred from Cr to Co through Cl)

Activated bridged intermediate

⇅ Electron transfer

$$[(NH_3)_5Co^{2+}\text{—}Cl\text{—}Cr^{3+}(H_2O)^{4+}]$$

$\downarrow +H_2O$

$$[Cr^{2+}(H_2O)_5Cl]^{2+} + [Co^{2+}(NH_3)_5(H_2O)]^{2+}$$

(Cr = +3)

$\downarrow +5H_2O^+$

$$[Co^{2+}(H_2O)_6]^{2+} + 5NH_4^+$$

(Co = +2)

It is obvious from this mechanism that the above reaction proceeds through the following steps :

(i) The labile nature of $[Cr(H_2O)_6]^{2+}$ allows this complex to lose a molecule of water readily to form an activated bridged intermediate which contains Co^{2+} and Cr^{2+} ions linked together through Cl^- ion which acts as a bridge between the two coordinate spheres. The bridging Cl^- ion is brought into the activated intermediate by the inert reactant *viz* $[Co(NH_3)_5Cl]^{2+}$. That $[Co(NH_3)_5Cl]^{2+}$ is the only source of Cl^- is proved by the following observation. If $[Co(NH_3)_5Cl]^{2+}$ containing radioactive $^{36}Cl^-$ is dissolved in a solution containing Cr^{2+} (*i.e.*, in $[Cr(H_2O)_6]^{2+}$) and unlabelled Cl^-, it is found that, after the reduction which is very fast, the product $[Cr(H_2O)_5Cl]^{2+}$ contains only labelled $^{36}Cl^-$. This proves that Cl^- ion is supplied by $[Co(NH_3)_5Cl]^{2+}$. The Cl^- bridge provides a good path between the two metals for electron transfer in a manner as copper wire connecting two electrodes provides a path for passing electric current.

(ii) In the activated intermediate an electron is transferred from Cr^{2+} to Co^{3+} through the bridging Cl^- ion to convert Cr^{2+} to G^{3+} and Co^{3+} to Co^{2+}.

(iii) The Cr^{3+} ion formed attracts Cl^- ion more strongly than does Co^{2+} and, therefore, Cl^- ion becomes a part of the complex of Cr^{3+}. Thus, we find that the electron is transferred from Cr^{2+} to Co^{3+} through the bridging Cl^-, but Cl^- ion goes from Co^{3+} to Cr^{2+} (I) and these two acts are mutually interdepent, *i.e.*, neither is possible without the other.

$$[(NH_3)_5Co^{3+}\text{—}Cl\rightarrow\text{—}Cr^{2+}(H_2O)_5]^{4+}$$

(e^- transferred from Cr to Co through Cl)

Activated bridged intermediate (I)

Thus, we find that after electron transfer the initial labile partner *viz* $[Cr(H_2O)_6]^{2+}$ becomes inert to substitution and the inert partner *viz* $[Co(NH_3)_5Cl]^{2+}$ becomes labile.

A direct transfer from $[Cr(H_2O)_6]^{2+}$ to $[Co(NH_3)_5Cl]^{2+}$ followed by the transfer of $^{36}Cl^-$ seems unlikely, since in this case unlabelled Cl^- from the solution would be readily incorporated into the Cr^{3+} complex as the $^{36}Cl^-$ is attached to cobalt.

The reaction is first-order with respect to the oxidant and the reductant.

$$v = k\,[\text{oxidant}]\,[\text{reductant}]$$
$$= k\,[Co(NH_3)_5Cl^{2+}]\,[Cr(H_2O)_6^{2+}]$$

Similar mechanism has been suggested for the following general reaction :

$$[Co^{2+}(NH_3)_5X]^{2+} + [Cr(H_2O)_6]^{2+} + 3H_3O^+ \longrightarrow [Co(H_2O)_6]^{2+} + [Cr(H_2O)_5X]^{2+} + 5NH_4^+$$

Here, $X = F^-, Cl^-, Br^-, I^-, SO_4^{2-}, NCS^-, N_3^-, PO_4^{4-}, P_2O_7^{4-}, CH_3COO^-$, etc. With these ligands which form bridges the rates of these reactions increase in the order : $SO_4^{2-} < Cl^- < Br^-$. The ions that form bridges most readily and provide the best path for electron produce fastest reactions.

There are some redox reactions in which multiple bridges are formed, *e.g.*, in the following reaction three oxygen atoms of EDTA serve as bridges.

$$\underset{(Co=+3)}{[Co^{3+}(EDTA)]^-} + \underset{(Cr=+2)}{Cr^{2+}} \longrightarrow \underset{(Co=+2)}{Co^{2+}} + \underset{(Cr=+3)}{[Cr^{3+}(H_2O)_3(EDTA)]^-}$$

In reactions with two bridging groups two ligands but only one electron are transferred. Conversely, in various Pt^{II}/Pt^{IV} exchanges two electrons but only one ligand is tranferred. There is given a reaction in which electron-transfer by an inner-sphere mechanism is not accompanied by ligand transfer, *e.g.*,

$$\underset{(Co=+2)}{[Co^{2+}(EDTA)]^{2-}} + \underset{(Fe=+3)}{[Fe^{3+}(CN)_6]^{3-}} \longrightarrow \underset{(Co=+3)}{[Co^{3+}(EDTA)]^-} + \underset{(Fe=+2)}{[Fe^{2+}(CN)_6]^{4-}}$$

Direct electron-transfer or outer-sphere mechanism

Here, we shall discuss the electron-transfer reactions in which only the formal valence states of the metal ions involved change. These reactions occur by direct electron transfer and the electron effectively hops from one species to the other and the ligands acts as electron-conduction media. Recent work on electron spin resonance of paramagnetic complexes has shown that unpaired electrons spend part of their time on ligands. Consequently electron transfer can oocur by a mechanism which involves movement of an electron from the outside of a ligand in one coordination sphere over the outside of a second sphere. This mechanism seems particularly appropriate with large conjugated ligands like **phenanthroline** and **bipyridine.**

In this mechanism direct transfer of an electron occurs. For this process to occur there is a critical requirement which is given by **Frank-Condon principle** which states that there can be no appreciable change of atomic arrangement during the time of an electronic transition, *i.e.,* very light electrons move much more rapidly than much heavier atoms. In order to understand its effect let us consider the transfer of an electron from $[Fe^{II}(CN)_4]^{4-}$ to $[Fe^{III}(CN)_6]^{3-}$. The rate of this redox reaction (which is actually no reaction at all) can be studied by labelling either of the complexes with a radioactive isotope of Fe or with ^{14}C.

e^-

$$[{}^*Fe^{2+}(CN)_6]^{4-} + [Fe^{3+}(CN)_6]^{3-} \longrightarrow$$

$[{}^*Fe^{2+}(CN)_6]^{4-}$	$[Fe^{3+}(CN)_6]^{3-}$
Ferrocyanide ion	Ferricyanide ion
Low-spin and inert	Low-spin and inert
$Fe^{2+} \to d^6$	$Fe^{3+} \to d^5$
$(t_{2g}^6 e_{2g}^0)$	$(t_{2g}^5 e_g^0)$
Fe—C bonds longer	Fe—C bonds shorter

$$[{}^*Fe^{3+}(CN)_6]^{3-} + Fe^{2+}(CN)_6]^{4-}$$

$[{}^*Fe^{3+}(CN)_6]^{3-}$	$Fe^{2+}(CN)_6]^{4-}$
Fe–C bonds longer	Fe–C bonds shorter

The above reaction is fast with second-order constant $\sim 10^5$ at 25°C and there is no heat change in the reaction, since we obtain the same products after the electron transfer. Both the anions are inert. $[Fe(CN)_6]^{4-}$ is a low-spin d^6 $(t_{2g}^6 e_g^0)$ system and $[Fe(CN)_6]^{3-}$ is a low-spin d^5 $(t_{2g}^5 e_g^0)$ system. Thus, the loss or exchange of CN^- or any substitution reaction is very fast. the possibility of electron transfer through a bridged activated complex is eliminated, since formation of the activated complex amounts to a substitution reaction. During this reaction none of the elements *viz.* Fe, C or N moves. The Fe–C bond in $[Fe(CN)_6]^{3-}$ is slightly shorter than that in $[Fe(CN)_6]^{4-}$. Thus, if an electron is to be transferred between the anions in their ground-state equilibrium configurations by the Franck-Condon principle, the product $[Fe(CN)_6]^{3-}$ would be expanded (*i.e.,* Fe–C bonds must become longer) and the $[Fe(CN)_6]^{4-}$ would be compressed (*i.e.,* Fe–C bonds must become shorter). For this to be so, the energy must be added to the system, *i.e.,* the products would be of higher energy than the reactants. This, however, contradicts the fact that there is no heat change associated with this electron transfer reaction.

It follows that an electron-transfer reactionc an only occur when the vibrations within the two anions have made them of identical geometries and electronic configurations. Then the products and the reactants in the electron-transfer process would be equivalent and no energy would be produced as a result of the electron transfer. Since both the anions are similar, a relatively small addition of energy (the activation energy) would make the anions alike. Thus, electron-transfer reaction can occur rapidly.

When both the reactants are inert as in the present case, the close approach of the metal atoms is impossible and hence the electron-transfer takes place by a **tunnelling** or **outer-sphere mechanism.** In this mechanism each complex retains its full coordination shell in the activated complex so that there is no ligand common to each central metal atom and an electron is believed to pass through both the coordination shells. This mechanism is sure to be correct when both the reactants exchange their ligands more slowly (*i.e.*, are inert) than they undergo electron transfer and differ only in their charges. Although for an isotopic change the equilibrium constant is nearly unity and $\Delta G°$ is nearly zero, activation energy is required (i) to overcome the electrostatic repulsion between ions of like charges (electrostatic energy) (ii) to distort the coordination shells of both species, and (iii) to modify the solvent structure around both species. Thus, activation energy is made up of the above three contributions.

Outer-sphere electron-transfer reactions are more rapid for complexes containing ligands such as *o*-phenanthroline and CN^- ion than for corresponding complexes with ligands like H_2O or NH_3.

Now, consider an electron-transfer between $[Co^{III}(NH_3)_6]^{3+}$ and $[Co^{II}(NH_3)_6]^{2+}$, both the complexes being octahedral. This reaction is slow.

$$\overset{e^-}{\longrightarrow}$$

$$\underset{\substack{\text{High-spin} \\ Co^{2+} \rightarrow d^7(t_{2g}^5 e_g^2)}}{[{}^*Co^{2+}(NH_3)_6]^{2+}} + \underset{\substack{\text{Low-spin} \\ Co^{2+} \rightarrow d^6(t_{2g}^6 e_g^0)}}{[Co^{3+}(NH_3)_6]^{3+}} \longrightarrow$$

$$\underset{Co^{3+} \rightarrow d^6(t_{2g}^5 e_g^1)}{[{}^*Co^{3+}(NH_3)_6]^{3+}} + \underset{Co^{2+} \rightarrow d^7(t_{2g}^6 e_g^1)}{[Co^{2+}(NH_3)_6]^{2+}}$$

These complexes do not differ greatly in size and hence one might expect that the electron-transfer reaction is fast. The two complexes, however, do differ in electronic configuration and Co–N bond lengths : $[Co(NH_3)_6]^{2+}$ is a high-spin $d^7(t_{2g}^5 e_g^2)$ system while $[Co(NH_3)_6]^{2+}$ is a low-spin $d^6(t_{2g}^6 e_g^0)$ system, Co—N bond lengths in $[Co(NH_3)_6]^{2+}$ and $[Co(NH_3)_6]^{3+}$ are 2.11 Å and 1.96 Å respectively.

After electron-transfer these configuration presumably become $t_{2g}^5 e_g^1$ and $t_{2g}^6 e_g^1$ respectively. Neither of these is the ground state configuration of the ion, *i.e.*, after electron-transfer reaction both the complexes will be electronically excited. This excess of energy will rapidly be lost either by radiation or more probably it will be converted into thermal energy. Because this electronic energy contributes to the activation energy of the process, the rate of electron-transfer reaction between $[Co(NH_3)_6]^{2+}$ and $[Co(NH_3)_6]^{3+}$ is much slower than that between $[Fe(CN)_6]^{3-}$ and $[Fe(CN)_6]^{4-}$.

Outer-sphere exchange reactions between complexes having different central metal ions with different oxidation states (*e.g.*, $[Os^{II}(dipy)_3]^{2+}$—$[Mo^{V}(CN)_8]^{3-}$ reaction) are usually faster than outer sphere exchange reaction between the complexes of the same metals with different oxidation states. For such reactions when excited states of the products are converted into ground states, the decrease in energy can appear as the free energy of the reaction ($\Delta G°$ must be negative or the reaction would not take place). This means that for such reactions the structure of the transition state is more like that of the reactants and consequently the activation energy is decreased and the rate is increased.

There are now a number of electron-transfer reactions such as those of $[Co^{III}(NH_3)_4X]^{2+}$ with $[Co^{II}(CN)_5]^{2-}$, where $X = F^-, CN^-, NO_3^-$ and NO_2^- and that of Cr^{2+} with $[IrCl_6]^{2-}$ in which the electron transfer takes place by both inner- and outer-sphere mechanisms.

Factors Affecting the Rates of Direct Electron-Transfer Reactions

The factors affecting the rates of direct electron-transfer reactions have been summarised by Halpern as follows :

(i) Electrostatic repulsion between ions of like charges

This contributes to the activation energy. Because of electrostatic repulsion the energy of activation also increases. The increase in activation energy tends to decrease the rate of exchange of electrons.

(ii) Identity and concentration of the cations present in solution

In several cases, the rate constants for the electron-transfer reactions have been found to depend on the identity and concentration of the cations present in the solution. Generally an increase in the concentration of the cations increases the rate, but certain cations are particularly effective. The general effect can be attributed to the formation of ion pairs which then decrease the electrostatic contribution to the activation energy.

(iii) Conductivity of the ligands

The greater the conductivity of the ligands, the more readily should electron-transfer proceed between the two complexes. Electron transfer between a variety of similar cyanide complexes has been found to be rapid. The same is true for the highly conducting complexes *viz.* $[M(\text{phen})_3]^{n+}$ and $[M(\text{bipy})_3]^{n+}$ relative to $[M(\text{en})_3]^{n+}$ and $[M(NH_3)_6]^{n+}$.

(iv) Reorganisation energy

The bond lengths in MnO_4^- and MnO_4^{2-} differ and the activated complex for exchange between these must involve a "stretched" MnO bond in MnO_4^-. Slow reactions are expected when the oxidant and the reductant have greatly different bond lengths, geometries or solvation shells. For octahedral complexes bond lengths are changed more drastically when e_g electrons are involved in the transfer as compared to t_{2g} electrons in the *d*-orbitals.

(v) Free energy change in the reaction

The greater the negative free energy change for the overall reaction, the faster the reaction.

Two Electron-Transfer Reactions

The electron-transfer reactions we have discussed so far involve the transfer of a single electron form one species to the other. Reactions in which two electrons are transferred are also known *e.g.*, the reaction :

$$^*Tl^+ + Tl^{3+} \longrightarrow {}^*Tl^{3+} + Tl^+$$

$$^*Pt^{2+} + Pt^{4+} \longrightarrow {}^*Pt^{4+} + Pt^{2+} \qquad \ldots(7)$$

have been studied in detail. In aqueous perchlorate solution, the rate-law for reaction (7) is

$$v = k_1\,[Tl^+]\,[Tl^{3+}] + k_2\,[Tl^+]\,[TlOH^{2+}]$$

In the presence of other anions like NO_3^-, Cl^-, CN^-, SO_4^{2-}, Br^- etc., more complicated rate-laws are found indicated that two-electron transfers occur through various Tl^{3+} complexes.

Ligand Substitution Reactions in Octahedral Complexes

Following are the important types of substitution reactions met with in coordination chemistry.

(i) Nucleophilic or ligand substitution (S_N) reactions. In these reactions, a nucleophile (*i.e.*, ligand, *L*) in a coordination complex, say ML_n is replaced by another nucleophile L'.

$$\underset{(\text{C.N.} = n)}{ML_n} + L' \longrightarrow \underset{(\text{C.N.} = n)}{ML_{n-1}L'} + L$$

(ii) Electrophilic or metal substitution (S_E) reactions. In these reactions an electrophile (*i.e.*, central metal atom) in a coordination complex is replaced by another electrophile, M'.

$$ML_n + M' \longrightarrow M'L_n + M$$

Although S_E reactions, such as that between Hg^{2+} and $[Co^{II}(NH_3)_5Cl]^+$ are known,they are much less common than S_N reactions and hence, will not be considered here.

Mechanism of Nucleophilic (Ligand) Substitution Reactions (S_N Reactions) in Octahedral Complexes

Two different paths of nucleophilic substitution reactions have been suggested :

(1) S_N1 or dissociation mechanism

S_N1 indicates substitution (S) nucleophilic (N) unimolecular or first order (1) reaction. The reaction is nucleophilic because the incoming ligand seeks a positive centre (like the nucleus of an atom), the metal ion. For a general ligand substitution reaction in an octahedral complex this mechanism can be shown as :

$$\underset{\substack{\text{Octahedral}\\\text{complex}\\(\text{C.N.} = 6)}}{MX_5Y} + Z \longrightarrow \underset{(\text{C.N.} = 6)}{MX_5Z} + Y$$

The above reaction actually procceds through a two-step mechanism.

(a) In this step which is a slow and rate-determining step, *Y* is lost and a five-coordinated intermediate (activated complex) is formed. This is a metal ligand bond breaking step and the reaction occuring in this step is unimolecular because this step which is the rate-determining step involves only one reactant species, MX_5Y to form the activated complex, MX_x which is an electron deficient intermediate. This has either square pyramidal or trigonal bipyramidal shape, since its coordination number is five.

Thus, on putting the values of $[ML^+]$, $[M^+]$ and $[L]$ from the above equations in

$$K_f = \frac{[ML^+]}{[M^+][L]}$$

the value of K_f can be evaluated. For the determination of $[ML^+]$, $[M^+]$ and $[L]$, the values of C_H, C_L, C_M, K_a and $[H^+]$ must be known. The last quantity, $[H^+]$, is generally determined potentiometrically using a pH meter.

In order to get precise results, the ligand must be a medium weak acid or base and the formation constant, K_f, should be within a factor of 10^5 of the value of the acid association constant of the ligand, K_a.

$$\underset{(\text{C.N.}=6)}{MX_5Y} \xrightarrow[\text{Unimolecular and rate-determing step}]{\text{Slow }(-Y)} \underset{\substack{\text{5-coordinated}\\ \text{intermediate}\\ (\text{C.N.}=5)}}{MX_5} + Y$$

In this step MX_5Y is dissociated to give MX_5. Hence, the name dissociation mechanism.

(b) In this step the short-lived penta-coordinated intermediate of very limited stability is attacked rapidly by the nucleophilic reagent, Z to give the complex, MX_5Z.

$$\underset{\substack{\text{5-coordinated}\\ \text{intermediate}}}{MX_5} \xrightarrow[+Z]{\text{Fast}} \underset{(\text{C.N.}=6)}{MX_5Z}$$

This is **fast** and **bimolecular** reaction. Normally the **activation energy** for the first step will be **high** and that for the second step will be **low.** The rate of overall reaction will depend on the concentration of MX_5Y and not on that of Z. Thus, the rate of reaction is first order with respect to MX_5Y and zero order with respect to Z. Hence,

$$\text{Rate of reaction} = k[MX_5Y]$$

The formation of MX_5Y can be shown by combining the two steps as :

$$\underset{(\text{C.N.}=6)}{MX_5Y} \xrightarrow[\text{Unimolecular and rate-determining step}]{\text{Slow }(-Y)} \underset{\substack{\text{5-coordinated}\\ \text{intermediate}\\ (\text{C.N.}=5)}}{MX_5} \xrightarrow{\text{Fast }(+Z)} \underset{(\text{C.N.}=6)}{MX_5Z}$$

These two steps are diagramatically shown in Fig. 9.38.

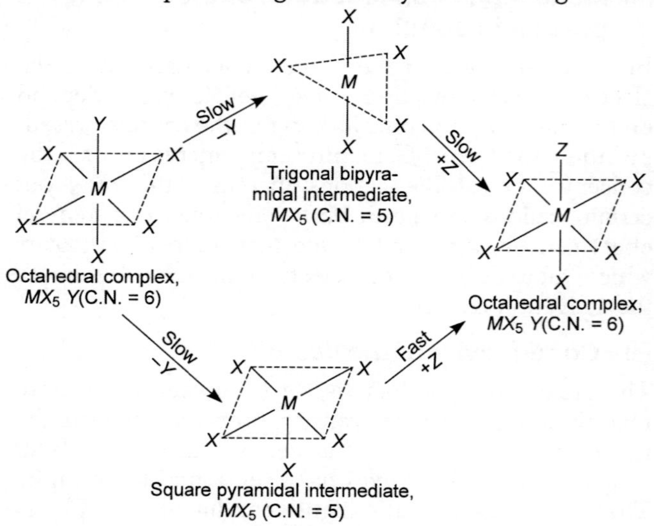

Fig. 9.38 S_N1 or dissociation mechanism for the substitution reaction.

$$MX_5Y + Z \longrightarrow MX_5Z + Y$$

(2) S_N2 or association or displacement mechanism

S_N2 stands to indicate substitution (S) nucleophilic (N) bimolecular or second order (2) reaction. This also proceeds through the two steps :

(a) This is a **slow** step and involves the attachment of the incoming nucleophile, Z to MX_5Y to form a seven-coordinated unstable intermediate (perhaps transition state) which is probably pentagonal bipyramidal in shape. Obviously it is a metal-ligand bond-making step.

$$\underset{(\text{C.N.}=6)}{MX_5Y} \xrightarrow[\text{Unimolecular and rate-determining step}]{\text{Slow }(+Z)} \underset{\substack{\text{Unstable seven}\\ \text{coordinated}\\ \text{intermediate}\\ (\text{C.N.}=7)}}{MX_5} + YZ$$

This reaction is **rate-determining** and **bimolecular because** two reactants *viz*, MX_5Y and Z are involved in this step. Thus, the rate of this rate-determining reaction is of second order : first order with respect to the complex, MX_5Y and first order with respect to the entering ligand, Z, *i.e.*,

$$\text{Rate of reaction} = k[MX_5Y][Z]$$

In this step Z associates with MX_5Y to form MX_5YZ. Hence, the name association mechanism.

(b) Either at the same time as Z adds to MX_5Y or shortly there after, Y leaves MX_5YZ rapidly to give MX_5Z. This is a fast step.

$$\underset{\substack{\text{Seven coordinated}\\ \text{unstable intermediates}\\ (\text{C.N.} = 7)}}{MX_5YZ} \xrightarrow[-Y]{\text{Fast}} \underset{(\text{C.N.} = 6)}{MX_5Z}$$

Both the steps can be represented as :

$$\underset{(\text{C.N.} = 6)}{MX_5Y} \xrightarrow[\substack{\text{Bimolecular and}\\ \text{rate-determining}\\ \text{step}}]{\text{Slow } (+Z)} \underset{\substack{\text{Seven-coordinated}\\ \text{unstable}\\ (\text{C.N.} = 7)}}{MX_5YZ} \xrightarrow[-Y]{\text{Fast}} \underset{(\text{C.N.} = 6)}{MX_5Z}$$

Both these steps are shown diagramatically in Fig. 9.39.

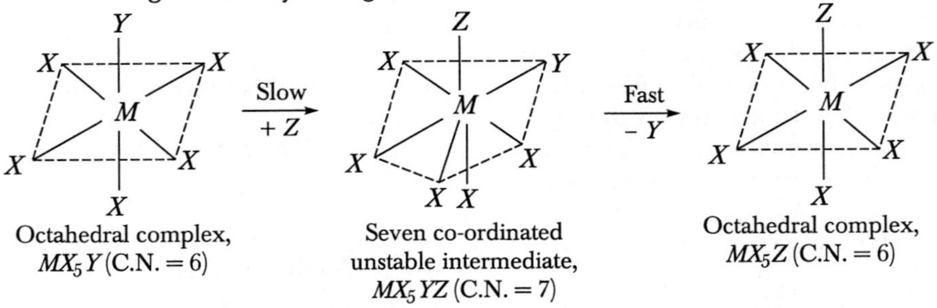

Fig. 9.39 S_N2 or association mechanism for the substitution reaction : $MX_5Y + Z \longrightarrow MX_5Z + Y$

S_N1 *vs* S_N2 mechanism

S_N1 and S_N2 mechanisms can be differentiated from each other by noting the following points :

(i) In S_N1 process the rate-determining slow step is a metal-ligand bond breaking step, since the coordination number of the complex, MX_5Y (= 6) is decreased to 5 which is the coordination number of the intermediate, MX_5. On the other hand in S_N2 process the rate-determining step involves a metal-ligand bond making step, since C.N. = 6 is increased to 7.

(ii) The rate of S_N1 mechanism is first order with respect to MX_5Y, *i.e.,* the rate-determining step in thismechanism is unimolecular. On the other hand the rate-determining step for S_N1 mechanism is bimolecular, *i.e.,* its rate of reaction is second order : first order with respect to MX_5Y and first order with repect to Z. Thus :

for S_N1 mechanism rate $= k[MX_5Y]$
and for S_N2 mechanism rate $= k[MX_5Y]\,[Z]$

Hydrolysis Reactions

These are the substitution reactions in which a ligand is replaced by a water molecule or by OH^- groups. The reactions in which an aquo complex is formed as a result of the replacement of a ligand by H_2O molecules are called **acid hydrolysis** or **aquation reactions** while those in which a hydroxo complex is formed by the replacement of a ligand by OH^- group are called **base hydrolysis reactions.** Acid hydrolysis reactions occur in neutral and acid solutions (pH < 3) while base hydrolysis reactions occur in acid solution (pH > 10). For intermediate pH ranges the reaction is referred to just as hydrolysis reactions. Examples of these reactions are given below :

$$\left.\begin{array}{l} [Co^{III}(NH_3)_5Cl]^{2+} + H_2O \longrightarrow \\ \qquad [Co^{III}(NH_3)_5(H_2O)]^{3+} + Cl^- \\ [Co^{III}(en)_2ACl]^{+} + H_2O \longrightarrow \\ \qquad [Co^{III}(en)_2A(H_2O)]^{2+} + Cl^- \\ (A = OH^-, Cl^-, NCS^-, NO_2^-) \end{array}\right\} \begin{array}{l}\text{Acid}\\ \text{hydrolysis}\\ \text{reactions}\end{array}$$

$$[Co(NH_3)_5Cl]^{2+} + OH^- \longrightarrow [Co(NH_3)_5(OH)]^{2+} + Cl^- \text{...... Base hydrolysis reaction}$$

Aquation or Acid Hydrolysis Reactions of Six-coordinated Co(III) Ammine Complexes

Ammine complexes of Co(III) have been most widely studied. Since work on these complexes has been done exclusively in water, the reactions of the complexes with solvent water had to be considered first. In general it has been observed that NH_3 or ammines like-ethylene diamine or its derivatives coordinated to Co(III) are replaced very slowly by H_2O molecules and hence in acid hydrolysis only the replacement of ligands other than ammines is usually considered.

The rates of hydrolysis of the reactions of the type

$$[Co(NH_3)_5X]^{2+} + H_2O \longrightarrow [Co(NH_3)_5(H_2O)]^{3+} + X^-$$

(X = any anion)

have been studied and found to be first order in the complex. Since in aqueous solution the concentration of water is always constant (about equal to 55.5 M), the effect of changes in water concentration on the rate of the reaction cannot be determined. Rate laws given below are experimentally indistinguishable in aqueous solution, since

$$k = k[H_2O] = K'[55.5]$$
$$\text{Rate} = k[Co(NH_3)_5X^{2+}]$$
$$= k'[Co(NH_3)_5X^{2+}][H_2O]$$
$$= k'[Co(NH_3)_5X^{2+}][55.5]$$

Thus, the rate law does not tell us whether H_2O is involved in the rate-determining step.

The rate-law given above does not indicate whether these reactions proceed by an S_N2 displacement of X^- by H_2O.

The rate of aquation of $[Co(NH_3)_5X]^{2+}$ corresponding to the replacement of X^- with H_2O molecule depends on the nature of X^- because the bond breaking step is important in rate-determing step. It has been observed experimentally that the reactivity of X^-groups decreases in the order :

$$HCO_3^- > NO_3^- > I^- > Br^- > Cl^- > SO_4^{2-} > F^- > CH_3COO^- > SCN^- > NO_2^-$$

This order corresponds to the order of the decreasing thermodynamic stability of the complexes formed with these groups. The results of various investigations are in favour of S_N1 mechanism. Bond-breaking is important in the activated complex.

Base Hydrolysis Reactions of Six-coordinated Co(III) Ammine Complexes

Most of the kinetic work has been done n six-coordinated Co(III) ammine complexes. For ammine complexes of Co(III) containing N—H bonds it has been seen that the rate of base hydrolysis is often as much 10^6 times faster than the corresponding rate of acid hydrolysis. Here we shall discuss the mechanism of the base hydrolysis reaction of $[Co(NH_3)_5Cl]^{2+}$ only. The base hydrolysis reaction represented by

$$[Co(NH_3)_5Cl]^{2+} + OH^- \rightarrow [Co(NH_3)_5(OH)]^{2+} + Cl^-$$

can proceed by any of the following two mechanisms :

(1) S_N2 displacement mechanism

According to this mechanism the reaction proceeds as

$$\underset{(C.N. = 6)}{[Co(NH_3)_5Cl]^{2+}} \xrightarrow[\text{Rate-determining step}]{\text{Slow }(+OH^-)} \underset{(C.N. = 7)}{[Co(NH_3)_5(OH)Cl]^+} \xrightarrow{\text{Fast }(-Cl^-)} \underset{(C.N. = 6)}{[Co(NH_3)_5(OH)]^{2+}} + Cl^-$$

The slow step which is a rate-determing step is a second-order reaction: first order with respect to the complex and first order with respect to the base. Thus :

$$\text{Rate of reaction} = k[\text{complex}]\,[\text{base}]$$
$$= k[Co(NH_3)_5Cl^{2+}][OH^-]$$

(2) S_N1 dissociation mechanism

This has been suggested by Garrick (1937). Before this mechanism could be applied,the complex which acts as a Bronsted acid is converted into its conjugate base (abbreviated as CB), $[Co(NH_3)_4(NH_2)Cl]^+$ which is obtained by removing a proton (H^+) from the amino group (NH_3) present in the complex. CB is an amido complex, since it contains an amido group : $:\ddot{N}H_2^-.OH^-$ which in a base is converted into its conjugated acid, H_2O.

Conjugate acid-base pair

$$\text{(a) } \underset{\substack{\text{Acid}_1 \\ \text{(Ammino complex)}}}{[Co(NH_3)_5Cl]^{2+}} + \underset{\text{Base}_2}{OH^-} \underset{}{\overset{\text{Fast}}{\rightleftharpoons}} \underset{\substack{\text{Base}_1 \\ \text{(Amido complex, CB)}}}{[Co(NH_3)_4(NH_2)Cl]^+} + \underset{\text{Acid}_2}{H_2O}$$

Conjugate acid-base pair

Obviously, if K = equilibrium constant for acid-base equilibrium (a), then

$$K = \frac{[CB]\,[H_2O]}{[Co(NH_3)_5Cl^{2+}]\,[OH^-]}$$

or

$$CB = \frac{K[Co(NH_3)_5Cl^{2+}]\,[OH^-]}{[H_2O]} \quad \ldots(8)$$

CB obtained as above is more labile than the original complex, $[Co(NH_3)_5Cl]^{2+}$ and hence undergoes S_N1 dissociation mechanism by a slow step to lose Cl^- ion and gives a 5-coordinated intermediate.

(b) $\underset{\text{(CB with C.N. = 6)}}{[Co(NH_3)_4(NH_2)Cl]^+} \xrightarrow[\substack{S_N1\text{ dissociation,}\\ \text{rate-determining}\\ \text{and-unimolecular}\\ \text{step}}]{\text{Slow }(-Cl^-)} \underset{\substack{\text{5-coordinated}\\ \text{intermediate}\\ \text{(C.N. = 5)}}}{[Co(NH_3)_4(NH_2)]^{2+}} + Cl^-$

This is the rate-determining and unimolecular step. Thus

$$\text{Rate} = k_1\,[BC]$$

$$= \frac{k_1K[Co(NH_3)_5]Cl^{2+}]\,[OH^-]}{[H_2O]}$$

[from Eq. (8)]

$$= K_B\ [\text{complex}]\ [\text{base}] \quad \ldots(9)$$

where, K_B = rate constant used for the dissociation of the conjugate base as in (b) step and is equal to $k_1K/[H_2O]$.

The intermediate formed as above reacts with the abundent solvent molecules (*i.e.*, H_2O molecules) to give the hydroxo complex, $[Co(NH_3)_5(OH)]^{2+}$. This is a relatively fast step.

(c) $\underset{\substack{\text{5-coordinated}\\ \text{intermediate}}}{[Co(NH_3)_4(NH_2)]^{2+}} \xrightarrow[(+H_2O)]{\text{Fast}} \underset{\text{Hydroxo complex}}{[Co(NH_3)_5(OH)]^{2+}}$

Although base hydrolysis involves an S_N1 mechanism, yet it is consistent with second-order : first order with respect to the complex and first order with respect to the base [see Eq. (9)].

Since the S_N1 dissociation step (b) which is the rate-determining step uses the conjugate base of the initial complex,the symbol S_N1 CB (substitution, nucleophile, conjugate-base) has been used by Garrick in place of S_N1 symbol.

Evidences in favour of S_N1 CB mechanism

The proposed rapid acid-base equilibrium (a) given above requires that the reacting complex should have at least one protonic hydrogen atom (H^+) on a non-leaving ligand so that H^+ may transfer to OH^- to form its conjugate acid, H_2O and conjugate base, $[Co(NH_3)_4(NH_2)Cl]^+$ of $[Co(NH_3)_5Cl]^{2+}$ which acts as an acid. Thus a complex having no proton (or no N—H hydrogen) should react with OH^- much more slowly and the rate of reaction would be independent of the concentration of OH^-, $[OH^-]$. In fact it has been observed that the complexes like $[Co(CN)_5Br]$ and *trans*-$[Co(py)_4Cl_4]^+$ which do not have N—H hydrogen undergo hydrolysis much more slowly in basic solution at a rate which is independent of $[OH^-]$ over a wide range. Thus in the absence of an acidic proton on the ligand an S_N1 CB mechanism is not possible. The failure of such complexes to undergo rapid base hydrolysis supports the S_N1 CB mechanism and the fact that the acid-base properties of the complexes are more important to the reaction rate than the nucleophilic properties of OH^-.

It may be noted that both the mechanisms *viz* S_N2 displacement and S_N1 CB give the same rate laws (second-order kinetics) and the same hydroxo products in aqueous solution, because water is a good coordinating agent and because proton shift is very fast.

However in a non-hydroxylic solvent (*i.e.*, non protonic solvent) different products are predicted to be formed for both the mechanisms under the condition that an excess of some nucleophile reagent other than OH^- ion or H_2O (*e.g.*, N_3^-, NO_2, SCN^-) is present,

Various steps to get $[Co(en)_2(NO_2)Y]^+$ from $[Co(en)_2(NO_2)Cl]^+$ based on S_N1 CB mechanism are :

(a) $\underset{\text{Acid}_1}{[Co(en)_2(NO_2)Cl]^+} + \underset{\text{Base}_2}{B} \overset{\text{Fast}}{\rightleftharpoons} \underset{\substack{\text{Base}_1\\ \text{(CB)}}}{[Co(en)\,(en-H)\,(NO_2)Cl]} + \underset{\text{Acid}_2}{BH^+}$

(b) $\underset{\text{(CB)}}{[Co(en)\,(en-H)\,(NO_2)Cl]} \xrightarrow[\substack{\text{Rate-determining}\\ \text{step}}]{\text{Slow }(-Cl^-)} \underset{\substack{\text{5-coordinated}\\ \text{intermediate}}}{[Co(en)\,(en-H)\,NO_2]^+} + Cl^-$

(c) $\underset{\text{intermediate}}{[Co(en)\,(en-H)\,NO_2]^+} + Y^- \xrightarrow{\text{Fast}} [Co(en)(en-H)(NO_2)Y]$

(d) $[Co(en)(en-H)(NO_2)Y] + BH^+ \xrightarrow{\text{Fast}} [Co(en)_2(NO_2)Y]^+ + B$

Anation Reactions

These are the reactions in which an aquo lignd (*i.e.,* H_2O molecule) from an aquo complex is replaced from the coordination shell by some anion.

$$\underset{\text{Aquo complex}}{[Co(NH_3)_5(H_2O)]^{3+}} + X^- \longrightarrow [Co(NH_3)_5X]^{2+} + H_2O$$

Thus we find that an anation reaction is the reverse of acid hydrolysis reaction (*i.e.,* aquation).

Kinetic studies of these reactions in aqueous solutions show that these are bimolecular reactions with a rate which depends on the concentration of the complex and X^-. However, this information alone is not sufficient to prove that these reactions are bimolecular. The same second-order kinetics would be observed for a unimolecular process such as :

$$\underset{\text{Aquo complex}}{[Co(NH_3)_5(H_2O)]^{+3}} \underset{\substack{\text{Fast} \\ (+H_2O)}}{\overset{\substack{\text{Slow} \\ (-H_2O)}}{\rightleftharpoons}} \underset{\substack{\text{5-coordinated} \\ \text{intermediate}}}{Co(NH_3)_5]^{3+}} \xrightarrow[+X^-]{\text{Fast}} [Co(NH_3)_5X]^{2+}\ H_2O$$

Substitution Reactions Without Breaking Metal-Ligand Bond

There are reactions in which ligand exchange takes place without breaking the metal-ligand bond. One well-known reaction is the preparation of an aquo complex, $[Co^{3+}(NH_3)_5(H_2O)]^{3+}$ from its corresponding carbonato complex, $[Co^{3+}(NH_3)_5CO_3]^+$ with the production of CO_2. When this reaction is carried out in the presence of $(H_3O^{18})^+$, none of O^{18} is found in the resulting aquo complex and CO_2. Hence, CO_2 is produced by the cleavage of C—O bond which keeps Co—O bond intact during the aquation reaction

$$\underset{\substack{\text{Carbonate} \\ \text{complex}}}{[(NH_3)_5Co^{3+}—O—CO_2]^+} + 3(H_2O^{18})^+ \longrightarrow \underset{\text{Aquo complex}}{[Co^{3+}(NH_3)_5(H_2O^{18})]^{3+}} + 2H_2O^{18} + CO_2$$

Mechanism

The most likely path for this reaction is believed to involve proton attack on the oxygen atom bonded to Co followed by the expulsion of CO_2 and H_2O and then protonation of the hydroxo complex.

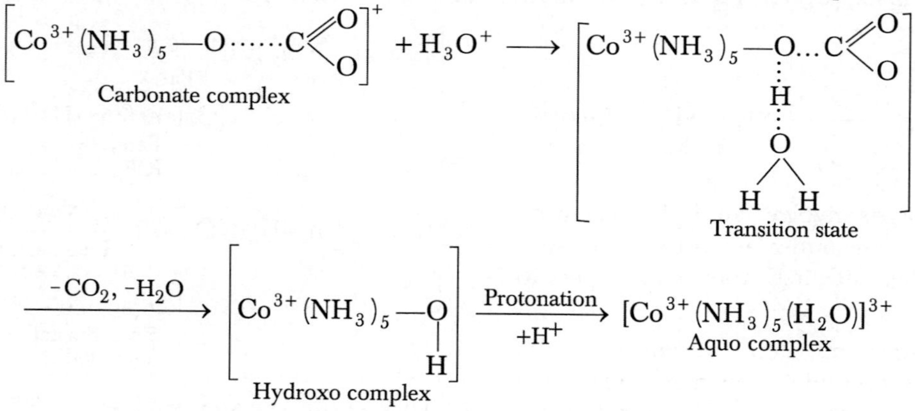

Thus, this is a decarboxylation reaction rather than an acid hydrolysis reaction.

Ligand Substitution Reactions in Square Planar Complexes

Consider the substitution reactions in Pt(II) square-planar complex, $[Pt(NO_2)Cl_3]^{2-}$ with NH_3 to yield $[Pt(NO_2)Cl_2(NH_3)]^-$. Theoretically there are two possible reaction products : (a) and (b) shown below :

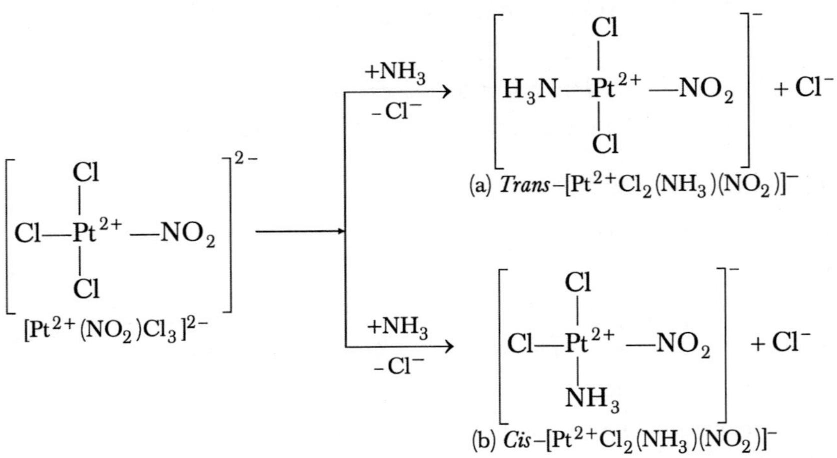

Experiments have, however, shown that it is only (a) (*i.e., trans*-isomer) which is formed. (a) is formed by the replacement of Cl^-lying *trans* to NO_2^- in $[Pt(NO_2)Cl_3]^{2-}$by NH_3. The formation of (a) is explained by saying that Cl^- ion lying *trans* to NO_2^- in $[Pt(NO_2)Cl_3]^{2-}$ is far more easily replaced by NH_3 than either of the two Cl^-ions lying *cis* to NO_2^- ion. The phenomena of such type of replacement is called ***trans*-effect.** Groups like NO_2^- which direct the entering ligand to occupy the position *trans* to them are called *trans* directing groups and the property of these groups due to which the groups lying *trans* to them are replaced far more readily by the entering ligand is called *trans*-directing character (or *trans*-directing influence or simply *trans*-effect).

Chatt et al have proposed that the *trans*-effect of a group coordinated to a metal ion is the tendency of that group to direct an incoming group to occupy the position trans to that group. Trans effect is also defined a the effect of a coordinated group on the rate of the replacement of a group lying trans to it in a metal complex, *e.g.,* in the trans form of square-planar complex, MLX_3 (L and X are *trans* to each other), if the ligand X which is *trans* to L is rapidly replaced by another group, say Y, to give MLX_2Y, L is said to have large *trans* effect or *trans* directing character. Thus, L has greater *trans* effect than X ($L > X$).

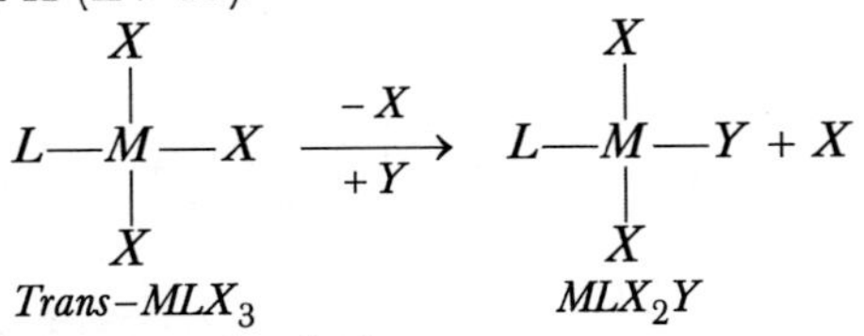

(L and X *trans* to each other)

By measuring rates a series of ligands can be put into an order of decreasing *trans*-effect. Such an order would not necessarily be invariant but might depend on the metal complex and also on the incoming group, Y. The approximate order of decreasing *trans*-effect of some common ligands is :

High end ⟶ *trans*-effect increasing ⟶ Low end

$$CN^-, CO, C_2H_4, NO > PR_3, H^- > CH^-, SC(NH_2)_2 > C_6H_5^-, NO_2^-, I^-,$$

$$SCN^-\text{(S-bonded)} > Br^-, Cl^- > py, NH_3, OH^-, H_2O.$$

The series given above is called ***trans*-effect series.**

The ligands lying at the high end of the series have vacant π or π^* orbitals which can accept electrons from metal orbital to form metal-ligand π-bond ($d\pi - d\pi$ or $d\pi - p\pi$ bond). These ligands are therefore, called π-bonding ligands.

The *trans*-directing ability of these π-bonding ligands increases with increase in their ability to form metal-ligand π-bonds.

The *trans*-effect of the ligands which are not able to form metal-ligand π-bonds increase with the increase of their polarisability, *e.g.*,

$$\xrightarrow{\text{Polarisability increases}}$$
$$Cl^- < Br^- > I^-$$
$$\xrightarrow{\textit{Trans}\text{-effect increases}}$$

Most of the work on *trans*-effect has been done on square planar Pt(II) complexes.

Uses of *Trans*-Effect

The following are important uses of this effect.

(1) Synthesis of Pt(II) complexes

The preparation of the following Pt(II) complexes illustrate the synthetic uses of *trans*-effect.

Synthesis of *cis*-and *trans*-$[PtA_2X_2]^0$. Here A = amine, NH_3, PR_3 and X = halide ion, NO_2^-, SCN^-. The synthesis of these isomers is based on the following facts :

(a) If the *trans*-effect of X^- is greater than that of A ($X^- > A$), the *cis*-isomer is obtained from $[PtX_4]^{2-}$ while the *trans*-isomer is isolated from $[PtA_4]^{2+}$ as shown below :

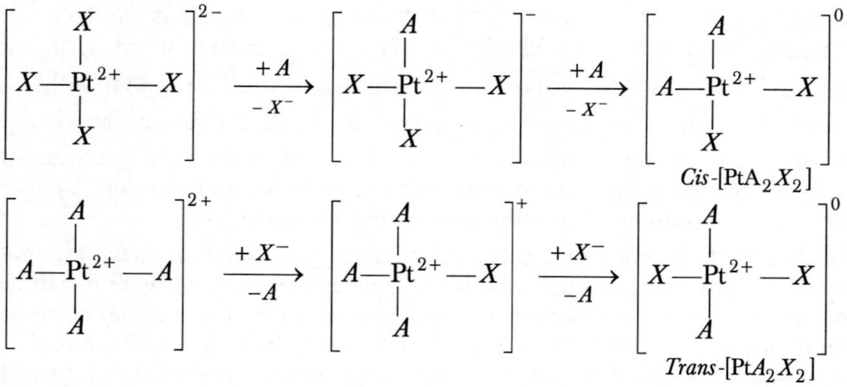

For the synthesis of *cis*- and *trans*-$[Pt(NH_3)_2Cl_2]$ where $Cl^- > NH_3$, the following scheme is applied.

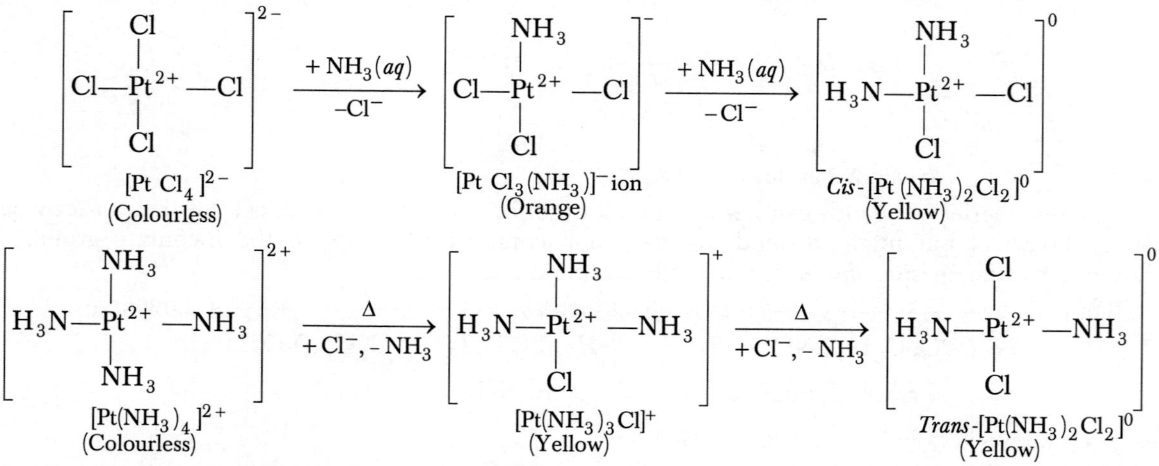

Cis-isomer is obtained by treating $[Pt^{II}Cl_4]^{2+}$ ion with NH_3. The reaction given the *cis*-isomer proceeds through the following two steps :

(i) In this step any of the four Cl^- ions is replaced by NH_3 molecule to given $[Pt^{II}(NH_3)Cl_3]^-$ ion.

(ii) In this step since Cl^- ion has a greater *trans*-directing influence than NH_3, $(Cl > NH_3)$, Cl^- ion lying *trans* to another Cl^- in $[PtCl_3(NH_3)]^-$ is readily replaced by NH_3 than is the Cl^- ion lying *trans* to NH_3.

The *trans*-isomer is obtained by heating $[Pt^{II}(NH_3)_4]^{2+}$ ion with Cl^- ion (*i.e.,* with HCl). Here also the reaction proceeds through two steps :

(i) In this step any of the four NH_3 molecules is replaced by Cl^- ion to give $Pt(NH_3)_3Cl]^+$ ion.

(ii) In this step since Cl^- ion has the superior *trans*-directing influence $(Cl^- > NH_3)$, the remaining NH_3 molecule to be most readity displaced is the one *trans* to Cl^- ion to give the *trans*-isomer. This can be said in other words that the superior *trans*-directing influence of Cl^- ion causes the second Cl^- ion to occupy a position *Trans* to the first one, producing *trans*-$[Pt^{II}(NH_3)_2Cl_2]^{10}$.

(b) If the *trans*-effect of $A > X^-$, then *cis*-isomer is obtained from $PtA_4]^{2+}$ while the *trans*-isomer is isolated from $[PtX_4]^{2-}$ as shown below :

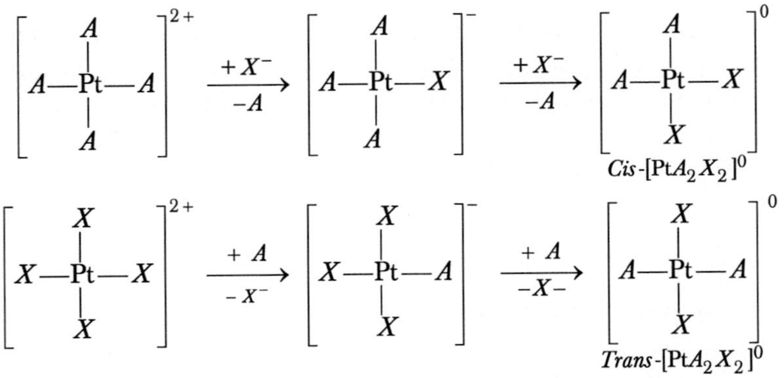

Synthesis of *cis*- and *trans*-$[PtCl_2(PR_3)_2]^{10}$ where $PR_3 > Cl^-$ is done according to the following scheme

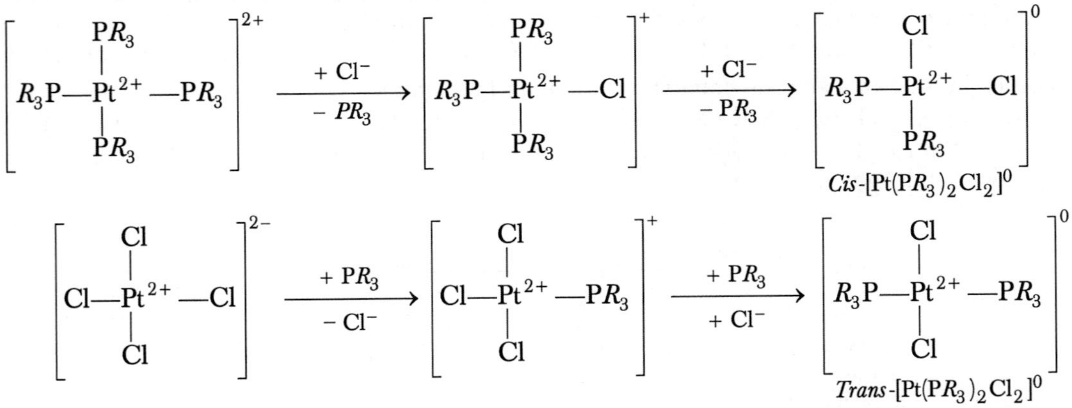

In the first reaction, PR_3 molecule lying *trans* to another PR_3 molecule is more easily replaced by Cl^-ion than is PR_3 molecule lying *trans* to Cl^-ion and thus *cis*-isomer is obtained. The formation of *cis*-isomer shows that PR_3 has greater *trans* effect than Cl^-ion. On the basis of similar reasoning the formation of *trans*-isomer can also be explained.

(2) To distinguish between *cis*- and *trans*-isomers of $[PtA_2X_2]^0$ type complexes

In addition to its utility in the synthesis of the desired Pt(II) complexes, the *trans*-effect has also been used by Russian chemists to distinguish between the *cis*- and *trans*- isomers of $[PtA_2X_2]^0$ type complexes $(A = NH_3$ or amine, X = a negative group), *e.g.*, *cis*- $[Pt(NH_3)_2Cl_2]^0$ reacts with thiourea, $NH_2 \cdot CS \cdot NH_2$ (abbreviated as *tu*) to give $[Pt(tu)_4]^{2+}$ whereas under the same conditions the *trans*-$[Pt(NH_3)_2Cl_2]^0$ gives $[Pt(tu)_2(NH_3)_2]^{2+}$.

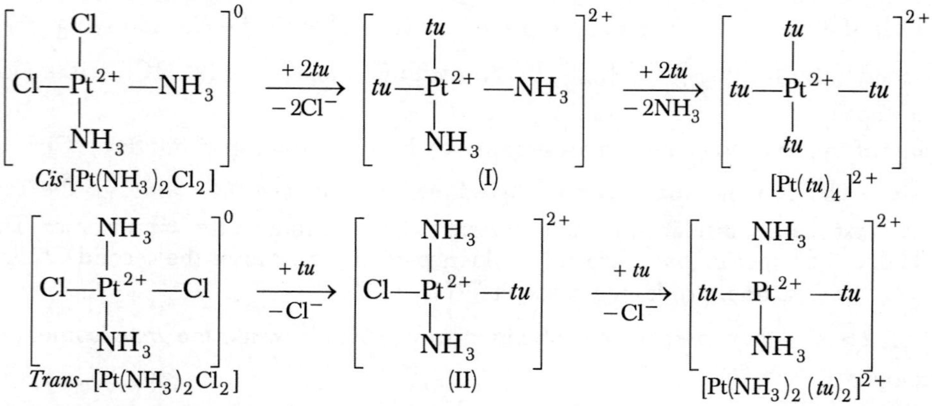

Compound (I) in the first reaction reacts further with *tu* to give the completely substituted product, $[Pt(tu)_4]^{2+}$ because of the larger *trans* effect of *tu* than NH_3. In (II) the *trans* effect of NH_3 being smaller than that of *tu*, NH_3 molecules are not sufficiently reactive to be replaced by *tu*. Thus Cl^- ion *trans* to *tu* in (II) is replaced by further *tu* molecule to form $[Pt(NH_3)_2(tu)_2]^{2+}$. The use of thiourea reaction, to assign structures is known as **Kurnakov's test**. Similar results have been reported for reactions of thiosulphate ion ($S_2O_3^{2-}$) instead of thiourea, *e.g.*, *cis*- and *trans*-$[Pt(NH_3)_2Cl_2]^0$ reacts with the excess of $S_2O_3^{2-}$ ion to form $[Pt^{II}(S_2O_3)_4]^{6-}$ and $[Pt^{II}(NH_3)_2(S_2O_3)_2]^{2-}$ respectively.

Mechanism of Substitution Reactions

Substitution reactions in Pt(II) square-planar complexes proceed by bimolecular displacement (S_N2) mechanism involving either the solvent or the entering ligand as the nucleophilic agent.

Experimental evidence in favour of S_N2 mechanism has been presented. Because of steric and electronic reasons the coordination number of the metal is increased to include the entering ligand. The metal is exposed for attack above and below the plane. Furthermore Pt(II) which is a d^8 system has a vacant p_z-orbital of relatively low energy which accepts the pair of electrons donated by the entering ligand.

Substitution reactions of *cis*-and *trans*-PtA_2LX with Y to yield PtA_2LY have been explained on the basis of nucleophilic attack of Y through *trigonal bipyramidal (tbp)* structrure. The process is entirely stereospecific : *cis*-Pt A_2LX yields *cis* product and *trans* gives *trans*.

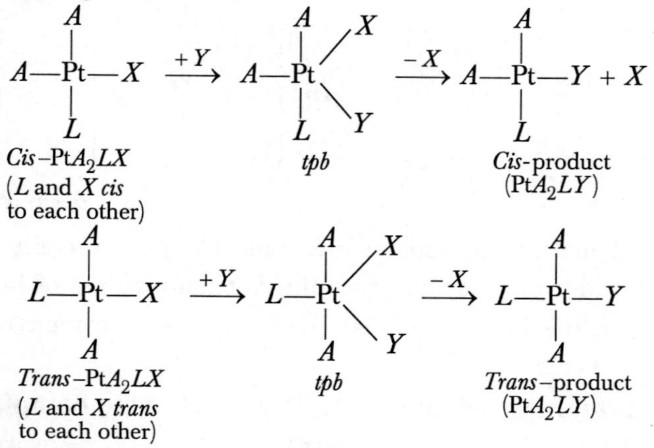

For the substitution reaction of square planar complex, $[PtA_3X]^{n+}$ with Y^- to yield $[PtA_3Y]^{n+}$ in water involves a complication, since the solvent water also behaves as a potential ligand.

$$[PtA_3X]^{n+} + Y^- \xrightarrow{H_2O} [PtA_3Y]^{n+} + X^-$$

For this reaction a two-term rate law is given by the expression :

$$\text{Rate} = k_1[PtA_3X^{n+}] + k_2[PtA_3X^{n+}][Y^-] \quad ...(10)$$

Here k_1 = first-order rate constant for solvent-controlled reaction,
and k_2 = second-order rate constant for reaction with Y^-.

A convenient analysis of rate constants can be made by running the reactions with a large excess of nucleophile, Y^-. Under this condition the observed rate-constant, k_{obs}, is pseudo first-order and is related to k_1 and k_2 as :

$$k_{obs} = k_1 + k_2[Y] \quad ...(11)$$

This equation shows that for the same complex with different reagents linear plots of k_{obs} against nucleophile concentration, [Y] should be obtained having the same intercepts, k_1 and different slopes, k_2 (see Fig. 9.40)

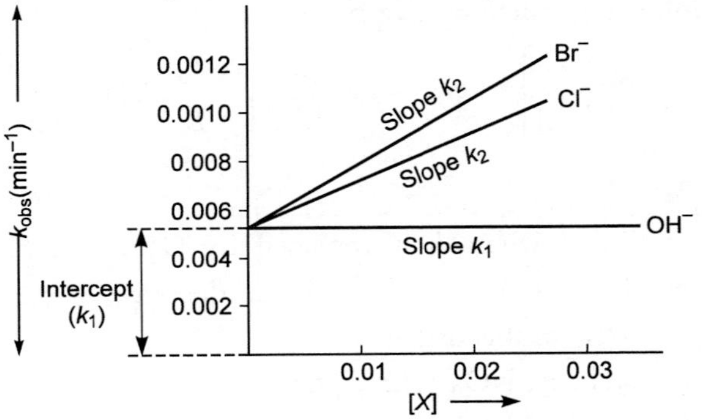

Fig. 9.40 Plot of observed rate-constant, k_{obs} for the reaction $[Pt^{2+}(dien)\,Cl]^+ + Y^- \xrightarrow[(Y = OH, Cl^-, Br^-)]{} [Pt^{2+}(dien)Y]^+ + Cl^-$ against concentration of the nucleophile, [Y]. dien ≡ $NH_2(CH_2)_2NH\,(CH_2)_2NH_2$

The rate-law represented by equation (11) indicates that the reaction of $[PtA_3X]^{n+}$ with Y^- to yield $[PtA_3Y]^{n+}$ is occurring by two path mechanism only one of which involves Y^- in the rate-determining step. These two paths are shown in fig. 9.41. The upper path is the solvent path (also called Y^- independent path) and the lower path is the direct path (reagent path). In the solvent path the solvent, H_2O replaces X^- in a slow and is subsequently replaced by Y^- in a rapid step. Experience shows that Y^- independent path is not an S_N1 process, but is a direct (S_N2) displacement of leaving group by nucleophile in probably the second-order path while the solvent path gives pseduo first-order kinetics.

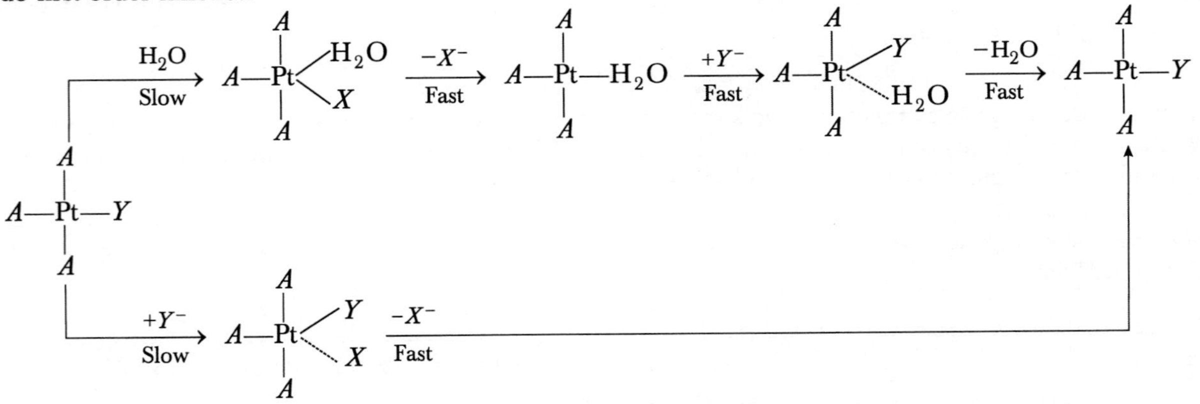

Fig. 9.41 Two-path mechanism proposed for the substitution reaction : $[PtA_3X] + Y \longrightarrow [PtA_3Y] + X$

The rate-constant, k_1 is due to the solvent path, while k_2 is due to the direct displacement of the leaving group by nucleophile. Thus, it becomes convenient to designate the solvent path k_1 as k_S and the direct displacement k_2 as k_Y so that equation (ii) becomes

$$k_{obs} = k_S + k_Y [Y^-] \quad \text{...(12)}$$

Factors Affecting the Rates of Substitution Reactions in Square Planar Complexes

Most of the kinetic data available deal with the effects of various factors on the rates of substitution reactions in Pt(II) square planar complexes. Some factors are :

(i) *Trans*-effect

In order to see the effect of ligands L *trans* to the leaving group, Cl^- in some analogous Pt(II) square-planar complexes, relative rates of the following reaction have been studied

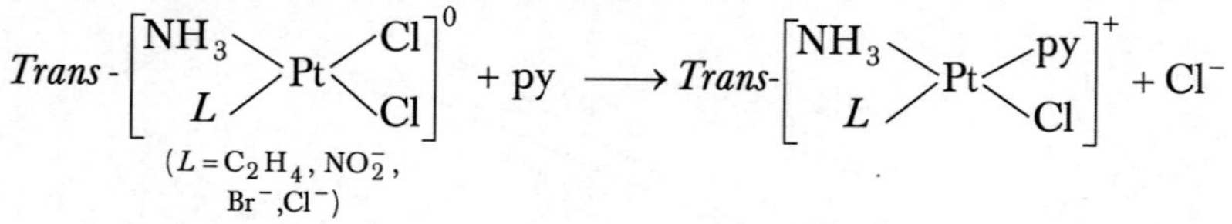

In this reaction, it has been found that when L is replaced by C_2H_4, NO_2^-, Br^- or Cl^- in the complex, $[Pt(NH_3)Cl_2L]^0$, the relative rates of reaction decrease with the decrease of relative *trans*-effect of these groups while the activation energies, E_a increase in this order.

Relative *trans*-effect :	C_2H_4	$\gg NO_2^-$	$> Br^-$	$> Cl^-$
Relative rates :	100	> 90	> 3	> 1
E_a (kcal/mol) :	–11	>	17	> 19

In order to see the *trans*-effect of some unusual ligands, the relative rates of the following reaction have been evaluated in ethanol solution at 25°C.

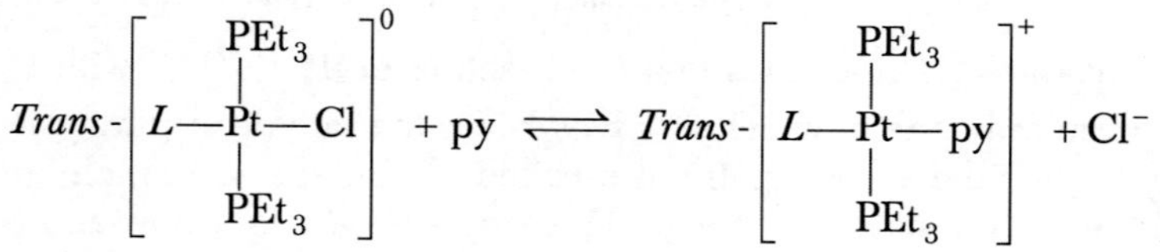

In this reaction only the ligand L which is *trans* to the leaving group *viz.* Cl^- group is changed by other groups like H^-, CH_3^-, $C_6H_5^-$ etc., Cl^- is replaced by py to yield *trans* $[Pt(PEt)_2 pyL]^+$. The rate data given below are in terms of k_1 and k_2 defined by the equation :

$$k_{obs} = k_1 + k_2 [Y]$$

These reactions do not go to completion. The approach to equilibrium is given by a pseudo first order process with a rate-constant given by the above equation. In this case k_1 and k_2 are composite quantities for forward and reverse reactions and both contribute to the over all observed rates.

Trans-directing ability of group L *trans* to Cl^- which is leaving group	H^- > methyl > phenyl ~*p*-chloro-phenyl~ *p*-methoxy phenyl > biphenyl > Cl^-
k_1 (min^{-1}) :	$1.1 > 1 \times 10^{-2} > 2 \times 10^{-3} \sim 1.7 \times 10^{-3} \sim> 1 \times 10^{-3} > 6 \times 10^{-5}$
k_2 (min^{-1}) :	$2.5 \times 10^{2} > 4 > 9.5 \times 10^{-1} \sim 9 \times 10^{-1} \sim 7.9 \times 10^{-1} 5.8 \times 10^{-1} > 2.4 \times 10^{-2}$

These results show that the effect on the rates of reaction of different L groups *trans* to Cl^- which is being replaced by py decreases in the following order :

$H^- >$ methyl > phenyl ~ *p*-chlorophenyl ~… . This is also the order of *trans*-effect of these groups.

(ii) Effect of leaving group

The reaction,

$$[Pt^{2+}(dien)X]^+ + py \longrightarrow [Pt(dien)(py)]^{2+} + X^-$$

$$X = NO_3^-, H_2O, Cl^- \text{ etc}).$$

has been studied and the rates of reaction have been obtained. The rates of reaction show that if the leaving group, X^- is replaced by NO_3^-; H_2O, Cl^-, Br^-, I^-, N_3^-, SCN^-, NO_2^- and CN^-, the rates decreases in the order :

$$NO_3^- > H_2O > Cl^- > Br^- > I^- > N_3^-, SCN^- > NO_2^- > CN^-$$

Note that in the square-planar complex, $[Pt(dien)X]^+$ three coordination positions are always occupied by the inert dien ligand while the fourth one is occupied by X^- which may be NO_3^-, H_2O, Cl^- etc.

(iii) Solvent effect

Since there is considerable evidence of the fact that in the solvent path, the solvent replaces X^- directly, it is to be expected that with the increase in the coordinating ability of the solvent, the contribution made by this path to the overall rate of reaction would also increase. This is in accordance with the experimental results of the solvent on the rate of $^{36}Cl^-$ exchange with *Trans* $[Pt(py)_2Cl_2]$. Some of the results are given in Table 9.15. Under the experimental condition *viz*, moderately low concentration of Cl^-, the solvents were divided into two categories :

(a) Those where the rate of exchange does not depend on $[Cl^-]$. These are poor coordinating solvents like H_2O, ROH and provide almost entirely a solvent path for exchange ($k_s >> k[Cl^-]$ or $k_1 >> k_2$.

(b) Those where the rate of exchange depends on the concentration of Cl^-. These are coordinating solvents like CCl_4, C_6H_6 and contribute little to the overall rate of reaction. The exchange occurs by Cl^- acting a nucleophile ($k_S < K_{Cl}$ $[Cl^-]$ or $k_1 < k_2$).

For good solvents it may be noted that the values of k_{obs} increase in the order : ROH < H_2O ~ CH_3NO_2 < $(CN_3)_2SO$ (Table 9.8). This series shows that the rate of exchange is faster in $(CH_3)_2SO$ than in water.

Table 9.8 **Effect of Solvent on the Rate of $^{36}Cl^-$ Exchange with *Trans*-$[Pt(py)_2Cl_2]$ at 25°C**

Solvents in which rate of exchange of independent of $[Cl^-]$	k_{obs} (min^{-1})	Solvents in which rate is dependent on $[Cl^-]$	k_{obs} (min^{-1})
H_2O	2.1×10^{-3}	CCl_4	1×10^{-4}
C_2H_5OH	8.5×10^{-4}	C_6H_6	2×10^{-4}
m-C_3H_7OH	2.5×10^{-4}	*m*-cresol	2×10^{-4}
$(CH_3)_2SO$	2.3×10^{-2}	*tert*-C_4H_9OH	1×10^{-3}
CH_3NO	1.9×10^{-3}		

(iv) Effect of charge on the complex

This has already been discussed under mechanism of substitution reactions.

Cis-trans Isomerisation in Planar Complexes

Cis-trans isomerisation in Pt(II) complexes are not common, yet they do occur. Unfortunately neither kinetic nor exchange studies have been made to obtain information in the mechanism of isomerisations. However some observations suggest that the isomerisation proceeds by an inter molecular process. The strongest evidence in support of this process is that a trace of some catalyst is required for these isomerisation.

Since substitution reactions of Pt(II) complexes are generally stereospecific (*i.e.,* they proceed with retention of configuration), *cis-trans* isomerisation is explained in terms of two-steps mechanism which is shown below in Fig. 9.42 for the isomerisation of *cis*-$[Pt(PR_3)_2Cl_2]^0$ in solution containing excess of PR_3 to the corresponding *trans*-isomer. In the first step Cl^- group is replace by the catalyst PR_3 to from $[Pt(PR_3)_3Cl]^+$. In the second step, the reverse happens and *trans*-$[Pt(PR_3)_2Cl_2]^0$ is formed along with the catalyst. Steps have been shown as (10) and (11).

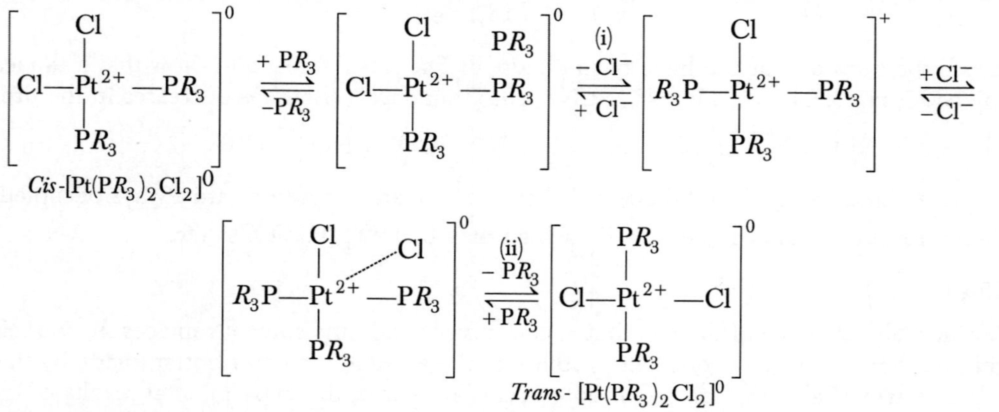

Fig. 9.42 Two-steps mechanism for isomerisation of *cis*-$[Pt[PR_3)_2Cl_2]^0$ to the corresponding *trans*-form.

Exercise 1

(For Part 'B')

1. Stabilization of highest oxidation states of transition metals by strong electronegative ligands is due to
(a) $p\pi(L) \longrightarrow d\pi(M)$ bonding
(b) $d\pi(M) \longrightarrow d\pi(L)$ bonding
(c) $p\pi(M) \longrightarrow d\pi(L)$ bonding
(d) $d\pi(L) \longrightarrow p\pi(M)$ bonding

2. In $TeCl_4$, the central atom tellurium involves
(a) sp^3 hybridisation (b) sp^3-d hybridisation
(c) sp^3d^2 hybridisation (d) sp^3d^3 hybridisation

3. The crystal field splitting energy for octahedral (Δ_o) and tetrahedral (Δ_t) complexes is related as
(a) $\Delta_t \simeq \frac{4}{9}\Delta_o$ (b) $\Delta_t \simeq \frac{1}{2}\Delta_o$
(c) $\Delta_o \simeq 2\Delta_t$ (d) $\Delta_o \simeq \frac{4}{9}\Delta_t$

4. The number of unpaired electrons in d^6, low spin octahedral complex is
(a) 0 (b) 1
(c) 2 (d) 3

5. Each of the compounds Pt $(NH_3)_6$ Cl_4, $Cr(NH_3)_6$ Cl_3, $Co(NH_3)_4Cl_3$ and K_2PtCl_6 has been dissolved in water to make its 0.001M solution. The order of their increasing conductivity in solution is
(a) $K_2PtCl_6 < Pt\,(NH_3)_6Cl_4 < Cr(NH_3)_6Cl_3 < Co\,(NH_3)_4Cl_3$
(b) $Pt(NH_3)_6Cl_4 < Cr(NH_3)_6Cl_3 < K_2PtCl_6 < Co(NH_3)_4Cl_3$
(c) $Cr(NH_3)_6Cl_3 < Co(NH_3)_4Cl_3 < K_2PtCl_6 < Pt(NH_3)_6Cl_4$
(d) $Co(NH_3)_4Cl_3 < K_2PtCl_6 < Cr(NH_3)_6Cl_3 < Pt(NH_3)_6Cl_4$

6. Among the following complexes, optical activity is possible in
(a) $[Co(H_2O)_2(NH_3)_2Cl_2]$ (b) $[Co(NH_3)_3(NO_2)Cl]^+$
(c) $[Co(CN)_5NC]^-$ (d) $[Cr(H_2O)_4Cl_2]^+$

7. Which one of the following acts as a π-acid ligand?
(a) F^- (b) O^{2-}
(c) CO (d) NH_3

8. The number of chloride ions which would be precipitated when the complex $PtCl_4 \cdot 4NH_3$ is treated with $AgNO_3$ solution is
(a) 1 (b) 2
(c) 3 (d) 4

9. Coordination number and oxidation state of Cr in $K_3[Cr(C_2O_4)_3]$ are respectively
(a) 3 and 0 (b) 3 and + 3
(c) 6 and + 3 (d) 4 and + 2

10. The complexes $[Co(NH_3)_5NO_2]Cl_2$ and $[Co(NH_3)_5ONO]Cl_2$ are examples of
(a) linkage isomers (b) ionisation isomers
(c) geometrical isomers (d) coordination isomers

11. Among the following ions which one has the highest paramagnetism?
(a) $[Zn(H_2O)_6]^{2+}$ (b) $[Cu(H_2O)_6]^{2+}$
(c) $[Fe(H_2O)_6]^{2+}$ (d) $[Cr(H_2O)_6]^{3+}$

12. How many isomers of $[Co(NH_3)_4(H_2O)_2]^{3+}$ can exist?
(a) 2 (b) 3 (c) 4 (d) 5

13. The number of ions per mole of the complex $CoCl_3 \cdot 5NH_3$ in aqueous solution will be
(a) 2 (b) 3 (c) 4 (d) 9

14. The number of unpaired electrons in tetrahedral $[Ni(CO)_4]$ complex is
(a) 0 (b) 2 (c) 3 (d) 4

15. In the square ligand field, the 3d-orbital will split into
(a) one level (b) two levels
(c) three levels (d) four levels

16. John-Teller effect is in the field of
(a) nuclear physics (b) vibronic interaction
(c) thermodynamics (d) kinetic theory of gases

17. Zeise salt is
(a) $K^+[PtCl_3(C_2H_4)]^-$
(b) $K_2[PtCl_3—\eta^2—C_3H_6]$
(c) $K^+[PtCl_3—\eta^2—(C_2H_4)]$
(d) $K^+[PtCl_2—\eta^2—(C_2H_4)]Cl^-$

18. Hybridised state of Fe in $[Fe(H_2O)_5NO]\,SO_4$ is
(a) sp^3d (b) sp^3d^2
(c) sp^3d^3 (d) dsp^2

19. $[Co(NH_3)_5Br]\,SO_4$ and $[Co(NH_3)_5SO_4]Br$ are examples of which type of isomerism?
(a) Linkage (b) Ionization
(c) Optical (d) Geometrical

20. Which one of the following is expected to be a paramagnetic complex?
(a) $[Ni(H_2O)_6]^{2+}$ (b) $[Ni(CO)_4]$
(c) $[Co(NH_3)_6]^{2+}$ (d) $[Zn(NH_3)_4]^{2+}$

21. Which complex has square planar structure?
(a) $[Ni(CN)_4]^{2-}$ (b) $[Ni(CO)_4]$
(c) $[NiCl_4]^{2-}$ (d) $[Cu(NH_3)_4]^{2+}$

22. Which of the following isomeric pair shows ionisation isomerism?
(a) $[Cr(H_2O)_6]Cl_3$ and $[Cr(H_2O)_5Cl]Cl_2 \cdot H_2O$
(b) $[Pt(NH_3)_2Cl_2]$ and $[Pt(NH_3)_4]$ $[PtCl_4]$
(c) $[Co(NH_3)_6]$ $[Cr(CN)_6]$ and $[Cr(NH_3)_6][Co(CN)_6]$
(d) $[Co(NH_3)_5Br]$ SO_4 and $[Co(NH_3)_5SO_4]Br$

23. Which of the following is hexadentate ligand?
(a) Acetyl acetonato
(b) 1, 10 phenonthraline
(c) Ethylene diamine
(d) Ethylene diamine tetraacetic acid

24. Which of the following system has maximum number of unpaired electrons?
(a) d^4 (octahedral, low spin)
(b) d^8 (octahedral, high spin)
(c) d^6 (tetrahedral, high spin)
(d) d^9 (octahedral)

25. Using valence bond theory predict which of the following complex does not have tetrahedral geometry?
(a) $[Ni(CO)_4]$ (diamagnetic)
(b) $[Ni(CN)_4]^{2-}$ (diamagnetic)
(c) $[NiCl_4]^{2-}$ (two unpaired electrons)
(d) $MnCl_4^-$ (diamagnetic)

26. The optical isomerism is not shown by the complex
(a) $[Cr(ox)_3]^{3-}$ (b) $[Co(EDTA)]^-$
(c) $[Co(en)(NH_3)_2Cl_2]^+$ (d) *trans*-$[Pt(NH_3)_2Cl_2]$

27. In the spectrochemical series, which ligand produces strong field?
(a) CO (b) H_2O (c) Cl^- (d) NO_2^-

28. Optical isomerism is shown by
(a) $[Ni(CO)_4]$ (b) $[Ni(CN)_4]^{2-}$
(c) $[Pt(NH_3)_4]^{2+}$ (d) $[Co(en)_3]^{3+}$

29. The isomerism shown by $[Cu(NH_3)_4]$ $[PtCl_4]$ and $[Pt(NH_3)_4]$ $[CuCl_4]$ is
(a) valence isomerism (b) ionisation isomerism
(c) coordination isomerism (d) linkage isomerism

30. Of the following, the species which is not blue or green is
(a) $CuSO_4 \cdot 5H_2O$ (b) $Cu(NH_3)_4^{2+}$
(c) $Cu(H_2O)_4^{2+}$ (d) $CuCl_2^{2-}$

31. The *d*-orbitals will split under trigonal bipyramidal ligand field into
(a) one level (b) two levels
(c) three levels (d) four levels

32. The CFSE (crystal field stabilization energy) for a high spin octahedral complex having d^1 configuration is
(a) 0.00 (b) $-0.4\Delta_0$ (c) $-0.6\Delta_0$ (d) $-0.8\Delta_0$

33. Low spin octahedral complexes are maximum distorted in which of the following state?
(a) $t_{2g}^3\, e_g^0$ (b) $t_{2g}^5 e_g$
(c) $t_{2g}^6 e_g^2$ (d) $t_{2g}^6 e_g^4$

34. Jahn-Teller effect is not observed in high spin complexes of
(a) d^4 (b) d^7 (c) d^8 (d) d^9

35. Δ_o in cm^{-1} is given for the following complexes : $[CrCl_6]^{3-}$, $[Cr(NH_3)_6]^{3+}$ $[Cr(CN)_6]^{3-}$ is 13500 cm^{-1}, 21600 cm^{-1}, 28200 cm^{-1} respectively. The number of unpaired electrons in the above complexes
(a) goes on decreasing with decreasing Δ_o
(b) goes on increasing with increasing Δ_o
(c) is the same in all the complexes
(d) cannot be predicted

36. For Mn^{3+} ion, $P = 28000\ cm^{-1}$, Δ_o for $[Mn(H_2O)_6]^{3+}$ and $[Mn(CN)_6]^{3-}$ are 21000 and 38500 cm^{-1} respectively. Then
(a) $[Mn(H_2O)_6]^{3+}$ and $[Mn(CN)_6]^{3-}$ both one low spin complex
(b) $[Mn(H_2O)_6]^{3+}$ is a high spin and $[Mn(CN)_6]^{3-}$ is a low spin complex
(c) $[Mn(H_2O)_6]^{3+}$ is a low spin and $[Mn(CN)_6]^{3-}$ is a high spin complex
(d) $[Mn(H_2O)_6]^{3+}$ and $[Mn(CN)_6]^{3-}$ both are high spin complex

37. The most unstable species among the following is
(a) $Ti(C_2H_5)_4$ (b) $Ti(CH_2Ph)_4$
(c) $Pb(CH_3)_4$ (d) $Pb(C_2H_5)_4$

38. On oxidative addition of O_2 to $Ir(CO)Cl(PPh_3)_2$ the oxidation state and coordination number of Ir changes by
(a) 1 and 3 (b) 2 and 2 (c) 3 and 1 (d) 2 and 3

39. $Ir(CO)Cl(PPh_3)_2$ is a coordination complex with geometry
(a) octahedral (b) tetrahedral
(c) square planar (d) distorted octahedral

40. Number of unpaired electrons present in $[CoCl_4]^{2-}$ is
(a) 1 (b) 2 (c) 0 (d) 3

41. Cu^{2+} complexes forms
(a) octahedral complexes only
(b) distorted octahedral complexes generally
(c) tetrahedral
(d) square planar

42. Which of the following compounds is optically active?
(a) $Pt(NH_3)_2Cl_2$ (b) *Trans*-$Co(en)_2Cl_2$
(c) $Ni(CO)_2(PPh_3)_2$ (d) *Cis*-$Co(en)_2Cl_2$

43. The complexes $[Co(1, 2\text{-diaminopropane})_2\ Cl_2]^+$ and $[Co\ (1, 3\text{-diaminopropane})_2\ Cl_2]^+$ represents an example of
(a) ligand isomerism
(b) linkage isomerism
(c) ionisation isomerism
(d) coordination isomerism

44. In Tanabe-Sugano diagrams the value for various electronic states of the metal ions are plotted against
(a) ligand field strength (b) frequency
(c) energy (d) partion function values

45. Two geometric isomers possible for $[Ru(H_2O)_3Cl_3]$ are
(a) ionisation and linkage
(b) hydrate and coordination
(c) ionisation and hydrate
(d) hydrate and linkage

46. "Any non-linear molecular system in a degenerate electronic state will undergo some kind of distortion which will lower its symmetry, thereby removing degeneracy". This statement is
(a) crystal field effect
(b) Jahn-Teller effect
(c) ligand-field effect
(d) tetrahedral distortion effect

47. For Cu^{2+} ion in $[Cu(H_2O)_4en]^{2+}$, $[Cu(H_2O)_2(en)_2]^{2+}$ and $[Cu(en)_3]^{2+}$ with the stability constant k_1, k_2 and k_3 respectively
(a) k_1 is far less than k_2 and k_3 and order is $k_1 < k_2 < k_3$
(b) $k_1 > k_2 > k_3$
(c) $k_2 < k_1 < k_3$
(d) k_3 is far less than k_2 and order is $k_1 > k_2$

48. In $[NiF_6]^{4-}$, $[FeF_6]^{3-}$, $[TiF_6]^{2-}$ and $[CrF_2]$
(a) all shows Jahn-Teller distortion
(b) $[NiF_6]^{4-}$ and $[TiF_6]^{2-}$ shows Jahn-Teller distortion
(c) only CrF_2 shows Jahn-Teller distortion
(d) None of the above

49. *d-p* mixing occurs in
(a) tetrahedral complexes only
(b) octahedral complexes only
(c) complexes with no centre of symmetry
(d) complexes with centre of symmetry

50. The formula for ethylene diamine tetra acetochromate (III) is
(a) $[Cr(EDTA)]^0$ (b) $[Cr(EDTA)]^-$
(c) $[Cr(EDTA)]^{2-}$ (d) $[Cr(EDTA)]^{3-}$

51. The magentic moment of octahedral Co(II) complex is 4.0 μ_B. The electronic configuration of the complex is
(a) $t_{2g}^3 e_g^4$ (b) $t_{2g}^5 e_g^2$ (c) $t_{2g}^6 e_g^1$ (d) $t_{2g}^4 e_g^3$

52. In $[FeF_6]^{3-}$ and $[CoF_6]^{3-}$
(a) $[FeF_6]^{3-}$ is coloured and $[CoF_6]^{3-}$ is colourless
(b) $[FeF_6]^{3-}$ is coloured and $[CoF_6]^{3-}$ is colourless
(c) $[FeF_6]^{3-}$ and $[CoF_6]^{3-}$ are both colourless
(d) $[FeF_6]^{3-}$ and $[CoF_6]^{3-}$ are both coloured

53. Which of the following compound is optically active?
(a) $Pt(NH_3)_2Cl_2$ (b) $Ni(CO)_2(PPh_3)_2$
(c) *Trans*-$Co(en)_2Cl_2$ (d) *Cis*-$Co(en)_2Cl_2$

54. The metal ion which is most likely to show the low spin-high-spin equilibria in its complexes has the electronic configuration
(a) d^3 (b) d^4 (c) d^6 (d) d^8

55. Among $(CH_3)_3P, NO^+, CN^-, I_3^-$ ligands, the one which is not a π-acceptor ligand is
(a) I_3^- (b) CN^-
(c) NO^+ (d) $(CH_3)_3P$

56. Among the followng complex ions, the one which is EPR active is
(a) $Ni(CO)_4$ (b) $[Co(NH_3)_5Cl]^{2+}$
(c) $[Cu(C_2O_4)_2]^{2-}$ (d) $[Mo(CO)_6]$

57. The complex with spin-only magnetic moment of ~4.9 BM is
(a) $[Fe(H_2O)_6]^{2+}$ (b) $[Fe(CN)_6]^{3-}$
(c) $Fe(CN)_6]^{4-}$ (d) $[Fe(H_2O)_6]^{3+}$

58. A compound which shows Jahn-Teller distortion is
(a) $[Mn(H_2O)_6]^{2+}$ (b) $[Mn(H_2O)_6]^{3+}$
(c) $[Cr(H_2O)_6]^{3+}$ (d) $[Fe(CN)_6]^{4-}$

59. The complexes $V(C_6H_6)_2$ and $Cr(C_6H_6)_2$ are both readily oxidized in air to their respective cations. The number of unpaired electrons, respectively in each are
(a) 0, 0 (b) 1, 0
(c) 0, 1 (d) 1, 1

60. The lowest energy *d–d* transitions in Cr(+3) complexes varies in the order
(a) $CrCl_6^{3-} < Cr(H_2O)_6^{3+} < Cr(en)_3^{3+} < Cr(CN)_6^{3-}$
(b) $CrCl_6^{3-} < Cr(en)_3^{3+} < Cr(H_2O)_6^{3+} < Cr(CN)_6^{3-}$
(c) $Cr(CN)_6^{3-} < CrCl_6^{3-} < Cr(H_2O)_6^{3+} < Cr(en)_3^{3+}$
(d) $Cr(H_2O)_6^{3+} < Cr(en)_3^{3+} < CrCl_6^{3-} < Cr(CN)_6^{3-}$

61. The most acidic aqua ion is
(a) $[Fe(H_2O)_6]^{3+}$ (b) $[Ti(H_2O)_6]^{3+}$
(c) $[Co(H_2O)_6]^{3+}$ (d) $[Cr(H_2O)_6]^{3+}$

62. Among the following, the strongest oxidising anion is
(a) CrO_4^{2-} (b) VO_4^{3-} (c) FeO_4^{2-} (d) MnO_4^{2-}

63. The existence of two different coloured complexes of $Co(NH_3)_4Cl_2$ is due to
(a) optical Isomerism (b) linkage
(c) geometrical isomerism (d) coordination

64. $[CoCl_4]^{2-}$ is
(a) more strongly coloured than $[Co(H_2O)_6]^{2+}$
(b) less strongly coloured than $[Co(H_2O)_6]^{2+}$
(c) (a) is correct and it is due to *d-p* mixing
(d) (b) is correct and it is due to *d-p* mixing

65. $KMnO_4$ is coloured due to
(a) *d–d* transitions
(b) $M \rightarrow L$ transitions or $M \rightarrow L$ charge transfer
(c) $L \rightarrow M$ transitions or $L \rightarrow M$ charge transfer
(d) None of the above

66. CrO_4^{2-} is
(a) colourless due to absence of *d–d* transitions
(b) coloured due to $M \rightarrow L$ charge transfer
(c) coloured due to $L \rightarrow M$ charge transfer
(d) None of the above

67. CrO_3 is bright orange in colour due to
(a) *d-d* transitions (b) CT transitions
(c) Both (a) and (b) (d) None of these

68. The zero magnetic moment of octahedral K_2NiF_6 is due to
(a) low spin d^6 Ni (IV) complex
(b) low spin d^8 Ni (II) complex
(c) high spin d^8 Ni (+2) complex
(d) high spin d^6 Ni (+4) complex

69. The absorption of $[Co(NH_3)_6]^{2+}$ is
(a) stronger than that of $[Co(NH_3)_5Cl]^{2+}$
(b) stronger than that of $[MnCl_4]^{2-}$
(c) weaker than that of $[MnCl_4]^{2-}$ but stronger than that of $[Co(NH_3)_5Cl]^{2+}$
(d) weaker than those of both $[MnCl_4]^{2-}$ and $[Co(NH_3)_5Cl]^{2+}$

70. The isomerism possible in Co(III) complexes $[Co(NH_3)_3(NO_2)_3]$ and $[Co(NH_3)_5NO_2]Cl_2$ are
(a) coordination and position
(b) geometric and linkage
(c) optical and linkage
(d) optical and optical

71. In tetrahedral geometry which one of the following sets of electronic configuration will have orbital contribution to the magnetic moment?
(a) d^3, d^4, d^8 and d^9 (b) d^3, d^4, d^7 and d^9
(c) d^1, d^6, d^7 and d^9 (d) d^1, d^3, d^4 and d^9

72. The complexes $[Co(NH_3)_4(H_2O)Cl]Br_2$ and $[Co(NH_3)_4Br_2]Cl \cdot H_2O$ are examples of
(a) ionisation isomerism (b) geometric isomerism
(c) linkage isomerism (d) optical isomerism

73. In the trigonal bipyramidal crystal field, the *d*-orbital with the highest energy is
(a) d_{xy} (b) d_{yz}
(c) $d_{x^2-y^2}$ (d) d_{z^2}

74. Magnetic moment of complex $K_3[CoF_6]$ is $5.0\mu_B$. The total stabilization energy will be
(a) $-0.4\Delta_o$ (b) $-0.4\Delta_o + P$
(c) $-2.4\Delta_o + 3P$ (d) $-1.8\Delta_o + 3P$

75. For the metal olefin complex (i) $[PtCl_3(C_2H_4)]^-$ and (ii) $[PtCl_3(C_2F_4)]^-$ the correct statement is
(a) C—C bond length is same in both (i) and (ii)
(b) C—C bond length in (i) is smaller than (ii)
(c) C—C bond length in (i) is larger compared to that of (ii)
(d) a metallocycle is formed in each complex

76. The experimental magnetic moment of $K_3[Fe(CN)_6]$ is $2.3\,\mu_B$ and is attributable to the
(a) spin only value of a low spin Fe
(b) spin only value of high spin Fe
(c) low-spin Fe with orbital contribution
(d) high spin Fe with orbital contribution

77. The set of ions expected to show Jahn-Teller distortion in their complexes is
(a) Ti(+3), Cu(+2), high spin Fe(+3)
(b) Cu(+I), Ni(+2), high spin Fe(+3)
(c) Cu(+2), low spin Fe(+3), Ti(+3)
(d) low spin Fe(+3), Mn(+2), Cu(+1)

78. The series with correct order of increasing Δ_o in their complexes is
(a) $I^{\ominus} < PR_3 < \overset{\ominus}{C}H_3 < CO$ (b) $PR_3 < \overset{\ominus}{C}H_3 < I^{\ominus} < CO$
(c) $\overset{\ominus}{C}H_3 < PR_3 < I^{\ominus} < CO$ (d) $I^{\ominus} < \overset{\ominus}{C}H_3 < PR_3 < CO$

79. Coordinated water molecules of Cd(II) complex can be successively replaced by $Br^{\ominus}$ finally to result in $[CdBr_4]^{2-}$. In this process the fourth equilibrium constant is observed and be higher than one because
(a) equilibrium constant for the last step is always the highest
(b) three molecules of H_2O are released during the 4th step
(c) the aquo-Cd(II) species is octahedral
(d) the anion $Br^{\ominus}$ replaces a neutral H_2O molecule from the coordination sphere

80. The correct order of rate of exchange of water molecules between the coordination sphere and bulk is

(a) $Cr^{3+} < Al^{3+} < Cr^{2+} < Ni^{2+}$
(b) $Cr^{3+} < Al^{3+} < Ni^{2+} < Cr^{2+}$
(c) $Cr^{3+} < Ni^{2+} < Cr^{2+} < Al^{3+}$
(d) $Cr^{3+} < Cr^{2+} < Al^{3+} < Ni^{2+}$

81. For an octahedral complex, which of the following *d*-electron configurations will give maximum crystal-field stabilization energy?
(a) High-spin d^6 (b) Low spin d^4
(c) Low- spin d^5 (d) High-spin d^7

82. Which one of the following does not obey EAN rule?
(a) $Fe(CO)_5$ (b) $V(CO)_6$
(c) $K_4[Fe(CN)_6]$ (d) $Mn_2(CO)_{10}$

83. Which one among the following exhibits optical isomerism?
(a) *Cis*-$[Co(NH_3)_4Cl_2]Cl$
(b) *Trans*-$[Co(NH_3)_4(Cl_2)]Cl$
(c) *Cis*-$[Co(en)_2Cl_2]Cl$
(d) *Trans*-$[Co(en)_2Cl_2]Cl$

84. Which one of the following is the spin-only magnetic moment of $K_3[Fe(CN)_6]$?
(a) 1.73 BM (b) 2.83 BM
(c) 4.90 BM (d) 5.92 BM

85. What is the IUPAC name of $[Co(NH_3)_3(NO_2)Cl(CN)]$ compound?
(a) Chloro cyano nitro triammine cobalt (III)
(b) Triammine chloro cyano nitro cobalt (III)
(c) Cyano chloro nitro triammine cobalt (III)
(d) Nitro chloro cyano triammine cobalt (III)

86. Among the following complex ions, the species containing Fe^{3+} in strongest ligand field is
(a) $[Fe(CN)_6]^{3-}$ (b) $[Fe(H_2O)_6]^{3+}$
(c) $[Fe(F)_6]^{3-}$ (d) $[Fe(CN)_6]^{3+}$

87. Which one of the following high-spin complexes has the largest CFSE (crystal field stabilization energy)?
(a) $[Mn(H_2O)_6]^{2+}$ (b) $[Cr(H_2O)_6]^{2+}$
(c) $[Mn(H_2O)_6]^{3+}$ (d) $[Cr(H_2O)_6]^{3+}$

88. Which one of the follownig is correct representation of tetraammine copper (II) hexacyanoferrate (III)?
(a) $[Cu(NH_3)_4][Fe(CN)_6]$
(b) $[Cu(NH_3)_4]_3[Fe(CN)_6]$
(c) $[Cu(NH_3)_4][Fe(CN)_6]_2$
(d) $[Cu(NH_3)_4]_3[Fe(CN)_6]_2$

89. The complex compound used in the chemotheraphy of cancer is
(a) *cis*-$[Pt^{IV}(NH_3)_4Cl_2]Cl_2$ (b) *cis*-$[Pt^{IV}(NH_3)_2Cl_4]$
(c) *cis*-$[Pt^{II}(NH_3)_4Cl_2]$ (d) *trans*-$[Pt^{II}(NH_3)_4Cl_2]$

90. An example of a hexadetntate ligand is
(a) 2, 2′-bipyridine
(b) ethylenediamineteracetate ion
(c) dimethlylyoxime
(d) iminodiacetate ion

91. Haemoglobin, a complex containing iron, is a constitutent of blood. The oxidation state of iron in the complex is
(a) zero (b) +1
(c) + 2 (d) + 3

92. The self-indicating silica gel (impregnated with cobalt chloride) turns pink on absorbing moisture and becomes blue on heating. The pink and blue colour are respectively due to
(a) $[Co(H_2O)_6]^{2+}$ and $[CoCl_4]^{2-}$
(b) $[Co(H_2O)_6]^{2+}$ and Co_2O_3
(c) $[Co(H_2O)_6]^{2+}$ and $[Co(H_2O)_6]^{3+}$
(d) Co^{2+} and Co^{3+}

Exercise 2

(For Part ‘C’)

1. The asymmetric nature of visible absorption bond of $[Ti(H_2O)_6]^{3+}$ is due to
(a) Laporte’s allowed transition
(b) Laporte’s forbidden transition
(c) Dynamic Jahn-Teller
(d) Intensity stealing transition

2. For the reaction

$$[Fe(CN)_6]^{4-} + [Mo(CN)_8]^{3-} \longrightarrow [Fe(CN)_6]^{3-} + [(Mo(CN)_8]^{4-}$$

the electron transfer takes place by
(a) inner sphere reaction
(b) outer sphere reaction
(c) induced electron transfer reaction
(d) None of the above

3. Which of the following ions has zero crystal field stabilization energy in octahedral field?
(a) Fe^{3+} (low spin) (b) Fe^{3+} (high spin)
(c) Cr^{3+} (high spin) (d) Co^{2+} (low spin)

4. The water soluble complex among the following is
(a) $[Ni(CO)_4]$ (b) $[Ni(HDMG)_2]$
(c) $[Ni(HDMG)_2Cl_2]$ (d) $[Co(NH_3)_3Cl_3]$

5. Amongst $[Ni(CO)_4]$, $[Ni(CN)_4]^{2-}$ and $[NiCl_4]^{2-}$
   (a) $[Ni(CO)_4]$ and $[NiCl_4]^{2-}$ are diamagnetic and $[Ni(CN)_4]^{2-}$ is paramagnetic
   (b) $[Ni(CO)_4]$ and $[Ni(CN)_4]^{2-}$ are diamagnetic and $[NiCl_4]^{2-}$ is paramagnetic
   (c) $[NiCl_4]^{2-}$ and $[Ni(CN)_4]^{2-}$ are diamagnetic and $[Ni(CO)_4]$ is paramagnetic
   (d) $[Ni(CO)_4]$ is diamagnetic and $[NiCl_4]^{2-}$ and $[Ni(CN)_4]^{2-}$ are paramagnetic

6. Which of the complexes is expected to have lowest Δ_o value?
   (a) $[CoF_6]^{3-}$ (b) $[Co(NH_3)_6]^{3+}$
   (c) $[Ir(NH_3)_6]^{3+}$ (d) $[Rh(NH_3)_6]^{3+}$

7. The total number of geometrical and optical isomers for the complex ion dichlorobsis (ethylene diamine) rhodium (III) is
   (a) 2 (b) 3 (c) 4 (d) 6

8. The purple colour of $KMnO_4$ is due to the transition
   (a) CT ($L \rightarrow M$) (b) CT ($M \rightarrow L$)
   (c) $p - d$ (d) $d - d$

9. Jahn-Teller effect affects the geometry of
   (a) $[Cu(NH_3)_4]^{2+}$ (b) $[MnCl_4]^{2-}$
   (c) $[Ni(NH_3)_6]^{2+}$ (d) None of these

10. Arrange the following metal complexes in order of increasing hydration energy
   (P) $[Mn(H_2O)_6]^{2+}$ (Q) $[V(H_2O)_6]^{2+}$
   (R) $[Ni(H_2O)_6[^{2+}$ (S) $[Ti(H_2O)_6]^{2+}$
   (a) P > S > Q > R (b) P < S < Q < R
   (c) P > R > S > Q (d) P < R < S < Q

11. The reaction of $[PtCl_4]^{2-}$ with NH_3 gives rise to
   (a) $[Pt\,Cl_4(NH_3)_2]^{2-}$ (b) *trans*-$[Pt\,Cl_2(NH_3)_2]$
   (c) $[Pt\,Cl_2(NH_3)_4]$ (d) *cis*-$[Pt\,Cl_2(NH_3)_2]$

12. The molecular orbital configuration of Re–Re bond in $[Re_2Cl_8]^{2-}$ is
   (a) $\sigma^2\pi^4\delta'\delta^{*1}$ (b) $\sigma^2\pi^2\delta^2\delta^{*2}$
   (c) $\sigma^2\pi^2\delta^2\pi^{*2}$ (d) $\sigma^2\pi^4\delta^2$

13. The square planar complex $[IrCl(PPh_3)_3]$ undergoes oxidative addition of Cl_2 to give two products which are
   (a) *fac*-and *mer*-isomer (b) *cis* and *trans*-isomer
   (c) enantiomer (d) linkage isomers

14. Reduction of $[CoCl(NH_3)_5]^{2+}$ by $[Cr(H_2O)_6]^{2+}$ is *via*
   (a) inner sphere mechanism
   (b) quater sphere mechanism
   (c) Both (a) and (b)
   (d) None of the above

15. Of Cu(II), Gc(II), Co(II), Ni(+3), Mn(+3) ions which shows Jahn-Teller distortion are
   (a) Only Cu(+2) and Cr(+2)
   (b) Only Cr(+2), Cu(+2), Co(+2)
   (c) Ni(+3) and Mn(+3)
   (d) All of the above

16. Consider the reaction
   I. $[Cr(H_2O)_6]^{2+} + [CoCl(NH_3)_5]^{2+} \longrightarrow [Co(NH_3)_5H_2O]^{2+} + [CrCl(H_2O)_5]^{2+}$
   II. $[Fe(CN)_6]^{4-} + [Mo(CN)_8]^{3-} \longrightarrow [Fe(CN)_6]^{3-} + [Mo(CN)_8]^{4-}$

   Which one of the following is correct statement?
   (a) Both involve inner sphere mechanism
   (b) Both involve outer sphere mechanism
   (c) Reaction I follows inner sphere mechanism and reaction II follows outer sphere mechanism
   (d) Reaction I follows outer sphere and reaction II follows inner sphere mechanism

17. Which one of the following complex ions shows minimum intensity of absorption in UV-visible region?
   (a) $[Cr(H_2O)_6]^{2+}$ (b) $[Mn(H_2O)_6]^{2+}$
   (c) $[V(H_2O)_6]^{2+}$ (d) $[Co(H_2O)_6]^{2+}$

18. CFSE will be highest for
   (a) CoF_6^{3-} (b) $[Mn(H_2O)_6]^{2+}$
   (c) $[Co(CNS)_4]^{2-}$ (d) $[Co(NH_3)_6]^{3+}$

19. The complex which exhibits lowest energy electronic absorption band is
   (a) $[NiCl_4]^{2-}$ (b) $[Ni(H_2O)_6]^{2+}$
   (c) $[Ni(CN)_4]^{2-}$ (d) $Ni(CO)_4$

20. Electron transfer from $[Fe(H_2O)_6]^{2+}$ to $[Fe(H_2O)_6]^{3+}$ is likely to occur *via*
   (a) *d-d* transition
   (b) inner sphere electron transfer
   (c) S_N1 mechanism
   (d) outer sphere electron transfer

21. Which of the following metal fragments d^n-ML_m is isolobal with CH?
   (a) $d^7 - ML_5$ (b) $d^9 - ML_3$
   (c) $d^8 - ML_4$ (d) $d^5 - ML_6$

22. The chromium (III) species formed soon after the electron transfer between $IrCl_6^{2-}$ and $[Cr(H_2O)_6]^{2+}$ is
   (a) $[Cr(H_2O)_6]^{3+}$ (b) $[Cr(H_2O)_5Cl]^{2+}$
   (c) $[CrCl_6]^{3-}$ (d) $Cr(H_2O)_3Cl_3$

23. Purple colour of iodine vapour is due to
(a) *d-d* transition (b) π-$\overset{*}{\sigma}$ transition
(c) *C-T* trasition (d) $\overset{*}{\pi}$ -$\overset{*}{\sigma}$ transition

24. $[FeF_6]^{3-}$ and $[FeBr_6]^{3-}$
(a) $[FeF_6]^{3-}$ is dark in colour than $[FeBr_6]^{3-}$
(b) $[FeF_6]^{3-}$ is yellow in colour and $[FeBr_6]^{3-}$ is colourless
(c) $[FeF_6]^{3-}$ is colourless and $[FeBr_6]^{3-}$ is brown
(d) Both are of some colour

25. $[NiX_4]^{2-}$, $[CoX_4]^{2-}$ and $[MnX_4]^{2-}$ where X is a halogen is
(a) coloured
(b) coloured due to $L \rightarrow MCT$
(c) colourless
(d) coloured due to $M \rightarrow LCT$

26. Lability of ions of Cr^{2+}, Mn^{2+} and V^{2+} should follow the order
(a) $Cr^{2+} > Mn^{2+} > V^{2+}$ (b) $Mn^{2+} > Cr^{2+} > V^{2+}$
(c) $Mn^{2+} > V^{2+} > Cr^{2+}$ (d) $V^{2+} > Cr^{2+} > Mn^{2+}$

27. The most suitable route to prepare the *trans*-isomer of $[PtCl_2(NH_3)PPh_3]$ is
(a) $[PtCl_4]^{2-}$ with PPh_3 followed by reaction with NH_3
(b) $[PtCl_4]^{2-}$ with NH_3 followed by reaction with PPh_3
(c) $[Pt(NH_3)_4]^{2+}$ with HCl followed by reaction with PPh_3
(d) $[Pt(NH_3)_4]^{2+}$ with PPh_3 followed by reaction with HCl

28. The number of absorption bands observed $[FeF_6]^{3-}$ and $[CoF_6]^{3-}$ respectively are
(a) 1 and 3 (b) 0 and 1 (c) 0 and 3 (d) 3 and 1

29. The rate of exchange of cyanide ligands in the complexes (i) $[Ni(CN)_4]^{2-}$, (ii) $Mn(CN)_6]^{3-}$ and (iii) $Cr(CN)_6]^{3-}$ by ^{14}CN follows the order
(a) ii > i > iii (b) iii > i > ii (c) i > iii > ii (d) i > ii > iii

30. The correct order of the soft character of central metal ion is
(a) $[CrO_4]^{2-} < [CrCl_4]^{-} < [Cr(bipy)_3] < [Cr(CO)_5]^{2-}$
(b) $[CrCl_4^-] < [Cr(bipy)_3] < [CrO_4]^{2-} < [Cr(CO)_5]^{2-}$
(c) $[CrO_4]^{2-} < [Cr(bipy)_3] < [Cr(CO)_5]^{2-} < [CrCl_4]^{\ominus}$
(d) $[CrCl_4]^{\ominus} < [CrO_4]^{2-} < [Cr(CO)_5]^{2\ominus} < [Cr(bipy)_3]$

31. $[Ru(2, 2' \text{ bipyridyl})_3]^{2+}$ when it absorbs at 452 nm is very good oxidising agent as well as reducing agent due to the formation of
(a) $[Ru^+ (2, 2' \text{ bipyridyl})_3]^+$
(b) $Ru^+ (2, 2' \text{ bipyridyl})_2 (2, 2' \text{ bipyridyl}^+)]^{2+}$
(c) $[Ru^{3+} (2, 2' \text{ bipyridyl})_3]^{3+}$
(d) $Ru^{3+} (2, 2' \text{ bipyridyl})_2 (2, 2' \text{ bipyridyl})]^{2+}$

32. Match the following Column I (compounds) with Column II (oxidation states of Co) and select the correct answer.

Column I		Column II	
A.	$[Co(NCS)(NH_3)_5](SO_3)$	1.	−1
B.	$Na[Co(CO)_4]$	2.	0
C.	$Na_4[Co(S_2O_3)_3]$	3.	+1
D.	$Co_2(CO)_8$	4.	+2
		5.	+3

	A	B	C	D
(a)	4	3	2	5
(b)	5	1	4	2
(c)	4	1	2	5
(d)	5	3	4	2

33. Arrange the following in order of decreasing number of unpaired electrons. (atomic number of Fe = 26)
I. $[Fe(H_2O)_6]SO_4H_2O$ II. $K_3[Fe(CN)_6]$
III. $K_4[Fe(CN)_6]$ IV. $[Fe(H_2O)_6]Cl_3$
Select the correct answer using the codes given below
Codes
(a) II III IV I
(b) I IV II III
(c) IV I III II
(d) IV I II III

34. Match Column I with Column II and select the correct answer.

Column I (Complexes)		Column II (CFSE values)	
A.	$Co(NH_3)_6^{3+}$	1.	$-20\Delta_q + 2P$
B.	$Cr(NH_3)_6^{3+}$	2.	$-12\Delta_q$
C.	FeF_6^{3-}	3.	$-24\Delta_q = 3P$
D.	$Fe(CN)_6^{3-}$	4.	$-4\Delta_q$
		5.	0

Codes

	A	B	C	D
(a)	3	2	4	5
(b)	2	3	1	4
(c)	4	5	2	3
(d)	3	2	5	1

35. Match Column I (Coordination compounds) with Column II (Types of isomerism) and select the correct answer.

Column I		Column II	
A.	$[Co(NH_3)_4Cl_2]^+$	1.	Optical isomerism
B.	*cis*-$[Co(end)_2Cl_2]^+$	2.	Ionization isomerism
C.	$[Co(end)_2(NO_2)Cl]SCN$	3.	Coordination isomerism
D.	$[Co(NH_3)_6][Cr(CN)_6]$	4.	Geometrical isomerism

Codes

	A	B	C	D
(a)	4	3	2	1
(b)	1	4	3	2
(c)	4	1	2	3
(d)	4	2	3	1

36. The reactions between $[Fe(CN)_6]^{3-}$ and $[Cr(NH_3)_5H_2O]^{2+}$ following an inner sphere mechanism. The possible intermediate is

(a) $[Cr(NH_3)_5OH—Fe(CN)_5]^0$

(b) $[Cr(NH_3)_5NC—Fe(CN)_5]^-$

(c) $[Cr(NH_3)_4(OH_2)NC—Fe(CN)_5]$

(d) $[Cr[NH_3]_5CN—Fe(CN)_5]^-$

37. While Ti^{3+}, V^{3+}, Fe^{3+} and Co^{2+} afford a large number of tetrahedral complexes, Cr^{3+} system plays the reason being

(a) Cr^{3+} forces high crystal field splitting with a varities of ligands

(b) Crystal field stabilization energy in octahedral *visa-vis* tetrahedral Cr^{3+}system plays the deciding role

(c) The ionic radius of Cr^{3+} is the largest among the other M^{3+} ionic mentioned

(d) Electronegativity of Cr^{3+} is the largest among these bivalent 3*d* metals and so chromium prefers to be associated with as many ligands as its ionic radius permit

38. Considred the following isomerisms

I. ionisation II. hydrate

III. coordinates IV. geometrical

V. optical

Which of the above isomerisms are exhibited by $[Cr(NH_3)_2(OH)_2Cl_2]^+$?

(a) I and V (b) II and III

(c) III and IV (d) IV and V

Directions (Q. Nos. 39 to 41)

Three different compounds (*A*, *B* and *C*) are known to have the empirical formula $CrCl_3 \cdot 6H_2O$ (*X*). When exposed to a dehydrating agent. *A* loses 2 moles of water per mole of the compound (*X*) *B* loses 1 mole of water and compounds *C* loses no water.

39. Thus, *A*, *B* and *C* are

	A	*B*
(a)	$[Cr(H_2O)_4Cl_2]Cl \cdot 2H_2O$	$[Cr(H_2O_5)Cl]Cl_2H_2O$ *C*. $[Cr(H_2O)_6]Cl_3$
(b)	$[Cr(H_2O)_2Cl_3] \cdot 4H_2O$	$[Cr(H_2O)Cl_3] \cdot 5H_2O$ *C*. $[CrCl_3] \cdot 6H_2O$
(c)	$[Cr(H_2O)_3Cl_3] \cdot 3H_2O$	$[Cr(H_2O)_4Cl_2] \cdot 2H_2O$ *C*. $[Cr(H_2O)_6]Cl_3$
(d)	$[Cr(H_2O)_6]Cl_3$	$[Cr(H_2O)_5Cl]Cl_2 \cdot H_2O$ *C*. $[Cr(H_2O)_4Cl_2]Cl \cdot 2H_2O$

40. Which is most conducting in aqueous solution?

(a) *A* (b) *B*

(c) *C* (d) Equal

41. One mole each of *A*, *B* and *C* is treated with excess of $AgNO_3$. There is formation of white precipitate of AgCl.

Moles of white precipitates are

	A	B	C
(a)	1	2	3
(b)	3	2	1
(c)	1	3	2
(d)	3	1	2

Directions (Q. No. 42 to 44)

The octahedral complex ions $[FeCl_6]^{3-}$ and $[Fe(CN)_6]^{3-}$ are both paramagnetic but the former is high spin and the latter is low spin.

42. High spin complex $[FeCl_6]^{3-}$ has the *d*-configuration as

(a) $t_{2g}^3 e_g^2$ (b) t_{2g}^5

(c) $t_{2g}^2 e_g^3$ (d) e_g^5

43. Low spin complex $[Fe(CN)_6]^{3-}$ has the *d*-configuration as

(a) $t_{2g}^3 e_g^2$ (b) t_{2g}^5 (c) $t_{2g}^2 e_g^3$ (d) e_g^5

44. CFSE for the complexes are

	$[FeCl_6]^{3-}$	$[Fe(CN)_6]^{3-}$
(a)	0	0
(b)	$-2\Delta_o$	0
(c)	0	$-2\Delta_o$
(d)	$-2\Delta_o$	$-2\Delta_o$

Directions (Q. Nos. 45 and 46)

The Alsatian-Swiss chemist Alfred Werner pioneered the field of coordination chemistry in the late ninteenth century. At that time, a number of compounds of cobalt (III) chloride with ammonia were known,with general formulae

$$CoCl_3 \cdot xNH_3 \qquad x = 3 \text{ to } 6$$

Treatment of these compounds with aqueous HCl acid did not remove the ammonia. However, treatment of the compounds with excess of $AgNO_3$ at 273 K gave white precipitate of AgCl in varying ratio depending on the structure. Also each complex had electrical conductivity of varying nature.

45. Which complex has the maximum electrical conductivity?

(a) $CoCl_3 \cdot 3NH_3$ (b) $CoCl_3 \cdot 4NH_3$

(c) $CoCl_3 \cdot 5NH_3$ (d) $CoCl_3 \cdot 6NH_3$

46. One mole of the compound gave three moles of white precipitate of AgCl, on reaction with aqueous $AgNO_3$. Thus, complex is

(a) $CoCl_3 \cdot 4NH_3$ (b) $CoCl_3 \cdot 5NH_3$

(c) $CoCl_3 \cdot 6NH_3$ (d) All of these

Directions (Q. Nos. 47 to 49)
Consider following reactions :

I. $[Co(NH_3)_6]^{2+}(aq) + 6H_3O^+(aq) \rightleftharpoons [Co(H_2O)_6]^{3+}(aq) + 6NH_4^+(aq)$

The products are favoured in the above reaction

II. $[Co(NH_3)_6]^{2+}(aq) + 6H_3O^+(aq) \rightleftharpoons [Co(H_2O)_6]^{2+}(aq) + 6NH_4^+(aq)$

This, reaction (II) takes place with H_2O in a matter of seconds.

47. Select the correct statement.
(a) $[Co(NH_3)_6]^{3+}$ is thermodynamically and kinetically stable relative to $[Co(H_2O)_6]^{3+}$
(b) $[Co(NH_3)_6]^{3+}$ is thermodynamically unstable but kinetically stable relative to $[Co(H_2O)_6]^{3+}$
(c) $[Co(NH_3)_6]^{3+}$ is thermodynamically and kinetically unstable relative to $[Co(H_2O)_6]^{3+}$
(d) $[Co(NH_3)_6]^{3+}$ is thermodynamically stable but kinetically unstable relative to $[Co(H_2O)_6]^{3+}$

48. Which is true in terms of $\Delta G°$?
(a) $\Delta G°_{\text{I}}$ is more negative than that of II
(b) $\Delta G°_{\text{I}}$ is less negative than that of II
(c) $\Delta G°_{\text{I}} = \Delta G°_{\text{II}} < 0$
(d) $\Delta G°_{\text{I}} = \Delta G°_{\text{II}} > 0$

49. Which is thermodynamically unstable and also kinetically labile?
(a) $Co(H_2O)_6]^{3+}$
(b) $[Co(H_2O)_6]^{2+}$
(c) $[Co(NH_3)_6]^{3+}$
(d) $[Co(NH_3)_6]^{2+}$

Directions (Q. Nos. 50 and 51)
The octahedral complex ion $[FeCl_6]^{3-}$ and $[Fe(CN)_6]^{3-}$ are both paramagnetic.

50. Select the correct statements.
(a) $[FeCl_6]^{3-}$ and $[Fe(CN)_6]^{3-}$ both are high-spin complex
(b) $[FeCl_6]^{3-}$ is high-spin and $[Fe(CN)_6]^{3-}$ is low-spin complex
(c) $[FeCl_6]^{3-}$ is low-spin $[Fe(CN)_6]^{3-}$ is high-spin complex
(d) $[FeCl_6]^{3-}$ and $[Fe(CN)_6]^{3-}$ both are low-spin complexes

51. Select the correct statement. The CFSE for
(a) $[FeCl_6]^{3-}$ is zero
(b) $[Fe(CN)_6]^{3-}$ is $-2\Delta_o$
(c) Both (a) and (b)
(d) None of the above is correct

Directions (Q. Nos. 52 to 54)
"A student in 1895 prepared three coordination compounds containing chromium with the following properties"

	Formula	Colour	Cl^- ions in solution per formula units
(A)	$CrCl_3 \cdot 6H_2O$	Violet	3
(B)	$CrCl_3 \cdot 6H_2O$	Light green	2
(C)	$CrCl_3 \cdot 6H_2O$	Dark green	1

52. IUPAC name of the complex A is
(a) hexaaquotrichlorochromium (III)
(b) hexaaquochromium (III) chloride
(c) pentaaquochlorochromium (III) chloride
(d) tetraaquodichlorochromium (III) chloride

53. Complex A, B, C are represented as
(a) $A: [Cr(H_2O)_6]Cl_3$
$B: [Cr(H_2O)_5Cl]Cl_2 \cdot H_2O$
$C: [Cr(H_2O)_4Cl_2]Cl \cdot 2H_2O$
(b) $A: [Cr(H_2O)_3Cl_3] \cdot 3H_2O$
$B: [Cr(H_2O)_4Cl_2]Cl \cdot 2H_2O$
$C: [Cr(H_2O)_5Cl]Cl_2 \cdot H_2O$
(c) $A: [Cr(H_2O)_6]Cl_3$
$B: [Cr(H_2O)_6]Cl_3$
$C: [Cr(H_2O)_6]Cl_3$
(d) None of the above

54. Conducting nature of these complexes in the increasing order is
(a) $A < B < C$
(b) $C < A < B$
(c) $B < A < C$
(d) $C < B < A$

Directions (Q. Nos. 55 and 56)
A rose coloured compound has the empirical formula $CoCl_4 \cdot 5NH_3 \cdot H_2O$. Two moles of this compound react with concentrated sulphuric acid to form HCl (g) and one mole of a new compound with empirical formula $Co_2(SO_4)_3 \cdot 10NH_3 \cdot 5H_2O$. When this new compound is dried at room temperature,it loses three moles of water per mol of $Co_2(SO_4)_3 \cdot 10NH_3 \cdot 5H_2O$.

55. What is the formula of the rose-coloured compound?
(a) $[Co(NH_3)_5Cl]Cl_2 \cdot H_2O$
(b) $[Co(NH_3)_5H_2O]Cl_2$
(c) $[Co(NH_3)_3(H_2O) \cdot Cl_2]Cl$
(d) None of the above

56. What is the structure of the new complex formed?
(a) $[Co—(NH_3)_5—Co—(NH_3)_5](SO_4)_3 \cdot 5H_2O$
(b) $[Co—(NH_3)_5—Co—(NH_3)_5(SO_4)](SO_4)_2 \cdot 5H_2O$
(c) $\left[(NH_3)_6Co\begin{smallmatrix}SO_4\\SO_4\end{smallmatrix}Co(NH_3)_4\right]SO_4 \cdot 5H_2O$
(d) None of the above

Directions (Q. Nos. 57 to 59)

A, *B* and *C* are three complexes of chromium (III) with the empricial formula $H_{12}O_6Cl_3Cr$. All the three complexes have water and chloride ions as ligands. Complex *A* does not react with concentrated H_2SO_4, whereas complexes *B* and *C* lose 6.75% and 13.5% of their original weight respectively, on treatment with concentrated H_2SO_4.

57. Complex *A* is
(a) $[Cr(H_2O)_6]Cl_3$
(b) $[Cr(H_2O)_5Cl]Cl_2 \cdot H_2O$
(c) $[Cr(H_2O)_4Cl_2]Cl \cdot 2H_2O$
(d) None of the above

58. Loss in weight on treatment with concentrated H_2SO_4 is due to
(a) Cl^- is lost as HCl
(b) Cr^{3+} is lost as $Cr_2(SO_4)_3$
(c) H_2O is lost due to absorption
(d) Cl^- is lost as Cl_2

59. Select the correct statement(s).
(a) Conductance in these complexes is in order $C < B < A$
(b) EAN and nuclear spin of chromium are identical in each complex
(c) Non-reactivty of *A* with conc. H_2SO_4 is due to absence of water molecules outside coordinated sphere
(d) All of the above are correct

Directions (Q. Nos. 60 and 61)

(*A*) When $Fe(CN)_2$ solution is treated with KCN solution, species formed, no longer, gives tests of Fe^{2+} and CN^-.
(*B*) When K_2SO_4 solution is treated with $Al_2(SO_4)_3$ solution, species formed gives tests of K^+, Al^{3+} and SO_4^{2-}.

60. Species formed in experiment *A* does not give test of Fe^{2+} and CN^-. It is due to formation of
(a) $K_2[Fe(CN)_4]$ (b) $K_3[Fe(CN)_5]$
(c) $K_3[Fe(CN)_6]$ (d) $K_4[Fe(CN)_6]$

61. When the species formed in (*A*) is treatd with $FeCl_3$, a blue colour is obtained. It is due to the formation of
(a) $Fe^{II}[Fe^{III}(CN)_6]^-$ (b) $Fe^{III}[Fe^{II}(CN)_6]^-$
(c) Both (a) and (b) (d) None of these

Directions (Q. Nos. 62 and 63)

Consider the following isomers of $[Cr(NH_3)_2Cl_4]^-$ and answer the questions

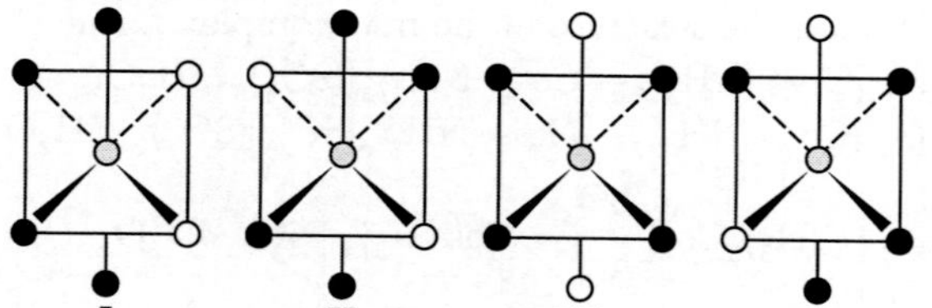

I II III IV

Cr = ○ NH_3 = ○ Cl = ●

62. Out of these isomers
(a) I and IV are *trans* and II and III are *cis*
(b) I and IV are *cis* and II and III are *trans*
(c) I and II are *cis* and III and IV are *trans*
(d) I and II are *trans* and III and IV are *cis*

63. Select the correct statement.
(a) Pair of I and IV are same and pari of II and III are also same
(b) All have chiral centres
(c) I and III are enantiomers
(d) II and IV are enantiomers

Directions (Q. Nos. 64 and 65)

A compound $Co(en)_2(NO_2)_2Cl$ has been prepared in a number of isomeric forms. One form undergoes no reaction with $AgNO_3$ or (en) and is optically inactive. A second form reacts with $AgNO_3$ but not with (en) and is optically inactive. A third form is optically active and reacts with both $AgNO_3$ and (en), complexes are :

I. 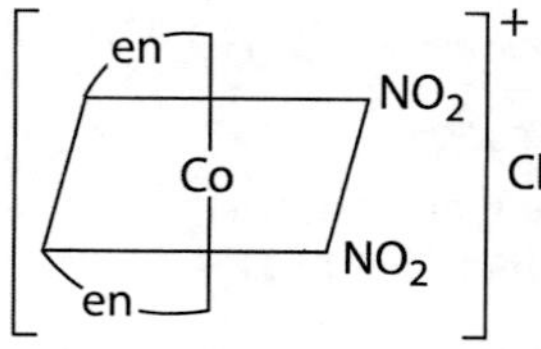

Cis-bis (ethylenediamine) dinitrocobalt (III) chloride

II. 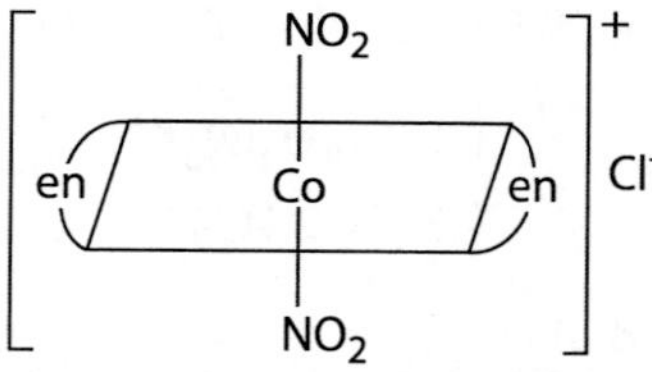

Trans-bis (ethylenendiamine) dinitrocobalt (III) chloride

III. 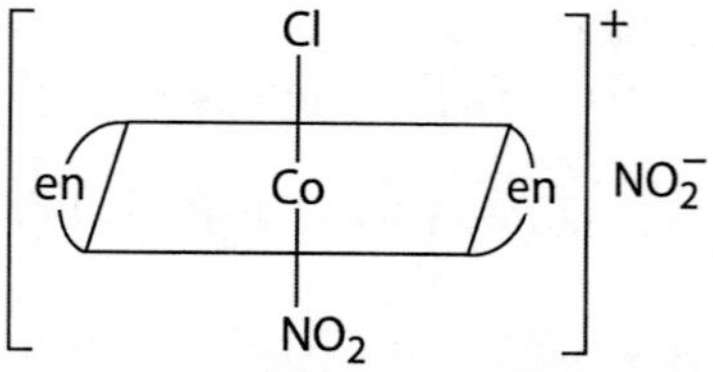

Trans-chloronitrobis (ethylenediamine) cobalt (III) nitrite

64. First form of the complex is
(a) I (b) II
(c) III (d) None of these

65. One of the complex turns KI-starch paper blue in acidic medium. This complex is
(a) III (b) II
(c) I (d) All of these

Answers

Exercise 1

1. (a)	**2.** (b)	**3.** (a)	**4.** (a)	**5.** (d)	**6.** (a)	**7.** (c)	**8.** (b)	**9.** (c)	**10.** (a)
11. (c)	**12.** (c)	**13.** (b)	**14.** (a)	**15.** (d)	**16.** (b)	**17.** (c)	**18.** (b)	**19.** (b)	**20.** (a)
21. (a)	**22.** (d)	**23.** (d)	**24.** (c)	**25.** (b)	**26.** (d)	**27.** (a)	**28.** (d)	**29.** (c)	**30.** (d)
31. (c)	**32.** (b)	**33.** (c)	**34.** (c)	**35.** (c)	**36.** (b)	**37.** (a)	**38.** (b)	**39.** (c)	**40.** (d)
41. (b)	**42.** (d)	**43.** (c)	**44.** (d)	**45.** (c)	**46.** (b)	**47.** (d)	**48.** (c)	**49.** (c)	**50.** (b)
51. (b)	**52.** (b)	**53.** (c)	**54.** (a)	**55.** (b)	**56.** (b)	**57.** (c)	**58.** (d)	**59.** (b)	**60.** (c)
61. (b)	**62.** (a)	**63.** (d)	**64.** (c)	**65.** (c)	**66.** (c)	**67.** (b)	**68.** (c)	**69.** (c)	**70.** (a)
71. (b)	**72.** (a)	**73.** (d)	**74.** (b)	**75.** (a)	**76.** (c)	**77.** (c)	**78.** (a)	**79.** (b)	**80.** (c)
81. (c)	**82.** (b)	**83.** (c)	**84.** (a)	**85.** (b)	**86.** (a)	**87.** (d)	**88.** (d)	**89.** (c)	**90.** (b)
91. (c)	**92.** (a)								

Exercise 2

1. (b)	**2.** (b)	**3.** (b)	**4.** (c)	**5.** (b)	**6.** (a)	**7.** (b)	**8.** (a)	**9.** (a)	**10.** (b)
11. (d)	**12.** (d)	**13.** (a)	**14.** (a)	**15.** (d)	**16.** (c)	**17.** (b)	**18.** (d)	**19.** (c)	**20.** (c)
21. (c)	**22.** (d)	**23.** (d)	**24.** (c)	**25.** (b)	**26.** (d)	**27.** (a)	**28.** (a)	**29.** (d)	**30.** (a)
31. (d)	**32.** (b)	**33.** (d)	**34.** (d)	**35.** (c)	**36.** (b)	**37.** (b)	**38.** (d)	**39.** (a)	**40.** (c)
41. (a)	**42.** (a)	**43.** (b)	**44.** (c)	**45.** (d)	**46.** (c)	**47.** (b)	**48.** (b)	**49.** (d)	**50.** (b)
51. (c)	**52.** (b)	**53.** (a)	**54.** (d)	**55.** (b)	**56.** (d)	**57.** (a)	**58.** (c)	**59.** (d)	**60.** (d)
61. (c)	**62.** (b)	**63.** (a)	**64.** (c)	**65.** (a)					

Hints & Solutions

Exercise 1

3. In an octahedral complex there is a ligand along each axis while in tetrahedral complex, no ligand lies directly along any axis, therefore, Δ_t is less than $\left(\Delta_t = \frac{4}{9}\Delta_o\right)$.

4. Configuration of d^6 (low spin) octahedral field is $t_{2g}^6 e_g^0$, *eg*,

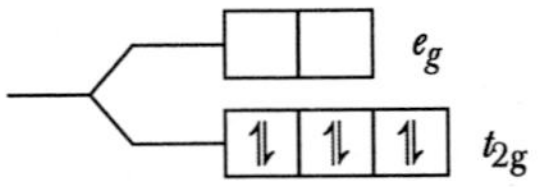

The number of unpaired electron is zero (0).

5. The conductivity of solution increases as the number of ions increases. Number of free ions in $[Co(NH_3)_4Cl_2]Cl$, $K_2[PtCl_6]$, $[Cr(NH_3)_6]Cl_3$ and $[Pt(NH_3)_6]Cl_4$ is 2, 3, 4 and 5 respectively. Therefore, increasing conductivity order is $2 < 3 < 4 < 5$.

6. Optical isomers of $[Co(NH_3)_2(H_2O)_2Cl_2]$ are :

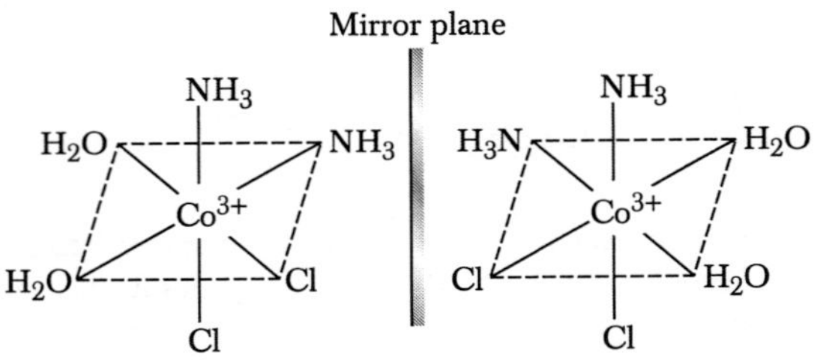

11. The compound or complex with maximum number of unpaired electrons will have highest paramagnetism.

14. $Ni = 3d^8 4s^2$

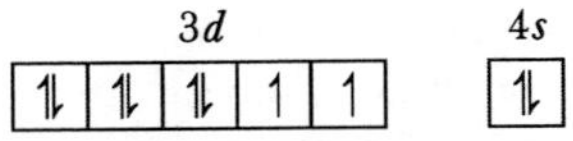

According to valence bond theory, under the influence of strong ligand field the pairing of electrons takes place.

Ni under the influence of CO ligand =

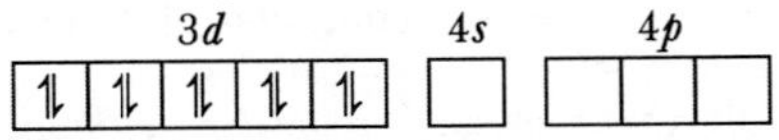

Thus, $[Ni(CO)_4]$ complex having no unpaired electron has tetrahedral structure with sp^3-hydridisation.

15. In a square field (D_4 symmetry), the five fold degenerate 3*d* level splits into four levels as follows; two fold degenerate state and non-degenerate states.

16. The Jahn-Teller effect is the separation of the degenerate electronic states in a given symmetry so as to remove degeneracy. (hanging the symmetry changes the vibrations of the molecules and consequently separates degenerate electronic states.)

20. $Ni^{2+} = 3d^8$, octahedral complexes of Ni^{2+} is outer orbital complex with sp^3d^2-hybridisation and two unpaired electrons.

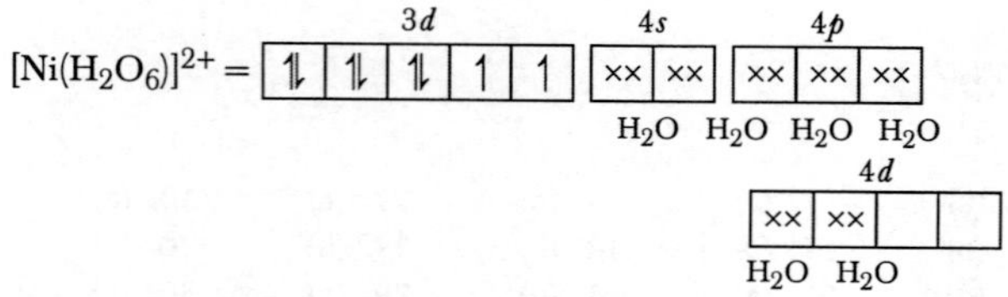

24. Distribution of *d*-electrons in weak field or high spin complex in tetrahedral field for d^6 ion is $t_{2g}^3e_g^3$, thus there are four unpaired electrons.

d^9 (octahedral) = $t_{2g}^6e_g^3$, No. of unpaired electron is one.

d^4 (octahedral, low spin) = $t_{2g}^4e_g^0$, No. of unpaired electrons is two.

d^7 (octahedral, high spin) = $t_{2g}^5e_g^2$, No. of unpaired electrons is three.

25. $[Ni(CN)_4]^{2-}$ has square planar geometry explained on the basis of dsp^2-hybridisation.

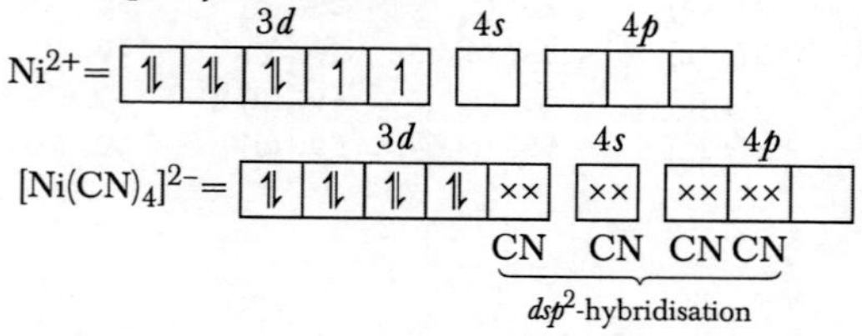

30. $CuCl_2^{2-}$ is yellow though solutions of it appear green because of the presence of blue $[Cu(H_2O)_6]^{2+}$ complexes, upon further dilution, the solution turns blue as H_2O replaces the Cl^- ions in the complexes.

31. In a trigonal bipyramidal field (D_{3h} symmetry) the five *d*-orbitals will split into three levels.

32. CFSE = $[0.4p + 0.6q]\,\Delta_o = [-4p + 6q]\,D_q$

where, p = electrons in e_g orbitals.

q = electrons in t_{2g} orbitals.

For d^1 (high spin) configuration $t_{2g}^1e_g^0$.

$$\text{CFSE} = [-0.4 \times 1 + 0.6 \times 0]\,\Delta_o = [-0.4 + 0]\,\Delta_o$$
$$= -0.4\Delta_o \text{ (or } 4D_q)$$

Note Configuration of d^1 in high spin or low spin is same.

33. Whenever e_g orbitals are unsymmetrical, *i.e.*, contain 1, 2 or 3 electrons in low spin complex, strong distortion occurs leading to tetragonal or square planar complexes. Since, the distortion of the e_g orbitals of the central metals ion correspond with the directions of the ligands disposed octahedrally around the metal ion. The octahedral arrangement of the ligands is likely to be more severely distorted by the dissymmetry of the e_g orbitals than that of the t_{2g} orbitals.

34. The configuration of d^8 ion of the high spin complex is $t_{2g}^6e_g^2$ which is a symmetrical arrangement therefore, Jahn-Teller effect is not observed in it.

36. For the complex ion $[Mn(H_2O)_6]^{3+}$, since $P > \Delta_o$ this is a high spin complex and its configuration is $t_{2g}^3e_g^1$ (Mn^{2+} ion is a d^4 system).

For the complex ion $[Mn(CN)_6]^{3-}$, since $P < \Delta_o$ the complex is low spin and its configuration is $t_{2g}^4e_g^0$.

37. $Ti(C_2H_5)_4$ is kinetically most unstable due to possibility of β-elimintion of hydride.

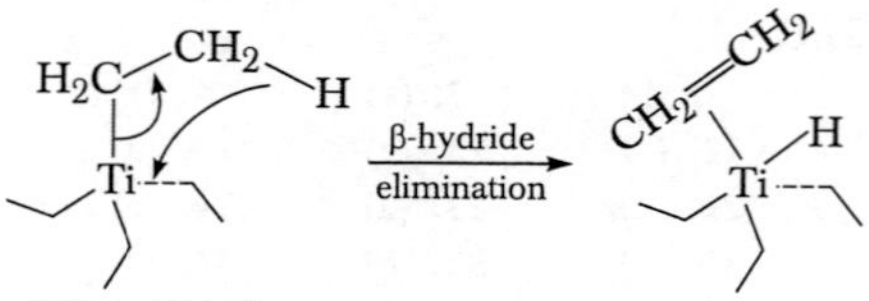

VE on Ti is 8

The reaction is simply the transfer of hydride (hydrogen atom) from the β-position on a ligand to the metal centre.

Hence, metal complexes containing ethyl ligands are kinetically less stable.

$Ti(CH_2Ph)_4$ is kinetically stable because it has no β-hydrogen.

$Pb(CH_3)_4$ and $Pb(C_2H_5)_4$ are thermally stable as Pb–C bond is relatively stable and *d*-orbitals are not available.

Metals with 18VE are more stable (VE-Valence Electrons)

18VE > 17VE > 16VE

38. During oxidative addition (not simple addition) of O_2 the oxidation state is changed from +1 to +3. The compound formed is $Ir(CO)ClO_2(PPh_3)_2$. It is octahedral (little bit distorted) and hence C.N. = 6. (contains 18 VE)

Dioxygen added is in peroxide from (O_2^{2-}) and not in superoxide form (O_2^-).

Both oxidation state and coordination no. is changed by 2.

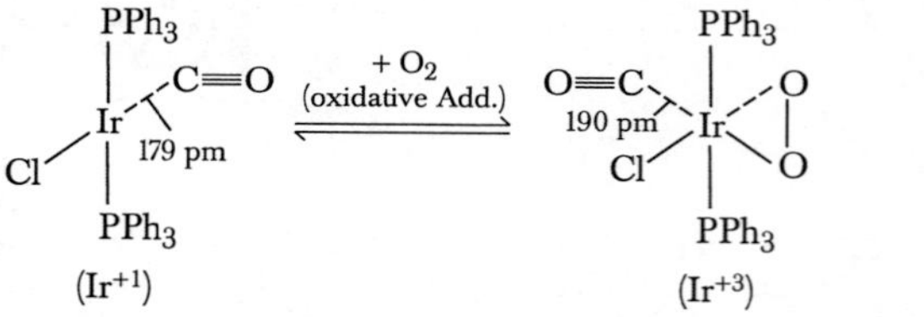

39. $Ir(CO)Cl(PPh_3)_2$ is a square planar complex which is often referred to as Vaska's compound. The oxidation state of Ir is +1. Coordination number is 4. It contains 16 VE.

47. Due to Jahn-Teller distortion of two en rings in $[Cu(en)_3]^{2+}$, it is highly unstable.

48. In $[NiF_6]^{4-}$ and $[FeF_6]^{3-}$ symmetric filling of electrons are there in t_{2g} and e_g orbitals while in $[TiF_6]^{2-}$ t_{2g} and e_g are vacant. For distortion asymmetric filling is necessary condition. Thus, only CrF_2 shows Jahn-Teller distortion.

52. Co_{27}–$4s^2$, $3d^7$

Fe_{26}–$4s^2$, $3d^6$

Fe^{3+}–$4s^0$, $3d^5$

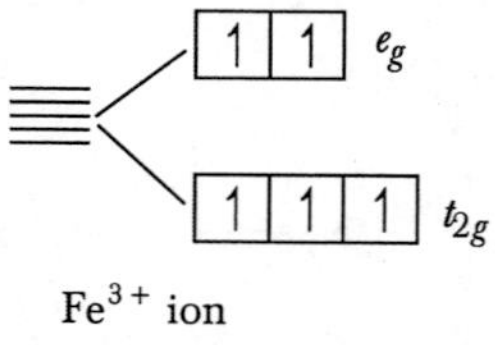

Fe^{3+} ion
spin forbidden
Laporte forbidden
so colourless

Co^{3+}–$4s^0$, $3d^6$

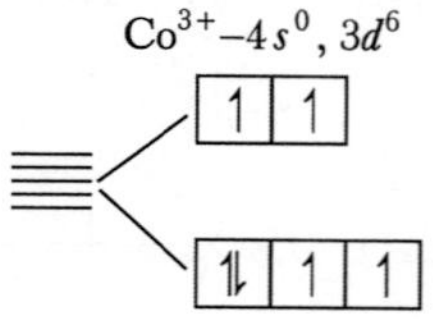

Laporte forbidden
but spin allowed
so more intense
absorption than
$[FeF_6]^{3-}$.

73. In trigonal bipyramidal crystal field *d*-orbitals splits as

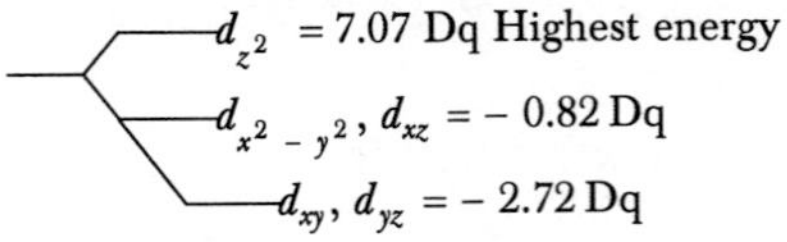

74. $K_3[CoF_6]$ $\quad$ $Co = (3d^7 4s^2)$

$Co^{3+} = 3d^6 4s^0$

$\mu = 5$

$\mu = \sqrt{n\,(n+2)}$

$25 = n\,(n+2)$

$25 = n^2 + 2n$

$n^2 + 2n - 25 = 0$

$$n = -\frac{2 \pm \sqrt{4 - 4 \times (-25)}}{2}$$

$$= \frac{-2 \pm \sqrt{124}}{2} = \frac{-2+11}{2} = 4.5 \sim 4$$

∴ 4 unpaired electron.

It means high spin complex.

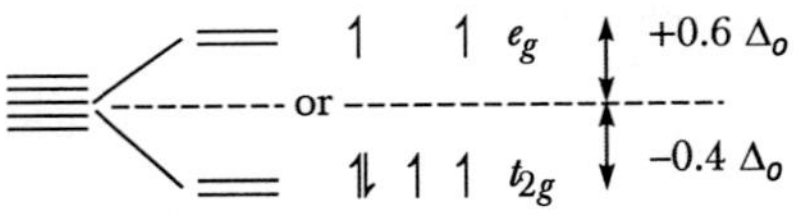

Total stabilisation energy.

$= (-0.4\Delta_o) \times 4 + (0.6\Delta_o) \times 2 + 1 \times P$

$= -1.6\Delta_o + 1.2\Delta_o + P$

$= -0.4\Delta_o + P.$

81. For an octahedral complex; five *d*-orbitals split into three t_{2g} and e_g orbitals. t_{2g} orbitals are more stable (lower in energy) than e_g orbitals : less stable (higher in energy).

Change in energy for $t_{2g}^x e_g^y$ configuration $= [-0.4x + 0.6y]\,\Delta_o$

(i) High-spin d^6

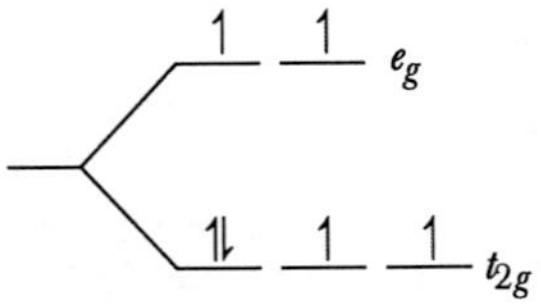

$[-0.4 \times 4 + 0.6 \times 2]\Delta_o$

$= -0.4\Delta_o$

(ii) Low-spin d^4

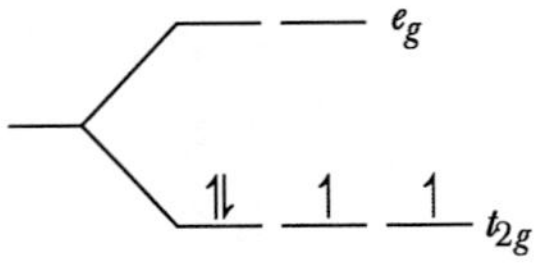

$[-0.4 \times 4]\Delta_o$

$= -1.6\Delta_o$

(iii) Low-spin d^5

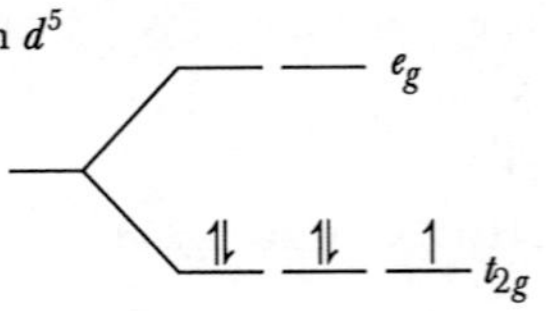

$[-0.4 \times 5]\Delta_o$

$= -2.0\Delta_o$

(iv) High-spin d^7

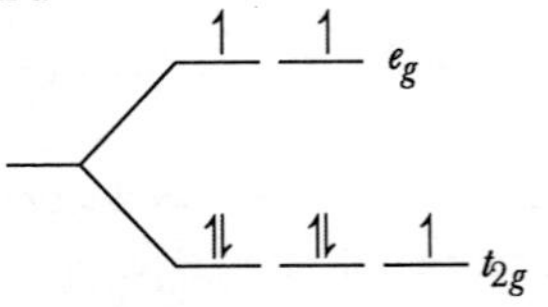

$[-0.4 \times 5 + 0.6 \times 2]$

$= -0.8\Delta_o.$

82. $V(CO)_6$ does not obey EAN rule. V(At. no. = 23) has 23 + 6 × 2 = 35 electrons. Each CO molecule contributes two electrons.

83. *Cis*-$[Co(NH_3)_4Cl_2]Cl$ and *trans*-$[Co(NH_3)_4Cl_2]Cl$ is optically inactive due to the presence of symmetry. *cis*-$[Co(en)_2Cl_2]Cl$ is optically active while *trans*-$[Co(en)_2Cl_2]$ is optically inactive because *cis*-isomer does not have any plane or centre of symmetry while *trans*-isomer has a plane of symmetry.

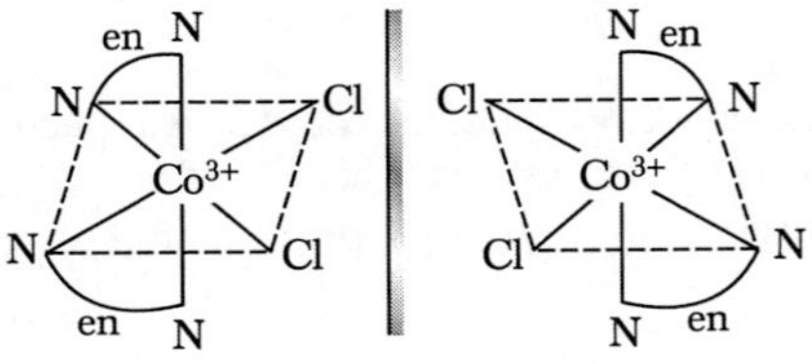

Cis-d-isomer $\quad$ *Cis-l*-isomer

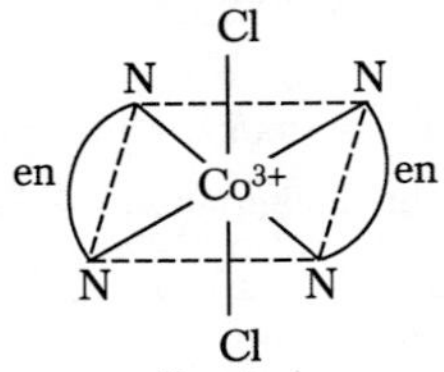

Trans-isomer

84. Spin-only magnetic moment $\mu = \sqrt{n(n+2)}$ BM where *n* is number of unpaired electrons in the central metal ion.

$K_3[Fe(CN)_6]$ or $[Fe(CN)_6]^{3-}$ oxidation state of Fe in $[Fe(CN)_6]^{3-}$ is $x - 6 = -3$; $x = +3$. (CN^- is strong field ligand.)

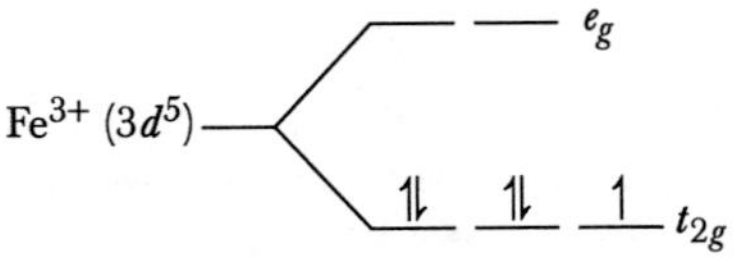

$(n = 1)$

$\mu = \sqrt{1\,(1+2)} = \sqrt{3} = 1.73$ BM

86. According to spectrochemical series CN^- is a stronger field ligand than NH_3, H_2O and F.

$CN > NH_3 > H_2O > F^-$

87. Change in energy (in terms of Δ_q) for $t_{2g}^p e_g^p$ configuration $= [-4p + 6q]\,\Delta_q$

(i) $[Mn(H_2O)_6]^{2+}$

Mn^{2+} (d^6), H_2O is a weak ligand.

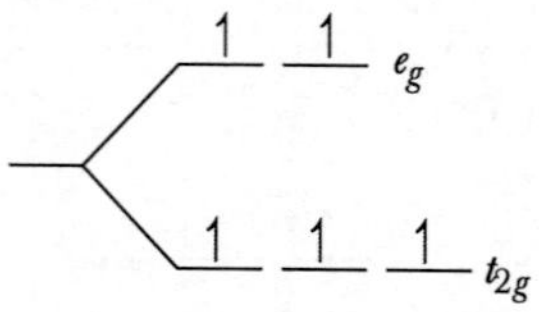

$$CFSE = -4 \times 3 + 6 \times 2 = 0\Delta_q$$

(ii) $[Cr(H_2O)_6]^{2+}$ and (iii) $[Mn(H_2O)_6]^{3+}$

Cr^{2+} and Mn^{3+} (d^4)

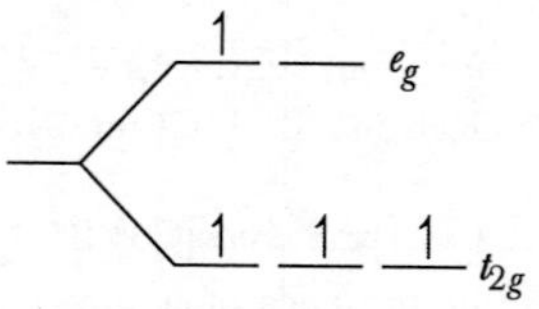

$$CFSE = -4 \times 3 + 6 \times 1 = -6\Delta_q$$

(iv) $[Cr(H_2O)_6]^{3+}$

Cr^{3+} (d^3)

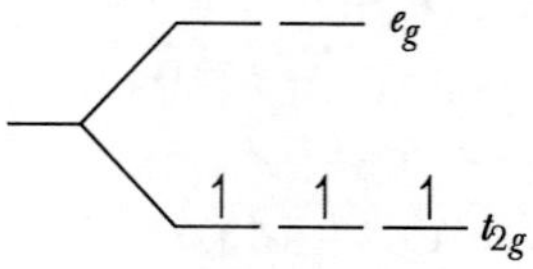

$$CFSE = -4 \times 3 = -12\Delta_q.$$

88. $[Cu(NH_3)_4]^{2+}$ $[Fe(CN)_6]^{3-}$.

89. *Cis*-$[Pt(NH_3)_4Cl_2]$ is called *cis*-platin and is used in the chemotherapy of cancer.

90. Ethylenediaminetetraacetate ion is hexadentate ligand.

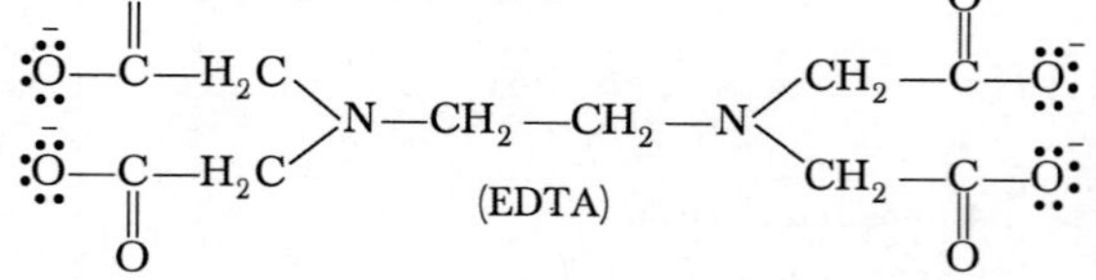

(EDTA)

91. It is Fe^{2+} porphyrin complex.

Exercise 2

2. In outer sphere reactions, the coordination sphere of the ions undergoing redox reaction is not altered

$$[Fe(CN)_6]^{4-} + [Mo(CN)_6]^{3-} \longrightarrow [Fe(CN)_6]^{3-} + [Mo(CN)_8]^{4-}$$

3. Cr^{3+} is d^3-system, in low or high spin state, its configuration is $t_{2g}^3 e_g^0$.

Co^{2+} is d^7-system. Its low spin configuration is $t_{2g}^6 e_g^1$ while high spin configuration will be $t_{2g}^5 e_g^2$.

Fe^{3+} and Fe^{2+} are d^5 and d^6 system respectively. There configurations are :

$d^5 = t_{2g}^5 e_g^0$ (low spin); $t_{2g}^3 e_g^2$ (high spin)

$d^6 = t_{2g}^6 e_g^0$ (low spin); $t_{2g}^4 e_g^2$ (high spin)

CFSE for Fe^{3+} (high spin) is CFSE for d^{p+q} ion

$$p = 3, q = 2$$

$$\therefore \quad CFSE = [-0.4p + 0.6q]\,\Delta_o = [-0.4 \times 3 + 0.6 \times 2] = 0$$

6. The magnitude of Δ_o varies from stronger to weaker ligands. According to spectrochemical series, F^- is a weaker while NH_3 is a stronger ligand. Stronger ligand gives a larger value of Δ_o.

7. Isomers of dichloro *bis* (ehtylenediamine) rhodium (II) $[Rh(en)_2Cl_2]^+$.

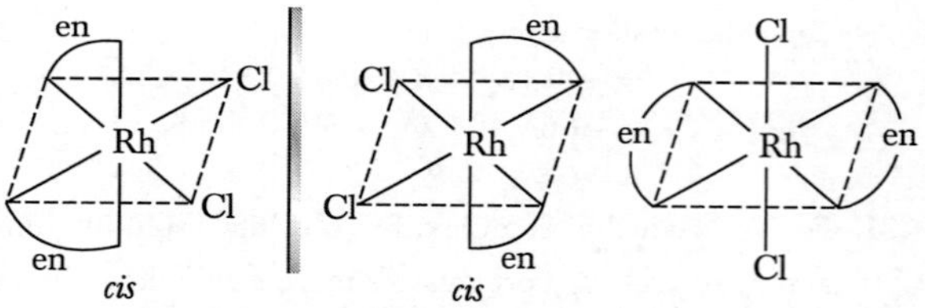

cis *cis*

9. In $[Cu(NH_3)_4]^{2+}$, the Cu^{2+} (d^9) ion has the configuration $t_{2g}^6 e_g^3$ in both the fields. So, two possible arrangement of electrons in t_{2g} and e_g orbitals are :

(i) $t_{2g}^6\,(d_{z^2})^2\,(d_{x^2-y^2})^1$

(ii) $t_{2g}^6\,(d_{z^2})^1\,(d_{x^2-y^2})^2$

Since, in both the configuration t_{2g} orbitals are completely filled, symmetry (distortion) is caused by incompletely filling of e_g orbitals.

10. Hydration energy is mainly proportional to CFSE

Ion	Configuration	CFSE
Mn^{2+}	$t_{2g}^3\,e_g^2$	$-0.0\,\Delta_o$
V^{2+}	$t_{2g}^3\,e_g^0$	$-1.2\,\Delta_o$
Ni^{2+}	$t_{2g}^6\,e_g^2$	$-1.2\,\Delta_o$
Ti^{2+}	$t_{2g}^2\,e_g^0$	$-0.8\,\Delta_o$

Increasing order of hydration energy is

$$P < S < Q < R.$$

11. *Trans* effect of Cl^- is greater than that of NH_3, the *cis*-isomer is obtained.

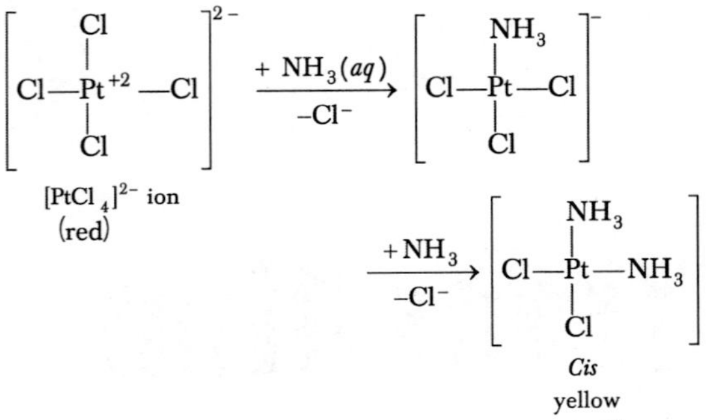

13. 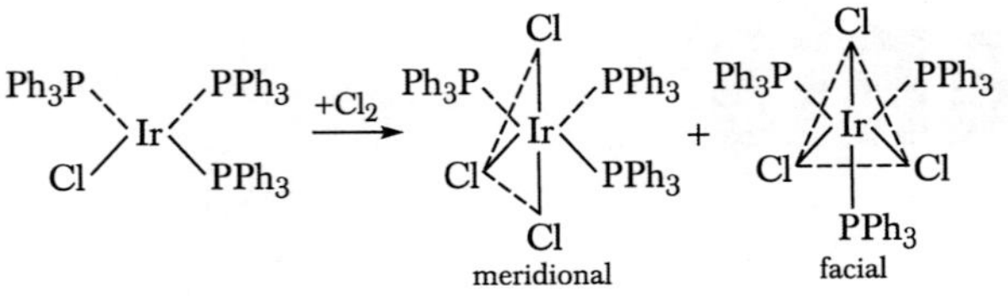

15. Asymmetric filling of e_g orbitals (that points directly towards the ligand) causes some ligands to be repelled more than others so distortion of regular octahedral shape occur.

d^4 (high spin-weak ligands)

[↑][↑][↑] [↑][ ] Mn^{3+}, Cr^{2+}

d^7 (low spin-strong ligand)

[↑↓][↑↓][↑↓] [↑][ ] Co^{2+}, Ni^{3+}

d^9 (both high and low spin)

[↑↓][↑↓][↑↓] [↑↓][↑] Cu^{2+}

17. $[Mn(H_2O)_6]^{2+}$ is practically colourless, since spin selection rule ($\Delta S = 0$) is not obeyed.

24. Replacement of F^- ions with Cl^- gives yellow solution, replacement of Br^- gives brown solution because of easier transfer of electrons from ligand to metal as we move from F^- to I^-.

26. Lability of cation is maximum for lowest atomic number.

29. It depends upon the crystal field activation energy (CAFE) CAFE should be negative or zero for labile.

10

Inner Transition Elements

The elements in which the additional electron enters in $(n-2)$ f-orbitals are called **inner transition elements.** The valence shell electronic configuration of these elements can be represented as $(n-2)f^{0,2...14}.(n-1)d^{0,1,2}.ns^2$. These are also called f-**block elements** because the extra electron goes to f-orbitals which belong to $(n-2)$ shell. f-block elements have been classifed as $4f$ and $5f$ block elements corresponding to the filling of $4f$ and $5f$-orbitals of $(n-2)$ shell.

The complete and valence shell electronic configurations of $4f$ and $5f$-block elements can be represented as (n represents the outermost shell).

Block elements	Complete configuration	Valence-shell configuration
$4f$-block elements or lanthanoids or first inner transition series.	2, 8, 18, $4s^2\,p^6\,d^{10}\,f^{0,2...14}$, $5s^2\,p^6d^{0,1}$, $6s^2$	$4f^{0,2...14}$, $5d^{0,1}$, $6s^2$ ($n=6$)
$5f$-block elements or actinides or actinones or second inner transition series	2, 8, 18, 32, $5s^2p^6d^{10}$ $f^{0,2...14}$, $6s^2\,p^6d^{0,1,2}$, $7s^2$	$5f^{0,2...14}6d^{0,1,2}$, $7s^2$ ($n=7$)

Lathanides (or) Rare Earths

$4f$-block elements are also called **lanthanides, lanthanones** or **rare earths.** The first two names are given because of their strong resemblance to lanthanum. The name rare earth was given to them because they were originally extracted from oxides for which ancient name is earth and which were considered to be rare. The term rare earths is avoided now because many of these elements are no longer rare but are abundant. Thus, strictly according to this definition of lanthanides only thirteen elements from Ce_{58} $(4f^2\,5d^0\,6s^2)$ to Yb_{70} $(4f^{14}\,5d^0\,7s^2)$ should be the members of lanthanide series. However, all the fifteen elements from La_{57} $(5d^1 6s^2)$ to Lu_{71} $(4f^{14}\,5d^1 6s^2)$ are considered as the members of lanthanide series, because all the fifteen elements have

Syllabus

- Introduction, Lanthanides and Actinides, General Characteristics, Spectral and Magnetic Properties, Redox Chemistry, Applications similar physical and chemical properties. In fact the name lanthanides has been derived from lanthanum which is the prototype of lanthanides.

Position of Lanthanides in the Periodic Table

All the fifteen lanthanides have atomic weights between those of barium (atomic number, $Z = 56$) and hafnium ($Z = 72$) and, therefore, must be placed between these two elements as was also proved by Moseley.

Barium has exactly the same outer electronic configuration as calcium and strontium and resembles them very closely. In a similar way hafnium is similar to zirconium ($Z = 40$). Therefore, Ba, must be placed below Sr (Group IIA) and Hf below Zr (Group IVB), thus leaving only one place between them, which lies exactly below Y ($Z = 39$, Group IIIB).

Since all the fifteen lanthanides resemble one another in many respects, these must be placed in the same group. These elements also resemble Y_{39} because of the following additional similarities : (a) Owing to lanthanide contraction (to be discussed subsequently), the ionic radius of Y^{3-} ion is almost similar to that of Er^{3+} ($Y^{3+} = 0.93$ Å, ${}^{r}Er^{3+} = 0.96$ Å). (b) 'Y' generally occurs in nature associated with the ores of heavier lanthanides and resembles Tb(III) and Dy(III) in its compounds. It, therefore, became necessary to accommodate all the fifteen lanthanides together at one place. This has been done by placing the first element *viz.* La_{57} below Y_{39} and remaining fourteen elements (*viz.* Ce_{58} to Lu_{71}) have been placed separately in the lower part of the Periodic Table.

Occurrence of Lanthanides

The lanthanides are not so scare in the earth's crust as the name rare earths implies. Potentially their sources are unlimited. Each lanthanide mineral contains all lanthanides, although some in traces only, excepting Pm which is an unstable radioactive element.

Classification of Rare-Earth Minerals

The rare earth minerals, like the earths themselves, fall into two distinct classes.

1. Cerium group minerals

These are also called cerite earth minerals or simply cerium earths and are rich in cerite-earths. This group of minerals contains largely elements of atomic numbers from 57 to 63 (*i.e.*, La_{57}—Eu_{63}), the light lanthanide elements. These are thus light rare earths.

Table 10.1 **Important Minerals of Lanthanides**

S. No.	Minerals	Composition
		1. Cerium group minerals.
(i)	Monazite Sand–Mixture of orthophosphates of Ce-earths, (Ce) PO_4	50-70% Ce-earths (*i.e.*, elements of atomic number 57 to 62 calculated as oxides)
		1-4% Y-earths (*i.e.*, elements of atomic number 63 to 71 calculated as oxides)
		5-10% TbO_2
		1-2% SiO_2
		22-30% P_2O_5
		Traces of U
(ii)	Bastaesite-cerium earth fluoro carbonate, (Ce) FCO_3	65-70% Ce-earths < 1% Y-earths
(iii)	Cerite–A hydrated silicate of the composition,	Traces of Thorium
	$(Ce)_3\ M^{II}\ H_3Si_3\ O_{11}$ (M = Ca, Fe)	51-72% Ce-earths
		7.6% Y-earths
		Traces of Tb, U, Zr
		2. Yttrium group minerals
(i)	Gadolinite or Ytterbite : A ytterium earth, iron and beryllium silicate,	35-48% Y-earths
		(Calculated as oxides)
	$(Fe, Be)_3\ (Y_2)_{Si_2}\ O_{10}$	2-17% Ce-earths
		Up to 11.6% BeO
		Traces of ThO_2

S. No.	Minerals	Composition
(ii)	Xenotime–An orthophosphate of Y-earth (analogous to monozite), (Y) PO_4	54-65% Y-earths
		~ 0.1% Ce-earths
		Up to 3% ThO_2, upto 3.5% U_3O_8 2-3% ZrO_2
(iii)	Euxenite–Mixture of titanates, niobates and tantalates of Y-earths,	13-35% Y-earths (Calculated as oxides)
	(Y) (Nb, Ta) $TiO_6 \cdot xH_2O$	2-8% Ce-earths (Calculated as oxides)
		20-23% TiO_2, 25-35% $(Nb, Ta)_2O_5$

2. Yttrium group minerals

These are also called yttrium earth minerals or simply *yttrium earths* and are rich in gadolinite earths. This group contains largely yttrium and lanthanides of atomic numbers from 64 to 71 (Gd_{64}—Lu_{71}), the heavier lanthanides. These are thus heavy rare-earths.

Some of the important minerals of these two groups, their composition and the places where their most important deposits are found are given in Table 10.1. In this table the symbols Ce and Y stand for any lanthanide atom of cerium group and ytterium group respectively. Both Euxenite and Gadolinite are quite abundant and are the future sources of yttrium earths.

Besides rare earth minerals there are many others, particularly the phosphates, arsenates, molybdates and tungstates of Ca, Sr, Fe and Pb which contain small amounts of rare earths. In some of these Sm, Gd and Eu are present in much larger quantities than in rare earth minerals.

Extraction of Lanthanides from Monazite Mineral

Lanthanides are mainly extracted from monazite mineral which is chiefly worked for thorium and the lanthanides are obtained as by-products. The operation consists of the following three steps :

I. Concentration of the Mineral

The concentration of monazite sand is usually begun with gravity separation on Wilfley tables, such as those which are used for gold. Since, monazite sand is much more heavier than quartz (sp. gravity of monazite = 5.5, sp. gravity of quartz = 2.6), the monazite sand gets caught up on the riffles and the quartz sand and other gangue material is washed off. The heavier material which contains monazite sand and other material sands (ilemenite and garnet)is dried and then passed through magnetic separator. The manozite, being much less magnetic than the other material sands, gets thereby separated from the rest. The refined monazite so obtained has an average composition ThO_2 = 7.5, Ce_2O_3 = 30%, other rare earths = 32%, P_2O_5 = 29% and SiO_2 = 1.5%.

II. Cracking of the Mineral

The concentrated monazite obtained as above is subjected to chemical treatment which is technically known as **"processing"** **"opening up"** or **"cracking"** of the mineral.

The chemical treatment of concentrated manazite is done either by conc. H_2SO_4 or by conc. NaOH solution.

Sulphuric acid *vs* caustic soda cracking

Although a greater variety of monazite sands can be processed by H_2SO_4 treatment than by the NaOH method, higher yields and cleaner separations are the main advantages of the latter process. However, the H_2SO_4 treatment method has the advantage over the NaOH process of being slightly cheaper to operate. In the NaOH cracking of monazite, concentration of the rare earths is achieved at relatively early stage of the process.

III. Separation of Individual Rare-Earth Elements

The long story of the methods used for the separation of the individual rare-earths may broadly be divided into two classes :

(a) **Old classical methods** are fractional crystallisation, fractional precipitation method, fractional thermal decomposition of oxy salts, change in oxidation states by selective oxidation or reduction.

(b) **Modern methods** are ion exchange method, solvent (liquid liquid) extraction method, paper chromatography, gas chromatography, and thin layer chromatography.

The classical methods were not only used by the early workers in the past, but still remain as very important methods for economical production of rare-earths on commercial scale.

(i) Ion-exchange method

This is the most effective method now available for the separation of lanthanide elements. This method utilises synthetic cation-exchange resins which are usually organic compounds containing sulphonic (—SO_3H) or carboxylic acid (–COOH) groups, the hydrogens of which are replaced by other cations. Thus, if an aqueous solution containing a mixture of tripositive lanthanide ions, $Ln^{3+}(aq)$ is allowed to pass down a column packed with a cation exchange resin (abbreviated as HR (solid)), the $Lu^{3+}(aq)$ ions replace H^+ ions of —SO_3H or —COOH group of the resin and thus get fixed on the resin.

$$Ln^{3+}(aq) + 3HR(\text{solid}) \longrightarrow LnR_3(\text{solid}) + 3H^+(aq)$$

Thus, all the $Ln^{3+}(aq)$ ions are attached with the resin as LnR_3 (solid). **Since, $Lu^{3+}(aq)$ is largest in size and $La^{3+}(aq)$ in smallest, $La^{3+}(aq)$ is attached to the resin in the column with maximum and $Lu^{3+}(aq)$ with minimum firmness.** In order to remove Ln^{3+} ions fixed as LnR_3 (solid) on the resin, the column is eluted (*i.e.,* leached) with a complexing agent in aqueous solution like a buffer solution of ammonium citrate-citric acid (pH = 4 to 7). Such complexing agents are called **eluants** or **eluates** or **eluting agents.** During elution process, NH_4^+ ions of the eluting agent replace Ln^{3+} ions from LnR_3 (solid) to give **Ln^{3+}** ions which react with citrate ion to form the Ln-citrate complex.

$$LnR_3 + NH_4^+ \longrightarrow NH_4R + Ln^{3+}$$

$$Ln^{3+} + \text{citrate ion} \longrightarrow \text{Ln-citrate complex}$$

We have seen that since $La^{3+}(aq)$ is attached to resin with maximum and $Lu^{3+}(aq)$ with minimum firmness, Lu-citrate complex comes out of the column first and La-citrate complex comes out last.

In actual practice the process of elution is to be repeated several times by careful control of concentration of ammonium citrate-citric acid solutions.

The yttrium group rare earths have been separated by Ketelle and Boyd on a column of Dowex 50 (270-325 mesh) using 5% (0.25 M) citric acid at pH 3.28. Mixtures of Eu—Sm and Y—Tb took eight hours for complete separation with 0.5 M citrate at pH 3.04 (87°C) and with 0.24 M lacatate at pH 5.0. Cunninghame *et. al.* reduced the separation time to four hours using 1 M lactate (pH = 3.25) at 87°C for a mixture of Y-Pr-Nd-Pm-Sm-Eu with a Zeokarb 225.

(ii) Solvent (liquid-liquid) extraction method

The separation of lanthanides by this method was first reported by Fischer. The method is based on the differences in the solubility of lanthanide salts in water and an immiscible or partially miscible organic solvent. These organic solvents are called **extracting solvents** or **extractants**. This method has been used on both tracer and macroscales. The technique consists of passing the aqueous solution of lanthanide salts counter-current to the organic solution which extracts the lanthanides from water. The most widely used extracting solvent is tri-n-butyl phosphate, TBP in an inert medium like kerosene or xylene to extract the lanthanides from nitric acid solutions. TBP forms complexes with $Ln^{3+}(aq)$ ions in the presence of NO_3^- ions.

$$Ln^{3+}(aq) + 3NO_3^-(aq) + 3TBP(org) \rightleftharpoons \underbrace{Ln(NO_3)_3(TBP)_3(org)}_{\text{Complex}}$$

where, (org) represents the organic phase.

The distribution between these two phases (*i.e.,* solvents) is described by distribution ratio (also called extraction coefficient), λ given by

$$\lambda = \frac{\text{Total concentration of solute in one solvent}}{\text{Total concentration of solute in the other solvent}} = \frac{C_{Ln(NO_3)_3(TBP)_3(org)}}{C_{Ln^{3+}(aq)}} \quad ...(1)$$

For two tripositive lanthanide ions, Ln'^{3+} and Ln^{3+}, the separation factor, α is given as

$$\alpha = \frac{\lambda'}{\lambda} = \frac{C_{Ln(NO_3)_3(TBP)_3(org)} \cdot C_{Ln^{3+}(aq)}}{C_{Ln(NO_3)_3(TBP)_3(org)} \cdot C_{Ln'^{3+}(aq)}} \quad ...(2)$$

Peppard has reported that an average separation factor for adjacent lanthanides for 15.8 M nitric acid–100% TBP system is about 1.5.

Equilibrium constant, K, is given by

$$K = \frac{C_{Ln(NO_3)_3(TBP)_3(org)}}{C_{Ln^{3+}(aq)} \cdot C^3_{NO_3^-(aq)} \cdot C^3_{TBP\,(org)}} \quad ...(3)$$

Combination of Eq. (3) with Eq. (1) gives Eq. (4), *viz.*

$$K = \frac{\lambda}{C^3_{NO_3^-(aq)} \cdot C^3_{TBP(org)}}$$

or

$$\lambda = K \cdot C^3_{NO_3^-(aq)} \cdot C^3_{TBP(org)} \quad ...(4)$$

Kilogram quantities of 95% pure lanthanides have been prepared by solvent extraction technique. Another organic solvent which is a better extracting than TBP is di (2-ethyl hexyl) phosphoric acid. For this extractant the average separation factor of 2.5 for adjacent lanthanides has been reported. Other extractants used in the separation process are : monoalkyl phosphoric acids : $RPO(OH)_2$ or RH_2PO_3, pyrophosphate esters : $(RO)_2$ P(O)—O—P(O) $(OR)_3$, phosphonates : $(RO)_2(R)$PO and (RO) (R) P(O) (OH) and 1, 3-diketones or 8-quinolinols.

Present status of solvent extraction technique The major uses of the solvent extraction process are that it can be used in separating the Ln^{3+} ions from Ln^{4+} ions such as Ce^{4+} and Th^{4+} and in the purification of Ce, Th and La. La is somewhat less readily extracted than other Ln^{3+} ions and it can thus be separated from them rather readily.

(iii) Paper chromatography

Cerrai and Testa separated some rare earths by ascending paper chromatography, using CRL/I papers treated with 0.1M dil. (2-ethylhexyl) orthophosphoric acid (HDEHP). Under the same conditions an increase in R_F value is noted with decreasing atomic number, Z, of the rare earths. For a given element the R_F value increases with the molarity of eluting acid (HCl) and with temperature, but decreases with the concentration of HDEHP. The following R_F values for 1 M HCl eluant have been reported :

Ln^{3+}	La	Ce	Pr	Sm	Eu	Gd	Dy	Er	Yb	Y	Sc
R_F	0.92	0.91	0.90	0.76	0.64	0.51	0.12	0.06	0.03	0.07	0.0

Later, Cerrai and Triulzi used a mixture of 3M HNO_3 and 80% CH_3OH as solvent on Whatman cellulose paper DE–20 to separate La, Ce, Pr, Nd, Sm and Gd. Whatman DE–20 is a cellulose anion exchanger, containing amine groups bonded to the cellulose matrix.

It has been found that a mixture of HCl and various aliphatic alcohols can successfully be used as eluant for the separation of rare earths by paper chromatography (Whatman No. 1).

(iv) Complex formation : oxalate precipitation in the presence of EDTA

In the presence of complexing reagent namely ethylene diamine tetra-acetic acid (EDTA), J.K. Marsh (1950-51) has been able to effect an efficient separation of rare-earths by precipitation as oxalates.

Lanthanide oxalates are insoluble in water, but they can be dissolved by complexing with EDTA.

These lanthanide-EDTA complexes differ in their stabilities. The stability of these complexes, as a rule, increases with an increase in atomic number as shown in Fig. 10.1. The difference in stabilities of these complexes may be made the basis of the separation of rare earths. Thus, if these complexes are treated with an acid, the least stable complex is destroyed first and changes to oxalate, while the most stable complex is destroyed last on the addition of an acid.

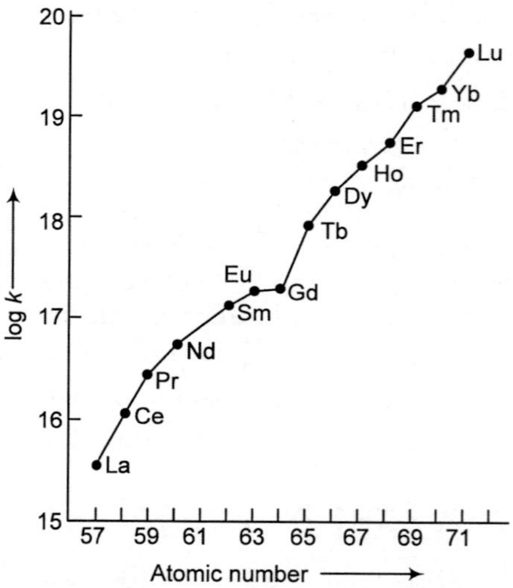

Fig. 10.1 Stability constants of lanthanides EDTA complexes in aqueous solutions at 20°C.

Preparation of the Metals

Because of the ease of oxidation of these metals, it is not a simple task to obtain the elements in the metallic state.

The following methods may be used for the preparation of metals :

(i) Thermal decomposition of lanthanide-mercury amalgam

Using a mercury cathode, an amalgam of the lanthanides may be prepared by the electrolysis of aqueous solutions. The amalgam thus formed is thermally decomposed to get the metals in a finely divided state, but complete elimination of mercury is difficult.

(ii) Electrolysis of fused chlorides

The anhydrous lanthanide (+3) chlorides are fused with sodium, potassium or calcium chloride by external heating and the molten mass is electrolysed in an iron pot or in a refractory lined pot which serves as the anode. Graphite cathodes are used. The molten metal collects as a pool at the bottom of the pot from where it is withdrawn and cast into ingots.

This method does not give the metals in high degree of purity required in modern technology.

(iii) Metallothermic reduction of the salts

In this method the anhydrous fluorides and chlorides of lanthanides are reduced with calcium in a tantalum container at about 1000°C. Calcium is volatilised from the lanthanide-calcium alloy. **This method is successful for all the lanthanides except Sm, Eu and Yb, because these metals form stable divalent fluorides**. However, these metals can be prepared by reducing their oxides with lanthanum metals at 1400°C in vacuum and distilling out Sm, Eu and Yb. These metals are more volatile than lanthanum.

The metals can be purified by vacuum distillation (pressure $\simeq 10^{-5}$ mm Hg) in tantalum apparatus.

General Properties of Lanthanides

Some of the important properties of lanthanides are discussed below.

1. Electronic Configuration

We know that at Ba_{56} 6*s*-orbital is completely filled ($Ba_{56} \longrightarrow [Xe]\,6s^2$) and at La_{57} 5*d*-orbital is singly occupied ($La_{57} \longrightarrow [Xe]\,5d^1\,6s^2$). But after La_{57} further filling of 5*d*-orbitals is discontinued. As the nuclear charge increases by one unit from La_{57} to Ce_{58}, 4*f*-orbitals which were higher in energy fall slightly below the 5*d*-level. 4*f*-orbitals, therefore, begin to fill and are completely filled up to Lu_{71} before the filling of 5*d*-orbitals is resumed. Electronic configurations of lanthanides are shown in Table 10.2.

Table 10.2 **Electronic Configuration of the Neutral Gaseous Atoms of Lanthanides**

Elements with atomic numbers	Complete configurations	Valence-shell configurations
La_{57}	*[Xe] $4f^0 5d^1 6s^2$	$4f^0 5d^1 6s^2$
Ce_{58}	[Xe] $4f^2 5d^0 6s^2$	$4f^2 5d^0 6s^2$
Pr_{59}	[Xe] $4f^3 5d^0 6s^2$	$4f^3 5d^0 6s^2$
Nd_{60}	[Xe] $4f^4 5d^0 6s^2$	$4f^4 5d^0 6s^2$
Pm_{61}	[Xe] $4f^5 5d^0 6s^2$	$4f^5 5d^0 6s^2$
Sm_{62}	[Xe] $4f^6 5d^0 6s^2$	$4f^6 5d^0 6s^2$
Eu_{63}	[Xe] $4f^7 5d^0 6s^2$	$4f^7 5d^0 6s^2$
Gd_{64}	[Xe] $4f^7 5d^1 6s^2$	$4f^7 5d^1 6s^2$
Tb_{65}	[Xe] $4f^9 5d^0 6s^2$	$4f^9 5d^0 6s^2$
Dy_{66}	[Xe] $4f^{10} 5d^0 6s^2$	$4f^{10} 5d^0 6s^2$
Ho_{67}	[Xe] $4f^{11} 5d^0 6s^2$	$4f^{11} 5d^0 6s^2$
Er_{68}	[Xe] $4f^{12} 5d^0 6s^2$	$4f^{12} 5d^0 6s^2$
Tm_{69}	[Xe] $4f^{13} 5d^0 6s^2$	$4f^{13} 5d^0 6s^2$
Yb_{70}	[Xe] $4f^{14} 5d^0 6s^2$	$4f^{14} 5d^0 6s^2$
Lu_{71}	[Xe] $4f^{14} 5d^1 6s^2$	$4f^{14} 5d^1 6s^2$

*[Xe] indicates the complete configuration of Xe atom which is 2, 8, 18, 18, 8.

From this table the following points may be noted :

(i) The complete electronic configuration of lanthanides can be represented by a general configuration *viz.*, 2, 8, 18 $4s^2 p^6 d^{10} f^{0-14}$ $5s^2 p^6 d^{0 \text{ or } 1}$, $6s^2$ (including La) which shows that the valence-shell configuration can be represented as $4f^{0,\,2\ldots 14}\,5d^{0 \text{ or } 1}\,6s^2$.

The valence-shell configuration indicates that the additional electron enters in the 4*f*-orbital without altering the electrons in the outermost 6*s*-orbital.

(ii) The filling of 4*f*-orbitals is not regular, *e.g.*, the additional electron in Gd_{64} does not enter in 4*f*-level but, instead, it goes to 5*d*-level. This is because the 4*f* and 5*d* orbitals in Gd are at about the same energy level and Gd atom has tendency to retain the configuration with half-filled $4f$-orbitals which are relatively more stable.

2. Oxidation States and Oxidation Potentials

Observed oxidation states of lanthanides noted either in solution or in insoluble compounds are given in Table 10.4 from which it may be noted that whatever be the electronic configurations of the lanthanides in the groud state, **all of the lanthanides form the tripositive lanthanide cations.** This fact is not directly evident from the electronic configurations, it is actually due to the fact that the magnitudes of the energy required to remove an electron from the gaseous ion in its lower oxidation state (*i.e.*, ionisation energy) and of that released when two gaseous ion combine with water to form the aquated species (*i.e.*, hydration energy) are such that all the tetrapositive species (except possibly Ce^{4+}) and all the dipositive species (except Eu^{2+}) revert to the tripositive species. **Thus, this leads to the conclusion that tripositive species are more stable than the di-and tetrapositive species in aqueous solutions.**

In the solid state too the combination of ionisation energy and the energy released when gaseous ions combine to produce crystalline solids (*i.e.*, the lattice or crystal energy) is more negative for the tripositive species than for di- and tetrapositive species. Consequently, the tripositive lanthanides are also the most common in the solid compounds.

Stability of various oxidation states

It is possible to correlate the stability of various oxidation states of lanthanides with the electronic configuration of their ions. On the basis of general rule that empty, half-filled and completely filled $4f$-orbitals are highly stable, the formation of Ce^{4+}, La^{3+} ($4f^0$), Tb^{4+}, Eu^{2+}, Gd^{3+} ($4f^7$) and Yb^{2+}, Lu^{3+} ($4f^{14}$) ions can be explained. It is, however, difficult to explain the stability of oxidation states of the cations other than those given above. It may thus be assumed that in addition to the special stability associated with $4f^0$, $4f^7$ and $4f^{14}$ configurations, there may be other factors such as thermodynamic and kinetic, in determining the stability of various oxidation states of lanthanides.

The stability order of + 2 state is Eu > Yb > Sm > Tm ~ Nd. LnI_2 solids (Ln = La, Ce, Pr and Gd) do not contain Ln^{2+} ions, but are metallic in nature. The stability order of + 4 state is Ce > Tb ~ Pr > Nd ~ Dy.

The ease of formation of the various oxidation states in solution is indicated by the values of the standard electrode potential, $E°$. These values (in volts) for different couples of lanthanides such as $Ln^0 \longrightarrow Ln^{3+} + 3e^-$, $Ln^{2+} \longrightarrow Ln^{3+} + e^-$ and $Ln^{3+} \longrightarrow Ln^{4+} + e^-$ for 1 M perchloric acid at 25°C are tabulated in Table 10.3. Here, Ln represents the elemental lanthanide. Ln^{2+}, Ln^{3+} and Ln^{4+} are the di-, tri- and tetrapositive lanthanide ions.

Table 10.3 **Various Oxidation States Shown by Lanthanides and Standard Oxidation Potentials, $E°$ (in Volt) for Various Couples of Lanthanide Elements in 1 M Perchloric Acid at 25°C**

Lanthanide elements	Oxidation states (less stable states are shown in brackets)			$E°$ values (in volts) for various couples (Estimated values are given in brackets)
La_{57}		+ 3		La^0/La^{3+} = 2.52 V
Ce_{58}		+ 3,	+ 4	Ce^0/Ce^{3+} = 2.48
Pr_{59}		+ 3,	+ 4	Pr^0/Pr^{3+} = 2.46, Pr^{3+}/Pr^{4+} = – 1.74
Nd_{60}	+ 2,	+ 3		Nd^0/Nd^{3+} = 2.43, Nd^{3+}/Nd^{4+} = (–2.86)
Pm_{61}		+ 3		Pm^0/Pm^{3+} = (2.42)
Sm_{62}	+ 2,		+ 4	Sm^0/Sm^{3+} = 2.41, Sm^{2+}/Sm^{3+} = 1.55
Eu_{63}	+ 2,	+ 3		Eu^0/Eu^{3+} = 2.40, Eu^{2+}/Eu^{3+} = 0.43
Gd_{64}		+ 3		Gd^0/Gd^{3+} = 2.39
Tb_{65}		+ 3,	+ 4	Tb^0/Tb^{3+} = 2.39
Dy_{66}		+ 3,	+ 4	Dy^0/Dy^{3+} = 2.35
Ho_{67}		+ 3		Ho^0/Ho^{3+} = 2.32, Ho^{2+}/Ho^{3+} = 0.57
Er_{68}		+ 3		Er^0/Er^{3+} = 2.30
Tm_{69}	+ 2,	+ 3		Tm^0/Tm^{3+} = 2.28
Yb_{70}	+ 2,	+ 3		Yb^0/Yb^{3+} = 2.27, Yb^{2+}/Yb^{3+} = 1.15
Lu_{71}		+ 3		Lu^0/Lu^{3+} = 2.25

From this table, we observe that :

(i) The high positive values of the oxidation electrode potentials for the couple $Ln^0(s)$ s $Ln^{3+}(aq) + 3e^-$ indicate that the elemental lanthanides are powerful reducing agents, *i.e.*, oxidation of the lanthanide metals to the tripositive state occurs readily and vigorously. The gradual decrease, though very slow, in the values of $E°$ indicates very slight decrease in chemical activity from one element to the next one.

(ii) The enhanced stabilities associated with the empty, half-filled and completely filled $4f$-orbitals is also indicated by these values. Thus, Ce^{4+} $(4f^0)$ is much less readily reduced to the tripositive ion, Ce^{3+} $(4f^1)$ than Pr^{4+} ion $(4f^1)$. Furthermore, the $4f^7$ species (*e.g.*, Eu^{2+} ion) and the $4f^{14}$ species (*e.g.*, Yb^{2+} ion) are the weakest reducing agents of the di-positive species.

(iii) The values of $E°$ for couple $Ln^0(s) \longrightarrow Ln^{3+}(aq) + 3e^-$ decreases with the increase of atomic number, as is evident from Table 10.4. The high values of $E°$ are in accordance with the electropositive character of lanthanides. The decrease in the values of $E°$ with the increase in atomic number (*i.e.*, a decrease in the electropositive character) is evidently inconsistent with the corresponding decrease in the ionic radius, *i.e.*, lanthanide contraction (to be described subsequently).

Chemistry of +3 state

In general, the lanthanides behave as active metals. Their electrode potential values are comparable to those of alkaline earths. All the metals act as strong reducing agents. They are all attacked by acids with the liberation of hydrogen. The metals dissolve slowly in cold but more rapidly in warm water and liberate hydrogen. They absorb hydrogen to form interstitial hydrides.

Nearly all known anions form the compounds with Ln^{3+} cation. These compounds are stable in solid as well as in solution state. Compounds of Ln^{2+} cation with the anions such as $OH^-, CO_3^{2-}, SO_4^{2-}$, $C_2O_4^{2-}, NO_3^-$ etc. decompose on heating, give first basic salts and finally oxides. Hydrated salts that contain thermally stable anions such as F^-, Cl^-, Br^-, PO_4^{3-} etc., also give similar products on heating because of hydrolysis.

Compounds of Ln^{3+} cation with the anions $Cl^-, Br^-, I^-, NO_3^-, CH_3COO^-, BO_3^{3-}$ are generally souble in water while those with $F^-, OH^-, O^{2-}, C_2O_4^{2-}, CO_3^{2-}, CrO_4^{2-}, PO_4^{3-}$ etc. are generally insoluble.

(a) **Oxides, Ln_2O_3** The oxides, Ln_2O_3 are formed by heating the metal in oxygen or by the thermal decomposition of the $Ln(OH)_3$ or oxy salts such as $Ln_2(CO_3)_3$ and $Ln(NO_3)_3$. The oxides resemble those of alkaline earth oxides. All the oxides are almost insoluble in water. They absorb CO_2 and H_2O from air to form carbonates and hydroxides respectively.

(b) **Hydroxides, $Ln(OH)_3$** The hydroxides are precipitated as gelatinous precipitates from aqueous solution by the addition of ammonia or dil. alkali to soluble salts of Ln^{3+} ion in solution. The precipitation of these hydroxides on the addition of an alkali or ammonia to their salts is as : Sc, Lu, Yb, Tm, Er, Ho, Dy, Tb, Sm, Gd, Eu, Y, Nd, Pr, Ce, La.

These hydroxides are not amphoteric. These are definite compounds with hexagonal structure and are not merely hydrous oxides. They absorb CO_2 to give normal carbonates.

The oxides and hydroxides are basic. The basicity decreases with increasing atomic number, Thus, La_2O_3 and $La(OH)_3$ are the most basic while Lu_2O_3 and $Lu(OH)_3$ are least basic. La_2O_3 is a strong base and slakes like CaO on addition of water. The hydroxides are decomposed on heating to form oxides.

(c) **Oxy salts** Lanthanide salts of most oxy acids (called oxy salts) such as sulphates, nitrates, perchlorates, bromates etc., are also known. These are generally soluble and crystallise as hydrates. Soluble oxy salts such as sulphates, nitrates and perchlorates can be prepared by dissolving the oxides, hydroxides or carbonates in the appropriate oxyacids. From the solution, hydrated salts can be crystallised out. The nitrates are often deliquescent and crystallise with $6H_2O$. Solutions of oxy salts furnish hydrated cations, $[Ln(H_2O)_x]^{3+}$ which tend to undergo slight hydrolysis in aqueous solution :

$$[Ln(H_2O)_x]^{3+} + H_2O \longrightarrow [Ln(H_2O)_{x-1}(OH)]^{2+} + H_3O^+$$

The smaller the ionic radius of Ln^{3+} ion, the greater is the tendency of the ion, $[Ln(H_2O)_x]^{3+}$, to hydrolyse. Thus, the tendency of the $[Ln(H_2O)_x]^{3+}$ ion to hydrolyse increases with increasing atomic number, since on passing from La^{3+} to Lu^{3+} there is a contraction in their ionic radii.

(d) **Double salts** Lanthanide salts form a large number of double salts. The most important double salts are :

(i) Double nitrates such as

$$2Ln(NO_3)_3 \cdot 3M^{II}(NO_3)_2 \cdot 24H_2O \quad (M^{II} = Mg, Zn, Ni, Mn)$$

and $Ln(NO_3)_3 \cdot 2NH_4NO_3 \cdot 4H_2O$.

(ii) Double sulphates such as $Ln_2(SO_4)_3 \cdot 3M_2^ISO_4 \cdot 12H_2O$ (M = alkali metal). The double sulphates, $Ln_2(SO_4)_3 \cdot 3Na_2SO_4 \cdot 12H_2O$ where, Ln = La—Eu are only sparingly soluble in Na_2SO_4, while those where Ln = Gd—Lu are appreciably soluble. Thus, a separation of lanthanides into two groups : **cerium group** having La_{57} to Eu_{82} lanthanides and **yttrium group** having Gd_{64}—Lu_{71} lanthanides is possible. Since the double salts crystallise well, these are used to separate the rare earths from one another.

(e) **Halides, LnX_3** Fluorides are precipitated by the addition of HF or a soluble fluoride to a Ln^{III} salts solution. The fluorides particularly of heavier lanthanides, are sparingly soluble in HF due to the formation of fluoro complexes.

The anhydrous chlorides can be prepared by the direct combination of the elements on heating. These are best prepared by heating the oxides with carbonyl chloride ($COCl_2$) or NH_4Cl.

$$Ln_2O_3 + 3COCl_2 \longrightarrow 2LnCl_3 + 3CO_2$$

$$Ln_2O_3 + 6NH_4Cl \xrightarrow{300^\circ} 2LnCl_3 + 3H_2O + 6NH_3$$

The anhydrous chlorides cannot be obtained from the hydrated chlorides, since these lose HCl on heating to give the oxychlorides, (LnOCl), more easily than they lose H_2O. ($ScCl_3 \cdot 3H_2O$ and $CeCl_4 \cdot 2H_2O$, however, give Sc_2O_3 and CeO_2). The chlorides are non-volatile, deliquescent solids, soluble in H_2O and alcohol. The hydrated chlorides are formed by dissolving the oxides or carbonates in HCl and concentrating the solution to crystallising point. They crystallise from solution usually as hexahydrates, $LnCl_3 \cdot 6H_2O$.

Bromides and iodides are rather similar to the chlorides. Iodides of the first few lanthanides are orthorhombic while those of the remaining lanthanides are hexagonal.

(f) **Carbonates, $Ln_2(CO_3)_3$** The normal carbonates can be prepared by passing CO_2 into an aqueous solution of $Ln(OH)_3$. They can also be prepared by adding Na_2CO_3 solution to Ln^{III} salt solution. The carbonates are insoluble in H_2O, but dissolve in acids with liberation of CO_2 and forming Ln^{III} salts.

(g) **Phosphates and oxalates** These are also insoluble in water. All lanthanides are quantitatively precipitated as oxalates from Ln^{3+} solution containing $C_2O_4^{2-}$ ion. The precipitate on drying and ignition give Ln_2O_3.

(h) **Compounds with non-metals and metalloids** The lanthanides also form well-defined compounds with non-metals and metalloids other than oxygen and halogens. These compounds can generally be prepared by the direct combination of the elements at elevated temperatures. Lanthanide nitrides (LnN), phosphides (LnP), arsenides (LnAs), anntimonides (LnSb) and bismuthides (LnBi) crystallise in the NaCl structure. The carbide (Ln_3C), is found for the lanthanides, Sm–Lu but not for La, Ce, Pr and Nd.

Chemistry of + 2 state

This is an anomalous oxidation state. The lanthanides showing + 2 oxidation state can be divided into + 2 two categories :

(a) **Sm_{62}, Eu_{63} and Yb_{70}** The dipositive ions of these lanthanides (*i.e.,* Sm^{2+}, Eu^{2+} and Yb^{2+}) exist in solution state. The standard oxidation potentials at 25°C, in acid solution, of these cations are given below :

$$Sm^{3+}(aq) + e^- \rightleftharpoons Sm^{2+}(aq) \quad -1.55\ V$$

$$Eu^{3+}(aq) + e^- \rightleftharpoons Eu^{2+}(aq) \quad -0.43\ V$$

$$Yb^{3+}(aq) + e^- \rightleftharpoons Yb^{2+}(aq) \quad -1.15\ V$$

These values indicate that Sm^{2+}, Eu^{2+} and Yb^{2+} ions are strong reducing agents and their reducing strength is in the order :

$$Sm^{2+} > Yb^{2+} > Eu^{2+}$$

Sm^{2+} and Yb^{2+} ions are rapidly oxidised by H_3O^+ ions (acidic solution), while Eu^{2+} ion is fairly stable and is only slowly oxidised by H_3O^+ ion.

$$2Sm^{2+}\ (\text{or } Yb^{2+}) + 2H_3O^+ \longrightarrow 2Sm^{3+}\ (\text{or } 2Yb^{3+}) + 2H_2O + H_2$$

All these cations are rapidly oxidised in the presence of oxygen, *e.g.*,

$$4Ln^{2+} + 4H_3O^+ + O_2 \longrightarrow 4Ln^{3+} + 6H_2O$$

where, Ln^{2+} may be Sm^{2+}, Eu^{2+} or Yb^{2+}.

The compounds of Sm^{2+}, Eu^{2+} and Yb^{2+} which are insoluble in H_2O are not oxidised by H_2O, while hydrated water-soluble compounds of Sm^{2+} and Yb^{2+} are oxidised by water. Hydrated water-soluble compounds of Eu^{2+} are more stable.

(b) **Ce_{58}, Nd_{60} and Tm_{69}** The compounds having these elements in + 2 oxidation state are known only as solid halides. These are immediately oxidised with air.

Of the divalent compounds of lanthanides, those of Eu^{2+} ion are most stable. The compounds of Ln^{2+}ion are not stable in solution. All the Ln^{2+} compounds decomposes water with the evolution of H_2.

$$2Ln^{2+} + 2H_2O \longrightarrow Ln^{3+} + 2OH^- + H_2\uparrow$$

The reaction is, however, sluggish; with Eu the reaction is so retarded that Eu^{2+} compounds may be regarded as fairly stable in aqueous solutions at an ordinary temperature.

Chemistry of + 4 state

This oxidation state is also an anomalous oxidation state. Double salts like $Ce(NO_3)_4 \cdot 2NH_4NO_3$ and $Ce(SO_4)_2 \cdot 2(NH_4)_2 SO_4 \cdot 2H_2O$ have also been prepared.

The standard oxidation potentials at 25°C, in acid solution of Ce^{4+} and Pt^{4+} ions are given as under :

$$Ce^{4+} + e^- \rightleftharpoons Ce^{3+} + 1.74 \text{ V}$$

$$Pr^{4+} + e^- \rightleftharpoons Pr^{3+} + 2.86 \text{ V}$$

These values show that Ce(IV) and Pr(IV) are strong oxidising agents, the latter being by far the stronger of the two. $Ce(SO_4)_2$is generally used in volumetric analysis. Ce^{4+} ion is readily reduced to Ce^{3+} ion.

The tetravalent ions of Ce are stable in the solid state as well as in solution; Pr^{IV}, Nd^{IV}, Tb^{IV} and Dy^{IV} are stable only in solution.

3. Atomic and Ionic Radii-Lanthanide Contraction

The atomic radii of the Ln atoms and the crystal or ionic radii of Ln^{2+}, Ln^{3+} and Ln^{4+} ions are given in the Table 10.3.

This table clearly show that as we move along the lanthanide series, there is a decrease in atomic and ionic radii. This steady decrease in the atomic and ionic radii is called **lanthanide contraction**. This decrease in size is regular in ions (Fig. 10.4) but not so regular in case of atoms.

Table 10.4 **Atomic and Ionic (or crystal) Radii of Lanthanides in Å**

Elements with atomic no.	Atomic radius (—Ln)	Crystal or ionic radii of		
		Ln^{2+} ion	Ln^{3+} ion	Ln^{4+} ion
Sc_{21}	1.64		0.68	
Y_{39}	1.80		0.88	
La_{57}	1.88		1.06	
Ce_{58}	1.82		1.03	0.92
Pr_{59}	1.83		1.01	0.90
Nd_{60}	1.82		0.99	
Pm_{61}	–		(0.98)	
Sm_{62}	1.80	1.11	0.96	
Eu_{63}	2.04	1.09	0.95	
Gd_{64}	1.80		0.94	
Tb_{65}	1.78		0.92	0.84
Dy_{66}	1.77		0.91	
Ho_{67}	1.77		0.89	
Er_{68}	1.76		0.88	
Tm_{69}	1.75	0.94	0.87	
Yb_{70}	1.94	0.93	0.86	
Lu_{71}	1.73		0.85	

Lanthanides

Fig. 10.3 clearly shows that the graph has two peaks, one at Eu_{63} and the other at Yb_{70}, which possess exceptionally high values for their atomic radii. This is regarded due to the difference is metallic bonding. **Each of the lanthanides is assumed to contribute three electrons for the formation of metallic bond, excepting Eu and Yb.** These two atoms contribute only two electrons towards bond formation, thus leaving behind half-filled and completely filled $4f$-orbitals respectively. The three vertical lines shown in the figure have been drawn just to mark of the lanthanide part of the curve and to divide the lanthanides into two portions marked as 1 and 2. The dividing line posses through Gd_{64} which has half-filled $4f$-shell (Gd $\longrightarrow$ $4f^7\ 5d^1\ 7s^2$). The right-hand half of the curve is obviously a duplicate pattern of left-hand half. The seven elements of portion 1 namely from Ce_{58} to Gd_{64} occupy a position corresponding to that occupied by the seven elements namely Tb_{65} to Lu_{71} of portion 2.

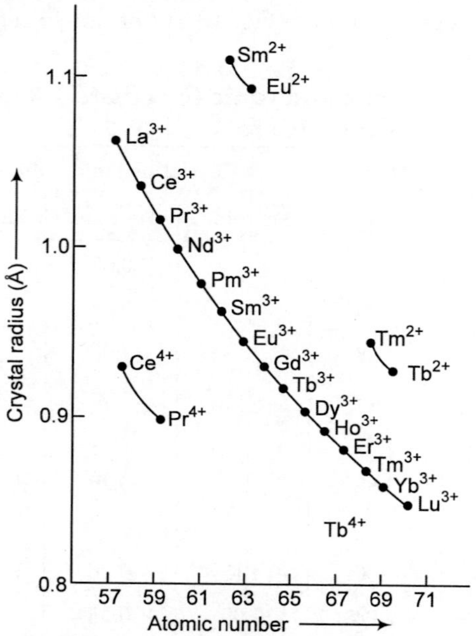

Fig. 10.2 Crystal radii of Ln^{2+}, Ln^{3+} and Ln^{4+} ions as a function of their atomic numbers.

Cause of lanthanide contraction

We have already seen that in lanthanides the additional electron enters in 4*f*-subshell but not in the valence-shell namely sixth shell. The shielding effect of one electron in 4*f*-subshell by another in the same subshell (*i.e.*, mutual shielding effect of 4*f*-electrons) is very little, being even smaller than that of *d*-electrons, because the shape of *f*-subshell is very much diffused. The nuclear charge (*i.e.*, atomic number), however, increases by unity at each step. While there is no comparable increase in the mutual shielding effect of 4*f*-electrons. Consequently the results in that electrons in the outermost shell experience increasing nuclear attraction from the growing nucleus. As a result of this the atomic and ionic radii go on decreasing as we move from La_{57} to Lu_{71}.

Some important consequences of the lanthanide contraction are summarised below

(i) Anomalous behaviour of post-lanthanide elements

The elements following lanthanides are called post-lanthanide elements. Thus, these are the elements of third transition series. Lanthanide contraction affects the properties of post-lanthanide elements. The following examples illustrate this point.

(a) **Atomic and ionic radii of post-lanthanide elements** Normally, in the same sub-group, the covalent radii increase as the atomic number increases. This fact is evident when we compare the covalent radii values of the elements of the first and second transition series as given in Table 10.4.

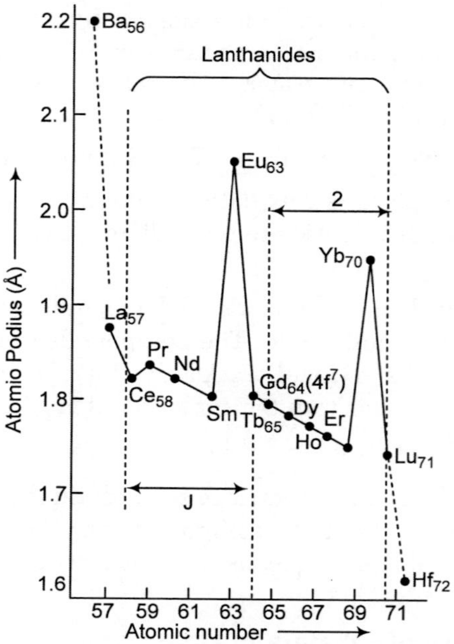

Fig. 10.3 Atomic radii of lanthanides, Ba and Hf as a function of their atomic numbers.

If we compare the covalent radii values of the elements of the second transition series with those of third series, we find that the normal increase in the covalent radii values from Sc_{22} to Y_{39} to La_{57} disappears after lanthanides and the pairs of elements; Zr—Hf, Na—Ta,……, Ag—Au, Cd—Hg possess almost same values. If the fourteen lanthanides had not been intervened between La_{57} and Hf_{72}, the value of covalent radius, for example, of Hf_{72} should have been greater than that of Zr_{40}, since Zr and Hf both are in the same sub-group IVB and Zr lies immediately above Hf. The occurrence of lanthanide contraction cancels the expected increase in the covalent radius value from Zr to Hf. This situation is also with other pairs of elements in the second and third series of transition elements.

Since the pairs of elements of second and third transition series, occurring after lanthanides; (*e.g.*, Zr—Hf, Nb—Ta etc., pairs) have almost similar size (which is due to lanthanide contraction), they are much more close to one another in properties than do the pairs of elements of first and second transition series, *e.g.*, solubilities of their salts are very much similar to one another.

(b) **High density of post-lanthanide elements** Because of lanthanide contraction, the atomic sizes of the post-lanthanide elements become very small. Consequently the packing of atoms in their metallic crystals become so much compact that their densities are very high. While the densities of the elements of second transition series are only slightly higher than those of the elements of first series, the densities of the elements of third transition series are almost double to those of the elements of second transition series.

(ii) Basic character of oxides, Ln_2O_3 and hydroxides, $Ln(OH)_3$

The chemical properties of an element or an ion depend on the size of the atom or ion. The greater the atomic or ionic radius, greater is the ease with which the species (*i.e.,* atom or ion) will lose electrons. Thus, the ease with which a species loses electrons is the measure of its basicity. Basicity decreases as the ionic radius decreases. Thus, basicity of Ln^{3+} ions may be expected to decrease in the order :

$$La^{3+} > Ce^{3+} > Pr^{3+} > Nd^{3+} > Pm^{3+} > Sm^{3+} > Eu^{3+} > Gd^{3-} > Tb^{3+} > Dy^{3+} > Ho^{3+} > Er^{3+} > Tm^{3+} > Yb^{3+} > Lu^{3+}$$

These differences in basicity are reflected in (a) thermal decomposition of oxy salts, *e.g.,* more basic oxy salts decomposes less easily, (*i.e.,* with difficulty) (b) hydrolysis of ions-more basic ions hydrolyse less readily (c) solubilities of salts (d) formation of complexes, and (e) decreasing ease of oxidation of the metals with increasing atomic number– oxidation potential for the couple, $Ln \longrightarrow Ln^{3+} + 3e^-$ regularly goes on decreasing.

Due to lanthanide contraction, the decrease in size of Ln^{3+} ions from La^{3+} to Lu^{3+} increases the covalent character (*i.e.,* decreases the ionic character) between Ln^{3+} and OH^- ions in Ln(III) hydroxides (Fajans rules). Thus, $La(OH)_3$ is the most basic while $Lu(OH)_3$ is the least basic.

Similarly there is a decrease in the basic strength of the oxides, Ln_2O_3 with the increase of atomic number of Ln atom.

Small variation in the properties on account of lanthanide contraction allows the separation of lanthanides by the methods based on fractional crystallisation and basicity differences.

(iii) Occurrence of Y with heavy lanthanides

The crystal radii of Y^{3+} and Er^{3+} are equal ($Y^{3+} = 0.93$ Å and $Er^{2+} = 0.96$ Å). This similarity in ionic size of these two cations coupled with the equality in ionic charge (= + 3 in both the ions) accounts for the invariable occurrence of Y with heavier lanthanides. The marked similarities in the crystal structure, chemical properties and solubility between yttrium compounds and the corresponding ones of the heavier lanthanides make it difficult to separate yttrium from the heavier lanthanides. It is because of these similarities that yttrium is regarded for all practical purposes as a member of lanthanide series.

4. Colour and Absorption Spectra of Ln^{3+} Ions

The striking colour characteristics of crystalline salts of a number of Ln^{3+} ions persist in aqueous and non-aqueous solutions and remain unaffected by the change of the anion present or by the addition of colourless complexing groups. Thus, it can be said that the colours are characteristic of Ln^{3+} ions themselves. Colours of Ln^{3+} ions are given in Table 10.6.

From Table 10.6 the following points may be noted :

(i) Ln^{3+} ions having x electrons add $(14 - x)$ electrons in $4f$-orbital have the same colour. For example Pr^{3+} and Tm^{3+} ions having 2 and $(14 - 2) = 12$ electrons in the $4f$-orbital respectively have the same colour namely green. Thus, we see that $4f$-orbitals are the source of colours of Ln^{3+} ions.

(ii) The colours of Ln^{3+} ions from La^{3+} to Gd^{3+} repeat themselves at least qualitatively, from Lu^{3+} back to Gd^{3+}. It can thus be concluded that the colours depend on the number of unpaired electrons in $4f$-orbitals, but the fact that Ln^{2+} (*e.g.,* Sm^{2+}, Eu^{2+}, Yb^{2+} ions) and Ln^{4+} ions (*e.g.,* Ce^{4+} ion) which are iso-electronic with Ln^{3+} ions have different colours suggests that the situation is somewhat more complex. For example, although both Eu^{3+} $(4f^6)$ and $Sm^{2+}(4f^6)$ ions have the same number of unpaired electrons in $4f$-orbitals (= 6), they have different colours (Eu^{3+}-colourless, Sm^{2+}-reddish). Other examples of pairs of cations having the same number of unpaired electrons in $4f$-orbitals but with different colours are :

(a) La^{3+} $(4f^0, n = 0)$-colourless, Ce^{4+} $(4f^0, n = 0)$ orange-red,

(b) $Gd^{3+}(4f^7, n = 7)$-colourless, Eu^{2+} $(4f^7, n = 7)$ -straw-yellow

(c) $Lu^{3+}(4f^{14}, n = 0)$-colourless, Yb^{2+} $(4f^{14}, n = 0)$-Green.

(iii) The colour of the Ln^{3+} cations can, to a large extent, be correlated with the electronic configuration of Ln^{3+} ions. Thus, as is evident from Table 10.6, the Ln^{3+} ions having no unpaired $4f$ electrons (*i.e.*, having either $4f^0$ or $4f^{14}$ electronic configuration) or half-filled $4f$-orbital (*i.e.*, $4f^7$ configuration) are colourless, *e.g.*, all the cations *viz.* La^{3+} ($4f^0$), Gd^{3+} ($4f^7$) and Lu^{3+} ($4f^{14}$) are colourless.

Origin of colour

The colour in due to Laporte-forbidden *ff* transitions, i.e., transitions between the J states of $4f^n$ configuration. Hence, the absorption bands of Ln^{3+} ions (except Ce^{3+} and Yb^{3+} ions) are very weak but sharp when compared to those of *d*-block elements. Many of these bands are line-like and become even narrower as the temperature is lowered. These narrow bands appear due to f–f transition and are independent of the nature of the anion present. As $4f$-electrons lie deep inside the atom, the colours of Ln^{3+} ions are not effected by changing the anion.

The colour one sees is the result of absorption of light of certain wavelengths and transmission of light of other wavelengths.

The coloured ions absorb in the visible region, and on occasion in the ultraviolet region. The colourless ions absorb either in the ultraviolet (Ce^{3+}, Gd^{3+} ions) or in the infrared region (Yb^{3+} ion). The Ln^{2+} ions absorb strongly in the ultraviolet. The only Ln^{4+} ion stable in aqueous solution, the Ce^{4+} ion, absorbs in the blue ultraviolet regions.

Laporte-permitted bands due to the transitions of $4f^n \longrightarrow 5d^1$ type have been observed in Ce^{3+}, Tb^{3+}, Sm^{2+}, Eu^{2+} and Yb^{2+}. These bands are strong and broader, since the transition is considerably

Table 10.5 **Colours and Wavelengths (in Å) of the Prominant Light Absorption Bands of Ln^{3+} Ions in Aqueous Solutions (n = No. of Unpaired Electrons in 4*f* Orbitals).**

Ln^{3+} ions with valence-shell configuration and number of unpaired electrons (n) in $4f$-orbitals	Colours and wavelengths (in Å)	Ln^{3+} ions with valence- shell configuration and number of unpaired electrons (n) in $4f$-orbitals	Colours and wavelengths (in Å)
$La^{3+}(4f^0, n=0)$	Colourless (No absorption in visible or infra-red region)	$Lu^{3+}(4f^{14}, n=0)$	Colourless (No absorption in visible, ultraviolet and infrared region)
$Ce^{3+}(4f^1, n=1)$	Colourless (No absorption in the visible region : strong bands in ultraviolet region–2105, 2220, 2380, 2520)	$Yb^{3+}(4f^{13}, n=1)$	Colourless (No absorption in visible region : strong bands in infrared-9750)
$Pr^{3+}(4f^2, n=2)$	Green (4445, 4690, 4822, 5885)	$Tm^{3+}(4f^{12}, n=2)$	Green (3600, 6825, 7800)
$Nd^{3+}(4f^3, n=3)$	Reddish (3540, 5218, 5745, 7395, 7420, 7975, 8030, 8680)	$Er^{3+}(4f^{11}, n=3)$	Reddish (3642, 3792, 4870, 5228, 6525)
$Pm^{3+}(4f^4, n=4)$	Pink-yellow (5485, 5680, 7025, 7355)	$Ho^{3+}(4f^{10}, n=4)$	Pink-yellow (2870, 3611, 4508, 5370, 6404)
$Sm^{3+}(4f^5, n=5)$	Pale-yellow (3625, 3745, 4020)	$Dy^{3+}(4f^9, n=5)$	Pale-yellow (3504, 3650, 9100)
$Eu^{3+}(4f^6, n=6)$	Pale-pink (nearly colourless) (3755, 3941)	$Tb^{3+}(4f^8, n=6)$	Pale-pink (nearly colourless) (3694, 3780, 4875)
$Gd^{3+}(4f^7, n=7)$	Colourless (No absorption in visible region, strong bands in ultraviolet region–2729, 2733, 2754, 2756)	$Gd^{3+}(4f^7, n=7)$	Colourless (No absorption in visible region, strong bands in ultraviolet region-2729, 2733, 2754, 2756)

influenced by the chemical environment. A charge transfer phenomena is also observed in certain lanthanide ions, *e.g.,* the orange-red colour of Ce^{4+} is due to the electronic transition from the ligand orbital to the f-orbital of cerium. Compounds of Eu^{3+} with reducing anions are yellow due to electron transfer from the metal.

5. Magnetic Properties

The paramagnetic property of an ion or an atom is due to the presence of unpaired electrons in it. Thus, since both La^{3+} $(4f^0\ 5d^0\ 6s^0)$ and Lu^{3+} $(4f^{14}\ 5d^0\ 6s^0)$ ions have no unpaired electrons, these are not paramagnetic. All other Ln^{3+} ions show paramagnetic property.

Since for most of Ln^{3+} ions, the energy difference between the two successive J levels of a multiplet (*i.e.,* multiplet width is large compared to kT, k = Boltzmann constant and T = absolute temperature), is a strong L-S coupling (see magnetic properties of transition elements). In these ions the unpaired electrons in $(n-2)\ f$ orbitals are quite deeply seated and hence are well shielded by $5s$ and $5p$ electrons from the effects of other atoms in their compounds (crystal field effect). Consequently the effective magnetic moments of Ln^{3+} ions, with the exception of Sm^{3+} and Eu^{3+} ions, are given by the following equation provided that the group state symbols of Ln^{3+} ions are known.

$$\mu_{eff} = \mu_J = g\sqrt{J(J+1)}\ \text{BM} \qquad \ldots(5)$$

where, g is the Lande splitting factor and is given by

$$g = 1 + \frac{J(J+1) + S(S+1) - L(L+1)}{2J(J+1)} \qquad \ldots(6)$$

S = resultant spin quantum number, L = resultant orbital quantum number and J = resultant inner quantum number which is obtained by coupling L and S.

Values of μ_{eff} of the sulphates of Ln^{3+} ions calculated from Eq. (5) and those found experimentally (*i.e.,* μ_{exp} values) are given in Table 10.7. From this table the following points may be noted :

1. Although for most of Ln^{3+} ions, there is an almost good agreement between the calculated and experimental values, for Sm^{3+} and Eu^{3+} ions the agreement is poor. This is due to the fact that in case of Sm^{3+} and Eu^{3+} ions, the energy difference (*i.e.,* multiplet width) between the successive J energy levels is comparable to kT and the J levels above the lowest energy J level are populated by atoms to some extent. The situation is actually not so simple as we have described here.
2. We know that for Ln^{3+} ions like $La^{3+}\ (4f^0)$, $Gd^{2+}\ (4f^7)$ and $Lu^{3+}\ (4f^{14})$ which have S term symbol, $L = 0$, *i.e.,* no orbit effect ($L = 0$ shows S term symbol). For these ions when $L = 0$, $J = S$ and hence $g = 2$. (From Eq. 5). Thus, Eq. (6) reduces to

$$\mu_{\text{eff}} = \mu_S = 2\sqrt{S(S+1)}$$

or

$$\mu_{\text{eff}} = \mu_{\text{spin only}} = 2\sqrt{\frac{n}{2}\left(\frac{n}{2}+1\right)} = \sqrt{n(n+2)}$$

The values of μ_{eff} calculated from these two equations are also given in Table 10.7 which shows that μ_J and μ_S values for La^{3+}, Gd^{3+} and Lu^{3+} ions are the same.

Example 1. *Calculate magnetic moment (μ) in BM of* Pr^{3+} *with outer configuration* $4f^2, 6s^0$.

Sol. The unpaired electrons are contained in the $4f$-orbitals. For determing the term symbols for the ground state of an atom. we write the box diagram of $4f$.

m_l =	3	2	1	0	−1	−2	−3
	1	1					

($4f$-orbitals)

In Pr^{3+}, $\quad L = 3 + 2 = 5$

and $\quad S = \frac{1}{2} + \frac{1}{2} = 2$

To determine ground state J, we take :

maximum J value if subshell is more than half-filled

and

minimum J value if subshell is less than half-filled.

$$J = |L+S|, |L+S-1| \ldots\ldots |L+S|$$
$$= |5+1|, |6-1|, |5-1| = 6, 5, 4$$

Since, $4f^2$ is less than half-filled, therefore, ground state $J = 4$.

Thus, we have $\quad S = 1;\ L = 5;\ J = 4$

From Eq. (6)

$$g = 1 + \frac{4(4+1) + 1(1+1) - 5(5+1)}{2 \times 4(4+1)}$$
$$= 1 + \frac{20 + 2 - 30}{40} = 1 - \frac{8}{40} = \frac{4}{5}$$
$$\mu = g\{J(J+1)\}^{1/2}$$
$$= \frac{4}{5}[4(4+1)]^{1/2} = \frac{4}{5}(20)^{1/2}$$
$$= \frac{4}{5} \times 4.47 = 3.58$$

μ = **3.58 BM**

Table 10.6 **Calculated and Experimental Values of Magnetic Moment, μ_{eff} (in BM) of the Sulphates of Ln^{3+} ions. (n = No. of Unpaired Electrons in 4f-orbitals)**

$$g = 1 + \frac{J(J+1) + S(S+1) - L(L+1)}{2S(S+1)}$$

Ln^{3+} ions with configurations	n	Term symbol	$S = n/2$	L	J	g	$\mu_J = g\sqrt{J(J+1)}$ BM	$\mu_S = 2\sqrt{S(S+1)}$ BM $= \sqrt{n(n+2)}$ BM	μ_{exp} (in BM)
$La^{3+}(4f^0)$	0	$^1S_0$	0	0	0	–	0.00	0.0	0.00 (diamagnetic)
$Ce^{3+}(4f^1)$	1	$^2F_{5/2}$	1/2	3	5/2	6/7	2.54	1.7	2.3–2.5
$Pr^{3+}(4f^2)$	2	$^3H_4$	1	5	4	4/5	3.58	2.8	3.4–3.6
$Nd^{3+}(4f^3)$	3	$^4I_{9/2}$	3/2	6	9/2	8/11	3.62	3.9	3.5–3.6
$Pm^{3+}(4f^4)$	4	$^5I_4$	2	6	4	3/5	2.70	4.9	–
$Sm^{3+}(4f^5)$	5	$^6H_{5/2}$	5/2	5	5/2	2/7	0.84	5.9	1.5–1.6
$Eu^{3+}(4f^6)$	6	$^7F_0$	3	3	0	–	0.00	6.9	3.4–3.6
$Gd^{3+}(4f^7)$	7	$^8S_{7/6}$	7/2	0	7/2	2	7.94	7.94	7.8–8.0
$Tb^{3+}(4f^8)$	6	$^7F_6$	3	3	6	3/2	9.70	6.9	9.4–9.6
$Dy^{3+}(4f^9)$	5	$^5H_{15/2}$	5/2	5	15/2	4/3	10.60	5.9	10.4–10.5
$Ho^{3+}(4f^{10})$	4	$^5I_8$	2	6	8	5/4	10.60	4.9	103–10.5
$Er^{3+}(4f^{11})$	3	$^4I_{15/2}$	3/2	6	15/2	6/5	9.60	3.9	9.4–9.6
$Tm^{3+}(4f^{12})$	2	$^3H_6$	1	5	6	7/6	7.60	2.9	7.1–7.4
$Yb^{3+}(4f^{13})$	1	$^2F_{7/2}$	1/2	3	7/2	8/7	4.50	1.7	4.4–4.9
$Lu^{3+}(4f^{14})$	0	$^1S_0$	0	0	0	–	0.00	0.0	0.00 (Diamagnetic)

6. Complex Formation

The lanthanides are moderate in their complex forming ability which increases to the right in the Periodic Table. The 4f-electrons of lanthanides are too well shielded to interact. Consequently each lanthanide ion is effectively an inert gas-type ion, like those of the alkaline earth metals, that attracts ligands only by overall electrostatic forces. On the basis, we expect and also observe a general decrease in case of complex ion formation with a specific ligand in the series $Ln^{4+} > Ln^{3+} > Ln^{2+}$.

The tendency of the anhydrous Ln^{3+} ions to form complexes increases from La^{3+} to Lu^{3+}, whereas that of the hydrated Ln^{3+} ions, $Ln^{3+}(aq)$, decreases in the same order. The difference in complexation tendencies of the anhydrous and hydrated ions is due to the fact that while the size of the Ln^{3+} ions decreases, that the $Ln^{3+}(aq)$ increases with the increasing atomic number.

Uses of Lanthanides and Their Compounds

(A) Uses of the Elements

(i) **Lanthanides are used in metallothermic reactions** due to their extraordinary reducing property (Ce is a stronger reducing agent than Al). Lanthanido-thermic processes can yield sufficiently pure Nb, Zr, Fe, Co, Ni, Mn, Y, W, U, B and Si. These metals are also used as de-oxidising agents particularly in the manufacture of Cu and its alloys.

(ii) Alloys of lanthanides are known as misch-metals. The major constituents of mish-metals are Ce (45–50%), La (25%), Nd (5%) and small quantities of other lanthanide metals and Fe and Ca impurities.

Misch-metals are used for the production of different brands of steel like heat resistant, stainless and instrumental steels. The addition of 0.75% of michh-metal to steel raises its yield point and its workability in heated state and improves its resistance to oxidation. Misch metal is an excellent scavenger for absorbed oxygen and sulphur in metallurgy.

Mg-alloys containing about 30% misch metal and 1% Zr are useful in making parts of jet engine. When alloyed with 30% iron, it is sufficiently pyrophoric to be useful in lighter flints.

(B) Uses of the Lanthanide Compounds

The uses of the compounds of lanthanides can broadly be classified as follows :

(i) Ceramic applications

CeO_2, La_2O_3, Nd_2O_3 and Pr_2O_3 are widely used for decolourising glass. Approximately 1% CeO_2 is used in the manufacture of protective transparent glass blocks to be used in nuclear technology because these blocks are not affected by prolonged exposure to radiations. Because lanthanide oxides can absorb ultra-violet rays, these are used as additive in glasses for speical purposes, *e.g.,* for making (a) sun-glasses (by adding Nd_2O_3) (b) goggles for glass blowing and welding work ($Nd_2O_3 + Pr_2O_3$) (c) glasses protecting eyes from neutron radiation ($Gd_2O_3 + Sm_2O_3$) etc.

The addition of more than 1% CeO_2 to a glass gives it a brown colour. Nd_2O_3 and Pr_2O_3, give respectively red and green colours, ($Nd_2O_3 + Pr_2O_3$) gives a blue colour.

(ii) Refractories

CeS (m.pt. = 2000°C) is used in the manufacture of a special type of crucibles which are used for melting metals in a reducing atmosphere at temperatures up to 1800°C. Borides, carbides and nitrides of lanthanides are also used as refractories.

(iii) Abrasives

Lanthanide oxides are used as abrasives for polishing glasses, *e.g.,* the mixture of oxides, CeO_2 (47%), $La_2O_3 + Nd_2O_3 + Pr_2O_3$ (51%) + SiO_2, CaO, Fe_2O_3 etc. (≃ 2%) which is called polirite has been used for polishing glasses.

(iv) Paints

Lanthanide compounds are used in the manufacture of lakes, dyes and paints for porcelain, *e.g.,* cerium molybdate gives light yellow colour, cerium tungstate gives greenish blue colour and salts of Nd give red colour.

(v) In textiles and leather industries

Ceric salts are used for dying in textile industries and as tenning agents in leather industries. $(Ce(NO_3)_4$ is used as a mordant for alizarin dyes. Chlorides and acetates of lanthanides make the fabrics water-proof and acid resistant.

Table 10.7 **Comparison of 4*f*- and 3*d*-Metal Ions**

S.No.	Properties	4*f*-metal ions (lanthanide ions)	3*d*-metal ions (Transition metal ions)
1.	Metal orbital	4*f*	3*d*
2.	Ionic radii	La^{3+} (= 1.06 Å), Lu^{3+}(= 0.85 Å)	0.75–0.6 Å
3.	Common coordination numbers	6, 7, 8 9	4-6
4.	Bonding	No metal-ligand orbital interaction	Strong metal-ligand orbitals interaction
5.	Bond direction	Little preference in bond directions	Strong direction bonding
6.	Bond strengths	Ligands bonds in order of electronegativity F^-, OH^-, H_2O, NO_3^-, Cl^-	Bond strengths determined by orbital interaction normally in the following order : CN^-, NH_3, H_2O , OH^-, F^-
7.	Solution complexes	Ionic, rapid ligand, exchange.	Often covalent, covalent complexes normally exchange slowly.

Actinides

The elements in which the extra electron enters in 5*f*-orbitals of (*n* – 2)th shell are known as 5*f*-block elements, actinides or actinones. Thus, strictly according to this definition of actinides only thirteen elements from Th_{90} $(5f^0\ 6d^2\ 7s^2)$ to No_{102} $(5f^{14}\ 6d^0\ 7s^2)$ should be the members of actinide series. However, all the fifteen elements from Ac_{89} $(5f^1\ 6d^1\ 7s^2)$ to Lr_{103} $(5f^{14}\ 6d^1\ 7s^2)$ are considered as the members of actinide series, since all these fifteen elements have similar physical and chemical properties. In fact the name actinides has been derived from actinium which is prototype of actinides as lanthanum is the prototype of lanthanides.

Position of Actinides in the Periodic Table

The existence of the lanthanide series helped the discoverers to predict that another series of elements resulting from the addition of electrons to an $(n-2)\,f$-shell (*i.e.,* $5f$-shell) should occur somewhere in the heavy elements region. Prior to the discovery of transuranium elements, the naturally occurring heaviest known elements namely Th_{90}, Pa_{91} and U_{92}, were placed below Hf_{72}, Ta_{73} and W_{74} in IVB, VB and VIB groups of the Periodic Table, because these elements showed + 4, + 5 and + 6 oxidation states and resembled Hf, Ta and W respectively in many of their properties. The then undiscovered transuranium elements with atomic numbers 93 to 100 were thus expected to occupy the positions in the Periodic Table below Re_{75}, Os_{76}, Ir_{77}, Pt_{78}, Au_{79}, Hg_{80}, Tl_{81} and Pb_{82} respectively.

Seaborg advanced the idea that the elements having atomic numbers greater than that of Ac_{89} might constitute a second series of inner-transition elements similar to the lanthanide series. The revised Periodic Table thus included the elements after Ac_{89} as a second inner transition series and these elements with the name *"actinide"* elements, were paired off with those in the already known lanthanide elements outside the body of the Periodic Table.

The new position of the actinides was further confirmed by the fact that all the predicted elements up to 103 were discovered by 1961. The actinides now occupy the same position in the Periodic Table as suggested in 1944 and the Periodic Table, as it looks now, is shown in Fig 10.4. The atomic numbers of the undiscovered "transactinide elements" (*i.e.,* the elements with atomic number greater than 103) have been shown in parentheses.

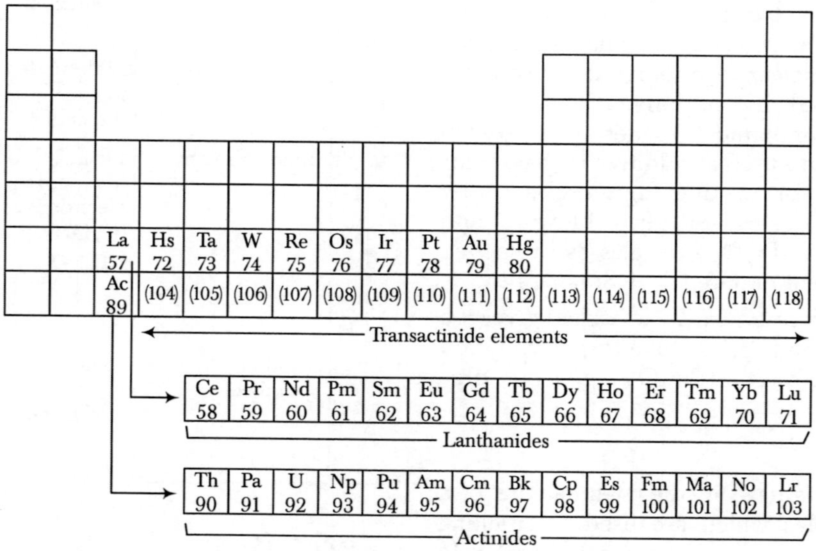

Fig. 10.4 The Periodic Table as it looks today.

Identification and Nuclear Synthesis of Transuranium Elements

Of all the naturally occurring elements, uranium has the highest atomic number equal to 92. For this reason this element continued to occupy the last position in the Periodic Table for a pretty long time. Since, 1940 eleven elements with atomic numbers equal to 93, 94, 95, 96, 97, 98, 99, 100, 101, 102 and 103 respectively have been identified and synthesised by the transformation of naturally occurring elements by nuclear reactions. These man-made eleven elements are placed beyond uranium in the Periodic Table and are collectively called **transuranium elements.**

The year of idenfication of the first isotope, the names of the discoverers, the method of identification and synthesis of these transuranium elements are summarised in Table 10.8.

Separation of Actinide Elements

Transuranium elements, produced as a result of nuclear reactions, are isolated from the target materials and irradiated nuclear fuels by the following methods :

1. Precipitation Method

Tri-and tetrapositive actinides can be precipitated as fluorides or phosphates from acidic solutions. Actinides in higher oxidation states either do not give a precipitate or form complexes. This method is particularly useful for the separation of the actinide elements of U-Am group. When the quantity of the actinide ion is insufficient to precipitate by itself, co-precipitation with a carrier like LaF_3 or $BiPO_4$ is adopted. The LiF_3-coprecipitation methods has been used for the separation of Np and Pu (obtained by neutron irradiation of uranium) from uranium and other fission products. The $BiPO_4$ coprecipitation method has been discovered by Thomson and Seaborg and is used for the large scale preparation of Pu from U and fission products. This is shown in flow-sheet 1.

$BiPO_4$-coprecipitation method for the separation of Pu from U and fission products. (FP's).

Flow sheet-I

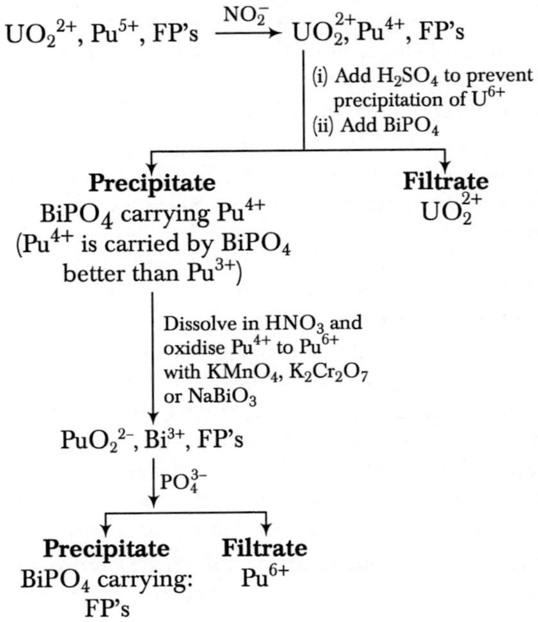

Table 10.8 **The Year of Identification of the First Isotope, the Names of the Discoverers and the Method of Identification and Synthesis of Transuranium Elements** (Np_{93} to Lw_{103})

Transuranium elements	First isotopes identified	Year	Source of synthesis	Discoverers
Neptunium ($_{93}Np$)	$_{93}Np^{239}$	1940	$_{92}U^{238} + _0n^1 \longrightarrow _{92}U^{239}$ $_{92}U^{239} \longrightarrow _{93}Np^{239} + _{-1}e^0$	Mcmillan and Abelson
Plutonium ($_{94}Pu$)	$_{94}Pu^{239}$	1941	$_{93}Np^{239} + _0n^1 \longrightarrow _{92}U^{239} + _{-1}e^0$	Seaborg, McMillian, Keenedy and Wahl
Americium ($_{95}Am$)	$_{95}Am^{241}$	1945	$_{92}U^{238} + _2He^4 \longrightarrow _{94}Pu^{241} + _0n^1$ $_{94}Pu^{241} \longrightarrow _{95}Am^{241} + _{-1}e^0$	Seaborg, James, Morgan and Ghiorso
Curium ($_{96}Cm$)	$_{96}Cm^{242}$	1944	$_{94}Pu^{239} + _2He^4 \longrightarrow _{96}Cm^{242} + _0n^1$	Seaborg, James and Ghiorso
Berkelium ($_{97}Bk$)	$_{97}Bk^{243}$	1949	$_{95}Am^{241} + _2He^4 \longrightarrow _{97}Bk^{243} + 2_0n^1$	Thomson, Ghiorso and Seaborg
Californium ($_{98}Cf$)	$_{98}Cf^{245}$	1950	$_{96}Cm^{242} + 2_2He^4 \longrightarrow _{98}Cf^{245} + _0n^1$	Thomson, Stred, Ghiorso and Seaborg
Einstenium ($_{99}Es$)	$_{99}Es^{255}$	1952	$_{92}U^{238} + 17_0n^1 \longrightarrow _{92}U^{255}$ $_{92}U^{255} \longrightarrow _{99}Es^{255} + 7_{-1}e^0$	Ghiorso and coworkers
Fermium ($_{100}Fm$)	$_{100}Fm^{255}$	1953	$_{92}U^{255} \longrightarrow _{100}Fm^{255} + 8_{-1}e^0$	Ghiorso and coworkers
Mendelevium ($_{101}Md$)	$_{101}Md^{256}$	1955	$_{99}Es^{253} + _2He^4 \longrightarrow _{101}Md^{256} + _0n^1$	Ghiorso and coworkers
Nobelium ($_{102}No$)	$_{102}No^{252}$	1958	$_{98}Cm^{246} + _6C^{12} \longrightarrow _{102}No^{252} + 6_0n^1$	Ghiorso, Sikkelaw, Walton and Seaborg
Lawrencium ($_{103}Lr$)	$_{103}Lr^{254}$	1961	$_{95}Cr^{245} + _5B^{10} \longrightarrow _{103}Lr^{254} + _0n^1$	Ghiorso and Coworkers

2. Solvent Extraction Method

This method depends on the extractability of the various oxidation states of actinide elements. This technique finds extensive application in the recovery of U and Pu from used-up nuclear fuels. This process is based on the distribution of metal between the aqueous solution and an organic solvent. Thus, with methyl isobutyl ketone (hexone) Np^{4+}, Np^{5+}, Pu^{6+} and U^{6+} are extracted while Pu^{3+} is not extracted. Diethyl ether and tri-n-butyl phosphate (TBP) are other solvents which are used as extractants. Because of the high viscosity and density, TBP is used as 20% solution in kerosene. The method is preferentially applied to nitrate systems, because other ions like sulphate, perchlorate, fluoride etc., are strongly complexing and tend to retain the metal in aqueous solution. Hexone and diethyl ether require a high concentration of NO_3^- ions in the aqueous phase and it is achieved by adding $Al(NO_3)_3$ which has a high salt-out action. TBP is resistant to nitric acid oxidation and acts by itself as a salt agent. Solvent extraction of Pu and U by hexone and TBP is shown in Flow-sheets 2 and 3 respectively.

Flow Sheet 2. Separation of Pu and U from fission products (FP's) by solvent extraction with hexane (Redox process).

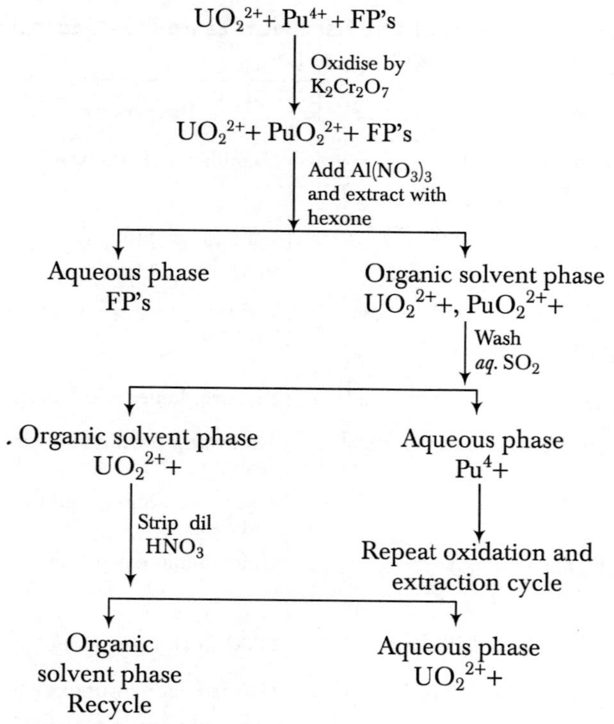

Flow Sheet 3. Separation of Pu and U from fission products (FP's) by solvent extraction with tributyl phosphate TBP (Purex process).

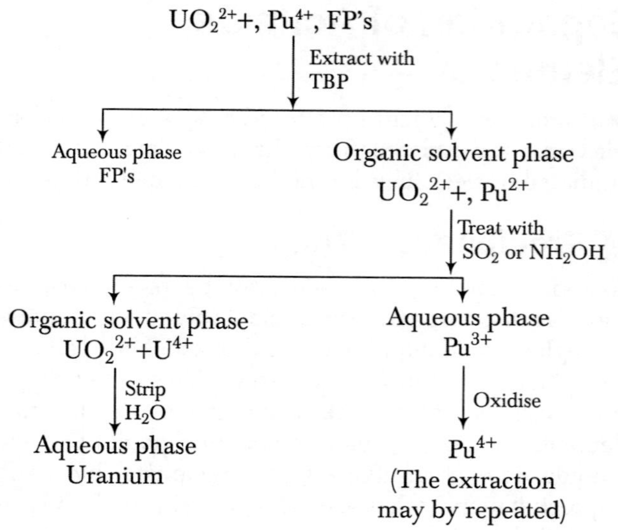

3. Ion-exchange Technique

Although this technique can be used to separate the actinide ions, this is best suited for separation of the trans- americium elements and also for some of the preceding elements, particularly for small amounts of material.

This method involves the following two steps.

(i) Lanthanide-actinide separation

The actinides as a group are separated from lanthanides by cation-exchange resin. Strong HCl is used as the eluting agent. The actinide ions form chloride complexes more easily and hence are eluted first.

Separation of actinides from lanthanides is now done on an anion-exchange resin with 10 M LiCl as eluent at elevated temperatures up to ~ 90° . With the exceptions of Gd, Ho and of Cm, Es, the elution sequences proceed in the order of increasing atomic number. Thus, La is absorbed least strongly.

(ii) Separation of individual actinide elements

The actinide ions, in general, can be separated from each other by removing from the cation exchange resin by elution with ammonium citrate, lactate, α-hydroxy isobutyrate and ethylene diamine tetracetate. If the activity is poltted against the number of drops of eluent, elution curves will be obtained as shown in Fig. 10.9. Lr (atomic number, $Z = 103$) is predicted to leave the column first, to be followed by No ($Z = 102$), and so on down the scale of atomic numbers. Elution positions for Md ($Z = 101$), Fm ($Z = 100$), and down to Am ($Z = 95$) are shown in the typical elution curves. Elution curves for lanthanides are also shown in the same figure for comparison. It may be noted that a very striking similarity occurs in the spacings of the corresponding elements in the two series (*e.g.,* Am and Eu, Cm and Gd, Bk and Tb etc). It is this similarity that made possible for scientists to predict the elution positions of the elements from Bk to Md before their discovery, and which also makes possible today to predict the elution positions of elements with $Z = 102$ and 103.

There is a distinct breakdown between Gd and Tb (lanthanide series) and between Cm and Bk (actinide series), which can be attributed to the small change in ionic radius occasioned by the half-filling of the $4f$- and $5f$-shells respectively. The elution order is not always as regular as shown in Fig. 10.5.

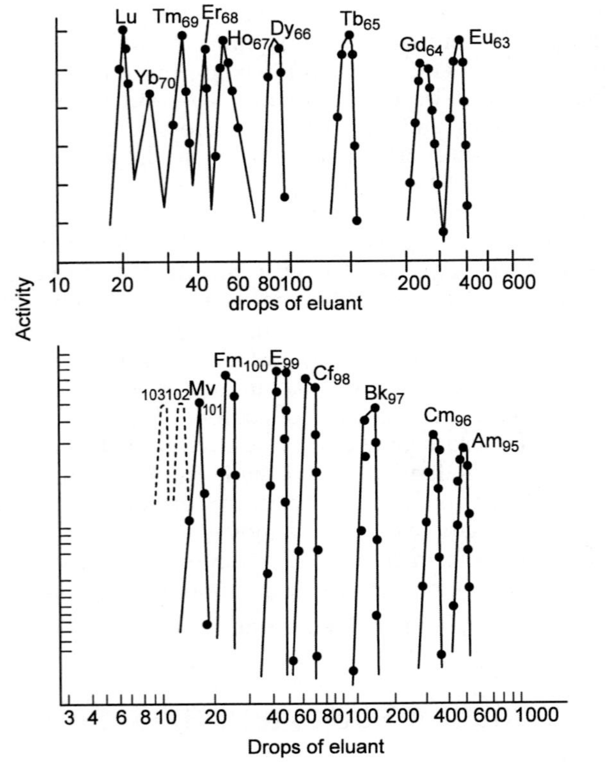

Fig. 10.5 Elution curves showing the elution positions of Ln^{3+} and An^{3+} ions eluted from Dowex-50 ion-exchange resin with ammonia alpha-hydroxy isobutyrate. The dotted elution curves indicate the predicted elution positions of the then undiscovered elements with atomic numbers 102 and 103.

General Properties of Actinides and Their Comparison with Lanthanides

Some of the important properties of actinides are discussed below.

1. Electronic Configuration and Nature of Bonding

According to modern view $5f$-orbitals in actinides start filling from protoactinium (Pa_{91}) and not from thorium (Th_{90}) as is evident from the valence-shell electronic configurations of actinides given in Table 10.10. For the sake of comparison the valence-shell configurations of lanthanides are also given in the same Table.

Table 10.9 **Electronic Configurations of the Neutral Gaseous atoms of Lanthanides and Actinides**

Lanthanides		Actinides		
Elements with atomic number	Valence shell configurations	Elements with atomic number	Complete configur-ations	Valence-shell configur-ations
La_{57}	$4f^0\ 5d^1\ 6s^2$	Ac_{89}	[Rn] $5f^0\ 6d^1\ 7s^2$	$5f^0\ 6d^1\ 7s^2$
Ce_{58}	$4f^2\ 5d^0\ 6s^2$	Th_{90}	[Rn] $5f^0\ 6d^2\ 7s^2$	$5f^0\ 6d^2\ 7s^2$
Pr_{59}	$4f^3\ 5d^0\ 6s^2$	Pa_{91}	[Rn] $5f^2\ 6d^1\ 7s^2$	$5f^2\ 6d^1\ 7s^2$
Nd_{60}	$4f^4\ 5d^0\ 6s^2$	U_{92}	[Rn] $5f^3\ 6d^1\ 7s^2$	$5f^3\ 6d^1\ 7s^2$
Pm_{61}	$4f^5\ 5d^0\ 6s^2$	Np_{93}	[Rn] $5f^4\ 6d^1\ 7s^2$	$5f^4\ 6d^1\ 7s^2$
Sm_{62}	$4f^6\ 5d^0\ 6s^2$	Pu_{94}	[Rn] $5f^6\ 6d^0\ 7s^2$	$5f^6\ 6d^0\ 7s^2$
Eu_{63}	$4f^7\ 5d^0\ 6s^2$	Am_{95}	[Rn] $5f^7\ 6d^0\ 7s^2$	$5f^7\ 6d^0\ 7s^2$
Gd_{64}	$4f^7\ 5d^1\ 6s^2$	Cm_{96}	[Rn] $5f^7\ 6d^1\ 7s^2$	$5f^7\ 6d^1\ 7s^2$
Tb_{65}	$4f^9\ 5d^0\ 6s^2$	Bk_{97}	[Rn] $5f^9\ 6d^0\ 7s^2$	$5f^9\ 6d^0\ 7s^2$
Dy_{66}	$4f^{10}\ 5d^0\ 6s^2$	Cf_{98}	[Rn] $5f^{10}\ 6d^0\ 7s^2$	$5f^{10}\ 6d^0\ 7s^2$

Lanthanides		Actinides		
Ho_{67}	$4f^{11}\ 5d^0\ 6s^2$	Es_{99}	[Rn] $5f^{11}\ 6d^0\ 7s^2$	$5f^{11}\ 6d^0\ 7s^2$
Er_{68}	$4f^{12}\ 5d^0\ 6s^2$	Fm_{100}	[Rn] $5f^{12}\ 6d^0\ 7s^2$	$5f^{12}\ 6d^0\ 7s^2$
Tm_{69}	$4f^{13}\ 5d^0\ 6s^2$	Md_{101}	[Rn] $5f^{13}\ 6d^0\ 7s^2$	$5f^{13}\ 6d^0\ 7s^2$
Y_{70}	$4f^{14}\ 5d^0\ 6s^2$	No_{102}	[Rn] $5f^{14}\ 6d^0\ 7s^2$	$5f^{14}\ 6d^0\ 7s^2$
Lu_{71}	$4f^{14}\ 5d^1\ 6s^2$	Lr_{103}	[Rn] $5f^{14}\ 6d^1\ 7s^2$	$5f^{14}\ 6d^1\ 7s^2$

Siilarity between lanthanoids and actinoids

Comparison of the electronic configurations of lanthanides and actinides shows both a substantial overall similarity and enhanced tendency for the lighter members namely Ac_{89} to Np_{93} to retain 6*d*-electrons. The later tendency results both from the even smaller energy separation between the 5*f* and 6*d*-orbitals in actinides than that between the 4*f* and 5*d*-orbitals in lanthanides and from the difference in change in binding energy of the weakest bound (*i.e.*, most readily removable) 6*d* and 5*f*-electrons in actinides with atomic number as shown in Fig. 10.10 in which a rough quantitative picture for the binding energies of the weakest bound 5*f* and 6*d*-electrons in actinides is shown. Spectroscopic chemical and other data tell that 5*f*-level becomes progressively lower in energy compared to the 6*d*-level with increasing atomic number. The relative point of change is thus different in the two series and also the fall in energy and shrinkage in size are not so precipitous for 5*f*-orbitals as for 4*f*-orbitals. The spatial extension of 5*f*-orbitals relative to 6*s* and 6*p*-orbitals is thus greater than that of 4*f* -orbitals relative to 5*s* and 5*p*-orbitals. The greater spatial extension of 5*f*-orbitals has also been shown experimentally.

Since, *f*-shell is being filled in lanthanides (4*f*-shell) and actinides (5*f*-shells), the elements of these two series have close relationship in properties with one another. Thus, Ac_{89} and La_{57} occupy corresponding positions as prototypes for the two series.

Difference between lanthanoids and actinoids

Although important similarities exist between the elements of the two series, very important differences also occur. These differences are due to mainly to the relatively lower binding energies and less effective sheilding of the 5*f*-electrons (in actinides) than those of 4*f*-electrons (in lanthanides).

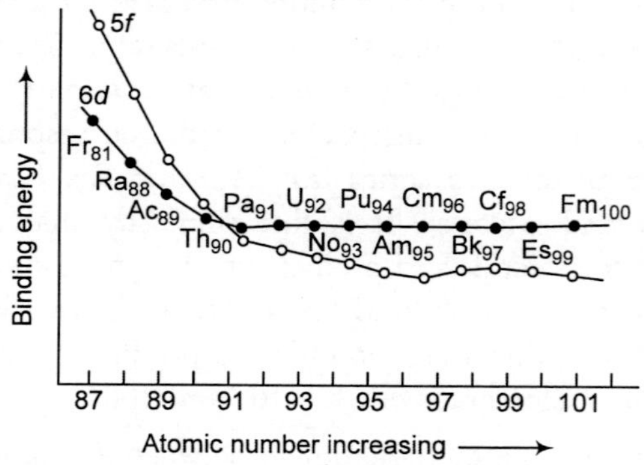

Fig. 10.6 Qualitative comparison of binding energies of 5*f*-and 6*d*-electrons.

The actinides have deeply seated incomplete 5*f*-orbitals compared to 4*f*-orbitals in lanthanides. 4*f* and 5*f*-orbitals differ in their radial distribution functions. The radial distribution of 4*f*-orbitals shows a small shell of electron density below the main 5*f*-orbital (compare, for example, 1*s* and 2*s* radial functions). Therefore, 5*f*-orbitals are more penetrating than 4*f*-orbitals. In lanthanides 4*f*-orbitals are well within the 6*s* and 5*p* orbital. Therefore, there is no question of an overlap between 4*f* and the surrounding ligands. The 5*f*-orbitals which are more penetrating than 4*f*-orbitals are little more diffuse at the periphery of the atom. Hence, these orbitals are somewhat disturbed by ligands. It is well known that the energy difference between different levels and sub-levels decreases with increasing atomic number. Thus, in the actinides the energies of 5*f*, 6*d*, 7*s* and 7*p* orbitals are equal. This results in that unlike lanthanides, the bonding in the compounds of actinides can involve any or all of these orbitals. This fact is realised when we find that while lanthanides virtually form no complexes or covalent compounds in which 4*f*-orbitals participate in bonding (lanthanides form mostly ionic compounds), the actinides form complexes not only with anions such as X^-, SO_4^{2-} etc., but also with π-bonding ligands such as alkyl phosphines, thioethers and cyclopentadiene by the use of 5*f*-orbitals.

2. Oxidation States and Oxidation Potentials

Observed oxidation states of acinide elements noted either in solution or in isolable compounds are summarised in Table 10.10.

Table 10.10 **Various Oxidation States Shown by Actinides and Standard Oxidation Potentials,** $E°$ **(in Volts) for Various Couples in 1 M Perchloric Acid at 25°C**

Actinides with atomic numbers	Oxidation states (less stable states are given in brackets)	$E°$ values (in volts) for various couples (Estimated values are given in brackets)
Ac_{89}	+ 3	$Ac^0 \xrightarrow{2.6\ V} Ac^{3+}$
Th_{90}	+ 4	$Th^0 \xrightarrow{1.90} Th^{4+}$
Pa_{91}	(+ 4), + 5	$Pa^0 \xrightarrow{(0.9)} Pa^{4+} \xrightarrow{0.1} PaO_2^+$
		$Pa^0 \xrightarrow{1.0} PaO_2^+$
U_{92}	(+ 3), (+ 4), (+ 5), + 6	$U^0 \xrightarrow{1.80} U^{3+} \xrightarrow{0.631} U^{4+} \xrightarrow{-0.58} UO_2^+ \xrightarrow{-0.063} UO_2^{2+}$
		$U^{4+} \xrightarrow{-0.32} UO_2^{2+}$
Np_{92}	(+ 3), (+ 4), + 5, (+ 6), (+ 7)	$Np^0 \xrightarrow{1.83} Np^{3+} \xrightarrow{-0.155} Np^{4+} \xrightarrow{-0.739} NpO_2^+ \xrightarrow{-1.137} NpO_2^{2+}$
		$Np^{3+} \xrightarrow{0.447} NpO_2^+$
		$Np^{4+} \xrightarrow{-0.938} NpO_2^{2+}$
Pu_{94}	(+ 3), + 4, (+ 5), (+ 6), (+ 7)	$Pu^0 \xrightarrow{2.03} Pu^{3+} \xrightarrow{-0.981} Pu^{4+} \xrightarrow{-1.172} PuO_2^+ \xrightarrow{-0.913} PuO_2^{2+}$
Am_{95}	+ 2, (+ 3), (+ 4), (+ 5), (+ 6)	$Am^0 \xrightarrow{(<2.7)} Am^{2+7} \xrightarrow{>1.5} Am^{3+} \xrightarrow{-2.4} Am^{4+} \xrightarrow{-1.04}$
		$AmO_2^+ \xrightarrow{-1.60} AmO_2^{2+}$
Cm_{96}	+ 3, (+ 4)	$Cm^0 \xrightarrow{(>-2.80)} Cm^{4+}$
Bk_{97}	+ 3, (+ 4)	$Bk^0 \xrightarrow{(-1.6)} Bk^{4+}$
Cf_{98}	+ 3	–
Es_{99}	+ 3	–
Fm_{100}	+ 3	–
Md_{101}	+ 3	$Md^{2+} \xrightarrow{(0.2)} Md^{3+}$
No_{102}	+ 3	$No^{2+} \xrightarrow{(-1.4)} No^{3+}$
Lr_{103}	+ 3	–

Comparison of the oxidation states of lanthanides with those of actinides indicates that + 3 oxidation state is the most common for both the series of elements. This oxidation state becomes increasingly more stable as the atomic number increases in the actinide series. The increasing stability of + 3 oxidation state is illustrated by the increasing difficulty of oxidation above + 3 oxidation state. This is clearly shown by the values of oxidation potentials ($E°$ values) listed in the same Table. $E°$ values have been recorded in 1M perchloric acid at 25°C. **The standard electrode potentials for the lanthanides couple, Ln^0 / Ln^{3+} become steadily more positive with the increase of atomic number (due to lanthanide contraction), while for the actinides couple An^0 / An^{3+} these values become more positive from Ac to U and become less positive till Am.** Am^{4+} is thus, a more powerful oxidising agent than Ce^{4+}, while Pu^{4+}, Np^{4+} and U^{4+} are less powerful. U^{3+} is a strong reducing agent.

As regards lanthanides, no definite rule can be give about whether or not the + 3 oxidation state of lanthanides increases in stability with the increase of atomic number.

Actinides show a greater multiplicity of oxidation states. Since in the first half of the actinide series (*i.e.*, lower actinides, the energy required for the conversion $5f \longrightarrow 6d$ is less than that required for the conversion

$4f \longrightarrow 5d$, the lower actinides should, on a comparative basis, show more higher oxidation states such as + 4, + 5, + 6 and + 7. Correspondingly, since in the second half of the actinide series (*i.e.,* higher actinides), the energy required for the conversion $5f \longrightarrow 6d$ is more than that required for the conversion $4f \longrightarrow 5d$, the higher actinides should show more lower oxidation states such as + 2. These expectations are in agreement with oxidation states given in Table 10.11. The second half of the series appears to parallel the lanthanides while the first halves of the two series are widely different from each other.

The tripositive oxidation state occurs widely in each series. The two groups of elements, however, are not entirely comparable in this respect. The +3 state, characteristic of lanthanides, does not appear in aqueous solution of Th and Pa and this oxidation state becomes the predominantly stable oxidation state in aqueous solution of the actinides only when we reach Am. The elements from U to Am have several oxidation states, while there is no analogous example among lanthanides . These differences can readily be explained on the basis of the assumption that 7*s*-, 6*d*- and 5*f*- levels have almost the same energies in this region.

Since, 5*f*-electrons are more easily removed than the 4*f*-electrons, for the actinide metals the lower oxidation states are less and the higher ions are more important compared to the lanthanide metals; *e.g.,* even Cm gives Cm (IV) oxidation state in solids CmO_2 and CmF_4, whereas only Gd(III) compounds are known. Cm^{4+} ion is also stable in solution.

+ 2 Oxidation state

Only americium (analogous to europium) is known to form a stable + 2 state. This state is stable in CaF_2 only and has been studied by optical and electron spin reasonance spectra. + 2 state is uncommon for other actinides. An^{2+} ions resemble Ln^{2+} ions in their general chemistry.

+ 3 Oxidation state

+ 3 state is a general oxidation state for most of the actinides. For Th and Pa, + 4 and + 5 states respectively are important. An^{4+} ions resemble Ln^{4+} ions in their properties. A large number of isomorphous salts are given by the elements of both the series. Trichlorides and trifluorides of Ac, U, Np, Pu and Am are isomorphous. On hydrolysis all the halides give oxyhalides.

Ac, Pu and heavier elements give the oxides of An_2O_3 type which are isomorphous with Ln_2O_3 oxides.

Nitrates, perchlorates and sulphates are soluble while hydroxides, fluorides and carbonates are insoluble. Like lanthanides, actinides also form complexes with EDTA. Lanthanide-EDTA complexes are less stable than the corresponding actinide-EDTA complexes.

+ 4 Oxidation state

This is the principal oxidation state for Th and is a stable oxidation state upto Am. Am^{4+} and Cm^{4+} exist only as complexes in concentrated fluoride solution of low acidity. General chemistry of An^{4+} ions is similar to that of Ln^{4+} ions. The hydrated fluorides and phosphates of both Au^{4+} and Ln^{4+} ions are insoluble. ThO_2, PaO_2, UO_2, NpO_2, AmO_2, CmO_2 and BkO_2 have fluorite structure. The tetrachlorides and tetrabromides of Th, Pa, U and Np are only known, while tetraiodides of Th, Pa and U have been isolated. Oxyhalides of Th, U and Np can be prepared by heating AnX_4 with Sb_2O_3. An^{4+} ions form complexes mostly with anionic ligands like HSO_4^-, NO_3^-, Cl^- etc.

+ 5 Oxidation state

This state is very important for Pa, Pa^{5+} resembles very much Na^{5+} and Ta^{5+}. U, Np, Pu and Am also exist in + 5 states, but these are less characterised. The only known pentahalides are those of Pa^{5+} and U^{5+}.

Fluoro anions of Pa, U, Np and Pu of the type AnF_6^-, AnF_7^{2-} and AnF_8^{3-} are known to exist in the solid state. Oxychlorides, $AnOCl_3$ (An = Pa, U and Np) are also known.

AnO_2^+ is the most important ion which contains An^{5+} cation. It has linear structure both in solid and solution. This monovalent dioxocation forms many complexes with anionic and neutral ligands.

+ 6 Oxidation state

U, Np, Pu and Am show + 6 oxidation state is divalent dioxo cation, AnO_2^{2+}. This cation is linear both in solid and solution. The simple molecular halide, UO_2F_3 has the linear O–U–O group with fluorine bridges. The O–U bond distance is 1.75 to 2.00 Å. The overall structure is a flattened octahedron. Although AnO_2^{2+} cation is linear in shape, it forms complexes with exceptional geometries, *e.g.,* four, five and six coordinated complexes are given by this cation.

+7 Oxidation states

+7 oxidation states is shown only by Np and Pu. Electrolysis or ozone oxidation of Np^{5+} or Np^{6+} in NaOH gives a green solution of NpO_5^{3-} which is slowly reduced to Np^{6+} at 25°C ($E°$ for $Np^{7+}/Np^{6+} = 0.58$ V in 1M NaOH). The existence of Np^{7+} ion has been confirmed by Mossbauer spectra.

Pu^{7+} ion is obtained by exposing a mixture of PuO_2 and Li_2O oxygen at 430°C when Li_5PuO_6 is formed. The chemistries of Np^{7+} and Pu^{7+} resemble those of Re^{7+} and Te^{7+}.

3. Atomic and Ionic Radii—Actinide Contraction

Crystal structure data have provided the basis for ionic radii of the actinide elements. In Table 10.11 atomic and ionic radii of the tripositive and tetrapositive actinide ions (*i.e.*, An^{3+} and An^{4+} ions) are summarised. The atomic radii of lanthanide atoms and ionic radii of Ln^{2+}, Ln^{3+} and Ln^{4+} ions are also included in the same table for comparison. It may be noted that for An^{3+} and An^{4+} ions there is an actinide contraction (*i.e.*, decrease in ionic radii of An^{3+} and An^{4+} ions), analogous to the lanthanide contraction, with increasing positive charge on the nucleus. **This actinide contraction is due to the addition of successive electrons to an inner *f*-shell (*i.e.*, 5*f*-shell), so that the imperfect screening of the increasing nuclear charge by the additional 5*f* electrons results in a contraction of the outer or valence orbital.**

It may also be noted that the tripositive actinide ion (An^{3+} ion) is always somewhat larger than the formally analogous Ln^{3+} ions as shown in Fig. 10.7. The slightly but readily detectable discontinuity at the Gd^{3+} ion does not have a parallel at the Cm^{3+} ion. Rather there is a continuing divergence in the size among the An^{3+} ions as the nuclear charge increases. The ionic radii of Ln^{4+} and An^{4+} cations are shown together in Fig. 10.18.

The jumps in contraction between the consecutive elements in the actinides in greater than in the lanthanides. The greater contraction is due to the lesser shielding of 5*f*-electrons which are therefore, pulled more strongly by the nucleus. **The actinide contraction, as usual, leads to a decrease in the basicity of the elements with increasing atomic number.**

Table 10.11 **Atomic and Ionic** (or crystal) **Radii of Lanthanides and Actinides in Å**

Lanthanides					Actinides			
Elements with atomic number	Atomic radius	Crystal or ionic radii of Ln^{2+} ion	Ln^{3+} ion	Ln^{4+} ion	Elements with atomic number	Atomic radius	Crystal or ionic radii of An^{3+} ion	An^{4+} ion
La_{57}	1.88		1.06		Ac_{89}	1.88	1.11	0.99
Ce_{58}	1.82		1.03	0.92	Th_{90}	1.80	(1.08)	0.96
Pr_{59}	1.83		1.01	0.90	Pa_{91}	1.61	(1.05)	0.93
Nd_{60}	1.82		0.99		U_{92}	1.38	1.03	0.92
Pm_{61}	–		(0.98)		Np_{93}	1.30	1.01	0.92
Sm_{62}	1.80	1.11	0.96		Pu_{94}	1.51	1.00	0.90
Eu_{63}	2.04	1.09	0.95		Am_{95}	1.73	0.99	0.89
Gd_{64}	1.80		0.94		Cm_{96}		0.98	0.88
Tb_{65}	1.78		0.92	0.84				
Dy_{66}	1.77		0.91					
Ho_{67}	1.77		0.89 (Decreasing ↓)					Decreasing ↓
Er_{68}	1.76		0.88				Decreasing ↓	
Tm_{69}	1.75	0.94	0.87					
Yb_{70}	1.94	0.93	0.86					
Lu_{71}	1.73		0.85					

*Predicted values are given in parentheses. In the octahedral fluorides, AnF_6, the An—F bond distance also decreases with increasing atomic number, namely, U–F = 1.99 Å, Np–F = 1.98 Å, Pu–F = 1.96 Å (Z for U, Np and Pu are 92, 93 and 94 respectively).

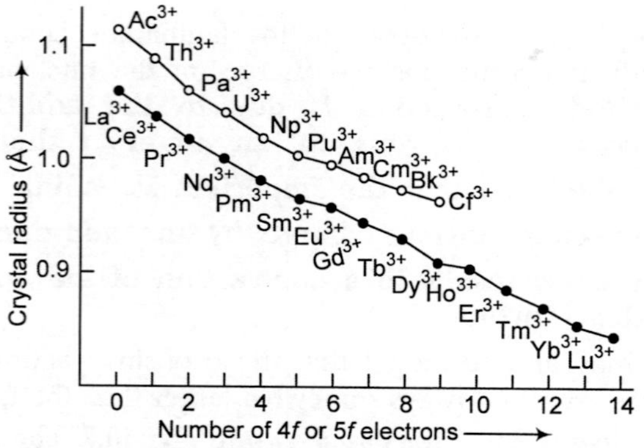

Fig. 10.7 Crystal radii of Ln^{3+} (shown by black circles) and An^{3+} ions (shown by hollow circles).

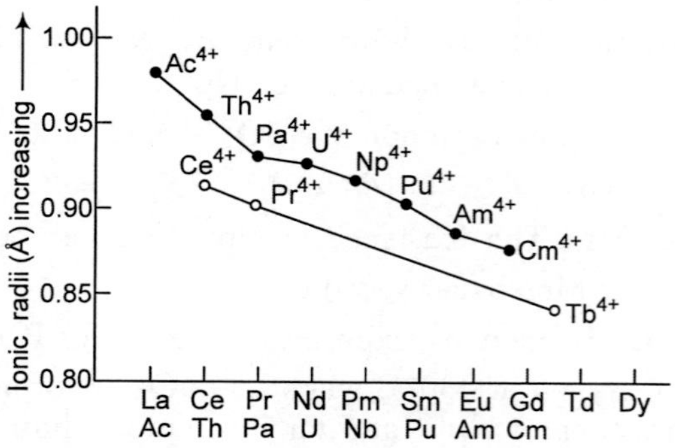

Fig. 10.8 Ionic radii of Ln^{4+} (shown by hollow circle) and An^{4+} ions (shown by black circles).

4. Colours and Absorption Spectra of Actinide Ions

Colours and the wavelengths of the more prominent light absorption bands of actinide ions like An^{3+}, An^{4+}, AnO_2^+ and AnO_2^{2+} are given in Table 10.12. It may be seen by comparing the colours of Ln^{3+} and An^{3+} ions, that the pairs of ions which have the same number of f electrons ($4f$ and $5f$-electrons) have roughly comparable colours. The pairs *viz.* (i) Nd^{3+} ($4f^2$-reddish) and U^{3+} ($5f^3$-red) and (ii) Gd^{3+} ($4f^7$-colourless) and Cm^{3+} ($5f^7$-colourless) illustrate this point. Ce^{3+} ($4f^1$) and Pa^{4+} ($5f^1$) ions are colourless.

The absorption spectra of actinide ions, in aqueous solution and in crystal, contain narrow bands in the visible, near-ultraviolet and near infrared regions of the spectrum. The bands seen in case of actinide ions arise from electronic transitions between energy states within the $5f$-electron subshell. It has been found, in general, that the absorption bands seen in case of actinide ions are about ten times sharper than those seen in case of lanthanide ions. The absorption spectra of lanthanide ions are observed due to electronic transitions between energy states within the $4f$-electron subshell.

Table 10.12 **Colours and Wavelengths (in Å) of more Prominent Light Absorption Bands of Actinide ions (An^{3+}, An^{4+}, AnO_2^+ and AnO_2^{2+}) in Aqueous Solution**

Elements	An^{3+} ions	An^{4+} ions	AnO_2^+ ions	AnO_2^{2+} ions
Ac	Colourless ($5f^0$) (No absorption)	–	–	–
Th	–	Colourless ($5f^0$) (No absorption)	–	–
Pa	–	Colourless ($5f^1$) (2240, 2550, 2760)	Colourless	–
U	Red ($5f^3$) (5200, 8800, 9000)	Green ($5f^2$) (5500, 6500)	–	Yellow (4000, 4110, 4250)
Np	Blue or purple ($5f^4$) (5520, 6610, 7875)	Yellow green ($5f^3$) (5040, 7430, 8250)	Green	Pink to red (4760, 5570)
Pu	Blue or violet ($5f^5$) (5600, 6000, 6030)	Tan to orange brown ($5f^4$) (4700, 6550, 8150)	Reddish purple	Yellow to pink- orange (8330, 9530, 9830)
Am	Pink ($5f^6$) (5027, 8200)	Rose ($5f^7$)	Yellow (5131, 7151)	Run- coloured (6660, 9950)
Cm	Colourless ($5f^7$) (2368, 2680, 2774)	–	–	–

Light absorption spectra of lanthanides are much more affected by environment.

Charge-transfer phenomena occur more frequently and the bands are more intense in the actinides because of lower energy involved in transitions. Moreover, the overlap of $5f$-orbitals with the ligand orbitals increases the intensity of absorption bands.

5. Magnetic Properties

In the $5f$-series, Pu^{3+} and Am^{3+} ions show that analogous behaviour as noted for Sm^{3+} and Eu^{3+} ions in $4f$-series.

The magnetic properties of the actinide ions are considerably more difficult to explain than those of the lanthanide ions. The values of magnetic moments found experimentally are usually lower than those calculated using Russell-Saunders coupling scheme. This is due perhaps to the inadequacy of the Russell-Saunders coupling scheme for $5f^n$ ions and also to more subtle ligand field effects which involve $5f$-orbitals to a greater extent than the $4f$-orbitals are involved in bonding the lanthanide complexes.

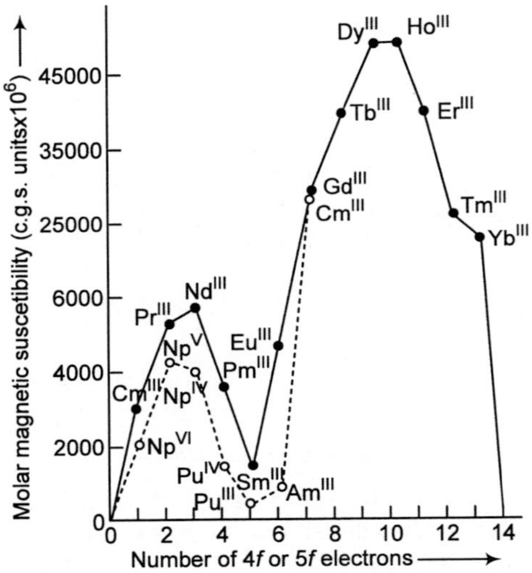

Fig. 10.9 Comparison of magnetic susceptibilities of lanthanide (shown by black circles) and actinide ions (shown by white circles).

An equation used for the calculation of molar susceptibility, χ_M, is given by

$$\chi_M = \frac{Ng^2\beta^2 J(J+1)}{3kT} + N\alpha$$

where, N = Avogadro's number,

g = Lande splitting factor which is given by

$$g = 1 + \frac{S(S+1) + J(J+1) - L(L+1)}{2J(J+1)}$$

β = Bohr magneton = $\frac{eh}{2\pi mc}$ = 9.27×10^{-21} erg/gauss,

J = Total angular momentum of atom = $|L + S|$,

k = Boltzmann constant,

T = absolute temperature,

and α = Small, temperature independent term due to second order Zeeman effect.

Strictly speaking the above equation can be applied only to gaseous ions in which the multiplet intervals are larger compared with
kT and the value of J to be used in it is taken from the ground state symbols of ions.

A comparison of the plots of molar magnetic susceptibilities of tripositive lanthanide and actinide ions against the number of $4f$- or $5f$-electrons (Fig. 10.10) reveals that there are remarkable similarities between the two plot. The plot of lanthanide ions has two humps while that of actinide ions has only one. In both the cases the first hump is, however, at the indentical place. The moments of the lanthanide ions agree closely with theoretical predictions but those of the transuranic ions are somewhat lower than expected (Fig. 10.10). This is because of $5f$-electrons of the transuranic ions are less effectively screened from the crystal field, which quenches the orbital contribution, than are the $4f$-electrons of the lanthanide ions.

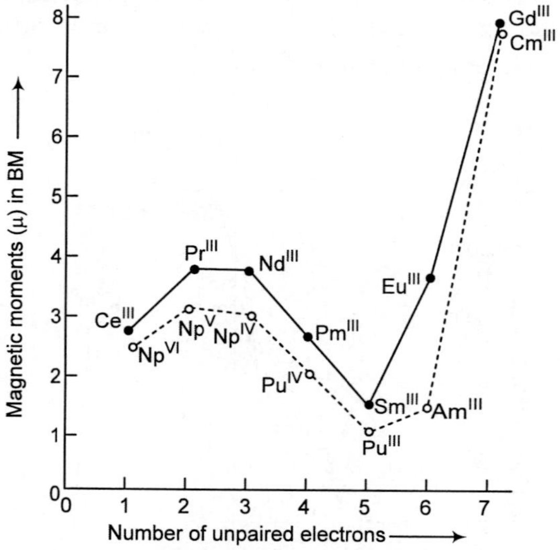

Fig. 10.10 Comparison of magnetic moments (in B.M.) of lanthanide (shown by black circles) and actinide ions (shown by hollow circles).

6. Complex Formation

The degree of complex formation decreases in the order :

$$An^{4+} > AnO_2^{2+} > An^{3+} > AnO_2^{+}$$

The complexing power of different singly charged and doubly charged anions follows the order :

Singly-charged anions : $F^- > NO_3^- > Cl^-$

Doubly-charged anions : $CO_3^{2-} > Ox^{2-} > SO_4^{2-}$

Actinides also form complexes with a large number of organic substances.

Exercise 1
(For Part 'B')

1. Due to lanthanide contraction
(a) all f-block ions have equal size
(b) all isoelectronic ions have equal size
(c) Zr and Hf have equal size
(d) Fe, Co and Ni have equal size

2. Which of the following statements concerning lanthanides elements is false?
(a) Ionic radii of trivalent lanthanides steadily increase with increase in the atomic number
(b) Lanthanides are separated from one another by ion exchange method
(c) All lanthanides are highly dense metals
(d) Move characteristic oxidation state of lanthanides elements is + 3

3. Which of the following statements is not correct?
(a) $La(OH)_3$ is less basic than $Lu(OH)_3$
(b) Atomic radius of Zr and Hf are same because of lanthanide contraction
(c) In lanthanide series ionic radius of Ln^{3+} ion decreases
(d) La is actually an element of transition series rather lanthanide

4. The lanthanide contraction is responsible for the fact that
(a) Zr and Zn have the same oxidation state
(b) Zn and Y have about the same radii
(c) Zr and Nb have similar oxidation state
(d) Zr and Hf have about the same radii

5. The electronic configuration of (Gd) (Nt, No 64) is
(a) $[Xe]4f^8, 5d^9, 6s^2$
(b) $[Xe]4f^7, 5d^1, 6s^2$
(c) $[Xe]4f^6, 5d^2, 6s^2$
(d) $[Xe]4f^3, 5d^3, 6s^2$

6. Which one of the following elements shows maximum number of different oxidation states in its compounds?
(a) La (b) Eu
(c) Am (d) Gd

7. Cerium $(Z = 58)$ is an important member of lanthanides. Which of the following statements about cerium is incorrect?
(a) Cerum IV acts as an oxidising agent
(b) The + 4 oxidation state of cerum is not known in solution
(c) The + 3 oxidation state is more stable than the + 4 state
(d) The common oxidation states of cerum are + 3 and + 4

8. Which of the following factors may be regarded as the main cause of lanthanide contraction?
(a) Poor shielding of one of $4f$-electrons by another in the subshell
(b) Greater shielding of $5f$-electrons by $4f$-electrons
(c) Poorer shielding of $5d$-electrons by $4f$-electrons
(d) Effective shielding of one $4f$-electrons by another in the subshell

9. The lanthanide contraction is due to
(a) filling of $5d$ before $4f$ (b) filling of $4d$ before $4f$
(c) filling of $4f$ before $5d$ (d) filling of $4f$ before $4d$

10. Elements after atomic number 92 are called
(a) actinoids
(b) lanthanoids
(c) inner-transition elements
(d) transuranium elements

11. Ln^{3+} (trivalent lanthanides ions) have electronic configurations
(a) $[Xe]4f^1$ to $[Xe]4f^{14}$
(b) $[Xe]4d^1\,4f^1$ to $[Xe]4d^1\,4f^{14}$
(c) $[Xe]4d^2\,4f^0$ to $[Xe]4d^1\,4f^{14}$
(d) $[Xe]4f^0$ to $[Xe]4f^{14}$

12. Which of the following have completely filled $5f$-orbitals?
(a) No (b) Lr
(c) Both (a) and (b) (d) None of these

13. An^{3+} (trivalent actinoid ions) have configuration
(a) $5f^0$ to $5f^{14}$ (b) $5f^1$ to $5f^{14}$
(c) $5f^2$ to $5f^{14}$ (d) $5f^0$ to $5f^{13}$

14. Select the correct statement(s).
(a) Maximum oxidation state of Np is + 7
(b) Pu^{4+} disproportionates to Pu^{3+} and PuO_2^{2+} in strongly acidic solutions
(c) UO_2^{2+} is stable
(d) All of the above are correct statement

15. Lanthanoids are
(a) 14 elements in the sixth period (at. no. to 103) that are filling $4f$ sub-level.
(b) 14 elements in the seventh period (at. no. = 90 to 103) that are filling $5f$ sub-level
(c) 14 elements in the sixth period (at. no. = 58 to 71) that are filling $4f$ sub-level
(d) 14 elements in the seventh period (at. no. = 58 to 71) that are filling $5f$ sub-level

16. The main reason for larger number of oxidation state exhibited by the actinoids than that corresponding lanthanides is
(a) lesser energy difference between $5f$ and $6d$ orbitals than between $4f$ and $5d$-orbitals
(b) greater reactive nature of the actinides than the lanthanides
(c) larger atomic size of actinides than the lanthanides
(d) more energy difference between $5f$ and $6d$-orbitals than between $4f$ and $5d$-orbitals

17. The common oxidation state of the elements of lanthanide series is
(a) $+1$ (b) $+3$
(c) $+4$ (d) $+6$

18. Lanthanide and actinides resemble in
(a) electronic configuration
(b) oxidation state
(c) ionization energy
(d) formation of complexes

19. Lanthanides for which + II and + III oxidation states are common is
(a) La (b) Eu
(c) Ce (d) Nd

20. Which of the following lanthanide is commonly used?
(a) Lanthanium (b) Thorium
(c) Cerium (d) Nobelium

21. The atomic size of cerium and promethium is quite close, due to
(a) f-electrons have poor shielding effect
(b) they are in same period in Periodic Table
(c) their electronic configuration is same
(d) nuclear charge is higher on cerium than promethuim

22. The trivalent ion having largest size is
(a) La (b) Ti
(c) Zr (d) Hf

23. Which of the following ions is paramagnetic?
(a) La^{3+} $(Z = 57)$ (b) Lu^{3+} $(Z = 71)$
(c) Yb^{2+} $(Z = 70)$ (d) Sm^{3+} $(Z = 62)$

24. The separation of lanthanides in ion exchange method is based on
(a) oxidation state of the ion
(b) size of the hydrated ions
(c) basicity of lanthanides
(d) the solubility of their nitrates

25. Which of the following forms stable $+4$ oxidation state?
(a) La $(Z = 57)$ (b) Ce $(Z = 58)$
(c) Eu $(Z = 63)$ (d) Sm $(Z = 62)$

26. Which of the following statement is not correct?
(a) f-block elements are called inner transition elements
(b) The tendency of d-block elements to form complexes is less than that of f-block elements
(c) The size of atoms and ions of d-block elements are relatively smaller than those of the f-block elements
(d) The oxides and hydroxides of d-block elements are less basic than those of f-block elements

27. Zr and Hf have similar atomic and ionic radii because
(a) both are in same group
(b) of diagonal relationship
(c) of lanthanide contraction
(d) they have similar chemical properties

28. Which element among the following has f-electrons?
(a) Arsenic (b) Indium
(c) Germanium (d) Thallium

29. Why are magnetic moments of trivalent lanthanide ions not affacted by ligand in comparison to those of $3d$-transition metals?
(a) f-electrons are more deep seated than d-electrons
(b) Lanthanides show high coordination number
(c) Properties of lanthanide ions are similar
(d) Lanthanides are heavier than $3d$-transition metals

30. The lanthanides have electronic configuration with $6s^2$ in common but with variable occupation of the
(a) $4d$ levels (b) $4f$ levels (c) $5p$ levels (d) $5d$ levels

31. In general, the configuration of lanthanides is $(n-2)\,f^{1-14}\;(n-1)\,s^2\,p^6\,d^{1\text{ or }0}\;ns^2$. It is observed that, with increase in atomic number of lanthanides, there is a decrease of ionic radii from La : 122 to Lu : 0.99 (Å).
The reason for decrease in atomic radii is increase in
(a) valence electrons
(b) electronegative character
(c) atomic volume
(d) nuclear attraction or valence electrons leading to inward shrinking of shells

32. Cerium oxide containing special variety glass, which cuts off ultraviolet rays, is known as
(a) crookes glass (b) jena glass
(c) flint glass (d) pyrex glass

33. The properties of zirconium and hafnium atoms and ions are almost the same because both
(a) are electropositive in nature
(b) have almost identical ionic radius and covalent radius
(c) have high melting point and belong to d-block element
(d) are metals are belong to the same period

34. Which one of the following is not true for lanthanides?
(a) Higher oxidation states are unusual among lanthanides
(b) Free lanthanide metals are more reactive and resemble alkaline earth and alkali metals rather than most transition metals
(c) Although + 3 is the characteristic oxidation state, + 4 state is also important in lanthanides
(d) Despite stable + 3 state, lanthanide elements do not closely resemble transition metals like chromium or cobalt

35. Cerite-earth minerals contains
(a) La_{57}—Eu_{63} (b) Gd_{64}—Lu_{71}
(c) Ce_{58}—Yb_{70} (d) Th_{90}—Pu_{94}

36. Which of the following is correct term-symbol of Ce^{3+} $(4f^1)$?
(a) $^2F_2$ (b) $^2F_5$
(c) $^2F_{5/2}$ (d) $^2F_0$

37. The additional electron in Gd_{64} enter in
(a) $4f$-orbital (b) $5d$-orbital
(c) $5p$-orbital (d) $6s$-orbital

38. The oxides of lanthanides resembles with
(a) alkali metals (b) alkaline earth metals
(c) transition metals (d) None of these

39. La_{57} shows the following oxidation state
(a) + 3 only (b) + 3 only + 4
(c) + 4 only (d) + 2 and + 4

40. Pr_{59} shows the following oxidation state in their compounds.
(a) + 3 only (b) + 3 only + 4
(c) + 4 only (d) + 2 and + 3

41. Nd_{60} shows the following oxidation state in their compounds
(a) + 2 only (b) + 3 only
(c) + 2 and + 3 (d) + 3 and + 4

42. Lanthanide elements and their compounds find many important nuclear uses as
(a) in nuclear fuel control
(b) shielding and fluxing devices
(c) Both (a) and (b)
(d) None of the above

43. The common coordination number of lanthanides and $3d$-metal ions is/are
(a) 4 only (b) 6 only
(c) 4 and 6 (d) 4, 6 and 7

44. Which one of the following is the correct source of synthesis of neptunium?
(a) ${}_{92}U^{238} + {}_0n^1 \longrightarrow {}_{92}U^{239} \longrightarrow {}_{93}Np^{239} + {}_{-1}e^1$
(b) ${}_{91}U^{238} + {}_{-1}e^0 \longrightarrow {}_{92}U^{238} \longrightarrow {}_{93}Np^{239} - {}_1p^1$
(c) Both (a) and (b)
(d) None of the above

45. Which one of the following is the correct source of synthesis of plutonium (Pu_{91})?
(a) ${}_{93}Np^{239} \longrightarrow {}_{94}Pu^{239} + {}_{-1}e^0$
(b) ${}_{92}U^{238} + {}_2He^4 \longrightarrow {}_{94}Pu^{242}$
(c) ${}_{94}Pu^{240} \longrightarrow {}_{94}Pu^{239} + {}_0n^1$
(d) None of the above

46. The magnetic moment (μ) in BM of Pr^{3+} with outer electronic configuration is dependent on
(a) $\mu = 2\sqrt{S(S+1)}$ (b) $\mu = g\sqrt{J(J+1)}$
(c) $\mu = Z\sqrt{L(L+1)}$ (d) $\mu = 0$

47. The magnetic moment of La^{3+} Gd^{2+}, Lu^{3+} can be given by
(a) $\mu = \sqrt{S(S+1)}$ (b) $\mu = g\sqrt{J(J+1)}$
(c) $\mu = 2\sqrt{S(S+1)}$ (d) $\mu = 2\sqrt{(n+2)}$

48. Uranium exhibits several oxidation states. This is because
(a) it is an inner-transition element
(b) its $5f$ orbitals participate in bonding
(c) its atomic number is high
(d) it forms strong bond with oxygen

49. The ligand field bands of lanthanide complexes are generally sharper than those of transition metal complexes because
(a) transitions are allowed for lanthanide complexes
(b) Intensity of the bands are higher for lanthanide complexes.
(c) f-orbitals have higher energy than d-orbitals
(d) p-orbitals compared to d-orbitals, interact less effectively with ligands.

50. The correct statement among the following that describes the property of lanthanides is
(a) they exhibit variable oxidation states either + 2 and + 3 or + 3 and+ 4.
(b) lanthanide elements are all coloured
(c) the magnetic moment of Ln depend only on their unpaired electrons
(d) the coordination number of aquated lanthanide ion is usually nine

51. An artifically synthesised element is
(a) Pm (b) Mo (c) Re (d) Tc

Exercise 2
(For Part 'C')

1. Consider the following statements.
   I. The size of the lanthanide M^{3+} ions decreases as the atomic number of M increases.
   II. Electronic spectra of lanthanides shows very broad bands.
   III. With transition metals, coordination number six is very common in lanthanide complexes.

   Which of the statements given above is/are correct?
   (a) I and II (b) II and III
   (c) I only (d) I and III

2. Uranium reacts with conc. HNO_3
   (a) to give U $(NO_3)_4$ and H_2
   (b) to give U $(NO_3)_2$ and NO_2
   (c) UO_2 $(NO_3)_2$ and H_2
   (d) None of the above

3. Which of the following statement(s) is/are not correct?
   (a) $La(OH)_3$ is less basic than $Lu(OH)_3$
   (b) Atomic radius of Zr and Hf are same because of lanthanide contraction
   (c) In lanthanide series ionic radius of Ln^{3+} ion increases
   (d) La is actually an element of transition series rather lanthanide

4. Consider the following statements.
   1. The size of the lanthanide M^{3+} ions decreases as the atomic number of M increases.
   2. Electronic spectra of lanthanides show very broad bond.
   3. As with transition metals, coordination number six is very common in lanthanide complexes.

   Which of the statements given above is/are correct?
   (a) 1 only (b) 3 only (c) 1 and 2 (d) 1 and 3

5. Which one of the following is the correct sequence of Ce^{3+}, La^{3+}, Pm^{3+} and Yb^{3+} in increasing order of their ionic radii?
   (a) $Yb^{3+} < Pm^{3+} < Ce^{3+} < La^{3+}$
   (b) $Pm^{3+} < La^{3+} < Ce^{3+} < Yb^{3+}$
   (c) $La^{3+} < Ce^{3+} < Pm^{3+} < Yb^{3+}$
   (d) $Ce^{3+} < La^{3+} < Yb^{3+} < Pm^{3+}$

6. Electronic configuration of Eu and Gd is
   (a) $[Xe]4f^7 5d^1 6s^2$, $[Xe]5d^2, 6s^0, 4f^7$
   (b) $[Xe]4f^7 5d^0 6s^2$, $[Xe]4f^7 5d^1 6s^2$
   (c) $[Xe]4f^7 5d^1 6s^2$, $[Xe]4f^8 5d^0 6s^2$
   (d) $[Xe]4f^8 5d^0 6s^2$, $[Xe]4f^9 5d^0 6s^2$

7. Which of the following ligands will bind to a tripositive lanthanide ion (Ln^{3+}) most strongly?
   (a) R_3S (b) NO_3^-
   (c) R_3P (d) I^-

8. Match Column I with Column II and select the correct answer.

Column I		Column II	
A.	Fullerene	1.	Lewis acid
B.	Promethium	2.	Actinide
C.	Water	3.	Lewis base
D.	Lawrencium	4.	Allotrope
		5.	Lanthanide

Codes

	A	B	C	D
(a)	4	5	3	2
(b)	2	3	5	4
(c)	1	2	3	4
(d)	4	3	2	1

9. Magnetic moment (μ) in BM of Pr^{3+} with outer electronic configuration is
   (a) zero (b) 3.58 BM
   (c) 1 BM (d) 2.58 BM

10. Sm^{2+}, Eu^{2+} and Yb^{2+} ions are strong reducing agents and their reducing strength is in the order
    (a) $Eu^{2+} > Yb^{2+} > Sm^{2+}$ (b) $Sm^{2+} > Yb^{2+} > Eu^{2+}$
    (c) $Yb^{2+} > Sm^{2+} > Eu^{2+}$ (d) $Eu^{2+} > Sm^{2+} > Yb^{2+}$

11. The stability order of + 2 oxidation state is
    (a) Eu > Yb > Sm > Tm (b) Tm > Sm > Yb > Eu
    (c) Sm ~ Tm > Yb > Eu (d) Eu ~ Tm > Yb ~ Sm

12. Only + 3 oxidation state is shown by
    (a) La_{57} (b) Pr_{59}
    (c) Pm_{61} (d) Lu_{71}

13. The order of the basicity of the following is correct
    (a) $La^{3+} > Ce^{3+} > Pr^{3+}$ (b) $Gd^{3+} > Dy^{3+} > Yb^{3+}$
    (c) $Ce^{3+} > Pr^{3+} > La^{3+}$ (d) $Dy^{3+} > Yb^{3+} > Gd^{3+}$

14. Lanthanides shows colours in their compounds due to
    (a) Laporte-forbidden f-f transitions
    (b) transitions between the J-states of $4f^n$ configuration
    (c) Both (a) and (b)
    (d) None of the above

15. Which of the followings are colourless?
    (a) La^{3+} (b) Ce^{3+}
    (c) Pr^{3+} (d) Pm^{3+}

16. Only + 3 oxidation state is shown by
(a) only Ac_{89} (b) only No_{102}
(c) Lr_{103} (d) None of these

17. The correct order of reducing strength is as follows of actinides
(a) $Ac_{89} > Th_{90} > U_{92}$ (b) $U_{92} > Th_{90} > Ac_{89}$
(c) $Th_{90} > U_{92} > Ac_{89}$ (d) $U_{92} > Ac_{89} > Th_{90}$

18. Ce^{3+} and Tb^{3+} are colourless but show strong absorption in UV region.This is due to
(a) *d*-*f* transition (b) *f* to *d* transition
(c) allowed *f*-*f* transition (d) *d*-*d* transition

19. Consider the following reagents.
I. $Eu(fod)_3$
II. $Eu(dpm)_3$
III. β-diketone complex of Eu^{3+}
Which of these can be used as shift reagent?
(a) I only (b) I and II only
(c) II and III only (d) I, II and III

20. Actinide oxides are mostly non-stoichiometric but lanthanide are not. This is due to the fact that
I. Actinide metals have large atomic radii.
II. Actinide have less difference between the energies of 5*f* and 6*s* electrons.
III. Lanthanides exhibit lesser oxidation states.
The correct statements are
(a) I and II only (b) II and III only
(c) I and III only (d) I, II and III

21. The calculated ground state magnetic moment of Sm^{3+} at room temperature is
(a) 0.84 BM (b) 5.97 BM
(c) 3.25 M (d) 7.9 BM

22. The oxy salt of which of the elements is highly stable?
(a) Pm (b) Gd (c) Tm (d) Ho

23. The ion that gets readily hydrolysed is
(a) Dy (b) Nd (c) Eu (d) Er

24. Consider the following statements.
I. Misch metal is added to steel to improve its strength and workability.
II. La_2O_3 is used in Crooke's glass.
III. $YBa_2Cu_2O_7$ is used as a lanthanide shfit reagent.
The correct statements is/are
(a) I only (b) I and II only
(c) II and III (d) II only

25. Lanthanoids are used for wavelength calibration of instruments because
I. *f*-orbitals are deep inside the atom.
II. The absorption bands are sharp.
III. Charge transfer spectra is possible.
The correct statements is/are
(a) I and II (b) II only
(c) I and III (d) I, II and III

26. Match oxidation states are geometry with most probable example of lanthanide ions and choose the correct answer using the codes given below :

	Oxidation state and geometry		Lanthanide complex/compound
A.	+3, octahdral	1.	$[Ce(NO_3)_5]^{2-}$
B.	+3, distorted square antiprism	2.	$[Er(NCS)_6]^{3-}$
C.	+3, bicapped dodrahedron	3.	Cs_2CeCl_6
D.	+4, octahedral	4.	$Y(acac)_3 \cdot 3H_2O$

Codes

	A	B	C	D
(a)	2	4	1	3
(b)	2	4	3	1
(c)	4	2	1	3
(d)	4	2	3	1

27. The shifts observed by two europium reagents and praseodymium reagent are respectively
(a) downfield and upfield
(b) upfield and downfield
(c) downfield and downfield
(d) upfield and upfield

28. Cerium (III) oxalate when heated in the presence of air, compound '*X*' is formed
I. *X* is white when pure.
II. *X* has antifluorite type structure.
III. *X* is soluble in acids but not in alkalies.
The correct statement(s) about *X* is/are
(a) II only (b) I only
(c) I and III (d) I, II and III

Directions (Q. Nos. 29 and 30)
Fractional thermal decomposition of oxysalts such as nitrates, sulphates and acetates of lanthanide elements at a given temperature decreases from La_{57} to Lu_{71}. If a mixture containing the nitrates of lanthanide elements is fused and then leached with water, the ytterium group of lanthanides rapidly concentrated and separate from cerium lanthanides.

29. From ammonium lanthanide double salt $[Ln(NO_3)_3 \cdot 2NH_4NO_3 \cdot 4H_2O]$, which will separate first?
(a) Cerium (b) Pe
(c) Nd (d) La

30. Yttterbium group of lanthanides rapidly concentrated and separate from cerium lanthanide due to
(a) being less acidic (b) being more acidic
(c) being more basic (d) being less basic

Directions (Q.No. 31 and 32)

Some of the lanthanides show + 2 and + 4 oxidation state in addition to + 3 state which is most characteristic of all elements of lanthanide series. The properties of Ln^{2+} and Ln^{4+} ions are different from those of usual Ln^{3+} ions.

A change in oxidation state results in remarkable change in properties.

31. To separate Ce from a mixture containing Ce^{3+} and other tripositive lanthanide cations, the mixture can be

(a) treated with some reducing agent
(b) treated with some oxidising agent
(c) treated with some reducing agent that will reduce other lanthanides (Ln^{3+})
(d) treated with oxidising agents that will oxidise Ce^{3+}

32. Ce^{4+} produced by treating mixture of tripositive lanthanide with $KMnO_4$ is

(a) More basic and more soluble
(b) less basic, more soluble
(c) more basic, less soluble
(d) less basic, less soluble

33. Which of the following statement is true?

(a) $EuSO_4$ is soluble in water
(b) Sulphate of all trivalent lanthanides are insoluble in water
(c) Sulphates of all trivalent lanthanides are soluble in water
(d) Zn-amalgam can bring about the reduction of Sm^{3+} and Eu^{3+}

34. Match the following and choose the correct answer using the codes given below.

	Column I		Column II
(I)	Ammonium citrate-citric acid	(p)	Cation exchange resin
(II)	Zn-amalgam	(q)	Anion exchange resin
(III)	tri-*n*-butyl phosphate	(r)	Liquid-liquid extraction
(IV)	Di(2-ethyl hexyl) phosphoric acid	(s)	Yb^{3+} to Yb^{2+}
		(t)	Sm^{3+} to Sm^{2+}
		(u)	Complexes with Ln^{3+} (*aq*) in the presence of NO_3^- ions.

Codes

(a) I-q, II-t, III-p, IV-r
(b) I-p, II-s, III-u, IV-r
(c) I-q, II-u, III-s, IV-q
(d) I-p, II-t, III-r, IV-u

35. TBP (Tri-*n* butyl phosphate) is an

(a) eluting agent like amonium citrate-citric acid
(b) reducing agent like Zn-amalgam
(c) extractant like pyrophosphates
(d) cellulose anion exchanger

36. Match the following and choose the correct answer using the codes given below.

	Column I (Chemicals)		Column II (Types of separation technique)
(I)	HDEHP	(p)	Thin-layer. chromatography.
(II)	$Ln(THD)_3$	(q)	Solvent extraction.
(III)	Silica gel H	(r)	Gas chromatography.
(IV)	8-quinolinols	(s)	Paper chromatography.

Codes

(a) I-p, II-q, III-r, IV-s
(b) I-q, II-p, III-s, IV-r
(c) I-s, II-r, III-q, IV-p
(d) I-s, II-r, III-p, IV-q

Assertion & Reason

Codes

(a) Both A and R are true and R is the correct explanation of A.
(b) Both A and R are true and R is not the correct explanation of A.
(c) A is true and R is false.
(d) A is false and R is true.

37. **Assertion (A)** The atomic and ionic sizes of lanthanides decrease with increase of atomic number.

Reason (R) Successive addition of electrons into 4*f* orbital provides strong screening effect.

38. **Assertion (A)** All the lanthanide elements exhibit a common oxidation state of + 3 in their compounds.

Reason (R) Tha atoms of the lanthanide elements contain three electrons in their outermost shell.

39. **Assertion (A)** Lu^{3+} (*aq*) ions are attached with resin as LnR_3 (solid). The Ln^{3+} replace H^+ ions of $—SO_3H$ or —COOH group of the resin and get fixed to resin.

Reason (R) La^{3+} ion is attached to resin with minimum firmness and eluted first.

40. **Assertion (A)** $La(OH)_3$ is the most basic, $Lu(OH)_3$ is least basic.

Reason (R) Due to lanthanide contraction, size decreases from La^{3+} to Lu^{3+}, covalent character increases.

41. The separation of trivalent lanthanide ions Lu^{3+}, Yb^{3+}, Dy^{3+}, Eu^{3+} can be effectively done by a cation exchange resin using ammonium *o*-hydroxy *iso*-butyrate as the eluent. The order in which the ions will be separated is

(a) $Lu^{3+}, Yb^{3+}, Dy^{3+}, Eu^{3+}$ (b) $Eu^{3+}, Dy^{3+}, Yb^{3+}, Lu^{3+}$
(c) $Dy^{3+}, Yb^{3+}, Eu^{3+}, Lu^{3+}$ (d) $Yb^{3+}, Dy^{3+}, Lu^{3+}, Eu^{3+}$

42. Ligand field stabilisation energies are smaller for lanthanides compared to transition metals is the same oxidation state because
(a) size of lanthanide ions are larger
(b) f orbitals interact less effectively with ligands
(c) size of lanthanide ions are smaller
(d) lanthanides favour oxygen donor ligands

43. The lanthanide complex (where, arac = acetylacetonate phen -1, 10-phenanthraline) that do not have square antiprismatic structure is
(a) $[Ce(NO_3)_6]^{2-}$ (b) $[La(acac)_3(H_2O)_2]$
(c) $[Ce(acac)_4]$ (d) $Eu(acac)_3$ (phen)]

Answers

Exercise 1

1. (c)	**2.** (a)	**3.** (a)	**4.** (d)	**5.** (b)	**6.** (c)	**7.** (b)	**8.** (a)	**9.** (c)	**10.** (d)
11. (a)	**12.** (c)	**13.** (b)	**14.** (d)	**15.** (c)	**16.** (d)	**17.** (b)	**18.** (b)	**19.** (b)	**20.** (c)
21. (a)	**22.** (a)	**23.** (d)	**24.** (b)	**25.** (b)	**26.** (b)	**27.** (c)	**28.** (d)	**29.** (a)	**30.** (b)
31. (d)	**32.** (a)	**33.** (b)	**34.** (c)	**35.** (a)	**36.** (c)	**37.** (b)	**38.** (b)	**39.** (a)	**40.** (b)
41. (c)	**42.** (c)	**43.** (b)	**44.** (a)	**45.** (a)	**46.** (b)	**47.** (b)	**48.** (b)	**49.** (d)	**50.** (a)
51. (d)									

Exercise 2

1. (a)	**2.** (a)	**3.** (a,c)	**4.** (d)	**5.** (a)	**6.** (b)	**7.** (c)	**8.** (a)	**9.** (b)	**10.** (b)
11. (a)	**12.** (a,c,d)	**13.** (a,b)	**14.** (c)	**15.** (a,b)	**16.** (a,b,c)	**17.** (b)	**18.** (b)	**19.** (d)	**20.** (d)
21. (a)	**22.** (c)	**23.** (d)	**24.** (b)	**25.** (a)	**26.** (a)	**27.** (a)	**28.** (b)	**29.** (d)	**30.** (d)
31. (d)	**32.** (d)	**33.** (c)	**34.** (b)	**35.** (c)	**36.** (d)	**37.** (a)	**38.** (c)	**39.** (c)	**40.** (a)
41. (a)	**42.** (b)	**43.** (a)							

Hints & Solutions

Exercise 1

23. $La = 4f^0\ 5d^1\ 6s^2$, $La^{3+} = 4f^0\ 5d^0\ 6s^0$
$Lu = 4f^{14}\ 5d^1\ 6s^2$, $Lu^{3+} = 4f^{14}\ 5d^0\ 6s^0$
$Yb = 4f^{14}\ 6s^2$, $Yb^{2+} = 4f^{14}\ 6s^0$
All are diamagnetic
$Sm = 4f^6\ 6s^2$, $Sm^{3+} = 4f^5\ 6s^0$
Paramagnetic.

25. Cerium show stable + 4 oxidation state because Ce^{4+} has $4f^0$ configuration, as in CeO_2.

26. The lanthanide ions have a high charge but their sizes being large they do not form complexes as readily as the transition metal ion.

29. The general electronic configuration of lanthanide is [Xe] $4f^{2-14}\ 5d^{0-1}\ 6s^2$.

The f-orbitals are deeply seated and covered by $5d, 6s$ orbitals hence, magnetic moments of trivalent lanthanide is not affected by ligands.

31. Due to poor shielding effect of $4f$ electrons, the nuclear charge increases from one element to another causes the decrease in atomic and ionic radii called lanthanide contraction.

36. $4f^1$

1						
+3	+2	+1	0	−1	−2	−3

$$S = n \times \frac{1}{2} = 1 \times \frac{1}{2} = \frac{1}{2}$$

$L = +3$, *i.e.*, orbital is F

$$J = L - S = 3 - \frac{1}{2} = \frac{5}{2}$$

Spin multiplicity $= (2S + 1)$
$$= \left(2 \times \frac{1}{2} + 1\right)$$
$$= 2$$

So the term symbol is $^2F_{5/2}$.

37. This is because the $4f$ and $5d$ orbitals in Gd are at about the same energy level and Gd atom has a tendency to retain the configuration with half-filled $4f$-orbitals which are relatively more stable.

39. The outer electronic configuration of La_{57} is $5d^1 6s^2$.

After losing 3 electrons, it achieves inert gas configuration, so it exhibit + 3 oxidation state.

Exercise 2

2. U + Conc. $HNO_3 \longrightarrow U(NO_3)_4) + H_2$

10. The standard oxidation potentials at 25°C, in acid solution, of these cations are given below :

$Sm^{3+}(aq) + e^- \longrightarrow Sm^{2+}(aq)$; O.P. = 1.55 V

$Eu^{3+}(aq) + e^- \longrightarrow Eu^{2+}(aq)$; O.P. = 0.43 V

$Yb^{3+}(aq) + e^- \longrightarrow Yb^{2+}(aq)$; O.P. = 1.15 V

These values indicate that their reducing strength is in the order : $Sm^{2+} > Yb^{2+} > Eu^{2+}$.

11. The stability order of + 2 state is

$$E_u > Y_b > S_m > T_m \sim N_d$$

as it is decided by their $E°$ values.

13. In case of lanthanoid ions, basicity decreases as the ionic radius decreases.

The order of ionic radii is

$La^{3+} > Ce^{3+} > Pr^{3+} > Nd^{3+} > Pm^{3+} > Sm^{3+} > Eu^{3+} > Gd^{3+}$

$> Tb^{3+} > Dy^{3+} > Ho^{3+} > Yb^{3+} > Lu^{3+}$

This is also the order of basicity.

15. La^{3+} No absorption in visible or infrared region (colourless) (No unpaired electron).

Ce^{3+} No absorption in the visible region; strong bands in ultraviolet region–2105, 2220, 2380, 2520 (colourless) (one unpaired electron).

Pr^{3+} Green (3 unpaired electrons).

Pm^{3+} Pink-yellow (four unpaired electrons).

18. Ce^{3+} and Tb^{3+} are colourless because they do not absorb in the visible region. However they exhibit exceptionally strong absorption in UV region because of the transitions from $4f$ to $5d$. This absorption is very strong.

21. Sm^{3+} has $4f^5$ configuration.

$$g = \frac{3}{2} + \frac{S(S+1) - L(L+1)}{2J(J+1)}$$

and $\mu_{eff} = g\sqrt{J(J+1)}$

For $4f^5$

1	1	1	1	1		
+3	+2	+1	0	−1		

$$L = \Sigma l = +3 + 2 + 1 - 1 + 0 = 5$$

$$S = n \times \frac{1}{2} = 5 \times \frac{1}{2} = \frac{5}{2}$$

$$J = L - S = 5 - \frac{5}{2} = \frac{5}{2}$$

Spin multiplicity $(2S + 1) = \left(2 \times \frac{5}{2} + 1\right) = 6$

For $L = 5$, orbital is H.

So ground state term symbol is ${}^6H_{5/2}$.

$$g = \frac{3}{2} + \frac{\frac{5}{2}\left(\frac{5}{2}+1\right) - 5(5+1)}{2 \times \frac{5}{2}\left(\frac{5}{2}+1\right)}$$

$$= \frac{3}{2} + \frac{\frac{35}{4} - 30}{\frac{35}{2}}$$

$$= \frac{3}{2} + \frac{\frac{35-120}{4}}{\frac{35}{2}}$$

$$= \frac{3}{2} + \frac{(-85)}{70}$$

$$= \frac{105 - 85}{70} = 0.286$$

$$\mu_{eff} = 0.286\sqrt{\frac{5}{2}\left(\frac{5}{2}+1\right)}$$

$$= 0.286\sqrt{\frac{35}{4}}$$

$$= 0.84 \text{ BM}$$

22. From La to Lu, basic character decreases becuase size decreases due to lanthanoid contraction and stability of oxysalt of lanthanide elements varies inversely with basicity, *i.e.*, increases from La to Lu.

Thus, the order of stability of oxysalt is

$$\text{Pm} < \text{Gd} < \text{Ho} < \text{Tm}.$$

23. A less basic salt gets hydrolysed more readily.

28. $Ce_2(C_2O_4)_3 + 2O_2 \longrightarrow 2CeO_2 + 6CO_2$

CeO_2 is white in its pure state. It has a fluorite type structure. It is insoluble in acids and alkalies.

41. As the atomic number of lanthanides increases, size of lanthanide ion (La^{3+}) decreases and a smaller lanthanide ion forms a stable complex with *o*-hydroxyisobutyrate ion.

Hence, a Lu^{3+} *o*-hydroxyisobutyrate complex ion comes out first and Eu^{3+} comes out last, *i.e.*, the order of separation is

$$Lu^{3+}\ Yb^{3+}\ Dy^{3+}\ Eu^{3+}$$

42. Electron in f-subshell does not screen the nucleus effectively, so the nuclear charge increases which results in decreased size and increased electronic repulsions. So, the chances of interaction wih the ligands becomes less and hence, LFSE are small.

43. $[Ce(NO_3)_6]^{2-}$ has icosahedral structure, other given complexes have coordination number 8 and thus, have square antiprismatic structure.

11

Organometallic Compounds

An organometallic compound is broadly defined as one that involves one or more carbon atoms of an organic group or molecule and a transition metal, lanthanide, actinide, or main group metal atom.

These are the compounds containing direct metal to carbon bonds, or at least one metal-carbon bond.

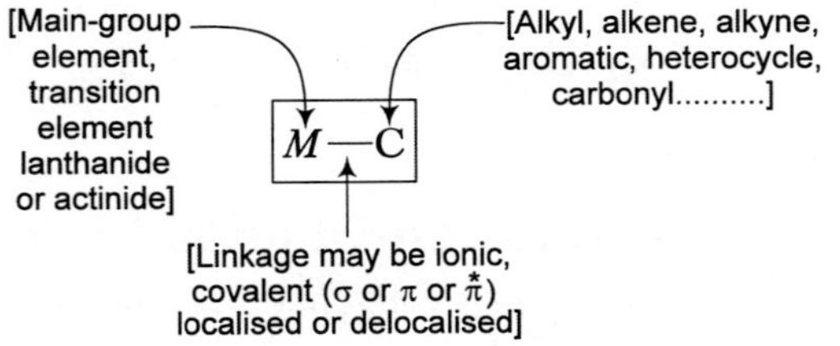

The bonding interaction between the metal atom and the organic moiety may be ionic, covalent, localised or delocalised in nature. Some common examples of organometallic compounds are tetraethyl lead, $(C_2H_5)_4Pb$, dimethylmercury, $(CH_3)_2Hg$, ferrocene $(C_5H_5)_2Fe$ etc. Despite this very broad and rigorous definition, the borderlines that distinguish between organometallic chemistry from other branches is often unclear. For example, carbon monoxide (CO) is a typical inorganic molecule, but metal carbonyls such as $Ni(CO)_4$ or $Fe(CO)_5$ are defined as organometallic compounds. These compounds show properties which are like those of other organometallic compounds. In this category are also included compounds formed by ligands such as CO_2, CS_2, *R*NC, CN^- with metals. Similarly, organoboron, organosilicon, organoarsenic compounds are classified as organometallic compounds even though boron, silicon, germanium, arsenic, antimony, selenium and tellurium are borderline metals.

Syllabus

- Types of Organometallic Compounds
- Classification of Ligands and their Uses
- 18 Electron Rule and Its Applications, EAN
- Synthesis, Bonding Structure and Reactivity
- Organometallics in Hhomogeneous Catalysis

Difference in Bonding between Main Group and Transition Metal Organometallic Compounds

Organometallic compounds involving main group elements such as Me_4Sn are formed between the metal and organic moiety by forming four σ-covalent bonds ($2c-2e$ bonds). The metal atom in the process acquires a completed octet, thus, Me_3Sn moiety is unstable and would not exist as tin does not complete an octet. The main group elements can form only $2c-2e$ bonds involving a single carbon atom. Main group elements form only electron-precise organometallic compounds.

However, transition metals are able to bond to more than one carbon atom of the same moiety. Also transition metals can bond to certain organic moieties through their π or $\overset{*}{\pi}$ electron densities (unlike $2c-2e$ sigma covalent bonds formed by main group metals only by accepting a lone pair donated by ligand) either by donating or by back accepting electron density. The formation of ferrocene $(C_2H_5)_2Fe$ is an example of multiple carbon atom bonding and involving overlap of π-electron density of cyclopentadienyl ion with iron. Complexes of transition metals with alkenes, alkynes, arenes, alkyl groups involve both donation of electron density (π-electrons) by ligand to metal and back acceptance from metal to ligand into $\overset{*}{\pi}$ (of the ligand) orbitals. We label these ligands as π-complexing ligands.

These special bonding interactions which involved π-acid ligands (CO, CN^-, NO, *R*NC etc.), π-complexing ligands (alkenes, alkynes, arenes etc.), came into existence only with transition metals and especially when these metals (or irons) are present in zero, negative or low positive oxidation states. Such bonding interactions are not feasible when the metal atom belongs to main-group as these elements do not contain suitable low energy filled *d*-orbitals for back donation of electron density to ligands.

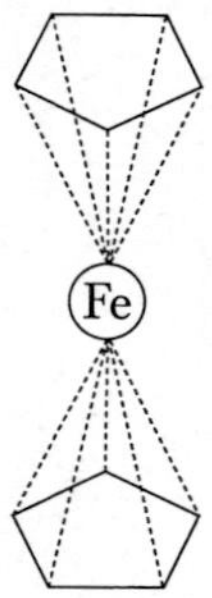

{ 'Ferrocene' exhibiting overlap with multiple carbon atoms }

Classification of Ligands

Representative metals form organometallic compounds with only a narrow range of ligands such as, alkyl, aryl and σ-cyclo-pentadienyl groups but transition metals form organometallic compounds with a very wide range of organic groups. Accordingly, it is more appropriate to classify these compounds according to the ligand type rather than the metal. It is, therefore, convenient to classify ligands according to the number of their carbon atoms involved in bonding to the metal atom. This is the most satisfactory way of classifying organometallic compounds. **The number of carbon atoms attached to metal atom is called the hapticity of the organic moiety**. For example, CH_3 group in $(CH_3)_4Sn$ is called monohapto group and is mentioned as η^1. Dihapto ligand like ethylene is referred to as $\eta^2—C_2H_4$ (in which the metal atom is attached to two carbon atoms of the same ligand) and pentahapto cyclopentadiene as $\eta^5—C_5H_5$.

One-Carbon-Bonded Ligands

One carbon-bonded ligands (one electron contributors) are molecules in which one carbon atom of the ligand is bound directly to the metal. Such ligands can be classified into three groups, such as hydrocarbons, acyl and carbene ligands.

Alkyls are typically very strong anionic σ-donors, second only to hydrides. They have virtually no π-acceptor ability.

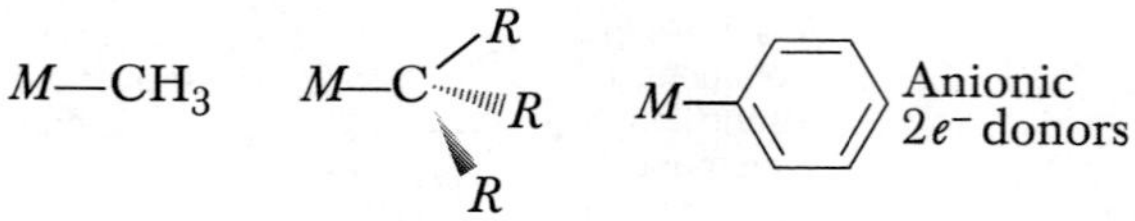

Two-Carbon-Bonded Ligands

Alkenes and alkynes (sometimes) act as two carbon-bonded ligands (two electron donors) because both the carbon atoms at each end of the multiple bond are involved in bonding to metal atom. The bonding of the ligand of metal (M) is indicated either by two dotted lines to the participating carbon atoms or a single solid line from the centre of the participating carbon atoms to the metal atoms as shown in Fig. 11.1.

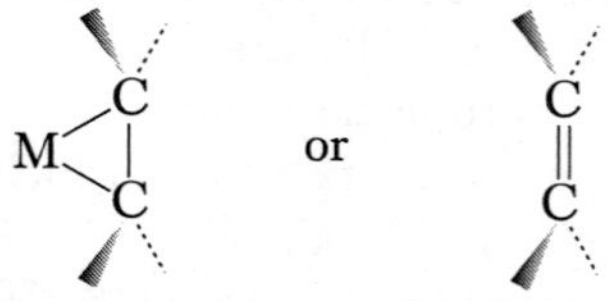

Metalloycloropropane π-bonded complex

Fig. 11.1 Alkene as a 2-electron, donor

The two carbon atoms involved in the bonding to the metal atom need not be equidistant from the metal atom. Such a behaviour is usually observed in the unsymmetrically substituted ligands such as $R—CH{=}CH_2$. Complexes of alkenes and alkynes are known for transition metals only.

Three-Carbon-Bonded Ligands

The allyl group (C_3H_5), bonded to transition metal through its three carbon atoms is known as π-allyl or π-eryl ligand. Here, allyl group acts as a 3 electron donor. The complexes are usually represented as (IV).

These may be distinguished from the σ-allyl complexes in which the allyl groups is bound as one-carbon bonded ligand (V).

(IV) π-allyl ($3e^-$ donor) (η^3)

(V) σ-allyl ($1e^-$ donor) (η^1)

Fig. 11.2

There are quite a few other organic molecules like the cycloheptatriene, C_7H_8 which can also act as three electron donors (three-carbon-bonded ligands) but shall not be discussed due to their complex nature.

Four-Carbon-Bonded Ligands

There are two main types of four carbon-bonded ligands (4-electron donors), (a) acyclic ligands such as 1, 3-butadiene, (VI) and (b) cyclic ligands, such as cyclobutadiene, C_4H_4, (VII).

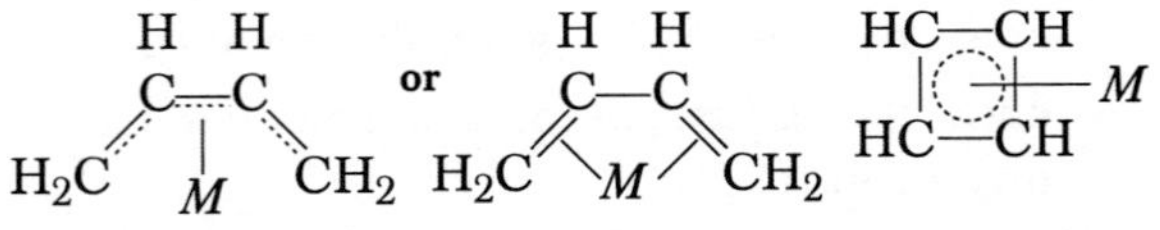

(Butadiene as a $4e^-$ donor) (VI)

(Cyclobutadiene as a $4e^-$ donor) VII

Fig. 11.3

Cyclobutadiene behaves as a four-carbon-bonded ligand but this may not hold good for butadienes. 1, 3-butadiene can act as a monoolefin or show more or less two independent monoolefin-metal interactions (Fig. 11.4)

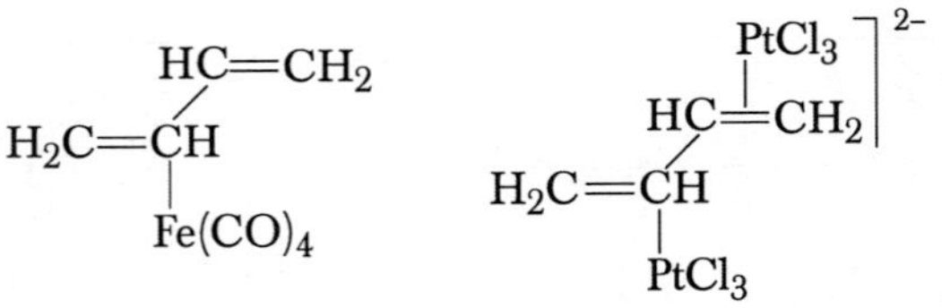

Fig. 11.4 Acyclic butadienes as donor.

Five-Carbon-Bonded Ligands

Acyclic dienyls $R_2C(CR)(CR)(CR)CR_2$ but more frequently cyclic dienyls behave as five electron donors, that is, five-carbon-bonded ligands (Fig. 11.5).

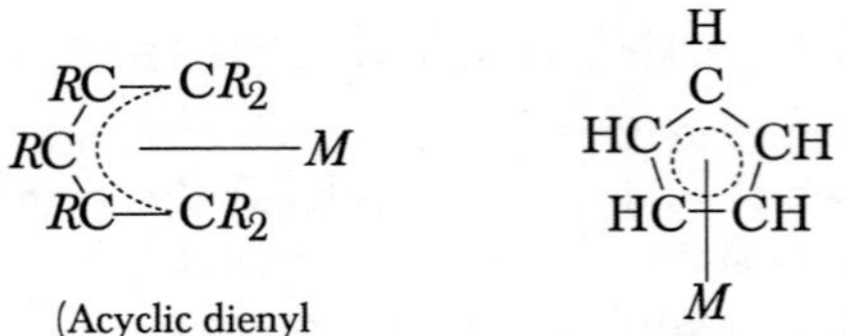

(Acyclic dienyl as a $5e^-$ donor)

(Cyclopentadienyl as a $5e^-$ donor)

Fig. 11.5

The five carbon bonded cylopentadienyles are referred as π-cyclopentadienyl ligands (to distinguish them from one-carbon bonded cyclopentadienyl, *i.e.*, σ-cyclopentadienyl ligand-1). These π-cyclopentadienyl ligands form complexes called metallocenes. The most important metallocene is the famous ferrocene $(\pi\text{-}C_5H_5)_2Fe$ in which the metal atom is sandwiched between two planar cyclopentadienyl rings (discussed subsequently). six-membered cyclic dienyls can also act as five-electron donors (five-carbon-bonded ligands), VIII.

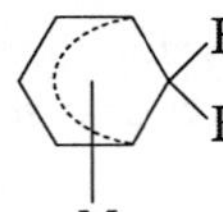

VIII

Six-Carbon-Bonded Ligands

Benzene is the most important six-carbon bonded (six electron donor) ligand. It forms sandwhich bonded compound with chromium named as dibenzene-chromium $(C_6H_6)_2Cr$ (Fig. 11.6).

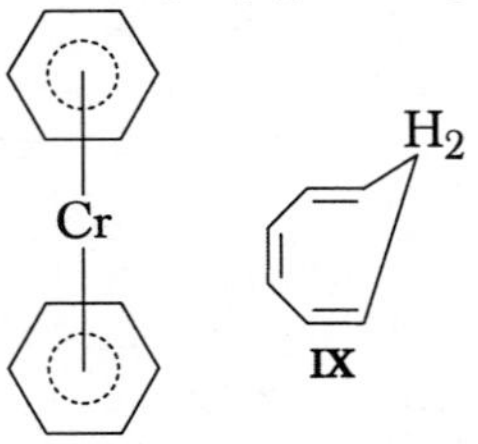

IX

Fig. 11.6 Sandwhich dibenzene chromium.

Cycloheptatriene, C_7H_8 and cyclooctatetraene, C_8H_8 can also act as six electron donor ligands when only six of the carbon atoms in the ring participate in bonding with the metal atom. Their detailed bonding is beyond our scope. Cycloheptatriene (IX) acts as a six electron donor through its three double bonds.

Seven-Carbon-Bonded Ligands

Cycloheptatrienyl ($—C_7H_7$) can act as a seven electron donor by participating all the seven carbon atoms in bond formation with transition metals. Such compounds are called π-cycloheptatrienyl complexes X.

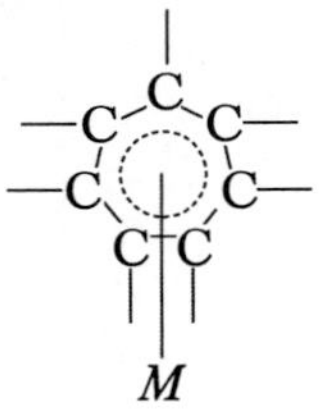

X

Eight-Carbon-Bonded Ligands

Cyclooctatetraene (C_8H_8) behaves as an eight electron donor in which it is planar with all the eight carbon atoms equidistant from the metal. It forms a well-known complex with uranium $U(C_8H_8)_2$ (Fig. 11.7).

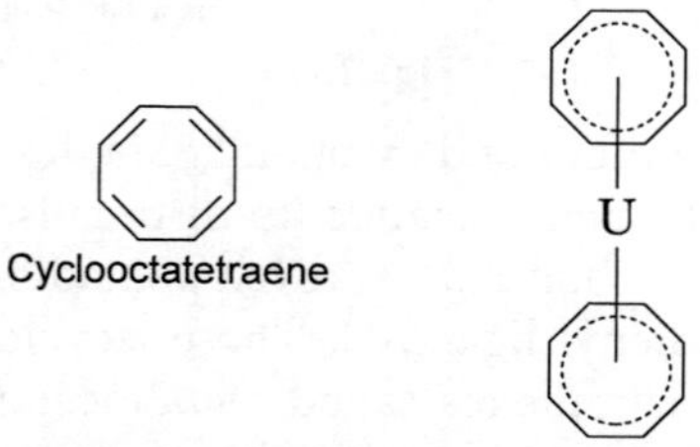

Fig. 11.7 Structure of dicyclooctatetraeneuranium.

Cyclooctatetraene can also act as a four electron donor (XI) or a six electron donor (XII).

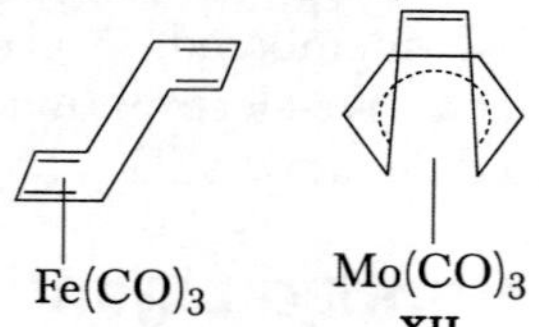

XI **XII**

Table 11.1 **Summary of Different Ligands**

Cationic $2e^-$ donors	NO (nitrosyl)
Neutral $2e^-$ donors	PR_3 (phosphine), CO (carbonyl), $R_2C{=}CR_2$ (alkenes), $RC{\equiv}CR$ (alkynes, can also donate $4e^-$), $N{\equiv}CR$ (nitriles)
Anionic $2e^-$ donors	Cl^- (chloride), Br^- (bromide), I^- (iodide), CH_3^- (methyl), CR_3^- (alkyl), Ph^- (phenyl), H^- (hydride)
Anionic $4e^-$ donors	$C_3H_5^-$ (allyl), O^{2-} (oxide), S^{2-} (sulphide), NR^{2-} (imide), CR_2^{2-} (alkylidene)
Anionic $6e^-$ donors	Cp^- (cyclopentadienyl)

18-Electron Rule and the Stability of Organometallic Complexes

It is generally observed that the stability of many organometallic complexes, particularly those involving the first row transition metals can be predicted by using the so-called 18-electron rule. This rule can be stated as, when a metal achieves an outer electron configuration of ns^2 $(n-1)\,d^{10}np^6$, there will be 18-electrons in the valence orbitals and a closed stable configuration is the result. It should be pointed here that for many second and third row transition metals 16-electron complexes are also found. The 18-electron rule is not sacrosanct. Rather, it may be used quite advantageously to predict the stability and existence of organometallic compounds. Let us see how to apply this a few examples.

Electron counting is the process of determining the number of valence electrons about a metal centre in a given transition metal complex.

To determine the electron count for a metal complex :

- Determine the oxidation state of the transition metal centre(s) and the metal centres resulting *d*-electron count. To do this one must :
  - note any overall charge on the metal complex.
  - know the charges of the ligands bounded to the metal centre.
  - know the number of electrons being donated to the metal centre from each ligand.
- Add up the electron counts for the metal centre and ligands.

Table 11.2 **Oxidation States of Transition Metals**

Group number (old)		IVa	Va	VIa	VIIa	VIII			Ib
Group number (new)		4	5	6	7	8	9	10	11
First row	3*d*	Ti	V	Cr	Mn	Fe	Co	Ni	Cu
Second row	4*d*	Zr	Nb	Mo	Te	Ru	Rh	Pd	Ag
Third row	5*d*	Hf	Ta	W	Re	Os	Ir	Pt	Au
Oxidation state	0	4	5	6	7	8	9	10	–
	I	3	4	5	6	7	8	9	10
	II	2	3	4	5	6	7	8	9
	III	1	2	3	4	5	6	7	8
	IV	0	1	2	3	4	5	6	7

(d^n)

[Many students made mistakes in *d*-electron counting. In many instances, the conept was correct but student did not make it right as the electron counting was wrong! If you are confused with metal *d*-electron counts, practice well and check with the Table 11.2 provided below]

Examples

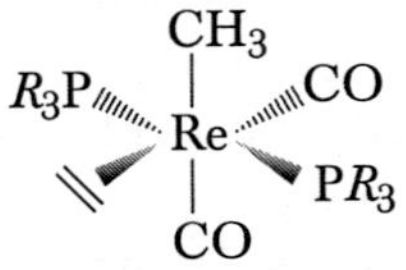

1. There is no overall charge on the complex.
2. There is one anionic ligand (CH_3^-, methyl group).
3. Since there is no overall charge on the complex (it is neutral), and since we have one anionic ligand present, the Re metal atom must have a +1 charge to compensate for the one negatively charged ligand. The +1 charge on the metal is also its oxidation state. So, the Re is in the +1 oxidation state. We denote this in two different ways : Re(+ 1), Re(1), or Re^{+1}.

Now, we can do our electron counting :

Re(+1)	d^6
$2PR_3$	$4e^-$
	$4e^-$
2CO	
	$2e^-$
CH_3	
$CH_2{=}CH_2$	$2e^-$
Total	$18e^-$

Example of 18-electrons systems

$[V(CO)_6]^-$; $[Cr(C_6H_6)_2]$; $[Mn(CO)_5]^-$; $[Fe(OH_2)_6]^{2+}$; $[Co(CN)_6]^{3-}$; $Ni(CO)_4$; $[Cu(NH_3)_4]^+$

$Cr(CO)_6$	Cr	6*e*	$Fe(CO)_5$	Fe	8*e*
	6CO	12*e*		5CO	10*e*
	Total	18*e*		Total	18*e*
$Ni(CO)_4$	Ni	8*e*	$Fe(CO)_4PPh_3$	Fe	8*e*
	4CO	10*e*		4CO	10*e*
	Total	18*e*		$IPPh_3$	2*e*
				Total	18*e*
$Fe(Cp)_2$	Fe(II)	6*e*	$Cr(C_6H_6)_2$	Cr	6*e*
	2Cp	12*e*		$2C_6H_6$	12*e*
	Total	18*e*			
$Cr(NO)_4$	Cr	6*e*	$Fe(CO)_2(NO)_2$	Fe	8*e*
	4NO	12*e*		2CO	4*e*
	Total	18*e*		2NO	6*e*
				Total	18*e*

The Effective Atomic Number Rule (EAN)

The nature of forces operating in coordination compounds was first thought of by Lewis in 1916 and Langmuir in 1919 in terms of coordinate bond, in which the ligand acts as the donor (Lewis base) and contributes both the bonding electrons. Lewis idea of electron pair bond formation was further extended to coordination compounds by Sidgwick in 1927. He suggested that a metal atom or ion formed a coordinate bond by accepting both the electrons from donors (ligands). That is, ligands were considered to be Lewis bases and metal ions as Lewis acids. He also suggested that transition metal ions will accept electron pairs from donors until the metal ion in the complex acquired an effective atomic number (EAN) of the nearest noble gas. That is, the sum of the electrons on the metal plus the electrons donated by the ligands was called the effective atomic number (EAN). When the total number of electrons thus counted is found to be 18 (Ar), 36 (Kr), 54 (Xe) or 86 (Rn), the EAN rule is said to be obeyed and the complexes are assumed to acquire greater stability.

Some Examples of EAN

(i) Hexaamminecobalt(III) ion, $[Co(NH_3)_6]^{3+}$

Atomic number of cobalt = 27

$\therefore Co^{3+}$ contains electrons = $24e^-$

$6NH_3$ ligands donate (6×2 electrons) = $12e^-$

EAN of $[Co(NH_3)_6]^{3+} = 36e^-$

Thus, it may be stated that the complex $[Co(NH_3)_6]^{3+}$ obeys EAN rule.

(ii) Hexacyanoferrate(II), $[Fe(CN)_6]^{4-}$

Atomic number of iron = 26

$\therefore Fe^{2+}$ contains electrons = $24e^-$

$6CN^-$ contribute $(6 \times 2) = 12e^-$

EAN of $[Fe(CN)_6]^{4-} = 36e^-$ (EAN rule is obeyed).

Table 11.3 **EAN Rule of some Stable Complex Ions**

Complex	Metal ion	No. of electrons in the metal ion	No. of electrons donated by ligands	EAN
$[Fe(CN)_6]^{3-}$	Fe^{3+}	23	12	35
$[Cr(NH_3)_6]^{3+}$	Cr^{3+}	21	12	33
$[Ni(NH_3)_6]^{2+}$	Ni^{2+}	26	12	38
$CoCl_4^{2-}$	Co^{2+}	25	8	33

Complex	Metal ion	No. of electrons in the metal ion	No. of electrons donated by ligands	EAN
$FeCl_4^-$	Fe^{3+}	23	8	31
$[FeF_6]^{3-}$	Fe^{3+}	23	12	35
$[Mn(CN)_6]^{4-}$	Mn^{2+}	23	12	35
$[Ni(CN)_4]^{2-}$	Ni^{2+}	26	8	34
$[Cu(NH_3)_4]^{2+}$	Cu^{2+}	27	8	35

If we look at Table 11.3, it is clear that a large number of well known stable coordination compounds do not obey EAN rule. However, the stability of many organometallic compounds can be correlated with the EAN rule. It also helps us in understanding structures of most of the carbonyl compounds and other organometallics containing organic groups as ligands. In metal carbonyls, the EAN is obeyed in almost 99% of the cases as elaborated below. Table 11.4 illustrates some examples of simple metal carbonyl complexes or complex ions which obey EAN rule. Vanadium hexacarbonyl, $V(CO)_6$ is a stable complex and does not obey EAN rule ($23 + 12 = 35$) due to odd number of electrons on the central V atom. On the other hand, $[V(CO)_7]^+$ obeys EAN $[22 + 14 = 36]$ but is unstable and is unknown. Perhaps the small vanadium V^+ is unable to accomodate more than six nearest neighbours. As indicated in Table 11.4. $[V(CO)_6]^-$ obeys EAN and consequently it is more stable than $V(CO)_6$.

Table 11.4 **Metal Carbonyls Obeying the EAN Rule**

Complex	Metal ion	No. of electrons in the metal ion	No. of electrons donated by ligands	EAN
$Cr(CO)_6$	Cr^0	24	12	36
$Fe(CO)_5$	Fe^0	26	10	36
$Ni(CO)_4$	Ni^0	28	8	36
$[Mn(CO)_5]^-$	Mn^{-1}	26	10	36
$[V(CO)_6]^-$	V^{-1}	24	12	36
$Mo(CO)_6$	Mo^0	42	12	54
$[Mn(CO)_6]^+$	Mn^{+1}	24	12	36
$Fe(CO)_4]^{2+}$	Fe^{2-}	28	8	36
$[Co(CO)_4]^-$	Co^{-1}	28	8	36

Just like $^{23}V(CO)_6$, other metal atoms with electrons such as ^{25}Mn, ^{27}Co and ^{29}Cu cannot satisfy EAN rule in their neutral mononuclear carbonyl complexes (which are not known). In order of satisfy EAN rule, such metal atoms have tendency to adopt other options.

Metal Carbonyl Compounds

Transition metal carbonyl complexes (metal carbonyls) are among the most well studies organometallic compounds. Almost all transition metals form carbonyls. Many of them comply with the 18-electron rule. For examples

$$V(CO)_6, Cr(CO)_6, Mn_2(CO)_{10}, Fe(CO)_5, Co_2(CO)_8, Ni(CO)_4$$

Table 11.5 **Examples of Neutral, Binary Metal Carbonyls**

4	5	6	7	8	9	10	11
Ti	$V(CO)_6$	$Cr(CO)_6$	$Mn_2(CO)_{10}$	$Fe(CO)_5$ $Fe_2(CO)_9$ $Fe_3(CO)_{12}$	$Co_2(CO)_8$ $Co_4(CO)_{12}$	$Ni(CO)_4$	Cu
Zr	Nb	$Mo(CO)_6$	$Te_2(CO)_{10}$	$Ru(CO)_5$ $Ru_3(CO)_{12}$	$Rh_4(CO)_{12}$ $Rh_6(CO)_{16}$	Pd	Ag
Hf	Ta	$W(CO)_6$	$Re_2(CO)_{10}$	$Os(CO)_5$ $Os_3(CO)_{12}$	$Ir_4(CO)_{12}$	Pt	Au

Standard Bonding Modes

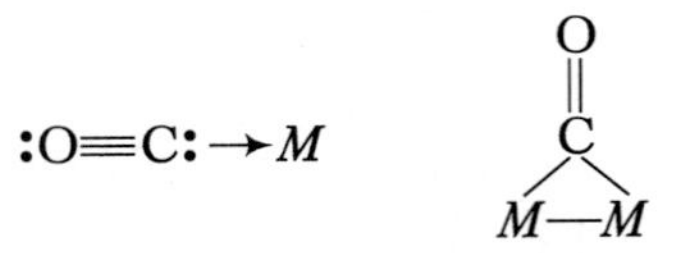

Terminal mode $2e^-$ neutral donor

μ_2–bridging mode $2e^-$ neutral donor

- Because of the π-acceptor ability of CO, a number of stable **anionic** metal carbonyls exists $Ti(CO)_6^{2-}$, $V(CO)_6^-$, $Cr(CO)_4^{2-}$, $Mn(CO)_5^-$, $Fe(CO)_4^{2-}$, $Co(CO)_4^-$.
- Some of them can be protonated to form metal **carbonyl hydrides** ($HCo(CO)_4$, $H_2Fe(CO)_4$, $HMn(CO)_5$ etc.) when often behave as strong protic acids in aqueous solutions.
- Since, CO is a weak σ-donor, cationic metal carbonyls are rare and very electrophilic *e.g.,* $Mn(CO)_6^+$, $Fe(CO)_6^{2+}$, $Co(CO)_5^+$, $Ir(CO)_6^{3+}$, $Hg(CO)_2^{2+}$.
- There is a variety of polynuclear **cluster** carbonyl compounds containing *M–M* bonds.

The structures of some of the carbonyl clustures are given below

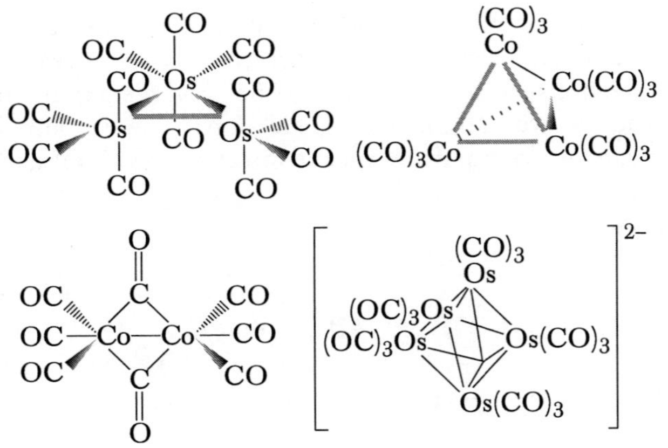

Molecular Orbital Diagram of CO

A simple MO diagram for CO is shown below. It would be sufficient if you concentrate on the highest occupied molecular orbital (HOMO) and lowest unoccupied molecular orbital (LUMO) at this level. The HOMO is the *s*σ lone pair orbital mainly centered on the carbon and weakly anti-bonding with respect to the C–O bond. The weak C–O anti-bonding nature of this MO, however, is clearly seen in the experimental data presented below. The LUMO is strongly $\overset{*}{\pi}$ anti-bonding and is low enough in energy to act as a good acceptor orbital for interacting with filled *d*-orbitals on metals.

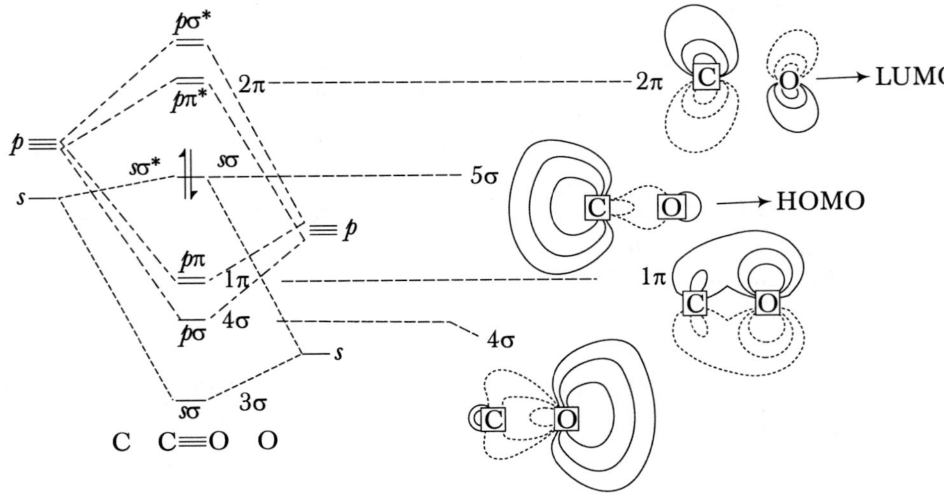

Table 11.6 **Experimental Data Supporting Nature of MO's in CO**

Species	Config	C–O Å	v_{CO} cm^{-1}	Comment
CO	$(5\sigma)^2$	1.13	2143	
CO^+	$(5\sigma)^1$	1.11	2184	5σ MO is weakly anti-bonding
CO*	$(5\sigma)^1\ (2\pi)^1$	T 1.21	1715	2π MO is strongly anti-bonding

Carbonyl ligand is considered as a weak 2-electron σ-donor and very strong π-acceptor. Two types of interactions are involved in the complexation of carbonyl with transition metal ion. The carbonyl donates its lone pair to vacant metal $d(\sigma)$ orbital and back-donation occurs metal $d\pi$ orbital to C—O $\overset{*}{\pi}$ orbital.

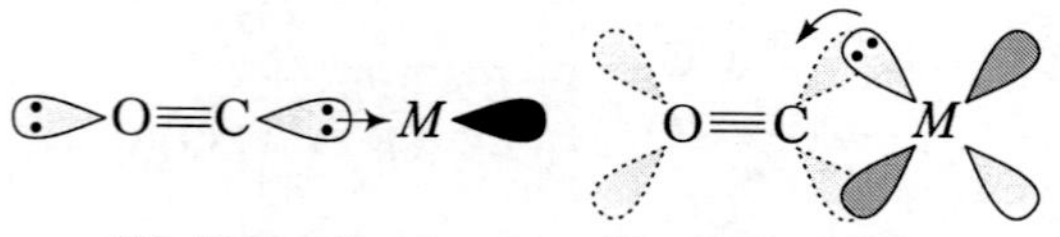

CO-*M* sigma bond *M* to CO π backbonding

Carbonyl IR Stretching Frequencies

The **position** of the carbonyl bands in the IR depends mainly on the bonding mode of the CO (terminal, bridging) and the amount of electron density on the metal being π-backbonded to the CO.

The **number** (and intensity) of the carbonyl bands one observes depends on the number of CO ligands present and the symmetry of the metal complex.

Bonding Modes

As one goes from a terminal CO-bonding mode to μ_2-bridging and finally μ_3-bridging, there is a relatively dramatic drop in the CO stretching frequency seen in the IR.

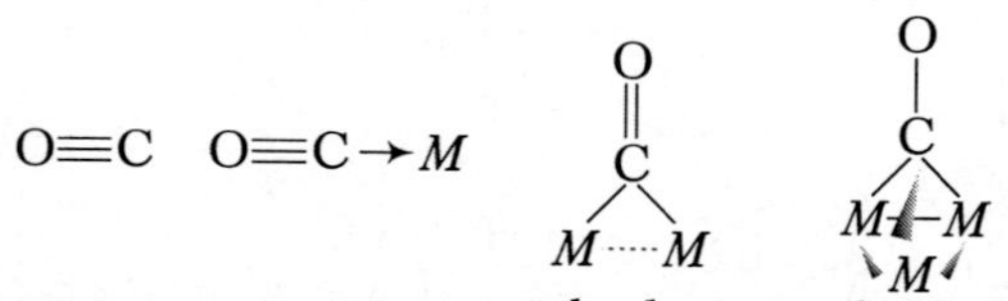

free CO terminal mode μ_2-bridging μ_3-bridging

ν_{CO}IR(cm^{-1}) 2143 2120-1850 1850-1720 1730-1500

(for neutral metal complexes)

As an example the IR spectrum of $[(\eta^5\text{-Cp})Fe(CO)_2]_2$ is shown to illustrate the clear difference in the region of absorptions of the two types of carbonyls. Note that the electron count cannot tell us about the existence (absence) of the bridging carbonyls. This has to found from the experiment.

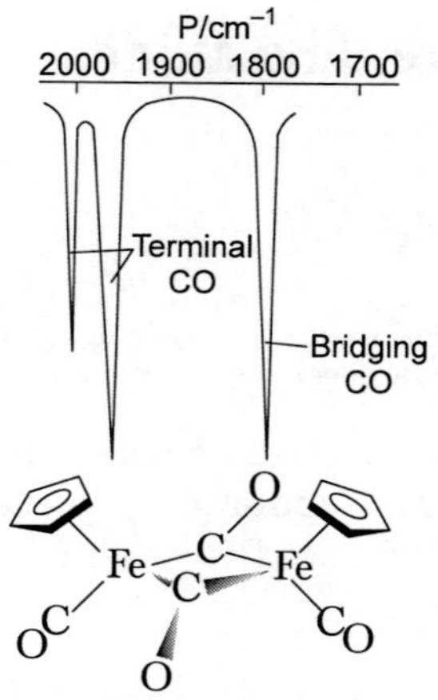

Effect of Electron Density on Metal

As the electron density on a metal centre increases, more π-backbonding to the CO ligand(s) takes place. This further weakens the C—O bond by pumping more electron density into the formally empty carbonyl $\overset{*}{\pi}$ orbital. This increases the *M*—CO bond strength making it more double-bond-like *i.e.,* the resonance structure *M*═C═O assumes more importance. This can clearly be seen on the table that illustrates the effect of charge and electronegativity on the amount of metal to CO π-backbonding and the CO IR stretching frequency. The variation in the ν_{CO} for the complexes given right can be readily explained by looking at charge on the central metal ion. As the positive charge increases, the metal is less likely (less effective) in the backbonding involving π-overlap. If there is less of π-bonding, the C—O bond has greater bond order; a higher value for the stretching frequency is consequently observed. Similarly, the higher negative charge on the metal increases the extent of π-backbonding, and hence the CO frequencies decreases.

d-count	Complex	ν_{CO} cm^{-1}
	free CO	2143
	$Ag(CO)^+$	2204
d^{10}	$Ni(CO)_4$	2060
	$Co(CO)_4^-$	1890
	$Fe(CO)_4^{2-}$	1790
	$Mn(CO)_6^+$	2090
d^6	$Cr(CO)_6$	2000
	$V(CO)_6^-$	1860

Ligand Donation Effects

Ligands that are *trans* to a carbonyl can have particularly large effect on the ability of the CO ligand on effectively π-backbond to the metal. For example, two *trans* π-backbonding ligands will partially complete for the same *d*-orbital electron density, weakening each others net $M—L$ π-backbonding. If both *trans* ligands are carbonyls, they will make equally strong *M-C* bonds.

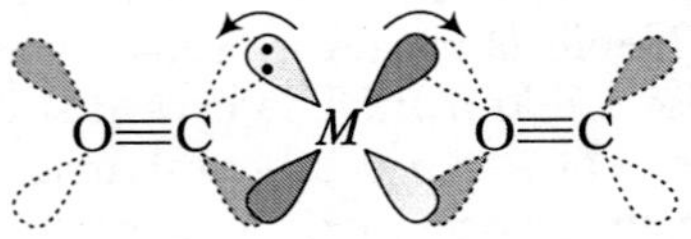

When the *trans* ligand is a σ-donating ligand, this can increase the *M*–CO bond strength (more $M{=}C{=}O$ character) by allowing unimpeded metal to CO π-backbonding. Pyridine and amines are not so strong σ-donors, but they are even worse π-backbonding ligands. So, the CO has virtually no competition for π-backdonation. Look at the IR stretching frequency of the CO group that is opposite to L in a series of complexes $W(CO)_5L$. The idea is as follows: if L is a weak π-accepting ligand, most of the electron density of the metal will be taken by the CO *trans* to it, and hence relatively low C—O stretching frequency.

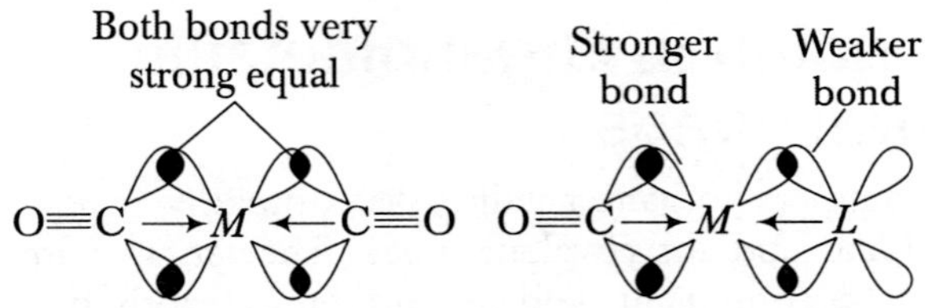

This is what happens when pyridine(py) is opposite CO. When PPh_3 is the opposite ligand, the competition for π-electron density increases and a slightly higher value is observed. With PF_3 as the opposite ligand, the value obtained for this compound is nearly the same for $W(CO)_6$. It indicates that the π-acceptor properties are nearly equal for CO and PF_3.

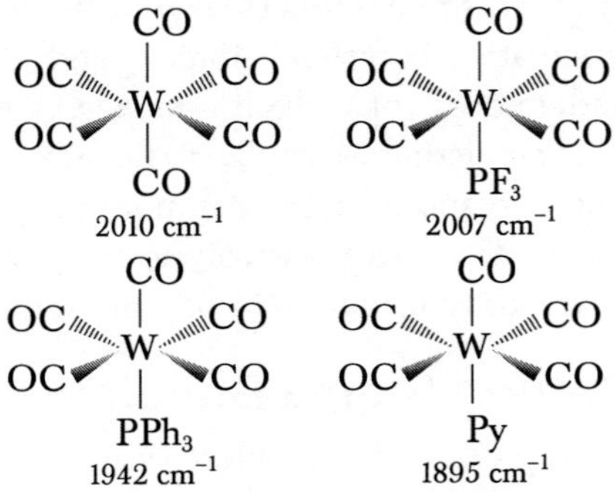

Based on CO IR stretching frequencies, the following ligands can be ranked from best π-acceptor to worst :

$$NO^+ > CO > PF_3 > RN{\equiv}C > PCl_3 > P(OR)_3 > PR_3 > RC{\equiv}N > NH_3$$

Table 11.7 **Properties of Metal Carbonyls**

$V(CO)_6$ Black green, 70° (*d*) Octahedral **Paramagnetic** ($1e^-$)	$Cr(CO)_6$ **White**, 130°(*d*) Octahedral	$Mn_2(CO)_{10}$ **Golden yellow,** m.p. 154°	$Fe(CO)_5$ **Colourless** m.p.-20° b.p.-103° tri-bipyramid	$Co_2(CO)_8$ **Orange red** m.p. 51°	$Ni(CO)_4$ **Colourless** m.p – 25°, b.p.-42° tetrahedral
			$Fe_2(CO)_9$ **Golden yellow,** 100° (d) $Fe_3(CO)_{12}$ **Green** 140°(*d*)	$Co_4(CO)_{12}$ **Black,** 60°,(*d*)	
	$Mo(CO)_6$ **White** 180° (*d*) Octahedral	$Tc_2(CO)_{12}$ **White** 160°	$Ru(CO)_5$ **Colourless** m.p.-22° trigonal bipyramid $Ru_3(CO)_{12}$ **Orange** m.p.-150°	$Ru_4(CO)_{12}$ **Red**, 150°(*d*)	
	$W(CO)_6$ **White** m.p. = 177° Octahedral	$Re_2(CO)_{10}$ **White** m.p. = 177°	$Os(CO)_5$ **Colourless** m.p.-15° trigonal bipyramidal $Os_3(CO)_{12}$ **yellow,** m.p. 224°	$Ir_4(CO)_{12}$ **Yellow**, 210° (*d*) tetrahedron of $Ir(CO)_3$ units.	

Bonding in Organometallic Compounds

Bonding in organometallics is primarily classified (a) ionic and (b) covalent types. The latter is much more predominant and is further categorised into (i) σ-bonding and (ii) multiple bonding.

Metal Carbon Ionic Bonding

This type of bonding is generally observed in organometallics of the most electropositive metals like sodium, potassium, rubedium and cesium. C_4H_9Na, CH_3K. However, some workers suggest the bonding to be intermediate between ionic and covalent. Cyclopentadienides of alkali metals, $M(C_5H_5)$, lanthanides and actinides $M(C_5H_5)_3$, are essentially ionic. Ionic organometallic compounds are quite reactive and undergo easy hydrolysis and oxidation in air. They are mostly insoluble in organic solvents.

Metal-Carbon Sigma Bonding

Metal alkyl represent the simplest systems containing metal carbon sigma bonds. Such metal carbon σ-bonds are not so unstable in main group metal derivatives such as $(CH_3)_4Sn$, $(CH_3)_6Al_2$, C_4H_9Li, etc., but are reported to be relatively unstable in case of transition metals. Although simple alkyl derivatives like $Ti(CH_3)_4$, $Nb(CH_3)_5$, $W(CH_3)_2$ are well known yet they are known to explode at or below room temperatures. Their stability may be enhanced in the presence of other ligands like CO, PR_3, amines etc. As for example, $TiMe_4$ decomposes violently around 250 K but the addition of dipyridine or diamine does not let it decompose up to room temperature. Similarly, the stability of $TaMe_5$ can be enchanced somewhat by the addition of a diphosphine ligand, dmpe ($Me_2PCH_2CH_2PMe_2$). **It has been observed that the higher alkyls are less stable than the lower alkyls but aryls are more stable than the methyls.** Although sufficient bond dissociation energy data of transition metal-carbon sigma bonded compounds are lacking, yet all direct or indirect bond energy estimates indicate thermodynamically stable metal carbon σ-bonds. For example, the mean bond dissociation energy of Ta–CH_3 in $TaMe_5$ is 260 kJ/mol. This is surprisingly substantially greater than the mean bond dissociation energy D(W–CO) of 180 kJ/mol in the much more stable (kinetically) $W(CO)_6$. These bond energy estimates indicate that the transition metal-carbon σ-bond is thermodynamically stable. Consequently, the instability of transition metal alkyls is kinetic. That is, there are easy pathways of decomposition. This means **they are possibly kinetically unstable but thermodynamically stable.**

Metal-Carbon Multiple Bonding

Another class of metal-carbon bonded system represents multiple bonding, wherein, carbene ($=CR_2$) or carbyne ($\equiv CR$) ligands may form double or triple bonds with metal atom. The first carbene complex $(CO)_5W[:C(R)(OMe)]$ was synthesized by E.O. Fisher (Noble laureate) in 1964 but now a large variety of these are known. The crystal structure of the above complex shows an octahedral arrangement with one of the positions occupied the carbene π-CR(OMe) (Fig. 11.8).

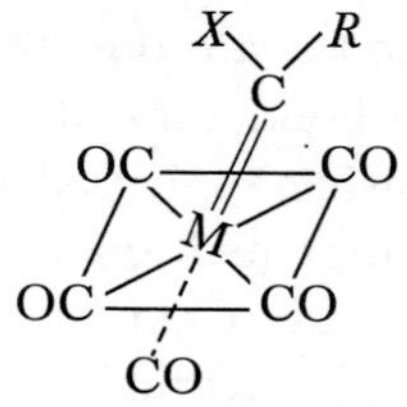

Fig. 11.8 Structure of $(CO)_5M(X)(R)$.

It has been found that the **metal-carbon bond is some what shorter than the normal metal alkyl σ-bond but noticeably longer than a metal-carbon double bond. This suggests only a limited double bond character M—C between the metal atom and the carbene ligand**. It is usually formulated as a metal carbon σ-bond supplemented by a weak π-bond resulting from the overlap of carbon p-orbital with suitable metal d-orbital (d_{xz}). Since, carbene complexes are usually stable with substituents (X = OMe or NMe_2) which can form π-bonding with the carbene carbon 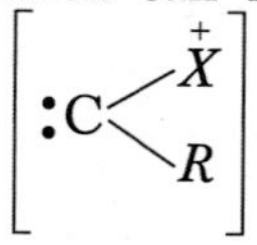 therefore resonance hybrid formulation assumes importance.

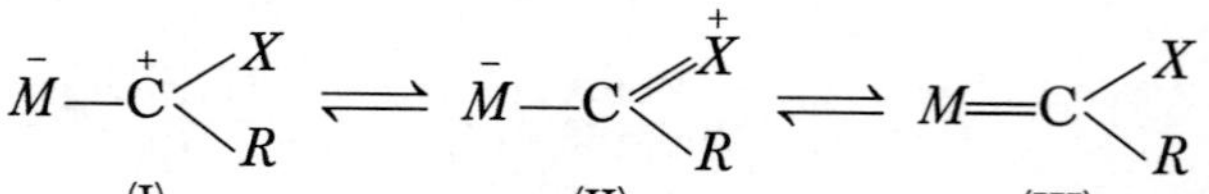

(I) (II) (III)

Structure(II) is considered to be more predominant and is supported by restricted rotation about the C—X bond. Structure(III) is also reported to have considerable importance in many cases.

Carbyne complexes of the type $(CO)_4M(\equiv CR)X$, (M = Cr, Mo, W; R = Me,. Et or Ph; X = Cl, Br or I) are the most important in this class of compounds and were first reported in 1973. The crystal structure of the complexes shows ≡CR group occupying position *trans* to halo ligand in an octahedral geometry as shown in Fig. 11.9.

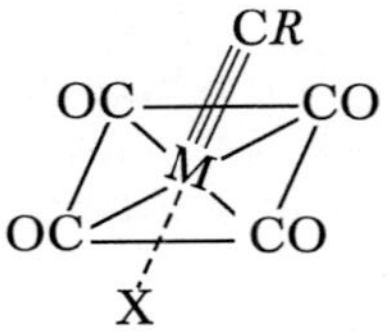

Fig. 11.9 Structure of $(CO)_4 \cdot M(\equiv CR)X$.

The bond angle M—C—R is 180° or less and the bond distance M—C ranges between 169 to 190 pm. In case of chromium complex the bond angle Cr—C—CH_3 is 180° and the bond distance Cr≡C is 169 pm (Cr—C single bond is around 220 pm and Cr═C double bond is around 190 pm). This suggests a chromium-carbon triple bond in the complex :

$$X(CO)_4Cr\equiv C—CH_3$$

Bonding in Alkenyl Complexes

Alkenes act as neutral $2e^-$ donors (per C═C double bond). Due to the presence of empty $\overset{*}{\pi}$ antibonding orbitals, there is the possibility of π-backbonding.

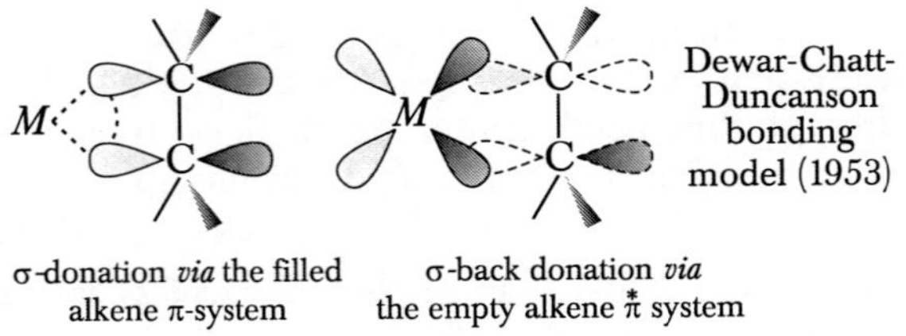

Alkenes are typically relatively weakly coordination ligands. They are also extremely important substrates for catalytic reactions. **The strongest alkene-metal bonds occur with third row metals** (as with almost all ligands) and when one can get more π-backbonding to occur.

The amount of π-backbonding depends strongly on how electron-rich the metal centre is and whether or not there are electron-withdrawing groups on the alkene to make it a better acceptor ligand.

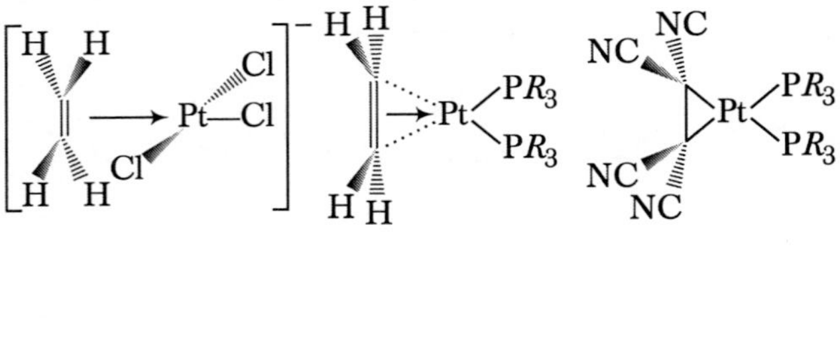

Pt(+2)	Pt(0)	Pt(+2)
C═C = 1.37Å	C═C = 1.37Å	C—C = 1.49Å
Zeiss's salt		Metallo cyclopropane

In extreme case, as shown above to the right, if the metal is electron-rich enough and if there are electron withdrawing groups on the alkene (like the CN's), one can actually get a formal oxidation of the metal *via* the transfer of 2*e*- to the alkene to form a dianionic metallocyclopropane ligand that is now coordinated *via* two anionic alkyl σ-bonds (thus the assignment of Pt(+2)).

Another interesting comparison is shown below where we have two different alkenes coordinating to the same metal centre. The electron withdrawing fluorine groups on the $F_2C═CF_2$ alkene makes it a better π-acceptor ligand. This weakens the C═C bond, but strengthens the alkene-metal bond.

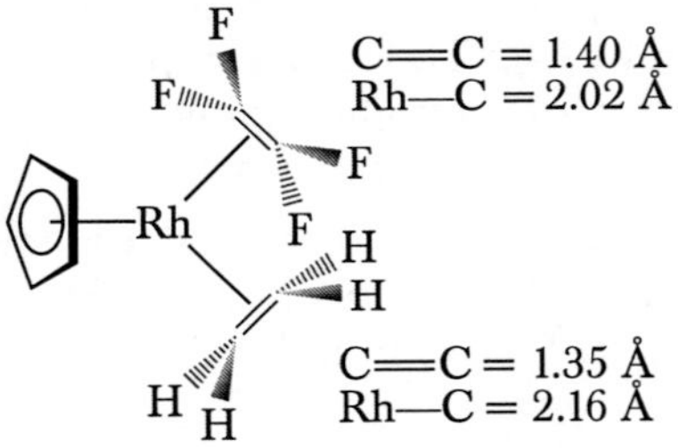

Another series of structures is shown below for butadiene, $Fe(\eta^4\text{-}C_4H_6)(CO)_3$ and $Cp_2Zr(\eta^4\text{-}C_4H_6)$.

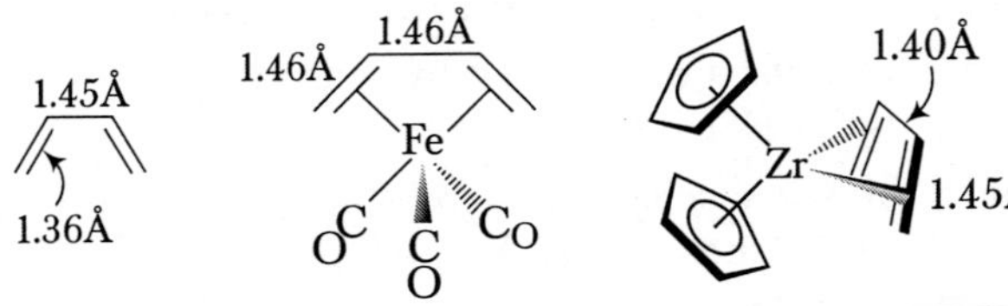

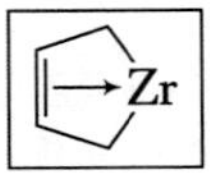

In this series one can see that the combination of π-backdonation from the Fe and σ-donation from the alkenes to the Fe weaken and lengthen the C═C bond. In the Zr complex, however, we see an interesting reversal where the single bond across the back of the butadiene shortens quite a bit. What is happening here is that the Zr is in a very low oxidation state (+2, but it really wants to be +4) and is, therefore, extremely electron-rich. The Zr transfers two electrons to the butadiene *via* the π-back donation and generates a metallocyclopentene resonance structure, shown schematically at the right.

Factors Providing Stability to Metal-Carbon Bond

(a) Avoidance of β-elimination

Instability due to β-elimination can be taken care of if metal-alkyls do not contain replaceable H-atom on the β-carbon atom. For example, metal alkyls like $M—CH_3$, $M—CH_2—CR_3$, $M—CH_2—Ar$, $M—CH_2—NR_2$, $M—CH_2—SiR_3$, etc. (where, β-hydrogen is absent) do not favour β-elimination. Consequently, it has been generally observed that metal-methyls are relatively more stable than metal higher *n*-alkyls. The most important examples of β-elimination stabilised alkyls are the trimethylsilylmethyls $M(—CH_2SiMe_3)_n$

(b) Increasing coordination number

Another stabilizing factor for metal alkyls is the presence of ligands which can occupy coordination positions firmly, *e.g.*, $TiMe_4$ decomposes below 253 K but the addition of bipyridine (bipy) increases stability up to 330 K due to the formation of $TiMe_4$ (bipy).

Introduction of oxygen to the coordination sphere greatly increases the stability of metal-carbon bond. For example, $Me_4Re^{VI}=O$ is thermally stable upto 473 K and $MeRe^{VII}(=O)_3$ is stable in air whereas Me_6Re and Me_7Re are unstable.

Vitamin B-12 containing a cobalt-carbon bonding is stabilized by five nitrogen donor atoms giving an octahedral arrangement around cobalt.

Platinum methyls are stabilized by acetylacetone ligand in the complex $[Me_3Pt(acac)]_2$.

Stability of metal alkyls is significantly enhanced by π-acid ligands such as CO, cyclopentadienyls and phophine ligands.

Examples Metal-alkyls or-aryls are not known for Fe, Ru and Os but the presence of π-acids stabilise derivatives like :

$$(\eta^5\text{-}C_5H_5)M(CO)_2R \text{ and } XMR(P—P)_2$$

where, M = Fe, Ru or Os ; X = halogen; R = alkyl and P—P disphosphine ligand like $Me_2P—CH_2—CH_2—PMe_2$.

Nickel, palladium and platinum alkyls (MR_2) are stabilized by monophosphines, PR_3 in complexes $R_2M(PR_3)_2$. Chromium, molybdenum and tungsten alkyls (MR) are stabilised by CO in the complex $(CH_3)Mn(CO)_5$.

(c) Chelation

Stability of metal-carbon sigma bond can be enhanced by involving it as a part of a chelate ring. A stable chelate ring may be formed either by donating through a terminal amino grouped metal alkyl chain (Fig. 11.10A) or by involving an orthocarbon in a benzyl amine derivative as shown as Fig. 11.9(B) or through donation from an *ortho*-amino group in a metal benzyl derivative (*C*).

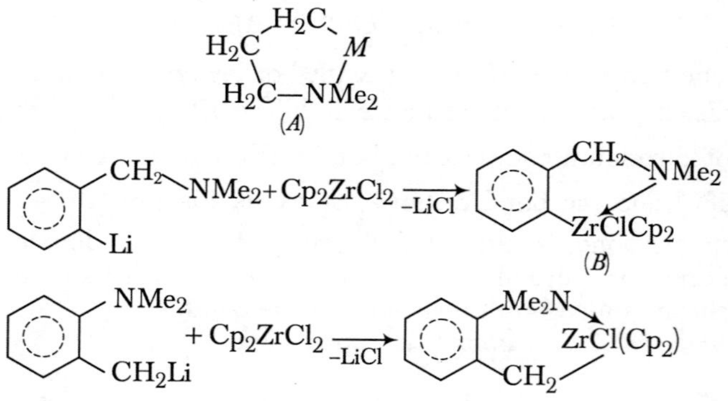

Fig. 11.10 Examples showing chelation ($C_P = C_5H_5$).

(d) **Delocalization of negative charge on carbon** In most of the cases, the metal-carbon σ-bond may acquire polarity ($M^{\delta+}—C^{\delta-}$) due to the difference in their electronegativities. Anything that can help in delocalization of the negative charge would help in stability of the metal-carbon bond. This is true for aromatic and halogen substituted carbon species like CF_3. It has been observed that $M—CF_3$ bonds are generally more stable than $M—C_6H_5$ which, in turn, are more stable than $M—CH_3$.

Cyclopentadienyl-Cp

The cyclopentadienyl ligand is one of the most common and popular ligands in organometallic chemistry.

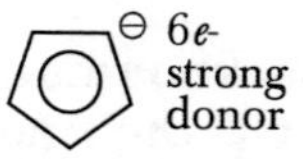

It is an anionic ligand that normally coordinates in an η^5 mode as a $6e^-$ donor, but it can adopt η^3- and η^1-coordination modes. The number of electrons donated is 6, 4 and 2 respectively.

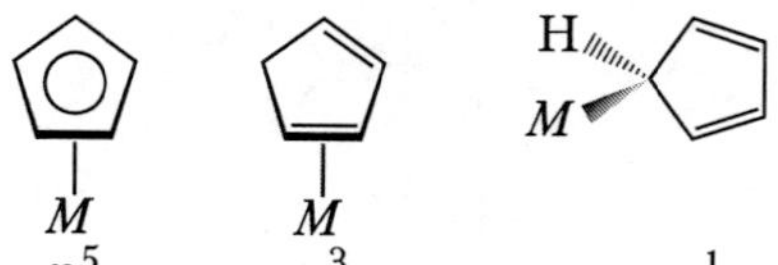

η^5 η^3 η^1

Ferrocene

Brief History

1951 Miller, Tebboth and Tremaine
Synthesis of $Fe(C_5H_5)_2$ from the reaction of C_5H_6 with freshly reduced Fe at 300°C

1951 Kealy and Pauson

$3C_5H_5MgBr + FeCl_3 \rightarrow Cp_2Fe +$ 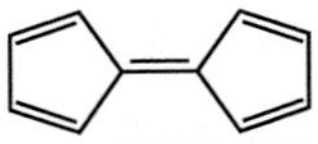 $+ 3MgBrCl$

They were trying to make fulvalene!
They proposed that they had made:

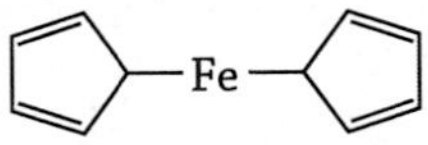

1952 Goeffrey Wilkinson and Robert Woodward proposed "Sandwich Structure"

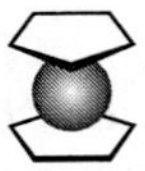

IR spectroscopy : It is diamagnetism, dipole moment = 0
Woodward noted that the Cp rings were susceptible towards electrophillic substitutions, similar to the aromatic behaviour of benzene. Thus, the common name is ferrocene

1973 Fischer and Wilkinson receive the Nobel Prize in Chemistry for their "discovery" of ferrocene, which played a key role in opening up the new area of organometallic chemistry.

Preparation

Ferrocene can be prepared by several methods, some of which are described below :

1. By the reaction of Fe (III) salts with appropriate Grignard reagent. Fe (III) is first reduced by the Grignard reagent to Fe (II) which then reacts to form ferrocene.
2. By the reaction of iron with cyclopentadiene in the presence of R_3NH^+Cl.

(i) $Fe + R_3NH^+Cl^- \longrightarrow FeCl_2 + 2R_3N + H_2$

(ii) $FeCl_2 + \underset{\text{Pentadiene}}{2C_5H_6} + R_3N \longrightarrow Fe(C_5H_5)_2 + 2R_3NH^+Cl^-$

Net reaction : $Fe + 2C_5H_6 \longrightarrow Fe(C_5H_5)_2 + H_2$

Ferrocene forms orange red crystals which melt at 174°C. The compound is thermally stable up to 500°C.

Aromatic Character of Ferrocene

Ferrocene cannot be hydrogenated under normal conditions nor does it undergoes the Diels-Alder reaction which is a characteristic property of conjugated dienes. This shows that the $C_5H_5^-$ rings to ferrocene behave as aromatic systems. This is supported by the fact that ferrocene has π delocalised MOs similar to the ones in aromatic systems. Ferrocene, therefore, gives almost all the reactions which are typical of aromatic systems.

Reactions of Ferrocene

Reactions of ferrocene can be divided into two groups : **A.** Reactions of the C_5H_5 rings. **B.** Reactions involving interaction of Fe atom with ring substituents.

Reactions of C_5H_5 rings : electrophilic substitution reactions

The mechanism of electrophilic substitution reactions in ferrocence is illustrated below :

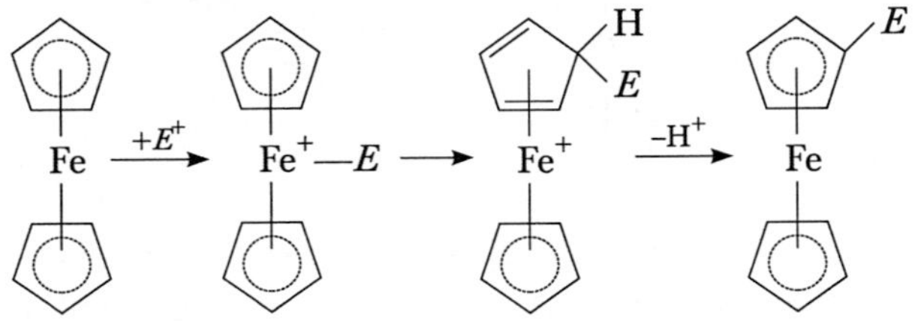

(i) **Nitration and Halogenation** Direct nitration and halogenation leads to the decomposition of ferrocene. The processes are, therefore, carried out indirectly as described below :

Nitration

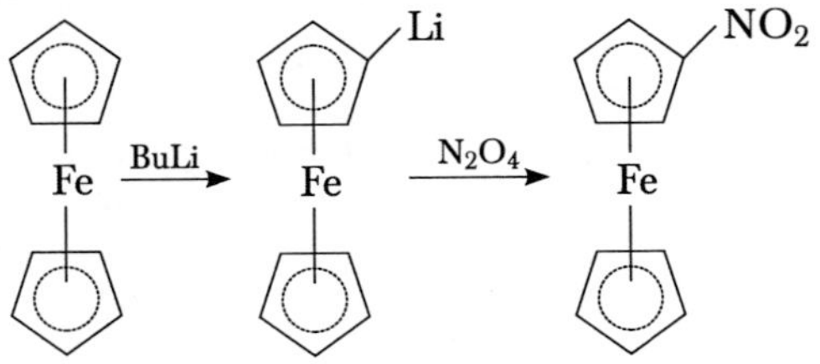

Nitroferrocene on reduction with Pd/HCl gives amino ferrocene.

Bromination

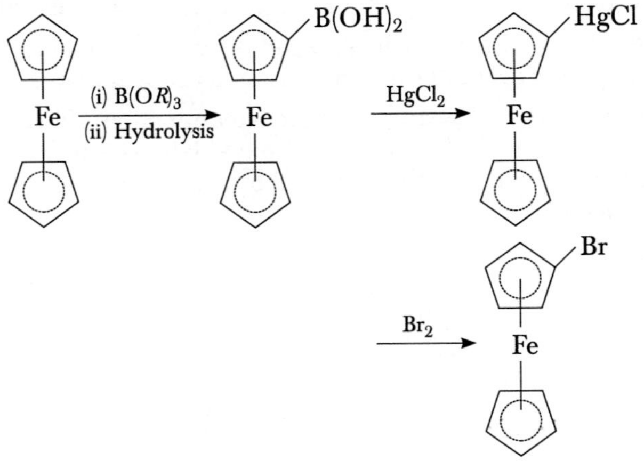

(ii) **Carboxylation** Ferrocene can also be carboxylated as shown

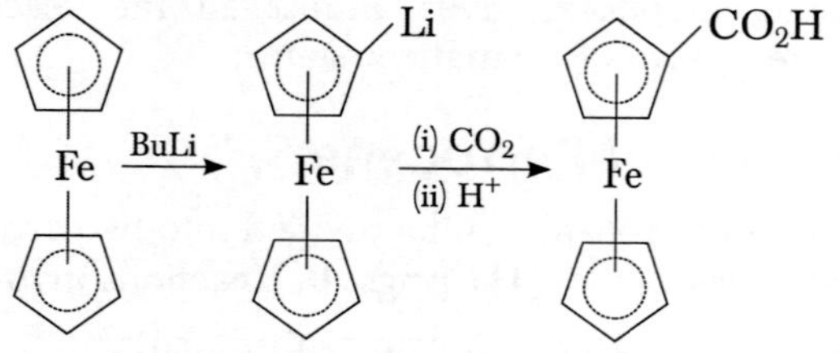

(iii) **Friedel-Crafts reaction** Ferrocene readily undegoes acylation as illustrated below :

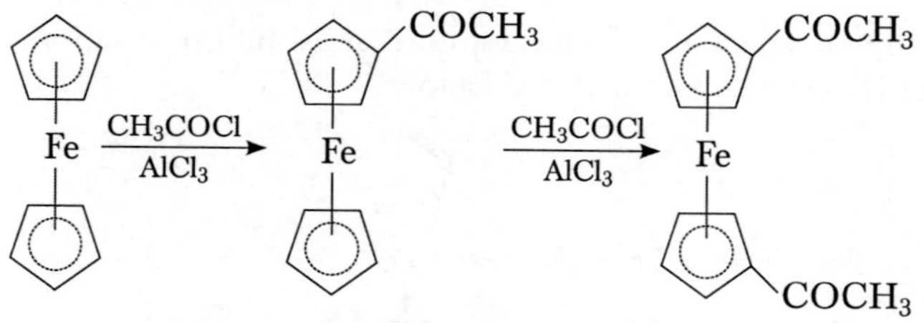

Ferrocene can also be **alkylated** in a similar manner. Alkylation of ferrocene can also be carried out as shown below

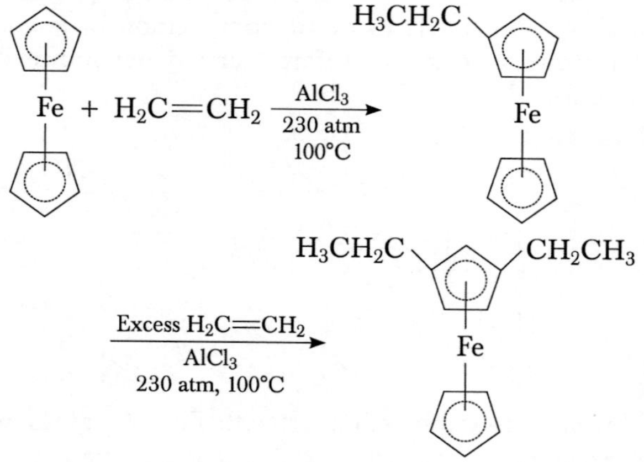

Since, the presence of an alkyl group increases the electron density on the $C_5H_5^-$ ring, hence, in the presence of excess of ligand, the disubstitution of alkyl group also occurs in the same ring, as shown above.

(iv) **Vilsmeir reaction** Ferrocence undergoes Vilsmeir reaction to yield ferrocene carboxyaldehyde which is a useful starting material for the preparation of the ferrocene derivatives.

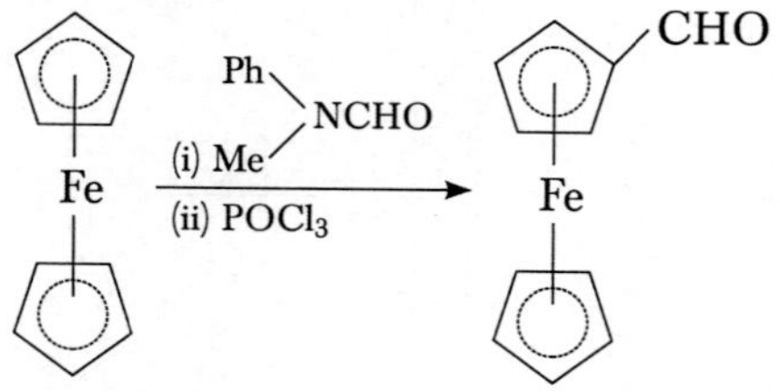

(v) **Mannich condensation** Ferrocene also undergoes Mannich condensation as shown below

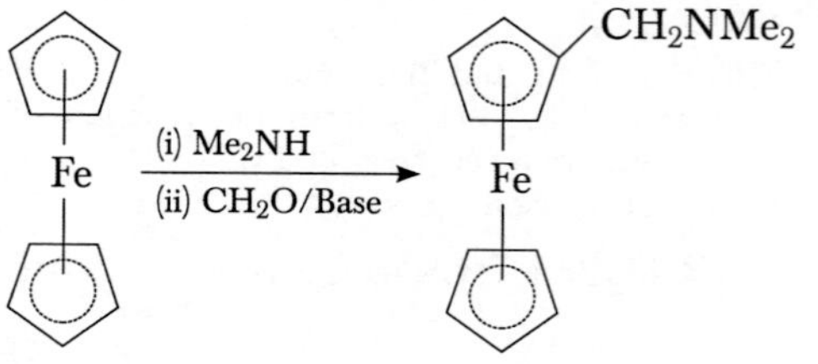

Note The Vilsmeir reaction and the Mannich condensation are reactions which are shown by those aromatic systems that are more reactive than benzene. It follows, therefore, that ferrocene is more aromatic than benzene.

B. Interaction of Fe atom with ring substituents α-carbonium ion stabilisation Ring substituted ferrocene reacts with acetic acid through the formation of a stable α-carbonium ion (intermediate) as shown below :

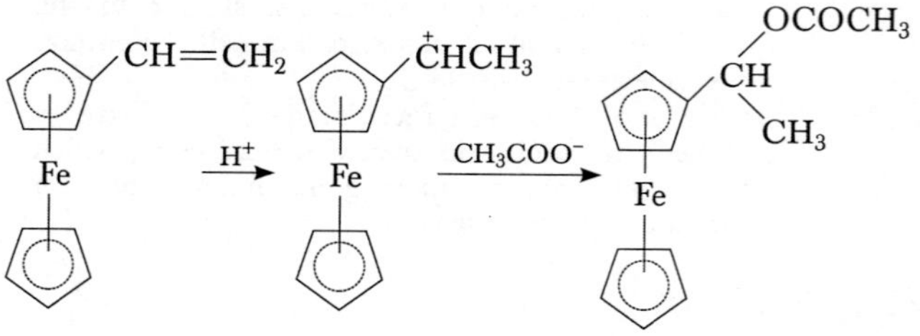

The stabilisation of the carbonium ion can be attributed to either the delocalisation of ring π-electrons to the vacant *p*-orbital of the α-carbonium ion of the same symmetry, as shown in (a) or to a direct interaction between lone orbitals of iron of proper symmetry and the *p*-orbital of the carbonium ion, as shown in (b). According to one view, both the above factors contribute towards the stabilisation of the carbonium ion.

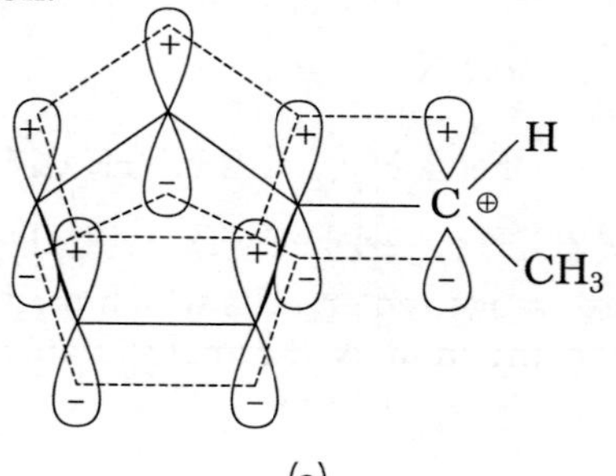

(a)

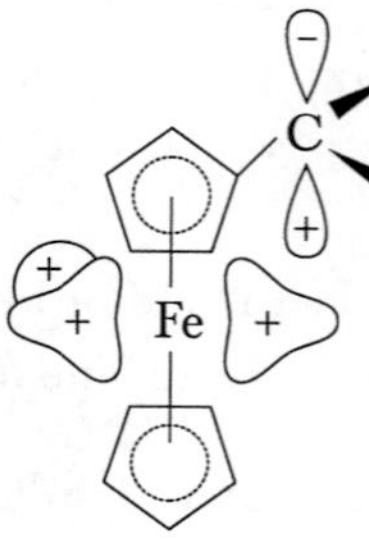

(b)

Bonding in Ferrocene

The molecular orbital energy level diagram for ferrocene is shown in figure below. As can be seen from this figure, there is room for 18 electrons in

BMOs and NBMOs of ferrocene. In terms of electron counting, these 18 electrons come from Fe^{II} ion (6 electrons) and two $C_5H_5^-$ anions ($2 \times 6 = 12$ electrons).

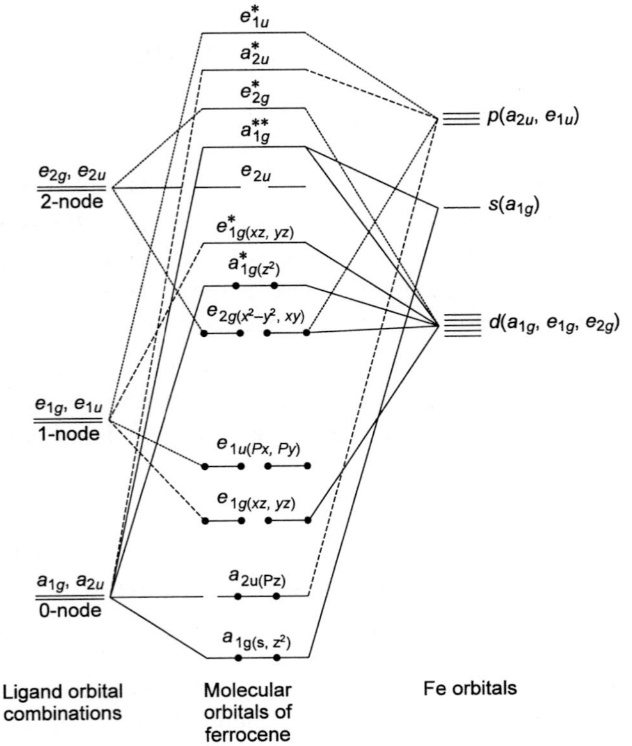

Fig. 11.11 The molecular orbital energy level diagram of ferrocene.

The stability of $Fe(C_5H_5)_2$ with 18 electrons compared to $Co(C_5H_5)_2$ with 19 electrons and $Ni(C_5H_5)_2$ with 20 electrons can be explained as follows : Cobalocene and nickelocene have one and two electrons, respectively, in their ABMO whereas ferrocene has none. The electrons in ABMO are easier to remove (why?) so that cobalocene and nickelocene are easily oxidisable compared to ferrocene.

Similarly, chromocene, $Cr(C_5H_5)_2$, with 16 electrons and vanadocene, $V(C_5H_5)_2$, with 15 electrons have unfilled BMO-NBMO set with the result that these systems can easily get reduced by accepting two and three electrons, respectively.

Structural Features

The parallel sandwhich structures have the following structural features :

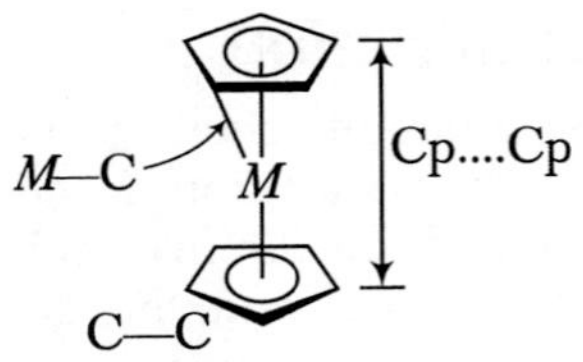

	Distances (Å)		
M	*M*–C	Cp...Cp	C–C
Fe	2.04	3.29	1.42
$[Fe]^+$	2.07	3.40	1.40
Ru	2.19	3.64	1.43
Co	2.10	3.44	1.41
$[Co]^+$	2.03	3.24	1.42
Ni	2.18	3.63	1.41

Note the various trends in the bond distances. The changes in the neutral Fe, Co, Ni metallocenes are a direct result of going from 18*e*- (Fe) to 19*e*- (Co) to 20*e*-(Ni) counts. The extra electrons for the Co and Ni complexes are going into *M*–Cp antibonding orbitals, which are delocalized and progressively weaken the *M*–Cp bonding, leading to the increase in bond distances. This in spite of the fact that the metal's covalent radius is decreasing as one goes from Fe ⟶ Ni (effective atomic number contraction effect).

Table 11.8 **Some Properties of Metallocenes**

Complex	Colour	m.p./°C	Stability
$V(C_5H_5)_2$	Purple	167	Highly air-sensitive, paramagnetic
$Cr(C_5H_5)_2$	Scarlet	173	Highly air-sensitive
$Mn(C_5H_5)_2$	Brown	173	Air-sensitive and easily hydrolyzed, interesting high-spin to low-spin inter- conversion
$Fe(C_5H_5)_2$	Orange	173	Air-stable, 18*e*-complex, can be oxidized to blue-green $[Fe(C_5H_5)_2]^+$, a good oxidizing agent.
$Co(C_5H_5)_2$	Purple-black	174	Air-sensitive, paramagnetic, 19*e*-complex, oxidized readily in the air to stable $18e^-$, yellow $[Co(C_5H_5)_2]^+$.
$Ni(C_5H_5)_2$	Green	173	20*e*- complex, unstable

β-Hydride Elimination

One of the most common "side' reactions of alkyls is called the β-hydride elimination reaction. The main driving force for β-hydride elimination is the formation of a stronger *M*–H bond and the generation of an alkene ligand that reduces the unsaturation of the metal complex. The reverse reaction, however, also can occur and is called a **migratory insertion.** This is very important in transition metal reaction chemistry and catalysis, as we will discuss this later.

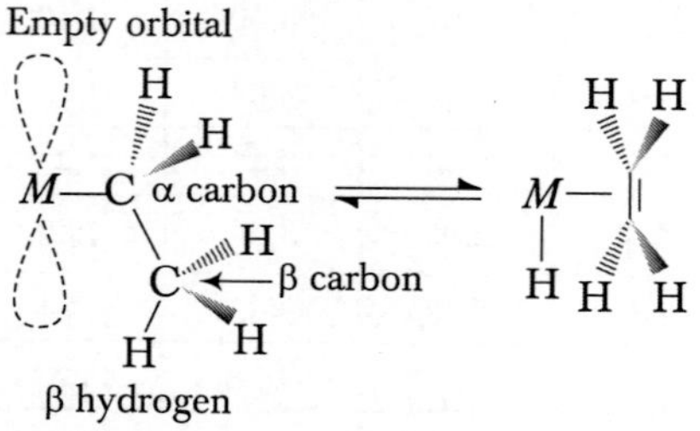

Note that in order to have a β-hydride elimination one must have an empty orbital on the metal cisoidal (next) to the alkyl ligand. One also must have β-hydrogens present on the alkyl. In order to prepare stable *M*-alkyl complexes one, therefore, often needs to stay away from alkyls with β-hydrogens (or avoid metals with empty coordination sites). Some common ligands used to avoid β-hydride elimination reactions are shown below.

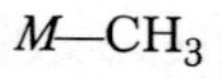

Methyl

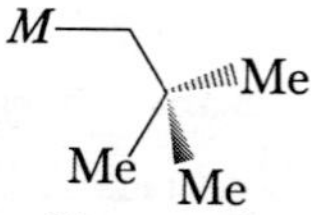

Neopentyl

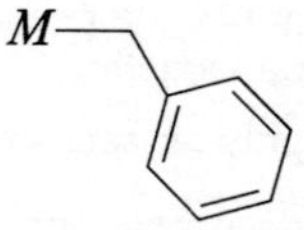

Benzyl

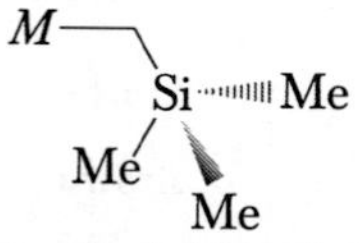

Trimethylsilylmethyl

Reactions of Organometallic Compounds

Oxidative Addition

An oxidative addition reaction is one in which (usually) a neutral ligand adds to a metal centre and in doing so oxidizes the metal, typically by $2e^-$. The transferring of the two electrons from the metal to the incoming ligand breaks a bond in that ligand forming two new anionic ligands. At least one of these new anionic ligands ends up bonded to the metal centre.

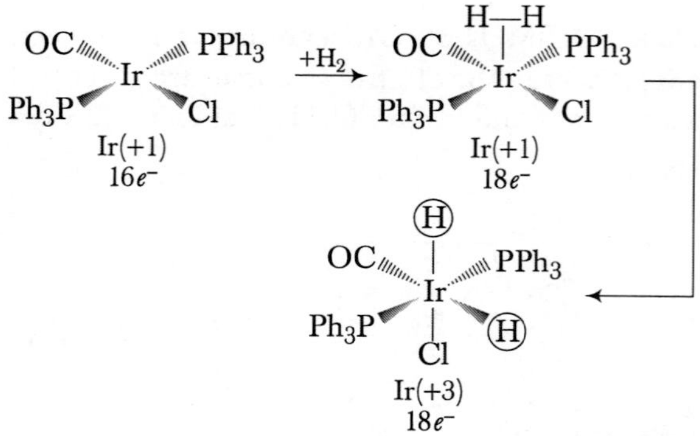

[The reverse of this reaction would be a **reductive elimination.** In the reverse reaction, the coordination number and the oxidation state of the metal decreases by the expulsion (elimination) of ligand(s)].

There are three main classes of molecules (substrates) that can perform oxidative additions to metal centres non-electrophilic, electrophilic, and intact. Below are the examples.

(a) Non-electrophilic

These molecules do not contain electronegative atoms and/or are not good oxidizing agents. A side from H_2, they are often considered to be "non-reactive" substrates. These molecules generally require the presence of an empty orbital on the metal centre in order for them to pre-coordinate prior to being activated for the oxidative addition reaction *e.g.*, **H_2, C—H bonds, S—H bonds, N–H bonds, S—S bonds, etc.**

H_2 is by far the most imortant for catalytic applications.

(b) Electrophilic

These molecules do contain electronegative atoms and are good oxidising agents. They are often considered to be "reactive" substrates. These molecules do not necessarily require the presence of an empty orbital (*i.e.*, may contain $18e^-$) on the metal centre in order to perform the oxidative addition reaction *e.g.*,

$$X_2\ (X = \text{Cl, Br, I}),\ R—X,\ \text{Ar}—X,\ \text{H}—X, \text{etc.}$$

The most common substrates used here are *R*–*X* (alkyl halides), Ar–*X* (aryl halides), and H–*X*. An example for the oxidative addition of CH_3Br to $IrCl(CO)(PPh_3)_2$ is shown below. Note that the starting metal complex in this case is $16e^-$:

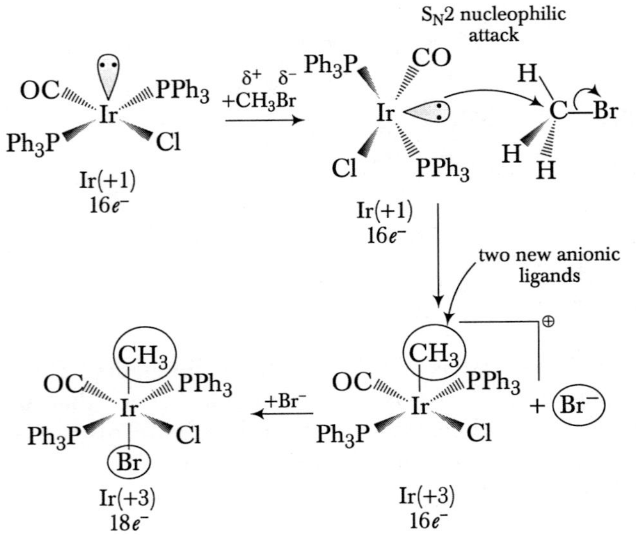

Note that the $H_3C—Br$ bond is broken on the oxidative addition reaction generating two new anionic ligands. CH_3^- and Br^-. If the starting metal complex is $16e^-$ (as shown above) both ligands will usually end up coordinated to the metal to make an $18e^-$ complex.

In the case of a starting $18e^-$ complex (shown below) only one of the two anionic ligands (usually the strongest binding) generated from the oxidative addition will end up coordinated to the metal unless a separate substitution reaction occurs.

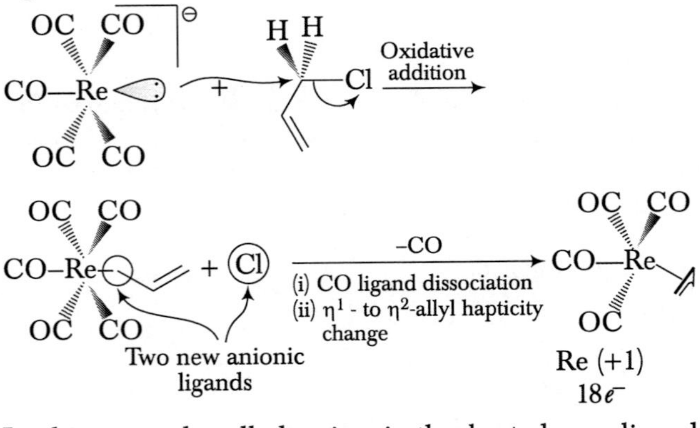

In this case, the alkyl anion is the best donor ligand compared to the more electronegative and poorly donating Cl^- anion. Note that the alkyl ligand ($—CH_2CH{=}CH_2$) initially coordinated to the Re after the oxidative addition is an η^1 -allyl ligand and that it can convert to the generally more stable η^3-allyl on CO ligand dissociation.

(c) Intact

These molecules may or may not contain electronegative atoms, but they do need to have a double or triple bond. Unlike most of the other substrate molecules that break a single bond and form two separate anionic ligands upon the oxidative addition, these ligands have double or triple bonds and only one of the π-bonds is broken leaving the σ-bond intact. The ligand does pick up two electrons from the metal and becomes a **dianionic** ligand.

One usually needs a metal centre with an empty orbital ($16e^-$ or lower count) in order to pre-coordinate the ligand before the oxidative addition occurs. The one notable exception to this is O_2, which can also act as an **electrophilic** substrate.

Typical "intact" ligands that can perform an oxidative addition without fragmenting apart are : alkenes, alkynes, and O_2.

One often needs to have electron withdrawing functional groups on the alkenes or alkynes in order to enhance their electron-withdrawing ability in order to help promote the transfer of electrons from the metal to the ligand.

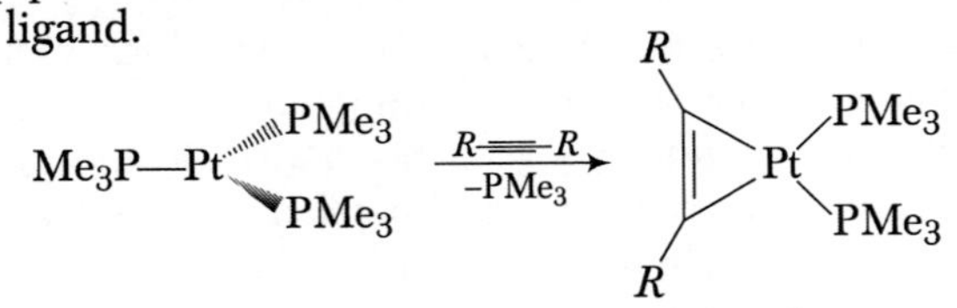

Metallocyclopropene

In this case we have oxidized the Pt centre from Pt(0) d^{10} to Pt(+2) d^8 and generated a new dianionic unsaturated alkenyl ligand. Note that we have broken one of the alkyne π-bonds.

General features of oxidative additions

Because oxidative addition involves oxidation (removal of electrons) of the metal centre, the more electron-rich the metal is, the easier the oxidative addition to the metal centre will be. So, in comparing two or more metal complexes to see which will be the most reactive towards a particular substrate for oxidative addition you would pick the metal centre with the strongest donor ligands, fewest π-acceptor ligands, or most negative charge. Also remember that the non-electrophilic ligands and "intact" ligands usually require that there is an empty orbital ($16e^-$ or lower) on the metal centre in order to react.

Reductive Elimination

A reductive elimination reaction is the reverse of an oxidative addition. It is a reaction in which two cisoidal anionic ligands on a metal centre couple together. Each anionic ligand pushes one electron back onto the metal centre (in the case of a monometallic complex) to reduce it by $2e^-$. The coupled anionic ligands then usually fall of the metal centre as a neutral molecule.

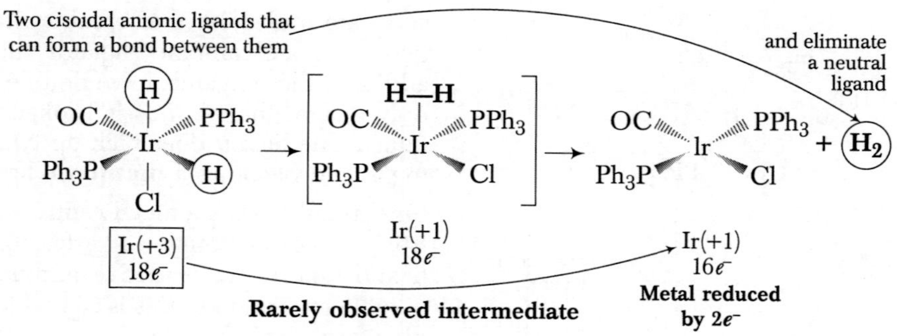

Since, electron-rich metal complexes favour oxidative addition, the reverse is true for reductive elimination. Since, reductive elimination involves pushing electrons back onto the metal centre from two anionic ligands that are usually more electronegative than the metal centre, it is best if the metal centre is electron deficient. This can be accomplished by having electron withdrawing ligands (*e.g.*, CO), cationic charge(s), and/or coordinative unsaturation (sub-$18e^-$ counts).

Migratory Insertion

A migratory insertion reaction is one in which a cisoidal anionic and neutral ligand on a metal complex couple together to generate a new coordinated anionic ligand. This new anionic ligand is composed of the original neutral and anionic ligands. There is no change in the oxidation state of *d*-electron count of the metal centre. But the overall electron-count on the metal decreases by $2e^-$. The empty orbital generated by the migratory insertion reaction can enable the reverse of a migratory insertion reaction, which is known as 'elimination' reaction. To stop the reverse elimination reaction from occurring after a migratory insertion, one often adds a neutral ligand to coordinate to this empty orbital thus stopping the elimination reaction from occurring. This is sometimes called the trapping ligand.

General features :

1. No change in formal oxidation state.
2. The two groups that react must be cisoidal to one another.
3. A vacant coordination site is generated by the migratory insertion. Therefore, a vacant site is required for the back elimination reaction (*e.g.*, β-hydride elimination). A trapping ligand is often needed to coordinate to the empty site formed from a migratory insertion in order to stop the back elimination reaction.
4. Migratory insertions are usually favoured on more electron-deficient metal centres.

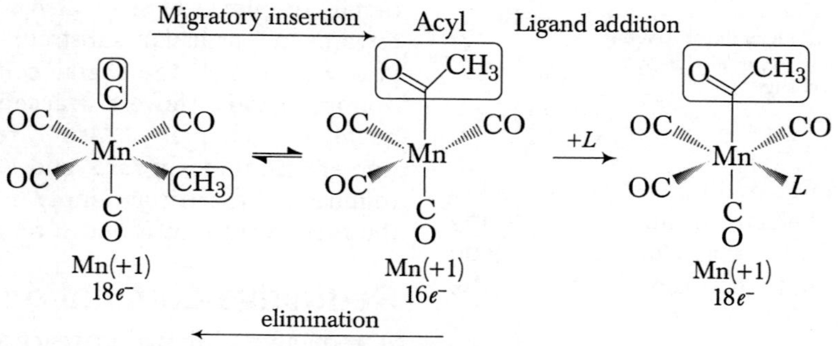

The following are common anionic and neutral ligands that can do migratory insertion reactions with one another.

Anionic

H^-, R^- (alkyl), Ar^- (aryl), $acyl^-$, O^{2-} (oxo) etc.

Neutral : CO, alkenes, alkynes, carbenes

- CO and alkyl migratory insertions (as shown above) are extremely important and are often generically referred to as **carbonylation reactions**. Hydride and CO migratory insertions to produce formyl groups are not common due to the thermodynamic instability of the formyl-metal interaction.
- Note that the acyl ligand formed is not as good a donor compared to the starting alkyl. But the metal has gained (replaced) an electron withdrawing CO ligand with a better donating phosphine. Thus, the overall reaction with a trapping ligand is usually towards the migratory insertion.
- The reason that more electron-deficient metals favour CO-alkyl migratory insertions is that it makes the carbon atom of the CO more electrophilic and susceptible to nucleophilic attack from the more electron rich alkyl group.

Mechanism

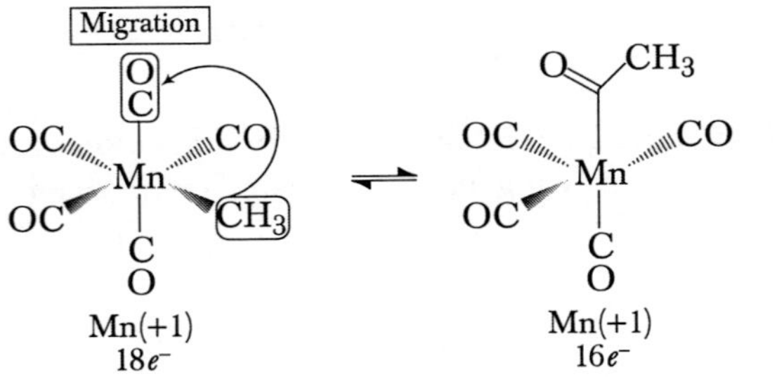

a **Migration** reaction involves the anionic ligand doing a nucleophile-like attack on the neutral ligand. This involves the anionic ligand moving to the site where the neutral ligand is coordinated. An empty coordination site is left behind.

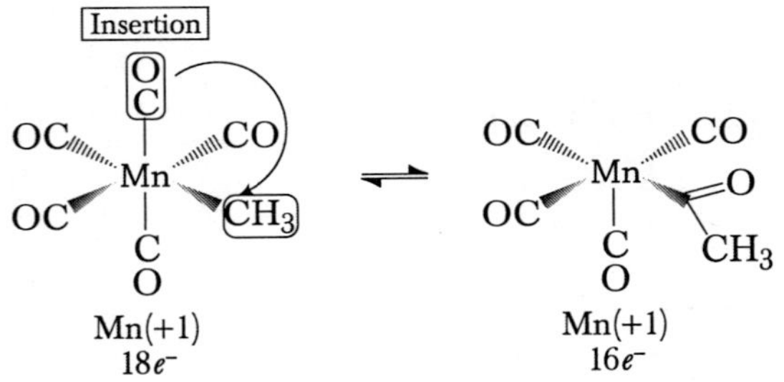

an **Insertion** reaction involves the neutral ligand moving over to where the anionic ligand is coordinated and "inserting" into the anionic ligand-metal bond to generate the new anionic ligand. An empty coordination site is left behind from where the neutral ligand originally was located.

We will not care in this course exactly how the reaction is proceeding. The redundant term "migratory insertion" is used to indicate that either directional pathway is fine. Many organometallic chemists short-cut this and just say insertion reaction. It does not necessarily mean that the mechanism is indeed insertion.

Alkene migratory insertions

An alkene and a hydride usually react *via* a migration of the hydride to the coordinated alkene ligand :

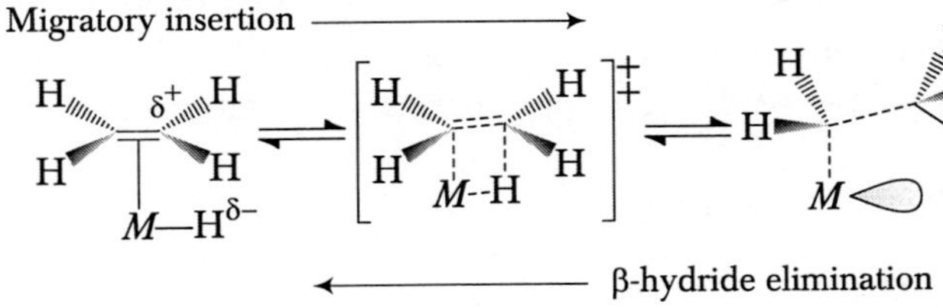

The backwards reaction, of course, is a β-hydride elimination and is usually quite favourable if there is an empty orbital *cis* to the alkyl ligand. Thus, the general importance of having a trapping ligand to coordinate to the empty orbital generated from the migratory insertion.

Alkene/alkyl migratory insertions are also extremely important and an example is shown below :

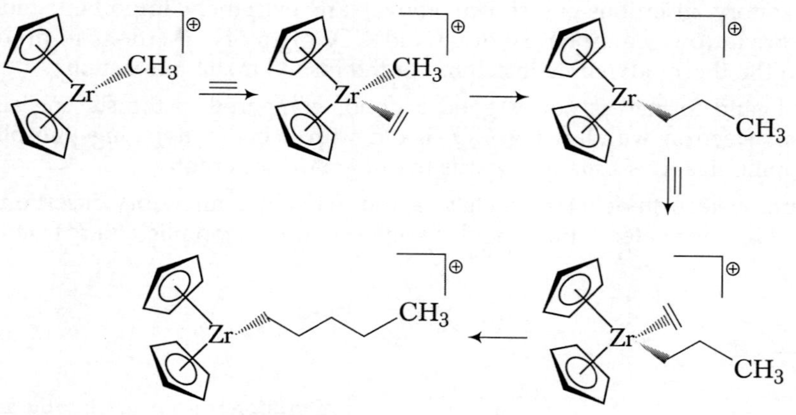

This is the basis for almost all transition metal-based polymerization catalysts. A polymerization reaction is just many, many migratory insertions of an alkene and alkyl (the growing polymer chain) interspaced with alkene ligand addition reactions.

Eliminations

Elimination reactions are just the reverse of migratory insertion reactions. The various common elimination reactions are as follows :

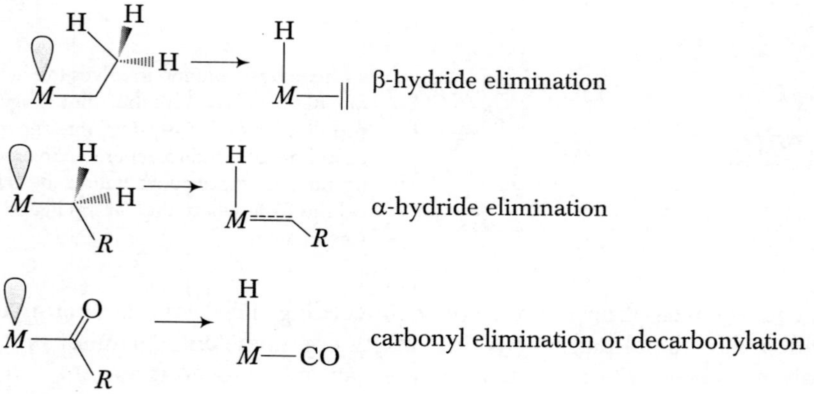

The key points to remember are :

1. No change in formal oxidation state (exception alkylidenes).
2. You must have an empty orbital that is cisoidal to the group that you are doing an elimination reaction on. Alternatively, a cisoidal labile ligand that can easily dissociate to open up an empty orbital.

One of the hardest elimination reactions is the breaking of a C—C bond. For example the following migratory insertion is quite common and plays a critical role in polymerization catalysis :

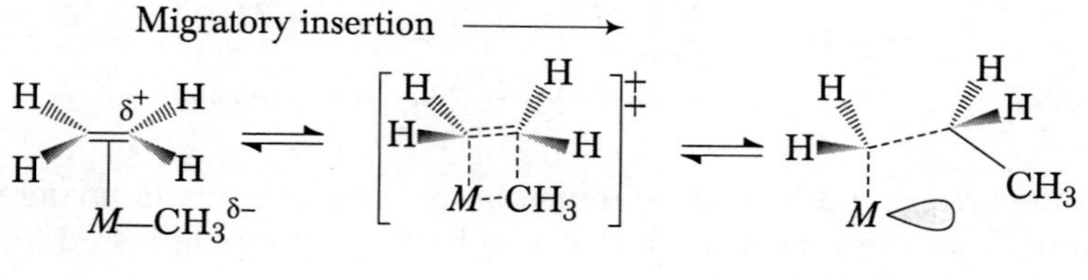

But the reverse methyl elimination reaction is very difficult :

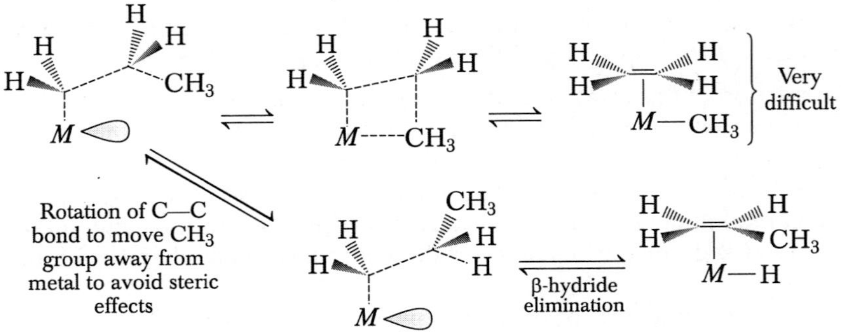

Homogeneous Catalysis

$$A + B \xrightarrow{[\text{Catalyst}]} C$$

Catalysis involves the use of a catalyst that accelerates the rate of a reaction. A catalyst does not alter the Gibbs free energy of the overall reaction (since, G is a state function). Therefore, reactions that are thermodynamically not favourable, cannot be made favourable by a catalyst. Another important feature is that stable catalytic intermediates do not occur in a catalytic cycle. If such a complex were formed it would not lead to a catalytic cycle. Catalyst poisons usually interfere with the catalytic cycle by the formation of such complexes.

In contrast to heterogeneous catalysts where the catalyst is an insoluble solid present in a different phase from the reagents, homogeneous catalysts are in the same phase as the reagents. Usually this implies that the reagents and the catalyst are dissolved in a solvent for carrying out the reaction. The advantage of such a procedure is that in principle all the catalyst used is available for the reaction. Also since the catalyst is soluble, the mechanism of the catalysis reaction can be more easily understood by the use of spectroscopic methods. This in turn allows for easier modification and modulation of catalyst design and activity. The disadvantage of the homogeneous catalyst is the separations of the catalyst from the reagents.

Advantages/Disadvantages of Homogeneous Catalysts Relative to Heterogeneous Catalysts

Homogeneous catalysts are :

Good	generally far more selective for a single product
	far more active
	far more easily studied from chemical and mechanistic aspects
	far more easily modified for optimizing selectivity
Bad	far more sensitive to permanent deactivation
	far more difficult for achieving product/catalyst separations

Heterogeneous catalysts dominate chemical and petrochemical industry. 95% of all chemical processes use heterogeneous catalysts.

Homogeneous catalysts are used when selectivity is critical and product-catalyst separation problems can be solved.

Olefin Hydrogenation using Wilkinson's Catalyst

Wilkinson's catalyst $RhCl(PPh_3)_3$ was the first highly active homogeneous hydrogenation catalyst and was discovered by Geoffrey Wilkinson (Nobel Prize winner for Ferrocene) in 1964. R. Coffey discovered it at about the same time while working for ICI (Imperial Chemical Industries). It was very simply prepared by reacting $RhCl_3 \cdot 3H_2O$ with excess PPh_3 in EtOH.

$$RhCl_3 \cdot H_2O + xsPPh_3 \longrightarrow RhCl(PPh_3)_3 + Ph_3P{=}O + \text{oxidized solvent}$$

Homogeneous Hydrogenation

- Wilkinson's catalyst is a Rh(I) complex, $Rh(PPh_3)_3Cl$ containing three phosphine ligands and one chlorine. Notice that the complex is a $16e^-$ species and the metal is in an oxidation state of + 1.
- The first step in the reaction of this catalyst is believed to be the dissociation of one of the phosphines to afford a vacant coordination site that is probably taken up very quickly by a weakly binding solvent molecule.
- This species undergoes oxidative addition reaction; the coordination number changes from four to six and the oxidation state of the metal increases to + 3. Also notice that the added hydrogens are in a *cis* orientation in the complex. This complex undergoes first a dissociation of the solvent molecule followed by the addition of the olefin. There is no change in the oxidation state, coordination number or the total number of valence electrons.
- As a result of the olefin insertion (hydrogen migration) we obtain a Rh(III), $16e^-$, five coordinate species. A solvent occupies the sixth coordination site to take it to a $18e^-$ species.
- Reductive elimination occurs to give the hydrogenated product and the catalytically active species. Notice that the fragments involved in the reductive elimination are *cis* to each other.

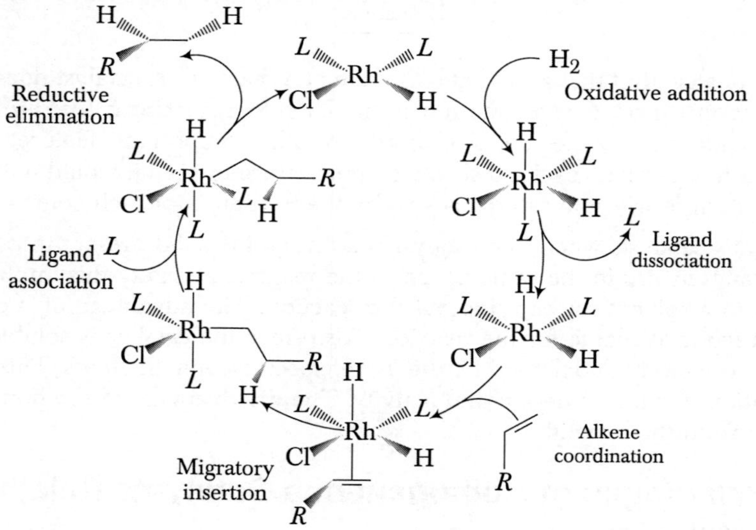

Hydroformylation

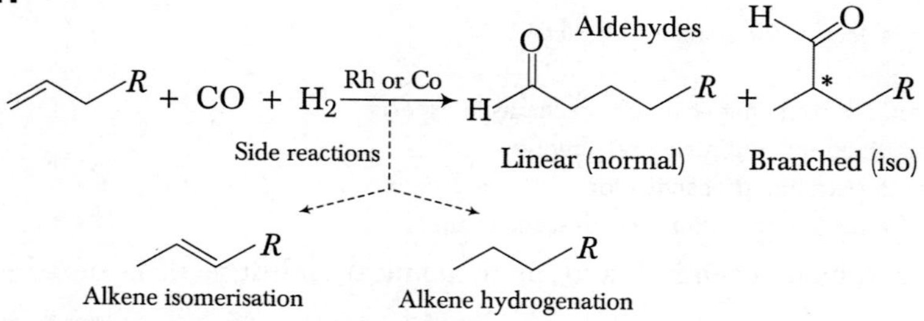

The reaction of an alkene with carbon monoxide and hydrogen, catalyzed by cobalt or rhodium salts to form an aldehyde is called hydroformylation. Hydroformylation was discovered by Otto Roelen in 1938. Roelen's observation that ethylene, H_2 and CO were converted into propanal, and at higher pressures, diethyl ketone, marked the beginning of hydroformylation catalysis. Cobalt catalysts completely dominated industrial hydroformylation until the early 1970's when rhodium catalysts were commercialized. In 1992, ~70% of all hydroformylation processes were based on rhodium triarylphosphine catalysts, which excel with C_8 or lower alkenes and where high regioselectivity to linear aldehydes is critical. Most aldehydes produced are hydrogenated to alcohols or oxidized to carboxylic acids. Esterification of the alcohols with phthalic anhydride produces dialkyl phthalate plasticizers that are primarily used for polyvinyl chloride plastics – the largest single end-use. Detergents and surfactants make up the next largest category, followed by solvents, lubricants and chemical intermediates.

Scheme 1. Heck/Breslow Hydroformylation Mechanism

The silent features of the mechanism of hydroformylation reaction are as follows :

- $HCo(CO)_4$ is generated by the oxidative addition of H_2 with cobalt octacarbonyl.
- $HCo(CO)_4$ is a $18e^-$ species; dissociation of CO is necessary to generate the coordinatively unsaturated catalytic species $HCo(CO)_3$. This latter species can add an olefin, which undergoes hydrogen migration to afford the $16e^-$ alkyl complex $RCo(CO)_3$.
- Addition of CO followed by CO insertion affords the acyl complex $RC(O)Co(CO)_3$. Hydrogen adds oxidatively to the latter complex to generate a $18e^-$ species. Reductive elimination from this compound affords the aldehyde and regenerates the catalytic species $HCo(CO)_3$.
- Note that branched aldehydes are also possible; this would depend where the hydrogen migrates in the alkene complex. Branched aldehydes are not desirable. It has been found that **addition of bulky phosphines can retard the branched aldehyde formation.**

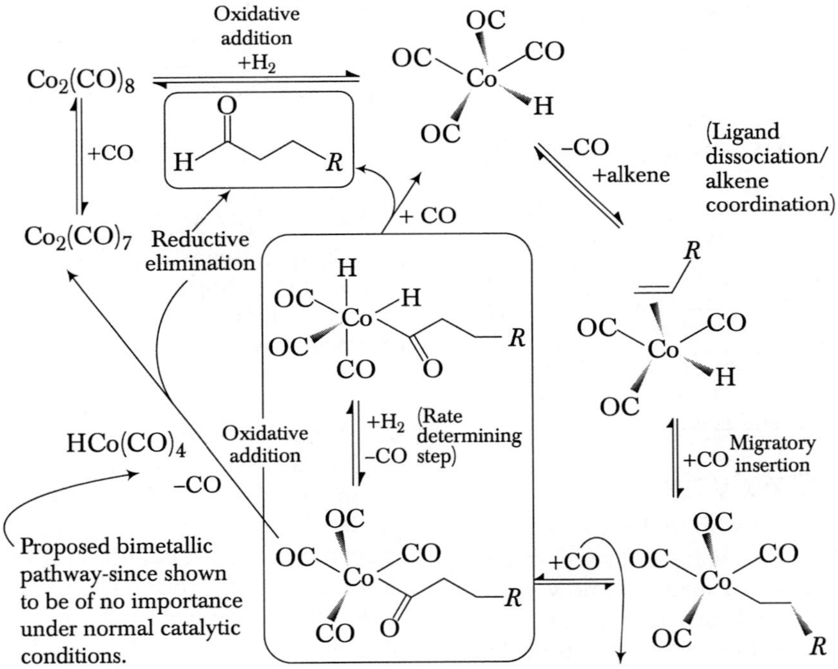

2.5 atm ™ 1.6 : 1 linear to branched

90 atm – 4.4 : 1 linear to branched

Increasing CO partial pressure keeps back reaction from occuring this limits alkene isomerisation and the corresponding opportunity for making branched aldehyde.

Monsanto Acetic Acid Process

Methanol is an important starting material obtained from the synthesis gas ($CO + H_2$). This can be converted into acetic acid by reaction with CO in the presence of a Rh(I) catalyst. The active catalyst in this process is $[Rh(CO)_2I_2]^-$ obtained by the reaction between $RhCl_3$, iodine and CO. The catalytic cycle is actually two cycles. In one of these, methanol is converted into methyl iodide, which enters the catalytic cycle involving the Rh(I) catalyst. The rhodium metal shuttles between the oxidation states of + 1 and + 3.

Wacker Process

This is one of the earliest industrial processes developed in Germany for the conversion of ethylene into acetaldehyde.

$$CH_2{=}CH_2 + \frac{1}{2}O_2 \xrightarrow{[PdCl_4]^{2-}} \underset{\text{Acetalydehyde}}{CH_3CHO}$$

In the reaction Pd^{2+} is reduced to palladium metal, which is reoxidized by Cu^{2+}. The reduced Cu^{+} is oxidized back by oxygen to Cu^{2+}. The overall mechanism for this reaction is outlined below.

Wacker process is more complex than the other catalytic processes described above.

- The first step in this the formation of the olefin complex $[Cl_3Pd(C_2H_4)]^-$.
- The metal activated olefin is susceptible to nucleophilic attack by water. This generates the complex $[Cl_3Pd{-}CH_2{-}CH_2{-}OH]^{2-}$.
- β-hydrogen transfer leads to the second olefin complex.
- The next step not understood properly, leads to the alkyl complex, where the alkyl complex has a hydroxyl substituent.
- This undergoes reductive elimination to afford the aldehyde, and Pd(0). Note that if there was no way of catalytically reoxidizing the Pd(0), the reaction will be dead now. Fortunately, Cu^{2+} is a good catalyst, which can oxidize Pd(0) to Pd^{2+}. The Cu^{+} thus generated is reoxidized by oxygen in another catalytic cycle. In this manner the expensive palladium reagent is reutilized.

Heterogeneous Catalysis

Polymers are large molecules with molecular weights in the range of 10^4 to 10^6. These consist of small building units known as monomers. For example, polyethylene is a made up of ethylene **monomers**. Poly vinylchloride is built from vinyl chloride and similarly polystyrene is made from styrene. In all of these cases a single monomer is repeated several times in the polymer chain. The number of repeating units determines the molecular weight of the polymer.

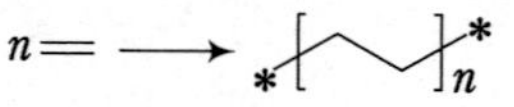

When only a few alkenes couple together to make a short chain, we refer to that as oligomerization (oligomers are very short polymers). There is typically three parts to most polymerizations :

Initiation

Generating the active catalyst from a less active catalyst precursor.

$$L_nM{-}Cl + AlR_3 \longrightarrow L_nM{-}R + AlR_2Cl$$
$$+ \text{MAO (methylalumoxane)} + ZnR_2$$

$$L_nM{-}Cl + H^- \longrightarrow L_nM{-}H + Cl^-$$

Propagation

The polymer chain growth portion of the reaction that occurs over and over again.

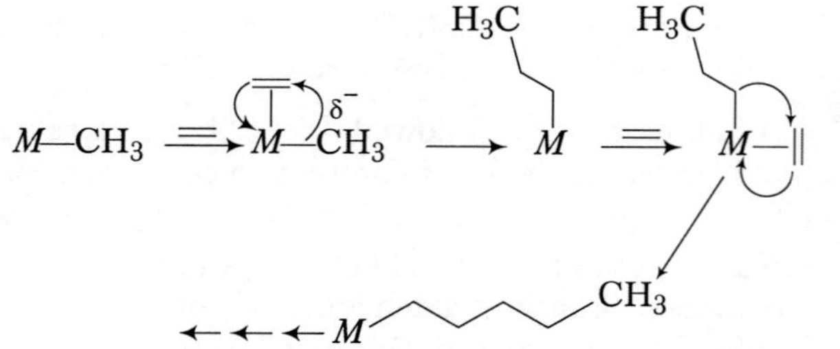

Termination

A reaction step that stops the polymer chain growth

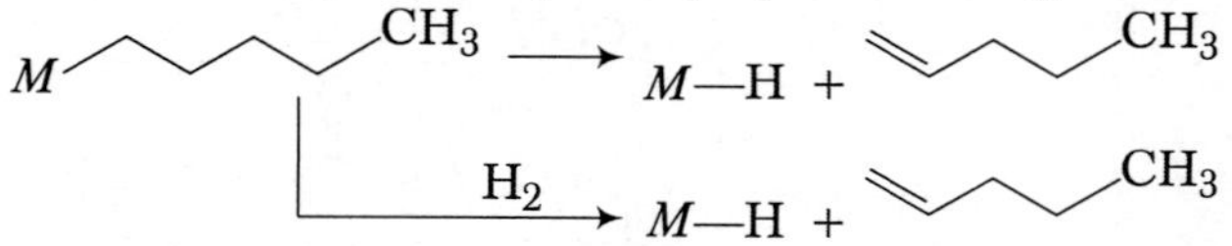

What is M_w / M_n? The average molecular weight of a polymer can be defined by M_n and M_w. M_n is the simple average of total mass of the chains divided by the number of chains. The weight average molecular weight M_w is the summation of the square of the molecular weights divided by the summation of the molecular weights of all the molecules present. In M_w more "weight" is provided to the higher molecular weight polymers, while M_n treats all of them the same. The basis for M_w is that the larger molecules contribute more to the properties of the polymer so they should have more importance. M_w is always greater than M_n and the narrower the distribution, the closer M_n and M_w are. The ratio of M_w to M_n is a measure of the distribution of different length polymer chains. The ratio is referred to as the **dispersity.** As the distribution narrows, the dispersivity approaches a minimum value of 1.0. Such a polymer referred to as mono disperse. Alternately as M_w / M_n for a polymer increases (10 or 20), it is a referred to as polydisperse.

Ziegler-Natta Catalysis for the Polymerization of Olefins

The German chemist Karl Ziegler (1898-1973) discovered in 1953 that when $TiCl_3(s)$ and $AlEt_3$ are combined together they produced an extremely active heterogeneous catalyst for the polymerization of ethylene at atmospheric pressure. Giulio Natta (1903-1979), an Italian chemist, extended the method to other olefins like propylene and developed variation of the Ziegler catalyst based on his findings on the mechanism of the polymerization reaction. The Ziegler-Natta catalyst family includes halides of titanium, chromium, vanadium, and zirconium, typically activated by alkyl aluminium compounds. Ziegler and Natta received the Nobel Prize in Chemistry for their work in 1963.

Mechanism

The first step is the alkylation of the titanium centre. Please note that since this is a heterogeneous catalyst we are looking at the surface of the catalyst. Obviously this implies coordination unsaturation at titanium. In the bulk sample the titanium has a coordination number of six. However, at the surface the coordination of titanium is incomplete. This site can be taken up by a ligand such as olefin. Subsequent steps are the olefin insertion and the creation of a long alkyl chain. The chain terminates by β-elimination.

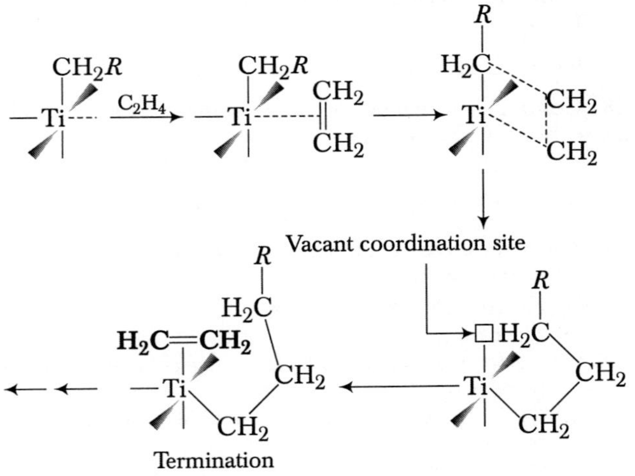

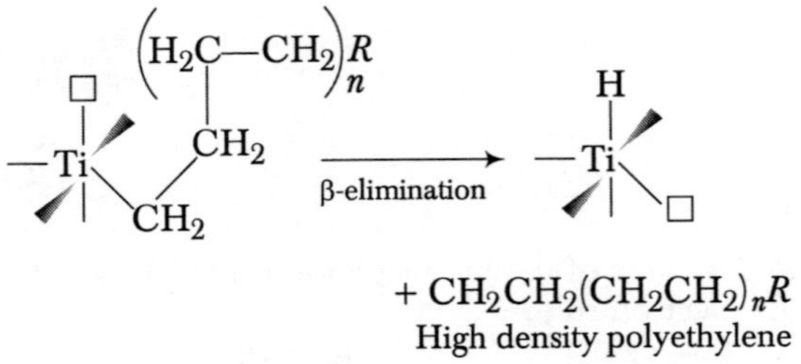

Polypropylene and Stereochemistry

The polymerization of propylene is slower and more complicated than ethylene due to increasing steric factors and the generation of stereochemistry on the polymer chain. It has been found that the Ziegler-Natta heterogeneous catalysts promote the formation of a linear chain polyethylene with a high amount of crystallinity (High Density Polyethylene). Also, if one use propylene as the monomer, isotactic polypropylene is preferred over the other two forms *viz.,* atactic and syndiotactic.

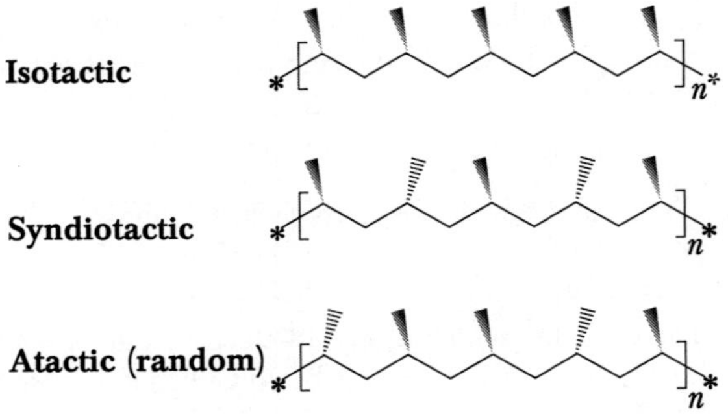

Exercise 1

(For Part 'B')

1. Which one of the following molecules does not obey 18-electron rule?
   (a) $[Mn(CO)_6]$ (b) $[Cr(CO)_5]^{2-}$
   (c) $Fe(CO)_5$ (d) $[Mn(CO)_4Cl_2]^{2+}$
2. An example of species having quaderpole bond is
   (a) $Mn_2(CO)_9$ (b) $Cr_2O_7^{2-}$
   (c) $[Re_2Cl_8]^{2-}$ (d) $Hg_2(CH_3COO)_2$
3. $MO_2(CH_3COO)_4$, $[Re_2Cl_8]^{2-}$ are examples of
   (a) quaderpole bonded compounds
   (b) $\sigma - \pi - S$ bonds
   (c) Both (a) and (b)
   (d) None of the above
4. The HOMO in CO is
   (a) π-bonding (b) σ-bonding
   (c) π-antibonding (d) σ-antibonding
5. Among the following the one which is EPR active is
   (a) $Ni(CO)_4$ (b) $[Cu(C_2O_4)]^{2-}$
   (c) $Mo(CO)_6$ (d) $[Co(NH_3)_5Cl]^{2+}$
6. Compound which obeys 18-electron rule is
   (a) $Mn(CO)_3$ (b) $Fe(CO)_4$
   (c) $V[CO]_6$ (d) $Cr(CO)_6$
7. The complex which obeys 18-electron rule is
   (a) $Fe(CO)_4$ (b) $Ni(CO)_3(Ph_3)$
   (c) $Cr(CO)_5$ (d) $Cr(C_2H_5)_2$
8. Polypropylene formed in absence of Ziegler-Natta catalyst is
   (a) atactic (b) Isotactic
   (c) syndiotatic (d) None of these
9. Wilkinson's catalyst in
   (a) $(Ph_3P)_3RhCl$ (b) (Ph_3P) RhCl
   (c) Ph_3P_3RhCl (d) $(Ph_3P)_2RhCl_2$
10. Waker's process uses the catalyst
    (a) Wilkinson's catalyst (b) Zeise's salt
    (c) Ziegler-Natta's catalyst (d) potash salt
11. Number of metal-metal bonds present in $Ir_4(CO)_{12}$ are
    (a) 4 (b) 5 (c) 6 (d) 8
12. Which of the following statements about ferrocene is false?
    (a) It obeys $18e^-$ rule
    (b) It is diamagnetic
    (c) It is an orange solid
    (d) It resists electrophilic reactions
13. The neutral complex which follows $18e^-$ rule is
    (a) $(\eta^5\text{-}C_5H_5)\,Fe(CO)_2$ (b) $(\eta^2\text{-}C_5H_5)\,Mo(CO)_3$
    (c) $(\eta^5\text{-}C_5H_5)_2Co$ (d) $(\eta^5\text{-}C_5H_5)\,Re(\eta^6\text{-}C_6H_6)$
14. Choose the $16e^-$ complex from the following
    (a) $Ni(CO)_4$ (b) $Fe(CO)_5$
    (c) $Rh(PPh_3)_3Cl$ (d) $(\eta^6\text{-}C_6H_6)_2Cr$
15. The species having metal-metal bond is
    (a) $Mn_2(CO)_{10}$ (b) $Al_2(OPr^i)_{12}$
    (c) $Al_2(CH_3)_6$ (d) V_2O_{12}
16. Number of bridging and terminal carbonyls present in $Co_4(CO)_{12}$ at low temperature are respectively
    (a) 3 and 9 (b) 6 and 6 (c) 4 and 8 (d) 0 and 12
17. Oxidation occurs very easily in case of
    (a) $(\eta^5\text{-}C_5H_5)_2Fe$ (b) $(\eta^5\text{-}C_5H_5)_2Co$
    (c) $(\eta^5\text{-}C_5H_5)_2Ru$ (d) $(\eta^5\text{-}C_5H_5)_2Co^+$
18. Complex in which organic ligand is having only σ-bond with metal is
    (a) $W(CH_3)_6$ (b) $(\eta^5\text{-}C_5H_5)_2Fe$
    (c) $K[PtCl_3(C_2H_4)]$ (d) $[(\eta^6\text{-}C_6H_6)_2Ru]$
19. The oxidative additon and reductive elimination steps are favoured by
    (a) electron rich metal centres
    (b) electron deficient metal centres
    (c) electron deficient and electron rich metal centres respectively
    (d) electron rich and electron deficient metal centres respectively
20. In $H_2Ru_6(CO)_{18}$ cluster, containing 8 coordinated Ru centres, the hydrogen atoms are
    (a) both terminal
    (b) one terminal and other bridging
    (c) both bridging between two Ru centres
    (d) both bridging between three Ru centres
21. $[Co(CO)_4]$ is isolobal with
    (a) CH_4 (b) CH_3 (c) CH_2 (d) CH
22. Number of metal-metal bonds in $[(C_5H_5)Fe(CO)_2]_2$ is
    (a) zero (b) one (c) two (d) three
23. Carbonyl groups in $Os_5(CO)_{16}$ and $Os_6(CO)_{18}$ are
    (a) All terminals carbonyls
    (b) All terminal except 3 carbonyls that are bridged
    (c) 4 bridged in $Os_5(CO)_{16}$ and 3 in $Os_6(CO)_{18}$
    (d) None of the above
24. $Os_6(CO)_{18}$ has
    (a) octahedral geometry (b) bicapped tetrahedron
    (c) bicapped octahedron (d) trigonal bipyramidal

25. $Rh_6(CO)_{16}$ has
(a) all terminal carbonyl groups
(b) ten terminal and 6 bridging groups
(c) four bridging and twelve terminal groups
(d) eight bridging and eight terminal groups

26. Generally octahedral clusters are formed by
(a) Se, Y, La (b) Zn, Cd, Hg
(c) Mo, Nb, Ta (d) Mo, Nb, Tl

27. Complexes having $t_{2g}^1, t_{2g}^2, t_{2g}^3 e_g^2$ configuration will be
(a) labile (b) inert
(c) Both (a) and (b) (d) None of these

28. The most unstable species among the following is
(a) $Ti(C_2H_5)_4$ (b) $Ti(CH_2Ph)_4$
(c) $Pb(CH_3)_4$ (d) $Pb(C_2H_5)_4$

29. $Ru(C_2H_5)Cl\ (PPh_3)_2$ is stable only under a pressure of ethene because
(a) it is a 16-electron complex
(b) it forms 18 electron adduct with ethene
(c) one of the decomposition product is ethene
(d) it prevents β-elimination of ethene

30. The square planar complex $[IrCl(PPh_3)_3]$ undergoes oxidative addition of Cl_2 to give two products
(a) *fac* and *mer* (b) *cis* and *trans*
(c) enantiomers (d) linkage isomerism

31. Which one of the mononuclear carbonyls does not obey EAN rule?
(a) $Fe(CO)_5$ (b) $V(CO)_6$ (c) $Ni(CO)_4$ (d) $Cr(CO)_6$

32. Indicate the organometallic complex that obeys EAN rule.
(a) $Ni(\pi\text{-}C_5H_5)_2$ (b) $(C_2H_5)W(CO)_2(\pi\text{-}C_5H_5)$
(c) $Co(C_6H_6)$ (d) $(\pi\text{-}C_5H_5)_2\ TiCl_2$

33. Which one of the following complex species does not obey EAN rule?
(a) $V(Co)_3\ (\pi\text{-}C_5H_5)(R_2C{=}CR_2)$
(b) $Co(CO)_3(\pi\text{-}C_5H_5)$
(c) $Fe(\sigma\text{-}C_5H_5)(\pi\text{-}C_5H_5)(CO)_3$
(d) $Cr(C_6H_6)(CO)_3$

34. Which one of these polynuclear carbonyls does not obey EAN rule?
(a) $Fe_2(CO)_8$ (b) $Mn_2(CO)_{10}$
(c) $Fe_3(CO)_{12}$ (d) $Co_4(CO)_{12}$

35. Which one of the following does not favour stabilization of metal-carbon bond?
(a) Chelation
(b) Increased coordinate number
(c) β-elimination
(d) Presence of π-acid ligands on the metal

36. Which one of the statements on ferrocene is incorrect?
(a) Ferrocene has a staggered configuration in the solid state
(b) Ferrocene has a sandwhiched structure with two parallel rings
(c) The stability of ferrocene is attributed to strong σ-bonds between iron and cyclopentadiene rings
(d) The cyclopentadiene rings have been found to rotate freely in solution of ferrocene

37. Which one of the statements concerning transition metal alkene complexes is incorrect?
(a) Bonding between metal atom and alkene is synergic
(b) A metal atoms must possess an empty p_z and d_{z^2} orbitals and a filled $d_{x^2-y^2}$
(c) Alkenes can also behave as divalent bidentate chelating agents in some complexes
(d) C_2H_4 group is not planar in its complexes with transition metals

38. Which one of the statements on complexation of alkynes with transition metal derivatives is not correct?
(a) Alkyne may behave as a 4-electrons donor in same cases
(b) Alkynes can also act as bidentate, divalent ligands
(c) The alkyne molecule containing a straight line arrangement in its complexes
(d) In some complexes, the —C≡C— group may lie above and at right angle to the metal-metal vector

39. Which one of the statements about alkyne complexes $PtCl_2(Bu_2C_2)$ is not correct?
(a) The alkyne behaves as a 2-electrons donor
(b) The molecule 'BuC≡CBu' is not longer a straight line
(c) The carbon-carbon bond is longer than a triple bond
(d) The molecules is a monomer with the —C≡C— perpendicular to the plane of coordination

40. Which one of the following is not important for the formation of stable metal carbonyls?
(a) Metals with low oxidation states
(b) Metals with small size
(c) Lowering of carbon-oxygen bond order
(d) EAN is obeyed

41. Which one of the following will have the lowest CO stretching frequency?
(a) $V(CO)_6^+$ (b) $Co(CO)_4^-$
(c) $Ni(CO)_4$ (d) $Fe(CO)_4^{2-}$

42. Which one of the following will have the highest CO stretching frequency?
(a) $Cr(CO)_6$ (b) $Mn(CO)_6^+$
(c) $[Mn(dien)\ (CO)_3]^+$ (d) $[Cr(dien)\ (CO)_3]$

43. The structure of $Fe_3(CO)_{12}$ shows
(a) no bridging and two terminal CO groups
(b) one bridging and eleven terminal CO groups
(c) two bridging and ten terminal CO groups
(d) three bridging and nine terminal CO groups

44. What about $V(CH_2SiMe_3)_3$ and $M(CH_2CMe_3)$ is true?
(a) Both are highly unstable organometallic compounds
(b) Both are stable organometallic compounds due to chelation
(c) Both are stable organometallic compound due to absence of β-elimination
(d) Metal neopentyls and trimethylsilylmethyles are stabilised due to the presence of β-elimination

45. $Co(C_5H_5)_2$ is
(a) green (b) purple black
(c) orange (d) brown

46. $Mn(C_5H_5)_2$ is
(a) green (b) brown
(c) purple black (d) orange

47. Which of the following is true about $Ni(C_5H_5)_2$
(a) It is unstable
(b) It is $20e^-$ complex
(c) It is green in colour
(d) All of the above

48. Reaction of $Me_3P{-}Pt(PMe_3)_2$ with $R{-}C{\equiv}C{-}R$ is an example of
(a) reductive elimination
(b) oxidative addition
(c) migratory insertion
(d) None of the above

49. Reaction of $Me_3P{-}Pt(PMe_3)_2$ with $R{-}C{\equiv}C{-}R$ is results in
(a) metallocyclopropene
(b) new alkenyl ligand is formed
(c) Pt goes from (0) to + 2 oxidation state
(d) All of the above

Exercise 2

(For Part 'C')

1. Which of the following forms bridged structures?
(a) $Fe_3(CO)_{12}$ (b) $Ru_3(CO)_{12}$
(c) $Os_3(CO)_{12}$ (d) $Mn_2(CO)_{10}$

2. Carbonyl group can bridge triangular arrays of three metal atoms in
(a) $Fe_3(CO)_{12}$ (b) $Os_3(CO)_{12}$
(c) $Ru_3(CO)_{12}$ (d) $Rh_6(CO)_{16}$

3. Carbonylate anions one formed by the action of
(a) Lewis acid such as $AlCl_3$ on CO and carbonyl halide
(b) halogen on $Fe(CO)_5$
(c) alkali on simple carbonyl
(d) by reduction of carbonyls with alkali metals, alkali metal amalgams or borohydrides

4. Arrange the following in increasing order of CO stretching
I. $Cr(CO)_6$ II. $[V(CO)_6]$
III. $[Mn(CO)_6]^+$ IV. CO
(a) I > II > III > IV (b) II < I < III < IV
(c) I < II < III < IV (d) II < I < III < IV

5. The value of CO stretching frequency of
I. $Ni(CO)_4$
II. $Ni(CO)_3P(CH_3)_3$ and
III. $Ni(CO)_2(PCH_3)_3)_2$
(a) I > II > III (b) III > II > I
(c) I > III > II (d) II > III > I

6. Match the following.

Column I	Column II
A. $(PPh_3)_3RhCl$	1. Friedel-Craft catalyst
B. $[Rh(CO)_2I_2]^-$	2. Ziegler-Natta catalyst
C. $[PdCl_4]^{2-}$	3. Monsanto catalyst
D. $[HCO(CO)_4]$	4. Oxo process or hydroformylation of alkenes
E. $Er_3Al : TiCl_3$	5. Wacker's process
	6. Hydrogenation catalyst

Codes

	A	B	C	D	E
(a)	6	1	4	5	3
(b)	1	6	5	2	3
(c)	6	3	5	4	2
(d)	2	6	4	5	3

7. Which pair follows effective atomic number rule (EAN)?
(a) $Cr(CO)_6$; $[Fe(CO)_8]^-$ (b) $Ni(CO)_4$; $[Mn(CO)_5]^-$
(c) $[Mn(CO)_5]$; $Ni(CO)_4$ (d) None of these

8. Solid $Co_2(CO)_8$ shows infrared CO stretching bands at 1857, 1886, 2001, 2031, 2044, 2059, 2071 and 2112 cm^{-1}. When $Co_2(CO)_8$ is dissolved in hexane, the carbonyl bands at 1887 and 1856 cm^{-1} disappears. These changes in infrared spectrum in hexane are due to

(a) loss of terminal CO
(b) structural changes of $CO_2(Co)_8$ involving conversion of terminal CO to bridging CO
(c) dissociation of $Co_2(CO)_8$ to $Co(CO)_4$
(d) structural changes of $Co_2(CO)_8$ involving conversion of bridging CO to terminal CO

9. For metal olefin complexes (i) $[PtCl_3(C_2H_4)]^-$ and $PtCl_3(C_2F_4)^-$, the correct statement is
(a) carbon-carbon bond length is same both in (i) and (ii)
(b) carbon-carbon bond length in (i) is smaller
(c) carbon-carbon bond length in (ii) is smaller
(d) a metallacycle is formed in each complexes

10. Olefin hydrogenation using Wilkinson's catalyst initiates with
(a) olefin addition to $Rh(PPh_3)_2Cl$
(b) olefin addition to $Rh(PPh_3)_3Cl$
(c) a phospine dissociation from $Rh(PPh_3)_3Cl$
(d) a phosphine addition to $Rh(PPh_3)_2Cl$

11. The maximum number of valence electrons of metal in these complexes are
$Mn_2(CO)_{10}$, $(\eta^5\text{-}C_5H_5)\,Mo(CO)_3Cl$, $(\eta^5\text{-}C_5H_5)_2Ni$ and $(\eta^5\text{-}C_5H_5)_2TiCl_2$
(a) 16 (b) 18
(c) 20 (d) 22

12. The highest oxidation state of the metal in the following compound
$(\eta^6\text{-}C_6H_6)_2Cr$, $Mn(CO)_5Cl$, $Na_2[Fe(CO)_4]$, $K[Mn(CO)_5]$ and $K[Mo(CO)_5Br]$ is
(a) 1 (b) 2
(c) −1 (d) −2

13. Identify the order according to increasing stability of the following organometallic compounds
$Ti(CH_3)_4$, $Ti(CH_2Ph)_4$, $Ti(i\text{-}Pr)_4$, $Ti(Et_4)$
(a) $Ti(CH_2Ph)_4 < Ti(iPr)_4 < TiEt_4 < Ti(Me)_4$
(b) $TiEt_4 < Ti(Me)_4 < Ti(i\text{-}Pr)_4 < Ti(CH_2Ph)_4$
(c) $Ti(i\text{-}Ph)_4 < Ti(Et)_4 < TiMe_4 < Ti(CH_2Ph)_4$
(d) $Ti(CH_3)_4 < TiEt_4 < Ti(i\text{-}Pr)_4 < Ti(CH_2\text{-}Ph)_4$

14. In the hydroformylation reaction the intermediate $CH_3—CH_2—CH_2—Co(CO)_4$
(a) forms an acyl intermediate

$$CH_3CH_2CH_2—\overset{\overset{\displaystyle O}{\|}}{C}o(CO)_3$$

(b) forms an adduct with an olefin reactant
(c) reacts with H_2
(d) eliminates propane

15. Which of the following reagent is best suited to prepare 1-phenyl butane from 1-bromo butane?
(a) C_6H_5Li (b) C_6H_5MgI
(c) $(C_6H_5)_2LiCu$ (d) $(C_6H_5)_2Zn$

16. $W(CO)_6$ reacts with MeLi to give an intermediate which upon treatment with CH_2N_2 gives a compound *X*. *X* is represented as
(a) $W(Me)_6$
(b) $(CO)_5W—Me$
(c) $(CO)_5W{=}C(Me)OCH_3$
(d) $(CO)_5W{\equiv}C\cdot Me$

17. In the reaction below, *X* and *Y* respectively are

$$Mn_2(CO)_{10} \xrightarrow{Na} X \xrightarrow{CH_3COCl} Y$$

(a) $[Mn(CO)_4]^{2-}$, $[CH_3C(O)Mn(CO)_5]^-$
(b) $[Mn(CO)_5]^-$, $[ClMn(CO)_5]$
(c) $[Mn(CO)_4]^{2-}$, $[ClMn(CO)_5]$
(d) $[Mn(CO)_5]^-$, $[CH_3C(O)Mn(CO)_5]$

18. Which of the following complexes are labile?
I. $[V(H_2O)_6]^{2+}$ II. $[V(H_2O)_6]^{3+}$
III. FeF_6^{3-} IV. $[Co(CN)_6]^{3-}$
V. $[CoF_6]^{3-}$
(a) I, II, III (b) I, IV, V
(c) II, III, V (d) II, III, IV

19. Which of the following statement about $[Re_2Cl_8]^{2-}$ and $Re_2(CO)_{10}$ is correct?
(a) Both have quadrapole bonding
(b) Both have Re–Re bond and carbonyl has D_{4d}
(c) Both have Re–Re bond and D_{4h} structure
(d) None of the above

20. Which is true about $Mn(CO)_4NO$?
(a) The complex is paramagnetic and follows $18e^-$ rule
(b) The complex is diamagnetic and follows $18e^-$ rule
(c) The complex is paramagnetic and does not follow $18e^-$ rule
(d) The complex is diamagnetic and does not follow $18e^-$ rule

21. Arrange the following in increasing order of C—O frequencies
I. CO II. $Mo(CO)_3(NH_3)_3$
III. $Mo(CO)_6$ IV. $Mo(CO)_3(PPh_3)_3$
(a) IV < III < II < I (b) III < IV < II < I
(c) I < II < III < IV (d) I > II > III > IV

22. Complex $Mo(py)_2(CO)_4$ has two forms. Which of the statement about these forms are true?
(a) *Cis*-form will give single band around 2000 cm^{-1} in IR and *trans* will give 4 bands
(b) *Cis*-form will give four bands and *trans* will give single band around 2000 cm^{-1} in IR
(c) Both *cis*- and *trans*- will give four bands
(d) Both *cis*- and *trans*- will give single band at 2000 cm^{-1}

23. Pyrolysis of dodeca-carbonyl triosmuim $[Os_3(CO)_{12}]$ gives
(a) $Os_6(CO)_{18}$ (b) $Os_8(CO)_{10}$
(c) $Os_5(CO)_{16}$ (d) $Os_4(CO)_{10}$

24. $Os_6(CO)_{18}$ and $Rh_6(CO)_{16}$ have
(a) octahedral and bicapped tetrahedral geometry
(b) octahedral geometry only
(c) bicapped tetrahedron and octahedral geometry
(d) None of the above

25. The reaction,
$$[(NH_3)_5Co(CO_3)]^+ + 2H_3O^+ \longrightarrow [(H_3N)_5Co(H_2O)]^{3+} + CO_2 + 2H_2O$$
is a
(a) substitution of CO_3^{2-} by H_2O
(b) substitution of CO_2 by H_2O
(c) substitution not at metal but at carbonate oxygen
(d) Both (b) and (c)

26. Arrange the following ligands in decreasing order of undergoing β-elimination in organometallics.
I. –Et II. –Ph
III. norbornyl IV. benzyl
(a) III > IV > II > I
(b) I > II > III > IV
(c) I > I > IV > III
(d) III > II > IV > I

27. On oxidative addition of O_2 to $Ir(CO)Cl(PPh_3)_2$ the oxidation state and coordination number of Ir changes respectively by,
(a) 1 and 3 (b) 3 and 1
(c) 2 and 2 (d) 2 and 3

28. Mammal condensation involves reaction of
(a) ferrocene with CH_3CoCl in the presence of $AlCl_3$
(b) ferrocene with butyllithium followed by reaction with N_2O_4
(c) ferrocene with $B(OR)_3$ followed by hydrolysis
(d) ferrocene with formaldehyde and amines

29. Which one of the following statements is incorrect?
(a) The 18 outer electrons in ferrocene are arranged in nine bonding and anti-bonding molecular orbitals
(b) Metalloncenes with more than 18 outer electrons are less stable than ferrocene
(c) Metallocenes with less than 18 other electrons are more reactive than ferrocene
(d) Bonds contributing the most of the stability of ferrocene have π-symmetry

30. Which one of the metal carbonyl is prepared by the direct interaction of finely divided metal with CO?
(a) $Fe(CO)_5$ (b) $Cr(CO)_6$
(c) $V(CO)_6$ (d) $Mn_2(CO)_{10}$

31. Which one of the following compounds is prepared by the photolysis of mononuclear carbonyl?
(a) $Co_2(CO)_8$ (b) $Co_4(CO)_{12}$
(c) $Fe_2(CO)_9$ (d) $Mn_2(CO)_{10}$

32. Nonacarbonyl diiron is prepared
(a) by the thermolysis of $Fe_3(CO)_{12}$
(b) by the photolysis of $Fe(CO)_5$
(c) by the reduction of $FeCl_3$ with Na and CO
(d) by the reaction of finally divided iron with CO

33. Decreasing trend of CO stretching frequency in the isoelectronic series $V(CO)_6^-$, $Cr(CO)_6$ and $Mn(CO)_6^+$ is
(a) $V(CO)_6^- > Mn(CO)_6^+ > Cr(CO)_6$
(b) $V(CO)_6^- > Cr(CO)_6 > Mn(CO)_6^+$
(c) $Mn(CO)_6^+ > Cr(CO)_6 > V(CO)_6^-$
(d) $Cr(CO)_6 > V(CO)_6^- > Mn(CO)_6^+$

34. $Co(C_5H_5)_2$ mettalocene is
I. Air sensitive
II. Paramagnetic
III. $19e^-$ complex
IV. Oxidised readily to yellow $[Co(C_5H_5)_2]^+$
The correct answer is
(a) I, II and III (b) II and III
(c) III and IV (d) All of the given

35. Which about ferrocene is true?
I. Ferrocene is diamagnetic
II. Dipole moment is zero
III. Kealy and Pauson synthesised ferrocene from C_5H_6 and freshly reduced Fe at 300°C
IV. Kealy and Pauson synthesised ferrocene from C_5H_5MgBr and $FeCl_3$.
The correct answer is
(a) III and IV only (b) I, II and III only
(c) I, II and IV only (d) II, III and IV only

36. Intact substrates are
I. oxidative addition substrates
II. reductive elimination substrates
III. double or triple bond is must
IV. double or triple bond and electronegative
The correct answer is
(a) I and III only (b) III only
(c) I and IV only (d) I, II and III only

37. Intact substrates for oxidative addition
(a) two separate anionic ligands are formed on oxidative addition
(b) only one of the π-bond is broken leaving σ-bond intact
(c) ligand pricks up two electrons from metal and becomes dianionic
(d) electron donating groups on alkenes enhances oxidative process

38. Which of the following is true for $Re(CO)_5$ reaction with $CH_2{=}CH{-}CH_2Cl$?
(a) Only one amonic ligand coordinate
(b) CO ligand dissociates
(c) Hapticity changes from η^1 to η^3
(d) Intact substrate oxidation addition

39. In metalocenes of Ni, Co, Fe the bond distances (Cp-Cp) are 3.63 Å, 3.44 Å, 3.29 Å respectively. Which of the following statements are true?
(a) Metal covalent radius is decreasing from Ni → Fe
(b) Metal covalent radius is decreasing from Fe → Ni
(c) Extra electron of Co and Ni are going in antibonding orbitals (*M*-Cp)
(d) Extra electron are going into empty *d*-orbitals of Co and Ni (Cp-*M*)

40. Which of the following statement(s) is true about stability of metal-C bond?
(a) Presence of H- at β carbon increases stability
(b) Compounds like $M{-}CH_2{-}SiR_3$ is more stable than $M{-}CH_2{-}CH_3$
(c) Stability of metal alkyls is enchanced by π-acid ligands
(d) Introduction of oxygen to coordination sphere decreases stability of *M*—C bond

41. Which of the following statements are true about *M*—C bonded compounds
(a) $Me_4Re^{VI}{=}O$ is stable up to 473 K while Me_6Re is unstable
(b) $MeRe^{VII}({=}O)_3$ is stable in air while Me_7Re is unstable
(c) $Ti(CH_3)_4$ decomposes below 253 K
(d) $Ti(CH_3)_4$(bipy) is stabilised up to 330K

42. Presence of empty orbitals on the metal centre in order to perform oxidative addition is generally required in
(a) non-electrophilic substrates
(b) electrophilic substrates
(c) intact substrates
(d) All of the above

43. In oxidative addition of $Ir(Co)(PPh_3)PPh_3Cl$ by CH_3Br, the starting material is
(a) $18e^-$ (b) $16e^-$
(c) $17e^-$ (d) $15e^-$

44. In $Re(CO)_5$ on reacting with $CH_2{=}CH{-}CH_2{-}Cl$ the starting material is
(a) $18e^-$ (b) $16e^-$
(c) $17e^-$ (d) $15e^-$

45. In $Re(CO)_5$ and $CH_2{=}CH{-}CH_2{-}Cl$ reaction result of oxidative addition is
(a) coordination of two anionic ligands
(b) coordination of one anion ligand
(c) CO ligand dissociation
(b) None of the above

Direrctions (Q. Nos. 46 and 47)
An oxidative addition reaction is one in which usually a neutral ligand adds to a metal centre and in doing so oxidises the metal, typically by $2e^-$. Transfering of two electrons from metal to incoming ligand breaks a bond in that ligand forming two new anionic ligands. At least one of these new anionic ligands end up bonded to the metal centre.There are three main classes of substrates that can perform oxidative additions to metal centres.

46. Which of the following is a result of oxidative addition on $[Ir(CO)(PPh_3), PPH_3, Cl]$?
(a) $[Ir(CO)(PPH_3), PPh_3(H)_2]$
(b) $[Ir(CO)(PPh_3)PPh_3Cl(CH_3)Br]$
(c) $[Ir(CO) PPh_3 PPh_3, Cl] + H_2$
(d) All of the above

47. In oxidative addition reactions alkene, alkynes and O_2 are examples of
(a) electrophilic substrates
(b) non-electrophilic substrates
(c) intact substrates
(d) Addition substrates

Directions (Q. Nos. 48 to 50)
Reverse of elimination reaction is migratory insertion reaction in which an anionic ligand moves and performs a nucleophilic like intramolecular attack on the electrophilic neutral ligand. Or when neutral ligand moves and inserts into bond between metal and anionic ligand. Most common anionic and neutral ligands that can do migratoryinsertion reactions are H^-, R^-, Ar^-, $acyl^-$, O^{2-}, oxo, CO, alkene, alkynes.

48. The two groups that react in migratory insertion to form new anionic ligand should be
(a) *Trans*
(b) Any of the two *cis* or *trans*
(b) *Cis*-oidal
(d) None of the above

49. Metal centre undergoes a change in oxidation state in migratory insertion from
(a) $+1 \rightarrow +2$
(b) $+2 \rightarrow +3$
(c) $2 \rightarrow +1$
(d) no change in oxidation state of metal atom

50. Trapping ligand is
(a) negative ligand on which migration takes place
(b) neutral ligands on which migration occurs
(c) negative ligands that binds with vacant orbitals generated by migratory insertion
(d) neutral ligands that binds with vacant orbitals generated by migratory insertion

Directions (Q. Nos. 51 to 54)
Migratory insertion reactions are those in which a cisoidal anionic and neutral ligands on the metal complex couples together to generate new coordinated anionic ligands. There is no change in oxidation state of *d*-electron count of metal centre and overall electron count on metal decreased by $2e^-$.

51. CO and alkyl migratory insertion reactions are also called
(a) substitution reactions
(b) formyl reactions
(c) carbonylation reactions
(d) addition elimination reactions

52. Insertion reactions is usually favoured by
(a) electron rich metal centres
(b) electron deficient metal centres
(c) empty d-orbitals on metal atoms
(d) None of the above

53. What is the product formed in the given reaction

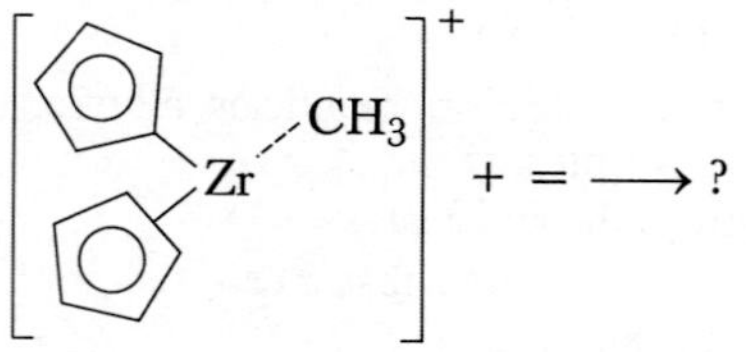

(a) $[(C_6H_5)_2\,Zr(CH_2CH_2CH_3)]^+$
(b) $[(C_6H_5)_2\,Zr(CH_3)\,(CH{=}CH_2)]^+$
(c) Both (a) and (b)
(d) None of the above

54. What is the product formed in the given reaction

$$H_2C{=}CH_2 + \text{Metal–H} \rightleftharpoons ?$$

(a) $CH_3—CH_2—$Metal (b) $H_2C—CH_2$ bridged by Metal (three-membered ring)

(c) $CH{=}CH$ bridged by Metal (three-membered ring) (d) None o these

Assertion & Reason

Codes
(a) Both A and R are true and R is the correct explanation of A.
(b) Both A and R are true and the R is not the correct explanation of A.
(c) A is true and R is false.
(d) R is false but A is true.

55. Assertion (A) In metalocenes of Fe, Co, Ni the bond distances $(C_P - C_P)$ are 3.29 Å, 3.44 Å, 3.63 Å.

Reason (R) As we move from Fe, Co to Ni, that is from $18e^-$, $19e^-$ to $20e^-$ count, the extra electron for Co and Ni complexes are going into M-C_P anti-bonding orbitals which are delocalised and progressively weaken the $M-C_P$ bonding, leading to increase in bond distance.

56. Assertion (A) Vacant coordinated site is generated by migratory insertion.

Reason (R) In a migratory insertion reaction amonic and neutral ligands on a metal complex couple to generate a new anionic coordinated ligand.

Matching Type

57. Match the following.

Column I (Compound)		Column II (Scientist)
A. First carbene complex	1.	Pairs, Cader
B. First organometallic $[(CH_3)_2As]_2O$	2.	Wilkinson and Coffey
C. $(PPh_3)_3RhCl$	3.	E.O. Fisher
D. Alkyl sodium, alkyl potassium, alkyl lithium compound.	4.	Ziegler, Gilman, Wittig

Codes

	A	B	C	D
(a)	3	1	2	4
(b)	4	2	3	1
(c)	1	3	2	4
(d)	4	3	2	1

58. Match the following.

Column I		Column II
A. Wilkinson catalyst	1.	Alkene + CO + H_2 + Co/Rh
B. Hydroformylation	2.	$CH_2{=}CH_2 + \frac{1}{2}O_2 \xrightarrow{PdCl_4}$
C. Wacker's process	3.	$[Rh(CO)_2I_2]^-$
D. Monsanto acetic acid	4.	$RhCl(PPh_3)_3$

Codes

	A	B	C	D
(a)	1	2	3	4
(b)	4	3	2	1
(c)	4	1	2	3
(d)	1	2	4	3

Answers

Exercise 1

1. (d)	**2.** (b)	**3.** (c)	**4.** (a)	**5.** (b)	**6.** (d)	**7.** (d)	**8.** (a)	**9.** (a)	**10.** (c)
11. (c)	**12.** (d)	**13.** (d)	**14.** (c)	**15.** (a)	**16.** (a)	**17.** (b)	**18.** (a)	**19.** (d)	**20.** (c)
21. (a)	**22.** (a)	**23.** (a)	**24.** (c)	**25.** (c)	**26.** (c)	**27.** (a)	**28.** (a)	**29.** (d)	**30.** (a)
31. (b)	**32.** (b)	**33.** (c)	**34.** (a)	**35.** (c)	**36.** (c)	**37.** (b)	**38.** (c)	**39.** (d)	**40.** (b)
41. (d)	**42.** (a)	**43.** (c)	**44.** (c)	**45.** (b)	**46.** (b)	**47.** (d)	**48.** (b)	**49.** (d)	

Exercise 2

1. (a)	**2.** (d)	**3.** (c)	**4.** (c)	**5.** (c)	**6.** (c)	**7.** (b)	**8.** (d)	**9.** (a)	**10.** (c)
11. (b)	**12.** (b)	**13.** (c)	**14.** (a)	**15.** (c)	**16.** (b)	**17.** (d)	**18.** (b)	**19.** (b)	**20.** (b)
21. (c)	**22.** (b)	**23.** (b)	**24.** (c)	**25.** (d)	**26.** (c)	**27.** (c)	**28.** (d)	**29.** (a)	**30.** (a)
31. (c)	**32.** (b)	**33.** (a)	**34.** (d)	**35.** (c)	**36.** (a)	**37.** (b,c)	**38.** (a,b,c)	**39.** (b,c)	**40.** (b,c)
41. (a,b,c,d)	**42.** (a,c)	**43.** (b)	**44.** (a)	**45.** (b,c)	**46.** (a,b)	**47.** (c)	**48.** (c)	**49.** (d)	**50.** (d)
51. (c)	**52.** (b)	**53.** (a)	**54.** (a)	**55.** (a)	**56.** (a)	**57.** (a)	**58.** (c)		

Hints & Solutions

Exercise 1

1. For $[Mn(CO)_4Cl_2]^{2+}$

Number of electrons $= 5 + 2 \times 4 + 2 \times 2 = 17e^-$

5. It is EPR active as contains unpaired electrons in the metal.

6. $Cr(CO)_6$ number of electron $= 6 + 2 \times 6 = 18$

11. Number of $M—M$ bonds are calculated as

$$2 \times m + An + 2L = Zn$$

where, m = number of $M—M$ bond

A = at. no. of metal atom

L = number of CO ligand

n = number of metals in the formula

$\therefore$ Number of $M—M$ bonds $= 2x + 77 \times 4 + 24 = 86 \times 4$

$$x = \frac{12}{2} = 6$$

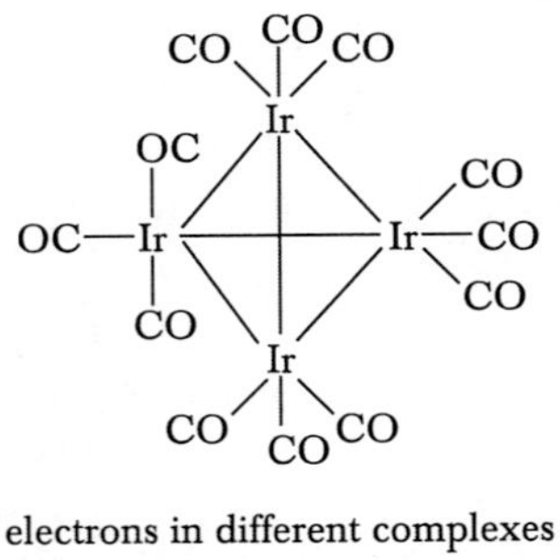

13. Number of electrons in different complexes can be calculated as

(a) $5 + 8 + 4 = 17$ (b) $5 + 6 + 6 = 17$

(c) $10 + 9 = 19$ (d) $5 + 7 + 6 = 18$

16. There are 9 terminal and 3 bridging CO's in the cobalt and rhodium clusters but in iridium all the 12CO's are terminal.

23. In $Os_6(CO)_{18}$ and $Os_5(CO)_{16}$ all carbonyls are terminal and they do not show IR bands, characteristics of bridging carbonyl groups.

24.

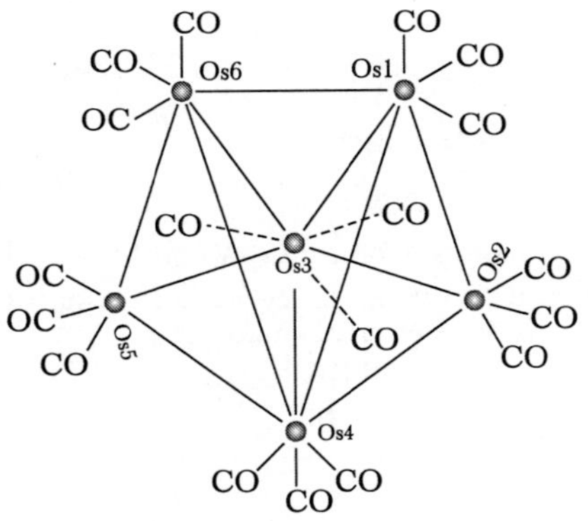

25.

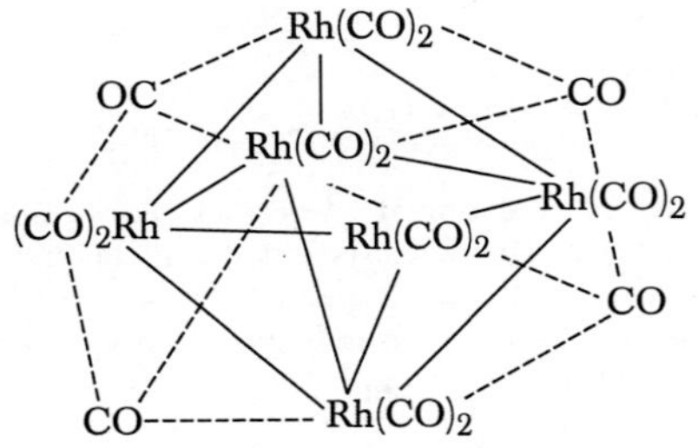

Octahedral arrays of $Rh(CO)_2$ units (each Rh having two terminal CO's) with remaining 4CO's bridging 4 faces of octahedron.

26. Clusters of 6-atoms of Mo, Nb, tantalum generally exist.

$$[M_6X_{12}]^{2+}\ M = \text{Nb or Ta}$$
$$X = \text{Cl}$$
$$[M_6Cl_8]^{4+}\ M = \text{Mo}$$

27. $t_{2g}^1, t_{2g}^2, t_{2g}^3\ e_g^2$ do not lose CFSE in the formation of activated complex to react fast (labile means easy substitution in $t_{2g}^3, t_{2g}^4, t_{2g}^5, t_{2g}^6$ there is CFSE loss in formation of activated complex so these ions react slowly.

28. $Ti(C_2H_5)_4$ is kinetically most unstable due to β-elimination of hydride.

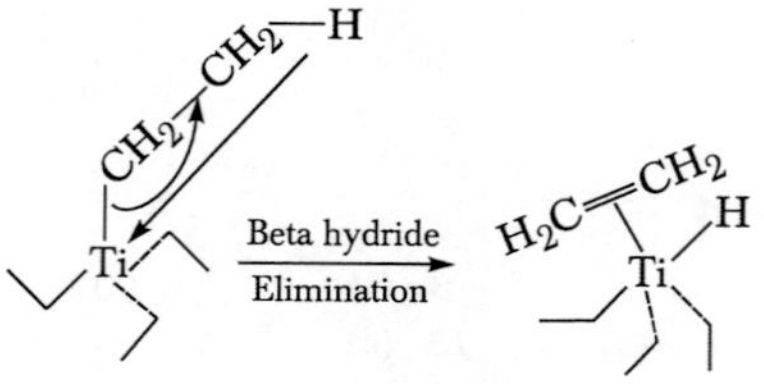

29. It prevents β-elimination under high pressure and backward reaction starts (Le-Chatelier's principle).

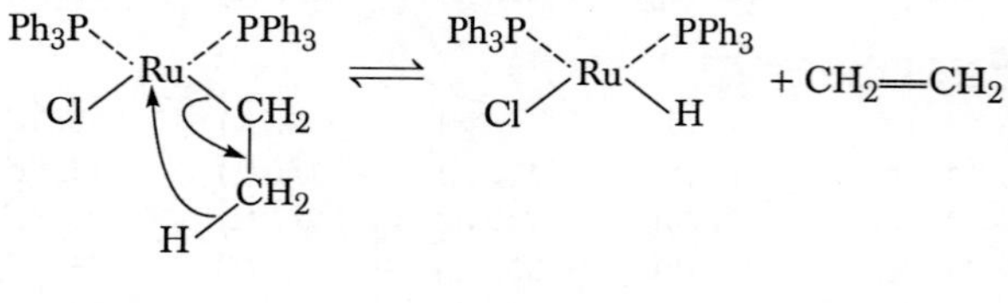

Exercise 2

1. Relative stabilities of bridged and non-bridged structures depends upon the size of metal atoms. Larger the metal atom, greater is the preference for non-bridged structure.

$Ru_3(CO)_{12}$, $Os_3(CO)_{12}$ have non-bridging structure while $Fe_3(CO)_{12}$ has two bridging COs · $Mn_2(CO)_{10}$ being having Mn-(larger atom) form only non-bridged structure.

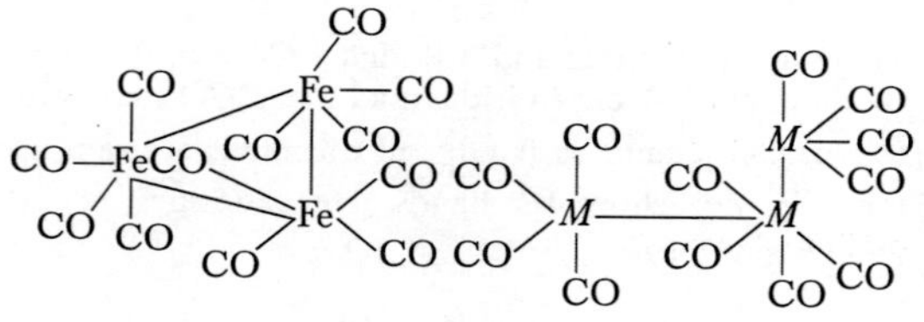

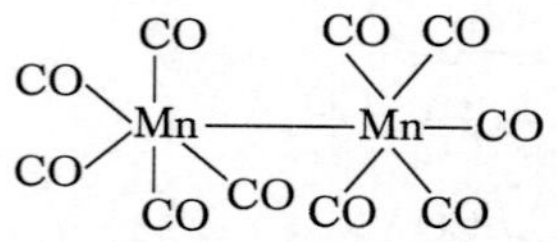

M= Os/Ru

3. Carbonylate anions are formed by two methods;
   (a) By action of NaOH on nitrogenous bases such as NH_3, amines, pyridines or metal carbonyls.

$$[Et_4N]_2^+\ [Fe(CO)]_{Et_4}^{2-} \xleftarrow[Et_4NI]{KOH} Fe(CO)_5$$
$$\downarrow NH_3/H_2O/Et_4NI$$
$$[Et_4N]^+[MFe(CO)_4]^{\ominus}$$

   (b) By reduction of carbonyl with alkali metals or alkali metal amalgams.

$$Co_2(CO)_3 \xrightarrow{Na-Hg} Na^+[Co(CO)_4]^{\ominus}$$

4. Positive charge on the metal decreases back bonding conversely, greater negative charge on the metal increases back bonding. Thus, increases metal-carbon bond order so, C—O bond weakens resulting in reduction in frequency.

$$[V(CO)_6]^- \sim 1860\ cm^{-1}$$
$$[Cr(CO)_6]^0 \sim 2000\ cm^{-1}$$
$$[Mn(CO)_6]^+ \sim 2090\ cm^{-1}$$
$$CO \sim 2143\ cm^{-1}$$

6. **Hydrogenation of alkene** (Homogeneous catalysis) $RhCl(PPh_3)_3$ (tristriphenyl phosphine) rhodium chloride or Wilkinson's catalyst.

$$>C{=}C< + \xrightleftharpoons{RhCl(PPh_3)_3\ +\ H_2} >\overset{H}{C}-\overset{H}{C}< + RhCl(PPh_3)_2$$
(Ethylene) (Ethane)

Ethylene to acrylaldehyde (Wacker's process)

$$\begin{matrix}H\\H\end{matrix}>C{=}C<\begin{matrix}H\\H\end{matrix} + [PdCl_4]^{2-} + H_2O \rightarrow CH_3CHO + Pd(O)$$
Zeise's salt
$$+\ 2HCl + 2Cl^-$$

Oxo reaction (hydroformylation)

$$RCH{=}CH_2 + H_2 + CO \xrightarrow{Catalyst} RCH_2CH_2CHO$$

Catalyst is dicobaltoctacarbonyl and rhodium complex $Rh(H)Co(PPh_3)_3$ or $[HCo(CO)_4]^-$

Conversion of methanol to acetic acid

$$CH_3OH + CO \xrightarrow{Catalyst} CH_3COOH$$

Process is monsanto process and catalyst is $[RhI_2(CO)_2]^{\ominus}$.

Polymerisation of alkenes Ziegler Natta catalyst

$$\text{Propylene} \xrightarrow[\text{Catalyst}]{\text{Ziegler-Natta}} \textit{Iso}\text{-polypropylene}$$

16. $$W(CO)_6 + LiMe \longrightarrow Li\left[(CO)_5W{-}C\begin{matrix}O^-\\CH_3\end{matrix}\right]$$
$$\downarrow \overset{+}{C}H_2N_2$$
$$(CO)_5W{=}C(CH_3)OCH_3$$
Carbene complex

17. $$Mn_2(CO)_{10} \xrightarrow{Na} 2[Mn(CO)_5]^- \xrightarrow{CH_3COCl} CH_3C(O)Mn(CO)_5$$
or $(CO)_5Mn \longrightarrow Mn(CO)_5$

18. $[V(H_2O)_6]^{2+}$ = inert (d^3) $[FeF_6]^{3-}$ = labile (d^5)
$[V(H_2O)_6]^{3+}$ = labile (d^2)

$Co(CN)_6]^{3-}$ = inert (low spin) d^6

$[CoF_6]^{3-}$ = labile (high spin) d^6

20. NO is 3 electron donor and hence $18e^-$ as

$$Mn^0 = 7e^-$$
$$4CO = 8e^-$$
$$\text{One NO} = 3e^- \; 18e^-$$

So, diamagnetic as all electrons are paired.

21. CO groups in $Mo(CO)_6$ are all terminal while.

NH_3 is electron donor so supplies electrons to Mo for back donation to $\overset{*}{\pi}$ orbitals of CO.

PH_3 is a weaker donor than NH_3.

25. $[(H_3N)_5Co\cdot O\cdot CO_2]^+ + H_3O^+ \rightarrow \left[(H_3N)_5Co{-}O{<}^{H}_{CO_2}\right]^{2+} + H_2O$

↓ Substitution of CO_2 at this oxygen

$$[(H_3N)_5\cdot Co(H_2O)]^{3+} + H_2O \xleftarrow{H_3O^+} [(NH_3)_5Co(OH)]^{2+} + CO_2$$

26. In cases of norbornyl, β-hydrogen not only has a difficult time approaching the metal centre but olefin generated would be highly strained.

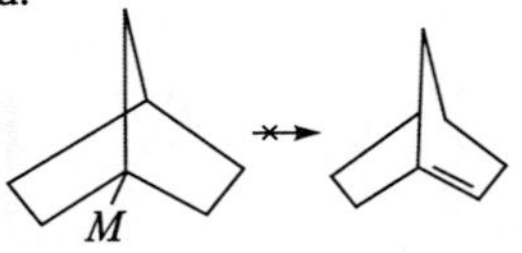

12

Analytical Chemistry

Syllabus

- Separation, Solvent Extraction
- Various Spectroscopic Techniques
- Chromatography
- Thermoanalytical Methods
- Electron Analytical Methods

Separation

Separation, as applied to chemical systems, means to part or divide a homogeneous or heterogeneous mixture or mass into components, individual units, or even into elements. Separations may be performed by making use of many different methods and techniques which are based on sound fundamental chemical and physical properties. A separation procedure may be used for purification, qualitative identification, or quantitative determination. Many different separation methods have been known and used for a long time (*e.g.,* gravimetry) and some have now been developed (*e.g.,* gas chromatography and thin layer chromatography).

Nature of the Separation Process

All separation methods have in common the distribution of the components in a mixture between two phases which subsequently can be mechanically separated.

If the ratio of the amount of a given component present in each phase (distribution ratio) differs significantly from that of another, a separation of the two is feasible, but the complexity of the method depends upon how great the distribution ratios, differ for the components from one another.

When the difference is extreme, a single stage process is sufficient for separation. For example, a single precipitation with Ag^+ ion is sufficient for the isolation of Cl^- ion from many other anions, because the ratio of the chloride ion in the solid phase to that in equilibrium in the aqueous phase is immense. The comparable ratios, *e.g.,* say NO_3^- or $HClO_4^-$ ions, approach zero.

A complex situation arises when the distribution ratio for one component is essentially zero, but the ratio for the other is not very large. In this case, a multistage process becomes necessary. For example, **uranium** (VI) can be extracted into ether from an aqueous HNO_3 solution. Although its distribution ratio in the two phases is only about unity for a single extraction, uranium (VI) can not be separated from other metal ions which have no tendency for transfer by **repeated or exhaustive extraction** of the aqueous solution with fresh portions of ether. The repeated extraction is readily automated. The Soxhlet extraction apparatus for removal of soluble components from a solid phase is an example of such a device.

Most complex procedures are needed when the distribution ratios for the species to be separated are greater than zero and approach one another in magnitude. In this case **multistage fraction** techniques are employed. These techniques are also based upon the differences in the distribution ratios of solutes between the two phases, but here, separation efficiency increases mainly due to the following reasons.

(a) The number of times that partitioning occurs between phases is increased enormously.

(b) Distribution is caused to occur between fresh portions of both phases.

Fractionation techniques have been applied to all combination of phases. Commonly, the continuous contact between the two phases is provided by flowing the one counter current to the other. As a result, the number of contacts increases enormously. In most separation methods, a **mobile phase** is forced through a fixed **immobile phase** in a column. However, in fractional distillation, the vapour phase is caused to move counter current to the condensed liquid phase inorder to provide multiple contact stages.

In general, separations are based on equilibrium processes and hence complete separation of an interference from the species of interest is never possible. However, separation may decrease the concentration of the interference to a tolerable level.

There are two important factors which are necessary to be considered in any separation.

(a) The completeness of the recovery of the species to be determined, and

(b) The degree of separation from the unwanted constituent.

These factors are expressed in terms of **recovery ratio** ***R***. If x is the amount of the required constituent A that is recovered in a separation, and x_0 is its amount in the original sample, then the recovery ratio is expressed as,

$$R_A = \frac{x}{x_0}$$

This ratio should be as close to one as possible. An incomplete recovery of A always results in a negative error.

Classification of Separation Methods

Separation methods can be classified in a number of ways. For example,

1. They can be classified according to whether they involve batch discrete equilibrium steps or continuos non-equilibrium steps.
2. They may also be classified according to the type of force involved.
3. Another method of classifying them is whether they are physical, chemical or mechanical in nature.
4. They can also be classified according to the type of heterogeneous equilibria involved.

All these approaches, however, suffer from one kind of limitation or the other. It is also impossible to scheme all separation techniques into one classification scheme, because of wide diverse properties on which separations are based. Many separation methods according to commonly used descriptive titles are given in table below.

Separation methods

	Method	Basis
1.	Precipitation	Difference in solubilities
2.	Distillation	Differences in volatility
3.	Sublimation	Differences in vapour pressure
4.	Extraction between two phases	Differences in solubility
5.	Crystallisation	Property of solubility usually at low temp.
6.	Floatation	Differences in density between substance and liquid.
7.	Ultrafiltration	Size of substance in comparison to filtering device.
8.	Dialysis	Osmosis; flow of a system through a membrane.
9.	Electro deposition	Electrolysis at inert electrodes.

Solvent Extraction

Liquid-liquid extraction is a separation technique; here an aqueous solution is brought in contact with a second solvent usually organic, immiscible with water in order to bring about a transfer of one or more of the solute into the second solvent. The separations are clean, rapid and convenient. The technique is applicable to trace level or large amounts of materials.

Theory For a solute 'A' to be distributed between two immiscible phases a and b, the Nernst Distribution Law states that,

$$\frac{\text{Concentration of solute in solvent } a}{\text{Concentration of solute in solvent } b} = \frac{[A]_a}{[A]_b} = K_D$$

K_D is called distribution or partition coefficient.

The law is valid provided the molecular state of solute is the same in both the liquids and the temperature is a constant; in other words the distributing species should not undergo dissociation or association in either phase.

The law does not take into account the activities of the various species and hence applies only to very dilute solution where the ratio of activities approaches unity.

In practical applications, the fraction of the total solute in one or other phase is important not if the solute would undergo dissociation or association or interaction with other dissolved species. It is more convenient to introduce the term distribution ratio, D (or extraction coefficient, E)

$$D = E = \frac{(C_A)_a}{(C_A)_b}$$

C_A is the concentration of A in all its forms as determined analytically. If the solution contains two solutes A and B, it often happens that under the conditions favouring the complete extraction of A some B is extracted as well. The effectiveness of separation increases with the magnitude of the separation coefficient or factor β which is related to the individual distribution ratio as follows :

$$\beta = \frac{[A]_0 / [B]_0}{[A]_\omega / [B]_\omega}$$

$$= \frac{[A]_0 / [A]_\omega}{[B]_0 / [B]_\omega}$$

$$= \frac{D_A}{D_B}$$

To have effective separation the relative value of D_A and D_B are of significance.

For *e.g.*,

$$D_A = 10$$

$$D_B = 0.1$$

A single extraction will remove 90.9% of A and 9.1% of B (ratio 10 : 1).

A second extraction of the same aqueous phase will bring the total amount of A extracted up to 99.2% but increase that of B to 17.4% (ratio 5 : 7 : 1). More complete extraction of A thus involves an increased contaminator by B.

It is very clear that when one of the distribution ratios is relatively large and other very small, almost complete separation can be quickly and easily achieved. When the extraction factor is large but the distribution ratio is of sufficient magnitude, extraction of both components occur. It is necessary to use other special technique to suppress the extraction of the unwanted component.

Choice of the Solvent

Solvent extraction is generally employed in analysis to separate a solute of interest from substances which interfere in the ultimate quantitative analysis. Sometimes the interfering solute are extracted selectively.

Solvent extraction is also used to concentrate a species which in aqueous solution is too dilute to be analysed.

The choice of solvent is decided by the following factors :

- A high distribution ratio for the solute and a low distribution ratio for the undesirable impurities.
- Low solubility in aqueous phase – Sufficiently low viscosity and sufficient density differences for the aqueous phase to avoid the formation of emulsions.
- Low toxicity and flammability.
- Ease of recovery of solute from the solvent for subsequent analytical processing.
- Sometimes mixed solvents may be used to improve the above properties.
- Salting-out agents may also improve extractability.

Factors Favouring Solvent Extraction

Ionic compounds would not be expected to extract into organic solvents from aqueous solution because of the larger loss in electrostatic solvation energy which would occur. The most obvious way to make an aqueous ionic species extractable is to neutralise its charge. **The larger and more hydrophobic the resulting molecular species, the better will be its extraction.**

This can be done by the formation of (i) a neutral metal chelate complex (ii) by ion association.

Formation of neutral metal chelate

The choice of a satisfactory chelating agent for a particular separation depends on the nature of the donor atoms, ring size and basic strength of the chelating group.

e.g., Copper (II) acetyl acetonate
Iron (III) cupferrate

Ion association complexes

They are formed when the solute species associate with oppositely charged ions to form neutral species which can be extracted. *e.g.*, tetraphenyl arsonium

$(C_6H_5)_2As^+$, tetrabutyl ammonium $(nC_4H_9)_4N^+$ form large ion aggregates with suitable oppositely charged ions, favouring solvent extraction.

These large and bulky ions do not have a primary hydration shell and cause disruption of the hydrogen bonded water structure and are "pushed" into the organic phase.

The principle of ion-pair formation has been used for the extraction of many metal ions.

The application of "crown ethers" which form stable complexes with metal ions and particularly alkali metal ions is a recent development. For example, the ion-pair extraction of Na^+, K^+ and Ca^{2+} with dicyclohexyl -18-crown-6 has been described.

Extraction

Extraction may be accomplished in either a batch operation or a continuous operation. Batch extraction the simplest and most widely used method is employed, where a **large distribution ratio** for the desired separation is readily obtainable.

For example, as in the case of separating funnel. When the **distribution ratio is low; continuous** methods of extraction are used. This procedure makes use of a continuous flow of immiscible solvents through the solution. If the solvent is volatile it is recycled by distillation.

Stripping Stripping is the removal of the extraction solute from the organic phase for further preparation of the detailed analysis. Sometimes stripping can be omitted when the concentration of the solute is determined directly in the organic phase. When the solute must be transferred to a more suitable medium, the simplest procedure is to add a small volume of water and evaporate the solvent on a water bath.

When the extracting solvent is non-volatile, the solute is removed by chemical means-shaking with water containing acid or other reagents.

Importance of Solvent Extraction

1. The technique of solvent extraction, permits the separation and often the pre-concentration of a particular element or substance. Following the quantitative determination by appropriate method is feasible.
2. Direct measurement of absorbance may be made with ion-association complexes.

   e.g., ferroinanionic detergent complex.
3. Improved results can be obtained by chelation.

   e.g., uranyl nitrate from nitric acid into tributyl phosphate and subsequent addition of dibenzoylmethane to form soluble coloured chelate.
4. Solvent extraction is probably the technique most widely used in **conjugation with AAS, and HPLC.**
5. A fully automated solvent extraction procedure using APDC for the **determination of trace metals in water** has been in commercial use.

Qualitative Spectrographic Analysis

In a qualitative analysis it is desirable to have a high sensitively so that the presence of trace elements may be revealed. The DC arc is preferred for the most difficult, excitable elements and for non-volatile and refractory compounds; a 'complete burn' of the sample may be obtained with comparative ease. A widely used system of qualitative spectrographic analysis is to arc the sample in a depression in a graphite electrode, using a pointed counter-electrode. The graphite electrode in air gives a cyanogen band spectrum (headings at 4216, 3883, and 3590 Å) in the near ultraviolet, which may mark some of the lines of interest. A sample of a few milligrams is sufficient; the exposure conditions must be determined by experiment. Non-conducting samples may be more easily excited by being mixed with an equal volume of graphite powder, and these, as well as all refractory materials, are often treated with a carrier to bring them into the arc stream. This carrier, usually a volatile salt such as ammonium chloride or ammonium sulphate, helps to propel the entire sample smoothly up into the arc gap.

The amount of an element that is detectable varies with its concentration, its relative volatility, the energy of excitation, etc. : approximate sensitivity figures with arc excitation for the common elements are summarised in the table below.

Arc sensitivities of some elements

Percentage detectable	Elements
0.1-1	As, Cs Nb, P, Ta, W
0.01-0.1	B, Bi, Cd, La, Rb, Sb, Si, Tl, Y, Zn, Zr
0.001-0.01	Al, Au, Ba, Be, Ca, Fe, Ga, Ge, Hg, Ir, K, Mn, Mo, Pb, Sc, Sn, Sr, Ti, V
0.0001-0.001	Ag; Co, Cr, Cu, In, Li, Mg, Na, Ni, Os, Pd, Pt, Rh, Ru

Raies ultimes

As one dilutes the amount of an element in an arc, the number of lines observable is reduced, and ultimately there remain only a few lines of the element which is diluted. These lines are referred to as the raies ultimes' or persistent lines. The identification of these lines will permit detection of elements present in low concentration, and all qualitative methods utilise the persistent lines.

R.U. Powder Method

It is the simplest and most direct procedure. The R.U. powder consists of small quantities of 50 elements incorporated in a base material composed of calcium oxide, magnesium oxide, and zinc oxide. The quantity of each element present has been carefully adjusted so that only the raies ultimes and the most important sensitive lines appear when the spectrum is excited. The excitation is done by placing 10-20 mg powder in the lower positive pole of an arc between graphite electrodes. A current of 5-7 A is used for an arc length of 6 mm. It is advisable not to expose for a longer time than the powder lasts, or else parts of the spectrum will be unnecessarily masked by the CN bands. The spectrum of the iron arc (together with the important wavelengths) is given alongside that of the R.U. powder; this enables the positions of the persistent lines relative to the iron-arc spectra to be seen immediately, and will also permit the position of any sensitive line to be found readily. A qualitative analysis is carried out by producing continuous arc spectra with the aid of a Hartmann diaphragm of the R.U. powder, the sample, and of a pure main element present in the sample. The plate is developed, and the lines present in both the R.U. powder and sample spectra are noted; the latter is most simply observed on a Rank Hilger projection comparator. The elements are tabulated with the number of lines appearing; three lines, which are free from interference, are considered proof of the presence of the element. With R.U. powder two lines may be acceptable for some elements; these include B, Cu, Au, P, Ag and Cs.

Another problem that frequently arises is to decide whether a substance contains a given element or a small number of specified elements.

Advantages that the spectrograph offers in the following operations.

(a) Rapid qualitative analysis of all the metallic constituents of a substance as a basis for planning a chemical analysis.

(b) Approximate analysis of minor components by sight (after some experience has been obtained).

(c) Examination of precipitates (after weighing) for freedom from constituents which should have been separated.

(d) Detection of traces of metallic impurities of constituents in inorganic residues and powders; in organic substances (foodstuffs, textiles etc.); in vitreous substances (glasses and slags); and in refractories and clays.

(e) Testing the purity of analytical reagents.

(f) Analysis of substances of which only small quantities are available.

(g) Detection of rare or trace metals in minerals.

Quantitative Spectrographic Analysis

If the excitation conditions are kept constant and the sample composition is varied over a narrow range, the energy emitted for a given spectral line of an element is proportional to the number of atoms that are excited and thus to the concentration of the element in the sample. The intensity of the light is usually measured by the photographic method. The concentration of the unknown is determined from the blackening of the plate for certain lines in the spectrum. The quantitative determination of the blackening of the individual lines is made with a microphotometer. Measurements are made of the light transmitted by the line and the light transmitted by the clear portion of the plate (I_0); the density D (strictly the density of blackening, also represented by B) may be defined by the expression $D = \log_{10}\left(\frac{I_0}{I}\right)$. It is assumed that the galvanometer deflection obtained on the microphotometer is directly proportional to the light falling on the photocell.

The density of the image of the spectral line should ideally be proportional to the concentration of the corresponding element in the sample if the exposure time and conditions of excitation, etc., are held constant. This is often not strictly true; hence, wherever possible, it is desirable to photograph spectra of several samples of varying known composition on the same plate with the unknown. The unknown may then be evaluated by interpolation on a graph of density against concentration. The fact that the unknown and all the standards are on the same plate prevents errors due to differences in sensitivity between plates as well as those due to differences in the time or temperature of photographic processing.

If one plots the density as a function of the logarithm of the exposure (the exposure of the photographic plate is defined as the product of the intensity of the light incident on the undeveloped plate and the time for which it is acting), a curve such as is shown in the figure results. It will be noted that there is a region BC over which the density is proportional to the logarithm of the exposure; this is the useful range of the plate. The slope of this linear portion of the curve is known as the gamma (or contrast) of the emulsion : $\gamma = \tan\theta$. Emulsions with a high gamma give images with strong contrast. The most common type of plate used for emission spectrography has a gamma of about 1.

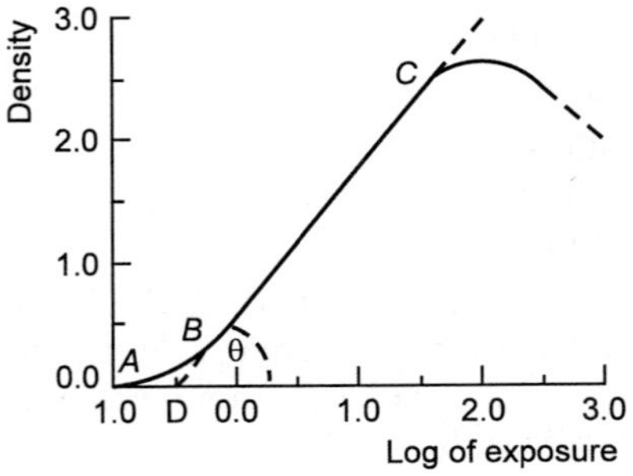

Fig. 12.1

Atomic Emission Spectroscopy

When certain metals are introduced as salts into the Bunsen flame, characteristic colours are produced : this procedure has long been used for detecting elements qualitatively. If the light from such a flame is passed through a spectroscope, several lines may be seen, each having a characteristic colour; calcium produces red, green and blue radiation, of which the red is largely responsible for the typical calcium flame colour. Although the flame colours of calcium, strontium and lithium are very similar, it is possible to differentiate them with certainty by observing their spectra, and it is possible to detect each in the presence of the others. By extending and simplifying the principles inherent in the qualitative flame test, analytical applications of emission spectrography have been developed. With electric spark or electric arc excitation, the spectra are recorded photographically by means of a spectrograph, and since the characteristic spectra of many elements occur in the ultraviolet region the optical system used to disperse the radiation is generally made of quartz.

Cause of Colour in Bunsen Flame

The quantum theory predicts that each atom or ion possesses definite energy states in which the various electrons can exist; In the normal or ground state the electrons have the lowest energy. Upon the application of sufficient energy by electrical, thermal or other means, one or more electrons may be removed to a higher energy state further from the nucleus; these excited electrons tend to return to the ground state, and in so doing emit the extra energy as a photon of radiant energy. Since, there are definite energy states and since only certain changes are possible according to the quantum theory, there are a limited number of wavelength possible in the emission spectrum. **The greater the energy of the exciting source, the higher the energy of the excited electrons, hence the greater the number of lines that may appear.**

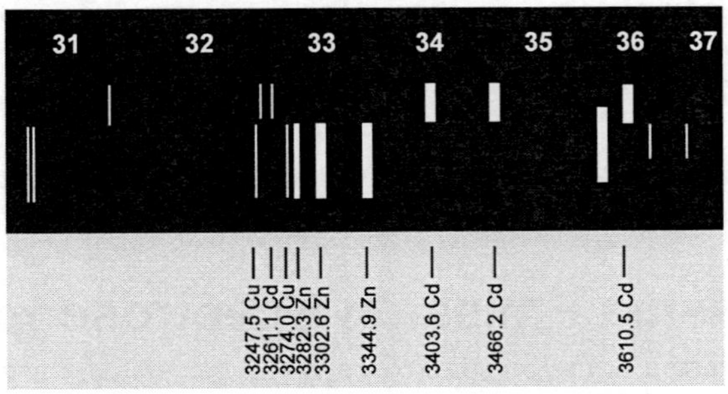

Fig. 12.2 Continuous spectra of cadmium, spelter and zinc.

The lines in the spectrum from any element always occur in the same positions relative to each other. **When sufficient amounts of several elements are present in the source of radiation, each emits its characteristic spectrum; this is the basis for qualitative analysis by the spectrochemical method.** Elements in an unknown spectrum may be identified by comparing the unknown spectrum with the spectrum of a known element. Fig. 12.2 shows part of the continuous spectra of cadmium, spelter and zinc. Examination of the three spectra will reveal whether cadmium is present or absent in the sample of spelter. In this example, cadmium is not detected in spelter, as no lines in the cadmium spectrum correspond with lines in the spelter spectrum.

The chief advantages of spectrographic method of analysis are

(a) The procedure is specific for the element being determined, although difficulties occasionally arise when a line of another element overlaps that of the unknown.

(b) The method is time-saving; a quantitative determination of traces of the elements in a sample, especially an alloy or a metal, may be made without any preliminary treatment. Most metals and some non-metals (*e.g.*, phosphorus, silicon, arsenic, and boron) may be determined.

(c) A permanent record may be obtained on a photographic plate.

(d) It may be (and is usually) applied to the determination of small quantities of added constituents or of traces of impurities where conventional methods of analysis are difficult, fail or give less accurate results. Lengthy and difficult separations by chemical methods, *e.g.,* of zirconium and hafnium and of niobium and tantalum, can be avoided.

(e) The accuracy and precision are not as high as gravimetric, titrimetric, and some spectrophotometric methods for elements present in quantities greater than 2-5 per cent of the total; indeed, spectrographic methods are not usually applied for elements presents to a greater extent than about 3 per cent.

Plasma Emission Spectroscopy

In plasma emission spectroscopy the gas, usually argon, is ionized by the influence of a strong electrical field either by a direct current or by radio frequency. Both types of discharge produce a plasma, the **direct current plasma** (DCP) or the **inductively coupled plasma** (ICP). Plasma sources operate at high temperatures somewhere between 70000 and 15000 K. Thus, the plasma source produces a greater number of exited emitted atoms, especially in the ultraviolet region, than that obtained by the relative low temperatures used in flame emission spectroscopy. Further, the plasma source is able to reproduce atomisation conditions with a far greater degree of precision than that obtained by classical arc and spark spectroscopy. This feature is especially important for the multi element determinations over a wide concentration range.

There are two basic types of instrument used in plasma emission analysis, namely the simultaneous and the sequential multi element spectrometer.

Multichannel instruments are capable of measuring the intensities of the emission lines of up to 60 elements simultaneously. To overcome the effect of possible non-specific background radiation, one or more additional wavelengths may be measured and background correction can be achieved.

The main advantage of photoelectric multichannel instruments is that with the modern computational facilities available rapid simultaneous analysis may be achieved with a better precision than that obtained from the spectrograph using a photographic plate. Thus, results for 25 elements may be obtained within a short time of about 1-2 minutes.

Atomic Absorption Spectroscopy and Atomic Fluorescence Spectroscopy (AAS and AFS)

When a solution containing a suitable compound of a metal is aspirated into a flame, the following events occur in rapid succession.

1. Evaporation of solvent leaving a solid residue.
2. Vaporization of the solid with dissociation into its constituent atoms, which initially will be in the ground state.
3. Some atoms may be excited by the thermal energy of the flame to higher energy levels and attain a condition in which they radiate energy characteristic of the metal.

In (3), the resulting emission spectrum thus consists of lines originating from excited atoms of ions. This is the basis of **flame emission spectroscopy** (FES or AFS), which was formerly referred to as flame photometry.

In the situation (2), the ground state atoms are capable of absorbing radiant energy of their own specific resonance wavelength. Hence, if light of the resonance wavelength is passed through a flame containing the atoms then part of the light will be absorbed and the extent of absorption will be proportional to the number of ground state atoms present in the flame. This is the underlying principle of atomic absorption spectroscopy (AAS).

The AFS is based on the re-emission of absorbed energy by free atoms.

These processes are represented in Fig. 12.3.

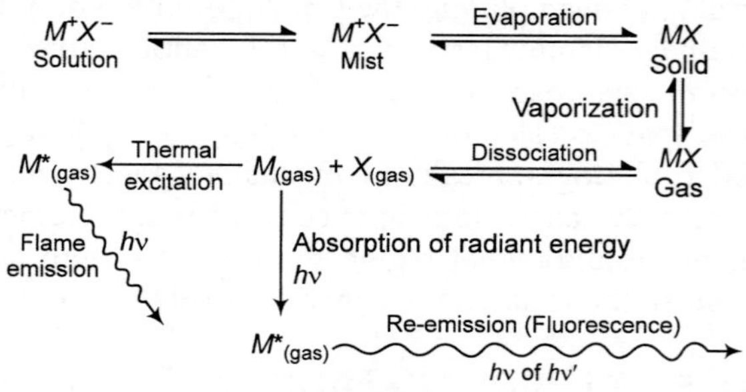

Fig. 12.3

Elementary Theory

Consider, the simplified energy-level diagram below, where E_0 represents the ground state in which the elements of a given atom, are at their lowest energy level and E_1, E_2, E_3 etc., represent highest or excited levels.

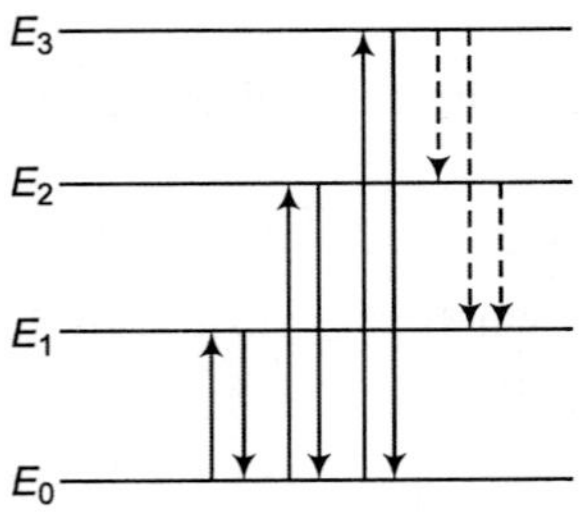

Transitions between two quantised energy levels, say from E_0 to E_1, correspond to the absorption radiant energy and the amount of energy absorbed (ΔE) is determined by Bohr's equation.

$$\Delta E = E_1 - E_0 = h\nu = \frac{hc}{\lambda}$$

where, c is the velocity of light, h is Planck's constant, v is the frequency and λ the wavelength of the radiation absorbed. Clearly, the transition from E_1 to E_0 corresponds to the emission of radiation of frequency v.

Since, an atom of a given element gives rise to a definite, characteristic line spectrum, it follows that there are different excitation states associated with different elements. The consequent emission spectra involve not only transitions from excited states to the ground state *e.g.,* E_3 to E_0, E_2 to E_0 (indicated by the full lines, but also transitions such as E_3 to E_2, E_3 to E_1, etc. (indicated by the broken lines). Thus, it follows that the emission spectrum of a given element may be quite complex. In theory it is also possible for absorption of radiation by already excited states to occur, *e.g.,* E_1 to E_2, E_2 to E_3, etc., but in practice the ratio of excited to ground state atoms is extremely small, and thus, the absorption spectrum of a given element is usually only associated with transitions from the ground state to higher energy states and is consequently much simpler in character than the emission spectrum. The relationship between the ground-state and excited-state populations is given by the Boltzmann equation $\frac{N_1}{N_0} = \left(\frac{g_1}{g_0}\right) e^{-\Delta E/kT}$

where,

N_1 = number of atoms in the excited state

N_0 = number of ground state atoms,

$\frac{g_1}{g_0}$ = ratio of statistical weights for ground and excited states,

ΔE = energy of excitation = hv,

k = the Boltzmann constant and

T = the temperature in Kelvin.

It can be seen from this equation that the ratio $\frac{N_1}{N_0}$ is dependent upon both the excitation energy ΔE and the temperature T. An increase in temperature and a decrease in ΔE (*i.e.,* when dealing with transitions which occur at longer wavelengths) will both result in a higher value for the ratio $\frac{N_1}{N_0}$.

Calculation shows that only a small fraction of the atoms are excited, even under the most favourable conditions, *i.e.,* when the temperature is high and the excitation energy is low.

Since, as already explained, the absorption spectra of most elements are simple in character as compared with the emission spectra, it follows that **atomic absorption spectroscopy is less prone to inter-element interferences than is flame emission spectroscopy.** Further, in view of the high proportion of ground state to excited atoms, it would appear that atomic absorption spectroscopy should also be more sensitive than flame emission spectroscopy. However, in this respect the wavelength of the resonance line is a critical factor, and elements whose resonance lines are associated with relatively low energy values are more sensitive as far as flame emission spectroscopy is concerned than those whose resonance lines are associated with higher energy values. Thus, sodium with an emission line of wavelength 589.0 nm shows, great sensitivity in flame emission spectroscopy, whereas zinc (emission line wavelength 213.9 nm) is relativity insensitive.

The integrated absorption is given by the expression

$$Kdv = f\ N_0 \left(\frac{\pi e^2}{mc}\right)$$

where, K is the absorption coefficient at frequency v,

e is the electronic charge,

m the mass of an electron,

c the velocity of light,

f the oscillator strength of the absorbing line (this is inversely proportional to the lifetime of the excited state),

N_0 is the number of metal atoms per mL capable of absorbing the radiation.

In this expression the only variable is N_0 and it is this which governs the extent of absorption. Thus, it follows that the **integrated absorption coefficient is directly proportional to the concentration of the absorbing species.**

The natural line width of an atomic spectral line is about 10^{-5} nm, but owing to the influence of Doppler and pressure effects, the line is broadened to about 0.002 nm at flame temperature of 2000-3000 ZK. To measure the absorption coefficient of a line thus broadened would require a spectrometer with a resolving power of 500000. This difficulty was overcome by Walsh, who used a source of sharp emission lines with a much smaller half width than the absorption line, and the radiation frequency of which is centred on the absorption frequency. In this way, the absorption coefficient at the centre of the line, K_{max}, may be measured. If the profile of the absorption line is assumed to be due to only Doppler broadening, then there is a relationship between K_{max} and N_0. Thus, the only requirement of the spectrometer is that it shall be capable of isolating the required resonance line from all other lines emitted by the source.

It should be noted that in atomic absorption spectroscopy, as with molecular absorption, the absorbance A is given by the logarithmic ratio of the intensity of the incident light signal I_0 to that of the transmitted light I_t, *i.e.*, $A = \log \frac{I_0}{I_t} = KLN_0$

where,

N_0 is the concentration of atoms in the flame (number of atoms per mL);

L is the path length through the flame (cm),

K is a constant related to the absorption coefficient.

For small values of the absorbance, this is linear function.

With flame emission spectroscopy, the detector response E is given by the expression

$$E = k\alpha c,$$

where,

k is related to a variety of factors including the efficiency of atomisation and of self-absorption,

α is the efficiency of atomic excitation,

c is the concentration of the test solution.

It follows that any electrical method of increasing E, as for example improved amplification, will make the technique more sensitive.

The basic equation for atomic fluorescence is given by

$$F = QI_o kc$$

where,

Q is the quantum efficiency of the atomic fluorescence process,

I_0 is the intensity of the incident radiation,

k is the constant which is governed by the efficiency of the atomisation process,

c is the concentration of the element concerned in the test solution.

It follows that the more powerful the radiation source, the greater will be the sensitivity of the technique.

To summarize, in both atomic absorption spectroscopy and in atomic fluorescence spectroscopy, the factors which favour the production of gaseous atoms in the ground state determine the success of the techniques. In flame emission spectroscopy, there is an additional requirement, namely the production of excited atoms in the vapour state. It should be noted that the conversion of the original solid *MX* into gaseous metal atoms (M_{gas}) will be governed by a variety of factors including the rate of vaporization, flame composition and flame temperature, and further, if *MX* is replaced by a new solid, *MY*, then the formation of M_{gas} may proceed in a different manner, and with a different efficiency from that observed with *MX*.

Procedures

The three flame spectrophotometric procedures require the following essential apparatus.

(a) For flame emission spectroscopy a **nebuliser-burner system** which produces gaseous metal atoms by using a suitable combustion flame involving a fuel gas-oxidant gas mixture is needed. Note however that with so called non-flame cells, the burner is not required.

(b) **A spectrophotometer system** which includes a suitable optical train, a photosensitive detector and appropriate display device for the output from the detector.

(c) For both atomic absorption spectroscopy and atomic fluorescence spectroscopy, a **resonance line source** is required for each element to be determined, these line sources are usually modulated.

A schematic diagram showing the disposition of these essential components for the different techniques is given in the Fig. 12.5. The components include within the frame drawn in broken lines represent the apparatus required for flame emission spectroscopy. For atomic absorption spectroscopy and for atomic fluorescence spectroscopy there is the additional requirement of a resonance line source. In atomic absorption spectroscopy this source is placed in line with the detector, but in atomic fluorescence spectroscopy it is placed in a position at right angles to the detector as shown in the diagram below.

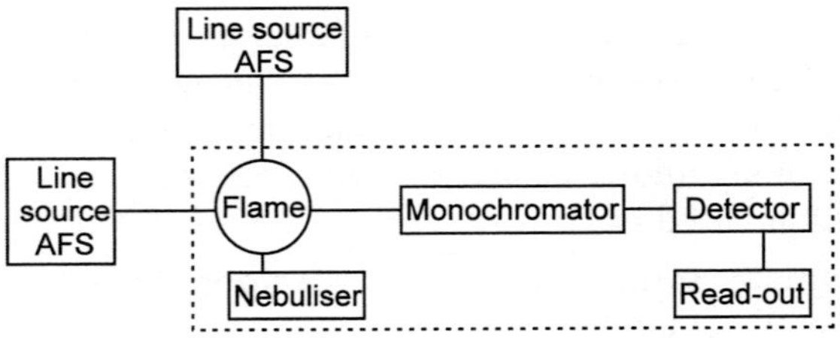

Fig. 12.4

Flames

The essential requirement is that the flame used shall produce a temperature of 2000 K. The flame temperature attained by the common fuel gases, burning in air and nitrous oxide are given in the Table 12.1 below.

Table 12.1 **Flame Temperatures with Various Fuels**

Fuel gas	Temperature K	
	Air	Nitrous oxide
Acetylene	2400	3200
Hydrogen	2300	2900
Propane	2200	3000

Non-Flame Techniques

In the Nebuliser a potential explosion hazard exists. Hence, it is possible in some cases to make use of non-flame methods.

(a) Involving the use of electrically heated graphite tubes or rods.

(b) Vapour techniques

Both find applications in atomic absorption spectroscopy and in atomic fluorescence spectroscopy.

Resonance Line Sources

For both atomic absorption spectroscopy and atomic fluorescence spectroscopy, a resonance line source is required, and the most important of these is the **hollow cathode lamp.** Multielement lamps are available in which the cathode is made from alloys, the electrode less discharge lamps give radiation intensities which are much greater than those given by hollow cathode lamps.

Monochromator

The purpose of a monochromator is (1) to select a given emissions line and to isolate it from other lines and molecular band emissions (2) to isolate the resonance line from all non-absorbed lines emitted by the radiation source. Diffraction, grating, interference filters and prisms are used as monochromators.

Detectors

A barrier-layer-cell is a sufficiently good detector. When improved spectral sensitivity is required photomultiplier are employed. The output from detector is fed to a suitable read-out system, like chart recorders and digital display.

Interferences

Various factors which lead to interference with the determination of the concentration of a given element are,

1. **Spectral interferences** in AAS arise mainly from overlap between the frequencies of selected resonance lines emitted by some other elements; in particular due to hydroxyl and cyanogen radicals.
2. **Chemical interferences** are due to stable compound formation and due to ionisation; both these inhibit ground-state gaseous atoms.
3. **Matrix effects** are due to physical factors like viscosity, density, surface tension and volatility and influence the amount of sample reaching the flame.

Background absorption is due to smoke and organic solvent molecules.

Chromatography

The term **Chromatography** (Greek : Khromtos - colour and graphos-written) and its principles were first discovered by Mikhail Tswett. In his experiment, a leaf extract sample in petroleum ether was allowed to pass through a column of $CaCO_3$. Pure ether was continued to flow through the column, as a result of which various chlorophyll pigments, etc., were separated into a series of differently coloured and easily distinguished zones.

Now various types of chromatographic techniques are possible and in its various forms, **chromatography is used for the separation, isolation, purification and identification of components of a mixture**. Chromatographic techniques can be used for very small samples or for components present at very low concentrations. Chromatographic techniques have been developed to analyse for air pollutants at concentrations of one part per million or less.

Chromatographic methods

	Method	**Basis**
1.	Adsorption column chromatography	Distribution of solute between a solid and liquid phase on a column.
2.	Partition column chromatography	Distribution of a solute between two liquids on a column.
3.	Paper chromatography	Partition on a sheet of paper.
4.	Thin layer chromatography	Adsorption or partition on thin sheets.
5.	Ion exchange chromatography	Exchange of ion.
6.	Molecular Sieves	Size of solute.
7.	Gel permeation	Size of solute.
8.	Gas chromatography	Distribution of gaseous solutes between a gas and liquid or solid phase.
9.	Zone electrophoresis	Separation on a sheet in the presence of an electric field.

General Concepts

Chromatographic separations can be carried out by the distribution of components in a mixture between a fixed moving phase. **The fixed phase is known as stationary phase, while the moving phase is known as mobile phase.** Separation between two substances begins to take place when one is held more strongly by the stationary phase than the other, which tends to move on faster in the mobile phase.

The main experimental procedure includes the following sequences

1. Preparation of the stationary phase.
2. Introduction of the sample.
3. Passing the sample over the stationary phase.
4. Collecting the individual components for qualitative purposes.

The chromatographic separations of analytical importance are often carried out in tubular columns of glass or metal that have been packed with a porous solid. The solid serves as a stationary phase itself or as a support for a stationary liquid phase. Instead of a packed column, the stationary phase may consists of strip of coarse paper or a finely ground solid supported by a glass plate. These alternatives are advantageous particularly when the amount of sample is small. The fundamental principles are the same for separation involving all these types of immobile phases.

Classification in Chromatography

The chromatography methods of analysis are classified by different features, namely by the state of aggregation of the phase used, by the nature of sorbate-sorbent interaction (the separation mechanism), by the technique used etc.

Chromatography can be divided into the following general areas

(1) Adsorption chromatography.

(2) Partition chromatography.

(3) Exclusion chromatography.

(4) Ion exchange chromatography.

It should be noted that partition can also be carried on paper (paper chromatography), in a column (column, partition, reversed phase and gas chromatography) or on a thin layer (thin layer chromatography). The fundamental principle of partition is, however, the same in all the techniques.

In adsorption chromatography, the stationary phase is a solid (*e.g.,* alumina, silica gel etc.). The solutes are adsorbed in different parts of the adsorbent column. The adsorbed components are then eluted by passing suitable solvents or eluents (mobile phase : liquid) through the column. When a column is used in such type of chromatography, the technique is known as **column chromatography.**

In partition chromatography, the stationary phase may be a liquid strongly adsorbed on a solid which acts as a support.

Thin layer chromatography (TLC) is a special type of adsorption chromatography in which a glass plate coated with a thin layer of the adsorbent is used as a stationary phase.

Phase combination in adsorption and partition chromatography are given in the Table 12.2

Table 12.2 **Classification of Multistage Fraction Procedures**

Phase type		Name of the process	Sample of phase	Second phase
Solid liquid	1.	Adsorption chromatography	Solution	Solid adsorbent
	2.	Thin layer chromatography	Solution	Fine powder supported on a glass plate
	3.	Ion exchange chromatography	Solution	Ion exchange resin
Liquid liquid	1.	Counter current separation	Solution	Immiscible solvent
	2.	Partition chromatography	Solution	Immiscible solvent on solid matrix
	3.	Paper chromatography	Solution	Immiscible solvent on solid paper matrix
	4.	Thin layer chromatography	Solution	Immiscible solvent on fine powder supported on a glass plate
	5.	Gel chromatography	Solution	Solvent held in the intersties of a polymetric solvent.
Liquid gas	1.	Fractional distillation	Gas	Condensed liquid
	2.	Gas liquid chromatography	Gas	Solvent held on solid matrix
Gas solid	1.	Gas solid chromatography	Gas	Solid adsorbent

Table 12.3

Stationary phase	Mobile phase	Types of chromatography
Solid	Liquid	Adsorption
Solid	Gas	Adsorption
Liquid	Liquid	Partition
Liquid	Gas	Partition

The adsorbents must have large surface area and high porosity. The distribution of solute takes place throughout the stationary phase and not only on the surface as in the case of adsorption. Here is partition, solubility of the solute in two phase is of great importance. **The process would, in general be identical to solvent extraction if the system is static rather than dynamic.**

It should be noted that forces which control adsorption are also those which can influence solubility in partitioning of the solute between the two phases. For example, solubility is greatly affected by hydrogen bonds, dipole interactions and charge transfer processes between solute and solvent molecules.

Fundamental Concepts

One of the most fundamental concepts, as well as one which is of great practical significance, is the relationship describing the amount of solute retained by one phase in relation to another phase. This relationship is usually known as **distribution coefficient,** K**,** and can be expressed as

$$K = \frac{C_1}{C_2} \qquad ...(1)$$

where, C_1 and C_2 are the concentrations of the solute in phase I and phase II respectively. The value of K depends upon temperature, pressure and independent of concentration. The value of K can be modified for a particular chromatographic technique.

In partition methods and also in solvent extraction, the distribution coefficient is called the partition coefficient, C_1 is then the concentration of solute in stationary phase (C_S) and C_2 is the concentration of solute in the mobile phase (C_M). Thus,

$$K_p = \frac{C_S}{C_M} \qquad ...(2)$$

The larger the K_p value, the greater is the retention of the solute in the stationary phase.

The **coefficient describing adsorption** is defined like the partition coefficient except that C_S is the amount of solute adsorbed by the stationary phase and C_M is the amount of solute in the mobile phase where both are expressed in the same units. Hence, a large adsorption coefficient indicates a high retention for the solute.

In ion exchange, the distribution coefficient is modified to account for the volume of solution and weight of resin. Thus,

$$K_D = \frac{\text{Amount of ion on resin per gm of resin}}{\text{Amount of ion in solution per mL of solution}} \qquad ...(3)$$

K_D **is referred to as batch distribution coefficient.**

In sheet methods, retention of solute, whether by partition or adsorption, is described by its migration relative to that of the eluting agent. This ratio has the symbol R_F and R_R, where, R_F is for linear flow in one direction and R_R is for linear flow in radial direction. Both are expressed as

$$R_F \text{ (or } R_R) = \frac{\text{Distance travelled by solute}}{\text{Distance travelled by mobile phase}} \quad \ldots(4)$$

As R_F increases, the retention of solute decreases.

The R_F values change with the type of migration, adsorbent and solvent. The concentration effects are minor in case of **partition**, while the R_F value generally decreases with decreasing solute concentration in **adsorption.** In addition, for getting reproducible R_F values, the experimental conditions, such as the nature and type of solvent, nature and type of adsorbent, porosity of the adsorbent, concentration, and temperature should be properly controlled.

Resolution

The effectiveness of the separation is determined by two general factors. Distance between zone centres as they migrate and compactness of zones.

As the distance between the zone centres increases the degree of separation increases and measure of this difference is called resolution.

As zones travel, however, they tend to spread and broaden and even though zone centres are well separated, overlapping of the bands can occur.

In general, resolution is affected by the distribution coefficient for the second component of the two component mixture, the selectivity, and the number of theoretical plates corresponding to the second component. As each of these increases, the separation of the two components increases.

Selectivity

It is a measure of the preference a stationary phase shows for one solute over another, and is expressed as,

$$\alpha = \frac{K_1}{K_2} \quad \ldots(5)$$

where, K_1 and K_2 are distribution coefficients for two different solutes. The choice of which is K_1 and K_2 is arbitrary, however, for the sake of convenience K_1 is usually referred as slower moving solute.

The selectivity α describes the relative rates of migration of two solutes and thus a direct measure of zone separation. The greater the difference between the distribution ratios, the larger the value of α and hence better the separation.

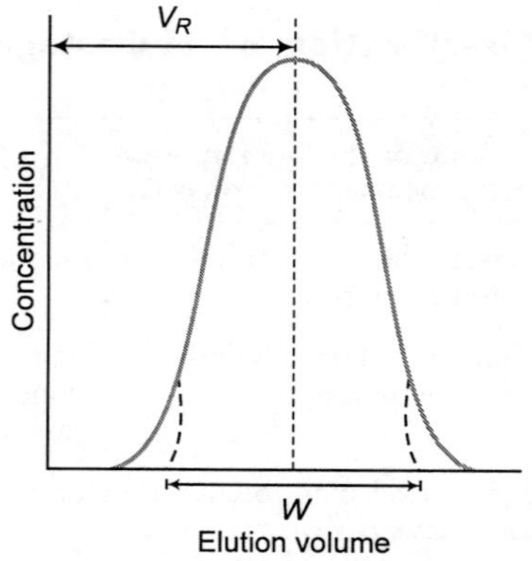

Calculation of the number of plates from an elution peak.

Efficiency

In chromatography, efficiency can be expressed in terms of number of theoretical plates N, or the height equivalent to a theoretical plate, H (or HETP). The two are related as,

$$H = \frac{L}{N} \quad \ldots(6)$$

where, L is the column length. In general, a **theoretical plate** is defined as that length of column in which the solute undergoes one complete equilibration between the two phases. The number of plates is given by

$$N = 16\left(\frac{V_R}{W}\right)^2 \quad \ldots(7)$$

where, V_R is the **retention volume** (= Retention time × flow rate of solvent) and W is the width of the elution peak in volume units. (See equation (iv)). Retention volume in equation (vii) can be replaced by **retention time** which means that the width is measured in time units.

The value of H is a measure of the efficiency of the chromatographic system. The smaller the value of H, the more efficient and better the resolution is for the particular column and experimental conditions. The value of H is thus a measure of the efficiency of the chromatographic systems. Since, N is inversely related to H, an increase in N improves the efficiency and resolution.

Assuming the system to be in equilibrium, ***H* is independent of length and depends on particle size of the stationary phase, diffusion coefficient of the solute in the mobile phase, rate of flow of mobile phase, and the kinetics of the system.** However, the value of N is directly proportional to length of band travel. So, an increase in the length increases the number of plates, which increases the resolution. It has been observed that **a 4 fold increase in the column length increases the peak to peak distance by 4 and the resolution by a factor of 2.**

It should be noted that the length of the column can not be increased without optimum limits, because increasing the length excessively often leads to broad bands. Since, the solute is diluted, it becomes more difficult to detect. Moreover, the separation can be much time consuming and very wasteful as far as eluting agent in concerned.

Chromatographic Development

Development is the process of passing of mobile phase over the adsorbent or support. During development sample components isolate themselves into zones or bands. The process of development is also called **elution**. Mobile phase used for the development is called **eluting agent**. The entire process represents a chromatogram in which the zones are detected or visualised.

Chromatographic development may be carried out by the following four techniques.

1. Elution development. 2. Gradient elution.
3. Frontal analysis.
4. Displacement development.

Although each of these techniques can be theoretically applied to all chromatographic procedures, yet in actual practice, elution has been used more widely than the others.

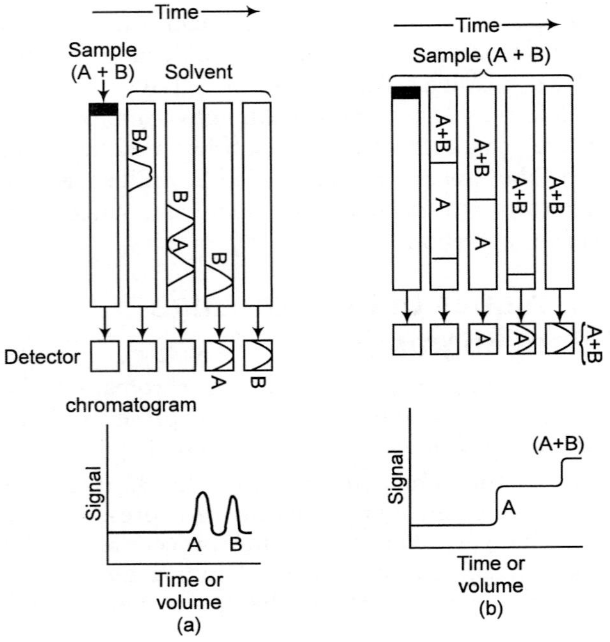

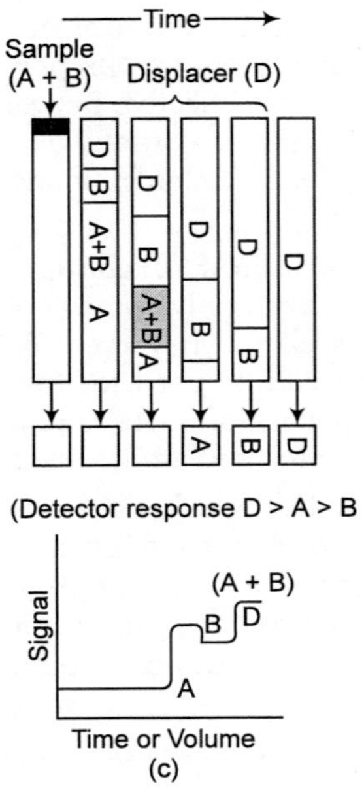

Fig. 12.4 Schematic diagram showing three methods of column operation. (a) Elution analysis (b) Frontal analysis (c) Displacement analysis.

Ion Exchange Chromatography

It is a process in which an interchange of ions of like sign takes place between a solution and essentially insoluble solid (ion exchanger) in contact with the solution. In ion exchange chromatography, a reversible exchange of ions is possible between ions in a liquid phase (**mobile phase**) and a solid, insoluble substance containing ionic sites **(called ion exchange resin).**

Ion exchange resins consists of beads of highly polymerised, crosslinked, organic materials containing large number of acidic or basic groups. Although the resins are insoluble in water, the active groups are hydrophilic and have varying degrees of affinity for ionic solutes.

There are four basic types of resins which are commonly used in ion exchange chromatography.

1. **Strongly acidic cation exchange resins** Sulphonated polystyrene resins belong to this class. They are useful between the pH range 1-14. These are used mainly in the fractionation of cations, inorganic separations, lanthanides, vitamins,peptides, and amino acids.
2. **Weakly acidic cation exchange resins** Carboxylic polymethacrylate is an example of such type of resins. They are effective between pH 5 and 14. These are useful in fractionation of cations, biochemical separations, transition elements, amino acids, antibiotics, and organic bases.

3. **Strongly basic anion exchange resins** Quaternary ammonium polystyrene belongs to this class and it is effective between pH 0 and 12. This type of resins are useful in fractionation of anions, halogens, alkaloids, vitamin B complex, fatty acids, etc.
4. **Weakly basic anion exchange resins** Phenol formaldehyde and polyamine polystyrene resins belong to this class. They are effective in the pH range 0-9 and can be used for the fractionation of anionic complexes of metals, anions of different valencies, vitamins and amino acids.

At pH below 5, the weak acid resins are highly dissociated and under such circumstances cation exchange becomes almost negligible. Similarly, weakly basic resins are so highly dissociated above pH 9 that anion exchange becomes negligible.

Ion exchangers, generally used now a days are synthetic polymers, most frequently copolymers of polystyrene and divinyl benzene. Cation exchangers contain groups such as RSO_3H, $RCOOH$ and R—OH in which the hydrogen can be replaced by cations. Anion exchangers contain groups such as A—$N(CH_3)_2$, A_2—NH and A—NH_2 capable of exchanging their anion (A) for anions in the solution.

A cation exchange process is illustrated with the equilibrium.

$$\underset{\text{Solid}}{xRSO_3^-H^+} + \underset{\text{Solution}}{M^{2+}} \longrightarrow \underset{\text{Solid}}{(RSO_3^-)^x M^{x+}} + \underset{\text{Solution}}{xH^+}$$

where, M^{x+} represents a cation and R represents a part of the resin molecule.

Similarly, a typical anion exchange reaction can be represented as,

$$\underset{\text{Solid}}{xRN(CH_3)_3^+OH^-} + \underset{\text{Solution}}{A^{x-}} \rightleftharpoons \underset{\text{Solid}}{(RN(CH_3)_3^+)_x A^{x-}} + \underset{\text{Solution}}{xOH^-}$$

The identity of the mobile ion attached to an ion exchange resin can be determined by the electrolyte content of the solution with which the resin is in contact. For example, the following exchange takes place when a sulphonic acid resin is treated with a solution of NaCl.

$$RSO_3^-H^+ + Na^+ \rightleftharpoons R\,SO_3^-Na^+ + H^+$$

Similarly, if anion exchange resin is treated with NaCl solution, the reaction,

$$RN(CH_3)_3^+OH^- + Cl^- \rightleftharpoons RN(CH_3)_3^+Cl^- + OH^+$$

is strongly favoured.

If a sulphonic acid resin is treated with Ca^{2+} ions, the equilibrium can be represented as,

$$(RSO_3^-H^+)_2 + Ca^{2+} \rightleftharpoons (RSO_3^-)_2Ca^{2+} + 2H^+$$

Thus, more than one functional units of the resin are also involved in exchange reactions with polyvalent ions.

Amphoteric electrolytes are the sorbents capable of both cation exchange and anion exchange.

Crosslinking is very important in ion exchange resins, because it affects swelling and strength of the resin. **As the crosslinking in the resin decreases, the resin swelling increases.** Divinyl benzene is the most commonly employed crosslinking agent and imparts strength to the polymer by joining the chains together at various positions. The structure of a typical cation and anion exchange resin are

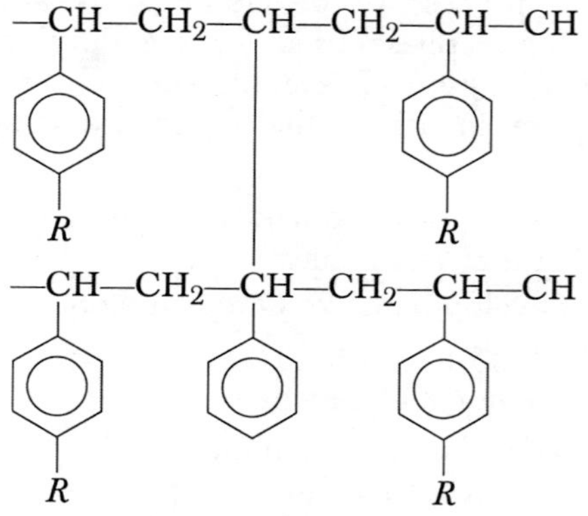

where, R is either —$SO_3^-H^+$ or —$CH_2N(RH_3)_3^+Cl^-$.

Particle size is also an important factor on which the effective separation is based. Finer and more uniform particles (particle size range of 50–100 mesh or 100–200 mesh) are most commonly employed for effective separation. Since, equilibrium constant upon which the separation depends is influenced by **temperature changes,** the latter also affects the effective separation.

Techniques of Ion Exchange Chromatography

In ion exchange chromatography, the chromatographic support contains ions which are capable of being exchanged with ionic solutes in the mobile phase.

A chromatographic column (Fig. 12.13) is packed with an ion exchanger so that no air is present in the ion exchanger layer. Before the procedure the ion exchanger should be converted into a definite ion exchange form (a cation exchanger is charged with

H^+ ions and an anion exchanger, with OH^- ions) by passing a definite amount of acid (base) through it. Excess of acid (or base) is then washed with water. The sample is percolated through the column at a definite rate, and the column is washed with water on another eluent. The ion exchanger must always be covered with a layer of liquid. The elute can be collected either as a whole or in fraction.

Ions adsorbed by the ion exchanger can be eluted with a suitable solvent. In practice, cation exchangers are regenerated by eluting with acids.

$$RM + H^+ \rightleftharpoons RH + M^+$$

while anion exchangers are eluted with an alkali.

$$RA + OH^- \rightleftharpoons ROH + A^-$$

Separation Factor

Ion exchange chromatography is based on the exchange of ions between a solid ion exchanger and ions present in the solution. The exchange of ions obeys the **law of mass action.** For example, the equilibrium between the ion exchanger and the solution can be represented as,

$$RA + B^+ \rightleftharpoons RB + A^+ \qquad \ldots(8)$$

The conditional ion exchange equilibrium constant in the first approximation can be expressed as,

$$\frac{[B^-]}{[A^-]} = K_{A,B} \frac{[B^+]}{[A^+]}$$

where, $[B^-]$ and $[A^-]$ are the concentrations of ions in the solid phase and $[B^+]$ and $[A^+]$ are the concentrations of ions in the liquid phase. $K_{A,B}$ is a conditional ion exchange equilibrium constant. It should be noted that **sorption of ions depends on the following important factors**

(a) Nature and structure of the ion exchanger.
(b) Nature of analysed substances.
(c) Experimental conditions such as pH, temperature, etc.

For dilute solutions, the activities may be replaced by the concentrations of exchanging ions in solution, because activity coefficients are equal to unity. The activities of ions in an ion exchanger may also be replaced by the concentrations if the ratio of activities of ions raised to powers corresponding to the reciprocal values of ionic charges is assumed to be a constant quantity. Thus, if ion exchange proceeds according to the equation,

$$Z_2 M_1 A_{Z_1} + Z_1 M_2^{Z_2+} \rightleftharpoons Z_1 M_2 A_{Z_1} + Z_2 M_1^{Z_1+}$$

where, Z_1 and Z_2 = Charges of exchanging ions

M_1 and M_2 = First and second exchanging ions of metals

A = Anion of resin

Applying law of mass action,

$$K = \frac{[M_2 Z_{Z_2}]^{Z_1} \, [M_1^{Z_1+}]^{Z_2}}{[M_1 A_{Z_1}]^{Z_2} \, [M_2^{Z_2+}]^{Z_1}} \qquad \ldots(9)$$

or

$$\frac{[M_2 A_{Z_2}]^{1/Z_2}}{[M_1 A_{Z_1}]^{1/Z_1}} = K_c \frac{C_2^{1/Z_2}}{C_1^{1/Z_1}} \qquad \ldots(10)$$

where, C_1 and C_2 are the concentrations of exchanging ions in solution and K_c is concentration exchange constant which depends on temperature and the chemical nature (the charge, and size of ions and their hydration) of exchanging ions and ion exchanger. It characterises the strength of incorporation of a given ion in the lattice of an ion exchange resin. For multicharged cations higher the exchange constant the greater is the charge of the cation and it increases with atomic number of the element involved.

Equation (10) is known as **Nikolsky equation** and is valid if the volume of the ion exchanger does not change in the course of an experiment, the ions in the solution do not react with the ion exchange radical, molecular and ionic sorption is absent, and the ions to be separated freely permeate into ion exchanger.

Each ion exchanger is capable of adsorbing a definite number of ions, *i.e.,* it exhibits a definite **capacity. Static exchange capacity** may be defined as the number of milligram equivalents of the ion adsorbed per a certain time interval by 1 g of the dry ion exchanger. **The thermodynamic exchange capacity** may be defined as the number of ions adsorbed by a layer of ion exchanger 20 cm high and 1 cm^2 in the cross section at the rate of migration of 0.5 dm^2 per hour.

The adsorptive effect of an ion is characterised by the distribution coefficient.

$$D = \frac{Cr \cdot m}{Cs \cdot V} \qquad \ldots(11)$$

Where Cr and Cs are the equilibrium concentrations of ions in the respective phase and m is the mass of the exchanger in grams. V is the volume of aqueous phase in cm^3.

The separation factor α is the ratio of the distribution coefficients of the two components (for ions of like charge). Thus,

$$\alpha = \frac{D_A}{D_B} \quad \ldots(12)$$

where, D_A and D_B are the distribution coefficients of two components.

Example 4. *How many grams of cation exchanger in the H^+ form are required to separate Ca^{2+} ions from 1 dm^3 of 0.1 N $CaCl_2$? The static exchange capacity in 0.1 N $CaCl_2$ is 4.5 mg equivalents.*

Sol. We know

$$D = \frac{Cr \cdot m}{Cs \cdot V} \quad \text{or} \quad m = \frac{D \cdot Cs \cdot V}{Cr}$$

The quantity Cr/D is the static exchange capacity of the cation exchanger. Hence,

$$m = \frac{0.1 \times 1000}{4.5} = \mathbf{22.22\ g}$$

Factors Affecting Separation Factor

Hydrated ions with a smaller radius as a greater charge have higher distribution coefficients and therefore similar elements are eluted from the column in the following sequence.

Li, Na, K, Rb, Cs

Mg, Ca, Sr, Ba,

Lu, Yb, Tu, Er, Ho, Dy, Tb, Gd, Eu, Sm, Pm, Ce, La

A considerably more complete separation can be achieved in complex forming elution. In this case, desorption can be accomplished with the help of a solution of a compound which, together with the cation absorbed by the resin, forms a complex ion bearing a charge of opposite sign. For example, in the desorption of the cations of rare earth elements by a citrate solution, the cations pass into solution as the complex ion, $M(C_6H_5O_7)_2^{3-}$.

Better separation takes place if there is an equilibrium between the ions in the solution and on the ion exchange resin. An increase in the surface area of the ion exchanger also improves the conditions for attainment of an equilibrium and separation. For good separation to be ensured, the solution must be passed slowly through the ion exchange resin. **The rate of attainment of equilibrium is also affected by the temperature.** A rise in temperature in many cases improves the result of separation. The temperature, however, changes also the equilibrium constant of the exchange, which may either improve or impair the separation conditions.

The separation is also influenced by the **composition of cation exchange resin.** Resins with high content of divinyl benzene have a high swelling ability and ion exchange capacity.

The length of column also plays an important role in separation process. For the separation to proceed more rapidly, the columns are expected to be short. Short columns are used for separation of anions and cations. Columns of greater length are needed for the separation of cations.

If cations, anions or complexes differ only slightly in their properties, columns of great length must be used.

Applications of Ion Exchange Chromatography

Ion exchange chromatography has proved to be an excellent tool for solving many complicated problems in the field of biology, organic and inorganic chemistry. Some important applications of ion exchange chromatography are briefly described below.

1. Determination of sodium and potassium in the mixture

According to **Beukenkamp and Reiman,** the separation of potassium and sodium ions in a mixture can be done by introducing the sample at the top of a column containing a sulphonic acid resin saturated with H^+ ions (acidic Form). The column is then eluted with a solution of 0.7 M HCl at a flow rate of 0.6 mL/sq min. Sodium ions, being the less strongly held, move down the column more rapidly and can be collected before potassium ions appear in the effluent. The solutions are evaporated to dryness and the alkali chlorides weighted. Divalent ions, if present, do not come out of the cation exchange resin until all the potassium ions have appeared in the effluent. Partition of the sodium ions in each theoretical plate of the column involves,

$$R^-H^+ + Na^+ \rightleftharpoons R^-Na^+ + H^+$$

The potassium ion behaves in a similar way but its partition coefficient is numerically larger. The alkali chlorides are then redissolved and analysed by titration of the Cl^- ion by the Mohr method.

A complete separation of Na^+ and K^+ ions is shown in the Fig. 12.5.

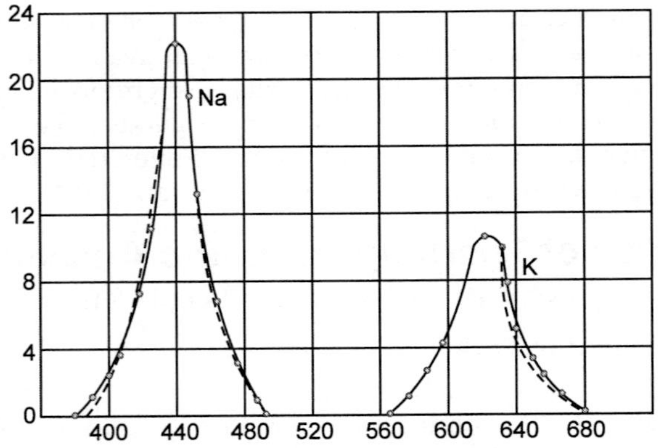

Fig. 12.5 Ion exchange separation of Na^+ and K^+ on a cation exchange resin.

2. **Separation of interfering ions of opposite charge**

Ion exchange resins have also been used for the removal of interfering ions, particularly where these ions have a charge opposite to the species being determined. For example, Fe (III), Al (III) and other cations cause interference in the determination of sulphate, because of their tendency to coprecipitate with barium sulphate. The solution to be analysed is passed through a column containing a cation exchange resin, as a result of which all cations are retained and corresponding number of protons (H^+) are liberated. The sulphate ion passes unhindered through the column and its analysis can be performed on the effluent.

Similarly phosphate ion, which interferes in the analysis of Ba^{2+} or Ca^{2+} can be removed by passing the sample solution through a column containing an anion exchange resin. Ion exchange chromatography has also been used to remove PO_4^{3-} from a solution in which cations are being determined by the acid-alkali or sulphide-alkali scheme of analysis, or M^{3+} is being determined quantitatively in the form of hydroxides; to remove trivalent metal cations from a solution where sulphate sulphur is determined by gravimetric techniques, and so on. In the first case, when the solution is passed through the cation exchanger, the cations are sorbed, while the phosphate ion remains in the solution. For the subsequent removal of the cations from the cation exchanger, HCl is used as the eluent. This acid shift the equilibrium of ion exchange (I) to the left, the cation exchanger again passes over into the H^+ form, and the cations enter the solution containing no PO_4^{3-} ions. While determining SO_4^{2-}, ions of trivalent metals are separated by passing the solution through a strongly acidic cation exchanger. H_2SO_4 remains in the solution, where it is determined.

3. **Separation of amphoteric metals from non-amphoteric metals**

Ion exchange chromatography has successfully been used in the separation of constituents of a mixture, separation of cations from anions, isolation of cations, isolation of anions, etc. In these cases amphoterism, complex formation and regulation of acidity of solutions are frequently used. For example, when **non-amphoteric metals** such as Fe, Cu, etc., are separated from **amphoteric metals** such as Zn, Sn, Al, etc., the mixture is passed through a column packed with a cation exchanger and then washed with an alkali solution. The non-amphoteric metals are adsorbed by the cation exchanger as hydroxides while the amphoteric metals are eluted as AlO_2^-, ZnO^{2-} ions, etc.

4. **Separation of metals, alloys and high alloy steels**

Pure metals, alloys and high alloy steels can be analysed using complexation processes. The method is based on the different stability of the complexes formed at a definite pH value. For example, addition of HCl to a mixture of Cu^{2+}, Zn^{2+}, Cd^{2+}, Pb^{2+} and Bi^{3+} ions produces the chloride complexes $[CuCl_4]^{2-}$, $[ZnCl_4]^{2-}$, $[CdCl_4]^{2-}$, $[PbCl_3]^-$ and $[BiCl_4]^-$. Their stability increases from copper to bismuth. The solution obtained is percolated through a column packed with an anion exchanger, which absorbs all the complexes. The metals are then eluted successively with dilute HCl, water and nitric acid. 2 N HCl elutes copper, 6 N HCl elutes zinc, 0.3 N HCl elutes cadmium, lead is eluted with water and bismuth is eluted with HNO_3.

5. **Identification of Ions**

The selectivity of colourless ion exchangers can be used to detect coloured ions in a mixture. Depending on their sorptivity, the ions are distributed in the cation exchanger by zones, namely, the lower the sorptivity of a cation, the lower in the column will its zone be. The separation of a mixture into differentially coloured zones, enables us to obtain a chromatogram with the characteristic colours of the relevant ions. For example, in the separation of simple ions (monovalent cations) on a strongly acidic exchanger, the relative affinities for water are $Li^+ < H^+ < Na^+ < NH_4^+ < K^+ < Rb^+ < Cs^+ < Ag^+$ and Ti^+. This shows that lithium ion is least strongly held on the resin. A comparable scale for divalent ions is :

$$UO_2^{2+} < Mg^{2+} < Zn^{2+} < Co^{2+} < Cu^{2+} < Cd^{2+} < Ni^{2+} < Ca^{2+} < Sr^{2+} < Pb^{2+} < Ba^{2+}$$

For ions carrying the same charge, the exchange ability increases with a decrease in the radius of the hydrated ion. For example,

$$Al^{3+} > Ni^{2+} \approx Co^{2+} > Cd^{2+} > Mg^{2+} > NH_4^{2+} \approx K^+ > Na^+$$

Methods for separating and identifying all the most important ions are developed. Methods for partial and complete analysis of mixtures of cations as well as anions have also been developed. The chromatograms so obtained are then examined visually, in UV light, with radioactive indicators, by measuring optical properties, dielectric constant, etc.

Thermometric or Thermoanalytical Methods

The thermometric methods are rather distinct analytical tools which involve techniques such as **thermogravimetric analysis (TGA), derivative thermogravimetric analysis (DTG), differential thermal analysis (DTA) and thermometric titrations (also called enthalpy titrations).** Data are obtained in the form of continuously recorded curves, which may be regarded as thermal data.

Table 12.4 **Thermoanalytical Methods**

	Designation	Property measured	Apparatus
1.	Thermogravimetric analysis (TGA)	Change in weight	Thermobalance
2.	Derivative thermogravimetric analysis (DTG)	Rate of exchange of weight	Thermobalance
3.	Differential thermal analysis (DTA)	Heat evolved or absorbe7d	DTA apparatus
4.	Thermometric titrations	Change of temperature	Titration calorimeter

In addition to the above thermoanalytical methods, other thermometric methods are also possible (which are less used at present). We shall discuss only the above analytical methods in some details.

Thermogravimetric Analysis (TGA)

The technique of thermogravimetric analysis is concerned with an analysis of the sample weight change curve. The technique involves change in weight of a system under examination as the temperature is increased at a predetermined and preferably at a linear rate. Although manual recording methods have been employed, but by the use of an automatic recording thermobalance, a curve of weight change of the sample *vs* sample temperature can be obtained directly. Thermogravimetric analysis has widely been used in recent years, because of the commercial availability of automatic, continuously recording thermobalances. These are reliable, rugged and very accurate. The first thermobalance was originated by **P. Chevenard (1944)** and extensively employed by **Duval et. al. (1953).**

Types of Thermogravimetric Analysis

Thermogravimetric analysis is usually of two types :

(i) Dynamic TGA

In this type of analysis, the sample is subjected to conditions of continuous increase in temperature usually linear with time.

(ii) Isothermal or static TGA

In this type of analysis, the sample is maintained at a constant temperature for a period of time during which any changes in weight are noted.

Principle and Method

The principle of the technique can be illustrated by the weight loss curve of a hypothetical compound $MCO_3 \cdot 2H_2O$ as shown in the Fig. 12.6.

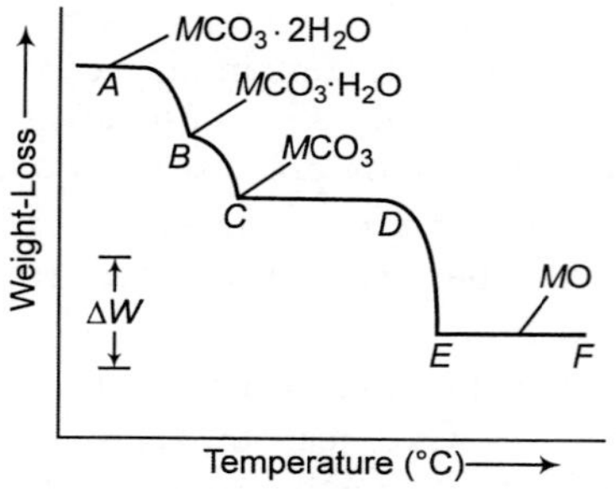

Fig. 12.6

It is evident from the Fig. 12.6 that water is evolved beginning at *A*. The temperature at *A* is called minimum weight loss temperature. A break is obtained in the curve at *B* due to the stoichiometry approaching that of $MCO_3 \cdot H_2O$. Further heating results in the formation of anhydrous MCO_3 weight levels from *C* to *D*. The drying temperature for MCO_3 should therefore be placed somewhere between *C* and *D*, the values of *C* and *D* depend upon heating rate of the furnace; a slower heating rate will shift these temperatures to lower values. At point *D*, the compound MCO_3 starts to evolve CO_2 giving *M*O weight level from *E* to *F*. The thermal stabilities of the original sample, the intermediate compounds and the final products can then be ascertained from an examination of the various regions in the curve. The curve is quantitative in that the calculation can be made to determine the stoichiometry of the compound at any given temperature.

The method of thermogravimetric analysis may be made more clear from the adjacent thermogram for calcium oxalate monohydrate (Fig. 12.7).

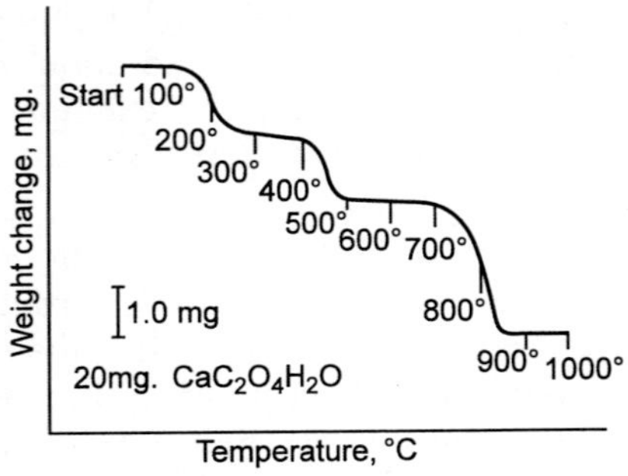

Fig. 12.7

The curve is known as decomposition curve. Plateaus, indicative of constant weight, represent stable phase over the particular temperature interval. Inflection in the curve represents either the formation of an intermediate compound or the absorption of a volatile compound on (or in) the new solid phase. In the figure 12.28 successive plateaus correspond to the anhydrous salt, calcium carbonate and calcium oxide.

An example is the analysis of copper silver alloys based on the relative stabilities of the nitrates.

$AgNO_3$ is stable up to 473°C, where it starts decomposing into NO_2 and O_2 and at 608°C only metallic silver is left behind. Cupric nitrate, $Cu(NO_3)_2$ however, decomposes into CuO in two steps. CuO remains stable up to 950°C.

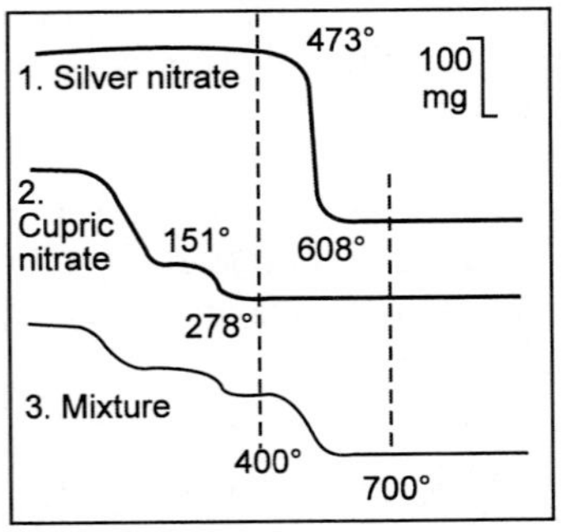

Fig. 12.8 Examples of curves taken with a thermobalance.

In the interpretation of the thermogravimetric curve, it should be noted that the decomposition temperature is a function of method, apparatus and procedure. Moreover, the balance must be calibratd preferably each time it is used by placing a known weight on the pan, to give a reference mark, such as that in the upper right corner of Fig. 12.8. Correction must also be applied for the apparent weight change of the empty sample pan to get the actual weight change taking place in the specimen. The apparent weight changes is usually caused by the interplay of a complex combination of various factors, such as container geometry, radiation effect, the atmosphere in the furnace, air buoyancy, conduction effects in the furnace, etc.

The shape of the corrected thermogravimetric curve depends upon the following factors

1. The rate of heating.
2. The crucible, and
3. The atmosphere.

It has been observed that at a particular temperature, the extent of decomposition is greater at a slow rate of heating than for a similar sample heated at a faster rate. The difference between the sample temperature and furnace temperature is also influenced by the heat of reaction.

If the reaction is exothermic, the sample temperature leads the furnace temperature, but if the reaction is endothermic, the furnace temperature leads the sample temperature. The use of a small finely divided sample is to be preferred.

Automatic Thermogravimetric Analysis

One of the useful contributions of the thermobalance has been the technique of automatic thermogravimetric analysis which is of great importance in analytical chemistry. The principle of this technique can be illustrated by using the following curves (Fig. 12.9).

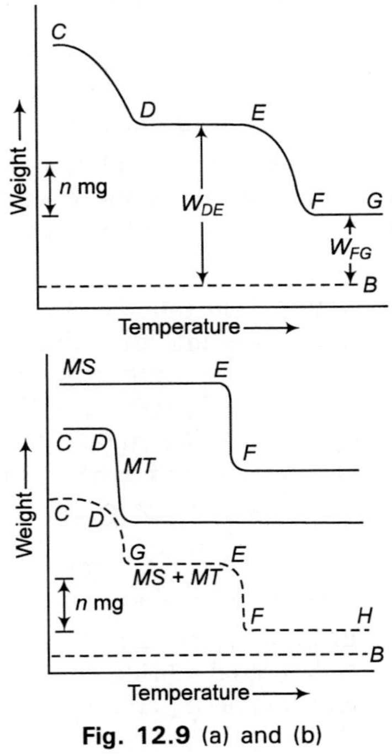

Fig. 12.9 (a) and (b)

In the case of a single component system, the base line of the thermobalance is first determined as indicated by the line B in the Fig. 12.30 (a). The wet sample is then placed in the sample container and heated. The weight change curve is recorded as usual and from the horizontal weight level DE, the weight W_{DE} can be obtained. Similarly, the weight W_{FG} can be obtained from weight level W_{FG}. Multiplication of W_{DE} and W_{FG} by appropriate gravimetric factors then gives the weight of metal ion present, since the weight levels DE and FG indicate that a definite compound stoichiometry has been attained.

For a binary mixture the same procedure is carried out. The weight loss curves for pure MS and MT and for a mixture of $MS + MT$ are indicated in Fig. 12.30 (b). Horizontal levels are obtained (in the curve for the mixture) at the same temperature as were found for the pure compounds. Thus, the amount of MT and MS can be obtained in the mixture curve from BG and EF respectively. The analysis of a binary and even ternary mixture can be carried out rapidly in this manner in a single operation.

Factors Affecting Results

There are two important factors upon which the TGA depends. These are

(i) Instrumental factors, (ii) Sample characteristics

(i) Instrumental factors

Furnace heating rate, recording chart speed, furnace atmosphere, geometry of sample holder, geometry of the furnace, sensitivity of recorder and recording balance and composition of sample container are the various factors which are instrumental.

For example, if a substance is allowed to heat at a **faster heating rate,** the decomposition temperature will be higher than that obtained at a **slower rate of heating.**

Furnace atmosphere also influences the TG curves. For example, decomposition of calcium carbonate takes place at a much higher temperature if it is carried out in an atmosphere of CO_2 instead of N_2. The effect of furnace atmosphere may be studied by considering the following reversible and irreversible reactions.

(a) X (Solid) $\rightleftharpoons$ Y (Solid) + Z (Gas)

(b) X (Solid) $\longrightarrow$ Y (Solid) + Z (Gas)

(c) X (Solid) + Y (Gas) $\longrightarrow$ Z (Solid) + Z (Gas)

The function of inert gas in the furnace is to remove the gaseous products liberated during thermogravimetric analysis in reactions (a) and (b) and to stop the reaction (c) from taking place.

The reaction (a) and not the reaction (b) is affected, if the atmosphere in the furnace has the same gas as is evolved during thermogravimetric analysis. If composition of gas (Y) in reaction (c) is changed, then the effect on the reaction will depend upon the nature of the gas in the atmosphere. For example, the TG curve will be affected by oxidisng or reducing gas introduced.

It is, however, desirable to maintain the nature of atmospheric gas as constant as possible throughout the experiment and it is achieved by heating the sample in vacuum. In thermogravimetric analysis, there, are, infact, three common furnace atmospheres. These are **static air** (air from air is passed through the furnace), **Dynamic air** (compressed air is allowed to flow through the furnace at a constant and measured rate of flow) and **inert atmosphere** (where oxygen free nitrogen gas is used as an inert atmosphere in the furnace).

The TG curve is also affeced by the **geometry of the sample holder.**

The shape of TG curve is not affected by the geometry of the sample holder when the atmosphere in the furnace is a gas evolved in the thermogravimetric analysis.

(ii) Sample characteristics

The important characteristics of the sample, which affect the TG curve or weight loss curve are the amount of sample, solubility of evolved gases in the sample, sample particle size, heat of decomposition of the reaction, sample packing, nature of the sample and thermal conductivity of the sample. For example, A deviation from linearity with the rise in temperature takes place especially in fast exothermic reaction, if a large sample is used. Liberation of CO during the decomposition of calcium oxalate to calcium carbonate is an example of this type.

$$CaC_2O_4 \longrightarrow CaCO_3 + CO$$
$$CaCO_3 \longrightarrow CaO + CO_2$$

Heat of decomposition of the reaction has also been found to affect the TG curves. Heat of decomposition has been found to change the difference between sample temperature and furnace temperature. If the decomposition is exothermic, the sample temperature leads the furnace temperature, but if the decomposition is endothermic, the sample temperature lags behind the furnace temperature.

Unfortunately, definite studies are lacking on many of the instrumental factors as well as sample characteristics. Many of these factors are fixed by the type of thermobalance. These include, sample holder geometry, recording speed, sensitivity of balance etc. It is, however, difficult to reproduce some of the sample characteristics which include, particle size, sample packing, and thermal conductivity (changes because of sintering and swelling).

Derivative Thermogravimetric Analysis (DTG)

In this type of thermodynamical method, the property measured is the rate of change of weight in a thermobalance. There is sometimes an advantage in being able to compare a thermogram with its first derivative. The Fig. 12.10 clearly indicates the relation between TGA and DTG curves for the pyrolysis of a mixture of calcium and magnesium carbonates.

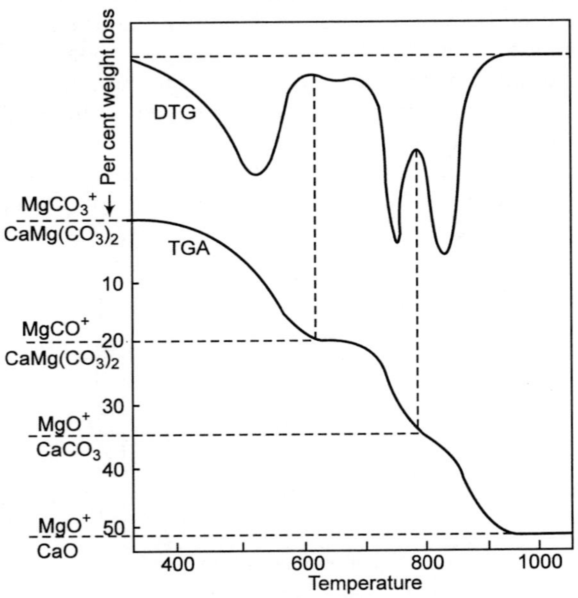

Fig. 12.10 Relation between TGA and DTG curves for the pyrolysis of mixed calcium and magnesium carbonates.

It is evident from the figure 12.10 that plateau in the thermogram at 700°C is quite clear, but the shoulder at about 870°C can only be made clear with the help of the derivative curve.

Commercial thermobalances have now been provided with electronic circuits to take the derivative automatically. Moreover, direct comparison of the DTG and TGA curve is possible with the help of a two pan recorder.

Applications

Thermogravimetric analysis has widely been used in the investigation of the following important analytical problems :

(i) Automatic gravimetric analysis.

(ii) New weighing compositions in gravimetric analysis and determination of their thermal stability ranges.

(iii) Weighing substances which are unstable at ambient temperatures such that those which absorb CO_2 and H_2O from air.

(iv) Determination of the composition of complex mixtures.

(v) Determination of the purity and thermal stability of analytical reagents, including primary and secondary standards.

(vi) Correction of errors in gravimetric analysis.

(vii) For studying the sublimation behaviour of various substances.

(viii) For deciding whether or not a precipitate should be dried or ignited.

(ix) Discovery of new methods of separation.

(x) For the evaluation of various filtration techniques, such as ignition of filter paper and so on.

(xi) For the study of properties of materials in relation to the methods useful for their preparation.

Some other applications are

1. Evaluation of suitable standards

In order to find some suitable standards in analytical chemistry, **Duval (1958)** combined TG studies with infrared absorption spectrophotometric studies and reached to the conclusion that large number of substances, such as magnesium ammonium chloride, ammonium bicarbonate and ammonium fluoride, etc., could not be used for preparing standard solutions, while compounds like sodium dichromate dihydrate, sodium cobaltinitrite, hydrazine chloride, ascorbic acid, etc., are most suitable for preparing standard solutions. He also proposed that the maximum temperature of heating of some compounds like EDTA, urea, NaF, $KHCO_3$ and $NiSO_4 \cdot 7H_2O$ should be 100°, 165°, 850°, 120° and 100°C respectively.

2. Testing of sample purity

Thermogravimetric analysis has also been used in sample purity testing. For example, an unusual weight loss below 100°C is shown in TG curve of impure sample of calcium oxalate. It was later on established by **Newkirk (1972),** that weight loss was due to some impurity in the sample, but not because of absorbed water.

3. **Study of organic compounds**

By making use of DTA in conjugation with TGA and using a derivatography, a large number of organic compounds have been studied in order to get various interesting results. For example, in the study of the decomposition of malonic acid simultaneously by TGA and DTA, it was observed that phase transition occured at 70°C with melting at 140°C followed by decomposition above 150°C.

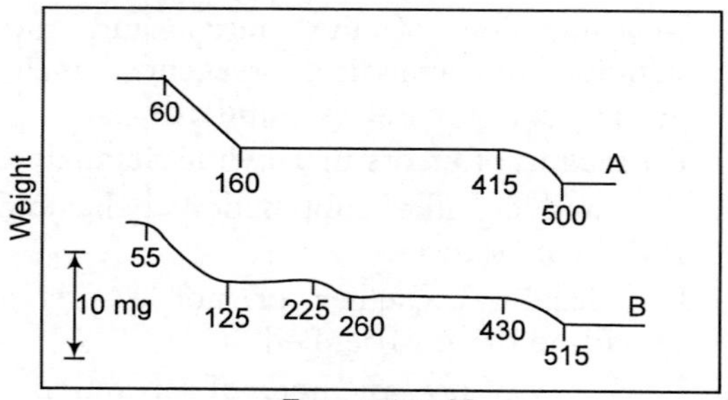

Fig. 12.11

$$COOH—CH_2—COOH \longrightarrow CO_2 + CH_3COOH$$

When glycine is studied by TGA and DTA, it is observed that during decomposition, the glycine undergoes foaming and melts with decomposition at about 220°C.

Differential Thermal Analysis (DTA)

This technique is also known as thermography. Differential thermal analysis is one in which heat effects, associated with chemical and physical changes of a substance are recorded when it is heated at a linear rate. In other words, differential thermal analysis is the technique in which the temperature difference between the sample and a thermally inert reference substance is continuously recorded as a function of furnace temperature or time. The measurement of changes in heat content is carried out by heating the two materials at elevated temperatures or cooling to subnormal temperature at a predetermined rate. The thermal effects may either be endothermic or exothermic and are caused by physical phenomena such, as fusion, crystalline structure inversions, boiling, vaporisation, sublimation and others. Some enthalpic effects are also caused by chemical reactions, such as dissociation or decomposition, oxidation, dehydration, reduction, combination, displacement, etc. In this manner endo and exothermal bands and peaks appearing on the thermograms give information regarding the detection of enthalpic changes. It has been found that most of the above transitions or reactions produce endothermic heat effects. Only a few, such as oxidation, some decomposition reactions, certain crystalline inversion reactions give exothermic heat effects. **It is also interesting to note that thermogravimetric analysis and differential thermal analysis are complementary techniques, because the information obtained by the application of the one approach is often enhanced by the application of the other method.**

Principle of Working

The principle of differential thermal analysis is based on the fact that the thermal effects associated with the physical and chemical changes described above are measured by a differential method in which the sample temperature is continuously compared against the temperature of the thermally inert reference material. The difference in temperature, called **differential temperature,** ΔT, is recorded as a function of reference material temperature (or furnace temperature) or time, assuming that the furnace temperature rise is linear with time.

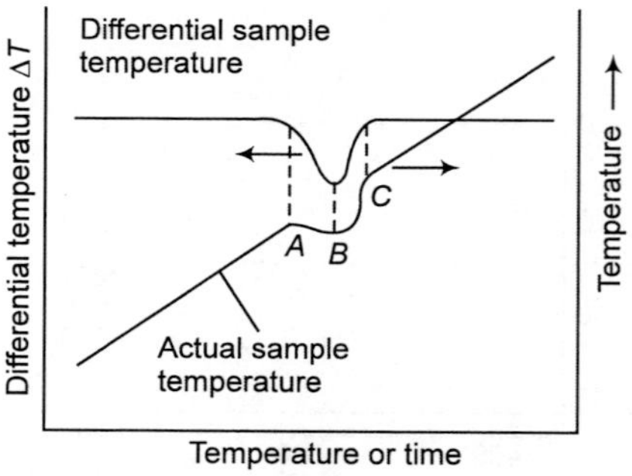

Fig. 12.12

In a typical experiment, a furnace is used which contains a sample holder or sample block, the latter of which has two identical and symmetrically located chambers. One set of thermocouple junctions is inserted into the inert material, such as aluminium oxide and the other set of thermocouple junction is placed in the other chamber containing the sample. Some other temperature detecting devices, which have also been employed, are thermistor, resistance thermometer or thermopile. The furnace and sample block temperature are then increased at a linear rate, and the temperature difference between the simple and reference material is continuously measured or recorded against the furnace or reference material temperature.

Suppose, the sample temperature and differential temperature are compared with each other as a function of time, then a curve of the type shown in Fig. 12.12 is obtained. At point *A*, it has been assumed that the sample undergoes some type of an endothermic reaction. It is also evident from the sample temperature curve that the sample temperature is no longer linear with respect to time, but lags the furnace temperature as a result of absorption of heat. The reaction becomes complete at *B* and the sample temperature increases and after sometime it becomes equal to the furnace temperature again at *C*. During the actual transition which begins at *A* the sample and reference material temperature differ ideally in the case of differential temperature curve. A peak *ABC*, with maximum at *B* is thus obtained in the curve. Beyond *B*, the curve returns to the base line $\Delta T = 0$ due to equalization of sample and reference temperatures. Although only an endothermic transition is illustrated here, the curve deviations would be in an opposite inverted position for an exothermic transition. Hence, each substance will, in general, give a curve whose number, shape and position of various endothermic and exothermic peaks act as a means of qualitative identification of the substance. The technique can also be used to evaluate quantitatively the amount of substance present by making use of the fact that the reaction is proportional to the amount of reacting substance.

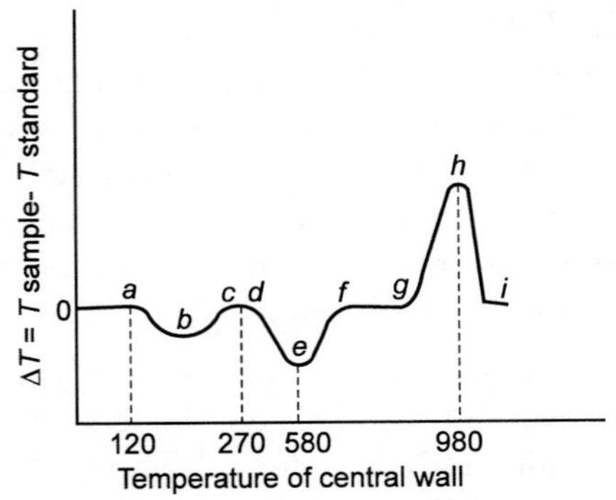

Fig. 12.13 Differential thermal curve of the clay mineral halloysite.

Let us consider the heating curve for the mineral halloysite $Al_2Si_2H_5(OH)_4$. In the figure 12.13, *a* represents the point at which water begins to evaporate off and the heat absorbed causes the thermocouple junction in the sample to lag in temperature behind the junction in the inert material. The loop *abc* on the curve represents the completion of this action. The decomposition of the mineral into water vapour, Al_2O_3 and Si_2O_3 has been represented by the deeper loop *def* in the curve. The crystallization of Al_2O_3, which is accompanied by the liberation of heat gives a sharp peak *ghi* on the curve. It is evident, therefore, that the upward loop results from an exothermic change, while downward loop results from an endothermic change.

Theory

For a sample block constructed from a metal, such as the nickel in which the sample holder geometry is a cylinder, **Boersma (1955)** derived the following equation for the peak area.

$$\int_{t_1}^{t_2} \theta \, dt = \frac{qa^2}{4\lambda} \quad \ldots(13)$$

where, t_1 and t_2 are the times at the beginning and end of the peak, θ is the differential temperature, a is the radius of the sample chamber, λ is the thermal conductivity of the sample and q is the heat of transition per unit volume.

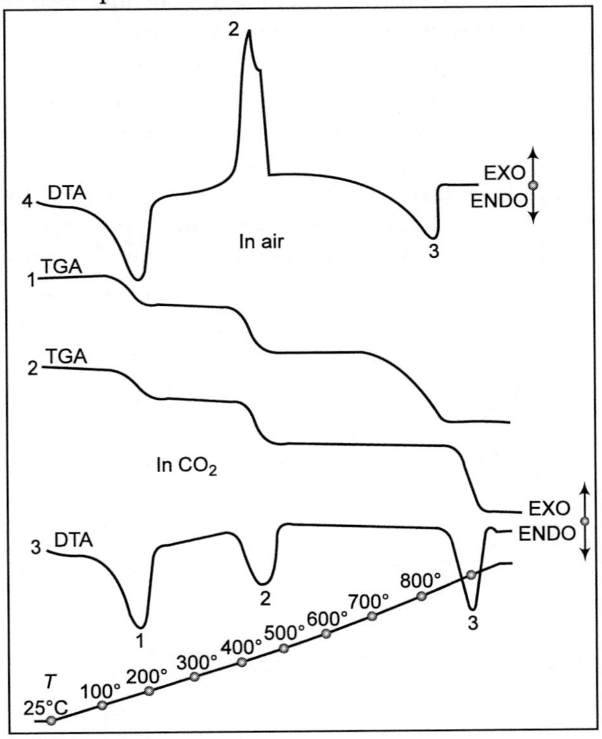

Fig. 12.14 Simultaneous DTA and TGA diagram of the decomposition of calcium oxalate monohydrate in air and in CO_2.

The sample is regarded as (i) a producer of heat, and (ii) a heat measuring resistance in which the flow of heat develops a temperature difference to be measured. Both these factors are in accordance with the above equation. To separate these two functions, **Boersma** recommended the use of metal sample and reference cups in which the temperature difference was measured from outside of the sample and reference material. Under these conditions, the peak area will be dependent upon the sample, heat of transformation and the calibration factor of the instruments. Hence, ΔH, the heat of reaction can be expressed as,

$$\Delta H = \frac{\psi}{m}\int_{1}^{2} \theta \, dt \qquad ...(14)$$

where, ψ is the experimentally determined constant and m is the mass of the sample. For a particular apparatus, if ψ is known, the heat of reaction or transformation can be calculated by using the above equation.

Simultaneous DTA-TGA Curves

The figure 12.14 indicates simultaneous DTA-TGA diagram of the decomposition of calcium oxalate monohydrate in air and in carbon dioxide.

It is evident from the curve 1 and 2 that they are identical up to the decomposition of $CaCO_3$, which requires now (in the CO_2 atmosphere) a higher temperature to decompose. Curve 3 is a differential thermogram (DTA curve) which shows the decomposition of calcium oxalate in an atmosphere of CO_2. The three points of weight loss in the curve

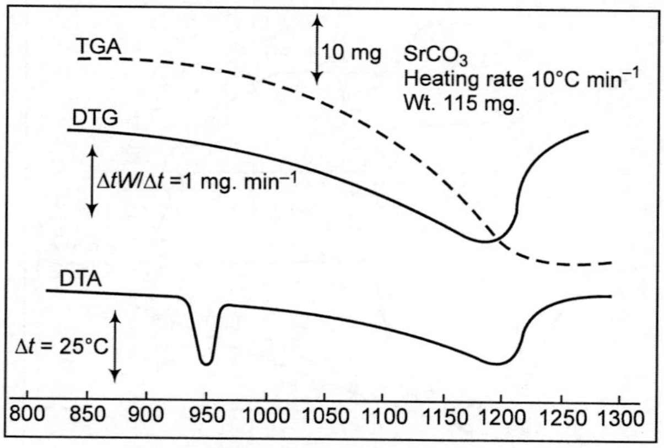

Fig. 12.15 Decomposition of $SrCO_3$ in air.

correspond to three endothermic processes. Now we come to the curve 4. It is DTA curve of calcium oxalate monohydrate in an atmosphere of air. In curve 3, all the three peaks indicate the endothermic processes, where energy is required to break the bonds in the successive elimination of H_2O, CO and CO_2. The second peak in curve 4 is sharply exothermic, but corresponds to the same weight loss as in presence of CO_2 atmosphere. The explanation for the difference lies in the exothermic burning of CO in air at the temperature of the furnace.

Now compare the Fig. 12.14 with Fig. 12.15. It is evident from both the figures that a degree of similarity exists between the curves obtained in DTG (derivative thermograms) and DTA (differential thermograms).

Derivative thermogravimetric analysis (DTG) provides information regarding the weight changes, while differential thermal analysis (DTA) gives information regarding changes in energy, irrespective of constancy or change in weight.

Applications

Differential thermal analysis is of great importance in the fields of ceramics, mineralogy and metalurgy, but it can also be useful with many other systems. Composition of mixed clays can be quickly identified. In organic studies it has been used in checking the thermal stabilities of the compounds. The analysis has also been used in checking the identities of compounds and to ensure that in a specific reaction a new compound is formed and that the producer is not simply the unreacted original product. Successful work on lubricating greases, such as lithium stearate has also been reported. Various organic systems have also been studied by **Morita (1957).**

The investigation of various solid phase reactions, phase transformation, and investigation regarding kinetics and phenomena associated with polymerisation, thermal and oxidative degradation, solvent extraction, etc., can be elegantly carried out by using differential thermal analysis.

The application of DTA to problems in **analytical chemistry** covers a broad area and includes its use as a control or routine technique for comparing similar but not identical materials.

As a **control technique,** it can be used to distinguish between raw materials quickly and easily in those cases where the treatment of the material must be modified if slight changes in the material are noticed.

As a **comparison technique,** DTA can be used to examine materials, that produce anomalous results by other methods. For example, if ΔH of the peak forming reaction is known, DTA can be used to determine the composition of mixtures containing this component.

Few illustrative example of the use of DTA are also given below.

Heat of reaction

The basic assumption of DTA is that the area enclosed by the curve peak be proportional to the heat of reaction. Taking into consideration this assumption, **Wittels (1951)** found that the peak areas obey a linear relationship to the weight of the sample, if calcite samples ranging in weight from 0.31–3.00 mg, are used. According to him curve peak area can be related with heating rate and sample mass according to the following relationship.

$$\Delta H = \frac{A}{\tan\left[\dfrac{\ln R(R-C)}{m}\right]}$$

where, R is heating rate, A peak area, m and C are constants. Maximum response of the instrument was obtained at a heating rate of 30°C per minute. The heat of reaction ΔH, can be determined, if peak area A and amount of the sample are known.

Determination of moisture content of powdered substances

Stone (1960) developed a method for the determination of moisture content of a nearly dry powdered substance by using the dynamic gas flow technique. The sample was placed in the DTA sample holder at room temperature and at atmospheric pressure. On evacuation of the sample chamber at fixed rate, the DTA curve peak began at the point (time) where the external water vapour pressure was less than the partial pressure of water vapour pressure of sample. The amount of moisture in the sample was then determined from the peak height using a calibration curve.

Linear polymer content of polyethylene

Clampitt (1963) had determined the linear polymer content of polyethylene by a DTA method. The DTA curve for the unannealed polyethylene sample obtained by him had an endothermic peak with a peak maximum temperature of 134°C, and also a small shoulder peak. After annealing the sample for half an hour at 120°C, the shoulder was resolved into two peaks with peak maximum temperatures of 115°C and 124°C. Only one peak with peak maximum temperature of 110° was obtained for a pure high pressure polyethylene sample. The area under the 115°C peak decreased, while the area under 124°C peak increased as the amount of linear polymer increased. Assuming that all of the linear polyethylene was crystallized, then using a proportionality constant and area under the 124°C peak, the amount of linear content of the sample was calculated.

Characterisation of rare earth chlorides

Wendeandt and Bear (1959) have successfully characterised the rare earth chloride hydrates by making use of DTA. They concluded, that on the basis of DTA curves, these compounds could be divided into four groups, each of which was characterised by the presence or absence of certain endothermic peaks.

Group I This group includes lanthanium, cerium (III), praseodymium and neodymium, and there are one or two small endothermic peaks which precede the large endothermic dehydration peak. Some exothermic peaks between 400–650°C, probably due to oxychloride formation, have also been observed with the exception of cerium III.

Group II This group contains samarium, curopium and gadolinium and the dehydration peaks contain just one maximum. Sharp endothermic peaks between 160–180° and broad endothermic peaks between 390–400°C have also been observed.

Group III This group which includes terbium, dysprosium, yttrium, holomium, erbium and thulium was characterised by the splitting of the dehydration into two peaks and also the splitting of the xychloride formation peaks.

Group IV This group which includes ytterbium and lutetium was characterised by the splitting of dehydration endothermic peak in addition to the peaks appeared in the 310–325°C temperature range.

Electroanalytical Techniques

The electro-analytical techniques include electro-gravimetry, polarography, coulometry, etc.

Electrogravimetry

It is a powerful technique in order to determine the concentration of metal ions in solutions. The experimental set-up is shown in the figure.

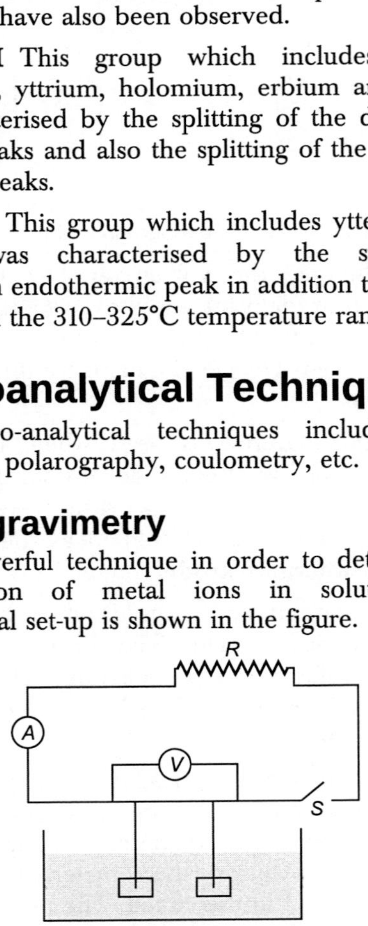

Fig. 12.16 Apparatus for electrogravimetry.

Power from an AC supply is stepped down to 3-15 volts and is rectified using a selenium bridge. Stirring is usually accomplished by facilitate circulation of electrolyte, reducing the concentration polarization.

The principle of electogravimetry is quantitative electrodeposition of the metal from a solution on a cathode. Weighing the cathode before and after the deposition enables one to calculate the concentration of metal ions in the solution.

Polarography

Polarography is an electroanalytical method of studying the composition of dilute electrolytic solutions by plotting current-voltage curves.

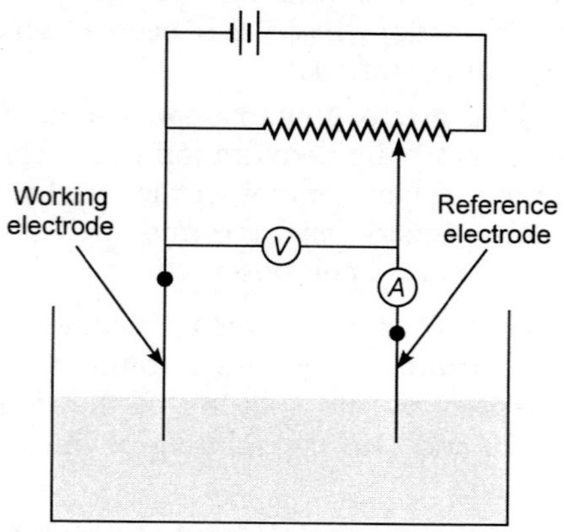

Fig. 12.17 Polarographic unit.

In this technique, the voltage applied to a small polarizable electrode is increased over a range of 0-2 V and the resulting changes in current through the solution are noted. The general name for this method is **voltammetry.**

The term polarography is used when a dropping mercury cathode is used. The dropping mercury electrode is referred to as **working electrode** in polarography. It is also referred to as the **indicator electrode** or **microelectrode.**

The term polarography is used when a dropping mercury cathode is used. The dropping mercury electrode is referred to as **working electrode** in polarography. It is also refferred to as the **indicator electrode** or **microelectrode.**

The experimental assembly used is shown above and is similar to the one used in potentiometry. The electrodes are connected to a variable voltage source. A very sensitive ammeter or galvanometer, provided with a shunt, is included in the circuit. The potential at the working electrode is measured by a voltmeter relative to the reference electrode.

The half-wave potential

It is a characteristic property of the electroactive material. This potential is found on the steeply rising portion of the current voltage curve and is one half of the distance between the residual and limiting currents.

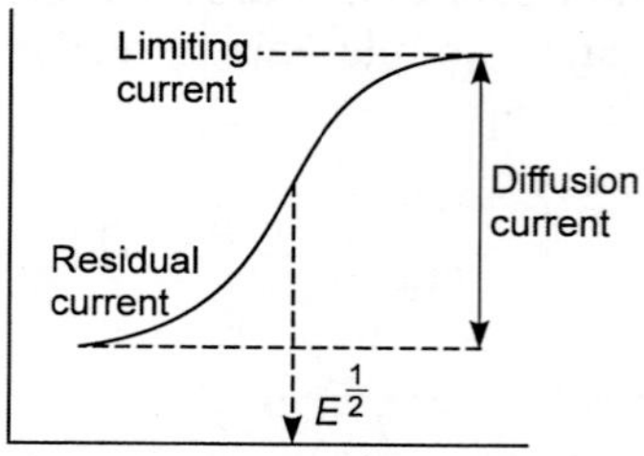

Applications of polarography

1. It can be used to estimate cations and anions in the presence of various interfering ions. For example, lithium having a negative half-wave potential can be estimated in the presence of other alkali metals, provided the latter metals are not of high concentration.
2. It is used in the determination of oxidation states of a metal ion in solution.
3. Ionic solutions of the various elements can be determined directly by it.
4. It is used in the direct determination of dissolved oxygen in solution, aqueous or organic.
5. It is used to determine the instability constants of complexes.

Conductometric Titrations

These can be applied to all titrations in which there occurs a sharp change in the conductivity at the end point. The determination of the end point of a titration by means of conductivity measurement is termed as conductometric titration.

In a conductometric titration, the titrant is added from the burette and the conductivity readings corresponding to various increments of titrant are plotted against the volume of titrant. Two curves will be obtained which will intersect each other at a point, called "end point" or "equivalence point".

Advantages of conductometric titrations

1. Such titrations are useful in the case of coloured or turbid liquids, where ordinary indicators cannot function.

2. These can be employed for the analysis of dilute solutions and also for very weak acids.
3. No special precautions are necessary as the titration approaches the equivalence point, since the latter is found graphically.
4. It is not necessary to measure the actual conductance, as we may use any quantity that is proportional to it, *e.g.,* the reading on a Wheatstone bridge or resistance box. The same can be directly plotted against the volume of the alkali solution used up.

Amperometric Titrations

A titration in which measurement of the current flowing at a voltammetric indicator electrode is used for the detection of end point is called an amperometric titration.

The experimental set-up is the same as the one used for polarographic studies. The potential is set corresponding to the diffusion plateau of a species (which may be a reactant or a product formed during the course of the titration) and the current is measured as a function of the volume of the titrant added.

Advanced Polarographic Techniques

The sample classical polarographic techniques discussed above assume that the electrode potential is always an equilibrium potential. However, new techniques have been introduced recently which are mainly based on the perturbation of equilibrium electrode potential by changing the scan rate or by using pulses. These techniques have been introduced for

(i) decreasing the time needed for the examination of a sample.

(ii) increasing sensitivity, and

(iii) investigating mechanisms of electrode reactions.

These methods could be broadly classified into the following groups :

1. Rapid-scan techniques
2. Pulse techniques
3. AC techniques

Exercise 1
(For Part 'B')

1. While studying the distribution law
   (a) the temperature should be constant throughout
   (b) there should be no association or dissociation of the solute
   (c) the concentration of the solute in solvents
   (d) All of the above
2. When a solute undergoes association in one of the solvent, the following expression of distribution law is applicable
   (a) $\frac{C_1}{C_2} = K_D$ (b) $\frac{C_1}{n\sqrt{C_2}} = K_D$
   (c) $\frac{C_1}{C_2^2} = K_D$ (d) $\frac{C_1}{\sqrt{C_2}} = K_D$
3. The modified distribution law for the solute undergoing dissociation in one of the solvents
   (a) $K_D = \frac{C_1}{\sqrt{C_2}}$ (b) $K_D = \frac{C_1}{C_1(1-\alpha)}$
   (c) $K_D = \frac{C_1}{C_2(\alpha - 1)}$ (d) $K_D = \frac{C_1}{C_2^2}$
4. The greater will be the distribution ratio in favour of organic solvents, the ……… will be the amount extracted in any one operation.
   (a) greater (b) lesser
   (c) equal to (d) None of these
5. When succinic acid and oxalic acid is shaken with ether and water it ……… in water.
   (a) associates to form dimer
   (b) dissociates into ions
   (c) dissolves with difficulty
   (d) does not dissolve at all
6. When a solute dissociates in aqueous layer (C_2) and exist as single molecule in ether (C_1), the degree of dissociation (or ionisation) K_D is
   (a) $\frac{C_2}{C_1(1-x)}$ (b) $\frac{C_2}{C_2(1-x)}$
   (c) $\frac{C_2}{C_1(x-1)}$ (d) $\frac{C_1}{C_2(1-x)}$
7. From an examination of the weight change *vs* temperature curve of a substance, information can be obtained regarding
   (a) thermal stability and composition of the original material
   (b) thermal stability and composition of the intermediate compounds
   (c) composition of the final product or residue
   (d) All of the above are correct
8. The most important requirements of a suitable recording thermobalance are
   (a) accuracy
   (b) reproducibility
   (c) insensitivity to ambient temperature changes
   (d) All of the above
9. The weight loss curve can be recorded
   (a) on a potentiometric strip chart recorder
   (b) on an *X-Y* recorder
   (c) on an X_2 -X_2 recorder
   (d) All the above are correct
10. In TGA, the weight loss curve depends on the following instrumental factors
    (a) furnace heating rate
    (b) recording or chart speed
    (c) furnace atmosphere
    (d) All of the above
11. The sample characteristics affecting the weight loss curve include
    (a) amount of sample
    (b) solubility of evolved gases in the sample
    (c) sample particle size
    (d) All of the above are correct
12. In DTA, thermal effects may be endothermic or exothermic. These are caused by
    (a) fusion
    (b) crystalline structure inversions
    (c) boiling and sublimation
    (d) All of the above
13. In DTA, thermal effects are caused by chemical reactions such as
    (a) dissociation or decomposition
    (b) oxidation or reduction
    (c) dehydration
    (d) All of the above are correct
14. In DTA most of the chemical reactions or transitions produce endothermic heat effects except
    (a) some oxidation reactions
    (b) some decomposition reactions
    (c) some crystalline inversions
    (d) All the above are correct
15. In DTA, the choice of a temperature detection device depends on
    (a) maximum temperature required
    (b) chemical reactivity of the sample
    (c) sensitivity of the d.c. amplifier
    (d) All of the above are correct

16. Thermocouples have been constructed from
(a) chromel *vs* alumel
(b) copper *vs* platinum, 10–13% rhodium
(c) Both (a) and (b)
(d) None of the above

17. Resistance elements are the most commonly used materials for heating the furnace in DTA. They are made of materials such as
(a) nichrome (b) platinum
(c) rhodium (d) All of these

18. The property measured in TGA is
(a) change in weight
(b) rate of change in weight
(c) heat evolved or absorbed
(d) change of temperature

19. The property measured in derivative thermogravimetric analysis (DTG) is
(a) change in weight
(b) rate of change in weight
(c) heat evolved or absorbed
(d) change in temperature

20. Light sources are required to emit spectra of the elements to be determined. The resulting spectra should have
(a) sharp lines (b) negligible background
(c) high stability (d) All of these

21. The most suitable source for atomic absorption spectroscopy is a hollow cathode tube. However, laboratory type discharge lamps can also be used for metals
(a) alkali metals (b) mercury
(c) zinc (d) All of these

22. The most widely used flame in atomic absorption is
(a) air-coal gas (b) air-propane
(c) air-acetylene (d) oxyacetylene

23. For the detection of lines in the spectra of the alkali metals, which of the following detection system is most suitable?
(a) Photoconductive cells
(b) Photovoltaic cells
(c) Red-sensitive photomultipliers
(d) All of the above

24. Analytical methods based on atomic absorption are highly specific because
(a) atomic absorption lines are very narrow
(b) transition energies are unique for each element
(c) Both (a) and (b) correct
(d) None of the above is correct

25. Which of the following devices is most commonly used for the formation of an atomic vapour in atomic absorption?
(a) Flame atomisation
(b) Electric arcs and sparks
(c) Sputtering devices
(d) Ovens

26. The region of the flame in which the maximum emission or absorption occurs depends upon
(a) droplet size
(b) type of flame used
(c) tendency for species to enter into oxide formation
(d) All of the above are correct

27. Low temperature flames such as natural gas-air can be used for determining the elements
(a) copper (b) lead
(c) zinc (d) All of these

28. For the analysis of alkali metals and some of the alkaline earth metals, a low temperature flame is desirable because
(a) with increasing flame temperatures some ionisation of the atoms can take place
(b) sufficient ionisation of these metals occurs in the hotter flame
(c) ionisation lowers significantly the number of absorbing particles
(d) All of the above are correct

29. The non-luminous air-acetylene flame at 2450°C is the best flame for routine determination of elements
(a) Mg (b) Ca
(c) Fe (d) All of these

30. The temperature of the flame obtained by burning acetylene in nitrous oxide is about
(a) 1000°C (b) 2000°C (c) 3000°C (d) 1500°C

31. Lean air acetylene flame (2300°C) is most suitable for
(a) alkaline earth metals (b) alkali metals
(c) transition metals (d) None of these

32. Which of the following statements are correct?
(a) Most universally useful flame is air acetylene
(b) Air propane can give better sensitivity for the alkali and other ionisable elements
(c) Nitrous oxide-acetylene flame is essential for elements which form refractory oxides
(d) All of the above are correct

33. Which of the following statements are correct?
(a) The resonance lines of most metallic elements lie within the range 190–850 mμ
(b) For economic reasons, the range of commercially available instruments is not usually extended to either lower or higher wavelengths
(c) Atmospheric absorbance occurs below 186 mμ and so prevents the determination of most non-metals
(d) All of the above are correct

34. Which of the following statements are correct?
(a) Alkali metals are almost completely ionised even at low concentrations in the air-acetylene or air-propane flame and do not absorb their resonance or ground state radiation
(b) When a small amount of another easily ionisable element is added to an alkali metal, the ionisation equilibrium is shifted towards the free atoms
(c) This shifting results in greater absorbance of radiation by the first metal
(d) All of the above are correct

35. In flame photometry, flame can be replaced by plasma produced electrically in argon gas, because
(a) the plasma that is formed is very energetic
(b) the plasma is capable of dissociating and activating a large number of elements
(c) the dissolved sample is aspirated into the plasma just as into a chemical flame
(d) All of the above are correct

36. The most important applications of flame photometry are
(a) Analysis of Na and K in biological fluids and tissues
(b) Analyse of those otherwise difficult to determine elements
(c) Both (a) and (b)
(d) None of the above

37. In flame emission spectroscopy, the flame acts
(a) to convert constituents of the liquid sample into the vapour state
(b) to decompose these constituents into atoms or simple molecules
(c) to electronically excite a fraction of the resulting atomic or molecular species
(d) All of the above are correct

38. In order to excite the spectra of many metals in flame photometry which of the following is/are good oxidants?
(a) Oxygen (b) Nitrogen
(c) Nitrous oxide (d) Hydrogen

39. Which of the following fuels produces hottest practical flame when combusted in oxygen?
(a) Acetylene (b) Cyanogen
(c) Hydrogen (d) Butane

40. Which of the following statements are correct for cyanogen flame?
(a) It is the hottest practical flame used in flame photometry
(b) It produces spectra that are almost arc-like in quality
(c) It permits the determination of elements having high excitation energies
(d) All of the above are correct

41. Which of the following statements are correct for high temperatures achieved with oxygen and nitrous oxide as oxidants?
(a) They are required to excite many elements
(b) They are required for most easily excited elements
(c) They usually provide enhanced emission intensities and thus higher sensitivity
(d) All of the above are correct

42. The analysis of alkali metals is performed with advantage with a low temperature flame, because
(a) these elements have low excitation energies
(b) the interference by other elements becomes greater at higher temperatures
(c) sensitivity may decrease at higher temperatures
(d) All of the above are correct

43. Which of the following statements are correct?
(a) All the fuels used in flame photometry produce both continuous background radiation as well as certain band spectra
(b) The nature and intensity of the spectrum for a given fuel depends upon the fuel to oxidant ratio and the flame temperature
(c) In analysis it is almost necessary to correct line intensities for the emission by the fuel
(d) All of the above are correct

44. Which of the following statements are correct?
(a) The continuous spectra associated with hydrocarbon flames are more intense than those of hydrogen
(b) For a high fuel to oxidant ratios black body radiation from carbon particles may contribute in hydrocarbon flames
(c) The combination of CO with atomic oxygen produces a continuum that may, under some circumstances, appear in a hydrocarbon flame
(d) All of the above are correct

45. Which of the following processes may occur in flames?
(a) Translational, vibrational and rotational motions
(b) Excitation
(c) Ionisation
(e) All of the above

46. Which of the following statements regarding ionisation in flames are correct?
(a) Ionisation of atoms and molecules is small in combustion mixtures involving air as oxidant
(b) Ionisation becomes important at the higher temperatures if oxygen or nitrous oxide is used as oxidant
(c) The degree of ionisation of a metal is strongly influenced by the presence of other ionisable metals in the flame
(d) All of the above are correct

47. Which of the following element can be used as ionisation suppressor?
(a) Cs (b) Cl
(c) Bi (d) Cu

48. Which of the following statements are correct?
(a) Flame excitation of many elements produces line spectra
(b) In general, only the lowest energy resonance lines of atoms rather than ions have sufficient intensity to be useful
(c) These characteristics of flame spectra arise directly from relatively low excitation energies involved
(d) All of the above are correct

49. Which of the following solvents are used to convey the sample into the flame?
(a) Low molecular weight alcohols
(b) Low molecular weight ketones
(c) Low molecular weight esters
(d) All of the above

50. Chromatographic analysis was first suggested by Tswett as an analytical tool for the separation of various pigments from plant extracts. This chromatographic technique was based on
(a) adsorption (b) absorption
(c) partition (d) ion exchange

51. Common materials used for tubing or column are
(a) stainless steel (b) glass
(c) teflon (d) All of these

52. A general discussion of column chromatography may be based on polarity of the solvent and on this basis reliable information can be gained regarding
(a) suitable supports (b) mobile phases
(c) stationary phases (d) All of these

53. Which of the following adsorbent used for column adsorption chromatography has maximum adsorptive power?
(a) Silica gel (b) Magnesium oxide
(c) Aluminium oxide (d) Calcium carbonate

54. Which of the following adsorbent used for column adsorption chromatography has maximum adsorptive power?
(a) Sucrose
(b) Magnesium carbonate
(c) Calcium oxide
(d) Calcium sulphate

55. Which of the following compounds is expected to have maximum polarity or maximum adsorption in adsorption chromatography?
(a) Hydroxy
(b) Aldehydic
(c) Unsaturated hydrocarbons
(d) Saturated hydrocarbons

56. Depending on the extent of drying and preparation, alumina may have the sites
(a) Al^{n+} (b) Al–OH
(c) AlO–H (d) All of these

57. Which of the following solvents have maximum eluting power?
(a) Pyridine (b) Acetone
(c) Chloroform (d) Methanol

58. Which of the following solvents is least polar in the chromatographic sense?
(a) Benzene (b) Water
(c) Ethyl ether (d) Ethanol

59. Which of the following solvents is most polar in chromatographic sense?
(a) Water (b) Carbon tetrachloride
(c) Chloroform (d) Toluene

60. Which of the following solvents has least eluting power?
(a) Cyclohexane (b) Ethyl ether
(c) Ethyl acetate (d) *n*-propanol

61. Separation of ions by exchange depends on
(a) nature and structure of the ion exchanger
(b) the nature of analysed substances
(c) temperature of the experiment
(d) All of the above are correct

62. Which of the following statements are correct?
(a) The pH effect on the ion exchange process depends on the chemical composition of the exchanger and the type of exchanger
(b) The exchange capacity of a cation exchanger is generally increased with increasing pH of the solution
(c) The exchange capacity of an anion exchanger decreases with an increase in pH of the solution
(d) All of the above are correct

63. An increase in pH causes an increase in the sorption capacity if an ion exchanger contains
(a) –COOH group (b) –OH group
(c) $-SO_3H$ group (d) All of these

64. The rate of cation exchange process depends on
(a) valence of the ions (b) charge on the ions
(c) degree of hydration (d) All of these

65. An ion exchange process is reversible. The equilibrium of this process depends on
(a) the acidity of the solution
(b) the concentration and charge of the cations participating in the exchange
(c) temperature
(d) All of the above

66. What is the pH range in which strongly basic anion exchangers can be used?
(a) 1-14 (b) 1-9 (c) 1-6 (d) 7-14

67. Synthetic ion exchange resins have widely been used for
(a) water softening (b) water deionisation
(c) ion separation (d) All of these

68. Anion exchange resins with similar ionogenic groups are
(a) quaternary ammonium bases
(b) tertiary amines
(c) quaternary sulphonium bases
(d) All of the above

69. Anion exchangers are high molecular compounds comprising a great number of basic groups such as
(a) $—NH_2$ (b) $—NH_3OH$
(c) $—NHR$ (d) All of these

70. Which of the following statements are correct?
(a) The mobility of H^+ and OH^- ions in the resin depends on the nature of ionogenic groups
(b) The H^+ ion moves freely in the resin phase of strong cation exchanger containing SO_3H group
(c) The H^+ ions freely changes places without disturbing the electrical neutrality
(d) All of the above are correct

71. When amino acids are separated on ion exchange resins, the following variables are taken into consideration
(a) choice of ion exchanger
(b) pH
(c) concentration of ionic species in the eluting agent
(d) All of the above are correct

72. Which of the following statements are correct regarding swelling?
(a) The concentration of electrolyte influences the degree of swelling
(b) Crosslinking provides mechanical strength to the resin and hence retards swelling
(c) If the internal portion of the resin is not available it indicates poor swelling and the rate of exchange is greatly reduced
(d) All of the above are correct

73. Which of the following statements are correct?
(a) Particle size and porosity surface area contribute directly to the rate of exchange
(b) The rate of exchange will increase with small particle size and large surface area
(c) The resins are not truly porous supports like alumina and zeolites
(d) All of the above are correct

74. The particle size in ion exchangers depends on
(a) column length
(b) column diameter
(c) gravity or pumping used to control the flow of mobile phase
(d) All of the above

75. Depending on the form of resin, cation resins strong acid) and anion resins (strong base) are stable to .... and .... °C respectively
(a) 150, 70 (b) 100, 50
(c) 250,150 (d) 500, 400

76. The commonly used chromatographic methods for qualitative drug analysis are
(a) GLC (b) TLC
(c) HPLC (d) All of these

77. Column for gas-liquid chromatography can be fabricated from
(a) glass (b) stainless steel
(c) copper (d) All of these

78. What are the important advantages of gas chromatography?
(a) Both qualitative and quantitative analyses are possible
(b) The time of analysis is short
(c) The instrument is simple and sensitivity is high
(d) All of the above are correct

79. By choosing proper column and conditions it is possible to separate the following with gas chromatography
(a) *Cis* and *trans* isomer (b) oxygen isotopes
(c) pesticides (d) All of these

80. Which of the following statements are correct?
(a) As the length of the column increases, the number of theoretical plates will increases
(b) An increase in surface area tends to increase the number of theoretical plates
(c) A decrease in particle size tends to increase the number of theoretical plates
(d) All of the above are correct

81. The maximum operable temperature for the column depends mainly on the factors such as
(a) vapour pressure of the liquid phase
(b) vapour pressure of the sample
(c) efficiency of separation
(d) All of the above

82. In comparison to TLC, the major limitations of paper chromatography are
(a) longer development times are required
(b) zones are not always sharply defined
(c) accuracy in quantitative analysis is only fair
(d) All of the above

83. Qualitative applications of paper chromatography are particularly important in
(a) natural product chemistry
(b) biological investigations
(c) pharmaceutical investigations
(d) All of the above are correct

84. Paper chromatography is more suited to
(a) adsorption (b) partition
(c) molecular sieving (d) ion exchange

85. The type of stationary phases that are used in paper chromatographic techniques includes
(a) aqueous systems (b) hydrophilic systems
(c) hydrophobic systems (d) All of these

86. Common hydrophilic solvents used as stationary phase in paper chromatography include
(a) methanol (b) formamide
(c) glycols (d) All of these

87. Which of the following are the basic mobile phases for paper chromatography?
(a) Water-phenol
(b) Formamide-chloroform
(c) Formamide-benzene
(d) All of the above

88. Numerous combination are possible for the mobile phase in paper chromatography. These include
(a) mixture of two, three, or more solvents
(b) solutions of salts
(c) solutions of buffers
(d) All of the above

89. Which of the following mobile phases are suitable for the separation of hydrophilic substances?
(a) Isopropanol-ammonia-water (9 : 1 : 2)
(b) *n*-butanol-acetic acid-water (4 : 1 : 5)
(c) Water-phenol
(d) All of the above

90. Which of the following mixtures are suitable for the separation of hydrophobic substances?
(a) Dimethyl formamide-cyclohexane
(b) Kerosene-70% isopropanol
(c) Paraffin oil-dimethylformamide-methanol-water
(d) All of the above

91. Which of the following materials are used as binders in TLC?
(a) Plaster of Paris (b) Starch
(c) Plastic dispersions (d) All of these

92. The R_F value of very sensitive to
(a) condition of sheet treatment
(b) conditions of development
(c) development techniques and parameters
(d) All of the above are correct

93. In a clinical laboratory, TLC can be used to identify
(a) the presence of illicit drugs
(b) poisons
(c) inks
(d) All of the above

94. Which of the following chromatographic techniques may involve solid as well as liquid as the stationary phase and liquid as mobile phase?
(a) Column (b) Thin layer
(c) Paper (d) All of these

95. In TLC, glass plates can be coated by
(a) spreading (b) pouring
(c) spraying (d) All of these

96. More accurate results can be obtained if precipitation process is combined with
(a) oxidation-reduction reactions
(b) complexing reactions
(c) Both (a) and (b)
(d) None of the above

97. Which among the following is/are polydentate ligands?
(a) Dithizone (b) 8-hydroxyquinoline
(c) Cupferron (d) All of these

98. Common adsorbents or stationary phases that can be used in adsorption column chromatography are
(a) alumina (b) silica gel
(c) cellulose powder (d) All of these

99. Which of the following statements is correct for paper chromatography?
(a) It is based on the principle which is partly partition and partly adsorption
(b) It is a sheet method
(c) In this technique a sheet or strip of paper acts as the adsorbent
(d) All of the above are correct

100. In which of the following techniques the sample phase is a gas?
(a) Fractional distillation
(b) Gas liquid chromatography
(c) Gas solid chromatography
(d) All of the above

101. Which of the following techniques are based on size of the solute?
(a) Molecular sieves (b) Gel filtration
(c) Gel permeation (d) All of these

102. Which of the following solvents can be used as the stationary phase on silica gel in partition chromatography?
(a) Aliphatic alcohols (b) Glycols
(c) Nitromethane (d) All of these

103. In LSC, which of the following solvents is most polar in the chromatographic sense for gradient elution?
(a) *n*-heptane (b) Chloroform
(c) Nitromethane (d) Acetone

Exercise 2
(For Part 'C')

1. K_D of I_2 between water and CS_2 is 0.0017. 1 L of aqueous solution containing 1 g of I_2 is shaken with 100 mL of CS_2 till equilibrium is reached. Amount of I_2 extracted by CS_2 is
   (a) 0.983 g (b) 0.893 g
   (c) 0.389 g (d) 0.888 g
2. An organic acid was dissolved in two immiscible solvents (*A*) and (*B*). At equilibrium, the concentration of acid in (*A*) and (*B*) was found to be 0.40 and 0.64 mol/L respectively. Distribution coefficient of organic acid in solvent (*B*) is
   (a) 0.2 (b) 0.3
   (c) 0.5 (d) 0.7
3. The air-propane flame at about 1950°C gives the best sensitivity for
   (a) alkali metals
   (b) certain elements whose compounds are not temperature stable
   (c) transition metals
   (d) elements which form highly refractory oxides
4. Which of the following statements are correct for flame photometry?
   (a) The presence of atom-ion equilibria in flames has a number of consequences
   (b) The intensity of atomic emission lines for the alkali metals are affected in a complex way by temperature
   (c) Increased temperature causes an increase in the population of excited atoms
   (d) All of the above are correct
5. Which of the following statements are correct?
   (a) Dissociation reactions involving metal oxides and hydroxides play an important part in determining not only the intensity but also the nature of emission by an element
   (b) Molecular bands arising from the presence of metal oxides or hydroxides in the flame thus constitute a prominent feature of their spectra
   (c) Except at very high temperatures, these bands are more intense than the lines for the atoms or ions
   (d) All of the above are correct
6. Which of the following statements are correct?
   (a) The intensification of lines by organic solvents is primarily due to their low viscosity and surface tension
   (b) Cooling by the solvent is decreased
   (c) Combustion of the organic solvent contributes to the temperature
   (d) All of the above are correct
7. Which of the following statements are correct?
   (a) Column diameter and packing can influence the resolution
   (b) The distance between the two zones is almost identical in the thin and the fat column
   (c) The zones appear to overlap as they emerge from the fat column, if the flow is non-uniform
   (d) All of the above are correct
8. Adsorption chromatography is preferred for the separation of mixtures whose components
   (a) differ in polarity
   (b) differ in structure
   (c) are very close in polarity
   (d) have almost similar structures
9. Arrange the following compounds in order of increasing polarity or increasing adsorption [*A*] Unsaturated hydrocarbons [*B*] Halogen compounds [*C*] Acids and bases [*D*] Aldehydes
   (a) $A < B < D < C$ (b) $B < A < C < D$
   (c) $A < C < B < D$ (d) $A < B < C < D$
10. Which of the following solvents has maximum eluting power?
    (a) Methanol (b) Toluene
    (c) Carbon tetrachloride (d) Ethanol
11. Which of the following chemical variables influence the separation factor in ion exchange process?
    I. pH of the solution.
    II. Nature of ions being separated.
    III. Conc. of ions in solution.
    (a) I, II (b) II, III (c) I, III (d) I, II, III
12. Ion exchange chromatography can be used in the separation of
    I. Cations of alkali and alkaline earth metals.
    II. Rare earth and transuranium elements.
    III. Zirconium and hafnium.
    IV. *cis-trans* isomeric complexes of cobalt and platinum.
    The correct answer is
    (a) I, II, III only (b) II, IV only
    (c) I, III only (d) I, II, III, IV
13. Which of the following statements are correct for cation exchangers containing strongly ionogenic groups such as $R—SO_3H$?
    I. The exhibit acidic properties in aqueous solutions within a broad range of pH.
    II. They are present in the deprotonised form.
    III. Such a cation exchanger is in the acidic form. (H^+ form) only in strongly acidic medium.
    (a) I, II (b) II, III (c) I, III (d) I, II, III

14. Which of the following statements are correct for weakly acidic cation exchangers?

I. They can be represented as *R*—COOH and *R*–OH.

II. They are deprotonised only in a neutral and alkaline medium.

III. They are in the H^+ form in weakly and strongly acidic medium.

(a) I, II (b) II, III (c) I, III (d) I, II, III

15. Cation exchangers with mixed functional groups occur in the combinations

I. Sulpho acid and hydroxyphenolic.

II. Sulpho acid and carboxylic.

III. Residues of phosphoric acid and hydroxyphenolic.

IV. Carboxylic and hydroxyphenolic.

V. Arsenic and hydroxyphenolic.

The correct answer is

(a) I, II, III, IV (b) II, IV, V
(c) I, III, V (d) All of the given

16. Which of the following statements are correct in case of resin swelling?

(a) The exchange sites are present primarily inside the resin bed and are available only if the resin swells
(b) When the resin swells, the polymer chains spread apart
(c) If the resin is placed in a polar solvent, swelling, occurs while if it is placed in a non-polar solvent contraction occurs
(d) All of the above are correct

17. Which of the following statements are correct for spray reagents used in the statement?

(a) Bromocresol green is used for carboxylic acids
(b) 2,4-dinitrophenyl hydrazine (2,4-DNP) is used for aldehydes and ketones
(c) Ferric chloride is used for phenols
(d) All of the above are correct

18. Which of the following statements are correct?

(a) Extraction separation of elements can be carried out in the form of chelates
(b) 8-hydroxyquinoline forms coordination saturated neutral chelates with most metals and these chelates are extracted by many organic solvents
(c) Acetylacetone is used as extractant in benzene or chloroform for the extraction separation of elements
(d) All of the above are correct

19. Which of the following statements are correct?

(a) Precipitation is based on the differences in solubility
(b) Distillation is based on the differences in volatility
(c) Sublimation is based on the differences in vapour pressure
(d) All of the above are correct

20. Which of the following statements are correct?

(a) In partition methods, the stationary liquid phase is held in a column of sheet by an inert support
(b) In some cases, the inert support may influence the action of the solute and act as adsorbent
(c) In adsorption, the adsorbent may retain some of the mobile liquid phase as a stationary phase and produce a partitioning effect
(d) All of the above are correct

21. Which of the following statements are correct?

(a) *LC* columns are generally operated at room temperature
(b) The rate of diffusion and hence speed of separation can be increased somewhat by high temperature operation, so a heating jacket or oven is sometimes required
(c) The temperature control in *LC* is not as significant as in gas chromatography
(d) All of the above are correct

22. Which of the following statements are correct for gradient elution?

(a) Gradient elution is a continuous alteration in the composition of the liquid phase and also known as solvent programming
(b) It causes a change in the partition coefficients of the components and leads to improved resolution
(c) Gradient elution is used to advantages in many *LC* applications
(d) All of the above are correct

23. Which of the following statements are correct for fluorescence detectors?

(a) These are especially important for the many biochemical applications of *LC*
(b) Excitation in them is usually with the 254 nm line of the mercury arc
(c) These detectors are highly selective and sensitive
(d) All of the above

24. Arrange the following solvents for gradient elution in LSC in order of increasing polarity.

I. Carbon tetrachloride II. 2-nitropropane

III. Propylacetate IV. Methanol

(a) I < II < III < IV (b) I < III < IV < II
(c) II < I < IV < III (d) IV < II < III < I

25. On a 1000 cm wall coated tabular column of 0.25 nm bore, the helium carrier gas velocity is 40 cm/s. The retention time for draw is 1.20 min and the peak width at half height is 0.88s. The retention time for a non-retained compound is

(a) 25 (b) 1.82 (c) 0.41 (d) 1.27

26. Substance *X* and *Y* were found to have a retention times of 17.30 and 19.92 minutes respectively on a 25 cm long column. The widths (at the base) for *A* and *B* were 1.10 and 1.22 minutes respectively. The column resolution is

(a) 3.25 (b) 2.26 (c) 1.25 (d) 1.29

27. On a 125 cm long column, operated at 160°C, these retention times were obtained :

Air peak 0.90, heptane 1.22; octane 1.43.

The base widths of the bands were 0.10 for heptane and 0.22 for octane. The relative retention and resolution for these bands are

(a) 1.66, 1.1 (b) 1.26, 1.82
(c) 1.82, 1.23 (d) 1.25, 1.1

28. How many gram of cation exchanger in the H^+ form are required to separate Ca^{2+} ions from 1 dm^2 of 0.1 N $CaCl_2$?

(The static exchange capacity in 0.1 N $CaCl_2$ is 4.5 mg equivalents)

(a) 15 (b) 18.2
(c) 22.22 (d) 20.56

29. The weight of Fe^{3+} left unextracted from 100 mL of a solution having 400 mg of Fe^{3+} in 6 M HCl after two extractions with 25 mL of diethyl ether is ($D = 150$)

(a) 0.333 mg (b) 0.269 mg
(c) 1.25 mg (d) 0.0629 mg

30. In the extraction of cerium (IV) with 2-thenoyl trifluoro acetone in benzene, the distribution ratio was 999. If the volume of organic phase was 20 mL and that of aqueous phase 50 mL, the percentage extraction was

(a) 90 % (b) 50 %
(c) 97 % (d) 99.7 %

Matching Type

31. Match Column I with Column II and choose the correct answer using the codes given below.

Column I (Wave forms of common excitation signals)		Column II (Types of voltametry)	
A.	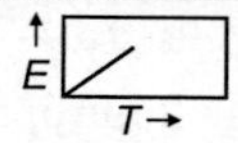	1.	Cyclic voltametry
B.	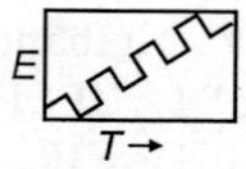	2.	Square wave voltametry
C.	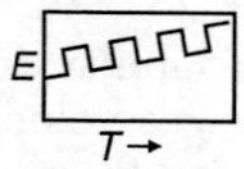	3.	Differential pulse polarography
D.	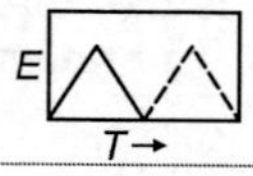	4.	Polarography

Codes

	A	B	C	D
(a)	4	3	2	1
(b)	4	2	3	1
(c)	1	2	3	4
(d)	1	3	4	2

32. In the determination of selenium in urine by AAS it was found that Beer's law applied up to the 2 ppm range. If the 2 ppm standard was set at 100 and a blank set at zero, what would be the selenium concentration of the sample that will read at 73?

(a) 0.73 ppm (b) 0.146 ppm
(c) 1.46 ppm (d) 7.3 ppm

33. Match Column I with Column II and choose the correct answer using the codes given below.

Column I (Quantity measured and variable controlled)		Column II (Name of method)	
A.	E, $i = 0$	1.	Conductometric titration
B.	E *vs* volume of titration $i = 0$	2.	In selective potentiometry
C.	i *vs* E, concentration	3.	Potentiometric titrations
D.	$1/R$ *vs* volume of titrant	4.	Voltametry

Codes

	A	B	C	D
(a)	2	3	4	1
(b)	3	2	4	1
(c)	2	3	1	4
(d)	3	2	1	4

34. Match Column I (conductometric titration curves) with Column II (proper statements) and choose the correct answer using the codes given below.

Column I		Column II	
A.	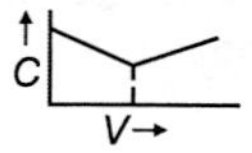	1.	Weak acid against a strong base
B.	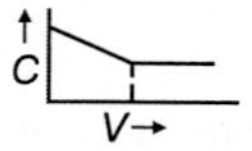	2.	Strong acid against strong base
C.	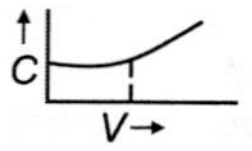	3.	Strong acid with a weak base
D.	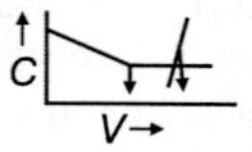	4.	Weak acid against weak base

(where, V = volume of titrant and C = conductance)

Codes

	A	B	C	D
(a)	2	3	4	1
(b)	2	3	1	4
(c)	3	2	4	1
(d)	3	2	1	4

35. Match the following.

	Column I		Column II
A.	Sulphonated polystyrene resin	1.	Anionic complexes of metals
B.	Carboxylic polymethacrylate	2.	Alkaloids
C.	Quartenary amonium polystyrene	3.	Antibiotics
D.	Phenol-formaldehyde	4.	Vitamins and lanthanides

Codes

	A	B	C	D
(a)	2	3	4	1
(b)	1	2	3	4
(c)	4	3	2	1
(d)	4	1	2	3

36. Which is the most common crosslinking agent in ion exchange resin?
(a) Polymethacrylate (b) Formic acid
(c) Divinyl benzene (d) Benzene

37. Which of the following statements is true about swelling of resins?
I. High content of divinyl benzene can cause high swelling of resin.
II. Crosslinking on decreasing increases swelling.
III. Swelling decreases with decrease in crosslinking.
(a) Only II is true (b) Only I & III are true
(c) Only I, II are true (d) Only I is true

Assertion & Reason

(a) Both A and R are true and R is the correct explanation of A.
(b) Both A and R are true but R is not the correct explanation of A.
(c) A is true but R is false.
(d) A is false but R is true.

38. Assertion (A) Exchange capacity of a cation exchange generally decreases with decrease in pH, while of anion exchange resin increases.
Reason (R) Ion exchanger containing weak acid groups as —COOH, —OH, sorbability, increases with increase in pH, charge, atomic masses, ionic radii.

39. Assertion (A) Selectivity of colourless ion exchangers can be used to detect coloured ions in the mixture.
Reason (R) Lower the sorptivity of a cation, lower will be its zone in the column.

40. Assertion (A) Separation of simple ions (monovalent cations) on a strongly acidic exchanger follows this order.

$$Li^+ < H^+ < Na^+ < \overset{+}{N}H_4 < K^+ < Rb^+ < Cs^+$$

Reason (R) Li ion is most strongly held on the resin.

41. Assertion (A) For ions of same charge the exchange ability follows this order

$$Al^{3+} > Ni^{2+} > Cd^{2+} > Mg^{2+} > \overset{+}{N}H_4 > K^+$$

Reason (R) Exchange ability decreases with decrease in the radius of hydrated ion.

Directions (Q. Nos. 42 and 43)
This technique is a separation technique that resembles column and paper chromatography. Here, partition occurs on a layer of finely divided adsorbent, which is supported on a glass plate. The common adsorbent used in TLC are silica gel, alumina, kieselguhr and powdered cellulose.

42. Which of the following is used to detect steroids by TLC?
(a) Bromocresol green (b) H_2O
(c) I_2 vapours (d) $SbCl_3$

43. Which of the following is used to detect non-volatile organic compounds?
(a) $SbCl_5$ is CCl_4
(b) Ninhydrin
(c) Chromic sulphuric acid solution
(d) I_2 vapours

Directions (Q. Nos. 45 to 48)
Ion-exchange is a process in which an interchange of ions like signs takes place between the solution and essentially insoluble solid (ion exchanger) in contact with the solution. Resins are though insoluble in water but active groups are hydrophilic and have varying degrees of affinity for ionic solutes.

44. Static exchange capacity is defined as
(a) number of mg equivalents of ions adsorbed per a certain time interval by 1 g of dry exchanger
(b) number of gm equivalents of ions adsorbed per a certain time interval by 1 g of dry exchanger
(c) number of ions adsorbed by 20 cm high and 1 cm^2 cross section
(d) number of ions adsorbed by 50 cm high and 1 m^2 cross section with 0.5 dm^2/h migration rate

45. Thermodynamic exchange capacity is
(a) number of ions adsorbed by 20 cm high and 1 cm^2 cross section with 0.5 dm^2/h migration rate ions exchanger
(b) number of ions adsorbed by 100 g of dry exchanger
(c) number of mg equivalents adsorbed by 1 g of dry exchanger
(d) number of ions adsorbed by 20 cm high and 1 m m^2 cross section with 0.5 dm^2/h migration rate

46. The exchanger capacity increases with increase of pH of
(a) cation exchange resin (b) anion exchanger resin
(c) Both (a) and (b) (d) All of these

47. Capacity of anion exchanger resin decreases with
(a) decrease in pH
(b) increase in pH
(c) at pH = 7
(d) not affected by pH

Directions (Q. Nos. 48 and 49)
Ion exchange is a physico-chemical process, both chemical and purely physical variables influence the separation factors chemical variables include pH, nature of ions being separated, conc. of ions in solution tendency of ions to hydrate, chemical composition of ion exchanger etc.

48. Exchange capacity of weak acid cation exchanger increases with
(a) increase in pH
(b) increase in atomic mass
(c) increase in charge
(d) All of the above

49. Sorbability of ions decreases with
(a) increase in charge
(b) increase in ionic radii
(c) increase in atomic mass
(d) decrease in pH

Answers

Exercise 1

1. (d)	2. (c)	3. (b)	4. (a)	5. (c)	6. (b)	7. (d)	8. (d)	9. (d)	10. (d)
11. (d)	12. (d)	13. (d)	14. (d)	15. (d)	16. (c)	17. (d)	18. (a)	19. (b)	20. (d)
21. (d)	22. (c)	23. (c)	24. (c)	25. (a)	26. (d)	27. (d)	28. (d)	29. (d)	30. (c)
31. (a)	32. (d)	33. (d)	34. (d)	35. (d)	36. (c)	37. (d)	38. (a)	39. (b)	40. (d)
41. (d)	42. (d)	43. (d)	44. (d)	45. (d)	46. (d)	47. (a)	48. (d)	49. (d)	50. (a)
51. (d)	52. (d)	53. (c)	54. (c)	55. (a)	56. (d)	57. (a)	58. (a)	59. (a)	60. (a)
61. (d)	62. (d)	63. (b)	64. (d)	65. (d)	66. (a)	67. (d)	68. (d)	69. (d)	70. (d)
71. (d)	72. (d)	73. (d)	74. (d)	75. (a)	76. (d)	77. (d)	78. (d)	79. (d)	80. (d)
81. (d)	82. (d)	83. (d)	84. (d)	85. (d)	86. (d)	87. (d)	88. (d)	89. (d)	90. (d)
91. (d)	92. (d)	93. (d)	94. (d)	95. (d)	96. (c)	97. (d)	98. (d)	99. (d)	100. (d)
101. (d)	102. (d)	103. (d)							

Exercise 2

1. (a)	2. (c)	3. (a,b)	4. (d)	5. (d)	6. (d)	7. (d)	8. (a,b)	9. (a)	10. (a)
11. (d)	12. (d)	13. (d)	14. (d)	15. (d)	16. (d)	17. (d)	18. (d)	19. (d)	20. (d)
21. (d)	22. (d)	23. (d)	24. (a)	25. (b)	26. (b)	27. (a)	28. (c)	29. (b)	30. (d)
31. (a)	32. (c)	33. (a)	34. (b)	35. (c)	36. (c)	37. (c)	38. (c)	39. (c)	40. (b)
41. (b)	42. (d)	43. (c)	44. (a)	45. (a)	46. (a)	47. (b)	48. (d)	49. (d)	

Hints & Solutions

Exercise 1

9. (a) As a function of time
(b) As a function of temperature
(c) Where furnace temperature is also recording as a function of time.

13. All these reactions cause heat effects in DTA.

14. All these reactions give exothermic heat effects.

16. Chromel-Alumel is a general purpose thermocouple used up to about 1100°C. For high temperature studies up to 1500°C, platinum couple is used and for fairly low temperatures, up to 300°C, the copper couple may be used.

21. These metals generally have low ionisation potentials and so can be vaporised easily.

22. Air acetylene flame is widely used.

23. Lines in the spectra of the alkali metals lie in the visible or near infrared region of the spectrum and for detection of such lines a photomultiplier is necessary.

24. Beer's law applies only for monochromatic radiation, so a linear relationship between absorbance and concentration can be expected if band width is narrow *wrt* the width of the absorption peak.

25. Flame atomisation has widely been used.

27. Because these elements are readily converted to atomic state.

28. Alkali and alkaline earth metals have low ionisation energies.

29. These elements form somewhat refractory oxides.

30. 3000°C, which is slightly lower than oxyacetylene.

31. It is best for alkaline earths and also suitable for many other elements.

34. Because the energy absorbed in ionising the first metal now becomes shared between the two metals. Sodium and potassium, or any pair of alkali metals mutually enhance in this way.

36. Because of convenience, speed and relative freedom from interference, flame emission spectroscopy has been applied with varying degrees of success to the determination of almost half of the elements in the Periodic Table.

39. $C_2N_2 + O_2 \longrightarrow 2CO + N_2$ (4550°C in oxygen). This reaction is highly exothermic and products of combustion are thermally stable at temperature less than 4000°C.

40. It produces a temperature of about 4500°C with oxygen as oxidant.

41. (a) The spectra of various metals require high temperature for excitation.

(b) If easily excited elements occur as refractory compounds in the sample.

(c) There are some instances, where the use of a low temperature flame is advantageous. For example, intensity of the atomic doublet line for K at about 767 nm is limited by the ease of ionisation of this element. As a consequence, little enhancement in sensitivity accompanies increase in temperature. Moreover, interference by other elements becomes greater at higher temperatures.

44. Because several processes contribute in hydrocarbon flame emission. $CO + O \longrightarrow CO_2 + h\nu$. A number of band spectra due to such species as OH radicals, CH radicals and C_2 molecules also occur in hydrocarbon flames. The intensities largely depend on the combustion conditions.

45. Theoretical and experimental evidence suggest that many of the processes occurring in the mantle of the flame are in approximate thermodynamic equilibrium. Thus, burned gases of the flame may be regarded as solvent medium to which thermodynamic calculations may be applied.

46. If the medium contains a metal *M* and their ionisable species *B*, the *M* and *B* are ionised as,

$$m \rightleftharpoons M^+ + e^- \qquad M \rightleftharpoons M^+ + e^-$$

At high temperature sufficient concentration of free electrons is present as a consequence of the equilibrium $M \rightleftharpoons M^+ + e^-$, but degree of ionisation of *M* will be decreased by the mass action effect of electrons.

47. Ionisation suppressor is an easily ionised element.

48. These line spectra are generally much less complex than the corresponding arc or spark spectra.

49. Use of these solvents tend to enhance line intensities by as much as a factor of 10 or more.

50. The first chromatographic technique proposed by Tswett was based on adsorption. The technique was developed to separate various coloured components of a plant extract.

51. All these substances have been used as materials for tubing.

53. The adsorptive power increase in the order : Calcium carbonate < silica gel < magnesium oxide < aluminium oxide.

54. Sucrose < calcium sulphate < magnesium carbonate < calcium oxide.

56. These sites are responsible for adsorption.

61. Separation depends on all these factors.

63. An increase in pH causes an increase in the sorption capacity if an ion exchanger contains weak groups like –COOH and –OH.

65. The equilibrium process depends on all these factors.

66. Strongly basic anion exchangers are used within a broad pH interval of 1-14 and weakly basic anion exchangers, within a narrower range of 1-9.

68. Sulphonium bases are coordination compounds, derivatives of thioethers, *e.g.,*

$$2C_2H_5I + K_2S \longrightarrow (C_2H_5)_2S + 2KI$$

Sulphur adds alkyl halides, salts, etc.

$$(C_2H_5)_2S + CH_3I \longrightarrow [(C_2H_5)_2S(CH_3)]I$$

71. All these variables are taken into consideration.

73. The small resin openings are a function of swelling and are not permanent channels or cavities.

76. All these techniques are commnly employed.

78. All these are the important advantages of gas chromatography.

79. The temperature should not be high enough to vapourise the stationary phase because it will destroy the uniformity of the column. The temperature has, however, to be high enough to maintain the sample in the vapour state.

82. All these are the limitations of paper chromatography.

83. Paper chromatography is more suited for partition.

84. In order to modify the chromatographic behaviour, the cellulose paper can be impregnated with all these materials. These kinds of papers will exhibit properties of these adsorbents and hence, influence the retention of the stationary liquid and the adsorption or partition sequence for a mixture.

85. All are hydrophilic solvents commonly used in paper chromatography.

86. The paper can be modified and be made hydrophobic by silicone treatment or by impregnating it with inert non-polar type organic polymers. All the given solvents are used as hydrophobic stationary phase.

87. All are suitable for the separation of hydrophobic substances.

91. All can be used as binders but calcium sulphate (plaster of Paris) is used most often.

94. When solid is stationary phase and liquid is mobile phase, the physical principles involved are adsorption, ion exchange, gel filtration, etc. When stationary and mobile phase both are liquids, the physical principles involved are partition and reversed phase partition.

95. Coating can be achieved by all these techniques but most uniform layers are obtained by spreading technique.

97. All are polydentate ligands.

98. All are used as adsorbents in adsorption column chromatography.

100. All these techniques involves gas as the sample phase.

103. Polarity increases in the order : *n*-heptane < chloroform < nitromethane < acetone.

Exercise 2

3. Alkali metals and certain elements whose compounds are not temperature stable.

4. According to Boltzmann relationship

$$\frac{N_j}{N_0} = \frac{P_j}{P_0} \exp\left[-\frac{E_j}{kT}\right]$$

Moreover under such conditions there is a decrease in concentration of atoms as a result of ionisation and a decrease in intensity of emission is observed in hotter flames.

5. For example, the alkaline earth oxides are relatively stable, with dissociation energies of the order of 5 eV.

6. (a) Low viscosity and surface tension result in higher flow rates of sample into the flame.

(b) Thus, the net effect is to increase the number of particles available for excitation without a corresponding adverse effect on flame temperature.

(c) Increase as great as 200°C have been reported for certain solvent.

8. For the separation of mixtures whose components differ widely in polarity and structure.

11. Since, ion exchange is a physicochemical process, the separation factor is influenced by all these variables.

12. Ion exchange chromatography can be used for the separation of substances possessing closely related properties.

20. Because of these reasons chromatographic process is not very often purely partition or adsorption.

25. Average linear velocity $v = \frac{L}{t_m}$.

where, L = column length, t_m = retention time for a non-retained compound.

$$t_m = \frac{L}{4} = \frac{1000 \text{ cm}}{40 \text{ cm s}^{-1}}$$

$$= 25 \text{ s or } 0.41 \text{ min}$$

The partition ratio, $K' = \frac{t'_R}{t_m}$

where, t'_R = adjusted retention time = $t_R - t_m$

$$\therefore \quad K = \frac{1.27 - 0.45}{0.45} = 1.82$$

26. Column resolution, $R_s = \frac{2\Delta Z}{w_A + w_B}$.

$$\Delta z = (19.92 - 17.30) = 2.62 \text{ min}$$

$$w_A = 1.10 \text{ min and } w_B = 1.22 \text{ min}$$

$$R_s = \frac{2 \times 2.62}{1.10 + 1.22}$$

$$= 2.26$$

27.
$$\alpha = \frac{(t'_R)_2}{(t'_R)_1} = \frac{t_{R_2} - t_M}{t_{R_1} - t_m}$$

$$= \frac{1.43 - 0.90}{1.22 - 0.90} = 1.66$$

The degree of separation or resolution of two adjacent bands is defined as the distance between band peaks divided by the average width, *i.e.*,

$$R_s = \frac{t_{R_2} - t_{R_1}}{0.5(w_2 + w_1)}$$

$$= \frac{1.43 - 1.22}{0.5(0.16 + 0.22)} = 1.10$$

28.
$$D = \frac{C_R \cdot m}{C_S \cdot V}$$

$$m = \frac{D.C_s.V}{C_r}$$

$$= \frac{0.1 \times 1000}{4.5}$$

($\because$ The quantity C_r/D is the static exchange capacity of the cation exchanger)

$$= 22.22 \text{ g}$$

29.
$$W_n = W\left(\frac{V_w}{DV_0 + V_w}\right)^n$$

where, w = amount of solute, V_w = volume of aqueous solution, $D = 150$, V_0 = volume of organic phase

$$W_n = 400\left(\frac{100}{150 \times 25 + 100}\right)^2 = 0.269 \text{ mg}$$

30.
$$D = \frac{(V_w/V_0)E}{(100 - E)} = 999$$

$$\frac{50/20.x}{(100 - x)} = 999$$

$$\therefore \quad 999 = \frac{2.5x}{100 - x}$$

$$x = 99.75\%$$

32. Selenium concentration in urine $= \frac{73}{100} \times 2$

$$= 1.46 \text{ ppm}$$

13 Bioinorganic Chemistry

Syllabus

- Porphyrins
- Metalloenzymes
- Metal Complexes in Medicine
- Oxygen Transport
- Electron Transfer Reaction
- Photosynthesis
- Nitrogen Fixation

Introduction to Bioinorganic Chemistry

"Bioinorganic chemistry" is at the gate-way of inorganic chemistry and biochemistry, *i.e.*, it describes the mutual relationship between these two sub-disciplines, with focus upon the function of inorganic substances in living systems, including the transport, speciation and eventually, mineralisation of inorganic materials, and including the use of inorganics in medicinal therapy and diagnosis. These substances can be metal ions (such as K^+, ferrous and ferric), composite ions (*e.g.*, molybdate), coordination compounds (like cisplatin and carbonyltechnetium), or inorganic molecules such as CO, NO, O_3.

The roles of inorganic elements, *i.e.*, general and transition metal ions in many biological processes are well recognized. In recent years, the field of bio-inorganic chemistry has grown very vast as a result of many recent findings. In this course, the discussion will be limited to the subtle role of a metal ion in an important biological process *viz.*, oxygen transport in living systems.

Haemoglobin and Myoglobin

There are two metalloproteins in vertebrates known as **haemoglobin and myoglobin,** which are responsible for oxygen uptake and transport. These are large polymeric entities. Haemoglobin picks up oxygen from lungs (or gills), transports it and delivers it to myoglobin, which is present in tissues. The role of myoglobin is to store the oxygen and release it for metabolic process. Also, it may serve as an oxygen reserve from which the organism can draw during increased metabolism or oxygen deprivation.

In 155 X-ray structures!

Haemoglobin (Hb)

- MW = 64500 g
- $\alpha_2\beta_2$
- a = 141 residues
- b = 146 residues
  active site : Fe(por)
- function : cooperatively binds and transports O_2

In 187 X-ray structures!

Myoglobin (Mb)

- MW = 17800 g
- α
- α = 161 residues

Both haemoglobin and myoglobin contain an **active centre or site** (where the function of the metalloprotein is carried out-in this case uptake and release of oxygen). This active site is wrapped up by the folding of the protein attached to it.

Notice that the haemolgobin is essentially a tetramer of myoglobin, *viz.*, there are four myoglobin like units in haemoglobin.

Active Site of Haemoglobin and Myoglobin

The active centre of haemoglobin and myoglobin is made of the **heme unit.** This consists of a macrocyclic ligand known as **porphyrin**, in the cavity of which is bound the iron atom. The porphyrin macrocycle is made up of four pyrrole rings with conjugated double bonds. The periphery of the macrocyclic ring can have several substituents. However, it may be noted that these substituents on the periphery can be used to tune the stereoelectronic properties of the complex. The inside of the **porphyrin ring** has four nitrogen atoms, two of which have hydrogens attached to them. It can be anticipated that these hydrogens can be quite readily deprotonated to generate a dianionic ligand (with a-2 charge). In this form the ligand can readily bind to a number of divalent metal ions. The distance from the centre of the porphyrin ring and the nitrogen atoms is about 2.0 Å, which corresponds to a normal *M*–N distance involving the first row transition metal ions. Because of the delocalization of electrons over the entire framework, the ring is planar and **rigid.** However, it can become non-planar to accomodate certain metal ions, which are either too small or too large to be fitted exactly in the cavity of the porphyrin ligand. Because of this versatility in terms of ligand properties the porphyrin ligand is present in a variety of biologically important system.

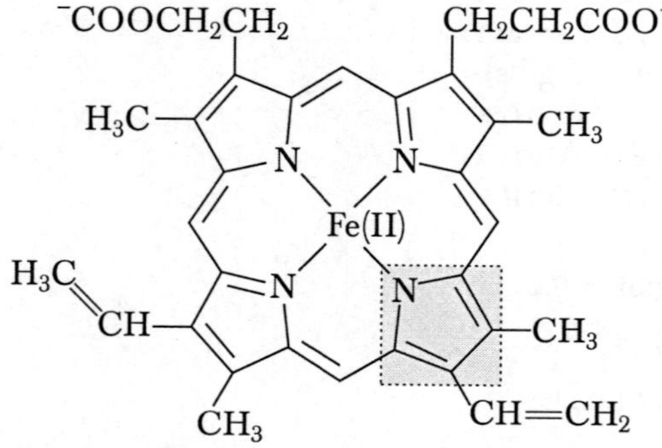

Fig. 13.1 The heme group in Hb/Mb.

The role of the protein

If free heme in an aqueous solution is exposed to oxygen, it is converted immediately into a μ-oxo dimer in a stepwise reaction sequence as shown below. Obviously it is important to be able to stop reactions 2, 3 and 4 if oxygen transport is to be successfully carried out in a continuous manner. The fact that the heme unit is wrapped around by the huge polymeric protein sheath has suggested to researchers that it may be functioning as a **steric block** to prevent the **reaction 2** from occurring. In order to test this hypothesis a model compound called **picket-fence porphyrin** was synthesized. Its design incorporated sterically hindered substituents on one side of the porphyrin. The Fe(II) complex of this porphyrin undergoes oxygenation reversibly without undergoing the irreversible reactions 2, 3 and 4. This means that the sterically hindered substituents prevent two such units to come together to form a μ-oxo complex. If we extend this logic to the naturally occurring system, **the role of the protein (at least one of the important roles) would be also to prevent the irreversible μ-oxo complex formation.**

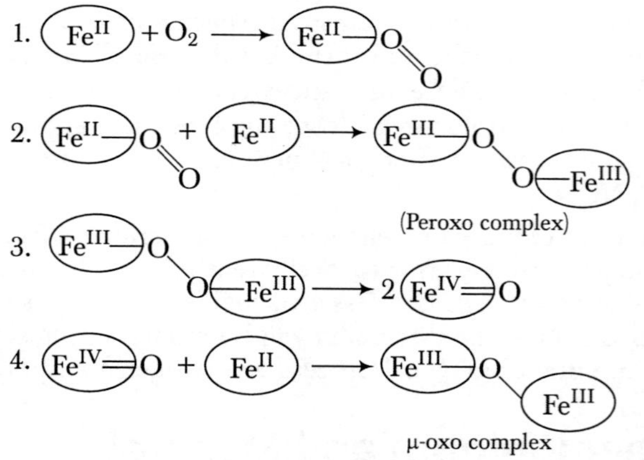

Coordination Environment of Fe(II) in Deoxymyoglobin and Oxymyoglobin

Iron (II) in deoxymyoglobin is in a high spin state. The coordination environment comprises of four nitrogens from the porphyrin ring, one imidazole nitrogen arising out of the amino acid residue, histidine, of the protein chain, and possibly a second distant imidazole nitrogen or a water molecule. (Notice that the coordination environment is very similar to the model picket-fence porphyrin). Note also that the Fe (II) is not present in the plane of the porphyrin ring but is about 0.4 Å above the plane.

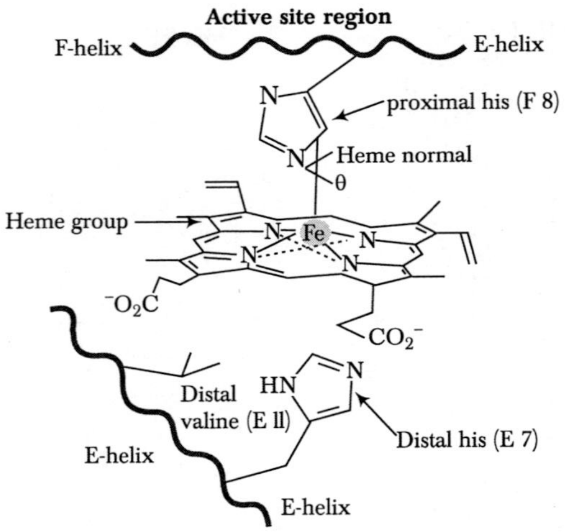

Fig. 13.2 Coordination of Fe(III) in deoxymyoglobin and myoglobin

Upon oxygenation the coordination number of iron goes up unambiguously to six. The oxygen ligand is found to bond to the iron atom in a bent manner. The Fe—O—O bond angle is about 150° and the Fe—O bond distance is about 1.8 Å. Secondly, the iron atom now sits in the plane of the four porphyrin nitrogens. Another important change is that the molecule becomes diamagnetic upon oxygenation.

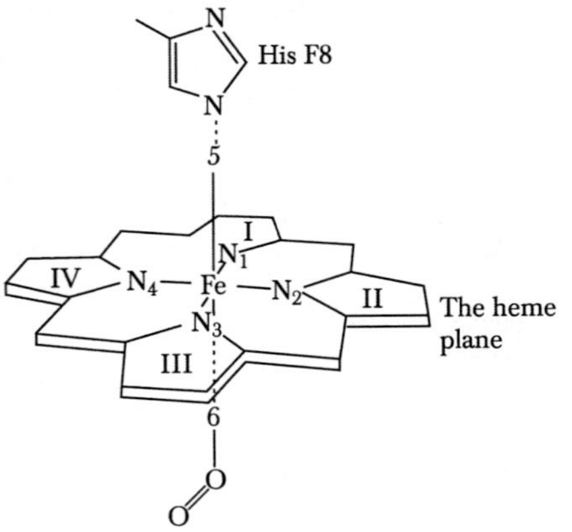

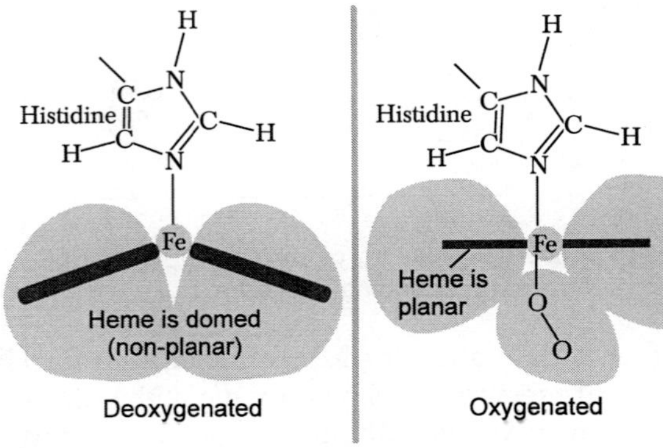

Fig. 13.3 Oxygenated and deoxygenated heme protein.

Diamagnetic Behaviour of the Oxygenated Complex

One possibility is that the Fe (II) is oxidized to Fe (III), which now becomes **low spin** and consequently t_{2g}^5 configuration. Oxygen, which picks up the electron is now O_2^-. This would contain an odd electron. The odd electron in Fe (III) and in O_2^- is coupled **anti-ferromagnetically** to afford a diamagnetic compound. In the model picket fence iron complex upon oxygenation the O—O stretching frequency has been measured and is found to be $1105\ cm^{-1}$. This value is much closer to the found for KO_2 ($1145\ cm^{-1}$) than for O_2 ($1560\ cm^{-1}$). Some recent vibrational studies on the oxyhaemoglobin also suggest that a similar situation is present. In short, the experimental fact is that **oxyhaemoglobin and oxymyoglobin become diamagnetic and the iron centres occupy the same plane as that of the porphyrin nitrogens.** This has a great bearing on the mechanism of oxygen transport, as we will see below.

Deoxy-Hb

Electronic spectrum λ_{max} ~ 400 (≥ 10000) nm

Soret band ($\pi \rightarrow \pi^*$)

Magnetism $S = 2$ (isolated paramagnet)

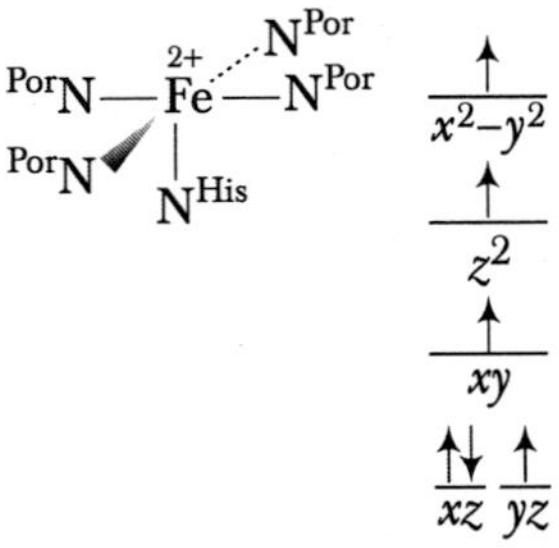

High-spin, $S = 2$

Oxy-Hb

Magnetism
- $S = 0$ (low T)
- increases towards $S = 1$ (higher T)

⇒ magnetic coupling

Resonance Raman

$$v_{O—O} = 1105\ cm^{-1}$$

	O_2	O_2^-	O_2^{2-}
$v_{O—O}$ (cm^{-1})	1560	~1100	850–740
	$S = 1$	$S = 1/2$	$S = 0$

Conclude

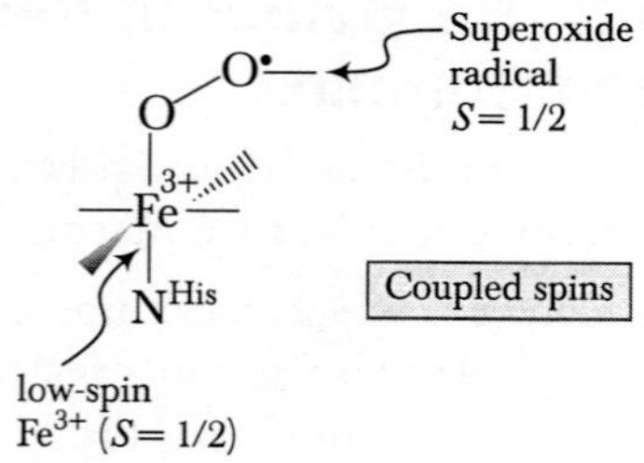

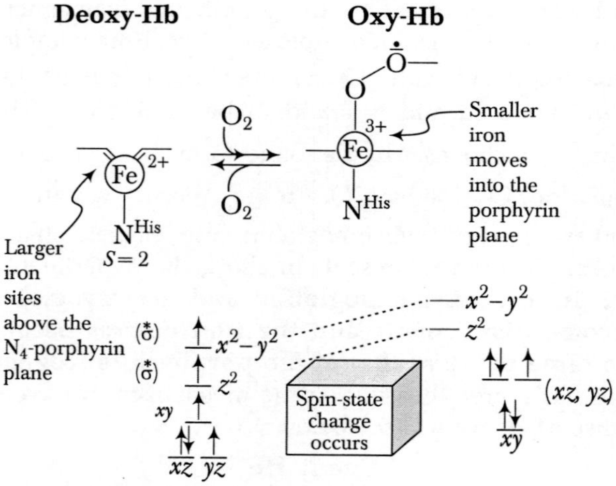

Conclude The proximal base increases O_2 affinity.

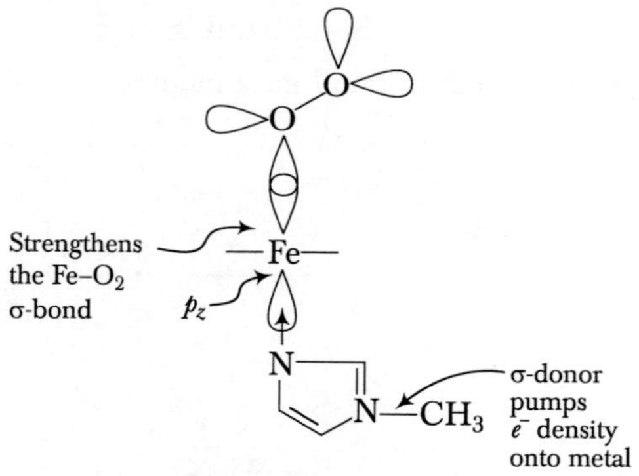

Role of the distal base

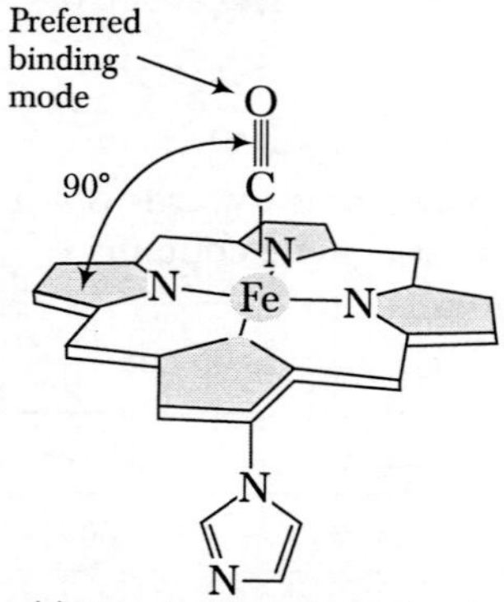

(a) Free heme with imidazole

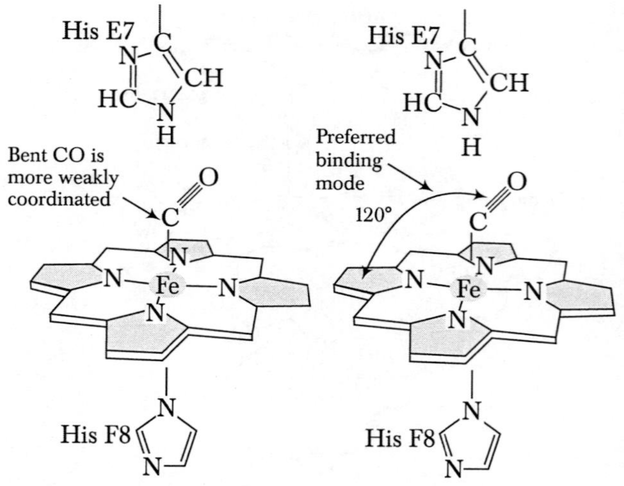

(b) Mb:CO complex (c) Oxymyoglobin

Fig. 13.4

The Mechanism of Oxygen Transport and Cooperativity

(a) Oxygen affinities of haemoglobin and myoglobin

The function of haemoglobin (Hb) is to bind oxygen in the lungs (at high oxygen partial pressures) and to carry it without any loss and release it to myoglobin (Mb) in the cellular tissues (at low oxygen partial pressures). This implies that Mb should have a greater affinity for oxygen at low partial pressures. Experimentally the oxygenation saturation curves for Hb and Mb are as shown in the figure.

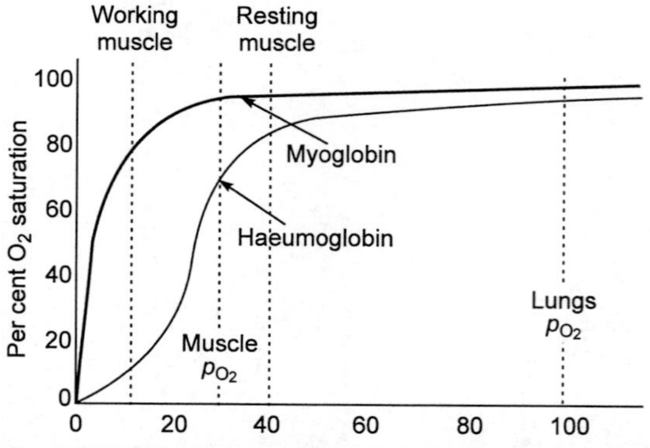

Fig. 13.5 Partial pressure of oxygen (p_{O_2} mm Hg) cooperative binding curve for Hb.

The degree of saturation for Mb is higher than for Hb at low partial pressures as shown by the comparison of the saturation curves for Mb and Hb at various partial pressures.

The shape of the curve is explained in terms of the equilibrium $Mb + O_2 \rightleftharpoons MbO_2$.

$$\therefore \qquad K = \frac{[MbO_2]}{[Mb]\,p}$$

where, p is the partial pressure of oxygen. The fractional oxygen saturation α is the ratio of the concentration of Mb present as MbO_2 to the total concentration of Mb.

$$\alpha = \frac{[MbO_2]}{[Mb] + [MbO_2]}$$

It follows that,

$$\alpha = \frac{K_p}{1 + K_p}$$

Mb curve only conforms to this equation but not the Hb curve. Another important feature of binding in Hb is that O_2 binding by Hb is pH depenent, in spite of the absence of an acid group at the heme site, and oxygen is released more readily at lower pH. Hence, **oxygen is released more readily in cells where metabolism is active and consequently a high concentration of CO_2 resulting in low pH.** Another observation is that the binding of organic phosphates to the protein of Hb far from the heme site also affects O_2 binding.

(b) Cooperativity in haemoglobin

Myoglobin is a monomer (one heme group) whereas haemoglobin is a tetramer (four heme groups). This difference is important, since it allows the four heme units of Hb to bind O_2 cooperatively; once one oxygen is bound to Hb the affinity for subsequent oxygen molecules increases. M.F. Perutz initially proposedthis mechanism. He argued that when a high spin Fe(II) that is about 0.4 Å above the plane of the porphyrin ring is bound to oxygen it shrinks in size (because it has been oxidized to Fe^{3+}) and is brought down into the plane. This causes a pulling of the histidine residue (imidazole group) along with protein attached to it. As a result the shape of the protein is adjusted and the binding characteristics of other sites are modified. This leads to greater oxygen affinity for the second iron centre and so on. During the release of oxygen from Hb to Mb also such cooperativity behaviour exists.

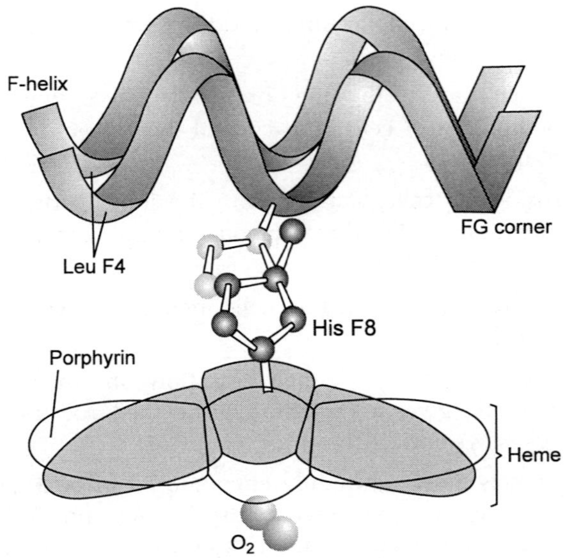

Fig. 13.6 Cooperativity in Hb.

The porphyrin ligand environment found in Hb and Mb, is also important in redox enzymes. A large class of biochemically important heme proteins have Fe-coordinated to a porphyrin ligand. The other iron-proteins are classified as non-heme. They constitute a large group of iron-sulphur-based proteins.

Among these a large group containing iron in a tetrahedral environment of four S-atoms are particularly important. They are involving conversion of NAD to NADH and N_2 to NH_3 and can generate H_2 from acid solutions.

Metal Ions in Biology

Several elements including metals play a very important role in biological systems. However, the order of importance of elements from the biological point of view has nothing to do with the order of their abundance in earth's crust. For example aluminium and silicon are very abundant in the earth's crust but have negligible importance in life systems. Certain elements which occur in trace quantities in the earth crust, play an important role in organisms. Copper and selenium are two examples. There are also other rare elements such as Be, Tl, V etc., which have no biological functions, investigations are being conducted and new discoveries are being made, and the importance of these elements may be realized in future.

The functions of elements can be classified as follows, in relation to their biological environment.

1. In the extracellular fluids and the outer faces of cell membranes.
2. In cell walls, the membranes which define the boundaries of cells, and control the exit and entry of materials.
3. Inside the cells, starting from the inner surface of membranes in the aqueous phase known as cytoplasmic fluid.
4. In the organelles inside cells including nuclei and mitochondria.

The identification of their location in the host environment gives a valuable clue to their role in the biological systems.

The metals most commonly encountered in biological systems such as enzymes etc., are K, Mg and Fe but cells generally discriminted against sodium and calcium.

Significance of Biologically Important Element

Na^+ and K^+ Most important free intra and extracellular cations. Regulation of the osmotic pressure, membrane potentials, enzyme activity, signalling.

Mg^{2+} Chlorophyll; anaerobic energy metabolism (ATP → ATP).

Ca^{2+} Signalling, muscle contraction, enzyme regulation. Main inorganic part of the endoskeletons (bones, teeth, enamel : hydroxyapatite; $Ca_5(PO_4)_3(OH)$. Exoskeletons of muscels, shells, corals, sea urchins etc., aragonite or clacite; $(CaCO_3)$.

$V^{IV/V}$, $Mo^{IV/VI}$, $W^{IV/VI}$, $Mn^{II/III/IV}$, $Fe^{II/III}$, $Ni^{I/II/III}$ $Cu^{I/II}$: active centres in electron-transport (redox) enzymes, oxygenases, dismutases.

Fe and Cu Transport of oxygen.

Fe^{III} Iron-storage proteins (ferritins).

$Fe^{II} + Fe^{III}$ in magnetite (Fe_3O_4) Orientation of magnetobacteria, pigeons, bees in Earth's magnetic field.

Co Synthases and isomerases (cobalamines, *e.g.*, vitamin-B_{12}); methylation of inorganics.

Zn^{2+} In the active centre of hydrolases, carboanhydrase, alcohol dehydrogenases, synthases; genetic transcription (zinc fingers), stabilisation of tertiary and quarternary structures of proteins; repair enzymes.

Si^{IV} ("silicate") Involved in the built-up bones. In the form of SiO_2/silica-gels as support in monocotyledonous plants (like grass) and the shells of diatoms.

P^V (phosphate) Constituent in hydroxy and fluoropatite ($Ca_5(PO_4)_3(OH/F)$); energy metabolism (ATP), NADPH, activation of organic substrate; phospholipids in cell membranes; phosphate esters (DNA, RNA,...).

Se^{-II} Selenocystein in special enzymes (*e.g.*, glutathionperoxidase)

F^- Fluoropatite ($Ca_5(PO_4)_3F$) in dental enamel.

Cl^- Along with hydrogencarbonate the most important free anion.

I Constituent of thyroid hormones (such as thyroxine).

Medicinal Relevant Elements

Li^+ Treatment of bipolar disorder (mavac depression) and hypertension.

Gd^{3+} Contrast agent in magnetic resonance tomography of soft tissue.

$BaSO_4$ Contrast reagent for X-ray tomography. Sun protection.

Pt^+ Chemotherapy (*e.g.*, with cisplatin *cis* $[Pt(NH_3)_2Cl_2]$ of cancer (ovary, testes)).

Au^I Therapy of rheumatic arthritis.

Sb^{II} Treatment of inflammatory skin pimples like acne.

Bi^{III} Treatment of gastritis.

Metallobiomolecules

The following tables give a survey of biomolecules which utilize metal ions. Many of these molecules are proteins. About 30% of enzymes are **Metalloenzmes;** *i.e.,* which have a metal atom in their active site. Metalloenzymes are involved in acid catalysed hydrolytic reactions, (involving hydrolases), redox reactions involving oxygenases and oxidases, processes involving rearrangement of C—C linkages (synthesis and isomerases). It is seen from the Table that metal ion containing molecules in general serve important functions as electron carriers, metal storage sites, oxygen binding and storage sites, etc. Metal ions are also involved in photoredox reactions, as in chlorophyll.

Table 13.1 **Classification of Some Biomolecules Containing Metal Ions**

Metallobiomolecules

- Proteins
  - Enzymes (see below)
  - Transport and storage proteins
    - Electron carriers
    - Metal storage and structural
    - O_2 binding
  - Signal transduction
    - Metal sensors and switching
- Non-proteins
  - Metal transport and structural
  - Photoredox

	Electron carriers	Metal storage and structural	O_2 binding	Metal sensors and switching	Metal transport and structural	Photoredox
Fe :	**Cytochrimes iron-sulpher**	**Ferritin Transferrin**	**Myoglobin Haemoglobin Hemerythrin**	**IRE-EP Fur**	**Siderophores**	
Cu :	Blue copper	Ceruloplasmin	Hemocyanin	Cup 2		
ZN, Hg :						**Chlorophyll**
Ca : Si :				Calmodulin	Skeletal	
Zn, Hg :		**Metallothionen**		**MerR**		

Enzymes

	Hydrolases	Oxido-reductases	Isomerases and synthetases
Fe :		**Oxygenases Hydrogenases**	**Aconitase Endo III**
Fe, Mo :		Nitrogenases	
Fe, Mo, Cu :		**Oxidases Reductases Hydroxylases**	
Mo, Cu, Zn :		Superoxide dismutases	
Co :			**Vitamin B_{12} coenzymes**
Zn :	Carboxypeptidase		
Zn, Cu, Mg :	**Phosphatases**		
Mg, Mn :	Aminopeptidases		

Some important metalloenzymes and their functions are as :

(a) Carbonic anhydrase

It is a zinc enzyme that catalyses the hydration of CO_2 and dehydration of carbonic acid (HCO_3^- to be more precise.)

The Lewis acidity of Zn^{2+} ion in carbonic anhydrase polarizes the coordinated H_2O molecule to the point of loss of H^+ ion to form coordinated OH group. It is the hydroxy form of the enzyme which is believed to reversibly hydrate CO_2 to HCO_3^-. The probable mechanism illustrating the role of the enzyme in the process is shown below.

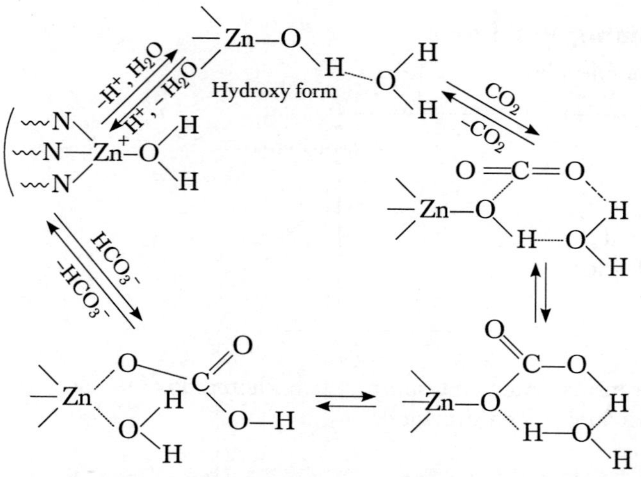

The probable mechanism for reversible hydration of CO_2.

Like all truly catalytic reactions, catalytic reversible hydration of CO_2 is a close loop. The clockwise cycle shows the hydration of CO_2 to HCO_3^- and the anti-clockwise cycle shows the release of CO_2 from HCO_3^-.

(b) Peroxidases

These form a class of enzymes which catalyse the oxidation of substrates by H_2O_2. The heme group containing high spin Fe(III) is the prosthetic group present in peroxidases. The heme group of a peroxidase is lodged deeply in a rather larger protein molecule with a histidine nitrogen coordinating to the fifth position of Fe(III). The sixth coordination site or Fe(III) of the heme group of the peroxidase can be occupied by a water molecule when the enzyme is at rest or by the substrate when it is in function. The mechanism illustrating the role of the enzyme in the process is as follows :

$$\underset{}{H_2O_2} + \underset{\text{Peroxidase enzyme}}{RFe^{III}} \longrightarrow R^{\bullet+}Fe^{IV}{=}O + H_2O$$

$$R^{\bullet+}Fe^{IV}{=}O + \underset{\text{(Substrate containing two removable hydrogens)}}{AH_2} \longrightarrow RFe^{III} + \underset{\text{(Oxidised substrate)}}{A} + H_2O$$

($R^{\bullet+}$ is the cation radical formed by the removal of a π electron from porphyrin part).

(c) Carboxy peptidase

It is also a zinc enzyme which hydrolyses the terminal peptide (amide) bond of the peptide chain from the side of its carboxy end, as shown below :

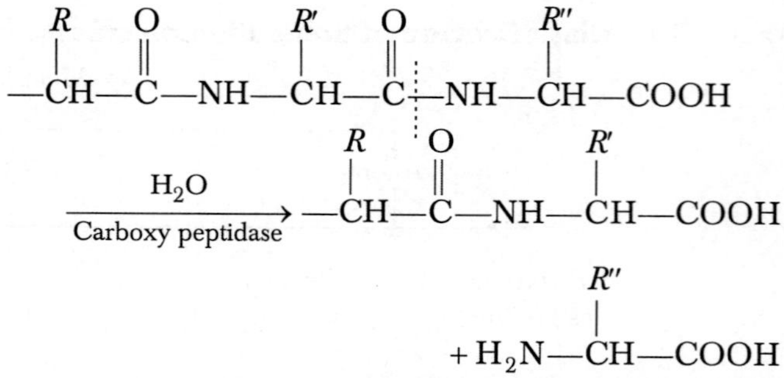

The enzyme is selective. **It hydrolyses those polypeptides in which the terminal amino acid segment has an aromatic or a branched chain aliphatic substituent *R*″.**

The active Zn^{2+} ion is located in a depression formed on the surface of the coiled epoenzyme.

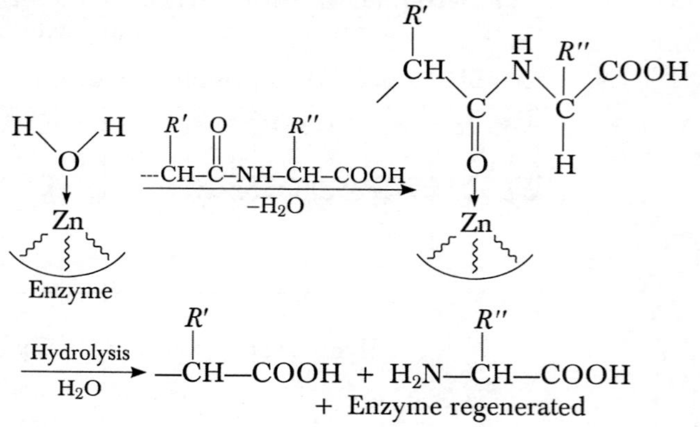

Mechanism for the hydrolysis of the peptide (amide) bond carried out by the enzyme carboxy peptidase.

It has been established that the Zn^{2+} ions can be replaced by Co^{2+} ions with the retention of enzyme activity. This is because the cobalt enzyme would show absorption bands in the visible region due to *d-d* transitions from which valuable information about metal ion environment in the enzyme can be obtained.

(d) Cytochrome P-450 enzymes

Cytochrome P-450 is the designation for a family of enzymes with iron porphyrin active sites which catalyse the addition of oxygen to a substrate. The most representative of the reaction brought about by these enzymes is the reaction involving insertion of O into the *R*—H linkage, which is a typical redox reaction. The reaction plays an important role in body's defence against hydrophobic compounds such as drugs, steroid precursors, and pesticides. The hydroxylation of *R*—H renders them water soluble and enables their easy elimination from the systems.

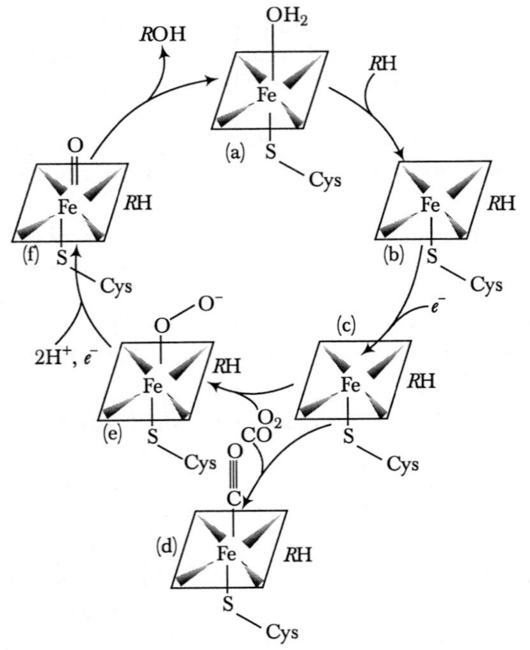

Fig. 13.7 The cycle of reactions of cytochrome P-450. The resulting state of the enzyme is (a) and the important Fe(IV) oxo species is (f).

The catalytic cycle which has proposed may be diagramatically represented by the following scheme.

The sequence begins at (a) with the enzyme in its resting state with iron present as Fe(III). The hydrocarbon substrate binds to (b) and one electron is transferred (c). The resulting complex contains Fe(II), and bond substrate proceeds to bind O_2 (e). At this point in the cycle a competing reaction with CO occurs, to give (d). The species formed is easily identified by its absorption at 450 nm, (which gives the family its name P-450). The key reaction is the reduction of the porphyrin ring of the oxygen complex (e) by a second electron which produces the ring radical anion. The uptake of two H^+ ions leads to the formation of the Fe(IV) complex (f) which attacks the substrate to insert oxygen. Loss of *R*OH and uptake of a H_2O molecule at the vacated coordination position bring the cycle to an end. The key to the cycle is the Fe(IV) oxo-complex.

The precise mechanism of the oxygenation has been investigated in detail. One mechanism involves the generation of an oxygen radical which can attack the C—H bond, and the other mechanism involves transfer of oxygen to a C—H bond. The oxidation involving a free radical entails certain unconventional features, since such reactions are not generally stereospecific. On the other hand, the oxidation brought about by P-450 enzymes are quite selective and preserve the optical activity of chiral substrate.

The other mechanism involves the attack of C—H bond, by the electrophilic positive oxygen centre. It is supported by the retention of stereochemical configuration and the reduction of activity in cases in which the substrate has substituents, that block the approach of the O atom to the C—H bond. The transfer of what is effectively a neutral oxygen atom leaves the iron porphyrin reduced from Fe(IV) to Fe(III) while the organic substrate is oxidized.

(e) Ferrodoxins

The ferrodoxins form an important class of enzymes which play a role in oxygen transfer. **They are of importance in lower organisms and are also involved in nitrogen fixation.** Ferrodoxin forms an important member of an interesting group of iron-sulphur proteins. It is a non-heme protein containing iron in a tetrahedral environment of S-atoms. The ferrodoxins contains non-heme iron and display reduction potentials from 0 to 0.5 V. They are involved in the reduction of NAD to NADH and N_2 to NH_3. They generate H_2 from acid solution.

One or more Fe atoms may participate at the active site in iron sulphur proteins. Examples are the isolated Fe atom, in tetrahedral environment of RS^- in cystine, 2Fe atom clusters formed with S^{2-} bridging atoms, known as two iron ferrodoxins. In addition there are also the 4 Fe 4 S ferrodoxins.

The Fe—S cluster is held in a fold of the protein. This enables control to be exercised over the access by substrates. The Fe—S cluster shows little change in bond length consequent on gain of an electron, in spite of the conversion of high spin Fe(III) to low spin Fe(II). As a result there is no barrier to electron transfer and the common function of these proteins is one electron transfer. The iron sulphur proteins are usually found in membranes or cytoplasm. Various side groups can render the protein molecule either water soluble or lipid souble, rendering it adaptable either to the cytoplasm or the membrane.

Certain compounds have been synthesised simulating the ferrodoxins. It has been found that the reaction of $FeCl_3$, $NaOCH_3$ and NaHS and benzylthiol in methanol yields a product $[Fe_4S_4(SCH_2Ph)_4]$. The electronic spectrum, magnetic susceptibility and redox properties are analogous to those of ferrodoxins. Oxidation number rules suggest two Fe(II) atoms and two Fe(III) atoms but all spectroscopic methods suggest four equivalent iron atoms. Consequently a delocalized electron description is the most appropriate and the electron transfer reaction involve orbitals which are delocalized over the clustre with S and Fe atoms both sharing the change in the oxidation state.

Ion Transport Through Membranes

The chief source of energy for cells is the phosphate polymer ATP (Adenosine triphosphate). This releases free energy through the cleavage of —P—O—P—bonds. The storage of energy in the form of ATP is very general and the means of synthesis of ATP is of central importance in the biochemistry of organisms.

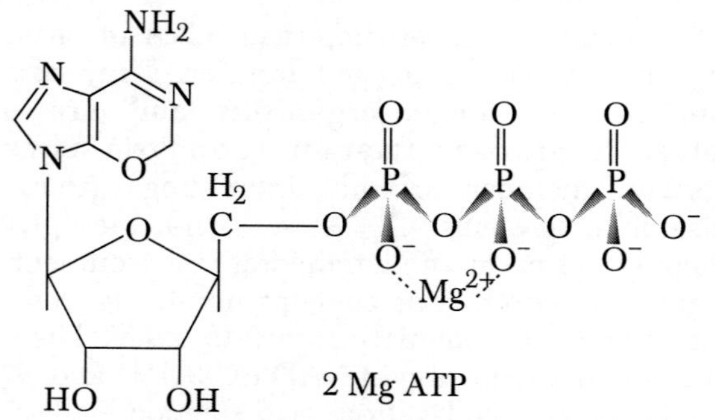

2 Mg ATP

The key features of conditions favouring the condensation of two —P—OH units are pH and electric charge. The PH and the charge gradient required are created across the cell membrane by reactions which exploit the electron acceptor properties of O_2 molecule and thus oxygen is ultimately responsible for driving, the buildup of the energy carrier of the cells. It is the intricate network of transport processes that sustain an organism.

The sodium and potassium pump constitutes to the active transport *i.e.,* the transport of ions through the membranes. The charge distribution established across the membrane by active transport results in an electric potential difference as well as a difference in the chemical composition of the fluids inside and outside the cell.

Most animal cells have higher concentration of K^+ ions inside the cell membranes and a higher concentration of Na^+ outside the cell. The immediate source of energy required to maintain this is ATP and a large amount of ATP is consumed to maintain this concentration gradient.

A valuable clue to the manner in which the ion pump functions, came in 1957, when an enzyme of molar mass 110 kg/mol was discovered by Jens Skou, which hydrolyses ATP only if Na^+ and K^+ ions are present in addition to Mg^{2+} required for all ADPases (enzymes catalysing the hydrolysis of ATP). The activity of this enzyme correlates quantitatively with the extent of ion transport. Another important clue was provided by the observation that this ATPase is phosphorylated at an aspartase site only in the presence of Na^+ and Mg^{2+} ions. The phosphorylated product is hydrolysed if K^+ ions are present. It has been also observed that the enzyme undergoes a conformational change when it is phosphorylated.

The mechanism shown in the following diagram has been proposed.

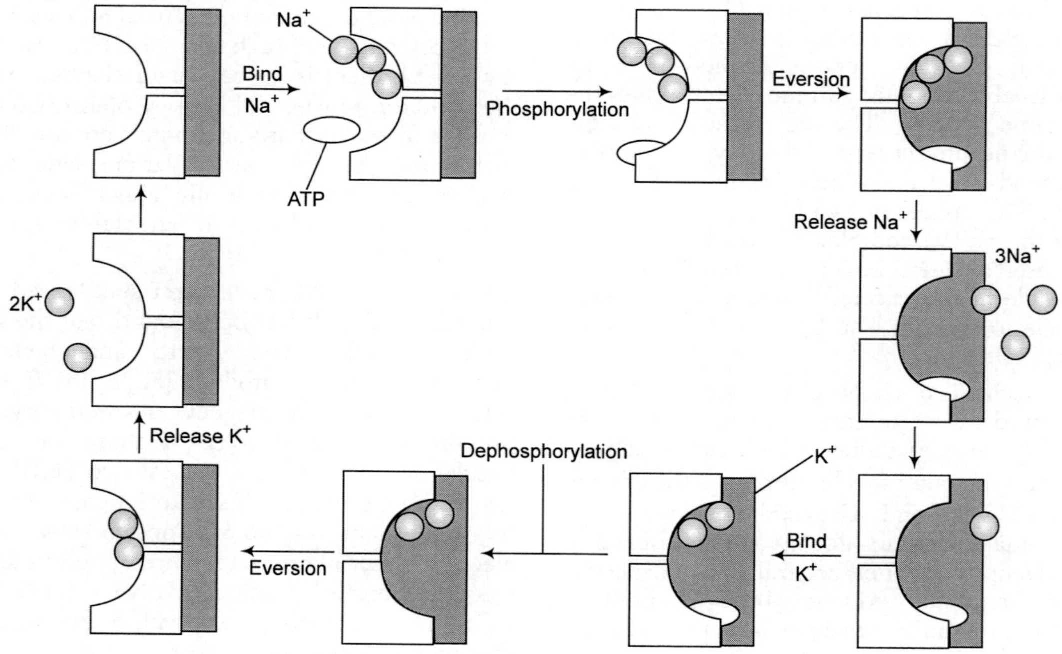

Fig. 13.8 Mechanism of ion transport through membrane.

At first ATP and three Na^+ ions bind to the inside of the membrane and the enzyme is phosphorylated. The product of the reaction by **eversion** brings the Na^+ ions outside of the cell membrane. These three ions are replaced by $2K^+$ ions. The attachment of K^+ ions induces dephosphorylation and hydrolysis of ATP to ADP produces a conformational change that carries two K^+ ions to the interior of the cell where they are released. This process builds up a charge gradient across the membrane, since $3Na^+$ ions are expelled for two K^+ ions incorporated and the out surface becomes relatively positively charged.

Support for the above mechanisms of ion transport comes from the observation that vanadate ions (VO_4^{3-}) can inhabit the operation of the enzyme ATPase. The difference between the PO_4^{3-} ion and VO_4^{3-} ion arises from the fact, that the 5-coordinate phosphate intermediated formed by the attack by water is unstable and readily breaks down and thus completing the hydrolysis. However in the case of VO_4^{3-} ion, 5-coordinated species is quite stable and does not break down, and consequently the conformational change does not take place and the bound K^+ ions remain on the outer part of the cell membrane.

The outstanding feature of the active transport is the selectivity of the comlexation process, between K^+ and Na^+. The enzyme is selective first to Na^+ and then to K^+ in its different conformations. The group I cation due to their large radii are not prone to strong complextion. **Selectivity is thus governed by coulombic forces and differences in ionic radii**.

The ion channels which permit transport of ions, are constructed from protein, polymers in helical conformations. These helices form the wall of cell channels and their precise conformations result in specific geometrical arrangements of a number of potential ligand-metal binding sites. There are striking differences between the channels, selectivity towards either Na^+ or K^+ ions.

1. Only Tl^+ approaches K^+ in permeability of K^+ channels. No other ion smaller or larger passes well.
2. The K^+ channels exclude NH_4^+ more rigorously than the Na^+ channels, inspite of the fact that K^+ and NH_4^+ have almost similar radii.
3. Large hydrogen bonded spherical molecules and ions pass the Na^+ channels. No methylated compounds *e.g.*, $CH_3 \cdot NH_3^+$ pass either channels.

These facts can be explained by the assumption that Na^+ channel is larger and hydrated. The more strongly hydrated Na^+ ion moves into sites in the channel while exchanging H_2O ligands to bind to the H_2O molecules in the channel interior. The larger and less strongly hydrated K^+ ions pass through a dehydrated channel where they complex to protein side chain anions. It is well known that solubilities of Na^+ salts of poorly hydrated anions such as ClO_4^-, are much greater than those of the cooresponding K^+ salts.

The role of the steric factors in iron transport is illustrated by considering a biochemically important ligand. It is known that crown ethers having antibiotic activity, increase the permeability of the cell membranes to cations. The chelating ligand binds both Na^+ and K^+ ions but strongly favours K^+ by a factor of nearly 100. The origin of selectivity is stereochemical since K^+ fits perfectly into the cavity of the hollow crown. Stereoselectivity is of imortance in complexation equilibria.

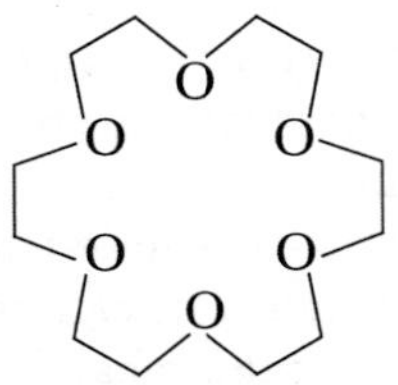

4 crown ether

Ionophores

Ion gradients play an important role in active transport and energy conservation. Natural products and drugs that cause a collapse of ion gradients across cellular membranes are poisons and also serve as antibiotics. The transport of ions is made possible by ionophores (ion bearers) which shuttle ions across membranes. There are cyclic peptides, that fold around metal ions and thus carry the metal ion down its concentration gradient. Valinomycin is a small cyclic peptide that fold around K^+ ion and thus neutralizes its positive charge. Valinomycin kills the 'microbial cells' by disrupting the secondry transport processes and energy conserving reactions.

Ionophores such as valinomycin uncouple oxidative phosphorylation by dissipating ion gradients across the inner mitochondrial membrane (where energy is released through redox reactions), eliminating the contribution of $\Delta\psi$ (transmembrane difference in electrical potential) to the proton motive force. A transmembrane electrical potential ($\Delta\psi$) exists because of unequal distribution of protons on either side. The ionophore valinomycin combines reversibly by combining with K^+ ions to form a membrane permeable complex which diffuses across the inner membrane and releases K^+ on the inside. This movement of charge reduces the value of $\Delta\psi$ and uncouples electron transfer from ATP synthesis. They thus act as **uncouplers**. Ionophores uncouple electron transfer from oxidative phosphorylation, by creating electrical short circuits across the mitochondrial membrane. The ionophores form lipid soluble complexes with K^+. While K^+ itself can penetrate the mitochondrial membrane slowly, the complex with K^+ can diffuse rapidly. The influx of positive ions neutralizes the excess of negative charge inside the matrix, thus diminishing the electrical component of the proton-motive force. Valinomycin slows mitochondrial ATP synthesis without blocking electron transfer to O_2.

Oxygen Transport

The most common oxygen carriers are all based on helical proteins. In haemoglobin the coiled proteins act like springs. The strain generated at one part by oxygen binding at one site is transmitted to other sites. The chemistry of oxygen transport can be a combination of oxygen complexation at the metal and of the alteration of the protein environment. **The oxygen carriers are selective to the identity of the incoming π-acceptor ligands, except in respect of size**. Thus, haemoglobin and myoglobin bind not only O_2, but also other ligands such as CN^-, NO, CO, *R*NC, N_3^-, SCN^- etc.

The proteins, haemoglobin (Hb) and myoglobin, are both complexes built around Fe(II). The oxidised forms met-myoglobin and met-haemoglobin containing Fe(III), do not bind O_2 and cannot play the role as oxygen transporters.

Naked 'heme' the Fe-porphyrin complex without the accompanying polypeptide is oxidised irreversibly by molecular oxygen, give ultimately a stable μO^{2-} complex which cannot function as an oxygen carrier. However, this unproductive reaction, which constitutes, a fatal flaw in its biological function is prevented by the protein environment in which heme is embedded in Hb or Mb. The proteins effectively protect the Fe(II) complex, which can survive long enough to bind and release oxygen. It is a typical example of the control of reaction environments that proteins can exercise. Deoxy Mb is a five coordinate high spin complex of Fe(II), four of the coordination positions being occupied by porphyrin ring N atoms. The fifth position is occupied by the N-atom of imidazole ligand of a histidine residue which couples the heme to the protein. Such five coordinate heme complexes of Fe(II) are always high spin. The diameter of the t_{2g}^4, e_g^2 (Fe II) ion is larger than that of the central hole of the porphyrin ring, and hence, the Fe(II) ion lies 0.4 Å above the plane of the ring.

When oxygen completes the six coordination environment, the high spin (Fe) II, gets converted into the spin Fe (II) with t_{2g}^6 configuration. The Fe(II) shrinks in size and moves into the plane of the porphyrin ring. These structural changes have been verified by X-ray diffraction.

Steric hindrance of dimer formation is achieved with the so called, Picket Fence Porphyrins the 'pickets' being a group of blocking substitutents projecting from one side of the planar ring. Coordination of a bulky ligand like N-alkyl-imidazole can occur only on the unhindered side. An imidazole is a σ-donor which favours coordination of π-acceptor lying trans to itself. It gives the complex an affinity for oxygen, similar to that of Mb and the blocking substituents create a pocket for O_2 and prevent formation of $[Fe(Porph)Im_2)]$. The pickets also prevent reaction with a second Fe-centre which would result in the inactive $\mu-O_2$ species.

The picket fence models, provide valuable guidance on Hb and Mb oxygen complexes.

Electron Transport System

Photosynthesis and respiration are two important biological processes. They involve primary energy conversion, and involve redox reactions. Such reactions may occur by electron transfer, atom transfer and group transfer. Metalloenzymes function in all these ways. The role of enzyme containing iron is illustrative and covers all forms of life.

Reduction and oxidation in cells do not take place directly, but involve a series of compounds known as mediators. Through them oxidation occurs in stages in a controlled manner.

Among the mediators, found in mitochondria (the organelles in which oxygen utilization is accomplished), we have the heme containing pigments namely the **cytochromes** and **flavoproteins**, which also function in the insertion of oxygen into organic molecules containing pigments known as **cytochromes.**

The chief source of energy in the organisms is derived from the oxidation of glucose and also fats. There are various steps leading to the liberation of energy by oxidation of glucose. Energy is finally stored by the formation of ATP from ADP. The conversion of ADP to ATP is known as **phosphorylation** and accompanies oxidation and is hence known as **oxidative phosphorylation.** However, **phosphorylation** may also take place without the accompaniment of oxidation.

The first step of this process involves the formation of pyruvic acid from oxaloacetic acid.

$$HOOC \cdot CO \cdot CH_2 \cdot COOH \xrightarrow{-CO_2} CH_3 \cdot CO \cdot COOH$$

This step is followed by the Kreb's cycle or citric acid cycle through the formation of acetyl coenzyme to which mitochondria are permeable.

The final stages involve electron transport resulting in the formation of water from oxygen. These stages involve the function of cytochromes. The oxidation is accompanied by phosphorylation of ADP.

Cytochromes function by shuttling iron between Fe(II) and Fe(III), at the active site and thus act as one electron agents. The Fe atoms are in the porphyrin ring coordination environments buried in the middle of the protein.

The net reaction involving oxidative phosphorylation can be expressed by the following equation

$$\text{glucose} + 6O_2 + 36ADP^{3-} + 36HPO_4^{2-} + 36H^+ \longrightarrow 6CO_2 + 36ATP^{2-} + 42H_2O$$

The sequence of reactions in the electron transportation in the mitochondria of the cells where oxygen is utilized may be diagrammatically represented as shown below.

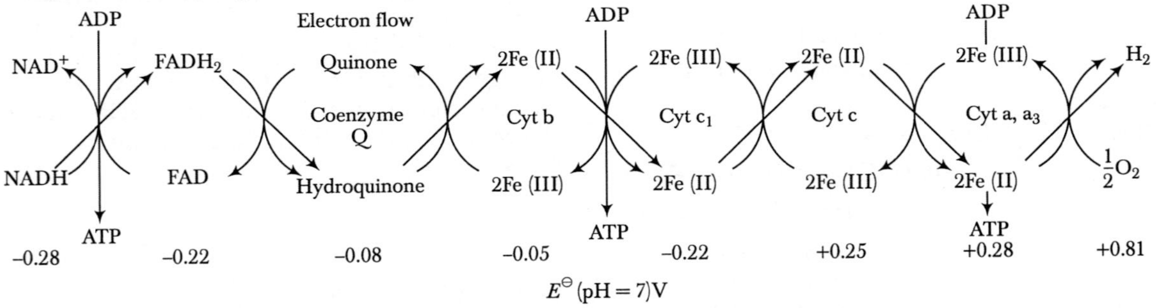

Fig. 13.9 The sequence of reactions in the electron transport chain in the mitochondria of cells where oxygen is utilized.

Photosynthesis

Photosynthesis results in reductive carbon fixation and production of oxygen, energy driven by light energy, $h\nu$

$$CO_2 + 2H_2O^* \xrightarrow{h\nu} \{CH_2O\} + O_2^* + H_2O$$

Carbon dioxide is reduced in a $4e^-$ reduction, to $\{CH_2O\}$. Here reducing agent is water, which is oxidised to O_2.

Instead of resorting to light as an energy source, chemical energy can be employed and sources for carbon other than CO_2, *e.g.*, CO or acetae, can be used.

In the photosynthetic process carried out by plants, one distinguishes between the light reaction and the light-independent (or dark) reaction on the one hand and, within the light reaction, between photosystems I and II (PSI and PSII, also referred to as light harvesting complexes LHC) on the other hand :

Light reaction :

PSII : $P_{680} + h\nu \longrightarrow [P_{680}]^+ + e^-$ (*via* phaeophytin, a "chlorophyll" depleted of Mg^{2+}) :

$$2[P_{680}]^+ + H_2O \longrightarrow 2P_{680} + \frac{1}{2}O_2 + 2H^+ \quad \text{(catalysed by water oxidase)}$$

The **water oxidase** (oxygen evolving centre, OEC), which catalyses the oxidation of water *via* P_{680}, contains 5 metal centres at its active site. Four of these metal ions (3 $Mn^{3+/4+}$ and one Ca^{2+}) form, together with $4O^{2-}$, a cubane-like cluster.

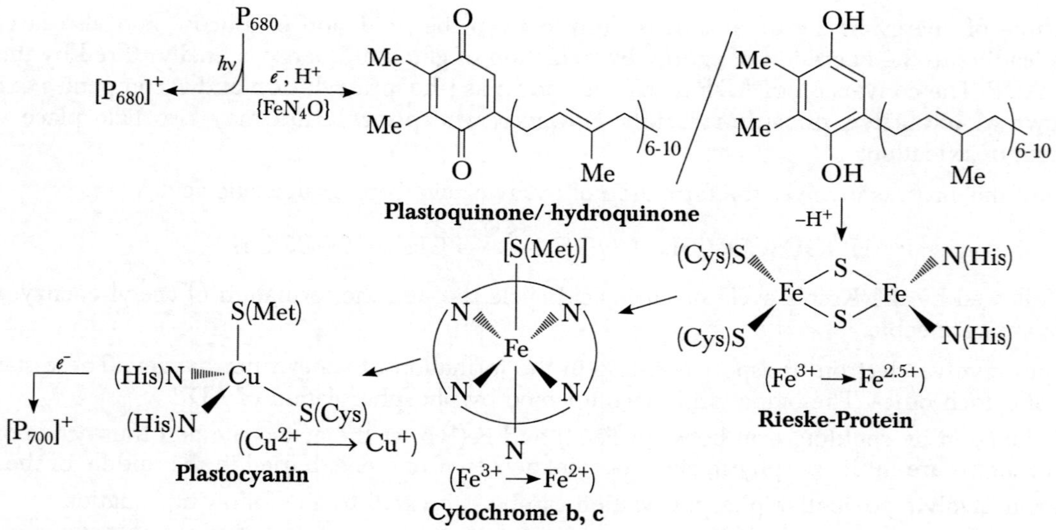

Fig. 13.10 Simplified representation of the electron transport chain between PSII and PSI.

PSI

$$P_{700} + h\nu \longrightarrow [P_{700}]^+ + e^-$$

$$[P_{700}]^+ + e^- \longrightarrow P_{700}$$

$$NADP^+ + 2e^- + 2H^+ \longrightarrow NADPH + H^+$$

(catalysed by[2 Fe, 2S])

Dark reaction

$$2(NADPH + H^+) + CO_2 \longrightarrow \{CH_2O\} + 2NADP^+ + H_2O$$

(energy driven by ATP)

The photosystems are collectives of pigment molecules (ca. 200), mainly chlorophyll-a and -b, carotinoids, anthocyanines and xantophylls. These pigments act as collectors over the complete spectrum of the (visible) sun light. The energy thus collected is transferred to the reaction centres, which represent specific molecules of chlorophyll-a, termed P_{680} in PSII, and P_{700} in PSI (see figure below)

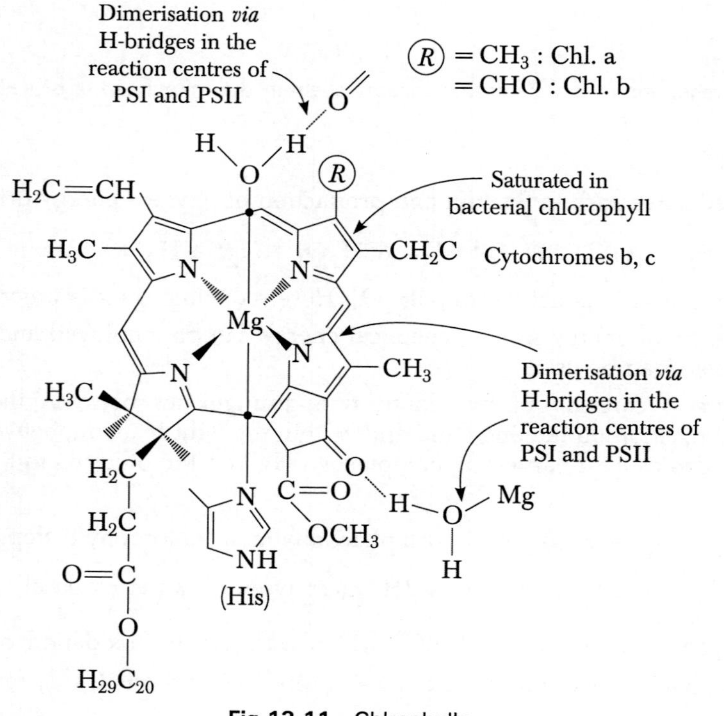

Fig.13.11 Chlrophylls.

Nitrogen Fixation

Nitrogen fixation is the biogenic and non-biogenic transformations of elemental N_2 into nitrogen compounds, affording to overcome the bonding energy between the two trebly bonded nitrogen atoms (949 kJ/mol). The biogenic fixation, carried out by free living nitrogen-fixing bacteria (*Azotobacter*) and cyanobacteria ("blue-green algae", *Anabaena*), some archaea, and by symbiotic bacteria associated with leguminous plants (*Rhizobium*), leads to ammonium ions. Biogencic fixation accounts for about 60% of the overall nitrogen supply. Non-biogenic non-anthropogenic fixation, which can occur by electric discharge (lightning) in the troposphere, and by cosmic radiation in the stratosphere [$N_2 \rightarrow 2N$; $N + O_2 \rightarrow NO + O \rightarrow NO_x$], accounts for 10%. The remaining 30% of world-wide N_2 fixation go back to the Haber-Bosch process and combustion of fossil fuels (natural gas, coal, crude oil) and products produced from crude oil (petrol, gasoline, diesel).

The biological process though less efficient, takes place under ordinary conditions of pressure and temperature. It essentially occur in anaerobic conditions.

The enzyme present in the nitrogen fixing bacteria, *i.e.*, nitrogenase complex is composed of proteins of two kinds, *i.e.*, reductase (Fe—S protein) and nitrogenase, (Fe—Mo—S protein). Reductase supplies electrons which are used by the nitrogenase to reduce the nitrogen to NH_4^+. The stoichiometry of the reaction catalysed by the nitrogenase complex is

$$N_2 + 6e^- + \underset{\text{(Adenosine triphosphate)}}{12\text{ATP}} \longrightarrow 2NH_4^+ + \underset{\text{(Adinosine diphosphate)}}{12\text{ADP}} + 4H^+$$

Recent studies suggest the following reaction sequence :

1. The reduced ferridoxine transfers its electrons to the reductase component of the nitrogenase complex.
2. ATP then binds to the reductase and thereby alters its conformation in such a way so that its reduction potential changes from – 0.30 V to – 0.40 V *i.e.*, it becomes more reducing.
3. Due to increased reducing power, it transfer its electrons to the nitrogenase component of the nitrogenase complex, which contains the bound nitrogen.
4. The ATP then gets hydrolysed and the nitrogen bound to the nitrogenase component get reduced to NH_4^+.

Exercise 1

(For Part 'B')

1. A well known naturally occurring organometallic compound is
(a) vit B_{12} coenzyme (b) chlorophyll
(c) cytochrome P-450 (d) myoglobin

2. Red colour of oxyhaemoglobin is mainly due to
(a) *d–d* transition
(b) metal to ligand CT transition
(c) interaligand $\pi - \pi^*$ transition
(d) ligand to metal CT transition

3. In biological systems, the metal ion involved in the dioxygen transport besides Fe is
(a) Co (b) Zn (c) Mg (d) Cu

4. Amino acid side chain high affinity for Ca^{2+} and Cu^{2+} in mettalo-protein is
(a) carboxylate in both the cases
(b) imidazole in both the cases
(c) carboxylate for Ca^{2+} and imidazole for Cu^{2+}
(d) imidazole for Ca^{2+} and carboxylate for Cu^{2+}

5. In biological system, the metal ions involved in electron transport are
(a) Na^+ and K^+ (b) Zn^{2+} and Mg^{2+}
(c) Ca^{2+} and Mg^{2+} (d) Cu^{2+} and Fe^{2+}

6. Iron-sulphur clusters in biological systems are involved in
(a) proton transfer (b) atom transfer
(c) group transfer (d) electron transfer

7. In photosynthesis, the predominent metal present in the reaction centre of photosystem II is
(a) Zn (b) Cu
(c) Mn (d) Fe

8. VO_4^{3-} or PO_4^{3-} which inhibits the operation of enzyme ATPase?
(a) Both (b) Only PO_4^{3-}
(c) Only VO_4^{3-} (d) None of these

9. Most animal cells have
(a) higher conc. of K^+ ions outside the cells membrane
(b) higher conc. of Na^+ ions inside the cell membrane
(c) higher conc. of K^+ ions inside and higher conc. of Na^+ ions outside the cell membrane
(d) higher conc. of Na^+ ions inside the cell and lower conc. of K^+ ion inside the cell

10. ADPase requires for its action
(a) Zn^{2+} (b) Mn^{2+}
(c) Ca^{2+} (d) Mg^{2+}

11. ATPase is phosphorylated at an aspartate side in presence of
(a) Na^+ and Mg^{2+} ions (b) K^+ and Mg^{2+} ions
(c) Na^+ and K^+ ions (d) Na^+ and Mn^{2+} ions

12. Inversion process ATP binds to
(a) two Na^+ ions (b) three Na^+ ions
(c) two K^+ ions (d) three K^+ ions

13. In oxygen transport element which are important are
(a) Fe and Cu (b) Fe and Co
(c) Fe and Mg (d) Fe and Mn

14. The inside of a cell is a
(a) reducing medium (b) oxidising medium
(c) neutral medium (d) None of these

15. Haemoglobin and myoglobin binds
(a) only O_2 (b) CN^-, NO, CO
(c) *R*NC, N_3^-, SCN^- (d) All of these

16. Oxyhaemoglobin has iron in
(a) Fe^{2+} state (b) Fe^{3+} state
(c) Both (a) and (b) (d) None of these

17. The metal ion present in carbonic anhydrase is
(a) Mn (b) Zn (c) Cu (d) Fe

18. In deoxy haemoglobin
(a) 5th position is coordinated with O_2
(b) 5th position is coordinated by porphyrin ring N-atom
(c) 5th position is occupied by N-atom of imidazole ligand of a histidine residue which couples heme to the protein
(d) None of the above

19. In deoxy haemoglobin
(a) Fe(+2) lies above the plane of the ring
(b) Fe(+3) lies above the plane of the ring
(c) Fe(+2) lies below the plane of the ring
(d) Fe(+3) lies below the plane of the ring

20. Degree of saturation for Mb is
(a) lower than for Hb (b) same as for Hb
(c) higher than for Hb (d) None of these

21. O_2 binding in Hb is
(a) pH dependent (b) pH independent
(c) O_2 binds at neutral pH (d) None of these

22. Release of O_2 from oxyhaemoglobin is favoured by
(a) high pH and low CO_2 conc
(b) low pH nd low CO_2 conc
(c) high pH and high CO_2 conc
(d) low pH and high conc. of CO_2

23. Myoglobin contains
(a) two heme groups
(b) Mb is a tetramer having 4 heme groups
(c) one heme groups
(d) three heme groups

24. Haemoglobin contains
(a) tetramer of Mb having four heme groups
(b) dimer of Mb having two heme groups
(c) trimer of Mb having three heme groups
(d) monomer having one heme group

25. Cytochromes acts as
(a) two electron transfer agents
(b) one electron transfer agents
(c) multielectron transfer agent
(d) None of the above

26. Ferrodoxins are enzymes which plays important role in
(a) oxygen transfer
(b) involved in nitrogen fixation
(c) reduction of NAD to NADH
(d) All of the above

27. What is not true about ferrodoxins?
(a) Involved in oxidation of NH_3
(b) Generate H_2 from acid solution
(c) Reduction potential is from 0 to 0.5 V
(d) It is Fe—S protein

28. Nitrogenase enzyme contains
(a) Fe—S protein (b) Mo Fe S protein
(c) Both (a) and (b) (d) None of these

29. Nitrogenase enzyme helps in
(a) nitrogen fixation
(b) works under anaerobic condition
(c) Fe—S protein and Mo—Fe—S protein acts as cofactors
(d) All of the above

30. Photosystem I has a
(a) chlorophyll a, structure
(b) Mg-dihydro porphyrin complex
(c) Both (a) and (b)
(d) None of the above

31. Oxidation of H_2O to O_2 occurs by
(a) oxidised form of PS I
(b) oxidised form of PS II
(c) reduced form of PS I
(d) reduced form of PS II

32. In the oxidation of H_2O to O_2 which element is essential or photolysis of H_2O involves
(a) Zn (b) Mg
(c) K (d) Mn

33. Manganese is converted from which state during photolysis of water
(a) Mn^{2+} to Mn^{4+} (b) Mn^{4+} to Mn^{2+}
(c) Mn^{2+} to Mn^{+} (d) Mn^{+} to Mn^{2+}

34. In the transformation of oxyhaemoglobin to deoxyhaemoglobin
(a) Fe^{2+} in the low spin state changes to Fe^{2+} in the high spin state
(b) Fe^{2+} in the low spin state changes to Fe^{2+} in the low spin state
(c) Fe^{2+} in the high spin state changes to Fe^{2+} in the low spin state
(d) Fe^{2+} in the high spin state changes to Fe^{2+} in the high spin state

35. Carboxypeptidase contains
(a) Fe (b) Mn (c) Zn (d) Cu

36. Vitamin B_{12} in an example of
(a) hydrolyses
(b) oxidoreductases
(c) isomerases and synthases
(d) siderophore

37. Calmodulin contains
(a) Ca (b) Si
(c) Both (a) and (b) (d) None of these

38. O_2 binding protein is
(a) haemoglobin (b) myoglobin
(c) hemerythrin (d) All of these

39. Superoxide dimutases contains
(a) Mo, Cu, Zn (b) C, Fe, Zn
(c) Mo, Cu, Fe (d) Cu, Fe, Mn

40. Oxygenases contains
(a) Zn, Fe (b) Mg, Fe
(c) Fe (d) Fe, Mo

41. Nitrogenases contains
(a) Fe, Mo (b) Mg, Fe
(c) Fe, Zn (d) Fe, Cu

42. What is common in oxidases, reductases, hydroxylases?
(a) They are oxido-reductases
(b) They contain Fe, Mo, Cu
(c) They are enzymes
(d) All of the above

43. Phosphatases contains
(a) Zn (b) Mg
(c) Cu (d) All of these

44. Ferritin and transferrin are
(a) hydrolyses
(b) metal storage and structural proteins
(c) electron carriers
(d) metal sensors

Exercise 2

(For Part 'C')

1. Among the following pair of metal ions present in nature, the first one functions as an electron transfer agent and the second one catalyses the hydrolysis reactions. The correct pair is
(a) Fe and Zn (b) Mg and Fe
(c) Co and Mo (d) Ca and Cu

2. Nature has chosen Zn (II) ion at the active site of many hydrolytic enzymes because
(a) Zn (II) is a poor Lewis acid
(b) Zn (II) does not have chemically accessible redox states
(c) Zn (II) forms both four and higher coordination complexes
(d) Zn (II) forms weak complexes with oxygen donor ligands

3. When the reduced cytochrome transfers an electron from its Fe (II) to the bound O_2
(a) bond order of O_2 is reduced by one and ν_{O_2} decreases
(b) a metal bound superoxide is formed and ν_{O_2} decreases
(c) A metal bound superoxide is formed and ν_{O_2} increases
(d) The bond order of O_2 is reduced by one and ν_{O_2} increases

4. Deoxyhaemoglobin is
(a) five coordinated complex
(b) high spin complex
(c) Fe^{2+} state and four of coordination position are occupied by porphyrin ring N-atom
(d) All of the above

5. Match the following.

Column I		Column II	
A.	Cytochromo C	1.	Mo
B.	Calmodulin	2.	K
C.	Chlorophyll	3.	Mg
D.	Alcohol dehydrogenase	4.	Zn
		5.	Fe
		6.	Ca

Codes

	A	B	C	D
(a)	1	2	3	4
(b)	2	3	4	5
(c)	5	4	6	2
(d)	5	6	3	4

6. Match the following.

Column I		Column II	
A.	Ferritin	1.	Electron transport
B.	Vitamin B_{12}	2.	Ionophore
C.	Cytochromes	3.	Oxygen transport
D.	Valiomycin	4.	Nitrogen fixation
		5.	Organometallic enzym
		6.	Iron storage

Codes

	A	B	C	D
(a)	6	4	2	1
(b)	1	3	6	4
(c)	3	5	4	6
(d)	6	5	1	2

Directions (Q. Nos. 7 to 11)
There are two metalloproteins in vertebrates known as haemoglobin and myoglobin, which are responsible for oxygen uptake and transport. These are large polymeric entities. Haemoglobin picks up oxygen from lungs (or gills) and transport it and delivers it to myoglobin which is present in tissues. The role of myoglobin is to store oxygen and release it for metabolic process.

7. Iron in deoxymyoglobin is in
(a) low spin state (b) zero oxidation state
(c) high spin state (d) +I oxidation state

8. Iron in deoxymyoglobin is in
(a) zero oxidation state (b) +I oxidation state
(c) +II oxidation state (d) +III oxidation state

9. Which of the following statement is true about iron in deoxymyoglobin?
(a) Fe is in +2 oxidation state
(b) Fe is in high spin state
(c) Fe is not present in plane of the porphyrin ring but is 0.4 Å above it
(d) All of the above

10. Upon oxygenation of myoglobin
(a) Iron atom goes in the plane of the four porphyrin nitrogens
(b) Coordination number of iron goes to 4
(c) The Fe(II) is not present in plane of porphyrin ring
(d) Molecule become paramagnetic

11. In oxyhaemoglobin and oxymyoglobin
(a) Fe is in +3 oxidation state in both
(b) Fe is in +3 and +2 oxidation state respectively
(c) Fe is in +2 oxidation state in both
(d) Fe is in +2 and +3 oxidation state respectively

Assertion & Reason

Codes

(a) Both A and R are true and R is the correct explanation of A.
(b) Both A and R are true and R is not the correct explanation of A.
(c) A is true but R is false.
(d) A is false but R is true.

12. **Assertion (A)** In oxyhaemoglobin Fe is in high spin state and paramagnetic.

Reason (R) In oxyhaemoglobin Fe is oxidised from +2 oxidation state to +3 oxidation state.

13. **Assertion (A)** Haemoglobin binds O_2 at high oxygen partial pressures and released more readily at lower pH.

Reason (R) In cells metabolic activities causes increase in pH.

14. Match the following.

Column I	Column II
A. Oxyhaemoglobin	1. α-141 residues, β-146 residues
B. Deoxyhaemoglobin	2. α-161 residue
C. Haemoglobin	3. Low spin and diamagnetic
D. Myoglobin	4. High spin and diamagnetic
	5. Fe^{2+} not present in plane of the ring

Codes

	A	B	C	D
(a)	3	5	2	1
(b)	4	3	2	1
(c)	3	5	1	2
(d)	4	3	1	2

15. Which of the following statement(s) is/are true?
(a) In haemoglobin the coiled proteins acts like springs
(b) Hb and myoglobin both contains Fe in + 2 state
(c) Met-myoglobin is oxidised form of myoglobin
(d) All of the above

16. Met-myoglobin and Met-haemoglobin are
(a) oxidised forms and do not have O_2 binding capacity
(b) reduced forms and do not have O_2 binding capacity
(c) oxidised form and have O_2 binding capacity
(d) reduced form and have O_2 binding capacity

Directions (Q. Nos. 17 to 21)
Function of haemoglobin (Hb) is to bind oxygen in lungs and to carry it without any loss and release it to myoglobin in the cellular tissues. The oxygen saturation curves of the Hb and Mb is shown as

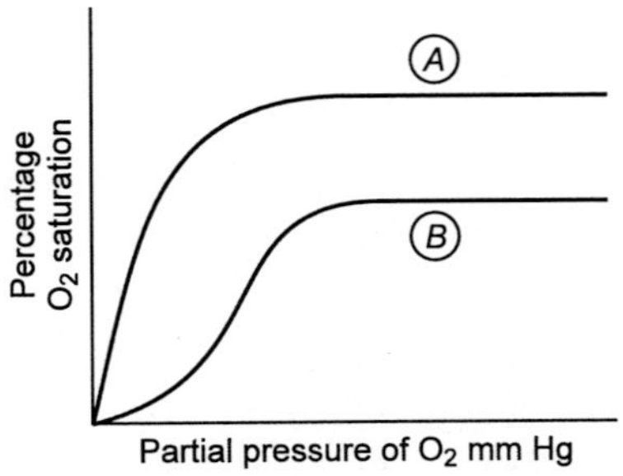

17. Curve *A* is of
(a) haemoglobin (b) myoglobin
(c) Both (a) and (b) (d) None of these

18. Curve *B* is of
(a) haemoglobin (b) myoglobin
(c) Both (a) and (b) (d) None of these

19. O_2 partial pressure for Mb in cellular tissue
(a) low
(b) high
(c) moderate
(d) can change depending upon the outer environment

20. In cell pH is
(a) high (b) low
(c) moderate (d) 7

21. Myoglobin is
(a) tetramer (b) trimer
(c) dimer (d) monomer

22. Consider the following metallobiomolecules.
1. Transferrin 2. Siderophores
3. Hydrogenase 4. Hydroxylases
5. Hemeerythrin
Which of these contain iron?
(a) 1, 3 and 4 (b) 1, 2 and 3
(c) 2, 4 and 5 (d) All of the given

23. Consider the following statement about calcium ion.
1. It help in muscle contraction.
2. It is the main inorganic part of exoskeleton but not of endoskeleton.
3. It helps in signalling.
The incorrect statement is/are
(a) 1 and 2 only (b) 2 only
(c) 3 only (d) 1, 2 and 3

24. Consider the following statements.
1. Hydration of carbon dioxide is catalysed by carbonic anhydrase.
2. Peroxidases contain Fe(III) in high spin state.
3. The fifth coordination site of Fe (III) of the peroxidase can be occupied by water when the enzyme is at rest.

The correct statement(s) is/are
(a) 1 and 2 only (b) 2 and 3 only
(c) 1 and 3 ony (d) 1, 2 and 3

Answers

Exercise 1

1. (a)	**2.** (b)	**3.** (d)	**4.** (c)	**5.** (d)	**6.** (d)	**7.** (c)	**8.** (c)	**9.** (c)	**10.** (d)
11. (a)	**12.** (b)	**13.** (a)	**14.** (a)	**15.** (d)	**16.** (b)	**17.** (b)	**18.** (c)	**19.** (a)	**20.** (c)
21. (a)	**22.** (d)	**23.** (c)	**24.** (a)	**25.** (b)	**26.** (d)	**27.** (a)	**28.** (c)	**29.** (d)	**30.** (a)
31. (b)	**32.** (d)	**33.** (b)	**34.** (a)	**35.** (c)	**36.** (c)	**37.** (c)	**38.** (d)	**39.** (a)	**40.** (c)
41. (a)	**42.** (d)	**43.** (d)	**44.** (b)						

Exercise 2

1. (a)	**2.** (d)	**3.** (b)	**4.** (d)	**5.** (d)	**6.** (d)	**7.** (c)	**8.** (c)	**9.** (d)	**10.** (a)
11. (a)	**12.** (d)	**13.** (c)	**14.** (c)	**15.** (d)	**16.** (a)	**17.** (b)	**18.** (a)	**19.** (a)	**20.** (b)
21. (d)	**22.** (d)	**23.** (b)	**24.** (a)						

14

Coordination Compounds, Part-II

Syllabus

- Term Symbols, Electronic Spectra of Transition Metal Complexes, Ligand field Theory

Introduction

Electronic spectra (*i.e.,* colour) of transition metal ions in complexes, refer to the absorption of light from the UV and visible regions of the electromagnetic spectrum. The interpretation of spectra (which result due to promotion of electron or electrons from one energy level (ground state) to higher energy level by absorption of particular amount of energy) provides a most useful method for knowing the energy levels present. The presence of these energy levels can be understood by a discussion of the **crystal field theory** of bonding of metal complexes.

Microstates

The different arrangement of electrons in a set of orbitals having slightly different energy is called **microstates.** p^2-electron can acquire 15 possible arrangements which are not of the same energy. In other words these 15 arrangements are also called 15 microstates of p^2-configuration. It is possible to write these combinations (as shown in Fig. 14.1) for a simple case like p^2 but it may be difficult to do so for configurations having higher number of electrons and for *d*-orbital configurations. For example, d^2-configuration has 45 microstates which are not easy to write otherwise. Therefore, it is better to calculate microstates by the formula :

$$\text{Number of microstates; } \binom{n}{r} = \frac{n!}{r!\,(n-r)!}$$

where, n = twice the number of orbitals

and r = the number of electrons

$n!$ and $r!$ are factorials of n and r, respectively. For example, for p^2-configuration there are three orbitals, hence, $n = 6$ and two electrons hence, $r = 2$.

$$\therefore \quad \text{Number of microstates; } \binom{n}{r} = \frac{6!}{2!\,(6-2)!}$$

$$\binom{6}{2} = \frac{6 \times 5 \times 4 \times 3 \times 2 \times 1}{2 \times 1\,(4 \times 3 \times 2 \times 1)} = 15 \text{ microstates}$$

For d^2-configuration = $n = 10$; $r = 2$

$$\text{No. of microstates} = \frac{10!}{2!\,(10-2)}$$

$$\binom{10}{2} = \frac{10 \times 9 \times 8 \times 7 \times 6 \times 5 \times 4 \times 3 \times 2 \times 1}{2 \times 1\,(8 \times 7 \times 6 \times 5 \times 4 \times 3 \times 2 \times 1)}$$

$= 45$ microstates

In this way we can calculate microstates for other configurations. The values for various p and d-configurations are given in Table 14.1 for your information.

Table 14.1 **Microstates for Different Electronic Configurations**

Electronic configuration	Number of microstates	Electronic configuration	Number of microstates
p^1	6	d^1	10
p^2	15	d^2	45
p^3	20	d^3	120
p^4	15	d^4	210
p^5	6	d^5	252
p^6	1	d^6	210
		d^7	120
		d^8	45
		d^9	10
		d^{10}	1

All these 15 arrangement are **not** of the same energy are also known as microstates. Even though the p-orbitals are of the same energy, *i.e.*, degenerate, the electrons present in them interact with each other and result in the formation of a **ground state** (lowest energy) and one or more higher (excited) energy states for the atom. The interelectronic repulsions for the arrangement in which two electrons are present in the same orbital p_x or p_y or p_z, (arrangement 13, 14 and 15 in Fig. 14.1) are higher than those in which 2 electrons are present in different orbitals (arrangement 1 to 12 in Fig. 14.1).

S. No.	p_x	p_y	p_z
1	↑	↑	
2		↑	↑
3	↑		↑
4	↓	↓	
5		↓	↓
6	↓		↓
7	↑	↓	
8		↑	↓
9	↑		↓
10	↓	↑	
11		↓	↑
12	↓		↑
13	↑↓		
14		↑↓	
15			↑↓

Fig. 14.1 Fifteen possible arrangements (microstates) of two electrons in p-subshell.

Term Symbols or *L-S* Coupling

In a multielectron system many energy states exist, which do not exist in a single electron system. We shall see in our subsequent discussions that the 15 arrangements can be grouped into **three energy** states (because many of these arrangements are degenerate). We shall also observe that the concepts of spin angular momentum (s) and orbital angular momentum (l) of the individual electrons do not hold good for the entire multi-electron system. These interact or couple together to give a resultant angular momentum for the entire multi-electron system in an atom. The resultant angular momentum and the energy of the system is represented as a **term symbol.** Thus, term symbols are used to define the electronic configuration and the resultant angular momentum of an atom.

The term symbol of an atomic state is expressed as :

$$^{2S+1}L_J$$

where,

S = resultant spin quantum number

$2S+1$ = the spin multiplicity of the state

L = resultant angular quantum number

J = total angular momentum quantum number (defined subsequently).

The resultant of all the l values is denoted by a new symbol L which defines the energy state for the atom. The states designated for a given L are given below :

L	=	0	1	2	3	4	5	6	7	...
State	=	S	P	D	F	G	H	I	K	...

In order to determine the resultant or total momentum quantum number J, two methods are used :

1. *L-S* or Russel-Saunders coupling scheme
2. *J-J* coupling scheme

Out of these two, we shall discuss only L-S coupling scheme here. This scheme is applicable to systems in which spin orbital interactions are negligible or relatively low as in cases of elements up to At. no. 30 and first transition series. In this scheme, the individual orbital angular momenta of the electrons couple to give a resultant angular momentum represented by quantum number L. The individual electron spin moments also couple to give a resultant spin momentum described by the quantum number, S. The L and S values determine the total angular momentum J which can take quantized positive values ranging from $|L+S|$ to $|L-S|$. In this method, the consecutive values are separated by one and J is always positive, *i.e.*, ≥ 0.

$$J = |L+S|, |L+S-1| \ldots |L-S|$$

We give below a systematic method for determining the various **term** (**energy states**) as defined by L, S and J values.

Coupling of Orbital Angular Momenta (l-l Coupling)

If two electrons with angular quantum number l_1 and l_2 interact, the resultant angular number L is given as :

$$L = (l_1 + l_2), (l_1 + l_2 - 1) \ldots |l_1 - l_2|$$

where the modulus sign | | indicates positive values. Let us take the case of p^2 configuration as in carbon atom. $(1s^2, 2s^2, 2p^2)$

Here $\quad l_1 = l_2 = 1$

$\therefore \quad L = (1+1), (1+1-1), (1-1)$

$\quad L = 2, \quad 1, \quad 0$

$\therefore \quad$ State $= D, \quad P, \quad S$

That is, p^2-electrons in carbon are represented by three S, P, D states corresponding to $L = 0$, 1 and 2, respectively. Thus, actually three energy states S, P and D represent the 15 arrangements for the two p-electrons shown earlier in Fig. 14.1.

Similarly, for d^2-configuration :

$l_1 = l_2 = 2$. These two vectors add to give a resultant L as shown above for carbon atom.

Hence, for d^2, we have

$$L = (2+2), (2+2-1), (2+2-2), (2+2-3), (2+2-4)$$

$$= 4, \quad 3, \quad 2, \quad 1, \quad 0$$

$\therefore$ State $= G, \quad F, \quad D, \quad P, \quad S$

Thus, a d^2-configuration is represented by five energy states S, P, D, F and G corresponding to $L = 0$, 1, 2, 3 and 4, respectively.

Coupling of Spin Angular Momenta (s-s Coupling)

For a single electron spin quantum number $m_s = \frac{1}{2}$. If two or more electrons are present in a subshell, their magnetic fields couple to produce resultant spin quantum number S (it should not be confused with state S for $L = 0$). The resultant spin angular momentum for p^2 or d^2 is given on the next page :

$$\left.m_S = \frac{1}{2} \uparrow\uparrow m_S = \frac{1}{2}\right\} \quad \text{Resultant } S = \frac{1}{2} + \frac{1}{2} = 1$$

$$\left.m_S = \frac{1}{2} \uparrow\downarrow m_S = -\frac{1}{2}\right\} \quad \text{Resultant } S = \frac{1}{2} - \frac{1}{2} = 0$$

(Resultant m_S terms for p^2 or d^2 configuration)

For p^3 or d^3 case, S has values $1\frac{1}{2}$ and $\frac{1}{2}$ as shown below.

$$\uparrow\uparrow\uparrow\} \quad \text{Resultant } S = \frac{1}{2} + \frac{1}{2} + \frac{1}{2} = 1\frac{1}{2}$$

$$\uparrow\uparrow\downarrow\} \quad \text{Resultant } S = \frac{1}{2} + \frac{1}{2} - \frac{1}{2} = \frac{1}{2}$$

Note That resultant S has +ve values only, *i.e.*, $S \geq 0$.

Spin multiplicity is given by the expression $2S + 1$. Spin multiplicity of 1 is called a singlet, three triplet, etc. This is summarized below :

Unpaired electrons	S	$2S + 1$	State
0	0	1	Singlet
1	$\frac{1}{2}$	2	Doublet
2	1	3	Triplet
3	$1\frac{1}{2}$	4	Quartet
4	2	5	Quintet

It is clear from the above that the multiplicity $(2S + 1)$ is always one more than the number of unpaired electrons.

Spin-Orbit Coupling, *L-S* Scheme

In an atom, the magnetic effects of the resultant angular momentum L, and the resultant spin quantum number, S couple together giving a new quantum number J called the **total angular momentum quantum number.** The J value is obtained by the vectorial combination of L and S. This coupling scheme is called **Russell-Saunders** or ***LS* coupling.**

$$J = (L + S), (L + S - 1), (L + S - 2), \ldots, |L - S|$$

Thus, J can acquire all quantized positive values ranging from $|L - S|$ to $|L + S|$. These values are separated by 1. The $|\ |$ sign indicates that absolute value of $|L - S|$ is employed and $J \geq 0$. The value of J is written as a **subscript in the term symbol.**

Derivation of terms for p^2 configuration

$$l_1 = 1 \text{ and } l_2 = 1$$

$$L = (1 + 1), (1 + 1 - 1), (1 + 1 - 2)$$

$$= 2, \ 1, \ 0$$

$\therefore$ State $= D, \ P, \ S$

In other words, states for p^2 are S, P and D

For two electrons in p^2,

$$S = 1, 0$$

$\therefore$ $2S + 1 = 3, 1$

Hence, for p^2-configuration, the six states are

$${}^3S, {}^3P, {}^3D, {}^1S, {}^1P, {}^1D$$

The different L and S values may now be coupled to give the total angular momentum quantum number J. As already stated, full spectroscopic term symbols are represented as ${}^{2S+1}L_J$.

Let us calculate J

(a) When $L = 2, 1$ and 0 but $S = 1$

(i) When $L = 2$; $S = 1$, *i.e.*, a ${}^3D$ state

$$J = (2 + 1), (2 + 1 - 1), (2 + 1 - 2)$$

$$J = 3, \ 2, \ 1$$

Full spectroscopic term symbols are :

$${}^3D_3, {}^3D_2 \text{ and } {}^3D_1$$

(ii) When $L = 1$; $S = 1$, *i.e.*, a ${}^3P$ state

$$J = (1 + 1), (1 + 1 - 1), (1 + 1 - 2)$$

$$J = 2, \ 1, \ 0$$

Full spectroscopic terms are :

$${}^3P_2, {}^3P_1 \text{ and } {}^3P_0$$

(iii) When $L = 0$; $S = 1$, *i.e.*, a ${}^3S$ state

$$J = 1 + 0$$

$$J = 1$$

Full spectroscopic terms is ${}^3S_1$

(b) When $L = 2, 1$ and 0 but $S = 0$

(i) When $L = 2$; $S = 0$, *i.e.*, a ${}^1D$ state

$$J = 2 + 0$$

$$J = 2$$

Full spectroscopic term is ${}^1D_2$

(ii) When $L = 1$; $S = 0$, *i.e.*, a ${}^1P$ state

$$J = 1$$

Full spectroscopic term is ${}^1P_1$

(iii) When $L = 0$; $S = 0$, *i.e.*, a ${}^1S$ state

$$J = 0$$

Full spectroscopic term is ${}^1S_0$

Thus, the total spectroscopic term symbols for p^2 configuration are :

$${}^3D_3, {}^3D_2, {}^3D_1, {}^3P_2, {}^3P_1, {}^3P_0, {}^3S_1, {}^1D_2, {}^1P_1$$

and ${}^1S_0$

These values indicated in a spectroscopic term are very useful. For example :

${}^3D_3$ means

D state, *i.e.*, $L = 2$: Spin multiplicity = 3, that is, $S = 1$ or two unpaired electrons and total quantum number $J = 3$.

All the spectroscopic terms derived from p^2-configuration may occur in an excited state of a carbon in which the two p electrons occupy different subshells (that is, say, $2p^1$ and $3p^1$). However, in the ground state, the number of states is restricted by the **Pauli exclusion principle.** According to Pauli exclusion principle, no two electrons in an atom can have the same value for all the four quantum numbers. In the ground state of carbon $1s^2, 2s^2, 2p^2$, the p-electrons have the same $n = 2$, same $l = 1$, so they must differ in at least one of the other quantum numbers m_l and m_s. This restriction reduces the number of terms for p^2 from six (${}^1S$, ${}^1P$, ${}^1D$, ${}^3S$, ${}^3P$, ${}^3D$) to three (${}^1S$, ${}^3P$, ${}^1D$) only. This can be achieved in the following ways.

Derivation of Term Symbols p^2-Configuration

All the different possible ways in which two electrons can be arranged with their spins in the *p*-orbitals are indicated by the *pigeon hole* diagram given in Fig. 14.2. Each vertical rectangle in Fig. 14.2 illustrates a box as used for representing a configuration.

The rules for constructing a **"pigeon hole"** are as follows :

1. Use one horizontal row for each value of m_l. Since, for $p(l = 1)$, m_l has values +1, 0, – 1, therefore, there are 3 rows with values +1, 0, – 1, as shown in Fig. 14.2.
2. In a given column place the first electron with spin up (↑) as in Fig. 14.2 (a).
3. The other electrons in a given column are placed in rows above that of the first electron. This avoids duplication of configuration.
4. In subsequent columns, systematically place the electrons in higher rows until all possibilities hence been exhausted.
5. The Pauli exclusion principle must be obeyed.
6. The procedure is carried on with paired spins (b) and opposite spins (c) as shown in Fig. 14.2.

m_l									
–1		↑	↑			⇅		↓	↓
0	↑		↑		⇅		↓		↑
+1	↑	↑		⇅			↑	↑	
m_L=	+1	0	–1	+2	0	–2	+1	0	–1
	(a)			(b)			(c)		

Fig. 14.2 Possible arrangements of two electrons in *p*-orbitals with (a) parallel spin, (b) paired spin, (c) opposite spin.

In Fig. 14.2 (a), we find that the resultant m_L values (Σm_l) are +1, 0, – 1 and $S\ (\Sigma m_s) = \frac{1}{2} + \frac{1}{2} = 1$ (because of parallel spins).

We know that when $m_l = +1, 0, -1$ the value of $l = 1$

Similarly when, $m_L = +1, 0, -1$ (Fig. 14.2 a); $L = 1$

Thus, we have $L = 1$; $S = 1$ or $(2S + 1 = 3)$

Hence, term symbol for these values is

$$\boxed{^3P}$$

In the part (b) and (c), the two electrons have opposite spin

$\therefore S = 0$ or $2S + 1$ is 1, and $m_L = +2, 0, -2, +1, 0, -1$

These m_L values can be rearranged to find out L by rewriting these as :

$m_L = +2, +1, 0, -1, -2$ with $L = 2$

and $m_L = 0$ with $L = 0$

For $L = 2$, state = D

$L = 0$ state = S

Since, both the electrons are paired,

and $2S + 1 = 1$ $(\because S = 0)$

Hence, the term symbols for

$L = 2, 2S + 1 = 1$ is

$$\boxed{^1D}$$

and for $L = 0$, $2S + 1 = 1$, it is

$$\boxed{^1S}$$

Hence, for p^2-configuration the term symbols that represent all the 15 arrangements are :

$$\boxed{^3P,\ ^1D,\ ^1S}$$

Determination of Ground State Term

The terms derived for a given configuration possess different energies. For example, the terms derived for p^2 configuration are ^3P, ^1D and ^1S. These three terms possess different energies. It is possible to arrange these terms in increasing order of energy as well as to know the ground state term (lowest energy term). This is done with the help of **Hund's rules.** These rules are as follows :

1. The terms are arranged depending on their spin multiplicities $(2S + 1)$ and their S values. The most stable state has the highest S value and the stability decreases as S value decreases. This means that the most **stable state (ground state) has electrons in parallel spins as far as possible–Hund's rule.**

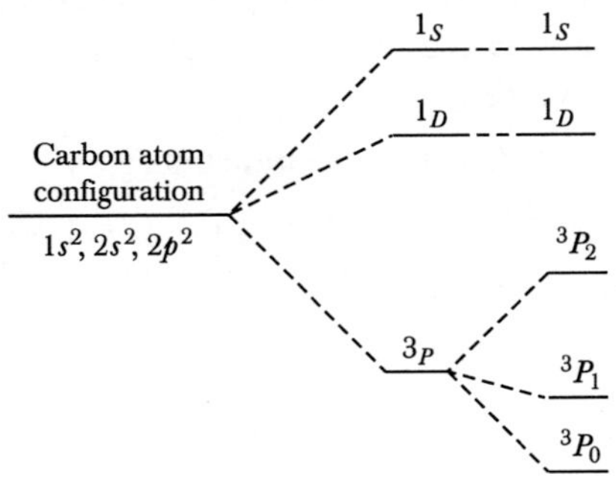

Fig. 14.3

2. For a given value of S, the state with the highest L value is the most stable, that is, if two or more states have the same S value, then the state with highest L will have the lowest energy.
3. The state with the maximum J value is the **ground state** if the sub-shell is more than half-filled. If the sub-shell is less than half-filled the term with the smallest J value is the lowest in energy.

$$\text{Ground State}\begin{cases}\text{Less than half- filled}: J\,\text{Minimum value}\\ \text{More than half- filled}: J\,\text{Maximum value}\end{cases}$$

If we apply these rules to the term derived for p^2 configuration of carbon atom which are ^1S, ^3P and ^1D, we find that ^3P is the only state with triplet multiplicity. This is the ground state. Among ^1S and ^1D, the second rule suggests that ^1D state with $L = 2$ is more stable than ^1S state which has ($L = 0$ and $S = 0$). Thus, the order of energy is $^3P < {}^1D < {}^1S$. The ^3P state has three terms $^3P_0$, $^3P_1$ and $^3P_2$ because the J values for ^3P states are 2, 1, 0. From the third rule $^3P_0$ is the lowest energy ($2p^2$ configuration of C is less than half-filled). The various terms are arranged in the above order (Fig. 14.3).

Hole Formalism

If a subshell is more than half-filled, it is easy to find out the terms by considering the holes, *i.e.,* vacancies in the orbitals rather than considering the large number of electrons. For example, Cu^{2+} ion with [Ar] $3d^9$ configuration may be treated as one vacancy. Similarly, oxygen atom with a $1s^2$, $2s^2$, $2p^4$ configuration may be treated as two holes, *i.e.,* same as carbon atom with a p^2 configuration, *i.e.,* ^1S, ^3P and ^1D terms. However, oxygen contains *more than half-filled subshell,* and hence, when we apply Hund's third rule, the energy of the ^3P state are reversed, *i.e.,* $^3P_2 < {}^3P_1 < {}^3P_0$. Thus, for oxygen atom $^3P_2$ is the ground state.

Table 14.2 contains ground state terms and other terms in increasing order of energy for s, p and d electronic configurations.

Table 14.2 **Ground States and Other States Order of Energy**

Electronic configuration	Ground state	Other states
s^1	^2S	–
s^2	^1S	–
p^1, p^5	^2P	–
p^2, p^4	^3P	^1D, ^1S
p^3	^4S	^2D, ^2P
p^6	^1S	–
d^1, d^9	^2D	–
d^2, d^8	^3F	^3P, ^1G, ^1D, ^1S
d^3, d^7	^4F	^4P, ^2H, ^2G, ^2F, ^2D, ^2P
d^4, d^6	^5D	^3H, ^3G, ^3F, ^3D, ^3P, ^1I, ^1G, ^1F, ^1D, ^1S
d^5	^6S	^4G, ^4F, ^4D, ^4P, ^2I, ^2H, ^2G, ^2F, ^2D ^2P, ^2S.
d^{10}	^1S	–

Derivation of the term symbol for closed-shell configuration (s^2, p^6 or d^{10} arrangements). If a subshell is completely filled with electrons, such as s^2, p^6 or d^{10} arrangements, then both S and L are zero. Thus, a closed shell always yield $^1S_0$ state.

Calculation of Ground State of an Atom Using *L-S* Coupling Scheme

The rules for determining the term symbol for the ground state according to L-S scheme are :

1. Maximize spin multiplicity $(2S + 1)$, that is, electrons occupy degenerate orbitals so as to retain parallel spins as long as possible(Hund's rule).
2. Maximize orbital angular momentum (L), that is, fill orbitals with the highest positive m_l values first.
3. Select maximum J for more than half-filled subshell and minimum J for less than half-filled.

Examples Let us determine term symbol for the ground state of carbon $1s^2$, $2s^2$, $2p^2$. We take the outer subshell $2p$ only because others are filled and calculate values of L and S as follows. Applying rules 1 and 2, we write the configuration of outer $2p^2$ as :

$$m_L = +1, 0, -1$$

2p | ↑ | ↑ | |

For L, add m_l values for all electrons in the incomplete outer $2p$-orbitals.

That is $L = 1 + 0 = 1 \quad \therefore$ State $= P$

For S, both have parallel spins, *i.e.*, $\frac{1}{2} + \frac{1}{2}$ or $S = 1$ and

$2S + 1 = 3$

Hence, term symbol is ^3P

For $S = 1$, $L = 1$, the values of J are :

$$J = |L + S| \ldots |L - S|$$
$$= 2, 1, 0$$

To find ground state we take minimum J for less than half-filled configuration. Hence, ground state term symbol of carbon is

$$^3P_0$$

Box diagram for V^{3+} (d^2) is

= +2 +1 0 −1 −2

| ↑ | ↑ | | | |

$$L = 2 + 1 = 3 \quad \therefore \text{ State } = F$$
$$S = \frac{1}{2} + \frac{1}{2} = 1 \quad \therefore \; 2S + 1 = 3$$
$$J = 4, 3, 2$$

d^2 is less than half-filled

$\therefore J$ is taken as 2

Hence, term symbol for ground state of V^{3+} is

$$^3F_2$$

Electronic Spectra of Transition Metal Complexes

The electronic spectra involve promotion of electron (or electrons) from one energy level (ground state) to a higher energy level. Such transitions of electrons are called **electronic transitions.** Electronic transitions are of high energy and are always accompanied by lower energy vibrational and rotational transitions. These vibrational and rotational levels are too close in energy to be resolved into separate peaks, but they cause considerable broadening of the absorption peaks.

Selection Rules

All theoretically predicted transitions are generally not observed. This may become clear by observing a number of **selection rules** which distinguish between allowed and forbidden transitions. The selection rules are :

1. Transitions in which **number of unpaired electrons changes** in going from a lower to a higher energy state are referred to as **spin** or **multiplicity forbidden.** This suggests that **transitions to only those excited states are to be considered which have the same spin multiplicity as the ground state.** Thus, for a d^2 configuration, the only terms which need to be considered are the ^3F (ground state) and ^3P (excited state). That is, a transition from ^3F to ^3P is allowed but from ^3F to ^1G or ^1D or ^1S is forbidden.

2. **Transitions which do not involve a change in the subsidiary quantum number,** ***i.e.***, $\Delta_l = 0$ are **Laporte forbidden if the molecule has centre of symmetry.** This rule suggests that transitions from one *d*-level to another *d*-level (*d-d* transitions) are not allowed **(Laporte forbidden transitions),** since, l remains the same or $\Delta l = 0$.

   Transitions which involve a change in l or $\Delta_l \neq 0$ are called **"Laporte allowed"** transitions. Such transitions are intense or have high absorbance.

As a result of this selection rule, *d-d* transitions in octahedral complexes are not allowed and therefore, many complexes would be **colourless** but for the following reasons :

(i) If the transition metal complex-ion does not have perfect octahedral structure, for example, all the six ligands may not be the same, so it has a slightly distorted octahedral structure, in that case its **centre of symmetry is destroyed** and mixing of *d* and *p* orbitals of the metal ion may occur, in which case transitions are no longer pure *d-d* transitions in nature. The intensity of such transitions is very weak often in the range $\varepsilon = 20$ to $50\ l\ mol^{-1}\ cm^{-1}$.

   Mixing of *d* and *p*-orbitals does not occur in **perfectly octahedral complexes which have a centre of symmetry** such as $[Co(NH_3)_6]^{3+}$. Complexes such as $MnCl_4^{2-}$ which is tetrahedral or $[Co(NH_3)_5Cl]^{2+}$ which is an irregular octahedron do not possess a centre of symmetry and are both coloured.

(ii) A complex which has a perfect octahedral structure can also exhibit absorption spectrum by the following mechanism : A molecule undergoes vibrations all the time and at any one time some molecules have a distorted octahedral symmetry. The *d* and *p* orbitals mix in the unsymmetrical configuration and an extremely low intensity transition results ($\varepsilon = 5$ to $25\ l\ mol^{-1}\ cm^{-1}$) such transitions are said to be vibronically **allowed transitions.**

For example, in the complex ion $[Mn(H_2O)_6]^{2+}$ (Mn^{II} with a $3d^5$ configuration), all transitions are both spin multiplicity and Laporte forbidden. But $[Mn(H_2O)_6]^{2+}$ ions are pale-pink in colour. This may be attributed to vibronic coupling which result in very low intensity transitions and are responsible for its pale-pink colour.

Some examples are given in the form of Table 14.3 to know which selection rule is responsible for the transitions in the following transition metal complexes.

Table 14.3 **Selection Rules in Some Complexes**

d^n	Example	Laporte transition	Spin multiplicity
d^7	$[CoBr_4]^{2-}$	Allowed	Allowed (^4F, ^4P)
d^5	$[MnBr_4]^{2-}$	Allowed	Forbidden
d^5	$[Mn(H_2O)_6]^{2+}$	Forbidden	Forbidden
d^2	$[V(H_2O)_6]^{3+}$	Forbidden	Allowed (^3F, ^3P)
d^3	$[Cr(H_2O)_6]^{3+}$	Forbidden	Allowed (^4F, ^4P)
d^8	$[Ni(NH_3)_6]^{2+}$	Forbidden	Allowed (^3F, ^3P)
d^7	$[Co(H_2O)_6]^{2+}$	Forbidden	Allowed (^4F, ^4P)

Splitting of Russel Saunders States in Octahedral and Tetrahedral Crystal Fields

In order to understand the nature of electronic transitions in transition metal complexes, let us study the splitting of electronic energy levels and spectroscopic terms into various components.

(i) An *s*-orbital is spherically symmetrical and hence is not affected by an octahedral or any other field. Similar is the case with spectroscopic term S.

(ii) The *p*-orbitals are directional and are affected by an octahedral field. However, since a set of three *p*-orbital are all affected equally, their energy levels remain equal and no splitting occurs. Similar is the case with spectroscopic term P.

(iii) A set of five *d*-orbitals is split by an octahedral field into two levels t_{2g} (d_{xy}, d_{yz}, d_{xz}) and e_g ($d_{x^2-y^2}$, d_{z^2}) . The difference in energy between the two is written as 10 Dq or Δ_o. The t_{2g} level is triply degenerate and e_g doubly degenerate. For a d^1 configuration, the ground state is ^2D ($\because L = 2;\ 2S+1 = 2$) and the t_{2g} and e_g electronic energy levels correspond with the T_{2g} and E_g spectroscopic states. Thus, the spectroscopic term D comprises of triply degenerate T and doubly degenerate E components.

(iv) A set of seven *f*-orbitals is split by an octahedral field into three levels. For an f^1-configuration, the ground state is a ^3F state which gets splitted into a triply degenerate T_{1g} state, a triply degenerate T_{2g} level and a single A_{2g} state. Thus, the spectroscopic term F comprises of two triply degenerate T_1 and T_2 and a singly degenerate A components.

Thus, we can say that in an octahedral field, the S and P states are not splitted, D states are splitted into two states, F states are splitted into three states and G states are splitted into four states. These states splitted by the external field are called **Mulliken symbols.** These symbols are used extensively in interpreting electronic spectra of transition metal complexes and are listed in Table 14.4.

Table 14.4 **Splitting of Terms of Free Ions or Atoms into Mulliken Symbols in an Octahedral or Tetrahedral Field**

Term	S	P	D	F	G
Mulliken Symbol	A_1	T_1	$E + T_2$	$A_2 + T_1 + T_2$	$A_1 + E + T_1 + T_2$
Term	H			I	
Mulliken Symbol	$E + T_1 + T_1 + T_2$			$A_1 + A_2 + E + T_1 + T_2 + T_2$	

The Mulliken symbols in a tetrahedral field are used as such as given in Table 14.4 but in an octahedral field these are distinguished by introducing the symmetry symbol g as given in Table 14.5.

Table 14.5 **Mulliken Symbols in an Octahedral Field**

Spectroscopic term	Mulliken symbol in an octahedral field
S	A_{1g}
P	T_{1g}
D	$E_g + T_{2g}$
F	$A_{2g} + T_{1g} + T_{2g}$
G	$A_{1g} + E_g + T_{1g} + T_{2g}$
H	$E_g + 2T_{1g} + T_{2g}$
I	$A_{1g} + A_{2g} + E_g + T_{1g} + 2T_{2g}$

Knowing spectroscopic terms *S, P, D,* etc., we can derive Mulliken symbols without resorting to unnecessary cramming. For example, term *S* stands for $L = 0$. The number of components of L (given by $2L + 1$) would be one because $L = 0$. This one component is singly degenerate represented by Mulliken symbol *A*. Similarly, term *P* means $L = 1$: number of components $(2L + 1) = 3$. Thus, it is triply degenerate and represented by symbol *T*. For term *D*; $L = 2$; $2L + 1 = 5$. The five components comprise a doubly degenerate *E* and a triply degenerate *T*.

For term *F*; $L = 3$; $2L + 1 = 7$. The seven components comprise a singly degenerate A + two triply degenerate components T_1 and T_2. For term *G*; $L = 4$; $2L + 1 = 9$. The nine components comprise a singly degenerate A + a doubly degenerate E + two triply degenerate T_1 and T_2.

You will notice in Tables 14.1 and 14.3 that sometimes singly degenerate is represented as A_1 and A_2 and triply degenerate as T_1 or T_2 and so on. The numbers 1 and 2 like *g* and *u* in t_{2g} or t_{1u}, etc., define symmetry of Mulliken symbol. This will not be discussed here and has to be remembered as such.

Spectra of d^1 and d^9 Ions

In a free gaseous metal ion the five *d*-orbitals are degenerate and therefore no electronic transition is possible. When this metal ion is in a complex form (*e.g.*, Ti^{3+} ion with d^1 configuration in aqueous solution exists as $[Ti(H_2O)_6]^{3+}$), the octahedral crystal field splits the *d*-orbitals into two groups t_{2g} and e_g as shown in Fig. 14.4. The symbol 2*D* is the ground state term for a free ion with a d^1-configuration. This term splits into two states $^2T_{2g}$ and ^2E_g as described by the Mulliken symbol (Table 14.3).

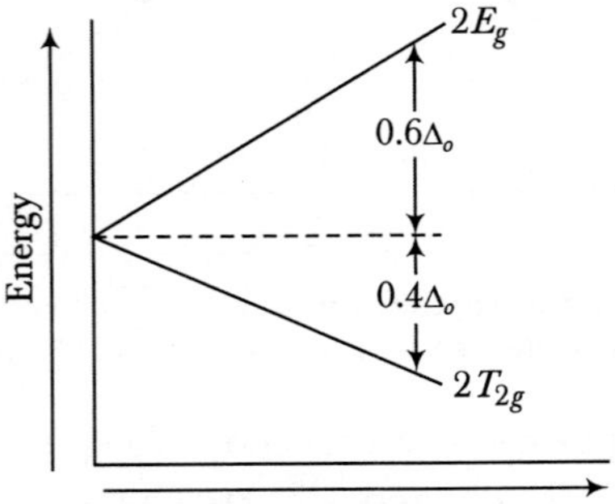

Fig. 14.4 (a)

The two states are separated more widely as the strength of the crystal field increases. The spectrum of $[Ti(H_2O)_6]^{3+}$ is shown in Fig. 14.4(b). Some characteristic features of the spectrum are its

(i) **position of the band**
(ii) **intensity of the band and**
(iii) **nature of the band.**

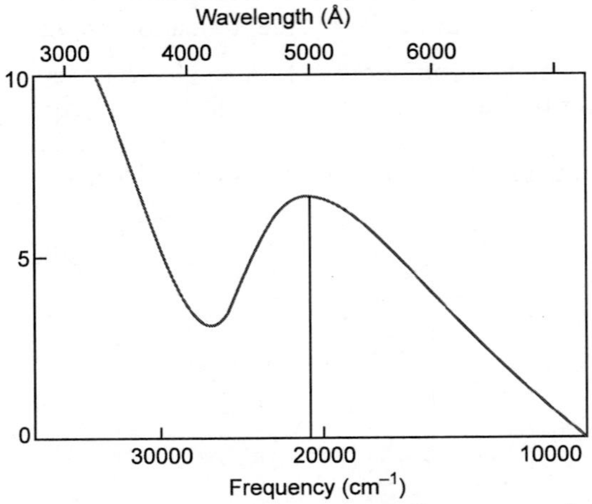

Fig. 14.4 (b) Splitting of energy levels for d^1 configuration in an octahedral field.

(i) The absorption band occurs at 5000 Å or 20000 cm^{-1} in the green and yellow region so these colours are filtered out. The blue and red light is transmitted and therefore Ti^{3+} solution looks purple.
(ii) The intensity of the absorption band is very weak ($\varepsilon \simeq 5 - 10$). This is due to the reason that transitions from one centrosymmetric *d*-orbital to another centrosymmetric *d*-orbital are forbidden by selection rules (Laporte forbidden). The molar absorbance value of such forbidden transitions (ε) are of the order of 1 to 10 whereas for allowed transitions, the ε values are close to 10,000, *i.e.*, peaks are very intense.
(iii) The peak is not a sharp line lying at the precise Δ_o value. The width of the transition is caused by the fact that the electronic transition is accompanied by a host of vibrational excitations which are spread over a range of thousand wave numbers.

The magnitude of the splitting, Δ_o depends on the nature of the ligands. This affects the energy of the transition and hence, the position of the absorption in the spectrum. For example, $[TiCl_6]^{3-}$ absorbs at 13000 cm^{-1}, $[Ti(CN)_6]^{3-}$ at 22300 cm^{-1}. This is related to spectrochemical series.

Octahedral complexes of ions with d^9-configuration Such as $[Cu(H_2O)_6]^{2+}$ can be explained in a manner similar to the Ti^{3+} octahedral complexes with d^1-configuration. In the d^1 case, there is a single electron in the lower energy T_{2g} level, whereas, in d^9 case, there is a **single hole** in the upper energy E_g level. Thus, the transition in case of d^9 involving promotion of an electron is actually described as the transfer of hole from E_g to T_{2g}. The energy level diagram of d^9 is; therefore, inverted as shown on the right hand side of Fig. 14.5.

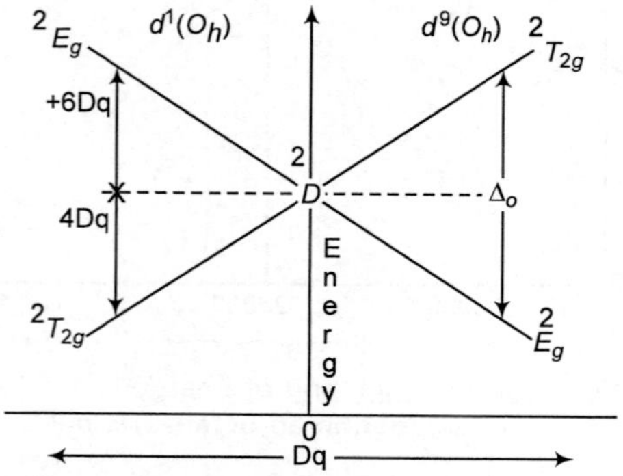

Fig. 14.5 Splitting of energy levels for d^1 and d^9-configurations in an octahedral field (O_h).

Tetrahedral complexes of ions with d^1 and d^9-configurations have energy levels **inverse of each other** (Fig. 14.6) as well as **inverse** of their **respective octahedral complexes.** Here the *d*-orbitals split into doubly degenerate *E*-orbitals of lower energy and triply degenerate T_2-orbitals of higher energy (Fig. 14.6). The other difference being lower splitting (4/9 of octahedral splitting) in a tetrahedral field, that is $\Delta_t = \frac{4}{9}\Delta_o$.

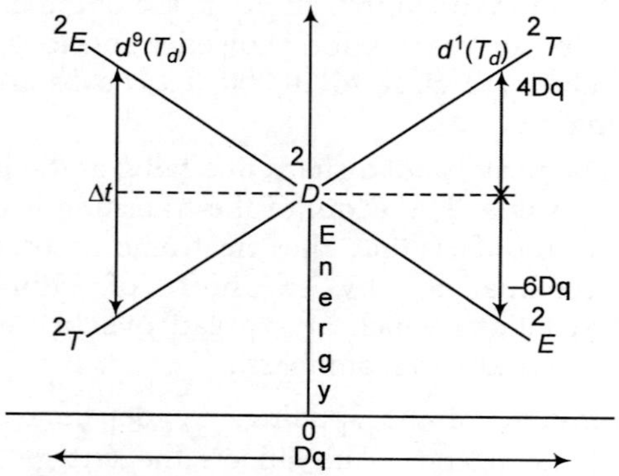

Fig. 14.8 Splitting of energy levels for d^1 and d^9-configurations in a tetrahedral field (T_d).

Besides that it has also been observed that the value of *L* or the state corresponding to it, is the same both for d^1 and d^6 configurations. It is $L = 2$; state = *D* for both d^1 and d^6. However, their spin multiplicities are different. In case of d^1, spin multiplicity = 2 and in case of d^6, spin multiplicity = 5. In other words, term symbol for d^1 is ^2D and for d^6, it is ^5D. State *D* is known to split into doubly degenerate term *E* and triply degenerate term *T* both in octahedral as well as tetrahedral fields and a single *d-d* transition can occur. Thus, the electronic transitions for d^1 and d^6 will be similar. Also the electronic transitions for $d^9(^2D)$ and $d^4(^5D)$ will also be similar. In other words, transitions in metal ions with a difference of five *d*-electrons in their configurations are similar for a given field (O_h or T_d). That means, d^1 and d^6 have similar transitions. Also d^9 and d^4 have similar transitions in a given field.

We can summarise that **electronic transitions** in

$$d^1(O_h) = d^6(O_h) \text{ but inverse of } d^9(O_h) = d^4(O_h)$$

Also, $d^1(T_d) = d^6(T_d)$ but inverse of $d^9(T_d) = d^4(T_d)$

We can represent all these in a single energy level diagram also called an **Orgel diagram.** Orgel diagram for d^1, d^4, d^6 and d^9 in both octahedral (O_h) as well as tetrahedral (T_d) fields is shown in Fig. 14.7.

$d^1_9, d^6_4\ (O_h)$ $\quad$ $d^9, d^4\ (O_h)$

$d^9, d^4\ (O_h)$ $\quad$ $d^1, d^6\ (T_d)$

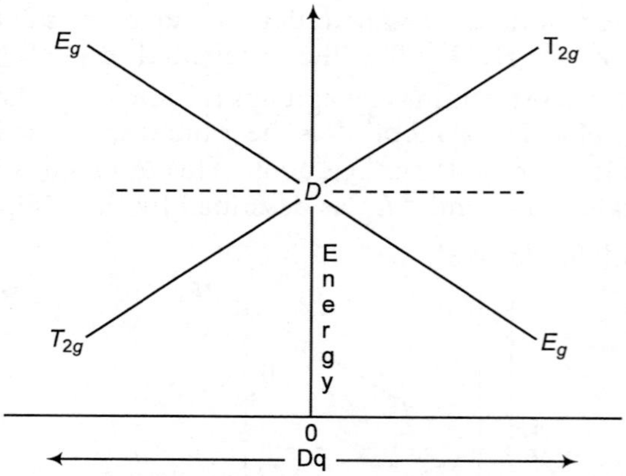

Fig. 14.7 Orgel diagram for d^1, d^4, d^6, d^9 complexes in octahedral (O_h) as well as tetrahedral (T_d) fields.

The splitting of states as a function of Dq for octahedral complexes with d^1 and d^6 configurations and for tetrahedral complexes with d^9 and d^4 configurations is described in the left hand side 7 Fig. 14.7.

The right hand side of the Orgel diagram applies to octahedral d^9 and d^4 as well as tetrahedral d^1 and d^6 complexes. The single *d-d* transition that occurs is assigned as $E_g \rightarrow T_{2g}$ for octahedral and as $E \rightarrow T_2$ for tetrahedral complexes. It may be mentioned again that *d–d* transitions in octahedral complexes are Laporte forbidden and hence such bands are normally very weak but these transitions for tetrahedral complexes are strong because *d–d* transitions in T_d field are allowed.

Spectra of d^2 and d^8 Ions

In an octahedral field, the *d*-orbitals are known to split into a triply degenerate set of orbitals t_{2g} and a doubly degenerate set e_g. The t_{2g} orbitals are lower in energy compared to the e_g orbitals which are higher in energy. The two *d*-electrons will prefer to occupy t_{2g} orbitals because of their lower energy. As we have already learnt the states of d^2-configuration are :

$$^3F,\ ^3P,\ ^1G,\ ^1D,\ ^1S$$

Applying Hund's rule, we find that ^3F is the ground state (lowest energy) and ^3P has higher energy than ^3F. We ignore ^1G, ^1D and ^1S states because transitions from ^3F to any of these singlet states in spin or multiplicity forbidden. Spin or multiplicity transitions are either not observed or are very weak. Hence, **we will consider ^3F and ^3P states only for determining transitions in a d^2 case.**

We know from Table 14.3 and 14.4 that the free ion term *P* does not split in an octahedral or a tetrahedral field and its Mulliken symbol is T_1. In other words, the Mulliken symbol of ^3P shall be $^3T_{1g}$ in an octahedral field and $^3T_1$ in a tetrahedral field (symbol *g* is missing because tetrahedral field does not possess symmetry *wrt* centre or *g* symmetry is absent in a tetrahedron). The free ion term *F* has Mulliken symbol $A_2 + T_1 + T_2$ (Table 14.4). That means, Mulliken symbols of ^3F are $^3A_{2g} + {}^3T_{1g} + {}^3T_{2g}$ in an octahedral field and $^3A_2 + {}^3T_1 + {}^3T_2$ in a tetrahedral field.

Out of $^3T_{1g}$, $^3T_{2g}$, $^3A_{2g}$, the former $^3T_{1g}$ has the lowest energy for a d^2-configuration in an octahedral field. This is because the lowest energy arangement of *d*-electron in an octahedral field is given by placing the two electrons in t_{2g} orbitals d_{xy}, d_{xz} and d_{yz} and the three degenerate possibilities of doing that are $d^1_{xy}, d^1_{xz}, d^0_{yz}, d^1_{xy}, d^0_{xz}, d^1_{yz}$ and $d^0_{xy}, d^1_{xz}, d^1_{yz}$.

This means that the lowest energy arrangement of d^2 electrons in an octahedral field is **triply degenerate** which means either $^3T_{1g}$ or $^3T_{2g}$ Mulliken symbol would represent ground state. Based on symmetry, the ground state for d^2-electrons in octahedral field is $^3T_{1g}(F)$.

The following information is conveyed by $^3T_{1g}(F)$

(i) the symbol *T* indicates orbital is triply degenerate.
(ii) superscript indicates spin multiplicity of three, that is, two unpaired electrons.
(iii) *g* indicates a gerade state, that is, symmetrical *wrt* centre.
(iv) the symbol *F* indicates that this state arose from the gaseous ion ^3F state. Similarly, $^3T_{1g}(P)$ indicates that this state arises from the gaseous ion ^3P state (See Fig. 14.8)

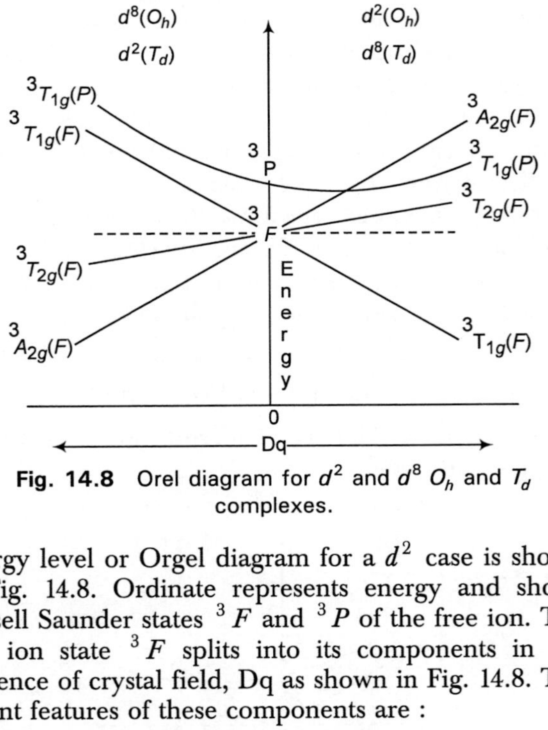

Fig. 14.8 Orel diagram for d^2 and d^8 O_h and T_d complexes.

Energy level or Orgel diagram for a d^2 case is shown in Fig. 14.8. Ordinate represents energy and shows Russell Saunder states ^3F and ^3P of the free ion. The free ion state ^3F splits into its components in the presence of crystal field, Dq as shown in Fig. 14.8. The salient features of these components are :

(i) State with identical designation never cross. For example, $^3T_{1g}(F)$ and $^3T_{1g}(P)$ are identical and will never cross each other.
(ii) Crystal field states have the same spin multiplicity as free ion. That is, the superscript remains three both on ^3F as well as its components $^3T_1$, $^3T_2$ and $^3A_2$.
(iii) States which are the only ones of their type have energies which depend linearly on the CFSE, whereas, when there are two or more

states of identical designation, their lines in general show curvature. This is because such states interact with one another as well as with the crystal field. This means identical states ä $^3T_{1g}(F)$ and $^3T_{1g}(P)$ interact with each other and with crystal field and may thus acquire curvature as shown prominantly for $^3T_{1g}(P)$ (Fig. 14.8).

Orgel energy level diagram of $d^2(O_h)$ is given on the right hand side of Fig. 14.8. The diagram is the same for $d^{10-2} = d^8(T_d)$ except that the subscript g is not used for tetrahedral field. The left hand side is inverse of the right hand side and corresponds to Orgel diagram of $d^8(O_h)$ and $d^2(T_d)$ as shown in Fig. 14.8.

As already observed (for spectra of d^1 and d^9) the transitions for d^1 and d^6 are similar in a given field and the only difference being spin multiplicity. Similarly, d^2 and d^7 (with a difference of 5d-electrons) have similar transitions. Also d^8 and d^3 have similar transitions. However, the spin multiplicity of d^3 and d^7 is different from that of d^2 and d^8. Both d^3 and d^7 have three unpaired electrons, therefore, their spin multiplicity value is 4. Hence, the free ion terms needed for determining their transitions are ^4F and ^4P with the former being the ground term. The Orgel diagram for $d^7(O_h)$ and $d^3(T_d)$ is given on the right hand side of Fig. 14.9 and of $d^3(O_h)$ and $d^7(T_d)$ on left hand side of Fig. 14.9. The left hand side is inverse of the right hand side.

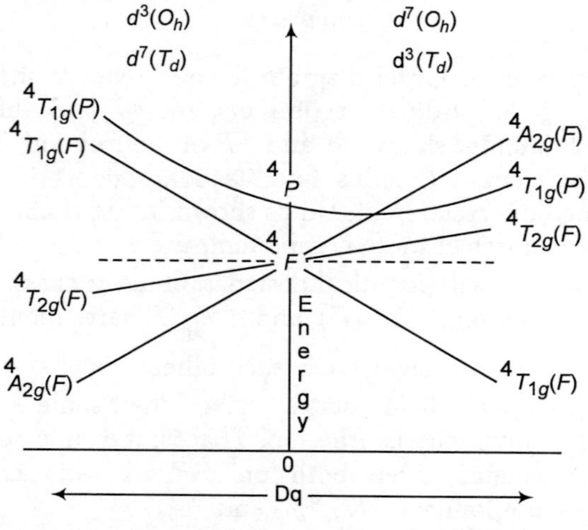

Fig. 14.9 Orel diagram for d^3 and d^7 O_h and T_d complexes.

Combined Spectra of d^2, d^3, d^7, d^8

A combined Orgel diagram for d^2, d^3, d^7 and d^8 in octahedral and tetrahedral fields is given in Fig. 14.10. The spin multiplicities of free ion terms F and P as well as those of Mulliken symbols are not given in Fig. 14.10 because it is not the same for all the cases. Besides, the subscript g should not be used when describing transitions in a tetrahedral field. Taking help of Fig. 14.10 or any of the Figs. 14.9 and 14.8, we can predict the electronic spectrum of any of these electronic configuration in O_h and T_d fields.

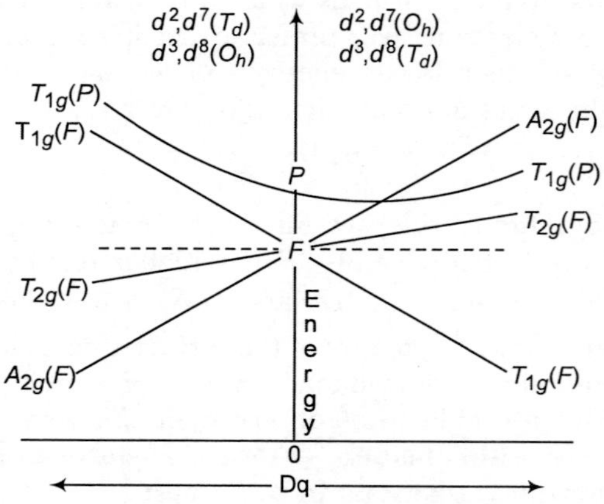

Fig. 14.10 Orel diagram for d^2, d^3, d^7, d^8 in O_h and T_d complexes.

Theoretically, three transitions are expected :

(i) $^3T_{1g}(F) \longrightarrow {}^3T_{2g}(F)$ (Lowest energy)

(ii) $^3T_{1g}(F) \longrightarrow {}^3A_{2g}(F)$

(iii) $^3T_{1g}(F) \longrightarrow {}^3T_{1g}(P)$ (Highest energy)

as shown in Fig. 14.11.

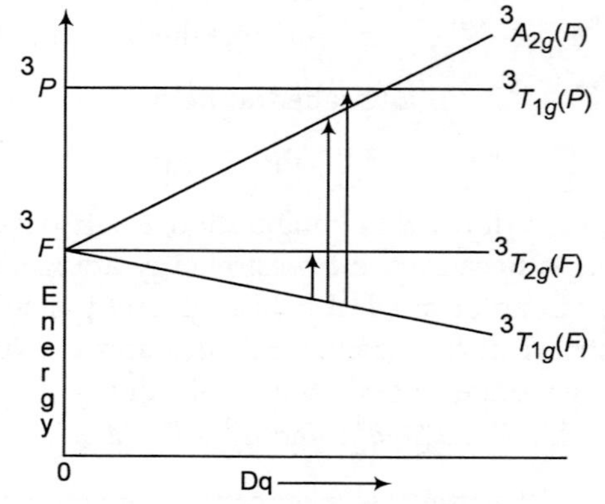

Fig. 14.11 Transitions in $[V(H_2O)]^{3+}$.

Depending upon the ligand field or Dq, the position of transitions or bands varies. If Dq is small, then the three bands indicated above appear with increasing order of energy : (i) < (ii) < (iii). However, if Dq is large then the order may change as :

(i) $^3T_{1g}(F) \longrightarrow {}^3T_{2g}(F)$ (Lowest energy)

(ii) $^3T_{1g}(F) \longrightarrow {}^3T_{1g}(P)$

(iii) $^3T_{1g}(F) \longrightarrow {}^3A_{2g}(F)$ (Highest energy)

In case Dq falls in the range where $^3T_{1g}(P)$ and $^3A_{2g}(F)$ tend to meet or cross over, then only two transitions may be observed.

Electronic spectrum of $[V(H_2O)_6]^{3+}$ shows only two bands assigned as :

$^3T_{1g}(F) \longrightarrow {}^3T_{2g}(F)$ at 17000 cm^{-1}

and $^3T_{1g}(F) \longrightarrow {}^3A_{2g}(F) = {}^3T_{1g}(F)$ at 24000 cm^{-1}

We do observe three bands with a stronger ligand like ammonia assigned as

$^3T_{1g}(F) \longrightarrow {}^3T_{2g}(F)$ 17200 cm^{-1}

$^3T_{1g}(F) \longrightarrow {}^3T_{1g}(P)$ 25600 cm^{-1}

$^3T_{1g}(F) \longrightarrow {}^3A_{2g}(F)$ 36000 cm^{-1}

d^2-(T_d). Although V^{3+} generally forms octahedral complexes, a few tetrahedral ions are known to exhibit bands attributed to :

$^3A_2(F) \longrightarrow {}^3T_1(F)$ 9000 cm^{-1} (Near infrared region)

$^3A_2(F) \longrightarrow {}^3T_1(P)$ 15000 cm^{-1}

The transition : $^3A_2(F) \longrightarrow {}^3T_2(F)$ is very low energy and does not fall in the visible region but exists in the infrared region and hence not observed in the electronic spectrum of d^2 (T_d).

$d^3(O_h)$ or $Cr^3(O_h)$

A common example is $[Cr(H_2O)_6]^{3+}$. The Orgel diagram Fig. 14.9 shows the Mulliken symbols for that on the left hand side. The spin multiplicity is 4 and the splitting of free ion terms of d^3 or Cr^{3+} are

$$^4A_{2g}(F) < {}^4T_{2g}(F) < {}^4T_{1g}(F) < {}^4T_{1g}(P)$$

in increasing order of their energies. Hence, theoretically expected transitions are :

$[Cr(H_2O)_6]^{3+}$

(i) $^4A_{2g}(F) \longrightarrow {}^4T_{2g}(F)$ 17400 cm^{-1}

(ii) $^4A_{2g}(F) \longrightarrow {}^4T_{1g}(F)$ 24500 cm^{-1}

(iii) $^4A_{2g}(F) \longrightarrow {}^4T_{1g}(P)$ 38600 cm^{-1}

The corresponding bands are shown on the right hand column for $[Cr(H_2O)_6]^{3+}$ and the energy level diagram is drawn in Fig. 14.12.

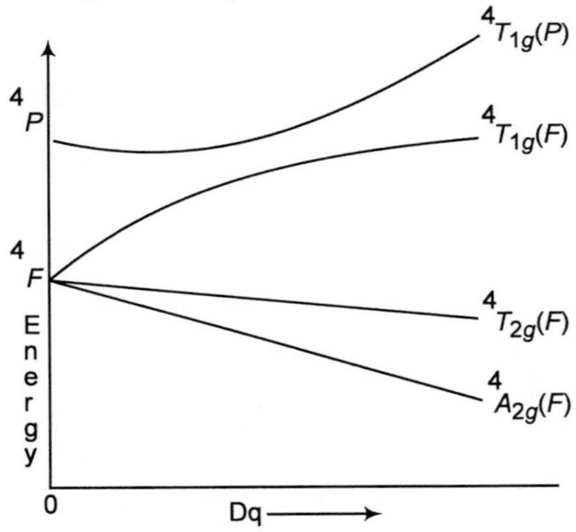

Fig. 14.12 Energy level diagram of d^3 (O_h).

Mulliken symbols $^4T_{1g}(F)$ and $^4T_{1g}(P)$ show curvature because being identical they interact and never cross each other.

Transitions between ground term and higher states and the corresponding bands (cm^{-1}) for some of the d^3 (Cr^{3+}) octahedral complexes are given in Table 14.6.

Table 14.6 **Electronic Transitions** (cm^{-1}) **of Some** Cr^{3+} (O_h) **Complexes**

Transition	$[CrF_6]^{3-}$ (Green)	$[Cr(H_2O)_6]^{3+}$ (Violet)	$[Cr(ox)_3]^{3-}$ (Red-violet)	$[Cr(en)_3]^{3+}$ (Yellow)	$[Cr(CN)_6]^{3-}$ (Yellow)
(i) $^4A_{2g} \to {}^4T_{2g}$	14900	17400	17500	21900	26700
(ii) $^4A_{2g} \to {}^4T_{1g}(F)$	22700	24500	23000	28500	32200
(iii) $^4A_{2g} \to {}^4T_{1g}(P)$	34400	38600	–	–	–

The highest energy transition : $^4A_{2g} \longrightarrow {}^4T_{1g}(P)$ falls usually in the ultraviolet region and is mostly overlapped by very strong charge transfer bands.

Transitions for $d^3(T_d)$ can be derived similarly from Fig. 14.9 (RHS) taking care to leave out subscript *g*. These are :

(i) $^4T_1(F) \longrightarrow {}^4T_2(F)$

(ii) $^4T_1(F) \longrightarrow {}^4A_2(F)$

(iii) $^4T_1(F) \longrightarrow {}^4T_1(P)$

$d^7(O_h)$ or $Co^{2+}(O_h)$ Orgel diagram for $d^7(O_h)$ is already given in Fig. 14.9 on the right hand side. The energy level diagram of $Co^{2+}(Oh)$ alone is given in Fig. 14.15 for greater clarity. Mulliken symbols $^4T_{1g}(F)$ and $^4T_{1g}(P)$, being identical, show curvature. Theoretically an octahedrally coordinated Co(II) should exhibit the following three spin allowed *d–d* transitions.

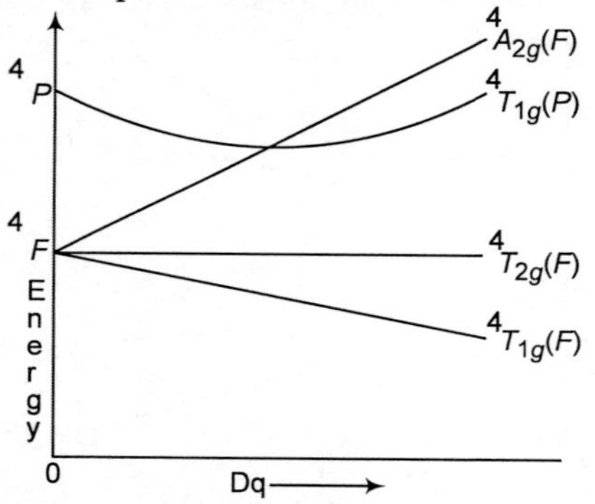

Fig. 14.13 Energy level diagram of $Co^{2+}(O_h)$.

	Transitions	$[Co(H_2O)_6]^{3+}$
(i)	$^4T_{1g}(F) \longrightarrow {}^4T_{2g}(F)$	8700 cm^{-1} (Near IR)
(ii)	$^4T_{1g}(F) \longrightarrow {}^4A_{2g}(F)$	16000 cm^{-1}
(iii)	$^4T_{1g}(F) \longrightarrow {}^4T_{1g}(P)$	19400 cm^{-1}

The actual spectrum of pale pink solution of $[Co(H_2O)_6]^{2+}$ is more complicated and is shown in Fig. 14.14.

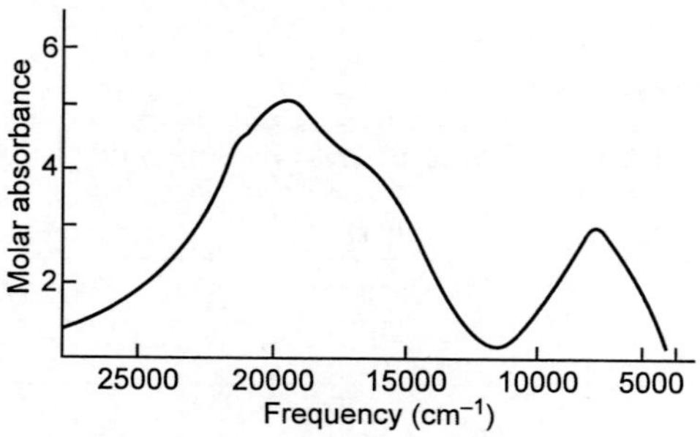

Fig. 14.14 Electronic spectrum of $[Co(H_2O)_6]^{2+}$.

The spectrum shows a weak, well defined low energy absorption at 8700 cm^{-1} which falls in the near infrared region. It is assigned to $^4T_{1g} \longrightarrow {}^4T_{2g}$. A multiple absorption band appearing at about 20000 cm^{-1} is more complicated and comprises of main band at 19400 cm^{-1} with shoulders at 16000 cm^{-1} and 21600 cm^{-1}. The main band at 19400 cm^{-1} is assigned to $^4T_{1g}(F) \longrightarrow {}^4T_{1g}(P)$ and the shoulder at 16000 cm^{-1} to $^4T_{1g}(F) \longrightarrow {}^4A_{2g}(F)$. This is tentative assignment because these transitions are close together because of cross-over point between the $^4A_{2g}$ and $^4T_{1g}(P)$. The extra shoulder is attributed to spin-orbit coupling in $^4T_{1g}(P)$ state.

Co(II) (T_d) or d^7 (T_d)

The blue complex anion $CoCl_4^{2-}$ is an example of $d^7(T_d)$. Orgel diagram Fig. 14.9 (LHS) shows that $d^7(T_d)$ and $d^3(O_h)$ have similar transitions. In other words, $CoCl_4^{2-}$ has transitions similar to $[Cr(H_2O)_6]^{3+}$, discussed already. These transitions are :

		$CoCl_4^{2-}$	
(i)	$^4A_2(F) \longrightarrow {}^4T_2(F)$	3300 cm^{-1}	(IR region)
(ii)	$^4A_2(F) \longrightarrow {}^4T_1(F)$	5800 cm^{-1}	(Near IR)
(iii)	$^4A_2(F) \longrightarrow {}^4T_1(P)$	15000 cm^{-1}	(Visible)

The blue colour of $CoCl_4^{2-}$ is attributed to transition $^4A_2 \longrightarrow {}^4T_1(P)$ occurring in the red part of the spectrum. The other two transitions (i) $^4A_2 \longrightarrow {}^4T_2$ falls in the infrared region and (ii) $^4A_2 \longrightarrow {}^4T_1(F)$ appears in the near infrared region. The actual electronic spectrum of $CoCl_4^{2-}$ is shown in Fig. 14.15.

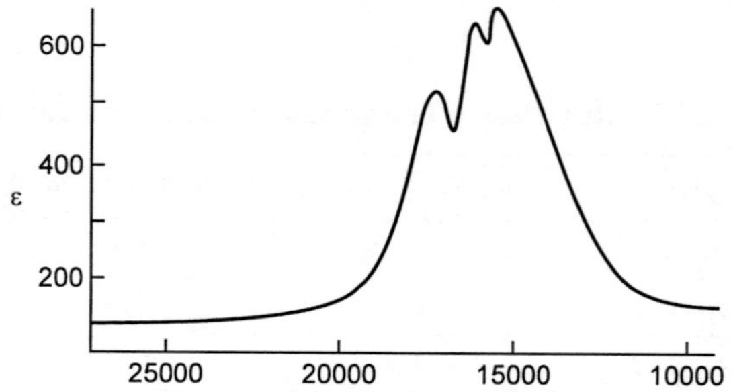

Fig. 14.15 Electronic spectrum of $CoCl_4^{2-}$.

The two shoulders on the higher energy side of the band at 15000 cm^{-1} are attributed to spin-orbit coupling. An important feature of this spectrum is the very intense band at 15000 cm^{-1} with molar absorbance of 600 l mol^{-1} cm^{-1} compared to $\varepsilon = 6\ l$ mol^{-1} cm^{-1} in $[Co(H_2O)_6]^{2+}$ shown in Fig. 14.16. That shows why $[Co(H_2O)_6]^{2+}$ has a light pink colour and $CoCl_4^{2-}$ a very intense blue colour. **The band in $CoCl_4^{2-}$** is intense because it is both spin allowed and Laporte allowed.

d^8 (O_h) or Ni(II) (O_h)

The configuration $d^8(O_h)$ shows transitions inverse of $d^2(O_h)$. Transitions for $d^8(O_h)$ are given in Fig. 14.8 (LHS) or Fig. 14.10 (LHS). The following transitions are expected to occur theoretically and their

Transitions	$[Ni(H_2O)_6]^{2+}$	$[Ni(NH_3)_6]^{2+}$
(i) $^3A_{2g}(F) \rightarrow {^3T_{2g}}(F)$	8500 cm^{-1}	10800 cm^{-1}
(ii) $^3A_{2g}(F) \rightarrow {^3T_{1g}}(F)$	15400 cm^{-1}	17500 cm^{-1}
(iii) $^3A_{2g}(F) \rightarrow {^3T_{1g}}(P)$	26000 cm^{-1}	28200 cm^{-1}

positions in the spectra of octahedral complexes of Ni(II) with H_2O and NH_3 are also listed. The actual spectrum of $[Ni(H_2O)_6]^{2+}$ is shown in Fig. 14.16.

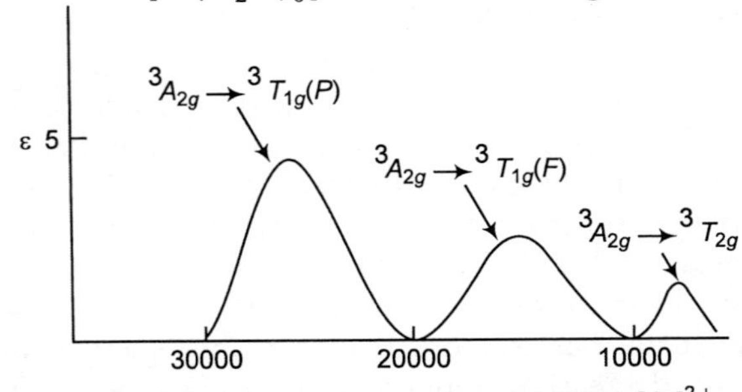

Fig. 14.16 Electronic spectrum of $[Ni(H_2O)_6]^{2+}$.

The spectrum shown in Fig. 14.16 is very simple and shows all the three transitions expected for $d^8(O_h)$. The molar absorbance is low (< 5 l mol^{-1} cm^{-1}) because the *d-d* transitions are Laporte forbidden.

Manganese(II) Octahedral Ions; d^5 (O_h)

Manganese(II) has d^5-configuration and in weak octahedral fields has $t_{2g}^3\ e_g^2$ electronic configuration. The ground state term is ^6S, *i.e.,* there are five unpaired electrons with parallel spins. Any electronic transition will lead to a reversal of spins, this will be a "spin forbidden" transition and this explains the pale-pink colour of Mn(II) compounds, as all such "spin forbidden" transitions are very weak. The spectra of Mn(II) salts are important as some fundamental issues are involved. The spectrum of $[Mn(H_2O)_6]^{2+}$ is shown in Fig. 14.17.

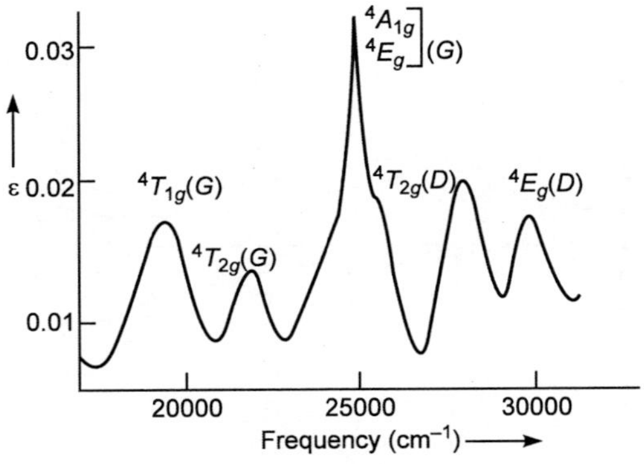

Fig. 14.17

Some special features of the spectrum are

(a) the **very weak** nature of the **bands,** *i.e.,* molar absorbance values are very low.

(b) the **large number of bands.**

(c) the **variation in the width of the bands,** *i.e.,* some are broad with one or two bands being very sharp.

(i) **The weakness of the bands The ^6S ground state** is not splitted by the field but acquires Mulliken symbol $^6A_{1g}$ as ground state in a weak octahedral field. This is the only sextuplet state $^6A_{1g}$ and any alteration in electron distribution results in the pairing of two spins, thus resulting in quartet states ^4G, ^4D, ^4F and ^4P which are of higher energy. Therefore, the excited states will have different spin multiplicity from the ground state and so **transitions** so these excited states **are spin-multiplicity forbidden.** However, due to weak spin-orbital interactions, these type of transitions are not totally forbidden, but give rise to very weak absorption bands shown in Fig. 14.18. The molar absorption coefficient ε is 0.02–0.03l mol^{-1} cm^{-1} as compared with 5-10 l mol^{-1} cm^{-1} for spin allowed transitions.

(ii) **Number of transitions** of the different transitions which can be formulated from the $^6S\ (t_{2g}^3\ e_g^2)$ state, the four quartets ^4G, ^4F, ^4D and ^4P involve the reversal of only one spin. The other states involve reversal of two spins leading to doublet states which obviously are of very high energy and are unlikely to be observed and are thus not included in the energy level diagram given in Fig. 14.18.

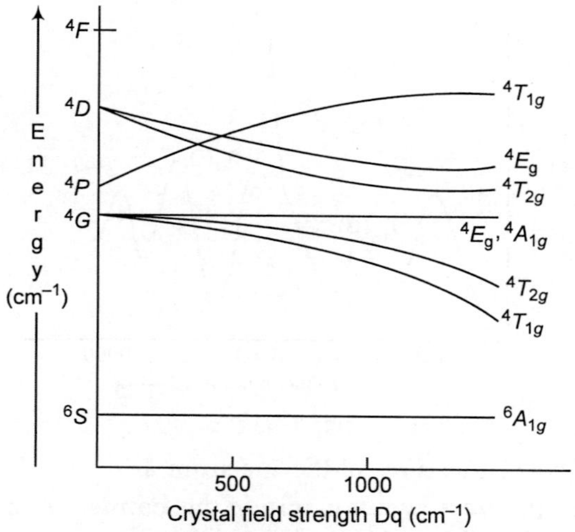

Fig. 14.18 Partial energy level diagram for the Mn^{II}, $[Mn(H_2O)_6]^{2+}$.

The following bands are assigned :

$$^6A_{1g} \longrightarrow {}^4T_{1g}(G) \quad 18900\ cm^{-1}$$
$$^6A_{1g} \longrightarrow {}^4T_{2g}(G) \quad 23100\ cm^{-1}$$
$$^6A_{1g} \longrightarrow {}^4E_g(G) \quad 24970\ cm^{-1}$$
$$^6A_{1g} \longrightarrow {}^4A_{1g}(G) \quad 25300\ cm^{-1}$$
$$^6A_{1g} \longrightarrow {}^4T_{2g}(D) \quad 28000\ cm^{-1}$$
$$^6A_{1g} \longrightarrow {}^4E_g(D) \quad 29700\ cm^{-1}$$

(iii) **Width of the bands** It has been theoretically shown that widths of the peaks for *d-d* transitions are proportional to the slope of the higher energy state relative to the slope of the ground state in the Orgel diagram. Since, the slope of the ground state term $^6A_{1g}$ is zero, and the slopes of the $^4E_g(G)$, $^4A_{1g}(G)$, $^4E_g(D)$ terms are also zero, transitions from the ground state to these states should give sharp peaks. By same argument, peaks due to transitions to $^4T_{1g}(G)$ and $^4T_{2g}(G)$ will give broad peaks.

The same diagram is applicable of d^5 tetrahedral complexes (minus the *g* subscripts). However, Mn^{II} tetrahedral complexes are yellow-green and are more intense (by a factor of 100) in colour than the octahedral complexes.

Evidence for Covalent Bonding in Complexes : Ligand Field Theory

By now we must appreciate that crystal theory does not take into consideration any contribution of covalence in the metal-ligand interactions. The metal-ligand orbital overlap is generally not very large and for most metal complexes, correct predictions can be made by the application of crystal field theory provided small modifications are introduced to account for orbital overlaps (covalence). **This modified CFT theory is given the name ligand field theory.** Before we consider the different modifications, we present here certain experimental evidences for covalent bonding in metal complexes. The evidence has been obtained in different experiments on a large number of complexes :

1. Absorption spectra
2. ESR spectra
3. NMR spectra and
4. Magnetic susceptibility results

1. Absorption Spectra

An evidence that metal orbitals and ligand orbitals overlap is given by the ehanced intensities of absorption bands attributed to *d-d* transitions. The observed intensities can be accounted for provided it is assumed that overlap and mixing of metal *d*-orbital and orbitals of the ligand atoms takes place. It has been observed that the repulsions between the *d*-electrons of the metal are less in the complex than in the free metal ion. In other words, we may say that *d*-electron cloud of the metal has expanded over to the ligand atoms thereby decreasing repulsions between them. This expansion of *d*-electron clouds can occur only provided the metal orbitals overlap with ligand orbital (covalence). This effect of ligands which expands the *d*-electron cloud of the metal is known as the **nephelauxetic effect**. Different ligands can cause cloud expansion to a different extent. The arrangement of ligands in the order of increasing ability of cloud expansion is termed as **nephelauxetic series** (just like the spectrochemical series).

Nephelauxetic series This order is

$$F^- < H_2O < NH_3 < Ox^{2-} < en < NCS^- < Cl^- < CN^- < Br^- < I^-$$

and is generally independent of the metal ion.

2. Electron Spin Resonance Spectra (ESR)

It has been observed in the ESR spectra of certain metal complexes that instead of a single band expected for the *d*-electrons (if localised only on the metal atom), a complex band (called sub-bands or hyperfine structure) is observed. The presence of hyperfine structure can be explained in terms of the overlap of metal orbitals and certain orbitals of the surrounding ligands such that the unpaired electron of the metal is not localized entirely on the metal but instead is also localised on the surrounding ligands. For example, the ESR spectrum of $[Ir^{IV}Cl_6]^{2-}$ can be explained if it is assumed that the iridium 4*d*-electron resides only 70% on iridium (instead of 100%) and 5% on each Cl^- on.

3. Nuclear Magnetic Resonance Spectra (NMR)

It has been observed that nuclear resonance of certain atoms in ligands of metal complexes are affected by the unpaired electron of the metal in a manner which can be explained only if it is assumed that some electron density from the metal is transferred into orbitals of the ligand atoms. For example, the resonance frequency of the ring proton (H_α) in *tris* (acetylacetonato) vanadium(III) is shifted from its position in a comparable diamagnetic compound, say in *tris* (acetylacetonato) aluminium(III).

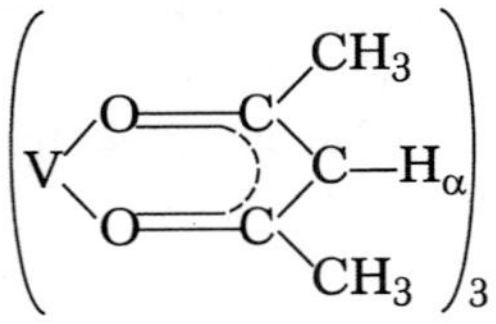

This shift can be explained if it is assumed that spin density of the unpaired vanadium electron gets transferred into the π-system of the 'acac' ligand and finally gets transferred into the 1*s* orbital of the hydrogen atoms (H_α).

4. Magnetic Susceptibility Results

The anti-ferromagnetism as observed in some ionic compounds like MnO, FeO, NiO cannot be explained in terms of pairing of electron spins within the individual ions but may be attributed to the alignment of magnetic moments of half the ions in a direction opposite to the other half of the ions. Such an anti-parallel alignment of the nearest metal ions separated by an oxide ion can be explained if overlap between the *d*-orbital of one metal ion which contains its unpaired electron and a π-orbital of the oxide ion is taking place. An electron from the oxide ion moves to and occupies the *d*-orbital of the metal. But this may happen only if it must have its spin opposed to that of *d*-electron (because of the Pauli exclusion principle). The other π-electron of the oxide ion must have its spin aligned parallel to the first metal ion.

$$M\downarrow\uparrow O\downarrow\uparrow M$$

If this π-electron moves into the *d*-orbital of the second metal ion which already contains its unpaired *d*-electron, the spin of the metal *d*-electron will have to be aligned opposite to that of the entering π-electron. Thus, the spins of the two metal atoms are aligned opposite to each other by the intervention of the oxide ion. This explanation is based on the fact that these oxides are not purely ionic ($—M^{2+}—O^{2-}—M^{2+}—$) but instead show significant degree of overlap between metal *d*-orbitals and ligand (anion) orbitals.

Ligand Field Theory

We have thus presented a lot of evidence to show that significant overlap exists between metal *d*-orbitals and ligand orbitals in metal complexes. It must thus be recognized that the basic assumption of crystal field theory that the metal ion and the surrounding ligand atoms interact with one another in an entirely electrostatic manner and no overlapping of their orbitals or mixing of their electrons take place is not true. The commonly employed method is to retain the basic features of crystal field theory and introduce interelectronic interaction parameters which take into account orbital overlap. The essential idea is that if the orbital overlap takes place then metal electrons come under the influence of the nuclei of ligand atoms. The metal electrons are drawn farther out thus lowering their mutual repulsions.

The three interaction parameters which are introduced are the **spin-orbit coupling constant,** λ and the **Racah parameters** *B* and *C*. The spin-orbit coupling constant plays an important part in determining magnetic properties of many transition metal ions and their complexes. The values of λ are about 70-80% of those for the free ions and we get good agreement between experimental and predicted results (on the basis of CFT) simply by using smaller λ values.

The Racah parameters *B* and *C* are measures of the energy separations of the various Russell-Saunders state (*L*-*S*) of an atom. The energy differences between different states in the complex are about 70% of the values expected for the free ion. Thus, in order to calculate an energy-level diagram or magnetic behaviour in ligand field theory, one proceeds in the same way as in crystal field theory except that, instead of using the free ion values of *A*, *B* and *C*, one uses approximately 70% (smaller) values.

Exercise 1

(For Part 'B')

1. The ground state term symbol for d^3 is
(a) $^4D_{5/2}$ (b) $^4P_{3/2}$
(c) $^4F_{9/2}$ (d) $^4F_{3/2}$

2. The lowest energy term for d^2 ion is
(a) ^3F (b) ^3P
(c) ^4P (d) ^1S

3. The state of d^2 configuration are
(a) $^3P, ^1S$ (b) $^3F, ^3P, ^2D$
(c) $^3F, ^3P, ^1G, ^1D, ^1S$ (d) $^3F, ^3P, ^3S, ^1P, ^1D, ^1S$

4. The term symbol for the ground state electronic configuration of chromium atom is
(a) ^6S (b) ^4F
(c) ^4S (d) ^5D

5. What are the values of L, S and J for a term symbol $^3F_2$?
(a) $L = 2, S = 3, J = 5$
(b) $L = 3, S = 2, J = 0, 1, 2, 3$
(c) $L = 3, S = 1, J = 4, 3, 2$
(d) $L = 1, S = 3, J = 4, 3, 2$

6. What is wrong in the atomic term symbol $^0D_1$?
(a) J cannot be equal to 1
(b) $2s + 1$ cannot be equal to 0
(c) D is not the letter used in atomic term symbol
(d) J cannot be equal to 0

7. The different values of L for d^1 to d^5 configuration are in the order
(a) $^2D, ^2D, ^3F\ ^3F\ ^0S$ (b) $^0S, ^2D, ^2D, ^3F, ^3F$
(c) $^2D, ^3F, ^3F, ^2D, ^0S$ (d) $^0S, ^2D, ^3F, ^3F, ^2D$

8. The term symbol for the lowest energy state of nitrogen is
(a) $^4S_0$ (b) $^4S_{3/2}$
(c) $^4S_{1/2}$ (d) $^2P_0$

9. Red and yellow ochres the colour is due to
(a) ligand to metal $3d$ (b) ligand to metal $4s$
(c) ligand to metal $5p$ (d) ligand to metal $6s$

10. Naples yellow is coloured due to
(a) CT spectra (b) ligand $p\pi$-metal $5s$
(c) ligand $p\pi$-metal $5p$ (d) All of these

11. Vermilion is coloured due to
(a) Ligand $\rightarrow$ metal $6s$, CT (b) Metal $\rightarrow$ Ligand CT
(c) Ligand $\rightarrow$ metal $5s$ CT (d) None of these

12. The atomic symbols for electrons for which $L = 2$ and $S = 1$ is
(a) $^2D_{3,2,1}$ (b) $^3D_{3,2,1}$
(c) $^3D_{0,1,2}$ (d) $^3D_{3/2,1/2,1}$

13. The ground state term symbol for p^3 and d^3 electronic configuration respectively are
(a) ^4S and ^4F (b) ^4D and ^4F
(c) ^1D and ^4F (d) ^4S and ^2G

14. The ground state of V^{3+} ion is
(a) $^3F_2$ (b) $^5D_0$
(c) $^3F_4$ (d) $^2D_{5/2}$

15. The lowest energy term symbol for the silicon atom is
(a) ^3P (b) ^3S
(c) ^3D (d) ^1P

16. The transition $^3A_2(F) \longrightarrow {^3T_2}(F)$ is fall in
(a) UV region (b) vision region
(c) microwave region (d) IR region

17. The number of microstates for d^3 configuration is
(a) 60 (b) 120
(c) 240 (d) 45

18. A transition is said to be spin forbidden, if it involves
(a) same number of electrons
(b) same number of unpaired electrons
(c) different number of electrons
(d) different number of unpaired electrons

19. ^3F to ^3P transition is
(a) Laporte allowed (b) spin allowed
(c) Laporte forbidden (d) spin forbidden

20. For the term D, the number of components are
(a) 2 (b) 3
(c) 4 (d) 5

21. A 'G term' consist of
(a) $A + E + T_{1g} + T_{2g}$ (b) $A + 2E + T_{1g}$
(c) $A + 2E_g + 2T_g$ (d) $E_g + 2T_{1g} + T_{2g}$

22. Which of the following statements are true?
(a) $d'(O_h) = d^6(O_h)$
(b) $d'(O_h)$ is inverse of $d^4(O_h)$
(c) $d'(T_d) = T^4(T_d)$
(d) All of the above

23. The number of microstates for p^5 configuration is
(a) 2 (b) 4
(c) 6 (d) 8

24. The number of possible spin allowed transitions for $[Ni(H_2O)_6]^{2+}$ is
(a) 0 (b) 1
(c) 2 (d) 3

25. Which of the following electronic transition corresponds to the lowest energy band in the absorption spectrum of Ni (ethylenediamine)$_3^{2+}$?
(a) $^3T_{2g} \leftarrow {}^2A_{2g}$ (b) $^3T_{1g}F \leftarrow {}^3A_{2g}$
(c) $^3T_{1g}(P) \leftarrow {}^3A_{2g}$ (d) $4A_{2g} \leftarrow {}^4T_{2g}$

26. The asymmetric nature of visible absorption band of $[Ti(H_2O)_6]^{3+}$ is due to
(a) Laporte's allowed transition
(b) Laporte's forbidden transition
(c) Dynamic Jahn-Teller effect
(d) Intensity stealing transition

27. Δ_o in cm^{-1} is given for the following complexes : $[CrCl_6]^{3-}$, $[Cr(NH_3)_6]^{3+}$, $[Cr(CN)_6]^{3-}$ is 135000 cm^{-1}, 21600 cm^{-1}, 28200 cm^{-1} respectively.
The number of unpaired electrons in the above complexes
(a) is the same in all the complexes
(b) goes on increasing with increasing Δ_o
(c) goes on increasing with decreasing Δ_o
(d) cannot be predicted

Exercise 2

(For Part 'C')

1. The increasing order of energies for the term symbols of Cr^{3+} ion are
(a) $^4A_{2g}(F) < {}^4T_{1g}(F) < {}^4T_{2g}(F) < {}^4T_{1g}(P)$
(b) $^4T_{1g}(P) < 4T_{2g}(F) < {}^4T_{1g}(F) < {}^4A_{2g}(F)$
(c) $^4T_{1g}(P) < {}^4A_{2g}(F) < {}^4T_{2g}(F) < {}^4T_{1g}(F)$
(d) $^4A_{2g}(F) < {}^4T_{2g}(F) < {}^4T_{1g}(F) < {}^4T_{1g}(F)$

2. In the energy level diagram of d^3 ion, the Mulliken symbols $^4T_{1g}(F)$ and $^4T_{1g}(P)$ show curvature and never cross each other. This is because
(a) they are identical
(b) they have same spin state
(c) they are gerade
(d) All of the above

3. For titanium complex $[Ti(H_2O)_5]^{3+}$ the absorption maximum is due to *d–d* transition is found at 20000 cm^{-1}. Therefore, the CFSE is
(a) –20000 cm^{-1} (b) $\frac{4}{9} \times 20000\ cm^{-1}$
(c) 8000 cm^{-1} (d) –8000 cm^{-1}

4. The crystal field splitting energy (Δ) for $(CoCl_6)^{4-}$ is 18000 cm^{-1} and Δ for $CoCl_4^{2-}$ will be
(a) 18000 cm^{-1} (b) 8000 cm^{-1}
(c) 16000 cm^{-1} (d) 2000 cm^{-1}

5. Electronic spectra of $KMnO_4$ and K_2CrO_4 shows broad bands at
(a) 20000 and 18000 cm^{-1}
(b) 18000 and 20000 cm^{-1}
(c) 26000 and 18000 cm^{-1}
(d) 18000 cm^{-1} and 26000 cm^{-1}

6. The crystal field stabilisation energy value for $[Ti(H_2O)_6]^{3+}$ that has as absorption maximum at 492 nm is
(a) 20325 cm^{-1} (b) 10162 cm^{-1}
(c) 8130 cm^{-1} (d) 12195 cm^{-1}

7. In an isoelectronic series VO_4^{3-}, CrO_4^{2-} and MnO_4^- all members have intense CT transitions. The incorrect statement is
(a) CT transitions are attributed to excitations of electrons from ligand σ to metal
(b) MnO_4^- exhibits CT at shortest wavelength among the three
(c) λ of transitions increases in the order of $VO_4^{3-} < CrO_4^{2-} < MnO_4^-$
(d) the charge on metal nucleus increases in the order $VO_4^{3-} < CrO_4^{2-} < MnO_4^-$

8. The increasing order of λ of the absorption for the complex ions
I. $[Cr(NH_3)_6]^{3+}$ II. $[CrCl_6]^{3-}$
III. $[Cr(OH_2)_6]^{3+}$ IV. $[Cr(CN)_6]^{3-}$
(a) IV < II < I < III (b) IV < I < III < II
(c) II < III < I < IV (d) IV < III < II < I

9. Strong UV absorption is observed in

(a) $[Co(NH_3)_6]^{3+}$ (b) $[Co(NH_3)_5Br]^{2+}$

(c) $[Co(NH_3)_5I]^{2+}$ (d) $[Co(NH_3)_5F]^{2+}$

10. $[(NH_3)_5Ru\text{-}pyz\text{-}Ru(NH_3)_5]^{5+}$ *pyz* is a bridging ligand has

(a) Ru in (II) oxidation state

(b) Ru in (III) oxidation state

(c) Ru in +2.5 oxidation state

(d) All of the above

11. The lowest energy Mulliken symbol for $Cr^{3+} (O_h)$ is

(a) $^4A_{2g}$ (b) $^3T_{1g}$ (c) $^4T_{2g}$ (d) $^4T_{1g}$

12. $^2P_{312}$ is the ground state of

(a) H (b) Li

(c) B (d) F

13. The number of microstates for d^5 configuration is

(a) 49×6^3 (b) 7×6^3

(c) 7×6^2 (d) 14×6^5

14. Which of the following complexes is coloured?

I. $[Co(NH_3)_6]^{3+}$ II. $[Co(NH_3)_5Cl]^{2+}$

III. $MnCl_4^{2-}$

(a) I and II (b) II and III

(c) I and III (d) I, II, III

15. The term symbol $^3T_{2g}$ gives the information that

I. It is doubly degenerate.

II. It has spin multiplicity 3.

III. It is symmetrical *wrt* centre.

The correct statements are

(a) I, II (b) II, III (c) III, I (d) I, II, III

16. Consider the following statements.

I. If subshell is less than half-filled, the state with maximum *J* value is the ground state.

II. If subshell is more than half-filled, the state with lowest *J* value is the ground state.

The true statement (*s*) is/are

(a) I only (b) II only

(c) Both I and II (d) Neither I nor II

Assertion & Reason

Codes

(a) A and R both are true and R is the correct explanation of A.

(b) A and R both are true and R is not the correct explanation of A.

(c) A is true and R is false.

(d) A is false and R is true.

17. **Assertion (A)** $V(H_2O)_6^{3+}$ shows only two bands.

Reason (R) H_2O is a weak field ligand.

18. **Assertion (A)** Carbon atom has six term symbols.

Reason (R) In accordance to Pauli exclusion principle, it contains only three term symbols.

19. **Assertion (A)** Angular momentum and energy of the multielectron system is represented by Term symbol. Which also represents electronic configuration.

Reason (R) Many energy states exist in multielectron system which do not exist in single electron system. Spin angular momentum and orbital angular momentum do not hold good for multi electron system.

Matching Type

20. Match the following.

Column I		Column II (Δ_o cm^{-1})	
A.	$[Co(NH_3)_6]^{3+}$	1.	10000
B.	$[Rh(NH_3)_6]^{3+}$	2.	23000
C.	$[Ir(NH_3)_6]^{3+}$	3.	34000
		4.	41000

Codes

	A	B	C
(a)	1	2	3
(b)	1	3	4
(c)	2	1	3
(d)	2	3	4

21. Match the following.

Column I (Complexes of Co^{3+})		Column II (Colour)	
A.	$[Co(NH_3)_6]^{3-}$	1.	Yellow
B.	$[Co(NH_3)_6]^{3+}$	2.	Violet
C.	$[Co(NH_3)_5H_2O]^{3+}$	3.	Orange
D.	$[Co(NH_3)_5Cl]^{2+}$	4.	Pink
E.	$[Co(NO_2)_6]^{2-}$	5.	Purple

Codes

	A	B	C	D	E
(a)	5	4	3	2	1
(b)	1	2	5	3	4
(c)	2	1	4	5	3
(d)	1	2	3	4	5

22. Match the following.

Column I (Configuration)		Column II (Ground state term)	
A.	d^1	1.	$^3P_0$
B.	f^1	2.	^2D
C.	d^2	3.	$^3F_2$
D.	p^2	4.	^3F

Codes

	A	B	C	D
(a)	1	4	3	2
(b)	1	2	3	4
(c)	2	4	3	1
(d)	4	3	2	1

Directions (Q. Nos. 23 and 24)

Transition metal form coloured complexes. Their complexes contain metal ions with incomplete *d*-subshells. Those transition metal ions which have completely filled or empty subshells of *d*-electrons will give colourless solutions.

The coloured ions are capable of absorbing radiations of particular wavelengths from visible region since differences in the energy between *d*-orbitals are of the same order of magnitude as energies of radiations constituting white light. $[Ti(H_2O)_6]^{3+}$ complex is pink in colour. Its spectrum shows a peak at 20000 cm^{-1} or 5000 Å.

23. What is the value of Δ_o for $[Ti(H_2O)_6]^{3+}$ complex.

(a) 293 cal/mol (b) 239 kJ/mol
(c) 293 kJ/mol (d) 239 cal/mol

24. Different complexes have different value of Δ_0 because

(a) Δ_o depends upon nature of metal ions
(b) Δ_o depends upon nature of ligands
(c) Δ_o depends upon difference between t_{2g} and *e.g.*, orbitals in octahedral complexes
(d) All of the above

Directions (Q. Nos. 25 and 26)

Trandition metals usually form coloured complexes and *d-d* transition (t_{2g}, e_g) are responsible for colour as the energy difference between t_{2g} and e_g, lies in the visible region. An allowed spectra is more intense as compared to forbidden one.

25. There is no *d-d* transition in Cu^+ but Cu_2O is coloured due to

(a) the presence of O^{2-} ion
(b) the presence of coloured Cu^+ ion
(c) CTLM spectra
(d) None of the above

26. Charge transfer spectra always produces more intense colour than *d-d* transition because

(a) charge transfer spectra is against Laporte-selection rules while *d-d* transition is according to selection rules $(\Delta l \pm 1)$
(b) charge transfer spectra is according to Laporte-selection rules while *d-d* transition are against the selection rules.
(c) Laporte selection rules are not applicable on charge transfer spectra so they are always more intense than *d-d* transitions
(d) Laporte selection rules are not applicable on *d-d* transitions and charge transfer spectra is according to Laporte selection rules.

27. Match the correct spin allowed ligand field transition with the complex.

	Column I		Column II
A.	$[Fe(H_2O)_6]^{2+}$	1.	0
B.	$[Ni(NH_3)_6)]^{2+}$	2.	many
C.	$Mn(H_2O)_6]^{2+}$	3.	1
D.	$Fe(CN)_6]^{4-}$	4.	3

The correct answer is

Codes

	A	B	C	D
(a)	3	1	4	2
(b)	3	4	1	2
(c)	1	2	3	4
(d)	4	3	2	1

Answers

Exercise 1

1. (d)	2. (a)	3. (c)	4. (a)	5. (c)	6. (b)	7. (c)	8. (b)	9. (a)	10. (d)
11. (a)	12. (b)	13. (a)	14. (a)	15. (a)	16. (d)	17. (b)	18. (d)	19. (a,b)	20. (d)
21. (a)	22. (d)	23. (c)	24. (d)	25. (a)	26. (b)	27. (a)			

Exercise 2

1. (d)	2. (a)	3. (d)	4. (b)	5. (d)	6. (c)	7. (b)	8. (c)	9. (d)	10. (d)
11. (a)	12. (d)	13. (c)	14. (b)	15. (b)	16. (d)	17. (a)	18. (b)	19. (c)	20. (d)
21. (c)	22. (c)	23. (b)	24. (d)	25. (c)	26. (c)	27. (b)			

Hints & Solutions

Exercise 1

4. $Cr = 3d^5 4s^1$

For d^5

1	1	1	1	1
+2	+1	0	−1	−2

$L = +2 + 1 + 0 - 1 - 2 = 0$

$S = n \times \frac{1}{2}$ (where, n = number of unpaired electron)

$= 5 \times \frac{1}{2} = \frac{5}{2}$

$(2S + 1) = \left(\frac{5}{2} \times 2 + 1\right) = 6$

Thus, the possible term is ^6S.

5. $^3F_2$ means $L = 3$ $\quad (\because {}^{2S+1}L_J)$

$2S + 1 = 3$

$J = 2$

This is for the configuration d^2.

1	1			

$L = 3 = F,\ S = \frac{2}{2} = 1,\ J = 4, 3, 2$

8. $N = 1s^2, 2s^2, 2p^3$

1	1	1
+1	0	−1

$L = 0$ and for $L = 0$ term symbol $= S$

Spin multiplicity $= 2S + 1 = 2 \times \frac{3}{2} + 1 = 4$

$J = L + S = 0 + \frac{3}{2} = \frac{3}{2}$

$\therefore$ Term symbol is $^4S_{3/2}$.

9. Red and yellow ochres is iron oxide (FeO)

$Fe^{3+}O^{2-} \xrightarrow{h\nu} Fe^{2+}O^{-}$ ligand $p\pi \rightarrow$ metal $3d$

10. Naples yellow is $[Pb_3(SbO_4)_2]$ $Sb^{5+}O^{2-} \xrightarrow[h\nu]{} Sb^{4+}O^{-}$

11. It has Ru in both (+2) and (+3) states. Metal electrons are sufficiently delocalised to give 2 equivalent Ru atoms in +2.5 O.S.

12. $L = 2$ means symbol is D.

Spin multiplictiy $= 2S + 1 = 2 \times 1 + 1 = 3$

and $J = (L + S)$ to $(L - S)$

$= (2 + 1)\ (2 + 1 - 1)\ (2 + 1 - 2)$

$= 3, 2, 1$

Therefore, term symbols are $^3D_3, {}^3D_2, {}^3D_1$ which are collectively written as $^3D_{3,2,1}$.

14. $V^{3+} = 3d^2$

1	1			
+2	+1	0	−1	−2

$L = \Sigma m_l = +2 + 1 = 3$ (*i.e.*, symbol is F)

$S = n \times \frac{1}{2} = \frac{2}{2} = 1$

spin multiplicity $(2S + 1) = (2 \times 1 + 1) = 3$

$J = (L - S)$

as it is less than half-filled.

$= 3 - 1 = 2$

Thus, the ground state term is $^3F_2$.

17. Number of microstates $\binom{n}{r} = \frac{10!}{3!(10-3)!}$

$= \frac{10 \times 9 \times 8 \times 7 \times 6 \times 5 \times 4 \times 3!}{3! \times 7!}$

$= \frac{10 \times 9 \times 8 \times 7 \times 6 \times 5 \times 4}{7 \times 6 \times 5 \times 4 \times 3 \times 2 \times 1}$

$= 120$

Exercise 2

7. $\lambda_{max} = 492$ nm or $\bar{\nu} = \frac{1}{\lambda} = \frac{1}{492 \times 10^{-7}\ \text{cm}}$

$= \frac{10^7}{492}\ \text{cm}^{-1} = 20325\ \text{cm}^{-1}$

CFSE for $Ti^{3+} = -0.4 \times \Delta_o = -0.4 \times 20325 = 8130\ \text{cm}^{-1}$

$Ti^{3+} = 4s^0, 3d^1$

8. Greater the oxidising power, lower the energy (higher the wavelength) at which charge transfer occur $(L \rightarrow M)$.

9. In the series of complexes $[Co(NH_3)_5X]^{2+}$ where X is a halogen, strong absorption in UV is observed with frequencies increasing in order X = I, Br, Cl, F (increase in ν) due to increasing difficulty in transferring electron from ligand to metal as we move from I to F.

12. $^2P_{3/2}$ represents,

$(2S + 1) = 2 \quad 2S = 1$ or $S = \frac{1}{2}$

$J = \frac{3}{2} = L + S = L + \frac{1}{2}$

$L = \frac{3}{2} - \frac{1}{2}$

$$= \frac{2}{2} = 1$$

The configuration of the given atoms are

$$H = 2s^1$$

$$Li = 1s^2$$

$$B = 1s^2, 2s^2 2p^1$$

$$F = 1s^2, 2s^2, 2p^5$$

In all these cases, $S = \frac{1}{2}$ but for B and F, L is larger than H and Li.

B is p^1 case while F is p^5 case. For both $L = 1$ so it is a p state. So, the terms symbol for B and F is $2p$. The possible J values are $(L + S)$ and $(L - S)$, *i.e.*, $\frac{3}{2}$ and $\frac{1}{2}$.

The term symbols are $^2P_{3/2}$ and $^2P_{1/2}$.

Here the larger value of J is $\frac{3}{2}$.

If this should correspond to the ground state, the p-orbital should be more than half-filled. Obviously this corresponds to F.

13. Number of microstates $\binom{n}{r} = \frac{n!}{r!(n-r)!}$

$$= \frac{10!}{5!(10-5)!}$$

(As d-orbital can accommodate maximum of 10 electrons.)

$$= \frac{10 \times 9 \times 8 \times 7 \times 6 \times 5!}{5! \times 5 \times 4 \times 3 \times 2 \times 1}$$

$$= 7 \times 6^2$$

15

Nuclear Chemistry

Discovery of Radioactivity

Shortly after the discovery of X-rays, French physicist, **Henri-Bacquerel,** in 1895, while trying to establish a possible relationship between the fluorescence of the glass wall of an X-ray tube and the phosphorescence of certain fluorescent salts caused by sunlight, left accidently a little pile of a uranium mineral on a photographic plate wrapped in a thick black paper lying in the dark room. On developing the plate he found a dark spot on it right below the position of the pile of the mineral. The black spot was a silhouette of the pile of the mineral. Bacquerel concluded that uranium emitted certain rays which penetrated paper wrapper and affected the photographic plate. These rays are invisible to naked eye and are given off by metallic uranium and also by uranium salts. These rays pass through thin sheets of glass or metal, produce ionisation in the cases through which they pass and rapidly discharge the charged leaves of a well-insulated electroscope. Bacquerel called these rays as radioactive rays (or radioactive emanations or radioactive radiations) and the property or phenomenon of giving out these rays is called **radioactivity**. The substances which emit these radioactive rays are called radioactive substances. The term radioactivity was first used by **Marie Curie.**

Radioactivity is essentially a nuclear phenomenon and is a drastic process because the element changes in kind. It is spontaneous and an irreversible self-disintegrating activity because the element breaks itself up to gain stability.

Types of Radioactive Rays

Rutherford and his co-workers, in 1904, passed the radiations emitted by radioactive elements through a strong electric field between parallel plates and thus separated them into three quite different kinds which are :

Syllabus

- Discovery of Radioactivity, Types, Properties
- Nuclear Reactions, Radioactive Disintegration, Nuclear Fission and Fusion
- Radioactive Equilibria
- Radioactive Series, Radioanalytical Techniques and Activation Analysis
- Magnetic Confinement
- Application of Radioisotopes

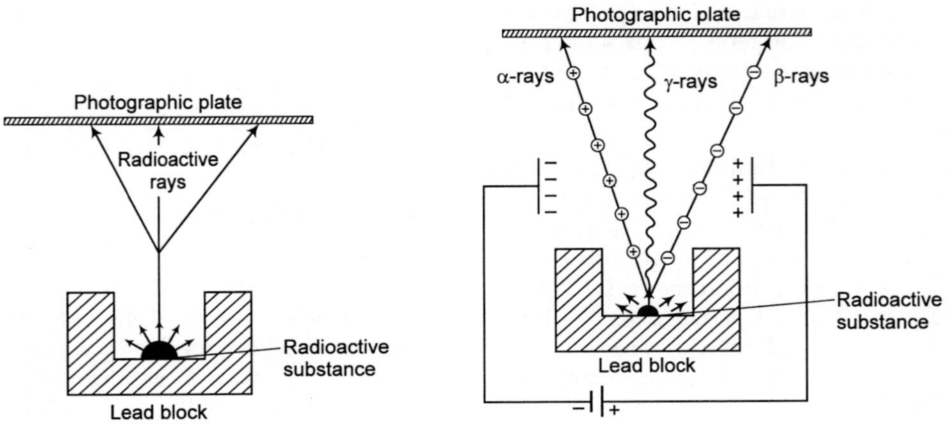

Fig. 15.1 Emission and separation of radioactive rays into α-, β-and γ-rays.

(i) Alpha (α) rays

The rays which are deflected towards the negative plate are positively charged and are called alpha (α) rays or alpha particles. These rays consist merely of helium nuclei.

(ii) Beta (β) rays

The rays which are deflected towards the positive plate are negatively charged and are called beta (β) rays or beta particles. These rays merely consist of electrons.

(iii) Gamma (γ) rays

These rays which are not deflected at all are neutral and are called gamma (γ) rays.

General Properties of Radioactive Radiations

(i) These radiations are highly penetrating. They affect photographic plates, ionize gases, cause scientillations on fluorescent screen, develop heat and produce chemical changes.

(ii) As radiations are given out, new elements are formed in an irreversible process–the new elements themselves being usually radioactive.

(iii) The emission of radiations is spontaneous and is not affected by external agents.

(iv) The emission is not instantaneous but is prolonged *i.e.,* it is extended over a period of time, otherwise it would not have been discovered at all.

(v) Except for radioactivity, there is nothing abnormal about the radioactive elements as regards their physical and chemical properties.

(vi) The rays are deflected by electric and magnetic fields showing that they are charged particles.

(vii) **They produce a heating effect** A quantity of radium always maintains itself at a temperature higher than that of the surroundings. The evolution of heat is due to the stoppage of α, β and γ-rays by the radioactive substance.

Properties of α-rays

(i) If a narrow beam of radioactive radiations proceeding from a deep cavity in a block of lead is subjected to an electric field between parallel plates, the α-particles are deflected towards the negative plate. This shows that α-rays consist of positively charged particles which have two units of positive charge and a mass four times the mass of hydrogen atom. In other words, α-particles are doubly charged helium ions, each consisting of two neutrons and two protons but having no electrons.

(ii) If a magnetic field is applied perpendicular to the plane of the paper and directed from top to bottom, the α-rays are deflected towards the left as shown in Fig. 15.2. (Application of Fleming's left hand laws)

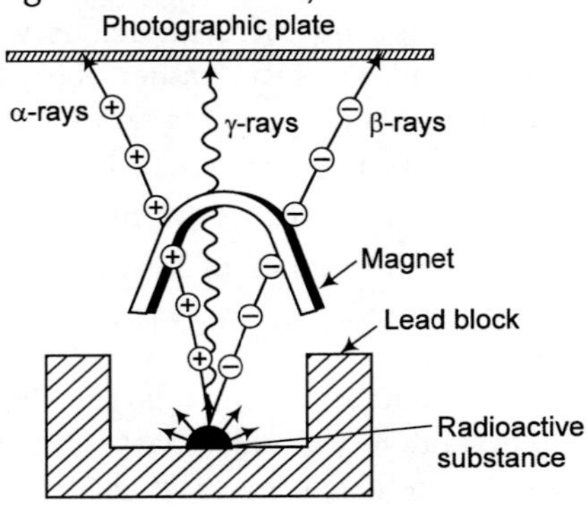

Fig. 15.2 Deflection of α, β and γ-rays in a magnetic field.

(iii) The ionisation first increases slightly, reahces a maximum and then suddenly drops almost to zero value, the distance at which the ionisation drops almost to zero gives the range of α-particles.

When the radioactive sample, say, polonium (*P*) is moved farther and farther away by pulling the rod (*R*) back, a point is reached when scientillations are no longer observed through the low-power microscope (*M*). The distance *d* where the α-particles just fail to reach the screen and hence produce no scientillation gives the range of the α-particles. (See Fig. 15.3.)

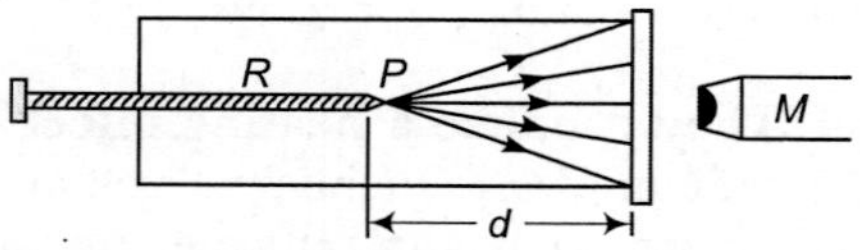

Fig. 15.3 Measurement of the range of an α-particle by scientillations produced on a fluorescent screen.
R = Rod; *P* = Radioactive sample, polonium; *S* = fluorescent screen; *M* = Low-power microscope; *d* = Range of α-particles.

(iv) The α-rays are scattered when they pass through thin sheets of mica, gold foil, etc. The divergence of α-particle from its straight line path is 2 to 3 degrees. Gieger and Marsden found that a few particles, sometimes, were deflected by more than 90°. This was explained by Rutherfored to be due to the repulsion between the α-particle and the nucleus of the atom scattering it.

(v) When exposed to α-rays the body suffers incurable burns.

Properties of β-rays

(i) **Velocity and range of β-rays** β-particles do not emerge out of the nucleus with the same range and velocity; rather they have a wide band of velocity ranging from 1 per cent to 99 per cent of the velocity of light.

(ii) **Ionisation in air** β-rays produce ionisation in air but the number of ions produced is hardly $\frac{1}{100}$th of those produced by α-rays. Although their velocity is very large, they possess a comparatively small mass and hence, have small kinetic energy. As β-particles change their path, their tracks in a Wilson cloud chamber are scattered, not continuous as are for the α-particles.

(iii) **Penetration** β-rays can penetrate through large thickness of matter, *e.g.,* they can easily pass through 1 cm thickness of aluminium sheet.

(iv) **Deflection** β-rays are deflected by electric and magnetic fields. Their direction of deflection shows that they are negatively charged particles. The e/m value has been found on the same lines as for cathode rays and this determination shows that β-rays are fast moving electrons which are of nuclear origin although they do not revolve in orbits as do the extra-nuclear electrons.

(v) **They are readily scattered when passing through matter** because of their extremely small mass. Generally, they undergo multiple scattering although single scattering also takes place by impact both with electrons and with nuclei.

(vi) They affect photographic plates more strongly than α-particles.

(vii) **They produce fluorescence** in barium platinocyanide, calcium tungstate, willemite etc.

Properties of γ-rays

(i) **Deflection** γ-rays are not deflected by electric and magnetic fields. This property shows that they are electromagnetic radiations which consist of very energetic photons. They are emitted by an excited nucleus and have extremely short wavelength ranging from 0.5 Å to 0.005 Å.

(ii) **Velocity** γ-rays possess the same velocity as that of light, *i.e.,* 3×10^{10} cm/s.

(iii) They are diffracted by crystals in the same way as X-rays.

(iv) **Ionisation in gas and generating power** They ionise the gas through which they pass, although the ionisation produced by them is comparatively small. Consequently, their penetrating power is very high as compared to that of β-rays, *e.g.,* they can pass easily through 30 cm, thickness of iron.

(v) They are capable of producing fluorescence and affecting photographic plates more intensely than β-rays.

Radioactive Disintegration

Atoms of heavy elements like uranium, thorium, polonium and radium etc., are constantly breaking up into fresh radioactive atoms with the emission of α-, β- and γ-rays from their nuclei. In this process, the original (or parent) atom disappears and gives rise to new (daughter) atom. These new atoms are also, in general, radioactive and hence spontaneously break up in their turn, thereby leading to a long chain of different radioactive elements in the form of a series until an inactive element (usually lead) is reached. This spontaneous breaking up of the nucleus is known as radioactive disintegration or radioactive decay.

Modes of Decay

The disintegration process may proceed in one of the following first two ways :

(i) α-particle emission

When an α-particle ($^{4}_{2}He$) is emitted from the nucleus of an atom (called parent element), the nucleus of the new element formed (called daughter element) possesses atomic weight or atomic mass number less by four units and nuclear charge (*i.e.,* atomic number) less by two units because α-particle has an atomic mass of four units and nuclear charge of two units. Thus, an atom of radium ($^{226}_{88}Ra$) changes on emission of an α-particle into an atom of radon ($^{222}_{86}Rn$). Here the subscript to the bottom left gives the atomic number, (*i.e.,* the number of protons or positive charges on the nucleus) and the superscript on the top left gives the atomic weight (*i.e.,* weight of the protons and neutrons put together) or atomic mass number.

Thus, the disintegration of $^{226}_{88}Ra$ into $^{222}_{86}Rn$ can be represented by the following equation which is called nuclear equation (or transmutation equation).

$$^{226}_{88}Ra \xrightarrow{-\alpha} {}^{222}_{86}Rn$$

or

$$^{226}_{88}Ra \longrightarrow {}^{222}_{86}Rn + {}^{4}_{2}He$$

In a balanced nuclear equation the sum of the mass numbers (*i.e.,* atomic mass numbers) of various species on the left (*i.e.,* reactants) is equal to the sum of the mass numbers of the species on the right (*i.e.,* products). Similarly, the sum of charge numbers (*i.e.,* atomic numbers) of various species on both the sides should be equal.

(ii) β-particle emission

A β-particle is just an electron and hence its symbol is $^{0}_{-1}e$. Since, ejection of a β-particle is also followed by the emission of γ-ray, γ-ray is also included in the equation. When a β-particle ($^{0}_{-1}e$) is emitted from the nucleus of an element, the nucleus of the new element formed possesses the same atomic weight but the positive charge, (*i.e.,* the atomic number) will be increased by one unit because the electron has one unit of negative charge with practically no mass.

Thus, the transformation of lead ($^{210}_{82}Pb$) into bismuth ($^{210}_{83}Bi$) can be shown as :

$$^{210}_{82}Pb \xrightarrow{-\beta} {}^{210}_{83}Bi + {}^{0}_{-1}e + \gamma\text{-ray}$$

However, it is now believed that **in a** β-particle emission, a neutron is converted into a proton ($^{0}_{+1}p$), an electron ($^{0}_{-1}e$) and a neutrino ($^{0}_{0}v$). The neutrino has zero mass and zero charge and is postulated to balance the spins. Thus,

$$\text{Neutron} \longrightarrow \text{Proton} + \text{Electron} + \text{Neutrino}$$

or

$$^{1}_{0}n \longrightarrow {}^{1}_{+1}p + {}^{0}_{-1}e + {}^{0}_{0}v$$

The electron produced escapes as a β-particle leaving the proton behind in the nucleus. The increase in the atomic number of the nucleus by one unit is due to this proton left in the nucleus.

(iii) γ-ray emission

We have already seen that γ-rays are short wave electro-magnetic radiations with no charge and no mass. Thus, the emission of γ-rays from a radioactive element will not produce a new element. The emission of γ-rays only results in decrease in energy of the nucleus. When α or β-particle is ejected from the nucleus, it is left in an excited state and emits γ-rays.

Laws of Radioactive Disintegration

Radioactive disintegration is found to obey the following two laws :

1. Atoms of all radioactive elements are undergoing spontaneous disintegration *i.e.,* are constantly breaking to form fresh radioactive products with the emission of α, β-and γ-rays.
2. The rate of breaking is not affected by external factors like temperature, pressure, chemical combination, etc., but depends entirely on the law of chance, *i.e.,* the number of atoms breaking per

second at any instant is proportional to the number present. In other words, the quantity of a radioactive element which disintegrates in units time is directly proportional to the amount of the radioactive element present.

Suppose an element A disintegrates into another element B. Let the number of atoms of A in the beginning (*i.e.,* at $t = 0$) be N_0. Now, as the time passes, the element A undergoes continuous disintegration into B and hence, the number of atoms of A goes on decreasing. Let the number of atoms of A left undisintegrated in time t be N. Thus,

$$A \longrightarrow B$$

At $t = 0$	N_0
At $t = t$	N

If dN atoms of A disintegrates in a small time dt, then the rate of disintegration (*i.e.,* rate of decrease) of A into B which is also called **activity** is equal to $-\dfrac{dN}{dt}$ which is proportional to N, *i.e.,*

$$-\frac{dN}{dt} \propto N$$

or
$$\frac{-dN}{dt} = \lambda N \qquad \ldots(1)$$

Here, λ is a constant of proportionality which has been called by Rutherford and Soddy as **radioactive (or decay or distintegration) constant.**

Since, the intensity and the number of atoms of A decrease with time, the rate of disintegration has been indicated by negative sign.

The differential equation (i) can be put in the form

$$\frac{dN}{N} = -\lambda dt$$

Integrating we have

$$\int \frac{dN}{N} = -\int \lambda dt + \text{constant of integration, } C$$

$$\log_e N = -\lambda t + C \qquad \ldots(2)$$

Now, when $t = 0,\ N = N_0$

$\because$ $\log_e N_0 = C$

Substituting the value of $\log_e N_0$ in Eq. (2), we get

$$\log_e \frac{N}{N_0} = -\lambda t$$

or
$$\frac{N}{N_0} = e^{-\lambda t}$$

$\because$
$$N = N_0 e^{-\lambda t} \qquad \ldots(3)$$

This decay equation may be used to find the number of the atoms of the original kind present at any time t.

If M_0 is the original mass of the material and M its present mass, then

$$M = M_0 e^{-\lambda t}$$

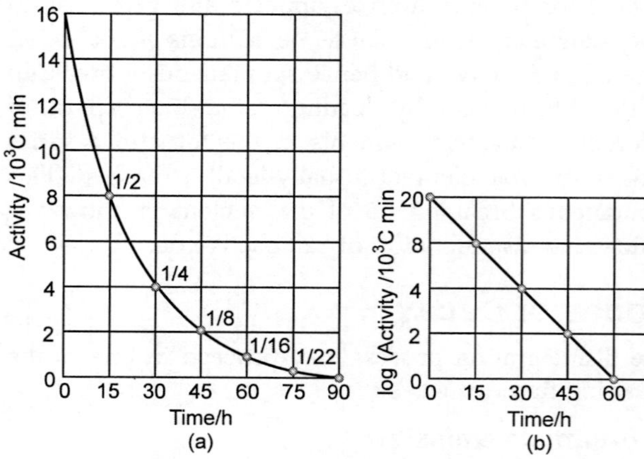

Fig. 15.4 Decay of ^{24}Na of half-life period 15.03 h.
(a) activity *vs* time
(b) log activity *vs* time

Radioactive constant (λ)

(a) Eq. (1) given above may be put as

$$\lambda = \frac{-dN/dt}{N}$$

Hence, radioactive constant may be defined as the ratio of the amount of the substance which disintegrates in a unit time to the amount of the substance present.

(b) Suppose, we put $t = 1/\lambda$ in Eq. (3) above. Then the number of the original atoms present after this time is

$$N = N_0 e^{-\lambda \times 1/\lambda} = N_0 e^{-1}$$

$$= \frac{N_0}{e} = \frac{N_0}{2.718}$$

$$N = 0.368\ N_0 \approx 0.37 N_0$$

Hence, radioactive constant may also be defined as the reciprocal of the time during which the number of atoms of a ratioactive substance falls to 37 per cent of its original value.

Half-Life Period ($t_{1/2}$ or T)

Suppose after time T (or $t_{1/2}$), half of the atoms of the radioactive element has disintegrated, *i.e.,*

when $t = T$, $N = N_0/2$

$$\frac{N_0}{2} = N_0 e^{-\lambda T}$$

or $$\frac{1}{2} = e^{-\lambda T}$$

or $$2 = e^{+\lambda T}$$

or $$\lambda T = \log_e 2$$

or $$T = \frac{\log_e 2}{\lambda}$$

Hence, $$t_{1/2} \text{ or } T = \frac{0.6931}{\lambda} \quad \ldots(4)$$

As is evident from Eq. (4), half-life period (T or $t_{1/2}$) of a radioactive substance is the time required to disintegrate one-half of the original amount of the substance. In other words, the half-life period of a radioactive substance is the time in which half of the radioactive substance will disintegrate.

In general, it may be said that at the end of time T, only 50% of the radioactive atoms remain unchanged, at the end of $2T$, only 25%, after $3T$, only 12.5%, after $4T$, only 6.25% and atthe end of $10T$, only 0.1% radioactive atoms remain unchanged. Hence, the life time of a radioactive element, though theoretically infinite, is finite for all practical purposes.

As already seen, λN represents the rate at which particles are emitted by N radioactive atoms.

∴ Rate of emission of particles or activity $= \lambda N = \frac{0.693N}{T}$.

If T is expressed in seconds, then the above equation gives the emission rate in terms of the number of particles expelled per second from N atoms of the given nuclide.

Evidently, half-life period of a given substance is independent of the amount of the substance present initially. It depends only on the disintegration constant (λ) of the element.

Half-life period of a radioactive substance is a measure of the radioactivity of the element, since shorter the half-life period of a radioactive element, larger the number of its atoms that are disintegrating in unit time.

Average Life Period (l)

This is also called **mean life period** or **life expectancy** and is defined as follows

Average life period of a radioactive element is the reciprocal of the disintegration constant (λ). Thus,

$$l = \frac{1}{\lambda} \quad \ldots(a)$$

We have already seen that

$$t_{1/2} = \frac{0.693}{\lambda}$$

or $$\frac{1}{\lambda} = \frac{t_{1/2}}{0.693} \quad \ldots(b)$$

Hence, from Eq. (a) and (b), we get

$$l = \frac{t_{1/2}}{0.693} = 1.44 \times t_{1/2}$$

Thus, average life period $(l) = 1.44 \times$ half-life period $(t_{1/2})$

Types of Radioactive Decay

Some important modes of nuclear decay are α-decay, β-decay, β^+-decay (this is accompanied by electron capture (EC)).

(i) In α-decay, two protons and two neutrons are emitted from the nucleus together as an α-particle. In other words, α-particle is nothing but a helium nucleus ($^4_2$He).

$$^{226}_{88}\text{Ra} \longrightarrow {}^{222}_{86}\text{Rn} + {}^{4}_{2}\alpha + Q$$

The energy released in the disintegration is represented by Q.

(ii) In β-decay, a negative electron is emitted by the nucleus and the atomic number is increased by one unit.

$$^{14}_{6}\text{C} \longrightarrow {}^{14}_{7}\text{N} + \beta + \bar{v} + Q$$

where $\bar{v}$ stands for the antineutrino.

(iii) Positron emission, also a β-decay process, results in a decrease by one unit in atomic number.

$$^{22}_{11}\text{Na} \longrightarrow {}^{22}_{10}\text{Ne} + \beta^+ + \bar{v} + Q$$

where, $\bar{v}$ represents the neutrino.

(iv) Electron capture (EC) is a third type of β-decay in which the atomic number is decreased by one unit, as in positron emission. One of the atomic electron (mostly K shell electron) is incorporated spontaneously into the nucleus.

In all the types of β-decay processes, since the atomic mass decreases very slightly, the mass number remains unchanged.

In addition to the above processes, there is one more radioactive decay mode called **spontaneous fission.** In this mode some heavy nuclei break up into two intermediate mass fragments and several neutrons.

$$^{252}_{98}\text{Cf} \longrightarrow {}^{140}_{54}\text{Xe} + {}^{108}_{44}\text{Ru} + 4n + Q$$

α-decay, β-decay and spontaneous fission may leave the nucleus in an excited state, which may de-excite by the emission of electromagnetic radiation called γ-rays which has neither mass nor charge.

Radioactive Equilibria

When a radioactive species disintegrates as a result of disintegration, another radioactive species or a stable species is produced. Suppose a radioactive species is formed, the behaviour of the two, namely parent and daughter can be studied as follows.

Let the parent be denoted by subscript 1 and the daughter be denoted by subscript 2. The behaviour of parent can be given by the equation

$$-\left(\frac{dN_1}{dt}\right) = \lambda_1 N_1 \qquad \ldots(5)$$

$$N_1 = N_1^0 e^{-\lambda_1 t}$$

$$N_1^0 = N_1 \qquad \text{when } t = 0$$

Similarly, the behaviour of daughter can be given by the equation

$$\frac{dN_2}{dt} = \lambda_1 N_1 - \lambda_2 N_2 \qquad \ldots(6)$$

$$\frac{dN_2}{dt} + \lambda_2 N_2 - \lambda_1 N_1^0 e^{-\lambda_1 t} = 0 \qquad \ldots(7)$$

The solution of this linear differential equation of the first order may be obtained by standard methods and is given by

$$N_2 = \frac{\lambda_1}{\lambda_2 - \lambda_1} N_1^0 (e^{-\lambda_1 t} - e^{-\lambda_2 t}) + N_2^0 e^{-\lambda_2 t} \ldots(8)$$

where, N_2^0 is the value of N_2 when $t = 0$.

In the Eq. (8), the first group of terms shows the growth of daughter from the parent and the decay of these daughter atoms; the last term gives the contribution at any time from the daughter atoms present initially.

Transient Equilibrium

When equation (8) is applied to radioactive pairs of parent and daughter, depending on the half-lives of the two, two general cases can be distinguished. If the parent is long lived than the daughter ($\lambda_1 < \lambda_2$; $(t_{1/2})_p > (t_{1/2})_d$) a state of so called radioactive equilibrium is reached; that is, after a certain time the ratio of the number of atoms and consequently, the ratio of the disintegration rates of parent and daughter become constant. This can be readily seen from the followng Fig. 15.5. After t becomes sufficiently large, $e^{-\lambda_2 t}$ is negligible compared with $e^{-\lambda_1 t}$ and $N_2^0 e^{-\lambda_2 t}$ also becomes negligible; then

$$N_2 = \frac{\lambda_1}{\lambda_2 - \lambda_1} N_1^0 e^{-\lambda_1 t}$$

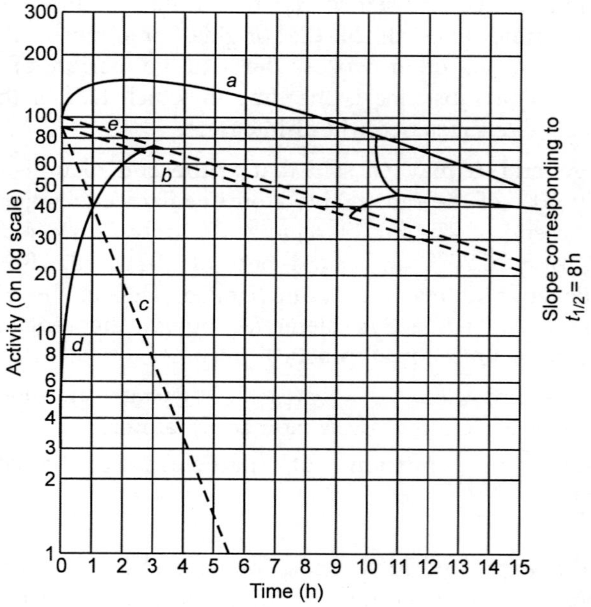

Fig. 15.5 Transient equilibrium :
(a) total activity of an initially pure parent fraction;
(b) activity due to parent ($t_{1/2}$ = 8.0 h);
(c) decay of freshly isolated daughter fraction ($t_{1/2}$ = 0.80 h);
(d) daughter activity growing in freshly purified parent fraction;
(e) total daughter activity in parent-plus-daughter fractions

and since $\quad N_1 = N_1^0 e^{-\lambda_1 t}$

$$\frac{N_1}{N_2} = \frac{\lambda_2 - \lambda_1}{\lambda_1} \qquad \ldots(9)$$

The relation of the two measured activities is found from $A_1 = C_1 \lambda_1 N_1$, $A_2 = C_2 \lambda_2 N_2$, to be

$$\frac{A_1}{A_2} = \frac{C_1 (\lambda_2 - \lambda_1)}{C_2 \lambda_2} \qquad \ldots(10)$$

In the special case of equal detection coefficients, $(C_1 = C_2)$ the ratio of the two activities, $A_1/A_2 = 1-(\lambda_1/\lambda_2)$, may have any value between 0 and 1, depending on the ratio of λ_1 to λ_2; that is, in equilibrium the daughter activity will be greater than the parent activity by the factor $\lambda_2/(\lambda_2-\lambda_1)$. In equilibrium both activities decay with the parent's half-life.

As a consequence of the condition of transient equilibrium $(\lambda_2 > \lambda_1)$, the sum of the parent and daughter disintegration rates in an initially pure parent fraction goes through a maximum before transient equilibrium is reached. This situation is illustrated in the Figure 15.8. The more general condition for the total measured activity $(A_1 + A_2)$ of an initially pure fraction to exhibit a maximum is found to be $C_2/C_1 > \lambda_1/\lambda_2$. This condition holds regardless of the relative magnitudes of λ_1 and λ_2. The condition $\frac{(\lambda_1-\lambda_2)}{\lambda_2} \le C_2/C_1 \le \lambda_1/\lambda_2$ will give a maximum in the total measured activity that occurs at a negative time.

Examples of transient equilibrium

1. $^{234}\text{Th} \xrightarrow[24.1d]{-\beta^-} {}^{234}\text{Pa} \xrightarrow[1.18\text{ min}]{-\beta^-}$ disintegration series
2. $^{232}\text{Rn} \xrightarrow[3.82d]{-\alpha} {}^{228}\text{Po} \xrightarrow[3.05\text{ min}]{-\alpha}$ disintegration series
3. $^{140}\text{Ba} \xrightarrow[12.8d]{-\beta^-} {}^{140}\text{La} \xrightarrow[40\text{ h}]{-\beta^-} {}^{140}\text{Ce}$ (stable)
4. $^{80m}\text{Br} \xrightarrow[\text{transition 4.4 h}]{\text{isomeric}} {}^{80}\text{Br} \xrightarrow[176\text{ min}]{-\beta^-} {}^{80}\text{Kr}$ (stable)

Secular Equilibrium

A limiting case of radioactive equilibrium in which $\lambda_1 << \lambda_2$ $((t_{1/2})_1 >> (t_{1/2})_2)$ and in which the parent activity does not decrease measurably during many daughter half-lives is known as secular equilibrium.

In this case of equilibrium, Eq. (vi) changes to

$$\frac{N_1}{N_2} = \frac{\lambda_2}{\lambda_1} \quad \text{or} \quad N_1\lambda_1 = N_2\lambda_2 \qquad \ldots(11)$$

and Eq. (vii) changes to

$$\frac{A_1}{A_2} = \frac{C_1}{C_2}$$

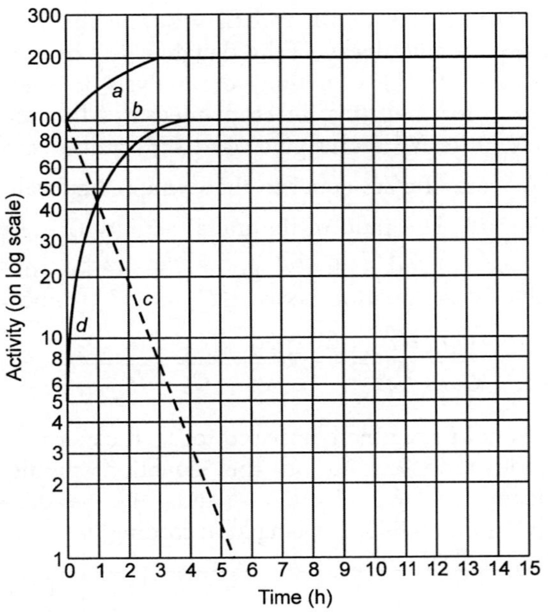

Fig. 15.6 Secular equilibrium :
(a) total activity of an initially pure parent fraction;
(b) activity due to parent ($t_{1/2} = \infty$); this is also the total daughter activity in parent-plus-daughter fractions;
(c) decay of freshly isolated daughter fraction ($t_{1/2}$=0.80 h);
(d) daughter activity growing in freshly purified parent fraction.

Fig. 15.6 is similar to Fig. 15.5 but it is for secular equilibrium. From the Fig. 15.6 it is apparent that as λ_1 becomes smaller compared to λ_2 the curves for transient equilibrium shift to approach more and more closely the limiting case.

Examples of secular equilibrium

1. $^{238}\text{U} \xrightarrow[4.5\times10^9 y]{-\alpha} {}^{234}\text{Th} \xrightarrow[24.1d]{-\beta^-}$ disintegration series
2. $^{226}\text{Ra} \xrightarrow[1600y]{-\alpha} {}^{222}\text{Rn} \xrightarrow[3.82d]{-\alpha}$ disintegration series
3. $^{90}\text{Sr} \xrightarrow[28.1y]{-\beta^-} {}^{90}\text{Y} \xrightarrow[64.1\ h]{-\beta^-} {}^{90}\text{Zr}$ (stable).

The Case of No Equilibrium

If the parent is shorter-lived than the daughter $(\lambda_1 > \lambda_2)$, it is evident that no equilibrium is attained at any time. If the parent is made initially free of the daughter, then as the parent decays the amount of daughter will rise, pass through a maximum, and eventually decay with the characteristic half-life of the daughter. This is illustrated in Fig. 15.7. For this plot we have taken $\lambda_1/\lambda_2 = 10$, and $C_1 = C_2$. In the Fig. the final exponential decay of the daughter is extrapolated back to $t = 0$. This method of analysis is useful if $\lambda_1 >> \lambda_2$, for then this intercept measures the activity $C_2\lambda_2 N_1^0$; the N_1^0 atoms give rise to N_2 atoms so early that N_1^0 may be set equal to the extrapolated value of N_2 at $t = 0$. The ratio of the initial activity $C_1\lambda_1 N_1^0$ to this extrapolated activity gives the ratios of the half-lives if the relation between C_1 and C_2 is known.

$$\frac{C_1\lambda_1 N_1^0}{C_2\lambda_2 N_1^0} = \frac{C_1}{C_2} \times \frac{\lambda_1}{\lambda_2} = \frac{C_1}{C_2} \times \frac{(t_{1/2})_2}{(t_{1/2})_1} \quad \ldots(12)$$

If λ_2 is not negligible compared to λ_1, it can be shown that the ratio λ_1/λ_2 in this equation should be replaced by $(\lambda_1 - \lambda_2)/\lambda_2$ and the expression involving the half-lives changed accordingly.

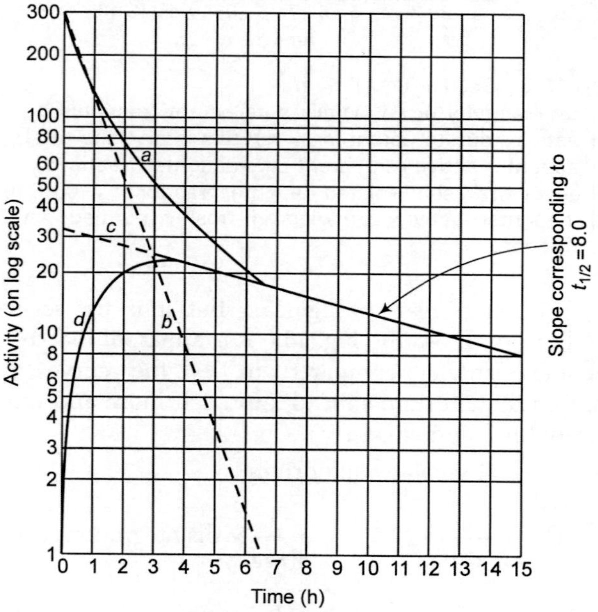

Fig. 15.7 The case of no equilibrium :
(a) total activity;
(b) activity due to parent ($t_{1/2} = 0.80$ h);
(c) exptrapolation of final decay curve to time zero;
(d) daughter activity in initially pure parent.

Both the transient-equilibrium and the no-equilibrium cases are sometimes analyzed in terms of the time t_m for the daughter to reach its maximum activity when growing in a freshly separated parent fraction. This time we find from the general Eq. (8) by differentiating;

$$\frac{dN_2}{dt} = \frac{\lambda_1^2}{\lambda_2 - \lambda_1} N_1^0 e^{-\lambda_1 t} + \frac{\lambda_1\lambda_2}{\lambda_2 - \lambda_1} N_1^0 e^{-\lambda_2 t} \ldots(13)$$

and setting $dN_2/dt = 0$ when $t = t_m$

$$\frac{\lambda_2}{\lambda_1} = e^{(\lambda_2 - \lambda_1)t_m} \text{ or } t_m = \frac{1}{\lambda_2 - \lambda_1} \ln \frac{\lambda_2}{\lambda_1} \quad \ldots(14)$$

At this time (t_m) the daughter decay rate $\lambda_2 N_2$ is just equal to the rate of formation $\lambda_1 N_1$. In Fig. 15.5 and 15.10, in which we assumed $C_1 = C_2$, we have the parent activity A, intersecting the daughter growth curve d at the time t_m. (The time t_m is infinite for secular equilibrium).

Table 15.1 **Comparison between Secular and Transient Equilibria**

S. No.	Secular equilibrium	Transient equilibrium
1.	$(t_{1/2})_1 >> (t_{1/2})_2$ and $(t_{1/2})_1 >>$ observation epoch	$(t_{1/2})_1 >> (t_{1/2})_2$ but $(t_{1/2})_1 \leq$ observation epoch
2.	As $(t_{1/2})_1 \longrightarrow \infty$ $(\lambda_1 \longrightarrow 0)$, $e^{-\lambda_1 t} \longrightarrow 1$	$(t_{1/2})_2$, λ_1 after finite $e^{-\lambda_1 t} < 1$
3.	$N_2 = \frac{\lambda_1 N_1^0}{\lambda_2 - \lambda_1}(e^{-\lambda_1 t} - e^{-\lambda_2 t})$ simplifies to $N_2 = \frac{\lambda_1}{\lambda_2} N_1^0 (1 - e^{-\lambda_2 t})$	The general equation remains same.
4.	After a sufficiently long time, $\frac{N_2}{N_1} = \frac{\lambda_1}{\lambda_2}$	After a sufficiently long time, $\frac{N_2}{N_1} = \frac{\lambda_1}{\lambda_2 - \lambda_1}$
5.	In the case of the series, $\frac{N_1}{(t_{1/2})_1} = \frac{N_2}{(t_{1/2})_2} = \ldots = \frac{N_n}{(t_{1/2})_n} =$ constant	No series is possible.

A Series of Successive Decays

In a chain of three or more radioactive products, the equations derived for N_1 and N_2 are valid, and N_3 may be found by solving the new differential equation.

$$\frac{dN_3}{dt} = \lambda_2 N_2 - \lambda_3 N_3 \quad \ldots(15)$$

This equation is very similar to the equation for $\frac{dN_2}{dt}$, but getting solution is very difficult as N_2 is a much more complicated function than N_1. Bateman, however, has given a solution for a chain of n members with the special assumption that at $t = 0$ the parent substance alone is present, that is, $N_2^0 = N_3^0 = \ldots = N_n^0 = 0$. This solution is

$$\left.\begin{aligned} N_n &= C_1 e^{-\lambda_1 t} + C_2 e^{-\lambda_2 t} + \ldots + C_n e^{-\lambda_n t} \\ C_1 &= \frac{\lambda_1 \lambda_2 \ldots\ldots \lambda_{n-1}}{(\lambda_2 - \lambda_1)(\lambda_3 - \lambda_1)\ldots\ldots(\lambda_n - \lambda_1)} N_1^0 \\ C_2 &= \frac{\lambda_1 \lambda_2 \ldots\ldots \lambda_{n-1}}{(\lambda_1 - \lambda_2)(\lambda_3 - \lambda_2)\ldots\ldots(\lambda_n - \lambda_2)} N_1^0 \\ &\vdots \\ C_n &= \frac{\lambda_1 \lambda_2 \ldots\ldots \lambda_{n-1}}{(\lambda_1 - \lambda_n)(\lambda_2 - \lambda_n)\ldots\ldots(\lambda_{n-1} - \lambda_n)} N_1^0 \end{aligned}\right] \ldots(16), \ldots(17)$$

Branching Decay

The case of branching decay occurs when a radioactive element can decay by more than one mode and is illustrated by

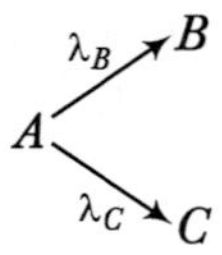

The two partial decay constants λ_B and λ_C must be considered when the general relations in either branch are studied because, for example, the substance B is formed at the rate.

$$\frac{dN_B}{dt} = \lambda_B N_A$$

but A is consumed at the rate

$$\frac{dN_A}{dt} = -(\lambda_B + \lambda_C) N_A$$

A is having only one half-life

$$t_{1/2}(A) = \frac{0.693}{\lambda_t} \qquad \ldots(18)$$

where, $\lambda_t = \lambda_B + \lambda_C + \ldots$ By definition the half-life is related to the total rate of disappearance of a substance, regardless of the mechanism by which it disappears.

Units of Radioactivity

The Curie (Ci) is a unit of radioactivity. It is defined as the quantity of an radioactive nuclide in which the number of disintegrations per second is 3.700×10^{10}. The SI unit of radioactivity is the becquerel, defined as 1 disintegration per second. The millicurie (mCi) and the microcurie (μCi) are practical units also in common use. The megacurie (MCi = 10^6 Ci) finds use in reactor technology.

Example 1. *1 g of radium is reduced by 2.1 mg in 5 yr by α decay. Calculate the half-life period of radium.*

Sol. Initial mass of radium $(N_0) = 1$ g

Mass of radium left behind $(N) = 1 - 0.0021$

$$= 0.9979 \text{ g}$$

$$\frac{N}{N_0} = e^{-\lambda t}$$

Here, $\dfrac{N}{N_0} = \dfrac{0.9979}{1}$

and $t = 5$ yr

Hence, $0.9979 = e^{5\lambda}$

or $e^{5\lambda} = \dfrac{1}{0.9979}$

$$5\lambda = 2.3026 \log_{10}\left[\frac{1}{0.9979}\right]$$

$$\lambda = \frac{2.3026 \times 0.0009}{5}$$

or $\lambda = 41.4468 \times 10^{-5}$ yr^{-1}

$$T = \frac{0.693}{\lambda}$$

$$= \frac{0.693}{41.4468 \times 10^{-5}} = 1672 \text{ yr}$$

Example 2. *^{227}Ac has a half-life of 21.8 yr. The decay follows two parallel paths, one leading to ^{227}Th and other to ^{223}Fr in the ratio 1.2% and 98.8% respectively. Calculate the rate constant in yr^{-1}, for each of the separate path.*

Sol. $\lambda_{Ac} = \dfrac{0.693}{t_{1/2}} = \dfrac{0.693}{21.8} = 3.18 \times 10^{-2}$ yr^{-1}

The overall rate constant λ_{Ac} is equal to sum of separate rate constant for Th and Fr.

$$\lambda_{Ac} = \lambda_{Th} + \lambda_{Fr}$$

The fractional yield is proportional to rate constant for that process.

$$\% \text{ yield of Th} = 1.2\% \text{ or } \frac{1.2}{100}$$

$$\lambda_{Th} = \frac{1.2}{100} \times 3.18 \times 10^{-2} = 3.82 \times 10^{-4} \text{ yr}^{-1}$$

Similarly, $\lambda_{Fr} = \dfrac{98.8}{100} \times 3.18 \times 10^{-2} = 3.14 \times 10^{-2}$ yr^{-1}.

Example 3. *Calculate the weight of C^{14} ($t_{1/2} = 5720$ yr) which gives 3.7×10^7 dps.*

Sol.

$$\lambda = \frac{0.693}{5720 \times 365 \times 24 \times 60 \times 60}$$

$$= 3.84 \times 10^{-12} \text{ s}^{-1}$$

$$-\frac{dN}{dt} = \lambda N$$

$$= \lambda \times \frac{W}{14} \times 6.02 \times 10^{23}$$

$$3.7 \times 10^7 = 3.84 \times 10^{-12} \times \frac{W}{14} \times 6.02 \times 10^{23}$$

On solving, $W = 2.24 \times 10^{-4}$ g

Example 4. *The half-life of* ^{22}Na *is 2.6 yr. 89% of it decays by* β^+ *emission and the rest by EC. Calculate (a) the partial decay constants and (b) the half-lives for each mode of decay.*

Sol. (a)

$$\lambda = \frac{0.693}{2.6} = 0.266 \text{ yr}^{-1}$$

$$\lambda_1 = 89\% \text{ of } \lambda = 0.237 \text{ yr}^{-1}$$

$$\lambda_2 = 0.266 - 0.237 = 0.029 \text{ yr}^{-1}$$

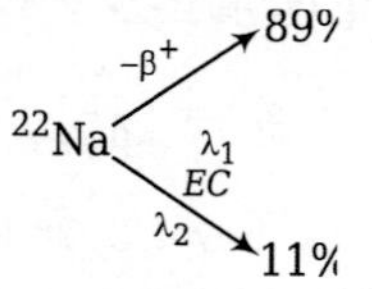

(b)

$$(t_{1/2})_1 = \frac{0.693}{0.237} = 2.92 \text{ yr}$$

$$(t_{1/2})_2 = \frac{0.693}{0.029} = 23.89 \text{ yr}$$

Example 5. *Calculate the proportions of* ^{238}U, ^{226}Ra *and* ^{222}Rn *in an ore which has attained equilibrium, the half-lives of these nuclides being* 4.47×10^9 yr, 1600 *yr and* 3.82 *days respectively.*

Sol.

$$^{238}\text{U} \xrightarrow[t_{1/2} = 4.47 \times 10^9 \text{ yr}]{\lambda_1} {}^{226}\text{Ra} \xrightarrow[t_{1/2} = 1600 \text{ yr}]{\lambda_2} {}^{222}\text{Rn} \xrightarrow[t_{1/2} = 3.82 \text{ days}]{\lambda_3}$$

$$\frac{N_2}{N_3} = \frac{N_{\text{Ra}}}{N_{\text{Rn}}} = \frac{\lambda_3}{\lambda_2}$$

$$= \frac{0.693 \times 1600 \times 365}{0.693 \times 3.82} = 1.53 \times 10^5$$

$$N_{\text{Ra}} : N_{\text{Rn}} = 1.53 \times 10^5 : 1$$

$$\frac{N_1}{N_2} = \frac{N_{\text{U}}}{N_{\text{Ra}}} = \frac{\lambda_2}{\lambda_1}$$

$$= \frac{0.693 \times 4.47 \times 10^9 \times 365}{0.693 \times 1600 \times 365} = 2.79 \times 10^6$$

$$\frac{N_{\text{U}}}{N_{\text{Ra}}} = 2.79 \times 10^6$$

$$\frac{N_{\text{U}}}{N_{\text{Rn}}} = 1.53 \times 10^5 \times 2.79 \times 10^6$$

$$= 4.27 \times 10^{11}$$

$$\text{Rn : Ra : U} = 1 : 1.53 \times 10^5 : 4.27 \times 10^{11}$$

Theory of Radioactive Disintegration— Stability of the Nucleus and Ratio of Neutrons and Protons

The stability of a nucleus depends qualitatively on the ratio of the number of neutrons (N) and protons (P) present in it. In case of elements with atomic numbers equal to 20, the ratio N/P is quite close to unity, *i.e.*, for such elements the number of neutrons is equal to that of protons. For the elements with higher atomic number ratio N/P increases progressively to about 1.6. In such elements the repulsion between them increases.

By plotting a graph between N and P for the nuclei of various elements it has been found that most of the stable nuclei (*i.e.*, non-radioactive nuclei) lie in a well-defined belt which is known as the **zone** or **belt of stability** because it contains the stable nuclei. (See Fig. 15.8). Nuclei whose N/P ratio lies above or below this belt, are unstable and, therefore, undergo spontaneous radioactive disintegration from one atom to another, giving α- or β- particles. This process of disintegration continues until a stable nucleus is obtained. For example, a radium nucleus changes successively into nine other nuclei emitting in all 5α and 4β particles and a stable nucleus of lead, Pb^{206} is obtained.

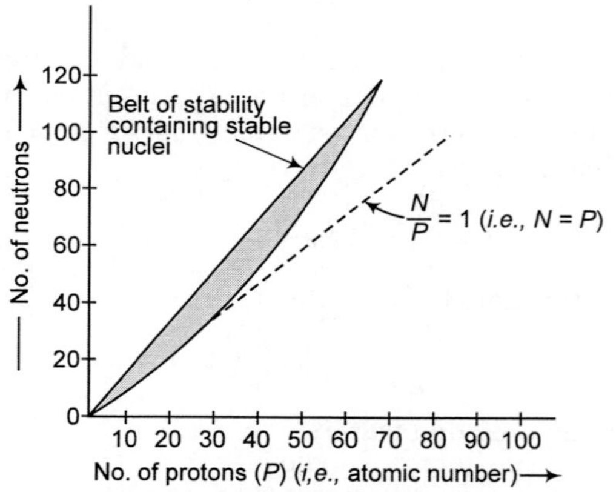

Fig. 15.8 A graph between the number of protons (P) and neutrons (N) having the belt of stability which contains stable nuclei. Nuclei whose N/P ratio lies above or below this belt are unstable and hence undergo spontaneous disintegration.

Group Displacement Law

The changes that occur when an α-particle or a β-particle is emitted from a radioactive element have been stated by **Fajan, Russel** and **Soddy** in 1913 in the form of a law which is known as **Group Displacement Law.** This law states as follows :

When an α-particle is emitted from a radioactive element (*i.e.*, parent element), the new element (*i.e.*, daughter element) formed has atomic number two units less and mass number four units less than the parent element. The element is consequently displaced two places (*i.e.*, two groups) to the left of the Periodic

Table. Similarly, when a β-particle is emitted, the new element has atomic number one unit more but its mass number remains the same as that of the parent element. Consequently the new element is displaced one place (*i.e.,* one group) to the right of the Periodic Table.

Examples to Illustrate the Law

$^{215}_{84}Po$ which is in group VIA of the Periodic Table, on losing an α-particle is transformed into radioactive lead, $^{211}_{82}Pb$ which belongs to group IVA. Thus, we see that the daughter element *viz.* $^{211}_{82}Pb$ is displaced two places to the left of the Periodic Table.

$$\begin{array}{ccc} \text{VIA} & & \text{IVA} \\ ^{215}_{84}Po & \xrightarrow{-\alpha} & ^{211}_{82}Pb \end{array}$$

Radioactive $^{211}_{82}Pb$ emits a β-particle to give radioactive $^{211}_{83}Bi$ which belongs to group VA, *i.e.,* one place to the right of the parent element *viz.,* $^{211}_{82}Pb$.

$$\begin{array}{ccc} \text{IVA} & & \text{VA} \\ ^{211}_{82}Pb & \xrightarrow{-\beta} & ^{211}_{83}Bi \end{array}$$

Radioactive bismuth, $^{211}_{83}Bi$ loses a β-particle resulting in the formation of $^{211}_{84}Po$ which belongs to group VIA, *i.e.,* one place to right of the parent element, $^{211}_{83}Bi$.

$$\begin{array}{ccc} \text{VA} & & \text{VIA} \\ ^{211}_{83}Bi & \xrightarrow{-\beta} & ^{211}_{84}Po \end{array}$$

The transformations shown above can be summarised as follows :

$$\begin{array}{ccccc} \text{IVA} & & \text{VA} & & \text{VIA} \\ ^{211}_{82}Pb & & \xleftarrow{\quad\quad -\alpha \quad\quad} & & ^{215}_{84}Po \\ \downarrow & & & & \\ \xrightarrow{-\beta} & & ^{211}_{83}Bi & \xrightarrow{-\beta} & ^{211}_{84}Po \end{array}$$

In the above example $^{215}_{84}Po$ and $^{211}_{84}Po$ are isotopes while $^{211}_{82}Pb$, $^{211}_{83}Bi$ and $^{211}_{84}Po$ are isobars. Thus, we conclude that a β-particle emission gives isobar while the combined emission of one α- and two β-particles results in the formation of an isotope.

Example 6. *Calculate the number of α- and β-particles emitted when $^{238}_{92}U$ changes into $^{206}_{82}Pb$.*

Sol. Let the element formed between $^{238}_{92}U$ and $^{206}_{82}Pb$ be *X*. The mass number of *X* should be the same as that of Pb because there is no loss in the mass number of the daughter element formed as a result of β-emission. Now let the number of α- and β-particles emitted be *x* and *y* respectively. The disintegration sequence will be as follows;

$$^{238}_{92}U \xrightarrow{-x\alpha} {}^{206}X \xrightarrow{-y\beta} {}^{206}_{82}Pb$$

Thus, $238 - 4x = 206$

∴ $x = 32/4 = 8$

The atomic number of

$$X = 92 - 2 \times 8 = 92 - 16 = 76$$

Consequently,

$$y = 82 - 76 = 6$$

Thus, the number of various particles emitted is

α-particles = 8

β-particles = 6.

Radioactive Series

Atoms of heavy elements like uranium, thorium, polonium and radium etc., are constantly breaking up into fresh radioactive atoms with the emission of α-, β- and γ-rays from their nuclei. In the process, the original (or parent) atoms disappears and gives rise to new (daughter) atoms. These new atoms are also, in general, radioactive and hence spontaneously break up in their turn, thereby leading to a long chain of different radioactive elements in the form of a series until an inactive element (usually lead) is reached. The series of elements thus obtained by the successive disintegration of the new atoms is known as **radioactive disintegration series** and the spontaneous breaking up the nucleus is known as **radioactive disintegration.**

All the naturally occurring radioactive elements belong to one of the following three series :

1. Uranium series [(4*n* + 2) series],
2. Thorium series [4*n* series],
3. Actinium series [(4*n* + 3) series].

These series have been named after the name of the element at or near the head of the respective series. All these three series which are also called **natural radioactive series** end with a stable isotope of lead.

Some elements of each series emit α-particles whereas some other elements emit β-particles. Although no one atom can go both ways, some atoms go either of the two ways and cause branches in the series. No matter which way the parent goes, the daughter goes otherway so that even though the series branch, they always come together again.

1. Uranium Series [(4*n* + 2) series]

This series is also called $(4n + 2)$ series because the mass number of the elements of this series are given by this expression in which n is an integer whose value decreases by unity when we go from one radioactive element to the next one below it. The mass numbers of the members of this series give a remainder of 2 when divided by 4. In this series $^{238}_{92}U$ is the parent element and through the successive disintegrations it is finally transformed into a stable isotopes of lead, $^{206}_{82}Pb$ (See Fig. 15.9).

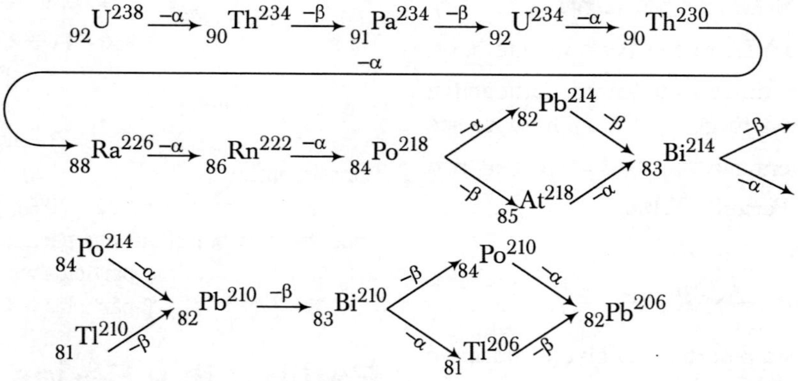

Fig. 15.9 Uranium or (4*n* + 2) series for naturally occuring elements.

2. Thorium Series (4*n* series)

This series is also known as $4n$ series because mass numbers of the members of this series are divisible by 4. This series starts with $^{232}_{90}Th$. As shown in Fig. 15.10 by a successive transmutation or disintegration it ends up in a stable isotope of lead, $^{208}_{82}Pb$.

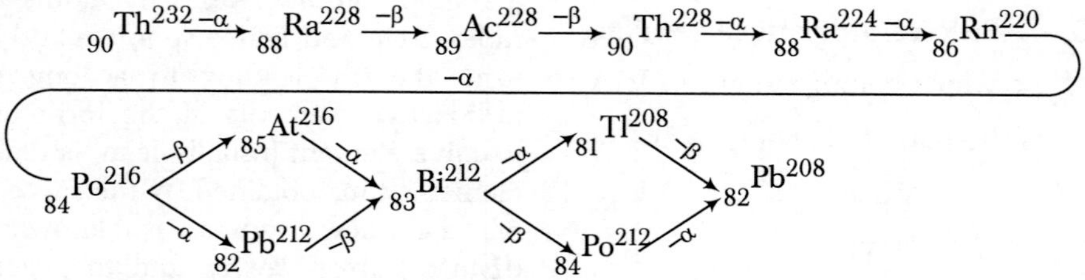

Fig. 15.10 Thorium or 4*n* series for natrually occuring elements.

3. Actinium Series [(4*n* + 3) series]

This series is also known as $(4n + 3)$ series because the mass numbers of the members of this series give a remainder of 3 when divided by 4. Actinium was one time thought to be the starting element of the series, but now it is known that the true starting element is $^{235}_{92}U$ which by successive transformations ends up in a stable isotope of lead, $^{207}_{82}Pb$. The whole chain of elements is shown in Fig. 15.11.

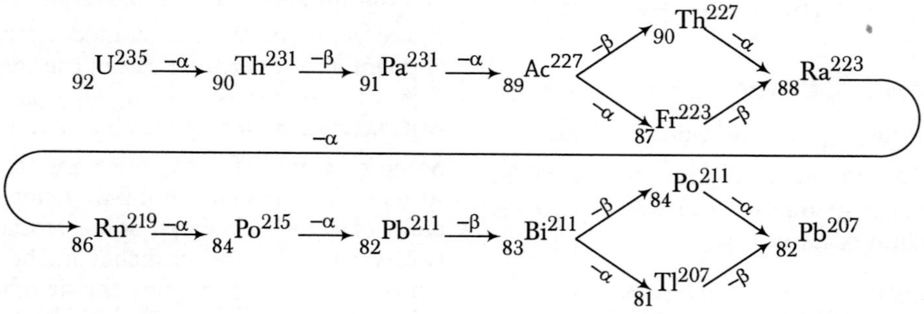

Fig. 15.11 Actinium or (4*n* + 3) series of naturally occurring elements.

Similarities between radioactive series

There are many points of similarity between three radioactive series :

(i) In all series, a product is formed which disintegrates in a branching process by emitting either α- or β-particle. The two substances thus produced are then transformed in such a way as to give a common product.

(ii) In all series, there is an element of atomic number 86 which has the properties of an inert gas and is called **emanation.**

(iii) The stable end-product in all the three series having an atomic number of 82, is an isotope of lead *i.e.*, Pb^{206}, Pb^{207} and Pb^{208}.

Neptunium Series [$(4n+1)$ series]

In addition to the three series described above, there is a fourth series which has been obtained from an artificially-produced radioactive material. The first stable element in this series is $^{237}_{93}Np$ after which it has been named and the stable end product is the ordinary bismuth $^{209}_{83}Bi$ rather than an isotope of lead as in the uranium, actinium and thorium series (See Fig. 15.12). This series is also known as $(4n+1)$ series. All the members of this series are either unknown or extremely rare in nature.

It is quite obvious from the study of these series that all the members of a particular series are characterised by having $(4n+q)$ nucleons, where q is one of the integers 0, 1, 2, 3 characteristic of a given series and n may be any integer. Evidently, $(4n+q)$ gives the mass number A of the members of the series. Thus,

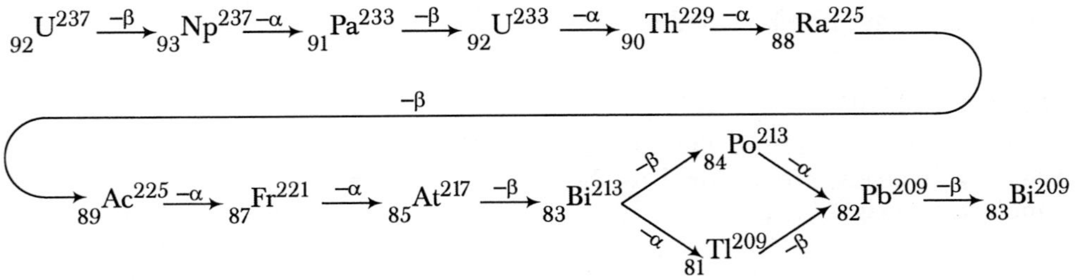

Fig. 15.12 Neptunium or $(4n+1)$ series obtained from an artificially produced radioactive material.

For thorium series $A = (4n+0)$, $q = 0$

For neptunium series $A = (4n+1)$, $q = 1$

For uranium series $A = (4n+2)$, $q = 2$

For actinium series $A = (4n+3)$, $q = 3$

Isotopes

Different kinds of atoms of the same element which have the same atomic number but different mass numbers or atomic masses (or atomic weights) are called isotopes of that element. Since, isotopes have the same atomic number, these can also be defined as different atoms of the same element which have the same number of protons but different number of neutrons in their respective nuclei.

The name isotope was first introduced by Soddy. The word isotopes has been derived from the Greek word meaning same position (isos = same; topes = position), since the isotopes occupy the same position in the Periodic Table. Isotopes have identical chemical properties and differ slightly only in respect of such properties as depend on their mass numbers.

As an exmple three isotpoes of carbon (at. no. = 6) having mass numbers equal to 12, 13 and 14 can be shown as :

(i) $^{12}_{6}C$ or ^{12}C (ii) $^{13}_{6}C$ or ^{13}C (iii) $^{14}_{6}C$ or ^{14}C

Some elements like beryllium and fluorine are found in nature as a single isotope. Such elements are called **monoisotopic. Only about 20 elements have been found to be monoisotopic.**

Calculation of the Actual Atomic Weight of an Element from Atomic Masses of Its Isotopes

The atomic weight of an element is a statistical mean of the atomic masses of different isotopes of the elements. The value of atomic weight depends on the relative proportions of the various isotopes. For example :

(i) The actual atomic weight of neon which is found to consist of $^{20}_{10}Ne$, $^{21}_{10}Ne$ and $^{22}_{10}Ne$ isotopes in the percentage : $^{20}Ne = 90.92\%$, $^{21}Ne = 0.26\%$ and $^{22}Ne = 8.82\%$ is :

$$= \frac{90.92 \times 20 + 0.26 \times 21 + 8.82 \times 22}{(90.92 + 0.26 + 8.82)}$$
$$= \frac{1818.40 + 5.46 + 194.04}{100} = \frac{2017.90}{100}$$
$$= 20.1790 \approx 20.18$$

(ii) Ordinary chlorine consists of 75.4% of ^{35}Cl isotope and 24.6% of ^{37}Cl isotope. Hence, its atomic weight is :

$$= \frac{75.4 \times 35 + 24.6 \times 37}{75.4 + 24.6} = 35.492$$

Separation of Isotopes

Since, all the isotopes of a given element have similar properties, it is almost impossible to separate them by chemical methods. However, some physical methods have been used for this purpose. **In these methods the difference in physical properties of the isotopes which depend on the mass of the atom has been utilised.** Some of the physical methods are discussed below :

1. Gaseous diffusion method

According to Grahm's law of diffusion, the rate of diffusion (r) of a gas is inversely proportional to the square root of its molecular weight (M), *i.e.,*

$$r \propto \sqrt{\frac{1}{M}}$$

Thus, **if a mixture consisting of two gaseous isotopes is allowed to diffuse through a porous partition, the lighter isotope passes through the porous partition more rapidly than the heavier one.** Gaseous ^{20}Ne and ^{22}Ne isotopes of neon and ^{16}O and ^{18}O isotopes of oxygen have been separated by this method. The separation of gases ^{16}O and ^{18}O isotopes has been shown in Fig. 15.13.

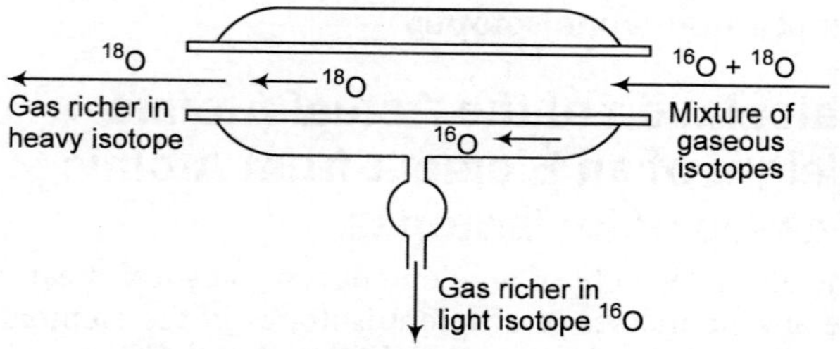

Fig. 15.13 Separation of gaseous ^{16}O and ^{18}O isotopes of oxygen by gaseous diffusion method.

The mixture of gaseous isotopes is passed through a porous tube sealed in an outer jacket. The lighter isotope (^{16}O isotope) passes into the jacket while the heavier isotope (^{18}O isotope) goes into the residual gas.

2. Thermal diffusion method

The apparatus used in this method consists of a long vertical cylindrical tube which is heated electrically to 600°C or above from inside by means of a thin platinum wire running down the axis of the tube (Fig. 15.14). **This method is based on the tendency of heavier molecules of a gas to concentrate in the cooler region of the vertical tube.** Thus, when a mixture of gaseous isotopes is introduced into the tube, the molecules of the lighter isotope diffuse more rapidly to the central hot region of the tube. Here, they are carried upwards by convection currents. The molecules of heavier isotope travel to the cooler inner surface of the tube and thus sink to the bottom. Thus, lighter isotope collects at the top while the heavier isotope collects at the bottom. The process is repeated several times. This method has been used by Clausius for the separation of ^{35}Cl and ^{37}Cl isotopes of chlorine.

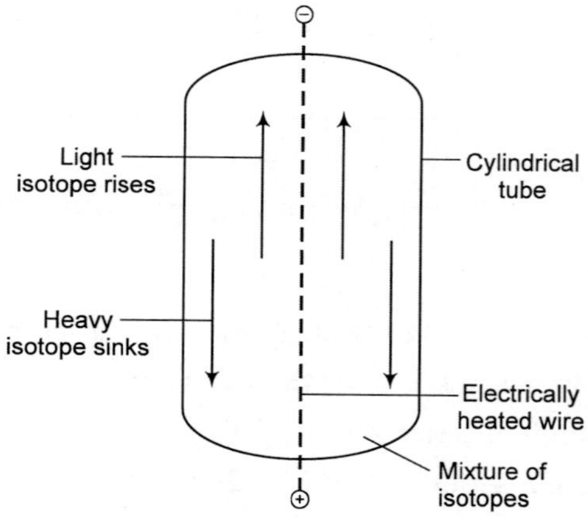

Fig. 15.14 Separation of isotopes by thermal diffusion method.

3. Fractional distillation and evaporation method

According to Graham's law of diffusion, the rate (r) of evaporation of a gas is inversely proportional to the square root of its density (d), *i.e.,*

$$r \propto \sqrt{\frac{1}{d}}$$

Thus, lighter isotope distills off first while the heavier isotope distills off last. For example, when liquid oxygen is distilled, the lighter isotope (^{16}O) comes off first and the heavier isotope (^{18}O) comes off in the end. The isotopes of neon have been separated by this method.

The separation of the two isotopes of Hg has been achieved by fractional evaporation of 40°C to 50°C in vaccum as shown in Fig. 15.15. The vapours of Hg are condensed on a surface cooled in liquid air which is placed a little above the evaporating Hg. After some time the liquid Hg left behind is found to consist of mostly heavier isotope which is taken out by opening stop-cock at the bottom. The frozen Hg collected at the cooler surface and consists of lighter isotope. It is removed, melted and evaporated under vaccum again. The whole process is repeated several times.

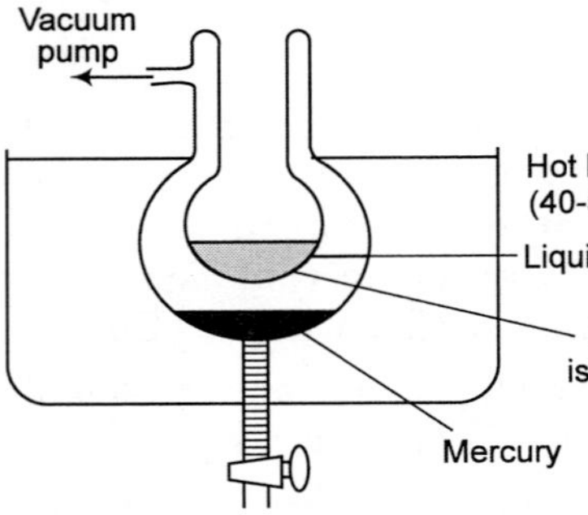

Fig. 15.15 Separation of the two isotopes of mercury by fractional evaporation.

4. Electromagnetic method

This method is based on the principle of Dempster's mass spectrograph. This method has been used for the separation of the three isotopes of neon. The beam of ions of the three isotopes of neon namely ^{20}Ne, ^{21}Ne and ^{22}Ne as obtained in dempster's mass spectrograph is passed between the poles of a magnet (Fig. 15.16). The different isotopes get deflected at different angles and are collected in cooled chambers which are placed in appropriate positions. The separation achieved by this method is complete, but the quantities of different isotopes obtained are very small.

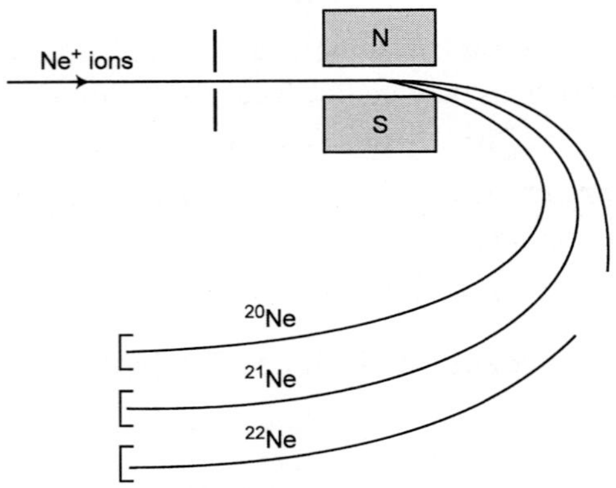

Fig. 15.16 Separation of the three isotopes of neon (^{20}Ne, ^{21}Ne and ^{22}Ne) by electromagnetic method making the use of Dempster's mass spectrography.

Isobars

The atoms of different elements which have the same mass number but different atomic number are called **isobars.** Since, isobars have the same mass number, these can also be defined as atoms of different elements which have the same sum of protons and neutrons in the nucleus of each of these atoms but different atomic number.

The word isobar has been derived from the Greek word meaning equally heavy (isos = equal; barys = heavy). $^{40}_{18}Ar$, $^{40}_{19}K$ and $^{40}_{20}Ca$ are the examples of isobars, since each of them has the same mass number *i.e.,* the sum of protons and neutrons is the same.

Isotones

The atoms of different elements which have the same number of neutrons but different atomic number are called **isotones.** Since, isotones have different atomic number, these can also be defined as the atoms of different elements which have the same number of neutrons but different number of protons and electrons. $^{14}_{6}C$, $^{15}_{7}N$ and $^{16}_{8}O$ are isotones, since each has the same number of neutrons *i.e.,* 8.

Nuclear Reactions or Nuclear Transmutation or Disintegration

Bethe's Notation A nuclear reaction is a transformation of a target atomic nucleus by bombarding it with projectiles like light nuclei, free nucleons, photons of adequate energy. The following type of equation is generally used to represent a nuclear reaction

$$^{A_1}_{Z_1}X + ^{A_2}_{Z_2}a \longrightarrow ^{A_3}_{Z_3}Y + ^{A_4}_{Z_4}b$$

In this equation '*X*' denotes the target nucleus, '*a*' denotes projectile which initiates the reaction, '*b*' represents the particle ejected or the ejectile and '*Y*' denotes recoil (product nucleus). Normally '*Z*'s are omitted in the equation unless the emphasis of nuclear charge conservation is required. Similarly, the values A_2 and A_4 are omitted unless *a* and *b* are uniquely indistinguishable. Bethe introduced a convenient notation to represent the nuclear reactions. As per this notation the above reaction can be represented as

$$^{A_1}X(a, b)\ ^{A_3}Y$$

The target nuclide is written first and the product last, with projectile and ejectile particles inside the parentheses separated by a comma.

(i) $^{24}Mg\ (d, \alpha)\ ^{22}Na$

(ii) $^{35}Cl\ (n, p)\ ^{35}S$

(iii) $^{23}Na\ (n, \gamma)\ ^{24}Na$

(iv) $^{63}Cu\ (p, p\ 3n\ 9\alpha)\ ^{24}Na$

In the last example, all the emitted particles are shown to the right of the comma.

Types of Nuclear Reactions

Based on the projectile and ejectile, the nuclear reactions can be classified as elastic scattering, inelastic scattering, photonuclear reactions and radiative capture. There are so many other types also like (n, p), (n, α), (α, n), (d, p), (d, n), (α, t), etc.

I. Classification based on Overall Energy Transmutation

(i) Capture reactions

In these reactions, the bombarding particle is captured or absorbed by the target nucleus with the emission of γ-rays. For example :

$$^{85}_{37}Rb + ^{1}_{0}n \longrightarrow ^{86}_{37}Rb + \gamma$$

$$^{12}_{6}C + ^{1}_{1}H \longrightarrow ^{13}_{7}N + \gamma$$

$$^{238}_{92}U + ^{1}_{0}n \longrightarrow ^{239}_{92}U + \gamma$$

(ii) Particle-particle reactions

In these reactions the bombarding particle is absorbed by the target nucleus to form the compound nucleus which breaks down to give the final product. For example :

$$^{24}_{11}Na + ^{4}_{2}He \longrightarrow \ ^{28}_{13}Al\ \longrightarrow ^{26}_{13}Al + 2\,^{1}_{0}n$$

$$^{27}_{13}Al + ^{1}_{0}n \longrightarrow \ ^{28}_{13}Al\ \longrightarrow ^{28}_{13}Al + \gamma$$

$$^{26}_{12}Mg + ^{2}_{1}H \longrightarrow \ ^{28}_{13}Al\ \longrightarrow ^{27}_{12}Mg + ^{1}_{1}H$$

$$^{27}_{12}Mg + ^{1}_{1}H \longrightarrow \ ^{28}_{13}Al\ \longrightarrow ^{24}_{11}Na + ^{4}_{2}He$$

($^{28}_{13}Al$: Compound nucleus)

(iii) Fission reactions

These are the reactions in which a heavier nucleus breaks down into two or more lighter nuclei of almost equal size and a large amount of energy is also liberated. For example $^{235}_{92}U$ breaks down into $^{144}_{56}Ba$ and $^{90}_{36}Kr$ nuclei by slow neutrons.

$$^{235}_{92}U + ^{1}_{0}n \text{ (slow)} \longrightarrow ^{144}_{56}Ba + ^{90}_{36}Kr + 2\,^{1}_{0}n + \text{Energy}$$

(iv) Fusion reactions

These are the reactions in which two lighter nuclei are combined or fused together to give a stable and heavier nucleus, and a large amount of energy is liberated. For example, the fusion or combination of deuterium ($^{2}_{1}H$) and tritium ($^{3}_{1}H$) gives a stable nucleus of helium ($^{4}_{2}He$) and energy equal to 17.6 MeV is also liberated.

$$^{2}_{1}H + ^{3}_{1}H \longrightarrow ^{4}_{2}He + ^{1}_{0}n + 17.6 \text{ MeV}$$

(v) Spallation reactions

These reactions were discovered by Seaborg and Perimen in 1947. In these reactions the high-speed bombarding particle is absorbed to form a normal nucleus and a large number of light particles. For example the bombardment of $^{63}_{29}Cu$ nucleus by high-speed α-particle having energy 400 MeV gives $^{37}_{17}Cl$ nucleus and 14 protons and 16 neutrons.

$$^{63}_{29}Cu + ^{4}_{2}He \longrightarrow ^{37}_{17}Cl + 14\,^{1}_{1}H + 16\,^{1}_{0}n$$

II. Classification Based on the Nature of the Bombarding Particle

This classification gives the following types of nuclear reactions :

(i) Nuclear reactions induced by alpha particles ($^{4}_{2}He$)

These reactions may be of following types :

(a) (α, p) **reactions** These reactions are common with the elements of low atomic number. Examples are

$$^{14}_{7}N + ^{4}_{2}He \longrightarrow ^{17}_{8}O + ^{1}_{1}H$$

$$^{10}_{5}B + ^{4}_{2}He \longrightarrow ^{13}_{6}C + ^{1}_{1}H$$

(b) (α, n) **reactions** By using more energetic α-particles these reactions may be obtained. Examples is

$$^{9}_{4}Be + ^{4}_{2}He \longrightarrow ^{12}_{6}C + ^{1}_{0}n$$

(c) (α, γ) **reactions** Following is a typical example of this type of reaction.

$$^{7}_{3}Li + ^{4}_{2}He \longrightarrow ^{11}_{5}B + ^{0}_{0}\gamma$$

(ii) Nuclear reactions induced by protons ($^{1}_{1}H$)

These reactions are of the following types :

(a) (p, α) **reactions** Examples are

$$^{7}_{3}Li + ^{1}_{1}H \longrightarrow ^{4}_{2}He + ^{4}_{2}He\ (p, 2\alpha)$$

$$^{19}_{9}F + ^{1}_{1}H \longrightarrow ^{16}_{8}O + ^{4}_{2}He$$

(b) (p, n) **reactions** If proton has sufficient energy, probability of (p, n) type reactions becomes high. Some examples are :

$$^{65}_{29}Cu + ^{1}_{1}H \longrightarrow ^{65}_{30}Zn + ^{1}_{0}n$$

$$^{23}_{11}Na + ^{1}_{1}H \longrightarrow ^{23}_{12}Mg + ^{1}_{0}n$$

(c) (p, γ) **reactions** With proton as the projectile, radiative capture processes of (p, γ) type have been observed for a number of lighter elements. Example are

$$^{7}_{3}Li + ^{1}_{1}H \longrightarrow ^{8}_{4}Be + \gamma$$

$$^{27}_{13}Al + ^{1}_{1}H \longrightarrow ^{28}_{14}Si + \gamma$$

$$^{50}_{24}Cr + ^{1}_{1}H \longrightarrow ^{51}_{25}Mn + \gamma$$

(d) (p, D) **reactions** These reactions are more common with heavier elements and protons are of fairly high energy.

$$^{9}_{4}Be + ^{1}_{1}H \longrightarrow ^{8}_{4}Be + ^{2}_{1}H \text{ or } D$$

$$^{7}_{3}Li + ^{1}_{1}H \longrightarrow ^{6}_{3}Li + ^{2}_{1}H \text{ or } D$$

(iii) Nuclear reactions induced by deutrons ($^{2}_{1}H$ or D)

Some of the nuclear reactions induced by deuterons are given below :

(a) (D, α) **reactions**

$$^{6}_{3}Li + ^{2}_{1}H \longrightarrow ^{4}_{2}He + ^{4}_{2}He$$

$$^{16}_{8}O + ^{2}_{1}H \longrightarrow ^{14}_{7}N + ^{4}_{2}He$$

(b) (D, p) **reactions**

$$^{31}_{15}P + ^{2}_{1}H \longrightarrow ^{32}_{15}P + ^{1}_{1}H$$

$$^{23}_{11}Na + ^{2}_{1}H \longrightarrow ^{24}_{11}Na + ^{1}_{1}H$$

(c) (D, n) **reactions**

$$^{12}_{6}C + ^{2}_{1}H \longrightarrow ^{13}_{7}N + ^{1}_{0}n$$

$$^{130}_{52}Te + ^{2}_{1}H \longrightarrow ^{131}_{53}I + ^{1}_{0}n$$

(d) (D, T) **reactions**

$$^{7}_{3}Li + ^{2}_{1}H \longrightarrow ^{6}_{3}Li + ^{3}_{1}T \text{ (or } ^{3}_{1}H)$$

$$^{109}_{47}Ag + ^{2}_{1}H \longrightarrow ^{108}_{47}Ag + ^{3}_{1}T$$

$$^{31}_{15}P + ^{2}_{1}H \longrightarrow ^{30}_{15}P + ^{3}_{1}T$$

(iv) Nuclear reactions induced by neutrons ($^{1}_{0}n$)

In these reactions the neutrons are captured resulting in the emission of any of the following : (a) γ-rays (b) α-particle (c) proton (d) neutron. Thus, these reactions may be of the following types :

(a) (n, γ) **reactions** Example is given below

$$^{238}_{92}U + ^{1}_{0}n \longrightarrow ^{239}_{92}U + \gamma$$

(b) (n, α) **reactions** Example is

$$^{6}_{3}Li + ^{1}_{0}n \longrightarrow ^{3}_{1}H + ^{4}_{2}He$$

(c) (n, p) **reactions** In these reactions the final product is a new element whose atomic number is one unit less than the target nucleus and atomic weight is the same. Example is

$$^{64}_{30}Zn + ^{1}_{0}n \longrightarrow ^{64}_{30}Zn + ^{1}_{1}H + ^{0}_{-1}e$$

Thus, we find that the final product is the same as the target nucleus and hence the overall effect is that the bombarding neutron splits up into a proton and an electron.

(d) $(n, 2n)$ **reactions** When the kinetic energy of the bombarding neutron is about 10 MeV, it is able to eject two neutrons from nucleus. For higher energies, more than two neutrons may be ejected. Example is

$$^{39}_{19}K + ^{1}_{0}n \longrightarrow ^{38}_{19}K + 2\,^{1}_{0}n$$

In such case the product nucleus invariably decays with the emission of a positron. For example :

$$^{38}_{19}K \longrightarrow ^{38}_{18}Ar + \underset{\text{Positron}}{^{0}_{+1}e}$$

(v) Nuclear reactions induced by tritons ($^{3}_{1}H$ or $^{3}_{1}T$)

The nuclear reactions induced by tritons are of the following types :

(a) (T, p) **reactions**

$$^{59}_{27}Co + ^{3}_{1}H \longrightarrow ^{61}_{27}Co + ^{1}_{1}H$$

(b) (T, d) **reactions**

$$^{6}_{3}Li + ^{3}_{1}H \longrightarrow ^{7}_{3}Li + ^{2}_{1}H$$

(c) (T, n) **reactions**

$$^{32}_{16}S + ^{3}_{1}H \longrightarrow ^{34}_{17}Cl + ^{1}_{0}n$$

(d) (T, α) **reactions**

$$^{7}_{3}Li + ^{3}_{1}H \longrightarrow ^{6}_{2}He + ^{4}_{2}He$$

(vi) Nuclear reactions induced by photons or γ-rays ($^{0}_{0}\gamma$)

The nuclear reactions induced by photons are called photo disintegration. The type of nuclear reaction induced by photons depends on the energy of the incident photon. Various types of reactions produced by photons are given below :

(a) (γ, n) **reactions**

$$^{2}_{1}H + ^{0}_{0}\gamma \longrightarrow ^{1}_{1}H + ^{1}_{0}n$$

(b) (γ, p) **reactions**

$$^{25}_{12}\text{Mg} + ^{0}_{0}\gamma \longrightarrow ^{24}_{11}\text{Na} + ^{1}_{1}\text{H}$$

(c) (γ, $2p$, n) **reactions**

$$^{27}_{13}\text{Al} + ^{0}_{0}\gamma \longrightarrow ^{24}_{11}\text{Na} + 2\,^{1}_{1}\text{H} + ^{1}_{0}n$$

Nuclear Reactions *vs* Chemical Reactions

Nuclear reactions differ from chemical reactions in the following respects :

(i) In chemical reactions rearrangement of outermost electrons of the atom takes place while the nuclei remain uneffected. Thus, no change occurs in the atomic species taking part in the chemical reaction. In other words, no new atomic species are formed in chemical reaction. On the other hand, in nuclear reactions, change in the number of nucleons present in the nucleus takes place and consequently there is formation of new atomic species. Thus, nuclear reactions bring about the atomic transmutation or transformation.

(ii) The amount of energy released in nuclear reactions is million times greater than that produced in chemical reactions. This is because of the fact that, in nuclear reaction, unlike in a chemical reaction, a small but measurable loss in mass takes place. This lose in mass is converted into energy, called nuclear reaction energy, in accordance with Eienstein's mass-energy relationship, $E = mc^2$ where, m = loss in mass, E = energy and c = velocity of light.

Mass Defect and Binding Energy of the Nucleus

It has been observed that the experimental value of atomic mass (A) of an isotope of an element is invariably less than the sum (M) of the masses of protons, neutrons (called nucleons) and electrons present in the atom of the element. The difference between the two masses is called mass defect and is denoted by ΔM. Thus,

Mass defect (ΔM) = sum of the masses of protons, neutrons and electrons (M) – experimental value of atomic mass of the isotope (A)

or $$\Delta M = M - A$$

When the nucleons are allowed to combine together to form the nucleus, some mass disappears in the form of energy, *i.e.*, in the combination of nucleons to form the nucleus, some amount of energy is released. The energy released in the formation of a nucleus from its constituent nucleons is called **binding energy of the nucleus**. Conversely, the same amount of energy will naturally be required to break the nucleus into its component nucleons.

If ΔM is the mass defect in amu, then binding energy of the nucleus in MeV is equal to $\Delta M \times 931$ MeV, since 1 amu or (u) = 931 MeV of energy. The greater the mass defect, the greater is the binding energy of the nucleus. The binding energy of a nucleus divided by the total number of nucleons (*i.e.*, neutrons + protons) is called the binding energy per nucleon in the atom, *i.e.*,

$$\text{Binding energy per nucleon} = \frac{\text{Binding energy}}{\text{Neutrons + Protons}}$$

The binding energy per nucleon is a measure of the stability of the nucleus. The greater the binding energy per nucleon, greater is the stability associated with the nucleus, *i.e.*, the greater the amount of binding energy per nucleon, greater is the force holding the nucleons in the nucleus together.

Calculation of Binding Energy

How the binding energy of a given nucleus can be calculated can be learnt from the following solved examples?

Example 7. *Calculate the binding energy of lithium nucleus, given that :*

mass of proton = 1.00814 u
mass of neutron = 1.00893 u
mass of lithium nucleus = 7.01822 u

Sol. Obviously, the lithium isotope considered is $_3\text{Li}^7$. It contains 3 protons and (7 – 3) = 4 neutrons.

Mass of 3 protons = $3 \times 1.00814 = 3.02442$ u

Mass of 4 neutrons = $4 \times 1.00893 = 4.03572$ u

Total mass of 7 nucleons, $M = 7.06014$ u

Mass of the lithium nucleus, $A = 7.01822$ u

Mass defect, $\Delta m = M - A = 7.06014 - 7.01822$

$= 0.04192$ u

$\therefore$ Binding energy = 931×0.04192 = **39 MeV**.

Example 8. *The mass of $_{17}\text{Cl}^{35}$ is 34.9800 u. Calculate its binding energy. What is the binding energy per nucleon?*

Mass of $_0n^1 = 1.008665$ u and $_1\text{H}^1 = 1.007825$ u.

Sol. The given chlorine atom has 17 protons and (35 – 17) = 18 neutrons.

Mass of 17 protons $= 17 \times 1.007825 = 17.133025$ u

Mass of 18 neutrons $= 18 \times 1.008665 = 18.155970$ u

Total mass of separate constituents = 35.288995 u

Mass defect, $\Delta m = 35.288995 - 34.9800$

$= 0.308995$ u

Now, 1 a = 931 MeV

∴ Binding energy of the nucleus

$= 931 \times 0.308995 = 288$ MeV

No. of nucleons (*i.e.*, protons and neutrons) = 35

∴ Binding energy per nucleon = 288/35 = **8.22 MeV.**

Binding Energies and Stability of Nuclei

If the binding energies per nucleon (in MeV) of a number of isotopes are plotted against their mass number (A), a graph of the type shown in Fig. 15.17 is obtained. This graph is called **binding energy** curve. The following conclusions may be drawn from this curve.

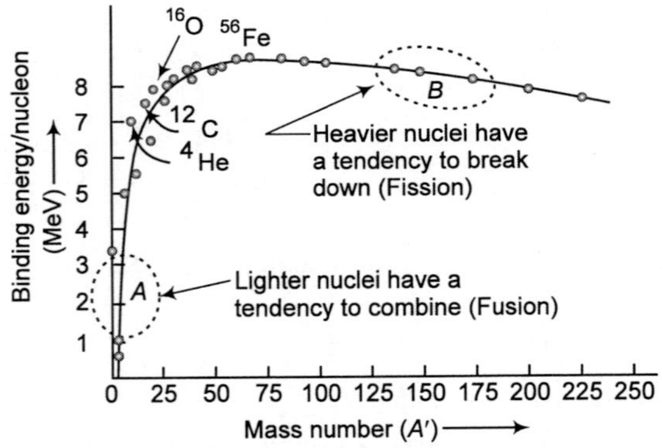

Fig. 15.17 Binding energy curve.The lighter nuclei (shown in region *A*) have a tendency to combine (fusion) while the heavier nuclei (shown in region *B*) have a tendency to break down (fission).

(i) Lighter nuclei have very small binding energy and hence are unstable. Therefore, such nuclei (shown in region A) have tendency to combine or fuse together (fusion) to give the nuclei of intermediate mass number (atomic weight) and higher binding energy or stability. Similarly, heavier nuclei are seen to have low binding energy and hence, are very unstable. Therefore, such nuclei (shown in region B) may break down (Fission) to form the nuclei of intermediate atomic weight that possess higher binding energies and greater stability.

(ii) The binding energies of some of the light nuclei are very small. The binding energy per nucleon rises sharply and reaches a maximum value of 8.7 MeV in the neighbourhood of a nucleus with mass number, $A = 56$ (Iron). Thus, nucleus of iron is thermodynamically most stable and hence is found in abundance in earth. The graph for the nuclei having mass numbers in the range of 50 to 100 is almost flat. Thus, the addition of a single nucleon to any nucleus in the range of $A = 50 - 100$ increases the binding energy roughly by the same amount. For the nuclei having high mass numbers the value decreases to 7.6 MeV for uranium.

(iii) The points for helium ($A = 4$), carbon ($A = 12$) and oxygen ($A = 16$) lie quite high in the graph. Thus, the nuclei of these elements are *exceptionally* stable.

(iv) Over a considerable range of mass numbers, the binding energy per nucleon is 8 MeV which is usually taken as the average value of binding energy for all nucleons.

Meson Theory of Nuclear Forces

We have already said that the neutrons and protons (*i.e.*, nucleons) are packed together in the nucleus in a very small space, since the nucleus is about $\frac{1}{10^5}$ in volume as compared to the entire atom. Moreover, the protons (positively-charged particles) should ordinarily repel each other, but they are present together in the nucleus. Therefore, a question arises here which is : What is the nature of forces that hold the protons and neutrons together in such a small space? The forces which hold protons and neutrons together in the nucleus are attractive forces and are called **nuclear forces.** These forces are different from electrostatic forces in that the former forces operate only within distances of approximately 0.10 fermi ($= 10^{-13}$ cm, 1 fermi $= 10^{-12}$ cm) while the latter operate over long range also. Nuclear forces fall rapidly to zero at distances greater than 1.4×10^{-13} cm and are referred to as short range forces. These forces do not obey the inverse square law.

The exact nature of the forces was explained by Hideki Yukawa, a Japanese theoretical physicist, who suggested in 1935 that the nucleons are surrounded by a cloud of negatively charged and positively charged π-mesons ($_{-1}\pi$ and $_{+1}\pi$ mesons) as shown in Fig. 15.18.

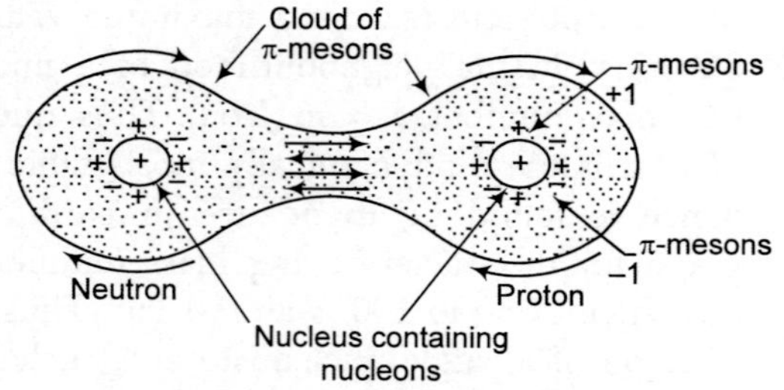

Fig. 15.18 Nature of nuclear forces holding nucleons in the nucleus.

These π-mesons rapidly jump back and forth between the neighbouring nucleons with a velocity approximately equal to that of light. This sort of jumping of mesons keeps the nucleons bound together in the nucleus. Negatively charged mesons ($_{-1}\pi$-mesons) interact with protons ($_{+1}p$) while positively-charged mesons ($_{+1}\pi$-mesons) interact with neutrons ($_0 n$) and by these interactions a proton is changed into a neutron and a neutron is changed in a proton. This change takes place for a part time only.

$$_{+1}p + {}_{-1}\pi \rightleftharpoons {}_0 n$$
$$_0 n + {}_{+1}\pi \rightleftharpoons {}_{+1}p$$

Value of a Nuclear Reaction

All types of nuclear reactions are accompained by either the absorption of energy or release of energy. The amount of energy absorbed or released in a nuclear reaction is generally called *Q*-value of the nuclear reaction. Thus, the following two cases arise :

(i) When the sum of the masses of the reactants (m_R) is less than that of the products (m_p) ($m_R < m_P$), energy is absorbed, *i.e.*, when there is an increase in the mass, energy is absorbed. For example in the nuclear reaction :

$$^{14}_{7}\text{N} + {}^{4}_{2}\text{He} \longrightarrow {}^{17}_{8}\text{O} + {}^{1}_{1}\text{H}$$

Since, the sum of the masses of the reactants (*i.e.*, mass of $^{14}_{7}$N + mass of $^{4}_{2}$He) is less than that of the masses of the products (*i.e.*, mass of $^{17}_{8}$O + mass of $^{1}_{1}$H), energy is absorbed in this reaction. Obviously *Q*-value (in MeV) is given by :

Q-value (Energy absorbed)

= Increase in mass (in amu) × 931 MeV

= $(m_P - m_R) \times 931$ MeV

Q-value which is absorbed is generally represented by a negative sign. Now, if *Q*-value is incorporated in the above reaction, the reaction can be written as :

$$^{14}_{7}\text{N} + {}^{4}_{2}\text{He} + Q \longrightarrow {}^{17}_{8}\text{O} + {}^{1}_{1}\text{H}$$
or $$^{14}_{7}\text{N} + {}^{4}_{2}\text{He} \longrightarrow {}^{17}_{8}\text{O} + {}^{1}_{1}\text{H} - Q$$
(Q is absorbed and hence is negative)

(ii) When the sum of the masses of the reactants is greater than that of products ($m_R > m_P$), energy is released, *i.e.*, when there is a decrease in the mass, energy will be released. For example in the nuclear reaction :

$$^{7}_{3}\text{Li} + {}^{1}_{1}\text{H} \longrightarrow {}^{4}_{2}\text{He} + {}^{4}_{2}\text{He}$$

Since, the sum of the masses of the reactants (*i.e.*, mass of $^{7}_{8}$Li + mass of $^{1}_{1}$H) is greater than that of the masses of the products (*i.e.*, masses of two $^{4}_{2}$He nuclei), energy is released in the above reaction. Obviously *Q*-value (in MeV) is given by :

Q-value (Energy released)

= Decrease in mass (in amu) × 931 MeV

= $(m_R - m_P) \times 931$ MeV

Q-value which is released in generally represented by a positive sign. Now, if *Q*-value is incorporated in the above reaction, the reaction can be written as

$$^{7}_{3}\text{Li} + {}^{1}_{1}\text{H} \longrightarrow 2\,{}^{4}_{2}\text{He} + Q$$
or $$^{7}_{3}\text{Li} + {}^{1}_{1}\text{H} - Q \longrightarrow 2\,{}^{4}_{2}\text{He.}$$
(Q is released and hence is positive)

Example 9. *Calculate Q-value of the following nuclear reactions*

(i) $^{14}_{7}\text{N} + {}^{4}_{2}\text{He} \longrightarrow {}^{17}_{8}\text{O} + {}^{1}_{1}\text{H}$

(ii) $^{7}_{3}\text{Li} + {}^{1}_{1}\text{H} \longrightarrow 2\,{}^{4}_{2}\text{He}$

$^{4}_{2}$He = 4.00387

$^{14}_{7}$N = 14.00753

$^{17}_{8}$O = 17.00450

$^{1}_{1}$H = 1.00814

$^{7}_{3}$Li = 7.01822

Sol. (i) $^{14}_{7}\text{N} + {}^{4}_{2}\text{He} \longrightarrow {}^{17}_{8}\text{O} + {}^{1}_{1}\text{H}$

The change in mass in atomic-mass-units (amu) can be found as follows :

Interacting particles	Product particles
$^{4}_{2}$He = 4.00387	$^{17}_{8}$O = 17.00450
$^{14}_{7}$N = 14.00753	$^{1}_{1}$H = 1.00814
Total = 18.01140 = m_R	Total = 18.01264 = m_P

Increase in mass = $(m_P - m_R)$ u

= 18.01264 − 18.01140 = 0.00124 u

∴ *Q*-value (Energy absorbed)

= 0.00124 × 931 = 1.15 MeV

Since, $m_R < m_P$, energy is absorbed in this reaction and hence ∴ value is negative, *i.e.*, *Q*-value = – 1.15 MeV.

(ii) $^7_3Li + ^1_1H \longrightarrow ^4_2He + ^4_2He$

Here, the mass values are as under :

Interacting particles	Product particles
$^1_1H = 1.00814$	$^4_2He = 4.00387$
$^7_3Li = 7.01822$	$^4_2He = 4.00387$
Total = $8.02636 = m_R$	Total = $8.0774 = m_P$

Decrease in mass = $(m_R - m_P)$ u

$= 8.02636 - 8.00774 = 0.01862$ u

∴ *Q*-value (Energy released)

$= 0.01862 \times 931$ MeV $= 17.3$ MeV

Since, $m_R > m_P$, energy is released in this reaction and hence *Q*-value is positive, *i.e.*, *Q*-value = + 17.3 MeV.

Q-Values and Reaction Thresholds

Sometimes, the *Q*-value of a reaction can be calculated even if the mases at the nuclei involved are not known, provided that the product nucleus is radioactive and decays back to the initial nucleus with known decay energy.

Consider the following nuclear reaction.

$$^{106}_{46}Pd + ^1_0n \longrightarrow ^{106}_{45}Rh + ^1_1H + Q$$

$$^{106}_{45}Rh \longrightarrow ^{106}_{46}Pd + \beta^- + \bar{\nu} + 2.54 \text{ MeV}$$

On adding the above two equations, we get the overall reaction as

$$^1_0n \longrightarrow ^1_1H + \beta^- + \bar{\nu} + Q + 3.54 \text{ MeV}$$

For energy balance

$$M_n = M_H + Q + 3.54 \text{ MeV}$$

where, $M_n = 1.008665$ u and $M_H = 1.007825$ u (sum of the masses of a proton and an electron).

Hence, $Q = (1.008665 - 1.007825) \times 931.5 - 3.54$

$= 2.76$ MeV

In the reaction $^{14}N(\alpha, p)^{17}O$, we have seen that the reaction is having a *Q*-value of – 1.19 MeV. However, α-particle bearing just 1.19 MeV of kinetic energy, cannot make the reaction feasible because during collision between α-particle and ^{14}N atom, for the conservation of momentum at least 14/18 of the kinetic energy of the α-particle will be retained by the products as the kinetic energy. Hence, only 14/18 of 1.19 MeV is available for the reaction and is less than the required value of 1.19 MeV. Hence, the Threshold energy of α-particles just capable of making the reaction energetically possible is $\frac{18}{14} \times 1.19 = 1.53$ MeV.

With the increase in the mass of the target nucleus, the fraction of the kinetic energy of the projectile retained by the target becomes less.

Barriers for charged particles There is another reason why the α-particle should have more energy than the *Q*-value to produce the reaction is the coulomb repulsion, between the α-particle and the target nucleus. Take the example of $^{14}N(\alpha, p)^{17}O$. The repulsion between α-particle and ^{14}N nucleus increases with decreasing distance between the two until the α particle comes within the range of the nuclear forces of ^{14}N nucleus. This coulomb repulsion gives rise to a potential barrier. The height (V_c) of this potential barrier around a spherical nucleus of charge Z_1e and radius R_1 for a particle of positive charge Z_2e and radius R_2 may be estimated as the energy of coulomb repulsion when the two particles are just in contact.

$$V_c = \frac{Z_1Z_2e^2}{(R_1 + R_2)}$$

If R_1 and R_2 are expressed in fermi than

$$V_c = 1.44\frac{Z_1Z_2}{R_1 + R_2} \text{ MeV}$$

Setting $R = 1.5\,A^{1/3}$ fermi in the equation we get a value of 3.4 MeV for this barrier height between ^{14}N and ^4He. Hence, an α-particle must have at least $\frac{18}{14} \times 3.4 = 4.4$ MeV of kinetic energy to enter a ^{14}N nucleus and produce the α, *p* reaction even though the threshold energy is only 1.53 MeV.

For the heaviest elements the potential barriers are about 12 MeV for proton and deutrons and about 25 MeV for α particles (because $V_c \propto Z^{2/3}$). Hence, to study the nuclear reactions involving heavy elements it is necessary to develop machines capable of accelerating charged particles to energies of many millions of electron volts.

Reaction Cross-Sections

Reaction cross-section in a nuclear reaction gives a quantitative consideration of reaction probabilities. Generally, the probability of a nuclear process is expressed in terms of a cross-section which is denoted by 'σ'. The probability for the reaction between a target nucleus and an impinging particle is proportional to the cross-sectional target area presented by the nucleus. For a beam of particles striking a thin target, the cross-section for a particular process is defined by the equation

$$R_i = I \cdot n\, x\sigma_i$$

where, R_i is the number of processes of the type under consideration occurring in the target per unit time, I is the number of incident particles per unit time, n is the number of target nuclei per cubic centimeter of target, σ_1 is the cross-section for the specified process expressed in square centimeters and x is the target thickness in centimeters.

Units of cross-section

The geometrical cross-section of a nucleus can be calculated assuming nucleus is a sphere. However, this geometrical cross-section will not give the value of total cross-section for a collision between the nucleus and the impinging particle. The total cross-section for the collision with a fast particle is never greater than twice the geometrical cross-sectional area of the nucleus and therefore fast-particle cross-sections are rarely much larger than 10^{-24} cm^2 which has been considered as a barn and used as the unit to denote the reaction cross-section and represented by '*b*'. **The commonly used units are millibarn (mb, 10^{-3} b), microbarn (μb, 10^{-6} b), and nanobarn (nb, 10^{-9} b).**

Cross-section and reaction rate

For a sample containing N nuclei in a flux of ϕ particles per square centimeter per second, the rate of reactions of type i, which have a cross-section σ_i is given by

$$R_i = \phi N\sigma_i$$

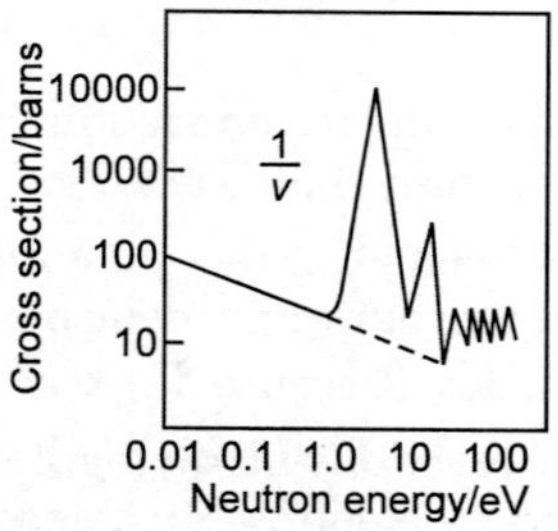

Fig. 15.19 Resonance capture for reaction ^{109}Ag (*n*, γ) ^{110}Ag.

On considering the de-Broglie wavelengths of neutrons of 1 eV energy, it clearly indicates that the wavelengths (2.86×10^{11} m) are much greater than the dimensions of the target nucleus. **For every increase of neutron energy by a factor of 10^2, the wavelength decreases by a factor of 10.** Thus, the wavelength of 1 MeV neutron becomes 2.86×10^{-14} m which is twice that of nuclear radius. Thus, a neutron wave of 1 eV energy surrounds a very large number of target nuclei resulting in a great capture cross-section. As the neutron energy increases, the wavelength diminishes and the number of nuclei surrounded by it, falls rapidly and hence the decrease of σ as per $1/v$ law.

This applies, regardless of the shape of the sample, provided that the particle flux is not appreciably attenuated by sample absorption anywhere in the sample. Moreover, the flux (ϕ) can be separated into two components of velocity (v cm s^{-1}) and their volume (n cm^3). Since, velocity is v cm s^{-1} it will be hit the target particle within a volume of v cm^3 (Fig. 15.20).

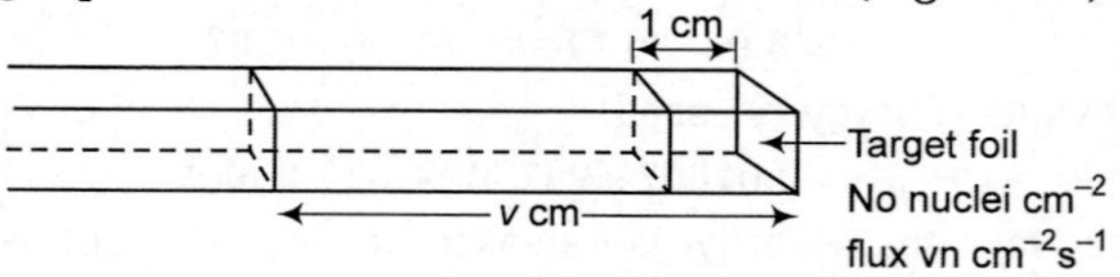

Fig. 15.20 Relationship between cross-section (σ) and reaction rate (*R*).

$$R = nv\sigma_i N$$

Based on this equation $\frac{1}{v}$ law was proposed. Lower energy particles have a longer wavelength and as a result they can surround a larger number of the target nuclei leading to larger reaction cross-section.

The slow neutron capture cross-section varies inversely as the neutron velocity. This is referred as $1/v$ law. The reaction cross-section, in otherwords, varies inversely with the square root of neutron energy.

Consider the reaction ^{10}B (n, α) ^{7}Li. When log σ is plotted against log neutron energy, a straight line is obtained (Fig. 15.21). Beyond a limit in the straight line sharp peaks are obtained due to resonance captures. The compound nucleus (nucleus formed by the target and neutron) has several excitation levels above the ground level. If the energy of the compound nucleus coincides with the energy of one of the excited states after the absorption of neutron, peaks are obtained in the graph and this is termed as **resonance capture**.

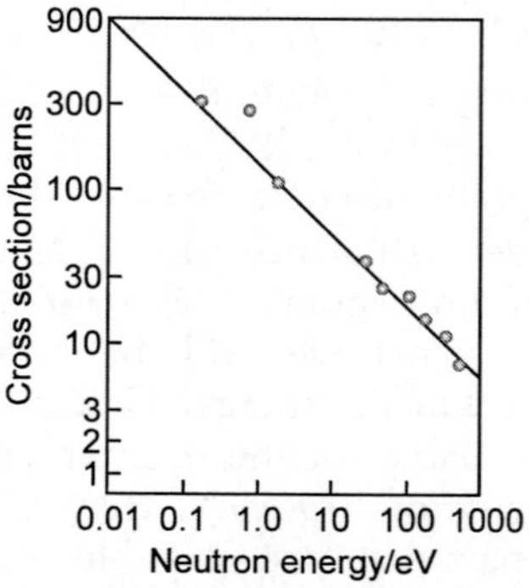

Fig. 15.21 Variation of neutron cross-section for the reaction ^{10}B (*n*, α) ^{7}Li.

Nuclear Fission

Nuclear fission was first discovered by **Otto Hahn** when uranium was split into barium and krypton. The proces of nuclear fission can be explained by two ways. One explanation is that after the capture of the neutron the nucleus may enlarge and split into two parts. The other explanation is that after the capture of the neutron the nucleus may lose the α-particle (Fig. 15.22).

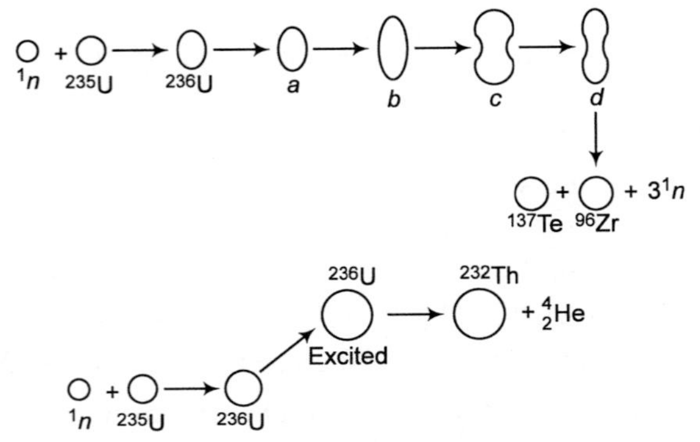

Fig. 15.22

The following theory explains the nuclear fission.

Nuclear Shape Distortion Following Excitation

As per this theory, the nucleus is considered as analogous to a drop of incompressible liquid and its size is proportional to the number of nucleus present in it. There are two forces acting in opposite directions. One is coulomb force which tends to distort the spherical shape due to inner-proton repulsion and the other is surface tension acting in opposite direction to restore the spherical shape. After the absorption of the neutron **if the excitation energy is not high enough, the nucleus gets de-excited by losing an α-particle. If the excitation energy is high enough the shape of the nucleus is distorted to ellipsoidal followed by dumb bell shape and finally the two halves separate out as fission fragments.**

Relationship between Fission Energy and Fission Barrier

When a nucleus $^A_Z N$ breaks into two halves yielding identical fragments ($^{A/2}_{Z/2} N$), the energy released is given as

$$E_f = [\,^A_Z N - 2\ ^{A/2}_{Z/2} N]\ 931\ \text{MeV}$$

Fission Yield

When a nucleus undergoes fission, there are several possibilities. For example, when $^{236}_{92}U$ undergoes fission, the following possibilities are there,

(a) $^{236}_{92}U \longrightarrow {}^{94}_{36}Kr + {}^{140}_{56}Ba + 2n$

(b) $^{236}_{92}U \longrightarrow {}^{95}_{38}Sr + {}^{139}_{54}Xe + 2n$

(c) $^{236}_{92}U \longrightarrow {}^{96}_{40}Zr + {}^{137}_{52}Te + 3n$

(d) $^{236}_{92}U \longrightarrow {}^{99}_{41}Nb + {}^{133}_{51}Sb + 4n$ and so on.

All the products of these fission are having excess neutrons than their stable isotopes and hence to obtain a stable $\frac{N}{Z}$ ratio, they will undergo successive β^- emissions.

For example, the products of possibility will have the following secondary fragmentation.

$$^{236}_{92}U \nearrow {}^{99}_{41}Nb \xrightarrow[2.6\ \text{min}]{-\beta^-} {}_{42}Mo \xrightarrow[66\ \text{h}]{-\beta^-} {}_{43}Tc \xrightarrow[2.1\times 10^5\ \text{y}]{-\beta^-} {}^{99}_{44}Ru\ (\text{stable})$$

$$^{236}_{92}U \searrow {}^{133}_{51}Sb \xrightarrow[2.3\ \text{min}]{-\beta^-} {}_{52}Te \xrightarrow[12.5\ \text{min}]{-\beta^-} {}_{53}I \xrightarrow[20.8\ \text{h}]{-\beta^-} {}_{54}Xe \xrightarrow[5.29\ \text{d}]{-\beta^-} {}^{133}_{55}Cs\ (\text{stable})$$

To explain the mass distribution between fission fragments a term called **cumulative chain fission yield**, is used. This can be defined as

$$Y(A) = \frac{\text{Number of product nuclei of mass number } (A)}{\text{Total number of nuclei fissioned}} \times 100$$

When fission mass yield is plotted against mass number (A), the following curve results (Fig. 15.23).

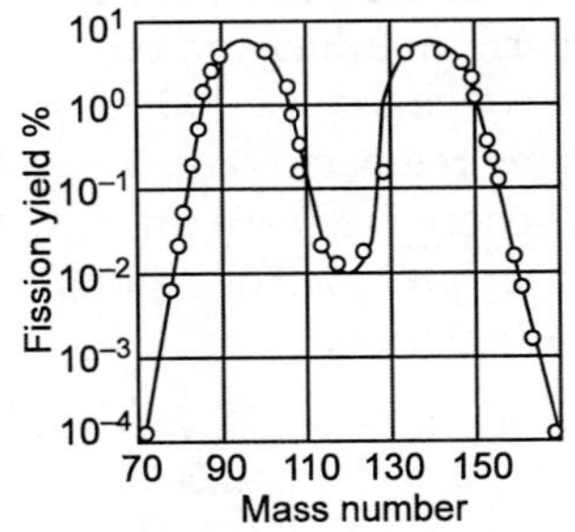

Fig. 15.23 Fission yield as a function of mass number in fission of ^{235}U.

The yield of any mass number is given by the yield of the final stable isotope of that mass number. Majority of the fissions are asymmetric, *i.e.*, $A_1 \neq A_2$. The fission yield curve shows two maxima, one in the region of $90-100$ for A_1 and the other in the region of $134-144$ for A_2 with an average loss of 2.5 neutrons per fission. The yield $\geq 1\%$ is the range of $85-105$ for A_1 and $130-150$ for A_2. The yield of symmetrical fission at $A_1 = A_2 = 117$ is the lowest (0.05 per cent). This is the case with thermal or low energy neutrons. When the energy of the neutron increases, the depth of the valley in the curve between two peaks diminishes and the two peaks approach each other till there is a single peak. This is clearly illustrated in Fig. 15.24.

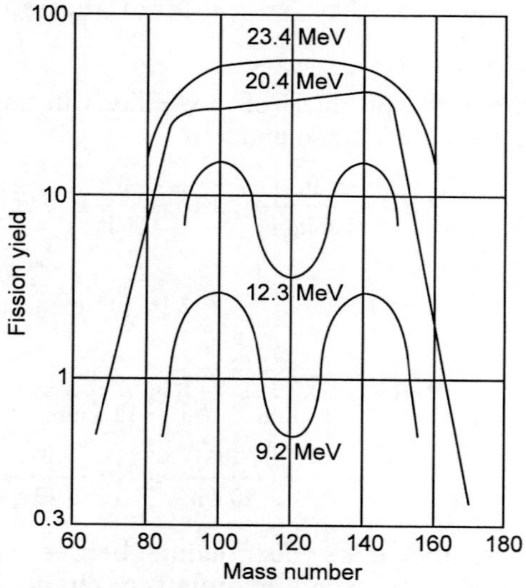

Fig. 15.24 Fission yield as a function of mass number in the fission of ^{239}Pu by deutrons

As the energy of the deutron increases from 9.2 MeV to 23.4 MeV, the valley disappears.

Fission Energy

Nuclear fission is accompanied by mass loss and the liberation of corresponding amount of energy. In fission the loss of mass is 100 times more when compared to other radioactive decays. This staggering amount of the energy release in fission makes the process, of special interest. For example, consider the following nuclear reaction.

$$\underset{235.0439}{{}^{235}_{92}U} + \underset{1.0087}{n} \longrightarrow \underset{94.9057}{{}^{95}_{42}Mo} + \underset{138.9061}{{}^{139}_{57}La} + \underset{2.0174}{2n} + 7\beta^- + 7\nu^- + x\gamma$$

Loss of mass $\Delta m = 0.2234$ u

Fission energy $= 931 \times 0.2234 = 208$ MeV

This total energy of 208 MeV is distributed between the products of fision as follows :

Light fragment	100	± 5 MeV
Heavy fragment	67	
2.5 neutrons each of 2 MeV energy	5	
α photons	12	
β^- and neutrons	16	
Total	200 ± 5 MeV	

Spontaneous Fission

All the nuclei with $A > 230$ suffer spontaneous fission due to the large coulombic repulsion in nucleus of high Z. The half lives vary over wide limits and are related to the fission parameter Z^2/A. The half-life decreases exponentially with Z^2/A, whereas the half-life for the competing mode of decay by γ and σ-emission varies in an inverse way. The ratio $\frac{t_{(1/2)sf}}{t_{(1/2)a}}$ is 10^{-11} for ^{234}U and 70 for ^{256}Fm. When $\log t_{1/2(sf)}$ is plotted against Z^2/A, (Fig. 15.25) a straight line results for even-even nuclei from ^{232}Th to ^{254}Fm. The half-lives of odd nuclei are much longer than even nuclei.

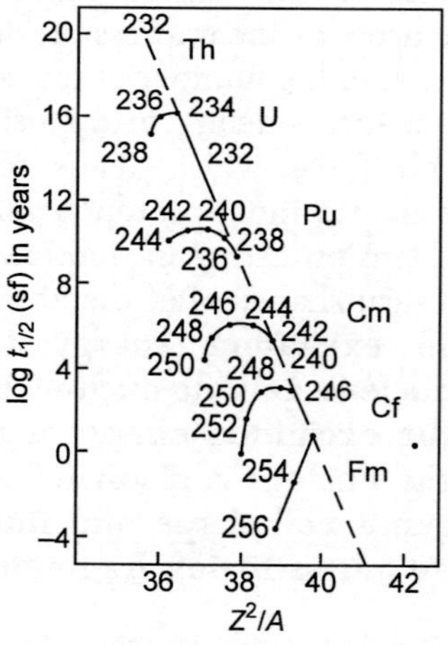

Fig. 15.25 $\log t_{1/2(sf)}$ *vs* Z^2/A for even-even nuclei.

The extrapolation of the curve in the above figure corresponds to zero half-life or 10^{-20} s, gives the critical maximum value of Z^2/A to be around 45. This hypothetical nucleus is referred to as cosmium. The fission parameter (Z^2/A) has been theoretically correlated to the deformation parameter (ε). The no-return or the scission stage is when the spherical nucleus of radius R gets deformed into a prolate ellipsoid of critical major and minor axes a and b related to R by

$$a = (1 + \varepsilon) R$$

and $$b = \frac{R}{(1+\varepsilon)^{1/2}}$$

ε^2 and the deformation energy become negative at the critical value

$$\frac{Z^2}{A} > \frac{2a_s}{a_c}$$

where, a_s and a_c are the surface and coulomb constants. Nuclei with Z^2/A exceeding 45-51 will all suffer spontaneous fission. Assuming A/Z to be around 2.59 in this region, cosmium would correspond to $Z = 116$ and $A = 300$.

Nuclear Fusion

The lighter nuclei have very small binding energies and hence are unstable. Therefore, two or more such nuclei have a tendency to combine or fuse together to give the nucleus of higher mass number (atomic weight) and higher binding energy or stability. Such a nuclear reaction in which two lighter nuclei are combined or fused together to form a heavier (and hence stabler) nucleus is called **nuclear fusion**. In this respect, nuclear fusion is the opposite of nuclear fission in which one heavier nucleus is split up into two lighter nuclei. In nuclear fusion also, large amount of energy is released because the mass of the product nucleus is less than the masses of the two nuclei which are fused together. Once fusion reaction is initiated, the energy released is sufficient to maintain the temperature and keep the reaction going on. Nuclear fusion occurs at reasonable rates only at very high temperatures. So, these are also called **thermonuclear reactions *i.e.,* temperature-dependent reactions.**

Uses of Nuclear Fusion

Nuclear fusion adequately explains (1) the energy of the solar system, called stellar energy, and (2) the basic principle of hydrogen bomb (Fusion bomb).

1. Stellar energy

Stellar energy is the energy of the sun and other stars of the main sequence. Van Weizsacher and Hans Beth (1932) proposed that stellar energy is due to a series of nuclear reactions involving carbon-hydrogen-nitrogen cycle which operates through the following six steps :

$$^{12}_{6}C + ^{1}_{1}H \longrightarrow ^{13}_{7}N + ^{0}_{0}\gamma + \text{Energy} \quad \ldots(i)$$

$$^{13}_{7}N \longrightarrow ^{13}_{6}C + \underset{\text{Positron}}{^{0}_{1}e} + \text{Energy} \quad \ldots(ii)$$

$$^{13}_{6}C + ^{1}_{1}H \longrightarrow ^{14}_{7}N + ^{0}_{0}\gamma + \text{Energy} \quad \ldots(iii)$$

$$^{14}_{7}N + ^{1}_{1}H \longrightarrow ^{15}_{8}O + ^{0}_{0}\gamma + \text{Energy} \quad \ldots(iv)$$

$$^{15}_{8}O \longrightarrow ^{15}_{7}N + ^{0}_{1}e + \text{Energy} \quad \ldots(v)$$

$$^{15}_{7}N + ^{1}_{1}H \longrightarrow ^{12}_{6}C + ^{4}_{2}He + \text{Energy} \quad \ldots(vi)$$

On adding the nuclear reactions from (i) to (vi) we have :

$$\underset{\text{Proton}}{4\,^{1}_{1}H} \longrightarrow \underset{\text{Helium}}{^{4}_{2}He} + \underset{\text{Positron}}{2\,^{0}_{1}e} + \text{Energy} \quad \ldots(19)$$

Nuclear reaction (19) indicates that the stellar energy is produced due to the fusion reaction in which four H-atoms (or protons) are fused together to produce one helium nucleus and two positrons. At the sun, the fusion of four H-nuclei into helium nucleus does not take place through a single step but takes place through deuterium ($^{1}_{1}H$) as shown below :

$$[2\,^{1}_{1}H \longrightarrow ^{2}_{1}H + ^{0}_{1}e + \text{Energy}] \times 2 \quad \ldots(i)$$

$$[^{2}_{1}H + ^{1}_{1}H \longrightarrow ^{3}_{2}He + \text{Energy}] \times 2 \quad \ldots(ii)$$

$$2\,^{3}_{2}He \longrightarrow ^{4}_{2}He + 2\,^{1}_{1}H + \text{Energy} \quad \ldots(iii)$$

$$\text{On adding : } 4\,^{1}_{1}H \longrightarrow ^{4}_{2}He + 2\,^{0}_{1}e + \text{Energy}$$

Energy Released in the nuclear fusion of 4 $^{1}_{1}H$ nuclei into one $^{4}_{2}He$ and two positrons ($^{0}_{1}e$)

The amount of energy, Q-released in the nuclear fusion reaction,

$$4\,^{1}_{1}H \longrightarrow ^{4}_{2}He + 2\,^{0}_{1}e$$

can be calculated by the mass-defect method as shown below (all the masses are given in amu)

$$4\,^{1}_{1}H \longrightarrow ^{4}_{2}He + 2\,^{0}_{1}e + Q$$

$$4 \times 1.0084167 = 4.003873 + 2 \times 0.000558 + Q$$

or $$4.0336668 = 4.003873 + 0.001115 + Q$$

or $$4.0336668 = 4.004988 + Q$$

$\therefore$ $$Q = 4.0336668 - 4.004988 = 0.028680 \text{ u}$$

$$= 0.028680 \times 931 \text{ MeV} = 26.7 \text{ MeV}$$

It is worth noting that the above energy release is less than that in a nuclear fission. However, its value is $26.7/4 = 6.7$ MeV per nucleon as compared to less than 1 MeV per nucleon in fission process.

2. **Hydrogen bomb** (Fusion bomb)

We have already seen that the nuclear fusion reaction is a temperature-dependent reaction, *i.e.,* the nuclear fusion reaction takes place only at drastically high temperature. Such a high temperature which is necessary for bringing about nuclear fusion reaction can be obtained only by the fission of ^{235}U nucleus which is an explosive chain reaction. This forms the principle of hydrogen bomb. In the preparation of hydrogen bomb a suitable quantity of all the isotopes of hydrogen ($_1^1H, _1^2H$ and $_1^3H$) is combined with an atomic bomb. The function of atomic bomb, as said above is to provide the high temperature which is necessary for bringing about the nuclear fusion reactions in hydrogen bomb.

In hydrogen bomb the following nuclear fusion reactions take place :

$$_1^1H + \underset{\text{Deuterium}}{_1^2H} \longrightarrow {}_2^3He + 5MeV$$

$$_1^2H + {}_1^2H \longrightarrow {}_2^3He + {}_0^1n + 3.2\ MeV$$

$$\underset{\text{Tritium}}{_1^3H} + {}_1^2H \longrightarrow {}_2^4He + {}_0^1n + 17.6\ MeV$$

We see that in each of the above nuclear fusion reactions energy is released. Thus, in hydrogen bomb isotopes of hydrogen are combined (fused) with deuterium ($_1^2H$) and form heavier nuclei with the release of enormous energy.

Hydrogen bomb is 1000 times more powerful than the atom bomb which is based on nuclear fission. Its more power is due to the rapid release of a tremendous amount of energy in the fusion reactions taking place in hydrogen bomb.

A fusion bomb is superior to a fission bomb because of the following reasons :

(i) The energy release in a hydrogen bomb is open-ended *i.e.,* it has no upper limit. It depends on how much fusible material is present in the bomb.

(ii) It has no limitation of a critical size of the fusible material unlike an atomic bomb. If the active material in an atomic bomb exceeds the critical size, spontaneous explosion results. Hydrogen bomb cannot explode unless 'ignited' *i.e.,* heated to critical ignition temperature and any amount of fusible material is safe until ignited. Thus, the amount of fusible material in a hydrogen bomb is not limited.

Basic Requirements for Controlled Thermonuclear Reactions

The major problem is achieving controlled fusion is the involvement of charged particles. The reaction is possible only if the reaction partners are having high energy to overcome the coulomb barriers. To obtain useful fusion power, the reactions must be self-substaining and this requires sufficiently high temperatures for the thermal velocities to bring about appreciable reaction rates. The temperature should be in the order of 10^8 K. At this high temperature gases are completely ionized resulting in the formation of high density gases of charged particles known as plasmas. A minimum condition for the production of practical fusion power is that the energy extracted from the thermonuclear reactions must exceed the energy required to heat and confine the plasma.

Threshold Conditions-Lawson's Criterion

The reaction between deuteron and tritium is bimolecular and the reaction rate is given by

$$R = n^2 < \sigma v > \text{reactions } m^{-3} s^{-1}$$

where, n is the concentration $[D] = [T] = 10^{20}$ m^{-3} and $< \sigma v >$ is the average value of the product of cross-section σ (m^2) and the particle velocity v (ms^{-1}). Another relevant quantity is the **energy confinement time** (T_c) which is given by

$$T_c = \frac{\text{Total energy of the surroundings}}{\text{Rate of energy loss to surroundings}}$$

T_c is the period where the given temperature of the plasma remains constant. For the energy balance (or the break-even point).

$$nT_c = 10^{20}\ sm^{-3}$$

This is known as Lawson's criterion.

Fusion Reactors : Magnetic Confinement

There are two ways to achieve the temperature and pressures necessary for hydrogen fusion to take place.

Magnetic Confinement (Pinch Effect)

Magnetic confinement fusion is an approach to generate fusion power which uses magnetic fields to confine the hot fusion fuel in the form of a plasma.

The plasma required is produced by subjecting the reaction partners to a high frequency, high voltage discharge in an endless ellipsoidal vessel. This plasma is confined to a narrow ribbon-like surface along the axis of the tube without touching the wall of the vessel at any point. This confinement is achieved by a powerful toroidal magnetic field which is all along normal to the tube axis and the plasma current. This leads to the plasma staying of the walls on all sides, the lines of force coiling on themselves in an endless helix. This is called **Pinch effect.** The toroidal field is countered by a poloidal field provided by an iron core transformer. Since, the plasma confinement is achieved by a magnetic field, the device is referred as magnetic bottle.

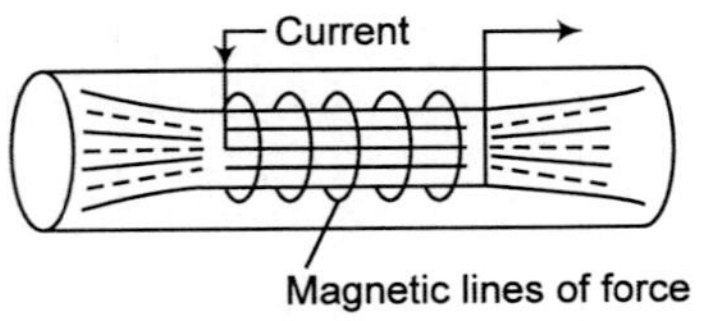

Fig. 15.26 The Pitch effect in plasma.

Inertial Confinement

In this type of confinement the deuteron-tritium fuel is taken in a solid form and sealed in a glass micro-shell coated with gold. On this 12 or more laser beams are focussed at pin-point from different directions. The glass shell is referred as cannon ball. Under the intense heat, the atoms on the surface of the shell evaporate and as each atom flies off its imparts its recoil momentum to the atoms underneath. The density under the terrific compression rises to a value of some 1000 times the normal leading to a temperature rise of the core of the shell to 10^6 K for a brief moment of 10^{-9} s. This results in an implosion (explosion inwards) and the fusion occurs. This device is referred as inertial confinement since the superhot particles are heldtogether by their own mass.

Neutron Activation Analysis (NAA)

The technique is used to measure the amount of a given element X in a particular sample.

Principle A known amount say x g of the sample containing N atoms of the element (mono-isotopic) is placed in a uniform flux of thermal neutrons for a sufficiently long period of time t seconds to produce measurable activity, say A_t. This activity A_t, is due to the isotope under study. If any other element present in the sample also becomes radioactive, the activity of the former is differentiated from the rest by its characteristic radiation, half-life etc. The activity A_t is given by

$$A_t = N\phi\sigma\,(1 - e^{-\lambda t})$$

where, ϕ is the neutron flux (number of neutrons in $cm^{-2}\,s^{-1}$), σ is the neutron capture cross section in cm^2 for the given target nucleus and λ is the decay constant in s^{-1} of the radioactive product. The number of the product nuclei produced, N' is given by A_t/λ. A_t is the activity of the product immediately at the end of the irradiation for time t. But it is not possible to measure it immediately at the end of the irradiation and there may be a time lapse of t'. Then

$$A_t' = A_t e^{-\lambda t'} = N\phi\sigma\,(1 - e^{-\lambda t})\,e^{-\lambda t'}$$

The weight (W) of the particular element present is calculated as follows :

$$W = \frac{NM}{L} = \frac{M}{L}\,\frac{A_t'}{\phi\sigma\,(1 - e^{-\lambda t})\,e^{-\lambda t'}}$$

where, M is the atomic weight of the element and L is the Avogadro number (6.023×10^{23}).

If $t_{1/2}$ (half-life) is very short, then the period of irradiation (t) can be prolonged to equal about six half-lives, when the factor $e^{-\lambda t} = e^{-0.693t/t_{1/2}} \approx 0$ as $t >> t_{1/2}$ and the expression simplifies.

In actual practice to avoid the use of complicated equations two samples, one containing a known amount (W_0) of the element (standard) and the other containing unknown amount (W) are irradiated and the resulting activities A_t^0 (known) and A_t (unknown) are measured.

$$\frac{W}{W_0} = \frac{A_t}{A_t^0}$$

Alternatively a series of known samples containing $W_1, W_2, W_3 \ldots W_n$ of the element and unknown are irradiated and a linear plot is drawn between W and A_t. From this, unknown amount is found out.

This method is useful in determining the amount of trace elements in minerals and ores. Elements which can be determined by neutron activation analysis are Na, P, Ca, Sc, Cr, Mn, Co, Cu, Zn, Ge, As, Se, Ag, In, W, Ir, Pt, Au, Sm, Eu, Gd, Dy, Ho, Yb, etc.

(i) Chromium content of ruby

The ^{50}Cr in natural chromium becomes ^{51}Cr by (n, γ) reaction. By irradiating with slow neutrons under identical conditions a chromium bearing ruby with a series a $Al_2O_3 + Cr_2O_3$ mixtures of varying, but known Cr-content, it was found that the rubies have 0.1 to 0.4% Cr.

(ii) Arsenic in hair (Slow arsenic poisoning)

The ^{75}As becomes ^{76}As which is having a $t_{1/2}$ of 26.3 hr by (n, γ) reaction.

Any arsenic entering the human body is known to accumulate in the roots of hair and move along the length of the hair as it grows, the normal rate of growth of hair in most people being 0.35 mm per day. In neutron activation method a single strand of hair is neutron activated and cut into short segments and the distribution of ^{76}As all along the hair length scanned and the pattern compared with the distribution of As in the hair of a normal person. While the normal hair would reveal about 0.8 ppm as distributed uniformly all along the length, the pattern for a person given periodic doses of As would show clear peaks and valley and the mean value would be much greater than 0.8 ppm.

Prompt Gamma Neutron Activation Analysis (PGNAA)

In this method instead of measuring the γ activities of the daughter products, the neutron capture γ photon emitted promptly within 10^{-15} s are detected. However, these photons are to be distinguished from the delayed γ emitted subsequently by the daughter nucleus. The prompt γ photon are characteristic of the emitter nuclide and serve as finger prints of the element. Thus, this technique permits the detection and estimation of the amount of the element in a given sample. This method is utilized for prospecting natural resources and also assessing vital elements as H, C, N, K, Ca, Fe and I in the whole body.

Counting Techniques

The property of charged particles ionizing gases has been utilised from the earliest times to measure radioactivity.

Electron Multiplication in a Gas

When an ionising agent enters a gas, marked ionisation occurs. If an external potential 'V' volts across electrodes 'l' cm apart is applied, the current 'i' is given by

$$i = ne(u_+ + u_-) V/l$$

where, 'n' is the number of electrons (= number of ions) per cm^3 and u_+ and u_- are the specific ionic mobilities of ions and electrons. This current is in the order of 10^{-13} A and hence cannot be easily measured.

As the potential is gradually raised, the field $X\left(\frac{V}{l}\right)$ and its ratio of pressure $\left(\frac{X}{p}\right)$ increases. A sharp increase is observed at a particular value called $\left(\frac{X}{p}\right)_{\text{critical}}$. When current '$i$' is plotted against l (the inter electrode distance) for $\frac{X}{p} > \left(\frac{X}{p}\right)_{\text{critical}}$, an exponentially rising curve (Fig. 15.27) is obtained. This can be given as

$$i = i_0 e^{\alpha t}$$

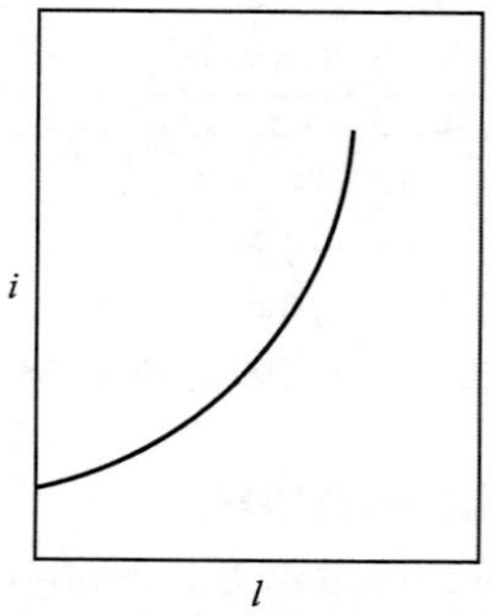

Fig. 15.27 Variation of 'i' with 'l'.

The corresponding equation for the number of ion pairs is

$$M = n_0 e^{\alpha l}$$

This equation is having the general form

$$M = n_0 \exp\left(\int_0^l \alpha \, dl\right)$$

Generally, $M = (10^3 - 10^4)\, n_0$

The α in the above Eqs. is a constant for a given $\left(\frac{X}{p}\right)$ and is found to be a function of $\left(\frac{X}{p}\right)$.

$$\left(\frac{\alpha}{p}\right) = f\left(\frac{X}{p}\right)$$

α is the number of new electron-ion pairs created by a primary electron in traversing a distance of 1 cm in the field direction. This represents electron multiplication in the gas. The energy which an electron acquires at the end of a mean free path (λ) is $E = Xe\lambda$. Generally, a part of this acquired energy is lost in the next elastic collision and the electron starts on a fresh journey.

However, if λ exceeds a critical value λ_i such that $Xe\lambda_i > E_i$ (the ionisation energy of the gas atom), the collision will be inelastic and the atom is ionised as follows :

$$A + e^- \longrightarrow A^+ + 2e^-$$

The primary electron has now doubled itself in going one mean free path in the direction of the field, which means no electron in traversing a distance l multiplied by $n_0 e^{\alpha l}$ as experimentally observed. The coefficient α is known as the Townsend coefficient. As per the Boltzmann distribution, the number of collisions with $\lambda > \lambda_i$ can be given as

$$Z_{\lambda i} = Z_0 \exp\left(\frac{\lambda_i}{\bar{\lambda}}\right)$$

where, $\bar{\lambda}$ is the average mean free path at the given pressure and temperture. Since, the mean free path varies inversely as gas pressure, (α / p) can be shown to be a function of (X/p) as observed.

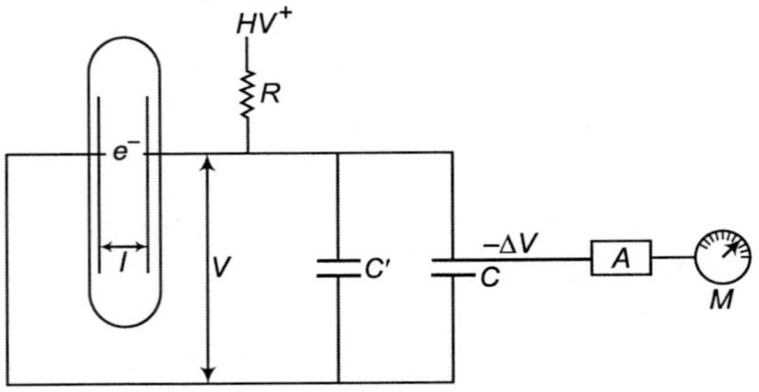

Fig. 15.28 Ionisation chamber.

HV^+	–	DC high voltage source
R	–	Resistance
C and C'	–	Condensers
$-\Delta V$	–	Negative voltage pulse (signal)
A	–	Amplifier
M	–	Recorder

The Gas Counter (Ionisation Counter)

The basic circuit of the gas counter is given in Fig. 15.37. The electrons generated by the incoming primary particle collect on the inner positive wire and this wire receives a charge $-Q$. If its capacity to earth is C then with a high resistance R in series, a negative voltage pulse ΔV (the signal) develops at its end as given by $\Delta V = -Q/C$.

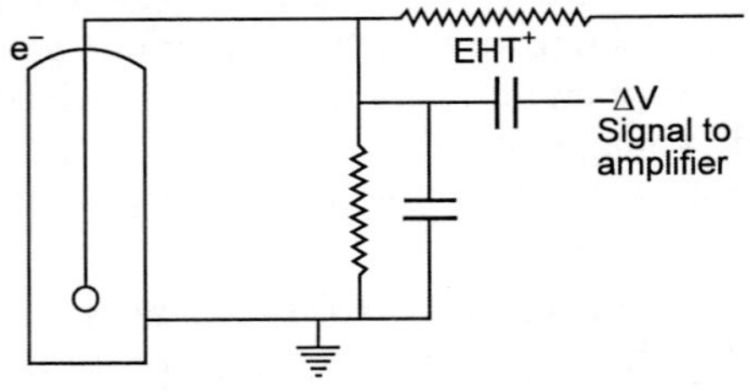

Fig. 15.29 The gas counter.

The Gieger-Muller Counter (GM Counter)

GM counters are severally designed to meet specific requirements. The most widely used types are end-window counter, thin walled line counter, and the liquid counter.

(i) The end-window counter

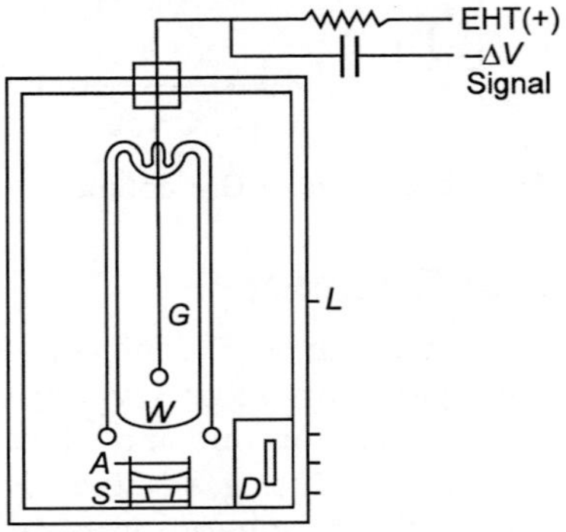

Fig. 15.30 End-window GM counter.

G	–	Gas filled GM tube
W	–	Thin window
T	–	Sample support stand
S	–	Source
A	–	Absorbers
L	–	Lead castle shielding
D	–	Door

This consists of a thin tungsten wire stretched along the axis of a metal or graphite coated glass cylinder, the bottom of which is covered with a thin foil of Al or mylor of $\approx 1 \text{ mg}/\text{cm}^2$ thickness. The source and absorbers are placed on a stand beneath. A 20 – 25 mm thick lead castle surrounds the counter to reduce background counts. The counter tube is filled with argon (90 mm pressure) and alcohol vapour, or halogen gas at a pressure of about 10 mm, for self-quenching. This is the most widely used type of GM counter for measuring β-γ activities in most radiochemical studies (Fig. 15.30)

(ii) The liquid counter

It is designed for counting activity in liquid samples. It consists of two coaxial glass tubes sealed at the bottom as shown in Fig. 15.31. The inner tube is filled with argon together with a halogen. A tungsten wire is stretched along the axis of the inner tube. This is connected to a positive high voltage source. The inner wall of the gas filled tube is silvered, which serves as the cathode, which is earthed. The annulus is filled with a fixed amount of $(5-10\ cm^3)$ of the liquid whose activity is to be measured. The rest of the electrical circuit is same as in other GM counters.

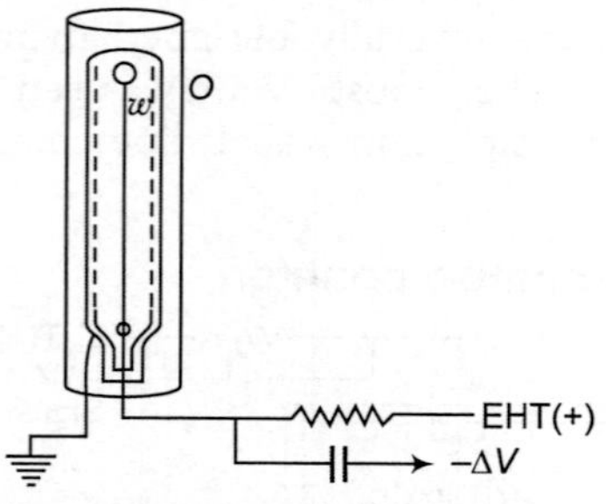

Fig. 15.31 Liquid GM counter.

Proportional Counter

A typical proportional counter is depicted in Fig. 15.40. Usually the filling gas is argon or krypton or methane or a mixture of 90% argon and 10% methane. Sometimes the domestic fuel gas butane is also used. All these are used at atmospheric pressure. However, all these gases should be free from electronegative impurities. At $V = 1.5-2.0$ kV, the electron multiplication is $10^2 - 10^3$ without external amplification. The sliding thin window W permits insertion of the sample inside the counter when necessary for 2π or 4π counting. The proportional counter is sensitive to X-rays and to lightly ionizing particles as β of ^3H, ^{63}Ni, ^{14}C, ^{35}S etc.

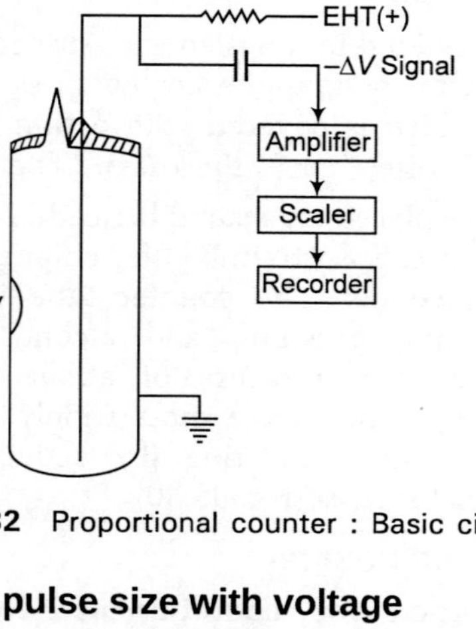

Fig. 15.32 Proportional counter : Basic circuit.

Variation of pulse size with voltage

The variation of the signal ΔV as a function of applied potential 'V' is shown in Fig. 15.33 for two primary ionising particles, as α and β, the ionizing power of α being much greater than that of β. The complete range of the signal strength *vs* 'V' consists of six characteristic ranges, described below.

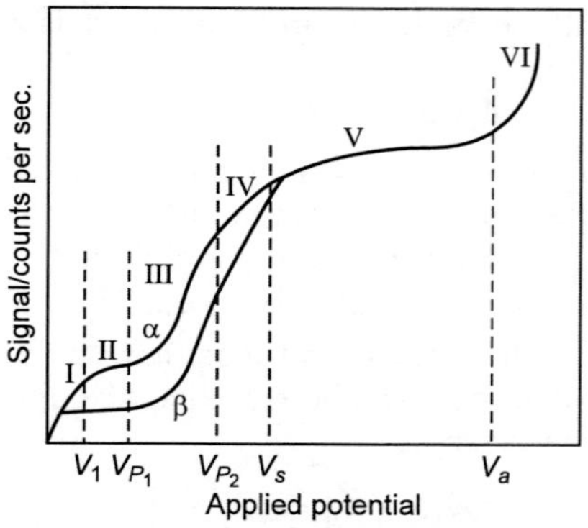

Fig. 15.33 Variation of signal with applied potential for particles of two different energies (α > β).

Stage I $V < V_i : V \propto n$;

Stage II Ionisation chamber range

Stage III Proportional counter range

Stage IV Limited proportionality range

Stage V Geiger-Muller counter range

Stage VI The discharge potential range.

Stage I Potential $< V_i$ Here, the pulse size depends on the difference of the number of ions collected over those removed by recombination and diffusion and $\Delta V \propto n$, the actual value of ΔV being very small.

Stage II Potential range $V_i - V_p$**, saturation range** This is the range relevant to the ionization chamber. Here, all the ions are collected, hence ΔV saturates. The voltage needed for saturation is higher for α than for β. Here, too pulse size is very small and large amplification is needed for measuring the same.

Stage III Potential range $V_{p_1} - V_{p_2}$ This stage begins with the onset of electron multiplication by collision, *i.e.,* the Townsend coefficient α becomes operative, leading to

$$M = n_0 \exp \int_{r_\alpha}^{r_m} \alpha dl = n_0 \exp [\alpha(r_m - r_\alpha)]$$

This is the range employed in a proportional counter where the pulse height is proportional to the energy of the primary particle. The pulse height is large enough to detect without any further amplification. However, during the operation of the proportional counter, the applied voltage should be constant to avoid any complication in detecting the energy of the primary particle.

Stage IV Limited proportionality potential $V_{p_2} - V_S$ In this stage, the proportionality is approximated or limited. Smaller pulses develop relatively more and the bigger ones will not be in proportion. At a particular potential V_S, pulses due to primary ionizing particles of all energies tend to equal up. Even the limited proportionality ceases and Gieger-Muller regime begins.

Stage V The Gieger-Muller Plateau region : Potential $V_S - V_d$ Each electron from the primary source entering the counter space grows into an avalanche and each avalanche grows into another resulting in all overall electron multiplication factor of the order of 10^7. The charge collected by the wire has a constant value, independent of the magnitude and location of the primary ionization. The discharge spreads along the whole length of the wire as a corona. The carriers are the photons produced by the process $A^* \longrightarrow A + h\nu$. The positive ion sheath keeps moving towards the cylinder reaching there in about $100 - 500\ \mu s$. This is the beginning of Geiger-Muller plateau region $V_S - V_d$, which is around 100 V, above which the pulse height remains constant, independent of the energy of the primary ionizing particle. The plateau has a very gently rising slope of around a few per cent. The GM counter is to be operated at a potential V_0 which is about midway between V_S and V_d, rather slightly to the left of the midpoint.

Stage VI The discharge potential $V \geq V_d$ At and above the potential V_d the counter goes into a continuous discharge. This is due to the creation of tertiary electrons which initiate the glow discharge. The potential should not be raised much above V_d which may lead to the loss of sensitivity of the counter.

Tracer Techniques

With the ready availability of radio isotopes, many applications are known.

1. Reaction Mechanisms

In the esterification reaction, whether the C—OH bond or O—H bond in the acid breaks can be determined using ^{18}O labelled alcohol.

$$RCOOH + HO^*R' \longrightarrow RCOO^*R' + H_2O$$

If the labelled oxygen is present in ester then it indicates that C—OH bond in the acid breaks.

2. Isotope Exchange Reactions

When an homogeneous isotope exchange reaction $AX + B^*X^- \longrightarrow A^*X + BX$ is considered, the rate of the reaction can be given by the equation

$$\frac{(a+b)}{ab} Rt = -\ln(1-F)$$

where, $a = [AX] + [A^*X]$

$b = [B^*X] + [BX]$

R = Rate constant

F = Fraction exchanged in time 't'

When $\ln(1-F)$ is plotted against time 't', a straight line passing through the origin is generally obtained. If there is a positive intercept in the ordinate, it indicates the exchange is either catalysed or follows two mechanisms, one of which is very fast. Example is the exchange between PCl_5 and Cl_2 dissolved in CCl_4. The three planar chlorine atoms are exchanged instantaneously whereas the chlorine atoms at the vertices exchange slowly. Similarly, if there is a negative intercept in the ordinate, it indicates that there is an induction period before the start of the exchange reaction. Example is radiation induced exchange between Br^- and BrO_3^-. This reaction is having a period of induction varying from 6 to 36 minutes.

Isotope Dilution Analysis

Isotope dilution analysis is used to determine the unknown amount of a given species of matter mixed up in a large sample. Examples are assessing the amount of an active component as auromycin in a large fermentation broth, or the volume of blood in a living being.

1. Direct Isotope Dilution Analysis (DIDA)

In this analysis, to the sample containing x g of the species, y g of a radioisotope form of the species of initial specific activity S_i counts $min^{-1}\ mg^{-1}$ is added and thoroughly mixed. Then a small amount of the species from the mixture is isolated and the final specific activity (S_f) is measured. According to the principle of the conservation of total activity, initial and final total activities should be equal.

Hence, $$(x+y)\,S_f = yS_i$$

$$x = y\left(\frac{S_i - S_f}{S_f}\right)$$

2. Inverse Isotope Dilution Analysis (IIDA)

This is just reverse of the previous analysis. In this analysis, to a small amount of a radioactive substance x g having initial specific activity, S_i, y g of the non-radioactive compound of the same substance is added and thoroughly mixed. Then a small amount of the mixture is isolated and final specific activity S_f is determined.

$$(x + y)\, S_f = xS_i$$

$$x = y\left(\frac{S_f}{S_i - S_f}\right)$$

Using this method the amount of a radioactive substance initially present can be measured.

3. Sub Stoichiometric Isotope Dilution Analysis (SSIDA)

In this method, an equal amount of extractant is added to two solutions one containing known amount (m_1) of labelled isotope and the other containing unknown original solution (m_2) and same amount (m_2) of labelled solution. After the extraction, the specific activity is measured in both the cases and from these activities the mass of the unknown substance is calculated.

Let S_1 be the specific activity of known stock solution containing the mass m_1 (known) and S_2 be the specific activity of mixture containing m_2 amount of unknown substance and m_1 amount of isotope.

$$(m_2 + m_1)\, S_2 = m_1 S_1$$

$$m_2 = m_1\left(\frac{S_1 - S_2}{S_2}\right)$$

This technique finds extensive application in **radio immunoassay.**

Artificial or Induced Radioactivity

There are many artificial transmutations (*i.e.,* nuclear reactions) in which the product nucleus is unstable (*i.e.,* radioactive isotope) and hence disintegrates spontaneously (*i.e.,* by itself) like naturally occurring radioactive elements such as uranium, radium etc., to give a stable isotope of some other element. The radioactive isotope while giving the stable isotope during its disintegration, emits usually either electrons $({}^{0}_{-1}e)$ or positrons $({}^{0}_{+1}e)$. The spontaneous disintegration of the radioactive isotope takes place according to the same laws that apply to the disintegration of naturally-occurring radioactive elements, Thus :

The process in which an element is converted into a new radioactive isotope (*i.e.,* unstable isotope) by artificial means (*i.e.,* by bombarding the element with fast moving particles like proton, deutron, helium etc.) is called **artificial or induced radioactivity.**

(i) Reactions emitting electrons $({}^{0}_{-1}e)$

Electrons are emitted in (n, γ), (n, p), (n, α) and (D, p) reactions. *e.g.,*

(a) (n, γ) $${}^{115}_{49}\text{In} + {}^{1}_{0}n \longrightarrow \underset{\text{Unstable}}{{}^{116}_{49}\text{In}} + {}^{0}_{0}\gamma$$

$${}^{116}_{49}\text{In} \longrightarrow \underset{\text{Stable}}{{}^{116}_{50}\text{Sn}} + {}^{0}_{-1}e \qquad (T = 13\text{ s})$$

(b) (n, p) $${}^{14}_{7}\text{N} + {}^{1}_{0}n \longrightarrow \underset{\text{Unstable}}{{}^{14}_{6}\text{C}} + {}^{1}_{1}\text{H}$$

$${}^{14}_{6}\text{C} \longrightarrow \underset{\text{Stable}}{{}^{14}_{7}\text{N}} + {}^{0}_{-1}e \qquad (T = 5568\text{ yr})$$

(ii) Reactions emitting positrons $({}^{0}_{+1}e)$

Positrons are emitted in (p, γ), (p, n), (α, n), (D, n) and (γ, n) reactions. *e.g.,*

(a) (p, γ) $${}^{12}_{6}\text{C} + {}^{1}_{1}\text{H} \longrightarrow \underset{\text{Unstable}}{{}^{13}_{7}\text{N}} + {}^{0}_{0}\gamma$$

$${}^{13}_{7}\text{N} \longrightarrow \underset{\text{Stable}}{{}^{13}_{6}\text{C}} + {}^{0}_{+1}e \qquad (T = 10\text{ min})$$

(b) (p, n) $${}^{58}_{28}\text{Ni} + {}^{1}_{1}\text{H} \longrightarrow \underset{\text{Unstable}}{{}^{58}_{29}\text{Cu}} + {}^{1}_{0}n$$

$${}^{58}_{29}\text{Cu} \longrightarrow \underset{\text{Stable}}{{}^{58}_{28}\text{Ni}} + {}^{0}_{+1}e \qquad (T = 2.6\text{ s})$$

Preparation of Transuranium Elements

Until recently, it was believed that there are only 92 elements (atomic number 1 to 92). As a result of study of radioactive processes, however, it was observed that atoms with atomic number higher than 92 could be produced. At present 13 elements with atomic weight higher than that of uranium (at. no. = 92) and with atomic numbers 93 to 105 are called **transuranium elements or transuranic elements** because they lie beyond uranium in the Periodic Table.

It was only in 1940 that the existence of these elements was definitely established.

The names, symbols and atomic numbers of these elements are given below. The numbers given on the bottom left of the symbols indicate their atomic numbers.

Neptunium $({}_{93}\text{Np})$, Plutonium $({}_{94}\text{Pu})$, Amercium $({}_{95}\text{Am})$, Curium $({}_{96}\text{Cm})$. Berkelium $({}_{97}\text{Bk})$, Californium $({}_{98}\text{Cf})$, Einsteinium $({}_{99}\text{Es})$, Fermium $({}_{100}\text{Fm})$, Mendelevium $({}_{101}\text{Md})$, Nobelium $({}_{102}\text{No})$, Lawrencium $({}_{103}\text{Lw})$, Kurchatovium $({}_{104}\text{Ku})$ and Hahnium $({}_{105}\text{Ha})$.

Uses of Radioisotopes

Some important uses of radioisotopes are given below :

Uses of Radioisotopes as Radioactive Tracers

First of all we should understand "What are radioactive tracers? Radioactive isotopes have a property due to which they can easily be detected and estimated quantitatively. Further, they reach almost exactly as the corresponding non-radioactive isotopes do. As such, if we want to trace the course of an atomic species in a chemical or a physical change, we mix a small quantity of the radioactive isotope with non-radioactive isotope. Here, we say that the radioactive isotope is acting as a **radioactive tracer** or **radioactive indicator** or simply as **labelled** or **tagged element.** The presence of radioactive tracer is later on detected in the products with the help of sensitive instruments. Some important uses of radioactive tracers are given below :

(i) Uses of tracers in studying reaction mechanisms

(a) **Photosynthesis** The mechanism of the process of photosynthesis taking place in plants has been studied by reacting carbon dioxide containing ^{18}O (CO_2^{18}) with H_2O. In this process the green plants take up CO_2 and H_2O in presence of sunlight and chlorophyll to form sugar and starch, giving out oxygen gas.

$$6CO_2 + 6H_2O \longrightarrow C_6H_{12}O_6 + 6O_2$$

Here, a very important question arises–whether the oxygen evolved in this process comes from CO_2 or from H_2O or from both. This question has been answered by the use of radioactive ^{18}O isotope. What we do is that H_2O is made to react with carbon dioxide containing ^{18}O (*i.e.*, CO_2^{18}) and it is found that the oxygen evolved does not contain ^{18}O, *i.e.*, O^{18} present in CO_2^{18} goes to sugar and water while that of water is evolved as free oxygen. Thus, oxygen evolved in the process of photosynthesis comes from H_2O and not from CO_2.

(b) **Functioning of thyroid gland** Radioisotope of iodine, I^{131} with $T = 8$ days is given to a patient with thyroid disorders. It decays β-rays. Detection of these rays gives an information regarding the functioning of the thyroid glands.

(c) **Disorders associated with pregnancy** Tracer iron has been used in studying the disorders associated with pregnancy.

(d) **Test of cancer growth** ^{60}Co emits high energy γ-rays which are used for testing deeply seated cancer growth.

(ii) Uses of tracers in industry

Radioactive isotopes have found many applications in industry both in research and in process control. Some of the examples are given below :

(a) **Determination of the wear of piston rings** The wear of piston rings and of gears in engines and its prevention by means of suitable lubricants have been studied by radioactivity. A steel piston ring is made radioactive by exposing it to neutrons in a nuclear reactor. The piston ring is then fitted into the cylinder of an internal combustion engine which is operated normally with a particular lubricating oil. By determining the radioactivity removed by the oil, the amount of piston wear can be determined.

(b) **Self-diffusion of metals** The phenomenon of self-diffusion in metals *i.e.*, the movement of the atoms of a metal within the crystal lattice has been studied with the help of isotopes.

(c) **Uniform mixing** Uniformity of mixing during the blending of petrols, lubricating oils and greases etc. has been achieved by labelling one of the constituents with a radioactive tracer.

(d) **As catalyst** γ-rays obtained from Co^{60} have been used as catalyst in the manufacture of C_2H_5Br from ethylene and HBr.

(e) **Effect of different phenomenon on metal** By incorporating radioactive isotope in the metal it is possible to know as to what happens when a metal is subjected to a particular treatment like age-hardening, annealing, quenching, coldroling etc.

(f) **Mechanism of effectiveness of lubricants** Radioactive isotopes have been used in studying the mechanism of the effectiveness of various lubricants.

(g) **Mechanisms of reactions** Radioactive carbon, C^{15} has been used as a tracer in studying mechanisms involved in many reactions of industrial importance such as alkylation, polymerisation, catalytic synthesis, etc.

(iii) Uses of tracers in agriculture

(a) **Uptake of phosphorus by plants** When a plant grows, it absorbs phosphorus both from the soil and from the added phosphatic fertilizer. In order to check the usefulness of the fertilizer, it is important to know what proportion of phosphorus comes from each source. Ordinary analytical methods cannot answer this question because phosphorus from both sources is exactly the same. However, if radiophosphorus (P^{32}), is added in the phosphatic fertilizer, the exact proportion taken up by the plant can be determined accurately.

The efficiency of different phosphatic fertilizers can be compared with the help of radioactive phosphorus being used as a tracer element. Fertilizer which is absorbed quickly is more efficient.

(b) **Transportation of mineral in plants** The transportation of mineral from roots to leaves and its subsequent redistribution within the plants can be followed through the use of radioactive isotopes by means of radioantography. By this technique the distribution of S^{35}, supplied in the form of sulphate, in sugar beet plants has been followed.

(c) **Irradiation of maize with radioactive cobalt** It produce 15% increase in the quantity of green part over those plants growing in the same field, but not irradiated. In some cases, solutions of radioactive substances are used in place of irradiation. The seeds are dipped in these solutions before planting. This also raises theyield of cane sugar, wheat, maize etc.

(iv) Uses of tracers in analytical chemistry

Suppose we want to determine the solubility of $PbSO_4$ in water. A known quantity of radioactive lead (Pb*) is mixed with ordinary lead (Pb) in a known proportion. The entire amount consisting of radioactive and ordinary lead is dissolved in dil. HNO_3 and then precipitated as lead sulphate on the addition of dil. H_2SO_4.

$$Pb^* + Pb \xrightarrow{HNO_3} Pb^*(NO_3)_2 + Pb(NO_3)_2$$

$$\xrightarrow{H_2SO_4} Pb^*SO_4 \downarrow + PbSO_4 \downarrow$$

After filtration, the radioactivity of the solution is measured and thus the amount of lead sulphate present in solution is calculated. This, of course, gives the amount of radioactive lead present in solution. If the ratio of the two varieties of lead originally taken is known, the amount of ordinary lead present in solution can be calculated.

(v) Uses of radioisotopes in the treatment of diseases (Radiotherapy)

The treatment of diseases by the use of radioisotopes is called radiotherapy. Some examples of radiotherapy are given below :

(a) **Treatment of thyroid complaints** Radioactive iodine I^{131} has been used for the treatment of certain thyroid complaints. Stable iodine and radioactive iodine are preferentially absorbed by the thyroid gland. This fact is ultilised in the treatment of hyper-thyroidism and cancer of the thyroid. Radioactive iodine destroys abnormal tissues in the thyroid gland more rapidly and in this way checks the abnormal growth.

(b) **Treatment of blood disorders** Radioactive phosphorus in the form of phosphate is widely used in the treatment of certain blood disorder.

(c) **Treatment of cancer growth** Radiocobalt (Co^{60}) produced by the action of neutrons from a nuclear pile, $T = 5.3$ days, γ-rays emitter and radiogold (Au^{198}), $T = 3$ days, γ-rays emitter are used in the treatment of some forms of cancer. Co^{69} has been called **Poor Man's Radium.**

(d) **Treatment of leukemia** Radioisotope of phosphorus is being used for the treatment of leukemia.

(e) **Treatment of skin diseases** Radiophosphorus (P^{30}), $T = 14.3$ days, β-emitter is found good for skin diseases.

(vi) Determination of the age of the earth by rock dating method

The age of a rock (*i.e.,* the time that elapsed since the rock crystallied from the molten state) gives an approximate idea of the age of the earth provided it is the assumed that the rock or the mineral under examination is as old as the earth. Let us consider a rock containing U-238 isotope formed many years ago. The age of this rock can be determined by considering its radioactive disintegration which, as we have already seen, is governed by the relation

$$N = N_0 \cdot e^{-\lambda t} \quad ...(20)$$

where, N_0 = amount of U-238 isotope originally present in a small quantity of the rock or mineral at the time the rock was formed, N = amount of U-238 still left undecayed after the lapse of time, t which represents the age of the rock, and λ = disintegration constant of U-238.

U-238 started to decay giving rise to U-238–Pb-206 series. Some of its quantity decayed into Pb-206 in time, t, while the remaining quantity of U-238 remained undisintegrated. If the quantity of U-238 remained undisintegrated is U^{238} (*i.e.,* U^{238} represents the quantity of U-238 existing at the present time in the rock) and that of Pb-206 formed as a result of disintegration of U-238 is Pb^{206} (*i.e.,* Pb^{206} represents the quantity of Pb-206 existing at present in the rock), then the quantity of U-238 present at zero time (*i.e.,* before disintegration started) is equal to $(U^{238} + Pb^{206})$. Thus,

$$N = U^{238} \text{ and } N_0 = (U^{238} + Pb^{206})$$

and hence Eq. (20) given above becomes :

$$U^{238} = (U^{238} + Pb^{206})\, e^{-\lambda t} \qquad \ldots(21)$$

or $$\frac{U^{238}}{(U^{238} + Pb^{206})} = e^{-\lambda t}$$

or $$e^{\lambda t} = \frac{U^{238} + Pb^{206}}{U^{238}} = \left(1 + \frac{Pb^{206}}{U^{238}}\right)$$

or $$\lambda t = 2.303 \log_{10}\left(1 + \frac{Pb^{206}}{U^{238}}\right)$$

Now, we know that the value of decay constant (λ) of U-238 is given by :

$$\lambda = \frac{0.693}{T_{50\%}}$$

where, $T_{50\%}$ is the half-life period of U-238.

Thus, $$t = \frac{2.303\, T_{50\%}}{0.693} \log_{10}\left(1 + \frac{Pb^{206}}{U^{238}}\right)$$

Since, the values of Pb^{206} and U^{238} can be determined experimentally, the value of t which is the age of the rock (or of earth) can be found out.

If, in place of rock containing U-238, we consider the rock containing U-235, then the isotope of lead obtained from the disintegration of U-235 is Pb-207 and the relation (ii) reduces to (iii) given below :

$$U^{236} = (U^{235} + Pb^{207})\, e^{-\lambda' t} \qquad \ldots(22)$$

where, λ′ is the disintegration constant of U-235 isotope.

Now, Eq. (21) can also be written as :

$$\frac{U^{238}}{U^{238}} = \left(\frac{U^{238}}{U^{238}} + \frac{Pb^{206}}{U^{238}}\right) e^{-\lambda t}$$

or $$1 = \left(1 + \frac{Pb^{206}}{U^{238}}\right) e^{-\lambda t}$$

or $$e^{\lambda t} = 1 + \frac{Pb^{206}}{U^{238}}$$

or $$(e^{\lambda t} - 1)\, U^{238} = Pb^{206} \qquad \ldots(23)$$

Likewise Eq. (22) reduces to :

$$(e^{\lambda' t} - 1)\, U^{235} = Pb^{207} \qquad \ldots(24)$$

On dividing Eqs. (23) and (24) by each other, we get

$$\frac{Pb^{206}}{Pb^{207}} = \frac{U^{238}}{U^{235}} \frac{(e^{\lambda t} - 1)}{(e^{\lambda' t} - 1)}$$

The present ratio, U^{238} / U^{235} is known to be 139 and hence

$$\frac{Pb^{206}}{Pb^{207}} = \frac{139\,(e^{\lambda t} - 1)}{(e^{\lambda' t} - 1)}$$

When the values of λ and λ′ as determined from the half-life periods of the isotopes *viz.* U-238 and U-235 and the ratio Pb^{206} / Pb^{207} as determined by a mass spectrometer are put in the above equation, we get the value of t which is the age of the rock or earth.

The above method is useful for dating minerals and rocks of considerable age.

Example 10. *The ratio of mass of* Pb^{206} *to the mass of* U^{238} *in a certain rock specimen is found to be* 0.5. *Assuming that the rock originally contained no lead, estimate its age. Half-life of uranium is* 4.5×10^9 *yr.*

Sol. We have already seen that the rleation between the existing masses of U^{238} and Pb^{206} in any rock specimen is given by

$$U^{238} = (U^{238} + Pb^{206})\, e^{-\lambda t}$$

or $$1 = \left(1 + \frac{Pb^{206}}{U^{238}}\right) e^{-\lambda t}$$

or $$1 = (1 + 0.5)\, e^{-\lambda t} = 1.5\, e^{-\lambda t}$$

∴ $$e^{\lambda t} = 1.5$$

or $$\lambda t = 2.3 \log_{10} 1.5 = 2.3 \times 0.1761$$

∴ $$\frac{0.693}{4.5 \times 10^9} \times t = 0.23 \times 0.1761$$

$$t = 2.63 \times 10^9 \text{ yr}$$

(vii) Determination of the age of recent objects by radio-carbon dating method

The age of recent objects such as those of animal or vegetable origin like a piece of wood or animal fossil can be determined by radio-carbon dating method, since rock dating method is useful only for the minerals or rocks of considerable age. This method was developed by Willard Libby who was awarded Nobel Prize for this brilliant work.

The determination of the age of a sample of wood (*i.e.,* the time which elapsed after the death of the living plant) consists of determining the ratio of the amount of ${}_6C^{14}$ to that of ${}_6C^{12}$ in both the pieces of wood, *i.e.,* in fresh (living) piece and dead (cut) piece. We know that the atmospheric carbon dioxide is a mixture of $C^{14}O_2$ and $C^{12}O_2$ which are present in a fixed ratio. Plants absorb carbon dioxide from the atmosphere and prepare cellulose (wood). As long as the plant is alive, the ratio of ${}_6C^{14}$ to ${}_6C^{12}$ atoms in the wood of the plant is the same as in the atmosphere but when the tree is cut (*i.e.,* when the plants dies), the ratio of ${}_6C^{14}$ to ${}_6C^{12}$ begins to decrease continuously due to the continuous decrease in the amount of ${}_6C^{14}$ in the plant. This decrease in the amount of ${}_6C^{14}$ is due to its continuous disintegration emitting β-radiations as shown :

$${}_6C^{14} \longrightarrow {}_7N^{14} + \beta\text{-particle} \qquad (T = 5568 \text{ yr})$$

Now, we know that

$$N = N_0 \cdot e^{-\lambda t}$$

or

$$t = \frac{2.303\ T_{50\%}}{0.693} \log_{10} \frac{N_0}{N}$$

On putting $N_0 = C^{14}/C^{12}$ ratio in the living (*i.e.,* fresh) plant, and $N = C^{14}/C^{12}$ ratio in the dead (*i.e.,* cut) plant, in the above equation, the age of the wood, t is given by :

$$t = \frac{2.303\,T_{50\%}}{0.693} \log\left[\frac{C^{14}/C^{12} \text{ ratio in the living plant}}{C^{14}/C^{12} \text{ ratio in the dead plant}}\right] \quad ...(25)$$

Here, $T_{50\%}$ is half-life period of ${}_6C^{14}$.

If the ratio of the amounts of C^{14}-isotope in the fresh and dead wood is known, then

$$t = \frac{2.303\ T}{0.693} \log\left[\frac{\text{Amount of } C^{14} \text{ in fresh wood}}{\text{Amount of } C^{14} \text{ in dead wood}}\right] \quad ...(26)$$

Example 11. *The amount of ${}_5C^{14}$ isotope in a piece of wood is found to be one-sixth present in a fresh piece of wood. Calculate the age of wood. Half-life of ${}_6C^{14} = 5577$ yr.*

Sol. With the help of Eq. (26) given above we get

$$t = \frac{2.303 \times 5577}{0.693} \log \frac{1}{1/6}$$

$$= \frac{2.303 \times 5577}{0.693} \log 6$$

$$= \frac{2.303 \times 5577 \times 0.7782}{0.693}$$

$$t = 20170 \text{ yr}$$

Exercise 1
(For Part 'B')

1. $^{238}_{92}U$ (IIIB) undergoes follows emissions

$$^{238}_{92}U \xrightarrow{-\alpha} A \xrightarrow{-\alpha} B \xrightarrow{-\beta} C$$

which is/are correct statements?
(a) A will be of IB group
(b) A will be of IIIA group
(c) B will be of IIA (alkaline earth metal) group
(d) C will be of IIIA (boron family) group

2. Radioactive disintegration rate is affected by
(a) temperature (b) pressure
(c) electric field (d) None of these

3. Carbon-14 dating method is based on the fact that
(a) carbon-14 is highly soluble
(b) carbon14 is highly insoluble
(c) carbon-14 fraction is same in all objects
(d) ratio of carbon -14 and carbon-12 remains constant during disintegration

4. Select the correct alternate.
(a) $^1_1p \longrightarrow {}^1_0n$ is positron emission
(b) $^1_1p \longrightarrow {}^1_0n$ is K-electron capture
(c) Both (a) and (b)
(d) None of the above

5. Mass defect of 1 g gives energy equal to
(a) 9×10^{13} J (b) 5.625×10^{32} eV
(c) Both (a) and (b) (d) None of these

6. Beta-emission takes place
(a) when neutron is converted to proton
(b) from the elements above the bond of stability
(c) with shifting of the new element one group towards right
(d) All the facts given above are true

7. Thorium is found in
(a) uranite (b) monazite
(c) pitchblende (d) malachite green

8. Little boy relates to
(a) U-bomb (b) H-bomb
(c) He-bomb (d) Pu-bomb

9. 'Fat man' relates to
(a) Pu-bomb
(b) U-bomb
(c) Th-bomb
(d) literary word from a book

10. Constituents of wine are carbon, hydrogen and oxygen. Half-lives of $^{13}C, {}^{15}O$ and ^3H are respectively 5730 yr, 124 s and 12.5 yr. A bottle of wine was sealed about 6 yr ago. To confirm its age, which of the isotopes would you choose to determine its age?
(a) ^3_1H (b) $^{13}_6C$
(c) $^{15}_8O$ (d) Any of these

11. Which is the correct combination?

	Change in			
	Emission	Atomic number	Mass number	Neutron number
(a)	α	– 2	– 2	– 2
(b)	β^+	– 1	0	0
(c)	β^-	+ 1	0	– 1
(d)	γ	0	0	– 1

12. After the emission of a β-particle followed by α-particle from $^{214}_{83}Bi$, the number of neutrons in the atom is
(a) 127 (b) 128
(c) 129 (d) 130

13. $^{238}_{92}U$ (IIIB) emits two α-particles, new element will be placed in
(a) IIA (b) IIB
(c) VIIA (d) VIIB

14. $^{14}_7N + {}^1_0n \longrightarrow {}^{14}_6C + {}^1_1H$ is written as
(a) $^{14}_7N\,(n, p)\,^{14}_6C$ (b) $^{14}_6C\,(p, n)\,^{14}_7N$
(c) $^{14}_7N\,(p, n)\,^{14}_6C$ (d) $^{14}_7N\,(n, e)\,^1_1H$

15. Water used as moderator in nuclear reactor is called
(a) hard water (b) heavy water
(c) nuclear water (d) critical water

16. Thiosulphate ion, $S_2O_3^{2-}$ on acidification changes to SO_2 along with precipitation of sulphur ^{35}S.

$$^{32}SO_3^{2-} + 2H^+ \longrightarrow H_2O + SO_2 + S$$

Which is the correct statement?
(a) ^{35}S is in sulphur (b) ^{35}S is in SO_2
(c) Both (a) and (b) (d) None of these

17. Which of the following nuclear reactions is an example of nuclear fusion?
(a) $^2_1H + {}^3_1H \longrightarrow {}^4_2He + {}^1_0n$
(b) $^{12}_6C + {}^1_1H \longrightarrow {}^{14}_7N + \gamma$
(c) $^{14}_7N + {}^1_0n \longrightarrow {}^{12}_6C + {}^1_1H$
(d) $^{235}_{92}U + {}^1_0n \longrightarrow {}^{142}_{56}Ba + {}^{91}_{36}Kr + 3\,{}^1_0n$

18. $A \xrightarrow[T_A]{k_A}$ Product (k = disintegration constant)

$B \xrightarrow[T_B]{k_B}$ Product

A and B are two radioactive elements with half-life periods T_A and T_B (in years) and k_A (yr^{-1}) and k_B (atom^{-1} yr^{-1}). If half-life periods are equal, disintegration would be

(a) 0.693 (b) $k_A T_A$
(c) Both (a) and (b) (d) None of these

19. There are 0.618 μg of ^{206}Pb and 0.238 μg of ^{238}U in a rock. If T_{50} of ^{238}U is 1.5× 10^9 yr, age of the rock is

(a) 0.75× 10^9 yr (b) 1.5× 10^9 yr
(c) 3.0× 10^9 yr (d) 4.5× 10^9 yr

20. If half-life period is 100 yr, average life is nearly

(a) 70 yr (b) 90 yr
(c) 100 yr (d) 144 yr

21. At radioactive equilibrium, the ratio between the atoms of two radioactive elements A and B was found to be 3.1× 10^9 : 1 respectively. If T_{50} of the element A is 2×10^{10} yr, then T_{50} of the element B is

(a) 6.45 yr (b) 2× 10^{10} yr
(c) 3.1× 10^9 yr (d) 6.2× 10^9 yr

22. In a series of three steps in radioactive disintegration sequence starting with $^{228}_{88}$Ra, the particles emitted are, successively, β^-, β^- and α-particles. The resulting product is an isotope of

(a) $_{90}$Th (b) $_{86}$Rn
(c) $_{92}$U (d) $_{88}$Ra

23. The half-life of ^{99}Tc is 6 h. Hence, average life is

(a) 3.0 h (b) 4.17 h
(c) 8.00 h (d) 8.66 h

24. Aluminium-25 decays by emitting a positron. The species immediately produced has

(a) $12p, 13n, 12e^-$ (b) $12p, 13n, 13e^-$
(c) $13p, 12n, 13e^-$ (d) $14p, 11n, 14e^-$

25. For an α-emitting isotope, the value of disintegration constant is 0.49× 10^{-10} per year. The amount of the isotope of a given sample will reduce to half its value after a period (in years) of nearly.

(a) 2.82× 10^{10} (b) 1.41× 10^{10}
(c) 0.9× 10^{10} (d) 0.45× 10^{10}

26. In uranium mineral, the atomic ratio $N_{U\text{-}238}/N_{Pb\text{-}206}$ is nearly equal to one. The age (in yr) of the mineral is nearly (half-life period of U-238 is 4.5× 10^9 yr)

(a) 3.0× 10^8 (b) 3.0× 10^9
(c) 4.5× 10^8 (d) 4.5× 10^9

27. The type of radiation that has the greatest penetrating power through matter is

(a) α (b) β^-
(c) γ (d) visible light

28. The radiation that produces the greatest number of ions as it passes through matter is

(a) α (b) β^-
(c) β^+ (d) γ

29. The most radioactive of the isotopes of an element is the one with the larget value of its

(a) atomic number (b) half-life
(c) decay constant (d) neutron number

30. Among the following nuclides, the highest binding energy per nucleon is found for

(a) $^3_1$H (b) $^{16}_8$O
(c) $^{56}_{26}$Fe (d) $^{235}_{92}$U

31. Of the following nuclides, the one most likely to decay by positron (β^+) emission is

(a) ^{68}Cu (b) ^{63}Cu
(c) ^{67}Cu (d) ^{59}Cu

32. One of the following elements has eight-naturally occurring stable isotopes.

(a) Cd (b) Br
(c) Ra (d) Au

33. Of the following nuclides, the one most likely to be radioactive is

(a) $^{14}_6$C (b) $^{14}_7$N
(c) $^{31}_{15}$P (d) $^{66}_{30}$Zn

34. A process that produces a one-unit increase in atomic number is

(a) α-emission (b) β^--emission
(c) γ-ray emission (d) electron-capture

35. Of the following types of radiations, the only one to be deflected in a magnetic field is

(a) X-ray (b) β-ray
(c) γ-ray (d) neutrons

36. Assuming that only particles emitted from atoms during natural ratioactive decay are α- and β-particles, which of the following atoms could not possibly result from the natural decay of $^{235}_{92}$U

(a) $^{207}_{82}$Pb (b) $^{227}_{89}$Ac
(c) $^{225}_{89}$Ac (d) $^{231}_{89}$Ac

37. The number of α- and β- particles lost when $^{238}_{92}$U changes to $^{206}_{82}$Pb are

(a) 6α, 6β (b) 6α, 8β
(c) 8α, 6β (d) 8α, 8β

38. $^{27}_{13}Al$ is a stable isotope. $^{29}_{13}Al$ is expected to disintegrate by
(a) α-emission (b) β-emission
(c) neutron emission (d) positron emission

39. A radioactive element decays by the sequence, and with half-lives, given below

$$X \xrightarrow[30\text{ min}]{\alpha} Y \xrightarrow[2\text{ days}]{2\beta} Z$$

Which of the following statements about this system are correct?
(a) Atomic number of X and Y are same
(b) After two hours, less than 10% of the initial X is left
(c) Maximum amount of y present at any time before 30 min is less than 50% of the initial amount of 'X'
(d) All of the above

40. In the chain reaction,

$$^{238}_{92}U \longrightarrow Ba + Kr + 3\,^{1}_{0}n + \text{energy } E$$

neutrons and energy produced at nth step will be
(a) $3n$, nE (b) 3^n, $3^{n-1}E$
(c) 3^{n-1}, nE (d) 3^n, nE

41. What is the average binding energy per nucleon, of helium nucleus,if its true mass defect is 0.030377 m_d?
(a) 22.65×10^{-13} J (b) 11.32×10^{-13} J
(c) 28.28×10^{-13} J (d) 28.281 eV

42. Which one is more biochemical important?
(a) $^{22}_{11}Na$ ($t_{1/2} = 22.8$ yr)
(b) $^{24}_{11}Na$ ($t_{1/2} = 28.7$ hr)
(c) Both are equally important
(d) None of the above

43. An accident occurs in a laboratory in which a large amount of radioactive material with a known $t_{1/2}$ of 20 days becomes embeded in floor. Tests show that the level of radiation is 32 times the permissible limit. The number of days after which the laboratory can be safely occupied will be
(a) 20 days (b) 50 days
(c) 60 days (d) 100 days

44. It is found that at 0°C and 1 atm pressure, 3.125×10^{-8} g-atoms of Rn are in equilibrium with 1g of radium. The disintegration constant of Rn is ($\lambda_{Ra} = 1.48 \times 10^{-11}\ s^{-1}$)
(a) $2.095 \times 10^{-6}\ s^{-1}$ (b) $2.96 \times 10^{-11}\ s^{-1}$
(c) $7.4 \times 10^{-11}\ s^{-1}$ (d) $4.736 \times 10^{-4}\ s^{-1}$

45. The effective neutron capture radius of a nucleus having a cross-section by 1.0 barn is
(a) 5.6×10^{-13} cm (b) 5.6×10^{-13}m
(c) 5.6×10^{-12} cm (d) 5.6×10^{-11} m

46. The average mass of chlorine is 35.5. The mass numbers of two isotopes are 35 and 37. What is the respective proportion of ^{35}Cl and ^{37}Cl in ordinary chlorine?
(a) 1 : 2 (b) 2 : 1
(c) 1 : 3 (d) 3 : 1

47. The ratio of the nuclear radii of the α-particle and the proton is
(a) 1.26 (b) 1.41
(c) 1.82 (d) 1.59

48. If an atom of $^{235}_{92}U$, after the absorption of slow neutrons, undergoes fission to produce ^{139}Xe and ^{94}Sr, what other particles are produced and how many?
(a) Two neutrons (b) Two positrons
(c) Three electrons (d) Three neutrons

49. A sample of river water was found to contain 8×10^{-18} tritium atoms $^{3}_{1}H$ per atoms of ordinary hydrogen. Tritium decomposes radioactively with a half-life of 12.3 yr. What will be the ratio of tritium to normal hydrogen atoms 49 yr after the original sample was taken if the sample is stored in a place where additional tritium atoms cannot be formed?
(a) 4×10^{-18} (b) 5×10^{-19}
(c) 1.6×10^{-17} (d) 5×10^{-18}

50. When an element is made radioactive by placing it in a homogeneous flux of energetic charged particles of neutrons, the activity produced in the element is given by
(a) $A = N\phi\left[1 - e^{\frac{1}{t_{1/2}}t}\right]$ (b) $A = N\phi\sigma\left(1 - e^{\frac{1}{t_{1/2}}t}\right)$
(c) $A = N\phi\sigma\left(1 - e^{\frac{0.693}{t_{1/2}}t}\right)$ (d) $A = N\phi\sigma\left(1 - e^{\frac{2.303}{t_{1/2}}t}\right)$

Exercise 2

(For Part 'C')

1. Which of these are the example (s) of transient equilibrium?

I. $^{234}Th \xrightarrow[24.1 \text{ days}]{\beta -} {}^{234}Pa \xrightarrow[1.18 \text{ min}]{\beta -}$ series

II. $^{140}Ba \xrightarrow[12.8 \text{ days}]{\beta -} {}^{140}La \xrightarrow[40 \text{ hr}]{\beta -} {}^{140}Ce_{(\text{stable})}$

III. $^{238}U \xrightarrow[4.5 \times 10^9 \text{ yr}]{\alpha} {}^{234}Th \xrightarrow[24.1 \text{ days}]{\beta -}$ series

IV. $^{90}Sr \xrightarrow[28.1 \text{ yr}]{\beta -} {}^{90}Y \xrightarrow[64.1 \text{ h}]{\beta -} {}^{90}Zr_{(\text{stable})}$

(a) I and III (b) I and II
(c) III and IV (d) All the given

2. The half-life of the nuclide ^{220}Rn is 54.5 s. The mass of Rn which is equivalent to 1 millicurie, is

(a) 1.06×10^{-13} g (b) 2.91×10^9 g
(c) 2.91×10^6 kg (d) 1.06×10^{-15} kg

3. With the help of approximate equation for the radius of the nucleus, calculate the density of the nucleus of $^{107}_{47}Ag$.

(a) 7.12×10^{-13} g/cm^3 (b) 1.78×10^{22} g/cm^3
(c) 1.18×10^{14} g/cm^3 (d) 1.51×10^{36} g/cm^3

4. The barrier height for an α-particle inside the $^{226}_{88}Ra$ nucleus is

(a) 931 MeV (b) 1.04×10^5 MeV
(c) 500 MeV (d) 31 MeV

5. Which of these reactions are not balanced?

I. $^{227}_{89}Ac \longrightarrow {}^{207}_{82}Pb + 5\,\alpha + 3\,\beta$

II. $^{223}_{91}Pa \longrightarrow {}^{209}_{83}Bi + 6\,\alpha + 4\,\beta$

III. $^{238}_{92}U \longrightarrow {}^{206}_{82}Pb + 8\,\alpha + 6\,\beta$

IV. $^{232}_{90}Th \longrightarrow {}^{208}_{82}Pb + 6\,\alpha + 4\,\beta$

The correct answer is

(a) I and II (b) III and IV
(c) I and III (d) I, II, III and IV

6. Match the following for detection of radioactivity.

Column I	Column II
A. Gaseous ion collection method	1. Scintillation counter
B. Semiconductor detectors	2. Cloud chamber
C. Detectors based on light emission	3. Geiger-Muller (GM) method
D. Track detectors	4. Solid ion chambers

The correct answer is

Codes

	A	B	C	D
(a)	1	2	3	4
(b)	3	4	1	2
(c)	4	3	1	2
(d)	3	4	2	1

7. The Q-value of the following nuclear reaction $^{14}_7N + {}^4_2He \longrightarrow {}^{17}_8O + {}^1_1H$ is

[$_2He^4 = 4.00387$, $^{14}_7N = 14.00753$, $^{17}_8O = 17.00450$]

(a) − 1.15 (b) + 1.15 (c) − 2.30 (d) + 2.30

8. Match the nature of decay curves with the appropriate statements.

Note *P*-Parent activity, *D*-Daughter activity, *T*-Total activity.

Column I	Column II
A. Daughter has a higher decay constant than the parent (secular equilibrium).	1. 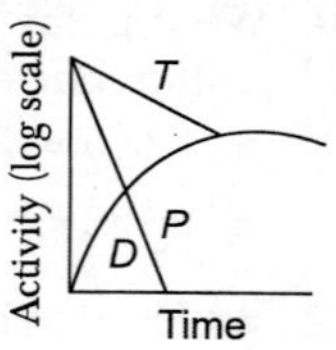
B. Parent has a higher decay constant.	2. 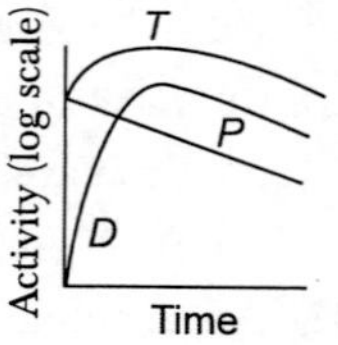
C. Daughter has higher decay constant than the parent. (Transient equilibrium)	3. 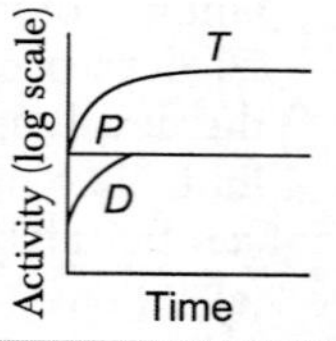

Codes

	A	B	C
(a)	1	2	3
(b)	2	3	1
(c)	3	1	2
(d)	3	2	1

9. Consider the following statements.

I. $^{16}_6C$ is more unstable than $^{16}_7N$.

II. ^{195}Hg, ^8B and ^{150}Ho are positrons emitters.

III. ^{30}Al and ^{95}Kr are beta emitters.

The true statements are

(a) I and II (b) II and III
(c) I and III (d) I, II and III

10. The Q-value for the $^{7}Li\ (p, n)^{7}$ Be reaction is
$[^{7}Li = 7.01822,\ ^{7}Be = 7.019465]$
(a) 1.64 eV (b) – 1.64 MeV
(c) 1.64 MeV (d) – 1.64 eV

11. The Q-value for the $^{3}He\ (n, p)$ reaction is 0.76 MeV. The mass of ^{3}He nuclide is
$[^{3}H = 3.01605]$
(a) 3.01 (b) 4.48 (c) 5.28 (d) 1.29

12. ^{14}C is believed to be made in upper atmosphere by an (n, p) process on ^{14}N. What is Q for this reaction?
$[^{14}N = 14.00753,\ ^{14}C = 14.00324]$
(a) 3.94 MeV (b) 4.48 MeV
(c) 5.28 MeV (d) 1.29 MeV

13. Calculate the energy needed to remove the least tightly bound neutron from $^{40}_{20}Ca$. It is given that

$$\text{Mass of } ^{40}_{20}Ca = 39.962589\ u$$
$$\text{Mass of } ^{39}_{20}Ca = 38.970691\ u$$
$$\text{Mass of } ^{1}_{0}n = 1.008665\ u$$

(a) 8.15 MeV (b) 10.89 MeV
(c) 13.25 MeV (d) 15.6 MeV

14. A nucleus $^{235}_{92}X$ splits into nuclei, which have mass numbers in the ratio of 2 : 1. Assuming $R = 1.5$ f, find out the ratio of radii of nuclei formed.
(a) 3 : 1 (b) 5 : 4 (c) 2 : 3 (d) 1 : 2

15. The binding energy per nucleus of ^{16}O is 7.79 MeV and that of ^{17}O is 7.75 MeV. Calculate the energy needed to remove a neutron from ^{17}O.
(a) 2.43 MeV (b) 8.46 MeV
(c) 4.23 MeV (d) 5.41 MeV

16. Calculate how long a 60 mg piece of Co wire has to be placed in a flux of 5×10^{13} thermal neutrons per square centimetre per second to make 1 mci (1 millicurie $= 3.7 \times 10^{7}$ dis s^{-1}) of 5.22-Y ^{60}Co. The cross-section for the reaction $^{59}Co\ (x, y)\ ^{60}Co$ is 37 b.
(a) 7.85×10^{2} s (b) 0.22 hr
(c) 7.85×10^{4} s (d) 2.2 hr

17. A thin sample of gold was irradiated in a thermal neutrons flux of 10^{12} neutrons $cm^{2}\ s^{-1}$ for 25.6 hr. In the reaction the nuclide ^{198}Au is produced with a half-life of 64 hr. If the thermal neutron absorption cross section is 98 barns, what is the specific activity of the sample?
(a) 1.96 Ci/g (b) 2.59 Ci/g
(c) 6.42 Ci/g (d) 0.895 Ci/g

18. The approximate mass of uranium that must undergo fission to produce the same energy as 10^{5} kg of coal is (Assume that heat of combustion of coal $= 8000$ cal g^{-1} and one fission of uranium releases 200 MeV)
(a) 235 g (b) 39 g (c) 32 g (d) 35 g

19. Red giant stars, which are coolar than the sun, produce energy by means of the reaction.

$$^{9}_{4}Be + ^{1}_{1}H \longrightarrow ^{6}_{3}Li + ^{4}_{2}He + \text{Energy}$$

The nuclidic mass of ^{9}Be is 9.01504 and of ^{6}Li is 6.0702, energy released in carbon cycle is 30 MeV and in solar-hydrogen cycle is 26.6 MeV).
$(^{4}He = 4.0015;\ ^{1}H = 1.00728)$
The energy released is
(a) lower than that released in carbon cycle
(b) higher than that released in solar helium-hydrogen cycle
(c) equal to the energy released in carbon cycle
(d) data insufficient

20. Calculate the energy released in a positron decay process

$$^{11}_{6}C \longrightarrow ^{11}_{5}B + ^{0}_{+1}\beta$$

$(^{11}C = 11.011443;\ ^{11}B = 11.009305)$
(a) 2.012 MeV (b) 1.984 MeV
(c) 4.282 MeV (d) 2.829 MeV

21. ^{13}N decays by β^{+} emission. The maximum kinetic energy of β^{+} is 1.20 MeV. The nuclidic mass of ^{13}N is
(a) 14.00258 (b) 13.0000
(c) 13.005874 (d) 13.00455

22. A mixture is to be assayed for penicillin. You add 10.4 mg of penicillin of specified activity 0.405 μc mg^{-1}. For this mixture you are able to isolate only 0.3 mg of pure crystalline penicillin and you determine its specific activity to be 0.035 μc mg^{-1}. What was the penicillin content of the original sample?
(a) 115 μg (b) 115 mg (c) 105 mg (d) 126 mg

23. Match the following and choose the correct answer using the codes given below.

	Column I		Column II
A.	$^{12}_{6}C + ^{1}_{1}H \longrightarrow ^{13}_{7}N + ^{0}_{0}\gamma$	1.	Spallation reaction
B.	$^{55}_{26}Fe \longrightarrow ^{55}_{25}Mn + \gamma$	2.	K-electron capture
C.	$^{118}_{50}Sn + ^{1}_{1}H \longrightarrow ^{72}_{31}Ga + 10^{4}_{2}He + 7^{1}_{0}n$	3.	Exo-ergic reaction
D.	$^{14}_{7}N + ^{4}_{2}He + Q \longrightarrow ^{17}_{8}O + ^{1}_{1}H$	4.	Capture reaction

Codes

	A	B	C	D
(a)	4	2	1	3
(b)	2	4	3	1
(c)	2	4	1	3
(d)	4	2	3	1

24. The nucleus and atom can be assumed to be spherical. The radius of the nucleus of mass number A is given by $1.25 \times 10^{-13} \times A^{1/3}$ cm. The atomic radius of atom is 1 Å. If the mass number is 64, what will be the ratio by the atomic volume that is occupied by the nucleus?

(a) 1.25×10^{-13} (b) 6.25×10^{-14}
(c) 2.50×10^{-13} (d) 5.0×10^{-13}

25. Calculate the cross-sectional area of the nucleus of a B atom assuming a spherical shape. Does the neutron have to make a direct hit in order to be captured?
(Cross-section for neutrons 3.99×10^{-21} cm^2.)

(a) 2.9×10^{-25} cm^2, no (b) 2.9×10^{-25} cm^2, yes
(c) 3.0×10^{-13} cm^2, no (d) 3.0×10^{-13} cm^2, yes

26. Consider the fission of $^{236}_{92}U$ represented by overall reaction

$$^{236}_{92}U \longrightarrow {}^{94}_{40}Zr + {}^{140}_{58}Ce + 6\,{}^{0}_{-1}e^- + 2\,{}^{1}_{0}n$$

Calculate the total energy released in the fission reaction. The masses in amu of various nucleides are as follows

$^{236}U = 236.0457$, $^{94}Zr = 93.90610$, $^{140}Ce = 139.9054$, ${}^{0}_{-1}e = 0.00055$, ${}^{1}_{0}n = 1.00867$

(a) 200 MeV (b) 2 MeV
(c) 20 MeV (d) 20 eV

27. An element with mass number 15 and isotopic mass 15.00486 u has mass defect of 0.124043 u. If mass of a proton and a neutron is 1.008145 u and 1.008986 u respectively, find out the atomic number of the element. Mass of the electron can be neglected.

(a) 6 (b) 7
(c) 8 (d) 5

28. A nucleus with $A = 235$ splits into two fragments whose mass numbers are in the ratio of 3 : 2. Find the separation between the fragments at the moment of splitting.

(a) 5.205 (b) 9.751
(c) 13.65 (d) 15.85

29. Select the correct statement (s).

(a) Neutron-proton ratio after a nuclide, $^{238}_{92}U$ loses an α-particle is 1.6
(b) Nuclear fusion reactions are known as thermonuclear reactions
(c) $^{27}_{13}Al$ can be converted to $^{30}_{15}P$ by (α, n) reaction
(d) Larger the value of disintegration constant, greater the stability of radioactive element

30. Two radioactive substance 'X' and 'Y' have disintegration constant in the ratio 2 : 1. If half-life of 'Y' is 4 days then after 12 days starting with equal mole-fraction of each in mixture of 'X' and 'Y'.

(a) mole-fraction of X is larger than that of Y
(b) mole-fraction of 'X' is smaller than that of Y
(c) mole-fraction of X and Y remains unchanged
(d) half-life of X is smaller than that of Y

31. In a nuclear reactor, oxides of which of the following metals are used as fuel material?

(a) Actinium (b) Uranium
(c) Thorium (d) Plutonium

32. Target nucleus 'A' is converted to product nucleus B by (p, n) as : $A(p, n)$ B.
In this case

(a) A and B are isotopes
(b) A and B are isobars
(c) A and B are isotones
(d) B has higher atomic number than that of A

33. Select the correct statement (s).

(a) ^{33}P isused for treatment of leukemia
(b) ^{59}Co cannot be used for treatment of cancer
(c) ^{131}I is used for the treatment of thyroid cancer
(d) Excessive use of radioactive elements cause cancer

34. Consider the following statement (s).

I. 'Carbon-dating' is based on the measurement of activity of ^{14}C.
II. ^{40}K is used to determine age of the objects upto 1 million years old.
III. The uranium-lead method is based on the natural uranium-238 decay series which ends up with the production of stable lead-206.

Select the correct statement (s).

(a) I, II (b) II, III
(c) I, III (d) I, II, III

36. Match the radioisotopes with their applications from the alternates given.

	Column I (Radioisotopes)		Column II (Applications)
A.	Cobalt-60	1.	Leukemia therapy
B.	Potassium-40	2.	Thyroid therapy
C.	Iodine-123	3.	Geological dating
D.	Phosphorus-32	4.	Cancer therapy
E.	Carbon-14	5.	Archaeological dating

Codes

	A	B	C	D	E
(a)	1	2	3	4	5
(b)	5	4	3	2	1
(c)	3	2	1	4	5
(d)	4	3	2	5	1

36. Which of the following are fissible isotope?

I. $^{238}_{92}U$ II. $^{233}_{92}U$ III. $^{239}_{94}Pu$ IV. $^{232}_{90}U$

Select the correct answer from the following.

(a) I and II (b) II and III
(c) I and IV (d) All of these

37. Match Column I and Column II and select the correct answer.

	Column I (Isotope)		Column II (Characteristics)
A.	$^{40}_{20}Ca$	1.	Unstable, α-emitter
B.	$^{133}_{53}I$	2.	Unstable, β-emitter
C.	$^{121}_{53}I$	3.	Unstable, positron emitter
D.	$^{232}_{90}Th$	4.	Stable

Codes

	A	B	C	D
(a)	4	2	3	1
(b)	1	2	3	4
(c)	4	3	2	1
(d)	2	3	4	1

38. Weight of ^{14}C to have radioactivity 1 curie [λ (disintegration constant) $= 4.4\times 10^{-12}\ s^{-1}$] is

(a) 0.9×10^{-4} kg (b) 1.7×10^{-4} kg
(c) 2.0×10^{-4} kg (d) 3.7×10^{-10} kg

39. 1 g of $^{200}_{79}Au$ (T_{50} = 13 days) emits a β-particle forming a stable Hg atom. Hg formed at the end of 52 days is

(a) 0.0625 g (b) 0.7500 g (c) 0.2500 g (d) 0.9375 g

40. Tritium, $^{3}_{1}H$ has a half-life of 12.26 yr. A 5.00 mL sample of tritiated water has an activity of 2.40×10^{9} cpm. How many years will it take for the activity to fall to 3.00×10^{8} cpm?

(a) 6.13 (b) 12.26
(c) 24.52 (d) 36.78

41. Match Column I with Column II and select the correct answer, using the codes given.

	Column I		Column II
A.	^{32}P	1.	Location of tumour in brain
B.	^{23}Na	2.	Location of blood clots and circulatory disorders
C.	^{60}Co	3.	Radiotherapy
D.	^{131}I	4.	Agriculture research

Codes

	A	B	C	D
(a)	1	2	3	4
(b)	4	3	2	1
(c)	4	2	3	1
(d)	4	3	1	2

42. Consider the following nuclear reactions.

I. $^{14}_{7}N + ^{4}_{2}He \longrightarrow ^{17}_{8}O + ^{1}_{1}H$

II. $^{9}_{4}Be + ^{1}_{1}H \longrightarrow ^{6}_{3}Li + ^{4}_{2}He$

III. $^{24}_{12}Mg + ^{4}_{2}He \longrightarrow ^{27}_{14}Si + ^{1}_{0}n$

IV. $^{10}_{5}B + ^{4}_{2}He \longrightarrow ^{13}_{7}N + ^{1}_{0}n$

Examples of induced radioactivity would include reactions

(a) I and II (b) III and IV
(c) I, II and IV (d) I, II, III and IV

43. In nuclear reaction

$$^{7}_{3}Li + ^{1}_{1}H \longrightarrow 2\,^{4}_{2}He$$

The mass loss is nearly 0.02 u. Hence, the energy released (in units of million kcal/mol) in the process is approximately

(a) 50 (b) 120
(c) 220 (d) 430

Assertion & Reason

Codes

(a) Both A and R are true and R is the correct explanation of A.
(b) Both A and R are true but R is not the correct explanation of A.
(c) A is true but R is false.
(d) A is false but R is true.

44. **Assertion (A)** Nuclear-fission is a chain reaction.
Reason (R) Extra electrons formed in the intermediate steps further attack the nuclei.

45. **Assertion (A)** Element formed by the successive emission of 1α-particle and 2β-particles is placed in the same group as the parent element.
Reason (R) α-particle is $[^{4}_{2}He]^{2+}$ while β-particle is $^{0}_{-1}e$.

46. **Assertion (A)** γ-rays produce a greater health hazard to those who work with radioactive element
Reason (R) γ-rays are extremely penetrating high energy electromagnetic radiations.

47. **Assertion (A)** Half-life period of the radioactive disintegration is independent of concentration.
Reason (R) 75% disintegration takes place in a time twice the 50% disintegration.

48. **Assertion (A)** When where is an emission of α-particle, new element is displaced two groups of the parent element.

Reason (R) Atomic mass decreases by 2 units due to α-particle emission.

49. **Assertion (A)** When there is emission of β-particle atomic number increases by one unit.

$$^{14}_{6}C \longrightarrow ^{14}_{7}N + ^{0}_{-1}e$$

Reason (R) Neutron is converted to proton

$$^{1}_{0}n \longrightarrow ^{1}_{1}p + ^{0}_{-1}e$$

Directions (Q. Nos. 50 and 51)

In a series of extraordinary events, a natural nuclear fission reactor operated at the time when the first life forms appeared on Earth. As is often the case in scientific endeavors, humans are not necessarily the innovators but merely the imitators of nature.

50. Nuclear-fission reaction is

(a) chain reaction (b) induced by neutrons
(c) related to Pu-bomb (d) related to U-bomb

51. Select the correct statements

(a) Sr-90 and Cs-137 are the other by-products of nuclear fission released through bomb testing
(b) Sr-90 and Cs-137 can produce cancer of the bone
(c) Sr-90 like Ca is incorporated into bone and thus produces bone-cancer
(d) Cs-137 though radioactive, is rapidly eliminated from the tissue being quite soluble like K

Directions (Q. Nos. 52 and 53)

Radiolysis of water yields H_2 as given below

$$2H_2O \longrightarrow H_2O_2 + H_2$$

In the analysis it is found that 1.7 molecules of H_2 are yielded per 100 eV of energy absorbed. A nuclear power reactor of 200 kW capacity has been installed based on this reaction.

52. What mass of heavy water is required to yield 448 kL of heavy hydrogen at STP?

(a) 996 kg (b) 448 kg
(c) 800 kg (d) 720 kg

53. Volume of H_2 produced per minute in the above reactor is

(a) 140 L (b) 70 L
(c) 35 L (d) 28 L

Directions (Q. Nos. 54 to 56)

To detect bombs that may be smuggled into airplanes, the Federal Aviation Administration (FAA) will soon require all major airports in the United States to install thermal neutron analysers. The thermal neutron analyser will bombard baggage with low-energy neutrons, converting some of the nitrogen-14 nuclei to nitrogen-15, with simultaneous emission of γ -rays. Because nitrogen content is usually high in explosives, detection of a high dosage of γ-rays will suggest that a bomb may be present.

54. Consider the following nuclear reactions

I. $^{14}_{7}N + ^{4}_{2}He \longrightarrow ^{17}_{8}O + ^{1}_{1}H$

II. $^{9}_{4}Be + ^{1}_{1}H \longrightarrow ^{6}_{3}Li + ^{4}_{2}He$

III. $^{24}_{12}Mg + ^{3}_{2}He \longrightarrow ^{27}_{14}Si + ^{1}_{0}n$

IV. $^{10}_{5}B + ^{4}_{2}He \longrightarrow ^{13}_{7}N + ^{1}_{0}n$

Examples of induced radioactivity would include reactions

(a) III and IV (b) I and II
(c) I, III and IV (d) I, II, III and IV

55. The sensitivity of the neutral activtion analysis depends on the

(a) neutron flux available for irradiation
(b) availability of nucleus to absorb a neutron
(c) energy of decay process
(d) All of the above are correct

56. Select the correct statement (s).

(a) Photon or particle is ionised and collected by the positive electrode in a Geiger counter
(b) A scintillation counter contains a phosphor, a substance that emits a flash of light when struck by a photon or particle
(c) Both (a) and (b)
(d) None of the above

Answers

Exercise 1

1. (b)	2. (a)	3. (d)	4. (c)	5. (a)	6. (d)	7. (b)	8. (a)	9. (a)	10. (a)
11. (c)	12. (b)	13. (a)	14. (a)	15. (b)	16. (a)	17. (a)	18. (c)	19. (c)	20. (d)
21. (a)	22. (d)	23. (d)	24. (b)	25. (b)	26. (d)	27. (c)	28. (a)	29. (c)	30. (c)
31. (d)	32. (a)	33. (a)	34. (b)	35. (b)	36. (c)	37. (c)	38. (c)	39. (d)	40. (c)
41. (b)	42. (b)	43. (d)	44. (a)	45. (a)	46. (d)	47. (d)	48. (d)	49. (b)	50. (c)

Exercise 2

1. (b)	2. (d)	3. (c)	4. (d)	5. (d)	6. (b)	7. (a)	8. (c)	9. (d)	10. (b)
11. (a)	12. (b)	13. (d)	14. (b)	15. (c)	16. (d)	17. (a)	18. (b)	19. (a)	20. (b)
21. (c)	22. (c)	23. (a)	24. (a)	25. (a)	26. (a)	27. (b)	28. (c)	29. (a,b,c)	30. (c,d)
31. (b,c,d)	32. (b,d)	33. (b,c,d)	34. (d)	35. (d)	36. (b,c)	37. (a)	38. (c)	39. (d)	40. (d)
41. (c,d)	42. (d)	43. (d)	44. (a)	45. (b)	46. (a)	47. (b)	48. (c)	49. (a)	50. (a,b,c)
51. (a,c,d)	52. (c)	53. (d)	54. (d)	55. (d)	56. (c)				

Hints & Solutions

Exercise 1

1. $$\underset{\text{(III B)}}{{}^{238}_{92}\text{U}} \xrightarrow{-\alpha} \underset{(A)}{{}^{234}_{90}\text{Th}} \xrightarrow{-\alpha} \underset{(B)}{{}^{230}_{88}\text{Ra}} \xrightarrow{-\beta} \underset{(C)}{{}^{230}_{89}\text{Ac}}$$

Th and Ac are also actinoids and all actinoids are placed in IIIB (or 3) group of the Periodic Table.

5. Mass defect is converted into energy as

$$E = mc^2$$

$$= 1\text{ g} \times (3\times10^{10})^2\ (\text{cm s}^{-1})^2$$

$$= 9\times10^{20}\text{ g cm}^2\text{ s}^{-2}$$

$$= 9\times10^{20}\times10^{-3}\times10^{-4}\text{ kg m}^2\text{ s}^{-2}$$

$$= 9\times10^{13}\text{ J} \qquad (1\text{ eV} = 1.9\times10^{-19}\text{ J})$$

$$= \frac{9\times10^{13}}{1.9\times10^{-19}}$$

$$= 4.74\times10^{32}\text{ eV}$$

12. $${}_{83}\text{Bi}^{214} \xrightarrow{-\beta} {}_{84}\text{Po}^{214} \xrightarrow{-\alpha} {}_{82}\text{Pb}^{210}$$

Number of neutrons in Pb = 210 – 82

= 128

13. $$\underset{\substack{\text{(III B)}\\\text{(3 group)}}}{{}^{238}_{92}\text{U}} \xrightarrow{-\alpha} {}^{234}_{90}\text{Th} \xrightarrow{-\alpha} \underset{\substack{\text{(II A)}\\\text{group}}}{{}^{230}_{88}\text{Ra}}$$

19. $$T = \frac{2.303}{\lambda}\log_{10}\left[1+\frac{\text{Pb}^{206}}{\text{U}^{238}}\right]$$

$$\lambda = \frac{0.693}{t_{1/2}} = \frac{0.693}{1.5\times10^9}\text{ yr}^{-1}$$

$$T = \frac{2.303\times1.5\times10^9}{0.693}\log_{10}\left[1+\frac{0.618}{0.238}\right]$$

$$= \frac{2.303\times1.5\times10^9}{0.693}\log_{10}[1+2.6]$$

$$= \frac{2.303\times1.5\times10^9}{0.693}\times0.56$$

$$= 2.7\times10^9\text{ yr}$$

$$\simeq 3\times10^9\text{ yr}$$

41. Binding energy = 931 × mass defect = 931 × 0.030377 MeV

$$= 28.281\text{ MeV } (= 45.31\times10^{-13}\text{ J})$$

Since, the nucleus contains two protons and two neutrons,

$$\text{Binding energy per nucleon} = \frac{45.31\times10^{-13}}{4}\text{ J}$$

$$= 11.327\times10^{-31}\text{ J}$$

42. ${}^{24}_{11}\text{Na}(t_{1/2} = 28.7\text{ h})$ has shorter half-life, so it is biochemically more important. (Shorter half-life ensures attainment of transient equilibrium faster.)

43. Since, the initial level of radiation is 32 times the permissible limit,

$$\frac{N}{N_0} = \frac{1}{32};\ t_{1/2} = 20\text{ days}$$

Disintegration constant, $\lambda = \frac{0.693}{20}\text{ day}^{-1}$

Suppose the laboratory becomes safe for use after t days. Then

$$\frac{N}{N_0} = e^{-\lambda t}$$

$$\frac{1}{32} = \exp\left(\frac{-0.693t}{20}\right)$$

$$\frac{0.693t}{20} = 2.303\log 32 = 2.303\times1.5051$$

$$t = \frac{2.303 \times 1.5051 \times 20}{0.693} = 100 \text{ days}$$

44. Number of atoms of ^{226}Ra in 1 g of ^{226}Ra

$$= \frac{1}{226} = 4.425 \times 10^{-3}$$

At equilibrium $\lambda_{Rn} \times N_{Rn} = \lambda_{Ra} \times N_{Ra}$

or $$\frac{\lambda_{Rn}}{\lambda_{Ra}} = \frac{N_{Ra}}{N_{Rn}}$$

$\therefore$ $$\lambda_{Rn} = \frac{N_{Ra}}{N_{Rn}} \times \lambda_{Ra}$$

$$= \frac{4.425 \times 10^{-3}}{3.125 \times 10^{-8}} \times 1.48 \times 10^{-11} \text{ s}^{-1}$$

$$= 2.095 \times 10^{-6} \text{ s}^{-1}$$

45. 1 barn $= 1.0 \times 10^{-24}$ cm^2

We know that area of a circle, $A = \pi r^2$

Hence, $$r = \sqrt{A/\pi}$$

$$= \sqrt{1.0 \times 10^{-24} \text{ cm}^2 / 3.14}$$

$$= 5.6 \times 10^{-13} \text{ cm}$$

46. Let the proportion of Cl-35 and Cl-37 be 1 : x.

Then the average mass would be $\dfrac{(35 \times 1) + (37 \times x)}{1 + x}$

But this is given to be 35.5

So, $$\frac{35 + 37x}{1 + x} = 35.5$$

$$35 + 37x = 35.5(1 + x)$$

$$35 + 37x = 35.5 + 35.5x$$

$$1.5x = 0.5$$

$$x = \frac{1}{3}$$

Therefore, the ratio is 1 : 1 / 3 or 3 : 1.

47. $_1H^1$ is proton and ^4_2He is α-particle

Radius equation $= R_0 A^{1/3}$

$$\frac{r(^4_2He)}{r(^1_1He)} = \frac{R_0(4)^{1/3}}{R_0(1)^{1/3}}$$

$$= 4^{1/3} = 1.587$$

48. The fission reaction is

$$^{235}_{92}U + ^1_0n \longrightarrow ^{139}_{54}Xe + ^{94}_{38}Sr + 3^1_0n$$

Thus, three neutrons are emitted.

49. 49 years is almost exactly four half-lives ($4 \times 12.3 = 49.2$Y), so we can avoid the log formula. The fractions of the tritium atoms remaining after four half-lives would be $(1/2)^4 = 1/16$. The normal hydrogen atoms are not radioactive and therefore, their number does not change. Thus, the final ratio of tritium to normal hydrogen will be

$$\left(\frac{1}{16}\right)(8 \times 10^{-18}) = 5 \times 10^{-19}$$

50. The activity produced in the element is given by

$$A = N\phi\sigma\left(1 - e^{\frac{0.693}{t_{1/2}}t}\right)$$

where,

N = the number of atoms of the nuclide in the same capable of forming radio isotope in question

ϕ = the neutron flux (*i.e.*, no. of neutrons cm^{-2} s^{-1})

σ = the neutron capture cross section in cm^2 for the given target nuclide.

t = time of irradiation

$t_{1/2}$ = half-life of nuclear species produced

λ = decay constant in s^{-1} of the radioactive product

Exercise 2

2. Disintegration constant, $\lambda = \dfrac{0.693}{t_{1/2}} = \dfrac{0.693}{54.5} = 1.27 \times 10^{-2} \text{ s}^{-1}$

$\because$ $$-\frac{dN}{dt} = \lambda N$$

$(\because 1 \text{ mci} = 3.7 \times 10^7 \text{ disintegration per sec} = -\dfrac{dN}{dt})$

$\therefore$ $$N = \frac{-dN/dt}{\lambda} = \frac{3.7 \times 10^7 \text{ s}^{-1}}{1.27 \times 10^{-2} \text{ s}^{-1}} = 2.91 \times 10^9$$

Mass of ^{220}Rn = Number of Rn nunclei × Mass of one Rn nucleus

$$= \frac{2.91 \times 10^9 \times 220 \text{ g mol}^{-1}}{6.02 \times 10^{23} \text{ mol}^{-1}} = 1.06 \times 10^{-12} \text{ g}$$

$$= 1.06 \times 10^{-15} \text{ kg}$$

3. The approximate equation for the radius is

$$r = R_0 A^{1/3}$$

$$= 1.5 \times 10^{-13} \times (107)^{1/3}$$

$$= 7.12 \times 10^{-13} \text{ cm}$$

Volume of the nucleus,

$$V = \frac{4}{3}\pi r^3 = \frac{4}{3}(7.12 \times 10^{-13} \text{ cm})^3$$

$$= 1.51 \times 10^{-36} \text{ cm}^3$$

Mass of the nucleus,

$$m = \frac{107 \text{ g/mol}}{6.02 \times 10^{23} \text{ atoms/mol}}$$

$$= 1.78 \times 10^{-22} \text{ g}$$

Density of the nucleus,

$$d = \frac{m}{V} = \frac{1.78 \times 10^{-22} \text{ g}}{1.51 \times 10^{-36} \text{ cm}^3} = 1.18 \times 10^{14} \text{ g/cm}^3$$

6. Barrier height $= \dfrac{2(z - 2)e^2}{R_0 A^{1/3}}$

$$= \frac{2 \times 86 \times (4.8 \times 10^{-10})^2}{1.3 \times 10^{-13} \times (226)^{1/3}} \times \frac{1}{1.6 \times 10^{-6} \text{ erg/MeV}}$$

$$= 31 \text{ MeV}$$

7. $^{14}_7N + ^4_2He \longrightarrow ^{17}_8O + ^1_1H$

The change is mass in atomic mass unit (amu) can be found as follows

For reactant particles,

$$^{4}_{2}He = 4.00387$$
$$^{14}_{7}N = 14.00753$$
$$\text{Total} = 18.01140 = m_R$$

For product particles

$$^{17}_{8}O = 17.00450$$
$$^{1}_{1}H = 1.00814$$
$$\text{Total} = 18.01264 = m_p$$
$$\text{Increased mass} = (m_p - m_R)\ u$$
$$= 18.01264 - 18.01140 = 0.00124\ u$$

$\therefore$ Q-value $= 0.000124 \times 931 = 1.15$ MeV

Since, $m_R < m_p$, energy is absorbed in this reaction and hence Q-value is negtive, *i.e.*, Q-value $= -$ 1.156 MeV.

9. $^{16}_{6}C$ has the ratio of neutron to protons farther above the belt of stability. It would emit a $^{0}_{-1}\beta$ particle to set n/p ratio back to the stable range.
The nuclide near the belt of stability are probably stable, those above the belt are beta emitters, those below, positron emitters. Thus, the beta emiters are ^{30}Al and ^{95}Kr, the positrons emitters are ^{195}Hg, ^{8}B and ^{150}Ho.

10. For reactants

$$^{7}_{1}Li = 7.01822$$
$$^{1}H = 1.00814$$
$$\text{Total} = 8.02636 = m_R$$

For products

$$^{7}Be = 7.019465$$
$$^{1}n = 1.008665$$
$$\text{Total} = 8.02813 = m_p$$
$$\text{Increase of mass} = m_p - m_R$$
$$= 8.02813 - 8.02636$$
$$= 0.00177\ u$$
$$Q = 0.00177 \times 931 = 1.64\ \text{MeV}$$

$\because$ $m_R < m_p$, energy is absorbed and hence Q-value $= -1.64$ MeV. This energy is supplied as kinetic energy of the bombarding proton and is part of the acceleration requirement for the proton supplied by the particle acceleration.

11. The reaction is $^{3}_{2}He + ^{1}_{0}n \longrightarrow ^{1}_{1}He + ^{3}_{1}H$

For reactants,

$$^{3}He = x$$
$$^{1}_{0}n = \mathbf{1.00865}$$
$$\text{Total} = x + 1.00865$$

For products,

$$^{1}H = 1.00814$$
$$^{3}H = 3.01605$$
$$\text{Total} = 4.02419$$

Mass defects $\Delta m = 0.761931 = 0.0008164$

Then $\quad (x + 1.00865) - 4.02419 = 0.0008164$

$$x = 3.01634$$

12. The reaction (n, p) is $^{14}_{7}N + ^{1}_{0}n \longrightarrow ^{1}_{1}H + ^{14}_{6}C$

For reactants,

$$^{14}N = 14.00753$$
$$^{1}_{0}n = 1.008665$$
$$\text{Total} = 15.016195 = m_R$$

For products,

$$^{1}H = 1.00814$$
$$^{14}C = 14.00324$$
$$\text{Total} = 15.01138 = m_p$$

Decrease in mass $= m_R - m_p$

$$= 15.016195 - 15.01138 = -\ 0.004815\ u$$
$$Q = 0.00481 \times 931 = 4.482\ \text{MeV}$$

13.
$$^{40}_{20}Ca \longrightarrow ^{39}_{20}Ca + ^{1}_{0}n$$

Suppose M represents the mass of $^{40}_{20}Ca$ and m' that of $^{39}_{20}Ca$. Let E energy is required to remove the least bound neutron from $^{40}_{20}Ca$. From the law of conservation of energy,

$$E = Mc^2 = m'c^2 + m_n c^2$$
$$E = (M^1 + m_n)C^2 - MC^2$$

where, m_n is the mass of neutron

$$= (38.970691\ u + 1.008665)\ 931.5\ \frac{\text{MeV}}{\text{amu}}$$
$$- (39.962589\ u)\ 931.5\ \frac{\text{MeV}}{\text{amu}}$$
$$= \mathbf{15.6\ MeV}$$

14. $r = R_0 A^{1/3}$

Given, $R_0 = 1.5$ f

For the two nuclei formed $r_1 = R_0 A_1^{1/3}$; $r_2 = R_0 A_2^{1/3}$

Since, the mass numbers of nuclei formed are in the ratio of 2 : 1, therefore,

$$r_1 = 1.5\ f \times (2 \times 235/3)^{1/3} = 8.086\ f$$
$$r_2 = 1.5\ f \times (1 \times 235/3)^{1/3} = 6.418\ f$$
$$\Rightarrow \quad \frac{r_1}{r_2} = \frac{8.086}{6.418}$$
$$= 5 : 4$$

15.
$$^{17}O \longrightarrow ^{16}O + ^{1}_{0}n$$

Energy needed to remove a neutron from ^{17}O,

E = energy equivalent of (mass of ^{16}O + mass of neutron − mass of ^{17}O)

$$= (8m_p + 8m_n - 7.97 \times 16) + m_n + 9m_n - 7.75 \times 17)$$

where, $\quad m_p$ = mass of proton, m_n = mass of neutron

$$= (7.75 \times 17 - 7.97 \times 16)\ \text{MeV} = 4.23\ \text{MeV}$$

16. Following the equation

$$R_i = \phi N \sigma_i$$
$$R = 5 \times 10^{13} \times \frac{0.060}{59} \times 6.02 \times 10^{23} \times 37 \times 10^{-24}$$
$$= 1.13 \times 10^{12}\ \text{atom s}^{-1}$$

From equation $\frac{dN}{dt} = \lambda N$ we calculate that 1 mci of ^{60}Co corresponds to 8.87×10^{15} atoms.

Thus, it will take $8.87 \times 10^{15}/1.13 \times 10^{12} = 7.85 \times 10^{3}$ s = 2.2 h to produce 1 mci of ^{60}Co.

17. $A = N\phi\,\sigma\left(1 - e^{\frac{0.693}{t_{1/2}} \times t}\right)$

Suppose 1 g of the gold was irradiated, then

$$N = \frac{1}{198} \times 6.023 \times 10^{23} \text{ atoms}$$

$\phi = 10^{12}$ neutrons cm^{-2} s^{-1}

$\sigma = 98$ barns $= 98 \times 10^{-24}$ cm^2

$t_{1/2} = 64$ hr and $t = 225.6$ hr

Substituting these values, we get

$$A = \frac{6.023 \times 10^{23}}{198} \times 10^{12} \times 98 \times 10^{-24}\left(1 - e^{\frac{0.693}{64} \times 25.6}\right)$$

$= 1.96$ curie/g

18. Mass of coal $= 10^5$ kg $= 10^8$ g

Heat of combustion of coal = 8000 cal g^{-1}

Total heat produced on combustion of 10^8 g coal

$= 8000 \times 10^8 = 8 \times 10^{11}$ cal

$= 8 \times 4.184 \times 10^{11}$ J $= 33.5 \times 10^{11}$ J

Energy released per fission = 200 MeV

$= 200 \times 10^6 \times 1.6 \times 10^{-19}$ J

$= 3.2 \times 10^{-11}$ J

Number of U-235 atoms needed to produce this amount of energy

$$= \frac{33.5 \times 10^{11}}{3.2 \times 10^{-11}} \approx 10^{23} \text{ atoms}$$

$\therefore$ Mass of 10^{23} atoms of U-235 $= \frac{235 \times 10^{23}}{6.02 \times 10^{23}} = 39$ g

19. The total mass of product = (6.01702 + 4.0015) = 10.0185

The total mass of the reactants = (9.01504 + 1.00728)

= 10.0223

Mass difference = 0.0038

Energy released = 0.0038 × 931.5 = 3.5 MeV

This value is much lower than the energy released in carbon cycle or solar helium-hydrogen cycle.

20. Mass defect = Mass of reactants – Mass of product

= 11.011443 – 11.009305 = 0.00213

$\therefore$ Energy released = 0.00213 × 913

= 1.984 MeV (Positron carries no mass)

21. $^{13}_{7}\text{N} \longrightarrow {}^{13}_{6}\text{C} + \beta^+$

Mass defect = [M (nucleus) for ^{13}N]

– [M (nucleus) for ^{13}C] – $M(e)$

$= [M(^{13}\text{N}) - 7M(e)] - [M(^{13}\text{C}) - 6M(e)] - M(e)$

$= M(^{13}\text{N}) - M(^{13}\text{C}) - 2M(e)$

$= M(^{13}\text{N}) - 13.00335 - 2(0.00055)$

$= M(^{13}\text{N}) - 13.00445$

This mass to equal to mass expressions of the kinetic energy of the β^+

$$\frac{1.20 \text{ MeV}}{932 \text{ MeV}} = 0.00129$$

Then $0.00129 = M(^{13}\text{N}) - 13.00455$

or $M(^{13}\text{N}) = 13.00574$

22. Given, mass $m' = 1.0$ mg

Specified activity, $S' = 0.405$ μc mg^{-1}

Specific activity, $S = 0.035$ μc mg^{-1}

Substituting these values in the following equations

$$m = m'\left[\frac{S'}{S} - 1\right] \text{mg}$$

$$= 10.0\left[\frac{0.405}{0.035} - 1\right] \text{mg}$$

$= 105.71$ mg

24. $\frac{\text{Volume of the nucleus}}{\text{Volume of the atom}} = \frac{4/3\,\pi r^3}{4/3\,\pi R^3}$

(where, r and R are the radii of the nucleus and atom respectively.)

$$= \frac{r^3}{R^3} = \frac{[1.25 \times 10^{-13} \times (64)^{1/3} \text{ cm}]^3}{(1 \times 10^{-8} \text{ cm})^3}$$

$= 1.25 \times 10^{-13}$

25. $r = 1.4\,A^{1/3} \times 10^{-13} = 1.4 \times (10)^{1/3} \times 10^{-13}$

$= 1.4 \times 2.15 \times 10^{-13} = 3.0 \times 10^{-13}$ cm

Area $= \pi r^2$

$= 3.14 \times (3.0 \times 10^{-13})^2$

$= 2.9 \times 10^{-25}$ cm^2

Compare to cross-section 3.99×10^{-21} cm^2, in capturing neutrons ^{10}B acts as if it has a much larger cross-section that its geometric cross-section *i.e.*, a direct hit is unnecessary

26. Mass of the reactants = 236.0457

Mass of the product = 93.90610

= 139.9053

0.00055 × 6

1.00867 × 2

235.83204

Mass defect = Mass of the reactants – Mass of the products

= 236.045 – 235.83204 = 0.21296

Energy released = 0.21296 × 931.5 MeV = 199 MeV

27. Let the element be represented as $^{15}_{a}X$, thus, the nucleus of the atom of this element has a proton and $(15 - a)$ neutrons.

Now, M' = mass of protons + mass of $(15 - a)$ neutrons

$= [a \times 1.008145 + (15 - a) \times 1.0089086]$ u

$M = 15.00486$

Mass defect $= M' - M$

or $0.124043 = 1.008145a + 1.008986 \times (15 - a) - 15.00486$

On solving this equation, we get $a = 7$

28. The separation between the fragments at the time of splitting is equal to the sum of their nuclear radii.

Atomic masses of fragments are :

(i) $\frac{235}{(3+2)} \times 3 = 141$ and (ii) $\frac{235}{(3+2)} \times 2 = 94$

Nuclear radius of fragment with $A = 141$

$$r_1 = r_0(141^{1/3})$$
$$= 5.205 r_0$$

Nuclear radius of fragment with $A = 94$

$$r_2 = r_0(94^{1/3})$$
$$= 4.546\, r_0$$

$\therefore$ Separation at the time of splitting $= r_1 + r_2$

$$= r_0(5.205 + 4.546)$$
$$= 9.751 r_0$$

Taking $r_0 = 1.4$ fermi

$$r = 13.65 \text{ fermi}$$

29. (a) $${}_{92}U^{238} \xrightarrow{-\alpha} {}_{90}X^{234}$$

Number of $p^+ = 90$

Number of $n^0 = 234 - 90$

$$\frac{n}{p} = \frac{144}{90} = 1.6$$

(b) Since very high temperature is required for the initiation of nuclear fusion reaction, these are called thermonuclear reactions.

(c) $${}_{13}Al^{27} + {}_{2}He^{4} \longrightarrow {}_{15}P^{30} + {}_{0}n^{1}$$

α-particle   Neutron

30. Mole fraction depends upon the number of moles present, so remains unchanged

$$\frac{\lambda_x}{\lambda_y} = \frac{(t_{1/2})_y}{(t_{1/2})_x} \qquad \left(\because \lambda = \frac{0.693}{t_{1/2}}\right)$$

$$\frac{2}{1} = \frac{4}{(t_{1/2})_x}$$

$(t_{1/2})_x = 2$ *i.e.*, it is smaller than the $t_{1/2}$ of *y*.

32. $${}_{x}^{y}A + {}_{1}H^{1} \longrightarrow {}_{x+1}^{\;\;y}B + {}_{0}n^{1}$$

As *A* and *B* have the same mass number but different atomic number, these are called isobars.

Atomic number of $A = X$ and of $B = X + 1$

So, At. no. of $B >$ At. no. of *A*.

37. $${}_{20}^{40}Ca = \frac{n}{p} = \frac{20}{20} = 1$$

So, it is highly stable.

$${}_{53}^{133}I, \quad \frac{n}{p} = \frac{80}{53} = 1.51$$

So, it is unstable and is a β-emitter because number of protons are higher than the number of neutrons.

$${}_{53}^{121}I, \frac{n}{p} = \frac{68}{53} = 1.3$$

It is also unstable and is a positron emitter.

$${}_{90}^{232}Th, \quad \frac{n}{p} = \frac{142}{90} = 1.58$$

It is also unstable and gain stability by emitting α-particle.

38. 1 curie $= 3.7 \times 10^{10}$ disintegration per second $= -\dfrac{dN}{dt}$

$$\lambda = 4.4 \times 10^{-12}\ s^{-1}$$

$$N = \frac{-dN/dt}{\lambda}$$

$$= \frac{3.7 \times 10^{10}}{4.4 \times 10^{-12}}$$

$$= 8.4 \times 10^{21}$$

$$\text{Mass of } {}^{14}C = \frac{8.4 \times 10^{21} \times 14}{6.02 \times 10^{23}}$$

$$= 1.9 \times 10^{-1}\ g$$

$$= 2.0 \times 10^{-4}\ kg$$

16 Quantum Mechanics or Wave Mechanics

Syllabus

- Basic Principles of Quantum Mechanics : Postulates, Operator Algebra; Exactly Solvable Systems-Particle-in-a-Box, Harmonic Oscillator and the Hydrogen Atom
- Approximate Methods of Quantum Mechanics; Variational Principle; Perturbation Theory up to Second Order in Energy Application

Introduction

The first positive suggestion for a new approach to the problem was made by the German physicist Max Born (1882-1879); his paper appeared in 1924, with the title "Zur Quantummechanik", this being the first time the term **quantum mechanics** had been used. In the spring of 1925 Werner Heisenberg (1901-1976), one of Born's research assistants, developed the first satisfactory system of quantum mechanics, but in a rather obscure form, involving matrix mechanics (about which Heisenberg knew nothing-he had reinvented it!). Born himself initially had difficulty with Heisenberg's treatment, but was soon able to convert it into a more understandable form. Later in 1925 the English physicist Paul Adrein Maurice Dirac (1902-1984) developed a similar system of quantum mechanics, based on Hamilton's methods of classical mechanics, which he transformed by means of postulates into a very versatile system of quantum mechanics.

Shortly afterwards the Austrian physicist Erwin Schrondinger (1887-1961) developed what appeared at first sight to be an entirely new system of quantum mechanics, and which was much easier to understand than the systems of Heisenberg and Dirac. Schrondinger soon proved that his system was mathematically equivalent to the other systems. Since, Schrodinger's method is easier to visualize and apply to chemical problems it is the system often used by chemists.

Wave Theory of Matter

de-Broglie (1924) suggested that any moving material particles has associated wave properties. He conceived the idea from Einstein's earlier suggestion that light quanta have properties of matter, among which one is momentum. From this suggestion, de-Broglie deduced that the laws of optics differ from the laws of ordinary mechanics only because the rest mass of the photon is zero. Hence, de-Broglie reasoned particles with small masses, such as electrons, protons, neutrons, atoms, molecules etc., show dual character. Therefore, he began with the assumption that every kind of material particle which is moving is carried by means of waves that are propagated in space according to laws similar to those obeyed by light waves. The wavelength associated with a moving particle is given by the equation

$$\lambda = \frac{h}{mu} \qquad \ldots(1)$$

where, λ is called de-Broglie's wavelength, h is Planck's constant, m is mass and u is velocity of the particle. This equation is known as **de-Broglie's wave equation.**

If an electron of charge e is accelerated by an applied potential, V (in esu), its kinetic energy is given by Ve. The magnitude of kinetic energy of an electron moving with a velocity u is also given by $\frac{1}{2}mu^2$. Thus, equating the two values, we get,

$$Ve = \frac{1}{2}mu^2 \quad \text{or} \quad u = \sqrt{\frac{2Ve}{m}}$$

On putting the value of v obtained as above in de-Broglie's equation $\left(\lambda = \frac{h}{mu}\right)$, we get

$$\lambda = h\sqrt{\frac{2Ve}{m}} \qquad \ldots(2)$$

Substituting the values of $h = 6.626 \times 10^{-34}$ Js, $e = 1.602 \times 10^{-19}$ C, $m = 9.108 \times 10^{-31}$ kg, for an electron, in the above equation, we get

$$\lambda = \frac{12.263}{\sqrt{V}} \text{ Å}$$

The Wave Equation

In the derivation of the so called wave equation, Schrodinger made use of the de-Broglie relationship between the momentum of a particle and the wavelength of the associated matter waves. This represents the essential postulatory basis of Schrodinger's approach to the new mechanics. In order to follow the development, it is convenient to consider the simplest type of wave motion, namely the vibrations of a stretched string. If ω is the amplitude of vibration at any point whose coordinate is x, at a time t, then the appropriate partial differential equation for the wave motion is

$$\frac{\partial^2 \omega}{\partial x^2} = \frac{1}{u^2} \cdot \frac{\partial^2 \omega}{\partial t^2} \qquad \ldots(3)$$

where, u is the velocity of propagation of the waves, sometimes called the phase velocity. The value of ω depends upon the two variables x and t. This differential equation may be solved by separating the variables. Thus, ω may be expressed in the form

$$\omega = f(x)\, g(t) \qquad \ldots(4)$$

where, $f(x)$ is a function of co-ordinate x only, while $g(t)$ is a function of the time t only. For the motion of the standing waves, *i.e.,* for stationary waves, such as which occurs in a stretched string, it is known that $g(t)$ may be represented by

$$g(t) = A \sin(2\pi v t) \qquad \ldots(5)$$

where, v is the vibrational frequency and A is a constant and is known as the **maximum amplitude.** The equation for ω may then be written as,

$$\omega = f(x)\, A \sin(2\pi v t) \qquad \ldots(6)$$

Differentiating Eq. (6) with respect to t,

$$\frac{\partial \omega}{\partial t} = f(x)\, A \cos(2\pi v t) \cdot 2\pi v$$

Similarly, $$\frac{\partial}{\partial t}\left(\frac{\partial \omega}{\partial t}\right) = \frac{\partial^2 \omega}{\partial t^2} = -f(x)\, A \sin(2\pi v t) \cdot 4\pi^2 v^2$$

or $$\frac{\partial^2 \omega}{\partial t^2} = -4\pi^2 v^2 f(x)\, g(t) \qquad \ldots(7)$$

From Eq. (4), we have

$$\frac{\partial^2 \omega}{\partial x^2} = \frac{\partial^2 f(x)}{\partial x^2} g(t) \qquad \ldots(8)$$

Combination of this equation with Eq. (3) and (7) gives

$$\frac{\partial^2 f(x)}{\partial x^2} = -\frac{4\pi^2 v^2}{u^2} f(x) \qquad \ldots(9)$$

The frequency of the vibrations, v and the velocity, u are related by the expression $u = \lambda v$, where, λ is the corresponding wavelength, hence from Eq. (9), we get

$$\frac{\partial^2 f(x)}{\partial x^2} = -\frac{4\pi^2}{\lambda^2} f(x) \qquad \ldots(10)$$

The above equation determines only the space part and not the time part of the amplitude. It is thus, a suitable starting point for setting up a wave function to describe wave mechanics.

The Schrodinger Wave Equation

The Schrodinger wave equation may be formulated, as shown below, by combining two relationships. One is on the purely mathematical property of waves, namely Eq. (10) and the other is on the wave property of matter as represented by de-Broglie equation, (*i.e.,* $\lambda = h/mu$).

The Eq. (10) represents wave motion in the direction only. It may be extended to movement in three directions represented by the coordinates x, y, z. If $f(x)$ for one coordinate is replaced by $\psi\ (x, y, z)$, which is the amplitude function for three coordinates, Eq. (10) takes the form,

$$\frac{\partial^2\psi}{\partial x^2}+\frac{\partial^2\psi}{\partial y^2}+\frac{\partial^2\psi}{\partial z^2}=-\frac{4\pi^2}{\lambda^2}\psi \quad \ldots(11)$$

where, ψ is a function of Cartesian coordinates (x, y, z). Replacing the symbol ∇^2 (pronounced as del square) for the differential (Laplacian) operator, *i.e.*,

$$\nabla^2=\frac{\partial^2}{\partial x^2}+\frac{\partial^2}{\partial y^2}+\frac{\partial^2}{\partial z^2}$$

we have,

$$\nabla^2\psi=-\frac{4\pi^2}{\lambda^2}\psi \quad \ldots(12)$$

The fundamental postulate of the Schrodinger treatment is that an equation of the type of Eq. (12) may be applied to all particles, including electrons, atoms and photons. Upon introducing de-Broglie relationship, $\lambda = h/mu$ in Eq. (12), we get

$$\nabla^2\psi=-\frac{4\pi^2m^2u^2}{h^2}\psi \quad \ldots(13)$$

where, m is the mass and u is the velocity of the particle. The kinetic energy of the particle, which is the difference between the total energy, E and the potential energy, V is equal to $\frac{1}{2}mu^2$; hence,

$$E-V=\frac{1}{2}mu^2$$

So,

$$u^2=-\frac{2(E-V)}{m}$$

$$\nabla^2\psi=\frac{-8\pi^2m(E-V)\psi}{h^2}$$

or

$$\nabla^2\psi+\frac{8\pi^2m}{h^2}(E-V)\psi=0 \quad \ldots(14)$$

Combination of this result with Eq. (13), gives

or

$$\frac{\partial^2\psi}{\partial x^2}+\frac{\partial^2\psi}{\partial y^2}+\frac{\partial^2\psi}{\partial z^2}+\frac{8\pi^2m}{h^2}(E-V)\psi=0 \quad \ldots(15)$$

These two Eq. (14) and (15) are the wave equations for a single particle. Either of these equations is called as **Schrodinger wave equation** which has been used to solve a number of problems related to atomic and molecular structure.

Eigen Values and Eigen Functions

In connection with the problem of standing waves in a stretched string, it is apparent that the solution $f(x)$ of Eq. (10) can have significance only for certain definite values of the wavelength, λ. These are the wavelengths corresponding to the normal modes of vibration of the string. The values are referred to as **eigen values.** The corresponding functions $f(x)$ which are the solutions of Eq. (10) are called the **eigen functions** or wave-functions. These functions must satisfy certain conditions which in the case of the stretched string are not difficult to understand. In the first place, $f(x)$ must be zero at each end of the string, since the system is fixed at these points and the vibration amplitude will be zero. In the second place, $f(x)$ must be single valued and finite between the limits of x represented by the two ends of the string. In other words, at every point on the vibrating string amplitude has a definite values at any given instant.

Just as the amplitude functions, $f(x)$ in Eq. (10) have significance only for certain definite values of λ, so the functions, ψ are satisfactory solutions of the wave Eq. (14) only for certain values, for eigen values, of the total energy, E. For an atom these eigen values are the equivalent of the discrete set of energy values postulated by the Bohr's theory. The occurrence of definite energy levels of the atom is thus a direct consequence of the wave mechanical treatment. The corresponding values of the function ψ are called as the **wave-functions** or **eigen-functions** of the Schrodinger equation. Like $f(x)$, the eigen functions, ψ of this equation must also satisfy certain conditions; that is they must be single valued, finite and continuous throughout the whole of the configuration space of the system under consideration, that is for all possible values of the coordinates x, y and z including infinity.

Physical significance of the wave-function

The only dependent variable in the Schrodinger equation is the wave amplitude of wave-function, ψ and it depends on the coordinates of the particle. In some cases, it may turn out to be a complex function of the form, $\psi = u + iv$, where, u and v are the functions of the coordinates and $i=\sqrt{-1}$. The complex conjugate of ψ is $\psi^* = u - iv$. Their product, $\psi\psi^* = u^2 + v^2$, and if ψ is real $\psi\psi^*$ is identical with ψ^2. Neither ψ nor ψ^* has any physical significance but $\psi\psi^*$ (or ψ^2, when ψ is real) has. In dealing with all forms of wave motion, such as light waves, sound waves, electrical fields or matter waves, the square of the wave amplitude at any point is interpreted as the intensity of the effect at that point. So the value of ψ^2 (ψ^2 can be used instead of $\psi\psi^*$, since most of the wave functions in atomic or molecular structure problems contain real terms only) at any point around the nucleus gives a measure of the electronic charge density at that point. This interpretation was originally suggested by Schrodinger. According to this view, the electron is to be regarded as smeared out forming a cloud of electricity, the density of which varies from point to point around the nucleus.

A statistical interpretation of the electron wave function was proposed by Max Born in 1926. This interpretation has been widely adopted since it has many advantages. According to this view, the electron is still considered as a particle, and the value of ψ^2 at any point is taken to represent the probability of finding the electron at the point at a given instant. It should be noted that consideration of the electron as a particle necessitates this statistical interpretation, for although a particle can only be in one position at a given instant, the Heisenberg uncertainty principle tells us that this position can never be precisely known. So, what we can do is only to state the probability of the electron being found at a given point in space. Thus, ψ^2 is interpreted as giving a direct measure of this probability. Consequently, the greater the wave amplitude, the greater is the probability of finding the electron at that point at a given instant or if a time interval is considered, the longer, on an average is the total time the electron spends at that point.

Schrodinger's Wave Equation for H-atom in Cartesian and Polar Coordinates

In H-atom, a single electron having charge $-e$ moves around the nucleus with charge equal to $+e$. The potential energy (V) of the electron in H-atom is equal to $\frac{(-e)\times(+e)}{r} = -\frac{e^2}{r}$.

1. **Wave equation in Cartesian coordinates (x, y, z)** Putting $V = -\frac{e^2}{r}$ in wave equation, we get the following form :

$$\left(\frac{\partial^2}{\partial x^2} + \frac{\partial^2}{\partial y^2} + \frac{\partial^2}{\partial z^2}\right)\psi + \frac{8\pi^2 m}{h^2}\left(E + \frac{e^2}{r}\right)\psi = 0 \quad \ldots(16)$$

2. **Wave equation in polar coordinates (r, θ, ϕ)**

   When Cartesian coordinates (x, y and z) in Eq. (16) are changed into polar coordinates (r, θ, ϕ) with the help of $z = r\cos\theta$, $y = r\sin\theta\sin\phi$ and $x = r\sin\theta\cos\phi$, we get the following form of Schrodinger's wave equation.

$$\left[\frac{\partial}{\partial r}\left(r^2\frac{\partial}{\partial r}\right) + \frac{1}{\sin\theta}\frac{\partial}{\partial\theta}\left(\sin\theta - \frac{\partial}{\partial\theta}\right) + \frac{1}{\sin^2\theta}\frac{\partial^2}{\partial\phi^2}\right]\psi + \frac{8\pi^2 m}{h^2}\left(E + \frac{e^2}{r}\right)\psi = 0$$

The Schrodinger equation can have several solutions, not all of which correspond to any physical or chemical reality. Such solutions or wave functions are, therefore, not acceptable. The acceptable wave functions must satisfy the following conditions :

1. The wave function ψ is single-valued, *i.e.*., for each value of the variables x, y, z, there is only one value of ψ. Suppose one of the variables is an angle θ. Then, single-valuedness of ψ requires that

   $\psi(\theta) = \psi(\theta + 2n\pi)$ where, n is an integer.

2. The wave function ψ and its first derivative with respect to its variables must be **continuous,** ***i.e.,*** there must not be any sudden change in ψ when its variables are changed.

3. For bound states, ψ must vanish at infinity, If ψ is a complex function, then $\psi^*\psi$ must vanish at infinity (ψ^* is the complex conjugate of ψ).

   Satisfying the above conditions, the Schrodinger equation yields **significant solutions for certain definite value of the total *E*.** These values are called eigen values. Thus, an eigen value equation and we can write it as

$$\hat{\mathbf{H}}\psi_n = E_n\psi_n \quad (n = 1, 2, 3\ldots) \quad \ldots(17)$$

   where, n is the quantum number. We express Eq. 17 saying that ψ_n are the eigen functions and E_n are the eigen values. For an atom, these eigen values correspond to discrete sets of energy values postulated by Bohr.

4. The eigen functions are said to form an orthonormal set if

$$\int \psi_n^*\psi_m\, d\tau = \begin{bmatrix} 0, & n \neq m \\ 1, & n = m \end{bmatrix} = \delta_{nm}$$

(called the Kronecker delta) ...(18)

They are orthogonal when

$$\int \psi_n^*\psi_m\, d\tau = 0 \quad \ldots(19)$$

are **normalised** when

$$\int \psi_n^*\psi_m\, d\tau = 1 \quad \ldots(20)$$

It is possible to identify regions of space around the nucleus where, there is **high probability** of locating an electron associated with a specific energy. This space is called an atomic orbital. An **atomic orbital,** thus, represents a definite region in three-dimensional space around the nucleus where, there is high probability of finding an electron of a specific energy *E*.

Statistical interpretation of ψ

It was Max Born (1882-1970), the German physicist, who gave statistical interpretation of the function ψ, naming it the **probability amplitude function.** Born won the 1954 Physics Nobel Prize for this interpretation. If $\psi(x)$ is the wave function of a particle, then, the probability of finding the particle within the range from x to $x + dx$ is given by

$$P(x)dx = \psi^* \psi \, dx = |\psi|^2 \, dx \qquad \ldots(21)$$

where, ψ^* denotes the complex conjugate of ψ. Note that $P(x)dx$ is the probability and $P(x)$ is the probability density.

We know that in the case of light waves, the intensity of the electromagnetic field is proportional to the square of the amplitude of the wave at that point. Likewise, in the case of a particle, the probability of its being found between the region x and $(x + dx)$ is proportional to the square of the wave function, *i.e.,* the square of the probability amplitude function at that point. Since, the total probability of locating the particle must be unity, we have

$$\int_{-\infty}^{\infty} P(x)\, dx = \int_{-\infty}^{\infty} \psi^* \psi \, dx = \int_{-\infty}^{\infty} |\psi|^2 \, dx = 1 \ldots(22)$$

For motion in the three-dimensions,

$$\int P(\vec{\mathbf{r}})\, dr^3 = \int |\psi(\vec{\mathbf{r}})|^2 \, dr^3 = 1 \qquad \ldots(23)$$

where, the integration is carried over the three-dimensional volume element $dr^3 = dx\, dy\, dz$.

It may be noted that in Bohr's theory, the electron associated with a definite energy is considered to be located at a definite distance from the nucleus. In wave mechanics, the equation for calculating the exact energy of the electron has been derived but there is a considerable uncertainty with regard to its exact location. This is in conformity with the Heisenberg uncertainty principle.

Further Mathematical Consideration of Schrodinger Wave Equation

1. Normalisation

The Schrodinger equation is a homogeneous differential equation whose solution gives a value for ψ, but when ψ is multiplied by a constant factor it would give the same differential equation. It is therefore, necessary to find some conditions which will indicate which constant factor is to be used.

As the electron must be found somewhere, one can say that the probability of finding an electron in the whole of space considered in a particular problem is unity. This may mathematically be written as

$$\int |\psi^2| \, d\Gamma = 1 \qquad \ldots(24)$$

where, Γ^- is the volume of the whole space. The integral determines by what constant ψ must be multiplied for the solution of a particular problem. This constant is known as the normalisation constant. An eigen function when has been completely evaluated in this manner is said to have been **'normalised'.**

The amplitude in the wave function is determined by using this normalisation condition. For ψ to represent a wave packet (*i.e.,* a group of waves) the above condition for normalisation should be satisfied. The numerical coefficient in ψ, the amplitude factor should be independent of time.

2. Orthogonality

Let us suppose two wave functions ψ_p and ψ_q which correspond to two values of the energy E_p and E_q. If these wave functions are separate solutions of the Schrodinger's equation, then $\int \psi_p \psi_q dT^- = 0$ and the wave functions ψ_p, ψ_q are said to be orthogonal. This property will be proved for one-dimension only.

Let us consider two Schrodinger equations which are written in one dimension only (for the motion of a particle in a straight line).

$$\frac{d^2\psi_p}{dx^2} + \frac{8\pi^2 m}{h^2}(E_p - V_p)\psi_p = 0$$

$$\frac{d^2\psi_q}{dx^2} + \frac{8\pi^2 m}{h^2}(E_q - V_q)\psi_q = 0$$

Multiplying the first equation by ψ_q and the second by ψ_p, and on subtracting we get

$$\frac{d}{dx}\left(\psi_q \frac{d\psi_p}{dx} - \psi_p \frac{d\psi_q}{dx}\right) + \frac{8\pi^2 m}{h^2}$$

$$(E_p - E_q - V_p + V_q)\psi_p\psi_q = 0$$

Integrating with respect to x over the whole of space from $(-\infty$ to $+\infty)$. Since, ψ and V are zero at infinity, the first term vanishes and second term becomes

$$\because \quad \frac{8\pi^2}{h^2}(E_p - E_q)\int_{-\infty}^{+\infty} \psi_p \psi_q \, dx = 0$$

$$E_p \neq E_q$$

$$\therefore \quad \int_{-\infty}^{+\infty} \psi_p \psi_q \, dx = 0 \qquad \ldots(25)$$

It is possible to make a line combination of orthogonal functions. (A proof extended to three dimensions is beyond the scope of this book).

3. Degeneracy

We have already proved that for every wave function ψ, there must be a corresponding energy value E, *i.e.,* for every eigen function there will be one eigen value. It means that each energy state must have a wave function which will be the characteristic of the system. If two different ψ's have the same value of energy then these two states (of different ψ's) are called **degenerate states.**

4. Forbidden transitions

When certain particular eigen functions are multiplied together, they give a zero product, *i.e.,* $\psi_p \psi_q = 0$. (This should not be confused with orthogonality). In such a case, the simultaneous execution of the two corresponding vibrations by the electron will not cause the emission of radiations. Such transitions are known as **forbidden transitions.** Due to these radiations, certain lines are missed in the spectral lines. In the presence of a strong electric or magnetic field, these lines may actually appear. In such a situation, the eigen functions are distorted by the strong fields, and so the product $\psi_p \psi_q$ is no longer zero.

5. Observables

On a physical system several observations and measurements can be made. These are called **observables.** Many of the observables are not the properties of a system but are characteristic of the measuring system which can be carried out on it. The measurement of an observable on a system gives a number.

The state of a physical system is represented by a function of certain variables, like space coordinates; time etc. From the rules of the quantum theory, information can be obtained from this function. The variables may be chosen in several ways. The function $\psi(r_1, r_2 \ldots r_n, t)$ is one which may represent a state, where the total number of variables is equal to the number of degrees of freedom of the system. At a given time, the state becomes a function of the space coordinates of the system only.

The quantum theory will be useful in solving the different problems in measuring an observable if two restrictions are made in selecting the function of the state.

1. **The functions should possess an integrable square** It should not give a value which is infinity.

$$\int \psi\psi^* dV < \infty \qquad \ldots(26)$$

Here, ψ is the function and ψ^* is its complex conjugate. dV is the volume element of the configuration space.

2. **The function ψ should be single valued** It ψ is a function of space coordinates, it should have a single value at a given point in space. For example, if ψ is a function of angle θ and if it is to be single valued it is necessary that the same value should be obtained if we add or subtract a multiple of 2π radians to angle θ. Therefore,

$$\psi(\theta) = \psi(\theta \pm 2n\pi) \qquad \ldots(27)$$

where, $n = 1, 2, 3 \ldots$ an integer.

6. Well defined functions (Well behaved functions)

In quantum mechanics, a function is well behaved or well defined if :

(i) It is single valued at all points.
(ii) It is finite at all points.
(iii) It is continuos at boundaries (Continuity means that the first derivative is the same as calculate from two sides).
(iv) It has definite parity.

7. Parity of wave function

The Schrondinger equation is

$$\hat{\mathbf{H}}\psi = E\psi \qquad \ldots(28)$$

where, $\hat{\mathbf{H}}$ = KE operator + PE operator

For one particle system in a central field

$$\hat{\mathbf{H}} = -\frac{h^2}{2m}\left(\frac{\partial^2}{\partial x^2} + \frac{\partial^2}{\partial y^2} + \frac{\partial^2}{\partial z^2}\right) + V(r)$$

where, $\qquad r = \sqrt{x^2 + y^2 + z^2}$

$\hat{\mathbf{H}}$ is symmetric in x, y and z, *i.e.,* if we replace x by $-x$, y by $-y$ and z by $-z$, then $\hat{\mathbf{H}}$ remains unchanged.

The wave function ψ is a function of x, y, z *i.e.,*

$$\psi = \psi(x, y, z)$$

If we replace x by $-x$, y by $-y$ and z by $-z$ in (28), then we have,

$$\hat{\mathbf{H}}\psi(-x, -y, -z) = E\psi(-x, -y, -z) \qquad \ldots(29)$$

From Eqs. (28) and (29), we see that both $\psi(x, y, z)$ and $\psi(-x, -y, -z)$ are wave functions of $\hat{\mathbf{H}}$ with same energy for non-degenerate forms.

So, $\psi(-x, -y, -z)$ is not different from $\psi(x, y, z)$, but it will be some multiple of $\psi(x, y, z)$, *i.e.,*

$$\psi(-x, -y, -z) = k\psi(x, y, z) \qquad \ldots(30)$$

In this equation replacing x by $-x$ and y by $-y$ and z by $-z$, then

$$\psi(x, y, z) = k\psi(-x, -y, -z) \qquad \ldots(31)$$

Solving (30) and (31), *i.e.*, putting $\psi(-x, -y, -x)$ from (30) in (31), we get

$$\psi(x, y, z) = k^2\psi(x, y, z) \quad \ldots(32)$$

or $$k^2 = 1$$

$$k = +-1$$

Putting these values of k in 30), we get

$$\psi(-x, -y, -z) = \pm\psi(x, y, z)$$

If $\psi(-x, -y, -z) = \psi(x, y, z)$, then we say that the wave function has **even parity.**

If $\psi(-x, -y, -z) = -\psi(x, y, z)$, then we say that wave function has **odd parity.**

8. Stationary state

A state is said to be in a stationary state, if the function determining the state does not include time. So, the function $\psi(x, y, z)$ is a stationary state, whereas function $\psi(x, y, z, t)$ is not.

9. Operators

An operator is a mathematical instruction or procedure to be carried out on a function.

It is written in the form,

(Operator) (function) = (Another function)

The function on which the operation is carried out is called **operand.** The left hand side of the above equation does not mean that the function is multiplied. with the operator. Evidently, an operator written alone has no significance.

A few examples are given below :

(i) $\frac{d}{dx}(x^4) = 4x^3$. Here $\frac{d}{dx}$ which stands for differentiation with respect to x is the operator. x^4 is the operand and $4x^3$ is the result of the operation.

(ii) $\int x^2\, dx = x^3/3 + C$. Here, $\int (\,)\, dx$ which stands for integration with respect to x is the operator, x^2 is the operand and $\frac{x^3}{3} + C$ is the result of the operation.

Similarly, taking the square or taking the square root or multiplication by a constant k etc., are different operations which can be carried out on any function (*i.e.*, the operand).

In case the symbol used for the operator is not self-explanatory, a suitably letter or some symbol for the operator is used with the symbol (Δ) over it.

Algebra of operator The operators follow certain rules similar to those of algebra. A few of these are given below :

(a) **Addition and subtraction of operators** If $\hat{\mathbf{A}}$ and $\hat{\mathbf{B}}$ are two different operators and f is the operand, then

$$(\hat{\mathbf{A}} + \hat{\mathbf{B}})f = \hat{\mathbf{A}}f + \hat{\mathbf{B}}f \quad \ldots(33)$$

and $$(\hat{\mathbf{A}} - \hat{\mathbf{B}})f = \hat{\mathbf{A}}f - \hat{\mathbf{B}}f \quad \ldots(34)$$

(b) **Multiplication of operators** If $\hat{\mathbf{A}}$ and $\hat{\mathbf{B}}$ are two different operators and f is the operand, then the expression $\hat{\mathbf{A}}\hat{\mathbf{B}}\,f$ means that first f is operated by the operator $\hat{\mathbf{B}}$ to get the result, say f', and then f' is operand by the operator $\hat{\mathbf{A}}$ to get the final result (say f''), *i.e.*, $\hat{\mathbf{A}}\hat{\mathbf{B}}\,f$ means that $\hat{\mathbf{B}}f = f'$ and then $\hat{\mathbf{A}}f' = f''$, so that we can write.,

$$\hat{\mathbf{A}}\hat{\mathbf{B}}\,f = f'' \quad \ldots(35)$$

Therefore, the order of using the operators is from right to left as written in the given equation.

If the same operation is to be done a number of times in succession, it is written by the power of the operator. For example,

If the same operation is to be done a number of times in succession, it is written by the power of the operator. For example,

$\hat{\mathbf{A}}\hat{\mathbf{A}}f$ is written as $\hat{\mathbf{A}}^2 f$

i.e., $$\hat{\mathbf{A}}\hat{\mathbf{A}}f - \hat{\mathbf{A}}^2 f \quad \ldots(36)$$

It may be noted that usually

$$\hat{\mathbf{A}}\hat{\mathbf{B}}f \neq \hat{\mathbf{B}}\hat{\mathbf{A}}f \quad \ldots(37)$$

This may be shown by the following example :

Suppose, $$\hat{\mathbf{A}} = x, \hat{\mathbf{B}} = \frac{d}{dx}$$

and $$f = f(x) = x^2$$

Then $$\hat{\mathbf{A}}\hat{\mathbf{B}}\,f = x\frac{d}{dx}(x^2) = x(2x) = 2x^2$$

$$\hat{\mathbf{B}}\hat{\mathbf{A}}\,f = x\frac{d}{dx}x(x^2) = \frac{d}{dx}x^3 = 3x^3$$

If, however, it is found that

$$\hat{\mathbf{A}}\hat{\mathbf{B}}\,f = \hat{\mathbf{B}}\hat{\mathbf{A}}f \quad \ldots(38)$$

i.e., the change of order of the operators gives the same result, the operators are said to commute. Therefore, this result is unlike algebra where, $xy = yx$.

(c) **Linear operators** An operator $\hat{\mathbf{A}}$ is said to be linear if for the two functions f and g are related as

$$\hat{\mathbf{A}}(f + g) = \hat{\mathbf{A}}f + \hat{\mathbf{A}}g$$

i.e., the operator on the sum of two functions gives the same result as the sum of two results obtained by carrying out the same operation on the two functions separately. For example, d/dx, d^2/dx^2 etc., are linear operators whereas 'taking the square', 'taking the square root' etc., are not-linear.

10. Laplacian operator

This is a very common operator used in quantum mechanics. It is represented by ∇^2 (pronounced as deal squared). It is mathematically defined as

$$\nabla^2 = \frac{\partial^2}{\partial x^2} + \frac{\partial^2}{\partial y^2} + \frac{\partial^2}{\partial z^2}$$

Thus, in terms of Laplacian operator the Schrodinger wave equation, *viz.,*

$$\frac{\partial^2 \psi}{\partial x^2} + \frac{\partial^2 \psi}{\partial y^2} + \frac{\partial^2 \psi}{\partial z^2} + \frac{8\pi^2 m\,(E - V)}{h^2}\psi = 0$$

may be written as

$$\nabla^2 \psi = -\frac{8\pi^2 m\,(E - V)}{h^2}\psi = 0$$

11. Hamiltonian operator

Schrodinger wave equation as written above may be rewritten as

$$\nabla^2 \psi = -\frac{8\pi^2 m\,(E - V)}{h^2}\psi$$

or $$\nabla^2 \psi = -\frac{8\pi^2 m}{h^2}(E\psi - V\psi)$$

or $$-\frac{h^2}{8\pi^2 m}\nabla^2 \psi + V\psi = E\psi$$

or $$\left(-\frac{h^2}{8\pi^2 m}\nabla^2 + V\right)\psi = E\psi \qquad \ldots(39)$$

This equation means that the operation $\left(-\frac{h^2}{8\pi^2 m}\nabla^2 + V\right)$ carried out on the function ψ, is equal to the total energy multiplied by the function ψ. The operation $\left(-\frac{h^2}{8\pi^2 m}\nabla^2 + V\right)$ is called **Hamiltonian operator** and is represented by $\hat{\mathbf{H}}$. So,

$$\hat{\mathbf{H}} = -\frac{h^2}{8\pi^2 m}\nabla^2 + V$$

Thus, Eq. (39) can be written as

$$\hat{\mathbf{H}}\psi = E\psi$$

This is another short-hand form of writing the Schrodinger wave equation.

Postulates of Quantum Mechanics

Postulate I

The physical state of a particle is described as fully as possible by an appropriate wave function $\psi(x, y, z, t)$.

Postulate II

The probability of finding the particle in the space within r and $r + dr$ is given by $\psi^* \psi\, dr$

where, $\psi(r)$ is the function and $\psi^*(r)$ is its complex conjugate.

The probability of finding the particle in a finite interval between r_1 and r_2 is given by

$$\text{Probability} = \int_{r_1}^{r_2} \psi^* \psi\, dr$$

Where there is only one particle which is present somewhere, the total probability of the particle at some place is given by,

$$\text{Probability} = \int_{-\infty}^{+\infty} \psi^* \psi\, dr = 1$$

Postulate III

The only possible values which a measurement of the observable whose operator is P, can give are the eigen values p_n of the equation.

$$P\psi = p_n \psi_n$$

This is true provided $\int \psi_n^* \psi_n\, dV < \infty$ and that ψ_n is single-valued.

As an example, consider the measurable value of linear momentum of the particle. If the particle is somewhere on the X-axis (*i.e.,* only one-dimensional) we have $p_x \to i\frac{\hbar}{2\pi}\frac{\partial}{\partial x}$ as the operator used. So, equation becomes, $-i\frac{\hbar}{2\pi}\frac{\partial \psi_n}{\partial x} = p_{x_n}\psi_n$

Here, p_{x_n} is the measurable value of the momentum. Similarly, for other components p_{y_n} and p_{z_n} are obtained using $\frac{\partial \psi_n}{\partial y}$ and $\frac{\partial \psi_n}{\partial z}$.

If we want to find the total momentum, the equation is

$$-i\frac{\hbar}{2\pi}\nabla\psi_n = p_n \psi_n$$

ψ_n is called an eigen function and p_n is an eigen value of the linear momentum.

The total momentum of the practice will be p_n. So,

$$p_n^2 = p_{x_n}^2 + p_{y_n}^2 + p_{z_n}^2$$
$$= p_{x_n} p_{x_n} + p_{y_n} p_{y_n} + p_{z_n} p_{z_n}$$

Postulate IV

The classical mechanical concepts such as position, velocity, linear momentum, angular momentum, energy and time occupy a central position in quantum mechanics. As in classical mechanics, they are regarded as the measurable properties of any system. However, the behaviour of these properties is quite different from that predicted by classical mechanics. In addition, certain new properties such as spin and symmetry with respect to the interchange of identical particles also appear. These properties do not appear in classical mechanics. So, all these variables are called as the **dynamical variables.**

Every dynamical variable can be assigned a linear operator Operators will be considered as latent observable leading to measurable quantities only when operate on the state function ψ, so that, we have the following table.

Since, all the physically measurable quantities are real, only linear and Hamiltonian operators are permissible in quantum mechanics. The operators in quantum mechanics do not necessarily commute. When they do commute, both the variables associated with them can be measured simultaneously and accurately. There will be no uncertainty in either of them.

If the two operators do not commute, the variables associated with them cannot be measured simultaneously and accurately. If one of them can be measured accurately, the other one cannot be measured simultaneously with accuracy.

The possible state function, ψ of a system is given by the solution of the differential equation, $\hat{\mathbf{H}}\psi = -\frac{\hbar}{i} \cdot \frac{\partial}{\partial t}\psi$, where, $\hat{\mathbf{H}}$ is the energy operator, the Hamiltonian operator for the system and $\hbar = \frac{h}{2\pi}$. This is the time dependent Schrodinger equation. One can expand this as :

$$\left[-\frac{\hbar}{2m}\nabla^2 + V(x, y, z, t)\right]\psi = -\frac{\hbar}{i}\frac{\partial}{\partial t}\cdot\psi$$

Postulate V

If A is the operator equivalent of an observable quantity, this will be the total energy and a is the precise value of that property in a given state of the system, then it is postulated that operation by A on the function ψ which is supposed to be suitable for this operator, is equivalent to multiplying ψ by the quantity a. Thus,

$$A\psi = a\psi$$

For the given state, known as the eigen state of the system, ψ is the eigen function for the operator A, and a is the corresponding eigen value. It may be mentioned that in certain cases two or more eigen functions correspond to the same eigen value and belong to the same eigen state. The state is then said to be **degenerate.** The operator A is also known as **Hermitial operator.**

Postulate VI

When a great many measurements of any dynamical variable are made on an assembly of system whose state function is ψ, the average value obtained is given by $< a >$.

$$< a > = \frac{\int_{-\infty}^{+\infty} \psi^* A\psi \, d\tau}{\int_{-\infty}^{+\infty} \psi^* \psi \, d\tau}$$

when, ψ is not normalized.

where, $d\tau$ represents an element in the configuration space. We have

$$< a > = \int_{-\infty}^{+\infty} \psi^* A\psi \, d\tau$$

when, ψ is normalised.

Here, A is the operator corresponding to the dynamical variable and integration is carried out over all the space.

Postulate VII

If ψ_i and ψ_j represent two different eigen functions both of which are satisfactory solutions of the wave equation for a given system, then these functions will be normalized if,

$$\int \psi_i \psi_i^* d\tau = 1$$

and

$$\int \psi_j \psi_j^* d\tau = 1$$

Further, if the two eigen functions have the property that

$$\int \psi_i \psi_j^* = 0$$

or

$$\int \psi_i^* \psi_j = 0$$

they are said to be **mutually orthogonal.**

Postulate VIII

If the two operators commute, then there exists a set of functions which are simultaneously eigen functions of both the operators.

Under such conditions, the operators yield real observable simultaneously. For example, $\hat{\mathbf{H}}$ and M_z commute and hence they have the same eigen function. Therefore, the observables or the eigen values associated with them can be measured simultaneously.

$$\therefore \qquad [\hat{\mathbf{H}}, M_z] = 0$$

$$\hat{\mathbf{H}}\psi = E\psi$$

and
$$M_z\psi = m\hbar\psi$$

$$\left[\frac{\hbar^2}{2m}\nabla^2 + V\right]\psi = E\psi$$

In spherical polar coordinates,

$$\therefore \qquad M_z \Rightarrow \frac{\hbar}{i}\frac{\partial}{\partial\phi}$$

Any two non-commuting operators cannot yield discrete or real observable simultaneously as they do not have the same eigen functions. For example, x and P_x, are non-commuting operators, so that

$$[x, P_x] = xP_x - P_x x = \frac{\hbar}{i} \neq 0$$

Table 16.1 **Wave Mechanical Operators for Evaluating Various Classical Variables**

Classical variable	Quantum mechanical operator	Operator	Operation
x	$\hat{\mathbf{x}}$	x	Multiplication by x.
p_x	$\hat{\mathbf{p}}_x$	$-i\hbar\frac{d}{\partial x}$	Taking derivative with respect to x and multiplying by $-i\hbar$
x^2	$\hat{\mathbf{x}}^2$	x^2	Multiplication by x^2
p_x^2	$\hat{\mathbf{p}}_x^2$	$-\hbar^2\frac{\partial^2}{\partial x^2}$	Taking second derivative with respect to x and multiplying by $-\hbar^2$
t	$\hat{\mathbf{t}}$		Multiplying by t
E	$\hat{\mathbf{E}}$	$i\hbar\frac{\partial}{\partial t}$	Taking derivative with respect to t and multiplying by $i\hbar$.

Operators in Quantum Mechanics

The concept of operators is very important in wave mechanics. We have already listed a few operators in the sixth postulate of quantum mechanics. Here, we shall briefly deal with the algebra of operators. If $\hat{\mathbf{A}}$ and $\hat{\mathbf{B}}$ are two operators and f is a function upon which they operate, then

$$(\hat{\mathbf{A}} + \hat{\mathbf{B}})f = \hat{\mathbf{A}}f + \hat{\mathbf{B}}f \qquad \ldots(40)$$

and
$$(\hat{\mathbf{A}} - \hat{\mathbf{B}})f = \hat{\mathbf{A}}f - \hat{\mathbf{B}}f \qquad \ldots(41)$$

Thus, we can generate new operators $\hat{\mathbf{A}} + \hat{\mathbf{B}}$ and $\hat{\mathbf{A}} - \hat{\mathbf{B}}$ by adding and subtracting $\hat{\mathbf{A}}$ and $\hat{\mathbf{B}}$. Also,

$$\hat{\mathbf{A}} + \hat{\mathbf{B}} = \hat{\mathbf{B}} + \hat{\mathbf{A}} \qquad \ldots(42)$$

$$\hat{\mathbf{A}} - \hat{\mathbf{B}} = -\hat{\mathbf{B}} + \hat{\mathbf{A}} \qquad \ldots(43)$$

The multiplication of operators can be carried out by doing successive operations with two or more operators on a function. If $\hat{\mathbf{A}}$ and $\hat{\mathbf{B}}$ are two operators and f is their **operand,** then we can obtain the quantity $\hat{\mathbf{A}}\hat{\mathbf{B}}f$ as follows : We first operate on f with $\hat{\mathbf{B}}$ to obtain f', that is, $\hat{\mathbf{B}}f = f'$. Then, f' is operated upon by $\hat{\mathbf{A}}$ to obtain f'', that is, $\hat{\mathbf{A}}f' = f''$. Thus, we have

$$\hat{\mathbf{A}}\hat{\mathbf{B}}f = f'' \qquad \ldots(44)$$

It should be remembered that the order of application of operators is always from left to right as they are written. Application of the same operator several times in succession is written with a power. Thus, we have

$$\hat{\mathbf{A}}\hat{\mathbf{A}}f = \hat{\mathbf{A}}^2 f \qquad \ldots(45)$$

Commutation of Operators

The algebra of operators should be distinguished from the algebra of ordinary numbers. If a and b are two numbers, then we know that

$$a \times b = b \times a \qquad \ldots(46)$$

However, if $\hat{\mathbf{A}}$ and $\hat{\mathbf{B}}$ are two operators, then their product $\hat{\mathbf{A}}\,\hat{\mathbf{B}}$ may or may not be equal to $\hat{\mathbf{B}}\,\hat{\mathbf{A}}$. If $\hat{\mathbf{A}}\,\hat{\mathbf{B}} = \hat{\mathbf{B}}\,\hat{\mathbf{A}}$, then the **commutator** of the two operators is defined as

$$[\hat{\mathbf{A}}, \hat{\mathbf{B}}] = \hat{\mathbf{A}}\,\hat{\mathbf{B}} - \hat{\mathbf{B}}\,\hat{\mathbf{A}} = 0 \qquad \ldots(47)$$

Example 1. *Show that*

(a) $[\hat{\mathbf{A}}, \hat{\mathbf{B}}] = -[\hat{\mathbf{B}}, \hat{\mathbf{A}}]$

(b) $[\hat{\mathbf{A}}^2, \hat{\mathbf{B}}] = \hat{\mathbf{A}}[\hat{\mathbf{A}}, \hat{\mathbf{B}}] + [\mathbf{A}, \hat{\mathbf{B}}]\hat{\mathbf{A}}$.

Sol. (a) $[\hat{\mathbf{A}}, \hat{\mathbf{B}}] = (\hat{\mathbf{A}}\,\hat{\mathbf{B}} - \hat{\mathbf{B}}\hat{\mathbf{A}}) = -(\hat{\mathbf{B}}\,\hat{\mathbf{A}} - \hat{\mathbf{A}}\,\hat{\mathbf{B}}) = [\hat{\mathbf{B}}, \hat{\mathbf{A}}]$

(b) R.H.S. $= \hat{\mathbf{A}}[\hat{\mathbf{A}}, \hat{\mathbf{B}}] + [\hat{\mathbf{A}}, \hat{\mathbf{B}}]\hat{\mathbf{A}}$

$= \hat{\mathbf{A}}(\hat{\mathbf{A}}\hat{\mathbf{B}} - \hat{\mathbf{B}}\hat{\mathbf{A}}) + (\hat{\mathbf{A}}\hat{\mathbf{B}} - \hat{\mathbf{B}}\hat{\mathbf{A}})\hat{\mathbf{A}}$

$= \hat{\mathbf{A}}^2\hat{\mathbf{B}} - \hat{\mathbf{A}}\hat{\mathbf{B}}\hat{\mathbf{A}} + \hat{\mathbf{A}}\hat{\mathbf{B}}\hat{\mathbf{A}} - \hat{\mathbf{B}}\hat{\mathbf{A}}^2$

$= \hat{\mathbf{A}}^2\hat{\mathbf{B}} - \hat{\mathbf{B}}\hat{\mathbf{A}}^2 = [\hat{\mathbf{A}}^2, \hat{\mathbf{B}}] =$ L.H.S.

Expressions for Operators

Expressions for operators can be obtained by operating with the operators on an operand and removing the operand at the end of the operation.

Example 2. *Find expressions for the following operators :*

(a) $\left(\frac{d}{dx}+x\right)^2$ (b) $\left(\frac{d}{dx}+x\right)\left(\frac{d}{dx}-x\right)$

(c) $\left(\frac{d}{dx}-x\right)\left(\frac{d}{dx}+x\right)$.

Sol. Let $\psi(x)$ be the operand.

(a)
$$\left(\frac{d}{dx}+x\right)^2\psi(x)=\left(\frac{d}{dx}+x\right)\left(\frac{d}{dx}+x\right)\psi(x)$$
$$=\left(\frac{d}{dx}+x\right)\left(\frac{d\psi}{dx}+x\psi\right)$$
$$=\frac{d^2\psi}{dx^2}+2x\frac{d\psi}{dx}+x^2\psi+\psi$$
$$=\left(\frac{d^2}{dx^2}+2x\frac{d}{dx}+x^2+1\right)\psi$$

Removing ψ from both sides of this equation, we have
$$\left(\frac{d}{dx}+x\right)^2=\frac{d^2}{dx^2}+2x\frac{d}{dx}+x^2+1$$

(b)
$$\left(\frac{d}{dx}+x\right)\left(\frac{d}{dx}-x\right)\psi(x)=\left(\frac{d}{dx}+x\right)\left(\frac{d\psi}{dx}-x\psi\right)$$
$$=\frac{d^2\psi}{dx^2}-\frac{d}{dx}(x\psi)+x\frac{d\psi}{dx}-x^2\psi$$
$$=\frac{d^2\psi}{dx^2}-\left(x\frac{d\psi}{dx}+\psi\frac{dx}{dx}\right)+x\frac{d\psi}{dx}-x^2\psi$$
$$=\frac{d^2\psi}{dx^2}-\psi-x^2\psi=\left(\frac{d^2}{dx^2}-1-x^2\right)\psi$$
$$(\because\ dx/dx=1)$$

Removing ψ from both sides of the equation, we have
$$\left(\frac{d}{dx}+x\right)\left(\frac{d}{dx}-x\right)=\frac{d^2}{dx^2}-1-x^2$$

(c)
$$\left(\frac{d}{dx}-x\right)\left(\frac{d}{dx}+x\right)\psi(x)=\left(\frac{d}{dx}-x\right)\left(\frac{d\psi}{dx}+x\psi\right)$$
$$=\frac{d^2\psi}{dx^2}+\frac{d}{dx}(x\,\psi)-x\frac{d\psi}{dx}-x^2\psi$$
$$=\frac{d^2\psi}{dx^2}+\left(x\frac{d\psi}{dx}+\psi\frac{dx}{dx}\right)-x\frac{d\psi}{dx}-x^2\psi$$
$$=\frac{d^2\psi}{dx^2}+\psi-x^2\psi=\left(\frac{d^2}{dx^2}+1-x^2\right)\psi$$

Removing ψ from both sides of the equation, we have,
$$\left(\frac{d}{dx}-x\right)\left(\frac{d}{dx}+x\right)=\frac{d^2}{dx^2}+1-x^2.$$

Example 3. *Show that ehe commutator* $\left[x,\frac{d}{dx}\right]=-1.$

Sol. By definition, $\left[x,\frac{d}{dx}\right]=x\frac{d}{dx}-\frac{d}{dx}x$

Let $\psi(x)$ be the operand, then operating on $\psi(x)$ by the right-hand side expression, we have
$$\left(x\frac{d}{dx}-\frac{d}{dx}x\right)\psi=x\frac{d\psi}{dx}-\frac{d}{dx}(x\psi)$$
$$=x\frac{d\psi}{dx}-x\frac{d\psi}{dx}-\psi\frac{dx}{dx}$$
$$=-\psi \qquad (\because\ dx/dx=1)$$

Removing ψ from both sides of this equation, we have
$$\left[x,\frac{d}{dx}\right]=-1.$$

Quantum Mechanics of Simple Systems

Here, we shall consider the simple systems for which the Schrodinger equation can be solved exactly. Considerations of these systems provided an insight into the methods of quantum mechanics and give results which are useful in the discussions of many problems of physical the chemical interests. Let us consider the following two systems.

(A) Systems with constant potential energy, *e.g.*,

1. Free particle.
2. Particle in a one-dimensional box.
3. Particle in a three-dimensional box.
4. The rigid rotator (or rotor).

(B) Systems for which potential energy is not constant, *e.g.*,

5. One-dimensional simple harmonic oscillator (SHO).
6. The hydrogen atom.

Systems where Potential Energy is Constant

1. Particle in a one-dimensional box

This is the simplest quantum mechanical problem. Here, a particle of mass *m* is confined to move in a one-dimensional box of length *a*, having infinitely high walls (Fig. 16.1).

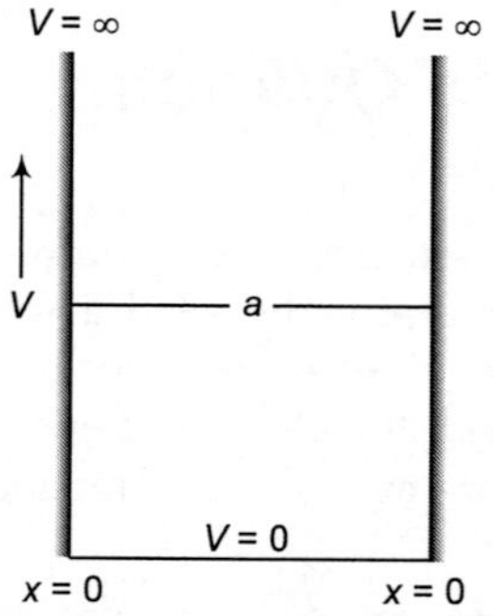

Fig. 16.1 Particle in a one-dimensional box.

It is assumed, for the sake of simplificy, that of potential energy of the particle is zero everywhere inside the box, that is

$$V(x) = 0 \quad \ldots(48)$$

Thus, inside the box the Schrodinger equation, *viz.*,

$$\left[-\frac{\hbar^2}{2m}(d^2/dx^2) + V(x)\right]\psi(x) = E\psi(x) \quad \ldots(49)$$

takes the form $-\frac{\hbar^2}{2m}(d^2\psi/dx^2) = E\,\psi(x)$ ...(50)

Our problem is to solve this equation for energy E and the wave-function $\psi(x)$.

Mathematically, Eq. 50 may be rewritten as

$$\frac{d^2\psi}{dx^2} + (2mE/\hbar^2)\,\psi = 0 \quad \ldots(51)$$

or as

$$\frac{d^2\psi}{dx^2} + k^2\psi = 0 \quad \ldots(52)$$

where, $k^2\ (= 2mE/\hbar^2)$ is a constant, independent of x.

Eq. 52 is an ordinary second-order differential equation which has solution of the form

$$\psi = A\cos kx + B\sin kx \quad \ldots(53)$$

where, A and B are constants. Before we proceed further, it should be pointed out that **outside** the box where, $V(x) = \infty$, the Schrodinger Eq. (49) is

$$\left[-\frac{\hbar^2}{2m}(d^2/dx^2) + \infty\right]\psi\,(x) = E\psi\,(x) \quad \ldots(54)$$

or

$$\frac{d^2\psi}{dx^2} + \frac{2m}{\hbar^2}(E - \infty)\,\psi = 0 \quad \ldots(55)$$

The equation is satisfied if ψ is zero everywhere **outside** the box. This is another way of saying that the particle cannot be found outside the box; it is confined within the box. This implies that ψ must be zero at the walls of the box, *i.e.*, at $x = 0$ and at $x = a$. Since, the postulate of quantum mechanics requires that ψ must be a continuous function of x, we are forced to conclude that in Eq. 53, A must be zero. Thus, the solution of Eq. 52 is of the form

$$\psi = B\sin kx \quad \ldots(56)$$

Since, $\psi = 0$ at $x = 0$ and at $x = a$, we have

$$B\sin ka = 0$$

or $\sin ka = 0$

or $ka = n\pi$

so that $k = n\pi/a$ ...(57)

where, $n\ (= 0, 1, 2, 3, 4 \ldots)$ is the quantum number. Hence, the allowed solutions of Eq. 52 are

$$\psi \equiv \psi_n = B\sin(n\pi x/a);\ (n = 1, 2, 3 \ldots) \quad \ldots(58)$$

$$\therefore \quad \Delta E = (2n + 1)\,E_0 = [2(3\times 10^{27}) + 1]$$

$$\frac{5.48\times 10^{-68}}{(0.001\text{ kg})\,(0.1\text{ m})^2}\text{J} = 3.3\times 10^{-35}\text{ J}$$

This implies that $E_1 = 5\times 10^{-8}$ J and

$$E_2 = 5\times 10^{-8}\text{ J} + 3.3\times 10^{-35}\text{ J} = 5\times 10^{-8}\text{ J}$$

Since, E_1 and E_2 are practically the same, it is not possible to observe quantization in the energy levels of macroscopic systems like the ball.

Example 4. *Calculate the expectation (average) value of the energy of a particle of mass m confined to move in a one-dimensional box of width a and infinite height with potential energy zero inside the box. The normalized wave function of the particle is* $\psi_n(x) = (2/a)^{1/2}$ $\sin(n\pi x/a)$ *where,* $n = 1, 2, 3 \ldots$

Sol. Total energy E of a particle is the sum of kinetic energy T and potential energy V. Since, the potential energy inside the box is zero. *i.e.*, $V = 0$, hence,

$$E = T$$

$$T = \frac{1}{2}mu^2 = m^2u_x^2/2m = p_x^2/2m$$

As shown in Table 16.1, the operator of p_x^2 is $-\hbar^2\,\partial^2/\partial x^2$, hence,

$$\hat{\mathbf{H}} = -(\hbar^2/2m)\,d^2/dx^2$$

$$\therefore \langle E\rangle = \int_0^a \psi_n(x)\,\hat{\mathbf{H}}\,\psi_n(x)\,dx$$

$$= -\frac{\hbar^2}{2m}\int_0^a \left(\frac{2}{a}\right)^{1/2}\sin\left(\frac{n\pi x}{a}\right)\frac{d^2}{dx^2}\left[\left(\frac{2}{a}\right)^{1/2}\sin\left(\frac{n\pi x}{a}\right)\right]dx$$

$$= -\frac{\hbar^2}{ma}\int_0^a \sin\left(\frac{n\pi x}{a}\right)\left[\frac{-n^2\pi^2}{a^2}\sin\left(\frac{n\pi x}{a}\right)\right]dx$$

$$= \frac{n^2h^2}{4ma^3}\int_0^a \sin^2\left(\frac{n\pi x}{a}\right)dx \qquad (\because\ \hbar = h/2\pi)$$

$$= \frac{n^2h^2}{4ma^3}\int_0^a \frac{1-\cos(2n\pi x/a)}{2}\,dx$$

$$= \frac{n^2h^2}{8ma^3}\left\{[x]_0^a - \frac{a}{2\pi n}\left[\sin\left(\frac{2\pi x}{a}\right)\right]_0^a\right\}$$

$$= \frac{n^2h^2}{8ma^3}(a - 0) = n^2h^2/8ma^2.$$

Notice that this is the same value as has been obtained by solving the Schrodinger equation for this system from first principles.

Example 5. *Verify that the wave functions of a particle in a one-dimensional box of width a and infinite height are orthogonal.*

Sol. We know that the wave functions of this system are

$$\psi_n(x) = \left(\frac{2}{a}\right)^{1/2} \sin\left(\frac{n\pi x}{a}\right); n = 1, 2, 3 \ldots \text{ (cf. Eq. 67)}$$

The orthogonality condition requires that

$$\int_0^a \psi_m^*(x)\,\psi_n(x)\,dx = 0 \qquad \text{(cf. Eq. 19)}$$

Since, the wave functions are real,

$$\psi_m^*(x) = \psi_m(x) = (2/a)^{1/2} \sin(m\pi x/a)$$

Hence, $\int_0^a \psi_m^* \psi_n\,dx = \int_0^a \left(\frac{2}{a}\right)^{1/2} \sin\left(\frac{m\pi x}{a}\right)\left(\frac{2}{a}\right)^{1/2} \sin n\pi x\,dx$

$$= \left(\frac{2}{a}\right) \int_0^a \sin\left(\frac{m\pi x}{a}\right) \sin\left(\frac{n\pi x}{a}\right) dx$$

We know from Trigonometry that

$$\sin A \sin B = \frac{1}{2}[\cos(A - B) - \cos(A + B)]$$

Notice that the $n = 0$ value of the quantum number, though allowed, is not acceptable since it implies that the wave function ψ is zero everywhere inside the box. This is not correct since the particle is taken to be inside the box, to begin with.

From Eqs. 52 and 63, we have

$$(2mE/h^2) = n^2\pi^2/a^2 \qquad \ldots(59)$$

or

$$E \equiv E_n = n^2\hbar^2\pi^2/2ma^2$$

$$= n^2 h^2/8ma^2$$

$$n = 1, 2, 3 \ldots (\hbar = h/2\pi) \qquad \ldots(60)$$

Eq. 60 gives the expression for the energy of the particle in a one-dimensional box. It should be committed to the memory. Since, energy depends upon the quantum number n, which can have an integral value, the energy levels of the particle in the box are quantized.

Before we discuss Eq. 60 further, let us determine the coefficient B in the wave function given by Eq. 58. This can be done by normalizing the wave function.

Normalisation of ψ

Since, the total probability of finding the particle within the box is 1, therefore, according to Born's interpretation of the wave function, the normalisation of ψ requires that

$$\int_0^a \psi_n^2\,dx = 1 \qquad \ldots(61)$$

Substituting the value of ψ_n from Eq. 58, we have

$$\int_0^a (B \sin n\pi x/a)^2\,dx = 1 \qquad \ldots(62)$$

or

$$B^2 \int_0^a \sin^2(*n\pi x/a)\,dx = 1 \qquad \ldots(63)$$

Since, $\sin^2\theta = \frac{1}{2}(1 - \cos 2\theta)$, hence from Eqs. 61 and 63, we have

$$\int_0^a \psi_n^2\,dx = B^2\left[\frac{1}{2}\int_0^a dx - \frac{1}{2}\int_0^a \cos\left(\frac{2n\pi x}{a}\right) dx\right] \ldots(64)$$

$$= B^2 [a/2 - 0] = 1 \qquad \ldots(65)$$

Hence, $B = (2/a)^{1/2}$ ...(66)

Thus, the normalized wave functions for the particle in a one-domensional box are

$$\psi_n(x) = (2/a)^{1/2} \sin(n\pi x/a);$$

$$n = 1, 2, 3 \ldots \qquad \ldots(67)$$

A few normalized wave functions and the corresponding probability functions for a particle in a one-dimensional box are given in Fig. 16.2.

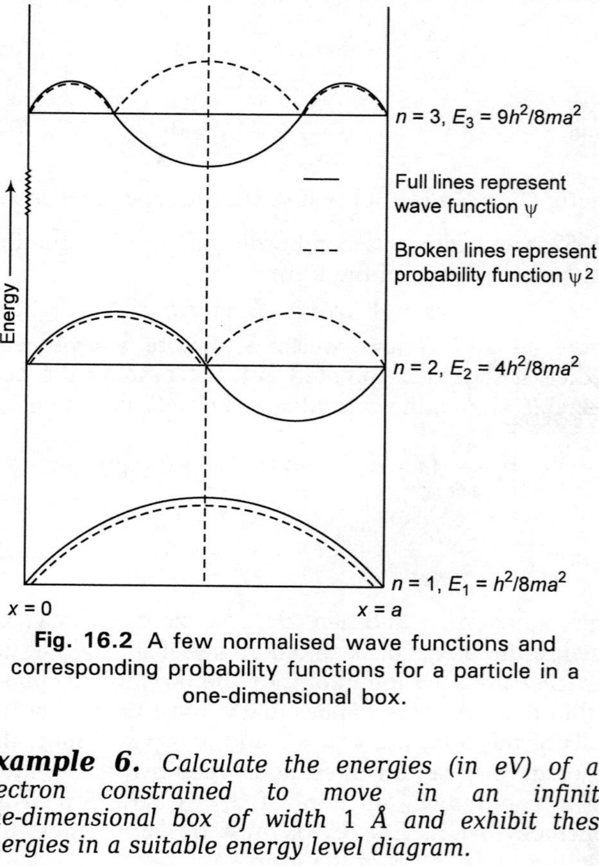

Fig. 16.2 A few normalised wave functions and corresponding probability functions for a particle in a one-dimensional box.

Example 6. *Calculate the energies (in eV) of an electron constrained to move in an infinite one-dimensional box of width 1 Å and exhibit these energies in a suitable energy level diagram.*

Sol. From Eq. 60, $E_n = n^2h^2/8ma^2$

Substituting the data in Eq. (39), we have

$$E_n = \frac{n^2 (6.626 \times 10^{-34}\text{ J s})^2}{(8)(9.109 \times 10^{-31}\text{ kg})(10^{-10}\text{ m})^2 (1.602 \times 10^{-19}\text{ J/eV})}$$

$$= 37.6n^2\text{ eV} \approx 38n^2\text{ eV}$$

Energies of the electron corresponding to different values of n are as follows :

$$n = 1,\quad E_1 = 38\text{ eV}$$

$$n = 2, \quad E_2 = 38\,(2)^2 = 152\text{ eV}$$

$$n = 3, \quad E_3 = 38\,(3)^2 = 342\text{ eV}$$

$$n = 4, \quad E_4 = 38\,(4)^2 = 608\text{ eV}$$

and so on.

The above energies are exhibited in the form of an energy level diagram in Fig. 16.3. Notice that the energy levels are sufficiently far apart; their quantization is thus distinctly evident.

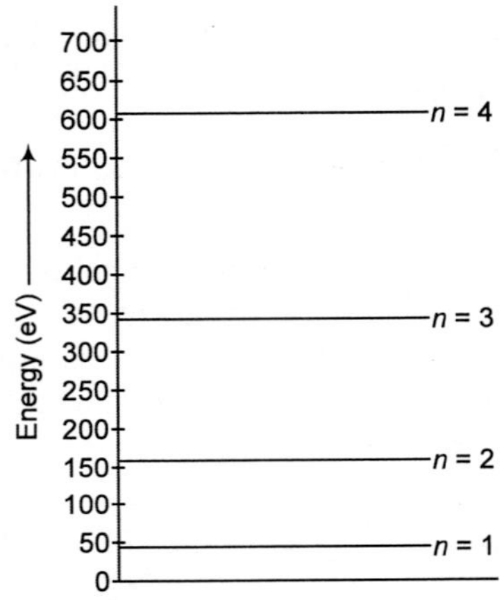

Fig. 16.3 Energies of an electron moving in a one-dimensional box.

Example 7. *A ball of mass* 1 g, *confined to a one-dimensional box of length* 0.1 m, *moves with a velocity of* 0.01 m s^{-1}. *Calculate the quantum number n. Is it possible to observe the quantization of energy levels of the ball?*

Sol. The kinetic energy of the ball equals the total energy since the potential energy within the box is zero. In the ground state, $n = 1$.

$$\therefore \quad E_1 = \frac{1}{2} m u_x^2 = \frac{1}{2} (0.001\text{ kg})\,(0.01\text{ ms}^{-1})^2$$

$$= 5 \times 10^{-8}\text{ J} \qquad (\text{J} = \text{kg m}^2\text{s}^{-2})$$

Since, from Eq. (60), $E_n = n^2h^2/8ma^2$

Hence, $\quad n^2 = 8ma^2E_n/h^2$

$$\therefore \quad n = [8ma^2E_n/h^2]^{1/2}$$

$$= (8mE_n)^{1/2}\,a/h$$

Substituting the various values, we have

$$n = [8\,(0.001\text{ kg})\,(5 \times 10^{-8}\text{ J})]^{1/2}$$

$$\left[\frac{0.1\text{ m}}{6.626 \times 10^{-34}\text{ J s}}\right] = 3 \times 10^{27}$$

Notice the fantastically high value of the quantum number n.

To see if the energy levels of the ball are quantized, let us calculate the difference in the successive energy levels, say, those characterized by the quantum numbers n and $n + 1$.

$$\Delta E = E_{n+1} - E_n = [(n+1)^2 - n^2]\,h^2/(8ma)^2 = (2n+1)\,E_0$$

where, $\quad E_0 = h^2/8ma^2 = (6.626 \times 10^{-34})^2/8ma^2$

$$= 5.48 \times 10^{-68}/ma^2\text{J}$$

Since, $\quad n = 3 \times 10^{27}, n + 1 = 3 \times 10^{27} + 1 = 3 \times 10^{27}$

(We can safely neglect 1 in comparison with 3×10^{27})

Hence, using this result.

$$\int_0^a \psi_m^* \psi_n dx = \frac{1}{a} \int_0^a \left(\cos (m-n) \frac{\pi x}{a} - \cos (m+n) \frac{\pi x}{a}\right) dx$$

which, on integration, yields

$$\int_0^a \psi_m^* \psi_n dx = \frac{1}{a} \left\{ \frac{a}{(m-n)\,\pi} \sin \left[(m-n) \frac{\pi x}{a}\right]_0^a - \frac{a}{(m+n)\,\pi} \sin \left[(m+n)\,\pi \frac{x}{a}\right]_0^a \right\} = 0$$

Hence the result. $\qquad$ ($\because$ m and n are integers).

Example 8. *Calculate the average value of* x, x^2, p_x *and* p_x^2 *for a particle in a one-dimensional box of width a and infinite height and verify that* $\Delta p_x \Delta x = h/2$, *where,* Δx *is the uncertainty in the positional coordinate x and* Δp_x *is the uncertainty in the linear momentum along the x-coordinate.*

Sol. We know that for the given system, the normalized wave functions are

$$\psi_n(x) = \left(\frac{2}{a}\right)^{1/2} \sin \left(\frac{n\pi x}{a}\right);\; n = 1, 2, 3 \ldots$$

and $\quad < x > = \int_0^a \psi_n\, \hat{\mathbf{x}}\, \psi_n dx \quad \left(\because\; < x > = \int_{-\infty}^{\infty} \psi^* \hat{\mathbf{x}}\, \psi\, dx\right)$

$$= \int_0^a \left(\frac{2}{a}\right)^{1/2} \sin \left(\frac{n\pi x}{a}\right) x \left(\frac{2}{a}\right)^{1/2} \sin \left(\frac{n\pi x}{a}\right) dx$$

$$= \frac{2}{a} \int_0^a x \sin^2 \left(\frac{n\pi x}{a}\right) dx$$

$$= \frac{2}{a} \int_0^a x \left[\frac{1 - \cos (2n\pi x/a)}{2}\right] dx$$

$$= (2/a)\,(a^2/4) = a/2$$

$$< x^2 > = \frac{2}{a} \int_0^a x^2 \sin^2 \left(\frac{n\pi x}{a}\right) dx$$

$$= \frac{2}{a} \int_0^a x^2 \left[\frac{1 - \cos (2n\pi x/a)}{2}\right] dx$$

$$= \frac{1}{a} \left[\int_0^a x^2 dx - \int_0^a x^2 \cos \left(\frac{2n\pi x}{a}\right) dx\right]$$

$$= \frac{1}{a} \left[\frac{a^3}{3} - \frac{a^3}{2n^2\pi^2}\right] = \frac{a^2}{3} - \frac{a^2}{2n^2\pi^2}$$

Since, the operator of p_x is $-i\hbar\, d/dx$ (Table 16.1), hence,

$$< p_x > = \int_0^a \psi_n \left(-i\hbar \frac{d}{dx}\right) \psi_n dx = -i\hbar \int_0^a \left(\frac{2}{a}\right)^{1/2}$$

$$\sin \left(\frac{n\pi x}{a}\right) \frac{d}{dx} \left[\left(\frac{2}{a}\right)^{1/2} \sin \left(\frac{n\pi x}{a}\right)\right] dx$$

$$= -(i\hbar)\left(\frac{2}{a}\right)\left(\frac{n\pi}{a}\right)\int_0^a \sin\left(\frac{n\pi x}{a}\right)\cos\left(\frac{n\pi x}{a}\right)dx = 0$$

$$< p_x^2 > = \int_0^a \psi_n\left[\left(-i\hbar\frac{d}{dx}\right)^2\right]\psi_n dx = -\hbar^2\int_0^a\left(\frac{2}{a}\right)^{1/2}$$

$$\sin\left(\frac{n\pi x}{a}\right)\frac{d^2}{ax^2}\left[\left(\frac{2}{a}\right)^{1/2}\sin\left(\frac{n\pi x}{a}\right)\right]dx$$

$$= \hbar^2\left(\frac{n\pi}{a}\right)^2\int_0^a\left(\frac{2}{a}\right)\sin^2\left(\frac{n\pi x}{a}\right)dx \quad ...(68)$$

The integral on RHS of Eq. (68) equals E_n, the energy of the particle so that

$$< p_x^2 > = \hbar^2 (n\pi/a)^2\ E_n = n^2h^2/4a^2 = 2mE_n$$

where, $E_n = n^2h^2/8ma^2$

We know that $(\Delta p_x)^2 = < p_x^2 > - < p_x >^2$

$$= < p_x^2 > = n^2h^2/4a^2 \qquad (\because < p_x >^2 = 0)$$

Again, $(\Delta x)^2 = < x^2 > - < x >^2$

$$= \frac{a^2}{3} - \frac{a^2}{2n^2\pi^2} - \left(\frac{a}{2}\right)^2$$

$$= \frac{a^2}{12} - \frac{a^2}{2n^2\pi^2}$$

Hence, $(\Delta p_x)^2 (\Delta x)^2 = \left(\frac{n^2h^2}{4a^2}\right)\left(\frac{a^2}{12} - \frac{a^2}{2n^2\pi^2}\right)$

$$= \frac{n^2h^2}{4}\left(\frac{1}{12} - \frac{1}{2n^2\pi^2}\right)$$

$$= \frac{h^2}{4}\left(\frac{n^2\pi^2}{3} - 2\right)$$

$\therefore$ $\Delta p\Delta x = (h/2)\,[(n^2\pi^2/3) - 2]^{1/2}$

or $\Delta p_x\,\Delta x > h/2$

($\because n^2\pi^2/3$ is always greater than 2)

The reader will recognize that here we have verified the Heisenberg uncertainty principle for the particle in a one-dimensional box.

Example 9. *What will happen if the walls of the one-dimensional box are suddenly removed?*

Sol. When the walls for the particle in a one-dimensional box are suddenly removed, it becomes free to move without any restriction on the value of the potential energy. If the potential energy is taken to be zero, then the solution of Schrodinger Eq. (55) is given by Eq. 57. However, the arbitrary constants A or B and k in Eq. 57 can have any values which may be assigned to them. Thus, the energy eigen values given by $E = k^2/h^2/8\pi^2$; m are not quantized. Hence, we conclude that a freely moving particle (which may be an electron) without any resriction has *continuous* energy spectrum.

Example 10. *What is the zero-point energy of a particle in a one-dimensional box of infinite height? Is the occurrence of zero-point energy in accordance with the Heisenberg uncertainty principle?*

Sol. Since, $E_n = n^2h^2/8ma^2$, the energy corresponding to $n = 1$, *viz.*, $E_1 = h^2/8ma^2$ is called the zero-point energy (Z.P.E.) of the particle. Since, Z.P.E. is finite (and not equal to zero) it means that the particle inside the box is not at rest even at 0 K. This being so, the position of the particle cannot be precisely known. Again, since only the expectation (and not exact) value of the kinetic energy $<\frac{1}{2}mu^2>$ is known, the linear momentum of the particle is also not precisely known. Thus, occurrence of Z.P.E. implies uncertainty in the position, Δx and also uncertainty in the x-component of the linear momentum Δp_x. This means that the occurrence of Z.P.E. is in keeping with the Heisenberg uncertainty principle.

2. Particle in a three-dimensional cubical box

Let us now consider the motion of a particle of mass m confined to a three-dimensional cubical box with edges of length a and volume equal to a^3. The potential is zero within the box and is infinite outside the box and at its boundaries. The time-independent Schrodinger equation for the particle is

$$\left[-\frac{\hbar^2}{2m}\left(\frac{\partial^2}{\partial x^2} + \frac{\partial}{\partial y^2} + \frac{\partial^2}{\partial z^2}\right)\right]\psi\,(x, y, z)$$

$$= E\psi\,(x, y, z) \quad ...(69)$$

Eq. 69 may be rewritten as

$$\frac{\partial^2\psi}{\partial x^2} + \frac{\partial^2\psi}{\partial y^2} + \frac{\partial^2\psi}{\partial z^2} + \left(\frac{2mE}{\hbar^2}\right)\psi = 0 \quad ...(70)$$

Assuming that the wave function ψ is a product of three parts which separately depend on x, y and z, we have

$$\psi(x, y, z) = X(x)\,Y(y)\,Z(z) \quad ...(71)$$

Hence,

$$\frac{\partial^2\psi}{\partial x^2} = YZ\frac{\partial^2 X}{\partial x^2} \quad ...(72)$$

$$\frac{\partial^2\psi}{\partial y^2} = XZ\frac{\partial^2 Y}{\partial y^2} \quad ...(73)$$

$$\frac{\partial^2\psi}{\partial z^2} = XY\frac{\partial^2 Z}{\partial z^2} \quad ...(74)$$

Substituting Eqs. (72)–(74) in Eq. (70) and dividing throughout by $(2m/h^2)XYZ$, we have

$$\frac{\hbar^2}{2m}\left[\frac{1}{X}\frac{\partial^2 X}{dx^2} + \frac{1}{Y}\frac{\partial^2 Y}{\partial y^2} + \frac{1}{Z}\frac{\partial^2 Z}{\partial z^2}\right] + E = 0 \quad ...(75)$$

We notice that the first term is a function of x only and is independent of y and z ; the second term is a function of y only and is independent of x and z and the third term is a function of z only and is independent of x and y. The fourth term E is a constant. If energy E is written as the sum of three contributions associated with the three coordinates, then Eq. 75 can be separated into three equations. Thus, for instance, for motion along the X-axis (where, X varies while Y and Z remain constant), the second and third terms on the left hand side of Eq. 75 remain constant. Let this constant be E_x. Accordingly, we can write

$$-\frac{\hbar^2}{2m}\left(\frac{1}{X}\frac{\partial^2 X}{\partial x^2}\right) = E_x \quad \ldots(76)$$

$$-\frac{\hbar^2}{2m}\left(\frac{1}{Y}\frac{\partial^2 Y}{\partial xy^2}\right) = E_y \quad \ldots(77)$$

$$-\frac{\hbar^2}{2m}\left(\frac{1}{Z}\frac{\partial^2 Z}{\partial xz^2}\right) = E_z \quad \ldots(78)$$

where, $E = E_x + E_y + E_z$.

We see that each of the Eqs. (76)–(78) is of the form of Eq. (50), the solution of which is given by Eq. (67), *i.e.*, we have

$$X(x) = (2/a)^{1/2} \sin (n_x \pi x/a);$$

$$n_x = 1, 2, 3 \ldots \quad \ldots(79)$$

and $$E_x = n_x^2 h^2/8ma^2 \quad \ldots(80)$$

Similar solutions exist for $Y(y)$ and $Z(z)$. Hence,

$$\psi(x, y, z) = X(x)\, Y(y)\, Z(z)$$

$$= (8/a^3)^{1/2} \sin (n_x \pi x/a) \sin (n_y \pi y/a) \sin (n_z \pi z/a) \quad \ldots(81)$$

and $$E = E_x + E_y + E_z = \frac{(n_x^2 + n_y^2 + n_z^2)\, h^2}{8ma^2} \quad \ldots(82)$$

where, $n_x, n_y, n_z = 1, 2, 3, 4 \ldots$

Degeneracy It is seen from Eq. 82 that the total energy depends upon the sum of the squares of three quantum numbers. It is evident tha groups of different states, each specified by a unique set of quantum numbers, can havethe isame energy. In such a case, the energy level and the corresponding independent states are said to be degenerate. Consider, for instance, the energy level having energy $= 14h^2/8ma^2$. There are six combinations of n_x, n_y and n_z which can give this value of energy :

n_x	1	1	2	3	2	3
n_y	2	3	1	1	3	2
n_z	3	2	3	2	1	1

This energy level is, therefore, 6-fold degenerate, *i.e.*, its degeneracy is equal to 6. Proceeding in this manner we can calculate degeneracy of the energy levels of a particle in a three-dimensional cubical box. The results are shown in Fig. 16.4.

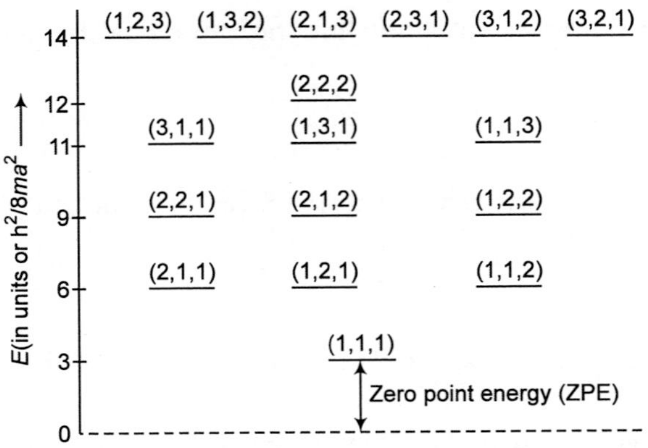

Fig. 16.4 Energy in units of ($h^2/8ma^2$) and degeneracy of a few states of a particle in a three-dimensional cubic box.

3. One-dimensional simple harmonic oscillator

A diatomic vibrating molecule can be represented by a simple model, the so called simple harmonic oscillator (S.H.O.) The force acting on the molecule is given by

$$f = -kx$$

where, x is the displacement from the equilibrium position and

k is a constant called the **force constant.** The potential energy $V(x)$ of this molecule is given by

$$V(x) = -\int_0^x f dx = \int_0^x kx\, dx = -\frac{1}{2}kx^2 \quad \ldots(83)$$

Eq. (99) is the equation of a parabola. Thus, if we plot potential energy of a particle executing simple harmonic oscillations as a function of displacement from the equilibrium position, we get a curve as shown in Fig. 16.5.

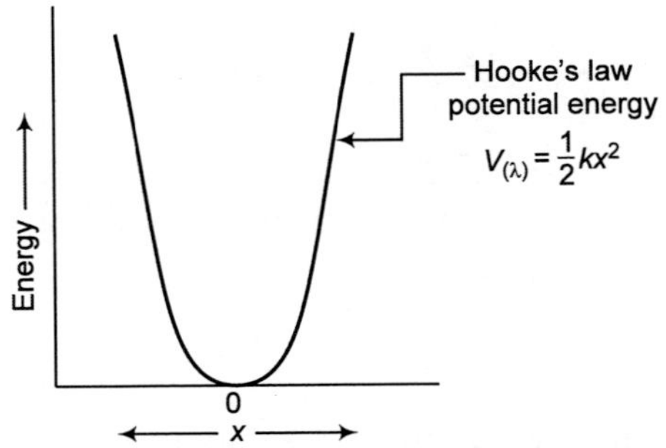

Fig. 16.5 Potential energy diagram for a simple harmonic oscillator.

The vibrational frequency of the oscillator of mass m is given by

$$\nu = \frac{1}{2\pi}\left(\frac{k}{m}\right)^{1/2} \quad \ldots(84)$$

It is more accurate to define the vibrational frequency as

$$v = \frac{1}{2\pi}\left(\frac{k}{\mu}\right)^{1/2} \qquad \ldots(85)$$

where, μ is the reduced mass of the diatomic molecule defined as

$$\frac{1}{\mu} = \frac{1}{m_1} + \frac{1}{m_2} \qquad \ldots(86)$$

where, m_1 and m_2 are the atomic masses of the two atoms.

Using the potential energy given by Eq. (83) for one-dimensional SHO, the Schrodinger equation is represented as

$$\left[-\frac{h^2}{2m}\left(\frac{d^2}{dx^2}\right) + \frac{1}{2}kx^2\right]\psi(x) = E\psi(x) \qquad \ldots(87)$$

Mathematically, Eq. (87) may be written as

$$\frac{d^2\psi}{dx^2} + \frac{2m}{h^2}\left(E - \frac{1}{2}kx^2\right)\psi = 0 \qquad \ldots(88)$$

Defining α and β as $\alpha = 2mE/h^2$ and $\beta = (mk)^{1/2}/h$ ...(89)

Eq. (88) becomes $\dfrac{d^2\psi}{dx^2} + (\alpha - \beta^2 x^2)\psi = 0$ ...(90)

Defining a new variable $\xi = \beta^{1/2}x$, the above equation becomes

$$\frac{d^2\psi}{d\xi^2} + \left(\frac{\alpha}{\beta} - \xi^2\right)\psi = 0 \qquad \ldots(91)$$

Eq. (91) has a solution of the form

$$\psi(\xi) = \phi(\xi)e^{-\xi^2/2} \qquad \ldots(92)$$

Using this solution Eq. (91) becomes

$$\frac{d^2\phi}{d\xi^2} - 2\xi\frac{d\phi}{d\xi} + \left(\frac{\alpha}{\beta} - 1\right)\phi = 0 \qquad \ldots(93)$$

Eq. (93) is identical in form to a well known second-order differential equation, called the **Hermite equation**, *viz.,*

$$\frac{d^2\phi}{d\xi^2} - 2\xi\frac{d\phi}{d\xi} + 2n\phi = 0 \qquad \ldots(94)$$

The Hermite equation has solutions which depend upon the value of n. These solutions are called Hermite polynomials, $H_n(\xi)$, *i.e.*, $\phi(\xi) \equiv H_n(\xi)$

The Hermite polynomial of degree n is defined as

$$H_n(\xi) = (-1)^n e^{\xi^2}\left\{\frac{\partial^n(e^{-\xi^2})}{\partial\xi^n}\right\} \qquad \ldots(95)$$

A few Hermite polynomials are given below :

$$H_0(\xi) = 1 \qquad H_3(\xi) = 8\xi^3 - 12\xi$$

$$H_1(\xi) = 2\xi \qquad H_4(\xi) = 16\xi^4 - 48\xi^2 + 12$$

$$H_2(\xi) = 4\xi^2 - 2$$

The normalized wave functions of the one-dimensional SHO are then written as

$$\psi_n(\xi) = \left[\frac{\beta^{1/2}}{2^n n!\sqrt{\pi}}\right]^{1/2} e^{-\xi^2/2}H_n(\xi)$$

where, $n = 0, 1, 2, 3, \ldots$ ...(96)

The first three wave functions (with $n = 0, 1, 2$) the corresponding energy levels and the probability functions ψ_n^2 for the SHO are shown in Fig. 16.6.

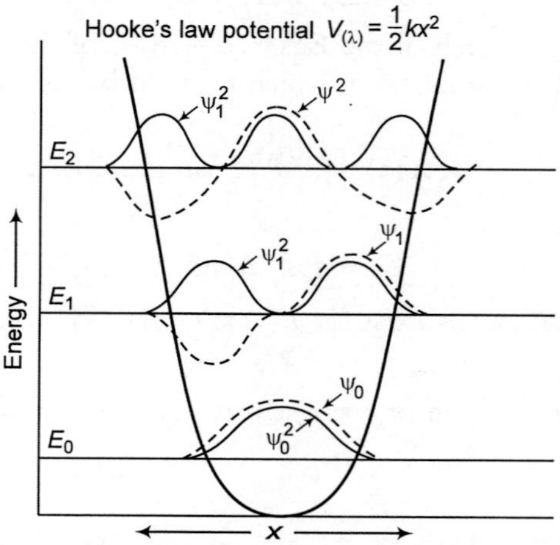

Fig. 16.6 The wave functions, the probability functions and the energy levels of a simple harmonic oscillator.

Energy of SHO The energy of the SHO is obtained by comparing Eqs. (93) and (117)), whence we find that

$$\alpha/\beta = 2n + 1 \qquad \ldots(97)$$

Substituting for α and β from Eq. (89), we have

$$(2mE/\hbar^2)(mk)^{1/2}/\hbar = 2n + 1 \qquad \ldots(98)$$

or

$$E = \left(n + \frac{1}{2}\right)\hbar\,(k/m)^{1/2} \qquad \ldots(99)$$

From Eq. (84), $(k/m)^{1/2} = 2\pi\nu$ ...(100)

Combining Eqs. (99) and (100), we have

$$E \equiv E_n = \left(n + \frac{1}{2}\right)\hbar\,(2\pi\nu)$$

$$= \left(n + \frac{1}{2}\right)h\nu;\ n = 0, 1, 2, 3, \ldots\ (\hbar = h/2\pi) \ldots(101)$$

The energy state with $n = 0$ is the vibrational ground state with energy

$$E_0 = \frac{1}{2}h\nu \qquad \ldots(102)$$

This energy is called the **zero point energy** of the oscillator. Classical mechanics predicts that the zero-point energy of the oscillator is zero whereas quantum mechanics predicts that the zero-point energy is non-zero. The occurrence of the zero-point energy is consistent with the Heisenberg uncertainty principle.

Example 11. *What is the restriction on α/β if the $n = 1$ wave function of a one-dimensional SHO has to satisfy wave equation $d^2\psi_1/d\xi^2 + (\alpha/\beta - \xi^2)\psi_1 = 0$? Given that $\psi = N\xi \exp(-\xi^2/2)$ where, N is a constant.*

Sol. $\psi_1 = N\xi e^{-\xi^2/2}$

$$\frac{d\psi_1}{d\xi} = N\xi(-\xi)e^{-\xi^2/2} + Ne^{-\xi^2/2} = -N\xi^2 e^{-\xi^2/2} + Ne^{-\xi^2/2}$$

$$\frac{d^2\psi_1}{d\xi^2} = -N\xi^2(-\xi)e^{-\xi^2/2} - 2N\xi e^{-\xi^2/2} - N\xi e^{-\xi^2/2}$$

$$= N\xi^3 e^{-\xi^2/2} - 3N\xi e^{-\xi^2/2}$$

Now $\dfrac{d^2\psi_1}{d\xi^2} + \left(\dfrac{\alpha}{\beta} - \xi^2\right)\psi_1$ will be equal to zero

if $\quad N\xi^3 e^{-\xi^2/2} - 3N\xi e^{-\xi^2/2} + \dfrac{\alpha}{\beta}N\xi e^{-\xi^2/2} - N\xi^3 e^{-\xi^2/2} = 0$

or if $\quad -3N\xi\, e^{-\xi^2/2} + (\alpha/\beta)\, N\xi e^{-\xi^2/2} = 0$

or if $\quad \alpha/\beta = 3$

which is the desired restriction.

Example 12. *According to the virial theorem for a diatomic SHO, the expectation (average) value of the kinetic energy, $<T>$, is equal to the expectation value of the potential energy, $<V>$. Verify this statement for the ground state of the SHO, given that the ground state wave function is*

$$\psi_0(x) = (\beta/\pi)^{1/4} \exp(-\beta x^2/2)$$

where, $\beta = (mk)^{1/2}/\hbar$ and $k = m\omega^2$; $\omega = 2\pi\nu$ where, ν is the vibrational frequency of the SHO.

Sol. Let us calculate $<\hat{T}>$ and $<\hat{V}>$

Here, the kinetic energy operator is $-\dfrac{\hbar^2}{2m}\dfrac{\partial^2}{\partial x^2}$ and potential energy $V(x) = \dfrac{1}{2}kx^2$ where, k is the force constant and x is the displacement of the SHO from the equilibrium position

$$<\hat{T}> = \int_{-\infty}^{\infty} \psi_0^*\hat{T}\psi_0 dx = \int_{-\infty}^{\infty} (\beta/\pi)^{1/4}e^{-\beta x^2/2} \left(-\frac{\hbar^2}{2m}\frac{d^2}{dx^2}\right)(\beta/\pi)^{1/4}e^{-\beta x^2/2}dx$$

$$= (\beta/\pi)^{1/2}(-\hbar^2/2m)\int_{-\infty}^{\infty} e^{-\beta x^2/2}\left(\frac{d^2}{dx^2}\right)e^{-\beta x^2/2}dx$$

$$= (\beta/\pi)^{1/2}(-h^2/2m)\int_{-\infty}^{\infty} e^{-\beta x^2/2}\left(\frac{d}{dx}\right)(-\beta x e^{-\beta x^2/2})dx$$

$$= (\beta/\pi)^{1/2}(-\hbar^2/2m)(-\beta)\int_{-\infty}^{\infty} e^{-\beta x^2/2}[1 - \beta x^2]\, e^{-\beta x^2/2})dx$$

$$= (\beta/\pi)^{1/2}(\hbar^2/2m)\left[\beta\int_{-\infty}^{\infty} e^{-\beta x^2}dx - \beta^2\int_{-\infty}^{\infty} x^2 e^{-\beta x^2}dx\right]$$

Using the standard integrals

$$\int_{-\infty}^{\infty} e^{-ax^2}dx = (\pi/a)^{1/2}$$

and
$$\int_{-\infty}^{\infty} x^2 e^{-ax^2}dx = \frac{1}{2a}(\pi/a)^{1/2}$$

we obtain $<\hat{T}>$

$$= (\beta/\pi)^{1/2}(\hbar^2/2m)\,[(\beta)(\pi/\beta)^{1/2} - (\beta^2)(1/2\beta)(\pi/\beta)^{1/2}]$$

$$= \frac{\beta\hbar^2}{2m} - \frac{\beta\hbar^2}{4m} = \frac{\beta\hbar^2}{4m} = \frac{\hbar\omega}{4} = \frac{h\nu}{4}$$

(since $\beta = (mk)^{1/2}/\hbar$; $k = m\omega^2$ and $\omega = 2\pi\nu$)

Again $<\hat{V}> = \int_{-\infty}^{\infty} \psi_0^*\hat{V}\psi_0\, dx$

$$= \int_{-\infty}^{\infty} (\beta/\pi)^{1/4}e^{-\beta x^2/2}\left(\frac{1}{2}kx^2\right)(\beta/\pi)^{1/4}e^{-\beta x^2/2}dx$$

$$= (\beta/\pi)^{1/2}\left(\frac{1}{2}k\right)\int_{-\infty}^{\infty} x^2 e^{-\beta x^2}dx$$

$$= (\beta/\pi)^{12}(k/2)\left(\frac{1}{2\beta}\right)(\pi/\beta)^{1/2}$$

$$= \frac{k}{4\beta} = \frac{m\omega^2}{4(mk)^{1/2}/\hbar} = \frac{m\omega^2\hbar}{4m\omega} = \frac{\hbar\omega}{4} = \frac{h\nu}{4}$$

We see that

$<\hat{T}> = <\hat{V}>$, which is the virial theorem.

Example 13. *Verify the Heisenberg uncertainty principle for the ground state of a one-dimensional SHO.*

Sol. We know that $\Delta x = [<x^2> - <x>^2]^{1/2}$

$$(\Delta p_x) = [<p_x^2> - <p_x>^2]^{1/2}$$

For an S.H.O., $\psi_0(x) = (\beta/\pi)^{1/4}e^{-\beta x^2/2}$

Now, $\quad <x> = \int_{-\infty}^{\infty} \psi_0^*\hat{x}\, dx$

$$= \int_{-\infty}^{\infty} (\beta/\pi)^{1/4}e^{-\beta x^2/2}\hat{x}\,(\beta/x)^{1/4}e^{-\beta x^2/2}dx$$

$$= (\beta/\pi)^{1/2}\int_{-\infty}^{\infty} xe^{-\beta x^2}dx = 0$$

(since the integrand is odd) ...(i)

Again $\quad <x^2> = \int_{-\infty}^{\infty} \psi_0^* x^2\psi_0 dx$

Proceeding as in Example 12, we find that

$$<x^2> = 1/2\beta \qquad \ldots(ii)$$

$$<\hat{p}_x> = \int_{-\infty}^{\infty} \psi_0^*(-i\hbar d/dx)\,\psi_0 dx$$

$$= (\beta/\pi)^{1/2}(-i\hbar(\int_{-\infty}^{\infty} e^{\beta x^2/2}[-\beta x e^{-\beta x^2/2}]\, dx$$

$= (\beta/\pi)^{1/2}(-i\hbar)(-\beta)\int_{-\infty}^{\infty} x\, e^{-\beta x^2}\, dx$

= 0 (because the integrand is odd) ...(iii)

Again, $\langle p_x^2 \rangle = \int_{-\infty}^{\infty} \psi_0^*(-\hbar^2 d^2/dx^2)\psi_0 dx$

$= (-\hbar^2)(\beta/\pi)^{1/2}\int_{-\infty}^{\infty} e^{-\beta x^2/2}(d^2/dx^2)\, e^{-\beta x^2/2} dx$

Proceeding as in Example 12, where we have evaluated $\langle \hat{T} \rangle$, we find that

$$\langle p_x^2 \rangle = \beta\hbar^2/2 \quad \text{...(iv)}$$

From Eqs. (i), (ii), (iii) and (iv) we find on simplification that

$$\Delta x \cdot \Delta p_x = \hbar/2$$

which is the Heisenberg uncertainty principle. A rigorous mathematical derivation gives the inequality.

$$\Delta x \cdot \Delta p_x \geq \hbar/2$$

4. The Schrodinger equation for hydrogen atom

Hydrogen atom is the simplest of all atoms. It is a three-dimensional system and the Schrodinger equation for this system is

$$\hat{H}\psi = E\psi \quad \text{...(103)}$$

where, $$\hat{H} = -\frac{\hbar^2}{2m}\nabla^2 + V(x, y, z) \quad \text{...(104)}$$

and where the Laplacian operator in Cartesian coordinates is given by

$$\nabla^2 = \frac{\partial^2}{\partial x^2} + \frac{\partial^2}{\partial y^2} + \frac{\partial^2}{\partial z^2} \quad \text{...(105)}$$

The potential energy of integration between the electron and the nucleus is given by

$$V(r) = -Ze^2/4\pi\varepsilon_0 r \quad \text{...(106)}$$

Since, this attractive potential has spherical symmetry depending only upon r, it is convenient to express the Schrodinger equation in terms of polar coordinates (r, θ, ϕ), rather than Cartesian coordinates (x, y, z). The Cartesian coordinates are related to polar coordinates (see Fig. 16.7) as follows :

$$x = r\sin\theta\cos\phi$$
$$y = r\sin\theta\sin\phi$$
$$z = r\cos\theta$$

The Schrodinger equation for hydrogen atom in terms of polar coordinates becomes

$$\frac{1}{r^2}\frac{\partial}{\partial r}\left(\frac{r^2\partial\psi}{\partial r}\right) + \frac{1}{r^2\sin\theta}\frac{\partial}{\partial\theta}\left(\sin\theta\frac{\partial\psi}{\partial\theta}\right) + \frac{1}{r^2\sin^2\theta}\cdot\frac{\partial^2\psi}{\partial\phi^2} + \frac{2\mu}{\hbar}\left(E + \frac{Ze^2}{4\pi\varepsilon_0 r}\right)\psi = 0 \quad \text{...(107)}$$

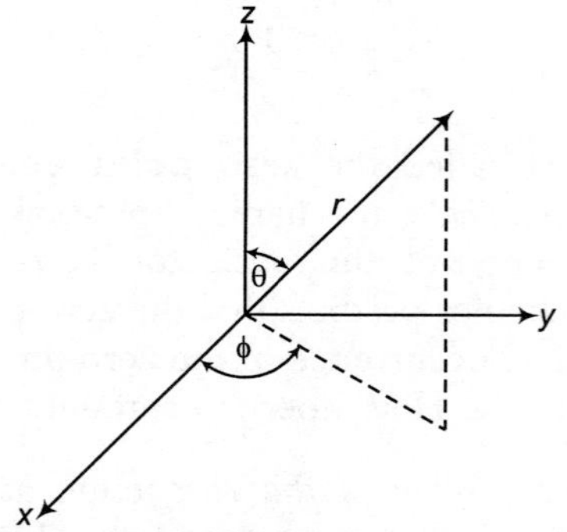

Fig. 16.7 The polar coordinate system for the motion of electron in hydrogen atom.

where, μ is the reduced mass of the electron and the nucleus, that is $\mu = m_e m_n/(m_n + m_e)$. Assuming that $V(r)$ is a function of r only, the above wave equation can be solved by separating the variables :

$$\psi(r,\theta,\phi) = R(r)\,\Theta(\theta)\,\Phi(\phi) \quad \text{...(108)}$$

where, $R(r)$ is the radial function which is a function of r only, and $\Theta(\theta)$ and $\Phi(\phi)$ are angular functions. Substituting Eq. (108) in Eq. (107) the we get an equation which can be separated into three equations which are

$$\frac{1}{r^2}\frac{d}{dr}\left(r^2\frac{dR}{dr}\right) - \frac{\beta}{r^2}R + \frac{2\mu}{\hbar^2}\left(E + \frac{Ze^2}{4\pi\varepsilon_0 r}\right)R = 0 \quad \text{...(109)}$$

$$\frac{1}{\sin\theta}\frac{d}{d\theta}\left(\sin\theta\frac{d\Theta}{d\theta}\right) - \frac{m^2\Theta}{\sin^2\theta} + \beta\Theta = 0 \quad \text{...(110)}$$

or $$\frac{d^2\Phi}{d\phi^2} + m^2\phi = 0 \quad \text{...(111)}$$

where, m and β are constants.

The complete solution of Eq. (107) comprises the solutions of Eqs. (109), (110) and (111). This will not be attempted here. It is found in standard books on quantum mechanics. Suffice it to mention here that the energy values of hydrogen-like atoms are found to be given by

$$E_n = -\frac{2\pi^2 Z^2\mu e^4}{(4\pi\varepsilon_0)^2(n^2h^2)} \quad \text{...(112)}$$

These energy levels are the same as those obtained from the Bohr theory. The normalized solutions of radial Eq. (111) are found to be

$$R_{n,l}(r) = -\left(\frac{(2Z/na_0)^3(n-l-1)!}{2n[n+l]^3!}\right)\exp(-\rho/2)\rho^l L_{n+l}^{2l+1}(\rho) \quad \text{...(113)}$$

where, $\rho = (2z/na_0)r$ and $a_0 = (4\pi\varepsilon_0)\hbar^2/\mu e^2$ ...(114)

$L_{n+l}^{2l+1}(\rho)$ are the associated Laguerre polynomials defined as

$$L_r^s(\rho) = \frac{d^s}{d\rho^s}\left[\frac{e^\rho d^r}{d\rho^r}(\rho^r e^{-\rho})\right] \qquad ...(115)$$

where, $s = 2l + 1$ and $r = n + l$ and $n = 1, 2, 3, 4, ...$

The number n is called the **principal quantum number** which determines the energies of different atomic orbitals and the distances of the electron from the nucleus.

The probability of finding the electron between r and $r + dr$ is given by the quantity $R^*(r)\, R(r) r^2\, dr$.

Angular functions The solution of Eq. (126) gives

$$\Theta_{l,m}(\theta) = \left[\frac{(2l+1)(l-|m|)!}{2(l+|m|)!}\right]^{1/2} P_l^{|m|}(\cos\theta) \quad ...(116)$$

where, $P_l^{|m|}(\cos\theta)$ are called **associated Legendre polynomials** defined as

$$P_l^{|m|}(\cos\theta) = \frac{1}{2^l\, l!}(1-\cos^2\theta)^{|m|/2}\, \frac{d^{l+|m|}(\cos^2\theta - 1)^l}{d\cos\theta^{l+|m|}} \qquad ...(117)$$

In the above equation, the quantum number $l\,(= 0, 1, 2, ...)$ is the **azimuthal quantum number**. It determines the shape of the atomic orbitals. The solution of Eq. (111) gives

$$\Phi_m(\phi) = \frac{1}{\sqrt{2\pi}}\exp(im\phi) \qquad ...(118)$$

where, $1/\sqrt{2\pi}$ is the normalization constant and $m = 0, \pm 1, \pm 2, ..., \pm l$ is the **magnetic quantum number**. This name is given to this quantum number because in the presence of the external magnetic field, the states having different values of m have different energies. The phenomenon of removal of degeneracy of an energy state by application of external magnetic field is known as **Zeeman effect**, after P. Zeeman (1865-1943) who was the co-winner (with H.A. Lorentz) (1853-1928) of the 1902 Physics Nobel Prize. These Dutch physicists were honoured for their work on the influence of magnetism upon radiation phenomena. (Lorentz also contributed to the theory of Relativity. Einstein held him in high esteem).

To sum up, the solution of the radial Eq. (109) gives quantum numbers n and l. The solution of the Θ Eq. (110) gives quantum numbers l and m and the solution of the Φ Eq. (111) gives quantum number m. In other words, the quantum numbers n, l and m follow directly from the wave mechanical treatment.

Example 14. *The unnormalized angular function, which is a solution of Eq. (138), is $\Phi(\phi) = N\, exp\,(im\phi)$. Normalize it.*

Sol. The wave function is normalized if

$$<\Phi(\phi)\,|\,\Phi(\phi)> \equiv \int_0^{2\pi} \Phi^*\Phi\, d\phi = 1$$

Substituting the value of $\Phi(\phi)$, we have

$$N^2\int_0^{2\pi} e^{im\phi}e^{-im\phi}d\phi = N^2\int_0^{2\pi} d\phi = N^2(2\pi) = 1$$

$$\therefore \qquad N = (1/2\pi)^{1/2}$$

Hence, the normalized angular function is

$$\Phi(\phi) = \frac{1}{\sqrt{2\pi}}\exp(im\phi)$$

Example 15. *Determine the radial functions $R_{n,l}(r)$ for (a) the 1s orbital (b) 2p orbital.*

Sol. (a) For the 1s-orbital, $n = 1, l = 0$. Hence, from Eq. (115) the associated Laguerre polynomial is

$$L_1^1(\rho) = \frac{d}{d\rho}\left[e^\rho\frac{d}{d\rho}(\rho e^{-\rho})\right] = \frac{d}{d\rho}(1-\rho) = -1$$

Hence, from Eq. (140)

$$R_{1,0}(r) = -\left(\frac{2Z}{a_0}\right)^{3/2}\left[\frac{0!}{2(1!)^3}\right]^{1/2} e^{-\rho/2}\rho^{-}(-1)$$

$$= 2\left(\frac{Z}{a_0}\right)^{32} e^{-\rho/2} = 2\left(\frac{Z}{a_0}\right)^{3/2} e^{-Zr/a_0}$$

(b) For the 2p-orbital, $n = 2, l = 1$. Hence, the associated Laguerre polynomial is

$$L_3^3(\rho) = \frac{d^2}{d\rho^3}\left[e^\rho\frac{d^3}{d\rho^3}(\rho^3 e^{-\rho})\right]$$

Now,

$$\frac{d^3}{d\rho^3}(\rho^3 e^{-\rho}) = \frac{d^2}{d\rho^2}[(3\rho^2 - \rho^3)e^{-\rho}]$$

$$= (6 - 18\rho + 9\rho^2 - \rho^3)\, e^{-\rho}]$$

Hence, we obtain

$$L_3^3(\rho) = \frac{d^3}{d\rho^3}[e^\rho(6 - 18\rho + 9\rho^2 - \rho^3)e^{-\rho}]$$

$$= \frac{d^3}{d\rho^3}(6 - 18\rho - 9\rho^2 - \rho^3) = -6$$

Hence, from Eq. (174)

$$R_{2,1}(r) = -\left(\frac{Z}{a_0}\right)^{3/2}\left[\frac{(2-1-1)!}{2\times 2\,[(2+1)!]^3}\right]^{1/2} e^{-\rho/2}\rho(-6)$$

$$= \left(\frac{Z}{a_0}\right)^{3/2}\frac{1}{2\sqrt{6}}\rho e^{-\rho/2}$$

$$= \frac{1}{2\sqrt{6}}\left(\frac{Z}{a_0}\right)^{5/2} re^{-Zr/2a_0} \qquad (\because \rho = 2Zr/a_0)$$

Example 16. *Show that the 1s wave function of hydrogen atom given by*

$$\psi_{1s} \equiv \psi_{1,0,0} = \frac{1}{\sqrt{\pi}a_0^{3/2}} \exp(-r/a_0) \text{ is normalized;}$$

a_0 is the Bohr radius.

Sol. For the wave function to be normalized the following condition holds

$$\int \psi_{1s}\psi_{1s}\, d\tau = 1$$

In polar coordinates (r, θ, ϕ), the volume element $d\tau = r^2 dr \sin\theta\, d\theta\, d\phi$. Using this expression for $d\tau$ and integrating between appropriate limits, we have

$$\int \psi_{1s}\psi_{1s}\, d\tau = \frac{1}{\pi a_0^3}\int_0^\infty r^2 e^{-2r/a_0} dr \int_0^\pi \sin\theta\, d\theta \int_0^{2\pi} d\phi$$

Each of these integrals can be evaluated seperately as follows

$$\int_0^{2\pi} d\phi = 2\pi \text{ and } \int_0^\pi \sin\theta\, d\theta$$

$$= [-\cos\theta]_0^\pi = -(-1) - (-1) = 2$$

The first integral is evaluated by using the result

$$\int_0^\infty x^n e^{-ax} ds = \frac{n!}{a^n + 1}, n \text{ is a positive integer; } a > 0$$

Thus, $$\int r^2 e^{-2r/a_0} dr = \frac{2}{(2/a_0)^3} = \frac{a_0^3}{4}$$

$\therefore$ $$\int \psi_{1s}\psi_{1s} d\tau = \left(\frac{1}{\pi a_0^3}\right)\left(\frac{a_0^3}{4}\right)(2)(2\pi) = 1$$

Hence, ψ_{1s} is normalized.

Example 17. *The un-normalized 1s wave function for hydrogen atom is given by*

$\psi_{1s} \equiv \psi_{1,0,0} = N \exp(-r/a_0)$, where a_0 is the Bohr radius. Determine the normalized wave function.

Sol. Here we have to determine the normalization constant, N. For the wave function to be normalized the following conditions holds

$$\int \psi_{1s}\, \psi_{1s}\, d\tau = 1$$

In polar coordinates (r, θ, ϕ) the volume element $d\tau = r^2 dr \sin\theta d\theta\, d\phi$. Using this expression for $d\tau$ and integrating between appropriate limits, we have

$$\int \psi_{1s}\psi_{1s}\, d\tau = N^2 \int e^{-2r/a_0} d\tau$$

$$= N^2 \int_0^\infty r^2 e^{-2r/a_0} dr \int_0^\pi \sin\theta d\theta \int_0^{2\pi} d\phi = 1$$

Each of these integrals can be evaluated separately as follows :

$$\int_0^{2\pi} d\phi = 2\pi$$

and $$\int_0^\pi \sin\theta\, d\theta = [-\cos\theta]_0^\pi = -(-1) - (-1) = 2$$

Using the result

$$\int_0^\infty x^n e^{-ax} dx = \frac{n!}{a^{n+1}} : n \text{ is a positive integer } a > 0, \text{ we obtain}$$

$$\int_0^\infty r^2 e^{-2r/a_0} dr = \frac{2!}{(2/a_0)^3} = \frac{a_0^3}{4}$$

Hence, $$N^2(a_0^3/4)(2)(2\pi) = 1$$

$\therefore$ $$N = 1/\sqrt{\pi}a_0^{3/2}$$

Hence, the normalized ground-state wave function is

$$\psi_{1s} = 1/\sqrt{\pi}a_0^{3/2} \exp(-r/a_0)$$

Note This example is the reverse of the last example.

Example 18. Show that the 1s and 2s wave functions of hydrogen atom, given by

$$\psi_{1s} \equiv \psi_{1,0,0} = \frac{1}{\sqrt{\pi}a_0^{3/2}} \exp(-r/a_0)$$

and $$\psi_{2s} \equiv \psi_{2,0,0} = \frac{1}{4\sqrt{2\pi}a_0^{3/2}}\left(2 - \frac{r}{a_0}\right) \exp(-r/2a_0)$$

are orthogonal to each other.

Sol. For the given wave functions to be orthogonal, they should satisfy the following condition

$$\int \psi_{1s}\, \psi_{2s}\, d\tau = 0$$

Since, in polar coordinates, $d\tau = r^2 dr \sin\theta\, d\theta\, d\phi$, we have, after integrating between appropriate limits

$$\int \psi_{1s}\psi_{2s} d\tau = \frac{1}{4\sqrt{2\pi}a_0^3}\left[2\int_0^\infty r^2 e^{-3r/2a_0} dr - \frac{1}{a_0}\int_0^\infty r^3 e^{-3r/2a_0} dr\right] \int_0^\pi \sin\theta \cdot d\theta \int_0^{2\pi} d\phi$$

Now, $$\int_0^\infty \sin\theta\, d\theta [-\cos\theta]_0^\pi = -(-1) - (-1)$$

$$= 2 \text{ and } \int_0^{2\pi} d\phi = 2\pi$$

Using the standard result $\int_0^\infty x^n e^{-ax} dx = \frac{n!}{a^{n+1}}$, we have

$$\int_0^\infty r^2 e^{-3r/2a} a_0 dr = \frac{2!}{(3/2a_0)^3} = \frac{16a_0^3}{27}$$

and $$\int_0^\infty r^3 e^{-3r/2a_0} dr \frac{3!}{(3/2a_0)^4} = \frac{32a_0^4}{27}$$

Using the above values of the various integrals we find that

$$\int \psi_{1s}\, \psi_{2s}\, d\tau = 0$$

Hence, the 1s and 2s wave functions of hydrogen atom are orthogonal.

Example 19. *Using the normalized wave function*

$$\psi_{1s} = (1/\pi a_0^3)^{1/2} \exp(-r/a_0)$$

for the ground state of hydrogen atom, calculate the probability for the electron to be confined in a sphere of radius $r = a_0$, the Bohr radius.

Sol. We have that from Bohr's interpretation of the wave function, the probability is given by

$$P(r)\, dr = \psi^* \psi\, d\tau$$

$\therefore$ Integrating, we obtain

$$\int P(r)\,dr = \int \psi^* \psi\, d\tau,$$

where, $d\tau = r^2 dr \sin\theta\, d\theta\, d\phi$

or
$$P = \frac{1}{\pi a_0^3}\int_0^{a_0} r^2 e^{-2r} dr \int_0^{\pi} \sin\theta\, d\theta \int_0^{2\pi} d\phi$$
$$= \frac{4}{a_0^3}\int_0^{a_0} r^2 e^{-2r} dr$$

Carrying out integration by parts, we obtain

$$P = \frac{4}{a_0^3}\left\{\left[\frac{a_0}{2} r^2 e^{-2r/a_0}\right]_0^{a_0} + \left[-\frac{a_0^2}{2} r e^{-2r/a_0}\right]_0^{a_0} + \left[-\frac{a_0^3}{4} e^{-2r/a_0}\right]_0^{a_0}\right\}$$
$$= 5e^{-2} + 1 = 0.323$$

Example 20. *Calculate the most probable distance r_{mp}, of the electron from the nucleus in the ground state of hydrogen atom, given that the normalized ground state wave function is*

$$\psi_{1s} = \frac{1}{\sqrt{\pi} a_0^{3/2}} \exp(-r/a_0)$$

Sol. Quantum mechanically, the probability of finding the electron in a spherical shell of the thickness dr at a distance r from the nucleus (Fig. 16.8) is given by

$$P(r)\,dr = 4\pi |\psi_{1s}|^2 r^2 dr$$
$$= 4\pi r^2 (1/\pi a_0^3)\, e^{-2r/a_0} dr$$

For the probability to be a maximum

$$dP(r)/dr = 0.$$

Thus,
$$\frac{dP(r)}{dr} = \frac{4}{a_0^3}\left(-\frac{2r^2}{a_0} + 2r\right) e^{-2r/a_0} = 0$$

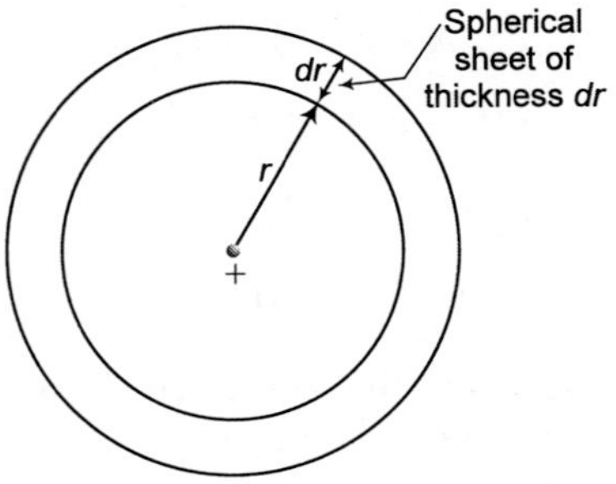

Fig. 16.8 Spherical shell of thickness *dr* at a distance *r* from the nucleus.

Since, the Bohr radius $a_0 \neq 0$ and the exponential is also $\neq 0$, hence,

$$-\frac{2r^2}{a_0} + 2r = 0$$

$$\therefore \quad r = r_{mp} = a_0$$

Example 21. *Calculate the average distance of the electron from the nucleus in the ground state of hydrogen atom given that the normalized ground state wave function is* $\psi_{1s} = \frac{1}{\sqrt{\pi} a_0^{3/2}} \exp(-r/a_0)$.

Sol. In quantum mechanics, the average (or expectation) value of dynamical variable r is given by

$$\langle r \rangle = \int \psi_n\, r\, \psi_n\, d\tau$$

In the present case, the average distance of the electron from the nucleus is given by

$$\langle r \rangle = \int \psi_{1s}\, r\, \psi_{1s}\, d\tau$$

Since, $d\tau = r^2 dr \sin\theta\, d\theta\, d\phi$, hence, integrating between appropriate limits, we get

$$\langle r \rangle = \frac{1}{\pi a_0^3}\int_0^{\infty} r^3 e^{-2r/a_0} dr \int_0^{\pi} \sin\theta\, d\theta \int_0^{2\pi} d\phi$$
$$= \frac{1}{\pi a_0^3}\left(\frac{3!}{(2/a_0)^4}(2)(2\pi)\right) = \frac{3}{2} a_0$$

Note The results of the last two examples are quite instructive. According to Bohr's theory of hydrogen atom, the distance of the electron from the nucleus in the ground state is exactly equal to a_0, the Bohr radius. But, according to Heisenberg's uncertainty principle, the electron cannot be exactly located in its orbit. Hence, quantum mechanically, while the most probable distance is a_0, the average distance is $3a_0/2$, *i.e.*, the average distance is 50% greater then the Bohr theory result ! The inescapable conclusion we draw from this is that we really do not know where the electron is located in its orbit at a given moment.

Example 22. *Show that the average of $1/r$ for an electron in the 1s-orbital of hydrogen atom is $1/a_0$, where, a_0 is the Bohr radius; given that*

$$\psi_{1s} = \frac{1}{\sqrt{\pi} a_0^{3/2}} \exp(-r/a_0)$$

Sol.
$$\langle 1/r \rangle = \int \psi_{1s} (1/r)\, \psi_{1s}\, d\tau$$

Since, $d\tau = r^2 dr \sin\theta\, d\theta\, d\phi$, hence, integrating between appropriate limits

$$\langle 1/r \rangle = \frac{1}{\pi a_0^3}\int_0^{\infty} r e^{-2r/a_0} dr \int_0^{\pi} \sin\theta\, d\theta \int_0^{2\pi} d\phi$$
$$= \frac{1}{\pi a_0^3}\left(\frac{1}{(2/a_0)^2}(2)(2\pi)\right) = \frac{1}{a_0}$$

Fine Structure in the Hydrogen Atomic Spectrum

We have seen that in the Bohr theory of hydrogen atom, the electronic transitions observed in the form of the various spectral series such as Lyman, Balmer, Paschen series, are governed by the selection rule that $\Delta n = 1, 2, 3, \ldots$ *i.e.*, the principal quantum number, n, may change by any integral value. However, observation of the spectrum under conditions of high resolution reveals many additional spectral lines.

Bohr's theory cannot explain these additional lines. Schrodinger's quantum mechanics has successfully accounted for these extra lines in the spectrum of hydrogen. It is found that the spectral transitions are governed by the selection rules :

(i) Δn = any integer, *i.e.,* 1, 2, 3, ...

(ii) $\Delta l = \pm 1$

Transitions which obey these selectrion rules are called **allowed transitions** and transitions which do not obey (or violate) these selection rules are known as **forbidden transitions.**

The Schrodinger Wave Equation for Multi-electron Atoms

The Schrodinger wave equation cannot be solved exactly for atoms beyond hydrogen atom in the Periodic Table. The troublesome term is the interelectron repulsion term in the Hamiltonian because of which the *n*-electron wave equation cannot be split into *n* one-electron wave equations. Hence, methods have been developed for the approximate solution of the multi-electron Schrodinger wave equation. In this book we shall deal briefly with these methods omitting mathematical details. One of these methods is based on the time independent perturbation theory and the other, called the variation method, involves the selection of a trial wave function.

1. Time-independent Perturbation Theory

The Schrodinger wave equation to be solved is

$$\hat{H}\psi = E\psi \qquad ...(119)$$

The Hamiltonian is decomposed into two parts as

$$\hat{H} = \hat{H}^{(0)} + \lambda\hat{H} \qquad ...(120)$$

where $\hat{H}^{(0)}$ is the unperturbed part and $\lambda\hat{H}$ is the perturbation where, λ is the perturbation parameter which measures the deviation of the problem of interest from the unperturbed system. It is further assumed that

$$\lambda\hat{H} << \hat{H}^{(0)} \qquad ...(121)$$

In general λ is set equal to unity which means that perturbation is fully applied.

Associated with $\hat{H}^{(0)}$ are a set of eigen values $E_1^{(0)}, E_2^{(0)}, ..., E_n^{(0)}$ and the corresponding eigen functions $\psi_1^{(0)}, \psi_2^{(0)}, ..., \psi_n^{(0)}$, *i.e.,*

$$\hat{H}\psi_n^{(0)} = E_n^{(0)}\psi_n{}^{(0)} \qquad ...(122)$$

It is assumed that the eigen functions ψ_n and the energy eigen values E_n of the total Hamiltonian $\hat{H}$ can be expressed in the form of a power series of λ

$$\psi_n = \psi_n^{(0)} + \lambda\psi_n^{(1)} + \lambda^2\psi_n^{(2)} + \lambda^3\psi_n^{3} + ... \qquad ...(123)$$

$$E_n = E_n^{(0)} + \lambda E_n^{(1)} + \lambda^2 E_n^{(2)} + \lambda^3 E_n^{(3)} + ... \qquad ...(124)$$

The first term in Eq. (123a) is the zeroth-order term, the second represents the first order correction : the third represents the second order correction, etc., to the unperturbed zeroth-order term. The eigen functions $\psi_n^{(1)}, \psi_n^{(2)}$, ... and the eigen values $E_n^{(1)}, E_n^{(2)}$, ... are independent of λ and $\psi_n^{(1)}, \psi_n^{(2)}$, ... are so chosen that they are orthogonal to $\psi_n^{(0)}$ which is assumed to be normalized. Omitting details when Eqs. (123) (a) and (b) are solved the results to the first-order in λ are

$$\psi_n = \psi_n^{(0)} + \lambda\psi_n^{(1)}$$

$$= \psi_n^{(0)} + \lambda \sum_{m \neq n} \frac{< \psi_n^{(0)} |\hat{H}'| \psi_n^{(0)} >}{E_n^{(0)} - E_m^{(0)}} \psi_m^{(0)}$$

$$E_n = E_n^{(0)} + \lambda E_n^{(1)}$$

$$= E_n^{(0)} + \lambda < \psi_n^{(0)}|\hat{H}|\psi_n^{(0)} > \qquad ...(125)$$

where, $E_n^{(0)} = < \psi_n^{(0)}|\hat{H}^{(0)}|\psi_n^{(0)} > \equiv \hat{H}_m^{(0)}$ ...(126)

It can be further shown that

$$E_n^{(1)} = < \psi_n^{(0)}|\hat{H}'|\psi_n^{(0)} > \qquad ...(127)$$

$$E_n^{(2)} = < \psi_n^{(0)}|\hat{H}'|\psi_n^{(1)} > \qquad ...(128)$$

$$E_n^{(3)} = < \psi_n^{(0)}|\hat{H}'|\psi_n^{(2)} > \qquad ...(129)$$

and $E_n^{(n)} = < \psi_n^{(0)} |\hat{H}'| \psi_n^{(n-1)} >$ ...(130)

These equations show that the calculation of *n*th order energy requires a knowledge of $(n-1)$th order eigen functions. Since, the contribution of second order, third order, etc., terms goes on successively decreasing, we are primarily interested in the first order correction.

Application of first-order perturbation theory to helium atom

We shall solve the Schrodinger wave equation for the ground state of helium atom using the first order time independent perturbation theory. In this case,

$$\hat{H}\psi = E\psi \qquad ...(131)$$

$$\hat{H} = \hat{H}^{(0)} + \hat{H}' \qquad ...(132)$$

where the unperturbed Hamiltonian, $\hat{H}^{(0)}$ is given by

$$\hat{\mathbf{H}}^{(0)} = -\frac{\hbar^2}{2\mu}(\nabla_1^2 + \nabla_2^2) - \frac{Ze^2}{4\pi\varepsilon_0}\left(\frac{1}{r_1} + \frac{1}{r_2}\right) \quad ...(133)$$

and the perturbation is the interelectron repulsion term

$$\hat{\mathbf{H}}' = e/4\pi\varepsilon_0 r_{12} \quad ...(134)$$

Here r_1 and r_2 are the distances of the two electrons from the helium nucleus of charge Ze, and r_{12} is the interelectron distance. We shall use atomic units, a.u. ($\hbar = e = \mu \approx m = 1/4\pi\varepsilon_0 = 1$), so that

$$\hat{\mathbf{H}}^{(0)} = -\frac{1}{2}(\nabla_1^2 + \nabla_2^2) - \left(\frac{2}{r_1} + \frac{2}{r_2}\right) \quad ...(135)$$

$$\hat{\mathbf{H}}' = 1/r_{12} \quad ...(136)$$

Since, $\hat{\mathbf{H}} << \hat{\mathbf{H}}^{(0)}$, it is pertinent to use perturbation theory.

Since, $\hat{\mathbf{H}}^{(0)}$ is the sum of two one-electron Hamiltonians, the unperturbed wave function $\psi^{(0)}(r_1, r_2)$ can be written as the product of two hydrogenic wave functions.

$$\psi^{(0)}(r_1, r_2) = \psi^{(0)}(r_1)\psi^{(0)}(r_2) \quad ...(137)$$

where, $\psi^{(0)}(r_i)$ is the wave function of the ith electron in a hydrogenic atom with nuclear charge = Ze. Thus,

$$\psi^{(0)}(r_1, r_2) = \left(\frac{Z^3}{\pi a_0^3}\right)^{1/2} e^{-Zr_1/a_0} \times \left(\frac{Z_3}{\pi a_0^3}\right)^{1/2} e^{-Zr_2/a_0}$$

$$= (Z^3/\pi)\, e^{-Z(r_1+r_2)} \text{ (in a.u.)} \quad ...(138)$$

The unperturbed ground state energy $E_0^{(0)}$ is euqal to the sum of the ground state energies of two hydrogenic atoms

$$E_0^{(0)} = (-Z^2/2) + (-Z^2/2) = -Z^2 \quad ...(139)$$

The first-order correction to the ground state energy is

$$E_0^{(1)} = <\psi^{(0)}|\hat{\mathbf{H}}'|\psi^{(0)}>$$

$$= \iint \psi^{*(0)}(r_1, r_2)\hat{\mathbf{H}}'\psi^{(0)}(r_1, r_2)\, d\tau_1 d\tau_2 \quad ...(140)$$

Substituting the value of $\psi^{(0)}(r_1, r_2)$ from Eq. (138) into Eq. (140), we obtain

$$E_0^{(1)} = \frac{Z^6}{\pi^2}\iint e^{-2Z(r_1+r_2)(1/r_{12})} d\tau_1 d\tau_2 \quad ...(141)$$

where, the volume elements of the two electrons (in spherical polar coordinates are) :

$$d\tau_1 = r_1^2 \sin\theta_1\, dr_1 d\theta_1 d\phi_1$$

$$d\tau_2 = r_2^2 \sin\theta_2 dr_2 d\theta_2\, d\phi_2$$

The evaluation of the interelectron repulsion integral Eq. (141) is rather tedious; it can be shown that it is given by

$$E_0^{(1)} = (5/8)Z \quad ...(142)$$

Notice that $E_0^{(1)}$ is positive, as was to be expected since the repulsion energy between two electrons is always positive.

Adding Eqs. (139) and (140), we have

$$E_0 = E_0^{(0)} + E_0^{(1)} = -Z^2 + \left(\frac{5}{8}\right)Z$$

$$= -\left(Z^2 - \frac{5}{8}Z\right) \text{(in a.u.)} \quad ...(143a)$$

Re-incorporating the original units we find that

$$E_0 = -\left(Z^2 - \frac{5}{8}Z\right)\frac{\mu e^2}{2\hbar^2} \quad ...(143b)$$

Recalling that the ground state energy of hydrogen atom is $-\frac{1}{2}$ a.u. or $-\mu e^4/2\hbar^2$ or -13.60 eV, we get for helium atom

$$E_0 = -\left(Z^2 - \frac{5}{8}Z\right)(27.2) \text{ eV}$$

$$= -2.75 \text{ a.u.}$$

$$= -74.80 \text{ eV} \quad ...(144)$$

The experimental value is -2.904 a.u. or -78.986 eV. The agreement between the theoretical and experimental values is not good. If the second-order and higher order contributions are included, the agreement improves but is still not very good.

Example 23. *Show that the first order Stark effect on the ground state of hydrogen atom is zero.*

Sol. This is another interesting application of the perturbation theory. In the Stark effect, named after the German physicist J. Stark, who won the 1919 Physics Nobel prize, the system, atom or molecule, is placed in an electric field. The energy levels are split by the field. Let F be the electric field applied in the z-direction, assuming that the hydrogen atom is placed at the origin of the three-dimensional Cartesian coordinate system. Hence, the perturbation is

$$\hat{\mathbf{H}}' = eFz = eFr\cos\theta \quad \text{(in polar coordinates)} ...(i)$$

$$\hat{\mathbf{H}} = \hat{\mathbf{H}}^{(0)} + \hat{\mathbf{H}} \quad ...(ii)$$

The eigen functions and eigen values of the unperturbed Hamiltonian, $\hat{\mathbf{H}}^{(0)}$, for the ground state of hyrdrogen atom are

$$E_0^{(0)} = -\frac{1}{2} \text{ (a.u.)} \quad ...(iii)$$

$$\psi_0^{(0)} = \psi_{1s}^{(0)} \equiv 1s = \frac{1}{\sqrt{\pi}} e^{-r} \text{ (in a.u.)} \quad ...(iv)$$

$$E_n = E_n^0 + E_n^{(1)} + E_n^{(2)} + ... \quad \text{(assuming } \lambda = 1)$$

For the ground state, $n = 0$ so that

$$E_0 = E_0^{(0)} + E_0^{(1)} + E_0^{(2)} + ... \quad ...(v)$$

From Eq. (127)

$$E_0^{(1)} = <\psi_0^{(0)}|\hat{H}'|\psi_0^{(0)}> \equiv 1s|\hat{H}'|1s>$$

$$= <1s|eFr\cos\theta|1s> = eF<1s|r\cos\theta|1s>$$

$$= eF\int \psi_{1s}^{*(0)} r\cos\theta\, \psi_{1s}^{(0)} d\tau \quad ...(vi)$$

Recalling that in spherical polar coordinates,

$$d\tau = r^2 \sin\theta\, dr\, d\theta\, d\phi \quad ...(vii)$$

we have from Eqs. (iv), (vi) and (vii)

$$E_0^{(1)} = eF(1/\pi)\int_0^\infty r^3 e^{-2r} dr \int_0^\pi \sin\theta\cos\theta\, d\theta \int_0^{2\pi} d\phi$$

$$= 2eF\int_0^\infty r^3 e^{-2r} dr \int_0^\pi \sin\theta\cos\theta\, d\theta \quad ...(viii)$$

We need not evaluate the first integral in Eq. (viii) because the second integral is zero

$$\int_0^\pi \sin\theta\cos\theta\, d\theta = \frac{1}{2}\int_0^\pi \sin 2\theta\, d\theta = 0 \quad ...(ix)$$

Hence, $$E_0^{(1)} = 0 \quad ...(x)$$

Thus, we see that there is no first-order Stark effect on the ground state of hydrogen atom.

2. Variation Method

According to the variation method, also called the variation theorem, if ψ is an approximate wave function of a quantum mechanical system an atom or a molecule, described by the Hamiltonian $\hat{H}$, then the energy eigen value of the system, approximately given by the integral

$$E = \frac{<\psi|\hat{H}|\psi>}{<\psi|\psi>} = \frac{\int \psi^* \hat{H}\psi\, d\tau}{\int \psi^*\psi\, d\tau} \quad ...(145)$$

or, if ψ is normalized (so that $<\psi|\psi> = 1$), by the integral

$$E = <\psi|\hat{H}|\psi> \equiv \int \psi^* \hat{H}\psi\, d\tau \quad ...(146)$$

is an upper bound to the ground state energy, E_0 of the system, *i.e.*,

$$E \geq E_0 \quad ...(147)$$

We shall not give the proof of the variation theorem here.

If the approximate wave function, also called the *trial function*, happens to be exact (true) wave function, then

$$E = E_0 \quad ...(148)$$

However, this is seldom the case since we have no idea of the exact wave function, to begin with. The application of the variation method involves the following steps :

(i) Choose a trial wave function ψ dependent on variable parameters.
(ii) Evaluate the integral $<\psi|\hat{H}|\psi>$
(iii) Minimise the above integral with respect to the variable parameters.
(iv) The function ψ with the optimum value of the parameters is the best approximation to the true wave function and the lowest value of $<\psi|\hat{H}|\psi>$ is the nearest approximation to the ture energy.

Application of variation method to helium atom

The Hamiltonian for He atom (in atomic units) is

$$\hat{H} = -\frac{1}{2}(\nabla_1^2 + \nabla_2^2) - \left(\frac{2}{r_1} + \frac{2}{r_2}\right) + \frac{1}{r_{12}} \quad ...(149)$$

where, the symbols have their usual meanings. As a result of screening, each electron (1 and 2) shields the other from the nucleus so that the two electrons do not "see" the same nuclear charge. Here it is natural to use a wave function with nuclear charge Z less than 2. That is, Z is a variation parameter which we shall determine from the variational calculation. It is important to remember that the Hamiltonian in Eq. (149) contains the exact value of $Z = 2$. The variational parameter appears only in the trial wave function.

$$\psi(r_1, r_2) = \left(\frac{Z^3}{\pi}\right)^{1/2} e^{-Zr_1} \times \left(\frac{Z^3}{\pi}\right)^{1/2} e^{-Zr_2} \quad ...(150)$$

$$= (Z^3/\pi)\exp[-Z(r_1 + r_2)] \quad ...(151)$$

$$E = <\psi|\hat{H}|\psi> \quad ...(152)$$

Substituting the value of $\hat{H}$ from Eq. (149) in Eq. (152)

$$E = -\frac{1}{2}<\psi + \nabla_1^2 + \psi> - \frac{1}{2}$$

$$<\psi + \nabla_2^2 + \psi> - 2<\psi\left|\frac{1}{r_1}\right|\psi>$$

$$-2<\psi\left|\frac{1}{r_2}\right|\psi> + <\psi\left|\frac{1}{r_{12}}\right|\psi> \quad ...(153)$$

The Laplacian operator in spherical polar coordinates (r, θ, ϕ) is given by

$$\nabla^2 = \frac{1}{r^2}\frac{\partial}{\partial r}\left(r^2\frac{\partial}{\partial r}\right) + \frac{1}{r^2\sin\theta}\frac{\partial}{\partial\theta}\left(\sin\theta\frac{\partial}{\partial\theta}\right)$$

$$+ \frac{1}{r^2\sin^2\theta}\frac{\partial^2}{\partial\phi^2} \quad ...(154)$$

Since, the trial function Eq. (150) does not depend upon angles θ and ϕ, differentiations with respect to

$\theta_1, \phi_1, \theta_2$ and ϕ_2 vanish so that for the first kinetic energy operator in Eq. (153), we get

$$-\frac{1}{2}<\psi|\nabla_1^2|\psi> = \left(\frac{Z^3}{\pi}\right)^2 \int e^{-Zr_1}\left[-\frac{1}{2r_1^2}\frac{\partial}{\partial r_1}\left(r_1^2\frac{\partial}{\partial r_1}\right)\right]$$

$$e^{-Zr_1} \times r_1^2 \sin\theta_1\, dr_1\, d\theta_1\, d\phi_1 \int e^{-2Zr_2} r_2^2 \sin\theta_2 dr_2 d\theta_2 d\phi_2 \quad \ldots(155)$$

The functions of r_2 are not affected by differentiation. Carrying out the integrations over all angles we obtain

$$-\frac{1}{2}<\psi|\nabla_1^2|\psi> = \left(\frac{Z^3}{\pi}\right)^2 (4\pi)^2$$

$$\int_0^\infty e^{-Zr_1}\left[-\frac{1}{2r_1^2}\frac{\partial}{\partial r_1}\left(r_1^2\frac{\partial e^{-Zr_1}}{\partial r_1}\right)\right] r_1^2 dr_1 \times \int_0^\infty e^{-2Zr_2} r_2^2 dr_2 \quad \ldots(156)$$

The second integral, evaluated using the standard integral, is equal to $2!/(2Z)^3$ so that Eq. (156) becomes

$$(4Z^3)^2\left(-\frac{1}{2}\right)\frac{2!}{(2Z)^3}\int_0^\infty e^{-Zr_1}\left[\frac{\partial}{\partial r_1}(-Zr_1^2 e^{-Zr_1})\right]dr_1$$

$$= (-2Z^3)\int_0^\infty e^{-Zr_1}(-2Zr_1 + Z^2 r_1^2)\, e^{-Zr_1}\, dr_1$$

$$= (-2Z^3)\left[-2Z\int_0^\infty r_1 e^{-2Zr_1} dr_1 + Z^2\int_0^\infty r_1^2 e^{-2Zr_1} dr_1\right]$$

$$= (-2Z^3)\left[-\frac{2Z}{(2Z)^2} + \frac{Z^2\, 2!}{(2Z)^3}\right] = \frac{Z^2}{2} \quad \ldots(157)$$

Similarly, the second kinetic energy operator term in Eq. (153) gives $Z^2/2$. The third and the fourth electron nulcear attraction energy terms can be handled easily. The third term, for instance, simplifies to

$$\left(\frac{Z^3}{\pi}\right)^2 \int e^{-Zr_1} e^{-Zr_2}\left[-\frac{2}{r_1}\right] e^{-Zr_1} e^{-Zr_2} r_1^2 \sin\theta_1 dr_1 d\theta_1 d\phi_1$$

$$\times\, r_2^2 \sin\theta_2 dr_2 d\theta_2 d\phi_2$$

$$= (4Z^3)^2(-2)\int_0^\infty r_1 e^{-2Zr_1} dr_1 \int_0^\infty r_2^2\, e^{-2Zr_2} dr_2$$

$$= -32Z^6 \times \frac{1}{(2Z)^2} \times \frac{2!}{(2Z)^3} = -2Z \quad \ldots(158)$$

Similarly, the fourth term in Eq. (153) gives $-2Z$. The fifth term, the interelectron repulsion energy integral, is somewhat more tedious. So, we will not go into details about its evaluation, merely stating that it evaluates to $(5/8)Z$. Combining all these contributions, Eq. (153) becomes

$$E = 2(Z^2/2) + 2(-2Z) + (5/8)Z = Z^2 - (27/8)Z \quad \ldots(159)$$

Using the variation method, we minimise the energy with respect to Z, obtaining

$$\partial E/\partial Z = 2Z - 27/8 = 0 \text{ whence } Z = 27/16 = 1.69$$

Substituting this value of Z in Eq. (159), we obtain the ground state energy of helium atom

$$E_0 = (27/16)^2 - (27/8)(27/16) = -2.8476 \text{ a.u.}$$

$$= -(2.8476)(27.21\text{ eV})$$

$$= -77.48\text{ eV} \quad [\because 1\text{ a.u.} = 27.21\text{ eV}] \quad \ldots(160)$$

This is much better than the first-order perturbation theory result, *viz.*, – 74.80 eV, we obtained in Eq. (144), the experimental value being – 2.904 a.u., *i.e.*, –78.986 eV. In 1929 E.A. Hyleraas, using a more complicated wave function and the concept of the so-called *electron correlation* which stipulates that electrons try to avoid each other, obtained a result for the ground state energy of helium which is very close to the experimental value. However, this is the realm of electronic computers and we shall not delve into the mathematical details which are beyond the scope of this book.

Example 24. *Using the normalized trial wave function $\psi = (\sqrt{30/a^{5/2}})\, x(a-x)$ for a particle of mass m moving inside an infinite one-dimensional box of width a, calculate the upper bound to the ground state energy and compare with the true value $h^2/8ma^2$.*

Sol. $<E> \int_0^a \psi^* \hat{\mathbf{H}} \psi\, dx$

where, $\hat{\mathbf{H}} = (-\hbar^2/2m)d^2/dx^2 \qquad 0 < x < a$

Thus, $$<E> = -\frac{30\hbar^2}{2ma^5}\int_0^a (ax - x^2)\frac{d^2}{dx^2}(ax - x^2)dx$$

$$= -\frac{30\hbar^2}{ma^5}\int_0^a (x^2 - ax)\, dx$$

$$= -\frac{30\hbar^2}{ma^5}\left|\frac{x^3}{3} - \frac{ax^2}{2}\right|_0^a = \frac{5h^2}{4\pi^2 ma^2}$$

Since, the true value $E_0 = h^2/8ma^2$, we see that $<E>$ is greater than E_0, which is as it should be according to the variation theorem.

$$\%\text{ error} = \frac{(5/4\pi^2 - 1/8)(h^2/ma^2)}{(1/8)(h^2/ma^2)} \times 100 = 1.3\%$$

Comment Though it is not a true variational calculation since it does not use a variation parameter, this examples does illustrate the fact that an approximate trial function always yields an **upper bound** to the true ground state energy.

Example 25. *The hydrogen atom problem has been solved quantum mechanically, the exact ground state wave function being of the form exp (–r) (in a.u.), neglecting the normalization factor; here r is the distance of the electron from the nucleus. Introduce a* *variational parameter α in the exponent to get a trial wave function exp (− αr) (in a.u.). Using variation method, estimate the ground state energy of the electron in hydrogen atom.*

Sol. The Schrodinger wave equation is

$$\hat{\mathbf{H}}\psi = E\psi \qquad \text{...(i)}$$

where, $\hat{\mathbf{H}} = -\frac{1}{2}\nabla^2 - \frac{1}{r}$ (in a.u.) since in a.u.,

$$\hbar = m_e = e = 1/4\pi\varepsilon_0 = 1 \qquad \text{...(ii)}$$

We know that the Laplacian operator ∇^2, in polar coordinates, is given by

$$\nabla^2 = \frac{1}{r^2}\frac{\partial}{\partial r}\left[r^2\frac{\partial}{\partial r}\right] + \frac{1}{r^2 \sin\theta}\frac{\partial}{\partial\theta}\left[\sin\theta\frac{\partial}{\partial\theta}\right] + \frac{1}{r^2\sin^2\theta}\frac{\partial^2}{\partial\phi^2}$$

We see that the trial function $\psi(r) = e^{-\alpha r}$ is spherically symmetric since if does not depend upon coordinates θ and ϕ. Hence, the partial derivatives $\partial\psi/\partial\theta$ and $\partial^2\psi/\partial\phi^2$ vanish, giving

$$\nabla^2 = \frac{1}{r^2}\frac{\partial}{\partial r}\left(r^2\frac{\partial}{\partial r}\right) \qquad \text{...(iii)}$$

Substituting in Eq. (ii) $\hat{\mathbf{H}} = -\frac{1}{2r^2}\frac{\partial}{\partial r}\left(r^2\frac{\partial}{\partial r}\right) - \frac{1}{r}$ ...(iv)

Instead of first normalizing the given trial function and then determining the energy from the relation

$$E = \langle\hat{\mathbf{H}}\rangle = \int \psi^*\hat{\mathbf{H}}\psi\, d\tau \equiv \langle\psi|\hat{\mathbf{H}}|\psi\rangle \qquad \text{...(v)}$$

We will keep it unnormalized and determine the energy using the relation

$$E \equiv \langle\hat{\mathbf{H}}\rangle = \frac{\langle\psi|\hat{\mathbf{H}}|\psi\rangle}{\langle\psi|\psi\rangle} \equiv \frac{\int \psi^*\hat{\mathbf{H}}\psi\, d\tau}{\int \psi^*\psi\, d\tau} \qquad \text{...(vi)}$$

We recall that in spherical polar coordinates (r, θ, ϕ) the volume element $d\tau = r^2\sin\theta\, dr\, d\theta\, d\phi$, where, $0 \le r \le \infty$; $0 \le \theta \le \pi$ and $0 \le \phi \le 2\pi$.

Let us first evaluate $\hat{\mathbf{H}}\psi$

$$\hat{\mathbf{H}}\psi = -\frac{1}{2r^2}\frac{\partial}{\partial r}\left(r^2\frac{\partial e^{-\alpha r}}{\partial r}\right) - \frac{1}{r}e^{-\alpha r}$$

$$\frac{\partial e^{-\alpha r}}{\partial r} = -\alpha e^{-\alpha r}$$

and

$$\frac{\partial}{\partial r}(-\alpha r^2 e^{-\alpha r}) = (-\alpha)\frac{\partial}{\partial r}(r^2 e^{-\alpha r})$$
$$= (-\alpha)(2r - \alpha r^2)\, e^{-\alpha r}$$
$$= (-2\alpha r + \alpha^2 r^2)\, e^{-\alpha r}$$

Thus,

$$\hat{\mathbf{H}}\psi = -\frac{1}{2r^2}(-2\alpha r + \alpha^2 r^2)\, e^{-\alpha r} - \frac{1}{r}e^{-\alpha r}$$
$$= \left(\frac{\alpha - 1}{r} - \frac{\alpha^2}{2}\right)e^{-\alpha r}$$

Substituting in Eq. (vi),

$$E = \frac{\int_0^\infty e^{-\alpha r}\left[\frac{\alpha-1}{r} - \frac{\alpha^2}{2}\right]e^{-\alpha r}r^2 dr \int_0^\pi \sin\theta\, d\theta \int_0^{2\pi} d\phi}{\int_0^\infty e^{-\alpha r}e^{-\alpha r}r^2 dr \int_0^\pi \sin\theta\, d\theta \int_0^{2\pi} d\phi}$$

Cancelling the common factors in the numerator and the denominator and simplifying

$$E = \frac{(\alpha-1)\int_0^\infty r e^{-2\alpha r}\, dr - \frac{\alpha^2}{2}\int_0^\infty r^2 e^{-2\alpha r}\, dr}{\int_0^\infty r^2 e^{-2\alpha r} dr}$$

The integrals occurring in the above equation can be evaluated using the standard integral

$$\int_0^\infty x^n e^{-ax}\, dx = \frac{n!}{a^{n+1}},$$

giving

$$E = \frac{(\alpha-1)\frac{1}{4\alpha^2} - \frac{\alpha^2}{2}\frac{2}{(2\alpha)^3}}{2/(2\alpha)^3}$$
$$= \frac{\frac{\alpha-1}{4\alpha^2} - \frac{1}{8\alpha}}{1/4\alpha^3}$$
$$= \frac{(2\alpha - 2 - \alpha)/8\alpha^2}{1/4\alpha^3} = \frac{1}{2}(\alpha^2 - 2\alpha) \qquad \text{...(vii)}$$

Using the variation method, differentiating E with respect to α and setting $(\partial E/\partial\alpha)_{\alpha_0} = 0$, we have $\partial E/\partial\alpha = (1/2)(2\alpha - 2) = \alpha - 1 = 0$, whence $\alpha = 1$, as expected. Substituting this value of the variational parameter in Eq. (vii),

$$E_0 = -\frac{1}{2} \text{ (a.u.)}$$

which, we recall, is the exact ground state energy of hydrogen atom corresponding to the exact ground state function $\psi = e^{-r}$ (in a.u.)

The Hartree and Hartree Fock Self-Consistent Field (SCF) Method

We have seen that the application of the above two approximate methods to the approximate solution of the Schrodinger wave equation for helium atom, the simplest two-electron system, does not give very accurate result. We expect that for the other atoms in the Periodic Table, the number of inter-electron repulsion terms in the Hamiltonian will increase thereby rendering the exact solution of the wave equation even more difficult. Thus, we need more powerful methods for the calculation of the ground state energy and wave functions of many electron atoms or ions. In 1928, the British physicist D.R. Hartree suggested that the wave function of an n-electron atom be written as the product of n one-electron wave functions.

$$\psi(1, 2, 3, \ldots, n) = \phi_1(1)\,\phi_2(2)\,\phi_3(3)\ldots\phi_n(n) \qquad \text{...(161)}$$

where, $\phi(i)$ are normalised and mutually orthogonal one-electron one-electron wave functions. Thus, $\phi_1(1)$ means that electron 1 occupies atomic orbital ϕ_1, etc. Hartree proposed the self-consistent field (SCF) method according to which each electron is assumed to move in a spherically symmetrical potential due to the nucleus and the average potential of all the electrons execpt the one under consideration. Thus, potential energy (in a.u.) of electron 1 can be written as

$$V_1 = -\frac{Z}{r_1} + \sum_{i \neq 1} \int \frac{\phi_i^2(i)}{r_{1i}} d\tau_i \qquad \ldots(162)$$

Similarly, for every other electron i in the atom

$$V_i = -\frac{Z}{r_i} + \sum_{j \neq 1} \int \frac{\phi_j^2(j)}{r_{ij}} d\tau_j \qquad \ldots(163)$$

where, the first term is the attractive potential energy between the ith electron and the nucleus; it is a negative term. It is the second term in Eq. (163) which represents the self consistent field; here r_{ij} is the distance between electrons i and j; the integral is over all space accessible to electron j and the summation is over all j electrons except $j = i$. The quantity $\phi_i^2(i)$ is the probability distribution of electron i.

Using the expression for V_i, the Schrodinger wave equation for the ith electron in an atom becomes

$$\left(-\frac{1}{2}\nabla_i^2 + V_i\right)\phi_i(i) = \varepsilon_i \phi_i \;\; (i = 1, 2, 3, \ldots, n) \quad \ldots(164)$$

where, ε_i is the energy of the ith orbital ϕ_i assumed to be normalized. The n non-linear simultaneous equations cannot be solved since V_i requires a prior knowledge of all other one electron wave functions ϕ_j. The SCF method is as follows : First, we choose an arbitrary set of *AOs* ϕ_j, ϕ_k, etc. The potential energy field V_i arising from all the electrons except the ith electron is calculated from this chosen set of functions and Eq. (164) is solved numerically on the computer to obtain ϕ_i. This procedure is repeated for each of the n electrons in the atom. In general, the calculated set of $\phi_i s$ is not identical with the original chosen set. The calculations are then repeated using the calculated set of orbitals. The process of *iteration* is continued until the assumed set of $\phi_i s$ and the calculated set are identical. This is expressed by saying that the set of Eq. (164) has been solved by the SCF method.

If $\phi_1'(1)$, $\phi_2'(2)$, $\phi_3'(3)$, ... are the self-consistent orbitals (one-electron wave functions) then the total wave function of the n-electron system is given by

$$\psi'(1, 2, 3, \ldots, n) = \phi_1'(1)\,\phi_2'(2)\,\phi_3'(3), \ldots \phi_n'(n) \quad \ldots(165)$$

The corresponding energy ε associated with this wave function is

$$\varepsilon = \langle \psi' | \hat{\mathbf{H}} | \psi' \rangle$$

$$= \left\langle \phi_1'(1)\,\phi_2'(2) \ldots \phi_n'(n) \left| -\frac{1}{2}\sum_i \nabla_i^2 - \sum_i \frac{Z}{r_i} + \frac{1}{2}\sum_{i \neq j} \frac{1}{r_{ij}} \right| \phi_1'(1)\,\phi_2'(2) \ldots \phi_n'(n) \right\rangle$$

$$= \sum_i \left\langle \phi_1'(1) \left| -\frac{1}{2}\nabla_i^2 - \frac{Z}{r_i} \right| \phi_1'(1) \right\rangle + \frac{1}{2}\sum_i \sum_j \left\langle \phi_i'(i)\,\phi_j'(j) \left| \frac{1}{r_{ij}} \right| \phi_i'(i)\,\phi_j'(j) \right\rangle \quad \ldots(166)$$

Omitting further mathematical details, the final result is

$$\varepsilon = \sum_i \varepsilon_i' - \frac{1}{2}\sum_{i\,j}\sum_{i\,j} \left\langle \phi_i'(i)\,\phi_j' \left| \frac{1}{r_{ij}} \right| \phi_i'(i)\,\phi_j'(j) \right\rangle \ldots(167)$$

In 1930, the Russian physicist V. Fock proposed that since the Hartree wave function Eq. (161) was the product of one-electron spatial functions, an improved wave function should include both the spatial part and the electron spin part. This suggestion had also been made by J.C. Slater (The details are discussed in the next section). Fock solved the many electron Schrodinger wave equation using such a wave function and the Hartree method. This technique is called the Hartree-Fock SCF method. Using this method E. Clementi obtained the SCF wave functions for atoms of various elements in the Periodic Table in 1965.

The Slater Determinant for *n*-Electron Atoms

It was proposed by J.C. Slater in 1930 that for a multi-electron atom (*i.e.*, all the atoms in the Periodic Table except hydrogen atom) the total wave function must consist of the spatial part and the spin part. He showed that the total atomic wave function, which is the product of the spatial wave function and the spin wave function, is antisymmetric (A) with respect to the interchange of electrons, *i.e.*,

$$\psi_{\text{total}} = \psi_{\text{space}} \times \psi_{\text{spin}} \text{ (antisymmetric)} \quad \ldots(168)$$

Thus, for helium atom with the ground state electronic configuration $1s^2$

$$\psi_{\text{space}} = 1s(1)\,1s(2) \qquad \ldots(169)$$

Interchanging the two electrons,

$$\psi_{\text{space}} = 1s(2)\,1s(1) \qquad \ldots(170)$$

That is ψ_{space} is symmetric (S); it does not change sign. If α and β are the spin wave functions for the upward ($\uparrow$) orientation and the downward ($\downarrow$) orientation, respectively, then

$$\psi_{spin} = \begin{cases} \alpha(1)\,\alpha(2);\ (S) \\ \frac{1}{\sqrt{2}}[\alpha(1)\,\beta(2) + \alpha(2)\,\beta(1)];\ (S) \\ \frac{1}{\sqrt{2}}[\alpha(1)\,\beta(2) - \alpha(2)\,\beta(1)];\ (A) \\ \beta(1)\,\beta(2);\ (s) \end{cases} \quad \ldots(171)$$

We see that there are three symmetric (S) and one antisymmetric (A) spin wave functions.

Thus $\psi_{total} = \psi_{space} \times \psi_{spin} = 1s(1)\,1s(2);$

$$(S) \times \begin{cases} \alpha(1)\,\alpha(2);\ (S) \\ \frac{1}{\sqrt{2}}[\alpha(1)\,\beta(2) + \alpha(2)\,\beta(1)];\ (S) \\ \frac{1}{\sqrt{2}}[\alpha(1)\,\beta(2) - \alpha(2)\,\beta(1)];\ (A) \\ \beta(1)\,\beta(2);\ (S) \end{cases} \quad \ldots(172)$$

Hence, the only combination which gives total antisymmetric wave function is the product of the symmetric space function and the antisymmetric spin function. Thus,

$$\psi_{total} \equiv \psi(1, 2) = 1s(1)\,1s(2)\left\{\frac{1}{\sqrt{2}}[\alpha(1)\,\beta(2) - \alpha(2)\beta(1)]\right\}$$

$$= \frac{1}{\sqrt{2}}[1s(1)\,\alpha(1)\,1s(2)\,\beta(2) - 1s(1)\,\beta(1)\,1s(2)\,\alpha(2)] \quad \ldots(173)$$

which can be written as a 2×2 determinant,

$$\psi(1, 2) = \frac{1}{\sqrt{2}}\begin{vmatrix} 1s(1)\,\alpha(1) & 1s(2)\,\alpha(2) \\ 1s(1)\,\beta(1) & 1s(2)\,\beta(2) \end{vmatrix} \quad \ldots(174)$$

This is called the **Slater determinant for helium atom.**

Interchanging electrons 1 and 2 in Eq. (208), we have

$$\psi(1, 2) = \frac{1}{\sqrt{2!}}\begin{vmatrix} 1s(2)\,\alpha(2) & 1s(1)\,\alpha(1) \\ 1s(2)\,\beta(2) & 1s(1)\,\beta(1) \end{vmatrix}$$

$$= -\psi(1, 2) \quad \ldots(175)$$

This result follows from the fact that if in a determinant two rows (or columns) are interchanged, it changes sign. What is true of a two-electron system is also true of polyelectron atoms and molecules. The polyelectron wave function also satisfies the antisymmetry rule. The solution of the Schrodinger wave equation for such systems must start from the appropriate Slatter determinant for a given electronic configuration. The Hartree-Fock SCF method, using Slater determinants has been succssfully employed by theoretical chemists and physicists. In 1951 the American physicist C.C.J. Roothaan extended it to molecules as well.

Example 26. *Write the Slater determinants for the ground states of (a) lithium atom ($1s^2\,2s^1$) and (b) carbon atom ($1s^2 2s^2 2p^2$).*

Sol. (a) $\psi(1, 2, 3) = \frac{1}{\sqrt{3!}}\begin{vmatrix} 1s(1)\,\alpha(1) & 1s(2)\,\alpha(2) & 1s(3)\,\alpha(3) \\ 1s(1)\,\beta(1) & 1s(2)\,\beta(2) & 1s(3)\,\beta(3) \\ 2s(1)\,\alpha(1) & 2s(2)\,\alpha(2) & 2s(3)\,\alpha(3) \end{vmatrix}$

(b) $\psi(1, 2, 3, 4, 5, 6)$

$$= \frac{1}{\sqrt{6!}}\begin{vmatrix} 1s(1)\,\alpha(1) & 1s(2)\,\alpha(2) & 1s(3)\,\alpha(3) & 1s(4)\,\alpha(4) & 1s(5)\,\alpha(5) & 1s(6)\,\alpha(6) \\ 1s(1)\,\beta(1) & 1s(2)\,\beta(2) & 1s(3)\,\beta(3) & 1s(4)\,\beta(4) & 1s(5)\,\beta(5) & 1s(6)\,\beta(6) \\ 2s(1)\,\alpha(1) & 2s(2)\,\alpha(2) & 2s(3)\,\alpha(3) & 2s(4)\,\alpha(4) & 2s(5)\,\alpha(5) & 2s(6)\,\alpha(6) \\ 2s(1)\,\beta(1) & 2s(2)\,\beta(2) & 2s(3)\,\beta(3) & 2s(4)\,\beta(4) & 2s(5)\,\beta(5) & 2s(6)\,\beta(6) \\ 2p_{+1}(1)\,\alpha(1) & 2p_{+1}(2)\,\alpha(2) & 2p_{+1}(3)\,\alpha(3) & 2p_{+1}(4)\,\alpha(4) & 2p_{+1}(5)\,\alpha(5) & 2p_{+1}(6)\,\alpha(6) \\ 2p_0(1)\,\alpha(1) & 2p_0(2)\,\alpha(2) & 2p_0(3)\,\alpha(3) & 2p_0(4)\,\alpha(4) & 2p_0(5)\,\alpha(5) & 2p_0(6)\,\alpha(6) \end{vmatrix}$$

There is no simple expression for the energy of a many electron atom. However, in contrast with the energy of the hydrogen atom, the energy of the polyelectronic atom can be written as

$$E_n = -\frac{2\pi^2 Z_{eff}^2 \mu e^4}{(4\pi\varepsilon_0)^2 n^2 h^2} \quad \ldots(176)$$

where, n is the effective principal quantum number, μ is the reduced mass and Z_{eff} is the effective nuclear charge, defined as $Z_{eff} = Z - \sigma$ where, Z is the atomic number (the true nuclear charge) and σ is the **screening constant** (or **shielding constant**) which depends upon the quantum numbers n and l.

J.C. Slater formulated the following empirical rules (known as **Slater's rules**) for estimating σ :

1. Electrons farther away from the nucleus than the electron under consideration do not contribute to α.
2. The electrons in the same group, *i.e., ns, np, nd* or *nf*-electrons contribute 0.35 to σ (except 1s-electron for which $\sigma = 0.30$).
3. In the case of electrons in the *ns* and *np* orbitals, all electrons in the $(n - 1)$ shell contribute 0.85 each and all electrons in the $(n - 2)$ shell contribute 1.0 each.
4. In the case of electrons in the *nd* and *nf* orbitals, each electron in the lower groups contributes 1.0 to σ.

Knowing the value of σ, Z_{eff} can be calculated.

Example 27. *Calculate the effective nuclear charge for (i) the 3s electron in sulphur (Z = 16) (ii) the 4s electron in potassium (Z = 19) (iii) a 3d and a 4s electron in vanadium (Z = 23)*

Sol. (i) Electronic configuration of S atom is

$$1s^2 2s^2 2p^6 3s^2 3p^4$$

For the 3s-electron

$$\sigma = (5 \times 0.35) + (8 \times 0.85) + (2 \times 1.00) = 10.55$$

$$\therefore \quad Z_{eff} = Z - \sigma = 16 - 10.55 = 5.45$$

(ii) Electronic configuration of K atom is

$$1s^3 2s^2 2p^6 3s^2 3p^6 4s^1$$

For the 4s electron $\sigma = 8 \times 0.85 + 1 \times 10 = 16.80$

$$\therefore \quad Z_{eff} = Z - \sigma = 19 - 16.80 = 2.20$$

(iii) Electronic configuration of V atom is

$$1s^2 2s^2 2p^6 3s^2 3p^6 3d^3 4s^2$$

For the 3d electron

$$\sigma = 2 \times 0.35 + 18 \times 1 = 18.70$$

$$\therefore \quad Z_{eff} = Z - \sigma = 23 - 18.70 = 4.30$$

For the 4s electron

$$\sigma = 0.35 \times 1 + 11 \times 0.85 + 10 \times 1$$

$$= 0.35 + 9.35 + 10 = 19.70$$

$$\therefore \quad Z_{eff} = 23 - 19.70 = 3.30$$

Example 28. *The energy of atoms and molecules, as obtained by solving the Schrodinger equation, is generally expressed in units of 'hartress' after Hartree who has done fundamental work in quantum mechanics. Verify that 1 hartree = 27.2 eV.*

Sol. 1 hartree = e^2/a_0 where, a_0, the Bohr radius, is given by $a_0 = \hbar^2/me^2$

$$\therefore \quad 1 \text{ hartree} = me^4/\hbar^2 \quad \text{(in CGS units)}$$

$$= \frac{me^4}{(4\pi\varepsilon_0)^2 \hbar^2} \quad \text{(in SI units)}$$

Let us solve this problem in both the units.

(i) In CGS units

$$1 \text{ hartree} = \frac{(9.107 \times 10^{-23} \text{g})\,(4.8 \times 10^{-10} \text{esu})^4}{(1.0545 \times 10^{-27} \text{ ergs})^2 (1.602 \times 10)^{-19} \text{ erg/eV})}$$

$$= 27.2 \text{ eV}$$

(ii) In SI units

$$1 \text{ hartree} = \frac{(9.107 \times 10^{-31} \text{kg})\,(1.602 \times 10^{-19} \text{C})^4}{(1.11264 \times 10^{-10} \text{C}^2\text{N}^{-1}\text{m}^{-2})^2 (1.0545 \times 10^{-34} \text{Js})^2 \; (1.602 \times 10^{-19} \text{J/eV}}$$

$$= 27.2 \text{ eV}$$

Note 1 hartree of energy is also called the atomic unit (a.u.) of energy.

1 hartree = 27.2 eV = 2 Ry where Ry = Rydberg.

Example 29. *Write the Hamiltonian for the following quantum systems : (a) Helium atom (b) Lithium atom (c) H_2^+ (d) H_2 (e) H_2^-. Which of the terms is hardest to handle in solving the Schrodinder equation in each case?*

Sol. (a) **He atom** It contains one nucleus and two electrons numbered 1 and 2 (Fig. 16.9). Here r_1 is the distance of electron 1 from the nucleus r_2 is the distance of electron 2 from the nucleus and r_{12} is the interelectron distance. The charge on the electron is e while that on the nucleus is Ze (Here, $Z = 2$).

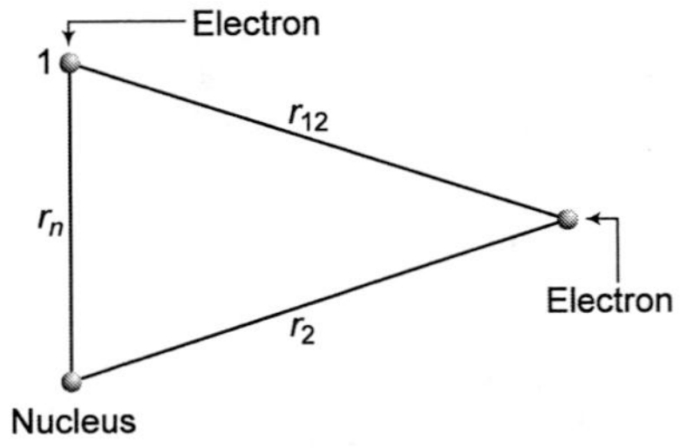

Fig. 16.9 The coordinate system for helium atom.

The Hamiltonian for the system is given by

$$\hat{\mathbf{H}} = -\frac{\hbar^2}{2m}\nabla_1^2 - \frac{\hbar^2}{2m}\nabla_2^2 - \frac{2e^2}{4\pi\varepsilon_0 r_1} - \frac{2e^2}{4\pi\varepsilon_0 r_2} + \frac{e^2}{4\pi\varepsilon_0 r_{12}} \quad \text{...(i)}$$

$$= -\frac{\hbar^2}{2m}(\nabla_1^2 + \nabla_2^2) + \frac{2e^2}{4\pi\varepsilon_0}\left(\frac{-1}{r_1} - \frac{1}{r_2}\right) + \frac{e^2}{4\pi\varepsilon_0 r_{12}} \quad \text{...(ii)}$$

In Eq. (i), the first two terms are the kinetic energy (Laplacian) operators for electrons 1 and 2 respectively; the third and fourth terms give the attraction of two electrons to the nucleus and the last term gives the repulsion between the two electrons; it is called the inter electron repulsion energy term.

(b) **Lithium atom** It contains one nucleus and three electrons 1, 2 and 3 (here, $Z = 3$). Hence,

$$\hat{\mathbf{H}} = -\frac{\hbar^2}{2m}(\nabla_1^2 + \nabla_2^2 + \nabla_3^2)$$

$$+ \frac{1}{4\pi\varepsilon_0}\left[-\frac{3e^2}{r_1} - \frac{3e^2}{r_2} - \frac{3e^2}{r_3} + \frac{e^2}{r_{12}} + \frac{e^2}{r_{232}} + \frac{e^2}{r_{31}}\right]$$

The interpretation of these terms is similar to that given in(a) above. The last three terms are interelectron repulsion energy terms.

(c) $\mathbf{H_2^+}$ It contains two nuclei A and B and one electron $Z = 1$ (Fig. 16.10)

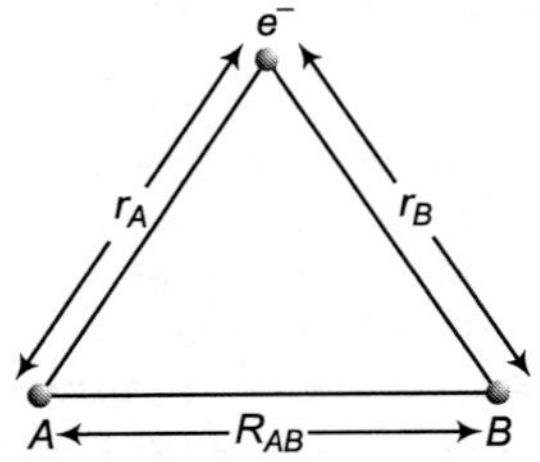

Fig. 16.10 The coordinate system for H_2^+.

The Hamiltonian is given by

$$\hat{\mathbf{H}} = -\frac{\hbar^2}{2m}\nabla^2 + \frac{1}{4\pi\varepsilon_0}\left[-\frac{e^2}{r_A} - \frac{e^2}{r_B} + \frac{e^2}{R_{AB}}\right]$$

There is no interelectron repulsion term here because the system contains only one electron. The last term is internuclear repulsion energy term.

(d) $\mathbf{H_2}$ It contains two nuclei A and B and two electrons 1 and 2. $Z = 1$ (Fig. 16.11). The Hamiltonian of the system is given by

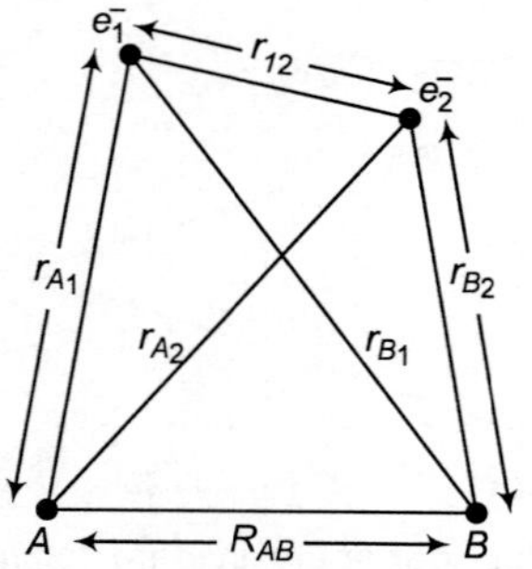

Fig. 16.11 The coordinate system for H_2.

$$\hat{\mathbf{H}} = -\frac{\hbar^2}{2m}(\nabla_1^2 + \nabla_2^2) + \frac{1}{4\pi\varepsilon_0}\left[-\frac{e^2}{r_{A_1}} - \frac{e^2}{r_{A_2}} - \frac{e^2}{r_{B_1}} - \frac{e^2}{r_{B_2}} + \frac{e^2}{r_{12}} + \frac{e^2}{R_{AB}}\right]$$

Here the term e^2/r_{12} is the intere-electron repulsion term and the last term is the internuclear repulsion.

(e) $\mathbf{H_2^-}$ It contains three electrons 1, 2, 3 and two nuclei A and B. Hence,

$$\hat{\mathbf{H}} = -\frac{\hbar^2}{2m}(\nabla_1^2 + \nabla_2^2 + \nabla_3^2) + \frac{1}{4\pi\varepsilon_0}\left[-\frac{e^2}{r_{A_1}} - \frac{e^2}{r_{A_2}} - \frac{e^2}{r_{A_3}} - \frac{e^2}{r_{B_1}} - \frac{e^2}{r_{B_2}} - \frac{e^2}{r_{B_3}} + \frac{e^2}{r_{12}} + \frac{e^2}{r_{13}} + \frac{e^2}{r_{23}} + \frac{e^2}{R_{AB}}\right]$$

Here the interelectron repulsion terms are (e^2/r_{12}), (e^2/r_{13}) and (e^2/r_{23}) while the last term is internuclear repulsion term.,

In all the above cases, the interelectron repulsion term is the most difficult to handle in solving the Schrodinger equation. For molecules, the internuclear term is considered a constant since the nuclei are infinitely heavier than the electrons.

Example 30. *Define the term degeneracy of an energy level. Calculate the degeneracies of the following systems : (i) third energy level of a particle in a one-dimensional box of infinite height (ii) the rigid diatomic rotor in the third rotational energy level (iii) the hydrogen atom in the third energy state and (iv) the hydrogen atom in the third excited state.*

Sol. When two or more wave functions (eigen functions) belong to the same energy state, *i.e..*, have the same energy, the energy level is said to be degenerate, *i.e.*, it is said to possess degeneracy, *e.g.*, degeneracy is a dimensionless quantity. An energy level with $g = 2$ is called two-fold degenerate and an energy level with $g = 3$ is called three fold degenerate, and so on.

(i) In this case, $g = 1$, *i.e.*, the energy level is **non-degenerate**. One dimensional systems are always non-degenerate in all the energy levels.

(ii) For a diatomic molecule rotating as a rigid rotor, the degeneracy is given by

$$g_J = 2J + 1;\ J = 0, 1, 2, 3, \ldots$$

where, J is the rotational quantum number.

Here, $J = 2$; hence $g_2 = 2 \times 2 + 1 = 5$, *i.e.*, the energy level is *five-fold degenerate*

(iii) For hydrogen atom, since the energy is given by $E_n = -R_H/n^2$ where, $n = 1, 2, 3, 4, \ldots$

the degeneracy is given by $g_n = n^2$

Here, $n = 3$, so that $g_3 = (3)^2 = 9$, *i.e.*, the energy level is **nin-fold degenerate**

(iv) Here, $n = 4$, so that $g_4 = (4)^2 = 16$, *i.e.*, the energy level is **16-fold degenerate.**

Example 31. *Calculate the degeneracies of a particle of mass m is a three-dimensional cubical box of width a having energies equal to (i) 6 (ii) 9 (iii) 12 and (iv) 14 in units of $(h^2/8ma^2)$.*

Sol. From Eq. 82

$$E_{n_x, n_y, n_z} = (n_x^2 + n_y^2 + n_z^2)(h^2/8ma^2),$$

where, $n_x, n_y, n_z = 1, 2, 3, \ldots$

Here we shall tabulate the various combinations of n_x, n_y and n_z which give rise to the energies given above.

(i) $n_x^2 + n_y^2 + n_z^2 = 6$

Three different combinations of n_x, n_y and n_z, *viz.*, (2, 1, 1) (1, 2, 1) and (1, 1, 2) give energy $= 6\,(h^2/8ma^2)$

n_x	n_y	n_z
2	1	1
1	2	1
1	1	2

n_x	n_y	n_z
2	2	1
2	1	2
1	2	2

Hence, $g = 3$, *i.e.*, the energy level is **three-fold degenerate.**

(ii) $n_x^2 + n_y^2 + n_z^2 = 9$

The combinations are (2, 2, 1), (2, 1, 2) and (1, 2, 2).

Hence, $g = 3$

(iii) $n_x^2 + n_y^2 + n_z^2 = 12$

$g = 1$ because only one combination (2, 2, 2) gives energy $= 12(h^2/8ma^2)$. The energy level is **non-degenerate**.

(iv) $n_x^2 + n_y^2 + n_z^2 = 14$

Here, six combinations, as shown, give energy

$$= 14(h^2/8ma^2)$$

Hence, $g = 6$. The eneregy level is thus **six-fold degenerate**.

n_x	n_y	n_z
1	2	3
1	3	2
2	1	3
3	1	2
2	3	1
3	2	1

Probability Distribution of Electrons Around the Nucleus

As mentioned before, the value of ψ in the Schrodinger wave equation is important since ψ^2 gives the probability of finding an electron of a given energy (*i.e.*, of known quantum numbers) at a given distance from the nucleus. Thus, by determining ψ^2 at different distances from the nucleus, it is possible to trace out a region of space around the nucleus where there is **high probability** of locating the electron. Each such region of space, as already pointed out, is called an orbital.

The probability of locating the electron at different distances from the nucleus can be represented graphically by plotting probability (ψ^2) against the distance (r) from the nucleus of the atom. However, electron probability distribution is generally expressed in the form of **radial probability distribution** which means the probability of finding an electron within a small radial space around the nucleus.

Let us suppose that the space around the nucleus is divided into a very large number of thin concentric shells of thickness dr at a distance r from the nucleus. The volume of a spherical shell between radii r and $r + dr$ will be given by $4\pi r^2 dr$. The probability of finding electron within this spherical shell will be given by $4\pi r^2 \psi^2 dr$. The radial probability at a distance r from the nucleus is thus given by the function, $4\pi r^2 \psi^2 dr$. In this function, while the probability factor ψ^2 decreases the volume factor $4\pi r^2 dr$ increaess with increase in the value of r. The radial probability distribution of the electron is thus obtained by plotting the function $4\pi r^2 \psi^2$ against the distance r from the nucleus.

The probability of finding an electron at zero distance from the nucleus is zero. The probability increases gradually as the distance increases, goes to a maximum and then begins to decrease. The peak of the curve gives the distance from the nucleus where the probability of finding the electron is maximum. This distance is called the **radius of maximum probability**. In the case of hydrogen atom, the radius of maximum probability is 0.529 Å.

Bohr's model restricts the electron to a definite orbit at a fixed distance from the nucleus. The wave mechanical model, however, gives merely the maximum probability of locating the electron at a given distance from the nucleus. In the case of hydrogen atom, for instance, according to Bohr's calculations, the electron under ordinary conditions always stays at a distance of 0.529 Å from the nucleus. According to the wave mechanical mode, however, the electron keeps on moving toward or away from the nucleus and the maximum probability of locating it lies at a radius of 0.529 Å from the nucleus.

Wave Mechanical Treatment of Probability Distribution for 1*s* Atomic Orbital of Hydrogen

Consider the 1*s* orbital wave function of hydrogen atom given by

$$\psi_{1s} = (1/\pi a_0^3)^{1/2} e^{-r/a_0} \qquad \ldots(177)$$

where, r is the distance of the electron from the nucleus. The probability density for an electron in this orbital is given by

$$\psi_{1s}^2 = (1/\pi a_0^3) e^{-2r/a_0} \qquad \ldots(178)$$

It may be noted that ψ_{1s}^2 is independent of θ and ϕ and hence the electron distribution in 1*s* orbital is spherically symmetrical. Graphically the plot of ψ_{1s}^2 against r is as shown by curve *a* in Fig. 16.12.

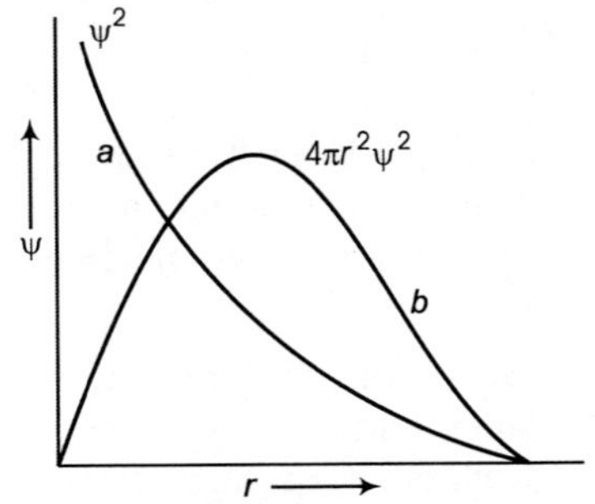

Fig. 16.12 The probability densities for the 1*s* atomic orbital of hydrogen.

There is also another procedure for describing the electron distribution in an atomic orbital. It consists in determining the probability of finding an electron in a spherical shell of thickness dr at distance r from the nucleus. This is called radial probability. The radial probability distribution of electron is given by

$$P(r)\,dr = 4\pi r^2 \psi_{1s}^2\,dr$$

$$= 4\pi r^2 \left(\frac{1}{\pi a_0^3}\right) e^{-2r/a_0}\,dr \quad \ldots(179)$$

The plot of $P(r)$, *i.e.*, of $4\pi r^2 \psi_{1s}^2$ against r is given by curve b in Fig. 16.12. The maximum of the curve is found by differentiating $P(r)$ with respect to r and setting the derivative equal to zero, *i.e.*,

$$\frac{dP(r)}{dr} = \frac{4}{a_0^3}\left(-\frac{2r^2}{a_0} + 2r\right) e^{-2r/a_0} = 0 \quad \ldots(180)$$

It readily follows from Eq. (180) that

$$r = a_0 \qquad (\because e^{-2r/a_0} \neq 0)$$

Thus, we find that the maximum radial probability occurs at a distance a_0, the Bohr radius. We, therefore, conclude that the most probable distance of the 1*s* electron from the nucleus is precisely what has been predicted by the Bohr theory. As already mentioned, while the Bohr model restricts the electron to a definite orbit at a fixed distance from the nucleus, the wave mechanical model gives merely the maximum probability of locating the electron at a given distance from the nucleus.

Physical Interpretation of the Hydrogenic Atomic Orbitals

According to the Bohr theory, the angular momentum L of an electron in an orbital is given by

$$L = n(h/2\pi);\ n = 1, 2, 3, \ldots \quad \ldots(181)$$

However, according to wave mechanics, the value of L is given by

$$L = [l\,(l+1)^{1/2}]\hbar = [l\,(l+1)]^{1/2}\left(\frac{h}{2\pi}\right) \quad \ldots(182)$$

Thus, while according to the Bohr theory the ground state angular momentum is equal to $h/2\pi$ since $n = 1$, (*ie.*, it is finite), according to wave mechanics its value is zero (since, $l = 0$).

Consider an electron of mass m_e moving about the nucleus at a distance r in an orbit with velocity u. The centrifugal force which keeps the electron away from the nucleus is given by

$$F = \frac{m_e u^2}{r} = \frac{m_e^2 u^2 r^2}{m_e r^3} = \frac{L^3}{m_e r^3} \quad \ldots(183)$$

where, $L = m_e ur$ is the angular momentum of the electron.

In terms of atomic units, frequently used in quantum mechanics, we set m_e as well as e and $\hbar = 1$. Hence, in atomic units we can write Eq. (182) as

$$L^2 = l(l+1) \quad \ldots(184)$$

Substituting for L^2 in Eq. (183), we have

$$F = l(l+1)/r^3 \quad \ldots(185)$$

The radial motion of an electron in an atom is controlled by the centrifugal force given by Eq. (185) as well as by the coulombic force of attraction, *viz.*, $-Ze^2/r^2$ (or $-Z/r^2$ in atomic units). For the atom to be stable,

$$\frac{l(l+1)}{r^3} - \frac{Z}{r^2} = 0 \text{ or } r = l(l+1)/Z \quad \ldots(186)$$

Eq. (186) shows that, other things being equal, an electron in an orbital of high angular momentum tends to say farther from the nucleus than an electron in a state of lower angular momentum. Fig. 16.13 shows the ratial parts of the hydrogenic wave functions for the principal quantum number $n = 3$. We see that the higher the value of l, the less likely it is to be found near the nucleus. Thus, for a given value of n, the size of the **orbit** increases with increase in the azimuthal quantum number, l.

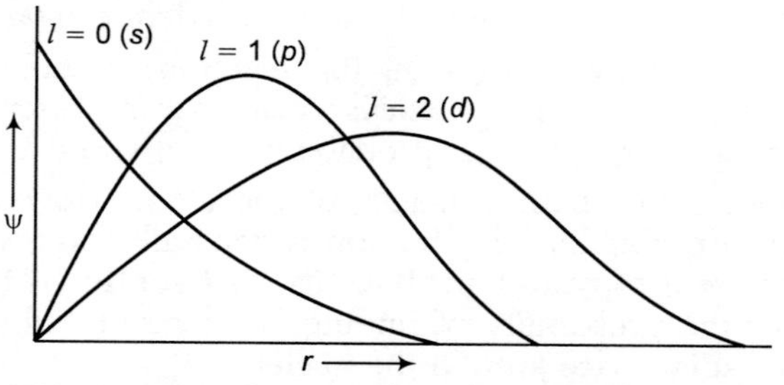

Fig. 16.13 Radial parts of the hydrogenic wave functions for the principal quantum number $n - 3$.

Example 32. *Calculate the probability of finding the electron in a sphere of radius $r = a_0$ (Bohr radius). Given that the 1s wave function of hydrogen atom is $\psi_{1s} = (1/\pi a_0^3)^{1/2}\exp(-r/a_0)$.*

Sol. The Probability is given by

$$P = \int \psi^*\psi\,d\tau = \frac{1}{\pi a_0^3}\int_0^{a_0} e^{-2r/a_0} r^2 dr \int_0^{\pi} \sin\theta\,d\theta \int_0^{2\pi} d\phi$$

$$= \frac{4}{a_0^3}\int_0^{a_0} e^{-2r/a_0} r^2 dr$$

After integrating by parts, we otbain

$$P = \frac{4}{a_0^3}\left\{\left[\frac{a_0}{2} r^2 e^{-2r/a_0}\right]_0^{a_0} + \left[-\frac{a_0^2}{2} r e^{-2r/a}\right]_0^{a_0} + \left[-\frac{a_0^3}{4} e^{-2r/a_0}\right]_0^{a_0}\right\}$$

$$= -5e^{-2} + 1 = 0.323 \qquad \text{(where, } e = 2.71\text{)}$$

Hermitian operators

Hermitian operators, named after the 19th century mathematician Charles Hermite, play a very important role in quantum mechanics. An operator $\hat{\mathbf{A}}$ is said to be Hermitian if

$$\int \overset{*}{\psi}_1 (\hat{\mathbf{A}}\psi_2) d\tau = \int (\hat{\mathbf{A}}\psi_1)\overset{*}{\psi}_2\, d\tau \qquad \ldots(187)$$

where, ψ_1 and ψ_2 are the eigen functions of the operator $\hat{\mathbf{A}}$. The asterisk shown as superscript represents the complex conjugate of the quantity. We shall prove a significant result that a Hermitian operator has real eigen values. Since, $\hat{\mathbf{A}}$ is an operator it obeys the eigen vealue equation

$$\hat{\mathbf{A}}\psi = \lambda\psi \qquad \ldots(188)$$

where, ψ is the eigen function of $\hat{\mathbf{A}}$ and λ is its eigen value. Multiplying both sides of Eq. (225) by the complex conjugate of ψ, *viz.*, $\overset{*}{\psi}$ and integrating over all space, we have

$$\int \overset{*}{\psi}\hat{\mathbf{A}}\psi\, d\tau = \lambda \int \overset{*}{\psi}\psi\, d\tau \qquad \ldots(189)$$

Taking the complex conjugate of every quantity in Eq. (188), we obtain

$$\hat{\mathbf{A}}^* \overset{*}{\psi} = \lambda^* \overset{*}{\psi} \qquad \ldots(190)$$

Multiplying both sides with ψ and integrating over all space, we obtain

$$\int \psi A^* \overset{*}{\psi}\, d\tau = \lambda^* \int \overset{*}{\psi}\psi\, d\tau \qquad \ldots(191)$$

According to the definition of the Hermitian operator, the left hand sides of Eqs. (189) and (191) an equal, so that

$$\lambda \int \overset{*}{\psi}\psi d\tau = \lambda^* \int \overset{*}{\psi}\psi\, d\tau \qquad \ldots(192)$$

i.e., $\lambda = \overset{*}{\lambda}$. This means that the eigen value λ is equal to its complex conjugate which is true only if λ is real. Since, most of the observables (observable quantities), which are physically measurable dynamical variables, are represented by Hermitian operators in quantum mechanics, they have real eigen values.

Secular Equations

In many examples, it is generally desirable to express the variation function in terms of a set of function ϕ. These functions are of class θ and are generally normalised. Therefore,

$$\psi = a_1\phi_1 + a_2\phi_2 + \ldots + a_n\phi_n \qquad \ldots(193)$$

where, $a_2, a_2, \ldots, a_n$ are arbitrary parameters. Their values can be varied to give a minimum in the energy. For the sake of simplicity, we will consider the variation function in terms of two functions only *i.e.*,

$$\psi = a_1\phi_1 + a_2\phi_2 \qquad \ldots(194)$$

From the variation method, we know

$$E = \frac{\int \overset{*}{\psi}\hat{\mathbf{H}}\psi\, d\tau}{\int \psi\overset{*}{\psi}\, d\tau} \qquad \ldots(195)$$

From Eqs. (194) and (195), we get

$$E = \frac{\int (a_1\phi_1^* + a_2\phi_2^*)\, H\, ((a_1\phi_1 + a_2\phi_2)\, d\tau}{\int (a_1\phi_1^* + a_2\phi_2^*)(a_1\phi_1 + a_2\phi_2)\, d\tau} \ldots(196)$$

or $$E = \int (a_1\phi_1^* + a_2\phi_2^*)(a_1\phi_1 + a_2\phi_2)\, d\tau$$

$$= \int (a_1\phi_1^* + a_2\phi_2^*)\, H\, (a_1\phi_1 + a_2\phi_2)\, d\tau$$

$$+ E\,(a_1^2 \int \phi_1^*\phi_1 d\tau + 2a_1a_2 \int \phi_1^*\phi_2 d\tau + a_2^2 \int \phi_2^*\hat{\mathbf{H}}\phi_2 d\tau)$$

$$= a_1^2 \int \phi_1^*\hat{\mathbf{H}}\phi_1 d\tau + a_1a_2 \int \phi_1^*\hat{\mathbf{H}}\phi_1 d\tau$$

$$+ a_2^2 \int \phi_2^*\hat{\mathbf{H}}\phi_2\, d\tau \quad \ldots(197)$$

In order to get the minimum value of E, it is required to minimise E with respect to both a_1 and a_2. For this, differentiation is used with respect to both a_1 and a_2. Differentiation Eq. (197) with respect to a_1, we get

$$E\,[2a_1 \int \phi_1^*\phi_1 d\tau + 2a_2 \int \phi_1^*\phi_2 d\tau]$$

$$+ \frac{\partial E}{\partial a_1}[a_1^2 \int \phi_1^*\phi_1 d\tau + 2a_1a_2 \int \phi_1^*\phi_2 d\tau + a_2^2 \int \phi_2^*\phi_2 d\tau]$$

$$= 2a_1 \int \phi_1^*\hat{\mathbf{H}}\phi_1 d\tau + 2a_2 \int \phi_2^*\hat{\mathbf{H}}\phi_2 d\tau \quad \ldots(198)$$

If we differentiate Eq. (197) with respect to a_2, we get an equation similar to Eq. (198).

According to the rules of differential calculus, the minimum value of E with respect to a_1 and a_2 is obtained by putting

$$\left(\frac{\partial E}{\partial a_1}\right)_{a_2} = \left(\frac{\partial E}{\partial a_2}\right)_{a_1} = 0 \qquad \ldots(199)$$

For the sake of simplicity, it is describe to introduce the symbolism

$$\hat{\mathbf{H}}_{iJ} = \int \phi_1{}^*\hat{\mathbf{H}}\phi_J d\tau \text{ and } S_{iJ} = \int \phi_i^*\phi_J d\tau$$

$$\ldots(200)$$

By applying the condition of Eq. (199), *i.e.,* $\partial E/\partial a_1 = 0$ to Eq. (198), we obtain an equation which on substitution according to Eq. (200) gives a new equation

$$(H_{11} - ES_{11})\, a_1 + (H_{12} - ES_{12})\, a_2 = 0 \quad ...(201)$$

The equivalent equation will be obtained by applying the condition $\partial E/\partial a_2 = 0$, *i.e.,*

$$(H_{21} - ES_{21}) a_1 + (H_{22} - ES_{22})\, a_2 = 0 \quad ...(202)$$

Eqs. (201) and (202) are known as **secular equations.** These equations are of the form

$$ax + by = 0 \text{ and } cx + dy = 0$$

In the determinantal form the above equations can also be put as

$$\begin{vmatrix} a & b \\ c & d \end{vmatrix} = 0$$

On applying the above condition applied to Eqs. (201) and (202), we get

$$\begin{vmatrix} \hat{\mathbf{H}}_{11} - ES_{11} & \hat{\mathbf{H}}_{12} - ES_{12} \\ \hat{\mathbf{H}}_{21} - ES_{21} & \hat{\mathbf{H}}_{22} - ES_{22} \end{vmatrix} = 0 \quad ...(203)$$

In order to express ψ in terms of n independent terms, the secular determinant of Eq. (203) can be expressed as

$$\begin{vmatrix} \hat{\mathbf{H}}_{11} - ES_{11} & \hat{\mathbf{H}}_{12} - ES_{12} \; ... & \hat{\mathbf{H}}_{1n} - ES_{1n} \\ \hat{\mathbf{H}}_{21} - ES_{21} & \hat{\mathbf{H}}_{22} - ES_{22} \; ... & \hat{\mathbf{H}}_{2n} - ES_{2n} \\ \hat{\mathbf{H}}_{n1} - ES_{n1} & \hat{\mathbf{H}}_{n2} - ES_{n2} \; ... & \hat{\mathbf{H}}_{nn} - ES_{nn} \end{vmatrix} = 0$$

...(204)

Important Theorems of Quantum Mechanics

1. **Theorem 1** Two eigen functions of a Hermitian operator with different eigen values are orthogonal.
2. **Theorem 2** If two operators commute, they have the same set of eigen functions.
3. **Theorem 3** Any arbitrary function can be arbitrarily expanded in a series of orthonormal functions.

Proof of theorem 1 Let $\hat{\mathbf{A}}$ be the Hermitian operator. Then its eigenvalue equations are

$$\hat{\mathbf{A}}\psi_1 = \lambda_1 \psi_1 \quad ...(205)$$

$$\hat{\mathbf{A}}\psi_2 = \lambda_2 \psi_2 \quad ...(206)$$

where, ψ_1 and ψ_2 are the eigen functions of $\hat{\mathbf{A}}$ with λ_1 and λ_2 the corresponding eigen values, respectively. Taking the complex conjugate of Eq. (205) and recalling that λ_1 is real,

$$\hat{\mathbf{A}}\psi_1^* = \lambda_1 \psi_1^* \quad ...(207)$$

Multiplying Eq. (207) on the left by ψ_2 and integrating

$$\int \psi_2 \hat{\mathbf{A}} \psi_1^* d\tau = \lambda_1 \int \psi_2 \psi_1^* \, d\tau \quad ...(208)$$

Again, multiplying Eq. (208) on the left by ψ_1^* and integrating,

$$\int \psi_1^* \hat{\mathbf{A}}\, \psi_2 \, d\tau = \lambda_2 \int \psi_1^* \psi_2 d\tau \quad ...(209)$$

Since, $\hat{\mathbf{A}}$ is a Hermitian operator, the left hand sides of Eqs. (208) and (209) are equal so that

$$\lambda_1 \int \psi_2 \psi_1^* d\tau = \lambda_2 \int \psi_1^* \psi_2 d\tau$$

or

$$(\lambda_1 - \lambda_2) \int \psi_1^* \psi_2 d\tau = 0 \quad ...(210)$$

Since, $\lambda_1 \neq \lambda_2$, $\int \psi_1^* \psi_2 d\tau = 0$. Thus, ψ_1 and ψ_2 are orthogonal.

Proof of theorem 2 Let $\hat{\mathbf{A}}$ be the operator whose eigen value equation is

$$\hat{\mathbf{A}}\psi_i = a_i \psi_i \quad ...(211)$$

where $\psi_i s$ are the set of eigen functions with $a_i s$ as the corresponding eigenvalues.

Since, $\hat{\mathbf{A}}$ and $\hat{\mathbf{B}}$ commute, hence

$$\hat{\mathbf{A}}\,\hat{\mathbf{B}} = \hat{\mathbf{B}}\,\hat{\mathbf{A}} \quad ...(212)$$

Operation on ψ_i,

$$\hat{\mathbf{A}}\,\hat{\mathbf{B}}\,\psi_i = \hat{\mathbf{B}}\hat{\mathbf{A}}\psi_i = \hat{\mathbf{B}}(a_i \psi_i) = a_i(\hat{\mathbf{b}}\psi_i) \quad ...(213)$$

This shows that $(\hat{\mathbf{B}}\psi_i)$ is an eigenfunction of $\hat{\mathbf{A}}$ with eigen value a_i. This is possible only if $(\hat{\mathbf{B}}\psi_i)$ is a multiple of ψ_i, *i.e.,*

$$\hat{\mathbf{B}}\psi_i = b_i \psi_i \quad ...(214)$$

In other words, ψ_i is also an eigen function of $\hat{\mathbf{B}}$

Proof of theorem 3 The proof of this theorem has not been rigorously established but it seems to be valid or Hermitian operators. This theorem states that

$$\psi = \sum_i c_i \, \phi_i \quad ...(215)$$

where, ψ is an arbitrary function and ϕ_i are orthonormal functions, *i.e.,* they are both orthogonal and normalized :

$$\left.\begin{array}{ll} \int \phi_i^* \phi_j \; d\tau = 0 & \text{(orthogonality condition)} \\ \int \phi_i^* \phi_i \; d\tau = 1 & \text{(normalization condition)} \end{array}\right\} \quad ...(216)$$

The two conditions, or criteria, can be summed up by the relation

$$\int \phi_i^* \phi_j \; d\tau = \delta_{ij} = \begin{cases} 1, & i = j \\ 0, & i \neq j \end{cases} \quad ...(217)$$

where, ψ_{ij} is called the Krnonecker delta in honour of the 19th centuray mathematician Leopold Kronecker.

4. **Virial theorem** According to the virial theorem, if the potential energy $V(x)$ of a quantum mechanical system moving in the x-direction is of the form

$$V(x) \propto x^s, \qquad ...(218)$$

where, s is a contant, then the expectation (average) value of the kinetic energy, $<\hat{\mathbf{T}}>$ and the expectation value of the potential energy, $<\hat{\mathbf{T}}>$ are related by

$$<\hat{\mathbf{T}}> = \frac{1}{2}s<\hat{\mathbf{V}}> \qquad ...(219)$$

Virial theorem is a very important theorem in quantum mechanics and is the real test of the accuracy of the wave function of the quantum mechanical system (atom or molecule), obtained by the solution of the Schrodinger wave equation by the Hartree-Fock Self-consistent field (SCF) method.

5. **Variation theorem** If ψ is the approximate wave function of a quantum mechanical system described by the Hamiltonian, $\hat{\mathbf{H}}$, then the expectation value of the energy, $<E>$ given by the integral

$$<E> = \int \psi^* \hat{\mathbf{H}}\psi \, d\tau \equiv <\psi^*|\hat{\mathbf{H}}|\psi> \qquad ...(220)$$

is an upper limit to the ground state energy, E_0, of the system, *i.e.,*

$$E \geq E_0 \qquad ...(221)$$

6. **Koopmanns' theorem** The ionization potential (energy) of a molecule is equal to the negative of the energy of the HOMO (highest occupied molecular orbital). This theorem was discovered by T. Koopmanns, the cowinner of the 1975 Nobel memorial Prize in Economics.

7. **Unsold's theorem** The electron density in a completely filled atomic orbital is spherically symmetric.

8. **The Hellmann-Feynman theorem** Discovered independently by Hellmann and R. Feynman, it states that the force acting on each nucleus of a molecule is exactly that calculated by classical electrostatics from the charges and positions of the other nuclei and the electrons. Since, at the equilibrium configuration of a molecule the resultant force acting on each nucleus vanishes, for this configuration the repulsion of a given nucleus by other nuclei is just balanced by its attraction by the electrons. This important theorem gives deeper insight into molecular electronic structure and has inspired considerable theoretical research activity.

9. **Kramer's theorem** It states that in the absence of the external magnetic field, the electronic states of any molecule or ion having an odd number of electrons are at least doubly degenerate. If follows that all complicated interactions (spin-spin interaction, spin-orbit interaction and ligand-field splitting) in transition metal ions cannot remove the degeneracy of a state with total electron spin $S = \frac{1}{2}, \frac{3}{2}, \frac{5}{2}$, etc., (Note that $2S + 1$) is the multiplicity of a state so that the states with $S = \frac{1}{2}, \frac{3}{2}, \frac{5}{2}$, etc. are doublet, quartet and sextet states, respectively.) The spin degeneracy of systems containing odd number of electrons is called Kramer's degeneracy. The spin levels are split even in the absence of the magnetic field, the splitting being referred to as zero-field splitting (ZFS).

10. **The Jahn-Teller theorem** According to this theorem a non-linear molecule in an electronically degenerate state always distorts itself into a less symmetric but more stable configuration in which the electronic degeneracy has been removed.

11. **Bohr's Correspondence (or complementarity) principle** It states that classical mechanics and quantum mechanics tend to give the same result when systems are in highly excited quantum states.

Since, science is an intellectual edifice based on theories, which must ultimately be tested by experiment, and theories imply the existence of theorems, important theorems such as those mentioned above are a part of the scientist's arsenal and must be on his/her fingertips.

Example 33. *Calculate the kinetic energy of an electron in the ground state confined to a box 3 Å in width and moving in one dimension (x-axis) only.*

Sol.

$$E = \frac{n^2h^2}{8ma^2} = \frac{1^2 \times (6.6 \times 10^{-27}\ \text{erg}^2, \text{s}^2)}{8 \times (9.1 \times 10^{-28}\text{g})\ (3 \times 10^{-8}\text{cm})^2}$$

$$= 6.6 \times 10^{-12}\ \text{erg/electron} \qquad [\because \text{erg} = \text{g cm}^2\ \text{s}^{-1}]$$

Example 34. *Calculate the transition energy when the electron in problem 1 moves from n = 2 to n = 1. What is the wavelength of the photon emitted?*

Sol. The general expression from problem 1 is

$$E = \frac{n^2h^2}{8ma^2} = n^2(6.6 \times 10^{-12})\ \text{erg/electron}$$

$$\Delta E = E_2 - E_1 = 6.6 \times 10^{-12}(n_2^2 - n_1^2)\ \text{per atom}$$

$$= 2.0 \times 10^{-11}\ \text{erg/atom}$$

According to Planck, $E = h\nu = \frac{hc}{\lambda}$

$$\therefore \quad \lambda = \frac{hv}{\Delta E} = \frac{(6.6\times10^{-27}\text{erg s})\,(3\times10^{10}\text{ cm/s})}{2.0\times10^{-11}\text{ erg}}$$

$$= 9.9\times10^{-6}\text{ cm} = 9.9\times10^{2}\text{ Å}$$

Example 35. *What is the degree of the degeneracy if the three quantum numbers n_1, n_2 and n_3 can have the values 1, 2 and 3?*

Sol. The following combinations are possible

123	132	213
231	312	321

There is therefore sixfold degeneracy.

Example 36. *An electron has a mass of* 9.11×10^{-31} *kg and a charge of* 1.602×10^{-19} *C. Calculate the de-Broglie wavelength of an electron that has been accelerated by a potential of* 100 V.

Sol. The kinetic energy of the electron is

$$100\times1.602\times10^{-19}\text{ V, C} = 1.602\times10^{-17}\text{ J}$$

The kinetic energy is $\frac{1}{2}mu^2$ and therefore

$$u = \sqrt{\frac{2\times1.602\times10^{-17}\text{ (J)}}{9.11\times10^{-31}\text{ (kg)}}} = 5.93\times10^{6}\text{ ms}^{-1}$$

The de-Broglie wavelength λ is

$$\frac{6.626\times10^{-34}\text{ (Js)}}{9.11\times10^{-31}\text{(kg)}\times5.93\times10^{6}\text{ (ms}^{-1})}$$

$$= 1.23\times10^{-19}\text{ m} = 123\text{ pm}$$

Example 37. *The operator x is the one-dimensional position operator and (h/2πi) (δ/δx) is the one-dimensional momentum operator. Do these operators commute?*

Sol. One way of dealing with this problem is to choose a function that is an eigen value of one of the operators and see if it is also an eigen value of the other. The function $2x$ is obviously an eigen value of x. Operating by the momentum operator gives

$$\frac{h}{2\pi i}\frac{\partial}{\partial x}(2x) = \frac{h}{\pi i}$$

Since, the result is not a constant times $2x$, the function $2x$ is not an eigen function for the momentum operator.

Alternatively, we can first operate on the function $2x$ by the operator x and then by the momentum operator. Then we can reverse the order of operation and see if the result is the same. Thus,

$$\frac{h}{2\pi i}\frac{\partial}{\partial x}(x)(2x) = \frac{h}{2\pi i}\frac{\partial}{\partial x}(2x^2) = \frac{2hx}{\pi i}$$

and
$$(x)\frac{h}{2\pi i}\frac{\partial}{\partial x}(2x) = (x)\frac{h}{\pi i} = \frac{hx}{\pi i}$$

Since, the result is different in the two cases, the operators do not commute.

Example 38. *Calculate the effective nuclear charge for a 2p electron in nitrogen.*

Sol. The electron configuration for nitrogen is $1s^2 2s^2 2p^3$ and it has a nuclear charge of 7. The shielding is 2(0.85) = 1.70 for the 1s electrons and $(4\times0.35) = 1.40$ for the two 2s and the two remaining 2p electrons. The effective nuclear charge for any 2p electron is thus, $Z - \sigma = 7 - (1.70 + 1.40) = 3.90$.

Example 39. *Estimate Z_{eff} for a 1s electron in He, if the first ionization energy of helium is 24.6 eV.*

Sol. In atomic units this ionization energy is

$$24.6/27.2 = 0.904\text{ au}$$

We know that

$$I = \frac{Z_{eff}^2}{2n^2}\text{ au}$$

where, I = Ionization energy

Z_{eff} = Effective charge

n = Number of shell

For the helium atom $n = 1$ and therefore,

$$0.904 = Z_{eff}/2 \quad\text{or}\quad Z_{eff} = 1.34$$

This is significantly less than 2, the Z value of He and shows that there is substantial screening by the other 1s electron.

Exercise 1

(For Part 'B')

1. The de-Broglie wavelength of a particle having KE E_k is given by

(a) $\lambda = \frac{h}{\sqrt{E_k}}$ (b) $\lambda = \frac{h}{\sqrt{2mE_k}}$

(c) $\lambda = \frac{h}{\sqrt{mE_k}}$ (d) $\lambda = \frac{h}{\sqrt{3mE_k}}$

2. The de-Broglie wavelength of a charge q and accelerated through a potential difference of V volts is

(a) $\lambda = \frac{h}{\sqrt{mqV}}$ (b) $\lambda = \frac{hm}{\sqrt{qV}}$

(c) $\lambda = \frac{h}{\sqrt{2mqV}}$ (d) $\lambda = \frac{h}{mqV}$

3. Which of the following statement is correct?

(a) Only charged particle in motion are accompanied by matter waves

(b) No particle in motion whether charged or uncharged is accompanied by matter waves

(c) No particle whether rest or in motion is ever accompanied by matter waves

(d) Only sub-atomic particles in motion are accompanied by matter waves

4. The de-Broglie hypothesis is associated with

(a) wave nature of electrons only

(b) wave nature of protons only

(c) wave nature of radiation

(d) wave nature of all material particles

5. Matter waves are

(a) longitudinal

(b) electromagnetic

(c) always travel with the speed of light

(d) show diffraction

6. According to Schrödinger, a particle is equivalent to a

(a) wave packet (b) single wave

(c) light wave (d) None of these

7. For a non-relativistic particle what is the relation between phase velocity v_p and group velocity v_g?

(a) $v_p = v_g$ (b) $v_p = \frac{v_g}{2}$ (c) $v_p = 2v_g$ (d) $v_p = 3v_g$

8. The Schrödinger time independent equation can be written as

(a) $H\psi = E\psi$ (b) $H\psi = (E - V)\psi$

(c) $H\psi = (E + V)\psi$ (d) $H\psi + E\psi = 0$

9. The probability of finding the particle in a volume dV can be written as

(a) $P(r, t)\, dV = |\psi(r, t)|\, dV$

(b) $P(r, t) = \psi(r, t)\, dV$

(c) $P(r, t)\, dV = |\psi(r, t)|^2\, dV$

(d) $P(r, t) = |\psi(r, t)|^3\, dV$

10. The wave function of a particle in a box of length L is

$$\psi(x) = \sqrt{\frac{2}{L}} \sin\frac{\pi x}{L},\ 0 < x < L$$

$$\psi(x) = 0,\ x < 0 \text{ and } x > L$$

the probability of the particle finding in the region $0 < x < \frac{L}{2}$ is

(a) 0.4% (b) 0.3% (c) 0.2% (d) 0.5%

11. If the probability that x lies between x and $x + dx$ is $P(x)\, dx = ae^{-ax}\, dx$, where $a < x < \infty$, $a > 0$, then the probability that x lies between x_1 and x_2 $(x_2 > x_1)$ is

(a) $(e^{-ax_1} - e^{-ax_2})$ (b) $a\,(e^{-ax_1} - e^{-ax_2})$

(c) $e^{-ax_2}\,(e^{-ax_1} - e^{-ax_2})$ (d) $e^{-ax_1}\,(e^{-ax_1} - e^{-ax_2})$

12. If the wave function of a particle trapped in space between $x = 0$ and $x = L$ is given by $\psi(x) = A \sin\left(\frac{2\pi x}{L}\right)$, where A is a constant for which value(s) x will the probability of the finding of particle be maximum.

(a) $\frac{L}{4}$ (b) $\frac{L}{2}$

(c) $\frac{L}{6}$ and $\frac{L}{3}$ (d) $\frac{L}{4}$ and $\frac{3L}{4}$

13. Which of the following is an allowed wave function for a particle in a bound state? N is a constant and $\alpha, \beta > 0$

(a) $\psi = \frac{Ne^{-\alpha r}}{r^3}$

(b) $\psi = N(1 - e^{-\alpha r})$

(c) $\psi = Ne^{-\alpha x} \times e^{-\beta(x^2 + y^2 + z^2)}$

(d) $\psi = \begin{cases} \text{non-zero constant} & \text{if } r < R \\ 0 & \text{if } r > R \end{cases}$

14. The wave function of a particle moving in a one-dimensional time independent potential $V(x)$ is given by $\psi(x) = e^{-iax + b}$, where a and b are constants. This means that the potential $V(x)$ is of the form

(a) $V(x) \propto x$ (b) $V(x) \propto x^2$

(c) $V(x) = 0$ (d) $V(x) \propto e^{-ax}$

15. The wave function of a particle is given by $\psi = C\exp(-x^2\sigma^2)$, $-\infty < x < \infty$, where C and σ are constants. The probability of finding the particle in the region $0 < x < \infty$

(a) 1 (b) $\frac{1}{3}$ (c) $\frac{1}{2}$ (d) $\frac{1}{4}$

16. Which of the following wave functions can be solutions of Schrödinger's equation for all values of x $(x > 0)$?

(a) $\psi = A\sec x$ (b) $\psi = A\tan x$
(c) $\psi = Ae^{x^2}$ (d) $\psi = Ae^{-x^2}$

17. For a particle moving in x-direction and having a wave function $\psi = A\sin(kx - \omega t)$, its energy is

(a) $\frac{k^2\hbar^2}{2m}$ (b) $\frac{k\hbar}{2m}$ (c) $\frac{\hbar^2k^2}{m}$ (d) $m^2\hbar^2$

18. The time independent Schrodinger's equation of a system represents the conservation of the

(a) total binding energy of the system
(b) total potential energy of the system
(c) total kinetic energy of the system
(d) total energy of the system

19. A free particle is moving in positive direction with a linear momentum p. The wave function of the particle normalized in a length L is

(a) $\frac{1}{\sqrt{L}}\sin\frac{p}{\hbar}x$ (b) $\frac{1}{\sqrt{L}}\cos\frac{p}{\hbar}x$
(c) $\frac{1}{\sqrt{L}}e^{-ip/\hbar}x$ (d) $\frac{1}{\sqrt{L}}e^{ip/\hbar}x$

20. A particle of mass m is represented by the wavefunction $\psi(x) = Ae^{ikx}$, where k is the wave vector and A is constant. The magnitude of the probability current density of the particle is

(a) $|A|^2\frac{\hbar k}{m}$ (b) $|A|^2\frac{\hbar k}{2m}$
(c) $|A|^2\frac{(\hbar k)^2}{m}$ (d) $\frac{|A|^2(\hbar k)^2}{2m}$

21. The value of A for $\psi = A\cos^2 x$ for $-\frac{\pi}{2} < x < \frac{\pi}{2}$ is

(a) $\sqrt{\frac{8}{3\pi}}$ (b) $\sqrt{\frac{3}{8\pi}}$ (c) $\frac{1}{\sqrt{2\pi}}$ (d) $\sqrt{\frac{3}{2\pi}}$

22. In case of wave function $\psi = \frac{e^{ikr}}{r}$, the probability current density is

(a) $\frac{v}{r^2}$ (b) $\frac{v}{r}$ (c) $\frac{v}{r^3}$ (d) v

23. For wave function $\psi(x) = \sqrt{\frac{2}{L}}\sin\frac{\pi x}{L}$, $0 < x < L$, the expectation value of P^2 is

(a) $\frac{\pi^2\hbar^2}{L^2}$ (b) $\frac{\pi^2\hbar}{L^2}$ (c) $\frac{\pi\hbar^2}{L^2}$ (d) $\frac{\pi^2\hbar^2}{L}$

24. The expectation value of momentum of a particle whose normalised wave function is

$$\psi(x) = Ne^{\left(-\frac{x^2}{2a^2}\right) + ikx}$$

(a) 0 (b) $\frac{\hbar k}{2}$ (c) $\hbar k$ (d) $\hbar^2k^2$

25. The probability of current density can be written as

(a) $S(r,t) = \frac{\hbar}{2im}(\psi^*\nabla\psi - \psi\nabla\psi^*)$
(b) $S(r,t) = \text{real part of } \psi^*\frac{h}{m}\psi$
(c) $S(r,t) = \text{imaginary part of } \psi^*\frac{h}{m}\psi$
(d) $S(r,t) = \frac{\hbar}{2m}\psi^*\nabla\psi$

26. The wave function in the ground state of H-atom is given by $\psi = \sqrt{\frac{1}{\pi a^3}}e^{-r/a}$, the average value of r is

(a) 0 (b) $\frac{3}{2}a$ (c) $\frac{a}{2}$ (d) $\frac{5}{2}a$

27. In momentum representation position operator $\hat{\mathbf{x}}_P$ can be written as

(a) $i\hbar\frac{\partial}{\partial P}$ (b) $-i\hbar\frac{\partial}{\partial P}$ (c) $\hbar\frac{\partial}{\partial P}$ (d) $-\hbar\frac{\partial}{\partial P}$

28. The eigen function in momentum representation for position operator $\hat{\mathbf{x}}_P$ can be writen as

(a) $\phi(P) = C\,e^{ipx/\hbar}$ (b) $\phi(P) = C\,e^{-ipx/\hbar}$
(c) $\phi(P) = C\,e^{Px/\hbar}$ (d) $\phi(P) = C\,e^{-px/\hbar}$

29. For a Gaussian wave packet described by

$$\psi(x) = A\exp\left(-\frac{x^2}{a^2}\right),$$

the value of momentum operator is

(a) 0 (b) $+a$
(c) $-a$ (d) undefined

30. The quantum mechanical operator for the momentum of a particle moving in one dimension is given by

(a) $i\hbar\frac{d}{dx}$ (b) $-i\hbar\frac{\partial}{\partial x}$
(c) $i\hbar\frac{\partial}{\partial t}$ (d) $-\frac{\hbar^2}{2m}\frac{d^2}{dx^2}$

31. The expectation value of the z-coordinate in the ground state of H-atom (wavefunction : $\psi_{100}(r) = A\,e^{-r/a_0}$, where A is the normalization constant and a_0 is Bohr radius) is

(a) a_0 (b) $\frac{a_0}{2}$ (c) $\frac{a_0}{4}$ (d) 0

32. The normalized ground state wave function of H-atom is given by $\psi(r) = \frac{1}{\sqrt{4\pi}} \frac{2}{a^{3/2}} e^{-r/a}$ where a is the Bohr radius and r is the distance of the electron from the nucleus located at origin. The expectation value of $\left\langle \frac{1}{r^2} \right\rangle$ is

(a) $\frac{8\pi}{a^2}$ (b) $\frac{4\pi}{a^2}$ (c) $\frac{4}{a^2}$ (d) $\frac{2}{a^2}$

33. A particle of mass m is confined in the ground state of a one-dimensional box extending from $x = -2L$ to $x = +2L$. The wave function of the particle in this state is $\psi(x) = \psi_0 \cos\frac{\pi x}{4L}$, where ψ_0 is constant. The energy of eigen value corresponding to this state is

(a) $\frac{\hbar^2\pi^2}{2mL^2}$ (b) $\frac{\hbar^2\pi^2}{4mL^2}$

(c) $\frac{\hbar^2\pi^2}{16mL^2}$ (d) $\frac{\hbar^2\pi^2}{32mL^2}$

34. The total energy operator can be written as

(a) $-i\hbar\frac{\partial}{\partial t}$ (b) $i\hbar\frac{\partial}{\partial t}$ (c) $-\hbar\frac{\partial}{\partial t}$ (d) $\hbar\frac{\partial}{\partial t}$

35. The wave function for a particle moving in x-direction $\psi(x) = A e^{ikx}$, $0 < x < L$, the value of normalization constant A is

(a) $\frac{2}{\sqrt{L}}$ (b) $\frac{1}{\sqrt{L}}$ (c) $L^{3/2}$ (d) $\frac{1}{L^{3/2}}$

36. For Gaussian wave function $\psi(x) = Ne^{-x^2/2\sigma^2}$, $-\infty < x < \infty$, the value of N is

(a) $\frac{1}{\pi\sigma^2}$ (b) $\pi\sigma^2$ (c) $\frac{1}{\sqrt{\pi\sigma^2}}$ (d) $\sqrt{\pi\sigma^2}$

37. If $\phi = A e^{im\phi}$, then value of A after normalization is

(a) $\frac{1}{\sqrt{\pi}}$ (b) $\frac{1}{\sqrt{2\pi}}$ (c) $\frac{1}{\sqrt{3\pi}}$ (d) $\frac{2}{\sqrt{\pi}}$

38. For the wave function $\psi(x) = N e^{-x^2/2a^2} + ikx$, the expectation value of momentum is

(a) $\hbar k$ (b) $\frac{\hbar}{2a}$ (c) $\frac{ka}{2}$ (d) $\frac{\hbar k}{4}$

39.

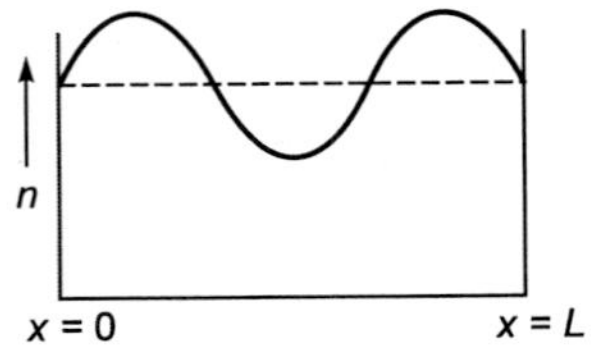

The above figure shows the plot of the wave function n for an electron confined in a box, from $x = 0$ to $x = L$. The quantum number n of the above state n is

(a) 2 (b) 1

(c) 5 (d) 3

40. If E_0 is the zero-point energy of a harmonic oscillator of frequency ν and h is Planck's constant then its energy in the $n = 2$ state will be

(a) $(E_0 + h\nu)$ (b) $2E_0$

(c) $4E_0$ (d) $(E_0 + 2h\nu)$

41. The figure shown in the energy level diagram corresponding to a

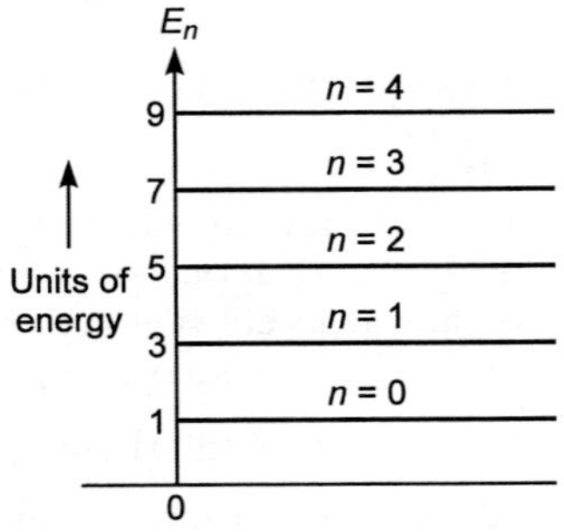

(a) particle in a box (b) particle tunnelling

(c) harmonic oscillator (d) hydrogen atom

42. In quantum mechanics a classical dynamical quantity is replaced by the corresponding quantum mechanical operator. Accordingly, the x-component of momentum, p_x is replaced by

(a) $\frac{h}{2\pi}\cdot\frac{\partial}{\partial x}$ (b) $\frac{ih}{2\pi}\cdot\frac{\partial}{\partial y}$

(c) $h^2\cdot\frac{\partial^2}{\partial x^2}$ (d) $\frac{ih}{2\pi}\cdot\frac{\partial}{\partial x}$

43. With symbols having the usual meaning, the wavelength of the electron of energy E is given by

(a) $2mhE$ (b) $\frac{2h}{mE}$

(c) $\frac{h}{\sqrt{2mE}}$ (d) $\frac{2\sqrt{2}\,mE}{h}$

44. An electron and a proton each having an energy 5 eV are incident on a barrier of 10 high and 1Å wide. The correct statement is

(a) The electron will have greater transmission probability
(b) The proton will have greater transmission probability
(c) Both electron and proton will have equal transmission probabilites
(d) Neither electrons nor protons can cross the barrier

45. If a 5 MeV α-as well as β-particles are incident on a potential barrier of height 10 MeV and width 2 fm, then the probability of transmission is

(a) higher for α-particle
(b) higher for β-particle
(c) equal for both α and β-particles
(d) zero for both α and β-particles

46. Consider the following statements.
In order that measurable properties (such as energy, linear momentum, etc.) of a quantum mechanical system be physically acceptable, it is essential that

I. the corresponding eigen function $\psi(x)$ and its derivative $\frac{d\psi(x)}{dx}$ must be single valued for all values of x.

II. $\psi(x)$ and $\frac{d\psi(x)}{dx}$ must be continuous for all the values of x.

III. $\psi(x)$ must have a finite value over the space $d\,I$ that the electron can occupy.

Which of the statements given above are correct?

(a) I, II and III (b) I and II
(c) I and III (d) II and III

47. Electrons with momentum p are incident at an angle of 30° with the crystal surface. If d is the separation between crystal atomic planes parallel to the surface, what is the smallest value of p in terms of d and Planck's constant h, for which the reflected beam will show a maximum intensity?

(a) $2h/d$ (b) $h/(2d)$
(c) d/h (d) h/d

48. A particle is described by a wave function $\psi(x) = e^{-|x|}$ in one-dimension. What is the probability that it will be found in the region $|x| \le a$, $a > 0$?

(a) e^{-a} (b) e^{-2a}
(c) $1 - e^{-a}$ (d) $1 - e^{-2a}$

49. Which one of the following is correct in respect of an electron and a proton having same de-Broglie wavelength of 2 Å?

(a) Both have same kinetic energy
(b) The kinetic energy of proton is more than that of electron
(c) Both have same velocity
(d) Both have same momentum

50. A particle of energy E is incident from the left on a potential step of height V_0 at $x = 0$. If $E < V_0$, what is the wave function in the region $x > 0$?

(a) $C \exp(-i\omega t + kx)$ (b) $C \exp(-i\omega t + ikx)$
(c) $C \exp(i\omega t - ikx)$ (d) $C \exp(-i\omega t - kx)$

51. If $\psi = \sqrt{\frac{2}{L}} \cos\frac{\pi x}{L}\, e^{-i\varepsilon t/\hbar}$, then $\langle x \rangle$ in the limit $-\frac{L}{2} < x < \frac{L}{2}$ is

(a) $\frac{3}{4L}$ (b) 0 (c) $\frac{1}{4L}$ (d) $\frac{L}{2}$

52. A particle is incident with a constant energy E on a one dimensional potential barrier as shown in the figure. The wavefunctions in the regions I and II are respectively

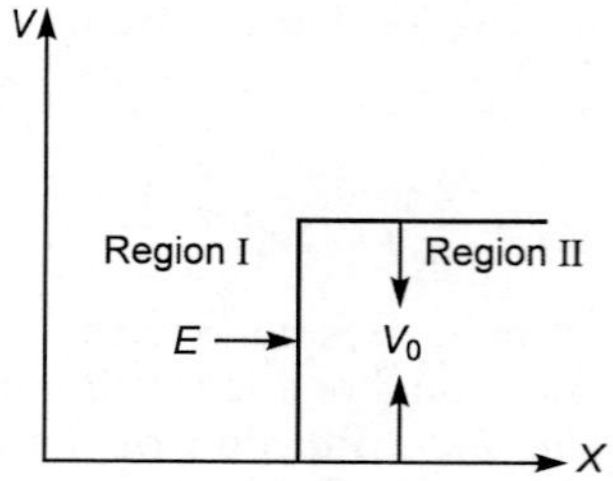

(a) decaying, oscillatory (b) oscillatory, decaying
(c) oscillatory, oscillatory (d) decaying, decaying

53. The wave function of a particle in one-dimensional potential at $t = 0$ is

$$\psi(x, t=0) = \frac{1}{\sqrt{15}}[2\psi_0(x) - \psi_1(x)]$$

where, $\psi_0(x)$ and $\psi_1(x)$ are the ground state and first excited states of the particle with corresponding energies E_0 and E_1. The wave function of the particle at time t is

(a) $\frac{1}{\sqrt{5}} e^{-i(E_0 E_1)t/2\hbar}[2\psi_0(x) - \psi_1(x)]$

(b) $\frac{1}{\sqrt{5}} e^{-iE_0 t/\hbar}[2\psi_0(x) - \psi_1(x)]$

(c) $\frac{1}{\sqrt{5}} e^{-iE_1 t/\hbar}[2\psi_0(x) - \psi_1(x)]$

(d) $\frac{1}{\sqrt{15}}[2\psi_0(x)\, e^{-iE_0 t/\hbar} - \psi_1(x)\, e^{-iE_1 t/\hbar}$

54. An electron with energy E is incident from left on a potential barrier, given by

$$V(x) = 0 \text{ for } x < 0$$
$$= V_0 \text{ for } x > 0$$

as shown in the figure

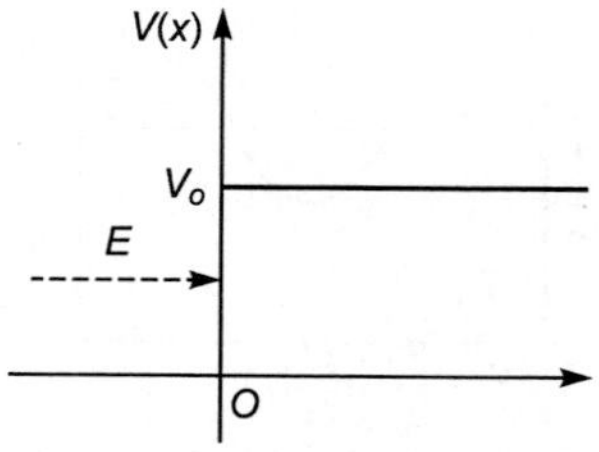

For $E < V_0$, the space part of the wave function for $x > 0$ is of the form of

(a) $e^{\alpha x}$ (b) $e^{-\alpha x}$
(c) $e^{i\alpha x}$ (d) $e^{-i\alpha x}$

55. Which of the functions given below represents the bound state eigen function of the operator $-\frac{d^2}{dx^2}$ in the region $0 \le x \le \infty$ with eigenvalue -4?

(a) $A_0\, e^{2x}$ (b) $A_0 \cosh 2x$

(c) $A_0\, e^{-2x}$ (d) $A_0 \sinh 2x$

56. A particle is confined in one-dimensional box with impenetrable walls at $x = \pm\, a$. Its energy eigen values is 2 eV and corresponding eigen function is shown below

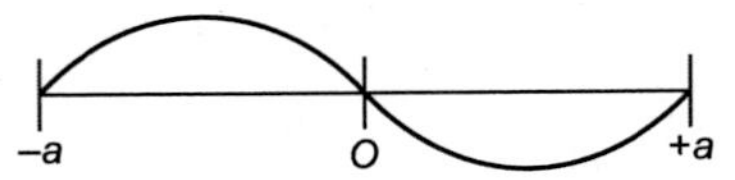

the lowest possible energy of the particle is

(a) 4 eV (b) 2 eV (c) 1 eV (d) 0.5 eV

57. The bound state eigenfunctions of an attractive finite range smooth potential, behave for larger r as

(a) $\exp\left(-\frac{r}{r_0}\right)$, where r_0 is positive constant

(b) $\frac{1}{r^n}\ n > 0$

(c) constant

(d) $\frac{\exp(ikr)}{r}$

58. A particle with energy $V_0/2$ coming in from the left encounters a potential $-3V_0/2$ at $x = 0$.

$$V(x) = 0 \text{ for } x < a$$
$$= -3V_0/2 \text{ for } x \ge a$$

What is the transmission coefficient?

(a) $\frac{1}{2}$ (b) $\frac{2}{3}$ (c) $\frac{4}{9}$ (d) $\frac{8}{9}$

59. Consider a particle in one-dimensional box between $x = 0$ and $x = a$

$$V(x) = 0 \text{ for } 0 < x < a$$
$$= \infty \text{ for } x \le 0 \text{ or } x \ge a$$

When it is in the ground state, what is the probability that it will be found in the region $(a/4) < x < (3a/4)$?

(a) 1/2 (b) $(1/2) + (1/\pi)$

(c) $(1/4) + (2/\pi)$ (d) $(1/4) + (1/\pi)$

60. For a particle described by the wavefunction $\psi = A(x + iy)e^{-r^2}$, where $r^2 = x^2 + y^2 + z^2$, the z-component of the angular momentum is

($\hbar = h/2\pi$, h = Planck's constant)

(a) zero (b) $\hbar$ (c) $2\hbar$ (d) $\hbar^2$

61. Which of the following phenomena can be explained by quantum mechanical tunnelling through the barrier?

I. α-decay

II. Field emission of electrons from a metal surface.

III. β-decay

Select the correct answer using the code given below.

(a) I, II and III (b) I only

(c) I and II only (d) II and III only

62. For what value of g is the function $x + gy$, an eigenfunction of L_z with eigen value $-\hbar$, where $\hbar = \frac{h}{2\pi}$ h being the Planck's constant?

(a) $g = 1$ (b) $g = -1$ (c) $g = i$ (d) $g = -i$

63. What is the fraction of a beam of electrons, each of energy $E = 0.08$ eV reflected from a step barrier of height $V_0 = 0.06$ eV and of infinite width?

(a) 0.11 (b) 0.33 (c) 0.67 (d) 0.89

64. The wave function of the ground state of hydrogen atom is $\psi(r) = Ae^{-r/a}$, where a is the Bohr radius and A is the normalization constant. What is the average value of r?

(Given that $\int_0^\infty e^{-t} t^{n-1}\, dt = (n-1)$, where n is a natural number)

(a) a (b) $\frac{3a}{2}$ (c) $2a$ (d) $\frac{a}{2}$

65. A particle of mass m is in a simple harmonic oscillator potential $V = x^2$. If the ground state wave function is Ae^{-ax^2}, what is the expression for constant a equal to?

(a) $\frac{2\pi(m/2)^{1/2}}{h}$ (b) $\frac{2\pi(1/m)^{1/2}}{h}$

(c) $\frac{h(m/2)^{1/2}}{(2\pi)}$ (d) $\frac{h(m)^{1/2}}{(2\pi)}$

66.

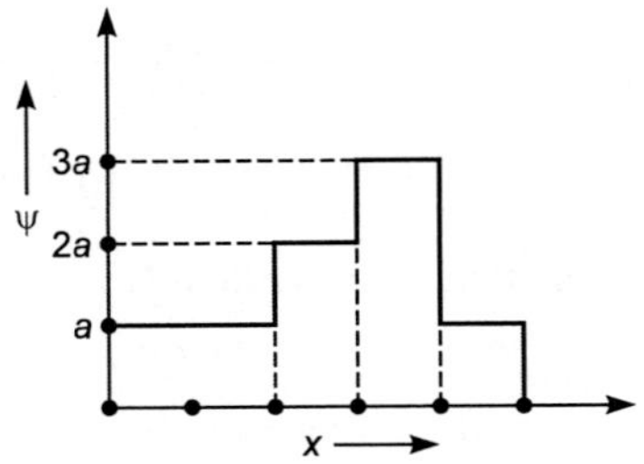

The wave function for a particle constrained to move in one dimension is shown in the graph above ($\psi = 0$ for $x \le 0$ and $x \ge 5$). What is the probability that the particle would be found between $x = 2$ and $x = 4$?

(a) $\frac{17}{64}$ (b) $\frac{25}{64}$ (c) $\frac{5}{8}$ (d) $\frac{13}{16}$

67. A particle of mass m and energy E is incident on a potential step of height V_0(at $x = 0$). If $E < V_0$, the wave function of the particle for $x > 0$ will be of the form

(a) e^{ikx} (b) zero

(c) e^{-kx} (d) $Ee^{ikx} + Ae^{-ikx}$

68. If n represents the number of eigen states of a hydrogen atom, then its discrete energy levels are proportional to

(a) n (b) n^2 (c) $1/n$ (d) $1/n^2$

69. For a particle of mass m in a one-dimensional box of length l, what is the average of momentum p_x for the ground state?

(a) zero (b) $h/(2l)$ (c) h/l (d) $h/(2\pi l)$

70. A particle constrained to move along the x-axis is described by the wave function

$$\psi(x) = 2x; \quad 0 < x < 1$$
$$\psi(x) = 0; \quad \text{elsewhere}$$

What is the probability of finding the particle within the interval (0, 0.4)?

(a) 0.85 (b) 0.085 (c) 0.0085 (d) 0.00085

71. If the perturbation $H' = ax$, where a is a constant, is added to infinite square well potential

$$V(x) = \begin{cases} 0 & \text{for } 0 \le x \le \pi \\ \infty & \text{otherwise} \end{cases}$$

The correction to the ground state energy to first order in a is

(a) $\frac{a\pi}{2}$ (b) $a\pi$ (c) $\frac{a\pi}{4}$ (d) $\frac{a\pi}{\sqrt{2}}$

72. The wave for one-dimensional oscillator is $\psi(x) = Ae^{-\alpha^2 x^2/2}$, for the ground state with energy $E_0 = \frac{\hbar\omega}{2}$, where $\alpha^2 = \frac{m\omega}{\hbar}$, when a perturbation $V(t) = E_0\left[\frac{\alpha x}{10}\right]^4$ is applied to the first order change in the ground state energy is

(a) $\frac{E_0}{2} \times 10^{-4}$ (b) $3E_0 \times 10^{-4}$

(c) $\frac{3}{4}E_0 \times 10^{-4}$ (d) $E_0 \times 10^{-4}$

73. The wave function for a particle is

$$\psi(x) = \begin{cases} e^{-kx}, & \text{for } 0 \le x < a \\ 0, & \text{otherwise} \end{cases}$$

When a perturbation $V(x) = Kx$ is applied on it, the first order change in ground state energy is

(a) $\frac{1}{4K^2} - e^{-2Ka}\left[\frac{1}{4K^2} + \frac{a}{2}\right]$

(b) $\frac{1}{4K^2} + e^{-2Ka}\left[\frac{1}{4K^2} + \frac{a}{2}\right]$

(c) $e^{-2Ka}\left[\frac{1}{4K^2} + \frac{a}{2}\right]$

(d) $\frac{1}{4K^2}e^{-2Ka}$

74. The wave function for a particle in one-dimensional potential well is given by $\sqrt{\frac{2}{a}}\sin\frac{n\pi x}{a}$, $0 < x < a$, when a potential of $V(x) = \frac{\cos \pi x}{a}$ is applied, the change in first order energy is

(a) zero (b) $\frac{a}{\pi}$ (c) $\frac{2\pi}{a}$ (d) $\frac{a}{2\pi}$

75. In the harmonic oscillator problem we consider a small perturbation bx, the first order energy correction to the nth energy level is

(a) $\frac{1}{2}\left(n + \frac{1}{2}\right)\frac{\hbar\omega}{mb}$ (b) $\frac{1}{2}\hbar\omega b$

(c) $\left(n + \frac{1}{2}\right)\hbar\omega b$ (d) 0

76. If a perturbation $\frac{1}{2}bx^2$ is given to a harmonic oscillator, the lowest order non-zero correction to the energy is

(a) $\frac{1}{2}\left(n + \frac{1}{2}\right)\frac{\hbar b}{m\omega}$ (b) $\left(n + \frac{1}{2}\right)\frac{\hbar b}{m\omega}$

(c) $-\frac{1}{8}\left(n + \frac{1}{2}\right)\frac{\hbar b}{m\omega}$ (d) $-\frac{1}{8}\left(n + \frac{1}{2}\right)\frac{\hbar b^2}{m^2\omega^2}$

77. Consider a charged harmonic oscillator having charge q in an electric field $\vec{E}$. The lowest order non-zero correction to the energy is

(a) $\frac{q^2E^2}{2m\omega^2}$ (b) $-\frac{q^2E^2}{2m\omega^2}$ (c) $\frac{q^2E^2}{m\omega^2}$ (d) $\frac{qE^2}{2m\omega^2}$

78. Consider the one-dimensional harmonic oscillator with a perturbation $H' = bx^4$. The first order correction to the energy is

(a) $\frac{-3b\hbar^2}{2m^2\omega^2}(n^2 + n + 1)$ (b) $\frac{-3b\hbar^2}{2m^2\omega^2}\left(n^2 + n + \frac{1}{2}\right)$

(c) $\frac{3b\hbar^2}{2m^2\omega^2}\left(n^2 + n + \frac{1}{2}\right)$ (d) $\frac{3b\hbar^2}{2m^2\omega^2}(n^2 + n + 1)$

79. Consider a two-dimensional harmonic oscillator with a perturbation $H' = bx_1x_2$, the first order correction to the energy is

(a) $\frac{\lambda\hbar}{2m\omega}$ (b) $\frac{-\lambda\hbar}{2m\omega}$ (c) $\pm\frac{\lambda\hbar}{2m\omega}$ (d) zero

80. Consider a harmonic oscillator of the form $H = \frac{P^2}{2m} + \frac{1}{2}m\omega^2x^2$. If it is subjected to a time independent perturbation $\lambda(xP + Px)$, where λ is real. The first order correction to the nth energy state is

(a) zero (b) $\lambda\hbar$ (c) $\lambda^2\hbar$ (d) $\frac{\lambda^2\hbar}{\omega}$

Exercise 2

(For Part 'C')

1. The eigen functions of hydrogen atom contain which of the following?

I. Legendre polynomials

II. Laguerre polynomials

III. Hermite polynomials

Select the correct answer using the code given below.

(a) I, II and III (b) I and II

(c) I only (d) II only

2. Consider the following statements.

A particle of energy E is incident from the left on a potential step of height V_0 at $x = 0$;

I. if $E < V_0$, wave function of the particle is zero for $x > 0$.

II. if $E < V_0$, wave function is not zero for $x > 0$.

III. if $E > V_0$, reflection coefficient is not zero.

Which of the statements given above is/are correct?

(a) I only (b) II only (c) I and II (d) II and III

3. A particle of mass m coming in from the left with energy $E > 0$, encounters a barrier potential

$$V(x) = V_0 \text{ for } |x| < a$$

and $$V(x) = 0 \text{ for } |x| > a$$

The wave function is given by

$$\psi(x) = e^{ikx} + Be^{-ikx} \text{ for } x < -a$$

$$= Ae^{ikx} \text{ for } x > a$$

The constants A and B satisfy which one of the following relations?

(a) $A + B = 1$ (b) $|A| + |B| = 1$

(c) $|A| = |B|$ (d) $|A^2| + |B|^2 = 1$

4. A barrier potential is defined as

$$V(x) = V_0, 0 < x < a$$

$$= 0, x < 0 \text{ and } x > a$$

The general solution in the region $0 < x < a$ when $E < V_0$ is

(a) $\psi(x) = A\,e^{-kx} + B\,e^{kx}, k = \sqrt{\frac{2m(V_0 - E)}{\hbar}}$

(b) $\psi(x) = A\,e^{-kx}, k = \sqrt{\frac{2m(V_0 - E)}{\hbar}}$

(c) $\psi(x) = B\,e^{kx}, k = \sqrt{\frac{2m(V_0 - E)}{\hbar}}$

(d) $\psi(x) = A\,e^{ikx} + B\,e^{-ikx}$

5. A particle incident on potential $[E \geq 0]$

$$V(x) = \infty, x < -\frac{a}{2} \text{ and } x > +\frac{a}{2}$$

and $$V(x) = 0, -\frac{a}{2} < x - \frac{a}{2}$$

the solution can be written as

(a) $\psi_n(x) = B_n \cos k_n x$ where, $k_n = \frac{n\pi}{a}$, $n = 1, 2, 3, \ldots$

(b) $\psi_n(x) = A_n \sin k_n x$, $n = 1, 2, 3, \ldots$

(c) $\psi_n(x) = B_n \cos k_n x$, $n = 1, 3, 5, \ldots$ and $\psi_n(x) = A_n \sin k_n x$, $n = 2, 4, 6, \ldots$

(d) $\psi_n(x) = B_n \cos k_n x$, $n = 2, 4, 6, \ldots$ and $\psi_n(x) = A_n \sin k_n x$, $n = 1, 3, 5, \ldots$

6. The energy separation between two successive states for a infinite potential well is given by

(a) $\Delta E \propto (2n + 1)$ (b) $\Delta E \propto n$

(c) $\Delta E \propto \sqrt{2n + 1}$ (d) $\Delta E \propto (2n - 1)$

7. A particle with energy E is in a time dependent double well potential as shown in figure, which of the following statement about the particle is not correct?

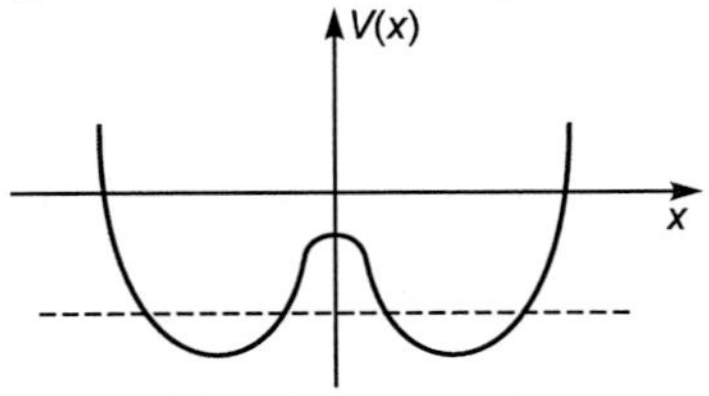

(a) The particle will always be in a bound state

(b) The probability of finding the particle in one well be time independent

(c) The particle will be confined to any one of the wells

(d) The particle can tunnel from one well to other and back

8. A particle of mass m is confined in the potential

$$V(x) = \begin{cases} \frac{1}{2} m\omega^2 x^2, & x < 0 \\ \infty, & x \geq 0 \end{cases}$$

Let wave function of the particle given by

$\psi(x) = -\frac{1}{\sqrt{5}}\psi_0 + \frac{2}{\sqrt{5}}\psi_1$, where ψ_0, ψ_1 are the wave functions of ground state and first excited states. The expectation value of energy is

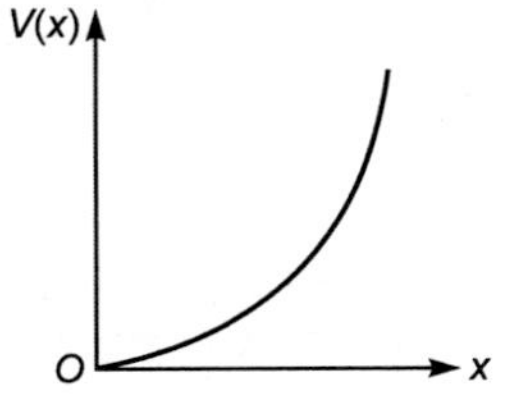

(a) $\frac{31}{10}\hbar\omega$ (b) $\frac{25}{10}\hbar\omega$ (c) $\frac{13}{10}\hbar\omega$ (d) $\frac{11}{10}\hbar\omega$

9. A particle is placed in a one-dimensional box of size L along x-axis, $(0 < x < L)$. Which of the following is true?

(a) In the ground state, the probability of finding the particle in the interval $\left(\frac{L}{4}, \frac{3L}{4}\right)$ is half

(b) In the first excited state, the probability of finding the particle in the interval $\left(\frac{L}{4}, \frac{3L}{4}\right)$ is half. This also holds for states with $n = 4, 6, 8, \ldots$

(c) For an arbitrary state, the probability of finding the particle in the left half of the well is half

(d) In the ground state, the particle has definite momentum

10. There are only three bound states for a particle of mass m in a one-dimensional potential well of the form shown in figure. The depth V_0 of the potential satisfies

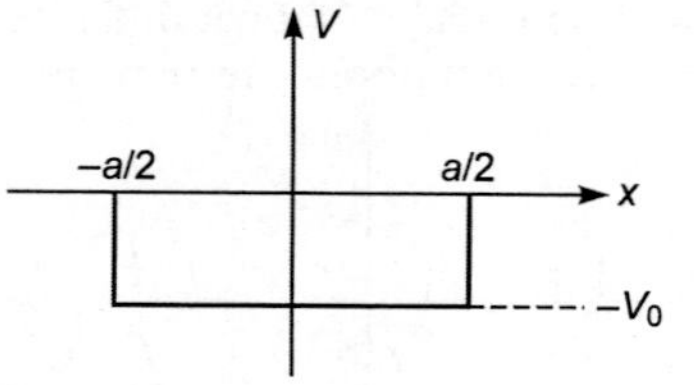

(a) $\frac{2\pi^2\hbar^2}{ma^2} < V_0 < \frac{9\pi^2\hbar^2}{2ma^2}$ (b) $\frac{\pi^2\hbar^2}{ma^2} < V_0 < \frac{2\pi^2\hbar^2}{ma^2}$

(c) $\frac{2\pi^2\hbar^2}{ma^2} < V_0 < \frac{8\pi^2\hbar^2}{ma^2}$ (d) $\frac{2\pi^2\hbar^2}{ma^2} < V_0 < \frac{50\pi^2\hbar^2}{ma^2}$

11. A one-dimensional harmonic oscillator is in the state

$$\psi(x) = \frac{1}{\sqrt{14}}[3\psi_0 x - 2\psi_1(x) + \psi_2(x)]$$

where $\psi_0(x)$, $\psi_1(x)$ and $\psi_2(x)$ are ground, first excited and second excited states, respectively. The probability of finding the oscillator in the ground state is

(a) zero (b) $\frac{3}{\sqrt{14}}$ (c) $\frac{9}{14}$ (d) 1

12. A particle has the wave function

$$\psi(x, t) = A[\exp(i\omega t)\cos kx]$$

Which one of the following is correct?

(a) This is an eigen state of both energy and momentum

(b) This is an eigen state of momentum only

(c) This is an eigen state of energy only

(d) This is not an eigen state for energy and momentum

13. A free particle with energy E whose wave function is a plane wave with wavelength λ enters a region of constant potential $V > 0$, where the wavelength of the particle is 2λ. The ratio $\left(\frac{V}{E}\right)$ is

(a) $\frac{1}{2}$ (b) $\frac{2}{3}$ (c) $\frac{3}{4}$ (d) $\frac{4}{5}$

14. The energy density of states of an electron in a one-dimensional potential wells of infinitely high walls is (The symbols have their usual meanings)

(a) $\frac{L\sqrt{m}}{[\pi\hbar\sqrt{2E}]}$ (b) $\frac{Lm}{\pi\hbar\sqrt{E}}$

(c) $\frac{Lm}{\pi\hbar\sqrt{2E}}$ (d) $\frac{L\sqrt{m}}{2\pi\hbar E}$

15. A system is known to be in a state described by the wavefunction

$$\psi(\theta, \phi) = \frac{1}{\sqrt{30}}[5Y_4^0 + Y_6^0 - 2Y_6^3]$$

where $Y_l^m(\theta, \phi)$ are the spherical harmonics. The probability of finding in a state with $l = 6$ is

(a) zero (b) $\frac{2}{15}$ (c) $\frac{1}{6}$ (d) $\frac{13}{15}$

16. A diatomic molecule is initially in the state

$$\psi(\theta, \phi) = \frac{(5Y_1^1 + 3Y_5^1 + 2Y_5^{-1})}{\sqrt{38}}$$

where, Y_l^m is a spherical harmonic. What is the probability of obtaining result $l = 5$?

(a) $\frac{36}{1444}$ (b) $\frac{9}{38}$ (c) $\frac{13}{38}$ (d) $\frac{34}{38}$

17. At $t = 0$, a one-dimensional harmonic oscillator is in a state given by

$$\psi(x, 0) = \frac{1}{2}u_0(x) + i\frac{\sqrt{3}}{2}u_1(x)$$

(a) the probability of finding the oscillator in state u_1 is $\frac{3}{4}$

(b) the probability of finding in state u_0 is $\frac{1}{2}$

(c) the average energy of oscillator is $2\hbar\omega$

(d) the average energy of oscillator is $5\hbar\omega$

18. The given figure shows the plot of the wave function u_n for an electron confined in a box from $x = 0$ to $x = L$, the quantum number of the above state ψ_n is

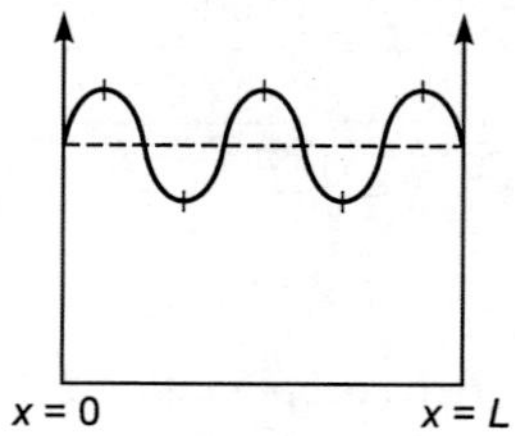

(a) 3 (b) 4 (c) 5 (d) 6

19. A particle is constrained to move along x-axis is described by the wave function

$$\psi(x) = 2x,\ 0 < x < 1$$
$$\psi(x) = 0, \text{ elsewhere}$$

the probability of finding between 0 and 0.4 is
(a) 0.85 (b) 0.085 (c) 0.0085 (d) 0.00085

20. What is the degeneracy of H-atom in state $n = 3$?
(a) 5 (b) 7 (c) 9 (d) 18

21. What is the fraction of beam reflected from the step barrier of V_0 if energy of electron E with $E > V_0$ and width of barrier is infinite, is given by
(a) $\frac{E}{V_0}$ (b) $\frac{E - V_0}{V_0}$
(c) $\frac{E - V_0}{2V_0}$ (d) $\frac{E + V_0}{E}$

22. Consider 8 electrons in a one-dimensional box of length a extending from $x = 0$ to $x = a$. What is the minimum allowed total energy using Pauli's exclusion principle for the system? (m = mass of electron)
(a) $\frac{10h^2}{ma^2}$ (b) $\frac{8h^2}{ma^2}$ (c) $\frac{15h^2}{4ma^2}$ (d) $\frac{15h^2}{2ma^2}$

23. A particle is described by a wavefunction $\psi(x) = e^{-|x|}$ in one-dimension. What is the probability that it will be found in the region $|x| \le a$, $a > 0$?
(a) e^{-a} (b) e^{-2a} (c) $1 - e^{-a}$ (d) $1 - e^{-2a}$

24. Consider a particle in one-dimensional box between $x = 0$ and $x = a$

$$V(x) = \begin{cases} = 0 & \text{for } 0 < x < a \\ = \infty & \text{for } x \le 0 \text{ or } x \ge a \end{cases}$$

When it is in ground state what is the probability that it will be found in the region $\frac{a}{4} < x < \frac{3a}{4}$?
(a) $\frac{1}{2}$ (b) $\frac{1}{2} + \frac{1}{\pi}$
(c) $\frac{1}{4} + \frac{2}{\pi}$ (d) $\frac{1}{4} + \frac{1}{\pi}$

25. A particle with energy $\frac{V_0}{2}$ coming from left encounters a potential $-\frac{3V_0}{2}$ at $x = 0$

$V(x) = 0$ for $x < a$ and $V(x) = -\frac{3V_0}{2}$ for $x > a$,

transmission coefficient is
(a) $\frac{1}{2}$ (b) $\frac{2}{3}$ (c) $\frac{4}{9}$ (d) $\frac{8}{9}$

26. A particle of mass m is confined to a one-dimensional box extending from $x = 0$ to $x = 9$. Assuming the particle in the first excited state, what is the position-probability density at $x = \frac{a}{8}$?
(a) $\frac{1}{a}$ (b) $\frac{2}{a}$
(c) $\frac{1}{2a}$ (d) $\frac{1}{4a}$

27. A particle of mass m coming in from the right with energy E encounters a potential $V(x) = 0$ for $x > 0$ and $\frac{E}{2}$ for $x \le 0$. What is the form of wave function for $x < 0$? Where,

$$k = 2\pi \frac{\sqrt{2mE}}{h}$$

(a) $A\,e^{-ikx/\sqrt{2}}$ (b) $A\,e^{ikx/\sqrt{2}}$
(c) $A\,e^{ikx}$ (d) $A\,e^{-ikx}$

28. Consider a potential barrier of width L and finite height U. For a particle having energy E ($E < U$), whose wave number inside the barrier is k_2, the transmission probability will be proportional to
(a) e^{-ik_2L} (b) e^{-2ik_2L}
(c) e^{-k_2L} (d) e^{-2k_2L}

29. If $\psi = \sqrt{\frac{2}{L}} \cos\frac{\pi x}{L}\, e^{-iEt/\hbar}$, then $<x>$ in the limit $-\frac{L}{2} < x < \frac{L}{2}$ is
(a) $\frac{3}{4L}$ (b) 0
(c) $\frac{1}{4L}$ (d) $\frac{L}{2}$

30. The average value of P_x, for the box normalized wave function

$$\psi(x) = \sqrt{\frac{2}{L}} \sin\left(\frac{3\pi x}{L}\right)$$

(a) $\frac{18\pi^2}{L}$ (b) $\frac{6\pi}{L} - 1$
(c) 0 (d) $\frac{18\pi^2}{L^2}$

31. A system is known to be in a state by the wave function

$$\psi(\theta, \phi) = \frac{1}{\sqrt{20}}[3Y_2^0 + \sqrt{7}\,Y_2^0 - 2Y_2^1],$$

the probability of finding the system in a state with $m = 0$ is
(a) $\frac{4}{5}$ (b) $\frac{1}{5}$
(c) $\frac{2}{5}$ (d) $\frac{3}{5}$

32. In case of H-atom the total degeneracy of the state of specified m is given by

(a) $N = n(2L+1)$ (b) $N = n^2$

(c) $N = l(l+1)$ (d) $N = 2L+1$

33. If ψ_{111} and ψ_{112} are the wave functions of the electrons in the two energy states 111 and 112 respectively in a cubical box of side a, then $\frac{\psi_{111}}{\psi_{112}}$ is

(a) $\dfrac{\sin\frac{\pi z}{a}}{\sin\frac{2\pi z}{a}}$ (b) $\dfrac{\sin\frac{2\pi z}{a}}{\sin\frac{\pi z}{a}}$

(c) $\dfrac{\sin\frac{\pi x}{a}}{\sin\frac{\pi y}{a}}$ (d) $\dfrac{\sin\frac{2\pi y}{a}}{\sin\frac{\pi y}{a}}$

34. A particle of mass m is confined in an potential well

$$V(x) = \begin{cases} 0, 0 < x < L \\ \infty, \text{otherwise} \end{cases}$$

It is subjected to a perturbing potential $V_P(x) = V_0 \sin\frac{2\pi x}{L}$ within the well. Let $E^{(1)}$ and $E^{(2)}$ be corrections in ground state energy and first and second order in V_0, which of the following is correct?

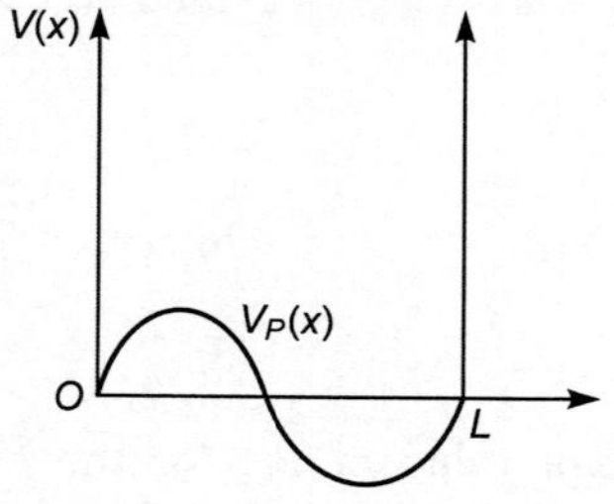

(a) $E^{(1)} = 0, E^{(2)} < 0$

(b) $E^{(1)} > 0, E^{(2)} = 0$

(c) $E^{(1)} = 0, E^{(2)}$ depends on the right of V_0

(d) $E^{(1)} < 0, E^{(2)} < 0$

35. An unperturbed two level system has energy eigen values E_1 and E_2 and eigen functions $\begin{bmatrix}1\\0\end{bmatrix}$ and $\begin{bmatrix}0\\1\end{bmatrix}$ when perturbed its Hamiltonian is represented by

$$\begin{bmatrix} E_1 & A \\ A^* & E_2 \end{bmatrix}$$

The first order correction to E_1 is

(a) $4A$ (b) $2A$

(c) A (d) zero

36. In the above question, the second order correction to E_1 is

(a) 0 (b) A

(c) $\dfrac{A^2}{E_2 - E_1}$ (d) $\dfrac{A^2}{E_1 - E_2}$

37. In Q. 35, the first order correction to eigen function $\begin{bmatrix}1\\0\end{bmatrix}$ is

(a) $\begin{bmatrix} 0 \\ A^*/E_1 - E_2 \end{bmatrix}$ (b) $\begin{bmatrix}0\\1\end{bmatrix}$

(c) $\begin{bmatrix} A^*/E_1 - E_2 \\ 0 \end{bmatrix}$ (d) $\begin{bmatrix}1\\1\end{bmatrix}$

38. The normalized eigen states of a particle in a one-dimensional potential well

$$V(x) = \begin{cases} 0, \text{ if } \le x \le a \\ \infty, \text{ otherwise} \end{cases}$$

are given by $\psi_n(x) = \sqrt{\frac{2}{a}} \sin\left(\frac{n\pi x}{a}\right)$

where, $n = 1, 2, 3, \ldots$

The particle is subjected to a perturbation

$$V(x) = V_0 \cos\left(\frac{\pi x}{a}\right) \text{for}$$

$$0 \le x \le \frac{a}{2} = 0; \text{otherwise}$$

The shift in the ground state energy due to perturbation, in the first order perturbation theory is

(a) $\dfrac{2V_0}{3\pi}$ (b) $\dfrac{V_0}{3\pi}$ (c) $-\dfrac{V_0}{3\pi}$ (d) $-\dfrac{2V_0}{3\pi}$

39. A one-dimensional harmonic oscillator of mass m, charge q and classical amplitude a is kept in an electric field of strength E along x. First order change in ground and first excited state are respectively

(a) $0, \dfrac{qEa}{2}$ (b) $0, qEa$ (c) $0, 0$ (d) $\dfrac{qEa}{\alpha}, qEa$

40. The wave function of a one-dimensional harmonic oscillator is $\psi_0 = A\exp\left[\frac{-\alpha^2 x^2}{2}\right]$ for the ground state $E_0 = \frac{\hbar\omega}{2}$, where $\alpha^2 = \frac{m\omega}{\hbar}$. In the presence of a perturbing potential of $E_0(\alpha x/10)^4$, the first order change in the ground state energy is

[Given $\Gamma(x+1) = \int_0^\infty t^x \exp(-t)\, dt$]

(a) $\left(\frac{1}{2}E_0\right)10^{-4}$ (b) $(3E_0)10^{-4}$

(c) $\left(\frac{3}{4}E_0\right)10^{-4}$ (d) $(E_0)10^{-4}$

41. A quantum harmonic oscillator is in the energy eigenstate $|n\rangle$. A time independent perturbation $1\lambda(a^t\ a)^2$ acts on the particle, where λ is a constant of suitable dimensions and a and a^t are lowering and raising operators respectively. Then, the first order energy shift is given by
(a) λn (b) $\lambda^2 n$ (c) λn^2 (d) $(\lambda n)^2$

42. Zeeman effect is
(a) the change in energy levels of an atom when it is placed in uniform external field
(b) the change in energy levels of an atom when placed in non-uniform external field
(c) the change in energy levels of an atom when placed in external electric field
(d) the change in energy levels of an atom when placed in non-uniform electric field

43. When a perturbation of cx^3 is applied in the Hamiltonian of harmonic oscillation, the shift in first order energy is
(a) zero (b) $\frac{3}{4}c\left(\frac{\hbar\omega}{k}\right)^2$
(c) $\frac{1}{2}c\left(\frac{\hbar\omega}{k}\right)^2$ (d) $c\frac{\hbar\omega}{k}$

44. Using perturbation theory second order energy correction can be written as
(a) $E''_x = \sum_L{}' \frac{|<K|H'|L>|^2}{E^\circ_K - E^\circ_L}$ (b) $E''_K = \sum_L{}' \frac{|<K|H'|L>|^2}{E^\circ_L - E^\circ_K}$
(c) $E''_K = \sum_L{}' \frac{|<K|H'|L>|^2}{E^\circ_K + E^\circ_L}$ (d) None of these

45. The first order perturbed Hamiltonian, when an external uniform electric field $\vec{\mathbf{E}}$ is applied to the z-axis on an atom is
(a) $H' = eEZ$ (b) $H' = -eEZ$
(c) $H' = \frac{eZ}{E}$ (d) $H' = \frac{-eZ}{E}$

46. The value of time dependent constants in perturbation theory is
(a) $\dot{a}_k = i\hbar \sum_n a_n <K|H'|n> e^{i\omega_{kn}t}$
(b) $\dot{a}_k = (i\hbar)^{-1} \sum_n a_n <K|H'|n> e^{i\omega_{kn}t}$
(c) $\dot{a}_k = (i\hbar)^2 \sum_n a_n <K|H'|n> e^{i\omega_{kn}t}$
(d) $\dot{a}_x = (i\hbar)^{-2} \sum_n a_n <K|H'|n> e^{i\omega_{kn}t}$

47. The transition probability per unit time in time dependent perturbation theory is
(a) $\omega = \frac{1}{t}\int |a_k^{(1)}(t)|^2 \rho_k dE_k$
(b) $\omega = \int |a_k^{(1)}(t)|^2 \rho_k dE_k$
(c) $\omega = \int |a_k^{(1)}(t)| \rho_k\, dE_k$
(d) ω = constant for all time

48. If ϕ is any normalized function, then
(a) $\int \phi^* H\phi\, d\tau \geq E_0$ (b) $\int \phi^* H\phi\, d\tau \leq E_0$
(c) $\int \phi^* H\phi\, d\tau \geq E_0^2$ (d) $\int \phi^* H\phi\, d\tau \leq E_0^2$

49. The system in a state $|i\rangle$ is perturbed by a potential

$$V(t) = \begin{cases} V, & t \geq 0 \\ 0, & t < 0 \end{cases}$$

The probability of transition to another state $|f\rangle$, where E_i and E_f are the energies of the eigenstates $|i\rangle$ and $|f\rangle$ is

(a) $P(t) = |V_{fi}|^2 \left[\frac{\sin\left\{\frac{(E_f - E_i)\,t}{2\hbar}\right\}}{\left(\frac{E_f - E_i}{2}\right)}\right]^2$

(b) $P(t) = |V_{fi}|^2 \left[\frac{\sin\left\{\frac{(E_f - E_i)t}{2\hbar}\right\}}{(E_f - E_i)}\right]^2$

(c) $P(t) = |V_{fi}|^2 \left[\frac{\sin (E_f - E_i)t}{2\hbar}\right]^2$

(d) None of the above

50. If $V(t)$ is a time dependent perturbation and $\rho(E)$ is the density of energy states in the range E and $E + dE$, then which of the following is correctly described Fermi's golden rule
(a) $\Gamma = \frac{\pi}{2\hbar}|V_{fi}|^2 \rho(E_f)$ (b) $\Gamma = \frac{2\pi}{\hbar}|V_{fi}|^2 \rho(E_f)$
(c) $\Gamma = \frac{4\pi}{\hbar}|V_{fi}|^2 \rho(E_f)$ (d) $\Gamma = \frac{2\pi}{\hbar}|V_{fi}|^2 \rho(E_f)^2$

51. Consider a sinusoidal time dependent perturbation

$$\vec{\mathbf{V}}(r, t) = V(\vec{\mathbf{r}})\cos\omega t$$

The transition probability between the energy states i and f, the energy difference being $\Delta E = \hbar\omega_0$ is given by

(a) $P(t) = \hbar^2 |V_{fi}|^2 \left[\frac{\sin\left(\frac{\omega_0 - \omega}{2}\right)t}{(\omega_0 - \omega)}\right]^2$

(b) $P(t) = \frac{1}{\hbar^2}|V_{fi}|^2 \left[\frac{\sin\left(\frac{\omega_0 - \omega}{2}\right)t}{(\omega_0 - \omega)}\right]^2$

(c) $P(t) = \frac{\pi}{\hbar^2}|V_{fi}|^2 \left[\frac{\sin\left(\frac{\omega_0 - \omega}{2}\right)t}{\left(\frac{\omega_0 - \omega}{2}\right)} \right]^2$

(d) $P(t) = \frac{1}{\hbar^2}|V_{fi}|^2 \left[\frac{\sin(\omega - \omega_0)t}{(\omega - \omega_0)} \right]^2$

52. The WKB (Wentzel, Kramers, Brillouin) approximation is valid, when

(a) $\frac{\hbar m \left|\frac{\partial V}{\partial x}\right|}{2m(E-V)^{3/2}} > 1$ (b) $\frac{\hbar m \left|\frac{\partial V}{\partial x}\right|}{[2m(E-V)]^{3/2}} > 1$

(c) $\frac{\hbar m \left|\frac{\partial V}{\partial x}\right|}{[2m(E-V)]^{3/2}} \leq 1$ (d) $\frac{\hbar m \left|\frac{\partial V}{\partial x}\right|}{[2m(E-V)]^{3/2}} < 1$

53. The wave function of a one-dimensional harmonic oscillator is $\psi_0 = A\exp\left(\frac{-\alpha^2 x^2}{2}\right)$ for the ground state $E_0 = \frac{\hbar\omega}{2}$, where $\alpha^2 = \frac{m\omega}{\hbar}$. In the presence of a perturbing potential of $E_0(\alpha x/10)^4$, the first order change in the ground state energy is

[Given, $\Gamma(x+1) = \int_0^\infty t^x \exp(-t)\,dt$]

(a) $\left(\frac{1}{2}E_0\right)10^{-4}$ (b) $(3E_0)10^{-4}$

(c) $\left(\frac{3}{4}E_0\right)10^{-4}$ (d) $(E_0)10^{-4}$

Matching Type

54. Match Column I (System) with Column II (Energy level) and select the correct answer using the codes given below

	Column I (System)		Column II (Energy level)
A.	Harmonic oscillator	1.	$E_n = \frac{2n-1}{2}$
B.	Hydrogen atom	2.	$E_n = n^2$
C.	Particle in a box	3.	E_n is continuous
D.	Free particle in motion	4.	$E_n \propto n^2$

Codes

	A	B	C	D
(a)	1	3	2	4
(c)	2	4	1	3
(c)	2	3	1	4
(d)	1	4	2	3

55. Data for the SiO diatomic molecule in the gas phase. $T = 1000$ K, mass $= 7.32 \times 10^{-26}$ kg vibration frequency $\tilde{\nu} = 1242\ \text{cm}^{-1}$, characteristic temperature, $\Theta_v = 1787$ K, rotation constant $\tilde{B} = 0.727\ \text{cm}^{-1}$, characteristic temperature $\Theta_r = 1.046$ K, electronic ground state, $E_0 = 0$, degeneracy $g_0 = 1$, electronic first excited state, $E_1 = 400$ KJ/mol, degeneracy $g_1 = 3$

Match the following.

	Matching quantity value		Quantity
A.	1.0	1.	Reduced mass μ in g/mol
B.	1.2	2.	q_{rot}
C.	10.2	3.	q_{trans}/V
D.	960	4.	q_{vib}
E.	2×10^{33}	5.	Symmetry number σ

Codes

	A	B	C	D	E
(a)	5	1	4	3	2
(b)	1	4	5	2	3
(c)	5	4	1	2	3
(d)	1	2	3	4	5

Assertion & Reason

Codes

(a) Both A and R are true and R is the correct explanation of A.

(b) Both A and R are true and the R is not the correct explanation of A.

(c) A is true and R is false.

(d) R is true and A is false.

56. Assertion (A) The orbital energy of the $2p$ electrons in flourine atoms is higher than that of $1s$ electron in hydrogen atoms.

Reason (R) The Z_{eff} for the $2pe^-$ in F is greater than Z_{eff} for H even when shielding of Z_{eff} for F occurs by $1s$, $2s$, $2pe^-$.

57. Assertion (A) A hydrogen atom in its $2p^2$ state can have a radial probability density r^2R_2, r^2.

Reason (R) The most probable r is the r at which the derivative of the radial probability density is zero.

Directions (Q. Nos. 58 to 60)

A beam of identical particles of mass m and energy E is incident from left on a potential barrier of width L (between $0 < x < L$) and height V_0 as shown in the figure ($E < V_0$).

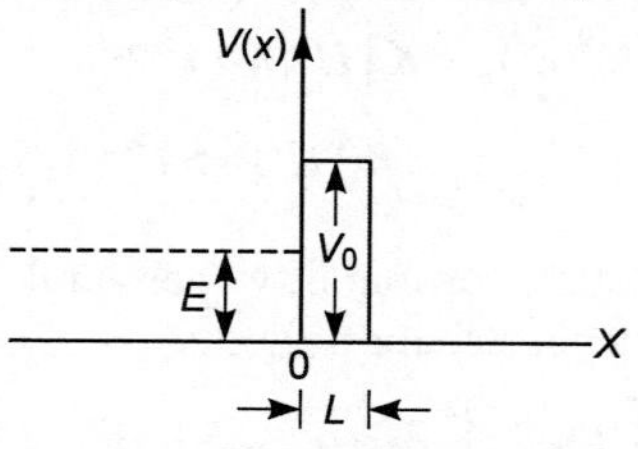

For $x > L$, there is tunnelling with a transmission coefficient $T > 0$. Let A_0, A_R and A_T denote the amplitudes for the incident, reflected and the transmitted waves respectively.

58. Throughout $0 < x < L$, the wave function
(a) can be chosen to be real
(b) is exponentially decaying
(c) is generally complex
(d) is zero

59. Let the probability current associated with the incident wave be S_0. Let R be the reflection coefficient. Then
(a) the probability current vanishes in the classically forbidden region
(b) the probability current is TS_0 for $x > L$
(c) for $x > L$, the probability current is $S_0(l + R)$
(d) for $x > L$, the probabilty current is complex

60. The ratio of the reflected to the incident amplitude A_R/A_0 is
(a) $1 - A_T/A_0$
(b) $\sqrt{(1-T)}$ in magnitude
(c) a real negative number
(d) $\sqrt{\left[1-\left|\frac{A_T}{A_0}\right|^2\right]\frac{E}{V_0 - E}}$

Directions (Q. Nos. 61 and 62)
A particle is located in a three-dimensional cubic well of width L with impenetrable walls.

61. The sum of the energies of the third and the fourth levels is
(a) $10\pi^2\hbar^2/mL^2$
(b) $10\pi^2\hbar^2/3mL^2$
(c) $11\pi^2\hbar^2/mL^2$
(d) $15\pi^2\hbar^2/mL^2$

62. The degeneracy of the fourth level is given by
(a) 1
(b) 2
(c) 3
(d) 4

Directionss (Q. Nos. 63 and 64)
The normalized wave functions ψ_1 and ψ_2 correspond to the ground state and the first excited state of a particle in a potential. You are given the information that the operator $\hat{A}$ acts on the wave functions as $\hat{A}\psi_1 = \psi_2$and $\hat{A}\psi_2 = \psi_1$.

63. The expectation value of A for the state
$\psi = (3\psi_1 + 4\psi_2)/5$ is
(a) − 0.32 (b) zero (c) 0.75 (d) 0.96

64. Which of the following are eigen functions of $\hat{A}^2$?
(a) ψ_1 and ψ_2
(b) ψ_2 and not ψ_1
(c) ψ_1 and not ψ_2
(d) Neither ψ_1 nor ψ_2

Direction (Q. Nos. 65 to 67)
An unperturbed two level system has energy eigen values E_1 and E_2 and eigen functions $\begin{bmatrix}1\\0\end{bmatrix}$ and $\begin{bmatrix}0\\1\end{bmatrix}$. When perturbed,its Hamiltonian is represented by $\begin{bmatrix}E_1 & A\\A^* & E_2\end{bmatrix}$.

65. The first order correction to E_1 is
(a) $4A$
(b) $2A$
(c) A
(d) zero

66. The second order correction to E_1 is
(a) zero
(b) A
(c) $\frac{A^2}{E_2 - E_1}$
(d) $\frac{A^2}{E_1 - E_2}$

67. The first order correction to the eigenfunction $\begin{bmatrix}1\\0\end{bmatrix}$ is
(a) $\begin{bmatrix}0\\A^*/(E_1 - E_2)\end{bmatrix}$
(b) $\begin{bmatrix}0\\1\end{bmatrix}$
(c) $\begin{bmatrix}A^*/(E_1 - E_2)\\0\end{bmatrix}$
(d) $\begin{bmatrix}1\\1\end{bmatrix}$

Directions (Q. Nos. 68 to 70)
The variation method is used to obtain the best function for a given Hamiltonian operator. If we use ψ as a trial function for the operator H where $\psi = \frac{(\phi_0 - \phi_1)}{(1+a^2)^{1/2}}$ and ϕ_0 and ϕ_1 are two lowest eigen functions with ε_0 and ε_1 eigen values of the Hamiltomian with $E_1 > E_0$.

68. Value of $\langle H \rangle$ is
(a) $\frac{E_0 + a^2E_1}{1+a^2}$
(b) $\frac{E_0 - a^2E_1}{1+a^2}$
(c) zero
(d) None of these

69. Value of $\langle H \rangle$ is
(a) greater than E_0
(b) greater than and equal to E_0
(c) lesser than E_0
(d) lesser than and equal to E_0

70. The value of a using variation method is :
(a) $a \geq 1$
(b) $a = 0$
(c) $a = 0$ to 1
(d) $a < 1$

Directions (Q. Nos. 71 and 72)
A wave function of a free particle can be given as $\psi(x) = \left(\frac{3}{5}\right)e^{ikx} - \left(\frac{4}{5}\right)e^{-ikx}$ where, k is a constant, $\hat{E}_x$ is the KE operator, m is mass of the particle.

71. Relation between ψ and $\hat{E}_k$ is
(a) ψ is an eigen value of $\hat{E}_k$
(b) ψ is an eigen function of $\hat{E}_k$
(c) $\hat{E}_k$ is an eigen value of ψ
(d) $\hat{E}_k$ is an eigen function of ψ

72. The relation between ψ and $\hat{E}_k$ is

(a) $\hat{E}_k\psi = \frac{\hbar^2}{2m}\psi$ (b) $\hat{E}_k\psi = \frac{\hbar^2 k^2}{2m}\psi$

(c) $\hat{E}_k\psi = \frac{\hbar^2 k^2}{m}\psi$ (d) $\hat{E}_k\psi = \frac{\hbar^2 k}{m^2}\psi$

73. The expected value of kinetic energy in terms of $\hbar$, k and m is

(a) $\hat{E}_k = \frac{\hbar}{2m}$ (b) $\hat{E}_k = \frac{\hbar^2 k^2}{m}$

(c) $\hat{E}_k = \frac{\hbar^2 k}{2m}$ (d) $\hat{E}_k = \frac{\hbar^2 k^2}{2m}$

Directions (Q. Nos. 74 to 78)

The natural abundance of ^{13}C is 1.1% and the abundance of deuterium (D or ^2H) is 0.015%. That is, for randomly sampled atoms,

$P(^{13}C) = 0.011$ $P(^{12}C) = 0.989$

$P(^1H) = 0.99985$ $P(D) = 0.00015$

Neglect any other isotope.

74. The probability of selecting $^1H-{}^{13}C-{}^1H$ from the sample of methylene diradicals, HCH, in the gas phase is

(a) 2.0×10^{-4} (b) 0.11

(c) 3.0×10^{-4} (d) 0.011

75. The probability of selecting $^1H-{}^{12}C-D$ or $D-{}^{12}C-{}^1H$ (*i.e.*, either end-to-end order) from large sample of methylene diradicals, HCH in gas phase is

(a) 2.0×10^{-4} (b) 3.0×10^{-4}

(c) 0.11 (d) 0.011

76. Total number of isotopomers of ethylene diradical are

(a) 4 (b) 6

(c) 8 (d) 10

77. Least probable isotopomer is

(a) $D-{}^{13}C-D$ (b) $^1H-{}^{13}C-{}^1H$

(c) $D-{}^{12}C-D$ (d) None of these

78. Probability of least probable isotopomer is

(a) $(0.00015)^2 \times 0.011$

(b) $(0.00015)^2 \times 0.989$

(c) $(0.99985)^2 \times 0.011$

(d) $0.99985 \times 0.00015 \times 0.989$

Answers

Exercise 1

1. (b)	2. (c)	3. (b)	4. (d)	5. (d)	6. (a)	7. (b)	8. (a)	9. (c)	10. (d)
11. (a)	12. (b)	13. (d)	14. (c)	15. (c)	16. (d)	17. (a)	18. (d)	19. (a)	20. (a)
21. (a)	22. (a)	23. (a)	24. (b)	25. (a)	26. (b)	27. (b)	28. (b)	29. (a)	30. (b)
31. (a)	32. (d)	33. (d)	34. (a)	35. (b)	36. (c)	37. (b)	38. (d)	39. (d)	40. (d)
41. (c)	42. (d)	43. (c)	44. (a)	45. (b)	46. (a)	47. (d)	48. (d)	49. (d)	50. (c)
51. (b)	52. (c)	53. (d)	54. (b)	55. (c)	56. (d)	57. (d)	58. (c)	59. (b)	60. (b)
61. (c)	62. (a)	63. (b)	64. (b)	65. (a)	66. (c)	67. (c)	68. (d)	69. (b)	70. (b)
71. (a)	72. (c)	73. (a)	74. (a)	75. (d)	76. (a)	77. (b)	78. (c)	79. (c)	80. (a)

Exercise 2

1. (b)	2. (d)	3. (d)	4. (a)	5. (c)	6. (a)	7. (c)	8. (c)	9. (c)	10. (c)
11. (c)	12. (a)	13. (c)	14. (a)	15. (b)	16. (c)	17. (a)	18. (c)	19. (a)	20. (c)
21. (b)	22. (c)	23. (d)	24. (a)	25. (c)	26. (a)	27. (b)	28. (d)	29. (b)	30. (c)
31. (a)	32. (a)	33. (a)	34. (c)	35. (c)	36. (c)	37. (c)	38. (a)	39. (d)	40. (c)
41. (b)	42. (a)	43. (a)	44. (a)	45. (b)	46. (b)	47. (a)	48. (b)	49. (a)	50. (b)
51. (a)	52. (d)	53. (c)	54. (d)	55. (c)	56. (c)	57. (a)	58. (a)	59. (b)	60. (a)
61. (a)	62. (c)	63. (d)	64. (a)	65. (c)	66. (c)	67. (c)	68. (a)	69. (b)	70. (b)
71. (b)	72. (b)	73. (d)	74. (d)	75. (b)	76. (b)	77. (a)	78. (a)		

Hints & Solutions

Exercise 1

2. $\lambda = \dfrac{h}{\sqrt{2mE_K}} = \dfrac{h}{\sqrt{2m\,qV}}$ $\qquad (\because E_K = qV)$

10. $$P = \int_0^{L/2} \frac{2}{L}\sin^2\frac{\pi x}{L}\,dx$$

$$= \frac{2}{L}\int_0^{L/2} \frac{1-\cos\dfrac{2\pi x}{L}}{2}\,dx$$

$$= \frac{1}{L}\left\{\left[\frac{L}{2}\right] - 0\right\} = \frac{1}{2} = 0.5\%$$

11. $P(x) = \int_{x_1}^{x_2} ae^{-ax}\,dx = a\left[\dfrac{e^{-ax}}{-a}\right]_{x_1}^{x_2}$

$$= (e^{-ax_1} - e^{-ax_2})$$

14. The wave function is $\psi(x) = e^{-iax+b}$

$\Rightarrow$ $\psi(x) = e^b\,e^{-iax} = B\,e^{-iax}$

This is the possible when $V(x) = 0$.

15. $\because$ $P = \int_0^{\infty} \psi^*\psi\,dx$

$\Rightarrow$ $P = \int_0^{\infty} C^2 \exp e^{-2a^2x^2}\,dx$

$\Rightarrow$ $P = \dfrac{C^2}{2\alpha}\left(\dfrac{\pi}{2}\right)^{1/2}$

$\because \int_{-\infty}^{\infty} P\,dx = 1$ on solving $p = \dfrac{1}{2}$

16. Only $\psi = A\,e^{-x^2}$ remain finite when $x \to \infty$ and $x \to -\infty$ hence, it is only solution.

19. Applying Schrodinger's equation

$$\frac{d^2\phi}{dx^2} + \frac{2m}{\hbar^2}(E - V)\,\phi = 0, \text{ we get}$$

$$\frac{d^2\phi}{dx^2} + \frac{2mE}{\hbar^2}\psi = 0$$

$\Rightarrow$ $\dfrac{d^2\psi}{dx^2} + \left(\dfrac{p}{\hbar}\right)^2\psi = 0$ $\qquad (\because p^2 = 2mE)$

Solution of this equation is

$$\psi = A\sin\frac{p}{\hbar}x + B\cos\frac{p}{\hbar}x$$

Applying boundary condition

$$\psi(0) = 0$$

$\Rightarrow$ $A\sin 0 + B\cos 0 = 0 \;\Rightarrow\; B = 0$

Hence, wavefunction is

$$\psi = A\sin\frac{p}{\hbar}x$$

Applying normalization, we get

$$\psi = \frac{1}{\sqrt{L}}\sin\frac{p}{\hbar}x$$

20. $\psi(x) = A\,e^{ikx} \Rightarrow \psi^*(x) = A\,e^{-ikx}$

$$J = \frac{\hbar}{m}\ln\left(\psi^*\frac{\partial\psi}{\partial x}\right)$$

On solving, we get

$$J = |A|^2\frac{\hbar k}{m}$$

21. $\int_{-\pi/2}^{\pi/2} \psi^*\psi\,dx = 1$

$\Rightarrow$ $A^2\int_{-\pi/2}^{\pi/2}\cos^4 dx = 1$

On solving, we get

$$A = \sqrt{\frac{8}{3\pi}}$$

22. We know that $J = \dfrac{\hbar}{m}\ln[\psi^*\nabla\psi]$

$\because$ Wave function depends upon only r

Hence, $J_r = \dfrac{\hbar}{m}\ln\left(\psi^*\dfrac{\partial\psi}{\partial r}\right)$

$$= \frac{\hbar}{m}\ln\left[\frac{e^{-ikr}}{r}\left(\frac{1}{r}ike^{ikr} - \frac{e^{ikr}}{r}\right)\right]$$

$$= \frac{\hbar}{m}\frac{k}{r^2} = \frac{v}{r^2} \qquad \because \frac{\hbar k}{m} = v$$

23. $$\langle p^2\rangle = \int \psi^*(\hat{\mathbf{p}})\psi\,dx$$

$$= \int \psi^*(\hbar^2)^2\frac{\partial^2}{\partial x^2}\psi\,dx$$

$$= -\hbar^2\int_0^L\left(\frac{2}{L}\right)^{1/2}\sin\frac{\pi x}{L}\frac{\partial^2}{\partial x^2}\left\{\left(\frac{2}{L}\right)^{1/2}\sin\frac{\pi x^2}{L}\right\}dx$$

$$= \frac{2}{L}\hbar^2\int_0^L\left(\sin\frac{\pi x}{L}\right)\left(\frac{\pi}{L}\right)\cdot\sin\frac{\pi x}{L}\,dx$$

$$= \frac{\pi^2\hbar^2}{L^3}\int_0^L\left[1 - \cos\frac{2\pi x}{L}\right]dx$$

$$= \frac{\pi^2\hbar^2}{L^2}\int_0^L 2\sin^2\frac{\pi x}{L}\,dx$$

$$= \frac{\pi^2\hbar^2}{L^3}\left[x - \left\{\frac{\sin 2\pi\dfrac{x}{2}}{2\pi\dfrac{x}{2}}\right\}\right]_0^L$$

$$= \frac{\pi^2\hbar^2}{L^3}\left[L - \frac{L}{2\pi}\cdot(\sin 2\pi - \sin 0)\right]$$

$$= \frac{\pi^2\hbar^2}{L^2}$$

29. $<P_x> = \int_{-\infty}^{\infty} A\,e^{-x^2/a^2}\left(-i\hbar\dfrac{\partial}{\partial x}\right)A\,e^{-x^2/a^2}\,dx$

$$= A^2\frac{2i\hbar}{a^2}\int_{-\infty}^{\infty} e^{-2x^2/a^2}\,x\,dx$$

$<P_x> = 0$

$\because$ Integrand is odd function of e.

32. $\left\langle \frac{1}{r^2} \right\rangle = \int_0^\infty \psi^*(r) \frac{1}{r^2} \psi(r)\, dv$

$\Rightarrow \left\langle \frac{1}{r^2} \right\rangle = \int_0^\infty \frac{1}{4\pi} \times \frac{4}{a^3} e^{-2r/a} 4\pi r^2\, dr$

$= \frac{4}{a^3} \int_0^\infty e^{-2r/a}\, dr$

$\because \int_0^\infty e^{-\alpha x} x^n\, dx = \frac{n!}{\alpha^{n+1}}$

$\Rightarrow \left\langle \frac{1}{r^2} \right\rangle = \frac{4}{a^3} \times \frac{0!}{\left(\frac{2}{a}\right)^{0+1}} = \frac{2}{a^2}$

33. Here, $k = \frac{\pi}{4L}$

But $k = \frac{\sqrt{2mE}}{\hbar}$

$\Rightarrow \frac{2mE}{\hbar^2} = \frac{\pi^2}{16L^2}$

$\Rightarrow E = \frac{\pi^2 \hbar^2}{32mL^2}$

38. $\langle P_x \rangle = \int_{-\infty}^{\infty} \psi^* \left(-i\hbar \frac{\partial}{\partial x}\right) \psi\, dx$

$= |N|^2 \int_{-\infty}^{\infty} \frac{i\hbar x}{a^2} e^{-x^2/a^2}\, dx + |N|^2 \int_{-\infty}^{\infty} \hbar k\, e^{-x^2/a^2}\, dx$

$\langle P_x \rangle = 0 + \frac{1}{a\sqrt{\pi}} \hbar k a \sqrt{\pi} = \hbar k$

39.

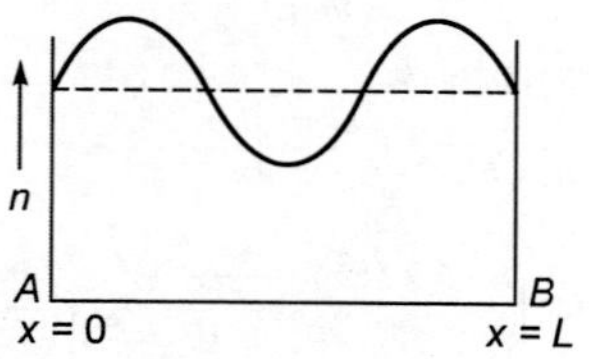

Quantum number of the state n is equal to number extreme points lying between the extreme points A and B.

40. The Schrodinger wave equation for one dimension harmonic oscillator is given as

$$\frac{d^2\psi}{dx^2} + \frac{2m}{\hbar}(E - V)\psi = 0$$

where E is kinetic energy and V is potential energy of the oscillator and is given as $V = \frac{1}{2}kx^2$

The energy of it of nth quantum is proportional to $\left(n + \frac{1}{2}\right)$

i.e., $E_n = \left(n + \frac{1}{2}\right) h\nu$ ...(i)

Zero point energy $E_0 = \frac{1}{2} h\nu$ ...(ii)

Then, the energy for $n = 2$ is

$E_2 = \left(2 + \frac{1}{2}\right) h\nu$

$= 2h\nu + \frac{1}{2} h\nu$

$= E_0 + 2h\nu$

41. (i) The energy of an electron in nth orbit of the hydrogen is proportional to $\frac{1}{n^2}$

(ii) Energy of a particle in a box $\propto n^2$

(iii) Energy of an oscillator is $\propto \left(n + \frac{1}{2}\right)$

Since, the energy difference between two consecutive n is 2 units $\Rightarrow$ a harmonic oscillator.

42. According to quantum theory. The p_x component of momentum is given as $p_x = \frac{ih}{2\pi} \cdot \frac{\partial}{\partial x}$ whereas energy is given as

$$E = \frac{h}{2\pi i} \frac{\partial}{\partial t}$$

43. de-Broglie law states that every moving body is associated with a wave of wavelength λ given as

$$\lambda = \frac{h}{mv} \quad \text{...(i)}$$

where, h is Planck's constant.

Kinetic energy $K = \frac{p^2}{2m} = \frac{(mv)^2}{2m}$

$\Rightarrow (mv)^2 = 2mE$

$\Rightarrow mv = \sqrt{2mE}$ ...(ii)

By Eqs. (i) and (ii), we get $\lambda = \frac{h}{\sqrt{2mE}}$

44. The probability of penetration of a barrier of width L and potential V_0 by a particle of mass m and kinetic energy E is given as

Probability $P = e^{-\frac{4\pi L}{h}[\sqrt{2m(V_0 - E)}]}$

The probability falls rapidly, if the mass m of the particle or the barrier width L or the energy difference $(V_0 - E)$ increases.

Electron will have greater transmission probability.

45. If a particle of mass m and kinetic energy E tries to penetrate a barrier of height V with $V_0 > E$, then probability of transmission or probability of penetration T is given as

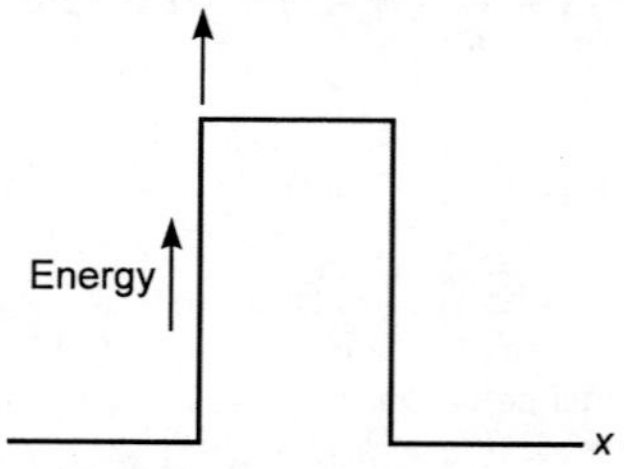

where, L is width of barrier.

It shows that probability of penetration drops exponentially for larger mass if other quantities remain constant.

Here,

$E = 5$ MeV

$V = 10$ MeV

Then probability is greater for smaller mass.

46. The wave function $\psi(x)$ has following properties.

(i) $\psi(x)$ and its derivative $\frac{d\psi}{dx}$ must be finite for all values of x

(ii) $\psi(x)$ and $\frac{d\psi}{dx}$ must be continuous for all values of x

(iii) ψ and $\frac{d\psi}{dx}$ must be single valued for all values of x

47. de-Broglie hypothesis wavelength λ associated with momentum p is given by $\lambda = \frac{h}{p}$.

According to Bragg's law,the condition of reflection is given by $2d \sin\theta = n\lambda$.

Then, $\quad 2d \sin 30° = n\lambda$

or $\quad 2d \times \frac{1}{2} = \frac{h}{p} \quad$ or $d = \frac{h}{p}$

Then $\quad p = \frac{h}{d}$

48. $\psi(x) = e^{-x}$ for $0 < x < a$

$= e^{x}$ fr $-a < x < 0$

Probability $= P = \int \psi^* \psi dx$

$$\therefore \quad P = \int_{-a}^{0} \psi^* \psi x + \int_{0}^{a} \psi^* \psi x$$

$$= \int_{-a}^{0} e^{x} \cdot e^{x} dx + \int_{0}^{a} e^{-x} \cdot e^{-x} dx$$

$$= \int_{-a}^{0} e^{2x} dx + \int_{0}^{a} e^{-2x} dx$$

$$= \left.\frac{e^{2x}}{2}\right|_{a}^{0} \left.\frac{e^{-2x}}{2}\right|_{0}^{a} = \frac{1}{2}[1 - e^{-2a}] - \frac{1}{2}[e^{-2a} - 1]$$

$$= \frac{1}{2}[1 - e^{-2a}] + \frac{1}{2}[1 - e^{-2a}]$$

$$= 1 - e^{-2a}$$

49. If the wavelength of proton and neutron having the same $= 2$ Å

$$\lambda = \frac{h}{p}$$

$p = \frac{h}{\lambda}$ for proton and electron

Then both having same momentum.

51. $\because$ Given function is odd.

56. Energy $E_n \propto n^2$

57. Since, it remain finite or becomes zero at $r = \pm\infty$.

58. $\quad n < a \quad x \geq a$

$V(x) = 0 \quad -3V_0/2$

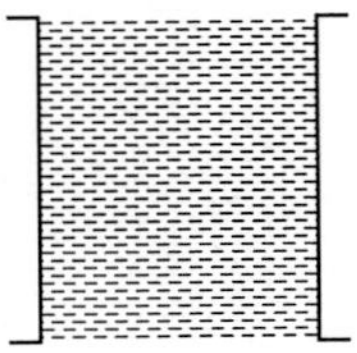

Transmission coefficient

$$= \frac{(V_0)^2}{\left(\frac{3V_0}{2}\right)^2} = \frac{V_0 \times 4}{9V_0^2}$$

$$= \frac{4}{9} = 4:9$$

59. $V(\alpha) = 0$ for $0 < x < a$

$V = \infty$ for $x \leq 0$ or $x \geq a$

When it is in ground state

at $\left(\frac{a}{4}\right) < x < \left(\frac{3a}{4}\right)$

then its probability $\left(\frac{3a}{4} - \frac{a}{4}\right) = \frac{2a}{4} = \frac{1a}{2}$

So, its value is $\left(\frac{a}{2} + \frac{1}{\pi}\right)$

60. If the wavefunction ψ for a particle is given as

$$\psi = A(x + iy)\, e^{-r^2}$$

$$r^2 = x^2 + y^2 + z^2$$

then, $\quad L_z = \frac{h}{2\pi} = \hbar$

61. α-decay and field emission of electrons are quantum mechanical tunnelling through the barrier as their energy are less than the barrier potential. While β-particle is emitted due to neutron decay, they are not already present in nucleus. Spectra of previous two is line while of β-ray is line spectra.

63. The fraction of beam reflected from the step barrier of V_0 if energy of electron is E with $E > V_0$ and width of barrier is ∞, is given as

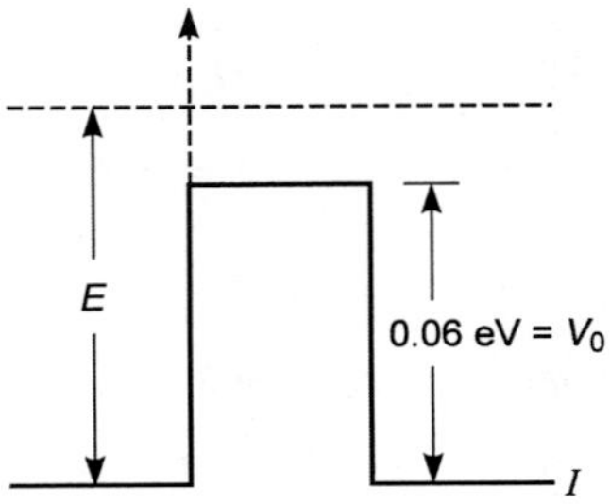

$$= \frac{E - V_0}{V_0}$$

Here, $\quad E = 0.08$ eV

$V = 0.06$ eV

$\Rightarrow \quad E - V_0 = 0.02$ eV

So, fraction of reflected beam $= \frac{0.02}{0.06}$

$$= \frac{1}{3}$$

$$= 0.33$$

65. Let us consider a wave mechanical harmonic oscillator. The Schrodinger equation for the oscillator is, with $V = x^2$

$$\frac{d^2\psi}{dx^2} + \frac{8\pi^2 m}{h^2}\left(E - \frac{1}{2}x^2\right)\psi = 0$$

If the ground state function is Ae^{-ax^2} then

$$\frac{8\pi^2 m}{h^2}\frac{1}{2}x^2 = 2a^2x^2$$

$$\Rightarrow \quad 2a^2 = \frac{4\pi^2 m}{h^2}$$

$$\Rightarrow \quad a = 2\pi \frac{(m/2)^{\frac{1}{2}}}{h}$$

66. It is given $\psi = 0 \begin{cases} x \le 0 \\ x \ge 5 \end{cases}$

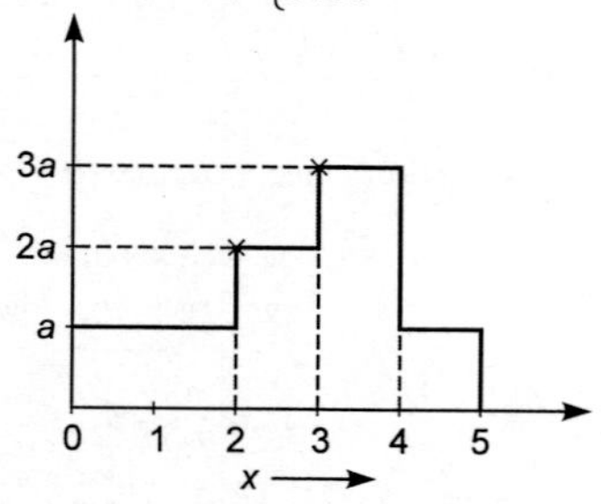

Since, $\int_x^{\infty} P dx = 1$

$\Rightarrow \int_0^5 P dx = 1$

$\Rightarrow (2 \times a) + (3-2) \times 2a + (4-3) \times 3a + (5-4) \times a = 1$

$\Rightarrow 2a + 2a + 3a + a = 1$

$\Rightarrow 8a = 1$

$\Rightarrow a = \frac{1}{8}$

Thus, probability to find between $x = 2$ to $x = 4$ is equal area of the probability distribution function between $x = 2$ to $x = 4$.

$= (3-2)\ 2a + (4-3) \times 3a$

$= 2a + 3a = 5a$

$= 5 \times \frac{1}{8} = \frac{5}{8}$

67. The Schrodinger wave equation for it is

$$\frac{d^2\psi}{dx^2} - k^2\psi = 0$$

So, $\psi = Ae^{-kx} + Be^{kx}$

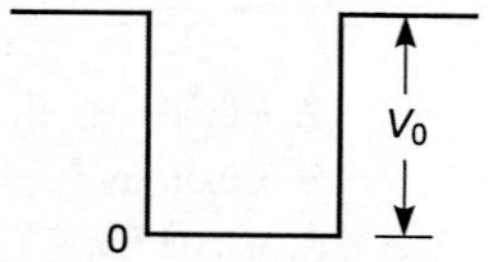

where, $-k^2 = E - V_0$

i.e., $k^2 = V_0 - E$

Sine, when $x \to \infty$, $e^{kx} \to \infty$ but ψ is finite so, we will put $B_0 = 0$. And hence ψ is written as

$$\psi = Ae^{-kr}$$

68. The energy in *n*th state of hydrogen atom is given as

$$E_n = \frac{13.6}{n^2} \text{eV}$$

$\Rightarrow E_n \propto \frac{1}{n^2}$

Thus, energy in hydrogen atom is proportional to the $\frac{1}{n^2}$.

69. A particle will lie in a box, if length of the box is an integral multiple of half wavelength

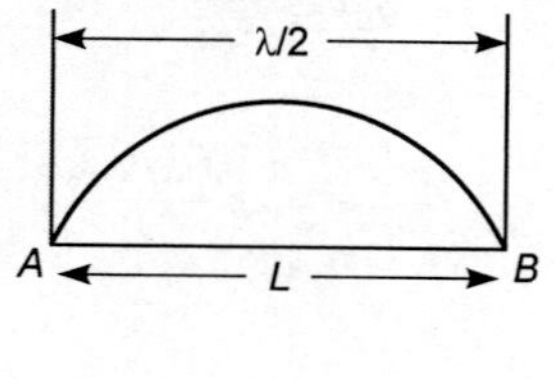

i.e., $L = n\ (\lambda/2),\ n = 1, 2, 3, ...$

$\Rightarrow \lambda = \frac{2L}{n}$

So,by de-Broglie wave equation

$p = \frac{2L}{\lambda}$

$\Rightarrow p = \frac{h}{(2L/n)}$

$\Rightarrow p = \frac{nh}{2L}$

For ground state $n = 1$

So, $p = \frac{h}{2L}$

70. If $\psi(x)$ is the wave function then probability of finding the particle in width dx is given as

$$P = |\psi(x)|^2 dx$$

we have, $\psi(x) = 2x\ \ 0 < x < 1$

$\psi(x) = 0$ elsewhere

Thus, $P = \int_0^{0.4} \psi^2 dx$

$\text{Probability} = \int_0^{0.4} (2x)^2 dx$

$= \frac{4}{3}[x^3]_0^{0.4}$

$= \frac{4}{3}(0.4)^3$

$= 0.085$

Thus, probability in interval (0, 0.4) is 0.085.

71. Here $V(x) = 0$, for $0 \le x \le \pi$

$= \infty$, otherwise

Applying Schrodinger equation

$$\frac{d^2\psi}{dx^2} + \frac{2m}{\hbar^2}(E - V)\psi = 0$$

$\Rightarrow \frac{d^2\psi}{dx^2} + \frac{2m}{\hbar^2}E\psi = 0 \quad$ for $0 \le x \le \pi$

$\Rightarrow \psi = A\cos kx + B\sin kx$

Applying boundry conditions $\psi(x) = \psi(\pi) = 0$

we get $A = 0$

$\Rightarrow \psi = B\sin kx$

Applying normalization

$$\int_0^{\pi} \psi\psi^* dx = 1$$

$\Rightarrow B^2 \int_0^{\pi} \sin^2 kx\ dx = 1$

$\Rightarrow B^2 \int_0^{\pi} \left[\frac{1 - \cos 2kx}{2}\right] dx = 1$

$\Rightarrow B^2 \left[\left(\frac{\pi}{2}\right) - \frac{1}{4k}(\sin 2kx)_0^{\pi}\right] = 1$

$\Rightarrow B = \sqrt{2/\pi}$

Hence, $\psi = \sqrt{\frac{2}{\pi}} \sin kx$

The energy correction due to $H' = ax$ is

$$<E> = \int_0^\pi \psi^* H' \psi dx$$

$$<E> = \frac{2a}{\pi} \int_0^\pi x \sin^2 kx \, dx$$

On solving this, we get

$$E = \frac{a\pi}{2}$$

Exercise 2

2. Hamiltonian for $E < V_0$

$$\frac{-\hbar^2}{2m} \frac{d^2\psi_1}{dx^2} = E\psi_1$$

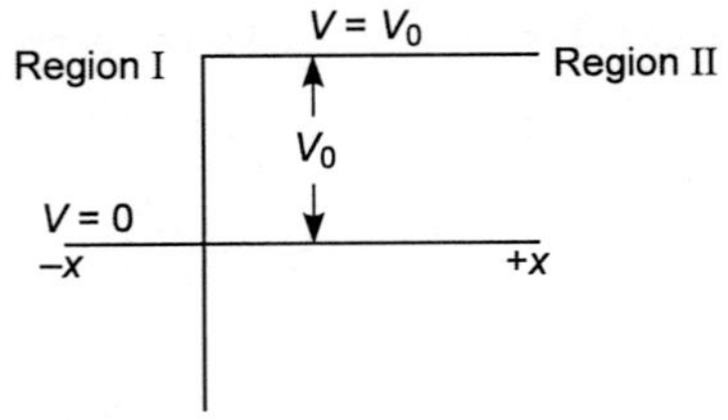

$$x = 0$$

or $$\frac{d^2\psi_1}{dx^2} + \frac{2mE}{\hbar^2}\psi_1 = 0$$

where $$\alpha = \frac{2mE}{\hbar^2}$$

or $$\psi_1 = ae^{i\alpha x} + Be^{-i\alpha x}$$

For second region

$$\frac{d^2\psi_{II}}{dx^2} + \frac{2m}{\hbar^2}(E - V_0)\psi_{II} = 0 \text{ but } V_0 > E$$

So, $$\frac{d^2\psi_{II}}{dx^2} + \frac{2m}{\hbar^2}(V_0 - E)\psi_{II} = 0,$$

where $$y = \frac{2m(V_0 - E)}{\hbar^2}$$

Solution is $$\psi_{II} = Ce^{yx} + De^{-yx}$$

For $x \to \infty$ in second region first term vanishes $\psi_{II} = De^{-yx}$. Thus wave function remains finite in second region $x > 0$.

Using boundary conditions $(\psi_I)_{x=0} = (\psi_{II})_{x=\infty}$ and $\left(\frac{d\psi_I}{dx}\right)_{x=0} = \left(\frac{d\psi_{II}}{dx}\right)_{x=0}$

we have $A + B = D$ and $i\alpha A - i\alpha B = -yD$

Finally $$B = \left(\frac{i\alpha + y}{i\alpha - y}\right)A$$

$$\therefore \text{Reflection coefficient } \frac{|B|^2}{|A|^2} = \frac{|(y + i\alpha)||(y - i\alpha)|}{|(i\alpha - y)||-i\alpha - y|} = 1$$

Thus, for $E < V_0$ reflection coefficient is non-zero for $E > V_0$

reflection coefficient $R = \left(\frac{\alpha - \beta}{\alpha + \beta}\right)^2 \neq 0$

3. The barrier potential is given as

$$V(x) = V_0 \text{ for } |x| < a$$

and $$V(x) = 0 \text{ for } |x| > a$$

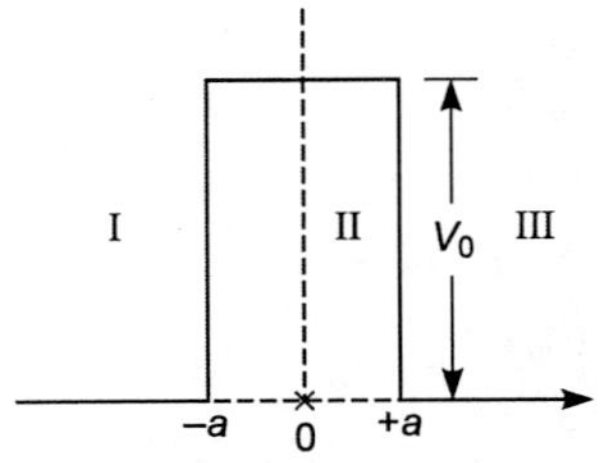

The wave function is given as

$$\psi(x) = e^{ikx} + Be^{-ikx} \text{ for } x < -a \quad \text{...(i)}$$

$$= Ae^{ikx} \text{ for } x > a \quad \text{...(ii)}$$

The quantity B in Eq. (i) represent the amplitude of reflected ray in medium I

and A in Eq. (ii) represents the amplitude of transmitted ray in medium III

Hence,

$$\text{Reflexivity } R = |A^2|$$

$$\text{and transmittivity } T = |B|^2$$

Since, $$R + T = 1$$

$$\Rightarrow \quad |A|^2 + |B|^2 = 1$$

10. For bound state

$$V_0 - |E| = \frac{n^2\pi^2\hbar^2}{2ma^2}$$

$$\Rightarrow \quad V_0 = \frac{n^2\pi^2\hbar^2}{2ma^2} + |E|$$

There are only three bound states.

Hence, $n = 2$ to $n = 4$

$$\Rightarrow \quad \frac{2\pi^2\hbar^2}{ma^2} < V_0 < \frac{8\pi^2\hbar^2}{ma^2}$$

13. For free particle

$$E = \frac{p^2}{2m} = \frac{h^2}{\lambda^2 2m} \quad \text{...(i)}$$

$$\text{KE} = E - V = \frac{h^2}{(2\lambda)^2 \cdot 2m} \quad \text{...(ii)}$$

Dividing Eq. (ii) by Eq. (i),

$$\Rightarrow \quad \frac{V}{E} = \frac{3}{4}$$

14. For one-dimensional potential well

$$E_n = \frac{n^2h^2}{8\pi nL^2} \Rightarrow n = \sqrt{\frac{8mL^2E}{h^2}}$$

$$\text{Energy density} = \frac{dn}{dE} = \frac{L\sqrt{m}}{\pi\hbar\sqrt{2E}}$$

18. Quantum number = number of maxima or minima of ψ

$= 5$

22. $\because \quad E_n = \dfrac{n^2h^2}{8ma^2}$

$\Rightarrow \quad E = E_1 + E_2 + \ldots + E_8$

$$E = \frac{h^2}{8ma^2}[1^2 + 2^2 + 3^2 + 4^2 + 5^2 + 6^2 + 7^2 + 8^2]$$

$\Rightarrow \quad E = \dfrac{15h^2}{4\pi ma^2}$

23. $\psi(x) = e^{-x}$ for $0 < x < a$

$= e^{x}$ for $-a < x < 0$

$$P = \int \psi^* \psi \, dx = \int_{-a}^{0} \psi^* \psi \, dx + \int_{0}^{a} \psi^* \psi \, dx$$

$$= \int_{-a}^{0} e^{x}e^{x} \, dx + \int_{0}^{a} e^{-x}e^{-x} \, dx$$

$$= 1 - e^{-2a}$$

24. When in ground state

$$\frac{a}{4} < x < \frac{3a}{4},$$

then its probability $= \dfrac{\left(\dfrac{3a}{4} - \dfrac{a}{4}\right)}{a} = \dfrac{1}{2}$

So, its value is $= \dfrac{1}{2} + \dfrac{1}{\pi}$

25. Transmission coefficient $= \dfrac{\left[\dfrac{V_0}{2} + \dfrac{3V_0}{2}\right]^2}{\left[\dfrac{3V_0}{2}\right]^2} = \dfrac{4}{9}$

34. We have $(E') = \int_0^L \dfrac{2V_0}{L} \sin^2 \dfrac{\pi x}{L} \sin \dfrac{2\pi x}{L} \, dx$

On solving, we get

$E' = 0$

Now, $\quad < E_2 > = V_0 + \dfrac{< E' >^2}{E_2 - E_1} = V_0 \qquad (\because E' = 0)$

35. First order correction to $< E_1 >$ is

$$< \psi^* | E | \psi > = [1, 0]\begin{bmatrix} E_1 & A \\ A^* & E_2 \end{bmatrix}\begin{bmatrix} 0 \\ 1 \end{bmatrix} = A$$

36. Second order correction is

$$= \frac{|< \psi^* | E | \psi >|^2}{E_2 - E_1} = \frac{A^2}{E_2 - E_1}$$

45. The force on electron is $F = (-e)E$

Hence, $\quad H' = (-eE)z.$

53. Here $\quad \psi_0 = A \exp\left(\dfrac{-\alpha^2 x^2}{2}\right)$

$\because \quad \int_{-\infty}^{\infty} \psi_0^* \psi_0 dx = 1$

$\Rightarrow \quad A^2 \int_{-\infty}^{\infty} \exp(-\alpha^2 x^2) \, dx = 1$

Now put $\quad \alpha x = y$

$\Rightarrow \quad dx = \dfrac{dy}{\alpha}$

$\Rightarrow \quad \dfrac{A^2}{\alpha} \int_{-\infty}^{\infty} \exp(-y^2) \, dy = 1$

$\because \quad \int_{-\infty}^{\infty} e^{-y^2} dy = \sqrt{\pi}$

$\Rightarrow \quad \dfrac{A^2}{\alpha}\sqrt{\pi} = 1$

$\Rightarrow \quad A = \left(\dfrac{\alpha}{\sqrt{\pi}}\right)^{1/2}$

Now, change in first order ground state energy is

$$E = \int_{-\infty}^{\infty} \psi_0^* E \psi_0 dx$$

$$= A^2 \int_{-\infty}^{\infty} E_0 \left(\frac{\alpha x}{10}\right)^4 \times \exp(-\alpha^2 x^2) \, dx$$

$$= \frac{\alpha}{\sqrt{\pi}} E_0 \frac{\alpha^4}{10^4} \int_{-\infty}^{\infty} x^4 \exp(-\alpha^2 x^2) \, dx$$

$$= \frac{2E_0}{\sqrt{\pi}} \frac{\alpha^5}{10^4} \int_0^{\infty} x^4 \exp(-\alpha^2 x^2) \, dx$$

Now, $\quad \alpha^2 x^2 = t$

$\Rightarrow \quad x = \dfrac{\sqrt{t}}{\alpha}$

and $\quad 2\alpha^2 x \, dx = dt$

$\Rightarrow \quad dx = \dfrac{dt}{2\alpha^2 \sqrt{\dfrac{t}{\alpha}}} = \dfrac{dt}{2\alpha\sqrt{t}}$

Putting these values, we get

$$E = \frac{E_0}{10^4\sqrt{\pi}} \int_0^{\infty} t^{3/2} e^{-t} dt$$

$\because \quad \Gamma x + 1 = \int_0^{\infty} t^x e^{-t} dt$

$\Rightarrow \quad E = \dfrac{E_0}{10^4\sqrt{\pi}} \times \Gamma 5/2$

$$= \frac{E_0}{10^4\sqrt{\pi}} \times \frac{3}{2} \times \frac{1}{2} \times \sqrt{\pi}$$

$$= \left(\frac{3}{4}E_0\right)10^{-4}$$

55. Details, in case one wants to see the calculations : rotational $\sigma = 1$ because Si–O is a heteronuclear diatomic molecule

$$q_{rot} = \frac{T}{\sigma\Theta_R} = \frac{1000 \text{ K}}{1 \times 1.046 \text{ K}} = 956$$

$$q_{vib} = \frac{1}{1 - e^{-\Theta_V/T}} = \frac{1}{1 - e^{1787/1000}} = \frac{1}{1 - e^{-1.787}}$$

$$= \frac{1}{1 - 0.167} = \frac{1}{0.833} = 1.201$$

$$q_{trans}/V = \frac{1}{\Lambda^3} \text{ where, } \Lambda = \frac{h}{\sqrt{2\pi mkT}} = 8.315 \times 10^{-12} \text{ m}$$

$$q_{trans}/V = \frac{1}{(8.315\times10^{-12})^3} = 1.74\times10^{33}$$

58. Here, $E < V_0$

Applying Schrödinger equation from $0 < x < L$

$$\frac{d^2\psi}{dx^2} + \frac{2m}{\hbar^2}(E - V_0)\psi = 0$$

$$\Rightarrow \quad \frac{d^2\psi}{dx^2} - \frac{2m}{\hbar^2}(V_0 - E)\psi = 0$$

$$\Rightarrow \quad \psi = Ae^{kx} + Be^{-kx}$$

where, $k = \sqrt{\frac{2m}{\hbar^2}(V_0 - E)}$

Hence, wave function through $0 < x < L$ is real.

59. $T = \frac{\text{Magnitude of transmitted current}}{\text{Magnitude of incident current}}$

$$= \frac{\text{Magnitude of transmitted current}}{S_0}$$

Probability current is TS_0 for $x > L$.

60. $\because \quad R + T = 1$

$$\Rightarrow \quad \frac{A_R}{A_0} + \frac{A_T}{A_0} = 1$$

$$\Rightarrow \quad \frac{A_R}{A_0} = 1 - \frac{A_T}{A_0}$$

61. The energy in three-dimensional cubic well can be written as

$$E_n = \frac{\hbar^2\pi^2}{2mL^2}[n_x^2 + n_y^2 + n_z^2]$$

For third state $n_x = 2$, $n_y = 2$ and $n_z = 1$

$$\Rightarrow \quad E_3 = \frac{\hbar^2\pi^2}{2mL^2}[2^2 + 2^2 + 1^2]$$

$$= \frac{9\pi^2\hbar^2}{2mL^2}$$

For fourth level $n_x = 3$, $n_y = n_z = 1$

$$\Rightarrow \quad E_4 = \frac{\hbar^2\pi^2}{2mL^2}[3^2 + 1^2 + 1^2] = \frac{11\hbar^2\pi^2}{2mL^2}$$

Now, $E = E_3 + E_4 = \frac{\pi^2\hbar^2}{2mL^2}[9 + 11]$

$$= \frac{10\pi^2\hbar^2}{mL^2}$$

62. For fourth level the possible values of n_x, n_y and n_z are (3, 1, 1), (1, 3,1) and (1,1, 3). Hence, degeneracy of this level is 3.

63. Here, $\psi = \frac{3\psi_1 + 4\psi_2}{5}$

$$A\psi_1 = \psi_2$$

and $A\psi_2 = \psi_1$

$$\Rightarrow \quad \int \psi^* A\psi\, dx = \int \frac{(3\psi_1 + 4\psi_2)}{5}\frac{A(3\psi_1 + 4\psi_2)}{5}dx$$

$$= \int \left(\frac{3\psi_1 + 4\psi_2}{5}\right)\left(\frac{3\psi_2 + \psi\psi_1}{5}\right)dx$$

$$= \frac{3\times4\int\psi_1^2\,dx + 4\times3\int\psi_2^2\,dx}{25}$$

$$= \frac{12+12}{25} = \frac{24}{25} = 0.96$$

64. $A^2\psi_1 = A(A\psi_1) = A(\psi_2) = \psi_1$

and $A_2\psi_2 = A(A\psi_2) = A(\psi_1) = \psi_2$

$\because \quad A^2\psi_1 = \psi_1$ and $A(\psi_1) = \psi_2$

Hence, ψ_1 and ψ_2 are eigen functions of A^2.

65. First order correction to E_1 is given by

$$<\psi_1^*|E|\psi> = [1, 0]\begin{bmatrix} E_1 & A_0 \\ E^* & E_2 \end{bmatrix}\begin{bmatrix} 0 \\ 1 \end{bmatrix}$$

$$= [1, 0]\begin{bmatrix} A \\ E_2 \end{bmatrix} = [A] = A$$

66. Second order correction

$$= \frac{<\psi_1^*|E|\psi>^2}{E_2 - E_1} = \frac{A^2}{E_2 - E_1}$$

67. Wave function correction to eigen function $\begin{bmatrix} 1 \\ 0 \end{bmatrix}$ is

$$\frac{<\psi_2^*|E|\psi>}{E_1 - E_2}$$

$$<\psi_2^*|H|\psi_1> = [0, 1]\begin{bmatrix} E_1 & A \\ A^* & E_2 \end{bmatrix}\begin{bmatrix} 1 \\ 0 \end{bmatrix}$$

$$= [0, 1]\begin{bmatrix} E_1 \\ A^* \end{bmatrix} = A^*$$

Hence, correction is $\begin{bmatrix} \frac{A^*}{E_1 - E_2} \\ 0 \end{bmatrix}$

74. $P = 0.99985\times0.011\times0.99985 = 0.011$

75. $P = 2\times0.99985\times0.989\times0.00015 = 3.0\times10^{-4}$

76. Here is the list of 6.

$^1H-^{13}C-H$	$^1H-^{13}C-D$	$D-^{13}C-D$
$^1H-^{12}C-^1H$	$^1H-^{12}C-D$	$D-^{12}C-D$

There are $2^3 = 8$ possibilities, because there are two independent possibilities for each atom. However, in the gas phase isotopomers that interconvert by rotation (such as the two shown in part b) are the same. Taking account of that reduces the number to 6.

17 Atomic Structure and Quantum Theory

Syllabus

- Basics of Atomic Structure
- Shape of Orbitals
- Hydrogen Atom Spectra

Atomic Structure

The essentials of Dalton's (John Dalton, 1809) atomic theory may be summarized in the following postulates :

1. All matter is composed of very small particles called atoms.
2. Atoms are indestructible, they cannot be sub-divided, created or destroyed.
3. Atoms of the same element are similar to one another and equal in weight.
4. Atoms of different elements have different properties and different weights.
5. Chemical combination results from the union of atoms in simple numerical properties.

Thus, according to Dalton, the atoms were solid, hard, impenetrable particles, as well as separate, unalterable individuals.

Discovery of Electron

Long after the discovery of cathode rays, Sir J.J. Thomson (1897) succeeded improving that they consists of particles carrying a charge of negative electricity with masses less than one-thousandth of the hydrogen atom. In this way, the existence of particles smaller than atoms was proved. Later it was concluded that these particles which were called as electrons were supposed to be constituent of all substances.

J.J. Thomson (1856-1940) determined the ratio *e/m* of electron by subjecting the beam of electrons produced in a discharge tube to magnetic as well as electric fields.

Robert Millikan determined the charge on electron by using the famous oil drop technique. Millikan carried out a number of experiments by varying the value of E and found that charge e^- was always equal; to a simple multiple of 1.6022×10^{-19} C. This indicates that oil droplet has captured one, two, three or more electrons, each carrying a charge equal to 1.6022×10^{-19} C. The American physicist Robert Millikan (1868-1953) was awarded the Physics

Nobel prize in 1923 for determining the charge on electron.

In recent years, the viscosity of air has been redetermined more accurately and the charge on electron is taken as 1.60206×10^{-19} C.

Since, $e = 1.60206 \times 10^{-19}$ C

and $e/m = 1.75875 \times 10^{11}$ C kg^{-1}

Hence, mass of electron

$$= \frac{e}{e/m} = \frac{1.60206 \times 10^{-19} \text{ C}}{1.75875 \times 10^{11} \text{ C kg}^{-1}}$$

$$= 9.1091 \times 10^{-31} \text{ kg} \qquad \ldots(1)$$

This is called the rest mass of the electron, *i.e.*, the mass which it possesses when it is moving with a velocity much smaller than that of light. The rest mass of electron is now taken as 9.1095×10^{-31} kg. At high speeds, the mass of electron, according to the theory of relativity, is given by

$$m = \frac{m_0}{(1 - u^2/c^2)^{1/2}} \qquad \ldots(2)$$

where, m is the mass of the electron moving with velocity u, c is the velocity of light and m_0 is the *rest mass* of the electron. Evidently, as u approaches c, m becomes infinity.

Discovery of Proton

Careful experiments with discharge tubes containing perforated cathode reveal the emission of another type of radiations which start from the side of the anode and pass through the holes of the cathode. These radiations, which carry positive charge, are called **positive rays** or **anode rays.** Further studies reveal that these rays consist of **positively charged particles** whose e/m ratio varies with the nature of the gas taken in the discharge tube. The positive particles are, infact, the positive residues of the gas left when one or more electrons are knocked out of the atoms of the gas. The smallest positive particle given out by the lightest element hydrogen is called the proton. It is another fundamental particle whose charge has been found to be equal in magnitude but opposite in sign to that of electron. Its mass is 1.6726×10^{-27} kg or 1.00722 u.

The charge on electron or proton is the smallest charge of electricity. It is usual to speak of the charge on an electron as unit negative charge and the charge on a proton as unit positive charge.

The Rutherford Scattering Experiment

In 1911, the British physicist Ernest Rutherford (1871-1937) directed a narrow beam of alpha particles obtained from polonium at an extremely thin sheet of a metal like silver and gold. After passing through the metal sheet, the alpha particles were made to strike a fluorescent screen. As a result of a series of experiments, Rutherford observed that

1. Most of the alpha-particles passing through the metallic sheet without suffering any change in their path showing that the atom consists predominantly of empty space.
2. An extremely small number of alpha particles get deflected through wider angles or even backwards showing the presence of a *heavy positively* charged body in each atom and that the volume of this body is only a minute fraction of the total volume of the atom.

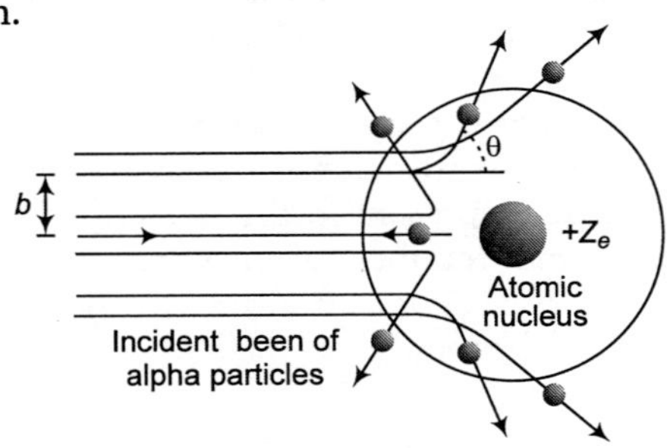

Fig. 17.1 Schematic representation of the scattering of alpha particles by an atom showing that the scattering angle θ decreases with increasing impact parameter, *b*. When *b* is zero, as in the case of perfect aim, the particle is deflected back along the line of approach. The extra-nuclear region of the atom is occupied by atomic electrons which, being so light, do not appreciably affect the motion of alpha particles.

The Rutherford Atomic Model

Based on his scattering experiments, Rutherford (the 1909 Nobel Laureate in Chemistry) suggested a model of the atom according to which an atom consists :

1. A minute positively charged body located at the centre, called the *nucleus* in which almost the entire mass of the atom is concentrated. Since, the mass of an atom is almost entirely due to protons, all the protons are present in the nucleus.
2. An equal number of extremely small negatively charged electrons distributed around the nucleus to balance its positive charge.

   In order to explain why the electrons do not fall into the nucleus on account of the mutual electrostatic attraction, Rutherford proposed that the electrons are revolving round the nucleus at extremely high speeds at great distances from the nucleus. The centrifugal force arising from this motion balances the force of electrostatic attraction. The electrons, therefore, do not fall into the nucleus.

Discovery of Neutron

James Chadwick (1891-1974), the British physicist, discovered in 1932 that when beryllium or boron is bombarded by alpha particles, new particles which carry no charge but have mass almost equal to that of a proton, are emitted. These particles are called **neutrons.** Chadwick won the Physics Nobel prize in 1935 for the discovery of neutron. The mass of neutron is now known to be 1.6749×10^{-27} kg or 1.00861 a.u.

All the neutrons are present in the nucleus along with protons. Because of the presence of protons, the nucleus carries a positive charge, as mentioned above. The number of unit positive charges carried by the nucleus of an atom is called the **atomic number** of the element. In other words, atomic number is equal to the number of protons present in the nucleus of the atom. The sum of the number of protons and neutrons present in the nucleus of an atom is called the **mass number** of the element.

Electromagnetic Radiation

Wavelength and Frequency

Visible light and many other apparently different types of radiation are all forms of *electromagnetic radiation,* and in a vacuum they all travel with the same speed, namely 2.998×10^8 metres per second (ms^{-1}). Electromagnetic radiation is characterized by a **wavelength** λ and a **frequency** ν. These two physical quantities are related to the speed of light c by the equation

$$\lambda\nu = c \qquad \ldots(8)$$

The SI unit of wavelength is the metre, although multiplies such as nanometres (nm) are frequently used, especially in spectroscopy. The SI unit of frequency is the reciprocal second (s^{-1}), which is also called the *hertz* (Hz).

Because of this relationship, all electromagnetic radiation can be classified in terms of either its wavelength or its frequency, as is done in Fig. 17.3. We see that long radio waves and electric waves may have wavelengths of many kilometres and very low frequencies, whereas γ (gamma) rays have very high frequencies and extremely short wavelengths.

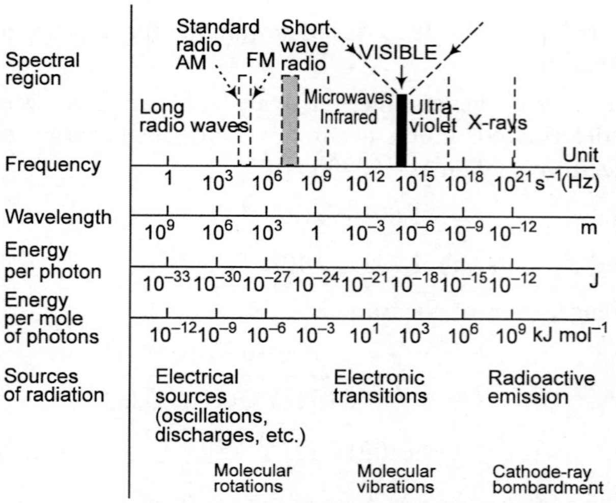

Fig. 17.2 The electromagnetic spectrum.

Electromagnetic radiation differs from certain other types of waves in a number of important respects. Sound waves, water waves, seismic waves, and waves in a plucked guitar string exist only by virtue of the medium in which they occur, whereas electromagnetic waves can travel in vaccum. Sound waves travelling through a gas, for example, consist of alternating zones of compression and rarefaction, and the molecular displacements that occur are in the direction in which the wave travels. As the wave passes a certain region, the gas molecules undergo changes in energy and momentum which then pass on to the next region. This type of wave propagation is also found with a seismic wave travelling through the earth.

Origin of the Quantum Theory

The quantum theory was originally formulated by Planck in 1900 in order to account for the observations on the distribution of energy in the radiation from a black body. A black body is generally understood to be a body which absorbs all the light falling upon it and accordingly can reflect none. Moreover, the black body is an ideal radiator so that the energy emitted per unit area at any temperature is equal to that absorbed. However, the nature of the radiation emitted by a black body depends on its temperature. Further more, Planck arrived at the conclusion that the radiation is emitted or absorbed discontinuously in integral multiples of a fundamental unit which he called as ***quantum***. The energy of this unit is proportional to the frequency of light. The conclusion led to the development of the quantum theory.

Black Body Radiation

A black body is one which absorbs the incident the radiations completely. Sometimes, this black body is referred to as a complete radiator. Although no actual body is perfectly black, it is possible to postulate a condition where radiation is completely enclosed in a space surrounded by thick walls at a constant temperature. Thus, we may imagine in a cavity inside a solid body containing a small hole in one wall whereby we may study the enclosed radiation without altering its character.

The inside walls of the cavity are emitted as well as absorbing radiant energy. If we try to increase the amount of light in the cavity by passing a beam of light through the hole, it would produce only a temporary change. The radiation would be absorbed in the walls of the enclosure and as a result their temperature is increased. But when the beam is redioved, the temperature would come down to its original value. It was postulated that the enclosure should be kept at a constant temperature, so that the same amount of light or radiation would remain in the cavity. The light emerging through the hole has a spectrum, usually referred to as the **black body spectrum.** If the energy emitted is plotted against its frequency or wavelength where, $\nu = c/\lambda$, where, c is the velocity of electromagnetic radiation, then the curve shows a maximum as indicated in Fig. (17.3).

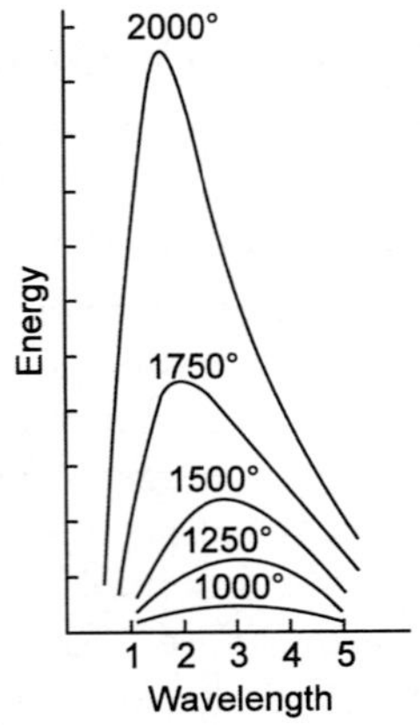

Fig. 17.3 Energy distribution for black body radiation at different absolute temperatures.

Quantum Theory of Radiation

The energy distribution in black body radiations could not be explained by the application of classical physics. The correct expression was derived by Planck on the basis of the quantum theory of radiation. According to this theory,

1. Radiant energy is emitted or absorbed discontinuously in the form of tiny bundles of the energy known as **quanta.**
2. Each quantum is associated with a definite amount of energy $E(= h\nu)$ where, E is the energy in joules, ν is the frequency of radiation in reciprocal seconds (s^{-1}) and h is a fundamental constant known as **Planck's constant.** The numerical value of h is 6.626×10^{-34} Js.

   The value of a quantum of energy is also given by $hc\bar{\nu}$ where, $\bar{\nu}$ is the **wave number** defined as the reciprocal of wavelength *i.e.,* $\bar{\nu} = (1/\lambda)$. Evidently, $\nu = c/\lambda = c\bar{\nu}$ and $E = hc\bar{\nu}$.
3. A body can emit or absorb energy only in whole number multiples of quantum, *i.e.,* $1h\nu$, $2h\nu$, $3h\nu$ ... $nh\nu$. Energy in fractions of a quantum cannot be lost or absorbed. This is known as quantization of energy.

Based on his theory, Planck obtained the following expression for energy density of black body radiation :

$$E(\nu)\, d\nu = \frac{8\pi h\nu^3}{c^3} \times \frac{d\nu}{\exp(h\nu/kT) - 1} \qquad ...(3)$$

Eq. 26 adequately accounts for the black body radiation curves at all wavelengths obtained at different temperatures, as shown in Fig. 17.3. Planck was awarded the Physics Nobel prize in 1918 for propounding the quantum theory of radiation.

Photoelectric Effect

J.J. Thomson, in some of his famous experiments, observed that when light of a certain frequency strikes the surface of a metal, electrons are ejected from the metal. This phenomenon is known as the **photoelectric effect**. A few metals show this effect under the action of visible light but many more show it under the action of more energetic ultraviolet light. Cesium, which amongst the alkali metals has the lowest ionisation energy, is also the metal from which electrons are ejected most easily by light. This metal is, therefore, used largely in photoelectric cells.

After making careful studies of photoelectric effect under different conditions, the following observations were made :

1. For each metal, a certain minimum frequency of incident light is needed to eject electrons. This is known as **threshold frequency**, ν_0. A light of

smaller frequency than this cannot eject electrons no matter how long it falls on the metal surface or how high is its intensity. The threshold frequency is different for different metals.

2. The kinetic energy of ejected electrons is independent of the intensity of the incident light but varies linearly with its frequency.
3. The number of ejected electrons from the metal surface depends upon the intensity of the incident radiation. The greater the intensity, the larger is the number of ejected electrons.

The photoelectric effect cannot be explained on the basis of the classical wave theory of light. According, to this theory, energy of light depends on its intensity. If this view is correct, then light of any frequency, if made sufficiently intense, can cause ejection of electrons. But this does not happen. The quantum theory of radiation affords an easy explanation for the photoelectric effect. According to this theory, light consists of bundles of energy called **photons**, the energy of each photon being equal to $h\nu$ where, ν is the frequency of the light. When a photon of light of frequency ν_0 (threshold frequency) strikes an electron in metal, it imparts its entire energy ($= h\nu_0$) to the electron. This energy enables the electron to break away from the atom by overcoming the attractive influence of the nucleus. Thus, each photon can eject one electron. If the frequency of the light is less than ν_0, there will be no ejection of electron. Now, suppose the frequency of the light falling on a metal surface is higher than the threshold frequency. Let it be ν. When photon of this light strikes a metal surface, some of its energy (which is equal to the energy binding the electron with the nucleus) is consumed to separate the electron from the metal and the remaining energy will be imparted to the ejected electron to give it certain velocity u (*i.e.*, kinetic energy $= \frac{1}{2} mu^2$). Einstein, applying quantum theory, showed that

$$h\nu = \phi + \frac{1}{2} mu^2 \qquad \ldots(4)$$

where, ϕ is the threshold energy (or the **work function**) of the metal and $\frac{1}{2} mu^2$ is the kinetic energy imparted to the ejected electron. Evidently,

$$\phi = h\nu_0 \qquad \ldots(5)$$

Substituting the above value of ϕ in Eq. 6 and rearranging, we have

$$\frac{1}{2} mu^2 = h(\nu - \nu_0) \qquad \ldots(6)$$

Eq. 6 is the **Einstein photoelectric equation.** Albert Einstein (1879-1955), the German physicist, won the Physics Nobel prize in 1921 for explaining the photoelectric effect and other contributions to mathematical physics. It may be mentioned that Einstein's contributions to the theory of relativity, considered controversial in those days, were not mentioned in the Nobel prize citation.

Eq. 6 was tested by Robert Millikan. The kinetic energies of the emitted electrons for various frequencies of light were determined by finding the opposing potential required to stop the photoelectric current. Knowing kinetic energy corresponding to a given incident light of frequency v and also knowing ν_0, *i.e.,* the threshold frequency required just to cause ejection of electrons, the value of h was calculated. It was found to be 6.570×10^{-34} J s. This is in excellent agreement with the value 6.626×10^{-34} J s obtained from experiments on black body radiations.

It is evident from the above discussion that photoelectric effect can be explained only on the basis of the corpuscular or particle theory of light. But certain phenomena, such as diffraction, interference and polarization of light, can be explained only on the basis of the classical wave theory of light. Thus, light is considered to have **dual character**. It behaves as a particle and also as a wave.

The Bohr's Theory of an Atom

In 1913, Niels Bohr, a Danish physicist, after working for a short time with Rutherford, advanced his own theory as to the structure of the atom.

Bohr adopted the Rutherford nuclear model of the atom with certain reservations and additional assumptions. Rutherford postulated that the atom consists of a positively charged nucleus containing practically all the mass, surrounded by a planetary system of electrons whose number is equal to the nuclear charge. Furthermore, Rutherford found it necessary to assume that the electrons were in rapid motion about the nucleus, so that the attractive force of the nucleus was exactly counter balanced by the outward centrifugal force produced by the motion of the electrons (Fig. 17.4). We have already pointed that such an atom would be extremely unstable, since according to the electromagnetic theory an electron in motion would emit radiation, thereby losing the kinetic energy, which should result in a constantly decreasing curvature of its path until the electron would eventually fall into the nucleus. To overcome the objections to the Rutherford's model, and also to explain the spectrum of atomic hydrogen, Bohr made the revolutionary suggestion that an electron could rotate in a stable orbital or stationary state with respect to nucleus, without emitting or absorbing energy. This suggestion with his other assumptions are contained in his postulates.

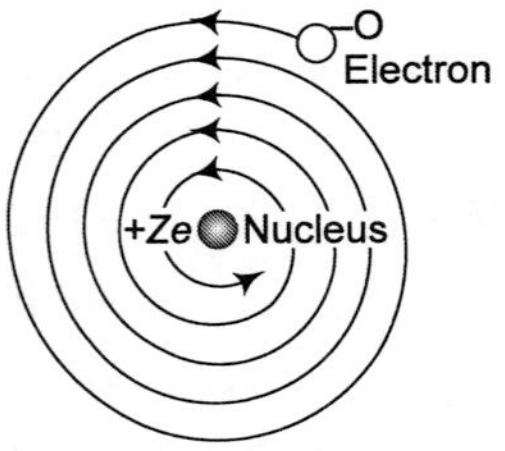

Fig. 17.4 An electron in the Rutherford atom spiral into the nucleus as it radiates energy due to acceleration.

The Bohr Postulates

1. An atom consists of positively charged nucleus responsible for almost the entire mass of the atom.
2. The electrons revolve round the nucleus in certain permitted circular orbitals of definite radii.
3. The permitted orbits are those for which the angular momentum of an electron is an integral multiple of $h/2\pi$ where, h is the Planck constant. If m is the mass and u is the velocity of the electron in a permitted orbit of radius, r, then

$$h = mu\,r = n\,\frac{h}{2\pi} \qquad \ldots(7)$$

where, $n = 1, 2, 3 \ldots$

where, L is the angular momentum and n is the number of the orbit. The integer n is called the principal quantum number. This equation is known as the **Bohr quantization postulate.**

4. When electrons move in permitted discrete orbits, they do not radiate energy. Such orbits are called stationary or non-radiating orbits. In this manner, Bohr overcame Rutherford's difficulty to account for the stability of the atom.
5. The energy is radiated when an electron jumps from higher to lower orbit and the energy is absorbed when it jumps from lower to higher orbit.

If E_i and E_f are the energies associated with orbital of principal quantum numbers n_i and n_f, respectively $(n_i < n_f)$, the frequency of the radiation emitted is given by

$$h\nu = \Delta E = E_f - E_i \qquad \ldots(8)$$

This equation is known as the Bohr frequency condition.

Let us now calculate the energy of electron in the Bohr hydrogen atom. Let the charge on the nucleus be $+ Ze$.

The electron with the charge $- e$ revolves round the nucleus of radius r with the velocity u (Fig. 17.5). The electrostatic force of attraction between the nucleus and the electron is given by

$$F_e \equiv \frac{1}{4\pi\varepsilon_0}\,\frac{Ze^2}{r^2}$$

The centripetal force, F_c, acquired by the electron is given by

$$F_c \equiv mu^2/r$$

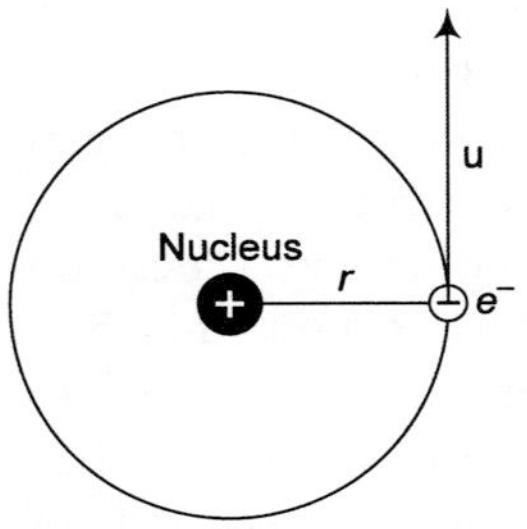

Fig. 17.5 Bohr's hydrogen atom.

Since, the electrostatic force of attraction between the nucleus and the electron provides the necessary centripetal force, hence, for the stable circular motion, $F_e = F_c$. Hence,

$$\frac{1}{4\pi\varepsilon_0}\,\frac{Ze^2}{r^2} = \frac{mu^2}{r}$$

$$mu^2 = (1/4\pi\varepsilon_0)\,(Ze^2/r) \qquad \ldots(9)$$

According to the Bohr quantization condition,

$$L = mu\,r = nh/2\pi \quad n = 1, 2, 3 \ldots$$

or

$$u = nh/2\pi mr \qquad \ldots(10)$$

Substituting for u

$$m\,(nh/2\pi mr)^2 = (1/4\,\pi\varepsilon_0)\,(Ze^2/r)$$

Hence, the radius r_n of the nth orbit is given by

$$r \equiv r_n = (4\pi\varepsilon_0)n^2h^2/4\pi^2 Zme^2\ ;$$

$$n = 1, 2, 3 \ldots \qquad \ldots(11)$$

We see that the radii of stationary orbits are directly proportional to the square of the principal quantum number.

The **Bohr radius** is defined as

$$r_1 \equiv a_0 = (4\pi\varepsilon_0)\,(h^2/4\pi^2 Zme^2) \qquad \ldots(12)$$

If the radius of the nth orbit is represented by r_n, then from the last equation, we can write.

$$r_n = \frac{n^2h^2}{4\pi^2 me^2 Z} \quad \ldots(13)$$

Using the known values of h, m and e, the radius of the first Bohr orbit, that is when n is equal to one is found to be 0.53×10^{-8} cm. It should then represent the radius of the normal hydrogen atom, that is when the electron occupied the lowest level. This so called **Bohr radius** is found to be the same order as the radius of hydrogen atom determined from the spectrum of hydrogen molecule.

Bohr's theory as outlined above gives the positions of the lines in the hydrogen spectrum in terms of one quantum number n, called as the **principal quantum number.** When observed with the spectroscopes of high resolving power, the hydrogen spectral line is found to have fine structure, *i.e.,* it appears as a set of closely spaced components. Therefore, it appears that the energy levels associated with the spectral lines fine structure. Further sub-division of spectral lines and hence of energy levels, also occurs if the substance under study is placed in a magnetic or an electric field. These are known as the **Zeeman** and **Stark effect,** respectively. It is thus obvious that one quantum number is inadequate and that additional quantum numbers are needed in order specify in detail the energy levels of atomic electrons. Actually four quantum numbers are necessary as we shall discuss them in detail later.

[I] Calculation of r_n

In SI system, the centripetal force is given by $\frac{1}{4\pi\varepsilon_0} \times \frac{Ze^2}{r^2}$ and the centrifugal force is $\frac{mv^2}{r}$. Therefore,

$$\frac{1}{4\pi\varepsilon_0} \times \frac{Ze^2}{r^2} = \frac{mv^2}{r}$$

or

$$v^2 = \frac{Ze^2}{mr} \times \frac{1}{4\pi\varepsilon_0}$$

$$mvr = \frac{nh}{2\pi}$$

or

$$v^2 = \frac{n^2h^2}{4\pi m^2 r^2}$$

From Bohr's second postulate,

$$\therefore \quad \frac{Ze^2}{mr} \times \frac{1}{4\pi\varepsilon_0} = \frac{n^2h^2}{4\pi^2 m^2 r^2}$$

or

$$r = \frac{n^2h^2 \times 4\pi\varepsilon_0}{4\pi^2 me^2 Z}$$

or

$$r_n = \frac{n^2h^2\varepsilon_0}{\pi me^2 Z}$$

On putting the values of h, π, m, e and ε_0 as $h = 6.626 \times 10^{-34}$ J s, $\varepsilon_0 = 8.85 \times 10^{-12}$ J^{-1} C^{2}m^{-1}, $\pi = 3.14$, $m = 9.108 \times 10^{-31}$ kg, $e = 1.602 \times 10^{-19}$ C and remembering that J = kg m^{2}s^{-2}, we have

$$r_n = \frac{n^2 \times (6.626 \times 10^{-34}\ \text{J s})^2 \times (8.85 \times 10^{-12}\ \text{J}^{-1}\ \text{C}^2\ \text{m}^{-1})}{(3.14) \times (9.108 \times 10^{-31}\ \text{kg})\,(1.602 \times 10^{-19}\ \text{C})^2 \times Z}$$

$$= \frac{n^2 \times 5.29 \times 10^{-11}}{Z} \times \frac{\text{J}^2\ \text{s}^2\ \text{J}^{-1}\text{C}^2\ \text{m}^{-1}}{\text{kg C}^2}$$

$$= \frac{n^2 \times 5.29 \times 10^{-11}}{Z} \times \frac{\text{J s}^2\ \text{m}^{-1}}{\text{kg}}$$

$$= \frac{n^2 \times 5.29 \times 10^{-11}}{Z} \times \frac{\text{kg m}^2\ \text{s}^2.\text{s}^2\ \text{m}^{-1}}{\text{kg}}$$

$$= \frac{0.529 \times 10^{-10} \times n^2}{Z}\ \text{m}.$$

[II] Relation between r_n and $(r_1)_H$

Here, r_n is the radius of the nth orbit of H-like species of atomic number Z, while $(r_1)_H$ is the radius of the first orbit ($n = 1$) of H-atom ($Z = 1$).

The values of r_n and $(r_1)_H$ in S.I. units are given as,

$$r_n = \frac{\varepsilon_0 h^2}{\pi me^2} \times \frac{n^2}{Z}$$

and

$$(r_1)_H = \frac{\varepsilon_0 h^2}{\pi me^2} \times \frac{(1)^2}{1}$$

On dividing,

$$\frac{r_n}{(r_1)_H} = \frac{\varepsilon_0 h^2}{\pi me^2} \times \frac{n^2}{Z} \times \frac{\pi me^2}{\varepsilon_0 h^2} = \frac{n^2}{Z}$$

or

$$r_n = \frac{n^2}{Z} \times (r_1)_H$$

or

$$r_n = 0.529 \times 10^{-10} \times \frac{n^2}{Z}\ \text{m}$$

[III] Number of Revolutions Made by an Electron Revolving in *n*th Orbit

The number of revolutions made by an electron with a velocity v_n in *n*th orbit is given by,

Number of revolutions $= \dfrac{v_n}{2\pi r_n}$

In SI units, the centrifugal force $\left(= \dfrac{mv^2}{r}\right)$ and centripetal force $\left(= \dfrac{Ze^2}{4\pi\varepsilon_0 d^2}\right)$ which are equal, we have,

$$\frac{mv^2}{r} = \frac{Ze^2}{4\pi\varepsilon_0 r^2}$$

or
$$v^2 = \frac{Ze^2}{4\pi\varepsilon_0 mr}$$

According to Bohr's postulate, $mvr = \dfrac{nh}{2\pi}$

or
$$v = \frac{nh}{2\pi mr}$$

On dividing,
$$\frac{v^2}{v} = \frac{Ze^2}{4\pi\varepsilon_0 mr} \times \frac{2\pi mr}{nh}$$

or
$$v = \frac{Ze^2}{2\varepsilon_0 nh}$$

Putting $e = 1.602 \times 10^{-19}$ C, $\varepsilon_0 = 8.85 \times 10^{-12}$ J^{-1} C m^{-1} and $h = 6.626 \times 10^{-34}$ Js and remembering J = kg m^{2}s^{-2}, we can show that

$$v_n = \frac{0.2185 \times 10^7 \times Z}{n} \text{ m s}^{-1}$$

We know,
$$r_n = \frac{0.529 \times 10^{-10} \times n^2}{Z} \text{ m}$$

∴ Number of revolutions

$$= \left[\frac{0.2185 \times 10^7 \times Z}{n} \text{ m s}^{-1}\right] \times \left[\frac{Z}{0.529 \times 10^{-10} \times n^2 \times 2\pi} \text{ m}\right]$$

$$= \frac{0.2185 \times 10^7 \times Z^2}{2 \times 3.14 \times 0.529 \times 10^{-10}\, n^3} \text{ s}^{-1}$$

$$= \frac{65.711 \times 10^{14} \times Z^2}{n^3} \text{ s}^{-1}$$

[IV] Velocity of the Electron

Substituting the value of r from Eq. 11 into Eq. 10, we obtain

$$u \equiv u_n = \frac{nh}{2\pi m}\left(\frac{1}{4\pi\varepsilon_0}\frac{4\pi^2 mZe^2}{n^2 h^2}\right)$$

$$= \frac{1}{4\pi\varepsilon_0}\frac{2\pi Ze^2}{nh} \qquad \ldots(14)$$

If c is the velocity of light, then Eq. 14 can be written as

$$u_n = \frac{1}{4\pi\varepsilon_0}\frac{2\pi Ze^2}{ch}\left(\frac{c}{n}\right)$$

The factor $(1/4\,\pi\varepsilon_0)(2\pi e^2/ch)$ is a constant called the fine structure constant, α. Its value is found to be 1/137. Thus, since $Z = 1$ for hydrogen atom, hence for $n = 1$ $u_n/c = \alpha/1 = 1/137$. We, thus, see that the velocity of the electron in the first orbit is equal to (1/137)th of the velocity of light.

[V] Energy of the Electron

Let E_k and E_p be the kinetic energy and the potential energy, respectively, of the electron in the *n*th orbit. Then, the total energy is given by

$$E = E_k + E_p = \frac{1}{2}mu^2 - \frac{Ze^2}{4\pi\varepsilon_0 r}$$

$$E_k = \frac{1}{4\pi\varepsilon_0}\frac{Ze^2}{2r}$$

Hence,
$$E = \frac{1}{4\pi\varepsilon_0}\frac{Ze^2}{2r} - \frac{1}{4\pi\varepsilon_0}\frac{Ze^2}{r}$$

$$= -\frac{1}{4\pi\varepsilon_0}\frac{Ze^2}{2r} \qquad \ldots(15)$$

Hydrogen Spectrum

The spectrum of hydrogen atom is comparatively simple. Hence, most of the applications of spectral data to the interpretation of atomic structure have been made from the spectrum of this element.

In 1885, Balmer pointed out that in case of ordinary spectrum of hydrogen atom there exists an interesting relationship between the different lines. This spectrum as shown in Fig. (9) consists of a series of lines known as H_α, H_β, H_γ, H_δ etc., extending from red to the ultraviolet region. Within of region of visible light and including the range of the longest ultraviolet wavelengths there is a group of lines called as the **Balmer series,** who discovered the relations of these lines to one another. However, Balmer found that the wavelengths of the hydrogen lines beginning with H_α could be expressed by means of the formula

$$\lambda = k \cdot \frac{n^2}{n^2 - 4}$$

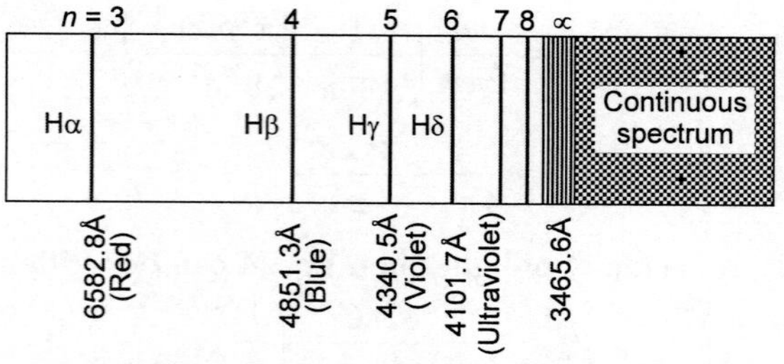

Fig. 17.6 Balmer series of atomic hydrogen excited by in electric discharge. The dark lines correspond to the bright emission lines of the spectrum.

where, λ is the wavelength in Angstroms, K is a constant, and n is an integer equal to 3, 4, 5, 6 etc., for the H_α, H_β, H_γ, H_δ lines, respectively.

From the above equation, it is seen that the value of n cannot be less than 2, since, λ would then be a negative number, which is meaningless. The value of n cannot be 2 either, since λ would then be infinite. If integer n becomes greater than 2, the corresponding wavelength λ becomes smaller. But when the value of n is already large, its further increase, causes λ to decrease only very slightly, the latter ultimately reaching the limiting value of K when n approaches infinity. This situation is reflected in the continuous radiation, at wavelengths less than that corresponding to this limit.

According to Bohr, the spectrum arises when the electron in the initial higher stationary orbit of principal quantum number n_i jumps to the final lower stationary orbit of principal quantum number n_f (*i.e.,* $n_i > n_f$), so that the difference of the energy associated with these orbits is emitted as *photon* of frequency ν. Accordingly,

$$h\nu = E_i - E_f = -\frac{1}{(4\pi\varepsilon_0)^2}\frac{2\pi^2 Z^2 me^4}{n_i^2 h^2} - \left[-\frac{1}{(4\pi\varepsilon_0)^2}\frac{2\pi^2 Z^2 me^4}{n_f^2 h^2}\right]$$

Hence, $$\nu = \frac{1}{(4\pi\varepsilon_0)^2}\frac{2\pi^2 me^4}{h^3}\left[\frac{1}{n_f^2} - \frac{1}{n_i^2}\right]$$

$$(Z = 1 \text{ for H atom}) \quad \ldots(16)$$

Since, the wavelength, λ, of the photon is related to ν by $\nu = c/\lambda$, hence

$$\frac{c}{\lambda} = \frac{1}{(4\pi\varepsilon_0)^2}\frac{2\pi^2 me^4}{h^3}\left[\frac{1}{n_f^2} - \frac{1}{n_i^2}\right]$$

or $$\bar{\nu} = \frac{1}{\lambda} = R_H\left[\frac{1}{n_f^2} - \frac{1}{n_i^2}\right] \quad \ldots(17)$$

where, R_H is called the **Rydberg constant** of the hydrogen atom. Evidently,

$$R_H = \frac{1}{(4\pi\varepsilon_0)^2}\frac{2\pi^2 me^4}{h^3 c} \quad \ldots(18)$$

Eq. 18 is called the Rydberg equation. Using this equation, the wave numbers of photons of the various spectral series are as follows :

1. Lyman series

In this series, the spectral lines correspond to the transition of the electron from some higher energy to the lower energy state corresponding to $n_f = 1$.

$$\bar{\nu} = R_H\left[\frac{1}{1^2} - \frac{1}{n_i^2}\right]; \; n_i = 2, 3, 4 \ldots \quad \ldots(19)$$

These lines are found in the ultraviolet region of electromagnetic spectrum.

2. Balmer series

In this series, the spectral lines correspond to the transition of the electron from some higher energy to the lower energy state corresponding to $n_f = 2$. Thus,

$$\bar{\nu} = R_H\left[\frac{1}{2^2} - \frac{1}{n_i^2}\right]; \; n_i = 3, 4, 5 \ldots \quad \ldots(20)$$

These lines are found in the visible region.

3. Paschen series

Here,

$$\bar{\nu} = R_H\left[\frac{1}{3^2} - \frac{1}{n_i^2}\right]; \; n_i = 4, 5, 6 \ldots \quad \ldots(21)$$

These lines are found in the infrared region.

4. Brackett series

Here,

$$\bar{\nu} = R_H\left[\frac{1}{4^2} - \frac{1}{n_i^2}\right]; \; n_i = 5, 6, 7 \ldots \quad \ldots(22)$$

These lines are also found in the infrared region.

5. Pfund series

Here,

$$\bar{\nu} = R_H\left[\frac{1}{5^2} - \frac{1}{n_i^2}\right]; \; n_i = 6, 7, 8 \ldots \quad \ldots(23)$$

These lines are found in the far infrared region.

6. Humphrey series

Here,

$$\bar{\nu} = R_H\left[\frac{1}{6^2} - \frac{1}{n_i^2}\right]; \; n_i = 7, 8, 9 \ldots \quad \ldots(24)$$

These lines are also found in the far infrared region.

The various spectral series are shown in Fig. 17.7.

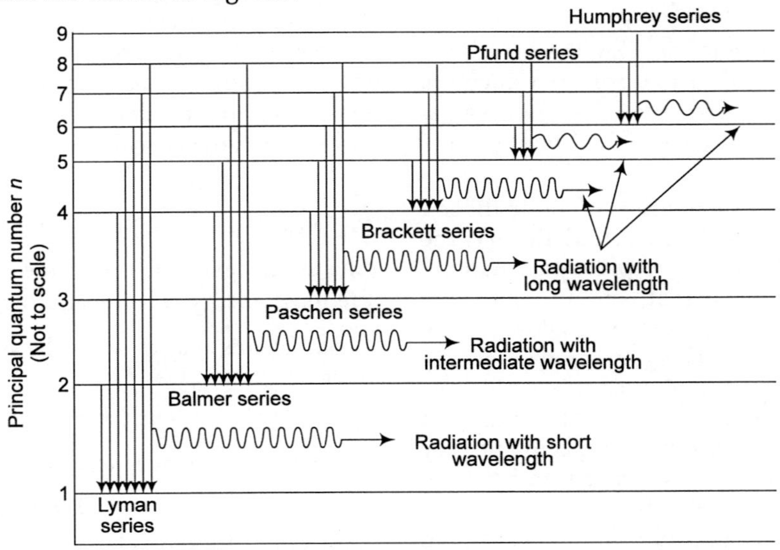

Fig. 17.7 The origin of the hydrogen spectrum.

The Bohr theory successfully accounts for the spectra of hydrogen atom and hydrogenic *i.e.,* hydrogen-like ions such as He^{+}, Li^{2+}, Be^{3+}, B^{4+}, etc.

The Sommerfeld Extension of the Bohr Theory

The Bohr theory of hydrogen atom enabled calculation of radii and energies associated with the permissible orbits in the hydrogen atom. The calculated values were found to be in good agreement with the experimental values. This theory could also explain successfully the positions of various series of spectral lines in the hydrogen spectrum. The theory was, therefore, largely accepted, However, a few years later, the use of spectroscopes of high resolving powers revealed the presence of fine structures (*i.e.,* groups of very fine spectral lines) in the line spectra of hydrogen. Bohr's, theory could not explain the occurrence of these fine spectral lines. The theory was, therefore, extended by Arnold Sommerfeld (1868-1951), the German mathematical physicist, by putting forward the idea of elliptical orbits.

According to Sommerfeld, an electron revolving around a central positively charged nucleus is so influenced by the nuclear charge that it is set into motion in elliptical orbits with the nucleus situated at one of the foci (Fig. 17.8). Thus, while according to Bohr's theory, electrons move in circular orbits, according to Sommerfeld's modification, electrons move in elliptical orbits. In the latter case, there will be a major axis and a minor axis having different lengths. As the orbit broadens, the lengths of the two axes become closer and they become equal when the orbit becomes circular, as shown in Fig. 17.8. Thus, the circular orbit is only a special case of elliptical orbits.

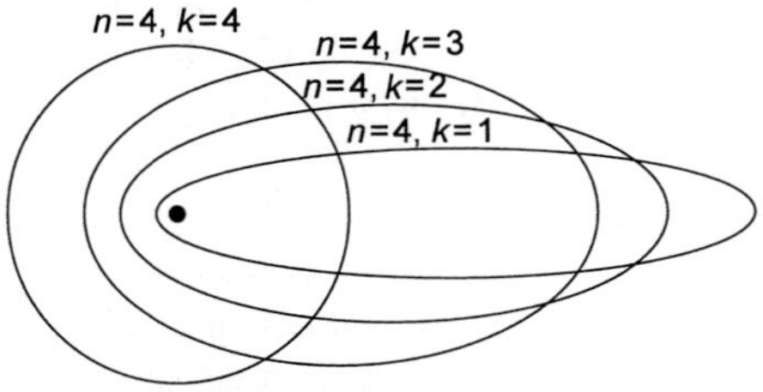

Fig. 17.8 Sommerfeld's elliptical electron orbits for $n = 4$.

The electron travelling in an elliptical orbit will have its angular momentum. The momentum, according to the quantum theory, must also be quantised and thus can have only a limited number of values given by the factor $kh/2\pi$ where, k is an integer known as the azimuthal quantum number. It can be shown that n, the principal quantum number, used by Bohr and k, the azimuthal quantum number used by Sommerfeld, are related to one another as

$$\frac{n}{k} = \frac{\text{length of major axis}}{\text{length of minor axis}} \qquad \ldots(25)$$

Thus, for any given values of n (except 1), k can have more than a single value. When $k = n$, the orbit must be circular. But, as k becomes smaller, the orbits become elliptical with greater and greater eccentricity. These facts are illustrated in Fig. 17.8. It may be noted that k cannot be zero because in that case minor axis would be zero which would imply linear motion of the electron passing through the nucleus.

As can be seen on reference to Fig. 17.8, the number of possible values of k is equal to the principal quantum number n. Thus, if n is 4, k can have four values varying from 4 to 1, *viz.*, 4, 3, 1 and 1. When n is 1, k can have only one value.

According to Sommerfeld's extension of Bohr theory, also referred to as the **Bohr-Sommerfeld theory**, the energy depends not only on n, the principal quantum number but also, to some extent, on the azimuthal quantum number, k. Hence, the transition of an electron from one energy level n_2 to another energy level n_1 will be slightly different as it would also depend upon the various possible values of k in the two states. This explains the occurrence of groups of very fine lines observed in the hydrogen spectrum by using highly refined spectroscopes. The frequencies of some of these fine spectral lines were found to be in agreement with the frequencies calculated from the Bohr-Sommerfeld theory.

Objection to the Bohr Model

Although Bohr's theory and its extension by Sommerfeld could explain atomic spectra of hydrogen, this model could not explain with mathematical exactness the spectra of atoms containing more than one electron.

The main objection of Bohr's model, however, ordinated from two additional sources. In 1923, Louis de-Broglie (1892-1987), the French physicist, suggested that electron, like light, has a dual character. It has particle (corpuscular) character as well as wave character. In Bohr's theory, there is no place for the wave character of electron. The second objection was raised by Heisenberg's uncertainty principle. According to the principle, it is impossible to determine simultaneously the exact position and the momentum or velocity of a small moving particle like an electron. This negates the idea of the movement of electron in definite orbits. These aspects are discussed below in some details.

Particle and Wave Character (Dual Character) of Electron

Einstein had suggested, in 1905, that light has a dual character; as wave and also as 'particle'. de -Broglie proposed that matter also has a dual character; as wave and as particle. de -Broglie was awarded the Physics Nobel prize in 1929.

In Bohr's theory, electron is treated as a particle. But, de -Broglie's theory suggested that matter and, therefore, electron also, has a dual character, both as a material particle and as a wave. He derived an expression for calculating the wavelength λ of a particle of mass m moving with velocity u according to which

$$\lambda = h/mu \quad \ldots(26)$$

Eq. 26 is known as the **de -Broglie equation.**

The de -Broglie equation can easily be derived by using the mass-energy relationship, *viz.*, $E = mc^2$.

Equating this energy with the energy of a photon, we have

$$h\nu = mc^2 \quad \ldots(27)$$

Since, $\nu = c/\lambda$, hence, $hc/\lambda = mc^2$ so that

$$\lambda = h/mc \quad \ldots(28)$$

Replacing c by the velocity of the electron, u, we have

$$\lambda = h/mu = h/p \quad \ldots(29)$$

where, p is the linear momentum of the particle.

Experimental Verification of de-Broglie's Relation

The verification of de -Broglie's equation is possible only by deriving from it certain consequences which may then be tested experimentally.

Let an electron of charge e^- be accelerated by a potential V. Then its kinetic energy would be Ve. The kinetic energy is also equal to $\frac{1}{2}mu^2$ where, u is velocity of the electron. Thus,

$$\frac{1}{2}mu^2 = Ve$$

or

$$u = (2Ve/m)^{1/2} \quad \ldots(30)$$

Substituting this value of v into de -Broglie's equation, we have

$$\lambda = h/(2meV)^{1/2} \quad \ldots(31)$$

Incorporating the numerical values of various quantities, we have

$$\lambda = \frac{6.626\times 10^{-34}\ \text{J s}}{[(2)\ (1.602\times 10^{-19}\ \text{C})\ (9.109\times 10^{-31}\ \text{kg})\ (V\ \text{volt})]^{1/2}}$$

$$= 12.26 \times 10^{-10}\ \text{V}^{-1/2}\ \text{metre} \quad \ldots(32)$$

where, V is the numerical value of the potential in volt.

If an electron is accelerated through a potential of 100 V, its wavelength should be 1.226×10^{-10} m, *i.e.*,

1.226 Å. If potentials are varied between 10 and 10000 V, λ should vary between 3.877 and 0.1226 Å. It is well known that X-rays have wavelengths of this order. It is also well known that crystalline solids can act as diffraction gratings for X-rays having wavelengths of the above order. Therefore, if de -Broglie's view regarding wave-particle duality of electron is correct, the crystalline solids should act as diffraction gratings for a beam of electrons as well. This has been verified experimentally.

The Heisenberg Uncertainty Principle

It states that *it is not possible to determine precisely both the position and the momentum (velocity) of a small moving particle.* In the words of the British cosmologist Stephen Hawking, "Even God is bound by the uncertainty principle and cannot predict the future exactly."

Consider a photon incident on a particle. If the particle is of reasonable size, its position or velocity will not be altered by the impact of light photons. Hence, it will be possible to know exactly both the position and velocity of the particle. But, this cannot be so when the particle is extremely minute, such as an electron. It will suffer a change in its velocity and path due to the impact of even a single photon of light used to observe it. The path and velocity of an electron, after the impact of light photons, may be quite different from the original path and velocity.

In view of the Heisenberg uncertainty principle, the Bohr model in which electrons are considered as particles revolving in definite orbits, *i.e.,* in well-defined paths, cannot hold good. It is more correct to say, therefore, that an electron belongs to a definite **energy level** and not that it belongs to a particular orbit.

For an electron moving in x-direction, the Heisenberg uncertainty principle is expressed mathematically as

$$(\Delta x)\,(\Delta p_x) \geq h/4\pi \qquad \ldots(33)$$

where, Δx is uncertainty with regard to the position and Δp_x is the corresponding uncertainty with regard to its momentum. Evidently, if Δx is very small, *i.e.,* the position of a particle is known more or less exactly, Δp would be large, *i.e.,* uncertainty with regard to momentum will be large. Similarly, if an attempt is made to measure exactly the momentum of the particle, the uncertainty with regard to position will become large. Werner Heisenberg (1900-1976), the German physicist, won the Physics Nobel prize in 1932.

The Compton Effect

Arthur Compton found that if monochromatic X-rays (*i.e.,* X-rays having one particular wavelength) are allowed to fall on carbon or some other light element, the scattered X-rays have wavelengths larger than the incident rays. In other words, the scattered X-rays have lower frequency, *i.e.,* lower energy than the incident X-rays. Since scattering is caused by electrons, it is evident that some interaction between X-rays and electrons has taken place and this has resulted in decrease in energy of the former. The decrease in energy or increase in wavelength of X-rays after scattering from the surface of an object is known as the **Compton effect.**

By applying the law of conservation of energy and the law of conservation of momentum and assuming X-rays to consist of photons, each possessing energy equal to $h\nu$, compton showed that

$$\Delta\lambda = (2h/mc)\sin^2(\theta/2) \qquad \ldots(34)$$

where, $\Delta\lambda$ is the increase in the wavelength (termed as **Compton shift**) produced as a result of the collision, m is the rest mass of the electron, c is the velocity of light and θ is the angle between the incident and the scattered X-rays.

According to this equation, Compton shift should be independent of the wavelength of the incident X-rays. This has been found to be so experimentally. Further, the values of Compton ship, as obtained from the above equation, by substituting the know values of h, c, m and θ, have been found to be close agreement with the experimental values.

Arthur Compton (1892-1962), the American physicist, shared the 1927 Physics Nobel prize with C.T.R. Wilson, the British physicist, who was honoured for this technique of making the paths of electrically charged particles visible by vapour condensation.

Compton effect provides a good illustration of the uncertainty principle. Suppose X-ray are used to determine the position of momentum of an electron. As a result of mutual interaction of X-rays and the electron, the wavelength of X-rays increases, *i.e.,* the frequency or energy of the X-rays decreases. This energy must have been transferred to the electron and, therefore, the momentum of the electron must have changed during the process. Consequently, the momentum of the electron cannot be determined with certainty.

Compton effect also provides evidence for the corpuscular or photon nature of radiation. The Compton Eq. (23) can be written as

$$\Delta\lambda = \lambda' - \lambda = \frac{h}{mc}(1 - \cos\theta) \qquad \ldots(35)$$

We see that the wavelength λ' of scattered X-rays is always greater than the wavelength λ of incident X-rays. The wavelength shift is independent of the nature of the substance and the wavelength of incident X-rays. It depends only on the scattering angle θ. The following three cases may be considered :

Case 1 $\theta = 0°$, *i.e.,* the scattered radiation is parallel to the incident radiation. In this case, $\cos\theta = 1$ so that $\Delta\lambda = 0$, *i.e.,* there is no wavelength shift.

Case 2 $\theta = 90°$, *i.e.,* the scattered radiation is perpendicular to the incident radiation. In this case, $\cos\theta = 0$ so that

$$\Delta\lambda = h/mc = 6.626 \times 10^{-34}\ \text{J s}/(9.109 \times 10^{-31}\ \text{kg})(3 \times 10^{8}\ \text{ms}^{-1})$$

$$= 0.02422 \times 10^{-10}\ \text{m} = 0.0242\ \text{Å} = 2.42\ \text{pm}$$

In the present case, $\Delta\lambda$ is referred to as the *Compton wavelength.*

Case 3 $\theta = 180°$, *i.e.,* the radiation is scattered in direction opposite to the incident radiation. In this case, $\cos\theta = -1$ so that

$$\Delta\lambda = 2h/mc = 0.0484\ \text{Å} = 4.84\ \text{pm}$$

This is twice the value of the Compton wavelength.

Shapes and Size of Orbitals

An orbital is the region of space around the nucleus within which the probability of finding an electron of given energy is maximum (90-95%). The shape of this region (electron cloud) gives the shape of the orbital. It is basically determined by the azimuthal quantum number (l), while the orientation of orbital depends on the magnetic quantum number (m). Let us now see the shapes of orbitals in the various subshells.

s-orbital

These orbitals are spherical and symmetrical about the nucleus. The probability of finding the electron is maximum near the nucleus and keeps on decreasing as the distance from the nucleus increases. There is vacant space between two successive *s*-orbitals known as radial node. But there is no radial node for 1*s* orbital since it is starting from the nucleus.

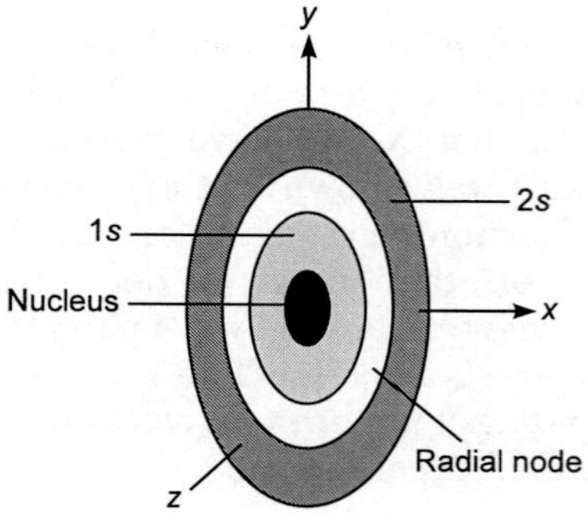

The size of the orbital depends upon the value of principal quantum number (n). Greater the value of n, larger is the size of the orbital. Therefore, 2*s*-orbital is larger than 1*s* orbital but both of them are non-directional and spherically symmetrical in shape.

p-orbital ($l = l$)

The probability of finding the *p*-electron is maximum in two lobes on the opposite sides of the nucleus. This gives rise to a dumb-bell shape for the *p*-orbital. For *p*-orbital $l = 1$. Hence, $m = -1, 0, +1$. Thus, *p*-orbital have three different orientations. These are designated as $p_x p_y$, and p_z depending upon whether the density of electron is maximum along the x y and z axis respectively. As they are not spherically symmetrical, they have directional character. The two lobes of *p*-orbitals are separated by a nodal plane, where the probability of finding the electron is zero.

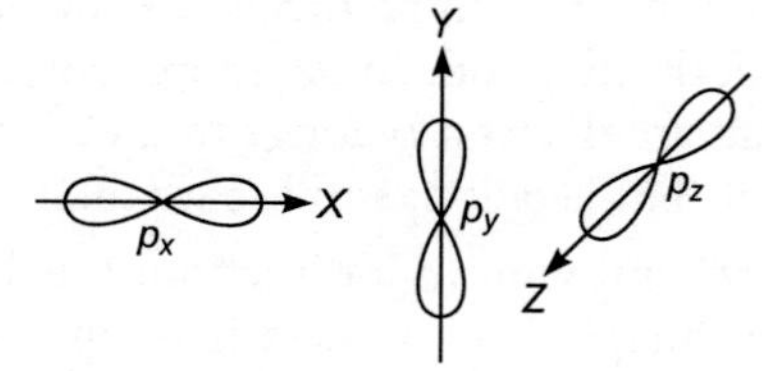

The three *p*-orbitals belonging to a particular energy shell have equal energies and are called degenerate orbitals.

d-orbital ($l = 2$)

For *d*-orbitals, $l = 2$. Hence, $m = -2, -1, 0, +1, +2$. Thus, there are 5*d* orbitals. They have relatively complex geometry. Out of the five orbitals, the three (d_{xy}, d_{yz}, d_{zx}) project in between the axis and the other two d_z^2 and d_{z-y}^{2-2} lie along the axis.

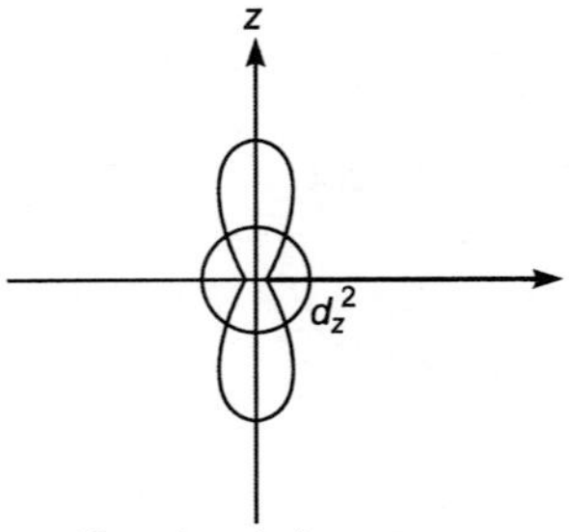

Dough-nut shape or Baby soother shape

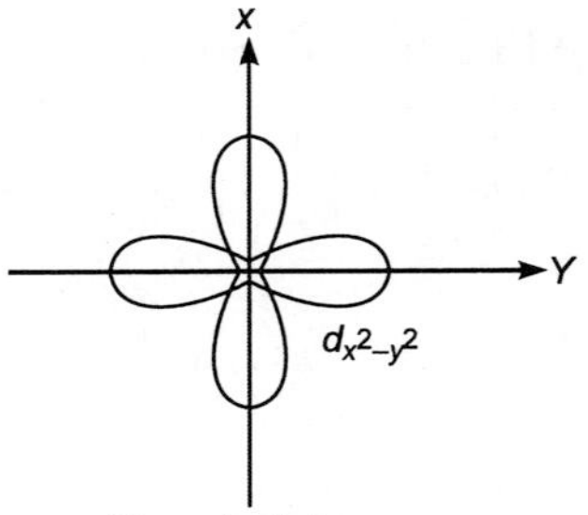

Clover leaf shape

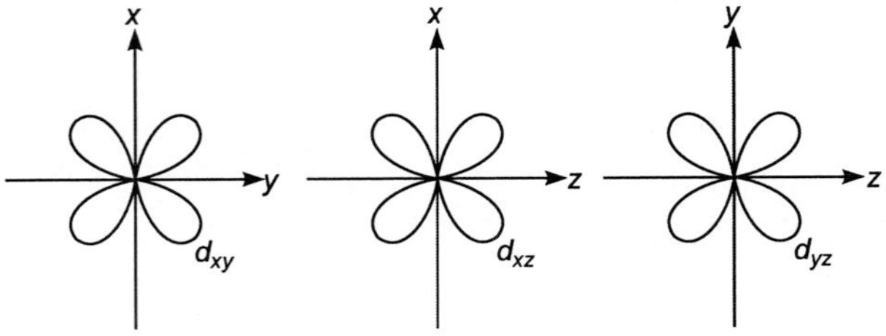

Mathematical forms of orbitals

1. For $n = 1$. There is only one atomic orbitals, *i.e.*, $1s = \psi_1,0,0$.
2. For $n = 2$ (energy –328 kJ/mol), there are four atomic orbitals.

$\psi_{2,0,0}$ — 2*s*-orbital

$\left.\begin{matrix}\psi_{2,1,+1}\\ \psi_{2,1,0}\\ \psi_{2,1,-1}\end{matrix}\right\}$ 2*p* orbitals

3. For $n = 3$ there are 9 orbitals

$\psi_{3,0,0}$ — 3*s* orbital

$\left.\begin{matrix}\psi_{3,1,+1}\\ \psi_{3,1,0}\\ \psi_{3,1-1}\end{matrix}\right\}$ 3*p* orbitals

$\left.\begin{matrix}\psi_{3,2,-2}\\ \psi_{3,2,-1}\\ \psi_{3,2,0}\\ \psi_{3,2,+1}\\ \psi_{3,2,-2}\end{matrix}\right\}$ 3*d* orbitals

4. Similarly, for $n = 4$ the total number of orbitals = 16 (including seven $4f$ orbitals)

Table 17.1 **Orbitals of Monoelectronic Atoms up to $n = 3$**

$n = 1, l = 0, m_l = 0$	$\psi_{1s} = \frac{1}{\sqrt{\pi}}\left(\frac{Z}{a_0}\right)^{3/2} e^{-\rho}\left[l = \frac{Zr}{a_0}\right]$
$n = 2, l = 0, m_l = 0$	$\psi_{2s} = \frac{1}{4\sqrt{2\pi}}\left(\frac{Z}{a_0}\right)^{3/2}(2-\rho)e^{-\rho/z}$
$n = 2, l = 1, m_l = 0$	$\phi\psi_{2pz} = \frac{1}{4\cdot\sqrt{2\pi}}\left(\frac{Z}{a_0}\right)^{3/2}\rho e^{-\rho/2}.\cos\theta$
$n = 2, l = 1, m_e = \pm 1$	$\psi_{2px} = \frac{1}{4\sqrt{2\pi}}\left(\frac{Z}{a_0}\right)^{3/2}\rho e^{-\rho/2}.\sin\theta\cos\phi$ $\psi_{2py} = \frac{1}{4\sqrt{2\pi}}\left(\frac{Z}{a_0}\right)^{3/2}\rho e^{-\rho/2}\sin\theta\sin\phi$
$n = 3, l = 0, m_l = 0$	$\psi_{3s} = \frac{2}{81\sqrt{3\pi}}\left(\frac{Z}{a_0}\right)^{3/2}(27-18\rho+2\rho^2)e^{-\rho/3}$
$n = 3, l = 1, m_l = 0$	$\psi_{3pz} = \frac{2}{81\sqrt{\pi}}\left(\frac{Z}{a_0}\right)^{3/2}(6\rho-\rho^2)e^{-\rho/3}.\cos\theta$
$n = 3, l = 1, m_l = \pm 1$	$\psi_{3px} = \frac{2}{81\sqrt{\pi}}\left(\frac{Z}{a_0}\right)^{3/2}(6\rho-\rho^2)e^{-\rho/3}\sin\theta\cos\phi$ $\psi_{3py} = \frac{2}{81\sqrt{\pi}}\left(\frac{Z}{a_0}\right)^{3/2}(6\rho-\rho^2)e^{-\rho/3}\sin\theta\sin\phi$
$n = 3, l = 2, m_l = 0$	$\psi_{3dz^2} = \frac{1}{81\sqrt{6\pi}}\left(\frac{Z}{a_0}\right)^{3/2}\rho^2 e^{-\rho/3}(3\cos^2\theta-1)$
$n = 3, l = 2, m_l = \pm 1$	$\psi_{3dxz} = \frac{\sqrt{2}}{81\sqrt{\pi}}\left(\frac{Z}{a_0}\right)^{3/2}\rho^2 e^{-\rho/3}\sin\theta\cos\theta\cdot\cos\phi$ $\psi_{3dyz} = \frac{\sqrt{2}}{81\sqrt{\pi}}\left(\frac{Z}{a_0}\right)^{3/2}\rho^2 e^{-\rho/3}\sin\theta\cos\theta\sin\phi$
$n = 3, l = 2, m_l = \pm 2$	$\psi_{3d_{x^2-y^2}} = \frac{1}{81\sqrt{2\pi}}\left(\frac{Z}{a_0}\right)^{3/2}\rho^2 e^{-\rho/3}\sin^2\theta\cdot\cos 2\phi$ $\psi_{3dxy} = \frac{1}{81\sqrt{2\pi}}\left(\frac{Z}{a_0}\right)^{3/2}\rho^2 e^{-\rho/3}\cdot\sin^2\theta\cdot\sin 2\phi$

Here, $a_0 = \dfrac{4p\varepsilon_0\hbar^2}{me^2} = 52\ 9$ pm is Bohr radius, equal to the radius of the first orbit in Bohr's model.

Also, *s*-orbitals are functions of r (and not of θ and ϕ), *i.e.*, each *s*-function has the same value for all points of space at a given distance r from the nucleus. They have spherical symmetry. We can see that $\psi \to 0$ as $r \to \infty$, through a factor $e^{-\rho/n}$ where, $\rho = \dfrac{Zr}{a_0}$.

For 1*s*, this is the only r dependent factor and the function decreases exponentially on increasing the electron-nucleus distance.

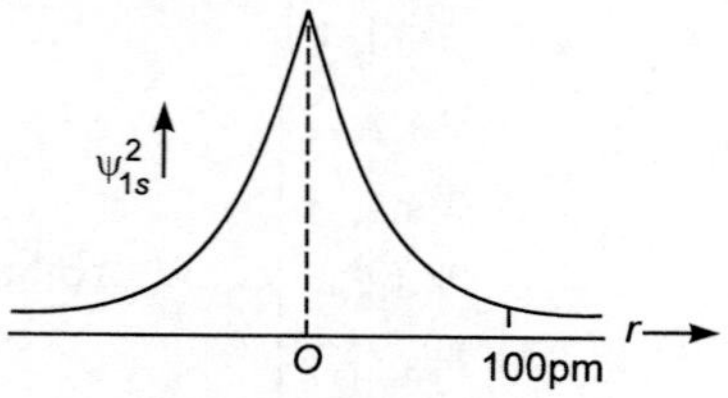

Graphical representation of ψ^2_{1s}

For 2*s*-orbital, the factor $(2 - \rho)$ vanishes for $\rho = Z$ (that is, $r = 2a_0$) and the spherical surface of radius $r = 2a_0$ is a nodal surface.

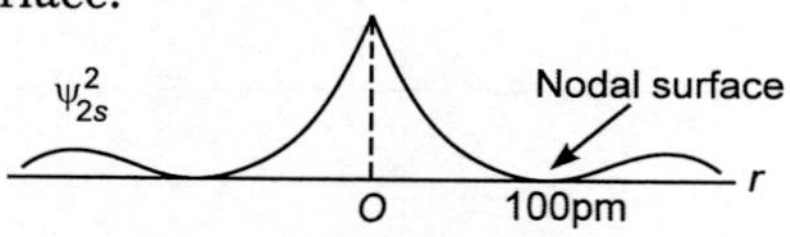

Graphical representation of ψ^2_{2s}

For a 3*s* orbital there are two nodal surfaces. For a 4*s* orbital there are three nodal surfaces.

$$\psi_{4s} = \frac{1}{1536\sqrt{\pi}}\left(\frac{Z}{a_0}\right)^{3/2} (192 - 144\rho + 24\rho^2 - \rho^3)\, e^{-\rho/4}$$

$$\psi_{5s} = \frac{1}{46875\sqrt{5\pi}}\left(\frac{Z}{a_0}\right)^{3/2} (9375 - 7500\rho + 1500\rho^2 - 100\rho^3 + 2\rho^4)\, e^{-\rho/5}$$

For 4*p* orbitals

$$\psi_{4pz} = \frac{1}{512\sqrt{5\pi}}\left(\frac{Z}{a_0}\right)^{3/2} (80\rho - 20\rho^2 + \rho^3) \cos\theta\, e^{-\rho/4}$$

$$\psi_{4py} = \frac{1}{512\sqrt{5\pi}}\left(\frac{Z}{a_0}\right)^{3/2} (80\rho - 20\rho^2 + \rho^3) \sin\theta \sin\phi\, e^{-\rho/4}$$

$$4px = \frac{1}{512\sqrt{5\pi}}\left(\frac{Z}{a_0}\right)^{3/2} (80\rho - 20\rho^2 + \rho^3) \sin\theta \cos\phi\, e^{-\rho/4}$$

While for 4*d* orbitals

$$\psi_{4dz^2} = \frac{1}{3072\sqrt{\pi}}\left(\frac{Z}{a_0}\right)^{3/2} (12\rho - \rho^3)(3\cos^2\theta - 1)\, e^{-\rho/4}$$

$$\psi_{4dx^2-y^2} = \frac{1}{3072}\left(\sqrt{\frac{3}{\pi}}\right)\left(\frac{Z}{a_0}\right)^{3/2} (12\rho - \rho^3) \sin^2\theta \cos 2\phi\, e^{-\rho/4}$$

$$\psi_{4dxy} = \frac{1}{3072}\sqrt{\frac{3}{\pi}}\left(\frac{Z}{a_0}\right)^{3/2} (12\rho - \rho^3) \sin^2\theta \sin 2\phi\, e^{-\rho/4}$$

$$\psi_{4dxz} = \frac{1}{1536}\sqrt{\frac{3}{\pi}}\left(\frac{Z}{a_0}\right)^{3/2} (12\rho - \rho^3) \sin\theta \cos\theta \cos\phi\, e^{-\rho/4}$$

$$\psi_{4dyz} = \frac{1}{1536}\sqrt{\frac{3}{\pi}}\left(\frac{Z}{a_0}\right)^{3/2} (12\rho - \rho^3) \sin\theta \cos\theta \sin\phi\, e^{-\rho/4}$$

For 4*f* orbital As there are seven 4*f* orbitals the simplest 4*f* can be visualized as $4f_z^3$ resembling a *p*-type orbital with two doughnuts of electron density ringing the nucleus.

$$\psi_{4fz^3} = \frac{1}{3072\sqrt{5\pi}}\left(\frac{Z}{a_0}\right)^{3/2} \rho^3 (5\cos\theta - 3\cos\theta)\, e^{-\rho/4}$$

Remaining six 4*f* orbitals contain either six lobes as the $4fyz^2$ orbital or eight lobes

$$\psi_{4fyz^2} = \frac{1}{6144}\sqrt{\frac{6}{5\pi}}\left(\frac{Z}{a_0}\right)^{3/2} \rho^3 (5\cos^2\theta - 1) \sin\theta \sin\phi\, e^{-\rho/4}$$

$$\psi_{4fxz^2} = \frac{1}{6144}\sqrt{\frac{6}{5\pi}}\left(\frac{Z}{a_0}\right)^{3/2} \rho^3 (5\cos^2\theta - 1) \sin\theta \cos\phi\, e^{-\rho/4}$$

$$\psi_{4fz(x^2-y^2)} = \frac{1}{3072}\sqrt{\frac{3}{\pi}}\left(\frac{Z}{a_0}\right)^{3/2} \rho^3 \sin^2\theta \cos\theta \cos 2\phi\, e^{-\rho/4}$$

$$\psi_{4fx(x^2-y^2)} = \frac{1}{6144}\sqrt{\frac{2}{\pi}}\left(\frac{Z}{a_0}\right)^{3/2} \rho^3 \sin^3\theta \cos 3\phi\, e^{-\rho/4}$$

$$\psi_{4fy(x^2-y^2)} = \frac{1}{6144}\sqrt{\frac{2}{\pi}}\left(\frac{Z}{a_0}\right)^{3/2} \rho^3 \sin^3\theta \sin 3\phi\, e^{-\rho/4}$$

$$\psi_{4fxyz} = \frac{1}{3072}\sqrt{\frac{3}{\pi}}\left(\frac{Z}{a_0}\right)^{3/2} \rho^3 \sin^2\theta \cos\theta \sin 2\phi\, e^{-\rho/4}$$

Quantum Numbers

To provide a complete description of an electron in an atom, four quantum numbers are needed. Morever, these quantum numbers describe the whole atomic state rather than particular orbits.

1. The Principal Quantum Number

This number designated as n is identical with Bohr's integers and was introduced by his to account for the restricted nature of an atom's energy levels. This number also denotes the major axis of the orbit of the particular electron. This principal quantum number is given by Bohr's theory by the following equation

$$mvr = n\frac{h}{2\pi}$$

The value of n for circular orbits indicates roughly the binding force and the distance between the nucleus and the electron. Hence, this quantum number represents the size of the electron orbit. For the first energy level $n = 1$, for the second energy level $n = 2$ etc. The first energy level is one which is nearest to the nucleus. Formerly, these energy levels were described as electron shells, and in the other notation the innermost shell was indicated as the K shell and the succeeding outer shells were assigned the letters L, M, N, O, P and Q.

According to Sommerfeld model.

$$\frac{n}{k} = \frac{\text{Length of major axis}}{\text{Length of minor axis}}$$

The principal quantum number n, thus, determines the major axis of the elliptical orbit, which is the same as the diameter of the Bohr circular orbit. The azimuthal quantum number k, on the other hand determines the minor axis of the elliptical orbit. The quantum number, k for a given value of n may have n values, *viz.*, $n, n-1, \ldots 1$. But k cannot be zero, because in that case the minor axis of the ellipse would be zero, that is the elliptical orbit would be reduced to a straight line passing through the nucleus of atom. However, this type of linear motion does not appear possible, if the electron is regarded as a particle moving in a definite path. Thus, there are n possible values of azimuthal quantum number k from n to 1, both inclusive. Thus, if n is 4, then the values of k can be 4, 3, 2 and 1. When k is equal to n, then the orbit is circular as shown in Fig. 17.9.

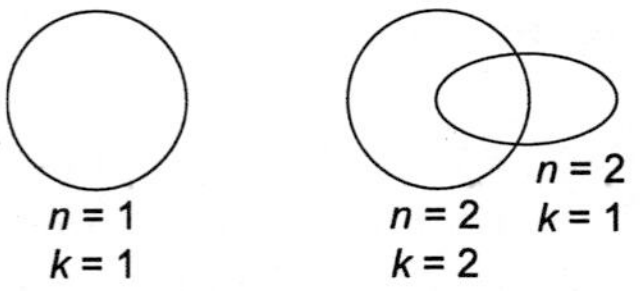

Fig. 17.9

But for other values, there result elliptical orbits with different eccentricities as shown in Fig (17.9) for hydrogen with various n values, for $k = 1$, 2 and 3.

2. The Magnetic Quantum Number

In a strong magnetic field the lines of the spectrum are split up, this is known as the Zeeman effect. If the spectrum is examined in a direction at right angles to the magnetic field then each line is seen to be split up into three, the middle one being polarised in a direction parallel to the field and the outer lines at right angles to it. When the lines are observed in the direction parallel to the field then each is found to be split into two components which are polarised circularly in opposite directions. To explain these phenomena by the Bohr's theory it was necessary to postulate an additional quantum which is termed as the magnetic quantum number, m where $mh/2\pi$ represents the component of the total angular momentum of the electron in the direction of the field. In the presence of a magnetic field, the orbital motion of the electron is disturbed in such a manner that the axis of the angular momentum will orient itself to form a definite angle with the direction of the applied field. The orbital angular momentum undergoes a Larmor processional motion, describing the surfaces of two cones whose axes are in the direction of the field. The Larmor procession of an electronic orbit in a magnetic field is indicated in Fig. (17.10).

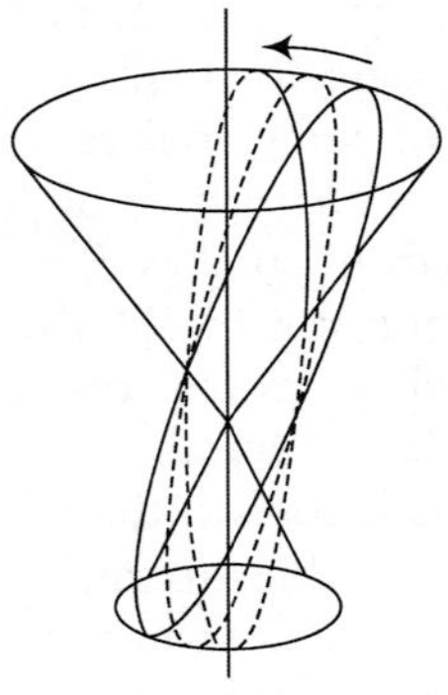

Fig. 17.10 Larmor procession of an electronic orbit in a magnetic field.

In this diagram, the upper circle represents the path of aphelion and the lower circle represents the path of perihelion. The frequency of the procession is proportional to the strength of the magnetic field. Furthermore, the electron axis processes only at certain angles with the direction field. The phenomenon is called as space quantisation and is shown in Fig. (17.11).

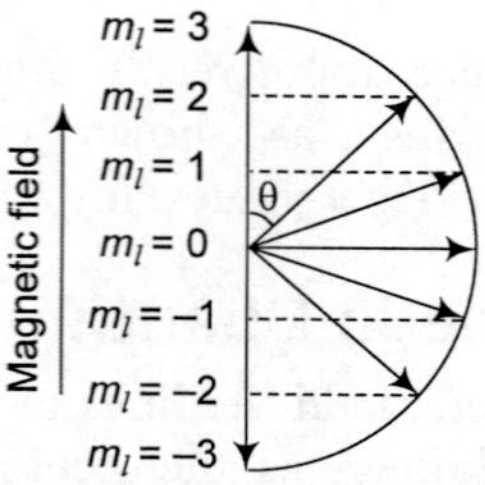

Fig. 17.11 Space quantisation in a magnetic field.

Here, l represents the axis of angular momentum of the electron and H the external field. The possible angles at which the vector quantity, l may process about H are given by the relation, $l \cos \theta = m$, where, m is the magnetic quantum number. The condition that $l \cos \theta$ must be a whole number gives rise to this quantum number called as the magnetic quantum number m, which was introduced by Laude in 1921. This m_1 will have the values $0, \pm 1, \pm 2, \ldots \pm l$ giving a total of $2l + 1$ possible values. In Fig. (17.11), the value of l, the azimuthal quantum number, which is also the vector of angular momentum, is taken as 3, and the possible angles are seven in all. As the diagram indicates, the positive values of m describe orbital angular momentum components which are in the direction of the applied magnetic field, and negative values are for those components which are oriented in a direction opposite to that of the field.

3. The Spin Quantum Number

Even the three quantum numbers n, l and m_1 were found to be inadequate for explaining the multiplicity and fine structure of some spectral lines that could be observed with a spectroscope of high resolving power. This idea of electron spin was then advanced by Uhlenbeck and Goudsmit in 1925 to account for this. An electron, according to this concept, can execute in addition to its orbital rotation, a spin around its own axis. The spin is analogous to the rotation of the earth as it moves along its orbit around the sun. Because of its spin, the electron has a spin angular momentum of magnitude $s\left(\frac{h}{2\pi}\right)$, where, s is the spin given by $+\frac{1}{2}$.

However, according to modern quantum theory the spin angular momentum is $\sqrt{\{s(s+1)\}} \cdot \frac{h}{2\pi}$ instead of $s\,\frac{h}{2\pi}$.

$$\therefore \qquad mvr = \sqrt{\{s(s+1)\}} \cdot \frac{h}{2\pi}$$

where, mvr denotes angular momentum. The rotating electron also has a magnetic moment and so will orient itself in an external magnetic field. The spectroscopic observations show that the electron may orient in an external magnetic field only in two ways, *viz.*, those in which the vector representing the spin angular momentum is either in the direction of the field or opposed to the field. The orientation of spin momentum with reference to orbital angular momentum is indicated diagrammatically in Fig. (17.12) shown below.

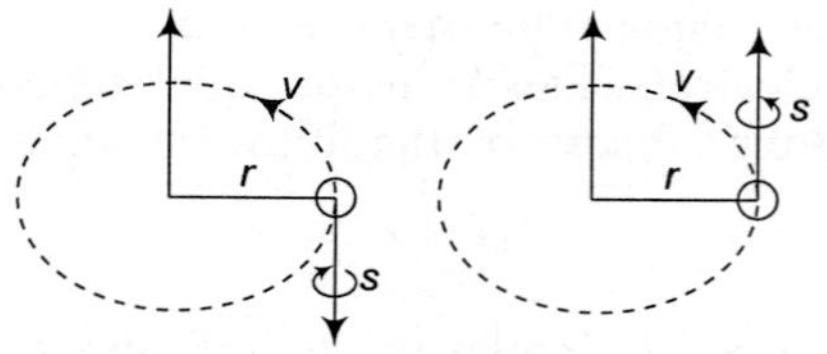

Fig. 17.12 Orientation of spin momentum with reference to orbital angular momentum.

Hence, the spin quantum number, m_s which is the component of the s vector in the direction of the field, can have only two values, $+\frac{1}{2}$ or $-\frac{1}{2}$.

Alkali Spectra

It is found that for many atoms especially belonging to the first three groups of the Periodic Table, the lines can be divided into at least four distinct series. These are referred to as sharp, principal, diffuse and fundamental series. The lines of sharp and diffuse series appear sharp and diffuse as their names indicate. But since the fundamental series is the not the really fundamental and so is often referred to as Bergamann series. Sometimes, the initial letters namely S, P, D and F have been employed to designate the series.

The absorption spectra of alkali vapour appear quite similar to the absorption spectrum of H-atom. The alkali spectra also consists of a series of lines with decreasing separation and also decreasing intensity. The series is called the principal series. It cannot be represented by the formula analogous to the Balmer formula. On the other hand, since the lines converge to a limit, we must be able to represent them as the differences between two terms. One of these terms is a constant T_{Ps}, known as fixed term and the other as the running term represented by $\frac{R}{(m+p)^2}$, where, R is the Rydberg constant, and p is a constant number < 1, and p is called the Rybderg correction. The running number, m takes the values from 2 to ∞. The quantity

$n^* = m + p$ is called the effective principal quantum number. Thus, the formula or the absorption principal series of the alkalies is given by,

$$v = T_{PS} - \frac{R}{(m+p)^2}$$

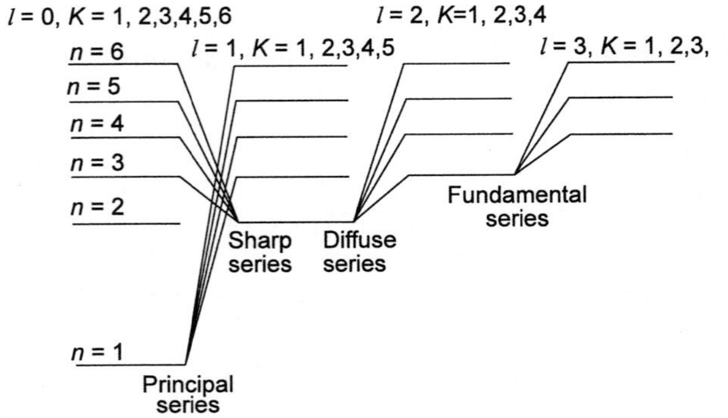

Fig. 17.13 Energy level diagram showing transistions of alkali metals.

In emission spectra, there are other three additional series apart from the principal series and they are diffuse, sharp and Bergamann series. The limits of these three series and, therefore, their limiting terms differ from the limiting terms of the principal series, but the sharp and diffuse series have a common limit. The T_{SS} is the common limiting term for the sharp and diffuse series. T_{BS} for the Bergmann series. The running terms are quite analogous to those of the principal series, but the Rydberg correction has a different value for each series. Thus, we have,

Principal series, $v = T_{PS} - \frac{R}{(m+p)^2}$,

where, $m = 2, 3 \ldots$

Sharp series, $v = T_{SS} - \frac{R}{(m+s)^2}$,

where, $m = 2, 3 \ldots$

Diffuse series, $v = T_{SS} - \frac{R}{(m+d)^2}$,

where, $m = 3, 4 \ldots$

Bergamann series, $v = T_{BS} - \frac{R}{(m+f)^2}$,

where, $m = 4, 5 \ldots$

The values found empirically show that

$$T_{PS} = \frac{R}{(1+s)^2} \cdot T_{SS} = \frac{R}{(2+p)^2} \cdot T_{BS} = \frac{R}{(3+d)^2}$$

i.e., the limiting terms belong to one of the series of running terms.

If we put p as a symbol for, $\frac{R}{(m+p)^2}$, ms for $\frac{R}{(m+s)^2}$ and so on, then the above series may be written as,

Principal series :	$v = 1s - mp$	$(m = 2, 3 \ldots)$
Sharp series :	$v = 2p - ms$	$(m = 2, 3 \ldots)$
Diffuse series :	$v = 2p - md$	$(m = 3, 4 \ldots)$
Bergamann series :	$v = 3d - mf$	$(m = 4, 5 \ldots)$

Theoretical Interpretation of Alkali Series

Hitherto it has been assumed that all lines in the spectral series are single. But closer examination shows that many of them have a multiplet structure. That is to say, the spectrum consists of groups of two, three or more lines very close together, that is unless a spectroscope of high resolving power is used, each group appears as a single line. A simple illustration of this is provided by yellow D-line of sodium. Careful examination has shown that it is actually a closely spaced doublet that is it consists of two separate lines. The frequency separation of two lines being almost constant in sharp and diffuse series, while in the principal series the separation becomes gradually smaller and the two lines coincide at the convergence limit.

The singly ionised atoms of the second group and doubly ionised atoms of the third group of the Periodic Table, each have a single optical electron and so behave spectroscopically like alkali atoms.

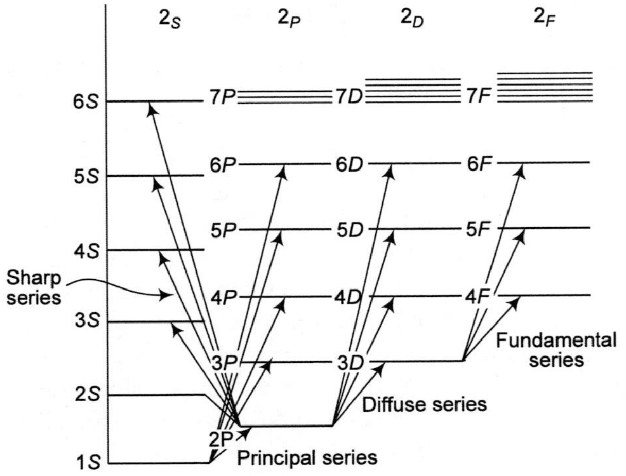

Fig. 17.14

From the four series of alkalies we have four sets of energy levels and they can be designated by S, P, D and F. These series are shown in Fig. 17.14 for Na-atom.

The ground state of the alkali atom is $1S$, since in the absorption, only the principal series appears, the S terms like $2S$, $3S$ follow after it. The lowest P state is $2P$ and it lies above the $1S$ term. The series of P-term follow it. The sharp series corresponds to the transition from higher S terms to the lower P terms. The lowest D terms lies still higher than the lowest P-terms and $4F$ term is higher than $3D$ term. All the term series go to the same limit.

When we examine the alkali spectra with spectral apparatus of greater dispersion, it is found that each of their lines is double as is known for D-line of sodium. The line splitting increases rapidly in the series Li, Na, K, Rb and Cs. This splitting can be detected for lithium only by using spectral apparatus of high dispersion. In the figure for sodium, the ground and other S terms are single, but the P terms are split. The splitting decreases with the increasing order number. If P states were assumed to be single then all the lines in the principal, sharp and diffuse series have same splitting. The splitting between D terms are so small that it makes scarcely any difference in case of potassium and sodium. Thus, it may be noted that many lines are actually multiples consisting of groups of two or three or more lines closer together. The interaction of fact was proved a matter of difficulty until 1925 when Goudsmit put forward that an electron rotates about it own axis, that is it spins and contributes to the total angular momentum. The spin quantum number is represented by s which is capable of having only two values $+\frac{1}{2}$ or $-\frac{1}{2}$. The resultant spin and azimuthal contribution to the angular momentum is obtained by adding l and s so that $j = l + s$, where, j is called inner quantum number. Since, $s = \pm 1/2$, so for every value of l, there are two values of j, *viz*., $j_i = l + 1/2$ and all s terms are, therefore, singlets. In the P-levels, l is 1, so that the corresponding j values are 3/2 and 1/2. In the D level, when $l = 2$, the j values are 5/2 and 3/2 and finally in F level, l is 3 and so the j values are 7/2 and 5/2. The doublet of the sharp series of the spectra may then be represented by the expression, $v_1 = 2P_{1/2} - mS$ and $v_2 = 2P_{3/2} - mS$, the S terms being a singlet and P terms, a doublet. The frequency separation of all the lines of sharp doublets is $2P_{1/2} - 2P_{3/2}$, which is clearly a constant as found experimentally. For principal series, the doublets are, $v_1 = 1S - mP_{1/2}$ and $v_2 = 1S - mP_{3/2}$, so that the frequency separation is $mP_{3/2} - mP_{1/2}$, which is not a constant, but increases as m increases. The lines of diffuse and fundamental series consist of triplets as shown below :

Diffuse series : $v_1 = 2P_{1/2} - mD_{3/2}$

$v_2 = 2P_{3/2} - mD_{3/2}$

$v_3 = 2P_{3/2} - mD_{5/2}$

Fundamental series : $v_1 = 3D_{3/2} - mF_{5/2}$

$v_2 = 3D_{5/2} - mF_{5/2}$

$v_3 = 3P_{5/2} - mF_{7/2}$.

Example 1. *Calculate the value of the Rydberg constant of hydrogen atom in eV.*

Sol.
$$R_H = \frac{1}{(4\pi\varepsilon_0)^2}\frac{2\pi^2 me^4}{ch^3}$$
$$\frac{1}{4\pi\varepsilon_0} = 9 \times 10^9 \text{ N m}^2\text{C}^{-2}$$

Substituting these values and the values of other constants and remembering that 1 eV = 8.0655×10^5 m^{-1}, we find that

$$R_H = 13.59 \text{ eV} \approx 13.60 \text{ eV}.$$

Example 2. *Calculate the radii of the second, third and fourth orbits of hydrogen atom (a = 0.53 Å).*

Sol. The radius of the nth orbit is given by

$$r_n = n^2 a_0 \; ; n = 1, 2, 3 \ldots \qquad \text{(Eqs. 16 and 17)}$$

1. $n = 2, r_2 = 2^2 (0.53 \text{ Å}) = 2.12 \text{ Å}$
2. $n = 3, r_3 = 3^2 (0.53 \text{ Å}) = 4.77 \text{ Å}$
3. $n = 4, r_4 = 4^2 (0.53 \text{ Å}) = 8.48 \text{ Å}$.

Example 3. *Calculate the value of the Bohr radius.*

Sol. The Bohr radius, *i.e.*, radius of the electron in the first orbit of hydrogen atom, is given by

$$a_0 = \frac{(4\pi\varepsilon_0)h^2}{4\pi^2 me^2}$$
$$= \frac{1.11265 \times 10^{-10} \text{ N}^{-1}\text{ C}^2\text{ m}^{-2}\,(6.626 \times 10^{-34}\text{ Js})^2}{(4)\,(3.14)^2\,(9.1 \times 10^{-31}\text{ kg})\,(1.6 \times 10^{-19}\text{ C})^2}$$
$$= 5.31 \times 10^{-11} \text{ m}$$
$$= 52.9 \text{ pm} = 0.529 \text{ Å}.$$

Example 4. *Calculate the short and the long wavelength limits of Lyman series in the spectrum of hydrogen atom. Given, R_H = 109677 cm^{-1}.*

Sol.
$$\bar{v} = \frac{1}{\lambda} = R_H\left[\frac{1}{1^1} - \frac{1}{n_i^2}\right]$$

For short wavelength limit,

$$\lambda = \lambda_s, n_i = \infty$$

Hence, we find that $\lambda_s = 911.6$ Å

For long wavelength limit,

$$\lambda = \lambda_i, n_i = 22$$

Hence, we find that $\lambda_i = 1.215$ Å.

Example 5. *Show that the ground state energy of electron in hydrogen atom is equal to the first excited state energy of electron in* He^+ *ion, assuming that their Rydberg constants are equal.*

Sol. $E_n = -R_H Z^2/n^2; (n = 1, 2, 3 \ldots)$

$$= -13.60\ Z^2/n^2 \text{ eV} \qquad \text{(from Ex. 2)}$$

For hydrogen atom in ground state,

$$Z = 1, \quad n = 1$$

$$\therefore \quad E_1 = -13.60 \text{ eV}$$

For He^+ ion in first excited state,

$$Z = 2, \quad n = 2$$

$$\therefore \quad E_2 = -13.60 \text{ eV}$$

Hence, the result.

Example 6. *Calculate the ground state energies of the electron (in eV) in the case of (i)* H *(ii)* He^+ *(iii)* Li^{2+} *(iv)* Be^{3+} *species, assuming that their Rydberg constants are equal.*

Sol. From Eqs. 20 and 23, $E_n = -R_H Z^2/n^2$. For ground state $(n = 1)$, $R_H = 13.60$ eV (from example 2)

(i) H $(Z = 1): E_1 = -13.60$ eV

(ii) H^+ $(Z = 2): E_1 = -(13.60)(2)^2 = -54.40$ eV

(iii) Li^{2+} $(Z = 3): E_1 = -(13.60)(3)^2 = -122.40$ eV

(iv) Be^{3+} $(Z = 4): E_1 = -(13.60)(4)^2 = -217.60$ eV.

Example 7. *Which state of the triply ionized beryllium* (Be^{3+}) *has the same orbital radius as that of the ground state of hydrogen atom?*

Sol. From hydrogen atom,

$$r_1 = (4\pi\varepsilon_0)h^2/(4\pi^2 me^2) \qquad \ldots\text{(i)}$$

For hydrogen-like atom

$$r'_n = (4\pi\varepsilon_0)\, n^2h^2/(4\pi^2 mZe^2) \qquad \ldots\text{(ii)}$$

Dividing Eq. (ii) by Eq. (i) we get

$$r'_n = r_1 = n^2/Z = n^2/4 \qquad (\because\ Z = 4 \text{ for } Be^{3+})$$

Since, $r'_n = r_1$, Hence, $n = 2$.

Thus, the second energy level (or the second orbit) of Be^{3+} has the same radius as that of the ground state of hydrogen atom.

Example 8. *Calculate the de-Broglie wavelength of a body of mass* 1 *kg moving with a velocity of* 2000 ms^{-1}.

Sol. $\lambda = \dfrac{h}{mu}$

$$= \frac{(6.626 \times 10^{-34} \text{ Js})}{(1 \text{ kg})\,(2000 \text{ ms}^{-1})}$$

$$= 3.313 \times 10^{-37} \text{ m} = 3.313 \times 10^{-27} \text{ Å}$$

$$(\text{J} = \text{kg m}^2\text{s}^{-2})$$

It may be noted that the above wavelength is too small to be measured by any conceivable technique.

Example 9. *A microscope using suitable photons is employed to locate an electron in an atom within a distance of* 0.1 Å. *What is the uncertainty involved in the measurement of its velocity? Mass of electron* $= 9.1 \times 10^{-31}$ kg. *Planck's constant* $(h) = 6.626 \times 10^{-34}$ Js.

Sol. From Eq. 41, $\Delta x \times \Delta p_x \geq h/4\pi$

or $\quad \Delta x \times m\Delta u_x \geq h/4\pi$

$$\therefore \quad 0.01 \times 10^{-10} \text{ m} \times 9.1 \times 10^{-31} \text{ kg} \times \Delta u$$

$$= 6.626 \times 10^{-34} \text{ Js}/4\pi$$

$$\Delta u = 0.579 \times 10^7 \text{ ms}^{-1} \qquad (\text{J} = \text{kg m}^2 \text{ s}^{-2}).$$

Example 10. *A cricket ball weighing* 100 *g is to be located within* 0.1 Å. *What is the uncertainty in its velocity? Comment on your result.*

Sol. From Eq. 41, $\Delta x \times \Delta p_x \geq h/4\pi$

or $\quad \Delta p_x \geq h/4\pi\Delta x$

$$\therefore \quad \Delta u_x = \Delta p_x/m = h/4\pi\Delta x m$$

$$= 6.626 \times 10^{-34}/4\pi(10^{-11})\,(0.1 \text{ kg})$$

$$= 0.527 \times 10^{-22} \text{ ms}^{-1} \qquad (\text{J} = \text{kg m}^2 \text{ s}^{-2})$$

Comparing this value with the typical velocity of a cricket ball, we find that this uncertainty in velocity is completely negligible. This means that we can disregard the uncertainty principle for the motion of macroscopic bodies. We can thus say that for such cases, both the position and velocity can be determined to a reasonable degree of precision.

Example 11. *Calculate the frequency and the energy associated with wavelength* 2000 Å.

Sol. (a) We know that,

$$\nu = \frac{c}{\lambda}$$

where, ν is frequency, c is velocity of light and λ is wavelength.

$$\nu = \frac{3.0 \times 10^{10} \text{ cm s}^{-1}}{200 \times 10^{-8} \text{ cm}} = 1.5 \times 10^{15} \text{ cm}^{-1}$$

(b) From Planck's relation, we have

$$E = h\nu = \frac{hc}{\lambda}$$

where, h is Planck's constant.

$$E = \frac{6.62 \times 10^{-27} \times 3.0 \times 10^{-10}}{2000 \times 10^{-8}}$$

$$= 9.93 \times 10^{-12} \text{ erg.}$$

Example 12. *An electron jumps from an outer orbit to an inner orbit with an energy difference of* 3.0 *eV. What will be the wavelength of the line emitted and in what region does the emission take place?* $(1 \text{ eV} = 1.6 \times 10^{-12}$ erg., $h = 6.62 \times 10^{-27}$ erg s).

Sol. We know that the energy is emitted in the form of quanta and is given by

$$\Delta E = h\nu = \frac{hc}{\lambda}$$

where, ΔE = energy emitted or absorbed

$$= 3.0 \times 1.6 \times 10^{-12} \text{ erg}$$

$$\lambda = \frac{hc}{\Delta E} = \frac{6.62 \times 10^{-27} \times 3 \times 10^{10}}{3.0 \times 1.6 \times 10^{-12}}$$

$$= 4.14 \times 10^{-5} \text{ cm} = 4.14 \times 10^{-5} \times 10^{8}$$

$$= 4140 \text{ Å}$$

Wavelength of the emitted line = 4140 Å.

This wavelength lies in the visible region, so, the emission takes place in the visible region.

Example 13. *Calculate the radius of the first and second orbit of hydrogen atom. Given, $h = 6.62 \times 10^{-27}$ erg s, mass of electron $= 9.1 \times 10^{-28}$ g; charge, $e = 4.8 \times 10^{-10}$ esu.*

Sol. From Eq. (10), we have

$$r = \frac{n^2h^2}{4\pi^2me^2}$$

(i) For first orbit, $n = 1$

$$\therefore \quad r_1 = \frac{1^2 \times (6.62 \times 10^{-27})^2}{4 \times (3.14)^2 \times 9.1 \times 10^{-28} \times (4.8 \times 10^{-10})^2}$$

$$= 0.5291 \times 10^{-8} \text{ cm}$$

$$\therefore \quad r_1 = 0.5291 \times 10^{-8} \times 10^{-8} = 0.5291 \text{ Å}$$

∴ Radius of first hydrogen orbit = 0.5291 Å.

(ii) For second orbit, $n = 2$

$$r_2 = \frac{2^2 \times (6.62 \times 10^{-27})^2}{4 \times (3.14)^2 \times 9.1 \times 10^{-28} \times (4.8 \times 10^{-10})^2}$$

$$= 2.1164 \times 10^{-8} \text{ cm}$$

$$= 2.1164 \times 10^{-8} \times 10^{8}$$

$$= 2.1164 \text{ Å}$$

∴ Radius of second hydrogen orbit = 2.1164 Å.

Example 14. *The radius of second orbit of hydrogen atom is 2.12 Å. Calculate the velocity of the electron rotating in this orbit. Given,*

Mass of electron $= 9.1 \times 10^{-28}$ g

Charge on electron $= e = 4.8 \times 10^{-10}$ esu.

Sol. We know that, $r = \dfrac{Ze^2}{mv^2}$

where, Z = number of protons = 1,

v = velocity of electron,

r = radius of the orbit.

$$\therefore \quad v = \sqrt{\left(\frac{Ze^2}{mr}\right)} = \sqrt{\left(\frac{e^2}{mr}\right)}$$

$$\therefore \quad v = \sqrt{\left(\frac{(4.8 \times 10^{-10})^2}{9.1 \times 10^{-28} \times 2.12 \times 10^{-8}}\right)}$$

$$= 1.092 \times 10^{8}$$

∴ Velocity of electron $= 1.092 \times 10^{8}$ cm s^{-1}.

Example 15. *Calculate the wavelength of H_α line of hydrogen spectrum in the Balmer series, given that the Rydberg constant is 109676 cm^{-1}.*

Sol. The wavelengths of the lines in the Balmer series are given by

$$\frac{1}{\lambda} = R\left(\frac{1}{2^2} - \frac{1}{n^2}\right)$$

where, λ = wavelength,

r = Rydberg constant,

n = any integer, which for Balmer series is equal to 3.

$$\frac{1}{\lambda} = 109676\left(\frac{1}{2^2} - \frac{1}{3^2}\right)$$

$$= 109676\left(\frac{9-4}{36}\right) = \frac{109676 \times 5}{36}$$

$$\therefore \quad \lambda = \frac{36}{109676 \times 5} = 6.561 \times 10^{-5} \text{ cm}$$

$$= 6.561 \times 10^{-5} \times 10^{8} = 6561 \text{ Å}$$

∴ Wavelength of H_α line = 6561 Å.

Example 16. *The electron of a hydrogen atom is excited to the third energy level. Find the frequencies of the lines produced in de-excitation from third level to second level and from third level to first level.*

$$h = 6.62 \times 10^{-27} \text{ erg s}, \quad m = 9.1 \times 10^{-28} \text{ g}$$

$$e = 4.8 \times 10^{-10} \text{ esu}.$$

Sol. The frequency of radiation emitted is given by

$$v = \frac{2\pi^2mZ^2e^4}{h^3}\left[\frac{1}{n_1^2} - \frac{1}{n_2^2}\right]$$

$$= \frac{2 \times (3.14)^2 \times 9.1 \times 10^{-28} \times 1^2 \times (4.8 \times 10^{-10})^4}{(6.62 \times 10^{-27})^3}\left(\frac{1}{n_1^2} - \frac{1}{n_2^2}\right)$$

(As Z = number of protons = 1)

$$v = 3.289 \times 10^{15}\left[\frac{1}{n_1^2} - \frac{1}{n_2^2}\right]$$

(a) For first transition from $n_1 = 2$ to $n_2 = 3$, we have

$$v = 3.289 \times 10^{15}\left(\frac{1}{2^2} - \frac{1}{3^2}\right)$$

$$= 3.289 \times 10^{15}\left(\frac{1}{4} - \frac{1}{9}\right)$$

$$= 4.567 \times 10^{14} \text{ s}^{-1}$$

∴ Frequency for the transition $= 4.567 \times 10^{14}$ s^{-1}.

(b) For second transition from $n_1 = 1$ to $n_2 = 3$, we have

$$\nu = 3.289 \times 10^{15}\left(\frac{1}{1^2} - \frac{1}{3^2}\right)$$
$$= 3.289 \times 10^{15}\left(1 - \frac{1}{9}\right)$$
$$= 2.9241 \times 10^{15}\ s^{-1}$$

∴ Frequency for the transition $= \mathbf{2.9241 \times 10^{15} s^{-1}}$

Example 17. *The first ionisation of a certain atom occurs with absorption of radiation of frequency* 1.5×10^{18} *cycles per second. Calculate the ionisation potential in calories per gram atom. Given,* $h = 6.62 \times 10^{-27}$ erg s, $N = 6.02 \times 10^{23}$.

Sol. We know that,

Ionisation energy per mole,

$$E = Nh\nu$$

∴ $$E = 6.02 \times 10^{23} \times 6.62 \times 10^{-27} \times 1.5 \times 10^{18} \text{ erg}$$
$$= 59.78 \times 10^{14} \text{ erg}$$

As $$4.18 \times 10^7 \text{ erg} \equiv 1 \text{ cal}$$

∴ $$E = \frac{59.78 \times 10^{14}}{4.18 \times 10^7} = 1.43 \times 10^8 \text{ cal}$$

∴ Ionisation potential $= 1.43 \times 10^8$ cal.

Example 18. *The ionisation potential of hydrogen atom is 13.60 eV. Calculate the energy required to produce one mole of* H^+ *ion. (1 eV* $= 23061$ cal mol^{-1}).

Sol. The ionisation potential 13.60 eV shows that 13.60 eV energy will have to be given to shed one electron from the hydrogen atom. One gram atom of H^+ ion will be obtained by shedding 6.02×10^{23} electrons.

$$H \longrightarrow H^+ + e^-$$

The energy per mole, $E = 13.6 \times 23061$

$$= 313629.6 \text{ cal}$$

∴ Energy required = 313.63 kcal.

Example 19. *The first and the second ionisation potentials of helium atom are 24.58 eV and 54.41 eV respectively. Calculate the energy required to produce 1 g atomic weight of* He^{2+} *ion. Given that* 1 eV $= 1.0 \times 10^{-12}$ *erg* $= 23061$ *cal mol*$^{-1}$.

Sol. We know that to get one gram atomic weight of He^{2+} $2 \times 6.02 \times 10^{23}$ electrons will have to be shedded.

From first ionisation potential, $He \longrightarrow He^+ + e^-$

∴ Energy per mole, $E_1 = 24.58 \times 23061$

$$= 566784.8 \text{ cal}$$

From second ionisation potential,

$$He^+ \longrightarrow He^{2+} + e^-$$

∴ Energy per mole, $E_2 = 54.41 \times 23061$

For the transition

$$He \longrightarrow He^{2+} + 2e^-$$

Total energy, $E = E_1 + E_2$

$$= 566784.8 + 1253376.1$$
$$= 1820.161 \text{ kcal}$$

Example 20. *A photon of wavelength 4000 Å strikes a metal surface, the work function of the metal being 2.13 eV. Calculate (i) the energy of the photon in eV (ii) the kinetic energy of the emitted photoelectron and (iii) the velocity of the photoelectron. Mass of electron* $= 9.109 \times 10^{-31}$ kg.

Sol. (i) Energy of the photon

$$u = c/\lambda = 3 \times 10^8 \text{ ms}^{-1} / 4000 \times 10^{-10}\text{m}$$
$$= 7.5 \times 10^{14} \text{ s}^{-1}$$
$$E = h\nu = (6.626 \times 10^{-34} \text{ Js})(7.5 \times 10^{14} \text{ s}^{-1})$$
$$= 4.97 \times 10^{19} \text{ J}$$

Since, $1 \text{ eV} = 1.602 \times 10^{-19}$ J

∴ $$E = 4.97 \times 10^{-19} \text{ J} / 1.602 \times 10^{-10} \text{ J/eV}$$
$$= 3.10 \text{ eV}$$

(ii) Kinetic energy of emitted photoelectron

$$\phi = 2.13 \text{ eV}$$

Hence, from Eq. 9,

$$KE = h\nu - \phi = 3.10 \text{ eV} - 2.13 \text{ eV} = 0.97 \text{ eV}$$

(iii) Velocity of photoelectron

$$KE = \frac{1}{2}mu^2 = 0.97 \text{ eV}$$
$$= 0.97 \times 1.602 \times 10^{-19} \text{ J}$$

∴ $$u = \left[\frac{2 \times 0.97 \times 1.602 \times 10^{-19} \text{ J}}{9.109 \times 10^{-31} \text{ kg}}\right]^{\frac{1}{2}}$$
$$= 5.85 \times 10^5 \text{ ms}^{-1} \qquad (\text{J} = \text{kg m}^2\text{s}^{-2})$$

Exercise 1
(For Part 'B')

1. Consider the following ions.
(1) Ni^{2+} (2) Cr^{2+} (3) Co^{2+} (4) Fe^{3+}
Correct sequence of increasing order of the number of unpaired electrons is
(a) 4, 3, 2, 1 (b) 4, 1, 2, 3
(c) 1, 2, 3, 4 (d) 1, 2, 4, 3

2. Consider the following statements.
The *d*-orbitals are having
1. Four lobes and one node.
2. Four lobes and two nodes.
3. Opposite lobes are having opposite signs.
4. Opposite lobes are having same signs.
Which of the above statements is/are correct?
(a) 1, 3 (b) 2, 4 (c) 2, 3 (d) 1, 4

3. In the Bohr's orbit, what is the ratio of total kinetic energy and total energy of the electron?
(a) 1 (b) −1 (c) + 2 (d) − 2

4. The ground state term symbol for p^3 and d^3 electronic configuration respectively are
(a) ^1D and ^4F (b) ^4S and ^4F
(c) ^4D and ^2G (d) ^4S and ^1D

5. The ground state energy of electron in H-atom and first excited state energy of electron in He^+ ion (assuming Rydberg constant are equal) are respectively
(a) −122.40 eV, +13.60 V (b) −13.60 eV, −13.60 eV
(c) −13.60 eV, +13.60 eV (d) None of these

6. Outer electronic configuration of technicium is $(Z = 43)$
(a) $4d^6\,5s^1$ (b) $4d^5\,5s^2$
(c) $3d^5\,4s^2$ (d) $4f^6\,6s^2$

7. The term symbol for ground state electronic configuration of nitrogen atom is
(a) ^6S (b) ^4S (c) ^5D (d) ^4F

8. The electronic configuration of an atom *M* is $1s^2, 2s^2, 2p^6, 3s^2, 3p^6, 3d^{10}, 4s^2, 4p^5$. The chemistry of *M* is, therefore, likely to be similar to that of
(a) chlorine (b) sulphur
(c) phosphorus (d) nitrogen

9. Which of the following are isoelectronic and isostructural?
$$SO_3, NO_3^-, ClO_3^-, CO_3^{2-}$$
(a) SO_3 and NO_3^- (b) CO_3^{2-} and SO_3
(c) NO_3^- and CO_3^{2-} (d) ClO_3^- and CO_3^{2-}

10. If the nitrogen atom had electronic configuration $1s^7$, it would have energy lower than that of normal ground state configuration $1s^2, 2s^2, 2p^3$ because the electrons would be closer to the nucleus yet $1s^7$ is not observed because it violates
(a) Hund's rule
(b) Heisenberg uncertainty principal
(c) Pauli's exclusion principle
(d) Bohr's theory

11. A substance A_xB_y crystallizes in a fcc lattice in which atoms *A* occupy each corner of cube and atoms *B* occupy the centres of each face of the cube. Identify the correct composition of substance A_xB_y
(a) A_4B_3
(b) AB_3
(c) A_3B
(d) Compound cannot be specified

12. A sudden large jump between the values of second and third ionisation potentials of an element would be associated with the electronic configuration
(a) $1s^2 \cdot 2s^2 \cdot 2p^6 \cdot 3s^2$ (b) $1s^2 \cdot 2s^2 \cdot 2p^6 \cdot 3s^1$
(c) $1s^2 \cdot 2s^2 \cdot 2p^6 \cdot 3s^2\,3p^2$ (d) $1s^2 \cdot 2s^2 \cdot 2p^6 \cdot 3s^2 \cdot 3p^1$

13. The 3*s* orbital has
(a) 1 node (b) 3 node
(c) 2 node (d) No node

14. Which of the following combination of atomic orbital is not possible (consider *Z*-axis as molecular axis) for forming molecular orbitals?
(a) $2p_y$ and $2p_y$ (b) 2*s* and 2*s*
(c) 2*s* and p_x (d) 2*s* and $2p_z$

15. The total energy of electron revolving round the nucleus is
(a) zero
(b) more than zero
(c) less than 0
(d) more than zero in certain atoms and less than zero in others

16. For an atomic orbital where angular dependence is given by $d_{xy} = A \sin^2\theta \sin 2\phi$ the electron density is maximum along
(a) *X*-direction (b) *Y*-direction
(c) *Z*-direction (d) Equal in all directions

17. The radial part of an atomic orbital wave function depends upon
(a) *n* and *l* (b) *l* and *m*
(c) *n*, *l* and *m* (d) *n* only

18. The diameter of an atom is how many times the diameter of the nucleus?
(a) 10^2 times (b) 10^3 times
(c) 10^4 times (d) 10^6 times

19. The electron octet rule is not obeyed in the case of
(a) H_2O (b) O_2 (c) CO_2 (d) NO^+

20. The maximum number of electrons with a dz^2 orbital can accommodate is
(a) 1 (b) 4 (c) 2 (d) 5

21. X-ray is produced when
(a) cathode rays are emitted
(b) canal rays are emitted
(c) an e^- is ejected from the outermost shell
(d) an e^- is ejected from inner shell

22. The ground state term symbol for d^9 configuration is
(a) ${}^2D_{3/2}$ (b) ${}^1S_0$ (c) ${}^4F_{9/2}$ (d) ${}^2D_{5/2}$

23. Different values of L for d^1 to d^5 configuration are in the order of
(a) $2D, 3F, 3F, 2D, 0S$ (b) $0S, 2D, 2D, 3F, 3F$
(c) $0S, 2D, 3F, 3F, 2D$ (d) $2D, 2D, 3F, 3F, 0S$

24. Number of nodes for $4s$ and $4d$ orbitals are
(a) 4, 4 (b) 3, 1 (c) 2, 2 (d) 1, 3

25. If the energy of an electron in the second level of hydrogen atom is $-E$, its value in the third energy level will be
(a) $-4E \times 9$ (b) $-9E/4$ (c) $-4E/9$ (d) $-2E \times 9$

26. If an electron travels with a velocity of $\frac{1}{100}$th the speed of the light in first Bohr's orbit, its velocity (relative still to the speed of light) in the 5th Bohr orbit is
(a) 0.5 (b) 0.025 (c) 0.25 (d) 0.002

27. What are the values of L, S and J for a term symbol ${}^3F_2$?
(a) $L = 3, S = 2, J = 0, 1, 2, 3$
(b) $L = 3, S = 1, J = 4, 3, 2$
(c) $L = 2, S = 3, J = 5$
(d) $L = 1, S = 3, J = 4, 3, 2$

28. Term symbol for the lowest energy state of nitrogen with configuration $1s^2 \cdot 2s^2 \cdot 2p^3$ is
(a) ${}^2P_0$ (b) ${}^4S_{1/2}$ (c) ${}^4S_0$ (d) ${}^4S_{3/2}$

29. 1 eV of energy is equivalent to a photon with a wavelength about
(a) 30 Å (b) 300 Å
(c) 1200 Å (d) 12000 Å

30. Out of X-rays, infrared rays, visible rays and micro waves, the largest frequency is of
(a) X-rays (b) infrared rays
(c) visible rays (d) micro waves

31. The s-orbitals of any atom are
(a) dependent on sin θ
(b) dependent on cos θ
(c) dependent on sin θ cos θ
(d) independent of angles

32. If a normal hydrogen molecule is 2.2 Å in diameter when both electrons are in the most stable Bohr orbit, the size of a hypothetical molecule in which the electrons were each in the third Bohr orbit is

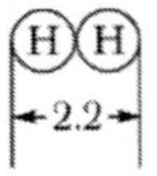

(a) 4.4 Å (b) 6.6 Å
(c) 8.8 Å (d) 19.8 Å

33. For a electron moving in the s-orbital, its total angular momentum is
(a) 0 (b) $\frac{1}{2}$
(c) 1 (d) $\frac{3}{2}$

34. The energy (in eV) of a photon having a wavelength of 0.1 Å is
(a) 1 eV (b) 12.4 eV
(c) 124 eV (d) 1.24×10^5 eV

35. Assuming that $n =$ principal quantum number, quantum mechanics postulates that the electron population of any energy level in an atom is limited to
(a) $2n$ (b) n (c) $2n^2 + 2$ (d) $2n^2$

36. The increasing order for the value of e/m for
(a) e, p, n, α (b) n, p, e, α (c) n, p, α, e (d) n, α, p, e

37. Which of the following electron transition in a hydrogen atom will require the largest amount of energy?
(a) From $n = 1$ to $n = 2$ (b) From $n = 2$ to $n = 3$
(c) From $n = \infty$ to $n = 1$ (d) From $n = 3$ to $n = 5$

38. The ionisation potential of hydrogen atom is 13.6 eV. The energy required to remove an electron in the $n = 2$ state of the hydrogen atom is
(a) 27.2 eV (b) 13.6 eV
(c) 6.8 eV (d) 3.4 eV

39. If each hydrogen atom is excited by giving 8.4 eV of energy, than the number of spectral lines emitted is equal to
(a) one (b) two (c) three (d) four

40. The number of d-electrons in Fe^{2+} (Z for Fe $= 26$) is not equal to that of the
(a) p-electrons in Ne ($Z = 10$)
(b) s-electrons in Mg ($Z = 12$)
(c) d-electrons in Fe
(d) p-electrons in Cl^- (Z of Cl $= 17$)

41. The uncertainty in position of an electron is zero. The uncertainty in its momentum would be
(a) zero (b) $> h/2\pi$
(c) $< h/2\pi$ (d) infinity

42. Which of the following statement is not correct for an electron that has the quantum numbers $n = 4$ and $m = 2$?
(a) The electron may have the quantum number $s = +1/2$
(b) The electron may have the quantum number $l = 2$
(c) The electron may have the quantum number $l = 3$
(d) The electron may have the quantum number $l = 0, 1, 2, 3$

43. Aufbau principle is not correct for
(a) Cu and Ar (b) Cu and Cr
(c) Cr and Ar (d) Mn and Cr

44. The correct ground state configuration for chromium is
(a) [Ar] $3d^4\,4s^2$ (b) [Ar] $3d^5\,4s^1$
(c) [Ne] $3d^5\,4s^1$ (d) [Ne] $3d^4\,4s^2$

45. The orbital diagram in which the Aufbau principle violated is

	2s	2p		
(a)	↑↓	↑↓	↑	
(b)	↑	↑↓	↑	↑
(c)	↑↓	↑	↑	↑
(d)	↑↓	↑↓	↑↓	↑

46. The electronic configuration of an element is $1s^2\,2s^2\,2p^5$. The ground state atomic term will be
(a) $^2P_{1/2}$ (b) $^2P_{3/2}$ (c) $^2S_{3/2}$ (d) $^3P_2$

47. The different J values for p^4 configuration are
(a) $\frac{3}{2}, \frac{1}{2}$ (b) 2, 1, 0 (c) 0 (d) $\frac{3}{2}$

48. The numerical value of Compton wavelength is
(a) 0.0242 m (b) 0.0243×10^{-8} Å
(c) 0.0242 Å (d) 0.0242 cm

49. A photon of wavelength 4000 Å strikes a metal surface, the work function of the metal being 2.13 eV. The kinetic energy of the emitted photoelectron is
(a) 0.97 eV (b) 9.7 eV (c) 5.23 eV (d) 3.10 eV

50. What is the wavelength of the electron in the *n*th Bohr orbit?
(a) $\lambda = (n \times 0.529)$ Å
(b) $\lambda = (n \times 2 \times 3.146 \times 0.529)$ Å
(c) $\lambda = (n \times 2 \times 3.14 \times 0.529)^2$ Å
(d) None of the above

51. The zero point energy of an electron is equal to
(a) $\frac{h^2}{2ma^2}$ (b) $\frac{h^2}{4ma^2}$ (c) $\frac{h^2}{8ma^2}$ (d) $\frac{h^2}{16ma^2}$

52. The uncertainty in the energy of the excited state for an atom with a mean life of 10^{-8} s
(a) 10^{-16} erg (b) 2×10^{-19} erg
(c) 6.6×10^{-19} erg (d) 10^{-19} erg

53. The number of orbitals possible for 5*g* sub shell is
(a) 7
(b) 9
(c) 5
(d) 5*g* subshell is not possible

54. The electronic configuration of the atom with atomic number 47 is
(a) [Kr] $4d^{10}\,5s^2$ (b) [Ar] $4d^{10}\,5s^1$
(c) [Kr] $4d^{10}\,5s^1\,5d^1$ (d) [Kr] $4d^{10}\,5s^1$

55. Which of the following statement regarding spectral series is correct?
(a) The lines in the Balmer series correspond to electron transition for energy levels higher than $n = 1$ energy level
(b) Paschen series appear in infrared region
(c) The lines of Lyman series appear in visible region
(d) Transition from higher energy levels to 4th energy level produce Pfund series which fall in IR region

56. A cricket ball weighing 100 g is to be located within 0.1 Å. The uncertainty in its velocity is
(a) 6.626×10^{-22} ms^{-1} (b) 66.26×10^{-22} ms^{-1}
(c) 0.6626×10^{-22} ms^{-1} (d) 6626×10^{-22} ms^{-1}

57. de-Broglie wavelength of a body of mass 1000 moving with a velocity of 3000 m/s is
(a) 2.208×10^{-31} m (b) 2.208×10^{-40} m
(c) 2.208×10^{-37} m (d) 220.8×10^{-37} m

58. The wavelength associated with a golf ball weighing 200 g and moving and a speed of 5 m/h is of the order
(a) 10^{-10} m (b) 10^{-20} m
(c) 10^{-30} m (d) 10^{-40} m

59. The principal and azimuthal quantum numbers of electrons in 4*f* orbitals are
(a) $n = 4, l = 2$ (b) $n = 4, l = 4$
(c) $n = 4, l = 3$ (d) $n = 3, l = 4$

60. The preference of three unpaired electrons in phosphorus in the ground state can be explained by
(a) Pauli exclusion principle (b) Aufbau principle
(c) Uncertainty principle (d) Hund's rule

61. How many possible combination of quantum numbers are there for N shell?
(a) 8 (b) 18 (c) 32 (d) 10

62. The outer configuration for gadolinium ($Z = 64$) can be written as
(a) $4f^7\ 5d^2\ 6s^1$ (b) $4f^7\ 5d^1\ 6s^2$
(c) $4f^8\ 5d^0\ 6s^2$ (d) $4f^7\ 6s^2\ 6p^1$

63. According to Seaborg the electronic configuration of the atom having atomic number 90 is
(a) $5f^2\ 7s^2$ (b) $6d^2\ 7s^2$
(c) $5f^1\ 6d^1\ 7s^2$ (d) $5f^2\ 6s^2$

64. If the ionisation potential for hydrogen atoms in 13.6 eV, than the ionisation potential for He^+ ion should be
(a) 13.6 eV (b) 6.8 eV (c) 79 eV (d) 54.4 eV

65. The zero-point energy is equal to
(a) kT (b) $\frac{1}{2}kT$ (c) $\frac{1}{2}h\nu$ (d) $h\nu$

66. The maximum number of electrons that may be found in the '*L*' shell of an atom is
(a) 6 (b) 8 (c) 32 (d) 18

67. Radius of the first orbital for hydrogen atom is
(a) 0.53×10^{-8} cm (b) 0.53×10^{-9} cm
(c) 0.53×10^{-10} cm (d) 0.53 cm

68. The ionisation potential of the He^+ ion compared to the ionisation potential of the H-atom (both species in gaseous state) is
(a) infinite (b) zero (c) same (d) greater

69. Atoms have radii closest in size to which one of the following?
(a) 1×10^{-4} cm (b) 1×10^{-8} cm
(c) 1×10^{-12} cm (d) 1×10^{-8} Å

70. Of the following, the compound that obeys the octet rule is
(a) CO_2 (b) BCl_3 (c) PCl_5 (d) OsF_8

71. How many are the possible results for the measurement of the z component of the orbital angular momentum of a hydrogen atom in a $3d$ state ($n = 3, l = 2$)?
(a) 1 (b) 2 (c) 3 (d) 5

72. The smallest ionic radius among the following is
(a) K^+ (b) Ca^{2+} (c) Sc^{3+} (d) Ti^{4+}

73. Which of the following is incorrect about the de-Broglie relationship?
(a) $h = \lambda \times p$ (b) $\frac{h}{\nu} = \lambda \times m$
(c) $E_{\text{kinetic}} = \frac{h\nu}{2\lambda}$ (d) $E_{\text{Kinetic}} = \frac{2h\nu}{\lambda}$

74. An electron travels with a velocity of ν ms^{-1}. For a proton to have the same de-Broglie wavelength, the velocity will be approximately
(a) $\frac{\nu}{1840}$ (b) $\frac{1840}{\nu}$ (c) 1840ν (d) ν

75. The number of nodal planes in a p_x-orbital is
(a) one (b) two (c) three (d) four

76. A $5f$-orbital has
(a) one node (b) two nodes
(c) three nodes (d) four nodes

77. Which of the following diatomic molecules would be stabilized by the removal of an electron?
(a) C_2 (b) CN (c) N_2 (d) O_2

78. The lowest energy term symbol for the Si atom is
(a) ^3P (b) ^3S (c) ^3D (d) ^1P

79. If the ionization energy of hydrogen atom is 13.6 eV, the expected third ionization energy of lithium atom is
(a) 13.6×3 eV (b) 13.6×2 eV
(c) 13.6×6 eV (d) 13.6×9 eV

80. The electrical resistivity of a semiconductor
(a) increases with temperature
(b) decreases with temperature
(c) increases at lower temperature and then decreases at higher temperature
(d) does not change with temperature

81. Which observation did not contribute to the development of the Bohr Model of the atom?
(a) Photons have a specific energy and wavelength
(b) The light emitted by hydrogen gas when electricity is passed through it
(c) The nuclear model of the atom
(d) The wave/particle dual nature of electrons

82. An orbital that has no radial nodes and has two angular nodes is
(a) $3s$ (b) $2s$ (c) $2p$ (d) $3d$

83. Which statement best describes a $4p$-orbital?
(a) It has one angular nodes with two regions of electron density
(b) It has two angular nodes with four regions of electron density
(c) It has two angular nodes with two regions of electron density
(d) It can hold a maximum of six electrons

84. How many electrons can have the quantum numbers $n = 3$, l = anything, $m_l = 1$, ms = anything?
(a) 2 (b) 4
(c) 1 (d) 6

85. Hydrogen atoms are excited from $n = 1 \rightarrow n = 2$. The electron in the $n = 2$ shell then returns to $n = 1$ emitting a photon. These emitted photons hit a piece of copper (work function, $\phi = 2.40$ eV) causing electron to be ejected. Calculate the energy of these ejected electrons in Joule.
(a) 1.63×10^{-18} J (b) 0.384×10^{-18} J
(c) 2.18×10^{-18} J (d) 1.25×10^{-18} J

86. You are given an electron with a de-Broglie wavelength of $\lambda = 76.3$ nm. What is the Kelvin temperature of this electron?
(a) 1.50 (b) 2.00 (c) 2.50 (d) 3.00

87. When the surface of a piece of potassium is irradiated with light of wavelength $\lambda_1 = 5000$ Å, the value of the stopping potential (voltage) necessary to stop the emitted electrons is $v_1 = 0.200$ V. When the wavelength is changed to $\lambda = 4000$ Å, the required stopping potential is, $V_2 = 0.600$ V. In this problem, you do not know the value of Planck's constant. Using this information calculate the Planck's constant.
(a) 4.27×10^{-34} (b) 3.60×10^{-34}
(c) 2.14×10^{-34} (d) 6.63×10^{-34}

88. A quantum numbers $+\frac{1}{2}$ and $-\frac{1}{2}$ for the electron spin represents.
(a) Rotation of the electron in clockwise and anticlockwise directions respectively
(b) Rotation of the electron in antoclockwise and clockwise direction respectively
(c) Magnetic movements of electron pointing up and down, respectively
(d) Two quantum mechanical spin states which have no classical analogoues

89. Rutherford's experiment, which established the nuclear model of atom, used a beam of
(a) β-particle, which impinged on a metal foil and got scattered
(b) γ-rays which impinged on a metal foil and got scattered
(c) helium atoms, which impinged on a metal foil and got scattered
(d) helium nuclei, which impigned on a metal foil and got scattered

90. If the nitrogen atom has electronic configuration $1s^7$. It would have energy lower than that of the normal ground state configuration $1s^2 2s^2 2p^3$, because the electrons would be closer to the nucleus. Yet $1s^7$ is not observed because it violates
(a) Heisenberg's uncertainty principle
(b) Hund's rule
(c) Pauli's exclusion principle
(d) Bohr's postulate of stationary orbit

91. The effective nuclear charge for 3*s* electrons in sulphur is
(a) 2.20 (b) 3.30 (c) 4.30 (d) 5.45

92. The effective nuclear charge for 4*s* electrons in potassium is
(a) 2.20 (b) 3.30
(c) 4.30 (d) 5.45

93. The effective nuclear charge for 3*d* and 4*s* electrons in vanadium is respectively
(a) 3.30 and 4.30 (b) 4.30 and 3.30
(c) 4.30 and 2.20 (d) 3.30 and 2.20

94. Energy of atoms and molecules as obtained by solving Schrodinger equation is expressed in Hartree. Value of 1 Hartree is equal to
(a) 27.2 eV
(b) 2 Rydberg
(c) $\frac{e^2}{a_0}$ where a_0 = Bohr's radius
(d) All of the above

95. Probability of finding an electron in a sphere of radius $r = a_0$ (Bohr radius) when 1*s* wave function of H-atom is

$$\psi_{1s} = \sqrt{\frac{1}{\pi a_0^3}}\, e^{-r/a_0} \text{ is}$$

(a) 1.0 (b) 2.71
(c) 0.0 (d) 0.323

96. The most probable distance at which 1*s* electron of H-like atom is found will be
(a) $\frac{Z}{a_0}$ (b) $\frac{Z^3}{a_0}$
(c) $\frac{a_0}{Z}$ (d) $\frac{a_0}{Z^3}$

97. de -Broglie wavelengths of a body of mass 1mg moving with a velocity of 10 m/s is
(a) 0.1226×10^{-20} nm (b) 5.8×10^5 m
(c) 3.4×10^{-30} m (d) 6.623×10^{-29} m

98. The factor $\frac{1}{4\pi\varepsilon_0}\frac{2\pi e^2}{Ch}$ is known as
(a) Rydberg constant (b) Planck's constant
(c) fine structure constant (d) work function

99. The average distance of the electron from the nucleus in the ground state of H-atom with normalised wave function $\psi_{1s} = \frac{1}{\sqrt{\pi}\, a_0^{3/2}} e^{-r/a_0}$ is
(a) a_0 (b) $\frac{a_0}{2}$
(c) $\frac{2a_0}{3}$ (d) $\frac{3}{2}a_0$

100. The average value of $\frac{1}{r}$ for an electron in 1*s*-orbital of H-atom where a_0 is Bohr's radius is
(a) a_0 (b) $2a_0$
(c) $\frac{a_0}{2}$ (d) $\frac{1}{a_0}$

Exercise 2
(For Part 'C')

1. The number of radial nodes of $3s$ and $2p$ orbitals are respectively
   (a) 2, 0 (b) 0, 2 (c) 1, 2 (d) 2, 1

2. Arrange the wavelengths (λ) of the following emission lines of H-atom in an increasing order
   (1) $n=3 \xrightarrow{\lambda_1} n=1$ (2) $n=5 \xrightarrow{\lambda_2} n=3$
   (3) $n=12 \xrightarrow{\lambda_3} n=10$ (4) $n=22 \xrightarrow{\lambda_4} n=20$
   (a) $\lambda_4 < \lambda_3 < \lambda_2 < \lambda_1$ (b) $\lambda_1 < \lambda_2 < \lambda_3 < \lambda_4$
   (c) $\lambda_1 < \lambda_2 < \lambda_4 < \lambda_3$ (d) $\lambda_1 < \lambda_3 < \lambda_4 < \lambda_2$

3. The size of an atomic nucleus is 10^{-14} m. What would be the uncertainty in speed (ms^{-1}) of an electron if it were to exist inside the nucleus? [$h = 6.625 \times 10^{-34}$ Js^{-1}, $m_e = 9.1 \times 10^{-31}$ kg]
   (a) 5.27×10^{-21} (b) 5.8×10^{-9}
   (c) 5.8×10^{9} (d) 1.725×10^{-10}

4. The de -Broglie's wavelength for an electron in 10th Bohr's orbit of H-atom is [$h = 6.625 \times 10^{-34}$ Js^{-1}, $m_e = 9.1 \times 10^{-31}$ kg and $a_0 = 0.529$ Å]
   (a) 33.2 Å (b) 16.6 Å (c) 66.4 Å (d) 332.4 Å

5. Which of the following was not concluded from Rutherford nuclear model of atom?
   (a) For a pure element, all the atoms are identical in mass, shape and size
   (b) Every atoms consists of a heavily, positively charged, centre in which entire mass of atom in concentrated
   (c) Negatively charged electrons revolve in circular orbits around the nucleus
   (d) This was the first model of established to existence of nucleus

6. Which of the following were observed in Rutherford experiment?
   (a) Most part of an atom is hollow
   (b) α-particle, due to its high mass and charge, suffers negligible deflection by an electron
   (c) A very few α-particles bounced back on their original path
   (d) Most of the α-particles suffer significant deflections from their original path

7. Which electronic transition in He^+ ion emits light of wavelength equal to the longest wavelength emitted in the Balmer series of Li^{2+} ion?
   (a) $4 \rightarrow 3$
   (b) $5 \rightarrow 3$
   (c) $3 \rightarrow 2$
   (d) No transition in He^+ matches this wavelengths

8. Which electronic transition in He^+ emits light of wavelength equal to the longest wavelength emitted in the Paschen series of H-atom?
   (a) $9 \rightarrow 6$ (b) $8 \rightarrow 6$ (c) $8 \rightarrow 5$ (d) $7 \rightarrow 3$

9. Which of the following statements concerning a radial wave function (ψ) of a H-like species is incorrect?
   (a) It has properties of standing wave
   (b) It changes sign when plotted against distance from nucleus
   (c) It is maximum at $r = 0$ (at nucleus)
   (d) It can have more than one maxima/minima when plotted against distance from nucleus

10. Which of the following statement concerning probability density (ψ^2) and radial distribution function ($4\pi r^2 \psi^2$) for a S-orbital of H-like species is correct?
    (a) ψ^2 is minimum at nucleus but $4\pi r^2 \psi^2$ is maximum at nucleus
    (b) ψ^2 is maximum at nucleus but $4\pi r^2 \psi^2$ is minimum at nucleus
    (c) Both ψ^2 and $4\pi r^2 \psi^2$ are maximum at nucleus
    (d) Both ψ^2 and $4\pi r^2 \psi^2$ are minimum at nucleus

11. Which of the following were concluded from Thomson's cathode ray discharged tube experiment?
    (a) Cathode rays are produced, have a characteristic independent of the identity of cathode
    (b) Electron is a fundamental particle present in the atoms of all elements
    (c) Electron has kinetic energy and therefore behaves like a particles
    (d) Conditions of pressure and temperature has no role to play in the experiment

12. Which statement(s) is/are correct regarding the photoelectric effect?
    (a) There is no electron ejection, regardless of intensity of the radiation unless the frequency, exceeds a Threshold value which is the characteistics of metals.
    (b) Kinetic energy of ejected electrons varies linearly with the frequency of incident radiation and its intensity
    (c) Even at low intensity, electrons are ejected immediately if the frequency of incident light is more than the threshold frequency
    (d) An intense and weak beam of monochromatic radiation differs in having number of photons and not in the energy of photons

13. If there were three possible values for spin quantum numbers $\left(+\frac{1}{2}, 0, -\frac{1}{2}\right)$ rather than the conventional two, which of the following is/are correct regarding a hypothetical Periodic Table based on this condition?
(a) First period would have only two vertical columns
(b) Second period would have 12 elements
(c) Periodic Table would have 27 groups
(d) Third period would have 12 elements

14. Which of the following is/are correct statement(s)?
(a) The ratio of wavelengths of *m*th and *n*th lines in Lyman series of a H-like species is

$$\frac{\lambda_m}{\lambda_m} = \left\{\frac{(m+1)^2}{(n+1)^2}\right\}\left\{\frac{(n+1)^2-1}{(m+1)^2-1}\right\}$$

(b) Kinetic energies of emitted electrons during photoelectric effect is lower than the energy of incident radiation
(c) Balmer lines are observed in visible region of electromagnetic spectrum for H-like species
(d) The scattering of α-particles involves a perfectly elastic collision

15. Consider the electronic configurations for the atoms

$$X \rightarrow [\text{Ar}]\,4s^1\;;(Y) \rightarrow [\text{Ar}]\,5s^1$$

Which of the following statement is/are incorrect?
(a) Energy is required to change *X* to *Y*
(b) *X* represents *K* atoms
(c) *X* and *Y* represent different elements
(d) More energy is required for removing an electron from *Y* and *X*

16. The number of regions of maximum probability is one for
(a) 1*s* (b) 3*p* (c) 3*d* (d) 4*f*

17. Which of the following is/are correct for an H-atom?
(a) $1s < 2p < 2p < 3s < 3p$ (b) $1s < 2s = 2p < 3s = 3p$
(c) $1s < 2p < 3d < 4s$ (d) $1s < 2s < 4s < 3d$

18. A sample of hydrogen atoms absorbs radiation of wavelength λ_0 and consequently emits radiations of six different wavelengths of which two wavelengths are shorter than λ_0. Choose the correct alternatives.
(a) The highest orbit occupied by the electron in the fourth orbit
(b) The initial orbit number of the electrons may be 2
(c) The initial orbit number of the electrons may be 3
(d) There are three transitions belonging to Lyman series

19. Let A_n be the area enclosed by *n*th orbit in the H-atom, the graph $\ln\left(\frac{A_n}{A_i}\right)$ against $\ln(n)$.
(a) will pass through origin
(b) will be straight line
(c) will be monotonically increasing non-linear curve
(d) will be a circle

20. Which of the followings are correct set of four quantum number for an electron in 4*d*-orbital?
(a) 4, 3, 2, $\frac{1}{2}$ (b) 4, 2, 1, 0
(c) 4, 2, − 2, $+\frac{1}{2}$ (d) 4, 2, 1, $-\frac{1}{2}$

21. Which of the followings are characteristics of wave function ψ?
(a) ψ must be single valued
(b) ψ must be finite and continuous
(c) $\int_{-\infty}^{+\infty} \psi^2\, dx\, dy\, dz = 1$
(d) ψ represents of standing wave

22. The number of scattered α-particles in Rutherford experiment is
(a) inversely proportional to square of kinetic energy of incident α-particle
(b) directly proportional to the square of atomic number (*Z*) of both the incidents α-particles(Z_α) and the target scattered [Z_t]
(c) directly proportional to the thickness of the thin target
(d) does not depend on the thickness of the thin target

23. If the Rutherford's experiment of α-particle scattering is repeated using β-particle, which of the following observations will be required to be corrected?
(a) Most part of atom is hollow
(b) Few β-particles will suffer large deflections from their original path
(c) Very few β-particles will bounce back on their original path
(d) Some thickness of the thin metal foil will work

24. Which of the following became basis of abandonment of Rutherford's nuclear model of atom?
(a) Classical theory of electromagnetic radiation
(b) Stability of the atom
(c) Failure to explain the emission spectrum of H-atom
(d) Electronegtivity of an atom

25. Which of the following were not taken into account in Bohr's model of an atom?
(a) Planck's quantum theory
(b) Stability of an atom
(c) Dual nature of electrons as wave and particle
(d) Results of Zeeman and Stark effects

26. According to Bohr's model
(a) energy of an electron is discrete-not continuous
(b) an electron revolves in a fixed orbit and does not loses energy during revolution
(c) angular momentum of an electron is quantized.
(d) when an electron jumps from a higher orbit to lower orbit. Energy equal to the energy of higher orbit's released in the form of photons

27. Which of the following is (are) true regarding a H-like species, on the basis of Bohr's model?

(a) Kinetic energy of an electron in nth Bohr orbit is $\dfrac{Ze^2}{8\pi\varepsilon_0 r}$

(b) Potential energy of an electron in nth Bohr's orbit $= -\dfrac{Ze^2}{4\pi\varepsilon_0 r}$

(c) Emission spectrum of H-atom is continuous

(d) Electron when passed through electric and magnetic field, get deflected.

28. Which of the following can be sets of four quantum numbers for the valence electrons of rubidium $(Z = 37)$?

(a) $n = 5, l = 0, m = 0, s = +\frac{1}{2}$

(b) $n = 5, l = 1, m = 0, s = +\frac{1}{2}$

(c) $n = 5, l = 1, m = 1, s = +\frac{1}{2}$

(d) $n = 5, l = 0, m = 0, s = -\frac{1}{2}$

29. If the radius of first Bohr's orbit of H-atom is X, which of the following is the correct conclusion?

(a) The de-Broglie wavelength in the third Bohr orbit of the H-atom $= 6\pi X$

(b) The fourth Bohr's radius of He^+ ion $= 8X$

(c) The de-Broglie wavelength in third Bohr's orbit of $Li^{2+} = 2X$

(d) The second Bohr's radius of $Be^{2+} = X$

30. If the shortest wavelength of transition of H-atom in Lyman series is X, then the correct conclusion is (are)

(a) The longest wavelength in Balmer series of He^+ is $\dfrac{X}{4}$

(b) The shortest wavelength in Balmer series of He^+ is X

(c) The longest wavelength in Lyman series of H-atom is $\frac{4}{3}X$

(d) The longest wavelength in Pashcen series of Li^{2+} is $\dfrac{16X}{7}$

31. The spin only magnetic moment of $V(Z = 23)$, $Cr(Z = 24)$ and Mn $(Z = 25)$ are X, Y and Z respectively. Which of the following is are correct relationship?

(a) $X > Y$ (b) $X > Z$

(c) $Y > Z$ (d) $X < Z$

32. Which of the followings can be concluded correctly from the solution of Schrodinger equation?

(a) For all orbitals, the radial wave-function (ψ) approaches to zero as r (distance from nucleus) approaches infinity

(b) The radial probability density (ψ^2) for 1s orbital is maximum at nucleus

(c) The radial distribution function $(4\pi r^2 \psi^2)$ for 1s orbital is minimum at nucleus

(d) In plot of radial wave function (ψ), ψ changes its sign at nodes

33. If the Aufbau principle is not followed, the first three quantum numbers (n, l and m) for the valence electron of K atom may take value

(a) $n = 3, l = 1, m = 0$ (b) $n = 3, l = 2, m = 0$

(c) $n = 3, l = 1, m = 1$ (d) $n = 3, l = 2, m = 1$

34. An electron in an atom can be located within 5×10^{-5} Å. Which of the following is/are true?

(a) The maximum uncertainty in its speed would be 10^{10}

(b) The uncertainty in measurements of kinetic energy would be 6.2×10^{-11} J

(c) Increasing frequency of light will increase uncertainty in position

(d) Decreasing frequency of light will increase in accuracy in measurement of speed

35. The uncertainties in measurement of position and momentum of an electron are equal. Choose the correct statement.

(a) The uncertainty in measurement of speed $= 8 \times 10^{12}$

(b) The uncertainty in measurement of kinetic energy $= \dfrac{h}{8\pi m}$

(c) The uncertainty in measurement of time $= 9.1 \times 10^{-31}$

(d) Increasing the wavelength of light used in the experiment will decrease uncertainty in position and increase the uncertainty in momentum

36. Which of the following graphs of radial part of wave-function (ψ) *versus* distance from nucleus is/are correctly labelled?

(a) 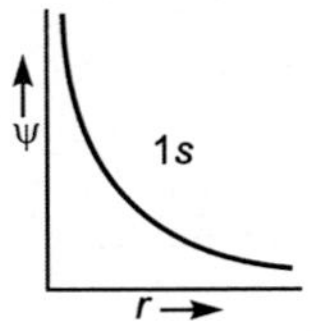

(b) 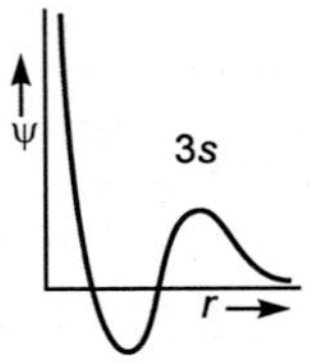

(c) 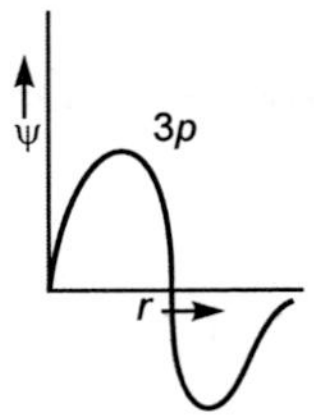

(d) 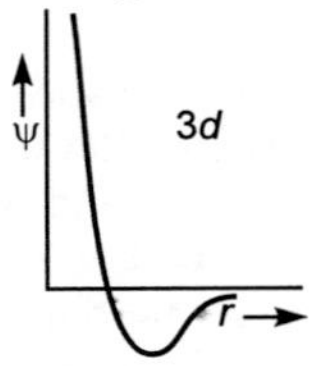

37. Which of the following plots of radial probability density (ψ^2) *versus* distance from nucleus is/are correctly labelled?

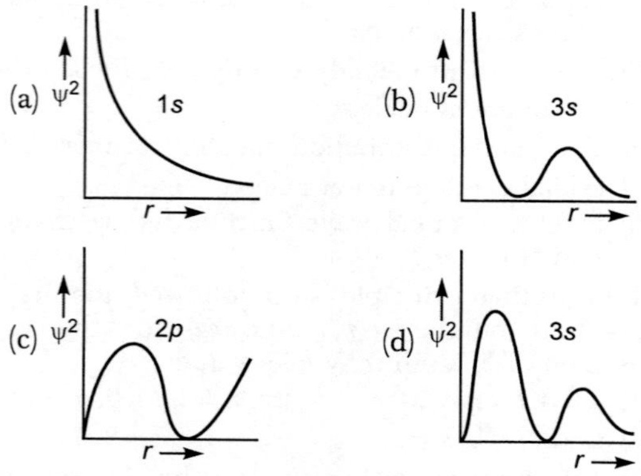

38. Which of the following plots of radial-probability function $4\pi r^2\psi^2$ is/are correctly labelled?

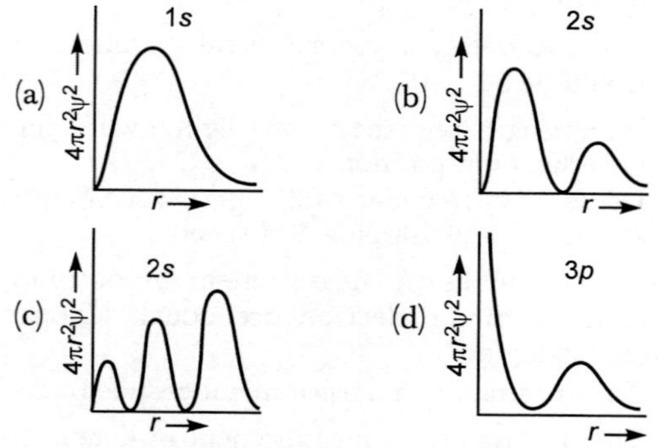

39. Which of the following can be concluded from the de-Broglie relationship?

(a) The kinetic energy of a de-Broglie electron of wavelength $\lambda = \dfrac{h^2}{2m\lambda^2}$

(b) The de-Broglie wavelength (λ) of an electron, after being accelerated by a potential difference of V volt, initially at rest $= \sqrt{\dfrac{h}{2meV}}$

(c) The number of de-Broglie waves formed in one complete revolution in a nth Bohr's orbit $= n$

(d) de-Broglie relation is derived from the observations of Zeeman and Stark effects exhibited by the electron in magnetic and electric fields, respectively

Assertion & Reason

Codes

(a) Both A and R are true and R is the correct explanation of A.

(b) Both A and R are true but R is not the correct explanation of A.

(c) A is true but R is false.

(d) A is false but R is true.

40. Assertion (A) Rutherford model of atom was discarded because it presented a model of unstable atom.

Reason (R) According to classical theory of electromagnetic radiation, moving charged body emits an energy continuously.

41. Assertion (A) Rutherford model predicted that most part of the atom is hollow.

Reason (R) High charge and mass of α-particles compared to the electron leads to negligible deflection in path of α-particles as they collide with electrons of an atom.

42. Assertion (A) Emission spectrum of a pure atom is line spectrum, not the continuous.

Reason Energy of the atoms are quantized.

43. Assertion (A) In the emission spectrum of hydrogen atom, lines are closely spaced in the region of large wavelengths.

Reason (R) In the reason of large wavelengths, electronic transitions occur more frequently.

44. Assertion (A) For 1*s* orbital of H-atom, the probability density (ψ^2) is maximum at nucleus but the probability of finding an electron $(4\pi r^2\psi^2)$is minimum at nucleus.

Reason (R) Nucleus has negligible volume compared to atomic volume.

45. Assertion (A) The maximum degeneracy of an electron for which azimuthal quantum number is '*l*' is$(2l+1)$.

Reason (R) For a given value of *l*, then magnetic quantum number (m) can have any value in the range of $-l \ldots 0 \ldots +l$.

46. Assertion (A) In the presence of electric and magnetic fields, the behaviour of cathode rays is not altered by changing the material of cathode.

Reason (R) The characteristics of cathode rays do not depend upon the material of cathode and nature of gases in the discharge tube.

47. Assertion (A) The radial wave function (ψ) for 1*s* atomic orbital is always greater than zero.

Reason (R) The radial part of wave function (ψ) never vanishes in the limit of finite value of distance (r) from nucleus.

48. Assertion (A) For H-atom, all Balmer lines in the emission spectrum have longer wavelengths than wavelength of any lines in Lyman series.

Reason (R) Transition energy is always greater what electrons come into an orbit with smaller '*n*' than in orbit with higher '*n*', no matter from which higher orbit the electron is coming.

49. Assertion (A) Orbital angular momentum for electron in *s*-orbital is zero.

Reason (R) For *s*-orbital, the value of azimuthal quantum number is zero.

50. Assertion (A) The energy of an electron depends only principal quantum number for H-atom and like species.

Reason (R) The energy of electron depends on azimuthal quantum number too for other non-hydrogen like species.

51. Assertion (A) The $3d_{x^2-y^2}$ orbital has zero probability of finding an electron along x and y axes.

Reason (R) The orbitals $d_{x^2-y^2}$ lies in x-y plane.

52. Assertion (A) The spin only magnetic moment of Zn is zero.

Reason (R) Electrons are lost from 4s atomic orbital leaving $3d^{10}$ configuration for Zn^{2+}.

53. Assertion (A) The two electrons is 1s orbital of He have anti-parallel spin.

Reason (R) One orbital cannot accommodate more than two electrons.

54. Assertion (A) Accurate measurement of both position and momentum can be done simultaneously for a macroparticle.

Reason (R) Heisenberg's uncertainty principle applicable of microparticles only.

55. Assertion (A) When a saddle of negligible mass and friction (revolving wheel about a fixed axis) is placed in the path of cathode rays in a discharge tube, it starts rotating.

Reason (R) Electrons have the properties of electromagnetic waves.

Matching Type

56. Match the following.

Column I		Column II	
I.	Velocity of an electron	p.	$-\frac{1}{(4\pi\varepsilon_0)^2}\frac{2\pi^2Z^2me^4}{n^2h^2}$
II.	Energy of electron in nth orbit	q.	$\frac{1}{(2\pi\varepsilon_0)}\frac{2\pi^2me^4}{h^3\cdot c}$
III.	Bohr's radius	r.	$4\pi\varepsilon_0\frac{h^2}{4\pi^2Zme^2}$
IV.	Rydberg equation	s.	$\frac{1}{4\pi\varepsilon_0}\frac{2\pi Ze^2}{nh}$

Codes

(a) I-r, II-p, III-q, IV-s
(b) I-s, II-p, III-r, IV-q
(c) I-r, II-s, III-p, IV-q
(d) I-p, II-q, III-r, IV-s

57. Match the following.

Column I		Column II	
I.	Short wavelength limit for Lyman series	p.	0.529 Å
II.	Bohr radius for H-atom for first orbit	q.	– 13.60 Å
III.	Bohr's radii for H-atom for second orbit	r.	2.12 Å
IV.	Energy of electron in first excited state in He^+ ion	s.	911.6 Å
		t.	1215 Å
		u.	+ 13.60 Å

Codes

(a) I-s, II-p, III-r, IV-u
(b) I-s, II-p, III-r, IV-q
(c) I-t, II-p, III-q, IV-r
(d) I-t, II-p, III-s, IV-r

Directions (Q.Nos. 58 to 61)
When two or more wave functions (eigen functions) belong to the same energy state *i.e.,* have the same energy, the energy level is said to be degenerate, *i.e.,* it is said to possess degeneracy 'g'. An energy level with $g=2$ is called to have two fold degenerate and energy level with $g=3$ is called three-fold degenerate and so on.

58. Unit of degeneracy is
(a) Joules (b) Rydberg
(c) cm^{-1} (d) dimensionless quantity

59. Degeneracy for H-atom in third energy state is
(a) 3 (b) 4 (c) 6 (d) 9

60. Degeneracy for H-atom in third excited state is
(a) 2 (b) 4
(c) 9 (d) 16

61. Degeneracy for rigid diatomic rotor in third rotational energy level is
(a) 4 (b) 5
(c) 6 (d) 9

Directions (Q.Nos. 62 and 63)
Bohr to account the stability of the atom introduced the concept of stationary orbits. Bohr postulated that : An atom consist of positively charged nucleus responsible for almost the entire mass of atom. The electrons revolve round the nucleus in certain permitted circular orbits of definite radii and permitted orbits are those for which angular momentum of an electron is integral multiple of $\frac{h}{2\pi}$.

62. Which of the following statement is true about Bohr's theory of H-atom?
(a) When electrons move in permittted discrete orbits they radiate energy
(b) Orbits radiating energy are called stationary orbits

(c) When electrons move in stationary orbits the radii of stationary orbits are directly proportional to the square of the principal quantum number

(d) $r_n = \dfrac{1}{4\pi\varepsilon_0} \dfrac{2\pi Z e^2}{n \cdot h}$

63. Radii of stationary orbits is equal to

(a) $4\pi\varepsilon_0 \dfrac{n^2 h^2}{4\pi^2 Z\, me}$ (b) $4\pi\varepsilon_0 \dfrac{nh^2}{4\pi^2 \cdot Z \cdot me^2}$

(c) $\dfrac{4\pi\varepsilon_0}{4\pi^2} \dfrac{n^2 h^2}{Zme^2}$ (d) $4\pi\varepsilon_0 \dfrac{nh}{4\pi^2 Z\, me^2}$

Directions (Q. Nos. 64 to 67)
According to Bohr, the spectrum arises when electron in the initial stationary orbit of principal quantum number n_i jumps to the final stationary orbit of principal quantum number n_f $(n_i > n_f)$ so,the difference of energy associated with these orbit is emitted as a photon of frequency ν.

64. The Rydberg constant of hydrogen atom is

(a) $\dfrac{1}{(4\pi\varepsilon_0)^2} \cdot \dfrac{2\pi^2 me^4}{h^2 c}$ (b) $\dfrac{1}{(4\pi\varepsilon_0)^2} \cdot \dfrac{2\pi^2 me^4}{h^3 c}$

(c) $\dfrac{1}{(2\pi\varepsilon_0)^2} \cdot \dfrac{2\pi^2 me^4}{h^2 c}$ (d) $\dfrac{1}{(2\pi\varepsilon_0)^2} \cdot \dfrac{2\pi^2 me^4}{h^3 c}$

65. The wave number of photons of spectral lines when electron jumps from higher to first energy state is

(a) $\bar{v} = R_H \left[1 - \dfrac{1}{n_i^2}\right]$ (b) $\bar{v} = R_H [n_i^2 - 1]$

(c) $\bar{v} = R_H [n_f^1 - 1]$ (d) $\bar{v} = R_H \left[\dfrac{1}{n_f^2} - 1\right]$

66. Paschen series lies in
(a) UV region (b) IR region
(c) visible region (d) microwave region

67. The spectral lines corresponding to transition of electron from some higher energy to lower energy state corresponding to $n_f = 2$ is
(a) Lyman (b) Balmer (c) Pfund (d) Paschen

Answers

Exercise 1

1. (c)	**2.** (b)	**3.** (b)	**4.** (b)	**5.** (b)	**6.** (a)	**7.** (b)	**8.** (a)	**9.** (c)	**10.** (c)
11. (b)	**12.** (a)	**13.** (c)	**14.** (a)	**15.** (c)	**16.** (c)	**17.** (d)	**18.** (c)	**19.** (a)	**20.** (c)
21. (d)	**22.** (d)	**23.** (a)	**24.** (b)	**25.** (c)	**26.** (d)	**27.** (b)	**28.** (d)	**29.** (d)	**30.** (a)
31. (d)	**32.** (d)	**33.** (b)	**34.** (d)	**35.** (d)	**36.** (d)	**37.** (a)	**38.** (d)	**39.** (a)	**40.** (d)
41. (d)	**42.** (d)	**43.** (b)	**44.** (b)	**45.** (b)	**46.** (b)	**47.** (b)	**48.** (c)	**49.** (a)	**50.** (b)
51. (c)	**52.** (d)	**53.** (b)	**54.** (d)	**55.** (b)	**56.** (a)	**57.** (c)	**58.** (c)	**59.** (c)	**60.** (d)
61. (c)	**62.** (b)	**63.** (c)	**64.** (d)	**65.** (c)	**66.** (b)	**67.** (a)	**68.** (d)	**69.** (b)	**70.** (a)
71. (d)	**72.** (d)	**73.** (d)	**74.** (a)	**75.** (a)	**76.** (a)	**77.** (d)	**78.** (a)	**79.** (d)	**80.** (b)
81. (d)	**82.** (d)	**83.** (d)	**84.** (b)	**85.** (d)	**86.** (c)	**87.** (a)	**88.** (d)	**89.** (d)	**90.** (c)
91. (d)	**92.** (a)	**93.** (b)	**94.** (d)	**95.** (d)	**96.** (c)	**97.** (d)	**98.** (c)	**99.** (d)	**100.** (d)

Exercise 2

1. (a)	**2.** (b)	**3.** (c)	**4.** (a)	**5.** (c)	**6.** (a,b,c)	**7.** (d)	**8.** (b)	**9.** (c)	**10.** (b)
11. (a,b,c)	**12.** (a,b,c,d)	**13.** (b,c,d)	**14.** (b,d)	**15.** (a,b,d)	**16.** (b)	**17.** (b,c)	**18.** (a,b,d)	**19.** (a,b)	**20.** (d)
21. (a,b,c,d)	**22.** (a,b,c)	**23.** (c,d)	**24.** (a,b)	**25.** (c,d)	**26.** (a,b,c)	**27.** (a,b)	**28.** (a,d)	**29.** (a,b)	**30.** (b,c,d)
31. (c,d)	**32.** (a,b,c,d)	**33.** (b,d)	**34.** (a,b,d)	**35.** (a,b,c)	**36.** (a,b)	**37.** (a,b)	**38.** (a,c)	**39.** (a,c)	**40.** (a)
41. (a)	**42.** (b)	**43.** (c)	**44.** (a)	**45.** (a)	**46.** (a)	**47.** (b)	**48.** (a)	**49.** (a)	**50.** (d)
51. (d)	**52.** (a)	**53.** (b)	**54.** (a)	**55.** (b)	**56.** (b)	**57.** (b)	**58.** (d)	**59.** (d)	**60.** (d)
61. (b)	**62.** (c)	**63.** (c)	**64.** (d)	**65.** (a)	**66.** (b)	**67.** (b)			

Hints & Solutions

Exercise 1

3. $$E_k = \frac{1}{4\pi\varepsilon_0} \cdot \frac{Ze^2}{2r}$$

$$E_{total} = -\frac{1}{4\pi\varepsilon_0} \cdot \frac{Ze^2}{2r}$$

$$\Rightarrow \quad \frac{E_k}{E_{total}} = -1$$

5. For ground state energy of H atom $(n = 1)$

$$E = -\frac{13.6}{n^2} \text{ eV} = -\frac{13.6}{1^2} \text{ eV} = -13.6 \text{ eV}$$

For first excited state of He^+ion $(n = 2, Z = 2)$

$$E = -\frac{13.6}{n^2} \cdot Z^2 \text{ eV} = -\frac{13.6 \cdot (2)^2}{(2)^2} = -13.6 \text{ eV}$$

8. Since, atomic number of atom

$$M = 2 + 2 + 6 + 2 + 6 + 10 + 2 + 5$$
$$= 35$$

So, chemistry of M is similar to chlorine.

15. $$E_{total} = -\frac{1}{4\pi\varepsilon_0} \cdot \frac{Ze^2}{2r} < 0$$

18. $$\frac{d_{atom}}{d_{nucleus}} = \frac{10^{-10} \text{ m}}{10^{-14} \text{ m}} = 10^4$$

26. $$v_n \propto \frac{C}{n}$$

$$\Rightarrow \quad \frac{v_5}{v_1} = \frac{1}{5}$$

$$\Rightarrow \quad v_5 = \frac{v_1}{5} = \frac{\frac{C}{100}}{5} \qquad \left(\because v_1 = \frac{C}{100}\right)$$

$$= \frac{C}{500} = 0.002 \text{ C}$$

29. $$\lambda = \frac{hc}{E} = \frac{6.6 \times 10^{-34} \text{ J-s} \times 3 \times 10^8 \text{ m-s}^{-2}}{1.0 \times 1.6 \times 10^{-19} \text{ J}}$$

$$= 12000 \times 10^{-10} \text{ m} = 12000 \text{Å}$$

41. $$\Delta p \times \Delta x \geq \frac{h}{4\pi}$$

$$\Delta p = \frac{h}{\Delta x}$$

$$\Delta x \longrightarrow 0$$

$$\Delta p \longrightarrow \infty$$

52. $$\Delta E \times \Delta t \geq \frac{h}{4\pi}$$

$$\Delta E \geq \frac{h}{4\pi \Delta t} \cdot \geq \frac{6.6 \times 10^{-34}}{4 \times 3.14 \times 10^{-8}} \text{J}$$

$$\geq 0.52 \times 10^{-26} \text{ J}$$

$$\geq 0.521^{-19} \text{ erg } (\because 1 \text{Joule} = 10^7 \text{ erg})$$

58. $$\lambda = \frac{h}{mv} = \frac{6.6 \times 10^{-34} \text{ J-s}}{(200 \times 10^{-3} \text{ kg}) \times \left(\frac{5 \text{m}}{3600 \text{ s}}\right)}$$

$$= 10^{-30} \text{ m (approx)}$$

68. For H atom, ionisation energy $\Delta E = E_\infty - E_1 = 0 - \left(-\frac{13.6}{1^2}\right)$

$$= 13.6 \text{ eV}$$

For He^+ ion, ionisation energy $\Delta E = E_\infty - E_1$

$$= 0 - \left(-\frac{13.6}{n^2} \cdot Z^2\right)$$

$$= \frac{13.6}{12} \cdot (2)^2 = 54.4 \text{ eV}$$

Hence, $\quad (IP)_{He^+} > (IP)_H$

74. For electron $\quad v = \frac{h}{m_e \lambda} \quad$ ...(i)

For proton $\quad v' = \frac{h}{m_p \cdot \lambda} \quad$ ...(ii)

$$\Rightarrow \quad \frac{v'}{v} = \frac{m_e}{m_p}$$

$$\Rightarrow \quad v' = \frac{v}{1840} \qquad \left(\because \frac{m_e}{m_p} = \frac{1}{1840}\right)$$

Exercise 2

2. For higher values of n, the energy gap between consecutive energy levels decreases and wavelength increases as $\Delta E \propto \frac{1}{\lambda}$.

So, $\quad \lambda_1, < \lambda_2 < \lambda_3 < \lambda_4$

4. $$v = \frac{0.22 \times 10^7 Z}{n} \text{ m/s}$$

$$= \frac{0.22 \times 10^7 \times 1}{10} \qquad (\because n = 10, Z = 1)$$

$$= 0.22 \times 10^6 \text{ m/s}$$

$$\lambda = \frac{h}{mv} = \frac{6.6 \times 10^{-34}}{9.1 \times 10^{-31} \times 0.22 \times \times 10^6}$$

$$= 33.2 \times 10^{-10} \text{m} = 33.2 \text{ Å}$$

7. For $Li^{2+}, Z = 3$ and $He^+ Z = 2$. Hence, no transition in He^+ matches this wavelength.

30. For shortest wavelength of Lyman series of H-atom is

$$\frac{1}{\lambda} = R\left(\frac{1}{1^2} - \frac{1}{\infty^2}\right) = R$$

$$\Rightarrow \quad \frac{1}{X} = R$$

$$\Rightarrow \quad X = \frac{1}{R} \qquad \text{...(i)}$$

(a) $$\frac{1}{\lambda_1} = RZ^2\left(\frac{1}{2^2} - \frac{1}{3^2}\right) = R\cdot(2)^2\left(\frac{5}{36}\right)$$

$$\frac{1}{\lambda_1} = \frac{5}{9}R$$

$$\Rightarrow \quad \lambda_1 = \frac{9}{5}X \qquad \text{[Using Eq. (i)]}$$

(b) $$\frac{1}{\lambda_2} = RZ^2\left(\frac{1}{2^2} - \frac{1}{\infty^2}\right) = R\cdot(2)^2 \times \frac{1}{2^2} = R$$

$$\lambda_2 = \frac{1}{R}$$

$$\Rightarrow \quad \lambda_2 = X \qquad \text{[Using Eq. (v)]}$$

(c) $$\frac{1}{\lambda_3} = R\left(\frac{1}{1^2} - \frac{1}{2^2}\right) = R\cdot\frac{3}{4}$$

$$\lambda_3 = \frac{4}{3R} = \frac{4}{3}X \qquad \text{[Using Eq. (i)]}$$

(d) $$\frac{1}{\lambda_4} = RZ^2\left(\frac{1}{3^2} - \frac{1}{4^2}\right) = R\cdot(3)^3\left(\frac{7}{16\times 9}\right) = \frac{7R}{16}$$

$$\lambda_4 = \frac{16}{7}X \qquad \text{[Using Eq. (i)]}$$

42. Assertion and reason both are true but reason is not the correct explanation.

50. $$E_n = -\frac{13.6Z^2}{n^2}\text{ eV} \qquad \text{...(i)}$$

$$E_n = -\frac{2\pi^2 Z^2 e^4}{h^2 (n_r + k)^2}\cdot\frac{m}{\left(1+\frac{m}{M}\right)} \qquad \text{...(ii)}$$

From Eq. (i) and (ii) it is clear that assertion is false and reason is true.

55. Due to kinetic energy of electrons, the saddle rotates and according to de -Broglie hypothesis moving electrons have the properties of waves.

So, the assertion and reason both are true but the reason is not the correct explanation of assertion.

18

Chemical Bonding in Diatomics

Syllabus

- Wave Mechanical Model, Variation Principle
- Elementary Concepts of MO and VB Theories; Huckel Theory for Conjugated π-electron Systems
- Dipole Moment, Hydrogen Bonding

Introduction

The idea of chemical bonding between two atoms based on sharing of electrons was given by G.N. Lewis in 1916. The Lewis picture of bonding is still relevant today but the quantum mechanical formulation, incorporating de-Broglie's wave particle duality, Pauli's exclusion principle and Heisenberg's uncertainty principle, gave a deeper insight into the nature of the chemical bond.

Broadly, there are two types of bonds between atoms :

1. **The ionic bond** in which electrons are transferred between atoms and the bond arises from the coulombic interactions between the resulting ions.
2. **The covalent bond** in which electron pairs are shared more or less equally between neighbouring atoms. The idea of **dative bond** or **covalent-coordinate bond,** in which one partner donates both the electrons of the shared pair, symbolized by $B \rightarrow A$, is now obsolete and the term 'covalent bond' signifies that a bond has been formed by electron-sharing irrespective of the donor of the electron pair.

Covalent bonds are also classified as single, double or triple. A single bond consists of one shared pair of electrons; a double bond consists of two shared pairs of electrons and a triple bond consists of three shared pairs of electrons. Quadruple bonds containing four shared pairs of electrons are rarely encountered though they occur quite frequently in the transition metal clusters.

Modern theories of chemical bonding have largely dispensed with the distinction between the various types of bonds. They consider bonding as a consequence of the lowering of energy that occurs when electrons occupy molecular orbitals that spread overall the atoms in the molecule. The bonding influence of an electron pair, according to MOT, may be distributed over many atoms. In fact, an electron-pair is not essential to bond formation but merely represents the maximum number of electrons that can occupy a given orbital thereby contributing to bonding.

Wave Mechanical Treatment of Covalent Bond

The Lewis concept of covalent bond based on sharing of electrons satisfactorily explains the bonding between atoms all of which have a tendency to gain electrons in order to acquire the stable noble gas configurations.

It cannot answer a number of questions such as

1. Why a covalent bond is formed at all?
2. How do the electrons distribute themselves in space around the central atom in a molecule?
3. What are the forces of attractive interaction in a covalent molecule?

Wave mechanics has provided satisfactory answers to most of these questions and has led ultimately to the development of more comprehensive theories of covalent bonding. These theories are : 1. **The Valence Bond Theory.** 2. **The Molecular Orbital Theory.** But, before we discuss the two theories, it would be worthwhile to elucidate the **wave mechanical principles** which are involved in their treatment. These principles are

1. If ψ_1 is a solution of the wave equation $\hat{\mathbf{H}}\psi = E\psi$, then $c_1\psi_1$ is also the solution of the same wave equation where c_1 is a constant known as coefficient of the wave function. This means that ψ_1 and $c_1\psi_1$ give the same value of energy E.
2. If ψ_1 and ψ_2 are separately the solutions of the wave equation $\hat{\mathbf{H}}\psi = E\psi$, then $c_1\psi_1$, $c_2\psi_2$ and $c_1\psi_1 \pm c_2\psi_2$ are also the solutions of the same wave equation. This means that $\psi_1, \psi_2, c_1\psi_1, c_2\psi_2$ and $c_1\psi_1 \pm c_2\psi_2$ would give the same value of energy E. The squares of the coefficients, *viz.* c_1^2 and c_2^2 give the contributions of ψ_1 and ψ_2, respectively, to the total wave function.
3. Several methods have been devised for finding out approximate ψ closest to the true ψ and the corresponding approximate energy closest to the true energy of multi-electron and multi-nucleus systems. One such method is based on the **variation principle.**

The Variation Principle

Consider the wave equation $\hat{\mathbf{H}}\psi = E\psi$. Multiplying each side of the wave equation by ψ and integrating it throughout the space, we get

$$\int_{-\infty}^{+\infty} \psi\hat{\mathbf{H}}\psi\, d\tau = \int_{-\infty}^{+\infty} \psi\, E\psi\, d\tau \qquad \ldots(1)$$

$$= E\int_{-\infty}^{+\infty} \psi^2 d\tau \quad (\because E \text{ is constant}) \qquad \ldots(2)$$

where, $d\tau$ is a small space element.

From Eq. (2)

$$E = \int_{-\infty}^{+\infty} \psi\hat{\mathbf{H}}\psi\, d\tau \Big/ \int_{-\infty}^{+\infty} \psi\, d\tau \qquad \ldots(3)$$

Thus, energy E of the system can be calculated if we know true ψ. If we do not true ψ, even then we can guess a wave function which is close to the true wave function ψ by using our chemical intuition. If this **approximate wave function** is ψ_1, then Eq. (3) takes the form

$$\varepsilon = \int_{-\infty}^{+\infty} \psi_1\, \hat{\mathbf{H}}\psi_1\, d\tau \Big/ \int_{-\infty}^{+\infty} \psi_1^2 d\tau \qquad \ldots(4)$$

where ε, known as **energy function,** will have the dimensions of energy but will **not be equal** to the true energy of the system.

According to the variation principle, if we are able to guess at a number of wave functions ψ_1, ψ_2, ψ_3, etc., which are thought to be close approximations of the true wave function ψ, then we can calculate the energy functions, ε_1, ε_2, ε_3 etc., with the help of Eq. (4). In such a case

1. All the energy functions calculated as above would have **higher values** than the true energy of the system.
2. Out of ε_1, ε_2, ε_3, etc., the energy function with the minimum value would be closest to the true energy E.
3. The wave function which gives the minimum value of energy function is the closest approximation of the true wave function ψ.

The approximate ψ can also be calculated with the help of **Ritz linear combination method** which too is based on the variation principle. Suppose we have reasons to believe that the wave function ψ has some characteristic of a known wave function ψ_1 and some characteristics of another known wave function ψ_2. The wave function ψ can then be written as a **linear combination** of ψ_1 and ψ_2, *i.e.*, as $\psi = c_1\psi_1 + c_2\psi_2$. Accordingly.

Energy function,

$$\varepsilon = \int_{-\infty}^{+\infty} \psi\hat{\mathbf{H}}\psi\, d\tau \Big/ \int_{-\infty}^{+\infty} \psi^2\, d\tau \qquad \ldots(5)$$

$$= \int_{-\infty}^{+\infty} (c_1\psi_1 + c_2\psi_2)\hat{\mathbf{H}}(c_1\psi_1 + c_2\psi_2)\, d\tau \Big/ \int_{-\infty}^{+\infty} (c_1\psi_1 + c_2\psi_2)^2\, d\tau \qquad \ldots(6)$$

The coefficient c_1 and c_2 are so adjusted in the total wave function ψ as to yield a **minimum value** of ε. **This is done by differentiating Eq. (6) with respect of c_1 and also with respect to c_2 and then putting $\partial\varepsilon/\delta c_1 = 0$ and also $\delta\varepsilon/\delta c_2 = 0$, as these are the conditions for minimization of ε. By doing so we get two equations containing ε, c_1 and c_2. From**

these, we can derive a quadratic equation in ε. The solutions of this quadratic equation gives ε, c_1 and c_2. Similarly, if we have reasons to believe that the true wave function ψ has characteristics of known wave functions ψ_1, ψ_2, ψ_3, etc., the actual ψ can then be written as $\psi = c_1\psi_1 + c_2\psi_2 + c_3\psi_3 + ...$ The coefficients c_1, c_2, c_3, etc., are so adjusted as to yield minimum value of the energy function.

This method has an advantage that if we guess at a wrong wave function (ψ_i), its coefficient (c_i) would automatically come out to be zero.

With the help of the wave mechanical principles elucidated above, it is possible to discuss at length the valence bond and the molecular orbital theories of covalent bonding.

Valence Bond Theory

The valence bond theory was first put forward by W.Heitler and F.London and extended further by J.C.Slater and L.Pauling. The theory utilises the following wave mechanical principles

1. If ψ_A and ψ_B are the wave functions for any two completely independent (non-interacting) systems *A* and *B*, then the total wave function ψ for these independent systems, taken together, would be given by :

$$\psi = \psi_A \psi_B \qquad ...(7)$$

and the total energy *E* of these non-interacting systems and the total Hamiltonian can be given as

$$E = E_A + E_B \text{ and } \hat{\mathbf{H}} = \hat{\mathbf{H}}_A + \hat{\mathbf{H}}_B$$

2. If the wave function for a many-electrons system has characteristics of several wave functions $\psi_1, \psi_2, \psi_3 ..... \psi_n$, then according to the Ritz principle of linear combination, the wave function ψ closest to the true wave function of the system is given by

$$\psi = c_1\psi_1 + c_2\psi_2 + c_3\psi_3 + ... c_n\psi_n \qquad ...(8)$$

where, $c_1, c_2 ... c_n$ are the various coefficients. As already mentioned, the square of the coefficient of a particular wave function gives the contribution of that wave function, generally called the **weightage** of that wave function, to the total wave function. These coefficients are so adjusted as to give a state of lowest energy, *i.e.*, a state of maximum stability. The function ψ should be normalised so that

$$c_1^2 + c_2^2 + c_3^2 + ... = 1 \qquad ...(9)$$

Valence bond theory can be elucidated by taking into consideration the formation of H_2 molecule.

Formation of Hydrogen Molecule

Consider two hydrogen atoms lying far apart from each other so that no interaction between them is possible. Let *A* and *B* represent the nuclei and e_1 and e_2 the two electrons. The two atoms of hydrogen may thus be represented as $H_A(e_1)$ and $H_B(e_2)$.

Let the wave functions for the electron (1) and (2) in the separated atoms be represented by $\psi_A(1)$ and ψ_B (2) respectively. According to Eq. (7) the combined wave function ψ for the two separated atoms of hydrogen can be written as

$$\psi = \psi_A(1)\psi_B(2) \qquad ...(10)$$

When the two atoms are brought closer together, their energy changes and consequently, the energy operator $\hat{\mathbf{H}}$ also changes. Assuming that the combined wave function ψ, as represented by Eq. (10) still describes the wave function for H_2 molecule, the energy of the hydrogen molecule, following Eq. (3) would be given by

$$E = \int_{-\infty}^{+\infty} \psi_A(1)\psi_B(2)\hat{\mathbf{H}}\psi_A(1)\psi_B(2)\,d\tau \Big/ \int_{-\infty}^{+\infty} [\psi_A(1)\psi_B(2)]^2\,d\tau... \qquad ...(11)$$

The energy changes that take place as the two H atoms are gradually brought closer to each other are shown graphically in Fig. (1).

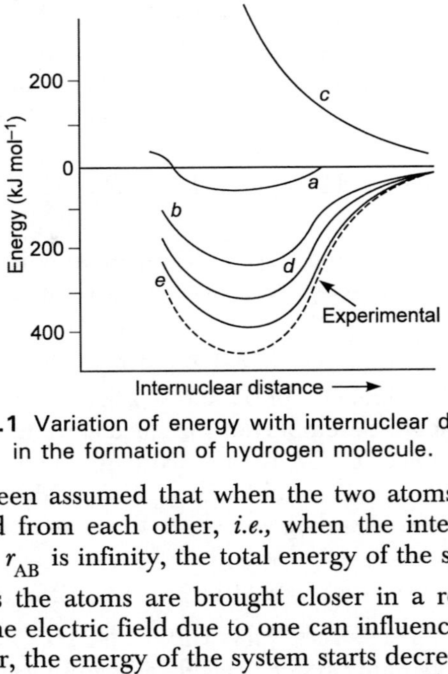

Fig. 18.1 Variation of energy with internuclear distance in the formation of hydrogen molecule.

It has been assumed that when the two atoms are far removed from each other, *i.e.,* when the internuclear distance r_{AB} is infinity, the total energy of the system is zero. As the atoms are brought closer in a region in which the electric field due to one can influence that of the other, the energy of the system starts decreasing till a certain minimum value is reached. This stage corresponds to the formation of H_2 molecule. The internuclear distance at this stage is designated as r_0.

When we calculate the energy of the system of the two hydrogen atoms by using Eq. (11) and plot these energies as a function of internuclear distance, the curve a is obtained. The bonding energy given by the minimum in potential energy curve a is only 24 kJ mol^{-1}. This is too far below the experimental value of 458 kJ mol^{-1} (represented by the minimum in the **dotted curve**). Moreover, the minimum is found at an internuclear distance of about 0.90 Å (curve a) whereas the experimental bond distance in hydrogen molecule is 0.74 Å. Evidently, the wave function $\psi_A(1)\psi_B(2)$, as applied to H_2 system, is not a good approximation. Apparently, some other interactions between the two hydrogen atoms are required to be taken into consideration to arrive at the correct wave function for the combined H_2 system. Some of these interactions are as follows.

1. Exchange of electrons

In arriving at Eq. (11), we had assumed that the electrons of the two hydrogen atoms could be distinguished from each other and therefore, the electron around nucleus *A* was labelled as e_1 and that around nucleus *B* was labelled as e_2. This assumption, however, is not correct because when a bond is formed, the two atomic orbitals overlap and the two electrons become indistinguishable from each other. We can no longer be sure that electron 1 will always be near the nucleus *A* and electron 2 will always be near the nucleus *B*. The system of two hydrogen atoms may then be represented by two different states, I and II, as shown below :

$$\underset{\text{(I)}}{H_A(e_1)H_B(e_2)} \qquad \underset{\text{(II)}}{H_A(e_2)H_B(e_1)}$$

If ψ_I and ψ_{II} are the wave functions representing states I and II, respectively, then, according to Eq. (9) we can write

$$\psi_I = \psi_A(1)\psi_B(2) \text{ and } \psi_{II} = \psi_A(2)\psi_B(1)$$

A linear combination of ψ_I and ψ_{II} (and not ψ_I or ψ_{II} alone) should be employed for calculating the energy of H_2 molecule. There are evidently two possible modes of linear combination, *viz.,* **additive and subtractive** according to which there are two wave functions, *viz.,* ψ_+ and ψ_-, given by

$$\psi_+ = \psi_I + \psi_{II} = \psi_A(1)\psi_B(2) + \psi_A(2)\psi_B(1) \ldots (12)$$

and $$\psi_- = \psi_I - \psi_{II} = \psi_A(1)\psi_B(2) - \psi_A(2)\psi_B(1) \ldots (13)$$

The energy of the system, calculated by using ψ_+ in the wave equation is shown by the curve b while that calculated from ψ_- is shown by the curve c in Fig. (1).

It is evident that ψ_-leads to increase of energy. Thus, bonding is not possible in ψ_-. We may, therefore, regard ψ_- as **repulsive state**. The wave function ψ_+, however, leads to fall of energy. Thus, bonding is possible in this state. We may, therefore, regard ψ_+ as a **bonding state**.

The wave function ψ_+ (Eq. (12) which represents the *bonding state* is also referred to as a **covalent wave function**. Therefore, it may be written as $\psi_{covalent}$. The reason for this terminology is that in state I as well as in state II, there is equal distribution of charge on both the nuclei *A* and *B*.

As mentioned above, the bonding energy calculated from Eq. (11). is only 24 kJ mol^{-1}. The bonding energy corresponding to ψ_+ (Eq. (12)) is 303 kJ mol^{-1} and the internuclear distance is 0.80 Å. The additional energy resulting from the exchange of electrons between the two hydrogen atoms is called the **exchange energy.** Thus, 303–24 = 279 kJ mol^{-1} is the exchange energy for H_2 molecule.

2. Screening effect of electrons

The wave function given by Eq. (12) is further improved by considering the screening effect of the electrons. When the two atoms come close to each other, the electron of one atom shields the electron of the other atom from the nucleus so that the electrons do not feel the full charge of the nucleus. The actual charge felt by an electron is termed as its effective nuclear charge. This will be, evidently, less than the actual nuclear charge. If we use the effective nuclear charge and improve the wave function given by Eq. (12) bonding energy of 365 kJ mol^{-1} is obtained. This is deplicted by the minimum in the curved *d.*

3. Ionic character of H—H bond

The bond energy of 365 kJ mol^{-1} is still appreciably smaller than the experimental value of 458 kJ mol^{-1}. This shows that ψ_+ still does not give the true wave function for H_2 molecule. An additional factor that has been suggested is the possibility that **momentarily both the electrons may simultaneously be present close to one nucleus or the other. This gives rise to ionic configurations** represented by states III and IV :

$$\underset{\text{III}}{\overset{e_2}{(e_1)H_A}H_B} \qquad \underset{\text{(IV)}}{H_A\overset{(e_2)}{H_B(e_1)}}$$

These two ionic structures may be represented as $H_A^-H_B^+$ and $H_A^+H_B^-$, respectively. However, the coulombic repulsion between the two electrons present so close to each other would far exceed the coulombic attraction between H_A^- and H_B^+ or between H_A^+ and H_B^-. This reduces the probability of the existence of these additional structures to a base minimum. Nevertheless, the incorporation of these structures as resonance structures does increase the stability of the hydrogen molecule and hence its bond energy.

The states III and IV are, amongst themselves, equally probable and the wave functions corresponding to state III (ψ_{III}) and state IV (ψ_{IV}) may be expressed as

$$\psi_{III} = \psi_A(1)\psi_A(2) \quad \ldots(14)$$

and

$$\psi_{IV} = \psi_B(1)\psi_B(2) \quad \ldots(15)$$

The total ionic wave function ψ_{ionic} may be expressed as a linear combination of ψ_{III} and ψ_{IV}, as

$$\psi_{ionic} = \psi_A(1)\psi_A(2) + \psi_B(1)\psi_B(2) \quad \ldots(16)$$

However, states III and IV are less probable than states I and II as the two electrons present on the same H atom would repel each other and make states III and IV less likely compared to states I and II.

Considering the possibilities of covalent as well as ionic structures, the combined wave function for H_2 molecule is written as

$$\psi = \psi_{covalent} + \lambda\psi_{ionic}$$
$$= [\psi_A(1)\,\psi_B(2) + \psi_A(2)\psi_B(1)] + \lambda\,[\psi_A(1)\psi_A(2) + \psi_B(1)\psi_B(2)] \quad \ldots(17)$$

where λ gives the extent to which the ionic structures contribute to the bonding. For H_2, λ is calculated to be 0.17. Knowing λ, we can find out the extent of the contribution of the ionic structures. The fraction λ is called the **mixing coefficient.**

With all these modifications, the calculated bond energy comes out to be about 388 kJ mol^{-1} which can be considered as reasonably close to the experimental value of 458 kJ mol^{-1}. The internuclear distance between hydrogen atoms now comes out to be 0.75 Å which is quite close to the experimental value of 0.74 Å.

Bond energies and bond lengths for H_2 molecule corresponding to various wave functions are summed up in Table 18.1.

Table 18.1 **Bond Energies and Bond Lengths for H_2 Molecule Corresponding to Various Wave Functions**

Wave function	Bond energy (kJ mol^{-1})	Bond length (Å)
$\psi = \psi_A(1)\psi_B(2)$	24	0.90
$\psi_{covalent} = \psi_A(1)\psi_B(2) + \psi_A(2)\psi_B(1)$	303	0.80
$\psi_{covalent}$ with screening effect	365	0.76
$\psi = \psi_{covalent} + \lambda\,\psi_{ionic} = [\psi_A(1)\psi_B(2) + \psi_A(2)\,\psi_B(1)] + \lambda[\psi_A(1)\psi_A(2) + \psi_B(1)\psi_B(2)]$	388	0.75
Experimental values	**458**	**0.74**

Example 1. *Write down the valence bond wave function for the HF molecule (assuming that it is formed from 1s orbital of H and $2p_z$ orbital of F) in the following three cases : (a) HF is purely covalent (b) HF is purely ionic and (c) HF is 80% covalent and 20% ionic.*

Sol. Let, the H atom be represented by *A* and F atom by *B*. Let, the electron numbered 1 be the 1*s* electron of H atom and the electron numbered 2 be the p_z electron of F atom.

(a) For purely covalent structure of HF, the wave function is written as

$$\psi_{covalent} = \phi_A(1)\,\phi_B(2) + \phi_A(2)\,\phi_B(1)$$

(b) For purely ionic structure H^+F^-, both the electrons are on the F atom so that

$$\psi_{ionic} = \phi_B(1)\,\phi_B(2)$$

(c) HF is a resonance hybrid shown as

$$\text{H—F} \longleftrightarrow \text{H}^+\text{F}^-$$

∴ $\psi = c_1\psi_{covalent} + c_2\psi_{ionic}$ with $c_1^2 + c_2^2 = 1$

Since, $c_1^2 = 0.80$

and $c_2^2 = 0.20$ (given), hence,

$$c_1 = \sqrt{0.80} = 0.89$$

and $c_2 = \sqrt{0.20} = 0.45$

∴ $\psi = 0.89\,[\phi_A(1)\,\phi_B(2) + \phi_A(2)\,\phi_B(1)] + 0.45\,[\phi_B(1)\,\phi_B(2)]$

Example 2. *Assuming that the ionic character in H—Br bond is 11%, calculate the fraction of the contribution of ionic character to the valence bond wave function.*

Sol. According to the equation, $\psi_{AB} = \psi_{covalent} + \lambda\psi_{ionic}$

The % ionic character is given by $\dfrac{\lambda^2}{1+\lambda^2} \times 100$

∴ $$11 = \frac{100\lambda^2}{(1+\lambda^2)}$$

or $$\lambda^2 = \frac{11}{89}$$

Hence, $$\lambda = \sqrt{\frac{11}{89}} = 0.35$$

Thus, the fraction of contribution of ionic character to ψ_{AB} is 0.35.

Molecular Orbital Theory (MOT)

The molecular orbital theory was put forth by F.Hund and R.S. Mullliken in 1930s and later further developed by I.E. Lennard-Jones and Charles Coulson.

According to MOT, the nuclei of the two atoms lie at appropriate distance and all the atomic orbitals of one atom overlap with all the atomic orbitals of the other atom provided the overlapping orbitals are of the same symmetry and of similar energy. The resulting polynuclear molecular Orbitals contain all the electrons of the molecule.

The basic **principles of molecular orbital theory** are as follows :

1. When nuclei of two atoms come close to each other, their atomic orbitals interact leading to the formation of **molecular orbitals.** The atomic orbitals of the atoms in a molecule completely lose their identity after the formation of molecular orbitals.
2. Each molecular orbitals is described by a wave function ψ, known as molecular orbital wave function.
3. Each molecular orbital wave function (ψ) is associated with a set of quantum numbers which determine the energy and the shape of the molecular orbital.
4. Each ψ is associated with a definite energy value and the total energy of the molecule is the sum of the energies of occupied molecular orbitals.
5. The molecular orbital wave function ψ is such that ψ^2 represents the probability density or electron charge density.
6. Electrons fill the molecular orbitals in the same way as they fill the atomic orbitals following the aufbau principle, Pauli's excision principle and the Hund's rule of maximum multiplicity.
7. Each electron in a molecular orbital belongs to all the nuclei present in the molecule.
8. Each electron moving in a molecular orbital has a spin of $+\frac{1}{2}$ or $-\frac{1}{2}$.

The basic **difference** between an atomic orbital and a molecular orbital is that while an electron in an atomic orbital is influenced by one positive nucleus only, an electron in a molecular orbital is influenced by all the nuclei of atoms **contained** in a molecule.

If we have a simple molecular system comprising of two electrons described by two one-electron molecular orbital wave functions ψ_1 and ψ_2, then the combined configurational wave function for the system, *i.e.*, the molecule, would be given by

$$\psi = \psi_1 \psi_2 \qquad \ldots(18)$$

If, in general, there are n electrons, then the configurational wave function for the system would be given by

$$\psi = \psi_1 \psi_2 \psi_3 \ldots \psi_n \qquad \ldots(19)$$

where ψ_1, ψ_2, ψ_3 etc., are one-electron molecular orbital wave functions*.

The individual one-electron molecular orbital wave functions such as $\psi_1, \psi_2, \psi_3, \ldots$ can be determined with the application of the wave mechanical principles, especially Ritz method of linear combination of atomic orbitals.

Linear Combination of Atomic Orbitals (LCAO). Molecular Orbital Treatment of Hydrogen Molecule Ion, H_2^+

We shall apply linear combination of atomic orbitals in the molecular orbital treatment of a simple species, *viz.*, H_2^+ ion, containing only one electron and then extend the treatment to more complicated systems.

Consider a H_2^+ ion consisting of two H nuclei designated as A and B (Fig. 18.2). The single electron is

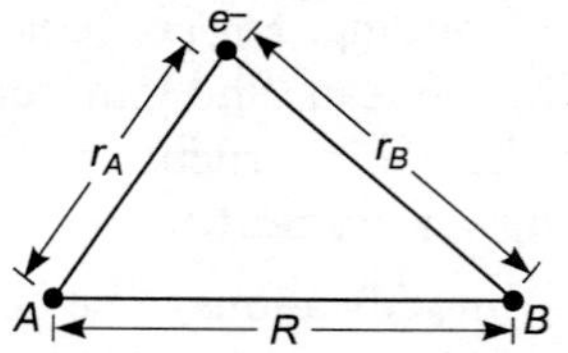

Fig. 18.2 Representation of H_2^+ ion.

supposed to be moving in a molecular orbital formed by the interaction of atomic orbitals of the two hydrogen atoms, H_A and H_B. The potential energy of the H_2^+ system would evidently, be given by

$$V = -\frac{e^2}{r_A} - \frac{e^2}{r_B} + \frac{e^2}{R} \qquad \ldots(20)$$

where r_A, r_B and R are the appropriate distances, as shown in Fig. (18.2).

As shown in previous chapter, the energy operator (*i.e.,* the Hamiltonian operator) $\hat{\mathbf{H}}$ for H_2^+ ion is represented as

$$\hat{\mathbf{H}} = -\frac{h^2}{8\pi^2 m}\nabla^2 + V \qquad \ldots(21)$$

$$= -\frac{h^2}{8\pi^2 m}\nabla^2 - \frac{e^2}{r_A} - \frac{e^2}{r_B} + \frac{e^2}{R} \qquad \ldots(22)$$

Accordingly, the wave equation $\hat{\mathbf{H}}\psi = E\psi$ becomes

$$\left(-\frac{h^2}{8\pi^2 m}\nabla^2 - \frac{e^2}{r_A} - \frac{e^2}{r_B} + \frac{e^2}{R}\right)\psi = E\psi \quad \ldots(23)$$

The electron in H_2^+ ion is moving in molecular orbital under the influence of both the nuclei *A* and *B*. When, at some instant, it comes nearer to nucleus *A* (situation I), the electron would behave as if it were moving in the atomic orbital of H_A. The motion of the electron would then be described by ψ_A (the unmixed atomic orbital of H_A). Similarly, when the electron is nearer to nucleus *B* (situation II), its motion would be described by ψ_B (the unmixed atomic orbital of H_B).

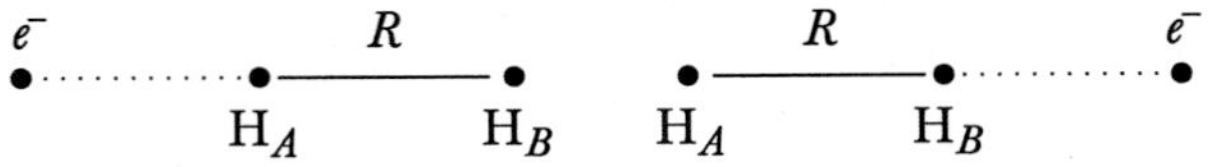

Situation I Situation II

In between the two situations, the electron would be under the influence of both the nuclei and its motion would be described by a wave function which is a linear combination of ψ_A and ψ_B. Thus,

$$\psi = c_A\psi_A + c_B\psi_B \qquad \ldots(24)$$

where c_A and c_B are the coefficients of the atomic orbital wave functions ψ_A and ψ_B, respectively. The squares of the coefficients, *viz.,* c_A^2 and c_B^2 give, respectively, the contributions of ψ_A and ψ_B to the wave function ψ.

The energy function ε corresponding to this wave function is given by

$$\varepsilon = \int_{-\infty}^{+\infty}\psi\hat{\mathbf{H}}\psi\, d\tau \Big/ \int_{-\infty}^{+\infty} d\tau\psi^2 \text{ (cf. Eq. (5))} \quad \ldots(25)$$

$$= \int_{-\infty}^{+\infty}(c_A\psi_A + c_B\psi_B)\hat{\mathbf{H}}(c_A\psi_A + c_B\psi_B)\, d\tau$$

$$\Big/ \int_{-\infty}^{+\infty}(c_A\psi_A + c_B\psi_B)^2\, d\tau \quad \ldots (26)$$

Differentiating Eq. (26) with respect to c_A only and then with respect to c_B only and applying the conditions of minimization of energy, *viz.,* $\partial\varepsilon/\partial c_A = 0$ and $\partial\varepsilon/\partial c_B = 0$, we get a quadratic equation in ε whose solution gives two values of energy function ε. Since these energy functions being of minimum energy are closest approximations of energy *E*, we may designate these two values of ε as E_+ and E_-.

Since, the probability of occurrence of situation I and situation II, described above, is the same, therefore, the weightages of ψ_A and ψ_B in overall ψ would be the same. Thus, $c_A^2 = c_B^2$.

In order that ψ is an acceptable wave function, it must be normalized, *i.e.,* it must satisfy the condition that $\int_{-\infty}^{+\infty}\psi^2 d\tau = 1$. The atomic orbital wave functions taken for the combination are already normalized, *i.e.,*

$$\int_{-\infty}^{+\infty}\psi_A^2\, d\tau = 1 \text{ and } \int_{-\infty}^{+\infty}\psi_B^2\, d\tau = 1$$

The above conditions of normalization give the relation

$$c_A^2 + c_B^2 = 1$$

But, as shown above, $\qquad c_A^2 = c_B^2$

$$\therefore \qquad c_A = \pm c_B = \pm(1/\sqrt{2}) \qquad \ldots(27)$$

Thus, we get two sets of values for c_A and c_B, *viz.,* $(+1/\sqrt{2}, +1\sqrt{2})$ and $(+1/\sqrt{2}, -1/\sqrt{2})$ and hence two linear combinations of ψ_A and ψ_B corresponding to each set of the values of c_A and c_B. Accordingly, we have

$$\psi_+ = +(1/\sqrt{2})\psi_A + (1/\sqrt{2})\psi_B = (1/\sqrt{2})(\psi_A + \psi_B) \qquad \ldots(28)$$

$$\psi_- = +(1/\sqrt{2})\psi_A - (1/\sqrt{2})\psi_B = (1/\sqrt{2})(\psi_A - \psi_B) \qquad \ldots(29)$$

In the above equations, ψ_+ corresponds to energy E_+ and ψ_- corresponds to energy E_-. The lower value of energy E_+ is lower that either of E_A and E_B (*viz.,* the energies of isolated H_A and H_B). the higher value of energy E_- is higher than either of E_A and E_B. Thus, we see that in the case of H_2^+ ion.

1. A linear combination of two atomic orbitals ψ_A and ψ_B leads to the formation of two molecular orbitals ψ_+ and ψ_-.
2. The energy E_+ of molecular orbital ψ_+ is lower than either of E_A and E_B. It is, therefore, designated as **bonding molecular orbital** (BMO).
3. The energy E_- of moleculr orbital ψ_- is higher than either of E_A and E_B. It is, therefore, designated as **anti-bonding molecular orbital** (ABMO).
4. The extent of lowering of energy of the bonding molecular orbital is equal to the extent of increase of energy of the antibonding molecular orbital, as shown in Fig. 18.3.

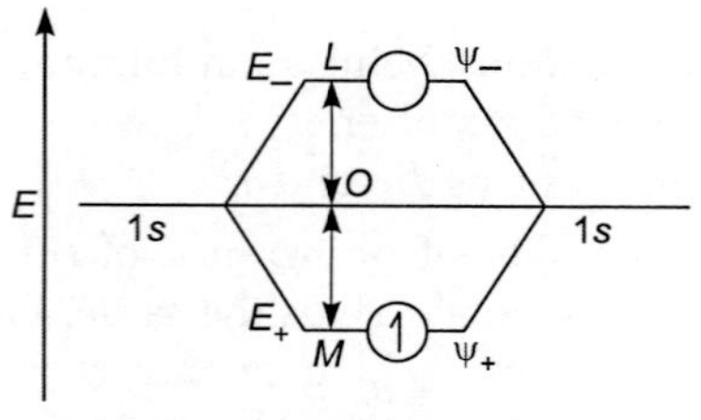

Fig. 18.3 Energies of bonding and anti-bonding molecular orbitals.

5. Detailed LCAO calculations show that the greater the overlap of the two combining atomic orbitals ψ_A and ψ_B, the lower would be the energy of the bonding molecular orbital (ψ_+) formed.
6. The combining atomic orbitals ψ_A and ψ_B are completely used up during the formation of the molecular orbitals ψ_+ and ψ_-. The electron occupying originally the 1s atomic orbital of H_A or H_B, now occupies the lower level molecular orbital ψ_+, losing energy $= OM$ and thus gaining in stability.
7. The BMO has high electron charge denisty in the overlap region whereas filled ABMO has no electron charge density in between the nuclei.

The molecular orbital treatment for H_2^+ ion, discussed above, can be extended to other homonuclear and heteronuclear systems. In general, whenever atomic orbitals ψ_A and ψ_B, of the same symmetry and of similar energies of two atoms A and B, overlap, two molecular orbitals ψ_+ and ψ_- would be formed by the linear combination of these atomic orbitals so that the equations for molecular orbitals would be

$$\psi_+ = N_+(\psi_A + \lambda\psi_B) \quad ...(30)$$

$$\psi_- = N_-(\lambda\psi_A - \psi_B) \quad ...(31)$$

where λ is called the **mixing coefficient** and N_+ and N_- are called **normalising constants. The values of these constants are adjusted in such a way that the normalising conditions, *viz.*, $\int_{-\infty}^{+\infty} \psi_+^2 d\tau = 1$ and $\int_{-\infty}^{+\infty} \psi_-^2 d\tau = 1$ are satisfied.**

If the molecule *AB* is homonuclear, the weightages of ψ_A and ψ_B in both ψ_+ and ψ_- would be the same, *i.e.*, $N_+^2 = \lambda^2 N_+^2$ and $N_-^2\lambda^2 = N_-^2$ (weightage of a wave function is related to square of its coefficient). It readily follows from above that $\lambda^2 = 1$ so that $\lambda = \pm 1$. In such a case, Eqs. (30) and (31) for molecular orbitals would reduce to Eqs. (28) and (29) respectively because $N_+ = N_- = 1/\sqrt{2}$ and $\lambda = \pm 1$.

If, however, the molecule *AB* is heteronuclear, the weightages of ψ_A and ψ_B would not be the same, *i.e.*, $N_-^2\lambda^2 \neq N_-^2$ and $N_+^2 \neq \lambda^2 N_+^2$ so that $\lambda^2 \neq 1$ and the equations for molecular orbitals would remain as Eqs. (30) and (31).

Example 3. *Write down the molecular orbital wave function for* H_2^- *molecule anion.*

Sol. H_2^- molecule anion contains three electrons which may be labelled as 1, 2 and 3. It contains two nuclei which may be designated as A and B.

$$\psi_{MO} = \psi_1\psi_2\psi_3$$

where,
$$\psi_1 = c_1\phi_A(1) + c_2\phi_B(1)$$
$$\psi_2 = c_3\phi_A(2) + c_4\phi_B(2)$$
$$\psi_3 = c_5\phi_A(3) + c_6\phi_B(3)$$

Example 4. *Construct a molecular orbital wave function for the bond between* H *and* Cl *in* HCl *assuming that the bond is formed from the* 1s *electron of* H *atom and a* 3p *electron of* Cl *atom.*

Sol. Let, H atom be designated by A and Cl atom by B. Let, the 1s electron of H atom be labelled as electron 1 and 3p electron of Cl atom be labelled as electron 2.

For notational convenience, we shall use the symbol ψ for MO and the symbol Φ for AO.

$$\psi_{MO} = \psi_1\psi_2$$

where,
$$\psi_1 = c_1\phi_A(1) + c_2\phi_B(1)$$
and
$$\psi_2 = c_1\phi_A(2) + c_2\phi_B(2)$$

$\therefore$
$$\psi_{MO} = \psi_1\psi_2 = [c_1\phi_A(1) + c_2\phi_B(1)]\ [c_1\phi_A(2) + c_2\phi_B(2)]$$
$$= c_1^2\,[\phi_A(1)\,\phi_A(2)] + c_1c_2\,[\phi_A(1)\,\phi_B(2) + \phi_A(2)\,\phi_B(1)] + c_2^2\,[\phi_B(1)\,\phi_B(2)]$$

As can be seen, the first and the last terms are ionic whereas the middle terms are covalent. Also the covalent terms have equal weight but the ionic terms have different weights from the covalent terms and also from each other.

Example 5. *Using the LCAO for the wave function for* H_2^+*, obtain the normalized wave function for the BMO and the AMBO.*

Sol. Using the LCAO-MO approximation, the wave function for H_2^+ is written as

$$\psi = N(c_1\phi_A + c_2\phi_B) \quad ...(i)$$

where, N is the normalization constant.

According to the normalization condition, for real ψ (using Dirac's 'bra' and 'ket' notation),

$$\psi^2 d\tau \equiv \langle \psi | \psi \rangle = 1 \quad ...(ii)$$

Incorporating the value of ψ from Eq. (i) in Eq. (ii), we have

$$N^2 \langle (c_1\phi_A + c_2\phi_B) | (c_1\phi_A + c_2\phi_B) \rangle = 1$$

or
$$c_1^2\,[\langle \phi_A | \phi_A \rangle] + c_2^2\,[\langle \phi_B | \phi_B \rangle] + 2c_1c_2\,[\langle \phi_A | \phi_B \rangle] = \frac{1}{N^2} \quad ...(iii)$$

Assuming that ψ_A and ψ_B are normalized, *i.e.*,

$$< \phi_A \mid \psi_A > \equiv \int \phi_A^2 \, d\tau = 1$$

and $$< \phi_B \mid \phi_B > \equiv \int \phi_B^2 \, d\tau = 1$$

We have $c_1^2 + c_2^2 + 2c_1c_2S = \frac{1}{N^2}$ where, S is the overlap integral defined as ...(iv)

$$S = < \phi_A \mid \phi_B > \equiv \int \phi_A\phi_B \, d\tau \qquad ...(v)$$

So, that $$N = (c_1^2 + c_2^2 + 2c_1c_2S)^{-1/2} \qquad ...(vi)$$

Hence, from Eq. (i),

$$\psi = (c_1^2 + c_2^2 + 2c_1c_2S)^{-1/2} \, (c_1\phi_A + c_2\phi_B) \qquad ...(vii)$$

We know that for BMO,

$$c_1 = c_2 \text{ and for ABMO, } c_1 = -c_2$$

Hence, from Eq. (vii),

$$\psi_{BMO} = \frac{1}{\sqrt{2(1+S)}} (\phi_A + \phi_B)$$

and $$\psi_{ABMO} = \frac{1}{\sqrt{2(1-S)}} (\phi_A - \phi_B)$$

Example 6. *Write down the wave function for the BMO for a heteronuclear diatomic molecule AB assuming that the electron on an average spends* 90% *of its time on nucleus A and* 10% *of its time on nucleus B.*

Sol. In the LCAO-MO scheme,

$$\psi_{MO} = c_A\phi_A + c_B\phi_B$$

where, the coefficients c_A and c_B are such that $[c_A]^2$ and $[c_B]^2$ determine the probability of finding the electron in the AOs ϕ_A and ϕ_B, respectively. Then, clearly,

$$[c_A]^2 = 90\% = 0.9$$

and $$[c_B]^2 = 10\% = 0.1$$

Hence, $$c_A = \pm\sqrt{0.9} = \pm 0.95$$

and $$c_B = \pm\sqrt{0.1} = \pm 0.32$$

Thus, $$\psi_{MO} = 0.95 \, \phi_A + 0.32 \, \phi_B$$

Example 7. *Write down the normalized VB wave function and MO wave function for* H_2 *molecule and comment on the expression obtained.*

Sol. H_2 molecule contains two electrons labelled 1 and 2 and two hydrogen nuclei labelled A and B. The pairing of electrons leads to the formation of a covalent bond. In the VB approach, if electron 1 is on nucleus A, then electron 2 would be on nucleus B and *vice-versa*. Since, however, the two electrons are indistinguishable, therefore, the VB wave function for H_2 molecule can be written as

$$\psi_{AB} = \left(\frac{1}{\sqrt{2}}\right) [\phi_A(1)\,\phi_B(2) + \phi_A(2)\,\phi_B(1)] \qquad ...(i)$$

where, $\frac{1}{\sqrt{2}}$ is the normalization constant obtained by normalizing ψ_{VB}.

In the MO theory, the MO wave function for H_2 molecule is given by

$$\psi_{MO} = \psi_1\psi_2 \qquad ...(ii)$$

where, ψ_1 and ψ_2 are the normalized wave functions for MOs of H_2 given by

$$\psi_1 = \left(\frac{1}{\sqrt{2}}\right) [\phi_A(1) + \phi_B(1)] \qquad ...(iii)$$

$$\psi_2 = \left(\frac{1}{\sqrt{2}}\right) [\phi_A(2) + \phi_B(2)] \qquad ...(iv)$$

Multiplying ψ_1 and ψ_2, we get the ψ_{MO} as

$$\psi_{MO} = \phi_1\phi_2 \, [\phi_A(1) + \phi_B(1)] \, [\phi_A(2) + \phi_B(2)] \qquad ...(v)$$

$$= \frac{1}{2} [\phi_A(1)\,\phi_A(2) + \phi_B(1)\,\phi_B(2)]$$

$$+ \frac{1}{2} [\phi_A(1)\,\phi_B(2) + \phi_B(1)\,\phi_A(2)] \qquad ...(vi)$$

In Eq. (vi), the first two terms represent the probability of finding both the electrons on the same atom at the same time. In other words, these terms represent the ionic structures of H_2 molecule which may be written as

$$\overset{+}{H}_A \overset{-}{H}_B \text{ and } \overset{-}{H}_A \overset{+}{H}_B$$

The last two terms in Eq. (vi) represents the covalent structure of the H_2 molecule.

Comparing ψ_{VB} and ψ_{MO}, we observe that while the wave function in VBT does not give any weightage to ionic structures, the MOT gives equal weightage to covalent and ionic structures.

Term Symbols for a Diatomic Molecule

The hydrogen molecule (and other diatomic molecules) have a large number of excited electronic states which are designated by **molecular term symbols.** As in an atom, in diatomic molecules the orbital angular momenta of electrons couple to give a resultant orbital angular momentum L and the electron spin momenta couple to give a resultant spin angular momentum S. The component of the orbital angular momentum along the axis of the molecule is given by

$$M_L = m_1 + m_2 + \ldots$$

where, $m_i = 0$ for a σ orbital and $m_i = \pm 1$ for a π orbital, and so on. The quantum number Λ is defined as the absolute value of M_L and is represented by the code letters

$$\Lambda = 0 \quad 1 \quad 2 \quad 3$$

$$\text{Symbol} = \Sigma \quad \Pi \quad \Delta \quad \Phi$$

in analogy to atomic term symbols. The multiplicity of an electronic state of a diatomic molecule is given by $2S + 1$ where, S is the sum of the spins of the electrons in the molecule. The term symbol of a molecule is represented by $^{2S+1}\Lambda$.

For, Σ terms, a superscript of plus or minus is added according to the behaviour of the wavefunction upon reflection in the plane containing the internuclear axis. A plus sign indicates that the wavefunction is invariant under this operation and a negative sign indicates that the wavefunction changes sign on reflection in this plane. If a diatomic molecule, such as a homonuclear diatomic, has a centre of symmetry, a right subscript of g or u is attached to the term symbol to denote the parity of the orbital. The parity of an orbital is determined by observing the inversion symmetry. When a point on an orbital is inverted an equal distance through the centre of the molecule, the orbital is said to be **gerade** (g) if it has the same sign at the two points; otherwise it is said to be **ungerade** (u); The reader can convince himself of the fact that in an atom an s orbital is g, a p orbital is u, a d orbital is g, and an f orbital is u. The parity of a multielectron molecule is obtained by noting g or u for every orbital and forming products, using the relations :

$$g \times g = g,\ g \times u = u,\ u \times u = g$$

Example 8. *Show that the ground state term symbol of H_2 is $^1\Sigma_g^+$.*

Sol. The H_2 molecule has the electronic configuration $(\sigma_s, 1s)^2$, *i.e.*, both the electrons are in the σ_g orbital. For the σ electrons, $m_1 = 0, m_2 = 0$ so that $M_L = 0$. Since, $s = |M_L|$, hence, $\Lambda = 0$. This means that the term symbol is Σ. Since, $S_1 = 1/2$ and $S_2 = -1/2$, hence, $S = S_1 + S_2 = 0$ so that multiplicity $2S + 1 = 1$ which corresponds to a singlet state. Since, the σ orbital is invariant under reflection in the plane containing the internucler axis, we use the superscript of plus (+). Again, since the orbital is gerade (g), we use the subscript g. Thus, the complete term symbol for H_2 is $^1\Sigma_g^+$.

Symmetry of Molecular Orbitals

Some of the possible combinations of atomic orbitals in the LCAO-MO scheme are shown in Fig. 18.4. Those orbitals which are cylindrically symmetrical about the internuclear axis are called σ orbitals, analogous to an s orbital of the highest symmetry. If the internuclear axis lies in the nodal plane, a π bond is formed. In δ bonds (encountered in the metal-metal quadruple bond in transition-metal chemistry), the internuclear axis lies in two mutually perpendicular nodal planes. All antibonding orbitals, identified with an *, possess an additional nodal plane perpendicular to the internuclear axis and lying between the nuclei. Also the MOs may or may not have a centre of symmetry. Thus, π_{p-p} orbitals are ungerade and $\overset{*}{\pi}_{p-p}$ orbitals are gerade.

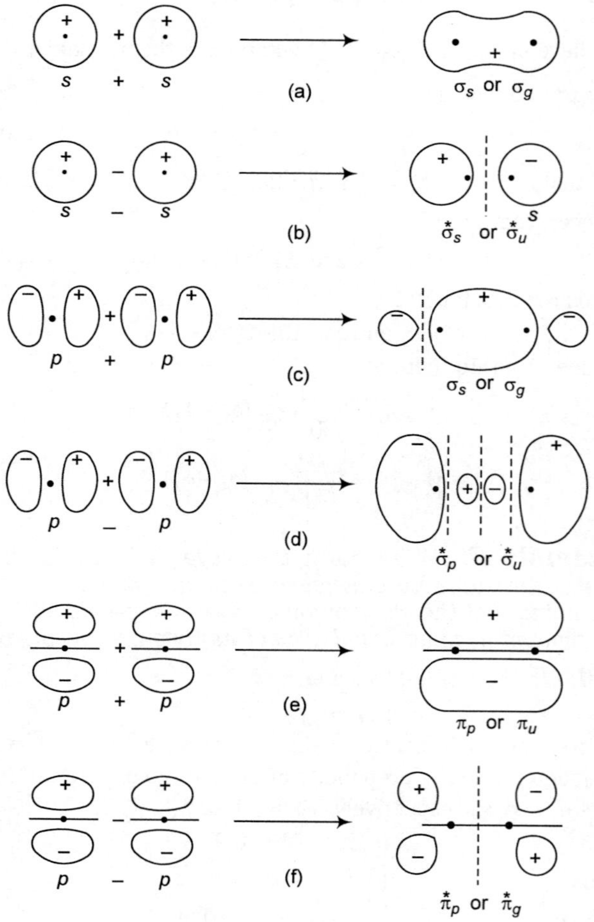

Fig. 18.4 Combinations of s, s and p, p atomic orbitals to form molecular orbitals of different symmetries. The figure displays the contours of the atomic and molecular orbitals. The traditional shapes of s and p orbitals arise from the projection of the contours on the respective axes.

Molecular Orbitals for Homonuclear Diatomic Molecules

The simplest molecules are those containing two atoms of the same element; these are called homonuclear diatomics. We shall now consider the LCAO-MO approximation for such molecules using the basis functions of the two atoms, such as the AOs $1s$, $2s$, $2p$, $3s$, etc. The two criteria that must be satisfied for the formation of BMOs are (i) the overlap between the AOs must be positive, (ii) the energies of the AOs must be approximately the same in order that there is effective interaction between the AOs of different atoms.

The molecules are built up by adding electrons to MOs in the same way as the atoms are built up by adding electrons to AOs. The principles involved in both cases are the same. The basic principles can be summed up as follows :

1. The MO with the lowest energy is filled first.
2. The maximum number of electrons in a MO cannot exceed two and the two electrons must be of opposite sign.
3. If there are two degenerate MOs, pairing of electrons will occur only after each degenerate MO has one electron.

The order of filling of molecular **orbitals is**

$$\sigma 1s, \overset{*}{\sigma} 1s, \sigma 2s, \overset{*}{\sigma} 2s, \sigma 2p_z, \pi 2p_x \approx \pi 2p_y\ \overset{*}{\pi} 2p_x$$

$$\approx \overset{*}{\pi} 2p_y\ \overset{*}{\pi} 2p_z \text{ (for molecules having } e^- > 14)$$

In case electrons are ≤ 14, the order is following :

$$\sigma 1s, \overset{*}{\sigma} 1s, \sigma 2s, \overset{*}{\sigma} 2s, \pi 2p_x \approx \pi 2p_y, \sigma 2p_z, \overset{*}{\pi} 2p_x$$

$$\approx \overset{*}{\pi} 2p_y, \overset{*}{\sigma} 2p_z$$

It is useful to define the term **bond order** that is roughly proportional to the strength of bonding. This is equal to one-half the difference between the number of bonding electrons and the number of anti-bonding electrons. Thus,

$$\text{Bond order} = \frac{1}{2}(N_b - N_a) \qquad \ldots(32)$$

where, N_b = number of electrons in bonding molecular orbitals.

N_a = number of electrons in anti-bonding MOs (represented by $\overset{*}{\sigma}$ or $\overset{*}{\pi}$)

Bond orders of 1, 2 and 3 signify single, double and triple bonds. Bond order of zero means that no bond is formed. The bond order of a molecule is directly proportional to its bond dissociation energy. This means that the higher the bond order, the larger the bond dissociation energy and the smaller the bond length. *e.g.*,

1. **H_2** $\sigma(1s)^2$; bond order $= \frac{1}{2}(2-0) = 1$. The molecule has a single bond.

   The bond dissociation energy of H_2 molecule has been found to be 458 kJ mol^{-1} and bond length equal to 0.74 Å.

2. **Hydrogen molecule ion, H_2^+** This molecule has been detected spectroscopically when electric discharge is passed through hydrogen gas under reduced pressure. The molecule has only one electron and its electronic configuration is

   $H_2^+\ \sigma(1s)^1$ and its bond order $= \frac{1}{2}(1-0) = \frac{1}{2}$

   The positive value of bond order indicates that the bond is formed and the molecule is stable. However, the bond in H_2^+ ion is weaker than that in H_2 molecule. The bond dissociation energy of H_2^+ ion (269 kJ mol^{-1}) is less than that of H_2 molecule (458 kJ mol^{-1}). The bond length in H_2^+ ion (1.04 Å) is larger than that in H_2 molecule (0.74 Å). These observations support the fact that the bond in H_2^+ ion is weaker than the bond in H_2 molecule.

3. **He_2** The electronic configuration of He_2 is

   $$He_2 : \sigma(1s)^2\ \overset{*}{\sigma}(1s^2)$$

   and its bond order $= \frac{1}{2}(2-2) = 0$

   The zero bond order indicates that the molecule does not exist. Calculations have shown that the anti-bonding effect of an anti-bonding MO is stronger than the bonding effect of a bonding MO. Consequently, there is no possibility whatsoever for the existence of He_2 molecule.

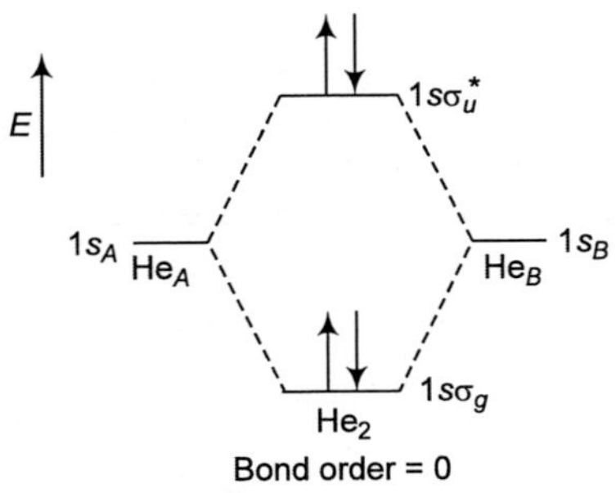

Fig. 18.5 The energies of bonding and antibonding orbitals for the He_2 molecule.

Diatomic molecules of the second row elements In these elements, the 1s orbitals are completely filled. In the formation of molecular orbitals, the electrons in the inner shells (*i.e.*, 1s electrons) of each atom remain essentially unperturbed in their respective atomic orbitals and may be kept out of consideration. In the formulation of electronic configurations of these molecules, the letters *KK* are generally used for denoting the fully filled inner shells (*K* shells) in the two atoms. *e.g.*,

4. **Li_2** The electronic configuration of lithium atom ($Z = 3$) is $1s^2\ 2s^1$. There are six electrons to be accommodated in lithium molecule. The four electrons are present in K shells and there are only two electrons to be accommodated in molecular orbitals. These two electrons go into $\sigma\ (2s)$ BMO which has lower energy and $\overset{*}{\sigma}\ (2s)$ ABMO remains empty. The electronic configuration of Li_2 molecule is thus represented as

$$Li_2 : KK\ \sigma\ (2s)^2$$

and its bond order $= \frac{1}{2}(2 - 0) = 1$

Thus, there is one Li–Li sigma bond. The bond dissociation energy of the molecule is quite low, being about 105 kJ mol^{-1}. The bond length is 2.67 Å.

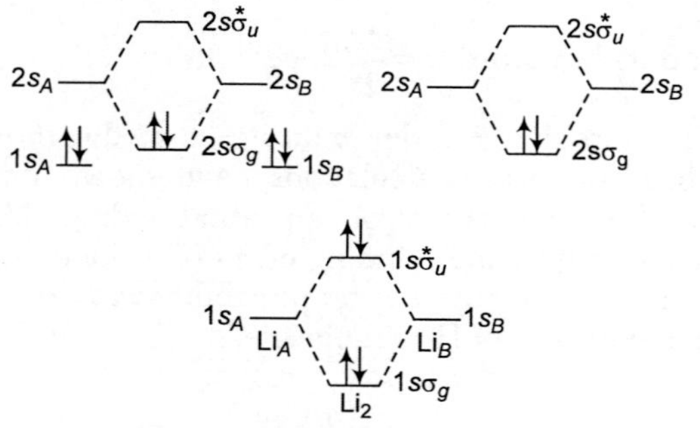

Fig. 18.6 Molecular-orbital descriptions for Li_2. In (a) the $1s$ electrons are regarded as remaining in atomic orbitals. In (b) they are in σ_g and $\overset{*}{\sigma}_u$ molecular orbitals.

5. **O_2** The electronic configuration of O_2 molecule is

$$O_2 : KK\ \sigma\ (2s)^2\ \overset{*}{\sigma}\ (2s)^2\ \sigma\ (2p_z)^2\ \pi\ (2p_x)^2\ \pi\ (2p_y)^2\ \overset{*}{\pi}\ (2p_x)^1\ \overset{*}{\pi}(2p_y)^1$$

Since, it contains two unpaired electrons, the oxygen molecule is paramagnetic.

Bond order $= \frac{1}{2}(8 - 4) = 2$. O_2 molecule, thus, contains a double bond.

Because of the presence of 4 electrons in ABMOs, O_2 molecule is less stable than N_2 molecule. Its bond dissociation energy is much less, being 494.6 kJ mol^{-1} and bond length is larger, being 1.21 Å.

Molecular Orbital Energy Level Diagrams of Heteronuclear Diatomic Molecules

The cases of heteronuclear diatomic molecules, in which the two atoms constituting a molecule are different, may now be considered. The principles involved in the distribution of electrons are the same as discussed before. However, the molecule orbital diagrams will not be symmetrical.

Let us discuss the electronic configurations and molecular orbital diagrams for some common heteronuclear diatomic molecules.

1. Carbon monoxide molecule, CO

The electronic configuration of carbon and oxygen atoms are :

$$C : 1s^2\ 2s^2\ 2p^2 \quad \text{and} \quad O : 1s^2\ 2s^2\ 2p^4$$

There are four electrons in the outermost shell of carbon atom and six electrons in the outermost shell of oxygen. Thus, a total of 10 electrons are to be accommodated in the molecular orbitals of CO molecule. The MO diagram for CO molecule may be drawn similar to NO molecule as shown in Fig. 18.10. Then the molecular orbital configuration may be written as :

$$CO : KK \left[\sigma 2s^2 \quad \overset{*}{\sigma}\ 2s^2 \quad \sigma 2p_z^2 \quad \begin{matrix} \pi 2p_x^2 \\ \pi 2p_y^2 \end{matrix} \right]$$

$$\text{Bond order} = \frac{8-2}{2} = 3$$

Thus, CO molecule has a **triple bond.** Its bond dissociation energy has been found to 1067 kJ mol^{-1} and bond length equal to 1.128 Å. However, it may be noted that the molecular orbital diagram of CO is somewhat complicated than NO molecule. The above configuration is not correct.

Oxygen is more electronegative than carbon and therefore, the atomic orbitals of oxygen are lower than those of carbon. Due to this difference, the $\overset{*}{\sigma}\ 2s$ MO is slightly higher in energy than $\sigma 2p_z$, $\pi 2p_x$ and $\pi 2p_y$ MOs. The diagram for CO molecule is shown in Fig. 18.7.

The better understanding of the structure is possible by comparison of CO and CO^+. CO^+ is formed by the loss of one electron from CO molecule. If the electronic configuration for CO molecule similar to NO, is correct, then electronic configuration for CO^+ is

$$CO: KK\left[\sigma 2s^2 \quad \overset{*}{\sigma} 2s^2 \quad \sigma 2p_z^2 \quad \begin{matrix}\pi 2p_x^2 \\ \pi 2p_y^1\end{matrix}\right]$$

$$\text{Bond order} = \frac{7-2}{2} = 2\frac{1}{2}$$

Thus, when CO is ionized to CO^+, then its bond order should be reduced to $2\frac{1}{2}$ and the bond length should be increased. However, the bond length in CO^+ is 1.115 Å and is less than in CO (1.128 Å). This means that the simple picture of CO molecule similar to other molecules is not correct. In fact, there is slight increase in bond order when CO is changed to CO^+. The most likely explanation for the increase in bond order or decrease in bond length is that the electron must have been removed from anti-bonding molecular orbital. This has been explained on the basis of energy levels of C and O atoms in Fig. 18.7.

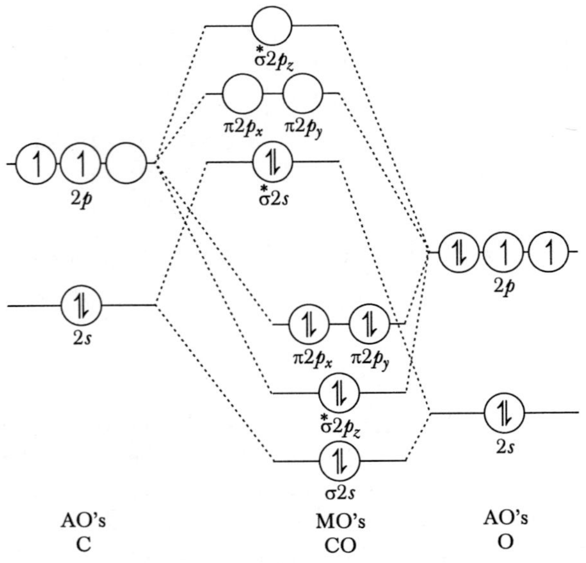

Fig. 18.7 Molecular orbitals diagram for CO molecule.

The above figure shows that $\overset{*}{\sigma} 2s$ MO is higher in energy than $\sigma 2p_z$, $\pi 2p_x$ and $\pi 2p_y$ MO's. Now when an electron is lost, it is removed from $\overset{*}{\sigma} 2s$ MO and therefore, bond order increases. As a result, CO^+ has slightly strong bond than does CO and bond length in CO^+ is less than that in CO molecule.

The molecular orbital configuration may be written as

$$CO: KK\left[\sigma 2s^2 \quad \sigma 2p_z^2 \quad \begin{matrix}\pi 2p_x^2 \\ \pi 2p_y^2\end{matrix} \quad \overset{*}{\sigma} 2s^2\right]$$

2. HF

The electronic configurations of hydrogen and fluorine are $1s^2$ and $1s^2 2s^2 p^5$, respectively. In the formation of HF molecule, only the $2p$ electrons of fluorine atom would combine effectively with the solitary electron of hydrogen atom. As has been already explained, only a p_z orbital is able to combine with an s orbital. The combination of a p_x or p_y orbital with an s orbital is ruled out on symmetry considerations. The $2p_z$ orbital of fluorine gives a highly effective overlap with the s orbital of hydrogen to form σ (sp) BMO and $\overset{*}{\sigma}$ (sp) ABMO.

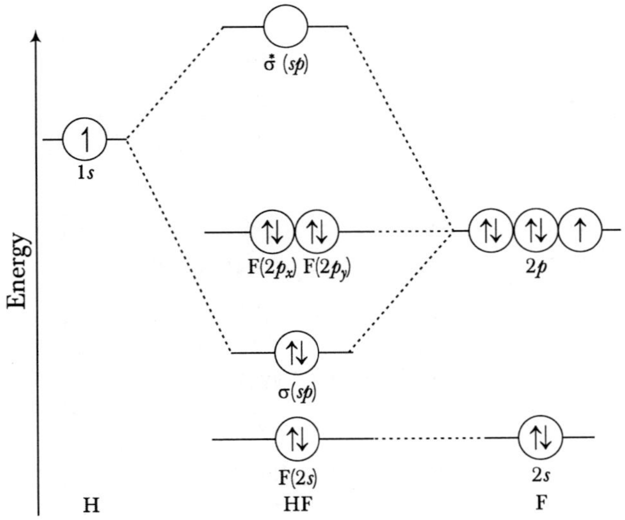

Fig. 18.8 Unsymmetrical shape of molecular orbital formed by the combination of 1s orbital of hydrogen with $2p_z$ orbital of fluorine.

The bonding molecular orbital is fully filled with two electrons. The rest of the electrons remain in their atomic orbitals. The MO formed in the case of HF molecule will not be symmetrical. The asymmetry occurs because the energies of H (1s) and F ($2p_z$) atomic orbitals are not the same. The MO diagram for HF molecule is shown in Fig. 18.8.

As can be seen, the bonding MO has an energy which is less closer to that of $2p_z$ orbital of fluorine than to that of higher energy 1s orbital of hydrogen.

3. HCl

The electronic configurations of H and Cl atoms are $1s^1$ and $1s^2, 2s^2, p^6, 3s^2, p^5$, respectively. In this case also, there is only one bonding MO and one anti-bonding MO formed by the combination of $1s$ orbital of hydrogen with $3p_z$ orbital of chlorine. The rest of the electrons of the chlorine atom remain in their respective AOs.

The electronic configuration of HCl may thus be represented as

$$\text{HCl}: KL\,(3s)^2, \sigma\,(sp)^2, (3p_x)^2, (3p_y)^2$$

Here, too, the MO formed will not be symmetrical. The MO energy level diagram of HCl molecule will be exactly similar to the one shown in Fig. 18.8 for HF molecule.

Table 18.2 gives the ground state electronic configuration of homonuclear diatomics (along with other relevant data), in a slightly different notation.

Table 18.2 **Ground State Electronic Configurations of Homonuclear Diatomics**

Molecule	Number of electrons	Electronic configuration	Term symbol	Bond order	R_e (pm)	D_e (eV)	D_e (kJ mol^{-1})
H_2^+	1	$(1\sigma_g)^1$	$^2\Sigma$	$\frac{1}{2}$	106.0	2.793	269.5
H_2	2	$(1\sigma_g)^2$	$^1\Sigma$	1	74.12	4.748	458.1
He_2^+	3	$(1\sigma_g)^2\,(1\sigma_u)$	$^2\Sigma$	$\frac{1}{2}$	108.0	2.5	238.0
He_2	4	$(1\sigma_g)^2\,(1\sigma_u)^2$	$^1\Sigma$	–	–	–	–
Li_2	6	$[He_2](2\sigma_g)^2$	$^1\Sigma$	1	267.3	1.14	110.0
Be_2	8	$[He_2](2\sigma_g)^2\,(2\sigma_u)^2$	$^1\Sigma$	0	–	–	–
B_2	10	$[Be_2](1\pi_u)^2$	$^3\Sigma$	1	158.9	~3.0	~290
C_2	12	$[Be_2](1\pi_u)^4$	$^1\Sigma$	2	124.2	6.36	613.8
N_2	14	$[Be_2](1\pi_u)^4\,(3\sigma_g)^2$	$^1\Sigma$	3	109.4	9.902	955.4
O_2^+	15	$[N_2](1\pi_g)^2$	$^2\Pi$	$2\frac{1}{2}$	112.27	6.77	653.1
O_2	16	$[N_2](1\pi_g)^2$	$^3\Sigma$	2	120.74	5.213	502.9
F_2	18	$[N_2](1\pi_g)^4$	$^1\Sigma$	1	143.5	1.34	118.8
Ne_2	20	$[N_2](1\pi_g)^4\,(3\sigma_u)^2$	$^1\Sigma$	0	–	–	–

4. The Water Molecule

The procedures for constructing molecular orbitals for more complicated molecules may be exemplified by a brief treatment of the water molecule, the symmetry elements for which are shown in Figure 18.10. The oxygen atom lies on all three of these symmetry elements, and in Figure 18.10(a). We show orbitals of the oxygen atom in relation to these elements. Since, the $1s$ and $2s$ orbitals are spherically symmetrical, none of the symmetry operations brings about any change in them and both are therefore of A_1 symmetry. The $2p_z$ orbital has a positive lobe in one direction along the Z axis and a negative lobe in the other. The C_2, σ_v, and σ'_v operations bring about no change in this orbital, which is therefore also of A_1 symmetry.

The $2p_x$ and $2p_y$ orbitals, however, behave differently. Reflection of the $2p_x$ orbital of the σ'_v plane interchanges the + and – lobes and therefore changes the sign, and the same happens with a C_2 rotation. Reflection in the σ_v plane brings about no change. The $2p_x$ orbital is therefore of B_1 symmetry. By similar arguments we find that the $2p_y$ orbital is of B_2 symmetry.

The situation with the orbitals on the hydrogen atoms in the water molecule is a little more complicated, since these atoms do not lie on all the symmetry elements of the molecule; they only lie in the σ'_v plane. The $1s$ orbital of the H_A atom, which we will write as $1s_A$, therefore does not correspond to the symmetry of the molecule, and the same is true of the $1s_B$ orbital. However, from these two orbitals we can construct orbitals that do have the right symmetry. Thus the sum of the atomic orbitals, $1s_A + 1s_B$, is unchanged when any of the symmetry operations is performed, and it is therefore of A_1 symmetry. The difference, $1s_A - 1s_B$, changes its sign when the C_2 operation is performed and when the σ_v operation is performed, but it remains unchanged when σ'_v is performed. It is therefore of B_2 symmetry.

The symmetry properties of the various orbitals on the H and O atoms are summarized in Figure 18.10 (b). The complete molecular orbital must correspond in symmetry to one of the symmetry species of the molecule, and this is impossible if we combine atomic orbitals of different symmetries. We can, however, obtain a molecular orbital of symmetry A_1 if we make a linear combination of $2s$, $2p_z$, and $1s_A + 1s_B$ orbitals, all of which are of A_1 symmetry. Such an orbital is designated a_1 (the lower case letter is used) and is of the form

$$a_1 = 1s_A + 1s_B + \lambda_1 2s + \lambda_2 2p_z \qquad \ldots(33)$$

where λ_1 and λ_2 are coefficients which could be determined by a variation procedure. This orbital is represented schematically in Figure 18.10.

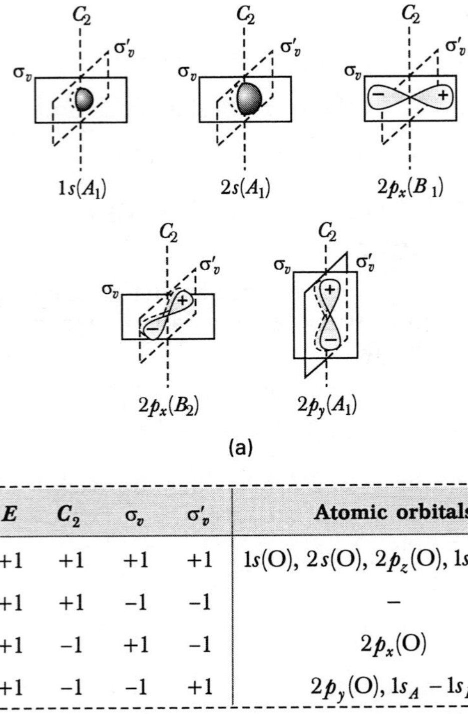

(a)

	E	C_2	σ_v	σ'_v	Atomic orbitals
A_1	+1	+1	+1	+1	$1s(O)$, $2s(O)$, $2p_z(O)$, $1s_A + 1s_B$
A_2	+1	+1	−1	−1	–
B_1	+1	−1	+1	−1	$2p_x(O)$
B_2	+1	−1	−1	+1	$2p_y(O)$, $1s_A - 1s_B$

(b)

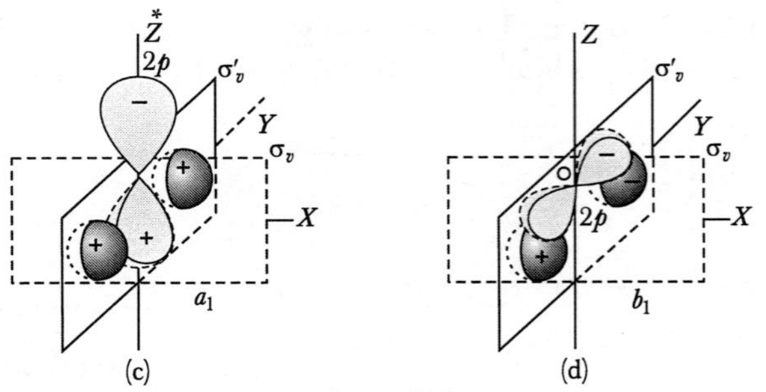

Fig. 18.9 Orbitals for the water molecule.
(a) The atomic orbitals and their symmetry species. The σ'_v plane is the plane of the molecule.
(b) The C_{2v} character table showing the symmetries of the atomic orbitals and the symmetry-adapted orbitals.
(c) and (d). The bonding molecular orbitals a_1 and b_2.

We can also construct the orbital

$$b_2 = 1s_A - 1s_B + \lambda 2p_y \qquad \ldots(34)$$

in which orbitals of B_2 symmetry are combined. This orbital is represented in Figure 18.10(d).

Both of these orbitals are bonding, since the atomic orbitals have been added together, and there is a piling up of charge between the nuclei. For each bonding molecular orbital there is an anti-bonding one, of the same symmetry, formed by subtracting the atomic orbitals. These are indicated by an asterisk. The anti-bonding molecular orbital corresponding to a_1 is

$$a_1^* = 1s_A + 1s_B - \lambda'_1 2s - \lambda'_2 2p_z \qquad \ldots(35)$$

That corresponding to b_2 is

$$b_2^* = 1s_A - 1s_B - \lambda' 2p_y \qquad \ldots(36)$$

There is also an anti-bonding orbital of B_1 symmetry, which consists only of $2p_x(O)$ itself; this cannot combine in any way with the hydrogen atom orbitals and, therefore, gives no bonding.

These conclusions are shown in Figure 18.11 in the form of an energy diagram. The order of the energy levels is that predicted by self-consistent field calculations. The $1s$ atomic orbital of the oxygen atom has a much lower energy than the other atomic orbitals, and it is therefore carried over as the lowest MO; electrons in this orbital are non-bonding. The $2s$ atomic orbital of the oxygen atom also forms an MO, designated a'_1, and electrons in this level are also non-bonding.

The assignment of the 10 electrons in the water molecule is shown in Figure 18.11. The 2 electrons in the $1s$ orbital of oxygen make no contribution to bonding. Two electrons are in each of the a_1 and b_2 orbitals, and these four electrons are responsible for the two O H bonds. The remaining four electrons are in the a'_1 and b_1 orbitals and constitute the two lone pairs.

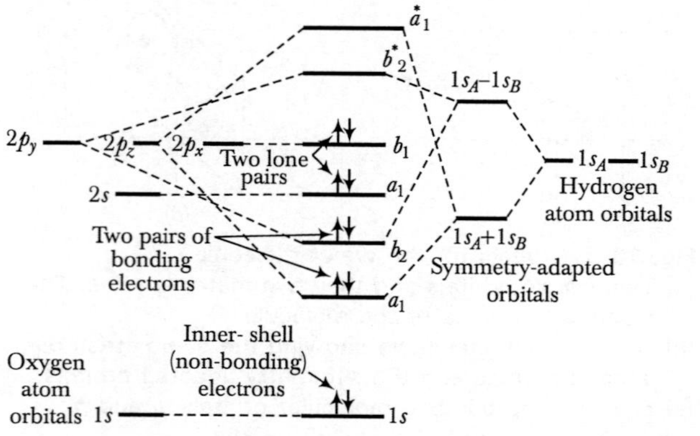

Fig. 18.10 The energy levels corresponding to the molecular orbitals for water, showing how they are derived from the atomic orbitals of oxygen and hydrogen (not to scale).

Example 9. *Of the following species, which has the shortest bond length :* NO, NO^+, NO^{2+}, NO^-?

Sol. We shall first calculate the bond orders for the given species from their electronic configurations.

NO $KK\ \sigma(2s)^2\ \overset{*}{\sigma}(2s)^2\ \sigma(2p_z)^2\ \pi(2p_x)^2\ \pi(2p_y)^2\ \overset{*}{\pi}(2p_x)^1$

$$\text{Bond order} = \frac{1}{2}(8-3) = 2\frac{1}{2}$$

NO^+ One electron is removed from the anti-bonding $\overset{*}{\pi}(2p_x)$ MO.

$$\text{Bond order} = \frac{1}{2}(8-2) = 3$$

NO^{2+} One electron is removed from the anti-bonding $\overset{*}{\pi}(2p_x)$ MO and the other electron is removed from the bonding $\pi(2p_y)$ MO.

$$\text{Bond order} = \frac{1}{2}(7-2) = 2\frac{1}{2}$$

NO^- One electron is added to the anti-bonding $\overset{*}{\pi}(2p_x)$ MO.

$$\text{Bond order} = \frac{1}{2}(8-4) = 2$$

Evidently, the species NO^+ has the highest bond order and thus has the **shortest bond length.**

Huckel Theory for Conjugated π-Electron Systems

This theory was originally introduced to permit qualitative study of the π-electron systems in planar, conjugated hydrocarbon molecules. It is thus most apropriate for molecules such as benzene or butadiene, but the approach and concepts have wider aplicability.

Basic Assumptions

1. The atomic orbitals contributing to the π-bonding in a planar molecule (*e.g.*, the so-called *pπ* orbitals in a molecule such as benzene) are anti-symmetric with respect to reflection in the molecular plane; they are therefore of a different symmetry to the atomic orbitals contributing to the σ-bonding and may be treated independently.

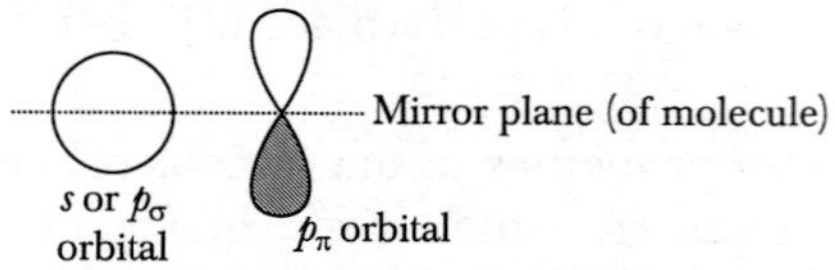

2. The Coulomb integrals for all the carbon atoms are assumed to be identical. *i.e.,* small differences in α-values due to the different chemical environment of C atoms in a molecule such as 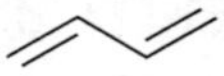 are neglected.
3. All reasonance integrals between directly-bonded atoms are assumed to be the same; whilst those between atoms that are not directly bonded are neglected.

   i.e., $\int \phi_i \hat{\mathbf{H}} \phi_i \cdot d\tau = \beta$ if atoms i and j are directly σ-bonded

   $= 0$: if atoms i and j are non-bonded.
4. All overlap integrals representing the overlap of atomic orbitals centred on different atoms are neglected.

   i.e., $\int \phi_i \phi_j \cdot d\tau = 0$: if $i \neq j$

Note $i = j$ then $\int \phi_i \phi_j \cdot d\tau = 1$ since it is assumed that the atomic orbitals are normalized

A Closer Look at the Secular Determinant

The basic form of the secular determinant for the bonding arising from the overlap of two orbitals is reproduced below.

$$\begin{vmatrix} \alpha_1 - E & \beta_{12} \\ \beta_{12} & \alpha_2 - E \end{vmatrix}$$

For three overlapping orbitals the approach leads to a secular determinant of the form :

$$\begin{vmatrix} \alpha_1 - E & \beta_{12} & \beta_{13} \\ \beta_{12} & \alpha_2 - E & \beta_{13} \\ \beta_{13} & \beta_{23} & \alpha_3 - E \end{vmatrix}$$

From a comparison of the two secular determinants given above, it is becoming clear that all such secular determinants have a characteristic structure

1. Each row and column may be associated with one of the atomic orbitals; thus the first row and first column contain information about the nature of orbital 1 and its interactions with the other orbitals, the second row and the second column contain informatin about the nature of orbital 2 and its interactions with the other orbitals.
2. The diagonal set of elements (comprised of those elements where row 1 intersects column 1, row 2 intersects column 2,... and so on) include the values of the relevant Coulomb integrals (α_1, α_2 etc.).
3. The off-diagonal elements (comprised of those elements having different row numbers and column numbers) are equal to the relevant resonance integrals (*e.g.*, β_{12} at the intersection of row 1 and column 2)

This structure is summarised below, where the rows and columns have been labelled with the numbers identifying the associated atomic orbital.

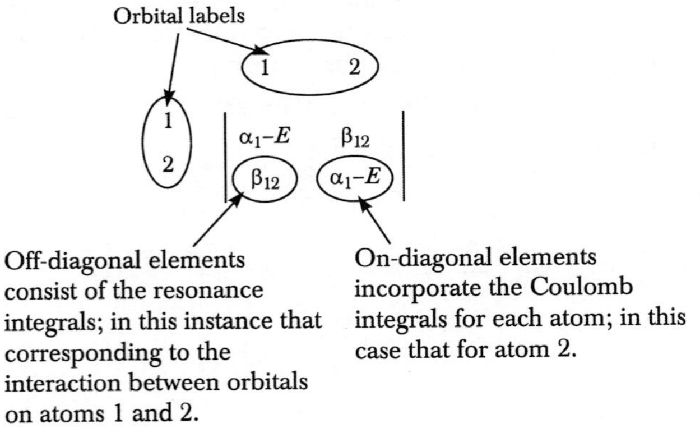

Linear Conjugated Hydrocarbons

C_3 Molecules (3-atom chain)

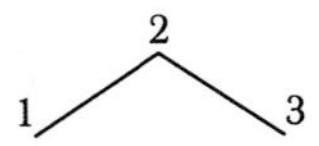

Secular Determinant/Equation

	1	2	3
1	$\alpha - E$	β	0
2	β	$\alpha - E$	β
3	0	β	$\alpha - E$

$= 0$

$$\Rightarrow \quad \begin{vmatrix} x & 1 & 0 \\ 1 & x & 1 \\ 0 & 1 & x \end{vmatrix} = 0 \quad \text{where } x = \frac{(\alpha - E)}{\beta}$$

$$\Rightarrow \quad x(x.x - 1.1) - 1(1.x - 1.0) + 0\,(1.1 - x.0) = 0$$

$$\Rightarrow \quad x^3 - x - x = 0$$

$$\Rightarrow \quad x^3 - 2x = 0$$

$$\Rightarrow \quad x(x^2 - 2) = 0$$

$$\Rightarrow \quad x = 0 \text{ or } x = \pm\sqrt{2}$$

i.e., $x = +\sqrt{2}, 0, -\sqrt{2}$

Now $E = \alpha - x\beta$

So the energies of the molecular orbitals are

$$E = \alpha - \sqrt{2}.\beta \text{ – Highest energy}$$

$$E = \alpha$$

$$E = \alpha + \sqrt{2}.\beta \text{ – Lowest energy}$$

The secular equations are

$$c_1(\alpha - E) + c_2\beta \qquad + 0 = 0$$

$$c_1\beta + c_2(\alpha - E) + c_3\beta = 0$$

$$0 + c_2\beta \qquad + c_3(\alpha - E) = 0$$

or, in terms of x,

$$c_1 x + c_2 + 0 = 0 \qquad \ldots(37)$$

$$c_1 + c_2 x + c_3 = 0 \qquad \ldots(38)$$

$$0 + c_2 + c_3 x = 0 \qquad \ldots(39)$$

For $x = 0$, (*i.e.*, $E = \alpha$)

(37) $\Rightarrow$ $c_2 = 0$

(38) $\Rightarrow$ $c_1 + c_3 = 0$

$\Rightarrow$ $c_1 = - c_3$

If we now apply the normalisation condition ($\Sigma c_i^2 = 1$)

$$\Rightarrow \quad |c_1| = |c_3| = \frac{1}{\sqrt{2}}$$

i.e.,

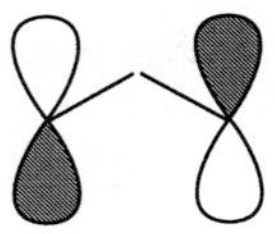

For $x = -\sqrt{2}$ (*i.e.*, $E = \alpha + \sqrt{2}.\beta$)

(37) – (39) $\Rightarrow$ $c_1 - c_3 = 0$

$\Rightarrow$ $c_1 = c_3$

(1) $\Rightarrow$ $-\sqrt{2}.c_1 + c_2 = 0$

$\Rightarrow$ $c_2 = \sqrt{2}.c_1$

If we now apply the normalisation condition ($\Sigma c_i^2 = 1$)

$$\Sigma c_i^2 = c_1^2 + c_2^2 + c_3^2 = c_1^2 + (\sqrt{2}c_1)^2 + c_1^2 = 4c_1^2 = 1$$

$$\Rightarrow \quad c_1^2 = \frac{1}{4}$$

$$\Rightarrow \quad c_1 = c_3 = \frac{1}{2} \qquad (= 0.500)$$

$\Rightarrow \qquad c_2 = \sqrt{2} \cdot \frac{1}{2} = \frac{1}{\sqrt{2}} \qquad (= 0.707)$

i.e.,

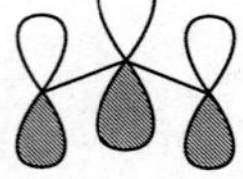

For $x = +\sqrt{2}$ (*i.e.,* $E = \alpha - \sqrt{2}.\beta$)

(37) – (39) $\Rightarrow \qquad c_1 - c_3 = 0$

$\Rightarrow \qquad c_1 = c_3$

(1) $\Rightarrow \qquad \sqrt{2}.c_1 + c_2 = 0$

$\Rightarrow \qquad c_2 = -\sqrt{2}.c_1$

If we now apply the normalisation condition ($\Sigma c_i^2 = 1$)

$\Rightarrow \qquad c_1 = c_3 = \frac{1}{2} \qquad (= 0.500)$

$\Rightarrow \qquad c_2 = \frac{-1}{\sqrt{2}} \qquad (= -0.707)$

i.e.,

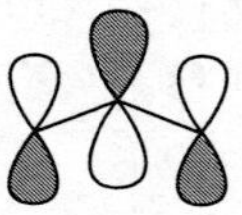

In summary,

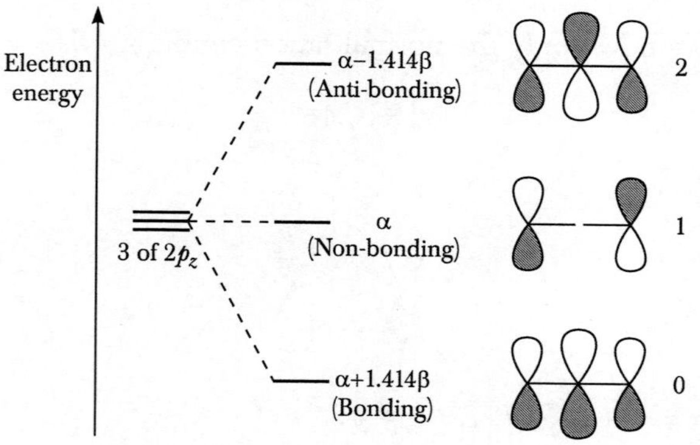

< *Lectures*-examples of bond order and charge distribution calculations for allylic species >

General Solution (*n*-atom chain; *e.g.,* $C_nH_{(n+2)}$ Conjugated polyenes)

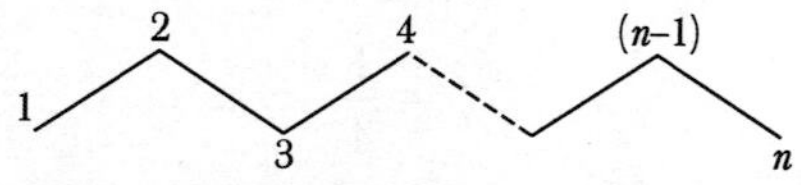

The secular determinant has the same basic form, whatever the chain length, as illustrated below :

	1	2	3			*n*	
1	*x*	1	0	0	...	0	
2	1	*x*	1				
3	0	1	*x*				= 0
	0						
					x	1	
n	0	...	...	...	1	*x*	

Consequently the solutions also have the same basic, form, whatever the chain length and it can be demonstrated that :

Orbital coefficients are given by

$$c_s \propto \sin\left(\frac{\pi ks}{n+1}\right) \qquad ...(40)$$

where,

n – total number of atoms in the conjugated chain

s – atom number (*i.e.,* 1, 2,.., n)

k – quantum number, identifying the MO (= 1, 2,..., n) and the constant of proportionality can be determined by applying the normalisation condition.

Example Consider the highest energy MO (k = 3) of the three carbon chain (n = 3).

$\Rightarrow \qquad c_s \propto \sin\left(\frac{3\pi s}{4}\right)$

i.e., $\quad c_1 \propto \sin\left(\frac{3\pi}{4}\right) = \frac{1}{\sqrt{2}}, \; c_2 \propto \sin\left(\frac{6\pi}{4}\right) = -1,$

$$c_3 \propto \sin\left(\frac{9\pi}{4}\right) = \frac{1}{\sqrt{2}}$$

These coefficients are not normalized to achieve this we need to multiply them all by the same constant value, chosen to ensure that the new values of the coefficients satisfy the condition that $\Sigma c_i^2 = 1$.

From the general expression for the coefficients given above it can be seen that the relative signs and sizes can also be visualised using the following trigonometric construction.

Procedure

1. Draw the n-regularly spaced atoms (1, 2,..., n) in a straight line and then add two imaginary atoms (labelled 0 and (n + 1)) at either end of the chain.
2. Sketch portions of sine waves between these two imaginary end atoms, ensuring that the imaginary end atoms correspond to nodes of the sine wave.
3. The lowest energy MO has no other nodes and corresponds to half a sine wave; the next MO has one-additional node in the middle and corresponds to a complete sine wave; the next MO has two additional nodes.... and so on.

e.g., for the third MO ($k = 3$) of the three carbon chain ($n = 3$).

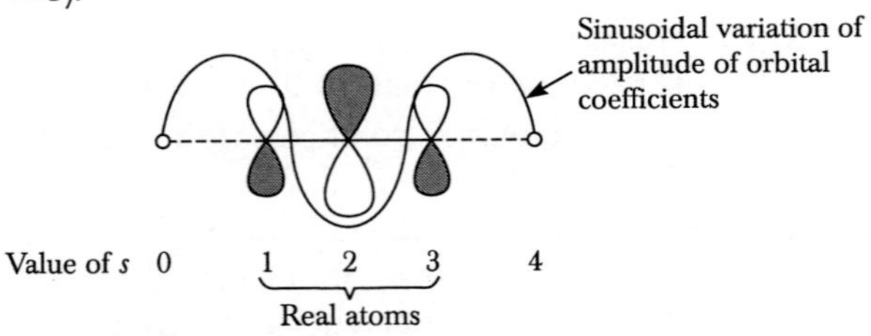

orbita energies are given by

$$E = \alpha + 2\beta \cos\left[\frac{\pi K}{n+1}\right] \qquad \ldots(41)$$

where, n-total number of atoms in the conjugated chain

k-quantum number, identifying the MO (= 1, 2, ..., n)

Note that the cosine function varies only between the limiting values of −1 and +1.

i.e., $$-1 \le \cos\left(\frac{\pi k}{n+1}\right) \le +1$$

hence, $$(\alpha + 2\beta) \le E \le (\alpha - 2\beta)$$

Consequently all molecular orbital energies must lie within an energy range of 4β, ±2β of the original atomic orbital energy.

Recall also that for an n-atom chain, in which each atom contributes one atomic orbital to the conjugated π-system, there will be n overlapping atomic orbitals giving rise to n molecular orbitals.

Since all these MOs are confined to a fixed energy range, it follows that the average energy separation must decrease as n increases. This is illustrated below in an electron energy diagram which also shows the electron occupancy (for the neutral molecule) for the first three members of the series :

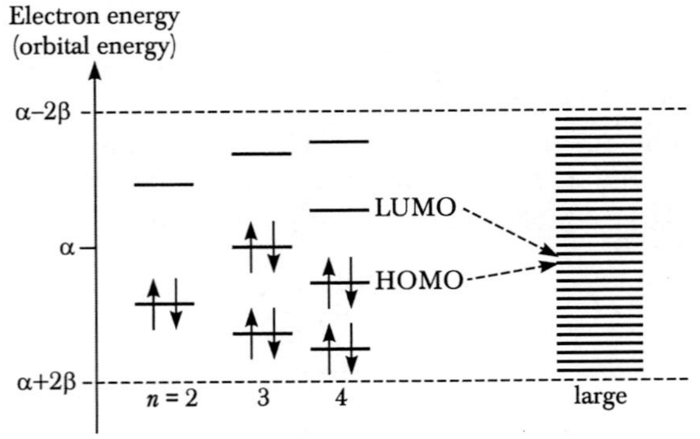

Note 1. As n increases : the HOMO-LUMO separation decreases-consequently the photon energy required to excite an electron from the HOMO to LUMO also decreases.

i.e., $h\nu = \Delta E = E_{HOMO} - E_{LUMO}$ decreases as n increases.

For conjugated carbon atom chains the photon energy changes from the UV (for small n) to the visible (large n). Consequently, molecules with extended conjugated systems are coloured.

2. As $n \to \infty$: the separation between any two energy levels decreases towards zero and the energy levels (although still discrete in principle) effectively merge to give a continuous band of energy levels. The width of this band is 4β and is therefore determined by the effectiveness of overlap of the individual atomic orbitals and hence the strength of interaction and the magnitude of the resonance integral β. The system approaches the *metallic state*-that is to say that electrical conduction can readily occur (since the HOMO-LUMO separation is essentially zero) and all wavelengths of visible light are readily absorbed.

Cyclic Conjugated Hydrocarbons

General solution (n-atom ring; C_nH_n cyclic conjugated hydrocarbons).

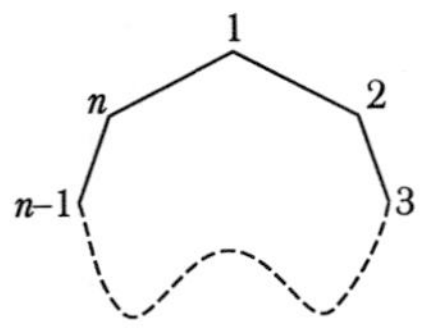

The secular determinant has the same basic form, whatever the ring size, as illustrated below

	1	2	3			n	
1	x	1	0	0	...	1	
2	1	x	1				
3	0	1	x				= 0
	0						
					x	1	
n	1	...	...	...	1	x	

Consequently the solutions also have the same basic form, whatever the ring size and it can be demonstrated that the :

Orbital energies are given by

$$E = \alpha + 2\beta \cos\left(\frac{2\pi k}{n}\right) \qquad \ldots(42)$$

where, n-total number of atoms in the conjugated ring system

k-quantum number, identifying the MO (= 0, 1, 2, ..., n − 1)

but, given the periodic and "even" (symmetrical about θ = 0) nature of the cosine function, this permitted range of k-values may also be written in the form

$$k = 0, \pm 1, \pm 2, \ldots, \left(\frac{n}{2}\right) \quad \text{for even } n$$

$$k = 0, \pm 1, \pm 2, \ldots, \pm\left(\frac{n-1}{2}\right) \quad \text{for odd } n$$

Note that the cosine function varies only between the limiting values of −1 and +1 and because the cosine function is an even function, the energy depends only on $|k|$.

i.e., $$-1 \leq \cos\left(\frac{2\pi k}{n}\right) \leq +1$$

hence $(\alpha + 2\beta) \leq E \leq (\alpha - 2\beta)$

It is possible to represent equation (6) as a geometrical construction and this is illustrated below. Consider $n = 6$ (*e.g.,* C_6H_6-benzene); then the expression for E is

$$E = \alpha + 2\beta \cos\left(\frac{2\pi k}{6}\right)$$

where, $k = 0, \pm 1, \pm 2, 3$ (since n is even)

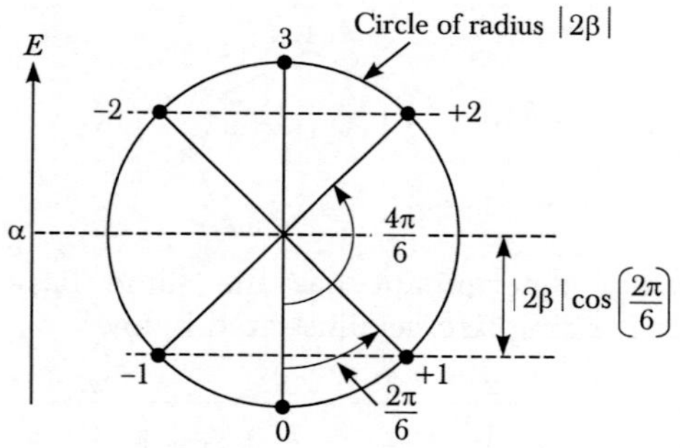

Whilst the above diagram highlights the relationship between the geometrical construction and the equation for E, it also suggests that the energies of the orbitals may also be obtained using a simpler construction-namely by drawing the corresponding regular polyhedron (*i.e.,* a hexagon for $n = 6$) inscribed inside the circle with one apex coincident with the bottom of the circle.

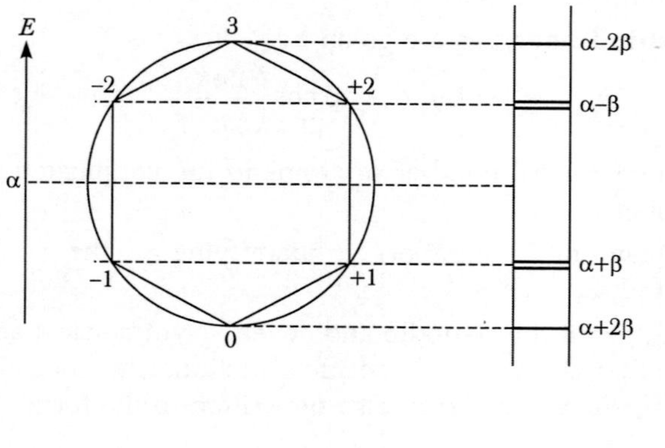

Note For these cyclic conjugated systems

1. The lowest-energy MO is always non-degenerate
2. The highest-energy MO may be non-degenerate (if n is even) or degenerate (if n is odd).
3. All the remaining solutions form pairs of degenerate MOs.

One consequence of this arrangement of the MOs is that only specific numbers of electrons can be accommodated if a stable molecule is to result-this is embodied in the … .

Huckel Rule

A stable, closed-shell conjugated cyclic structure is obtained for $(4N + 2)$ electrons. *i.e.,* stable structure are obtained for 2, 6, 10, …electrons.

- The MO of lowest energy $(k = 0)$ is always non-degenerate (irrespective of whether n is even or odd) and has the same coefficient for each and every contributing atomic orbital-there are therefore no angular nodes in the wave function. *e.g.,* for $n = 6$.

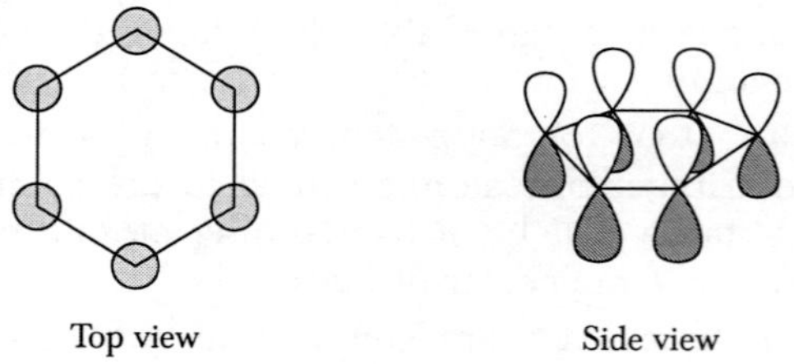

The molecular plane is a nodal plane for all the π-MOs, but for this particular MO there are no angular nodal planes in the wavefunction and all the interactions between orbitals on adjacent atoms are of a bonding nature.

- The highest-energy MO of even n systems is also non-degenerate.

  The magnitude of the coefficient is the same for each and every contributing atomic orbital but the sign changes between adjacent atoms. *e.g.,* for $n = 6$

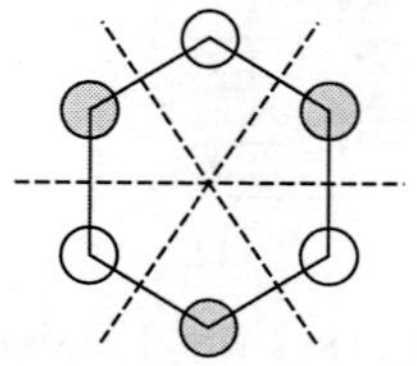

In this case there are three angular nodal planes as marked (---) on the diagram. The wave function thus changes sign between each pair of atoms and all the interactions between orbitals on adjacent atoms are of an anti-bonding nature.

- The remaining degenerate pairs of solutions are complex wave functions but it is possible to generate completely real linear combinations of these which are still solutions of the Schrodinger equation with the same energies (in the same way that the p_x and p_y atomic orbitals may be constructed from the p_+ and p_- atomic orbitals).

The coefficients for the real functions are

$$\psi_{k+} \propto \sum_s \left[\cos\left(\frac{2\pi ks}{n}\right)\right]\phi_s$$

$$\psi_{k-} \propto \sum_s \left[\sin\left(\frac{2\pi ks}{n}\right)\right]\phi_s$$

e.g, for $n = 6$

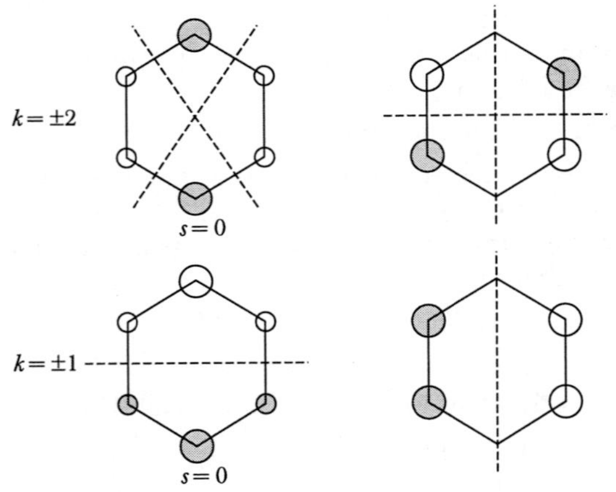

Symmetry and Hybridisation

As the size of a molecule increases then the solution of the secular equations can become rather difficult...but consideration of molecular symmetry can be used to greatly simplify the problem.

To illustrate this consider a simple example - a diatomic molecule H*X*.

(where X = Li, Be, B, C, N, O, F)

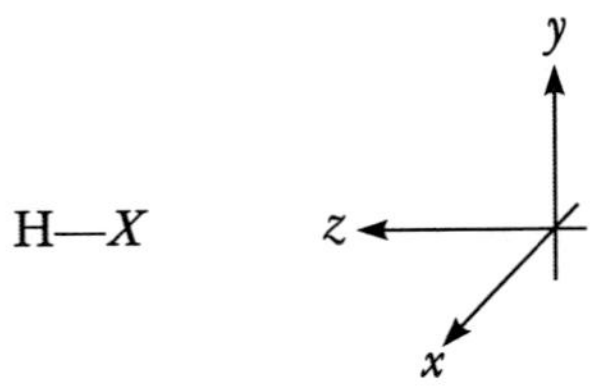

The valence orbitals of the atoms concerned are :

$$H = 1s$$
$$X = 2s, 2p_x, 2p_y, 2p_z$$

The interactions of the five valence orbitals can be described using a (5×5) secular determinant.

	$1s$	$2s$	$2p_z$	$2p_y$	$2p_x$
$1s$	$\alpha_{1s} - E$	β_{ss}	β_{sp}	0	0
$2s$	β_{ss}	$\alpha_{2s} - E$	0	0	0
$2p_z$	β_{sp}	0	$\alpha_{2p} - E$	0	0
$2p_y$	0	0	0	$\alpha_{2p} - E$	0
$2p_x$	0	0	0	0	$\alpha_{2p} - E$

H $1s$ will only give a non-zero resonance integral when it overlaps with the $2s$ and $2p_z$ orbitals of the X atom-see below.

AOs of the X-atom are orthogonal-hence they "can't interact with each other".

The off-diagonal elements in the determinant may be obtained by noting that :

(i) Integrals involving two different orbitals of the X-atom are exactly zero, since the atomic orbitals are orthogonal to one another.

(ii) The resonance integrals due to the interactions of the H $1s$ orbital with the orbitals of the X-atom are only non-zero if the orbitals have the "same symmetry" (that is, the same symmetry within the point group of the molecule).

Conversely, if the two overlapping orbitals are of different symmetries then any constructive overlap of the orbitals is always exactly counter balanced by an equal amount of destructive overlap and the net interaction is always exactly zero.

These two contrasting situations are illustrated below

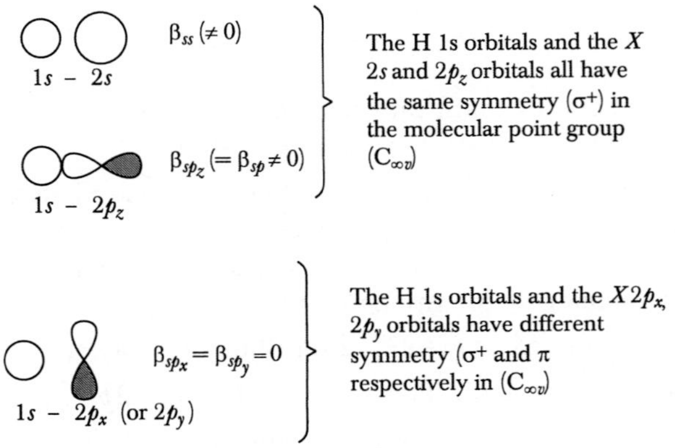

Consequently, in this case, rows 4 and 5 have no (non-zero) off-diagonal elements, because the $2p_x$ and

$2p_y$ orbitals are of different symmetry to the H 1*s* orbital. The (5×5) secular determinant can therefore be simplified to two trivial (1×1) determinants and a (3×3) determinant.

$$|(5\times 5)| = 0 \begin{cases} |\alpha_{2p} - E| = 0 \quad \Rightarrow \quad E = \alpha_{2p_x} \\ |\alpha_{2p} - E| = 0 \quad \Rightarrow \quad E = \alpha_{2p_y} \\ \begin{vmatrix} \alpha_{1s} - E & \beta_{ss} & \beta_{sp} \\ \beta_{ss} & \alpha_{2s} - E & 0 \\ \beta_{sp} & 0 & \alpha_{2p} - E \end{vmatrix} = 0 \end{cases}$$

We can conclude that in this molecule, the $2p_x$ and $2p_y$ orbitals of the *X*-atom are non-bonding and more generally that it is only necessary to consider interactions between orbitals possessing the same symmetry in the molecular environment.

Solution of the (3×3) Determinant

Strictly and solution necessarily involves both the 2*s* and $2p_z$ orbitals of the *X*-atom-however, the extent to which each is involved depends upon the energies of the orbitals relative to that of the 1*s* orbital of the H atom and this varies significantly across the Periodic Table.

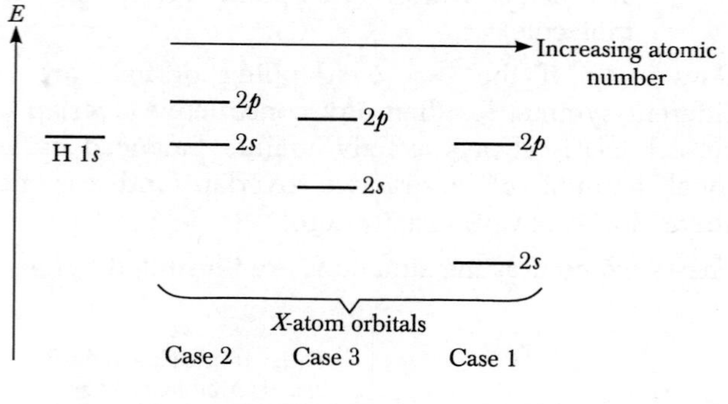

The above diagram illustrates how the relative orbital energies might vary for different *X*-atoms;

There is only a significant bonding interaction between two orbitals if the energy separation, $|\alpha_2 - \alpha_1|$ is not large compared to the interaction energy, as represented by the resonance integral, β_{12}.

We can therefore identify three "limiting" cases;

Case 1. The main interaction is H 1*s* – *X* $2p_z$...and if we completely neglect any interaction with *X* 2*s* then the problem simplifies to a (2×2) determinant.

e.g.,

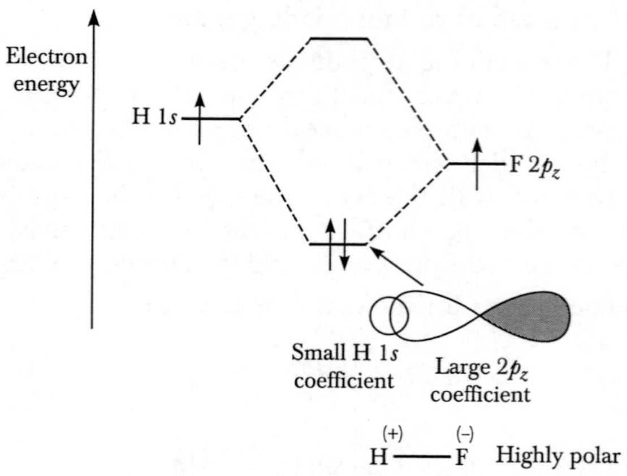

Case 2. The main interaction is H 1*s* – *X* 2*s*... and if we completely neglect any interaction with *X* $2p_z$ then the problem again simplifies to a (2×2) determinant-this limiting case is most closely aproached for LiH.

Case 3. ...is the intermediate case.

To illustrate what sort of solutions might be obtained in this case we can consider a "model" system (obtained by making some drastic simplifying assumptions)-let us suppose that :

$$\alpha_{2s} = \alpha_{1s} + 1/2\beta$$
$$\alpha_{2p} = \alpha_{1s} - 1/2\beta$$

and $\beta_{ss} = \beta_{sp}$ (and for simplicity, just call this β)

Then, $$\begin{vmatrix} \alpha_{1s} - E & \beta_{ss} & \beta_{sp} \\ \beta_{ss} & \alpha_{2s} - E & 0 \\ \beta_{sp} & 0 & \alpha_{2p} - E \end{vmatrix} = 0$$

simplifies to

$$\begin{vmatrix} \alpha - E & \beta & \beta \\ \beta & \left(\alpha + \frac{1}{2}\beta\right) - E & 0 \\ \beta & 0 & \left(\alpha - \frac{1}{2}\beta\right) - E \end{vmatrix} = 0$$

where α is the value for α_{1s}.

$$\Rightarrow \quad \begin{vmatrix} x & 1 & 1 \\ 1 & \left(x + \frac{1}{2}\right) & 0 \\ 1 & 0 & \left(x - \frac{1}{2}\right) \end{vmatrix} = 0$$

To which the solutions ar

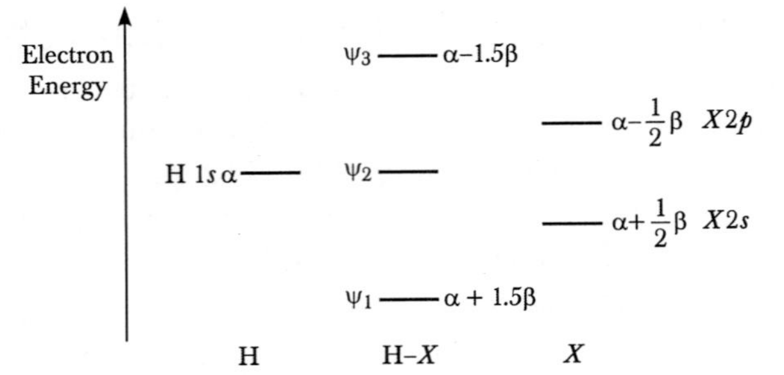

Now consider the MO coefficients

	H $1s$	$X2s$	$X2p_z$
ψ_3	0.67	0.33	0.67
ψ_2	0.33	–0.67	0.67
ψ_1	0.67	0.67	0.33

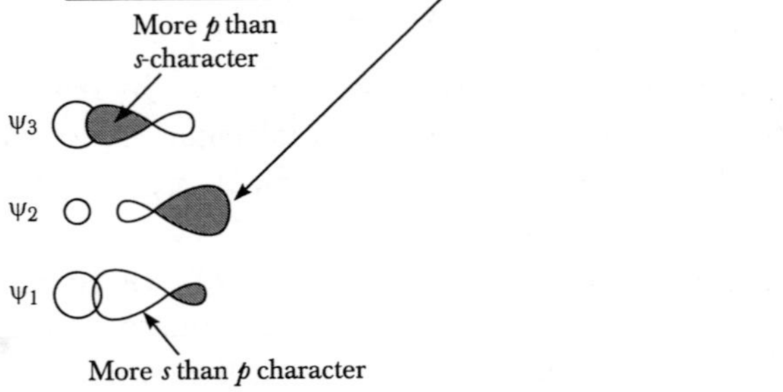

Note that similar, but **not** identical, MO energies and orbital coefficients would be predicted using a valence bond approach (as illustrated below) in which we first "hybridise" the $2s$ and $2p_z$ orbitals of the X atom to give two sp hybrid orbitals and then let the one pointing towards the H-atom interact with the H $1s$ orbital whilst the other is considered to undergo no interaction with the H $1s$ orbital and may thus be labelled a non-bonding orbital,

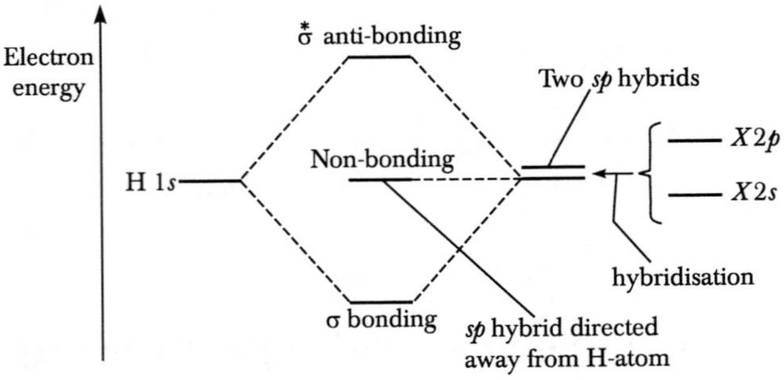

Minimization of the Expression for the Orbital Energy

Rearrangement of the equation for determining the expectation value of the orbital energy yields :

$$E\int \psi^2 \cdot d\tau = \int \psi \hat{\mathbf{H}} \psi \cdot d\tau$$

Which may (for two orbital overlap) be written in the form.

$$E(c_1^2 + c_2^2 + 2c_1c_2S) = c_1^2\alpha_1 + 2c_1c_2\beta_{12} + c_2^2\alpha_2 \qquad \ldots(43)$$

To minimize *E* with respect to c_1 We need to differentiate Eq. (43) with respect to c_1 and set $\frac{\partial E}{\partial c_1} = 0$.

Derivative of LHS

$$= E(2c_1 + 2c_2S) + \frac{\partial E}{\partial c_1}(c_1^2 + c_2^2 + 2c_1c_2S)$$

(using the chain rule)

Derivative of RHS $= 2c_1\alpha_1 + 2c_2\beta_{12}$

Hence, when we set $\frac{\partial E}{\partial c_1} = 0$, the differentiated form of Eq. (43) becomes

$$E(2c_1 + 2c_2S) = 2c_1\alpha_1 + 2c_2\beta_{12}$$

$$\Rightarrow \quad c_1(\alpha_1 - E) + c_2(\beta_{12} - ES) = 0$$

To minimize *E* with respect to c_2 We need to differentiate Eq. (43) with respect to c_2 and set $\frac{\partial E}{\partial c_2} = 0$.

Derivative of LHS

$$= E(2c_2 + 2c_1S) + \frac{\partial E}{\partial c_2}(c_1^2 + c_2^2 + 2c_1c_2S)$$

(using the chain rule)

Derivative of RHS $= 2c_2\alpha_2 + 2c_1\beta_{12}$

Hence, when we set $\frac{\partial E}{\partial c_2} = 0$, the differentiated form of Eq. (43) becomes

$$E(2c_2 + 2c_1S) = 2c_2\alpha_2 + 2c_1\beta_{12}$$

$$\Rightarrow \quad c_1(\beta_{12} - ES) + c_2(\alpha_2 - E) = 0$$

Example 10. *Set up the Huckel secular equation for cyclobutadiene, calculate the energies of the π orbitals and determine the DE (delocalization energy).*

Sol. See figure.

Cyclobutadiene

The Huckel secular equation is

$$\begin{vmatrix} x & 1 & 0 & 1 \\ 1 & x & 1 & 0 \\ 0 & 1 & x & 1 \\ 1 & 0 & 1 & x \end{vmatrix} = 0 \qquad \text{...(i)}$$

(where $x = (\alpha - E)/\beta$)

which upon expansion gives the polynomial equation

$$x^4 - 4x^2 = 0 \text{ or } x = 0 \text{ (twice); } \pm 2 \qquad \text{...(ii)}$$

Hence, the energy levels are

$x = -2$: $E = \alpha + 2\beta$ (BMO) ...(iii)

$x = 0$: $E_2 = E_3 = \alpha$ (degenerate pair); (NBMO) ...(iv)

$x = 2$: $E_4 = \alpha - 2\beta$ (ABMO) ...(v)

The molecular diagram for cyclobutadiene as shown in figure.

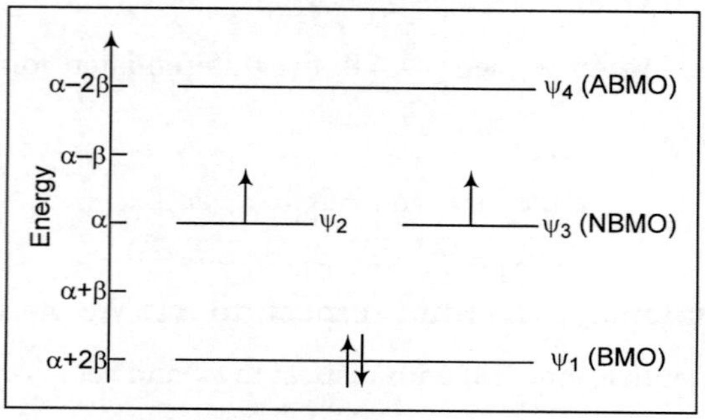

HMO diagram for cyclobutadiene

Hydrogen Bond

"It is a weak electrostatic force of covalently bonded hydrogen atom and covalently bonded highly electronegative atom (having small atomic size) within the molecule or between the molecules", *e.g.*, H_2O, HF, NH_3, *o*-nitrophenol, *p*-nitrophenol, etc.

(i) **Water** (H_2O)

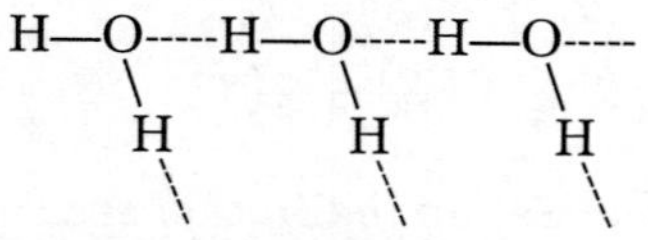

(ii) **Hydrogen fluoride** (HF)

-----H—F-----H—F-----H—F-----H—F-----

(iii) ***o*-nitrophenol**

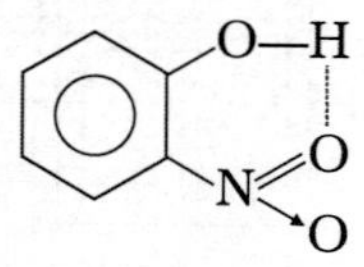

Hydrogen bonding is of two types :

1. Intermolecular Hydrogen Bonding

When hydrogen bonding takes place between the molecules of the same or different compounds, it is called intermolecular hydrogen bonding, *e.g.*,

(i) Various molecules of the same compound like HF, H_2O, alcohol, carboxylic acid, etc.

(ii) Various molecules of the different compounds like water and alcohol or water and ammonia :

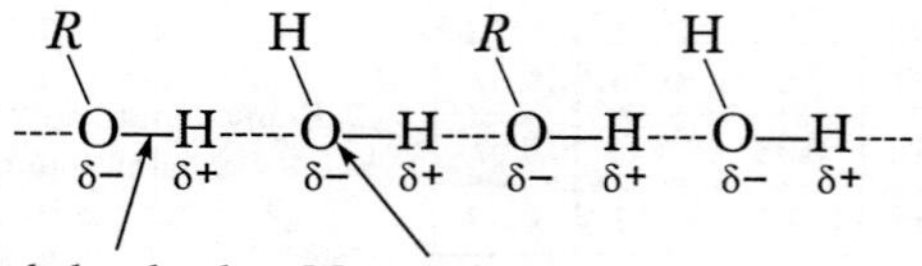

Consequences of intermolecular hydrogen bonding Formation of an intermolecular hydrogen bond influences the properties of various substances in the following manner :

(i) **Association** The molecules of carboxylic acids exist as dimers due to intermolecular hydrogen bonding. Therefore, their molecular masses are found to be double than calculated from their simple formula. For example, the molecular mass of acetic acid is found to be 120.

(ii) **Dissociation** Among halogens, only fluorine forms hydrogen bonding because of its small size and high electronegativity. In aqueous solution, hydrogen fluoride dissociates and gives the difluoride ion (HF_2^-) instead of fluoride ion (F^-). This supports the existence of KHF_2; however, formation of $KHCl_2$, $KHBr_2$ and KHI_2 is not possible.

(iii) **High melting and boiling points** The compounds having intermolecular hydrogen bonding show abnormally high melting and boiling points. For example :

2. Intramolecular Hydrogen Bonding (Chelation)

When hydrogen bonding occurs within the same molecule, it is termed as intramolecular hydrogen bonding. Common examples of intramolecular hydrogen bonding are given below :

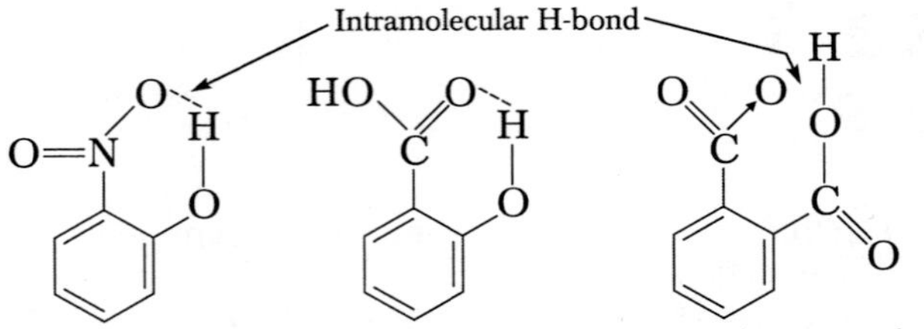

o-nitrophenol Salicyclic acid *o*-nitrobenzoic acid

Consequences of intramolecular hydrogen bonding Effect of intramolecular hydrogen bonding on physical properties of compounds is described below :

(i) **Low melting point** Compounds having an intramolecular hydrogen bond (*i.e., o*-isomers) have a lower melting point than the other isomers (*meta* or *para* isomers). This is due to the formation of an intramolecular hydrogen bond in the *o*-isomer whereas the *m*- and *p*-isomers have intramolecular hydrogen bonding.

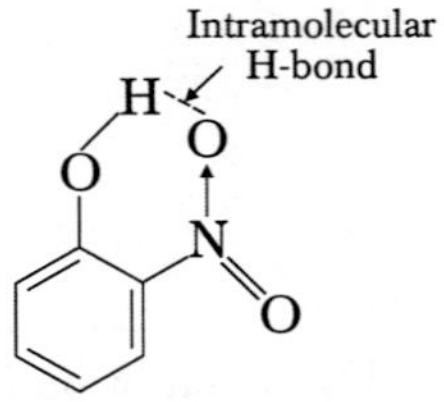

o-Nitrophenol

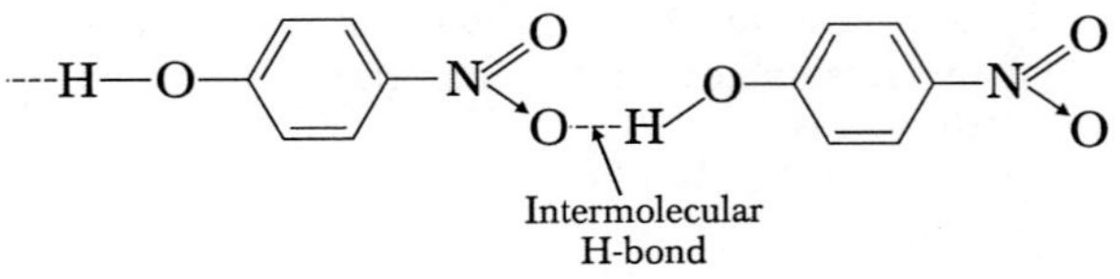

p-Nitrophenol

(ii) **Solubility in non-polar solvents** Compounds involved in chelation become non-polar, *i.e.,* salicylaldehyde. Consequently, such compounds are soluble in non-polar solvents like ether, benzene, etc., and are only sparingly soluble in water, whereas the corresponding *meta* and *para* isomer are more soluble in water and less soluble in non-polar solvents.

Exercise 1

(For Part 'B')

1. The MOT
(a) puts equal importance on both ionic and covalent structures
(b) overestimates the importance of ionic structures
(c) underestimates the importance of covalent structures
(d) None of the above

2. The VBT
(a) underestimates the importance of covalent structures
(b) overestimates the importance of covalent structure
(c) underestimates the importance of ionic structure
(d) puts equal emphasis on both ionic and covalent structures

3. If electronegativity difference between atoms *A* and B is 1.5, percentage ionic character of $A - B$ bond is
(a) 8 (b) 24.22
(c) 28.22 (d) 31.88

4. Hydrogen bonding is maximum in
(a) $(CH_3)_3N$ (b) CH_3Cl
(c) $(C_2H_5)_2O$ (d) C_2H_5OH

5. The non-polar molecule is
(a) *cis* 1,2-dichloroethane
(b) 1,3-dichlorobenzene
(c) NH_3
(d) *trans* 1,2-dichloroethene

6. The dipole moment is maximum for
(a) HF (b) HCl
(c) HBr (d) HI

7. In the change of NO^+ to NO, the electron is added to
(a) π orbital (b) $\overset{*}{\pi}$ orbital
(c) σ orbital (d) $\overset{*}{\sigma}$ orbital

8. If *Z*-axis is the molecular axis, which of the following combination is not allowed for the formation of MO?
(a) p_x and p_x (b) s and p_z
(c) p_z and p_z (d) s and p_x

9. According to the molecular orbital model, the highest occupied molecular orbital of O_2 is
(a) $\sigma\, 2s$ (b) $\overset{*}{\sigma}\ 2p$
(c) $\pi\, 2p$ (d) $\overset{*}{\pi}\ 2p$

10. In monomeric BH_3, let an axis definition place the molecule in the *xz* plane. Which atomic orbital on *B* is non-bonding?
(a) $2s$ (b) $2p_x$
(c) $2p_y$ (d) $2p_z$

11. Which of the following best represents the 3-dimensional view of H_2N^-?

(a) 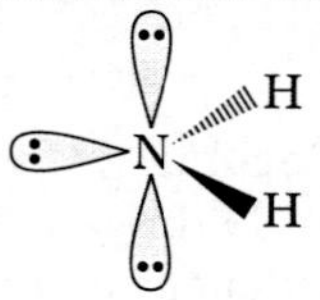

(b) 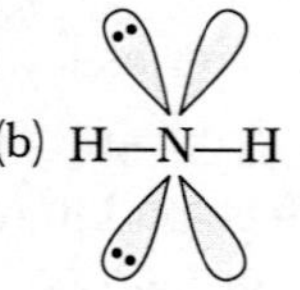

(c) 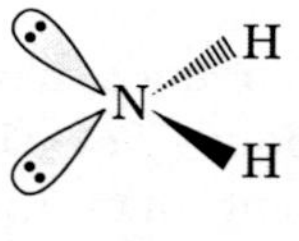

(d) 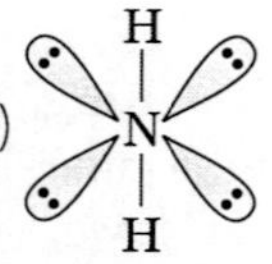

12. Considering the one electron He—H^{2+} ion system, the Hamiltonian (Born oppenheiner approximation) for the electronic energy in atomic units is

(a) $\hat{\mathbf{H}} = -\frac{1}{2}\nabla^2 + \frac{1}{r_H} - \frac{2}{r_{He}}$

(b) $\hat{\mathbf{H}} = \frac{1}{2}\nabla^2 + \frac{1}{r_H} + \frac{2}{r_{He}}$

(c) $\hat{\mathbf{H}} = -\frac{1}{2}\nabla^2 - \frac{1}{r_H} + \frac{2}{r_{He}}$

(d) $\hat{\mathbf{H}} = -\frac{1}{2}\nabla^2 - \frac{1}{r_H} - \frac{2}{r_{He}}$

13. How many molecular orbitals may be constructed from the valence shell orbitals of the constituent atoms in CH_4?
(a) 7 (b) 8 (c) 4 (d) 6

14. What is the symmetry of the anti-bonding molecular orbital formed by a linear combination of the p_x or p_y atomic orbitals in a homonuclear diatomic molecule?
(a) σ_g (b) σ_u
(c) π_u (d) π_g

15. For a diatomic molecule whose internuclear axis lies along the *z*-axis, what is the value of the overlap integral for the overlap between an p_z orbital on one atom and a p_y orbital on the other?
(a) 1 (b) 0
(c) $+\sqrt{2}$ <= ""label=""> (d) $-\sqrt{2}$ <= ""label="">

16. Use molecular orbital theory to determine the bond order for the O_2^+ ion.
(a) 3 (b) $1\frac{1}{2}$ (c) $2\frac{1}{2}$ (d) 2

17. The Pauling electronegativity of hydrogen is 2.1. Use the definition of Pauling electronegativity to estimate the electronegativity of chlorine given that the dissociation energy of an H—Cl bond is

427 kJ mol^{-1}, for a H–H bond is 432 kJ mol^{-1} and for a Cl–Cl bond is 239 kJ mol^{-1}.
(a) 3.0 (b) 1.1 (c) 2.1 (d) 4.2

18. The number of ionic terms present in the molecular orbital wave function for the bond between H and Cl in HCl (assuming that the bond is formed from the 1*s* electron of H atom and a 3*p* electron of Cl atom) is
(a) 0 (b) 1 (c) 2 (d) 3

19. For *n*-chain atoms, as the *n* increases, the HOMO-LUMO separation
(a) increases
(b) decreases
(c) first increases then decreases
(d) remains the same

20. For a cyclic conjugated hydrocarbon, the orbital energies are given by
(a) $E = \alpha + 2\beta \cos\left(\frac{2zk}{n}\right)$ (b) $E = \alpha + \beta \sin\left(\frac{2zk}{n}\right)$
(c) $E = \alpha - \beta \cos\left(\frac{2z}{n}\right)$ (d) $E = \alpha - 2\beta \sin\left(\frac{2zk}{2n}\right)$

21. Which of the following statements is correct?
(a) Bonding molecular orbital have higher energy than the combining atomic orbitals
(b) Bonding molecular orbital has high electron charge density than the anti-bonding molecular orbital
(c) Bonding molecular orbitals are the result of substractive interaction
(d) All of the above

22. Select the correct statement.
(a) Bond length of C–O bond is higher in CO than in CO^+.
(b) Bond order of C–O bond is higher in CO than in CO^+.
(c) Bond strength of C–O bond is higher in CO than in CO^+.
(d) (b) and (c) both

23. The HOMO of CO is
(a) $\pi 2p_x, \pi 2p_y$ (b) $\sigma 2p_z$
(c) $\sigma 2s$ (d) $\overset{*}{\pi}\ 2p_x, \overset{*}{\pi}\ 2p_y$

24. The term symbol for He_2^+ is
(a) °∧ (b) $^2\Sigma$
(c) 2π (d) $^3\Sigma$

25. The term symbol of O_2^+ is
(a) °∧ (b) $^1\Sigma$ (c) 2π (d) 3ϕ

26. The normalised wave function can be represented as
(a) $\int_0^{+\alpha} \psi^2 d\tau = 0$ (b) $\int_{-1}^{+1} \psi^2 d\tau = 0$
(c) $\int_{-\infty}^{+\infty} \psi^2 d\tau = 0$ (d) $\int_{-\infty}^{0} \psi^2 d\tau = 0$

27. For five electrons, the configurational wave function for the system would be given by
(a) $\psi = \psi + \psi_2 + \psi_3 + \psi_4 + \psi_5$
(b) $\psi = \psi_1\psi_2\psi_3\psi_4\psi_5$
(c) $\psi = \frac{\psi_1 + \psi_2 + \psi_3}{\psi_4 + \psi_5}$
(d) $\psi_0 = \psi_1\psi_2\psi_3 - \psi_4\psi_5$

28. For HCl molecule,
(a) $\lambda^2 N_-^2 = N_-^2$ (b) $N_+^2 \neq \lambda^2 N_+^2$
(c) $\lambda^2 = 1$ (d) $N_+ = \frac{1}{\sqrt{2}}$

29. In a diatomic molecules the *d*-orbitals contribute to
(a) σ orbitals only (b) π orbitals only
(c) σ and π orbitals both (d) None of these

30. The number of *p*-function perpendicular to the molecular plane in case of butadiene is
(a) 2 (b) 3
(c) 4 (d) 6

31. The delocalisation energy of butadiene can be given as
where, Bu = butadiene and Et = ethylene
(a) E_z (Bu) – E_z (Et) (b) E_z (Bu) + E_z (Et)
(c) E_z (Bu) – $2E_x$ (Et) (d) E_z (Bu) + $2E_x$ (Et)

32. A homonuclear diatomic MO is given by $\varphi = 2p_{z,a} + 2p_{z,b}$, where, the *z* axis is the same as the internuclear axis. Which one of the following statements about φ is correct?
(a) φ is an anti-bonding MO, symbolized σ*u*
(b) φ is a bonding MO, symbolized π*u*
(c) φ is an anti-bonding MO, symbolized π*g*
(d) φ is a bonding MO, symbolized σ_g

33. For the three species N_2, N_2^+, N_2^-, which one of the following orders for the bond energy (*i.e.,* bond strength) is most reasonable?
(a) $N_2 > N_2^+ > N_2^-$ (b) $N_2^+ > N_2 > N_2^-$
(c) $N_2^- > N_2 > N_2^+$ (d) $N_2^- > N_2^+ > N_2$

34. According to the LCAO-MO model, which one of the following second period diatomic molecules has a double bond in the ground electronic state?
(a) Li_2 (b) Be_2
(c) B_2 (d) C_2

35. For a planar unsaturated hydrocarbon having formula C_xH_y, where, all the carbon are part of the unsaturated frame work, how many pi MOs are there?
(a) $1 - y$ (b) x
(c) y (d) 2

Exercise 2

(For Part 'C')

1. Maximum bond strength is in
(a) O_2^{2-} (b) O_2^-
(c) O_2^+ (d) O_2

2. The paramagnetic molecule is
(a) O_2 (b) N_2
(c) Cl_2 (d) ClO_3

3. The molecule containing one unpaired electron is
(a) CO (b) CN^-
(c) NO (d) O_2

4. In which set of diatomic molecules, the bond order is 2.5?
(a) NO, CN, CN^- (b) O_2^+, N_2^+, CN^+
(c) O_2^-, CN^-, NO^- (d) CN, NO, N_2^+

5. Arrange the following in decreasing order of bond length–$O_2^{2-}, O_2^+, O_2, O_2^-, O_2^{2+}$
(a) $O_2^{2-} > O_2^- > O_2^{2+} > O_2^+ > O_2$
(b) $O_2^{2-} > O_2^- > O_2 > O_2^+ > O_2^{2+}$
(c) $O_2^{2+} > O_2^+ > O_2 > O_2^- > O_2^{2-}$
(d) $O_2^{2+} > O_2^+ > O_2 > O_2^{2-} > O_2^{2-}$

6. Arrange the following in decreasing order of bond dissociation energies $O_2^{2+}, O_2^+, O_2, O_2^-, O_2^{2-}$
(a) $O_2^{2-} > O_2^- > O_2 > O_2^+ > O_2^{2+}$
(b) $O_2^{2-} > O_2^- > O_2^+ > O_2^{2+} > O_2$
(c) $O_2^{2+} > O_2^+ > O_2 > O_2^- > O_2^{2-}$
(d) $O_2^{2+} > O_2^+ > O_2^{2-} > O_2^- > O_2$

7. Arrange the following in increasing order of reactivity $O_2^{2+}, O_2^+, O_2, O_2^-, O_2^{2-}$
(a) $O_2^{2-} < O_2^- < O_2^{2+} < O_2^+ < O_2$
(b) $O_2^{2-} < O_2^- < O_2 < O_2^+ < O_2^{2+}$
(c) $O_2^{2+} < O_2^+ < O_2 < O_2^- < O_2^{2-}$
(d) $O_2^{2+} < O_2^+ < O_2^- < O_2^{2-} < O_2$

8. Which of the following species is/are paramagnetic?
(a) O_2^{2-} (b) CN^- (c) NO^- (d) CO^+

9. In beaker *A*, an ice cube of pure D_2O is to be placed in pure liquid H_2O. In beaker *B*, an ice cube of pure H_2O is to be placed in pure liquid D_2O. Which of the following is the correct statement?
(a) Ice cube will float in both the beakers *A* and *B*
(b) Ice cube will sink in both the beakers *A* and *B*
(c) Ice cube will sink in beaker *A* but float over in *B*
(d) Ice cube will sink in baker *B* but float over in *A*

10. In the molecule HSCN, the hybridisation around S, C and N are respectively
(a) sp, sp^2, sp^3 (b) sp^3, sp^2, sp
(c) sp^3, sp, sp (d) sp^3, sp^2, sp^2

11. The molecular orbital diagram for the carbide ion (C_2^{2-}) would show which of the following molecular orbitals?
(a) $\sigma 1s^2, \overset{*}{\sigma} 1s^2, \sigma 2s^2, \overset{*}{\sigma} 2s^2, \pi 2p^4$
(b) $\sigma 1s^2, \overset{*}{\sigma} 1s^2, \sigma 2s^2, \overset{*}{\sigma} 2s^2, \pi 2p^4, \sigma 2p^2$
(c) $\sigma 1s^2, \overset{*}{\sigma} 1s^2, \sigma 2s^2, \overset{*}{\sigma} 2s^2, \pi 2p^4, \sigma 2p^2, \overset{*}{\pi} 2p^2$
(d) $\sigma 1s^2, \overset{*}{\sigma} 1s^2, \sigma 2s^2, \overset{*}{\sigma} 2s^2, \pi 2p^4, \sigma 2p^2, \overset{*}{\pi} 2p^4$

12. The Huckel molecular orbital energies of the planar radical (*i.e.*, 1 non-paired electron) CH_2CHCH_2 is
(a) $\alpha + \beta, \alpha, \alpha - \beta$ (b) $\alpha + \beta, \alpha, \alpha + 2\beta$
(c) $\alpha + \sqrt{2}\beta, \alpha, \alpha - \sqrt{2}\beta$ (d) $\alpha + 2\beta, \alpha, \alpha - 2\beta$

13. The two lowest electron states of H_2 can be understood in terms of the MO theory using spatial function of the form

$$\psi_{\pm} = \frac{1}{\sqrt{2(1 \pm 2)}}[1s_A \pm 1s_B]$$

The number of possible two electron functions which are anti-symmetric with respect to electron exchange of
(a) 4 (b) 6
(c) 8 (d) 2

14. The normalised wave function for ψ_+ is
(a) $\frac{1}{\sqrt{2(1+s)}}(1s_A - 1s_B)$ (b) $\frac{1}{\sqrt{(1+s)}}(1s_A + 1s_B)$
(c) $\frac{1}{\sqrt{2(s-1)}}(1s_A - 1s_B)$ (d) $\frac{1}{\sqrt{2(1+s)}}(1s_A + 1s_B)$

15. The energy levels for allyl radical and allyl anion are respectively $2(\alpha + \sqrt{2}\beta)$, α, 3α and $2(\alpha + \sqrt{2}\beta)$, 2α, 4α. The delocalisation energy for the allyl radical and allyl anion are respectively.
(a) 0.828α and 1.414β (b) 0.828β and 0.828β
(c) 0.828β and 2β (d) 2β and 0.828β

16. For ethylene molecule, the coefficient of atomic orbital wave functions are
(a) $\frac{1}{2}, -\frac{1}{2}$ (b) $\frac{1}{\sqrt{2}}, -\frac{1}{\sqrt{2}}$
(c) $\frac{1}{4}, -\frac{1}{4}$ (d) $\frac{1}{2\sqrt{2}}, -\frac{1}{2\sqrt{2}}$

17. Match Column I (molecules) with Column II (π energy levels) and choose the correct answer using the codes given below :

	Column I (Molecule)		Column (E_π)
A.		1.	$4\alpha + 5.123\,\beta$
B.	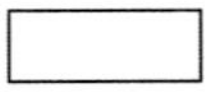	2.	$4\alpha + 4\,\beta$
C.	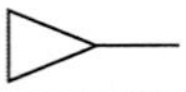	3.	$4\alpha + 4.962\,\beta$
D.	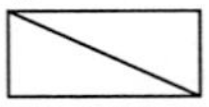	4.	$6\alpha + 6.988\,\beta$

Codes

	A	B	C	D
(a)	3	2	1	4
(b)	3	1	2	4
(c)	3	4	1	2
(d)	1	2	3	4

18. The valence bonding molecular orbital of a hydrogen chloride, HCl molecule may be described as the linear combination of the hydrogen 1*s* and chlorine 3*p* atomic orbitals

$\psi = 0.23\psi_H + 0.77\psi_{Cl}$

Calculate the probability of finding an electron in a 1*s* orbital on hydrogen.

(a) 59% (b) 77% (c) 23% (d) 54%

19. Predict, by analogy with benzene, the Huckel energies of the π molecular orbitals for cyclobutadiene, C_4H_4.

(a) $\alpha + \beta, \alpha, \alpha, \alpha - \beta$
(b) $\alpha + 2\beta, \alpha, \alpha, \alpha - 2\beta$
(c) $\alpha + \beta, \alpha + \beta, \alpha - 2\beta, \alpha - 2\beta$
(d) $\alpha + 2\beta, \alpha + 2\beta, \alpha - 2\beta, \alpha - 2\beta$

20. The valence bond wave function for a hypothetical molecule X_4 (if it is formed from 1*s* orbital of *X* and p_z orbital of *Y*), if the bond is 65% covalent is

(a) $0.80\,[\psi_x(1)\,\psi_y(2) + \psi_x(2)\,\psi_y(1)] + 0.59\,[\psi_y(1)\,\psi_y(2)]$
(b) $0.59\,[\psi_x(1)\,\psi_y(2) + \psi_x(2)\,\psi_y(1)] + 0.80\,[\psi_y(1)\,\psi_y(2)]$
(c) $0.80\,[\psi_1(1)\,\psi_x(2) + \psi_y(2)\,\psi_y(1)] + 0.59\,[\psi_x(1)\,\psi_x(2)]$
(d) $0.59\,[\psi_x(1)\,\psi_y(1) + \psi_x(2)\,\psi_y(2)] + 0.59\,[\psi_y(1)\,\psi_y(2)]$

21. If $\hat{H}$ is the Hamiltonian and usind the trial function for H_2^+ molecular ion, the energy of anti-bonding orbital is given by

(a) $\dfrac{H_{aa} + H_{ab}}{1 - S_{ab}}$ (b) $\dfrac{H_{aa} + H_{ab}}{1 + S_{ab}}$
(c) $\dfrac{H_{aa} - H_{bb}}{1 - S_{bb}}$ (d) $\dfrac{H_{aa} - H_{ab}}{1 - S_{ab}}$

22. In the above question the magnitude of coefficient of wave function is

(a) $\dfrac{1}{(1+s)^{1/2}}$ (b) $\dfrac{1}{(1+2s)^{1/2}}$
(c) $\dfrac{1}{(2+2s)^{1/2}}$ (d) $\dfrac{1}{(2+3s)^{1/2}}$

23. In the equation,

$$\psi' + N\{\psi_{1s}(A) + \psi_{1s}(B)\}$$

the normalisation factor for molecular orbital is

(a) $\dfrac{1}{(1+s)^{1/2}}$ (b) $\dfrac{1}{(1+2s)^{1/2}}$
(c) $\dfrac{1}{\sqrt{2}\,(1+s)^{1/2}}$ (d) $\dfrac{1}{2\,(1+s)^{1/2}}$

Directions (Q. Nos. 24 and 25)

Given, the integral

$$\frac{1}{\pi}\int \exp.(-2r_A)\cdot\frac{1}{r_B}\cdot r_A^2\,dr_A, \sin\theta\, d\theta\phi = \frac{1}{R}[1 - (1+R)e^{-2R}]$$ here

R, is the internuclear distance.

24. The expected value of the Hamiltonian for H_2^+ using the ground state wave function of H atom is

(a) 1 au (b) 0.5 au
(c) -0.5 au (d) -1 au

25. At an intermediate value of *R*, the total energy of H_2^+ is

(a) $\dfrac{1}{2} + \left(1 + \dfrac{1}{R}\right)e^{-2R}$ (b) $-\dfrac{1}{2} - \left(1 + \dfrac{1}{R}\right)e^{-2R}$
(c) $\dfrac{1}{2} - \left(1 + \dfrac{1}{R}\right)e^{-2R}$ (d) $-\dfrac{1}{2} + \left(1 + \dfrac{1}{R}\right)e^{-2R}$

26. For ethene molecule, the secular determinant are

$$\begin{pmatrix} \alpha - E & \beta \\ \beta & \alpha - E \end{pmatrix}\begin{pmatrix} c_1 \\ c_2 \end{pmatrix} = 0$$

The energies for this molecule is

(a) $\alpha - \beta, \alpha + \beta$ (b) $\alpha - 2\beta, \alpha + 2\beta$
(c) $\alpha - \beta, \alpha$ (d) $\alpha - \sqrt{2}\beta, \alpha + \sqrt{2}\beta$

27. The π-stabilisation energy for ethene is

(a) β (b) 2β
(c) 3β (d) $\sqrt{2}\beta$

28. The wave function for non-bonding molecular orbitals of diborane in terms of its orbitals is

(a) $\dfrac{1}{2}[\phi(B_1) + \phi B_2] + \dfrac{1}{\sqrt{2}}\phi(H)$

(b) $\dfrac{1}{\sqrt{2}}[\phi(B_1) + \phi(B_2)]$

(c) $\dfrac{1}{\sqrt{2}}(\phi(B_1) - \phi(B_2)]$

(d) $\dfrac{1}{2}[\phi(B_1) + \phi(B_2)] - \dfrac{1}{\sqrt{2}}\phi(H)$

29. The compound which has zero dipole-moment is/are

(a) BF_3 (b) NF_3
(c) PF_2Cl_2 (d) CH_2Cl_2

30. Which of the following compounds possesses zero dipole moment?

(a) Benzene (b) Carbon tetrachloride
(c) Boron trifluoride (d) Water

31. Which of the following have identical bond-order?
(a) CN^- (b) CN^+ (c) NO^+ (d) O_2^{2+}

32. The total pi energy of cycloheptatrienyl radical $(C_7H_7)^+$ is $7\alpha + 8.5429\beta$. The bond order of any bond in this molecule assuming it to be heptagonal is
(a) 8.5429 (b) 0.6102 (c) 4.2714 (d) 1.2204

33. Consider the following statements for Huckel approximation.
I. All overlaps are set to zero.
II. All diagonal term are set equal to Coulomb integral α.
III. All resonance integrals between neighbours are set to zero.
The correct statements are
(a) I and II (b) II and III
(c) I and III (d) I, II and III

34. Match Column I with Column II and choose the correct answer using the codes given below.

Column I (Molecule)		Column II (Delocalisation energy)	
A.	Butadiene	1.	0
B.	Cyclobutadiene	2.	0.83 β
C.	Benzene	3.	2β
D.	Allyl cation	4.	0.48 β

Codes

	A	B	C	D
(a)	4	1	3	2
(b)	3	4	1	2
(c)	4	3	1	2
(d)	4	1	2	3

Answers

Exercise 1

1. (b)	2. (c)	3. (d)	4. (d)	5. (d)	6. (a)	7. (b)	8. (d)	9. (a)	10. (b)
11. (c)	12. (d)	13. (b)	14. (d)	15. (b)	16. (c)	17. (a)	18. (c)	19. (b)	20. (a)
21. (b)	22. (a)	23. (c)	24. (b)	25. (c)	26. (a)	27. (b)	28. (b)	29. (c)	30. (c)
31. (c)	32. (a)	33. (a)	34. (d)	35. (b)					

Exercise 2

1. (c)	2. (a)	3. (c)	4. (d)	5. (b)	6. (c)	7. (c)	8. (c)	9. (a)	10. (c)
11. (d)	12. (c)	13. (b)	14. (d)	15. (b)	16. (b)	17. (a)	18. (a)	19. (b)	20. (a)
21. (d)	22. (c)	23. (c)	24. (c)	25. (d)	26. (a)	27. (b)	28. (c)	29. (a,c)	30. (a,b)
31. (c)	32. (b)	33. (a)	34. (a)						

Hints & Solutions

Exercise 1

13. There are four atomic orbitals, one *s* and three *p*, in the valence shell of carbon, whilst each of the four hydrogen atoms possesses one orbital in its valence shell. There are therefore eight atomic orbitals in total and eight molecular orbitals.

14. The p_x and p_y atomic orbitals are by convention, those that are perpendicular to the internuclear axis in a diatomic molecule. These orbitals have π symmetry in a linear molecule. The anti-bonding combination, in which the two atomic orbitals combine constructively. For this molecular orbital, the sign of the wave function does not change on inversion. The anti-bonding π-orbital must therefore be of *g* inversion symmetry, making it π_g overall.

16. The O_2^+ ion has 15 electrons of which 11 are valence electrons. Filling the molecular orbitals using the building-up principle leads to the electronic configuration.

$$1\sigma_g^2 1\sigma_u^2 2\sigma_g^2 1\pi_u^4 1\pi_g^1$$

Of these orbitals, the $1\sigma_g$, $2\sigma_g$ and $1\pi_u$ orbitals are bonding and the $1\sigma_u$ and $1\pi_g$ orbitals are anti-bonding. There are therefore 8 bonding electrons and 3 anti-bonding electrons. The bond order is therefore

$$b = \frac{1}{2}(8 - 3) = 2\frac{1}{2}$$

17. The Pauling electronegativity is defined on a relative scale through equation as

$$|\chi_H - \chi_{Cl}| = 0.102 \times (\Delta E/\text{kJ mol}^{-1})^{1/2}$$

with $\Delta E = E(\text{H–Cl}) - \frac{1}{2}\{E(\text{H—H}) + E(\text{Cl—Cl})\}$

Thus, for hydrogen chloride,

$$|\chi_H - \chi_{Cl}| = 0.102 \times \left\{472 - \frac{1}{2}(432 + 239)\right\}^{1/2} = 0.98$$

Thus, because we know that chlorine is more electronegative than hydrogen

$$|\chi_{Cl} = \chi_H + |\chi_H - \chi_{Cl}| = 2.1 + 1.0 = 3.1$$

18. Let H atom be designated by A and Cl atom by B. Let the $1s$ electron of H atom be labelled as electron 1 and $3p$ electron of Cl atom be labelled as electron 2.

$$\Psi_{MO} = \Psi_1\Psi_2$$

where $\quad \psi_1 = C_1\psi_A(1) + C_2\psi_A(2)$

and $\quad \psi_2 = C_1\psi_A(2) + C_2\psi_B(2)$

$$\therefore \; \psi_{MO} = [C_1\psi_A(1) + C_2\psi_B(1)]\,[C_1\psi_A(2) + C_2\psi_B(2)]$$
$$= C_1^2\,[\psi_A(1)\psi_A(2)] + C_1C_2[\psi_A(1)\,\psi_B(2)]$$
$$+ [C_1C_2\psi_A(2)\psi_B(1)] + C_2^2\,[\psi_B(1)\,\psi_B(2)]$$

The first and last terms are ionic and the middle terms are covalent.

23. In CO, $\sigma 2s$ orbital is filled after $\pi 2p_x$ and $\pi 2p_y$ orbitals.

24. $He_2^+(3) = \sigma 1s^2, \sigma 2s^1$

For σ orbital $m_l = 0$ so $M_L = 0$

Thus, it is represented by the symbol Σ $S = \frac{1}{2}$. So spin multiplicity, $2s + 1 = 2$. So the term symbol is $^2\Sigma_g$.

25. $O_2^+ \; (8 + 8 - 1 = 15) = KK\,\sigma 2s^2, \overset{*}{\sigma} 2s^2, \sigma 2p_z^2,$

$$\pi 2p_x^2 \approx \pi 2p_y^2, \overset{*}{\pi} 2p_x^1$$

Thus, $\quad M_L = m_1 + m_2 + m_3 + m_4 \ldots\ldots\ldots m_7$

$$= 1 + 1 + 0 + 0 + (-1) + (-1) + 1 = 1$$

Thus, term symbol is π and $2s + 1 = 2$

$\therefore$ The complete term symbol is $2\pi_u$.

28. HCl is a heteroatomic molecule and for a heteroatomic molecule,

$$N_+^2 \neq \lambda^2 N_+^2,\; N_-^2 \neq \lambda^2 N_+^2,\; \lambda \neq \pm 1$$

30. The p_x orbital is the p-function perpendicular to the molecular plane. For butadiene, there are four p_x orbitals.

Exercise 2

12. We can set up the secular equations in the same way as outlined for ethene.

Thus, we may write

$$(\alpha - E)c_A + \beta c_B = 0$$
$$\beta c_A + (\alpha - E)c_B + \beta c_C = 0$$
$$\beta_{c_B} + (\alpha - E)c_C = 0$$

or, introducing the parameter

$$x = (\alpha - E)/\beta$$

in matrix form as

$$\begin{vmatrix} x & 1 & 0 \\ 1 & x & 1 \\ 0 & 1 & x \end{vmatrix} = 0$$

Evaluating this determinant

$$x\begin{vmatrix} x & 1 \\ 1 & x \end{vmatrix} - 1\begin{vmatrix} 1 & 1 \\ 0 & x \end{vmatrix} + 0\begin{vmatrix} 1 & x \\ 0 & 1 \end{vmatrix} = 0$$

$$x(x^2 - 1) - x = 0$$

$$x^2 - 2x = 0$$

The roots of this equatioin are

$$x = 0$$

Corresponding to an energy of

$$E = \alpha$$

and $\quad x = \pm\sqrt{2}$

Corresponding to energies of

$$E = \alpha \pm \sqrt{2}\beta$$

18. The squares of the coefficients may be used to determine the electron density on each atom. Thus the probability of finding an electron in a $1s$ orbital on hydrogen is $0.77^2 = 59\%$.

19. We should expect the π-system of cylobutadiene to consist of four molecular orbitals because it is made up from the contributions from the four out-of-plane p orbitals on the four carbon atoms. One of these orbitals will correspond to a completely bonding orbital in which the coefficients of each of the orbitals are the same. Comparison with the result for benzene shows that for a cyclic system, this orbital has an energy of $\alpha + \beta$. There will also be a corresponding anti-bonding orbital in which the magnitudes of the coefficients of the atomic orbitals are the same but the signs alternate around the ring. This anti-bonding orbital must have an energy of α-β. In benzene, the remaining molecular orbitals are arranged in degenerate pairs and this is also true for cyclobutadiene. The two remaining molecular orbitals can only therefore each have an energy of α. Thus the energies of the orbitals are $\alpha + 2\beta$, α, α-2β. It is possible to obtain the same results by setting up and solving the secular equations, but use of symmetry arguments and knowledge of similar systems makes this unnecessary.

20. Let $1s$ electron be labelled as 1 and p_z electron be as 2.

For purely covalent structure of xy, the wave function is written as

$$\psi_{covalent} = \psi_A(1)\,\psi_B(2) + \psi_A(2)\,\psi_B(1)$$

For purely ionic structure, both the electron are on the more electronegative y atom, so

$$\psi_{ionic} = \psi_y(1)\,\psi_y(2)$$

Net $\quad \psi = C_1\,\psi_{covalent} + C_2\psi_{ionic}$

with $\quad C_1^2 + C_2^2 = 1$

Since, $\quad C_1^2 = 0.65$

$\therefore \quad C_2^2 = 0.35$

$$C_1 = \sqrt{0.65} = 0.80$$
$$C_2 = 0.35 = 0.59$$

$$\therefore \quad \psi = 0.80\,[\psi_x(1)\,\psi_y(2) + \psi_x(2)\psi_y(1)] + 0.59[\psi_y(1)\psi_y(2)]$$

21. The average energy of H_2^+ ion using the trial wave function $\psi = C_1\phi_a(1) + C_2\phi_b(1)$ can be written as

$$\bar{\varepsilon} = \frac{\int [C_1\phi_a(1) + C_2\phi_a(1)]\,\hat{\mathbf{H}}\,[C_1\phi_a(1) + C_2\phi_b(1)]d\tau}{\int [C_1\phi_a(1) + C_2\phi_a(1)]\,[C_1\phi_a(1) + C_2\phi_b(1)]d\tau}$$

$$= \frac{C_1^2 \int \phi_a(1)\,\hat{\mathbf{H}}\,\phi_a(1)\,d\tau + C_2^2 \int \phi_b(1)\,\hat{\mathbf{H}}\,\phi_b(1)\,d\tau + C_1C_2 \int \phi_a(1)\,\hat{\mathbf{H}}\,\phi_b(1)\,d\tau + C_1C_2 \int \phi_b(1)\,\hat{\mathbf{H}}\,\phi_a(1)\,d\tau}{C_1^2 \int \phi_a(1)\,\phi_a(1)\,d\tau + C_2^2 \int \phi_b(1)\,\phi_b(1)\,d\tau + C_1C_2 \int \phi_a(1)\,\phi_b(1)\,d\tau + C_1C_2 \int \phi_b(1)\,\phi_a(1)\,d\tau} \quad ...(1)$$

Let

$\int \phi_a(1)\,\hat{\mathbf{H}}\,\phi_a(1)\,d\tau = H_{aa}$; $\int \phi_b(1)\,\hat{\mathbf{H}}\,\phi_b(1)\,d\tau = H_{bb}$

$\int \phi_a(1)\,\hat{\mathbf{H}}\,\phi_b(1)\,d\tau = H_{ab}$; $\int \phi_b(1)\,\hat{\mathbf{H}}\,\phi_b(1)\,d\tau = H_{ba}$

$\int \phi_a(1)\,\phi_a(1)\,d\tau = S_{aa}$; $\int \phi_b(1)\,\phi_b(1)\,d\tau = S_{bb}$

$\int \phi_a(1)\,\phi_b(1)\,d\tau = S_{ab}$; $\int \phi_b(1)\,\phi_a(1)\,d\tau = S_{ba}$

Now, both ϕ_a and ϕ_b are normalized $1s$ atomic orbital wave functions, $H_{aa} = H_{bb}$, $S_{aa} = S_{bb} = 1$.

It can also be shown that $H_{ab} = H_{ba}$. The equation (1) becomes

$$\bar{\varepsilon} = \frac{C_1^2 H_{aa} + C_2^2 H_{aa} + 2C_1C_2H_{ab}}{C_1^2 + C_2^2 + 2C_1C_2S_{ab}} \quad ...(2)$$

Using the variation theorem and minimising the energy with respect to C_1 and C_2. The equation obtained after rearranging and setting

$$\frac{d\bar{\varepsilon}}{dC_1} = 0$$

and $$\frac{d\bar{\varepsilon}}{dC_2} = 0,$$

we get $(H_{aa} - \varepsilon)\,C_1 + (H_{ab} - \varepsilon S_{ab})C_2 = 0 \quad ...(3)$

$(H_{ab} - \varepsilon S_{ab})\,C_1 + (H_{aa} - \varepsilon)C_2 = 0 \quad ...(4)$

The solution of these equation other that $C_1 = C_2 = 0$, is if the following determinant is zero, *i.e.*,

$$\begin{vmatrix} H_{aa} - \varepsilon & H_{ab} - \varepsilon S_{ab} \\ H_{ab} - \varepsilon S_{ab} & H_{aa} - \varepsilon \end{vmatrix} = 0 \quad ...(5)$$

or, $(H_{aa} - \varepsilon)^2 - (H_{ab} - \varepsilon S_{ab})^2 = 0$

This is called 'Secular determinant'. The solutions of the quadratic equation (5) are

$$\varepsilon_1 = \frac{H_{aa} + H_{ab}}{1 + S_{ab}} \quad \text{(for BMO)} \quad ...(6)$$

$$\varepsilon_2 = \frac{H_{aa} - H_{ab}}{1 - S_{ab}} \quad \text{(for ABMO)} \quad ...(7)$$

22. Substituting the value of ε_1 in equation (3) of the above answer we get

$$\left(H_{aa} - \frac{H_{aa} + H_{ab}}{1 + S_{ab}}\right)C_1 + \left(H_{ab} - \frac{H_{aa}S_{ab} + H_{ab}S_{ab}}{1 + S_{ab}}\right)C_2 = 0$$

or, $$\left(\frac{H_{aa}S_{ab} - H_{ab}}{1 + S_{ab}}\right)C_1 + \left(\frac{H_{ab} - H_{aa}S_{ab}}{1 + S_{ab}}\right)C_2 = 0$$

or, $C_1 = C_2 = C$

IIIrd for $\varepsilon = \varepsilon_2$, $C_1 = -C_2 = C$

Since the total probability is unity, with $C_1 = C_2$ and ψ, we get

$$1 = \int \psi^* \psi\, d\tau \quad \text{all space}$$

$$= \int C^2 [\phi_a(1) + \phi_b(1)]\,[\phi_a(1) + (1)]\,d\tau$$

$$= C_2 [\int \phi_a(1)\,\phi_a(1)\,d\tau + \int \phi_b(1)\,\phi_b(1)\,d\tau + 2\int \phi_a(1)\,\phi_b(1)\,d\tau]$$

$$= C^2 (2 + S)$$

or, $$C = \frac{1}{\sqrt{2 + 2S}}$$

Similarly for

$C_1 = -C_2 = C$, the value of C will be

$$C = \frac{1}{\sqrt{2 - 2S}}$$

23. We need to find the factor N in the given equation that ensures that

$$\int \psi^2 d\tau = 1$$

To proceed we substitute LCAO into this integral and make use of the fact that the atomic orbitals are individually normalized. The additional integral required is the overlap integral (S)

$$S = \int \psi_A^* \psi_B d\tau = 0$$

When we substitute the wave function we find

$$N^2 \{\int \psi_{1s}(A)^2\,d\tau + \int \psi_{1s}(B)^2\,d\tau + 2\int \psi_{1s}(A)\,\psi_{1s}(B)\,d\tau)\}$$

$$= N^2 \{1 + 1 + 2s\} = 1$$

$\therefore$ The normalization factor is

$$N = \left(\frac{1}{2(1 + S)}\right)^{1/2}$$

or $$= \frac{1}{\sqrt{2}(1 + s)^{1/2}}$$

24. $$E_{H_2^+} = \int 1S_A\left[-\frac{1}{2}\nabla^2 - \frac{1}{r_A} - \frac{1}{r_B}\right]1S_A d\tau$$

$$= \int 1S_A\left(-\frac{1}{2}\nabla^2 - \frac{1}{r_A}\right)1S_A d\tau - \int 1S_A \cdot \frac{1}{r_B} 1S_A d\tau$$

$$= E_H - \frac{1}{\pi}\int \exp(-2r_A)\frac{1}{r_B}.r_A^2.dr_A.\sin\theta\, d\theta\, d\phi$$

$$= -\frac{1}{2} - \frac{1}{R}[1 - (1 + R)\,e^{-2R}] \quad \text{(in a.u.)}$$

When, $R \to \infty$ $\quad E_{H_2^+} = E_H = -\frac{1}{2}$ au

25. When R is a very small, $e^{-2R} \approx 1 - 2R$,

then $(1 + R)e^{-2R} \approx 1 - R - 2R^2$

and $$E_{H_2^+} \approx E_H - (1 + 2R) \approx -\frac{1}{2} + 1$$

$$= +\frac{1}{2} a.u$$

At an intermediate value of R, addition of the internuclear repulsion energy $\frac{1}{R}$ gives the total.

$$E_{H_2^+} = -\frac{1}{2} + \left(1 + \frac{1}{R}\right)e^{-2R}$$

32. The total π-bond order must be 8.5429 or 4.2714. These result from several identical bonds, so each bond order is $\frac{4.2714}{7} = 0.6102$.

19 Molecular Symmetry and Group Theory

Syllabus

- Symmetry Elements and Symmetry Operations
- Point Group : Multiplication and Application
- Grand Orthogonality Theorem
- Character Table and Selection Rules

Symmetry is a very fascinating phenomenon in nature. It is found in geometrical figures such as a cube, a sphere, an equilateral triangle, a rectangle, a square, a regular pentagon, a regular hexagon, etc. Its importance was recognized by eminent Greek philosophers Pythagoras and Plato. However, in this chapter we shall be concerned with the symmetry found in molecules and solids. Mathematical study of symmetry is called **group theory**. Its foundations were laid in the 19th century by the French mathematician E. Galois and European mathematicians Jordan, Frobenius, Sylvester, Sylow, Cayley, Lie and Abel. In the 20th century, applications of group theory to physics and chemistry were pioneered by H. Weyl and the 1963 Physics Nobel Laureate. E.P. Wigner, the Hungarian-American mathematical physicist. Murray Gell-Mann, the American theoretical physicist, was awarded the 1969. Physics Nobel Prize for applying symmetry to the classification of elementary particles and the postulation of quarks which are the constituents of baryons and hadrons.

Symmetry Elements and Symmetry Operations

Symmetry element

A symmetry element is a geometrical entity such as a point, a line or a plane about which a symmetry operation is performed.

Symmetry operation

A symmetry operation is the movement of a molecule about the symmetry element in such a manner that the resulting configuration of the molecule is indistinguishable from the original. The molecule may assume an equivalent configuration or an identical configuration.

There are five types of symmetry element : E, C_n, σ, S_n and i. E is called the identity; C_n is the n-fold proper axis of rotation; σ is the plane of symmetry; S_n is the n-fold improper axis of rotation and i is the centre of symmetry (or the inversion centre). These symmetry elements and the corresponding symmetry operations are listed in Table 19.1.

Table 19.1 **Symmetry Elements and Symmetry Operations**

	Symmetry element	Symmetry operation
1.	Identity (E)	The operation leaves the molecule unchanged.
2.	Proper axis of notation (C_n)	Rotation by an angle $\theta = 2\pi/n$ about the axis.
3.	Plane of symmetry (σ)	Reflection in the plane.
4.	Improper axis of rotation or rotation-reflection axis, S_n.	Rotation about the axis followed by reflection in a plane perpendicular to the axis.
5.	Inversion centre or centre of symmetry (i)	Inversion of all atoms in the molecule through the inversion centre.

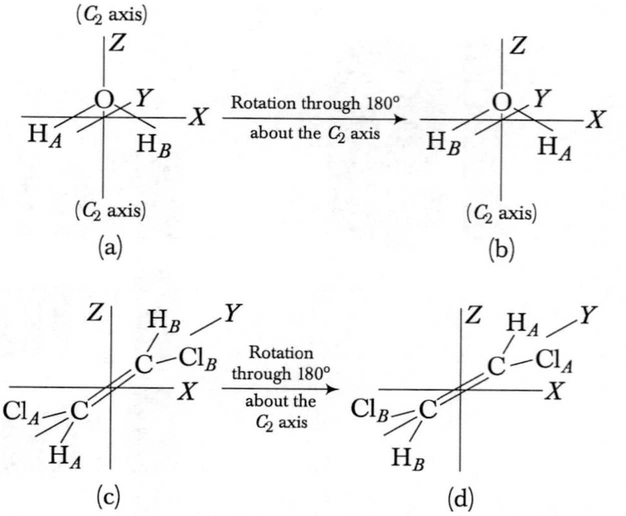

Fig. 19.1 Two molecules having a C_2 rotational axis (a) and (b). The water molecule. (c) and (d) *trans*-dichloroethylene. In both cases rotation through 180° about the Z axis leads to an indistinguishable configuration.

1. Symmetry Axis (C_n)

Rotation about a symmetry axis A molecule may have one more axes about which a rotation leads to a configuration that is indistinguishable from the original one. Such an axis is a symmetry element and is called a **symmetry axis** or a **rotational axis.** A rotation about a symmetry axis is a symmetry operation. A simple example is provided by the water molecule, shown in Fig. 19.1 (a) and (b). We can draw the Z axis through the oxygen atom, bisecting the angle between the two O—H bonds. The X axis can be drawn through the centre of gravity of the molecule and in the plane of the molecule, and the Y axis is at right angles to these two axes. The X and Y axes are not symmetry axes, but the Z axis is a symmetry axis because a 180° rotation about this axis leads to an indistinguishable configuration. To show this we have labelled the two hydrogen atoms A and B. If Fig. 19.1 (a) represents the original configuration, Fig. 19.1 (b) represents the configuration after rotation through 180°. Since, the labels are only mental constructs, the configuration in Fig. 19.1 (b) is indistinguishable from that in Fig. 19.1 (a).

If a molecule is rotated through an angle θ in order to achieve the indistinguishable configuration, the axis is said to be a $360°/\theta$ fold rotational axis and to have an order p of $360°/\theta$; such an axis is designated C_p. In the example of water, $p = 360°/180° = 2$ and the designation is therefore C_2; the axis is said to be a two fold rotational axis. The planar molecule *trans*-dichloroethylene also has a two fold (C_2) axis, as shown in Fig. 19.1 (c). All molecules remain the same if they are rotated through 360°, so that all molecules have C_1 axes, and these needed not be specified.

The non-planar ammonia molecule has a three fold (C_3) axis; its order is $360°/120° = 3$. If we label the hydrogen atoms A, B and C, Fig. 19.2 (a) shows one configuration, and Fig. 19.2 (b) shows the configuration after a rotation though 120°; Fig. 19.2 (c) shows the result of a further rotation through 120°.

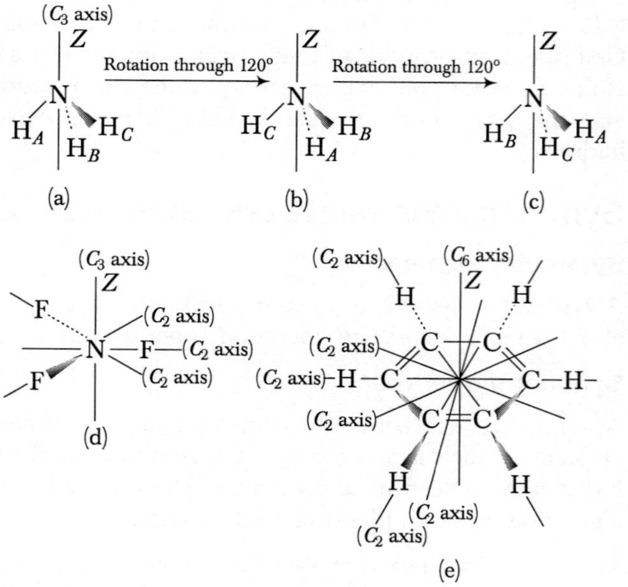

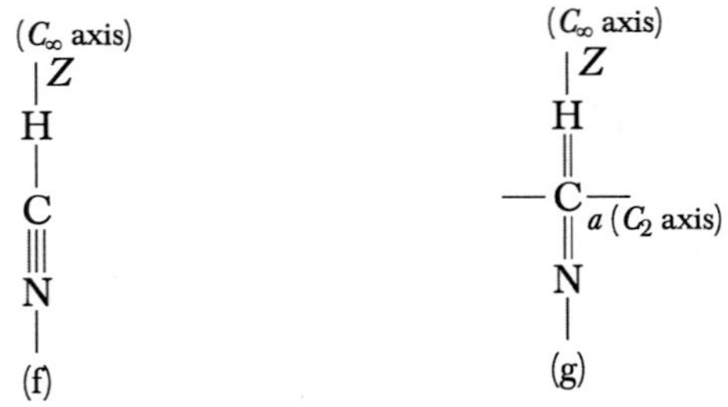

Fig. 19.2 (a), (b) and (c) The non-planar ammonia molecule, having a C_3 axis. (d) The planar BF_3 molecule, which has a C_3 axis and three C_2 axes. (e) Benzene, having a C_6 axis and six C_2 axes. (f) The linear molecule HCN, having a C_∞ axis. (g) The linear molecule CO_2, which has a C_∞ axis and an infinite number of C_2 axes.

The planar molecule BF_3 [Fig. 19.2 (d)] has a three fold axis at right angles to the plane of the molecule and passing through the boron atom. In addition, each of the bonds lies along a two fold rotational axis; there are thus three C_2 axes we well as the one C_3 axis. When a molecule has symmetry axes of different orders, a useful convention is to take an axis of the highest order as the Z axis and to draw it vertically. The axis of highest order is often called the **principal axis**. Thus, in the example of BF_3, shown in Fig. 19.2 (d), the C_3 axis is taken to be the vertical Z axis, so that the molecule lies in a horizontal plane.

Benzene, shown in Fig. 19.2, is a molecule having a C_6 axis. It also has six C_2 axes at right angles to the C_6 axis. The C_6 axis is thus the principal axis. All linear molecules have a C_∞ rotational axis, since, an infinitesimal rotation about the axis of the molecule leaves the molecule unchanged; thus $\theta \to 0$ and $p = 360°/\theta \to \infty$. An example is H—C≡N, shown in Fig. 19.2 (f). The linear symmetrical molecule CO_2 has, in addition to the C_∞ axis, which is the principal axis, an infinite number of C_2 axes, since any axis through the carbon atom and at right angles to the C_∞ axis is a C_2 axis [see Fig. 19.2 (g)].

2. Centre of Symmetry (i)

Inversion about a centre of symmetry A molecule has a **centre of symmetry**, designated i (for inversion), if a straight line drawn from every atom through the centre and extended in the same direction encounters an equivalent atom equidistant from the centre. Such a centre of symmetry, which can also be called a centre of inversion, is another example of a symmetry element. Fig. 19.3 shows some examples of molecules having a centre of symmetry. In each case there are pairs of atoms equidistant from the centre and situated in opposite directions from the centre.

3. Plane of Symmetry (σ)

Reflection through a plane of symmetry For some molecules there is a plane such that if the molecule is reflected in the plane, it is indistinguishable from the original. Such a plane, which is another symmetry element, is called a **plane of symmetry** and is denoted by the symbol σ (sigma); it is also often called a **mirror plane**. Several types of mirror planes may be distinguished according to their orientation. Consider, for example, the water molecule, shown again in Fig. 19.4 (a). We have seen that there is one axis of symmetry, a C_2 axis, and that this is conventionally taken as the Z axis and drawn vertically. Both planes of symmetry pass through this axis and are therefore vertical planes. One of them is the plane of the molecule itself; we take it to be the YZ plane and denote it by the symbol σ_v. The other planes of symmetry is at right angles to this σ'_v plane and is the XZ plane; we denote it by the symbol σ_v. In this example of water there are only two planes and both pass through the axis of symmetry. Some molecules

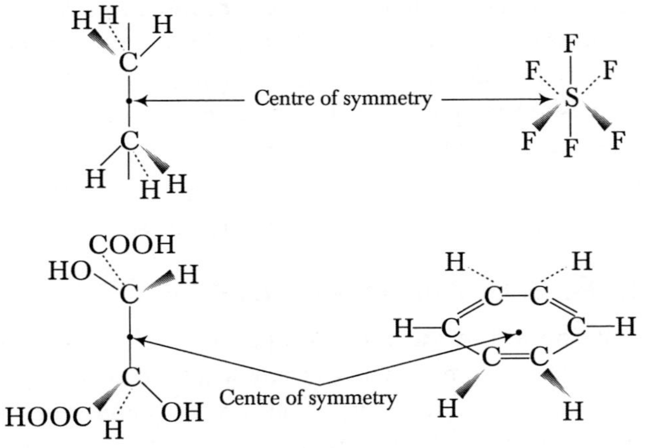

Fig. 19.3 Four molecules having a centre of symmetry. Heavy wedged lines represent bonds projecting toward the reader out of the plane of the paper. Dashed lines represent bonds projecting behind the plane of the paper.

have a plane that is perpendicular to the principal axis of symmetry. Since, this axis is conventionally taken to the vertical, this type of plane is horizontal and is designated σ_h. An example of such a plane is found in benzene, as shown in Fig. 19.4.

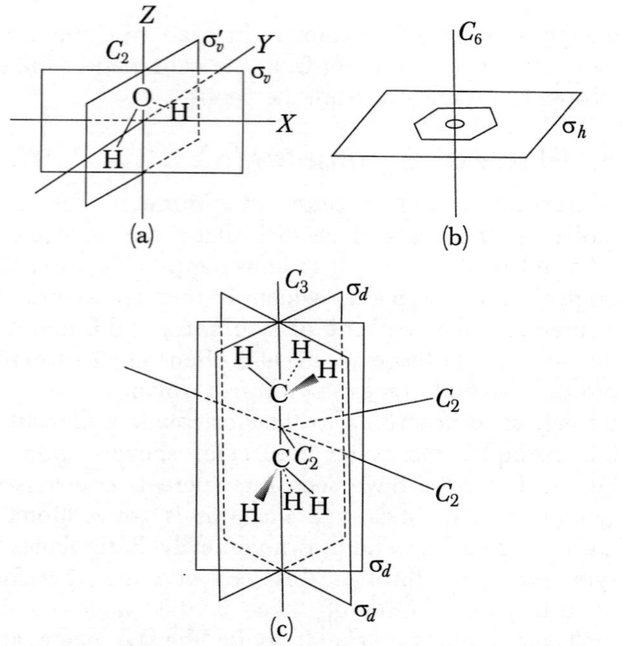

Fig. 19.4 Some molecules having planes of symmetry (a) H_2O : the σ_v' plane is the plane of the molecule : the σ_v plane is at right angles to the σ_v' plane. (b) Benzene, C_6H_6, which has a σ_h plane. (c) Staggered ethane, which has three dihedral (σ_d) planes; these bisect the angles between the three C_2 axes.

Another type of plane, called the **dihedral** plane and given the symbol σ_d, is found in ethane in the staggered conformation [Fig. 19.4 (c)]. In this molecule there is a principal C_3 axis, and there are also three C_2 axes at right angles to the C_3 axis.

The three dihedral planes contain the principal axis and also bisect the angles between the three C_2 axes.

4. Axis of Improper Rotation (S_n)

Rotation about an axis followed by reflection in a Plane The symmetry of some molecules is such that if there is first a rotation about an axis and then a reflection in a plane perpendicular to this axis, the result is superimposable on the original. Such an axis is known as an axis of improper rotation, or a rotation-reflection axis. The designation used for such an axis is S_p; p is equal to 360°/θ, where, θ is the angle through which the molecule is rotated in order for the reflection to give a superimposable form. Methane has an S_4 rotation-reflection axis, as shown in Fig. 19.5.

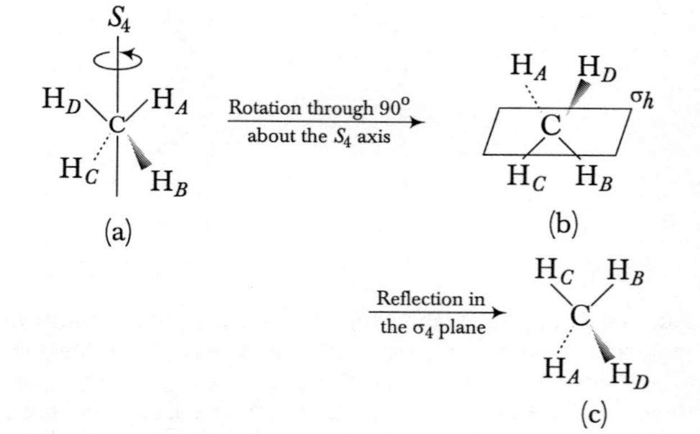

Fig. 19.5 Methane, which has an S_4 rotation reflection axis. (a) The original form. (b) After rotation through 90° (*i.e.*, a C_4 rotation). (c) After reflection in the horizontal plane perpendicular to the S_4 axis.

5. The Identity of Element (E)

The identity operation we have seen that all molecules have a C_1 axis of symmetry, since, rotation through 360° restores anything to its original condition. The same is, of course, true if we perform no operation at all; we then say that we are performing the identity operation. This operation is included for mathematical completeness, and the symbol E is used for it.

If an operation $\hat{A}$ is performed and is followed by an operation $\hat{B}$, we write the combined operation as $\hat{B}\hat{A}$. If a C_2 operation is performed, and then another C_2 operation, the combined operation is written as C_2^2. Since, C_2 rotates about 180°, C_2^2 rotates about 360° and is therefore equal to C_1 and to E.

Group Postulates

The complete set of operations forms a mathematical group. In order that the symmetry elements A, B, C ... form a mathematical group G, the following conditions must be satisfied :

1. Two elements A and B of a group combine to give the third element C, which is also an element of the group.

$$AB = C$$

   It means that the application of B followed by A is equivalent to the application of C. If $AB = BA$, the elements A and B are said to commute.

2. An element combines with itself to form another element of the group.

3. The group must contain the identity element E which commutes with all the elements and leaves them unchanged.

$$EA = AE = A$$
$$EB = BE = B, \text{ etc.}$$

4. Every element of the group obeys the associative law of combination.

$$A(BC) = (AB)C$$

5. Every element A of a group has an inverse A^{-1} which is also an element of the group.

$$AA^{-1} = A^{-1}A = E$$

Example 1. *Show that the set of rational numbers from zero to infinity forms a mathematical group.*

Sol. Let 5 and 7 be any two rational numbers. Then $5 \times 7 = 7 \times 5 = 35$. The numbers 5 and 7 are in the same group and 35 is also in the same group. Also, $1 \times 4 = 4 \times 1 = 4$. The number 4 is in the same group and the identity element E is 1. Again, $3 \times \frac{1}{3} = \frac{1}{3} \times 3 = 1$. $\frac{1}{3}$ is the inverse of 3. Further, $4 \times (5 \times 6) = (4 \times 5) \times 6$. Hence, the set of rational numbers between 0 and ∞ forms a group.

Types of Groups

Abelian and non-Abelian groups

A group is said to be Abelian if all the elements commute and non-Abelian if all the symmetry elements do not commute with one another. We shall later show that H_2O molecule belongs to an Abelian group and NH_3 to a non-Abelian group.

Cyclic groups

A group is said to be cyclic if all its elements can be generated from one symmetry element. Thus, $A, A^2, A^3, \ldots A^n$ form the elements of a cyclic group; here, $A^n = E$, the identity element. In general, the roots of the equation $x^n - 1 = 0$ form a cyclic group. Note that all cyclic groups are Abelian.

Point Groups and Multiplication Tables

All the symmetry operations in a molecule can be combined to form a molecular group. This group is called **point group** since, all the symmetry elements of the molecule intersect at a common point which remains fixed under all the symmetry operations. Crystals have very high symmetry. In fact, they have translational symmetry which is not found in gaseous molecules. The molecular point groups are represented by the Schoenflies symbols whereas the point groups for crystals are denoted by Hermann-Mauguin symbols. Table 19.2 lists some molecular point groups which are of interest to chemists.

(i) Order of a group

The number of elements in a group is known as its order (h). For a symmetry group the order is therefore the number of operations that leave the molecule unchanged. An important property of a mathematical group is that the product of any pair of operations in the group results in another operation that is also a member of the group. This result is helpful in that by taking products of known symmetry operations for a molecule we may discover other symmetry operations that were not at once apparent.

(ii) Sub-group

This is a group within a group. If any selection or subset of the elements of a group satisfies the definition of a group, then this subset of element is called a subgroup. A subgroup must necessarily include the identity element E.

(iii) Similarity transformation and conjugate element

If A and X are two elements of a group obeying the relation

$$X^{-1}AX = B \qquad \ldots(1)$$

Where, B is also in the same group, then B is called the similarity transformation of A by X and A and B are said to be conjugate to each other.

(iv) Multiplication table

Point groups are defined with respect to the particular symmetry elements involved. Table 19.2, lists the more important point groups and gives some examples. A molecule having no symmetry at all, such as CHClBrI [Fig. 19.6 (a)], is said to belong to the C_1 point group. The hydrogen peroxide molecule, in which the two O—H bonds do not lie in the same plane [Fig. 19.6 (b)], has a two fold (C_2) axis of symmetry. Its symmetry operations are therefore C_2 and E, and it said to belong to the C_2 point group. Since, the identity operation E does nothing, EC_2 and C_2E are both equal to C_2, and the C_2 operation performed twice ($i.e.$, C_2^2) is equal to E.

A multiplication table for a point group shows all possible products of the symmetry operations and such a table is included in Fig. 19.6 (b).

The water molecule contains the symmetry elements E, C_2, σ_v and σ'_v and is said to belong to the point group C_{2v}. Fig. 19.6 (c) gives the multiplication table.

Table 19.2 **Some Molecular Point Groups**

Point group	Symmetry elements	Examples
C_1	E	CHFClBr
C_2	E, C_2	H_2O_2
C_3	E, C_3	C_2H_6
C_5	E, σ_v	NOCl
C_{2v}	$E, C_2, 2\sigma_v$	H_2O, $CH_2{=}O$, pyridine
C_{3v}	$E, C_3, 3\sigma_v$	NH_3, $CHCl_3$, PH_3
$C_{\infty v}$	$E, C_\infty, \infty\sigma_v$	HCl, NO, CO
C_{2h}	E, C_2, σ_h, i	*trans* CHCl$=$CHCl
D_{2h}	$E, 3C_2, 3\sigma, i$	$CH_2{=}CH_2$, naphthalene
D_{3h}	$E, 2C_3, 3C_2$ ($\perp$ to C_3), $3\sigma_v, \sigma_h, 2S_3$	BF_3 (trigonal planar)
D_{4h}	$E, C_4, 4C_2$ ($\perp$ to C_4), $2\sigma_v, 2\sigma_d, \sigma_h, C_2, S_4$ (coincident with C_4), i	$[PtCl_4]^{2-}$ (square planar)
D_{6h}	$E, 2C_6, 6C_2$ ($\perp$ to C_6), $3\sigma_v, 3\sigma_d, \sigma_h, C_2$, $2C_3, 2S_6, 2S_3, i$	C_6H_6
T_d	$E, 4C_3, 3C_2, 3S_4$ (coincident with C_2), $6\sigma_d$	CH_4
O_h	$E, 3C_4, 4C_3, 3S_4$ and $3C_2$ (both coincident with the C_4 axes), $6C_3, 4S_6, 3\sigma_6, 6\sigma_d$	SF_6

The reader should verify the individual entries in this table. Consider, for example, the item

$$\sigma'_v C_2 = \sigma_v \qquad \ldots(2)$$

This means that rotation by 180° about the C_2 axis followed by reflection in the σ'_v plane is equivalent to reflection in the σ_v plane.

Ammonia [Fig. 19.5 (d)] has the symmetry elements E and C_3 and it has there vertical planes that we may designate σ_1, σ_2 and σ_3. Its point group is called C_{3v}, and its multiplication table is shown in Fig. 19.6 (d). One special point that arises hereis the direction of rotation. If we take C_3 to mean a clockwise rotation through 120°, then C_3^2 means a clockwise rotation through 240°; this however is equivalent to an anticlockwise rotation through 120°, an operation that can be written as $\overline{C}_3$. Thus, $C_3^2 = \overline{C}_3$. In the multiplication table it is therefore necessary to include both C_3 and $\overline{C}_3$.

Structure	Symmetry elements	Point group	Multiplication table
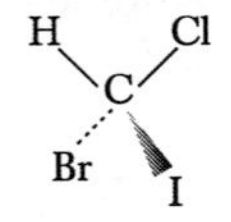 (a) CHClBrI	E only (no symmetry)	C_1	
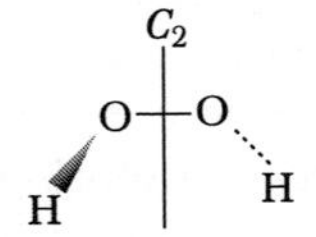 (b) Hydrogen peroxide	E, C_2	C_2	See table (b) below
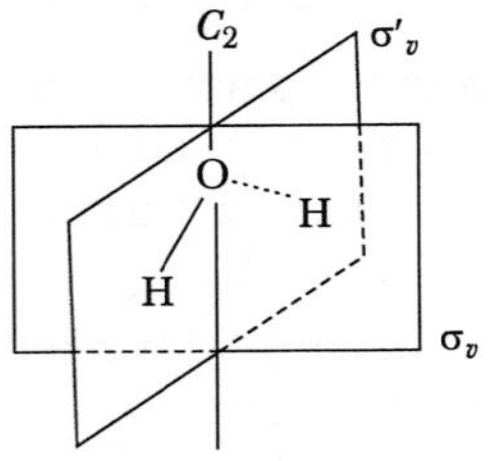 (c) Water	E, C_2, σ_v, σ'_v	C_{2v}	See table (c) below
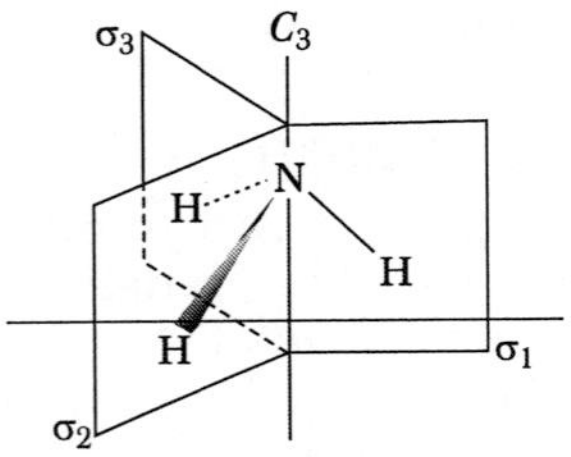 (d) Ammonia	E, C_3, $\overline{C}_3 (= C_3^2)$, σ_1, σ_2, σ_3	C_{3v}	See table (d) below

Multiplication table for C_2:

Second operation	First operation	
	E	C_2
E	E	C_2
C_2	C_2	E

Multiplication table for C_{2v}:

Second operation	First operation			
	E	C_2	σ_v	σ'_v
E	E	C_2	σ_v	σ'_v
C_2	C_2	E	σ_v	σ_v
σ_v	σ_v	σ'_v	E	C_2
σ'_v	σ'_v	σ_v	C_2	E

Multiplication table for C_{3v}:

Second operation	First operation					
	E	C_2	$\overline{C}_3$	σ_1	σ_2	σ_3
E	E	C_3	$\overline{C}_3$	σ_1	σ_2	σ_3
C_3	C_3	$\overline{C}_3$	E	σ_3	σ_1	σ_2
$\overline{C}_3$	$\overline{C}_3$	E	C_3	σ_2	σ_3	σ_1
σ_1	σ_1	σ_2	σ_3	E	C_3	$\overline{C}_3$
σ_2	σ_2	σ_3	σ_1	$\overline{C}_3$	E	C_3
σ_3	σ_3	σ_1	σ_2	C_3	$\overline{C}_3$	E

Fig. 19.6 Examples of the point groups C_1, C_2, C_{2v}, and C_{3v}, with their multiplication tables.

(v) Representation

The essential feature of group theory is that the symmetry operations are replaced by numbers or matrices that multiply in the same way as the operations themselves. These sets of numbers and matrices are known as representations or as symmetry species, and we will first give some examples for the point group C_{2v}.

The multiplication table for this point group is shown in Fig. 19.6 (c). There are four operations, E, C_2, σ_v and σ'_v, and we ask what sets of numbers multiply in the same way as the actual operations. One obvious possibility is to replace all the operations by unity :

$$E \rightarrow 1,\ C_2 \rightarrow 1,\ \sigma_v \rightarrow 1,\ \sigma'_v \rightarrow 1$$

Another is to replace E and C_2 by unity, and σ_v and σ'_v by -1

$$E \rightarrow 1,\ C_2 \rightarrow 1,\ \sigma_v \rightarrow -1,\ \sigma'_v \rightarrow -1$$

We can easily verify that this representation also leads to the same multiplication table; for example, $\sigma_v \sigma'_v = C_2$ and $(-1)(-1) = 1$. Two other representations are also shown in Table 19.2. The four representations have been designated A_1, A_2, B_1, and B_2. The A designation means that there is no change on rotation about the principal axis; B means that there is a change.

(vi) Irreducible representations

It turns out that there are certain representations that are the most fundamental and useful, and these are known as **irreducible representations.** The symmetry species shown in Table. 19.3 are in fact all the irreducible representations for this point group.

(vii) Classes

For the point group C_{2v} there are four different types of operation; the identity operation (E), rotation (C_2), and two reflections (σ_v and σ'_v). We refer to these types of operation as **classes**. Sometimes, (although not in the present example) there is more than one operation in a class, and we then speak of the degeneracy of the class. An important theorem in group theory is that the number of irreducible representations is equal to the number of classes. Thus, for the C_{2v} point group there are four classes, E, C_2, σ_v and σ'_v and, therefore, four irreducible representations as listed in Table 19.3.

(viii) Character table

Tables such as Table 19.3 are known as **character tables**. The numbers + 1, – 1, etc., that appear in these tables are known as **characters**. In the appendix to this chapter we give character tables for some of the more common point groups. In these tables we have made use of symbols such as A_1, B_2 and Σ_g^+, and these are part of a scheme proposed by the American chemical physicist Robert S. Mulliken (1896-1986).

Table 19.3 **Representations** (Symmetry species) **for the Point Group C_{2v}**

Designation of symmetry species	E	C_2	$\sigma_v(xz)$	$\sigma'_v(yz)$
A_1	+1	+1	+1	+1
A_2	+1	+1	−1	−1
B_1	+1	−1	+1	−1
B_2	+1	−1	−1	+1

The modern convention is to take the $\sigma'_v(yz)$ plane to be the plane of the molecule. For the B_1, species there is therefore antisymmetry with respect to a reflection in the plane of the molecule.

They are also known as traces. The word character is then reserved for the set of traces that are given in a character table.

(ix) Parity

The terms symmetric and antisymmetric are used to refer to the characters +1 and – 1, respectively, for a particular operation. For example, suppose that a molecular orbital is such that it retains its sign when a rotation is carried out; the character is +1 and the orbital is said to be symmetric with respect to that rotation. If it changes sign, the character is – 1 and the function is said to be antisymmetric. A particular notation is used if the molecule (*e.g.,* a homonuclear diatomic molecule) has a centre of symmetry, in which case one of the symmetry elements is inversion. If the symmetry species is such that inversion brings about no change of sign, the species is symmetric with respect to inversion and the subscript g (German gerade) is added to the symbol. An example, is the Σ_g^+ species shown in the appendix to this chapter for point group D_{coh}. If, one of the other hand, inversion brings about a change of sign, the subscript is u (German ungerade). An example is the symmetry species Σ_u^+ found in the point group $D_{\infty h}$. The word parity is used with reference to inversion about a centre of symmetry, and therefore relates to the g-u classification. Other features of the notation for the symmetry species of diatomic molecules are considered in molecular orbitals.

Basis for a Representation

Many of the applications of group theory to molecular problems depend on the fact that certain simple functions behave, with respect to the symmetry operations, in the same way as certain symmetry species. Such a function is said to be a **basis** for the particular species.

Consider, for example, the point group C_{2v}, which is shown in Fig. 19.6 (c). A z-coordinate is unchanged by a rotation about the C_2 axis and by reflections in the σ_v and σ'_v planes. It therefore behaves in the same way as the species A_1;

E	C_2	σ_v	σ'_v
+1	+1	+1	+1

A z coordinate is therefore a basis for the A_1 representation, An x coordinate, however, changes its sign on a C_2 rotation and on reflection in the σ'_v plane; reflection in the σ_v plane, however, does not affect it. It therefore, transforms according to the scheme.

E	C_2	σ_v	σ'_v
+1	−1	+1	−1

and it is therefore a basis for the B_1 representation (Table 19.3). A y coordinate can similarly be shown to be a basis for the B_2 representation.

Rotations can be considered from the same point of view. Suppose that the water molecule shown in

Fig. 19.4 (a) is rotating about the Z axis. The direction of rotation is unchanged by the C_2 operation, whereas it is reversed by reflections in the σ_v and σ'_v planes. The rotation R_z therefore, transforms according to the scheme

E	C_2	σ_v	σ'_v
+1	+1	−1	−1

and the function R_z therefore, belongs to the A_2 symmetry species. Rotation about the X axis is unchanged by the σ'_v operation but is reversed by C_2 and by σ_v and R_x therefore, transforms according to

E	C_2	σ_v	σ'_v
+1	−1	−1	+1

The function R_x therefore belongs to the B_2 symmetry species. Similarly, R_y belongs to the B_1 species.

These and other relationships are shown in the character tables given in the appendix to this chapter. We shall see in Chapter 13 that the x, y and z relationships are relevant to infrared vibrational spectra; R_x, R_y and R_z to infrared rotational spectra; and x^2, y^2, z^2, xy, xz and yz to Raman spectra.

Details for Representations of Molecular Point Groups

Representations of molecular point groups

The five kinds of symmetry operations, *viz.*, E, C_n, σ, S_n, i can be represented by matrices. It can be shown (we omit the derivation) that if these operations operate on a two-dimensional position vector

$$\bar{r} = x\hat{\mathbf{i}} + y\hat{\mathbf{j}} \qquad \ldots(3)$$

where, $\hat{\mathbf{i}}$, $\hat{\mathbf{j}}$ are the unit vectors along the x and y axes, respectively, they generate five 2×2 matrices :

$$\begin{bmatrix} x' \\ y' \end{bmatrix} = \underbrace{\begin{bmatrix} \quad\quad\quad \end{bmatrix}}_{2 \times 2 \text{ matrix}} \begin{bmatrix} x \\ y \end{bmatrix} \qquad \ldots(4)$$

Here, we have written the position vector as a column vector and the transformed vector as a primed column vector. The matrices are :

$$E = \begin{bmatrix} 1 & 0 \\ 1 & 0 \end{bmatrix}; C_2 = \begin{bmatrix} \cos\theta & \sin\theta \\ -\sin\theta & \cos\theta \end{bmatrix};$$

$$\sigma_{yz} = \begin{bmatrix} -1 & 0 \\ 0 & 1 \end{bmatrix}; \text{ etc.} \qquad \ldots(5)$$

On the other hand, if the same operations operate on a three-dimensional position vector they generate five 3×3 matrices :

$$\bar{r} = x\hat{\mathbf{i}} + y\hat{\mathbf{j}} + z\hat{\mathbf{k}} \qquad \ldots(6)$$

$$E = \begin{bmatrix} 1 & 0 & 0 \\ 0 & 1 & 0 \\ 0 & 0 & 1 \end{bmatrix}; C_n(z) = \begin{bmatrix} \cos\theta & \sin\theta & 0 \\ -\sin\theta & \cos\theta & 0 \\ 0 & 0 & 1 \end{bmatrix};$$

$$\sigma_{yz} = \begin{bmatrix} -1 & 0 & 0 \\ 0 & 1 & 0 \\ 0 & 0 & 1 \end{bmatrix}; \qquad \ldots(7a)$$

$$S_n = \sigma_{xy} C_n(z) = \begin{bmatrix} \cos\theta & \sin\theta & 0 \\ -\sin\theta & \cos\theta & 0 \\ 0 & 0 & -1 \end{bmatrix};$$

$$i = \begin{bmatrix} -1 & 0 & 0 \\ 0 & -1 & 0 \\ 0 & 0 & -1 \end{bmatrix}; \sigma_{xy} = \begin{bmatrix} 1 & 0 & 0 \\ 0 & 1 & 0 \\ 0 & 0 & -1 \end{bmatrix}; \text{ etc.} \qquad \ldots(7b)$$

The sum of the diagonal elements of a matrix is called the trace or character χ of the matrix. The character of the various matrices corresponding to the symmetry operations described above are given in Table 19.4.

Table 19.4 **Characters of the Symmetry Operations**

Symmetry operation (R)	Character of R, $\chi(R)$
E	$\chi(E) = 3$
C_n	$\chi(C_n) = 2\cos\theta + 1$
σ	$\chi(\sigma) = 1$
S_n	$\chi(S_n) = 2\cos\theta - 1$
i	$\chi(i) = -3$

We can verify the remarkable fact that these matrices combine like the symmetry operations themselves. Thus, for instance,

$$\sigma_{xz}\sigma_{yz} = \begin{bmatrix} 1 & 0 & 0 \\ 0 & -1 & 0 \\ 0 & 0 & 1 \end{bmatrix} \begin{bmatrix} -1 & 0 & 0 \\ 0 & 1 & 0 \\ 0 & 0 & 1 \end{bmatrix}$$

$$= \begin{bmatrix} -1 & 0 & 0 \\ 0 & -1 & 0 \\ 0 & 0 & 1 \end{bmatrix} = C_2(z) \qquad \ldots(8)$$

The set of matrices corresponding to the symmetry operations (or the symmetry elements) of a group is called its **representation**. It must be borne in mind that this set of matrices is not a unique set. For a point group of a molecule these can be many other sets of matrices (and hence many representations) which combine in the same way as the symmetry operations themselves. We are, however, interested in the most fundamental representation from which other representations can be derived.

Representations can be classified into (a) Reducible representations (reps) and (b) irreducible representations (irreps).

Reps. Let A, B, C ... be the matrices which form the representation of a group and let X be the similarity transformation matrix of this group such that

$$X^{-1}AX = A' \qquad \ldots(9)$$

$$X^{-1}BX = B' \quad ...(10)$$

$$X^{-1}CX = C' \quad ...(11)$$

Then, if X is the proper transformation matrix, we have

$$X^{-1}AX = A' = \begin{bmatrix} \boxed{a'_1} & & & 0 \\ & \boxed{a'_2} & & \\ 0 & & \boxed{a'_3} & \\ & & & \boxed{a'_4} \end{bmatrix} \quad ...(12)$$

The new matrix A' is now blocked out along the diagonal into smaller matrices a'_1, a'_2, a'_3, a'_4 etc., with the off-diagonal elements equal to zero. Similarly, we have

$$X^{-1}BX = B' = \begin{bmatrix} \boxed{b'_1} & & & 0 \\ & \boxed{b'_2} & & \\ 0 & & \boxed{b'_3} & \\ & & & \boxed{b'_4} \end{bmatrix} ;\text{ etc.} \quad ...(13)$$

This is expressed by saying that the given sets of matrices form a reducible representation (rep).

Irreps. If it is not possible to find a similarity transformation which will reduce the matrices $A, B, C, ...$ to block-diagonalized form, the representation is called in irreducible representation (irrep).

Grand/Great Orthogonality Theorem (GOT)

This is the most important theorem of group theory. It concerns the matrix elements (*i.e.,* elements of the matrices) which constitute the irreps of a point group. Mathematically it is stated as follows :

$$\sum_R \Gamma_i (R)_{mn} \Gamma_j (R)^*_{m'n'} = \frac{h}{\sqrt{l_i l_j}} \delta_{ij} \delta_{mm'} \delta_{nn'} \quad ...(14)$$

Here, Γ_i and Γ_j are the ith and jth irreps of a point group of order h with dimensions l_i and l_j, respectively; $\Gamma_i(R)_{mn}$ is the mnth matrix element corresponding to the symmetry operation R belonging to the ith irrep and $\Gamma_j(R)^*_{m'n'}$ is the complex conjugate of the $m'n'$th matrix element corresponding to the symmetry operation R belonging to the jth irrep. The δs are the well known 'Kronecker deltas' which have the following property :

$$\delta_{ij} = \begin{cases} 1, & i = j \\ 0, & i \neq j \end{cases}; \quad \delta_{mm'} = \begin{cases} 1, & m = m' \\ 0, & m \neq m \end{cases};$$

$$\delta_{nn'} = \begin{cases} 1, & n = n' \\ 0, & n \neq n' \end{cases} \quad ...(15)$$

The summation is performed over all the symmetry operations R of the molecules. If the matrix elements are real, then

$$\Gamma_j (R)^*_{m'n'} = \Gamma_j (R)_{m'n'} \quad ...(16)$$

The following three cases arise for the G.O.T. assuming that the matrix elements are real :

1. For two different irreps, $i \neq j$, $m = m'$ and $n = n'$
$$\sum_R \Gamma_i (R)_{mn} \Gamma_j (R)_{mn} = 0 \quad ...(17)$$
2. For the same irrep, $i = j$, $m \neq m'$ and $n \neq n'$
$$\sum_R \Gamma_i (R)_{mn} \Gamma_j (R)_{mn'} = 0 \quad ...(18)$$
3. For an irrep i and for $m = m'$, $n = n'$,
$$\sum_R [\Gamma_i (R)_{mn}]^2 = h/l_i \quad ...(19)$$

In practice, we do not use the GOT in the form given above but in a slightly different form involving the characters of the irreps, as shown in the next section.

Important Properties of Irreducible Representations (Irreps)

The properties of the irreps can be derived from the GOT. Consider a point of order h. Recall that h is the number of symmetry operations of a point group. Let the h symmetry operations be divided into k classes. We shall denote the irreps by $\Gamma_1, \Gamma_2, \Gamma_3 ... \Gamma_k$ and their dimensions by $l_1, l_2, l_3 ... l_k$. Using the GOT the following properties of the irreps can be obtained :

1. The number of irreps in a point group is equal to the number of its symmetry classes.
2. The sum of the squares of the dimensions of the irreps of a group is equal to h, the order of the group. Thus,
$$\sum_{i=1}^{k} l_i^2 = h \quad ...(20)$$
3. The sum of the squares of the characters of the identity operation in the irreps is equal to h, the order of the group :
$$\sum_{i=1}^{k} (\chi_i (E))^2 = h \quad ...(21)$$
4. The character of the symmetry operations in two different irreps satisfy the relation

$$\sum_{p=1}^{k} g_p \chi_i (R_p) \chi_j (R_p) = h\delta_{ij} \quad \ldots(22)$$

where, δ_{ij} is the Kronecker delta :

$$\delta_{ij} = \begin{cases} 1, & i = j \\ 0, & i \neq j \end{cases} \quad \ldots(23)$$

For $i \neq j$, this relation reduces to

$$\sum_{p=1}^{k} g_p \chi_i (R_p) \chi_j (R_p) = 0 \quad \ldots(24)$$

and for $i = j$, it becomes

$$\sum_{p=1}^{k} g_p (\chi_i (R_p))^2 = h \quad \ldots(25)$$

In these equations, g_p refers to the number of symmetry operations in the pth class; R_p is the symmetry operation of the pth class and $\chi_i (R_p)$ and $\chi_j (R_p)$ are the characters of the matrix for the symmetry operation R_p in the i and j irreps. respectively.

5. The characters of all matrices belonging to the symmetry operations in the same class are identical.

Use of GOT to Construct Character Tables for the Molecular Point Groups

Let us use the GOT to construct the character table for the C_{3v} point group to which NH_3 belongs. This point group has three symmetry elements, E, C_3 and $3\sigma_v$; the corresponding six symmetry operations can be divided into the following three classes : $E(C_3^2, C_3^2)\ 3\sigma_v$.

According to rule 1, the three symmetry classes give rise to three irreps. From rule 2.

$$\sum_{i=1}^{3} l_i^2 = l_1^2 + l_2^2 + l_3^2 = 6 \quad \ldots(26)$$

where, the order of the group is 6.

The only positive integral values of l_i that satisfy Eq. 25 are 1, 1 and 2. Here, we state a very important property that every point group possesses a totally symmetric irrep in which all the symmetry operations have character equal to 1. From rule 3,

$$\sum_i [\chi_i (E)]^2 = [\chi_1(E)]^2 + [\chi_2(E)]^2 + [\chi_3(E)]^2 = 6 \quad \ldots(27)$$

which is satisfied only if

$$\chi_1(E) = 1, \chi_2(E) = 1 \text{ and } \chi_3(E) = 2 \quad \ldots(28)$$

We can now draw up the following table for the characters of different representations :

Table 19.5 **Characters of Different Representation**

Irrep	$\chi(E)$	$\chi(C_3)$	$\chi(\delta_v)$
Γ_1	1	1	1
Γ_2	1	p	q
Γ_3	2	r	s

We have to determine the values of the unknown characters p, q, r and s in the irreps Γ_2 and Γ_3. Applying rule 4 to irreps Γ_1 and Γ_2, we have

$$\sum_{p=1}^{k} g_p \chi_i (R_p) \chi_j (R_p) = 0 \quad \ldots(29)$$

$$\sum_{p=1}^{3} g_p \chi_1 (R_p) \chi_2 (R_p) = g_1 \chi_1 (E) \chi_2 (E)$$

$$+ g_2 \chi_1 (C_3) \chi_2 (C_3) + g_3 \chi_1 (\sigma_v) \chi_2 (\sigma_v) = 0 \quad \ldots(30)$$

From Table 19.5, remembering that $g_1 = 1$, $g_2 = 2$ and $g_3 = 3$, we obtain

$$1 + 2p + 3q = 0 \quad \ldots(31)$$

Applying Eq. 24 to the irrep Γ_2, we obtain

$$1 + 2p^2 + 3q^2 = 6 \quad \ldots(32)$$

Solving Eqs. 30 and 31, we obtain

$$p = 1 \text{ and } q = -1$$

Proceeding similarly, we obtain from the irreps Γ_1 and Γ_3, the following equations :

$$2 + 2r + 3s = 0 \quad \ldots(33)$$

and

$$4 + 2r^2 + 3s^2 = 6 \quad \ldots(34)$$

Solving Eqs. 32 and 33, we obtain

$$r = -1 \text{ and } s = 0$$

Using the values of p, q, r and s in Table 19.5, we obtain the desired character table (Table 19.6) for C_{3v} point group.

The symbols Γ_1, Γ_2 and Γ_3 are the Bethe notation for the irreps and A_1, A_2 and E are the Mulliken notation for the irreps.

Table 19.6 **Character Table for C_{3v} Point Group**

C_{3v}	E	$2C_3$	$3\sigma_v$
$\Gamma_1 \equiv A_1$	1	1	1
$\Gamma_2 \equiv A_2$	1	1	−1
$\Gamma_3 \equiv E$	2	−1	0

Character tables for point groups

For practical purposes, it is sufficient to know only the characters of each symmetry class of a point group to which a molecule belongs. A character table lists the characters of all the symmetry classes for all the irreps of a group. Character tables for the C_{2v} and C_{3v} point groups are given in Tables 19.7 and 19.8.

Table 19.7 **Character Table for C_{2v} Point Group**

C_{2v}	E	$C_2(z)$	$\sigma_v(xz)$	$\sigma'_v(yz)$		
I			II		III	IV
A_1	1	1	1	1	z	x^2, y^2, z^2
A_2	1	1	1	−1	R_z	xy
B_1	1	−1	1	−1	x, R_y	xz
B_2	1	−1	1	1	y, R_x	yz

Table 19.8 **Character Table for C_{3v} Point Group**

C_{3v}	E	$2C_3$	$3\sigma_v$		
I		II		III	IV
A_1	1	1	1	z	x^2+y^2, z^2
A_2	1	1	−1	R_z	
E	2	−1	0	$(x, y)(R_x, R_y)$	$(x^2-y^2, xy)(xz, yz)$

The character tables can be obtained from the properties of the irreps given above. We can explain the character table by dividing it into four sections I, II, III and IV.

Section I In the top row, the Schoenflies symbol for the point group is given. The section also lists the Mulliken symbols for the different irreps. Symbols A and B are used to label one-dimensional irreps and E and T to label two-dimensional and three-dimensional irreps, respectively. The nomenclature E should not be confused with the identity operation. A is used when the character for the rotation about the principal axis is +1 and B when it is −1. In other words, A stands for symmetric and B for antisymmetric to such rotation. For a molecule having a centre of symmetry, the subscripts g and u are used to label the irreps that are respectively symmetric and antisymmetric to inversion through the centre of symmetry. Subscripts 1 and 2 are used to label the irreps that are respectively symmetric and antisymmetric to reflection in a horizontal plane σ_h.

Section II This section gives the characters for all the symmetry operation of different irreps. The characters of the identity operation for the one-dimensional, two-dimensional and three-dimensional irreps are, respectively, 1, 2 and 3.

Section III It gives the transformation properties of the Cartesian coordinates x, y, z (and the p_x, p_y, p_z atomic orbitals) and rotations R_x, R_y, R_z about these axes.

Section IV It gives the transformation properties of the binary products of Cartesian coordinates xy, yz, zx, etc., and the squares of the coordinates x^2, y^2, z^2, x^2+y^2, $x^2+y^2+z^2$ etc. The Cartesian coordinates, their squares and binary products, etc., listed in sections III and IV are referred to as the basis functions on which the symmetry operations operate.

It is important to recognize the point groups of some common molecules. Homonuclear diatomic molecules (H_2, N_2, O_2, Cl_2, etc.) and linear molecules with a centre of symmetry (CO_2, HC≡CH) belong to the point group $D_{\infty h}$. On the other hand heteronuclear diatomic molecules and other linear molecules that do not have a centre of symmetry (HCl, CO, NO, OCS, NNO) belong to the point group $C_{\infty v}$. Tetrahedral (T_d) and octahedral (O_h) molecules have more than one non-collinear principal axis of symmetry a tetrahedral molecule such as CH_4 has four non-collinear C_3 axes, one along each C—H bond. A closely related group, the icosahedral group I_h which characterizes the icosahedron has non-collinear five-fold axes. The icosahedral group I_h occurs prominently in boron compounds and for fullerence (C_{60}) molecule.

A regular tetrahedron has four equilateral triangles for its faces, an octahedron has eight, a dodecahedron twelve and an icosahedron has twenty faces.

Table 19.9 lists the point groups of some common molecules along with their geometry and general formulae.

Table 19.9 **Point Groups and Geometry of Some Common Molecules**

Molecule/complex ion	General formula	Point group	Geometry
H_2	A_2	$D_{\infty h}$	Linear with i
HF	AB	$C_{\infty v}$	Linear without i
CO_2	AB_2	$D_{\infty h}$	Linear with i
COS	ABC	$C_{\infty v}$	Linear without i
H_2O	A_2B	C_{2v}	Angular
C_2H_2	A_2B_2	$D_{\infty h}$	Linear with i
CH_2Cl_2	AB_2C_2	C_{2v}	Tetrahedral
$CHCl_3$	ABC_3	C_{3v}	Tetrahedral
NH_3	AB_3	D_{3h}	Pyramidal
CH_4	AB_4	T_d	Tetrahedral
PCl_5	AB_5	D_{3h}	Trigonal bipyramidal
SF_4	AB_4	C_{2v}	Angular
$[PtCl_4]^{2-}$	$[AB_4]^{2-}$	D_{4h}	Square planar

Molecule/complex ion	General formula	Point group	Geometry
BrF_5	AB_5	C_{4v}	Square pyramidal
SF_6	AB_6	O_h	Octahedral
IF_7	AB_7	D_{5h}	Pentagonal bipyramidal
$[B_{12}H_{12}]^2$	$[A_{12}B_{12}]^{2-}$	I_h	Icosahedral

Applications of Group Theory

Group theory is a very powerful tool at the hands of a chemist, a theorist and a spectroscopist. It finds many applications the details of which are beyond the scope of this book. Some important applications of the group theory are listed below :

1. Construction of hybrid orbitals.
2. Construction of SALCs (symmetry adapted linear combinations of atomic orbitals). SALCs are used in molecular orbital theory (MOT) of chemical bonding.
3. Determination of the irreps to which the vibrational modes of molecules belong.
4. Determining which spectral transition in infrared and Raman spectra are allowed or forbidden.
5. Determining the selection rules for $n \to \overset{*}{\pi}$ and $\pi \to \overset{*}{\pi}$ transitions in carbonyl compounds and other chromophores. It is found that the former transitions are forbidden whereas the latter are allowed.
6. Simplifying the so-called secular equation which is a special feature of the quantum mechanical calculations in both VBT and MOT. From the symmetry of the molecule it is possible to predict which integrals or matrix elements occurring in the secular equation will vanish. This aspect of group theory is of paramount importance in quantum mechanics and it reduces the computational labour and cost of calculations and the digital computer which may otherwise run into thousands of dollars!
7. Determining optical activity of molecules.
8. Determining which molecules are polar or non-polar.
9. Classification of elementary particles into fermions and bosons in quantum mechanics.

We shall briefly discuss the last three applications here. A molecule will be chiral *i.e.,* optically active if it does not possess the S_n axis of any order. This implies that it should not have the reflection plane (S_1 axis), the centre of inversion (S_2 axis) and any improper axis of order n. A molecule is not chiral if it belongs to the point groups D_{nh} or D_{nd} or to cubic point groups T and O (and their modifications).

Again, a molecule cannot be polar if it has a centre of inversion and belongs to any of the D groups including D_n, D_{nh} and D_{nd}. It will be polar if it belongs to C_n, C_s, C_{nv} or the infinite $C_{\infty,v}$ point group. The dipole moment lies along the C_n axis in the C_n and C_{nv} point groups; in the case of the C_s point-group, it lies in the reflection plane.

As an application of group theory to quantum mechanics, consider the Schrodinger equation for helium atom.

$$\hat{\mathbf{H}}\psi = E\psi$$

where, $$\hat{\mathbf{H}} = -\frac{1}{2}(\nabla_1^2 + \nabla_2^2) - \frac{2}{r_1} - \frac{2}{r_2} + \frac{1}{r_{12}}$$

(in atomic units)

(See Fig. 19.7 for the definition of the coordinates of the two electrons.)

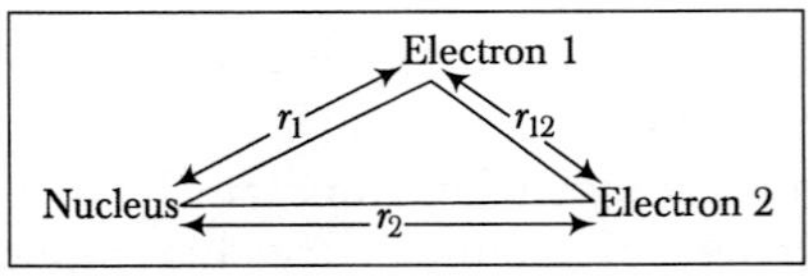

Fig. 19.7 Coordinates for helium atom.

If we use a symmetry operation called parity, $\hat{\mathbf{P}}$, which interchanges the coordinates of the two electrons, we find that $\hat{\mathbf{H}}$ remains unchanged. This is expressed in group-theoretical language by saying that the Hamiltonian (and hence the energy E) is invariant under the symmetry operation $\hat{\mathbf{P}}$. In fact the Hamiltonian operator $\hat{\mathbf{H}}$ is invariant under all the symmetry operations of the point group of an atom or a molecule, since, it commutes with them, *i.e.,*

$$[\hat{\mathbf{H}}, \hat{\mathbf{P}}] = \hat{\mathbf{H}}\hat{\mathbf{P}} - \hat{\mathbf{P}}\hat{\mathbf{H}} = 0 \quad \ldots(36)$$

Applying the parity operation to both sides of Eq. 35 and using Eq. 36, we have

$$\hat{\mathbf{P}}\hat{\mathbf{H}}\psi = \hat{\mathbf{H}}\hat{\mathbf{P}}\psi \quad \ldots(37)$$

Hence, $$\hat{\mathbf{H}}(\hat{\mathbf{P}}\psi) = E(\hat{\mathbf{P}}\psi) \quad \ldots(38)$$

This means that $\hat{\mathbf{P}}\psi$ is also a solution of Eq. 35 with the eigen value E. Thus, assuming the absence of degeneracy (*i.e.,* no two wave functions have the same energy), we can say that there is no difference between $\hat{\mathbf{P}}\psi$ and ψ.

Let us next consider the effect parity on ψ. Consider the eigen value equation,

$$\hat{\mathbf{P}}\psi = \lambda\psi \quad \ldots(39)$$

where, λ is the eigen value of $\hat{\mathbf{P}}$. Operating on Eq. 39 again with $\hat{\mathbf{P}}$, we obtain

$$\hat{\mathbf{P}}^2\psi = \hat{\mathbf{P}}\lambda\psi \qquad \ldots(40$$

or $$\psi = \lambda\hat{\mathbf{P}}\psi = \lambda^2\psi \qquad \ldots(41)$$

i.e., $$\lambda^2 = 1 \qquad \ldots(42)$$

$\therefore$ $$\lambda = \pm 1$$

Substituting in Eq. 39, we find that

$$\hat{\mathbf{P}}\psi = \pm\psi \qquad \ldots(43)$$

Eq. 43 has the following significance. It implies that ψ must be either symmetric (does not change sign) or antisymmetric (changes sign) to exchange of any pair of electrons.

Particles such as electrons and protons which have half-integral spin are classified as fermions because their wave function is antisymmetric to exchange of their coordinates, and particles such as photons and photons which have integral spin are classified as bosons since their wave function is symmetric to exchange of their coordinates. Fermions obey Fermi-Dirac statistics and bosons obey Bose-Einstein statistics.

From the above discussion we see that since, ψ and $\hat{\mathbf{P}}\psi$ both belong to the energy level E, the parity operation $\hat{\mathbf{P}}$ transforms the eigen functions of E into each other. In the language of group theory this implies that we can choose the eigen functions of $\hat{\mathbf{H}}$ with energy E as a basis set for the irreps of the point group.

Crystallographic Symmetry

We shall know in the chapter on the solid state that there are seven crystal systems, fourteen Bravais lattices, thirty two classes (or point groups) and 230 space groups. A crystallographer must determine to which crystal system, Bravais lattice, point group and space group a given unknown crystal belongs. This can prove to be a very arduous task, indeed. The additional symmetry which ultimately produces space groups in crystals is a consequence of unique features not found in molecules.

It can be shown from purely geometrical considerations that a crystal can possess only 1-, 2-, 3-, 4- or 6-fold axis of symmetry but not a 5-fold axis of symmetry. Every crystal possesses external symmetry and internal symmetry. The former is determined by the symmetry elements and the interfacial angles of the crystal whereas the latter is determined by the arrangement of atoms in the lattice.

External Symmetry of Crystals

This symmetry is described by ten basic symmetry elements : n (where, $n = 1, 2, 3, 4$ and 6) and $\bar{n}$ (where, $\bar{n} = \bar{1}, \bar{2}, \bar{3}, \bar{4}$ and $\bar{6}$). Here, n is the n-fold proper axis and $\bar{n}$ is the n-fold proper axis combined with the operation of inversion through a central point on the axis. In other words, $\bar{n}$ is the n-fold rotation-inversion axis. On the basis of external symmetry, crystals are classified into 32 point groups which are listed in Table 10 in both the Hermann-Mauguin (HM) notation, (preferred by crystallographers) and in Schoenflies notation, reserved for molecules.

Table 19.10 **The 32 Crystallographic Point Groups**

Hermann-Mauguin notation	Schoenflics notation	Hermann-Mauguin notation	Schoenflies notation
$n(1, 2, 3, 4, 6)$	$C_n\ (C_1, C_2, C_3, C_4, C_6)$	$n/m\ 2/m\ 2/m$ (n is even)	D_{nh} (n is even)
$n(\bar{1}, \bar{2}, \bar{3}, \bar{4}, \bar{6})$	$(C_1, C_5, S_6, S_4, S_3)$	$(2/m\ 2/m\ 2/m,\ 4/m\ 2/m\ 2/m$	
$n\ 22$ (n is even)	D_n (n is even)	$6/m\ 2/m\ 2/m)$	(D_{2h}, D_{4h}, D_{6h})
(222, 422, 622)	(D_2, D_4, D_6)	$\bar{6}\ 2m$	D_{3h}
32	D_3	$\bar{4}\ 2m$	D_{2d}
nmm (n is even)	C_{nv} (n is even)	$\bar{3}\ 2/m\ (\bar{3}\ m)$	D_{3d}
$(2mm, 4mm, 6mm)$	(C_{2v}, C_{4v}, C_{6v})	23	T
$3m$	C_{3v}	$\bar{4}\ 3m$	T_d
n/m (n is even)	C_{nh} (n is even)	$2/m\ \bar{3}$	T_h
$(2/m, 4/m, 6/m)$	(C_{2h}, C_{4h}, C_{6h})	432	O
		$4/m\ \bar{3}\ 2/m$	O_h

We shall now explain the rather unfamiliar Hermann-Mauguin (HM) notation for the crystallographic point groups. Crystals containing the proper axis of symmetry alone are denoted by the symbol *n*. The HM notation for crystals possessing the centre of symmetry alone is $\bar{1}$. The symbol $\bar{2}$ stands for the crystal having rotation-inversion axis of order 2. As shown below, $\bar{2}$ is equivalent it σ_h, the horizontal reflection plane :

$$\bar{2} = C_2^1 i = C_2^1 C_2^1 \sigma_h = E\sigma_h = \sigma_h \quad \ldots(43)$$

The crystallographic point group having a mirror plane is denoted by the symbol *m*. A crystal which possesses to rotation-inversion axis of order 3 is denoted by the notation $\bar{3}$. $\bar{3}$ can be shown to be equivalent to the rotation-reflection axis of order 6 as follows :

$$\bar{3} = C_3^1 i = C_3^1 C_2^1 \sigma_h = C_6^2 C_6^3 \sigma_h = C_6^5 \sigma_h = S_6^5 \quad \ldots(44)$$

A crystal possessing a rotation-inversion axis of order 4 is denoted by the symbol $\bar{4}$ which is equivalent to a rotation-reflection axis of order 4 :

$$\bar{4} = C_4^1 i = C_4^1 C_2^1 \sigma_h = C_4^1 C_4^2 \sigma_h = C_4^3 \sigma_h = S_4^3 \quad \ldots(45)$$

And finally, the $\bar{6}$ group has the rotation-inversion axis of order 6 :

$$\bar{6} = C_6^1 i = C_6^1 C_2^1 \sigma_h = C_6^1 C_6^3 \sigma_h = C_6^4 \sigma_h = C_3^2 \sigma_h = S_3^5 \quad \ldots(46)$$

D_n groups are denoted by the symbol *n* 22 when the principal axis is of even order; here, *n* refers to the principal axis and 22 corresponds to two sets of C_2 axes in different classes. D_3 group is denoted by 32 which implies the presence of C_3 axis and 2-fold axes; the 2-fold axes are in the same class.

C_{nv} groups are denoted by *nmm* when the principal axis *n* is of even order; *mm* denotes two sets of vertical planes in different classes. C_{3v} group is denoted by 3*m*; here 3 stands for 3-fold principal axis and *m* for vertical planes all of which are in the same class. C_{nh} symmetry is referred to as n/m when *n* is even (2, 4 or 6). The n/m point groups contain C_n axis and a horizontal plane σ_h, $\bar{6}$ is the HM notation for the C_{3h} point group.

If a crystal with D_{nh} symmetry contains a C_n axis of even order, then the HM notationis $n/m\ 2/m\ 2/m$. It denotes the presence of the C_n axis, two sets of C_2 axes in different classes and the horizontal plane. The notation $\bar{6}\ 2m$ corresponds to D_{3h} point group. It means that the crystal has an $S_3(\bar{6})$ axis. C_2 axes and mirror planes. The $\bar{6}$ axis generates C_3 axis. σ_h and identity operation *E*. The HM notation for D_{2d} and D_{3d} point groups is $\bar{4}\ 2m$ and $\bar{3}\ 2/m$; respectively. The D_{2d} point group possesses a $\bar{4}$ axis, C_2 axes and dihedral planes, whereas the D_{3d} point group possesses the S_6 axis, C_2 axes and dihedral planes. A crystal cannot have the D_{4d} symmetry since, $\bar{8}$ or S_8 axis cannot occur.

The *T* group is denoted by 23 which means the presence of 2-fold axes and 3-fold axes. If, in addition, *i*, C_2 and C_3 axes are also present, the point group obtained is T_h whose HM notation is $2/m\ \bar{3}$. T_d group is denoted by $\bar{4}\ 3m$; it contains $\bar{4}$ axis, 3-fold axes and mirror planes. The point group *O* is represented by 432; it contains C_4, C_3 and C_2 axes whereas the HM notation for the point group O_h is $4/m\ \bar{3}\ 2m$; it implies the presence of C_4 axes. C_2 axes S_6 axes and mirror planes.

Crystal Systems

It is known that the unit cell of a crystal is specified by the six unit cell parameters *a*, *b*, *c*, α, β and γ where, *a*, *b*, *c* are the crystallographic axes and α, β, γ are the angles at which these axes intersect one another. The 32 point groups are grouped into seven crystal systems, *viz.,* cubic (isometric), tetragonal, hexagonal, rhombohedral (trigonal), orthorhombic, monoclinic and triclinic.

The cube which belongs to the O_h point group has the maximum symmetry and the trilinic system has the minimum symmetry. The cube and the octahedron are mutual polyhedra.

Table 19.11 lists the various *n*-fold rotation axes *n* and the *n*-fold rotation-inversion axes $\bar{n}$ possessed by the seven crystal systems :

Table 19.11 **The *n* or $\bar{n}$-axes of the Seven Crystal Systems**

Crystal system	*n* or $\bar{n}$-axis	Crystal system	*n* or $\bar{n}$-axis
Cubic	Many 3-fold or $\bar{3}$ axes	Orthorhombic	2 or many 2-fold axes
Tetragonal	4 or $\bar{4}$ axes	Moniclinic	2 or $\bar{2}$ axes
Hexagonal	6 or $\bar{6}$ axes	Triclinic	1 or $\bar{1}$ axis
Trigonal	3 or $\bar{3}$ axes		

Table 19.12 lists the 32 point groups corresponding to seven crystal systems :

Table 19.12 **The 32 Point Groups Corresponding to the Seven Crystal Systems**

System	Example	Unit cell parameters	Point groups (HM notation)
Cubic	NaCl	$a = b = c$	23, $2/m\ \bar{3}$, $\bar{4}$
		$\alpha = \beta = \gamma = 90°$	$3m$, 432, $4/m$, $\bar{3}\ 2m$
Tetragonal	SnO_2	$a = b \neq c$	4, $\bar{4}/m$, $4mn$, $\bar{4}$ $2m$
		$\alpha = \beta = \gamma = 90°$	422, $4/m\ 2/m$ $2/m$
Hexagonal	SiO_2	$a = b \neq c$	6, $\bar{6}$, $6/m$, $6mm$, 622
		$\alpha = \beta = 90°$, $\gamma = 120°$	$\bar{6}\ 2m$, $6/m\ 2/m$ $2/m$
Trigonal	$CaCO_3$	$a = b = c$	3, $\bar{3}\ 3m$, 32, $\bar{3}$ $2/m$
		$\alpha = \beta = \gamma \neq 90°$	
Orthorhombic	KNO_3	$a \neq b \neq c$	$2mm$, 222, $2/m$ $2/m\ 2/m$
		$\alpha = \beta = \gamma = 90°$	
Monoclinic	$CaSO_4 \cdot 2H_2O$	$a \neq b \neq c$	2, m, $2/m$
		$\alpha = \beta = 90°$, $\gamma \neq 90°$	
Triclinic	$K_2Cr_2O_7$	$a \neq b \neq c$	1, 1
		$a \neq \beta \neq \gamma \neq 90°$	

Internal Symmetry of Crystals

On the basis of the arrangement of atoms or ions in the lattice. Auguste Bravias, the 19th century French crystallographer, determined that only fourteen space lattices, now referred to as the Bravias Lattices, are possible for the seven crystal systems. When combined with the symmetry operations, they generate 230 space groups (Table 19.13).

Table 19.13 **14 Bravias Lattices and 230 Space Groups**

System	Number of space lattices*	Number of space groups
Cubic	3 (*P*, *I*, *F*)	36
Tetragonal	2 (*P*, *I*)	68
Hexagonal	1 (*P*)	27
Trigonal (Rhombohedral)	1 (*R*)	25
Orthorhombic	4 (*P*, *F*, *I*, *C*)	59
Monoclinic	2 (*P*, *C*)	13
Triclinic	1 (*P*)	2
	Total : 14	**Total : 230**

**P* Primitive, *I* Body-centred, *F* Face-centred *C* End-centred, *R* Rhombohedral

Two types of space groups result depending upon the presence or absence of translational elements of symmetry in a crystal. It is found that the 230 space groups can be grouped into 73 space groups containing no translational elements of symmetry and 157 space groups involving translational elements of symmetry.

1. Space Groups without Translational Elements of Symmetry

The symbol for such a space group is described by mentioning the space lattice and the symmetry point group of the crystal in the Hermann-Mauguin (HM) notation.

A few examples of space groups are *I* 23 (in the cubic system), *P* 6 *mm* (in the hexagonal system), *F* $2/m\ 2/m$ $2/m$ (in the orthorhombic system) and *C* $2/m$ (in the monoclinic system). They denote, respectively, the body-centred Bravais lattice with point groups 23, the primitive Bravais lattice with point group 6 *mm*, the face-centred Bravais lattice with point group $2/m\ 2/m$ $2/m$ and the side-centred Bravais lattice with point group $2/m$.

2. Space Groups with Translational Elements of Symmetry

In order to describe such space groups we must first describe what is translational symmetry. Translational symmetry is defined by two symmetry elements, *viz.*, the screw axis and the glide plane.

Screw Axis

Let us consider a set of equivalent atoms, say, a_1, a_2, a_3, a_4, a_5, a_6 within a crystal structure. A screw axis is defined by an operation which combines a rotation corresponding to 2-, 3-, 4- or 6-fold axis with a translation parallel to the axis. Fig. 19.8 (a) shows a normal 2-fold axis in which atom a_1 is related to atom a_2 by a rotation about the rotation axis through 180°. Fig. 19.8 (b), on the other hand, shows a 2-fold screw

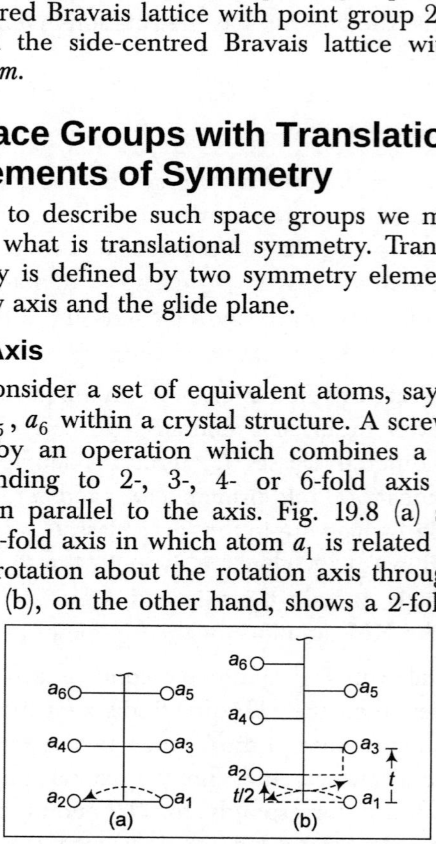

Fig. 19.8 The symmetry elements in a space group (a) The normal 2-fold axis (b) The 2-fold screw axis.

axis, denoted by 2_t, in which atom a_1 is related to atom a_2 by rotation through 180° about the rotation axis followed by $t/2$ translation parallel to the axis. This is expressed by saying that a 2-fold axis generates a 2_t screw axis.

Similarly, a 3-fold axis generates two screw axes 3_1 and 3_2; the former corresponding to a 120° rotation about the axis followed by a translation $t/3$, and the latter corresponding to a 240° rotation about the axis followed by a translation $2t/3$. Similarly, a 4-fold axis generates three screws axes 4_1, 4_2 and 4_3 while a 6-fold axis generates 6_1, 6_2, 6_3, 6_4 and 6_5 screw axes.

Glide planes

Consider again a set of equivalent atoms a_1, a_2, a_3, a_4, a_5, a_6, a_7, a_8 within a crystal structure. A glide plane is defined by an operation which involves a translation $t/2$ parallel to the reflection plane followed by reflection across the plane. Here, t is the distance between the successive atoms. Fig. 19.9(a) shows a normal mirror plane and Fig. 19.9(b) shows the glide plane. The glide planes are further classified into three kinds, *viz.*, axial glides, diagonal glides and diamond glides.

Axial glides are planes having glide component parallel to a crystallographic axis a, b or c and with length equal to $a/2$, $b/2$ or $c/2$. They are denoted as a glide, b glide or c glide. Diagonal glides, denoted by the symbol n, correspond to planes whose glide component is the vector sum of any of the two vectors $a/2$, $b/2$ or $c/2$. The diamond glides, denoted by the symbol d, correspond to planes whose glide component is the vector sum of any of the two vectors $a/4$, $b/4$ or $c/4$.

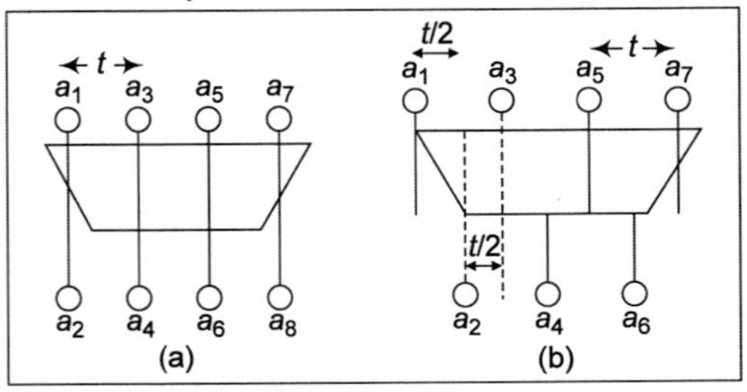

Fig. 19.9 The symmetry elements in a space group : (a) Normal mirror plane (b) Glide plane with glide component $t/2$.

The space group for a crystal containing translational symmetry elements is described by mentioning the Bravais lattice, the symmetry point group of the crystal in the HM notation, and the translational symmetry elements. Thus, for instance, the space group $P\ 2_t/b\ 2_t/a\ 2/m$ for an orthorhombic crystal has the following interpretation : It means that (i) the Bravais lattice is primitive; (ii) the a-axis is a 2_t screw axis having a b-glide plane normal to it; (iii) the b-axis is also a 2_t screw axis with an a-glide plane normal to it; (iv) the c-axis is the ordinary 2-fold axis and (v) the ordinary mirror plane is normal tothe 2-fold axis. All the 230 space groups of the seven crystal systems have similar notation and interpretation.

Molecular Symmetry and Crystallographic Symmetry

Table 19.14 gives the comparison between molecular and crystallographic symmetry.

Table 19.14 **Comparison between Molecular and Crystallographic Symmetry**

	Molecular symmetry	Crystallographic symmetry
1.	C_n axis of order n (where, $n = 1, 2, 3, 4 \ldots \infty$) is present.	C_n axis of order n ($n = 1, 2, 3, 4, 6$) is present. Note that 5-fold axis is not present.
2.	Rotation-reflection axis is present.	Rotation-inversion axis is present.
3.	The number of point groups is not limited.	The number of point groups is 32.
4.	Schoenflies notation is used to denote point groups.	Hermann-Mauguin (HM) notation is used to denote point groups.

Quasicrystals

Recently, quasicrystals have been prepared by metallurgists. A quasicrystal has 5-fold axis of symmetry. The best known quasicrystal is an alloy of solidified aluminium and a transition metal such as chromium, manganese or iron. It possesses the icosahedral symmetry (the icosahedral point group I_h consists of twelve 5-fold axes of symmetry). A quasicrystal occurs primarily as a metastable phase and its dimension is so small that it cannot be investigated by the conventional X-ray single crystal diffractometry. Quasicrystals can be prepared by techniques such as rapid solidification of alloys, rapid pressurization of the melt and precipitation from solid solutions. They can be studied by transmission electron microscopy. Quasicrystals having the symmetry of such polyhedra as icosahedron, pentagonal dodecahedron and triacontahedron have been prepared. They have generated considerable interest in materials science and engineering.

Example 2. *The similarity transformation diagonalises a square matrix. Let us consider a 2×2 matrix A and the transformation matrix X, defined by*

$$A = \begin{bmatrix} -7 & 6 \\ -18 & 14 \end{bmatrix};\ X = \begin{bmatrix} 2 & 1 \\ 3 & 2 \end{bmatrix}$$

Using the similarity transformation, diagonalise A.

Sol. In this example we assume that the reader has familiarity with matrix algebra and knows how to determine the inverse of a matrix. The similarity transformation is defined as

$$X^{-1}AX = B$$

The inverse X^{-1} of matrix X is given by

$$X^{-1} = \text{adj } X/|X|$$

where, adj X is the adjoint of X and $|X|$ is the determinant of X ($|X| \neq 0$) :

$X = \begin{bmatrix} 2 & 1 \\ 3 & 2 \end{bmatrix}$. It can be easily shown that $X^{-1} = \begin{bmatrix} 2 & -1 \\ -3 & 2 \end{bmatrix}$

Hence, $X^{-1}AX = \begin{bmatrix} 2 & -1 \\ -3 & 2 \end{bmatrix}\begin{bmatrix} -7 & 6 \\ -18 & 14 \end{bmatrix}\begin{bmatrix} 2 & 1 \\ 3 & 2 \end{bmatrix} = \begin{bmatrix} 2 & 0 \\ 0 & 5 \end{bmatrix}$

We see that B is a diagonal matrix. Thus, matrix A has been diagonalized.

Example 3. *Verify that the characters given in the C_{2v} point group obey the properties of the irreps.*

Sol. Refer to the character table for the C_{2v} point group. We find that

(i) The number of irreps is equal to the number of classes (in this case 4) of the group.

(ii) All the four irreps are one-dimensional, so that

$$\sum_{i=1}^{4} l_i^2 = l_1^2 + l_2^2 + l_3^2 + l_4^4$$

$$= (1)^2 + (1)^2 + (1)^2 + (1)^2 = 4$$

which is the order of the group.

(iii) $\sum_{i=1}^{4} (\chi_i(E))^2 = (\chi_{A_1}(E))^2 + (\chi_{A_2}(E))^2 + (\chi_{B_1}(E))^2 + (\chi_{B_2}(E))^2$

$$= (1)^2 + (1)^2 + (1)^2 + (1)^2 = 4$$

(iv) $\sum_{p=1}^{4} g_p \chi_i(R_p)\, \chi_j(R_p) = h\delta ij.$

For the A_1 and A_2 irreps, we obtain

$$(1)(1)(1) + (1)(1)(1) + (1)(1)(-1) + (1)(1)(-1) = 0$$

and for the B_1 irrep, we obtain.

$$(1)(1)^2 + (1)(-1)^2 + 1(1)^2 + 1(-1)^2 = 4$$

and so on. Hence, the result.

Example 4. *Verify that the characters given in the C_{3v} point group obey the properties of the irreps.*

Sol. Refer to the character able for the C_{3v} point group. We find that

(i) The number of irreps is equal to the number of classes (in this case 3) of the group.

(ii) Two irreps A_1 and A_2 are one-dimensional, *i.e.*, $l_1 = l_2 = 1$ and the third is two-dimensional, *i.e.*, $l_3 = 2$. Thus,

$$\sum_{l=1}^{3} l_i^2 = l_1^2 + l_2^2 + l_3^2$$

$$= (1)^2 + (1)^2 + (2)^2 = 6$$

which is the order of the group.

(iii) $\sum_{l=1}^{4} (\chi_i(E))^2 = (\chi_{A_1}(E))^2 + (\chi_{A_2}(E))^2 + (\chi_E(E))^2$

$$= (1)^2 + (1)^2 + (2)^2 = 6$$

(iv) $\sum_{p=1}^{3} g_p \chi_1(R_p)\chi_i(R_p) = h\delta_{ij}$

For the irreps A_2 and E (say), this relation gives

$$(1)(1)(2) + (2)(1)(-1) + 3(-1)(0) = 0$$

For the irreps A_1 and A_2 (say), it gives $(1)(1)(1) + (2)(1)(1) + (3)(1)(-1) = 0$ and for the irrep

$$E = (1)(1)(2)^2 + 2(-1)^2 + 3(0)^2$$

$$= 6 \text{ and so on}$$

Hence, the result.

Example 5. *List the symmetry elements and locate as many of them as possible (in the molecule) for the following molecules :*

(a) CH_4 *(b)* $[PtCl_4]^{2-}$

(c) H_2 *(d)* HF,

(e) HCN *and* *(f)* C_2H_2

Sol. (a) CH_4 (tetrahderal) It belongs to the T_d point group. The symmetry elements are $E, 4C_3, 3C_2, 3S_4$ and $6\sigma_d$ (Fig. 19.10).

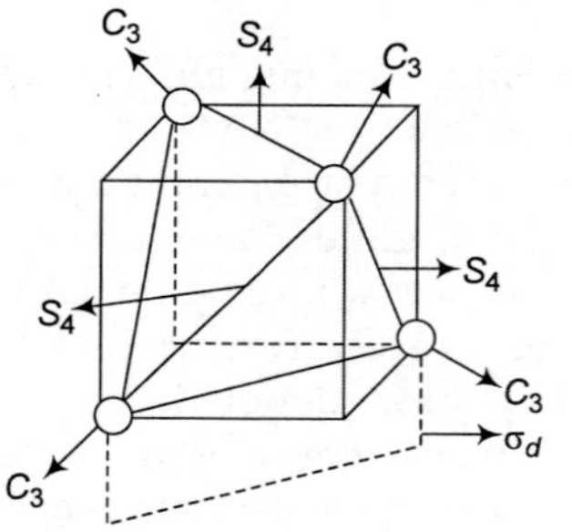

Fig. 19.10 Symmetry elements of the T_d point group.

(b) $[PtCl_4]^{2-}$ (square planar) This molecule has the general formula AB_4 and belongs to the D_{4h} point group. The symmetry elements are $E, C_4, S_4, 4C_2, 4\sigma_v, \sigma_h$ and i (Fig. 19. 11).

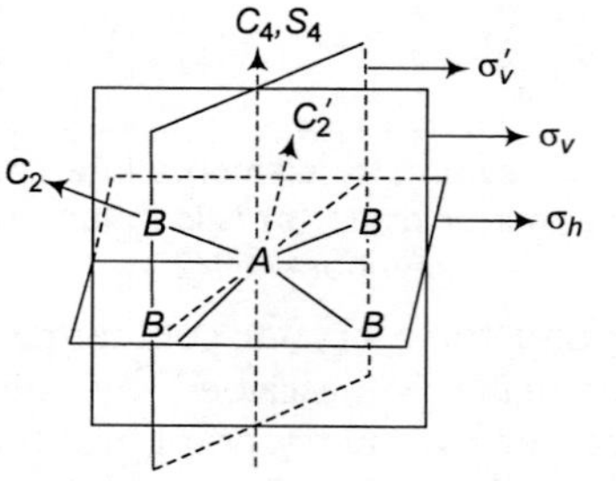

Fig. 19.11 Symmetry elements of the D_{4h} point group.

(c) H_2 (linear with a centre of symmetry) (*i*) It belongs to the $D_{\infty h}$ point group. It has the symmetry elements E, $2C\infty, \infty\sigma_v, \sigma_h, i, 2S_\infty$ and ∞C_2 (Fig. 19.12).

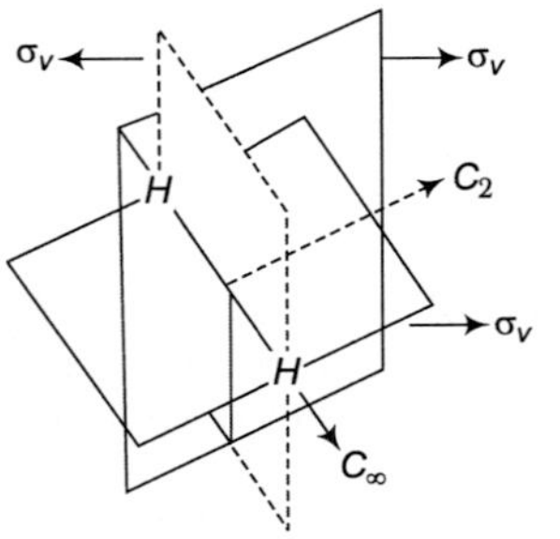

Fig. 19.12 Symmetry elements of the $D_{\infty h}$ point group.

(d) HF (linear without centre of symmetry) (*i*) It belongs to the $C_{\infty v}$ point group, and has the symmetry elements E, C_∞ and $\infty\sigma_v$ (Fig. 19.13).

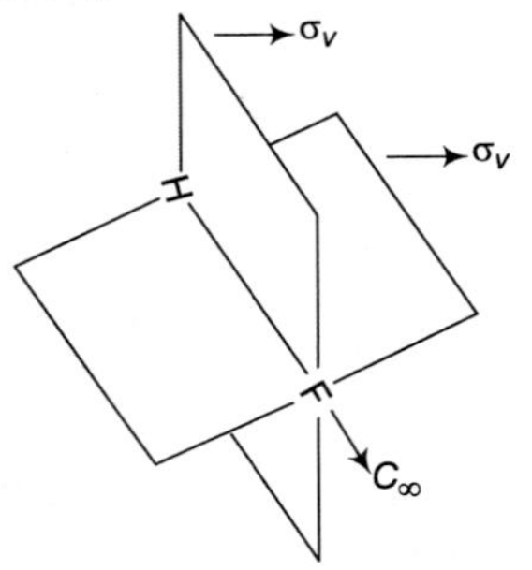

Fig. 19.13 Symmetry elements of the $C_{\infty v}$ point group.

(e) HC≡N (linear without centre of symmetry) (*i*) It belongs to $C_{\infty v}$ point group and possesses the symmetry elements E, C_∞ and $\infty\sigma_v$ (Fig. 19.14).

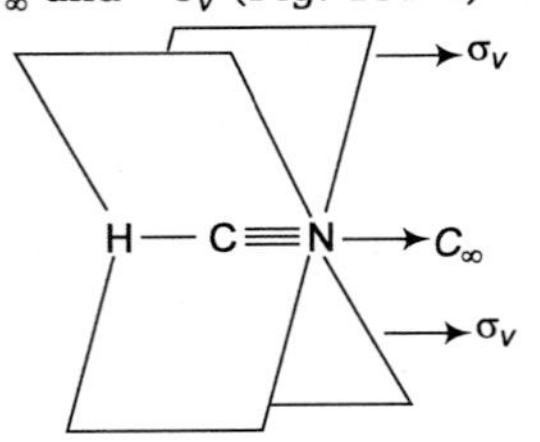

Fig. 19.14 Symmetry elements of the $C_{\infty v}$ point group.

(f) HC≡CH (linear with centre of symmetry) (*i*) It belongs to the $D_{\infty h}$ point group, and has the symmetry elements $E, 2C_\infty, \infty\sigma_v, \sigma_h, i, 2S_\infty$ and ∞C_2 (Fig. 19.15).

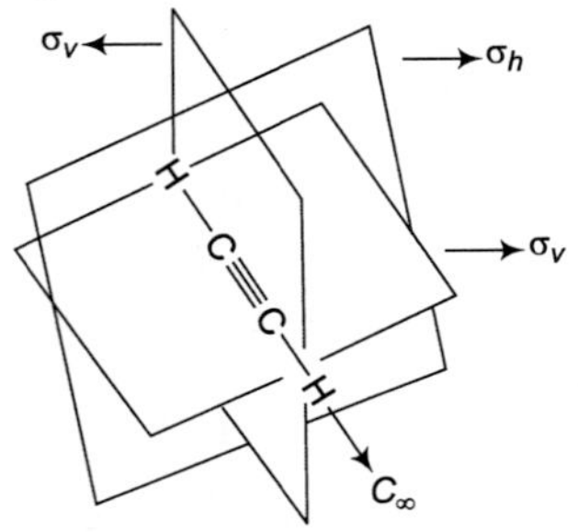

Fig. 19.15 Symmetry elements of the $D_{\infty h}$ point group.

Example 6. *Illustrate diagrammatically that* H_2O *molecule is Abelian whereas* NH_3 *molecule is non-Abelian.*

Sol. A molecule is said to be Abelian if all the symmetry elements commute with one another and non-Abelian if they do not commute with one another.

H_2O molecule See Fig. 19.16.

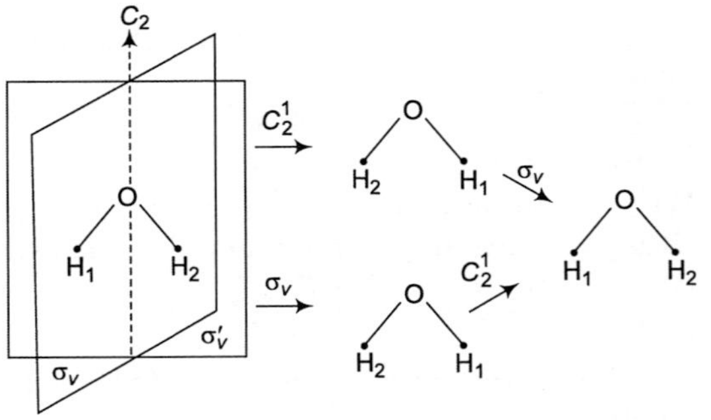

Fig. 19.16 Illustration of a an Abelian group.

We see that the application of C_2^1 followed by σ_v gives the same configuration as the application of σ_v followed by C_2^1.

Hence, C_2^1 and σ_v commute, *i.e.*, $\sigma_v C_2^1 = C_2^1 \sigma_v$

Thus, H_2O molecule belongs to an Abelian point group (C_{2v}).

NH_3 molecule See Fig. 19.17.

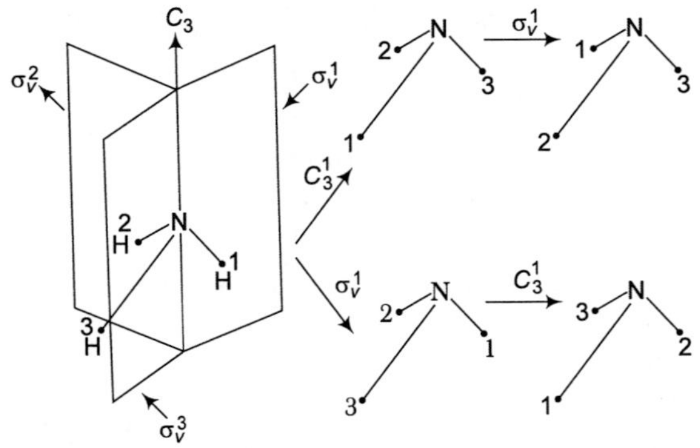

Fig. 19.17 Illustration of a non-Abelian group.

Here, we find that application of C_3^1 followed by σ_v^1 gives a different configuration of NH_3 molecule than the application of σ_v^1 followed by C_3^1, *i.e.*,

$$\sigma_v^1 C_3^1 \neq C_3^1 \sigma_v^1$$

so that the two symmetry operations do not commute. Thus, NH_3 molecule belongs to a non-Abelian point group (C_{3v}).

Exercise 1

(For Part 'B')

1. Eclipsed form of ferrocene belongs to the following point group
(a) T_d (b) C_{5v}
(c) D_{5h} (d) D_{5d}

2. Staggered form a ferrocene belongs to the following point groups
(a) C_{5v} (b) D_{5d}
(c) D_{5h} (d) C_{4v}

3. When a molecule AB_6 belongs to O_h point group, changes to *trans*-AB_4C_2 results in which point group?
(a) C_{4v} (b) D_{4h}
(c) O_h (d) T_d

4. Centre of inversion is absent in the following point group
(a) D_{2h} (b) D_{4h}
(c) D_{6h} (d) T_d

5. *Trans*-N_2F_2 belongs to the point group
(a) C_{2h} (b) $C_{\infty v}$
(c) D_{2h} (d) $D_{\infty h}$

6. NO belongs to the following point group
(a) D_{2h} (b) C_{2v}
(c) $D_{\infty h}$ (d) $C_{\infty v}$

7. $[PtCl_4]^{2-}$ belongs to the following point group
(a) O_h (b) T_d
(c) D_{4h} (d) C_{4v}

8. CO_2 belongs to the following point groups
(a) D_{2h} (b) $D_{\infty h}$
(c) C_{2v} (d) $D_{\infty v}$

9. BF_3 molecule belongs to the following point group
(a) C_{2v} (b) D_{3d}
(c) C_{3v} (d) D_{3h}

10. H_2O molecule belongs to the following point group
(a) D_{2h} (b) D_{2d}
(c) C_{3v} (d) C_{2v}

11. Which of the following belongs to C_{2v} group?
(a) H_2S, PCl_3
(b) Thiophene, IF_5
(c) 1, 2 dichlorobenzene, H_2S
(d) 1, 2 dichlorobenzene, PCl_3

12. Which of the following belong to C_{2v} point group?
(a) $CH_2{=}O$ (b) 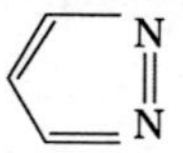
(c) H_2S (d) All of these

13. Which of the following belongs to C_{2v} point group?
(a) H_2S, $CH_2{=}O$, thiophene, 1, 2-dichlorobenzene
(b) H_2S, $CH_2{=}O$, thiophene, IF_5
(c) H_2S, $CH_2{=}O$, IF_5, PCl_3
(d) H_2S, $CH_2{=}O$, PCl_3, 1, 2-dichlorobenzene

14. Match the following.

(i) PCl_3 (pyramidal)	(a) D_{2h}
(ii) IF_5 (square pyramidal)	(b) D_{3h}
(iii) B_2H_6	(c) $D_{\infty h}$
(iv) CO_3^{2-}	(d) C_{4v}
(v) XeF_2	(e) C_{3v}
(vi) H—C≡C—Na	(f) $C_{\infty v}$

(a) (i)-(e), (ii)-(d), (iii)-(a), (iv)-(b), (v)-(c), (vi)-(f)
(b) (i)-(d), (ii)-(e), (iii)-(a), (iv)-(b), (v)-(f), (vi)-(c)
(c) (i)-(e), (ii)-(d), (iii)-(b), (iv)-(c), (v)-(a), (vi)-(f)
(d) (i)-(d), (ii)-(a), (iii)-(e), (iv)-(b), (v)-(f), (vi)-(c)

15. *Para* dichlorobenzene and naphthalene belongs to which point groups?
(a) D_{2h}, D_{3h} respectively
(b) D_{3h}, D_{2h} respectively
(c) Both D_{2h}
(d) Both D_{3h}

16. SiF_4, BF_4^- belongs to which point groups?
(a) O_h (b) T_d
(c) C_{2v}, D_{2h} (d) D_{2h}, C_{2v}

17. Ketene ($CH_2{=}C{=}O$) and B_2H_6 belongs to
(a) D_{2h}, C_{2v} (b) Both C_{2v}
(c) C_{2v}, D_{2h} (d) Both D_{2h}

18. *Gauche* CH_2—Cl | CH_2—Cl belongs to which point group?
(a) C_{2v} (b) $C_{\infty v}$
(c) C_2 (d) C_{4v}

19. 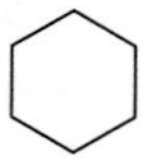 (cyclohexane) belong to which point group?
(a) D_{2h} (b) D_{4h}
(c) D_{3d} (d) $D_{\infty h}$

20. Which of the following molecules and ions have S_4 axis?
(a) SO_4^{2-} (b) BF_3
(c) C_2H_2 (d) CO_2

21. Molecule AB_6 belongs to O_h point group, changes to AB_5C and *cis*-AB_4C_2 results in point groups
(a) Both C_{4v} (b) C_{4v}, C_{2v}
(c) C_{4v}, D_{4h} (d) C_{2v}, D_{4h}

22. IO_6^{5-} (octahedral) belongs to
(a) T_d (b) C_{2v}
(c) D_{2h} (d) O_h

23. $CF_2{=}CF_2$ belongs to which point groups?
(a) D_{3d} (b) $D_{\infty h}$
(c) D_{2h} (d) D_{3h}

24. *Cis*-AB_4C_2 and *trans*-AB_4C_2 belongs to which point groups?
(a) Both D_{4h} (b) Both C_{2v}
(c) Both C_{4v} (d) C_{2v} and D_{4h}

25. In the solid state PCl_5 exists as an ionic solid composed of PCl_4^+ cations and PCl_6^- anions but the vapour is molecular. To what point groups do the ionic species in the solid belong?
(a) T_d only (b) O_h only
(c) T_d and O_h respectively (d) O_h and T_d respectively

26. *Trans* 1, 2-dichloroethylene and *cis* 1, 2-dichloroethylene belongs to
(a) C_{2h}, C_{2v} point groups
(b) C_{2h} only
(c) C_{2v} only
(d) C_{2v} and C_{2h} point groups respectively

Exercise 2

(For Part 'C')

1. Which of the following does not contain a C_3 axis?
(a) $POCl_3$ (b) $[NH_4]^+$
(c) $[H_3O]^+$ (d) ClF_3

2. Which of the following symmetry elements does *cis*-N_2F_2 contain?
(a) A C_2-axis (b) A σ_h-plane
(c) An inversion centre, i (d) An S_2-axis

3. Which of the following species possesses both C_3 and C_2 axes?
(a) SO_3 (b) NH_3
(c) PCl_3 (d) $[H_3O]^+$

4. Which two species belong to the same point group?
(a) XeF_2 and OF_2
(b) H_2O and CO_2
(c) H_2S and OF_2
(d) $[NO_2]^+$ and $[NO_2]^-$

5. Which of the following belongs to the C_{3v} point group?
(a) SO_3 (b) BBr_3
(c) NH_3 (d) $AlCl_3$

6. Which molecule does not have T_d symmetry?
(a) SiF_4 (b) P_4
(c) CH_4 (d) XeF_4

7. Which molecule or ion has D_{3h} symmetry?
(a) $[H_3O]^+$ (b) $CHCl_3$
(c) $[CO_3]^{2-}$ (d) NF_3

8. SO_2 belongs to which point group?
(a) C_{2v} (b) C_2
(c) $D_{\infty h}$ (d) C_{2h}

9. Which of the following molecules or ions possesses a C_4 principal axis?
(a) XeF_4 (b) CF_4
(c) SF_4 (d) $[PF_4]^+$

10. Which of the following molecules or ions possesses an inversion centre (centre of symmetry)?
(a) $[PF_6]^-$ (b) SiH_4
(c) BF_3 (d) PF_5

11. Which of the following molecules or ions belong to the C_{4v} point group?
(a) SF_5Cl (b) $[BF_4]^-$
(c) XeF_4 (d) *Trans*-Cl_2F_4

12. Which statement is true about the change in symmetry on going from BF_3 to $[BF_4]^-$?
(a) The point group changes from D_{3h} to T_d
(b) The point group changes from D_{3v} to T_d
(c) The point group changes from D_{3h} to D_{4h}
(d) The point group changes from D_{3h} to C_{3v}

13. CO_2 has
(a) 3 vibrational modes
(b) 4 vibrational modes, 2 of which are degenerate
(c) stretching modes only
(d) an IR active symmetric stretch

14. The number of degrees of vibrational freedom possessed by CH_4 is
(a) 10 (b) 6
(c) 4 (d) 9

15. Which of the following gives the correct description of the vibrational modes of SO_3, and how many absorptions do these vibrational modes give rise to in the IR spectrum of SO_3?

(a) Symmetric stretch; asymmetric stretch (doubly degenerate); one absorption
(b) Symmetyric stretch; asymmetric stretch (doubly degenerate); two absorptions
(c) Symmetric stretch; aymmetric stretch; two absorptions
(d) Symmetric stretch; asymmetric stretch; one absorption

16. Which of the following statements is correct?
(a) The symmetric stretching mode of PCl_3 is IR active and Raman inactive
(b) The symmetric stretching mode of PCl_3 is IR active and Raman active
(c) The symmetric stretching mode of PCl_3 is IR inactive and Raman active
(d) The symmetric stretching mode of PCl_3 is IR inactive and Raman inactive

17. The symmetric stretching mode of the SiF_4 molecule
(a) is IR active
(b) is IR inactive
(c) generates a change in molecular dipole moment
(d) gives rise to a strong absorption in the IR spectrum

18. An O_h XY_6 molecule exhibits two T_{1u} IR active modes. Which statement is true?
(a) Each T_{1u} mode is triply degenerate, and each gives rise to one absorption in the IR spectrum of XY_6
(b) Each T_{1u} mode is triply degenerate, and each gives rise to three absorptions in the IR spectrum of XY_6
(c) Each T_{1u} mode is non-degenerate, and gives rise to one absorption in the IR spectrum of XY_6
(d) One of the T_{1u} modes is the symmetric stretching mode of XY_6

19. Which pairing of molecule and point group is correct?
(a) BCl_3, C_{3v} (b) $SiCl_4$, D_{4h}
(c) H_2S, C_{2v} (d) SF_4, C_{4v}

20. Which pairing of molecule and point group is correct?
(a) CH_2Cl_2, T_d (b) $CHCl_3$, C_{3v}
(c) CCl_4, D_{4d} (d) CCl_2Br_2, C_{2h}

21. The orbital shown below is a

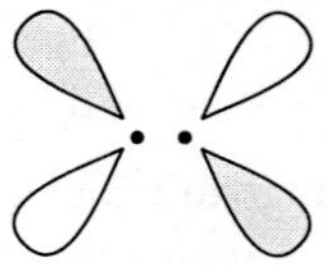

(a) σ_u^* (b) σ_g
(c) σ_g^* (d) π_g^*

22. BF_3 is more stable than the separated B and F atoms because
(a) boron is more electronegative than fluorine
(b) molecular orbitals are always more stable than atomic orbitals
(c) the bonding electron pairs are attracted to, and stabilized by two nuclei as opposed to one
(d) the Pauli exclusion principle requires this

23. The point group of the molecule shown below is

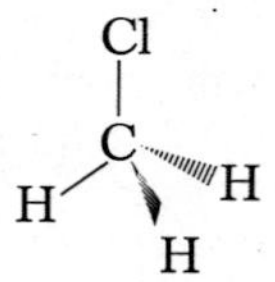

(a) C_{2v} (b) D_{3d}
(c) D_{2d} (d) C_{3v}

24. The following metal ion(s) would possess an $S = 1/2$ spin-state in a weak-field (π-donor) octahedral metal complex
(a) Fe^{3+} (b) Ni^{2+}
(c) Cu^{2+} (d) Co^{2+}

25. π-donor complexes of d^3 ions tends to be more reactive than d^3 π-acceptor complexes because
(a) the LFSE is more negative for the π-donor complex
(b) the LFSE is less negative for the π-donor complex
(c) the π-donor complex has more filled anti-bonding orbitals than the π-acceptor complex
(d) the π-donor complex has fewer filled anti-bonding orbitals than the π-acceptor complex

Answers

Exercise 1

1. (c)	**2.** (b)	**3.** (b)	**4.** (d)	**5.** (a)	**6.** (d)	**7.** (c)	**8.** (b)	**9.** (d)	**10.** (d)
11. (c)	**12.** (d)	**13.** (a)	**14.** (a)	**15.** (c)	**16.** (b)	**17.** (c)	**18.** (c)	**19.** (c)	**20.** (a)
21. (b)	**22.** (d)	**23.** (c)	**24.** (d)	**25.** (c)	**26.** (a)				

Exercise 2

1. (d)	**2.** (a)	**3.** (a)	**4.** (c)	**5.** (c)	**6.** (d)	**7.** (c)	**8.** (a)	**9.** (a)	**10.** (a)
11. (a)	**12.** (a)	**13.** (b)	**14.** (d)	**15.** (a)	**16.** (b)	**17.** (a)	**18.** (a)	**19.** (c)	**20.** (b)
21. (d)	**22.** (c)	**23.** (d)	**24.** (c)	**25.** (b)					

20 Molecular Spectroscopy

Syllabus

- Basic Principles and Applications of Spectroscopy
- Rotational and Vibrational Spectra of Diatomic Molecules, Electronic Spectra
- IR and Raman Activities, Selection Rules
- Basic UV-Visible, Principles of Magnetic Resonance (NMR, ESR, NQR Mossbauer) MS PES

Spectroscopy

Spectroscopy deals with the transitions that a molecule undergoes between its energy levels upon absorption of suitable radiations determined by quantum mechanical selection rules.

Let us consider how a spectrum arises. Consider two molecular energy levels E_n and E_m, as shown in Fig. 20.1.

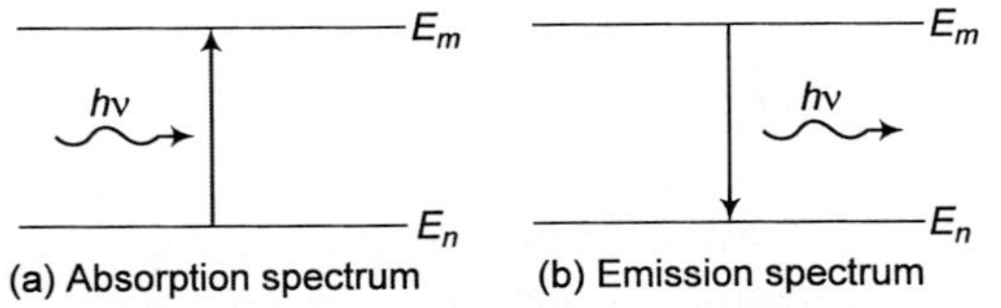

Fig. 20.1 Spectroscopic transitions between molecular energy levels.

If a photon of frequency ν falls on a molecule in the ground state and its energy $h\nu$ is exactly equal to the energy difference $\Delta E \; (= E_m - E_n)$ between the two molecular energy levels, then the molecule undergoes a transition from the lower energy level to the higher energy level with the absorption of a photon of energy $h\nu$. The spectrum thus, obtained is called the **absorption spectrum.** If the molecule falls from the excited state to the ground state with the emission of a photon of energy $h\nu$, the spectrum obtained is called the **emission spectrum.**

Basic Features of Different Spectrometers

The schematic diagram of the apparatus for absorption spectroscopy is given in Fig. 20.2.

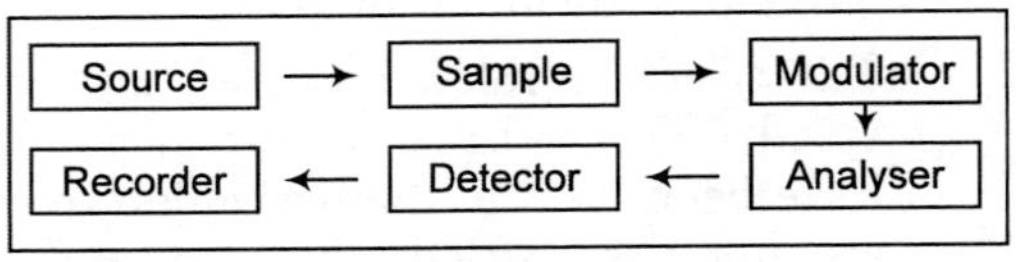

Fig. 20.2 Apparatus for absorption spectroscopy.

Source

The spectrometer is used when absorption occurs in infrared and ultraviolet regions of the electromagnetic spectrum. The source in a spectrometer produces radiation spanning a range of frequencies, but in a few cases (such as lasers), it is almost a monochromatic radiation. The radiation source in an absorption spectrometer is a heated ceramic filament coated with rare-earth oxides (a Nernst emitter or filament) for the infrared region. The source for the visible region of the spectrum is a tungsten filament which gives out intense white light : for the ultraviolet region the source is a hydrogen discharge lamp. A *klystron* (which is also used in radar installations and microwave ovens) or more commonly, a semiconductor device called *Gunn diode*, is used to generate microwaves. The radio-frequency radiation is generated by causing an electric current to oscillate in a coil of wire.

Dispersing Elements or Analyser

The variation of absorption with frequency is determined, traditionally, by analyzing the spectral radiation by means of a dispersing element which separates different frequencies into rays that travel in different directions. The simplest dispersing element is a glass or quartz prism but a diffraction grating is more widely used.

Detector

The third component of spectrometers is the detector, a device that converts the spectral radiation into an electrical signal that is passed on to a recording device operating synchronously with the analyzer, thus producing either a trace on a chart recorder or a computer record of the spectrum. Common detectors are the radiation-sensitive semiconductors. The radiation is chopped by a shutter that rotates in the beam so that an alternating signal is obtained from the detector (an oscillating signal is easier to amplify than a steady signal). A modulator is introduced to convert the signal to an alternating character. The procedure enables more AC electronics to be employed in the recording stages. In the microwave region the source frequency is varied and the analyser is not necessary.

Sample

The highest resolution is obtained when the sample is gaseous and at such low pressure that collisions between molecules are infrequent. Gaseous samples are essential for microwave (pure rotational) spectroscopy for molecules can freely rotate only in the gaseous state. In order to achieve sufficient absorption, the path lengths of gaseous samples must be very long, of the order of metres. Long path lengths are achieved by multiple passage of the beam between two parallel mirrors at each end of the sample cavity. For infrared spectroscopy, the sample is typically a liquid held between windows of sodium chloride (which is transparent down to 700 cm^{-1}) or potassium bromide (down to 400 cm^{-1}). Other ways of preparing the sample include grinding it into a paste with 'Nujol', a hydrocarbon oil, or passing it into a solid disk, with powdered potassium bromide.

Fourier Transform Technique

Now-a-days, it is a common practice to use Fourier transform technique in spectroscopy, particularly with infrared (IR) and nuclear magnetic resonance (NMR) spectroscopies. In Fourier-transform infrared (FTIR) spectroscopy, a Michelson-type interferometer is used to analyse the spectrum. It functions by producing an interferogram which is the superposition of a series of waves, each of which represents a component in the spectrum in terms of intensity and wave number. A Fourier transformation of the interferogram then produces a well-resolved absorption spectrum of the species, with a good signal-to-noise (S/N) ratio, also abbreviated as SNR.

Selection Rules

The molecular spectra are governed by the so-called **selection rules** which specify the changes in the quantum numbers accompanying a particular transition. The chemist is lucky that selection rules exist which determine a spectrum. It there were no selection rules. The resulting spectrum would by very chaotic, indeed ! The selection rules are, in fact, the 'backbone' of spectroscopy and are obtained from the quantum theory of interaction of radiation with matter. Let us enumerate a few examples which would later be elucidated. For a diatomic molecule, such as H_2, NO, CO, etc., the selection rule for a pure rotational transition is $\Delta J = \pm 1$, where, J is the rotational quantum number. The selection rule for a pure vibrational transitioin is $\Delta V = \pm 1$, where, V is the vibrational quantum number.

The selection rules, however, are not always obeyed strictly. This is because certain approximations which have been used in the derivation of the selection rules are not valid strictly. The spectral transitions which obey a given selection rule are called **allowed transitions** whereas those which violate a selection rule are called **forbidden transitions.** In general, the allowed transitions are more intense (stronger) than the forbidden transitions which are weak.

The natural line width (or line-time broadening) of a spectral line is determined by the Heisenberg uncertainty principle, $\Delta E \Delta t \geq h / 4\pi$, where, ΔE is the uncertainty in the energy and Δt is the uncertainty in the life-time of the energy level. Since, for a photon $E = h\nu$ so that $\Delta E = h\Delta\nu$, hence the natural line width, $\Delta\nu$, is given by

$$\Delta\nu \geq (4\pi\Delta t)^{-1} \qquad \ldots(1)$$

Width and Intensity of Spectral Lines

When we analyse the spectrum of a molecule, the first thing we wish to know is how sharp and how intense (strong) is the spectral line. These two quantities are common to all branches of spectroscopy. Fig. 20.3(a) shows sharp spectral line having no width while Fig. 20.3(b) shows a spectral line having a width ΔE at half-height. The chemist would, indeed, be a happy person if the spectral lines were all very sharp and very intense. In practice, this is not so.

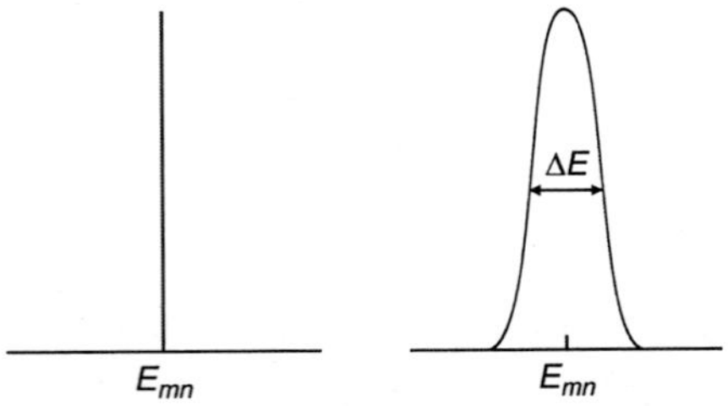

Fig. 20.3 (a) Sharp spectral line,
(b) Spectral line having a width.

Two factors contribute to broadening of a spectral line : (i) The collision broadening and (ii) the Doppler broadening. The **collision broadening** is largely responsible for the width of spectral lines in the ultraviolet (UV) and visible regions. These transitions mostly take place between electrons in the outer shells in a molecule. When molecules in the gaseous or liquid phase collide with one another, they deform the charge clouds of the outer electrons thereby slightly perturbing the energy levels of these electrons. Hence, the spectral transitions between these perturbed energy levels are broadened.

The **Doppler broadening** arises when the molecule under investigation has a velocity relative to the observer or observing instrument. This is generally, the case with gaseous samples where the molecules are undergoing random motion according to the postulates of the kinetic theory of gases. If the molecule is moving towards the measuring instrument with velocity u, then the frequency v' of radiation 'seen' by the molecule is given by

$$v' = v(1 + u / c) \qquad \ldots(2a)$$

where, v is the radiation frequency and c is the velocity of light. If, on the other hand, the molecule is moving away from the measuring instrument, the frequency of radiation 'seen' by the molecule is given by

$$v' = v\,(1 - u / c) \qquad \ldots(2b)$$

Rearrange Eq. (2a), we obtain

$$(v - v') / v = \Delta v / v = -u / c \qquad \ldots(3a)$$

Similarly, rearranging Eq. (2b), we obtain

$$(v - v')/v = \Delta v / v = u / c \qquad \ldots(3b)$$

The quantity Δv is the Doppler broadening. From the kinetic theory of gases, it can be shown that the Doppler broadening of the spectral line of a molecule of mass m is given by

$$\Delta v / v = (2 / c)\,(2kT \ln 2 / m)^{1/2} \qquad \ldots(4)$$

Since, $\Delta v / v$ is directly proportional to $T^{1/2}$, Doppler broadening can be reduced (and spectral lines of maximum sharpness can be obtained) by working with cold gaseous samples.

Intensity of spectral lines

The intensity of a spectral line is determined by (i) the Boltzmann population of the energy levels and (ii) the transition probability between the energy levels.

According to Boltzmann, if, at temperature T, N_0 is the number of molecules in the ground state, then the number of molecules, N, in the excited state is given by

$$N = N_0 e^{-\Delta E/kT} \qquad \ldots(5)$$

where, ΔE is the energy difference between the ground and excited states and k is the Boltzmann constant. The relative population at equilibrium is, thus, given by

$$N / N_0 = e^{-\Delta E/kT} \qquad \ldots(6)$$

Evidently, if ΔE is large, N/N_0 is small, *i.e.,* the number of molecules in the excited state is less than that in the ground state. In fact, at room temperature, most of the molecules are in the ground state. Hence, the spectral lines originating from transitions from the ground state to a higher, say, third excited state would be more intense than those originating from transitions from the first excited state to the third excited state.

Pure Rotation (Microwave) Spectra

The investigation of pure rotation spectra provides a powerful method of finding molecular parameters of simple molecules that may be obtained in the gas phase. A rotating diatomic molecule whose nuclei are considered as being separated by a definite mean distance may be treated as a rigid rotator with free axis. As a suitable model for the interpretation of pure rotation spectra, we may consider two atoms of masses m and M, respectively at a fixed distances of r_1 and r_2 from the centre of gravity as shown in Fig. 20.5.

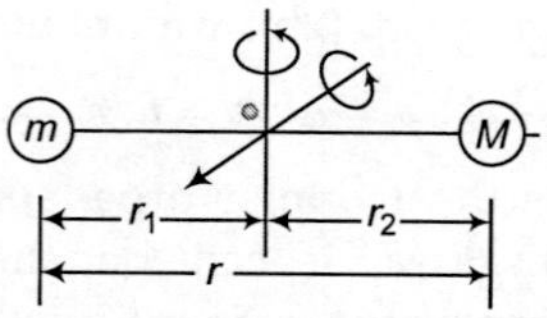

Fig. 20.4 Rotation of a diatomic molecule about its centre of gravity.

If this molecule rotates about an axis perpendicular to the internuclear axis through the centre of gravity O, then moment of inertia is given by

$$I = mr_1^2 + Mr_2^2 \quad \ldots(7)$$

or

$$I = \sum_i m_i r_i^2$$

where, r_i is the distance of ith particle from the centre of gravity of the system.

For a diatomic molecule, for instance, the masses and distances of the above figure lead to the centre of gravity being located so that,

$$mr_1 = Mr_2 \quad \text{(By law of momentum)}$$

or since, $r_1 + r_2 = r$, to the relations,

$$r_1 = \frac{M}{m+M} r$$

and

$$r_2 = \frac{m}{m+M} r$$

Substituting these values in Eq. (7) we obtain

$$I = \frac{mM^2}{(m+M)^2} r^2 + \frac{m^2 M}{(m+M)^2} r^2$$

$$= \frac{mM}{m+M} r^2$$

$$\therefore \quad I = \mu r^2$$

where, μ the reduced mass is defined as,

$$\mu = \frac{mM}{m+M}$$

The kinetic energy of a system of moving particles is given by

$$T\text{ (KE)} = \sum_i \frac{1}{2} m_i v_i^2$$

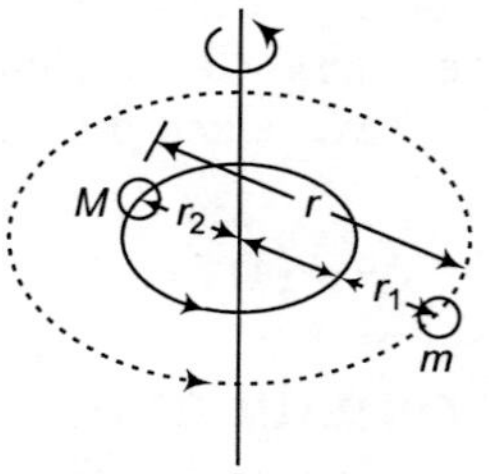

Fig. 20.5 Rotating dumbell.

If the system performs a rotational motion then the particle velocities are more conveniently treated in terms of the angular velocity ω of the system, so that we can write the kinetic energy T, as

$$T = \frac{1}{2} \sum m_i v_i^2$$

or

$$T = \frac{1}{2} \sum m_i \omega^2 r_i^2$$

$$= \frac{1}{2} \omega^2 \sum m_i r_i^2$$

$$T = \frac{1}{2} I\omega^2 \quad \ldots(8)$$

Thus, the rotation of any system is most conveniently treated in terms of the angular velocity, ω and the moment of inertia, I.

The above equation is the classical expression for the rotational kinetic energy of the rigid rotator model.

By analogy with linear momentum, which is defined as the product of the linear velocity and mass, the angular momentum is defined as the product of angular velocity and moment of inertia. Denoting the angular momentum by P we can write

$$P = I \cdot w$$

and so the expression for KE becomes

$$\text{KE} = P^2/2I \quad \ldots(9)$$

In Eq. (9), the allowed amount of angular momentum are multiples of the quantity $h/2\pi$ where, h is Planck's constant. Thus, the angular momentum will be given by,

$$P = \sqrt{(J(J+1))} \cdot h/2\pi \quad \ldots(10)$$

in which J is a rotational quantum number having only integral values, 0, 1, 2, ... The expression for allowed rotational energies for a diatomic molecule is then obtained by substituting (10) into (9). Denoting the rotational energy for a molecule by E_R, the expression becomes

$$E_R = J(J+1)\frac{h^2}{8\pi^2 I} \qquad \ldots(11)$$

where, I is the moment of inertia which is the characteristic of the molecule.

If a rotational transition occurs, from an upper level with quantum number J' to lower level of quantum number J'', the energy emitted is given by

$$E'_R - E''_R = \frac{h^2}{8\pi^2 I}(\{J'(J'+1) - J''(J''+1)\} \ldots(12)$$

The frequency of corresponding spectral line should be

$$v = \frac{E'_R - E''_R}{h}$$

or $\quad \omega\,(\text{cm}^{-1}) = \dfrac{E'_R - E''_R}{hc}$, in wave number.

Substituting the value of $E'_R - E''_R$ in the above equation we obtain

$$\omega\,(\text{cm}^{-1}) = \frac{1}{hc} \times \frac{h^2}{8\pi^2 I}\{J'(J'+1) - J''(J''+1)\}$$

$$= \frac{h^2}{8\pi^2 Ic}\{J'(J'+1) - J''(J''+1)\} \quad \ldots(13)$$

The selection rule for rotational transitions of linear molecules that occur with absorption or emission of electromagnetic radiation is $\Delta J = \pm 1$, where, ΔJ is equal to $J' - J''$.

For studies of the absorption of rotation, the experiment that is invariably done when rotational spectra are obtained, the appropriate part of the selection rule is, $\Delta J = +1$ or $J' - J'' = +1$ or $J' = J'' + 1$. Now, substituting the value of J' in Eq. (13), we get

$$\omega\,(\text{cm}^{-1}) = \frac{h}{8\pi^2 Ic}\{(J''+1)(J''+1+1) - J''(J''+1)\}$$

$$= \frac{2h}{8\pi^2 Ic}(J''+1)$$

For the sake of simplicity, writing J instead of J'' we have,

$$\omega\,(\text{cm}^{-1}) = \frac{h}{8\pi^2 Ic}(J+1)$$

or $\quad \omega\,(\text{cm}^{-1}) = 2B(J+1)$

where, $\quad B = \dfrac{h}{8\pi^2 Ic}\,\text{cm}^{-1}$

and this B is called the rotational constant of the molecule and is a characteristic property of the molecule. We can expect the absorptions of radiation at frequencies of $2B, 4B, 6B, \ldots$ etc., for the levels with $J = 0, 1, 2, \ldots$ etc. Therefore, the lines are spaced equally and the constant frequency separation between successive line is equal to $2B$, *i.e.*, $\dfrac{h}{4\pi^2 Ic}$.

According, to classical electrodynamics, an intermolecular motion leads to a radiation of light if a changing dipole moment is associated with it. For a rigid rotator this can be caused by the rotating mass having a permanent dipole moment, that lies in the direction perpendicular from the mass point to the axis of rotation. This applies to all diatomic molecules that consist of unlike atoms like CO, NO, HCl, etc. For such molecules the centres of positive and negative charges do not coincide, *i.e.*, such molecules have a permanent dipole moment. During rotation, the component of dipole changes in a fixed direction with rotational frequency, *i.e.*, classically light of frequency, v_{rot} should be emitted.

For molecules consisting of two like atoms (homonuclear) such as H_2, O_2, N_2, no dipole moment arises and, therefore, no light is emitted. Conversely, **only if a permanent dipole moment is present, then an infrared frequency can be absorbed and thereby a rotation of the system be produced.**

Thus, a rigid rotator is assumed by making all these derivations and the expression for a rigid planar rotator can also be written as :

$\dfrac{E_R}{hc} = \dfrac{h}{8\pi^2 Ic}\cdot J(J+1)$, where, $\dfrac{E_R}{hc}$ values are called rotational terms or sometimes the spectroscopic terms of the molecules.

Example 1. *The pure rotational (microwave) spectrum of gaseous HCl consists of a series of equally spaced lines separated by 20.80 cm^{-1}. Calculate the internuclear distance of the molecule. The atomic masses are :* $^{1}\text{H} = 1.673 \times 10^{-28}$ *kg :*

$^{35}\text{Cl} = 58.06 \times 10^{-27}$ *kg.*

Sol. The spacing between the lines $= 2B = 20.80\ \text{cm}^{-1}$

$$\therefore \quad B = \frac{20.80}{2} = 10.40\ \text{cm}^{-1}$$

$$B = \frac{h}{8\pi^2 Ic}\,\text{cm}^{-1}$$

$$I = \frac{h}{8\pi^2 Bc}$$

$$= \frac{6.626 \times 10^{-34}\ \text{J s}}{(8\pi^2)\ (10.40\ \text{cm}^{-1})\ (3 \times 10^{10}\ \text{cm s}^{-1})}$$

$$= 0.2689 \times 10^{-46}\ \text{kg m}^2 \qquad (\text{J} = \text{kg m}^2\ \text{s}^{-2})$$

The reduced mass is given by

$$\mu = \frac{m_1 m_2}{m_1 + m_2}$$

where, m_1 and m_2 are the atomic masses of H and Cl, respectively. Thus,

$$\mu = \frac{(1.673 \times 10^{-27}\ \text{kg})\ (58.06 \times 10^{-27}\ \text{kg})}{(1.673 + 58.06) \times 10^{-27}\ \text{kg}}$$

$$= \frac{(1.673 \times 58.06)\ 10^{-27}}{59.73}\ \text{kg} = 1.626 \times 10^{-27}\ \text{kg}$$

Since, $I = \mu r^2$

hence, $r = \left(\frac{I}{\mu}\right)^{1/2}$

$$= \left[\frac{0.2689 \times 10^{-46}\ \text{kg m}^2}{1.626 \times 10^{-27}\ \text{kg}}\right]$$

$$= 1.29 \times 10^{-10}\ \text{m} = 129\ \text{pm}.$$

Example 2. *Compare the first excited state rotational energy of CO molecule obtained in the last example with its thermal energy at room temperature and comment on the result.*

Sol. Thermal energy of CO molecule at room temperature, *i.e.*, 25°C = kT

$$= \frac{1.38 \times 10^{-23}\ \text{J K}^{-1})\ (298\ \text{K})}{1.602 \times 10^{-19}\ \text{J (eV)}^{-1}} = 2.6 \times 10^{-2}\ \text{eV}$$

Comparing it with the first excited state rotational energy of CO (*viz.*, 4.76×10^{-4} eV), obtained in the last example, we find that the thermal energy is far greater. Hence, we conclude that at room temperature, all the molecules in the gaseous sample of carbon monoxide are in the excited rotational energy levels.

Relative Intensities of Rotational Spectral Lines

The relative intensities of spectral lines depend upon the relative populations of the energy levels. Since, the energy level population is given by the Boltzmann distribution, the intensity of rotational lines is evidently proportional to the Boltzmann distribution of molecules in the rotational energy levels, *i.e.*,

$$\text{Intensity} \propto N_J / N_0 = e^{-E_J/kT} \qquad \ldots(14)$$

Rotational energy levels are, however, degenerate, their degeneracy (g_J) for a diatomic molecule being given by

$$g_J = 2J + 1 \qquad \ldots(15)$$

In other words, for a given value of J, the energy level is $(2J + 1)$-fold degenerate. For $J = 0$, $g_J = 1$; for $J = 1$, $g_J = 3$; for $J = 2$, $g_J = 5$; and so on.

Hence, the intensity of the rotational spectra is determined by the product of the degeneracy factor and the Boltzmann exponential factor. Thus,

$$\text{Intensity} \propto N_J / N_0 = (2J + 1)\ e^{-E_J/kT} \qquad \ldots(16)$$

Since, $E_J = hcF(J)$ ...(17)

and $F(J) = BJ\ (J + 1)$ ...(18)

we have, $N_J / N_0 = (2J + 1)\ e^{-BJ(J+1)hc/kT}$ ...(19)

The quantity N_J / N_0 is plotted *versus* J for a rigid diatomic molecule at room temperature in Fig. 20.6.

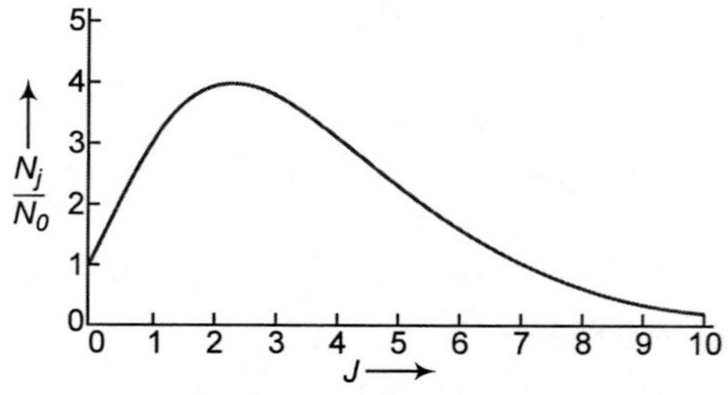

Fig. 20.6 Plot of the relative Boltzmann population *versus* J for a rigid diatomic molecule.

We see that the relative intensity passes through a maximum. It can be shown that the value of J corresponding to the maximum in population is given by

$$J_{\max} = \left(\frac{kT}{2hc\,B}\right)^{1/2} - \frac{1}{2} \qquad \ldots(20)$$

The $J_{\max}$ should be rounded off to the nearest integral value.

Example 3. *Calculate $J_{\max}$ for a rigid diatomic molecule for which at 300 K, the rotational constant is 1.566 cm^{-1}.*

Sol. $J_{\max} = \left(\frac{kT}{2hcB}\right)^{1/2} - \frac{1}{2}$ [From Eq. (20)]

$$= \left[\frac{(1.38 \times 10^{-23}\ \text{JK}^{-1})\ (300\ \text{K})}{2\ (6.626 \times 10^{-34}\ \text{Js})(3 \times 10^{10}\text{cms}^{-1})(1.566\text{cm}^{-1})}\right]^{1/2} - \frac{1}{2}$$

$$= 7.56 = 8$$

Rotational Spectra of Polyatomic Molecules

The diatomics have only one bond distance and hence only one moment of inertia, polyatomic molecules have more than one bond distance and hence several moments of inertia. In fact, the Cartesian coordinate system (x, y, z), there are nine components of the moment of inertia.

However, in the so-called principal axis system (a, b, c), these components reduce to three moments of inertia I_a, I_b, I_c, where, I_a, I_b and I_c are, respectively, the principal moments of inertia about the a, b and c axes. Thus, polyatomic molecules in microwave spectroscopy are classified into different types of rotators (rotors) as shown in Table 20.1.

Table 20.1. **Classification of Polyatomic Molecules**

Moment of inertia	Type of rotor	Examples
$I_a = I_b, I_c = 0$	Linear	HX, O=C=S, H—C≡N
$I_a = I_b = I_c$	Spherical top	CH_4, SF_6, UF_6
$I_a < I_b = I_c$	Prolate symmetric top	NH_3, $CHCl_3$, CH_3Cl
$I_a = I_b < I_c$	Oblate symmetric top	
$I_a \neq I_b \neq I_c$	Asymmetric top	H_2O

In case of non-linear molecules, we recognise that there are three rotational degrees of freedom, therefore, we can expect three moments of inertia to describe the motion. These three moments are generally chosen to coincide with rotation about the three principal molecular axes. Accordingly, non-linear molecules are divided into three classes, depending upon the relation between the moments of inertia about the Cartesian axes.

Vibrational (Infrared) Spectra of Diatomic Molecules

A diatomic molecule with atomic massess m_1 and m_2 joined by a chemical bond vibrates as a one-dimensional simple harmonic oscillator (SHO). Classically, the vibrational frequency of a mass point m connected by a spring of force constant k is given by

$$v = \frac{1}{2\pi}\left(\frac{k}{m}\right)^{1/2} \quad \ldots(21)$$

In the case of a diatomic molecule, the masses m_1 and m_2 vibrate back and forth relative to their centre of mass in opposite directions (Fig. 20.7).

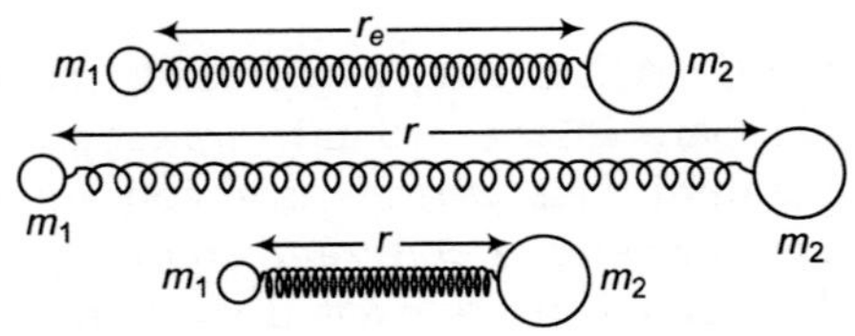

Fig. 20.7 Vibration of a diatomic molecule.

The two masses reach the extreme of their respective motions at the same time. The vibrational frequency of the molecule is given by a relation analogous to that of Eq. (21) with m replaced by the reduced mass μ

$$v = \frac{1}{2\pi}\left(\frac{k}{\mu}\right)^{1/2} \text{ s}^{-1} \quad \ldots(22)$$

Two convert the frequency v from s^{-1} (hertz) to cm^{-1}, we divide by c, the velocity of light. Thus,

$$\bar{v} = \frac{1}{2\pi c}\left(\frac{k}{\mu}\right)^{1/2} \text{ cm}^{-1} \quad \ldots(23)$$

The units of the force constant are dyn cm^{-1} in the c.g.s. system and Nm^{-1} in SI system. The potential energy of the simple harmonic oscillator (SHO) as a function of displacement from the equilibrium configuration is given by the parabolic Hooke's law equation, *viz.*,

$$V(x) = \frac{1}{2}k(r - r_e)^2 = \frac{1}{2}kx^2 \quad \ldots(24)$$

where, $x\,(= r - r_e)$ is the displacement, r_e being the equilibrium bond length. The Hooke's law potential energy is shown in Fig. 20.8.

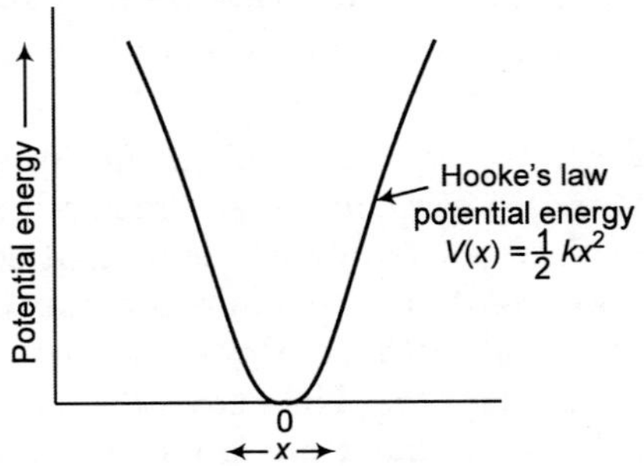

Fig. 20.8 The Hooke's law potential energy for a diatomic vibrator.

The solution of the Schrodinger equation for a simple harmonic oscillator gives the quantized vibrational energy levels,

$$E_v = \left(v + \frac{1}{2}\right)hv' \,;\; v = 0, 1, 2, 3 \ldots \quad \ldots(25)$$

where, v is the vibrational quantum number and v' is the vibrational frequency given by Eq. 22. Notice that the energy of the lowest vibrational level of the oscillator is not zero but is equal to $\frac{1}{2}hv$; this is called zero-point energy (Z.P.E.). The energy levels of the SHO are equally spaced, the spacing being equal to hv. To convert the energy from joules to cm^{-1} we divide by hc, obtaining

$$G(v) = E_v/hc = \left(v + \frac{1}{2}\right)v/c = \left(v + \frac{1}{2}\right)\omega_e \quad \ldots(26)$$

where, ω_e is the equilibrium vibrational frequency. $G(v)$ is called the **vibrational term.**

The selection rule for a vibrational transition in the simple harmonic oscillator is

$$\Delta v = \pm 1 \quad \ldots(27)$$

The operative part of the selection rule for the absorption spectrum is $\Delta v = +1$, *i.e.,* the vibrational quantum number changes by unity. Using the selection rule, the frequency of the vibrational transition is given by

$$\bar{v} = G(v \rightarrow v+1) = \left(v + 1 + \frac{1}{2}\right)\omega_e - \left(v + \frac{1}{2}\right)\omega_e = \omega_e \quad \ldots(28)$$

At room temperature, most of the molecule are in the ground vibrational state $(v = 0)$ so that the only transition of interest is that which takes place from $v = 0$ to $v = 1$. The vibrational frequency corresponding to this transition is called **fundamental vibrational frequency.** Diatomic molecules have only one vibrational frequency. This is a stretching vibrational frequency. Diatomic molecules do not have a bending vibrational frequency.

Vibrational spectra are observed in the infrared (IR) region. There is a very important requirement for a molecule to show an infrared spectrum. It states that the **dipole moment of the molecule must change during the vibration.** Homonuclear diatomic molecules such H_2, O_2, N_2, etc., do not have a permanent dipole moment nor does the stretching of the bond between the two atoms change the dipole moment from zero. Hence, **homonuclear diatomics do not show IR spectra. On the other hand, heteronuclear diatomic molecules such as CO, NO, CN, HCl, do possess a dipole moment which changes when the bond length changes. Hence, they show IR spectra. Thus, homonuclear diatomics are IR-inactive while heteronuclear diatomics are IR-active.**

In 1929, P.M. Morse suggested an empirical expression for the potential energy of an an harmonic diatomic oscillator, given by

$$V(r) = D_e\,[1 - \exp a\{r - r_e\}]^2 \quad \ldots(29)$$

Here, a is a constant and D_e is the dissociation energy of the molecule. The Morse potential energy is sketched in Fig. 20.9.

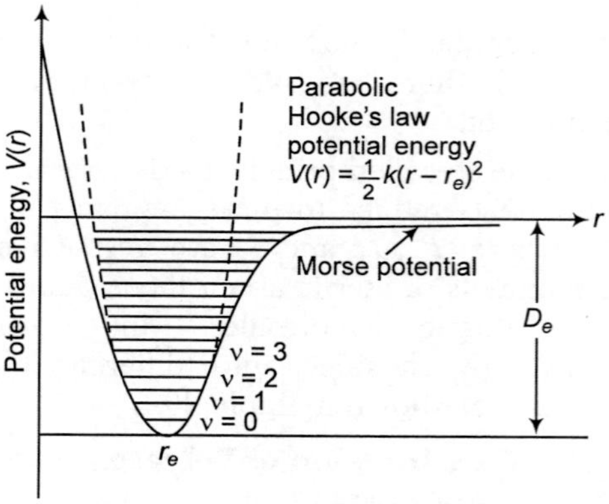

Fig. 20.9 Morse potential energy for an anharmonic diatomic oscillator.

It may be pointed out that the dissociation energy D_e in the Morse potential energy curve is measured from the bottom of the potential well. The experimentally measured dissociation energy D_0 is measured from the ground level $(v = 0)$ to the top. Thus,

$$D_e = D_0 + h\nu/2 \quad \ldots(30)$$

When the Schrodinger equation for an **anharmonic oscillator** is solved using the Morse potential energy, the energy levels are given by

$$G(v) = \left(v + \frac{1}{2}\right)\omega_e - \left(v + \frac{1}{2}\right)^2 \omega_e x_e\,; \quad (v = 0, 1, 2, 3 \ldots) \quad \ldots(31)$$

where, $\omega_e x_e$ is called the **anharmonicity constant**. As expected, $\omega_e x_e << \omega_e$. The consequence of an harmonicity is that the vibrational energy levels of the SHO are all slightly lowered and the spacing between them is no longer constant but goes on steadily decreasing with increase in vibrational quantum number. Also, because of anharmonicity, the rule for vibrational transitions is no longer $\Delta v = \pm 1$. Instead, transitions corresponding to $\Delta v = \pm 2, \pm 3$, etc., are also observed in the IR spectra. These are called the first overtone, the second overtone, etc., respectively. The intensity of an overtone is dependent on the anharmonicity of the vibration. Compared with the highly intense fundamental vibrational frequency, the overtones are very weak, *i.e.,* of considerably low intensity.

We see that $kT < \Delta E$. Hence, we conclude that most of the molecules are in the ground vibrational state at room temperature. This situation is in contrast with the rotational states where, $kT > \Delta E$ and consequently most of the molecules are in the excited rotational states at room temperature.

Example 4. *The force constant of* CO *is* 1840 *N m*$^{-1}$. *Calculate the vibrational frequency in cm*$^{-1}$ *and the spacing between the vibrational energy levels in eV. Compare this spacing with the thermal energy at room temperature and comment on your result. The atomic masses are* $^{12}C = 19.9 \times 10^{-27}$ *kg;* $^{16}O = 26.6 \times 10^{-27}$ *kg,* 1 *eV* = 8066 *cm*$^{-1}$.

Sol. The reduced mass of CO is given by

$$\mu = \frac{m_1 m_2}{m_1 + m_2}$$

$$= \frac{(19.9 \times 10^{-27} \text{ kg}) \times (26.6 \times 10^{-27} \text{ kg})}{(19.9 + 26.6) \times 10^{-27} \text{ kg}}$$

$$= 11.4 \times 10^{-27} \text{ kg}$$

$$\bar{\nu} = \frac{1}{2\pi c}\left(\frac{k}{\mu}\right)^{1/2} = \frac{1}{2(3.1416)(3 \times 10^{10} \text{ cms}^{-1})}$$

$$\left(\frac{1840 \text{ kg s}^{-2}}{11.4\ 10^{-27} \text{ kg}}\right) = 2140 \text{ cm}^{-1}$$

The spacing between energy levels,

$$\Delta E = E_{v+1} - E_v = h\nu \text{ joules}$$

$$= h\nu/hc = \nu/c = \bar{\nu} = 2140 \text{ cm}^{-1}$$

Since, $\qquad 1 \text{ eV} = 8066 \text{ cm}^{-1}$

$$\therefore \qquad \Delta E = \frac{2140 \text{ cm}^{-1}}{8066 \text{ cm}^{-1}/\text{eV}} = 0.265 \text{ eV}$$

$$\text{Thermal energy} = kT = \frac{(1.38 \times 10^{-23} \text{ J K}^{-1})(300\text{K})}{1.602 \times 10^{-19} \text{ J/eV}}$$

$$= 2.6 \times 10^{-2} \text{ eV} = 0.026 \text{ eV}.$$

Example 5. *For the molecule* BH, $\omega_e = 2368$ cm^{-1} *and the anharmonicity constant* $\omega_e x_e = 49$ *cm*$^{-1}$. *Calculate the vibrational terms of the first four vibrational levels and determine the spacing between them.*

Sol. From Eq. 31

$$G(v) = \left(v + \frac{1}{2}\right)\omega_e - \left(v + \frac{1}{2}\right)^2 \omega_e x_e$$

$$G(0) = \left(0 + \frac{1}{2}\right) \times 2368 - \left(0 + \frac{1}{2}\right)^2 \times 49$$

$$= 1184 - 12 = 1172 \text{ cm}^{-1}$$

$$G(1) = \left(1 + \frac{1}{2}\right) \times 2368 - \left(1 + \frac{1}{2}\right)^2 \times 49$$

$$= 3552 - 110 = 3442 \text{ cm}^{-1}$$

$$G(2) = \left(2 + \frac{1}{2}\right) \times 2368 - \left(2 + \frac{1}{2}\right) \times 49$$

$$= 5920 - 306 = 5614 \text{ cm}^{-1}$$

$$G(3) = \left(3 + \frac{1}{2}\right) \times 2368 - \left(3 + \frac{1}{2}\right) \times 49$$

$$= 8288 - 600 = 7688 \text{ cm}^{-1}$$

The spacing between the energy levels are :

$$G(1) - G(0) = 3442 - 1172 = 2770 \text{ cm}^{-1}$$

$$G(2) - G(1) = 5614 - 3442 = 2172 \text{ cm}^{-1}$$

$$G(3) - G(2) = 7688 - 5616 = 2074 \text{ cm}^{-1}$$

Notice that the energy levels are not equally spaced and the spacing goes on steadily decreasing with increase in the vibrational quantum number.

Example 6. *The force constant of* H_2 *is* 510 *N m*$^{-1}$ *and its dissociation energy is* 4.5 *eV. Assuming that it vibrates as a simple harmonic oscillator, calculate the vibrational quantum number corresponding to its dissociation energy.*

Sol. From the given value of the force constant, the frequency of vibration can be easily calculated; it is found to be 4159 cm^{-1}. Since, vibrational levels of an S.H.O. are equally spaced, the dissociation energy of 4.5 eV (*i.e.*, $4.5 \times 8066 \text{ cm}^{-1} = 36297 \text{ cm}^{-1}$) corresponds to

$$\frac{36297 \text{ cm}^{-1}}{4159 \text{ cm}^{-1}} = 8.7 = 9\text{th energy level}$$

Hence, the vibrational quantum number corresponding to the given dissociation energy is 8.

Rotation-Vibration (IR) Spectra of Diatomic Molecules

Pure vibrational spectra can be observed only in liquids where interactions between molecules inhibit rotation. Since, rotational energies are considerably smaller than vibrational energies, **the freely moving molecules in the gaseous state are almost always rotating regardless of their vibration state. Hence, molecules in gaseous state show rotation-vibration spectra**. The rotation and vibration are, to a first approximation, independent of each other. Ignoring the effect of centrifugal distortion and taking into account the anharmonicity, the **rotation-vibration term,** $S(v, J)$, for vibrating rotator is given by

$$S(v, J) = F(J) + G(v) \qquad \ldots(32)$$

$$S(v, J) = BJ(J+1) + \left(v + \frac{1}{2}\right)\omega_e - \left(v + \frac{1}{2}\right)^2 \omega_2 x_e \text{ cm}^{-1} \qquad \ldots(33)$$

The selection rules for combined vibrational and rotational transitions are

$$\Delta v = \pm 1 \text{ and } \Delta J = \pm 1 \qquad \ldots(34)$$

It is customary to designate the lower energy state by doubly prime and the upper energy state by a single prime. Using the energy level expression (33) and the selection rule (34), we have

$$\Delta S\,(v, J) = \left[BJ'\,(J' + 1) + \frac{3}{2}\,\omega_e - \frac{9}{4}\,\omega_e x_e\right]$$
$$- \left[BJ''\,(J'' + 1) + \frac{1}{2}\,\omega_e - \frac{1}{4}\,\omega_e x_e\right]$$
$$= \omega_0 + B\,(J' - J'')\,(J' + J'' + 1)\ \text{cm}^{-1} \qquad ...(35)$$

where, $\omega_0 = \omega_e\,(1 - 2x_e)$

Here, we have assumed that the rotational constant B is the same in the upper and lower vibrational states, an assumption that is justified by the fact that rotation and vibration are, to a first approximation, independent. Since, most of the molecules are in the ground vibrational state at room temperature, only the $v = 0$ to $v = 1$ transition is of interest,

(i) For the $\Delta J = +1$ transition, $J' = J'' + 1$, *i.e.*, $J' - J'' = +1$ so that

$$\Delta S\,(v, J) = \omega_0 + 2B\,(J'' + 1)\ \text{cm}^{-1}\ ;$$
$$J'' = 0, 1, 2, 3\,... \qquad ...(36)$$

(ii) For the $\Delta J = -1$ transition, $J'' = J' + 1$, *i.e.*, $J' - J'' = -1$ so that

$$\Delta S\,(v, J) = \omega_0 + 2B\,(J'' + 1)\ \text{cm}^{-1}\ ;$$
$$J' = 0, 1, 2, 3\,... \qquad ...(37)$$

The frequency ω_0, called the *band centre*, does not appear in the rotation-vibration spectrum which consists of equally spaced lines with spacing equal to $2B$ on each side of the band centre (Fig, 20.10). The lines corresponding to $\Delta J = -1$ are called the ***P*-branch** while those corresponding to $\Delta J = +1$ are called the ***R*-branch.**

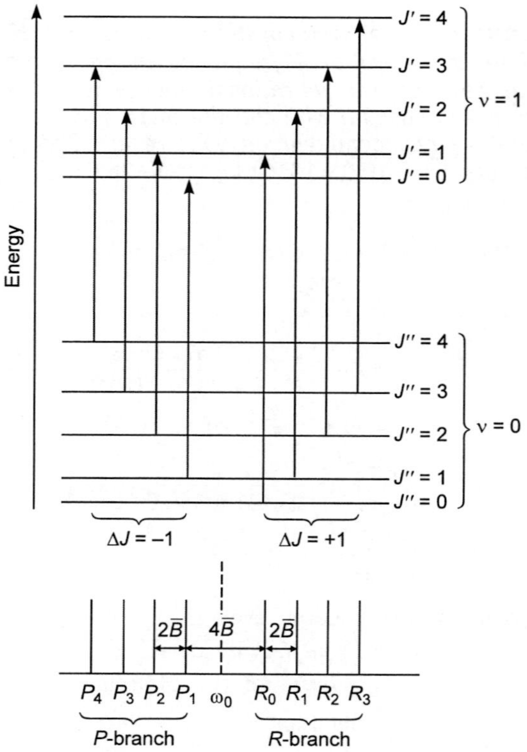

Fig. 20.10 The rotation-vibration spectrum of a diatomic molecule.

Vibrational Spectra of Polyatomic Molecules

In order to study the vibrational spectra of polyatomic molecules, we have to investigate the vibrations of polyatomic molecules for which we start with the classical model of a molecule where the atoms (or nuclei) are represented by mathematical mass points. Each point requires three coordinates (such as x, y, z in a Cartesian coordinate system) to define its position. This is expressed by saying that there are three independent **degrees of freedom** in the x, y and z directions. For a molecule containing n atomic nuclei, there will be $3n$ degrees of freedom for all the nuclear masses in the molecule.

We need three coordinates to specify the centre of gravity of the molecule. Thus, the centre of gravity of the molecule has **three** independent **translational** degrees of freedom. For a non-linear molecule in its equilibrium configuration, three rotational coordinates are needed to specify the molecular orientation about the centre of gravity. These can be the three angular coordinates specifying rotation about three mutually perpendicular axes, each passing through the centre of gravity. Thus, a non-linear molecule has three independent rotational degrees of freedom. On the other hand, a linear molecular has only *two* independent rotational degrees of freedom about the two mutually perpendicular axes which are perpendicular to the molecular axis.

If we substract the translational and rotational degrees of freedom from the total $3n$ degrees of freedom, we find that we are left with **$3n - 6$ *internal* degrees of freedom for a non-linear molecule and $3n - 5$ *internal* degrees of freedom for a linear molecule.**

The three normal modes of vibration (*i.e.*, fundamental vibrational frequencies) of H_2O molecule are shown in Fig. 20.11.

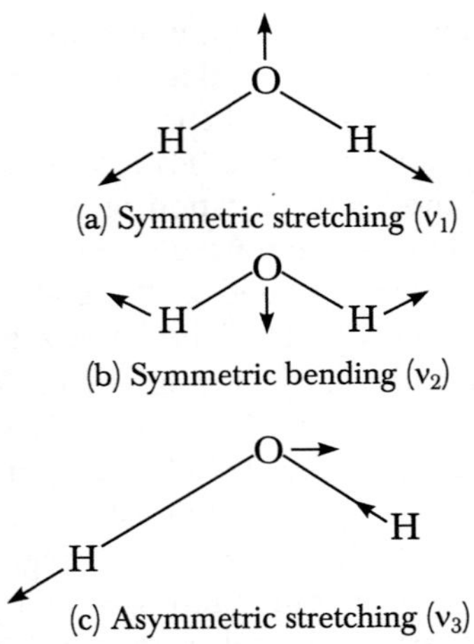

Fig. 20.11 The normal modes of vibration of water molecule.

The value of these frequencies are in the order symmetric stretching > Asymmetric stretching > Symmetric bending

The linear CO_2 molecule has $3 \times 3 - 5 = 4$ fundamental vibrational frequencies while the linear acetylene molecule has $3 \times 4 - 5 = 7$ fundamental vibrational frequencies. These are shown schematically in Fig. 20.12 and Fig. 20.13 respectively.

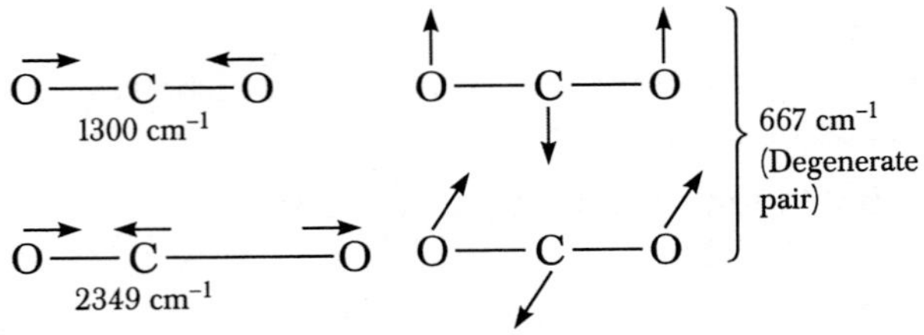

Fig. 20.12 The normal modes of vibration of CO_2.

Of the four fundamental vibrations of CO_2, two have the same frequency and are said to be **degenerate.** The symmetric stretching frequency $\bar{\nu}_1$ is not observed in the IR spectrum of CO_2 since it is not accompanied by a change in the dipole moment of the molecule with vibration.

Since the nuclei in a polyatomic molecule do not always vibrate in a simple harmonic manner, there arises **anharmonicity** in molecular vibrations. The harmonic vibrations give rise to $3n - 5$ (or $3n - 6$) fundamental vibrational frequencies as said above. On the other hand, the anharmonic vibrations give rise to the so called **overtones** and **combination bands.** The overtones occur as multiplies of a given fundamental frequency. Thus, for H_2O molecule which has three fundamental vibrational frequencies $\bar{\nu}_1, \bar{\nu}_2$ and $\bar{\nu}_3$, the overtones would occur at (or near) $2\bar{\nu}_1, 3\bar{\nu}_1, \ldots, 2\bar{\nu}_2, 3\bar{\nu}_2 \ldots, 2\bar{\nu}_3, 3\bar{\nu}_3, \ldots,$ etc. The first overtone of $\bar{\nu}_1$ is designated as $2\bar{\nu}_1$, the second as $3\bar{\nu}_1$, the third as $4\bar{\nu}_1$ and so on. The **combination bands** are merely the sum of two or more fundamental frequencies or overtones while the difference bands are the differences of two or more fundamental frequenceis or overtones. Thus, combination bands are $\bar{\nu}_1 + \bar{\nu}_2, 2\bar{\nu}_1 + \bar{\nu}_2, \bar{\nu}_1 + \bar{\nu}_2 + \bar{\nu}_3$, etc. while the difference bands are $\bar{\nu}_1 - \bar{\nu}_2, 2\bar{\nu}_1 - \bar{\nu}_2, \bar{\nu}_1 - \bar{\nu}_2 + \bar{\nu}_3, \bar{\nu}_1 + \bar{\nu}_2 - \bar{\nu}_3$, etc. The overtones and combination bands have low intensity.

Table 20.2 **IR Spectrum of H_2O Vapour**

$\bar{\nu}$ (cm^{-1})	Intensity	Assignment
1595.0	Very strong	$\bar{\nu}_2$
3151.4	Medium	$2\bar{\nu}_2$
3651.6	Strong	$\bar{\nu}_1$
3755.8	Very strong	$\bar{\nu}_3$
5332.0	Medium	$\bar{\nu}_2 + \bar{\nu}_3$
6874.0	Weak	$2\bar{\nu}_2 + \bar{\nu}_3$

The complete IR spectrum of a polyatomic molecule, therefore, consists of the highly intense fundamental vibrational frequencies and the less intense overtones, combination bands and difference bands. **The overtones and combination bands arise as a result of the violation of the selection rule for harmonic vibrations.** The analysis of the IR spectrum of water vapour is given in Table 20.2.

Sometimes it may happen that a fundamental mode of vibration becomes **accidentally degenerate** with an overtone or a combination band. As a result, the intensity of the overtone or the combination band which is otherwise very low is enhanced by a resonance phenomenon, known as **Fermi resonance,** after E. Fermi who first observed it. The classic example of Fermi resonance is furnished by CO_2 molecule where, $\bar{\nu}_1 = 1330$ cm^{-1} and $2\bar{\nu}_2 = 1334$ cm^{-1}.

Quantum mechanically it can be shown that, as a result of Fermi resonance, the higher frequency is raised whereas the lower frequency is depressed. The two bands of CO_2 mentioned above are not observed in IR but they are observed in the Raman spectrum at 1285 cm^{-1} and 1385 cm^{-1}, respectively. Their mean is near 1330 cm^{-1}.

Rotation-Vibration (IR) Spectra of Polyatomic Molecules

1. Linear molecules

Linear molecules such as CO_2 and HCN, whether they possess permanent electric dipole moment or not, are IR-active if some of their vibrations produce an oscillating dipole moment. Consider CO_2 molecule. It has two types of IR-active vibrations :

(i) The oscillating dipole is parallel to the molecular axis :

$$\overset{\rightarrow}{\mathrm{O}}—\overset{\leftarrow}{\mathrm{C}}—\overset{\rightarrow}{\mathrm{O}}\quad \overset{\leftarrow}{\mathrm{O}}—\overset{\rightarrow}{\mathrm{C}}—\overset{\leftarrow}{\mathrm{O}}$$

Such a vibration produces the so-called **parallel band**. The selection rules are $\Delta v = \pm 1$ and $\Delta J = \pm 1$.

(ii) The oscillating dipole is perpendicular to the molecular axis :

$$\overset{\uparrow}{\mathrm{O}}—\underset{\downarrow}{\mathrm{C}}—\overset{\uparrow}{\mathrm{O}}\,;\ \overset{\oplus}{\mathrm{O}}—\overset{\ominus}{\mathrm{C}}—\overset{\oplus}{\mathrm{O}}$$

(Here, $\ominus$ indicates vibration of C atom perpendicular to the plane of the paper downwards and $\oplus$ indicates vibration of O atom perpendicular to the plane of the paper upwards). Such a vibration gives rise to a **perpendicular band.** The selection rules are $\Delta v = \pm 1$ and $\Delta J = 0, \pm 1$.

2. Symmetric top molecules

Ignoring anharmonicity and centrifugal distortion, the energy levels of a symmetric top molecule such as CH_3Cl are given by

$$E_{J,K} = \left(v + \frac{1}{2}\right)\omega_e + B_v\, J(J+1) + (A - B)\, k^2$$

Parallel band : $\Delta J = 0, \pm 1, \Delta k = 0$

Perpendicular band : $\Delta J = 0, \pm 1, \Delta k = \pm 1$

3. Asymmetric top molecules

Since the solution of the Schrodinger wave equation for the asymmetric top molecules is very difficult, we shall not deal with them here.

Vibrational Frequencies of Different Functional Groups

In general, the bond lengths and bond angles for given moieties of various compounds remain approximately constant. However, small changes occur in these parameters according to other species present in the molecule. These factors give rise to characteristic ranges of vibrational wave numbers and intensities for functional groups in molecules. Assignment of these wave numbers in an infrared spectrum often provides a rapid method for the identification of a compound. Some normal modes of vibration of organic molecules can be regarded as motions of individual functional groups ; others are regarded as the collective motions of the molecule as a whole. The latter are generally of low frequency and occur below about 1500 cm^{-1} in the spectrum. The resulting whole-molecule region of the absorption spectrum is called a **finger print region** of the spectrum since it is characteristic of the molecule. The matching of the finger print region with the spectrum of a known compound in a library of infrared spectra is a very powerful way of confirming the presence of a particular substance.

From studies over a range of compounds, charts have been developed that give the vibrational wave number ranges for most functional groups in different compounds. These wave numbers that occur outside the finger print region are very useful for the identification of an unknown compound. Table 20.3 lists some of the assignments for a selection of the common functional groups encountered in organic chemistry. Lower frequency bending modes usually occur in the finger print region and so are less easily identified.

The infrared spectrum of a molecule can be regarded as made of several regions :

1. Hydrogen stretching vibrations, 3700-2500 cm^{-1}

These vibrations occurs at higher wave numbers because of the low mass of the hydrogen atom. If H atom is replaced by D atom (*i.e.,* deuterium atom), the vibrational wave number falls by a factor of $1/\sqrt{2}$ because of the greater reduced mass of the deuterium molecule : $\bar{v}(\mathrm{O—D}) / \bar{v}\,(\mathrm{O—H}) = 1/\sqrt{2}$. If an –OH group is not involved in hydrogen bonding, it usually has a vibrational wave number in the vicinity of 3700-3600 cm^{-1}. Hydrogen bonding causes this wave number to drop by 300-1000 cm^{-1} or more.

2. Triple-bond region, 2500-2000 cm^{-1}

These bonds have high vibrational wave numbers because of the large force constants. The C≡C group usually causes absorption between 2300 and 2050 cm^{-1} but this absorption may be weak or absent because of the symmetry of the molecule. The C≡N group absorbs near 2300-2200 cm^{-1}.

Table 20.3 **Typical Vibrational Wave Number for Functional Groups**

Group	Mode	Range (cm^{-1})	Intensity
$>CH_2$ $-CH_3$ $\geqslant C-H$	C—H (s)	3000-2850	*s*
$>CH_2$		2900-2880	*w*
$-CH_3$	C—H (b)	1470-1430	*m*
$-CH_3$	CH_3 (sb)	1390-1370	*m*
$>CH_2$	CH_2 (r)	700-750	*w*
$-C\equiv C-H$	CH (s)	3300	*s*
$RHC=CHR$	CH (s)	960-980	*s*
$>C=C<$	C=C (s)	1680-1620	*s*
—O—H	O—H (b)	1410-1260	*s*
—O—H	O—H (s)	3650-3590	*s*
$>C-OH$	C—OH (s)	1150-1050	*s*
$>N-H$ $=N-H$	N—H (ss/as)	3500-3300	*m*
$>C=O$	C=O (s)	1780-1680	*vs*
Hydrogen bonds	O—H (s)	3570-3200	*s*

Key s, stretch; b, bend; sb, symmetric bend; r, rock; ss, symmetric stretch; as, asymmetric stretch; vs, very strong; s, strong; m, medium; w, weak.

3. Double-bond region, 2000-1600 cm^{-1}

Absorption bands of substituted aromatic compounds fall in this range and are a good indicator of the position of the substitution. Carbonyl groups, (C=O), of ketones, aldehydes, acids, amides and carbonate usually show strong absorption in the vicinity of 1700 cm^{-1}. Alkenes, C=C, may show absorption in the vicinity of 1650 cm^{-1}.

4. Single-bond stretch and bend region, 500-1700 cm^{-1}

This region is not diagnostic for particular functional groups but it is a useful finger print region since it shows differences between similar molecules.

Raman Spectroscopy

Quantum Theory of Raman Scattering

In contrast with other conventional branches of spectroscopy, Raman spectroscopy deals with the **scattering of light** and not with its absorption. Consider a photon of frequency v falling on a molecule. If the collision is **elastic**, then the scattered photon will have the same energy as the incident photon. If, on the other hand, the collision is **inelastic**, the scattered photon will have either a higher or a lower energy than the incident photon. If we further assume that the kinetic energy of the photon and the molecule remains unchanged before and after the collision, then, from the law of conservation of energy,

$$h\nu + E = h\nu' + E' \quad \ldots(38)$$

where, $h\nu$ is the energy of the incident photon and $h\nu'$ is the energy of the scattered photon after collision; E is the energy of the molecule (rotational, vibrational and electronic) before collision and E' is the molecular energy after collision. Rearranging Eq. 38, we obtain

$$(E' - E)/h = \nu - \nu'$$

Consider now the following cases :

Case I $\nu = \nu'$ so that $E = E'$

Case II (a) $\nu < \nu'$ so that $E > E'$

Case II (b) $\nu > \nu'$ so that $E < E'$

Case I is referred to as **Rayleigh scattering** and cases II(a) and II(b) as **Raman scattering** or **Raman effect.**

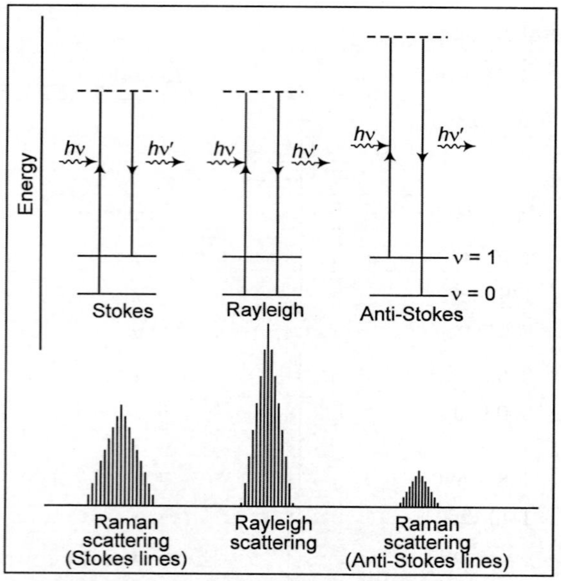

Fig. 20.13 The Rayleigh scattering and the Raman scattering.

When the molecule, excited to the higher unstable vibrational state, returns to the original vibrational state, we get Rayleigh scattering. If it returns to a different vibrational state, this gives rise to Raman scattering (Stokes lines). When the molecule, initially in the first excited vibrational state, is promoted to a higher unstable vibrational state and returns to the ground state, this again gives rise to Raman scattering (anti-Stokes lines). Thus, **the Raman spectrum of a molecule consists of Stokes lines and anti-Stokes lines, situated symmetrically about the Rayleigh line.**

The Rayleigh line is far more intense than the Stokes lines which, in turn, have greater intensity than the anti-Stokes lines. The anti-Stokes lines are very difficult to observe in the conventional Raman spectroscopy because they correspond to the return of a molecule from the unstable excited vibrational state to the ground state and initially there are very few molecules in the excited vibrational state.

We can write Eq. 38 as

$$E' - E = h\,(\nu - \nu') = h\,\Delta\nu_{\text{Raman}} = hc\,\Delta\bar{\nu}_{\text{Raman}} \quad \ldots(39)$$

The shifts in frequency $(\nu - \nu')$ are called **Raman shifts.**

The Raman shifts fall in the range 100–4000 cm^{-1} for vibrational energy changes. Their values are smaller for rotational energy changes.

Since, $\bar{\nu} = 1/\lambda$,

we have $\bar{\nu}\ (\text{in cm}^{-1}) = \dfrac{10^8}{\lambda\ (\text{in Å})}$

Hence, Raman shift (in cm^{-1}) is given by

$$\Delta\bar{\nu} = \frac{10^8}{\lambda_{\text{exc}}\ (\text{in Å})} - \frac{10^8}{\lambda_{\text{Raman}}\ (\text{in Å})} \quad \ldots(40)$$

where, λ_{exc} is the wavelength corresponding to the exciting (incident) frequency.

Classical Theory of Raman Scattering

The classical theory of Raman effect, also called the polarizability theory, was developed by G. Placzek in 1934. The Raman spectrum of a vibrating molecule consists of a relatively intense band at the incident frequency and two very weak bands at frequencies slightly above and below that of the intense band.

Homonuclear diatomic molecules such as H_2, N_2, O_2, which do not show IR spectra since they do not possess a permanent dipole moment, **do show Raman spectra since their vibration is accompained by a change in polarizability of the molecule.** As a consequence of the change in polarizability, there occurs a change in the induced dipole moment at the vibrational frequency.

The selection rule for the vibrational Raman spectrum of a diatomic molecule is

$$\Delta v = \pm 1 \quad \ldots(41)$$

On the other hand, the selection rule for pure rotational Raman spectrum of a diatomic molecule is

$$\Delta J = 0, \pm 2 \quad \ldots(42a)$$

The operation part of the rotational selection rule is

$$\Delta J = +2 \quad \ldots(42b)$$

Since, $\Delta J = 0$ corresponds to Rayleigh scattering and $\Delta J = -2$ transition can be ignored as the rotational quantum number of the upper state must be greater than that of the lower state. Using the selection rule (Eq. 42) with the energy level expression for rigid diatomic rotor, *viz.,*

$$F(J) = BJ\,(J+1)\ \text{cm}^{-1}\ (J = 0, 1, 2, 3 \ldots),$$

we find that

$$\Delta F(J) = F(J+2) - F(J) = B(4J+6)\ \text{cm}^{-1} \ldots(43)$$

It is customary to call the $\Delta J = +2$ transitions as S-branch lines. Thus,

$$\Delta F(J) = B(4J+6)\ \text{cm}^{-1}\ (J = 0, 1, 2, 3 \ldots) \quad \ldots(44)$$

where, J is the quantum number of the lower rotational energy level. Hence, the Raman spectral lines appear at the wave numbers given by the following equation :

$$\bar{v}_S = \bar{v}_{exc} \pm \Delta F(J) = \bar{v}_{exc} \pm B(4J+6)\ \text{cm}^{-1} \quad ...(45)$$

where, v_{exc} is the exciting (incident) frequency, the negative sign refers to the Stokes lines and the positive sign to the anti-Stokes lines.

The energy level diagram and the rotational Raman spectrum for a diatomic molecule are shown in Fig. 20.14.

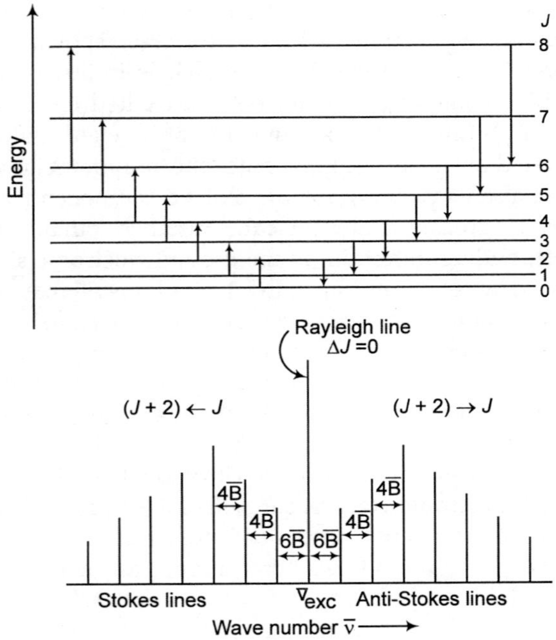

Fig. 20.14 Rotational Raman spectrum of a rigid diatomic molecule.

We see that the first Stokes line (or the first anti-Stokes line) appears at a distance of $6B$ from the exciting Rayleigh line. This is evident from Eq. 44, where putting $J = 0$ we obtain $\Delta F(J) = 6B$. The separation of the successive Raman lines is, however, $4B$, as can be easily verified by putting $J = 1, 2, 3$ etc., in Eq. 45.

Rotation-Vibration Raman Spectrum

Let us now briefly consider the rotational transitions accompanying a vibrational Raman transition of a diatomic molecule. The selection rules now involve the changes in both the vibrational and the rotational quantum number. For a diatomic molecule, the selection rules are,

$$\Delta v = +1;\ \Delta J = 0, \pm 2 \quad ...(46)$$

Since, at room temperature most of the molecules are in the ground vibrational state ($v = 0$), only the vibrational transition, $v = 0$ to $v = 1$, is of interest. The transitions with $\Delta J = 0$ form a Q**-branch**; those with $\Delta J = +2$ form an S-branch and those with $\Delta J = -2$ form an O-branch. The rotational Raman transitions accompanying a $0 \rightarrow 1$ vibrational transition are shown in Fig. 20.15. Here, $\Delta\bar{v}$ measures the displacement from the exciting mercury line. The Q-branch exhibits an intense 'narrow line' at $\bar{v}_{exc}$ that is usually unresolved while the S and O-branches form weak wings which extend to lower and higher wave numbers, respectively, from the intense narrow line.

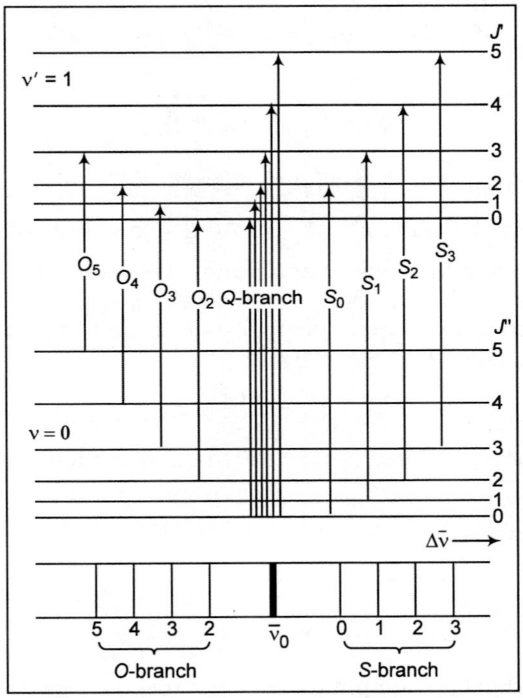

Fig. 20.15 The rotation-vibration transitions in the Raman spectrum of a diatomic molecule.

Example 7. *At what wavelength in Å would the anti-Stokes line appear in the Raman spectrum?*

Sol. The anti-Stokes line will appear at a frequency $460\ \text{cm}^{-1}$ higher than the frequency (in cm^{-1}) associated with 4358 Å Hg line used as a source of excitation. Now,

$$\bar{v}_{exc}\ (\text{cm}^{-1}) = \frac{10^8}{\lambda_{exc}\ (\text{Å})} = \frac{10^8}{4.358 \times 10^3}$$

$$= 2.295 \times 10^4\ \text{cm}^{-1}$$

Hence,
$$\bar{v}_{\text{anti-Stock}} = (2.295 \times 10^4\ \text{cm}^{-1}) + (460\ \text{cm}^{-1})$$

$$= 2.341 \times 10^4\ \text{cm}^{-1}$$

∴
$$\lambda\ (\text{in Å}) = \frac{10^8}{\bar{v}\ (\text{cm}^{-1})} = \frac{10^8}{2.341 \times 10^4} = 4227\ \text{Å}$$

Electronic Spectra

The electronic band spectra of molecules are observed in the ultraviolet and visible regions of the electromagnetic spectrum. Their complexity arises from the fact that a transition between two electronic states is almost invariably accompained by simultaneous transitions between the vibrational and rotational energy levels as well. This is expressed by saying that electronic spectra have **vibrational fine structure** and **rotational fine structure.** According to the Born-Oppenheimer approximation, the total energy of molecule in the lower (ground) state is given by

$$E'' = E''_{el} + E''_{vib} + E''_{rot} \quad ...(47)$$

neglecting the translational energy, E''_{tr}, which is not quantized. Here, E''_{el}, E''_{vib} and E''_{rot} are respectively, the electronic, vibrational and rotational energies. Assuming that the Born-Opphenheimer approximation is valid in the upper (excited) state as well, the excited state energy E' is given by

$$E' = E'_{el} + E'_{vib} + E'_{rot} \quad ...(48)$$

The energy change for an electronic transition is given by

$$\Delta E = E' - E'' = (E'_{el} - E''_{el}) + (E'_{vib} - E''_{vib}) + (E'_{rot} - E''_{rot}) \quad ...(49)$$

$$= \Delta E_{el} + \Delta E_{vib} + \Delta E_{rot} \quad ...(50)$$

Considerable simplification of spectra results by recognizing that

$$\Delta E_{el} >> \Delta E_{vib} >> \Delta E_{rot} \quad ...(51)$$

The frequency for the electronic transition is given by the **Bohr frequency condition,** *viz.,*

$$\bar{v} = \frac{\Delta E}{hc} = \frac{\Delta E_{el} + \Delta E_{vib} + \Delta E_{rot}}{hc} \text{ cm}^{-1} \quad ...(52)$$

Eq. 52 shows how an electronic transition possesses the vibrational and rotational fine structure.

Franck-Condon Principle

A very useful guiding principle for investigating the vibrational structure of electronic spectra is provided by the well known **Franck-Condon principle** which states that **an electronic transition takes place so rapidly that a vibrating molecule does not change its internuclear distance appreciably during the transition.** This principle is, to a first approximation, true since the electrons move so much faster than the nuclei that during the electronic transition the nuclei do not change their position. Hence, **an electronic transition may be represented by a vertical line on a plot of potential energy *versus* the internuclear distance.**

Let us demonstrate the Franck-Condon principle for the electronic transition of a diatomic molecule. Consider Fig. 20.27. where we have shown two potential energy curves for the molecule in the ground electronic state (E_0) and in the first excited electronic state (E_1). Since, the bonding in the excited state is weaker than in the ground state, the minimum in the potential energy curve for the excited state occurs at a slightly greater internuclear distance than the corresponding minimum in the ground electronic state. Also, quantum mechanically it is known that the molecule is in the *centre* of the ground vibrational level of the ground electronic state. Thus, when a photon falls on the molecule, the most probable electronic transition, according to the Franck-Condon principle, takes place from $v'' = 0$ to $v' = 2$ (written schematically as $0 \rightarrow 2$). Transitions to other vibrational levels of the excited electronic state occur with lower probabilities so that their relative intensities are smaller than the intensity of the $0 \rightarrow 2$ transition, as shown in Fig. 20.17.

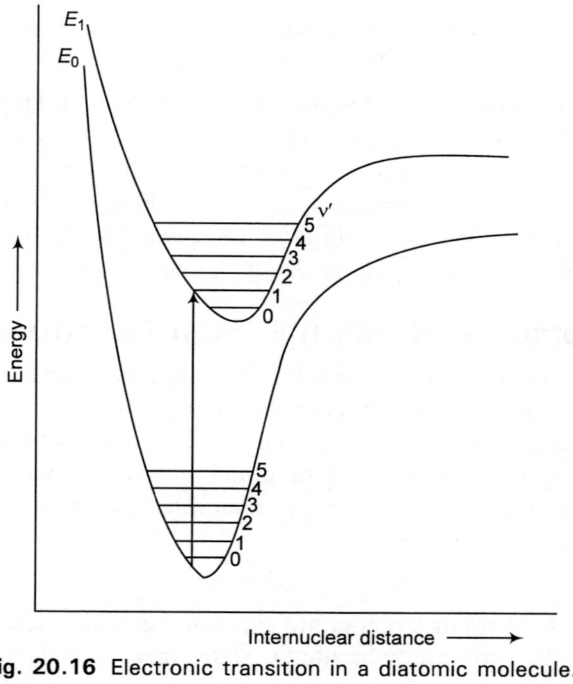

Fig. 20.16 Electronic transition in a diatomic molecule.

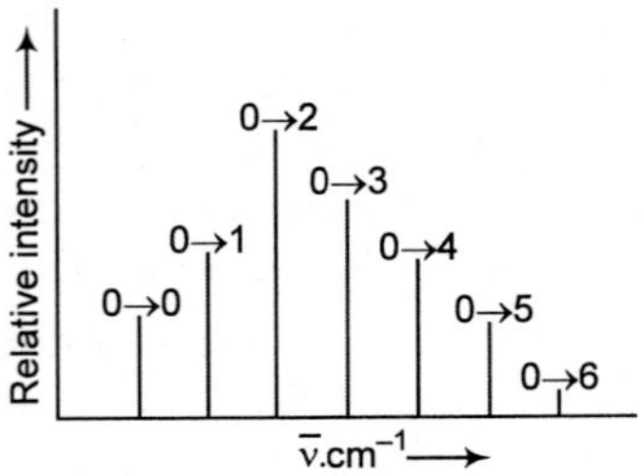

Fig. 20.17 Electronic spectrum of a diatomic molecule.

Consider now a slightly different case of a diatomic molecule which has a potential energy curve E_0 in ground state and two potential energy curves E_1 and E_2 in excited states.

The potential energy curve E_2 does not have a minimum, as shown in Fig. 20.17.

The equilibrium internuclear distance is longer in E_1 than in E_0 since the bond is weaker in the excited state. The transition indicated by arrow *a* has, according to the Franck-Condon principle, maximum intensity. Other possible transitions are from the first excited vibertional level of the ground electronic state; they are indicated by the duplication of the vertical arrows b_1 and b_2. The transition b_1 ends in the lowest vibrational level of the first excited electronic state where the molecule is still held firmly. However, the transition b_2 promotes the molecule to a point where its energy is far above the potential energy plateau of state E_1 at large distance with the result that the molecule dissociates.

The molecule will also dissociate if it is excited to a level below the plateau in E_1 but above point *c* where the potential energy curves for E_1 and E_2 cross. At an internuclear distance corresponding to the point *c*, the molecule may undergo a crossover from one state to the other without energy change and continue to dissociate.

Types of Electronic Transitions

Organic compounds, particularly those containing groups like C═C, C═O, —N═N— and extensively conjugated systems, form a special class of polyatomic molecules whose electronic spectra are amenable to simple interpretation even though the investigation of their detailed spectral features may require knowledge of quantum mechanics and group theory. On the basis of the molecular orbital theory (MOT), the electrons can be classified as σ, π or n (non-bonding) depending upon the MOs they occupy. For organic carbonyl compounds, the electronic transitions involve promotion of the electrons in n, σ and π orbitals in the ground state to $\overset{*}{\sigma}$ and $\overset{*}{\pi}$ ABMOs in the excited state (Fig. 20.18). In other words, only the transitions of the type $\overset{*}{\sigma} \leftarrow \sigma$, $\overset{*}{\pi} \leftarrow \pi$ and $\overset{*}{\pi} \leftarrow n$ are allowed. Since, electrons in the n orbitals are not involved in bond formation, there are no ABMOs associated with them.

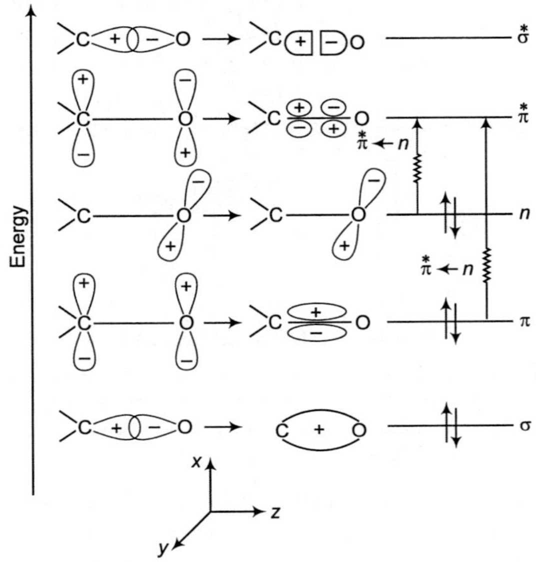

Fig. 20.18 Localized molecular orbitals and electronic transitions for the carbonyl group.

The $\overset{*}{\sigma} \leftarrow \sigma$ transitions occurring in saturated hydrocarbons and other types of compounds in which all valence shell electrons are involved in single bonds, are found in ultraviolet region since they involve very high energy.

The $\overset{*}{\pi} \leftarrow \pi$ and the $\overset{*}{\pi} \leftarrow n$ transitions, on the other hand, are found either in the UV or visible regions. The unsaturated molecules containing C═C and C═O groups (such as aldehydes and ketones) show $\overset{*}{\pi} \leftarrow n$ and $\overset{*}{\pi} \leftarrow \pi$ transitions. For aldehydes and ketones the more intense band near 1800 Å (180 nm) is due to $\overset{*}{\pi} \leftarrow \pi$ transition and the weaker band around 2850 Å (285 nm) is due to $\overset{*}{\pi} \leftarrow n$ transition. Olefinic hydrocarbons show a $\overset{*}{\pi} \leftarrow \pi$ transition in the wavelength 160-170 nm. Acetylene shows an absorption near 180 nm.

Functional groups such as C═C, —N═N— which absorb at wavelengths longer than 180 nm, are called **chromophores.** Other chromophores are nitro, nitroso, crbonyl, thiocarbonyl, sulphoxide groups as well as aromatic rings.

Molecules such as methyl amine and methyl iodide which do not contain a π orbital, show $\overset{*}{\sigma} \leftarrow n$ transitions.

In extensively conjugated systems, the π-electrons are delocalized over the entire skeletal frame-work. Such systems are treated in terms of the 'free-electron model' and it is found that the **absorption bands shift to longer wavelengths as the extent of conjugation increases.** Thus, in the compound $C_6H_5—(CH{=}CH)_n—C_6H_5$, the $\pi^* \leftarrow \pi$ transition lies in the UV region when $n = 1$ or 2. As n increases, the electronic transition shifts to the visible region. This aspect is dealt with later in the chapter. This phenomenon is shown schematically in Fig. 20.19.

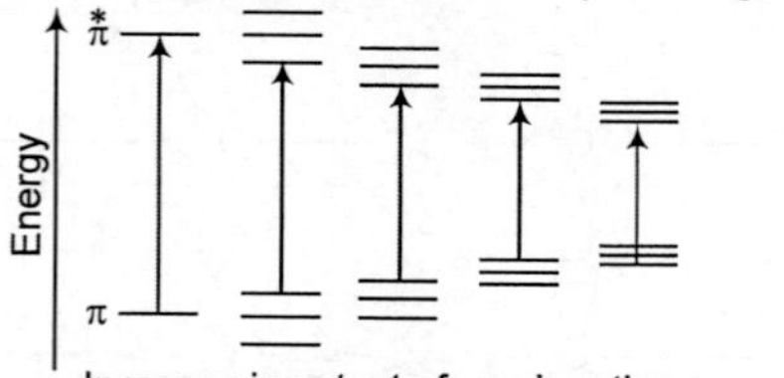

Fig. 20.19 Energy level diagram showing that in a conjugated π-electron system, the wavelength of absoprtion maximum is directly proportional to the extent of conjugation.

The intensity of an electronic band is determined by the extent of overlap of the wave functions in the ground and excited states. Since, there is very poor overlap of wave functions of the ground and excited states in the $\pi^* \leftarrow n$ transition and there is considerable overlap of the corresponding wave functions in the $\pi^* \leftarrow \pi$ transitions, the $\pi^* \leftarrow n$ transitions are less intense (*i.e.,* weaker) than the $\pi^* \leftarrow \pi$ transitions. Also, in strongly acidic media, the $\pi^* \leftarrow n$ band disappeards due to the protonation to lone pair of electrons. In fact, **the protonation may increase the excitation energy to such an extent that the $\pi^* \leftarrow n$ transition may shift far out into UV region and may not be observed.** The protonation of a functional group introduces profound changes in the spectra. Thus, the spectrum in such cases is strongly dependent upon pH. Solvent effects, too, are useful in identifying the nature of these transitions. The $\pi^* \leftarrow n$ transitions are altered by the solvent effects in cases where the lone pair electrons in oxygen or nitrogen-containing systems interact with polar solvents. It is customary in spectroscopic literature to refer to the shifts in absorption bands and their intensity changes as follows :

1. **Bathochromic shift** (or, the red shift) a shift of λ_{max} to longer wavelengths.
2. **Hypsochromic shift** (or, the blue shift) a shift of λ_{max} to shorter wavelengths.
3. **Hyperchromic shift** an increase in the intensity of an absorption band, usually with reference to its molar extinction coefficient, ε_{max}.
4. **Hypochromic shift** a decrease in the intensity of an absorption band with reference to ε_{max}.

The term **auxochrome** refers to an atom or a group of atoms which does not give rise to an absorption band on its own but, when in conjugation with a chromophore, causes a bathochromic shift and a hyperchromic effect. For instance, >C=C< group is a chromophore in ethylene; when one of the hydrogens is replaced by a halogen atom, a bathochromic shift and a hyperchromic effect are produced. This is because the lone pair on the halogen atom conjugates with the alkene double bond. We conclude that the halogen atom acts as an auxochrome.

As said earlier, solvent effects are important in identifying $\pi^* \leftarrow \pi$ and $\pi^* \leftarrow n$ transitions. **Polar solvents often stabilize the ground state of $\pi^* \leftarrow n$ transition more than the excited state, causing blue shifts (Fig. 20.20(a)). On the other hand, for $\pi^* \leftarrow \pi$ transitions the excited state is stabilized more than the ground state, causing red shifts (Fig. 20.20(b)).**

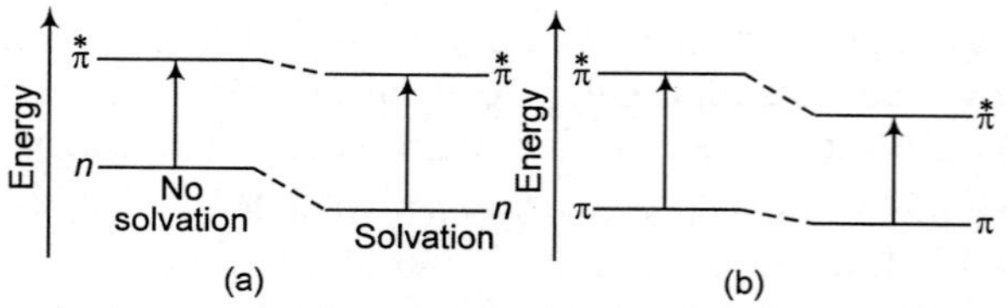

Fig. 20.20 Solvent effects on (a) $\pi^* \leftarrow n$ and (b) $\pi^* \leftarrow \pi$ transitions.

One of the most important applications of UV spectroscopy, based on the Lambert-Beer law, is in quantitative analysis. According to the Labert-Beer law, the absorbance A of a compound of concentration c is given by $A = \varepsilon bc$ where, b is the path length and ε is the molar extinction coefficient. Consider the following equilibrium $X \rightleftharpoons Y$. If X and Y have absorption bands that overlap and if at some wavelength over the overlapped region both X and Y have equal absorbance, then there will be no change in the absorbance at this wavelength as the ratio $[Y]/[X]$ is varied. This gives rise to the so-called isosbestic point. When there is more than one isosbestic point present, we have

$$A_1 = b\,(\varepsilon_X^{(1)} c_X + \varepsilon_Y^{(1)} c_Y)$$

$$A_2 = b\,(\varepsilon_X^{(2)} c_X + \varepsilon_Y^{(2)} c_Y)$$

where, 1 and 2 indicate the two wavelengths. Since, A_1 and A_2 can be measured, the concentrations of X and Y, viz., c_X and c_Y (and hence the equilibrium constant $K = [Y]/[X]$ can be calculated if the various extinction coefficients $\varepsilon_X^{(1)}, \varepsilon_X^{(2)}, \varepsilon_Y^{(1)}$ and $\varepsilon_Y^{(2)}$ are known.

Finally, we may mention that UV spectroscopy has an advantage over IR spectroscopy as far as applications to biological systems are concerned. Most biological systems have high water contents and since water absorbs strongly in the IR, its use is severely limited. On the other hand, aqueous solutions can be conveniently investigated by UV spectroscopy. UV spectra have also better resolution than IR spectra of biochemical systems.

Electronic Spectra of Conjugated Molecules

The electronic spectra of conjugated systems using free-electron molecular orbital (FEMO) theory is based on the theory proposed in the 1930s by Pauling and, independently, by Kathleen Lonsdale and H. Kuhn, that the pi-electrons are delocalized over the entire carbon skeletal framework. Thus, there is no true carbon-carbon single bond or carbon-carbon double bond and we can use the particle-in-a-one dimensional box-approach for such systems. We know that for an electron in a one-dimensional box with width equal to a and infinite height, with potential energy equal to zero everywhere inside the box,

$$E_n = n^2h^2/(8m_e a^2)\ (n = 1, 2, 3 \ldots) \qquad \ldots(53)$$

The electrons in the π MOs are filled according to the Pauli principle and Hund's rule. Thus, if N is the number of π-orbitals, only $N/2$ π-orbitals are filled in the ground state.

The **longest wavelength** transition involves the excitation of the π-electron from the $N/2$ HOMO to $(N/2)+1$ LUMO. Hence, the frequency of the electronic transition is given by

$$v = \frac{E_{(N/2)+1} - E_{N/2}}{h} = \frac{h}{8m_e a^2}\left[\left(\frac{N}{2}+1\right)^2 - \left(\frac{N}{2}\right)^2\right]$$

$$= h(N+1)/8m_e a^2 \qquad \ldots(54)$$

$$\therefore \qquad \bar{v} = v/c = h(N+1)/(8m_e a^2 c) \qquad \ldots(55)$$

Let us now estimate the value of the chain length *a* of the conjugated system (*i.e.,* the width of the box). Since, there is a residual free valence at each of the two terminal carbon atoms, hence

a = number of actual C—C bonds between N carbon atoms + 2

$$= (N - 1 + 2)\, l = (N + 1)\, l \qquad \ldots(56)$$

where, l is the C—C bond length, assumed to be equal to 139 pm. Here, we have made allowance for the molecular orbitals to extend one bond length l past each terminal carbon atom which is a very plausible assumption. Substituting for a in Eq. 65, we have

$$\bar{v}\ (\text{cm}^{-1}) = \frac{h(N+1)}{8m_e c(N+1)^2 l^2} = \frac{h}{8m_e c(N+1)l^2}$$

$$= 148137.6/(N+1)$$

(after substituting various constants) ...(57)

A more realistic approach is the use of sinusoidal form of potential energy with a minimum at the centre of double bond considered. Eq. 67 is then modified to

$$\bar{v}\ (\text{cm}^{-1}) = \frac{153000}{N+1} + 16000\left(1 - \frac{1}{N}\right) \qquad \ldots(58)$$

Example 8. *Derive an expression for the lowest frequency (i.e., highest wavelength) transition from HOMO to LUMO for polymethine dyes.*

Sol. The general formula of polymethine dyes is

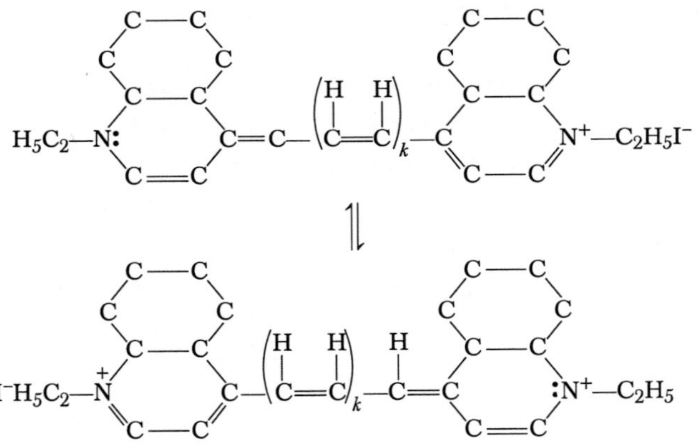

Using the FEMO theory,

$$\bar{v}\ (\text{cm}^{-1}) = \frac{h(N+1)}{8m_e a^2 c} \qquad \text{[Eq. (55)]}$$

If n_c is the number of carbon atoms in the polymethine dye, then N (the total number of π-electrons)= $n_c + 3$. The three electrons are due to two nitrogen atoms, two due to one and one to the other N atom. Assuming, as before, that the molecular orbitals extend by one bonds length on either side and all bond are equal.

$$a = (n_c + 2 - 1 + 2)l$$

or $$a = (n_c + 3)l \qquad \ldots\text{(i)}$$

Substituting the values of a and N Eq. (55) becomes

$$\bar{v} = \frac{h(n_c + 3 + 1)}{8m_e c(n_c + 3)^2 l^2} = \frac{(n_c + 4) \times 1.48 \times 10^5}{(n_c + 3)^2}\ \text{cm}^{-1} \qquad \ldots\text{(ii)}$$

Example 9. *Assuming that* $k = 1$ *in the polymethine dye given above, calculate the wave number and the wavelength of the lowest energy HOMO-to-LUMO electronic transition.*

Sol. If $k = 1$, then $n_c = 9$.

Hence, from Eq. (ii) of Example 8, we obtain

$$\bar{\nu} = 1.3361 \times 10^4\ cm^{-1} \quad \text{and} \quad \lambda = 748.4\ nm$$

Woodward-Fieser Rules for Calculating Absorption Maximum

(a) In dienes

Woodward formulated certain empirical rules for calculating the λ_{max} * in case of dienes. These rules were later modified by Fieser in 1948.

The various rules for calculating the absorption maximum in case of dienes and trienes are summarised in the Table 20.4.

Table 20.4 **Conjugated Dienes and Trienes**

Solvent-ethanol Transition involved-$\pi \rightarrow \overset{*}{\pi}$	
Parent value for butadiene system or a cyclic conjugated diene	217 mμ
Acyclic triene	245 mμ
Homoannular conjugated diene	253 mμ
Heteroannular conjugated diene	215 mμ
Increment for each substituent	
Alkyl substituent or ring residue	5 mμ
Exocyclic double bond	5 mμ
Double bond extending conjugation	30 mμ
Auxochrome	
—OR	+6 mμ
—SR	+30 mμ
—Cl*, —Br*	+5 mμ
$—NR_2$	+60 mμ
$OCOCH_3$	0 mμ

Example 10. *Calculate the absorption maximum in the ultraviolet spectrum of 2, 4 hexadiene.*

Sol. The basic unit in 2, 4 hexadiene is butadiene. There are two alkyl substituents (one on each double bond) on it. Thus,

$$(CH_3—CH{=}CH—CH{=}CH—CH_3)$$

Basic value	= 217 μμ
2-alkyl substituents (2 × 5)	= 10 mμ
Calculated value	= **227 mμ**

The observed value** is also found to be 227 mμ.

Example 11. *Calculate* λ_{max} *for*

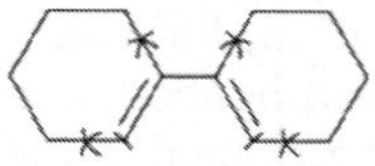

Sol. It is an example of heteroannular diene and there are four ring residues on the double bonds. Thus,

Basic value	= 215 mμ
Four ring residues (4 × 5)	= 20 mμ
Calclated value	= **235 mμ**

(represented by *X*)

The observed value is also found to be 234 mμ.

(b) Bicyclic compounds

If a diene system is present in a bicyclic compound, then due to the strain in the bicyclic compound, 15 mμ is added as the ring strain correction in the calculated value of absorption maximum.

Example 12. *Calculate the absorption maximum in the ultraviolet spectrum of* 2, 3-*dimethylene bicyclo* [2, 2, 1] *heptane.*

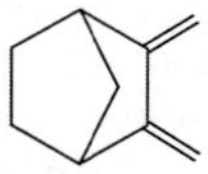

Sol. The value of absorption maximum for this compound is calculated as :

Basic value	= 217 mμ
2-ring residues	(2 × 5) = 10 mμ
2-exocyclic double bonds	= 10 mμ
1-bicyclic system (strain correction)	= 15 mμ
Calculated value	= **252 mμ**
Observed value	= 254 mμ

(c) In α, β-unsaturated carbonyl compounds

The various rules in case of these compounds are

(i) The basic value of α, β-unsaturated ketone is taken as 215 mμ. The α, β-unsaturated ketone may be a cyclic or six membered.

For a compound, = CH—CO*X*, basic value is 215 mμ, if *X* is an alkyl group.

If *X* = H, basic value becomes 207 mμ. The basic value is 193 mμ, if *X* is OH or O*R*.

(ii) If the double bond and the carbonyl group are contained in a five membered ring (cyclopentanone), then for such an α, β-unsaturated ketone, the basic value becomes 202 mμ. The ε_{max} for such compounds are generally above 10000.

The structural increments for estimating λ_{max} for a given α, β-unsaturated carbonyl compound are as follows :

(i) For each exocyclic double bond +5 mμ

(ii) For each double bond endocyclic in five or seven membered ring except cyclo-pent-2 enone +5 mμ

(iii) For each alkyl substituent or ring residue at the

α-position +10 mμ

β-position + 12 mμ

γ- or δ- or higher position +18 mμ

(iv) For each double bond extending conjugation +30 mμ

(v) For a homoannular conjugated diene +39 mμ

(vi) Increments for various auxochromes in the various α-, β-, γ- etc., positions are given in the following table.

Table 20.5 **Chromophore Increments in Carbonyl Compounds**

	Chromophore increment in nm (or mμ) for position wrt the carbonyl group			
	α-	β-	γ-	δ- or higher
—OH	+35	+30	–	+50
—OAc	+6	+6	+6	+6
—Cl	+15	+12	–	–
—Br	+25	+35	–	–
—OR	+35	+30	17	31
—SR	–	+85	–	–
—NR_2	–	+95	–	–

Example 13. *Calculate λ_{max} for the following structure.*

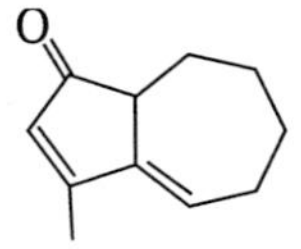

Sol. It is an α, β-unsaturated cyclopentanone system.

Basic value	=	202 mμ
1 β-alkyl substitution	=	12 mμ
1 exocyclic double bond	=	15 mμ
1 double bond extending conjugation	=	30 mμ
1 γ-ring residue	=	18 mμ
1 δ-ring residue	=	18 mμ
Calculated value	=	**285 mμ**
Observed value	=	287 mμ

(d) For derivatives of acyl benzenes

These rules help in estimating the position of absorption maximum in ethanol in a number of monosubstituted aromatic ketones, aldehydes, acids and esters.

For a compound of the type

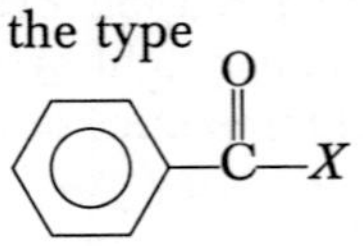

(i) The basic value is 246 mμ if *X* is an alkyl group or alicyclic residue.

(ii) If *X* is hydrogen atom, the basic value becomes 250 mμ and

(iii) The basic value is 230 mμ if *X* is OH or O*R*. The structural increments in mμ for further substitution on the aromatic ring in the *ortho, meta* and *para* positions are given in the Table.

Table 20.6. **Auxochrome Acting as a Substituent**

Auxochrome	Increment in mm position of the substituent		
	Ortho	*Meta*	*Para*
Alkyl	+3	+3	+10
OH, O*R*	+7	+7	+25
Cl	0	0	+10
Br	+2	+2	+15
NH_2	+13	+13	+58
NHAc	+20	+20	+45
NR_2	+20	+20	+85
O^-	+11	+20	+75

Note It is important to note that the effect of the *para* substituent is more pronounced for the bathochromic shift.

Example 14. *Calculate the absorption maximum in ethanol for p-chloroacetophenone.*

Sol. In this case, *X* is an alkyl group and thus the basic value is 246 mμ.

Basic value	= 246 mμ
Cl-substitution at *para* position	= 10 mμ
Calculated value	= **256 mμ**

The observed value is found to be 254 mμ.

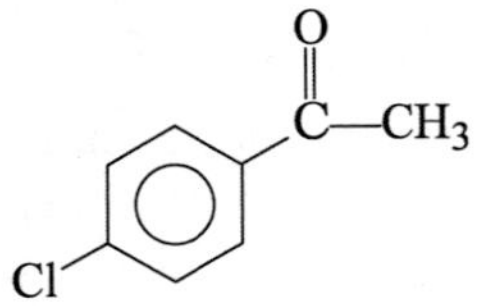

Fluorescence and Phosphorescence

Fluorescence is the light of comparatively longer wavelength emitted from a molecule after it has absorbed light of different and short wavelength.

On the other hand, the phenomenon of phosphorescence is said to occur when the substance continues to emit the radiation of longer wavelength even when the irradiating light is removed. To study the phenomenon of fluorescence and phosphorescence, let us study the one electron excitation process (see Fig. 20.21).

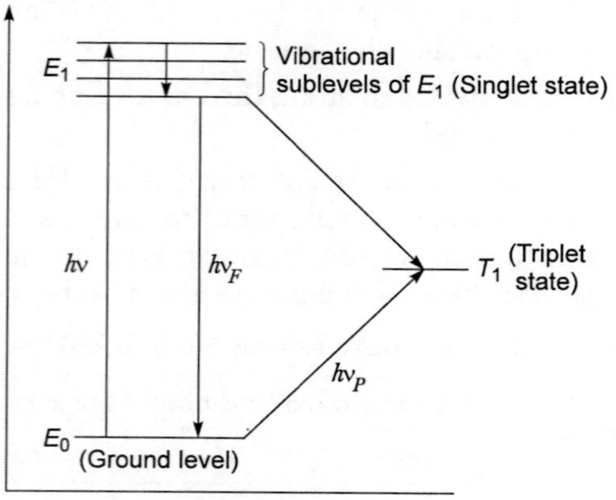

Fig. 20.21 Mechanism of fluorescence and phosphorescence.

Magnetic Resonance Spectroscopy

Magnetic resonance spectroscopy is classified into (a) Nuclear magnetic resonance (NMR) spectroscopy and (b) Electron spin resonance (ESR) spectroscopy (also sometimes called electron paramagnetic resonance (EPR) spectroscopy). Both these branches are essentially similar, being based upon the same principles. However, whereas **NMR spectra are experimentally observed in the radiofrequency (rf) region, ESR spectra are observed in the microwave region of the electromagnetic spectrum**. The application of ESR is limited to species containing unpaired electrons such as organic and inorganic free radicals and the ions of the *d*-block and *f*-block elements.

NMR Spectroscopy

All atomic nuclei possess nuclear spin, *I*, which may be integral (*i.e.* 1, 2, 3, etc.) or half-integral (*i.e.* 1/2, 3/2, 5/2, 7/2 etc.). The proton and the neutron each has spin $\frac{1}{2}$. Since a nucleus contains nucleons (collective term for protons and neutrons), it is evident that the spin of the nucleus may be considered as the resultant of the spins of protons and neutrons comprising it. Consider, for instance, the deuteron nucleus, ^2D, which contains one proton and one neutron. Now, depending upon whether the spins of the proton and the neutron are aligned parallel (↑↑) or antiparallel (↑↓) the deuteron is expected to have a spin of 1 or 0. It is however, found that in the ground state, deuteron has spin of 1 which means that the proton and neutron spins are aligned parallel to each other. The angular momentum associated with a nuclear spin is given by $[I(I+1)]^{1/2}(h/2\pi)$.

It is difficult to predict the spin of a nucleus. The following rules are, however, helpful in predicting the nuclear spin :

(i) If the mass number *A* is odd, nuclear spin *I* is half integral. Thus, in the case of ^1H, ^{15}N, ^{19}F, ^{31}P, $I = \frac{1}{2}$ and in the case of ^{11}B, $I = 3/2$.

(ii) If the mass number *A* and the atomic number *Z* are both even, the spin is zero. Thus, in the case of ^4_2He, $^{12}_6O$, $^{16}_8O$, $I = 0$.

(iii) If the mass number *A* is even but the atomic number *Z* is odd, the spin is integral. Thus, the spin of ^2_1H and $^{14}_7N$ is 1 while that of $^{10}_5B$ is 3.

Since a nucleus possesses an electric charge, the spinning nucleus gives rise to a magnetic field whose axis coincides with the axis of spin. Thus, each nucleus can be thought of being equivalent to a minute magnet having a magnetic moment μ. Each nucleus with $I > 0$ has magnetic moment. However, $^{12}_6C$ and $^{16}_8O$ having $I = 0$ do not posses a magnetic moment, *i.e.,* they are non-magnetic.

Nuclei possessing $I \geq 1$ have also a nuclear electric quadrupole moment, *Q*, which is a measure of the deviation of the nuclear charge distribution from spherical symmetry. Some common quadrupolar nuclei are ^2_1H (deuteron) and $^{14}_7N$ both of which have $I = 1$.

The nuclear quadrupole moment interacts with the electric field gradient (EFG) created at the nucleus by the bonding and non-bonding electrons in a molecule. The quantity e^2Qq (where, *e* is the electronic charge and *q* the *EFG*) is known as the nuclear quadrupole coupling constant. Quadrupolar nuclei not only 'spoil' their own NMR spectra but also the NMR spectra of nuclei attached to them in a molecule. Thus, the NMR spectra of quadrupolar nuclei are generally very broad and not at all sharp.

When a magnetic nucleus is placed in a uniform magnetic field, the magnetic dipole associated with the magnetic moment assumes only a discrete set of orientations. This is expressed by saying that the nuclear spin (and hence the magnetic moment associated with it) is quantized with respect to the direction of the applied magnetic field. The magnetic nucleus assumes any one of the $2I + 1$ orientations with respect to the direction of the applied magnetic field. Suppose that a nucleus with spin I is placed in an external magnetic field B_z, applied along the z-direction. Then, as a result of quantization of spin, the observable component m_I of the spin I along the direction of the field is given by

(i) $m_I = I, I-1, I-2, \ldots 0, \ldots, -(I-2), -(I-1), -I$ (for integral spins)

(ii) $m_I = I, I-1, I-2, \ldots, 1/2, -1/2, -3/2, \ldots, -I$ (for half-integral spins)

In each case, there are $(2I + 1)$ values of m_I.

As mentioned earlier, a nucleus with spin has associated with it a magnetic dipole moment (or simply magnetic moment) μ that is proportional to the angular momentum $\vec{\mathbf{I}}$ whose magnitude is given by $(I(I+1)^{1/2}(h/2\pi)$. Thus,

$$\vec{\mu} = g_N \mu_N \vec{\mathbf{I}} \quad \ldots(59)$$

where, g_N is called the nuclear g-factor and μ_N is the nuclear megneton defined as $\mu_N = eh/4\pi m_p$, where, e is the electronic charge, m_p is the mass of the proton. Substituting the various values,

$$\mu_N = \frac{(1.602 \times 10^{-19}\text{C}) \times (6.626 \times 10^{-34}\ \text{Js})}{(4\pi) \times 1.673 \times 10^{-27}\ \text{kg}}$$

$$= 5.05 \times 10^{-27}\ \text{JT}^{-1}$$

The magnitude of the nuclear magnetic moment is thus given by

$$\mu = g_N \mu_N [I(I+1)]^{1/2} \quad \ldots(60)$$

Also, since the magnetic moment μ and the angular momentum I can be parallel or antiparallel vectors, g_N can have a positive, or a negative value. It should be noted that whereas the value of the electron g-factor, g_e has been very accurately calculated to be equal to 2.0023, the value of the nuclear g-factor, g_N, can only be obtained from experiment and is different for different nuclei.

Example 15. *Calculate the nuclear spin angular momentum and the magnetic moment for a proton, given that* $I = \frac{1}{2}$, g_N *for proton is* 5.585 *and* $\mu_N = 5.05 \times 10^{-27}\ \text{JT}^{-1}$.

Sol. The nuclear spin angular momentum

$$= [I(I+1)]^{1/2}(h/2\pi)$$

$$= \left[\frac{1}{2}\left(\frac{1}{2}+1\right)\right]^{1/2} \times (1.055 \times 10^{-34}\ \text{Js})$$

$$= 0.866 \times 1.055 \times 10^{-34}\ \text{Js}$$

$$= 0.914 \times 10^{-34}\ \text{Js}$$

The nuclear magnetic moment is given by

$$\mu = g_N \mu_N [I(I+1)]^{1/2}$$

$$= (5.585) \times (5.05 \times 10^{-27}\ \text{JT}^{-1}) \left[\frac{1}{2}\left(\frac{1}{2}+1\right)\right]^{1/2}$$

$$= 2.44 \times 10^{-26}\ \text{JT}^{-1}$$

NMR of a 'Bare' Nucleus

A 'bare' nucleus is, of course, an ideality. Actually, nuclei are parts to atoms and molecules. However, it is useful of consider the NMR of a bare nucleus. From quantum mechanics it is known that the energy of integration of nuclear magnetic moment μ with an external magnetic field B_z, applied in the z-direction, is given by

$$E = -\vec{\mu}\vec{\mathbf{B}}_z \quad \ldots(61)$$

Substituting the value of $\vec{\mu}$ from Eq. 59, we find that

$$E = -g_N \mu_N \vec{\mathbf{B}}_z \vec{\mathbf{I}} \quad \ldots(62)$$

As already mentioned, the nuclear spin I is quantized in the presence of the magnetic field and the energy of nuclear spin is defined only by its component m_I. We may thus write :

$$E_{m_I} = -g_N \mu_N B_z m_I \quad \ldots(63)$$

Consider a bare proton $_1$H with $I = 1/2$ so that $m_I = \pm 1/2$. Thus, for $m_I = 1/2$, the energy

$$E_{1/2} = -\frac{1}{2} g_N \mu_N B_z \quad \ldots(64)$$

and for $m_I = -\frac{1}{2}$, the energy

$$E_{-1/2} = \frac{1}{2} g_N \mu_N B_z \quad \ldots(65)$$

It should be noted that in the absence of the external magnetic field, the two components of the proton spin have the same energy (*i.e.,* they are degenerate). However, in the presence of the magnetic field, the components have different energies given by Eqs. (64) and (65). This is expressed by saying that **the magnetic field lifts** or **removes the degeneracy of the spin components.** This is called **Zeeman splitting** of energy levels. The energy difference is given by

$$\Delta E = E_{-1/2} - E_{1/2} = g_N \mu_N B_z \qquad ...(66)$$

This is illustrated in Fig. 20.22.

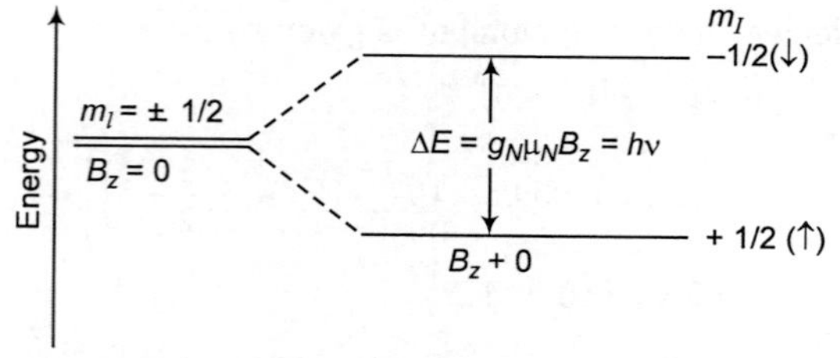

Fig. 20.22 Splitting of nuclear energy levels of a bare proton in a magnetic field when the magnetic field is kept constant and frequency is varied.

In order to induce transitions between the two energy levels $E_{-1/2}$ and $E_{1/2}$, *i.e.,* in order to let the nuclear spin 'flip' from the upward direction (↑) to the downward direction (↓), we must apply an oscillating radiofrequency field perpendicular to the direction of B_z. The nuclear spin flips, provided the energy $h\nu$ of the radiofrequency photon of frequency ν is exactly equal to ΔE, *i.e.,*

$$\Delta E = g_N \mu_N B_z = h\nu \qquad ...(67)$$

This is called the **Bohr frequency condition**. Thus, the NMR frequency of a **bare proton** (or a bare nucleus with $I = 1/2$) is given by

$$\nu = \frac{\Delta E}{h} = \frac{g_N \mu_N B_Z}{h} \qquad ...(68)$$

It may be noted that g_N can be positive or negative but v must be positive. Hence, only the absolute value of g_N should be used in calculating ν.

Eq. 68 shows that ν is directly proportional to B_z. We thus see that the NMR spectra can be recorded in two ways, *viz.,* (i) keeping the magnetic field B_z fixed and varying the frequency ν (Fig. 20.22) or (ii) keeping ν fixed and varying B_z (Fig. 20.23). The latter mode is preferred in modern NMR spectrometers.

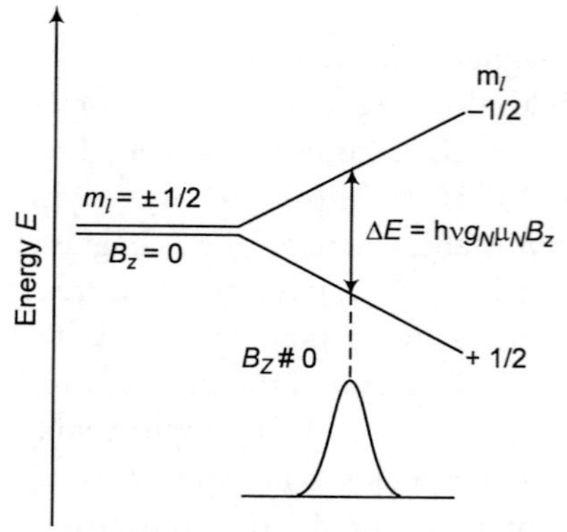

Fig. 20.23 Energy level diagram showing the splitting of nuclear energy levels of a bare proton in a magnetic field when the frequency is kept fixed and the magnetic field is varied.

Example 16. *Calculate the NMR frequency (in MHz) of the proton (^{1}H) in a magnetic field of intensity* 1.4092 *tesla, given that* $g_N = 5.585$ *and* $\mu_N = 5.05 \times 10^{-27}$ JT^{-1}.

Sol.
$$\nu = \frac{g_N \mu_N B_z}{h}$$
$$= \frac{(5.585) \times (5.05 \times 10^{-27}\ \text{JT}^{-1}) \times (1.4092\ \text{T})}{6.626 \times 10^{-34}\ \text{Js}}$$
$$= 60 \times 10^6\ s^{-1} = 60 \times 10^6\ \text{Hz} = 60\ \text{MHz}$$

This frequency lies in the radiofrequency region.

Example 17. *Calculate the magnetic field strength required to observe the NMR frequency for fluorine* (^{19}F) *at 60 MHz. Given,* g_N *for* $^{19}\text{F} = 5.257$ *and* $\mu_N = 5.05 \times 10^{-27}$ JT^{-1}.

Sol. Since, $\nu = g_N \mu_N B_z / h$, we have

$$B_z = \frac{h\nu}{g_N \mu_N} = \frac{(6.626 \times 10^{-34}\ \text{Js})\ (60 \times 10^6\ \text{s}^{-1})}{(5.257)\ (5.05 \times 10^{-27}\ \text{JT}^{-1})}$$
$$= 1.4973\ \text{T}$$

It should be borne in mind that nuclei such as $^{12}_{6}$C and $^{16}_{6}$C have no spin ($I = 0$) so that they have no magnetic moment; they are called **non-magnetic** nuclei. **Non-magnetic nuclei do not show NMR spectra because, their magnetic moment being zero, their energy levels do not exist**. Thus, if an organic compound contains hydrogen, carbon and oxygen, only hydrogen nuclei ($I = 1/2$) will show NMR spectra.

Some nuclear properties and NMR frequencies of a few nuclei in a magnetic field of intensity 1.4092 T are given in Table 20.7.

Table 20.7 **Nuclear Magnetic Properties of Some Nuclei**

Nucleus	% Abundance	Spin, I	g_N	NMR frequency v in MHz at 1.4092 T
^{1}H	99.99	$\frac{1}{2}$	5.585	60.000
^{2}D	0.01	1	0.857	9.210
^{10}B	18.83	3	0.600	6.448
$_{11}B$	81.17	$\frac{3}{2}$	1.792	19.248
^{13}C	1.11	$\frac{1}{2}$	1.404	15.086
^{14}N	99.63	1	0.404	4.334
^{15}N	0.36	$\frac{1}{2}$	0.566	6.079
^{17}O	0.037	$\frac{5}{2}$	- 0.757	8.134
^{19}F	100	$\frac{1}{2}$	5.255	56.444
^{29}Si	4.70	$\frac{1}{2}$	- 1.110	11.919
^{31}P	100	$\frac{1}{2}$	2.261	24.286
^{35}Cl	75.41	$\frac{3}{2}$	0.547	5.879
^{37}Cl	24.60	$\frac{3}{2}$	0.455	4.893
^{127}I	100	$\frac{5}{2}$	1.118	12.005

A nucleus having a magnetic moment μ behaves as a bar magnet which spins on its axis. In the presence of the magnetic field B_z, the interaction of μ and B_z produces a torque. This torque causes μ to precess about B_z, as shown in Fig. 20.24. This phenomenon is called Larmor precession and the angular frequency of precession is referred to as the **Larmor frequency,** ω (expressed in radians per second). Mathematically, Larmor frequency is given by

$$\omega = \gamma B_z \qquad \ldots(69)$$

where, γ is the **magnetogyric ratio (formerly called gyromagnetic ratio) of the nucleus. It is defined as the ratio of the nuclear magnetic moment μ and the nuclear spin angular momentum $I(h/2\pi)$,** *i.e.,*

$$\gamma = \frac{\mu}{I(h/2\pi)}$$

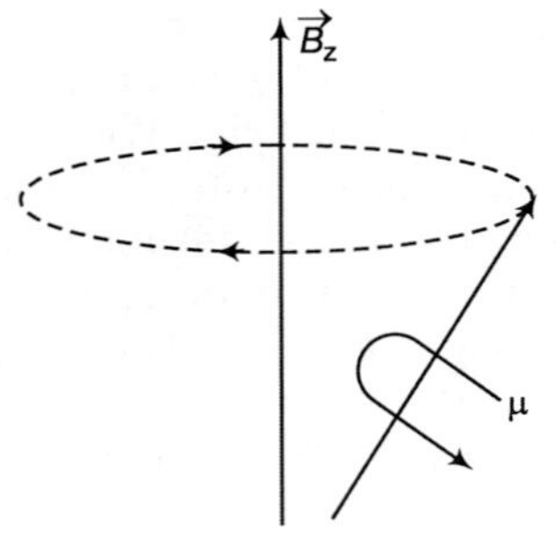

Fig. 20.24 Larmor precession of a nucleus in a magnetic field.

It is expressed in terms of radians T^{-1} s^{-1} (or, simply at T^{-1} s^{-1}). Note that $\omega = 2\pi\nu$ where, ν is the NMR frequency.

Example 18. *In a spectrometer operating at 1 T, the NMR frequency of ^{19}F is 40.06 MHz. Calculate the magnetogyric ratio of ^{19}F.*

Sol.
$$\gamma = \frac{\omega}{B_z} = \frac{2\pi\nu}{B_z}$$
$$= \frac{2 \times (3.1416) \times (40.06 \times 10^6 \ s^{-1})}{1 \ T}$$
$$= 2.517 \times 10^8 \ T^{-1} s^{-1}$$

Example 19. *The magnetic moment of ^{31}P is equal to 1.1305 nuclear magnetons, i.e., 1.1305 μ_N. Calculate its magnetogyric ratio and the g-factor. Given, $\mu_N = 5.05 \times 10^{-27}$ JT^{-1} and nuclear spin of ^{31}P is 1/2.*

Sol.
$$\gamma = \frac{\mu}{I(h/2\pi)}$$
$$= \frac{1.1305 \times (5.05 \times 10^{-27} \ JT^{-1}) \times (2 \times 3.1416)}{(1/2) \times (6.626 \times 10^{-34} Js)}$$
$$= 1.083 \times 10^8 \ T^{-1} s^{-1}$$

We know that $\mu = g_N \mu_N I$

For ^{31}P, $\quad \mu = 1.305 \ \mu_N$ and $I = \frac{1}{2}$ (given)

$\therefore \quad 1.1305 \ \mu_N = \frac{1}{2} g_N \mu_N$

$\therefore \quad g_N = 2 \times 1.1305 = 2.261$

The Chemical Shift

In practice, one does not investigate the NMR spectra of 'bare' nuclei. Nuclei are essential parts of the molecules held together by the electrons of the chemical bonds. The magnetic field at which a free or 'bare' nucleus resonates is quite different from the field at which the same nucleus in a molecule resonates. It is thus clear that the electrons in a molecule affect the NMR frequency of a given nucleus in the molecule. The electrons are said to **shield** or **deshield** nucleus from the applied magnetic field, depending upon whether the magnetic field generated by their motion opposes or reinforces the field. We shall discuss this aspect a little later in this chapter. Suffice it to mention here that the applied external magnetic field affects the motion of the electrons surrounding the nuclei thereby inducing local magnetic fields. The magnitude of the local magnetic field is determined by the electron distribution around a nucleus. The difference between the magnitudes of the magnetic field at which 'free' nuclei and molecular nuclei resonate is called **chemical shift.**

For measuring chemical shifts it is not possible to use a free nucleus as a reference. Instead, chemists use those compounds that exhibit only a **single sharp resonance line** as a reference for measuring chemical shifts. The most frequently employed reference compound is tetramethylsilane (TMS) having the formula, $Si(CH_3)_4$.

The local magnetic field B_{local} experienced by a nucleus in a molecule is related to the external magnetic field B_0 by

$$B_{local} = B_0(1 - \sigma) \qquad \ldots(70)$$

where σ, a dimensionless quantity, is called the screening constant (or the shielding constant).

For two nuclei *A* and *B* in a molecule, the local fields are

$$B_A = B_0(1 - \sigma_A) \qquad \ldots(71)$$

$$B_B = B_0(1 - \sigma_B) \qquad \ldots(72)$$

where, σ_A and σ_B are the respective screening constants, Thus,

$$B_B - B_A = B_0(1 - \sigma_B) - B_0(1 - \sigma_A) = B_0(\sigma_A - \sigma_B) = B_0\delta_{AB} \qquad \ldots(73)$$

where, δ_{AB} (or simply, δ) is the chemical shift of nucleus *A* with respect to nucleus *B*. In practice, we define chemical shift of a sample as

$$\delta = \frac{B_{sample} - B_{ref}}{B_0} \times 10^6 \text{ ppm} \qquad \ldots(74)$$

Since, $B \propto \nu$, hence

$$\delta = \frac{\nu_{sample} - \nu_{TMS}}{\nu_0} \times 10^6 \text{ ppm} \qquad \ldots(75)$$

where the reference compound is TMS. The chemical shift is expressed in parts per million (ppm).

The reasons for using TMS as the reference are as follows :

1. It has 12 equivalent protons; this can be seen from its structure $Si(CH_3)_4$.

   Since, all the protons are in the same environment, TMS gives a single intense peak in its NMR spectrum.
2. It has a low boiling point (27°C) and thus can be easily recovered after the spectrum is recorded.
3. It is chemically inert.
4. The methyl groups in TMS are highly shielded by their electrons from the external magnetic field. Consequently, TMS shows NMR at a very high magnetic field strength compared to other protons.

It is pertinent to mention here that two chemical-shift scales, *viz.,* the δ-scale and the τ-scale are used in recording NMR signals. They are related by the expression

$$\delta + \tau = 10$$

i.e.,

$$\tau = 10 - \delta \qquad \ldots(76)$$

On the δ-scale, δ is set equal to zero at the reference peak (or signal) of TMS and it **increases downfield.** This scale has the disadvantage that a large value of δ implies that a proton undergoes a resonance at low field. Hence, it implies a low-shielding of the nucleus by the external magnetic field.

In the τ-scale, τ is set equal to 10 at the reference peak of TMS and it **decreases downfield.** Thus, a low value of τ implies that a proton undergoes a resonance at low field. Hence, it implies a low-shielding of the nucleus by the external magnetic field. It follows that a higher value of τ means a more shielded nucleus and hence a high-field resonance.

The τ-values for most organic compounds lie between 0 and 10. They are highly characteristic of the chemical environment of the megnetic nuclei. Thus, they can help in locating different kinds of protons in an organic molecule. The τ-values for some protons in different environments are given in Table 20.8.

Table 20.8 **Typical Chemical Shifts For Protons in Different Environments**

		Chemical shift (*I*, in spin)
Primary	$R—CH_3$	9.1
Vinylic	C═C—H	5.4–4.1
Acetylenic	C≡C—H	8–6.5
Aromatic	Ar—H	4–1.0
Aluorides	H—C—F	6–5.5
Chlorides	HC—Cl	7–6
Alcohols	H—C—OH	6.0–6
Ethers	H—C—O*R*	6.7–6
Esters	H—C—COO*R*	8–7.8
Acids	H—C—COOH	8–7.5
Aldehydic	*R*CHO	1–0
Hydroay	*R*—OH	9–4.5
Phenolic	Ar—OH	6 to –2
Carboxylic	*R*COOH	–0.5 to –2

Example 20. *A compound shows a proton -NMR peak at 240 Hz down-field from the TMS peak in a spectrometer operating at 60 MHz. What are the values of the chemical shifts δ and τ in the ppm relative to TMS?*

Sol. From Eq. 75,

$$\delta = \frac{\nu_{\text{sample}} - \nu_{\text{TMS}}}{\nu_0} \times 10^6 \text{ (ppm)}$$

$$= -\frac{240 \text{ s}^{-1}}{60 \times 10^6 \text{ s}^{-1}} \times 10^6$$

$$= 4 \text{ ppm}$$

From Eq. 76, $\tau = 10 - \delta = 6$ ppm

Shielding and Deshielding of Protons

The concept of chemical shift, introduced above, is closely linked with the shielding or deshielding of protons in a molecule. A **bare** photon, when exposed to a radiofrequency proton, 'flips' its spin from lower energy level to a higher energy level, *i.e.,* its spin changes its orientation from (↑) to (↓). However, all protons do not change or flip their spins at the same applied magnetic field because their energy depends upon the chemical environment of the protons. The magnetic field 'sensed' by a proton in a molecule is not the same as the applied magnetic field since the electrons in the bond close to the proton and the neighbouring electrons in other bonds **induce** their own magnetic field. This induced field may oppose or reinforce the applied magnetic field. The field experienced by the proton is thus the resultant of the applied and induced fields, as shown in Fig. 20.25. When the two fields reinforce, as in Fig. 20.25(b), a smaller field must be applied to flip the proton. Such a proton is said to be **deshielded** and absorbs more **down-field** (*i.e.,* at lower magnetic field strength). On the other hand when the fields oppose, as in Fig. 20.25(c), a stronger field must be applied. The proton is now **shielded** and absorbs more **upfield** (*i.e.,* at higher magnetic field strength).

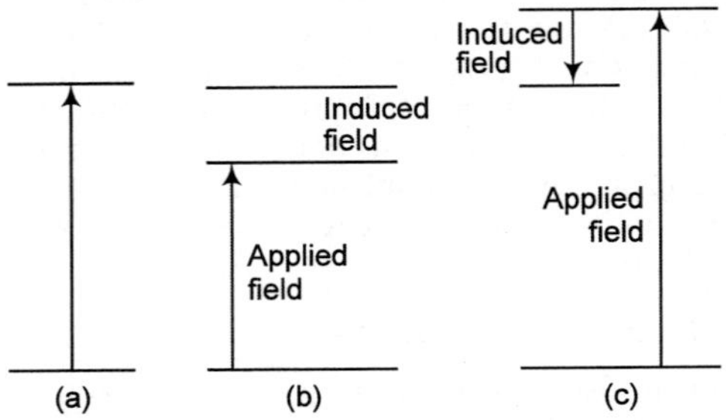

Fig. 20.25 Shielding and deshielding of protons.

Nuclear Spin-Spin Interaction

When the NMR spectrum of **acidified** ethanol is examined under high resolution, the peaks for CH_2 and CH_3 groups are seen to be split into multiples as shown in Fig. 20.26.

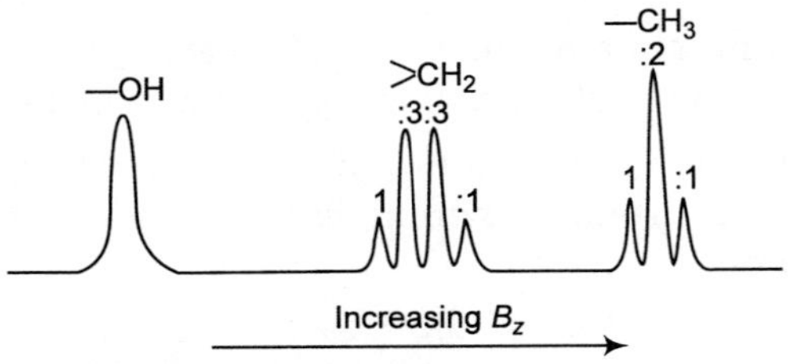

Fig. 20.26 High-resolution NMR spectrum of acidified ethanol.

The magnitude of the splitting between the lines of a given multiplet is given by the **spin-spin coupling constant *J*** (measured in units of Hz).

There are some general rules about spin-spin interactions which are helpful in calculating the number of lines expected in the NMR spectra. These are :

1. Protons of the same group do not interact among themselves to cause observable splitting (*eg.,* the three protons in the CH_3 group do not interact with one another).
2. The multiplicity of the peak of a group of equivalent protons is determined by the *neighbouring* protons. In general, if n equivalent protons interact or couple with the protons on an adjacent carbon atom, the resonance peak is split into $n + 1$ peaks or signals.
3. The intensities are symmetric about the mid-point of the group and the relative intensities of the $n + 1$ peaks are given by the coefficients of the binomial expansion of order n, *i.e.,* $(1 + x)^n$. These coefficients can be arranged in the so-called *Pascal's triangle* as shown in Table 20.8.

Table 20.8 **Pascal's Triangle giving Intensities of NMR Signals**

Number of protons, n	Number of NMR lines	Relative intensities
0	1	1
1	2	1 1
2	3	1 2 1
3	4	1 3 3 1
4	5	1 4 6 4 1
5	6	1 5 10 10 5 1
6	7	1 6 15 20 15 6 1

It may be noted that the spin-spin interaction is **independent** of the applied magnetic field strength whereas the chemical shift depends on the field strength.

The proton NMR spectrum of a molecule thus gives information about

(a) The **number of peaks** which enables us to know about the kinds of protons present in a molecule.

(b) **The positions of the peaks** which tell us about the electronic environment of each kind of proton.

(c) **The intensities of the peaks** which tell us about the number of protons of each kind that are present and

(d) The **splitting of a peak into several peaks** which tells us about the environment of a proton with respect to other nearby protons in the molecule.

Example 21. *Predict the proton NMR spectrum of ethyl acetate using the three rules mentioned earlier.*

Sol. The molecule has the structure

$$CH_3—CO—O—CH_2—CH_3$$

(a) From rule 1, there is no splitting due to spin-spin interaction of the protons in either of the two methyl groups or in the methylene group.

(b) From rule 2, the CH_2 protons split the CH_3 peak into three lines (*i.e.*, a triplet) and the CH_3 protons split the CH_2 peak into four lines (*i.e.*, a quartet).

(c) From rule 3, the intensities of the CH_3 triplet are given by the coefficients of the expansion $(1+x)^2 = 1 + 2x + x^2$, *i.e.*, by the ratio of 1 : 2 : 1 and the intensities of the CH_3 quartet are given by the coefficients of the expansion $(1+x)^3 = 1 + 3x + 3x^2 + x^3$, *i.e.*, by the ratio of 1 : 3 : 3 : 1.

Chemical shift-equivalent and magnetically equivalent nuclei

If nucleus have exactly the same chemical shift, they are called **chemical shift-equivalent nuclei** and designated by the same letter. Chemical shift-equivalent nuclei can be interchanged by one of the symmetry operations of a molecule. Thus, all the protons in benzene are chemical shift equivalent since they can be interchanged by the six-fold symmetry axis of benzene.

If nuclei are coupled in exactly the same way to every other nucleus in the molecule, they are called **magnetically equivalent nuclei**. Thus, in *para*-fluoronitrobenzene,

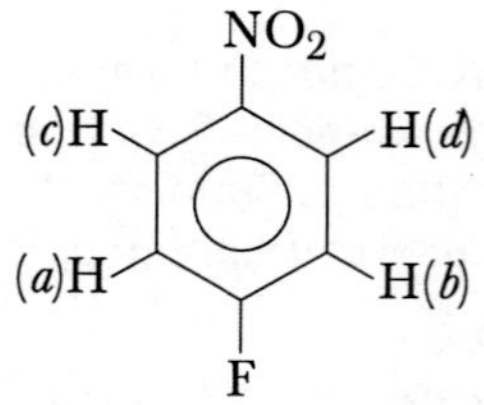

the protons (a) and (b) are chemical shift-equivalent since they are related by the mirror plane which bisects the molecule. The nuclear spin of F is $I = \frac{1}{2}$. Since, F has identical bond distances and angles with respect to protons (a) and (b), these protons are identically coupled to F. However, protons (a) and (b) are not identically coupled to protons (c) and (d). Hence, they are not magnetically equivalent. Similarly, protons (c) and (d) are not magnetically equivalent.

Another way to decided the equivalence of two protons is by replacing each alternately by a group *X*. If the *X* derivatives are the same, the protons are equivalent. If the replacement of each H in a CH_2 gives 2 diastereomers, the protons are not equivalent.

Example 22. *Determine which of the following molecules will show spin-spin coupling in their NMR spectra. If the coupling or splitting is observed, give the multiplicity of each kind of proton, i.e., give the number of lines arising from each proton :*

(a) $ClCH_2CH_2Cl$ (b) $ClCH_2CH_2I$

(c) 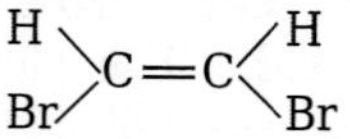

(d) 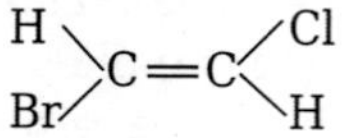

(e) 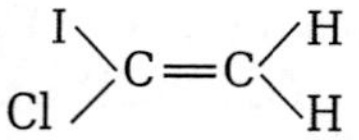

(f) $CH_3—CH{=}O$

(g) 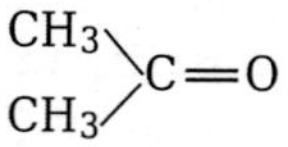

(h) $CH_3—C(Cl_2)—CH_3$

Sol. Spin-spin splitting is not observed in (a), (c), (g) and (h) which have only equivalent protons. The protons of the CH_2 groups in (b) are non-equivalent each being split into a 1 : 2 : 1 triplet. In (d) the two protons are not equivalent and each is split into a doublet. The vinyl protons in (e) are not equivalent since one is *cis* to Cl and the other is *cis* to I so that each is split into a doublet. Notice that in this case the protons undergoing spin-spin interaction are on the same carbon. In (f) the protons of CH_3 and the proton of the $—CH{=}O$ group are not equivalent; the CH_3 resonance is split into a doublet and the $—CH{=}O$ resonance is split into a 1 : 3 : 3 : 1 quartet.

Spin-spin coupling constant

The magnitude of the coupling *J* is also intimately related to the geometrical relationship of the bonds over which the coupling is transmitted. Thus, in the system H—C—C—H, the H—H coupling constant, known as the vicinal coupling constant, depends upon the dihedral angle ϕ between the C—H bonds. The angle ϕ is the angle between the projections of the two C—H bonds viewed along the C—C bonds axis. It is found that

$$J_{vic} = 4.22 - 0.5 \cos \phi + 4.5 \cos 2\phi \quad \ldots(76)$$

The is called the **Karplus relation.**

The variation of the vicinal coupling constant, J_{vic}, with the dihedral angle ϕ between the two vicinal C—H bonds, is shown in Fig. 20.27.

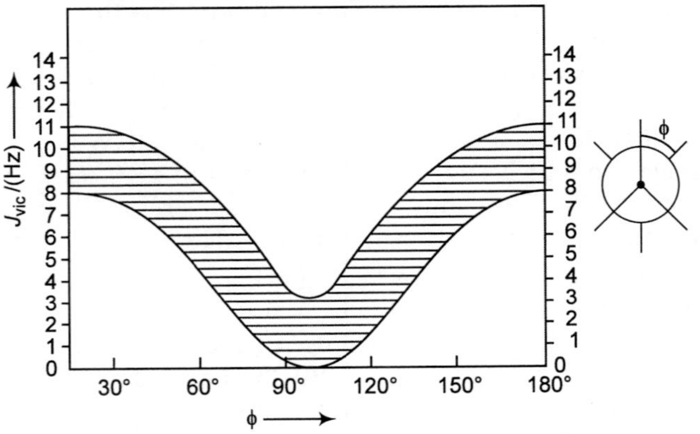

Fig. 20.27 Variation of vicinal coupling constant and dihedral angle.

Some typical J-values are given in Table 20.9.

Table 20.9. **Spin-Spin Coupling Constnts of Some Systems**

System	J (Hz)	System	J (Hz)
H—H	276	—C(H)=C(H)—O	7 to 10
H—F H—C C(H)(H)	521 120 – 260 – 20 to + 6	H—C=C—H	12 to 19
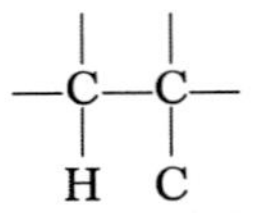	5.5 to 7.5	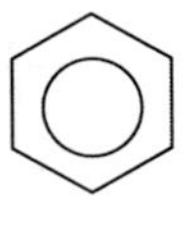	*ortho*, 6 to 9 *meta*, 0.5 to 4 *para*, 0 to 2.5

Largest vicinal couplings arise with the protons in the *trans* coplanar positions ($\phi = 180°$). Vicinal couplings for *cis* coplanar protons are almost as large ($\phi = 0$). Very small coiuplings arise between protons which are 90° to each other.

NMR Spectra of Other Nuclei

Besides protons, other nuclei having nuclear spin $I = \frac{1}{2}$ m, such as ^{13}C, ^{19}F, ^{29}Si and ^{31}P, have also been investigated by NMR spectroscopy. **The NMR spectra of ^{1}H and ^{19}F are most easily obtained because of their high natural abundance and large magnetogyric ratios**. Spectra of other nuclei provide structural information about compounds in the same way as the proton magnetic resonance (p.m.r.) spectra do. While ^{1}H-chemical shifts extend only over a small range of the order of 15 ppm, ^{31}P-chemical shifts have a span of about 400 ppm and ^{19}F-chemical shifts have a still wider span of 600 ppm. This wider range can be attributed to the greater number and mobility of extranuclear electrons which produce greater variation in diamagnetic shielding.

In recent years, the ^{13}C-NMR spectroscopy has emerged as good structural tool although there is considerable difficulty in recording the ^{13}C-NMR spectra. This is due to the fact that ^{13}C has a very small natural abundance and a small value of the magnetogyric ratio.

Example 23. *Peredict the NMR spectrum of borohydride ion* BH_4^-. *The nuclear spin of* ^{11}B *is 3/2.*

Sol. The four protons in BH_4^- are equivalent. Thus, the ^{11}B resonance splits into a quintet with the relative intensity ratio 1 : 4 : 6 : 4 : 1. Since, the nuclear spin, I of ^{11}B is 3/2, in the presence of magnetic field its four components are + 3/2, + 1/2, – 1/2 and – 3/2. Thus, this proton resonance is split into a quartet by interaction with the ^{11}B nucleus, the four lines being equally intense.

Example 24. *The* ^{31}P*-NMR spectrum of phosphonic acid gives a doublet whereas that of phosphinic acid gives a triplet. Write the structures of the two acids, justifying them.*

Sol. Phosphonic acid, 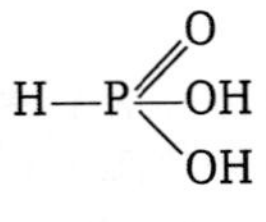

Phosphinic acid, 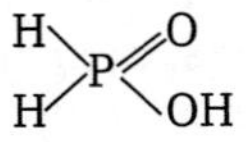

Both ^{1}H and ^{31}P have nuclear spin $I = 1/2$. In phosphonic acid, the P atom is attached to one proton which causes its resonance to be split into a doublet. In phosphinic acid, the P atom is attached to two protons which cause its resonance to be split into a triplet in the intensity ratio 1 : 2 : 1.

Example 25. *Describe the proton and deuteron-NMR spectra of* HD.

Sol. For ^1H, $I = 1/2$ and for ^2D, $I = 1$. In the presence of magnetic field, the proton spin has two components, $m_I = 1/2$ and $-1/2$, whereas, the deuteron spin has three components $m_I = +1, 0, -1$. Thus, the deuteron resonance is split by the proton into a doublet and the proton resonance is split by the deuteron into a triplet (1 : 2 : 1).

Example 26. *Describe the proton and phosphorus-NMR spectra of phosphonium ion,* PH_4^+.

Sol. Both ^1H and ^{31}P have $I = 1/2$. Thus, the P atom splits the resonance of the four equivalent protons in PH_4^+ ion into a doublet and the protons split the phosphorus resonance into a quintet in the intensity ratio 1 : 4 : 6 : 4 : 1.

Example 27. *Describe the proton- and nitrogen-NMR spectra of the ammonium ion,* NH_4^+.

Sol. ^1H has $I = 1/2$, whereas ^{14}N has $I = 1$. In the presence of the magnetic field, the ^{14}N-spin has three components : $m_I = +1, 0, -1$. Thus, the N-atom splits the resonance of the four equivalent protons in NH_4^+ ion into a 1 : 1 : 1 triplet. The protons split the nitrogen resonance into 1 : 4 : 6 : 4 : 1 quintet.

Example 28. *Why is NMR spectrum of* NH_3 *broad whereas that of* NH_4^+ *ion is sharp?*

Sol. We know that ^{14}N ($I = 1$) is a quadrupolar nucleus. The electric field gradient (EFG) at this nucleus due to the bonding electrons and the lone pair electrons on N-atom interacts with the nuclear quadrupole moment of ^{14}N in NH_3, thereby broadening the NMR spectrum of ^{14}N which, in turn, broadens the spectrum of ^1H. However, in the case of NH_4^+ ion which is spherically symmetrical, the EFG vanishes (this is a result of quantum mechanics), so that there is no nuclear qudrupole interaction of EFG with the quadrupole moment of ^{14}N. Hence, the NMR spectrum of NH_4^+ ion is sharp.

Fourier-Transform NMR Spectroscopy

In 1966, R.R. Ernst and W.A. Anderson published a remarkable paper on the Fourier-Transform (FT) NMR spectroscopy. In this technique spectra are presented in the time-domain as against the conventional continuous wave (CW) NMR where the spectra are presented in the frequency domain. In the frequency domain, the intensity of the radiation at the detector is a function of frequency, *i.e.*, $I(v)$, and in the time-domain, the intensity is a function of time, *i.e.*, $F(t)$, $I(v)$ can be transofrmed by the mathematical technique known as Fourier transform into $F(t)$ as follows :

$$F(t) = \int_{-\infty}^{\infty} e^{2\pi/vt} I(v)\, dv \qquad \ldots(77)$$

Conversely, $F(t)$ can be transformed into $I(v)$ by the inverse Fourier transofrm :

$$I(v) = \int_{-\infty}^{\infty} e^{-2\pi/vt} F(t)\, dt \qquad \ldots(78)$$

These transforms are carried out by a computer attached to the NMR aparatus. $F(t)$ contains all the information about the NMR spectrum that $I(\nu)$ does. Now, the question arieses : Why do we need $F(t)$ if $I(v)$ can do the job? The reason is that to measure the NMR spectrum in the frequency domain, one has to scan a very broad range of frequencies, which is time-consuming. On the other hand, to record the spectrum in the time-domain, one can apply all the frequencies in a very short time. Thus, a CW-NMR spectrum which takes, say, 25 minutes to scan, can be scanned in 25 seconds as FT-NMR spectrum. Clearly, FT-NMR is vastly faster than CW-NMR.

In order to excite FT-NMR, the band of frequencies required is obtained by applying a short, approximately squre-wave pulse of radiofrequency (rf) power in the *xy* plane. Fig. 20.28 shows the Fourier synthesis of a square wave which is a superposition of several sinosoidal waves. Better approximation to square wave can be achieved by including more sine waves. Conversely, the analysis of $F(t)$ into its Fourier components yields a whole spectrum of different superimposed harmonic (sinosoidal) waves. In the pulse FT-NMR spectrometer, the pulse B_1 is supplied by a radiofrequency field that has the Larmor (NMR) frequency v_0 which is of the order of 100 MHz for ^1H NMR. The Fourier components add to, or substract from, this **carrier frequency.** Suppose the length of the pulse is t_p ($\approx 100\ \mu s$). The sample receives a range of frequencies of about $\nu_0 \pm 1/t_p$ which, in the present example, are 100 MHz ± 10 kHz.

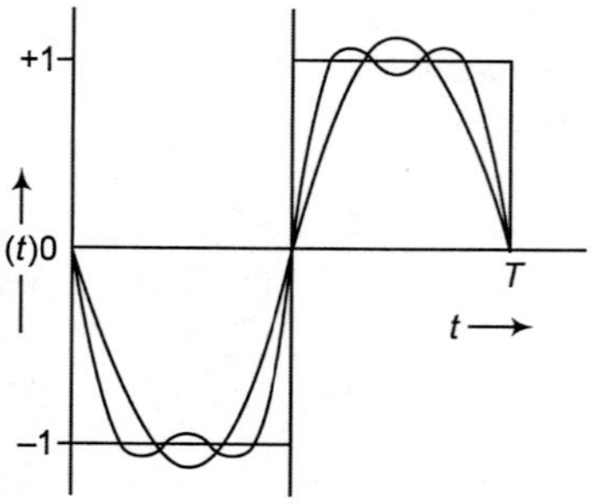

Fig. 20.28 Fourier synthesis of a square wave pulse in FT-NMR.

As soon as the radiofrequency pulse B_1 terminates, the magnetization vector (of all the magnetic nuclei in the sample) in the *xy*-plane starts decaying. This important process is called free **induction decay** (FID) because the nuclei are freely precessing about the Zeeman field, B_0, in the absence of the radio frequency field B_1. Without going into details, we may remark that in order to improve the **signal-to-noise** (S/N) **ratio**, several consecutive pulses can be applied to the sample thereby considerably enhancing the intensity of the signal. The FIDs are collected in the computer and averaged before being Fourier-transformed to give the $I(\nu)$ spectrum.

Thermal Equilibrium of Nuclear Spins and the Relaxation Processes in Magnetic Resonance

The Zeeman splitting of the nuclear or electron spins obtained by applying magnetic fields at room temperature, is very small. The relative Boltzmann population of the nuclear spins in the upper state and the lower state is given by

$$n_{\text{upper}}/n_{\text{lower}} = \exp(-\Delta E/kT) = \exp(-g_N\mu_N B_0/kT) \quad \ldots(79)$$

where, n_{upper} and n_{lower} are the numbers of spins in the upper and lower energy states. At room temperature, $g_N\mu_N B_0 << kT$ so that the exponential can be approximated by a power series :

$$n_{\text{upper}}/n_{\text{lower}} \approx 1 - (g_N\mu_N B_0/kT) \quad \ldots(80)$$

The excess population in the lower state is then given by

$$\frac{n_{\text{lower}} - n_{\text{upper}}}{n_{\text{lower}} + n_{\text{upper}}} = \frac{g_N\mu_N B_0}{2kT} \quad \ldots(81)$$

which, for ordinary temperatures and magnetic field B_0, is very small. Now, only the spins in the low energy state can absorb radiation which has to be of the right frequency to be absorbed. Since, the excess population in the lower energy state is directly proportional to the magnetic flux density, B_0, the intensity of the NMR signal increases as B_0 increases. To record and NMR spectrum there occurs a process known as **relaxation which removes the excitation energy from the upper state to restore the excess population in the ground state** so that the energy can be continuously absorbed from the radiofrequency field, B_1.

The transition from the lower to upper energy state corresponds to flipping of the nuclear magnetic moment vector from one allowed orientation to the other in the large Zeeman field B_0. In the ground state, the proton spins are aligned so that the *z*-components of the magnetic moment μ_z are in the direction of B_0. The radiofrequency field B_1 flips the nuclear moments to the opposite direction as the energy is absorbed. The relaxation process flips them back to the original orientation with the result that **the spin system returns to the ground state by transferring its energy of excitation to the random thermal motions in the surroundings.** In other words, the nuclear spin system becomes **cooler** and its surroundings become **warmer** as a result of the energy transfer.

If the excess number of nuclei in the lower energy level is represented by n and the initial number is n_0, the approach to the new equilibrium n_{eq} is described by

$$n - n_{eq} = (n_0 - n_{eq})\exp(-t/T_1) \quad \ldots(82)$$

where, t is the time and T_1 is called the **spin-lattice relaxation time.** The name **spin-lattice relaxation** originates from the fact that the first experiments were carried out on solid samples where the relaxation was brought about by the transfer of spin excitation energy to the lattice vibrations. The terms spin-lattice relaxation has been retained but it refers to relaxation due to fluctuating magnetic field arising from random motions in the surroundings of the spin system. This, in brief, is the basis of the so-called **Bloembergen-Purcell-Pound (BPP) theory** of relaxation processes in magnetic resonance, proposed in 1948. The most common cause of the T_1-relaxation is the magnetic dipole-dipole interaction. Paramagnetic substances, if present in the sample, **increase** the efficiency of the nuclear spin relaxation and thus **decrease** T_1.

Example 29. *Calculate the relative Boltzmann population of the proton spins in the lower state to that in the upper state in a magnetic field of flux density 1 T at room temperature. What is the excess population in the lower state?*

Sol.

$$\frac{n_{\text{lower}}}{n_{\text{upper}}} = 1 + \frac{g_N\mu_N B_0}{kT}$$

$$= 1 + \frac{(5.585)(5.05 \times 10^{-27}\ \text{J T}^{-1})(1\ \text{T})}{(1.38 \times 10^{-23}\ \text{J K}^{-1})(298\ \text{K})}$$

$$= 1 + 6.686 \times 10^{-6}$$

$$\frac{n_{\text{lower}} - n_{\text{upper}}}{n_{\text{lower}} + n_{\text{upper}}} = \frac{g_N\mu_N B_0}{2kT} = 3.343 \times 10^{-6}$$

Electron Spin Resonance (ESR) Spectra

It is also called electron paramagnetic resonance (EPR). NMR and ESR are similar in their theoretical principles. The systems which can be investigated by ESR spectroscopy are organic or inorganic free radicals and ions of transition metals which contain unpaired *d* or *f* electrons. One of the most important uses of ESR technique lies in the detection of extremely short-lived (transient) free radical intermediates in chemical reactions.

ESR Spectrum of an Unpaired Electron

As is well known, an electron possesses a spin S whose value is $\frac{1}{2}$. The magnetic moment associated with this spin is given by

$$\vec{\mu} = -g_e \mu_B \vec{\mathbf{S}} \quad ...(83)$$

where, g_e is the Lande'g-factor and μ_B is the Bohr magneton. The value of g_e is 2.0023. $\mu_B = eh/4\pi m_e$ where, e is the electronic charge and m_e is the mass of the electron. Substituting various values, μ_B is equal to 9.273×10^{-24} J T^{-1}.

The energy associated with electron spin S in the magnetic field B_z, applied along the z-axis, is given by

$$E = -\vec{\mu}\,\vec{\mathbf{B}}_z \quad ...(84)$$

The component of spin S along the field direction is m_s. Hence, from Eqs. 94 and 95.

$$E_{ms} = g_e\,\mu_B B_z m_s \quad ...(85)$$

Since, $m_S = \pm\frac{1}{2}$, we have

$$E_{+1/2} = \frac{1}{2} g_e\,\mu_B B_z \quad ...(86)$$

$$E_{-1/2} = -\frac{1}{2} g_e\,\mu_B B_z \quad ...(87)$$

Here, too, as in the case of a bare proton, while in the absence of the applied magnetic field the two energy levels are degenerate, the degeneracy is removed in the presence of the field, as shown in Fig. 20.29.

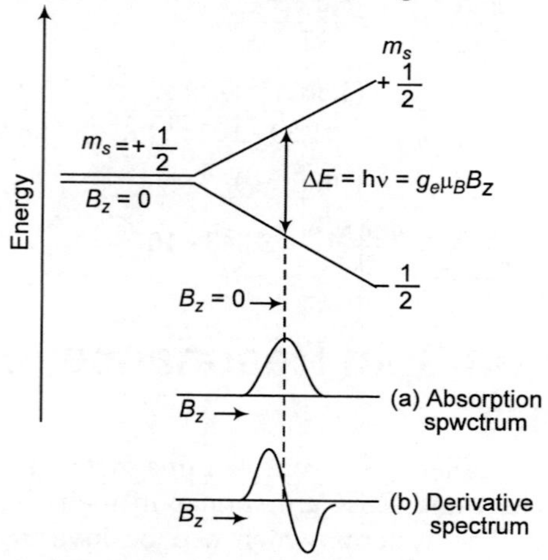

Fig. 20.29 Energy level diagram showing the ESR spectrum of an electron.

Application of an oscillating field perpendicular to the direction of B_z induces transitions between the two sub-energy levels provided the frequency of the oscillating field satisfies the Bohr-Einstein condition, *viz.,*

$$\Delta E = E_{1/2} - E_{-1/2} = g_e\mu_B B_z = h\nu \quad ...(88)$$

Thus, the ESR frequency of the odd electron is given by

$$v = \Delta E/h = g_e\mu_B B_z/h \quad ...(89)$$

In Fig. 20.29 is shown the ESR spectrum of the odd electron in two modes : (a) the absorption mode and (b) the derivative mode. Since, the ESR spectra are generally broad (*i.e.,* not sharp), it is difficult to locate the peak in the absorption mode but it is quite easy to locate it in the derivative mode. Hence, the ESR spectra are generally recorded in the derivative mode.

Example 30. *Calculate the ESR frequency of an unpaired electron in a magnetic field of* 0.33 T *given that for the free electron,* $g_e = 2$ *and* $\mu_B = 9.273 \times 10^{-24}$ J T^{-1}.

Sol. $v = g_e\mu_B B_z/h$

$$= \frac{(2)\,(9.273 \times 10^{-24}\text{ J T}^{-1})\,(0.33\text{ T})}{6.626 \times 10^{-34}\text{ J s}} \quad \text{[Eq. 89]}$$

$= 9000 \times 10^6$ s^{-1} $= 9000 \times 10^6$ Hz

$= 9.00$ GHz.

Hyperfine Structure in ESR Spectra

Hyperfine structure (HFS) occurs as a result of the magnetic interaction between the electronic spin S and the nuclear spin l. The hyperfine interaction in ESR spectra is analogous to the fine structure, *i.e.,* nuclear spin-spin interaction in NMR spectra. As a result of this interaction, the ESR signals or peaks are split into several lines (HFS).

Let us consider the hyperfine interaction in the following seven cases : (1) hydrogen atom (2) methyl radical, $CH_3^{\bullet}$ (3) the $(SO_3)_2NO^-$ radical anion (4) 1,4-benzosemiquinone radical anion (5) naphthalene negative ion (6) anthracene negative ion and (7) triphenylmethyl radical. The selection rule for hyperfine transitions is

$$\Delta m_S = \pm 1;\ \Delta m_I = 0 \quad ...(90)$$

This selection rule may be interpreted by saying that the nuclear motion is much slower than the electronic motion so that during the time electron changes its spin orientation, the nucleus, being heavier, has no time to reorient its spin so that $\Delta m_I = 0$.

1. Hydrogen atom

It contains an unpaired electron with $S = \frac{1}{2}$ and a proton with nuclear spin $I = \frac{1}{2}$. Thus, $m_S = \pm\frac{1}{2}$ and $m_I = \pm\frac{1}{2}$. In the absence of magnetic field ($B_z = 0$), the electron spin energy levels are degenerate, *i.e.*, have the same energy. Application of B_z removes the degeneracy between them, the $m_S = -\frac{1}{2}$ sublevel going down and the $m_S = +\frac{1}{2}$ sublevel going up (see Fig. 20.30). Each of these electron sublevels interacts with the nucleus giving four sublevels designated by the value of m_I. This is hyperfine interaction. Using the selection rule, two ESR lines, *i.e.*, a doublet, are observed, as shown in the experimental spectrum. They are equally intense, the spacing between them gives the **hyperfine coupling constant**, a expressed in units of tesla or millitesla.

2. Methyl radical, CH_3

It contains an unpaired electron with $S = \frac{1}{2}$ and three equivalent protons. Since, for a proton, $I = \frac{1}{2}$, it is evident that for three equivalent protons, $m_I = +\frac{3}{2}, +\frac{1}{2}, -\frac{1}{2}, -\frac{3}{2}$. Also, $m_S = \pm\frac{1}{2}$. This interpretation of the ESR spectrum (Fig. 20.55) is similar to that of H-atom given in Fig. 20.30. The ESR spectrum contains four equally spaced lines, *i.e.*, a quartet.

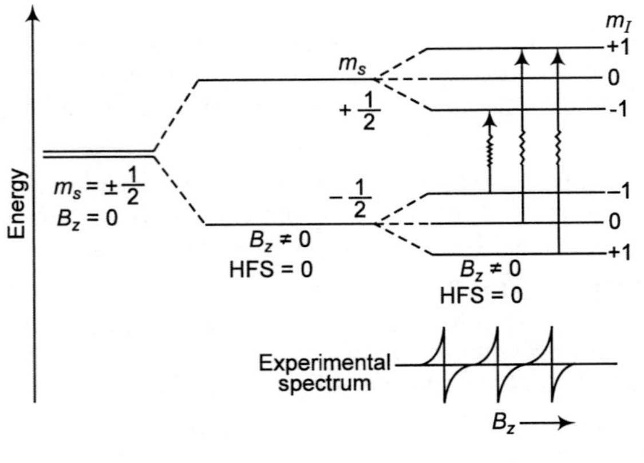

Fig. 20.30 The hyperfine structure in the ESR spectrum of hydrogen atom.

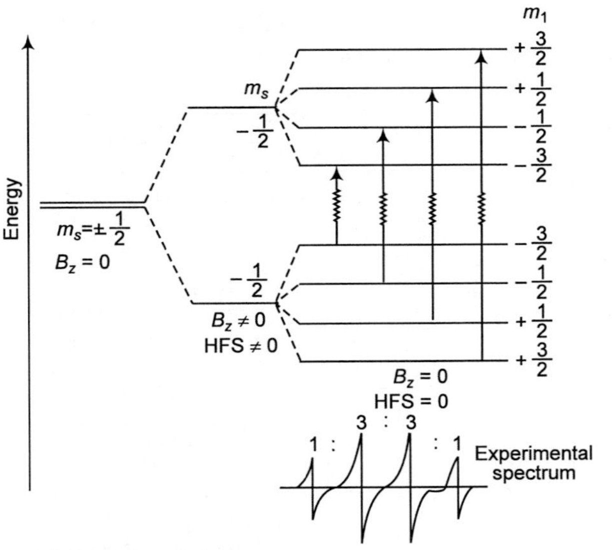

Fig. 20.31 The hyperfine structure in the ESR spectrum of the methyl radical $\dot{C}H_3$.

3. $(SO_3)_2NO^-$ anion

In this anion, the unpaired electron interacts with the nitrogen nucleus with $I = 1$. Here, $m_S = \pm\frac{1}{2}$ and $m_I = +1, 0, -1$. The ESR spectrum (Fig. 20.32) contains three equally spaced lines, *i.e.*, a triplet.

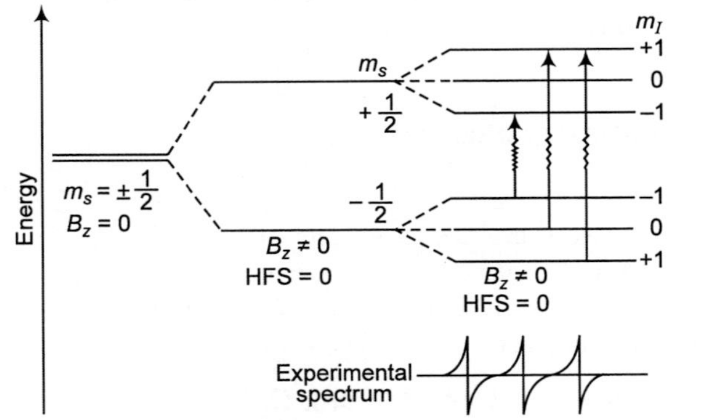

Fig. 20.32 The ESR spectrum of the $(SO_3)_2NO^-$ radical anion.

4. 1, 4-benzosemiquinone radical anion

This anion, having the structure 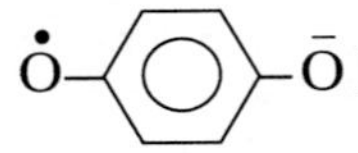 has one unpaired electron $\left(S = \frac{1}{2}\right)$, interacting with four equivalent protons. Since, for a proton $I = \frac{1}{2}$, it is evident that for four equivalent protons, $m_I = +2, 1, 0, -1, -2$.

The ESR spectrum (Fig. 20.33) contains a quintet, *i.e.,* five equally spaced lines.

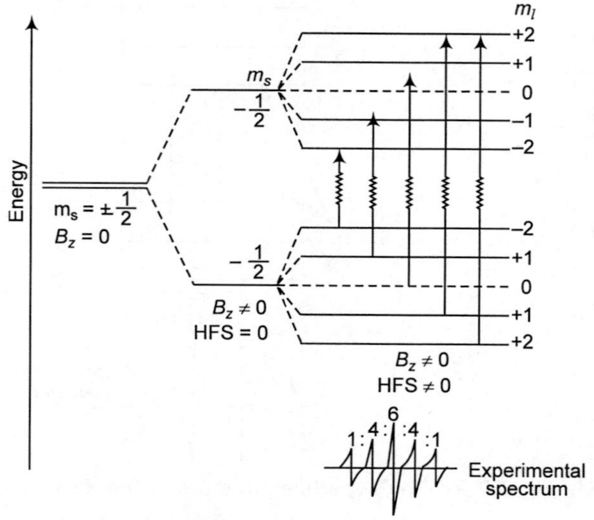

Fig. 20.33 The hyperfine structure in the ESR spectrum of *p*-benzosemiquinone radical anion.

5. **Naphthalene negative ion**

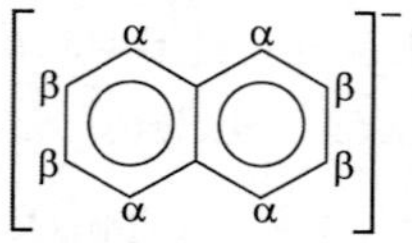

In this case, there are two sets (α and β) of four equivalent protons each. The ESR spectrum would thus, show $(4 + 1) \times (4 + 1) = 25$ lines.

6. **Anthracene negative ion,**

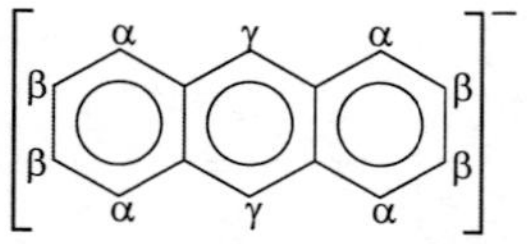

In this case there are three sets of equivalent protons : sets α and β consist of four equivalent protons each and set γ consists of two equivalent protons. The ESR spectrum consists of $(4 + 1)(4 + 1)(2 + 1) = 75$ lines.

7. **Triphenylmethyl radical, $C(C_6H_5)_3$**

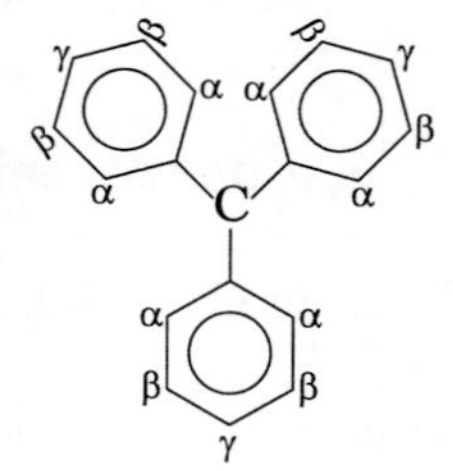

It has also three sets of eqivalent protons : sets α and β consist of six equivalent protons each and set γ consists of three equivalent protons. The ESR spectrum consists of $(6 + 1)(6 + 1)(3 + 1) = 196$ lines. It is a triumph of theory that all 196 lines have been observed. One can imaging the complexity of this spectrum!

The hyperfine structure in ESR spectra of complicated organic radicals ions may consist of a very large number of lines all of which can be interpreted in a manner similar to the above.

In general, the ESR spectrum of a system where the unpaired electron interacts with n equivalent protons, contains $n + 1$ lines and their relative intensities are given by Pascal's triangle, discussed earlier. Thus, we have for (i) H atom, 2 lines (*i.e.,* a doublet) of equal intensity (ii) for CH_3 radical, 4 lines (*i.e.,* a quartet) in the intensity ratio 1 : 3 : 3 : 1, (iii) for the 1, 4-benzosemiquinone anion, 5 lines (*i.e.,* a quintet) in the intensity ratio 1 : 4 : 6 : 4 : 1 and for benzene radical anion, a septet in the relative intensity ratio 1 : 6 : 15 : 20 : 15 : 6 : 1 since here the unpaired electron interacts with six equivalent protons.

For nuclei with $I > 1/2$, other rules apply. Thus, the ^{14}N nucleus in $(SO_3)_2NO^-$, with $I = 1$, gives a hyperfine pattern of 3 lines (triplet) of equal intensity. Similarly, a ^{63}Cu nucleus $\left(I = \frac{3}{2}\right)$ interacting with an odd electron gives a hyperfine pattern of four lines (quartet) of equal intensity.

The hyperfine coupling constant a in hydrogen atom is 50.68 mT. This coupling is due entirely to the **Fermi contact interaction**, being proportional to the probability density of the 1*s* electron at the nucleus. In aromatic free radicals where the unpaired electron is delocalized over the molecular orbitals extending over the entire molecule, the probability of finding the electron on a given nucleus is evidently small : hence, the hyperfine coupling constant is also small. Thus, the ESR spectrum of benzene radical anion, $C_6H_6^-$, containing six equivalent protons, is a septet with $a = 0.375$ mT. For CH_3, consisting of a quartet, $a = 2.3$ mT.

Note ESR spectrum can be used to map the molecular orbital occupied by the unpaired electron. This mapping is aided by the **McConnell Equation,**

$$q = Q\rho, \text{ where } Q = 2.25 \text{ mT} \qquad ...(91)$$

Here, ρ is the unpaired elecron spin density on a C atom and a is the hyperfine splitting constant observed for the H atom to which it is attached.

Example 31. *The hyperfine constants in the ESR spectrum of (naphthalene) at the α and β positions are $a = 0.490$ mT and $a = 0.183$ mT, respectively. Map the unpaired electron spin density around the ring.*

Sol. Using Eq. 91 and the given a values, we find the following mapping of the unpaired electron spin density at the α and β positions :

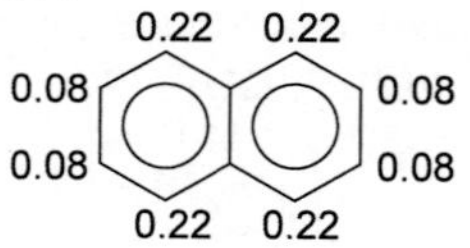

Notice that the unpaired electron spin density is greater at the α positions than at β positions because the hyperfine coupling constants at the α positions are greater than at the β positions.

Mossbauer Spectroscopy

The discovery of **Mossbauer effect** or Mossbauer spectroscopy (also known as the recoilless nuclear gamma resonance fluorescence (NRF) spectroscopy) in 1958 by the German physicist Rudolf Mossbauer was hailed as a break through in nuclear and solid state physics. Mossbauer spectroscopy has found wide application in elucidating the nature of the chemical bond in inorganic solid state chemistry and biological science, for instance, bonding in haemoglobin and oxyhaemoglobin.

Basic Principle of NRF Spectroscopy

Consider the original experiment performed by Mossbauer. here ^{57}Co decays to the excited state of iron, ^{57}Fe* by electron capture (EC), which further decay to the stable ^{57}Fe by the emission of delayed gamma ray (Fig. 20.34). This latter phenomenon is called **γ-ray fluorescence.** In the presence of a target nucleus ^{57}Fe, this gamma ray can be resonantly absorbed. Since the excited state ^{57}Fe* has a finite life-time (τ)m the uncertainty in the energy of the emittd γ-ray is governed by the Heisenberg uncertainty principle, $\Delta E \Delta t \sim \hbar$, which can be rewritten in a slightly different notation as

$$\Gamma\tau \sim \hbar \quad \ldots(92)$$

where, Γ is the line width and τ is the life-time of the excited state. From Eq. 92 we see that since 10^{-11} s $< \tau < 10^{-4}$ s, $10^{-4} < \Gamma < 10^{-11}$ 4 eV.

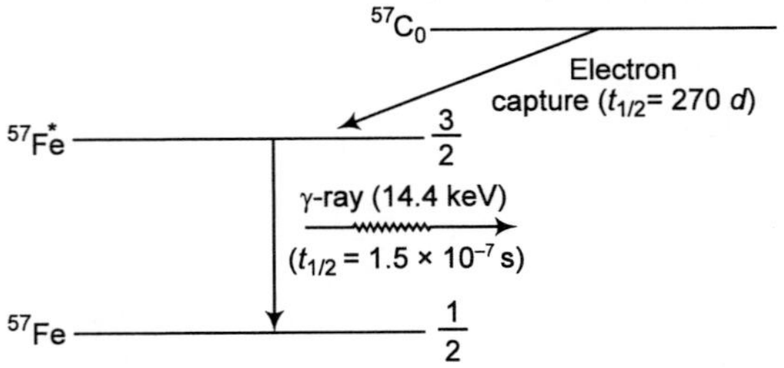

Fig. 20.34 Schematic simplified diagram showing the decay of the radioactive ^{57}Co to ^{57}Fe.

The momentum of the emitted γ-ray is given, according to the de Broglie relation, by

$$P = h/\lambda \quad \ldots(93)$$

where, λ is the γ-ray wavelength. Since, linear momentum must be conserved, the nucleus must recoil in the opposite direction, with the recoil energy R given by

$$R = P^2/2M \quad \ldots(94)$$

where, M is the mass of the recoiling nucleus. The target nucleus, too, must recoil with energy R on receiving the γ-ray, with the result that some of the energy of the γ-ray transition, E_γ, is converted into the recoil energy. Thus, for the emitting nucleus

$$E = E_\gamma - R \quad \ldots(95)$$

and for the absorbing nucleus (absorber)

$$E = E_\gamma + R \quad \ldots(96)$$

We see that the emission and absorption lines are centred $2R$ apart.

Since, $$E_\gamma = h\nu = hc/\lambda = Pc \quad \ldots(97)$$

we have, from Eqs. 94 and 95.

$$2R = E_\gamma^2/Mc^2 \quad \ldots(98)$$

For the resonance absorption to occur, Γ must be greater than or equal to the loss in γ-ray energy due to recoil, *i.e.,*

$$\Gamma \sim 2R \quad \ldots(99)$$

The plot of the number of the emitted γ-rays *versus* energy is given in Fig. 20.35.

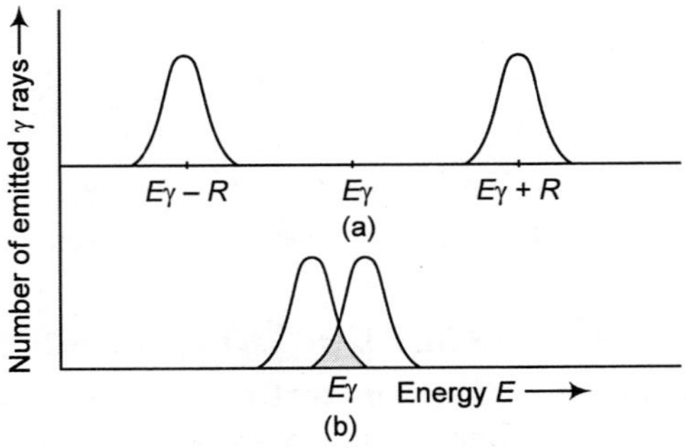

Fig. 20.35 (a) Rosonance absorption and emission curves for $2R > \Gamma$.
(b) Resonance absorption and emission curves for $2R \sim \Gamma$.

It should be noted that Mossbauer effect cannot be observed in liquids and gases because the recoil energy cannot be dissipated in these states of matter.

The Mossbauer Experiment

The set-up that Mossbauer designed for his experiment is very simple (Fig. 20.36). The Doppler motion is given to the source, *i.e.,* the source is moved towards the absorber with velocity *v* by means of the velocity drive. The intensity of the emitted gamma rays is measured as a function of the Doppler velocity, *v*. It must be remembered that the Doppler velocity given to the source relative to the absorber is necessary to bring the source and the absorber lines closer to meet the resonance absorption condition; it is *not* required to compensate the recoil energy because the recoil has already been eliminated by taking the sample in the form of a solid. When the source and the absorber move towards each other, the sign of Doppler velocity is taken to be positive. A typical Mossbauer spectrum is shown in Fig. 20.37.

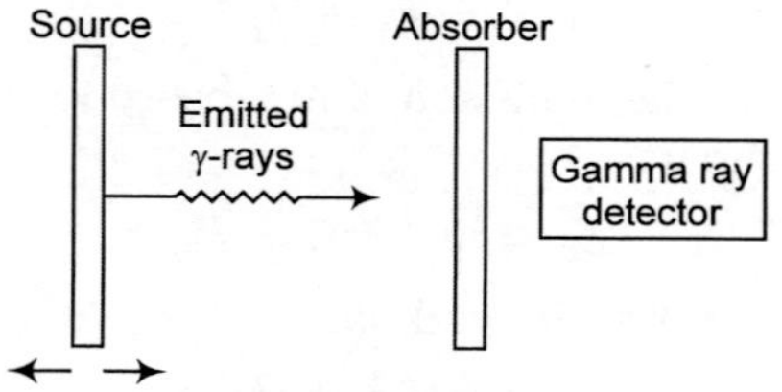

Fig. 20.37 The Mossbauer spectrometer.

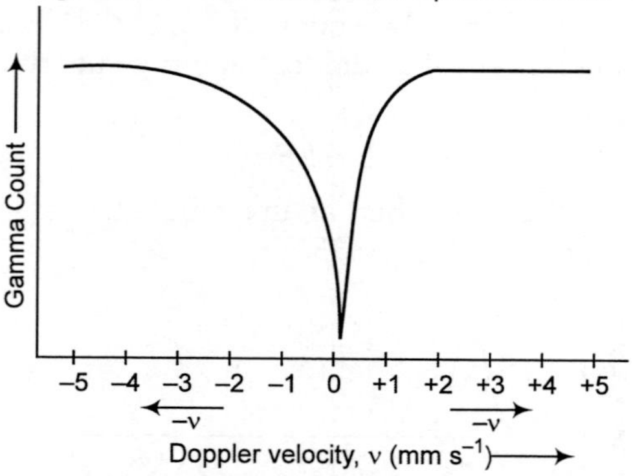

Fig. 20.38 A typical Mossbauer spectrum.

Theory of Mossbauer Spectroscopy

There quantities, called **hyperfine interactions,** are studied by Mossbauer spectroscopy, *viz.,* chemical (isomer) shift (δ); nuclear electric quadrupole splitting (ΔE_Q) and nuclear Zeeman splitting.

1. Chemical (Isomer) shift

As a result of the electrostatic interaction between the nucleus and the electrons in a solid, the nuclear energy levels are shifted in both the source and the absorber. The shift, called the **isomer shift**, is given by

$$\delta = \frac{2\pi}{5} Ze^2 [|\psi_a(0)|^2 - |\psi_s(0)|^2](R_{ex}^2 - R_{gd}^2) \quad \ldots(100)$$

where, *e* is the electronic charge, *Z* the atomic number and R_{ex} and R_{gd} are the radii of the nucleus in the excited and the ground states, respectively. $|\psi_a(0)|^2$ is the corresponding quantity for the source. Since, only *s* electrons have a finite wave function at the nucleus and the *p* and *d* electrons have vanishing wave functions at the nucleus, it is only the *s* electrons which are responsible for the isomer shift.

2. Nuclear electric quadrupole splitting, ΔE_Q

Sometimes, as the case of ^{57}Fe, the excited state has a nuclear spin > 1; here, $I = 3/2$. If the quadrupole moment *eQ* of the ^{57}Fe nucleus in the absorber interacts with the *EFG* (electric field gradient, *eq*) that is not spherically symmetric, the resulting interaction splits the excited state energy levels into two lines, the splitting being called electric quadrupole splitting, ΔE_Q. The quantity e^2Qq is called **nuclear electric quadrupole coupling constant**. Fig. 20.39 illustrates the concepts of isomer shift and electric quadrupole splitting.

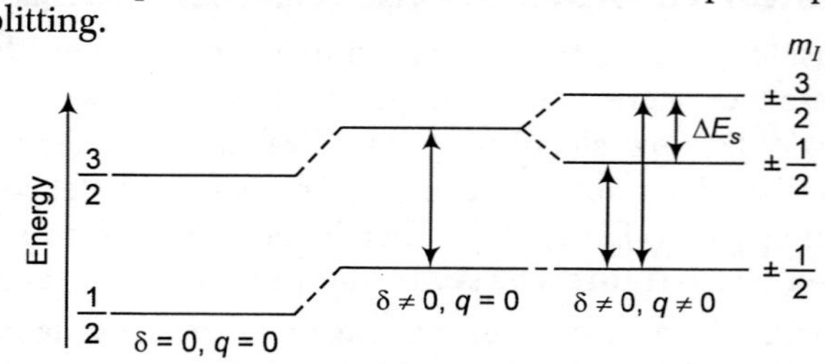

Fig. 20.39 Isomer shift and electric quadrupole splitting in ^{57}Fe energy levels.

Example 32. *The Mossbauer spectrum of* $K_4[Fe(CN)_6]$ *consists of one line whereas that of* $K_3[Fe(CN)_5NO]$ *consists of two lines. Draw these spectra qualitatively and account for their appearance.*

Sol. (a) $K_4[Fe(CN)_6]$. A single line Mossbauer spectrum shows only the effect of isomer shift because for the $[Fe(CN)_6]^{4-}$ anion, being spherically symmetric, $q = 0$ (Fig. 20.40). Also, refer to Fig. 20.39.

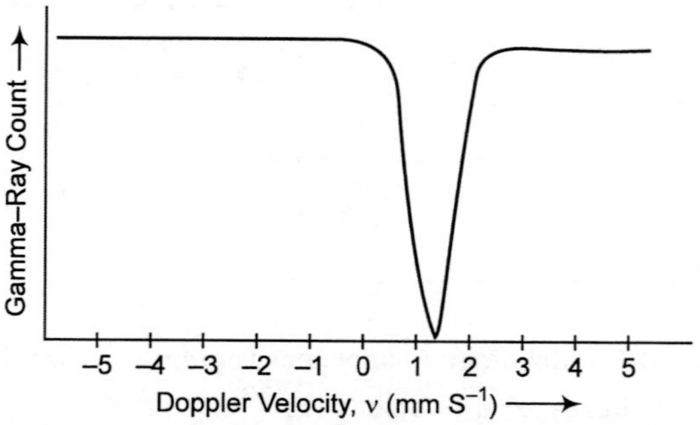

Fig. 20.40 The Mossbauer spectrum of $K_4[Fe(CN)_6]$. $\delta \neq 0, q = 0$

(b) $K_3[Fe(CN)_5NO]$. A two-lines spectrum shows the effect of both the isomer shift and the quadrupole splitting because for the $[Fe(CN)_5NO]^{3-}$ anion, being not spherically symmetric, $q \neq 0$ (Fig, 20.41). Also, refer to Fig. 20.39.

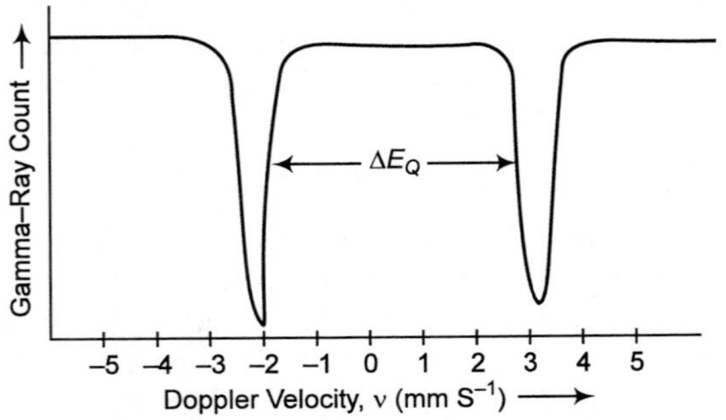

Fig. 20.41 The Mossbauer spectrum of $K_3[Fe(CN)_5NO]$. Here $\delta \neq 0$, $q \neq 0$.

3. Nuclear Zeeman splitting (also called magnetic hyperfine splitting)

The external nuclear Zeeman splitting is caused by the splitting of the nuclear energy levels by the magnetic field, *B*. Infact, in the metallic state of iron very large internal magnetic field of the order of about 30 T, exists; this field, too, causes huge splitting. Fig. 20.42 shows the combined effect of isomer shift ($\delta \neq 0$) and magnetic field ($\delta \neq 0$, $B \neq 0$) on the Mossbauer spectrum of ^{57}Fe. The selection rule $\Delta m_I = 0, \pm 1$ gives six lines in the spectrum.

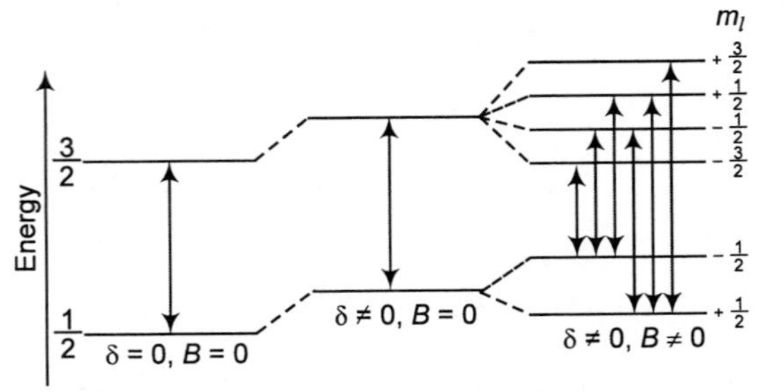

Fig. 20.42 Isomer shift and nuclear Zeeman splitting in ^{57}Fe energy levels.

Photoelectron Spectroscopy (PES)

Photoelectron spectroscopy is a very important technique for determining the atomic and molecular energy levels and hence the ionization energies (or the binding energies) of atoms and molecules. Consider a few energy levels of an atom containing electrons with paired spins (Fig. 20.43). The ionization energy (IE), or preferably, the binding energy (BE) of the atom is defined as the **least** energy required to remove an electron from the highest occupied orbital. The elecrons are classified as the **valence electrons** and the **core electrons.** When the atom (or the molecule) is irradiated with ultraviolet (UV) radiation, photoionization occurs by the ejection of the valence electrons which carry away certain kinetic energy (KE). On the other hand, irradiation by the highly energic X-rays results in the ejection of the core electrons. The former technique is known as UV-PES or simply UPES and the latter XPES. In each case, we have

$$h\nu = \text{BE} + \text{KE} \qquad \ldots(101)$$

where, $h\nu$ is the photon energy. Thus,

$$\text{BE} = h\nu - \text{KE} \qquad \ldots(102)$$

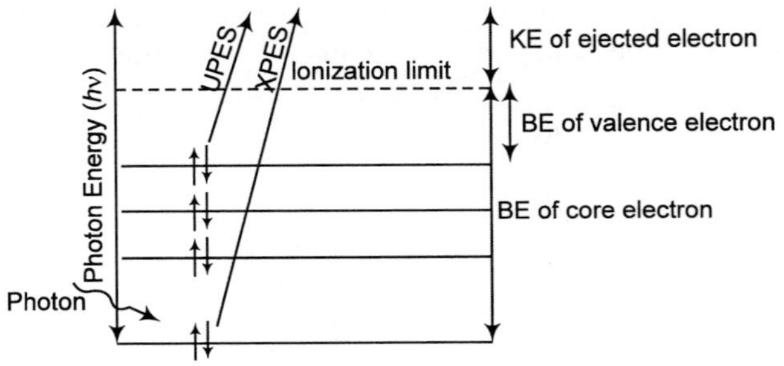

Fig. 20.43 Schematic diagram illustrating UPES and XPES.

It follows that knowing $h\nu$ and measuring KE, BE can be calculated. It may be mentioned that PES is the technique derived from Einstein's photoelectric effect where, a beam of monochromatic photons, incident on a metal, removes the electrons from the bulk of the metal (the metal is a "sea" of electrons), which carry away the excess kinetic energy. The work function of the metal, which is the energy required to remove the bulk electrons to the surface of the metal, is the analogue of the ionization energy of the atom (or the molecule) in PES.

In UPES the most commonly used source of UV photons is a helium gas discharge tube; the most intense line has a wavelength of 58.4 nm which corresponds to an energy of 21.22 eV. **In XPES we use an X-ray source of higher energy to ionize the inner core electrons**. Here, the X-ray beam is produced by electron bombardment of a metal target such as aluminium or magnesium. The K_α line for aluminium occurs at 1486.6 eV. Photoelectron spectra are interpreted in terms of **Koopmans' theorem** which states that the ionization energy, IE, is equal to the negative of the energy of the orbital (usually the HOMO) from which the electron is ejected, *i.e.*, $(\text{IE})_i = -\text{E}_i$. This very important theorem is, however, only an approximation since it ignores the fact that the remaining electrons adjust their distributions when ionization occurs.

Siegbahn's experimental technique of PES consists in measuring the kinetic energies of the photoelectrons using an electrostatic deflector which produces different deflections in the paths of the photoelectrons as they pass between charged plates. With the increase in field strength, electrons of different speeds and hence different kinetic energies, reach the detector. The photoelectron spectrum is recorded with intensity of electron flux as a function of the kinetic energy.

(a) Atomic PES

The photoelectron spectra of inert gases argon, krypton and xenon, excited by the helium resonane radiation ($h\nu = 21.22$ eV), are the simplest spectra. In each case a two-line spectrum with roughly 2 : 1 intensity is obtained (Fig. 20.44). For argon, we have

$$Ar + h\nu \longrightarrow Ar^{+} + e^{-}$$

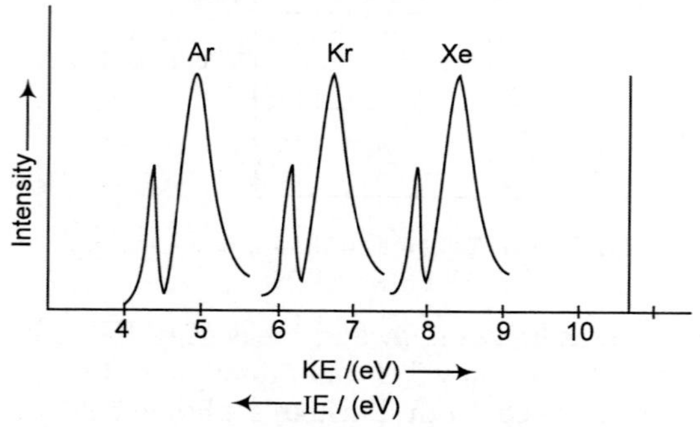

Fig. 20.44 Photoelectron spectra of Ar, Kr and Xe.

The term symbol of the ground state of Ar is $^1S_0$ while the term symbols of Ar^+ are $^2P_{1/2}$ and $^2P_{3/2}$. The two-line spectrum corresponds to the two transitions $^2P_{1/2} \leftarrow {}^1S_0$ and $^2P_{3/2} \leftarrow {}^1S_0$. For argon, KE = 5.40 eV (as shown in Fig. 20.44), so that IE = (21.22 – 5.40) eV = 15.82 eV.

(b) Molecular PES

The principle of molecular PES is similar to that of the atomic PES except that the PES spectrum is more complex showing vibrational structure. From the spectrum we can determine the ionization potential of the molecule.

Nuclear Quadrupole Resonance (NQR) Spectroscopy

NQR spectroscopy are observed in the solid state. They are observed in the radiofrequency region. All nuclei having integral and half integral spins $\left(I = 1, \frac{3}{2}, 2, \frac{5}{2}, 3, \frac{7}{2}, \text{etc.}\right)$ possess nuclear electric quadrupole moments, designated as eQ (or simply as Q), where, e is the electronic charge. Q is a measure of the deviation of nuclear charge from spherical symmetry; it is defined as

$$Q = \int \rho r^2 \,(3\cos^2\theta - 1)\, dr \qquad \ldots(103)$$

where, ρ is the nuclear charge density, r is the distance from the origin to the element dr and θ is the angle between r and the spin axis. The quadrupole moment Q(or eQ) interacts with electric field gradient (*EFG*), designated as q (or eq), created at the quadrupolar nucleus by the asymmetric charge distribution arising from the extranuclear electrons or the non-bonding electrons in the molecule of which the nucleus forms a part. **The product of eQ and eq, *i.e.*, e^2Qq is called nuclear quadrupole coupling constant, also sometimes designated as *QCC*.**

If is assumed that the nucleus is centred at the origin of an arbitrarily oriented coordinate system (x, y, z). The time-averaged electrostatic potential, V, is produced at the nucleus by all charges outside it. The electric field of all those charges is defined by

$$E = E_x\hat{\mathbf{i}} + E_Y\hat{\mathbf{j}} + E_z\hat{\mathbf{k}} \qquad \ldots(104)$$

where, $\hat{\mathbf{i}}, \hat{\mathbf{j}}, \hat{\mathbf{k}}$ are the unit vectors which specify the directions of the axes x, y and z, respectively. The components of the electric field are defined as

$$E_x = -\left(\frac{\partial V}{\partial X}\right)$$

$$E_y = -\left(\frac{\partial V}{\partial Y}\right)$$

$$E_z = -\left(\frac{\partial V}{\partial Z}\right)$$

The electric field gradient components are defined as

$$q_{xx} = \left(\frac{\partial E_X}{\partial X}\right) = \frac{\partial^2 V}{\partial X^2}$$

Similarly,

$$q_{yy} = \left(\frac{\partial^2 Y}{\partial Y^2}\right)$$

$$q_{zz} = \left(\frac{\partial^2 V}{\partial Z^2}\right)$$

Also,

$$q_{xy} = \left(\frac{\partial^2 V}{\partial X \partial Y}\right)$$

$$q_{yz} = \left(\frac{\partial^2 V}{\partial Y \partial Z}\right); \text{ etc.}$$

The nine electric field gradient components may be written as a 3 × 3 **matrix (or tensor)** :

$$\begin{bmatrix} q_{xx} & q_{xy} & q_{xz} \\ q_{yx} & q_{yy} & q_{yz} \\ q_{zx} & q_{zy} & q_{zz} \end{bmatrix} \quad ...(105)$$

They are found to be a **symmetric tensor** with $q_{ij} = q_{ji}$, so that

$$q_{xy} = q_{yx}\,;\; q_{xz} = q_{xz}\;;\; q_{yz} = q_{zy} \quad ...(106)$$

Hence, the *EFG* tensor given by Eq. 105 can be written as

$$\begin{bmatrix} q_{xx} & q_{xy} & q_{xz} \\ q_{xy} & q_{yy} & q_{yz} \\ q_{xz} & q_{yz} & q_{zz} \end{bmatrix} \quad ...(107)$$

The diagonal components of this tensor are known to obey the **Laplace equation.**

$$q_{xx} + q_{yy} + q_{zz} = 0 \quad ...(108)$$

ie.,
$$\frac{\partial^2 V}{\partial x^2} + \frac{\partial^2 V}{\partial y^2} + \frac{\partial^2 V}{\partial z^2} = 0$$

or
$$\nabla^2 V = 0$$

where,
$$\nabla^2 = \frac{\partial^2}{\partial x^2} + \frac{\partial^2}{\partial y^2} + \frac{\partial^2}{\partial z^2} \quad ...(109)$$

is the Laplacian operator. The four relations given by Eqs. 106 and 108 reduce the number of independent tensor components from nine to five. In general, it is convenient to choose a coordinate system (x, y, z) in which the **cross components,** q_{ij} are zero. Such a coordinate system is called **principle axis system** and the *EFG* components in this system are designated as q_{xx}, q_{yy}, q_{zz}. In the principal axis system we define

$$|q_{zz}| \geq |q_{yy}| \geq |q_{xx}| \quad ...(110)$$

The modulus sign | ... | stands for the absolute value of the components. The largest *EFG*, q_{zz} is in the z-direction and the smallest *EFG*, q_{xx} is in the x-direction. From Eq. 108 the sum of the *EFG* components is zero. It follows, therefore, that only two parameters are needed to specify the *EFG* tensor. An important quantity, the **asymmetry parameter,** η, is defined as

$$\eta = (q_{xx} - q_{yy})/q_{zz} \quad ...(111)$$

From Eqs. 108, 110 and 111 we see that the asymmetry parameter lies between 0 and 1, *i.e.*, $0 < \eta < 1$. When $\eta = 0$, we speak of a case of axial symmetry around the z-axis. In this case

$$q_{xx} = q_{yy} = -\frac{1}{2} q_{zz} \quad ...(112)$$

The *EFG* is said to be spherical if $q_{xx} = q_{yy} = q_{zz}$. In this case there is no interaction of the nuclear quadrupole moment, Q, with the electronic charge distribution. The *EFG* is said to be nonsymmetric if $q_{xx} \neq q_{yy} \neq q_{zz}$. The following points should be borne in mind about NQR spectroscopy :

1. It is observed for nuclei with $I \geq 1$. When $I < 1$, the nuclei do not possess eQ so that there is no nuclear quadrupole interaction with eq.
2. NQR is observed in the solid state. In the gaseous and the liquid state, because of very fast molecules collisions resulting in a fast tumbling motion, the axis of rotation changes continuously so that *EFG*, q, averages to zero. Thus, there is no NQR interaction.
3. The quantities e^2Qq, q and η are three most important quantities in NQR spectroscopy. η is a measure of the non-sysmmetry of the *EFG*.

With this digression on *EFG*, we are now ready to discuss the basic theory of NQR. the solution of the Schrodinger wave equation for a quadrupolar nucleus having both the integral and hall-integral spin $(I \geq 1)$ gives the following expression for NQR energy levels :

$$E_{m_I} = \frac{e^2 Qq}{4I(2I-1)}[3m_I^2 - I(I+1)]$$
$$= A(3m_I^2 - I(I+1)$$

where,
$$A = \frac{e^2 Qq}{4I(2I-1)} \quad ...(113)$$

Here, $m_I = -I, -I+1 ..., +I$; m_I is the component of the nuclear spin I along the axis of quantization, assumed to be the z-axis. The NQR energy level expression involves m_I^2 term; hence, the NQR energy levels are **doubly degenerate**. The selection rule for NQR transitions is $\Delta m_I = \pm 1$. Expression (113) holds for an **axially symmetric** EFG, *i.e.*, $\eta = 0$.

We shall consider that NQR spectra of the follownig nuclei, assuming that $\eta = 0$; ${}^{14}_{7}N(I = 1)$; ${}^{11}_{5}B\left(I = \frac{3}{2}\right)$; ${}^{35}_{17}Cl\left(I = \frac{3}{2}\right)$; the radioactive isotope ${}^{36}_{17}Cl^*(I = 2)$; ${}^{27}_{13}Al\left(I = \frac{5}{2}\right)$; ${}^{132}_{53}Cs\left(I = \frac{7}{2}\right)$.

1. ${}^{14}_{7}N : (I = 1)$, so that $m_I = -1, 0, 1$. But $m_I = -1$ and $m_I = +1$ levels are degenerate. Hence, $I \rightarrow 0, \pm 1$. Substituting these values of m_I in Eq. 113, we obtain $E_0 = -\left(\frac{2}{4}\right)e^2Qq$, $E_{\pm 1} = \left(\frac{1}{4}\right)e^2Qq$. The selection rule $\Delta m_1 = \pm 1$ gives only one NQR frequency (Fig. 20.45).

$$\nu(0 \to \pm 1) = (E_{\pm 1} - E_0)/h = \frac{3}{4}(e^2Qq/h) \quad \ldots(114)$$

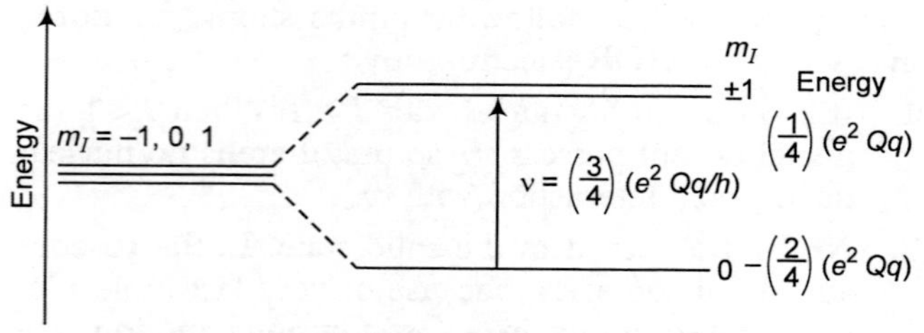

Fig. 20.45 NQR transition in $^{14}_{7}N$ nucleus ($\eta = 0$).

2. $^{11}_{5}B: I = \frac{3}{2}$ so that $m_I = -\frac{3}{2}, -\frac{1}{2}, \frac{1}{2}, \frac{3}{2}$. Because of the m_I^2 term in the energy expression, the NQR interaction splits the $I = \frac{3}{2}$ level into two doubly-degenerate pairs of sublevels, $m_I = \pm\frac{1}{2}$ and $m_I = \pm\frac{3}{2}$. Thus, $I = \frac{3}{2} \to \pm\frac{1}{2}, \pm\frac{3}{2}$. Substituting these values of m_I in Eq. 113 we obtain $E_{\pm\frac{1}{2}} = -\left(\frac{1}{4}\right)(e^2Qq)$ and $E_{\pm\frac{3}{2}} = \left(\frac{1}{4}\right)(e^2Qq)$. The selection rule $\Delta m_I = \pm 1$ gives only one NQR frequency (Fig. 20.46).

$$\nu\left(\pm\frac{1}{2} \longleftrightarrow \pm\frac{3}{2}\right) = (E_{\pm 3/2} - E_{\pm 1/2})/h$$

$$= \left(\frac{1}{2}\right)(e^2Qq/h) \quad \ldots(115)$$

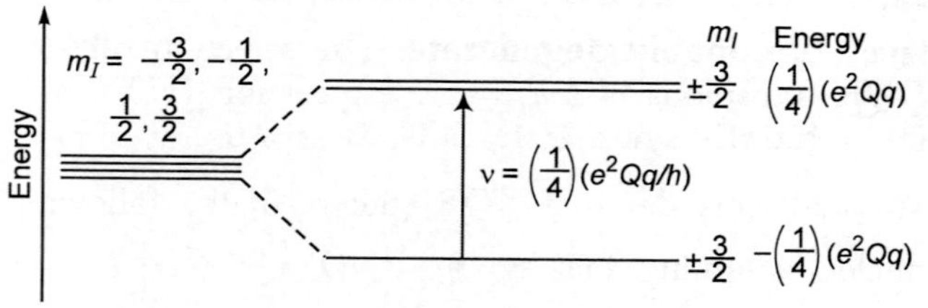

Fig. 20.46 NQR transition in $^{11}_{5}B$ nucleus ($\eta = 0$).

3. $^{35}_{17}Cl: I = \frac{3}{2}$. The frequency is the same as in part (2) above.

4. $^{36}_{17}Cl^*: I = 2$. The NQR interaction gives the following pairs of energy sublevels : $m_I = 0, \pm 1, \pm 2$. (The $m_I = 0$ sublevel is non-degenerate).

$$E_0 = -\left(\frac{1}{4}\right)(e^2Qq)$$

$$E_{\pm 1} = -\left(\frac{1}{8}\right)(e^2Qq)$$

$$E_{\pm 2} = \left(\frac{1}{4}\right)(e^2Qq)$$

The selection rule $\Delta m_I = \pm 1$ gives two NQR frequencies (Fig. 20.47)

$$\nu_1\ (0 \longleftrightarrow \pm 1) = (E_1 - E_0)/h = \left(\frac{1}{8}\right)(e^2Qq/h) \quad \ldots(116)$$

$$\nu_2(\pm 1 \longleftrightarrow \pm 2) = (E_{\pm 2} - E_{\pm 1})/h = \left(\frac{3}{8}\right)(e^2Qq/h)$$

We see that $\nu_1 : \nu_2 = 1 : 3$.

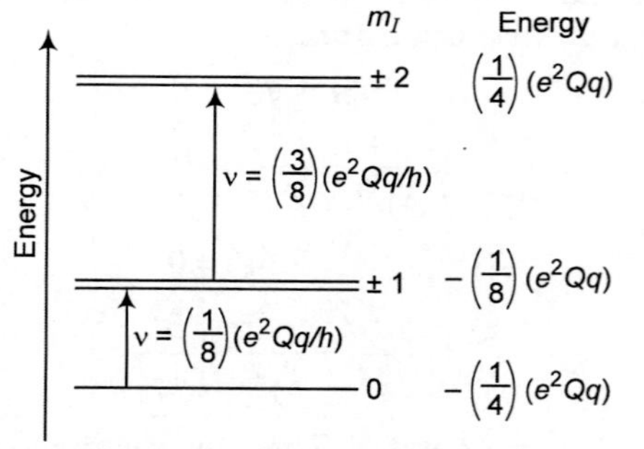

Fig. 20.47 NQR transition in $^{36}_{17}Cl^*$ nucleus ($\eta = 0$).

5. $^{27}_{13}Al: I = \frac{5}{2}$. The NQR interaction gives the following pairs of degenerate energy sublevels : $m_I = \pm\frac{5}{2}, \pm\frac{3}{2}, \pm\frac{1}{2}$.

Substituting these values of m_I in Eq. 113 we obtain

$$E_{\pm\frac{1}{2}} = \left(-\frac{1}{5}\right)(e^2Qq)$$

$$E_{\pm\frac{3}{2}} = -\left(\frac{1}{20}\right)(e^2Qq)$$

$$E_{\pm\frac{5}{2}} = \left(\frac{1}{4}\right)(e^2Qq)$$

The selection rule $\Delta m_I = \pm 1$ gives two frequencies (Fig. 20.48)

$$\nu_1\left(\pm\frac{1}{2} \longleftrightarrow \pm\frac{3}{2}\right) = (E_{\pm 3/2} - E_{\pm 1/2})/h$$

$$= \left(\frac{3}{20}\right)(e^2Qq/h)$$

$$\nu_2\left(\pm\frac{3}{2} \longleftrightarrow \pm\frac{5}{2}\right) = (E_{\pm 5/2} - E_{\pm 3/2})/h$$

$$= \left(\frac{6}{20}\right)(e^2Qq/h)$$

We see that $\nu_1 : \nu_2 = 1 : 2$.

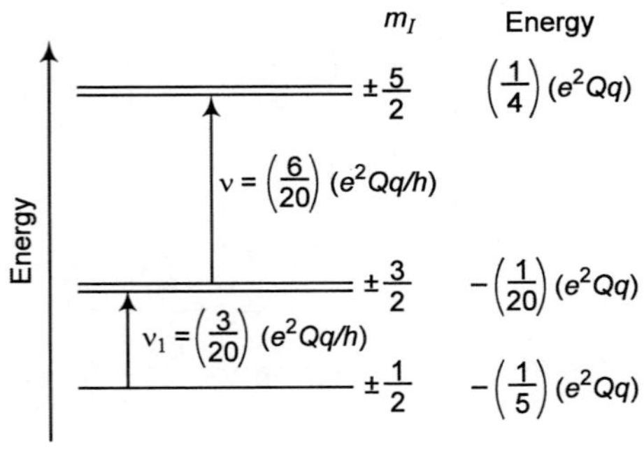

Fig. 20.48 NQR transitions in $^{27}_{13}Al$ ($\eta = 0$)

6. $^{133}_{53}Cs$: $I = \frac{7}{2}$. The NQR interaction gives the following pairs of degenerate energy sublevels : $m_I = \pm\frac{7}{2}, \pm\frac{5}{2}, \pm\frac{3}{2}, \pm\frac{1}{2}$.

$$E_{\pm 7/2} = \left(\frac{1}{4}\right)(e^2Qq) = \left(\frac{21}{84}\right)e^2Qq$$

$$E_{\pm 5/2} = \left(\frac{3}{84}\right)(e^2Qq)$$

$$E_{\pm 3/2} = -\left(\frac{9}{84}\right)(e^2Qq)$$

$$E_{\pm 1/2} = -\left(\frac{15}{84}\right)(e^2Qq)$$

The selection rule : $\Delta m_I = \pm 1$ gives three frequencies (Fig. 20.49)

$$\left.\begin{aligned}
\nu_1\left(\pm\frac{1}{2} \longleftrightarrow \pm\frac{3}{2}\right) &= (E_{\pm 3/2} - E_{\pm 1/2})/h \\
&= \left(\frac{6}{84}\right)(e^2Qq/h) \\
\nu_2\left(\pm\frac{3}{2} \longleftrightarrow \pm\frac{5}{2}\right) &= (E_{\pm 5/2} - E_{\pm 3/2})/h \\
&= \left(\frac{12}{84}\right)(e^2Qq/h) \\
\nu_3\left(\pm\frac{5}{2} \longleftrightarrow \pm\frac{7}{2}\right) &= (E_{\pm 7/2} - E_{\pm 5/2})/h \\
&= \left(\frac{18}{84}\right)(e^2Qq/h)
\end{aligned}\right\} \quad \ldots(117)$$

We see that $\nu_1 : \nu_2 : \nu_3 = 1 : 2 : 3$.

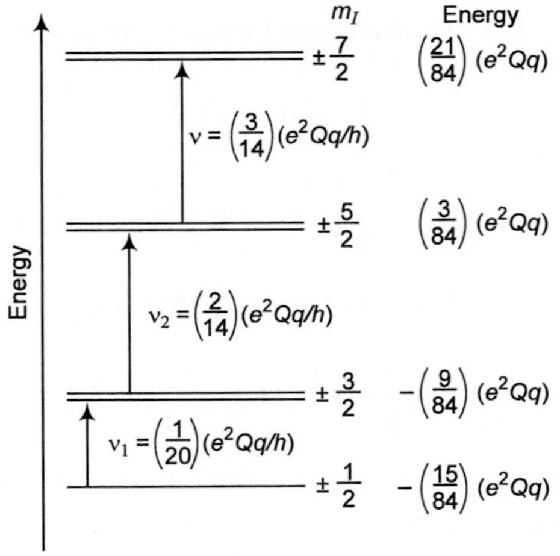

Fig. 20.49 NQR transitions in ^{133}Cs ($\eta = 0$).

NQR spectra when *EFG* is not axially symmetric, *i.e.*, $\eta \neq 0$ The NQR spectra in the presence of non-axially symmetric *EFG* are very complex. The NQR energy level expression contains terms involving η and power of η. For instance, for $I = 1$, the energy levels are given by

$$E_0 = -\frac{1}{2}(e^2Qq)$$

and

$$E_1 = \frac{1}{2}(e^2Qq)(1 \pm \eta)$$

The Bohr frequency condition and the selection rule $\Delta m_I = \pm 1$ gives the following two NQR frequencies (Fig. 20.50).

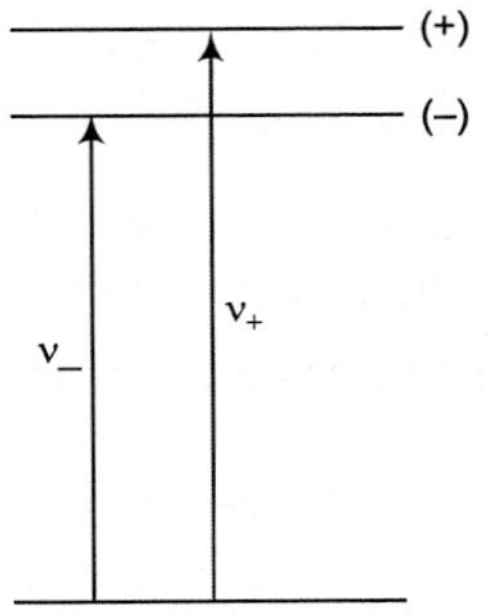

Fig. 20.50 NQR transitions for $I = 1$ ($\eta \neq 0$).

$$\left.\begin{aligned}
\nu_+ \,(0 \rightarrow +1) &= \frac{3}{4}(e^2Qq/h)\left(1 + \frac{1}{3}\eta\right) \\
\nu_- \,(0 \rightarrow -1) &= \frac{3}{4}(e^2Qq/h)\left(1 - \frac{1}{3}\eta\right)
\end{aligned}\right\} \quad \ldots(118)$$

They are separated by an amount, Δv, given by $\Delta v = \frac{1}{2}(e^2Qq/h)\eta$. Thus, experimental measurement of the two frequencies yields the value of both e^2Qq and η.

For $I = \frac{3}{2}$, the two doubly degenerate energy levels are

$$E_{\pm 1/2} = -\frac{1}{4}(e^2Qq)\left(1+\frac{1}{3}\eta^2\right)^{1/2}$$

$$E_{\pm 3/2} = +\frac{1}{4}(e^2Qq)\left(1+\frac{1}{3}\eta^2\right)^{1/2}$$

The selection rule $\Delta m_I = \pm 1$ gives only one NQR frequency

$$\nu\left(\pm\frac{1}{2} \longleftrightarrow \pm\frac{3}{2}\right) = \frac{1}{2}(e^2Qq/h)\left(1+\frac{1}{3}\eta^2\right)^{1/2}$$

Since, this eqution contains two unknowns, e^2Qq and η, measurement of the NQR frequency does not permit them to be determined separately. If, however, from structural considerations η is known to be very small, it can be neglected and e^2Qq determined with sufficient accuracy. When $\eta > 0.3$, the frequency expressions for $I = \frac{5}{2}, \frac{7}{2}, \frac{9}{2}$, etc., cannot be rigorously applied. Also, when $I \geq \frac{5}{2}$ we get two or more frequencies the measurement of which can yield both e^2Qq and η. When η is large, it is possible to observe some of the forbidden transitions ($\Delta m_I =$`$+-2$), in addition to the strongly allowed transitions ($\Delta m_I = \pm 1$).

Zeeman Effect in NQR Spectra

The determination of both e^2Qq and η for the special case of $I = \frac{3}{2}$, which yields only one NQR frequency, can be done by using Zeeman effect. The applied magnetic (Zeeman) field removes the degeneracy of the $\pm\frac{1}{2}$ and $\pm\frac{3}{2}$ energy sublevels. It is theoretically found that whereas the $-\frac{3}{2}$ sublevel is raised in energy and the $+\frac{3}{2}$ sublevel is lowered, exactly similar splitting does not occur for the doubly degenerate sublevels $\pm\frac{1}{2}$. There occurs considerably **mixing of state** so that the $+\frac{1}{2}$ sublevel partakes of some character of $-\frac{1}{2}$ sublevel and *vice-versa*. The resulting sublevels are designated as + and –, respectively. The Zeeman splitting for the case $I = \frac{3}{2}$ is shown schematically in Fig. 20.51.

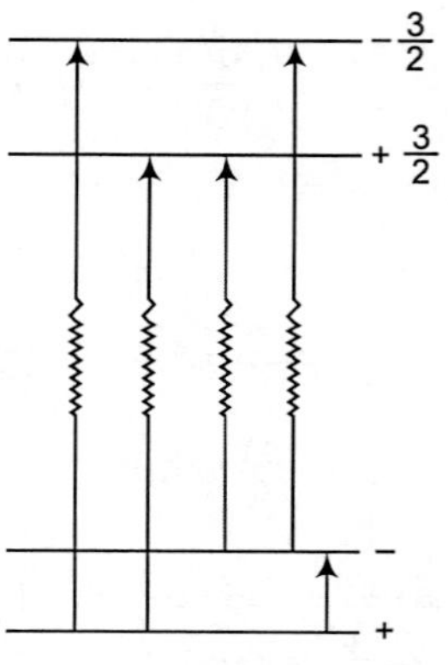

Fig. 20.51 Zeeman splitting for $I = \frac{3}{2}$ ($\eta \neq 0$).

The application of radiofrequency (*r.f.*) field brings about transitions between the different sublevels. The $+ \rightarrow -$ transition, shown by the dotted arrow, is of no interest since, it involves a frequency much smaller than the NQR frequency. When the Zeeman field is of the order of 0.01 T, as is the case with several nuclei of chemical interest, this frequency is of the order of 0.1 MHz (or even less). This $+ \rightarrow -$ frequency between the mixed states $\psi_\pm$ corresponds to the selection rule $\Delta|m_I| = 0$. The $\Delta|m_I| = 0$ transition, $\pm\frac{3}{2} \longleftrightarrow -\frac{3}{2}$, not shown in Fig. 20.50, too, is of no interest. The $\Delta|m_I| = \pm 1$ transitions between the mixed states $\psi_\pm$ and the $\psi_{\pm\frac{3}{2}}$ states give rise to the following four frequencies :

$$\nu_\alpha \equiv \nu\left(+\longrightarrow +\frac{3}{2}\right);\ \nu_{\alpha'} \equiv \nu\left(-\longrightarrow +\frac{3}{2}\right)$$

$$\nu_\beta \equiv \nu\left(+\longrightarrow -\frac{3}{2}\right);\ \nu_{\beta'} \equiv \nu\left(-\longrightarrow -\frac{3}{2}\right) \quad \ldots(119)$$

The four frequencies are symmetric about the pure NQR frequency, ν_Q. The inner pair of lines ν_α and

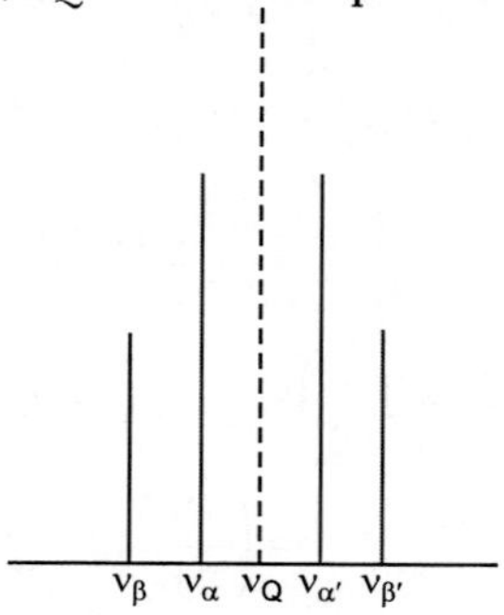

Fig. 20.51 The four frequencies for $I = \frac{3}{2}$ in the presence of Zeeman field.

$\nu_{\alpha'}$ has equal intensity. Likewise, the outer pair of lines ν_β and $\nu_{\beta'}$ has equal intensity. However, the α, α'-pair is more intense than the β, β'-pair (Fig. 20.51).

For a given orientation of the Zeeman field, both pairs of components α, α' and β, β' have maximum intensity when the *r.f.* field is perpendicular to the symmetry axis of the *EFG* tensor. Also, the intensity of the two pairs depends upon the orientation of the Zeeman field. Omitting the details of intensity of the spectral lines, suffice it to say that from the Zeeman study the two unknowns e^2Qq and η can be determined from the four known frequencies.

Mass Spectrometry (MS)

Mass spectrometry is the most accurate method for determining the molecular mass of the compound and its elemental composition. In this technique, molecules are bombarded with a beam of energetic electrons. The molecules are ionised and broken up into many fragments, some of which are positive ions. Each kind of ion has a particular ratio of mass to charge, *i.e., m/e* ratio (value). For most ions, the charge is one and thus, *m /e* ratio is simply the molecular mass of the ion.

Thus, for Neopentane

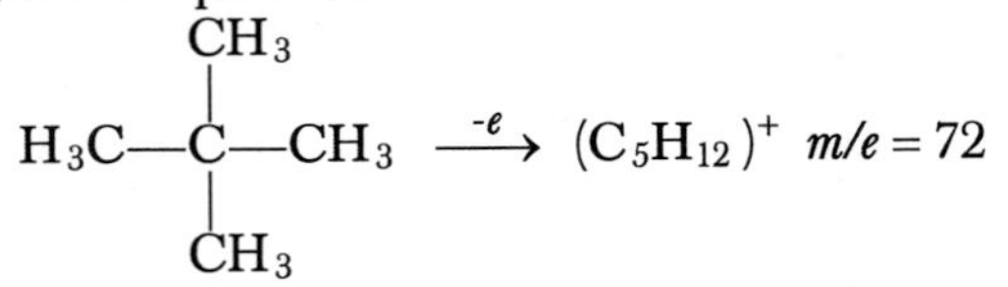

Molecular ion

Fragmentation

	$C_4H_9^+$	$C_3H_5^+$	$C_2H_5^+$	$C_2H_3^+$
	57	41	29	27
Relative intensity	100	41.5	38.5	15.7

The molecular ion (here $C_5H_{12}^+$) is called parent ion and is usually designated as M^+. It is positively charged molecule with an unpaired electron.

The set of ions (fragment ions or daughter ions) are analysed in such a way that a signal is obtained for each value of *m/e* that is represented. The intensity of each signal represents the relative abundance of the ion producing the signal. The largest peak in the structure is called the **base peak** and its intensity is taken as 100. The intensities of other peaks are represented relative to the base peak.

Neutral particles, produced in the process of fragmentation (whether neutral molecules or radicals) cannot be detected in the mass spectrometer.

Mass Spectrum

It is a record of the masses and the relative abundances of the molecular ion and the positively charged fragments formed from it by the electron bombardment. The *m/e* ratios are taken along the abscissa while the relative abundances are taken along the ordinate. Base peak is the highest peak or the most intense peak in the spectrum. Relative abundance of an ion means the percentage of the total ion current.

The mass spectrum of neopentane is known as follows.

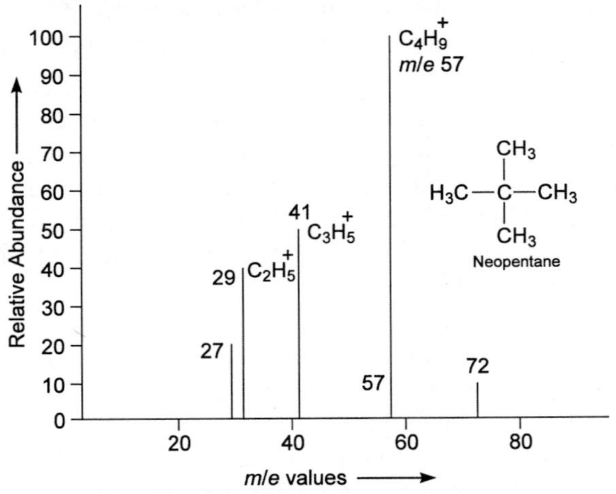

Fig. 20.52 Mass spectrum of neopentane.

Some important features of the parent ion peak are as follows :

(a) The molecular ion peak in aromatic compounds is relatively much intense due to the presence of π-electron system.

(b) Conjugated olefines show more intense molecular ion peak as compared to the corresponding non-conjugated olefines with the same number of unsaturation. Conjugated olefines are more stable than the corresponding non-conjugated olefines.

(c) Unsaturated compounds give more intense peak as compared to the saturated or the cyclic molecule.

(d) The relative abundance of the saturated hydrocarbon is more than the corresponding branched chain compound with the same number of carbon atoms. For example, the molecular ion peak for *n*-pentane is more intense than that of neopentane.

(e) The substituent groups like —OH, —OR, —NH_2, etc., which lower the ionisation potential increase the relative abundance in case of aromatic compounds. Also the groups like —NO_2, —CN, etc., which increase the ionisation potential, decrease the relative abundance of the aromatic compounds.

(f) Absence of molecular ion peak in the mass spectrum means that the compound under examination is highly branched or tertiary alcohols. Primary and secondary alcohols give very small molecular ion peaks.

(g) In case of chloro or bromo compounds, isotope peaks are also formed alongwith the molecular ion peak. In case of bromo compounds, M^+ and $(M^+ + 2)$ peaks are formed in the intensity ratio 1 : 1. In case of chloro compounds, M^+ and $(M^+ + 2)$ peaks are formed in the intensity ratio 1 : 3.

Important Nitrogen containing compounds with an odd number of nitrogen atoms in the molecule must have an odd molecular mass. An even number of nitrogen atoms or absence of nitrogen atoms in the compound show that the molecular mass of the compound must be even.

In some cases, a McLafferty rearrangement ion peak gives an important clue in the determination of molecular formula of the compound. For example, all straight chain aldehydes containing a γ-hydrogen atom form a base peak at *m/e* 44 (McLafferty rearrangement ion peak). Also in aldehydes a fairly abundant M^+ peak (parent peak) follows a less abundant $(M^+ - 1)$ peak.

Let us consider a simple mass spectrum having *m/e* values at 72, 71, 44 (100%), 43, 29, etc.

McLafferty rearrangement

It involves the migration of γ-hydrogen atom followed by the cleavage of a β-bond. The rearrangement leads to the elimination of neutral molecules from aldehydes, ketones, amines, unsaturated compounds, substituted aromatic compounds, etc. The rearrangement proceeds through a sterically hindered six membered transition state. Consider a general compound (ketone).

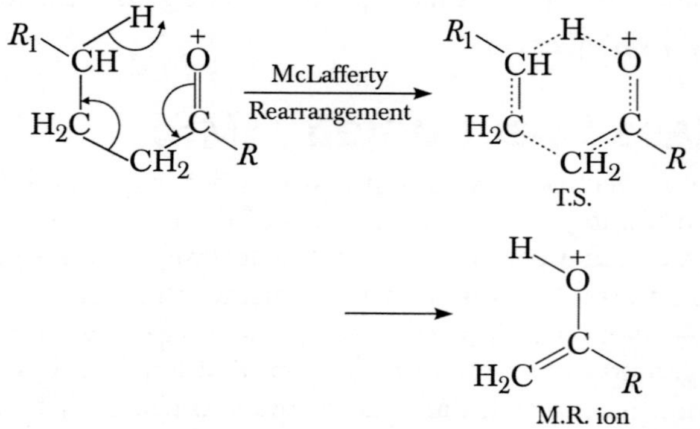

M.R. ion

Butanal contains a γ-hydrogen atom. The McLafferty rearrangement ion formed in this case is shown below :

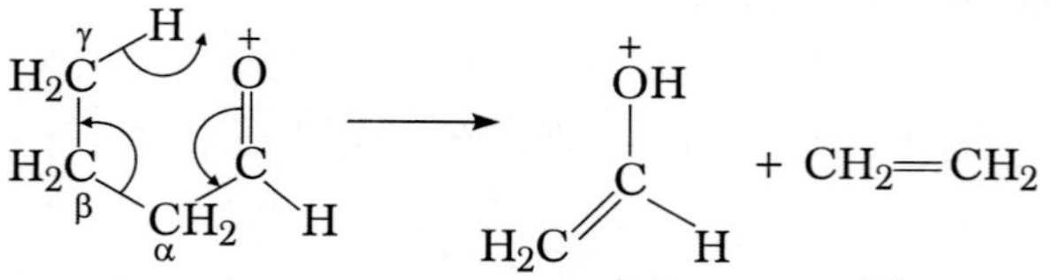

Butanal | *m/e* 44 (MR ion) | Ethene (neutral molecule)

Exercise 1
(For Part 'B')

1. The Mossbauer spectra of $K_4[Fe(CN)_6]$ and $K_3[Fe(CN)_3NO]$ consists of, respectively
(a) 1 line each (b) 2 lines each
(c) 1 and 2 lines (d) 2 and 4 lines

2. The ESR spectrum of anthracene radical anion consists of
(a) 25 lines (b) 50 lines
(c) 75 lines (d) 100 lines

3. Intensity of a spectral line is proportional to
(a) $|<\psi_n|\mu|\psi_m>|^4$ (b) $|<\psi_n|\mu|\psi_m>|^2$
(c) $<|\psi_n|\mu|\psi_m>$ (d) $|<\psi_n|\mu|\psi_m>|^{3/2}$
Where $<|\psi_n|\mu|\psi_m>$ is the transition moment integral of the electric dipole moment μ between the eigen function states ψ_n and ψ_m.

4. The electrons which contribute to isomer shift in Mossbauer spectroscopy are
(a) *s*-electrons (b) *p*-electrons
(c) *d*-electrons (d) *f*-electrons

5. In Raman spectroscopy, using mercury vapour lamp
(a) the stokes line is more intense than the anti-stokes line
(b) the anti-stokes line is more intense than the stokes line
(c) the stokes and anti-stokes lines are equally intense
(d) None of the above

6. The ESR spectrum of CD_3 free-radical (the nuclear spin of $^2D=1$) consists of
(a) four lines
(b) 1 : 2 : 3 : 2 : 1 quintet
(c) 1 : 6 : 15 : 20 : 15 : 6 : 1 septet
(d) 1 : 3 : 6 : 7 : 6 : 3 : 1 septet

7. If force constant, *k*, of a diatomic SHO is equal to
(a) $4\pi^2c^2\,\bar{v}\,\mu^2$ (b) $4\pi^2c^2\bar{v}^2\mu$
(c) $4\pi^2c\nu^2\mu$ (d) None of these

8. The molecule which is IR-inactive but Raman-active is
(a) N_2 (b) HCl
(c) SO_2 (d) protein

9. The difference between the incident and scattered frequencies in the Raman spectrum is called the
(a) Stokes line (b) Anti-Stokes line
(c) Raman frequency (d) *P*-branch

10. Number of translational, rotational and vibrational degrees of freedom in CO_2 are, respectively
(a) 2, 3, 4 (b) 4, 3, 2
(c) 3, 2, 4 (d) 4, 2, 3

11. ESR spectra are observed in .... region.
(a) microwave (b) radiofrequency
(c) X-ray (d) UV/VIZ

12. Both NMR and NQR spectra are observed in .... region.
(a) microwave (b) radiofrequency
(c) X-ray (d) UV/VIZ

13. Raman effect is
(a) elastic scattering of light
(b) inelastic scattering of light
(c) emission of light
(d) absorption of light

14. Mossbauer and NQR spectra are observed in
(a) solid state (b) liquid state
(c) gaseous state (d) liquid crystalline state

15. The ESR spectrum of *p*-benzosemiquinone radical anion consists of a
(a) 1 : 2 : 3 : 2 : 1 quintet
(b) 1 : 3 : 3 : 1 quartet
(c) 1 : 4 : 6 : 4 : 1 quintet
(d) equally intense quintet

16. The ESR spectrum of naphthalene radical anion consists of :
(a) 15 lines (b) 25 lines
(c) 30 lines (d) 40 lines

17. The photon of wavelength 400 nm corresponds to
(a) $20000\ cm^{-1}$ (b) $25000\ cm^{-1}$
(c) $40000\ cm^{-1}$ (d) $50000\ cm^{-1}$

18. In the Born-Oppenheimer approximation
(a) $E_{el} > E_{vib} > E_{rot} > E_{tr}$ (b) $E_{fr} > E_{rot} > E_{vib} > E_{el}$
(c) $E_{vib} > E_{tr} > E_{rot} > E_{el}$ (d) $E_{el} > E_{rot} > E_{tr} > E_{vib}$

19. Zero point energy of diatomic SHO of vibrational frequency ν is
(a) $h\nu$ (b) $\frac{1}{2}h\nu$ (c) $\frac{1}{4}h\nu$ (d) $\frac{2}{3}h\nu$

20. The relation between D_e and D_0, the two dissociation energies, of an SHO is
(a) $D_e = D_0 + \frac{h\nu}{2}$ (b) $D_e = D_0 + 2h\nu$
(c) $D_e = D_0 + h\nu$ (d) $D_0 = D_e + \frac{h\nu}{2}$

21. The compound DPPH, used for calibrating ESR sectra, shows ESR spectrum consisting of a
(a) 1 : 4 : 6 : 4 : 1 quintet
(b) 1 : 3 : 3 : 1 quartet
(c) 1 : 2 : 3 : 2 : 1 quintet
(d) equally intense quartet

22. The *pmr* spectrum of BH_4^- (with nuclear spin of ^{11}B equal to 3/2) is
(a) *a* 1 : 3 : 3 : 1 quartet
(b) *a* 1 : 4 : 6 : 4 : 1 quntet
(c) *a* 1 : 2 : 3 : 2 : 1 quintet
(d) an equally intense quartet

23. The ^{31}P-nmr spectrum of PH_4^+ consists of
(a) *a* 1 : 3 : 3 : 1 quartet
(b) *a* 1 : 4 : 6 : 4 : 1 quintet
(c) a triplet
(d) an equally intense quintet

24. A compound shows a *pmr* peak at 240 Hz downfield from the TMS peak in a spectrometer operating at 60 MHz. The chemical shift (in ppm) is
(a) 1 (b) 2 (c) 3 (d) 4

25. The rotational (microwave) spectrum of a rigid diatomic rotor consists of equally spaced lines with spacing equal to
(a) B (b) $\frac{B}{2}$ (c) $\frac{3B}{2}$ (d) $2B$
(where, B is the rotational constant)

26. The vibrational rotational spectrum is observed in .... region.
(a) near infrared (b) microwave region
(c) visible region (d) radiofrequency region

27. When the oscillating molecule is in its lowest vibrational level, its energy is equal to $\frac{1}{2}k\nu_0$ and is called ....
(a) zero point energy (b) rotational energy
(c) electronic energy (d) vibrational energy

28. In the Raman spectrum, the lines scattering at right angles with frequencies lower than the original are called .... while those with higher frequencies are called .... lines.
(a) Stoke, anti-stoke (b) anti-stoke, Stoke
(c) Stoke, *p*-branch (d) *p*-branch, Stoke

29. In a rotational spectrum, transitions are only observed between rotational levels of ΔJ =......
(a) ± 1 (b) ± 2 (c) $\pm \frac{1}{2}$ (d) ± 3

30. Vibrational transitions are always accompanied by .... transitions.
(a) vibrational (b) rotational
(c) electronic (d) None of these

31. Raman frequency is .... the frequency of incident light and is characteristic only of the substance exposed to the incident light.
(a) lower than (b) higher than
(c) equal to (d) independent of

32. Which of the following statement(s) is/are correct?
(a) In the Raman spectrum the stokes lines have higher frequencies than the antistokes lines
(b) Electronic band spectra are observed in visible and UV regions
(c) The spectral lines in rotational spectra are equally spaced with spacing equal to $\frac{q}{8\pi^2 IC}$
(d) In a polyatomic linear molecule with N atoms, there are $3N-6$ normal modes of vibration

33. Choose the correct alternative in the following :
(a) electronic excitation
(b) increase in potential energy
(c) increase in vibration
(d) decrease in rotational energy

34. Reversal of electron spin absorption spectrum in radio frequency is due to
(a) parallel spin of nuclei
(b) nuclear spin
(c) reversal of electron spin
(d) ncrease in rotational energy

35. The increase in rotational energy shows absorption spectrum in
(a) IR region (b) UV region
(c) visible region (d) microwave region

36. The frequency of UV radiation is greater than
(a) IR radiation (b) microwaves
(c) Both (a) and (b) (d) None of these

37. The increase in vibrational energy leads to absorption spectrum in
(a) microwave region (b) visible region
(c) IR region (d) UV region

38. The frequency of UV radiation is greater than
(a) microwaves (b) IR radiation
(c) Both (a) and (b) (d) None of these

39. State which of the following molecules can show a pure rotational microwave spectrum.
(a) N_2 (b) CO_2
(c) OCS (d) HCl

40. Which of the following molecules may show absorption in the infrared?
(a) N_2 (b) H_2
(c) Cl_2 (d) $CH_3 \cdot CH_3$

41. Which of the following diatomic molecules will not give a rotational spectrum?
(a) N_2 (b) CO
(c) NO (d) HF

42. The selection rule of the translational energy levels in the Raman spectrum is
(a) $\Delta J = \pm 1$ (b) ± 2
(c) $+1$ (d) $+2$

43. The population (N) distribution over states (n) of a diatomic molecule corresponds to

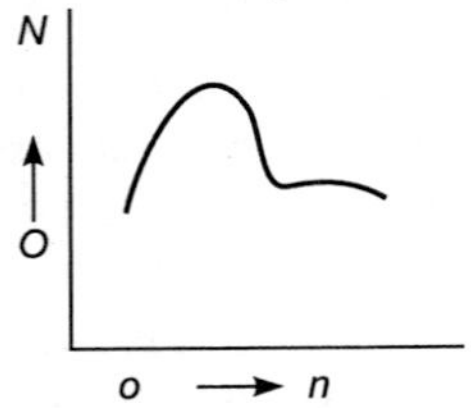

(a) translation (b) rotation
(c) vibration (d) electronic

44. Which one of the complex will exhibit lowest energy electronic absorption band?
(a) $[NiCl_4]^{2-}$ (b) $[Ni(H_2O)_6]^{2+}$
(c) $[Ni(CN)_4]^{2-}$ (d) $Ni(CO)_4$

45. Among the following diatomic molecules, which one will show EPR signal?
(a) Li_2 (b) B_2 (c) C_2 (d) N_2

46. $\sigma \to \overset{*}{\sigma}$ transition λ lies in
(a) IR region (b) visible region
(c) UV region (d) None of these

47. What is the main factor on which chemical shift depends in Mossbauer spectra?
(a) Electron density (b) Transition energy
(c) Intensity of light (d) All of these

Exercise 2
(For Part 'C')

1. The expected position of the λ_{max} in the following trienones is

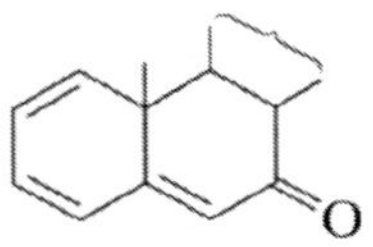

(a) 244 nm (b) 349 nm (c) 305 nm (d) 360 nm

2. The frequency shift of the carbonyl absorption in the cyclohexane carboxaldehyde is
(a) 1700 cm^{-1} (b) 1835 cm^{-1}
(c) 1730 cm^{-1} (d) 1600 cm^{-1}

3. The frequency shift of the carbonyl absorption in the salicylaldehyde is
(a) 1600 cm^{-1} (b) 1700 cm^{-1}
(c) 1750 cm^{-1} (d) 1666 cm^{-1}

4. Which of the compounds I and II is expected to have a lower C=O stretching frequency?

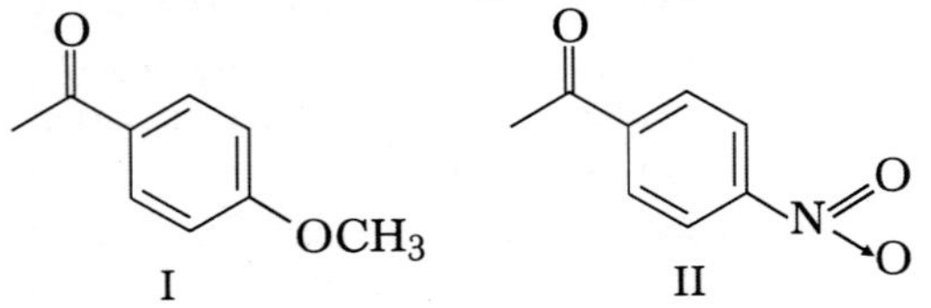

I II

(a) I
(b) II
(c) both have equal frequency
(d) Nothing can be said

5. The rotational spectrum of HI is found to contain a series of lines with a separation of 12.8 cm^{-1}. Moment of for the molecule is
(a) 4.36×10^{-40} g cm^2 (b) 1.13×10^{-39} g cm^2
(c) 2.23×10^{-40} g cm^2 (d) 8.72×10^{-40} g cm^2

6. In the Q. 5, the internuclear distance is
(a) 1.45 Å (b) 1.62 Å
(c) 2.64 Å (d) 1.13 Å

7. The bond length in CN^+ is 0.129 nm. The position of second line in the microwave spectrum is
(a) 6.264 cm^{-1} (b) 3.132 cm^{-1}
(c) 9.396 cm^{-1} (d) 12.528 cm^{-1}

8. Carbon monoxide, in an inert solvent, absorbs radiation at a wavelength of 4.68 μ. Find the force constant for the molecule
(a) 1.138×10^6 dyne cm^{-1} (b) 0.641×10^8dyne cm^{-1}
(c) 18.5×10^5 dyne cm^{-1} (d) 2.451×10^5 dyne cm^{-1}

9. Among the singlet (S), doublet (D) and triplet (T) electronic states, phosphorescence involves transition between
(a) $S \to S$ (b) $D \to D$
(c) $T \to S$ (d) $S \to T$

10. For pure vibrational spectra, the selection rule is
(a) 0 (b) ± 1
(c) 0, ± 1 (d) ± 1, 2

11. The molar absorbancy index ε of a solute is 44000 L mol^{-1} cm^{-1}. The absorption cross-section σ is
(a) 1.7×10^{-20} (b) 8.56×10^{-21}
(c) 1.252×10^{-19} (d) 0.855×10^{-21}

12. The value of the nuclear magneton is
(a) 50.50×10^{-25} JT^{-1} (b) 50.50×10^{-26} JT^{-1}
(c) 50.50×10^{-28} JT^{-1} (d) 5.050×10^{-28} JT^{-1}

13. The percentage transmittance of an aqueous solution of disodium fumarate at 250 nm and 25°C in 19.2% for a 5×10^{-4} mol L^{-1} solution in a 1 cm cell. The molar absorption coefficient, ε is
(a) 1.43×10^5 L mol^{-1} cm^{-1}
(b) 1.42×10^{-5} L mol^{-1} cm^{-1}
(c) 1.43×10^{-3} L mol^{-1} cm^{-1}
(d) 1.43×10^3 L mol^{-1} cm^{-1}

14. The length of the π-bond system is about 0.95 nm. The lowest absorption frequency for octatetraene (C_8H_{10}) that contain a series of four conjugated double bond is
(a) 15100 cm^{-1} (b) 30200 cm^{-1}
(c) 12800 cm^{-1} (d) 7550 cm^{-1}

15. The J_{max} for a rigid diatomic molecule for which at 300 K, the rotational constant is 1.566 cm^{-1}, is
(a) 4 (b) 6
(c) 8 (d) 10

16. The internuclear distance for $H^{35}Cl$ is 0.13 nm and the force constant is 500 Nm^{-1}. The first excitation energy in cm^{-1} of $H^{35}Cl$ molecule in the harmonic approximation is
(a) 5802 cm^{-1} (b) 1259 cm^{-1}
(c) 2259 cm^{-1} (d) 2951 cm^{-1}

17. The NMR frequency (in MHz) of the proton in a magnetic field of intensity 1.4092 tesla is (given $g_N = 5.585$ and $\mu_N = 5.05 \times 10^{-27}$ JT^{-1})
(a) 60 (b) 30
(c) 120 (d) 90

18. The g value for the benzene radical anion is 2.0025. At what field would you search for resonance in a spectrometer operating at 9.302 GHz?
(a) 0.432 T (b) 0.332 T
(c) 0.872 T (d) 0.243 T

19. Magnetic moment of phosphorus-31 is $1.1305\,\mu_N$. Its magnetogyric ratio is
(Given, $\mu_N = 5.05 \times 10^{-27}$ JT^{-1} and nuclear spin of ^{31}P is 1/2)
(a) 1.98×10^{12} $T^{-1}s^{-1}$ (b) 1.08×10^8 $T^{-1}s$
(c) 1.98×10 Ts^{-1} (d) 1.08×10^8 $T^{-1}s^{-1}$

20. In the above question, the g factor is
(a) 1.39 (b) 2.3
(c) 4.2 (d) 0.59

21. The normal modes of vibrations of N_2O is
(a) 1 (b) 3
(c) 4 (d) 7

22. The fundamental vibration frequency and rotational constant of carbon monoxide molecule are 6.5×10^{13} s^{-1} and 1.743×10^{11} s^{-1} respectively. The rotational quantum number, for which the CO molecule will have the same energy as it would have in its first vibrational state with no rotation energy is
(a) 10 (b) 9 (c) 19 (d) 25

23. Calculate the frequency at which the transition between the two spin states of a free electron may be observed at a field strength of 0.3000 T.
(a) 8.4×10^9 s^{-1} (b) 5.39×10^8 s^{-1}
(c) 4.82×10^6 s^{-1} (d) 1.93×10^{10} s^{-1}

24. A series of rotational lines are measured in the far IR region. The intensity of the fifth line is 6.38 times the intensity of second rotational line. What is the temperature of the sample? (B = 55.35 GHz)
(a) 273 K (b) 22°C
(c) −22°C (d) −273 K

25. For the selection rules $\Delta n = 1, 2, 3, 4, \ldots$, $\Delta l = \pm 1$, consider the following transitions :
I. $1s \rightarrow 2p$
II. $2s \rightarrow 3s$
III. $2p \rightarrow 3s$
IV. $3p \rightarrow 3d$
The allowed transitions are
(a) I, II and IV (b) I, II and III
(c) I, III and IV (d) I, II, III and IV

26. Mossbauer effect will occur when
I. The γ-ray energy is small
II. The temperature of the crystal source is small
III. The Debye temperature of the crystallatic is high
The correct answer is
(a) I and II (b) II and III
(c) I and III (d) I, II and III

27. The pure rotational (microwave) spectrum of the gaseous molecule CN consists of a series of equally spaced lines separated by 3.7978 cm^{-1}. The internuclear distance of the molecule is [Molar masses are $^{12}C = 12.011$ and $^{14}N = 14.007$ g mol^{-1}]
(a) 130 pm (b) 117 pm
(c) 150 pm (d) 93 pm

28. Which sets of the following nuclei do not show nuclear magnetic resonance?
^1H, ^2H, ^{12}C, ^{13}C, ^{14}N, ^{15}N, ^{16}O, ^{19}F, ^{31}P
I. ^{12}C, ^{16}O, ^{32}S
II. ^{14}N, ^{31}P, ^{12}C
III. ^2H, ^{14}C, ^{16}O

(a) I and II (b) I only
(c) II and III (d) III and I

29. The number of line observed in the low resolution NMR and high resolution NMR spectrum of acetone are respectively
(a) 0, 1 (b) 1, 0
(c) 1, 1 (d) 1, 2

30. In an ESR spectrometer operating at 9.302 GHz, the ESR spectrum of hdyrogen atom gave two lines, one at 357.3 mT and the other at 306.6 mT. The hyperfine coupling constant of hdyrogen atom is
(a) 2.3 mT (b) 4.6 mT
(c) 1.15 mT (d) None of these

Assertion & Reason

Codes
(a) A and R both are true and R is the correct explanation of A.
(b) A and R both are true and R is not the correct explanation of A.
(c) A is true and R is false.
(d) A is false and R is true.

31. Assertion The deuteron resonance is split by the proton into a doublet.

Reason Proton and deuteron have two spin components.

32. Assertion Nitrous oxide is a triatomic molecules.

Reason Nitrous oxide contain 12 degrees of freedom.

33. Assertion All γ-emitters are suitable for Mossbauer study.

Reason For Mossbauer study, the γ-emission half-life of the excited source should be within the limits 10^{-6} s > T > 10^{-10} s.

34. Match Column I (molecules) with Column II (fundamental vibrational frequency) and choose the correct answer using the codes given below.

	Column I (Molecules)		Column II (Fundamental vibrational frequency)
A.	CO_2 (Linear)	1.	30
B.	C_6H_6	2.	4
C.	*Trans* N_2F_2	3.	7
D.	Linear C_2F_2	4.	6
		5.	3

Codes

	A	B	C	D
(a)	5	1	4	3
(b)	5	1	3	2
(c)	4	1	3	2
(d)	2	1	4	3

35. Match Column I with Column II and choose the correct answer using the codes given below.

	Column I		Column II
A.	Pure rotational spectra	1.	NH_3
B.	Vibrational spectra	2.	HCl
C.	Rotational Raman spectra	3.	CH_4
D.	Vibrational Raman spectra	4.	CH_3Cl
		5.	SF_6

Codes

	A	B	C	D
(a)	1	2	4	3
(b)	2	4	3	5
(c)	2	3	4	1
(d)	1	2	4	5

36. Match Column I (expression of I) with Column II (molecular giving rotational spectra) and choose the correct answers using the codes given below.

	Column I		Column II
A.	CO_2	1.	$I_{xx} = I_{yy} \neq I_{zz}$ (complicated)
B.	CH_4	2.	$I_{xx} \neq I_{yy} \neq I_{zz}$
C.	Benzene	3.	$I_{xx} = I_{yy} = 2mR^2$, $I_{zz} = 0$ (mass of central atom is not involved)
D.	H_2O	4.	$I_{xx} = I_{yy} = I_{zz} = \frac{8}{3} m_1 R^2$

Codes

	A	B	C	D
(a)	3	4	2	1
(b)	3	2	4	1
(c)	3	4	1	2
(d)	2	3	4	1

37. Match Column I (techniques) with Column II (regions) and choose the correct answer using the codes given below.

	Column I (Spectroscopy)		Column II (Region)
A.	Vibrational	1.	Microwave
B.	Rotational	2.	γ-rays
C.	Mossbauer	3.	Radiofrequency
D.	NMR	4.	IR

Codes

	A	B	C	D
(a)	3	4	2	1
(b)	4	3	2	1
(c)	4	2	3	1
(d)	4	1	2	3

38. Match the various ways in which an electronically excited molecule can lose energy and choose the correct answer using the codes given below.

	Column I		Column II
A.	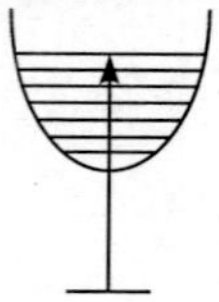	1.	Fluorescence
B.	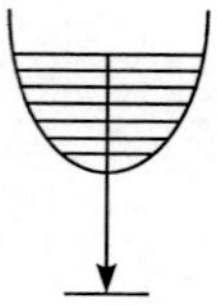	2.	Phosphorescence
C.	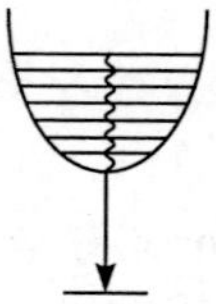	3.	Re-emission
D.	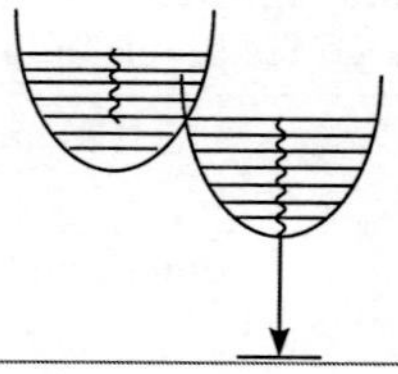	4.	Absorption

Codes

	A	B	C	D
(a)	4	3	2	1
(b)	4	3	1	2
(c)	3	4	2	1
(d)	3	4	1	2

39. Match Column I (transitions) with Column II (selection rules in term of quantum numbers) and choose the correct answer using the codes given below.

Column I (Spectroscopy)	Column II (Selection rule)
A. Vibrational	1. $\Delta V = \pm 1$
B. Pure rotational (for linear molecule)	2. $\Delta J = \neq 1$
C. NMR	3. $\Delta m_I = \pm 1$
D. EPR	4. $\Delta m_s = \pm 1$

Codes

	A	B	C	D
(a)	1	2	3	4
(b)	1	3	2	4
(c)	4	3	2	1
(d)	1	4	3	2

40. Match Column I (methods used in kinetic studies) with Column II (ranges of life times that can be investigaged) and choose the correct answer using the codes given below.

Column I	Column II
A. ESR	1. 10^{-11} s
B. Mossbauer (Fe)	2. $10^{-4} \sim 10^{-8}$ s
C. IR and Raman	3. 10^{-18} s
D. Photoelectron spectroscopy	4. 10^{-7} s

Codes

	A	B	C	D
(a)	2	4	1	3
(b)	4	3	2	1
(c)	1	2	3	4
(d)	2	3	1	4

41. Match Column I (molecules) with Column II (modes of vibrations) and choose the correct answer using the codes given below

	Column I (Molecule)		Column II (Normal modes of vibrations)
A.	HCl	1.	7
B.	SO_2	2.	4
C.	CO_2	3.	3
D.	C_2H_2	4.	1

Codes

	A	B	C	D
(a)	1	2	3	4
(b)	1	3	2	4
(c)	4	3	2	1
(d)	4	2	3	1

Directions (Q. Nos. 42 to 44)

Pure rotational spectra provides a powerful method of finding molecular parameters of simple molecules.

A rotating diatomic molecule whose nuclei are considered as being separated by a definite mean distance may be treated as a rigid rotator with free axis. Selection rule for rotational transitions of linear molecules that occur with absorption or emission of electromagnetic radiation is $\Delta J = \pm 1$.

42. The rotational constant is

(a) $\dfrac{h^2}{8\pi^2 I} J(J+1)$ (b) $\dfrac{h}{2\pi}\sqrt{J(J+1)}$

(c) $\dfrac{h}{8\pi^2 Ic}$ (d) $\dfrac{h^2}{8\pi^2 I}$

43. Frequency of absorption for transition from $2 \to 3$ energy level will be

(a) $3B$ (b) $4B$

(c) $5B$ (d) $6B$

44. Rotational energy or rotational term can be written as

(a) $2B(J+1)$ (b) $\dfrac{h^2}{8\pi^2 I} J(J+1)$

(c) $J(J+1)$ (d) $\dfrac{h}{8\pi^2 Ic}(J+1)$

Directions (Q. Nos. 45 to 47)
Rotational spectra result from transitions between the rotational energy levels of a gaseous molecule on absorption of radiations falling in microwave region. Microwave spectra occur in spectral range of 1–100 cm^{-1}. Vibrational spectras occur in spectral range of 500 – 4000 cm^{-1} while Raman spectra is observed in range of 12500–25000 cm^{-1}.

45. Rotational spectra is shown by
(a) H_2 (b) Cl_2
(c) CO_2 (d) CO

46. Necessary condition for compounds to show rotational spectra is
(a) Molecule should be symmetric
(b) Molecule should undergo a change in dipole moment during rotational transitions
(c) Molecule should possess a permanent dipole moment
(d) None of the above

47. Raman spectra is observed in
(a) UV region (b) visible region
(c) IR region (d) microwave region

Directions (Q. Nos. 48 to 50)
Relative Boltzmann population of rotational energy levels of a diatomic molecule is given by

$$\frac{N_J}{N_0} = g_J \exp\frac{\left(-\frac{E_J}{kT}\right)}{g_0 \exp\left(-\frac{E_0}{kT}\right)}$$

If $I = 5.08 \times 10^{-47}$ kg/m^2 and temperature is 25°C, $N_0 = 100$, answer the following questions based on this data.

48. Value of N_J can be expressed as
(a) $(J+1)\,N_0\,e^{E_J/kT}$ (b) $(J+1)\,N_0 e^{-E_J/RT}$
(c) $(2J+1)\,N_0 e^{E_J/RT}$ (d) $(2J+1)\,N_0 e^{-E_J/kT}$

49. If $J = 1$ and $J = 2$ N_J for DCl^{35} will be
(a) 285, 100 (b) 100 and 426
(c) 100 and 285 (d) 426 and 100

50. Rotational quantum number for the rotational spectrum of diatomic molecule for maximum populated level is given by
(a) $\frac{kT}{2h\cdot c\cdot B} - \frac{1}{2}$ (b) $\sqrt{\frac{kT}{2h\cdot c\cdot B}}$
(c) $\sqrt{\frac{kT}{2h\cdot cB}} - \frac{1}{2}$ (d) one

Directions (Q. Nos. 51 to 53)
The internuclear distance (bond length) of carbon monoxide molecule is 1.13 Å. Atomic masses of $^{12}C = 1.99 \times 10^{-26}$ kg and $^{16}O = 2.66 \times 10^{-26}$ kg.

51. The energy in joules of CO molecule in first excited rotational level is
(a) 4.76×10^{-4} J (b) 7.61×10^{-23} J
(c) 4.67×10^{-23} J (a) zero

52. Angular velocity of CO molecule in first excited rotational level is
(a) 2.6×10^{-2} rad/s (a) 3.23×10^{11} rad/s
(c) 4.76×10^{-4} rad/s (d) None of these

53. Thermal energy of CO molecule compared to first excited state rotational energy of CO molecule will be
(a) less (b) zero
(c) can be greater or lesser (d) far greater

Answers

Exercise 1

1. (c)	**2.** (c)	**3.** (b)	**4.** (a)	**5.** (a)	**6.** (d)	**7.** (b)	**8.** (a)	**9.** (c)	**10.** (c)
11. (a)	**12.** (b)	**13.** (b)	**14.** (a)	**15.** (c)	**16.** (b)	17. (b)	**18.** (a)	**19.** (b)	**20.** (a)
21. (c)	**22.** (d)	**23.** (b)	**24.** (d)	**25.** (d)	**26.** (a)	**27.** (a)	**28.** (a)	29. (a)	**30.** (b)
31. (d)	**32.** (b,c)	**33.** (a)	**34.** (c)	**35.** (d)	**36.** (c)	**37.** (a)	38. (c)	39. (d)	**40.** (d)
41. (a)	**42.** (b)	**43.** (b)	**44.** (d)	**45.** (b)	**46.** (c)	**47.** (a)			

Exercise 2

1. (b)	**2.** (c)	**3.** (d)	**4.** (b)	**5.** (a)	**6.** (b)	**7.** (a)	**8.** (c)	**9.** (c)	**10.** (b)
11. (a)	**12.** (c)	**13.** (d)	**14.** (b)	**15.** (c)	**16.** (d)	**17.** (a)	**18.** (b)	**19.** (b)	**20.** (b)
21. (c)	**22.** (c)	**23.** (a)	**24.** (b)	**25.** (c)	**26.** (d)	**27.** (b)	**28.** (b)	**29.** (c)	**30.** (a)
31. (c)	**32.** (c)	**33.** (d)	**34.** (d)	**35.** (a,d)	**36.** (c)	**37.** (d)	**38.** (b)	**39.** (a)	**40.** (a)
41. (a)	**42.** (b)	**43.** (d)	**44.** (c)	**45.** (d)	**46.** (c)	**47.** (b)	**48.** (d)	**49.** (b)	**50.** (c)
51. (c)	**52.** (b)	**53.** (d)							

Hints & Solutions

Exercise 2

1.

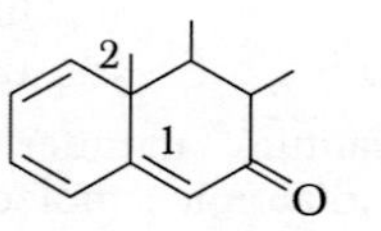

Parent value	215 nm
β-substituent 1	12 nm
w-substituent 2	18 nm
2 × extended conjugation	60 nm
Homoannular diene component	39 nm
Exocyclic double bond	5 nm
	349 nm

3. In salicylaldehyde, the internal (chelated) hydrogen bonding causes a large frequency shift to around 1666 cm^{-1}.

4. Presence of *p*-OMe (+*M*) group in I assists the mesomeric shift to decrease the bond order of C═O bond leading to lower C═O stretching frequency. A *p*-NO_2 (− *M*) group tends to oppose these trends and thus in II, the C═O stretching frequency is higher than I.

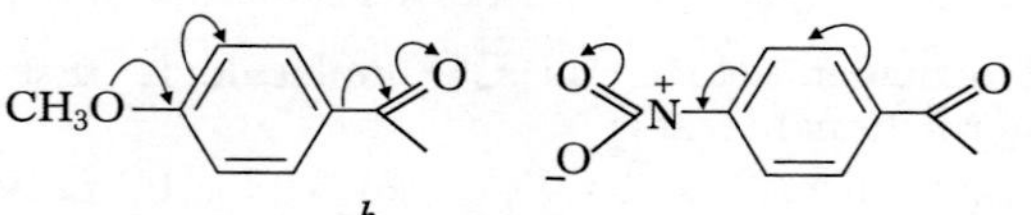

5.
$$B = \frac{h}{8\pi^2 Ic}$$

$$2B = 12.8\ cm^{-1},\ i.e.,\ B = 6.4\ cm^{-1}$$

$$\therefore \quad 6.4\ cm^{-1} = \frac{6.62 \times 10^{-27}\ \text{erg-s}}{8 \times (3.143)^2\ I \times 3 \times 10^{10}\ \text{cm s}^{-1}}$$

$$\therefore \quad I = \frac{6.62 \times 10^{-27}\ \text{erg-s}}{6.4 \times 8 \times (4.143)^2 \times 3 \times 10^{10}}$$

$$= 4.36 \times 10^{-40}\ \text{g cm}^2$$

6.
$$r^2 = \frac{I}{\mu}$$

$$\text{Reduced mass, } \mu = \frac{1 \times 127}{6.023 \times 10^{-23}} = 0.165 \times 10^{-23}\ \text{g}$$

$$r^2 = \frac{I}{\mu} = \frac{4.36 \times 10^{-40}}{0.165 \times 10^{-23}}$$

$$= 2.64 \times 10^{-16}\ \text{cm}^2$$

$$\therefore \quad r = 1.62 \times 10^{8}\ \text{cm} = 1.62\ \text{Å}$$

8. The reduced mass of CN^+, (atomic mass C = 12 and N = 14)

$$\mu = \frac{12 \times 10^{-3} \times 14 \times 10^{-3}}{(6.023 \times 10^{23}) \times 26 \times 10^{-3}}\ \text{kg}$$

$$= 1.073 \times 10^{-26}\ \text{kg}$$

$$I = \mu r^2$$

where, $r = 0.129 \times 10^{-9}\ \text{m} = 1.29 \times 10^{-10}\ \text{m}$

$$I = 1.073 \times 10^{-26} \times (1.29 \times 10^{-10})^2\ \text{kg m}^2$$

$$= 1.786 \times 10^{-46}\ \text{kg m}^2$$

$$B(\text{m}^{-1}) = \frac{h}{8\pi^2 Ic} = \frac{6.626 \times 10^{-34}\ \text{J-s}}{8 \times (3.14)^2 \times 1.786 \times 10^{-46} \times 2.998 \times 10^8}$$

$$= 156.6\ \text{m}^{-1} = 1.566\ \text{cm}^{-1}$$

$$\therefore \text{Second line, } \overline{V}_2 = 4B = 4 \times 1.566$$

$$= 6.264\ \text{cm}^{-1}$$

11. Absorption cross-order, $\sigma = \dfrac{2.303\ \varepsilon cl}{Nx}$

$$C = \frac{N}{N_A (10^3\ \text{Lm}^{-3})}$$

$$l = x(10^2\ \text{cm m}^{-1})$$

$$\therefore \quad \sigma = \frac{2.303 \times (44000\ \text{L mol}^{-1}\ \text{cm}^{-1}) \times 10^2\ \text{cm m}^{-1}}{(6.02 \times 10^{23}\ \text{mol}^{-1})(10^3\ \text{Lm}^{-3})}$$

$$= 1.7 \times 10^{-20}\ \text{m}^2$$

12.
$$\mu_N = \frac{e\hbar}{2mP} \qquad \left(\text{where } \hbar = \frac{h}{2\pi}\right)$$

$$= \frac{(1.602 \times 10^{-19}\ \text{C})(6.626 \times 10^{-34}\ \text{J-s})}{4\pi\ (1.672 \times 10^{-27}\ \text{kg})}$$

$$= 50.50 \times 10^{-28}\ \text{JT}^{-1}$$

The nuclear magneton is 1/1836 of the Bohr magneton.

13. Absorbance, $A = \log \dfrac{I_0}{I} = \log \dfrac{100}{19.2} = 0.717$

$$\varepsilon = \frac{A}{lc} = \frac{0.717}{(1\ \text{cm})(5 \times 10^{-4}\ \text{mol/L})}$$

$$= 1.43 \times 10^3\ \text{L mol}^{-1}\ \text{cm}^{-1}$$

14. The absorption frequency in term of wave numbers is given by

$$\bar{\nu}_{\min} = \frac{\Delta E}{hc} = \frac{h(N+1)}{8cm_e a^2}$$

where, N = number of π-electrons

$$\therefore J_{\min} = \frac{(6.62 \times 10^{-34}\ \text{J-s})(9) \times 10^{-2}\ \text{m cm}^{-1}}{8 \times (3 \times 10^8\ \text{m/s})(9.11 \times 10^{-31}\ \text{kg})(0.95 \times 10^{-9}\ \text{m})^2}$$

$$= 30200\ \text{cm}^{-1}$$

15.
$$J_{\max} = \sqrt{\frac{kT}{2hcB}} - \frac{1}{2}$$

$$= \sqrt{\frac{1.38 \times 10^{-23} \times 300}{2 \times 6.626 \times 10^{-34} \times 3 \times 10^{10} \times 1.566}} - \frac{1}{2}$$

$$\approx 8$$

16. Frequency of oscillator,

$$\bar{\nu} = \frac{1}{2\pi c}\sqrt{\frac{k}{\mu}}$$

$$k = 500 \text{ Nm}^{-1} = 5 \times 10^5 \text{ dyne cm}^{-1}$$

$$\therefore \quad \bar{\nu} = \frac{1}{2 \times 3.14 \times 3 \times 10^{10}} \sqrt{\frac{5 \times 10^5}{1.6145 \times 10^{-24}}}$$

$$\left[\mu = \frac{1}{6.022 \times 10^{23}} \left(\frac{35}{36}\right) \text{g} = 0.16145 \times 10^{-23} \text{ g}\right]$$

$$= 2.951 \times 10^3 \text{ cm}^{-1} = 2951 \text{ cm}^{-1}$$

For harmonic oscillator, $E_{v=0 \text{ to } v=1} = hc\omega$ (ω in cm^{-1})

Thus, energy in term of wave number unit = ω = 2951 cm^{-1}

17. $\nu = \frac{\Delta E}{h} = \frac{g_N \mu_N B_z}{h} = \frac{5.585 \times 5.05 \times 10^{-27} \times 1.4092}{6.626 \times 10^{-34}}$

$$= 60 \times 10^6 \text{ s}^{-1} = 60 \times 10^6 \text{ Hz}$$

or $= 60$ MHz

18. $\Delta E = h\nu = 6.626 \times 10^{-34} \text{ Js} \times 9.3 \times 10^9 \text{ s}^{-1}$

$$= 6.164 \times 10^{-24} \text{ J}$$

$$\Delta E = g\mu_B B$$

or $B = \frac{\Delta E}{g\mu_B}$

$$= \frac{6.164 \times 10^{-24} \text{ J}}{(2.0025)(9.2741 \times 10^{-24} \text{ JT}^{-1})}$$

$$= 0.332 \text{ T}$$

19. Magnetogyric ratio, $Y = \frac{\mu}{I\left(\frac{h}{2\pi}\right)}$

$$= \frac{1.1305 \times 5.05 \times 10^{-27} \text{ JT}^{-1} \times 2 \times 3.14 \times 2}{1 \times 6.626 \times 10^{-34} \text{ J-s}}$$

$$= 1.083 \times 10^8 \text{ T}^{-1}\text{s}^{-1}$$

20. $\mu = g_N \mu_N I$

Given, $\mu = 1.1305 \, \mu_N$

$$\therefore \quad 1.1305 \, \mu_N = \frac{1}{2} g_N \mu_N$$

$$\therefore \quad g_N = 2.261 \approx 2.3$$

22. Rotational constant in term of frequency units

$$= \frac{h}{8\pi^2 I} = 1.743 \times 10^{11} \text{ s}^{-1}$$

$$E = \frac{h}{8\pi^2 I} J(J+1) = (1.743 \times 10^{11} \text{ s}^{-1}) \, J(J+1)$$

where,

E = fundamental vibrational frequency, *i.e.*, $= 6.5 \times 10^{13}$ s^{-1}

$$6.5 \times 10^{13} \text{ Hz} = (1.743 \times 10^{11} \text{ Hz}) \, J(J+1)$$

$$\therefore \quad J(J+1) = \frac{6.5 \times 10^{13}}{1.743 \times 10^{11}} = 372.9$$

or $J^2 + J - 372.9 = 0$

$a = 1, b = +1, c = -372.9$

$$J = \frac{+b \pm \sqrt{b^2 + 4ac}}{2 \times a}$$

$$= \frac{-1 \pm \sqrt{1 + 4 \times 372.9}}{2}$$

$$= 18.82 \approx 19$$

23. $\Delta E = h\nu = g_e \mu_B N$

$$\nu = \frac{g_e \mu_B B}{h}$$

$$= \frac{2.002 \times 9.274 \times 10^{-24} \text{ JT}^{-1} \times 0.3000 \text{ T}}{6.626 \times 10^{-34} \text{ J-s}}$$

$$= 8.406 \times 10^9 \text{ s}^{-1}$$

24. The fifth rotational line corresponds to $J = 4$ to $J = 5$ transition and the second one corresponds to $J = 1$ to $J = 2$ transition.

$$\therefore \quad \frac{5N_4}{2N_1} = \frac{I(5 \leftarrow 4)}{I(2 \leftarrow 1)} = 6.38 \text{ (where, } I = \text{intensity)}$$

$$\frac{N_4}{N_1} = 2.55$$

From the Boltzmann distribution law,

$$\frac{N_J}{N'_J} = \frac{2J+1}{2J'+1} = e^{-(E_J - E'_J)\,kT}$$

$$2.55 = \frac{9}{3} \exp \frac{-B(20-2)}{kT}$$

$$0.163 = \frac{18B}{kT}$$

The rotational constant,

$$B_J = Bh = (55.35 \times 10^9 \text{ s}^{-1})(6.62 \times 10^{-34} \text{ Js})$$

$$= 3.66 \times 10^{-23} \text{ J}$$

$$T = \frac{18B}{0.163\,k} = \frac{18 \times 3.66 \times 10^{-23}}{0.163 \times 1.38 \times 10^{-23}}$$

$$= 295 \text{ K or } 22°\text{C}$$

31. In the presence of magnetic field, the proton spin has two components 1/2 and −1/2 whereas the deuteron spin has three components, $m_I = +1, 0, -1$. Thus, the deuteron resonance is split by the proton into a doublet and the proton resonance is split by the deuteron into triplet (1 : 1 : 1).

21 Thermodynamics

Basics of Thermodynamics

Thermodynamics is an experimental science that is based on a very small number of principles. It gives a macroscopic description of a system in terms of a few measurable properties, suggested more or less by our sense perceptions. Thermodynamics provide relations between the measurable properties and tells which few of these properties must be determined experimentally in order to find all the properties of the system. The basic difference between kinetic theory and statistical mechanics is that kinetic theory applies the laws of mechanics (classical or quantum) to individual constituents and to understand the properties of the system while in statistical mechanics, the consideration of individual molecules is ignored and one applies the principles of statistics to find the distribution of particles which may, in turn, be used to find the properties of the system.

The importance of thermodynamics lies in the fact that it is based on a few measurable macroscopic properties based on our sense perceptions. As long as our sense perceptions remain unchanged, thermodynamics relations will remain unchanged. The microscopic description assumes the internal structure of matter and the structure of matter keeps on changing. So, the microscopic view is constantly being changed.

If matter and energy do not cross the boundary then, it is called an **isolated system**. If matter do not cross but there is a transfer of energy then, it is called a **closed system**. If both matter and energy can pass through the boundary then, it is called an **open system**. Once, we choose a system and specify whether it is open or closed or isolated, the next step is a description of the system through some experimentally measurable quantities, which are called **thermodynamic variables.** Thermodynamic variables may be either intensive or extensive. If a thermodynamic variable y is such that by introducing a partition into two chambers I and II, $y = y_{\text{I}} + y_{\text{II}}$, then it is called an extensive variable but if $y_{\text{I}} = y_{\text{II}}$, then it is called an intensive variable. For example, volume, mass and charge are extensive variables while temperature and pressure are intensive variables.

Syllabus

- Relativistic Quantum Mechanics : Klein-Gordon and Dirac Equations
- Spin Angular Momentum
- Semi-classical Theory of Radiation
- Selection Rules

The Zeroth Law of Thermodynamics

Two systems are not in thermal equilibrium. Their measurable properties continue to change and at thermal equilibrium, there is no change in the measurable properties. We may infer that there is some property which determines whether or not two bodies are in thermal equilibrium. This property is called **temperature.** If two bodies are not in thermal equilibrium, their temperatures must be different and *vice-versa.* If two bodies are separately in thermal equilibrium with a third, will the two bodies when placed in contact be in thermal equilibrium.

This observation is generally called the zeroth law of thermodynamics (due to Fowler) stated as follows

If two systems are separately in thermal equilibrium with a third, they will also be in thermal equilibrium.

From zeroth law, we may deduced that in thermal equilibrium, a property called temperature exists and are equal in equilibrium. Consider three system describable in terms of pressure p and volume V.

Let systems 1 and 2 be in thermal equilibrium. So, there is some relation

$$f_{12}(p_1, V_1, p_2, V_2) = 0 \qquad \ldots(1)$$

Let systems 2 and 3 be also in thermal equilibrium, so there is some relation

$$f_{23}(p_2, V_2, p_3, V_3) = 0 \qquad \ldots(2)$$

From these two relations, one may solve for p_2 to get,

$$p_2 = g(p_1, V_1, V_2) = h(p_3, V_3, V_2)$$

We may solve for $p_3 = \psi\,(p_1, V_1, V_2, V_3)$ ...(3)

By zeroth law, systems 1 and 3 are also in thermal equilibrium, so there is a relation

$$f_{13}(p_1, V_1, p_3, V_3) = 0$$

We may solve for $p_3 = \phi_{13}\,(p_1, V_1, V_3)$ ...(4)

So, p_3 is a function only of p_1, V_1 and V_3. But $p_3 = \psi\,(p_1, V_1, V_2, V_3)$. Hence, V_2 must appear in the expression for p_3. Hence, V_2 must cancel out in the equality

$$g(p_1, V_1, V_2) = h(p_3, V_3, V_2)$$

Therefore, g must be of the form

$$g(p_1, V_1, V_2) = T_1(p_1, V_1)\,\alpha_1(V_2) + \beta_1(V_2) \qquad \ldots(5)$$

and similarly for h

$$h(p_3, V_3, V_2) = T_3(p_3, V_3)\,\alpha\,(V_2) + \beta\,(V_2) \qquad \ldots(6)$$

So, the equality of g and h gives

$$T_1(p_1, V_1) = T_3(p_3, V_3) \qquad \ldots(7)$$

This is the condition for thermal equilibrium between 1 and 3.

In general, we may get

$$T_1(p_1, V_1) = T_2(p_2, V_2) = T_3(p_3, V_3)$$

Thus, temperature is a function of pressure and volume,

$$T = T(p, V)$$

This is called the **equation of state.**

Work Done in Various Process

In mechanics, work done by a force $\vec{\mathbf{F}}$ on a particle is defined as $\int \vec{\mathbf{F}} \cdot d\vec{\mathbf{r}}$ where, $d\vec{\mathbf{r}}$ is the small displacement produced due to the action of $\vec{\mathbf{F}}$. Consider a p-V system in hydrostatic equilibrium with the surroundings.

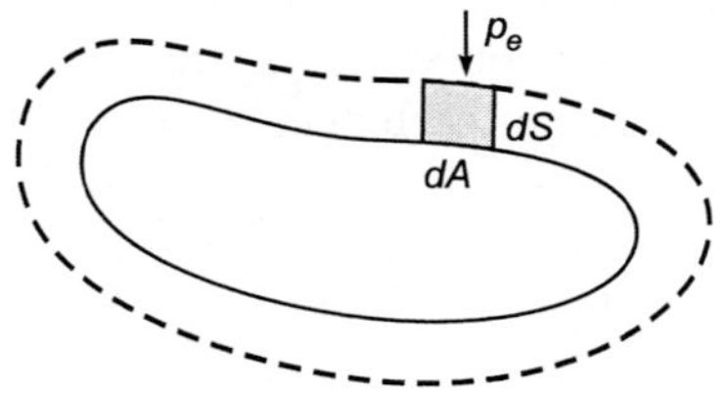

Let p_e be the external pressure applied on the surface of the system. So, work done by external surroundings

$$d'W = p_e \int dA\, ds = p_e\, dV$$

We take the convention in thermodynamics that work done by a system is positive and therefore work done on the system is negative. $d'W = -p_e\, dV$ for a quasistatic process, the pressure extend by the system differs infinitesimally from the external pressure. Hence, the work done by the system is $d'W = p\, dV$.

For a finite quasistatic process

$$W = \int_{V_1}^{V_2} p\, dV$$

At this stage, we may define some special processes

(i) **Isothermal process** A process in which the temperature remains same throughout.

For isothermal process

$$W = \int p\, dV = \int \frac{nRT}{V}\, dV$$

$$= nRT \ln\left(\frac{V_2}{V_1}\right)$$

(ii) **Isochoric process** A process in which volume remains same throughout.

For an isochoric process

$$W = \int p\, dV = 0$$

(iii) **Isobaric process** A process in which pressure remains same throughout.

For an isobaric process

$$W = \int p\, dV = p(V_2 - V_1)$$

Free Expansion

Imagine a cylinder with a membrane mid-way inside the cylinder, in which one side is vacuum and the other side is filled with a gas. If the membrane is punctured, gas flows out and fills the entire cylinder. The end state would be the same, if the membrane were replaced by a very light piston. Then, the process is called a free expansion. Let us compute the work done in a free expansion then, the pressure external to the gaseous system is zero (vacuum). Hence, $p_e = 0$

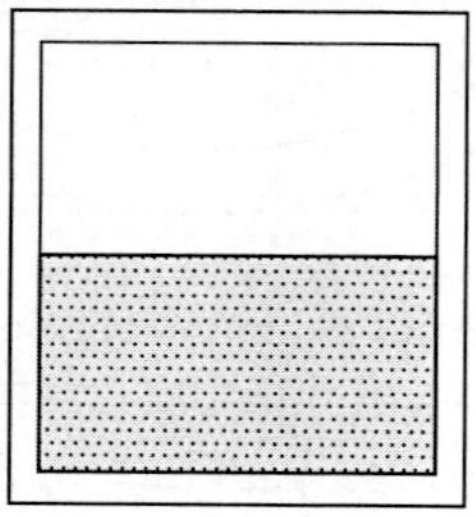

$$W = \int p_e\, dV = 0$$

Therefore, work done in a free expansion is zero.

This work done $W (= \int p\, dV)$ depends on the path.

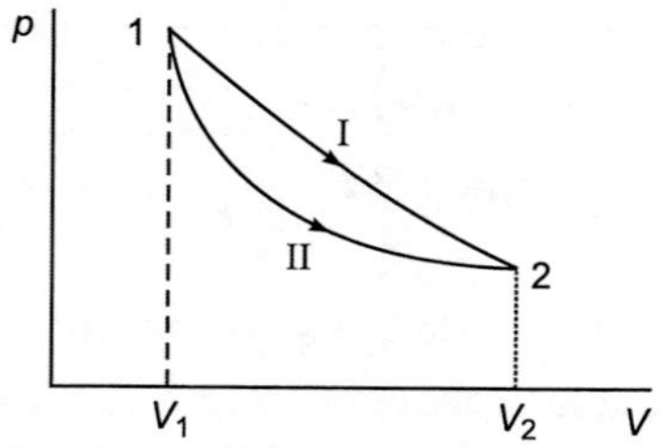

$\int p\, dV$ depends on whether the path is I or II. We say $d'W$ is an inexact differential because $\int p\, dV$ is path dependent. Work is a path function and not a point function. In fact $\oint p\, dV \neq 0$.

First Law of Thermodynamics

The first law of thermodynamics is usually referred to the conservation of energy and goes on to state that heat added to a system equals the increase in internal energy plus work done by the system.

Let us consider some thermodynamic processes with an initial state *a* and a final state *b*. Among adiabatic paths there are many possible paths from *a* to *b*. It may be a reversible expansion from *a* to *b*, or a reversible expansion from *a* to *c* followed by a free expansion from *c* to *b* or it may be a free expansion from *a* to *d* followed by a reversible expansion and followed by some dissipative process from *e* to *b*. Let us also assume that there is no change in the kinetic and potential energy of the system.

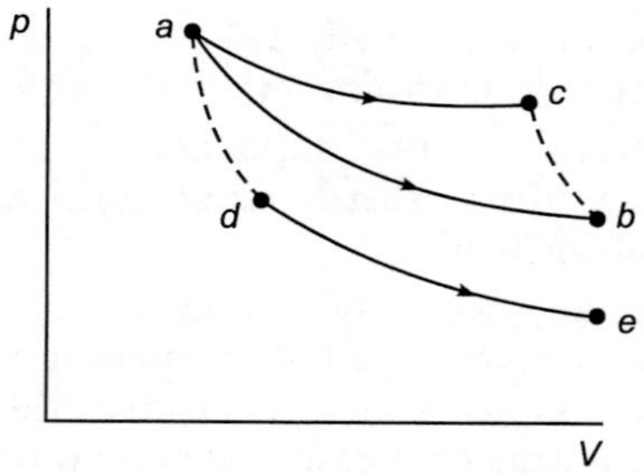

It is found that the total work done from *a* to *b* is the same for all paths. Thus, the first law of thermodynamics may be stated as

The total work done is same for all adiabatic paths between two equilibrium states that have the same potential and kinetic energy.

This means $d'W_{ad}$, the differential in the adiabatic work is a perfect differential. So, we may write $d'W_{ad} = -dU$ (the minus sign is by convention)

U is a function of state because dU is a perfect differential. This function of state, U is called the internal energy of the system.

Now, let us consider non-adiabatic processes. We have seen that the total work done between any two equilibrium states by adiabatic processes are the same regardless of the choice of the adiabatic path taken and $d'W_{ad} = -dU$. For non-adiabatic processes $d'W \neq -dU$. In other words, between any two equilibrium paths, the loss of internal energy does not appear in the form of work done while in adiabatic processes, it appears in the form of adiabatic work done. Thus, we may conclude that the energy has been transfered by means other than the performance of work. We may define heat flow in terms of work as $d'Q = d'W - d'W_{ad}$, for a path whose work done is $d'W$.

Thus, when a system at temperatures different from its surroundings undergoes a process, the energy transfer by non-mechanical means is called heat.

So,
$$dQ = d'W + dU$$

This is called the mathematical formulation of the first law of thermodynamics. Thus, the first law is not simply the law of conservation of energy. It contains three related ideas

(i) The existence of an internal energy function.
(ii) The principle of conservation of energy.
(iii) The definition of heat as energy in transit due to temperature difference.

Imagine two systems separated by a diathermic wall and the whole system is insulated. Applying the first law

$$Q_1 = W_1' + \Delta U_1 \quad \text{(for system 1)}$$

and

$$Q_2 = W_2' + \Delta U_2 \quad \text{(for system 2)}$$

Adding, we get

$$Q_1 + Q_2 = (W_2' + W_2') + (\Delta U_1 + \Delta U_2)$$

$(W_1' + W_2')$ is the total work done on the system.

$(\Delta U_1 + \Delta U_2)$ is the change in the internal energy of the system. Hence, $(Q_1 + Q_2)$ is the total heat added into the system since, it is insulated, $Q_1 + Q_2 = 0$

or

$$Q_1 = -Q_2$$

In other words, heat lost by a system is equal to heat gained.

Heat capacity

Heat capacity at constant volume and heat capacity at constant pressure can be denoted by

$$C_V = \left(\frac{d'Q}{dT}\right)_V \quad \text{and} \quad C_p = \left(\frac{d'Q}{dT}\right)_p$$

Experimentally, it is C_p that is generally found and C_V is more convenient theoretically. The measurement of heat capacity is very important to the theoretical physicist because it provides a test for the underlying assumptions behind the structure of matter and the behaviour of specific heat gives an insight into the nature of the intermolecular forces and molecules themselves.

Relation Between C_p and C_v

From the first law

$$\delta Q = dU + \delta W$$
$$= dU + p\,dV$$

Taking U as a function of T and V

$$dU = \left(\frac{\partial U}{\partial T}\right)_V dT + \left(\frac{\partial U}{\partial V}\right)_T dV$$

Therefore,

$$\delta Q = \left(\frac{\partial U}{\partial T}\right)_V dT + \left[p + \left(\frac{\partial U}{\partial V}\right)_T\right] dV$$

Now, divide both sides by dT at constant volume $dV = 0$

$$\left(\frac{\delta Q}{dT}\right)_V = \left(\frac{\partial U}{\partial T}\right)_V$$

By definition,

$$\left(\frac{\delta Q}{dT}\right)_V = C_V$$

So,

$$C_V = \left(\frac{\partial U}{\partial T}\right)_V$$

Instead of dividing by dT at constant V, if it is done at constant p, then

$$\left(\frac{\delta Q}{dT}\right)_p = C_V + \left[p + \left(\frac{\partial U}{\partial V}\right)_T\right]\left(\frac{\partial V}{\partial T}\right)_p$$

or

$$C_p - C_V = \left[p + \left(\frac{\partial U}{\partial V}\right)_T\right]\left(\frac{\partial V}{\partial T}\right)_p$$

An ideal gas defined by the equation $pV = nRT$. The internal energy is a function purely of the temperature may be derived from this and using the second law but for now let us assume that the equations $pV = nRT$ and $U = U(T)$ define an ideal gas.

So,

$$\left(\frac{\partial U}{\partial V}\right)_T = 0$$

As U is a function of temperature only.

So,

$$C_p - C_V = p\left(\frac{\partial V}{\partial T}\right)_p$$
$$= p \cdot \frac{nR}{p} = nR$$

For one mole of gas, $C_p - C_V = R$

This is called **Mayer's formula.**

Example 1. *Consider an ideal gas having thermodynamic variables (p,V,T). Let it undergo an adiabatic process from state 1 to state 2. Obtain the adiabatic curves on a p-V diagram, also called an indicator diagram. Also, find the work done.*

Sol. For an adiabatic process $\delta Q = 0$

So, the first law reduces to

$$0 = dU + p\,dV$$
$$= C_V\,dT + p\,dV$$
$$= C_V\,dT + \frac{RT}{V}dV$$

(For one mole of an ideal gas)

or

$$C_V\frac{dT}{T} = -\frac{R\,dV}{V}$$

On integrating, we get

$$C_V \ln T + R \ln V = \text{constant}$$
$$\ln T + (\gamma - 1)\ln V = \text{constant}$$

where, $\frac{C_p}{C_V} = \gamma$

or $$TV^{\gamma-1} = \text{constant}$$

Using the equation of state, we may eliminate T in favour of p and V, to get

$$pV^{\gamma} = \text{constant}$$

We may get the work done in such an adiabatic process as follows

$$W = \int_1^2 p\, dV = \int_1^2 kV^{-\gamma}\, dV$$

(where, $pV^{\gamma} = k$ and k is a constant)

$$= k\left.\frac{V^{1-\gamma}}{1-\gamma}\right|_{V_1}^{V_2} = \frac{k(V_2^{1-\gamma} - V_1^{1-\gamma})}{(1-\gamma)}$$

$$= \frac{p_2V_2 - p_1V_1}{1-\gamma} = \left(\frac{p_1V_1 - p_2V_2}{\gamma - 1}\right)$$

Prove that $C_p = \left(\frac{\partial H}{\partial T}\right)_p$, where $H = U + pV$ called the enthalpy

$$H = U + pV$$

Taking differentials on both sides

$$dH = dU + p\, dV + V\, dp$$
$$= d'Q + V\, dp$$

Dividing both sides by dT at constant p, $dp = 0$

$$\left(\frac{\partial H}{\partial T}\right)_p = \left(\frac{\delta Q}{dT}\right)_p = C_p$$

Example 2. *Adiabatic lapse rate — the variation of temperature in the atmosphere as a function of height may be explained by adiabatic expansion. The air near the surface is heated due to sun's radiation and also due to radiation reflected from the surface of the earth. Hot air from the lower region rises upwards where, there is lower pressure. Therefore, it expands. As air is a poor conductor of heat, the expansion may be considered adiabatic. Find the temperature gradient.*

Sol. For an adiabatic process,

$$p^{1-\gamma}T^{\gamma} = \text{constant}$$

(an equivalent form of $pV^{\gamma} = \text{constant}$)

Assuming the air to behave like an ideal gas.

Taking logarithmic derivatives, we get

$$(1-\gamma)\frac{dp}{p} + \gamma\frac{dT}{T} = 0$$

As we go up, the pressure decreases. From hydrostatics, we know

$$dp = -\rho g dh$$

and $$p = nRT$$

where n = number of moles per unit volume

So, $$(1-\gamma)\frac{\rho g dh}{nRT} = \gamma\frac{dT}{T}$$

or $$\frac{dT}{dh} = -\left(1 - \frac{1}{\gamma}\right)\frac{\rho g}{nR}$$
$$= -\left(1 - \frac{1}{\gamma}\right)\frac{Mg}{R}$$

where, M is the molar mass.

This is the required expression for the adiabatic lapse rate.

Taking $\gamma = 1.4$, $g = 9.8\ \text{ms}^{-2}$, $R = 8.31\ \text{J mol}^{-1}\ \text{K}^{-1}$

$$M = 0.029\ \text{kg mol}^{-1}$$

$$\frac{dT}{dh} = -10^{-2}\ \text{km}^{-1}$$

The temperature drop in 1 km is about 10°C, a value somewhat higher than the observed 5-6°C per km.

Example 3. *Prove that*

(i) $\left(\frac{\partial U}{\partial p}\right)_V = \frac{C_V k}{\alpha}$

(ii) $\left(\frac{\partial U}{\partial V}\right)_p = \frac{C_p}{V\alpha} - p$

where, α is the coefficient of volume expansion, $\frac{1}{V}\left(\frac{\partial V}{\partial T}\right)_p$ *and k is the bulk modulus,* $-\frac{1}{V}\left(\frac{\partial V}{\partial p}\right)_T$.

Sol. From the first law,

$$\delta Q = dU + p\, dV$$

$$= \left(\frac{\partial U}{\partial V}\right)_p dV + \left(\frac{\partial U}{\partial p}\right)_V dp + p\, dV$$

(i) Let $dV = 0$ and divide both sides by dT

$$C_V = \left(\frac{\partial U}{\partial p}\right)_V \left(\frac{\partial p}{\partial T}\right)_V$$

or $$\left(\frac{\partial U}{\partial p}\right) = C_V\left(\frac{\partial T}{\partial p}\right)_V$$

$$= -C_V\left(\frac{\partial T}{\partial V}\right)_p\left(\frac{\partial V}{\partial p}\right)_T$$

$$= -C_V\frac{\frac{1}{V}\left(\frac{\partial V}{\partial p}\right)_T}{\frac{1}{V}\left(\frac{\partial V}{\partial T}\right)_p}$$

$$= \frac{C_V k}{\alpha}$$

(ii) Let $dp = 0$ and divide both sides by dT

$$C_p = \left(\frac{\partial U}{\partial V}\right)_p\left(\frac{\partial V}{\partial T}\right)_p + p\left(\frac{\partial V}{\partial T}\right)_p$$

$$\left(\frac{\partial U}{\partial V}\right)_p = C_p\left(\frac{\partial T}{\partial V}\right)_p - p$$

$$= \frac{C_p}{V} V \left(\frac{\partial T}{\partial V}\right)_p - p$$

$$= \frac{C_p}{V\alpha} - p$$

Example 4. *The molar heat capacity at constant pressure of a gas varies with temperature as $C_p = a + bT - \frac{C}{T^2}$, where a, b and c are constants. How much heat is transferred during the isobaric process in which n moles of gas undergo a temperature rise from T_1 to T_2?*

Sol. For an isobaric process

$$\int \delta Q = \int C_p \, dT$$

So,
$$Q = n \int_{T_1}^{T_2} \left(a + bT - \frac{C}{T^2}\right) dT$$

$$= n\left\{a(T_2 - T_1) + b(T_2^2 - T_1^2) + C\left(\frac{1}{T_2} - \frac{1}{T_1}\right)\right\}$$

Enthalpy (Heat Content)

If ΔU is replaced by $U_B - U_A$ and the increase in volume (ΔV) by $V_B - V_A$ (where, A and B represent the initial and the final states of the system, respectively), then heat absorbed at constant pressure becomes

$$q_p = (U_B - U_A) \;\; p(V_B - V_A)$$
$$= (U_B - pV_B) - (U_A + pV_A) \quad \ldots(8)$$

The factors p and V are the properties of the state of the system. Hence, it is evident that the quantities $(U_B + pV_B)$ or $(U_A + pV_A)$, like the energy U must be dependent only on the state of the system and not on the previous history of the system. Therefore, we may define a new quantity by the equation,

$$H = U + pV$$

where, H is known as **heat content** or **enthalpy** of the system. Therefore,

$$H_B = U_B + pV_B \text{ and } H_A = U_A + pV_A$$

$$\therefore \quad q_p = H_B - H_A = \Delta H \quad \ldots(9)$$

where, ΔH is the increase in the heat content of the system. It (ΔH) may, therefore, be defined as the amount of heat absorbed at constant pressure.

Enthalpy of gaseous system

If the system is composed of ideal gases and if n_1 and n_2 are the number of moles before and after a chemical change, then

$$pV_1 = n_1 RT \text{ and } pV_2 = n_2 RT$$

$$\therefore \quad p\Delta V = p(V_2 - V_1)$$
$$= (n_2 - n_1)RT = \Delta nRT \quad \ldots(10)$$

From Eqs. (8) and (9)

$$q_p = \Delta H = \Delta U + p\Delta V$$

Hence, from Eq. (10), we have

$$\Delta H = \Delta U + \Delta nRT \quad \ldots(11)$$

The internal energy of an ideal gas does not depend upon the volume, but depends upon temperature, therefore, at constant temperature, $\left(\frac{dU}{dV}\right)_T = 0$.

At constant temperature, the pressure varies with volume. Since, for ideal gases

$$\left(\frac{dU}{dV}\right)_T = 0, \text{ hence } \left(\frac{dU}{dp}\right)_T = 0$$

Further, we know $H = U + pV$, *i.e.*,

$$\left(\frac{\partial H}{\partial p}\right)_T = \left(\frac{dU}{dp}\right)_T + \left[\frac{\partial(pV)}{\partial p}\right]_T \quad \ldots(12)$$

Since, ideal gases obey Boyle's law, therefore

$$\left[\frac{\partial(pV)}{\partial p}\right]_T = 0$$

Equation (12) now becomes $\left(\frac{\partial H}{\partial p}\right)_T = 0$ and also $\left(\frac{\partial H}{\partial V}\right)_T = 0$.

The Second Law of Thermodynamics

The branch of thermodynamics started as a discipline to find ways for better efficiency of heat engines and interconversion of work and heat energy. We are interested in a device to convert heat into work by means of series of processes by means of which such conversion may continue indefinitely without any change in the state of the system. The essential ingredients of a heat engine are–

(i) source of heat (a reservoir)
(ii) sink
(iii) working substance

Heat engine absorbs heat energy at a higher temperature, delivers work and rejects heat energy at a lower temperature. The thermal efficiency of a heat engine is

$$\eta = \frac{\text{Work output}}{\text{Heat input}}$$

$$= \frac{W}{Q_1} = \frac{Q_1 - Q_2}{Q_1}$$

$$= 1 - \frac{Q_2}{Q_1}$$

where, Q_1 = heat absorbed by the system
Q_2 = heat rejected by the system
W = work done by the system

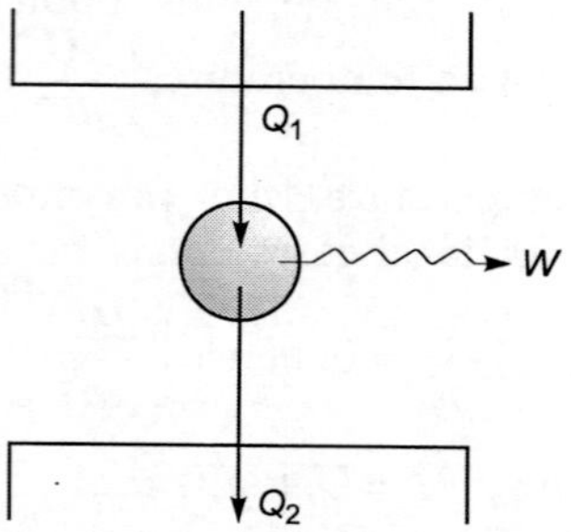

Fig. 21.1 Schematic diagram of a heat engine.

For better working of the heat engine, we want the efficiency η to be as close to one as possible. However, no engine has even been developed which absorbs heat and delivers work without the rejection of heat at some lower temperature. This experimental observation constitutes one form of the second law of thermodynamics. We will discuss the Kelvin, Planck and Clausius statements of the second law.

Kelvin-Planck Statement

"No process is possible whose sure result is the absorption of heat and the complete conversion of this heat into work."

What Kelvin-Planck statement says that the efficiency η is always less than one. It may be noticed that even if there is 100% conversion of heat into work, it would not violate the first law of thermodynamics.

If a heat engine were operated in the reverse order extracting heat energy at a lower temperature reservoir and rejecting a larger quantity of heat at a higher temperature reservoir by doing work on the system, such a device is called a refrigerator.

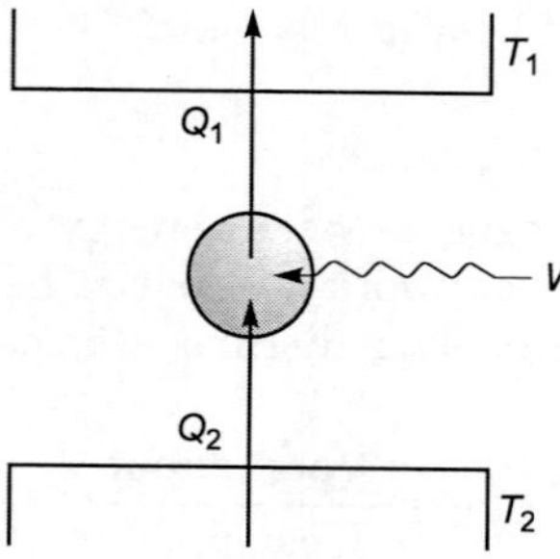

Here, the output is the amount of heat extracted Q_2 and input is the work done W. Hence, the efficiency of a refrigerator is

$$\eta = \frac{\text{Heat extracted}}{\text{Work done}}$$

$$= \frac{Q_2}{W} = \frac{Q_2}{Q_1 - Q_2}$$

Experimentally, it is found that work is always necessary to extract heat from a cold reservoir and deliver it to a higher temperature reservoir.

Clausius Statement

'No process is possible whose sure result is the transfer of heat from a cold body to a hot body'.

Equivalence of Kelvin-Planck and Clausius Statement

We will show that Kelvin-Planck statement implies Clausius statement and Clausius statement implies Kelvin-Planck statement, or equivalently, the violation of Clausius statement implies the violation of Kelvin Planck statement and the violation of Kelvin-Planck statement implies the violation of Clausius statement.

(i) Let Clausius statement be violated. So, there is a transfer of heat Q_2 from reservoir T_2 to reservoir T_1 without doing any work.

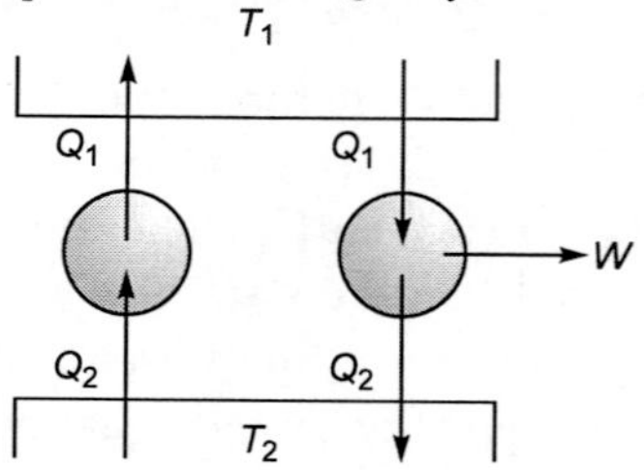

Let us consider a heat engine working between the two reservoirs, extracting heat Q_1 at temperature T_1 and rejecting heat Q_2 to temperature T_2 and delivering work W. When the refrigerator and the heat engine are combined and looked as a single device, it extracts heat $Q_1 - Q_2$ from reservoir at temperature T_1 and delivers work W with no rejection of heat to reservoir at temperature T_2. The combined device violates Kelvin-Planck statement of the second law.

(ii) Let the Kelvin-Planck statement be violated. Then, there is extraction of heat energy Q_1 from reservoir at temperature T_1 delivering work Q with no rejection of heat at reservoir at temperature T_2.

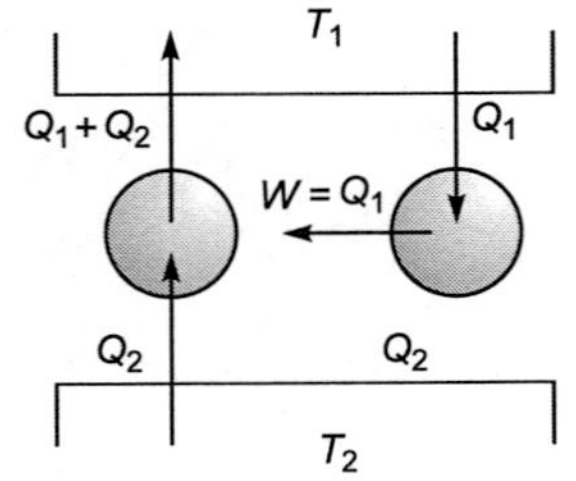

Consider a refrigerator which extracts heat Q_2 at T_2, receive work done $W\ (= Q_1)$ on the system and delivers heat $(Q_2 + Q_1)$ at T_1. As a combined system, the net effect is to extract heat Q_2 at T_2 and deliver Q_2 at T_1 without the expenditure of work. This violates Clausius statement of the second law.

Hence, Kelvin-Planck statement and Clausius statement are equivalent.

Carnot Cycle

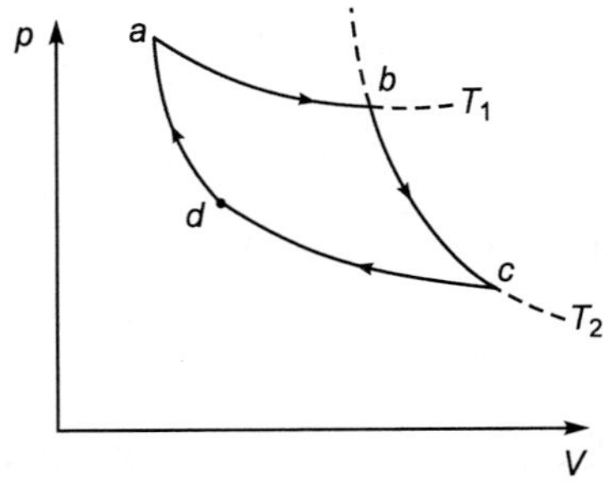

Consider the closed cyclic path as shown above. The path $(a \rightarrow b)$ is an isothermal expansion process; $(b \rightarrow c)$ is an adiabatic expansion process; $(c \rightarrow d)$ is isothermal compression process and $(d \rightarrow a)$ is adiabatic compression process. Such a cycle bounded by two isothermals and two adiabatics is called a Carnot cycle. All processes are assumed to be reversible.

For correctness, imagine a cylinder filled with a gas maintained at temperature T_1.

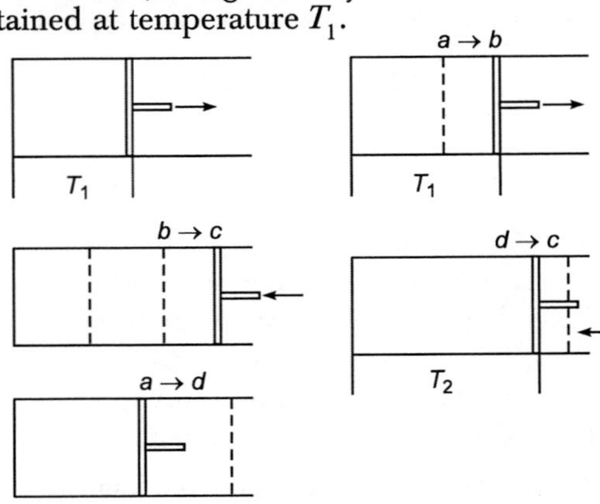

Let it undergo reversible isothermal expansion at T_1, from a to b in the indicator diagram. The cylinder is insulated and let it undergo reversible adiabatic expansion to state C, which have the system at temperature T_2. By placing in contact with a heat reservoir at temperature T_2, it is made to undergo reversible isothermal contraction, from c to d. It is insulated and made to undergo adiabatic contraction till the initial state a is reached. During the process, $a \rightarrow b$, heat Q_1 is absorbed by the system and during the process $c \rightarrow d$, heat Q_2 is released by the system. Assuming an ideal gas as the working substance

$$|Q_1| = \int p\, dV$$

(as $\int dU = 0$ as the temperature is kept constant)

$$= \int \frac{nRT_1}{V}\, dV = nRT_1 \ln\left(\frac{V_b}{V_a}\right) \qquad \ldots(13)$$

and
$$|Q_2| = \int p\, dV = \int \frac{nRT_2}{V}\, dV$$

$$= -nRT_2 \ln\left(\frac{V_d}{V_c}\right) \qquad \ldots(14)$$

Now, the points b and c lie on an adiabatic line hence,

$$T_1 V_b^{\gamma-1} = T_2 V_c^{\gamma-1} \qquad \ldots(15)$$

and points d and a lie on an adiabatic line hence,

$$T_2 V_d^{\gamma-1} = T_1 V_a^{\gamma-1} \qquad \ldots(16)$$

Eliminating T_1 and T_2, we get

$$V_b V_d = V_c V_a$$

or
$$\frac{V_b}{V_a} = \frac{V_c}{V_d}$$

So, efficiency $\eta = 1 - \dfrac{|Q_2|}{|Q_1|}$

$$= 1 - \frac{T_2}{T_1} \frac{\ln\left(\frac{V_d}{V_c}\right)}{\ln\left(\frac{V_b}{V_a}\right)}$$

$$\eta = 1 - \frac{T_2}{T_1}$$

Thus, the efficiency of a Carnot engine depends only on the temperature of the two reservoirs, the nature of the working substance plays no role in its efficiency.

Carnot's Theorem

"Of all heat engines working between the same temperature, the reversible Carnot engine has the maximum efficiency."

Proof Suppose, there is a heat engine whose efficiency is greater than that of a reversible Carnot engine. We may consider the heat engine and a reversed Carnot engine; a refrigerator to act as a single device as shown below.

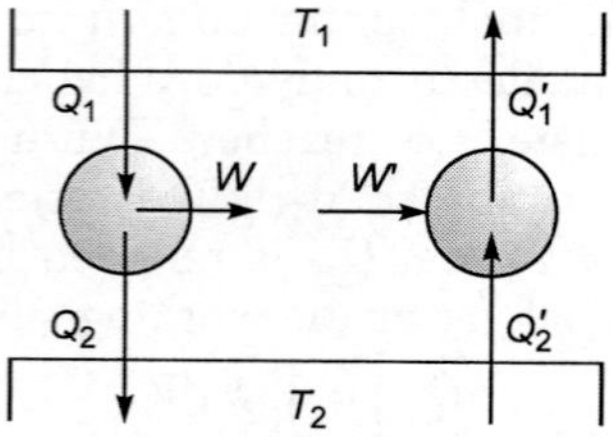

On the left is a heat engine whose efficiency is greater than the Carnot engine on the right.

So, $$\frac{W}{Q_1} > \frac{W'}{Q_1'}$$

Let $W = W'$, then $Q_1' - Q_1 > 0$

Also, $$W = Q_1 - Q_2$$

and $$W = W' = Q_1' - Q_2'$$

So, $$Q_1' - Q_1 = Q_2' - Q_2$$

Since, $$Q_1' - Q_1 > 0$$
$$Q_2' - Q_2 > 0$$

Hence, the overall effect is to transfer $Q_2' - Q_2$ amount of heat from a reservoir at temperature T_2 and delivering the same amount of heat at a higher temperature without the expenditure of any work, thus violating Clausius form of the second law. Thus, the above hypothesis is wrong and Carnot engine has the highest efficiency of all heat engines working between the same temperatures.

Entropy

We have seen that for a Carnot cycle operating between the thermodynamic temperatures T_1 and T_2, the ratio of heats exchanged equals $\frac{Q_1}{Q_2}$

or $$\boxed{\frac{Q_1}{Q_2} = \frac{T_1}{T_2}} \quad \text{...(17)}$$

Q_1 is heat added to the system and Q_2 is heat rejected by the system. For consistency in signs, we should write $-Q_2$ instead of Q_2.

So, $$\frac{Q_1}{T_1} + \frac{Q_2}{T_2} = 0$$

Now, we claim that any reversible cycle may be thought of as made up of a number of Carnot cycles. This may be easily seen from the diagram below.

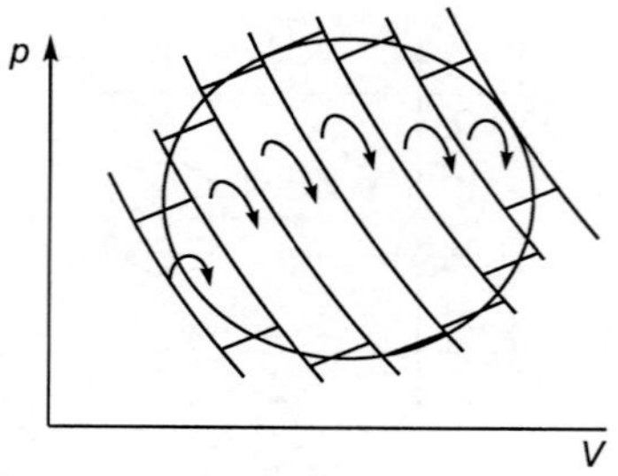

For each Carnot cycle, $\frac{\delta Q}{T} = 0$

For the entire complete reversible cycle

$$\int \frac{\delta Q}{T} = 0$$

This implies $\frac{\delta Q}{T}$ is a perfect differential. Hence, there exists a function of state S called the entropy such that

$$\frac{\delta Q}{T} = dS$$

By integrating, we may find the differences in entropy between any two equilibrium states. Within the framework of the second law, it is only possible to find differences in the value of entropy; it is not possible to find the absolute value of entropy.

Entropy Changes in Reversible Processes

Consider first a reversible adiabatic process

$$\delta Q = 0$$

So, $$\int dS = \int \frac{\delta Q}{T} = 0$$

Thus, the entropy remains constant in a reversible adiabatic process. It is also called an isentropic process.

Now, consider a reversible isothermal process

So, $$\int dS = \int \frac{\delta Q}{T} = \frac{Q}{T}$$

or $$S_2 - S_1 = \frac{Q}{T} \quad \text{...(18)}$$

The increase in entropy equals the heat added reversibly divided by temperature in an isothermal process. The change in phase at constant pressure is a reversible isothermal process. For example, change of phase from solid to liquid or liquid to vapour etc. The heat Q is called the latent heat of transformation.

In a reversible isothermal process, the net change of entropy of the universe (system plus surrounding) is zero. This is because, when the temperature of the system and surroundings are equal, heat inflow equals heat outflow and the entropy change of the system is equal but opposite to the entropy change of the surrounding.

Entropy Change in Irreversible Process

Almost all processes in nature are irreversible. Hence, it is essential to know the nature of entropy change in such irreversible processes. Before discussing this, let us take up a relation known as Clausius inequality.

We know the efficiency of a Carnot engine is higher than any other heat engine working between the same two temperatures.

i.e., $$1-\frac{Q_2}{Q_1}<1-\frac{T_2}{T_1}$$

(Note Q_1 and Q_2 are taken positive.)

or $$\frac{Q_2}{Q_1}>\frac{T_2}{T_1}$$

or $$\frac{Q_1}{T_1}-\frac{Q_2}{T_2}<0 \qquad \ldots(19)$$

Taking the sign convention that heat outflow is negative, Q_2 is to be taken negative,

So, $$\oint\frac{\delta Q}{T}<0$$

For reversible heat engines, $$\oint\frac{\delta Q}{T}=0$$

So, for irreversible processes, $$\oint\frac{\delta Q}{T}<0 \qquad \ldots(20)$$

Now, we are ready to take up the question of entropy change in an irreversible process.

Consider a closed path consisting of a path I from 1 to 2 which is irreversible and path II from 2 to 1 which is reversible. Overall, the closed path is irreversible,

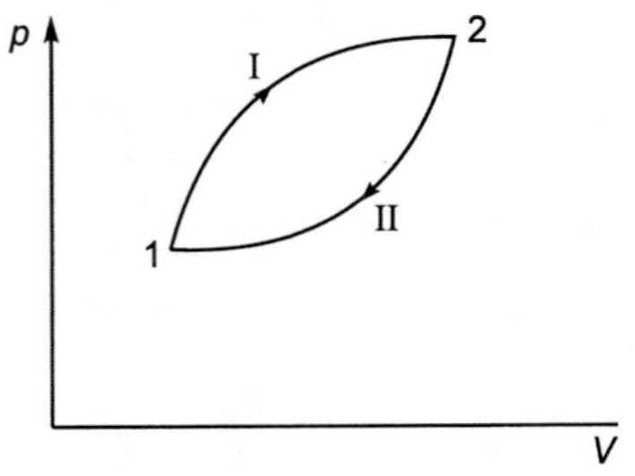

So, $$\oint\frac{\delta Q}{T}<0 \text{ and } \int_1^2\frac{\delta Q}{T}+\int_2^1\frac{\delta Q}{T}<0$$

For path II we know the answer,

$$\int_2^1\frac{\delta Q}{T}=S_1-S_2=-\Delta S$$

where, $$\Delta S=S_2-S_1$$

So, $$\int_1^2\frac{\delta Q}{T}-\Delta S<0$$

or $$\Delta S>\int_1^2\frac{\delta Q}{T} \qquad \ldots(21)$$

This shows that entropy always increases in all irreversible processes.

Consider an irreversible process in which a system at temperature T_1 is placed in contact with a heat reservoir at temperature $T_2(T_2>T_1)$ at constant pressure. Assuming as C_p is constant in the temperature range, we may find the entropy change.

$$\Delta S \text{ for the body}=\int\frac{\delta Q}{T}$$

$$=\int_{T_1}^{T_2}C_p\frac{dT}{T}=C_p\ln\frac{T_2}{T_1}$$

$$\Delta S \text{ for the reservoir}=\int\frac{\delta Q}{T}=\frac{1}{T_2}\int\delta Q$$

Heat lost by the reservoir is equal to the heat gained by the body.

So, $$\delta Q=\int C_p\,dT=C_p\,(T_2-T_1)$$

So, $$\Delta S_{\text{reservoir}}=-\frac{C_p(T_2-T_1)}{T_2} \qquad \ldots(22)$$

Hence, $$\Delta S=\Delta S_{\text{body}}+\Delta S_{\text{reservoir}}$$
$$=C_p\left[\ln\frac{T_2}{T_1}-\frac{T_2-T_1}{T_2}\right]$$

which is always positive for $T_2>T_1$.

Thus, the entropy of the universe increases.

Even for an isolated system, $\Delta Q=0$ whenever there is an irreversible process, $\Delta S>0$.

The Principle of Increase of Entropy

We have such that entropy of an isolated system remains constant in all reversible processes and increases in all irreversible processes. This is known as the principle of increase of entropy and is a part of the second law of thermodynamics. We may compare and contrast with the principle of conservation of energy. While the energy conservation principle forbids creation of energy or destruction of energy, the second law says that while entropy can be created it can never be destroyed in a isolated system.

Example 5. *An ideal gas engine operates in a cycle which when represented on a p-V diagram is a rectangle as shown.*

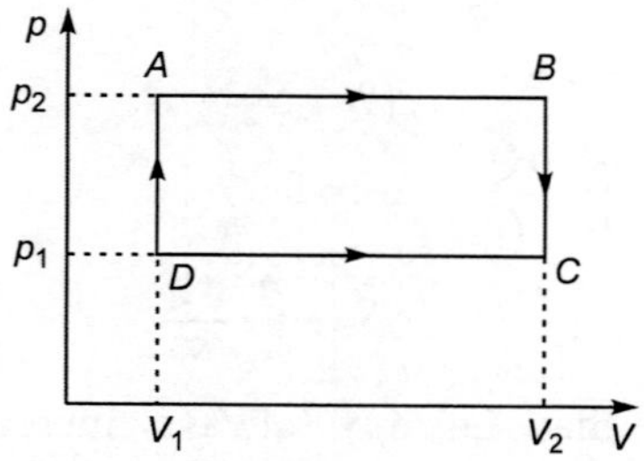

Find the efficiency of the heat engine.

Sol. Net work done

$$= p_2(V_2 - V_1) - p_1(V_2 - V_1)$$
$$= \Delta p\, \Delta V \quad \text{...(23)}$$

where, $\Delta p = p_2 - p_1$

and $\Delta V = V_2 - V_1$

Heat is absorbed by the system during the path $A \to B$ and $C \to D$.

$$\Delta Q_{A\to B} = \Delta U + p_2\, \Delta V \quad \text{...(24)}$$

Now, $pV = RT$

(For one mole of an ideal gas)

$$p_2\, \Delta V = R\, \Delta T$$

So, $\Delta U = C_V\, \Delta T$

(since $U = U(T)$ for an ideal gas)

$$= C_V \frac{p_2\, \Delta V}{R}$$

So,
$$\Delta Q_{A\to B} = C_V \frac{p_2\, \Delta V}{R} + p_2\, \Delta V$$
$$= p_2\, \Delta V\left(1 + \frac{C_V}{R}\right)$$
$$= p_2\, \Delta V\left(\frac{\gamma}{\gamma - 1}\right) \quad \text{...(25)}$$

and $\Delta Q_{C\to D} = \Delta U$ (since, $\int p\, dV = 0$)

Again from $pV = RT$ ...(26)

$$\Delta p\, V_1 = R\, \Delta T$$

So,
$$\Delta U = C_V \frac{V_1\, \Delta p}{R}$$
$$\Delta Q_{C\to D} = C_V \frac{\Delta p\, V_1}{R}$$

So, Q_1 = heat added

$$= \Delta Q_{A\to B} + \Delta Q_{C\to D}$$
$$= p_2\, \Delta V\left(\frac{\gamma}{\gamma - 1}\right) + \frac{\Delta p\, V_1}{(\gamma - 1)} \quad \text{...(27)}$$

So, efficiency
$$\eta = \frac{W}{Q_1} = \frac{\Delta p\, \Delta V}{p_2 \frac{\Delta V\, \gamma}{\gamma - 1} + \frac{\Delta p\, V_1}{\gamma - 1}}$$

or
$$\eta = \frac{\gamma - 1}{\frac{\gamma p_2}{p_2 - p_1} + \frac{V_1}{V_2 - V_1}}$$

Example 6. *1 g of steam is condensed at 100°C and 1 atmosphere pressure. Calculate the entropy change. (Given latent heat of steam is $2.238 \times 10^6\ J\ kg^{-1}$.)*

Sol. Consideration of steam is an isothermal process.

So,
$$\Delta S = \int \frac{dQ}{T} = \frac{1}{373} 10^{-3} \times 2.238 \times 10^6\ \text{JK}^{-1}$$
$$= 6\ \text{JK}^{-1}$$

Example 7. *m_1 gram of water at temperature T_1 is isobarically and adiabatically mixed with m_2 gram of water at temperature T_2. Find the entropy change.*

Sol. After mixing, let T be the final temperature and $T_2 > T_1$. So, $T_1 < T < T_2$ the mass of water initially at temperature T_1 will gain heat energy while the mass of water initially at T_2 will lose heat.

But heat lost = heat gained

$$m_2C_p(T_2 - T) = m_1C_p(T - T_1)$$

where, C_p is the specific heat at constant pressure

So,
$$T = \frac{m_2C_pT_2 + m_1C_pT_1}{(m_2 + m_1)C_p}$$
$$= \left(\frac{m_2T_2 + m_1T_1}{m_2 + m_1}\right)$$

Entropy change $\Delta S = \Delta S_1 + \Delta S_2$

$$= m_1C_p \int_{T_1}^{T} \frac{dT}{T} + C_pm_2 \int_{T_2}^{T} \frac{dT}{T}$$
$$= m_1C_p \ln\left(\frac{T}{T_1}\right) - m_2C_p \ln\left(\frac{T_2}{T}\right)$$

Example 8. *A body of constant heat capacity C_p and at a temperature T_i is put in contact with a reservoir at a higher temperature T_f. Assuming the pressure to remain constant, find the entropy change of the universe after the body has come to an equilibrium.*

Sol. Entropy change of the body,

$$\Delta S_{\text{body}} = \int \frac{\delta Q}{T}$$
$$= C_p \int \frac{dT}{T} = C_p \ln\left(\frac{T_f}{T_i}\right)$$

Heat absorbed $Q = \int C_p\, dT = C_p(T_f - T_i)$

Now, heat lost by the reservoir equals heat gained by the body

$$\Delta S_{\text{reservoir}} = -\int \frac{\delta Q}{T} = -\frac{1}{T_f}\int \delta Q$$
$$= -C_p \frac{(T_f - T_i)}{T_f}$$

So, $\Delta S = \Delta S_{\text{body}} + \Delta S_{\text{reservoir}}$

$$= C_p \left[\ln\left(\frac{T_f}{T_i}\right) - \frac{T_f - T_i}{T_f} \right]$$

Let $T_f = T_i(1 + x)$

where, $x > 0$ as $T_f > T_i$

$$\Delta S = C_p \left[\ln(1 + x) - \frac{x}{1 + x} \right]$$

We will show that $\Delta S > 0$

Differentiating ΔS with respect to x, we get

$$\frac{d}{dx}\Delta S = C_p \left[\frac{1}{1 + x} - \frac{1}{1 + x} + \frac{x}{(1 + x)^2} \right]$$

$$= C_p \frac{x}{(1 + x)^2} > 0 \qquad (\text{Since, } x > 0)$$

So, $\Delta S(x) > \Delta S \qquad (x = 0)$

So, $\Delta S > 0$

Consequences of the First and Second Laws

The mathematical formulation of the first law is

$$\delta Q = dU + \delta W$$

This is true for both reversible as well as irreversible processes.

From the second law, for a reversible process between two equilibrium states,

$$T\,dS = \delta Q$$

For a reversible process in p-V system

$$\delta W = p\,dV$$

Combining all these, in a reversible process for a p-V system

$$T\,dS = dU + p\,dV$$

This is a relation between two nearby equilibrium states. Since, it expresses the relation between properties of a system between two nearby equilibrium states, it is true for all pairs of nearby equilibrium states whatever be the nature of process between them whether reversible or irreversible.

Using the above, we may derive thermodynamic relations which are applicable to almost any system. The importance of such thermodynamic relations lies in the fact that once a few thermodynamic properties have been found either experimentally or by using an assumed structure of matter, all other thermodynamic properties may be obtained. Besides thermodynamic properties such as internal energy and entropy cannot be measured experimentally. So, their behaviour have to be understood through other properties.

The Maxwell Relations

The combined form of the first and the second law is

$$dU = T\,dS - p\,dV$$

Considering U as a function of thermodynamic variables x and y.

Dividing by dx at constant y, we get

$$\left(\frac{\partial U}{\partial x}\right)_y = T\left(\frac{\partial S}{\partial x}\right)_y - p\left(\frac{\partial V}{\partial x}\right)_y$$

Dividing by dy at constant x, we get

$$\left(\frac{\partial U}{\partial y}\right)_x = T\left(\frac{\partial S}{\partial y}\right)_x - p\left(\frac{\partial V}{\partial y}\right)_x$$

Also, $$\frac{\partial^2 U}{\partial x\,\partial y} = \frac{\partial^2 U}{\partial y\,\partial x}$$

So, $$\left(\frac{\partial T}{\partial y}\right)_x \left(\frac{\partial S}{\partial x}\right)_y - \left(\frac{\partial p}{\partial x}\right)_x \left(\frac{\partial V}{\partial x}\right)_y = \left(\frac{\partial T}{\partial x}\right)_y \left(\frac{\partial S}{\partial y}\right)_x - \left(\frac{\partial p}{\partial x}\right)_y \left(\frac{\partial V}{\partial y}\right)_x$$

Other terms are cancelled out.

or $$\left(\frac{\partial p}{\partial x}\right)_y \left(\frac{\partial V}{\partial y}\right)_x - \left(\frac{\partial p}{\partial y}\right)_x \left(\frac{\partial V}{\partial x}\right)_y = \left(\frac{\partial T}{\partial x}\right)_y \left(\frac{\partial S}{\partial y}\right)_x - \left(\frac{\partial T}{\partial y}\right)_x \left(\frac{\partial S}{\partial x}\right)_y$$

or in Jacobian form

$$\frac{\partial(p, V)}{\partial(x, y)} = \frac{\partial(T, S)}{\partial(x, y)}$$

(i) We may take $x = T$ and $y = V$

$$\left(\frac{\partial p}{\partial T}\right)_V = \left(\frac{\partial S}{\partial V}\right)_T$$

(ii) We may take $x = T$ and $y = p$

$$\left(\frac{\partial V}{\partial T}\right)_p = -\left(\frac{\partial S}{\partial p}\right)_T$$

(iii) We may take $x = S$, $y = V$

$$\left(\frac{\partial p}{\partial S}\right)_V = -\left(\frac{\partial T}{\partial V}\right)_S$$

(iv) We may take $x = S$ and $y = p$

$$\left(\frac{\partial V}{\partial S}\right)_p = \left(\frac{\partial T}{\partial p}\right)_S$$

The above relations (i), (ii), (iii) and (iv) are known as Maxwell relations. We may remember three things about Maxwell relations

(a) The cross-multiplication of variables in any relation gives the dimensions of energy. For example p and V; T and S.

(b) The conjugate variables are taken as constants.

(c) If p and T occur together in one side, the sign is positive otherwise it is negative.

The Clausius-Clapeyron Equation

The Clausius-Clapeyron equation is an important relation describing the variation of pressure with temperature for a system containing two phases in equilibrium.

Consider a cylinder containing liquid and some of its vapour in equilibrium. The saturated vapour pressure is a function of temperature only. We have the first Maxwell relation

$$\left(\frac{\partial S}{\partial V}\right)_T = \left(\frac{\partial p}{\partial T}\right)_V$$

Multiplying throughout by T,

$$T\left(\frac{\partial S}{\partial V}\right)_T = T\left(\frac{\partial p}{\partial T}\right)_V$$

Let the system expand a little at constant temperature T. More space is created and as the temperature remains constant, more liquid will evaporate to fill the extra space. This will require absorption of an amount of heat $\delta Q = \delta mL$ where, L is the latent heat of vaporization.

So, the Clausius-Clapeyron equation may be written as

$$T\left(\frac{\partial S}{\partial V}\right)_T = \left(\frac{\delta Q}{\partial V}\right)_T = \frac{L}{v_{\text{vap}} - v_{\text{liq}}} = T\left(\frac{\partial p}{\partial T}\right)_V$$

where, $v = \dfrac{V}{m}$ = specific volume.

If we keep volume constant and increase temperature, more liquid will evaporate and a new saturated vapour pressure will be attained. Hence.

$$\left(\frac{\partial p}{\partial T}\right)_V = \left(\frac{dp}{dT}\right)_{\text{sat}}$$

So,
$$\left(\frac{dp}{dT}\right)_{\text{sat}} = \frac{L}{T(v_{\text{vap}} - v_{\text{liq}})}$$

This is the Clausius-Clapeyron equation for liquid vapour equilibrium. As $v_{\text{vap}} > v_{\text{liq}}$,

$$\left(\frac{dp}{dT}\right)_{\text{sat}} > 0$$

In other words, if pressure is increased, the boiling point temperature will increase. We may similarly get relations for solid vapour equilibrium and solid liquid equilibrium.

Example 9. *Prove that the ratio of adiabatic elasticity to isothermal elasticity equals* $\dfrac{C_p}{C_V} = \gamma$.

Sol. Elasticity is defined as $V\left(\dfrac{\partial p}{\partial V}\right)$

Under appropriate conditions

$$\frac{E_S}{E_T} = \frac{V\left(\frac{\partial p}{\partial V}\right)_S}{V\left(\frac{\partial p}{\partial V}\right)_T}$$

$$= -\frac{V\left(\frac{\partial p}{\partial S}\right)_V\left(\frac{\partial S}{\partial V}\right)_p}{V\left(\frac{\partial p}{\partial V}\right)_T} \quad \left(\text{Since, }\left(\frac{\partial x}{\partial y}\right)_z = -\left(\frac{\partial x}{\partial z}\right)_y \cdot \left(\frac{\partial z}{\partial y}\right)_x\right)$$

$$= -\frac{\left(\frac{\partial S}{\partial T}\right)_p\left(\frac{\partial T}{\partial V}\right)_p}{\left(\frac{\partial p}{\partial V}\right)_T\left(\frac{\partial S}{\partial T}\right)_V\left(\frac{\partial T}{\partial p}\right)_V} \quad \left[\text{Since, }\left(\frac{\partial x}{\partial y}\right)_z = \frac{1}{\left(\frac{\partial y}{\partial x}\right)_z}\right]$$

and
$$C_p = T\left(\frac{\partial S}{\partial T}\right)_p$$

$$C_V = T\left(\frac{\partial S}{\partial T}\right)_V$$

$$= -\frac{C_p}{C_V}\frac{1}{\left(\frac{\partial p}{\partial V}\right)_T\left(\frac{\partial T}{\partial p}\right)_V\left(\frac{\partial V}{\partial T}\right)_p}$$

$$= \frac{C_p}{C_V} \quad \left[\text{Since, }\left(\frac{\partial x}{\partial y}\right)_z\left(\frac{\partial y}{\partial z}\right)_x\left(\frac{\partial z}{\partial x}\right)_y = -1\right]$$

Example 10. *Prove that* $K_S - K_T = -\dfrac{\alpha^2 VT}{C_p}$

where, K is compressibility.

Sol. We know $\dfrac{E_S}{E_T} = \dfrac{K_T}{K_S} = \dfrac{C_p}{C_V}$

$$\frac{K_S - K_T}{K_T} = \frac{C_V - C_p}{C_p}$$

$$K_S - K_T = -\frac{K_T}{C_p}(C_p - C_V)$$

$$= -\frac{K_T}{C_p}T\left(\frac{\partial p}{\partial T}\right)_V\left(\frac{\partial V}{\partial T}\right)_p$$

$$= -\frac{K_T}{C_p} T \left(\frac{\partial p}{\partial V}\right)_T \left(\frac{\partial V}{\partial T}\right)_p^2$$

$$= \frac{T}{VC_p}\left(\frac{\partial V}{\partial T}\right)_p^2 = \frac{VT\alpha^2}{C_p}$$

$$\left[\text{Since, } K_T = -\frac{1}{V}\left(\frac{\partial V}{\partial p}\right)_T \text{ and } \alpha = \frac{1}{V}\left(\frac{\partial V}{\partial T}\right)_p\right]$$

Example 11. *Show that the ratio of adiabatic to isobaric volume expansivity is* $\frac{1}{1-\gamma}$.

Sol. Volume expansivity is defined as $\frac{1}{V}\left(\frac{\partial V}{\partial T}\right)$.

So,
$$\frac{\alpha_S}{\alpha_p} = \frac{\left(\frac{\partial V}{\partial T}\right)_S}{\left(\frac{\partial V}{\partial T}\right)_p}$$

$$= -\frac{\left(\frac{\partial V}{\partial S}\right)_T \left(\frac{\partial S}{\partial T}\right)_V}{\left(\frac{\partial V}{\partial T}\right)_p}$$

$$= -\frac{\left(\frac{\partial S}{\partial T}\right)_V}{\left(\frac{\partial S}{\partial V}\right)_T \left(\frac{\partial V}{\partial T}\right)_p}$$

$$= -\frac{C_V}{T\left(\frac{\partial p}{\partial T}\right)_V \left(\frac{\partial V}{\partial T}\right)_p}$$

$$= -\frac{C_V}{C_p - C_V} = \frac{1}{1-\gamma}$$

Example 12. *Show that*

(i) $C_p = T\left(\frac{\partial V}{\partial T}\right)_p \left(\frac{\partial p}{\partial T}\right)_S$

(ii) $C_V = -T\left(\frac{\partial p}{\partial T}\right)_V \left(\frac{\partial V}{\partial T}\right)_S$

Sol. (i) $C_p = T\left(\frac{\partial S}{\partial T}\right)_p = -T\left(\frac{\partial S}{\partial p}\right)_T \left(\frac{\partial p}{\partial T}\right)_S$

or
$$C_p = T\left(\frac{\partial V}{\partial T}\right)_p \left(\frac{\partial p}{\partial T}\right)_S$$

$$\left[\text{Using Maxwell relation } \left(\frac{\partial S}{\partial p}\right)_T = -\left(\frac{\partial V}{\partial T}\right)_p\right]$$

(ii) $C_V = T\left(\frac{\partial S}{\partial T}\right)_V = -T\left(\frac{\partial S}{\partial V}\right)_T \left(\frac{\partial V}{\partial T}\right)_S$

$$= -T\left(\frac{\partial p}{\partial T}\right)_V \left(\frac{\partial V}{\partial T}\right)_S$$

$$\left[\text{Using Maxwell relation } \left(\frac{\partial S}{\partial V}\right)_T = \left(\frac{\partial p}{\partial T}\right)_V\right]$$

Thermodynamic Potentials

For an isolated system, the entropy always increases or remains constant. For a system in contact with a heat reservoir, it is no longer isolated, maximization of entropy for the system is not the criterion but a criterion for equilibrium for the system plus reservoir.

Consider a system in contact with a reservoir at temperature T. For two equilibrium states at the same temperature T

$$\Delta S_{\text{system}} + \Delta S_{\text{reservoir}} \geq 0$$

and
$$\Delta S - \frac{Q}{T} \geq 0$$

where, Q is the amount of heat gained by the system.

or
$$Q \leq T\,\Delta S \qquad \ldots(28)$$

Now by the first law,

$$Q = U_2 - U_1 + W$$

$$U_2 - U_1 + W \leq T(S_2 - S_1)$$

$$W \leq (U_1 - TS_1) - (U_2 - TS_2)$$

or
$$W \leq F_1 - F_2 \qquad \ldots(29)$$

where, $F = U - TS$ called the **Helmholtz free energy.**

Thus, the decrease in the Helmholtz free energy sets an upper limit to the maximum work that may be done by the system, in any process between any two equilibrium states.

For generality, we can consider W as a sum of pdV work and non-$p\,dV$ work which is denoted by W_{pV} and $W_{\text{non-}pV}$ respectively.

At constant volume

$$W_{\text{non-}pV} \leq F_1 - F_2 \qquad \ldots(30)$$

$(F_1 - F_2)$ sets an upper limit to the non-$p\,dV$ work obtainable from the system. If it is only $p\,dV$ work, then $F_1 - F_2 \geq 0$ or $F_1 \geq F_2$ or Helmholtz free energy always decreases or remain constant in a system at constant temperature and constant volume.

If it is at constant pressure

$$W_{\text{non-}pV} + p(V_2 - V_1) \leq F_1 - F_2$$

$$W_{\text{non-}pV} \leq (U_1 - TS_1 + pV_1) - (U_2 - TS_2 + pV_2)$$

$$W_{\text{non-}pV} \leq G_1 - G_2 \qquad \ldots(31)$$

where, $G = U - TS + pV$ is called the Gibbs free energy. The decrease in the Gibbs free energy sets an upper limit to non-$p\,dV$ work obtainable for systems between two equilibrium states at constant temperature and pressure.

If there is no non-$p\,dV$ work done then, $G_1 - G_2 \geq 0$

or
$$G_1 \geq G_2$$

or the Gibbs free energy either remains constant or decreases.

We have also defined the enthalpy H as

$$H = U + pV \quad ...(32)$$

Let us take the differentials of U, F, G, H

(i) $dU = T\,dS - p\,dV$ (for a p-V system)

So, $T = \left(\frac{\partial U}{\partial S}\right)_V$ and $p = -\left(\frac{\partial U}{\partial V}\right)_S$

(ii) $dF = dU - T\,dS - S\,dT = -p\,dV - S\,dT$

$$p = -\left(\frac{\partial F}{\partial V}\right)_T \text{ and } S = -\left(\frac{\partial F}{\partial T}\right)_V$$

(iii) $dG = dU - T\,dS - S\,dT + p\,dV + V\,dp$

$$= -S\,dT + V\,dp$$

$$S = -\left(\frac{\partial G}{\partial T}\right)_p \text{ and } V = \left(\frac{\partial G}{\partial p}\right)_T$$

The functions U, F, G, H are called thermodynamic potentials. p, V, T, S are obtained as partial derivatives of one or more of the above functions just as the electric field is the partial derivative of the electric potential. Hence, they are called thermodynamic potentials.

Example 13. *Show that* $H = \left[\frac{\partial (G/T)}{\partial (1/T)}\right]_p$

Sol. By definition $G = U - TS + pV$

Taking differentials

$$dG = dU - T\,dS + p\,dV - S\,dT + V\,dp$$
$$= -S\,dT + V\,dp$$

So, $V = \left(\frac{\partial G}{\partial p}\right)_T$, $S = -\left(\frac{\partial G}{\partial T}\right)_p$

$$H = U + pV \quad \text{(by definition)}$$
$$= G + TS$$
$$= G - T\left(\frac{\partial G}{\partial T}\right)_p$$
$$= G\left(\frac{\partial T}{\partial T}\right)_p - T\left(\frac{\partial G}{\partial T}\right)_p$$
$$= -T^2\frac{\partial}{\partial T}\left(\frac{G}{T}\right) = \frac{\partial (G/T)}{\partial (1/T)}$$

Example 14. *Prove that* $dF = -(pV\alpha + S)dT + pVk\,dp$ *where,* α *is the coefficient of volume expansion and* k *is the compressibility.*

Sol. $dF = -p\,dV - S\,dT$

$$= -p\left(\frac{\partial V}{\partial T}\right)_p dT - p\left(\frac{\partial V}{\partial p}\right)_T dp - S\,dT$$
$$= -pV\,\alpha\,dT - S\,dT + pV\,k\,dp$$

Example 15. *Show that for n moles of an ideal gas*

$$F = \int C_V\,dT - T\int \frac{C_V}{T}dT - nRT\ln V - a_1T + a_2$$

where, a_1 *and* a_2 *are constants.*

Sol. F is given by $F = U - TS$

Taking U and S as functions of T and V,

$$dU = \left(\frac{\partial U}{\partial T}\right)_V dT + \left(\frac{\partial U}{\partial V}\right)_T dV$$
$$dU = C_V\,dT$$

Since, for an ideal gas $\left(\frac{\partial U}{\partial V}\right)_T = 0$

and $$dS = \left(\frac{\partial S}{\partial T}\right)_V dT + \left(\frac{\partial S}{\partial V}\right)_T dV$$
$$= \frac{C_V}{T}dT + \left(\frac{\partial p}{\partial T}\right)_V dV$$
$$= \frac{C_V}{T}dT + \frac{nR}{V}dV$$

On integrating, we get $U = \int C_V\,dT + a_1$

and $$S = \int \frac{C_V}{T}dT + nR\ln V + a_2$$

Substituting into the expression for F,

$$F = U - TS$$
$$= \int C_V\,dT - T\int\frac{C_V}{T}dT - nRT\ln V + a_1 - a_2T$$

where a_1, a_2 are constants of integration.

Gibbs-Helmholtz Equation

From Gibbs free energy function, $G = H - TS$, a relation between the quantities, ΔG, ΔH and ΔS can be obtained. Similarly, the quantities ΔA, ΔE and ΔS can be related with the work function, $A = E - TS$.

The relations between the above thermodynamic functions lead to two important relations. Each of the two relations is known as **Gibbs-Helmholtz equation.** It is one of the most important relations in chemical thermodynamics, because it helps us towards a better understanding of the driving force behind chemical reactions. The two relations may be derived as under

We know that at constant pressure,

$$dG = Vdp - SdT$$
$$dG_p = -SdT_p$$

or $$\left(\frac{\partial G}{\partial T}\right)_p = -S \quad ...(33)$$

If the value of S is substituted in $G = H - TS$, we have

$$G = H + T\left(\frac{\partial G}{\partial T}\right)_p \quad ...(34)$$

Similarly, from equation (*i.e.,* $dA = -pdV - SdT$) at constant volume, we have

$$dA_v = -SdT_v$$

or
$$\left(\frac{\partial A}{\partial T}\right)_V = -S \qquad \ldots(35)$$

Combining equation (35 with $A = E - TS$, we get,

$$A = E + T\left(\frac{\partial A}{\partial T}\right)_V \qquad \ldots(36)$$

Equations (35) and (36) are generally known as Gibbs-Helmholtz equations.

Dividing equation (36) by T^2, we get,

$$\frac{G}{T^2} = \frac{H}{T^2} + \frac{1}{T}\left(\frac{\partial G}{\partial T}\right)_p$$

This on rearrangement becomes,

$$\left[\frac{\partial (G/T)}{\partial T}\right]_p = -\frac{H}{T^2} \qquad \ldots(37)$$

Similarly, the following expression can also be derived from equation (36) after dividing it by T^2 and rearranging.

$$\left[\frac{\partial (A/T)}{\partial T}\right]_V = -\frac{E}{T^2} \qquad \ldots(38)$$

The above forms of Gibbs-Helmholtz equations are not frequently used by scientists. Alternative forms which are frequently used can also be derived as follows

For an isothermal process, equation can be written for initial and finals states as

$$G_1 = H_1 - TS_1 \text{ and } G_2 = H_2 - TS_2$$

where the subscripts 1 and 2 represent the initial and final states, respectively. Now,

$$G_2 - G_1 = (H_2 - H_1) - T(S_2 - S_1)$$

or
$$\Delta G = \Delta H - T\Delta S \qquad \ldots(39)$$

Similarly, equation (39) can be written as

$$\left(\frac{\partial G_1}{\partial T}\right)_p = -S_1 \text{ and } \left(\frac{\partial G_2}{\partial T}\right)_p = -S_2$$

or
$$\left(\frac{\partial G_2}{\partial T}\right)_p - \left(\frac{\partial G_1}{\partial T}\right)_p = -S_2 + S_1$$

$$= -(S_2 - S_1) = -\Delta S \qquad \ldots(40)$$

Combining equations (39) and (40), we get

$$\Delta G = \Delta H + T\left[\left(\frac{\partial G_2}{\partial T}\right)_p - \left(\frac{\partial G_1}{\partial T}\right)_p\right]$$

$$\Delta G = \Delta H + \left(\frac{\partial (G_2 - G_1)}{\partial T}\right)_p$$

$$\Delta G = \Delta H + T\left[\frac{\partial (\Delta G)}{\partial T}\right]_p \qquad \ldots(41)$$

Equation (41) can be represented as,

$$\Delta A = \Delta E + T\left[\frac{\partial (\Delta A)}{\partial T}\right]_V \qquad \ldots(42)$$

Equation (41) and (42) are useful forms of **Gibbs-Helmholtz equation.**

Dividing equation (43) by T^2, we get,

$$\frac{\Delta G}{T^2} = \frac{\Delta H}{T^2} + \frac{1}{T}\left[\frac{\partial (\Delta G)}{\partial T}\right]_V \qquad \ldots(43)$$

On rearrangement, we obtain,

$$\left[\frac{\partial (\Delta G / T)}{\partial T}\right]_p = -\frac{\Delta H}{T^2} \qquad \ldots(44)$$

Equation (46) represents the variation of $\Delta G / T$ with temperature.

Similarly from equaton (65) we can obtain the expression,

$$\left[\frac{\partial (\Delta A / T)}{\partial T}\right]_V = -\frac{\Delta E}{T^2} \qquad \ldots(45)$$

Equation (46) represents the variation of ΔA or $\Delta A / T$ with temperature.

Integrated form of Gibbs-Helmholtz equation On rearranging equation (65), we get,

$$\frac{1}{T}\left[\frac{\partial (\Delta G)}{\partial T}\right]_p - \frac{\Delta G}{T^2} = -\frac{\Delta H}{T^2}$$

or
$$\frac{\partial}{\partial T}\left(\frac{\Delta G}{T}\right) = -\frac{\Delta H}{T^2}$$

or
$$\int d\left(\frac{\Delta G}{T}\right) = \int -\frac{\Delta H}{T^2}\, dT$$

i.e.,
$$\frac{\Delta G}{T} = -\int \frac{\Delta H}{T^2}\, dT + X_p \qquad \ldots(46)$$

where,
$$X_p = f(p)$$

If equation (46) is integrated between limits T_1 and T_2, we get,

$$\frac{\Delta G_2}{T_2} - \frac{\Delta G_1}{T_1} = -\int_{T_1}^{T_2} \frac{\Delta H}{T^2}\, dT \qquad \ldots(47)$$

From (47) it is possible to calculate ΔG_2 at T_2 from the known values of ΔG_1 at T_1 and heat of reaction (ΔH).

Equations (46) and (47) are known as integrated forms of Gibbs-Helmholtz equation.

Significance of Gibbs-Helmholtz Equation

(i) It helps us to calculate the heat change in a reaction form the E.M.F.'s of galvanic cells. We know that the change in the free energy produced by the passage of *n* Faradays, *i.e., nF* coulombs through a reversible cell is given by, $-\Delta G = nFE$, where E denotes the reversible E.M.F. The negative sign implies that there is a decrease of free energy when the E.M.F. is positive. Hence, combining the last expression with equation (46), we get

$$E = -\frac{\Delta H}{nF} + T\left(\frac{\partial E}{\partial T}\right)_p$$

Whether the electrical work is greater than, equal to or less than ΔH depends on the sign of $\partial E / \partial T$, *i.e.,* temperature coefficient of E.M.F. It will thus be seen that if E and $\partial E / \partial T$ are known, the heat of reaction of the process occurring in the cell can be evaluated.

(ii) If the standard potential of an electrode is known at two or more temperatures, the entropy of the reversible ion can be determined by using a suitable form of Gibbs-Helmholtz equation.

(iii) By means of Gibbs-Helmholtz equation, the entropy changes and enthalpy changes can also be calculated.

Third Law of Thermodynamics

It is known, that it is impossible to attain the temperature 0 K. The approach to within 1×10^{-6} degrees of absolute zero does not mean that there remains only a small step, which will be soon taken. On the other hand, it is practically unattainable.

In cooling by means of isothermal magnetization and adiabatic demagnetization, the temperature obtained in each stage steadily decreases. If, however, a perfect reversibility is achieved, we would attain absolute zero at the limit of an infinite series of steps. We, therefore, postulate the third law of thermodynamics as a generalisation and can be stated as follows **(first form)**

"It is impossible by any method no matter how idealised, to reduce the temperature of any system to absolute zero in a finite number of operations."

We know that during the nineteenth century the first and second law of thermodynamics were formulated and applied to many problems of scientific nature. The first and second laws have led to the development of the concepts of energy content and entropy, respetively. In the first decade of the twentieth century, the investigations constituted the third law of thermodynamics. This law, however, differs from the first law in the respect that it leads to no new concepts. It, however, places some limitations upon the value of the entropy. It was due to this fact, that some writers hesitated to refer it to as a third law of thermodynamics. As deduced earlier, we have

$$\lim_{T=0} \Delta C_p = 0$$

$$\lim_{T=0} [C_p(\text{products}) - C_p(\text{reactants})] = 0$$

Therefore, the heat capacities of produts and reactants become identical at 0 K. This leads to suggest that "at absolute zero, all substances have the same heat capacity." From quantum theory, the heat capacities of solids should tend to zero at 0 K. Hence, Nernst's heat theorem can be extended to,

$$\lim_{T=0} C_p = 0$$

or

$$\lim_{T=0} \Delta S = 0$$

In other words, the absolute entropies of products and reactants in solid state are identical. Hence, we can conclude that at absolute zero, all solid substances have the same entropy. Planck on the basis of quantum theory suggested that the entropies of pure solids and liquids approach zero at 0 K, i.e.,

$$\lim_{T=0} S = 0$$

This law may also be stated in the words of Lewis and Randall that, "every substance has a finite positive entropy, but at absolute zero of temperature the entropy may become zero and does so become in the case of perfectly crystalline substances."

This statement of the third law of thermodynamics is similar to the heat theorem proposed by W. Nernst (1906). Nernst asserted that the entropy change for reactions between pure crystalline substances.

Consequences of Third Law of Thermodynamics

From the third law of thermodynamics we can arrive at a number of generalisations, all of which are not derivable from the Nernst's theorem.

[I] The entropy change of a system due only to a small pressure-change, for a process near 0 K may be expressed, as

$$\Delta S = \int \left(\frac{\partial S}{\partial p}\right)_T dp$$

But at 0 K, $\Delta S = 0$, so $\left(\frac{\partial S}{\partial p}\right)_T = 0$

From Maxwell's relations,

$$\left(\frac{\partial S}{\partial p}\right)_T = -\left(\frac{\partial V}{\partial T}\right)_p$$

Hence, at 0 K $\left(\frac{\partial V}{\partial T}\right)_p = 0$

or $\lim_{T=0}\left(\frac{\partial V}{\partial T}\right)_p = 0$

[II] For a small volume-change of the system,

$$\Delta S = \int \left(\frac{\partial S}{\partial V}\right)_T dV$$

Hence, at 0 K $\left(\frac{\partial S}{\partial V}\right)_T = 0$

From Maxwell's relations,

$$\left(\frac{\partial p}{\partial T}\right)_V = \left(\frac{\partial S}{\partial V}\right)_T$$

At absolute zero, $\left(\frac{\partial p}{\partial T}\right)_V = 0$

or $\lim_{T=0}\left(\frac{\partial p}{\partial T}\right)_V = 0$

[III] We know that,

$$C_p = \left(\frac{\partial q}{\partial T}\right)_p = \left(\frac{TdS}{dt}\right)_p$$

$$dS = C_p \frac{dT}{T}$$

$$\int_0^T dS = \int_0^T C_p \frac{dT}{T}$$

$$S_T - S_0 = \int_0^T C_p \frac{dT}{T}$$

Since, $\left(\frac{C_p}{T}\right)$ is a finite quantity, we can say $(S_T - S_0)$ must be a positive quantity, *i.e.*, $S_T > S_0$. In other words, **the entropy of a substance at an temperature must be greater than its entropy at absolute zero. S_T is called absolute entropy of a substance at temperature T.**

Now, the third law states that the value of S_T must be finite at all temperatures. This means that at absolute zero ($T = 0$ K), C_p must be zero, otherwise, if at 0 K, C_p is finite, then S_T cannot be finite. Therefore,

$$\lim_{T=0} C_p = 0$$

Similarly, at constant volume, it can be shown that,

$$\lim_{T=0} C_V = 0$$

[IV] We know that, $G = H - TS$

$$\begin{aligned} dG &= dH - TdS - SdT \\ &= d(E + pdV) - TdS - SdT \\ &= dE + pdV + Vdp - TdS - SdT \\ &= (dq - pdV) + pdV + Vdp - TdS - SdT \\ \therefore \quad &= TdS - pdV + pdV + Vdp - TdS - SdT \\ \therefore \quad dG &= Vdp - SdT \end{aligned}$$

According to Maxwell's relations,

$$-\left(\frac{\partial S}{\partial p}\right)_T = \left(\frac{\partial V}{\partial T}\right)_p$$

According to third law of thermodynamics,

$$\left(\frac{\partial S}{\partial p}\right)_{T=0} = 0$$

$$\therefore \quad \lim_{T=0}\left(\frac{\partial V}{\partial T}\right)_p = 0$$

[V] We know that, $A = E - TS$

$$dA = -SdT - pdV$$

According to Maxwell's relations,

$$\left(\frac{\partial S}{\partial V}\right)_T = \left(\frac{\partial p}{\partial T}\right)_V$$

But $\left(\frac{\partial S}{\partial V}\right)_{T=0} = 0$

$$\therefore \quad \lim_{T=0}\left(\frac{\partial p}{\partial T}\right)_V = 0$$

Perfect crystal In a perfect crystal, at absolute temperature, each atom must be at a crystal lattice point and it must have lowest energy. This means that this state is of perfect order or of zero entropy. Therefore, perfect crystals have no disorder and have zero entropy at absolute zero. In the case of glassy solids or liquids, there exists some randomness in the arrangement of atoms or molecules, therefore, the entropy of such substances is never zero. Hence, the third law is only true for perfectly crystalline solids.

Entropies of Real Gases

From one of the Maxwell relations, we can show

$$\left(\frac{\partial S}{\partial p}\right)_T = -\left(\frac{\partial V}{\partial T}\right)_p \quad ...(48)$$

$$dS = -\left(\frac{\partial V}{\partial T}\right)_p dp \quad ...(49)$$

Integrating between p_1 and p_2 at constant T, we get

$$\int_1^2 dS = -\int_{p_1}^{p_2}\left(\frac{\partial V}{\partial T}\right)_p dp \quad ...(50)$$

A real gas behaves ideally at low pressures. Let, this pressure be p. Let, $(S_r)_1$ be the entropy of the real gas at 1 atm pressure and $(S_r)_p$ be the entropy at pressure p, the temperature remaining constant. Then, from equaton (50),

$$(S_r)_1 - (S_r)_p = -\int_p^1\left(\frac{\partial V}{\partial T}\right)_p dp \quad ...(51)$$

For an ideal gas, $\left(\frac{\partial V}{\partial T}\right)_p = \frac{R}{p}$. If $(S_i)_1$ and $(S_i)_p$ are the entropies of an ideal gas at 1 atm and p atmosphere, respectively, then equation (51) can be written as,

$$(S_i)_p - (S_i)_1 = \int_p^1\left(\frac{R}{p}\right)dp \quad ...(52)$$

We can equate $(S_r)_p$ with $(S_i)_p$ because at low pressure p, the real gas behaves ideally.

Combining equations (52) and (53), we get,

$$(S_i)_1 - (S_r)_1 = S° - S = \int_p^1\left[\left(\frac{\partial V}{\partial T}\right)_p - \frac{R}{p}\right]dp \quad ...(53)$$

where, $S°$ is the standard entropy and S is the entropy of real gas both determined at 1 atm. We have to determine $S°$. So, S is given by,

$$S = \frac{1}{3}a(T^*)^3 + \int_{T^*}^{T_f}\frac{C_{p(s)}}{T}dT + \frac{\Delta H_f}{T_f}$$

$$+\int_{T_f}^{T_b}\frac{C_{p(l)}}{T}dT + \frac{\Delta H_V}{T_b} + \int_{T_b}^{T}\frac{C_{p(g)}}{T}dT \quad ...(54)$$

Though the integrals in equation (54) can be evaluated graphically, it is more convenient to do so with the use of an equation of state. Berthelot equations of state, *viz.*,

$$\left(p + \frac{a}{TV^2}\right)(V - b) = RT \quad ...(55)$$

is more appropriate to use than the van der Waals' equation of state.

Multiplying and rearranging, we get

$$pV = RT + pb - \frac{a}{TV} + \frac{ab}{TV^2} \quad ...(56)$$

The term ab/TV^2 in the above equation is negligible as compared to other terms since, the Berthelot constants a and b are small.

Thus, equation (56) becomes

$$pV = RT + pb - \frac{a}{TV}$$

$$= RT\left[1 + \frac{pb}{RT} - \frac{ap}{R^2T^3}\right]$$

$$[\because V \approx RT/p] \quad ...(57)$$

For Berthelot's equation of state, the constants a, b and gas constant R can be written in terms of critical constants. Accordingly,

$$a = \left(\frac{16}{3}\right)p_cV_c^2T_c;\ b = \frac{V_c}{4};\ R = \left(\frac{32}{9}\right)\frac{p_cV_c}{T_c} \quad ...(58)$$

So, equation (57) becomes,

$$pV = RT\left[1 + \frac{9}{128}\frac{pT_c}{p_cT}\left(1 - \frac{6T_c^2}{T^2}\right)\right] \quad ...(59)$$

Dividing the above equation by p, we have

$$V = \frac{RT}{p} + \frac{9}{128}\frac{RT_c}{p_c} - \frac{27RT_c^3}{64p_cT^2}$$

$$\therefore \quad \left(\frac{\partial V}{\partial T}\right)_p = \frac{R}{p} + \frac{27RT_c^3}{32p_cT^3}$$

Substituting the value of $\left(\frac{\partial V}{\partial T}\right)_p$ in equation (58), we get

$$S° = S + \frac{27}{32}\frac{RT_c^3}{p_cT^3}\int_p^1 dp$$

$$= S + \frac{27}{32}\frac{RT_c^3}{p_cT^3}(1 - p)$$

$$= S + \frac{27}{32}\frac{RT_c^3}{p_cT^3} \quad (\because p << 1) \quad ...(60)$$

As mentioned earlier, S is given by equation (55). In equation (60), the second term is the correction term that should be added to S to give $S°$, the standard entropy of a real gas.

Entropy Changes in Chemical Reactions

We can calculate the $\Delta S°$ value of a chemical reaction from the tabulated standard entropy values for the reactants and products at 298 K. This is one of the most important applications of the third law of thermodynamics. For a reaction

$$aA + bB + \ldots \rightarrow lL + mM + \ldots$$

occurring in the standard state, the standard entropy change, $\Delta S°$, is given by

$$\Delta S° = [lS°_L + mS°_M + \ldots] - [aS°_A + bS°_B + \ldots]$$
$$= \Sigma S°_{\text{products}} - \Sigma S°_{\text{reactants}} \qquad \ldots(61)$$

where, $S°$s are the molar standard entropies of the species involved and a, b, l, m, etc., are the stoichiometric coefficients.

From the tabulated values of $S°$, $\Delta S°$ for the reaction at 298 K can be calculated. The $\Delta S°$ value at any other temperature can be calculated by the Kirchhoff-type equation, *viz.*,

$$\left[\frac{d(\Delta S°)}{dT}\right]_p = \Sigma\left(\frac{\partial S°_{\text{products}}}{\partial T}\right)_p - \Sigma\left(\frac{\partial S°_{\text{reactants}}}{\partial T}\right)_p \qquad \ldots(62)$$

Since, $\left(\frac{\partial S}{\partial T}\right)_p = \frac{C_p}{T}$, we have

$$\left[\frac{d(\Delta S°)}{dT}\right]_p = \Sigma\left(\frac{C_p}{T}\right)_{\text{products}} - \Sigma\left(\frac{C_p}{T}\right)_{\text{reactants}} \qquad \ldots(63)$$

Rearranging and integrating between 298 K and T K, we have

$$\int_{298}^{T} d(\Delta S°) = \int_{298}^{T} \left(\frac{\Delta C_p}{T}\right) dT = \int_{298}^{T} \Delta C_p \, d \ln T$$

or $$\Delta S°_T = \Delta S°_{298} + \int_{298}^{T} \Delta C_p \, d \ln T \qquad \ldots(64)$$

Eq. (64) is applicable to chemical reactions involving solids, liquids or gases.

Exercise 1

(For Part 'B')

1. All natural process are irreversible. This is a direct consequence of
(a) first law of thermodynamics
(b) second law of thermodynamics
(c) third law of thermodynamics
(d) Gibb's paradox

2. Third law of thermodynamics implies that
(a) $T = 0°K$ cannot be attained even by infinite numbers of process
(b) $T = 0°K$ cannot be attained by infinite numbers of processes
(c) T cannot be negative
(d) even at $T = 0$, there is non-zero entropy

3. Which of the following statement is true?
(a) Third law of thermodynamics and quantum mechanics are not consistent
(b) Third law of thermodynamics and quantum mechanics are consistent
(c) Third law of thermodynamics is valid only for interacting system
(d) Third law of thermodynamics is valid only for non-interacting system

4. A given amount of heat cannot be completely converted into work. However, it is possible to convert a given amount of work completely into heat. This statement results from the
(a) zeroth law of thermodynamics
(b) first law of thermodynamics
(c) second law of thermodynamics
(d) third law of thermodynamics

5. The temperature of the surface of the sun is approximated 6000 K. If we take a big lens and focus the sun rays and produce a temperature of 8000 K. This will violate
(a) zeroth law (b) first law
(c) second law (d) third law

6. For any process, the second law of thermodynamics requires that the change of entropy of the universe by
(a) positive only (b) positive or zero
(c) zero only (d) negative or zero

7. The first law of thermodynamics is conservation of
(a) momentum (b) energy
(c) Both (a) and (b) (d) None of these

8. The combined form of first and second law of thermodynamics is given by
(p = Pressure, V = Volume, T = Temperature, U = Internal energy, S = Entropy, Q = Quantity of heat)
(a) $TdS = dU + pdV$ (b) $dQ = TdS + pdV$
(c) $dU = TdS + dQ$ (d) $TdS = dU - pdV$

9. If a system A is in thermal equilibrium separately with B and C, then B and C are also in thermal equilibrium with each other. This is the statement of
(a) zeroth law of thermodynamics
(b) first law of thermodynamics
(c) second law of thermodynamics
(d) third law of thermodynamics

10. A piston containing an ideal gas is originally in the state X (see figure). The gas is taken through a thermal cycle $X \to Y \to X$ as shown

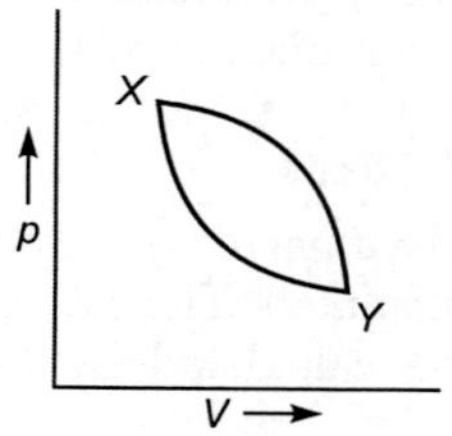

The work done by the gas is positive, if the direction of the thermal cycle is
(a) clockwise
(b) counter-clockwise
(c) neither clockwise nor counter-clockwise
(d) clockwise from $X \to Y$ and counter-clockwise from $Y \to X$

11. If W is work done by a system against its surrounding, what will $-W$ stand for?
(a) Work done on the system by its surroundings
(b) Work done by the system on its surroundings
(c) Work done is zero
(d) None of the above

12. Let ΔW_i = amount of work done by the gas when compressed isothermally to volume V, ΔQ = amount of heat absorbed by the gas during the process, ΔW_a = amount of work done by the gas when expanded adiabatically to volume V; ΔE = change in internal energy of the gas due to complete process. So, ΔE is given by
(a) $\Delta W_i + \Delta Q + \Delta W_a$
(b) $\Delta Q + \Delta W_a - \Delta W_i$
(c) $\Delta Q - \Delta W_i - \Delta W_a$
(d) None of the above

13. In a cyclic process
(a) work done is zero
(b) work done by the system is equal to the quantity of heat given to the system
(c) work done does not depend on the quantity of heat given to the system
(d) the internal energy of the system increases

14. In the pV diagram below which is the correct statement?

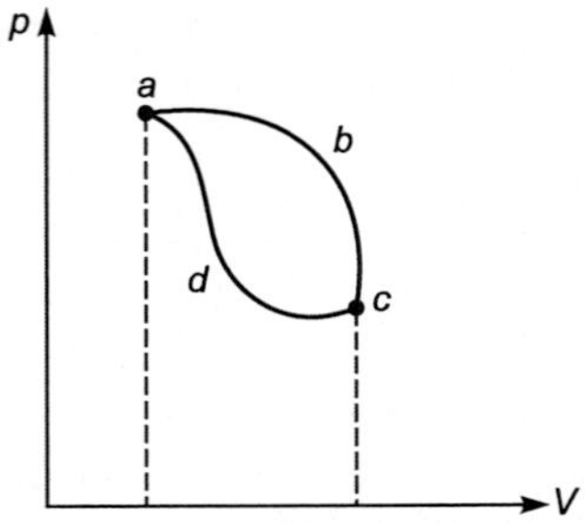

(a) Any point on the line *abc* represents a higher temperature than any point on the line *adc*
(b) The area *abcda* represents the work done by the system for the process
(c) Heat is lost to the surroundings during the process is represented by path *adc*
(d) The path *abc* and *adc* represent isothermals

15. The work done by the gas in adiabatic expansion is represented in the diagram

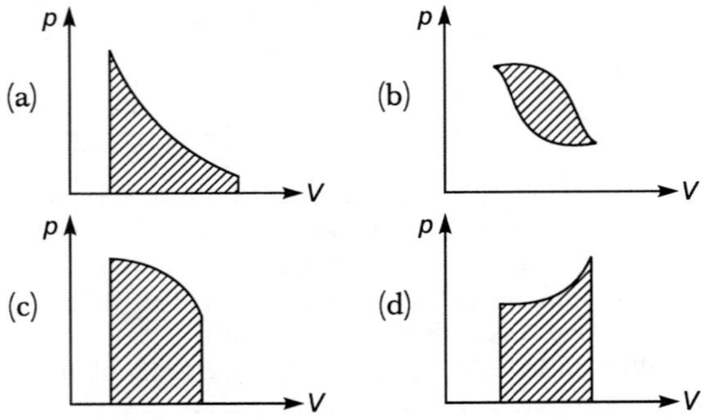

16. For a thermodynamic system, work done in a process depends upon
(a) the path (b) state of the system
(c) external pressure (d) nature of the system

17. In case a system goes reversibly from an initial state to a final state adiabatically
(a) the work done differs for neighbouring adiabatic paths connecting these states
(b) the work done is same for all neighbouring adiabatic paths connecting those states
(c) there is no work done because there is no heat flow
(d) the total energy of the system does not change

18. Which of the following is not an exact differential?
(a) dQ (Q = heat absorbed)
(b) dU (U = internal energy)
(c) dS (S = entropy)
(d) dF (F = free energy)

19. One mole of a perfect gas expands adiabatically. As a result of this, its pressure, temperature and volume change from p_1, T_1, V_1 to p_2, T_2 and V_2 respectively. If molar specific heat at constant volume is C_V, then the work done by the gas is

(a) $2.303 p_1 V_1 \log \frac{V_2}{V_1}$ (b) $RT_1 \log \frac{V_2}{V_1}$
(c) $\frac{p_1^2 V_1^2 - p_2^2 V_2^2}{R(T_2 - T_1)}$ (d) $C_V(T_1 - T_2)$

20. A thermos bottle containing coffee is vigorously shaken and thereby the temperature of coffee rises. Regard the coffee as the system
(a) $Q = 0; W = -$ ve; $\Delta U = +$ ve
(b) $Q = 0; W = +$ ve; $\Delta U = +$ ve
(c) $Q = 0; W = -$ ve; $\Delta U = -$ ve
(d) $Q = 0; W = +$ ve; $\Delta U = -$ ve

21. A resistor immersed in running water carries an electric current. Consider the resistor as the system
(a) $Q = 0; W = -$ ve; $\Delta U = -$ ve
(b) $Q = 0; W = -$ ve; $\Delta U = +$ ve
(c) $Q = 0; W = +$ ve; $\Delta U = -$ ve
(d) $Q = 0; W = +$ ve; $\Delta U = +$ ve

22. In a refrigerator, the heat exhausted to the outer atmosphere is
(a) less than that absorbed from the contents of the refrigerator
(b) same as that absorbed from the contents
(c) more than that absorbed from the contents
(d) any of the above depending upon the working substance

23. A system consists of 10^{24} atoms and is at a temperature of 300 K. Assuming that there is no interatomic energy in the system, its total internal energy is
(a) 12.4 kJ (b) 12.4 J
(c) 4.12 kJ (d) 4.12 J

24. In a heat engine, the maximum heat that can be converted into mechanical work
(a) depends upon friction
(b) depends upon working temperatures
(c) is 100%
(d) depends upon the working

25. In case of isothermal expansion forbidden process will be
(a) $W < W_{max}$ (b) $W = W_{max}$
(c) $W > W_{max}$ (d) $W = 0$

26. When a perfect gas is supposed to expand freely against vacuum in an insulated vessel, the gas has undergone
(a) an increase in pressure
(b) a change in temperature
(c) a change in entropy
(d) a change in phase

27. In an isothermal change, the internal energy of molecules
(a) may increase or decrease
(b) does not change
(c) increases
(d) decreases

28. When a liquid is heated but its state remains unchanged, its molecule gain
(a) potential energy (b) kinetic energy
(c) Both (a) and (b) (d) None of these

29. The internal energy of a perfect monatomic gas at 27°C is
(a) only kinetic
(b) only potential
(c) partly potential and partly kinetic
(d) only vibrational

30. A gas obeys Boyle's law, the shape of the graph between pV and p is
(a) a straight line parallel to pV axis
(b) a straight line parallel to p axis
(c) a hyperbola
(d) a straight line passing through origin and inclined at 45° to the axis

31. The critical temperature of a gas is
(a) $T_C = \frac{8}{27bR}$ (b) $T_C = \frac{27}{8}\frac{a}{bR}$
(c) $T_C = \frac{a}{27b^2}$ (d) $T_C = \frac{8}{27}\frac{a}{bR}$

32. The Boyle temperature of a gas is
(a) $\frac{a}{bR}$ (b) $\frac{a}{27b^2}$
(c) $\frac{8a}{27bR}$ (d) $\frac{8a}{27b}$

33. The relation between Boyle's temperature and critical temperature is
(a) $2T_B = \frac{8}{27}T_C$ (b) $T_B = \frac{27}{8}T_C$
(c) $T_B = \frac{3}{2}T_C$ (d) $3T_B = \frac{5}{13}T_C$

34. The p-V relation for a monatomic ideal gas undergoing an adiabatic process
(a) $pV^{1/3}$ = constant (b) $pV^{2/3}$ = constant
(c) $pV^{4/3}$ = constant (d) $pV^{5/3}$ = constant

35. In the near future, when the world population becomes 6 billion, how many moles of humans will be there on earth?
(a) 1×10^{-12} mol (b) 1×10^{-14} mol
(c) 1×10^{12} mol (d) 1×10^{14} mol

36. The work done W during an isothermal process in which the gas expands from an initial volume V_1 to a final volume V_2 is given by
(R = Gas constant, T = Temperature)
(a) $R(V_2 - V_1)\log_e\left(\frac{T_1}{T_2}\right)$ (b) $R(T_2 - T_1)\log_e\left(\frac{V_2}{V_1}\right)$
(c) $RT\log_e\left(\frac{V_2}{V_1}\right)$ (d) $RT\log_e\left(\frac{V_1}{V_2}\right)$

37. An ideal gas in a cylinder is compressed adiabatically to one-third of its initial volume. During this process, 20 J work is done on the gas by compressing agent. Which of the following statements is true for this case?
(a) Change in the internal energy in this process is zero
(b) The internal energy increases by 20 J
(c) The internal energy decreases by 20 J
(d) Temperature of the gas decreases

38. A gas obeys the equation of state $p(V - b)\ RT$ where, b is a constant. For this gas, a plot of V *versus* T at constant p (isobar) will be

(a)
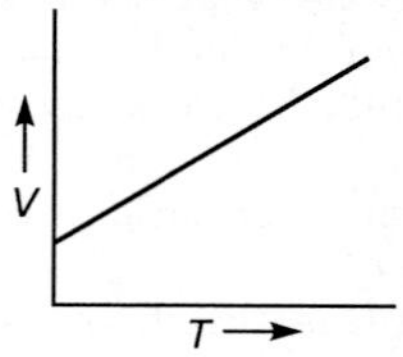

(b)
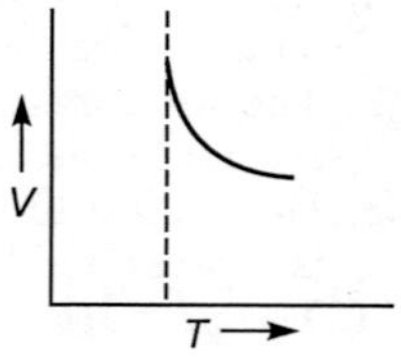

(c)
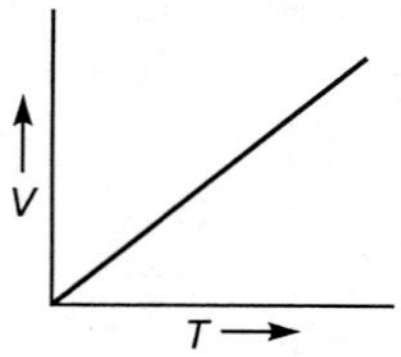

(d)
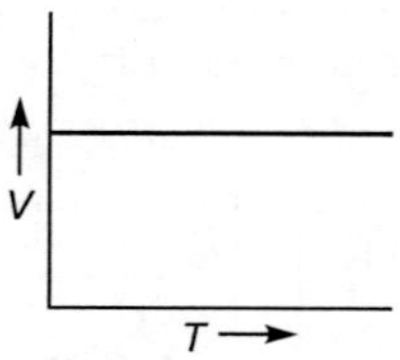

39. For liquefying a gas, it is essential that the gas
(a) should be above its temperature of inversion
(b) should be above its critical temperature
(c) should be below its temperature of inversion but above the critical temperature
(d) should be below its temperature of inversion and also below its critical temperature

40. $C_p > C_V$ (where, C_p = specific heat of a gas at constant pressure and C_V = specific heat of the same gas at constant volume) because at constant pressure
(a) the attraction between the molecules is larger
(b) the coefficient of expansion differs
(c) work is done by the expanding gas
(d) None of the above

41. The relation connecting pressure and volume in an adiabatic expansion is given by pV^n = constant. If the specific heat at constant pressure is l and the specific heat at constant volume is m, then n is given by
(a) $\frac{m}{l}$ (b) $\frac{l}{m}$
(c) $l - m$ (d) $m - l$

42. A perfect gas is expanded from 10 m^3 to 20 m^3 at a constant pressure of 10^5 N/m^2. The temperature before the expansion was 100°C. Temperature after the expansion is
(a) 473 K (b) 473°C
(c) 200°C (d) 746°C

43. Which of the following statements is correct?
(a) It is possible to transfer heat from lower to higher temperature
(b) All the reversible processes are cyclic
(c) Work done in a cyclic process is zero
(d) Cooling is produced in adiabatic expansion of a gas

44. The quantity remaining constant in the isothermal expansion of an ideal gas is
(a) heat
(b) internal energy
(c) pressure
(d) temperature and pressure

45. The potential energy of the molecules of an ideal gas is
(a) equal to their kinetic energy
(b) equal to the internal energy
(c) zero
(d) equal to the external work

46. The ratio of two specific heats of a diatomic gas is
(a) 1.66 (b) 1.33
(c) 1.40 (d) 1.52

47. Boyle's law can be expressed in differential form as
(a) $\frac{dV}{dp}=1$ (b) $\frac{dV}{dp}=\frac{V}{p}$
(c) $\frac{dV}{dp}=\frac{p}{V}$ (d) $\frac{dV}{dp}=-\frac{V}{p}$

48. Specific heat of a gas at constant volume (C_V) and at constant pressure (C_p) are related as
(a) $\frac{C_p}{C_V}=1-\frac{R}{J}$ (b) $C_p-C_V=\frac{R}{J}$
(c) $C_p-C_V=\frac{J}{R}$ (d) $C_p+C_V=\frac{R}{J}$

49. For polyatomic gases such as hydrogen the corresponding degree of freedom would be
(a) two, three (b) five, six
(c) Three, nine (d) three, four

50. Choose the correct alternatives.
(a) Internal energy of a van der Waals' gas at given temperature increases as the volume increases
(b) Internal energy of a perfect gas at a given temperature increases as the volume increases
(c) Internal energy of a Fermi gas at a given temperature increases as the volume increases
(d) Internal energy of a Fermi gas at a given temperature decreases as the volume increases

51. The equation of states of a dilute gas at very high temperature is described by $\frac{pV}{k_BT}=1+\frac{B(T)}{V}$, where, V is the volume per particle and $B(T)$ is a negative quantity. One can conclude that this is a property of
(a) a van der Waals' gas (b) an ideal Fermi gas
(c) an ideal Bose gas (d) an ideal inert gas

52. Which of the following is correct?
(a) $\frac{T_1}{H_2}+\frac{T_2}{H_1}=0$ (b) $\frac{H_1}{T_1}=\frac{H_2}{T_2}$
(c) $H_1T_1=H_2T_2$ (d) $H_1T_1+H_2T_2=0$

53. T-S diagram for a Cannot cycle is
(a) rectangle
(b) circle
(c) ellipse
(d) quadilateral type but not rectangle

54. A Carnot engine operating between 27°C and 127°C has efficiency equal to
(a) 21% (b) 22% (c) 24% (d) 25%

55. A heat pump working on the Carnot cycle maintains the inside temperature of a house at 22°C by supplying 450 kJ/s. If the outside temperature is 0°C, the heat taken, in kJ/s, from the outside air is approximately
(a) 487 (b) 470 (c) 467 (d) 417

56. A Carnot cycle operates on a working substance between two reservoirs at temperatures T_1 and T_2, where, $T_1>T_2$. During each cycle, an amount of heat Q_1 is extracted from the reservoir at T_1 and an amount Q_2 is delivered to the reservoir at T_2. Which of the following statements is incorrect?
(a) Work done in one cycle is Q_1-Q_2
(b) $\frac{Q_1}{T_1}=\frac{Q_2}{T_2}$
(c) Entropy of the hotter reservoir decreases
(d) Entropy for the universe (consisting of the working substance and the two reservoirs) increases

57. An engine absorbs heat at temperature of 100 K and rejects heat at 600K. If the engine operates at maximum possible efficiency, the amount of work performed by the engine for 200 J heat input is
(a) 1600 J (b) 1200 J (c) 800 J (d) 400 J

58. A sample of an ideal gas with initial pressure p and volume V is taken through an isothermal expansion proceed during which the change in entropy is found to be ΔS. The universal gas constant is R. Then, the work done by the gas is given by
(a) $(pV\Delta S)/(nR)$ (b) $nR\Delta S$
(c) pV (d) $(p\Delta S)/(nRV)$

59. For the thermodynamic process shown in the figure, corresponding T-S diagram is

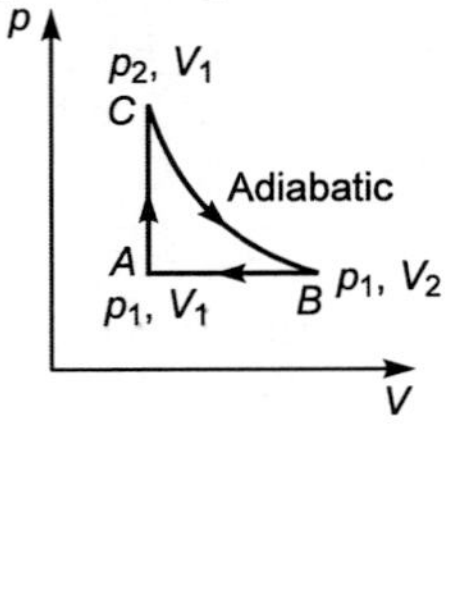

(a) 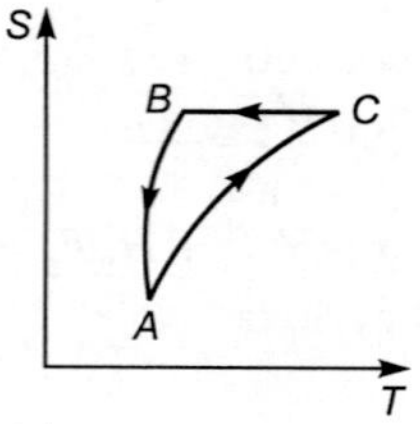

(b) 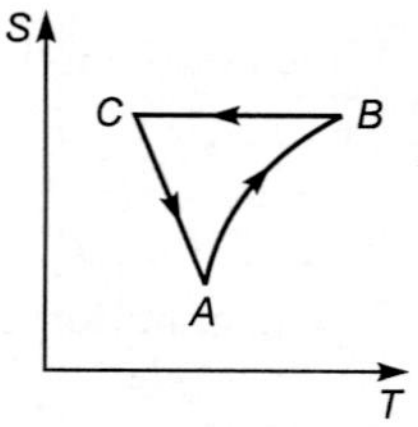

(c) 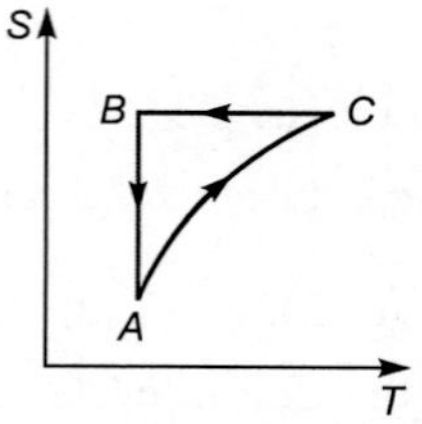

(d) 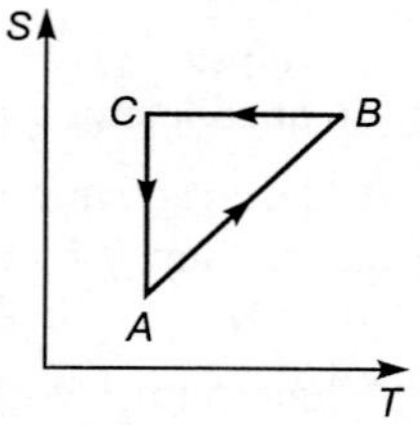

60. An amount of heat Q is transferred from a heat reservoir at temperature T_A to another heat reservoir at temperature T_B. What is the change in the entropy ΔS of the combined system?

(a) $Q\left(\frac{1}{T_B}-\frac{1}{T_A}\right)$ (b) $Q\left(\frac{1}{T_A}+\frac{1}{T_B}\right)$

(c) $\frac{Q}{\sqrt{T_A T_B}}\ln\frac{T_B}{T_A}$ (d) $Q\left(\frac{1}{T_A}-\frac{1}{T_B}\right)$

61. The efficiency of a heat engine working between heat reservoirs at temperature 327°C and 27°C respectively

(a) 25% (b) 50% (c) 75% (d) 100%

62. The T-S diagram of two cycles for the operation of an engine are shown in figure below.

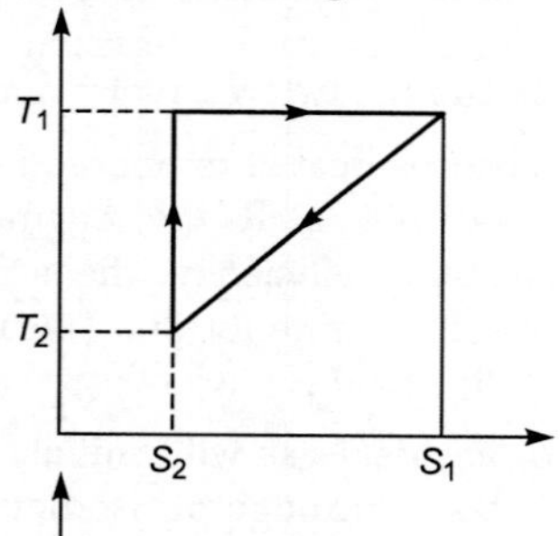

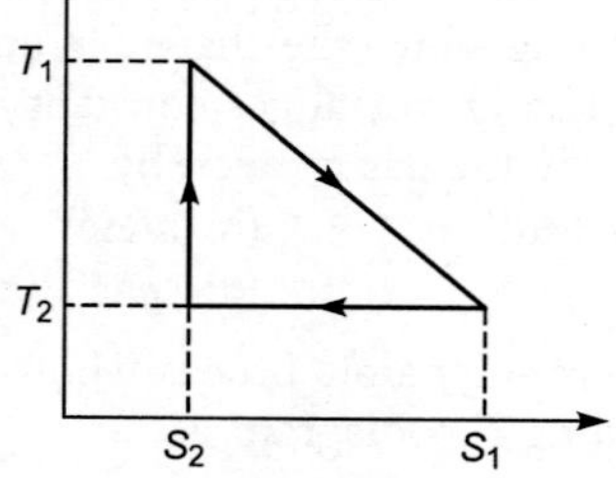

The numerical values of the parameters T_1, T_2, S_1 and S_2 in the two figures are the same which cycle has greater efficiency?

(a) First
(b) Second
(c) Both have equal efficiency
(d) None of the above

63. The efficiency of a reversible heat engine performing this cycle is

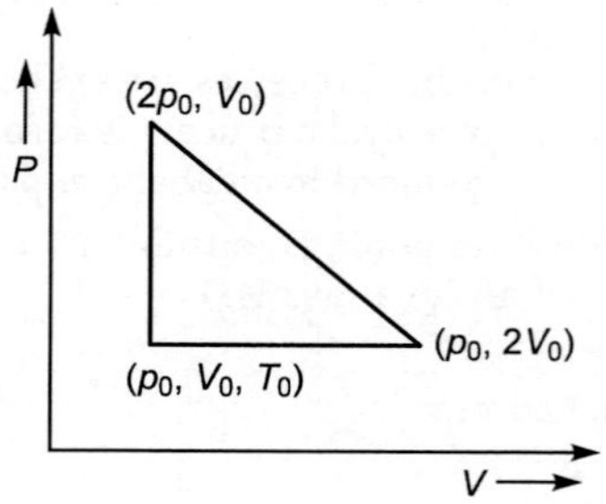

(a) $\frac{1}{4}$ (b) $\frac{1}{6}$ (c) $\frac{1}{8}$ (d) $\frac{1}{10}$

64. A reversible engine cycle is shown in the following T-S diagram. The efficiency of the engine is

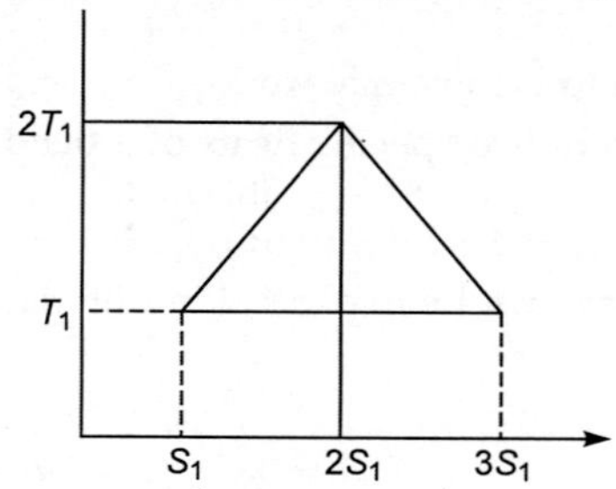

(a) $\frac{1}{3}$ (b) $\frac{1}{2}$ (c) $\frac{1}{5}$ (d) $\frac{1}{4}$

65. Out of three Carnot engines, operating between reservoir temperature of (i) 400 and 500 K (ii) 600 and 800 K (iii) 400 and 600 K which has the greatest thermal efficiency?

(a) (i)
(b) (ii)
(c) (iii)
(d) All the above have same efficiency

66. To increase the coefficient of performance of an ideal refrigerator, which will be the greatest coefficient of performance? The magnitude of the temperature changes are to be same in all the four cases

(a) running the cold water chamber at a slightly higher temperature
(b) running the cold water chamber at a slightly lower temperature
(c) Both (a) and (b)
(d) None of the above

67. If T_1 and T_2 are the temperatures of two reservoirs (where, $T_1 > T_2$) and a Carnot engine being operated between them will have the efficiency

(a) $\frac{(T_1-T_2)}{T_2}$ (b) $\frac{(T_1-T_2)}{T_1}$

(c) $\frac{T_1}{(T_1-T_2)}$ (d) $\frac{T_2}{(T_1-T_2)}$

68. The area of the Carnot cycle on a T-S diagram represents
(a) heat absorbed from the source
(b) work done in a cycle
(c) heat rejected to the sink
(d) efficiency of the engine

69. A reversible heat engine can have 100% efficiency if the temperature of sink is
(a) less than that of source
(b) equal to that of source
(c) 0°C
(d) 0 K

70. For a cyclic process, the value of $\oint \frac{dQ}{T}$ is
(a) always equal to zero
(b) always positive
(c) always negative
(d) either positive or negative

71. Internal energy of an ideal gas varies with volume as $U = \alpha V^{\beta}$ the work done by the gas as its internal energy increases by Δu is (γ is adiabatic exponent).
(a) $\frac{\Delta U(\gamma+1)}{\beta}$ (b) $\frac{\Delta U(\gamma-1)}{\beta+1}$
(c) $\frac{\Delta U(\gamma-1)}{\beta}$ (d) $\frac{\Delta U(\gamma-1)}{\beta-1}$

72. The internal energy of n moles of a gas is given $E = \frac{3}{2}nRT - \frac{a}{V}$, where V is the volume of the gas at temperature T and a is a positive constant. One mole of the gas in state (T_1, V_1) is allowed to expand adiabatically into vacuum to a final state (T_2, V_2). The temperature T_2 is
(a) $T_1 + \frac{a}{R}\left(\frac{1}{V_2} + \frac{1}{V_1}\right)$ (b) $T_1 - \frac{2}{3}\frac{a}{R}\left(\frac{1}{V_2} - \frac{1}{V_1}\right)$
(c) $T_1 + \frac{2}{3}\frac{a}{R}\left(\frac{1}{V_2} - \frac{1}{V_1}\right)$ (d) $T_1 - \frac{1}{3}\frac{a}{R}\left(\frac{1}{V_2} - \frac{1}{V_1}\right)$

73. Which of the following expresses the second law of thermodynamics? All the symbols have their usual meanings.
(a) $\Delta S \le 0$ (b) $\Delta S < \frac{Q}{T}$
(c) $\Delta U = Q + W$ (d) $\Delta F \le W$

74. For any process, the second law of thermodynamics requires that the change of entropy of the universe be
(a) positive only (b) positive or zero
(c) zero only (d) negative or zero

75. If a system can exchange entropy with a reservoir, then which of the following variables will have same value for both the system and reservoir?
(a) Pressure (b) Temperature
(c) Chemical potential (d) Particle energy density

Exercise 2
(For Part 'C')

1. One mole of helium and one mole of oxygen contained in two vessels of same volume have same entropy. If temperature of He be 300 K, what is the temperature of oxygen?
(a) 300 K (b) 100 K (c) 37.5 K (d) 75 K

2. Consider a system of N atoms of an ideal gas of type A at temperature T and volume V. It is kept in diffusive contact with another system of N atoms of another ideal gas of type B at the same temperature T and volume V. Once the combined system reaches equilibrium,
(a) the total entropy of final system is less than the sum of the initial entropies of the two gases
(b) the entropy of mixing is $2NK_B \ln 2$
(c) entropy of final system is equal to the sum of individual entropies
(d) the entropy of mixing is non-zero when the atoms A and B are of the same type

3. One kilogram of ice melts at 0°C into water at the same temperature. The change in entropy is (in cal/K)
(a) ∞ (b) 0 (c) 0.293 (d) 293

4. Change in entropy depends
(a) only on the transfer of heat
(b) only on change of temperature
(c) on transfer of mass
(d) on the thermodynamic state

5. Two ends of a rod are kept at 127°C and 227°C. When 2000 cal of heat flows in this rod, then the change in entropy is
(a) 1.0 cal/K (b) 20 cal/K (c) 6.9 cal/K (d) 0.7 cal/K

6. In a reversible cycle, the value of the integral $\oint \frac{dQ}{T}$ is
(a) $\oint \frac{dQ}{T} > 0$ (b) $\oint \frac{dQ}{T} < 0$
(c) $\oint \frac{dQ}{T} = 0$ (d) $\oint \frac{dQ}{T} = \text{constant}$

7. Water is heated on a stove, which has the greatest change in entropy of the water as its temperature rises
(a) from 20°C to 30°C
(b) 30°C to 35°C

(c) 80°C to 85°C
(d) All of them have same entropy change

8. An ideal gas has temperature T_1 at the initial state i shown in the p-V diagram here. The gas has a higher temperature T_2 at final states a and b, which it can reach along the path shown. The entropy change along the path to state a is

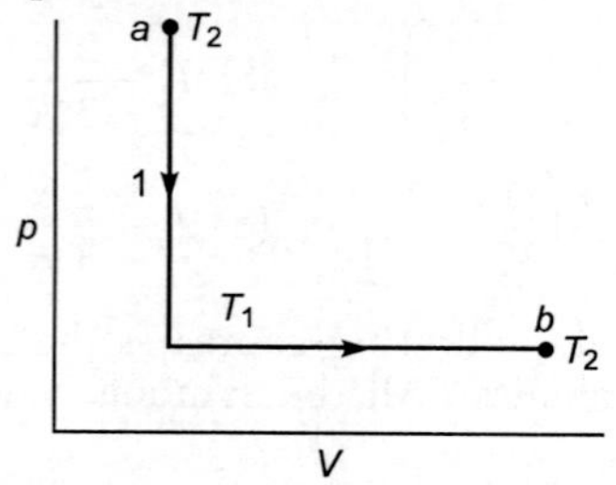

(a) larger than b
(b) smaller than b
(c) same as that along b
(d) zero

9. Which of the following is a property of entropy?
(a) Entropy increases during an irreversible operation
(b) Net change in entropy in a reversible cycle is zero
(c) Change in entropy during an adiabatic opertion is zero
(d) All of the above

10. At 0 K, fluids are assumed to have
(a) minimum entropy
(b) maximum entropy
(c) zero entropy
(d) fixed value of entropy

11. The difference in entropy between a state of volume V_i and a state of volume V_f (temperature and number of molecules remaining constant) is equal to
(a) $nR \log \frac{V_f}{V_i}$
(b) $nR \log \frac{V_i}{V_f}$
(c) $nR^2 \log \frac{V_f}{V_i}$
(d) $nR^2 \log \frac{V_i}{V_f}$

12. An electric current of 3 A flows through a resistance of 10 ohm. It is being cooled by running water and is kept at temperature 300 K, change in entropy per second of the resistance
(a) 0.3 J deg^{-1}
(b) 3 J deg^{-1}
(c) No change
(d) Zero

13. The entropy of an isolated system
(a) remains unchanged in any process
(b) remains unchanged or increase during any process
(c) remains unchanged in an irreversible process
(d) the entropy of non-isolated systems always increase

14. The two ends of a rod of thermal conductivity K, length L and cross-section A are immersed in two heat reservoirs at temperature T_1 and T_2. The rod is thermally insulated from the surroundings. In a steady state, the entropy of the universe increases per unit time at the rate
(a) $[(T_1 - T_2)^2 / T_1T_2](kA/L)$
(b) $[(T_1 + T_2)^2 / T_1T_2](kA/L)$
(c) $[(T_1 - T_2)/\sqrt{T_1T_2}](kA/L)$
(d) $[(T_1 + T_2)/\sqrt{T_1T_2}](kA/L)$

15. A mass m of water at temperature T_1 K is isobarically and adiabatically mixed with an equal mass of water at T_2 K. The entropy change of the inverse is
(a) $2m\,C_p \frac{T_1}{T_2}$
(b) $2m\,C_p \ln \frac{T_1 + T_2}{2\sqrt{T_1T_2}}$
(c) $2m\,C_p \ln \frac{(T_1 + T_2)}{2}$
(d) None of these

16. In a reversible process, the entropy of the system
(a) increases
(b) decreases
(c) zero
(d) remains constant

17. In an irreversible process, the entropy of the universe
(a) remains constant
(b) increases
(c) decreases
(d) sometimes increases sometimes decreases

18. In a complete Carnot cycle, the change in the entropy of the Universe is
(a) positive (b) negative (c) zero (d) infinite

19. Entropy remains constant in
(a) isothermal process
(b) adiabatic process
(c) cyclic process
(d) isobaric process

20. A gas is compressed isothermally to its volume of that at NTP, then change in entropy
(a) 0.56 cal/K
(b) 0 cal/K
(c) – 56 cal/K
(d) 9.9 cal/K

21. Steam at 100°C is mixed with 1500 g of water at 15°C so that the final temperature of the mixture is 80°C. The mass of steam is
(a) 1250 g (b) 625 g (c) 175 g (d) 350 g

22. Each of the two isolated vessels A and B of fixed volumes contain N molecules of a perfect gas (monatomic) at pressure p. The temperature of A and B are T_1 and T_2 respectively. The two vessels are brought into thermal contact. At equilibrium, the change in entropy is
(a) $\frac{3}{2} NK_B \ln \left[\frac{T_1^2 + T_2^2}{4T_1T_2}\right]$
(b) $NK_B \ln \left(\frac{T_2}{T_1}\right)$
(c) $\frac{3}{2} NK_B \ln \left[\frac{(T_1 + T_2)^2}{4T_1T_2}\right]$
(d) $2NK_B$

23. A fluid at high pressure is throttled through a narrow porous opening in a region of lower pressure without any transfer of heat. In such a process
(a) the entropy does not change
(b) the Gibb's free energy remains constant
(c) the entropy is decreased
(d) the enthalpy of the fluid is constant

24. 1 g of perfect gas at volume V_A, pressure p_A and temperature T_A changes from state A to state B when volume is V_B, pressure is p_B and temperature T_B. The change in entropy is

(a) $C_V \log_e \frac{V_B}{V_A} + R \log_e \frac{T_B}{T_A}$

(b) $C_V \log_e \frac{T_B}{T_A} + R \log_e \frac{V_B}{V_A}$

(c) $C_V \log_e \frac{V_A}{V_B} + R \log_e \frac{T_A}{T_B}$

(d) $C_V \log_e \frac{T_A}{T_B} + R \log_e \frac{V_A}{V_B}$

25. An oil bath kept at 27°C is being supplied heat at the rate of 100 Js^{-1}. Assuming the process to be quasi-static, the rate of increase of entropy of the system is approximately

(a) $3.7\,JK^{-1}\,s^{-1}$ (b) $3.7\,JK^{-1}\,s^{-2}$
(c) $0.33\,JK^{-1}\,s^{-1}$ (d) $0.33\,JK^{-1}\,s^{-2}$

26. Which among the following sets for Maxwell relation is correct? (U-internal energy, H-enthalpy, A-Helmholtz free energy and G-Gibb's free energy)

(a) $T = \left(\frac{\partial U}{\partial V}\right)_S$ and $p = \left(\frac{\partial U}{\partial S}\right)_V$

(b) $V = \left(\frac{\partial H}{\partial p}\right)_S$ and $T = \left(\frac{\partial H}{\partial S}\right)_p$

(c) $p = -\left(\frac{\partial G}{\partial V}\right)_T$ and $V = \left(\frac{\partial G}{\partial p}\right)_S$

(d) $p = -\left(\frac{\partial A}{\partial S}\right)_T$ and $S = -\left(\frac{\partial A}{\partial p}\right)_V$

27. The thermodynamical relation expressing the change at temperature with volume at constant entropy is

(a) $\left(\frac{\partial T}{\partial V}\right)_S = -T\left(\frac{\partial p}{\partial Q}\right)_V$ (b) $\left(\frac{\partial T}{\partial V}\right)_S = T\left(\frac{\partial p}{\partial Q}\right)_V$

(c) $\left(\frac{\partial T}{\partial V}\right)_S = -V\left(\frac{\partial p}{\partial Q}\right)_T$ (d) $\left(\frac{\partial T}{\partial V}\right)_S = T\left(\frac{\partial p}{\partial Q}\right)_T$

28. The thermodynamical relation expressing TdS equation

(a) $TdS = C_V dT - T\left(\frac{\partial p}{\partial T}\right)_V dV$

(b) $TdS = C_V dT + T\left(\frac{\partial p}{\partial T}\right)_V dV$

(c) $TdS = C_V dT - T\left(\frac{\partial S}{\partial V}\right)_T$

(d) $TdS = C_V dT + T\left(\frac{\partial S}{\partial V}\right)_T$

29. The Gibb's function G in thermodynamics is defined as

$$G = H - TS$$

(where, H = Enthalpy, T = Temperature, S = Entropy)

In an isothermal, isobaric,reversible process, G

(a) remains constant but not zero
(b) varies linearly
(c) varies non-linearly
(d) is zero

30. The enthalpy of unit mass for any system is

(a) $H = U + pV + S$ (b) $H = U + pV - S$
(c) $H = U + pV$ (d) None of these

31. The Gibb's potential is defined as

(a) $G = U - pV + TS$ (b) $G = U + pV + TS$
(c) $G = U - pV - TS$ (d) $G = U + pV - TS$

32. According to consequences of the second law of thermodynamics (Symbols have their usual meaning)

(a) $T = \left(\frac{\partial U}{\partial S}\right)_V$ and $p = -\left(\frac{\partial U}{\partial V}\right)_S$

(b) $T = \left(\frac{\partial U}{\partial S}\right)_V$ and $p = \left(\frac{\partial U}{\partial V}\right)_S$

(c) $T = \left(\frac{\partial U}{\partial V}\right)_S$ and $p = -\left(\frac{\partial V}{\partial S}\right)_V$

(d) $T = -\left(\frac{\partial U}{\partial V}\right)_S$ and $p = \left(\frac{\partial V}{\partial S}\right)_V$

33. The thermodynamical potential enthalpy $H = U + pV$, then which of the following relation hold true?

(a) $T = -\left(\frac{\partial H}{\partial S}\right)_V$ and $V = \left(\frac{\partial H}{\partial p}\right)_S$

(b) $T = \left(\frac{\partial H}{\partial S}\right)_V$ and $V = \left(\frac{\partial H}{\partial p}\right)_S$

(c) $T = -\left(\frac{\partial H}{\partial p}\right)_S$ and $V = \left(\frac{\partial H}{\partial S}\right)_V$

(d) $T = \left(\frac{\partial H}{\partial p}\right)_S$ and $V = \left(\frac{\partial H}{\partial S}\right)_V$

34. Helmholtz free energy is given as $F = U - TS$, then which of the relation hold true?

(a) $C_V = -T\left(\frac{\partial^2 F}{\partial T^2}\right)_V$ (b) $C_V = T\left(\frac{\partial^2 F}{\partial T^2}\right)_V$

(c) $C_V = -T\left(\frac{\partial^2 F}{\partial V^2}\right)_T$ (d) $C_V = T\left(\frac{\partial^2 F}{\partial V^2}\right)_T$

35. Gibb's thermodynamical potential can be represented as $G = H - TS$. Which relation hold true? [where, H = Enthalpy; S = Entropy]

(a) $\left(\frac{\partial S}{\partial V}\right)_{U,N} = -\frac{p}{T}$ (b) $\left(\frac{\partial S}{\partial V}\right)_{U,N} = \frac{p}{T}$

(c) $\left(\frac{\partial S}{\partial U}\right)_{V,N} = -\frac{p}{T}$ (d) $\left(\frac{\partial S}{\partial U}\right)_{V,N} = \frac{p}{T}$

36. Gibb's thermodynamical potential can be represented as $G = H - TS$ (Symbols have their usual meaning) which relation holds true?

(a) $\left(\frac{\partial S}{\partial U}\right)_{V,N} = \frac{1}{T}$ and $\left(\frac{\partial S}{\partial N}\right)_{U,V} = \frac{\mu}{T}$

(b) $\left(\frac{\partial S}{\partial U}\right)_{V,N} = \frac{\mu}{T}$ and $\left(\frac{\partial S}{\partial N}\right)_{U,V} = \frac{1}{T}$

(c) $\left(\frac{\partial S}{\partial U}\right)_{V,N} = \frac{1}{T}$ and $\left(\frac{\partial S}{\partial N}\right)_{U,V} = -\frac{\mu}{T}$

(d) $\left(\frac{\partial S}{\partial U}\right)_{V,N} = -\frac{1}{T}$ and $\left(\frac{\partial S}{\partial N}\right)_{U,V} = \frac{\mu}{T}$

37. Helmholtz free energy, $F = U - TS$. Which relation holds true?

(where, U = Internal energy; S = Entropy)

(a) $\left(\frac{\partial F}{\partial V}\right)_T = -p$ and $\left(\frac{\partial F}{\partial T}\right)_V = -S$

(b) $\left(\frac{\partial F}{\partial V}\right)_T = p$ and $\left(\frac{\partial F}{\partial T}\right)_V = S$

(c) $\left(\frac{\partial F}{\partial V}\right)_T = -p$ and $\left(\frac{\partial F}{\partial T}\right)_V = S$

(d) $\left(\frac{\partial F}{\partial V}\right)_T = p$ and $\left(\frac{\partial F}{\partial T}\right)_V = -S$

38. In one of the Maxwell's relations $\left(\frac{\partial S}{\partial p}\right)$ equals

(a) $\left(\frac{\partial V}{\partial T}\right)_V$ (b) $-\left(\frac{\partial V}{\partial T}\right)_p$ (c) $-\left(\frac{\partial T}{\partial V}\right)_S$ (d) $\left(\frac{\partial p}{\partial T}\right)_V$

39. Which of the following is not Maxwell's equation?

(a) $\left(\frac{\partial S}{\partial V}\right)_T = \left(\frac{\partial p}{\partial T}\right)_V$ (b) $\left(\frac{\partial T}{\partial V}\right) = -\left(\frac{\partial p}{\partial S}\right)_V$

(c) $\left(\frac{\partial V}{\partial p}\right)_S = \left(\frac{\partial T}{\partial S}\right)$ (d) $\left(\frac{\partial T}{\partial p}\right)_S = \left(\frac{\partial V}{\partial S}\right)_p$

40. Under equilibrium conditions, the thermodynamic variable associated with black body radiation at temperature T which reduces to zero is

(a) entropy (b) Helmholtz free energy
(c) Gibb's free energy (d) pressure

41. For a thermodynamic system, Helmholtz free energy is a function of

(a) S, V (b) V, T
(c) T, p (d) S, p

42. For an isolated thermodynamical system- p, V, T, U, S and F represent the pressure, volume, temperature, internal energy, entropy and free energy respectively. Then, the following relation is true

(a) $\left(\frac{\partial F}{\partial T}\right)_V = -S$ (b) $\left(\frac{\partial F}{\partial T}\right)_p = -S$

(c) $\left(\frac{\partial U}{\partial S}\right)_p = T$ (d) $\left(\frac{\partial U}{\partial V}\right)_T = -p$

43. Which of the following statements is correct?

(a) Chemical potential cannot be defined for photon
(b) Chemical potential for photon is zero
(c) Chemical potential for photon is positive
(d) Chemical potential for photon is negative

44. If the equation of state for a gas with internal energy V is $pV = \frac{1}{3}U$, then the equation for an adiabatic process is

(a) $pV^{1/3}$ = constant (b) $pV^{2/3}$ = constant
(c) $pV^{4/3}$ = constant (d) $pV^{3/5}$ = constant

45. Entropy of a system can be expressed as,

(a) $V\left(\frac{\partial p}{\partial T}\right)_\mu$ (b) $\frac{V^2}{T}\left(\frac{\partial p}{\partial V}\right)_\mu$

(c) $V\left(\frac{\partial p}{\partial T}\right)_\mu$ (d) $-\frac{V^2}{T}\left(\frac{\partial p}{\partial V}\right)_\mu$

46. Helmholtz free energy function and internal energy U are related as

(a) $U = -T\frac{\partial F}{\partial T}$ (b) $U = -T^2\frac{\partial^2 F}{\partial T^2}$

(c) $U = -T^2\frac{\partial}{\partial T}[F/T]$ (d) $U = T^2\frac{\partial^2 F}{\partial T^2}$

47. Two system A and B at temperatures T_A and T_B and chemical potential μ_A and μ_B respectively are allowed to exchange both energy and particles keeping their volumes fixed. The minimum value of chemical potential attained by the system A is

(a) $\frac{\mu_A T_A + \mu_B T_B}{T_A + T_B}$ (b) $\frac{\mu_A T_B - \mu_B T_A}{T_B - T_A}$

(c) $\frac{\mu_A T_A - \mu_B T_B}{T_A - T_B}$ (d) $\frac{\mu_A T_B + \mu_B T_A}{T_A + T_B}$

48. Each of the two isolated vessels, A and B of fixed volumes, contains N molecules of a perfect monoatomic gas at a pressure p. The temperatures of A and B are T_1 and T_2, respectively. The two vessels are brought into thermal contact. At equilibrium, the change in entropy is

(a) $\frac{3}{2}Nk_B \ln\left[\frac{T_1^2 + T_2^2}{4T_1T_2}\right]$ (b) $Nk_B \ln\left(\frac{T_2}{T_1}\right)$

(c) $\frac{3}{2}Nk_B \ln\left[\frac{(T_1 + T_2)^2}{4T_1T_2}\right]$ (d) $2Nk_B$

49. The mean internal energy of a one-dimensional classical harmonic oscillator in equilibrium with a heat bath of temperature T is

(a) $\frac{1}{2}k_BT$ (b) k_BT

(c) $\frac{3}{2}k_BT$ (d) $3k_BT$

50. Denoting temperature, entropy and internal energy by T, S and U respectively and their initial and final values by subscripts i and f respectively, the Joule-Thomson expansion of an ideal gas can be expressed as

(a) $U_f \neq U_i : T_f = T_i : S_f \neq S_i$

(b) $U_f \neq U_i : T_f = T_i ; S_f = S_i$

(c) $U_f = U_i : T_f \neq T_i : S_f \neq S_i$

(d) $U_f = U_i : T_f = T_i ; S_f \neq S_i$

51. The volume of a perfect gas of N atoms is doubled the energy being held constant. Change in entropy is

(a) $N \log 2$ (b) $N^2 \log 2$

(c) $N \log \frac{1}{2}$ (d) $N^2 \log \frac{1}{2}$

52. Out of the following, identify the correct entry for the value of P_F, the radius of the Fermi sphere of a degenerate free electron gas at zero temperature, having N particles and contained in volume V

(a) $(3\pi^2)^{1/3}(N/V)^{1/6}\hbar$ (b) $(3\pi^2)^{1/3}(N/V)^{1/3}\hbar$

(c) $(3\pi^2)^{1/3}(N/V)^{2/3}\hbar$ (d) $(3\pi^2)^{1/3}(N/V)\hbar$

53. For a stable thermodynamic system, the temperature dependence of the internal energy U (T) is represented as

(a)
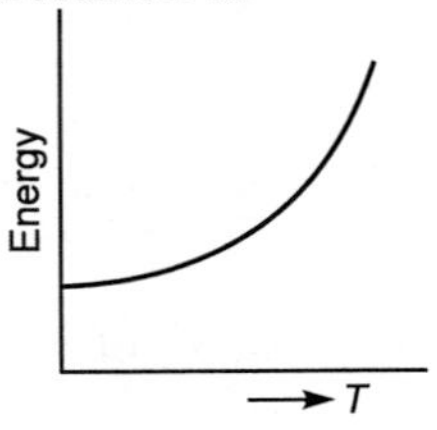

(b)
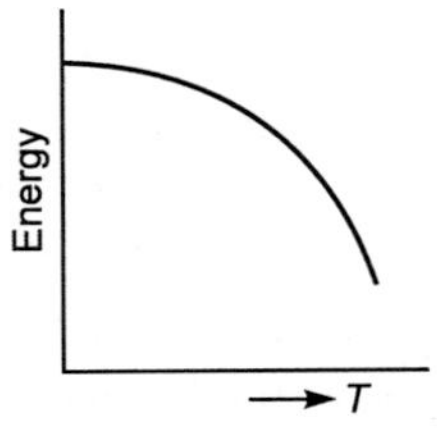

(c)
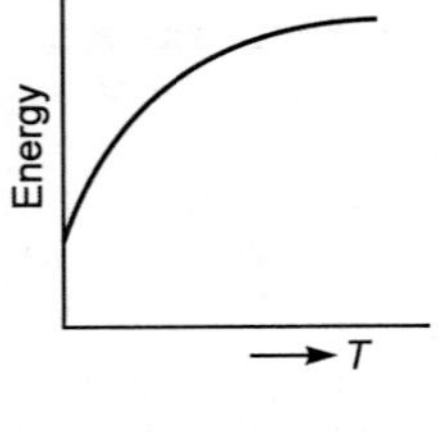

(d)
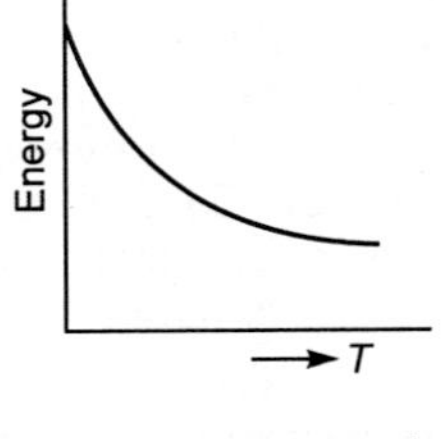

54. With U and F as thermodynamic potentials, the Gibb's Helmholtz equation is given as

(a) $U = F - T\left(\frac{\partial F}{\partial T}\right)_V$ (b) $U = F + T\left(\frac{\partial F}{\partial T}\right)_V$

(c) $S = F - T\left(\frac{\partial F}{\partial T}\right)_V$ (d) $S = F + T\left(\frac{\partial F}{\partial T}\right)_V$

55. The free energy of a photon gas enclosed in a volume V is given by $F = -\frac{1}{3}aVT^4$, where a is a constant and T is the temperature of the gas. The chemical potential of the photon gas is

(a) 0 (b) $\frac{4}{3}aVT^3$

(c) $\frac{1}{3}aT^4$ (d) aVT^4

56. For a particle equilibrium, chemical potential μ_i may be defined as

(a) $\frac{\mu_i}{\tau} = \left(\frac{\partial \sigma}{\partial n_i}\right)_{U,V}$ (b) $\frac{\tau}{\mu_i} = \left(\frac{\partial \sigma}{\partial n_i}\right)_{U,V}$

(c) $-\frac{\mu_i}{\tau} = \left(\frac{\partial \sigma}{\partial n_i}\right)_{U,V}$ (d) $-\frac{\tau}{\mu_i} = \left(\frac{\partial \sigma}{\partial n_i}\right)_{U,V}$

57. Consider the following statements.

A gas can be liquefied by increasing the pressure

1. above the critical pressure only.
2. only when the temperature of the enclosed gas in below the critical temperature.
3. only when the volume of the enclosed gas is below the critical volume.

Which of the statements given above is/are correct?

(a) 1 and 2 (b) 2 only

(c) 3 only (d) 2 and 3

58. Consider the following statements.

When a compressed real gas is allowed to pass through a narrow hole, the temperature

1. always falls 2. falls for some gases
3. rises for some gases

Which of the statements given above is/are correct?

(a) 1 only (b) 2 only

(c) 3 only (d) 2 and 3

59. Consider the following statements.

1. The value of $C_p/(C_p + C_v)$ for helium is $8/3(\gamma = 5/3)$
2. The value of $(C_p - C_V)/(C_p + C_V)$ for H_2 is $1/6(\gamma = 7/5)$

Which of the statements given above is/are correct?

(a) 1 only (b) 2 only

(c) Both 1 and 2 (d) Neither 1 nor 2

60. Consider the following statements with reference to thermodynamics

1. Heat (Q) is a state function
2. Work (W) is a state function
3. $Q + W$ is a state function

Which of the above statements is/are correct?

(a) 2 only (b) 3 only

(c) 1 and 2 only (d) 1,2 and 3

61. Consider the following statements related to kinetic theory of gases

1. The molecules of a gas are all alike in size and shape and are hard, smooth, spherical particles.

2. The size of the molecules is very small compared to the volume occupied by the gas.
3. The molecules exert no appreciable force on one another except during a collision.
4. The collisions of the molecules with the walls of the containing vessel are inelastic.

Which of the above statements are correct?
(a) 1, 2, and 3 (b) 2 and 4
(c) 3 and 4 (d) 2, 3 and 4

62. Consider the following statements relating to a heat reservoir.
1. Total heat content in a reservoir is considered as unchanged in a thermodynamical process.
2. Temperature of reservoir remains unchanged even after absorbing or supplying large amount of heat.
3. A black body is an example of heat reservoir.

Which of the statements given above are correct?
(a) 1, 2 and 3 (b) 1 and 2 only
(c) 2 and 3 only (d) 1 and 3 only

63. Two gases, nitrogen and hydrogen are at the same temperature (27°C). Assume both of them to be ideal gases. Which one of the following is correct?
(a) The kinetic energy of nitrogen gas molecule is 14 times that of hydrogen gas molecule
(b) The kinetic energy of nitrogen gas molecule is 28 times that of hydrogen gas molecule
(c) The kinetic energy of nitrogen gas molecule is 1/14 times that of hydrogen gas molecule
(d) The kinetic energy of nitrogen gas molecule is equal to that of hydrogen gas molecule

64. Consider the following statements pertaining to entropy.
1. Net gain in entropy of working substance in Carnot's cycle is negative.
2. Entropy remains constant in a reversible process.
3. Entropy remains constant in an adiabatic process.

Which of these statements is/are correct?
(a) 1, 2 and 3 (b) 2 and 3
(c) 2 only (d) 3 only

65. Consider the following statements regarding the characteristics of entropy
1. Entropy is a measure of disorder.
2. Entropy changes during a reversible adiabatic process.
3. Entropy of a system decreases in all irreversible processes.
4. Change in entropy for a complete reversible thermodynamic cycle is zero.

Which of the above statements are correct?
(a) 1 and 2 (b) 2 and 3
(c) 3 and 4 (d) 1 and 4

66. The following processes are used for cooling
1. adiabatic expansion
2. adiabatic demagnetisation
3. Joule-Thomson effect
4. evaporation

The correct sequence of these processes in order of their ability to produce lower and lower temperature is
(a) 4, 1, 2, 3 (b) 4, 1, 3, 2
(c) 1, 4, 2, 3 (d) 1, 4, 3, 2

67. Consider the following statements regarding the transition of a system from one thermodynamics state to another.
1. The heat absorbed by it along any reversible path is independent of the path.
2. The change of entropy of the system in a reversible process is independent of the path.
3. The change of entropy of the system in a irreversible process is also independent of the path.

Of these statements
(a) 1 and 2 are correct (b) 2 and 3 are correct
(c) 2 alone is correct (d) 1 alone is correct

68. Consider the following statements.
1. The entropy change during a reversible adiabatic process is zero.
2. Entropy is a state function.
3. The entropy of a thermally isolated system never decreases.
4. The entropy change during an irreversible adiabatic process is zero.

Of these statements
(a) 1 and 3 are correct (b) 2, 3 and 4 are correct
(c) 2 and 4 are correct (d) 1, 2 and 3 are correct

Assertion & Reason

Codes
(a) Both A and R are true and R is the correct explanation of A.
(b) Both A and R are true but R is not the correct explanation of A.
(c) A is true but R is false.
(d) A is false but R is true.

69. Assertion (A) The total ordered energy could be converted into disordered energy but the total disordered energy could not be converted into ordered energy.
Reason (R) This is the implication of the second law of thermodynamics.

70. Assertion (A) A solid ball rolling to and from a table ultimately comes to rest, converting whole kinetic energy into heat, but a heated ball kept at rest does not start moving itself.
Reason (R) Although the first law of thermodynamics allows this, the second law of thermodynamics does not permit it.

71. Assertion (A) The change of internal energy with respect to volume in free expansion of a perfect gas is zero,

i.e., $$\left(\frac{\partial U}{\partial V}\right)_T = 0$$

Reason (R) This is an implication of the experimental observation of joule that $\Delta T = 0$ in such a process.

72. **Assertion (A)** The pressure exerted by a gas is the same and independent of the finite size of the molecules.
Reason (R) Molecular collisions will invariably change the velocities of individual molecules but the number of molecules having any particular velocity will remain unaltered.

73. **Assertion (A)** With the help of a reversible engine it is possible to extract heat from a source and convert all of it into mechanical work.
Reason (R) Thermal energy and mechanical energy are different forms of energy.

74. Match Column I with Column II and select the correct answer using the codes given below the Column.

Column I	Column II
A. Isothermal process	1. No heat exchange
B. Isentropic process	2. Constant temperature
C. Isochoric process	3. Constant pressure
D. Isobaric process	4. Constant volume
	5. Constant enthalpy

Codes

	A	B	C	D
(a)	2	1	3	5
(b)	1	2	3	5
(c)	2	1	4	3
(d)	1	2	4	3

75. Match Diagram I with Diagram II and select the correct answer using the codes given below the Diagrams.

Diagram I ($p - V$)	Diagram II ($T - S$)
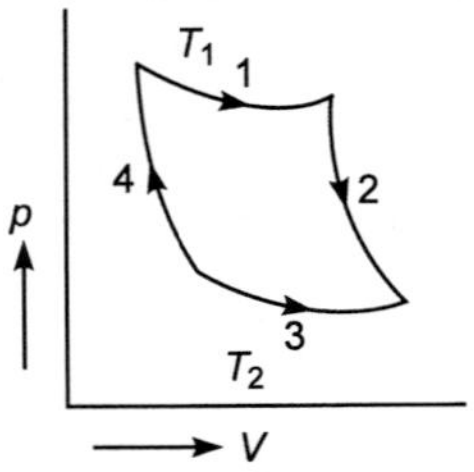	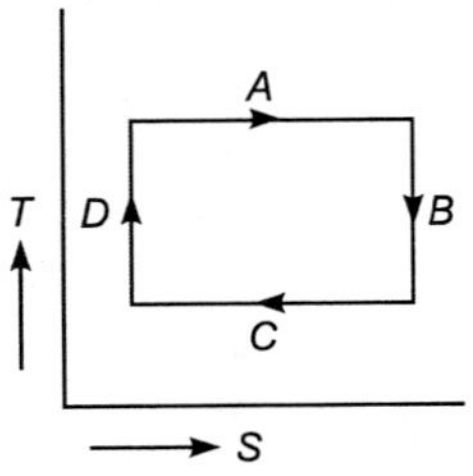

(Diagram I and Diagram II represent reversible cycle)

Codes

	A	B	C	D
(a)	1	2	3	4
(b)	2	3	4	1
(c)	3	4	1	2
(d)	4	1	2	3

76. Match Column I with Column II and select the correct answer using the codes given below the Column.

Column I	Column II
A. Temperature of inversion in Joule-Thomson effect is related to	1. $\left(\frac{\partial U}{\partial V}\right)_T = 0$
B. For perfect gases	2. $\left(\frac{\partial T}{\partial p}\right)_H = \frac{1}{C_p}\left[\frac{2a}{RT} - b\right]$
C. For a perfect gas Joule-Thomson effect vanishes because	3. $\frac{\partial}{\partial p}(pV)_T \neq 0$
D. Deviation from Boyle's law implies	4. $\left(T\frac{\partial V}{\partial T} - V\right) = 0$

Codes

	A	B	C	D
(a)	2	4	1	3
(b)	3	1	4	2
(c)	2	1	4	3
(d)	3	4	1	2

77. Match Column I (Thermodynamic process) with Column II (Governing equation) and select the correct answer using the codes given below the Column.

Column I (Thermodynamic process)	List II (Governing equation)
A. Constant volume process	1. $TdS = dE + dW$
B. Reversible process	2. $dE = C_V dT$
C. Irreversible process	3. $dE - dW - TdS = 0$
	4. $TdS - dE - dW > 0$

Codes

	A	B	C
(a)	4	1	2
(b)	2	3	4
(c)	4	3	2
(d)	2	1	4

Answers

Exercise 1

1. (b)	**2.** (b)	**3.** (b)	**4.** (c)	**5.** (c)	**6.** (b)	**7.** (b)	**8.** (a)	**9.** (a)	**10.** (a)
11. (a)	**12.** (c)	**13.** (b)	**14.** (b)	**15.** (a)	**16.** (a)	**17.** (b)	**18.** (a)	**19.** (d)	**20.** (a)
21. (b)	**22.** (c)	**23.** (a)	**24.** (b)	**25.** (c)	**26.** (b)	**27.** (b)	**28.** (b)	**29.** (a)	**30.** (b)
31. (d)	**32.** (a)	**33.** (b)	**34.** (d)	**35.** (b)	**36.** (c)	**37.** (b)	**38.** (a)	**39.** (d)	**40.** (c)
41. (b)	**42.** (b)	**43.** (c)	**44.** (b)	**45.** (c)	**46.** (c)	**47.** (d)	**48.** (b)	**49.** (a)	**50.** (d)
51. (a)	**52.** (b)	**53.** (a)	**54.** (d)	**55.** (d)	**56.** (b)	**57.** (c)	**58.** (a)	**59.** (a)	**60.** (a)
61. (b)	**62.** (b)	**63.** (b)	**64.** (a)	**65.** (c)	**66.** (a)	**67.** (b)	**68.** (b)	**69.** (d)	**70.** (b)
71. (c)	**72.** (c)	**73.** (d)	**74.** (b)	**75.** (b)					

Exercise 2

1. (c)	**2.** (c)	**3.** (d)	**4.** (d)	**5.** (b)	**6.** (c)	**7.** (a)	**8.** (b)	**9.** (d)	**10.** (c)
11. (a)	**12.** (c)	**13.** (b)	**14.** (a)	**15.** (b)	**16.** (c)	**17.** (b)	**18.** (c)	**19.** (b)	**20.** (a)
21. (c)	**22.** (a)	**23.** (d)	**24.** (b)	**25.** (c)	**26.** (b)	**27.** (a)	**28.** (b)	**29.** (a)	**30.** (c)
31. (d)	**32.** (a)	**33.** (b)	**34.** (a)	**35.** (b)	**36.** (c)	**37.** (a)	**38.** (b)	**39.** (c)	**40.** (c)
41. (b)	**42.** (a)	**43.** (b)	**44.** (d)	**45.** (c)	**46.** (c)	**47.** (b)	**48.** (c)	**49.** (b)	**50.** (d)
51. (a)	**52.** (c)	**53.** (a)	**54.** (a)	**55.** (a)	**56.** (c)	**57.** (b)	**58.** (d)	**59.** (b)	**60.** (b)
61. (b)	**62.** (a)	**63.** (b)	**64.** (b)	**65.** (d)	**66.** (b)	**67.** (b)	**68.** (d)	**69.** (a)	**70.** (a)
71. (a)	**72.** (d)	**73.** (c)	**74.** (c)	**75.** (a)	**76.** (c)	**77.** (d)			

Hints & Solutions

Exercise 1

5. The creation of a temperature of 8000 K by transferring heat from a colder body (sun at 6000 K) by means of a lens is a violation of **second law of thermodynamics.**

8. According to first law of thermodynamics

$$dQ = dU + pdV \quad \ldots(i)$$

According to second law of thermodynamics

$$dS = \frac{dQ}{T} \quad \ldots(ii)$$

Combined form of Eqs. (i) and (ii) we get,

$$TdS = dU + pdV$$

10. Since, work done = Area between p-V curve and volume axis.

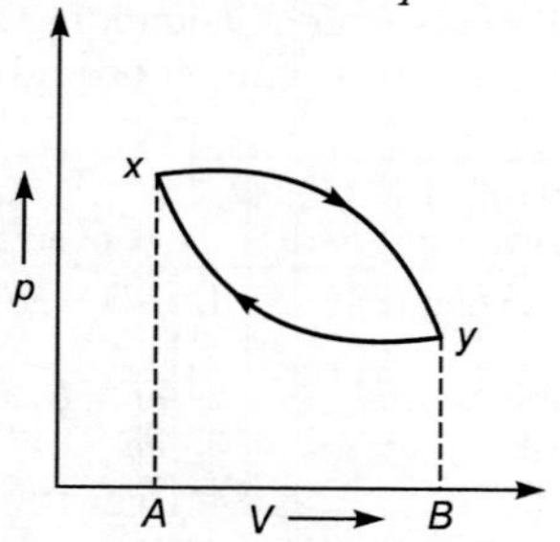

Hence, work in positive direction is clockwise.

$\therefore$ W_{xy} = Area $xyBA$

and W_{yx} = Area $yBAx$

and $W_{xy} > W_{yx}$.

12.
$$dU = dQ - dW$$

$\Rightarrow$
$$\Delta V = \Delta Q - \Delta W$$
$$\Delta W = \Delta W_i + \Delta W_a$$

ΔW, work done by gas when compressed isothermally is +ve. Similarly, ΔW_a is also a +ve quantity.

$$\Delta U = \Delta Q - (\Delta W_i + \Delta W_a)$$
$$= \Delta Q - \Delta W_i - \Delta W_a$$

13. From first law of thermodynamics

$$dQ = dU + dW$$

In cyclic process, $dU = 0$ (because initial state = final state)

$\therefore$ $dQ = dW$

19. Work done in adiabatic expansion of one mole of a perfect gas

$$= \frac{R}{\gamma - 1}(T_1 - T_2) = C_V(T_1 - T_2)$$

20. The heat has not been transferred to coffee which is thermally insulated.

By shaking work has been done on coffee (system) against the viscous forces in it.

According to first law;

$$\Delta U = Q - W$$

Here, $Q = 0$

and W is negative as work is done on the system so that

$$\Delta U = 0 - (-W)$$
$$= W$$

i.e., ΔU is positive. The internal energy of system (coffee) increases.

$$Q = 0;\ W = -\text{ ve};\ \Delta U = +\text{ ve}$$

21. There is no flow of heat into the resistor and work is done on the resistor (system).

According to first law as applied to the system, we write

$$\Delta U = Q - W$$

For resistor $Q = 0$,

W is negative. Thus,

$$\Delta U = 0 - (-W) = W$$

$\therefore$ $Q = 0;\ W = -\text{ ve};\ \Delta U = +\text{ ve}$

23. The internal energy of a system is given by

$$U = \frac{3N}{2\beta}$$

N = Number of atoms and $\beta = \frac{1}{kT}$

$$\therefore \quad \beta = \frac{1}{1.38 \times 10^{-23}\ \text{JK}^{-1} \times 300\ \text{K}}$$
$$= 2.42 \times 10^{20}\ \text{J}^{-1}$$

$$\therefore \quad U = \frac{3 \times 10^{24}}{2.42 \times 10^{20}}\ \text{J}$$
$$= 12.4\ \text{kJ}$$

25. Let $p_{sun}\, dV$ work done by an ideal gas in the three types of expansion

Since, $$W = -\int_{V_1}^{V_2} p_{surr}\, dV$$

The maximum work is done when the gas pressure

$$p_g = p_{surr}$$

For reversible expansion

$$W_{max} = -\int_{V_1}^{V_2} p_g\, dV \quad \text{(Path 1)}$$

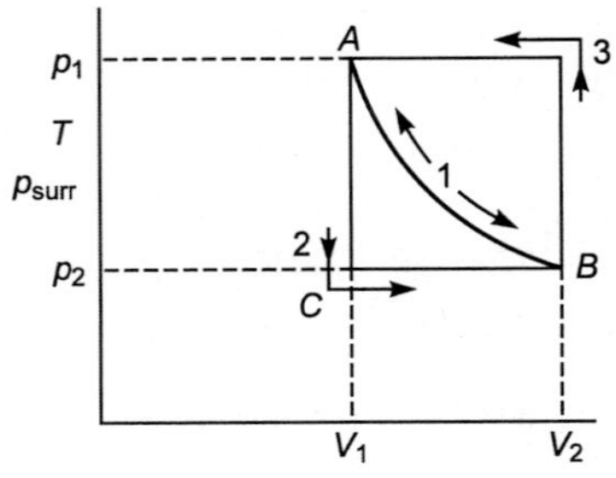

Path 2 Corresponds to a permitted or irreversible expansion, in this case work done

$$W = -p_2(V_2 - V_1) \quad (p_{surr} = p_2 = \text{constant})$$

In a forbidden expansion; *i.e.,* one against an external pressure greater than the gas pressure, the work done by the gas would have to be greater than the maximum work, such an expansion is never observed.

∴ In case of isothermal expansion

Permitted process : $W < W_{max}$

Reversible process : $W = W_{max}$

Forbidden process : $W > W_{max}$

34. E = internal energy

$$dE = -dW \quad \text{for adiabatic process}$$

$$\text{Energy } E = \frac{3}{2}NkT$$

Which gives

$$dE = \frac{3}{2}NkdT$$

$$dW = pdV = \frac{NkT}{V}dV$$

$$\frac{3}{2}NkdT = -\frac{NkT}{V}dV$$

$$\frac{dT}{T} + \frac{2}{3}\frac{dV}{V} = 0$$

$$\ln T + \frac{2}{3}\ln V = \text{constant}$$

or $$TV^{2/3} = \text{constant}$$

or $$pV^{5/3} = \text{constant}$$

35. $$\frac{6 \times 10^9 \text{ people}}{6 \times 10^{23} \text{ people/mol}} = 1 \times 10^{-14} \text{ mol}$$

36. Work done W, is given by

$$W = \int_{W_1}^{W_2} pdV$$

Since, the expansion is isothermal

$$pV = RT$$

or $$p = \frac{RT}{V}$$

∴ $$W = RT\int_{V_1}^{V_2}\frac{dV}{V}$$

$$= RT[\log_e V]_{V_1}^{V_2}$$

$$W = RT \log_e \frac{V_2}{V_1}$$

37. First law of thermodynamics

$$dU = dQ - dW$$

During adiabatic process heat exchange is zero

∴ $$dQ = 0$$

and $$dU = -dW$$

Since, work has been done on the system, internal energy will increase by 20 J.

38. $$p(V - b) = RT$$

or $$V - b = \frac{RT}{p}$$

or $$V = b + \frac{RT}{p}$$

42. We know,

$$p_1 = \frac{nRT_1}{V_1}$$

after expansion

$$p_2 = \frac{nRT_2}{V_2}$$

Since, the pressure is constant $p_1 = p_2$

or $$\frac{nRT_1}{V_1} + \frac{nRT_2}{V_2}$$

or $$T_2 = \frac{V_2}{V_1}T_1$$

$$T_1 = 273 + 100 = 373 \text{ K}$$

∴ $$T_2 = \frac{20}{10} \times 373 \text{ K}$$

$$= 746 \text{ K}$$

or $$T_2 = (746 - 273)°\text{C}$$

$$T_2 = 473°\text{C}$$

47. Boyle's law is given by

$$pV = \text{constant}$$

Differentiating Eq. (i), we get

$$pdV + Vdp = 0$$

or $$pdV = -Vdp$$

or $$\frac{dV}{dp} = -\frac{V}{p}$$

51. van der Waals' equation

$$\left(p + \frac{a}{V^2}\right)(V - b) = RT$$

⇒ $$p = -\frac{a}{V^2} + \frac{RT}{V - b}$$

$$pV = -\frac{a}{V} + RT \quad \text{(Since, } b \text{ is very small)}$$

$$R = Nk_B$$
$$N = 1$$
$$pV = -\frac{a}{V} + k_B T$$
$$pV = k_B T\left[1 - \frac{a}{k_B TV}\right]$$
$$\frac{pV}{k_B T} \approx 1 + \frac{B(T)}{V}$$
$$-\frac{a}{k_B T} = BT$$

53. Rectangle

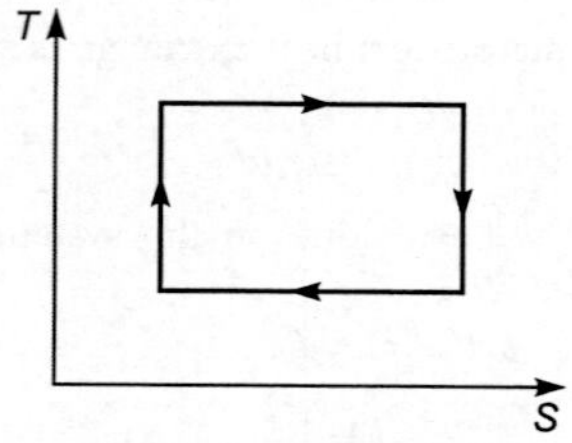

54.
$$T_1 = (27 + 273)\text{ K} = 300\text{ K}$$
$$T_2 = (127 + 273)\text{ K} = 400\text{ K}$$
$\therefore$ Efficiency $= 1 - \dfrac{T_1}{T_2}$
$$= 1 - \frac{300}{400} = \frac{1}{4} = 25\%.$$

55. The efficiency of Carnot heat engine may be defined as
$$\eta = \frac{Q_1 - Q_2}{Q_1} = \frac{T_1 - T_2}{T_1}$$
where, Q_1 is the heat taken from the source by working substance and Q_2 is the heat given by working substance to sink respectively, T_1 and T_2 are the temperatures of source and sink respectively.

Hence, in question
$$Q_1 = 450\text{ kJ/s}, Q_2 = ?$$
$$T_1 = 22 + 273 = 295\text{ K},$$
$$T_2 = 273\text{ K}$$
Hence, $= \dfrac{450 - Q_2}{450}$
$$= \frac{295 - 273}{295}$$
or $Q_2 = \dfrac{273 \times 450}{295}$
$$= 416.44\text{ kJ/s} \cong 417\text{ kJ/s}$$

58. By ideal gas equation,
$$pV = nRT \quad \ldots(i)$$
and $\Delta S = \dfrac{\Delta Q}{T} \quad \ldots(ii)$

Multiplying Eqs. (i) and (ii),
$$pV\Delta S = nR\Delta Q$$
$\Rightarrow$ $\Delta Q = \dfrac{pV\Delta S}{nR}$

$\because$ For isothermal expansion $\Delta V = 0$

$\Rightarrow$ $W = \Delta Q = \dfrac{pV\Delta S}{nR}$

60. Conventionally, heat given to the system is taken to be positive and heat extracted from the system is taken to be negative.

$\therefore$ $\Delta S_A = \dfrac{\Delta Q}{T_A} = \dfrac{-Q}{T_A}$
$$\Delta S_B = \frac{\Delta Q}{T_B} = \frac{+Q}{T_B}$$
$$\Delta S = \Delta S_A + \Delta S_B$$
$$= Q\left(\frac{1}{T_B} - \frac{1}{T_A}\right)$$

61.
$$T_1 = 327°\text{C}$$
$$= 327 + 273 = 600\text{ K}$$
$$T_2 = 27°\text{C}$$
$$= 27 + 273 = 300\text{ K}$$
$$\eta = \frac{T_1 - T_2}{T_1}$$
$$= \frac{600\text{ K} - 300\text{ K}}{600\text{ K}}$$
$$= \frac{300}{600} = 0.5 \text{ or } 50\%.$$

62. Efficiency $\eta = \dfrac{W}{Q_1} = \dfrac{Q_1 - Q_2}{Q_1}$
$$= \frac{\text{Available energy}}{Q_1}$$

For curve

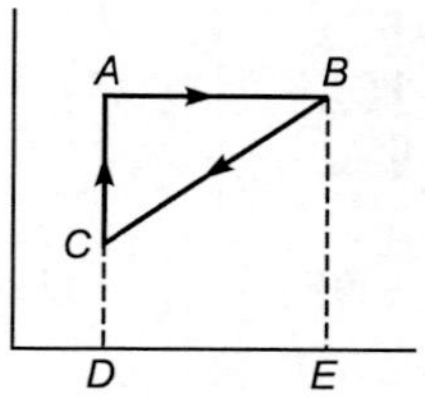

Fig. 1

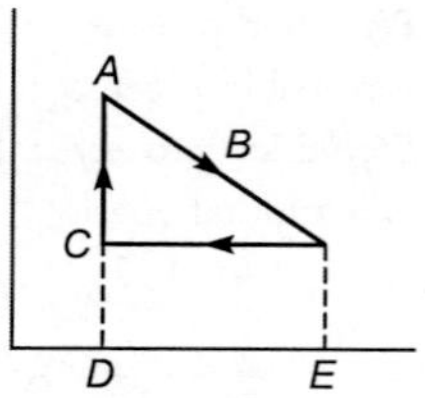

Fig. 2

Available energy per cycle is
$$Q_1 - Q_2 = \text{Area of curve } (ABC)$$
$$Q_1 = \text{Total area of curve } (ABED)$$
$\Rightarrow$ Area of curve is same for both figures, but total area is more for Fig. 1.
$$\text{Efficiency} \propto \frac{1}{\text{Total area of figure}}$$
Hence, second figure has greater efficiency.

64. In given figure,
available energy per cycle is
$$Q_1 - Q_2 = \left[2T_1 \times S_1 + T_1 \times \frac{1}{2} 2S_1\right] - 2T_1 S_1$$
$$= T_1 S_1$$
and $Q_1 = 3T_1 S_1$

efficiency $\eta = \dfrac{Q_1 - Q_2}{Q_1}$
$$= \frac{T_1 S_1}{3T_1 S_1} = \frac{1}{3}$$

67. Efficiency $\eta = \frac{\text{Output}}{\text{Input}} = \frac{W}{H_1}$

Now, $$H_1 = RT_1 \log_e \frac{V_2}{V_1}$$

$$\eta = \frac{W}{H_1} = \frac{H_1 - H_2}{H_1}$$

$$= \frac{R(T_1 - T_2)\log_e \frac{V_2}{V_1}}{RT_1 \log_e \frac{V_2}{V_1}}$$

$\therefore$ $$\eta = \frac{T_1 - T_2}{T_1}$$

71. Given, $u = \alpha V^{\beta}$

and we know that $u = n \cdot \frac{1}{2} \cdot RT$

where, f is degree of freedom

$\therefore$ $$f = \frac{2}{\gamma - 1}$$

$\therefore$ $$\alpha Vp = \frac{nRT}{\gamma - 1}$$

$\therefore$ $$T = \frac{(\gamma - 1)}{nR} \alpha V^{\beta}$$

$\therefore$ From ideal gas equation

$$pV = nRT$$

$\therefore$ $$pV = nR \cdot \frac{(\gamma - 1)}{nR} \cdot \alpha V^{\beta}$$

or $$p = (\gamma - 1)\alpha V^{\beta - 1}$$

Work done $= \int pdV = (\gamma - 1) \propto \left[\frac{V^{\beta}}{\beta}\right]_{V_1}^{V_2}$

$$= \left(\frac{\gamma - 1}{\beta}\right) \alpha \, [V_2^{\beta} - V_1^{\beta}]$$

$$= \frac{\gamma - 1}{\beta} \Delta U$$

72. During adiabatic expansion, the system does not exchange any heat amount with the surroundings *i.e.,* $\Delta Q = 0$. Hence, if gas expands adiabatically, then the temperature of the system decreases because internal energy used to overcome by the intermolecular attraction

$$E_1 = E_2 = \frac{3}{2} RT_1 - \frac{a}{V_1} = \frac{3}{2} RT_2 - \frac{a}{V_2}$$

(For one mole of gas)

or $$\frac{3}{2} R(T_2 - T_1) = a\left(\frac{1}{V_2} - \frac{1}{V_1}\right)$$

or $$T_2 = \frac{2a}{3R}\left(\frac{1}{V_2} - \frac{1}{V_1}\right) + T_1$$

74. In reversible process, change in entropy is zero but in irreversible process, change in entropy is positive. So, for any process, the change of entropy of the universe will be positive or zero.

Exercise 2

1. Entropy of a gas containing N particles is given

$$\delta = Nk\left[\ln\left(\frac{2\pi mkT}{h^2}\right)^{3/2} + \frac{5}{2}\right]$$

where, m is mass of particles

$\therefore$ For the given situation ($N = Na$ = Avogadro's number)

$$N_a k\left[\ln\left(\frac{2\pi m_{He}\, kT_{He}}{h^2}\right)^{3/2} + 5/2\right]$$

$$= N_a k\left[\ln\left(\frac{2\pi m_0 kT_0}{h^2}\right)^{3/2} + \frac{5}{2}\right]$$

$\therefore$ $$m_0 T_0 = m_{He} T_{He}$$

$$T_0 = \frac{m_{He} T_{He}}{m_0}$$

$$= \frac{4}{32} \times T_{He}$$

$$= \frac{T_{He}}{8} = \frac{300}{8} = 37.5 \text{ K}.$$

3. Change in entropy

$$dS = \frac{dQ}{T}$$

$$= \frac{1000 \times 80}{273} = 293 \text{ cal/K}$$

$$dQ = mL$$

L = Latent heat of vaporization.

5. Change in entropy

$$\Delta S = \frac{dQ}{dT} = \frac{2000}{500 - 400}$$

$$= \frac{2000}{100} \text{ cal/K}$$

$$\Delta S = 20 \text{ cal/K}.$$

8. Because Q is smaller.

12. There is no change in the entropy of the resistance because there is no change in the state of wire.

14. Since the rod is thermally insulated from the surroundings and its two ends are immersed in two heat reservoirs.

then, $$Q = KA\frac{T_1 - T_2}{l} \quad \ldots\text{(i)}$$

where, K = thermal conductivity

Now, increase in entropy is given by

$$S_2 - S_1 = \frac{Q}{T_2} - \frac{Q}{T_1}$$

$$= \frac{(T_1 - T_2)Q}{T_1 T_2} \quad \ldots\text{(ii)}$$

From Eq. (i), substitute for Q

$$\Delta S = \frac{(T_1 - T_2)^2}{T_1 T_2} \cdot \frac{KA}{l}$$

15. A point to note is that, since the process is adiabatic there is no change of the surroundings. We know that for isobaric (constant pressure process), the change in entropy is given by

$$\Delta S = mC_p \ln \left(\frac{T_{\text{final}}}{T_{\text{initial}}} \right)$$

Now, $Q_{T_1} = mC_p (T_f - T_1)$

and $Q_{T_2} = mC_p (T_f - T_2)$

Also, the higher temperature loses heat and the water at the lower temperature gains heat, we can write

$$Q_{T_1} = -Q_{T_2}$$

$$mC_p (T_f - T_1) = -mC_p (T_f - T_2)$$

$$\Rightarrow \quad T_f = \frac{T_1 + T_2}{2}$$

Since, $\Delta S_{T_1} = mC_p \ln \left(\frac{T_f}{T_1} \right)$

and $\Delta S_{T_2} = mC_p \ln \left(\frac{T_f}{T_2} \right)$

Total entropy or entropy change of universe

$$\Delta S = mC_p \ln \left(\frac{T_f}{T_1} \right) + mC_p \ln \left(\frac{T_f}{T_2} \right)$$

$$= mC_p \left[\ln \left(\frac{T_f^2}{T_1 T_2} \right) \right]$$

$$= mC_p \left[\ln \left(\frac{(T_1 + T_2)^2}{4T_1 T_2} \right) \right]$$

$$\Delta S = 2mC_p \ln \frac{T_1 + T_2}{2\sqrt{T_1 T_2}}.$$

21. Here, $m_1 = ?$ $m_2 = 1500$ g

$$T_1 = 373 \text{ K}, \; T_2 = 273 + 15 = 288 \text{ K}$$

The final temperature of mixture be $T = 273 + 80 = 353$ K.

$$\therefore \quad m_1 \times 540 + m_1 (373 - 353) = 1500 (353 - 288)$$

$$(540 + 20) m_1 = 1500 \times 6.5$$

or $m_1 = 175$ g

24. From first law of thermodynamics

$$dQ = dU + dW$$

$$= C_V dT + pdV$$

Change in entropy $S_B - S_A = \int_A^B \frac{dQ}{T}$

$$= \int_A^B \frac{C_V dT + pdV}{T}$$

$$= \int_A^B \frac{C_V dT}{T} + \int_A^B \frac{pdV}{T}$$

$$pV = RT$$

or $\frac{p}{T} = \frac{R}{V}$

$$\therefore \quad S_B - S_A = C_V \log_e \frac{T_B}{T_A} + R \log_e \frac{V_B}{V_A}.$$

25. Change in entropy

$$= \frac{dQ}{T \text{ (ln } K)} = \frac{100 \text{ J-s}^{-1}}{(273 + 27) \text{ K}}$$

$$= \frac{100}{300} \text{ J-s}^{-1} \text{ K}^{-1}$$

$$= 0.33 \text{ J}^{-1} \text{ s}^{-1} \text{ K}^{-1}.$$

28. Let the entropy S of a thermodynamic system be a function of temperature T and volume V, *i.e.,*

$$S = f(T, V)$$

Since, dS is perfect differential, we can write

$$dS = \left(\frac{\partial S}{\partial T} \right)_V dT + \left(\frac{\partial S}{\partial V} \right)_T dV$$

Multiplying by T, we get

$$TdS = T \left(\frac{\partial S}{\partial T} \right)_V dT + T \left(\frac{\partial S}{\partial T} \right)_T dV$$

For any substance, the specific heat at constant volume is given by

$$C_V = \left(\frac{\partial Q}{\partial T} \right)_V = T \left(\frac{\partial S}{\partial T} \right)_V$$

Using $dQ = TdS$

Also from Maxwell's equation, we have

$$\left(\frac{\partial S}{\partial V} \right)_T = \left(\frac{\partial p}{\partial T} \right)_V$$

$$\therefore \quad TdS = C_V dT + T \left(\frac{\partial p}{\partial T} \right)_V dV.$$

29. Condition for a change to occur in any processess

$$dU - TdS \le -pdV$$

$$d(U + pV - TS) \le 0$$

$$d(H - TS) \le 0$$

as $[H = U + pV]$

$$G = H - TS$$

or $dG \le 0$

It means in isothermal, isobaric and reversible process

$$dG = 0 \text{ or } G = \text{constant}$$

32. $dQ = dU + pdV$

Second law of thermodynamics is

$$dS = \frac{dQ}{T}$$

$\therefore$ Eq. (i) becomes

$$TdS = dU + pdV$$

$$dU = TdS - pdV$$

$$\Rightarrow \quad T = \left(\frac{\partial U}{\partial S} \right)_V$$

and $p = -\left(\frac{\partial U}{\partial V} \right)_S.$

51. $\frac{\Delta \Gamma_2}{\Delta \Gamma_1} = \frac{V_2^N}{V_1^N}$

$$\therefore \quad \Delta \sigma = \log V_2^N - \log V_1^N$$

$$= \log \left(\frac{V_2}{V_1} \right)^N$$

$$= N \log \left(\frac{2V}{V} \right) = N \log 2$$

55. Chemical potential $\mu = \frac{\partial F}{\partial N}$

and $F = -\frac{1}{3} aVT^4$

No term depends on N

Hence, $$\mu = \frac{\partial}{\partial N}\left(-\frac{1}{3}aVT^4\right)$$

$$\mu = 0.$$

57. When temperature of a gas is above a fixed temperature, known as critical temperature, the gas cannot be liquid whatever the pressure is applied. If temperature of the gas is equal to or smaller than the critical temperature, then it can be liquefied.

58. The fall of temperature is given as

$$dT = \frac{dp}{C_p}\left(\frac{2a}{RT} - b\right)$$

$$\Rightarrow \quad T_i = \frac{2a}{Rb}$$

Thus, temperature $T > T_i$ then heating effect, if temperature $T < T_i$ then cooling effect.

Temperature falls for some gases whereas increases for some other.

59. The ratio of C_p and C_V is known as coefficient of adiabatic expansion. Hence,

$$\gamma = \frac{C_p}{C_V}$$

(I) So, for helium $\gamma = \frac{5}{3}$

Hence, $$\frac{C_p}{C_p + C_V} = \frac{1}{1 + \frac{C_V}{C_p}}$$

$$= \frac{1}{1 + \frac{5}{3}}$$

$$\frac{C_p}{C_p + C_V} = \frac{3}{8}$$

(II) For hydrogen $\gamma = \frac{7}{5}$

$$\frac{C_p - C_V}{C_p + C_V}$$

Dividing by C_V the numerator and denominator, we get

$$\frac{C_p - C_V}{C_p + C_V} = \frac{C_p/C_V - 1}{C_p/C_V + 1}$$

$$= \frac{\gamma - 1}{\gamma + 1}$$

$$= \frac{7/5 - 1}{7/5 + 1}$$

$$= \frac{7 - 5}{7 + 5}$$

$$= \frac{2}{12}$$

$$\Rightarrow \quad \frac{C_p - C_V}{C_p + C_V} = \frac{1}{6}$$

Thus, first statement is wrong whereas second is right. Hence, right answer is (b)

60. First law of thermodynamics is given as

$$\delta Q = dU \text{ and } \delta W \qquad \ldots\text{(i)}$$

where $\delta Q \rightarrow$ amount of heat absorbed. This does not depend on initial and final positions hence it is not a state function.

$dU \rightarrow$ change in internal energy. This depends on initial and final position of the system, hence it is a state function.

$\delta W \rightarrow$ work done it is also not a state function

By Eq. (i) $\quad dU = \delta Q - \delta W$

Hence, $\pm\, dU \Rightarrow$ state function

$\Rightarrow \quad \delta Q$ and δW is state function

62. Reservoir which is a hot body at fixed temperature T_1 is calld source and its heat content is fixed after liberation or absorption. Reservoir which is a cold body at fixed temperature $T_2\,(<T_1)$ in which any amount of heat can be rejected is called sink. A black body is a good emitter and absorber of heat by Kirchhoff's law and Stefan's law. Emitted radiation is proportional to fourth power of temperature.

64. Entropy is a physical quantity defined as

$$dS = \frac{\delta Q}{T}$$

(i) The change in entropy in a reversible process is zero hence in reversible process entropy remains constant.

(ii) For adiabatic $\delta Q = 0 \Rightarrow dS = 0$

$\Rightarrow$ no change in entropy

$\Rightarrow$ entropy remains constant

Change in entropy of a system can never be negative.

65. Entropy of a system is a function of thermodynamical coordinates defining the state of the system *viz.,* the pressure, the volume, the temperature or internal energy and its change between two states is equal to the $\int \frac{\delta Q}{T}$.

This is a measure of disorder and is constant during a reversible adiabatic process whereas it increases in all reversible processes. Since, for complete reversible process

$$\Rightarrow \quad \delta Q = 0$$

$$\Rightarrow \quad dS = 0$$

66. The ability to produce lower and lower temperature is given as

(i) evaporation.
(ii) adiabatic expansion.
(iv) Joule Thomson effect.
(iv) adiabatic demagnetization.

67. The change in entropy in a reversible process is independent of the path.

68. Entropy it is a state function and is defined as

$$dS = \frac{\delta Q}{T}$$

where, $\delta Q \rightarrow$ amount of used heat. If this taken in by a system then change in entropy is positive and so entropy of the system increases.

The entropy change during an reversible adiabatic process is zero.

The entropy change during an irreversible process is positive. Hence in given statements (i), (ii) and (iii) are right.

69. Kelvin-Planck statement of the second law say that; it is impossible to construct a device which is operating in a cycle, has the sole effect of extracting heat from a reservoir and performing an equivalent amount of work. In term of entropy, which is a measure of disorderness, II law is given as

$$TdS = \delta Q$$

Thus, total energy of order system can be converted into disorder and converse is not possible.

70. First law of thermodynamics

$$\delta Q = \delta U + \delta W$$

According to second law we cannot obtain a continuous supply of work from a single supply of heat. Thus, heat of the rolling body cannot be converted into work.

71. From first law of thermodynamics

$$\partial Q = \partial U + \partial W = \partial U + p\partial V; \partial Q = T\partial S$$

$$\partial U = T\partial S - p\partial V$$

$$\left(\frac{\partial U}{\partial V}\right)_T = T\left(\frac{\partial S}{\partial V}\right)_T - p$$

Using Maxwell's second relation

$$\left(\frac{\partial S}{\partial V}\right)_T = \left(\frac{\partial S}{\partial V}\right)_V$$

$$\therefore \quad \left(\frac{\partial U}{\partial V}\right)_T = T\left(\frac{\partial p}{\partial T}\right)_V - p$$

For perfect gas $pV = RT$ then $\frac{\partial p}{\partial T} = \frac{R}{V}$

$$T\left(\frac{\partial p}{\partial T}\right) = \frac{RT}{V} = \frac{pV}{V} = p$$

$$\therefore \quad \left(\frac{\partial U}{\partial V}\right)_T = p - p = 0$$

Using this relation the Joule's coefficient $\eta = \frac{(\partial U/\partial V)_T}{(\partial U/\partial T)_V} = 0.$

This represent free expansion.

Then, if temperature of flask A is rising surely temperature of flask B will falls and change in temperature $\Delta T = 0$.

72. The pressure exerted a gas depends on the size of molecules. This is reason that the ideal gas equation $pV = RT$ has to be corrected by van der Waals'.

73. According to the second law of thermodynamics. It is impossible to convert heat into work by taking heat from a sink at lower temperature.

Thus, assertion is wrong.

74. (i) Isothermal process

$\Rightarrow$ $\delta T = 0$

$\Rightarrow$ no change of temperature

$\Rightarrow$ temperature is constant.

(ii) Isoentropic process $\Rightarrow dS = 0 \Rightarrow$ entropy is constant

(iii) Isochoric process $\Rightarrow dV = 0 \Rightarrow$ volume is constant

(iv) Isobaric process $\Rightarrow dp = 0 \Rightarrow$ pressure is constant

Hence right answer is (c).

75.

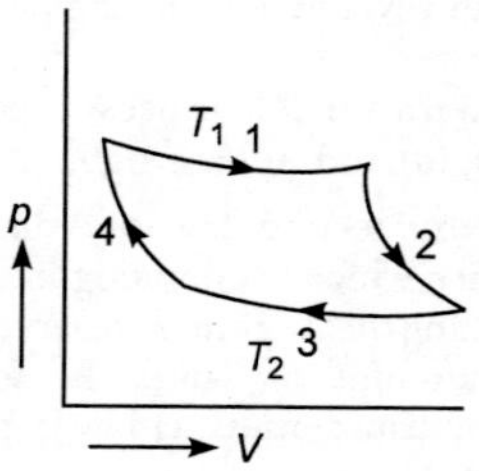

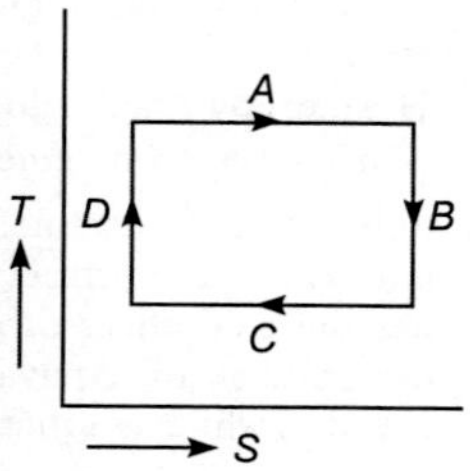

Path (1) Expansion of constant temperature

$\Rightarrow$ heat is absorbed

$\Rightarrow$ $dQ = +$ ve

$\Rightarrow$ corresponding to A.

Path (2) Adiabatic expansion

$\Rightarrow$ $dQ = 0$

$\Rightarrow$ S is constant

$\Rightarrow$ corresponding to B.

Path (3) Isothermal compression

$\Rightarrow$ $dQ = -$ ve

$\Rightarrow$ S is decrease

$\Rightarrow$ corresponding to C.

Path (4) Adiabatic compression

$\Rightarrow$ $dQ = 0$

$\Rightarrow$ S is constant

$\Rightarrow$ corresponding to D.

76. (i) The temperature of inversion in Joule-Thomson effect is the temperature above of which all gases show heating effect. Below of this all gases show colling effect and at the temperature of inversion no effect. This is given as

$$\left(\frac{\partial T}{dp}\right)_H = \frac{1}{C_p}\left(\frac{2a}{RT} - b\right)$$

(ii) The internal energy of perfect gas does not depend on volume this depends only on temperature. Thus,

$$\left(\frac{\partial U}{\partial V}\right)_T = \left(\frac{\partial U}{\partial p}\right)_T = 0$$

For real gases $\left(\frac{\partial U}{\partial V}\right)_T = \frac{a}{V^2}$

(iii) For a perfect gas Joule-Thomson effect vanishes because $\left(T\frac{\partial V}{\partial T} - V\right) = 0$

(iv) The pressure p and pV is related as

$$pV = A + BP + CP^2 + DP^3 + \ldots$$

$A > B > C > D\ldots$ are virial constants.

The Boyle's law is applied when p is very low hence when

$$pV = A$$

$$\Rightarrow \quad \frac{\partial}{\partial p}(pV) = 0$$

So, deviation from Boyle's law

$$\Rightarrow \quad \frac{\partial}{\partial p}(pV)_T \neq 0$$

77. (i) At constant volume $C_V = \frac{dE}{dT}$

$\Rightarrow$ $dE = C_V dT$

(ii) For reversible process $dS = 0$

$\Rightarrow$ $TdS = 0$

$\Rightarrow$ $(dE + dW) - TdS = 0$

(iii) For irreversible process $TdS > 0$

$\Rightarrow$ $TdS - (dE + dW) > 0$

$\Rightarrow$ $TdS - dE - dW > 0$

22

Statistical Thermodynamics

Syllabus

- Microstates and Macrostates, Thermodynamic Probability
- Partition Function and their Relation to Thermodynamic Quantities Calculation for Model System
- Classical and Quantum Statistics
- Ideal Bose and Fermi Gases
- Maxwell Velocity Distribution

Statistical Thermodynamics

In statistical thermodynamics, we deal with systems involving a very large number of particles. Classically, the state of such a system at any future time may be known if the initial positions and initial momenta are known and the laws governing their interaction. Such a description of position and momenta is known as specification of the state of the system. Consider the phase diagram in q coordinate and momenta p.

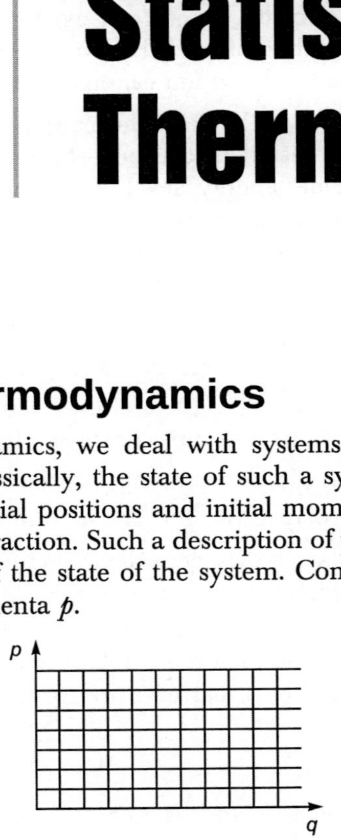

For a one-dimensional problem, the state of the system is represented by a point (q, p) in the phase space. As the system involves in time, the point (q, p) moves in the phase space. In order to better describe the state of the system, we may divide each variable q and p into equal small intervals Δq and Δp and say that the system point lies in some rectangle $\Delta q \, \Delta p = h$ where, h has the dimensions of angular momentum. Classically, h may be taken as small as the phase but in quantum mechanics, the product $\Delta q \, \Delta p$ is limited by the uncertainty principle. The smallest value of $\Delta q \, \Delta p$ can never be less than Planck's constant. Thus classically, the specification of the state of a system means specifying the cell in the phase space in which the representative point of the system is located. Quantum mechanically, the state of any system is described by a wave function ψ. Given ψ at some time t, ψ at any later time can be obtained through the Schrödinger's equation in principle. A number of quantum states may exist for the system. Specification of the state of the system means specifying the quantum state in which the system is found.

Microstates and Macrostates

The particles in a system are either distinguishable or indistinguishable. If the particles are indistinguishable, a complete specification of the system would be the specification of the total number of particles in each quantum state of some energy. We cannot say which particles are in which energy state because they are indistinguishable. If the particles are distinguishable, a complete specification would mean which particles are occupying which energy state. Such description is said to define a microstate of the assembly of particles. A macrostate is the average of the sum total of its various microstates. There may be a number of microstates for a given microstate. This number is called the statistical weight for that macrostate.

While a system may have a number of macrostates, we observe some microstates more than others. Thus, the most probable macrostate is that macrostate which has the maximum number of microstates since, all accessible microstates are equally probable.

Thermodynamic Entropy and Probability

Canonical, Microcanonical and Grand Canonical Ensemble

Consider a system A in contact with a heat reservoir A' at temperature T. The whole system $(A + A')$ is isolated. Hence, its total energy is conserved (The number of particles is also conserved). The system A can be found in any energy E and the A' in corresponding $(E° - E)$. We are interested in the probability of finding the system A in a state having energy E_i. When A is definitely in a state of energy E_i, the number of states accessible to the whole system is simply the number of states accessible by the system A' which is equal to $\Omega'(E° - E_i)$ when its energy lies in some narrow range δE around $E° - E_i$.

So,
$$P(E_i) = C\,\Omega'(E° - E_i) \quad ...(1)$$

Since, A' is a heat reservoir, we may take

$$E_i << E°$$

So,
$$\Omega'(E° - E_i) = e^{\ln \Omega'(E° - E_i)}$$

$$= e^{\ln \Omega'(E°) - E_i \left.\frac{\partial \ln \Omega(E°)}{\partial E}\right|_{E°}}$$

$$= e^{\ln \Omega'(E°)}\, e^{-\beta E_i}$$

Thus,
$$P(E_i) = C\, e^{-\beta E_i} \quad ...(2)$$

where, C is some constant of proportionality which is to be determined by the condition $\sum_i P(E_i) = 1$.

The exponential factor $e^{-\beta E}$ is called the Boltzmann factor. An ensemble systems of which can exchange energy with a reservoir (but not particles) are said to be a canonical ensemble, and the corresponding probability distribution is called a canonical distribution. When the system is isolated, the ensemble of such systems is said to be a microcanonical and when the system can exchange both heat energy and number of particles, the ensemble of such systems is said to be grand canonical ensemble.

Coming back to the canonical distribution, if we are interested in the probability of finding the system in some energy level E, then we must sum over all probabilities in all states whose energy lies in $E + dE$ and E

$$P(E) = C\,\Omega(E)\, e^{-\beta E} \quad ...(3)$$

where, $\Omega(E)$ is the number density of states; the number of energy states per unit energy in the range $E + dE$ and E.

$\Omega(E)$ is a rapidly increasing function of E while $e^{-\beta E}$ is a rapidly decreasing function of E. Hence, $\Omega(E)\, e^{-\beta E}$ is shaped pressed arrow some energy value E.

Now, let us consider a grand canonical ensemble in which we have an ensemble of systems in contact with a large reservoir which can exchange both energy and particles. For the whole system, the total energy and the number of particles are fixed.

$$E + E' = E°$$
$$N + N' = N° \quad ...(4)$$

where E and N refer to the energy and number of particles in system A respectively. As before, the probability of finding the system A in a state having energy E_i and number of particles N_i is $P(E_i, N_i) = C\,\Omega'(E° - E_i, N° - N_i)$, where Ω' refers to the number of microstates in system A' where energy lies in a range δE around $E° - E_i$ and the number of particles lie in a range δN around $N° - N_i$.

$$\Omega'(E° - E_i, N° - N_i) = e^{\ln \Omega(E° - E_i, N° - N_i)}$$

$$= e^{\ln \Omega(E°, N°) - E_i \left.\frac{\partial \ln \Omega(E, N)}{\partial E}\right|_{E_0} - N_i \left.\frac{\partial \ln \Omega}{\partial N}\right|_{N_0}}$$

So,
$$P(E_i, N_i) = C\, e^{-\beta E_i - \alpha N_i} \quad ...(5)$$

where,
$$\beta = \frac{\partial \ln \Omega}{\partial E}, \; \alpha = \frac{\partial \ln \Omega}{\partial N}$$

We may write $\alpha = \beta\mu$

So, $$P(E_i, N_i) = C\, e^{-(E_i - \mu N_i)/kT} \quad ...(6)$$

The Occupation Number, < *n* >

Let us calculate the occupation number $<n>$ for a quantum state in a variety of cases.

In some state S of the system,

Let there be n_i particles in ith state. We also assume negligible interaction between the particles so,

$$E_S = \sum_i n_i \varepsilon_i \quad ...(7)$$

where, ε_i is the energy of a particle in state i

and $$N_S = \Sigma n_i$$

So, $$\bar{n}_S = \frac{\Sigma n_S e^{-\beta E_S}}{\Sigma e^{-\beta E_S}} \quad ...(8)$$

The condition $\Sigma n_i = N$ causes a complication. One easy way out of this is to consider a grand canonical ensemble. So, $\bar{n}_S$ is given by

$$\bar{n}_S = \frac{\sum_i n_S e^{-\beta(E_S - \mu n_S)}}{\sum_i e^{-\beta(E_S - \mu n_S)}}$$

$$= \frac{\sum_i n_S e^{-n_i \beta(\varepsilon_i - \mu_i)}}{\sum_i e^{-n_i \beta(\varepsilon_i - \mu)}}$$

With no restriction on n_i's.

For weakly interacting particles, we may write

$$\bar{n}_S = \frac{\sum_i n_S e^{-n_i \beta(\varepsilon_i - \mu)}}{\sum_i e^{-n_i \beta(\varepsilon_i - \mu)}}$$

$$= \frac{\sum_{n_S} n_S e^{-n_S \beta(\varepsilon_S - \mu)}}{\Sigma e^{-n_S \beta(\varepsilon_S - \mu)}}$$

Let, $\beta(\varepsilon_S - \mu) = \alpha_S$

So, $$\bar{n}_S = \frac{\sum_i n_S e^{-n_S \alpha_S}}{\sum_i e^{-n_S \alpha_S}}$$

$$= -\frac{\partial}{\partial \alpha_S} \ln(\Sigma e^{-n_S \alpha_S})$$

$$= -\frac{\partial}{\partial \alpha} \ln Z \quad ...(9)$$

where, $Z = \sum_S e^{-n_S \alpha_S}$

Let us consider two special cases

1. When n_S is either 0 or 1, which is the case for Fermi-Dirac statistics.
   - When $n = 0$ or 1, then

$$Z = \sum_{n_S} e^{-n_S \alpha_S} = 1 + e^{-\alpha_S}$$

So, $$\boxed{\bar{n}_S = \frac{e^{-\alpha_S}}{1 + e^{-\alpha_S}} = \frac{1}{e^{\beta(\varepsilon_S - \mu)} + 1}}$$

which is the Fermi-Dirac distribution.

2. n_S can range from 0 to infinity which is the case for Bose-Einstein statistics.
   - When $n_S = 0$ to ∞,

then, $$Z = \sum_{n_S} e^{-n_S \alpha_S} = \frac{1}{1 - e^{-\alpha_S}}$$

$$\bar{n}_S = -\frac{\partial}{\partial \alpha_S}(\ln Z) = \frac{e^{-\alpha_S}}{1 - e^{-\alpha_S}}$$

$$= \frac{1}{e^{\alpha_S} - 1}$$

or $$\boxed{\bar{n}_S = \frac{1}{e^{\beta(\varepsilon_S - \mu)} - 1}}$$

which is the Bose-Einstein distribution.

Example 1. *Consider a quantum harmonic oscillator having characteristic frequency ω, in thermal contact with a heat reservoir at temperature T ($kT << \hbar\omega$).*

(a) Find the ratio of probability of the oscillator being in the first excited state to the probability of its being in the ground state.

(b) Find the mean energy of the oscillator assuming that only the states up to the first excited states are appreciably filled.

Sol. Let $P(\varepsilon)$ denote the probability of finding the particle in a state of energy ε.

So, $$\frac{P(\varepsilon)}{P(0)} = \frac{e^{-\varepsilon/kT}}{1}$$

(a) In the first excited state $\varepsilon = \frac{3}{2}\hbar\omega$

So, $$\frac{P(\varepsilon_1)}{P(\varepsilon_0)} = e^{-\frac{3}{2}\hbar\omega/kT}$$

(b) Mean energy,

$$\bar{\varepsilon} = \frac{\Sigma \varepsilon_n e^{-\varepsilon_n/kT}}{\Sigma e^{-\varepsilon_n/kT}}$$

$$= \frac{\frac{\hbar\omega}{2} e^{-\frac{\hbar\omega}{2kT}} + \frac{3\hbar\omega}{2} e^{-\frac{3\hbar\omega}{2kT}}}{e^{-\frac{\hbar\omega}{2kT}} + e^{-\frac{3\hbar\omega}{2kT}}}$$

$$= \frac{\hbar\omega}{2}\left[\frac{1+3e^{-\frac{\hbar\omega}{kT}}}{1+e^{-\frac{\hbar\omega}{kT}}}\right]$$

Example 2. *A wire of radius r_0 is coincident with the axis of a metal cylinder of radius R and length L. The wire is maintained at a positive potential V with respect to the cylinder. The whole system is at some high temperature T. As a result, electrons are emitted from the wire and form a dilute gas filling the cylindrical container. Assuming that the density of electrons is so low, that their mutual electrostatic mutual interaction may be neglected. Find the equilibrium charge density as a function of radial distance.*

Sol. Let σ be the uniform charge density on the surface of the wire.

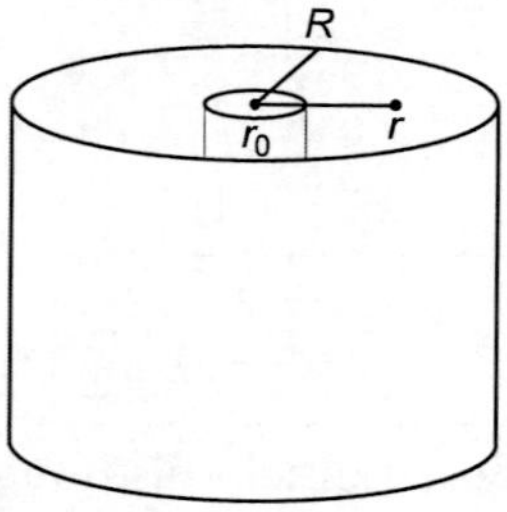

So, by Gauss's law

$$\int \vec{\mathbf{E}}\cdot d\vec{\mathbf{S}} = \frac{q}{\varepsilon_0} \qquad \text{(enclosed)}$$

$$E\, 2\pi r = \frac{\sigma\, 2\pi r_0}{\varepsilon_0}$$

$$E(r) = \frac{\sigma r_0}{\varepsilon_0 r}, \qquad (r_0 \le r \le R)$$

and $$\int_{r_0}^{R} E(r)\cdot dr = V$$

So, $$V = \frac{\sigma r_0}{\varepsilon_0} \ln\left(\frac{R}{r_0}\right)$$

This determines σ in terms of V.

And $$\int_{r_0}^{r} E(r)\, dr = V(r_0) - V(r)$$

$$= V - V(r)$$

$$\frac{\sigma r_0}{\varepsilon_0} \ln\left(\frac{r}{r_0}\right) = V - V(r)$$

$$V(r) = \frac{\sigma r_0}{\varepsilon_0}\left\{\ln\left(\frac{R}{r_0}\right) - \ln\left(\frac{r}{r_0}\right)\right\}$$

$$V(r) = \frac{\sigma r_0}{\varepsilon_0} \ln\left(\frac{R}{r}\right) \qquad (r_0 \le r \le R)$$

Now, the energy of each electron at a distance r is

$$eV(r) = \frac{e\,\sigma r_0}{\varepsilon_0} \ln\left(\frac{R}{r}\right)$$

So, probability of finding n electrons at a radial distance r

$$P(r) = C\, e^{-\frac{ne\,\sigma r_0}{\varepsilon_0 kT} \ln\left(\frac{R}{r}\right)}$$

where, C is a constant.

Electron number density

$$\bar{n} = \frac{\sum_n n e^{-n\alpha}}{\sum e^{-n\alpha}}$$

where, $$\alpha = \frac{e\,\sigma r_0}{\varepsilon_0 kT} \ln\left(\frac{R}{r}\right)$$

So, $$\bar{n} = \frac{1}{\left(e^{\frac{e\,\sigma r_0}{\varepsilon_0 kT} \ln\left(\frac{R}{r}\right)} - 1\right)}$$

Or in terms of V $$\bar{n} = \frac{1}{\left(e^{\frac{eV}{kT}\frac{\ln(R/r)}{\ln(R/r_0)}} - 1\right)}$$

Therefore, the density of electron is

$$\rho(r) = \bar{n} m$$

where, m is the mass of an electron

$$\rho(r) = \frac{m}{\left(e^{\frac{eV}{kT}\frac{\ln(R/r)}{\ln(R/r_0)}} - 1\right)}$$

The Partition Function

Let us consider an assembly of ideal gas molecules obeying classical statistics. Let the distribution of gas molecules be such that n_i molecules occupy the ith state with energy between ε_i and $\varepsilon_i + d\varepsilon_i$ and degeneracy (*i.e.*, the number of energy levels) g_i. Then, from Maxwell-Boltzmann distribution law.

$$n_i = g_i e^{-\alpha} e^{-\varepsilon_i/kT} \qquad \ldots(10)$$

Let us substitute $e^{-a} = A$. Then

$$n_i = g_i A e^{-\varepsilon_i/kT}$$

If the total number of gas molecules in the assembly is N, then

$$N = \sum_i n_i = \sum_i g_i A e^{-\varepsilon_i/kT}$$

$$= A \sum_i g_i e^{-\varepsilon_i/kT} \qquad \ldots(11)$$

The term $A\,(= e^{-\alpha})$ has been taken out of the summation sign because α is a constant, the Lagrangian undetermined multiplier.

From Eq.(11), we get

$$\frac{N}{A} = \sum_i g_i e^{-\varepsilon_i/kT} = Z \text{ (say)} \qquad ...(12)$$

The quantity Z is called the Boltzmann partition function or simply the partition function. Therefore, the quantity Z indicates how the gas molecules of an assembly are distributed or partitioned among the various energy levels.

If the energy of the ith level is ε_i then keeping in mind that the weight of an individual level is unity Eq. (12) can be written as

$$Z = \sum_i e^{-\varepsilon_i/kT} \qquad ...(13)$$

Partition Function for a Gas Molecule

Classically, a gas molecule is assumed to be a structureless identity and the total energy of the gas molecule is practically equal to the sum of the kinetic energies of individual molecules. In classical treatments, the distribution of energy states is considered continuous. The number of energy levels in the momentum range p and $p + dp$ is given by

$$g(p)dp = \frac{V \cdot 4\pi p^2 dp}{h^3}$$

Therefore, the number of energy levels between energy ε and $\varepsilon + d\varepsilon$ is now written by substituting $p^2 = 2m\varepsilon$ and $dp = \frac{m d\varepsilon}{\sqrt{(2m\varepsilon)}}$ in above equation, *i.e.*,

$$g(\varepsilon)d\varepsilon = \frac{V.4\pi 2m\varepsilon}{h^3} \cdot \frac{m d\varepsilon}{\sqrt{(2m\varepsilon)}}$$

or

$$g(\varepsilon)\, d\varepsilon = \frac{2\pi V}{h^3}(2m)^{3/2}\varepsilon^{1/2} d\varepsilon \qquad ...(14)$$

Since, here the distribution of energy states is continuous, Eq. (12) may be written as

$$Z = \sum_i g_i e^{-\varepsilon_i/kT}$$

$$= \int_0^\infty g(\varepsilon)d\varepsilon . e^{-\varepsilon/kT}$$

$$= \int_0^\infty \frac{2\pi V}{h^3}(2m)^{3/2}\varepsilon^{1/2} d\varepsilon . e^{-\varepsilon/kT}$$

[Using Eq. (14)]

$$= \frac{2\pi V(2m)^{3/2}}{h^3} \int_0^\infty \varepsilon^{1/2} e^{-\varepsilon/kT} d\varepsilon$$

The definite integral can be shown to have the value

$$\int_0^\infty \varepsilon^{1/2} e^{-\varepsilon/kT} d\varepsilon = \frac{\sqrt{\pi}}{2}.(kT)^{3/2}$$

$$\therefore \qquad Z = \frac{2\pi V(2m)^{3/2}}{h^3} \cdot \frac{\sqrt{\pi}}{2}(kT)^{3/2}$$

i.e.,

$$Z = \frac{V}{h^3}(2\pi mkT)^{3/2} \qquad ...(15)$$

This equation gives the translational partition function for a gas molecule.

Partition Function and Thermodynamical Quantities

The entropy of an assembly and the weight of the most probable configuration are related by the equation.

$$S = k \log \Omega_{\max} \qquad ...(16)$$

The weight of the configuration for a classical system is given by

$$\Omega = N! \prod_i \frac{g_i^{ni}}{n_i!}$$

Therefore, $\log \Omega = \log N! + \Sigma_i (n_i \log_{g_i} - \log n_i!)$

Now, using Stirling approximation, $\log n! = n \log n - n$, we get

$$\log \Omega = N \log N - N + \sum_i (n_i \log g_i - n_i \log n_i + n_i) \qquad ...(17)$$

According to Maxwell-Boltzmann distribution law for a most probable configuration

$$n_i = g_i e^{-\alpha} e^{\beta \varepsilon_i} \qquad ...(18)$$

As the total number of molecules is constant, we have

$$N = \sum_i n_i \qquad ...(19)$$

Substituting these values in Eq. (16), we get

$$\log \Omega_{\max} = N \log N - N + \Sigma[n_i \log g_i - n_i \log (g_i e^{-\alpha} e^{-\beta\varepsilon_i}) + n_i]$$

$$= N \log N - N + \sum_i n_i \log_{g_i} - \sum_i n_i \log_{g_i} + \sum_i n_i \alpha + \sum_i n_i \beta \varepsilon_i + \sum_i n_i$$

$$= N \log N + \alpha N + \beta \sum_i n_i \varepsilon_i \qquad ...(20)$$

$$\left(\text{since, } N = \sum_i n_i\right)$$

If the total energy of the gas molecules of the assembly is E, then

$$E = \sum_i n_i \varepsilon_i \qquad ...(21)$$

So, Eq. (14) may be written as

$$\log \Omega_{\max} = N \log N + N + \alpha N + \beta E \qquad ...(22)$$

Let us substitute $A = e^{-\alpha}$, *i.e.*, $\alpha = -\log A$

So, Eq. (22) may be written as

$$\log \Omega_{\max} = N \log N - N \log A + \beta E$$

$$= n \log \frac{N}{A} + \beta E = N \log Z + \beta E \quad \ldots(23)$$

$$\left(\text{since partition function, } Z = \frac{N}{A}\right)$$

But $\beta = \dfrac{1}{kT}$, so

$$\log \Omega_{max} = N \log Z + \frac{E}{kT} \quad \ldots(24)$$

Therefore, the entropy of the ensemble (or assembly), is given by

$$S = k \log \Omega_{max}$$

$$S = Nk \log Z + \frac{E}{T} \quad \ldots(25)$$

For an ideal gas, we have

$$E = \frac{3}{2} NkT$$

Therefore, Eq. (25) yields

$$S = Nk \log Z + \frac{3}{2} Nk \quad \ldots(26)$$

The equation gives the expression for the entropy of the assembly of ideal gas molecules. The other thermodynamical functions, can now be evaluated easily as follows.

Helmholtz free energy *F* The Helmholtz free energy F is given by

$$F = E - TS$$

Using Eq. (25), we get

$$F = E - T\,(Nk \log Z + E/T)$$

$$F = NkT \log_e Z \quad \ldots(27)$$

This is the required expression for Helmholtz free energy E in terms of partition function.

Total energy *E*. If $\bar{\varepsilon}$ is the average energy of a system of an assembly of N such independent systems, then

$$\bar{\varepsilon} = \frac{E}{N} = \frac{\sum_i n_i \varepsilon_i}{\sum_i n_i}$$

Using Maxwell-Boltzmann distribution law, we get

$$\bar{\varepsilon} = \frac{\sum_i g_i e^{-\alpha} e^{-\beta \varepsilon_i} \varepsilon_i}{\sum_i e^{-\alpha} e^{-\beta \varepsilon_i}} = \frac{\sum_i g_i \varepsilon_i e^{-\beta \varepsilon_i}}{\sum_i g_i e^{-\beta \varepsilon_i}}$$

$$= \frac{\sum_i g_i \varepsilon_i e^{\varepsilon_i / kT}}{\sum_i g_i e^{-\varepsilon_i / kT}} \qquad \left(\text{since } \beta = \frac{1}{kT}\right)$$

$$= \frac{\sum_i g_i \varepsilon_i e^{-\varepsilon_i / kT}}{Z} \quad \ldots(28)$$

Since, partition function

$$Z = \sum_i g_i e^{-\beta \varepsilon_i} = \sum_i g_i e^{-\varepsilon_i / kT} \quad \ldots(29)$$

We have $\left(\dfrac{\partial Z}{\partial T}\right)_V = \sum_i g_i \dfrac{\varepsilon_i}{kT^2} e^{-\varepsilon_i / kT}$

$$= \frac{1}{kT^2} \sum_i g_i \varepsilon e^{\varepsilon_i} / kT$$

For isothermal isochoric transformation.

Therefore, for isothermal isochoric transformation, we have

$$\bar{\varepsilon} = \frac{kT^2}{Z} \left(\frac{\partial T}{\partial Z}\right)_V$$

$$\bar{\varepsilon} = kT^2 \left(\frac{\partial(\log Z)}{\partial T}\right)_V$$

Therefore, $E = N\bar{\varepsilon}$

$$= NkT^2 \left[\frac{\partial(\log Z)}{\partial T}\right]_V \quad \ldots(30)$$

This is the expression for total energy of an ensemble in terms of partition function.

Enthalpy *H* The enthalpy H is given by

$$H = E + pV$$

For an ideal gas, we have $pV = RT$

Therefore, $H = E + RT$

Using Eq. (35), we get

$$H = NkT^2 \left[\frac{\partial(\log Z)}{\partial T}\right]_V + RT \quad \ldots(31)$$

Gibb's potential *G* The Gibb's potential G is given by

$$G = H - TS \quad \ldots(32)$$

Using Eqs. (31) and (32), we get

$$G = NkT^2 \left(\frac{\partial(\log Z)}{\partial T}\right)_V + RT - T \left(Nk \log Z + \frac{3}{2} Nk\right)$$

$$= NkT^2 \left[\frac{\partial(\log Z)}{\partial T}\right]_V + RT - NkT$$

$$\log Z - \frac{3}{2} NkT \quad \ldots(33)$$

Pressure of a gas *p* The pressure (p) of a gas is given by

$$p = -\left(\frac{\partial F}{\partial V}\right)_T$$

Using Eq. (27), we get

$$p = NkT\left[\frac{\partial(\log Z)}{\partial V}\right]_T \quad \ldots(34)$$

Specific heat at constant volume C_V For an isothermal isochoric transformation, the internal energy U of the assembly is equal to its total energy E.

Therefore, $$C_V = \left(\frac{\partial E}{\partial T}\right)_V$$

Using Eq. (30), we get

$$C_V = \frac{\partial}{\partial T}\left\{NkT^2\left(\frac{\partial(\log Z)}{\partial T}\right)_V\right\}$$

$$= Nk\left[2T\frac{\partial(\log Z)}{\partial T} + T^2\frac{\partial^2(\log Z)}{\partial T^2}\right]_V \quad \ldots(35)$$

Example 3. *Show that if the partition function is given by Z, the mean energy $\bar{\varepsilon}$ is given by*

$$\bar{\varepsilon} = \frac{\partial \log Z}{\partial \beta} \quad \textit{where, } \beta = \frac{1}{kT}$$

Sol. If $\bar{\varepsilon}$ is the mean energy of a system of an ensemble consisting N such independent systems, then

$$\bar{\varepsilon} = \frac{E}{N}$$

where, E is total energy of the ensemble.

$$= \frac{\sum_i g_i n_i}{\sum_i n_i}$$

According to Maxwell-Boltzmann distribution law, we have

$$n_i = g_i e^{-\alpha} e^{-\beta\varepsilon_i}$$

where, $$\beta = \frac{1}{kT}$$

Therefore, $$\bar{\varepsilon} = \frac{\sum_i \varepsilon_i g_i e^{-\alpha} e^{-\beta\varepsilon_i}}{\sum_i g_i e^{-\alpha} e^{-\beta\varepsilon_i}}$$

Since, α is a constant being Lagrangian undetermined multiplier, we have

$$\bar{\varepsilon} = \frac{\sum_i g_i \varepsilon_i e^{-\beta\varepsilon_i}}{\sum_i g_i e^{-\beta\varepsilon_i}}$$

$$= \frac{\sum_i g_i \varepsilon_i e^{-\beta\varepsilon_i}}{Z} \quad \ldots(i)$$

Since, partition function

$$Z = \Sigma g_i e^{-\beta\varepsilon_i} \quad \ldots(ii)$$

From Eq. (ii), we have

$$\frac{\partial Z}{\partial \beta} = \sum_i g_i \varepsilon_i^{-\beta\varepsilon_i} \quad \ldots(iii)$$

Using Eq. (iii) and Eq. (i) may by written as

$$\bar{\varepsilon} = -\frac{(\partial Z / \partial \beta)}{Z}$$

or mean energy $$\bar{\varepsilon} = -\frac{\partial(\log Z)}{\partial \beta} \quad \ldots(iv)$$

where, $$\beta = \frac{1}{kT}$$

This is the required expression.

Classical and Quantum Statistics

The study of statistical mechanics can be divided into two main classes :

1. Classical Statistics or Maxwell-Boltzmann Statistics.
2. Quantum Statistics

1. Classical Statistics

Let there be total N particles out of which n_i particles are in ε_ith energy level having g_i states (or having degeneracy g_i). Let us label the g_i cells. The first particle may occupy any of the g_i cells. The second particle may occupy any of the meaning $(g_i - 1)$ cells etc. Thus, the total number of ways of accommodating all n_i particles in g_i cells is $g_i^{n_i}$.

Taking into account for the fact that there are n_i particles in g_i cells for each $i = 1, 2, 3, \ldots$. The total number of ways is $\prod_i g_i^{n_i}$. The total number of particles is N. So, preventing all the particles in which n_i are alike $(i = 1, 2, 3, \ldots)$ is $\frac{N!}{\prod_i n_i!}$.

So, the total number of microstates is

$$\Omega = \frac{N!}{\prod_i n_i!}\prod_i g_i^{n_i} \quad \ldots(36)$$

Having found the number of microstates, we are ready to find the most probable state. We maximise $\ln \Omega$ subject to the two constraints

$$\sum_i n_i = N \quad \ldots(37)$$

$$\sum_i n_i\varepsilon_i = E \quad \ldots(38)$$

where, N and E are constants.

$$\delta(\ln \Omega) = \delta \ln\left(\frac{N!}{\prod_i n_i!}\prod g_i^{n_i}\right)$$

$$= \delta\left[\ln N! + \Sigma n_i \ln g_i - \Sigma \ln n_i!\right]$$

$$= \delta\,[\ln N! + \Sigma\, n_i \ln g_i - \Sigma\,(n_i \ln n_i - n_i)]$$
$$= \sum_i (\delta n_i \ln g_i - \delta n_i - \delta n_i \ln n_i + \delta n_i)$$
$$= \sum_i \left[\delta n_i \ln\left(\frac{g_i}{n_i}\right)\right]$$

Again as before, let α and β be Lagrange multipliers,

So, $$\sum_i \left[\delta n_i \ln \frac{g_i}{n_i} + \alpha\, \delta n_i - \beta\varepsilon_i\, \delta n_i\right] = 0$$

or $$\ln \frac{g_i}{n_i} + \alpha - \beta\varepsilon_i = 0$$

or $$\frac{g_i}{n_i} = e^{-\alpha}\, e^{\beta\,\varepsilon_i}$$

or $$n_i = g_i e^{-(\beta\,\varepsilon_i - \alpha)}$$

which is the classical or Maxwell-Boltzmann distribution.

2. Bose-Einstein Statistics

This statistics is obeyed by identical, indistinguishable particles of integral spin (bosons) that have symmetrical wave function and is so named as it was derived by Bose for light quanta and generalized by Einstein.

Consider a system having n indistinguishable particles. Let these particles be divided into quantum groups or levels such that there are $n_1, n_2, \ldots n_i$ number of particles in groups whose approximate constant energies are $\varepsilon_1, \varepsilon_2, \ldots, \varepsilon_i \ldots$ respectively. Let g_i be the number of eigen states (*i.e.* degeneracy or statistical weight) of the ith level (for a non degenerate case $g_i = 1$).

For finding Bose-Einstein distribution consider a box divided into g_i sections (or cells) and n_i indistinguishable particles are to be distributed among these sections. The choice that which of the sections will head the sequence can be made in g_i ways. Once this has been done the total number of permutations of n_i particles and the remaining $(g_i - 1)$ sections is $(n_i + g_i - 1)$. Thus, the total number of possible ways in which n_i particles can be distributed in g_i sections is

$$g_i[(n_i + g_i + 1)!] \qquad \ldots(39)$$

Since the particles are indistinguishable the permutations of particles among themselves will not give rise to indistinguishable arrangements. Obviously these are $n_i!$ such permutations, hence expression (39) must be divided by $n_i!$. Further, the distributions which arise by mere permutations of sections among themselves do not produce different states. Obviously there are $g_i!$ such permutations hence expressions must also be divided by $g_i!$

Thus, the required number of ways in which n_i particles are to be distributed among g_i sub-levels of ith quantum group is

$$\frac{[g_i(n_i + g_i - 1)!]}{n_i!\,g_i!} = \frac{(n_i + g_i - 1)!}{n_i(g_i - 1)!}$$

Similar expressions can be found for various other quantum states. Considering all the available quantum groups, with n_1 particles in first group of energy ε_1, n_2 particles in second group of energy ε_2 and so on, the total number of distinguishable arrangements are given by

$$G = \frac{(n_1 + g_1 - 1)}{n_1!(g_1 - 1)!} \cdot \frac{(n_2 - g_2 - 1)!}{n_2!(g_2 - 1)!} \cdot \frac{(n_i + g_i - 1)!}{n_i!(g_i - 1)!} \cdots$$
$$= \prod_i \frac{(n_i + g_i - 1)}{n_i!(g_i - 1)!} \qquad \ldots(40)$$

As n_i and g_i are large numbers, we may neglect one in above expression therefore, equation (40) may be written as

$$G = \prod_i \frac{(n_i + g_i)!}{n_i!(g_i)!} \qquad \ldots(41)$$

In accordance with the postulate of equal a priori probability of states,the probability Ω of the system for occuring with the specified distribution is proportional to the total number of eigen states, *i.e.*,

$$\Omega = \prod_i \frac{(n_i + g_i)!}{n_i!\,g_i!} \times \text{constant.} \qquad \ldots(42)$$
$$= C \prod_i \frac{(n_i + g_i)!}{n_i!\,g_i!} \quad \text{where } C \text{ is constant}$$

The distribution law of Bose-Einstein statistics can now be obtained by determining the most probable distribution as in classical statistics.

Taking log of Eq. (42), we have

$$\log \Omega = \log C \prod_i \frac{(n_i + g_i)!}{n_i!\,g_i!}$$
$$= \log C + \sum_i [\log(n_i + g_i)]$$
$$\log n! = \log_i n_i - \log g_i! \qquad \ldots(43)$$

As n_i and g_i are very large numbers, we can use stirling approximation. So, we get

$$\log n! = n \log n - n$$
$$\log\, [\Omega = \log C + \sum_i [n_i + g_i) \log (n_i + g_i) \ldots n_i \log n_i - g_i \log g_i] \ldots(44)$$

Differentiation of above equation gives

$$\delta(\log \Omega) + \sum_i (\log(n_i + g_i) - \log n_i\}\delta n_i$$
$$\delta\,(\log \Omega) = -\sum_i \left\{\log \frac{n_i}{n_i + g_i}\right\}\delta n_i \qquad \ldots(45)$$

For most probable distribution $\Omega = \Omega_{max}$: so $\delta(\log \Omega_{max}) = 0$. Thus, the condition of most probable distribution gives

$$\sum_i \left\{ \log \frac{n_i}{n_i + g_i} \right\} \delta n_i = 0 \qquad \ldots(46)$$

The two subsidiary conditions are

1. Total number of particles of the system is constant *i.e.*,

$$n = \sum_i n_i = \text{constant}$$

i.e.,
$$\delta n = \sum_i \delta n_i = 0 \qquad \ldots(47)$$

2. Total energy of the system is constant *i.e.*,

$$E = \sum_i n_i \varepsilon_i = \text{constant}$$

i.e.,
$$\delta E = \sum_i \varepsilon_i \delta n_i = 0 \qquad \ldots(48)$$

Now we are shall apply the Lagrangian method of undetermined multipliers. For this, we multiply Eq. (47) by α, Eq. (48) by β and add the resulting expression to Eq. (46); so that we get

$$\sum_i \left[\log \frac{n_i}{n_i + g_i} \right] + \alpha + \beta\varepsilon_i = 0. \qquad \ldots(49)$$

As the variations δn_i are independent of each other, we get

$$\log\left(\frac{n_i}{n_i + g_i} \right) + \alpha + \beta\varepsilon_i = 0$$

or
$$\frac{n_i}{n_i + g_i} = e^{-(\alpha + \beta\varepsilon_i)}$$

i.e.,
$$\frac{n_i + g_i}{n_i} = e^{\alpha + \beta\varepsilon_i}$$

i.e.,
$$1 + \frac{g_i}{n_i} = e^{\alpha + \beta\varepsilon_i}$$

i.e.,
$$\frac{g_i}{n_i} = e^{\alpha + \beta\varepsilon_i} - 1$$

i.e.,
$$n_i = \frac{g_i}{e^{\alpha + \beta\varepsilon_i} - 1}$$

This equation represents the most probable distribution of the particles among various energy levels for a system obeying Bose-Einstein statistics and is therefore known as Bose-Einstein's distribution law.

Fermi-Dirac Statistics

This statistics is obeyed by indistinguishable particles of half-integral spin that have anti-symmetric wave functions and obey Pauli exclusion principle.

Consider a system having n indistinguishable particles. Let these particles be divided into quantum groups or levels such that there are $n_1, n_2, \ldots n_i \ldots$ number of particles in groups whose approximate constant energies are $\varepsilon_1, \varepsilon_2, \ldots \varepsilon_i \ldots$ respectively. Let g_i denote the degeneracy or statistical weight (*i.e.*, number of sublevels) of ith level.

Since due to Pauli's principle, no cell can occupy more than one particle, therefore among g_i cells only n_i cells are occupied by one particle each and the remaining $(g_i - n_i)$ cells are empty. The possible number of such a distribution is given by $g_i!$ corresponding to the permutations of the g_i cells. But as the particles are indistinguishable, therefore all the occupied n_i cells are similar to each other. Hence $n_i!$ permutations of occupied cells will not give rise to indistinguishable arrangements. Further $(g_i - n_i)!$ permutations of empty cells among themselves also give rise to indistinguishable arrangements. Hence, the number of distinguishable arrangements of n_i particles in g_i cells are

$$\frac{g_i}{n!\,(g_i - n_i)} \qquad \ldots(50)$$

Similar expressions can also be found for various other quantum states. Considering all the available quantum groups, with n_i particles in first group of energy ε_1 ; n_2 particles in second group of energy ε_2 and so on and keeping in mind that due to indistinguishability of particles, the division of total number of n particles into groups of $n_1, n_2, \ldots n_i \ldots$ particles can be done in only one way; the total number of eigen states for the whole system is given by

$$G = \prod_i \frac{g_i!}{n_i!(g_i - n_i)!} \qquad \ldots(51)$$

In accordance with the postulate of equal a priori probability of states, the probability Ω of the system for occurring with the specified distribution is proportional to the total number of eigenstates *i.e.*,

$$\Omega = \prod_i \frac{g_i!}{n_i!(g_i - n_i)!} \times \text{constant.}$$

$$= C \prod_i \frac{g_i!}{n_i!(g_i - n_i)!} \qquad \ldots(52)$$

where, C is a constant.

The Fermi-Dirac distribution law can be obtained by determining the most probable distribution

Taking log of Eq. (52), we get

$$\log \Omega = \log \left\{ C \prod_i \frac{g_i!}{n!(g_i - n_i)!} \right\}$$

$$= \log C + \sum_i \log g_i! - \log n_i! - \log(g_i - n_i)! \qquad \ldots(53)$$

As n_i and g_i are large numbers, therefore using Stirling approximation. Eq. (53) reduces to

$$\log \Omega = \log C + \sum_i [g_i \log g_i - g_i - n_i \log n_i + n_i - (g_i - n_i) \log (g_i - n_i) + (g_i - n_i)]$$

$$= \log C + \sum_i [(n_i - g_i) \log(g_i - n_i) + g_i \log g_i - n_i \log n_i] \quad ...(54)$$

The differentiation of above equation gives

$$\delta(\log \Omega) = \sum_i \{\log(g_i - n_i) - \log n_i\} \delta n_i$$

$$= \sum_i \left\{ \log \frac{n_i}{g_i - n_i} \right\} \delta n_i. \quad ...(55)$$

For most probable distribution $\Omega = \Omega_{max}$; so

$$\delta(\log \Omega_{max}) = 0$$

Thus, the condition of most probable distribution gives

$$\sum_i \left\{ \log \frac{n_i}{g_i - n_i} \right\} \delta n_i = 0 \quad ...(56)$$

The two subsidiary conditions are :

1. The total number of particles of the systems is constant

$$n = \sum_i n_i = \text{constant}$$

i.e., $$\delta n = \delta n_i = 0 \quad ...(57)$$

2. Total energy of the system is constant

i.e., $$E = \sum_i n_i \varepsilon_i = \text{constant}$$

i.e., $$\delta E = \sum_i \varepsilon_i \delta n_i = 0 \quad ...(58)$$

Now to apply the Lagrangian method of undetermined multipliers, we multiply Eq. (57) by α and Eq. (58) by β and add the resulting expression to Eq. (56); so that we get

$$\sum_i \left\{ \left(\log \frac{n_i}{g_i - n_i} \right) + \alpha + \beta \varepsilon_i \right\} \delta n_i = 0 \quad ...(59)$$

As the variations δn_i are independent of each other, we get

$$\log \frac{n_i}{g_i - n_i} + \alpha + \beta \varepsilon_i = 0$$

or $$\frac{n_i}{g_i - n_i} = e^{-(\alpha + \beta \varepsilon_i)}$$

i.e., $$\frac{g_i - n_i}{n_i} = e^{\alpha + \beta \varepsilon_i}$$

i.e., $$\frac{g_i}{n_i} - 1 = e^{\alpha + \beta \varepsilon_i}$$

i.e., $$\frac{g_i}{n_i} = e^{\alpha + \beta \varepsilon_i} + 1$$

i.e., $$n_i = \frac{g_i}{e^{\alpha + \beta \varepsilon_i} + 1}$$

This equation represents the most probable distribution of the particles among various energy levels for a system obeying Fermi-Dirac statistics and is therefore known as Fermi-Dirac distribution law.

Comparison of Three Statistics

The expressions for the most probable distributions in the three statistics are

(i) Maxwell-Boltzmann Statistics

$$n_i = \frac{g_i}{e^{\alpha + \beta \varepsilon_i}}$$

(ii) Bose-Einstein Statistics $n_i = \dfrac{g_i}{e^{\alpha + \beta \varepsilon_i} - 1}$

(iii) Fermi-Dirac Statistics

$$n_i = \frac{g_i}{e^{\alpha + \beta \varepsilon_i} + 1}$$

It is to be note that if g_i / n_i is very large in comparison to unity, we may write

$$\frac{g_i}{n_i} \approx \frac{g_i}{n_i} + 1 \approx \frac{g_i}{n_i} - 1$$

i.e., for large values g_i / n_i Bose-Einstein and Fermi-Dirac distributions approach the Maxwell-Boltzmann distribution.

Ideal Bose Gas

An assembly of bosons (*i.e.*, indistinguishable elementary particles of zero or integral spin) is termed as Bose-Einstein gas or Bose gas.

Consider a perfect Bose-Einstein gas of n bosons. Let these particles be distributed among quantum groups or states such that there are $n_1, n_2, ..., n_i, ...$ number of particles in quantum states whose approximate constant energies are $\varepsilon_1, \varepsilon_2 ..., \varepsilon_i ...$ respectively.

If g_i is the degeneracy or statistical weight of ith quantum state then according to Bose-Einstein distribution law the most probable distribution is given by

$$n_i = \frac{g_i}{e^{\alpha + \beta \varepsilon_i} + 1} \quad ...(60 \text{ a})$$

where $$\alpha = -\frac{\mu}{kT} \text{ and } \beta = \frac{1}{kT}$$

Eq. (60 a) may be written as

$$n_i = \frac{g_i}{\frac{1}{A}e^{\beta \varepsilon_i} - 1} \qquad \ldots(60\text{ b})$$

where $$A = e^{-\alpha} \qquad \ldots(61)$$

As the number of particles in a state cannot be negative, we must always have $n_i \geq 0$. This requires

$$e^{\alpha + \beta \varepsilon_i} = \frac{1}{A}.e^{\alpha + \beta \varepsilon_i} \geq 1 \qquad \ldots(62)$$

If the ground state (or lowest energy state) is taken to be at zero energy. Then

$$e^{\alpha} = e^{-\mu kT} = \frac{1}{A} \geq 1 \qquad \ldots(63)$$

i.e., $$\alpha \geq 0 \,;\, \mu \leq 0 \leq A \leq 1 \qquad \ldots(64)$$

The constant α can be determined by the condition

$$n = \sum_i n_i = \sum_i \frac{g_i}{e^{\alpha + \beta \varepsilon_i} - 1} \qquad \ldots(65)$$

$$= \sum_i \frac{g_i}{\frac{1}{A} \cdot e^{\beta \varepsilon_i} - 1}$$

It is known that for the particles in a box of normal size, the translational levels are spaced closely enough so that we can integrate over phase space instead of summing over particle states.

The number of particle states $g(p)dp$ lying between momentum p and $p + dp$ is given by

$$g(p)\, dp = g_s \frac{4\pi p^2 dp}{h^3 / V} \qquad \ldots(66)$$

where, $g_s = (2s + 1)$ is the spin degeneracy factor caused by the particle spin s. For simplicity let use take $s = 0$ *i.e.*, $g_0 = 1$, then Eq. (66) becomes

$$g(p)dp = \frac{4\pi V}{h^3} P^2 dp \qquad \ldots(67)$$

According to Eq. (66) for most probable distribution the number of particles in the momentum range p and $p + dp$ is given by

$$dn\,(p) = \frac{g(p)dp}{e^{\alpha + \beta \varepsilon_i} - 1} \qquad \ldots(68)$$

Now remembering that for perfect gas (non-interacting) particles

$$\varepsilon = \frac{p^2}{2m} \qquad \ldots(69)$$

and using Eq. (67), we get

$$dn(p) = \frac{4\pi V}{3} \cdot \frac{p^2 dp}{e^{\alpha + p^2/2mkT} - 1} \left\{ \text{since}\, \beta = \frac{1}{kT} \right\} \qquad \ldots(70)$$

Using Eqs. (69) and (70), the number of particles lying between energy range ε and $\varepsilon + d\varepsilon$ may be written as

$$dn(\varepsilon) = \frac{4\pi V}{h^3} \cdot \frac{(2m\varepsilon)\left\{\frac{m}{2\varepsilon}\right\}^{1/2} d\varepsilon}{e^{\alpha + \varepsilon/kT} - 1} \qquad \ldots(71)$$

Now, let us substitute

$$x = \frac{\varepsilon}{kT}$$

or $$dx = \frac{d\varepsilon}{kT} \qquad \ldots(72)$$

So that Eq. (71) may be expressed as

$$dn(\varepsilon) = \frac{4\pi m V}{h^3} \cdot (2m)^{1/2} \frac{(kTx)^{1/2}(kT\ dx)}{e^{\alpha + x} - 1}$$

$$= \frac{V}{h^3}(2\pi\, mkT)^{3/2} \frac{2}{\sqrt{\pi}} \frac{x^{1/2} dx}{e^{\alpha + x} - 1} \qquad \ldots(73)$$

Now, keeping in mind the closely spaced levels in this case, the total number of particles are given by

$$n = \int dn\,(\varepsilon)$$

$$= \frac{V}{h^3}(2\pi mkT)^{3/2} \cdot \frac{2}{\sqrt{\pi}} \int_0^{\infty} \frac{x^{1/2} dx}{e^{\alpha + x} - 1}$$

$$= \frac{V}{h^3}(2\pi\, mk\, T)^{3/2} f_1(\alpha) \qquad \ldots(74)$$

where, $$f_1\,(\alpha) = \frac{2}{\sqrt{\pi}} \int_0^{\infty} \frac{x^{1/2} dx}{e^{\alpha + x} - 1} \qquad \ldots(75)$$

The total energy of the system is given by

$$E = \int \varepsilon\, dn(\varepsilon) = \int kTx.dn(\varepsilon) \qquad \text{[using Eq. (71)]}$$

$$= \frac{V}{h^3}(2\pi mkT)^{3/2}$$

$$kT \frac{2}{\sqrt{\pi}} \int_0^{\infty} \frac{x^{3/2} dx}{e^{\alpha + x} - 1} \qquad \text{[using Eq. (73))}$$

$$= \frac{3}{2^3} \cdot \frac{V}{h^3} (2\pi m\ kT)^{3/2} kTf_2(\alpha) \qquad \ldots(76)$$

where, $$f_2(\alpha) = \frac{4}{3\sqrt{\pi}} \int_0^{\infty} \frac{x^{3/2} dx}{e^{\alpha + x} - 1} \qquad \ldots(77)$$

For $A < 1$, the integral functions $f_1(\alpha)$ and $f_2(\alpha)$ may be evaluated by expanding the series as follows

$$f_1(\alpha) = \frac{2}{\sqrt{\pi}} \frac{x^{1/2}dx}{e^{\alpha+x}-1} = \frac{2}{\sqrt{\pi}} \int_0^\infty x^{1/2}\left(\frac{e^x}{A}-1\right)^{-1} dx$$

$$= \frac{2}{\sqrt{\pi}} \int_0^\infty x^{1/2} Ae^{-x}(1-Ae^{-x})^{-1}\, dx$$

$$= \frac{2}{\sqrt{\pi}} \int_0^\infty x^{1/2} Ae^{-x}(1+Ae^{-x}+A^2e^{-2x}+\ldots)\, dx$$

$$= \frac{2}{\sqrt{\pi}}\left[\int_0^\infty x^{1/2}e^{-x}\,dx + A^2\int_0^\infty x^{1/2}e^{-2x}\,dx+\ldots\right]$$

$$= \frac{2}{\sqrt{\pi}}\left[\frac{\sqrt{\pi}}{2}\left(A+\frac{A^2}{2^{3/2}}+\frac{A^3}{3^{3/2}}+\ldots\right)\right]$$

$$= A+\frac{A^2}{2^{3/2}}+\frac{A^2}{3^{3/2}}+\ldots = \sum_{r=1}^{\infty}\frac{A^r}{r^{3/2}} \qquad \ldots(78)$$

Similarly, we can write

$$f_2(\alpha) = A+\frac{A^2}{2^{5/2}}+\frac{A^3}{3^{5/2}}+\ldots = \sum_{r=1}^{\infty}\frac{A^r}{r^{5/2}} \qquad \ldots(79)$$

Therefore, the expressions for total number of particles and total energy of perfect Bose-Einstein gas become

$$n = \frac{V}{h^3}(2\pi\, mkT)^{3/2}\sum_{r=1}^{\infty}\frac{A^r}{r^{3/2}}$$

$$n = \frac{V}{h^3}(2\pi\, mkT)^{3/2}\left(A+\frac{A^2}{2^{3/2}}+\frac{A^3}{3^{3/2}}+\ldots\right)$$

$$E = \frac{3}{2}\frac{V}{h^3}(2\pi m\, kT)^{3/2}kT\sum_{r=1}^{\infty}\frac{A^r}{r^{5/2}}$$

$$= \frac{3}{2}\frac{V}{h^3}(2\pi\, mkT)^{3/2}kT\left(A+\frac{A^2}{2^{5/2}}+\frac{A^3}{3^{5/2}}+\ldots\right)$$

Dividing E by n, we get

$$\frac{E}{n} = \frac{3}{2}kT\left(A+\frac{A^2}{2^{5/2}}+\frac{A^3}{3^{5/2}}+\ldots\right)\left(A+\frac{A^2}{2^{3/2}}+\frac{A^3}{3^{3/2}}+\ldots\right)^{-1}$$

$$E = \frac{3}{2}nkT\left[1-\frac{A}{2^{5/2}}-\frac{A}{3^{5/2}}-\ldots\right]$$

Ideal Fermi Gas

An assembly of fermions (*i.e.*, indistinguishable particles of half integral spin obeying Pauli exclusion principle) is known as Fermi-Dirac gas or Fermi Gas

Consider a perfect Fermi-Dirac of n fermions. Let these particles be distributed among quantum groups or states such that there are $n_1, n_2, \ldots, n_i \ldots$ number of particles in quantum states whose approximate constant energies are $\varepsilon_1, \varepsilon_2, \ldots \varepsilon_i \ldots$ respectively.

If g_i is the degneracy or statistical weight of ith quantum state, then according to Fermi-Dirac distribution law, the most probable distribution is given by

$$n_i = \frac{g_i}{e^{\alpha+\beta\varepsilon_i}+1} \qquad \ldots(80)$$

where, $\alpha = -\dfrac{\mu}{kT}$

and $\beta = \dfrac{1}{kT}$

Eq. (80) may be written as

$$n_i = \frac{g_i}{\frac{1}{A}e^{\beta\varepsilon_i}+1} \qquad \ldots(81)$$

where, $A = e^{-\alpha}$ ...(82)

As in the denominator of Eq. (80) a positive sign appears before one, α need not be restricted to positive values as in Bose-Einstein case; but may be positive or negative. The number of particle states lying between momentum p and $p + dp$ is given by

$$g(p)dp = g_s \cdot \frac{4\pi p^2\,dp}{h^3/V} = g_s \cdot \frac{4\pi Vp^2\,dp}{h^3} \qquad \ldots(83)$$

where, g_s is the spin degeneracy factor caused by the particle spin s and given by

$$g_s = (2s+1) \qquad \ldots(84)$$

Since, $\varepsilon = \dfrac{p^2}{2m}$

or $dp = \left(\dfrac{m}{2\varepsilon}\right)^{1/2} d\varepsilon,$

The number of states between energy ε and $\varepsilon + d\varepsilon$ is given by

$$g(\varepsilon)d\varepsilon = g_i \cdot \frac{4nV(2m\varepsilon)\left(\frac{m}{2\varepsilon}\right)^{1/2}d\varepsilon}{h^3} \qquad \ldots(85)$$

For a gas of fermions at temperature T in a volume V, the mean number of fermions in the energy range between ε and $\varepsilon + d\varepsilon$ is given by

$$dn(\varepsilon) = g_s \cdot \frac{4\pi mV}{h^3}\sqrt{(2m)} \cdot \frac{\varepsilon^{1/2} de}{e^{\alpha + \varepsilon/kT} + 1} \quad ...(86)$$

The total number of particles in Fermi-Dirac gas is given by

$$n = \Sigma dn(\varepsilon) = \int dn\,(e) = g_s \cdot \frac{4\pi mV}{h^3}\sqrt{(2m)}\int_0^\infty \frac{\varepsilon^{1/2} d\varepsilon}{e^{\alpha+\varepsilon/kT} + 1} \quad ...(87)$$

and the total integral energy is given by

$$E = \int_0^\infty \varepsilon dn(\varepsilon)$$

$$= g_s \cdot \frac{4\pi mV}{h^3}\sqrt{(2m)} \cdot \int_0^\infty \frac{\varepsilon^{3/2} d\varepsilon}{e^{\alpha + \varepsilon/kT} + 1} \quad ...(88)$$

Now substituting $x = \frac{\varepsilon}{kT}$ or $dx = \frac{d\varepsilon}{kT}$; ...(89)

Eqs. (87) and (88) take the form

$$n = g_s \cdot \frac{V}{h^3}(2\pi mkT)^{3/2} \frac{2}{\sqrt{\pi}}\int_0^\infty \frac{x^{1/2} dx}{e^{\alpha + x} + 1}$$

$$= g_s \cdot \frac{V}{h^3}(2\pi\, mkt)^{3/2} f_1(\alpha) \quad ...(90)$$

$$\text{where } f_1(\alpha) = \frac{2}{\sqrt{\pi}}\int_0^\infty \frac{x^{1/2} dx}{e^{\alpha + x} + 1}$$

$$= \frac{2}{\sqrt{\pi}}\int_0^\infty \frac{x^{1/2} dx}{\frac{1}{A}e^x + 1} \quad ...(91)$$

and $$E = \frac{3}{2} \cdot g_s \cdot \frac{V}{h^3}(2\pi\, mkT)^{3/2} \cdot \frac{4}{3\sqrt{\pi}}\int_0^\infty \frac{x^{3/2} dx}{e^{\alpha + x} + 1}$$

$$= \frac{3}{2} \cdot g_s \frac{V}{h^3}(2\pi\, mkT)^{3/2} kT f_2(\alpha) \quad ...(92)$$

where, $$f_2(\alpha) = \frac{4}{3\sqrt{\pi}}\int_0^\infty \frac{x^{3/2} dx}{e^{\alpha + x} + 1}$$

$$= \frac{4}{3\sqrt{\pi}}\int_0^\infty \frac{x^{3/2} dx}{\frac{1}{A}e^x + 1} \quad ...(93)$$

The integrals $f_1(\alpha)$ and $f_2(\alpha)$ must be evaluated for both positive and negative values of α.

It is often convenient to introduce the Fermi-distribution function $f(\varepsilon)$ defined by

$$f(\varepsilon) = \frac{n(\varepsilon)}{g(\varepsilon)} = \frac{1}{e^{\alpha + \varepsilon/kT} + 1}$$

$$= \frac{1}{e^{(\varepsilon - \varepsilon_F)/kT} + 1} \quad ...(94)$$

where α in terms of chemical potential μ or Fermi-energy $\varepsilon_F(T)$ at temperature T is given by

$$\alpha = -\frac{\mu}{kT} = -\frac{\varepsilon_F(T)}{kT} \quad ...(95)$$

At $T = 0$ K

$$\left.\begin{aligned} f(\varepsilon) &= 1, \text{ for } \varepsilon_F < \varepsilon_F(0) \\ &= 0, \text{ for } \varepsilon_F > \varepsilon_F(0) \end{aligned}\right\} \quad ...(96)$$

This is shown in figure by solid line

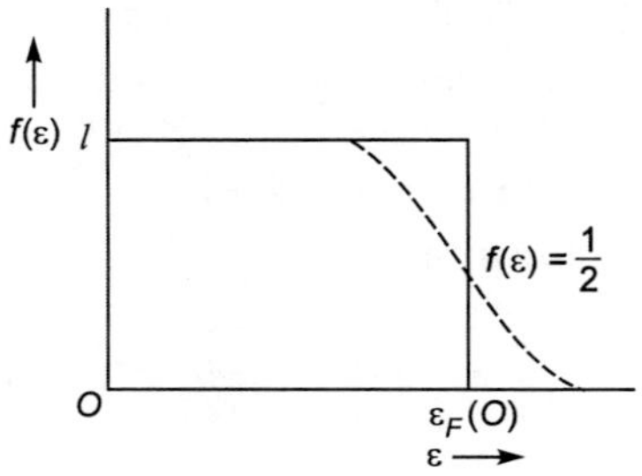

At any temperature T,

$$f(\varepsilon) = \frac{1}{2} \text{ for } \varepsilon = \varepsilon_F$$

This value of ε_F is determined by the condition that the total number of particles is constant at a given temperature T.

The expression for the number of fermions with energy between ε and $\varepsilon + d\varepsilon$ is written as

$$dn(\varepsilon) = f(\varepsilon)g(\varepsilon)d\varepsilon$$

$$= g_s \cdot \frac{4\pi mV}{h^3}\sqrt{(2m)}\frac{\varepsilon^{1/2} d\varepsilon}{e^{\varepsilon - \varepsilon_F/kT} + 1} \quad ...(97)$$

Thus at absolute zero all states with $0 < \varepsilon < \varepsilon_F(0)$ are completely filled and all states with $\varepsilon > \varepsilon_F(0)$ are empty.

The value $\varepsilon_F(0)$ of ε_F at $T = 0$ K is determined by

$$n = \int_0^{\varepsilon_F(0)} dn(\varepsilon) f(\varepsilon) g(\varepsilon) d\varepsilon$$

$$= \int_0^{\varepsilon_F(0)} g(\varepsilon) d\varepsilon$$

$$= \int_0^{\varepsilon_F(0)} g_s \cdot \frac{4\pi mV}{h^3}(2m)^{1/2}\varepsilon^{1/2} d\varepsilon = g_s \cdot \frac{4\pi mV}{h^3}$$

$$(2m)^{1/2} \cdot \frac{2}{3}[\varepsilon_F(0)]^{3/2}$$

i.e., $$\varepsilon_F(0) = \frac{h^2}{2m}\left[\frac{3n}{4\pi V g_s}\right]^{2/3} = \mu_F \quad \ldots(98)$$

This represents the energy of the highest level occupied at

$$T = 0 \text{ K}$$

For particles of spin $\frac{1}{2}$ (*e.g.*, electrons, protons, etc.) the spin degeneracy factor g_s is 2. This means that each level can be occupied by two particles, one with spin up and the other with spin down (↑↓).

(a) Degeneracy

(i) **Weak degeneracy** As $T > T_F$ (*i.e.*, at intermediate temperatures), the Fermi gas is said to be slightly degenerate. In this case $kT > \varepsilon_F(0)$, then ε_F is negative or α is positive and $A < 1$

For $A < 1$, we can write

$$\frac{1}{\frac{1}{A}e^x + 1} = \left\{\frac{1}{A}e^x + 1\right\}^{-1} = Ae^{-x}(1 + Ae^{-x})^{-1}$$

$$= Ae^{-x}(1 - Ae^{-x} + A^2e^{-2x} - \ldots)$$

Therefore, $$f_i(\alpha) = \frac{2}{\sqrt{\pi}}\int_0^\infty \frac{x^{1/2}dx}{\frac{1}{A}e^x + 1}$$

$$= \frac{2}{\sqrt{\pi}}\left[A\int_0^\infty e^{-x}x^{1/2}dx - A^2 \int_0^\infty e^{-2x}x^{1/2}dx + A^3 \int_0^\infty e^{-3x}x^{1/2}dx - \ldots\right]$$

$$= A - \frac{A^2}{2^{3/2}} + \frac{A^3}{3^{3/2}} - \quad \ldots(99)$$

Similarly, $$f_2(\alpha) = A - \frac{A^2}{2^{5/2}} + \frac{A^3}{3^{5/2}} - \quad \ldots(100)$$

Using these values of f_1 (α) and (α), Eq. (90) and (92) take the form

$$n = g_s \frac{V}{h^3}(2\pi mkT)^{3/2}\left[A - \frac{A^2}{2^{3/2}} + \frac{A^3}{3^{3/2}} - \ldots\right] \quad \ldots(101)$$

$$E = \frac{3}{2}g_s \cdot \frac{V}{h^3}(2\pi mkT)^{3/2} KT\left[A - \frac{A^2}{2^{5/2}} + \frac{A^3}{3^{5/2}} - \ldots\right] \quad \ldots(102)$$

Dividing Eq. (101) by (100), we get

$$\frac{E}{n} = \frac{3}{2}kT\left[A - \frac{A^2}{2^{5/2}} + \frac{A^3}{3^{5/2}} - \ldots\right] \left[A - \frac{A^2}{2^{3/2}} + \frac{A^3}{3^{3/2}} - \ldots\right]$$

i.e., $$E = \frac{3}{2}nkT\left[1 + \frac{A}{2^{5/2}} - \frac{A^2}{3^{5/2}} + \ldots\right] \quad \ldots(103)$$

To the first approximation, we can write

$$n = g_s \cdot \frac{V}{h^3}(2\pi mkT)^{3/2} A$$

$$E = \frac{3}{2}g_s \cdot \frac{V}{h^3}(2\pi mkT)^{3/2} kTA$$

i.e., $$\frac{E}{n} = \frac{3}{2}kT \text{ or } E = \frac{3}{2}nkT \quad \ldots(104)$$

which is well known relation for a perfect gas in classical statistics.

A comparison of Eqs. (103) and (104) shows that ideal Fermi-Dirac gas deviates from perfect gas behaviour and this deviation, as we know, is called degeneracy.

(ii) **Strong degeneracy** We shall discuss this case of strong degeneracy at absolute zero *i.e.*, when $T = 0$. When $T \to 0$, $A \to \infty$.

In this case, the Fermi-Dirac gas is completely degenerate.

At $$T = 0,$$

we have $$f(\varepsilon) = \frac{1}{\frac{1}{A}e^{\varepsilon/kT} + 1} = \frac{1}{e^{(\varepsilon - \varepsilon_F)/kT} + 1}$$

$$= 1 \text{ for } 0 \le \varepsilon \le \varepsilon_F(0)$$

$$= 0 \text{ for } \varepsilon > \varepsilon_F(0)$$

So that $$dn = g_s \cdot \left(\frac{4\pi mV}{h^3}\right)(2m)^{1/2}\varepsilon^{1/2}d\varepsilon$$

For $0 \le \varepsilon \le \varepsilon_F(0)$

$= 0$ for $\varepsilon > \varepsilon_F(0)$

Now, the total internal energy of perfect Fermi-Dirac gas at $T = 0$ *i.e.*, zero point energy of Fermi gas is

$$E_0 = \int_0^{\varepsilon_F(0)} \varepsilon dn = g_s \cdot \left(\frac{4\pi mV}{h^3}\right)(2m)^{1/2}\int_0^{\varepsilon_F(0)} \varepsilon^{3/2}d\varepsilon$$

$$= g_s \cdot \left(\frac{4\pi mV}{h^3}\right)(2m)^{1/2}\left[\frac{\varepsilon^{5/2}}{5/2}\right]_0^{\varepsilon_F(0)}$$

$$= \frac{2}{5} g_s \left(\frac{4\pi mV}{h^3}\right)(2m)^{1/2} [\varepsilon_F(0)]^{5/2}$$

Using Eq. (98), above equation gives

$$E_0 = \frac{3nh^2}{10m}\left[\frac{3n}{4\pi V g_s}\right]^{2/3} = \frac{3}{5} n\varepsilon_F(0) \quad ...(105)$$

Now, the pressure at $T = 0$ (*i.e.*, zero point pressure) is given by

$$P_0 = \frac{2}{3}\frac{E_0}{V}\left[\text{Since } P = -\left(\frac{\partial E}{\partial T}\right)_{T,S} = \frac{2E}{3V}\right]$$

$$= \frac{1}{5}\frac{n}{V}\frac{h^2}{m}\left(\frac{3n}{4\pi g_s V}\right)^{2/3} \quad ...(106)$$

From Eqs. (105) and (106) it is obvious that as strongly degenerate Fermi-Dirac gas possesses energy and exerts a pressure even at 0K, quite unlike a Bose-Einstein and classical gases where the energy and pressure at absolute zero are zero.

Maxwell's Velocity Distribution of Molecules in a Perfect Gas

Molecules have different speeds ranging from zero to infinity. It is a legitimate question to ask how many molecules have velocity between $\vec{\mathbf{v}} + d\vec{\mathbf{v}}$ and $\vec{\mathbf{v}}$. Let us proceed to find such a velocity distribution. We make a few assumptions

1. There is no mass motion.
2. There is complete randomness of velocity of the molecules.
3. The probability that a molecule has a given velocity component depends on the given velocity component and the width of that internal and is independent of other velocity components.
4. The energy is the form of pure translational energy.

The probability that a molecule has the *x*-component of velocity in the range $v_x + dv_x$ and v_x is $f(v_x)\,dv_x$, where f is some function to be determined and similarly for the *y* and *z*-components. The probability that a molecule has got velocity components in the ranges $v_x + dv_x$ and v_x, $v_y + dv_y$ and v_y and $v_z + dv_z$ and v_z simultaneously is the product of $f(v_x)\,dv_x$, $f(v_y)\,dv_y$, $f(v_z)\,dv_z$ because probabilities of independent events are multiplicative.

So, $\quad F(\vec{\mathbf{v}}) = dv_x\, dv_y\, dv_z$

$$= f(v_x)\, f(v_y)\, f(v_z)\, dv_x\, dv_y\, dv_z \quad ...(107)$$

where, F is some other function to be determined.

Now, since F cannot depend on the direction of $\vec{\mathbf{v}}$ as it would amount to a preferential choice of the coordinate axis, F must be a function of v^2.

So, $$F(v^2) = f(v_x)\, f(v_y)\, f(v_z) \quad ...(107)$$

At constant v^2 $\quad dF(v^2) = 0$

or $$\frac{f'(v_x)}{f(v_x)} dv_x + \frac{f'(v_y)}{f(v_y)} dv_y + \frac{f'(v_z)}{f(v_z)} dv_z = 0$$

These were obtained subject to the conditions

$$dv^2 = 0$$

or $$v_x\, dv_x + v_y\, dv_y + v_z\, dv_z = 0 \quad ...(108)$$

Taking B as a Lagrange multiplier

$$\left[\frac{f'(v_x)}{f(v_x)} + Bv_x\right] dv_x + \left[\frac{f'(v_y)}{f(v_y)} + Bv_y\right] dv_y + \left[\frac{f'(v_z)}{f(v_z)} Bv_z\right] dv_z = 0$$

We may choose B such that

$$\frac{f'(v_z)}{f(v_z)} + Bv_z = 0$$

and out of v_x, v_y and v_z, we may let v_x and v_y be independent variables. So,

$$\frac{f'(v_x)}{f(v_x)} + Bv_x = 0 \text{ and } \frac{f'(v_y)}{f(v_y)} + Bv_y = 0$$

After integrating, we get

Probability that a molecule has velocity in the range $\vec{\mathbf{v}} + d\vec{\mathbf{v}}$ and $\vec{\mathbf{v}}$ is

$$p(\vec{\mathbf{v}})\, dv_x\, dv_y\, dv_z = A\, e^{-Bv^2} dv_x\, dv_y\, dv_z$$

where, A is a constant of integration which can be determined

Using $\int P(\vec{\mathbf{v}})\, dv_x\, dv_y\, dv_z = 1$

$$A \int_{\infty}^{\infty} e^{-Bv_x^2} dv_x \int_{-\infty}^{\infty} e^{-Bv_y^2} dv_y \int_{-\infty}^{\infty} e^{-Bv_z^2} dv_z = 1$$

$$A\left(\sqrt{\frac{\pi}{B}}\right)^3 = 1$$

So, $$A = \left(\frac{B}{\pi}\right)^{3/2} \quad ...(109)$$

Multiplying by N, the total number of molecules. We get the number of molecules having velocities in the range $\vec{\mathbf{v}} + d\vec{\mathbf{v}}$ and $\vec{\mathbf{v}}$.

$$dN = N\left(\frac{B}{\pi}\right)^{3/2} e^{-Bv^2}\, dv_x\, dv_y\, dv_z$$

$N\left(\frac{B}{\pi}\right)^{3/2} e^{-Bv^2}$ is called **Maxwell's velocity distribution function**. We may express it in terms of speed or the number of molecules possessing speed between $v + dv$ and v

$$dN = N\left(\frac{B}{\pi}\right)^{3/2} e^{-Bv^2}\, 4\pi v^2\, dv$$

The function $N\left(\frac{B}{\pi}\right)^{3/2} e^{-Bv^2}\, 4\pi v^2$ is called **Maxwell's speed distribution function.**

The constant B may be fixed using the relation

$$v_{\text{rms}} = \sqrt{\frac{3kT}{m}}$$

$$v_{\text{rms}}^2 = \frac{\int v^2\, dN}{\int dN}$$

$$= \frac{\int_0^\infty v^4 - e^{-Bv^2}\, dv}{\int_0^\infty v^2 e^{-Bv^2}\, dv}$$

$$= -\frac{\partial}{\partial B}\left[\ln \int_0^\infty v^2 e^{-Bv^2}\, dv\right]$$

Let $\qquad Bv^2 = t$

So, $\qquad \int_0^\infty v^2 e^{-Bv^2}\, dv = \int_0^\infty \frac{t}{B} e^{-t} \frac{1}{\sqrt{B}} \frac{dt}{2\sqrt{t}}$

$$= \frac{1}{B^{3/2}} \frac{1}{2} \int_0^\infty t^{1/2} e^{-t}\, dt$$

Thus, $\qquad -\frac{\partial}{\partial B}\left[\ln \int_0^\infty v^2 e^{-Bv^2}\, dv\right] = -\frac{\partial}{\partial B} \ln B^{-3/2} = \frac{3}{2B}$

So, $\qquad \frac{3}{2B} = \frac{3kT}{m}$

or $\qquad B = \frac{m}{2kT} \qquad \ldots(110)$

Thus, the speed distribution becomes

$$dN = N\left(\frac{m}{2\pi kT}\right)^{3/2} e^{-\frac{mv^2}{2kT}}\, 4\pi v^2\, dv$$

$$= f(v)\, dv$$

We may plot $f(v)$, the **Maxwell's speed distribution function as a function of speed** v

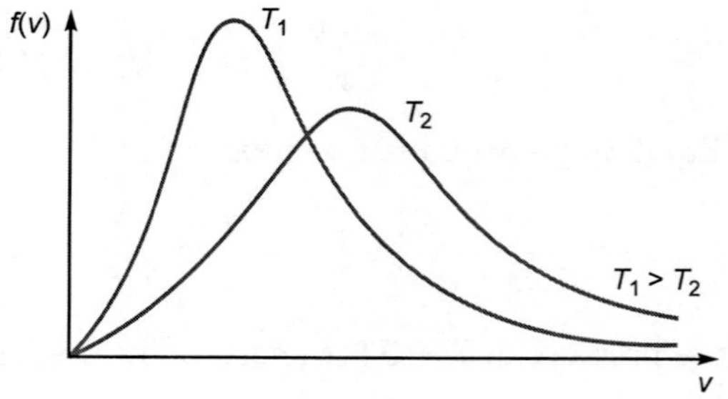

$f(v)$ has a maximum, say at v_p and decreases exponentially for large v. The curves of $f(v)$ at different temperatures have different v_p but their areas under the curve are all equal.

We may find an expression for v_P

$$\frac{\partial}{\partial v} f(v) = 0$$

or $\qquad 2v\, e^{-\frac{mv^2}{2kT}} - v^2 \frac{me^{-\frac{mv^2}{kT}}}{kT} = 0$

or $\qquad v_p = \sqrt{\frac{2kT}{m}} \qquad \ldots(111)$

and $\qquad f(v_p) = 4\pi N\left(\frac{m}{2\pi kT}\right)^{3/2} e^{-1}\left(\frac{2kT}{m}\right)$

$$= 4N\left(\frac{m}{2\pi kT}\right)^{1/2} e^{-1} \qquad \ldots(112)$$

Average speed $\bar{v}$ is defined as

$$\bar{v} = \frac{\int_0^\infty v\, dN}{\int_0^\infty dN} = \frac{\int_0^\infty e^{-\frac{mv^2}{2kT}} v^3\, dv}{\int_0^\infty e^{-\frac{mv^2}{2kT}} v^2\, dv}$$

$$= \sqrt{\frac{8kT}{\pi m}} \qquad \ldots(113)$$

(Using the gamma function $\int_0^\infty x^{n-1} e^{-x}\, dx$ evaluate the integrals)

As an exercise in integration, we may find the average value of $\frac{1}{v}$

$$\overline{\frac{1}{v}} = \frac{\int \frac{1}{v}\, dN}{\int dN}$$

$$= \frac{\int_0^\infty e^{-Bv^2} v\, dv}{\int_0^\infty e^{-Bv^2} v^2\, dv}$$

$$= \frac{1}{2B \int_0^{\infty} e^{-Bv^2} v^2 \, dv}$$

Let $Bv^2 = t$

So, $\int_0^{\infty} e^{-t} \frac{t}{B} \frac{dt}{\sqrt{B}\, 2\sqrt{t}} = \frac{1}{2B^{3/2}} \int_0^{\infty} t^{1/2} e^{-t} \, dt$

$$= \frac{1}{2B^{3/2}} \Gamma\left(\frac{3}{2}\right) = \frac{\sqrt{\pi}}{4B^{3/2}}$$

So, $$\overline{\frac{1}{v}} = \frac{1}{2B} \frac{4B\sqrt{B}}{\sqrt{\pi}}$$

$$= \frac{2\sqrt{B}}{\sqrt{\pi}} = 2\sqrt{\frac{\pi}{2\pi kT}} \qquad \ldots(114)$$

Instead of finding the number of molecules having speeds in a given range $v + dv$ and v, we may find the number of molecules possessing energy in a given range $\varepsilon + d\varepsilon$ and ε.

Let $\varepsilon = \frac{1}{2} mv^2$

So, $$dv = \sqrt{\frac{2}{m}} \frac{d\varepsilon}{2\sqrt{\varepsilon}}$$

So, $$dN_{\varepsilon} = N\left(\frac{m}{2\pi kT}\right)^{3/2} e^{-\varepsilon/kT} \, 4\pi \frac{2\varepsilon}{m} \frac{d\varepsilon}{\sqrt{2m\varepsilon}}$$

or we may say

$$dN_{\varepsilon} \propto e^{-\varepsilon/kT} \sqrt{\varepsilon} \, d\varepsilon$$

or $$dN_{\varepsilon} = C\sqrt{\varepsilon}\, e^{-\varepsilon/kT} \, d\varepsilon \qquad \ldots(115)$$

where, C is a constant which may be fixed using the condition $\int dN_{\varepsilon} = N$

Mean energy $\bar{\varepsilon}$ is defined by $\bar{\varepsilon} = \frac{\int \varepsilon \, dN_{\varepsilon}}{\int dN_{\varepsilon}}$

Most probable energy ε_P is defined as the energy at which $\sqrt{\varepsilon}\, e^{-\varepsilon/kT}$ is maximum.

Example 4. *Find the mean energy for a system of molecules whose speeds are distributed in a Maxwell's speed distribution function.*

Sol. By definition $\bar{\varepsilon} = \frac{\int \varepsilon \, dN_{\varepsilon}}{\int dN_{\varepsilon}}$

$$= \frac{\int_0^{\infty} \varepsilon^{3/2} e^{-\varepsilon/kT} \, d\varepsilon}{\int_0^{\infty} \varepsilon^{1/2} e^{-\varepsilon/kT} \, d\varepsilon} = \frac{\int \varepsilon^{3/2} e^{-\beta\varepsilon} \, d\varepsilon}{\int \varepsilon^{1/2} e^{-\beta\varepsilon} \, d\varepsilon}$$

where, $\beta = \frac{1}{kT}$

$$= -\frac{\partial}{\partial\beta}\left(\ln \int_0^{\infty} \varepsilon^{1/2} e^{-\beta\varepsilon} \, d\varepsilon\right)$$

If we let $\beta\varepsilon = x$

Then, $$\int_0^{\infty} \varepsilon^{1/2} e^{-\beta\varepsilon} \, d\varepsilon = \int \sqrt{\frac{x}{\beta}}\, e^{-x} \frac{dx}{\beta}$$

$$= \beta^{-3/2} \int x^{1/2} e^{-x} \, dx$$

So, $$-\frac{\partial}{\partial\beta}\left(\ln \int \varepsilon^{1/2} e^{-\beta\varepsilon} \, d\varepsilon\right) = \frac{3}{2\beta} = \frac{3kT}{2}$$

Therefore, the average energy, $\bar{\varepsilon} = \frac{3kT}{2}$

Exercise 1

(For Part 'B')

1. Spins of boson is equal to
(a) positive integer
(b) integer
(c) positive integral multiple of $\frac{1}{2}$
(d) any fraction

2. Distribution function for a photon gas is
(a) $\exp\left(-\frac{\varepsilon}{kT}\right)$
(b) $\frac{1}{\exp\left(\frac{\varepsilon}{kT}\right)+1}$
(c) $\frac{1}{\exp\left(\frac{\varepsilon}{kT}\right)-1}$
(d) $\frac{1}{\exp\left(-\frac{\varepsilon}{kT}\right)-1}$

3. For a two-dimensional free electron gas, the electronic density n and the Fermi energy E_F, are related by
(a) $n=\frac{(2mE_F)^{3/2}}{3\pi^2\hbar^3}$
(b) $n=\frac{mE_F}{\pi\hbar^2}$
(c) $n=\frac{mE_F}{2\pi\hbar^2}$
(d) $n=\frac{2^{3/2}(mE_F)^{1/2}}{\pi\hbar}$

4. The specific heat of an ideal Fermi gas in three-dimensions at very low temperature (T) varies at
(a) T
(b) $T^{3/2}$
(c) T^2
(d) T^3

5. Which of the following gives condition for stable equilibrium of a thermodynamic system?
(a) $dS=0$ and $d^2S<0$
(b) $dE=0$ and $d^2E>0$
(c) Both (a) and (b)
(d) None of these

6. Which of the following statements is true?
(a) Fermions are distinguishable whereas bosons are not
(b) Bosons are distinguishable whereas fermions are not
(c) Both fermions and bosons are distinguishable
(d) Both fermions and bosons are indistinguishable but classical particles are distinguishable

7. The equation of state of a dilute gas at very high temperature is described by $\frac{pV}{k_BT}\approx 1+\frac{B(T)}{V}$, where V is the volume per particle and $B(T)$ is a negative quantity. One can conclude that this is a property of
(a) a van der Waals' gas
(b) an ideal Fermi gas
(c) an ideal Bose gas
(d) an ideal inert gas

8. Consider the Fermi-Dirac distribution function $f(E)$ at room temperature (300 K), where E refers to energy. If E_F is the Fermi energy, which of the following is true?
(a) $f(E)$ is a step function
(b) $f(E_F)$ has a value of $\frac{1}{2}$
(c) States with $E<E_F$ are filled completely
(d) $f(E)$ is large and tends to infinity as E decreases much below E_F

9. Gibb's paradox states that when $\frac{N}{2}$ molecules of two gases kept at temperature T and having same volume are mixed to have the same final temperature and total volume then entropy of mixing is equal to $Nk_B \ln 2$. This paradox arise because of a factor missing in the Boltzmann's formula of entropy. That factor is equal to
(a) N
(b) $\frac{1}{N}$
(c) $N!$
(d) $\frac{1}{N!}$

10. If Z be the partition function and $\beta=\frac{1}{k_BT}$, then average energy of the system is given by
(a) $\frac{\partial}{\partial\beta}\ln Z$
(b) $-\frac{\partial}{\partial\beta}\ln Z$
(c) $\beta\frac{\partial}{\partial\beta}\left[\frac{\ln(Z)}{\beta}\right]$
(d) $-\beta\frac{\partial}{\partial\beta}\left[\frac{(\ln Z)}{\beta}\right]$

11. Which of the following plots correctly represents the variation of average energy of N spin-half isolated using magnets kept in magnetic field and maintained at temperature T?

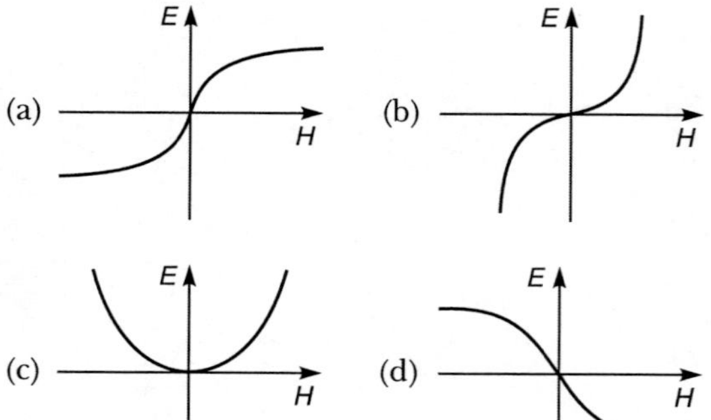

12. For a Fermi gas of N particles in three dimensions at $T=0$ K, the Fermi energy E_F is proportional to
(a) $N^{2/3}$
(b) $N^{3/2}$
(c) N^3
(d) N^2

13. A system of N non-interacting classical point particles is constrained to move on the two-dimensional surface of a sphere. The internal energy of the system is

(a) $\frac{3}{2}Nk_BT$ (b) $\frac{1}{2}Nk_BT$

(c) Nk_BT (d) $\frac{5}{2}Nk_BT$

14. The total energy per particle of a collection of free fermions is 3 eV. The Fermi energy of the system is
(a) 1.8 eV (b) 3 eV
(c) 4 eV (d) 5 eV

15. The wave functions of two identical particles in stated n and s are given by $\phi_n(r_1)$ and $\phi_s(r_2)$, respectively. The particles obey Maxwell-Boltzmann statistics. The state of the combined two particles system is expressed as
(a) $\phi_n(r_1)+\phi_s(r_2)$
(b) $\frac{1}{\sqrt{2}}[\phi_n(r_1)\,\phi_s(r_2)+\phi_n(r_2)\,\phi_s(r_1)]$
(c) $\frac{1}{\sqrt{2}}[\phi_n(r_1)\,\phi_s(r_2)-\phi_n(r_2)\,\phi_s(r_1)]$
(d) $\phi_n(r_1)\,\phi_s(r_2)$

16. Choose the correct alternative
(a) A fermions gas will exert the greatest pressure
(b) A boson gas will exert the greatest pressure
(c) A fermion gas will exert the least pressure
(d) A boson gas will exert the least pressure

17. Gibb's paradox arises due to
(a) indistinguishability of classical particles
(b) distinguishability of classical particles
(c) absence of inter-particle interaction
(d) ommittance of quantum nature of the particles

18. Which of the following statements is true for black body radiation?
(a) As temperature increases, peak of energy distribution curve decreases in height and shifts to longer wavelength
(b) As temperature increases, peak of energy distribution curve increases in height and shifts to lower wavelength
(c) As temprature increases, peak of energy distribution curve increases in height and shifts to longer wavelength
(d) A temperature increases, the peak of energy distribution curve decreases in height and shifts to lower wavelength

19. The number of states for a system of N identical free particles in a three-dimensional space having total energy between E and $E+\delta E$ ($\delta E << E$), is proportional to
(a) $(E^{3N/2-1})\,\delta E$ (b) $E^{N/2}\delta E$
(c) $NE^{1/2}\delta E$ (d) $E^{N}\delta E$

20. A system of N non-interacting and distinguishable particles of spin 1 is in thermodynamic equilibrium. The entropy of the system is
(a) $2k_B \ln N$ (b) $3k_B \ln N$
(c) $Nk_B \ln 2$ (d) $Nk_B \ln 3$

21. It is necessary to apply quantum statistics to a system of particles, if
(a) there is substantial overlap between the wave functions of the particles
(b) the mean free path of the particles is comparable to the inter-particle separation
(c) the particles have identical mass and charge
(d) the particles are interacting

22. Two particles are said to be distinguishable when
(a) the average distance between them is large compared to their de-Broglie wavelengths
(b) the average distance between them is small compared to their de-Broglie wavelengths
(c) they have overlapping wavepackets
(d) their total wave function is symmetric under particle exchange

23. The free energy of a photon gas enclosed in a volume V, is given by $F=-\frac{1}{3}aVT^{-4}$, where a is a constant and T is the temperature of the gas. The chemical potential of the photon gas is
(a) zero (b) $\frac{4}{3}aVT^3$ (c) $\frac{1}{3}aT^{-4}$ (d) aVT^{-4}

24. Hamiltonian of a system consists of contribution from three different modes and is written as $H=H_t+H_v+H_e$. If Z_t, Z_v and Z_e be the corresponding partition functions, the partition function of the system is written as
(a) $Z=Z_t\times Z_v\times Z_e$ (b) $Z=Z_t+Z_v+Z_e$
(c) $Z=Z_t\times Z_v\div Z_e$ (d) $Z=Z_t+Z_v-Z_e$

25. Hydrogen molecules (mass m) are in thermal equilibrium at a temperature T. Assuming classical distribution of velocity, the most probable speed at room temperature is
(a) $\frac{(k_BT)}{m}$ (b) $\frac{2k_BT}{m}$
(c) $\left(\frac{\sqrt{2k_B T}}{m}\right)$ (d) $\frac{m}{(\sqrt{2k_B T})}$

26. A system of non-interacting Fermi particles with Fermi energy E_F, has the density of states proportional to $\sqrt{E}$, where E is the energy of a particle. The average energy per particle at temperature $T=0$ is
(a) $\frac{1}{6}E_F$ (b) $\frac{1}{5}E_F$
(c) $\frac{2}{5}E_F$ (d) $\frac{3}{5}E_F$

27. The mean free path of the particles of a gas at a temperature T_0 and pressure p_0 has a value λ_0. If the pressure is increased to $1.5p_0$ and the temperature is reduced to $0.75T_0$, the mean free path
(a) remains unchanged (b) is reduced to half
(c) is doubled (d) is equal to $1.125\lambda_0$

28. Which of the following relations between the particle number density n and temperature T must hold good for a gas consisting of non-interacting particles to be described by quantum statistics?

(a) $\frac{n}{T^{1/2}} << 1$

(b) $\frac{n}{T^{3/2}} << 1$

(c) $\frac{n}{T^{3/2}} >> 1$

(d) $\frac{n}{T^{1/2}}$ and $\frac{n}{T^{3/2}}$ can have any value

29. An ensemble of quantum harmonic oscillators is kept at a finite temperature $T = \frac{1}{k_B \beta}$. The partition function of a single oscillator with energy levels $\left(n + \frac{1}{2}\right)\hbar\omega$ is given by

(a) $Z = \frac{e^{-\beta\hbar\omega/2}}{1 - e^{-\beta\hbar\omega}}$ (b) $Z = \frac{e^{-\beta\hbar\omega/2}}{1 + e^{-\beta\hbar\omega}}$

(c) $Z = \frac{1}{1 - e^{-\beta\hbar\omega}}$ (d) $Z = \frac{1}{1 + e^{-\beta\hbar\omega}}$

30. An ensemble of quantum harmonic oscillators is kept at a finite temperature $T = \frac{1}{k_B \beta}$, then the average number of energy quanta of the oscillators is given by

(a) $< n > = \frac{1}{e^{-\beta\hbar\omega} - 1}$ (b) $< n > = \frac{e^{-\beta\hbar\omega}}{e^{-\beta\hbar\omega} - 1}$

(c) $< n > = \frac{1}{e^{\beta\hbar\omega} + 1}$ (d) $< n > = \frac{e^{-\beta\hbar\omega}}{e^{\beta\hbar\omega} + 1}$

31. Each of the two isolated vessels, A and B of fixed volumes, contains N molecules of a perfect monatomic gas at pressure p. The temperatures of A and B are T_1 and T_2 respectively. The two vessels are brought into thermal contact. At equilibrium, the change in entropy is

(a) $\frac{3}{2} Nk_B \ln\left[\frac{T_1^2 + T_2^2}{4T_1T_2}\right]$ (b) $Nk_B \ln\left(\frac{T_2}{T_1}\right)$

(c) $\frac{3}{2} Nk_B \ln\left[\frac{(T_1 + T_2)^2}{4T_1T_2}\right]$ (d) $2Nk_B$

32. Consider a two levels quantum system with energies $\varepsilon_1 = 0$, $\varepsilon_2 = \varepsilon$. The Helmholtz free energy of the system is given by

(a) $-k_BT \ln(1 + e^{-\varepsilon/k_BT})$ (b) $k_BT \ln(1 + e^{-\varepsilon/k_BT})$

(c) $\frac{3}{2} k_BT$ (d) $\varepsilon - k_BT$

33. An ensemble of N three level systems with energies $\varepsilon = -\varepsilon_0$, 0, $+\varepsilon_0$ is in thermal equilibrium at temperature T. Let $\beta = (k_BT)^{-1}$. If $\beta\varepsilon_0 = 2$, the probability of finding the system in the level $\varepsilon = 0$ is

(a) $\frac{(\cosh x)}{2}$ (b) $(\cosh x)^{-1}$

(c) $(2\cosh x)^{-1}$ (d) $(1 + 2\cosh x)^{-1}$

34. An ensemble of N three level systems with energies $\varepsilon = -\varepsilon_0$, 0, $+\varepsilon_0$ is in thermal equilibrium at temperature T. Let, $\beta = (k_BT)^{-1}$.

The free energy of the system at high temperature (*i.e.*, $x = \beta\varepsilon_0 << 1$) is approximately

(a) $-Nk_BTx^2$

(b) $-Nk_BT\,[\ln 2 + x^2/2]$

(c) $-Nk_BT\,[\ln 3 + x^2/3]$

(d) $-Nk_BT \ln 3$

35. Two identical particles have to be distributed among three energy levels. Let r_B, r_F and r_C represents the ratios of probability of finding two particles to that of finding one particle in a given energy state. The subscripts B, F and C correspond to whether the particles are bosons, fermions and classical particles respectively. The $r_B : r_F : r_C$ is equal to

(a) $\frac{1}{2} : 0 : 1$ (b) $1 : \frac{1}{2} : 1$ (c) $1 : \frac{1}{2} : \frac{1}{2}$ (d) $1 : 0 : \frac{1}{2}$

36. A photon gas is at thermal equilibrium at temperature T. The mean number of photons in an energy state $\varepsilon = \hbar\omega$ is

(a) $\exp\left(\frac{\hbar\omega}{k_BT}\right) + 1$ (b) $\exp\left(\frac{\hbar\omega}{k_BT}\right) - 1$

(c) $\left[\exp\left(\frac{\hbar\omega}{k_BT}\right) + 1\right]^{-1}$ (d) $\left[\exp\left(\frac{\hbar\omega}{k_BT}\right) - 1\right]^{-1}$

37. Consider a system of N atoms of an ideal gas of type A at temperature T and volume V. It is kept in diffusive contact with another system of N atoms of another ideal gas of type B at the same temperature T and volume V. Once the combined system reaches equilibrium

(a) the total entropy of the final system is the same as the sum of the entropy of the individual system always

(b) the entropy of mixing is $2Nk_B \ln 2$

(c) the entropy of the final system is less than that of sum of the initial entropies of the two gases

(d) the entropy of mixing is non-zero, when the atoms A and B are of the same type

38. Consider a system of two non-interacting classical particles which can occupy any of the three energy levels with energy values $E = 0$, ε and 2ε having degeneracies $g(E) = 1$, 2 and 4 respectively. The mean energy of the system is

(a) $\varepsilon\left[\frac{4\exp\left(\frac{-\varepsilon}{k_BT}\right) + 8\exp\left(\frac{-2\varepsilon}{k_BT}\right)}{1 + 2\exp\left(\frac{-\varepsilon}{k_BT}\right) + 4\exp\left(\frac{-2\varepsilon}{k_BT}\right)}\right]$

(b) $\varepsilon\left[\dfrac{2\exp\left(\dfrac{-\varepsilon}{k_BT}\right)+8\exp\left(\dfrac{-2\varepsilon}{k_BT}\right)}{1+2\exp\left(\dfrac{-\varepsilon}{k_BT}\right)+4\exp\left(\dfrac{-2\varepsilon}{k_BT}\right)}\right]$

(c) $\varepsilon\left[\dfrac{2\exp\left(\dfrac{-\varepsilon}{k_BT}\right)+4\exp\left(\dfrac{-2\varepsilon}{k_BT}\right)}{1+2\exp\left(\dfrac{-\varepsilon}{k_BT}\right)+4\exp\left(\dfrac{-2\varepsilon}{k_BT}\right)}\right]$

(d) $\varepsilon\left[\dfrac{\exp\left(\dfrac{-\varepsilon}{k_BT}\right)+2\exp\left(\dfrac{-2\varepsilon}{k_BT}\right)}{1+\exp\left(\dfrac{-\varepsilon}{k_BT}\right)+\exp\left(\dfrac{-2\varepsilon}{k_BT}\right)}\right]$

39. In a gas, relative magnitudes of the most probable speed (v_p), the average speed $\bar{v}$ and root mean square speed (v_{rms}) of the molecule are

(a) $v_{\text{rms}} > \bar{v} > v_p$ (b) $\bar{v} > v_{\text{rms}} > v_p$
(c) $v_p > \bar{v} > v_{\text{rms}}$ (d) $v_p > v_{\text{rms}} > \bar{v}$

40. The average translational kinetic energy of the molecules of a gas will be doubled if

(a) at constant volume, its pressure is doubled
(b) at constant volume, its pressure is halved
(c) at constant temperature, its pressure is doubled
(d) at constant temperature, its pressure is halved

41. In a Maxwellian gas, if v_{rms} is the root mean square velocity, then the most probable velocity v_p is

(a) $\sqrt{\dfrac{1}{3}}\,v_{\text{rms}}$ (b) $\sqrt{\dfrac{2}{3}}\,v_{\text{rms}}$
(c) $\sqrt{\dfrac{3}{2}}\,v_{\text{rms}}$ (d) None of these

42. The mean free path λ of a gas molecule as given by Maxwell is related to its radius a, as

(a) $\lambda=\dfrac{1}{\sqrt{2}\cdot 4\pi a^2 n}$ (b) $\lambda=\dfrac{1}{\sqrt{2}\cdot \pi a^2 n}$
(c) $\lambda=\dfrac{1}{\sqrt{2}\cdot 2\pi^2 a^2 n}$ (d) $\lambda=\dfrac{1}{\sqrt{2}\cdot 2\pi a^2 n}$

43. According to Maxwell's law of distribution of velocities of molecules, the most probable velocity is

(a) greater than the mean velocity
(b) equal to the mean velocity
(c) equal to root mean square velocity
(d) less than the root mean square velocity

44. The mean translational kinetic energy per molecule of an ideal gas is

(a) kT (b) $\dfrac{1}{2}kT$ (c) $\dfrac{3}{2}kT$ (d) $\dfrac{2}{3}kT$

45. The root mean square speed, average speed and most probable speed for a gas are in the ratio

(a) $\sqrt{3}:2\sqrt{2}:3\sqrt{2}$ (b) $2:2\sqrt{2}:\sqrt{3}$
(c) $\sqrt{3}:\sqrt{2}:2\sqrt{2}$ (d) $\sqrt{3}:2\sqrt{2}:\sqrt{2}$

46. In relation to statistical mechanics
(Choose incorrect statement)

(a) all particles of a given kind are treated as mutually indistinguishable
(b) the phase space for n degrees of freedom will have $2n$ dimensions and its unit cell volume will be h^n
(c) with a system having $N \sim 10^{23}$ particles, probability of two halves of a box having particle density difference of 0.001% is negligibly small
(d) photons may be treated as following Fermi-Dirac statistics

47. The figure further shows the probability distribution P_α of molecules of a gas against a parameter α. In this figure two curves are shown for temperatures T_1 and T_2. Which of the following is true, if C refers to molecular speed and v_x to one of the cartesian components of velocity?

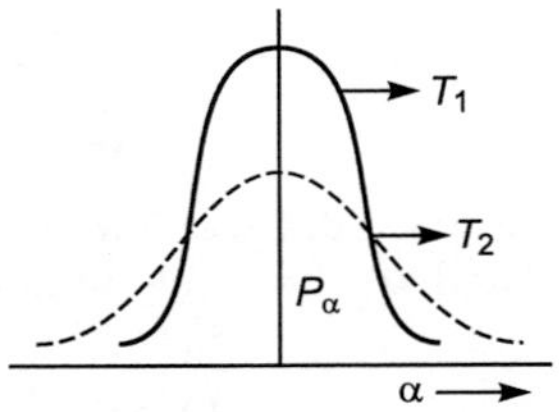

(a) $\alpha = v_x$ and $T_2 > T_1$ (b) $\alpha = v_x$ and $T_2 < T_1$
(c) $\alpha = C$ and $T_2 > T_1$ (d) $\alpha = C$ and $T_2 < T_1$

48. Following figure shows two distributions for a given gas at two temperatures, for a parameter α undefined

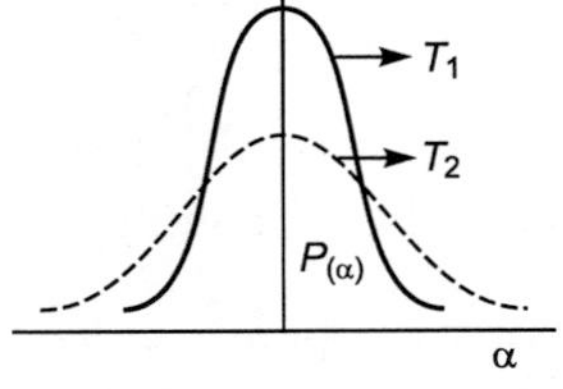

(a) α stands for P (b) α stands for C
(c) α stands for P_x (d) T_2 is less than T_1

49. Following curve shows the distribution of ε for one gas. For another gas of higher molecular mass, T remaining unchanged, the distribution will

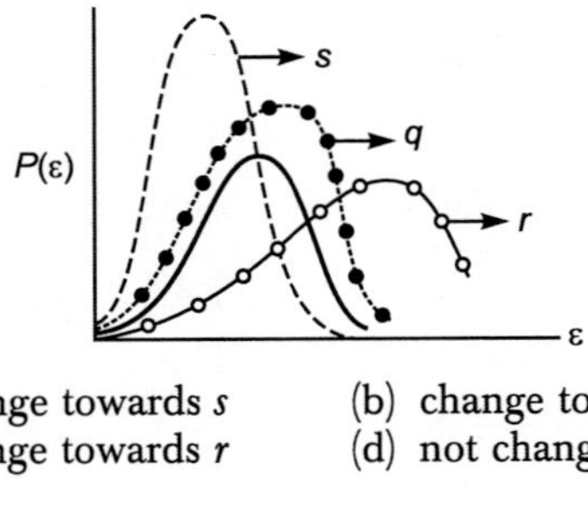

(a) change towards s (b) change towards q
(c) change towards r (d) not change

50. Following figure shows the distribution of C for a given gas. For the same gas, as the temperature rises, the curve would change with

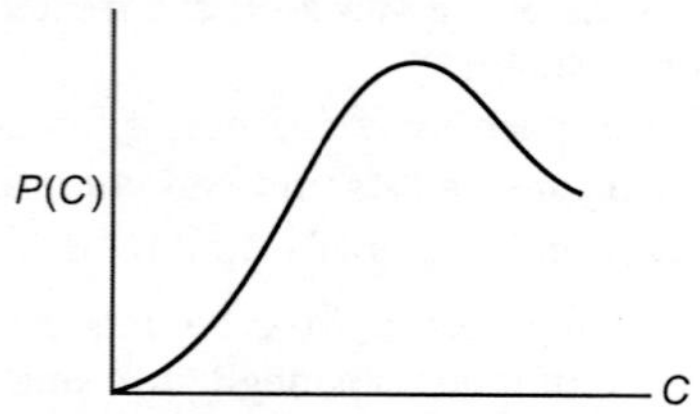

(a) peak shifting to left, height rising
(b) peak shifting to right, height falling
(c) peak shifting to right, height rising
(d) $P(C)$ increasing for all C values

51. For the phase representing a single particle is mass m in a volume V, the number of phase cell in energy range 0 to E, if volume of each phase cell is h_0^3

(a) $\frac{4\pi V}{3h_0^3}(2mE)^{3/2}$ (b) $\frac{4\pi V}{3h_0^3}(2mE)^{1/2}$
(c) $\frac{4\pi V}{3h_0^3}(2mE)^{2/3}$ (d) $\frac{4\pi V}{3h_0^3}(2mE)^{1/3}$

52. In statistical physics, the absolute temperature T of a system is related to the total number of accessible states Ω as

(a) $kT = \frac{\partial \Omega}{\partial E}$ (b) $kT = \frac{\partial \log \Omega}{\partial E}$
(c) $\frac{1}{kT} = \frac{\partial \Omega}{\partial E}$ (d) $\frac{1}{kT} = \frac{\partial \log \Omega}{\partial E}$

53. The average value of v_x in Maxwellian distribution is given as

(a) 0 (b) $\frac{1}{2\alpha}$
(c) $\frac{kT}{m}$ (d) $\sqrt{\frac{kT}{m}}$

54. The Maxwell velocity distribution is valid for a classical gas

(a) in equilibrium irrespective of the nature of particle interaction
(b) strictly under contact interaction amongst particles
(c) under a steady flow of particles
(d) only in the absence of interparticle interactions

55. The quantum statistics reduces to classical statistics under the following condition

(a) $\rho\lambda^3 \approx 1$ (b) $\rho\lambda^3 >> 1$ (c) $\rho\lambda^3 << 1$ (d) $\rho = 0$

56. If the partition function of a harmonic oscillator with frequency ω at a temperature T is $\frac{kT}{\hbar\omega}$, then the free energy of N such independent oscillators is

(a) $\frac{3}{2}NkT$ (b) $kT \ln \frac{\hbar\omega}{kT}$
(c) $NkT \ln \frac{\hbar\omega}{kT}$ (d) $NkT \ln \frac{\hbar\omega}{2kT}$

57. A system of N localized, non-interacting spin $\frac{1}{2}$ ions of magnetic moment μ each is kept in an external magnetic field H. If the system is in equilibrium at temperature T, the Helmholtz free energy of the system is

(a) $Nk_BT \ln\left(\cosh \frac{\mu H}{k_BT}\right)$
(b) $-Nk_BT \ln\left(2\cosh \frac{\mu H}{k_BT}\right)$
(c) $Nk_BT \ln\left(2\cosh \frac{\mu H}{k_BT}\right)$
(d) $-Nk_BT \ln\left(2\sinh \frac{\mu H}{k_BT}\right)$

58. Consider a radiation cavity of volume V at temperature T. The density of states at energy E of the quantized radiation (photons) is

(a) $\frac{8\pi V}{h^3c^3}E^2$ (b) $\frac{8\pi V}{h^3c^3}E^{3/2}$
(c) $\frac{8\pi V}{h^3c^2}E$ (d) $\frac{8\pi V}{h^3c^2}E^{1/2}$

59. The average number of photons in equilibrium inside the cavity (in Q. 67) is proportional to

(a) T (b) T^2
(c) T^3 (d) T^4

60. Choose the correct alternative.

At the same temperature
(a) a fermion gas will exert the greatest pressure
(b) a boson gas will exert the greatest pressure
(c) a fermion gas will exert the least pressure
(d) a gas obeying MB statistics

61. Consider a system of 2 identical particles each of which can be in any one of 3 single particles states. The number of states of the systems are possible in B-E statistics

(a) 9 (b) 3 (c) 6 (d) 1

62. Which statistics will apply to deuterons and α paricles?

(a) B-E (b) F-D
(c) M-B (d) None of these

63. The average energy of an electron in a metal at $T = 0$

(a) $\frac{2}{5}E_F(0)$ (b) $\frac{3}{5}E_F(0)$ (c) $\frac{4}{5}E_F(0)$ (d) $\frac{1}{5}E_F(0)$

64. If f is the Fermi-Dirac distribution function, then

$$\int_{-\infty}^{\infty}\left(-\frac{\partial f}{\partial E}\right)dE$$

(a) 1 (b) 0 (c) f (d) $-f$

65. According to the Fermi-Dirac statistics the number of particles in a phase cell can be

(a) any number (b) only two
(c) only three (d) only one

66. Fermi energy gives the value of energy in a Fermi-Dirac system upto which all the energy states are

(a) occupied (b) vacant
(c) partly filled (d) None of these

67. The pressure for a non-interacting Fermi gas with internal energy U at temperature T is

(a) $p = \frac{3}{2}\frac{U}{V}$ (b) $p = \frac{2}{3}\frac{U}{V}$
(c) $p = \frac{3}{5}\frac{U}{V}$ (d) $p = \frac{1}{2}\frac{U}{V}$

68. A system of non-interacting Fermi particles with Fermi energy E_F, has the density of state proportional to $\sqrt{E}$, where E is the energy of a particles. The average energy per particle at temperature $T = 0$ is

(a) $\frac{1}{6}E_F$ (b) $\frac{1}{5}E_F$
(c) $\frac{2}{5}E_F$ (d) $\frac{3}{5}E_F$

69. The Fermi energy of a free electron gas depends on the electron density ρ as

(a) $\rho^{1/3}$ (b) $\rho^{2/3}$
(c) $\rho^{-1/3}$ (d) $\rho^{-2/3}$

70. The probability that a state which is 0.2 eV above the Fermi energy in a metal atom at 700 K is

(a) 96.2% (b) 62.3%
(c) 3.5% (d) 37.7%

71. A system of N particles is enclosed in a volume V at a temprature T. The logarithmic of the partition function is given by $\ln Z = N \ln \{(V - bN)(k_BT)^{3/2}\}$, where b is a constant with appropriate dimensions. The internal energy of the gas is given by

(a) $U = \left(\frac{1}{2}\right)k_BT$ (b) $U = Nk_BT$
(c) $U = \frac{3}{2}Nk_BT$ (d) $U = 2Nk_BT$

72. In Fermi-Dirac statistics, the degeneracy parameter is given by

(a) $A = \frac{h^2}{2mkT}\left(\frac{3N}{8\pi}\right)^{2/3}$ (b) $\ln A = \frac{h^2}{2mkT}\left(\frac{3N}{8\pi V}\right)^{2/3}$
(c) $\ln A = \frac{h^3}{2mk}\left(\frac{3NV}{8\pi}\right)^{2/3}$ (d) $\ln A = \frac{h^2}{2mk}\left(\frac{3NV}{8\pi}\right)^{2/3}$

73. In Fermi-Dirac statistics, the volume of phase cell is

(a) h (b) h^2
(c) h^3 (d) not fixed

74. An assembly has only two particles, which are to be arranged in three phase cells. The possible number of arrangements in B-E statistics is

(a) two (b) nine
(c) six (d) three

75. The rotational partition function for a diatomic molecule of moment of inertia I at a temperature T is given by

(a) $\frac{Ik_BT}{\hbar^2}$ (b) $\frac{2Ik_BT}{\hbar^2}$
(c) $\frac{3Ik_BT}{\hbar^2}$ (d) $\frac{Ik_BT}{2\hbar^2}$

76. The entropy of a photon gas is proportional to

(a) T (b) T^2
(c) T^3 (d) T^4

77. A quantity of heat ΔH is transferred from a large heat reservoir at temperature T_1 to another large heat reservoir at temperature T_2, with $T_1 > T_2$ required for spontaneous transfer. The heat reservoir have such large capacities that there is no observable change in their temperature. The entropy of the entire system has

(a) increased (b) decreased
(c) remains unchanged (d) zero

78. The number of classical states, ds_v, in the speed interval between v and $v + dv$, then the density of states $g(v)$ is proportional to

(a) v (b) $v^{1/2}$
(c) v^2 (d) $v^{3/2}$

79. The most probable distribution of $N = 5$ distinguishable particles among $r = 3$ cells if the intrinsic probabilities for the cells are $g_1 = g_2 = g_3 = \frac{1}{3}$ is

(a) 3, 2, 0 (b) 3, 1, 1
(c) 4, 1, 0 (d) 2, 2, 1

80. In (Q. 79) if the energy of a particle in cell 1 is zero, in cell 2 is ε and in cell 3 is 2ε, the most probable distribution is if the total energy is fixed at $E_{tot} = 3\varepsilon$ is

(a) 3, 1, 1 (b) 2, 3, 0
(c) 3, 2, 0 (d) 1, 3, 1

81. Six distinguishable particles are to be distributed into 3 cells. Find the number of different combinations of particles that can produce the distribution (4, 1, 1)

(a) 1 (b) 12
(c) 20 (d) 30

82. For a two state system with energies ε and 2ε, the most probable distribution for the average energy is, $g_1 = g_2 = \frac{1}{2}$

(a) $\frac{2\varepsilon e^{-2\beta\varepsilon} + \varepsilon e^{-\beta\varepsilon}}{e^{-2\beta\varepsilon} + e^{-\beta\varepsilon}}$ (b) $\frac{e^{-2\beta\varepsilon} + e^{-\beta\varepsilon}}{2\varepsilon e^{-2\beta\varepsilon} + \varepsilon e^{-\beta\varepsilon}}$
(c) $\frac{\varepsilon e^{-2\beta\varepsilon} + 2\varepsilon e^{-\beta\varepsilon}}{e^{-2\beta\varepsilon} + e^{-\beta\varepsilon}}$ (d) None of these

83. The normalization condition, that the total number of particles is a fixed number, for the low temperature an expression for the Fermi energy E_f of an electron gas in terms of E_{f0}, the Fermi energy at $T = 0\,\text{K}$ is $E_f = E_{f0}\left[1 - \frac{\pi^2}{12}\left(\frac{kT}{E_{f_0}}\right)^2\right]$, where E_{f_0} is

(a) $\frac{h^2}{8m}\left(\frac{\pi}{3}\frac{V}{N}\right)^{2/3}$ (b) $\frac{h^2}{8m}\left(\frac{3V}{\pi N}\right)^{2/3}$

(c) $\frac{h^2}{8\pi}\left(\frac{3}{\pi}\frac{N}{V}\right)^{2/3}$ (d) $\frac{h^2}{8m}\left(\frac{3}{\pi}\frac{V}{N}\right)^{1/3}$

84. What is the density of photon states in the energy interval between E and $E + dE$ in a cubical cavity of volume $V = l^3$

(a) $\frac{8\pi VE}{hC}$ (b) $\frac{8\pi VE^2}{hC}$

(c) $\frac{8\pi VE^2}{(hC)^3}$ (d) $\frac{8\pi VE^3}{(hC)^2}$

85. What is the order of degeneracy of the $57E_0$ level of a three-dimensional cubical infinite well?

(a) 2 (b) 3 (c) 6 (d) 10

86. In a quantum mechanical two state system with energy levels $E_1 = 0$ and $E_2 = \varepsilon$, the probability of finding a particle in a state of energy E is proportional to the Boltzmann's factor $e^{-E/kT}$, the total energy of a system of N particles is

(a) $E_T = \frac{N\varepsilon e^{-\varepsilon/kT}}{1 + e^{-\varepsilon/kT}}$ (b) $E_T = \frac{Ne^{-\varepsilon/kT}}{1 + e^{-\varepsilon/kT}}$

(c) $E_T = \frac{N\varepsilon e^{-\varepsilon/kT}}{1 - e^{-\varepsilon/kT}}$ (d) $E_T = \frac{Ne^{-\varepsilon/kT}}{1 - e^{-\varepsilon/kT}}$

Exercise 2

(For Part 'C')

1. The common between classical and quantum mechanical fundamental distribution function is

(a) they are all depend upon the quantity that define state only
(b) they all depend only upon the energy of state only
(c) they all depend both on energy and quantity defining state
(d) nothing is common in them

2. For 1 mole of copper, $\varepsilon_{F0} = 7\,\text{eV}$, find out the density of states $g(\varepsilon)$, by taking $\varepsilon = 7\,\text{eV}$

(a) 1.3×10^{13} states/eV (b) 1.3×10^{20} states/eV

(c) 1.3×10^{23} states/eV (d) 1.3×10^{26} states/eV

3. The Fermi temperature of a system is defined as $T_F =$

(a) $\frac{3}{5}\frac{\varepsilon_{F0}}{k}$ (b) $\frac{2}{3}\frac{\varepsilon_{F0}}{k}$ (c) $\frac{\varepsilon_{F0}}{k}$ (d) $\frac{k}{\varepsilon_{F0}}$

4. In the equilibrium state

(a) probability is maximum
(b) β parameter of two systems are equal
(c) Both (a) and (b)
(d) None of the above

5. Four phase points are distributed in two cells (i and j) in phase space. Then the thermodynamical probability for the macrostate $n_i = 3$, $n_j = 1$ is

(a) 2 (b) 4 (c) 6 (d) 24

6. The rotational partition function is

(a) $\left[n \times \frac{8\pi^2 IkT}{h^2}\right]$ (b) $\left[\frac{8\pi^2 IkT}{h^2}\right]^n$

(c) $\frac{V^n}{h^{3n} n!}(2\pi mkT)^{3n/2}$ (d) $\frac{1}{2\sinh(h\nu/2kT)}$

7. For a stable thermodynamic system, the temperature dependence of the free energy $\frac{F}{(T)}$ is represented by

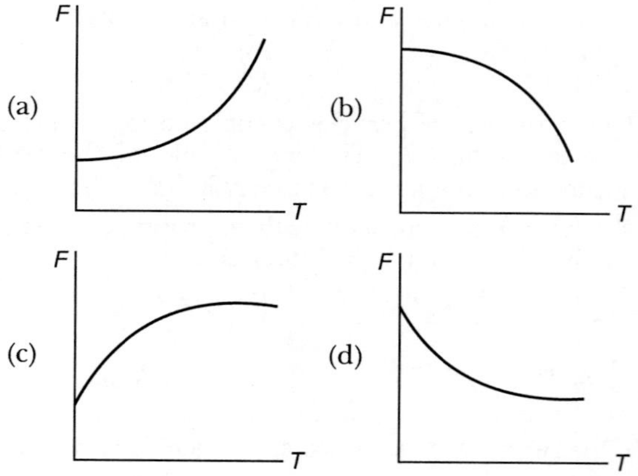

8. A system containing 10 distinguishable spin-1/2 particles is kept in a magnetic field $\vec{\mathbf{B}}$. The system has an energy $-2\mu_B B$. The distinct possible configurations are

(a) 210 (b) 720
(c) 1024 (d) 10!

9. The total number of accessible states of N non-interacting particles of spin $\frac{1}{2}$ is

(a) 2^N (b) N^2
(c) $2^{N/2}$ (d) N

10. Which of the following relations between total energy E and the microcanonical partition function Z, is true?

(a) $E = -N\dfrac{\partial}{\partial T}\log Z$ (b) $E = NkT^2\left[\dfrac{\partial(\log Z)}{\partial T}\right]_V$

(c) $E = -NkT\log Z$ (d) $E = NkT\dfrac{\partial}{\partial V}\log Z$

11. Which of the following relation between pressure p and the microcanonical partition function Z, is true?

(a) $p = -N\left(\dfrac{\partial}{\partial V}\log Z\right)_T$ (b) $p = -NkT\log Z$

(c) $p = NkT\left(\dfrac{\partial(\log Z)}{\partial V}\right)_T$ (d) $p = NkT^2\left(\dfrac{\partial(\log Z)}{\partial V}\right)_T$

12. If the two sub-systems 1 and 2 are in thermal equilibrium and the entropy σ of the total system must have maximum value with respect to small transfer of energy from one subsystem to the other, then the statistical temperature τ is defined as

(a) $\dfrac{1}{\tau} = \left(\dfrac{\partial\sigma}{\partial U}\right)$ (b) $\dfrac{1}{\tau} = -\left(\dfrac{\partial\sigma}{\partial U}\right)$

(c) $\tau = \left(\dfrac{\partial\sigma}{\partial U}\right)$ (d) $\tau = -\left(\dfrac{\partial\sigma}{\partial U}\right)$

13. Fermi function $f(\varepsilon) = \dfrac{1}{e^{(\varepsilon-\varepsilon_f)/kT}+1}$

gives the probability of occupation of electrons per energy state. Then the probability of number of electrons at absolute temperature ($T = 0\,\text{K}$) when $\varepsilon = \varepsilon_f$ is

(a) 1 (b) 0 (c) ∞ (d) $\dfrac{1}{2}$

14. For two assemblies of equal volumes and at same temperature and pressure, the entropy on removing partition becomes

$$S_T = 2S + 2Nk\ln 2$$

The factor $2Nk\ln 2$ arises due to

(a) the indistinguishability of classical particles
(b) the distinguishability of classical particles
(c) the steady flow of particles
(d) the absence of interparticle interaction

15. Plot for Fermi-Dirac distribution is

(a) 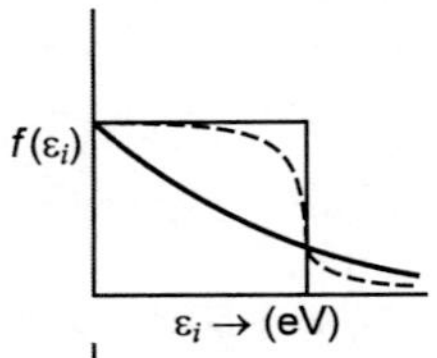

(b) 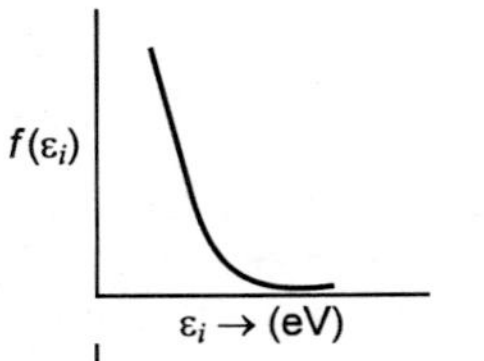

(c) 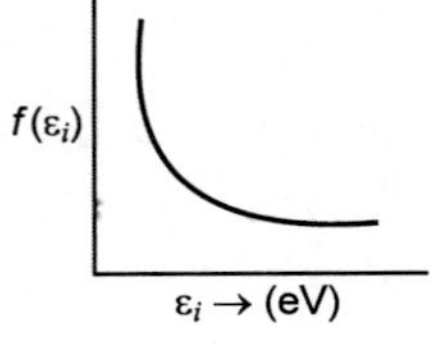

(d) 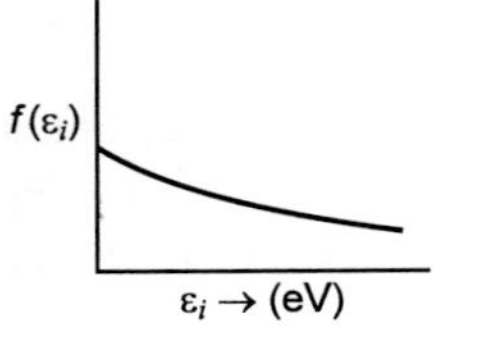

16. The Fermi-Dirac occupation index is given as

$$f_{\text{F-D}}(\varepsilon_i) = \frac{1}{e^{(\varepsilon_i-\varepsilon_f)/kT}+1}$$

where, ε_f is called the Fermi energy.

The value of $f_{\text{F-D}}(\varepsilon_i)$ at the absolute zero of temperature and $\dfrac{(\varepsilon_i-\varepsilon_F)}{kT} = -\infty$ (or $\varepsilon_i < \varepsilon_f$) is

(a) 1 (b) 0

(c) ∞ (d) $\dfrac{1}{2}$

17. The Fermi energy for a non-degenerate gas is given by

(a) $kT\ln\left[\dfrac{(2\pi mkT)^{3/2}Nh^3}{2V}\right]$

(b) $kT\ln\left[\dfrac{Nh^3}{2V(2\pi mkT)^{3/2}}\right]$

(c) $kT\ln\left[\dfrac{2V}{(2\pi mkT)^{3/2}Nh^3}\right]$

(d) $kT\ln\left[\dfrac{2V(2\pi mkT)^{3/2}}{Nh^3}\right]$

18. Which of the following relations between free energy F and the microcanonical partition function Z, is true?

(a) $F = -N\dfrac{\partial}{\partial T}(\log Z)$ (b) $F = NkT\log Z$

(c) $F = NkT^2\log Z$ (d) $F = Nk\dfrac{\partial}{\partial V}(\log Z)$

19. Which of the following relations between free energy F and the canonical partition function Z, is true?

(a) $F = -kT\log Z$ (b) $F = -kT^2\log Z$

(c) $F = kT\log Z$ (d) $F = kT^2\log Z$

20. Which of the following relations between entropy S and the canonical partition function Z, is true?

(a) $S = k\left[\ln Z + T\left(\dfrac{\partial(\ln Z)}{\partial T}\right)_V\right]$

(b) $S = k\left[\ln Z - T\left(\dfrac{\partial(\ln Z)}{\partial T}\right)_V\right]$

(c) $S = k\left[\ln\left(\dfrac{1}{Z}\right) + T\left(\dfrac{\partial(\ln Z)}{\partial T}\right)_V\right]$

(d) $S = k\left[\ln\left(\dfrac{1}{Z}\right) - T\left(\dfrac{\partial(\ln Z)}{\partial T}\right)_V\right]$

21. Which of the following relations between free energy F and the canonical partition function Z, is true?

(a) $F = -\dfrac{\partial}{\partial T}\log Z$ (b) $F = k_BT^2\dfrac{\partial}{\partial T}\log Z$

(c) $F = -kT\log Z$ (d) $F = kT\dfrac{\partial}{\partial V}\log Z$

22. The probability that an energy level ε at a temperature T is unoccupied by a fermion of chemical potential μ is given by

(a) $\frac{1}{e^{(\varepsilon-\mu)/k_BT}+1}$ (b) $\frac{1}{e^{(\varepsilon-\mu)/k_BT}-1}$

(c) $\frac{1}{e^{(\mu-\varepsilon)/k_BT}+1}$ (d) $\frac{1}{e^{(\mu-\varepsilon)/k_BT}-1}$

23. Thermal wavelength of a particle is defined as $\lambda = \frac{h}{(2\pi mkT)^{1/2}}$. If n be the densities of the particles, which of the following represents condition for quantum effects to be important

(a) $n\lambda^3 >> 1$ (b) $n\lambda^3 << 1$

(c) $n\lambda << 1$ (d) $n\lambda >> 1$

24. For a classical system having N indistinguishable particles, which have coordinates q_i and momenta p_i, partition function is given by

(a) $\frac{1}{h^{3N}} \int d^{3N}p\, d^{3N}q\, e^{-\beta H(p,q)}$

(b) $\frac{1}{h^{N}} \int d^{N}p\, d^{N}q\, e^{-\beta H(p,q)}$

(c) $\frac{1}{h^{3N}N!} \int d^{3N}p\, d^{3N}q\, e^{-\beta H(p,q)}$

(d) $\frac{1}{h^{N}N!} \int d^{N}p\, d^{N}q\, e^{-\beta H(p,q)}$

25. If the number of electrons per unit volume with energy between E and $E + dE$ is dn and the density of states $g(E)$ is given by $\frac{1}{2\pi^2}(2m/\hbar^2)^{3/2}\, E^{1/2}$, the total number of electrons N is given by

(a) $N = \frac{2C}{3}[E_F(0)]^{1/2}$

(b) $N = \frac{2C}{3}[E_F(0)]^{3/2}$

(c) $N = \frac{3C}{5}[E_F(0)]^{2/3}$

(d) None of the above

26. At high temperature, entropy of a spin half system is equal to

(a) Nk (b) $Nk \ln 2$

(c) $\frac{Nk}{2}$ (d) $2Nk$

27. Virial of a system is defined as $V = \sum_i q_i p_i$, where q_i is a generalized coordinate and p_i conjugate momentum. Value of V for a system consisting of N particles at temperature T is equal to

(a) $-2kNT$ (b) $-3NkT$

(c) $-NkT$ (d) $-\frac{3}{2}NkT$

28. For $x << 1$ $\coth x - \frac{1}{x}$ upto second lowest order, is equal to

(a) $\frac{x}{3}+\frac{x^3}{45}$ (b) $\frac{x}{3}-\frac{x^3}{45}$ (c) $\frac{x}{5}-\frac{x^3}{3}$ (d) $\frac{x}{5}+\frac{x^3}{3}$

29. Which of the following represents the variation of specific heat of a spin half system with temperature?

(a)
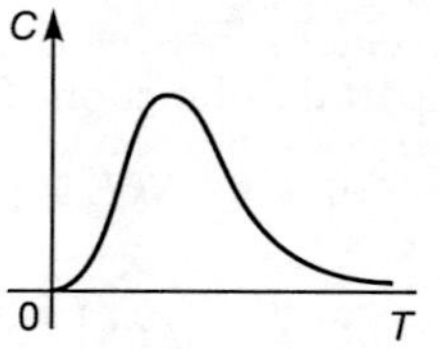

(b)
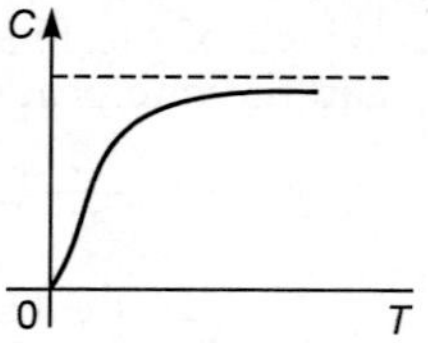

(c)
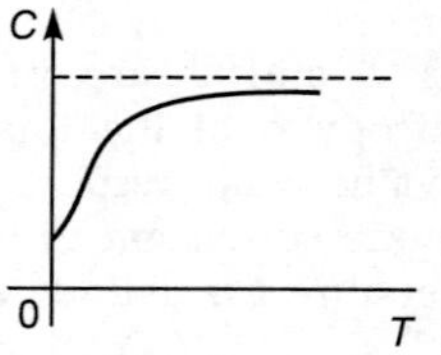

(d)
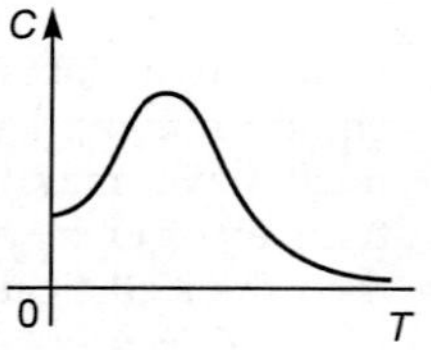

30. If U be the internal energy, p pressure and V volume of a gas. The relation $U = \frac{3}{2}pV$ holds for

(a) Bose gas
(b) Fermi gas
(c) classical Boltzmann gas
(d) All of the above

31. If P_r represents canonical probability, then entropy of system in terms of P_r can be expressed as

(a) $S = k \sum_r \ln P_r$ (b) $S = -k \sum_r \ln P_r$

(c) $S = -k \sum_r P_r \ln P_r$ (d) $S = -2k \sum_r P_r^2 \ln P_r$

32. For a Fermi gas (in 8 dimension) value of the ratio $\frac{C_p}{C_V}$ is

(a) $\frac{2}{3}$ (b) $\frac{3}{2}$

(c) $\frac{4}{3}$ (d) $\frac{5}{3}$

33. The partition function of two Bose particles, each of which can occupy any of the two energy levels 0 and ε is

(a) $1 + e^{-2\varepsilon/kT} + 2e^{-\varepsilon/kT}$ (b) $1 + e^{-2\varepsilon/kT} + e^{-\varepsilon/kT}$

(c) $2 + e^{-2\varepsilon/kT} + e^{-\varepsilon/kT}$ (d) $e^{-2\varepsilon/kT} + e^{-\varepsilon/kT}$

34. For the partition function of above question, what is average energy of the system

(a) $2\varepsilon\,[e^{-\varepsilon\beta} + e^{+\varepsilon\beta}]$ (b) $-2\varepsilon\,[e^{-\varepsilon\beta} + e^{+\varepsilon\beta}]$

(c) $2\varepsilon\,[e^{-\varepsilon\beta} + e^{-2\varepsilon\beta}]$ (d) $2\varepsilon\,[e^{-\varepsilon\beta} - e^{-2\varepsilon\beta}]$

35. What is the chemical potential of the above system

(a) $\varepsilon\,[e^{-\varepsilon\beta} + 2e^{-2\varepsilon\beta}]$ (b) $\varepsilon\,[e^{-\varepsilon\beta} - e^{-2\varepsilon\beta}]$

(c) $\varepsilon\,[2e^{-\varepsilon\beta} + e^{-2\varepsilon\beta}]$ (d) $\varepsilon\,[e^{-\varepsilon\beta} + e^{-2\varepsilon\beta}]$

36. For non-interacting fermions, entropy varies with temperature as (for $T \to 0$)
(a) $S \propto T^3$ (b) $S \propto T$
(c) $S \propto T^2$ (d) $S \propto T^{1/2}$

37. A system has two energy levels with energies ε and 2ε. The lower level is 4-fold degenerate while the upper level is doubly degenerate. If there are N non-interacting classical particles in the system, which is in thermodynamic equilibrium at temperature T, the fraction of particles in the upper level is

(a) $\dfrac{1}{1+e^{-\varepsilon/k_BT}}$ (b) $\dfrac{1}{1+2e^{\varepsilon/k_BT}}$

(c) $\dfrac{1}{2e^{\varepsilon/k_BT}+4e^{2\varepsilon/k_BT}}$ (d) $\dfrac{1}{2e^{\varepsilon/k_BT}-4e^{2\varepsilon/k_BT}}$

38. f represents the distribution function for particles. f *vs* ε plot at $T \neq 0$, which of the following is true?

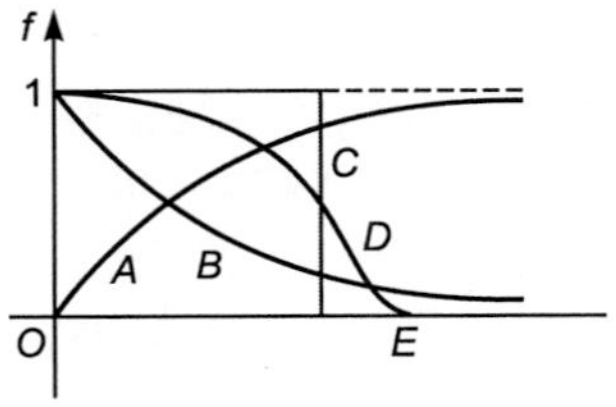

(a) A and C represent classical and Fermi distributions respectively
(b) B and C represent classical and Fermi distribution respectively
(c) A and D represent classical and Fermi distribution respectively
(d) B and D represent classical and Fermi distribution respectively

39. Entropy of a system of N classical harmonic oscillator having frequency ω and at temperature T is given by

(a) $Nk \ln\left(\dfrac{kT}{\hbar\omega}\right)$ (b) $Nk\left[\ln\left(\dfrac{kT}{\hbar\omega}\right)-1\right]$

(c) $Nk\left[\ln\left(\dfrac{kT}{\hbar\omega}\right)+1\right]$ (d) $Nk\left(\dfrac{\hbar\omega}{kT}\right)$

40. In the above question, chemical potential of the system is given by

(a) $kT \ln\left(\dfrac{\hbar\omega}{kT}\right)$ (b) $kT\left[\ln\left(\dfrac{\hbar\omega}{kT}\right)+1\right]$

(c) $kT\left[\ln\left(\dfrac{\hbar\omega}{kT}\right)-1\right]$ (d) $\hbar\omega$

41. In Q. 39, if classical oscillators are replaced by quantum oscillators, then chemical potential of the system will be

(a) $\dfrac{1}{2}\hbar\omega + kT \ln\{1-e^{-\frac{\hbar\omega}{kT}}\}$ (b) $kT \ln\{1-e^{-\frac{\hbar\omega}{kT}}\}$

(c) $\dfrac{\hbar\omega}{2} - kT \ln\{1-e^{-\frac{\hbar\omega}{kT}}\}$ (d) $\dfrac{\hbar\omega}{2}$

42. The equation of state of an ideal gas is given by $pV = RT$. Then the value of Z is
(a) p (b) p^2
(c) $\dfrac{1}{p}$ (d) $\dfrac{1}{p^2}$

43. An approximate equation of state of a real gas at moderate pressure is $p(V-b) = RT$, where R and b are constants. The partition function Z is given by

(a) $Z = \dfrac{1/p}{1+bp/RT}$ (b) $Z = \dfrac{p}{1+bT}$

(c) $Z = \dfrac{p^2}{1-bT}$ (d) None of these

44. Six distinguishable particles are distributed over three non-degenerate levels of energies 0, E and $2E$. The total energy of the distribution for which the probability is a maximum, is
(a) $6E$ (b) $4E$
(c) $2E$ (d) $0E$

45. Five identifiable particles are distributed in three non-degenerate levels with energies 0, E and $2E$. The most probable distribution for a total energy $3E$ is
(a) $N_1 = 2, N_2 = 2, N_3 = 1$ (b) $N_1 = 4, N_2 = 1, N_3 = 0$
(c) $N_1 = 3, N_2 = 1, N_3 = 1$ (d) $N_1 = 2, N_2 = 1, N_3 = 2$

46. Two identical particles have to be distributed among three energy levels. Let, r_B, r_F, r_C represent the ratio of probability of finding two particles to that finding one particles in a given energy state. The subscripts B, F, C correspond to whether the particles are bosons, fermions and classical particles respectively. The $r_B : r_F : r_C$ is equal to

(a) $\dfrac{1}{2}:0:1$ (b) $1:\dfrac{1}{2}:1$ (c) $1:\dfrac{1}{2}:\dfrac{1}{2}$ (d) $1:0:\dfrac{1}{2}$

47. In a system of two particles, each particle can be in any one of three possible quantum states. The ratio of the probability, that the two particles occupy the same state to the probability, that the two particles occupy different states for M-B statistics is

(a) $\dfrac{2}{3}$ (b) $\dfrac{1}{2}$

(c) $\dfrac{1}{3}$ (d) None of these

48. In (Q. 47) the ratio of the probability that the two particles occupy the same state to the probability that the two particles occupy different states for F-D statistics is

(a) $\dfrac{1}{2}$ (b) 0 (c) $\dfrac{1}{3}$ (d) $\dfrac{1}{4}$

49. In (Q. 46), the ratio of the probability that the two particle occupy same state to the probability that the two particle occupy different state for B-E statistics is

(a) 1 (b) $\frac{1}{2}$

(c) $\frac{2}{3}$ (d) $\frac{1}{3}$

50. If f is the Fermi-Dirac distribution function, then choose the correct answer/answers

(a) At Fermi level $-\frac{\partial f}{\partial E}$ is maximum

(b) At Fermi level $-\frac{\partial f}{\partial E}$ is minimum

(c) At Fermi level $-\frac{\partial f}{\partial E}$ is symmetric

(d) At Fermi level $-\frac{\partial f}{\partial E}$ is not symmetric

51. The volume of a mole of liquid He^4 is 27×10^{-6} m^3 and the mass of a He^4 atom is 6.65×10^{-27} kg. Assuming that liquid He^4 is an ideal boson gas with zero spin then

(a) the concentration of boson in the volume is 2.2×10^{28} m^{-3}

(b) the concentration of boson in this volume is 4.2×10^{26} m^{-3}

(c) The boson temperature is 6.4 K

(d) The boson temperature is 3.1 K

52. Choose the correct matching pair of elementary particles with the associated statistics

(a) Bosons	Photons, Electron, Proton
(b) Bosons	Photons, Phonons, Mesons
(c) Fermions	Photon, Neutron, Positrons
(d) Fermions	Photon, Electron, He atom

Assertion & Reason

Codes

(a) Both A and R are true and R is the correct explanation of A.

(b) Both A and R are true and the R is not the correct explanation of A.

(c) A is true and R is false.

(d) R is true and A is false.

53. Assertion (A) Three bosons can be distributed in four energy levels *a, b, c, d* in possible 20 ways.

Reason (R) Bosons are distinguishable particles having half integral spin.

54. Assertion (A) The rapid increase in the population of the ground state below the critical temperature T_0 for a Bose-Einstein gas is called Bose-Einstein condensation.

Reason (B) An assembly of bosons which have integral spin is termed as Bose-Einstein gas.

Directions (Q. No. 55)

The partition function for a gas of photons is given by

$$l_n Z = \frac{\pi^2}{45} \frac{V(k_B T)^3}{\hbar^3 c^3}$$

55. The pressure of the photon gas is

(a) $\frac{\pi^2}{15} \frac{V(k_B T)^3}{\hbar^3 c^3}$ (b) $\frac{\pi^2}{8} \frac{V(k_B T)^4}{\hbar^3 c^3}$

(c) $\frac{\pi^2}{45} \frac{V(k_B T)^4}{\hbar^3 c^3}$ (d) $\frac{\pi}{45} \frac{V(k_B T)^{3/2}}{\hbar^3 c^3}$

Directions (Q. Nos. 56 and 57)

Consider a two-dimensional electron gas of N electrons of mass m each in a system of size $L \times L$.

56. The density of states between energy ε and $\varepsilon + d\varepsilon$ is

(a) $\frac{4\pi L^2 m}{h^2} d\varepsilon$ (b) $\frac{4\pi L^2 m}{h^2} \frac{1}{\sqrt{\varepsilon}} d\varepsilon$

(c) $\frac{4\pi L^2 m}{h^2} \sqrt{\varepsilon}\, d\varepsilon$ (d) $\frac{4\pi L^2 m}{h^2} \varepsilon\, d\varepsilon$

57. The ground state energy E_0 of the system in terms of the Fermi energy E_F and the number of electrons N is given by

(a) $\frac{1}{3} NE_F$ (b) $\frac{1}{2} NE_F$

(c) $\frac{2}{3} NE_F$ (d) $\frac{3}{5} NE_F$

Directions (Q. Nos. 58 to 61)

For copper atomic weight = 63.5, density = 8.95 g cm^{-3} and compressibility $\beta = 7.3 \times 10^{-13}$ cm^2/dyne. Using this data deduce the following.

58. The mass of copper atoms is

(a) 1.05×10^{-22} g (b) 1.05×10^{-12}

(c) 4.06×10^{-22} (d) None of these

59. The interatomic distance (α) assuming simple cubic lattice is

(a) 1.426 Å (b) 2.281 Å

(c) 3.025 Å (d) 9.910 Å

60. The frequency of vibration, $\nu = \frac{1}{2\pi}\sqrt{\frac{3\alpha}{\beta m}}$ is

(a) 4.723×10^8 Hz (b) 6.025×10^{17} Hz

(c) 1.972×10^{11} Hz (d) 4.757×10^{12} Hz

61. Using result of Q. 61, the temperature above which the classical theory result $C_V = 3R$ should be valid for copper

(a) 293 K (b) 273 K

(c) 230 K (d) 100 K

Answers

Exercise 1

1. (c)	**2.** (b)	**3.** (c)	**4.** (a)	**5.** (c)	**6.** (d)	**7.** (a)	**8.** (a)	**9.** (d)	**10.** (b)
11. (c)	**12.** (a)	**13.** (a)	**14.** (a)	**15.** (d)	**16.** (c)	**17.** (b)	**18.** (a)	**19.** (c)	**20.** (c)
21. (d)	**22.** (a)	**23.** (a)	**24.** (a)	**25.** (c)	**26.** (d)	**27.** (b)	**28.** (b)	**29.** (a)	**30.** (c)
31. (a)	**32.** (a)	**33.** (d)	**34.** (d)	**35.** (d)	**36.** (d)	**37.** (d)	**38.** (d)	**39.** (a)	**40.** (a)
41. (b)	**42.** (b)	**43.** (d)	**44.** (c)	**45.** (d)	**46.** (d)	**47.** (a)	**48.** (c)	**49.** (d)	**50.** (b)
51. (a)	**52.** (d)	**53.** (a)	**54.** (a)	**55.** (c)	**56.** (c)	**57.** (d)	**58.** (a)	**59.** (c)	**60.** (a)
61. (c)	**62.** (a)	**63.** (b)	**64.** (a)	**65.** (d)	**66.** (a)	**67.** (b)	**68.** (d)	**69.** (b)	**70.** (c)
71. (d)	**72.** (b)	**73.** (c)	**74.** (c)	**75.** (b)	**76.** (c)	**77.** (a)	**78.** (c)	**79.** (d)	**80.** (a)
81. (d)	**82.** (a)	**83.** (c)	**84.** (c)	**85.** (c)	**86.** (a)				

Exercise 2

1. (c)	**2.** (c)	**3.** (c)	**4.** (c)	**5.** (b)	**6.** (b)	**7.** (a)	**8.** (c)	**9.** (d)	**10.** (b)
11. (c)	**12.** (a)	**13.** (d)	**14.** (b)	**15.** (a)	**16.** (a)	**17.** (b)	**18.** (b)	**19.** (a)	**20.** (a)
21. (c)	**22.** (c)	**23.** (a)	**24.** (c)	**25.** (b)	**26.** (b)	**27.** (b)	**28.** (b)	**29.** (a)	**30.** (d)
31. (c)	**32.** (d)	**33.** (c)	**34.** (c)	**35.** (d)	**36.** (b)	**37.** (d)	**38.** (d)	**39.** (c)	**40.** (a)
41. (a)	**42.** (c)	**43.** (a)	**44.** (a)	**45.** (c)	**46.** (a)	**47.** (b)	**48.** (b)	**49.** (a)	**50.** (a,c)
51. (a,d)	**52.** (c)	**53.** (c)	**54.** (b)	**55.** (c)	**56.** (a)	**57.** (d)	**58.** (a)	**59.** (b)	**60.** (d)
61. (c)									

Hints & Solutions

Exercise 1

7. The gas equation for real gas can be written as

$$\left(p + \frac{a}{V^2}\right)(V - b) = RT \quad \ldots\text{(i)}$$

where, a and b are known as van der Waals' coefficients and equation is known as van der Waals' gas equation.

By rearranging the above equation, we have

$$\Rightarrow \quad p = \frac{-a}{V^2} + \frac{RT}{V - b}$$

Multiplying by volume V on both sides in the above equation,

$$pV = \frac{-a}{V} + \frac{RTV}{V - b}$$

$$\approx \frac{-a}{V} + RT \quad (\because V >> b)$$

$$= k_B T - \frac{a}{V}$$

$[R = Nk_B$ and for one mole gas we have $R = k_B]$

$$\text{or} \quad \frac{pV}{k_B T} = 1 - \frac{a}{k_B TV}$$

$$\Rightarrow \quad \frac{pV}{k_B T} \simeq 1 + \frac{B(T)}{V} \quad \left[\text{where, } \frac{-a}{k_B T} = B(T)\right]$$

8.

$$f(E) = \frac{1}{\exp\left[(E - E_F)/kT + 1\right]}$$

For $E = E_F$

$$f(E_F) = \frac{1}{\exp[0] + 1} = \frac{1}{2}$$

9. Factor $\frac{1}{N!}$ is missing in classical boson formula, this is because classically particles are treated as distinguishable, whereas quantum particles are indistinguishable.

10. Average energy of a system is defined as

$$< E > = \frac{\sum_r E_r e^{-\beta E_r}}{Z} \quad \text{where,} \quad Z = \sum_r e^{-\beta E_r}$$

$$\therefore \quad < E > = -\frac{\partial}{\partial \beta} \ln Z$$

11. Average energy of the spin system is given by

$$E = N\mu_B \tanh\left(\frac{\mu_B}{k_B T}\right)$$

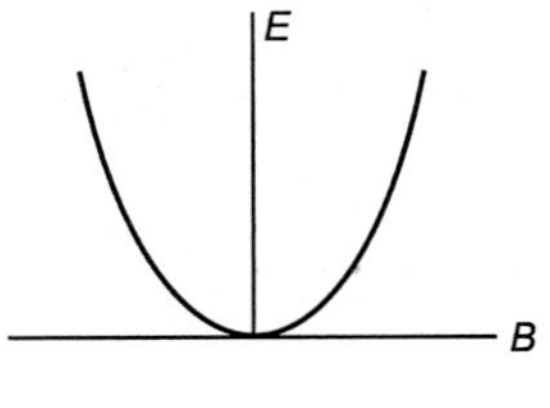

12. The Fermi energy is given by

$$E_F = \frac{\hbar^2}{2m}(3\pi^2 N)^{2/3}$$

$$\Rightarrow \quad E_F \propto n^{2/3}$$

13. Since, particle is moving on two-dimensional surface, its degree of freedom = 2

Hence, for N non-interacting particle total degree of freedom = $2N$

The energy per degree of freedom $= \frac{1}{2} k_B T$

Hence, Total energy $U = 2N \times \frac{1}{2} k_B T$

$$U = Nk_B T$$

28.

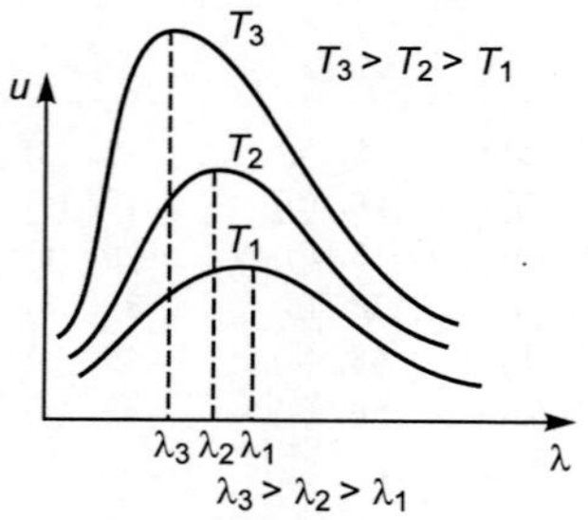

20. Number of microstates $\Omega = 3^N$

Entropy is given by $S = k \ln \Omega$

$\therefore \quad S = Nk_B \ln 3$

23. Chemical potential of the photon gas

$$\mu = -\frac{1}{\beta}\frac{\partial}{\partial N}(F)$$

$$= \frac{\partial}{\partial N}\left(-\frac{1}{3} aVT^{-4}\right)$$

$\because$ F is not an explicit function of N.

25. The probability that molecule will possess a speed v is

$$P(v) = 4\pi\left(\frac{m}{2\pi kT}\right)^{3/2} v^2 e^{-mv^2/(2kT)}$$

For the most probable speed, the probability of the speed must be maximum. Therefore, we differentiate the above equation with respect to v for equating it to zero, *i.e.*,

$$\frac{\partial P(v)}{\partial v} = 4\pi\left(\frac{m}{2\pi kT}\right)^{3/2}\left[2ve^{-mv^2/2kT} - \frac{v^3 m}{kT} \times e^{-mv^2/2kT}\right] = 0$$

or $\quad v_{mp} = \sqrt{\frac{2kT}{m}}$

where, $k (= k_B)$ is Boltzmann constant.

26. We know that $E = \frac{U}{N}$

where, $\quad E = \frac{\pi}{5}\left[\frac{8ma^2}{n^2}\right]^{3/2}(E_F)^{5/2}$

and $\quad N = \frac{\pi}{3}\left[\frac{8m}{n^2}\right]V(E_F)^{3/2}$

$$E = \frac{3}{5}E_F$$

27. Mean free path of the particle of a gas at a temperature T_0 may be given as

$$\lambda = \frac{1}{\sqrt{2}\,\pi\sigma^2 n}$$

where, σ is the diameter of the molecule and n be the number of molecules per unit volume.

For pressure p_0 and temperature T_0, the mean free path λ_0 may be given as

$$\lambda_0 = \frac{1}{\sqrt{2}\,\pi\sigma^2 N}$$

where, $\quad n = \frac{p}{kT}$

So, $\quad \lambda_0 = \frac{kT_0}{\sqrt{2}\,\pi\sigma^2 p_0}$

For $p_1 = 1.5p_0, T_1 = 0.75T_0$, we have

$$\lambda_1 = \frac{kT_1}{\sqrt{2}\,\pi\sigma^2 p_1} = \frac{k \times 0.75T_0}{\sqrt{2}\,\pi\sigma^2\, 1.5p_0}$$

$$= 0.5\left[\frac{kT_0}{\sqrt{2}\,\pi\sigma^2 p_0}\right] = \frac{\lambda_0}{2}$$

28. The particle density and temperature T are related as

$$\frac{n}{T^{3/2}} << 1$$

29.

$$\beta = \frac{1}{k_B T}$$

$$\frac{\partial}{\partial\beta}(\log Z) = -E$$

$$\log Z = \int E\,\partial\beta$$

$$Z = e^{-\int E\,\partial\beta}$$

$$\Rightarrow \quad Z = \frac{e^{-\beta\hbar\omega/2}}{1 - e^{-\beta\hbar\omega}}$$

30. $<n> = \frac{1}{e^{\beta\hbar\omega} + 1}$

31. If T_F is the final temperature, we have

$$mC(T_1 - T_F) = mC(T_F - T_2)$$

$$\Rightarrow \quad T_F = \frac{T_1 + T_2}{2}$$

$$\Delta S = \frac{3}{2}k_B N \log\left(\frac{T_F}{T_i}\right)$$

$$= \frac{3}{2}k_B N \log\left(\frac{T_F^2}{T_1 T_2}\right)$$

$$= \frac{3}{2}k_B N \log\left[\frac{(T_1 + T_2)^2}{4T_1 T_2}\right]$$

32. $F = -k_B T \log[e^{-\varepsilon_1/k_B T} + e^{-\varepsilon_2/k_B T}]$

$\because \quad \varepsilon_1 = 0, \varepsilon_2 = \varepsilon$

$$F = -k_B T \log[1 + e^{-\varepsilon/k_B T}]$$

33. The probability of finding the system in the energy state with energy ε_i may be defined as

$$P(\varepsilon_i) = \frac{e^{-\beta\varepsilon_i}}{\sum_i e^{-\beta\varepsilon_i}}$$

But $\varepsilon = 0, -\varepsilon_0, +\varepsilon_0$, hence, the probability of finding the system with $\varepsilon = 0$ is

$$P(0) = \frac{e^0}{(e^{\beta\varepsilon_0} + e^0 + e^{-\beta\varepsilon_0})}$$

In question $\beta\varepsilon_0 = 2$, so

$$P(0) = \frac{e^0}{(1 + e^2 + e^{-2})}$$

But $\qquad \dfrac{e^x + e^{-x}}{2} = \cosh x$

Hence, $\qquad P(0) = \dfrac{1}{(1 + 2\cosh x)}$

34. The Helmholtz free energy of N particles in terms of partition function may be defined as

$$F = -Nk_BT \log Z$$

where, Z is known as partition function.

Since, $\quad Z = \Sigma e^{-\beta\varepsilon_i} = 1 + e^{-\beta\varepsilon_0} + e^{+\beta\varepsilon_0}$

$= 1 + e^{-x} + e^{+x} \qquad$ (where, $x = \beta\varepsilon_0$)

For high temperature $\beta\varepsilon_0 << 1 \Rightarrow x << 1, \left(\beta = \dfrac{1}{kT}\right)$

Therefore, $e^{-x} \approx (1 - x)$ and $e^{+x} \approx (1 + x)$

And $\qquad Z = 1 + (1 - x) + (1 + x) = 3$

$\Rightarrow \qquad F = -Nk_BT \log 3$

38. Total energy $= 0 \times e^{-0/k_BT} + 2e^{-\varepsilon/k_BT} + 4e^{-2\varepsilon/k_BT}$

$= 0 + 2e^{-\varepsilon/k_BT} + 4e^{-2\varepsilon/k_BT}$

$= 2\,[e^{-\varepsilon/k_BT} + 2e^{-2\varepsilon/k_BT}]$

Mean energy $= \dfrac{\varepsilon\,[\exp(-\varepsilon/k_BT) + 2\exp(-2\varepsilon/k_BT)]}{[1 + \exp(-\varepsilon/k_BT) + \exp(-2\varepsilon/k_BT)]}$

43. Maxwell's distribution of velocities law yields

Root mean square velocity,

$$v_{rms} = \sqrt{\frac{3kT}{m}}$$

Mean velocity, $\quad v_{mean} = \sqrt{\dfrac{6kT}{\pi m}}$

Most probable velocity,

$$v_p = \sqrt{\frac{2kT}{m}}$$

It is clear that, $\quad v_p < v_{rms}$

45. rms speed : Average speed : Most probable speed

$$= \sqrt{\frac{3kT}{m}} : \sqrt{\frac{8kT}{\pi m}} : \sqrt{\frac{2kT}{m}}$$

$$\sqrt{3} : \frac{2\sqrt{2}}{\sqrt{\pi}} : \sqrt{2}$$

$$\sqrt{3} : 2\sqrt{2} : \sqrt{2}$$

$$\sqrt{\pi} = \sqrt{3.14} = 1.7$$

46. Photons are Bose-Einstein particles.

47. C cannot have negative values but v_x can. Then, at higher T molecules go from $v_x = 0$ to higher magnitudes.

48. P and C refer to magnitudes, which will not have negative values. So, α can stand for P_x only. Curve for T_2 extends to higher magnitudes of $|P_x|$, so T_2 is higher, not lower than T_1.

49. ε, at a given T is the same for all gases. Curve q violates the rule that area under the curve must be invariant. p and r do not violate that, but statistics would not choose between them;

The conclusion : not only ε but the entire distribution unchanged.

50. With rise of T, ε is to increase. So, more molecules go to higher C, which means less left at lower C. Since, area under the curve is to stay constant, only (b) fits in.

51. 3 translational degrees of freedom : three position coordinates q_x, q_y, q_z and three momentum coordinates p_x, p_y, p_z.

$\therefore$ Phase space volume is

$$\iiiiiint dp_x\, dp_y\, dp_z\, dq_x\, dq_y\, dq_z$$

where, $\iiint dq_x\, dq_y\, dq_z$ = Volume V

and $\iiint dp_x\, dp_y\, dp_z$ is limited by

$$(p_x^2 + p_y^2 + p_z^2)_{max} = 2mE = p_{max}^2$$

$$\therefore \qquad \iiint dp_x\, dp_y\, dp_z = \frac{4\pi}{3}(p_{max}^3)$$

Hence, volume of phase space $= V \cdot \dfrac{4\pi}{3} p_{max}^3$

$= V \cdot \dfrac{4\pi}{3}(2mE)^{3/2}$

As $\qquad p_{max}^2 = 2mE$

Hence, number of phase cells $= \dfrac{\text{Volume of phase space}}{\text{Volume of one cell}}$

$= \dfrac{\frac{4\pi}{3} V(2mE)^{3/2}}{h_0^3}$

Number of phase cells $= \dfrac{4\pi V}{3h_0^3}(2mE)^{3/2}$

53. We have, $(v_{max})_{mean} = \int_{-\infty}^{\infty} v p_x(v_x)\, dv_x$

$= \int_{-\infty}^{\infty} v_x \left(\dfrac{m}{2\pi kT}\right)^{1/2} e^{-mv_x^2/2kT}\, dv_x$

as $p_x(v_x) = \sqrt{\dfrac{m}{2\pi kT}}\, e^{-mv_x^2/2kT}$

$= \left(\dfrac{m}{2\pi kT}\right)^{1/2} \int_{-\infty}^{\infty} v_x\, e^{-mv_x^2/2kT}\, dv_x$

$= 0 \left(\text{Since, } \int_{-\infty}^{\infty} xe^{-\alpha x^2}\, dx = 0\right)$

55. We know, $\qquad \delta q\, \delta p >> h$

or $\qquad r_{av}\, p_{av} >> h$

Since $\qquad p = \dfrac{h}{\lambda}$

$r_{av} >> \lambda_{av}$

in classical limit.

Since $r_{av}^2 N = V$

or $r_{av} = \left(\frac{V}{N}\right)^{1/3}$

or $r_{av} = \left(\frac{1}{\rho}\right)^{1/3}$

Substitute in condition

$$\left(\frac{1}{\rho}\right)^{1/3} >> \lambda_{av}$$

$$\frac{1}{\rho} >> \lambda^3$$

or $1 >> \rho\lambda^3$

56. Helmholtz free energy F is given by

$$F = U - TS = -kT \ln Z$$

Here $Z = \frac{kT}{h\omega}$

$\therefore$ $F = -kT \ln \frac{kT}{h\omega}$

or $Z = kT \ln \frac{h\omega}{kT}$

57. Partition function

$$Z = \Sigma e^{-n_i \varepsilon_i / kT}$$

Vibrational partition function in this case

$$Z = \sum_{n=0}^{\infty} \exp\left[-\beta (n+1) \mu H\right] \qquad \text{where } \beta = \frac{1}{k_B T}$$

$$= \exp(-\beta\mu H)\left[1 + \exp(-\beta\mu H) + \exp(-2\beta\mu H) + \ldots\right]$$

$$= \exp\left(-\frac{\mu H}{2k_B T}\right)\left[1 - \exp\left(-\frac{\mu H}{k_B T}\right)\right]^{-1}$$

$$= \left[2 \sinh\left(\frac{\mu H}{2k_B T}\right)\right]$$

For the whole system

$$Z(\nu) = [Z(\nu)]^N$$

Helmholtz free energy

$$F = -Nk_B T \ln Z$$

$$= -Nk_B T \ln\left[2 \sinh\left(\frac{\mu H}{k_B T}\right)\right]$$

$$F = -Nk_B T \ln\left[2 \sinh\left(\frac{\mu H}{k_B T}\right)\right]$$

58. For photon, B-E statistics is applicable

For photons $p = \frac{h}{\lambda} = \frac{h\nu}{c}$

$$dp = \frac{hd\nu}{c}$$

The density of states for photons between p and $p + dp$ is

$$g(p)\, dp = \frac{4\pi p^2 dp}{h^3 / \nu}$$

$$g(\nu)\, d\nu = 4\pi V \cdot \frac{\nu^2}{c^3}\, d\nu$$

Since, two independent direction of polarization

$$g(\nu)\, d\nu = \frac{8\pi V}{c^3} \cdot \nu^2\, d\nu$$

Since, $h\nu = E$

$$h \cdot d\nu = dE$$

$\therefore$ $g(E)\, dE = \frac{8\pi V E^2}{h^2 c^3} \cdot \frac{dE}{h}$

$$= \frac{8\pi V}{h^3 c^3} E^2\, dE$$

59. For average number of photons

$$n = \frac{8\pi V}{c^3} \int \frac{\nu^2\, d\nu}{c^3 (e^{h\nu/kT} - 1)}$$

$$\frac{h\nu}{kT} = x$$

or $\nu = \frac{kT}{h} x$

$$d\nu = \frac{kT}{h} dx$$

$$n = \frac{8\pi V}{c^3} \int \left(\frac{kT}{h}\right)^2 \frac{x^2 \cdot \frac{kT}{h} dx}{e^x - 1}$$

or $n = \frac{8\pi V}{h^3 c^3} T^3 k^3 \int_0^{\infty} \frac{x^2\, dx}{e^x - 1}$

or $n \propto T^3 \quad \left[\text{Since, } \int_0^{\infty} \frac{x^2\, dx}{e^x - 1} = \text{constant number}\right]$

60. A gas of fermions will exert the greatest pressure since, the proportion of high energy particles in the Fermi distribution is larger than that in the other two distributions. A gas of boson will exert the least pressure since, the proportions of low energy particles in the Bose distribution is larger than that in the other distribution.

61. The total number of ways W, of distributing 2 identical particles (1) and (2) is

$$W = \prod_{i=1}^{n} \frac{(N_i + g_i - 1)!}{n_i!(g_i - 1)!}$$

$$N_i = 2$$

$$g_i = 3$$

$$W = \frac{(2 + 3 - 1)!}{2!(3-1)!}$$

$$= \frac{4!}{2!\,2!} = \frac{4 \times 3 \times 2 \times 1}{2 \times 2} = 6$$

63. The total number of cells upto energy level

$$E = \frac{4\pi}{3} \frac{V}{h^3} (2mE)^{3/2}$$

Thus, the number of cells corresponding to energy interval E and $E + dE$ is given by

$$g(E)\, dE = \frac{4\pi}{3} \frac{V}{h^3} \frac{3}{2} (E)^{1/2} \cdot (2m)^{3/2}\, dE$$

and multiply by 2 to take account of the two possible spins of electron so that

$$g(E)\,dE = \frac{4\pi}{3}\,V(2m)^{3/2}\,E^{1/2}\,dE$$

The total number of cells between energy levels 0 and E_f at $T = 0$, are equal to the total number of particles, *i.e.*,

$$N = \int_0^{E_{f0}} g(E)\,dE$$

$$= \frac{4\pi V}{h^3}(2m)^{3/2}\int_0^{E_{f0}} E^{1/2}\,dE$$

Thus, $$E_{f_0} = \frac{1}{2m}\left[\frac{3Nh^3}{8\pi V}\right]^{2/3}$$

[E_{f_0} is value of E_f at $T = 0$]

The average kinetic energy of the particles at $T = 0$ is given by

$$\bar{E} = \frac{1}{N}\int_0^{E_{f0}} n_i\,E\,dE$$

$$= \frac{1}{N}\int_0^{E_{f0}} g(E)\,E\,dE$$

$$= \frac{4\pi V}{Nh^3}(2m)^{3/2}\int_0^{E_{f0}} E^{3/2}\,dE$$

$$\bar{E} = \frac{3}{5}\,E_f(0)$$

64. Introduce a function $\lambda(E)$, such that $\lambda(0) = 0$ and evaluate the integral

$$I = \int_0^{\infty} f(E)\,\frac{d\lambda(E)}{\partial E}\,dE$$

where $f(E)$ is the F-D distribution. Integrating by parts

$$I = [f(E)\,\lambda(E)]_0^{\infty} - \int_0^{\infty}\lambda(E)\,\frac{\partial F}{\partial E}\,dE$$

$$= -\int_0^{\infty}\lambda(E)\,\frac{\partial F}{\partial E}\,dE$$

$\lambda(E)$ expanding by Taylor's series

$$\lambda(E) = \lambda(E_F) + (E - E_F)\left(\frac{\partial\lambda}{\partial E}\right)_{E_F} + \frac{1}{2}(E - E_F)^2\left(\frac{\partial^2\lambda}{\partial E^2}\right)_{E_F} + \ldots$$

Writing $I_i = -\frac{1}{i!}\int_0^{\infty}(E - E_F)^i\,\frac{\partial f}{\partial E}\,dE$

or $$I = A_0\lambda(E_F) + A_1\left(\frac{\partial\lambda}{\partial E}\right)_{E_F} + A_2\left(\frac{\partial^2\lambda}{\partial E^2}\right)_{E_F} + \ldots$$

or $$\frac{\partial f}{\partial E} = -\frac{f(1-f)}{k_BT}$$

Thus, $\frac{\partial f}{\partial E}$ is significant near $E = E_F$ and will be zero for energies removed from E_1, since either f or $(1 - f)$ will be zero for such energies.

If $E_f >> k_BT$, the lower limit may, therefore, be shifted to $-\infty$. Then

$$A_0 = -\int_{-\infty}^{\infty}\frac{\partial f}{\partial E}\,dE = [-f]_{-\infty}^{\infty} = 1$$

$f \rightarrow$ F-D distribution

67. The mean pressure of the perfect Fermi gas can be written as

$$P = \Sigma P_i\left[-\frac{\partial E_i(N_1V)}{\partial V}\right] \quad \ldots\text{(i)}$$

The average energy of the system is

$$U = \sum_{\text{states}} P_iE_i \quad \ldots\text{(ii)}$$

For an ideal fermions in a cubical box, the energy of single particle states are given by

$$E = \left(\frac{h^2\pi^2}{2mV^{2/3}}\right)(n_x^2 + n_y^2 + n_z^2)$$

If there is no interaction

$$E_i = \left[\frac{h^2\pi^2}{2mV^{2/3}}\right]\Sigma\,[n_x^2 + n_y^2 + n_z^2]_s$$

[$E_i \Rightarrow$ energy of ith micro state of the system]

$$\therefore \quad P = \Sigma P_i\,\frac{2}{3}\left(\frac{h^2\pi^2}{2m}\right)V^{-1/2}\quad\Sigma\,[n_x^2 + n_y^2 + n_z^2]_s$$

or $$= \frac{2}{3}\,\Sigma\,\frac{P_iE}{V}$$

$$P = \frac{2}{3}\frac{U}{V} \quad \text{[using Eq. (ii)]}$$

69. The Fermi energy of free electron gas is given by

$$E_F(0) = \frac{h^2}{2m}\left(\frac{3N}{4\pi Vg_s}\right)^{2/3}$$

with $g_s = 2$ and density gas $\rho = \left(\frac{Nm}{V}\right)$ kg/m^3

$$E_F(0) = \frac{h^2}{2m^{1/3}}\left(\frac{Nm}{V}\right)^{2/3}\cdot\left(\frac{3}{8\pi}\right)^{2/3}$$

or $$E_F(0) \propto \rho^{2/3}$$

70. Probability of occupancy of a given state with energy E is given by the Fermi-Dirac distribution formula which is

$$f(E) = \frac{1}{1 + \exp\{(E - E_F)/k_BT\}}$$

$$= \frac{1}{1 + \exp\left(\dfrac{0.2\times1.6\times10^{-19}}{1.38\times10^{-23}\times700}\right)}$$

$$f(E) = 3.5\%$$

71. $$U = k_BT^2\left(\frac{\partial \ln Z}{\partial T}\right)$$

$$= k_BT^2\,\frac{\partial}{\partial T}\,[N\ln\{V - bN\}\,(k_BT)^{3/2}]$$

$$= k_BT^2\left[\frac{N\cdot\frac{3}{2}k^{3/2}\,B\,T^{1/2}\,(V - bN)}{(V - bN)\,(k_BT)^{3/2}}\right]$$

$$U = \frac{3}{2}\,Nk_BT$$

75. For a diatomic molecule, the rotational energy levels are

$$\varepsilon(r) = \left(\frac{h^2}{2I}\right) J(J+1);\ J = 0, 1, 2, \ldots$$

The degeneracy of each level of a two dimensional rotation is $g(r) = (2J+1)$. Since, there are $2J+1$ values of the z component of angular momentum

$$\therefore \quad Z = \sum_J (2J+1) \exp\left[-\beta\left(\frac{h^2}{2I}\right) J(J+1)\right]$$

or $$Z(r) = \int_0^\infty \exp\left[-\beta\left(\frac{h^2}{2I}\right) J(J+1)\right](2J+1)\, dJ$$

Using $$\int_0^\infty x e^{-ax^2}\, dx = \left(\frac{1}{2a}\right)$$

[where we have neglected unity in comparison of J]

or $$Z(r) = \frac{2IkT}{h^2}$$

76. For photon gas

$$Z_{ph} = \prod_{i=0}^{\infty} \frac{1}{1-\exp(-\beta\varepsilon_i)}$$

$$F(T, V) = -kT \ln Z_{ph}(T, V)$$

Since, $$\ln Z_{ph} = -\int \ln[1-\exp(-\beta h\nu)]\, g(\nu)\, d\nu$$

$$= -\frac{8\pi V}{c^3}\int_0^\infty \nu^2\, d\nu \ln[1-\exp(-\beta h\nu)]$$

$$F(T, V) = \frac{8\pi VkT}{c^3}\int_0^\infty \nu^2\, d\nu \ln[1-\exp(-\beta h\nu)]$$

$$= \frac{8\pi VkT}{c^3\beta^3 h^3}\int_0^\infty x^2\, dx \ln(1-e^{-x})$$

$$F(T, V) = -\frac{1}{3} bVT^4$$

$$\left[\text{Since, } \frac{1}{3}\int_0^\infty d(x^3)\ln(1-e^{-x}) = -\frac{\pi^4}{45}\right]$$

Entropy $$S = -\left(\frac{\partial F}{\partial T}\right)_V$$

$$S = \frac{4}{3} bVT^3$$

or Entropy $\propto T^3$

77. $$\Delta S_1 = \frac{\Delta H_1}{T_1} = -\frac{\Delta H}{T_1}$$

$$\Delta S_2 = \frac{\Delta H_2}{T_2} = \frac{\Delta H}{T_2}$$

$$\Delta S = -\frac{\Delta H_1}{T_1} + \frac{\Delta H}{T_2}$$

$$= \Delta H \frac{(T_1 - T_2)}{T_1 T_2}$$

Since $T_1 > T_2$

Therefore, ΔS increases.

79. $$P_n = \frac{5!}{n_1!\, n_2!\, n_3!}\left(\frac{1}{3}\right)^5$$

Most probable state can be checked by

$$X = \frac{5!}{n_1!\, n_2!\, n_3!}$$

n_1	n_2	n_3	X
5	0	0	1
4	1	0	5
3	2	0	10
3	1	1	20
2	2	1	30

So, 2, 2, 1 is most probable state.

Exercise 2

2. $$g(\varepsilon) = \frac{3N\varepsilon^{1/2}}{2\varepsilon_F^{3/2}}$$

$$N = N_A = 6.02 \times 10^{23}$$

$$\varepsilon_{F_0} = 7 \text{ eV}$$

$$g(\varepsilon_{F_0}) = \frac{3 \times 6.02 \times 10^{23}}{2 \times (7)^{3/2}}(7)^{1/2}$$

$$= 1.3 \times 10^{23} \text{ states/eV}$$

8. The distinct possible configurations are

$$= 2^{10}$$

$$= 1024$$

12. If σ_1 and $\sigma_2 \rightarrow$ entropies of the sub-systems 1 and 2, then additive property of entropy

$$\sigma = \sigma_1 + \sigma_2 \quad \ldots\text{(i)}$$

Also, $$\sigma = \sigma(U_1, U_2) \quad \ldots\text{(ii)}$$

and $$U = U_1 + U_2 \quad \ldots\text{(iii)}$$

Then $$\delta\sigma = \delta\sigma_1 + \delta\sigma_2$$

$$= \left(\frac{\partial\sigma_1}{\partial U_1}\right)\delta U_1 + \left(\frac{\partial\sigma_2}{\partial U_2}\right)\delta U_2 \quad \ldots\text{(iv)}$$

and $$\delta U = \delta U_1 + \delta U_2 \quad \ldots\text{(v)}$$

For thermal equilibrium, we have

$$\delta U = \delta U_1 + \delta U_2 = 0$$

or $$\delta U_2 = -\delta U_1 \quad \ldots\text{(vi)}$$

and $$\delta\sigma = \left(\frac{\partial\sigma_1}{\partial U_1}\right)\delta U_1 + \left(\frac{\partial\sigma_2}{\partial U_2}\right)\delta U_2 = 0 \quad \ldots\text{(vii)}$$

From Eqs. (vi) and (vii)

$$\delta\sigma = \left[\frac{\partial\sigma_1}{\partial U_1} - \frac{\partial\sigma_2}{\partial U_2}\right]\delta U_1 = 0$$

δU_1 is arbitrary variation, hence, $\delta U_1 \neq 0$

$$\therefore \quad \frac{\partial\sigma_1}{\partial U_1} = \frac{\partial\sigma_2}{\partial U_2}$$

or we can define quantity τ by

$$\frac{1}{\tau} = \left(\frac{\partial\sigma}{\partial U}\right)$$

13. $$f(\varepsilon) = \frac{1}{e^{(\varepsilon - \varepsilon_f)/kT} + 1}$$

at $T = 0\,\text{K}$

and $\varepsilon = \varepsilon_f$

$$e^{(\varepsilon - \varepsilon_f)/kT} = e^0 = 1$$

$$\text{Probability} = \frac{1}{1+1} = \frac{1}{2}$$

16. $$f_{\text{F-D}}(\varepsilon_i) = \frac{1}{e^{(\varepsilon_i - \varepsilon_f)/kT} + 1} = \frac{1}{e^{-\infty} + 1} = \frac{1}{0+1} = 1 \quad [\because e^{-\infty} = 0]$$

17. Total number of particles

$$N = \int_0^\infty n(\varepsilon)\, d\varepsilon$$

$$n(\varepsilon)\, d\varepsilon = \frac{7\sqrt{2\pi}\, Vm^{3/2}\, \varepsilon^{1/2}\, d\varepsilon}{h^3(e^{(\varepsilon - \varepsilon_f)/kT} + 1)}$$

$$\therefore \quad N = \frac{8\sqrt{2\pi}\, m^{3/2}\, V}{h^3} \int_0^\infty \varepsilon^{1/2}\, e^{-\frac{\varepsilon - \varepsilon_f}{kT}}\, d\varepsilon$$

$$= \frac{8\sqrt{2\pi} m^{3/2} V e^{\varepsilon f/kT}}{h^3} \int_0^{\Delta_0} \varepsilon^{1/2} e^{-\varepsilon/kT}\, d\varepsilon$$

Let $\frac{\varepsilon}{kT} = x$

$$N = \frac{8\sqrt{2\pi}\, m^{3/2}\, Ve^{\varepsilon_f/kT}}{h^3} \int_0^\infty (kT)^{3/2}\, x^{1/2}\, e^{-x}\, dx$$

$$= \frac{8\sqrt{2\pi}\, m^{3/2}\, Ve^{\varepsilon_f/kT}}{h^3} (kT)^{3/2} \frac{\sqrt{\pi}}{2}$$

$$= 2\left[\frac{2\pi mkT}{h^2}\right]^{3/2} Ve^{\varepsilon_f/kT}$$

or $$e^{-\varepsilon_f/kT} = \frac{2V}{Nh^3}(2\pi mkT)^{3/2}$$

and $$\varepsilon_f = kT \ln\left[\frac{Nh^3}{2V(2\pi mkT)^{3/2}}\right]$$

22. Probability of occupying is given by Fermi function

$\therefore$ Probability of not occupying is given by

$$1 - f(\varepsilon) = 1 - \frac{1}{\varepsilon^{\beta(\varepsilon - \mu)} + 1}$$

$$= \frac{e^{\beta(\varepsilon - \mu)}}{e^{\beta(\varepsilon - \mu)} + 1}$$

$$= \frac{1}{e^{-\beta(\varepsilon - \mu)} + 1}$$

$$= \frac{1}{e^{\beta(\mu - \varepsilon)} + 1}$$

23. Quantum effects are important when interparticle distance $(r) \le \lambda$

Since $r \le \frac{1}{n^{1/3}}$

$$\therefore \quad \frac{1}{n^{1/3}} \le \lambda$$

or $n^{1/3}\,\lambda \ge 1$

or $n\lambda^3 \ge 1$

$\therefore$ Quantum effects are important when $n\lambda^3 >> 1$

25. dn is given by

$$dn = g(E)\, f(E)\, dE$$

By substituting $f(E) = \dfrac{1}{\exp\left(\dfrac{E - E_F}{kT}\right) + 1}$

and $g(E)$ is given, we obtain

$$dn = \frac{1}{2\pi^2}\left(\frac{2m}{\hbar^2}\right)^{3/2} \frac{E^{1/2}\, dE}{\exp\left(\frac{E - E_F}{kT}\right) + 1}$$

$$= \frac{CE^{1/2}\, dE}{\exp\left(\frac{E - E_F}{kT}\right) + 1}$$

$f(E) = 0$ for $E > E_F$

$f(E) = 1$ for $E < E_F$

Thus, all states are filled up to E_F and g_E is determined in terms of the number of electrons per unit volume N by

$$\int dn = \int \frac{CE^{1/2}\, dE}{\exp\left(\frac{E - E_F}{kT}\right) + 1}$$

or $$N = \frac{2C}{3}[E_F(0)]^{3/2}$$

26. At high temperature

$$\cosh(\beta\mu H) \simeq 1$$

and $\mu H\beta\,[\tanh(\beta\mu H)] \simeq 0$

$\therefore$ Entropy for spin $\frac{1}{2}$ system which is given by

$$S = Nk\,[\ln\{2\cosh(\beta\mu H)\} - \beta\mu H \tanh(\beta\mu H)]$$

Reduces to $S = Nk \ln 2$

27. Virial theorem states that

$$V = -2\,\text{KE}$$

Since $\text{KE} = \frac{3}{2}NkT$

$$\therefore \quad V = -3NkT$$

28. $$\cot\text{h}\, x = \frac{e^x + e^{-x}}{e^x - e^{-x}}$$

$$= \frac{\left(1 + x + \frac{x^2}{2} + \frac{x^3}{6}\right) + \left(1 - x + \frac{x^2}{2} - \frac{x^3}{6} + \dots\right)}{\left(1 + x + \frac{x^2}{2} + \frac{x^3}{6}\right) - \left(1 - x + \frac{x^2}{2} - \frac{x^3}{6} + \dots\right)}$$

$$= \frac{2\left(1 + \frac{x^2}{2} + \frac{x^4}{24}\right)}{2\left(x + \frac{x^3}{3} + \frac{x^5}{120}\right)}$$

$$= \frac{1}{x}\left(1 + \frac{x^2}{2} + \frac{x^4}{24}\right)\left(1 + \frac{x^2}{6} + \frac{x^4}{120}\right)^{-1}$$

$$= \frac{1}{x}\left(1+\frac{x^2}{2}+\frac{x^4}{24}\right)\left[1-\left(\frac{x^2}{6}+\frac{x^4}{120}\right)+\left(\frac{x^2}{6}+\frac{x^4}{120}\right)^2\ldots\right]$$

$$= \frac{1}{x}\left(1+\frac{x^2}{2}+\frac{x^4}{24}\right)\left[1-\left(\frac{x^2}{6}+\frac{x^4}{120}\right)+\frac{x^4}{36}\ldots\right]$$

$$= \frac{1}{x}\left(1+\frac{x^2}{2}+\frac{x^4}{24}\right)\left[1-\frac{x^2}{6}+\frac{7x^4}{360}\right]$$

$$= \frac{1}{x}\left[1+\frac{x^2}{2}+\frac{x^4}{24}-\frac{x^2}{6}-\frac{x^4}{12}+\frac{7x^4}{360}\right]$$

$$= \frac{1}{x}\left[1+\frac{x^2}{3}-\frac{x^4}{45}\right] = \frac{1}{x}+\frac{x}{3}-\frac{x^3}{45}$$

$\therefore$ $$\coth x - \frac{1}{x} = \frac{x}{3} - \frac{x^3}{45}$$

29. For a spin half system of magnetic moment μ placed in a magnetic field $\vec{H}$, partition function is given by

$$Z_1 = e^{\beta\mu H} + e^{-\beta\mu H}$$
$$= 2\cosh(\beta\mu H)$$

For N particle,

$$Z = (Z_1)^N$$
$$= (2\cosh\beta\mu H)^N$$

$\therefore$ Helmholtz free energy function is given by

$$F = -kT\ln Z$$
$$= -NkT\ln(2\cosh\beta\mu H)$$

$\therefore$ Entropy of the system

$$S = -\frac{\partial F}{\partial T}$$

$$= Nk\ln(2\cosh\beta\mu H) + NkT\tanh(\beta\mu H)\cdot\left(\frac{-\beta}{T}\right)\mu H$$

$$= Nk\ln(2\cosh\beta\mu H) - Nk\beta\tanh(\beta\mu H)$$

$$= Nk\ln(2\cosh(\beta\mu H)) - Nk\beta\mu H\tan(\beta\mu H)$$

$\therefore$ Internal energy $E = F + TS$

$$= -Nk\beta T\tanh(\beta\mu H)\times\mu H$$
$$= -N\mu H\tanh(\beta\mu H)$$

$\therefore$ $$C = \frac{\partial E}{\partial T} = Nk(\mu H)^2\,\mathrm{sech}^2(\beta\mu H)$$

Plot of $\frac{C}{Nk}$ *vs* $\frac{kT}{\mu H}$ is shown below.

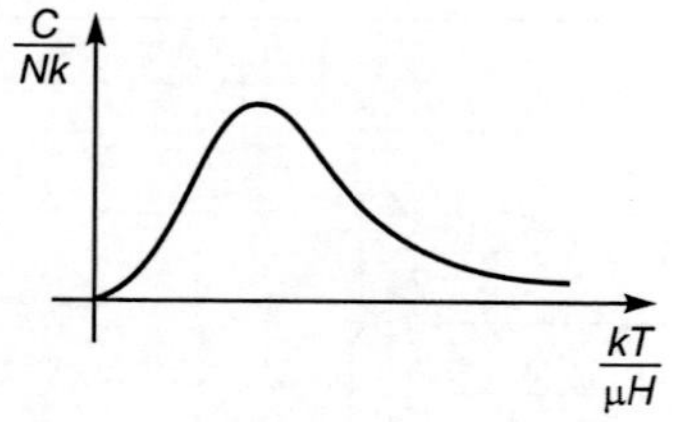

31. $$P_r = \frac{e^{-\beta E_r}}{\sum_r e^{-\beta E_r}} = \frac{e^{-\beta E_r}}{Z}$$

or $$\ln P_r = -\beta E_r - \ln Z \quad \ldots(i)$$

$$S = -\frac{\partial F}{\partial T} = +\frac{\partial}{\partial T}(kT\ln Z)$$

$$= k\ln Z - \frac{1}{T}\frac{\partial}{\partial\beta}\ln Z$$

$$= k\left[\ln Z - \beta\frac{\partial}{\partial\beta}\ln Z\right] \quad \ldots(ii)$$

$$= -\beta^2 k\frac{\partial}{\partial\beta}\left[\frac{\ln Z}{\beta}\right]$$

From Eq. (i) $$\Sigma P_r\ln P_r = -\beta\,\Sigma E_r P_r - \Sigma P_r\ln Z$$

$$= +\beta\cdot\frac{\partial}{\partial\beta}\ln Z - \ln Z\,\Sigma P_r$$

$$= \beta\frac{\partial}{\partial\beta}\ln Z - \ln Z \quad \ldots(iii)$$

(Since, $\Sigma P_r = 1$)

$\therefore$ From Eqs. (ii), we get [using Eq. (iii)]

$$S = -k\sum_r P_r\ln P_r$$

32. Average energy of Fermions is given by

$$E = \frac{3}{5}N\varepsilon_F$$

$\therefore$ $E \propto k_F^2$ (Since, $k_F \propto \rho^{1/3}$)

or $E \propto \rho^{2/3}$ $\left(\rho = \frac{N}{V}\right)$

or $E \propto V^{-2/3}$

$\therefore$ $$p = -\frac{\partial E}{\partial V}$$

$\therefore$ $p \propto V^{-5/3}$

or $pV^{5/3} = \text{constant}$

$\Rightarrow$ $$\gamma = \frac{5}{3} \text{ or } \frac{C_p}{C_V} = \frac{5}{3}$$

33. Partition function is given by

$$Z = \Sigma e^{-\varepsilon_i n_i/kT}$$

where ε_i is energy of quantum state occupied by n_i particle

$\Rightarrow$ Now two Bose particles 1 and 2 (indistinguishable) two energy levels 0 and ε

$\therefore$ $$Z = e^{-\frac{0}{kT}\times 2} + e^{-\frac{0}{kT}\times 1} + e^{-\frac{\varepsilon}{kT}\times 2} + e^{-\frac{\varepsilon}{kT}\times 1}$$

$$= 1 + 1 + e^{-\frac{\varepsilon}{kT}} + e^{\frac{-2\varepsilon}{kT}}$$

$$Z = 2 + e^{-\frac{\varepsilon}{kT}} + e^{\frac{-2\varepsilon}{kT}}$$

34. Average energy of the system is

$$\langle E\rangle = -\frac{\partial}{\partial\beta}\ln Z = 2\varepsilon\left[e^{-\varepsilon\beta} + e^{-2\varepsilon\beta}\right]$$

35. Chemical potential of non-interacting system is given as

$$\mu = \frac{\langle E\rangle}{N}$$

$\therefore$ $$\mu = \varepsilon\left[e^{-\varepsilon\beta} + e^{-2\varepsilon\beta}\right]$$

36. For black body radiation,

$$U \propto T^4 \text{ (Stefan's Boltzmann's law)}$$

$$\therefore \quad S \sim \frac{U}{T} \propto T^3$$

For $T \to 0$ internal energy $\propto T^2$

$$\therefore \quad S \propto T$$

39. For Harmonic oscillator

$$H(p_i, q_i) = \frac{1}{2} m\omega^2 q_i^2 + \frac{1}{2m} p_i^2$$

$\therefore$ Single-oscillator partition function

$$Z_1 = \int_{-\infty}^{+\infty}\int_{-\infty}^{+\infty} e^{-\beta\left\{\frac{1}{2} m\omega^2 q_i^2 + \frac{p_i^2}{2m}\right\}} \frac{dq_i dp_i}{h} = \frac{2\pi}{\beta\omega h}$$

$\therefore$ N-oscillator partition function

$$Z = (Z_1)^N$$

$$Z = \left(\frac{2\pi}{\beta\omega h}\right)^N$$

$\therefore$ Helmholtz free energy function

$$F = -kT \ln Z$$

$$= +NkT \ln\left(\beta\omega \frac{h}{2\pi}\right)$$

$$= NkT \ln\left(\frac{\hbar\omega}{kT}\right)$$

$\therefore$ Entropy $\quad S = -\frac{\partial F}{\partial T}$

$$= Nk\left[-\ln\left(\frac{\hbar\omega}{kT}\right) + 1\right]$$

$$= Nk\left[\ln\left(\frac{kT}{\hbar\omega}\right) + 1\right]$$

40. Chemical potential of the system is defined as

$$\mu = \left(\frac{\partial F}{\partial N}\right)_T$$

$$\therefore \quad \mu = kT \ln\left(\frac{\hbar\omega}{kT}\right)$$

41. For quantum oscillators

$$E_n = \hbar\omega\left(n + \frac{1}{2}\right)$$

Single-oscillator partition function is

$$Z_1 = \sum_n e^{-\beta E_n} = e^{-\frac{\beta\hbar\omega}{2}} \sum_n e^{-\beta\hbar\omega\, n}$$

$$= \frac{e^{-\frac{\beta\hbar\omega}{2}}}{1 - e^{-\beta\hbar\omega}} = \frac{1}{e^{\frac{\beta\hbar\omega}{2}} - e^{-\frac{\beta\hbar\omega}{2}}}$$

$\therefore$ N-oscillator partition function

$$Z = Z_1^N = [e^{\frac{\beta\hbar\omega}{2}} - e^{-\frac{\beta\hbar\omega}{2}}]^{-N}$$

$$F = -kT \ln Z$$

$$= NkT \ln [e^{\frac{\beta\hbar\omega}{2}} - e^{-\frac{\beta\hbar\omega}{2}}]$$

$$= NkT\left\{\ln 2 + \ln\left[\sinh\left(\frac{\beta\hbar\omega}{2}\right)\right]\right\}$$

$\therefore$ Chemical potential

$$\mu = \left(\frac{\partial F}{\partial N}\right)_T$$

$$\therefore \quad \mu = kT\left\{\ln 2 + \ln\left[\sinh\left(\frac{\beta\hbar\omega}{2}\right)\right]\right\}$$

or

$$\mu = kT\left\{\ln 2 + \ln\left[\frac{e^{\frac{\hbar\omega\beta}{2}} - e^{-\frac{\hbar\omega\beta}{2}}}{2}\right]\right\}$$

$$= kT \ln \{e^{\frac{\hbar\omega\beta}{2}} [1 - e^{-\hbar\omega\beta}]\}$$

$$= kT\left[\ln (1 - e^{-\hbar\omega\beta}) + \frac{\hbar\omega\beta}{2}\right]$$

$$= \frac{\hbar\omega}{2} + kT \ln (1 - e^{-\hbar\omega\beta})$$

42. For an ideal gas, $Z = -\left(\frac{1}{V}\right)\left(\frac{\partial V}{\partial p}\right)_T$

From $pV = RT$; $\left(\frac{\partial V}{\partial p}\right)_T = -\frac{RT}{p^2}$

$$\therefore \quad Z = -\frac{1}{V} \times -\frac{RT}{p^2}$$

$$= \frac{pV}{Vp^2}$$

or

$$Z = \frac{1}{p}$$

43. From $p(V - b) = RT, V = \frac{RT}{p} + b$

Then, $\quad \left(\frac{\partial V}{\partial p}\right)_T = \frac{-RT}{p^2}$

Substitute for Z, where

$$Z = -\left(\frac{1}{V}\right)\left(\frac{\partial V}{\partial p}\right)_T$$

Hence, $\quad Z = -\frac{1}{V} \cdot \frac{-RT}{p^2}$

$$\Rightarrow \quad Z = \frac{p}{RT + pb} \cdot \frac{RT}{p^2}$$

$$= \frac{RT}{p(RT + pb)}$$

or

$$Z = \frac{\frac{1}{p}}{1 + \frac{bp}{RT}}$$

44. Since, the levels are non-degenerate, there is only one state associated with each energy.

Let, the number of particles in the three energy states be N_1, N_2 and N_3 respectively, where

$$N_1 + N_2 + N_3 = 6$$

As the particls are distinguishable, the number of microstates, *i.e.*, the number of ways of choosing N_1, N_2 and N_3 particles from 6 particles is

$$W = \frac{6!}{N_1!N_2!N_3!}$$

$W \rightarrow$ thermodynamic probability. It is maximum when $N_1!N_2!N_3!$ is a minimum.

By inspection we find that $N_1!N_2!N_3!$ is a minimum when $N_1 = N_2 = N_3 = 2$

The corresponding total energy of the distribution is

$$0 \times N_1 + EN_2 + 2E \times N_3 = 2E + 4E = 6E$$

45. As the levels are non-degenerate, there is only one state for each energy.

Let, the number of particles occupying the three energy states be N_1, N_2 and N_3 respectively, where

$$N_1 + N_2 + N_3 = 5$$

The particles are identifiable, the number of ways of choosing the particles is

$$W = \frac{5!}{N_1!N_2!N_3!}$$

The energy of the system is

$$0N_1 + EN_2 + 2EN_3 = 3E \text{ (given)}$$

or $$N_2 + 2N_3 = 3 \quad \text{...(i)}$$

Now, the most probable distribution is the one in which W is a maximum, subject to the constraint given by Eq. (i). Thus,

if $N_2 = 1$, $\quad N_3 = \frac{3-1}{2} = 1$

and $\quad N_1 = 5 - (N_2 + N_3) = 5 - 2 = 3$

if $N_2 = 3$, $\quad N_3 = \frac{3-3}{2} = 0$

and $\quad N_1 = 5 - (3 + 0) = 2$

No other distributions are possible.

For $N_1 = 3$, $\quad N_2 = 1$

and $\quad N_3 = 1$

$$W = \frac{5!}{3!}$$

$$1!1! = 20$$

For $N_1 = 2$, $\quad N_2 = 3$

and $\quad N_3 = 0$

$$W = \frac{5!}{2!\,3!\,0!} = 10$$

So, the most probable distribution is $N_1 = 3$, $N_2 = 1$ and $N_3 = 1$.

46. Two fermions cannot be found in same energy level

$\therefore \quad r_F = 0$

If P_r be the probability of two classical particles to be found together, then corresponding probability for bosons is given by

$$\frac{P_r}{2!} = \frac{P_r}{2}$$

$\therefore \quad r_B : r_F : r_C = \frac{1}{2} : 0 : 1$

47. Let, r be the desired ratio

$W_1 \rightarrow$ the number of ways in which two particles occupy the same state.

$W_2 \rightarrow$ the state in which they occupy different state then

$$r = \frac{W_1}{W_2}$$

For M-B statistics The particles are distinguishable and $W_1 = 3$

Now, one particle can be in any one of the 3 quantum states and the remaining particles can be in any one of the 2 quantum states that are available to it. So,

$$W_2 = 3 \times 2 = 6$$

Therefore, $$r = \frac{W_1}{W_2} = \frac{3}{6} = \frac{1}{2}$$

48. For F-D statistics The particles are indistinguishable, $W_1 = 0$ since, the two particles cannot be in the same quantum states.

Here $$W_2 = {}^3C_2 = 3$$

So, $$r = \frac{W_1}{W_2} = \frac{0}{3} = 0$$

49. For B-E statistics Again, the particles are indistinguishable

$$W_1 = 3 \text{ and } W_2 = {}^3C_2 = 3$$

So $$r = \frac{W_1}{W_2} = \frac{3}{3} = 1$$

50. We have $$f = \frac{1}{1 + e^{(E - E_F)/k_BT}}$$

$$= \frac{1}{1 + e^x}$$

where, $x = \frac{E - E_F}{k_BT}$, $E_F \rightarrow$ Fermi level

So, $$\frac{\partial f}{\partial E} = \frac{\partial f}{\partial x} \cdot \frac{\partial x}{\partial E}$$

$$= -\frac{e^x}{k_BT\,(1 + e^x)^2}$$

or $$-\frac{\partial f}{\partial E} = \frac{1}{k_BT}\frac{e^x}{(1 + e^x)^2} \quad \text{...(i)}$$

and $$-\frac{\partial^2 f}{\partial E^2} = -\frac{d}{dx}\left(\frac{\partial f}{\partial E}\right)\frac{\partial x}{\partial E}$$

$$= \frac{1}{k_BT}\frac{d}{dx}\left(-\frac{\partial f}{\partial E}\right)$$

$$= \frac{1}{(k_BT)^2}\frac{(1 + e^x)^2 e^x - 2e^x(1 + e^x)\,e^x}{(1 + e^x)^4}$$

$-\frac{\partial f}{\partial E}$ is maximum when $-\frac{\partial^2 f}{\partial E^2} = 0$

or $$(1 + e^x)^2 - 2e^x(1 + e^x) = 0$$

or $$(1 + e^x)(1 + e^x - 2e^x) = 0$$

or $$(1 + e^x)(1 - e^x) = 0$$

or $$1 - e^{2x} = 0$$

$\Rightarrow$ $$e^{2x} = 1 = e^0$$

or $$x = 0$$

$$= \frac{E - E_F}{k_BT}$$

or $$E = E_F$$

Thus, $-\frac{\partial f}{\partial E}$ is maximum at the Fermi level.

If E is below E_F by the same amount, x is replaced by $-x$, the

$$-\frac{\partial f}{\partial E} = \frac{1}{k_B T}\frac{e^{-x}}{(1+e^{-x})^2}$$

$$= \frac{1}{k_B T}\frac{e^{x}}{(1+e^{x})^2}$$

Thus, $-\frac{\partial f}{\partial E}$ is unchanged upon the reversal of the sign of x.

Hence, $-\left(\frac{\partial f}{\partial E}\right)$ is symmetric about $x = 0$, *i.e.*, about $E = E_F$.

51. Concentration of boson $= \frac{N}{V} = \frac{6.02 \times 10^{23}}{27 \times 10^{-6}\ \text{m}^3}$

$$= 2.2 \times 10^{28}\ \text{m}^{-3}$$

Now, $g_s = 2S + 1 = 1 \quad (\because S = 0)$

Boson temperature $T_b = \frac{2\pi\hbar^2}{mk}\left(\frac{N}{2.612 \times gV}\right) = 3.1\ \text{K}$

53. Number of possible ways using Bose-Einstein statistics

$$= \frac{g_i(n_i + g_i - 1)!}{n_i!\, g_i!}$$

$$= \frac{4(4+3-1)!}{3!\,4!} = \frac{4 \times (6)!}{3!\,4!}$$

$$= \frac{4 \times 5 \times 6}{2 \times 3} = 20$$

55. $p = \frac{\log Z}{\beta} = k_B T \times \frac{\pi^2}{45}\frac{V(k_B T)^3}{\hbar^3 C^3} = \frac{\pi^2}{45}\frac{V(k_B T)^4}{\hbar^3 C^3}$

56. $g(\varepsilon)\, d\varepsilon = \frac{4\pi^2}{h} m \times L^2 d\varepsilon$

57. $E_0 = \frac{3}{5} N\varepsilon_F$

58. Mass of copper atom,

$$m = \frac{\text{Atomic weight}}{\text{Avogadro number}}$$

$$= \frac{63.5}{6.02 \times 10^{23}} = 1.05 \times 10^{-22}\ \text{g}$$

59. Interatomic distance, $\alpha = \frac{nA}{N\rho}$

Here,

n = Lattice points per unit cell = 1 for simple cubic lattice

A = Atomic weight = 63.5

N = Avogadro number = 6.02×10^{23}

ρ = Density of copper = 8.95 g cm^{-3}

$$\therefore \quad a = \left(\frac{1 \times 63.5}{6.02 \times 10^{23} \times 8.95}\right)^{1/2}$$

$$\log a = \frac{1}{3}[\log 63.5 - \log 6.02 - 23 - \log 8.95]$$

$$= \frac{1}{3}[1.8028 - 0.7796 - 23 - 0.9513]$$

$$= \bar{8}.3572.$$

$$\therefore \quad a = 2.281 \times 10^{-8}\ \text{cm} = 2.281\ \text{Å}$$

60. $\nu = \frac{1}{2\pi}\sqrt{\frac{3a}{\beta m}}$

$$= \frac{1}{2 \times 3.14}\sqrt{\left(\frac{3 \times 2.281 \times 10^{-8}}{7.3 \times 10^{-13} \times 1.05 \times 10^{-22}}\right)}$$

$$\log \nu = -\log 2 - 3.14 + \frac{1}{2}[\log 3 + \log 2.81 - 8 - \log 7.3 - 13 - \log 1.05 + 22]$$

$$= -0.3010 - 0.4969 + \frac{1}{2}[0.4771 + 0.3581 - 8.9633 + 13 - 0.0212 + 22]$$

$$= 12.6774$$

$$\nu = 4.757 \times 10^{12}\ \text{cycles/sec}$$

61. According to Einstein's theory of atomic heat C_V aproaches the value $3R$ if $\frac{h\nu}{kT} << 1$, *i.e.*, if, $\frac{h\nu}{k} < T$, *i.e.*, if $T > \frac{h\nu}{k}$.

Here $\frac{h\nu}{k} = \frac{(6.62 \times 10^{-34}\ \text{J sec.}) \times (4.75 \times 10^{12}\ \text{s}^{-1})}{1.38 \times 10^{-23}\ \text{J/K.}}$

$$= 230\ \text{K.}$$

Therefore, for copper classical theory result

$$C_V = 3R \text{ is valid if } T > 230\ \text{K}$$

23

Electrochemistry

Syllabus

- Electrolytic Conductance-Kohlrausch's Law and its Applictations
- Debye-Huckel Theory
- Electrochemical Cell, Nernst Equation, Redox Systems
- Ionic Equilibria; Conductometric and Potentiometric Titrations

Electrolytic Conductance

In a metallic conductor, flow of electric current is due to flow of electrons. It is known as electronic conductance. The flow of current through an electrolytic solution gives electrolytic conduction which occurs only if ions of the electrolyte are free to move. Cations move towards cathode while anions move towards anode.

Conductance (*G*)

It measures the ease with which the current flows through a conductor. It is the reciprocal of the electrical resistance ($G = 1/R$). Unit of conductance is Siemen, S or ohm^{-1}, Ω^{-1}.

Specific Resistance or Resistivity

It is defined as the resistance in ohm of a conductor having length equal to 1 cm and 1 cm^2 area of cross-section.

$$R = \rho \frac{l}{a} \quad \text{or} \quad \rho = \frac{Ra}{l}$$

Its SI unit is ohm metre, Ω m but quite often ohm cm is also used.

Specific Conductance (Conductivity)

The reciprocal of specific resistance, $1/\rho$ is known as specific conductance. It is denoted by κ.

$$\kappa = \frac{1}{\rho} = \frac{l}{a} \times \frac{1}{R} = \frac{l}{a} \times \text{conductance}$$

The units of specific conductance are Sm^{-1}.

Equivalent Conductance

It is defined as the conducting powers of all the ions produced by dissolving one gram equivalent of an electrolyte in solution placed between two large electrodes one centimetre apart.

$$\Lambda_{eq} = \frac{\kappa \times 1000}{C_{eq}} = \frac{\kappa \times 1000}{\text{Normality}}$$

Λ_{eq} is expressed practically in the unit of S cm^2 equivalent^{-1}.

Molar Conductance

It is defined as the conducting powers of all the ions produced by dissolving 1 g-mol of the electrolyte placed between two large electrodes at one centimeter apart.

$$\Lambda_m = \frac{\kappa \times 1000}{C_m} = \frac{\kappa \times 1000}{\text{Molarity}}$$

Λ_m is expressed in the unit of S cm^2 mol^{-1}.

The equivalent as well as molar conductance of the electrolytes depend upon, the nature of electrolyte, temperature and concentration of electrolyte in the solution.

Note Cell constant $= \frac{\text{Specific conductance}}{\text{Conductance}}$

The unit of cell constant is m^{-1} and cm^{-1}.

Variation of Molar Conductivity and Equivalent Conductivity with Concentration

In the lower concentration range, for a strong electrolyte the variation is given by **Huckel Onsagar equation.**

$$\Lambda = \Lambda_m^\circ - b\sqrt{C}$$

where, b is a constant depending on the nature of solvent and temperature and Λ_m° is the molar conductance at infinite dilution. At infinite dilution, the concentration, C tends to be zero. $\lim_{c \to 0} \Lambda_m = \Lambda_m^\circ$. If we plot molar conductivity against $\sqrt{C}$, the graph is linear in lower concentration range for strong electrolyte. Λ_m° can be obtained by extrapolation. Λ_m decreases slightly with $\sqrt{C}$ and this decrease is due to change in the interionic attractions.

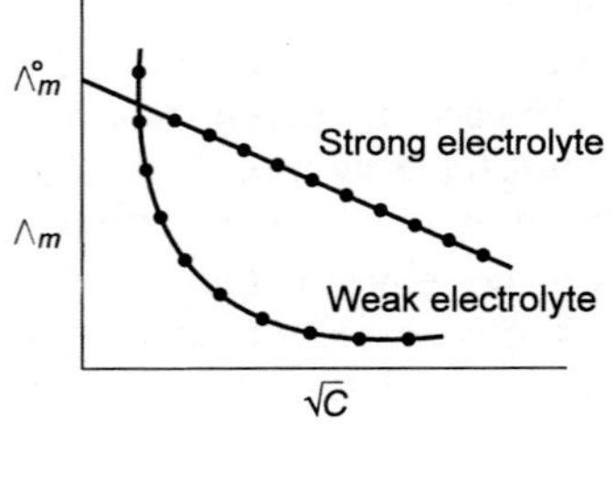

In case of weak electrolyte Λ_m is low due to very small ionization. But Λ_m increases sharply when solution is diluted in lower concentration range because degree of ionization rises sharply.

Kohlrausch's Law

According to this law, at infinite dilution, when ionization is complete, each ion makes its contribution towards equivalent conductance (or molar conductance) of the electrolyte and at infinite dilution equivalent or molar conductance is given by the sum of the equivalent conductances of two ions (cations and anions).

$$\Lambda_m^\circ = \Lambda_+^\circ + \Lambda_-^\circ$$

where, Λ_+° and Λ_-° is the contribution of the cation and anion respectively towards the equivalent or molar conductance at infinite dilution. It is applied in calculation of molar conductance at infinite dilution for weak electrolytes.

Calculation of Molar Conductance

Transport number of cation, $t_+^\circ = u_+^\circ / (u_+^\circ + u_-^\circ)$

where, u_+° and u_-° are the mobility of cation and anion respectively at infinite dilution.

$$\Lambda^\circ \propto u^\circ$$

$\therefore$ $t_+^\circ = \Lambda_+^\circ / (\Lambda_+^\circ + \Lambda_-^\circ)$ $(\Lambda_+^\circ + \Lambda_-^\circ = \Lambda_m^\circ)$

$t_+^\circ = \Lambda_+^\circ / \Lambda_m^\circ$

similarly, $t_-^\circ = \Lambda_-^\circ / \Lambda_m^\circ$

Relation between Molar Ionic Conductance and Ionic Mobility

Ionic mobility is defined as the distance travelled by an ion per second under a potential gradient of 1 volt per metre.

Ionic mobility (for either ion), $u^\circ = \Lambda^\circ / F$, where, $F = 96493$ C mol^{-1}.

Example 1. *A dilute solution of* KCl *was placed between two platinum electrodes* 10.0 *cm apart, across which a potential of* 6.0 *V was applied. How far would the* K^+ *ion move in two hours at* 25°C? *Molar ionic conductance of* K^+ *ion at infinite dilution at* 25°C *is known to be* 73.52×10^{-4} S m^2 mol^{-1}.

Sol. Λ_+° for K^+ ion $= 73.52 \times 10^{-4}$ S m^2 mol^{-1}

$$u_+^\circ = \Lambda_+^\circ / F$$

$$= 73.52 \times 10^{-4} \text{ S m}^2\text{mol}^{-1} / 96493 \text{ C mol}^{-1}$$

$$u_+^\circ = 7.619 \times 10^{-8} \text{ m}^2 \text{ V}^{-1} \text{ s}^{-1}$$

Potential gradient (z Vm^{-1}) = 6.0 V/10 cm

$$= 0.6 \text{ V cm}^{-1} = 0.6 \times 10^2 \text{ Vm}^{-1}$$

Speed of K^+ ion

$$= 7.619 \times 10^{-8} \text{ m}^2\text{V}^{-1}\text{s}^{-1} \times 0.6 \times 10^2 \text{ Vm}^{-1}$$

$$= 4.5714 \times 10^{-6} \text{ ms}^{-1}$$

Distance travelled by K^+ ion in 2 h ($60 \times 60 \times 2$ s)

$$= 4.5714 \times 10^{-6} \text{ ms}^{-1} \times 60 \times 60 \times 2$$

$$= 3.2914 \times 10^{-2} \text{ m}$$

Diffusion and ionic mobility

Diffusion involves the migration of a component in solution down a gradient of its own concentration (from a region of higher concentration to a region of lower concentration. Diffusion coefficient, D measures the mobility of the ion due to its thermal energy kT.

$$D = ukT/ez$$

(e = electronic charge, z = charge number of the ion). This equation is known as **Nernst-Einstein equation.**

Molar ionic conductance and viscosity

$\Lambda^\circ_\pm \eta_0$ = constant, This is called Walden's rule. The larger the viscosity of the medium the lesser would be the mobility and hence the lesser would be the conductance of the ions. Larger ions such as $(CH_3)_4N^+$ obey Walden's rule satisfactorily.

Applications of Kohlrausch's Law

1. Calculation of degree of ionization and ionization constant

$$\text{Degree of ionization, } \alpha = \frac{\Lambda_c}{\Lambda_0}$$

where, Λ_c = molar conductance of solution at any concentration

Λ_0 = molar conductance at infinite dilution

$$\text{Ionization constant, } k = \frac{C\alpha^2}{(1-\alpha)}$$

2. Calculation of solubility product of a sparingly soluble salt

Since, the solution is saturated at infinite dilution $\Lambda_o = \Lambda^\circ_m$ and molarity = solubility.

$$\Lambda^\circ_m = \frac{\kappa \times 1000}{\text{Molarity}}$$

$$\therefore \quad \text{Solubility (mol L}^{-1}) = \frac{\kappa \times 1000}{\Lambda^\circ_m}$$

Λ_0 can be computed by the use of Kohlrausch's law.

$$\Lambda_0 = \Lambda^\circ_{\text{cation}} + \Lambda^\circ_{\text{anion}}$$

3. Calculation of equivalent or molar conductance of weak electrolyte at infinite dilution

The main application of the law is to calculate the equivalent or molar conductance of a weak electrolyte at ∞ dilution. Such electrolyte are not completely ionic at any dilution therefore their equivalent or molar conductance cannot be determine experimently. In such cases the equivalent or molar conductance at ∞ dilution can be calculated with the help of Kohlrausch's law.

Let us calculate the limiting molar conductivity for CH_3COOH. According to Kohlrausch's law $\Lambda^\circ_{CH_3COOH} = \Lambda^\circ_{CH_3COO^-} + \Lambda^\circ_{H^+}$

This equation can be obtained by the knowledge of molar conductivity at infinite dilution for some strong electrolytes. For example, consider the strong electrolytes HCl, NaCl and CH_3COONa.

$$\Lambda^\circ_{CH_3COONa} = \Lambda^\circ_{CH_3COO^-} + \Lambda^\circ_{Na^+}$$

$$\Lambda^\circ_{HCl} = \Lambda^\circ_{H^+} + \Lambda^\circ_{Cl^-}$$

$$\Lambda^\circ_{NaCl} = \Lambda^\circ_{Na^+} + \Lambda^\circ_{Cl^-}$$

It is clear that

$$\Lambda^\circ_{CH_3COO^-} + \Lambda^\circ_{H^+} = [\Lambda^\circ_{CH_3COO^-} + \Lambda^\circ_{Na^+}] + [\Lambda^\circ_{H^+} + \Lambda^\circ_{Cl^-}] - [\Lambda^\circ_{Na^+} + \Lambda^\circ_{Cl^-}]$$

or

$$\Lambda^\circ_{CH_3COOH} = \Lambda^\circ_{CH_3COONa} + \Lambda^\circ_{HCl} - \Lambda^\circ_{NaCl}$$

Similarly we have

$$\Lambda^\circ_{NH_4OH} = \Lambda^\circ_{NH_4Cl} + \Lambda^\circ_{NaOH} - \Lambda^\circ_{NaCl}$$

Debye-Huckel Theory of Strong Electrolytes

According to this theory strong electrolytes completely ionized in solution at all concentration. If the solvent has high dielectric constant, the interionic forces become very small and the ions will lie far apart from each other. But in case of solvent having low dielectric contant, due to appreciable interionic forces, some ions remain in pairs known as ionic doublets.

In case of strong electrolytes molar conductance increases with increase in dilution. It is due to the increase in mobilities of ions due to weak inter ionic attractions. Similarly, decrease in molar conductance with increase in concentration is not due to fall in the degree of ionization but to decrease in the mobilities of ions due to greater interionic effect.

Debye and Huckel derived an equation which enabled them to calculate the magnitude of the interionic effect. Three factors which help to qualitatively explain the variation in the mobility of ions are (i) asymmetry effect (ii) electrophoretic effect (iii) viscous effect. Debye, Huckel and Onsager derived the following expression for the molar conductivity, Λ_m of a very dilute solution of a strong electrolyte.

$$\Lambda_m - \Lambda_m^\circ - [A + B\,\Lambda_m^\circ]\sqrt{C}$$

where, A and B are called Debye-Huckel constants.

$$A = \frac{82.4}{(DT)^{1/2}\,\eta},\ B = \frac{8.20\times10^5}{(DT)^{3/2}}$$

D and η are dielectric constant and coefficient of viscosity of the medium respectively at temperature $T(K)$ and C is the molar concentration (mol L^{-1}).

The values of A and B for water at 25°C come out to be 60.2 and 0.229 respectively.

$$\Lambda_m = \Lambda_m^\circ - (60.2 + 0.229\,\Lambda_m^\circ)\sqrt{C}$$

A plot of Λ *versus* $\sqrt{C}$, on the basis of this equation, is expected to be linear and it is so observed in low concentration region for various strong electrolytes. In case of weak electrolyte the graph is not linear and it reaches the y-axis with a sharp rise.

Activity coefficients of electrolytes

$$\underset{\text{Uni-univalent electrolyte}}{MA} \rightleftharpoons M^+ + A^-$$

Applying the law of chemical equilibrium,

$$K = \frac{(a_{M^+})(a_{A^-})}{a_{MA}}$$

Activity, $a = \gamma m$

(m = molarity and γ = activity coefficient).

$$K = \frac{(\gamma_{M^+}\, m_{M^+})(\gamma_{A^-}\, m_{A^-})}{\gamma_{MA}\cdot m_{MA}}$$

$$K = \frac{\gamma_{M^+}\,\gamma_{A^-}}{\gamma_{MA}}\cdot\frac{m_{M^+}\, m_{A^-}}{m_{MA}}$$

Mean ionic activity coefficient

$$M_xA_y \rightleftharpoons xM^+ + yA^-$$

The activity and mean ionic activity of the electrolyte M_xA_y type is defined as :

$$a = (a_+)^x\,(a_-)^y = (a\,\pm)^{x+y}$$

$$a = (x\gamma + m)^x\,(y\gamma - m)^y$$

$$a = x^x y^y \cdot \gamma_+^x \cdot \gamma_-^y\, m^{x+y} = x^x y^y\,(\gamma_\pm\, m)^{x+y}$$

$\gamma_\pm$ is the mean molar ionic activity coefficient, $(\gamma_\pm)^{x+y} = (\gamma_+)^x\,(\gamma_-)^y$ for uni-univalent electrolytes like NaCl, KCl, $x = 1$ and $y = 1$

$$a = (\gamma_\pm\, m)^2$$

for uni-bivalent electrolytes like K_2SO_4, Na_2SO_4, $BaCl_2$, $Zn(NO_3)_2$

$$x = 2 \text{ and } y = 1$$

$$a = 2^2 \times 1^1\,(\gamma_\pm\, m)^{2+1}$$

$$a = 4\gamma_\pm^3\, m^3.$$

The activity coeffcient of each electrolyte is taken as unity at infinite dilution.

Example 2. *Relate $a_\pm$ to a and $\gamma_\pm$ to m in the case of* KCl *and* $CaCl_2$ *solution.*

Sol. For KCl solution

Here, $x = 1$ and $y = 1$

$\therefore\quad a_\pm = (a_+^1 \cdot a_-^1)^{1/2} = a^{1/2}$, where '$a$' is the total activity.

$m_\pm = (m_+^1 \cdot m_-^1)^{1/2}$. But $m_+ = m_- = m$, the molality of KCl

$\therefore\quad m_\pm = m$

$\therefore\quad \gamma_\pm = \dfrac{a_\pm}{m_\pm} = \dfrac{a_\pm}{m}$

For $CaCl_2$ solution

$x = 1$ and $y = 1$

$\therefore\quad a_\pm = (a_+^1 \cdot a_-^2)^{1/3}$ or $a^{1/3}$

$m_\pm = (m_+^1 \cdot m_-^2)^{1/3}$.

But $m_+ = m$ and $m_- = 2m$, where 'm' is the molality of $CaCl_2$ solution.

$\therefore\quad m_\pm = (m \cdot 4m^2)^{1/3} = 4^{1/3}\cdot m$

$\gamma_\pm = \dfrac{a_\pm}{m_\pm} = \dfrac{a_\pm}{4^{1/3}\cdot m}$

Example 3. *Calculate $a_\pm, m_\pm$ and $\gamma_\pm$ of* $CaCl_2$ *in a* 0.01 *molal solution. γ_+ and γ_- may be assumed to be* 0.5 *and* 0.8 *respectively.*

Sol. Here $x = 1, y = 2$

$$m_+ = 0.01;\quad m_- = 0.02$$

$$a_+ = m_+ \cdot \gamma_+ = 0.01 \times 0.5 = 0.005$$

$$a_- = m_- \cdot \gamma_+ = 00.2 \times 0.8 = 0.016$$

$$a_\pm = (a_+^x \cdot a_-^y)^{\frac{1}{x+y}} = (0.005 \times 0.016^2)^{1/3} = 0.01086$$

$$m_\pm = (m_+^1 \cdot m_-^2)^{1/3} = (0.01 \times 0.02^2)^{1/3} = 0.01587$$

$$\gamma_\pm = (\gamma_+^x \cdot \gamma_-^y)^{\frac{1}{x+y}} = (0.5 \times 0.8^2)^{1/3} = 0.684$$

Molality of the electrolyte solution = m

Electrolyte valence type	Example	x	y	$m_\pm$	$a_\pm = m_\pm \cdot \gamma_\pm$
1–1	NaCl	1	1	m	$m \cdot \gamma_\pm$
2–2	$CuSO_4$	1	1	m	$m \cdot \gamma_\pm$
3–3	$AlPO_4$	1	1	m	$m \cdot \gamma_\pm$
1–2	Na_2SO_4	2	1	$m \cdot (4)^{1/3}$	$m \cdot \gamma_\pm \cdot (4)^{1/3}$
2–1	$BaCl_2$	1	2	$m \cdot (4)^{1/3}$	$m \cdot \gamma_\pm \cdot (4)^{1/3}$
1–3	Na_2PO_4	3	1	$m \cdot (27)^{1/4}$	$m\ \gamma_\pm\ (27)^{1/4}$
3–1	$La(NO_3)_3$	1	3	$m \cdot (27)^{1/4}$	$m \cdot \gamma_\pm (27)^{1/4}$

Ionic strength The interionic attraction in an electrolyte depends on the valences and concentrations of the ions. These two factors are combined in a single entity, known as ionic strength.

$$I = \frac{1}{2}(m_1 z_1^2 + m_2 z_2^2 + m_3 z_3^2 + \ldots)$$

(where, m_1, m_2 ... are molarities and z_1, z_2 ... are valencies of the various ions in the solution).

$$I = \frac{1}{2} \Sigma\, m_i z_i^2$$

Modifications of the Debye-Huckel Limiting Law

Correction for ion size

The Debye-Huckel limiting law holds good only at extremely low concentration and at such concentration, the ions may be treated nearly as point charges, since the size of the ion becomes negligible compared to the thickness of th ions atmosphere, $\frac{1}{b}$ (refer to the expression for 'b'–the lower the concentration of solution, the smaller the value of b and hence the larger the value of $\frac{1}{b}$). At moderate and high concentrations, the thickness of the ionic atomsphere becomes small and the size of the ion cannot be neglected and the modified Debye-Huckel expression, as already seen, is.

$$\log \gamma_\pm = -|z_+ z_-| \frac{AI^{1/2}}{1 + B\sigma I^{1/2}}$$

where 'σ', according to Debye-Huckel, is the mean distance of approach of ions, also known as the closest distance of approach.

The factor '$B\sigma$' in the denominator of the above expression increases $\gamma_\pm$. This is also understandable qualitatively. An increase in the size of the ion would mean an increase in the closest distance of approach of the two oppositely charged ions, and hence a decrease in interionic attraction. In other words, $\gamma_\pm$ would increase.

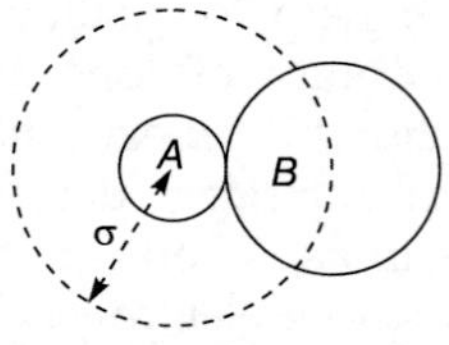

Mean distance of approach of ions.

2. Correction for linearisation of the P-B equation

With reference to the Poisson-Boltzmann equation, we came across the expression,

$$\rho = \Sigma n_i^0\ q_i e^{-\varepsilon_i/kT}$$

which was linearised for very diluted solution. This is permitted since in dilute solution, interionic attractions are very small and hence $\varepsilon_i\ (= q_i \psi) << kT$. At high concentration linearisation cannot be done and the exponential has to be expanded to a series and as many terms as possible, depending on the accuracy needed, have to be retained. If too many terms are retained, the Poisson-Boltzmann differential equation cannot be easily solved for ψ and the mathematical process becomes discouragingly messy.

3. Correction for ion-association

In concentrated solutions, interionic attractions is large and oppositely charged ions to some extent, form what are called ion pairs. There is an equilibrium between the ion-pairs and free ions.

$$A^+ + B^- \rightleftharpoons A^+B^-$$

The ion-pairs, in a way, behave lime neutral molecules, since they do not contribute to electrical conduction and colligative properties.

According to Bjerrum, the critical distance of separation between two oppositely charge ions ion-pair formation is

$$x = \frac{e^2\ |z_+ z_-|}{2DkT}$$

A greater critical distance means greater tendency for ion-pair formation. The above expression indicates that the greater the product of the valences of the ions and the smaller the dielectric constant of the medium, the greater the ease of ion-pair formation. If m is the initial concentration of the ions A^+ and B^- and if θ is the fraction converted to ion-pairs.

$$\log \gamma_{\pm} = -\frac{A|z_+ z_-|}{1 + Bx\sqrt{(1-\theta)\,m}} \cdot \sqrt{(1-\theta)\,m}$$

x is the critical distance mentioned earlier, compare it with the previous expression,

$\log \gamma_{\pm} = -\dfrac{A|z_+ z_-|\sqrt{m}}{1 + B\sigma\sqrt{m}}$ that assume the absence of ion-pairs. (Note that m is used in the place of 1, since the electrolyte is of 1 : 1 valence type.)

The Debye-Huckel Theory of Mean Ionic Activity Coefficients

Poisson equation It is an expression for the variation of electrostatic potential, ψ_r with charge density ρ_r at a distance r from the central ion. In rectangular coordinates, the Poisson equation is $\nabla^2\psi = \dfrac{-4\pi\rho}{D}$ (D = dielectric constant of the medium) for spherically symmetrical situation, the Poisson equation assumes the special form,

$$\nabla^2\psi = \frac{1}{r^2}\frac{d}{dr}\left(r^2\frac{d\psi}{dr}\right) = \frac{-4\pi\rho}{D}$$

where, ψ and ρ depend on the distance r from the central ion and not on direction.

Poisson-Boltzmann equation

$$\nabla^2\psi = \frac{1}{r^2}\cdot\frac{d}{dr}\left(r^2\frac{d\psi}{dr}\right) = \frac{-4\pi\rho}{D}$$

$$= +\frac{4\pi\psi}{D}\frac{\Sigma n_i^0 q_i^2}{KT} = b^2\psi \qquad \left(\rho = \frac{\Sigma n_i^0 q_i^2 \psi}{KT}\right)$$

The use of term $b\left(b^2 = \dfrac{4\pi}{DKT}\Sigma n_i^0 q_i^2\right)$ reduces the tedium of writing.

Thus, $$\nabla^2\psi = b^2\psi$$

Free energy of interaction The free energy of interaction between the ionic atmosphere and the central ion may be equated to the work done in charging the particle i from $q_i = 0$ to $q_i = q_i$.

$$\Delta G_{\text{electrostatic}} = -\frac{bq_i^2}{2D} \text{ per ion}$$

or $-\dfrac{Nbq_i^2}{2D}$ per mole of the ion.

Activity coefficient and interionic attraction

$$RT\ln\gamma_i = \frac{-Nbq_i^2}{2D}$$

or $$\ln\gamma_i = \frac{-Nbq_i^2}{2RTD}.$$

Mean activity coefficient of the electrolyte related to ionic strength

$$\log\gamma_{\pm} = -0.509\,|z_+ z_-|I^{1/2}$$

This equation is known as **Debye-Huckel limiting law.**

Some empirical corrections for Debye-Huckel equation have been suggested to make it applicable also to solutions which are not so dilute. One corrected form is

$$\log\gamma_{\pm} = -A_{z_+ z_-}\sqrt{I} + CI$$

(where, C is an empirical constant).

Example 4. *Calculate the ionic strength of (i) 0.2 molal $BaCl_2$ solution and (ii) solution which is 0.1 molal in KCl and 0.2 molal in K_2SO_4.*

Sol. $$I = \frac{1}{2}(m_1z_1^2 + m_2z_2^2 + m_3z_3^2 + \ldots)$$

(i) For 0.2 molal $BaCl_2$ solution

$$m_+ = 0.2,\ m_- = 2\times0.2 = 0.4$$

$$z_+ = 2,\ z_- = 1$$

$$I = \frac{1}{2}(0.2\times2^2 + 0.4\times1^2) = 0.6$$

(ii) In a solution which is 0.1 molal in KCl and 0.2 molal in K_2SO_4; the total molality of K^+ ions,

$$m_1 = 0.1 + 2\times0.2 = 0.5,\ z_1 = 1$$

molality of Cl^- ions,

$$m_2 = 0.1,\ z_2 = 1$$

molality of SO_4^{2-} ions,

$$m_3 = 0.2,\ z_3 = 2$$

$$I = \frac{1}{2}(0.5\times1^2 + 0.1\times1^2 + 0.2\times2^2) = 0.7.$$

Electrochemical or Voltaic (Galvanic) Cells

A galvanic cell is a device in which free energy of a chemical process is converted into electrical energy. If a cell is constructed with two metals, each dipped in its own ions, more electropositive metals acts as anode and other acts as cathode. If a cell is constructed with zinc and copper electrodes, the cell reaction is given as

$$Zn(s) + Cu^{2+}(aq) \rightleftharpoons Cu(s) + Zn^{2+}(aq)$$

Cell notation

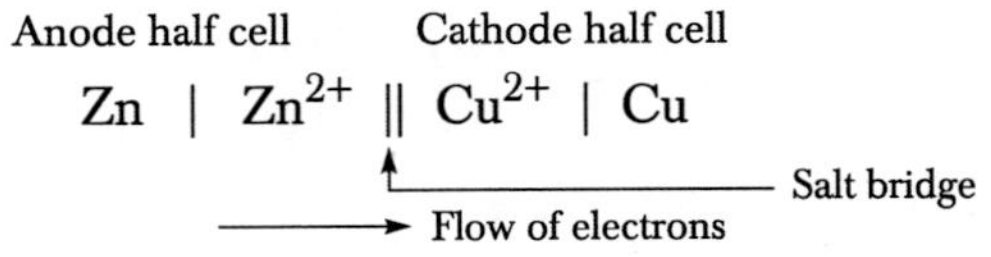

- In galvanic cell oxidation occurs at anode while reduction occurs at cathode. Anode is negative plate while cathode is positive plate. Electrons flow in the external circuit from anode to cathode while conventional current flows from cathode to anode. Two half cells in a galvanic cell are connected by a salt bridge. Salt bridge is a U-shaped glass tube filled with a gel like substance *agar-agar* mixed with an inert electrolyte such as Na_2SO_4. Salt bridge is necessary to complete the electrical circuit and to maintain electrical neutrality in both compartments by flow of ions.

Electrode Potential

Potential difference between the metal and the metal ion in which electrode is dipped, is called electrode potential (E) in a given state and standard electrode potential ($E°$) in a standard state.

$$E^\circ_{Zn|Zn^{2+}} = E^\circ_{ox}$$

(Standard oxidation potential of Zn | Zn^{2+})

$$E^\circ_{Cu^{2+}|Cu} = E^\circ_{red}$$

(Standard reduction potential of Cu^{2+} | Cu)

$$E^\circ_{cell} = E^\circ_{ox} + E^\circ_{red}$$

(Take $E°$ values according to reaction)

$$E_{cell} = E_{ox} + E_{red}$$

Reference Electrode

Standard hydrogen electrode (SHE) and calomel electrodes are used as reference (half cells) electrodes. Potential of the standard hydrogen electrode is taken as zero.

Nernst Equation

It gives a relationship between the electrode potential and ionic concentration of the electrolyte solution.

For a reduction reaction occurring at an electrode M^{n+}/M

$$M^{n+} + ne^- \longrightarrow M(s)$$

$$E = E^\circ - \frac{RT}{nF} \ln \frac{[M]}{[M^{n+}]}$$

(Molar concentration of pure solids and liquids is taken as unity)

$$E = E^\circ - \frac{RT}{nF} \ln \frac{1}{[M^{n+}]}$$

or

$$E = E^\circ + \frac{RT}{nF} \ln [M^{n+}]$$

or

$$E = E^\circ + \frac{0.0591}{n} \log [M^{n+}] \text{ at } 25°C.$$

Relationship between the EMF of the Cell and Ionic Concentration of the Electrolyte

For a general electrochemical cell reaction,

$$aA + bB \longrightarrow cC + dD$$

$$E_{cell} = E^\circ_{cell} - \frac{2.303RT}{nF} \log \frac{[C]^c\,[D]^d}{[A]^a\,[B]^b}$$

For a cell reaction in equilibrium, $E_{cell} = 0$

$$0 = E^\circ_{cell} - \frac{2.303RT}{nF} \log K_c$$

$$E^\circ_{cell} = \frac{2.303RT}{nF} \log K_c$$

$$E^\circ_{cell} = \frac{0.0591}{n} \log K_c \text{ at } 25°C.$$

- **EMF of a cell and free energy**

  $\Delta G = -\,nFE$ in a given state.

  $\Delta G^\circ = -\,nFE^\circ$ in a standard state.

- **Free energy and equilibrium constant**

  $$\Delta G^\circ = -\,2.303RT \log K_c$$

- $\Delta G^\circ_1 + \Delta G^\circ_2 = \Delta G^\circ_3$ when different number of electrons are involved.

  $$E^\circ_3 = \frac{n_1 E^\circ_1 + n_2 E^\circ_2}{n_3}$$

  and if equal number of electrons are involved $E^\circ_1 + E^\circ_2 = E^\circ_3$.

- **Thermodynamic properties from EMF data** From EMF of reversible cells, we can evaluate ΔG, ΔS and ΔH of the cell reactions. Thus,

  $$\Delta G = -\,nFE$$

  $$\Delta S = nF\left(\frac{\partial E}{\partial T}\right)_p$$

  $$\Delta H = -\,nFE + nFT\left(\frac{\partial E}{\partial T}\right)_p$$

  where, E is the EMF of cell, $\left(\frac{\partial E}{\partial T}\right)_p$ is the temperature coefficient of EMF, n is the number of electrons involved in the cell reaction.

Table 23.1 **Various Types of Half Cells**

	Type	Example	Half cell reaction	$Q =$	Reversible to	Electrode potential (oxidation), $E =$
1.	Gas-ion half cell	$Pt(H_2)\,|\,H^+(aq)$	$\frac{1}{2}H_2(g) \longrightarrow H^+(aq) + e^-$	$[H^+]$	H^+ ion	$E° - 0.0591 \log [H^+]$
		$Pt(Cl_2)\,|\,Cl^-(aq)$	$Cl^-(aq) \longrightarrow Cl_2(g) + e^-$	$\frac{1}{[Cl^-]}$	Cl^- ion	$E° + 0.0591 \log [Cl^-]$
2.	Metal-metal ion half cell	$Ag\,|\,Ag^+(aq)$	$Ag(s) \longrightarrow Ag^+(aq) + e^-$	$[Ag^+]$	Ag^+ ion	$E° - 0.0591 \log [Ag^+]$
3.	Metal-insoluble salt anion half cell	$Ag, AgCl\,|\,Cl^-(aq)$	$Ag(s) + Cl^-(aq) \longrightarrow AgCl(s) + e^-$	$\frac{1}{[Cl^-]}$	Cl^- ion	$E° + 0.0591 \log [Cl^-]$
4.	Calomel electrode	$Hg, Hg_2Cl_2\,|\,Cl^-(aq)$	$2Hg(l) + 2Cl^-(aq) \longrightarrow Hg_2Cl_2(s) + 2e^-$	$\frac{1}{[Cl^-]^2}$	Cl^- ion	$E° + 0.0591 \log [Cl^-]$
5.	Metal-metal oxide hydroxide half cell	$Hg, HgO\,|\,OH^-(aq)$	$Hg(l) + 2OH^-(aq) \longrightarrow HgO(s) + H_2O(l) + 2e^-$	$\frac{1}{[OH^-]^2}$	OH^- ion	$E° + 0.0591 \log [OH^-]$
6.	Oxidation-reduction half cell	$Pt\,|\,Fe^{2+}(aq), Fe^{3+}(aq)$	$Fe^{2+}(aq) \longrightarrow Fe^{3+}(aq) + e^-$	$\frac{[Fe^{3+}]}{[Fe^{2+}]}$	Fe^{2+}, Fe^{3+} ions	$E° - 0.0591 \log \frac{[Fe^{3+}]}{[Fe^{2+}]}$
7.	Mercury-mercury sulphate half cell	$Hg, HgSO_4\,|\,SO_4^{2-}(aq)$	$SO_4^{2-}(aq) + Hg(l) \longrightarrow HgSO_4(s) + 2e^-$	$\frac{1}{[SO_4^{2-}]}$	SO_4^{2-}	$E° + \frac{0.0591}{2} \log [SO_4^{2-}]$
8.	Quinhydrone half cell	$Pt\,|\,Quinhydrone\,|\,H^+(aq)$	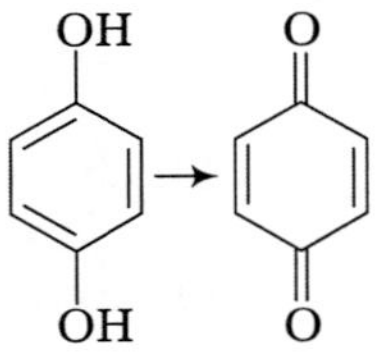 $+ 2H^+ + 2e^-$	$[H^+]^2$	H^+	$E° - 0.0591 \log [H^+]$

Concentration Cells

A cell in which both the electrodes are of the same type but the solutions of electrolyte in which they dip have different concentration is called concentration cell. In concentration cells, the EMF arises not from any chemical reaction but from a transfer of matter from one electrode to another electrode, which occurs due to difference in concentration of the same species at the two electrodes. Concentration cells are of two types :

1. Electrode concentration cells
2. Electrolyte concentration cells
   (a) Cells without liquid junction or transport
   (b) Cells with liquid junction or transport.

Electrode Concentration Cells

Examples gas electrode and amalgam electrode.

Gas electrode

$$\overset{\ominus}{Pt}, \underset{(p_1)}{H_2(g)}\,|\,H^+\,|\,\underset{(p_2)}{H_2(g)}, \overset{\oplus}{Pt}$$

Cell reaction $\frac{1}{2}\underset{(p_1)}{H_2(g)} \longrightarrow \frac{1}{2}\underset{(p_2)}{H_2(g)}$

$$E_{cell} = \frac{RT}{F} \ln \left(\frac{p_1}{p_2}\right)^{1/2}$$

$$E_{cell} = \frac{RT}{2F} \ln \frac{p_1}{p_2} \quad (E^\circ_{cell} = 0)$$

Amalgam electrode

$$\overset{\ominus}{Cd}\underset{(a_1)}{(Hg)}\,|\,Cd^{2+}\,|\,Cd\underset{(a_2)}{(Hg)}^{\oplus}$$

Cell reaction $\underset{(a_1)}{Cd} \longrightarrow \underset{(a_2)}{Cd}$

$$E_{cell} = \frac{RT}{2F} \ln \frac{a_1}{a_2}$$

In above expression, E°_{cell} does not appear.

Electrolyte Concentration Cells without Liquid Junction

Each half cell of this type of cell is actually a full or complete cell, namely a chemical cell without liquid junction.

Example Consider, a cell consisting of two cells connected back to back through silver electrodes.

$$\overset{(-)}{\text{Pt}};\ \underset{(1\text{ atm})}{H_2},\ \underset{(a_1)}{\text{HCl}},\ \text{AgCl}(s), \text{Ag} \mid \text{Ag}, \text{AgCl}(s), \underset{(a_2)}{\text{HCl}},\ \underset{(1\text{ atm})}{H_2};\ \overset{(+)}{\text{Pt}}$$

The electrode reactions are :

$$\text{RHS}\quad \text{Ag}(s) + \underset{\text{HCl }(2)}{H^+ + Cl^-} \longrightarrow \underset{(1\text{ atm})}{\tfrac{1}{2}H_2} + \text{AgCl}(s)$$

$$\text{LHS}\quad \underset{(1\text{ atm})}{\frac{1}{2}H_2} + \text{AgCl}(s) \longrightarrow \text{Ag}(s) + \underset{\text{HCl}(1)}{H^+ + Cl^-}$$

The overall cell reaction :

$$\underbrace{\underset{(a_2)}{H^+} + \underset{(a_2)}{Cl^-}}_{\text{HCl}(1)} \rightleftharpoons \underbrace{\underset{(a_1)}{H^+} + \underset{(a_1)}{Cl^-}}_{\text{HCl}(2)}$$

Thus, overall reaction involves no chemical change. It consists only of the transfer of HCl from solution of activity a_2 to solution of activity a_1.

$$E_{\text{cell}} = \frac{-RT}{F}\ln\frac{a_{\text{HCl}(1)}}{a_{\text{HCl}(2)}} = \frac{RT}{F}\ln\frac{a_2}{a_1}$$

$$a_{\text{HCl}} = a_{H^+}\cdot a_{Cl^-} = a^2_{\pm(\text{HCl})}$$

Therefore,

$$E_{\text{cell}} = \frac{RT}{F}\ln\frac{a^2_{\pm(2)}}{a^2_{\pm(1)}} = \frac{2RT}{F}\ln\frac{a_{\pm(2)}}{a_{\pm(1)}}$$

(where, $a_\pm$ is the mean activity of HCl)

If the activity coefficient, are neglected,

$$E_{\text{cell}} = \frac{RT}{F}\ln\frac{C^2_{\text{HCl}(2)}}{C^2_{\text{HCl}(1)}} = \frac{2RT}{F}\ln\frac{C_2}{C_1}$$

(where, C_1 and C_2 are respective concentration of HCl on the two sides).

For such cases cell EMF is positive if $C_2 > C_1$. In above cell, the extreme electrodes are reversible with respect to the cation, H^+. The extreme electrodes may also be reversible with respect to the anion (Cl^-), when the above cell is written in a reverse way.

$$\overset{(-)}{\text{Ag}}, \text{AgCl}(s);\ \underset{(a_1)}{\text{HCl}},\ \underset{(1\text{ atm})}{H_2(g)}, \text{Pt} \mid \text{Pt}, \underset{(1\text{ atm})}{H_2(g)},\ \underset{(a_2)}{\text{HCl}};\ \text{AgCl}(s), \overset{(+)}{\text{Ag}}$$

$$E_{\text{cell}} = \frac{2RT}{F}\ln\frac{C_1}{C_2}$$

Cell EMF is positive if $C_1 > C_2$.

Electrolyte Concentration Cells with Liquid Junction or Transport

In a cell, if two electrolytic solutions of different concentrations are in contact with each other, a potential difference develops across the boundry of the two solutions. It is called liquid junction potential or the diffusion potential across the interface of two electrolytes.

Example $\overset{(-)}{\text{Pt}}, \underset{(1\text{ atm})}{H_2(g)},\ \underset{(a_1)}{\text{HCl}} \ \vdots\ \underset{(a_2)}{\text{HCl}},\ \underset{(1\text{ atm})}{H_2(g)},\ \overset{(+)}{\text{Pt}}$

$$E_{\text{cell}} = 2t_-\frac{RT}{F}\ln\frac{a_{\pm(2)}}{a_{\pm(1)}}$$

Electrolyte concentration cell with liquid junction, the junction potential being almost completely eliminated by the use of salt bridge

$$\overset{(-)}{\text{Pt}}, \underset{(1\text{ atm})}{H_2(g)},\ \underset{(a_1)}{\text{HCl}} \parallel \underset{(a_2)}{\text{HCl}},\ \underset{(1\text{ atm})}{H_2(g)},\ \overset{(+)}{\text{Pt}}$$

$$E_{\text{cell}} = \frac{RT}{F}\ln\frac{a_{\pm(2)}}{a_{\pm(1)}}$$

Fuel Cells

Fuel cells are galvanic cells in which chemical energy of fuels is directly converted into electrical energy. These cells convert about 75% of the available chemical energy into electrical energy.

Hydrogen-Oxygen Fuel Cell

Electrodes are made of porous carbon impregnated with metallic catalysts (Pt, Ag or metal oxide), electrolyte is hot aqueous KOH.

Oxidation half cell

$$H_2 + 2OH^- \rightleftharpoons 2H_2O + 2e^-] \times 2$$

Reduction half cell

$$O_2(g) + 2H_2O + 4e^- \rightleftharpoons 4OH^-$$

Overall fuel cell reaction

$$2H_2(g) + O_2(g) \rightleftharpoons 2H_2O(l)$$

In place of KOH or NaOH, phosphoric acid can also be used as an electrolyte.

Hydrocarbon-Oxygen Fuel Cells

Fuel cells based on the combustion of hydrocarbons such as CH_4, C_2H_6, C_3H_8 etc., in presence of suitable catalysts as Pt.

Oxidation half cell

$$C_3H_8 + 20OH^- \longrightarrow 3CO_2 + 14H_2O + 20e^-$$

Reduction half cell

$$O_2 + 2H_2O + 4e^- \rightleftharpoons 4OH^-] \times 5$$

Overall fuel cell reaction

$$C_3H_8 + 5O_2 \rightleftharpoons 3CO_2 + 4H_2O$$

Coal-Fired Fuel Reaction

Coal is converted into H_2 and CO by gassification at about 650°C. These gases serve as fuel in molten sodium carbonate electrolyte in presence of catalyst made of alloy of Pt or Cr or V or Ti.

Coal gassification

$$C + H_2O \xrightarrow{O_2} CO + H_2$$

Anode reaction

$$H_2 + CO + 2CO_3^{2-} \longrightarrow 3CO_2 + H_2O + 4e^-$$

Cathode reaction

$$4e^- + 2CO_2 + O_2 \longrightarrow 2CO_3^{2-}$$

Overall fuel cell reaction

$$CO + H_2 + O_2 \longrightarrow CO_2 + H_2O$$

(55% efficient)

Reacently a **zinc-air fuel cell (ZAFC)** has been developed for automobiles.

This uses zinc as fuel in place of hydrogen.

Anode reaction

$$2Zn + 4OH^- \rightleftharpoons 2ZnO + 2H_2O + 4e^-$$

Cathode reaction

$$O_2 + 2H_2O + 4e^- \rightleftharpoons 4OH^-$$

Overall reaction $2Zn + O_2 \rightleftharpoons 2ZnO$

ZnO produced dissolves in the electrolyte. The spent electrolyte is pumped out and subjected to special treatment to regenerate zinc and electrolyte.

Hydrazine-Oxygen Fuel Cell

Hydrate hydrazine is used as a fuel. The fuel electrode is palladium activated porous nickel and the oxygen electrode is porous silver or porous carbon base with small amount of catalysts like Pt black.

Anode reaction

$$N_2H_4 + 4OH^- \longrightarrow N_2 + 4H_2O + 4e^-$$

Cathode reaction

$$O_2 + 2H_2O + 4e^- \longrightarrow 4OH^-$$

Overall cell reaction

$$N_2H_4 + O_2 \longrightarrow N_2 + 2H_2O$$

Actually N_2H_4 acts as a source of H_2 in the cell.

$$N_2H_4 \longrightarrow N_2 + 2H_2$$

and the overall cell reaction is

$$2H_2(g) + O_2(g) \longrightarrow 2H_2O(l)$$

Batteries

The term battery is generally used for two or more galvanic cells connected in series. Thus a battery is an arrangement of electrochemical cells used as an energy source.

Lead Storage Batteries

Anode-a series of lead grids packed with spongy lead, **cathode**-a series of grid packed with PbO_2 and **electrolyte**-38% H_2SO_4 by weight. The overall cell reaction is :

$$Pb(s) + PbO_2(s) + 2H^+ + 2HSO_4^-(aq) \underset{\text{Recharge}}{\overset{\text{Discharge}}{\rightleftharpoons}} 2PbSO_4(s) + 2H_2O(l),\ E° = 1.924\ V$$

Nickel-Cadmium Batteries

Anode-cadmium metal, **cathode**-nickel III compound like NiO(OH) supported on Ni and **electrolyte**-KOH solution. The overall cell reaction is :

$$Cd(s) + 2NiO(OH)(s) + 2H_2O(l) \underset{\text{Recharge}}{\overset{\text{Discharge}}{\rightleftharpoons}} Cd(OH)_2(s) + 2Ni(OH)_2(s)$$

Lithium Batteries

Anode-lithium metal, **cathode**-metal oxide + Li ions and **electrolyte**-$LiClO_4$ in organic solvent.

The overall reaction is

$$MnO_2(s) + Li(s) \underset{\text{Recharge}}{\overset{\text{Discharge}}{\rightleftharpoons}} LiMnO_2(s)$$

Mercury Cell

Anode-zinc, **cathode**-graphite, **electrolyte**-HgO + KOH (moist). The overall cell reaction is

$$Cd(s) + 2Ni(OH)_3 \underset{\text{Recharge}}{\overset{\text{Discharge}}{\rightleftharpoons}} CdO(s) + 2Ni(OH)_2(s) + H_2O(l)$$

Dry Battery

Anode-zinc, **cathode**-graphite and **electrolyte**-$MnO_2 + C$ (touching cathode) $NH_4Cl + ZnCl_2$ (touching anode).

The overall cell reaction is

$$2MnO_2 + 2H_2O + Zn \longrightarrow Zn^{2+} + 2MnO(OH) + 2OH^-$$

Faraday's Laws of Electrolysis

First Law of Electrolysis

The amount of any substance deposited or liberated at any electrode is directly proportional to the quantity of electricity passed through the electrolytic solution.

$$w \propto Q$$

$$w = ZQ = Z\,it$$

where, Z = electrochemical equivalent

Q = charge

Second Law of Electrolysis

It states that when same quantity of electricity is passed through different electrolytic solutions connected in series, the weights of the substance produced at the electrodes are directly proportional to their chemical equivalent weights.

$$\frac{\text{Weight of metal } A}{\text{Weight of metal } B} = \frac{\text{Eq. wt. of } A}{\text{Eq. wt. of } B}$$

Example When same current is passed through copper sulphate and silver nitrate solutions which are connected in series, the weights of Cu and Ag deposited are :

$$\frac{\text{Weight of Cu deposited}}{\text{Weight of Ag deposited}} = \frac{\text{Eq. wt. of Cu}}{\text{Eq. wt. of Ag}}$$

Applications of EMF Measurements

1. In determination of activity coefficients of electrolytes.
2. In determination of transport numbers.
3. In determination of valency of ions in doubtful cases.
4. In determination of the solubility products.
5. In determination of pH.
6. In potentiometric titrations.

Ionic Equilibria

Equilibrium is a dynamic process. It is established in a system when reactants combine to form products at the same rate at which products combine to form reactants. For a reaction in equilibrium.

$$aA + bB \rightleftharpoons cC + dD$$

$$K_c = \frac{[C]^c\,[D]^d}{[A]^a\,[B]^b} \text{ in terms of active mass}$$

$$K_p = \frac{[p_C]^c\,[p_D]^d}{[p_A]^a\,[p_B]^b} \text{ in terms of partial pressure}$$

$$K_x = \frac{[x_C]^c\,[x_D]^d}{[x_A]^a\,[x_B]^b} \text{ in terms of mole fraction}$$

Partial pressure of solid is taken as unity and in calculation of partial pressure of solids their number of moles are not considered.

Relation between K_p, K_c and K_x

$$K_p = K_c\,(RT)^{\Delta n_g}$$

$$K_p = K_x\,(p)^{\Delta n_g}$$

$$\Delta n_g = (c + d) - (a + b)$$

(while determining Δn_g, take only gaseous species).

Ostwald Dilution Law

For a weak acid by Ostwald dilution law

$$K_a = \frac{C\alpha^2}{1-\alpha} \approx C\alpha^2$$

Similarly, for a weak base,

$$K_b = \frac{C\alpha^2}{(1-\alpha)} \approx C\alpha^2$$

$$[H^+] = \sqrt{K_a C}, \quad pH = \frac{1}{2}[pK_a - \log C]$$

$$[OH^-] = \sqrt{K_b C}, \; p^{OH} = \frac{1}{2}[pK_b - \log C]$$

$$\% \text{ dissociation} = \frac{[H^+]_{eq} \times 100}{[HA]_o}.$$

Henderson-Hasselbalch Equation for Buffer

Acidic buffer $pH = pK_a + \log \frac{[\text{Conjugate base}]}{[\text{Weak acid}]}$

Basic buffer $p^{OH} = pK_b + \log \frac{[\text{Conjugate acid}]}{[\text{Weak base}]}$

Buffer range $pH = pK_a \pm 1$

Common Ion Effect

The decrease in the ionization of a weak electrolyte by the presence of a common ion from a strong electrolyte is called common ion effect.

Example 5. *The ionization constant of propanoic acid is 1.32×10^{-5}. Calculate the degree of ionization of the acid in its 0.05 M solution and also its pH. What will be its degree of ionization if the solution is 0.01 M HCl also?*

Sol. $\underset{\text{Propanoic acid}}{CH_3CH_2COOH} + H_2O \rightleftharpoons CH_3CH_2COO^- + H_3O^+$

By Ostwald's dilution law,

Degree of ionization, $\alpha = \sqrt{\frac{K_a}{C}}$

$$\alpha = \sqrt{\frac{1.32 \times 10^{-5}}{0.05}} = 0.0162$$

$$[H_3O^+] = \sqrt{K_a C} = \sqrt{1.32 \times 10^{-5} \times 0.05}$$

$$[H_3O^+] = 8.124 \times 10^{-4} \text{ M}$$

$$pH = -\log [H_3O^+] = 3.09$$

$$K_a = \frac{[CH_3CH_2COO^-][H_3O^+]}{[CH_3CH_2COOH]}$$

In presence of 0.01 M HCl, ionization of weak acid is decreased.

$$\therefore \quad 1.32 \times 10^{-5} = \frac{(0.05 \times \alpha)\, 0.01}{0.05}$$

$$1.32 \times 10^{-5} = 0.01\,\alpha$$

$$\alpha = 1.32 \times 10^{-3}.$$

The Solubility Product Constant, K_{sp}

A solubility product constant expression is the product of the concentrations of the ions appearing in the chemical equation for a solubility equilibrium, with each term raised to the power given by the coefficient in the chemical equation.

$$BaSO_4(s) \rightleftharpoons Ba^{2+}(aq) + SO_4^{2-}(aq)$$

$$K_{sp} = [Ba^{2+}][SO_4^{2-}] = s^2$$

For a solute A_xB_y (giving $(x+y)$ ions)

$$A_xB_y(s) \rightleftharpoons \underset{xs}{xA^{y+}} + \underset{ys}{yB^{x-}}$$

$$K_{sp} = [A^{y+}]^x [B^{x-}]^y$$

$$K_{sp} = (xs)^x (ys)^y = x^x y^y \cdot (s)^{x+y}$$

- Solute AB is precipitated if $[A^+][B^-] > K_{sp}$,

Salt Hydrolysis

- A salt is acidic due to hydrolysis of cation of the salt of weak base and strong acid.

$$NH_4^+ + H_2O \rightleftharpoons NH_4OH + H^+$$

Degree of hydrolysis, $h = \sqrt{\frac{K_w}{K_b C}}$

Hydrolysis constant, $K_h = \frac{K_w}{K_b}$

$$pH = 7 - \frac{pK_b}{2} - \frac{\log C}{2}$$

- A salt is basic due to hydrolysis of anion of the salt of weak acid and strong base.

$$CH_3COO^- + H_2O \rightleftharpoons CH_3COOH + OH^-$$

$$h = \sqrt{\frac{K_w}{K_a C}}$$

$$K_h = \frac{K_w}{K_a}$$

$$pH = 7 + \frac{pK_a}{2} + \frac{\log C}{2}$$

- A salt is neutral due to hydrolysis of salt of weak acid and weak base.

$$CH_3COO^- + NH_4^+ + H_2O \rightleftharpoons CH_3COOH + NH_4OH$$

$$h = \sqrt{\frac{K_w}{K_a K_b}}$$

$$K_h = \frac{K_w}{K_a \cdot K_b}$$

$$pH = 7 + \left(\frac{pK_a - pK_b}{2}\right)$$

$pH = 7$ if $pK_a = pK_b$, $pH < 7$ if $pK_a < pK_b$ and $pH > 7$ if $pK_a > pK_b$.

For amphiprotic anion like HCO_3^-, $pH = \frac{pK_1 + pK_2}{2}$

Conductometric Titrations

Titration in which end point can be determined by measuring conductance at each addition of the titre solution is called **conductometric titration**. The principle involved is that electrical conductance depends upon the number and mobility of ions. Consider the titration of a strong acid (HCl) with a strong base (NaOH).

$$HCl(aq) + NaOH(aq) \rightleftharpoons NaCl(aq) + H_2O$$

$$H^+(aq) + OH^-(aq) \rightleftharpoons H_2O$$

Initially, there is maximum conductance due to HCl (free H^+). As NaOH (OH^-) is added, equivalent H^+ is neutralised and conductance falls. This decrease appears till all the HCl is neutralized. After complete neutralization, further addition of NaOH results in increase in conductance.

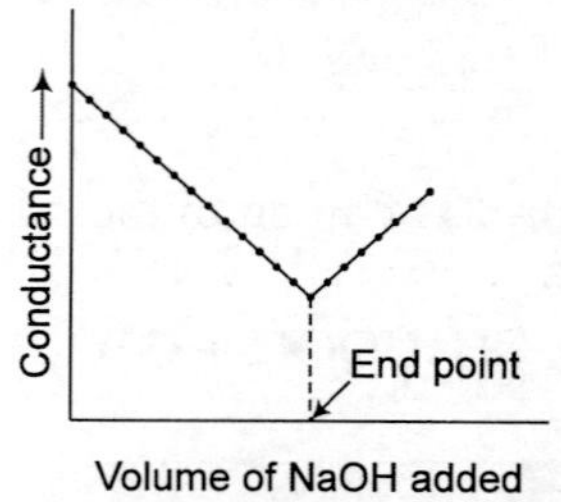

Titration of a strong acid against a strong base.

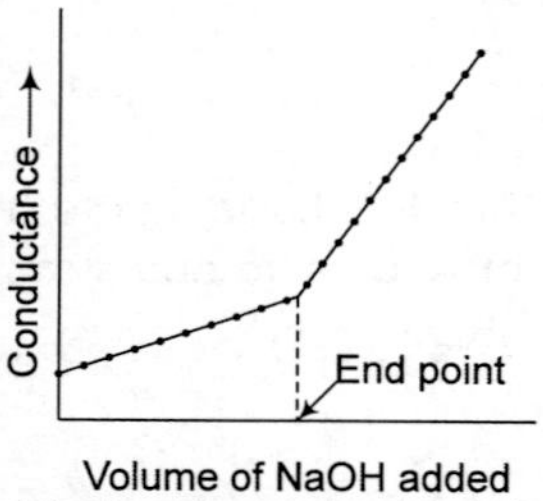

Titration of a weak acid against a strong base.

Potentiometric Titrations

These titrations involve the measurement of electrode potentials with the addition of titrant. There is a sharp change in the potential at the electrode at the equivalence point.

1. Redox Titrations

Let us consider the following redox reaction;

$$Fe^{2+}(aq) + Ce^{4+}(aq) \rightleftharpoons Fe^{3+}(aq) + Ce^{3+}(aq)$$

During titration, these ionic species will be in equilibrium at the electrode. Suppose Ce^{4+} is the titrant added to Fe^{2+} in a beaker in acidic medium. Prior to the addition of Ce^{4+} ions, the solution contains only the Fe^{2+} ions. On adding a small amount of Ce^{4+} ions to the solution, a small amount Fe^{2+} ions is oxidised to Fe^{3+} ions. Before the attainment of the equivalence point, $[Ce^{4+}]$ in the equilibrium mixture is extremely small with the presence of both the Fe^{2+} and Fe^{3+} ions, the electrode behaves as an oxidation-reduction electrode.

$$E_{Pt|Fe^{3+},Fe^{2+}} = E^\circ_{Pt|Fe^{3+},Fe^{2+}} - \frac{RT}{F}\ln\frac{[Fe^{2+}]}{[Fe^{3+}]}$$

During the titration, the ratio $\frac{[Fe^{2+}]}{[Fe^{3+}]}$ decreases and hence electrode potential increases. At the equivalence point, $[Fe^{2+}] = [Ce^{4+}]$ and $[Fe^{3+}] = [Ce^{3+}]$, so that the electrode potential at the equivalent point,

$$E_{eq} = \frac{(E^\circ_{Fe^{3+},Fe^{2+}} + E^\circ_{Ce^{4+},Ce^{3+}})}{2}$$

Once the end point is crossed, $[Fe^{3+}] \approx 0$, as a result of which the electrode potential thereafter is controlled only by the $[Ce^{4+}]/[Ce^{3+}]$ ratio. The electrode potential

$$E_{Pt|Ce^{4+},Ce^{3+}} = E^\circ_{Pt|Ce^{4+},Ce^{3+}} - \frac{RT}{F}\ln\frac{[Ce^{3+}]}{[Ce^{4+}]}$$

With addition of Ce^{4+} there is an increase in E, which becomes gradual on addition of a few drops of the titrant after the end point.

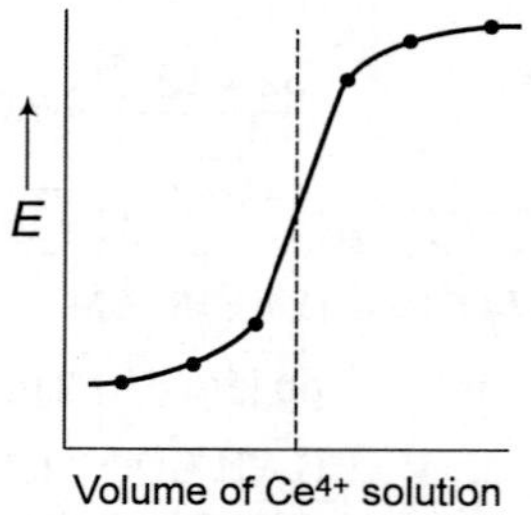

2. Acid Base Titration

Example Titration of HCl against NaOH. An electrode whose potential depends upon H^+ ion concentration like hydrogen electrode is placed in HCl solution. It is connected to reference electrode like calomel electrode to form galvanic cell.

$$Pt, \underset{(1\ atm)}{H_2}, H^+ (C = \text{unknown}) \,||\, \underset{\text{Saturated solution}}{KCl} \;;\; Hg_2Cl_2(s), Hg$$

$$E = E_{calomel} - E_{hydrogen} = 0.2422 - 0.0591 \log H^+$$

$$E = 0.2422 + 0.0591 \text{ pH}$$

As the alkali is added to acid present at the electrode, the H^+ ion concentration decreases and pH of the solution increases. This results in increase in EMF of cell. Actually the EMF of the cell changes slowly at first but more and more rapidly as the equivalence approaches. After the end point, the increase in pH is again gradual.

3. Precipitation Reaction

Example Titration of $AgNO_3$ against KCl solution. In this case silver electrode is used as the indicator electrode.

$$Ag^+ + e^- \longrightarrow Ag$$

$$E = E° + \frac{RT}{F} \log [Ag^+]$$

As $AgNO_3$ is added to the KCl solution at the electrode, at the equivalence point, the potential $E_{Ag^+|Ag}$ sharply increases.

Redox Indicators

These are the organic compounds which can exist in reduced form as well as in oxidised form in equilibrium. Their oxidised and reduced forms have different colours. These indicators when added in small amount to any other redox system say $Fe^{3+}|Fe^{2+}$, they spontaneously adjusted themselves to the same potential as that of the latter. Therefore, the potential of any redox system can be easily obtained by noting the colour shade developed visually or by means of colorimeter. Diphenyl amine is used as a redox indicator in the titration of Fe^{2+} against $K_2Cr_2O_7$ in acidic medium. It shows a sharp change of colour at the equivalence point from colourless to violet, through green as a possible intermediate.

Irreversible Electrode Processes

(i) Over Voltage

In electrolysis, the potential at which the metal ion start depositing at cathode is very close to standard reduction potential of that metal. However, in some cases specially in the case of evolution of gases, the potential required for their liberation is much higher than their standard reduction potential. Therefore, the difference between the potential required for the liberation of a gas and the standard reduction potential of that gas is called over voltage or bubble over voltage.

(ii) Polarography

It is based on the electrolysis of a minute fraction of a solution. The electrolytic cell used in this process consists of a polarizable microelectrode like a dropping mercury electrode and a non-polarizable current carrying electrode like a calomel electrode. The data are obtained by measuring current as a function of applied voltage.

The current-voltage curve are known as polarogram.

Exercise 1
(For Part 'B')

1. Electrolysis of dilute aqueous NaCl solution was carried out by passing 10 mA current. The time required to liberate 0.01 mol of H_2 gas at the cathode is (1 Faraday $= 96500\ C\ mol^{-1}$)

(a) 9.65×10^4 s (b) 19.3×10^4 s
(c) 28.95×10^4 s (d) 38.6×10^4 s

2. Given, $E^\circ_{Fe^{3+}/Fe} = -0.036$ V, $E^\circ_{Fe^{2+}/Fe} = -0.439$ V
The value of standard electrode potential for the charge, $Fe^{3+}(aq) + e^- \longrightarrow Fe^{2+}(aq)$ will be

(a) -0.072 V (b) 0.385 V
(c) 0.770 V (d) -0.270 V

3. The molar conductivities Λ°_{NaOAc} and Λ°_{HCl} at infinite dilution in water at 25°C are 91.0 and 426.2 S cm^2/mol respectively. To calculate Λ°_{AcOH}, the additional value required is

(a) $\Lambda^\circ_{H_2O}$ (b) Λ°_{KCl}
(c) Λ°_{NaOH} (d) Λ°_{NaCl}

4. Given the data at 25°C

$$Ag + I^- \longrightarrow AgI + e^-; \quad E^\circ = 0.152 \text{ V}$$
$$Ag \longrightarrow Ag^+ + e^-; \quad E^\circ = -0.800 \text{ V}$$

What is the value of $\log K_{sp}$ for AgI? $\left(2.303\frac{RT}{F} = 0.059 \text{ V}\right)$

(a) -8.12 (b) $+8.612$ (c) -37.83 (d) -16.13

5. For strong electrolytes the plot of molar conductance *vs* $\sqrt{C}$ is

(a) parabolic (b) linear
(c) sinusoidal (d) circular

6. The molar conductivities of KCl, NaCl and KNO_3 are 152, 128 and 111 S cm^2 mol^{-1} respectively. What is the molar conductivity of $NaNO_3$?

(a) 101 S cm^2 mol^{-1} (b) 87 S cm^2 mol^{-1}
(c) -101 S cm^2 mol^{-1} (d) -391 S cm^2 mol^{-1}

7. What will be the proportion of moles of metal (Cu : Ni : Ag) at cathode according to the second law of Faraday?

(a) 1 : 2 : 1 (b) 2 : 2 : 1
(c) 1 : 2 : 2 (d) 1 : 1 : 2

8. The standard emf of a cell, involving one electron change is found to be 0.591 V at 25°C. The equilibrium constant of the reaction is
($F = 96500\ C\ mol^{-1}$)

(a) 1.0×10^1 (b) 1.0×10^5
(c) 1.0×10^{10} (d) 1.0×10^{30}

9. For the redox reaction,
$Zn(s) + Cu^{2+}(0.1M) \longrightarrow Zn^{2+}(1M) + Cu(s)$ taking place in a cell, E°_{cell}, is 1.10 V. E_{cell} for the cell will be $\left(2.303\frac{RT}{F} = 0.0591\right)$

(a) 2.14 V (b) 1.80 V (c) 1.07 V (d) 0.82 V

10. Aluminium oxide may be electrolysed at 1000°C to furnish aluminium metal (atomic mass = 27 u; 1F = 96500 C). The cathode reaction is

$$Al^{3+} + 3e^- \longrightarrow Al^0$$

To prepare 5.12 kg of aluminium metal by this method would require

(a) 5.49×10^1 C of electricity
(b) 5.49×10^4 C of electricity
(c) 1.83×10^7 C of electricity
(d) 5.49×10^7 C of electricity

11. Simultaneous oxidation and reduction, according to the reaction

$$2Cu^+(aq) \rightleftharpoons Cu^{2+}(aq) + Cu(s)$$

choose correct E° for above reaction if
$E^\circ_{Cu^{2+}/Cu} = 0.34$ V and $E^\circ_{Cu^{2+}/Cu} = 0.15$ V

(a) -0.38 V (b) $+0.49$ V
(c) $+0.38$ V (d) -0.53 V

12. EMF of reduction hydrogen electrode in term of pH is (at 1 atm pressure).

(a) $E_{H_2} = \frac{RT}{F} \times \text{pH}$ (b) $E_{H_2} = \frac{RT}{F} \times \frac{1}{\text{pH}}$
(c) $E_{H_2} = \frac{2.303RT}{F}\text{pH}$ (d) $E_{H_2} = -0.0591$ pH

13. The standard E°_{red} values of *A*, *B* and *C* are $+0.68$ V, -2.54 V, -0.50 V respectively. The order of their reducing power is

(a) $A > B > C$ (b) $A > C > B$
(c) $C > B > A$ (d) $B > C > A$

14. The ionic conductance of Ba^{2+} and Cl^- are respectively 127 and 76 ohm^{-1} cm^2 at infinite dilution. The equivalent conductance (in ohm^{-1} cm^2) of $BaCl_2$ at infinite dilution will be

(a) 139.5 (b) 203
(c) 279 (d) 101.5

15. The one which decreases with dilution is

(a) conductance (b) specific conductance
(c) equivalent conductance (d) molar conductance

16. When a quantity of electricity is passed through $CuSO_4$ solution, 0.16 g of copper gets deposited. If the same quantity of electricity is passed through acidulated water, then the volume of H_2 liberated at STP will be [Given, atomic weight of Cu = 64]

(a) 4.0 cm^3 (b) 56 cm^3
(c) 604 cm^3 (d) 8.0 cm^3

17. Solubility product constant (K_{sp}) of salts of types MX, MX_2 and M_3X at temperature 'T' are 4.0×10^{-8}, 3.2×10^{-14} and 2.7×10^{-15}, respectively.

Solubilities (mol dm^{-3}) of the salts at temperature 'T' are in the order

(a) $MX > MX_2 > M_3X$
(b) $M_3X > MX_2 > MX$
(c) $MX_2 > M_3X > MX$
(d) $MX > M_3X > MX_2$

18. Solid $Ba(NO_3)_2$ is gradually dissolved in a 1.0×10^{-4} M Na_2CO_3 solution. At what concentration of Ba^{2+} will a precipitate begin to form? (K_{sp} for $BaCO_3 = 5.1 \times 10^{-9}$)

(a) 4.1×10^{-5} M (b) 5.1×10^{-5} M
(c) 8.1×10^{-8} M (d) 8.1×10^{-7} M

19. The pK_a of a weak acid, HA, is 4.80. The pK_b of a weak base, BOH, is 4.78. The pH of an aqueous solution of the corresponding salt, BA, will be

(a) 9.58 (b) 4.79
(c) 7.01 (d) 9.22

20. In a saturated solution of the sparingly soluble strong electrolyte $AgIO_3$ (Molecular mass = 283) the equilibrium which sets in is

$$AgIO_3(s) \rightleftharpoons Ag^+(aq) + IO_3^-(aq)$$

If the solubility product constant K_{sp} of $AgIO_3$ at a given temperature is 1.0×10^{-8}, what is the mass of $AgIO_3$ contained in 100 mL of its saturated solution?

(a) 28.3×10^{-2} g (b) 2.83×10^{-3} g
(c) 1.0×10^{-7} g (d) 1.0×10^{-4} g

21. 10^{-6} M NaOH is diluted 100 times. The pH of the diluted bases is

(a) between 5 and 6 (b) between 6 and 7
(c) between 10 and 11 (d) between 7 and 8

22. A monobasic acid solution of 0.005 M has a pH of 5. The degree of ionization of acid is

(a) 0.1×10^{-2} (b) 0.2×10^{-2}
(c) 0.5×10^{-4} (d) 0.6×10^{-6}

23. The standard reduction potentials of $Zn^{2+}|Zn$, $Cu^{2+}|Cu$ and $Ag^+|Cu$ and $Ag^+|Ag$ are respectively −0.76, 0.34 and 0.8 V. The following cells were constructed

1. $Zn|Zn^{2+}||Cu^{2+}|Cu$ 2. $Zn|Zn^{2+}||Ag^+|Ag$
3. $Cu|Cu^{2+}||Ag^+|Ag$

What is the correct order of E°_{cell} of these cells?

(a) 2 > 3 > 1 (b) 2 > 1 > 3
(c) 1 > 2 > 3 (d) 3 > 1 > 2

24. The specific conductivity of 0.1 N KCl solution is 0.0129 ohm^{-1} cm^{-1}. The resistance of the solution in the cell is 100 Ω. The cell constant of the cell will be

(a) 1.10 cm^{-1} (b) 1.29 cm^{-1}
(c) 0.56 cm^{-1} (d) 2.80 cm^{-1}

25. $Zn^{2+} \longrightarrow Zn(s)$; $E^\circ = -0.76$ V

$Cu^{2+} \longrightarrow Cu(s)$; $E^\circ = -0.34$ V

Which of the following is spontaneous?

(a) $Zn^{2+} + Cu \longrightarrow Zn + Cu^{2+}$
(b) $Cu^{2+} + Zn \longrightarrow Cu + Zn^{2+}$
(c) $Zn^{2+} + Cu^{2+} \longrightarrow Zn + Cu$
(d) None of the above

26. Two electrochemical cells $Zn|Zn^{2+}||Cu^{2+}|Cu$ and $Fe|Fe^{2+}||Cu^{2+}|Cu$ are connected in series.

What will be the net emf of the cell at 25°C given $Zn^{2+}|Zn = -0.76$ V, $Cu^{2+}|Cu = +0.34$ V, $Fe^{2+}|Fe = -0.41$ V

(a) 1.10 V (b) 1.85 V (c) 0.75 V (d) −1.85 V

27. A cell is represented by

$Zn|Zn^{2+}(aq)||Cu^{2+}(aq)|Cu$.

Given, $Cu^{2+} + 2e^- \longrightarrow Cu$, $E^\circ = +0.35$ V and $Zn^{2+} + 2e^- \longrightarrow Zn$, $E^\circ = -0.763$ V. Write the cell reactions, emf of the cell and state whether the cell reaction will be spontaneous or not?

	Cell reaction	emf	Spontaneous
(a)	$Zn + Cu^{2+} \longrightarrow Cu + Zn^{2+}$	1.113 V	Yes
(b)	$Zn + Cu^{2+} \longrightarrow Cu + Zn^{2+}$	−1.113 V	Yes
(c)	$Zn + Cu^{2+} \longrightarrow Cu + Zn^{2+}$	−1.113 V	No
(d)	$Cu + Zn^{2+} \longrightarrow Zn + Cu^{2+}$	−1.113 V	No

28. A current of 12 A is passed through an electrolytic cell containing aqueous $NiSO_4$ solution. Both Ni and H_2 gas are formed at the cathode. The current efficiency is 60%. What is the mass of nickel deposited on the cathode per hour?

(a) 7.883 g (b) 3.941 g
(c) 5.91 g (d) 2.645 g

29. The cell reaction of a cell is
$Mg(s) + Cu^{2+}(aq) \longrightarrow Cu(s) + Mg^{2+}(aq)$. If the standard reduction potentials of Mg and Cu are -2.37 and $+0.34$ V respectively. The emf of the cell is
(a) 2.03 V (b) -2.03 V
(c) $+2.71$ V (d) -2.71 V

30. In the electrochemical reaction,
$$2Fe^{3+} + Zn \longrightarrow Zn^{2+} + 2Fe^{2+}$$
increasing the concentration of Fe^{2+}
(a) increases cell emf
(b) increases the current flow
(c) decrease the cell emf
(d) alter the pH of the solution

31. Which one of the following has the highest molar conductivity?
(a) Diaminedichloroplatinum (II)
(b) Tetraaminedichlorocobalt (III) chloride
(c) Potassium hexacynoferrate (II)
(d) Hexaaquochromium (III) bromide

32. On the basis of the following $E°$ values, the strong oxidising agent is
$$[Fe(CN)_6]^{4-} \longrightarrow [Fe(CN)_6]^{3-} + e^- \quad ; E° = -0.35$$
$$Fe^{2+} \longrightarrow Fe^{3+} + e^-; \quad E° = -0.77$$
(a) $[Fe(CN)_6]^{4-}$ (b) Fe^{2+}
(c) Fe^{3+} (d) $[Fe(CN)_6]^{3-}$

33. If $E°_{Fe^{2+}/Fe} = -0.441$ V, and $E°_{Fe^{3+}/Fe^{2+}} = 0.771$ V, the standard emf of the reaction
$$Fe + 2Fe^{3+} \longrightarrow 3Fe^{2+}$$
will be
(a) 0.330 V (b) 1.653 V
(c) 1.212 V (d) 0.111 V

34. Approximate relationship between dissociation constant of water (K) and ionic product of water (K_w) is
(a) $K_w = K$ (b) $K_w = 55.6 \times K$
(c) $K_w = 18 \times K$ (d) $K_w = 14 \times K$

35. What volume of M/10 NaOH is added in 50 mL $\frac{M}{10}$ acetic acid solution to get a buffer solution having highest buffer capacity?
(a) 50 mL (b) 25 mL
(c) 10 mL (d) 40 mL

36. In a mixture of acetic acid and sodium acetate the ratio of concentration of the salt to the acid is increased ten times. Then, the pH of the solution
(a) increases by one (b) decreases by one
(c) decreases ten fold (d) increases ten fold

37. A buffer solution is prepared by mixing equal concentration of acid (ionization constant K_a) and a salt. The pH of buffer is
(a) $pK_a + 7$ (b) $14 - pK_a$
(c) pK_a (d) $pK_a + 1$

38. A weak monobasic acid is half neutralized by a strong base if the pH of the solution is 5.4, its p^{K_a} is
(a) 5.4 (b) 4×10^{-5}
(c) 8.6 (d) 4×10^{-8}

39. Which of the following will decrease the pH of a 50 mL solution of 0.01 M HCl?
(a) Addition of 5 mL of 1 M HCl
(b) Addition of 50 mL of 0.01 M HCl
(c) Addition of 50 mL of 0.002 M HCl
(d) Addition of Mg

40. Calculate the number of H^+ ions present in 1 mL of a solution whose pH is 10.
(a) 1×10^{-13} (b) 6.02×10^{10}
(c) 1×10^{-10} (d) 6.02×10^{13}

41. At 30°C the solubility of Ag_2CO_3 ($K_{sp} = 8 \times 10^{-12}$) would be greatest in 1 L of
(a) 0.05 M Na_2CO_3 (b) 0.05 M $AgNO_3$
(c) pure water (d) 0.05 N NH_3

42. The solubility of Sb_2S_3 in water is 1.0×10^{-5} mol/L at 298 K. What will be its solubility product?
(a) 108×10^{-25} (b) 1.0×10^{-25}
(c) 144×10^{-25} (d) 126×10^{-24}

43. A weak acid, HA, has a K_a of 1.00×10^{-5}. If 0.100 mol of this acid is dissolved in 1 L of water, the percentage of acid dissociated at equilibrium is closest to
(a) 99.0% (b) 1.00%
(c) 99.9% (d) 0.100%

44. What is the $[OH^-]$ in the final solution prepared by mixing 20.0 mL of 0.050 M HCl with 30.0 mL of 0.10 M $Ba(OH)_2$?
(a) 0.40 M (b) 0.0050 M
(c) 0.12 M (d) 0.10 M

45. The pH of 0.1 M solution of the following salts increases in the order
(a) $NaCl < NH_4Cl < NaCN < HCl$
(b) $HCl < NH_4Cl < NaCl, < NaCN$
(c) $NaCN < NH_4Cl < NaCl < HCl$
(d) $HCl < NaCl < NaCN < NH_4Cl$

46. The standard emf of a galvanic cell involving cell reaction with $n = 2$ fould to be 0.295 V at 25°C. The equilibrium constant of the reaction would be
(a) 2×10^{11} (b) 4×10^{12}
(c) 1×10^{2} (d) 1×10^{10}

47. When lead storage battery is charged
(a) lead dioxide dissolves
(b) sulphuric acid is regenerated
(c) the lead electrode becomes coated with lead sulphate
(d) the amount of sulphuric acid decrease

48. $Zn(s) + Cl_2\ (1\,atm) \longrightarrow Zn^{2+} + 2Cl^-$, E°_{cell} of the cell is 2.12 V. To increase E
(a) $[Zn^{2+}]$ should be increased
(b) $[Zn^{2+}]$ should be decreased
(c) $[Cl^-]$ should be decreased
(d) p_{Cl_2} should be decreased

49. The standard potentials at 25°C for the half reactions given against them below

$$Zn^{2+} + 2e^- \longrightarrow Zn\,; \qquad E^\circ = -0.762$$

$$Mg^{2+} + 2e^- \longrightarrow Mg\,; \qquad E^\circ = -2.37$$

When Zn dust is added to a solution of $MgCl_2$
(a) magnesium is precipitated
(b) zinc dissolves in the solution
(c) zinc chloride is formed
(d) no reaction takes place

50. 4.5 g of aluminium (atomic mass 27 u) is deposited at cathode from a molten electrolyte containing Al^{3+} ions by a certain quantity of electric charge. The volume of hydrogen produced at STP from H^+ ions in a solution by the same quantity of electric charge will be
(a) 44.8 L (b) 11.2 L
(c) 22.4 L (d) 5.6 L

51. The resistance of N/10 solution is found to be 2.5×10^3 ohm. The equivalent conductance of the solution is (cell constant $= 1.25\ cm^{-1}$)
(a) $2.5\ ohm^{-1}\ cm^2\ equiv^{-1}$
(b) $5.0\ ohm^{-1}\ cm^2\ equiv^{-1}$
(c) $2.5\ ohm^{-1}\ cm^{-2}\ equiv^{-1}$
(d) $5.0\ ohm^{-1}\ cm^{-2}\ equiv^{-1}$

52. The specific conductance of a saturated solution of silver chloride at 25°C after subtracting the specific conductance of water is $2.28 \times 10^{-4}\ S\ m^{-1}$. Calculate the solubility of silver chloride in grams per dm^3 at this temperature.

$$\Lambda^\circ_{m\ AgCl} = 138.3 \times 10^{-4}\ S\ m^2\ mol^{-1}$$

and $$M_{(AgCl)} = 143.5\ g\ mol^{-1}$$

(a) $2.365 \times 10^{-3}\ g\ dm^{-3}$
(b) $0.2365 \times 10^{-3}\ g\ dm^{-3}$
(c) $23.65 \times 10^{-3}\ g\ dm^{-3}$
(d) $236.5\ g\ dm^{-3}$

53. The mean activity coefficient $\gamma_\pm$ of NaCl at the molality of 0.01 is
(a) 0.226 (b) 0.443
(c) 0.669 (d) 0.889

54. The dissociation constants of formic and acetic acids are 1.77×10^{-4} and 1.75×10^{-5}, respectively. The relative strengths of the two acids will be
(a) 3.18 : 1 (b) 3.18 : 2
(c) 5.50 : 3 (d) 7.46 : 3

55. 25 mL of 4×10^{-5} M solution of $Ba(NO_3)_2$ is mixed with 500 mL of 5×10^{-5} M solution of Na_2SO_4. A precipitate of $BaSO_4$ is formed because ionic product is (K_{sp} ($BaSO_4$) $= 1.08 \times 10^{-10}\ M^2$).
(a) less than K_{sp} (b) more than K_{sp}
(c) equal to K_{sp} (d) None of these

56. Calculate the liquid junction potential at 25°C between two solutions of HCl having mean ionic activities of 0.01 and 0.001, respectively. The transference number of H^+ ion (t_+) in HCl may be taken as 0.83.
(a) 0.039 V (b) 0.0039 V
(c) 0.39 V (d) 3.9 V

57. The mean activity coefficient of 0.001 molal Na_2SO_4 solution is
(a) 0.879 (b) 0.246
(c) 0.571 (d) 0.369

58. Cu^{2+}/Cu^+, $E^\circ = 0.15$ V; $Cu^{2+}\,|\,Cu$, $E^\circ = 0.34$ V. E° for the disproportionation of Cu^+ is
(a) -0.19 V (b) 0.19 V
(c) 0.38 V (d) -0.38 V

59. Titration curve if a strong base is titrated with strong acid is

(a)
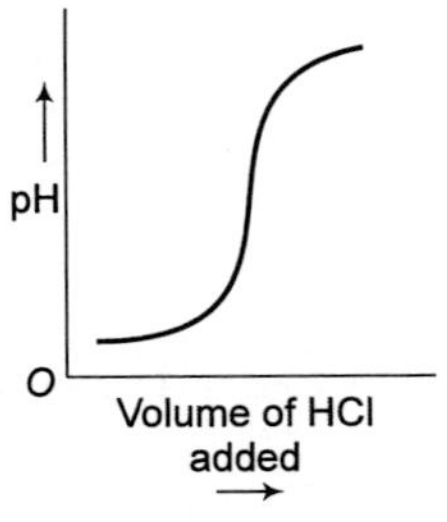

(b)
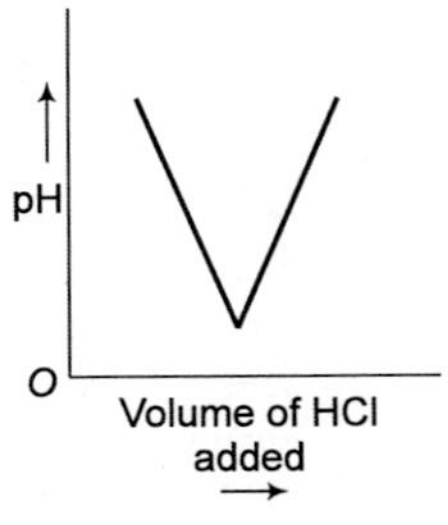

(c)
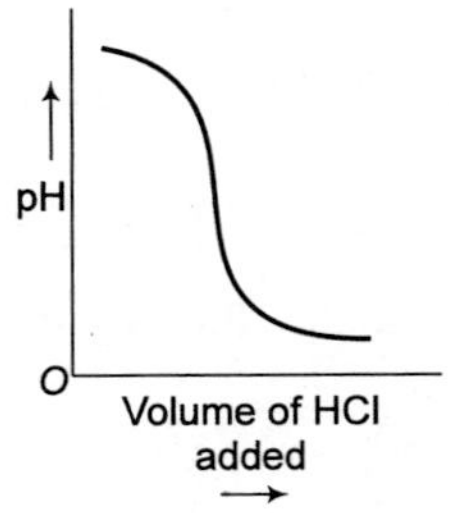

(d)
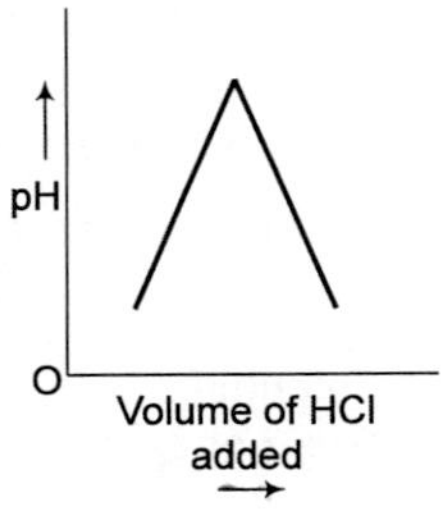

60. An old hand book lets the equivalent conductance of 0.01 N solution of $CaCl_2$ as 120.36 mho cm^2 $equiv^{-1}$. The molar conductance in $ohm^{-1}\ m^2\ mol^{-1}$ is
(a) 2.4072 (b) 240.72
(c) 24.072 (d) 2407.2

61. Under what pressure of $H_2(g)$, half cell Pt $(H_2)|H_2O$ will be have like SHE?
(a) 1×10^{-6} atm (b) 1×10^{-8} atm
(c) 1×10^{-10} atm (d) 1×10^{-14} atm

62. (M^{n+}) solution was electrolyzed for 75 min by a current of 0.30 A. The weight of the metal deposited was 0.958 g. The value of *n* if atomic weight of *M* is 137 is
(a) 1 (b) 2
(c) 3 (d) 4

63. A zinc rod is placed in 0.1 M solution of zinc sulphate at 25°C. Assuming that the salt is dissociated to the extent of 95 per cent at this dilution. The potential of the electrode at 25°C is $(E^\circ_{Zn^{2+}|Zn} = -0.76\ V)$
(a) −0.76 V (b) +0.76 V
(c) +0.79 V (d) −0.79 V

64. Use the Debye-Huckel limiting law to calculate the mean activity coefficient for the ions in an aqueous solution of potassium sulphate, K_2SO_4, of molality 0.010 mol kg^{-1} at 25°C.
(a) 0.943 (b) 1.074
(c) 1.023 (d) 0.932

65. The pK_a of hydrocyanic acid, HCN, is 9.218 at 293 K. Calculate the conductivity of an queous solution of perchloric acid of concentration 0.15 mol dm^{-3}, given that the ionic conductivity of H^+ ions is 35 mS m^2 mol^{-1} and of CN^- ions is 82 mS m^2 mol^{-1}.
(a) 12 m S m^2mol^{-1} (b) 24×10^{-2}m S m^2mol^{-1}
(c) 8.1×10^{-1} m S m^2mol^{-1} (d) 15×10^{-2} m S m^2mol^{-1}

66. For a galvanic cell, which of the following statements is never true?
(a) The potential of cathode is higher than that of the anode
(b) The electrons flow in the external circuit from the anode to the cathode
(c) Reduction takes place at cathode
(d) Oxidation takes place at the anode

67. The standard reaction Gibbs energy for the electrochemical reation

$$Cr_2O_7^{2-} + 2Fe + 14\ H^+ \longrightarrow 2Cr^{3+} + 2Fe^{3+}\ 7H_2O$$

is −793 kJ mol^{-1}. Calculate the standard cell potential.
(a) + 1.37 V (b) + 4.11 V
(c) + 2.74 V (d) + 2.05 V

68. The standard cell potential for the reaction, $2\ NO + \frac{1}{2}O_2 + H_2O \longrightarrow 2NHO_2$ was measured to be + 0.240 V. Calculate the standard reaction Gibbs energy.
(a) − 11 .6 kJ mol^{-1} (b) − 23 .2 kJ mol^{-1}
(c) − 46 .3 kJ mol^{-1} (d) − 96 .5 kJ mol^{-1}

69. The standard cell potential for the reaction $Cu^{2+}(aq) + Fe^{2+}(aq) + I^-(aq) \rightleftharpoons CuI(s) + Fe^{3+}(aq)$ is + 0.090 V. Use the Nernst equation on calculate the electrochemical potential at 298.15 K for the cell Pt (*s*) | CuI_2 (*aq*, 0.010 mol dm^{-3}) | CuI(*s*) | $FeSO_4$ (*aq*, 0.010 mol dm^{-3}), $Fe_2(SO_4)_3$ (*aq*, 0.020 mol dm^{-3})| Pt (*s*)
(a) − 0.147 V (b) − 0.129 V
(c) − 0.309 V (d) − 0.090 V

70. Calculate the equilibrium constant for the reaction $S_2O_8^{2-}(aq) + 2Fe^{2+}(aq) \rightleftharpoons 2Fe^{3+}(aq) + 2SO_4^{2-}(aq)$ at 25°C, given that the standard cells potentials for the two half reactions at this temperature are

$$S_2O_8^{2-}(aq) + 2e^- \rightleftharpoons SO_4^{2-}(aq);\ E^\circ = +2.08\ V$$

$$Fe^{3+}(aq) + e^- \rightleftharpoons Fe^{2+}(aq);\ E^\circ = +0.77\ V$$

(a) 102 (b) 2×10^{96}
(c) 2×10^{44} (d) 2×10^{48}

71. The standard cell potential for the Daniell cell, $Zn(s) + Cu^{2+}(aq) \longrightarrow Zn^{2+}(aq) + Cu(s)$ is +1.102 V at 298 K and +1.095 V at 363 K. Calculate the standard reaction entropy.
(a) + 20.8 J K^{-1} mol^{-1} (b) − 20.8 J K^{-1} mol^{-1}
(c) + 10.4 J K^{-1} mol^{-1} (d) − 10.4 J K^{-1} mol^{-1}

72. Resistance of 0.2 M solution of an electrolyte is 50 Ω. The specific conductance of the solution is 1.3 S m^{-1}. It resistance of the 0.4 M solution of the same electrolyte is 260 Ω, its molar conductivity is
(a) 62.5 S m^2 mol^{-1} (b) 6250 S m^2 mol^{-1}
(c) 6.25×10^{-4} S m^2 mol^{-1} (d) 625×10^{-4} S m^2 mol^{-1}

73. E_1, E_2 and E_3 are the emf values of the three galvanic cells respectively.
I. $Zn|Zn^{+2}_{1m}\ ||\ Cu^{2+}_{0.1m}|\ Cu$
II. $Zn|Zn^{2+}_{1m}\ ||\ Cu^{2+}_{1m}|\ Cu$
III. $Zn|Zn^{+2}_{0.1m}\ ||\ Cu^{2+}_{1m}|\ Cu$
Which one of the following is true?
(a) $E_2 > E_3 > E_1$ (b) $E_3 > E_2 > E_1$
(c) $E_1 > E_2 > E_3$ (d) $E_1 > E_3 > E_2$

74. The standard emf of galvanic cell involving 3 moles of electrons is its redox reaction is 0.59 V. The equilibrium constant for the reaction of the cell is

(a) 10^{25} (b) 10^{20}
(c) 10^{15} (d) 10^{30}

75. An increase in equivalent conductance of a strong electrolyte with dilution is mainly due to
(a) increase in both *i.e.,* number of ions and ionic mobility of ions.
(b) increase in number of ions
(c) increase in ionic mobility of ions
(d) 100% ionization of electrolyte at normal dilution

76. The Gibbs energy for the decomposition of Al_2O_3 at 500°C is at least
(a) 2.5 V (b) 5.0 V
(c) 4.5 V (d) 3.0 V

77. The equivalent conductances of two strong electrolytes at infinite dilution in H_2O (where ions move freely through a solution) at 25°C are given below

$$\overset{\circ}{\Lambda}_{CH_3COONa} = 91.0 \text{ cm}^2\text{/equiv}$$

$$\overset{\circ}{\Lambda}_{HCl} = 426.2 \text{ S cm}^2\text{/equiv}$$

What additional information/quantity one needs to calculate Λ° of an aqueous solution of acetic acid?
(a) Λ° of NaCl
(b) Λ° of CH_3COOK
(c) The limiting equivalent conductance of H^+ ($\overset{\circ}{\lambda}_{H^+}$)
(d) Λ° of chloroacetic acid ($ClCH_2COOH$)

78. Resistance of conductivity cell filled with a solution of an electrolyte of concentration 0.1 M is 100 Ω. The conductivity of this solution is 1.29 S m^{-1}. Resistance of the same cell when filled with 0.2 M of the same solution is 520 Ω. The molar conductivity of 0.02 M solution of the electrolyte will be
(a) 124×10^{-4} S m^2 mol^{-1} (b) 1240×10^{-4} S m^2 mol^{-1}
(c) 1.24×10^{-4} S m^2 mol^{-1} (d) 12.4×10^{-4} S m^2 mol^{-1}

79. Saturated solution of KNO_3 is used to make 'salt bridge' because
(a) velocity of K^+ is greater than that of NO_3^-
(b) velocity of NO_3^- is greater than that of K^+
(c) velocity of both K^+ and NO_3^- are nearly the same
(d) KNO_3 is highly soluble in water

80. For the electrochemical cell

$$M \mid M^+ \parallel X^- \mid X, E°[M^+ \mid M] = 0.44 \text{ V}$$

and $$E°[X \mid X^-] = 0.33 \text{ V}$$

From the data one can deduce that
(a) $M + X \rightarrow M^+ + X^-$ is the spontaneous reaction
(b) $M^+ + X^- \rightarrow M + X$ is the spontaneous reaction
(c) $E_{cell} = 0.77$ V
(d) $E_{cell} = -0.77$ V

81. The standard reduction potential $E°$ for half reactions are
$Zn = Zn^{2+} + Zn$; $E° = +0.76$ V
$Fe = Fe^{2+} + Ze$; $E° = +0.41$ V
The EMF of the cell reaction $Fe^{2+} + Zn = Zn^{2+} + Fe$ is
(a) −0.35 V (b) + 0.35
(c) + 1.17 V (d) −1.17 V

82. Consider the following cell reaction

$$2Fe(s) + O_2(g) + 4H^+(aq) \longrightarrow 2Fe^{2+}(aq) + 2H_2O\,(l); E° = 1.67 \text{ V}$$

At $[Fe^{2+}] = 10^{-3}$ M, $P(O_2) = 0.1$ atm and pH = 3, the cell potential at 25° C is
(a) 1.47 V (b) 1.77 V
(c) 1.87 V (d) 1.57 V

83. The reduction potenital of hydrogen half-cell will be negative if
(a) $p(H_2) = 2$ atm and $[H^+] = 2.0$ M
(b) $p(H_2) = 1$ atm and $[H^+] = 2.0$ M
(c) $p(H_2) = 1$ atm and $[H^+] = 1.0$ M
(d) $p(H_2) = 2$ atm and $[H^+] = 2.0$ M

84. Given $E^{\circ}_{Cr^{3+}/Cr} = -0.72$ V, $E^{\circ}_{Fe^{2+}/Fe} = -0.42$V. The potential for the cell Cr / Cr^{3+} (0.1 M) || Fe^{2+} (0.01 M) | Fe is
(a) −0.26 V (b) 0.26 V
(c) 0.339 V (d) −0.339 V

85. The hydrogen electrode is dipped in a solution of pH 3 at 25°C. The potential would be (the value of 2.303 *RT/F* is 0.059 V)
(a) 0.177 V (b) 0.087 V
(c) 0.059 V (d) − 0.177 V

86. The rusting of iron takes place as follows

$$2H^+ + 2e^- + \frac{1}{2}O_2 \longrightarrow H_2O(l); E° = +\ 1.23 \text{ V}$$

$$Fe^{2+} + 2e^- \longrightarrow Fe\ (s); E° = -\ 0.44 \text{ V}$$

(a) − 332 kJ mol^{-1} (b) −161 kJ mol^{-1}
(c) −152 kJ mol^{-1} (d) −76 kJ mol^{-1}

87.

Electrolyte	KCl	KNO_3	HCl	NaOAc	NaCl
Λ_∞ (S cm^2 mol^{-1})	149.5	145	426.2	91	126.5

Calculate Λ^{∞}_{NaOAc} using appropriate molar conductances of the electrolytes listed above at infinite dilution in H_2O at 25°C
(a) 517.2 (b) 552.7
(c) 390.7 (d) 217.5

88. Zn | Zn^{2+} ($a = 0.1$M) || Fe^{2+} ($a = 0.01$M) | Fe. The emf of the above cell is 0.2905 V. Equilibrium constant for the cell reaction is

(a) $10^{0.32/0.0591}$ (b) $10^{0.32/0.0295}$
(c) $10^{0.26/0.0295}$ (d) $e^{0.32/0.295}$

89. In a cell that utilizes the reaction $Zn(s) + 2H^{+}(aq) \longrightarrow Zn^{2+}(aq) + H_2(g)$ addition of H_2SO_4 to cathode compartment, will :
(a) lower the E and shift equilibrium to the left
(b) lower the E and shift the equilibrium to the right
(c) increase the E and shift the equilibrium to the right
(d) increase the E and shift the equilibrium to the left

90. The electrical conductivity of a new material was measured at different temperature and found to very as below. What is the best description of the conduction properties of the material?

T/K	300	400	500	600
Conductivity/ S m^{-1}	0.004	0.047	0.202	0.535

(a) Insulator
(b) Semiconductor
(c) Conductor
(d) It is not possible to infer anything about the properties of the material.

91. The fuel cell reaction generates electricity directly from H_2 and O_2. The net reaction is $2H_2 + O_2 \longrightarrow 2H_2O$. What potential should the battery generate (under standard conditions)?
(a) 0.40 (b) 0.43
(c) 0.68 (d) 1.23

92. If the electrochemical cell

$$Ba(s)|Ba^{2+}(aq)||Al^{2+}(aq)|Al(s)$$

has "died" and an outside voltage is applied
(a) The concentration of $Ba^{2+}(aq)$ increases
(b) The concentration of $Al^{3+}(aq)$ increases
(c) Nothing happens
(d) The amount of $Al(s)$ increases

93. What are the electrolysis products when a volgate is applied to a molten mixture of MgF_2, KI and Na_2O?
(a) $Mg(s)$ at the cathode $I_2(s)$ at the anode.
(b) $K(s)$ at the cathode $I_2(s)$ at the anode.
(c) $Na(s)$ at the cathode $F_2(g)$ at the anode.
(d) $K(s)$ at the cathode $O_2(g)$ at the anode.

94. Which voltaic cell has the greatest standard potential E°_{cell}?
(a) $Zn(s) \mid Zn^{2+}(aq) \mid\mid Sn^{4+}(aq), Sn^{2+}(aq)$ graphite
(b) $Zn(s)|Zn^{2+}(aq)||Cu^{4+}(aq)|, Cu^{+}(aq)$ graphite
(c) $Ag(s)|Ag^{2+}(aq)||Fe^{3+}(aq)|, Fe^{2+}(aq)$ graphite
(d) $Ba(s)|Ba^{2+}(aq)||Al^{3+}(aq)|, Al(s)$

95. For the balanced cell reaction $Cu(s) + 2Ag^{+}(aq) \longrightarrow Cu^{2+}(aq) + 2\,Ag(s)$, by how much will the voltage of the cell change if the activity of $Ag^{+}(aq)$ is doubled? You may take RT/F to be 0.026 V.
(a) $\Delta E = 0.052\ \ln(1/4)$ V
(b) $\Delta E = -0.026$ V
(c) $\Delta E = 0.013\ \ln(4)$ V
(d) $\Delta E = 0.026\ \ln(4)$ V

96. The below equation defines the standard reduction potential of the normal hydrogen electrode to be zero. What is the approximate pH of the aqueous solution in the normal hydrogen electrode?

$$E^{\circ}_{red}\,[H_2\ (f = 1\ \text{bar})|\,H^{+}\ (a_{\pm} = 1) = 0$$

(a) −1 (b) 0
(c) 1 (d) 7

97. Standard reduction potentials are shown for 2 half-cells below. What is the standard notation for a full cell constructed from these two half cells, the standard potential for the full cell, and the correct value of n to be used in relating the potential to free energy?

$$Cd^{2+}(aq) + 2e^{-} \longrightarrow Cd(s);\ E^{\circ} = -0.40\ V$$

$$In^{3+}(aq) + 3e^{-} \longrightarrow In(s);\ E^{\circ} = -0.34\ V$$

(a) $In\ (s)\,|\,In\ (NO_3)_3(aq)\,||\,CdCl_2(aq)\,|\,Cd(s)$, $E^{\circ} = 0.12\ V, n = 1$
(b) $In\ (s)\,|\,In\ (NO_3)_3(aq)\,||\,CdCl_2(aq)\,|\,Cd(s)$, $E^{\circ} = 0.01\ V, n = 6$
(c) $In(s)\,|\,In(NO_3)_3(aq)\,||\,CdCl_2(aq)\,|\,Cd(s)$, $E^{\circ} = 0.06\ V, n = 1$
(d) $Cd(s)\,|\,CdCl_2(aq)\,||\,In\ (NO_3)_3(aq)\,|\,In(s)$, $E^{\circ} = 0.06\ V, n = 6$

98. Given, the electrochemical cell reaction $H_2(g) + PbSO_4(s) \rightleftharpoons 2H^{+}(aq) + SO_4^{2-}(aq) + Pb(s)$ which of the following changes would not decrease the cell voltage?
(a) Increase in the size of the lead electrode
(b) Decreased solution pH
(c) Dissolution of K_2SO_4
(d) Dissolution of HBr

99. The standard voltage E_0 for this battery, is 1.1 V. The relative concentration of Zn^{+2} (in its container) to Cu^{+2} (in its container) when the battery is dead. (Assume that you do not run out of either Cu of Zn metal) will be
(a) 1.7×10^{28} (b) 1.7×10^{30}
(c) 1.7×10^{20} (d) 1.7×10^{38}

Exercise 2
(For Part 'C')

1. Resistance of a conductivity cell filled with a solution of an electrolyte of concentration 0.1 M is 100 Ω. The conductivity of this solution is 1.29 S m^{-1}. Resistance of the same cell when filled with 0.02 M of the same solution is 520 Ω. The molar conductivity of 0.02 M solution of the electrolyte will be
(a) 124×10^{-4} S m^2 mol^{-1}
(b) 1240×10^{-4} S m^2 mol^{-1}
(c) 1.24×10^{-4} S m^2 mol^{-1}
(d) 12.4×10^{-4} S m^2 mol^{-1}

2. (E°_{cell} = 1.10 V), was allowed to be completely discharged at 298 K. The relative concentration of Zn^{2+} to Cu^{2+} *i.e.,* $\left(\frac{[Zn^{2+}]}{[Cu^{2+}]}\right)$ is
(a) antilog (24.08) (b) 37.3
(c) $10^{37.3}$ (d) 9.65×10^4

3. 2.5 mL of $\frac{2}{5}$ M weak monoacidic base ($K_b = 1 \times 10^{-12}$ at 25°C) is titrated with $\frac{2}{15}$ M HCl in water at 25°C. The concentration of H^+ at equivalence point is ($K_w = 1 \times 10^{-14}$ at 25°C)
(a) 3.7×10^{-13} M (b) 3.2×10^{-7} M
(c) 3.2×10^{-2} M (d) 2.7×10^{-2} M

4. The pK_a of a weak acid (*HA*) is 4.5. The pOH of an aqueous buffer solution of *HA* in which 50% of the acid ionized is
(a) 4.5 (b) 2.5
(c) 9.5 (d) 7.0

5. Solubility product of a salt *AB* is 1×10^{-8} M^2 in a solution in which the concentration of A^+ ions is 10^{-3} M. The salt will precipitate when the concentration of B^- ions is kept
(a) between 10^{-8} M to 10^{-7} M
(b) between 10^{-7} M to 10^{-8} M
(c) $> 10^{-5}$ M
(d) $< 10^{-8}$ M

6. 30 cc of $\frac{M}{3}$ HCl, 20 cc of $\frac{M}{2}$ HNO_3 and 40 cc of $\frac{M}{4}$ NaOH solutions are mixed and the volume was made upto 1 dm^3. The pH of the resulting solution is
(a) 2 (b) 1
(c) 3 (d) 8

7. The concentration of oxalic acid is '*x*' mol L^{-1}. 40 mL of this solution reacts with 16 mL of 0.05 M acidified $KMnO_4$. What is the pH of '*x*' M oxalic acid solution? (Assume that oxalic acid dissociates completely)
(a) 1.3 (b) 1.699
(c) 1.0 (d) 2.0

8. pH of a buffer solution decreases by 0.02 units when 0.12 g of acetic acid is added to 250 mL of a buffer solution of acetic acid and potassium acetate at 27°C. The buffer capacity of the solution is
(a) 0.1 (b) 10
(c) 1 (d) 0.4

9. 20 mL of 0.1 M acetic acid is mixed with 50 mL of potassium acetate. K_a of acetic acid $= 1.8 \times 10^{-5}$ at 27°C. Calculate concentration of potassium acetate if pH of the mixture is 4.8.
(a) 0.1 M (b) 0.04 M
(c) 0.4 M (d) 0.02 M

10. For the following cell reaction,

$$Ag | Ag^+ | AgCl | Cl^\ominus, | Cl, Pt$$

$$\Delta G^\circ_f \text{ (AgCl)} = -109 \text{ kJ/mol}$$

$$\Delta G^\circ_f \text{ } (Cl^\ominus) = -129 \text{ kJ/mol}$$

$$\Delta G^\circ_f \text{ } (Ag^+) = 78 \text{ kJ/mol}$$

E° of the cell is
(a) −0.60 V (b) 0.60 V
(c) 6.0 V (d) None of these

11. If the H^+ concentration is decreased from 1 M to 10^{-4} M at 25°C for the couple MnO_4^-/Mn^{2+}, then the oxidising power of the MnO_4^-/Mn^{2+} couple changes by
(a) −0.18 V (b) 0.18 V
(c) 0.38 V (d) −0.38 V

12. The potential of the cell for the reaction,
$M(s) + 2H^+ \text{ (1M)} \longrightarrow H_2(g) \text{ (1 atm)} + M^{2+} \text{ (0.1 M)}$
is 1.500 V. The standard reduction potential for $M^{2+}/M(s)$ couple is
(a) 0.1470 V (b) −1.470 V
(c) 14.70 V (d) None of these

13. An alloy of Pb-Ag weighing 1.08 g was dissolved in dilute HNO_3 and the volume made to 100 mL. A silver electrode was dipped in the solution and the emf of the cell set up $Pt(s), H_2(g) | H^+ \text{ (1M)} || Ag^+(aq) | Ag(s)$ was 0.62 V. If E°_{cell} = 0.80 V what is

the percentage of Ag in the alloy? [At 25°C, $RT/F = 0.06$]
(a) 25 (b) 2.50
(c) 10 (d) 50

14. The equivalent conductance of $\frac{M}{32}$ solution of a weak monobasic acid is 8.0 mho S cm^2 and at infinite dilution is 400 mho S cm^2. The dissociation constant of this acid is
(a) 1.25×10^{-6} (b) 6.25×10^{-4}
(c) 1.25×10^{-4} (d) 1.25×10^{-5}

15. For a concentrated solution of a weak electrolyte $A_x B_y$ of concentration 'C', the degree of dissociation 'α' is given as
(a) $\alpha = \sqrt{K_{eq}/C(x+y)}$
(b) $\alpha = \sqrt{K_{eq}C/(xy)}$
(c) $\alpha = (K_{eq}/C^{-x+y-1}x^x y^y)^{1/(x+y)}$
(d) $\alpha = \frac{K_{eq}}{Cxy}$

16. Solubility product of $Mg(OH)_2$ at ordinary temperature is 1.96×10^{-11}. pH of a saturated solution of $Mg(OH)_2$ will be
(a) 10.53 (b) 8.47
(c) 6.94 (d) 3.47

17. The solubility product of a salt having formula M_2X_3 is 2.2×10^{-20}. If the solubility of an another salt having formula M_2X is twice the molar solubility of M_2X_3, the solubility product of M_2X is
(a) 3×10^{-12} (b) 9.16×10^{-5}
(c) 4.58×10^{-5} (d) 2.76×10^{-18}

18. The emf of Daniell cell at 298 K is E_1
$Zn \mid ZnSO_4\ (0.01\,M) \mid\mid CuSO_4\ (1.0\,M) \mid Cu$
When the concentration of $ZnSO_4$ is 1.0 M and that of $CuSO_4$ is 0.01 M, the emf changed to E_2. What is the relation between E_1 and E_2?
(a) $E_1 = E_2$ (b) $E_2 = 0 \neq E_2$
(c) $E_1 > E_2$ (d) $E_1 < E_2$

19. Standard free energies of formation (in kJ/mol) at 298 K are −237.2, −394.4 and −8.2 for $H_2O(l)$, $CO_2(g)$ and pentane (g), respectively. The value of E°_{cell} for the pentane-oxygen fuel cell is
(a) 1.968 V (b) 2.0968 V
(c) 1.0968 V (d) 0.0968 V

20. Two concentration cells of Ag and Ag electrode in $AgNO_3$. In first cell concentration of one electrode is 1 M and other electrode is 0.1 M and emf is 0.06 V. In second cell concentration of one electrode is 1 M and other electrode is 0.01 M, calculate emf of second cell
(a) 0.12 V (b) 0.06 V
(c) 0.09 V (d) 0.16 V

21. In an experiment 0.04 F was passed through 400 mL of a 1 M solution of NaOH. What would be the pH of the solution after the electrolysis?
(a) 8.00 (b) 10.00
(c) 13.95 (d) 0.046

22. The molar conductances at infinite dilution of HCl, NaCl and NaZ (sodium crotonate) are 425×10^{-4}, 125×10^{-4} and 80×10^{-4} S m^2 mol^{-1}, respectively. The specific conductance of 0.001 M aqueous solution of crotonic acid (HZ) is 3.8×10^{-3} S m^{-1}. Calculate the degree of dissociation and the dissociation constant of the acid.
(a) 2.22×10^{-5} mol dm^{-3} (b) 1.11×10^{-5} mol dm^{-3}
(c) 1.11×10^{-3} mol dm^{-3} (d) 2.22×10^{-3} mol dm^{-3}

23. A buffer solution contains 0.2 mole of acetic acid and 0.25 mole of potassium acetate per litre. Calculate the change in pH of the solution if 0.5 mL of 1 M HCl is added to it. The dissociation constant of acetic acid at room temperature is 1.75×10^{-5}. (The volume change on the addition of HCl may be neglected).
(a) 0.001 (b) 0.002
(c) 0.003 (d) 0.004

24. The dissociation constants of aniline, acetic acid and water at 25°C are 3.83×10^{-10}, 1.75×10^{-5} and 1.008×10^{-14}. The percentage hydrolysis of aniline acetate in a decimolar solution is
(a) 17.43 (b) 29.25
(c) 54.95 (d) 66.17

25. EMF of the cell Cd(s), $CdCl_2$ ($m = 0.02$) |AgCl(s), Ag(s) is found to be 0.780 V at 25°C. Using the standard potentials $E^\circ_{Cd^{2+}/Cd} = -0.403$ V and $E^\circ_{AgCl/Cl^-} = 0.222$ V, the mean ionic activity coefficient of $CdCl_2$ at 25°C is
(a) 0.036 (b) 0.227
(c) 0.437 (d) 0.558

26. EMF of the concentration cell with transference Pt/H_2 (1 atm), HCl ($a_\pm = 0.0090$) : HCl ($a_\pm = 0.018$), H_2 (1 atm)/Pt is 0.028 V at 25°C. The EMF of the corresponding cell without transference is 0.017 V. The transference number of H^+ ion is
(a) 0.8 (b) 0.2
(c) 0.4 (d) 0.6

27. The amount of $(NH_4)_2SO_4$ in gram which must be added to 500 mL of 0.2 M NH_4OH to yield a solution of pH 9.35 is (Given pK_a of $NH_4^+ = 9.26$)
(a) 2.66 g (b) 3.45 g
(c) 5.35 g (d) 7.01 g

28. Calcium lactate is a salt of weak organic acid and strong base, represented as $Ca(LaC)_2$. A saturated solution of Ca $(LaC)_2$ contains 0.13 mole of this salt in 0.50 L solution. The pOH of this solution is 5.60. Assuming a complete dissociation of the salt, calculate K_a of lactic acid.
(a) 8.3×10^{-2} (b) 8.3×10^{-4}
(c) 8.3×10^{-6} (d) 8.3×10^{-8}

29. Calculate the pH at the equivalence point when a solution of 0.01 M CH_3COOH is titrated with a solution of 0.01 M NaOH. pK_a of CH_3COOH is 4.74.
(a) 2.11 (b) 4.22 (c) 6.22 (d) 8.22

30. The ionization constant of benzoic acid is 6.46×10^{-5} and K_{sp} for silver benzoate is 2.5×10^{-13}. How many times is silver benzoate more soluble in a buffer of pH 3.19 compared to its solubility in pure water?
(a) 1.6 (b) 3.2 (c) 4.8 (d) 6.4

31. The normal electrode potential of zinc is -0.76 V and that of silver is 0.8 V (both referred to normal hydrogen electrode). Calculate the EMF of the cell at 25°C.

$$\overset{\ominus}{Zn} \mid \underset{0.5\ N}{Zn(NO_3)_2} \parallel \underset{0.1\ N}{AgNO_3} \mid \overset{\oplus}{Ag}$$

The mean activity coefficient of $Zn(NO_3)_2$ and $AgNO_3$ are 0.5 and 0.8 respectively.
(a) 4.267 V (b) 3.953 V
(c) 2.501 V (d) 1.513 V

32. The molar solubility of $Zn(OH)_2$ in 1 M ammonia solution at room temperature is (K_{sp} $Zn(OH)_2$ $=1.8 \times 10^{-17}$; K_{stab} $[Zn(NH_3)_4]^{2+} = 1.64 \times 10^{10}$)
(a) 6.653×10^{-3} mol dm^{-3} (b) 6.653×10^{-2} mol dm^{-3}
(c) 6.653×10^{2} mol dm^{-3} (d) 6.653×10^{3} mol dm^{-3}

33. At 25°C the specific conductance of distilled water is 58.0×10^{-7} S m^{-1} the Λ_m° values for H^+ and OH^- ions are 349.8×10^{-4} and 198.5×10^{-4} S m^2 mol^{-1} respectively. Assuming that Λ_m differs very little from Λ_m°. The ionic product of water at 25°C is
(a) 1.0×10^{-14} mol^2 dm^{-6} (b) 1.12×10^{-14} mol^2 dm^{-6}
(c) 1.12×10^{-13} mol^2 dm^{-6} (d) 1.0×10^{-13} mol^2 dm^{-6}

34. A conductivity cell, when filled with an aqueous solution of 0.02 M KCl at 25°C, had a resistance of 250 ohm. Its resistance, when filled with 6×10^{-5} M NH_4OH solution was 10^5 ohm. The specific conductance of 0.02 M KCl was 0.277 S m^{-1}. The molar conductances at infinite dilution of NH_4^+ and OH^- ions are 73.4×10^{-4} and 198.0×10^{-4} S m^2 mol^{-1}, respectively. The degree of dissociation of 6×10^{-5} M NH_4OH solution is
(a) 0.424 (b) 0.526
(c) 0.601 (d) 0.703

35. Calculate the EMF of the cell at 25°C
$Ag \mid \frac{N}{25}\ AgNO_3 \mid$ bridge solution $\mid \frac{N}{1000}\ AgNO_3 \mid Ag^+$;
activity coefficient of $\frac{N}{100}$ solution is 0.8
(a) -0.023 V (b) -0.341 V
(c) -0.079 V (d) -0.086 V

36. Consider the Zn/Cu battery described by : $Zn \mid Zn^{+2} \parallel Cu^{2+} \mid Cu$. The battery, when new has a measured potential of 1 V.
Electrical work that we can get from this battery, when the battery is run at a current of 0.1 A for 1000 s (about 20 min). (An amp, 1, is a coul/sec. Assume that the loss of material is small enough that the potential of the battery does not change significantly) will be
(a) 1000 J (b) 100 J
(c) 10 kJ (d) 100 kJ

37. An electrochemical cell consists of a standard hydrogen electrode and a copper metal electrode. If you wish to constructed a combination curve to show now the cell potential varies with $|Cu^{2+}|$, what should you plot to obtain a straight line and slope ?
(a) Voltage on ordinate and Cu concentration on abscissa and slope is + 20 mV.
(b) Voltage on abscissa and Cu concentration on ordinate and + 30 mV slope
(c) Voltage on ordinate and log of Cu concentration on abscissa and + 30 mV slope
(d) Voltage on abscissa and log of Cu concentration on ordinate and slope is 20 mV.

38. For the reduction of NO_3^- ion in an aqueous solution $E°$ is + 0.96 V. Values of $E°$ for some metal ions are given below :

$V^{2}_{(aq)} + 2e^- \longrightarrow V;$ $E° = -1.19$ V

$Fe^{3+}_{(aq)} + 3e^- \longrightarrow Fe;$ $E° = -0.04$ V

$Au^{3+}_{(aq)} + 3e^- \longrightarrow Au;$ $E° = +1.40$ V

$Hg^{2+}_{(aq)} + 2e^- \longrightarrow Hg;$ $E° = +0.86$ V

The pair(s) of metals that is (are) oxidized by NO_3^- in aqueous solution is (are)
(a) V and Hg (b) Hg and Fe
(c) Fe and Au (d) Fe and V

39. Which of the following decreases with increase in concentration?
(a) Conductance
(b) Specific conductance
(c) Equivalent conductance
(d) Molar conductance

Mathcing Type

40. Match the terms (in Column I) with corresponding units (in Column II).

Column I		Column II	
A.	Transport number	1.	$cm^2\ v^{-1}\ s^{-1}$
B.	Ionic mobility	2.	$ohm^{-1}\ cm^2\ mol^{-1}$
C.	Ionic conductivity	3.	$ohm^{-1}\ cm^{-1}$
D.	Cell constant	4.	unit-less
		5.	cm^{-1}

Codes

	A	B	C	D
(a)	3	2	4	1
(b)	4	1	2	5
(c)	5	2	3	1
(d)	2	3	4	1

41. Match the physical term (in Column I) with the unit (in Column II).

Column I		Column II	
A.	Conductance	1.	Siemen m^2 mo^{-1}
B.	Resistivity	2.	m^{-1}
C.	Conductivity	3.	Volt per ampere
D.	Molar conductivity	4.	Siemen
E.	Cell constant	5.	Siemen m^{-1}
F.	Resistance	6.	ohm metre

Codes

	A	B	C	D	E	F
(a)	4	6	5	1	2	3
(b)	6	5	4	3	2	1
(c)	5	6	4	3	1	2
(d)	2	3	5	1	4	6

42. Match the effect of addition of 1 M NaOH to 100 mL. 1 M CH_3COOH (in Column I) with pH (in Column II).

Column I		Column II	
A.	25 mL of NaOH	1.	pK_a
B.	50 mL of NaOH	2.	$pK_a + \log 3$
C.	75 mL of NaOH	3.	$pK_a - \log 3$
D.	100 mL of NaOH	4.	$\frac{1}{2}[pK_w + pK_a - \log 2]$

Codes

	A	B	C	D
(a)	3	1	2	4
(b)	2	1	4	3
(c)	4	3	2	1
(d)	4	2	1	3

43. Match the salt (in Column I) with its equation of pH (in Column II).

Column I (Salt)		Column II (pH)	
A.	Weak acid and strong base	1.	$\frac{1}{2}pK_w$
B.	Strong acid and weak base	2.	$\frac{1}{2}[pK_w + pK_a - pK_b]$
C.	Weak acid and weak base	3.	$\frac{1}{2}[pK_w - pK_b - \log C]$
D.	Strong acid and strong base	4.	$\frac{1}{2}[pK_w + pK_a + \log C]$

Codes

	A	B	C	D
(a)	3	4	1	2
(b)	4	3	2	1
(c)	2	1	4	3
(d)	4	1	3	2

Assertion & Reason

(a) Both A and R are true and R is the correct explanation of A.
(b) Both A and R are true but R is not the correct explanation of A.
(c) A is true but R is false.
(d) A is false but R is true.

44. **Assertion (A)** The aqueous solution of CH_3COONa is alkaline in nature.

Reason (R) Acetate ion undergoes anionic hydrolysis.

45. **Assertion (A)** For the Daniel cell $Zn|Zn^{2+}||Cu^{2+}|Cu$ with $E°_{cell} = 1.1$ V, the application of opposite potential greater than 1.1 V results into flow of electron from cathode to anode.

Reason (R) Zn is deposited at anode and Cu is deposited at cathode.

46. **Assertion (A)** Equivalent conductivity of a weak electrolyte at infinite dilution can be found be Kohlrausch law.

Reason (R) Kohlraush law is applicable only to weak electrolyte.

47. **Assertion (A)** Equivalent conductance of all electrolytes decreases with increasing concentration.

Reason (R) Lesser number of ions are available per g equivalent at higher concentration.

Directions (Q. Nos. 48 to 51)

The overall reaction in the lead battery is

$$Pb(s) + PbO_2(s) + 2H^+(aq) + 2HSO_4^-(aq) \rightarrow 2PbSO_4(s) + 2H_2O(l)$$

where, $E^0_{cell} = 2.04$ V

One of the half reactions is

$$PbSO_4(s) + 2e^- + H^+(aq) \longrightarrow Pb(s) + HSO_4^-(aq)$$

48. Number of electrons transferred during the reaction per unit reaction is
(a) 1 (b) 3 (c) 2 (d) 4

49. When the concentration of the sulphuric acid is 5 M. Assume the sulphuric acid is a strong acid, dissociating the first proton only, therefore $[H^+] = [HSO_4^-] = 5$ M. The value of E_{cell} at 25°C and 1 atm will be
(a) 1.96 V (b) 2.123 V (c) −1.96 V (d) −2.123 V

50. For the cell chemical reaction, at −40°C, the free energy of reaction is $\Delta G = -377.5$ kJ, E_{cell} athis new temperature. (You may assume that all species are at unit molar concentration) will be
(a) 1.96 V (b) 2.123 V (c) − 1.96 V (d) − 2.123 V

51. What will be the pH of the lead storage battery when the battery has a measured voltage of 1.5 V?
(a) 0.54 (b) 1.18 (c) 4.6 (d) 5.4

Directions (Q. Nos. 52 to 55)

$2Cu^{2+}(aq) + Zn(s) \longleftrightarrow 2Cu^+(aq) + Zn^{2+}(aq)$ at 298

52. What is the standard cell potential, $E°_{cell}$?
(a) 1.10 V (b) 0.91 V
(c) 0.61 V (d) 0.0 V

53. What is the equilibrium constant, K?
(a) 6×10^{30} (b) 70
(c) 2×10^{-30} (d) 2×10^{15}

54. What is the standard Gibbs free energy, $\Delta G°$?
(a) −80 kJ (b) 80 kJ
(c) − 200 kJ (d) 200 kJ

55. If the concentrations of ions are $[Cu^+] = 2M$, $[Zn^{2+}] = 1M$, $[Cu^{2+}] = 1 \times 10^{-7}$ M, then
(a) the reaction is spontaneous in the forward direction
(b) the reaction is nonspontaneous in the forward direction
(c) the reaction is at equilibrium.
(d) None of the above

Directions (Q. Nos. 56 to 59)

Consider a battery made with a beaker (*A*) containing a solution of $AgNO_3 \longrightarrow Ag^+(aq) + NO_3^-(aq)$ with a silver electrode and a second beaker (*B*) containing a solution of $Cu(NO_3)_2 \longrightarrow Cu^{2+}(aq) + 2NO_3^-(aq)$ and a copper electrode. Both salts completely dissociate. Initially the concentration of each of the two metals in the ionic form is 1 M.

56. Standard free energy $\Delta G°$, of the cell above will be
(a) 0.46 kJ (b) −88.8 kJ
(c) −0.46 kJ (d) +88.8 kJ

57. Standard voltage of the cell is
(a) 0.46 V (b) 1.14 V
(c) − 0.46 V (d) − 1.14 V

58. A new battery is made up using 0.01 M $AgNO_3$ in solution in beaker *A* and 0.0001 M $Cu(NO_3)_2$ in beaker *B*. What is the voltage of this new cell?
(a) 0 (b) 0.46 V
(c) 1.14 V (d) − 1.14 V

59. Now NaCl is added to beaker *A* of the battery described in Q. 58 so that the concentration should be 0.01 M NaCl. However the chloride ion combines with the silver ion to precipitate in the reaction :

$Ag^+(aq) + Cl^-(aq) \rightleftharpoons AgCl(solid)\downarrow$, leaving behind sodium ions at 0.01 M Na^+. [Nothing is changed in beaker *B* from Q. 58]. After the addition of the sodium chloride the battery voltage reads 0.28 V. What is the concentration of silver ions remaining in solution in beaker *A*?
(a) 5.5×10^{-5} M (b) 9.8×10^{-5} M
(c) 9.8×10^{-6} M (d) 8.9×10^{-6} M

Directions (Q. Nos. 60 to 65)

The overall reaction and equilibrium constant value of a hydrogen-oxygen fuel cell at 298 K is $2H_2(g) + O_2(g) \longrightarrow 2H_2O(l)$ $K = 1.28 \times 10^{83}$

60. Calculate $E°$ at 298 K for the fuel cell reaction.
(a) 12.3 V (b) 1.23 V
(c) 0.123 V (d) .00123 V

61. $\Delta G°_{exn}$ at 298 K for the above fuel cell will be
(a) −113 kJ (b) − 226 kJ
(c) +113 kJ (d) + 226 kJ

62. The signs of ΔH and ΔS for fuel cell will be
(a) Both negative
(b) ΔH negative, ΔS = positive
(c) ΔH positive, ΔS = negative
(d) Both zero

63. In the above fuel cell which of the following statements is true
(a) $\Delta S = 0$
(b) ΔS = positive as gas going to liquid
(c) ΔS = negative as gas going to liquid
(d) None of the above

64. As temperature increases does the maximum amount of work obtained from the fuel cell reaction will
(a) decrease
(b) increase
(c) remains same
(d) can increase or can decrease

65. Consider the cell described as $Al | Al^{3+}$ (1.00 M) || Pb^{2+} (1.00 M) | Pb, the cell potential at the start of runing the battery and change in cell potential after the reaction has operated long enough for $[Al^{3+}]$ to have change by 0.2 mol/L (Assuming $T = 25°C$) will be respectively.
(a) 1.53 V and + 6 mV (b) − 1.79 V and + 9 mV
(c) 1.53 V and − 6 mV (d) − 1.79 V and − 9 mV

Answers

Exercise 1

1. (b)	**2.** (c)	**3.** (d)	**4.** (d)	**5.** (b)	**6.** (b)	**7.** (d)	**8.** (c)	**9.** (c)	**10.** (d)
11. (d)	**12.** (d)	**13.** (d)	**14.** (a)	**15.** (b)	**16.** (b)	**17.** (d)	**18.** (b)	**19.** (c)	**20.** (b)
21. (d)	**22.** (b)	**23.** (b)	**24.** (b)	**25.** (b)	**26.** (d)	**27.** (a)	**28.** (a)	**29.** (c)	**30.** (c)
31. (c)	**32.** (c)	**33.** (c)	**34.** (b)	**35.** (b)	**36.** (a)	**37.** (c)	**38.** (a)	**39.** (d)	**40.** (b)
41. (d)	**42.** (a)	**43.** (b)	**44.** (d)	**45.** (b)	**46.** (d)	**47.** (b)	**48.** (b)	**49.** (d)	**50.** (d)
51. (a)	**52.** (a)	**53.** (d)	**54.** (a)	**55.** (a)	**56.** (a)	**57.** (a)	**58.** (c)	**59.** (c)	**60.** (a)
61. (d)	**62.** (b)	**63.** (d)	**64.** (d)	**65.** (b)	**66.** (a)	**67.** (a)	**68.** (c)	**69.** (a)	**70.** (c)
71. (b)	**72.** (c)	**73.** (b)	**74.** (d)	**75.** (c)	**76.** (a)	**77.** (a)	**78.** (d)	**79.** (c)	**80.** (b)
81. (b)	**82.** (d)	**83.** (d)	**84.** (b)	**85.** (d)	**86.** (a)	**87.** (c)	**88.** (b)	**89.** (c)	**90.** (b)
91. (d)	**92.** (b)	**93.** (a)	**94.** (d)	**95.** (c)	**96.** (b)	**97.** (b)	**98.** (a)	**99.** (d)	

Exercise 2

1. (a)	**2.** (c)	**3.** (c)	**4.** (c)	**5.** (c)	**6.** (a)	**7.** (c)	**8.** (d)	**9.** (b)	**10.** (a)
11. (d)	**12.** (b)	**13.** (d)	**14.** (d)	**15.** (c)	**16.** (a)	**17.** (a)	**18.** (c)	**19.** (c)	**20.** (a)
21. (c)	**22.** (b)	**23.** (b)	**24.** (c)	**25.** (d)	**26.** (a)	**27.** (c)	**28.** (b)	**29.** (d)	**30.** (b)
31. (d)	**32.** (a)	**33.** (b)	**34.** (a)	**35.** (c)	**36.** (b)	**37.** (c)	**38.** (a,b,d)	**39.** (a,c,d)	**40.** (b)
41. (a)	**42.** (a)	**43.** (b)	**44.** (b)	**45.** (a)	**46.** (c)	**47.** (c)	**48.** (c)	**49.** (b)	**50.** (a)
51. (c)	**52.** (b)	**53.** (a)	**54.** (c)	**55.** (a)	**56.** (d)	**57.** (a)	**58.** (c)	**59.** (d)	**60.** (c)
61. (c)	**62.** (a)	**63.** (c)	**64.** (a)	**65.** (b)					

Hints & Solutions

Exercise 1

1. $2H_2O + 2e^- \longrightarrow H_2 + OH^-$

$$w = Zit$$

$$Z = \frac{\text{Molar mass}}{\text{Electrons} \times 96500}$$

$$= \frac{2}{2 \times 96500} = \frac{1}{96500}$$

$$w = 0.01 \text{ mole} = 0.02 \text{ g } H_2$$

$$i = 10 \times 10^{-3} \text{ A}$$

$$t = ?$$

$$0.02 = \frac{1 \times 10^{-2} \times t}{96500}$$

$$t = 2 \times 96500 \text{ s}$$

$$= 19.3 \times 10^4 \text{ s}$$

4.

$$AgI(s) + e^- \rightleftharpoons Ag(s) + I^-; \; E° = -0.152$$

$$Ag(s) \longrightarrow Ag^+ + e^-; \; E° = -0.8$$

$$AgI(s) \longrightarrow Ag^+ + I^-; \; E° = -0.952$$

$$E°_{cell} = \frac{0.059}{n} \log K_{sp}$$

$$-0.952 = \frac{0.059}{1} \log K_{sp}$$

$$\log K_{sp} = \frac{-0.952}{0.059} = -16.135.$$

9. $E_{cell} = E°_{cell} - \dfrac{0.0591}{n} \log Q$

$$\underset{0.1\,M}{Cu^{2+}} + Zn \longrightarrow \underset{1\,M}{Zn^{2+}} + Cu$$

$$Q = \frac{[Zn^{2+}]}{[Cu^{2+}]} = \frac{1}{0.1} = 10$$

$$E_{cell} = 1.10 - \frac{0.0591}{2} \log 10$$

$$E_{cell} = 1.10 - 0.0295 = 1.0705 \text{ V}.$$

11. $\Delta G° = -nFE°$

(i) $Cu(s) \longrightarrow Cu^{2+}(aq) + 2e^-; \; \Delta G_1° = -2 \times (-0.34) \times F$

(ii) $Cu^{2+}(aq) + e^- \longrightarrow Cu^+(aq); \; \Delta G_2° = -1 \times (0.15)\, F$

On addition :

$$Cu(s) \longrightarrow Cu^{2+}(aq) + e^-;$$

$$\Delta G_3° = -1 \times E° \times F$$

$$\Delta G_3° = \Delta G_1° + \Delta G_2°$$

$$\Delta G_3° = (-2 \times -0.34 \times F) + (-1 \times 0.15 \times F)$$

$$\Delta G_3° = 0.68\,F - 0.15\,F = 0.53\,F$$

$$E° = -0.53.$$

20. $AgIO_3(s) \rightleftharpoons Ag^+(aq) + IO_3^-(aq)$

Let solubility of $AgIO_3$ be s

$$K_{sp} = [Ag^+][IO_3^-]$$

$$1.0 \times 10^{-8} = s^2$$

$$s = 1 \times 10^{-4} \text{ mol L}^{-1}$$

In 1000 mL, mole of $AgIO_3$ dissolved $= 1 \times 10^{-4}$ mol

In 100 mL, mole of $AgIO_3$ dissolved $= 1 \times 10^{-5}$ mol

Mass of $AgIO_3$ in 100 mL $= 1 \times 10^{-5} \times 283 = 2.83 \times 10^{-3}$ g

25. Specific conductivity (κ) $= \frac{1}{R} \times$ cell constant

Cell constant $= \kappa \times R$

$= 0.0129 \times 100 = 1.29\ \text{cm}^{-1}$.

29. $Ni^{2+} + 2e^- \longrightarrow Ni$ at cathode

Equivalent weight of Ni $= \frac{\text{Mol. wt.}}{\text{Gain electron}} = \frac{58.7}{2} = 29.35$

$i = 12$ A, $t = 1$ h $= 60 \times 60$ s

$$Z = \frac{\text{Eq. wt.}}{96500}$$

Weight of Ni deposited $= \frac{Zit \times \text{efficiency}}{100}$

$$= \frac{29.35 \times 12 \times 60 \times 60 \times 60}{96500 \times 100}$$

$$= 7.883\ \text{g}$$

37. Mixture of acetic acid and sodium acetate is an acidic buffer. Hence,

$$\text{pH} = \text{p}K_a + \log\frac{[\text{Salt}]}{[\text{Acid}]}$$

Initially $\frac{[\text{Salt}]}{[\text{Acid}]} = 1$

$$\text{pH} = \text{p}K_a$$

On increasing [salt] ten time of that of [acid].

$$\text{pH} = \text{p}K_a + \log\frac{10}{1} = \text{p}K_a + 1$$

∴ pH increases by one.

43.

$$Sb_2S_3 \rightleftharpoons 2Sb^{3+} + 3S^{2-}$$

s mol L^{-1} $2s$ $3s$

$$K_{sp}(Sb_2S_3) = [Sb^{3+}]^2 [S^{2-}]^3$$

$$K_{sp} = (2s)s \cdot (3s)^3$$

$$= 108\ s^5$$

$$K_{sp} = 108 \times (1.0 \times 10^{-5})^5$$

$$K_{sp} = 108 \times 10^{-25}.$$

47.

$$E^\circ_{\text{cell}} = \frac{2.303RT}{nF}\log K_{\text{eq}}$$

$$0.295 = \frac{2.303 \times 8.314 \times 298}{2 \times 96500}\log K_{\text{eq}}$$

$$\log K_{\text{eq}} = \frac{2 \times 96500 \times 0.295}{2.303 \times 8.314 \times 298} = 10$$

$$K_{\text{eq}} = \text{antilog}\, 10 = 1 \times 10^{10}\ .$$

49. According to Nernst's equation

$$E_{\text{cell}} = E^\circ_{\text{cell}} - \frac{nRT}{F}\log\frac{C_1}{C_2}$$

For $\quad Zn(s) + Cl_2\ (1\ \text{atm}) \longrightarrow Zn^{2+} + 2Cl^-$

Hence, to increase E, C_1 should be decreased and C_2 should be increased *i.e.,* $[Zn^{2+}]$ should be decreased and Cl_2 should be increased.

53.

$$\Lambda^\circ_m = K/C$$

$$138.3 \times 10^{-4}\ \text{S m}^2\ \text{mol}^{-1} = 2.28 \times 10^4\ \text{S m}^{-1}/\text{C}$$

$$C = 0.01648\ \text{mol m}^{-3} = 1.648 \times 10^{-2}\ \text{mol m}^{-3}$$

$$C = 1.648\ \times 10^{-5}\ \text{mol dm}^{-3}$$

(Concentration of AgCl in aqueous solution = solubility of AgCl)

Hence, solubility in g per dm^3

$$= 1.648 \times 10^{-5}\ \text{mol dm}^{-3} \times 143.5\ \text{g mol}^{-1}$$

$$= 2.365 \times 10^{-3}\ \text{g dm}^{-3}.$$

54. Ionic strength of 0.01 molal NaCl solution,

$$I = \frac{1}{2}(m_+z_+^2 + m_-z_-^2) = \frac{1}{2}(0.01 \times 1^2 + 0.01 \times 1^2) = 0.01$$

Mean activity coefficient, $\gamma_\pm = -Az_+z_-\sqrt{I}$

For water at 25°C, the constant $A = 0.509$

$$\log\gamma_\pm = -0.509 \times 1 \times 1 \times \sqrt{0.01} = -0.0509$$

$$\gamma_\pm = 0.889.$$

56. $[Ba^{2+}] = 4 \times 10^{-5}\ \text{M} \times 25/525 = 1.90 \times 10^{-6}\ \text{M}$

$[SO_4^{2-}] = 5 \times 10^{-5}\ \text{M} \times 500/525 = 4.76 \times 10^{-5}\ \text{M}$

Ionic product $= [Ba^{2+}][SO_4^{2-}]$

$$= 1.90 \times 10^{-6}\ \text{M} \times 4.76 \times 10^{-5}\ \text{M}$$

$$= 9.04 \times 10^{-11}\ \text{M}^2$$

Ionic product is less then K_{sp} ($BaSO_4$), the precipitate of $BaSO_4$ will not be formed.

57.

$$t_+ = 0.83,\ t_- = 1 - t_+ = 0.17$$

$$(a_\pm)_1 = 0.01,\ (a_\pm)_2 = 0.001$$

$$E_l = (t_- - t_+)\frac{RT}{F}\ln\frac{(a_\pm)_2}{(a_\pm)_1}$$

$$E_l = (0.17 - 0.83)\ 0.059\log\frac{0.001}{0.01}$$

$$E_l = 0.039\ \text{V}.$$

65. The Debye-Huckel limiting law, allows the mean activity coefficients of the ions in a dilute aqueous solution to be calculated from the ionic strength

$$\log\gamma_+ = -A\,|\,z_+\,z_-|\sqrt{I}$$

where, $A = 0.509$

The ionic strength of a solution is

$$I = \frac{1}{2}\Sigma\, z_i^2\, b_i b^0$$

where the summation is over all positive and negative ions. In this case, the molality of potassium ions in solution, $K^+(aq)$, is $2b$ because each mole of potassium sulphate that disolves yields two moles of potassium ions. The molality of sulphate ions, $SO_4^{2-}(aq)$, is b.

Thus $\quad I = \frac{1}{2}[\{(+1^2 \times 2 \times 0.010\ \text{mol kg}^{-1}\}$

$$+ \{(-2)^2 \times 0.010\ \text{mol kg}^{-1}\}]/1\ \text{mol kg}^{-1} = 0.030$$

and so $\quad \log\gamma_+ = -A|z_+\,z_-|\sqrt{I}$

$$= -0.509 \times |+1 \times -2| \times 0.030 = -0.031$$

Thus $\quad \gamma_+ = 10^{-0.031} = 0.932$

66. Hydrocyanic acid is a weak acid. For the dissociation of weak acid, the fraction of acid molecules that are present as ions is

$$\alpha = \frac{[A^-]}{[HA]}$$

So that because $[HA] \approx [HA]_0$

and $\quad [H^+] = [A^-]$

Then $\quad K_a = \frac{[H^+][A^-]}{[HA]} \approx \frac{[H^+][A^-]}{[HA]_0} = \frac{[A^-]^2}{[HA]_0}$

Thus $\quad [A^-] \approx (K_a[HA]_0)^{1/2}$

and so $\quad \alpha = \frac{(K_a(HA]_0)^{1/2}}{[HA]_0} = \left(\frac{K_a}{[HA]_0}\right)^{1/2} = \left(\frac{10^{-\text{p}K_a}}{[HA]_0}\right)^{1/2}$

The molar conductivity of a solution of completely dissociated acid would be given by the sum of the molar conductivity of the ions

$$\Lambda_m^0 = \lambda_{H^+} + \lambda_{CN^-}$$

However, because the acid is only partially dissociated, the molar conductivity is

$$\Lambda = \alpha\Lambda_m^0$$

$$= \left(\frac{10^{-pK_a}}{[HCN]_0}\right)^{1/2} (\lambda_{H^+} + \lambda_{CN^-})$$

$$= \left(\frac{10^{-9.218}}{0.015}\right)^{1/2} (35 + 82)\ \text{mS m}^2\,\text{mol}^{-1}$$

$$= 24 \times 10^{-2}\ \text{mS m}^2\,\text{mol}^{-1}$$

68. The standard cell potential is related to the standard reactions Gibbs energy as $E^\circ_{cell} = -\frac{\Delta_r G^\circ}{vF}$

We can see by expressing the reaction in terms of two half reactions,

$$Cr_2O_7^{2-} + 14H^+ + 6e^- \longrightarrow 2Cr^{3+} + 7H_2O$$

$$2Fe^{3+} + 6e^- \longrightarrow 2Fe$$

that the overall cell reaction is written as a six-electron process, $v = 6$, so that

$$E^\circ_{cell} = \frac{-793 \times 10^3\ \text{J mol}^{-10}}{6 \times 96485\ \text{C mol}^{-1}} = +1.37\ \text{V}$$

69. The standard cell potential is related to the standard reactions Gibbs energy is as $\Delta_r G^\circ = -vFE^\circ_{cell}$

We can see by expressing the reaction in terms of two half reactions,

$$\frac{1}{2}O_2 + 2H^+ + 2e^- \longrightarrow H_2O$$

$$2\,HNO_2 + 2H^+ + 2e^- \longrightarrow 24NO + 2H_2O$$

that the overall cell reaction is written as a two-electron process, $v = 2$, so that

$$\Delta_r G^\circ = -2 \times 96485\ \text{C mol}^{-1} \times 0.240\ \text{V}$$

$$= -46.3\ \text{kJ mol}^{-1}$$

70. The Nernst equation, allows us to calculate the potential of a cell when the reactants and products are not in their standard states.

$$E_{cell} = E^0_{cell} - \frac{RT}{vF}\ln Q$$

The reaction quotient, Q, is

$$Q = \frac{a_{CuI}\,a_{Fe^{3+}}}{a_{Cu^{2+}}\,a_{Fe^{2+}} + a_{I^-}}$$

We know that $a_{CuI} = 1$ because the copper iodide, CuI, is present as a solid and is therefore in its standard state. For dilute aqueous solution such as this, we may use the approximation that

$$a_{Fe^{3+}} \approx [Fe^{3+}]/C^\circ$$

and replace that activities of all of the ions in solution by their concentrations. As written, the reaction is a one-electron process so that

$$E_{cell} = E^\circ_{cell} - \frac{RT}{F}\ln\frac{[Fe^{3+}]}{[Cu^{2+}][Fe^{2+}][I^-]}$$

where we have omitted the terms in the standard concentration, C°, for clarity.

Thus, $$E_{cell} = 0.090\ \text{V} - \frac{8.3145\ \text{J K}^{-1}\text{mol}^{-1} \times 298.15\ \text{K}}{96485\ \text{C mol}^{-1}}$$

$$\ln\frac{0.020}{0.010 \times 0.010 \times 0.040} = -0.147\ \text{V}$$

71. For the reaction as written, the standard cell potential is

$$E^\circ_{cell} = +2.08\ \text{V} - 0.77\ \text{V} = +1.31\ \text{V}$$

The equilibrium constant is related to the standard cell potential as $\ln K = \frac{vFE^\circ_{cell}}{RT}$

As written, the cell reaction is a two-electron process so that

$$\ln K = \frac{2 \times 96485\ \text{C mol}^{-1} \times 1.31\ \text{V}}{8.3145\ \text{J K}^{-1}\ \text{mol}^{-1} \times (25.0 + 273.15)\ \text{K}} = 102.0$$

so that $K = 2 \times 10^{44}$

72. The relationship between the entropy of reaction and the cell potential is as

$$\Delta_r S^\circ = \frac{vF(E^\circ_{cell} - E^\circ_{cell})}{T - T'}$$

As written, the reaction is a two-electron process, so that

$$\Delta_r S^\circ = \frac{2 \times 96485\ \text{C mol}^{-1} \times (1.102 - 1.095)\ \text{V}}{(298 - 363)\ \text{K}}$$

$$= -20.8\ \text{J K}^{-1}\ \text{mol}^{-1}$$

100. $$E = E^\circ - \frac{RT}{v_e F}\ln Q = 0$$

$$Cu^{+2} \rightleftharpoons Zn^{2+}$$

$$Q = \frac{a(Zn^{2+})\,a(Cu)}{a(Zn)\,a(Cu^{2+})} = \frac{[Zn^{2+}]}{[Cu^{2+}]}$$

$$E^\circ = \frac{RT}{v_e F}\ln Q$$

$$1.1 = \frac{25 \cdot 10^{-3}}{2}\ln Q$$

$$Q = e^{88} = 1.7 \cdot 10^{38}$$

basically all the Cu ions are used up.

Exercise 2

2. Cell is completely discharged, it means equilibrium gets established, $E = 0$

$$Zn/Zn^{2+}\ (1\ M)\ ||\ Cu^{2+}\ (1\ M)\ |\ Cu$$

$$\text{Cell reaction, } Zn + Cu^{2+} \rightleftharpoons Zn^{2+} + Cu$$

$$K_{eq} = \frac{[Zn^{2+}]}{[Cu^{2+}]}$$

$$E_{cell} = E^\circ_{cell} - \frac{0.0591}{n}\log K_{eq}$$

$$E^\circ_{cell} = \frac{0.0591}{n}\log K_{eq}$$

$$1.10 = \frac{0.0591}{2}\log K_{eq}$$

$$K_{eq} = \frac{[Zn^{2+}]}{[Cu^{2+}]} = \text{antilog}\ \frac{2.20}{0.0591}$$

$$K_{eq} = \text{antilog } 37.3 = 10^{37.3}.$$

3. $$N_1V_1 = N_2V_2$$

Base Acid

$$2.5 \times \frac{2}{5} = \frac{2}{15} \times V_2$$

$$V_2 = \frac{15}{2}\text{ mL} = 7.5\text{ mL}$$

$$BOH + HCl \longrightarrow BCl + H_2O$$

2.5 mL of $\frac{2}{5}$ M base contains $= 2.5 \times \frac{2}{5} = 1$ mmol base

∴ Salt BCl formed = 1 mmol

Volume of solution = 2.5 mL + 7.5 = 10 mL

Concentration of salt, BCl in the solution $= \frac{1}{10}$ M = 0.1

For salt of weak base and strong acid,

$$[H^+] = \sqrt{\frac{K_wC}{K_b}} = \sqrt{\frac{10^{-14} \times 0.1}{10^{-12}}}$$

$$= 3.2 \times 10^{-2}\text{ M.}$$

7. Oxalic acid = x mol L^{-1}

Dibasic acid = $2xN$

$$KMnO_4 = 0.05\text{ M} = 0.05 \times 5 = 0.25\text{ N}$$

$$MnO_4^- + 8H^+ + 5e^- \longrightarrow Mn^{2+} + 4H_2O$$

$$C_2O_4^{2-} \longrightarrow 2CO_2 + 2e^-$$

∴ Eq. wt. of $MnO_4^- = \frac{\text{Mol. wt.}}{5}$

and normality = 5 × molarity.

For oxalic acid, normality = 2 × molarity

$$N_1V_1 = N_2V_2$$

$$H_2C_2O_4 = MnO_4^-$$

$$2x \times 40 = 16 \times 0.25$$

$$x = 0.05$$

$$H_2C_2O_4 = 0.05\text{ mol L}^{-1}$$

$$[H^+] = 0.05 \times 2 = 0.10\text{ N}$$

$$pH = -\log H^+ = -\log 0.1 = 1.0.$$

8. Buffer capacity, $\beta = \frac{dC_{HA}}{d_{pH}}$

dC_{HA} = number of moles of acid added per litre

d_{pH} = change in pH

$$dC_{HA} = \frac{\text{Mole of acetic acid}}{\text{Volume}}$$

$$dC_{HA} = \frac{0.12/60}{250/1000} = \frac{1}{125}$$

$$B = \frac{1/125}{0.02} = \frac{1}{2.5} = 0.4.$$

11. $MnO_4^- + 8H^+ + 5e^- \longrightarrow Mn^{2+} + 4H_2O$

$[H^+] = 1$ M;

$$E_{MnO_4^-/Mn^{2+}} = E^\circ_{MnO_4^-/Mn^{2+}} - \frac{0.0591}{5}\log\frac{1}{[H^+]^8}$$

$$= E^\circ_{MnO_4^-/Mn^{2+}} - \frac{0.0591}{5}\log\frac{1}{[1]^8}$$

$$= E^\circ_{MnO_4^-/Mn^{2+}} - \frac{0.0591}{5}\log 1^{-8}$$

For $[H^+] = 10^{-4}$ M

$$E'_{MnO_4^-/Mn^{2+}} = E^\circ_{MnO_4^-/Mn^{2+}} - \frac{0.0591}{5}\log\frac{1}{(10^{-4})^8}$$

$$= E^\circ_{MnO_4^-/Mn^{2+}} - \frac{0.0591}{5}\log 10^{+38}$$

or $$E'_{MnO_4^-/Mn^{2+}} = E^\circ_{MnO_4^-/Mn^{2+}} - 0.378$$

$$E'_{MnO_4^-/Mn^{2+}} - E^\circ_{MnO_4^-/Mn^{2+}} = -0.378$$

13. $Pt(s), H_2(g) \mid H^+ (1\text{ M}) \parallel Ag^+(aq) \mid Ag(s)$

EMF of cell = 0.62 V, E°_{cell} = 0.80 V

$H_2 \longrightarrow 2H^+ + 2e^-$ (at anode)

$2Ag^+ + 2e^- \longrightarrow 2Ag$ (at cathode)

$H_2 + 2Ag^+ \longrightarrow 2Ag + 2H^+$ (overall reaction)

$$E_{cell} = E^\circ - \frac{2.303RT}{2F}\log\frac{[H^+]^2}{[Ag^+]^2\,[H_2]}$$

$$E_{cell} = E^\circ - \frac{2.303RT}{2F}\log\frac{1}{[Ag^+]^2}$$

$$0.62 = 0.80 - \frac{2.303 \times 0.06}{2}\log\frac{1}{[Ag^+]^2}$$

$$0.62 = 0.80 + \frac{2 \times 2.303 \times 0.06}{2}\log[Ag^+]$$

$$-0.18 = 0.1382\log[Ag^+]$$

$$[Ag^+] = 0.05\text{ M}$$

∴ Mole of Ag^+ in 100 mL $= 0.05 \times \frac{100}{1000}$

Weight of Ag^+ in 100 mL $= 0.05 \times \frac{100}{1000} \times 108$

% of Ag in 1.08 g alloy $= \frac{0.05 \times 100 \times 108 \times 100}{1000 \times 1.08} = 50\%.$

15. The weak electrolyte A_xB_y dissociates as follows :

$$A_xB_y \rightleftharpoons xA^{y+} + yB^{x-}$$

Initial conc.	C	0	0
Equal conc.	$C(1-d)$	$x\,Cd$	$y\,Cd$

$$K_{eq} = \frac{[A^{y+}]^x\,[B^{x-}]^y}{[A_xB_y]}$$

$$= \frac{[xC\alpha]^x\,[yC\alpha]^y}{C\,(1-\alpha)}$$

$$= \frac{x^x \cdot C^x \cdot \alpha^x \cdot y^y \cdot C^y \cdot \alpha^y}{C} \quad \because [(1-\alpha) = 1]$$

$$K_{eq} = x^x \cdot y^y \cdot \alpha^{x+y} \cdot C^{x+y-1}$$

$$\alpha^{x+y} = \frac{K_{eq}}{x^x \cdot y^y \cdot C^{x+y-1}}$$

$$\alpha = \left(\frac{K_{eq}}{x^x \cdot y^y \cdot C^{x+y-1}}\right)^{\left(\frac{1}{x+y}\right)}.$$

16. $$Mg(OH)_2 \rightleftharpoons Mg^{2+} + 2OH^-$$

s $2s$

$$K_{sp}\ Mg(OH)_2 = [Mg^{2+}][OH^-]^2$$

$$K_{sp}\ Mg(OH)_2 = 4s^3$$
$$1.96\times10^{-11} = 4s^3$$
$$s = \left(\frac{1.96\times10^{-11}}{4}\right)^{1/3}$$
$$s = (4.9\times10^{-12})^{1/3} = 1.69\times10^{-4}$$

So, concentration of $[OH^-] = 2s$

$$[OH^-] = 3.38\times10^{-4}$$
$$pOH = -\log[OH^-] = -\log 3.38\times10^{-4}$$
$$pOH = 3.471$$
$$pH = 14 - pOH$$
$$= 14 - 3.471 = 10.529.$$

17. $$M_2X_3 \rightleftharpoons 2M^{3+} + 3X^{2-}$$
$$K_{sp} = (2s)^2\cdot(3s)^3 = 108s^5$$
$$2.2\times10^{-20} = 108s^5$$

or $$s = 4.59\times10^{-5}$$

For M_2X, $$M_2X \rightleftharpoons \underset{2s}{2M^+} + \underset{s}{X^{2-}}$$
$$K_{sp} = (2s)^2\cdot s = 4s^3$$
$$K_{sp} = 4\,(2\times4.59\times10^{-5})^3 = 3\times10^{-12}$$

(because solubility of $M_2X = 2X$ solubility of M_2X_3).

18. Case I $[Zn^{2+}] = 0.01$ M

$[Cu^{2+}] = 1.0$ M

and $n = 2$

$$E_1 = E^\circ_{cell} - \frac{0.0591}{2}\log\frac{[Zn^{2+}]}{[Cu^{2+}]}$$
$$E_1 = E^\circ_{cell} - \frac{0.0591}{2}\log\frac{0.01}{1}$$
$$E_1 = E^\circ_{cell} + 0.0591$$

Case II $[Zn^{2+}] = 1.0$ M, $[Cu^{2+}] = 0.01$ M and $n = 2$

$$E_2 = E^\circ_{cell} - \frac{0.0591}{2}\log\frac{[Zn^{2+}]}{[Cu^{2+}]}$$
$$E_2 = E^\circ_{cell} - \frac{0.0591}{2}\log\frac{1}{0.01}$$
$$E_2 = E^\circ_{cell} - 0.0591$$

Thus, $E_1 > E_2$.

19. $$\Delta G^\circ_{H_2O(l)} = -237.2$$
$$\Delta G^\circ_{CO_2(g)} = -394.4$$
$$\Delta G^\circ_{C_5H_{12}(g)} = -8.2$$
$$C_5H_{12} + 16O_2 \longrightarrow 5CO_2 + 6H_2O$$
$$\Delta G^\circ = 5\times\Delta G^\circ_{CO_2} + 6\Delta G^\circ_{H_2O} - (\Delta G^\circ_{C_5H_{12}} + \Delta G^\circ_{O_2})$$
$$\Delta G^\circ = 5\times(-394.4) + 6\times(-237.2) - (-8.2) + 0$$
$$\Delta G^\circ = -3387\ \text{kJ mol}^{-1}.$$

In pentane-oxygen fuel cell 32 electrons are involved.

$$\Delta G^\circ = -nFE^\circ_{cell}$$
$$-3387\times10^3 = -32\times96500\times E^\circ$$
$$E^\circ = \frac{+3387\times10^3}{32\times96500} = 1.0968\ \text{V}.$$

22. $$HCl + NaZ \longrightarrow NaCl + \underset{\text{Crotonic acid}}{HZ}$$

(where, Z = crotonate ion)

$$\Lambda^\circ_m(HZ) = \Lambda^\circ_m(HCl) + \Lambda^\circ_m(NaZ) - \Lambda^\circ_m(NaCl)$$
$$= (425 + 80 - 125)\times10^{-4}\ \text{S m}^2\ \text{mol}^{-1}$$
$$= 380\times10^{-4}\ \text{S m}^2\ \text{mol}^{-1}$$
$$_m = \frac{k}{C} = \frac{3.8\times10^{-3}\ \text{S m}^{-1}}{0.001\times10^3\ \text{mol m}^{-3}} = 38.0\times10^{-4}\ \text{S m}^2\ \text{mol}^{-1}$$
$$\alpha = \frac{\Lambda_m}{\Lambda^\circ_m} = \frac{38.0\times10^{-4}\ \text{S m}^2\ \text{mol}^{-1}}{380\times10^{-4}\ \text{S m}^2\ \text{mol}^{-1}} = 0.10$$

By Ostwald's dilution law,

$$K_a = \frac{C\alpha^2}{1-\alpha} = \frac{1.0\times10^{-3}\ \text{mol dm}^{-3}\times(0.10)^2}{1-0.10}$$
$$K_a = 1.11\times10^{-5}\ \text{mol dm}^{-3}.$$

24. $$K_h = \frac{K_w}{K_a\times K_b}$$
$$K_h = \frac{x^2}{(1-x)^2}$$
$$\frac{h^2}{(1-h)^2} = \frac{K_w}{K_a\cdot K_b}$$
$$\frac{h}{(1-h)} = \sqrt{\frac{K_w}{K_a\cdot K_b}}$$
$$\frac{h}{(1-h)} = \sqrt{\frac{1.008\times10^{-14}}{1.75\times10^{-5}\times3.83\times10^{-10}}}$$
$$\frac{h}{(1-h)} = 1.219$$
$$h = 0.5495$$

% hydrolysis = 54.95.

19. Cathode $2AgCl(s) + 2e^- \rightleftharpoons 2Ag(s) + 2Cl^-$; $E^\circ = +0.222$ V

Anode $2Cd(s) \rightleftharpoons Cd^{2+}(aq) + 2e^-$;

$E^\circ = -0.403$ V

Overall reaction

$$Cd(s) + 2AgCl(s) \rightleftharpoons Cd^{2+}(aq) + 2Ag(s) + 2Cl^-(aq)$$
$$E^\circ_{cell} = E^\circ_{cathode} - E^\circ_{anode} = 0.222 - (-0.403)$$
$$E^\circ_{cell} = +0.625\ \text{V}$$
$$CdCl_2(aq) \rightleftharpoons Cd^{2+}(aq) + 2Cl^-(aq)$$

Total number of ions produced by the ionization of $CdCl_2$ are 3 ($x = 1$ and $y = 2$)

$$a(CdCl_2) = (a_\pm)^{x+y} = (a_\pm)^3$$
$$a_+ = \gamma_+ m$$
$$a_- = \gamma_- m\times2 = 2\gamma_- m$$
$$a(CdCl_2) = (a_\pm)^3 = (\gamma_+ m)(2\gamma_- m)^2 = 4(\gamma_\pm)^3 m^3$$
$$E_{cell} = E^\circ - \frac{0.0591}{2}\log(a_\pm)^3$$
$$0.780 = 0.625 - \frac{0.0591}{2}\log[4(\gamma_\pm)^3 m^3]$$
$$\log[4(\gamma_\pm)^3 m^3] = -5.2542 = \bar{6}.7458$$
$$\gamma(\gamma_\pm)^3 m^3 = 5.57\times10^{-6}$$

$$\gamma_{\pm} = \frac{5.57 \times 10^{-6}}{4 \times (0.02)^3} = 0.558.$$

26.
$$E_l = \text{EMF}_{\text{cell w.t.}} - \text{EMF}_{\text{cell w.o.t}}$$
$$E_l = 0.028 \text{ V} - 0.017 \text{ V} = 0.011 \text{ V}$$
$$E_l = (t_- - t_+) \frac{RT}{F} \ln \frac{(a_\pm)_2}{(a_\pm)_1}$$
$$0.011 = (t_- - t_+)\, 0.059 \log \frac{0.009}{0.018}$$
$$0.011 = (t_- - t_+)\, 0.059 \log \frac{1}{2}$$
$$(t_- - t_+) = -0.61$$

or $(t_+ - t_-) = 0.61$

because $t_+ + t_- = 1$

so $2t_+ = 1.61$

$t_+ = 0.8$

Transference number of H^+ ion = 0.8.

31. Cell reaction is, $Zn + 2Ag^+ \longrightarrow Zn^{2+} + 2Ag$

$$E_{\text{cell}} = E° - \frac{0.0591}{2} \log \frac{a_{Zn^{2+}}}{a^2_{Ag^+}}$$
$$E° = E_R - E_L = 0.8 - (-0.76) = 1.56 \text{ V}$$

Activity of Zn^{2+}, $a_{Zn^{2+}}$ = activity coefficient × concentration

$$= 0.5 \times 0.5 = 0.25$$

Similarly, $a_{Ag^+} = 0.8 \times 0.1 = 0.08$

$$E_{\text{cell}} = 1.56 - \frac{0.0591}{2} \log \frac{0.25}{(0.08)^2}$$
$$E_{\text{cell}} = 1.56 - 0.0295 \log 39.06$$
$$E_{\text{cell}} = 1.56 - 0.0295 \times 1.5917 = 1.513 \text{ V}.$$

35. For aqueous solution A (constant) = 0.509

$$\log \gamma_{\pm} = -A \,|\, Z_+ Z_- \,|\, \sqrt{I} + CI$$
$$\log 0.8 = -0.509 \times 1 \times 1\, \sqrt{0.01} + C \times 0.01$$
$$-0.09691 = -0.0509 + 0.01C$$
$$0.01C = -0.09691 + 0.0509$$
$$C = -4.6$$

For $\frac{N}{1000}$ solution,

$$\log \gamma_{\pm} = -0.509 \,|\, Z_+ Z_-\, \sqrt{0.001} + (-4.6) \times 0.001$$
$$\log \gamma_{\pm} = -0.509 \times 1 \times 1 \times 0.0316 + -4.6 \times 0.001$$
$$\log \gamma_{\pm} = -0.02068 = \bar{1}.9793$$
$$\gamma_{\pm} = 9.535 \times 10^{-1} = 0.9535$$
$$a_2 = 0.001 \times 0.9535 = 9.535 \times 10^{-4}$$

Similarly for $\frac{N}{25}$ solution,

$$\log \gamma_{\pm} = -0.509 \times 1 \times 1 \times \sqrt{0.04} + -4.6 \times 0.04$$
$$\log \gamma_{\pm} = -0.2858 = \bar{1}.7142$$
$$\gamma_{\pm} = 0.5178$$

Activity, $a_1 = 0.5178 \times 0.04 = 0.02071$

$$E = \frac{RT}{nF} \ln \frac{a_2}{a_1}$$
$$E = 0.0591 \log \frac{9.535 \times 10^{-4}}{0.02071}$$
$$E = 0.0591 \log 0.0460$$
$$E = -0.0591 \times 1.337 = -0.079 \text{ V}$$

(With reversed polarities, EMF would be positive).

36.
$$w = \Delta G = (0 - v_e FE) dX$$
$$Q = Idt = 1.10^3 = 10^2 \text{ Coul}$$
$$Q = v_e FdX$$
$$w = \Delta G = (-v_e FE)\, dX = -EQ = 1.100 \text{ J} = 100 \text{ J}$$

37.
$$E_{\text{cell}} = E°_{\text{cell}} - \frac{0.0591 \text{ V}}{n} \log(Q)$$
$$= 2.04 \text{ V} - \frac{0.0591 \text{ V}}{2} \log\left(\frac{1}{[H^+]^2\, [HSO_4^-]^2}\right)$$
$$= 2.04 \text{ V} + \frac{2 \cdot 0.0591 \text{ V}}{2} \log([H^+]\,[HSO_4^-])$$
$$= 2.04 \text{ V} + 0.0591 \text{ V} \log(25) = 2.123 \text{ V}$$

38.
$$\Delta G = -nFE_{\text{cell}}$$
$$E_{\text{cell}} = \frac{\Delta G}{-nF} = \frac{377.5 \text{ kJ}}{2 \times 96.84 \text{ kJ/V}} = 1.96 \text{ V}$$

51.
$$E_{\text{cell}} = 1.5 \text{ V} = 2.04 \text{ V}$$
$$= -\frac{0.0591 \text{ V}}{2} \log\left(\frac{1}{[H^+]^2\, [HSO_4^-]^2}\right)$$
$$0.54 \text{ V} = -\frac{0.0591 \text{ V}}{2}\, 4 \log([H^+]) = -0.118 \text{ V}$$
$$\log([H^+]) = 0.118 \text{ V pH}$$
$$\text{pH} = \frac{0.54}{0.118} = 4.6$$

56.
$$\Delta G° = -nF\Delta E = -2 \times 96.485 \times 0.46 \text{ kJ}$$
$$= 88.8 \text{ kJ}$$

58.
$$E_{\text{cell}} = E°_{\text{cell}} - \frac{0.059}{n} \log Q = 0.46 - \frac{0.059}{n} \log Q$$
$$= 0.46 - \frac{0.059}{n} \log \frac{[Cu^{2+}]}{[Ag^+]^2} = 0.46 - \frac{0.059}{2} \log \frac{10^{-4}}{(10^{-2})^2}$$
$$= 0.46 \text{ V}$$

59.
$$E_{\text{cell}} = E°_{\text{cell}} - \frac{0.059}{n} \log\left\{\frac{[Cu^{2+}]}{[Ag^+]^2}\right\}$$
$$0.28 = 0.46 - \frac{0.059}{2} \log \frac{10^{-4}}{[Ag^+]^2} = 0.46 - 0.059 \log \frac{10^{-2}}{[Ag^+]}$$
$$\log \frac{10^{-2}}{[Ag^+]} = \frac{0.18}{0.059} = 3.05$$
$$\frac{10^{-2}}{[Ag^+]} = 10^{3.05}$$
$$[Ag^+] = 8.9 \cdot 10^{-6} \text{ M}$$

64.
$$2\{Al^0 \longrightarrow Al^{3+} + 3e^-\}\, 1.66$$
$$3\{Pb^{2+} + 2e^- \longrightarrow Pb^0\} - 0.13$$
$$E° = 1.66 - 0.13 = 1.53 \text{ V}$$
$$\Delta E = E - E° = -\frac{RT}{nF} \ln Q$$
$$= -\frac{0.06}{6} \log Q = -0.01 \cdot \log \frac{[Al^{3+}]^2}{[Pb^{2+}]^3}$$
$$= -0.01 \cdot \log \frac{[1 + 2\Delta X]^2}{[1 - 3\Delta X]^3}$$
$$[Al^{3+}] = 1 + 2 = 1 + 2\Delta X \Rightarrow \Delta X = 0.1$$
$$\Delta E = -0.01 \cdot \log \frac{[1.2]^2}{[0.7]^3}$$
$$= -0.01 \cdot 0.62 = -6 \text{ mV}$$

24

Chemical Kinetics

Chemical kinetics concerns with measurement of rates of reactions occurring under given conditions of temperature, pressure and concentrations. Kinetic studies help us in determining the factors which influence rates of reactions as well as in understanding mechanisms of a number of reactions.

Syllabus

- Empirical Rate Laws
- Arrhenius Equations
- Theories of Reaction Rates
- Determination of Reaction Mechanism
- Experimental Techniques for Fast Reactions

Rate of a Chemical Reaction

It is defined as the amount of change in concentration divided by the corresponding time interval.

$$\frac{\Delta x}{\Delta t} = \frac{dx}{dt} = \frac{x_1 - x_2}{t_2 - t_1}$$

where, Δx or dx is the concentration change $(x_1 - x_2)$ in the time interval Δt or $dt\,(t_2 - t_1)$.

Concentration is generally expressed in active mass, *i.e.*, mol L^{-1}.

For a simplest reaction,

$$\text{Reactant } (R) \longrightarrow \text{Product } (P)$$

$$\frac{-\Delta\,[R]}{(\Delta t \to 0)\,\Delta t} = \frac{\Delta\,[P]}{\Delta t}$$

or

$$\text{Instant rate} = \frac{-d\,[R]}{dt} = \frac{d\,[P]}{dt}$$

Instant rate can be determined by drawing a tangent at a given time, t on the curve R (reactant) *versus* time, t or P (product) *versus* time, t.

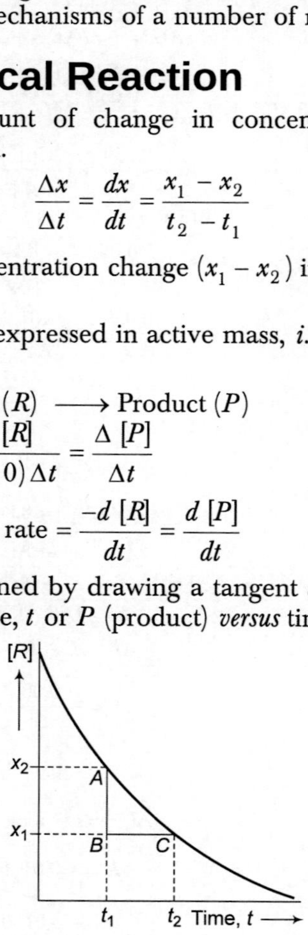

Thus, instant rate = – slope (for reactant R) $= -\dfrac{d[R]}{dt}$

$$= \frac{AB}{BC} = \frac{\Delta x}{\Delta t}$$

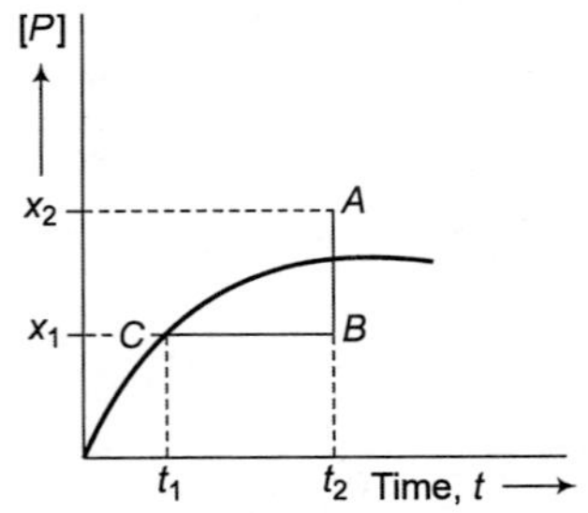

Instant rate = slope (for product P) $= +\dfrac{d[P]}{dt}$

$$= \frac{AB}{BC} = \frac{\Delta x}{\Delta t}$$

For the reaction, $aA + bB \longrightarrow cC + dD$

Rate of disappearance of a reactant is negative and rate of formation of product is positive.

$$\frac{dx}{dt} = -\frac{1}{a}\frac{d[A]}{dt} = -\frac{1}{b}\frac{d[B]}{dt} = \frac{1}{c}\frac{d[C]}{dt} = \frac{1}{d}\frac{d[D]}{dt}$$

Law of Mass Action and Rate Constant

The rate at which a substance reacts is directly proportional to its active mass and the rate at which a reaction proceeds is proportional to the product of the active masses of the reacting substances.

$$A + B \longrightarrow C + D$$

$$-\frac{d[A]}{dt} \propto [A] \quad \text{and} \quad -\frac{d[B]}{dt} \propto [B]$$

So, that rate of the reaction,

$$\frac{dx}{dt} \propto [A][B]$$

or

$$\frac{dx}{dt} = k[A][B]$$

where, k is called rate constant or velocity constant and $[A]$ and $[B]$ are active masses or molar concentration of the reactants A and B.

- At a time when $[A] = [B] = 1 \text{ mol L}^{-1}$; $\dfrac{dx}{dt} = k$

  Rate constant, k is also called specific reaction rate.
- Temperature, concentration of reacting substance, radiation, surface area of the reacting solids and the presence of a catalyst affect the rate of reaction.

Rate Law, Molecularity and Order of Reaction

Total number of molecules of the reactants involved in the reaction as shown by chemical equation is termed its **molecularity**. It is always an integral value and is never zero.

$$A + 2B \longrightarrow \text{Product}$$

For the above reaction molecularity is three (termolecular).

Rate, $\dfrac{dx}{dt} = k[A]^x [B]^y$

Above equation is called **rate law**. It describes the functional dependence of the reaction rate upon concentration of the various reactants.

The order of the reaction *wrt* some component is the power to which the concentration of the components is raised in the rate law.

Sum of exponents, *i.e.*, $x + y$ gives the overall **order of a reaction** whereas x and y represent the order with respect to the reactants A and B respectively. Order of a reaction can be 0, 1, 2, 3 and even a fraction.

The rate law may not depend on the concentration of every reactant or product of the reaction.

The rate law may depend on the concentration of species (*e.g.*, catalyst) which do not appear in the equation for the overall reaction.

For relatively simple reactions or isolated reactions in which the reactants are directly transformed into products without any intermediate step, their molecularity is same as their order. But in several reactions, when one of the reactants is present in large excess, the second order reaction confirms to the first order and is known as **pseudounimolecular reaction**. The examples are hydrolysis of ethyl acetate and inversion of cane sugar in aqueous solutions.

$$CH_3COOC_2H_5 + \underset{\text{(Excess)}}{H_2O} \xrightarrow{H^+} CH_3COOH + C_2H_5OH$$

$$\underset{\text{Sucrose}}{C_{12}H_{22}O_{11}} + \underset{\text{(Excess)}}{H_2O} \xrightarrow{H^+} \underset{\text{Glucose}}{C_6H_{12}O_6} + \underset{\text{Fructose}}{C_6H_{12}O_6}$$

Order and Molecularity of a Complex Reaction

Complex reactions occur in two or more steps. Each step of the reaction, however, is a simple reaction, *i.e.*, an elementary reaction. For such reactions, molecularity of each elementary step is taken into account and not that of overall reaction. The order of a complex reaction is given by the order of the slowest step in the sequence of various steps involved in that reaction. For example decomposition of N_2O_5 represented as

$$2N_2O_5 \longrightarrow 4NO_2 + O_2$$

has been found to be first order and is believed to have the mechanism as given

(i) $N_2O_5 \xrightarrow{\text{Slow}} NO_2 + NO_3$

(ii) $NO_2 + NO_3 \longrightarrow NO_2 + O_2 + NO$

(iii) $NO + N_2O_5 \longrightarrow 3NO_2$

(iv) $NO_2 + NO_3 \longrightarrow N_2O_5$

Steps (ii), (iii) and (iv) are bimolecular and step (i) is unimolecular. But often the molecularity of the slowest step in the sequence of the steps is found to be the order of the overall reaction.

Integrated Equation for Rate Constants of Different Order Reactions

Zero Order Reaction

	A $\longrightarrow$	Product
At $t = 0$	a	0
At time t	$a - x$	x

Rate law is $\dfrac{dx}{dt} = k_0\,[A]^0 = k_0$

$$dx = k_0\,dt$$

$$x = k_0 t$$

In terms of disappearance of the reactant, $\dfrac{-d\,[A]}{dt}$

$$[A]_t = -k_0 t + [A]_0$$

$$(a - x) = -k_0 t + a$$

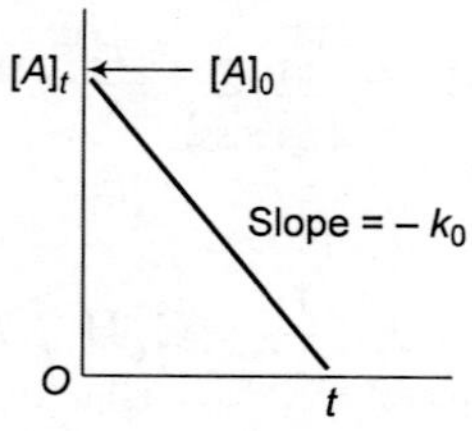

$\therefore$ $$k_0 = \frac{x}{t}$$

If concentration of the product is x_1 at time t_1 and x_2 at time t_2, then

$$k_0 = \frac{x_1 - x_2}{t_1 - t_2}$$

Half-life period, $t = t_{1/2}$, $x = \dfrac{a}{2}$

$\therefore$ $$t_{1/2} = \frac{a}{2k_0}$$

$$t_{1/2} \propto a \quad \therefore \quad t_{1/2} \propto \frac{1}{k_0}$$

At $t = t_{3/4}$ (which is the time required by the reactant to decompose 75%) $x = \dfrac{3}{4}a$

$$t_{3/4} = \frac{3a}{4k_0} = 1.5\,t_{1/2}$$

Thus, $t_{3/4}$ or $t_{1/2} \propto a$

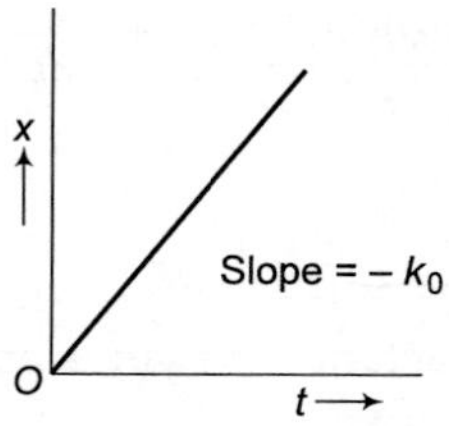

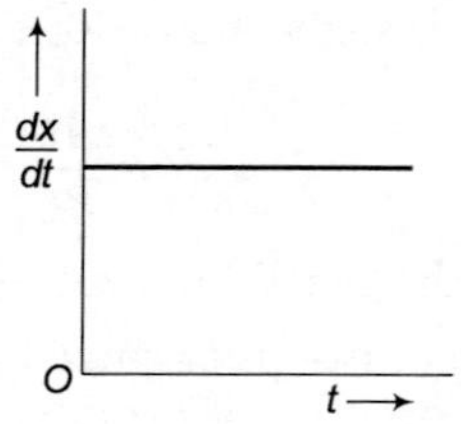

- A graph between x (along y-axis) and time, t (along x-axis) is linear of slope k_0. A graph between $\dfrac{dx}{dt}$ and time, t is a straight line parallel to t-axis showing $\dfrac{dx}{dt} = k_0$.
- Photochemical reactions like ($H_2 + Cl_2 \longrightarrow 2HCl$) and decomposition of various gases on the surface of metallic catalysts, such as decomposition of HI on gold surface also exhibits zero order kinetics. Zero order reactions generally take place in a heterogeneous system.

$$CH_2{=}CH_2(g) + H_2(g) \xrightarrow{Ni(s)} CH_3{-}CH_3(g)$$

First Order Reaction

	A $\longrightarrow$	Product
At $t = 0$	$a = C_0 = N_0$	0
At time t	$(a - x) = C = N$	x

Rate law is $\dfrac{dx}{dt} = k\,[A] = k_1(a - x)$

$$\frac{dx}{a - x} = k_1\,dt$$

Integration of this equation gives

$\therefore$ $$k_1 = \frac{1}{t}\log_e\left(\frac{a}{a - x}\right)$$

$$k_1 = \frac{2.303}{t} \log_{10} \left(\frac{a}{a-x} \right)$$

Also
$$\log_e (a-x) - \log_e a = -k_1 t$$
$$\log_e C - \log_e C_0 = -k_1 t$$
$$\log_e \left(\frac{C}{C_0} \right) = -k_1 t$$
$$C = C_0 e^{-k_1 t}$$
$$N = N_0 e^{-k_1 t}$$

Thus, concentration of the reactant A varies exponentially with time (as shown in the figure). This equation is called Wilhelmy's equation.

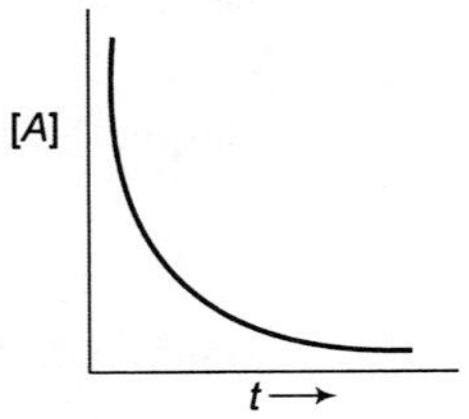

- If concentrations of reactant are $(a - x_1)$ and $(a - x_2)$ at time t_1 and t_2 respectively, then
$$k_1 = \frac{2.303}{(t_2 - t_1)} \log_{10} \left(\frac{a - x_1}{a - x_2} \right)$$
- If $t = t_{1/2}$, $x = \frac{a}{2}$, $(a - x) = \frac{a}{2}$
then half-life period of first order reaction is
$$t_{1/2} = \frac{2.303 \log 10^2}{k_1}$$
$$t_{1/2} = \frac{2.303 \times 0.3010}{k_1} = \frac{0.693}{k_1}$$

A graph between $\log_{10}(a - x)$ and time t is a straight line

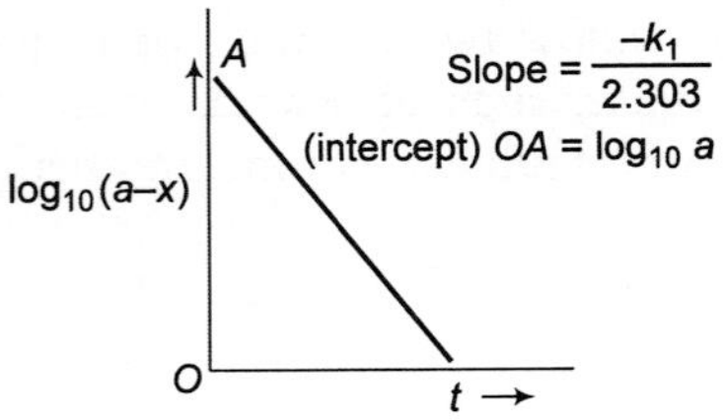

Following are some examples of first order reactions

(i) $H_2O_2(s) \longrightarrow H_2O(l) + \frac{1}{2} O_2(g)$

(ii) $2N_2O_5(g) \xrightarrow{\Delta} 4NO_2(g) + O_2(g)$

(iii) $(CH_3)_3CCl + OH^-(aq) \longrightarrow (CH_3)_3COH + Cl^-(aq)$

Note All radioactive decays are first order reactions.

- k_1^{-1} is called average life, $t_{av.}$ of first order reaction
$$t_{av} = \frac{1}{k_1} = \frac{t_{1/2}}{0.693} = 1.443\, t_{1/2}$$
- t_{av} is sometimes referred to as the natural life time of reactant A.
- During one t_{av}, the concentration of the reactant A decreases to $\frac{1}{e}$ of the original value (C_0). After two average life, concentration of the reactant A is reduced to $\frac{1}{e^2}$ of the original value (C_0).

Second Order Reaction

$$A + A \longrightarrow \text{Product}$$

or
$$A + B \longrightarrow \text{Product}$$

At $t = 0$	a	a	0
At time t	$(a - x)$	$(a - x)$	x

Rate law is $\frac{dx}{dt} = k_2 [A]^2 = k_2 [A][B]$

or $\frac{dx}{dt} = k_2 (a - x)^2$

Rate constant k_2 of second order reaction is

$$k_2 = \frac{1}{t} \left[\frac{1}{(a-x)} - \frac{1}{a} \right] = \frac{1}{t} \frac{x}{a(a-x)}$$

If concentrations of reactant A are $(a - x_1)$ and $(a - x_2)$ at time t_1 and t_2 respectively, then

$$k_2 = \frac{1}{(t_2 - t_1)} \left[\frac{1}{(a - x_2)} - \frac{1}{(a - x_1)} \right]$$
$$k_2 = \frac{1}{(t_2 - t_1)} \left[\frac{(x_2 - x_1)}{(a - x_1)(a - x_2)} \right]$$

If reactants A and B have different concentrations, a and b respectively, then

$$k_2 = \frac{2.303}{t(a-b)} \log_{10} \frac{b(a-x)}{a(b-x)}$$

If reactant A is in excess $(a >> b)$, then $(a - b) \approx a$, $(a - x) \approx a$, the above equation reduces to

$$k_2 = \frac{2.303}{ta} \log_{10} \left(\frac{b}{b-x} \right)$$
$$k'_2 = k_2 a = \frac{2.303}{t} \log_{10} \left(\frac{b}{b-x} \right)$$

This is the rate constant of the first order reaction. This is an example of pseudo-unimolecular reaction.

- Equation of second order can be written as

$$\frac{1}{(a-x)} = k_2 t + \frac{1}{a}$$

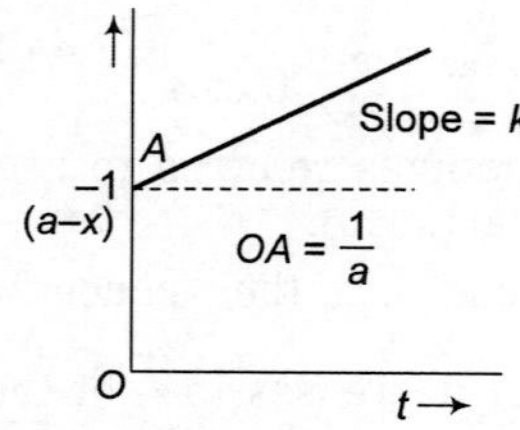

A graph between $(a-x)^{-1}$ and time t is a straight line of slope $= k_2$ and intercept on y-axis $= \frac{1}{a}$.

$$k_2 t = \frac{1}{(a-x)} - \frac{1}{a}$$

$$k_2 t_{1/2} = \frac{1}{a/2} - \frac{1}{a}$$

or $$k_2 t_{1/2} = \frac{1}{a} \quad \text{or} \quad t_{1/2} = \frac{1}{k_2 a}$$

$$t_{1/2} \propto \frac{1}{a}$$

Following are some examples of the second order reaction

(i) $CH_3COOC_2H_5 + OH^-(aq) \longrightarrow CH_3COO^-(aq) + C_2H_5OH$

(ii) $2CH_3CHO \longrightarrow 2CH_4 + 2CO$

(iii) $\underset{\text{Persulphate}}{S_2O_8^{2-}} + 2I^- \longrightarrow 2SO_4^{2-} + I_2$

*n*th Order Reaction

$$A \longrightarrow \text{Product}$$

Rate law is $\frac{dx}{dt} = k[A]^n = k(a-x)^n$

$$k_n = \frac{1}{(n-1)t}\left[\frac{1}{(a-x)^{n-1}} - \frac{1}{a^{n-1}}\right] \quad \text{but } n \geq 2$$

- k is expressed in the unit of conc.$^{(1-n)}$ time^{-1}.
- Time t required to complete a particular fraction of a reaction

$$t \propto (a)^{1-n}$$

- $t_{1/2}$ of nth order reaction is $(n \geq 2)$

$$= \frac{2^{n-1} - 1}{(n-1)k_n (a)^{n-1}}$$

- If concentration is changed to m times, new rate will be m^n times.

Order	Equation	Unit of the rate constant	Equation for half-life
0	$k = \frac{x}{t}$	mol dm^{-3} s^{-1}	$\frac{a_0}{2k}$
$\frac{1}{2}$	$k = \frac{2}{t}[a_0^{1/2} - (a_0 - x)^{1/2}]$	mol$^{1/2}$dm$^{-3/2}$s^{-1}	–
1	$k = \frac{1}{t}\ln\left[\frac{a_0}{a_0 - x}\right]$	s^{-1}	$\frac{0.693}{k}$
$\frac{3}{2}$	$k = \frac{2}{t}\left[\frac{1}{(a_0 - x)^{1/2}} - \frac{1}{a_0^{1/2}}\right]$	dm$^{3/2}$mol$^{-1/2}$s^{-1}	–
2	$k = \frac{2}{ta_0(a_0 - x)}$	dm^3 mol^{-1}s^{-1}	$\frac{1}{k \cdot a_0}$
3	$k = \frac{2a_0x - x^2}{2ta_0(a_0 - x)^2}$	dm^{6}mol^{-2}s^{-1}	$\frac{3}{2ka_0^2}$
⋮	⋮	⋮	⋮
n	$k = \frac{1}{t(n-1)}\left[\frac{1}{(a_0 - x)^{n-1}} - \frac{1}{a_0^{n-1}}\right]$	dm^{3n-3}mol^{1-n}s^{-1}	$\frac{2^{n-1} - 1}{k_n(n-1)\,a_0^{n-1}}$

Composite Reactions (Complex Reactions)

Composite reactions occur from the intervention of many simple reactions which act either simultaneously (opposing and parallel reactions) or successively (successive or consecutive reactions.)

Side Reactions, Parallel Reactions or Concurrent Reactions

In such reactions, the reacting substances, instead or proceeding along one path to yield a given set of products, also follow two or more other paths to give different products, such as where, B and C may not have any chemical affinity for one another.

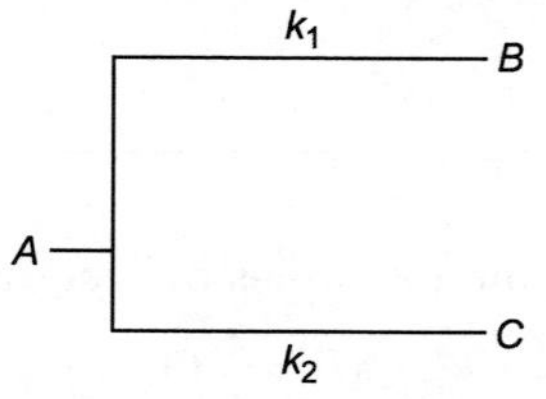

Let a be the initial concentration of A and x be the amount transformed in time t. If y and z be the amounts of B and C formed in time t, then we have the rates of formation of B and C given by $\frac{dy}{dt}$ and $\frac{dz}{dt}$ respectively.

Since, both B and C are formed from A, we have

$$\frac{dx}{dt} = \frac{dy}{dt} + \frac{dz}{dt} \quad \ldots(1)$$

If the reaction is unimolecular and k_1 is the velocity constant for the formation of B from A, then

$$\frac{dy}{dt} = k_1(a - x)$$

Similarly, the rate of formation of C is given by

$$\frac{dz}{dt} = k_1(a - x)$$

where, k_2 = velocity constant for the formation of C. Hence, from equation (1), we have

$$\frac{dx}{dt} = k_1(a - x) + k_2(a - x) = (k_1 + k_2)(a - x)$$

On integration, we have

$$k_1 + k_2 = K \text{ (say)} = \frac{1}{t} \log \frac{a}{a - x} \quad \ldots(2)$$

Now in order to evaluate k_1 and k_2 separately, we must know some relationship between them. The amounts of B and C formed at any time will depend upon the rates of the two reactions, *i.e.*,

$$\frac{\text{Amount of } B \text{ at any stage}}{\text{Amount of } C \text{ at any stage}} = \frac{\frac{dy}{dt}}{\frac{dz}{dt}}$$

$$= \frac{k_1(a - x)}{k_2(a - x)} = \frac{k_1}{k_2} = K'\text{(say)} \quad \ldots(3)$$

The relative amounts of B and C can be determined at the end of the reaction, the ratio of the relative amounts giving the value of K. The values of k_1 and k_2 can be calculated separately from equations (2) and (3) in terms of K and K' which are directly measurable quantities. We have

$$k_1 + k_2 = K \text{ and } \frac{k_1}{k_2} = K'$$

Therefore, $K = K'k_2 + k_2 = k_2(1 + K')$

or $$k_2 = \frac{K}{1 + K'}$$

Similarly, $$k_1 = \frac{KK'}{1 + K'}$$

Consecutive Reactions, Simultaneous or Parallel Reactions

Chemical reactions which proceed from reactants to products through one or more intermediate stages are called **consecutive reactions**. The simplest case arises when both the consecutive reactions are of the same order, *viz.*

$$A \xrightarrow{k_1} B \xrightarrow{k_2} C$$

Suppose we start with a mole of A. Let after a time t, x moles of A are left behind, giving y moles of B and z moles of C. Therefore, x, y and z are connected as,

$$x + y + z = a \quad \ldots(11)$$

The rate of disappearance of A, *i.e.*, $\left(-\frac{dx}{dt}\right)$ is given by

$$\frac{-dx}{dt} = k_1 x \quad \ldots(12)$$

where, k_1 = rate constant for transformation of A to B

The rate of formation of C, *i.e.*, $\left(\frac{dz}{dt}\right)$ is given by

$$-\frac{dx}{dt} = k_2 y \quad \ldots(13)$$

k_2 = rate constant for the formation of C from B

The rate at which B accummulates, *i.e.*, $\left(\frac{dy}{dt}\right)$ in the system is thus the difference between the rate of formation of B from A and the rate of transformation of B into C. Therefore,

$$\frac{dy}{dt} = -\frac{dx}{dt} + \left(\frac{dz}{dt}\right)$$

$$= k_1 x - k_2 y \quad \ldots(14)$$

On integrating equation (12), and finding the proper value of integration constant, as usual, we have

$$-\int \frac{dx}{x} = \int k_1 dt$$

Therefore, $$-\log x = k_1 t - \log a$$

$$\frac{x}{a} = e^{-k_1 t}$$

$$\frac{x}{a} = e^{-k_1 t}$$

or $$x = ae^{-k_1 t}$$

This shows that $[A]$ decreases exponentially with time as in first order reactions.

To get the value of $[B]$, *i.e.*, y, substitute the value of x in equation (13). So,

$$\frac{dy}{dt} = k_1 a e^{-k_1 t} - k_2 y$$

This is a linear differential equation of the first order, whose solution is

$$y = e^{-k_2 t}\left[\frac{k_1 a e^{(k_1 - k_2)t}}{(k_2 - k_1)} + c\right]$$

When $t = 0$, $y = 0$. So, $c = -k_1 a/(k_2 - k_1)$

$$\therefore \quad y = e^{-k_2 t}\left[\frac{k_1 a e^{(k_2 - k_1)t}}{(k_2 - k_1)} - \frac{k_1 a}{k_2 - k_1}\right]$$

or $$y = \frac{a k_1}{(k_2 - k_1)}(e^{-k_1 t} - e^{-k_2 t}) \quad \ldots(15)$$

Substituting the values of x and y in equation (33, we get

$$z = a - x - y$$

or $$z = a - a e^{-k_1 t} - \frac{a k_1}{(k_2 - k_1)}[e^{-k_1 t} - e^{-k_2 t}]$$

or $$z = \left(1 - \frac{k_2 e^{-k_1 t} - k_1 e^{-k_2 t}}{(k_2 - k_1)}\right) \quad \ldots(16)$$

Reaction Mechanisms

Two approximations (i) the equilibrium approximation (ii) the steady state approximation are generally used for elucidating the mechanism of a complex reaction.

The Equilibrium Approximation

Consider a reaction in which reactant gives rise to product through the formation of a number of intermediates $I_1, I_2, I_3, \ldots, I_n$.

$$R \xrightarrow{k_0} I_1 \xrightarrow{k_1} I_2 \xrightarrow{k_3} I_3 \ldots\ldots\ldots\ldots I_n \xrightarrow{k_n} P$$

In order to derive the rate equation for the complex reaction, we assume that rate determining step (slowest step) exists and all the steps preceeding the rate determining step are in equilibrium.

The Steady State Approximation

In this approximation the reactions are investigated under such conditions that the rate determining step does not exist and we assume the steady state approximation for the intermediate. In such a mechanism, the rate of formation of an intermediate is equal to the rate of its decomposition.

$$R \xrightarrow{k_0} I_1 \xrightarrow{k_1} I_2 \xrightarrow{k_2} I_3 \xrightarrow{k_{n-1}} I_n \xrightarrow{k_n} P$$

$$\frac{d[I_1]}{dt} = \frac{d[I_2]}{dt} = \frac{d[I_n]}{dt} = 0$$

Simple Reaction Mechanisms

The sequence of a number of steps proposed to account for an overall reaction is called mechanism of reaction. The experimentally observed rate law helps us to propose a mechanism.

Reaction between NO_2 and F_2

$$2NO_2 + F_2 \longrightarrow 2NO_2F$$

It obeys the following rate law,

$$-\frac{1}{2}\frac{d[NO_2]}{dt} = k[NO_2][F_2]$$

This suggests that one molecule of each of NO_2 and F_2 is involved in the rate determining step. The proposed mechanism is

$$NO_2 + F_2 \xrightarrow{k_1} NO_2F + F \quad \text{(slow)}$$

$$F + NO_2 \xrightarrow{k_2} NO_2F \quad \text{(fast)}$$

Reaction between hypochlorite and iodide ions in alkaline medium

$$OCl^- + I^- \xrightarrow{OH^-} OI^- + Cl^-$$

The reaction obeys the following rate law

$$-\frac{d[I^-]}{dt} = k\frac{[OCl^-][I^-]}{[OH^-]}$$

Presence of $[OH^-]$ in denominator indicates that the rate of reaction is retarded in the presence of $[OH^-]$ ions. The proposed mechanism is

(a) $$OCl^- + H_2O \underset{k_{-1}}{\overset{k_1}{\rightleftharpoons}} HOCl + OH^- \quad \text{(fast)}$$

(b) $$I^- + HOCl \xrightarrow{k_2} HOI + Cl^- \quad \text{(slow)}$$

(c) $$OH^- + HOI \underset{k_{-3}}{\overset{k_3}{\rightleftharpoons}} H_2O + OI^- \quad \text{(fast)}$$

Step (b) is slow, so we may write

$$-\frac{d[I^-]}{dt} = k_2[I^-][HOCl]$$

$$[HOCl] = \frac{k_1}{k_{-1}}\frac{[OCl^-][H_2O]}{[OH^-]}$$

$$-\frac{d[I^-]}{dt} = \frac{k_2 k_1 [I^-][OCl^-][H_2O]}{k_{-1}[OH^-]}$$

$$-\frac{d[I^-]}{dt} = \left(\frac{k_2 k_1}{k_{-1}} \cdot [H_2O]\right)\frac{[I^-][OCl^-]}{[OH^-]}$$

$$-\frac{d[I^-]}{dt} = k\frac{[I^-][OCl^-]}{[OH^-]}$$

Effect of Temperature on Reaction Rate

It has been found that for a chemical reaction with rise in temperature by 10°C, the rate constant is nearly doubled. **Temperature coefficient** of a reaction is defined as the ratio of rate constants at two temperatures differing by 10 K (generally 25°C and 35°C). Observed value usually lies between 2 and 3 for most of the reactions.

The temperature dependence of the rate of a chemical reaction can be accurately explained by Arrhenius equation,

$$k = Ae^{-E_a/RT}$$

where, E_a is called the Arrhenius activation energy and A is called the Arrhenius pre-exponential factor or frequency factor. A has the same units as the rate constant k because it is dimensionless.

In Arrhenius equation, the factor $e^{-E_a/RT}$ corresponds to the fraction of molecules that have kinetic energy greater than E_a.

$$\ln k = -\frac{E_a}{RT} + \ln A$$

The plot of ln k *vs* $\frac{1}{T}$ gives a straight line according to the equation.

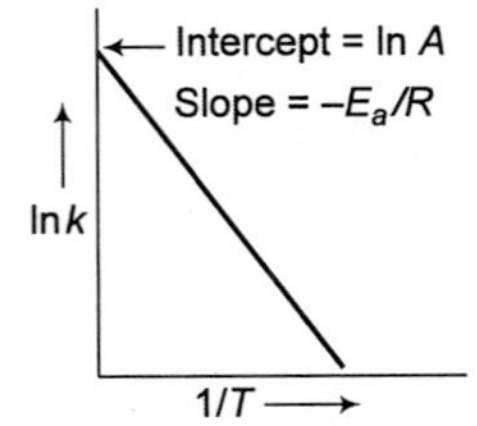

If k_1 and k_2 are the values of rate constants at temperatures T_1 and T_2 respectively then,

$$\ln\frac{k_2}{k_1} = \frac{E_a}{R}\left[\frac{T_2 - T_1}{T_1 \cdot T_2}\right]$$

This is integrated Arrhenius equation. By knowing the rate constants at two different temperatures, the energy of activation can be readily determined.

Collision Theory of Chemical Reactions

It was developed by Arrhenius and van't Hoff. According to this theory, the reactant molecules must collide with each other before they react. The number of collisions per second per unit volume of the reaction mixture is known as collision frequency (Z).

$$Z_{AA} = 2n^2 d^2 \left(\frac{8\pi kT}{\mu}\right)^{1/2} \quad \ldots(17)$$

(When collisions among molecules of one species)

$$Z_{AB} = n_A n_B (d_{av})^2 \left(\frac{8\pi kT}{\mu}\right)^{1/2} \quad \ldots(18)$$

(When collision between unlike molecules)

$$Z_{AB} = n_A n_B (d_{av})^2 \left[\frac{(M_A + M_B)\, 8\pi RT}{M_A M_B}\right]^{1/2} \quad \ldots(19)$$

where, Z_{AB} = collision frequency of reactants A and B. n_A and n_B are the numbers of A and B molecules, d_{av} = average collision diameter defined as $\frac{(d_A + d_B)}{2}$

and μ = reduced mass $\left(\mu = \frac{M_A \cdot M_B}{M_A + M_B}\right)$.

According to the hard sphere collision theory, the collision number multiplied by Arrhenius factor $e^{-E_a/RT}$ gives the rate of formation of the products of the reaction in terms of the number of molecules formed per unit volume and per unit time.

$$\text{Rate} = n_A n_B (d_{av})^2 \left(\frac{8\pi kT}{\mu}\right)^{1/2} \cdot e^{-E_a/RT}$$

Division by $n_A n_B$ and multiplication by Avogadro constant L gives a rate constant in molar units $(m^3 mol^{-1} s^{-1})$

$$k = Z_{AB} e^{-E_a/RT}$$

because $Z_{AB} = Ld^2 \left(\frac{8\pi kT}{\mu}\right)^{1/2}$

Steric Factor

Collision must occur in order for a chemical reaction to proceed but they do not guarantee that a reaction will occur. If colliding molecules have improper orientations, they do not react even though they may possess sufficient energy. To account for effective collisions, another factor P, called steric factor is introduced. The fraction of collisions having proper orientation for conversions of reactants to products is called steric factor, P.

$$k = PZ_{AB} \cdot e^{-E_a/RT}$$

Absolute Reaction Rate Theory or Transition State Theory or Activated Complex Theory

It is developed by Erying, Polanyi and Evans in 1935. According to this theory bimolecular reaction between two molecules takes place through the formation of the activated complex.

$$\underset{\text{Reactants}}{A + B} \rightleftharpoons \underset{\substack{\text{Transition state} \\ \text{(Activated complex)}}}{[AB]^*} \longrightarrow \text{Products}$$

The activation energy, E_a is the additional energy that must be absorbed by the reactants in their ground states to allow them to reach the transition state. If they do possess sufficient energy to reach the transition state, the reaction can proceed.

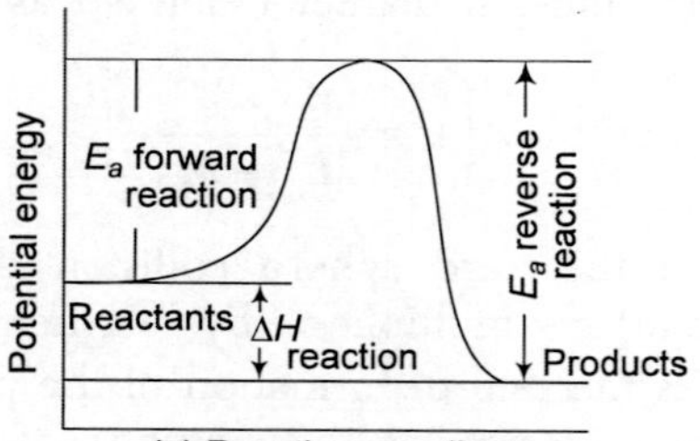

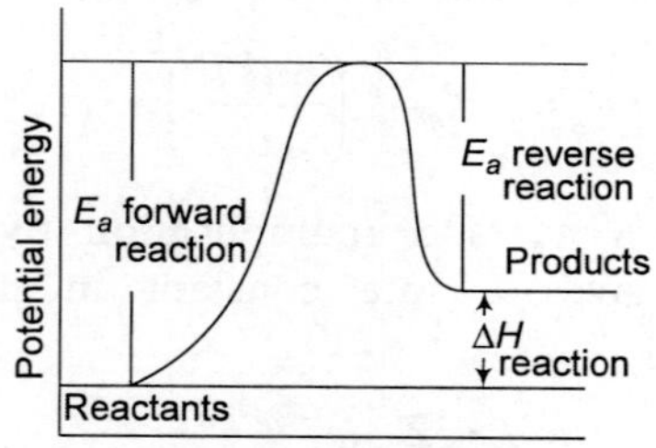

Fig. 24.1 Potential energy diagram
(a) for exothermic reaction.
(b) endothermic reaction.

Rate of reaction = frequency of crossing energy barrier × concentration of activated complexes at the top of energy barrier × probability of crossing the barrier

$$\text{Rate of reaction} = \frac{1}{\delta} \times \left(\frac{kT}{2\pi m}\right)^{1/2} \times C^* \times \frac{(2\pi mkT)^{1/2}\,\delta}{h}$$

$$= C^* \frac{kT}{h} \qquad \ldots(20)$$

$\frac{kT}{h}$ = Universal frequency with dimension of time^{-1}. Its value depends only on temperature.

Rate of formation of activated complex = Rate of decomposition of activated complex

$$k_S C_A C_B = C^* \frac{kT}{h}$$

(k_S = Specific reaction rate, C_A and C_B are the concentration of A and B respectively)

$$k_S = \frac{C^*}{C_A C_B} \cdot \frac{kT}{h} \qquad \ldots(21)$$

On applying law of mass action to the following equilibrium

$$A + B \rightleftharpoons [AB]^*$$

$$K^* = \frac{C^*}{C_A C_B} \quad (K^* = \text{equilibrium constant})$$

On substituting the value of C^* in equation (21), we get

$$k_S = \frac{kT}{h} \cdot K^* \qquad \ldots(22)$$

From statistical mechanics, the value of equilibrium constant can be written in terms of partition function as

$$K^* = \frac{q^*}{q_A q_B} \cdot e^{-\Delta E_0/RT} \qquad \ldots(23)$$

where, q^*, q_A and q_B are partition functions of the activated complex and reactants A and B respectively, ΔE_0 = heat of activation.

On substituting the value of K^* in equation (22), we get

$$k_S = \frac{kT}{h} \cdot \frac{q^*}{q_A q_B} \cdot e^{-\Delta E_0/RT} \qquad \ldots(24)$$

Eyring's Equation

The equation of the theory of absolute reaction rate can be expressed in terms of thermodynamical functions instead of partition functions.

$$k_S = \frac{kT}{h} \cdot e^{-\Delta H^*/RT} \cdot e^{\Delta S^*/R}$$

The above equation is known as Eyring's equation.

Transmission Coefficient

It is not necessary that every activated complex is converted into the products. To allow for this possibility, it is convenient to introduce a transmission coefficient K in equation (24)

$$k_s = K \frac{kT}{h} \frac{q^*}{q_A q_B} e^{-\Delta E_0/RT}$$

For many reactions the value of transmission coefficient is unity. It means that every activated complex becomes a product. However, the value of K is less than unity in the following types of reactions.

1. Reactions in which there is a change from one type of electronic state to another.
2. Bimolecular atom recombination in the gas phase.
3. The reverse decomposition of atomic molecules.

In certain cases the value of K is greater than unity due to quantum mechanical tunnelling.

Comparison of Absolute Reaction Rate Theory With Eyring's Equation

The absolute reaction rate theory based on statistical mechanics does not provide a quantitative treatment of the steric factor P in bimolecular reaction.

But in the case of Eyring's equation based on **thermodynamic formulation** a quantitative treatment of the steric factor P in bimolecular reaction is provided.

$$k_s = PZe^{-E/RT}$$

From Eyring's equation

$$k_s = \frac{kT}{h} e^{\Delta S^*/R} \cdot e^{\Delta H^*/RT}$$

On comparing these two equations for k_s we get

$$PZe^{-E/RT} = \frac{kT}{h} e^{\Delta S^*/R} \cdot e^{-\Delta H^*/RT}$$

But $\quad E = \Delta H^*$

$$PZ = \frac{kT}{h} e^{\Delta S^*/R}$$

$$\therefore \quad P = \frac{kT}{Zh} e^{\Delta S^*/R}$$

Thus, the steric factor P is related to the entropy of activation ΔS^*.

Similarly, Eyring's equation can be applied to determine the rate constants of unimolecular and termolecular processes in addition to bimolecular reaction. It can also be applied to reactions in solution. However, these are not possible with the equation derived using statistical mechanics.

Comparison or Absolute Reaction Rate Theory With Arrhenius Equation

Arrhenius equation is given as

$$k_S = Ae^{-E_a/RT} \quad \ldots(25)$$

where, 'A', the pre exponential factor is known as the "frequency factor'. However the physical significance of the frequency factor could not be explained. But the physical significance of 'A' can be explained using Absolute Reaction Rate (ARR) theory.

Consider equation (24)

$$k_S = \frac{kT}{h} \cdot \frac{q^*}{q_A q_B} e^{-\Delta E_0/RT}$$

Replacing ΔE_0 by E_a, energy of activation, we get

$$k_S = \frac{kT}{h} \cdot \frac{q^*}{q_A q_B} e^{-E_a/RT}$$

On comparing the above equation with equation (25), the value of 'A' can be obtained as

$$A = \frac{kT}{h} \frac{q^*}{q_A q_B} \quad \ldots(26)$$

From thermodynamics,

$$q_A = \frac{(2\pi m_A kT)^{3/2}}{h^3} \quad \ldots(27)$$

$$q_B = \frac{(2\pi m_B kT)^{3/2}}{h^3} \quad \ldots(28)$$

$$q^* = \left[\frac{(2\pi(m_A + m_B)kT)^{3/2}}{h^3}\right]\left[\frac{8\pi^2 IkT}{h^2}\right] \quad \ldots(29)$$

where, I is the moment of inertia and its value is given as

$$I = \sigma^2 \left[\frac{m_A m_B}{m_A + m_B}\right]$$

where, σ is the mean diameter of the activated complex. Substituting the values of q_A, q_B, q^* and I in equation (26) we get

$$A = \frac{kT \times \dfrac{(2\pi(m_A + m_B)kT)^{3/2} \cdot \dfrac{8\pi^2 m_A m_B \sigma^2 kT}{(m_A + m_B)h^2}}{h^3}}{h \times \dfrac{(2\pi m_a kT)^{3/2}}{h^3} \cdot \dfrac{(2\pi m_B kT)^{3/2}}{h^3}}$$

$$A = \left[\frac{8\pi(m_A + m_B)}{m_A m_B} kT\right]^{1/2} \sigma^2$$

$$A = \left[\frac{8\pi(Nm_A + Nm_B) \cdot kTN}{Nm_A \cdot Nm_B}\right]^{1/2} \sigma^2$$

$$A = \left(8\pi \frac{M_A + M_B}{M_A \cdot M_B} RT\right)^{1/2} \sigma^2$$

where, $Nm = M$ and $R = Nk$ ...(30)

This equation for A indicates its physical significance.

Unimolecular Reactions

In these reactions activated complex is formed from a single reactant molecule. There are two types of unimolecular reactions namely elementary unimolecular reactions and unimolecular reactions involving free radical mechanism.

The Lindemann Theory of Unimolecular Reactions

The process of forming an activated molecule A^* having sufficient energy to undergo reaction is known as the energization process. This process involves collision between two molecules of A. The energized molecule A^* may undergo either de-energization by collision with a normal molecule or a unimolecular reaction to form products. These three processes are distinct and can be explained as follows.

$$A + A \underset{k_{-1}}{\overset{k_1}{\rightleftharpoons}} A^* + A$$

$$A^* \xrightarrow{k_2} \text{Products.}$$

The rate of energization $= k_1[A]^2$

The rate of de-energization $= k_{-1}\ [A^*][A]$

The rate of conversion into products $= k_2\,[A^*]$

At high pressure

The rate of de-energization will be greater than the rate of product formation, $k_2\,[A^*]$. When this is the case, the energized molecules A^* are essentially in equilibrium with normal molecules, and the concentration $[A^*]$ is thus proportional to the first power of $[A]$, being given by

$$[A^*] = \frac{k_1}{k_{-1}}[A]$$

Thus, the rate of reaction, equal to $k_2\,[A^*]$, is also proportional to $[A]$

$$\text{rate } v = k_2\,[A^*] = k_2\,\frac{k_1}{k_{-1}}[A] \qquad ...(31)$$

The kinetics are first order.

Change of order with pressure

The rate of de-energization will be very much less than the rate at which products are formed. There is no longer an equilibrium involving A^*. Instead the rate of product formation is almost equal to the rate at which A^* molecules are formed, since now these molecules nearly always become products. The rate of reaction therefore equals the rate of energization, which is $k_1[A]^2$. The kinetics are second order.

As per this theory there should be an observable transition from first order kinetics to second-order kinetics When the kinetics are first order, the rate of the reaction is given by equation (i). This is possible only if the rate of de-energization is considerably greater than the rate of conversion of A^* into products.

$$\text{rate } v = k'_\infty\ [A] \qquad ...(32)$$

where, $k'_\infty = \dfrac{k_1 k_2}{k_{-1}}$ (from equation (32)

Consider the situation when the rate of de-energization and of product formation are equal : the condition is

$$k_{-1}[A^*]\,[A]_{1/2} = k_2\,[A^*]$$

where, $[A]_{1/2}$ is the concentration at which this situation is attained. Now A^* has only 50% chance of becoming products and the rate is just half of the rate given by equation (31). Thus

$$v_{1/2} = \frac{1}{2}k_2\,\frac{k_1}{k_{-1}}\,[A]_{1/2}$$

$$= \frac{1}{2}k'_\infty\,[A]_{1/2} \qquad ...(33)$$

The first order rate coefficient k', defined under any condition by $v = k'[A]$ has fallen to one half of its limiting (high pressure) value of k'_∞.

On applying steady state hypothesis, the concentration $[A^*]$ becomes constant with time, so that $d[A^*]/dt = 0$. Hence, we can have

$$\frac{d[A^*]}{dt} = k_1[A]^2 - k_{-1}[A^*][A] - k_2[A^*] = 0$$

$$[A^*] = \frac{k_1[A]^2}{k_{-1}\ [A] + k_2}$$

The rate of formation of products

$$v = k_2\ [A^*] = \frac{k_1 k_2 [A]^2}{k_{-1}\ [A] + k_2} \qquad ...(34)$$

At sufficiently high concentrations (high pressure) $k_{-1}\ [A] >> k_2$, and the rate is

$$v = \frac{k_1 k_2}{k_{-1}}[A] = k'_\infty\,[A] \qquad \text{[equation (31)]}$$

At low pressure

At low concentrations (low pressure) $k_2 > k_{-1}[A]$ and $v = k_1[A]^2$ (from equation (34))

The kinetics becomes second order.

From equation (34) the first order rate coefficient is given as

$$k' = \frac{k_1 k_2 [A]}{k_{-1}[A] + k_2}$$

The above equation can be written as

$$k' = \frac{k_2 (k_1/k_{-1})}{1 + k_2/k_{-1}[A]} \qquad \ldots(35)$$

According to the equation (v), a plot of k' *versus* $[A]$ is a hyperbola, as shown in Figure 24.2. The first order coefficient k' is constant at higher concentration range but falls off at lower concentrations.

$$k' = k'_\infty/2 \qquad \text{when } k_{-1}[A] = k_2$$

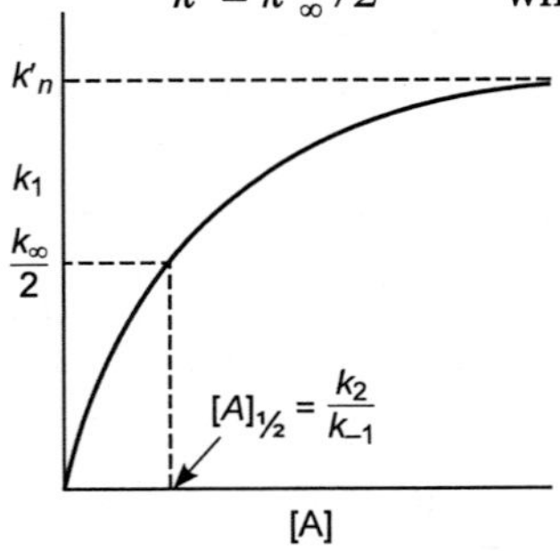

Fig.24.2 Plot of k' *versus* $[A]$ (according to equation (35))

At this situation the concentration is given as $[A]_{1/2}$.

Hence, $$[A]_{1/2} = \frac{k_2}{k_{-1}} = \frac{k'_\infty}{k_1}$$

Criticism of Lindemann's theory

The value of k'_∞ is an experimental quantity. It was though that the value of k_1 could be estimated easily on the basis of simple collision theory, from the equation $k_1 = Z_1 e^{-E_1/RT}$ where Z_1 is the collision frequency factor, E_1 is the activation energy. However, the experimental values of $[A]_{1/2}$ were always much smaller than those estimated in this way. Since k'_∞ is an experimental quantity, the error must be in the determination of k_1. Thus a modification is required to allow k_1 to be much larger than $Z_1 e^{-E_1/RT}$.

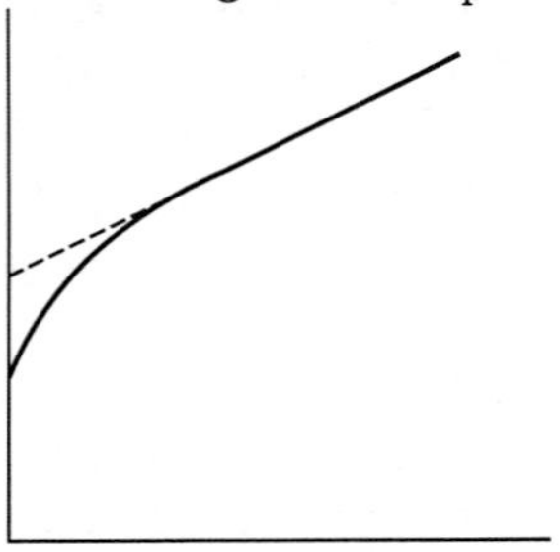

Fig. 24.3 Plot of $\frac{1}{k'}$ *vs* $\frac{1}{[A]}$

Secondly equation (35) can be written by taking the reciprocal as

$$\frac{1}{k'} = \frac{k_{-1}}{k_1 k_2} + \frac{1}{k_1[A]}$$

As per this equation a plot of $\frac{1}{k'}$ against $\frac{1}{[A]}$ should give a straight line. However, deviations from linearity is found as shown in the above figure.

Hinshelwood's Theory

Hinshelwood proposed his theory to overcome the difficulties in Lindemann theory. He pointed out that the expression $Ze^{-E/RT}$ only applies if energy is distributed among two degrees of freedom. However, for some unimolecular reactions the number of degrees of freedom '*s*' is considerable. The activation energy is distributed initially among these degrees of freedom, and there are many ways in which the distribution may be effected. Once the energy is in the molecule, distributed in any way among '*s*' vibrational degrees of freedom, the molecule is in a position eventually to react. After a number of vibrations of the energized molecule A^* –which may be a very considerable number–the energy may find its way into appropriate degrees of freedom so that A^* can pass at once into products.

Hinshelwood derived an equation for the fraction of molecules having energy in excess of ϵ_0^* using statistical mechanics as

$$f^* = \frac{1}{(s-1)!}\left(\frac{\epsilon_0^*}{kT}\right)^{s-1} \cdot e^{-\epsilon_0^*/kT} \qquad \ldots(36)$$

where s is the number of degrees of freedom. The rate constant k_1 can be given as

$$k_1 = \frac{1}{Z_1 (s-1)!}\left(\frac{\epsilon_0^*}{kT}\right)^{s-1} \cdot e^{-\epsilon_0^*/kT} \qquad \ldots(37)$$

In this equation in addition to $Z_1 e^{-\epsilon_0^*/kT}$, an additional factor of $\frac{1}{(s-1)!}\left(\frac{\epsilon_0^*}{kT}\right)^{s-1}$ has appeared. If '*s*' is sufficiently great this will be greater than unity by many powers of 10. Hence, there is a difference between the activation energy predicted by simple collision theory and Hinshelwood formulation for k_1. Equation (37) can be written as

$$k_1 \propto T^{1/2}\left(\frac{1}{T}\right)^{s-1} \cdot e^{-\epsilon_0^*/kT}$$

This equation leads to

$$\frac{d\ln k_1}{dT} = \frac{(3/2 - s)\,kT + \epsilon_0^*}{kT^2}$$

Since by the definition of the experimental activation energy

$$\frac{d\ln k_1}{dT} = \frac{E_a}{RT^2} = \frac{\epsilon_0}{kT^2}$$

where ϵ_a is the experimental activation energy per molecule and is related to ϵ_0^* as

$$\epsilon_0^* = \epsilon_a + (s - 3/2)\,kT \qquad \ldots(38)$$

Equation (37) gives much higher rates of activation and therefore much higher $\frac{k_1}{k_{-1}}$ values than simple collision theory.

Criticism of Hinshelwood's theory

1. The number '*s*' of degree of freedom required to give agreement with experiment on the basis of Hinshelwood's proposal usually turns out to be only about one-half of the total number of vibrational modes. No satisfactory explanation has been given for this.
2. According to Hinshelwood's treatment k'_∞ is given by
$$k'_\infty = \frac{k_1 k_2}{k_{-1}} = k_2 \frac{1}{(s-1)!}\left(\frac{\epsilon_0^*}{kT}\right)^{s-1} \cdot e^{-\epsilon^*/kT}$$
From this equation it is clear that the pre-exponential factor has a strong temperature dependence. But there is no experimental evidence for this.
3. Hinshelwood's treatment does not affect the argument that a plot of $\frac{1}{k'}$ *versus* $\frac{1}{[A]}$ should be linear (Figure 24.3). The lack of linearity found experimentally still calls for an explanation.
$$k' = \frac{k_2(k_1/k_{-1})}{1 + k_2/k_{-1}[M]} \qquad \ldots(39)$$

In Hinshelwood's theory both k_2 and $\frac{k_1}{k_{-1}}$ are treated as independent of ϵ_0^* the amount of energy in the energized molecule. Hinshelwood's formula (equation (37) involves only the critical energy ϵ_0^* and not ϵ^*.

Rice and Ramsperger and Kassel proposed RRK theory which involves the dependency of k_2 and $\frac{k_1}{k_{-1}}$ on ϵ^*, the amount of energy in the energized molecule. Equation (39) can be modified by replacing k_2 by $k_2(\epsilon^*)$ and $\frac{k_1}{k_{-1}}$ by $f(\epsilon^*)$ which is a distribution function. Then,

$$dk' = \frac{k_2(\epsilon^*)\,f(\epsilon^*)}{1 + k_2(\epsilon^*)/k_{-1}[M]}\,d\epsilon^* \qquad \ldots(40)$$

This equation gives a microcanonical constant relating to energized molecules having energy between ϵ^* and $\epsilon^* + d\epsilon^*$. To obtain the ordinary rate coefficient k', the expression can be integrated from ϵ_0^* (the minimum energy that can lead to reaction to infinity.

$$k' = \int_{\epsilon_0^*}^{\infty} \frac{k_2(\epsilon^*)\,f(\epsilon^*)}{1 + k_2(\epsilon^*)/k_{-1}[M]}\,d\epsilon^* \qquad \ldots(41)$$

In this theory a molecule is regarded as a system of loosely coupled oscillators. In the energized molecule A^* an amount of energy ϵ^* is distributed among the normal modes of vibration. Since he modes are coupled loosely, the energy can flow between them. After a sufficient number of vibrations the critical amount of energy ϵ_0^* may be in a particular normal mode and reaction can occur. For example, energy in an energized molecule of ethane, $C_2H_6^*$ may pass into a normal mode which corresponds to an extension of the C–C bond. If the energy is sufficiently great the bond will break with the formation of two methyl radicals.

RRK theory considers that the energy is distributed randomly among the normal modes. That is the energized molecules A^* have random lifetimes. The process of energised molecules A^* becoming activated molecules $A^\#$ depends entirely on statistical factors. In other words, the process by which A^* is formed does not lead to a species in which the energy is more likely to be in certain normal modes. Hence, there may be a higher or lower probability of forming $A^\#$.

Collisions which form A^* and which lead to deactivation of A^* are **strong collisions.** Activation occurs in a single collision than in successive collisions. When an energized molecule A^* undergoes a collision, it is assumed in the strong collision theory that de-energization is almost inevitable.

The dependency of k_2 on $\in^*$ can be explained as follows. The statistical weight of a system of '*s*' degrees of vibrational freedom containing '*j*' quanta of vibrational energy is equal to the number of ways in which '*j*' objects can be divided among '*s*' boxes, each of which can contain any number. The number of such ways is

$$w = \frac{(j+s-1)!}{j!\,(s-1)}$$

The statistical weight for states in which the '*s*' oscillators have '*j*' quanta among them and one particular oscillator has '*m*' quanta can be given as

$$w' = \frac{(j-m+s-1)!}{(j-m)!\,(s-1)!}$$

The probability that a particular oscillator has '*m*' quanta and all '*s*' oscillators have '*j*' quanta is the ratio of these.

$$\frac{w'}{w} = r = \frac{(j-m+s-1)!\; j!}{(j-m)!\,(j+s-1)!}$$

If Sterling approximation ($n! = n^n/e^n$) is applied to this expression, the terms in e^n cancel out, and the result is

$$r = \frac{(j-m+s-1)^{j-m+s-1}\, j^{\,j}}{(j-m)^{j-m}\,(j+s-1)^{j+s-1}}$$

If $j - m >> s - 1$, this reduces to

$$r = \frac{(j-m)^{j-m+s-1}\, j^{j}}{(j-m)^{j-m}\; j^{j+s-1}}$$

$$= \left(\frac{j-m}{j}\right)^{s-1}$$

The total number of quanta '*j*' may be taken as proportional to $\in^*$, the total energy of the molecule, while '*m*' is proportional to $\in_0^*$, the minimum energy that a molecule must have for decomposition to take place. Hence

$$r = \left(\frac{\in^* - \in_0^*}{\in^*}\right)^{s-1}$$

The rate with which the required energy $\in_0^*$ passes into this particular oscillator is proportional to this quantity. Hence,

$$k_2 = k^{\#}\left(\frac{\in^* - \in_0^*}{\in^*}\right)^{s-1} \qquad \ldots(41)$$

where $k^{\#}$ is the rate constant corresponding to the free passage of the system through the dividing surface; when $\in^*$ is sufficiently large, the energized molecule is essentially an activated molecule and therefore can pass immediately into the final state. The variation of k_2 with $\in^*/\in_0^*$, according to equation (41) is shown in Figure. 24.4.

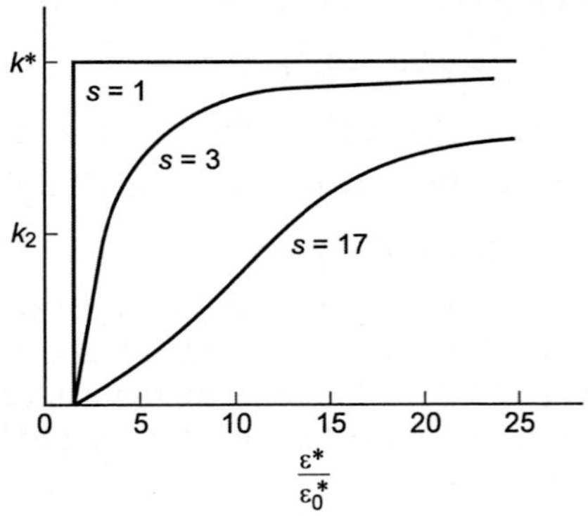

Fig. 24.4 Variation of k_2 with $\in^*/\in_0^*$ as given by equation (41) for different values of *s*, the number of degrees of freedom.

RRK theory also treats the distribution function $f(\in^*)$ as dependent on $\in^*$. If the energy $\in^*$ is distributed among *s* normal modes of vibration, from the Boltzmann distribution of energies, we get

$$f(\in^*) = \frac{1}{(s-1)!}\left(\frac{\in^*}{kT}\right)^{s-1}\frac{1}{kT}e^{-\in^*/kT}\cdot d\in^*$$

Introduction of this expression into equation (41) the general rate equation gives

$$k' = \int_{\in_0^*}^{\infty} \frac{k^{\#}\left(\dfrac{\in^* - \in_0^*}{\in^*}\right)^{s-1}\dfrac{1}{(s-1)!}\left(\dfrac{\in^*}{kT}\right)^{s-1}\dfrac{1}{kT}e^{-\in^*/kT}\cdot d\in^*}{1+\dfrac{k^{\#}}{k_{-1}[M]}\left(\dfrac{\in^* - \in_0^*}{\in^*}\right)^{s-1}}$$

This equation may be reduced by making the following substitutions :

$$x = \frac{\in^* - \in_0^*}{kT};\; b = \frac{\in_0^*}{kT}$$

Changing $d\in^*/dT$ to dx and integrating within the limits we get

$$k' = \int_0^{\infty}\frac{1/[(s-1)!]e^{-(x+b)}k^{\#}x^{s-1}dx}{1+(k^{\#}/k_{-1}[M])\,[x/(x+b)]^{s-1}}$$

$$= \frac{k^{\#}e^{-b}}{(s-1)!}\int_0^{\infty}\frac{x^{s-1}e^{-x}\,dx}{1+(k^{\#}/k_{-1}[M]\,[x/(x+b)]^{s-1}}$$

$$k' = \frac{k^{\#} e^{-\epsilon_0^*/kT}}{(s-1)!} \int_0^{\infty} \frac{x^{s-1} e^{-x} dx}{1 + (k^{\#}/k_{-1}[M])\,[x/(x+b)]^{s-1}} \quad \ldots(42)$$

When $[M]$ is very large (at the high pressure first-order limit) this expression reduces approximately to

$$k'_{\infty} = k^{\#} e^{-\epsilon_0^*/kT}$$

For given values of $[M]$, ϵ_0^* and s, the integral in equation (42) can be obtained by numerical methods.

Criticism of RRK theory

Equation (42) gives a reasonable agreement with experiment if 's' is taken to be about one-half of the total number of normal modes in the molecule. It is impossible to predict what value of 's' should be taken for a given reaction.

This theory also predicts a pre exponential factor of about $10^{13}\ s^{-1}$ for all unimolecular reactions. This is true for some reactions, but for many reactions the values are very much greater than this. There is no explanation for such high values.

Slater's treatment

Slater made a dynamical approach to explain the unimolecular reactions, According to him the bond breaks only when it becomes extended by a critical amount due to number of normal mode vibrations coming phase. This can be explained using the following equation.

$$C_2H_6 \longrightarrow 2CH_3$$

When the ethane molecule is energized as a result of collisions, the energy is distributed among the 18 normal modes of vibration. The C—C bond can break only if the bond expands by a critical amount.

Slater's theory could be successfully applied to explain the isomerisation reaction of cyclopropane. Slater was able to obtain good agreement with experimental value, since he considered that all 21 normal modes of vibration contribute to reaction.

Failures of Slater's treatment

Reactions like the dissociation of hydrogen peroxide and the decomposition of cyclobutane could not be explained by Slater's treatment. This theory gave low-pressure second-order rate constants which were much lower than experimental values. This problem is due to the assumption that all the modes contribute to reaction, but in reality certain modes are not contributing to reaction.

Marcus's extension of the RRK theory (RRKM)

According to this theory individual vibrational frequencies of the energized species and activated complexes are considered explicity. The way the various normal mode vibrations and rotations contribute to reaction is taken into account and allowance is made for the zero-point energies.

The total energy contained in a molecule is classified as active or inactive. The inactive energy is the energy remaining in the same quantum state without contributing to the breaking of bonds, essential for a reaction. The zero point energy containing overall translation and rotation energy is considered as inactive energy whereas the vibrational energy and the energy of internal rotations are considered active energy.

In this theory the distribution function $f(\epsilon^*)$ is given as

$$f(\epsilon^*)d\epsilon^* = \frac{N(\epsilon^*)\, e^{-\epsilon^*/kT} d\epsilon^*}{\int_0^{\infty} N(\epsilon^*) e^{-\epsilon^*/kT} d\epsilon^*}$$

where, $N(\epsilon^*)$ is the density of states having energy between ϵ^* and $\epsilon^* + d\epsilon^*$. The density of states is defined as the number of states per unit energy range. The denominator is the partition function relating to the active-energy contributions.

The expression for $k_2(\epsilon^*)$ in RRKM theory is

$$k_2(\epsilon^*) = \frac{l^{\#} \Sigma P(\epsilon^*_{\text{active}})}{hN(\epsilon^*)F_r}$$

where, $l^{\#}$ is the statistical factor, $\Sigma P(\epsilon^*_{\text{active}})$ is the number of vibration-rotational quantum states of the activated molecule, corresponding to all energies upto and including $\epsilon^*_{\text{active}}$. The factor F_r is introduced to correct for the fact that the rotations may not be the same in the activated molecule as in the energized molecule.

This theory gives the same expression for the limiting high-pressure first-order rate constant that is given by conventional transition-state theory.

$$k'_{\infty} = \frac{kT}{h} \frac{q_{\#}}{q_i} e^{-\epsilon_0^*/kT} \quad \ldots(43)$$

where $q_{\#}$ and q_i are the partition functions for activated and initial states. Thus, the theory can explain the abnormally high pre-exponential factor that are sometimes obtained.

Influence of foreign gases

The rate of a unimolecular gas reaction can be influenced by the addition of a non-reaction or 'foreign' gas which contributes to energization.

If the reaction is occurring in the low-pressure region where there is a fall-off in the first-order rate coefficient, the addition of a foreign gas may raise the rate coefficient to its high pressure limiting value.

If a gas A is undergoing reaction and a foreign gas M is added, the reactions are

$$A + A \underset{k_{-1}}{\overset{k_1}{\rightleftharpoons}} A^* + A$$

$$A + M \underset{k_{-1}}{\overset{k'_1}{\longrightarrow}} A^* + M$$

$$A^* \xrightarrow{k_2} \text{Product}$$

With the simple Lindemann-Christiansen-Hinshelwood assumptions, the steady state treatment leads to

$$u = \frac{k_2 (k_1 [A]^2 + k'_1 [A][M])}{k_{-1}[A] + k'_{-1}[M] + k_2}$$

By studying rates at various concentration of A and M, it is possible to obtain k'_1/k_1 and k'_{-1}/k_{-1}. These ratios represent the relative effectiveness with which M and A transfer energy to A.

Figure 24.5 represents the energy scheme for Lindemann, Hinshelwood, RRK and RRKM mechanisms.

Figure 24.6 summarises the way in which the theories arise from this general equation.

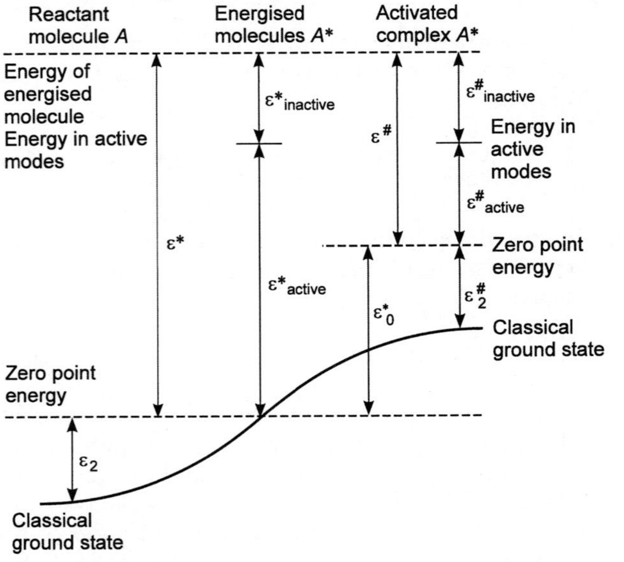

Fig. 24.5 Energy scheme for Lindemann, Hinshelwood, RRK and RRKM mechanisms.

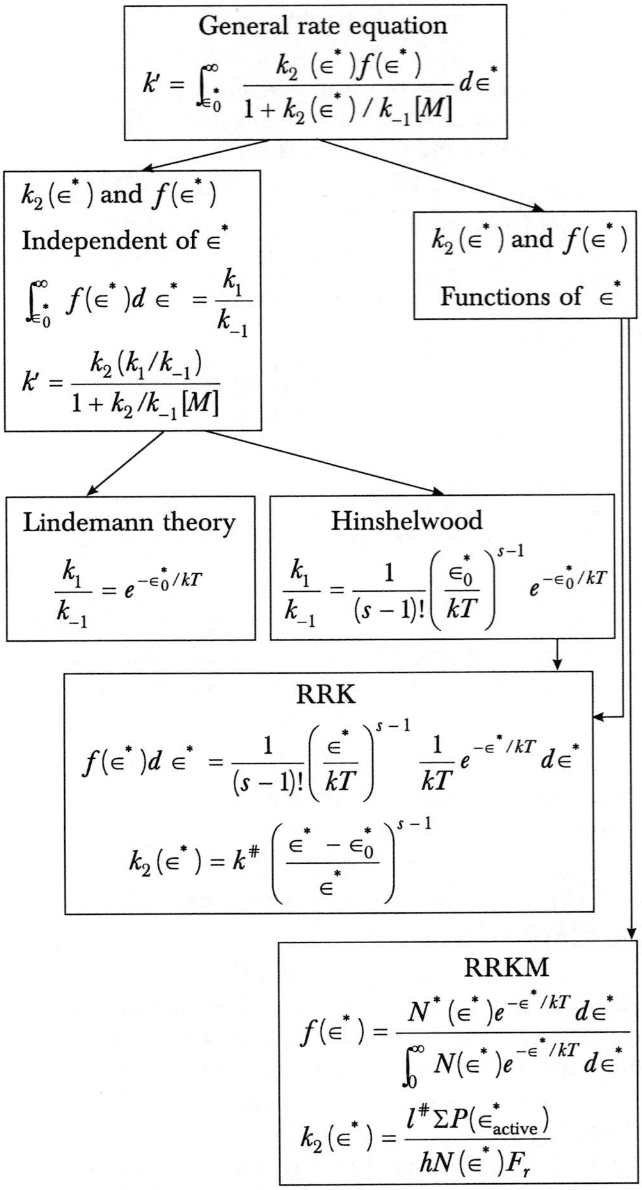

Fig. 24.6 Relationship between some of the theories of unimolecular gas reactions.

Enzyme Kinetics

Formation of the enzyme-substrate complex

$$\underset{\text{(Enzyme)}}{E} + \underset{\text{(Substrate)}}{S} \underset{k_{-1}}{\overset{k_1}{\rightleftharpoons}} \underset{\substack{\text{Complex} \\ \text{(enzyme-substrate complex)}}}{ES} \quad \text{(fast)}$$

Decomposition of the complex

$$ES \xrightarrow{k_2} \underset{\text{Product}}{P} + \underset{\text{Enzyme (free)}}{E}$$

On applying steady state treatment,

$$k_1[E][S] - k_{-1}[ES] - k_2[ES] = 0$$

The total concentration of the enzyme $[E]_0$ is equal to the concentration of free enzyme $[E]$ + the concentration of the complex, $[ES]$.

$$[E]_0 = [E] + [ES] \quad \text{or} \quad [E] = [E]_0 - [ES]$$

$$k_1([E]_0 - [ES])[S] - (k_{-1} + k_2)[ES] = 0$$

Hence, $$ES = \frac{k_1[E]_0[S]}{k_{-1} + k_2 + k_1[S]}$$

The rate of reaction,

$$r = k_2[ES] = \frac{k_1 k_2 [E]_0 [S]}{k_{-1} + k_2 + k_1[S]}$$

$$r = \frac{k_2[E]_0[S]}{(k_{-1} + k_2)/k_1 + [S]}$$

$$r = \frac{k_2[E]_0[S]}{k_m + S}$$

[where, $k_m = (k_{-1} + k_2)/k_1$]

This equation is known as Michaelis Menton equation and k_m is known as the Michaelis constant.

$$r = \frac{k_2[E]_0[S]}{k_m}$$

when $[S]$ is sufficiently small, the kinetics is first order in substrate concentration.

$$r = k_2[E]_0$$

when $[S] >> k_m$, the kinetics is zero order

When $[E]_0 = [ES]$,

$$r_{max} = V_{max} = k_2[E]_0$$

(The constant k_2 is called turn over number of the enzyme. It is defined as the number of molecules converted in unit time by one molecule of enzyme.)

V_{max} is the maximum rate, using the notation of enzymology.

The Michaelis Menton equation can be written as

$$\text{rate} = \frac{V_{max}[S]}{(k_m + [S])}$$

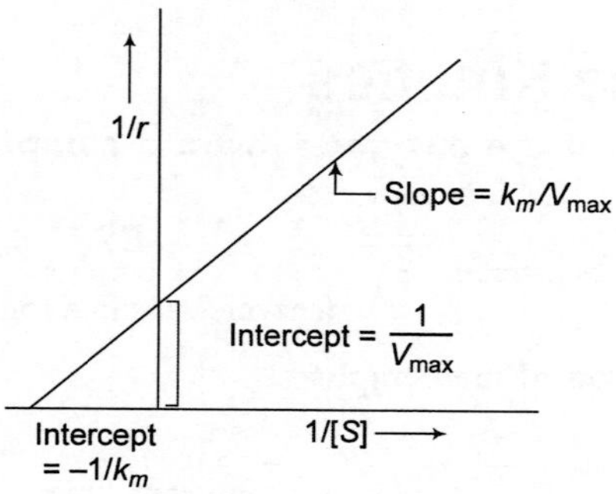

If $k_m = [S]$, $$\text{rate} = \frac{V_{max}[S]}{[S] + [S]} = \frac{V_{max}}{2}$$

A plot of $\frac{1}{r}$ *versus* $\frac{1}{[S]}$ gives a straight line with intercept on the X-axis and Y-axis $= \left(-\frac{1}{k_m}\right)$ and $\frac{1}{V_{max}}$ respectively and slope $= \frac{k_m}{V_{max}}$.

Homogeneous Catalysis

A catalyst is defined as a substance which increases the rate of the reaction without undergoing any change and the phenomenon is known as catalysis. In **homogeneous catalysis** reactants and catalyst are in the same phase, *e.g.,*

$$2SO_2(g) + O_2(g) \xrightarrow{NO(g)} 2SO_3(g)$$

In heterogeneous catalysis reactants and catalyst are in different phases. *e.g.,*

$$2H_2O_2(l) \xrightarrow{Pt(s)} 2H_2O + O_2$$

Theory of Homogeneous Catalysis

Catalysts allow reactions to occur *via* alternative pathways that increase reaction rates by lowering activation energies. The activation energy is lowered in all catalyzed reaction. A catalyst does take part in the reaction, but all of it is regenerated in later steps. The theory of homogeneous catalysis contains the following postulates

1. An intermediate compound is formed by catalyst with one of the reactants and this reactant is called substrate.

$$\underset{\text{Substrate}}{S} + \underset{\text{Catalyst}}{C} \underset{k_{-1}}{\overset{k_1}{\rightleftharpoons}} \underset{\text{Intermediate compound}}{SC} \qquad \text{(fast)}$$

2. Intermediate compound then reacts with the other reactant molecule 'R' to form the product (P) the catalyst (C).

$$SC + R \xrightarrow{k_2} P + C \qquad \text{(slow)}$$

$$r = k_2[SC][R] \qquad \ldots(43)$$

3. The catalyst generated above further undergo the first two steps to form more and more of the products. Therefore, in homogeneous catalysis rate of reaction depends upon the concentration of the catalyst.

Rate of formation of intermediate, SC

$$\frac{d[SC]}{dt} = k_1[S][C] - k_{-1}[SC] - k_2[SC][R]$$

On applying steady state treatment;

$$\frac{d[SC]}{dt} = k_1[S][C] - k_{-1}[SC] - k_2[SC][R] = 0$$

$$[SC] = \frac{k_1[S][C]}{k_{-1} + k_2[R]}$$

Substituting for $[SC]$ in equation (44)

rate of reaction, $$r = \frac{k_1 k_2[S][C][R]}{k_{-1} + k_2[R]}$$

If $k_{-1} << k_2$ $[R]$, then $r = k_1[S]$ $[C]$

If $k_{-1} >> k_2[R]$, then $$r = \frac{k_1 k_2[S][C][R]}{k_{-1}}$$

Photochemical Reactions

These reactions can occur by the absorption of photons of suitable energy, *e.g.*, photochemical decomposition of HI.

$$2HI \xrightarrow{hv} H_2 + I_2$$

Photochemical combination of H_2 and Cl_2 to form HCl.

$$H_2 + Cl_2 \xrightarrow{hv} 2HCl$$

Two basic laws of photochemistry are :

1. The Grothuss-Draper Law

This law states that only those radiations which are absorbed by the reacting system are effective in producing chemical change.

2. Law of Photochemical Equivalence

This law states that each light absorbing molecule in a photochemical reaction absorbs only one quantum of light which causes the activation.

Hydrogen and Chlorine Reaction

The photochemical reaction between hydrogen and chlorine is initiated by the light absorbed by chlorine in the region of 4785 Å. This reaction is very much influenced by oxygen. The chain mechanism of this reaction is explained in two ways (i) Combination of hydrogen and chlorine in the absence of oxygen and (ii) Combination of hydrogen and chlorine in the presence of oxygen.

Mechanism in the absence of oxygen

When a mixture of hydrogen and chlorine is exposed to light in the region of chlorine spectrum, chlorine molecule dissociates into atoms.

Chain initiation

(a) $$Cl_2 + hv \xrightarrow{k_1} 2Cl$$

Chain propagation

(b) $$Cl + H_2 \xrightarrow{k_2} HCl + H$$

(c) $$H + Cl_2 \xrightarrow{k_3} HCl + Cl$$

Chain termination

(d) $$Cl + \text{wall} \xrightarrow{k_4} \frac{1}{2}Cl_2$$

Derivation of rate law

The formation of hydrogen chloride is given by reactions (b) and (c). Therefore, its rate of formation is given by

$$\frac{d[HCl]}{dt} = k_2\,[Cl][H_2] + k_3[H][Cl_2] \qquad ...(54)$$

The formation of chlorine atoms is given by steps (a) and (c) and the removal of chlorine atom is given by steps (b) and (d). Therefore, the net rate of formation of [Cl] atoms is given by

$$\frac{d[Cl]}{dt} = k_1 I_{abs} + k_3\,[H][Cl_2] - k_2[Cl][H_2] - k_4[Cl] \qquad ...(55)$$

Similarly, for hydrogen atoms were can write as

$$\frac{d[H]}{dt} = k_2\,[Cl]\,[H_2] - k_3\,[H][Cl_2] \qquad ...(56)$$

When the stationary state is reached, it follows that

$$\frac{d[H]}{dt} = \frac{d[Cl]}{dt} = 0$$

Hence, $$k_1 I_{abs} + k_3[H][Cl_2] - k_2[Cl][H_2] - k_4[Cl] = 0 \qquad ...(57)$$

$$k_2[Cl][H_2] - k_3[H][Cl_2] = 0 \qquad ...(58)$$

On adding equations (57) and (58), we get

$$k_1 I_{abs} - k_4[Cl] = 0$$

$$[Cl] = \frac{k_1 I_{abs}}{k_4}$$

Similarly form equation (58), we get

$$[H] = \frac{k_2[Cl][H_2]}{k_3[Cl_2]}$$

On substituting this value of [H] in equation (54), we get

$$\frac{d[\text{HC}]}{dt} = k_2\ [\text{Cl}]\ [\text{H}_2] + k_2 [\text{Cl}][\text{H}_2] \quad \ldots(59)$$

On substituting the value of [Cl] in equation (59), we get

$$\frac{d[\text{HCl}]}{dt} = \frac{k_1 k_2}{k_4} \text{I}_{\text{abs}}\ [\text{H}_2] + \frac{k_1 k_2}{k_4} kI_{\text{abs}} [\text{H}_2]$$

$$= 2\left(\frac{k_1 k_2}{k_4}\right) I_{abs}\ [\text{H}_2] \quad \ldots(60)$$

This equation is in perfect agreement with experimental data.

In the presence of oxygen

When the reaction is carried out in the presence of oxygen, the mechanism is as follows.

(a) $\text{Cl}_2 + h\nu \xrightarrow{k_1} 2\text{Cl}$ (b) $\text{Cl} + \text{H}_2 \xrightarrow{k_2} \text{HCl} + \text{H}$

(c) $\text{H} + \text{Cl}_2 \xrightarrow{k_3} \text{HCl} + \text{Cl}$ (d) $\text{H} + \text{O}_2 \xrightarrow{k_4} \text{HO}_2$

(e) $\text{Cl} + \text{O}_2 \xrightarrow{k_5} \text{ClO}_2$ (f) $\text{Cl} + X \xrightarrow{k_6} \text{Cl}X$

In step (f) X is the substance which removes chlorine atom.

The formation of hydrogen chloride is given by steps (b) and (c). Thus,

$$\frac{d[\text{HCl}]}{dt} = k_2 [\text{Cl}][\text{H}_2] + k_3 [\text{H}][\text{Cl}_2]$$

Since, the reaction (c) is much faster than (b)

$$\frac{d[\text{HCl}]}{dt} = k_3 [\text{Cl}_2][\text{H}]$$

Chlorine atoms are formed at steps (a) and (c) and removed at steps (b), (e) and (f). Thus,

$$\frac{d[\text{Cl}]}{dt} = k_1 \text{I}_{\text{abs}} + k_3 [\text{H}]\ [\text{Cl}_2] - k_2 [\text{Cl}][\text{H}_2] - k_5 [\text{Cl}][\text{O}_2] - k_6 [\text{Cl}][X]$$

Applying steady state

$$\frac{d[\text{Cl}]}{dt} = k_1 \text{I}_{\text{abs}} + k_3 [\text{H}]\ [\text{Cl}_2] - k_2 [\text{Cl}]\ [\text{H}_2] - k_5 [\text{Cl}]\ [\text{O}_2] - k_6 [\text{Cl}][X] = 0$$

$$[\text{Cl}] = \frac{k_1 \text{I}_{\text{abs}} + k_3 [\text{H}]\ [\text{Cl}_2]}{k_2 [\text{H}_2] + k_5 [\text{O}_2] + k_6 [X]} \quad \ldots(61)$$

Similarly,

$$\frac{d[\text{H}]}{dt} = k_2 [\text{Cl}][\text{H}_2] - k_3 [\text{H}][\text{Cl}_2] - k_4 [\text{H}][\text{O}_2] = 0$$

From this

$$[\text{Cl}] = \frac{k_3 [\text{H}][\text{Cl}_2] + k_4 [\text{H}][\text{O}_2]}{k_2 [\text{H}_2]} \quad \ldots(62)$$

Equating equations (61) and (62), we get

$$\frac{k_1 \text{I}_{\text{abs}} + k_3 [\text{H}][\text{Cl}_2]}{k_2 [\text{H}_2] + k_5 [\text{O}_2] + k_6 [X]} = \frac{k_3 [\text{H}][\text{Cl}_2] + k_4 [\text{H}]\ [\text{O}_2]}{k_2 [\text{H}_2]}$$

$$(k_2 [\text{H}_2])\ (k_1 \text{I}_{\text{bas}} + k_3 [\text{H}][\text{Cl}_2])$$

$$= (k_2 [\text{H}_2] + k_5 [\text{O}_2] + k_6 [X]\ (k_3 [\text{H}][\text{Cl}_2] + k_4 [\text{H}][\text{O}_2])$$

$$k_2 [\text{H}_2] k_1 \text{I}_{\text{abs}} + k_2 k_3 [\text{H}][\text{H}_2][\text{Cl}_2]$$

$$= k_2 [\text{H}_2] k_3 [\text{H}][\text{Cl}_2] + k_2 [\text{H}_2] k_4 [\text{H}][\text{O}_2] + k_5 [\text{O}_2] k_3 [\text{H}][\text{Cl}_2] + k_5 [\text{O}_2] k_4\ [\text{H}][\text{O}_2] + k_6 [X] k_3 [\text{H}][\text{Cl}_2] + k_6 [X] k_4\ [\text{H}][\text{O}_2]$$

After omitting the term $k_4 k_5 [\text{O}_2]^2 [\text{H}]$ which is very small, the equation becomes

$$k_2 [\text{H}_2] k_1 \text{I}_{\text{abs}} + k_2 k_3 [\text{H}][\text{H}_2][\text{Cl}_2]$$

$$= k_2 [\text{H}_2] k_3 [\text{H}][\text{Cl}_2] + k_2 [\text{H}_2] k_4 [\text{H}][\text{O}_2] + k_5 [\text{O}_2] k_3 [\text{H}][\text{Cl}_2] + k_6 [X] k_3 [\text{H}][\text{Cl}_2] + k_6 [X] k_4 [\text{H}][\text{O}_2]$$

$$[\text{H}] = \frac{k_1 k_2 [\text{H}_2] \text{I}_{\text{abs}}}{k_2 k_4 [\text{H}_2][\text{O}_2] + k_3 k_5 [\text{O}_2][\text{Cl}_2] + k_6\ [X] k_3 [\text{Cl}_2] + k_6 [X] k_4 [\text{O}_2]}$$

$$= \frac{k_1 k_2 [\text{H}_2] \text{I}_{\text{abs}}}{k_3 k_6 [\text{Cl}_2][X] + [\text{O}_2][k_2 k_4 [\text{H}_2] + k_3 k_5\ [\text{Cl}_2] + k_4 k_6 [X]]} \quad \ldots(63)$$

On introducing [H] in equation (i), we get

$$\frac{d[\text{HCl}]}{dt} = \frac{k_3 k_1 \text{I}_{\text{abs}}\ k_2 [\text{H}_2][\text{Cl}_2]}{k_3 k_6 [\text{Cl}_2][X] + [\text{O}_2](k_2 k_4 [\text{H}_2] + k_3 k_5 [\text{Cl}_2] + k_4 k_6 [X])} \quad \ldots(64)$$

On dividing the numerator and denominator of the right hand side by $k_2 k_4$, we get

$$\frac{d[\text{HCl}]}{dt} = \frac{\left(\frac{k_1 k_3}{k_4}\right) \text{I}_{\text{abs}}\ [\text{H}_2][\text{Cl}_2]}{\frac{k_3 k_6}{k_2 k_4} [\text{Cl}_2][X] + [\text{O}_2]\left([\text{H}_2] + \frac{k_3 k_5}{k_2 k_4} [\text{Cl}_2] + \frac{k_6}{k_2} [X]\right)} \quad \ldots(65)$$

$$= \frac{k\text{I}_{\text{abs}}\ [\text{H}_2][\text{Cl}_2]}{m[\text{Cl}_2] + [\text{O}_2]\left([\text{H}_2] + \frac{[\text{Cl}_2]}{10} + \frac{k_6}{k_2}[X]\right)} \quad \ldots(66)$$

where $k = \frac{k_1 k_3}{k_4}$, $m = \frac{k_3 k_4 [X]}{k_2 k_4}$ and $\frac{1}{10} = \frac{k_3 k_5}{k_2 k_4}$

Equation (66) is in full agreement with the experimental rate equation.

Photolysis of Acetaldehyde

While studying this reaction the following points are to be kept in mind.

1. The quantum yield increases with increase in temperature.
2. The quantum yield of carbon monoxide formation increases with decreasing wavelength.
3. The quantum yield of carbon monoxide formation at room temperature increases with decreasing pressure at 3130 Å.
4. The photolysis of acetaldehyde in the light of 2500 – 3100 Å wavelength yields methane, carbon monoxide, ethane and number of other products.

$$CH_3CHO + h\nu \longrightarrow CH_4 + C_2H_6 + CO + \text{other products}$$

To account for the above facts, the following mechanism has been proposed.

(a) $CH_3CHO + h\nu \xrightarrow{k_1} CH_3 + CHO$

(b) $CH_3CHO + CH_3 \xrightarrow{k_2} CH_4 + CH_3CO$

(c) $CH_3CO \xrightarrow{k_3} CO + CH_3$

(d) $CH_3 + CH_3 \xrightarrow{k_4} C_2H_6$

Carbon monoxide is formed only in step (c), hence, the rate of formation is given as

$$\frac{d[CO]}{dt} = k_3[CH_3CO] \quad ...(67)$$

The CH_3CO is formed in step (b) and removed in step (c). Hence, the net rate of formation is given as

$$\frac{d[CH_3CO]}{dt} = k_2\,[CH_3CHO]\,[CH_3] - k_3[CH_3CO] ...(68)$$

Similarly CH_3 is formed in steps (a) and (c) and removed in steps (b) and (d). Hence, its rate of formation is given as

$$\frac{d[CH_3]}{dt} = k_1 I_{abs} + k_3[CH_3CO] - k_2[CH_3CHO][CH_3] - k_4[CH_3]^2 \quad ...(69)$$

Applying steady state treatment to $[CH_3CO]$, we obtain

$$d\frac{[CH_3CO]}{dt} = k_2\,[CH_3CHO]\,[CH_3] - k_3[CH_3CO] = 0 \quad ...(70)$$

Similarly on applying steady state treatment to $[CH_3]$, we get

$$\frac{d[CH_3]}{dt} = k_1 I_{abs} - k_2[CH_3CHO][CH_3] + k_3[CH_3CO] - k_4[CH_3]^2 = 0 ...(71)$$

By adding equations (70) and (71), we get

$$k_1 I_{abs} - k_4[CH_3]^2 = 0$$

$$= [CH_3] = \left(\frac{k_1 I_{abs}}{k_4}\right)^{1/2}$$

On substituting the value of $[CH_3]$ in equation (72) we get

$$k_2[CH_3CHO]\left(\frac{k_1 I_{abs}}{k_4}\right)^{1/2} - k_3[CH_3CO] = 0$$

$$k_3[CH_3CO] = k_2[CH_3CHO]\left(\frac{k_1 I_{abs}}{k_4}\right)^{1/2} \quad ...(73)$$

Substituting this value of $k_3[CH_3CO]$ in equation (67), we get

$$\frac{d[CO]}{dt} = k_2[CH_3CHO]\left(\frac{k_1 I_{abs}}{k_4}\right)^{1/2}$$

$$= \left(\frac{k_1}{k_4}\right)^{1/2} k_2\,[CH_3CHO]\,(I_{abs})^{1/2}$$

$$= k[CH_3CHO]\,(I_{abs})^{1/2} \quad ...(68)$$

where $k = k_2\left(\frac{k_1}{k_4}\right)^{1/2}$

Quantum yield

If the rate of formation of carbon monoxide is divided by the intensity of absorbed radiation, the value of quantum yield is obtained. Thus

$$\text{Quantum yield} = \frac{d[CO]/dt}{I_{abs}} = \frac{k(I_{abs})^{1/2}[CH_3CHO]}{I_{abs}} = \frac{k[CH_3CHO]}{(I_{abs})^{1/2}} \quad ...(69)$$

General discussion

From equation (69) it is clear that the quantum yield of carbon monoxide formation increases with decrease in light intensity. CHO is formed from CH_3CHO by the absorption of light at 3130 Å. At this wavelength CHO does not posses enough energy to decompose spontaneously. At high pressure CHO may combine to form glyoxal. At low pressure CHO may diffuse to the walls to form carbon monoxide.

Kinetics of Polymerization

There are two main types of polymerization, condensation polymerization and addition polymerization.

Condensation Polymerization

Consider a general reaction,

$$M_m + M_n \longrightarrow M_{m+n}$$

m and n are integers greater than one.

The rate of disappearance of the monomer takes place by combination of either two monomer units or a monomer and a dimer or a monomer and a trimer and so on.

$$-\frac{d[M_1]}{dt} = k[M_1]^2 + k[M_1][M_2] + \ldots$$

Thus, $$-\frac{d[M_1]}{dt} = k[M_1]\sum_{n=1}^{\infty}[M_n]$$

The net rate of production of the dimer is

$$\frac{d[M_2]}{dt} = \frac{1}{2}k[M_1]^2 - k[M_2]\sum_{n=1}^{\infty}[M_n]$$

(The factor $\frac{1}{2}$ is included in the rate of production because one dimer molecule is formed from two monomer molecules). Similarly, net rate of production of polymer containing n monomers is

$$\frac{d[M_n]}{dt} = \frac{1}{2}k\sum_{s=1}^{s-n-1}[M_s][M_{n-s}] - k[M_n]\sum_{n=1}^{\infty}[M_n]$$

$$\frac{d\sum_{n=1}^{\infty}[M_n]}{dt} = -\frac{1}{2}k\left[\sum_{n=1}^{\infty}[M_n]^2\right]$$

If $[M_1]_0$ is the total concentration of monomer at $t = 0$ and $\sum_{n=1}^{\infty}[M_n]$ the concentration of all species together at t, then we define,

$$f = \frac{[M_n]_0 - \sum_{n=1}^{\infty}[M_n]}{[M_1]_0}$$

$$\frac{df}{dt} = \frac{1}{2}[M_1]_0\, k(1-f)^2$$

On integration, we get $$f = \frac{[M_1]_0\, kt}{2 + [M_1]_0\, kt}$$

The concentration of polymer containing n monomers

$$[M_n] = [M_1]_0\, f^{n-1}(1-f)^2$$

Kinetics of Addition Polymerization

Consider the catalytic polymerization of a monomer vinyl chloride, $CH_2{=}CHCl$. Polymerization reaction proceed through free radical mechanism.

Chain initiation step

The initiator molecule I produces a free radical R.

$$I \xrightarrow{k_1} R$$

The rate of production of the free radical,

$$r = K_1 I \quad \ldots(72)$$

Chain propagation step

Free radical R reacts with monomer molecules and generates new free radicals.

$$R + CH_2{=}CHCl \xrightarrow{k_2} RCH_2{-}CHCl$$

$$RCH_2{-}CHCl + CH_2{=}CHCl \longrightarrow$$

$$R{-}(CH_2{-}CHCl)_2 \text{ and so on.}$$

Rate of disappearance of monomer, M

$$-\frac{d[M]}{dt} = k_2[R][M] \quad \ldots(73)$$

Chain termination step

Recombination of two free radicals

$$R{-}(CH_2{-}CHCl)_n + (ClCH{-}CH_2)_2{-}R \xrightarrow{k_3}$$

$$R{-}(CH_2{-}CHCl)_n{-}(ClCH{-}CH_2)_n{-}R$$

Since, the free radicals have very low concentration, the rate of appearance of free radicals = rate of disappearance of free radicals.

$$k_1[I] = k_3[R]^2 \quad \ldots(74)$$

$$[R] = \left(\frac{k_1}{k_3}\right)^{1/2} I^{1/2} \quad \ldots(75)$$

By putting the value of $[R]$ in equation (73), we get

$$-\frac{d[M]}{dt} = k_2\left(\frac{k_1}{k_3}\right)^{1/2}[I]^{1/2}[M]$$

$$-\frac{d[M]}{dt} = k[I]^{1/2}[M]$$

Kinetic chain length, $$\gamma = \frac{\text{Overall rate}}{\text{Rate of initiation step}}$$

$$\gamma = \frac{-d[M]/dt}{r} = \frac{-d[M]/dt}{k_1[I]}$$

γ can also be defined as the number of repeating chain units in the polymer chain.

Exercise 1

(For Part 'B')

1. Choose the correct statement.
(a) The $t_{1/2}$ of a first order reaction is independent of the initial concentration.
(b) Order is always equal to molecularity of reaction.
(c) The units of second order rate constant are mol dm^{-3} s^{-1}.
(d) The rate constant of a reaction decreases with T.

2. The pseudo first order reaction rate for the reaction,
$C_2H_5OH + OH^- \longrightarrow C_2H_5O^- + H_2O$, studied in 0.1 M NaOH solution is given by $-d[C_2H_5OH]/dt = k[C_2H_5OH]$. If k is 2.95×10^{-5} s^{-1}, second order rate constant is
(a) 2.95×10^6 dm^3 mol^{-1} s^{-1}
(b) 2.95×10^4 dm^3 mol^{-1} s^{-1}
(c) 2.95×10^2 dm^3 mol^{-1} s^{-1}
(d) 2.95×10^{-6} dm^3 mol^{-1} s^{-1}

3. If E_a of a reaction is zero, k is equal to (A is the frequency factor)
(a) zero (b) infinity
(c) A^2 (d) A^{-1}

4. The rate constant, $k = 1.2 \times 10^3$ mol^{-1} L s^{-1} and $E_a = 2.0 \times 10^2$ kJ mol^{-1}. When $T \to \infty$
(a) $A = 2.0 \times 10^2$ kJ mol^{-1}
(b) $A = 1.2 \times 10^3$ mol^{-1} L s^{-1}
(c) $A = 1.2 \times 10^3$ mol L^{-1} s^{-1}
(d) $A = 2.4 \times 10^3$ kJ mol^{-1} s^{-1}

5. At a certain temperature, the first order rate constant k_1 is found to be smaller than the second order rate constant k_2. If the $E_a(1)$ of the first order reaction is greater than $E_a(2)$ of the second order reaction, then as temperature is raised
(a) k_2 will increase faster than k_1
(b) k_1 will increase faster than k_2 but will always remain less than k_2
(c) k_1 will increase faster than k_2 and become equal to k_2
(d) k_1 will increase faster than k_2 and become greater than k_2

6. The rate of a chemical reaction generally increases rapidly even for small temperature increase because of rapid increase in the
(a) collision frequency
(b) fraction of molecules with energies in excess of the activation energy
(c) activation energy
(d) average kinetic energy of molecules

7. Select correct statement.
(a) A collision between reactant molecules must occur with a certain minimum energy before it is effective in yielding product molecules.
(b) $\dfrac{d(\log_{10} k)}{dt} = \dfrac{E_a}{2.303\,RT^2}$ is called Arrhenius equation.
(c) Both (a) and (b)
(d) None of the above

8. Graph between concentration x of the product and time of the reaction $A \longrightarrow B$ is of the following type,

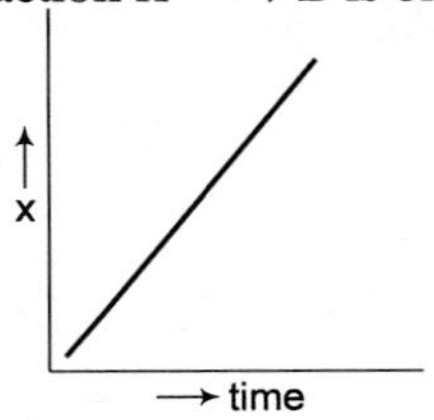

Hence, graph between $-\dfrac{d[A]}{dt}$ and time will be of the type

(a)
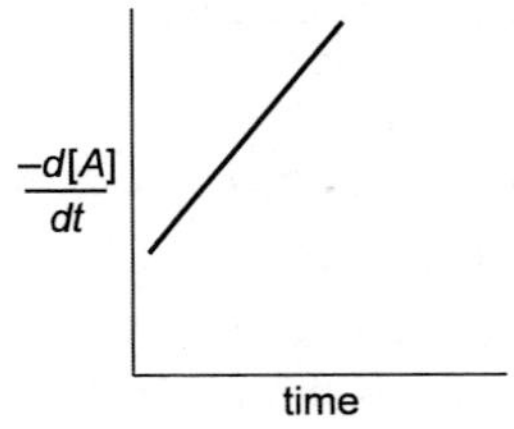

(b)
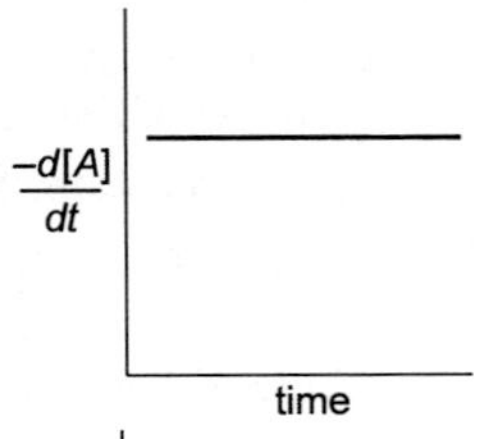

(c)
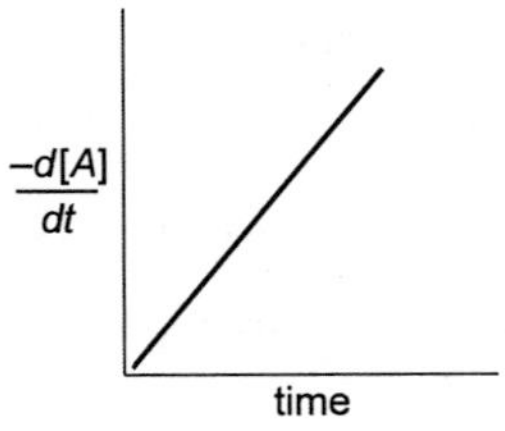

(d)
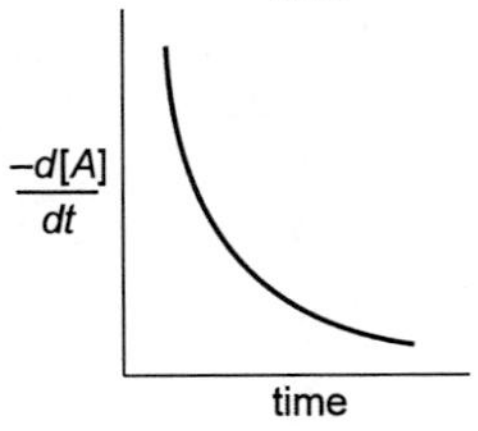

9. The reaction,
$H_2(g) + 2ICl(g) \longrightarrow I_2(g) + 2HCl(g)$ has a second order rate law, rate $= k[H_2][ICl]$.
Hence, rate determining step is
(a) $H_2(g) + ICl(g) \longrightarrow HCl(g) + HI(g)$
(b) $HI(g) + ICl(g) \longrightarrow HCl(g) + I_2(g)$
(c) Both (a) and (b)
(d) None of the above

10. Consider the first order decomposition of A molecules in three vessels of equal volume

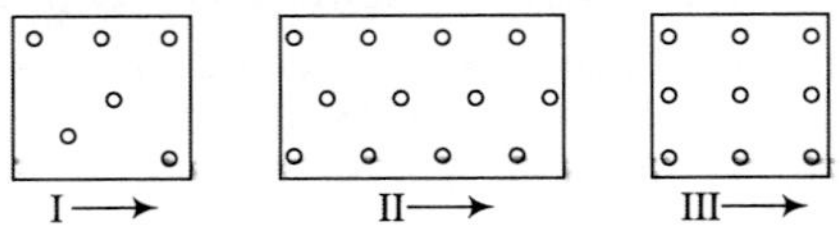

Relative rates of decomposition in I, II and III are
(a) 1 : 2 : 1.5 (b) 1 : 1 : 1
(c) 1 : 3.5 : 2 (d) 2 : 4 : 1

11. For the reaction,

$$A_2 + 2B \longrightarrow 2AB$$

$[A_2]$	$[B]$	$-\dfrac{d[A_2]}{dt}$
0.1 M	0.2 M	1×10^{-2} Ms^{-1}
0.2 M	0.2 M	2×10^{-2} Ms^{-1}
0.2 M	0.4 M	8×10^{-2} Ms^{-1}

Order of reaction *wrt* A_2 and B are respectively
(a) 1, 2 (b) 2, 1
(c) 1, 1 (d) 2, 2

12. In presence of catalyst, E_a is lowered by 2 kcal at 27°C. Hence, rate will be
(a) 20 times (b) 14 times
(c) 28 times (d) 2 times

13. 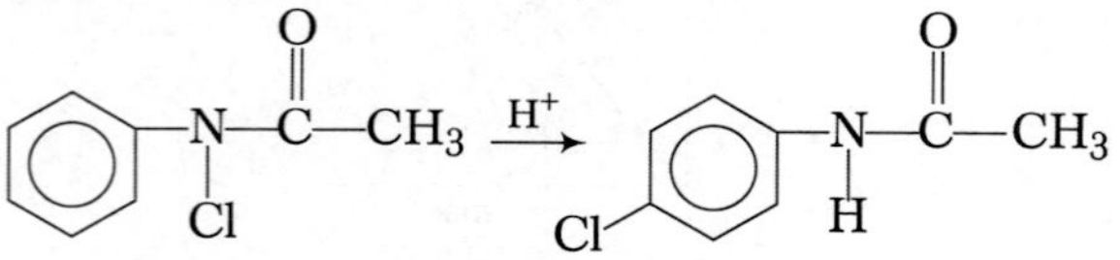

Reaction kinetics can be studied by
(a) measurement of pH
(b) titration with hypo after adding KI
(c) Both (a) and (b) are correct
(d) None of the above is correct

14. For the reaction, $3BrO^- \longrightarrow BrO_3^- + 2Br^-$
in alkaline aqueous solution, the value of the second order (in BrO^-) rate constant at 80°C in the rate law $-\Delta[BrO^-]/\Delta t$ was found to the 0.056 L mol^{-1} s^{-1}. Rate constant when the rate law is written for $\dfrac{\Delta[BrO_3^-]}{\Delta t}$ is
(a) 0.056 L mol^{-1} s^{-1} (b) 0.056/3 L mol^{-1} s^{-1}
(c) $0.056\times\dfrac{2}{3}$ L mol^{-1} s^{-1} (d) 0.028 L mol^{-1} s^{-1}

15. $2N_2O_5 \longrightarrow 4NO_2 + O_2$
If $-\dfrac{\Delta[N_2O_5]}{\Delta t} = k_1[N_2O_5]$, $\dfrac{\Delta[NO_2]}{\Delta t} = k_2[N_2O_5]$, $\dfrac{\Delta[O_2]}{\Delta t} = k_3[N_2O_5]$, then
(a) $k_1 = k_2 = k_3$ (b) $2k_1 = k_2 = 4k_3$
(c) $2k_1 = 4k_2 = k_3$ (d) None of these

16. A reaction is catalyzed by H^+ ion. In presence of HA rate constant is 2×10^{-3} min^{-1} and in presence of HB rate constant is 1×10^{-3} min^{-1}. HA and HB (both strong acids) have relative strength as
(a) 0.5 (b) 0.002
(c) 0.001 (d) 2

17. For the first order reaction $(C = C_0 e^{-k_1 t})$ and $T_{av} = k_1^{-1}$. After two average lives, concentration of the reactant is reduced to
(a) 25% (b) 75% (c) $\dfrac{100}{e}$ % (d) $\dfrac{100}{e^2}$ %

18. The rate law for the dimerization of NO_2 into N_2O_4 is

$$-\frac{d[NO_2]}{dt} = k[NO_2]^2$$

Which of the following changes will change the value of the specific rate constant k?
(a) Doubling the total pressure
(b) Decreasing the pressure
(c) Changing the volume of the flask
(d) Changing the temperature

19. When temperature of a reaction is changed from T_1 and T_2, half-life is found to decrease. Thus,
(a) $T_1 > T_2$ and reaction is endothermic
(b) $T_2 > T_1$ and reaction is exothermic
(c) $T_1 > T_2$ and reaction is exothermic
(d) $T_2 > T_1$ and reaction can be exothermic or endothermic

20. Following reaction takes place by mechanism

$$NO_2 + CO \longrightarrow NO + CO_2$$

Step I $NO_2 + NO_2 \xrightarrow{k_1,\text{ slow}} NO_3 + NO$

Step II $NO_3 + CO \xrightarrow{k_2,\text{ fast}} NO_2 + CO_2$

Hence, $\left(\dfrac{dx}{dt}\right)$ for the given reaction is
(a) $k_1[NO_2]^2 - k_2[NO_3][CO]$
(b) $k_1[NO_2]^2 + k_2[NO_3][CO]$
(c) $k_1[NO_2]^2$
(d) $k_1[NO_2] + k_2[CO]$

21. For the reaction

$$2Fe^{2+} + H_2O_2 \longrightarrow 2Fe^{3+} + 2OH^-,$$

$\dfrac{d[Fe^{3+}]}{dt} = k[Fe^{2+}][H_2O_2]$, hence, slow step is
(a) $Fe^{2+} + H_2O_2 \longrightarrow Fe^{3+} + OH^- + OH$
(b) $Fe^{2+} + OH \longrightarrow Fe^{3+} + OH^-$
(c) $2Fe^{2+} + H_2O_2 \longrightarrow 2Fe^{3+} + 2OH^-$
(d) $Fe^{2+} \longrightarrow Fe^{3+} + e^-$

22. For the reaction,
$2H_2(g) + 2NO(g) \longrightarrow N_2(g) + 2H_2O(g)$ rate law is rate $= k[NO]^2[H_2]$. Mechanism is given by

Step I $2NO \longrightarrow N_2O_2$
Step II $N_2O_2 + H_2 \longrightarrow N_2O + H_2O$
Step III $N_2O + H_2 \longrightarrow N_2 + H_2O$

Rate law is true if
(a) Step I is the slow step
(b) Step II is the slow step
(c) Step III is the slow step
(d) Step I and II are slow steps

23. A chemical reaction is said to take place through the various stages with $\Delta G°$ values indicated by the graph

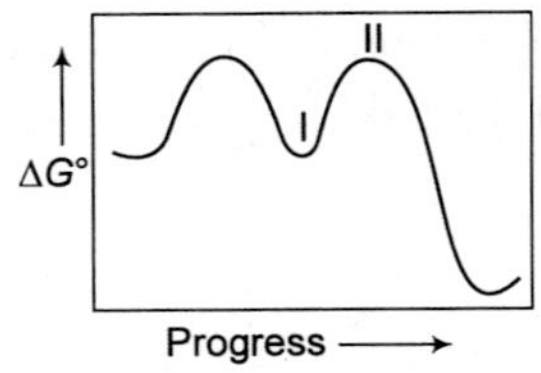

Stages I and II represent respectively.

	I	II
(a)	activated complex	activated complex
(b)	reaction intermediate	activated complex
(c)	activated complex	reaction intermediate
(d)	reaction intermediate	reaction intermediate

24. The reaction of $NO_2(g)$ and $O_3(g)$ is first order in $NO_2(g)$ and $O_3(g)$

$$2NO_2(g)+O_3(g) \longrightarrow N_2O_5(g)+O_2(g)$$

The reaction can take place by mechanism

Step I $NO_2 + O_3 \xrightarrow{\text{Slow}} NO_3 + O_2$

$NO_3 + NO_2 \xrightarrow{\text{Fast}} N_2O_5$

Step II $O_3 \xrightarrow{\text{Fast}} O_2 + O$

$NO_2 + O \xrightarrow{\text{Slow}} NO_3$

$NO_3 + NO_2 \xrightarrow{\text{Fast}} N_2O_5$

Select the correct mechanism.
(a) I only (b) II only
(c) Both I and II (d) None of I and II

25. The rates of many chemical reactions double for a ten degree rise in temperature. Which of these factors does not contribute to this change in the rate with increasing temperature?
(a) The average kinetic energy of the reactant species
(b) The number of collisions in a given time
(c) The number of very energetic spector
(d) The activation energy

26. If I is the intensity of absorbed light and C is the concentration of AB for the photochemical process.
$AB + h\nu \longrightarrow AB^*$, the rate of formation of AB^* is directly proportional to
(a) C (b) I
(c) I^2 (d) $C \cdot I$

27. The data for the reaction $A + B \longrightarrow C$, is

Exp.	$[A]_0$	$[B]_0$	Initial rate
1	0.012	0.035	0.10
2	0.024	0.070	0.80
3	0.024	0.035	0.10
4	0.012	0.070	0.80

The rate law corresponds to the above data is
(a) rate $= k[B]^3$ (b) rate $= k[B]^4$
(c) rate $= k[A][B]^3$ (d) $k[A]^2[B]^2$

28. For a given reaction,

$$2H_2O_2 \longrightarrow 2H_2O + O_2$$

Graph between $\log[H_2O_2]$ and time t is of the type.

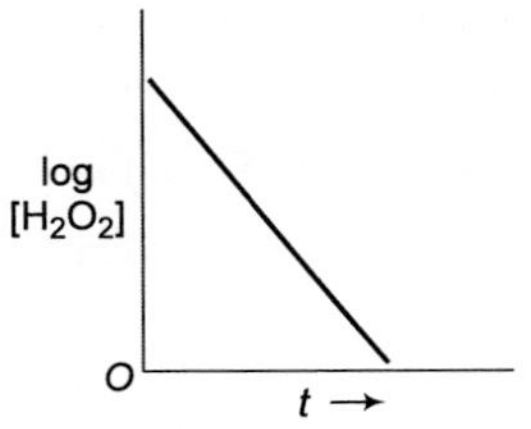

Thus, rate law is
(a) $k[H_2O_2]^2$ (b) $k[H_2O_2]$
(c) $k[H_2O_2]^0$ (d) $k[H_2O_2]^{-1}$

29. For the following sequential reaction,

$$A \xrightarrow{k_A} B \xrightarrow{k_B} C$$

$k_A = 2k_B = 0.1\ s^{-1}$

Time at which $[B]$ is maximum is
(a) 13.9 s (b) 10 s
(c) 6.0 s (d) 16.7 s

30. For the case $n \geq 2$, $\left(\dfrac{dC}{dt}\right) = -kC^n$ then

(a) $\dfrac{1}{C^{n-1}} = \dfrac{1}{C_0^{n-1}} + (n-1)kt$

(b) $k = \dfrac{1}{(n-1)t}\left[\dfrac{1}{C^{n-1}} + \dfrac{1}{C_0^{n-1}}\right]$

(c) T_{50} (half-life) $= \dfrac{2^{n-1}-1}{(n-1)kC_0^{n-1}}$

(d) All of the above are true relations

31. Rate of the reaction in terms of the pressure of the reactant (assume rate as an extensive property) is

$CH_3CHO \longrightarrow CO + CH_4$

(a) $-\dfrac{V}{RT}\dfrac{dp_{CH_3CHO}}{dt}$ (b) $-\dfrac{1}{RT}\dfrac{dp_{CH_3CHO}}{dt}$

(c) $-\dfrac{1}{RTV}\dfrac{dp_{CH_3CHO}}{dt}$ (d) $\dfrac{n_{CH_3CHO}}{V}\dfrac{dp_{CH_3CHO}}{dt}$

32. The half-life period of a first order chemical reaction is 6.93 min. The time required for the completion of 99% of the chemical reaction will be ($\log 2 = 0.301$)
(a) 230.3 min (b) 23.03 min
(c) 46.06 min (d) 460.6 min

33. A reaction was found to be second order with respect to the concentration of carbon monoxide. If the concentration of carbon dioxide is doubled, with everything else kept the same, the rate of reaction will
(a) remain unchanged
(b) triple
(c) increases by a factor of 4
(d) double

34. The temperature dependence of rate constant (k) of a chemical reaction is written in terms of Arrhenius equation, $k = Ae^{-E_a/RT}$. Activation energy (E_a) of the reaction can be calculated by plotting
(a) $\log k$ *vs* $\frac{1}{T}$ (b) $\log k$ *vs* $\frac{1}{\log T}$
(c) k *vs* T (d) k *vs* $\frac{1}{\log T}$

35. For the reaction system,
$$2NO(g) + O_2(g) \longrightarrow 2NO_2(g)$$
volume is suddenly reduced to half its value by increasing the pressure on it. If the reaction is of first order with respect to O_2 and second order with respect to NO; the rate of reaction will
(a) diminish to one-fourth of its initial value
(b) diminish to one eighth of its initial value
(c) increase to eight times of its initial value
(d) increase to four times of its initial value

36. The concentration of a reactant X decreases from 0.1 M to 0.005 M in 40 min. If the reaction follows first order kinetics, the rate of reaction when the concentration of X is 0.01 M will be
(a) 1.73×10^4 M min^{-1} (b) 3.47×10^{-4} M min^{-1}
(c) 3.47×10^{-5} M min^{-1} (d) 7.5×10^{-4} M min^{-1}

37. The rate constant of a first order reaction at 27°C is 10^{-3} min^{-1}. The temperature coefficient of this reaction is 2. What is the rate constant (in min^{-1}) at 17°C for this reaction?
(a) 10^{-3} (b) 5×10^{-4}
(c) 2×10^{-3} (d) 10^{-2}

38. For a first order reaction at 27°C, the ratio of time required for 75% completion to 25% completion of reaction is
(a) 3.0 (b) 2.303
(c) 4.8 (d) 0.477

39. The rate constant for a second order reaction is 0.001 L mol^{-1} s^{-1}. Its value, expressed in units of mL molecule^{-1} min^{-1} is
(a) 9.96×10^{23} (b) 9.96×10^{-23}
(c) 10^3 (d) 0.001

40. Graph between $\log k$ and $\frac{1}{T}$ (k is rate constant in s^{-1}) and T is temperature in K) is a straight line. If $OX = 5$ and slope of the line $= -\frac{1}{2.303}$ then E_a is

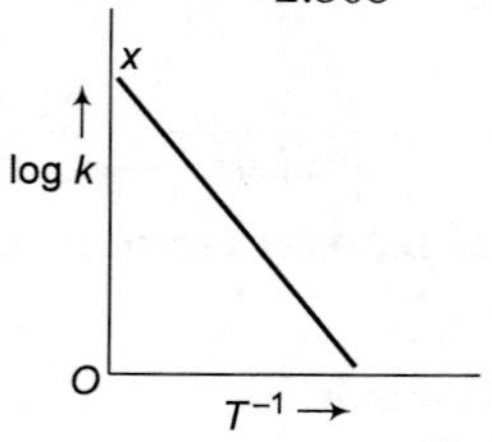

(a) 2.303×2 cal (b) $\frac{2}{2.303}$ cal
(c) 2 cal (d) None of these

41. A reaction takes place by the following mechanism
$$A + BC \longrightarrow AC + B$$
$$AC + D \longrightarrow A + CD$$
The potential energy profile for this is shown below

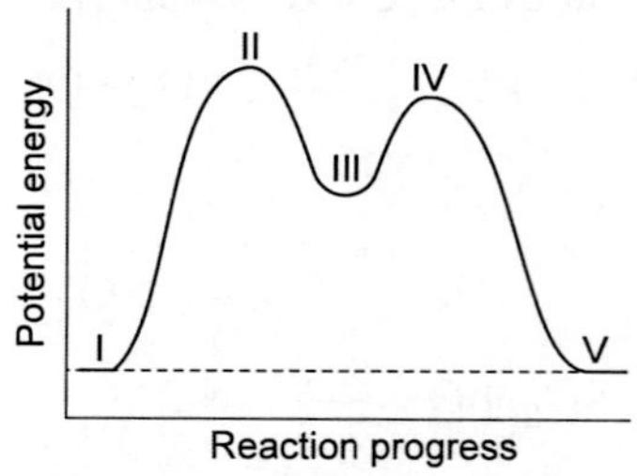

Transition states are shown by
(a) I, V (b) II, IV
(c) II, III, IV (d) III only

42. The esterification of acetic anhydride (A) by ethyl alcohol (B) can be shown as
$$\underset{A}{(CH_3CO)_2O} + \underset{B}{C_2H_5OH} \longrightarrow CH_3COOC_2H_5 + CH_3COOH$$
Select the correct statement.
(a) In dilute hexane solution, rate is $k[A][B]$
(b) In ethyl alcohol as solvent, rate is $k[A]$
(c) In ethyl alcohol, reaction is pseudo first order
(d) All the above are correct statements

43. If in the fermentation of sugar in an enzymatic solution that is initially 0.12 M the concentration of the sugar is reduced to 0.06 M in 10 h and to 0.03 M in 20 h, then, order of the reaction is
(a) zero (b) one
(c) two (d) three

44. If $\left(\frac{dx}{dt}\right) = k\,[H^+]^n$ and rate becomes 100 times when pH changes from 2 to 1. Hence, order is
(a) 1 (b) 2
(c) 3 (d) 0

45. Which is not true for a second order reaction?
(a) It can have rate constant 1×10^{-2} L mol^{-1} s^{-1}
(b) Its half-life is inversely proportional to its initial concentration
(c) Time to complete 75% reaction is twice of half-life
(d) $T_{50} = \frac{1}{k_a}$

46. Two reactions with different activation energies have the same rate at room temperature. Which statement correctly describes the rates of these two reactions at the same higher temperature?
(a) The reaction with the greater activation energy will be faster
(b) The reaction will the smaller activation energy will be faster
(c) The two reactions will have the same rate
(d) Temperature range is also required

47. The following mechanism has been proposed for the reaction of NO with Br_2 to form NOBr

$$NO(g) + Br_2(g) \rightleftharpoons NOBr_2(g)$$
$$NOBr_2(g) + NO(g) \longrightarrow 2NOBr(g)$$

If the second step is the rate determining step, the order of the reaction with respect to NO(*g*) is
(a) 1 (b) 0
(c) 3 (d) 2

48. The reaction, $2SO_2(g) + O_2(g) \rightleftharpoons 2SO_3(g)$ is carried out in a 1 dm^3 vessel and 2 dm^3 vessel separately. The ratio of the reaction velocities will be
(a) 1 : 8 (b) 1 : 4
(c) 4 : 1 (d) 8 : 1

49. Which one of the following is wrongly matched?
(a) Saponification of $CH_3COOC_2H_5$ – Second order reaction
(b) Hydrolysis of CH_3COOCH_3 – Pseudo unimolecular reaction
(c) Decomposition of H_2O_2 – First order reaction
(d) Combination of H_2 and Br_2 to give HBr – First order reaction

50. A chemical reaction proceeds following the formula $k = PZe^{-E_a/RT}$. Which of the following process will increase the rate of reaction?
(a) Lowering of E_a
(b) Lowering of *P*
(c) Lowering of *Z*
(d) Independent of all the above factors

51. If the volume of the vessel in which the reaction, $2NO + O_2 \longrightarrow 2NO_2$ is occurring is diminished to $\frac{1}{3}$rd of its initial volume. The rate of the reaction will be increased by
(a) 3 times (b) 9 times
(c) 27 times (d) 36 times

52. The reaction of hydrogen and iodine monochloride is given as

$$H_2(g) + 2ICl(g) \longrightarrow 2HCl(g) + I_2(g)$$

This reaction is of first order with respect to $H_2(g)$ and ICl(*g*) following mechanism were proposed
Mechanism I :
$$H_2(g) + 2ICl(g) \longrightarrow 2HCl(g) + I_2(g)$$
Mechanism II :
$$H_2(g) + ICl(g) \longrightarrow HCl(g) + HI(g);\ \text{slow}$$
$$HI(g) + ICl(g) \longrightarrow HCl(g) + I_2(g);\ \text{fast}$$
Which of the above mechanism(s) can be consistent with the given information about the reaction?
(a) II only (b) I and II both
(c) Neither I nor II (d) I only

53. The rate constant is given by the equation $k = P \cdot Ze^{-E/RT}$. Which factor should register a decrease for the reaction to proceed more rapidly?
(a) *T* (b) *Z*
(c) *E* (d) *P*

54. Plots showing the variation of the rate constant (*k*) with temperature (*T*) are given below. The plot that follows Arrhenius equation is

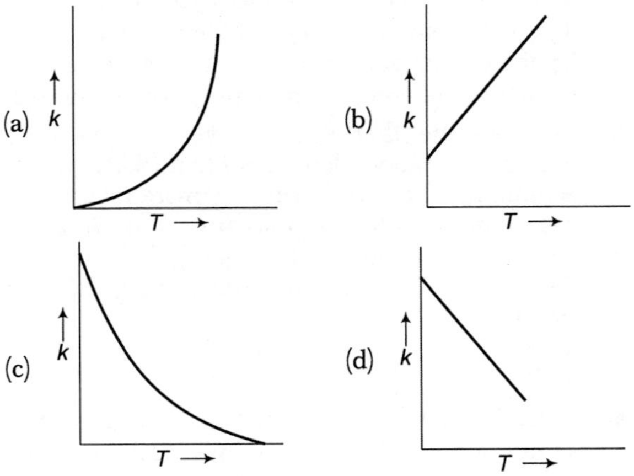

55. $A(g) \longrightarrow B(g)$ is a first order reaction. The initial concentration of *A* is 0.2 mol L^{-1}. After 10 min, the concentration of *B* is found to be 0.18 mol L^{-1}. After 10 min, the concentration of *B* is found to be 0.18 mol L^{-1}. The rate constant (in min^{-1}) for the reaction is
(a) 0.2303 (b) 2.303
(c) 0.693 (d) 0.01

56. For a first order reaction, to obtain a positive slope, we need to plot {where [*A*] is the concentration of reactant *A*}

(a) $-\log_{10}[A]$ *vs* t (b) $-\log_e[A]$ *vs* t
(c) $\log_{10}[A]$ *vs* $\log t$ (d) $[A]$ *vs* t

57. Which of the following is the correct statement?

(a) Order of a reaction has always an integral value
(b) Mechanism of a reaction proposed is always final
(c) Zero order reactions are multistep reactions
(d) Order of reaction can be predicted even without knowing the rate law

58. For the first order reaction,

$$2N_2O_5(g) \longrightarrow 4NO_2(g) + O_2(g)$$

Which one of the following option is not correct?

(a) The concentration of the reactant decreases exponentially with time
(b) The half-life of the reaction decreases with increasing temperature
(c) The half-life of the reaction depends on the initial concentration of the reactant
(d) The reaction proceeds of 99.6% completion in eight half-life duration

59. High quantum yields of photochemical reactions are due to

(a) lowering of activation energy
(b) high frequency of collision
(c) accompanying side reactions
(d) formation of free radicals

60. During the course of chemical reaction, the frequency factor *A* in Arrhenius equation is directly related to

(a) the entropy change in the reaction
(b) the free energy change in the reaction
(c) the energy of activation in the reaction
(d) change in entropy and free energy in the reaction

61. Let's assume that you got very drunk the night before. You blood alcohol content (BAC) was 0.20%. Assuming that the **rate constant** for alcohol degradation $k = 0.015$ (units involving % and hours, depending on order of kinetics), how many hours would it take to be suitable for driving $BAC < 0.08\%$) assuming

(a) 8 h (b) 30 h
(c) 45 h (d) 60 h

62. Consider a mixture of O_2 gas and He gas. Temperature is 555 K. Volume $= 0.23\ m^3$. Data are given at below.

	P(Pa)	m(amu)	r(nm)
O_2	432	32.0	0.17
He	9876	4.00	0.13

$$Z_{12} = \left(\frac{p_1}{k_BT}\right)\left(\frac{p_2}{k_BT}\right)\sigma\left(\frac{8k_BT}{\pi\mu}\right)^{\frac{1}{2}}$$

Recall the formulae for total collision frequencies

and $$Z_{11} = \frac{1}{\sqrt{2}}\left(\frac{p_1}{k_BT}\right)^2 4\pi r_1^2 \left(\frac{8k_BT}{\pi m_1}\right)^{1/2}$$

where, $\sigma = \pi(r_1 + r_2)^2$ and $\mu = \dfrac{m_1 m_2}{m_1 + m_2}$

For every O_2–O_2 collision, how many O_2–He collisions occur?

(a) 46 (b) 56
(c) 76 (d) 230

63. The rate of O_2 formation by photosystem II was measured by Joachim Buchta, et al., as shown in figure. At 20°C, the rate coefficient was 600/s or 0.600 ms^{-1}. Rate coefficients are graphed *versus* $1000/T$ at right. Note that the scale on the ordinate is logarithmic, not linear. The activation energy for production of O_2 (in kJ/mol) is

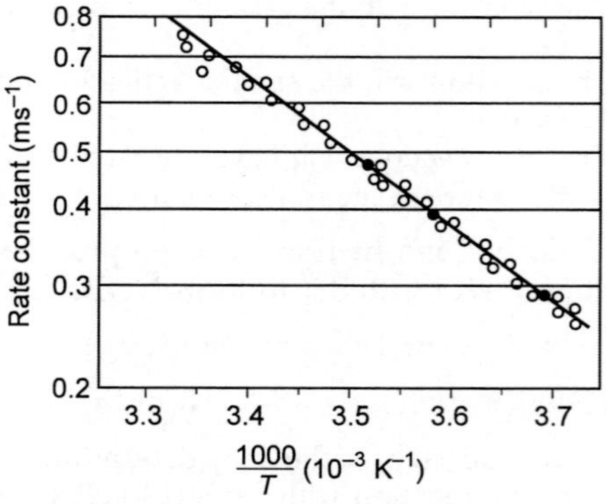

(a) −10 (b) 2.3
(c) 10 (d) 20

64. Graphed at right are concentrations [*A*], [*B*] and [*C*] from one of the mechanisms below, $k_1 1 = 0.1$, $k_2 = 0.2$. Which mechanism matches the graph ?

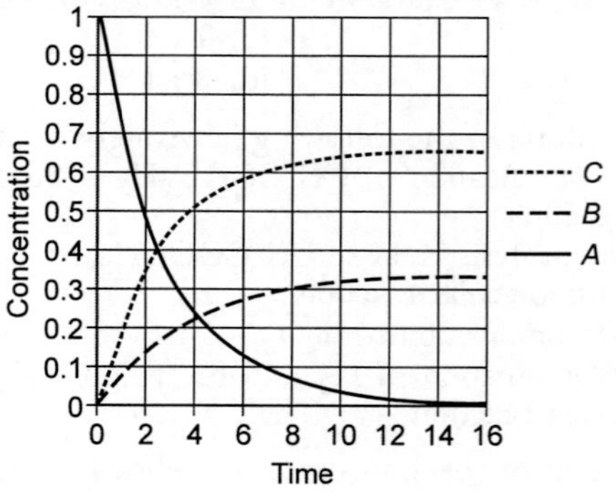

(a) $A \xrightarrow{k_1} B \xrightarrow{k_2} C$ (b) $A \underset{k_2}{\overset{k_1}{\rightleftarrows}} B + C$

(c) $A \xrightarrow{k_1} B,\ A \xrightarrow{k_2} C$ (d) $A \xrightarrow{k_1} B \underset{k_1}{\overset{k_2}{\rightleftarrows}} C$

65. A possible mechanism for the overall reaction, $OH + NO_2 \longrightarrow HNO_3$ in the presence of N_2 is

$$OH + NO_2 \underset{k_{-1}}{\overset{k_1}{\rightleftharpoons}} (HO \cdot NO_2)^{\#}$$

$$(HO \cdot NO_2)^{\#} + N_2 \xrightarrow{k_2} HNO_3 + N_2$$

Apply the steady state approximation to the mechanism. With the approximation, which one of the following rate laws is correct?

(a) $\text{Rate} = \dfrac{k_1 k_2 [OH][NO_2][N_2]}{k_{-1} + k_2[N_2]}$

(b) $\text{Rate} = \dfrac{k_1}{k_{-1}} k_2 [OH][NO_2][N_2]$

(c) $\text{Rate} = \dfrac{k_1 k_2}{k_{-1}} [OH][NO_2] \dfrac{[N_2]}{[HNO_3]}$

(d) $\text{Rate} = (k_1 - k_{-1})([OH][NO_2] + k_2[N_2])$

66. In this mechanism, what is the role of N_2?

$$OH + NO_2 + \underset{k_{-1}}{\overset{k_1}{\rightleftharpoons}} (HO \cdot NO_2)^{\#}$$

$$(HO \cdot NO_2)^{\#} + N_2 \xrightarrow{k_2} HNO_3 + N_2$$

(a) N_2 carries away the released bond energy.
(b) N_2 donates a nitrogen atom to the activated complex.
(c) N_2 extract a hydrogen atom from the hydroxyl radical
(d) N_2 maintains constant reaction temperature.

67. The initial rate of hydrolysis of lactose was measured at two lactose concentrations and at pH= 3.0 and 2.4. Results are at right. Applying the method of initial rates, the rate law will be

Initial rate ($M^{-1}s^{-1}$)	$[\text{Lactose}]_n$ (M)	$[H^+]$ (M)
0.012	0.010	0.0010
0.023	0.020	0.0010
0.046	0.010	0.0040

(a) $\text{Rate} = k[\text{lactose}]^0 [H^+]^0$ (b) $\text{Rate} = k[\text{lactose}]^0 [H^+]^1$
(c) $\text{Rate} = k[\text{lactose}]^1 [H^+]^0$ (d) $\text{Rate} = k[\text{lactose}]^1 [H^+]^1$

68. For $A + B \longrightarrow C$ the kinetic expression for the appearance of C as a function of $[A]$ and $[B]$ will be

Rate/ms^{-1}	$[A]$/M	$[B]$/M
1.2×10^{-5}	0.02	0.01
0.3×10^{-5}	0.02	0.005
0.6×10^{-5}	0.01	0.01

(a) $\dfrac{dc}{dt} = k[A][B]$ (b) $\dfrac{dc}{dt} = k[A][B]^2$

(c) $\dfrac{dc}{dt} = k[A]^2[B]$ (d) $\dfrac{dc}{dt} = k[A]^{\frac{1}{2}}[B]^{\frac{1}{2}}$

69. Using a catalyst, the E_a is reduced 4 fold, so that now $E_a = 25$ kJ/mol./ Now approximately what fraction of the molecules are able to react at $T = 270$ K?

(a) 10^{-20} (b) $\dfrac{1}{2}$
(c) 10^{-5} (d) 0.1

70. Which of the following statements about the kinetics of the reaction $H_2(g) + Br_2(g) \rightarrow 2HBr(g)$ is definitely true?
(a) The reaction is first order with respect to bromine, Br_2
(b) The reaction is second order overall.
(c) The presence of hydrogen bromide, HBr, inhibits the rate of the reaction.
(d) It is not possible to determine anything about the kinetics of the reaction from the stoichiometry.

71. Which statement explains why the speed of some chemical reactions is increased when the surface area of the reactant is increased?
(a) This change increases the density of the reactant particles.
(b) This change increases the concentration of the reactant
(c) This change exposes more reactant particles to a possible collision.
(d) This change alters the electrical conductivity of the reactant particles.

72. If the following concentrations were measured as a function of time for the reaction of N_2 with H_2. What is the order of the reaction for H_2? (Time is in milliseconds.)

Time	20	40	60	80	100	120
$[N_2]$	10.00	10.00	10.00	9.99	9.99	9.99
$[H_2]$	0.0256	0.0218	0.0186	0.0158	0.0135	0.0115

(a) first order because the log of the concentration is a linear function of time.
(b) second order because the log of the concentration is a linear function of time.
(c) first order because the reciprocal of the concentration is a linear function of time.
(d) second order because the reciprocal of the concentration is a linear function of time.

73. The rate constant for the reaction

$$H_2 + OH \longrightarrow H + H_2O$$

which is an important step in the hydrogen-oxygen reaction mechanism, has the value $k_r = 3.52 \times 10^6\ mol^{-1}\ dm^3 s^{-1}$? What is the equivalent value expressed in units of $molecules^1\ cm^{-1}\ s^{-1}$?

(a) 2.12×10^{27} $molecule^{-1}\ cm^3 s^{-1}$
(b) 5.85×10^{-15} $molecule^{-1}\ cm^3 s^{-1}$
(c) 5.85×10^{-21} $molecule^{-1}\ cm^3 s^{-1}$
(d) 2.12×10^{-15} $molecule^{-1}\ cm^3 s^{-1}$

74. In an experiment to investigate the mechanism of the condensation reaction between acrolein and 1,3-butadiene, the initial rate was measured spectrophotometrically for various different partial pressures of the reactants. The table below shows the initial rates of reaction, v_0, for various partial pressures of acrolein, p, at a temperature of 560 K with 1,3-butadiene being in excess.

p/Pa	1260	3310	4930	6610
$v_0/(10^{12}$ Pa $s^{-1})$	3.88	9.32	14.40	10.86

Use the method of initial rates to determine the order of the reaction with respect to acrolein.
(a) 0 (b) 1
(c) 2 (d) 3

75. In an investigation of the first-order decomposition reaction,

$$C_2H_5I \longrightarrow C_2H_4 + HI$$

at a temperature of 400 K, the partial pressure of C_2H_5I, p was found to vary with time, t, as shown below. Determine the rate constant of the reaction.

p/Torr	74.0	57.1	44.0	34.0	26.2
t/s	0	10.0	20.0	30.0	40.0

(a) 0.0259 s^{-1} (b) 38.6 s^{-1}
(c) 0.175 s^{-1} (d) 0.455 s^{-1}

76. In a chemical reaction, a catalyst changes the
(a) potential energy of the products
(b) potential energy of the reactants
(c) heat of reaction
(d) activation energy

77. The rate constant for the substitution reaction

$$C_4H_9Cl + H_2O \longrightarrow C_4H_9OH + HCl$$

increases by a factor of 10.6 when the temperature is increased from 298 K to 308 K. Calculate the activation energy of the reaction.
(a) 180 kJ mol^{-1} (b) 78.2 kJ mol^{-1}
(c) 809 kJ mol^{-1} (d) 2.14 kJ mol^{-1}

78. The half-life for the acid-catalysed hydrolysis of sucrose to form glucose and fructose, which is first order overall, is 3.20 h at 25°C. What is the rate constant for the reaction at this temperature?
(a) 6.02×10^{-5} s^{-1} (b) 8.68×10^{-5} s^{-1}
(c) 0.217 s^{-1} (d) 2.16×10^{-5} s^{-1}

79. The rate constant for the second order reaction between iodomethane, CH_3I, and ethoxy anions, $C_2H_5O^-$, in ethanol solution is $9.86 \times 10^{-5} dm^{-3}$ s^{-1} mol at 298 K and 6.17×10^{-3} mol dm^{-3} s^{-1} at 338 K. Calculate the activation energy.
(a) 300 kJ mol^{-1} (b) 116 kJ mol^{-1}
(c) 10.4 kJ mol^{-1} (d) 86.6kJ mol^{-1}

80. Predict the Arrhenius pre-exponential factor for the reaction

$$H_2 + CO \longrightarrow H_2CO$$

at 298.15 K, given that the collision cross section of H_2 is given that the collision cross section of H_2 is 0.0452 nm^2 and of CO 0.0804 nm^2
(a) 69.2×10^6 mol^{-1} m^3s^{-1} (b) 192×10^6 mol^{-1} m^3s^{-1}
(c) 67.8×10^6 mol^{-1} m^3s^{-1} (d) 271×10^6 mol^{-1} m^3s^{-1}

Exercise 2
(For Part 'C')

1. Acid hydrolysis of ester is first order reaction and rate constant is given by

$$k = \frac{2.303}{t} \log \frac{V_\infty - V_0}{V_\infty - V_t}$$

where, V_0, V_t and V_∞ are the volume of standard NaOH required to neutralise acid present at a given time, if ester is 50% neutralized then
(a) $V_\infty = V_t$ (b) $V_\infty = (V_t - V_0)$
(c) $V_\infty = 2V_t - V_0$ (d) $V_\infty = 2V_t + V_0$

2. For the reaction, $A(g) \longrightarrow B(g) + C(g)$

rate law is $-\frac{d[A]}{dt} = k[A]$

At the start, pressure is 100 mm and after 10 min, pressure is 120 mm, hence rate constant (min^{-1}) is
(a) $\frac{2.303}{10} \log \frac{6}{5}$ (b) $\frac{2.303}{10} \log 5$
(c) $\frac{2.303}{10} \log \frac{5}{4}$ (d) $\frac{2.303}{10} \log \frac{5}{6}$

3. For the reaction, $A(g) + 2B(g) \longrightarrow C(g) + D(g)$

$$\frac{dx}{dt} = k[A][B]^2$$

Initial pressure of A and B are respectively 0.60 atm and 0.80 atm. At a time when pressure of C is 0.20 atm, rate of the reaction, relative to the initial value is
(a) $\frac{1}{6}$ (b) $\frac{1}{48}$ (c) $\frac{1}{4}$ (d) $\frac{1}{24}$

4. For the reaction, $aA + bB \longrightarrow$ Product

$$\frac{dx}{dt} = k\,[A]^a\,[B]^b$$

If concentration of A is doubled, rate is four times. If concentration of B is made four times, rate is doubled. Hence,

(a) $-\frac{d[A]}{dt} = -\frac{d[B]}{dt}$ (b) $\frac{-d[A]}{dt} = -\frac{d[B]}{dt}$

(c) $-4\frac{d[A]}{dt} = -\frac{d[B]}{dt}$ (d) None of these

5. For the reaction, $A + B \longrightarrow C$

	$[A]$	$[B]$	$-\frac{d[A]}{dt}$
1.	1.0 M	1.0 M	0.25 M min^{-1}
2.	2.0 M	1.0 M	0.50 M min^{-1}
3.	1.0 M	2.0 M	0.25 M min^{-1}

Hence, rate law is

(a) $k\,[A][B]$ (b) $k\,[A][B]^{1/2}$

(c) $k\,[A]$ (d) $k\,[B]$

6. $C_6H_5N_2Cl + H_2O \xrightarrow{\Delta} C_6H_5OH + N_2 + HCl$

This reaction is pseudomolecular *wrt* $C_6H_5N_2Cl$. 50 mL of 1 M benzene diazonium chloride (A) is taken. After 1 h, 1.226 L of N_2 gas at 1 atm and 300 K is obtained. Rate constant is

(a) 9.2×10^{-2} min^{-1} (b) 9.2×10^{-3} min^{-1}

(c) 9.2×10^{2} min^{-1} (d) 9.2×10^{3} min^{-1}

7. The reaction between nitric oxide and hydrogen has been investigated by measuring the initial rate of decrease of pressure in known mixture of gases. The following results were obtained at 700°C.

S. No.	Initial pressure/atm		Initial rate of decrease of pressure/atm min^{-1}
	NO	H_2	
(i)	0.5	0.2	0.0048
(ii)	0.5	0.1	0.0024
(iii)	0.25	0.2	0.0012

The rate constant for the overall reaction at 700°C is

(a) 0.096 atm^{-2} min^{-1} (b) 0.96 atm^{-2} min^{-1}

(c) 9.6 atm^{-2} min^{-1} (d) 96.0 atm^{-2} min^{-1}

8. A radioactive substance decays 20% in 10 min. If at the start there are 5×10^{20} atoms present, after what time will the number of atoms be reduced to 10^{18} atoms?

(a) 46.5 h (b) 0.465 h

(c) 4.65 h (d) 465 h

9. The rate of gaseous reaction,

$$A(g) + B(g) \longrightarrow \text{Product}$$

is given by expression $\frac{dx}{dt} = k\,[A][B]$

If the volume of the reaction vessel is suddenly reduced to one fourth of the initial volume, then the ratio of the final rate to initial rate is

(a) 2 : 1 (b) 4 : 1

(c) 8 : 1 (d) 16 : 1

10. A hydrogenation reaction is carried out at 500 K. If the same reaction is carried out in presence of a catalyst at the same rate, the temperature required is 400 K. If the catalyst lowers the activation barrier by 20 kJ mol^{-1}, then the activation energy of the reaction is

(a) 50 kJ mol^{-1} (b) 100 kJ mol^{-1}

(c) 150 kJ mol^{-1} (d) 200 kJ mol^{-1}

11. Following is the graph between $(a-x)^{-1}$ and time t for a second order reaction

$$\theta = \tan^{-1}(0.5)$$

$$OA = 2\ \text{L mol}^{-1}$$

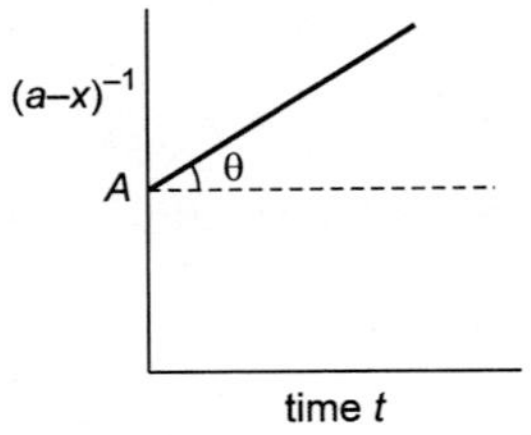

Hence, rate at the start of the reaction is

(a) 1.25 mol^{-1} min^{-1} (b) 0.5 mol L^{-1} min^{-1}

(c) 0.125 mol L^{-1} min^{-1} (d) 1.25 mol L^{-1} min^{-1}

12. Rate constant k varies with temperature as given by equation

$$\log k\,(\text{min}^{-1}) = 5 - \frac{2000\ \text{K}}{T}$$

Consider the following about this equation

I. Pre-exponential factor is 10^5

II. E_a is 9.212 kcal

III. Variation of $\log k$ with $\frac{1}{T}$ is linear

Select the correct statement.

(a) I, II, III (b) I, III

(c) II, III (d) I, II

13. Consider the following reaction.

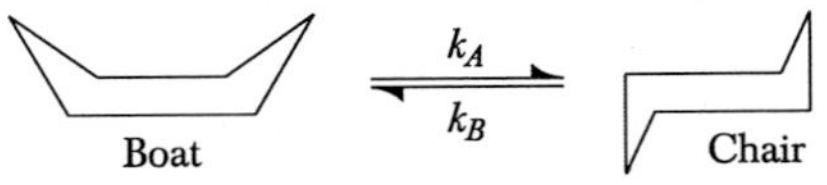

The reaction is first order in each direction, with an equilibrium constant of 10^4. For the conversion of chair form to boat form $e^{-E_a/RT} = 4.35 \times 10^{-8}$ at 298 K with pre-exponential factor of 10^{12} s^{-1}. Apparent rate constant $(= k_A + k_B)$ at 298 K is

(a) 4.35×10^4 s^{-1}
(b) 4.35×10^8 s^{-1}
(c) 4.35×10^{-8} s^{-1}
(d) 4.35×10^{12} s^{-1}

14. For *n*th order reaction,

$$\frac{dx}{dt} = \text{Rate} = k\,[A]_0^n$$

Graph between log (rate) against $\log [A]_0$ is of the type

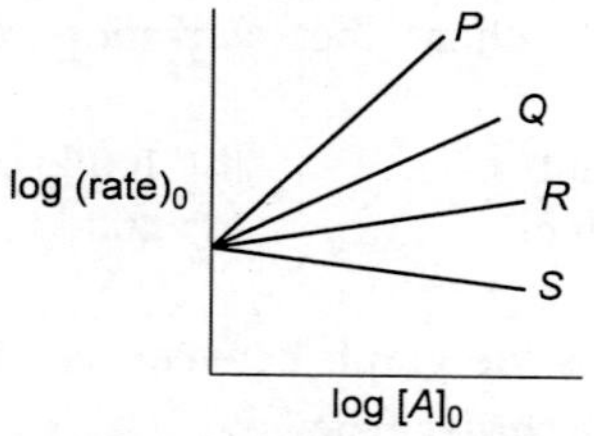

Lines *P, Q, R, S* are for the order

	P	*Q*	*R*	*S*
(a)	0	1	2	3
(b)	3	2	1	0
(c)	1	2	3	0
(d)	0	3	2	1

15. For the second order reaction, concentration (x) of the product at time t starting with initial concentration $[A]_0$ is

(a) $\dfrac{kt\,[A_0]^2}{1 + kt\,[A_0]}$
(b) $\dfrac{k + [A_0]^2}{1 + kt}$
(c) $\dfrac{1 + kt\,[A_0]^2}{k + [A_0]^2}$
(d) None of these

16. Time constant, τ is the required for the concentration of a reactant to fall to $\frac{1}{e}$ of its initial value, then

(a) $k\tau = 2.303$
(b) $k\tau = \dfrac{1}{2.303}$
(c) $k\tau = 1$
(d) $k\tau = \log_{10} e$

17. For a first roder reaction, $A \longrightarrow P$. The temperature (T) dependent rate constant (k) was found to follow the equation

$$\log k = -(2000)/T + 6.0$$

The pre-exponential factor A and the activation energy E_a, respectively are

(a) 1.0×10^6 s^{-1} and 9.2 kJ mol^{-1}
(b) 6.0 s^{-1} and 16.6 kJ mol^{-1}
(c) 1.0×10^6 s^{-1} and 16.6 kJ mol^{-1}
(d) 1.0×10^6 s^{-1} and 38.3 kJ mol^{-1}

18. Under the same reaction conditions, initial concentration of 1.386 mol dm^{-3} of a substance becomes half in 40 s and 20 s through first order and zero order kinetics, respectively. Ratio $\left(\dfrac{k_1}{k_0}\right)$ of the rate constants for the first order k_1 and zero order (k_0) of the reaction is

(a) 0.5 mol^{-1} dm^{-3}
(b) 1.0 mol dm^{-3}
(c) 1.5 mol dm^{-3}
(d) 2.0 mol^{-1} dm^3

19. Consider a reaction, $aG + bH \longrightarrow$ Products. when concentration of both the reactants G and H is doubled, the rate increases by eight times. However, when concentration of G is doubled keeping the concentration of H fixed, the rate is double. The overall order of the reaction is

(a) zero
(b) one
(c) two
(d) three

20. For the two gaseous reactions, following data are given

$$A \longrightarrow B; \quad k_1 = 10^{10}\, e^{-20000/T}$$
$$C \longrightarrow D; \quad k_2 = 10^{12}\, e^{-24606/T}$$

the temperature at which k_1 becomes equal to k_2 is

(a) 400 K
(b) 1000 K
(c) 800 K
(d) 1500 K

21. The energies of activation for forward and reverse, reactions for $A_2 + B_2 \rightleftharpoons 2AB$ are 180 kJ mol^{-1} and 200 kJ mol^{-1} respectively. The presence of a catalyst lowers the activation energy of both (forward and reverse) reactions by 100 kJ mol^{-1}. The enthalpy change of the reaction $(A_2 + B_2 \longrightarrow 2AB)$ in the presence of catalyst will be (in kJ mol^{-1})

(a) −300
(b) −120
(c) +280
(d) −20

22. A hypothetical reaction, $A_2 + B_2 \longrightarrow 2AB$ follows the mechanism as given below,

$$A_2 \rightleftharpoons A + A \text{ (fast)}$$
$$A + B_2 \longrightarrow AB + B \text{ (slow)}$$
$$A + B \longrightarrow AB \text{ (fast)}$$

The order of the overall reaction is

(a) 2
(b) 1
(c) $1\frac{1}{2}$
(d) 0

23. For a reaction taking place in three steps, the rate constants are k_1, k_2 and k_3. The overall rate constant, $k = \dfrac{k_1 k_2}{k_3}$. If the energy of activation values for the first, second and third stages are respectively 40, 50 and 60 kJ mol^{-1} then the overall energy of activation in kJ mol^{-1} is

(a) 30
(b) 40
(c) 60
(d) 50

24. The rate constant for a first order reaction becomes six times when the temperature is raised from 350 K to 400 K. Calculate the activation energy for the reaction ($R = 8.314\ \mathrm{JK^{-1}\ mol^{-1}}$).

(a) 41.7 kJ $\mathrm{mol^{-1}}$ (b) 4.17 kJ $\mathrm{mol^{-1}}$
(c) 417 kJ$\mathrm{mol^{-1}}$ (d) 4170 kJ $\mathrm{mol^{-1}}$

25. The Arrhenius equations for the rate constant of decomposition of methyl nitrite and ethyl nitrite are

$$k_1\ (\mathrm{s^{-1}}) = 10^{13} \exp\left(\frac{-152300\ \mathrm{J\ mol^{-1}}}{RT}\right)$$

and $$k_2\ (\mathrm{s^{-1}}) = 10^{14} \exp\left(\frac{-157700\ \mathrm{J\ mol^{-1}}}{RT}\right)$$

respectively. Find the temperature at which the rate constants are equal.

(a) 232 K (b) 382 K
(c) 282 K (d) 482 K

26. The gas phase decomposition of NOBr is second order in [NOBr], with $k = 0.810\ \mathrm{M^{-1}\ s^{-1}}$ at 10°C. We start with 4.00×10^{-3} M NOBr in a flask at 10°C. How many seconds does it take to use up 1.50×10^{-3} M NOBr?

$$2NOBr(g) \longrightarrow 2NO\ (g) + Br_2\ (g)$$

Rate $= k\ [NOBr]^2$

(a) 92.6 s (b) 9.26 s
(c) 926 s (d) 0.926 s

27. The frequency factors for a unimolecular gas reaction occurring at 473 K is $2.5 \times 10^{13}\ \mathrm{s^{-1}}$. The entropy of activation is

(a) –572 $\mathrm{JK^{-1}\ mol^{-1}}$ (b) –57.2 $\mathrm{JK^{-1}\ mol^{-1}}$
(c) –5.72 $\mathrm{JK^{-1}\ mol^{-1}}$ (d) –0.572 $\mathrm{JK^{-1}\ mol^{-1}}$

28. The rate constant for the first order decomposition of ethylene oxide into CH_4 and CO follows the equation,

$$\log k\ (\text{in s}^{-1}) = 14.34 - (1.25 \times 10^4\ \text{k})/T$$

The activation energy of the reaction is

(a) 0.23913 kJ $\mathrm{mol^{-1}}$ (b) 2.3913 kJ$\mathrm{mol^{-1}}$
(c) 23.913 kJ $\mathrm{mol^{-1}}$ (d) 239.3 kJ $\mathrm{mol^{-1}}$

29. The acid catalyzed reaction of acetic acid with ethanol,

$$CH_3COOH + C_2H_5OH \xrightarrow{H^+} CH_3COOC_2H_5 + H_2O$$

follows the rate law $-d\,[CH_3COOH]/dt = k\,[H^+]\,[CH_3COOH]\,[C_2H_5OH]$

If $[CH_3COOH]_0 = [C_2H_5OH]_0 = 0.2$ M, pH = 3 and $t_{1/2} = 50$ min, the apparent rate constant and the true rate constant are

(a) $k_{app} = 0.1\ \mathrm{M^{-1}\ min^{-1}}$; $k = 1.0 \times 10^2\ \mathrm{M^{-2}\ min^{-1}}$
(b) $k_{app} = 1.0\ \mathrm{M^{-1}\ min^{-1}}$; $k = 1.0 \times 10^2\ \mathrm{M^{-2}\ min^{-1}}$
(c) $k_{app} = 10.0\ \mathrm{M^{-1}\ min^{-1}}$; $k = 10.0\ \mathrm{M^{-2}\ min^{-1}}$
(d) $k_{app} = 10.0\ \mathrm{M^{-1}\ min^{-1}}$; $k = 1.0 \times 10^3\ \mathrm{M^{-2}\ min^{-1}}$

30. If activation energy of a reaction is 80.9 kJ $\mathrm{mol^{-1}}$, calculate the fraction of molecules at 400°C which have enough energy to form products

(a) 526×10^{-7} (b) 52.6×10^{-7}
(c) 5.26×10^{-7} (d) 0.526×10^{-7}

31. For the decomposition of gaseous CH_3CHO, rate constants at 430°C and 460°C were 0.0111 and 0.0350 respectively. The energy of activation for the reaction is ($R = 1.987\ \mathrm{cal\ K^{-1}\ mol^{-1}}$ or $8.314\ \mathrm{JK^{-1}\ mol^{-1}}$)

(a) 39.2 kcal (b) 67.4 kcal
(c) 3.92 kcal (d) 6.74 kcal

32. Consider the following Lindemann mechanism for the unimolecular decomposition of a molecule A in the presence of an inert gas molecule M

$$A + A \underset{k_{-1}}{\overset{k_1}{\rightleftharpoons}} A^* + A$$

$$A + M \underset{k_{-2}}{\overset{k_2}{\rightleftharpoons}} A^* + M$$

$$A^* \xrightarrow{k_3} P$$

Applying the steady state approximation to A^*, the rate law for the formation of the product is

(a) $r = k_3[A^*] = \dfrac{k_3k_1[A]^2 + k_2[A][M]}{k_{-1}[A] + k_{-2}[M] + k_3}$

(b) $r = k_3[A^*] = \dfrac{k_3k_{-1}[A] + k_{-2}[M] + k_3}{k_1[A]^2 + k_2[A][M]}$

(c) $r = k_3[A^*] = \dfrac{k_3k_1[A]^2 - k_2[A][M]}{k_{-1}[A] + k_{-2}[M] + k_3}$

(d) $r = k_3[A^*] = \dfrac{k_3k_1[A]^2 + k_2[M][A]}{k_{-1}[A] - k_{-2}[M] + k_3}$

33. In the temperature range of 250 K to 450 K, the pre-exponential factor, A, for the reaction. $Cl(g) + H_2(g) \longrightarrow HCl(g) + H(g)$ is found to be equal to $1.20 \times 10^{10}\ \mathrm{dm^3\ mol^{-1}\ s^{-1}}$. If $M\,(Cl) = 35.453\ \mathrm{g\ mol^{-1}}$, $M\,[H_2] = 2.016\ \mathrm{g\ mol^{-1}}$, $d\,(Cl) = 200$ pm and $d\,[H_2] = 150$ pm, the value of the steric factor, P is

(a) 0.11 (b) 0.33
(c) 0.55 (d) 0.77

34. The activation energy of a non-catalysed reaction at 37°C is 83.68 kJ mol^{-1} and activation energy of the same reaction catalysed by an enzyme is 25.10 kJ mol^{-1}. The ratio of the rate constants of the enzyme-catalysed and non-catalysed reactions, $\frac{k_e}{k_n}$ is

(a) 10^2 (b) 10^5
(c) 10^{10} (d) 10^{23}

35. The following data were obtained for the decomposition of a compound at 580°C

a_0 (mol dm^{-3})	0.50	1.10	2.48
$t_{1/2}$ (s)	4280	885	174

The order of reaction and the rate constant are
(a) zero order, $k = 1.40 \times 10^{-3}\ dm^6\ mol^{-2}\ s^{-1}$
(b) 1st order, $k = 3.36 \times 10^{-3}\ dm^6\ mol^{-2}\ s^{-1}$
(c) 2nd order, $k = 3.36 \times 10^{-3}\ dm^6\ mol^{-2}\ s^{-1}$
(d) 3rd order, $k = 1.40 \times 10^{-3}\ dm^6\ mol^{-2}\ s^{-1}$

36. Inversion of sucrose is studied by measuring angle of rotation at any time t

$$\underset{\text{Sucrose}}{C_{12}H_{22}O_{11}} + H_2O \xrightarrow{H_3O^+} \underset{\text{Glucose}}{C_6H_{12}O_6} + \underset{\text{Fructose}}{C_6H_{12}O_6}$$

It is found that $(r_\infty - r_0) \propto a$ and $(r_\infty - r_t) \propto (a - x)$ where, r_0, r_t and r_∞ are the angle of rotation at the start, at the time t and at the end of the reaction respectively. From the following values calculate rate constant and the time at which solution is optically inactive

Time/min	0.0	46.0	∞
Rotation of polarized light/degree	24.1	10.0	−10.7

(a) $k = 0.011\ min^{-1}$, $t = 107.2$ min
(b) $k = 0.11\ min^{-1}$, $t = 107.2$ min
(c) $k = 1.1 \times 10^2\ min^{-1}$, $t = 304$ min
(d) $k = 2.1 \times 10^2\ min^{-1}$, $t = 304$ min

37. At room temperature (20°C) milk turns sour in about 64 h. In a refrigerator at 3°C milk can be stored three times as long before it sours. How long should it take milk to sour at 40°C?

(a) 10.20 h (b) 15.40 h
(c) 20.51 h (d) 25.20 h

38. During nuclear explosion, one of the products is ^{90}Sr with half-life is 28.1 yr. If 1 μg of ^{90}Sr was absorbed in the bones of a newly born baby instead of calcium, how much of it will remain after 10 yr if it is not lost metabolically?

(a) 0.2278 μg (b) 0.4345 μg
(c) 0.7815 μg (d) 0.9336 μg

39. Select the incorrect statement.
(a) Larger the value of E_a, smaller the value of rate constant (k).
(b) Larger the value of E_a, greater is the effect on the value of k for a given temperature change.
(c) At lower temperature, increase in temperature causes more change in the value of k than at higher temperature.
(d) k is affected by change in concentration.

40. Which factors would increase the rate of a chemical reaction?

I. Increasing the temperature.
II. Removing products as they are formed.
III. Adding a catalyst.

(a) I and II (b) II and III
(c) I, II and III (d) I only

41. The hydrolysis of t-bromobutane, C_4H_9Br, by hydroxide, OH^-, ions in aqueous solution follows an S_N1 reaction mechanism in which the rate-determining step is the loss of a bromide, Br^-, ion, followed by rapid reaction with hydroxide ions. Which of the following rate laws is consistent with this mechanism?

(a) Rate = $k[C_4H_9Br]$ (b) Rate = $k\,[C_4H_9BrOH^-]$
(c) Rate = $k[C_4H_9Br^2]$ (d) Rate = $k[OH^-]$

42. Which of the following statements is in accordance with collision theory?

I. Rate is directly proportional to collision frequency.
II. Rate depends upon orientation of atoms.
III. Temperature determines the rate.

(a) Only III (b) Only I and II
(c) Only II and III (d) All of these

43. The following homogeneous gaseous reactions were experimentally found to be second order overall

I. $2NO \longrightarrow N_2 + O_2$
II. $3O_2 \longrightarrow 2O_3$
III. $N_2O_3 \longrightarrow NO + NO_2$
IV. $H_2 + I_2 \longrightarrow 2HI$

Which of these are most likely to be elementary reactions that occur in one step?

(a) III only (b) I, III
(c) I, IV (d) III, IV

44. Which one of the following statements is incorrect about order of reaction?
(a) Order of reaction is determined experimentally
(b) Order of reaction is equal to sum of the power of concentration terms in differential rate law
(c) It is not affected with stoichiometric coefficient of the reactants
(d) Order cannot be fractional

45. Which among the following plots are linear? $(a - x)$ is the concentration of reactant remaining after time, t.

(a) $(a - x)$ *vs* t, for a first order reaction
(b) $(a - x)$ *vs* t, for a zero order reaction
(c) $(a - x)$ *vs* t, for a second order reaction
(d) $\frac{1}{(a-x)}$ *vs* t, for a second order reaction

46. Consider the following statements.

An increase in the rate of a reaction for a rise in temperature is due to

I. the increase in the number of collisions
II. the shortening of the mean free path
III. the increase in the number of activated molecules
IV. the increase in pressure of the system

Which of the statements given above correct?

(a) I, II (b) II, III
(c) I, III (d) I, III, IV

Assertion & Reason

(a) Both A and R are true and R is the correct explanation of A.
(b) Both A and R are true but R is not the correct explanation of A.
(c) A is true but R is false.
(d) A is false but R is true.

47. Assertion (A) In rate laws, the exponents for concentration do not necessarily match the stoichiometric coefficients.

Reason (R) It is the mechanism and not the balanced chemical equation for the overall change that governs the reaction rate.

48. Assertion (A) The Arrhenius equation explains the temperature dependence of rate of a chemical reaction.

Reason (R) Plots of $\log k$ *vs* $\frac{1}{T}$ are linear and the energy of activation is obtained from such plots.

49. Assertion (A) The rate of a chemical reaction increases as the temperature is increased.

Reason (R) The collision frequency between the reactant molecules increases on increasing temperature.

50. Match order of reaction in Column I with its property in Column II.

Column I (Order of reaction)		Column II (Property)	
A.	Zero	1.	Half-life $\propto \frac{1}{a^2}$
B.	First	2.	Half-life $\propto \frac{1}{a}$
C.	Second	3.	Half-life is doubled on doubling the initial concentration.
D.	Third	4.	50% reaction takes same time even if concentration is halved or doubled.

Codes

	A	B	C	D
(a)	3	4	2	1
(b)	4	2	3	1
(c)	2	1	4	3
(d)	2	3	4	1

51. Match order of the reaction in Column I with corresponding rate constant Column II.

Column I (Order)		Column II (Rate constants)	
A.	Zero	1.	$k = \frac{1}{2t}\left[\frac{1}{(a-x)^2} - \frac{1}{a^2}\right]$
B.	First	2.	$k = \frac{1}{t}\left[\frac{1}{(a-x)} - \frac{1}{a}\right]$
C.	Second	3.	$k = \frac{x}{t}$
D.	Third	4.	$k = \frac{1}{t}\log_e\left(\frac{a}{a-x}\right)$

Codes

	A	B	C	D
(a)	3	4	2	1
(b)	4	2	3	1
(c)	2	1	4	3
(d)	2	3	4	1

52. Match the given reaction of various order (in Column I) with method of study of kinetics (in Column II)

	Column I (Reactions)		Column II (Method)
A.	$2N_2O_5(g) \rightarrow 2N_2O_4(g) + O_2(g)$	1.	Titration by $Na_2S_2O_3$
B.	$S_2O_8^{2-} + 2I^- \rightarrow 2SO_4^{2-} + I_2$	2.	Titration by $KMnO_4$
C.	$2H_2O_2 \rightarrow 2H_2O + O_2$	3.	Titration by NaOH
D.	$C_{12}H_{22}O_{11} + H_2O \rightarrow C_6H_{12}O_6 + C_6H_{12}O_6$	4.	Measuring pressure of the mixture in inert medium.
E.	$CH_3CHO(g) \rightarrow CH_4(g) + CO(g)$	5.	Measuring angle of rotation.
F.	$CH_3COOC_2H_5 + H_2O \xrightarrow{H^+} CH_3COOH + C_2H_5OH$	6.	Measuring pressure of the gas in CCl_4 medium.

Codes

	A	B	C	D	E	F
(a)	6	1	2	5	4	3
(b)	3	4	5	6	1	2
(c)	2	1	4	3	6	5
(d)	4	5	6	1	2	3

53. The rate law for the multistep chain reaction

$$H_2 + Br_2 \longrightarrow 2HBr$$

is

$$\text{Rate} = \frac{d[\text{HBr}]}{dt} = \frac{k_{r1}[\text{H}_2][\text{Br}_2]^{3/2}}{[\text{Br}_2] + k_2[\text{HBr}]}$$

Which of the following expresses the rate law in the limit of high pressures of bromine, Br_2?

(a) Rate $= k_{r1}[\text{Br}_2]^{3/2}$

(b) Rate $= k_{r1}[\text{H}_2][\text{Br}_2]^{3/2}$

(c) Rate $= k_{r1}[\text{H}_2][\text{Br}_2]^{1/2}$

(d) Rate $= k_{r1}[\text{H}_2][\text{Br}_2]$

54. The kinetics of many radical-radical recombination reactions are diffusion controlled. Calculate the rate constant for a diffusion-controlled bimolecular reaction in water at 77°C. The viscosity of water at this temperature is $\eta = 0.60 \times 10^{-4}$ kg m^{-1}s^{-1}.

(a) 2.47×10^6 mol^{-1} m^{3}s^{-1}

(b) 8.72×10^6 mol^{-1} m^{3}s^{-1}

(c) 7.42×10^6mol^{-1} m^{3}s^{-1}

(d) 11.3×10^6 mol^{-1} m^{3}s^{-1}

55. The table below shows how, for the myosin-catalysed hydrolysis of ATP, the rate of reaction varies with substrate concentration.

$v/(10^{-6}$ mol dm^{-3}s$^{-1})$	0.067	0.095	0.119	0.149
$[S]/(10^{-5}$ mol dm$^{-3})$	7.5	12.5	20.0	32.5

By constructing a Lineweaver-Burk plot, determine the value of the Mishaelis constant.

(a) 7.935 s

(b) 4.307×10^6 mol^{-1}dm^{3}s^{-1}

(c) 1.84×10^{-6} mol dm^{-3}

(d) 537.6 mol^{-1} dm > 3

56. The isomerisation of *cis* to *trans*-but-2-ene, C_4H_8, follows a Lindemann mechanism. At high pressure, the pseudo first-order rate constant for the isomerisation is 2×10^{-5} s^{-1} at 500°C. Given that, at this temperature, collisional activation occurs with an efficiency that is 10^{11} times slower than that of collisional deactivation, determine the rate constant for the final step of the mechanism.

(a) 5×10^5 s^{-1} (b) 2×10^{-5} s^{-1}

(c) 2×10^{-16} s^{-1} (d) 5×10^{-7} s^{-1}

57. The thermal decomposition of acetone, $(CH_3)_2CO$, proceeds *via* the formation of the stable intermediate ketene, CH_2CO

$$(CH_3)_2CO \longrightarrow CH_2CO + CH_4$$

$$CH_2CO \longrightarrow \frac{1}{2}C_2H_4 + CO$$

The rate constant for the initial decomposition of acetone is $k_a = 5.25 \times 10^{-3}$ s^{-1}, whilst the rate constant for the subsequent decomposition of ketene is $k_b = 15.23 \times 10^{-3}$ s^{-1}, at a temperature of 600°C. Calculate the time after which the ketene intermediate has reached its maximum concentration.

(a) 10 s (b) 20 s

(c) 46 s (d) 107 s

58. From the following mechanism the overall equilibrium constant for the reaction $A_2 + 2B \overset{k}{\longleftrightarrow} 2AB$ in terms of the four rate constants for the mechanism will be

Step	Reaction
#1	$A_2 + B \overset{k_{1f},\,k_{1b}}{\longleftrightarrow} AB + A$
# 2	$A + B \overset{k_{2f},\,k_{2b}}{\longleftrightarrow} AB$

(a) $\frac{k_{1f}}{k_{1b}} \cdot \frac{k_{2b}}{k_{2f}}$ (b) $\frac{k_{1f} \cdot k_{2f}}{k_{1b} \cdot k_{2b}}$

(c) $\frac{k_{1b} \cdot k_{2b}}{k_{1f} \cdot k_{2f}}$ (d) zero

Directions (Q. Nos. 59 to 62)

Questions are based on the proposed reaction mechanism for uncatalyzed ammonia production :

$$H_2 \longrightarrow 2H \text{ (fast)}$$

$$N_2 + H \longrightarrow NH + N \text{ (slow)}$$

$$N + H_2 \longrightarrow NH + H \text{ (fast)}$$

$$NH + H_2 \longrightarrow NH_3 \text{ (fast)}$$

59. What is the rate law for this reaction?

(a) Rate $= k[\text{H}_2]$ (b) Rate $= k[\text{N}_2][\text{H}]$

(c) Rate $= k[\text{N}_2][\text{H}_2]^3$ (d) Rate $= k[\text{N}_2][\text{H}_2]^{1/2}$

60. What is the order with respect to N_2?

(a) 1 (b) $\frac{3}{2}$

(c) $\frac{1}{2}$ (d) 2

61. What is the order with respect to H_2?

(a) 1 (b) $\frac{3}{2}$

(c) $\frac{1}{2}$ (d) 2

62. What is the overall reaction order?

(a) 1 (b) $\frac{3}{2}$

(c) $\frac{1}{2}$ (d) 2

Directions (Q. Nos. 63 to 66)
Deal with a simpler suggested mechanism due to the presence of a catalyst :

$$N_2 + H_2 \longrightarrow 2NH \quad \text{slow (on catalytic surface)}$$

$$NH + H_2 \longrightarrow NH_3 \quad \text{fast (off the surface)}$$

63. What is the rate law for this reaction ?

(a) Rate $= k[H_2]$ (b) Rate $= k[N_2][H_2]$

(c) Rate $= k[N_2][H_2]^3$ (d) Rate $= k[NH][H_2]$

64. What is the order with respect to N_2?

(a) 1 (b) $\frac{3}{2}$

(c) $\frac{1}{2}$ (d) 2

65. What is the order with respect to H_2?

(a) 1 (b) $\frac{3}{2}$

(c) $\frac{1}{2}$ (d) 2

66. What is the overall reaction order?

(a) 1 (b) $\frac{3}{2}$

(c) $\frac{1}{2}$ (d) 2

Directions (Q. Nos. 67 to 68)

Time (min)	$[N_2O_5]$ (M)
20	0.010
40	0.004

The decomposition of N_2O_5 (a heterodimer) into NO_2 and NO_3 is thought to be either first order in N_2O_5 or second order.

The (scant) data) (right) was collected :

67. The rate constant for the loss of N_2O_5 if the reaction is first order will be

(a) $0.92\ s^{-1}$ (b) $0.046\ s^{-1}$

(c) $9.2\ s^{-1}$ (d) $0.46\ s^{-1}$

68. The rate constant for loss of N_2O_5 if the reaction is second order is

(a) $0.75\ (\text{mol s})^{-1}$ (b) $7.5\ (\text{mol s})^{-1}$

(c) $0.75\ \text{mol}^{-1}\ \text{s}$ (d) $7.5\ \text{mol}^{-1}\ \text{s}$

Direction (Q. Nos. 69 to 70) In the following reaction

$$2N_2H_4(g) + N_2O_4(g) \rightleftharpoons 3N_2(g) + 4H_2O(g)$$

69. If the rate of appearance of $H_2O(g)$ at 150 K is 4.6×10^{-2} M/s, what is the rate of disappearance of $N_2O_4(g)$?

(a) 4.6×10^{-2} M/s (b) 1.55×10^{-2} M/s

(c) 2.3×10^{-2} M/s (d) 1.15×10^{-2} M/s

70. If the activation barrier energy is 48 kJ/mol. The rate of appearance of $H_2O(g)$ at 300 K will be

(a) 4.6×10^{-2} M/s (b) 0.46×10^{-2} M/s

(c) 22×10^6 M/s (d) 2.2×10^6 M/s

Answers

Exercise 1

1. (a)	2. (a)	3. (c)	4. (b)	5. (a)	6. (b)	7. (c)	8. (b)	9. (a)	10. (a)
11. (c)	12. (c)	13. (b)	14. (b)	15. (b)	16. (d)	17. (d)	18. (d)	19. (d)	20. (c)
21. (a)	22. (b)	23. (b)	24. (c)	25. (d)	26. (b)	27. (a)	28. (b)	29. (c)	30. (d)
31. (b)	32. (c)	33. (c)	34. (a)	35. (c)	36. (d)	37. (b)	38. (c)	39. (b)	40. (c)
41. (b)	42. (d)	43. (b)	44. (a)	45. (c)	46. (a)	47. (d)	48. (d)	49. (d)	50. (a)
51. (c)	52. (b)	53. (c)	54. (a)	55. (a)	56. (b)	57. (d)	58. (c)	59. (d)	60. (c)
61. (d)	62. (c)	63. (d)	64. (c)	65. (a)	66. (a)	67. (d)	68. (b)	69. (c)	70. (d)
71. (c)	72. (a)	73. (b)	74. (b)	75. (a)	76. (d)	77. (a)	78. (a)	79. (d)	80. (c)

Exercise 2

1. (c)	2. (c)	3. (a)	4. (b)	5. (c)	6. (a)	7. (a)	8. (c)	9. (d)	10. (b)
11. (c)	12. (a)	13. (b)	14. (b)	15. (a)	16. (c)	17. (d)	18. (a)	19. (d)	20. (b)
21. (d)	22. (c)	23. (a)	24. (a)	25. (c)	26. (a)	27. (d)	28. (d)	29. (a)	30. (c)
31. (a)	32. (a)	33. (a)	34. (c)	35. (d)	36. (a)	37. (c)	38. (c)	39. (a,b,c)	40. (c)
41. (a)	42. (c)	43. (c)	44. (a,b,c)	45. (b,d)	46. (c)	47. (a)	48. (b)	49. (a)	50. (a)
51. (a)	52. (a)	53. (c)	54. (d)	55. (c)	56. (c)	57. (d)	58. (b)	59. (b)	60. (a)
61. (c)	62. (b)	63. (b)	64. (a)	65. (a)	66. (d)	67. (c)	68. (c)	69. (d)	70. (b)

Hints & Solutions

4. $k = Ae^{-E_a/RT}$ when $T \to \infty$

$$k = Ae^0 = A$$

$$A = k = 1.2 \times 10^3 \text{ mol}^{-1} \text{ L s}^{-1}$$

12. k (no catalyst) $= A \cdot e^{-E_a/RT}$

k' (catalyst present) $= A \cdot e^{-(E_a - 2)/RT}$

$$\frac{k'}{k} = e^{2/RT} = e^{2/0.002 \times 300} = e^{3.33} = 28$$

$$k' = 28 \text{ K}$$

27. Assume rate law as

$$\left(\frac{dx}{dt}\right) = k[A]^a [B]^b$$

By general rule if order $= n$

Multiple of concentration $= m$

Then rate becomes $= m^n$ times

On comparison of values of sets (1) and (4)

Concentration of B has been doubled keeping $[A]$ constant, and rate becomes 8 times.

Thus, $$(2)^b = 8 = 2^3$$

$$b = 3$$

On comparison of values of stes (1) and (3)

$$(2)^a = 1 = (2)^0$$

$$a = 0$$

31. $pV = nRT$ or $p = \frac{n}{V} RT$

$$p_{CH_3CHO} = [CH_3CHO] RT$$

$$[CH_3CHO] = \frac{p_{CH_3CHO}}{RT}$$

$$\therefore \quad \frac{-d[CH_3CHO]}{dt} = -\frac{1}{RT} \frac{dp_{CH_3CHO}}{dt}$$

36. $$k = \frac{2.303}{t} \log \frac{A_0}{A} = \frac{2.303}{40} \log \frac{0.1}{0.005}$$

$$= \frac{2.303}{40} \log 20 = 0.075 \text{ min}^{-1}$$

Rate of reaction when concentration of X is 0.01 M will be

$$0.075 \times 0.01 = 7.5 \times 10^{-4} \text{ M min}^{-1}$$

37. Temperature coefficient $= \frac{k_t + 10}{k_t}$

$$2 = \frac{10^{-3}}{k_t}$$

or $$k_t = \frac{10^{-3}}{2} = 5 \times 10^{-4} \text{ min}^{-1}$$

38. For a first order reaction,

$$t = \frac{2.303}{k} \log_{10} \frac{a}{a - x}$$

Let, initial amount of reactant is 100.

$$\frac{t_1}{t_2} = \frac{\log \frac{100}{100 - 75}}{\log \frac{10}{100 - 25}} = \frac{\log 4}{\log \frac{4}{3}}$$

$$\frac{t_1}{t_2} = \frac{0.6020}{0.6020 - 0.4771} = 4.81$$

40. $$\log_{10} = \log_{10} A - \frac{E_a}{2.303\, RT}$$

$$\text{Slope} = -\frac{E_a}{2.303\, R} = -\frac{1}{2.303}$$

$$E_a = R = 2 \text{ cal}$$

44. $$\text{pH} = 2, [H^+] = 10^{-2} \text{ M}$$

$$\text{pH} = 1, [H^+] = 10^{-1} \text{ M}$$

$$\left(\frac{dx}{dt}\right) = k(10^{-2})^n$$

$$100\left(\frac{dx}{dt}\right) = k(10^{-1})^n$$

$$100 = (10)^n$$

$$(10)^2 = (10)^n$$

$$n = 2$$

47. $$\text{Rate} = k[NOBr_2][NO] \quad \ldots(i)$$

But $NOBr_2$ is in equilibrium

$$K_{eq} = \frac{[NOBr_2]}{[NO][Br_2]}$$

$$[NOBr_2] = K_{eq}[NO][Br_2] \quad \ldots(ii)$$

Putting the $[NOBr_2]$ in equation (i)

$$\text{Rate} = k \cdot k_{eq} [NO][Br_2][NO]$$

$$\text{Rate} = k \cdot k_{eq} [NO]^2 [Br_2]$$

$$\text{Rate} = k'[NO]^2 [Br_2] (\text{where, } k' = k \cdot K_{eq})$$

61. First order kinetics

$$\ln([A]_1) = \ln([A]_0) - kt$$

$$\Rightarrow \quad t = \frac{\ln([A]_0/[A]_1)}{k} = \frac{\ln(0.2/0.08)}{0.015} = 60 \text{ h}$$

62. Note that $\mu_{0.2,\,He} = (32 \times 4)/36 = 3.56$ u

$$\frac{Z_{O_2,He}}{Z_{O_2,O_2}} = \sqrt{2}\, \frac{p_{He}}{p_{O_2}} \frac{\sigma}{4\pi r_{O_2}^2} \left(\frac{m_{O_2}}{\mu_{O_2,\,He}}\right)^{\frac{1}{2}}$$

$$= \sqrt{2}\left(\frac{9876}{432}\right) \frac{(0.13 + 0.17)^2}{4 \times 0.17^2} \left(\frac{32.0}{3.56}\right)^{1/2}$$

$$\frac{Z_{O_2,He}}{Z_{O_2,O_2}} = \sqrt{2}\,(22.9) \frac{0.0900}{0.1156} \sqrt{9.00}$$

$$= \sqrt{2} \times 22.9 \times 0.78 \times 3.00 = 76$$

63. $$E_a = -R \times \frac{d\ln(k)}{d(1/T)} = -R \times 10^3 \frac{d\ln(k)}{d(1000/T)}$$

$$E_a = 8.314 \times 10^3 \frac{J}{\text{mol}\cdot\text{K}} \times \frac{\ln(0.8) - \ln(0.3)}{3.67 - 3.32}$$

$$E_a = 8314 \times \frac{0.981}{0.35} + 8314\,\text{J/mol} \times 2.8$$

$$= 23\text{ kJ/mol or } 240\text{ me V}$$

64. The graph shows B and C forming in parallel and $[A]$ going to zero. Because $\frac{k_2}{k_1} = 2, \frac{[C]}{[B]} = 2.$

66. Nitrogen is the buffer gas.It stabilizes the new bond by carrying away the bond energy.

67. Doubling initial lactose increases the rate by a factor of 2, so the order with respect to lactose is 1. A four-fold increase in $[H^+]$ increases the rate by a factor of 3.8 so the order with respect to protons is also 1.

70. The reaction between hydrogen, H_2, and bromine, Br_2, has been found to proceed by a complicated multistep radical reaction. The differential rate law, which is given as equation 10, does not therefore have a simple form. In general, it is not possible to make any deductions about the kinetics of a reaction simply from the stoichiometry. Instead, it is necessary to consider the mechanism by which the reaction occurs.

71. Reaction rate of affected by nature and concentration of reactants, temperature, surface area and a catalyst. Increasing surface area exposes more particles to contact with reactants, increasing the number of particle collisions. Imagine a cube of chocolate 3 feet by 4 feet and 2 inches thick. Take the same block and make it into a 24 candy bars. A class of chemistry students could eat the bars faster than the single chocolate block.

73. To convert between units, we must note that

$$1\text{ dm}^3 = 10^3\text{ cm}^3$$

and that, because Avogadro's number is the number of molecules in 1 mole,

$$1\text{ mole} = 6.022 \times 10^{23}\text{ molecule}$$

$$\text{then, } k_2 = 3.52 \times 10^6 \times \left(\frac{1}{6.022 \times 10^{23}\text{ molecule}}\right) \times (10^3\text{ cm}^3)\,\text{s}^{-1}$$

$$= 5.85 \times 10^{-15}\text{ molecule}^{-1}\text{ cm}^3\text{ s}^{-1}$$

75. For a first-order process, the integrated form of the rate law is :

$$\ln[A] = \ln[A]_0 - k_r t$$

Since, for a gas, concentration is proportional to partial pressure

$$[A] \propto p_A$$

and so we can write

$$\ln p = \ln p_0 - k_r t$$

This has the form of straight-line graph

$$y = c + mx$$

Thus, a graph of $\ln p$ against t should be a straight line with a gradient $- k_r$. As can be seen from the following plot, this is indeed the case.

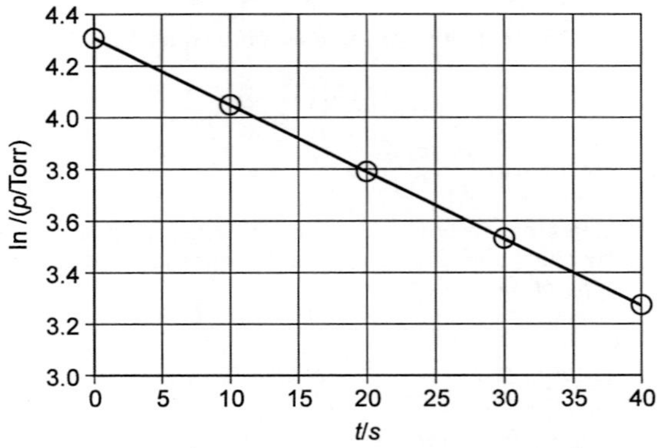

The gradient of the line is $m = - k = - 0.0259\text{ s}^{-1}$, so that $k = 0.0259\text{ s}^{-1}$.

77. $$\ln \frac{k_r(T')}{k_r(T)} = \frac{E_a}{R}\left(\frac{1}{T} - \frac{1}{T'}\right) = \frac{E_a}{R}\left(\frac{T' - T}{T \times T'}\right)$$

to derive an expression for the activation energy

$$E_a = R \ln \left\{\frac{k_r(T')}{k_r(T)}\right\} \times \left(\frac{T \times T'}{T' - T}\right)$$

Thus, since $\left\{\frac{k_r(T')}{k_r(T)}\right\} = 10.6$

Then, $E_a = 8.3145\text{ JK}^{-1}\text{ mol}^{-1} \times \ln 10.6 \times \left(\frac{298 \times 308}{308 - 298}\right)\text{K}$

$$= 180 \times 10^3\text{ J mol}^{-1} = 180\text{ kJ mol}^{-1}$$

78. The half-life for a first-order reaction does not vary with composition and is related to the rate constant by the following equation

$$t_{1/2} = \frac{\ln 2}{k_r}$$

Rearranging, and remembering to convert from hours to seconds,

$$kr_{1/2} = \frac{\ln 2}{t_{1/2}} = \frac{0.693}{(3.20 \times 3600)\text{ s}} = 6.02 \times 10^{-5}\text{ s}^{-1}$$

79. $\because$ $$\ln k_r = \ln A - \frac{E_a}{RT}$$

to write two simultaneous equations, one for each temperature. Thus, if we neglect the units of the rate constants for clarity, we obtain.

$$\ln 9.86 \times 10^{-5} = \ln A - \frac{E_a}{8.3145\text{ JK}^{-1}\text{mol}^{-1} \times 298\text{ K}}$$

$$- 9.224 = \ln A - \frac{E_a}{2477\text{ J mol}^{-1}}$$

and $$\ln 6.17 \times 10^{-3} = \ln A - \frac{E_a}{8.3145\text{ JK}^{-1}\text{ mol}^{-1} \times 338\text{ K}}$$

$$- 5.088 = \ln A - \frac{E_a}{2810\text{ J mol}^{-1}}$$

If we subtract the second equation from the first we obtain

$$- 9.224 - (- 5.088) = - (E_a / \text{J mol}^{-1}) \times \left(\frac{1}{2477} - \frac{1}{2810}\right)$$

$$- 4.136 = 4.784 \times 10^{-5} \times (E_a/\text{J mol}^{-1})$$

$$E_a = 86.6 \times 10^3\text{ J mol}^{-1} = 86.6\text{ kJ mol}^{-1}$$

80. For a reaction $A + B \longrightarrow$ Products

the kinetic theory of gases leads to equation

$$A = \sigma\left(\frac{8kT}{\pi\mu}\right)^{1/2} N_A$$

where, $\mu = \dfrac{m_A m_B}{m_A + m_B}$

The cross section for a collision is the target area presented by one molecule to the other. For collisions between the same type of molecule,

$$\sigma_{AA} = \pi d_{AA}^2 = 4\pi r_A^2$$

so that $\quad r_A = \sqrt{\dfrac{\sigma_{AA}}{4\pi}}$

and similarly for collisions between two B molecules. For collisions between different types of molecule

$$\sigma_{AB} = \pi(r_A + r_B)^2$$

$$= \pi\,(r_A^2 + 2r_A r_B + r_B^2)$$

$$= \frac{1}{4}\,(\sigma_{AA} + 2\sqrt{\sigma_{AA}\,\sigma_{BB}} + \sigma_{BB})$$

Thus for this reaction,

$$\sigma = \frac{1}{4}\,(0.0452 + 2\sqrt{0.0452 \times 0.084} + 0.0804)\ \text{nm}^2$$

$$= 0.0615\ \text{nm}^2 = 0.0615 \times 10^{-19}\ \text{m}^2$$

Note that it is not appropriate to take the cross section for collision as simply the arithmetic mean of the cross sections of the two individual molecules.

Since, $\quad m_{H_2} = (2 \times 1.01)\ m_u = 2.02\ m_u$

and $\quad m_{CO} = (12.01 + 16.00)\ m_u = 28.01\ m_u$

$$\mu = \frac{2.02 \times 28.01}{2.02 + 28.01}\ m_u$$

$$= 1.88\ m_u$$

$$= 1.88 \times 1.661 \times 10^{-27}\ \text{kg}$$

$$= 3.13 \times 10^{-27}\ \text{kg}$$

Then $\quad A = 0.0165 \times 10^{-19}\ \text{m}^2$

$$\times \left(\frac{8 \times 1.381 \times 10^{-23}\ \text{JK}^{-1} \times 298.15\ \text{K}}{\pi \times 3.13 \times 10^{-27}\ \text{kg}}\right)^{1/2}$$

$$\times 6.022 \times 10^{23}\ \text{mol}^{-1}$$

$$= 67.8 \times 10^{6}\ \text{mol}^{-1}\ \text{m}^3\text{s}^{-1}$$

Exercise 2

1. $RCOOR' + H_2O \xrightarrow{H^+} RCOOH + R'OH$

At $t = 0$:	a	0	0
At time t :	$(a - x)$	x	x
At time ∞ :	$(a - a)$	a	a

At $t = 0$, V_0 = volume of NaOH due to H^+ catalyst

$$V_t = V_0 + x$$

$$V_\infty = V_0 + a$$

If 50% ester is hydrolyzed then $x = \dfrac{a}{2}$

$$V_t = \frac{a}{2} + V_0$$

$$a = 2V_t - 2V_0$$

$$V_\infty = 2V_t - 2V_0 + V_0 = 2V_t - V_0$$

5. $\dfrac{dx}{dt} = k\,[A]^a\,[B]^b$

$$0.25 = k\,[1.0]^a\,[1.0]^b \quad \text{...(i)}$$

$$0.50 = k\,[2.0]^a\,[1.0]^b \quad \text{...(ii)}$$

$$0.25 = k\,[1.0]^a\,[2.0]^b \quad \text{...(iii)}$$

Divide values of (ii) by that of (i) and (iii) by that of (i)

$$2 = (2)^a = a = 1$$

$$1 = (2)^b$$

$$2^0 = (2)^b = b = 0$$

$$\frac{dx}{dt} = k\,[A]$$

7. The initial rate of decrease of pressure

$$-\frac{dp}{dt} = kp_{NO}^a\,p_{H_2}^b$$

where, a and b are the order of reaction *wrt* NO and H_2 respectively and p_{NO} and p_{H_2} are initial pressures.

Order *wrt* H_2, $b = \dfrac{\log_{10}\left(\dfrac{R_1}{R_2}\right)}{\log\left[\dfrac{(p_{H_2})_1}{(p_{H_2})_2}\right]}$ (from van't Hoff's diferential method)

where, R_1 and R_2 are the rates of decrease of pressure in (i) and (ii).

$$b = \frac{\log\left(\dfrac{0.0048}{0.0024}\right)}{\log\left(\dfrac{0.2}{0.1}\right)} = 1$$

Similarly, order *wrt* NO [by using values in (i) and (iii)]

$$a = \frac{\log_{10}\left(\dfrac{R_1}{R_3}\right)}{\log\left[\dfrac{(p_{NO})_1}{(p_{NO})_3}\right]}$$

$$a = \frac{\log_{10}\left(\dfrac{0.0048}{0.0012}\right)}{\log\left(\dfrac{0.5}{0.25}\right)} = 2$$

Thus, order *wrt* H_2 = 1 and *wrt* NO is 2 and overall order is

$$a + b = 3$$

Rate law, $\quad -\dfrac{dp}{dt} = kp_{NO}^2\,p_{H_2}$

$$k = \frac{-dp/dt}{p_{NO}^2 \cdot p_{H_2}} = \frac{0.0048\ \text{atm min}^{-1}}{(0.5)^2 \times 0.2\ \text{atm}^3}$$

$$k = 0.096\ \text{atm}^{-2}\ \text{min}^{-1}$$

12. $\log k\ (\text{min}^{-1}) = 5 - \dfrac{2000\ \text{K}}{T}$

$$\log k = \log_{10} A - \frac{E_a}{2.303\ RT}$$

(I) $\log A = 5,\ A = 10^5$ true

$$\frac{E_a}{2.303\ R} = 2000$$

(II) $E_a = 2000 \times 2.303 \times 0.002$ kcal = 9.212 kcal, true

(III) Equation represents straight line, hence, true.

13. $$k_B = A_e^{-E_a/RT} = 10^{12} \times 4.35 \times 10^{-8}$$

$$= 4.35 \times 10^4\ s^{-1}$$

Equilibrium constant $= \frac{k_A}{k_B} = 10^4$

$$k_A = k_B \times 10^4 = 4.35 \times 10^8\ s^{-1}$$

14. $$\left(\frac{dx}{dt}\right) = k\,[A]_0^n$$

$$\log\left(\frac{dx}{dt}\right) = n \log [A]_0 + \log k$$

Thus, n = slope = order

Greater the order, larger the slope.

Thus, $P = 3, Q = 2, R = 1, S = 0$

15. $$k = \frac{1}{t}\left[\frac{1}{a-x} - \frac{1}{a}\right]$$

$$k = \frac{1}{t}\frac{x}{(a-x)\,(a)}$$

$$k = \frac{1}{t}\frac{x}{[A]\,[A_0]} \quad \text{or} \quad x = kt\,[A]\,[A_0]$$

Also, $$k = \frac{1}{t}\left[\frac{1}{[A]} - \frac{1}{[A_0]}\right]$$

$$kt = \left[\frac{1}{[A]} - \frac{1}{[A_0]}\right]$$

$$kt + \frac{1}{[A_0]} = \frac{1}{[A]}$$

$$\frac{kt\,[A_0] + 1}{[A_0]} = \frac{1}{[A]}$$

$$[A] = \frac{[A_0]}{kt\,[A_0 + 1]}$$

$$x = \frac{kt\,[A_0]^2}{kt\,[A_0] + 1}$$

17. Comparing the slope and intercept of the given equation with the following Arrhenius equation.

$$\log k = -\frac{E_a}{2.303\ RT} + \log A$$

Hence, $\log A = 6$, *i.e.,* $A = 10^6\ s^{-1}$

Comparing slope gives $E_a = 2000 \times 2.303\ R$

$$= 2000 \times 2.303 \times 8.3143 \times 10^{-3}$$

$$= 38.3\ kJ$$

20. $$k_1 = 10^{10}\ e^{-20000/T}$$

$$k_2 = 10^{12}\ e^{-24606/T}$$

$$k_1 = k_2,$$

so, $$e^{-\frac{20000}{T} + \frac{-24606}{T}} = 10^2$$

or $$e^{4606/T} = 10^2$$

On taking log both sides

$$\frac{4604}{2.303\,T} = \log 10^2$$

$$2 \log 10 \times T = \frac{4606}{2.303}$$

$$T = \frac{4606}{2.303 \times 2} = 1000\ K$$

22. From slow step, rate = $k\,[B_2]\,[A]$

From 1st equation, $K_{eq} = \frac{[A]^2}{[A_2]}$

$$[A] = \sqrt{K_{eq}\,[A_2]} = K_{eq}^{1/2}\,[A_2]^{1/2}$$

$$\text{Rate} = k\,[B_2]\,K_{eq}^{1/2}\,[A_2]^{1/2}$$

$$\text{Rate} = k'\,[A_2]^{1/2}\,[B_2]$$

$$\text{Order} = 1\frac{1}{2}$$

25. At temperature T K, rate constants are equal, hence

$$10^{13} \exp\left(\frac{-152300\ J\ mol^{-1}}{RT}\right) = 10^{14} \exp\left(\frac{-157700\ J\ mol^{-1}}{RT}\right)$$

$$\exp\left(\frac{157700 - 152300}{RT}\right) = 10$$

$$\log_e \exp\left(\frac{157700 - 152300}{RT}\right) = \log_e 10$$

$$= 2.303 \log_{10} 10$$

or $$\frac{157700 - 152300}{8.314\ T} = 2.303$$

Thus, $T = 282$ K

26. Initial $[NOBr]_0 = 4.00 \times 10^{-3}$ M

after time t, $[NOBr]_t = [NOBr]_0 - [NOBr]_{used}$

$[NOBr]_t = 4.00 \times 10^{-3} - 1.50 \times 10^{-3} = 2.50 \times 10^{-3}$

$$k = \frac{1}{2t}\left[\frac{1}{[NOBr]_t} - \frac{1}{[NOBr]_0}\right]$$

$$0.810 = \frac{1}{2t}\left[\frac{1}{2.50 \times 10^{-3}} - \frac{1}{4.00 \times 10^{-3}}\right]$$

$$t = \frac{1}{2 \times 0.810}\left[\frac{(4.00 - 2.50) \times 10^{-3}}{2.50 \times 10^{-3} \times 4.00 \times 10^{-3}}\right]$$

$$t = 92.6\ s$$

30. $$\frac{\Delta N}{N_{av}} = e^{-E_a/RT}$$

$$= e\left(\frac{80.9 \times 10^3\ J\ mol^{-1}}{8.314\ kJ\ mol^{-1} \times 673\ K}\right) = e^{-14.459}$$

$$= 5.257 \times 10^{-7}$$

32. Rate of formation of product, P

$$r = k_3[A^*] \quad \ldots(i)$$

Applying steady state approximation to A^*, we obtain

$$k_1[A]^2 - k_{-1}[A^*]\,[A] + k_2[A]\,[M] - k_{-2}[A^*]\,[M] - k_3[A^*] = 0$$

$$k_1[A]^2 + k_2[A][M] = [A^*]\{k_{-1}[A] + k_{-2}[M] + k_3\}$$

$$[A^*] = \frac{k_1[A]^2 + k_2[A][M]}{k_{-1}[A] + k_{-2}[M] + k_3}$$

Putting the value of $[A^*]$ in equation (i)

$$r = k_3[A^*] = \frac{k_3k_1[A]^2 + k_2[A][M]}{k_{-1}[A] + k_{-2}[M] + k_3}$$

33. For bimolecular reaction between unlike molecules

$$A = (2.753 \times 10^{29})\, P(d_{av})^2 \left[\frac{T(M_A + M_B)^{1/2}}{M_A M_B}\right] \text{dm}^3 \text{ mol}^{-1} \text{ s}^{-1}$$

$$\text{Steric factor, } P = \frac{1.20 \times 10^{10}}{1.142 \times 10^{11}} = 0.11$$

34. From Arrhenius equation, $k = Ae^{-E_a/RT}$

Let, k_e and k_n be the rate constants for enzyme catalyzed reactions and non-catalyzed reactions.

$$\frac{k_e}{k_n} = \frac{e^{-E_a/RT}}{e^{-E_a/RT}}$$

$$= \exp\left(\frac{83.68 \text{ kJ mol}^{-1} - 25.10 \text{ kJ mol}^{-1}}{8.314 \times 10^{-3} \text{ kJ K}^{-1} \text{ mol}^{-1} \times 310}\right)$$

$$\frac{k_e}{k_n} = e^{22.728}$$

or

$$\ln \frac{k_e}{k_n} = 22.728$$

$$\frac{k_e}{k_n} = 10^{10}$$

37.

$$\frac{k_{(293)}}{k_{(276)}} = 3$$

$$E_a = \frac{2.303\, RT_1T_2}{(T_2 - T_1)} = \log \frac{k_{293}}{k_{273}}$$

$$E_a = \frac{2.303 \times 8.314 \times 10^{-3} \times 276 \times 293}{17} \times \log 3$$

$$E_a = 43.46 \text{ kJ mol}^{-1}$$

$$E_a = \frac{2.303\, RT_2T_3}{(T_3 - T_2)} \log \frac{k_{T_3}}{k_{T_2}} \quad (T_2 = 293\text{ K}, T_3 = 313\text{ K})$$

$$43.46 = \frac{2.303 \times 8.314 \times 10^{-3} \times 293 \times 313}{(313 - 293)} \log \frac{k_{T_3}}{k_{T_2}}$$

$$\frac{k_{T_3}}{k_{T_2}} = 3.126 = \frac{t_2}{t_3} \quad \left(\because k \propto \frac{1}{\text{time}}\right)$$

$$\therefore t_3, \text{ time required at } T_3 = \frac{t_2}{3.126} = \frac{64}{3.126}$$

$$= 20.51 \text{ h}$$

38.

$$t_{1/2} = 28.1 \text{ yr}$$

$$k = \frac{0.693}{28.1} = 2.4662 \times 10^{-2} \text{ yr}^{-1}$$

^{90}Sr after 10 yr = $a - x$

$$a = 1\ \mu\text{g}$$

$$k = \frac{2.303}{t} \log\left(\frac{a}{a-x}\right)$$

$$2.4662 \times 10^{-2} = \frac{2.303}{10} \log\left(\frac{1}{a-x}\right)$$

$$\log\left(\frac{1}{a-x}\right) = 0.107086$$

$$\frac{1}{a-x} = 1.2796$$

$$(a - x) = 0.7815\ \mu\text{g}$$

52. The rate-determining step of an S_N1 reaction is unimolecular dissociation. We need not consider the rate of the subsequent addition step because it is so much quicker than the initial dissociation that we may assume that every ion thus formed reacts instantaneously. The rate law of the reaction may therefore the taken as the rate law of the first step.

$$\text{Rate} = k\,[C_4H_9Br]$$

53. For high pressures of bromine,

$$[Br_2] >> [HBr]$$

so that

$$[Br_2] + k_{r2}\,[HBr] \approx [Br_2]$$

and therefore

$$\frac{d[HBr]}{dt} = \frac{k_{r1}\,[H_2]\,[Br_2]^{3/2}}{[Br_2] + k_{r2}\,[HBr]}$$

$$= \frac{k_{r1}\,[H_2][Br_2]^{3/2}}{[Br_2]}$$

$$= k_{r1}\,[H_2]\,[Br_2]^{1/2}$$

so that $\quad \text{Rate} = k_{r1}\,[H_2][Br_2]^{1/2}$

54. The rate constant for the rate-determining step, and hence, the entire mechanism, of a diffusion controlled reaction is given by

$$k_{r,d} = \frac{8RT}{3\eta}$$

Thus, because the viscosity of water is $\eta = 6.90 \times 10^{-4}$ kg m^{-1} s^{-1} at 350 K,

$$k_{r,d} = \frac{8 \times 8.3145 \text{ JK}^{-1} \text{ mol}^{-1} \times (77 + 273.15)\text{ K}}{3 \times 6.9 \times 10^{-4} \text{ kg m}^{-1}\text{s}^{-1}}$$

$$= 11.3 \times 10^6 \text{ mol}^{-1} \text{ m}^3\text{s}^{-1}$$

55. For enzyme-catalysed reactions that follow a Michaelis-menten mechanism, the relationship between the rate of reaction and enzyme substrate,

$$\frac{1}{v} = \frac{1}{v_{max}} + \left(\frac{K_M}{v_{max}}\right)\frac{1}{[S]}$$

This expression has the form of a straight-line graph

$$y = c + mx$$

A plot of $\frac{1}{v}$ against $\frac{1}{S}$ should therefore have a gradient of $\frac{K_M}{v_{max}}$ and an intercept of v_{max}. The value of the Mischaelis constant is therefore given by the ratio of the gradient to the intercept

$$\frac{m}{c} = \frac{(K_M/v_{max})}{1/v_{max}} = K_M$$

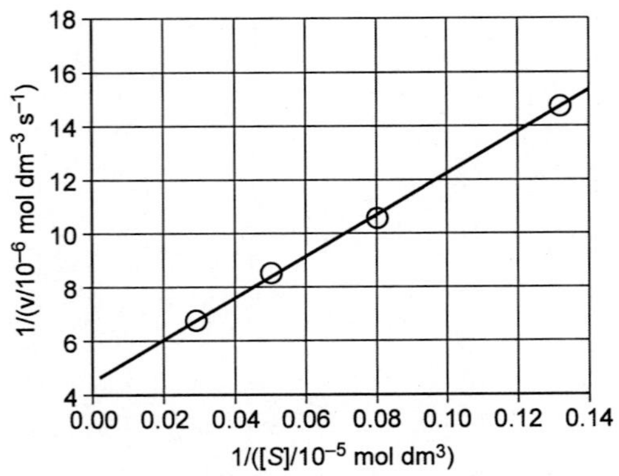

The gradient of the Lineweaver-Burk plot is 7.935 s and the intercept 4.307×10^6 mol^{-1} dm^3 s^{-1}, so that

$$K_M = \frac{7.935 \text{ s}}{4.307 \times 10^6 \text{ mol}^{-1} \text{ dm}^3 \text{ s}^{-1}}$$

$$= 1.84 \times 10^{-6} \text{ mol dm}^{-3}$$

In determining the gradient and intercept, it is important to take care to include the appropriate multipliers.

56. At high pressure, the rate law for a reaction that follows the Lindemann mechanism is given by

$$k_r = \frac{k_a k_b}{k'_a}$$

so that the rate constant of the final step of the mechanism is

$$k_b = \frac{k'_a}{k_a} \times k_r$$

If collisional activation is 10^{-11} times slower than collisional deactivation, it follows that $\frac{k_a}{k'_a} = 10^{-11}$

so that $k_b = \frac{k'_a}{k_a} \times k_r = 10^{-11} \times 2 \times 10^{-5}$ s^{-1}

$$= 2 \times 10^{-16} \text{ s}^{-1}$$

57. It is seen that the concentration of the intermediate in a two-step reaction reaches a maximum after a time given

$$t = \frac{1}{k_a - k_b} \ln \frac{k_a}{k_b}$$

So that

$$t = \frac{1}{(5.25 - 15.23) \times 10^{-3} \text{ s}^{-1}} \ln \frac{5.25}{15.23} = 107 \text{ s}$$

58. $K = \frac{k_{1f}\, k_{2f}}{k_{1b}\, k_{2b}}$ because $\frac{k_{1f}}{k_{1b}} = \frac{[AB][A]}{[A_2][B]}$ and $\frac{k_{2f}}{k_{2b}} = \frac{[AB]}{[A][B]}$

67. $\ln(A) = \ln(A_0) - kt.$

Solve for $k = \ln(0.004/0.01)/20 = 7.5 = 0.046$ s^{-1}.

68. $\frac{1}{A} = \frac{1}{A_0} + kt.$

Solve for $k = (1/0.004 - 1/0.01)/20 = 7.5$ (mol-s)$^{-1}$

69. $-1\frac{d[N_2O_4(g)]}{dt} = \frac{1}{4}\frac{d[H_2O(g)]}{dt} = \frac{1}{4}\, 4.6 \cdot 10^{-2}$ M/sec as a disappearance, then

$$\frac{d[N_2O_4(g)]}{dt} = 1.15 \cdot 10^{-2} \text{ M/s}$$

70. $$\frac{\text{Rate}(300)}{\text{Rate}(150)} = \frac{k_{300}}{k_{150}} = \frac{Ae^{-\left\{\frac{E_0}{R300}\right\}}}{Ae^{-\left\{\frac{E_0}{R150}\right\}}} = e^{-\left\{\frac{E_a}{R300} - \frac{E_0}{R150}\right\}}$$

here $\frac{E_a}{R300} = 48/2.4 = 20$

$$\text{rate}(300) = \text{rate}(150) \cdot e^{-(20-40)}$$

$$= 4.6 \cdot 10^{-2} e^{20}$$

$$= 4.6 \cdot 10^{6.68} = 22 \times 10^6 \text{ M/s}$$

25

Surface Chemistry

Colloids

A colloid is a heterogeneous system in which finely divided particles of any substance with diameter lying within 1 to 100 nm range is dispersed (dispersed phase) in any medium called dispersion medium. Colloidal solutions are intermediate between true solutions and suspensions. Colloidal system is a two phase system consisting of a continuous phase or dispersion medium in which minute particles of second substance known as discontinuous phase or dispersed phase are suspended. The dispersed phase and dispersion medium may be solid, liquid and gas. Colloidal system is called aerosol when dispersion medium is a gas and sol when dispersion medium is liquid (hydrosol-water, alcosol-alcohol and benzosol-benzene).

Syllabus

- Colloids : Classification, Preparation and Properties
- Coagulation and Hardy-Schulze Rule
- Protective Colloids Sol and Gold Number
- Stability of Sols
- Adsorption : Types and Various Theories of Isotherm
- Structure of Solid Surface

Classification of Colloids

Lyophilic colloids

The colloidal solutions in which dispersed phase particles have a great affinity for dispersion medium are called lyophilic colloids. These are reversible colloids. They are much stable.

Lyophobic colloids

The colloidal solutions in which dispersed phase particles have no affinity for dispersion medium are called lyophobic colloids. These are irreversible colloids. They are much less stable.

Types of Solutions

Depending upon the size of dispersed phase particles in dispersion medium, solutions are divided into three classes :

1. True solutions–size smaller than 1 nm.
2. Colloidal solutions–size in between 1 nm to 100 nm.
3. Suspensions–size greater than 100 nm.

Preparation of Colloidal Solutions

Dispersion methods

(a) **Mechanical dispersion** The substance is grinded to the size of colloidal particles by the help of colloidal mill.

(b) **Electrical dispersion** (Bredig's arc method) Colloidal solutions of metals are prepared by this method. An arc is struck between two electrodes of a metal (electrodes are made of metals whose solutions are to be prepared) like Pt, Au in water containing traces of an alkali, when the metal passes into colloidal solution.

(c) **Peptization** It involves conversion of a freshly formed precipitate into a sol by addition of a small amount of a suitable electrolyte.

$$\underset{\text{Fresh ppt.}}{Fe(OH)_3} + \underset{\text{Electrolyte}}{FeCl_3} \longrightarrow [Fe(OH)_3 \cdot Fe]^{3+} + 3Cl^-$$

Peptization action is due to the preferential adsorption of the common ion of the electrolyte and the precipitate to be dispersed. For example, AgI is peptized by the addition of $AgNO_3$ or KI

$$AgI + AgNO_3 \longrightarrow [AgI]\,Ag^+ : NO_3^-$$
(Ag^+ is adsorbed)

$$AgI + KI \longrightarrow [AgI]\,I^- : K^+$$
I^- is adsorbed

Cellulose nitrate is peptized by organic solvents such as ethyl alcohol and product is called collodion.

2. Chemical Methods/Condensation Methods

(a) **Double decomposition**

$$As_2O_3 + 3H_2S \longrightarrow As_2O_3 + 3H_2O$$

(b) **Hydrolysis**

$$2FeCl_3 + 6H_2O \xrightarrow{\Delta} \underset{\text{Red sol of hydrated ferric oxide}}{Fe_2O_3 \cdot 3H_2O} + 6HCl$$

(c) **By oxidation**

$$Br_2 + H_2S \longrightarrow 2HBr + \underset{\text{Colloidal sol}}{S}$$

$$2H_2S + SO_2 \longrightarrow 2H_2O + 3S$$

(d) **By reduction**

$$2H[AuCl_4] + 5K_2CO_3 \longrightarrow 2KAuO_2 + 5CO_2$$

$$2KAuO_2 + 2HCHO + K_2CO_3 \xrightarrow{\Delta} 2Au\ (sol) + 3HCOOK + KHCO_3$$

$KAuO_2$ acts as stabilizer.

(e) **Exchange of solvents and excessive cooling** are the other physical methods that can be employed to prepare colloidal solutions.

Purification of Colloidal Solutions

Presence of impurities renders the sol unstable. These must be eliminated by

Dialysis

It involves keeping the sol in a bag made of parchment or cellophane and suspending the bag in the pure water. Small molecules and ions (impurities) can pass through the membrane, but the sol is retained. When an electric field is applied during dialysis, the process is known as **electrodialysis**.

Ultrafiltration

The ultrafilters allow only the electrolytes to pass through under the influence of pressure or suction pump.

Ultracentrifugation

Under the influence of high speed, the colloidal particles settle down at the bottom while impurities remain in solution.

Multimolecular, Macromolecular and Associated Colloids

Multimolecular colloids consist of aggregates of atoms or small molecules with diameter of less than 1 nm. *e.g.*, gold sol, sulphur sol. In macromolecular colloids, the dispersed particles are themselves large molecules having dimensions comparable to those of colloidal particles, *e.g.*, polymers. Micelles or associated colloids behave as normal electrolytes at low concentrations, but exhibit colloidal properties at higher concentrations. Surface active agents like soaps and synthetic detergents belong to this class.

- Critical micelle concentration, CMC is the lowest concentration at which micelle formation appears. At higher concentration they form **lamellar** micelles.
- In concentrated solutions, micelles take the form of long clinders packed in hexagonal arrays and are called **lytotropic mesomorphs.**
- Micelles from ionic surfactants such as sodium stearate ($C_{17}H_{35}COONa$) can be formed only above a certain temperature called the **Kraft temperature.**
- Increasing the hydrophobic part of surfactant molecules favours micelle formation.
- The cleansing action of soap is due to affinity of soap anions, *e.g.*, $C_{17}H_{35}COO^-$. The anionic carboxylic group is hydrophilic and hydrocarbon chain ($C_{17}H_{35}$) is hydrophobic. This hydrophobic part dissolves in grease deposit while hydrophilic

part has an affinity with water, thus micelle is formed, which in turn is removed by rinsing with water.

- Soaps are known as emulsifying agents because they reduce oil and greasy dirt to colloidal particles (an emulsion).

Properties of Colloids

Heterogeneous nature

Colloidal sols are heterogeneous in nature.

Colligative properties

Colloidal solutions also exhibit colligative properties. But due to formation of associated molecules, observed values of colligative properties are smaller than expected.

Brownian movement

It involves motion of colloidal particles in *zig-zag* paths. This type of motion is due to the moving molecules of the dispersion medium constantly colliding with colloidal particles. This motion is independent of the nature of the colloid, but is more rapid in case of smaller size and in less viscous dispersion medium. It offers explanation for the stability of colloidal solutions.

Electrical properties

(a) **Electrophoresis** Colloidal particles possess some type of electric charge. Depending on the charge they move towards a positive or negative electrodes when an electric field is applied to colloidal dispersion. This is called electrophoresis.

(b) **Electroosmosis** When the movement of the dispersed particles are prevented by some suitable means, it is observed that dispersion medium itself begins to move in an electric field. This phenomenon is called eletroosmosis.

The rate at which colloidal particles migrate in an electric field is expressed in electrophoretic mobility. It is defined as the distance travelled by them in one second under a potential gradient of $1\ \text{V cm}^{-1}$. Different colloidal material have different mobilities.

Determination of size of colloidal particles

(i) By using ultrafilters.

(ii) From Brownian movement

$$\frac{RT}{N_A}\ln\left(\frac{n_1}{n_2}\right)=\frac{4}{3}\pi r^3/(h_2-h_1)(\rho-\rho')$$

where, n_1 and n_2 are number of particles at two depths h_1 and h_2 of the vertical column. ρ and ρ' are the densities of particles and of liquid medium.

(iii) From scattering of light

Volume of colloidal phase, $\frac{m}{\rho}=\frac{4}{3}\pi r^3\times n$

$$r=\left(\frac{3m}{4\pi\rho n}\right)^{1/3}$$

where, m is the mass of colloidal particles per unit volume and n is the number of particles per unit volume.

Optical properties

When light passes through a sol, its path become visible because of scattering of light by particles. It is called **Tyndall effect** and the illuminated path is known as **Tyndall cone**. The intensity of the scattered light depends on the difference between refractive indices of the dispersed phase and the dispersion medium. In lyophobic colloids, the difference is appreciable and the Tyndall effect is well defined in comparison to lyophilic colloids.

Charge on Colloidal Particles

Colloidal particles are either positively charged or negatively charged. This charge is due to preferential adsorption of either positive or negative ions on their surface. There is adsorption of common ion present in excess. For example, positive charge on colloidal sol of ferric hydroxide is due to adsorption of $\mathbf{Fe}^{3+}$ ions.

$$Fe(OH)_3 + FeCl_3 \longrightarrow \underset{\text{Fixed part}}{[Fe(OH)_3]\,Fe^{3+}} : \underset{\text{Diffused part}}{Cl^-}$$

Similarly, As_2S_3 sol is negatively charged due to the adsorption of S^{2-} ions.

$$As_2S_3 + H_2S \longrightarrow \underset{\text{Fixed part}}{[As_2S_3]\,S^{2-}} : \underset{\text{Diffused part}}{2H^+}$$

SnO_2 in acidic medium forms positively charged colloidal sol due to adsorption of Sn^{4+} ions, while in basic medium it forms negatively charged colloidal sol due to adsorption of SnO_3^{2-} ions.

$$SnO_2 + Sn^{4+} \longrightarrow [SnO_2]\,Sn^{4+}$$

(Acidic medium)

$$SnO_2 + SnO_3^{2-} \longrightarrow [SnO_2]\,SnO_3^{2-}$$

(Basic medium)

There is formation of an electrical double layer of opposite charges on the surface of colloidal particles. The combination of the two layers of opposite charges around the colloidal particle is called **Helmholtz**

electrical double layer. The first layer is fixed and second layer is mobile which is called diffused layer. Potential difference of this electrical double layer is called **zeta potential** or **electro kinetic potential,** Z.

$$Z = \frac{4\pi\eta u}{D}$$

where, η = coefficient of viscosity, D = dielectric constant of medium, u = velocity of colloidal particles when an electric field is applied.

(Fixed layer is known as the **stern layer** and diffused layer is known as **Gouy-Chapmann layer**).

The value of Zeta potential decreases when an ion of opposite charge to that of the colloidal particle is adsorbed. This reduces the mutual repulsion between the similar charged colloidal particles. Due to this colloidal particles come closer to each other and form bigger aggregates. This process of changing colloidal state to suspension state is called coagulation, precipitation or flocculation of colloidal solutions. Lyophobic colloids are stable due to the presence of electrical charge on the colloidal particles while lyophilic colloids are stable due to the presence of electrical charge on the colloidal particles and solvation.

Charge on acidic dyestuff is due to ionization to form H^+ and negatively charged dyes particles.

$$\underset{\text{D-dye}}{DH} \rightleftharpoons \underset{\text{Dye particle}}{D^-} + H^+$$

Similarly, basic dyestuff on ionization forms positively charged dye particles.

$$DOH \rightleftharpoons \underset{\text{Dye particle}}{D^+} + OH^-$$

Coagulation and Hardy-Schulze Rule

The phenomenon of change of colloidal state to suspended state is known as **coagulation** or **flocculation** of colloidal solutions. It can take place by the addition of suitable electrolyte. *e.g.,* coagulation of positively charged sol takes place by the addition of negative ion of suitable electrolyte and *vice-versa.*

$$[Ag\,I]\,Ag^+ + I^- \longrightarrow 2AgI$$

$$2\,[AgI]\,Ag^{3-} + SO_4^{2-} \longrightarrow 2AgI + Ag_2SO_4$$

$$3\,[AgI]\,Ag^+ + PO_4^- \longrightarrow 3AgI + Ag_3PO_4$$

Thus, larger the charge on the coagulating ion, larger the coagulation.

$$I^- < SO_4^{2-} < PO_4^{3-}$$

Similarly, addition of Ag^+, Pb^{2+}, Fe^{3+} and Si^{4+} causes coagulation of negatively charged colloidal sol in 1 : 2 : 3 : 4 molar ratio.

$$Ag^+ < Pb^{2+} < Fe^{3+} < Si^{4+}$$

Hardy-Schulze rule states that the greater the valency of the coagulating ion added, the greater is its power to cause coagulation. The minimum concentration of an electrolyte required to cause coagulation or flocculation of a sol is called its **flocculation value.** It is expressed in millimoles per litre.

If two oppositely charged colloidal sols are mixed, coagulation takes place.

$$[AgI]\,Ag^+ + [AgI]\,I^- \longrightarrow 3AgI$$

- Quantitatively, the efficacy of an ion to cause coagulation varies directly as the square of the valency of the ion. Therefore, Mg^{2+} ion is four times more effective and an Al^{3+} ion is nine times more effective than a Na^+ ion in flocculating (coagulating) a negative colloidal sol.
- Flocculation value of HCl (30 millimoles per litre) and $KBrO_3$ (31 millimoles per litre) for As_2S_3 sol and $Fe(OH)_3$ sol are relatively low. It is due to the strong adsorption of H^+ ions on As_2S_3 sol particles and BrO_3^- ion on $Fe(OH)_3$ sol particles.
- Flocculation values of potassium citratte, potassium acetate and potassium formate for As_2S_3 sol should be about same, but their observed flocculation values are 270, 115 and 85 millimoles per litre respectively. Actually citrate, acetate and formate ions are adsorbed to different extents on the surface of As_2S_3 particles. This increase the negative Zeta potential of the particles to the different extents. Therefore, different concentrations of effective K^+ ions are required to cause coagulation of As_2S_3 sol.

$$Mg^{2+} > Ca^{2+} > Ba^{2+} > Na^+ > K^+$$

$$SO_4^{2-} > Cl^- > NO_3^- > ClO_3^- > I^-$$

Protective Colloidal Sols and Gold Number

Lyophilic colloidal sols are called protective sols. These protects lyophobic colloidal sols from precipitation, *e.g.,* gelatin (lyophilic) protects gold sol (lyophobic) from coagulation on addition of NaCl solution. Protective powers of different colloidal sols are measured in terms of **gold number.** It is defined as the amount of protective sol in milligrams that prevents the coagulation of 10 mL of a given gold sol on adding 1 mL of 10% NaCl solution.

- Smaller the gold number of a lyophilic sol, greater is the protective power.
- Gold number of some lyophilic colloidal sols are as :

Gelatin	–	0.005–0.01
Casein	–	0.01
Haemoglobin	–	0.03
Gum arabic	–	0.15
Potato starch	–	25

Stability of Sols

Preventing coagulation of a colloidal solution by any manner or means is known as stabilising the colloid. Bencroft (1915) gave the position with regard to stability. He said that 'Any substance may be brought into a colloidal state, provided the particles of the dispersed phase are so small that the Brownian movement keeps the particles suspended and provided the coagulation of the particles is prevented by a suitable surface film.

It was observed that lyophobic sols are stable due to their electric charge. As most of the lyophobic sols are prepared by preferential adsorption of ions, the mutual repulsion of particles is responsible for their stability. The sols become unstable, as soon as they are robbed of their charge. However, in case of lyophilic sols, the stability is due to electric charges as well as solvation–a phenomenon in which the colloid particle is surrounded by a thin film of the solvent. This layer of the solvent forms an envelope around each colloidal particle and thus prevents the particles from coming together. Groups like —COOH and —NH_2 in proteins and —OH in hydroxides and polysaccharides can bind water molecules. Lyophilic sols are coagulated when first the solvent layer and then the charge of the ion is removed.

Factors affecting stability

There are numerous factors which confer stability on the colloidal system.

(a) **Brownian movement** As a result of this movement, the particles are in constant rapid motion where by aggregation of particles is prevented, so that the sol remains stable. But as soon as Brownian motion ceases, the sol becomes unstable. It is, therefore, expected that a sol will be more stable, the higher the disparity and greater the charge on the particles.

(b) **Addition of electrolytes** A sol becomes unstable by the addition of suitable quantity of electrolytes. It is now established that the presence of electrolytes has a powerful effect on the potential difference between the particles of the dispersed phase and the dispersion medium and that this potential difference is closely connected with the stability of sols.

(c) **Effect of concentration of the sol** Gosh and Dhar (1927) showed that a number of positively charged sols follow the rule that, greater the concentration of the sol the greater the amount of electrolyte required to coagulate the sol. In other words, the greater the concentration of the sol greater is its stability.

(d) **Effect of dilution** Choudhury (1928) showed that the dilution of a sol also affects the stability, which is decreased. The reason is the diminution of the charge and the total surface of sol particles with dilution decrease the stability of the sol. Mukherjee (1930) attempted to find out a relation between dilution and stability of a sol by measuring the migration velocity of the particles, but found the relation to be complicated.

(e) **Rate of addition of the electrolyte** Dhar (1925) showed that the amount of electrolyte required to confer stability on a sol depends upon the rate at which it is added–this phenomenon is known as **'acclimatization of sols'**. There are two types of acclimatizations : in some cases, less electrolyte is required, when it is added slowly or in small quantities at a time, and in other cases the amount required is more. The former and latter are known as **positive** and **negative acclimatization**, respectively. this phenomenon is probably due to changes occurring in the stabilising by electrolytes.

(f) **Effect of temperature** It is seen that decrease of temperature confers more stability on the sols. Reid and Burton (1928) showed that heat alone is sufficient to cause coagulation.

(g) **Mechanical agitation** It has been seen that mechanical agitation decreases the stability of sols. Freundlich and Loehmann (1922) showed that the sol of CuO was found to be coagulated by mechanical agitation. The rate of coagulation is proportional to the square of the rate of stirring.

(h) **Ultra-violet light and X-ray radiations** Many lyophobic sols are coagulated by UV light and X-rays of even from radiations of radium. It is seen that the coagulating effect of the rays is independent of the sign of the colloid. Lal and Ganguly (1930) studied the coagulating influence of UV light on sols of AgI, Au, Ag, V_2O_5, $Th(OH)_2$, As_2S_3 etc.

(i) **Charge on the particle** The presence of charge on the colloid particles also confers stability on sols. If the charge is removed (as shown in cataphoresis) be any manner, the sol becomes unstable.

(j) **Stabilization by protecting films** A typical example of protection by a film is shown by preparing two sols of hydrous ferrous oxide, the first by adding dropwise a few drops of conc. $FeCl_3$ to boiling water and the second by adding a small amount of 1% gelatin to the $FeCl_3$ before using. The relative stability of the two sols will be shown by the greater amount of electrolyte required to coagulate the second sol. The reason for this is that gelatin forms a protective layer around each sol particle and thus prevents it to some extent from being precipitated. Generally, lyophilic colloids are used for this purpose.

Emulsions

An emulsion is a colloidal system of two immiscible liquids in which one liquid acts as the dispersed phase while the other liquid acts as the dispersion medium. Depending on the nature of the dispersed phase, the emulsions are of two types :

1. Oil in water emulsion = oil-dispersed phase, water dispersion medium. **Example** milk and vanishing cream.
2. Water in oil emulsion = water-dispersed phase, oil-dispersion medium. **Example** cold cream and butter.

Identification of the type of emulsions

(a) Dilution test
(b) Dye test
(c) Electrical conductivity test
(d) Spreading test
(e) Viscosity test

Emulsifiers or emulsifying agent

Emulsions formed by merely shaking the two immiscible liquids together, is highly unstable. For stabilization of an emulsion, a third component called emulsifying agent is usually added. The emulsifying agent forms an interfacial film between suspended particles and the medium. The emulsifiers or emulsifying agents consist of ionic as well as non-ionogenic surfactants. Some lyophilic colloids such as proteins, gums, gelatin and agar-agar also act as emulsifiers. These substances form a multi molecular film around the droplets of the dispersed phase, while ionic surfactants get adsorbed at the interface between the dispersed droplets and the dispersion medium in the form of mono molecular layer and lower the interfacial tension between oil and water.

Surfactants

Surfactants are substances which get preferentially adsorbed at the air-water, oil-water and solid-water interfaces, forming an oriented monolayer where in the hydrophilic groups point towards the aqueous phase and hydrocarbon chains point towards the air or towards the oil phase. Surfactants are of three types; anionic surfactants, cationic surfactants and non-ionogenic surfactants.

Bancroft's Rule

Hydrophilic emulsifiers promote the formation of an o/w emulsion and hydrophobic emulsifiers favour the formation of a w/o emulsion. This is called Bancroft's rule.

Adsorption

The phenomenon of higher concentration of any molecular species at the surface than in the bulk of a solid or liquid is known as **adsorption.** As a result of adsorption, there is a decrease of surface energy. The substance adsorbed is known as **adsorbate** and the substance on which adsorption takes place is called **adsorbent**.

- The removal of the adsorbed substance from a surface is called **desorption.**
- In some cases, adsorption and absorption take place simultaneously, the term **sorption** is used in such cases.

Types of Adsorption

Physisorption

In physisorption, adsorbate is held to the adsorbent by weak van der Waals' forces of attraction.

Chemisorption

In chemisorption, adsorbate is held to the adsorbent by strong chemical bonds.

After adsorption the gas molecules are restricted to two dimensional motion. Therefore, adsorption is accompanied by a decrease in entropy. It also results in decrease in free energy (ΔH-negative). The adsorption of a gas by a solid is an exothermic process.

Initially only physical adsorption takes place since no activation energy is involved and there is a gradual transition to chemisorption.

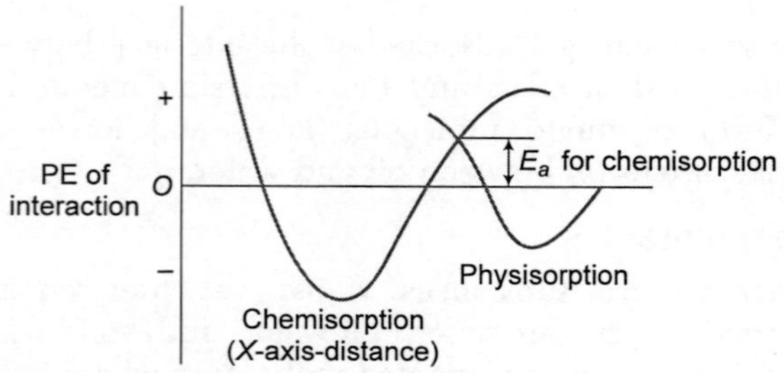

Fig. 25.1 PE curves for adsorption.

As shown in Fig. 25.1, the transition from physisorption, to chemisorption takes place where the two curves meet. The energy at this point is equal to the activation energy for chemisorption. The magnitude of this activation energy depends on the shape of the two curves and varies from system to system.

Factors Influencing Adsorption

The magnitude of the gaseous adsorption depends upon the following four factors

1. Temperature
2. Pressure
3. Nature of the gas
4. Nature of the adsorbent

- Decrease of temperature and increase of pressure both tend to cause increase in the mgnitude of adsorption of a gas on a solid.
- Greater the surface area per unit mass of adsorbent, the greater is its capacity for adsorption under the given conditions of temperature and pressure.

Desorption Activation Energy

$$k_{\text{desorption}} = Ae^{-E_a/RT}$$

$\dfrac{1}{k_{\text{desorption}}}$ is called life time, τ of the adsorbate molecule on the surface, therefore,

$$\tau = \tau_0 e^{E_a/RT}$$

where, $\tau_0 = \dfrac{1}{A}$ is known as the pre-exponential factors

and E_a = desorption activation energy of adsorbate.

Adsorption Isotherm

The variation of adsorption with pressure at a given constant temperature is generally expressed graphically. Each curve is known as adsorption isotherm for the particular temperature.

Freundlich Adsorption Isotherm

The variation of adsorption with pressure can be represented by the equation, commonly known as **Freundlich adsorption isotherm.**

$$\frac{x}{m} = kp^{1/n}$$

where, $\dfrac{x}{m}$ = amount of gas adsorbed per unit mass of the adsorbent at pressure p. k and n are constants depends upon the nature of the gas and nature of adsorbent ($n > 1$).

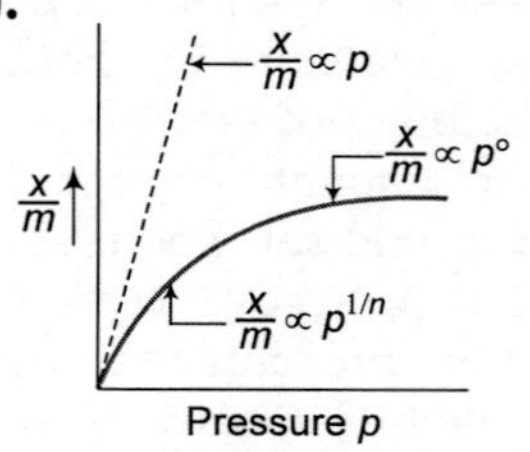

The Freundlich plot.

$$\log\frac{x}{m} = \log k + \frac{1}{n}\log p$$

A graph between $\log\dfrac{x}{m}$ and $\log p$ is a straight line with slope $\dfrac{1}{n}$ and intercept $\log k$.

Langmuir Adsorption Isotherm

The simplest situation is when the gas atoms or molecules occupy single sites on the surface and are not dissociated, the process can be represented as

$$A(g) + M(\text{surface}) \underset{k_d}{\overset{k_a}{\rightleftharpoons}} AM$$

Let, θ is the fraction of the surface covered. At equilibrium, the rate of adsorption is equal to the rate of desorption.

$$k_a p_A (1-\theta) = k_d\theta$$

where, k_a and k_d are the rate constants for adsorption and desorption respectively. The rate of adsorption is proportional to the pressure of A gas, *viz.*, p_A.

$$\theta = \frac{kp_A}{1 + kp_A}$$

This equation is called Langmuir adsorption isotherm.

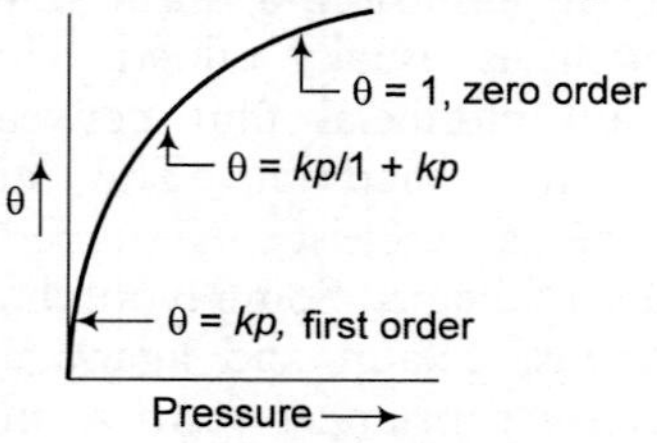

The Langmuir plot.

- At low pressures, $kp_A << 1$ so that $\theta = kp_A$. It means the fraction of the surface covered is directly proportional to the partial pressure of the gas molecules (1st order reaction).
- At high pressures, $kp_A >> 1$, so that $\theta = 1$, it means the entire surface gets covered by a monomolecular layer of the gas and the reaction rate becomes independent of the pressure (zero order reaction).

The Langmuir adsorption isotherm applies to ideal case of chemisorption on a perfectly smooth surface with no interactions between adsorbed molecules.

Deviations from the Langmuir isotherm are often observed. This may be because (i) the surface is not uniform (ii) there may be interactions between adsorbed molecules (iii) there may be adsorption in more than one layer.

BET Adsorption Isotherm for Multimolecular adsorption

The theory of Brunauer, Emmett and Teller is an extension of the Langmuir treatment to allow for multilayer adsorption on non-porous solid surfaces. Physical adsorption is not limited to a monomolecular layer. Since, the forces operating are similar to those in liquefaction, the adsorption of molecules can continue until a multimolecular layer of liquid covers the adsorbent surface. It is assumed that energy of adsorption in the first layer, E_1 is constant and the energy of adsorption in succeeding layers is assumed to be the same as E_L, the energy of liquefaction of the gas. The BET equation is written in the form

$$\frac{p}{V\,(p_0 - p)} = \frac{1}{V_{\text{mono}}C} + \frac{C-1}{V_{\text{mono}}C}\left(\frac{p}{p_0}\right)$$

where, p_0 is the saturation vapour pressure, V_m is the monolayer capacity and $C = \exp\,(E_1 - E_L)/RT$

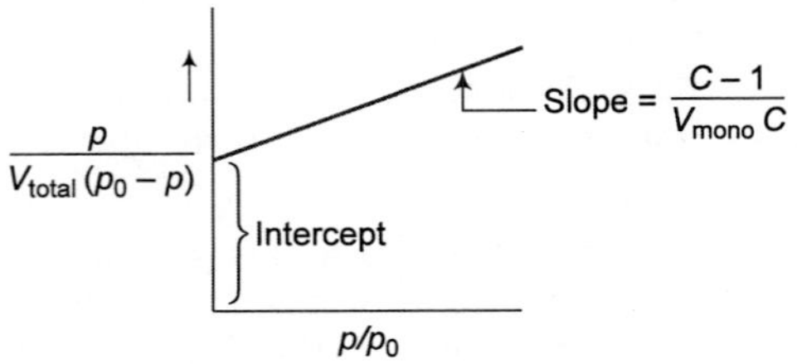

Determination of surface area

$$V_{\text{mono}} = \frac{1}{\text{slope} + \text{intercept}}$$

By knowing V_{mono}, the surface area of the adsorbent can be easily calculated.

Surface area (covered by adsorbate molecule) of adsorbent = No. of molecules in V_{mono} × area of cross-section of one molecule

Area of cross-section '*a*' of the molecule,

$$a = \pi r^2 = \pi\left[\frac{3M}{4\pi N_A \rho}\right]$$

where, M = molar mass of adsorbate,
ρ = density of the adsorbate,
N_A = Avogadro number

Adsorption from Solution Phase

Freundlich's equation describes the behaviour of adsorption from solution with a difference that instead of pressure, concentration of the solution is taken.

$$\frac{x}{m} = kC^{1/n}$$

C is the equilibrium concentration when adsorption is complete.

$$\log\frac{x}{m} = \log k + \frac{1}{n}\log C$$

Plotting $\log\frac{x}{m}$ against $\log C$, a straight line is obtained which shows the validity of Freundlich isotherm.

Gibbs Adsorption Isotherm

$$\Gamma_2 = -\frac{1}{RT}\left(\frac{\partial\gamma}{\partial\ln C_2}\right)_T = -\frac{C_2}{RT}\left(\frac{\partial\gamma}{\partial C_2}\right)_T$$

where, γ is the surface energy which is numerically the same as the surface tension, C_2 is the concentration of the solution and Γ_2 is the surface excess concentration. For a solute that lowers the surface tension, the surface excess concentration Γ_2 is positive and for a solute that raises the surface tension, Γ_2 is negative.

Types of Adsorption Isotherms

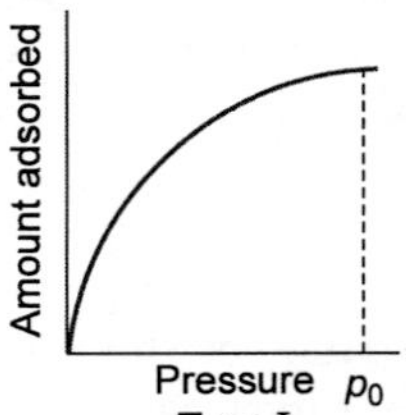

Type I

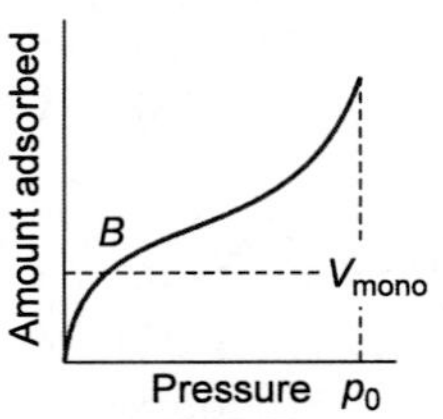

Type II

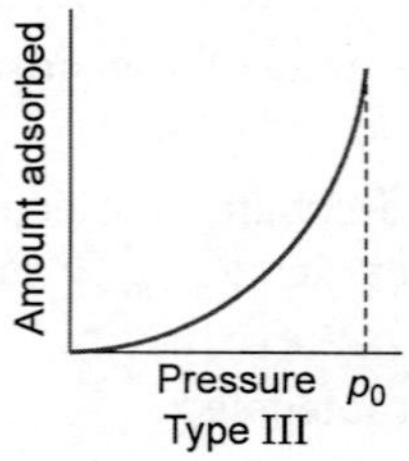

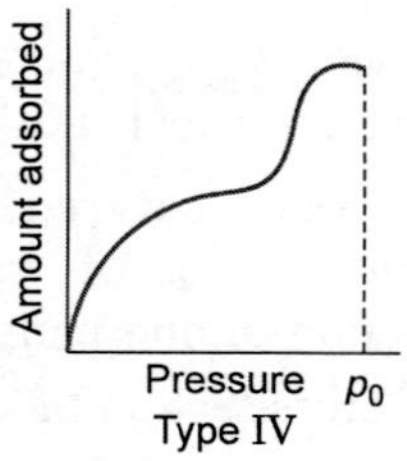

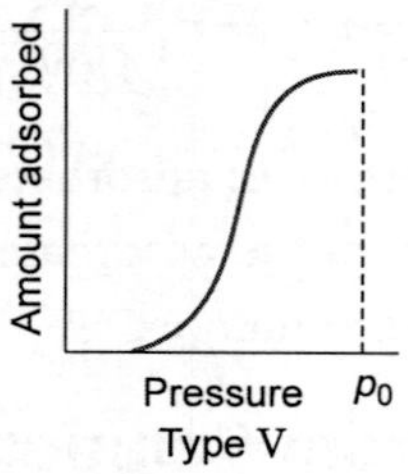

The relationship at a given temperature between the amount of the gas adsorbed and equilibrium pressure is known as an adsorption isotherm.

- Type I isotherms show a fairly rapid rise in the amount of adsorption with increasing pressure upto a limiting value (Langmuir-type isotherm). **Example** adsorption of H_2 and N_2 on charcoal at −180°C.
- Type II isotherms represent multilayer physical adsorption on non-porous solids. Point B represents the formation of an adsorbed monolayer. **Example** adsorption of N_2 on silica gel.
- Type III isotherms show amount of adsorption keeps on rising in each case with increase in pressure. **Example** adsorption of Br_2 on silica or alumina gel at 80°C.
- Type IV and type V are observed in those cases where there is capillary condensation in porous solids. **Example** of type IV: adsorption of benzene on silica gel at 50°C and **example** of type V: adsorption of water vapour on activated carbon at 100°C.

Relation between adsorption and energy of liquefaction of the gaseous adsorbate More readily soluble and easily liquefiable gases such as NH_3, HCl, Cl_2 and SO_2 are adsorbed more than so called permanent gases like H_2, N_2 and O_2.

Catalysis

A catalyst is a substance which enhances the rate of a chemical reaction without itself getting used up in the reaction. The phenomenon using catalyst is known as **catalysis.** In homogeneous catalysis, the catalyst is in same phase as are the reactants, and in heterogeneous catalysis, the catalyst is in different phase from that of the reactants.

Heterogeneous Catalysis, Surface Reactions

The theory of heterogeneous catalysis is based upon the phenomenon of adsorption. The action of a heterogeneous catalyst is due to the presence of free valencies present on the surface.

Reactions between gaseous reactants are catalyzed by solid-state catalysts. According to the Langmuir-Hinshelwood mechanism, a gaseous reaction taking place on the surface of a solid catalyst (surface reaction) can be divided into the following five steps.

1. Diffusion of reactants to the surface of the catalyst.
2. Adsorption of reactant molecules on the surface of the catalyst.
3. Occurrence of chemical reaction on the catalyst's surface through the formation of an intermediate.
4. Desorption of reaction products from the catalyst surface, and there by, making the surface available again for more reaction to occur.
5. Diffusion of reaction products away from the catalyst's surface.

These steps are consecutive. If any of them has a slower rate constant than the other steps, it will become the rate determining step. With the help of above theory, the following facts can be explained.

1. **Action of finely divided catalyst** With the increase of surface area of the adsorbent (catalyst), free valencies or active centres increase, which are responsible for the increase in adsorption of reactants. Therefore, catalytic activity is greatly enhanced if catalyst is finely divided.
2. **Action of promoters** Promoters get adsorbed on the surface of the catalyst and produce discontinuity. As a result of this number of active centres increases which in turn increases the catalytic activity.
3. **Action of poisons** Poisons are preferentially adsorbed by active centres present on the surface of the catalyst and reduces the number of active centres present on the surface of a catalyst.
4. **Specific action of the catalyst** For a particular reaction, a specific catalyst is used. The specific action of the catalyst is due to the affinity between

the catalyst and the reactants. This affinity determines the subsequent conversion of reactants into products.

Quantitative Treatment of Adsorption Theory of Heterogeneous Catalysis on Reactants

According to Langmuir's theory of adsorption, the concentration of the adsorbed molecules on the surface of the catalyst is proportional to the area occupied by the reactants. It θ is the area covered by the reactants then.

Rate of reaction, $$r = \frac{dx}{dt} \propto \theta$$

$$r = \frac{dx}{dt} = Z_1\theta$$

where, Z_1 is a constant.

Area covered by the reactant is related to the pressure of the gas p.

$$\theta = \frac{k_1 p}{1 + k_1 p} \qquad \text{where, } k_1 \text{ is a constant}$$

$$r = \frac{dx}{dt} = Z_1 \frac{k_1 p}{1 + k_1 p}$$

When there is only one reactant it will be absorbed on the surface and after the reaction it will be desorbed. But when there are two reactants, their molecules are adsorbed on adjacent sites and reaction proceeds. Let us consider both the cases.

Unimolecular surface

Dissociation of a single gaseous substance on a solid surface.

Rate of reaction, $$r = \frac{-dp}{dt} = Z_1 \frac{k_1 p}{1 + k_1 p}$$

- **When pressure is low,** the value of p becomes negligible compared to unity

$$-\frac{dp}{dt} = Z_1 k_1 p = Z_2 p \qquad (Z_2 = Z_1 k_1)$$

On integration, $$Z_2 = \frac{1}{t} \ln \frac{p_0}{p}$$

where p_0 is the initial pressure of the gas. The order of reaction is one.

- **When pressure is high,** $k_1 p > 1$ and $\theta \to 1$ (reactant is strongly adsorbd)

So, $$\frac{-dp}{dt} = Z_1 \frac{k_1 p}{k_1 p} = Z_1$$

Therefore, the reaction rate becomes independent of pressure and the reaction is zero order.

- **At moderate pressure**

$$\frac{-dp}{dt} = \textbf{constant} \times p^n$$

Value of n varies from 0 to 1 and is a fraction. The order of reaction become fractional one.

Bimolecular surface reactions

A bimolecular reaction involves a reaction between two molecules A and B on a surface. According to Langmuir-Hinshelwood mechanism, the two molecules A and B are adsorbed on adjacent active centres. Let, θ_A and θ_B be the area covered by A and B respectively. At equilibrium, rate of adsorption = rate of desorption.

$$k_1 [1 - (\theta_A + \theta_B)]\, p_A = k'_1 \theta_A \qquad \ldots(1)$$

$$k_2 [1 - (\theta_A + \theta_B)]\, p_B = k'_2 \theta_B \qquad \ldots(2)$$

where, p_A and p_B are partial pressures of reactants A and B respectively.

On dividing equation (2) by (1), we get

$$\theta_B = \frac{k_2 k'_1\, p_B \cdot \theta_A}{k_1 k'_2\, p_A} \qquad \ldots(3)$$

On substituting equation (3) in equation (1), we get

$$\theta_A = \frac{k_1 p_A}{K'_1 + k_1 p_A + \dfrac{k_2 k'_1 \cdot p_B}{k'_2}} \qquad \ldots(4)$$

From equation (3)

$$\theta_A = \frac{\theta_B \cdot k_1 k'_2\, p_A}{k_2 k'_1\, p_B} \qquad \ldots(5)$$

On substituting equation (4) in eq. (2)

$$\theta_B = \frac{k_2 p_B}{k'_2 + k_2 p_B + \dfrac{k_1 k'_2}{k'_1} p_A} \qquad \ldots(6)$$

Rate of reaction, $r = \dfrac{-dp}{dt} = Z\theta_A \theta_B$

On sustituting the value of θ_A and θ_B from equation (4) and (6), we get

$$\frac{-dp}{dt} = Z \times \frac{k_1 p_A}{k'_1 + k_1 p_A + \dfrac{k_2 k'_1}{k'_2} p_B} \times \frac{k_2 p_B}{k'_2 + k_2 p_B + \dfrac{k_1 k'_2}{k'_1} p_A} \qquad \ldots(7)$$

Let us consider the following three cases

1. **When *A* and *B* both are weakly adsorbed** In this case, θ_A and θ_B become negligible as compared to unity. Hence, in equation (7), the terms involving p_A and p_B in denominator becomes negligible.

$$-\frac{dp}{dt} = Z\frac{k_1 p_A k_2 p_B}{k'_1 + k'_2} = k_A p_A p_B \qquad \ldots(8)$$

$$\left(\text{where, } k_A = \frac{Zk_1 k_2}{k'_1 + k'_2}\right)$$

The reaction is second order overall.

2. **When *A* is adsorbed more strongly than the *B*** In this case, θ_A is relatively larger than θ_B but θ_A is less than unity. Hence, in equation (7), the terms involving p_B in denominator becomes negligible.

$$\frac{-dp}{dt} = Z\frac{k_1 p_A}{k'_1 + k_1 p_A} \times \frac{k_2 p_B}{k'_2 + \frac{k_1 k'_2}{k'_1} p_A} \qquad \ldots(9)$$

$$\frac{-dp}{dt} = Z\frac{k_1 k'_1 k_2 p_A p_B}{k'_2 (k'_1 + k_1 p_A)^2} = \frac{k_B (p_A \cdot p_B)}{(1 + b_{p_A})^2} \qquad \ldots(10)$$

where, $k_B = \frac{Zk_1 k_2}{k'_2}$ and $b = \frac{k_1}{k'_1}$

3. **When one reactant is very strongly adsorbed (Reactant *A* is adsorbed strongly)** In such a case, θ_A is almost equal to unity.

$$\frac{-dp}{dt} = Z\theta_A\theta_B = Z\frac{k'_1 k_2 p_B}{k_1 k'_2 p_A} \qquad (\text{Because } \theta_A = 1)$$

$$\frac{-dp}{dt} = k_C\frac{p_B}{p_A} \qquad \left(k_C = \frac{Zk'_1 k_2}{k_1 \cdot k'_2}\right)$$

The rate is inversely proportional to the concentration of the very strongly adsorbed component.

Exercise 1
(For Part 'B')

1. Eletro-osmosis is observed when
   (a) dispersion medium begins to move in an electric field
   (b) dispersed phase begins to move in an electric field
   (c) Both (a) and (b)
   (d) None of the above

2. Potential difference of the electrical double layer formed in a colloidal sol is called
   (a) EMF (b) Zeta potential
   (c) Brownian potential (d) Nernst potential

3. SnO_2 is taken in basic medium and current is passed. Colloidal sol migrates towards
   (a) anode (+ve plate) (b) cathode (−ve plate)
   (c) Both (a) and (b) (d) None of these

4. Fixed parts of a colloidal sol of AgI are respectively [AgI] Ag^+ and [AgI] I^- in presence of
   (a) KI and $AgNO_3$ (b) KI and KI
   (c) AgI and KI (d) $AgNO_3$ and KI

5. Following is the variation of physical adsorption with temperature

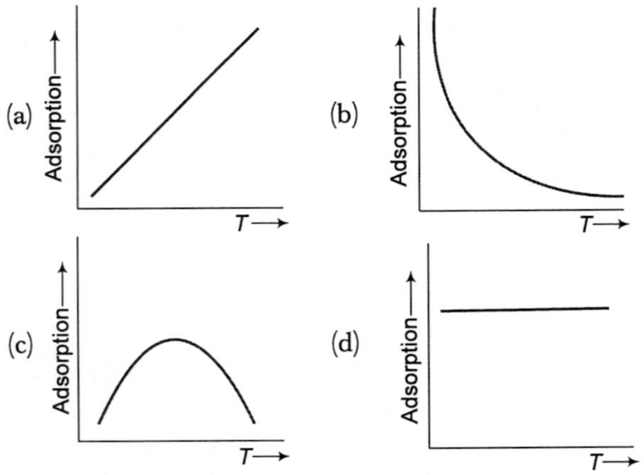

6. Select correct statement(s).
   (a) Residual force-field on a surface is responsible for adsorption.
   (b) Rate of adsorption is very rapid in the beginning but decreases until equilibrium is attained.
   (c) Desorption and adsorption are two opposite terms.
   (d) All of the above are correct statements.

7. Which gas is adsorbed to maximum extent on the given surface?
   (a) NH_3 (b) H_2
   (c) N_2 (d) O_2

8. The Langmuir adsorption isotherm is deduced using the assumption
   (a) the adsorbed molecules interact with each other
   (b) The adsorption takes place in multilayers
   (c) The adsorption sites are equivalent in their ability the particles.
   (d) The heat of adsorption varies with coverage.

9. Adsorption is
   (a) an exothermic process hence increase in temperature decreases adsorption in cases where van der Waals' forces exist between adsorbate and adsorbent
   (b) an endothermic process hence increase in temperature increases adsorption
   (c) an exothermic process hence increase in temperature increases adsorption
   (d) None of the above

10. Lake test of aluminium ion is based on adsorption of blue litmus on
    (a) solid surface of Al
    (b) solid surface of $Al(OH)_3$
    (c) solid surface of Al_2O_3
    (d) solid surface of $AlCl_3$

11. A plot of log x/m *versus* $\log p$ for the adsorption of a gas on a solid gives a straight line with slope equal to
    (a) n (b) $\frac{1}{n}$
    (c) $\log k$ (d) $-\log k$

12. In the following isotherm

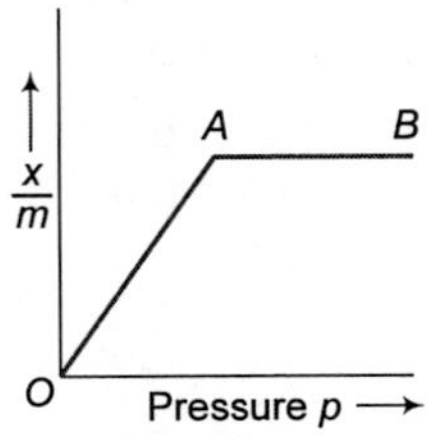

    (a) $\frac{x}{m} \propto p^0$ when point A is reached
    (b) desorption may start along AB
    (c) $\frac{x}{m} \propto p^{1/n}$ along OA
    (d) All of the above

13. Which pair is correctly matched?
    (a) $[Fe(OH)_3] : Fe^{3+}$
    (b) $[As_2S_3] : As^{3+}$
    (c) $[SnO_2] : SnO_3^{2-}$ in acidic medium
    (d) $[AgI] : I^-$ in excess of $AgNO_3$

14. Zeta potential or electrokinetic potential is dependent on
(a) viscosity
(b) dielectric constant
(c) velocity of the colloidal particles when an electric field is applied
(d) All of the above

15. Colloidal sulphur particles are negatively charged with $S_2O_3^{2-}$ and other ions on the surface of sulphur. Hence, most effective electrolyte in coagulating colloidal sulphur is
(a) NaCl (b) $MgCl_2$
(c) $AlCl_3$ (d) Na_2SO_4

16. Aluminium hydroxide forms a positively charged sol. Which of the following ionic substances should be most effective in coagulating the sol?
(a) NaCl (b) $Fe_2(SO_4)_3$
(c) $CaCl_2$ (d) K_3PO_4

17. $[AgI]\,I^-$ colloidal sol can be coagulated by the addition of a suitable cation. 1 mol of $[AgI]\,I^-$ requires mol of $AgNO_3$, $Pb(NO_3)_2$ and $Fe(NO_3)_3$ as
(a) 1, 1, 1 (b) 1, 2, 3
(c) $1, \frac{1}{2}, \frac{1}{3}$ (d) 6, 3, 2

18. Flocculation value of a coagulating electrolyte is expressed in
(a) millimol L^{-1} (b) mol L^{-1}
(c) mg K^{-1} (d) microgram mL^{-1}

19. In Freundlich Adsorption isotherm, the value of $\frac{1}{n}$ is
(a) 1 in case of physical adsorption
(b) 1 in case of chemisorption
(c) between 0 and 1 in all cases
(d) Between 2 and 4 in all cases

20. When MnO_4^- is added to oxalic acid rate of the reaction with time (oxidation of MnO_4^- by oxalic acid) may follow graph

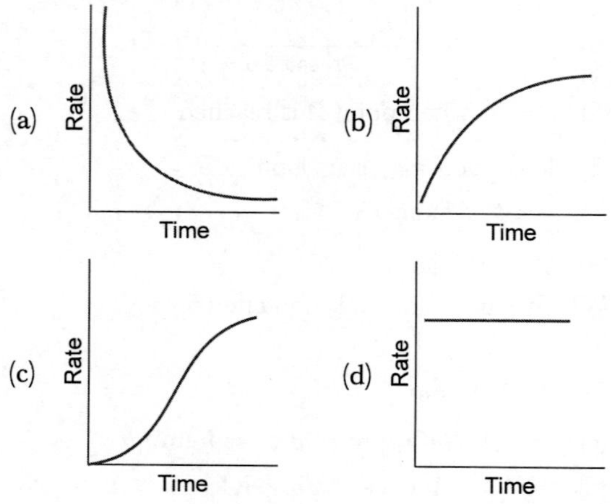

21. In Langmuir's model of adsorption of a gas on a solid surface
(a) the adsorption at a single site on the surface may involve multiple molecules at the same time
(b) the mass of gas striking a given area of surface is proportional to the pressure of the gas.
(c) the mass of gas striking a given area of surface is independent of the pressure of the gas
(d) the rate of dissociation of adsorbed molecules from the surface does not depend on the surface covered.

22. A catalyst accelerate the rate of reaction by
(a) decreasing energy of activation
(b) increasing Arrhenius constant
(c) increasing both
(d) decreasing both

23. It is instructed that automobiles with catalytic converter must use unleaded gasolines because
(a) leaded gasolines may give more fumes
(b) surface of the catalyst is rendered ineffectively by adsorption of lead
(c) automobiles with catalytic converter cannot run on leaded-gasolines
(d) unleaded-gasoline is cheaper

24. Gold number of some lyophilic sols are

I. Casein	0.01
II. Haemoglobin	0.03
III. Gum arabic	0.15
IV. Sodium oleate	0.40

Which has maximum protective power?
(a) I (b) II
(c) III (d) IV

25. Which is not the correct matching of emulsions?
(a) Milk : O/W
(b) Cold cream : W/O
(c) Butter : O/W
(d) Vanishing cream : O/W

26. An emulsion can be diluted with H_2O (dispersion medium), then it is
(a) O/W type (b) W/O type
(c) Both (a) and (b) (d) None of these

27. Rubber plating and chrome tanning of leather are based on
(a) electro-osmosis (b) Tyndall effect
(c) electrophoresis (d) Brownian motion

28. Water carrying impurities is purified by addition of potash alum. Al^{3+} of the potash alum causes
(a) peptization of negatively charged turbidity
(b) coagulation of negatively charged turbidity
(c) peptization of positively charged turbidity
(d) coagulation of positively charged turbidity

29. Milk is an emulsion of fat dispersed in water. It is stabilized by
(a) casein–a lyophilic colloidal sol
(b) casein–a lyophobic colloidal sol
(c) lactose–a lyophilic colloidal sol
(d) lactose–a lyophobic colloidal sol

30. Which one of the following statements is wrong about adsorption?
(a) It is a selective and specific process
(b) It is a reversible process
(c) An increase in the gaseous adsorbate causes increase in adsorption. However, at high pressure, the adsorption becomes constant
(d) It is an endothermic process

31. 1 mole of [AgI] Ag^+ sol is coagulated by
(a) 1 mole of KI
(b) 500 mL of 1 M K_2SO_4
(c) Both (a) and (b)
(d) None of the above

32. Arsenic (III) suphide forms a sol with a negative charge. Which of the following ionic substances should be most effective in coagulating the sol?
(a) KCl (b) $MgCl_2$
(c) $Al_2(SO_4)_3$ (d) Na_3PO_4

33. Aluminium hydroxide forms a positively charged sol. Which of the following ionic substances should be most effective in coagulating the sol?
(a) NaCl (b) $CaCl_2$
(c) $Fe_2(SO_4)_3$ (d) K_3PO_4

34. The colligative property of a colloidal sol compared to solution of non-electrolyte of same concentration will be
(a) same (b) higher
(c) lower (d) higher or lower

35. Which of the following can act as a protective colloid?
(a) Gelatin (b) Silica gel
(c) Oil-in-water emulsion (d) All of these

36. If a freshly formed ppt. of SnO_2 is peptized by a small amount of NaOH, these colloidal particles may be represented as
(a) $[SnO_2]\,SnO_3^{2-} : 2Na^+$ (b) $[SnO_2]\,Sn^{4+} : O^{2-}$
(c) $[SnO_2]\,Na^+ : OH^-$ (d) $[SnO_2]\,Sn^{4+} : OH^-$

37. On adding $AgNO_3$ solution into KI solution, a negatively charged colloidal sol is obtained when they are in
(a) 100 mL of 0.1 M $AgNO_3$ + 100 mL of 0.1 M KI
(b) 100 mL of 0.1 M $AgNO_3$ + 100 mL of 0.2 M KI
(c) 100 mL of 0.2 M $AgNO_3$ + 100 mL of 0.1 M KI
(d) 100 mL of 0.15 M $AgNO_3$ + 100 mL of 0.15 M KI

38. Smoke has generally blue tinge. It is due to
(a) scattering (b) coagulation
(c) Brownian motion (d) electro-osmosis

39. Adsorption is the phenomenon in which a substance
(a) accumulates on the surface of the other substance
(b) goes into the body of the other substances
(c) remains close to the other substance
(d) None of the above

40. Sorption is the term used when
(a) adsorption takes place
(b) absorption takes place
(c) Both (a) and (b)
(d) desorption takes place

41. Amount of gas adsorbed per gram of adsorbent increases with pressure, but after certain limit is reached, adsorption becomes constant. It is where
(a) multilayers are formed
(b) desorption takes place
(c) temperature is increased
(d) absorption also starts

42. Softening of hard water is done using sodium aluminium silicate (zeolite). This causes
(a) adsorption of Ca^{2+} and Mg^{2+} ions of hard water replacing Na^+ ions
(b) adsorption of Ca^{2+} and Mg^{2+} of hard water replacing Al^{3+} ions
(c) Both (a) and (b)
(d) None of the above

43. In 'lake-test' of Al^{3+} ion, there is formation of coloured floating-lake. It is due to
(a) adsorption of litmus by $Al(OH_4)^-$
(b) adsorption of litmus by $Al(OH)_3$
(c) adsorption of litmus by H_2O
(d) None of the above

44. Compared to common colloidal sols micelles have
(a) higher colligative properties
(b) lower colligative properties
(c) same colligative properties
(d) None of the above

45. Which is not the correct statement for a catalyst?
(a) It does not alter E_a
(b) The surface of a catalyst adsorbs reactants
(c) Catalyst may form intermediates with the reactants
(d) Action of enzyme catalyst is always specific

46. The ability of the catalyst to direct the reaction to yield particular product is called
(a) reactivity (b) selectivity
(c) activity (d) fugacity

47. Which of the following is an example of zeolite?
(a) ZSM-5 (b) $AgNO_3$
(c) $Mg(OH)_3$ (d) $Co(OH)_3$

48. Colloidal solutions of gold prepared by different methods are of different colours because of
(a) different diameters of colloidal gold particles
(b) variable valency of gold
(c) different concentration of gold particles
(d) impurities produced by different methods

49. Bleeding is stopped by the application of ferric chloride. This is because
(a) the blood starts flowing in opposite direction
(b) the blood reacts and forms a solid, which seals the blood vessel
(c) the blood is coagulated and thus the blood vessel is sealed
(d) the ferric chloride seals the blood vessel

50. Lyophilic colloids are stable due to
(a) small size of the particle
(b) large size of the particle
(c) layer of dispersion medium on the particle
(d) charge on the particle

51. The physical adsorption of gases on the solid surface is due to
(a) covalent bond (b) hydrogen bond
(c) ionic bond (d) van der Waals' forces

52. Among the electrolytes Na_2SO_4, $CaCl_2$, $Al_2(SO_4)_3$ and NH_4Cl, the most effective coagulating agent for Sb_2S_3 sol is
(a) Na_2SO_4 (b) $CaCl_2$ (c) $Al_2(SO_4)_3$ (d) NH_4Cl

53. Among the following, the surfactant that will form micelles in aqueous solution at the lowest molar concentration at ambient conditions is
(a) $CH_3(CH_2)_{15}N^+(CH_3)_3Br^-$
(b) $CH_3(CH_2)_{11}OSO_3^-Na^+$
(c) $CH_3(CH_2)_6COO^-Na^+$
(d) $CH_3(CH_2)_{11}N^+(CH_3)_3Br^-$

54. Which of the following statements is incorrect regarding physisorption?
(a) It occurs because of van der Waals' forces
(b) More easily liquefiable gases are adsorbed readily
(c) Under high pressure it results into multi molecular layer on adsorbent surface
(d) Enthalpy of adsorption ($\Delta H_{adsorption}$) is low and positive

55. Gold numbers of protective colloids *A*, *B*, *C* and *D* are 0.50, 0.01, 0.10 and 0.005, respectively. The correct order of their protective powers is
(a) $D < A < C < B$ (b) $C < B < D < A$
(c) $A < C < B < D$ (d) $B < D < A < C$

56. In Langmuir's model of adsorption of a gas on a solid surface
(a) the rate of dissociation of adsorbed molecules from the surface does not depend on the surface covered
(b) the adsorption at a single site on the surface may involve multiple molecules at the same time
(c) the mass of gas striking a given area of surface is proportional to the pressure of the gas
(d) the mass of gas striking a given area of surface is independent of the pressure of the gas

57. $2SO_2(g) + O_2(g) \xrightleftharpoons{V_2O_5}$ is an example for
(a) neutralization reaction (b) homogeneous catalysis
(c) heterogeneous catalysis (d) irreversible reaction

58. When a sulphur sol is evaporated sulphur is obtained. On mixing with water sulphur sol is not formed. The sol is
(a) lyophilic (b) reversible
(c) hydrophobic (d) hydrophilic

59. The physical states of dispersing phase and dispersion medium in colloid like pesticide spray respectively, are
(a) gas, liquid (b) solid, gas
(c) liquid, solid (d) liquid, gas

60. In an electrical field, the particles of a colloidal system move towards cathode. The coagulation of the same sol is studied using K_2SO_4 (I), Na_3PO_4 (II), $K_4[Fe(CN)_6]$ (III) and NaCl (IV). Their coagulating power should be
(a) (I) > (II) > (III) > (IV) (b) (III) > (II) > (I) > (IV)
(c) (III) > (I) > (II) > (IV) (d) (IV) > (III) > (I) > (II)

Exercise 2

(For Part 'C')

1. Following are some of the properties of the colloidal sols
I. Tyndall effect
II. Brownian motion
III. Maxwell distribution of molecules
These valid properties are
(a) I, II, III (b) I, II
(c) I, III (d) II, III

2. For the adsorption of solution on a solid surface $\frac{x}{m} = kC^{1/n}$. Adsorption isotherm of $\log\left(\frac{x}{m}\right)$ and $\log C$ was found of the type

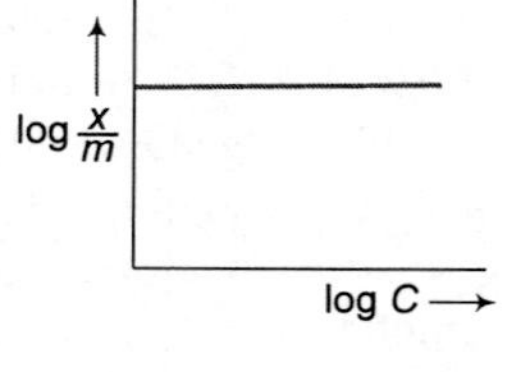

This is when

(a) $C = 0$ (b) $\frac{1}{n} = 0$

(c) $C =$ constant (d) $C = 2$ M

3. When saturation is attained in terms of adsorption, variation of $\left(\frac{x}{m}\right)$ and C (concentration) is given by the portion of the isotherm

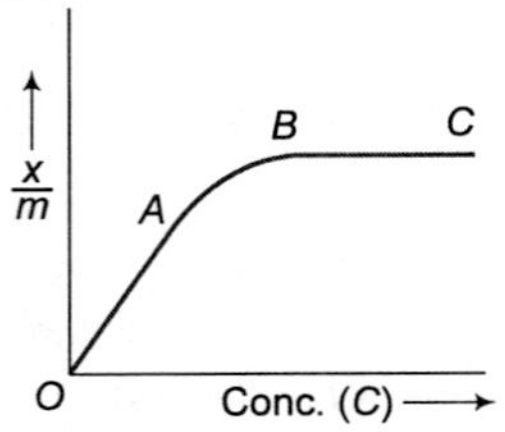

(a) OA (b) OB
(c) AB (d) BC

4. Coagulation or de-emulsification can be done by some of the methods given below

I. By addition of a substance which would destroy the emulsifier

II. By addition of an electrolyte which would destroy the charge

III. By heating, freezing and centrifuging

Select correct methods.

(a) I, II (b) I, II, III
(c) II only (d) III only

5. Some of the properties of emulsions are

I. Emulsions scatter light and thus exhibit Tyndall effect.

II. Oily emulsions are more viscous than the aqueous emulsions.

III. Electrical conductance of aqueous emulsions is higher than that of oily emulsion and increases on the addition of electrolyte.

Select correct properties.

(a) I, II (b) I, III
(c) II, III (d) I, II, III

6. Which of the following statements is/are true for hydrophilic sols?

(a) They do not require electrolytes for stability
(b) Their coagulation is reversible
(c) Their viscosity is of the order of that of water
(d) Their surface tension is usually lower than that of dispersion medium

7. Match Column I (catalyst) with Column II (process).

	Column I		Column II
A.	SiO_2	1.	Cracking of hydrocarbon
B.	Pt	2.	Alkylation of benzene
C.	Zeolites	3.	Automobile converter

Codes

	A	B	C
(a)	1	2	3
(b)	3	2	1
(c)	2	3	1
(d)	3	1	2

8. Match reaction (in Column I) with catalyst employed (in Column II).

	Column I		Column II
A.	Hydrogenation of oil	1.	Iron
B.	Friedel-Crafts reaction	2.	Anhydrous $AlCl_3$
C.	Oxidation of SO_2 to SO_3 by contact process	3.	Vanadium pentoxide
D.	Haber process	4.	Nickel
		5.	Zinc

Codes

	A	B	C	D
(a)	4	2	3	1
(b)	3	4	2	1
(c)	2	1	4	1
(d)	4	3	1	2

9. Match Column I with Column II.

	Column I (Term)		Column II (Related property)
A.	Coagulation	1.	Scattering of light
B.	Lyophilization	2.	Washing of precipitate
C.	Peptisation	3.	Purification of colloids
D.	Tyndall effect	4.	Electrolyte

Codes

	A	B	C	D
(a)	2	1	4	3
(b)	4	3	2	1
(c)	3	2	1	4
(d)	2	3	4	1

Assertion & Reason

Codes

(a) Both A and R are true and R is the correct explanation of A.
(b) Both A and R are true but R is not the correct explanation of A.
(c) A is true but R is false.
(d) A is false but R is true.

10. **Assertion (A)** Micelles are formed by surfactant molecules above the critical micellar concentration (CMC).

Reason (R) The conductivity of a solution having surfactant molecules decreases sharply at the CMC.

11. **Assertion (A)** The conversion of fresh precipitate to colloidal state is called peptization.

Reason (R) It is caused by addition of common ions.

12. Assertion (A) Colloidal solutions are stable but colloidal particles do not settle down.

Reason (R) Brownian movement counters the force of gravity actively on colloidal particles.

13. If $\left(\frac{x}{m}\right)$ is the mass of adsorbate adsorbed per unit mass of adsorbent. p is the pressure of the adsorbate gas and a and b are constants, which of the following represents "Langmuir adsorption isotherm"?

(a) $\log\left(\frac{x}{m}\right) = \log\left(\frac{a}{b}\right) + \frac{1}{a}\log p$

(b) $\frac{x}{m} = \frac{b}{a} + \frac{1}{ap}$

(c) $\frac{x}{m} = \frac{1+bp}{ap}$

(d) $\frac{1}{(x/m)} = \frac{b}{a} + \frac{1}{ap}$

14. Which one of the following graphs represents Freundlich adsorption isotherm?

(a)

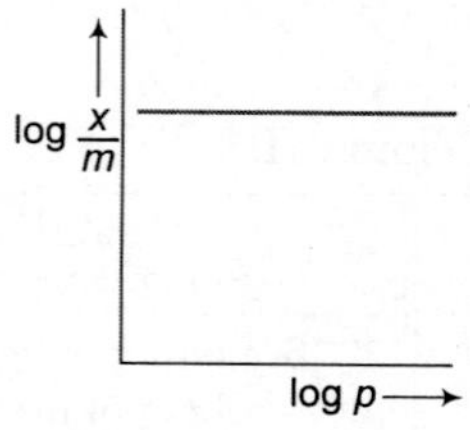

(b)

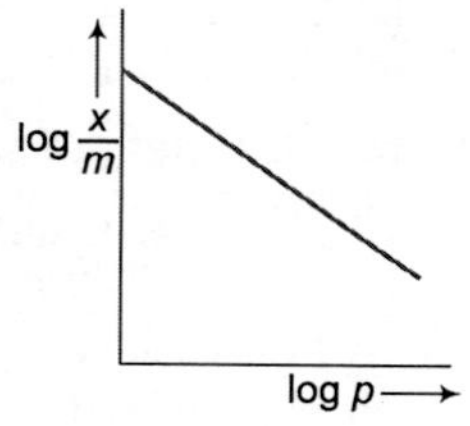

(c)

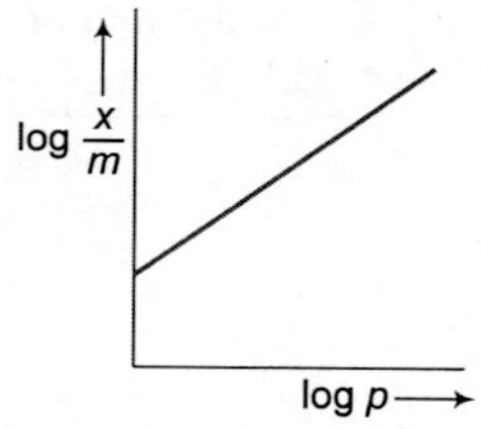

(d)

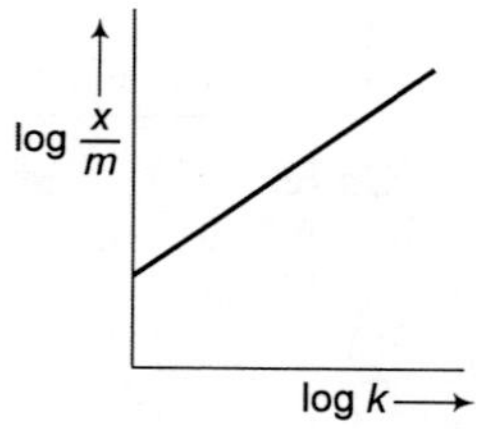

15. Select the incorrect statement.

(a) Physical adsorption is reversible while chemical is irreversible

(b) High pressure favours physical adsorption while low pressure favours chemical adsorption

(c) Physical adsorption is specific while chemical is specific

(d) High activation energy is involved in chemical adsorption

16. Select the correct statement.

(a) If a very small amount of $AlCl_3$ is added to gold sol, coagulation occurs, but if a large quantity of $AlCl_3$ is added, there is no coagulation.

(b) Organic ions are more strongly adsorbed on charged surfaces in comparison to inorganic ions.

(c) Both emulsifier and peptising agents stabilise colloids but their actions are different.

(d) Colloidal solutions are thermodynamically stable.

17. Which of the following is incorrect matching?

	Name of colloidal solution	Examples	Dispersed phase	Dispersion medium
(a)	Foam	Soap leather, soda water	Gas	Liquid
(b)	Solid foam	Rubber bread	Gas	Solid
(c)	Aerosol	Mist, fog, cloud	Liquid	Solid
(d)	Emulsion	Milk, cod liver oil	Liquid	Liquid

18. Which among the following statements are correct with respect to adsorption of gases on a solid?

I. The extent of adsorption is equal to kp^n according to Freundlich isotherm.

II. The extent of adsorption is equal to $kp^{1/n}$ according to Freundlich isotherm.

III. The extent of adsorption is equal to $(1+bp)/ap$ according to Langmuir isotherm.

IV. The extent of adsorption is equal to $ap/(1+bp)$ according to Langmuir isotherm.

(a) I, III (b) I, IV
(c) II, III (d) II, IV

19. Graph between $\log\left(\frac{x}{m}\right)$ and $\log p$ is a straight line at angle 45° with intercept OA as shown. Hence, $\left(\frac{x}{m}\right)$ at a pressure of 0.2 atm is

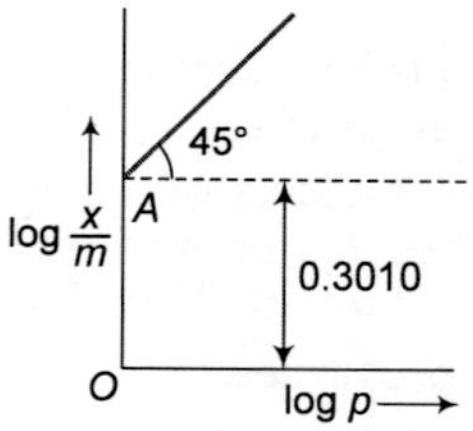

(a) 0.2 (b) 0.4
(c) 0.6 (d) 0.8

20. 50 mL of 1 M oxalic acid (molar mass =126) is shaken with 0.5 g of wood charcoal. The final concentration of the solution after adsorption is 0.5 M. What is the amount of oxalic acid adsorbed per gram of carbon?

(a) 3.15 (b) 1.575
(c) 6.30 (d) 12.60

21. Gold number of haemoglobin is 0.03. Hence, 100 mL of gold sol will require haemoglobin so that gold is not coagulated by 10 mL of 10% NaCl solution

(a) 0.03 mg (b) 30 mg
(c) 0.30 mg (d) 3 mg

22. Plot of $\log \frac{x}{m}$ against $\log p$ is straight line inclined at an angle of 45°. When the pressure is 0.5 atm and Freundlich parameter, k is 10, the amount of solute adsorbed per gram of adsorbent will be ($\log 5 = 0.6990$)
(a) 1 g (b) 2 g (c) 3 g (d) 5 g

23. The coagulation of 200 mL of a positive colloid took place when 0.73 g HCl was added to it without changing the volume much. The flocculation value of HCl for the colloid is
(a) 0.365 (b) 36.5 (c) 100 (d) 150

24. A sample of charcoal weighing 6.00 g was brought into contact with a gas contained in a vessel of 1 L capacity at 27°C. The pressure of the gas was found to fall from 700 to 400 mm. Calculate the volume of the gas (reduced to STP) that is adsorbed per gram of the adsorbent under the condition of the experiment (density of charcoal sample is 1.5 g cm^{-3})
(a) 60.19 mL (b) 11.56 mL
(c) 125.67 mL (d) 22.4 mL

25. Calculate how long a hydrogen atom will remain on the surface of a solid at 1000 K if its desorption activation energy is 15 kJ mol^{-1}. Assume that $\tau_0 = 10^{-13}$ s.
(a) 1.5×10^{-10} s (b) 4.2×10^{-11} s
(c) 5.7×10^{-12} s (d) 6.1×10^{-13} s

26. The mass x of a solute adsorbed per gram of a solid adsorbent is given by the Freundlich adsorption isotherm as $x = kk^n$, where, k and n are 0.160 and 0.431, respectively. Calculate the amount of acetic acid ($M = 60.05$ g mol^{-1}) that 1 kg of charcoal would adsorb from a 0.837 M vinegar solution.
(a) 1.08 mol (b) 1.97 mol (c) 2.47 mol (d) 2.83 mol

27. 1 g of charcoal adsorbs 100 mL of 0.5 M acetic acid to form a monolayer and there by the molarity of acetic acid reduces to 0.49. Calculate the surface area of the charcoal adsorb by each molecule of acetic acid. Surface area of charcoal is 3.01×10^2 $m^2 g^{-1}$.
(a) 5.0×10^{-19} m^2 (b) 5.0×10^{20} m^2
(c) 6.0×10^{-19} m^2 (d) 6.0×10^{20} m^2

28. At 0°C and 1 atm pressure, the volume of nitrogen gas required to cover a sample of silica gel, assuming Langmuir monolayer adsorption, is found to be 130 $cm^3 g^{-1}$ of the gel. Calculate the surface area per gram of silica gel. Given that the area occupied by a nitrogen molecule is 0.162 nm^2.
(a) 5658 $m^2 g^{-1}$ (b) 565.38 $m^2 g^{-1}$
(c) 56.58 $m^2 g^{-1}$ (d) 5.658 $m^2 g^{-1}$

29. For a 1.0×10^{-4} M aqueous solution of n-butanoic acid $\frac{d\gamma}{dC} = -0.080$ $Nm^2 mol^{-1}$ at 25°C. Using the Gibbs adsorption equation, determine the average surface area available to each molecule.
(a) 2.4×10^{-19} m^2 (b) 3.5×10^{-19} m^2
(c) 4.7×10^{-19} m^2 (d) 5.2×10^{-19} m^2

30. 20% of surface sites are occupied by nitrogen molecules. The density of surface site is 6.02×10^{14} cm^{-2} and total surface area is 1000 cm^2. The catalyst is heated to 300 K while nitrogen is completely desorbed into a pressure of 0.001 atm and volume 2.46 cm^3. What is the number of active sites occupied by each nitrogen molecule?
(a) 4 (b) 3 (c) 2 (d) 1

31. Calculate the collisional flux of hydrogen, H_2, molecules on a solid tungsten surface if the pressure of hydrogen is 15 Pa and the temperature is 25°C.
(a) 1.61×10^{24} m^{-2} s^{-1} (b) 5.56×10^{24} $m^{-2} s^{-1}$
(c) 2.79×10^{24} $m^{-2} s^{-1}$ (d) 9.81×10^{24} $m^{-2} s^{-1}$

32. A monolayer of carbon monoxide, CO, molecules is allowed to desorb from the surface of a sample of charcoal. The volume of the gas produced is 128 cm^3 at a temperature of 0°C and 1.00 bar. Deduce the effective number of surface sites.
(a) 3.11×10^{21} (b) 3.40×10^{22}
(c) 3.11×10^{23} (d) 3.40×10^{21}

33. In an experiment to study the adsorption of hydrocarbons onto silica gel, the amount of butane adsorbed onto the gel surface was measured for various pressures of gas at a temperature of 303 K. Use the following data to demonstrate that the adsorption follows a Langmuir isotherm and determine the amount that corresponds to complete surface coverage.

p/atm	0.1	0.2	0.3	0.4	0.5
n/mmol g^{-1}	0.36	0.68	0.98	1.24	1.49

(a) 14.0 mmol g^{-1} (b) 2.67 mmol g^{-1}
(c) 4.62 mmol g^{-1} (d) 7.15 mmol g^{-1}

34. The adsorption of a gas on a solid surface was found to follow a Langmuir isotherm with $K = 3.76$ kPa^{-1} at a temperature of 25°C. Determine the pressure of gas required to achieve a fractional surface coverage of 10%.
(a) 27 Pa (b) 30 Pa (c) 38 Pa (d) 270 Pa

35. The partial pressure of ethene, C_2H_4, in equilibrium above a nickel surface was measured at different temperature for a constant surface coverage. Use the following data to determine the isosteric ethalpy of adsorption.

T/K	280	285	290	295
p/Pa	0.67	6.11	28.29	170.35

(a) – 239 kJ mol^{-1} (b) – 155 kJ mol^{-1}
(c) – 249 kJ mol^{-1} (d) – 427 kJ mol^{-1}

36. The multilayer adsorption of nitrogen, N_2, on a titanium dioxide, TiO_2, surface follows a BET isotherm at low temperatures. Experiments have shown that the enthalpy of desorption from the surface is very much greater than the enthalpy for vaporization of the liquid. The data below shows how the volume of nitrogen gas adsorbed, corrected to a temperature of 298 K and pressure of 1 bar, varies with pressure. B plotting a graph, use the data to determine the volume that corresponds to monolayer coverage.

p/Torr	7.6	15.2	22.8	30.4
V/cm^3	684.8	691.8	698.9	706.2

(a) 124 cm^3
(b) 548 cm^3
(c) 163 cm^3
(d) 678 cm^3

37. Calculate the rate of absorption of nitrogen, N_2, molecules on a tungsten (320) surface for a pressure of 0.10 kPa and temperature of 298 K, given that the sticking probability is 0.74.
(a) $7.37\times 10^{24}\ s^{-1}m^{-2}$
(b) $2.13\times 10^{24}\ s^{-1}m^{-2}$
(c) $2.88\times 10^{24}\ s^{-1}m^{-2}$
(d) $1.28\times 10^{24}\ s^{-1}m^{-2}$

38. Which of the following involve coagulation?
(a) Peptization
(b) Formation of delta regions
(c) Treatment of drinking water by potash alum
(d) Clotting of blood by the use of ferric chloride

39. Which of the following statements is/are correct regarding physisorption?
(a) It occurs because of van der Walls' forces
(b) More easily liquefiable gases are adsorbed readily
(c) Under high pressure it results into multimolecular layer on adsorbent surface
(d) Enthalpy of adsorption ($\Delta H_{adsorption}$) is low and positive

Answers

Exercise 1

1. (a)	**2.** (b)	**3.** (a)	**4.** (d)	**5.** (b)	**6.** (d)	**7.** (a)	**8.** (c)	**9.** (a)	**10.** (b)
11. (b)	**12.** (a)	**13.** (a)	**14.** (d)	**15.** (c)	**16.** (d)	**17.** (c)	**18.** (a)	**19.** (c)	**20.** (c)
21. (b)	**22.** (a)	**23.** (b)	**24.** (a)	**25.** (c)	**26.** (a)	**27.** (c)	**28.** (b)	**29.** (a)	**30.** (d)
31. (c)	**32.** (c)	**33.** (d)	**34.** (c)	**35.** (a)	**36.** (a)	**37.** (b)	**38.** (a)	**39.** (a)	**40.** (c)
41. (a)	**42.** (a)	**43.** (b)	**44.** (b)	**45.** (a)	**46.** (b)	**47.** (a)	**48.** (a)	**49.** (c)	**50.** (c)
51. (d)	**52.** (c)	**53.** (a)	**54.** (d)	**55.** (c)	**56.** (c)	**57.** (c)	**58.** (c)	**59.** (d)	**60.** (b)

Exercise 2

1. (b)	**2.** (b)	**3.** (a)	**4.** (b)	**5.** (d)	**6.** (a,b,d)	**7.** (c)	**8.** (a)	**9.** (b)	**10.** (b)
11. (b)	**12.** (a)	**13.** (d)	**14.** (c)	**15.** (b,c)	**16.** (b,c,d)	**17.** (c)	**18.** (d)	**19.** (b)	**20.** (c)
21. (c)	**22.** (d)	**23.** (c)	**24.** (a)	**25.** (d)	**26.** (c)	**27.** (a)	**28.** (b)	**29.** (d)	**30.** (c)
31. (a)	**32.** (d)	**33.** (d)	**34.** (b)	**35.** (c)	**36.** (d)	**37.** (b)	**38.** (b,c,d)	**39.** (a,b,c)	

Hints & Solutions

Exercise 2

19. $\log\left(\frac{x}{m}\right) = \log k + \frac{1}{n}\log p$

$\log k = 0.3010 =$ intercept on Y-axis

$\frac{1}{n} = \tan 45 = 1$ slope

$$\log\left(\frac{x}{m}\right) = 0.3010 + 1\log 0.2$$

$$\log\left(\frac{x}{m}\right) = \log 2 + \log 0.2$$

$$\frac{x}{m} = kp^{1/n} = 2\times(0.2)^1$$

$$\frac{x}{m} = 0.4$$

22. Freundlich adsorption isotherm equation is

$$\frac{x}{m} = kp^{1/n}$$

$$\log\frac{x}{m} = \log k + \frac{1}{n}\log p$$

$$\log\frac{x}{m} = \log 10 + \frac{1}{n}\log 0.5$$

$\because$ Slope $= \frac{1}{n} = \tan\theta = \tan 45° = 1$

$$\log \frac{x}{m} = 1 + \frac{1}{1}\log(5 \times 10^{-1})$$

$$\log \frac{x}{m} = 1 - 0.6990 + 1 = 0.6990$$

$$\frac{x}{m} = 5.00 = 5 \text{ g}$$

23. Molarity $= \frac{0.73}{36.5} \times \frac{1000}{200} = 0.1$ M

This means that a minimum of 0.1 mole or $0.1 \times 1000 = 100$ millimoles are required for coagulating 1 L of colloid. The minimum concentration of an electrolyte required to cause coagulation of a sol is called flocculation value. Hence, flocculation value of HCl for the colloid is 100.

24. The adsorption is taking place in a close vessel hence, if pressure falls there is correspondingly increase in volume and to keep volume constant, excess of the volume of the gas would be adsorbed.

$$p_1V_1 = p_2V_2 \quad \text{or} \quad V_2 = \frac{700 \times 1000}{400} = 1750 \text{ mL}$$

Actual volume of the flask = 1000 – volume of charcoal

$$= 1000 - \frac{6.00}{1.50} = 996 \text{ mL}$$

Volume of gas adsorbed = 1750 – 996 = 754 mL

Volume of gas adsorbed per gram of charcoal

$$= \frac{754}{6} = 125.67 \text{ mL g}^{-1}$$

Volume of gas adsorbed per gram at STP,

$$\frac{p_1V_1}{T_1} = \frac{p_2V_2}{T_2}$$

$$V_2 = \frac{125.67 \times 400 \times 273}{300 \times 760} = 60.19 \text{ mL}$$

25.

$$\tau = \tau_0 \cdot e^{E_a/RT}$$

$$\tau = (10^{-13} \text{ s}) \exp\left(\frac{15 \times 10^3 \text{ J mol}^{-1}}{8.314 \text{ JK}^{-1}\text{mol}^{-1} \times 1000 \text{ K}}\right)$$

$$\tau = (10^{-13} \text{ s})\, e^{1.81} = 6.1 \times 10^{-13} \text{ s}$$

27. Number of moles of acetic acid in 100 mL of 0.5 M acetic acid

$$n = \frac{M \times 100}{1000} = \frac{0.5 \times 100}{1000} = 0.05 \text{ mole } (CH_3COOH)$$

After adsorption, moles of acetic acid = 0.049 mol

∴ Moles of acetic acid adsorbed by 1 g charcoal

= 0.05 – 0.049 = 0.001 mol

Molecules of acetic acid $= 6.02 \times 10^{23} \times 0.001$

$= 6.02 \times 10^{20}$ molecules

Surface area of 1 g charcoal $= 3.01 \times 10^2 \text{ m}^2$

Surface area of charcoal adsorbed by each molecule

$$= \frac{\text{Surface area of 1 g charcoal}}{\text{Molecules of acetic acid}}$$

$$= \frac{3.01 \times 10^2 \text{ m}^2}{6.02 \times 10^{20} \text{ molecules}} = 5 \times 10^{-19} \text{ m}^2$$

28. $V_{mono} = 130 \text{ cm}^3/\text{g} = 0.130 \text{ dm}^3/\text{g}$

$$V_m = 22.414 \text{ dm}^3\text{mol}^{-1}$$

Number of molecules present in V_{mono}

$$= \frac{6.02 \times 10^{23} \text{ mol}^{-1} \times 0.130 \text{ dm}^3\text{g}^{-1}}{22.414 \text{ dm}^3\text{mol}^{-1}}$$

$$= 3.49 \times 10^{21} \text{ g}^{-1}$$

Area of cross section of 1 molecule $= 0.162 \text{ (nm}^2)$

$= 0.162 \times 10^{-18} \text{ m}^2$

Area covered by 3.49×10^{21} molecules, (surface area)

$= 0.162 \times 10^{-18} \text{ m}^2 \times 3.49 \times 10^{21} \text{ g}^{-1}$

$= 565.38 \text{ m}^2\text{g}^{-1}$

29. From Gibbs adsorption equation

$$\Gamma_2 = -\frac{C}{RT}\frac{d\gamma}{dC}$$

$$\Gamma_2 = -\frac{(1.0 \times 10^{-4} \text{ mol dm}^{-3})(10^3 \text{ dm}^3\text{m}^{-3})}{(8.314 \text{ JK}^{-1}\text{mol}^{-1})(298 \text{ K})}(-0.080 \text{ Nm}^2\text{mol}^{-1})$$

$$\Gamma_2 = 3.2 \times 10^{-6} \text{ mol m}^{-2}$$

Average surface area available to each molecule

$$= \frac{1}{3.2 \times 10^{-6} \times 6.02 \times 10^{23}}$$

$$= 5.2 \times 10^{-19} \text{ m}^2$$

31. The collisional flux of molecules colliding with a surface is given by the following equation, so that, remembering to express the temperature in units of kelvins,

$$Z_w = \frac{p}{(2\pi mkT)^{1/2}}$$

$$= \frac{15 \text{ Pa}}{\{2\pi \times (2.02 \times 1.661 \times 10^{-27} \text{ kg}) \times 1.381 \times 10^{-23} \text{ JK}^{-1} \times 298.15 \text{ K}\}^{1/2}}$$

$$= 1.61 \times 10^{24} \text{ m}^{-2}\text{s}^{-1}$$

32. We may calculate the amount of gas adsorbed onto the surface of the charcoal using the perfect gas equation,

$$pV = nRT$$

So that the number of molecules is

$$N = n \times N_A = \frac{pVN_A}{RT}$$

$$= \frac{10^6 \text{Pa} \times 128 \times (10^{-2} \text{ m})^3 \times 6.022 \times 10^{23} \text{ mol}^{-1}}{8.3145 \text{ JK}^{-1} \text{ mol}^{-1} \times 273 \text{ K}}$$

$$= 3.40 \times 10^{21}$$

Because the molecules formed a monolayer on the surface, this must also be the number of surface sites.

33. The surface coverage may be expressed in terms of the amount of gas adsorbed relative to the amount that corresponds to complete monolayer coverage. Thus

$$\theta = \frac{n}{n_\infty}$$

and so, from the Langmiur isotherm,

$$\frac{n}{n_\infty} = \frac{kp}{1 + kp}$$

or, transforming

$$\frac{n_\infty}{n} = \frac{1 + kp}{kp}$$

So that $$\frac{1}{n} = \frac{1}{n_\infty kp} + \frac{1}{n_\infty}$$

A plot of $\frac{1}{n}$ against $\frac{1}{p}$ should therefore have an intercept of $\frac{1}{n_\infty}$.

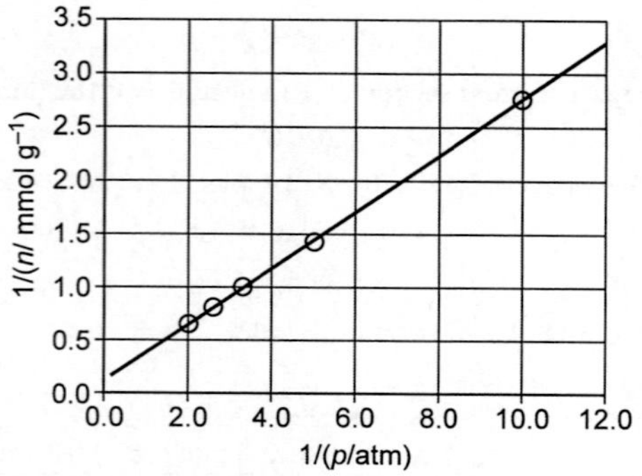

The plot of the data given has an intercept of 0.140 m mol^{-1} g, which corresponds to

$$n_\infty = \left(\frac{1}{0.140}\right) \text{mol}^{-1}\ \text{g}^{-1} = 7.15\ \text{mmol}^{-1}\ \text{g}^{-1}$$

34.

$$\theta = \frac{kp}{1 + kp}$$

in order to determine the pressure required for a given surface coverage. Thus

$$p = \frac{\theta}{(1-\theta)k} = \frac{0.10}{(1-0.10) \times 3.76\ \text{kPa}^{-1}} = 30\ \text{Pa}$$

36. The temperature variation of the equilibrium constant for adsorption follows the vant Hoff equation, Example shows how data for the pressure of a gas in equilibrium with molecules adsorbed onto a surface at different temperatures may be used to determine the enthalpy of adsorption. Plotting in p against $\frac{1}{T}$ should result in a straight-line graph with a gradient of $\Delta_{\text{ads}}H°/R$

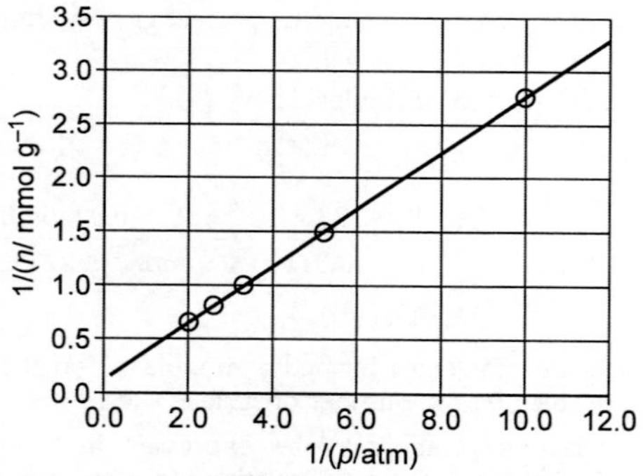

The gradient of the graph produced by plotting the data above is -29.92×10^3 K, so that $\frac{\Delta_{\text{ads}}H°}{R} = -29.92 \times 10^3$ K

and therefore $\Delta_{\text{ads}}H° = -249\ \text{kJ mol}^{-1}$

36. For system for which the enthalpy of desorption from the surface is very much greater than the enthalpy for vaporization of the liquid, BET isotherm,

$$\frac{V}{V_{\text{mon}}} = \frac{cz}{(1-z)\{1\ (1-c)z\}}$$

$$\frac{V}{V_{\text{mon}}} = \frac{1}{1-z}$$

Substituting

$$\frac{1}{V} = \frac{1}{V_{\text{mon}}} - \frac{P}{p \cdot V_{\text{mon}}}$$

So that a plot of $\frac{1}{V}$ against p should be a straight line with an intercept of $\frac{1}{V_m}$.

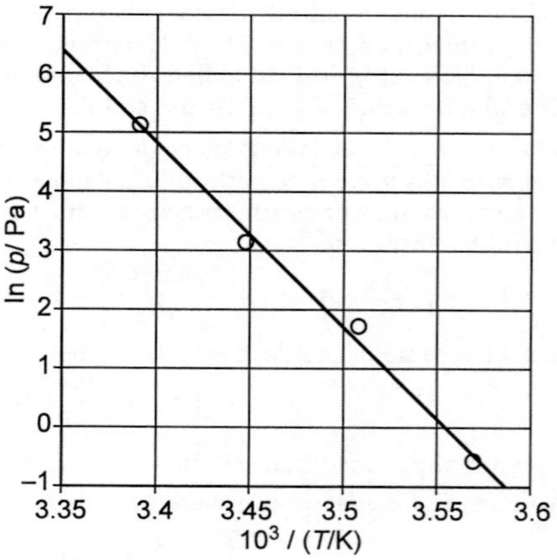

The intercept of the plot is

$$\frac{1}{V_{\text{mon}}} = 1.475 \times 10^{-3}\ \text{cm}^{-3}$$

So that

$$V_{\text{mon}} = 678\ \text{cm}^3$$

37. The sticking probability for adsorption is defined by

$$s = \frac{\text{Rate of adsorption of particles by the surface}}{\text{Rate of collision of particles with the surface}}$$

The rate of collision of the gas molecules with the metal surface may be calculated using collision theory. The flux is

$$Z_W = \frac{p}{(2\pi mkT)^{1/2}}$$

so, that because the mass of a nitrogen molecules is

$$m = 2 \times 14.01 \times 1.661 \times 10^{-27}\ \text{kg}$$

$$= 4.56 \times 10^{-26}\ \text{kg}$$

the rate of collision per unit area is

$$Z_W = \frac{p}{(2\pi mkT)^{1/2}}$$

$$= \frac{100\ \text{Pa}}{(2\pi \times 4.65 \times 10^{-26}\ \text{kg} \times 1.381 \times 10^{-23}\ \text{JK}^{-1} \times 298\ \text{K})^{1/2}}$$

$$= 2.88 \times 10^{24}\ \text{s}^{-1}\text{m}^{-2}$$

The rate of adsorption is therefore,

$$s \times Z_W = 0.74 \times 2.88 \times 10^{24}\ \text{s}^{-1}\text{m}^{-2}$$

$$= 2.13 \times 10^{24}\ \text{s}^{-1}\text{m}^{-2}$$

26

Solid State

Syllabus

- Classification of Solids
- Symmetry in Crystals
- Crystallography and its Law
- Miller Indices and Bravais Lattices
- Close Packed Structures
- Density, Radius Ratio and Coordination Number
- Bragg's Equation and its Applications
- Electron and Neutron Diffraction
- Imperfection in Solids.
- Band Model of Bonding in Metals
- Semiconductors : Their Types and Applications
- Electrical, Thermal, Magnetic and Dielectric Properties
- Superconductors : Properties and Applications

Characteristics of Solids

Solids are characterised by definite mass, volume and shape, high density, rigidity, low compressibility and mechanical strength. These properties indicates that constituent particles of solid are closely packed. These particles are held together by strong forces of attraction and have fixed positions. These can still oscillate about their mean positions.

Amorphous and Crystalline Solids

Solids can be classified as crystalline or amorphous on the basis of the nature of order present in the arrangement of their constituent particles. In a crystal, constituent particles (atoms, ions or molecules) are arranged in a definite pattern throughout the entire three dimensional network so it has long range order. Sodium chloride and quartz are typical examples of crystalline solids.

In amorphous solid, the constituent particles are arranged irregularly along all the directions. It has short range order. In such an arrangement, a regular and periodically repeating pattern is observed over short distances only. Glass, rubber and plastics are typical examples of amorphous solids.

Table 26.1 **Difference between Crystalline and Amorphous Solids**

	Crystalline solids	Amorphous solids
1.	They have definite characteristic shape and sharp melting point.	They have irregular and do not have sharp melting point.
2.	They undergo clean cleavage.	They undergo irregular cleavage.
3.	They are anisotropic in nature.	They are isotropic in nature.
4.	They are true solids.	They are supercooled liquid or pseudo solids.

There is no unique way of classifying all the solids found in nature. A consideration of the chemical, thermal, electrical and magnetic characteristics of solid materials provides a basis for the following classification

(i) Metals (ii) Ionic crystals (iii) Valence crystals or Covalent crystals (iv) Semiconductors (v) Molecular crystals.

(i) Metals have excellent electrical and thermal conductivity. They have moderately high melting points and they are malleable and ductile. They are formed by the combination of atoms of electropositive elements.

(ii) Ionic crystals are exemplified by NaCl, KNO_3, etc. They have high melting points. They are brittle and show good cleavage. They exhibit good electrical conductivity in the fused state and have strong infrared absorption spectra. Generally, they are soluble in polar solvents like water and their solutions exhibits ionic conductivity. They are formed by a combination of highly electropositive and highly electronegative elements.

(iii) Valence crystals have poor electronic and ionic conductivity, great hardness and poor cleavage. They have high melting points and may be described as giant molecules. They are formed by combination of the lighter elements in the middle columns of the Periodic Table. Diamond and carborundum are examples of this type.

(iv) Semiconductors are exemplified by zinc oxide and cuprous oxide. They show low electronic conductivity which increases with temperature. Their conducting properties depend on the presence of impurities in them or on their compositions slightly deviating from correct stoichiometry.

(v) Molecular crystals have low melting points and are easily sublimed. They are electrical insulators and are usually brittle. Examples are solids formed from rare gases or saturated molecules. They have low boiling points and evaporate in the form of stable molecules.

Table 26.2 **Classification of Solids**
(On the basis of nature of intermolecular forces operating in them).

S. No.	Type of solid	Constituent particles	Bonding attractive forces	Examples	Physical nature	Electrical conductivity	Melting point
1.	Molecular						
	(i) Non-polar	Molecules	Dispersion or London forces	Ar, CCl_4, H_2, I_2, CO_2	Soft	Insulator	Very low
	(ii) Polar		Dipole-dipole interactions	HCl, SO_2	Soft	Insulator	Low
	(iii) Hydrogen bonded		Hydrogen bonding	H_2O (ice)	Hard	Insulator	Low
2.	Ionic solids	Ions	Coulombic or electrostatic	NaCl, MgO, ZnS, CaF_2	Hard but brittle	Insulators in solid state but conductors in molten state and in aqueous solutions	High
3.	Metallic solids	Positive ions in a sea of delocalized electrons	Metallic bonding	Fe, Cu, Ag, Mg	Hard but malleable and ductile	Conductors in solid state as well as in molten state	Fairly high
4.	Covalent or network solids	Atoms	Covalent bonding	SiO_2 (quartz), SiC, C (diamond), AlN, C (graphite)	Hard Soft	Insulators Conductor (exception)	Very high

Faces, Edges and Interfacial Angle of a Crystal

Crystals are bound by plane surfaces. These surfaces are called faces and where two faces intersect an edge is obtained. The angle between any two faces is called an interfacial angle.

Law of Constancy of Interfacial Angles

Any carefully-grown large crystal has well developed faces which give it a particular shape. This external shape is called crystal habit. The formation of the faces is often a matter of the kinetics of crystal growth and the presence of impurities in the solution in which crystallisation takes place. Sodium chloride crystallised from water gives cubic crystals. If the water solution contains appreciable quantities of urea, then the crystals of NaCl are octahedral. Thus different crystals will have different shapes (crystal habits) especially under conditions of rapid crystallization. But the angles between the faces are always the same for the same crystalline substance whatever the crystal shape.

This is referred to as the law of constancy of interfacial angles.

Symmetry in Crystal Systems

Symmetry is an important property of crystals. There are various types of symmetry, only three of which will be discussed here. These are plane of symmetry, axis of symmetry and centre of symmetry.

Plane of symmetry

When an imaginary plane can divide a crystal into parts such that one part is the mirror image of the other part, the crystal is said to have a plane of symmetry.

Axis of symmetry

An axis of symmetry is a line about which the crystal may be rotated such that it represents similar or same appearance more than one during one complete rotation. For example, in the case of a cube, an axis passing perpendicularly through the centre is such that when the cube is rotated it represents similar appearance in three rotation of 90° each and the same appearance in fourth rotation. This type of axis is called a four fold axis. A crystal can have only two fold, three fold, four fold and six fold axis of rotation. The angle through which the crystal will have to be rotated to get similar or same appearance will be 180°, 120°, 90° and 60° respectively.

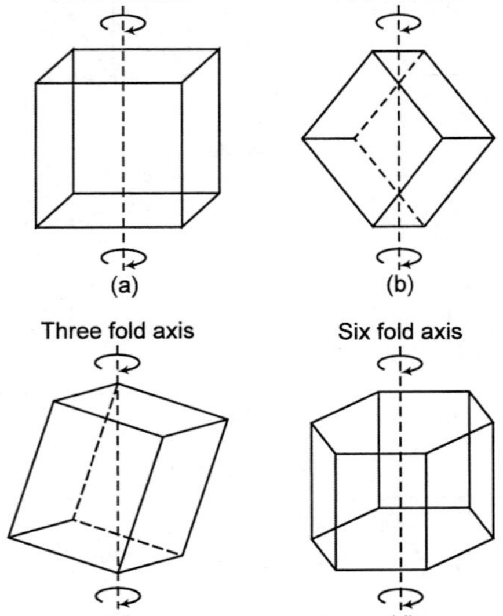

Fig. 26.1 Various axes of symmetry.

Centre of symmetry

It is a point in a crystal if any line drawn through it intersect the surface of the crystal at equal distances in both directions. A crystal has only one centre of symmetry.

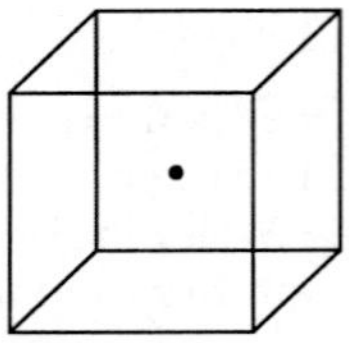

Fig. 26.2 Centre of symmetry.

Elements of symmetry

The total number of planes, axis and centre of symmetries possessed by a crystal is known as elements of symmetry of a crystal. For example, a cubic system has 23 symmetry elements.

Planes of symmetry = 3 + 6 = 9 elements

Axis of symmetry = 3 + 4 + 6 = 13 elements

Centre of symmetry = 1 element

Total number of symmetry elements = 23

Crystallography and Its Laws

Crystallography is the branch of science which deals with the study of structure, geometry and properties of crystals. It is based upon three fundamental laws. These are as follows :

Law of constancy of interfacial angles (Steno's Law)

It states that angle between adjacent corresponding faces of the crystal of a particular substance is always constant inspite of different shapes and sizes.

Law of constancy of symmetry

It states that all crystals of the same substance possess same elements of symmetry.

Law of rational indices

It states that the intercepts of any face of a crystal along the crystallographic axis are either equal to unit intercepts a, b, c or some simple whole number multiples of them *e.g.,* na, $n'b$, $n''c$ where, n, n' and n'' are simple whole numbers. The whole numbers n, n' and n'' are called Weiss indices. In the given figure 26.3, the simple multiplies are 2, 2 and 3.

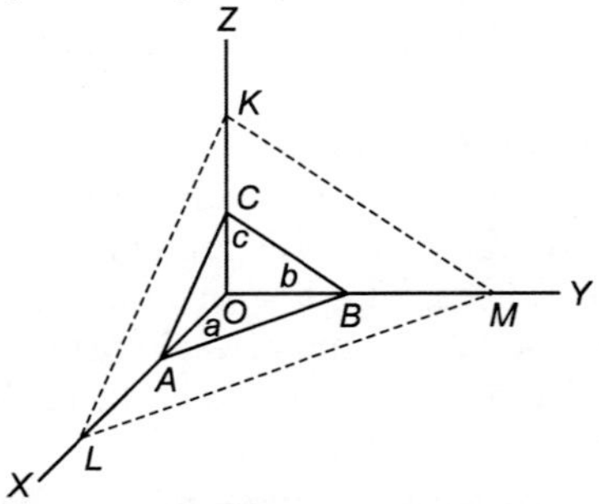

Fig 26.3 Crystallographic axes and the law of rational indices.

Miller Indices

The use of Miller indices is more advantageous instead of Weiss indices. In Miller indices, we take the reciprocal of the three Weiss indices and then multiply them by the smallest number to make them all integers. The three resultant integers are known as Miller indices. These are represented as *h*, *k* and *l*.

Designation of crystal forces-law of rational indices

The geometry of the crystal may be conveniently studied with a choice of proper axes taking into consideration the symmetry of the crystal. Let a lattice point be chosen as the origin *O*, with axes as shown in the Figure 26.4. The lattice points nearest to *O* along the chosen axes are *D*, *E*, *F*. The plane *DEF* is called the unit plane or the standard plane. Consider now any other plane *A*, *B*, *C* with intercepts *OA*, *OB* and *OC* on the axes. *A*, *B* and *C* are also lattice points. Thus *OA* is

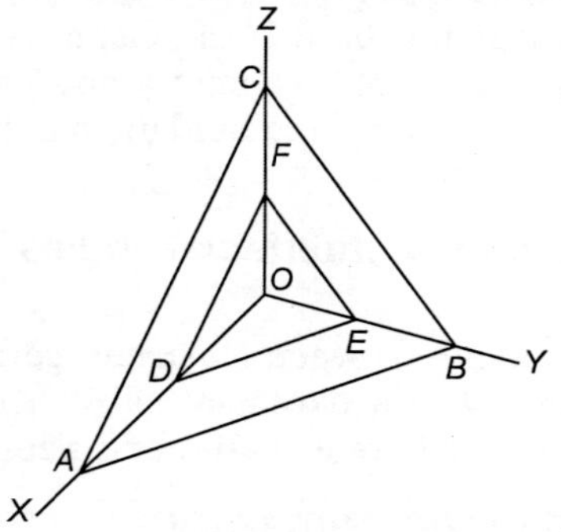

Fig. 26.4

an integral multiple of *OD* and similarly *OB* and *OC* are integral multiples of *OE* and *OF* respectively. The ratio $\frac{OA}{OD} = n_1$, $\frac{OB}{OE} = n_2$ and $\frac{OC}{OF} = n_3$ are simply the intercepts of any possible crystal plane *ABC* on the chosen axes expressed as multiples of the intercepts of the unit plane. Taking reciprocals we have $\frac{1}{n_1}, \frac{1}{n_2}, \frac{1}{n_3}$

Multiply by *N*, the 1 cm of n_1, n_2, n_3 thus getting $\frac{N}{n_1}, \frac{N}{n_2}, \frac{N}{n_3}$ *i.e.*, *h*, *k*, *l* which are also integers. The integers, *h*, *k* and *l* are known as the Miller indices of the plane *ABC* and indeed for the whole set of planes parallel to *ABC*. Each possible face of the crystal has its set of Miller indices. The law of rational indices states that any possible face of the crystal corresponds to a set of 3 indices and the most likely faces have indices which are small whole numbers.

It is possible that a crystal plane may be parallel to one of the axes, the corresponding Miller index is zero *e.g.*, (1, 0, 0) corresponds to a plane parallel to the *Y* and *Z* axes. (1, 1, 0) corresponds to a plane to the *Z*-axis.

Important planes of cubic lattices

Figures 26.5 1*A*, 1*B* and 1*C* represent the planes of a simple cubic lattice; Figures 26.5 2*A*, 2*B* and 2*C* indicate the planes of a body-centred cubic lattice and Figures 26.5 3*A*, 3*B* and 3*C*,the planes of a face-centred cubic lattice. For the simple cubic lattice, the planes 100, 110, and 111 completely describe the lattice structure; for the body-centred and face-centred cubic lattices, there are additional planes. For instance, in the body-centred and face-centred lattices, we have the additional plane 200 parallel to the 100 plane and passing through the body-centred or face-centred points, as the case may be. Although this plane 200 may still be called the 100 plane from the external crystallographic point of view, it is better to call it a 200 plane from the point of view of the internal unit cell concept, since the intercept made by this plane is one half of the side of the unit cell. If '*a*' is the side of the unit cell of the cubic lattice, the interplanar distance is

$$d_{hkl} = \frac{a}{\sqrt{h^2 + k^2 + l^2}}$$

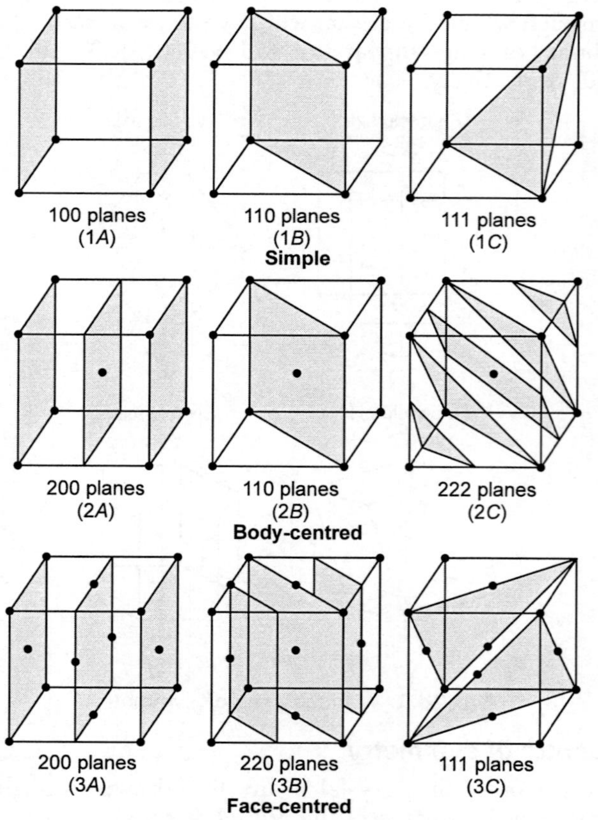

Fig. 26.5 Units cells with the lattice points and lattice planes.

Space Lattice

If the three dimensional arrangement of constituent particles in a crystal is represented diagrammatically, in which each particle is depicted as a point, the arrangement is called space lattice (or crystal lattice). Therefore, a regular three dimensional arrangement of points in space is called a space lattice. The following are the characteristics of a crystal or space lattice.

(i) Each point in a lattice is called lattice point or lattice site.

(ii) Each point in a lattice represents one constituent particle which may be an atom, a molecule or an ion.

(iii) Lattice points are joined by straight lines to bring out the geometry of the lattice.

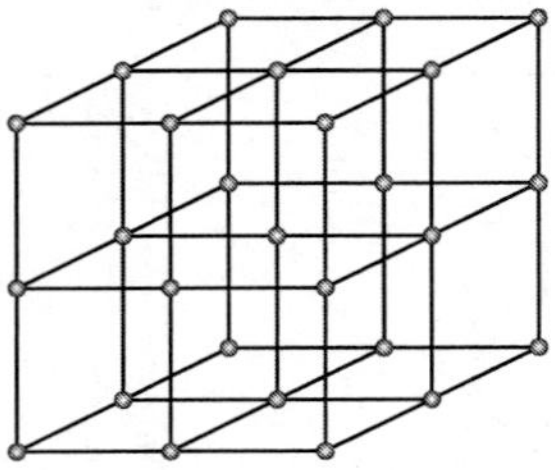

Fig. 26.6 A part of a three dimensional cubic lattice and its unit cell.

Seven Crystal Systems

The morphological study of crystals of different symmetries showed that they can be classified into seven crystal systems based on the presence of certain rotation axes. Some detailed descriptions of these seven crystal systems are as follows :

Table 26.3 **The Seven Crystal Systems**

S. No.	Crystal system	Bravais lattices	Minimum symmetry elements	Parameters of unit cell		Examples
				Cell dimensions	Crystals angles	
1.	Cubic	Primitive, face-centred, body-centred = 3	Four 3-fold axes : Three 4-fold axes	$a = b = c$	$\alpha = \beta = \gamma = 90°$	NaCl, zinc blende, Cu
2.	Orthorhombic	Primitive, face-centred, body-centred, end-centred = 4	Three mutually perpendicular 2-fold axes	$a \neq b \neq c$	$\alpha = \beta = \gamma = 90°$	Rhombic sulphur, KNO_3, $BaSO_4$
3.	Tetragonal	Primitive, body-centred = 2	One 4-fold axis	$a = b \neq c$	$\alpha = \beta = \gamma = 90°$	White tin, SnO_2 , TiO_2, $CaSO_4$
4.	Monoclinic	Primitive, end-centred = 2	One 2-fold axis	$a \neq b \neq c$	$\alpha = \gamma = 90°$ $\beta \neq 90°$	Monoclinic sulphur, $Na_2SO_4 \cdot 10H_2O$
5.	Triclinic	Primitive = 1	One 1-fold axis	$a \neq b \neq c$	$\alpha \neq \beta \neq \gamma \neq 90°$	$K_2Cr_2O_7$, $CuSO_4 \cdot 5H_2O$, H_3BO_3
6.	Hexagonal	Primitive = 1	One 6-fold axis	$a = b \neq c$	$\alpha = \beta = 90°$ $\gamma = 120°$	Graphite, ZnO, CdS
7.	Rhombohedral or trigonal	Primitive = 1	One 3-fold axis	$a = b = c$	$\alpha = \gamma = \beta \neq 90°$	Calcite ($CaCO_3$), HgS (cinnabar)

The Fourteen Bravais Lattices

There are only 14 possible three dimensional lattices. These are called Bravais lattices (after the French mathematician, Auguste Bravais who first described them). In contrast to the crystal system, the Bravais lattice type cannot be recognized from the external form of the crystal.

Types of Bravis Lattices

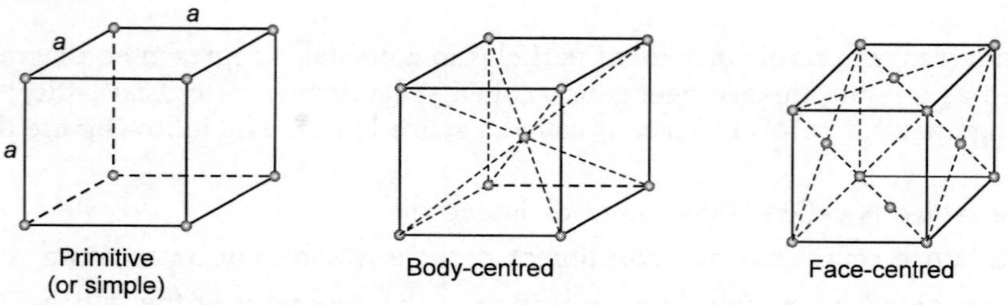

The three cubic lattices : all sides of same length, angles between faces all 90°

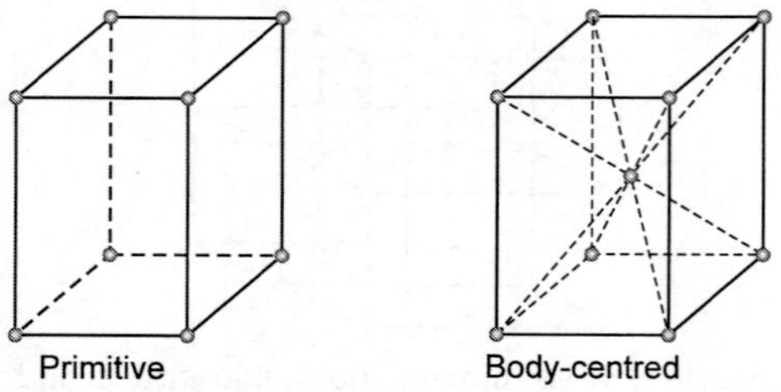

The two tetragonal : one side different in length to the other two, angles between faces all 90°

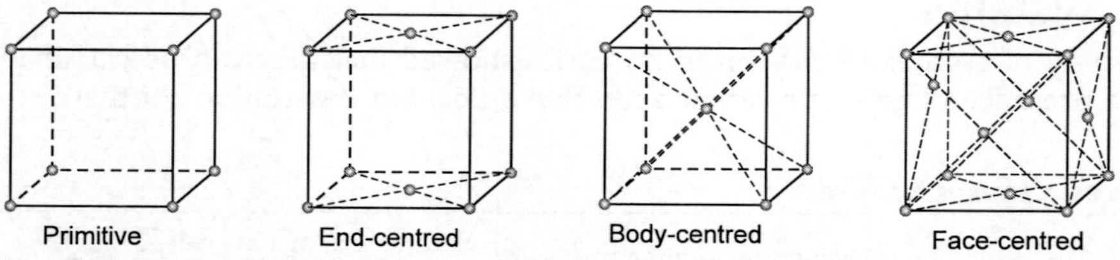

The four orthorhombic lattices : unequal sides, angles between faces all 90°

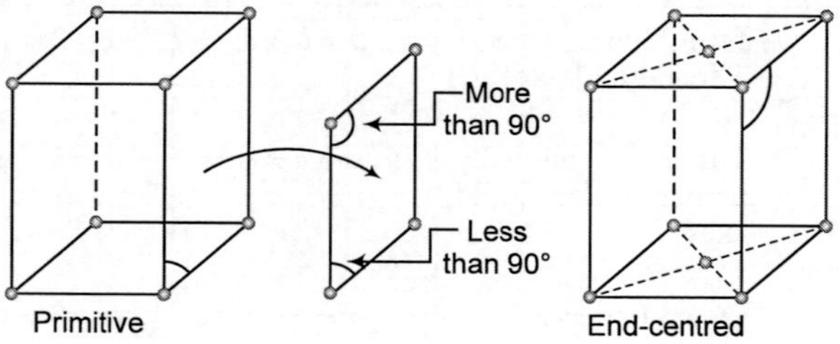

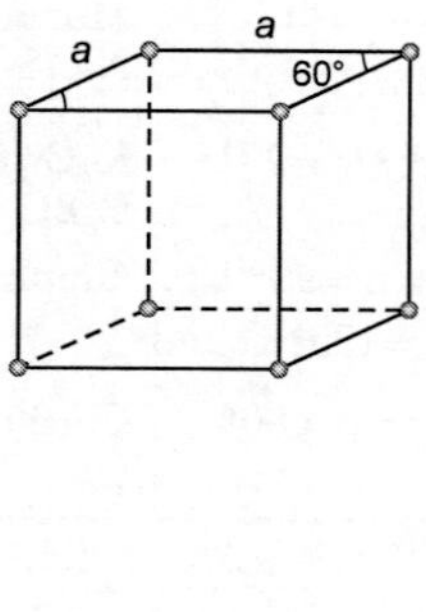

Hexagonal lattice one side different in length to the other two, the marked angles on two faces are 60°

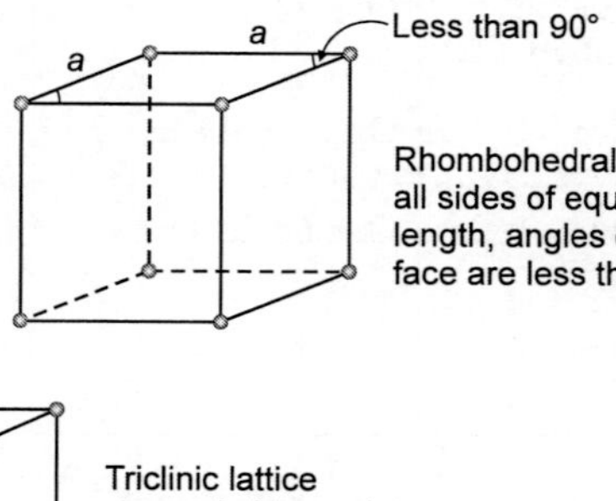

Rhombohedral lattice one all sides of equal length, angles on two face are less than 90°

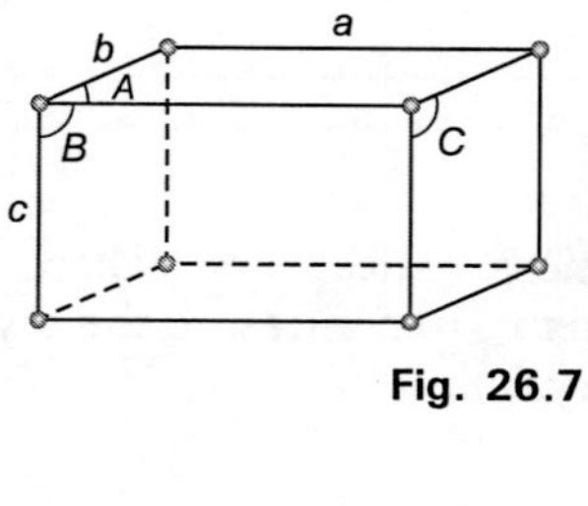

Triclinic lattice unequal sides *a*, *b*, *c*. *A*, *B*, *C* are unequal angles with none equal to 90°

Fig. 26.7

Unit Cell

It is the smallest portion of a crystal lattice which, when repeated in different directions, generates the entire lattice.

Cell Parameters

(i) A unit cell is characterised by, its dimensions along the three edges *a*, *b* and *c*. These edges may or may not be mutually perpendicular.

(ii) Angles between the edges, α (between *b* and *c*) β (between *a* and *c*) and γ (between *a* and *b*). Thus, a unit cell is characterised by six parameters *a*, *b*, *c*, α, β and γ.

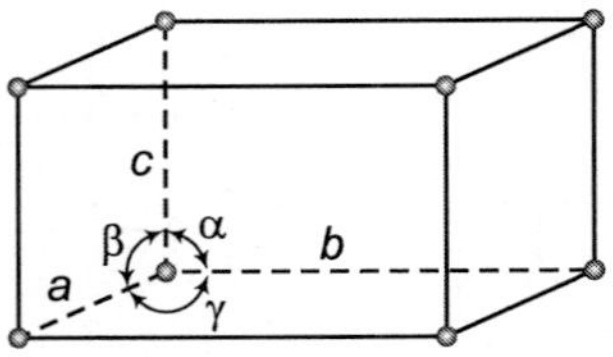

Fig. 26.8 Parameters of a unit cell.

Primitive and Centred Unit Cells

Unit cells can be broadly divided in two categories, primitive and centred unit cells.

(a) Primitive unit cells

In a primitive unit cell, constituent particles are present only on the corner positions.

(b) Centred unit cells

These are of three types :

(i) **Body-centred unit cells** It contains constituent particles at its corners as well as one constituent particle at its body centre.

(ii) **Face-centred unit cells** It contains constituent particles at its corners as well as the centre of each face.

(iii) **End-centred unit cells** It contains constituent particles at its corners and at the centre of any two opposite faces.

Number of Particles Per Unit Cell

Contribution of a particle present at the corner $= \frac{1}{8}$

Contribution of a particle present at the face $= \frac{1}{2}$

Contribution of a particle present at the body centre = 1

Contribution of a particle present at the centre of an edge $= \frac{1}{4}$

Number of atoms in a primitive unit cell $= \frac{1}{8} \times 8 = 1$

Number of atoms in the face-centred unit cell (FCC)

$$= \frac{1}{8} \times 8 + \frac{1}{2} \times 6 = 4$$

Number of atoms in the body-centred unit cell (BCC)

$$= \frac{1}{8} \times 8 + 1 = 2$$

Number of atoms in the end-centred unit cell (ECC)

$$= \frac{1}{8} \times 8 + \frac{1}{2} \times 2 = 2$$

Close Packed Structures

In solids, the constitutent particles are close packed, leaving minimum vacant space. Let us consider the constituent particles identical hard spheres and build up the three dimensional structures in three steps :

(i) Close packing in one dimension

In this arrangement, each sphere is in contact with two of its neighbours therefore, the coordination number is 2.

Fig. 26.9 Close packing of spheres in one dimension.

(ii) Close packing in two dimensions

This can be done in two different ways :

(a) **Square close packing** In this arrangement, each sphere is in contact with four of its neighbours. Thus, the two dimensional coordination number is 4. In this arrangement only 52.4% of the available space is occupied by spheres.

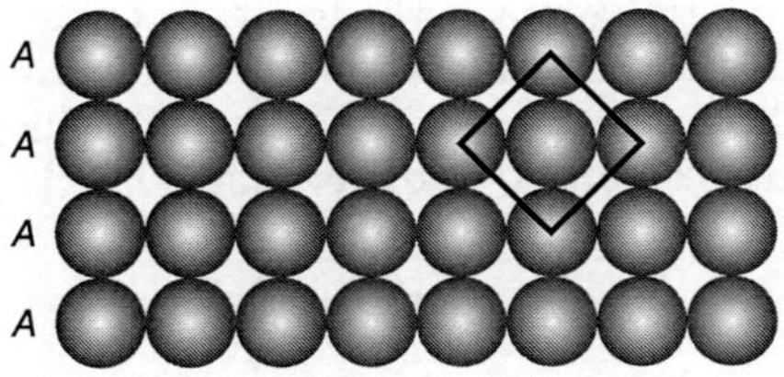

Fig. 26.10 Square close packing of spheres in two dimensions.

(b) **Hexagonal close packing** In this arrangement, each sphere is in contact with six of its neighbours and two dimensional coordination number is 6. In this arrangement only 60.4% of the available is occupied by spheres hence, hexagonal close packing is more efficient.

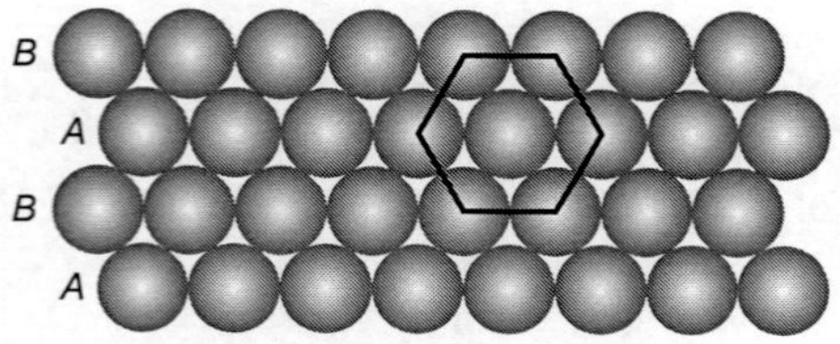

Fig. 26.11 Hexagonal close packing of spheres in two dimensions.

(iii) **Close packing in three dimensions**

These can be obtained by stacking two dimensional layers one above the other.

(a) **Three dimensional close packing from two dimensional square close packing** In this arrangement, spheres of second layer are placed exactly above the spheres of the first layer. If the arrangement of spheres in the first layer is called '*A*' type, all the layers have the same arrangement. Thus, this lattice has *AAA* type pattern. The lattice thus, generated is the simple cubic lattice and its unit cell is the primitive cubic unit cell. In this type of packing only 52% space in the crystal is filled.

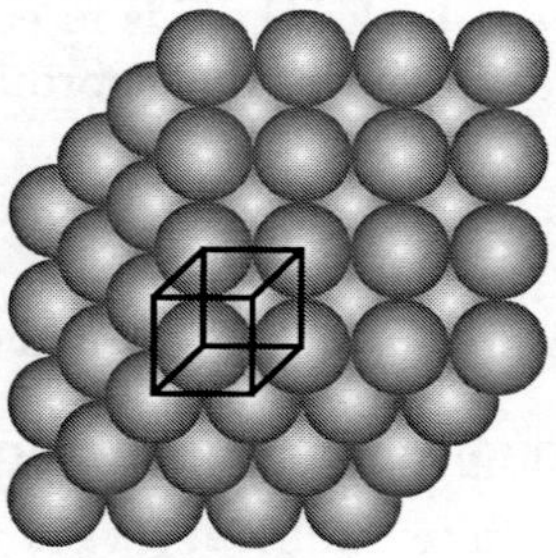

Fig. 26.12 Simple cubic lattice formed by *AAA*... arrangement.

- In this arrangement, spheres of second layer are placed exactly in the hollow at the junction of four spheres below it. The third layer then rests on these in arrangement which corresponds exactly to that in the first layer. This type of arrangement gives-body centred cubic lattice. In this type of packing 68% space in the crystal is filled.

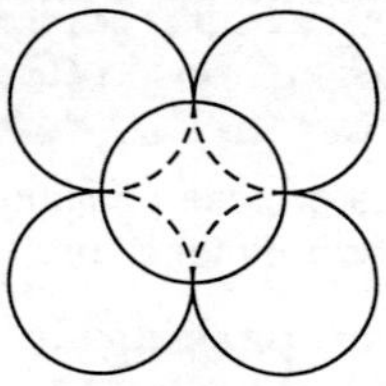

Fig. 26.13 Body-centred cubic lattice.

(b) **Three dmensional close packing from two dimensional hexagonal close placking** The two common types of close packing in three dimensional hexagonal close placked layers are :

- *ABAB*...pattern gives hexagonal close packing (hcp). This sort of arrangement of atoms is found in many metals like magnesium and zinc.
- *ABC ABC* ... pattern givens cubical close packing or face centred cubic (ccp or fcc). Metals such as copper and silver crystallize in this structure.

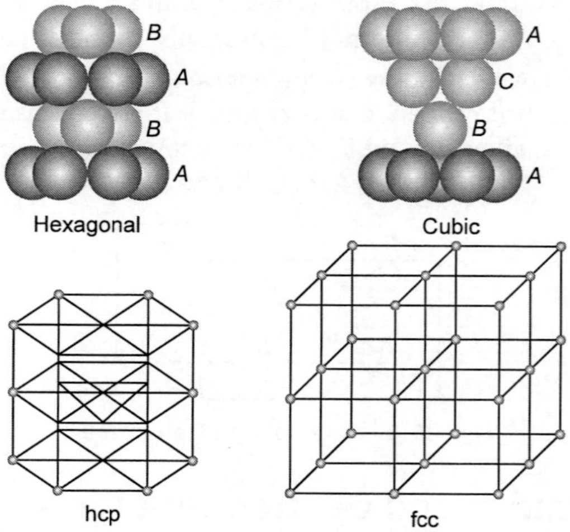

Fig. 26.14

Both these types of close packing are highly efficient and 74% space in the crystal is filled and the coordination number is 12 in either of these two structures.

Coordination Number and Radius Ratio

Radius ratio (r^+/r^-)	Coordination number	Structural arrangement	Examples
0.15-0.225	3	Planar triangular	B_2O_3
0.225-0.414	4	Tetrahedral	ZnS, SiO_4^{4-}
0.414-0.732	6	Octahedral	NaCl, AgCl
0.732-1.000	8	Body-centred cubic	CsCl, CsBr

Relation between number of voids and spheres in close packing

In close packing of N spheres

Number of octahedral voids = N

Number of tetrahedral voids = $2N$

Relation between radius of a void (r) and the radius of the spheres in the close packing

For a tetrahedral void, $r = 0.225R$

For an octahedral void, $r = 0.414R$

Relation between atomic radius (r) and edge length (a) for cubic unit cell (Pure elements)

Simple cubic, $r = a/2$

Body-centred cubic, $r = \sqrt{3}a/4$

Face-centred cubic, $r = \sqrt{2}a/4$

Interplanar distance ratios for the three cubic lattices

Cubic lattice type	Interplanar distance ratio
Simple cubic	$d_{100} : d_{110} : d_{111} = a : \frac{a}{\sqrt{2}} : \frac{a}{\sqrt{3}}$
Body-centred cubic	$d_{200} : d_{110} : d_{222} = \frac{a}{2} : \frac{a}{\sqrt{2}} : \frac{a}{2\sqrt{3}}$ $= 1 : 1.414 : 0.577$
Face-centred cubic	$d_{200} : d_{220} : d_{111} = \frac{a}{2} : \frac{a}{2\sqrt{2}} : \frac{a}{\sqrt{3}}$ $= 1 : 0.707 : 1.154$

Calculations of density (d) of a cubic crystal from its edge length (a)

$$\text{Density of the unit cell} = \frac{\text{Mass of unit cell}}{\text{Volume of unit cell}}$$

$$d = \frac{ZM}{a^3 \cdot N_A}$$

where, Z is the number of atoms present in one unit cell and M is molar mass.

Structures of Some Compounds and Elements

Structure of Salts of the Type *MX*

There are four basic structures in which salts of the formula MX commonly crystallise. They are sodium chloride, cesium chloride, zinc sulphdie (zinc blende or sphalerite) and zinc sulphide (wurtzite) types. The first three have cubic symmetry, while the last one has hexagonal symmetry.

Structure of Sodium Chloride (NaCl)

Determination of the type of lattice The external form of the sodium chloride crystal indicates that it has a cubic lattice. We have to decide the nature of the cubic lattice, that is, whether it is simple cubic or face-centred or body-centred. As indicated in the earlier section, the interplanar distance for each set of planes in the crystal is determined, using Bragg's law. Taking the 100 planes, for the first order reflection maximum, $\lambda = 2d_{100} \sin\theta_1$ or $d_{100} = \frac{\lambda}{2\sin\theta_1}$. Similarly for 110 and 111 planes, we have $d_{110} = \frac{\lambda}{2\sin\theta_2}$ and $d_{111} = \frac{\lambda}{2\sin\theta_3}$: where θ_2 and θ_3 are the glancing angles for the set of planes 110, 111 respectively, both for the first order reflection (*i.e.*, $n = 1$). Therefore, the interplanar distance ratio, $d_{100} : d_{110} : d_{111} = \frac{1}{\sin\theta_1} : \frac{1}{\sin\theta_2} : \frac{1}{\sin\theta_3}$. The angles θ_1, θ_2 and θ_3 have been measured with the X-ray spectrometer and the above ratio evaluated as 1 : 0.70 : 1.15, which corresponds to face-centred cubic. Thus NaCl has face-centred cubic lattice in Na^+ as well as in Cl^- ions.

Sodium chloride is an ionic compound. The chloride ions (Cl^-) adopt cubic close packed arrangement. This arrangement is also regarded as face centred cubic arrangement. The sodium ions occupy all the octahedral sites. The coordination number of Na^+ ion and Cl^- ion are 6 and 6 in NaCl. The NaCl structure is also called rock salt structure.

Evaluation of lattice dimension Refer to an earlier section for the Figure 26.15 representing the unit cell of NaCl. The edge or the side of the unit cell (a) is the distance between two consecutive Na^+ ions or Cl^- ions lying on the edge of cube. This can be calculated from the molar volume (V_m) and the Avogadro number (N).

It can be shown that each unit cell contains effectively four Na^+ ions and four Cl^- ions thus :

Referring to the diagram, the eight corners of the cube are occupied by eight Cl^- ions and since each corner is common to eight cubes, the effective contribution is $\frac{1}{8} \times 8 = 1$ chloride ion. Similarly we have six Cl^- ions occupying the centres of the six faces and since each face is common to two cubes, the effective contribution is $\frac{1}{2} \times 6 = 3$ chloride ions. Thus each unit cell (*i.e.*, cube) effectively contains four Cl^- ions. Now for the Na^+ ions, we have one Na^+ ion at the centre of each edge of the cube and we have thus twelve Na^+ ions corresponding to the twelve edges. Each edge is common to four cubes and hence the effective contribution is $\frac{1}{4} \times 12 = 3$ sodium ions. Also there is one Na^+ ion at the centre of the cube which is not shared by any other cube. Thus the unit cell effectively contains four Na^+ ions.

The molar volume of the crystal, $V_m = \frac{M}{\rho}$, where M is the molar mass and ρ the density. This volume contains N molecules (Avogadro number). Hence, the volume corresponding to 4 molecules (*i.e.*, 4 Na^+ and 4 Cl^- ions) $= V_m \times \frac{4}{N} = \frac{M}{\rho} \times \frac{4}{N}$. This must be the volume of the unit cell, since each unit cell contains effectively 4 Na^+ and 4 Cl^- ions. Hence, side of the unit cell, $a = \left(\frac{M}{\rho} \times \frac{4}{N}\right)$. The interplanar distance d_{100} or more correctly $d_{200} = \frac{a}{2} = \frac{1}{2}\left(\frac{M}{\rho} \times \frac{4}{N}\right)^{1/3} = \left(\frac{M}{2N_\rho}\right)^{1/3}$.

Making use of the interplanar distance, we can calculate the wavelength of the X -radiation used, through the Bragg equation, $n\lambda = 2d \sin\theta$.

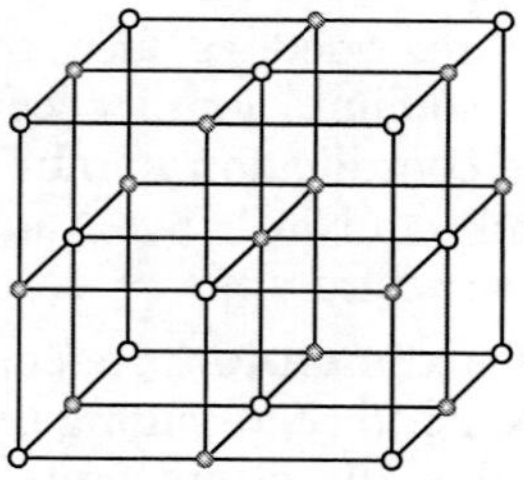

Fig. 26.15

e.g., LiX, KX, AgCl, MgO and CaO etc.

Structure of Zinc Blende (ZnS)

Zinc blende (sphalerite) is ionic compound. S^{2-} ions are present in face centred cubic arrangement and Zn^{2+} ions occupy alternate (one half) tetrahedral voids. The coordination numbers of Zn^{2+} and S^{2-} in ZnS crystal are 4 and 4 respectively. *e.g.*, CuCl, CuBr, CuI and BeS etc.

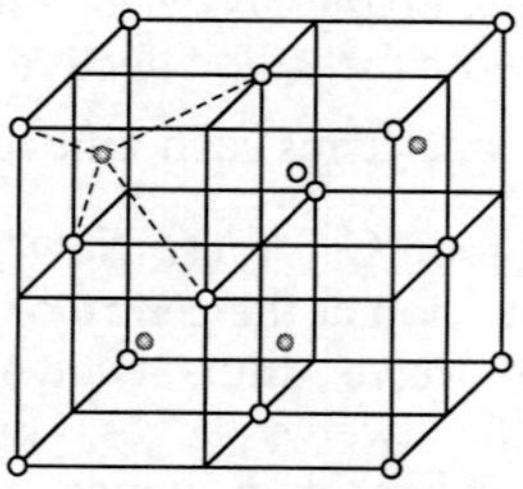

Fig. 26.16

Structure of Cesium Chloride (CsCl)

Cesium chloride is an ionic compound. The Cl^- ions are present in simple cubic arrangement (at all the corners of a cube). Cs^+ ions occupy the cubic voids *i.e.*, the Cs^+ are present at the body centre of the cube. The coordination numbers of Cs^+ and Cl^- ions in CsCl crystals are 8 and 8 respectively.

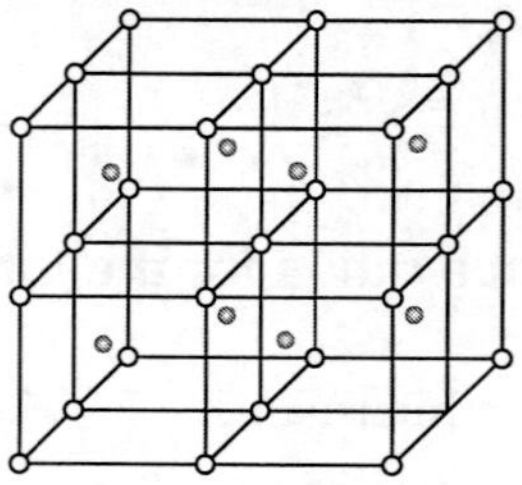

Fig. 26.17

e.g., CsBr, CsI etc.

Structure of Calcium Fluoride (CaF_2)

It is an ionic solid and also known as fluorite. The Ca^{2+} ions are arranged in ccp or fcc arrangement. F^- ions occupy all the tetrahedral sites. In this structure the coordination numbers of Ca^{2+} and F^- ions are 8 and 4 respectively. *e.g.*, BaF_2, $BaCl_2$, PbF_2 and SrF_2 etc.

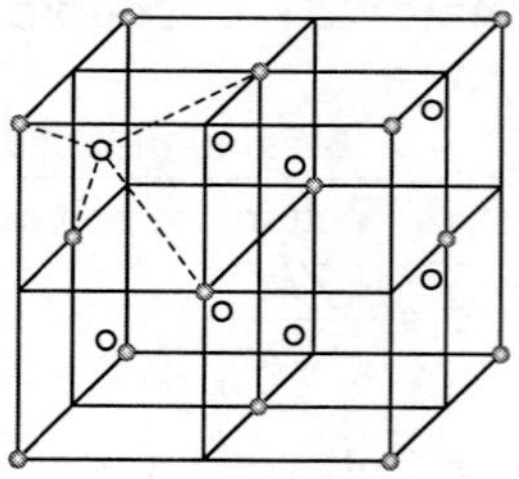

Fig. 26.18

Structure of Sodium Oxide or Antifluorite (Na_2O)

Na_2O is an ionic compound. O^{2-} ions are present in ccp or fcc arrangement and Na^+ ions occupy all the tetrahedral sites. In this structure the coordination numbers of Na^+ ions and O^{2-} ions are 4 and 8 respectively. *e.g.*, Li_2O, K_2O, Rb_2O, Rb_2S and K_2S respectively.

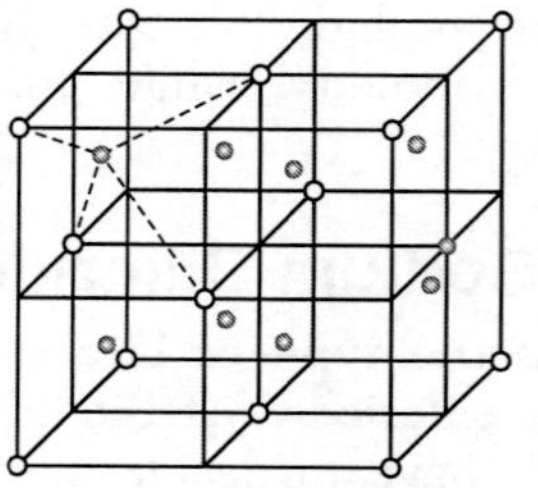

Fig. 26.19

Structure of Iron Oxide (FeO)

It has rock salt structure. However, this oxide is always non-stiochiometric $Fe_{0.95}O$ (Wustite). This composition can be obtained if a small number of Fe^{2+} ions are replaced by two thirds or many Fe^{3+} ions in octahedral sites.

Normal Spinel Structure

General formula of the compounds adopting spinel structure is AB_2O_4. In this type of structure negative ions are present in ccp or fcc arrangement and positive ions occupy voids. The dipositive ions are in tetrahderal voids while tripositive ions are in octahedral voids. *e.g.,* $MgAl_2O_4$, $MgCr_2O_4$ and $ZnFe_2O_4$ etc.

Inverse Spinel Structure

In this type of structure negative ions are present in ccp and fcc arrangement and dipositive ions are present in octahedral voids while tripositive ions are equally distributed between tetrahderal and octahedral voids. *e.g.,* Fe_3O_4 (magnetite or load stone), $MgFe_2O_2$ and $MgIn_2O_4$ etc.

Corundum Structure

In this type of structure anions are present in hexagonal close packing. Cations occupy $\frac{2}{3}$ of octahedral voids. *e.g.,* Fe_2O_3, Al_2O_3 and Cr_2O_3.

Structure of Diamond

It is a covalent solid. Carbon atoms are arranged in fcc pattern as well as half of the tetrahderal voids are also ccupied by carbon atoms. Every atom in this structure is surrounded tetrahedrally by four others. The entire crystal is a giant molecule. *e.g.,* germanium silicon and grey tin.

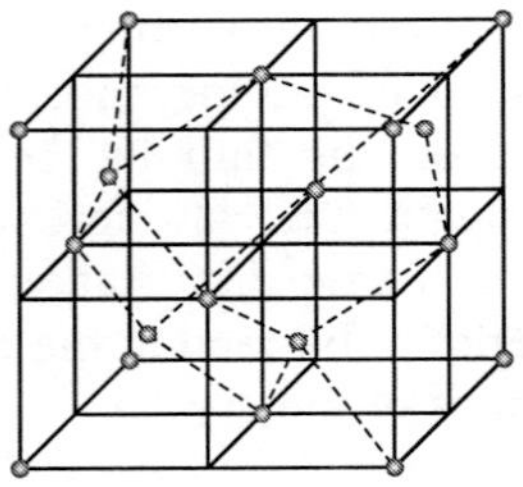

Fig. 26.20 Structure of diamond.

Graphite Structure

It is an example of a covalent solid. It is more stable than diamond. Carbon atoms are present as hexagonal system in layer lattice. Different layers are held by weak van der Walls' forces. Due to this crystals of graphite is slippery and flaky in nature. *e.g.,* arsenic, antimony, black phosphorus and mica.

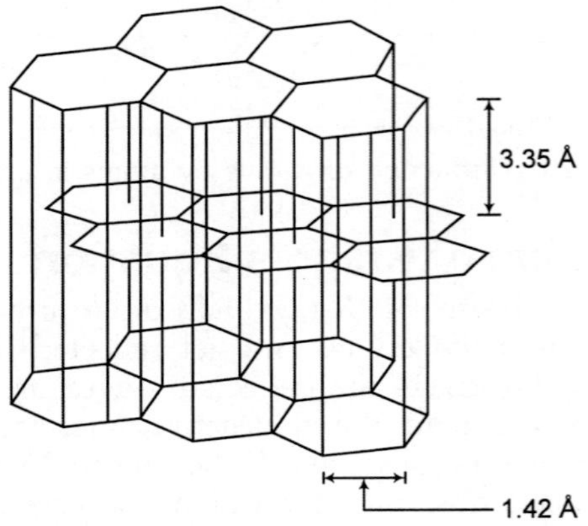

Fig. 26.21 Structure of graphite.

Diffraction of X-rays by Crystals

In 1912 Max Von Laue suggested if a beam of non-homogeneous X-rays were passed through a crystal a diffraction pattern would be observed. The diffraction pattern can be obtained by placing a photographic film behind the crystal. From the position of Laue spots, it is possible to determine the shape and size of the unit cell.

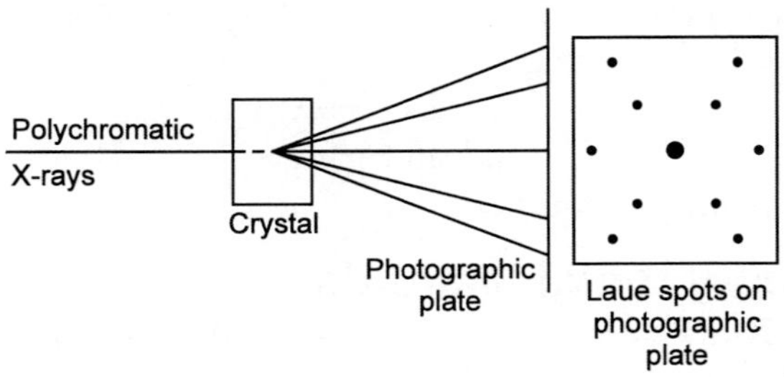

Fig. 26.22

Bragg's Equation

A fundamental equation which gives a simple relation between the wavelength of the X-rays used and the interplanar distance in the crystal and the angle of reflection is known as the Bragg's equation.

$$n\lambda = 2d \sin \theta$$

where, n = order of diffraction and its value equal to 1, 2, 3, 4, 5 ... etc.,

λ = wavelength of X-rays used,

θ = angle of diffraction and

d = distance between planes in the crystal parallel to the surface examined.

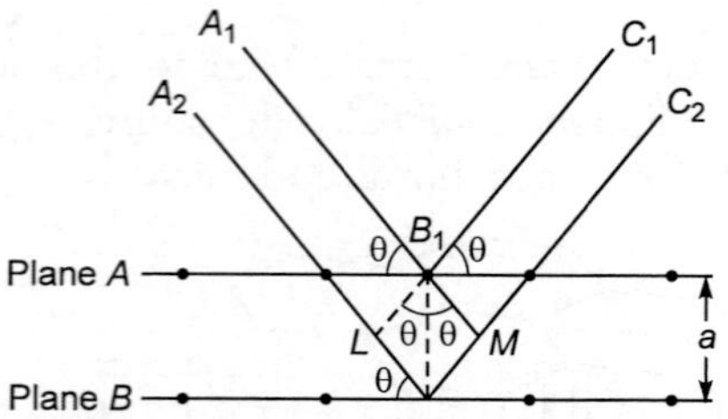

Fig. 26.23 Diffraction of X-rays by atoms in a crystal.

Derivation of Bragg's Equation

Suppose a beam of X-rays fall on a crystal and penetrate into the crystal and get reflected from the successive layers. If the reflected waves are out of phase, then due to the destructive interference, no diffraction will be observed. If the reflected waves are in phase, a diffraction spot will be observed due to constructive interference.

In the above figure (26.23) horizontal lines represent parallel planes in the crystal structure separated from one another by the ditance d. Two parallel beams of monochromatic X-rays A_1B_1 and A_2B_2 are incident at points B_1 and B_2 at an angle θ and are reflected along B_1C_1 and B_2C_2. The waves are in phase after reflection, the difference in distance travelled by two rays (path difference) must be an integral multiple of wavelenth.

Path difference = $B_2L + B_2M = n\lambda$

Since, triangles B_1LB_2 and B_1MB_2 are congruent, hence $B_2L = B_2M$

$$2B_2L = n\lambda$$

$$2d \sin\theta = n\lambda$$

This is Bragg's equation.

Experimental Methods

The X-ray diffraction techniques used in the study of crystals are of two types :

(i) rotating crystal technique
(ii) powder technique.

Rotating crystal technique

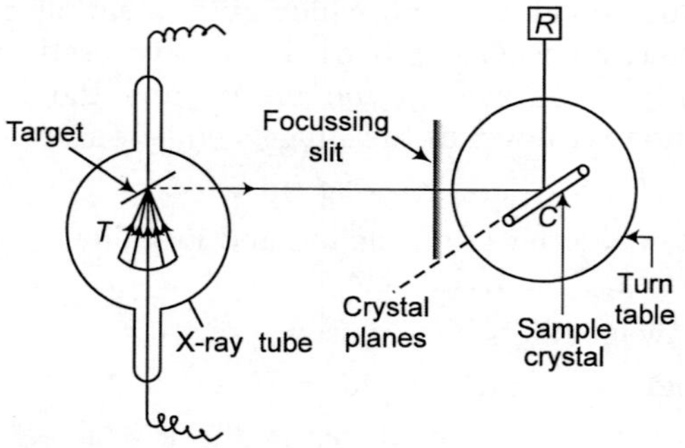

Fig. 26.24 An X-ray spectrometer.

The X-rays are generated in tube A by bombarding cathode rays on suitable target metals such as Cu, Mo and Cr. X-rays are passed through slits and filters to obtain a sharp monochromatic beam and it is then allowed to strike a single crystal mounted on the turn table. The crystal is rotated gradually by means of turn table and the intensities of reflected rays are measured by the help of electrometer. The variation in intentisy of diffracted beam is due to the variation in density of atoms in different sets of planes.

The experiment is repeated at various incident angles of X-rays and the angle at which maximum reflection occurs is determined. The process is carried out for each plane of the crystal. The lowest angle for which maximum reflection occurs corresponds to $n = 1$ (first order reflection) and the next higher angle for which maximum reflection occurs again corresponds to $n = 2$ (second order reflection)

Powder diffraction method

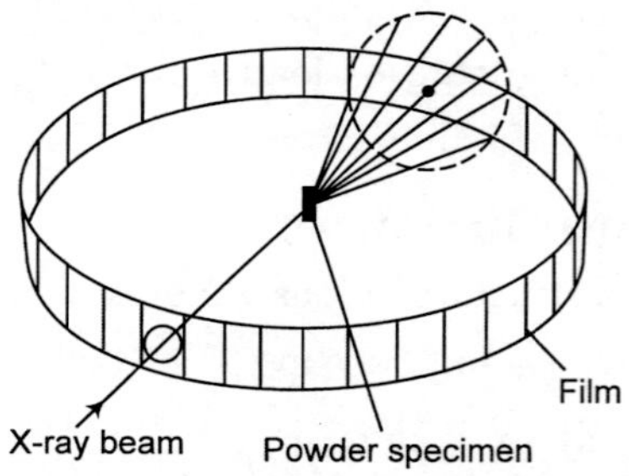

Fig. 26.25 The powder method for X-ray diffraction.

The powder pattern is mainly used in the study of relatively simple crystal structure. Since, the powder consists of many small crystals which are oriented in all possible directions, no rotation is necessary.

In this method given substance is taken in a thin walled capillary tube in the powder form. A narrow beam of X-rays is allowed to fall on the powder. The diffracted X-rays strike a strip of photographic film and it will leave impressions on the film in the form of either circular arc or straight lines at diferent distances from the incident beam. These distances can be converted into scattering angles to be used in the Bragg's equation for diffraction planes of the crystal.

Electron Diffraction

The diffraction of an electron by molecules of a gas can be used to determine the structure of molecules. When the beam of electron interact strongly with atoms of the sample, diffraction patterns are obtained.

An electron diffraction pattern consists of a pattern of rings of varying intensity. The accuracy of bond length and bond angles obtained from electrical diffraction studies is comparable to that obtained from X-ray diffraction studies for simple molecules. Electron beam is not scattered very effectively by hydrogen atoms. The position of such atoms in a molecule cannot be determined easily by this method. The neutron diffraction method overcome this difficulty since protons have a large scattering cross section for neutrons.

Neutron Diffraction

X-rays are scattered by the electrons that surround each atom of an ion or molecule. Because atomic scattering factors are approximately proportional to atomic number so the position of hydrogen atoms generally determined by neutron diffraction.

The two main uses of neutron scattering are in refining molecular structures that have been mostly determined by X-ray diffraction and in polymer characterization using small-angle neutrons scattering. For the three types of diffraction methods, neutrons are unique as they have magnetic moment and are therefore, sensitive to magnetic ordering in solids.

A neutron beam is obtained from thermal neutrons of a neutron reactor, when it is passed through a velocity selector device a monochromatic beam is obtained. The crystal whose structures are known, except for the positions of hydrogen atoms are studied by this technique.

Imperfections in a Crystal

An ideally perfect crystal is one which has the same unit cell and same lattice points throughout the crystal. Imperfection or defects means deviation from regular arrangement of constituent particles. Two types of defects are generally observed in crystals. These are point defects and line defects.

Point Defects

Point defects are the irregularities or deviations from ideal arrangement around a point or an atom in a crystalline substance. Point defects are of the three types; (A) stiochiometric defects (B) impurity defects (C) non-stoichiometric defects.

(A) Stoichiometric defects

These are the point defects that do not disturb the stiochiometry of the solid. Basically these are of two types, vacancy defects and interstitial defects.

(i) **Vacancy defect** This type of defect can develop when a substance in heated. In this type of defect some of the lattice sites are vacant, this results in decrease in density of the substance.

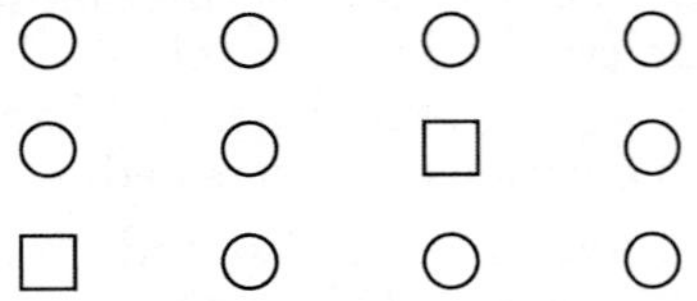

Fig. 26.26 Vacancy defect.

(ii) **Interstitial defect** In this type of defect some constituent particles (atoms or molecules) occupy an interstitial site. This results in increase in density of the substance.

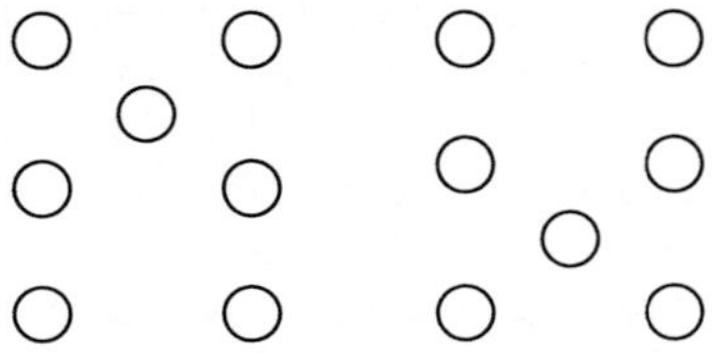

Fig. 26.27 Interstitial defect.

Vacancy and interstitial defects are shown by non-ionic solids. Ionic solids show these defects as Frenkel and Schottky defects.

(iii) **Schottky defect** It is caused when equal number of cations and anions are missing from their lattice sites. Due to this defect density decreases.

e.g., NaCl, KCl, CsCl and AgBr. At room temperature there are approximately 106 Schottky pairs per cm^3 in NaCl crystal.

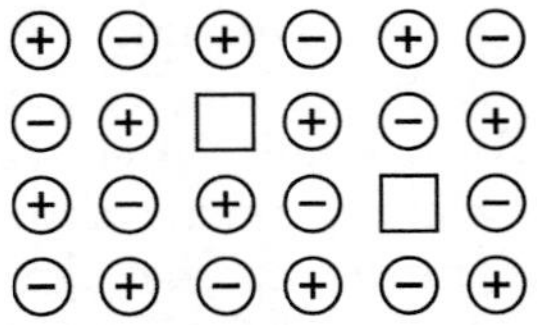

Fig. 26.28 Schottky defect.

(iv) **Frenkel defect** It is caused when the cations are missing from their lattice sites and occupy interstitial sites and the density remain unchanged. Due to this defect dielectric constant value increases.

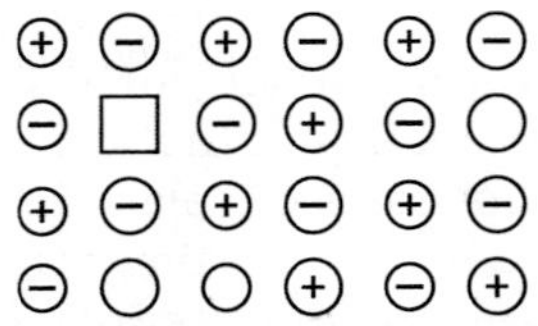

Fig. 26.29 Frenkel defect.

e.g., ZnS, AgCl, AgBr and AgI. It may be noted that AgBr shows both, Frenkel as well as Schottky defects.

(B) Impurity defects

These defects are caused by the presence of an impurity in the crystal. In ionic solids, when the ionic impurity has a different valence than the main compound some vacancies are created.

e.g., (i) solid solution of $SrCl_2$ and NaCl, (ii) solid solution of $CdCl_2$ and AgCl.

(C) Non-stoichiometric defects

These deflects are of two types; metal excess defect and metal deficiency defect.

(i) **Metal excess defect** Metal excess defect due to anionic vacancies. It has been observed that if NaCl crystal is heated in Na vapours it acquires yellow colour. The Cl^- ions diffuse to the surface of the crystal and combine with Na^+ ions to give NaCl and the vacant anionic (Cl^-) sites are occupied by unpaired electrons.

The anionic sites which are occupied by electrons are called *F*-centres or colour centres. *e.g.,* excess lithium makes LiCl crystals pink and excess of potassium makes KCl crystals violet.

Metal excess defect due to presence of extra cations in interstitial sites.

For example, on heating zinc oxide crystal it loses oxygen and turns yellow. The excess Zn^{2+} ions move to interstitial sites and the electrons to the neighbouring interstitial sites.

(ii) **Metal deficiency defect** This type of defect is generally found amongst the comounds of transition metals which can exhibit variables valency. For example, in crystals of FeO some Fe^{2+} cations are missing and loss of positive charge is made up by the conversion of required number of Fe^{2+} ions to Fe^{3+} ions.

Line Defects

These are the irregularities or deviations from ideal arrangement in enter rows of lattice points. The most common type of line defect within a crystal is a dislocation.

(i) **Edge dislocation** (Taylor dislocation) In an edge dislocation, an extra half plane of atoms is inserted along the slip plane in the lattice. This extra plane is accomodated through a displacement of top portion of the lattice by one interatomic distance. As the distance from dislocation increases, the effect dies down.

(ii) **Screw dislocation** In screw dislocation (Burger's dislocation), part of set of lattice planes has been displaced relative to the adjacent to the adjacent planes by one or more lattice points.

Alloys have edge dislocations so they require greater shear force for permanent deformation than the pure metals. On the other hand screw dislocations are responsible for the high malleability and ductility of metals.

The concentration of defects

Energy is required to form a defect : this means that the formation of defects is always an **endothermic process.** It may seem surprising then that defects exist in crystals, at all and yet they do even at low temperatures, albe it in very small concentrations. The reason for this is that the formation of defects produces a commensurate gain in entropy. The enthalpy of formation of the defects is thus balanced by the gain in entropy such that, at equilibrium, the overall change in free energy of the crystal due to the defect formation is zero according to the equation :

$$\Delta G = \Delta H - T\Delta S$$

The interesting point is that the thermodynamically we do not expect a crystalline solid to be perfect, contrary, perhaps to our common sense expectation of symmetry and order. At any particular temperature there will be an equilibrium population of defects in the crystal.

The number of Schottky defects in a crystal of composition *MX* is given by

$$n_s \approx N\exp - (\Delta H_s / 2kT), \qquad \text{...(1)}$$

where, n_s is the number of Schottkey defects per m^3, at *T*K, in a crystal with *N* cation and *N* anion sites per m^3 ΔH_s, is the enthalpy required to form one defect. It is a quite simple mater to derive these equations for the equilibrium concentration of Schottky defects by considering the change in entropy of a perfect crystal due to the introduction of defects. The change in entropy will be due to the variations of atoms around the defects and also to the arrangement of the defects. It is possible to estimate this latter quantity, the **configurational entropy**, using the methods of statistical mechanics.

If the number of Schottky detects is n_s per m^3 at *T*K, then there will be n_s cation vacancies and n_s anion vacancies in a crystal containing *N* possible cation sites and *N* possible anion sites per m^3 . The **Boltzmann**

formula tells us that the entropy of such a system is given by :

$$S = k \ln W \quad \ldots(2)$$

where W is the number of ways of distributing n_s defects over N possible sites at random, and k is the Boltzmann constant (1.380622×10^{-23} JK^{-1}). Probability theory shows that W is given by

$$W = \frac{N!}{(N-n)!\,n!} \quad \ldots(3)$$

where $N!$ is called factorial N and is mathematical shorthand for

$$N \times (N-1) \times (N-2) \times (n-3) \ldots \times 1$$

So, the number of ways we can distribute the cation vacancies will be

$$W_c = \frac{N!}{(N-n_s)!\,n_s!}$$

and similarly for the anion vacancies

$$W_a = \frac{N!}{(N-n_s)!\,n_s!}$$

The total number of ways of distributing these defects, W, is given by the product of W_c and W_a :

$$W = W_c W_a$$

and the change in entropy due to introducing the defects into a perfect crystal is thus :

$$\Delta S = k \ln W = k \ln \left(\frac{N!}{(N-n_s)!\,n_s!} \right)^2$$

$$= 2k \ln \frac{N!}{(N-n_s)!\,n_s!}$$

We can simplify this expression using **Stirling**'s approximation that $\ln N! \approx N \ln N - N$

and the expression becomes (after manipulation)

$$\Delta S = 2k\,(N \ln N - (N-n_s) \ln (N-n_s) - n_s \ln n_s)$$

If the enthalpy change for the formation of a single defect is ΔH_s and we assume that the enthalpy change for the formation of n_s defects is $n_s \Delta H_s$, then the Gibbs free energy change is given by

$$\Delta G = n_s\,\Delta H_s - 2kT\,\{N \ln N - (N-n_s) \ln (N-n_s) - n_s \ln n_s)\}$$

At equilibrium, at constant T the Gibbs free energy of the system must be a minimum with respect to changes in the number of defects n_s; thus

$$\left(\frac{d\Delta G}{dn_s} \right) = 0$$

So,
$$\Delta H_s - 2kT \frac{d}{dn_s} [N \ln N - (N-n_s) \ln (N-n_s) - n_s \ln n_s] = 0$$

$N \ln N$ is a constant and hence, its differential is zero; the differential of $\ln x$ is $\frac{1}{x}$ and of $(x \ln x)$ is $(1 + \ln x)$. On differentiating we get :

$$\Delta H_s - 2kT\,[\ln (N-n_s) + 1 - \ln n_s - 1] = 0$$

Hence,
$$\Delta H_s = 2kT \ln \left[\frac{(N-n_s)}{n_s} \right]$$

and
$$n_s = (N-n_s) \exp(-\Delta H_s/2kT)$$

as $N > n_s$ we can approximate $(N-n_s)$ by N, finally giving :

$$n_s = N \exp(-\Delta H_s/2KT) \quad \ldots(4)$$

If we express this equation in molar quantities it becomes

$$n_s \approx N \exp(-\Delta H_s/2RT) \quad \ldots(5)$$

where now ΔH_s is the enthalpy required to form one mole of Schottky defects and R is the gas cosntant, 8.314 JK mol^{-1} the units of ΔH_S are J mol^{-1}.

By a similar analysis we find that the number of Frenkel defects present in a crystal MX is given by the expression :

$$n_F = (NN_i)^{1/2} \exp(-\Delta E_F/2kT) \quad \ldots(6)$$

where n_F is the number of Frenkel defects per m^3, N is the number of lattice sites and N_i the number of interstitial sites available. ΔH_F is the enthalpy of formation of one Frenkel defect. If ΔH_F is the enthalpy of formation of one of Frenkel defects the expression becomes :

$$n_F = (NN_i)^{1/2} \exp(-\Delta H_F/2RT) \quad \ldots(7)$$

Whether Schottky or Frenkel defects are found in a crystal depends in the main on the value of ΔH, the defect with the lower ΔH value predominating. In some crystal it is possible for both types of defect to be present.

Table 26.4 **Value of $\frac{n_s}{N}$**

T(K)	$\Delta H_S = 5 \times 10^{-19}$ J	$\Delta H_S = 1 \times 10^{-19}$ J
300	6.12×10^{-27}	5.72×10^{-6}
1000	1.37×10^{-8}	2.67×10^{-2}

First, we have seen from the above calculation, that raising the temperature introduces more defects. We would have expected this to happen because defect formation is an endothermic process and Le-Chatelier's principle tell us that increasing the temperature of an endothermic reaction will favour the products, in this case defects. Second, if it were possible to decrease the enthalpy of formation of a defect, ΔH_S or ΔH_F, this would also increase the proportion of defects present. A simple calculation a gain using equation (4), but now with a lower value for ΔH_S says 1×10^{-19} J allows us to see this. Table above compares the results. This has had a dramatic effect on the numbers of defects! At 1000 K we are now finding of the order of three in every hundred. It is difficult to see how the value of ΔH could be manipulated within a crystal, but we do find crystals where the value of ΔH is lower than usual due to the nature of the structure, and this can be exploited. This is true for one of the systems that we shall look at in detail later, α – AgI. Third, if we introduce impurities into a crystal selectively, we can increase the defect population.

Extrinsic defects Extrinsic point defects are inevitable because perfect purity is unattainable in crystals of any size. Extremely pure silica glass used in optical fibres contain 1 part in 10^9 metal impurities. Extrinsic defects are also deliberatively created with a purpose in view. In ZrO_2 lattice Ca^{2+} is introduced in the cation sub-lattice and the charge neutrality is maintained by an O^{2-} ion vacancy. Incorporation of Li^+ in a Ni^{2+} lattice site of NiO results in the oxidation of an Ni^{2+} into Ni^{3+}.

Electrical conduction in solids on account of point defects is not rare. In a perfect crystal, the ions stay put in their positions and no diffusion can occur at ambient temperatures. Thus, movement of ions can occur only through defect mobility. An ion may jump or hop from a lattice position to an adjacent vacant site. This is known as vacancy mechanism. Or, an interstitial ion may jump or hop to an equivalent adjacent site. This is called interstitial mechanism. (Figure 26.30 (a) and (b)).

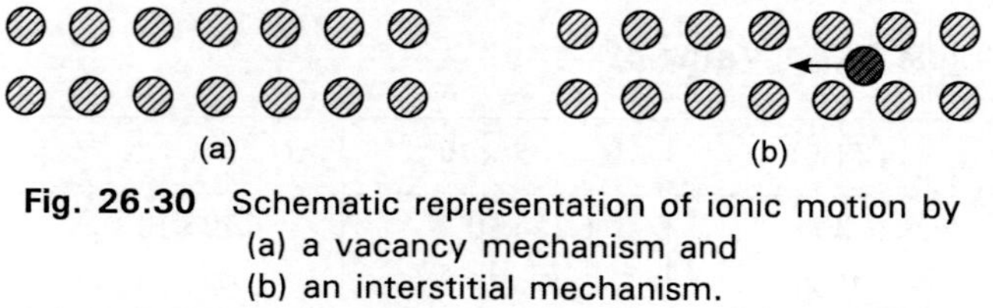

Fig. 26.30 Schematic representation of ionic motion by (a) a vacancy mechanism and (b) an interstitial mechanism.

Ionic conductivity in a solid is given by, $\mu = n\,Ze$, where, n = number of charge carriers per unit volume, Ze is either charge, and μ = their mobility, which is the drift velocity in an applied electrical field. The fact that ionic solids have a conductivity range which is several orders of magnitude lower than that of metals shows that electric current in ionic solids is carried only by the defects. Therefore, n is closely related to the concentration of defects in the crystal. In NaCl, for example, Na^+ ions can easily move because they are smaller than the Cl^- anions. Even here, the Na^+ ion has to pass through a route which would as far as possible avoid coming very close to Cl^- ions (route 4). When the Na^+ ions move through route 1-2-3, its coordination number changes from the normal 6 to lower numbers before finally returning to 6 again as it occupies the normal lattice site. Since, the ion has to pass through an energy barrier, its mobility is governed by an Arrhenius equation.

$$\mu = \mu_0 \exp(-E_a/RT)$$

The pre-exponential factor, μ_0 depends on the attempt frequency *i.e.,* the number of times the ion attempts to move in one second, the distance moved by the ion, and the extent of the electrical field. A similar equation emerges for the electrical conductivity of the crystal :

$$\sigma = \left(\frac{\sigma_0}{T}\right)\exp\left(-\frac{E_a}{RT}\right)$$

Here σ_0 includes n and Ze, as well as the jump distance

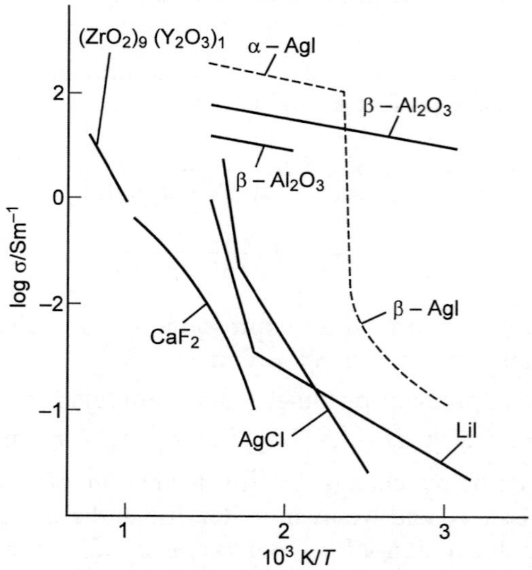

Fig. 26.31 The conductivities of selected solid electrolytes over a range of temperature.

and attempt frequency. The Arrhenius plot is shown in Figure 26.31. In some crystals, such as LiI, there is a change in slope indicating that the mechanism of conduction changes over from one temperature region to another. This can be explained as follows : Even a pure crystal contains some impurities. The line corresponding to low temperatures is due to extrinsic vacancies. At low temperatures the concentration of intrinsic vacancies is very low and can be neglected. Therefore, the conduction is due to extrinsic vacancies in the low temperature region. For a particular amount of impurity the number of vacancies present will be essentially constant. The mobility in this region thus depends only on the cation mobility on account of extrinsic defects, the temperature dependence of mobility is given by $\mu = \mu_0 \exp(-E_a/RT)$.

At the higher temperature region, the concentration of intrinsic defects has increased to such an extent that it is greater than the concentration of extrinsic defects. Unlike extrinsic defects, intrinsic defects do not stay constant in concentration and will vary as follows :

$$\mu_S = N \exp(-\Delta H_s/2RT)$$

In this intrinsic region, a plot of $\frac{\ln \sigma}{T}$ against $\frac{1}{T}$ will indicate a higher value for the activation energy. This is the sum of two E_a^S : one for the cation jump and another for the creation of a Schottky defect. A similar expression can be had for Frenkel defects.

$$E_S = E_S + \frac{1}{2}\Delta H_S \; ; \; E_F = E_A + \frac{1}{2}\Delta H_F$$

Though the number of defects and hence the conductivity of the crystal can be increased by raising the temperature, the same end can be achieved better by finding materials with low activation energies.

Some solids have conductivities comparable with that of a 40% aqueous solution of sulphuric acid, $0.8\ \Omega^{-1}\ \text{cm}^{-1}$. In $RbAg_4I_5$ a simple cube of I^- ions has O_h holes filled by Rb^+ and part of the t_a holes occupied by Ag^+ ions. The latter being smaller more in a rigid lattice of the other two kinds of ions. A second example is provided by β-alumina containing Na^+ ions in between spiral layers.

Dislocation in Solids

A dislocation is a linear defect resulting from the non-alignment of one group of atoms from an adjacent group. Two types are frequently encountered; edge dislocation and serew dislocation. In an edge dislocation (also called a Taylor dislocation), an extra half-plane of atoms is inserted along the slip plane in the lattice. This extra plane is accommodated through a displacement of the top portion of the lattice by one interatomic distance. The top portion gets squeezed and gets distorted, the distortion concentrating mainly at the edges of the dislocation. As the distance from the dislocation increases the effect dies down.

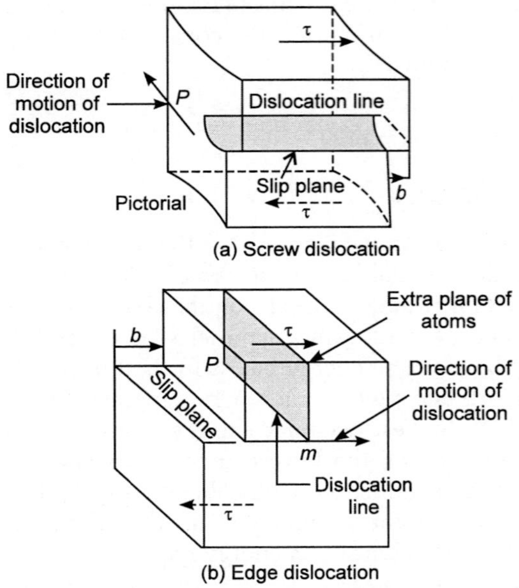

Fig. 26.32 Screw dislocation, with edge dislocation for comparison.

In the screw dislocation (Burger's dislocation), part of a set of lattice planes has been displaced relative to the adjacent planes, by one or more lattice points. These dislocations are responsible for the high malleability and ductility of metals. Compared to the number of lattice points covered by a full circle around a regular lattice, the number of lattice points covered around a dislocation is higher. This difference in length is known as the Burger's vector of the dislocation. Burger's vector is parallel to the dislocation in the edge type, and perpendicular to the dislocation in the screw type. (Figure 26.32). Random planar defects are known as Wadsley defects.

Electrical Properties of Solids

Solids are classified into following classes depending on the extent of conducting nature. Conductivities

(i) Conductors (metals) 10^8 ohm^{-1} m^{-1}

(ii) Insulators 10^{-20} to 10^{-10} ohm^{-1} m^{-1}

(iii) Semiconductors 10^{-6} to 10^4 ohm^{-1} m^{-1}

Conductivity of solids may be due to the movement of electrons, holes or ions or due to the presence of vacancies and other defects. Metals show electronic conductivity. Most metals crystallize in closed packed structures. The ability of metals to conduct electricity and heat must result from strong electronic interactions among 8 to 12 nearest neighbours. Bonding in metals is called metallic bonding. It is due to the electrical attractions among positively charged metal ions and mobile, delocalised electrons belonging to the crystal as a whole. Two models are considered to explain metallic bonding.

(a) Band model

(b) Electron sea model

Band Model

It is based on molecular orbital theory. According to this model a metal lattice consists of a large number of atoms. The atomic orbitals of these atoms with the same energy and same symmetry overlap to form energy bands. The energy bands formed from different atomic orbitals may overlap or be separated from each other. The highest occupied energy band is called the valence band and the lowest unoccupied energy band is called the conduction band. The energy gap between the bottom of the conduction band and top of the valence band is known as energy gap. *e.g.,*

- In case of **conductors** such as metals, the valence band is half filled or it overlaps with a higher energy unoccupied conduction band. Only a small amount of energy suffices to allow electrons to move within the conduction band. This movement of electrons within conduction band constitutes electrical conduction.

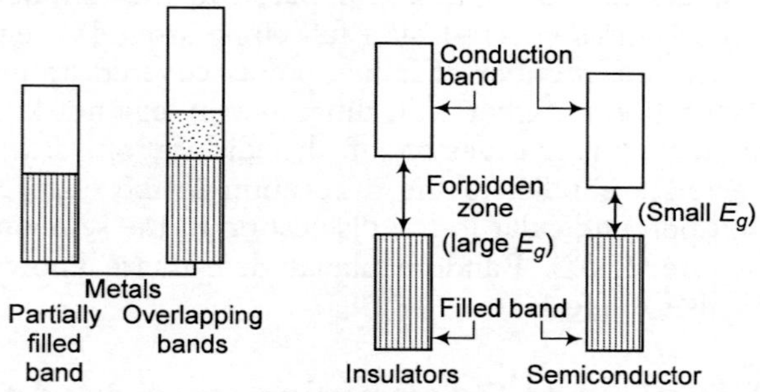

Fig. 26.33

- In case of **insulators**, the valence band is full and energy gap is very large. Therefore, the vacant conduction band is not available to the electrons of completely filled valence band. Rubber is an example of an insulator.
- In case of **semiconductors**, the gap between the valence band and conduction band is small. Therefore, some electrons of valence band can jump to the conduction band and show some conductivity. Electrical conductivity of semiconductors increases with rise in temperature, since, more electrons can jump to conduction band.

The conductivity of these intrinsic semiconductors (a semonconductor in 'its own right', it means no impurity has been added to it) is too low to be of practical use. The best known intrinsic semiconductors are silicon and germanium. Their conductivity is increased by adding an appropriate amount of suitable impurity. This process is called doping. Doping can be done with an impurity which is electron rich or electron deficient as compared to the intrinsic semiconductor such as Si or Ge.

Band Theory-Quantum Mechanical Aspect

In the free electron theory, it was assumed that the potential energy of the electrons is constant. This gave the result that the total energy of the electrons rises as a parabolic function of the quantum number n. Although the assumption of constancy of the potential energy was not so bad for metals, it is not tenable for ionic and covalent solids. In such solids, the valence electrons are localized at the atoms. Hence, the potential energy will vary periodically as an electron moves through the crystal.

The Schrodinger equation for a free electron moving in x direction is

$$\frac{d^2\psi}{dx^2} + \frac{8\pi^2 m}{h^2}(E - V)\psi = 0 \quad \ldots(8)$$

This, as we know, leads to the solution

$$\psi = \text{C}e^{\pm}\ 2\pi \frac{\sqrt{2m\,(E - V)}}{h}\, x \quad \ldots(9)$$

Let us now define, wave number $k = \frac{2\pi}{\lambda}\cdot$ Since, the kinetic energy $(E - V) = \frac{p^2}{2m}$, applying de-Broglie relation; we get $p = \frac{hk}{2\pi}$. This gives

$$E - V = \frac{h^2 K^2}{8\pi^2 m} \quad \ldots(10)$$

Substituting this in the Schrodinger equation, we obtain the general solution for a free electron moving at constant potential as

$$\psi(x) = \text{C}e^{\pm ikx} \quad \ldots(11)$$

According to the band theory, however, the potential energy V is not a constant but it is function of x and the Schrodinger equation is written as

$$\frac{d^2\psi}{dx^2} + \frac{8\pi^2 m}{h^2}[E - V(x)]\psi \qquad ...(12)$$

The solution of this equation was obtained by Bloch

$$\psi(x) = w_x(x)\, e^{\pm ikx} \qquad ...(13)$$

Where u_k is a periodic function. when the electron is moving in the x direction, the magnitude of $u_k(x)$ changes but has the same value at two points separated by the lattice spacing. this means.

$$u_k(x + a) = u_k(x) \qquad ...(14)$$

Where a is the lattice constant. $\psi(x)$ is known as Bloch function. The form of $u_k(x)$ depends on the direction in the crystal.

Kronig and Penney made the assumption that the potential energy is zero near the nucleus and is maximum V_0 at the point half way between two neighbouring nuclei. Further, they assumed the product of the potential height and the width ($V_0\ a$) as constant. They obtained the relation

$$\cos k\alpha = p\frac{\sin \alpha a}{\alpha a} + \cos \alpha a \qquad ...(15)$$

where $P = \frac{4\pi^2\ ma}{h^2} V_0\ \omega$ and $\alpha = \frac{2\pi}{h}\sqrt{2mE}$. Now, $\cos k\alpha$ can vary between $+1$ and -1 if k is real. This implies that only certain values of α are allowed which in turn, means that all values of energy E are not allowed.

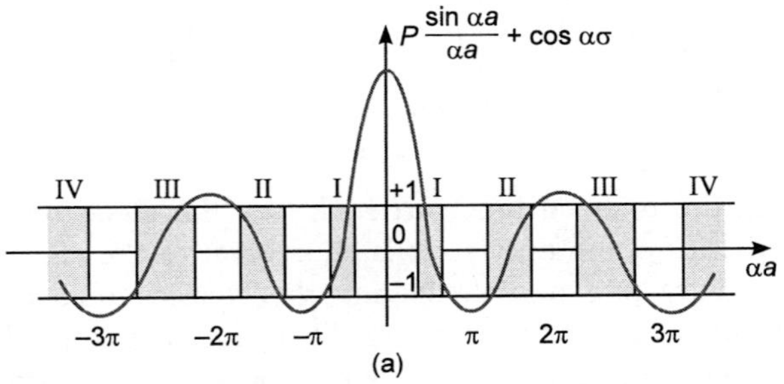

Fig. 26.34 Allowed values of αa arising due to the reason that $\cos k\alpha$ can only vary between + 1 and – 1.

Figure 26.34 represents the graphical solution of the equation (15). The allowed values of $\cos k\alpha$ are shown by the shaded regions. The permitted values of electron energy can be calculated from the relation between α and E. It can be seen that as energy increases, the width of the allowed energy zone increases. The width depends on the magnitude of P too. If $P \to \infty$, the allowed zone narrows to become discrete levels at $\alpha a = n\pi$ where n is a positive or negative integer. When $P \to 0$, the forbidden region disappears and the electron behaves like a free electron.

We see that if the electron in the crystal moves in a periodic field, it can only have energies lying within a certain zone. the electrons occupying the different energy levels (1*s*, 2*s*, 2*p*, 3*s*, 3*p*, 3*d* etc.) in the isolated atoms will form different allowed zones in the solid where these electrons experience a periodically changing potential. A plot of energy E against k for the different wave functions will show the periodic fluctuations as shown in Figure 26.35. Such plots are known as dispersion curves. It can be seen that for a linear chain of atoms arranged periodically, the possible energy values show distinct breaks at the lattice points. The dashed curve shows the energy variation according to the free electron model. In general, the higher the atomic energy level greater is the overlap of the atomic orbitals and broader is the energy band. This is why the higher atomic energy levels lead to the band formation and the lower energy levels essentially remain as in isolated atoms.

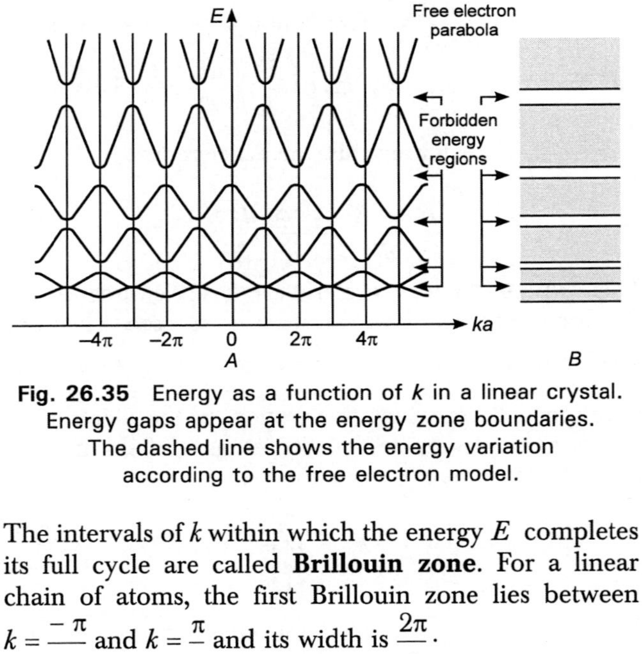

Fig. 26.35 Energy as a function of k in a linear crystal. Energy gaps appear at the energy zone boundaries. The dashed line shows the energy variation according to the free electron model.

The intervals of k within which the energy E completes its full cycle are called **Brillouin zone.** For a linear chain of atoms, the first Brillouin zone lies between $k = \frac{-\pi}{a}$ and $k = \frac{\pi}{a}$ and its width is $\frac{2\pi}{a}$.

Instead of showing the actual dispersion curve that bounds the various energy bands, parallel lines are drawn tangentially from the top and bottom of the energy bands. These two lines represent the upper and lower boundaries of an energy band and two such bands are separated by a forbidden energy gap E_g.

Effective mass of the electron From de-Broglie relation, we have $p = hK$ and the velocity of the electron $V = \frac{p}{m} = \left(\frac{h}{m}\right)k$. We have also seen earlier that for the free electron $E = \frac{h^2}{2m}k^2$. Differentiating with respect to k, we get

$$k = \frac{m}{h^2}\frac{dE}{dk} \quad ...(16)$$

From this, we get $p = \frac{m}{h}\frac{dE}{dk}$ and $v = \frac{1}{h}\frac{dE}{dk}$. These expressions for momentum and velocity are valid not only for the free electron but also for the electron moving in a periodic lattice.

In an external field ε is applied in the crystal, the force acting on the electron is

$$F = -q\varepsilon \quad ...(17)$$

The acceleration,

$$\frac{dv}{dt} = \frac{1}{h}\frac{d^2E}{dk^2}\frac{dk}{dt} \quad ...(18)$$

The work done by the force F in the interval dt is $dW = Fvdt = \frac{F}{h}\frac{dE}{dk}dt$. This amount of work increases the electron energy by $dE = \left(\frac{F}{h}\right)\left(\frac{dE}{dk}\right)dt$. This gives $\frac{F}{h} = \left(\frac{dk}{dt}\right)$. Substituting this, the acceleration

$$\frac{F}{h^2}\frac{d^2K}{dk^2} = \frac{-q\varepsilon}{h^2}\frac{d^2E}{dk^2} \quad ...(19)$$

This expression for acceleration is an expression of Newton's second law. If it was a free electron, acceleration would be given by $\frac{-q\varepsilon}{m}$. A similar equation will represent the motion of the electron in the periodic lattice under the external field if m is replaced by some m_{eff} such that

$$m_{eff} = \frac{h^2}{\frac{d^2E}{dk^2}} \quad ...(20)$$

The quantity m_{eff} is called the effective mass of the electron. By replacing m by m_{eff}, it is now possible to treat the electron moving in the periodic potential in the same way as one would treat a free electron with mass m. It encompasses all the details of electron movement in the lattice and can be either positive or negative. It can be either many times greater or many times smaller than the rest mass m.

In can be shown that m_{eff} is positive when an electron energy is close to the bottom of an energy band and negative when it is close to the top of an energy band and its absolute value is determined by the band width. Why does the electron behave in this manner?

The work done by the external field external field acting on a free electron goes only to increase its kinetic energy as it has no potential energy of any kind. Work done $W = E_k = \frac{mv^2}{2} = \frac{h^2}{2m}k^2$. Differentiating E_k with respect to k and substituting in the equation (20), we see that $m_{eff} = m$, the rest mass of the electron. In the case of electron in a periodic potential, the work done by the application of the external field goes to increase the kinetic energy as well as the potential energy of the electron. Since, the increase in kinetic energy and hence velocity is less than that of a free electron, the acceleration will be less as if the weight of the electron has increased. If the emitter work done by the external force is converted to potential energy, the effective mass will be infinite. If in the course of its motion a part of the initial kinetic energy along with the entire work done is converted to potential energy, the velocity of the electron will be decreasing and the effective mass will become negative as happens when the energy is close to the top of a band.

The hole The current due to the movement of the electron is $i_e = -$ ev. For a group of electrons it will be

$$i = -e\sum_s V_s \quad ...(21)$$

If the band is full, $i = 0$, because for every electron with velocity V_s, there is an electron with velocity $-V_s$. Suppose that all the states but one in a band are occupied. The total current now

$$i = -e\sum_{S\neq i} V_S = -e\sum_S V_S + eV_i \quad ...(22)$$

This gives the total current

$$i = +eV_i \quad ...(23)$$

Thus, the total current carried by all the electrons in band with one empty state is equivalent to the current carried by one particle having the charge equal and opposite to that of an electron. This particle is termed a hole. The concept of hole makes it possible to consider the complex motion of a large number of electrons to a much simplified picture of motion of a fewer number of holes. The effective mass of the hole is the same as that of the electron that occupied the state.

n-type Semiconductor

When silicon and germanium (14th group elements) doped with a group 15 element like phosphorus or arsenic, which contains five valence electrons, they occupy some of the lattice sites in Si or Ge crystal. Four out of five valence electrons are used in the formation of four covalent bonds with the four neighbour Si atoms. The fifth electron is extra and becomes delocalized. These delocalized electrons increase the conductivity of doped Si or Ge. Since, current is carried by excess electrons this is known as ***n*-type semiconduction** and the Si or Ge doped with electron rich impurity is known as *n*-type semiconductor. Electrons of donor atoms (P or As) are localized and form filled donor band which lies below empty conduction band of the lattice.

The magnitude of semiconductivity in an extrinsic semiconductor is far greater than that in an intrinsic pure semiconductor.

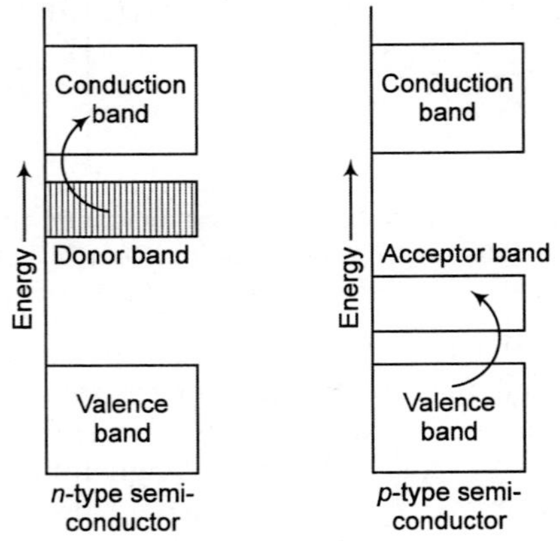

Fig. 26.36

In ZnO, the lattice consists of an excess of zinc atoms in the interstitials resulting in a formula of $Zn_{(1+X)}O$. Each such excess atom has two valence electrons forming a donor level just below the conduction band. The electrons can jump from the Zn atom to a neighbouring Zn ion making it an atom, while itself becoming an ion. The electron hops from atom to ion in this way under an applied electrical field. This metal-excess type (*n*-type) also occurs in TiO_2. In general, if a metal ion in a compound has an easily accessible lower oxidation state, it would be an *n*-type semiconductor.

p-type Semiconductor

When silicon or germanium doped with a group 13 element like boron, aluminium or gallium which contains three valence electrons they occupy some of the lattice sites in Si or Ge crystal. Each B or Al or Ga atom form three covalent bonds with three neighbour Si atoms. One bond is incomplete and the site which remains unoccupied because of missing electron is called a positive hole. The dopant atoms form a very narrow empty **acceptor band** which lies above the full silicon or germanium valence band. At zero kelvin, the acceptor band is empty but as the temperature increases from zero kelvin, it can accept thermally excited electrons from Si or Ge valence band. As a result of this new positive holes are formed in Si valence band and the holes appear to move in a direction opposite to the motion of electrons. Since, the charge carriers are positively charged holes, this type of conduction is known as ***p*-type semiconduction** and the Si or Ge doped with electron deficient impurity is known as *p*-type semiconductor.

NiO provides an example of the *p*-type semiconduction through non-stoichiometry. In the Ni^{2+} lattice, a vacancy occasionally occurs; in order to maintain charge balance, two Ni^{2+} positions are replaced by Ni^{3+} ions. The extra charge on the Ni ion is known as a hole (absence of an electron). An electron from a neighbouring Ni^{2+} can migrate to this Ni^{3+} making it an Ni^{2+}, and rendering the Ni^{2+} into an Ni^{3+}. This in effect is a hole movement from Ni^{3+} to Ni^{2+}.Oxides such has CuO, Ag_2O and FeO exemplify this *p*-type semiconduction. These are metal -deficient oxides of the general formula $M_{(1-x)}O$, or $M(2-x)O$. Metal ion in a lattice with an easily accessible higher oxidation state available would form this type of semiconductors. Through oxide-excess (oxygen atoms in interstitials) can also result in a *p*-type semiconduction, this is very scarce because of the larger size of the oxide anion which would not fit into an interstitial. Non-stoichiometric compounds are found to exist over a wide range of composition and throughout this range the electrical conductivity and the unit cell size varies smoothly with composition without any change in symmetry (Vegard's law).

Application of *n*-type and *p*-type Semiconductors

Various combinations of *n*-type and *p*-type semiconductors are used for making electronic components. Diode is a combination of *n*-type and *p*-type semiconductors and is used as rectifier.

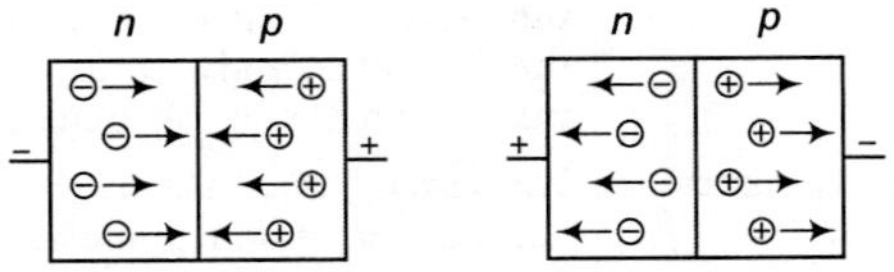

Fig. 26.37 Semiconductor acting as rectifier.

Transistors used to detect or amplify radio or audio signals are made by sandwiching a layer of one type of semiconductor between two layers of the other type of semiconductor (*n*-*p*-*n* and *p*-*n*-*p* type transistor).

A large variety of solid state materials have been prepared by combination of groups 13 and 15 or 12 and 16 to stimulate average valence of four as in Ge or

Si. Typical compounds of groups 13-15 are InSb, AlP and GaAs. ZnS, CdS, CdSe and HgTe are examples of groups 12-16 compounds.

Effect of Temperature on Conductivity

The conductivity of metals usually decreases with rise in temperature, while that of semiconductors increases. The conductivity of insulators, however increases to very small extent.

Some oxides of elements of fourth period of Periodic Table have electrical behaviour as metals (*M*) insulator (*I*) and a transition from metal to insulator (*T*) behaviour at certain temperature. Table 26.5).

Table 26.5

TiO(*M*)	VO(*M*)		MnO(*I*)	FeO(*I*) CoO(*I*) NiO(*I*) CuO(*I*)
$Ti_2O_3(T)$ $TiO_3(I)$	$V_2O_3(T)$ $VO_2(T)$ $V_2O_5(I)$	$Cr_2O_3(I)$ $CrO_2(M)$	$Mn_2O_3(I)$ $MnO_2(I)$	$Fe_2O_3(I)$

Sulphides of above elements bahave similarly. It has been observed that those transition metal oxides (*M*O) which have similar NaCl structure have different electrical properties. Some of these behave as metals, while some others behave as semiconductors or insulators.

Magnetic Properties

Every substance has some magnetic properties associated with it. The origin of these properties lies in electron. Each electron in an atom has magnetic moment arising as a result of its orbital motion around the nucleus and its spin around its own axis.

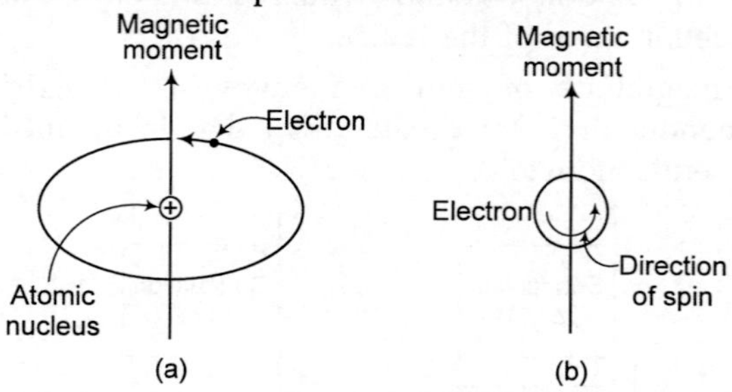

Fig. 26.38 Demonstration of the magnetic moment associated with (a) an orbiting electron and (b) a spinning electron.

Thus, each electron in an atom may be thought of as being a small magnet having permanent orbital and spin magnetic moments. The fundamental magnetic moment is the Bohr Magneton, μ_B ($= 9.27 \times 10^{-24}$ Am^2). On the basis of their magnetic properties, substances can be classified into five categories.

Table 26.6

S. No.	Properties	Description	Alignment of magnetic dipoles	Examples	Applications
1.	Diamagnetic	Feebly repelled by the magnetic fields. Non-metallic elements (except O_2, S) inert gases and species with paired electrons are diamagnetic.	All paired electrons ↑↓↑↓↑↓	TiO_2, V_2O_5, NaCl, C_6H_6 (benzene)	Insulator
2.	Paramagnetic	Attracted by the magnetic field due to the presence of permanent magnetic dipoles (unpaired electrons). In magnetic field, these tend to orient themselves parallel to the direction of the field and thus, produce magnetism in the substances.	↑↓↑↑ at least one unpaired electron	O_2, Cu^{2+}, Fe^{3+}, TiO, Ti_2O_3, VO, VO_2, CuO	Electronic appliances
3.	Ferromagnetic	Permanent magnetism even in the absence of magnetic field. Above a temperature called **Curie** temperature, there is no ferromagnetism.	Dipoles are aligned in the same direction ↑↑↑↑↑	Fe, Ni, Co, CrO_2	CrO_2 is used in audio and video tapes
4.	Antiferromagnetic	This arises when net dipole alignment is zero due to equal and opposite alignment.	↑↓↑↓↑↓	MnO, MnO_2, Mn_2O, FeO, Fe_2O_3, NiO, Cr_2O_3, CoO, Co_3O_4	—
5.	Ferrimagnetic	This arises when there is net dipole moment.	↑↓↓↓↑↓	Fe_3O_4, ferrites	—

Dielectric Properties

When a non-conducting material is placed in an electrical field, the electrons and the nuclei in the atom or molecule of that material are pulled in the opposite directions and negative and positive charges are separated and dipoles are generated. In an electric field these dipoles may align themselves in the same direction, so that there is net dipole moment in the crystal or these dipoles may align themselves in such a manner that the net dipole moment in the crystal is zero.

Table 26.7

S. No.	Property	Description	Alignment of electric dipoles	Examples	Applications
1.	Piezoelectricity	When polar crystal is subjected to a mechanical stress, electricity is produced-a case of piezoelectricity. Reversely if electric field is applied, mechanical stress is developed. Piezoelectric crystal acts as a mechanical electrical transducer.			Record players
		• Piezoelectric crystals with permanent dipoles are said to have **ferroelectricity.**	↑↑↑↑↑	$BaTiO_3$, KH_2PO_4 Rochelle salt	
		• Piezoelectric crystals with zero dipole are said to have **antiferroelectricity.**	↑↓↑↓↑↓	$PbZrO_3$	
2.	Pyroelectricity	Small electric current is produced due to heating of some of polar crystals a case of pyroelectricity.	—		

Superconductors

Introduction

Superconductors which can function well above absolute zero of temperature were discovered by Bednorz and Muller in 1936.

Superconductors have two unique properties First, they have zero electrical resistance and so carry current with no energy loss : this could revolutionize the national grid for instance, and is already exploited in the windings of superconducting magnets as used in NMR experiments. Second, they expel all magnetic flux from their interior and so are forced out of a magnetic field. The superconductors can float or 'levitate' above a magnetic field : the Japanese have an experimental frictionless train that floats above magnetic rails and has achieved speeds of over 500 kmh^{-1} (300 mph). The posibilites are exciting, but until recently there has always been the major snag that superconductivity was observed only at temperatures close to absolute zero. Until 1986, the highest temperature a superconductor operated at was 23 K, and so they all had to be cooled by liquid helium (boiling temperature ≈ 4 K).

For many years, efforts were on to find a superconductor that will operate at the very least at liquid nitrogen temperatures (above 77 K) so as to be commercially viable, hoping, eventually for a room-temperature superconductor. The events of recent years have brought the operating temperatures above the liquid nitrogen temperature, and there may be evidence for superconductivity being observed above 200 K. A room temperature superconductor, has not been reported yet.

In 1908, Kamerlingh Onnes succeeded in liquefying helium, and this paved the way for many new experiments to be performed on the bahaviour of materials at low temperatures : For a long time, it had been known from conductivity experiments that the electrical resistance of a metal decreases with temperature. In 1911, Onness was measuring the variation of the electrical resistance of mercury with temperature when he was amazed to find that at 4.2 K the resistance suddenly dropped to zero. He called this effect **superconductivity** and the temperature at which it occurs is known as the (superconducting) critical temperature, T_c. This effect is illustrated for tin in Figure 26.39. One effect of the zero resistance is that there is no power loss in an electrical circuit made from a superconductor.

For more than 20 years, little progress was made in the understanding of superconductors and only more substances exhibiting the effect were found. More than

20 metallic elements can be made superconducting under suitable conditions (Figure 26.40), as can thousands of alloys. It was not until 1933 that a new effect was observed by Meissner.

The Magnetic properties of Superconductors

Meissner and Ochsenfeld found that when a superconducting material is cooled below its critical temperature, T_c, it expels all magnetic flux from within its interior (Figure 26.41 (a)); the magnetic flux, B is thus zero inside a superconductor. Since $B - \mu_0 H(1 + \chi)$, when $B = 0$, χ must equal – 1, *i.e.,* superconductors are perfect diamagnets. If a magnetic field is applied to a superconductor, the magnetic flux is excluded (Figure 26.41 (b) and the superconductor repels a magnet.

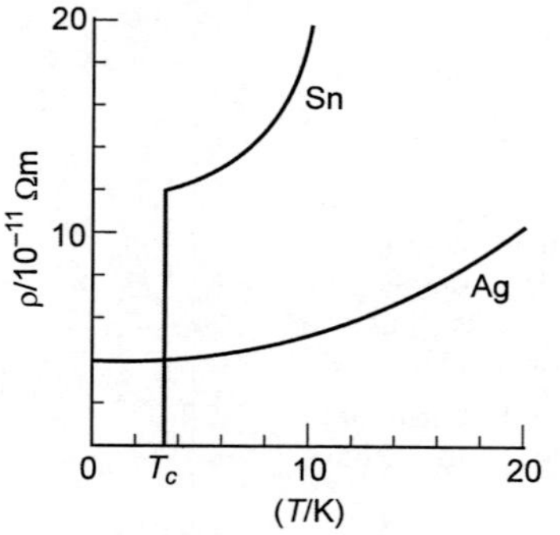

Fig. 26.39 A plot of resistivity, ρ *versus* temperature *T*, showing the drop to zero at the critical temperature. T_c, for a superconductor, and the finite resistivity of a normal metal at absolute zero.

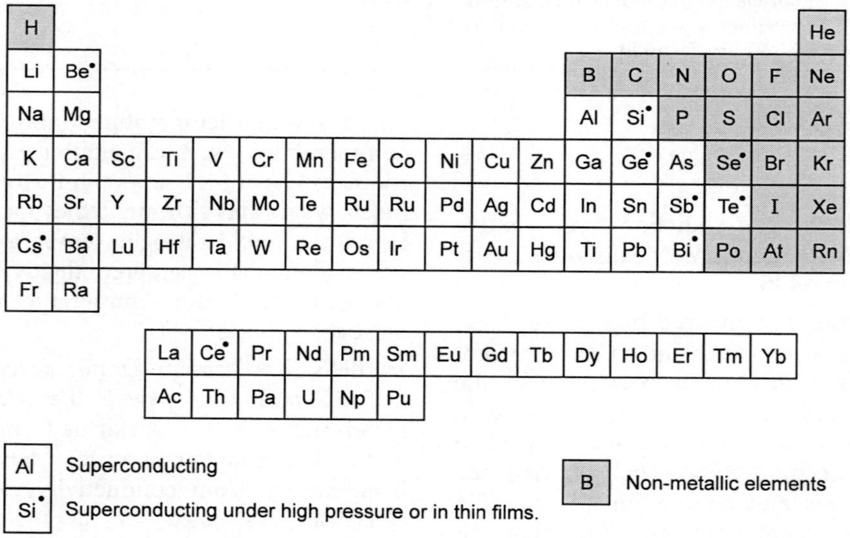

Fig. 26.40 The superconductivity elements.

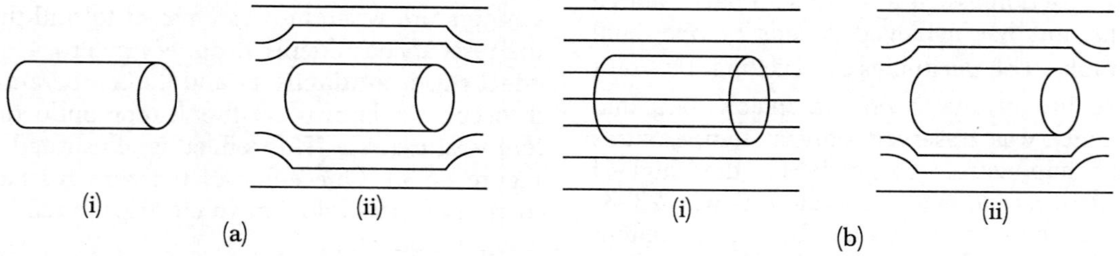

Fig. 26.41 (a) (i) Superconductor with no magnetic field. When a field is applied in (ii) the magnetic flux is excluded. (b) (i) Superconducting substance above the critical temperature, T_c, in a magnetic field. When the temperature drops below the critical temperature (ii), the magnetic flux is expelled from the interior. Both are called Meissner effects.

It is also found that T_c, changes in the presence of a magnetic field. *A* typical plot of T_c against increasing magnetic field is shown in Figure. 26.42. as the applied field increases, the critical temperature drops. It follows that a superconducting material can be made non-superconducting by the application of a large enough magnetic field. The minimum value of the field strength required to bring about this change is called the **critical field strength.**H_c; its value depending on the material in question and on the temperature.

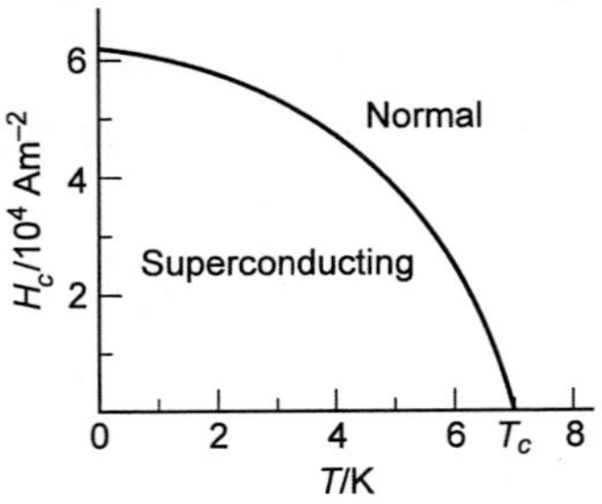

Fig. 26.42 The variation with temperature of the critical field strength, H_c, for lead. Note that H_c is zero when the temperature, T, equals the critical temperature T_c.

Similarly, if the current in the superconductor exceeds a **critical current,** the superconductivity is destroyed. This is known as the **Silsbee effect.** The size of the critical current is dependent on the nature and geometry of the particular sample.

The Theory of Superconductivity

To begin with, it looked as through the lattice played no part in the superconducting mechanism as X-ray studies showed that there was no change in either the symmetry or the spacing of the lattice when superconductivity occurred. However, in 1950, an **isotope effect** was first observed : for a particular metal, the critical temperature was found on the isotopic mass, M, such that

$$T_c \propto \frac{1}{\sqrt{M}}$$

The frequency v, of vibration of a diatomic molecules is known to be given by

$$v = \frac{1}{2\pi}\sqrt{\frac{k}{\mu}}$$

where μ is the reduced mass of the molecule, and k the force constant of the bond. We can see that a vibration also changes frequency on isotopic substitution such that the frequency, v is proportional to $\frac{1}{\sqrt{\text{mass}}}$. This suggested to physicists that superconductivity was in some way related to the vibrational modes of the lattice and not just to the conduction electrons. The vibrational modes of a lattice are quantized, as are the modes of an isolated molecule, the quanta of the lattice vibrations being called **phonons.**

Frohlich suggested that there could be a strong phonon-electron interaction in a superconductor that leads to an attractive force between two electrons that is strong enough to overcome the Coulomb repulsion between them. Very simply, the mechanism works like this : as a conduction electron passes through the lattice, it can disturb some of the positively charged ions from their equilibrium positions, pushing them together and giving a region of increased positive charge density. As these oscillate back and forth, a second electron passing this moving region of increased positive charge density is attracted to it. The net effect is that the two electrons have interacted with one another, using the lattice vibration as an intermediary. Furthermore, the interaction between the electrons is attractive because each of the two separate steps involved an attractive Coulomb interaction.

It is the scattering of conduction electrons by the lattice vibrations, phonons that produces electrical resistance at room temperature. (At low temperatures it is predominantly the scattering by lattice defects that gives electrical resistance.) Contrary to what we might have expected intuitively, a superconductor will have high resistance at room temperature, because it has strong electron-phonon interactions. Indeed, the best room-temperature electronic conductors, silver and copper, do not superconduct at all ! Superconductors do not have low electrical resistance above the superconducting T_c.

In 1957, Bardeen, Cooper and Schrieffer published their theory of superconductivity, known as the **BCS theory.** It predicts that under certain conditions, the attraction between two conduction electrons due to a succession of phonon interactions can slightly exceed the repulsion that they exert directly on one another due to the Coulomb interaction of their like charges. The two electrons are thus weakly bound together forming a so-called **Copper pair.** It is these Cooper pairs that are responsible for superconductivity.

BCS theory shows that there are several conditions that have to be met for a sufficient number of Cooper pairs to be formed and superconductivity to be achieved. The electron-phonon interaction must be strong and low temperature favours pair formation, hence, high temperature superconductors are not presdicted by BCS theory.

Cooper pairs are weakly bound, with typical separations of 10^6 pm for the two electrons. They are also constantly breaking up and reforming (usually with other partners). There is thus enormous overlap between different pairs and the pairing is a complicated dynamic process. The ground state of a superconductor therefore is a collective state, describing the ordered motion of large numbers of Cooper pairs. When an external electrical field is applied, the Cooper pairs move through the lattice under its influence. However, they do so in such a way that the ordering of the pairs is maintained. The motion of each pair is looked to the motion of all the others, and none of them can be individually scattered by the lattice. Because the pairs cannot be scattered by the lattice, the resistance is zero and the system is a superconductor.

Josephson Effect

In 1962 Josephson predicted that if two superconducting metals were placed next to each other separated only by a thin insulating layer (such a their surface oxide coating) then a current would flow in the absence of any applied voltage. This effect is indeed observed because if the barrier is not too thick then electron pairs can cross the junction from one superconductor to the other without dissociating. This is known as the **d.c. Josephson effect.** He further predicted that the application of a small d.c. electric potential to such a junction would produce a small alternating current, the **a.c. Josephson effect.** These two properties are of great interest to the electronics and computing industries where they can be exploited for fast-switching purposes.

The Search for a High-Temperature Superconductor

By 1973, the highest temperature found for the onset of superconductivity was 23.3 K. This was for a compound of niobium and germanium, Nb_3Ge, and here it stayed until 1986 when Georg Bednorz and Alex Muller reported their findings. Their Nobel Prize citation states 'Last year, 1986, Bednorz and Muller reported finding. Superconductivity in an oxide material at a temperature 12°C higher than previously known'. The compound that prompted their initial paper has been shown to be $La_{2-x}Ba_xCuO_4$, where $x = 0.2$, with a structure based on that of K_2NiF_4, a perovskite-related layer compound : they observed the onset of superconductivity at 35 K. The insight that they brought to this field was to move away from the investigation of metals and their alloys and to study systematically the solid state about physics and chemistry of metallic oxides.

The idea was soon born that it might be possible to raise the temperature even further by substitution with different metals. Using this technique, it was Chu's group at Houston, Taxes that finally broke through the liquid nitrogen temperature barrier with the superconductor that is now known as '1-2-3' (from the proportions of the metal atoms in the compound). This superconductor replaces lanthanum with yttrium and has the formula $YBa_2Cu_3O_{7-x}$. The onset of superconductivity for 1-2-3 occurs at 93 K.

The Crystal Structures of High-Temperature Superconductors

The perovskite structure is named after the mineral $CaTiO_3$. Many oxides of general formula ABO_3 adopt this structure (also fluorides, ABF_3 and sulphide, ABS_3)

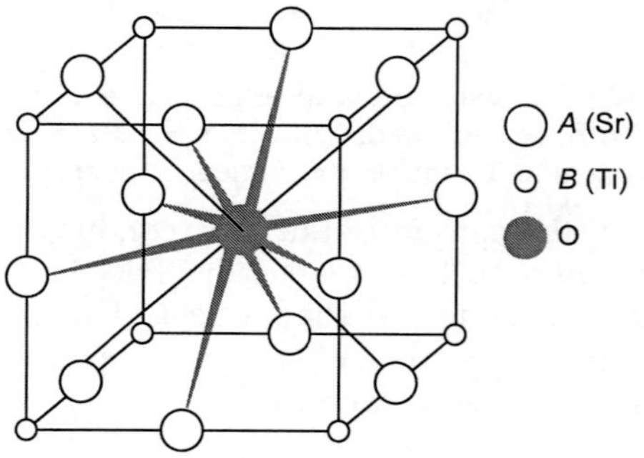

Fig. 26.43 The *A*-type unit cell of perovskite structure for compounds ABO_3, such as $SrTi_2O_3$.

The so-called perovskite *A*-type unit cell (with the *A*-type atom in the centre of the cell) is shown in Figure 26.43. The central *A* atom (Sr) is coordinated by eight titaniums at the corners of the cube and by 12 oxygens at the mid-points of the edges. The perovskite structure can be equally well represented by moving the origin of the unit cell to the body centre. This has the effect of putting Sr (*A*) atoms at each corner, Ti (*B*) atoms at the body centre and an O atom in the centre of each face (Figure 26.44)

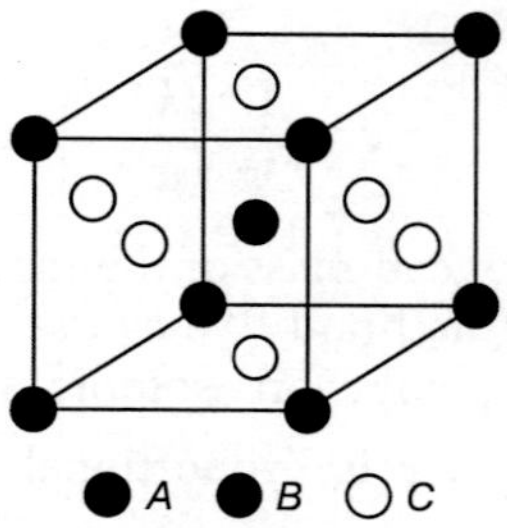

Fig. 26.44 *B*-type cell for the ABO_3 perovskite structure.

The K_2NiF_4 structure is adopted by the Bednorz/Muller superconductor $La_{2-x}Ba_xCuO_4$. Its unit cell, and its relationship to the perovskite structure is illustrated in Figure 26.45. The structure has a body centred tetragonal cell. We can get more in sight into the structure by dividing it up into three sections along its *c* direction (Figure 26.45 (a)). The central section is a *B*-type perovskite unit cell, and this is sandwiched by two *A*-type cells that have their bottom and top layers, respectively, missing (they are shown by dotted atomic positions). The lanthanum and barium atoms are similar in size and they are randomly distributed amongst the K (*A*) atom positions in the structure. Cu takes the Ni (*B*) positions. Notice that the *A*-type atoms (K or La/Ba) are surrounded only by nine oxygens in this structure whereas *A* was coordinated by 12 equidistant oxygens in the basic perovskite structure.

For the sake of simplicity each section of the unit cell has been shown as a cube. In practice, the central section is slightly elongated in the *c* direction and the Cu atoms are coordinated by an elongated octahedron of six Os (and by eight La/Bask at the corners). This elongation is a Jahn-Teller effect and is the reason that Bednorz and Muller chose to investigate these copper oxides for superconductivity. The copper atoms and the four closest oxygen atoms lie in the *ab* planes forming networks of the copper and oxygen atoms separated by planes of other atoms. It is this planar arrangement of copper and oxygen atoms that confers the superconducting properties on the crystal.

The parent compound La_2CuO_4 (without any barium in the lattice) has no superconductivity. This is because the parent compound is anti-ferromagnetic. This crystal contains Cu^{2+} ions and the unpaired electrons on the copper ions align anti-parallel throughout the structure. The presence of this interaction locks the electrons to the lattice stopping both conductivity and superconductivity very effectively. When some barium (Ba^{2+}) is introduced into the lattice replacing lanthanum (La^{3+}), obviously some charge compensation has to be made in order to preserve electrical neutrality. For every Ba^{2+} present, one Cu^{II} must be oxidized to Cu^{III} and this breaks up the alignment of the unpaired spins. When the average valence of the copper atoms reaches a critical value of ≈ 2.2 the antiferromagnetism disappears and superconductivity appears. (Substitution with strontium or calcium also produces superconductivity.) It has been observed that if pressure is applied to the compound, such that the Cu–O distance decreases, then T_c increases. There is also a general correlation of higher T_c with higher Cu (III) content : a Cu (III)–O bond is shorter than a CU (II)–O bond because the electron is removed from an anti-bonding e_g orbital. These two observations are not necessarily related because the high-pressure studies show an increase of T_c

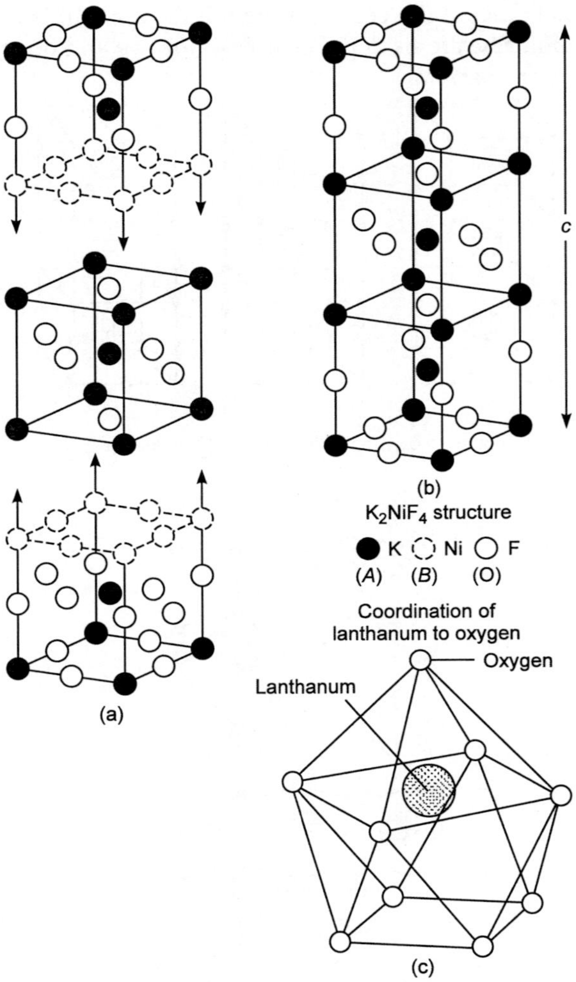

Fig. 16.45 (a) and (b) show the K_2NiF_4 structure derived from perovskite type (ABO_3) unit cells as adopted by $La_{2-x}Ba_xCuO_4$ (c) The nine-fold coordination of lanthanum by oxygen in this structure.

with decrease in Cu–O distance, without any change in the Cu (III) content of the compound.

The crystal structure of the 1-2-3 superconductor, $YBa_2Cu_3O_{7-x}$ is shown in Figure 26.46. Figure 26.46 (a) shows only the positions of the metal atoms : note the strong similarity between this and the structure of $La_{2-x}Ba_xCuO_4$. If, as before we discuss it in terms of the perovskite structure ABO_3, where B = Cu the central section is now an *A*-type pervoskite unit cell and above and below it are also *A*-type perovskite unit cells with their bottom and top layers missing. This gives copper atoms at the unit cell corners and on the unit cell edges at fractional coordinates $\frac{1}{3}$ and $\frac{2}{3}$. The atom at the body centre of the cell (*i.e.*, in the centre of the middle section) is now yttrium. The atoms in the centres of the top and bottom cubes are barium.

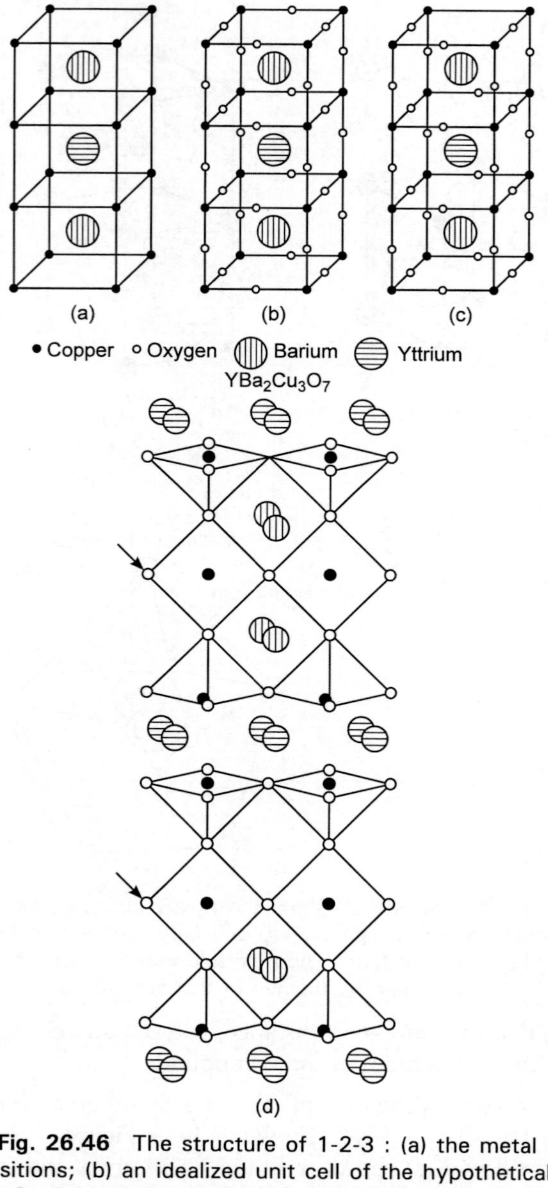

Fig. 26.46 The structure of 1-2-3 : (a) the metal positions; (b) an idealized unit cell of the hypothetical $YBa_2Cu_3O_9$, based on three pernovskite *A*-type unit cells; (c) indealized structure of $YBa_2Cu_3O_{7-x}$ (d) the structure of $YBa_2Cu_3O_7$, showing copper-oxygen planes formed by the bases of the pyramids, with copper-oxygen diamonds in between.

If in this structure, all three sections were based exactly on perovskite unit cells, we would expect to find the oxygen atoms in the middle of each cube edge (Figure 24.46 (b)). This would give an overall formula of $YBa_2Cu_3O_9$. This formula is improbable because it gives an average oxidation state for the three copper atoms of $\frac{11}{3}$ implying that the unit cell contains both Cu (III) and Cu(IV), which is unlikely as Cu(IV) complexes are extremely rare. The unit cell in fact contains only approximately seven oxygen atoms ($YBa_2Cu_3O_{7-x}$). When $x = 0$, then oxygen atoms on the vertical edges of the central cube are not here and there are also two missing from both the top and bottom faces. (Figure 26.46 (c)). A unit cell containing seven oxygen atoms has an average copper oxidation state of 2.33 indicating the presence of Cu (II) and Cu (III) in the unit cell (but no longer Cu (IV).

In the 1-2-3 structure (when $x = 0$) the yttrium atom is coordinated by eight oxygens and the barium atoms by 10 oxygens. The oxygen vacancies in the 1-2-3 superconductor create sheets and chains of linked copper and oxygen atoms running through the structure (this is known slightly idealized in the diagrams as, in practice, the copper atoms lie slightly out of the plane of the oxygens); the copper is in four-fold square-planar or five-fold square-pyramidal coordination. (Figure 26.46 (d). The superconductivity is found in directions parallel to the copper planes which are created by the bases of the Cu–O pyramids and which are separated by layers of yttrium atoms. These Cu–O nets seem to be a common feature of all the new high-temperature superconductors. If this superconductor is made more deficient in oxygen, at $YBa_2Cu_3O_{6.5}$ ($x = 0.5$) the superconducting T_c, drops to 60 K and at $YBa_2Cu_3O_6$ the superconductivity disappears. The oxygen is not lost at random but goes from specific sites, gradually changing the square-planar coordination of the copper along the *c* direction into the two-fold linear coordination characteristic of Cu^+. The sites from which the oxygen atoms are lost are indicated by arrows in (Figure 26.46 (d)). The arrangement of the copper and oxygen atoms in the base of the pyramids is not affected. However, when the formula is $YBa_2Cu_3O_6$ all the square planar units along *c* have become chains containing Cu^+ and the pyramid bases contain only Cu^{2+}; the unpaired spins of the Cu^{2+} are aligned antiparallel and the compound is antiferromagnetic. It is not until the oxygen content is increased to $YBa_2Cu_3O_{6.5}$ that the antiferromagnetic properties are destroyed and the compound becomes a superconductor. It is thought that this compound contains copper in all three oxidation states : I, II and III. $YBa_2Cu_3O_7$ contains Cu (II) and Cu (III) both in the sheets and the chains. Clearly the oxidation state of the coppers in the structure (and thus their bonding connections and bond lengths) is extremely important in determining both, whether superconductivity occurs at all, and the temperature below which it occurs (T_c).

In both of the superconductors discussed here the average oxidation state of the copper is greater than two and as a result positive holes are formed in the valence bands. The charge is carried by the positive holes and as a consequence these materials are known as ***p*-type superconductors.** Until 1988, all the high temperature superconductors that had been found were *p*-type and it was assumed by many that this would be a feature of high-temperature superconductor. However, some *n*-type superconductors have now also been discovered where the charge carriers are electrons. The first to be found was based on the compound Nd_2CuO_4 with small amounts of the three-valent neodymium substituted by four-valent cerium, $Nd_{2-x}Ce_xCuO_{4-y}$ where $x = 0.17$ (samarium, europium or aseodymium can also be substituted for the neodymium). Other similar compounds have since been found based on this structure where the three-valent lanthanide is substituted by, for example, four-valent thorium in $Nd_{2-x}Th_xCuO_{4-y}$. The superconductivity occurs at $T_c \leq 25$ K for these compounds.

Till 1991 the superconductors with the highest known critical temperatures are formed from thallium, barium, calcium, bismuth, copper and oxygen. Again the characteristic Cu–O planes are present, interspersed by ones containing thallium and oxygen. The highest T_c reported so far for this series of compounds is 125 K for $Tl_2Ba_2CaCu_3O_{10}$.

It seems clear that these new ceramic superconductors all have a common feature : the presence of Cu–O layers sandwiched between layers of other elements. The superconductivity takes place in these planes and the other elements present and the spacings between the planes change the superconducting transition temperature; exactly how is not yet understood. Theoretical physicists have been working hard to try and explain the phenomenon of high-temperature superconductivity, but with no clear consensus so far. It has been hoped that the later discovery of *n*-type superconductors will shed some light on the problem. BCS theory does not account for all the evidence concerning high-temperature superconductors; first, the net attraction resulting from the lattice does not appear to be strong enough to account for the high T_c values and second, although there is evidence that pairs of electrons are still responsible for high-temperature superconductivity, it is not yet clear whether they interact with each other *via* a lattice vibration, because the isotopic substitution data are contradictory.

Potential Uses of High-Temperature Superconductors

In order to be useful in many of the possible applications of superconductors the new high-temperature superconductors have to meet some fairly stringent criteria : they have to be able to carry currents of more than 10^9 Am^{-2} (100000 A cm^{-2}); withstand strong magnetic field (up to 5T) and be physically strong enough to be used in motors and generators. For some of the uses bulk samples will not be useful and the material will need to be available in the form of wire, tape or thin film. Added to this, the benefits of using the new materials (better performance or cheaper running costs, for instance) have to outweigh any extra capital costs that may be needed to change to the new technology.

Making useful products in the form of wire or tape has proved to be difficult. They are made from a powdered mixture of superconductor and polymer which is formed into the appropriate shape, sintered, then annealed; unfortunately the product tends to be brittle. Another problem is that the 1-2-3 superconductor tends to lose oxygen, and therefore its superconductivity at the same time; other ceramics may not have this same problem. It has proved possible to make thin films that can carry large currents-of the order of 10^6 A cm^{-2} (10^{10-} Am^{-2}) and it may be feasible to mount these films on a backing tape that can be wound or shaped.

The uses of superconductors are based around four main properties the Meissner effect, the lack of electrical resistance, the ability to create superconducting magnets and the Josephson effect. We will look at each area in turn.

The property of superconductors that has received most publicity is the Meissner effect, the ability to expel magnetic flux from the interior and so float or levitate above a magnet. The Japanese have been developing a magnetically levitating train, the so called **'maglev,'** using low-temperature superconducting magnets. USe of the new high-temperature superconductors instead, should reduce the refrigeration costs of the project. Unfortunately, refrigeration is only a very small percentage of both the capital and running costs and so will probably not make the difference as to whether this becomes a viable node of transport or not. The hope is to produce a train that can travel at several hundreds of kilometers per hour and so compete with flying over short and medium length journeys.

Conventional electromagnets (made by passing an electric current through insulated copper wire wound around an iron core) can produce fields of about two tesla. Low-temperature superconducting magnets are manufactured from both NbTi and Nb_3Sn wires which can carry much higher currents than copper wire (≈ 400000 A cm^{-2}) and so eliminate the need for the amplifying iron core. Such superconducting magnets are both lighter and more powerful (≈ 10 T) than their conventional counterparts, consume very little power, and produce little heat, but they have to be cooled to 4 K to become superconducting. If the windings could be replaced by high-temperature superconductors the liquid helium coolant (priced in pounds per litre) would be replaced by liquid nitrogen (priced in pence per litre) thus dramatically reducing the running costs. It might also be possible to produce even larger value magnetic fields than currently achieved.

Low-temperature superconducting magnets are currently employed for several important uses. Strong magnets are used to remove impurities from food and raw materials; for instance, the magnetic impurities in China clay discolour the manufactured product if not removed. The latest NMR spectrometers employ superconducting magnets to provide large magnetic fields, so improving sensitivity. They are an important tool in fundamental scientific research, and are increasingly being used in body scanners for NMR imaging used in medical diagnosis. However, the prospect of high-temperature supermagnets still seems a long way off, until a wire is developed that can carry the kind of current densities possible for the niobium alloys.

Electrical generators produce power, by spinning a magnet inside a coil; an electrical current is produced in the coil. it is thought that the use of a superconducting magnet would make the process more efficient and the electricity a little cheaper. As with many of the other possible uses for the high-temperature superconductors, the percentage savings would be quite small,perhaps 1%, and whether this will ever offset the immense capital investment required is not clear.

Although superconductors carry direct current (d.c.) with no loss of power and without generating heat, there is a small loss of power when they carry alternating current (a.c.) due to the production of radio waves. This absence of electrical resistance could be extremely useful in the distribution of electricity throughout the country, as the copper and aluminium wires now used loss 5-8% of the power due to the resistance of these elements. The superconducting wire (once it could be manufactured) is unlikely to be strong enough to be suspended from pylons, this mean to all the cables, together with the cooling system, would have to be at ground level or buried underground-an expensive capital outlay! On the hand, the environmental pressure groups would be greatly in favour of this, both for esthetic and for safety reasons.

A supermagnetic energy storage unit (SMES) has seen designed that could store a massive amount of direct current with no energy loss. This design currently uses NbTi alloy and the liquid helium calling system. It would be used to store electricity generated at times of low demand, at night or in the summer for instance. A liquid nitrogen cooling system would be cheaper to build and to run.

Josephson junctions have been of great interest to the electronics industry because they can be used for switching voltages very quickly. As they do so, they consume very little power and thus do not heat up. This means that they can be packed very close together without the need for elaborate cooling, giving the potential for making smaller and faster computers. IBM expended much time and research on building a Josephson computer based on these junctions. Sadly, the project was eventually abandoned because they found the memory cells unereliable. Japanese workers are still continuing the research,but in the meantime semiconductor technology reigns supreme.

Josephson junctions are used in Superconducting Quantum Interference Devices (SQUIDs). These consist of a loop of superconductive wire with either one built in Josephson junction (RFSQUID) or two (DCSQUID). The device is extremely sensitive to changes in magnetic field, and can measure voltages as small as 10^{-18} V, current of 10^{-18} A and magnetic field of 10^{-14} T. SQUIDs are being used in medical research to detect small changes in magnetic field in the brain. Geologists are able to employ SQUIDs in prospecting for minerals and oil where deposits can cause small local changes in the earths magnetic field.

Solid State Reactions

Manu useful solids are prepared by reactions between and a liquid or between a solid and a gas. It has been found useful to classify such a reaction based on the physical state of the reactants and the products involved in the reaction as shown below :

Type I : $A(s) \longrightarrow B(s) + C(g);$

Type II : $A(s) + B(s) \longrightarrow C(s);$

Type III : $A(s) + B(s) \longrightarrow C(s) + D(g);$

Type IV : $A(s) + (B)(g) \longrightarrow C(s);$

Type V : $A(s) + B(g) \longrightarrow C(s) + D(g);$

Type VI : $A(s) \longrightarrow B(g) + C(g)$

Here (s) and (g) stand for solid and gas respectively. Most of these reactions take place when the reactants are subjected to heating.

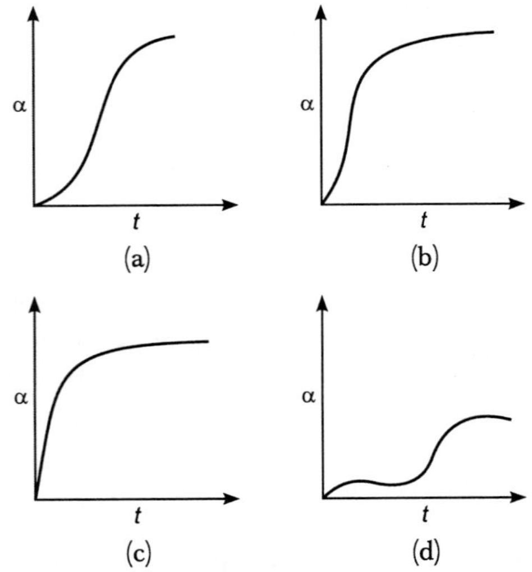

Fig. 26.47 Fraction of the solid decomposed *versus* time : (a) self-catalyzed, (b) short induction followed by rapid decomposition (c) no induction period, (d) initial slow gas evolution.

Thermal Decompostion Reactions

Reactions types I and VI belongs to thermal decomposition.

In type I reaction, decomposition of a solid A to give a new solid B on heating may or may not have an induction period. Typical plots of the fraction (α) of A decomposed *versus* time (t) may be represented by any of the four curves shown in Figure 26.47. At some stage of heating, nuclei of B will be formed that will be embedded in A. Since the structure of B is generally different from that of A, at some stage of growth of B sufficient local deformation will be present giving rise to strain energy. There exists a critical size of B at which the thermodynamics stability of B will overcome the strain energy created by its formation. Upto this size, nuclei of B will revert back to A. If the nuclei of B are bigger than the critical size, transformation of A to B will continue.

Free energy of the reaction

$$\Delta G = m\Delta G_b + a_\gamma \qquad \ldots(24)$$

where m is the number of molecules in the nucleus of B, ΔG_b is the bulk free energy of the reaction, a is a shape factor and γ is the strain energy per unit area of the interface between A and B. If the particles are spherical, $a + 4\pi r^2$ and $m = \dfrac{4\pi r^3}{3v_m}$ where r is the radius of the nucleus of B and v_m is the volume per molecule of the phase B. In equation (1) ΔG_b is a negative quantity and γ is positive. So the growth of B makes opposite contribution to the free energy ΔG of the reaction. there is a critical value of m, *i.e.,* m^* at which $\Delta G = 0$.

Jacobs and Tomkins have found that

$$m^* = \left(\frac{2\gamma}{3\Delta\, G_b}\right)^3 36\pi v_m^2 \qquad \ldots(25)$$

When $m > m^*$, $\dfrac{\partial\, \Delta G}{\partial_m}$ is negative and the reaction will proceed, the nucleus of B will grow. When $m < m^*$, the change of ΔG with m becomes positive and B will revert back to A. This is shown in Figure 26.48.

If the formation of the nuclei is followed by rapid growth, it will be autocatalytic in nature. If the activation energy of the reaction is less than that of the formation of the nuclei, the reaction will proceed only at a few nuclei as is the case for many dehydration reactions. When the activation energy of nucleation and growth are comparable, there will be practically no induction period. These cases are shown in Figure 26.47 (a-c). Figure 26.47 represents two stages of the reaction. Initially, a number of nuclei are formed after which growth proceeds rapidly all over. We see that the α *versus* t plots can be explained in terms of the nucleation and growth of the newly formed solid phase. it should be realised that for reactions of Type I, nucleation can occur only at the surface so that the gaseous product can escape.

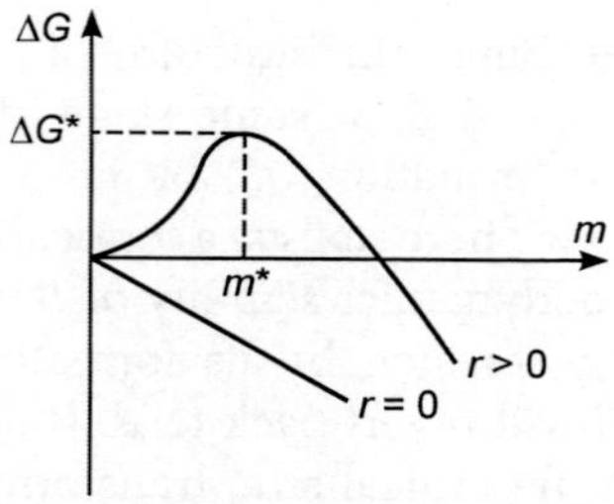

Fig. 26.48 ΔG of the reaction, $A(s) \rightarrow B(s) + C(g)$ as a function of number of molecules per nuclei of B. m^* is the critical number.

Laws Governing Nucleation

Nuclei of the product solid will be formed in the reactant solid matrix at different points if the local fluctuations of the atoms are sufficient to overcome the energy of activation of nucleation. Nucleation generally occurs at some lattice defects. If nucleation requires decomposition of a single molecule, it can be shown that

$$\frac{dN}{dt} = k_1 N_0 \exp((k_1 t) \qquad ...(26)$$

where, N is is the number of nuclei present at time t, N_0 is the number of potential nucleation sites and κ_1 is a rate constant. If the energy of activation of nucleation is large, κ_1 is small and it becomes.

$$\frac{dN}{dt} = \kappa_1 N_0 \qquad ...(27)$$

Under these conditions, the number of nuclei increases linearly with time. If κ_1 is very large,

$$N = N_0 \qquad ...(28)$$

This occurs when nucleation is instantaneous. If nucleation involves stepwise decomposition of two or three molecules, the rate follows a power law such as

$$\frac{dN}{dt} = At^{\beta - 1} \qquad ...(29)$$

where, A is a constant and β is equal to two or three.

Growth of Nuclei

If nucleation follows per law and growth is linear, it can be shown that

$$\alpha = Ct^n \qquad ...(30)$$

where, C and n are constants. For reactions of Type I, the pressure (p) developed in a closed system is proportional to α.

$$\therefore \quad P = Dt^n \qquad ...(31)$$

where, D is a third constant.

The power law equation holds good for many reactions of Type I such as decomposition of barium and calcium azides, aged mercury fulminate and aged silver oxalate.It has been found at times that n changes if the temperature of decomposition is varied, and with finely powdered crystals. This is explained by assuming that the growth is much slower if the crystals are small. In order to explain the observed high values of n (between 11.2 and 22.8) in the case of the decomposition of mercury, fulminate, Garner and Hailes assumed that the nuclei are linear branching chains. The assumption let to the expression.

$$\alpha = Ce^{kt} \qquad ...(32)$$

where, k is a branching coefficient.

The pressure developed during decomposition inside a closed system is

$$p = De^{kt} \qquad ...(33)$$

The equation (32) holds good for values of α between 0.1 and 0.5 depending upon the reaction.

If the branched chains interfere with each other, the fraction decomposed can be expressed as

$$\log \frac{\alpha}{1-\alpha} = kt + C \qquad ...(34)$$

which gives

$$\log \frac{p}{pf - p} = kt + C \qquad ...(35)$$

where, pf is the final pressure in the system after complete decomposition of the solid and C is a constant. This is one of many equations developed.

Towards the end of the reaction, the difference of the molecular volumes of the reactant and the product solids may bring about a collapse of the interface between them. This will give blocks of reactant in which there may not be any product nuclei. If each molecule in such blocks has some probability of decomposition, the rate of the reaction will be proportional to the amount of the reactant left. Hence,

$$\frac{d\alpha}{dt} = \kappa(1-\alpha) \qquad ...(36)$$

which gives

$$\log \frac{1}{1-\alpha} = \kappa t \qquad ...(37)$$

Type-I reactions may be endothermic or exothermic. The most commonly studied endothermic reactions is the dehydration of a metal salt hydrate and the decomposition of the metal carbonates.

The decomposition product of some metal hydrates has a crystal lattice identical with that of the parent solid. In some cases, the product is devoid of any well defined crystal structure. In a few others, the product shows a distinctly different phase. The process may be imagined to be as follows. The dehydration of the crystalline hydrate forms a highly disordered product. Rearrangement of this may give a new crystalline phase. During the reaction, they are present as shown in Figure 26.49. There is a shrinkage in the volume due to the new phase giving rise to cracks of molecular dimensions through which the water molecules will have to escape. Slow diffusion through the cracks slows down the rate of dehydration. This possibly is the reason why there is an initial fall in the rate of dehydration of $CuSO_4 \cdot 5H_2O$.

The rate of dehydration depends not only on the rate at which water is lost at the interface between the reactant and the product solids, but also on the rate of diffusion of the water vapour. If the product is amorphous, it hardly can develop any crack to give a diffusion path. This will make diffusion difficult as found in the case of the dehydration of copper sulphate hydrate. If the product is highly crystalline as found in the case of the dehydration of chrome alum, large radial cracks develop in the new phase facilitating diffusion and thereby dehydration.

Decomposition of the metal carbonates is another widely studied solid state reaction. Many carbonates decompose to the corresponding oxides with the formation of a basic carbonate as an intermediate. In many cases, the rate follows a first order law and the energy of activation is nearly actual to the heat of the reaction. A typical example is the decomposition of calcium carbonate.

$$CaCO_3(s) \longrightarrow CaO(s) + CO_2(g)$$

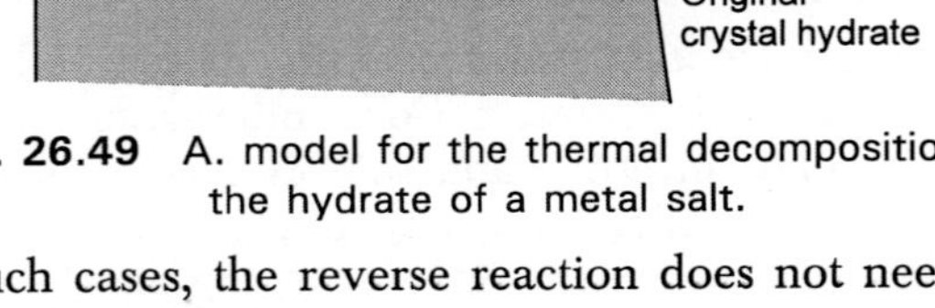

Fig. 26.49 A. model for the thermal decomposition of the hydrate of a metal salt.

In such cases, the reverse reaction does not need any activation energy.

A large number of Type I reactions are exothermic. Typical examples are the decomposition of metal azides, metal oxalates and metal hydrides. Since these reactions proceed with gas evolution, they have been studied by recording the time *versus* pressure curves. The reactions generally involve three major steps. These are (i) initial reaction at the surface of the solid A, (ii) the formation of the nuclei of the product solid B and (iii) the reaction at the interface between A and B.

The metal azides are highly sensitive explosives although some such as sodium azide are quite stable. They generally decompose giving metal and nitrogen and give a variety of pressure-time curves.

Reaction Between two Solids

The Type II reaction

$$A(s) + B(s) \longrightarrow C(s)$$

is considerably different from the reactions taking place in the gas phase or in a solution. Whereas the reaction in the gas phase or in solution depends on the chance of the reactant molecules meeting each other, the solid state reactions of Type II takes place between two solid phases in which the atoms have very restricted movement. The reaction can take place only at the points of contact of the two phases and a product layer builds up. Further reaction depends on the diffusion of the reactants through this product layer. Rate of a solid-solid reaction depends on the rate of transfer of atoms or ions through this layer. For a reaction to take place, the free energy ΔG should be negative. Since the entropy change in such a process is small, the change in enthalpy determines whether the reaction is possible. This means that the enthalpy change of the process should be negative making reactions of Type II exothermic in nature. If the solids A and B do not form a solid solution to any appreciable extent, ΔG will remain unchanged during the reaction and equilibrium will not be reached. The reaction will go to completion.

Studying the kinetics of such reactions is often difficult as there is no mass loss or gas evolution. The reaction is generally followed by observing the X-ray diffraction (XRD). This is difficult if the product has poor crystallinity. Kinetic study becomes more difficult if the product is formed through some intermediate.

Since these reactions are exothermic, temperature of the sample rises during the reaction due to inefficient heart transfer from the sample to the surroundings, resulting in an increase in the rate of the reaction. The temperature at which the reaction rate is maximum is generally taken as the reaction temperature. It is convenient to follow such reactions by differential thermal analysis (DTA) where the temperature of the DTA peak is taken as the reaction temperature.

Because the reaction proceeds by diffusion of the reactants through the initially formed product layer, the reaction depends on the structure of the product phase *B*. The diffusion path can be effectively shortened by using finely divided particles of the reactants. The newly formed phase is often poorly crystalline and contains a large concentration of defects that makes diffusion easy.

The growth of the product *C* (*s*) depends on the rate of diffusion of *A* and *B* through *C*. Three cases may be distinguished depends on the ability of *A* and *B* to diffuse through the bulk of *C*. These are (i) *A* diffuses through the bulk of the product of react with *B*, (ii) *B* diffuses and reacts and (iii) both *A* and *B* diffuse through the product to react.

Representative of Type II reaction is the addition reaction such as

$$ZnO + Al_2O_3 \longrightarrow ZnAl_2O_4$$
$$2AgI + HgI_2 \longrightarrow Ag_2HgI_4$$

Zinc aluminate has the spinel structure in which only a fraction of the available tetrahedral and octahedral sites are occupied. Diffusion of zinc and aluminium ions are facilitated through the vacant sites. In the second reaction, both Ag^+ and Hg^{2+} diffuse at high rates. There are three cations for every four cationic sites in the product Ag_2HgI_4 and diffusion takes place through these cationic vacancies.

Improving Reactivity of Solids

One of the incentives to study solid state reactions is to improve the reactivity of solids so that the product can be obtained in a shorter time and under milder conditions. This can be achieved in several ways. Single phase oxides with multiple cations are generally prepared by thoroughly grinding and mixing the individual oxides and then firing at high temperature. It is possible to obtain the new phase following this ceramic technique provided the new phase is stable at the heating temperature. The long diffusion path of the cation makes it a time consuming process and the product is highly sintered which may not be always desired. The reaction can be achieved under mild conditions by adopting a few modifications.

Increasing the Surface Area

Since solid state reactions being at the surface of the reactant, increasing its surface area is always helpful. In case of the reaction between two solids, this gives a larger area of contact between them where the reaction begins. Small particle size of the high surface area material also reduces the diffusion path. Thus, it is advantageous to use solid reactants with high surface area.

High surface area oxides can be prepared in a number of ways. Since oxides are generally prepared by thermal decomposition of precursor solid, it is easy to prepare an oxide with high surface area by the decomposition of a precursor also with high surface area. The precursor with high surface area can be prepared in a number of ways. It can be achieved by precipitation of a precursor that has low solubility in the medium used. It can also be done by spray drying or freeze drying. The precursor may be a metal hydroxide or a carboxylate or some other compound that decomposes at a relatively low temperature to give the oxide.

Preparation of Ternary Oxides Through Single Phase Precursor

When it is desired to prepare a compound containing two different metal ions, it can be done first first by preparing a single phase precursor that contains both the metal ions. In a reaction between the two phases, reacting ions may have to travel through a distance of several thousand angstroms. By using a single phase precursor, this may be brought down to abut 10 Å. This situation is shown in Figures 26.50. Many divalent metal carbonates crystallize with the calcite structure.

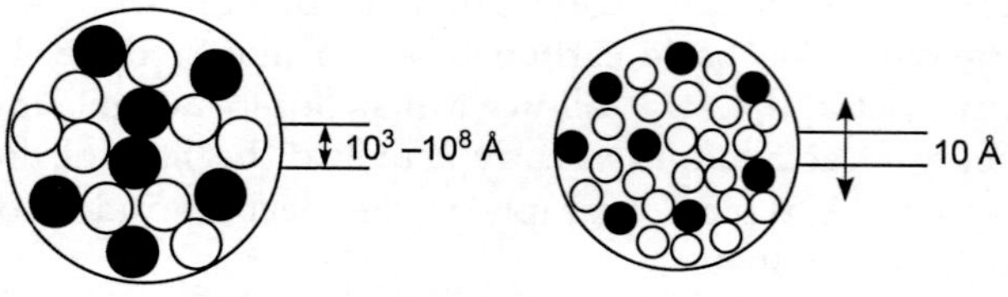

Fig. 26.50 Diffusion paths in (a) a biphasic and (b) a monophasic precursor.

It is possible to precipitate mixed metal carbonates as a single calcite phase. By thermal decomposition of $Ca_{1-x}Mn_xCO_3$, Longo and Horowitz prepared a number of mixed metal oxides with perovskite and related structures under comparatively mild conditions.

Addition of Impurities

Impurities may be introduced in a solid during crystallization deliberately or otherwise. These impurities play an important, role in determining the reactivity of the solid. They may introduce a distortion in the crystal structure thereby weakening the chemical bonds. The impurity cation may be present as an interstitial defect. If it is present at a substitutional position but has a higher cationic charge than that of the host lattice cation,it will produce cation vacancies. The diffusion of the ions may then be enhanced due to the presence of the defects by any of the diffusion mechanisms. Thus, it has been found that when silver oxalate is doped with divalent copper, there is a linear decrease in the decomposition rate constant with the concentration of the copper ion. Doping with Cu^{2+} ions increases cation vacancy concentration which in turn decreases the interstitial cation concentration. This brings down the decomposition rate.

Doping affects the rate of reduction of nickel oxide. Generally, doping with cations with higher than + 2 charge enhances reduction. Doping with a monovalent cation, on the other hand, decreases the rate of reduction.

Structural Effects

The reactivity of a solid is related to its structure. this has led to the investigation of solid state reactions just below and above the temperature of its polymorphic transformation. Such changes in reactivity has been observed even in the cases of second. Order phases transformation for example, in the antiferromagenetic to paramagnetic transition of NiO.

Coupling Effect

This general term stants for combining the effect on one transformation in the solid with another reaction. In this general sense, the higher reactivity of a solid at the temperature of its phase transition is also a coupling effect. The coupling effect, however, relates to the higher reactivity of a newly formed solid. Suppose instead of mixing two metal oxides and heating them to obtain a new single phase mixed oxide we heat their carbonates or the oxalates. The carbonates (or) oxalates will initially decompose to the respective oxides. These instantaneously formed oxides will react much more rapidly giving the product.

Effect of High Energy Radiation

High energy radiations like α-rays neutron beam or γ-rays cause extensive radiation damage in a solid by knocking off the atoms from their normal sites. But the displaced atoms generally do not move far from their normal sites and revert back once the radiation source is withdrawn. Neverthless, high energy radiation has been found to influence the reactivity of solids. The effect is particularly important in the case of organic solids due to the formation of free radicals. Radiation induced polymerization is also well known.

Applications of superconductivity Super conductors find use in electronics, in transmission, in preparing magnets and in trains which move in air without rails (levitation transportation).

Thermal properties of solids One of the most well-defined thermal properties of a solid is its specific heat unit volume C_v. The classical result relating to C_v is the Dulong and Petit's law which states $C_v = 3R$.

Classical physics justified this law on the following basis. Atoms in a solid have three degrees of freedom. They vibrate about their equilibrium position. For each degree of freedom, there is $\frac{kT}{2}$ of potential energy and $\frac{kT}{2}$ of kinetic energy per atom by the law of equipartition of energy.

Hence, $2kT$ is the total energy per atom of $3NkT$ per mole if N is Avogadro's number. Hence, $C_v = \left(\frac{\partial U}{\partial T}\right)_v = 3Nk = 3R$. Classical physics did not predict any temperature dependence for C_v, but experiments towards the end of the last century observed considerable decreases in specific heat of all solids at low temperatures.

Einstein's theory of specific heat was the first application of the quantum theory to a solid state problem.

He assumed that a solid element containing N atoms could be represented by N harmonic oscillators of the same frequency. The Planck formula for the mean energy of an oscillator is $< E > = \frac{h\nu}{e^{h\nu/kT} - 1}$

Hence, the vibrational energy of a solid element composed of N atoms is equal to $E = 3N\frac{h\nu}{(e^{h\nu/kT} - 1)}$

$$C_v \text{ is therefore } \frac{\partial E}{\partial T} = 3R\left(\frac{h\nu}{kT}\right)^2 \frac{e^{\frac{h\nu}{kT}}}{(e^{h\nu/kT} - 1)^2}$$

When $kT >> h\nu$, the Einstein formula reduces to the classical value

$$\left[\text{when } x << 1,\ e^x = 1 + x, \text{ where } x = \frac{h\nu}{kT}\right]$$

At low temperatures, the specific heat decreases.

Einstein in his 1907 paper in Annalen der Physik calculated the molar specific heat of diamond for a frequency

$\omega = \left(\frac{kT_E}{h}\right)$ for a characteristic temperature

$T_E = 1320$ K

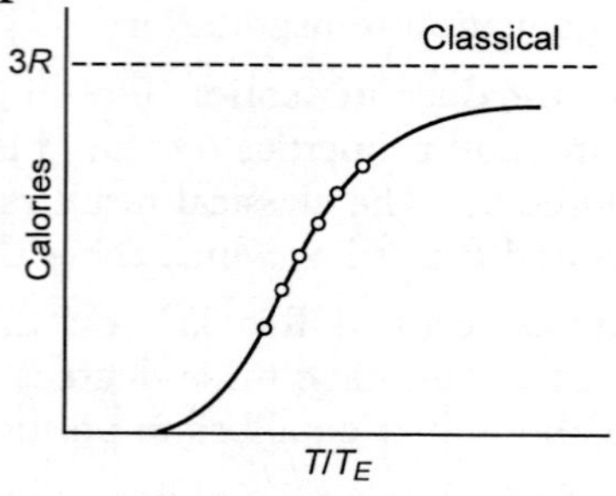

Fig. 26.51

There is good agreement with experiment at higher temperature. The Einstein curve falls of more rapidly at low temperature than it should. The reason for the discrepancy is that the use of a single frequency is too simplistic. The phonon spectrum covers a wide range of frequencies.

Debye's calculation of C_v Debye suggested that a more accurate way to get the vibrational modes of a crystal is to treat crystal as an isotropic continuous medium.

The wave equation in solid may be written as

$$\frac{\partial^2 u}{\partial x^2} + \frac{\partial^2 u}{\partial y^2} + \frac{\partial^2 u}{\partial z^2} = \frac{1 \partial^2 u}{v_s \partial t^2}$$

where, v_s = velocity of propagation of the waves in this solid. [Actually in a solid one longitudinal and two transverse waves can propagate. We can take care of this refinement later.]

Assuming a solid in the shape of a cube of side L, the possible stationary wave solutions are of the form

$$u(x, y, z, t) = A \sin\left(\frac{n_x \pi x}{L}\right) \sin\left(\frac{n_y \pi y}{L}\right) \sin\left(\frac{n_z \pi z}{L}\right)$$

$\cos 2\pi vt$ where n_x, n_y, n_z are positive integers > 1.

Substituting this solution into the wave equation,we get

$$\frac{\pi^2}{L^2}(n_x^2 + n_y^2 + n_z^2) = \frac{4\pi v^2}{v_s^2} = \frac{4\pi^2}{\lambda^2}$$

The possible frequencies are determined by this triplet of integers. Consider a cartesian n-space, each point in the network is determined by the three integers.

$$\text{Writing } R^2 = n_x^2 + n_y^2 + n_z^2 = \frac{4L^2 \nu^2}{v_s^2}$$

Since each point in the n-space occupies unit volume the number of points in the spherical shell between R and $R + dR$ is $\frac{1}{8} 4\pi R^2 dR$.

Expressing R^2 in terms of ν,

$G(\nu)\, d\nu = \frac{4\pi V}{v_s^3} \nu^2 d\nu$ where $V = L^3$ is the volume of the solid. Taking care of the refinement stated above

$$G(\nu)\, d\nu = 4\pi V \left(\frac{2}{v_t^3} + \frac{1}{v_t^3}\right) v^2 d\nu$$

In a cubic crystal, $v_t = \sqrt{\frac{C_{11}}{p}}$ and $v_t = \left(\frac{C_{11} - C_{12}}{2p}\right)^{1/2}$

The Debye approximation A solid is not a continuum, but as long as the wave is large compared with the interatomic distance, the crystal looks like a continuum from the point of view of the wave. This is the justification for employing the continuum model to get the number of possible vibrational modes of the crystal.

The function $G(\nu)$ is normalised by limiting the total number of vibrational modes to $3N$, N being the total number of atoms. The cut-off procedure leads to a maximum frequency, the Debye frequency, common to the longitudinal and transverse modes.

$$\int_0^{\nu_D} G(\nu)\, d\nu = \int_0^{\nu_D} 4\pi V \left(\frac{2}{v_t^3} + \frac{1}{v_i^3}\right) \nu^2 d\nu = 3N$$

$$\nu_D^3 = \frac{9N}{4\pi V}\left(\frac{2}{v_t^3} + \frac{1}{v_i^3}\right)$$

Associating each vibrational mode, a harmonic oscillator and the Plank formula for the average energy of an oscillator, we have

$$E = \int_0^{\nu_D} G(\nu) \frac{h\nu}{e^{h\nu/kT} - 1} d\nu = 9N\left(\frac{kt}{h\nu_D}\right)^3 kT \int_0^{x_m} \frac{x^3 dx}{e^x - 1}$$

where, $x = \frac{h\nu}{kT}$ and $x_m = \frac{h\nu_m}{kT}$.

Example 1. *CsBr crystallises in bcc (body-centred cubic type) lattice with the side of the unit cell 4.29 Å. Calculate the angles at which the II order reflection maxima may be expected from the planes 100, 110 and 111, when X-rays of $\lambda = 0.50$ Å are used.*

Sol. Refer to an earlier diagram representing the three types of planes in a body-centred cubic lattice.

(i) d_{100} or more precisely $d_{200} = \frac{a}{2} = \frac{4.29}{2} = 2.145$ Å

$$n\lambda = 2d \sin\theta; \text{ Here } n = 2.$$

$$\therefore \quad 2 \times 0.5 \text{ Å} = 2 \times 2.145 \text{ Å} \times \sin\theta$$

$$\sin\theta = \frac{1}{4.29} = 0.2331$$

$$\therefore \quad \theta = 13.48°$$

(ii) $d_{110} = \frac{a}{\sqrt{2}} = \frac{4.29}{\sqrt{2}} = 3.024$ Å

$$2 \times 0.5 = 2 \times 3.034 \times \sin\theta;\ \sin\theta = \frac{1}{6.068} = 0.1648$$

$\therefore \quad \theta = 9.49°$

(iii) d_{111} or more precisely $d_{222} = \frac{a}{2\sqrt{3}} = \frac{4.29}{2\sqrt{3}} = 1.238$ Å

$$2 \times 0.5 = 2 \times 1.238 \times \sin\theta;\ \sin\theta = \frac{1}{2.476} = 0.4039$$

$\therefore \quad \theta = 23.82°$

Example 2. *Caesium bromide has* CsCl *structure (body-centred cubic type of lattice). Its density is* 4.49 cc^{-1}. Calculate the side of the unit cell.

Sol. Adopting the procedure indicated for NaCl (see determination of lattice dimension), we can show in an analogous manner that the unit cell of CsBr contains effectively one molecule of CsBr. Molar mass of CsBr is 212.8 (*i.e.*, 212.8 g mol^{-1}).

$$\text{Molar volume} = \frac{212.8}{4.49} = 47.39 \text{ cm}^3$$

N molecules (6.023×10^{23}) correspond to 47.39 cm^3

1 molecule corresponds to $\frac{47.39}{6.023 \times 10^{23}}$

$$= 7.868 \times 10^{-23} \text{ cm}^8$$

i.e., the volume of the unit cell $= 7.868 \times 10^{-23}$ cm^3

$\therefore$ Side of the unit cell $= (7.868 \times 10^{-23})^{1/3}$

$$= 4.285 \times 10^{-8} \text{ cm or } 4.285 \text{ Å}$$

Example 3. *Aluminium metal (atomic weight* $= 26.08$*) crystallises in the cubic system with* $a = 4.05$ Å. *Its density is 2.7 g* cm^{-3}. *Determine the unit type. Calculate the radius of aluminium atom.*

Sol. Assume that the unit cell effectively contains 'n' atoms of Al.

$$\text{Molar volume} = \frac{6.023 \times 10^{23}}{n} \times (4.05)^3 \times 10^{-24} \text{ cm}^3$$

$$= \frac{26.08}{2.7}$$

$\therefore \quad n = 4.14 \approx 4$

That is, the unit cell effectively contains 4 atoms of Al. Hence the cubic lattice belong to the face-centered type.

Diagonal of any face $= a\sqrt{2}$

$$= 4.05\sqrt{2} = 5.727 \text{ Å};$$

$$4r = 5.727 \text{ Å}$$

$\therefore \quad r = 1.432$ Å

Example 4. *The* I *order reflection of a beam of X-rays from a given crystal occurs at 5°15′. At what angle the third order reflection will occur?*

Sol. $n\lambda = 2d\sin\theta$; $1\lambda = 2d\sin 5°\,15'$; $3\lambda = 2d\sin\theta$, where θ is the required angle.

$$3 = \frac{\sin\theta}{\sin 5°\,15'} = \frac{\sin\theta}{0.0915} \ \sin\theta = 0.2745\ \theta = 15°\,57'$$

Example 5. *Density of* NaCl $= 2.17\, g\, cc^{-1}$ *(at 20°C); molar mass* $= 58.45$. *Calculate the interplanar distance* (d_{200}). *The first order reflection maximum of the* K_α *rays of palladium from the 200 planes of* NaCl *occurs at a glancing angle* 5.90°. *Calculate the wavelength of the X-radiation.*

Sol. Method $d_{200} = \left(\frac{M}{2N\rho}\right)^{1/8} = \left(\frac{58.45}{2 \times 6.023 \times 10^{23} \times 2.17}\right)^{1/3}$

$$= (2.236 \times 10^{-23})^{1/3}$$

$$= 2.32 \times 10^{-8} \text{ cm} = 2.82 \text{ Å}$$

$$n\lambda = 2d\sin\theta;\ n = 1;\ d = 2.82 \text{ Å}$$

and $\quad \sin\theta = \sin 5.9° = 0.1028$

$$\lambda = 2 \times 2.82 \times 0.1028 = 0.5797 \text{ Å}$$

Exercise 1

(For Part 'B')

1. At very low temperature, oxygen O_2, freezen and forms a crystalline solid. Which term best describes the solid?
(a) Covalent network (b) Molecular crystals
(c) Metallic (d) Ionic

2. The mass of a unit cell of NaCl corresponds to
(a) 1 Na^+ and 6 Cl^- (b) 1 Cl^- and 6 Na^+
(c) 1 Na^+ and 1 Cl^- (d) 4 Cl^- and 4 Na^+

3. Edge length of M^+X^- (fcc structure) is 7.2 Å. Assuming $M^+ \rightarrow X^-$ contact along the cell edge, radius of X^- ion is (r_{M^+} =1.6 Å)
(a) 2.0 Å (b) 5.6 Å
(c) 2.8 Å (d) 3.8 Å

4. In a solid '*AB*' having the NaCl structure, '*A*' atoms occupy the corners of the cubic unit cell. If all the face-centred atoms along one of the axes are removed, then the resultant stoichiometry of the solid is
(a) AB_2 (b) A_2B
(c) A_4B_3 (d) A_3B_4

5. A substance A_xB_y crystallizes in a face centred cubic (fcc) lattice in which atoms '*A*' occupy each corner of the cube and atoms '*B*' occupy the centres of each face of the cube. Identify the correct composition of the substance A_xB_y.
(a) AB_3
(b) A_4B_3
(c) A_3B
(d) Composition cannot be specified

6. Which of the following fcc structure contains cations in alternate tetrahedral voids?
(a) NaCl (b) ZnS
(c) Na_2O (d) CaF_2

7. A metallic element crystallizes into a lattice containing a sequence of layers of *AB AB AB*... Any packing of layers leaves out voids in the lattice. The percentage of this lattice empty space is
(a) 26% (b) 46% (c) 68% (d) 74%

8. A mineral having the formula AB_2 crystallizes in the ccp lattice with the *A* atoms occupying the lattice points. Fraction of the tetrahedral sites occupied by *B* atoms is
(a) 50% (b) 75%
(c) 100% (d) 66.67%

9. The diffraction of barium with X-radiation of wavelength 2.29 Å gives a first order reflection at 30°. The distance between the diffracted planes is
(a) 2.29 Å (b) 1.145 Å
(c) 4.58 Å (d) 0.765 Å

10. A group of 13 element if added in small amounts to Ge crystal. The doped crystal acts as
(a) *n*-type semiconductor (b) *p*-type semiconductor
(c) insulator (d) rectifier

11. If the three inter axial angles defining the unit cell are equal in magnitude, the crystal cannot belong to the
(a) orthorhombic system (b) cubic system
(c) hexagonal system (d) tetragonal system

12. The melting point of RbBr is 682°C while that of NaF is 988°C. The principal reason that the melting point of NaF is much higher than that of RbBr is that
(a) the two crystals are not isomorphous
(b) the molar mass of NaF is smaller than that of RbBr
(c) the bond an RbBr has more covalent character than the bond in NaF
(d) the internuclear distance is greater for RbBr than for NaF

13. A solid has a structure in which W atoms are located at the cube corners of the unit cell, O atoms are located at the cube edges, and Na atoms are at the cube centres. Hence, formula of the compound is
(a) $NaWO_3$ (b) $NaWO_2$
(c) $NaWO_4$ (d) NaW_2O_3

14. Hexagonal closest-packed structure and a cubic closest packed structure for a given element would be expected to have
(a) the same coordination number
(b) the same packing fraction
(c) Both (a) and (b)
(d) None of the above

15. It is stated that ZnS does not crystallizes in the NaCl structure. It is due to
(a) The $\frac{r^+}{r^-}$ ration is 0.402, too low to avoid anion-anion contact in the NaCl structure
(b) ZnS is water insoluble, NaCl is water soluble
(c) ZnS is water soluble, NaCl is water insoluble
(d) ZnS belongs to *d*-block, Na belongs to *s*-block

16. In a face centred cubic arrangement of *A* and *B* atoms, where, *A* atoms are at the corners of the unit cell and *B* atoms at the face centres, one of the *A* atoms is missing from one corner in each unit cell. The simplest formula of the compound
(a) A_3B_4 (b) AB_6
(c) A_2B_3 (d) A_7B_{24}

17. The number of atoms in different cubic unit cells of monoatomic substances is
(a) simple cubic-1 (b) bcc-2
(c) fcc-4 (d) All are correct

18. 8 : 8 coordination of CsCl is found to change into 6 : 6 on
(a) applying high pressure
(b) increase in temperature
(c) Both (a) and (b)
(d) None of the above

19. Antifluorite structure is for
(a) ThO_2 (b) Na_2O
(c) Both (a) and (b) (d) None of these

20. Which is true of radius ratio of $\frac{r^+}{r^-}$?
(a) Is in range 0.732 to 0.414, CN is 6 and is octahedral
(b) Is above 0.732, CN is 8 and is cubic
(c) Is 0.225 to 0.155, CN is 3 and is triangular
(d) All of the above

21. Schottky defect is due to
(a) missing of electron from normal lattice site
(b) missing of an atom from normal lattice site
(c) Both (a) and (b)
(d) None of the above

22. Which is true?
(a) Piezoelectricity is due to net dipole moment
(b) Some electric current is produced on heating polar crystals, is is pyroelectricity
(c) Ferroelectricity is due to alignment of dipole in same direction
(d) All of the above

23. Ferrimagnetic is converted into ferromagnetic at
(a) 300 K (b) 400 K
(c) 600 K (d) 850 K

24. *ABC ABC* types of arrangement of different layers, in a closest packed structure is called
(a) hcp (b) bcc
(c) fcc (d) cubic closest packed (ccp)

25. Zinc blende structure is obtained when Zn^{2+} occupies
(a) all tetrahedral sites (b) half tetrahedral sites
(c) all octahedral site (d) half octahedral sites

26. Frenkel defect appears in
(a) AgI (b) ZnS
(c) AgBr (d) All of these

27. The presence of *F*-centres in a crystal makes it
(a) conducting (b) colourless
(c) coloured (d) non-conducting

28. An electron trapped in an anion vacancy within the crystal is called
(a) *n*-type conductor (b) *p*-type conductor
(c) *F*-centre (d) insulator

29. The point defect which lowers the density of the material is
(a) Schottky (b) Frenkel
(c) Both (a) and (b) (d) None of these

30. The *p*-type semiconductor is obtained when Si is doped with
(a) Al (b) Ge
(c) Ga (d) As

31. Amorphous solids
(a) do not have sharp melting points
(b) are isotropic
(c) have same mechanical strength, electrical and optical properties in all directions
(d) all the facts given in (a), (b) and (c) are correct about them

32. It is stated that uncharged atoms or molecules never crystallize in simple cubic structures because,
(a) they are water insoluble
(b) they are water insoluble
(c) they pack more efficiently in closest packed structure
(d) None of the above

33. Numbers of formula units in unit cells of MgO (rock salt), ZnS (zinc blende) and Pt (fcc) respectively are
(a) 4, 3, 2 (b) 4, 3, 4
(c) 4, 4, 4 (d) 4, 3, 1

34. Ferrimagnetism is in
(a) ↑↑↑↑↑ (b) ↑↓↑↓
(c) ↑↑↑↓↓ (d) None of these

35. A Schottky defect may involve all but one of the following which one is incorrect?
(a) A vacant cation and a vacant anion in a *MX* lattice
(b) Vacant cation : anion sites in ratio in an MX_2 lattice
(c) Vacant cation : anion sites in ratio 2 : 1 in an M_2X lattice
(d) Random vacancy in any lattice

36. In NaCl type of unit cell of *AB*, the statement which is (are) always true
(a) coordination number of both *A* and *B* are 6
(b) number of *A* in the nearest neighbour of $A = 12$
(c) $4r_B = \sqrt{2}a$
(d) $2(r_A + r_B) = \sqrt{3}a$

37. The correct statement(s) regarding defects in solids is (are)
(a) Frenkel defet is usually favoured by a very small differene in the size of cation and anion
(b) Frenkel defect is a dislocation defect
(c) Trapping of an electron in the lattice leads to the formation of *F*-centre
(d) Schottky defects have no effect on physical properties of solids

38. Sapphire is aluminium oxide. It crystallizes with aluminium ions in two thirds of octahedral holes in a closest packed array of oxide ions. Hence, the simple formula of aluminium oxide is
(a) Al_2O_3 (b) AlO_2
(c) Al_4O_6 (d) None of these

39. A cubic crystal possess several axes of symmetry, several planes of symmetry and
(a) a C_5-axis
(b) a C_7-axis
(c) a centre symmetry
(d) None of the above

40. No Bragg reflection of X-rays from a crystal will be observed if d_{hkl} is small than
(a) $\lambda/4$ (b) $\lambda/3$
(c) $\lambda/2$ (d) λ

41. In the X-ray diffraction pattern for a bcc lattice, h, k, l can have
(a) any value (b) even value
(c) $h + k + l$ even (d) odd values

42. For a first order Bragg reflection, $d_{khl}/\lambda = 1/2$, the Bragg angle of incidence is
(a) 30° (b) 60°
(c) 45° (d) 90°

43. A tetragonal crystal possesses the following axis of symmetry
(a) two fold (b) three fold
(c) four fold (d) six fold

44. A crystal which possess no element of symmetry (*i.e.*, a triclinic crystal) is
(a) $CuSO_4 \cdot 5H_2O$ (b) CsCl
(c) NaCl (d) KNO_3

Assertion & Reason

Codes
(a) Both A and R are true and R is the correct explanation of A.
(b) Both A and R are true but R is not the correct explanation of A.
(c) A is true but R is false.
(d) A is false but R is true.

45. Assertion (A) In any ionic solid (MX) with Schottky defects, the number of positive and negative ions are same.

Reason (R) Equal number of cation and anion vacancies are present.

46. Assertion (A) Band gap in germanium is small.

Reason (R) The energy spread of each germanium atomic energy level is infinitesimally small.

47. For a first order Bragg reflection, if the Bragg angle of incidence is 30°, then d_{hkl} is equal to
(a) 2 (b) 1
(c) $\frac{1}{2}$ (d) $\frac{1}{4}$

48. The smallest interplanar spacing in a crystal which will give nth order Bragg reflection is
(a) $d_{hkl} = n$ (b) $d_{hkl} = n/2$
(c) $d_{hkl} = n/3$ (d) $d_{hkl} = n/4$

49. All crystals except ……… are anisotropic.
(a) trigonal (b) orthorhombic
(c) hexagonal (d) cubic

50. A crystal having unit cell dimensions $a \neq b \neq c$, $\alpha = \beta = \gamma = 90°$ is
(a) tetragonal (b) orthorhombic
(c) cubic (d) hexagonal

51. For a fcc lattice, which of the following statements is correct?
(a) h, k, l values are all odd or all even
(b) h, k, l values are all even
(c) h, k, l values are all odd
(d) $h + k + l$ are all even

52. In the CsCl structure, the number of ions in a unit cell is
(a) 2 (b) 4 (c) 6 (d) 8

53. Which one of the following has the largest band gap energy?
(a) Germanium (b) Silicon
(c) Tellurium (d) Diamond

54. Calcium fluoride crystallizes in fluorite structure. The coordination number for the cation and anion is respectively
(a) 6, 6 (b) 6, 4
(c) 4, 6 (d) 8, 4

55. In a close packed (hcp, ccp) arrangement of a lattice comprising of n atoms of a kind, the number of tetrahedral and octahedral holes present respectively are
(a) $2n, 2n$ (b) n, n (c) $n, 2n$ (d) $2n, n$

56. An element crystallizes both in fcc and bcc lattices. If the density of the element in the two forms is the same, the ratio of unit cell length of fcc to that of bcc lattice is
(a) $(2)^{1/3}$ (b) $\left(\frac{1}{2}\right)^{1/3}$ (c) $4^{1/3}$ (d) $\left(\frac{1}{4}\right)^{1/3}$

57. According to band theory of bonding, conduction occurs in very good conductors because
(a) valence band is full
(b) valence band and conduction band overlap
(c) band gap is appreciable
(d) band gap is small

58. Which of the following, when doped into a crystal of ultrapurified germanium, will convert it into a p-type semiconductor?
(a) C (b) As (c) In (d) Na

59. Icosohedral structure is generally exhibited by
(a) C (b) Si (c) Ge (d) B

60. Consider an orthorhombic unit cell of dimensions $a = 450$ pm, $b = 650$ pm and $c = 400$ pm. The perpendicular distance between the (110) planes is
(a) 650 pm (b) 450 pm
(c) 370 pm (d) 500 pm

61. Sodium metal crystallizes in the body-centred cubic lattice with cell edge (a). The radius of the sodium atom is
(a) $a/\sqrt{2}$ (b) $a\sqrt{3}/2$
(c) $a\sqrt{3}/4$ (d) $a/2\sqrt{2}$

62. The number of manganese ions in tetrahedral and octahedral sites, respectively in Mn_3O_4 are
(a) one Mn^{2+} and two Mn^{3+}
(b) one Mn^{3+} and two Mn^{2+}
(c) two Mn^{3+} and one Mn^{2+}
(d) two Mn^{2+} and one Mn^{3+}

63. Gold crystallizes in face-centred cubic lattice. The atomic weight and density of gold are 196.97 and 19.4 g/cm^3 respectively. The length of the unit cell is
(a) 2.563 Å (b) 3.230 Å
(c) 4.070 Å (d) 8.140 Å

64. The spinels $CoFe_2O_4$ and $FeFe_2O_4$ respectively are
(a) inverse and inverse (b) inverse and normal
(c) normal and normal (d) normal and inverse

65. The incorrect statement for solid sodium chloride is that
(a) both sodium and chloride ions adopt inert gas configuration
(b) the conduction band is full
(c) the conduction band is empty
(d) the valence band is full

66. The atomic radius (in cm) of an element with a body-centred cubic unit cell of volume 75.8 cm,^{3} mol^{-1}, molecular weight 137.3 and density 3.62 g cm^{-3} is
(a) 1.5×10^{-8} (b) 1.6×10^{-8}
(c) 2.0×10^{-8} (d) 2.2×10^{-8}

67. The arrangement of sulphur in zinc blende and wurtzite structure respectively are
(a) hexagonal close packing and cubic close packing
(b) cubic close packing and hexagonal close packing
(c) simple cubic close packing in both the structures
(d) hexagonal close packing in both the structures

68. The lattice parameters for a monoclinic crystal are
(a) $a \neq b \neq c$; $\alpha = \gamma = 90°$, $\beta \neq 90°$
(b) $a = b \neq c$; $\alpha \neq \beta \neq \gamma$
(c) $a \neq b \neq c$; $\alpha \neq \beta \neq \gamma$
(d) $a = b = c$; $\alpha = \gamma = 90°$

69. Band theory predicts that magnesium is an insulator. However, in practice it acts as a conductor due to
(a) presence of filled 3s-orbital
(b) overlap of filled 2p and filled 3s-orbital
(c) overlap of filled 3s and empty 3p-orbital
(d) presence of unfilled 3p-orbital

70. The band structure in an n-type semiconductor is

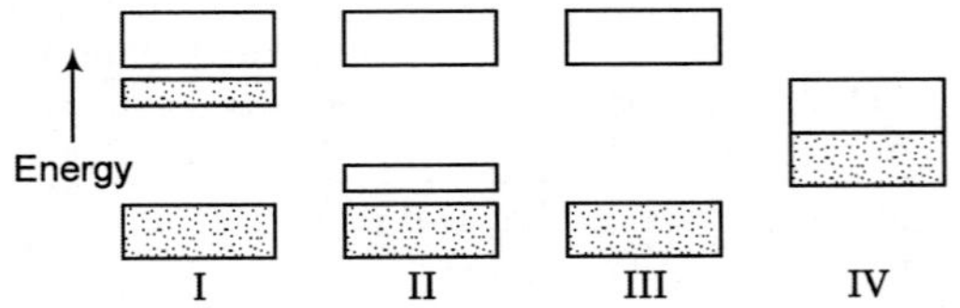

(a) I (b) II
(c) III (d) IV

Exercise 2
(For Part 'C')

1. A metal crystallizes into two cubic phases, face-centred cubic (fcc) and body-centred cubic (bcc) whose unit cell lengths are 3.5 and 3.0 Å, respectively. The ratio of densities of fcc and bcc is
(a) 0.26 (b) 1.26
(c) 2.26 (d) 1.76

2. The density of solid argon is 1.64 g per mL at –233°. If the argon atom is assumed to be a sphere of radius 1.54×10^{-8} cm. The percentage of solid argon is apparently empty space is (Ar = 40)
(a) 28% (b) 38%
(c) 62% (d) 74%

3. When an electron in an excited M_0 atom, falls from L to K shell, an X-ray is emitted. These X-rays are diffracted at angle 7.75° by planes with a separation of 2.64 Å. The difference in energy between Kshell and L shell in M_0 assuming a first order diffraction is (sin 7.75° = 0.1349).
(a) 2.788×10^{-16} J (b) 27.88×10^{-16} J
(c) $2.788 \times 10^{+16}$ J (d) $27.88 \times 10^{+16}$ J

4. The packing efficiency of the two dimensional square unit cell shown below is

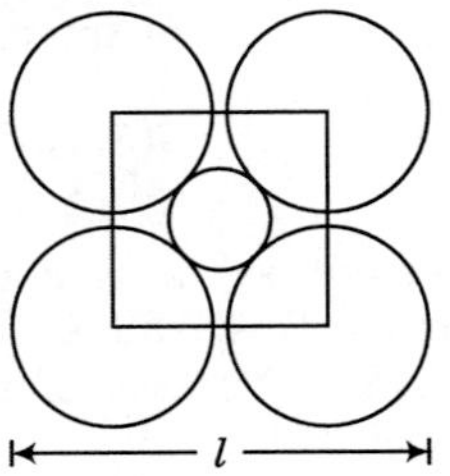

(a) 39.27% (b) 68.02%
(c) 74.05% (d) 78.54%

5. KCl has the same structure as NaCl. If the volume of the unit cell is 247.7 cubic Angstroms. The distance between adjacent K^+ and Cl^- centres is
(a) 1.24 Å (b) 2.48 Å (c) 3.14 Å (d) 6.28 Å

6. The number of hexagonal faces that are present in truncated octahedron is
(a) 2 (b) 4 (c) 6 (d) 8

7. Silver (atomic weight = 108 g mol^{-1}) has a density of 10.5 g cm^{-3}. The number of silver atoms on a surface of area 10^{-12} m^2 can be expressed in scientific notation as 4×10^x. The value of x is
(a) 3 (b) 5 (c) 7 (d) 9

8. Match crystal system/unit cells mentioned in Column I with their characteristic features mentioned in Column II.

	Column I		Column II
A.	Simple cubic and face centred cubic	p.	have these cell parameters $a = b = c$ and $\alpha = \beta = \gamma$
B.	Cubic and rhombohedral	q.	are two crystal systems
C.	Cubic and tetragonal	r.	have only two crystallographic angles of 90°
D.	Hexagonal and monoclinic	s.	belong to same crystal system

(a) A-p, s B-p, q: C-q; D-q,r
(b) A-s; B-r,s; C-p; D-q,s
(c) A-q; B-q,r; C-p; D-p,s
(d) A-q; B-r; C-s; D-p

9. The crystal *AB* (rock salt structure) has molecular weight 6.023 *y*u. where, *y* is an arbitrary number in u . If the minimum distance between cation and anion is $y^{1/3}$ nm and the observed density is 20 kg/m^3. Find the type of defect.
(a) Schottky defect (b) Frenkel defect
(c) Metal excess defect (d) *F*-centre defect

10. Marbles of diameter 10 mm are to be put in a square area of side 40 mm so that their centres are within this area. Maximum number of marbles per unit area are
(a) 5 (b) 10 (c) 15 (d) 25

11. An element crystallizes in fcc lattice having edge length 400 pm. The maximum diameter of atom which can be placed in interstitial site without distorting the structure is
(a) 117 pm (b) 110 pm
(c) 217 pm (d) 11.7 pm

12. A metallic element exists as a cubic lattice. Each edge of the unit cell is 2.88 Å. The density of the metal is 7.20 g cm^{-3}. Number of unit cells in 100 g of the metal will be
(a) 6.022×10^{23} (b) 2.78×10^{23}
(c) 5.82×10^{23} (d) 2.88×10^{10}

13. Iron (II) oxide, FeO, crystal has a cubic structure and each edge of the number cells is 5.0 Å. Density of the oxide is 4.0 g cm^{-3}. Number of Fe^{2+} and O^{2-} ions present in each cell will be
(a) one Fe^{2+} ions and one O^{2-} ions
(b) two Fe^{2+} ions and two O^{2-} ions
(c) three Fe^{2+} ions and three O^{2-} ions
(d) four Fe^{2+} ions and four O^{2-} ions

14. Lithium borohydride, $LiBH_4$, crystallizes in an orthorhombic system. The unit cell dimensions are $a = 6.81$ Å, $b = 4.43$ Å and $c = 7.17$ Å. If the molar mass, *M* of the lithium borohydride ($LiBH_4$) is 21.76 g mol^{-1}, the density of the crystal will be
(a) 0.668 g cm^{-3} (b) 6.68 g cm^{-3}
(c) 66.8 g cm^{-3} (d) 0.0668 g cm^{-3}

15. The parameters of an orthorhombic unit cell are $a = 50$ pm, $b = 100$ pm, $c = 150$ pm. The spacing between the (123) planes will be
(a) 50 pm (b) 29 cm
(c) 19 pm (d) 75 pm

16. The element chromium exists as a bcc lattice whose unit cell edge is 2.88 Å. The density of chromium is 7.20 g/cc. Number of atoms present in 52.0 g of chromium are
(a) 6.05×10^{23} (b) 6.05×10^{24}
(c) 6.05×10^{22} (d) 6.05×10^{28}

17. Gold (197) crystallizes in a 'fcc' unit cell. The second-order reflection ($n = 2$) of X-rays for the planes that makes up the tops and bottoms of the unit cells is at $\theta = 22.20°$. The wavelength of the X-rays is 1.54 Å. The density of the metallic gold is (sin 22.20° = 0.3778)
(a) 19.33 g/cm^3 (b) 1.933 g/cm^3
(c) 19.33 kg/m^3 (d) 1.933 kg/m^3

18. KF has NaCl (fcc) structure with density 2.475 g/cm^3. Determine interionic distance in crystal of KF ($M = 58$ g mol^{-1})
(a) 134.5 pm (b) 26.9 pm
(c) 269 pm (d) None of these

19. X-rays of wavelength 0.154 nm are diffracted from a crystal at angle of 14.17°. Assuming that $n = 1$, calculate the distance between layers in the crystal.
(a) 0.3145 nm (b) 3.145 nm
(c) 31.45 nm (d) 314.5 nm

20. The distance between layers in a NaCl crystal is 282 pm. X-rays are diffracted from these layers at an angle of 23.0°. Assuming that $n = 1$, calculate the wavelength of the X-rays in nm.
(a) 2204 nm (b) 220.4 nm
(c) 22.04 nm (d) 0.2204 nm

21. A group IVA element with density of 11.35 g/cm^3 crystallize in a face-centred cubic lattice whose unit cell edge length is 4.95 Å. What is the element?
(a) Copper (b) Lead
(c) Chromium (d) Iron

22. A newly synthesized copper complex with molecular formula $C_{11}H_{29}N_5B_2Cu$ is found to crystallize in the orthorhombic system with $a = 14.709$ Å, $b = 17.604$ Å and $c = 13.907$ Å. The density is 1.17 g cm^{-3}. Number of molecules per unit cell will be [B = 11, Cu = 63.5]
(a) 2 (b) 4 (c) 6 (d) 8

23. Tantalum (181 g mol^{-1} density 16.7 g/cm^3) crystallizes in a cubic lattice whose unit cell edge length is 3.32 Å. How many atoms are in one unit cell? The types of cubic crystall lattice is
(a) fcc
(b) bcc
(c) simple unit cell lattice
(d) None of the above

24. What is the fraction of the unit cell as shown?

(a) 0.52 (b) 0.68
(c) 0.74 (d) 0.907

25. Calculate the atomic volume of an element whose atoms have a radius 1.414 Å when the atoms are in cubic closest packed structure.
(a) 96.32 cm^3/mol (b) 9.632 cm^3/m
(c) 963.2 cm^3/mol (d) 0.9632 cm^3/mol

26. The edge length of the unit cell of LiCl (NaCl-like structure, fcc) is 5.14 Å. Assuming that the lithium ion is small enough that the chloride ions are in contact, calculate the ionic radius for the chloride ions.

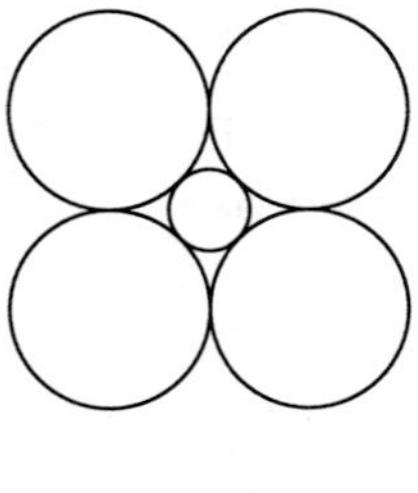

(a) 181.73 Å (b) 18.173 Å
(c) 1.8173Å (d) 0.18173 Å

27. What is the per cent by mass of titanium in rutile, a mineral that contains Ti and oxygen if structure can be described as a closest packed array of oxide ions with titanium ions in one-half of the octahedral holes.
(a) 20% (b) 40%
(c) 60% (d) 80%

28. What fraction of calcium atoms lies on the surface of a cubic crystal that is 1.00 cm in length? Calcium has fcc lattice with edge lengh 0.556 nm.
(a) 1.67×10^{-7} (b) 1.67×10^{8}
(c) 4.39×10^{-7} (d) 3.34×10^{-7}

29. Sodium metal crystallizes in body-centred cubic lattice with the cell edge, $a = 4.29$ Å. The radius of sodium atom is
(a) 1.8576 Å (b) 18.576 Å
(c) 185.76 Å (d) 0.18576 Å

30. Analysis shows that nickel oxide formula $Ni_{0.98}O_{1.00}$. What fractions of the nickel exist as Ni^{2+} ions?
(a) 4.08% (b) 20.16%
(c) 75% (d) 95.92%

31. If NaCl is doped with 10^{-3} mol % of $SrCl_2$, what is the concentration of cation vacancies?
(a) 6.02×10^{23} mol^{-1} (b) 6.02×10^{22} mol^{-1}
(c) 6.02×10^{20} mol^{-1} (d) 6.02×10^{18} mol^{-1}

32. A beam of X-rays from a copper target, with wavelength 154.1 pm is passed at low angles onto the surface of a silver crystal. As the angle is increased from the glancing angle, a beam of reflected X-rays is observed at $\theta = 22.20°$. The spacing between the planes of silver atoms that give rise to this reflection is
(a) 51 pm (b) 102 pm
(c) 204 pm (d) 255 pm

33. Density of NaCl = 2.17 g cc^{-1} at 20°C; molar mass = 58.45. Calculate the interplanar distance (d_{200}). The first order reflection maximum of the X-rays of palladium from 200 planes of NaCl occurs at the glancing angle 5.90°. The wavelength of the X-radiation is
(a) 0.2456 Å (b) 0.5797 Å
(c) 0.6891 Å (d) 0.9132 Å

Answers

Exercise 1

1. (b)	2. (d)	3. (a)	4. (d)	5. (a)	6. (b)	7. (a)	8. (c)	9. (a)	10. (b)
11. (c)	12. (d)	13. (a)	14. (c)	15. (a)	16. (d)	17. (d)	18. (b)	19. (b)	20. (d)
21. (d)	22. (d)	23. (d)	24. (d)	25. (b)	26. (d)	27. (c)	28. (c)	29. (a)	30. (c)
31. (d)	32. (c)	33. (c)	34. (c)	35. (d)	36. (b)	37. (b,c)	38. (a)	39. (c)	40. (c)
41. (c)	42. (d)	43. (c)	44. (a)	45. (a)	46. (c)	47. (b)	48. (b)	49. (d)	50. (b)
51. (a)	52. (a)	53. (d)	54. (d)	55. (d)	56. (a)	57. (b)	58. (c)	59. (c)	60. (b)
61. (c)	62. (a)	63. (c)	64. (b)	65. (c)	66. (d)	67. (b)	68. (a)	69. (c)	70. (a)

Exercise 2

1. (b)	2. (c)	3. (b)	4. (d)	5. (c)	6. (d)	7. (c)	8. (a)	9. (c)	10. (d)
11. (a)	12. (c)	13. (d)	14. (a)	15. (b)	16. (a)	17. (a)	18. (c)	19. (a)	20. (d)
21. (b)	22. (d)	23. (b)	24. (d)	25. (b)	26. (c)	27. (c)	28. (a)	29. (a)	30. (d)
31. (d)	32. (c)	33. (b)							

Hints & Solutions

Exercise 1

3. In fcc structure edge length,

$$a = 2(r_{M^+} + r_{X^-})$$
$$7.2 = 2(r_{M^+} + r_{X^-})$$
$$(r_{M^+} + r_{X^-}) = 3.6$$
$$r_{X^-} = 3.6 - 1.6 = 2.0\text{ Å}$$

4. In NaCl, Na^+ occupies body centre and edge centres while Cl^- occupies corners and face centres, giving four Na^+ and four Cl^- per unit cell. In the present case. 'A represent Cl^- and B represents Na^+. Two face centres lies on one axis.

Number of A removed $= 2 \times \frac{1}{2} = 1$

Number of B is not removed because it is not present on face centres.

$$A \text{ remaining } = 4 - 1 = 3$$
$$B \text{ remaining } = 4$$
$$\text{Formula} = A_3B_4$$

5. In cubic system number of A atoms present at corners of a unit cell $= \frac{1}{8} \times 8 = 1$

Number of B atoms present at the centre of a faces of a unit cell $= \frac{1}{2} \times 6 = 3$

Formula $= AB_3$

7. The given arrangement $AB\ AB\ AB$ represents hexagonal close packed unit cell in which there are six atoms per unit cell. Also volume of a unit cell $= 24\sqrt{2}r^3$

$$\text{Packing fraction} = \frac{\text{Volume occupied by atoms}}{\text{Volume of a unit cell}}$$
$$= 6 \times \frac{4}{3}\pi r^3 \times \frac{1}{24\sqrt{2}r^3} = 0.74$$

Per cent empty space $= 100 - (1 - 0.74) = 26\%$

9. $2d \sin\theta = n\lambda$ (Bragg's equation)

$$d = \frac{n\lambda}{2\sin\theta}$$
$$= \frac{2.29}{2 \times \sin 30°} = 2.29\text{ Å}$$

16. Number of A atoms from the corners of the unit cell $= \frac{7}{8}$

No of B atoms from the faces of unit cell = 3

Thus, $A : B :: \frac{7}{8} : 3$

$$A_{7/8}B_3$$

Hence, the simplest formula is A_7B_{24}.

Exercise 2

1.
$$d = \frac{ZM}{N_A \cdot a^3}$$
$$d \propto \frac{Z}{a^3}$$
$$\frac{d_1}{d_2} = \frac{Z_1}{Z_2}\left(\frac{a_2}{a_1}\right)^3$$
$$= \frac{4}{2}\left(\frac{3}{3.5}\right)^3 = 1.26$$

2. Volume of one molecule $= \frac{4}{3}\pi r^3$

$$= \frac{4}{3}\pi(1.54 \times 10^{-8})^3 \text{ cm}^3$$
$$= 1.53 \times 10^{-23} \text{ cm}^3$$

Volume of all the molecules in 1.65 g Ar

$$= \frac{1.65}{40} \times N_A \times 1.53 \times 10^{-23} \text{ cm}^3$$

$$= 0.380 \text{ cm}^3$$

Volume of solid Ar containing 1.65 g = 1 cm^3

$$\text{Empty space} = 1 - 0.380 = 0.620$$

$$\% = 62\%$$

7. Ag crystallizes in fcc unit cell with 4 atoms per unit cell

$$d = \frac{4 \times 108}{6.023 \times 10^{23} \times a^3} = 10.5 \text{ g cm}^{-3}$$

Volume of a unit cell,

$$a^3 = 6.83 \times 10^{-23} \text{ cm}^3$$

$$a = 4 \times 10^{-8} \text{ cm} = 4 \times 10^{-10} \text{ m}$$

Surface area of unit cell = $a^2 = 1.6 \times 10^{-19}$ m^2

Number of unit cells on 10^{-12} m^2 surface

$$= \frac{10^{-12}}{1.6 \times 10^{-19}} = 6.25 \times 10^6$$

There are two atoms (effectively) on one face a unit cell. Number of atoms on 10^{-12}m^2 surface = 2 × number of unit cell

$$= 1.25 \times 10^7$$

$$x = 7$$

9. In rock salt like crystal *AB*, there are four *AB* units per unit cell. Therefore, density, *d* is

$$d = \frac{4 \times 6.023y}{6.023 \times 10^{23} \times 8y \times 10^{-27}}$$

$$(\because\ a = 2y^{1/3} \text{ nm} = 2y^{1/3} \times 10^{-9} \text{ m})$$

$$= 5 \times 10^3 \text{ g / m}^3$$

$$= 5 \text{ kg / m}^3$$

Since, the observed density is greater than expected theoretical density there must be some excess metal occupying interstitial spaces. This type of defect is known as metal excess defect.

11. If r_1 is the radius of void and r_2 is the radius of atom creating these voids then

for octahedral void, $r_1 = 0.414r_2$

for tetrahedral void, $r_1 = 0.225r_2$

$r_1 = 0.414r_2$ (because octahedral void has larger radius)

In fcc, $4r_2 = \sqrt{2}a$

Diameter required $(2r_1) = (2r_2) \times 0.414$

$$= \frac{a}{\sqrt{2}} \times 0.414$$

$$= \frac{400 \times 0.414}{\sqrt{2}} = 117 \text{ pm}$$

12. Volume of a unit cell = $(2.88 \text{ Å})^2 = 23.9 \times 10^{-24}$ cm^3

Volume of 100 g of the metal = $\frac{100\text{g}}{7.20 \text{ g cm}^{-3}} = 13.9 \text{ cm}^3$

Number of unit cells in 100 g metal

$$= \frac{13.9 \text{ cm}^3}{23.9 \times 10^{-24} \text{ cm}^3}$$

$$= 5.82 \times 10^{23}$$

13. Volume of the unit cell = $(5 \times 10^{-8})^3$ cm^3

$$= 1.25 \times 10^{-22} \text{ cm}^3$$

Density of FeO = 4.0 g cm^{-3}

Mass of the unit cell = $d \times V$

$$= 1.25 \times 10^{-22} \times 4.0$$

$$= 5.0 \times 10^{-22} \text{ g}$$

Mass of one molecule of FeO = $\frac{\text{molar mass (g)}}{6.022 \times 10^{23}}$

$$= \frac{72}{1.195 \times 10^{-22}} = 1.195 \times 10^{-22} \text{ g}$$

Number of FeO molecules per unit cells

$$= \frac{5.0 \times 10^{-22}}{1.195 \times 10^{-22}} = 4.19 \approx 4$$

Hence, there are four Fe^{2+} ions and four O^{2-} ions in each unit cell.

15. For an orthorhombic unit cell, the inter planar distance, d_{hkl}

$$\frac{1}{(d_{hkl})^2} = (h^2/a^2) + (k^2/b^2) + (l^2/c^2)$$

$$= (1/50)^2 + (2/100)^2 + (3/150)^2$$

$$= 3\,(1/50)^2$$

$$\frac{1}{d_{123}} = \sqrt{3}/50$$

$$d_{123} = 50/\sqrt{3} = 29 \text{ pm}$$

16. $$d = \frac{ZM}{a^3 N_A}$$

$$M = \frac{dN_A a^3}{Z}$$

$$= \frac{7.2 \times 6.02 \times 10^{23} \times (2.88 \times 10^{-8})^3}{2}$$

$$= 51.77 \text{ g mol}^{-1}$$

$$\therefore \quad 52.0 \text{ g Cr} = \frac{52.0}{51.77} \text{ mol} = \frac{52\,N_A}{51.77}$$

$$= 6.05 \times 10^{23} \text{ atoms}$$

17. For 'fcc' unit cell number of atoms in unit cell = 4

Also by Bragg's equation $2d \sin\theta = n\lambda$

$$d = \frac{n\lambda}{2 \sin\theta}$$

$$= \frac{2 \times 1.54 \times 10^{-8}}{2 \times \sin 22.2}$$

$$= 4.076 \times 10^{-8} \text{ cm}$$

$$d = \frac{M_z}{N_A a^3}$$

$$= \frac{197 \times 4}{6.02 \times 10^{23} \times (4.076 \times 10^{-8})^3}$$

$$= 19.33 \text{ g / cm}^3$$

18. Interionic distance = $(r_+ + r_-) = \frac{a}{2}$

$$a^3 = \frac{M_z}{dN_A}$$

$$= \frac{58 \times 4}{2.475 \times 6.02 \times 10^{23}}$$

$$\therefore \quad a = 5.38 \times 10^{-8} \text{ cm}$$

$$= 538 \text{ pm}$$

$$(r_+ + r_-) = \frac{a}{2}$$

$$= 269 \text{ pm}$$

19. $2d \sin \theta = n\lambda$

$$d \text{ (distance between layers)} = \frac{n\lambda}{2 \sin \theta}$$

$$= \frac{1 \times 0.154}{2 \sin (14.17)} = 0.3145 \text{ nm}$$

20.

$$2d \sin \theta = n\lambda$$

$$\lambda = \frac{2d \sin \theta}{n}$$

$$= \frac{2 \times 282 \times \sin 23°}{1}$$

$$= 220.37 \text{ pm}$$

$$= 220.37 \times 10^{-12} \text{ m}$$

$$= 220.37 \times 10^{-9} \times 10^{-3} \text{ m}$$

$$= \frac{220.37}{1000} \text{ nm}$$

$$= 0.2204 \text{ nm}$$

21.

$$\text{Density } d = \frac{Mz}{N_A a^3}$$

$$M = \frac{dN_A a^3}{z}$$

$$= \frac{11.35 \times 6.02 \times 10^{23} \times (4.95 \times 10^{-8})^3}{4}$$

$$= 207.18 \text{ g mol}^{-1}$$

Element is lead.

23.

$$\text{Density} = \frac{\text{Mass of unit cell}}{\text{Volume}}$$

$$= \frac{Mz}{VN_A} = \frac{Mz}{a \times b \times c \times N_0}$$

$$\therefore \quad z = \frac{a \times b \times c \times d \times N_A}{M}$$

$$= \frac{14.749 \times 10^{-8} \times 17.604 \times 10^{-8} \times 13.907 \times 10^{-8} \times 1.17 \times 6.02 \times 10^{23}}{316.5}$$

$$= 8$$

24.

$$\text{Packing fraction} = \frac{\text{Area occupied by circles}}{\text{Area of the unit cell}}$$

Area occupied by parallelograms = $2R(\sqrt{3}R) = 2\sqrt{3}R^2$

The unit cell content is the total number of atoms contained within the unit cell. From fig. it is clear that only part of each circle is contained within the parallelogram unit cell. Adding all these (shaded) part, we get one circle. Thus, area of one circle $(Z = 1) = \pi R^2$.

$$\therefore \text{ Packing fraction} = \frac{\pi R^2}{2\sqrt{3}R^2} = 0.907$$

25. Structure is cubic closest packed (fcc)

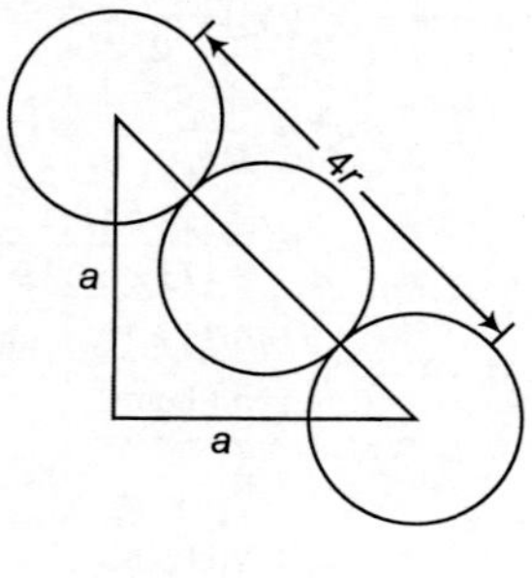

Thus, $z = 4$

Also diagonal $= 4 \times r$

$$= \sqrt{a^2 + a^2} = \sqrt{2}a$$

$$\therefore \quad a = \frac{4r}{\sqrt{2}} = 2\sqrt{2}r$$

$$= 2\sqrt{2} \times 1.414 \text{ Å}$$

$$= 4 \text{ Å}$$

Thus, volume of four atoms $= N_A a^3$

$$\therefore \quad \text{Atomic volume} = \frac{N_A a^3}{4}$$

$$= \frac{6.02 \times 10^{23} \times (4 \times 10^{-8})^3}{4}$$

$$= 9.632 \text{ cm}^3 \text{ / mol}$$

26. Li^+ ion is so small that all the ions in the structure touch as shown :

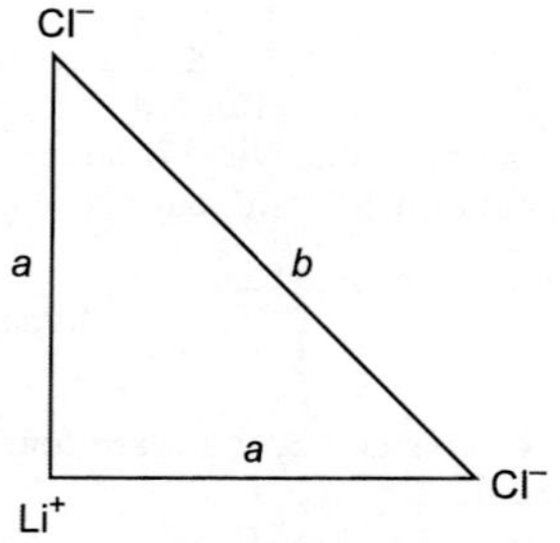

Let a = distance between the centres of Li^+ and Cl^- ions, then

$$a = \frac{5.14}{2} = 2.57 \text{ Å}$$

b = distance between the centres of two Cl^- ions then

$$b = \sqrt{a^2 + a^2} = \sqrt{2}a = \sqrt{2} \times 2.57 \text{ Å}$$

$$= 3.6345 \text{ Å}$$

$$\therefore \quad r_{Cl^-} = \frac{b}{2} = 1.8173 \text{ Å}$$

27. Let the number of oxide ions = 1

Titanium ions occupy half of the octahedral holes so, number of titanium ions $= \frac{1}{2} \times 1 = \frac{1}{2}$

(there is one octahedral hole for one oxide ion)

Chemical formula for rutile $= Ti_{1/2}O$

$$= TiO_2$$

Total molar mass of TiO_2 $= 48 + 32 = 80 \text{ g mol}^{-1}$

$$\% \text{ of Ti} = \frac{48}{80} \times 100 = 60\%.$$

28. The number of unit cells present in the crystals is $= \frac{V_{(\text{crystal})}}{V_{(\text{unit cell})}}$

$(1 \text{ nm} = 10^{-9} \text{ m} = 10^{-7} \text{ cm})$

$$= \frac{(1.00)^3}{(0.556 \times 10^{-7})^3}$$

$$= 5.82 \times 10^{21}$$

Number of atoms present $= 4 \times 5.82 \times 10^{21}$

$$= 23.28 \times 10^{21}$$

$$\text{Number of surface cells} = \frac{\text{Area (crystal) of six faces}}{\text{Area (unit cell)}}$$

$$= \frac{(1)^2 \times 6}{(0.556 \times 10^{-7})^2}$$
$$= 1.94 \times 10^{15}$$

On the surface of a unit cell, there are two atoms-the face centred atom and one-fourth of each of the four corner atoms.

Thus, number of atoms present on the surface

$$= 1.94 \times 10^{15} \times 2 = 3.88 \times 10^{15}$$

Thus, fraction of the atoms on the surface is

$$\frac{N_{(surface)}}{N_{(crystal)}} = \frac{3.88 \times 10^{15}}{23.28 \times 10^{21}}$$
$$= 1.67 \times 10^{-7}$$

29. For bcc structure :

$$r = \frac{\sqrt{3}}{4} a$$
$$= \frac{\sqrt{3}}{4} \times 4.29 \text{ Å}$$
$$= 1.8576 \text{ Å}$$

30. From the valency of nickel as Ni(II) and Ni(III), it is clear that three Ni(II) ions will be replaced by two Ni(III) ions, thus, causing a loss of one nickel ion.

Total loss of nickel from one molecule of NiO = 1 – 0.98
= 0.02

Total nickel (III) present in one molecule of NiO

$$= 0.02 \times 2 = 0.04$$

Thus, percentage of Ni(III) $= \frac{0.04}{0.98} \times 100$

$$= 4.08\%$$

and Ni(II) = 95.92%.

31. Due to addition of $SrCl_2$, each Sr^{2+} ion replaces two Na^+ ions, but occupied only one Na^+ lattice point. This makes one cationic vacancy.

100 moles of NaCl contains cation vacancies $= 10^{-3}$ mol

Thus, 1 moles of NaCl contains cation vacancies $= 10^{-5}$ mol

Total cation vacancies $= N_A \times 10^{-5}$
$$= 6.02 \times 10^{23} \times 10^{-5}$$
$$= 6.02 \times 10^{18} \text{ mol}^{-1}.$$

32. $n\lambda = 2d \sin \theta$

$$\sin \theta = \frac{n\lambda}{2d}$$

Smallest angle reflection is the first order reflection.

So, $n = 1$

$$d = \frac{n\lambda}{2 \sin \theta}$$
$$= \frac{1 \times 154.1}{2 \sin 22.20°}$$
$$d = \frac{1 \times 154.1}{2 \times 0.3778} = 204 \text{ pm}$$

33. Interplanar distance, $d_{200} = \left(\frac{M}{2NP}\right)^{1/3}$

$$= \left(\frac{58.45}{2 \times 6.023 \times 10^{23} \times 2.17}\right)^{1/3}$$
$$= (2.236 \times 10^{-23})^{1/3}$$
$$= 2.82 \times 10^{-8} \text{ cm} = 2.82 \text{ Å}$$
$$n\lambda = 2d \sin \theta$$
$$1 \times \lambda = 2 \times 2.82 \times \sin 5.9°$$
(sin 5.9° = 0.1028)
$$\lambda = 2 \times 2.82 \times 0.1028 = 0.5797 \text{ Å}$$

27

Data Analysis

Syllabus

- Types of Errors
- Accuracy
- Mean and Standard Deviation
- Distribution of Random Errors
- Correlation and Regression

Introduction

The function of the analyst is to obtain a result as close to the true value as possible by the correct application of the analytical procedure employed. He is always interested in knowing the cause and magnitude of errors in his measurement which is always present. Since, measurements involve recording of data which are always associated with a certain amount of uncertainty, the proper handling of data obtained by measuring the quantities is very important.

Types of Errors

Errors which affect an experimental result may be divided into two groups, (i) systematic or determinate errors and (ii) random or indeterminate errors.

(i) Systematic or determinate errors

These types of errors can be avoided or their magnitude can be determined. The most important of them are as follows :

(a) **Operational and personal errors** For these types of errors only individual analyst is responsible. These errors are not connected with the method or procedure. These errors are usually physical in nature and occur when sound analytical technique is not followed. *e.g.,* overwashing or underwashing the precipitates, ignition of precipitate at improper temperature, insufficient cooling of crucibles before weighing, mechanical loss of materials in various steps of analysis and use of reagents containing harmful impurities. Personal errors may arise also due to the inability of a person to make certain observations accurately.

(b) **Instrumental and reagent errors** These errors arise due to faulty construction of chemical balances, improperly calibrated weights, burette, and other glass wares and instruments, the attack of reagents upon porcelain, glass ware etc. (which results in addition of foreign materials) and use of reagents containing impurities.

(c) **Errors of method** These types of errors arise due to incorrect sampling and due to incompleteness of a reaction. *e.g.,* in titrimetric analysis errors may arise due to failure of reactions to proceed to completion, occurrence of induced or side reactions and a difference between the observed end point and stoichiometric equivalence point of a reaction. In gravimetric analysis errors may arise due to coprecipitation, post precipitation, appreciable solubility of precipitates and decomposition or volatilisation of precipitate during ignition and precipitation of undesired substances.

(d) **Additive and proportional errors** The absolute value of an additive error is independent of the amount of the substance being determined *e.g.,* loss in weight of crucible in which a precipitate is ignited, error in weights and solubility of precipitate. The absolute value of proportional error depends upon the amount of substance present *e.g.,* presence of impurities in a standard substance results in wrong value of normality of the standard solution.

(ii) Random or indeterminate errors

These errors are usually small and irregular. An analyst has hardly any control over these errors. These errors are due to the limitations in the equipment used and the limited skill of the observer.

Accuracy

Accuracy is the agreement of a particular value to the true value of the result *e.g.,* if the true value of a result is 2.00 g and a student '*A*' takes two measurements and reports the results as 2.01g and 1.99 g. These values are accurate. Accuracy is expressed in terms of either absolute or relative error.

- **Absolute error** It is the difference between the measured value and true value.

Absolute error, $E = x_i - x_t$;

where, x_1 = measured value

and x_i = true value of the quantity.

A low value produces a negative error and a high value produces a positive one.

Relative error It is more useful quantity than the absolute error. The per cent relative error,

$$E_R = \frac{x_i - x_t}{x_t} \times 100$$

It is also expressed in parts per thousand (ppt).

Precision It refers to the closeness of various measurements for the same quantity. Accuracy expresses the correctness of a measurement and precision the reproductibility of a measurement. Ideally all measurements should be both accurate and precise. Measurements are frequently repeated to improve accuracy and precision. Average values obtained from several measurements are usually more reliable than individual measurements. Significant figures indicate how accurately measurement have been made.

Minimisation of errors Systematic errors can be reduced by one of the following methods :

- Calibration of apparatus and application of corrections.
- Running a blank determination.
- Running a control determination using primary standards.
- Running parallel determinations.
- Use of independent method of analysis.
- Standard addition
- Internal standards
- Amplification method
- Isotopic dilution

Significant Figures

The total number of digits in the number is called the number of significant figures (SF). It equals the number of digits written including the last one, even though its value is uncertain. The following rules should be followed in counting of (SF) in a given measured quantity :

(i) All digits are significant except zero at the beginning of the number.

(ii) The zeros to the right of the decimal point are significant.

Thus, zero between non-zero digits are significant.

Digit	SF	Rule
101	3	i
0.101	3	i
0.0101	3	i
101.0	4	ii
101.00	5	ii

(iii) The above rules prepurpose that the numbers are expressed in scientific notation. In this term, every number is written as $N \times 10^n$.

where, N = a number with a single non-zero digit to the left of the decimal point.

n = an integer.

We can write 20000 in scientific notation as

	2×10^4	2.0×10^4	2.00×10^4
having	1 S.F.	2 S.F.	3 S.F.

(iv) Zero at the end of a number and before the decimal point may or may not be significant.

- Any number can be conveniently transformed to scientific notation by moving the decimal point in the number to obtain a new number, A greater than or equal to 1 and less than 10. If the decimal point is moved to the left, you multiply A by 10^n, when, n equals the number of places moved. If the decimal point is moved to the right, you multiply A by 10^{-n}.

SF in Numerical Calculations

To express the result of an experiment, we have often **add**, **subtract**, **multiply** or **divide** the number obtained in different measurements. It usually happens these different numbers do not have the same precision. The following rules should be followed to obtain the proper numbr of S.F. in any calculation.

Rule I S.F. rule in multiplication/division

The result of multiplication and/or division may carry no more S.F. than the least precisely known quantity in the calculation. In the following **multiplication**, the result should be in **three S.F.**

$$\underset{(4\text{ S.F.})}{14.79} \times \underset{(4\text{ S.F.})}{12.11} \times \underset{(3\text{ S.F.})}{5.05} = 904.\cancel{48985} = 904$$

$$= \underset{(3\text{ S.F.})}{9.04} \times 10^2$$

Rule II S.F. rule in addition/subtraction

The result of addition and/or subtraction must be expressed with the same number of decimal places as the term carrying the smallest number of decimal places. In the following addition the result should be reported only up to one digit after the decimal point.

$$22.2 + 2.22 + 0.222 = 24.6\cancel{42} = 24.6.$$

Rule III S.F. rule for each exact number

Exact numbers can be considered to have an **unlimited number** of S.F.

Rule IV

If $Q = Kx^a$, where, K is a constant and a is an accurately known constant component, then

$$\frac{\Delta Q}{Q} = a\frac{\Delta x}{x}$$

i.e., the fractional uncertainty in Q is equal to the fractional uncertainty in x multiplied by the exponent a.

Rule V

The number of significant digits in x determines the number of decimal places (the mantissa) in log x, and conversely.

This rule is illustrated by following example.

If we take $[H^+] = 3.75 \times 10^{-5}$ M

then $pH = -\log[H^+] = -[0.574 - 5] = 4.426$

Here, three decimal places are kept in the mantissa (0.574) because $[H^+]$ is given to three significant digits (3.75).

On the other hand, if it is given that pH = 10.7, then

$$[H^+] = 10^{-pH} = 10^{-10}\ 10^{-0.7}$$
$$= 10^{-11} \times 10^{0.3}$$
$$= 2 \times 10^{-11}$$

Where, we evaluate the antilog of 0.7 to one significant digit since 0.7 has only one decimal place).

"Rounding Off" the Numerical Results

To three S.F., we should express 15.453 as 15.5 and 14755 as 1.48×10^4. It is called **"Rounding off"** the result.

- If the first digit you remove is less than 5, round down by dropping it and all following digits. Thus, 5.663507 becomes 5.66 when rounded off to three S.F. because first of the dropped digits (3) is less than 5.
- If the first digit you remove is 6 or greater than 6 round off by adding 1 to the digit on the left. Thus, 5.663507 becomes 5.7 when rounded off to four S.F.
- If the first digit you remove is 5 and there are more non-zero digits following round up. Thus, 5.663507 becomes 5.664 when rounded off to four S.F.
- If the digit you remove is 5 and there is no digit after, then **add one** to the preceeding digit if it is **odd**, otherwise write as such if it **is even**.

Thus, 4.7475 becomes 4.748 when rounded off to four S.F.

(odd digit before 5)

and 4.7465 becomes 4.746 when rounded off to four S.F.

(even digit before 5)

Mean and Standard Deviation

The mean is the numerical value obtained by dividing the sum of a set of measurements by the total number of measurements. It is also known as arithmetic mean. Let the series of n observations arranged in ascending order of magnitude; $x_1, x_2, x_3 \ldots x_{n-1}, x_n$, the arithmetic mean is given by

$$\bar{x} = \frac{x_1 + x_2 + x_3 + \ldots + x_{n-1} + x_n}{n}$$

Median

It is defined as the middle most or central value of the variate when the observations are arranged in ascending or descending order of their magnitudes. Let n be the number of observations in the series.

- If n is odd, then

$$M_e = \left(\frac{n+1}{2}\right) \text{th term}$$

- In n is even, then

$$M_e = \frac{\left(\frac{n}{2}\right)\text{th term} + \left(\frac{n}{2}+1\right)\text{th term}}{2}$$

The mean and median may or may not be the same. If data is irregular near median than it would not be a true representative.

Mean Deviation

Mean deviation or average deviation is the arithmetic mean of deviation of all the values taken from a statistical average (mean, median or mode) of the series. Let the series be $x_1, x_2 \ldots x_n$ and let M be any average ($\bar{x}$ or M_e or M_0) of the series. Then the mean deviation is defined as :

$$\text{MD} = \frac{1}{n}\sum_{i=1}^{n} |x_i - M|$$

where, x_i = ith observation of the series and n = number of observations.

Relative Mean Deviation

It is the mean deviation divided by the mean. It is expressed in terms of percentage or parts per thousand.

Standard Deviation

It is the square root of the arithmetic mean of the squared deviations of various values from their arithmetic mean.

Let the series be $x_1, x_2 \ldots x_n$ and mean of the given series be $\bar{x}$, then the standard deviation is defined as

$$\text{SD} = +\sqrt{\frac{1}{N}\sum_{i=1}^{n}(x_i - \bar{x})^2}$$

or

$$\text{SD} = \sigma = +\sqrt{\frac{\sum_{i=1}^{n} x_i^2}{n} - (\bar{x})^2}$$

where, x_i = ith observation of the series,

$\bar{x}$ = arithmetic mean

and n = number of observations.

The square of the standard deviation is called **variance.**

The relative measure of dispersion based on standard deviation is called coefficient of the standard deviation and is defined as,

$$\text{Coefficient of SD} = \frac{\sigma}{\bar{x}}$$

Coefficient of variation is equal to $\text{CV} = \frac{\sigma}{\bar{x}} \times 100$

The mean of several reading $(\bar{x})$ will make a more reliable estimate of the true mean (μ) than is given by one observation.

Distribution of Random Errors

If a large number of replicate readings, at least 50 are taken of a continuous variable, *e.g.*, a titrimetric end point the results obtained will usually be distributed about the mean in a roughly symmetrical manner. The mathematical model that best satisfies such a distribution of random errors is called **Normal or Gaussian distribution**. The bell shaped curve satisfies the equation,

$$\frac{1}{\sigma\sqrt{2\pi}} e - \frac{(x-\mu)^2}{2\sigma}$$

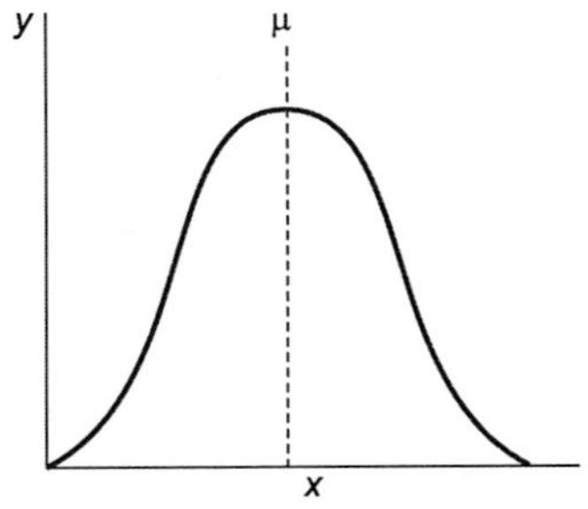

Normal distribution

where,

σ = standard deviation

and μ = mean of total population, s and $\bar{x}$ are used for samples of populations.

Reliability of Results

Analysis of the results can be considered in two main categories (i) reliability of the results (ii) comparison of the results with the true value. Q test

$$Q = \frac{|\text{questionable value} - \text{nearest value}|}{\text{largest value} - \text{smallest value}}$$

If the value of Q exceeds the critical value given in the Q-table, then the questionable value may be rejected.

Confidence Interval

Confidence limits of μ, for n replicate measurement,

$$\mu = \bar{x} \pm \frac{t_s}{\sqrt{n}};$$

where, t is a parameter that depends upon the number of degrees of freedom (v) and confidence level required.

Comparison of Results

- **Students t-test** $t = \frac{(\bar{x} - \mu)\sqrt{n}}{s}$
- ***F*-test** $F = \frac{s_A^2}{s_B^2}$

Comparison of the means of two samples

$$t = \frac{\bar{x}_1 - \bar{x}_2}{s_p\sqrt{\frac{1}{n_1} + \frac{1}{n_2}}};$$

where, s_p is the pooled standard deviation.

$$s_p = \sqrt{\frac{(n_1 - 1)\, s_1^2 + (n_2 - 1)\, s_2^2}{n_1 + n_2 - 2}}$$

Correlation and Regression

There are two statistical tests that should be applied to a calibration curve;

(i) to ascertain if the graph is linear, or in the form of a curve.

(ii) to evaluate the best straight line (or curve) throughout the data points.

Correlation coefficient

Pearson's correlation coefficient,

$$r = \frac{n\,\Sigma x_1 y_1 - \Sigma x_1\, \Sigma y_1}{\sqrt{[n\,\Sigma x_1^2 - (\Sigma x_1)^2]\,[n\,\Sigma y_1^2 - (\Sigma y_1)^2]}}$$

where, x_1 and y_1 are two variables and n is the number of data points. The value of r must lie between + 1 and − 1 (there is a definite linear relationship between variables x and y).

Linear Regression

The equation of straight line is

$$y = ax + b;$$

where, y is dependent variable and x is the independent variable. To obtain the regression line y on x, the slope of the line (a)

$$= \frac{n\,\Sigma x_1 y_1 - \Sigma x_1\, \Sigma y_1}{n\,\Sigma x_1^2 - (\Sigma x_1)^2}$$

and the intercept on the y axis $(b) = \bar{y} - a\bar{x}$ where, $\bar{x}$ and $\bar{y}$ are mean of all values of x_1 and y_1 respectively.

Exercise

1. The number of significant figures in 0.0500 are
(a) one (b) three
(c) two (d) four

2. The correctly reported answer of the addition of 29.4406, 3.2 of 2.25 will have significant figures
(a) three (b) four
(c) two (d) five

3. On dividing 0.25 by 22.1176, the actual answer is 0.011303. The correctly reported answer will be
(a) 0.011 (b) 0.01
(c) 0.0113 (d) 0.013

4. Two students X and Y report the mass of the same substance as 7.0 g and 7.00 g respectively. Which of the following statement is correct?
(a) Both are equally accurate
(b) X is more accurate than Y
(c) Y is more accurate than X
(d) Both are inaccurate scientifically

5. In which of the following numbers all zeros are significant?
(a) 0.0005 (b) 0.0500
(c) 50.000 (d) 0.0050

6. Two students performed the same experiment separately and each one of them recorded two readings of mass which are given below. Correct reading of mass is 3.0 g. On the basis of given data, mark the correct option out of the following statements.

Student	Reading	
	(i)	(ii)
A	3.01	2.99
B	3.05	2.95

(a) Results of both the students are neither accurate nor precise
(b) Results of student *A* are both precise and accurate
(c) Results of student *B* are neither precise nor accurate
(d) Results of student *B* are both precise and accurate

7. If the density of a solution is 3.12 g mL^{-1}, the mass of 1.5 mL solution in significant figures is
(a) 4.7 g (b) 4680×10^{-3} g
(c) 4.680 g (d) 46.80 g

8. How many significant figures should be present in the answer of the following calculations?
$$\frac{2.5 \times 1.25 \times 3.5}{2.01}$$
(a) 2 (b) 3
(c) 4 (d) 5

Assertion & Reason

Codes
(a) Both A and R are true and R is the correct explanation of A.
(b) Both A and R are true but R is not the correct explanation of A.
(c) A is true but R is false.
(d) A is false but R is true.

9. **Assertion (A)** Significant figures for 0.200 is 3 where as for 200 it is 1.
Reason (R) Zero at the end or right of a number are significant.

10. Determinate error can be obtained by
(a) experimentally
(b) theoretically
(c) both experimentally and theoretically
(d) None of the above

11. 17000000 cm can be expressed by two significant numbers as
(a) 170 km (b) 1.7×10^7 cm
(c) 0.0170×10^9 cm (d) 0.15×10^6 m

12. With the increase in absolute error the value of the relative error
(a) increases
(b) decreases
(c) remains same
(d) first decreases then increases

13. Which of the following statements is correct?
(a) Additive error is an example of indeterminate error
(b) Erratic error is an example of determinate error
(c) Determinate error is also known as accidental error
(d) Indeterminate error is also known as random

14. For a set of experimental data standard deviation is determined to be 1.5. Thus, the mean deviation would be approximately
(a) 1.2 (b) 2.2
(c) 3.2 (d) 4.2

15. A precipitate is ignited in a crucible and the error varies due to the loss of weight of the crucible concerned. This type of error is
(a) methodic error (b) personal error
(c) instrumental error (d) proportional error

16. Accuracy cannot be determined by the method
(a) comparative (b) absolute
(c) minimal (d) None of these

17. Accuracy expresses the
(a) deviation from experiment
(b) correctness of an experiment
(c) feasibility of an experiment
(d) reproducibility of an experiment

18. Amongst the following coefficients of variance for four sets of experiments whose values are given below, the most consistent one is
(a) 1.12 (b) 1.22 (c) 1.21 (d) 2.12

19. Which of the following is determinate error?
(a) Erratic error (b) Personal error
(c) Absolute error (d) Relative error

20. Two sets of experiments have equivalent absolute errors but the number of measurements taken are different. Thus, they would have
(a) equivalent mean deviations
(b) equivalent standard deviations
(c) equivalence variance
(d) None of the above

21. A sample of iron weighs 6.5425 g and its density is 8.8 g cm^{-3}. What is the volume? The answer in terms of significant number is
(a) 0.7 cm^3 (b) 0.74 cm^3
(c) 0.743 cm^3 (d) 0.74346 cm^3

22. The mean deviation expressed as a fraction of the mean value in percentage is known as
(a) standard deviation
(b) relative deviation
(c) standard mean deviation
(d) None of the above

23. Proportional error is an example of
(a) relative error (b) absolute error
(c) determinate error (d) indeterminate error

24. A set of measurement of an experimental data shows the values 28.7, 28.9 and 28.8 while the true value is 24.4, thus, the experimental data shows
(a) poor accuracy but good precision
(b) poor accuracy and poor precision
(c) good accuracy and good precision
(d) good accuracy and poor precision

25. The percentage of a constituent x in a compound was found to be 48.32, 48.36 and 48.22. The mean deviation would be
(a) 0.053 (b) 0.53 (c) 5.3 (d) 0.0053

26. Which of the following errors are not an example of constant error?
(a) Reagent errors (b) Erratic errors
(c) Personal error (d) Additive errors

27. Keeping all the parameter same if the standard deviation is doubled, variance would be
(a) halved (b) remain same
(c) doubled (d) quadrupled

28. Which one of the following statements is correct?
(a) Accuracy is the measurement of systematic error
(b) Precision expresses reproducibility of a measurement of an experiment under identical set of condition
(c) Mistakes are absolute errors
(d) Indeterminate errors are constant

29. Which of the following errors cannot be avoided?
(a) Instrumental errors (b) Additive errors
(c) Personal errors (d) Indeterminate errors

30. Keeping the mean deviation constant, if the arithmetic mean is doubled, the relative deviation would be
(a) halved (b) doubled
(c) quadrupled (d) remain same

31. Which type of error effects to the same degree the results of a series of determinations?
(a) Indeterminate (b) Accidental
(c) Determinate (d) Errratic

32. Evaluate 3.728 – log (1.1×10^{-7}) and round off your answer to the proper number of significant figures.
(a) 10.69 (b) 10.687
(c) 10.6870 (d) None of these

33. 57.675 is rounded off to in four significant figures as
(a) 5.768×10^1 (b) 57.68
(c) 5.767 (d) 0.5767×10^2

34. Which choice best describes the degree of uncertainty in the measurement 16.30 g?
(a) The uncertainty cannot be determined without additional information
(b) The quantity is exact
(c) ± 0.10 g
(d) ± 0.01 g

35. Which choice best describes the degree of uncertainty in the measurement 4.0032 g?
(a) The quantity is exact
(b) The uncertainty cannot be determined with additional information
(c) The measurement is between 4.002 and 4.004 g
(d) The measurement is between 4.0031 and 4.0033 g

36. Least count of an analytical balance is 0.0002 g. Which of the following is the correct recorded value?
(a) 9.3171 g (b) 9.317 g
(c) 9.3175 g (d) 9.3170 g

37. The mercury thermometer commonly used in the doctor's office may be accurate to ±0.1°C. In degree celsius express the per cent error expected in measuring person's body temperature of 38.9°C.
(a) 0.257% (b) 0.098%
(c) 0.076% (d) 0.045%

38. Find the mean deviation from the following data.

Weight (g)	Deviation
15.11	0.17
15.38	0.10
15.32	0.04
15.36	0.08
15.23	0.05

(a) 1.88 (b) 0.188 (c) 18.8 (d) 0.088

39. In the above question what is relative mean deviation?

(a) 5.75 ppt (b) 57.5 ppt
(c) 575 ppt (d) 0.575 ppt

40. Mathematically the standard deviation is represented by

(a) $\sigma = \sqrt{\frac{\Sigma (x_i - \bar{x})^2}{N}}$ (b) $\sigma = \sqrt{\frac{\Sigma (x_i - \bar{x}^2)}{N}}$

(c) $\sigma = \sqrt{\frac{\Sigma (x_i - \bar{x})}{N}}$ (d) $\sigma = \sqrt{\frac{\Sigma (x_i^2 - \bar{x})}{N}}$

Answers

1. (b)	**2.** (a)	**3.** (a)	**4.** (c)	**5.** (c)	**6.** (b)	**7.** (a)	**8.** (a)	**9.** (c)	**10.** (c)
11. (b)	**12.** (a)	**13.** (d)	**14.** (a)	**15.** (c)	**16.** (c)	**17.** (b)	**18.** (a)	**19.** (b)	**20.** (d)
21. (b)	**22.** (b)	**23.** (c)	**24.** (a)	**25.** (a)	**26.** (b)	**27.** (d)	**28.** (b)	**29.** (d)	**30.** (a)
31. (c)	**32.** (a)	**33.** (b)	**34.** (d)	**35.** (d)	**36.** (d)	**37.** (a)	**38.** (d)	**39.** (a)	**40.** (a)

Hints & Solutions

32. The number of decimal places in the log term is limited to two.

$$3.728 - \log(1.1 \times 10^{-7})$$
$$= 3.728 + 6.959 = 10.687 = 10.69$$

Answer is expressed in two decimal places as there are two significant digits in log term.

36. Result should be reported up to four decimal places such that fourth decimal digit should be even number including zero.

28 IUPAC Nomenclature of Organic Compounds

Introduction

The simplest organic compounds containing carbon and hydrogen only are called hydrocarbons and when combined with a hetero atom are called hydrocarbon derivatives. The properties of an organic compound chiefly depend upon the presence of functional group which contains a hetero atom (O, N, S, *X*, etc). Each homologous series containing a specific functional group show similar properties. Organic compounds are named by the rules quoted by IUPAC (International Union of Pure and Applied Chemistry).

Syllabus

- IUPAC Nomenclature of Organic Molecules Including Regio-isomers and Stereoisomers

Naming of Organic Compounds

The International Union of Pure and Applied Chemistry (IUPAC) system of naming is primarily based on :

1. Word root
2. Suffix (primary and secondary)
3. Prefix (primary and secondary)

Word Root

The number of carbon atoms present in the longest chain of the compound is the basis of word root.

Table 28.1 **Word Root for Different Carbon Chains**

Length of chain	Word root	Length of chain	Word root
C_1	Meth	C_{10}	Dec
C_2	Eth	C_{11}	Undec
C_3	Prop	C_{12}	Dodec
C_4	But	C_{13}	Tridec
C_5	Pent	C_{20}	Eicos
C_6	Hex	C_{21}	Heneicos
C_7	Hept	C_{22}	Doicos
C_8	Oct	C_{30}	Triacont
C_9	Non	C_{31}	Hentriacont

Suffix

Primary suffix indicates the unsaturation in carbon chain. *e.g.,*

Unsaturation	Primary suffix
C—C	ane
C═C	ene
C≡C	yne

If the parent chain contains two or more double bonds then the numerical prefixes like di, tri, tetra etc., are added before the primary suffix. *e.g.,*

For two ═ bonds : diene
For three ═ bonds : triene
For two ≡ bonds : diyne
For three ≡ bonds : triyne

The secondary suffix indicates the functional group present in the organic compond. *e.g.,*

Functional group	Secondary suffix
Alcohol (—OH)	ol
Aldehyde (—CHO)	al

Prefix

In case of cyclic compounds, the primary prefix, cyclo is added before the word root of the parent chain of the compound. *e.g.,*

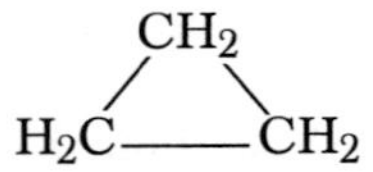

Cyclopropane

The secondary prefixes indicate the substitution of groups (other than functional group) in place of hydrogen atoms in the compound. *e.g.,*

Atom/Group	Name
—F	Fluoro
—Cl	Chloro
—OCH_3	Methoxy

Some suffix and prefix for functional groups are given in Table 28.2.

Table 28.2 **Suffix and Prefix for Functional Groups**

Group	Structure	Prefix	Suffix
Acid	—C(=O)—OH	Carboxy	Carboxylic or –oic
Acid amide	—C(=O)—NH_2	Carbamoyl	Amide or carbonamide
Acid chloride	—C(=O)—Cl	Chloroformyl	Oyl or carbonyl
Alcohol	—OH	Hydroxy	ol
Aldehyde	—C(=O)—H	formyl, aldo, oxo	al
Amine	—NH_2	Amino	amine
Carbonitric (nitrile)	—CN	cyano	carbonitrile (nitrile)
Double bond	C═C	—	ene
Ester	—C(=O)—O(*R*)	Alk (yl) oxocarbonyl	carboxylate
Ether	—O—*R*	Alkoxy	—
Ethylene oxide, etc. (oxirane)	—C—C— (bridged by O)	Epoxy	—
Halide	—*X*	Halo	—
Ketone	C—C(=O)—C	oxo, keto	one
Nitro derivative	—NO_2	Nitro	—
Nitro derivative	—NO	Nitroso	—
Sulphide	—S—*R*	Alkyl thio	—
Sulphonic derivative	—SO_3H	Sulpho	sulphonic acid
Mercaptan	—SH	Mercapto	thiol
Triple bond	C≡C	—	yne
Anhydride	—O—C(=O)—CH_3	Acetoxy or Acetyloxy	oic anhydride

General Rules for IUPAC Nomenclature of Organic Compounds

Nomenclature of Saturated Hydrocarbons (Alkanes)

1. Selection of the longest carbon chain which is called parent chain.
2. Number of the carbon atoms in the parent chain as 1, 2, 3... etc., starting from the end which gives smaller number to the carbon atoms carrying the substituent.

   When two or more substituents attached to the parent chain, then the end of the parent chain which gives **lowest set of the locants** is preferred for numbering.

3. If two or more substituents are present on the parent chain, they are named in the alphabetical order. If more than one locants of similar types are present at the same or different positions di, tri, tetra etc., are prefixed before the locants.

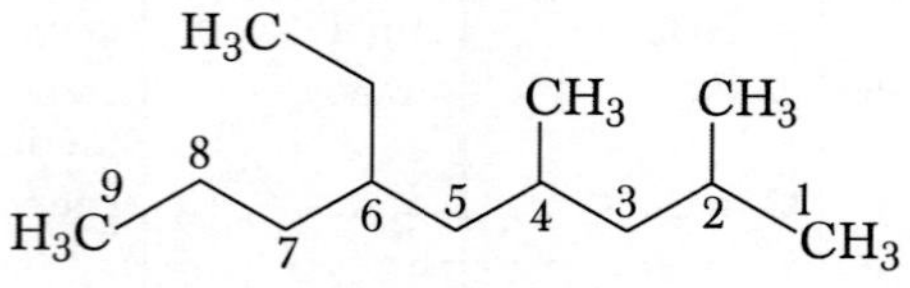

6-ethyl-2, 4-dimethyl nonane
(not 2, 4-dimethyl-6-ethylnonane)

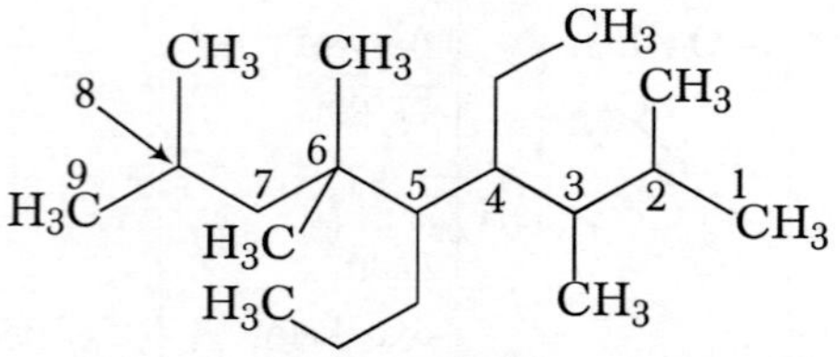

4-ethyl-2, 3, 6, 6, 8-pentamethyl-5-propylnonane
(not 6-ethyl-2, 4, 4, 7, 8-pentamethyl-5-propylnonane)

4. When two different alkyl locants are equidistant from the two ends of main chain, they are numbered in alphabetical order as

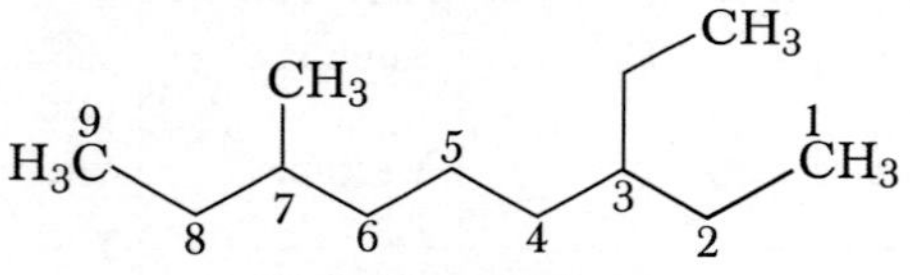

3-ethyl-7-methylnonane
(not 3-methyl-7-ethylnonane)

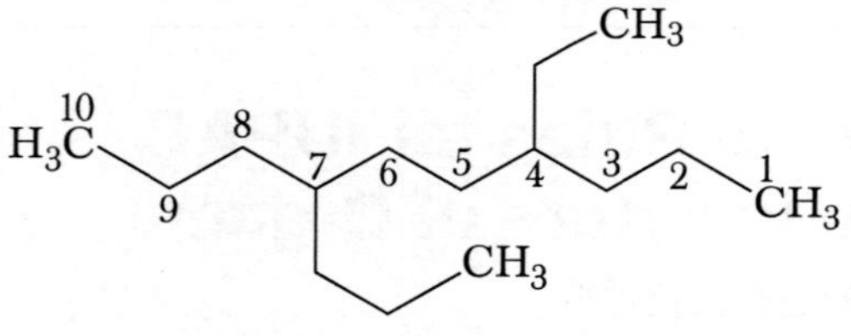

4-ethyl-7-propyldecane
(not 7-ethyl-4-propyldecane)

Note When the same complex substituents occur more than once, it is indicated by multiplying prefix bis, tris, tetrakis etc.

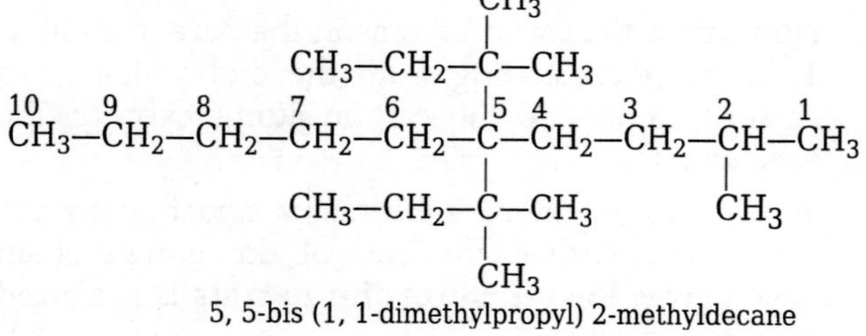

5, 5-bis (1, 1-dimethylpropyl) 2-methyldecane

Nomenclature of Unsaturated Hydrocarbons (Alkenes and Alkyne)

1. The longest chain determined must have multiple bond.
2. The suffix 'ane' of the corresponding alkane is replaced by 'ene' and 'yne' for double and triple bonds respectively.
3. If a compound contains two or more double bonds or triple bonds, the letter '*a*' should be added to word root.

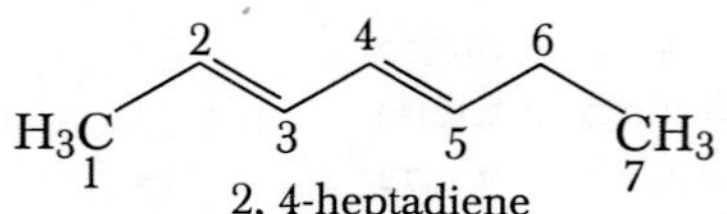

2, 4-heptadiene

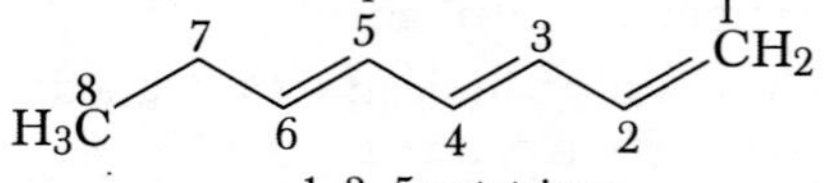

1, 3, 5-octatriene

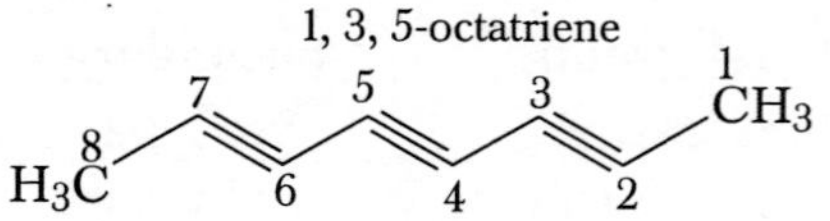

2,4,6-octatriyne

4. The numbering of atoms in parent chain is done in such a way that the carbon atom containing the = bond or ≡ bond gets the lowest number.
5. Unsaturated unbranched acyclic hydrocarbons, having both double and triple bonds are named by replacing ending "ane" from the name of the corresponding saturated hydrocarbons by "enyne", "adienyne", "atrienyne" "enediyne" etc. Numbers as low as possible are given to double and triple bonds even though at this time gives "yne" a lower number than "ene".

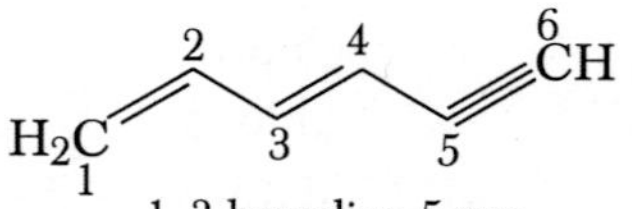

1, 3-hexadien-5-yne

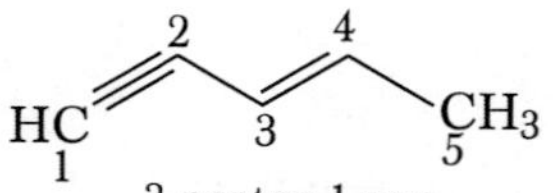

3-penten-1-yne

6. When there is a choice in numbering between double and triple bond (this occur when double and triple bonds are equidistant from the two terminal), the double bonds are given lowest number (ene comes before yne in alphabetical order).

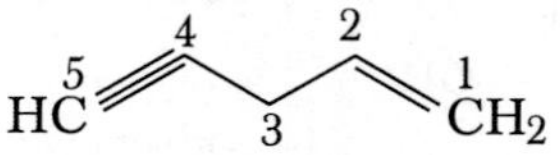

1-penten-4-yne

7. All the rules for naming the substitutent are same as that of alkane.

Nomenclature of Compounds Containing Functional Group

1. Select the longest continuous chain containing the carbon atom having the functional group.
2. The numbering of atoms in the parent chain is done in such a way that the carbon atom bearing the functional group gets the lowest number.

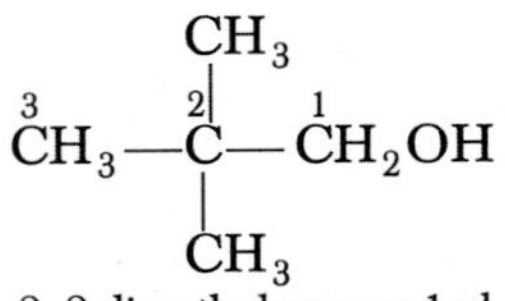

2, 2-dimethylpropan-1-ol

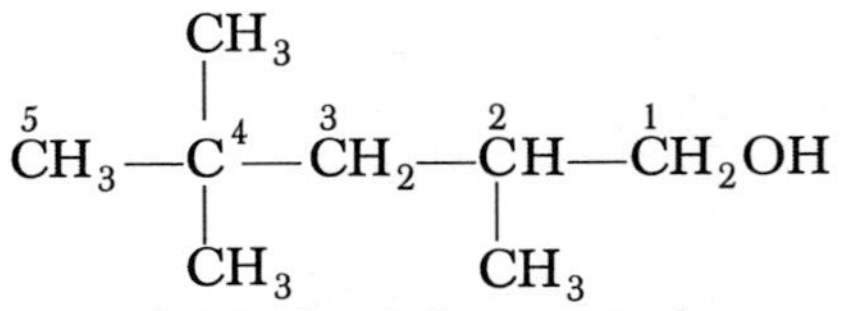

2, 4,4-trimethylpentan–1–ol

Note The functional group should get the lowest number even if it violates the lowest set rule or lowest sum rule.

3. The functional groups such as —CHO, —COOH, —$CONH_2$, —CN etc., always start the numbering of the parent chain.
4. All the rules for naming the substituents are same as that of alkane.
5. If a compound contains several functional groups, the senior most functional group will be considered as a principal functional group (suffix) while all other groups should be treated as prefix. The order for preference of principal functional group is :

Sulphonic acid > carboxylic acids > acid anhydrides > esters > acid chlorides > amides > nitriles > aldehydes > ketones > alcohols > amines > ethers.

All the remaining groups such as halo, nitro, nitroso and alkoxy are always treated as substitutent groups.

Some examples of compounds containing more than one type of functional groups.

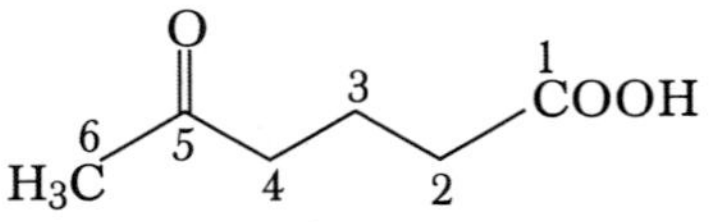

5-oxohexanoic acid

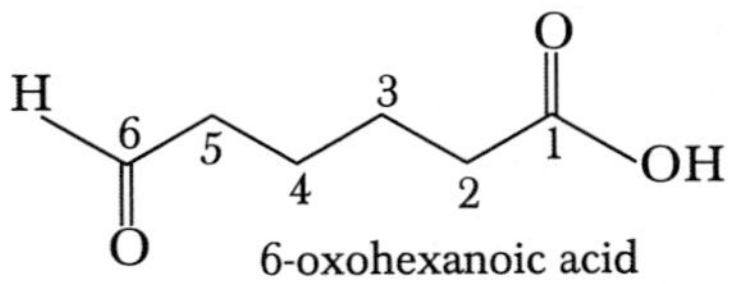

6-oxohexanoic acid

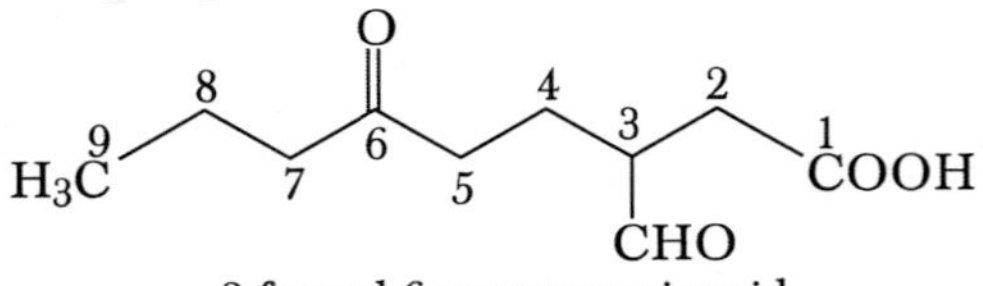

3-formyl-6-oxononanoic acid

Nomenclature of Alicyclic Compounds

1. The name of the alicyclic compound is obtained by adding the prefix **cyclo** to the name of the corresponding straight chain hydrocarbon (alkane, alkene or alkyne).

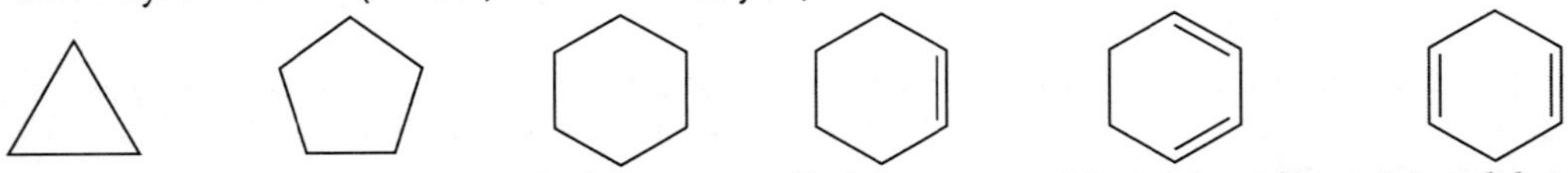

Cyclopropane Cyclopentane Cyclohexane Cyclohexene 1,3-cyclohexadiene 1,4-cyclohexadiene

2. If only one substituent is present, it is not necessary to designate its position. If two or more substituents are present in the ring, their positions are indicated by arabic numerals (1, 2, 3, 4...) while numbering the ring the substituent which comes first in alphabetical order is given the lowest number and the ring is numbered in the direction that gives the next substituent the lowest number possible. When three or more substituents are present, we begin from the substituent which leads to the lowest set of locants.

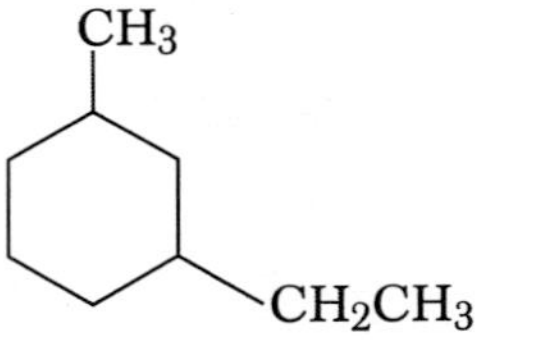

1-ethyl-3-methylcyclohexane
(not 1-ethyl-5-methyl cyclohexane)

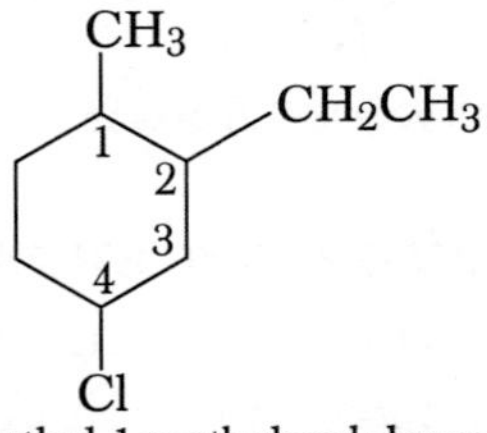

4-chloro-2-ethyl-1-methylcyclohexane
(not 1-chloro-3-ethyl-4-methylcyclohexane)

3. When a single ring system is attached to a single chain with a greater number of carbon atoms, or when more than one ring system is attached to a single chain, then they are named as cycloalkylalkane.

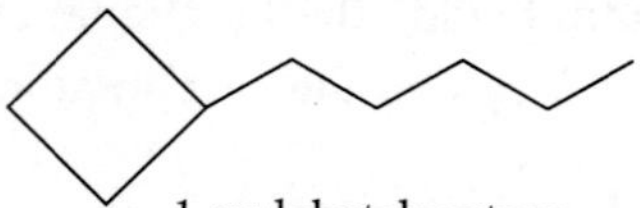

1-cyclobutylpentane

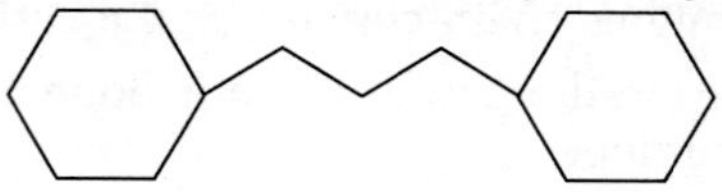

1,3-dicyclohexylpropane

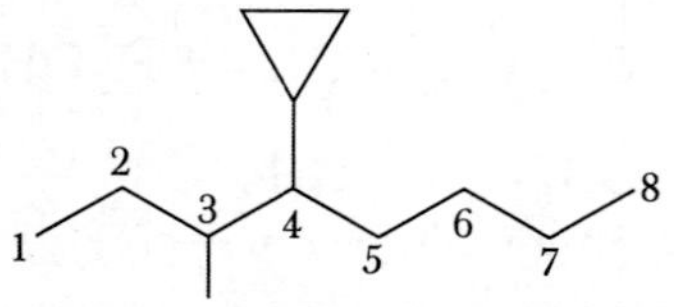

4-cyclopropyl-3-methyloctane

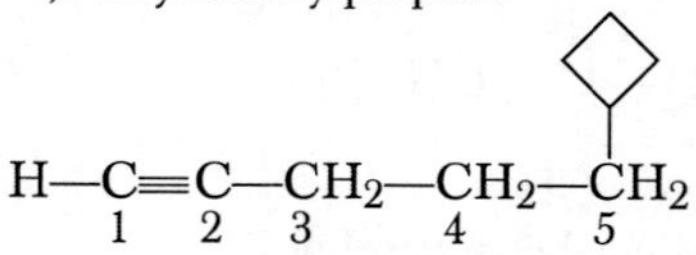

5-cyclobutyl-1-pentyne
or 5-cyclobutylpent-1-yne

Nomenclature of Bicyclic Compounds

Cycloalkanes consisting of two rings only and having two or more atoms in common are named by taking the prefix **bicyclo** followed by the name of the alkane. In between bicyclo and alkane, number of carbon atoms representing the bridge (except bridge head positions) are written within bracket. The carbon atoms common to both the ring are called bridgeheads and each bond or chain of atoms connecting the bridge head atoms is called a bridge.

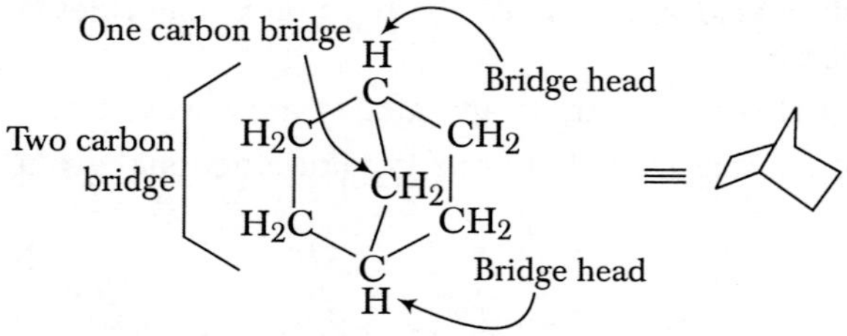

A bicycloheptane

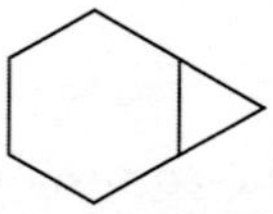

Bicyclo [4, 1, 0] heptane

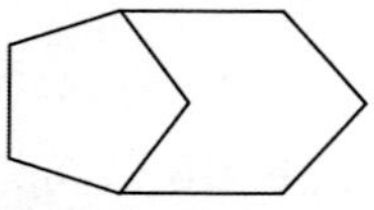

Bicyclo [3, 2, 1] octane

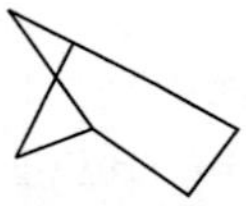

Bicyclo [2, 1, 1] hexane

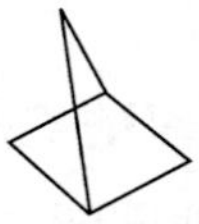

Bicyclo [1, 1, 1] pentane

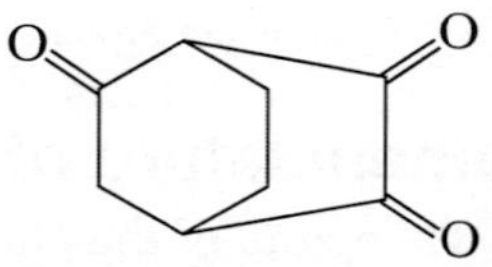

Bicyclo [2, 2, 2] octane
2,3,5-trione

If substituents are present, we number the bridged ring system beginning at one bridgehead, proceeding first along the longest bridge to the other bridgehead, then along the next longest bridge back to the first bridgebead. The shortest bridge is numbered last.

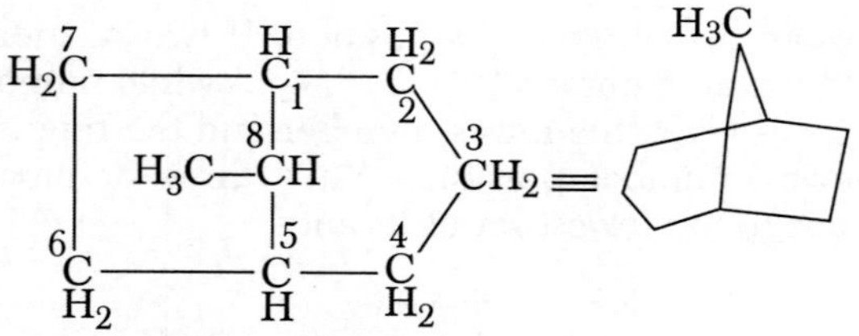

8-methylbicyclo [3,2,1] octane

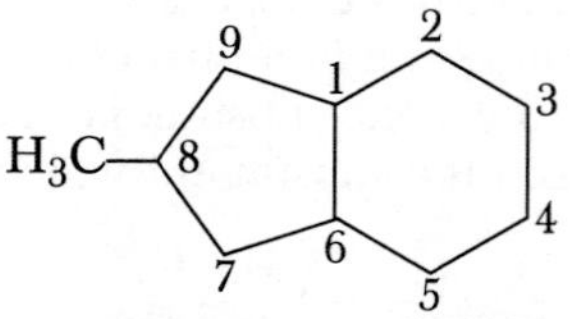

8-methylbicyclo [4.3.0] nonane

Nomenclature of Spiro Compounds

Two rings with one common atom–spiro ring system.

The ring system in spiro compounds is indicated by the word “spiro” (instead of “cyclo”), followed by brackets indicating how many atoms are contained in each path around the rings, ending with the alkane name describing how many carbons are in the ring systems including the spiro carbon. Numbering follows the smaller path first, passing through the spiro carbon and around the second ring.

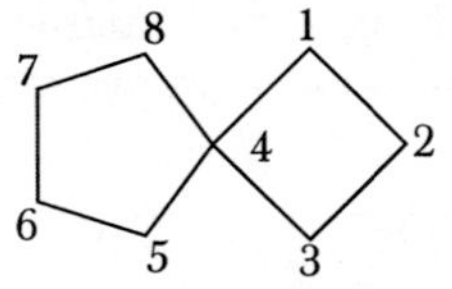

Spiro[3,4] octane

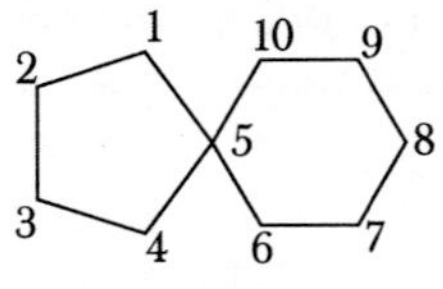

Spiro[4,5]decane

Substituents and functional groups are indicated in the usual ways. Spiro ring systems are always numbered smaller before larger, and numbered in such a way so as to give the highest priority functional group the lower position number.

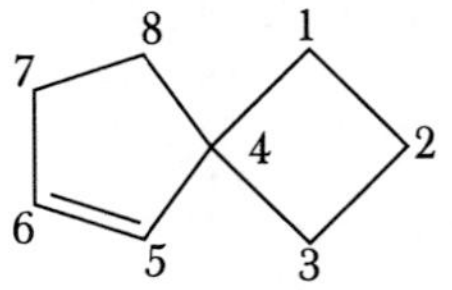

Spiro[3,4]oct-5-ene

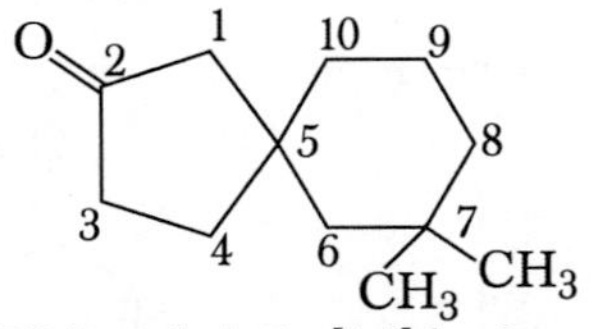

7,7-dimethylspiro[4.5]dec-2-one

IUPAC Nomenclature of Aromatic Compounds

Substituted aromatic hydrocarbons

Following names for the substituted monocyclic aromatic hydrocarbons are retained.

Benzene

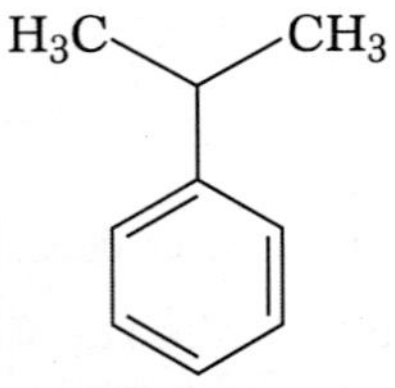

Cumene

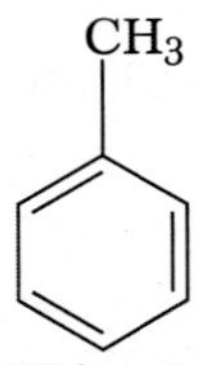

Toluene

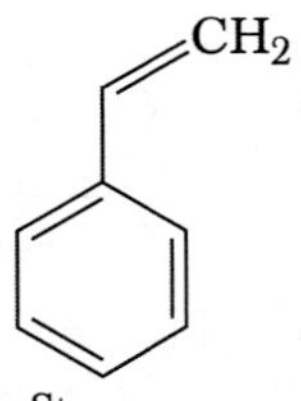

Styrene

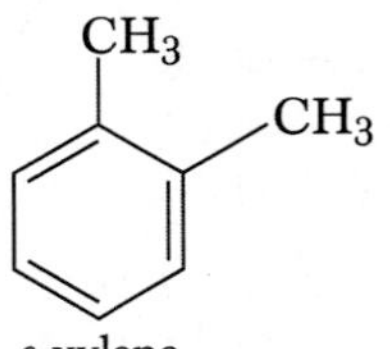

o-xylene

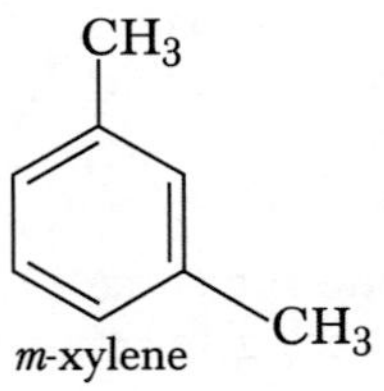

m-xylene

p-xylene

Other monocyclic substituted hydrocarbons are named as derivatives of benzene or one of the compounds listed above. However, if the substituent introduced into such a compound is identical with already present in that compound, then the substituted compound is named as derivatives of benzene as :

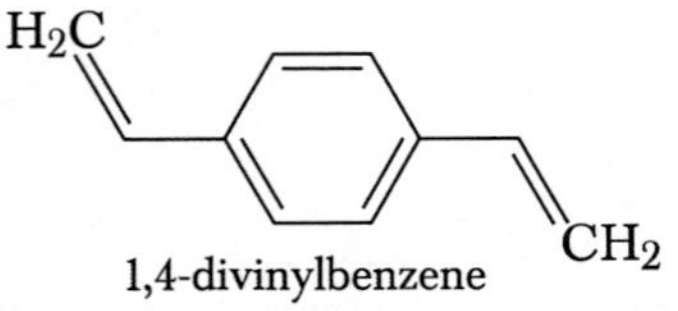

1,4-divinylbenzene

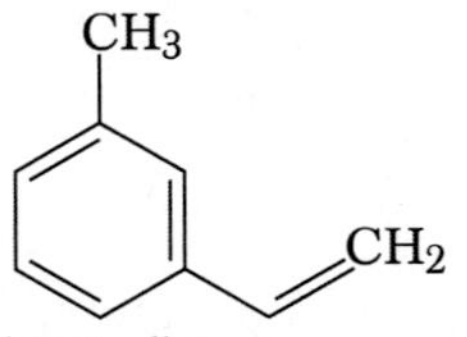

1-methyl-3-vinylbenzene

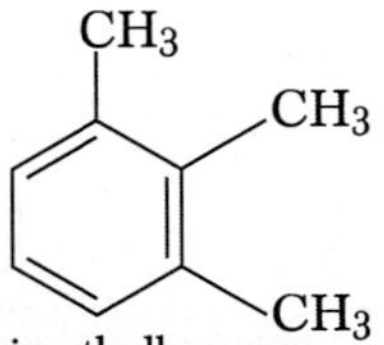

1,2,3-trimethylbenzene

The positions of substitutents are indicated by numbers except *o*-(*ortho*), *m*-(*meta*), *p*-(*para*) may be used in place of 1, 2-, 1, 3- and 1, 4-respectively, when only two substituents are present. The lowest possible number given to the substitutent coming first in alphabetical order.

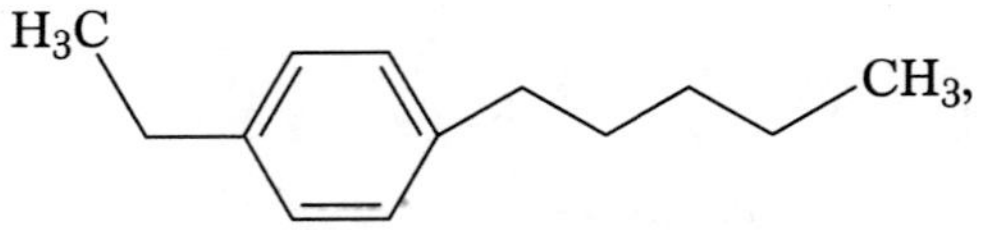

1-ethyl-4-pentylbenzene

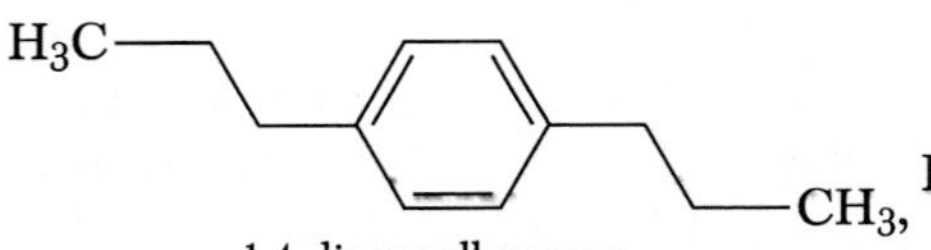

1,4-dipropylbenzene

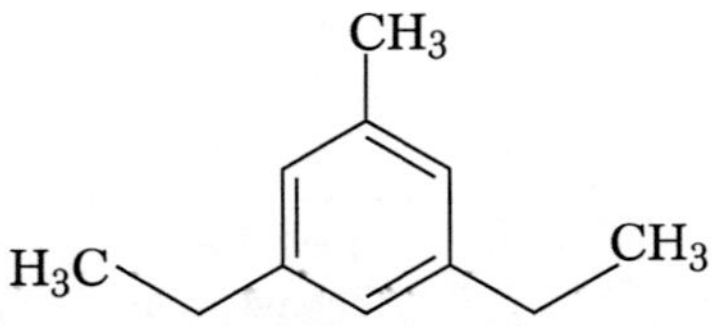

3,5-diethyltoluene

Benzene derivatives

The nomenclature of substituted benzene ring compounds is less systematic than that of the alkanes, alkenes and alkynes. A few mono-substituted compounds are named by using a group name as a prefix to "benzene", as shown by the combined names listed below. A majority of these compounds, however, are referred to by singular names that are unique.

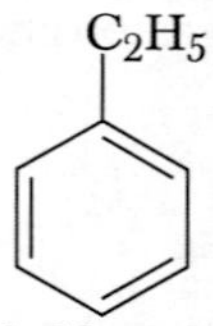

Ethyl benzene

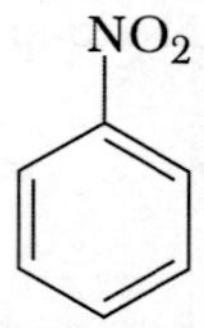

Nitrobenzene

} Combined name

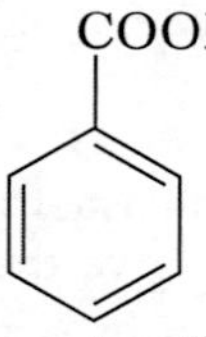

Benzoic acid

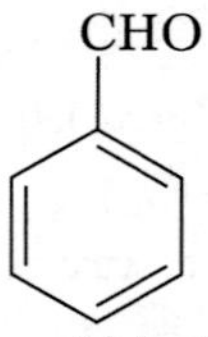

Benzaldehyde

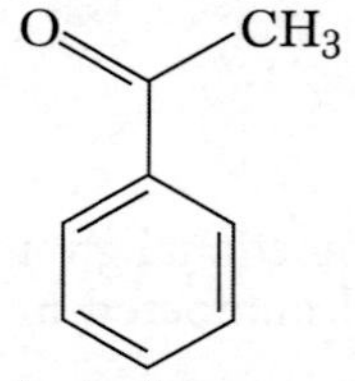

Acetophenone

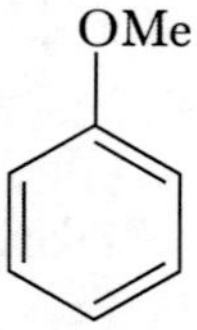

Anisole

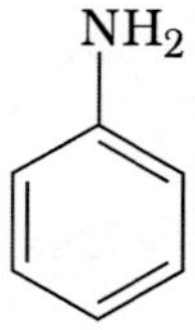

Aniline

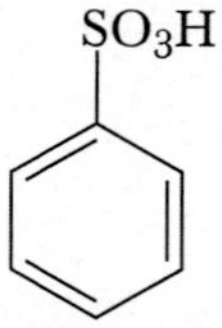

Benzene sulphonic acid

} Singular name

Note Two commonly encountered substitutent groups that incorporate a benzene ring are **phenyl** and **benzyl.**

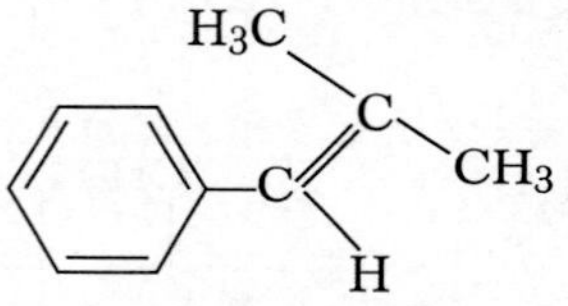

2-methyl-1-phenyl propene

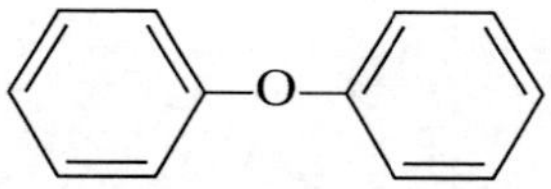

Diphenyl ether

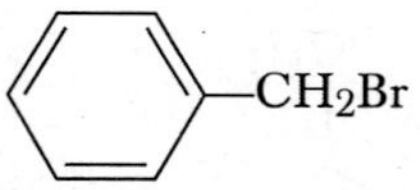

Benzyl bromide

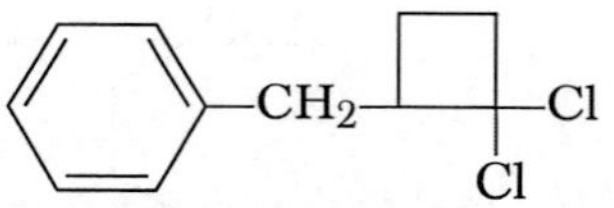

2-benzyl-1,1-dichlorocyclobutane

When more than one substituent is present on a benzene ring, the relative locations of the substituents must be designated by numbering the ring carbons or by some other notation. In the case of disubstituted benzenes, the prefixes *ortho, meta* and *para* are commonly used to indicate a 1, 2- or 1, 3- or 1, 4- relationship respectively.

Finally, if there are three or more substituent groups, the ring is numbered in such a way as to assign the subtituents the lowest possible numbers. The substituents are listed alphabetically in the final name. If the substitution is symmetrical numbering corresponding to the alphabetical order.

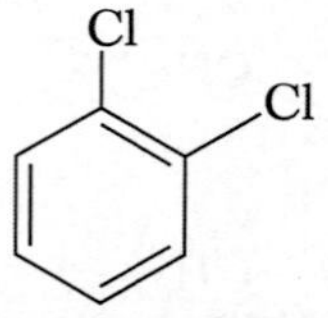

1, 2-dichlorobenzene
ortho-dichlorobenzene

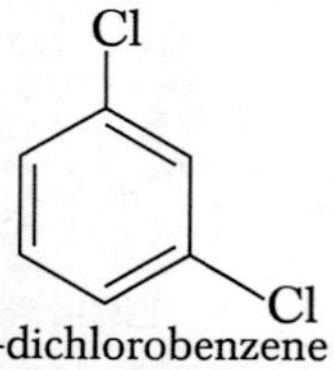

1,3-dichlorobenzene
meta-dichlorobenzene

1,4-dichlorobenzene
para-dichlorbenzene

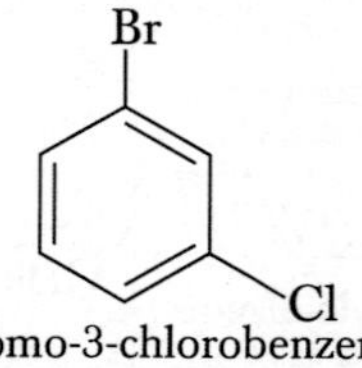

1-bromo-3-chlorobenzene
meta-chlorobromobenzene

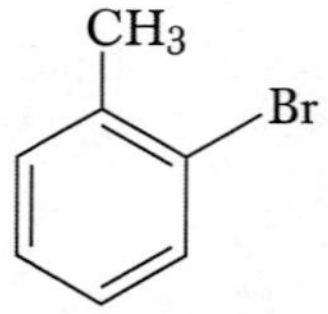

2-bromo toluene
ortho-bromo toluene

When large and complex groups are attached to the benzene ring it is common practice to name the molecule as an alkane, alkene, etc., and benzene as side chain derivative written as phenyl (C_6H_5, ϕ—, Ph).

ϕ—C≡CH
Phenylethyne

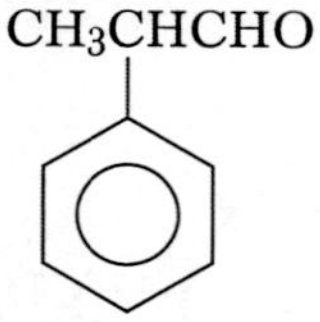

2-pehnylpropanal

ϕ—CH_2—ϕ
Diphenylmethane

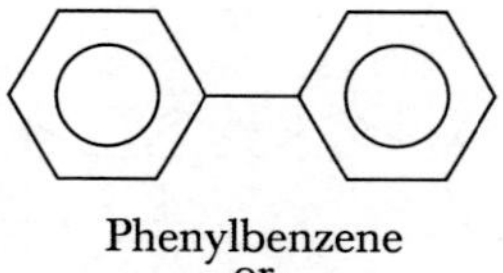
Phenylbenzene
or
biphenyl

Regioisomers

The type of isomerism which is produced as a result of the different outcomes of chemical reactions in which there are different orientations or sites to choose from. For example, when addition reactions between unsymmetrical **reagents** and unsymmetrical double or triple bonds occur, two outcomes are possible. As part of the original observations of this chemistry, wherein one of the atoms added was a hydrogen and the other was some distinctive, non-hydrogen atom, the placement of this distinctive atom was said to occur at one region or other of the molecule, hence, the formation of regioisomers. Based on the mechanism of the chemical reaction, the selectivity for one of these regioisomers forming faster than the other can be predicted. With the addition of simple mineral acids, for example, the product derived from a faster protonation giving a more stable **intermediate** is referred to as the Markownikoff's regioselectivity.

Regioselectivity in the formation of regioisomers is also observed in electrophilic aromatic substitution reactions. In the case of monosubstituted benzene derivates, there are three possible regioisomeric products that form at different rates, based on the mechanism of the reaction.

One of the most fundamental reactions in organic chemistry is the addition of H*X* to an unsymmetrical alkene. In those cases, two different 'regioisomers' could be formed. The reaction is according to Markownikoff's rule.

The addition of HCl to propene is shown below

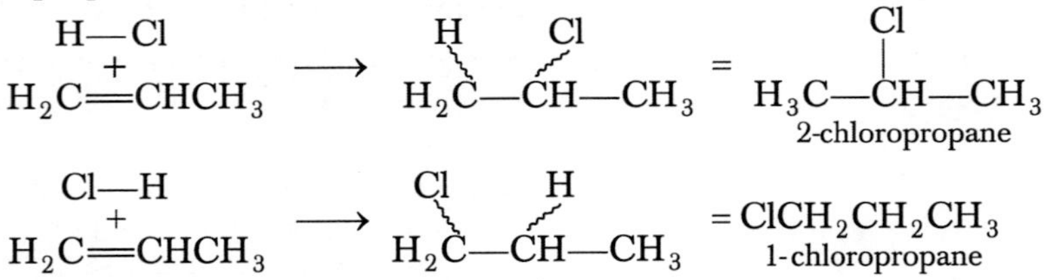

In fact, the only product that is formed in the reaction of propene with HCl is 2-chlorpropane. None of the regioisomer 1-chloropropane is formed. As such, we call this a "regiospecific" reaction, since only one of several possible regioisomers was formed.

Note The structural isomers, functional isomers and positional isomers are also called regioisomers. Tautomers are the subcategory of functional isomers.

IUPAC name of some position isomers is as :

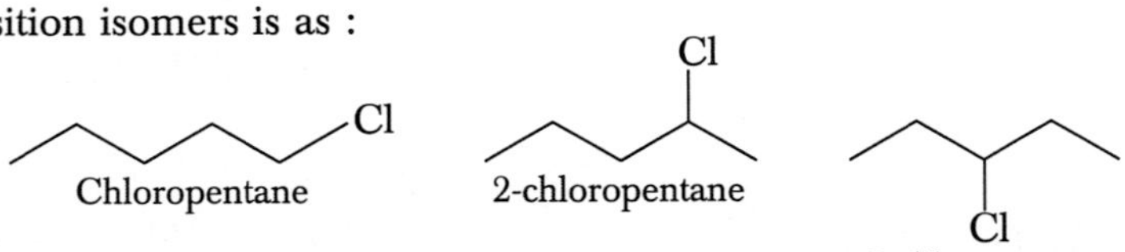

Chloropentane 2-chloropentane 3-chloropentane

R, S Nomenclature for Stereoisomers

The different stereoisomers of a molecule can be expressed in terms of *R* and *S* configuration. This method was proposed by Cahn, Ingold and Prelog. This method has been accepted by IUPAC. The method involves the following steps :

Step I Identify the centre of chirality in the molecule.

Step II The four atoms or groups of atoms joined to the asymmetric carbon atom are assigned as sequence of the priority by the sequence rules. These are also called Cahn, Ingold, Prelog (CIP) rules. These rules are as follows :

1. The four substituents are listed in order of decreasing atomic number of the atom directly attached to the chiral carbon atom. *e.g.,*

Priority order : I, Br, Cl, H Priority order : Br, Cl, D, H

If two atoms are isotopes of the same element, the atom of higher mass number has the higher priority.

2. If the relative priority of two groups is not decided by rule I (on the basis of the atomic number of the atoms that are directly attached to the asymmetric carbon atom), then the next atoms are considered for priority assignment.

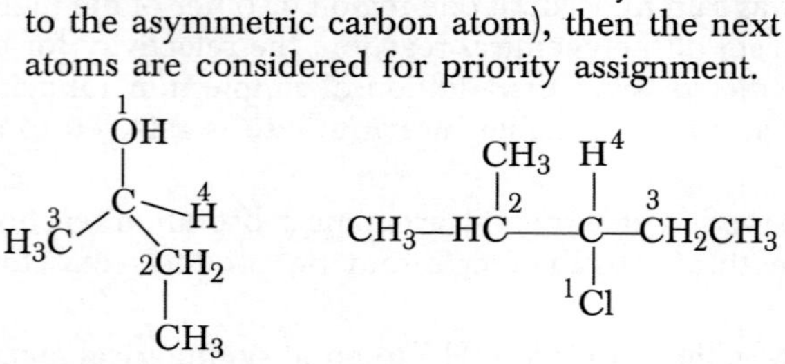

3. Where there is a double bond or triple bond, both atoms are considered to be duplicated or triplicated.

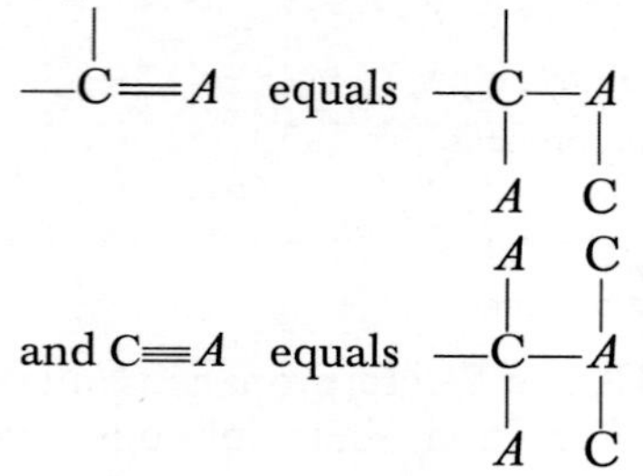

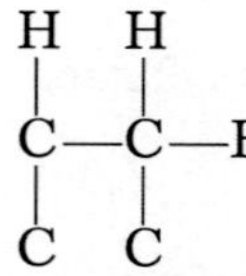 has higher priority than

Vinyl group

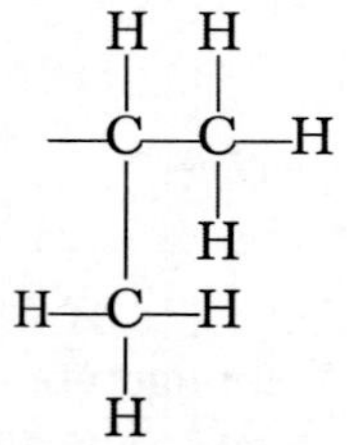

Isopropyl group

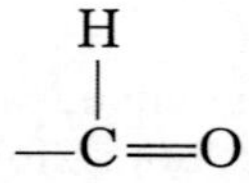 has higher priority than $—CH_2OH$.

4. All atoms except hydrogen are formally given a valence of four. If the actual valence is less than four as in case of nitrogen, oxygen, etc. phantom atoms are used [designated by a subscript (o)]. These phantom atoms are assigned zero atomic number and ranked the lowest in priority sequence.

According, to the above sequence rule of *R*–S notation, a list of common atoms and groups in the increasing order of priority is as :

I > Br > Cl > SO_2R > SOR > SR > SH > F > $OCOR$ > OR > OH > NO_2 > NO > $NHCOR$ > NR_2 > NHR > NH_2 > CX_3 (X = halogen) > $COOX$ > CO_2R > $CONH_2$ > COR > CHO > CR_2OH > $CHOHR$ > CH_2OH > $C{\equiv}CR$ > C_6H_5 > $CH{\equiv}C$ > $CR{=}CR_2$ > CR_3CHR_2 > CH_2R > CH_3 > D > H > Phantom atoms.

Step III After assigning the priorities to the four groups or atoms attached to the asymmetric C-atom, the molecule is visualized to be in a position where the atom or group of atoms of lowest priority is directed away from us. Then we trace the path from atom/group in the decreasing order of priorities.

R is given to the isomer if sequence is left to right *i.e.,* clockwise (*R* stands for **rectus**, a Latin word for right).

S is given to the isomer if sequence is right to left *i.e.,* anticlockwise (*S* stand for **sinister**, a Latin word for left).

Note When the molecule contains more than one chiral centre, configuration of each centre is determined separately following same the sequence rule.

Let us consider some examples.

(i) Butan-2-ol : 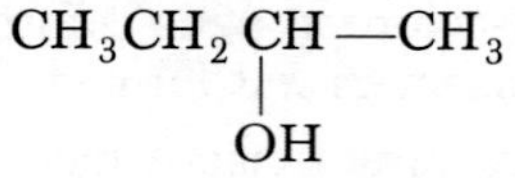

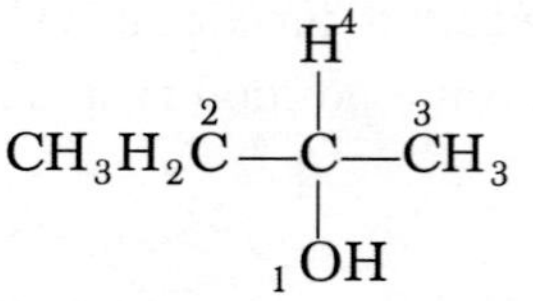

Priority order : OH, CH_2CH_3, CH_3, H

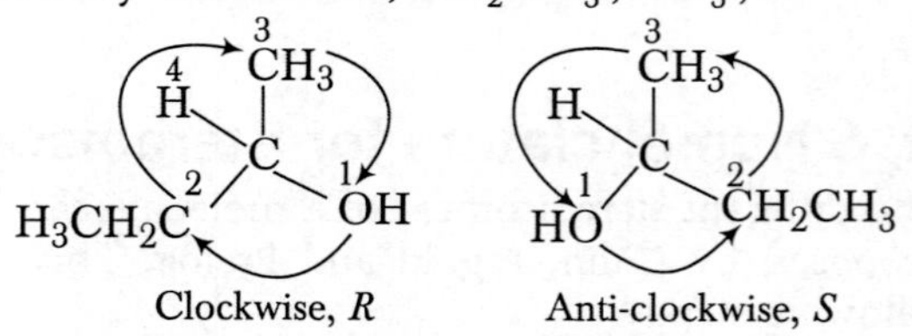

Clockwise, *R* Anti-clockwise, *S*

(ii) 1-aminoethanol 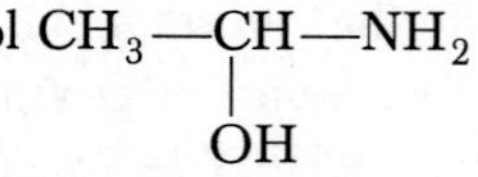

Priority order : OH, NH_2, CH_3, H

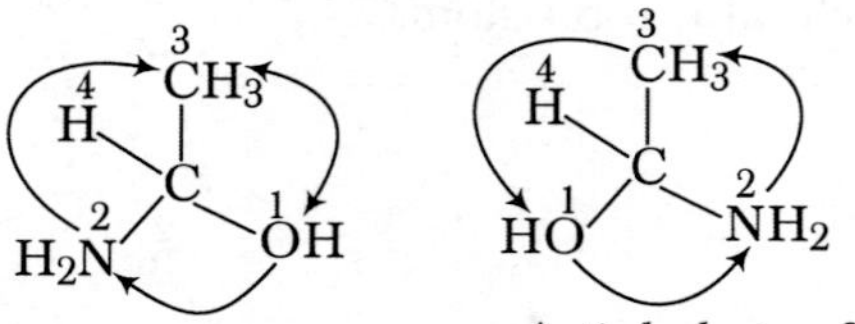

Clockwise, *R* Anti-clockwise, *S*

(iii) 3-bromobutan-2-ol

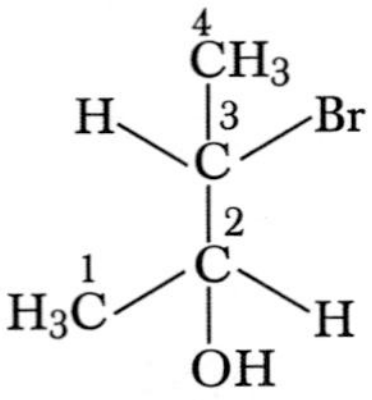

Designation of configuration of C-2 and C-3

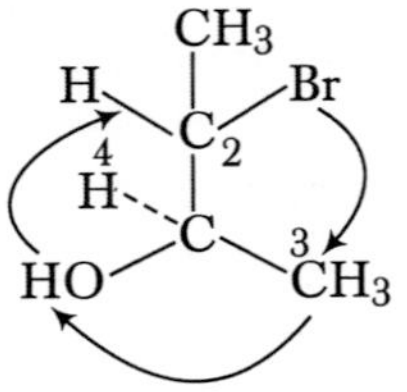

R

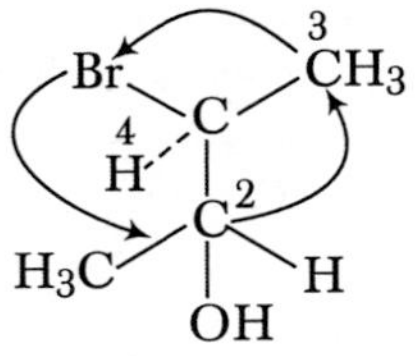

S

Hence, the molecule may be represented as (2*R*, 3*S*).

E-Z-System of Nomenclature for Geometrical Isomers

When there are three or four different groups attached to the carbon atoms of a double bond, it becomes difficult to assign *cis* and *trans* designation to isomers. To overcome this problem, Cahn-Ingold-Prelog developed the *E-Z* system which is based on the assignment of priorities to atoms or groups attached to each carbon of the double bond. According to priority sequence rule by Cahn-Ingold-Prelog the priority of the substituents is determined for each carbon atom. (These rules are same as given earlier for *R*, *S* nomenclature system).

If the two higher priority groups are on the same side of the double bond, the isomer is called ***Z*** (German Zusammen meaning together) and if the two higher priority groups are on the opposite side of the double bond, the isomer is called ***E*** (German, Entgegen meaning opposite).

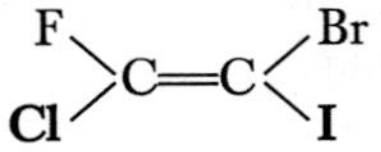

(*Z*)

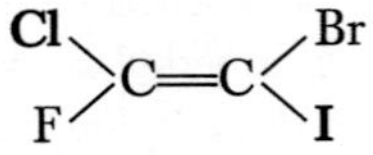

(*E*)

(Priority : Cl > F and I > Br)

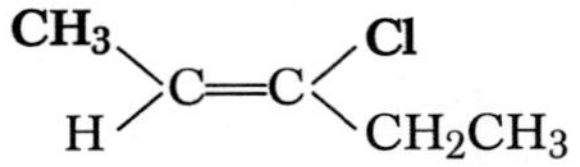

(*Z*)

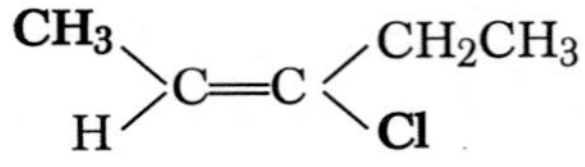

(*E*)

(Priority : CH_3 > H and Cl > CH_2CH_3)

Some other examples of *E* and *Z* nomenclature are as

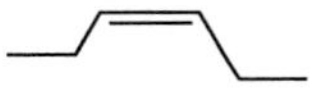

(*Z*)-3-hexene

(2*Z*, 4*Z*)–2, 4 hexadiene

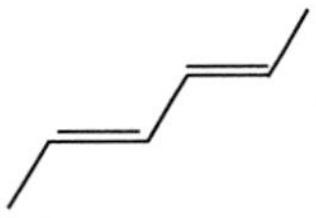

(2*E*, 4*E*)–2, 4 hexadiene

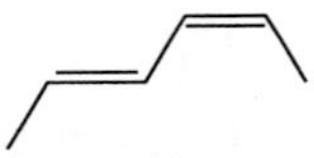

(2*Z*, 4*E*)–2, 4-hexadiene

Exercise 1
(For Part 'B')

1. 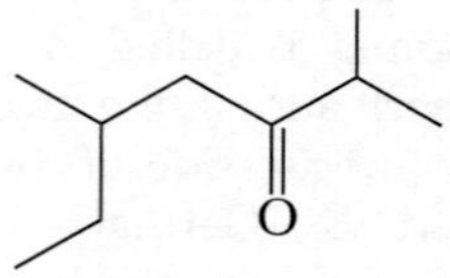

(a) 5-ethyl-2-methylhexan-3-one
(b) 2, 5-dimethylheptan-3-one
(c) 3, 6-dimethylheptan-5-one
(d) 2-ethyl-5-methylhexan-4-one

2. 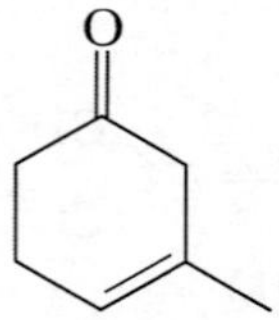

(a) 5-methyl-cyclohex-4-en-1-one
(b) 3-methyl-cyclohex-3-en-1-one
(c) 1-methyl-cyclohex-1-en-5-one
(d) 2-methyl-cyclohex-1-en-4-one

3. $CH_3CH_2CH_2CH_2CH(CH(CH_3)_2)CH_2CH_2CH_2CH_3$ (the $H_3C-CH-CH_3$ group is attached to the CH of the chain)

(a) 2-methyl-3-butyloctane
(b) 5-isopropylnonane
(c) 5-(1-methylethyl) nonane
(d) isododecane

4. Formula of N,N-dimethylethanamide is

(a) $H_3C-CO-N(CH_3)_2$
(b) $H_3C-NH-COCH_3$
(c) $H_3C-CH_2CON(CH_3)_2$
(d) $H_3C-CO-C(CH_3)_2NH_2$

5. The IUPAC name for

$CH_3-CH_2-C(OH)[CH(CH_3)_2][CH(CH_3)CH_2-CH_3]$

(a) *i*-propyl-*sec*-butyl propanol
(b) 2, 4-dimethyl-3 ethyl-3-hexanol
(c) 3, 5-dimethyl-5 ethyl-4-hexanol
(d) 3-ethyl 2,4-dimethyl-3-hexanol

6. The IUPAC name for

$CH_3-CH_2-C(=O)-CH_2CH_2-C(=O)-OCH_3$ is

(a) ethyl-4-oxoheptanoate
(b) methyl-4-oxoheptanoate
(c) ethyl-4-oxohexanoate
(d) methyl-4-oxohexanoate

7. Which of the structural formulae have correct IUPAC name?

(a) $CH_3-C(CH_3)_2-CH_2-CH_2-CH_2-CH_3$
2, 2-dimethyl 3-propylbutane

(b) $CH_3-CH(CH_2-CH_3)-CH_3$
2-methyl butane

(c) $(H_3C)_2CH-CH_2-CH_2-CH_3$
1-isopropyl propane

(d) $CH_3-CH_2-CH(CH_3)-C(CH_3)_2-CH_2-CH_2-CH_3$
4, 4, 5-trimethyl heptane

8. The correct IUPAC name of the following hydrocarbon is

(a) 4, 5-diisopropyl-3-methylheptane
(b) 3-methyl-4, 5-diisopropylheptane
(c) 5-ethyl-4-isopropyl-3, 6-dimethylheptane
(d) 3-ethyl-4-isopropyl-2, 5-dimethylheptane

9. The correct IUPAC name of the compound below is

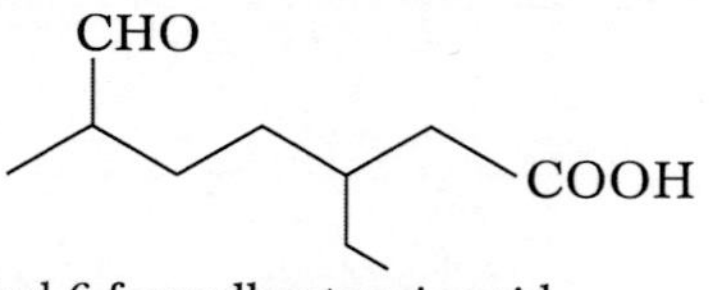

(a) 3-ethyl-6-formylheptanoic acid
(b) 3-ethyl-6-methyl-7-oxoheptanoic acid
(c) 3-ethyl-6-methyl heptan-7-aloic acid
(d) 5-ethyl-2-methyl-1-oxoheptanoic acid

10. IUPAC name of the following compound is

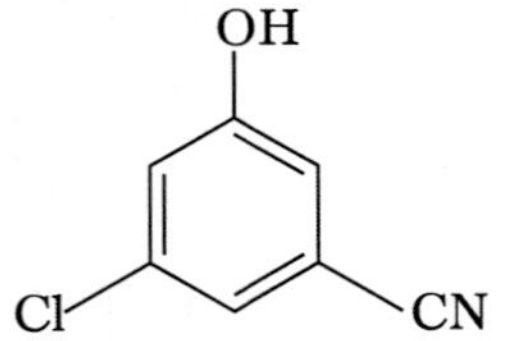

(a) 3-hydroxy-5-chlorobenzonitrile
(b) 3-chloro-5-hydroxybenzonitrile
(c) 3-chloro-5-cyanophenol
(d) 3-cyano-5-chlorophenol

11.

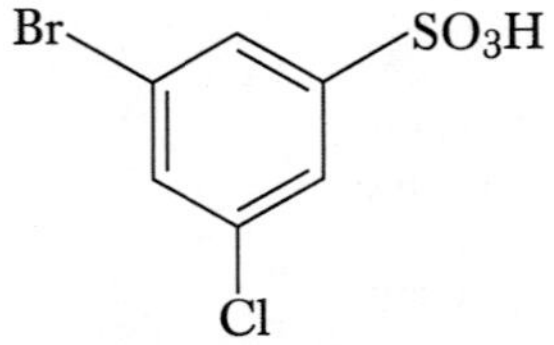

This compound can be named according to IUPAC conventions as
(a) *meta*chloro-*meta*bromo benzene sulphonic acid
(b) *meta*bromo-*meta*chloro benzene sulphonic acid
(c) 3-bromo-5-chloro benzene sulphonic acid
(d) 5-bromo-3-chloro benzene sulphonic acid

12. What is the correct IUPAC name of the following compound?

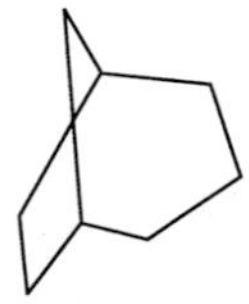

(a) Bicyclooctane (b) Tricyclooctane
(c) Bicyclo[3, 2, 1]octane (d) Bicyclo[1,2,3]octane

13. The correct structure of 3-carboxy-1, 5-pentanedioic acid is

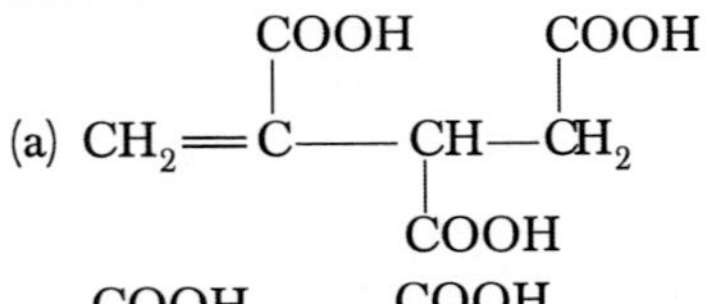

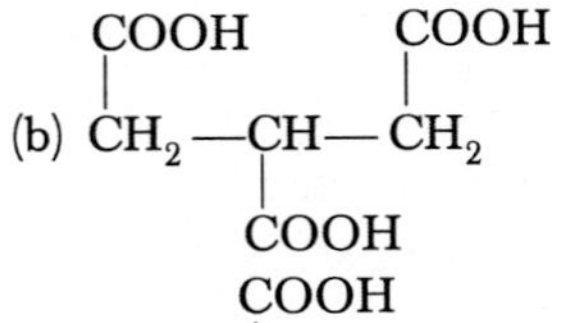

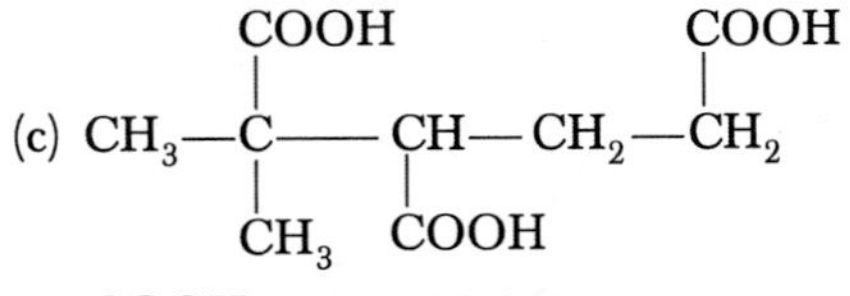

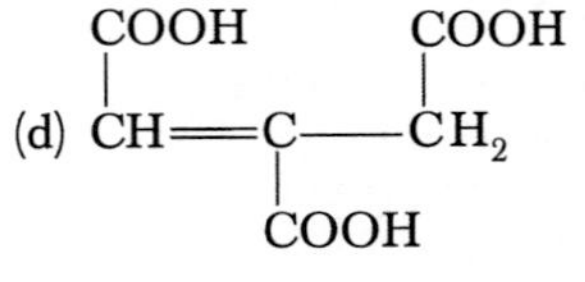

14. The correct structure for the compound 3-hepten-5-yn-2-one is

(a) $H_3C-HC=CH-CH\equiv CH-\overset{\overset{O}{\|}}{C}-CH_3$

(b) $H_2C=\underset{H}{C}-CH_2-CH=CH-\overset{\overset{O}{\|}}{C}-CH_3$

(c) $H_3C-HC=CH-CH=CH-\overset{\overset{O}{\|}}{C}-CH_3$

(d) $H_3C-C\equiv C-CH=CH-\overset{\overset{O}{\|}}{C}-CH_3$

15. IUPAC name of the compound

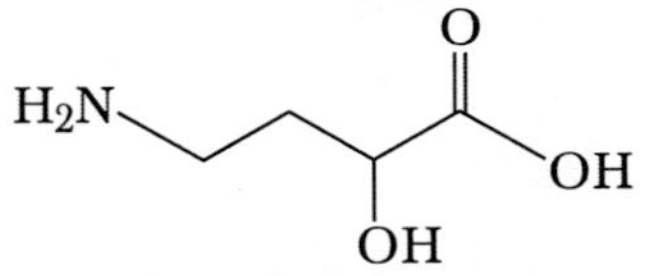

(a) γ-amino-α-hydroxybutyric acid
(b) 4-amino-2-hydroxybutanoic acid
(c) α-amino-γ-hydroxybutyric acid
(d) 1-amino-3-hydroxybutanoic acid

16. 3-butenoic acid (or But-3-enoic acid) is represented as

(a) 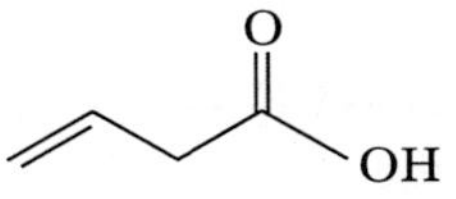 (b) 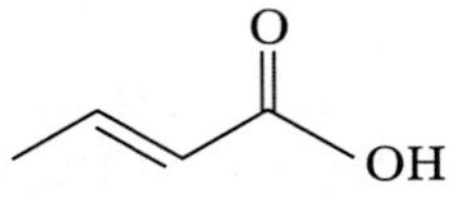

(c) 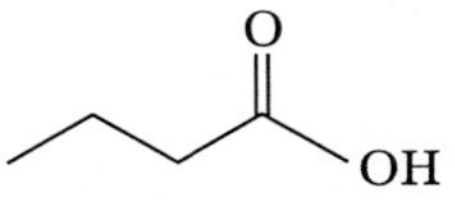 (d) None of these

17. IUPAC name of the following compounds is

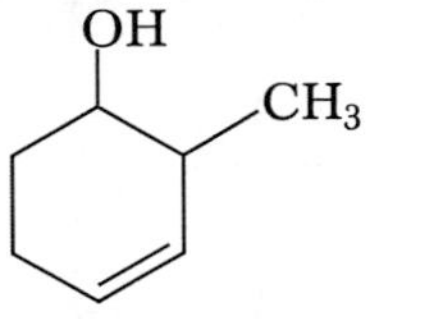

(a) 2-methyl-3-cyclohexenol
(b) 3-methyl-1-cyclohexen-4-ol
(c) 4-hydroxy-3-methyl-1-cyclohexene
(d) 2-hydroxy-1-methyl cyclohexene

18. Systematic nomenclature of the following cycloalkane is

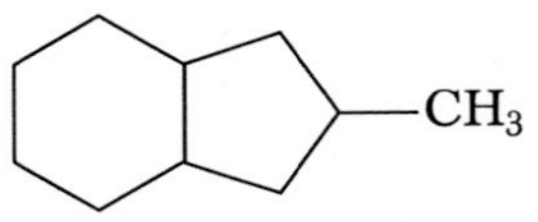

(a) 1-methylbicyclo (4, 3, 0) nonane
(b) 8-methylbicyclo (4, 3, 0) nonane
(c) 3-methylbicyclo (4, 3, 0) nonane
(d) 4-methylbicyclo (4, 3, 0) nonane

19. 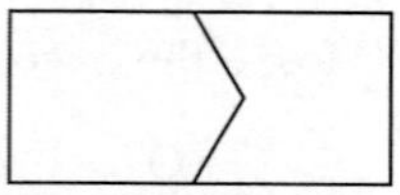

The IUPAC name of the above compound is
(a) bicyclo (2, 2, 1) heptane
(b) bicyclo (2, 2, 0) hexane
(c) bicyclo (2, 1, 0) hexane
(d) bicyclo (2, 1, 0) heptane

20. Which class represent oxiranes?
(a) 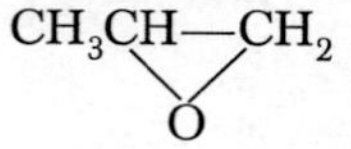

(b) 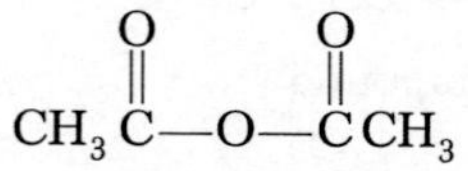

(c) 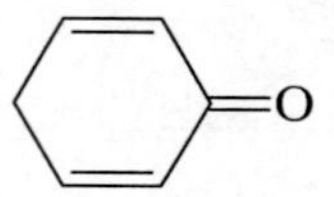

(d) ---SiO_2 O SiO_2---

21. The IUPAC name for

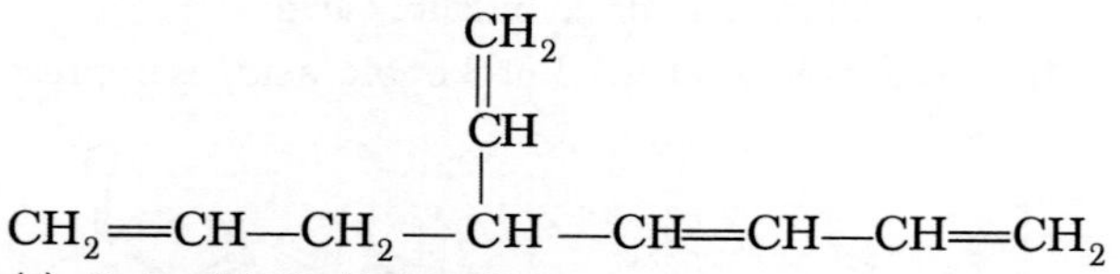

(a) 5-vinyl 1, 3, 7-octatriene
(b) 4-vinyl 1, 6, 8-octatriene
(c) 4-vinyl 2, 5, 7-octatriene
(d) 5-vinyl 2, 4, 7-octatriene

22. The IUPAC name of the compound

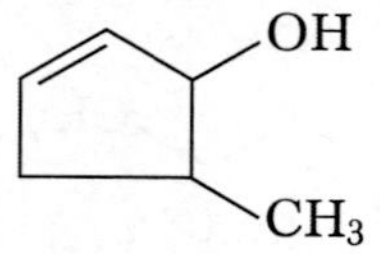

(a) 4-methylcyclopent-1-en-2-ol
(b) 5-methylcyclopent-2-en-1-ol
(c) 2-methylcyclopent-4-en-1-ol
(d) 3-methylcyclopent-1-en-2-ol

23. The IUPAC name for the compound is

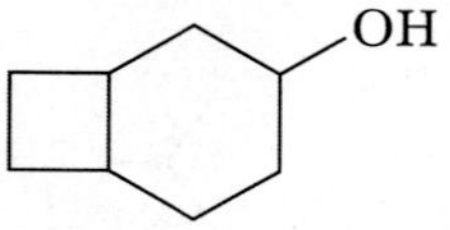

(a) bicyclo [4, 2, 0] octan-6-ol
(b) bicyclo [4, 2, 0] octan-3-ol
(c) bicyclo [2, 2, 2] octan-4-ol
(d) bicyclo [4, 2, 0] octan-4-ol

24. Bicyclo [2, 2, 2] is

(a) 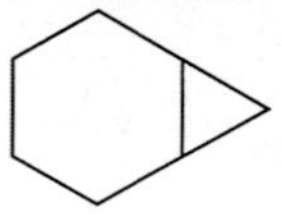
(b) 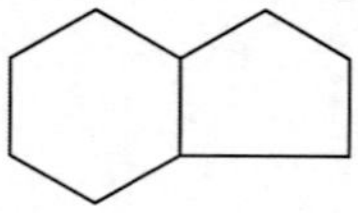
(c) 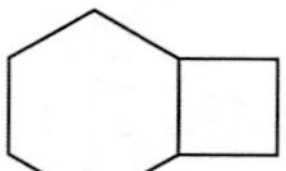
(d) 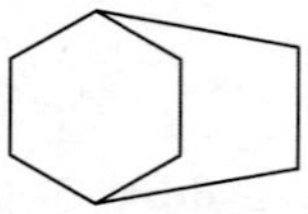

25. IUPAC name of the following compound is

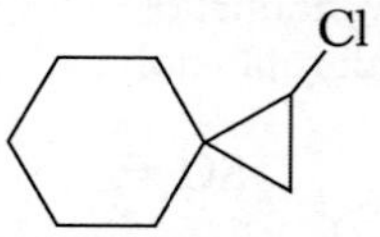

(a) 1-chlorospiro [2, 5] octane
(b) 2-chlorospiro [2, 5] octane
(c) 7-chlorospiro [2, 5] octane
(d) 1-chlorospiro [5, 2] octane

26. The correct IUPAC name of the compound is

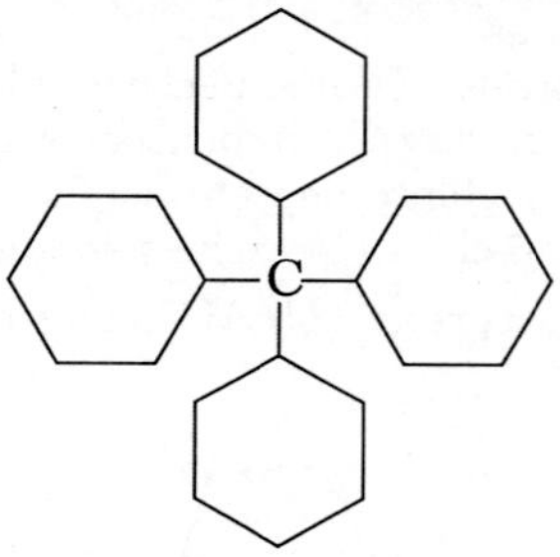

(a) tetraphenyl methane
(b) 1, 1, 1, 1-tetraphenyl methane
(c) 1, 1, 1, 1-tetracyclohexyl methane
(d) methyl-1, 1, 1, 1-tetracyclohexane

27. The IUPAC name of the compound is

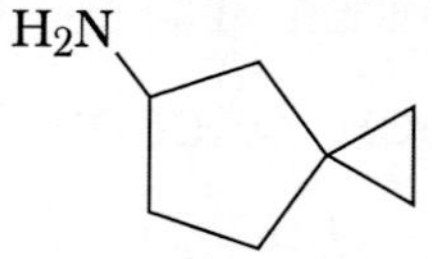

(a) 2-aminospiro [4, 2] heptane
(b) 2-aminospiro [2, 4] heptane
(c) 5-aminospiro [4, 2] heptane
(d) 5-aminospiro [2, 4] heptane

28. The IUPAC name of the compound is

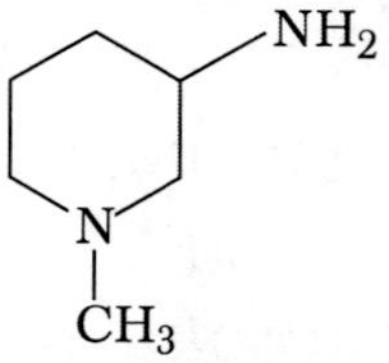

(a) 1-methyl-3-amino-1-azacyclohexane
(b) 2-amino-N-methyl piperidine
(c) 4-methyl-2-amino-1-azacyclohexane
(d) *para* methyl-amino piperidine

29. Rank the following groups in order of *R*, *S* precedence (4 is highest)

$-CH(CH_3)_2$ $-CH_2CH_2Br$ $-CH_2Br$ $-C(CH_3)_3$
A *B* *C* *D*

	4	3	2	1
(a)	*C*	*B*	*D*	*A*
(b)	*A*	*D*	*B*	*C*
(c)	*C*	*D*	*A*	*B*
(d)	*C*	*D*	*B*	*A*

30. 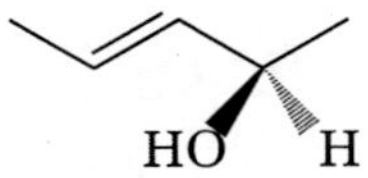

is named as
(a) (2*R*, 3*E*)-pent-3-en-2-ol
(b) (2*S*, 3*E*)-pent-3-en-2-ol
(c) (2*E*, 3*R*)-pent-2-en-3-ol
(d) (2*E*, 3*S*)-pent-2-en-3-ol

31. The correct IUPAC name of the spiro compound

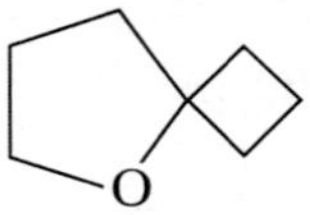 is

(a) 1-oxaspiro [4, 3] octane
(b) 5-oxospiro [3, 4] octane
(c) 1-oxospiro [3, 4] octane
(d) 5-oxaspiro [3, 4] octane

32. The name of the following compound by the aza system is

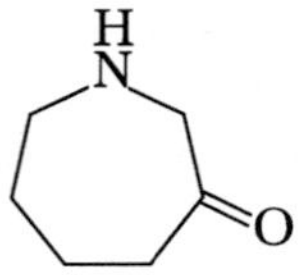

(a) 3-azacycloheptan-1-one
(b) 1-azacycloheptan-3-one
(c) 3-oxo-1-azacycloheptane
(d) 1-oxo-3-azacycloheptane

33. The IUPAC name of the following compound is

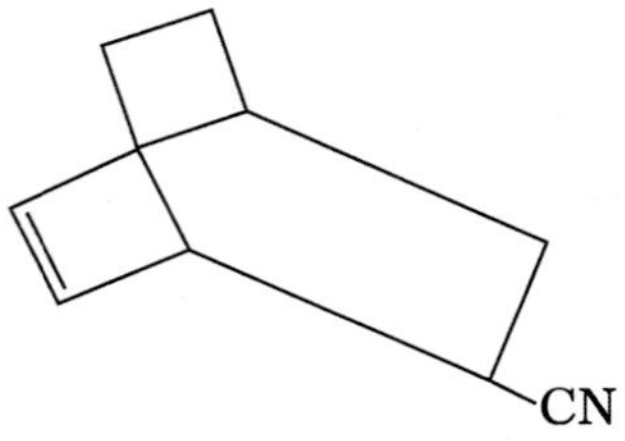

(a) bicyclo [2, 2, 2] oct-2-en-5-nitrile
(b) bicyclo [2, 2, 2] oct-5-en-2-carbonitrile
(c) 3-cyanobicyclo [2, 2, 2] oct-5-ene
(d) 2-cyanobicyclo [2, 2, 2] oct-5-ene

34. The absolute configuration of the following compound is

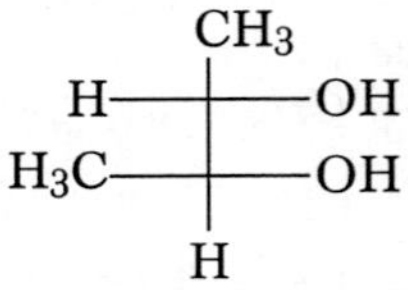

(a) 2*S*, 3*S* (b) 2*S*, 3*R*
(c) 2*R*, 3*S* (d) 2*R*, 3*R*

35. The absolute configuration of the following structure

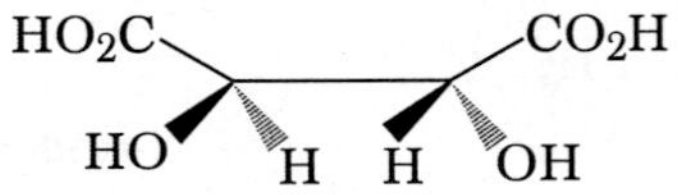

is
(a) *S*, *S* (b) *R*, *R*
(c) *R*, *S* (d) *S*, *R*

36. The IUPAC name of the following compound is

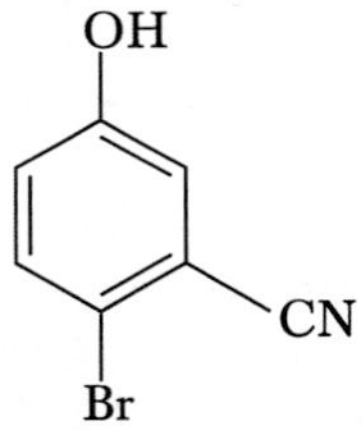

(a) 4-bromo-3-cyanophenol
(b) 2-bromo-5-hydroxybenzonitrile
(c) 2-cyano-4-hydroxybromobenzene
(d) 6-bromo-3-hydroxybenzonitrile

37. The absolute configuration of the following structure is

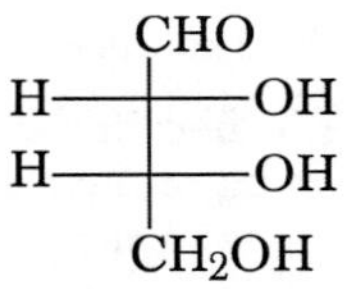

(a) 2*R*, 3*R* (b) 2*R*, 3*S*
(c) 2*S*, 3*R* (d) 2*S*, 3*S*

38. The absolute configuration of the following compound is

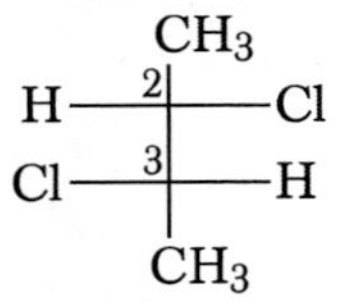

(a) 2*S*, 3*R* (b) 2*S*, 3*S*
(c) 2*R*, 3*S* (d) 2*R*, 3*R*

39. The IUPAC name of
$CH_3-CH=C(CHO)-CH_2-CH_3$ is

(a) 3-formyl-2-pentene (b) 2-ethylbut-2-enal
(c) 3-ethylbut-3-enal (d) 2-ethyl crotonaldehyde

40. Which of the following compound has wrong IUPAC name?

(a) $CH_3—CH_2—CH_2—COO—CH_2CH_3$
Ethyl butanoate

(b) $CH_3—CH(OH)—CH(CH_3)—CH_3$ 2-methyl-3-butanol

(c) $CH_3—CH(CH_3)—CH_2—CHO$ 3-methylbutanal

(d) $CH_3—CH(CH_3)—C(=O)—CH_2—CH_3$

2-methyl-3-pentanone

41. The correct IUPAC name of the following compound is

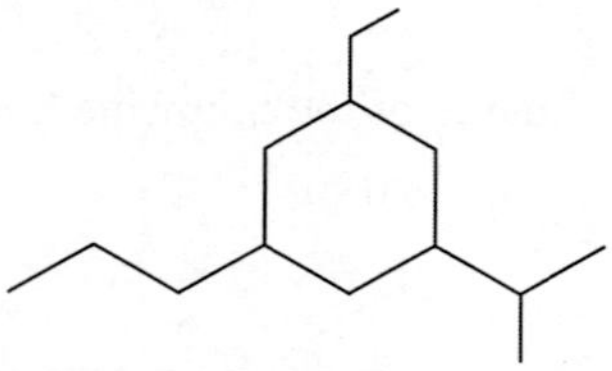

(a) 1-ethyl-3-isopropyl-5-propylcyclohexane
(b) 1-propyl-3-isopropyl-5-ethylcyclohexane
(c) 3-ethyl-5-isopropyl propylcyclohexane
(d) 3-ethyl-5-propyl isopropylcyclohexane

42. Consider the following compounds and its name

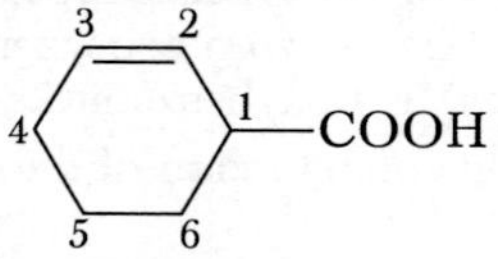

2-cyclohexenoic acid

Something wrong is their in the given name. What is the mistake in naming of the above compound?

(a) Numbering is done wrongly
(b) Position of double bond is not specified in the name
(c) Position of —COOH is not specified in the name
(d) Suffix is used wrongly

43. According to IUPAC convention, name of the following compound is

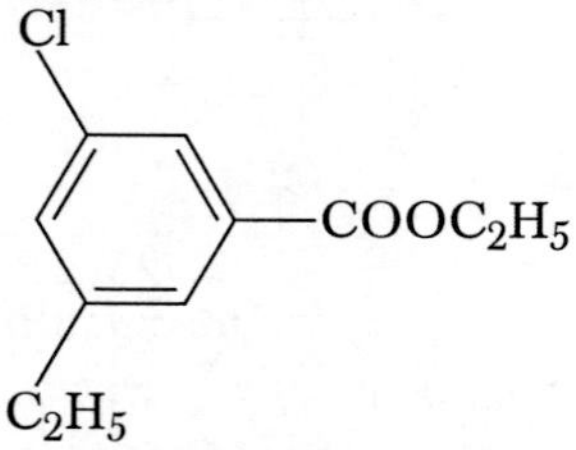

(a) 3-chloro-5-ethyl ethylbenzoate
(b) ethyl-3-chloro-5-ethylbenzoate
(c) metachloro-metaethyl ethylbenzoate
(d) Both 'b' and 'c' are correct

44. The IUPAC name of the following compound is

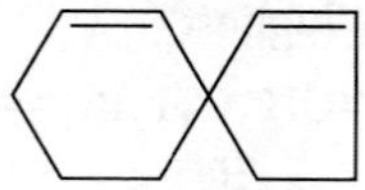

(a) spiro [4, 5] deca-1, 6-diene
(b) spiro [5, 4] deca-1, 6-diene
(c) 1, 6-diene spiro [4, 5] decane
(d) 1, 6-diene spiro [5, 4] decane

45. The IUPAC name of the following compound

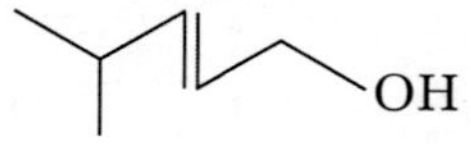

is

(a) 2-methyl hex-3-enol
(b) 4-methyl pent-2-en-1-ol
(c) 2-methyl hexanol
(d) 5-methyl-hex-3-enol

46. The IUPAC name of

$CH_3—C(=O)—CH_2—CH(OH)—CHO$ is

(a) 5-oxo-4-hydroxy-2-pentanone
(b) 4-hydroxy-5-al-2-pentanone
(c) 2-hydroxy-4-oxopentanal
(d) 1-al-4-oxo-2-pentanol

47. Identify the wrongly named compound

(a) $CH_3—CH(CH_3)—CH_2—CH_2—CHO$

4-methyl-1-pentanal

(b) $CH_3—CH(CH_3)—C{\equiv}C—COOH$

4-methyl-2-pentyn-1-oic acid

(c) $CH_3CH_2CH_2—CH(CH_3)—COOH$

2-methyl-1-pentanoic acid

(d) $CH_3CH_2—CH{=}CH—C(=O)—CH_3$

3-hexen-5-one

48. IUPAC name of the following compound is

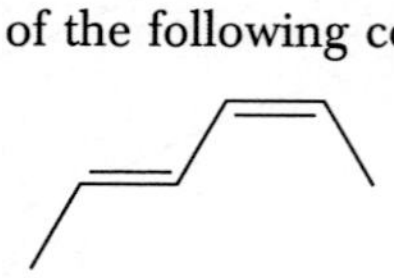

(a) (2*Z*, 4*E*)-2, 4-hexadiene
(b) (2*E*, 4*E*)-2, 4-hexadiene
(c) (2*Z*, 4*Z*)-2, 4-hexadiene
(d) (2*E*, 4*Z*)-2, 4-hexadiene

49. IUPAC name of the following compound is

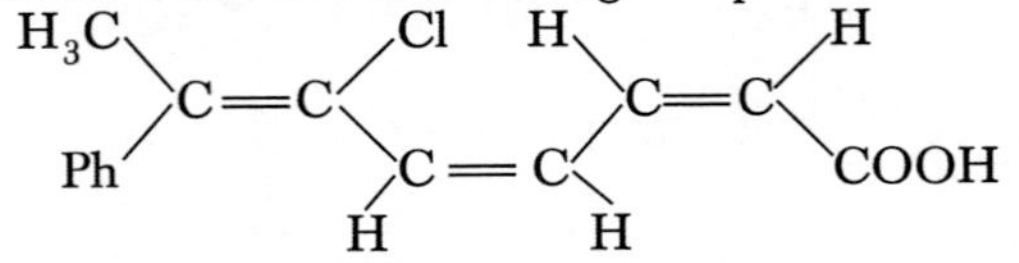

(a) 7-phenyl octa-2*E*, 4*Z*, 6*E*-trienoic acid
(b) 7-phenyl octa-2*Z*, 4*E*, 6*E*-trienoic acid
(c) 7-phenyl octa 2*Z*, 4*Z*, 6*Z*-trienoic acid
(d) 7-phenyl octa-2*Z*, 4*Z*, 6*E*-trienoic acid

50. The IUPAC name of the compound

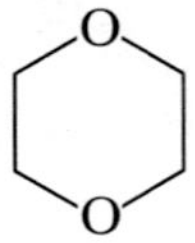

is

(a) dioxane
(b) diethylene-1, 4-dioxide
(c) 1, 4-dioxocyclohexane
(d) 1, 4-dioxacyclohexane

Exercise 2

(For Part 'C')

1. IUPAC name of the following compound

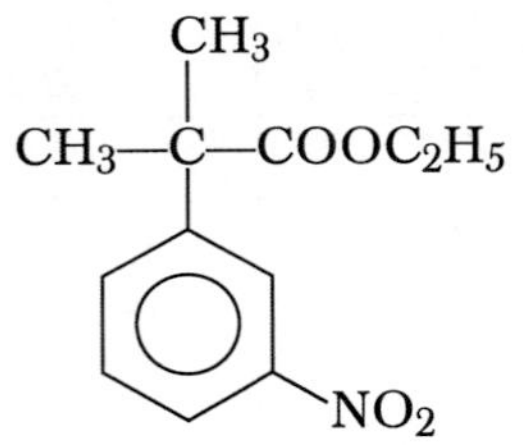

(a) ethyl 2-methyl-2-(*m*-nitrophenyl) propionate
(b) ethyl 2-methyl-2-(*m*-nitrophenyl) propanoate
(c) ethyl 2-methyl-2-(3-nitrophenyl) propionic acid
(d) ethyl 2-methyl-2-(3-nitrophenyl) propanoate

2. Which of the following compounds is not correctly named?

(a) 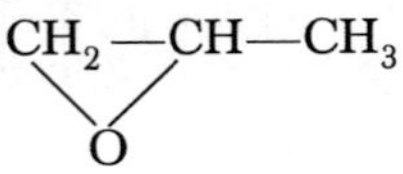 1, 2-epoxypropane

(b) 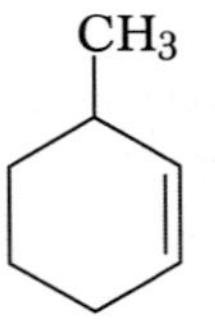 3-methylcyclohexene

(c) 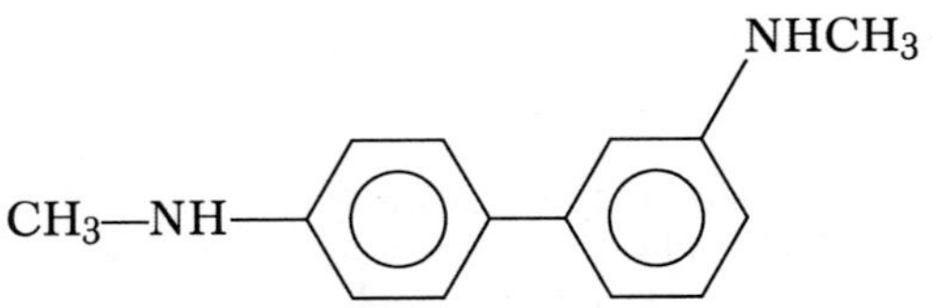

3, 4-bis (N-methylamino) biphenyl

(d) 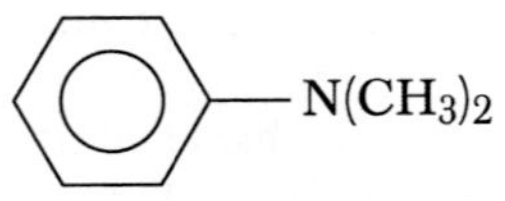

N-phenyldimethylamine

3. The correct IUPAC name of the compound

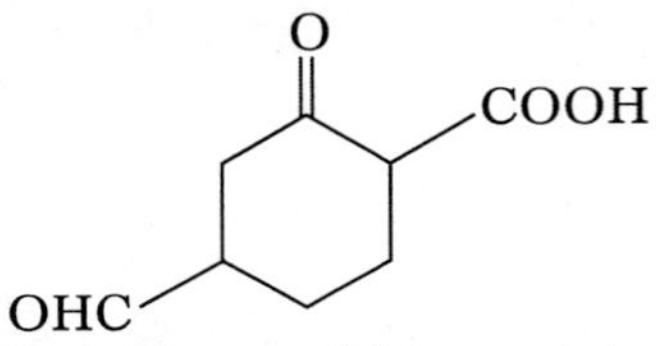

is

(a) 5-carboxy-3-oxocyclohexane carboxaldehyde
(b) 2-carboxy-5-formylcyclohexane
(c) 4-formyl-2-oxocyclohexane carboxylic acid
(d) 4-carboxy-3-oxocyclohexanal

4. The IUPAC name of the compound

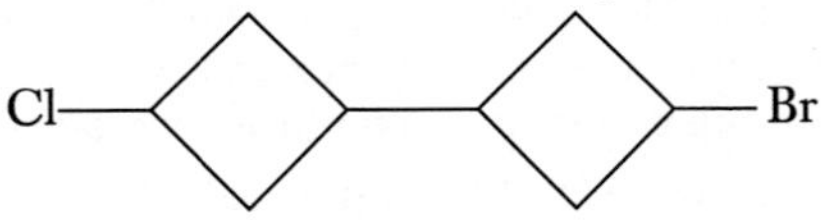

is

(a) 3-bromo-3′-chloro-1, 1′-bicyclobutane
(b) 1-bromo-1′-chloro-4, 4′-bicyclobutane
(c) 1-bromo-1′-chloro-3, 3′-bicyclobutane
(d) 4-(4′-chlorocyclobutyl)-1-bromocyclobutane

5. The compound, 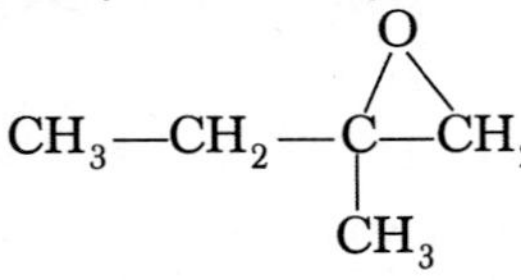 may be named as

(a) 2-ethyl-2-methyloxirane
(b) 1, 2-epoxy-2-methylbutane
(c) Both (a) and (b)
(d) None of the above

6. By acidic hydrolysis —CN group changes to $-\overset{\overset{\large O}{\|}}{C}OH$ as given

I. $CH_3\underset{\underset{\large CN}{|}}{C}HCHO \xrightarrow{H_3O^+} CH_3\underset{\underset{\large COOH}{|}}{C}HCHO$

II. $CH_3\underset{\underset{\large OH}{|}}{C}HCN \xrightarrow{H_3O^+} CH_3\underset{\underset{\large OH}{|}}{C}HCOOH$

III. $CH_3\overset{O}{\overset{\|}{C}}CN \xrightarrow{H_3O^+} CH_3\overset{O}{\overset{\|}{C}}COOH$

In which case(s), preference group of nomenclature changes?

(a) I, II (b) I, III
(c) II, III (d) I

7. Following reactions are possible

I. $CH_2{=}CHCOOH \xrightarrow{\Delta} CH_2{=}CH_2$

II. 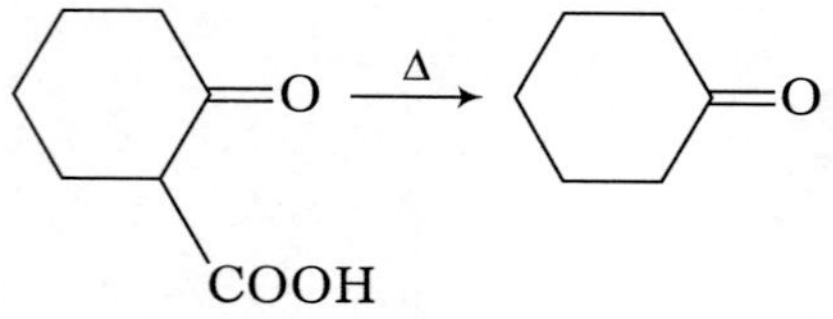

III. $CH_3CH(COOH)_2 \xrightarrow{\Delta} CH_3CH_2COOH$

In which case(s), principal group loses its prefrence?

(a) I, II (b) I, II, III
(c) II, IIII (d) I, III

8. The IUPAC name of the compound

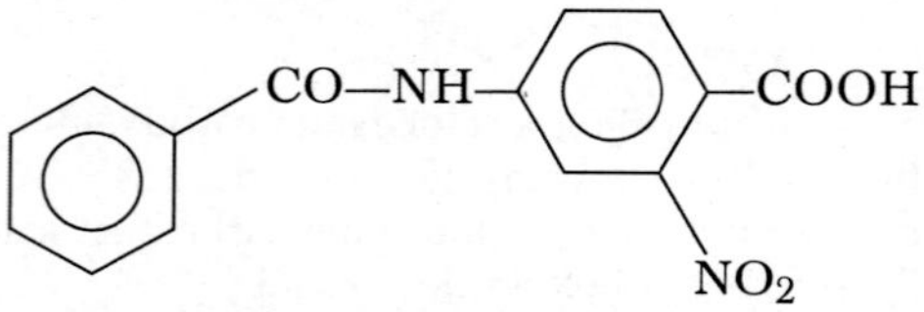

is

(a) 4-(benzoylamino)-2-nitrobenzoic acid
(b) 4-(benzamido)-2-nitrobenzoic acid
(c) 4-(benzoylamino)-6-nitrobenzoic acid
(d) 4-benzene carboxamide-6-nitrobenzoic acid

9. The correct IUPAC name of the following hydrocarbon

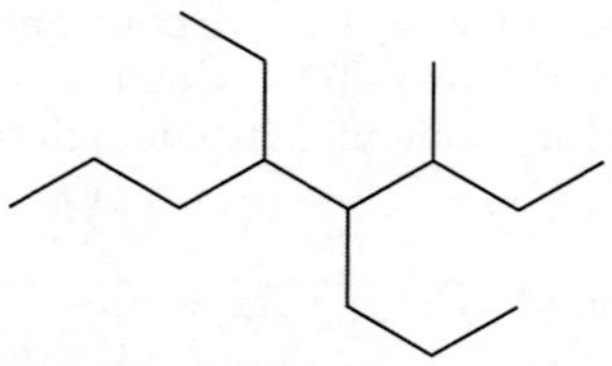

is

(a) 4-ethyl-6-methyl-5-propyloctane
(b) 3-methyl-4-propyl-5-ethyloctane
(c) 5-ethyl-3-methyl-4-propyloctane
(d) 5-ethyl-4-propyl-3-methyloctane

10. What is the IUPAC name of the following compound?

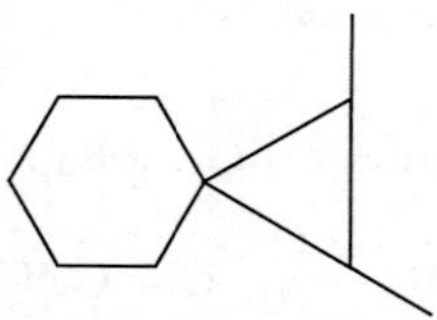

(a) 1, 2-dimethylcyclopropyl cyclohexane
(b) 1, 2-dimethyl spiro [2, 5] octane
(c) 7, 8-dimethyl spiro [5, 2] octane
(d) 1, 2-dimethyl bicyclo [5, 2] octane

11. The IUPAC name of the compound

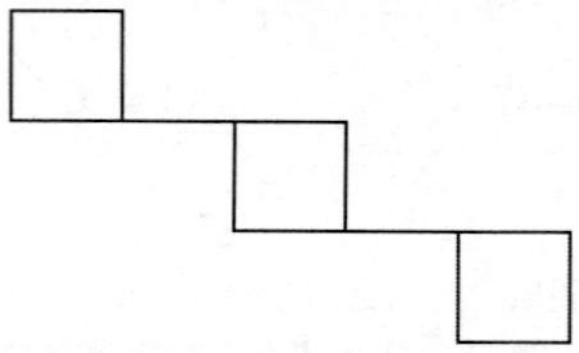

is

(a) 1, 3-bis cyclobutyl cyclobutane
(b) 1, 3-dicyclobutyl cyclobutane
(c) 1, 1′, 3′,1′′-tricyclobutane
(d) 1, 1′, 3′, 1′′-tercyclobutane

12. Match the Column I with Column II.

Column I		Column II	
A.	$CH_2{=}\overset{\mid}{C}{-}CH_3$	1.	2-methylpropyl
B.	$-CH_2C(CH_3)_3$	2.	1,1-dimethyl ethyl
C.	$-C(CH_3)_3$	3.	3-methyl butyl
D.	$-CH_2CH_2CH(CH_3)_2$	4.	iso-propynyl
E.	$-CH_2CH(CH_3)_2$	5.	2,2-dimethylpropyl

Codes

	A	B	C	D	E
(a)	4	5	3	2	1
(b)	4	5	2	3	1
(c)	5	4	3	2	1
(d)	4	5	2	1	3

13. The IUPAC name of the compound

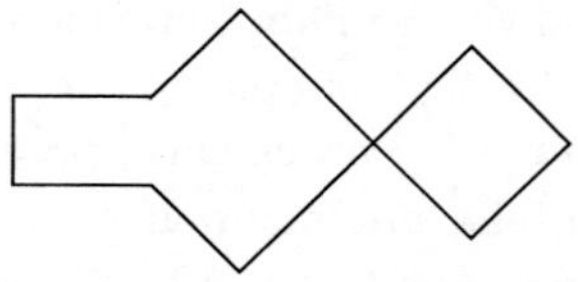

is

(a) 1, 1-cyclobutyl heptane (b) bicyclo [6, 3, 0] nonane
(c) spiro [3, 6] decane (d) spiro [6, 3] decane

14. The IUPAC name of citric acid is

(a) 1, 2, 3-tricarboxy-2-propanol
(b) 3-carboxy-3-hydroxy-1, 5-pentanedioic acid
(c) 2-hydroxypropane-1, 2, 3-tricarboxylic acid
(d) 3-hydroxy-1, 2, 3-tricarboxypropane

15. The IUPAC name of the compound

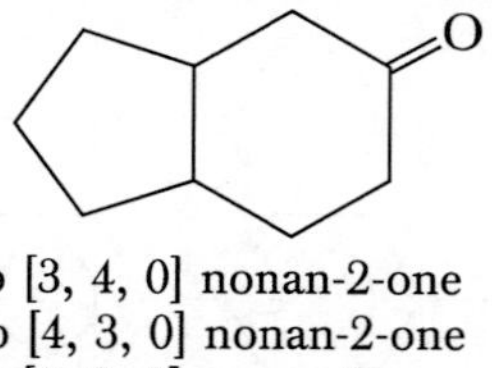

is

(a) Bicyclo [3, 4, 0] nonan-2-one
(b) Bicyclo [4, 3, 0] nonan-2-one
(c) Bicyclo [4, 3, 0] nonan-3-one
(d) Bicyclo [4, 3, 0] nonan-6-one

16. IUPAC name of following compound is $(HOCH_2CH_2O)_2CH{-}COOH$

(a) 2, 2-bis (2-hydroxyethoxy) ethanoic acid
(b) 4-carboxy-3, 5-dioxaheptane-1, 7-diol
(c) 2, 2-bis (2-hydroxyethoxy) acetic acid
(d) None of the above

Assertion & Reasons

Codes

(a) Both A and R are true and R is the correct explanation of A.
(b) Both A and R are true but R is not the correct explanation of A.
(c) A is true but R is false.
(d) A is false but R is true.

17. **Assertion (A)** The IUPAC name for is 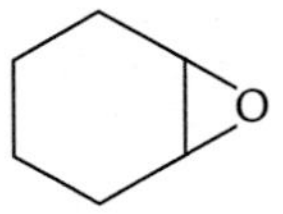 is 7-oxabicyclo [4, 1, 0] heptane.

Reason (R) The prefix oxo is used for the C=O group.

18. **Assertion (A)** The IUPAC name for the compound $NCCH_2CH_2COOH$ is butane-3-nitrile-1-oic-acid.

Reson (R) COOH is considered as substituent group while CN is considered as the principal functional group.

19. **Assertion (A)** The compound $C_6H_5CH{=}CHCl$ is called β-chlorostyrene.

Reason (R) In organic halides the carbon atom attached to the halogen atom is designated as α.

20. The stereochemical descriptors for the chiral centre and olefin in the compound given below, are

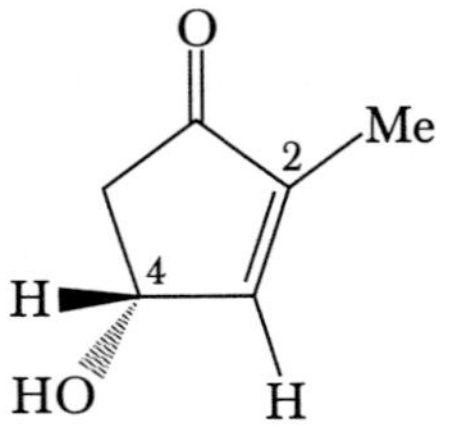

(a) 4*R*, 2*Z* (b) 4*S*, 2*Z*
(c) 4*R*, 2*E* (d) 4*S*, 2*E*

21. According to CIP system of nomenclature following compound will be named as

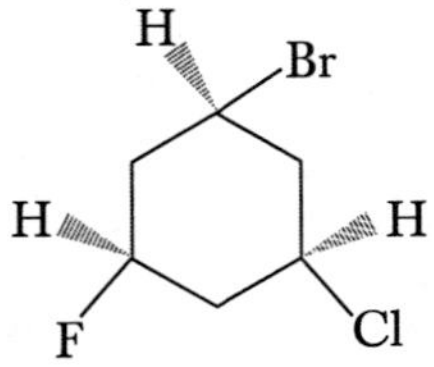

(a) 1-(*R*)-bromo-3-(*R*)-chloro-5-(*R*)-fluorocyclohexane
(b) 1-(*R*)-bromo-3-(*S*)-chloro-5-(*R*)-fluorocyclohexane
(c) 1-(*S*)-bromo-3-(*S*)-chloro-5-(*S*)-fluorocyclohexane
(d) 1-(*S*)-bromo-3-(*R*)-chloro-5-(*S*)-fluorocyclohexane

22. Designate the absolute configuration of the following compound

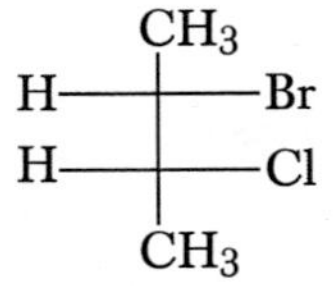

(a) 2*R*, 3*R*-2-bromo-3-chlorobutane
(b) 2*S*, 3*S*-2-bromo-3-chlorobutane
(c) 2*S*, 3*R*-2-bromo-3-chlorobutane
(d) 2*R*, 3*S*-2-bromo-3-chlorobutane

23. The IUPAC name of the compound

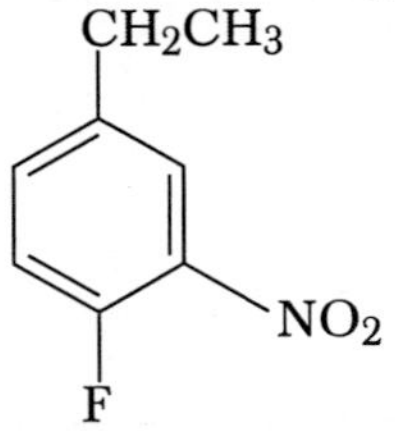

is

(a) 4-ethyl-1-fluoro-2-nitrobenzene
(b) 5-ethyl-2-fluoro-1-nitrobenzene
(c) 1-ethyl-5-fluoro-4-nitrobenzene
(d) 4-ethyl-1-fluoro-6-nitrobenzene

24. The structure of 3-ethylpentane-2, 4-dione is

(a) 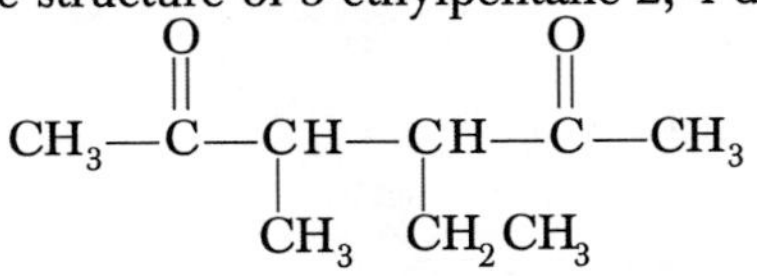

(b) 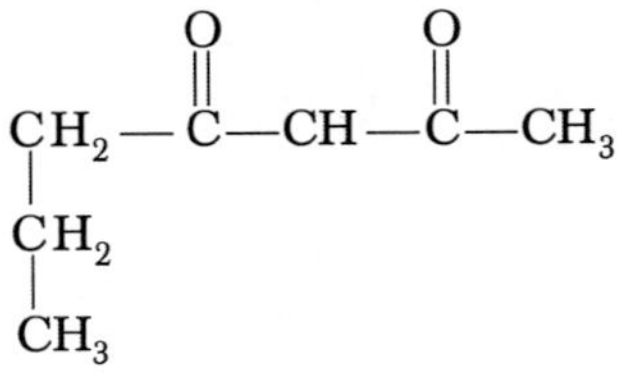

(c) 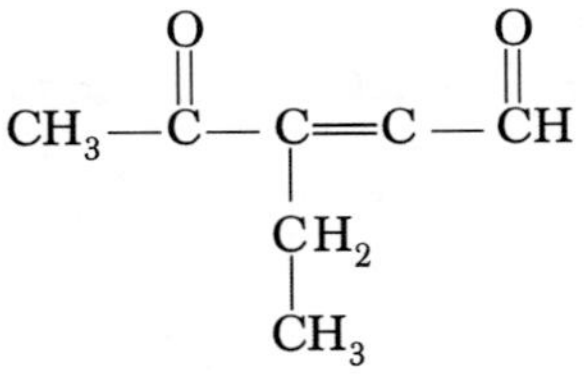

(d) 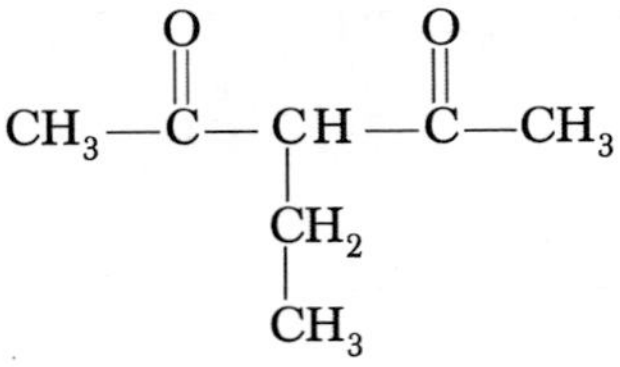

25. D(+) glucose is
(a) 2(*S*), 3(*R*), 4(*R*), 5(*R*), 6-pentahydroxy hexanal
(b) 2(*R*), 3(*S*), 4(*R*), 5(*R*), 6-pentahydroxy hexanal
(c) 2(*R*), 3(*R*), 4(*S*), 5(*R*), 6-pentahydroxy hexanal
(d) 2(*R*), 3(*R*), 4(*R*), 5(*S*), 6-pentahydroxy hexanal

26. Match the Column I with Column II.

	Column I		Column II
A.	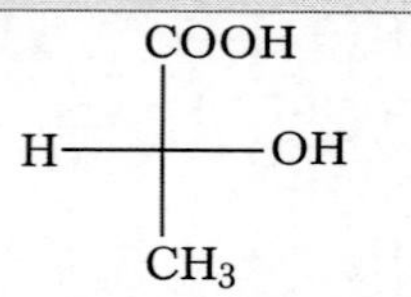	1.	2*R*, 3*S*
B.	$CH_3-\underset{OH}{CH}-\underset{Cl}{CH}-CH_3$	2.	2*S*, 3*R*
C.	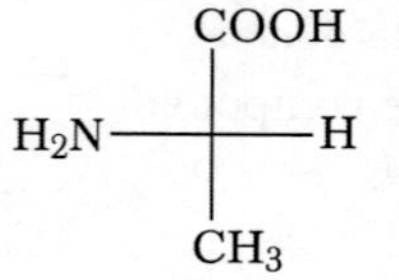	3.	*R*
D.	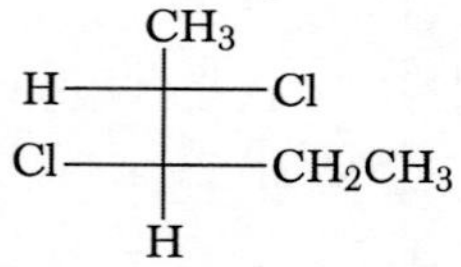	4.	*S*

Codes

	A	B	C	D
(a)	4	2	3	1
(b)	3	1	4	2
(c)	3	1	2	4
(d)	4	2	1	3

27. The IUPAC name of

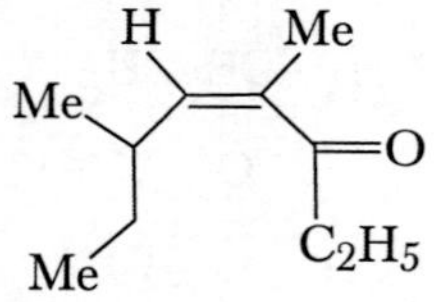

is

(a) (*Z*)-4, 6-dimethyloct-4-en-3-one
(b) (*E*)-4, 6-dimethyloct-4-en-3-one
(c) (*Z*)-3, 5-dimethyloct-4-en-6-one
(d) (*E*)-3, 5-dimethyloct-4-en-6-one

28. The compound $CH_3—C≡C—CH_3$ can be named as

(a) dimethylacetylene (b) crotonylene
(c) but-2-yne (d) allylene

29. The compound 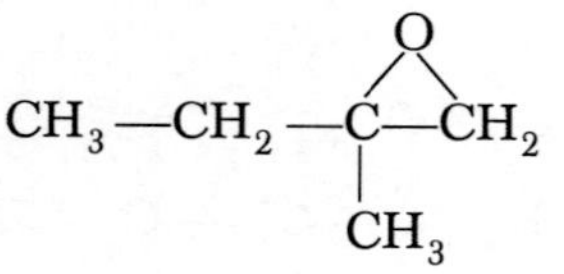 may be named as

(a) 2-ethyl-2-methyloxirane
(b) 1,2-epoxy-2-methylbutane
(c) 1,2-oxapentane
(d) 2-methyl-1,2-butoxide

30. Which of the following names are not correct for $\underset{CHO}{CH_2}—\underset{CHO}{CH}—\underset{CHO}{CH_2}$?

(a) 3-formylpentane, 1,5-dial
(b) 1,2,3-triformylpropane
(c) 2-formylmethylbutane-1,4-dial
(d) propane-1,2,3-tricarbaldehyde

31. The compound $C_6H_5CH{=}CHCOOH$ may be called as

(a) succinic acid
(b) 2-phenylprop-2-en-1-oic acid
(c) mandelic acid
(d) cinnamic acid

32. Match the Column I with Column II.

	Column I (Group)		Column II (Suffix)
A.	Alcohol	1.	one
B.	Aldehyde	2.	ol
C.	Acid chloride	3.	al
D.	Ketone	4.	oyl

Codes

	A	B	C	D
(a)	4	3	2	1
(b)	2	3	1	4
(c)	2	3	4	1
(d)	3	2	4	1

Directions (Q. Nos. 33 to 35)

In 1993 the IUPAC published a guide to nomenclature of organic compound recommendations 1993, R. Panico, W.H. Powell and Jean Claude Richer, Blackwell science. This publication advocated one major change that affects the nomenclature of relatively simple compounds. The 1993 recommendations prefer the principal group or multiple bond position with a number preceding the suffix itself whereas the 1979 recommendations take into account the principal group or multiple bond position with a number preceding the hydrocarbon name. **The 1993 recommendations have not been generally adopted, thus names that adhere to either set of recommendations are acceptable.**

33. IUPAC stands for

(a) Indian Union of Pure and Applied Chemists
(b) International Union of Pure and Applied Chemistry
(c) International Union of Pure and Applied Chemists
(d) Italian Union of Pure and Applied Chemists

34. $CH_3CH{=}CHCH_3$ is named as based on 1993 recommendations

(a) 2-butene (b) but-2-ene
(c) Both (a) and (b) (d) None of these

35. $NC—CH_2—\overset{CN}{CH}—CH_2—CN$ is named as based on 1993 recommendations.

(a) Propane-1,2,3-tricarbonitrile
(b) 3-cyaanopropane-1,5-dinitrile
(c) Propane-1,2,3-carbonitrile
(d) 3-cyanopropane-1,5-nitrile

Answers

Exercise 1

1. (b)	**2.** (b)	**3.** (c)	**4.** (a)	**5.** (d)	**6.** (d)	**7.** (b)	**8.** (d)	**9.** (b)	**10.** (b)
11. (c)	**12.** (c)	**13.** (b)	**14.** (d)	**15.** (b)	**16.** (a)	**17.** (a)	**18.** (b)	**19.** (a)	**20.** (a)
21. (a)	**22.** (b)	**23.** (b)	**24.** (d)	**25.** (a)	**26.** (c)	**27.** (d)	**28.** (a)	**29.** (c)	**30.** (a)
31. (d)	**32.** (a)	**33.** (b)	**34.** (a)	**35.** (b)	**36.** (b)	**37.** (c)	**38.** (b)	**39.** (b)	**40.** (b)
41. (a)	**42.** (d)	**43.** (b)	**44.** (a)	**45.** (b)	**46.** (c)	**47.** (d)	**48.** (a)	**49.** (d)	**50.** (d)

Exercise 2

1. (d)	**2.** (d)	**3.** (c)	**4.** (a)	**5.** (c)	**6.** (d)	**7.** (a)	**8.** (a)	**9.** (c)	**10.** (b)
11. (d)	**12.** (b)	**13.** (c)	**14.** (c)	**15.** (c)	**16.** (a)	**17.** (b)	**18.** (d)	**19.** (b)	**20.** (b)
21. (b)	**22.** (c)	**23.** (a)	**24.** (d)	**25.** (b)	**26.** (b)	**27.** (a)	**28.** (a,b,c)	**29.** (a,b)	**30.** (b,c)
31. (b,d)	**32.** (c)	**33.** (b)	**34.** (b)	**35.** (a)					

Hints & Solutions

Exercise 1

2.

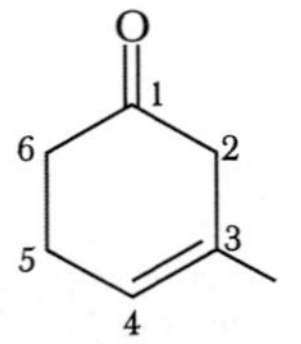

3-methyl-cyclohex-3-en-1-one

5.

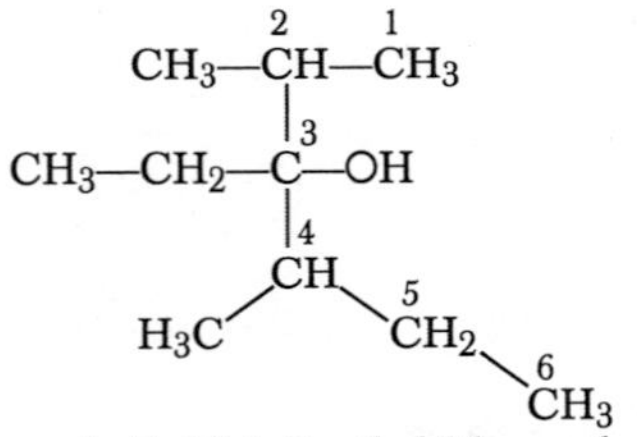

3-ethyl 2,4-dimethyl-3-hexanol

9.

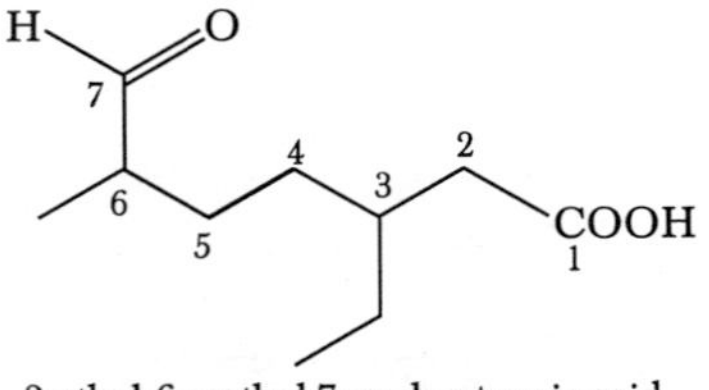

3-ethyl-6-methyl-7-oxoheptanoic acid

The selected chain is the longest chain and has more number of locants than the other seven membered chain.

11.

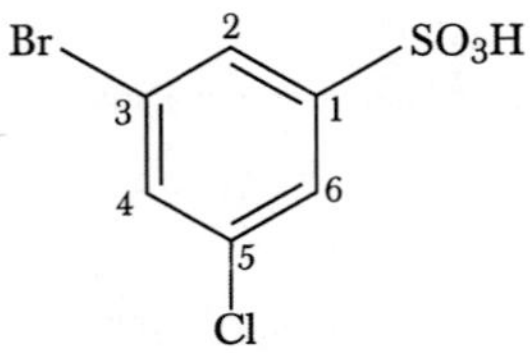

3-bromo-5-chloro benzene sulphonic acid

13. The correct structure of 3-carboxy-1, 5-pentane dioic acid is as

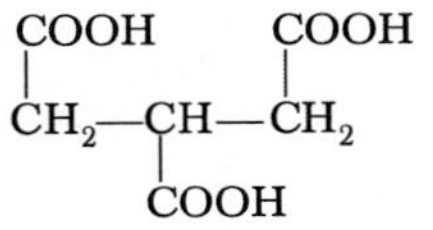

18.

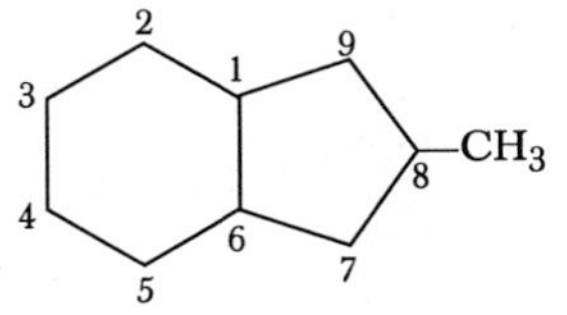

8-methyl bicyclo [4, 3, 0] nonane

23.

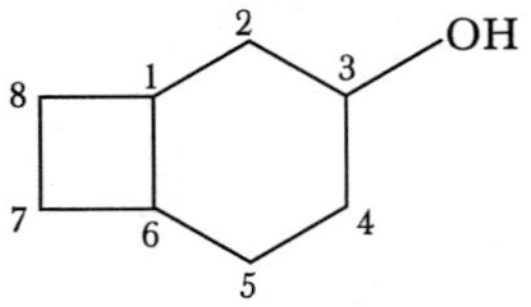

(Bicyclo [4, 2, 0] octan-3-ol)

27.

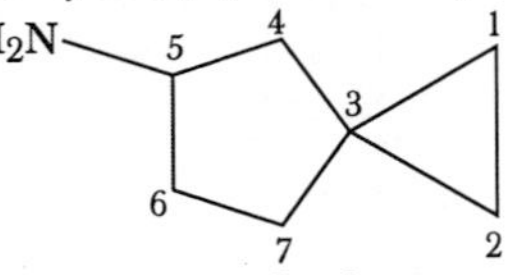

5-aminospiro [2, 4] heptane

31.

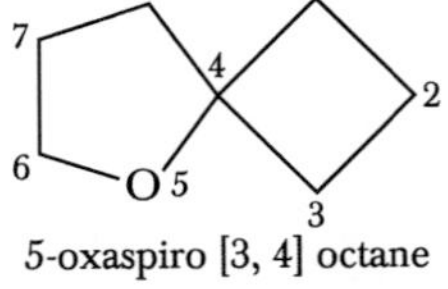

5-oxaspiro [3, 4] octane

33.

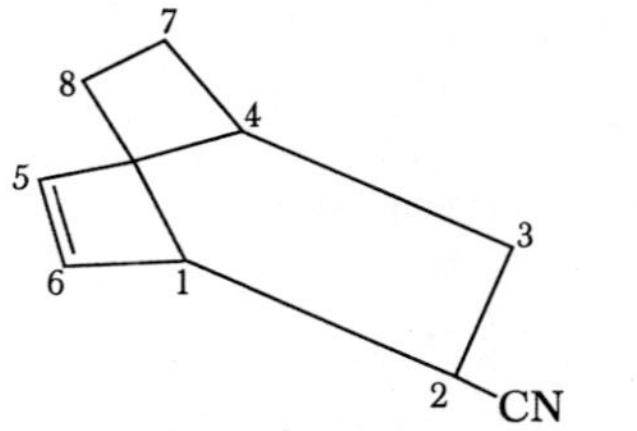

Bicyclo [2, 2, 2] oct-5-en-2-carbonitrile

34. 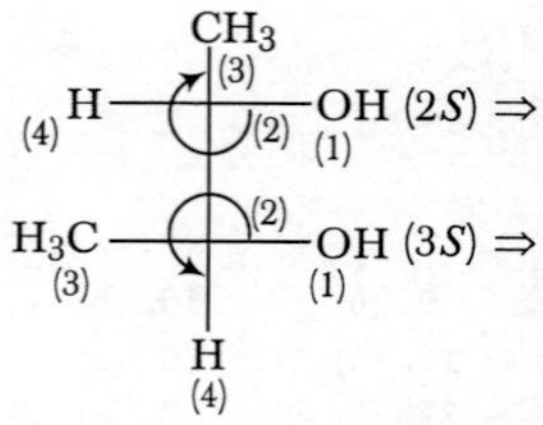

R and change to S hence, 2S (H is on horizontal position)

S and does not change hence, 3S (H is on vertical position)

Hence, the absolute configuration is (2S, 3S).

38. 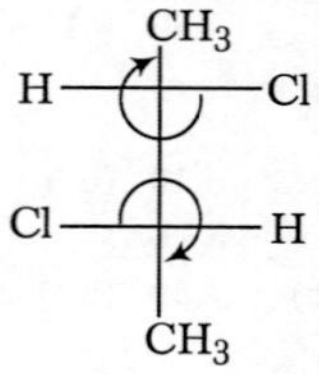

R and change to S hence 2S

R and change to S hence 3S.

Hence, absolute configuration is (2S/3S).

42. When —COOH is not the part of numbering system of the parent chain, suffix carboxylic acid, rather than -oic acid is used.

45. 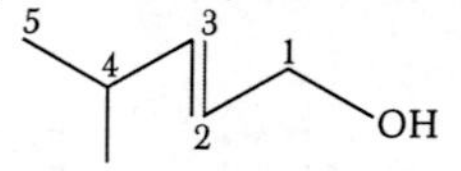

4-methyl pent-2-en-1-ol

49. 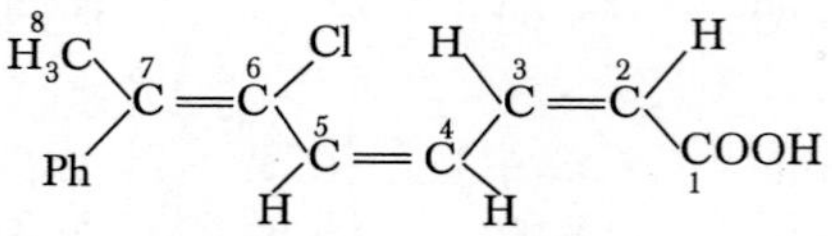

7-phenyl-2Z, 4Z, 6E-trienoic acid

Exercise 2

2. 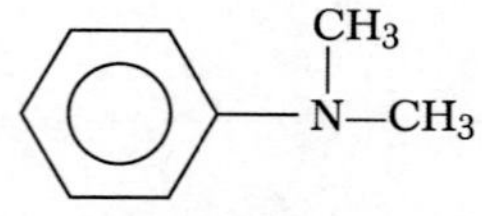

N, N-dimethyl benzenamine
or, N,N-dimethylaniline

4. 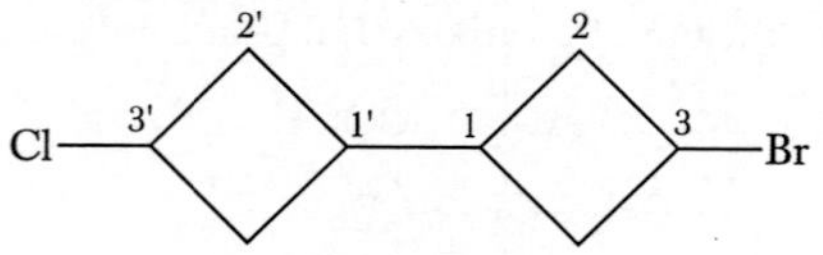

Br gets preference over Cl

3-bromo-3'-chloro-1, 1'-bicyclobutane

8. 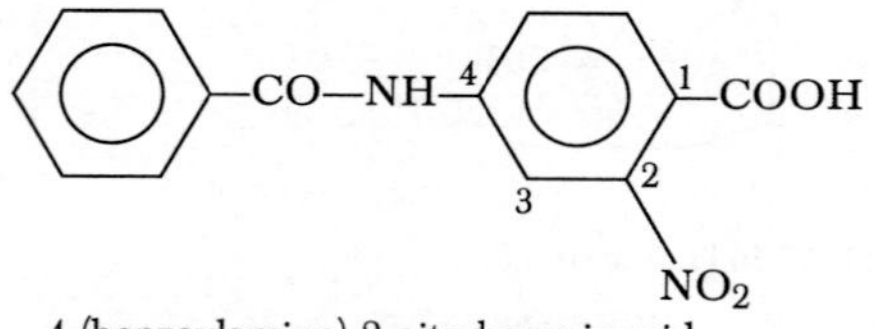

4-(benzoylamino)-2-nitrobenzoic acid

11. 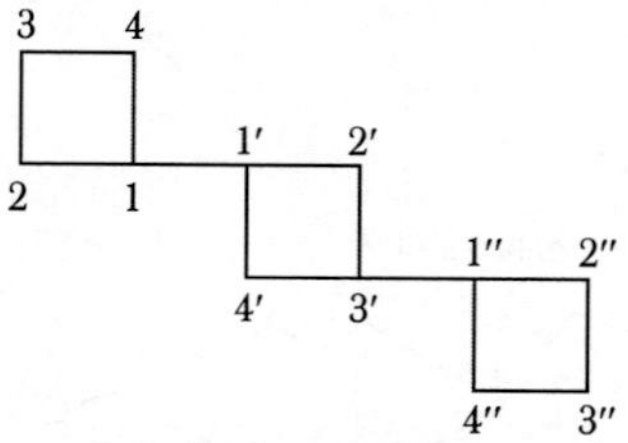

1, 1′, 3′, 1″-tercyclobutane

14. 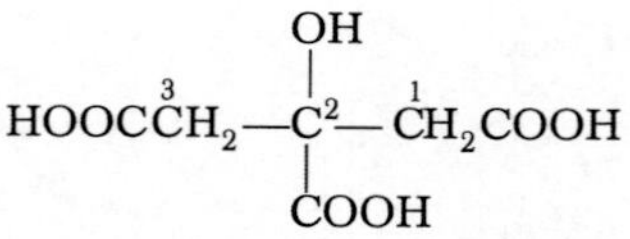

2-hydroxypropane-1, 2, 3-tricarboxylic acid

16. 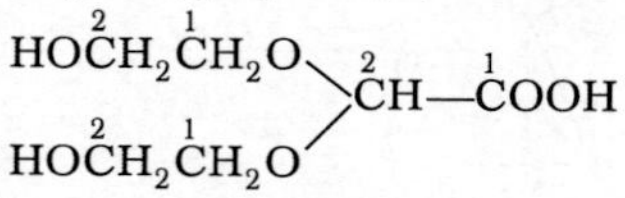

2, 2-bis (2-hydroxyethoxy)-ethanoic acid

20. 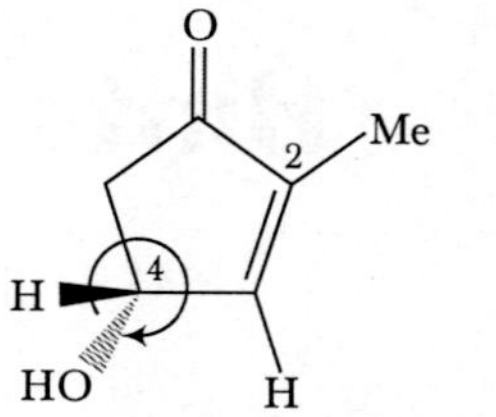

2 = Z, because the first priority groups are on one side and second priority groups are on the other.

4 = S, The rotation is clockwise with group with lowest priority (*i.e.,* H) is pointing to us. Hence, it is "S". Hence, 4S, 2Z.

23. 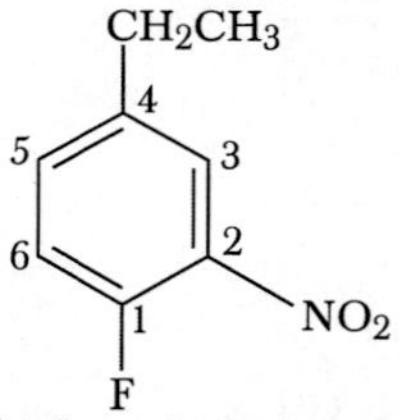

4-ethyl-1-fluoro-2-nitrobenzene

25. 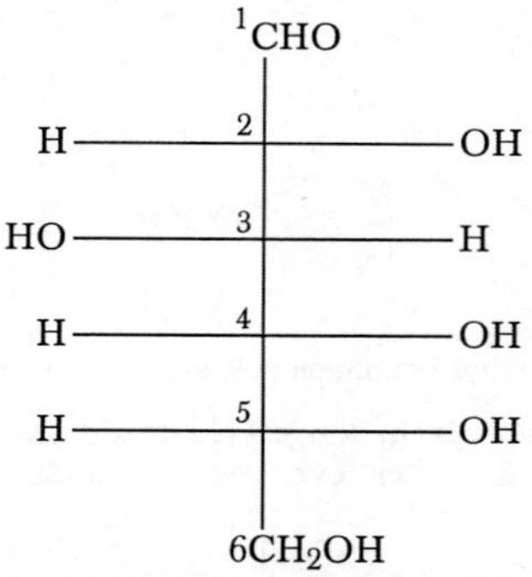

2(R), 3(S), 4(R), 5(R), 6-pentahydroxy hexanal

29. 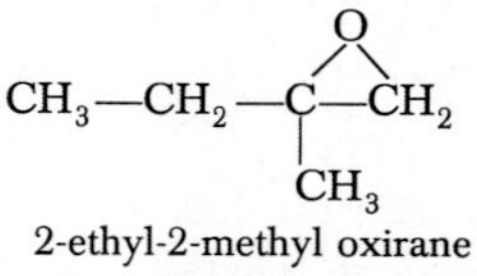

2-ethyl-2-methyl oxirane
or 1,2-epoxy-2-methyl butane

30. 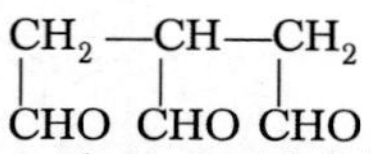

3-formyl pentane-1,5-dial
or propane-1,2,3-tricarbaldehyde

29

Stereochemistry

Syllabus

- Principles of Stereochemistry
- Configurational and Conformational Isomerism in Acyclic and Cyclic Compounds
- Stereogenicity, Stereoselectivity, Enantioselectivity, Diastereoselectivity and Asymmetric Induction

Introduction

The branch of chemistry concerned with three dimensional arrangements of atoms in a molecule and the chemical effect of stereoisomerism is known as stereochemistry. Stereoisomers are the isomers which have similar constitution *i.e.*, similar bonding pattern or connectivity but differ in the arrangements of atoms or groups in three dimensional space and the phenomenon involved is collectively known as stereoisomerism. On the basis of nature of arrangements of atoms or groups stereoisomerism are further classified into two categories :

1. Configurational isomerism
2. Conformational isomerism

Configurational Isomerism

It arises due to different configuration at one or more stereocentre. The isomers are known as configurational isomers. These are non-superimposable and non-interconvertible by rotation around single bonds. They can be interconverted by breaking and making bonds. Configurational isomerism are of two types :

1. Geometrical isomerism
2. Optical isomerism

The main condition for the existence of geometrical isomerism is that the atoms or groups of atoms at either end of the carbon-carbon double bond be different from each other whereas the main requirement for a compound to exhibit optical isomerism is that the molecule to be asymmetric as a whole.

Geometrical Isomerism

Geometrical isomerism arises due to restricted rotation of atoms or groups about a covalent bond. There are two important classes of organic compounds where rotation about a covalent bonds are restricted, they are (i) compound containing multiple bonds and (ii) cyclic compounds.

Geometrical isomerism is further classified into two categories as *cis-trans* isomerism and $E-Z$ isomerism.

Cis-trans isomerism

(a) ***Cis-trans* isomerism in acyclic compounds** *Cis-trans* isomerism in acyclic compound can be observed due to restricted rotations of atoms or groups about carbon-carbon double bond or in compound containing double bond between carbon and other atoms *viz* "N" or double bond between two atoms which may be similar or different.

- In the compound containing carbon-carbon double bond, if identical atoms or groups lies on the same side of a π-plane, the stereoisomer is known as ***cis*-isomer,** and if identical atoms or groups lies on opposite side of a π-plane, the stereoisomer is known as ***trans*-isomer** as shown below :

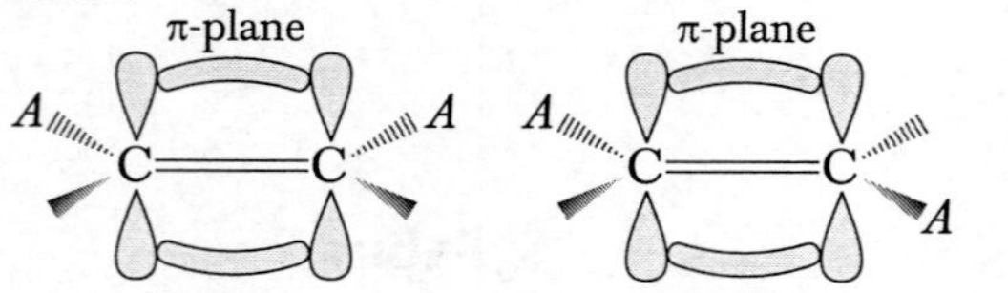

Cis-isomer *Trans*-isomer

In the above shown structures, it is evident that π-plane is perpendicular to the molecular plane. In *cis*-isomer, the identical groups *A* are on same side to the π-plane *i.e.,* behind the π-plane. In the *trans*-isomer the identical groups *A* are on the opposite side of plane *i.e.,* one behind the π-plane and one in the front side of π-plane. *i.e.,*

Cis-2-butene *Trans*-2-butene

Note The main conditions for geometrical isomerism are.

- The molecule must have a double bond.
- The two atoms or groups attached to the same carbon atom must be different.

- There are several functional groups, when present in a compound, involve geometrical isomerism although they do not contain carbon-carbon double bond. They are :

(i) Oximes contain C=N and may give rise to geometrical isomerism. All aldo-oxime (except formaldoxime) show geometrical isomerism.

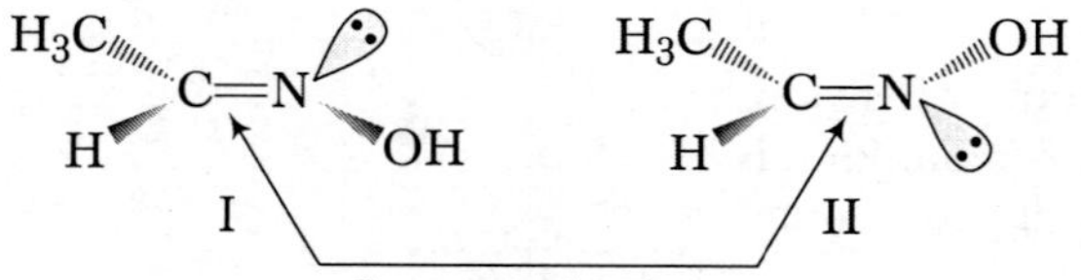

Geometrical isomers

Here, structure I and II represents different configuration and they are non-interconvertible due to restricted rotation about carbon-nitrogen double bond.

In case of ketones, symmetrical ketones will not form stereoisomers after formation of keto-oxime, but all unsymmetrical ketones will result in the formation of two stereoisomers of keto-oxime after condensation with hydroxyl amine.

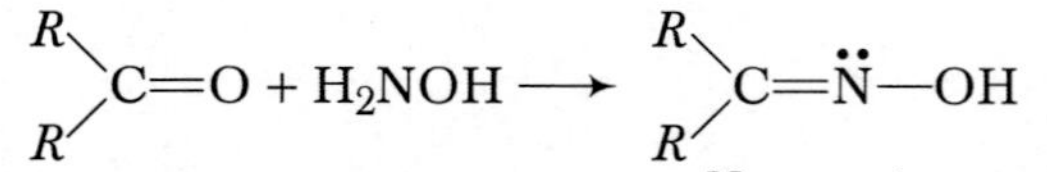

Symmetrical ketone No stereoisomers

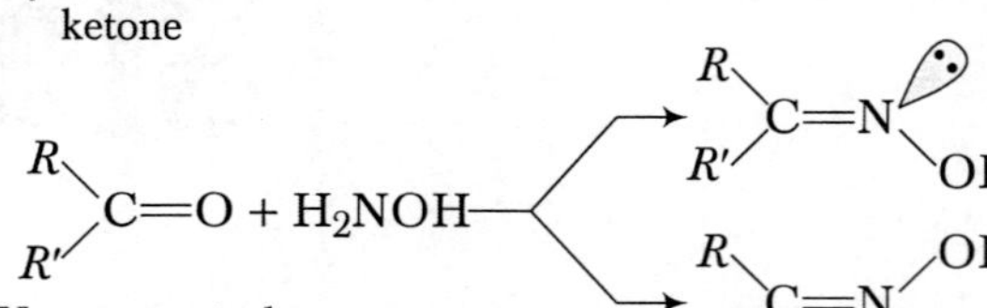

Unsymmetrical ketone Stereoisomers

(ii) Imines, also contain C=N and may give rise to geometrical isomerism as

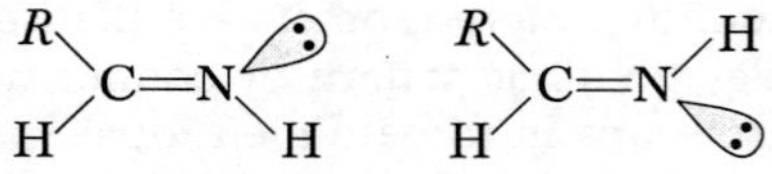

Geometrical isomers

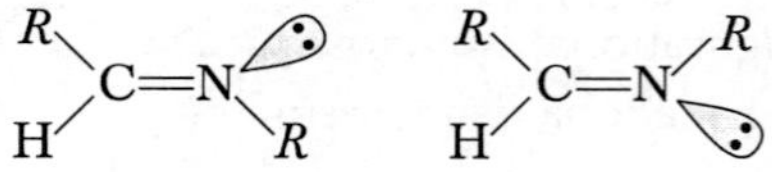

Geometrical isomers

(b) ***Cis-trans* isomerism in cycloalkenes** The smaller cycloalkenes are rigid and exists predominantly in their *cis*-forms. If the ring size becomes large enough, flexibility increases and possibility of existence of *trans*-isomers increases. The smallest cycloalkene for which *trans*-isomer exist in practice is cyclo-octene as

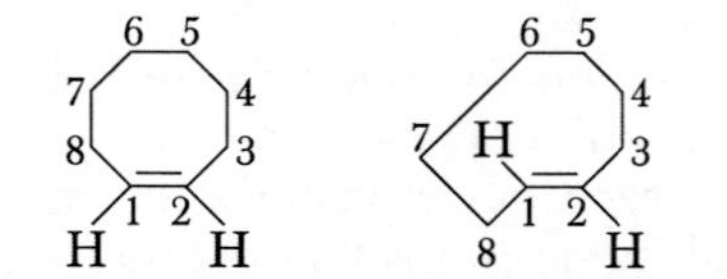

Cis-cyclo-octene *Trans*-cyclo-octene

In larger, cycloalkenes, *trans*-forms are well existent.

(c) ***Cis-trans* isomerism in substituted cycloalkanes** The smaller cycloalkanes are rigid rings, and if substituted properly, they may exhibit phenomena of *cis-trans* or geometrical isomerism.

In case of cycloalkanes, if identical atoms or groups are on the same side of plane of the ring, they are called *cis*-isomer provided its *trans*-form exist independently.

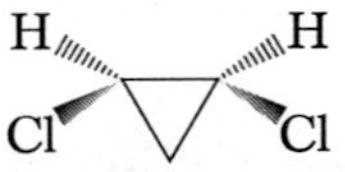

Cis-1,2-dichlorocyclopropane

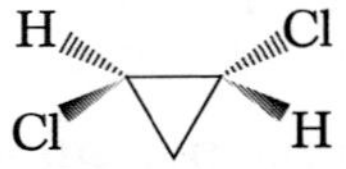

Trans-1,2-dichlorocyclopropane

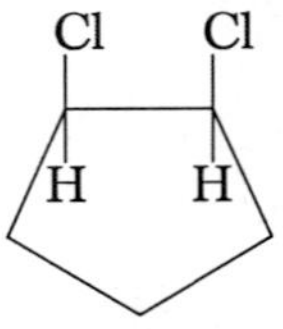

Cis-1, 2-dichlorocyclopentane

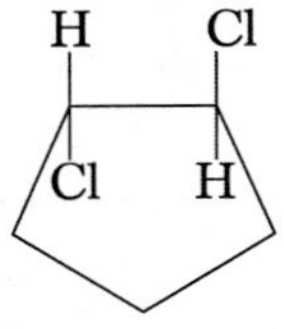

Trans-1, 2-dichlorocyclopentane

E and *Z* isomerism

It is another type of geometrical isomerism, arises when all four atoms or groups bonded to stereocentres are different *e.g.,* FClC═CBrI. In such type of compounds, geometrical isomers are classified as *E* and *Z* isomers. If the group of similar priority are on the opposite side of the π-plane, the isomer is known as ***E*-isomer** (German word Entgegen meaning opposite) while if the groups of similar priority are the same side of π-plane, the isomer is known as ***Z*-isomer** (German word Zusammen meaning together).

The priority of the substituents is determined for each carbon atom is according to the priority sequence rule given by Cahn-Ingold, Prelog.

e.g.,

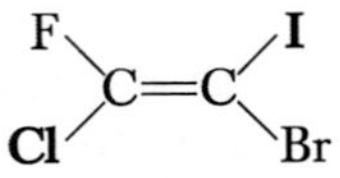

E-isomer

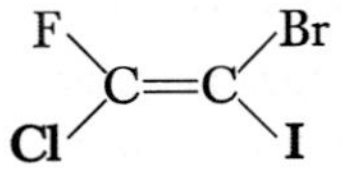

Z-isomer

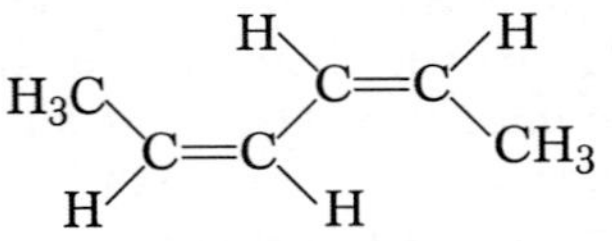

Z, Z-isomer

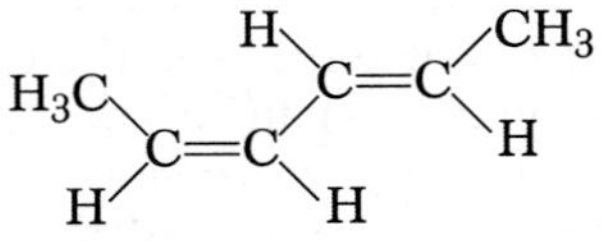

Z, E-isomer

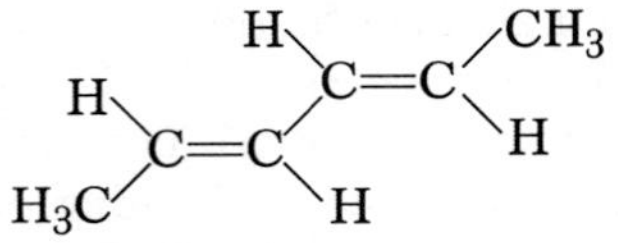

E, E-isomer

Note The *E-Z* nomenclature can also be used to designate cyclic compounds when the two higher priority groups age on the same side of the ring the compound is *Z* and when these are on opposite sides of the ring it is *E*.

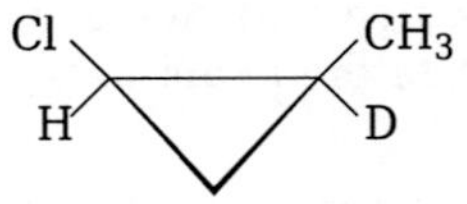

Z

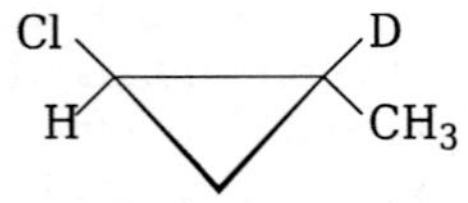

E

Optical Isomerism

It is another type of configurational isomerism. A substance which is not superimposable on its mirror image is known as optically active substance and the phenomenon is called optical isomerism. Optical activity of an optically active substance is measured with the help of an instrument known as **"Polarimeter"**. Stereoisomers which rotate the plane polarized light right (clockwise) to the viewer is called **"Dextrorotatory"** and the other which rotate plane polarized light left (anticlockwise) to the viewer, is called **"Laevorotatory"**. Dextrorotatory isomer is designated as "*d*" or (+) and laevorotatory as "*l*" or (–).

Chirality

A pure compound that rotates the plane of plane polarized light is called optically active compound and it is found that the molecule is non-superimposable on its mirror image. On the other hand, if the molecule is superimposable on its mirror image, the compound does not rotate the plane of plane polarized light and is called optically inactive. Hence, the molecules which are not superimposable or their mirror images are called **chiral** molecules. The property of non-superimposability of a structure on its mirror image is called **chirality.** Similarly, molecules which are superimposable on their mirror images are called **achiral** molecules.

The carbon which is bonded to form different atoms or groups of atoms is called **chiral** or **asymmetric** carbon atom. It is generally indicated by asterisk as C*. A modern term for chiral carbon is **stereogenic centre** or **stereocentre.**

e.g., In 2-butanol C-2 is chiral hence it shows optical isomerism.

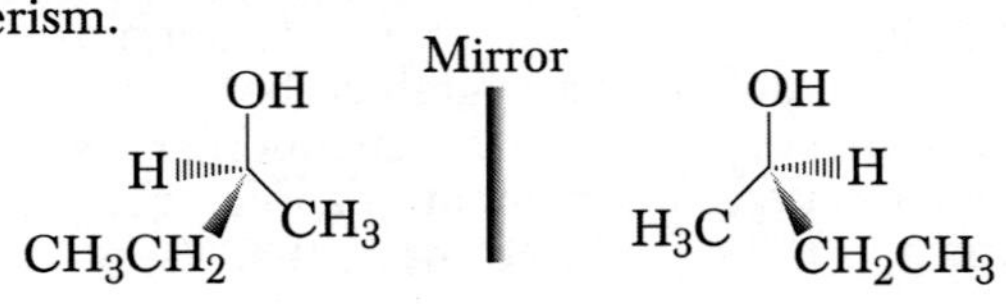

A *B*

The two structures represent

(+)-2-butanol $[\alpha]_D^{25°C} = +13.52°$

(–)-2-butanol $[\alpha]_D^{25°C} = -13.52°$

The two structures of 2-butanol, *A* and *B* are non-superimposable mirror images of one another, hence, they are optically active and stereo chemically different compounds. *A* rotate the plane polarized light to right and *B* to left.

A carbon atom is **achiral** if it has two or more identical atoms or groups attached to it and it would be superimposable on its mirror image.

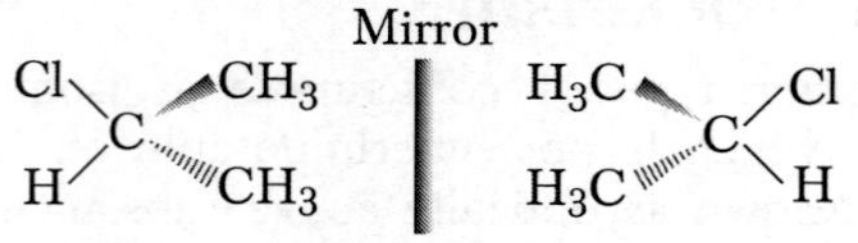

Superimposable mirror image

Enantiomers

Stereoisomers which are non-superimposable mirror images of one another are known as "enantiomers". *e.g.,* 2-butanol, 2-chlorobutane, lactic acid, 3-methylhexane etc., form non-superimposable mirror images and exist as enantiomers.

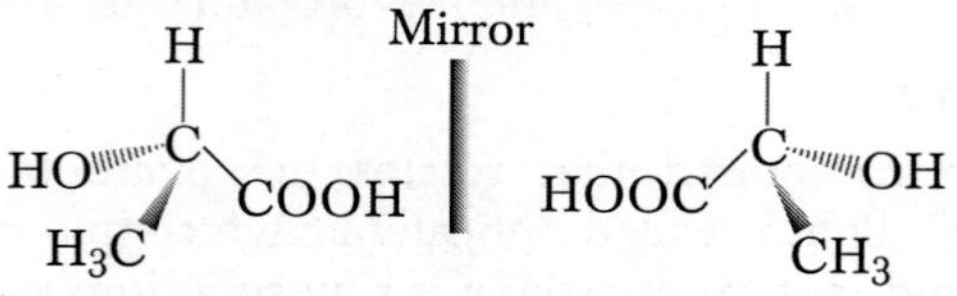

Non-superimposable mirror images of lactic acid.

Enantiomers show the following properties :

(a) Enantiomers have identical physical properties *i.e.,* same melting points, solubility in a standard solvent, same refractive index, densities (if liquid at room temperature), same surface-tension, same viscosity etc.

(b) Enantiomers have equal magnitude of specific optical rotation but differ in sign (*i.e.,* direction of rotation of plane polarized light).

(c) Enantiomers have similar chemical action with optically inactive (achiral) substances.

(d) Enantiomers differ in their chemical action with optically active substance. This difference in chemical action with optically active substance has a great significance in medicinal chemistry *i.e.,* one enantiomer may help in healing; other may have adverse effect *i.e.,* an important drug "Thalidomide" has a chiral carbon and exist as enantiomers. One of its enantiomer was milk sedative used to combat nausea in pregnant women, other enantiomer has lethal effect.

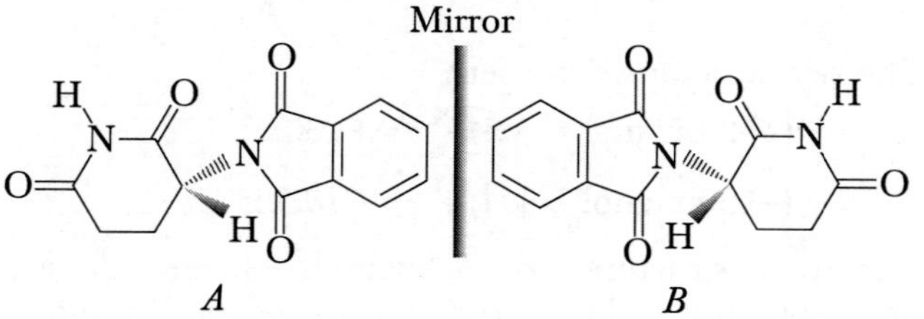

A *B*

A and *B* are enantiomers and one of them is useful ingredient of a drug while its enantiomer has adverse (negative) effect. The usefulness of a specific enantiomer in medicinal chemistry owes from the fact that most of the protein and enzymes found in human body are themselves chiral.

Optical isomerism in compounds containing more than one chiral centre

When a molecule has two chiral carbons, there are four different configurations are possible.

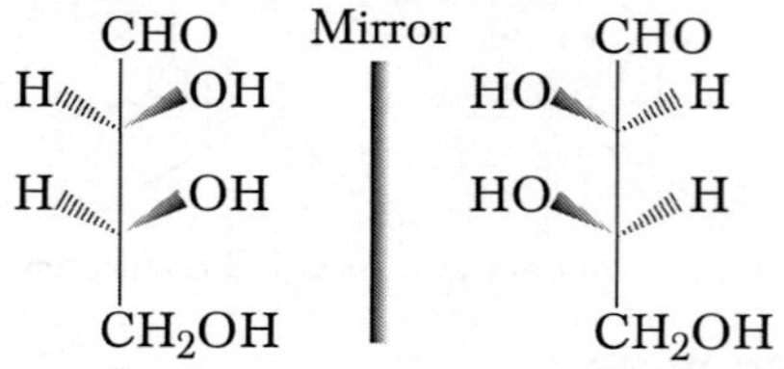

I II

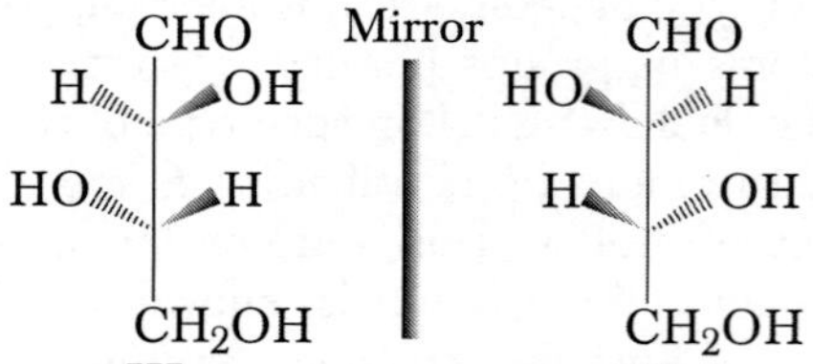

III IV

The above shown four structures (I, II, III and IV) of 2, 3, 4-trihydroxybutanal are all stereoisomers. All these have different configuration at the chiral centre. Therefore, it can be concluded that maximum number of different configurations possible for a molecule with "n" chirality centre is 2^n. Also; I and II and III and IV are pair of **enantiomer**.

A pair of stereoisomers which has no mirror image relationship is known as pair of **disastereomers**. In the given example, all those pair I and III, I and IV and II and III, II and IV are pairs of diastereomers. Also all four structures are optically active, therefore, both isomers in pair of diastereomers are also optically active, but it is not an essential requirement for diastereomerism. In a pair of diastereomers, both counterparts may be optically active as in the present case, one of the pair may be optically active and other may be optically inactive, or both of them, in a pair of diastereomers may be optically inactive. Some important characteristics of diastereomers are mentioned below :

(a) Diastereomers have different physical properties *i.e.,* different melting and boiling points, different refractive indices, different solubility in standard solvent etc.

(b) Optical rotations of diastereomers are not at all related in either magnitude or in directions.

(c) Diastereomers differ in their chemical reaction with both optically active and inactive substances.

Note Stereochemistry of cyclic compounds with two or more chiral centres is similar to those of acyclic compounds. The number of stereoisomers is usually given by 2^n. However, in bridged compounds, the number of stereoisomers is lesser than expected. Some diastereomers cannot be formed due to steric reasons. Thus, twistane has four equivalent chiral centres exists only in two enantiomeric forms.

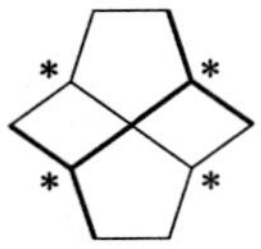

Twistane

Meso compounds

A molecule with two chiral carbons will not always have four possible stereomers. Sometimes there may be three only. This is because some molecules with chiral centres are overall achiral. To understand this, let us consider an example of 2, 3-dichlorobutane which has two chiral carbons C-2 and C-3.

$$H_3C—\overset{*}{C}H—\overset{*}{C}H—CH_3$$
$$\quad\;\; | \qquad\;\; |$$
$$\quad\; Cl \qquad Cl$$

The different structures of 2,3-dichlorobutane are as :

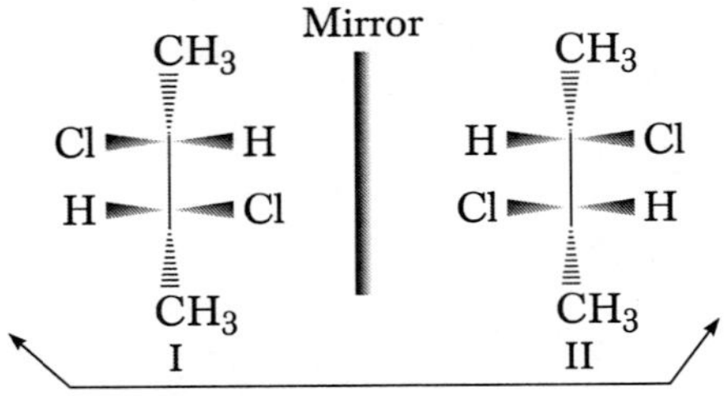

A pair of enantiomers
(Non-superimposable)

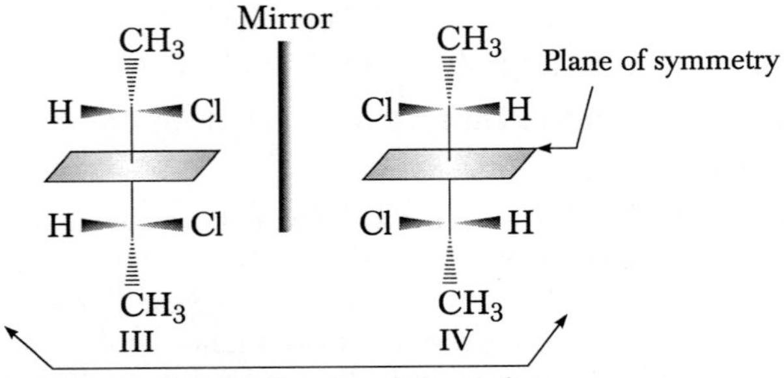

Not a pair of enantiomers (Identical)

These structures I and II are non-superimposable mirror images, hence these represent a pair of enantiomers. The structures III and IV are superimposable. Structure III coincides exactly with IV. This means that inspite of its chiral centres, III is not chiral *i.e.,* optically inactive. Such molecules are called ***meso*** **compounds**. Thus, "*meso* compounds are those whose molecules are superimposable on their mirror images even though they contain chiral centres, due to presence of the element of symmetry." Compound III possesses a plane of symmetry hence it is optically inactive and called *meso*-form of 2, 3-dichlorobutane.

A *meso*-form of a compound has permanent optical inactivity and this is due to internal compensation of optical rotation.

Note Racemic mixture is a mixture containing equal amount of enantiomers. It is optically inactive due to external compensation of optical rotation. It has temporary optical inactivity and can be resolved by proper chemical treatment.

Chiral carbon and optical isomerism in cyclic compounds

If a carbon of cyclic compound is sp^3-hybridized, two of its valencies are satisfied by ring carbons and remaining two by the substituent as :

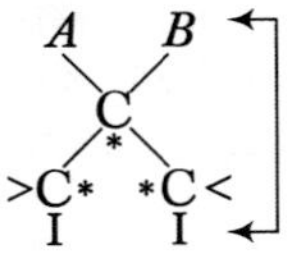

Here, starred carbons are part of cyclic rings. If *A* and *B* are different and different groups are present at equal distance at any two carbons of the ring with respect to the >*CAB*, then this carbon will be chiral. Let us consider 1, 2-and 1, 3-dimethylcyclobutane.

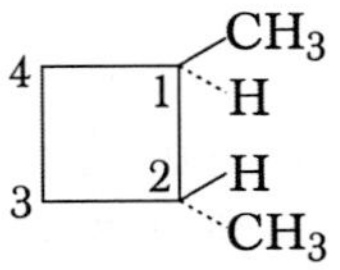

Now, let us investigate C-1 of the ring C-2 and C-4 are equidistant from C-1, and they are differently substituted, C-2 has *a*-H and *a*-CH_3 substituent while C-4 has CH_2 group. Hence, C-1 is a chiral carbon. Same will be true for C-2. Hence, both C-1 and C-2 are chiral carbons.

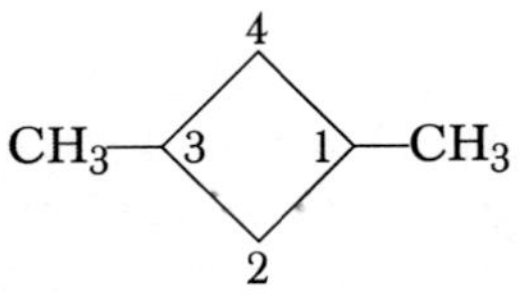

In 1,3-dimethyl cyclobutane, there is no chiral carbon, with respect to C-1, equisdistant carbons C-2 and C-4 are identical and C-3 is equidistant from the two side *i.e.,* from clockwise and from counter clockwise direction, hence, it has no chiral carbon.

Example, dichlorocyclobutane

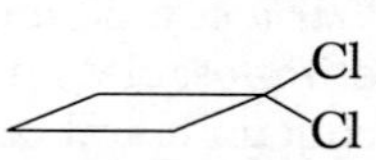

1,1-dichlorocyclobutane
No chiral carbon

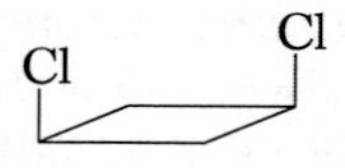

1,3-dichlorocyclobutane
No chiral carbon

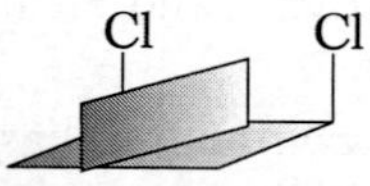

Cis-1,2-dichlorocyclobutane
has a plane of symmetry,
superimposable on its mirror
image, optically inactive (*meso*)

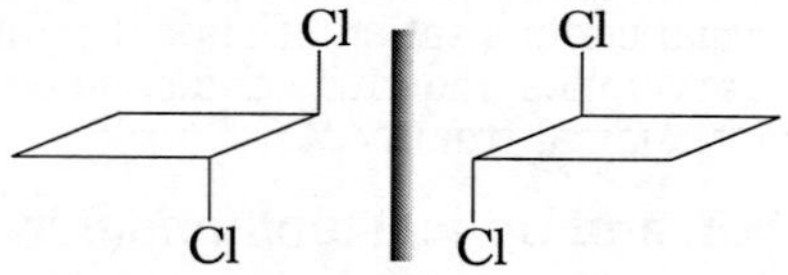

Non-superimposable mirror images,
optically active, a pair of enantiomers

Optical activity due to chiral axis

There are several compounds which do not have chiral centre or chiral carbon, but still are optically active. **Example,** allenes and spiro compounds.

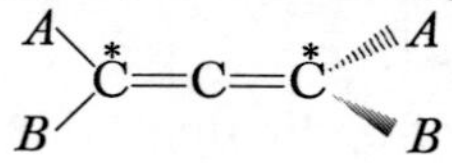

(a)

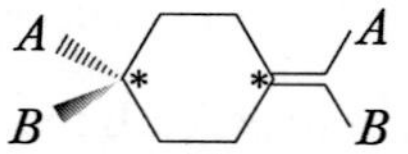

(b)

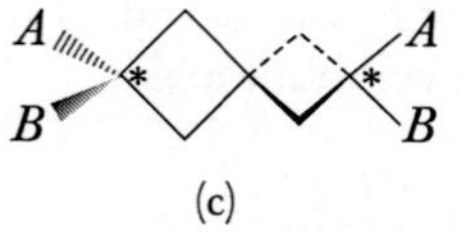

(c)

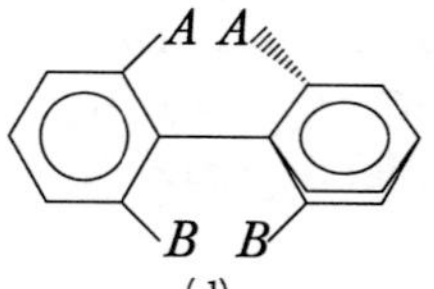

(d)

(a) **Allenes** The two strained carbon atoms lie in planes perpendicular to each other. This is also the case with alkylidenecycloalkane (b) and spirane (c) In the biphenyl system (d) the two benzene rings are perpendicular to each other. When viewed along the carbon atoms, allenes look like.

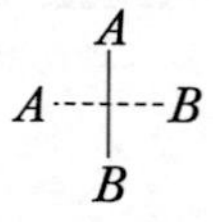

These molecules are chiral and not superimposable on their mirror images, and exists as enantiomers despite the absence of asymmetric carbon atoms.

Designation of configuration In addition to sequence rule, another rule is needed for molecules with chiral axis which states that the two near groups precede the two far groups.

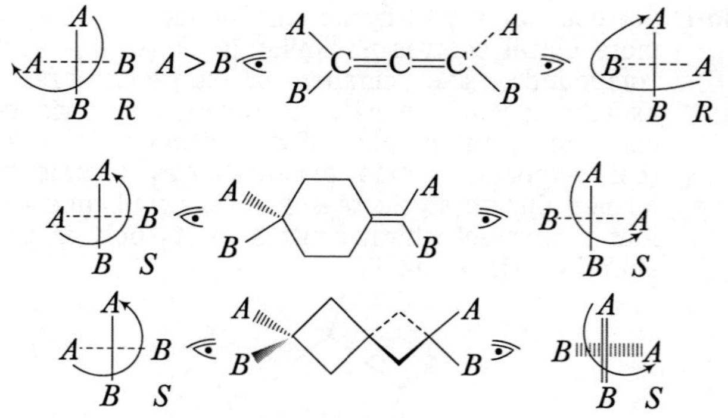

In case of biphenyls, when bulky groups are present in *ortho* positions they can exist as stable stereoisomers. The configuration of substituted biphenyls is assigned in the same way as for allenes and spiranes. The molecule is viewed from either end of the chiral axis and projection formulae are drawn. Only C_2, C_6, C_2' and C_6' are considered. The priority order is through substituents to the four carbon atoms.

Groups at the near end are given precedence over groups at the far end. When there are H at *ortho* positions, the H nearer to a substituent gets precedence.

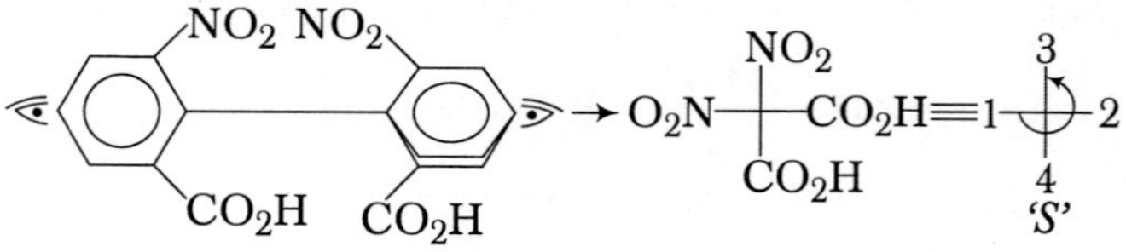

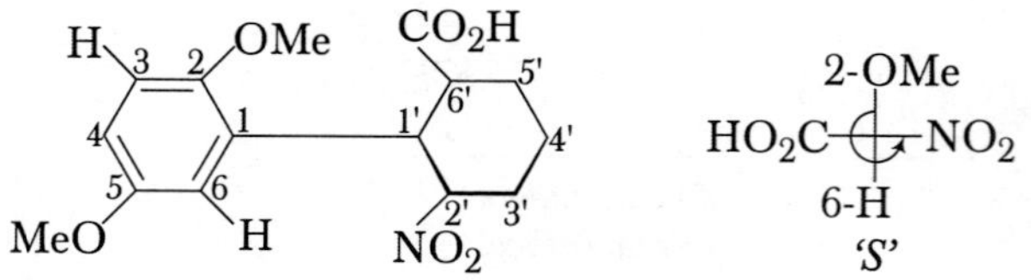

The molecule when viewed from the left side along 1 – 1′ bond gives projection with *S* configuration.

Chiral molecules without a chiral atoms or centre

Certain molecules are chiral despite the absence of a chiral centre or chiral axis. These are non-superimposable on their mirror images. The ether derivative of 2-bromohydroquinone (I) and paracyclophane (II) are optically active due to chirality of the whole molecule.

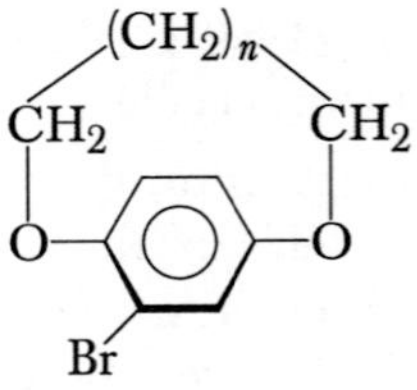

I

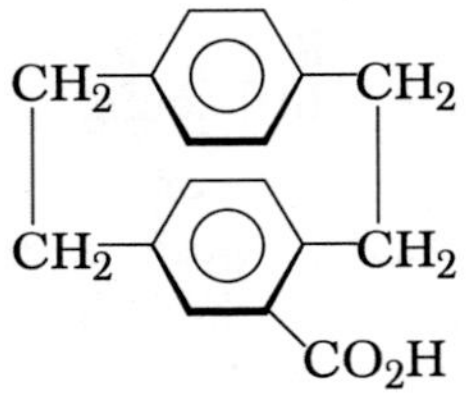

II

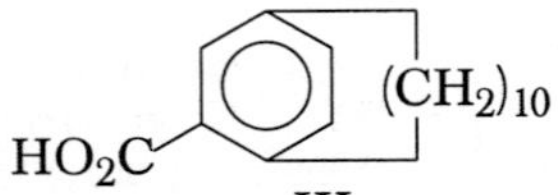

III

If two *para* positions of an aromatic ring are attached to a polymethylene chain through hetero-atoms, they are called **ansa compounds** (I).

Cyclophanes are similar to ansa compounds usually two aromatic rings are joined together to give paracyclophanes (II).

In assigning configurations to these compounds a pilot atom is selected first. This atom is directly attached to an atom in the chiral plane, though this is not in the plane. This is the first out of plane atom, chosen from the most preferred side of the plane. The sequence starts from the first in plane atom and continues through atoms along the bonds leading to the most preferred atom by shortest route. Thus, in I viewed from the pilot atom if the order appears clockwise the configuration is '*R*' and if anticlockwise it is '*S*'.

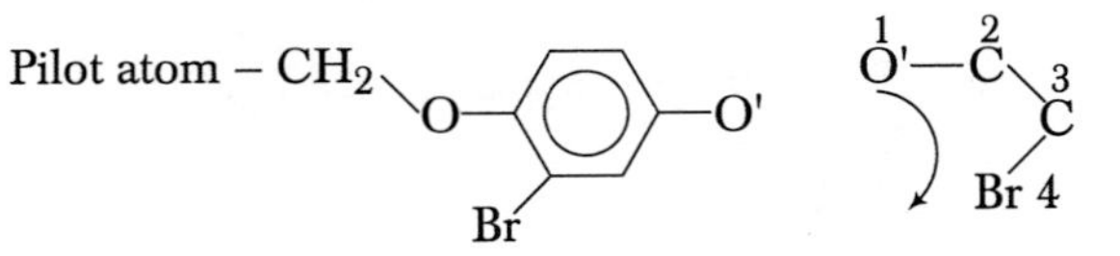

(Most preferred atom)

In II

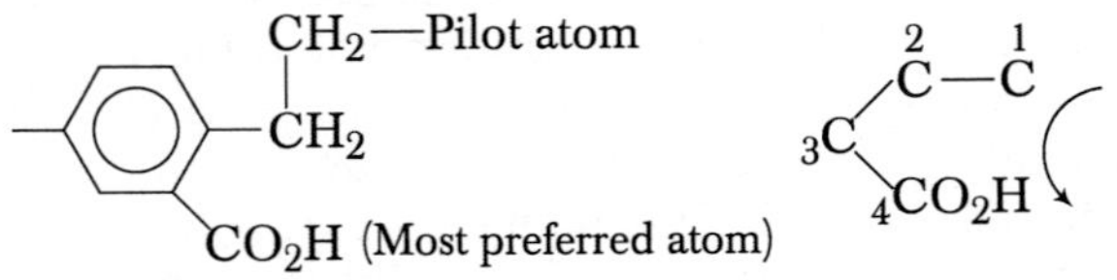

'*S*' configuration

In III

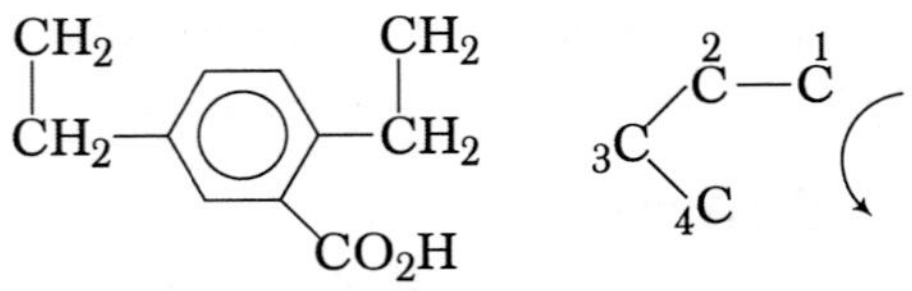

'*S*' configuration

Fischer projections

It is a representation of tetrahedral carbon atoms as a two-dimensional structure on paper. To construct a Fischer projection, the molecule is first arranged with the horizontal bonds to its chiral centre projecting above the plane of the page and the vertical bonds projecting behind the page. Most important functional group is placed at the top and the main chain of the molecule is vertical. In the Fischer projection the bonds are projected into the plane of the page, resulting in a cross with the chiral centre at its centre.

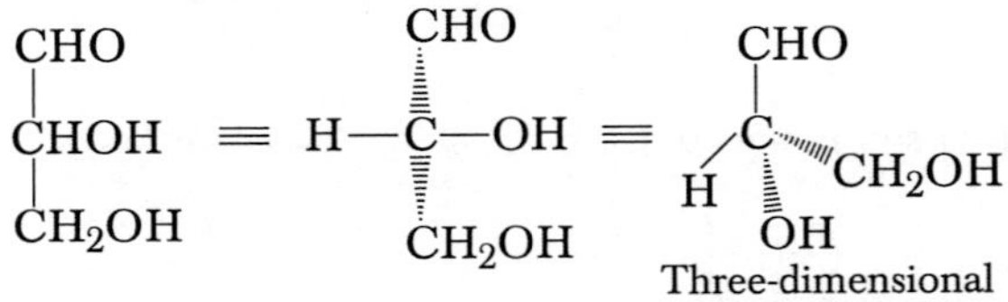

Three-dimensional representation

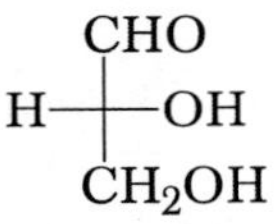

Projected form
(Fischer projection)

Even number of interchanges do not result in change of configuration. Similarly, rotation of the projection through 180° does not change the configuration; odd number of interchanges or rotation through an angle of 90° inverts the configuration.

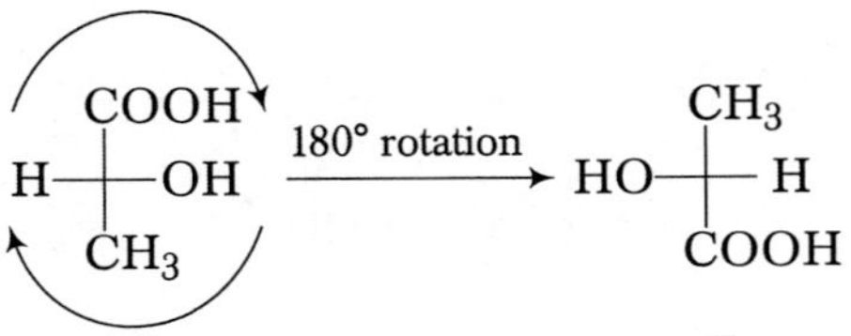

I II

In this case the groups into and coming out of paper remain the same. Hence, I and II are identical molecules.

R-S system of nomenclature

There are two different stereoisomers for a molecule that has a centre of chirality; **absolute configuration** in such cases is expressed in terms of *R* and *S* configuration devised by **Cahn, Ingold and Prelog.** The *R*, *S* system of nomenclature indicates the configuration of a chirality centre. For any pair of enantiomers with a chirality centre, one will have the *R* configuration and the other will have the ***S* configuration.**

R is given to the isomer if sequence is left to right (*R* stands for ***Rectus***, a Latin word for right)

S is given to the isomer if sequence is right to left (*S* stand for ***Sinister,*** a latin word for left)

Priority sequence is decided by the sequence rule. These are also called CIP rules.

Atoms directly attached to the chiral carbon are arranged in decreasing atomic number.

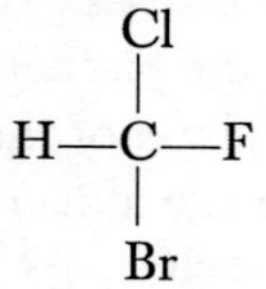

For this sequences will be $\overset{a}{Br} \longrightarrow \overset{b}{Cl} \longrightarrow \overset{c}{F} \longrightarrow \overset{d}{H}$

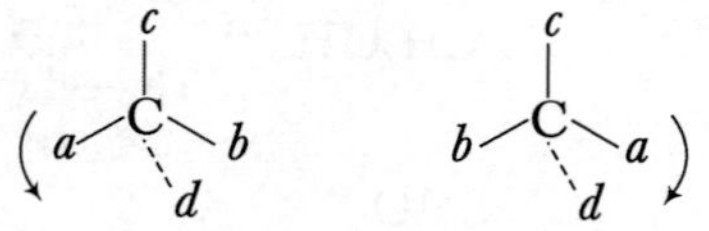

Viewing side (*S*) | Viewing side (*R*)

If the sequence $a \longrightarrow b \longrightarrow c$ traces a clockwise turn, configuration is ***R***. If the sequence $a \longrightarrow b \longrightarrow c$ traces an anti-clockwise turn, the configuration is ***S***.

Example $CH_3—CH_2CHCHO$ (with CH_3 on the CH)

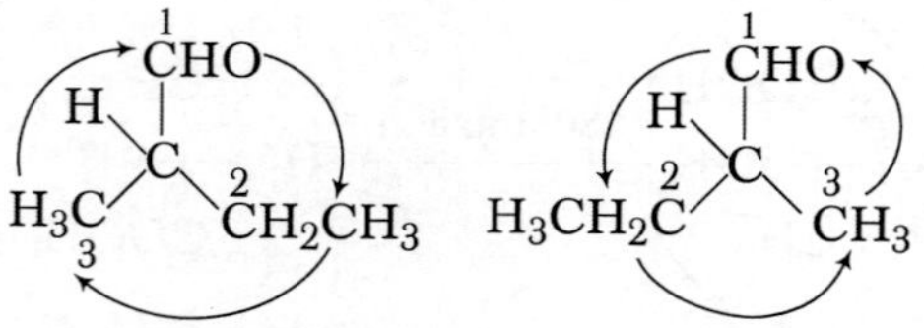

Clockwise, *R* | Anti-clockwise, *S*

Priority order : CHO, C_2H_5, CH_3, H

Assigning *R* and *S* configuration from Fischer projections

Fischer projections are very helpful to assign *R* and *S* configuration especially in case of compounds containing more than one chiral centre. There is a very simple way to predict the configuration (*R* or *S*) from Fischer projection.

(a) Assign priorities to four atoms or groups attached to the chiral centres.

(b) If the atom or group of lowest priority occupies vertical position (upward or downward) in the Fischer projection then the observed configuration is the actual configuation of the molecule.

(c) If the atom or group of lowest priority occupies horizontal position (right or left) in the Fischer projection, then change the observed configuration from *R* to *S* and *vice-versa.* This gives the correct configuration.

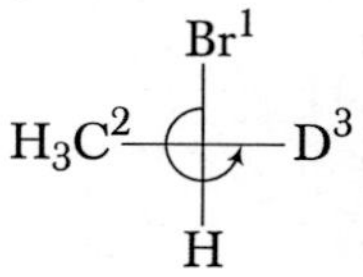

Observed configuration is *S*. Since, H lies on vertical position. Hence, the actual configuration is same *i.e.,* *S*.

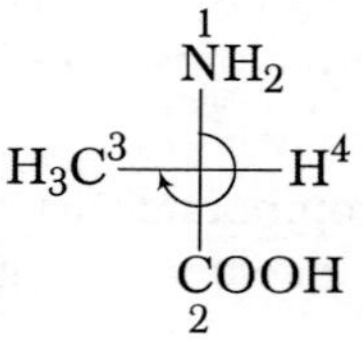

Observed configuration is *R*,. Since H lies on horizontal position. Hence, the actual configuration is *S*.

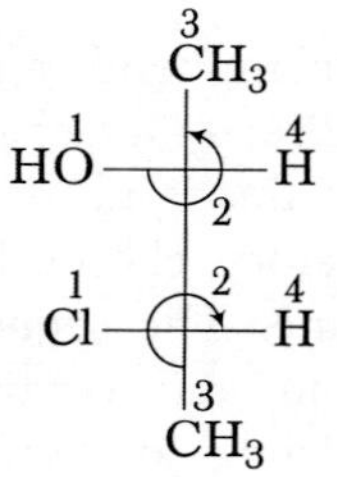

S and change to *R* hence (H is on horizontal position).

R and change to *S* hence 3*S* (H is on horizontal position)

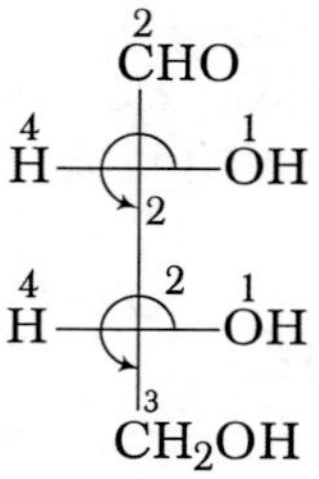

S and change to *R* hence 2*R*.

S and change to *R* hence 3*R*.

Conformational Isomerism

Isomers that have the same skeletons but differ from each other with relative positions of some atoms in three-dimensional space by virtue of rotation about σ-bonds are called conformational isomers or conformers and phenomenon is known as conformational isomerism. The study of various aspects of these infinite temporary conformers is known as conformational analysis. The stability of a conformation is dependent on torsional strain, angle strain, van der Waals' or steric strain and dipole-dipole interaction.

Torsional Strain

The bond pair-bond pair repulsion is called torsional strain. Greater is the torsional strain, lower is the stability of the conformation. Torsional strain is the least in *anti*-form.

Angle Strain

Deviations from the usual bond angle of the bonding orbitals due to molecular geometry is known as angle strain. The usual bond angles for sp^3, sp^2 and sp-hybridized carbon atoms are 109°28′, 120° and 180° respectively. Greater the deviation of the bond angle from the above usual values due to structural rigidity, greater is the angle strain and consequently less stable is the conformation. The angle deviation could be either positive or negative with respect to usual value.

van der Waals' or Steric Strain

If the distance between any two substituents is less than the sum of their van der Waals' radii, a repulsive force generates known as van der Waals' strain or steric strain. Usually the fully eclipsed conformation has the highest van der Waals' strain and least in case of *anti* conformation.

Dipole-Dipole Interaction

Any two non bonded substituents in a molecule can undergo dipole-dipole interactions which can even lead to hydrogen bonding. The attractive dipole-dipole interaction between opposite partial charges stabilizes the conformations while repulsive dipole-dipole interaction due to similar partial charge on the substituent destablizes the conformations.

Conformations of Acyclic System

Conformation of ethane

The ethane molecule contains only one carbon-carbon single bond about which free rotation is possible. Rotation about ($C \overset{\sigma}{—} C$) bond in ethane can give various conformers.

In structure A_1 or B_1, C—H flagpoles at C-1 completely overlap each other at C-2. It is called **eclipsed conformation.**

Name of conformer	Sawhorse projection	Newman projection
Eclipsed conformer	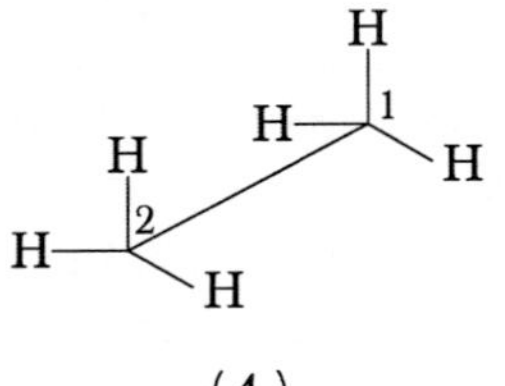 (A_1)	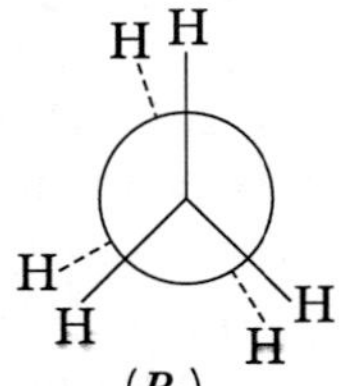 (B_1)
Staggered conformer	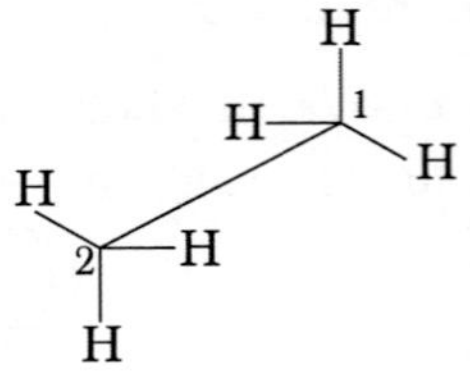 (A_2)	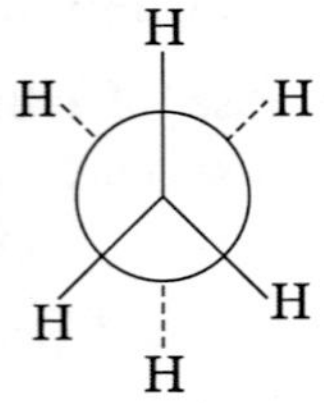 (B_2)

In structure A_2 or B_2, C—H flagpoles at C-1 is fixed at 60° dihedral angle so that it is exactly between two C—H flagpoles at C-2. This is called **staggered conformation.** Various other structures in between eclipsed and staggered conformations are called **skew conformation.**

Eclipsed form can be converted into staggered by rotation of 60° about ($C \overset{\sigma}{—} C$) bond.

$$\underbrace{\text{Eclipsed} \xrightarrow{60°} \text{Staggered} \xrightarrow{60°} \text{Eclipsed}}_{120°}$$

Thus, total rotation of 120° about ($C \overset{\sigma}{—} C$) bond will give same conformation in ethane.

Energy of eclipsed form is greater than that of staggered form due to steric hindrance and thus staggered form is more stable than eclipsed form (Fig. 29.1).

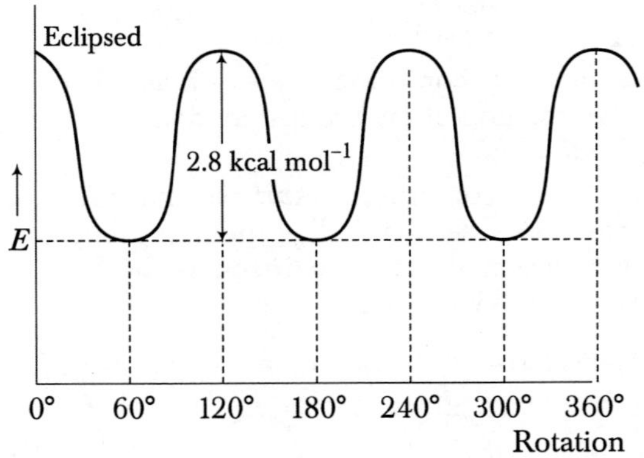

Fig. 29.1 Potential-energy change by rotation about ($C \overset{\alpha}{—} C$) bond.

Note In propane, rotation about ($C \overset{\sigma}{—} C$) bond again gives staggered and eclipsed conformations but due to one —CH_3 group extra, torsional strain is increased. Again a rotation of 60° about ($C \overset{\sigma}{—} C$) bond converts eclipsed form into staggered form a *vice-versa*.

Conformations of butane

In case of *n*-butane rotation about ($C_2 \overset{\sigma}{—} C_3$) bond gives various conformation as given below.

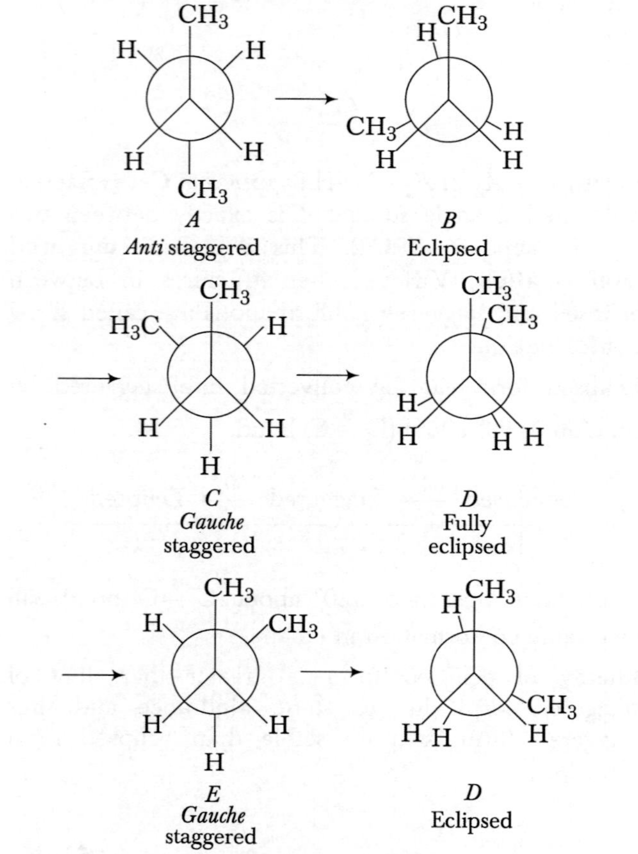

The above six conformers are obtained on each successive rotation of the groups bonded to rear carbon by an angle of 60°.

Among these conformers ***Anti*** is the most stable conformer because the bulky methyl groups are at maximum distance. **Fully eclipsed** is the least stable because the bulky methyl groups are closest, providing maximum repulsion, has highest potential energy. The stability order of these conformers is shown in Fig. 29.2.

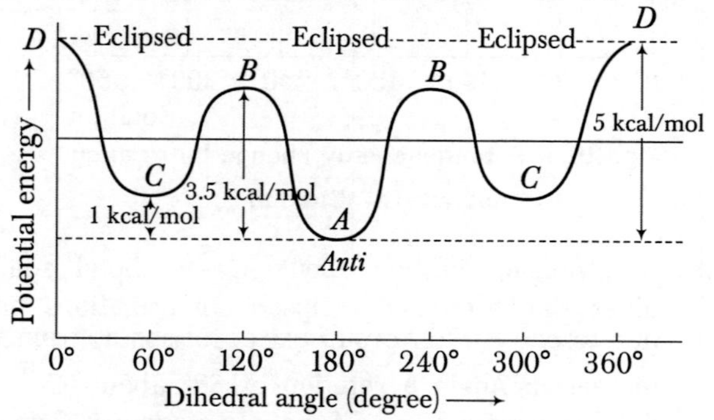

Fig. 29.2 Energy profile diagram for butane conformations with different dihedral angle.

Conformations of Cyclic System

Conformations of cyclohexane

Sasche proposed two non-planar models for cyclohexane, in which the bond angles were 109°28′. These models are free of Bayer's strain. One form called chair form and it is fairly rigid form. The other form is called boat form and it is more flexible form.

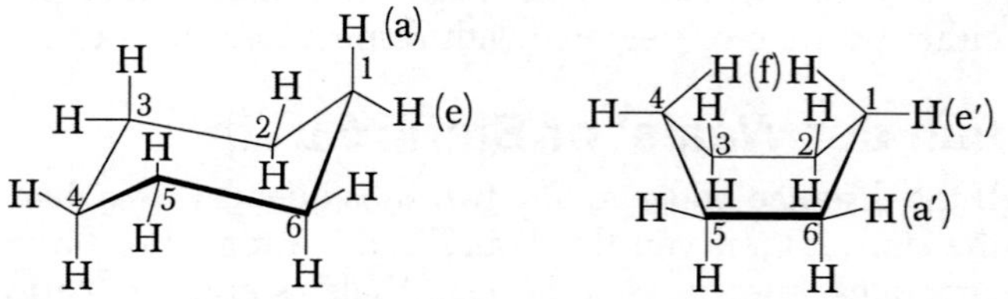

Chair conformation with 6-fold alternating axis of symmetry

Boat conformation 2-fold axis of symmetry (flagpole interaction)

Sawhorse projection

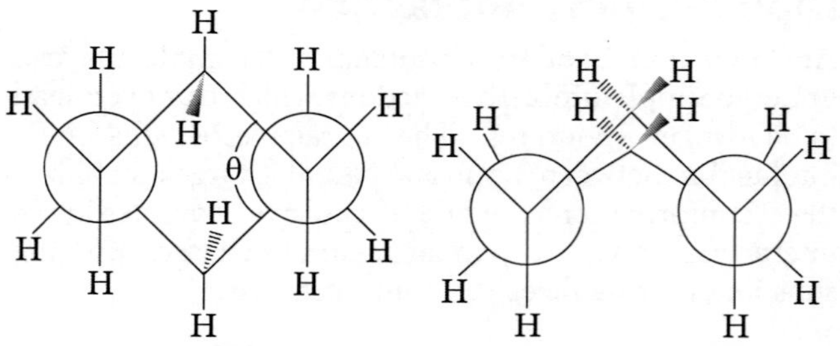

Chair conformation

Boat conformation

Newman projection

- Each carbon atom of cyclohexane is bonded to two hydrogens. Hydrogens lying in the plane of the ring are called equatorial hydrogens because they are situated essentially along the equator of the ring. The bonds holding such hydrogens are called the equatorial bonds. The hydrogens lying above or below the plane of the ring are called the axial hydrogens because they are situated along an axis perpendicular to the plane of the ring. The bonds holding such hydrogens are referred to as axial bonds. Each carbon in the chair conformation has one equatorial and one axial bond. Axial bonds have been marked '*a*' and equatorial bonds '*e*'.
- In chair forms, C—H flagpoles at C_1 and C_4 are in *trans* side thus minimising strain and thus increasing stability.

- In boat form, there is some repulsion between C—H flagpoles at C_1 and C_4 being on same side and thus steric hindrance is increased and stability is decreased Fig. 29.3 represents diagram showing the conformations of cyclohexane (and their relative energies) as one chair conformation interconverts to the other chair conformation.

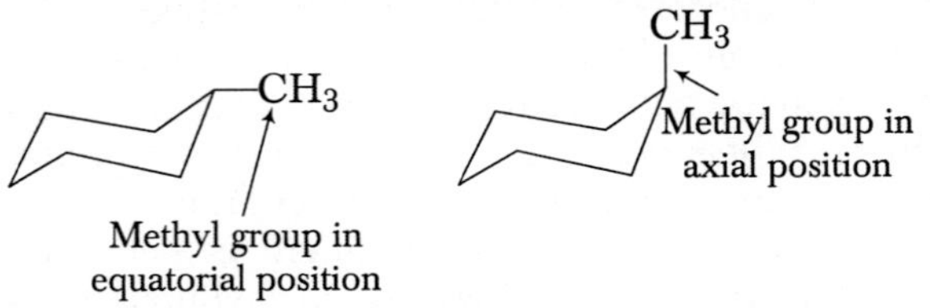

Cyclohexane with methyl group in the equatorial position is more stable than in the axial position.

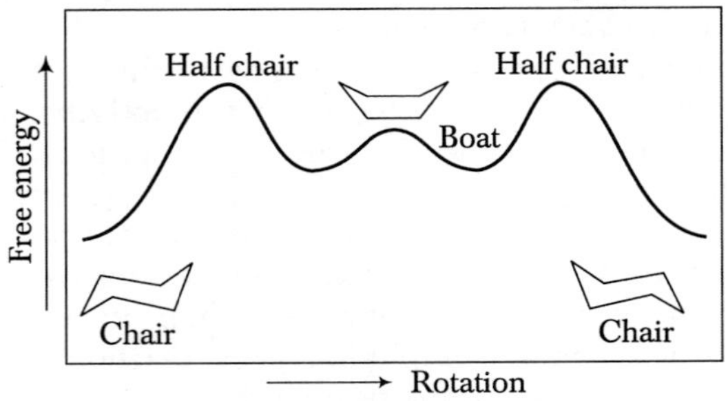

Fig. 29.3

Note At room temperature a chair form of cyclohexane undergoes ring inversion called ring flipping spontaneously to another chair form-the mirror image of the former.

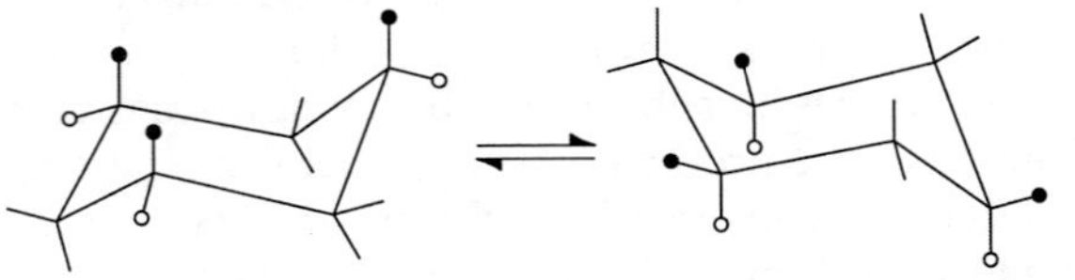

Projections of Conformations

To understand the stereochemistry of a molecule the three-dimensional arrangement of the atoms or groups is required. However, it is not feasible to describe all the molecules three-dimensionally by writing on paper. Hence, some equivalent two dimensional molecular projections are required to represent the stereochemistry of the molecule.

The conformations of the molecule can be projected on a paper two dimensionally in the following ways :

1. Fischer projection
2. Newman projection
3. Sawhorse projection
4. Flying-Wedge projection (not in syllabus).

Interconversion of Fischer, Newman and Sawhorse projections

Conversion of Fischer projection of a molecule containing two asymmetric carbon atoms to Sawhorse projection can easily be carried out starting with proper numbering of the carbon atoms otherwise the transformation may lead to a mirror image *i.e.,* enantiomer. Numbering the carbon atoms from top to bottom in Fischer projection is converted to Sawhorse projection by taking the bottom chiral carbon as the front carbon atom in Sawhorse projection. Whereas the topmost chiral carbon in Fischer projection is taken as the rear carbon in Sawhorse projection. While the substituents are placed infront and behind in Sawhorse projection for the lower and upper as implied in Fischer projection. The Sawhorse projection thus formed is taken as eclipsed. For the staggered Sawhorse projection the front carbon is simply rotated through 180°.

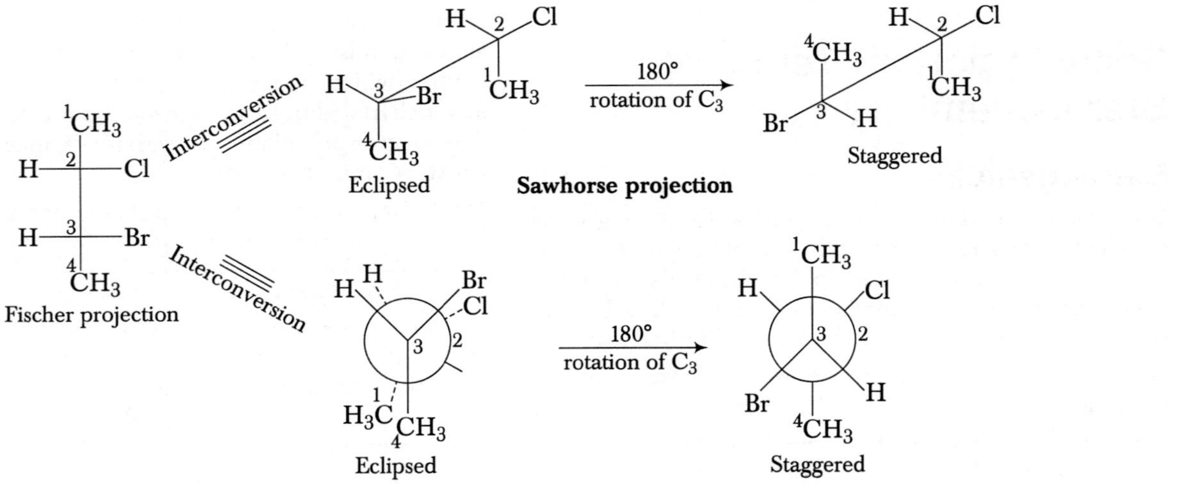

Newman projection

Conversion of Fischer projection to Newman projection is carried out in a similar fashion to the eclipsed form which can subsequently be transformed to staggered Newman projection by simply rotating the front carbon athrough 180°.

The Sawhorse projection and Newman projection can likewise be converted into Fischer projection by reversing the above procedure.

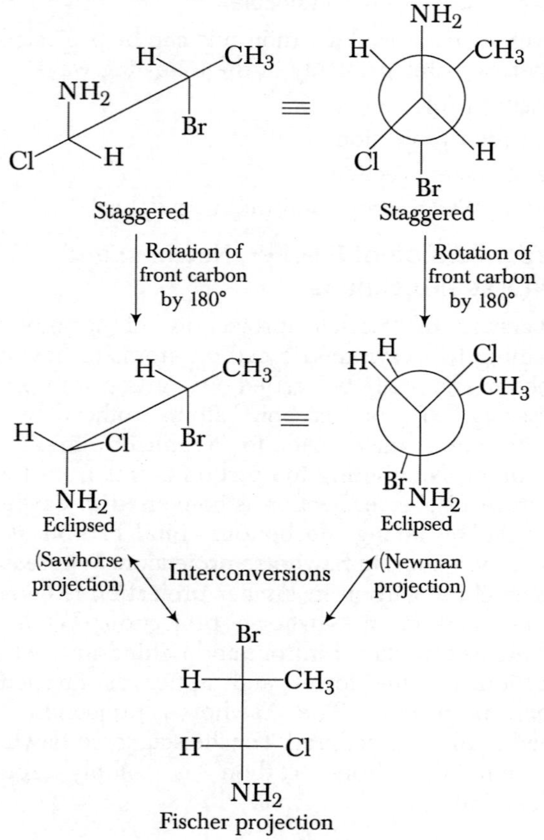

Some Important Terms of Stereochemistry

Stereogenicity

Compound, in which an atom has all the four groups different is said to have chirality or stereogenicity and this centre (carbon) is said to be chiral (asymmetric) centre or stereogenic centre or stereocentre. Hence, stereogenic centre is also known as a chiral centre.

A chiral centre is a generalised extension of an asymmetric carbon atom which is a carbon atom bonded to four different entities such that an interchanging of any two groups gives rise to an enantiomer.

Stereoselectivity, Enantioselectivity and Diastereoselectivity

In chemistry **stereoselectivity** is the property of a chemical reaction in which a single reactant forms an unequal mixture of stereoisomers during non-stereospecific creation of a new stereocentre or during non-stereospecific transformation of a pre-existing one. The selectivity arises from differences in steric effects and electronic effects in the mechanistic pathways leading to the different products. Stereoselectivity can vary in degree but it can never be total since the activation energy difference between the two pathways is finite. However, in favourable cases, the minor stereoisomer may not be detectable by the analytic methods used.

An **enantioselective** reaction is one in which one enantiomer is formed in preference to the other and this process is said to be **enantoselectivity**. In a reaction that creates an optically active product from an achiral starting material using either a chiral catalyst, an enzyme or a chiral reagent. The degree of selectivity is measured by the **enantiomeric excess**. An important variant is kinetic resolution in which a pre-existing chiral centre undergoes reaction with a chiral catalyst, an enzyme or a chiral reagent such that one enantiomer reacts faster than the other and leaves behind the less reactive enantiomer, or in which a pre existing chiral centre influences the reactivity of a reaction centre elsewhere in the same molecule.

A **diastereoselective** reaction is one in which one diastereomer is formed in preference to another (or in which a subset of all possible diastereomers dominates the product mixture) establishing a preferred relative stereochemistry and this process is said to be **diastereoselectivity**. In this case either two or more chiral centres are formed at once such that one relative stereochemistry is favoured or a pre-existing chiral centre (which needs not be optically pure) biases the stereochemical outcome during the creation of another. The degree of relative selectivity is measured by the **diastereomeric excess.**

Note Stereoconvergence can be considered an opposite of stereoselectivity, when the reaction of two different stereoisomers yield a single product stereoisomer.

The quality of stereoselectivity is concerned solely with the products and their stereochemistry of a number of possible stereoisomeric products, the reaction selects one or two to be formed. An example of modest stereoselectivity is the dehydrogenation of 2-iodobutane which yields 60% *trans*-2-butene and 20% *cis*-2-butene. Since, alkene geometric isomers are also classified as diastereomers, this reaction would also be called diastereoselective.

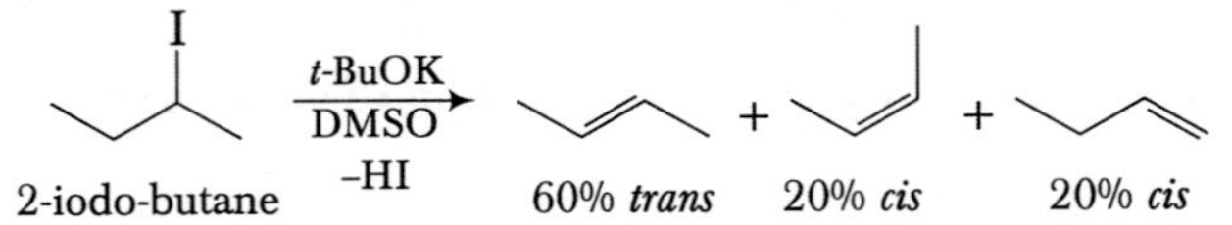

The addition of formic acid to norbornene is also stereospecific because the exoisomer is formed exclusively without any of the endoisomer.

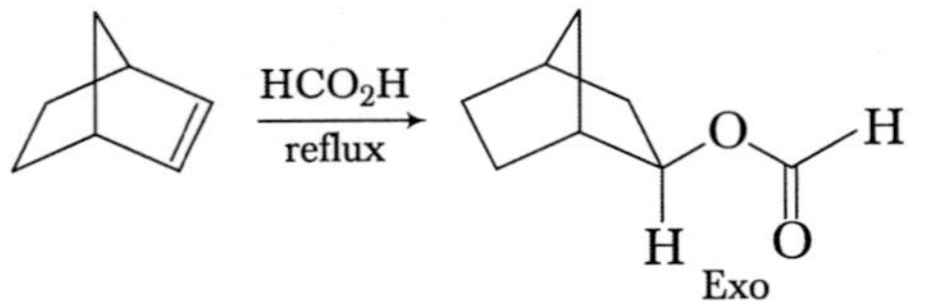

Cram's rule predicts the major diastereomer resulting from the diastereoselective nucleophilic addition to a carbonyl group next to a chiral centre. The chiral centre need not be optically pure as the relative. Stereochemistry will be the same for both enantiomers. *e.g.,* the (S) aldehyde reacts with a thiazole to form the (S, S) diastereomer but a small amount of the (S, R) diastereomer.

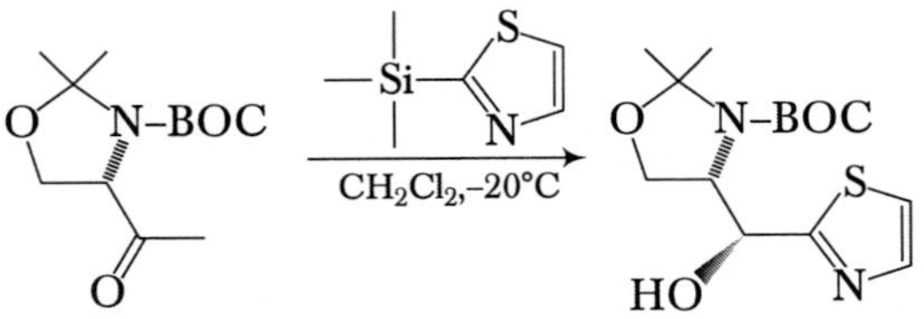

(S) (S, S) 92% *anti*

The sharpless epoxidation is an example of an enantioselective process in which an achiral allylic alcohol substrate is transformed into an optically active epoxy alcohol. In the case of chiral allylic alcohols, kinetic resolution results. Another example is sharpless asymmetric dihydroxylation. In the example below the achiral alkene yields only one of possible 4 stereoisomers.

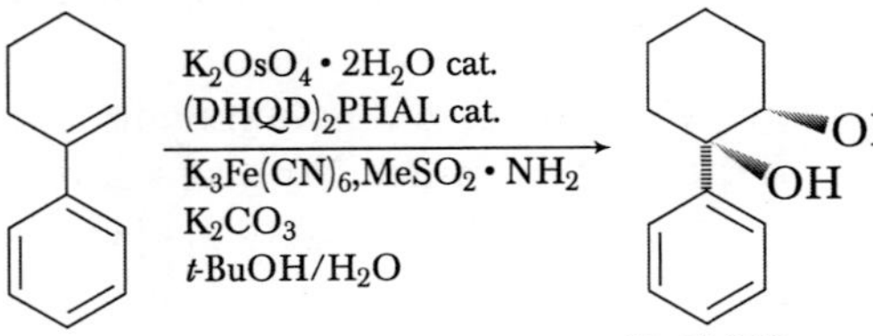

(R, R) 98%

With a stereogenic centre next to the carbocation the substitution can be stereoselective in inter and intramolecular reactions. In the reaction given below the nucleophile (furan) can approach the carbocation formed from the least shielded side away from the bulky *t*-butyl group resulting in high facial diastereoselectivity.

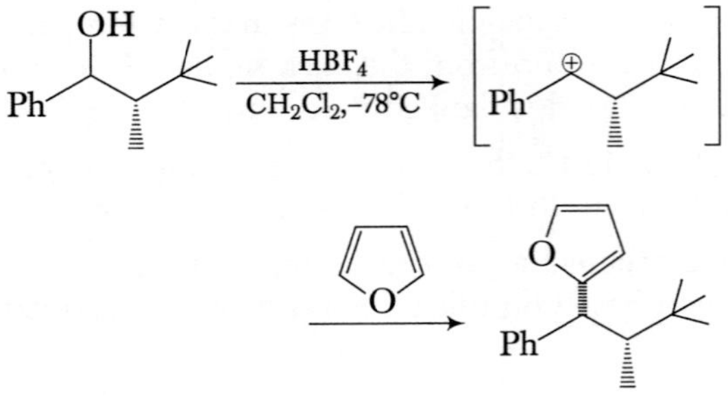

Asymmetric Induction

If a reaction is carried out using a chiral or optically active reagent, only one of the enantiomer or an excess of one enantiomer can be formed. This introduction of chirality or asymmetry is called asymmetric induction. In other words asymmetric induction converts a achiral reactant to a chiral product having an excess of one of the enantiomers with the help of a chiral reagent or a chiral catalyst. This principle can be used for resolving racemic mixtures into *d*-or-*l*-forms.

Asymmetric induction (also enantio induction) in stereochemistry describes the preferential formation in a chemical reaction of one enantiomer or diastereoisomer over the other as a result of the influence of a chiral feature present in the substrate, reagent catalyst or environment. Asymmetric induction is a key element in asymmetric synthesis. Several types of induction exist.

Internal asymmetric induction makes use of a chiral centre bound to the reactive centre through a covalent bond and remains so during the reaction. The starting material is often derived from chiral pool synthesis. In **relayed asymmetric induction** the chiral information is introduced in a separate step and removed again in a separate chemical reaction. Special synthons are called **chiral auxiliaries.** In **external asymmetric induction** chiral information is introduced in the transition state through a catalyst of chiral ligand. This method of asymmetric synthesis of economically most desirable.

Carbonyl 1, 2 asymmetric induction

Several models exist to describe chiral induction at carbonyl carbons during nucleophilic additions. These models are based on a combination of steric and electronic considerations and are often in conflict with each other. Models have been devised by Cram (1952), Cornforth (1959), Felkin (1969) and others.

The **Cram's rule of asymmetric induction** developed by **Donald J. Cram** (1952) is an early concept relating to the prediction of stereochemistry in certain acyclic system. In full the rule is :

In certain non-catalytic reactions that diastereomer will predominate, which could be formed by the approach of the entering group from the least hindered side when the rotational conformation of the C—C bond is such that the double bond is flanked by the two least bulky groups attached to the adjacent asymmetric centre.

The rule indicates that the presence of an asymmetric centre in a molecule induces the formation of an asymmetric centre adjacent to it based on steric hindrance.

Cram presented a large number of reactions for which the conformation of the reaction products could be explained based on this rule and he also described an elaborate experiment making his case.

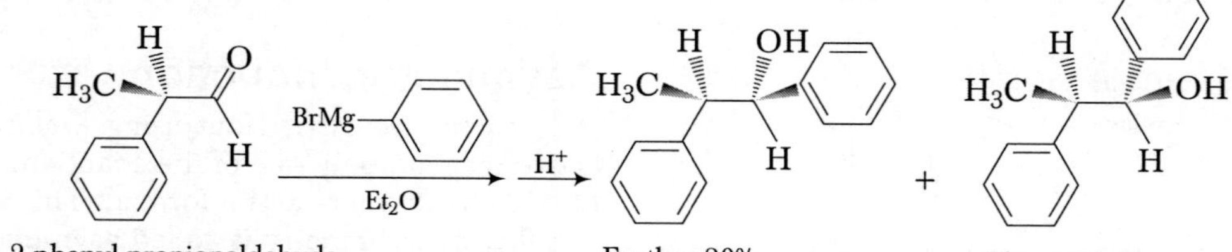

2-phenyl propionaldehyde — Erythro 20% — Threo 80%

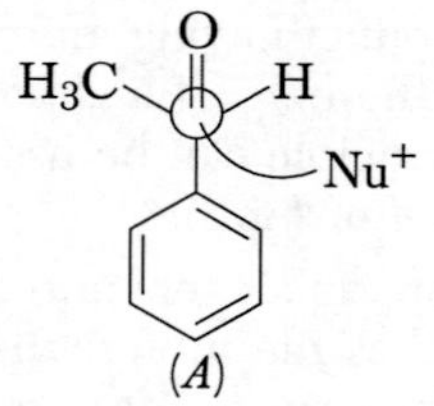

(A)

Fischer projection

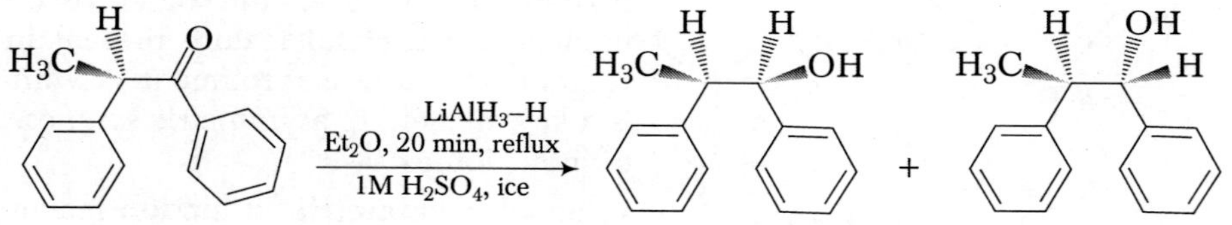

Erythro 80% — Threo 20%

The experiments involved two reactions. In first experiment 2-phenylpropionaldehyde (racemic but (*R*)-enantiomer shown) was reacted with the Grignard reagent of bromobenzene to 1, 2-diphenyl-1-propanol as a mixture of diastereomers, predominantly the **threo isomer** (see for explanation the Fischer projection).

The preference for the formation of the threo isomer can be explained by the rule stated above by having the active nucleophilic in this reaction attacking the carbonyl group from the least hindered side (see Newman projection *A*) when the carbonyl is positioned in a staggered formation with the methyl group and the hydrogen atom, which are the two smallest substitutents creating a minimum of steric hindrance, in a *gauche* orientation and phenyl as the most bulky group in the *anti*-conformation.

The second reaction is the organic reduction of 1, 2-diphenyl-1-propanone with lithium aluminium hydride, which results in the same reaction product as above but now with preference for the erythro isomer. Now, a hydride anion (H^-) is the nucleophile attacking from the least hindered side (imagine hydrogen entering from the paper plane).

Exercise 1
(For Part 'B')

1. C_6H_6 molecule has the point group
   (a) D_{4h} (b) D_{2d}
   (c) D_{6h} (d) D_{3d}
2. CHBrFCl has only one symmetry element which is
   (a) inversion centre (b) identity element
   (c) S_1 axis (d) C_2 axis
3. Absence of an S_n axis denotes
   (a) geometrical isomerism
   (b) optical activity
   (c) a *trans* isomer
   (d) a tetrahedral point group
4. What is the number of possible stereoisomer having the structure below?

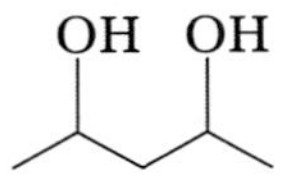

   (a) Two optically active and one *meso*
   (b) One optically active and one *meso*
   (c) Four optically active
   (d) Two optically active and two *meso*
5. Which of the alkenes below can exist as stereoisomer?
   (a) 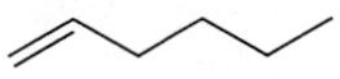 (b) 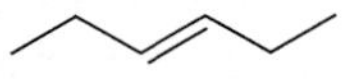
   (c) 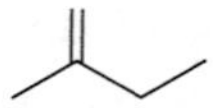 (d) $(CH_3)_2C{=}C(CH_3)_2$
6. What is the stereochemical relationship between the following compounds?

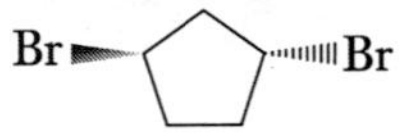

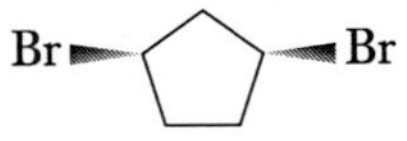

   (a) Enantiomers (b) Diastereomers
   (c) Both are *meso* (d) Same compound
7. Which of the compound is chiral?
   (a) 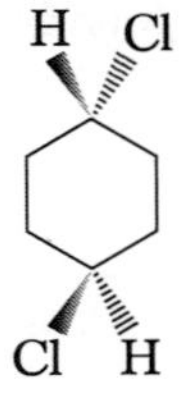

   (b) 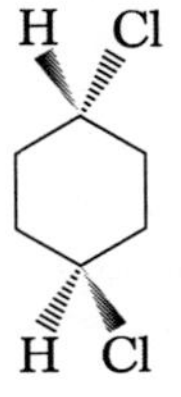

   (c) 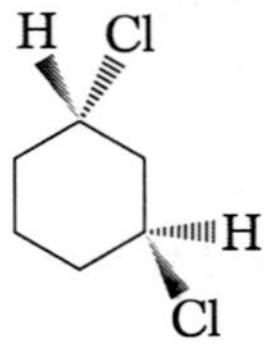

   (d) 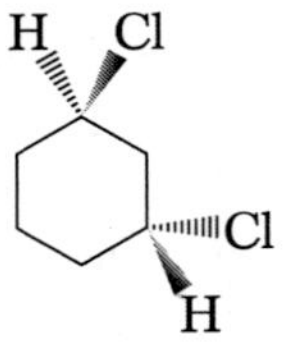

8. An example of an optically active molecule is
   (a) 2-methyl-1-propanol
   (b) 2-methyl-2-propanol
   (c) 1-butanol
   (d) 1-butanol-1-*D*
9. 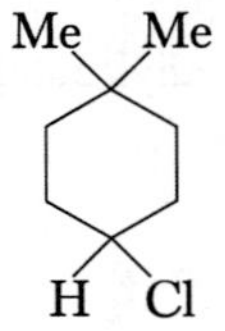

(*A*)
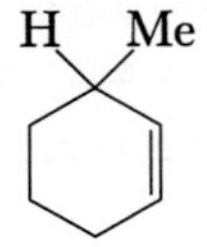

(*B*)

   Select the correct statement.
   (a) *A* is optically active, while *B* is optically inactive
   (b) *B* is optically active while *A* is optically inactive
   (c) Both *A* and *B* are optically inactive
   (d) Both *A* and *B* are optically active
10. The two compounds shown in the figure below are

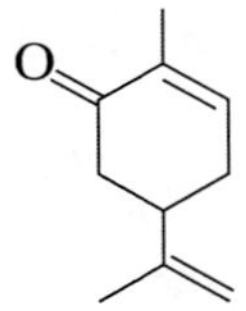

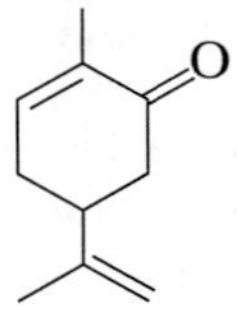

   (a) diastereomers (b) enantiomers
   (c) epimers (d) regioisomers
11. Which one of the following compounds is optically active?

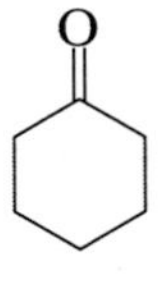

I
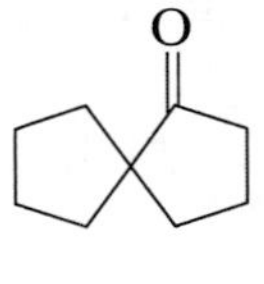

II
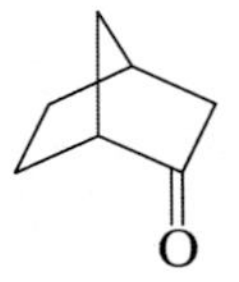

III
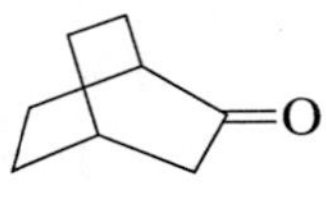

IV

   (a) I (b) II
   (c) III (d) IV
12. In erythro-2,3-dihydroxy butanoic acid, if the methyl group is replaced by a carboxyl group, the results is
   (a) *dl*-tartaric aci (b) *d*-tartaric acid
   (c) *l*-tartaric acid (d) *meso*-tartaric acid
13. Which of the following cannot be optically active?
   (a) 2-hydroxypropanoic acid
   (b) 2-hydroxybutanedioic acid
   (c) 3-hydroxypropanoic acid
   (d) 2, 3-dihydroxybutane dioic acid

14. The Newman projection below represents

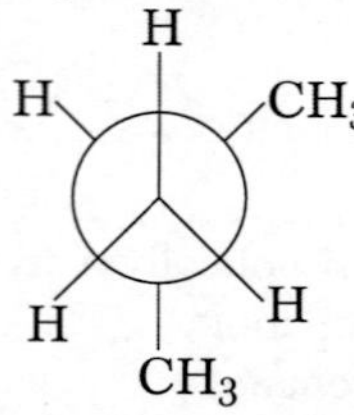

(a) A staggered form of 2-methyl propane
(b) A gauche form of butane
(c) An eclipsed form a 2-methyl propane
(d) A most stable conformation of 2-methyl butane

15. How many stereoisomers are there for molecule drawn?

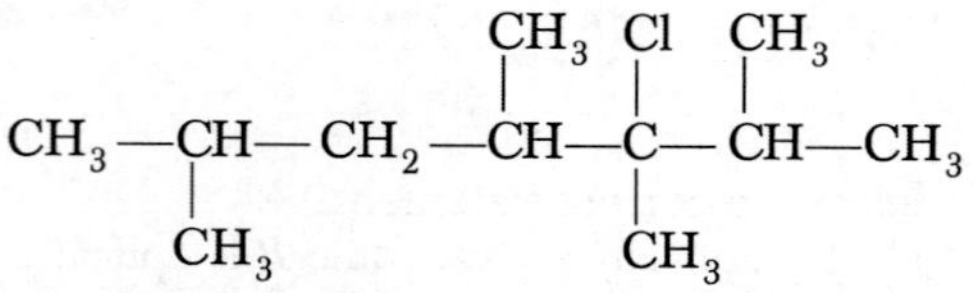

(a) Two (b) Four (c) Six (d) Eight

16. Choose the correct configuration in *E*-1-bromo-1-chloropropane.
(a) H and Br are on opposite side of the double bond
(b) —CH_3 and Cl are on the same side of the double bond
(c) H and Cl are on same side of the double bond
(d) —CH_3 and Cl are on opposite side

17. Choose the correct order of the stability of the different conformations of cyclohexane.
(a) Chain form > boat form > twist boat form
(b) Boat form > twist boat form > chair form
(c) Chair form > twist boat form > boat form
(d) Twist boat form > boat form > chair form

18. Which of the following molecules will not show optical activity?

(a)
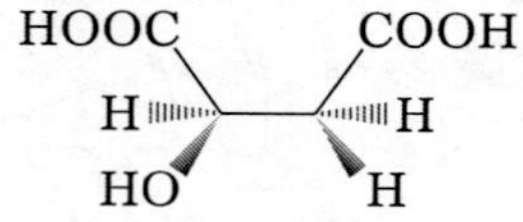

(b)
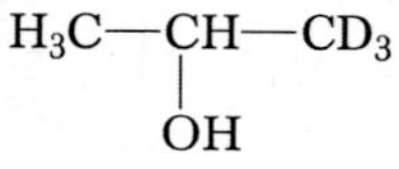

(c)
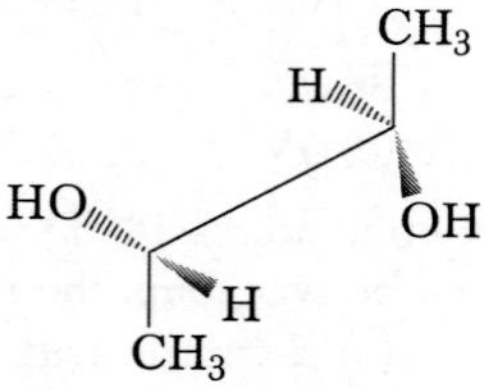

(d)
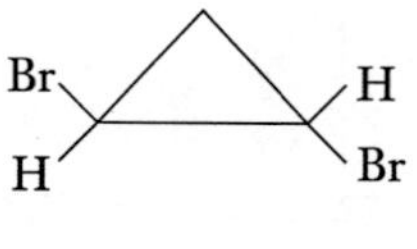

19. In 3-methyl pentane-1-ol

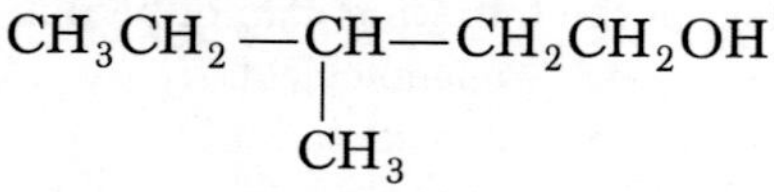

the priority sequence for *R* and *S* notations is

(a) $CH_3CH_2OH > CH_3CH_2 > CH_3 > H$
(b) $CH_3CH_2 > CH_2CH_2OH > CH_3 > H$
(c) $CH_3 > CH_3CH_2 > CH_2CH_2OH > H$
(d) $H > CH_3 > CH_3CH_2 > CH_2CH_2OH$

20. The dihedral angle between C—H (as viewed along the carbon-carbon bond axis) in a staggered form of ethane is
(a) 240° (b) 180°
(c) 120° (d) 60°

21. The structural representation of tartaric acid as shown here has

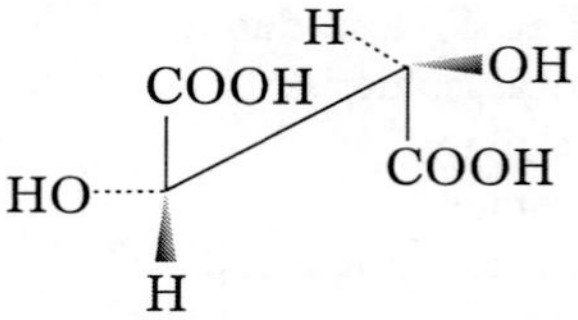

(a) a plane of symmetry
(b) a centre of symmetry
(c) no symmetry
(d) both plane of symmetry and centre of symmetry

22. The preferred conformation of *trans*-1, 4-dimethylcyclohexane has the cyclohexane ring in the
(a) chair form with both methyl groups in the equatorial positions
(b) chair form with both methyl groups in the axial positions
(c) chair form with one methyl group in the axial and the other in the equatorial positions
(d) boat form with the methyl groups in the flag poles

23. The one which will show optical isomerism is

(a)
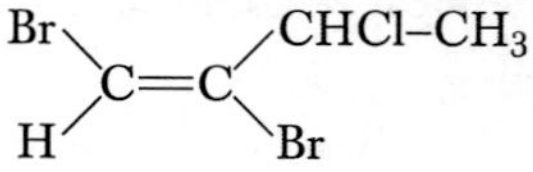

(b)
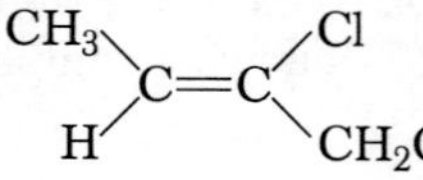

(c)
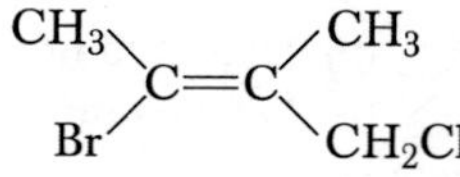

(d)
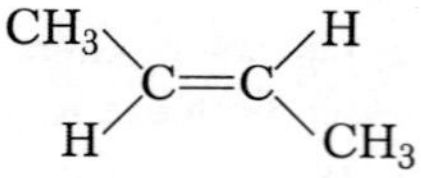

24. Which of the following compound contains diastereotropic protons?
(a) Ethyl chloride
(b) 1, 2-dichloropropane
(c) 2-methyl propene
(d) 1, 2-dichloroethane

25. The reaction of erythro 1-bromo 1, 2-diphenyl propane with alcoholic KOH gives
(a) (*Z*)-1, 2-diphenyl-1-propene
(b) (*E*)-1, 2-diphenyl-1-propene
(c) both (*Z*) and (*E*)-1, 2-diphenyl-1-propene
(d) 1, 2-diphenyl-1-propanol

26. The proper designation for the chiral centre and the geometrical configuration of this molecule would be

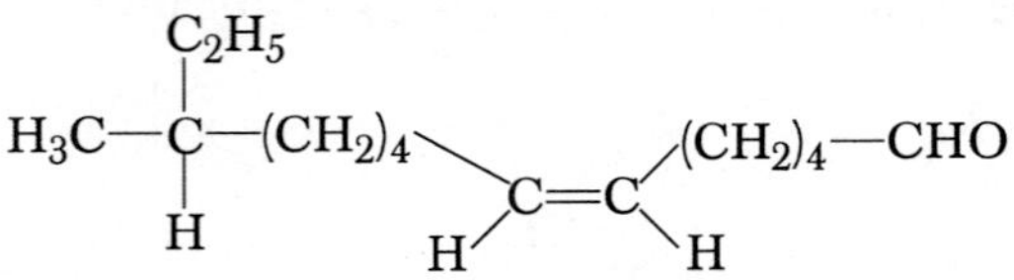

(a) *R* and *Z* (b) *R* and *E*
(c) *S* and *trans* (d) *S* and *Z*

27. Which of the following is resolvable into enantiomers?
(a) *Trans*-1, 3-cyclohexane diol
(b) *Trans*-1, 4-cyclohexane diol
(c) *Cis*-1, 2-cyclohexane diol
(d) *Cis*-1, 4-cyclohexane diol

28. The most stable conformation of 1, 4-dimethyl cyclohexane is

(a) 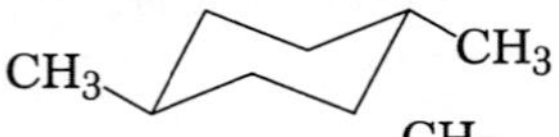

(b) 

(c) 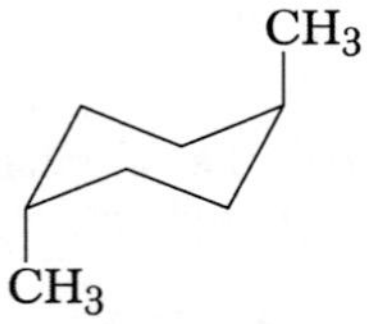

(d) 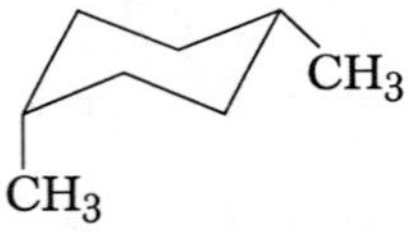

29. Addition of bromine to *cis*-2-butene yields
(a) *meso*-2, 3-dibromobutane
(b) racemic 2, 3-dibromobutane
(c) *d*-2, 3-dibromobutane
(d) *l*-2, 3-dibromobutane

30. Which of the following is best explanation for the relative stabilities of the conformations?

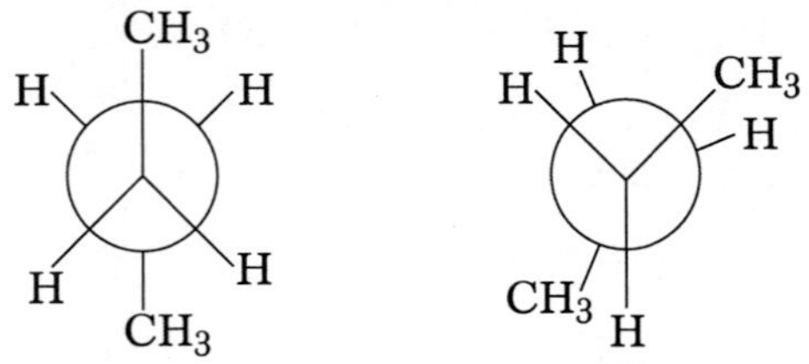

I II

(a) I has more torsional strain
(b) II has more torsional strain
(c) I has more steric strain
(d) both have more steric strain

31. Which of the following represent the lowest energy conformer of 2-methylhexane considering the rotation about C-3, C-4?

(a) 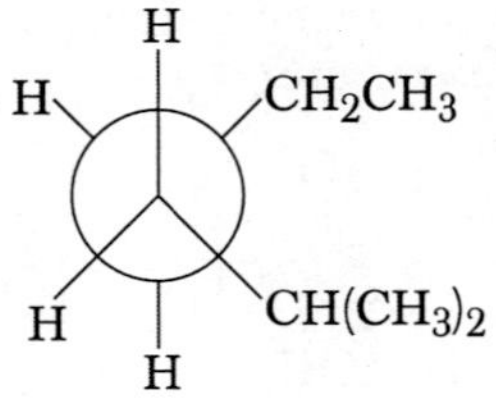

(b) 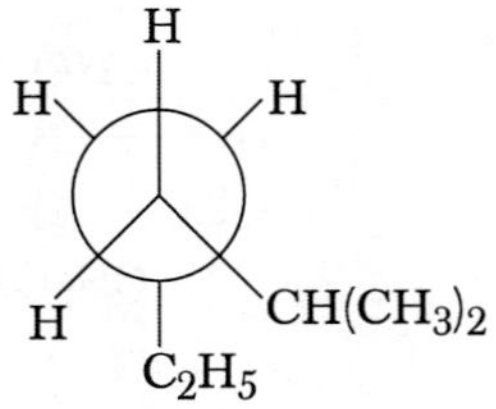

(c) 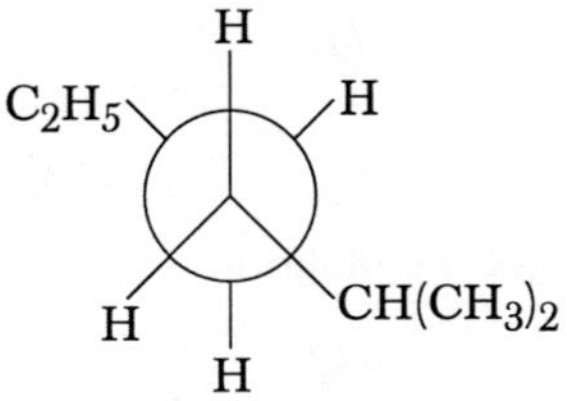

(d) 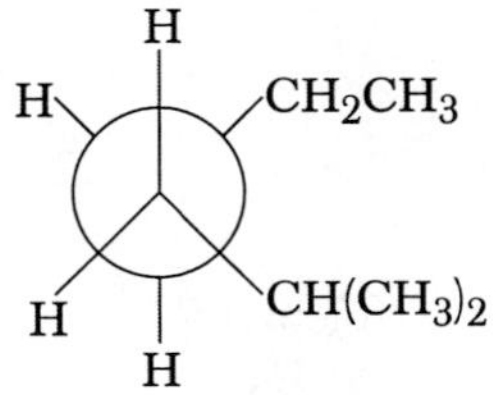

32. 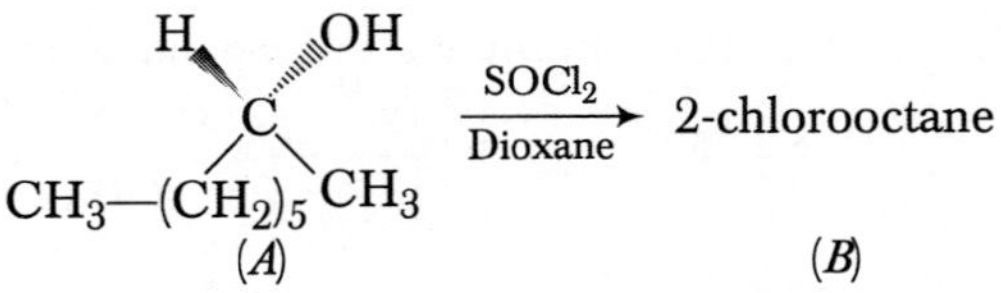

(*A*) (*B*)

The statement that is true is true about the reaction is
(a) *A* and *B* are both *R*-isomers
(b) *A* and *B* are both *S*-isomers
(c) *A* is *R*-isomer and *B* is *S*-isomer
(d) *A* is *S*-isomer and *B* is *R*-isomer

33. The most stable conformer of *meso*-1, 2-dibromo-1, 2-dichloro ethane is

(a) 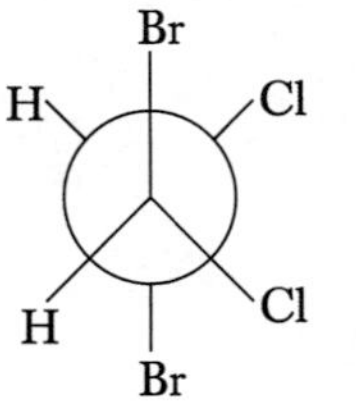

(b) 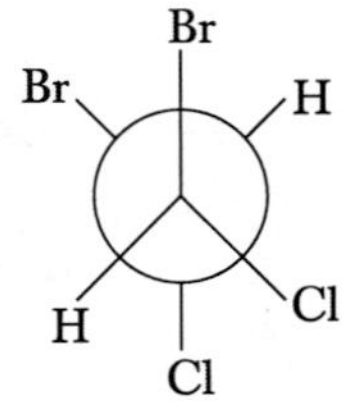

(c) 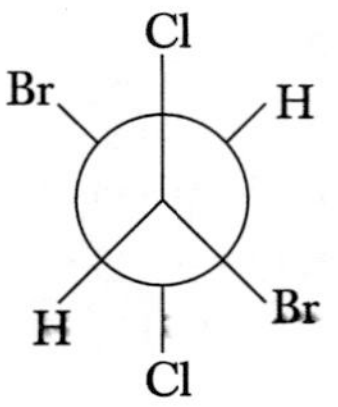

(d) 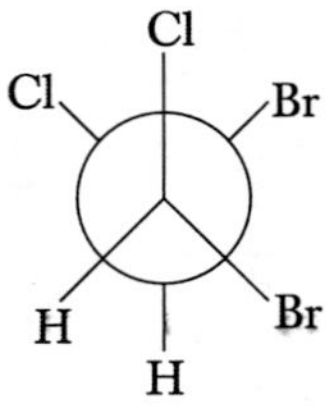

34. Which of the Fischer projection formula correspond to the following stereostructure?

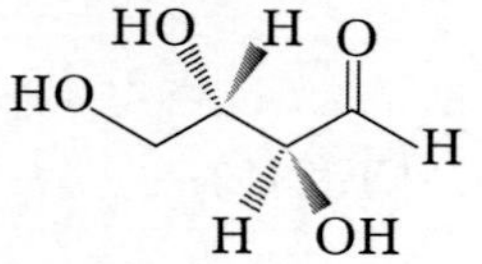

(a)
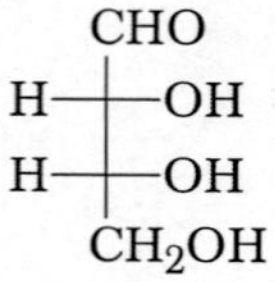
(b)
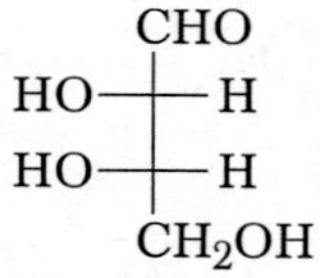

(c)
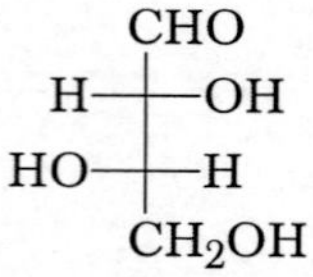
(d)
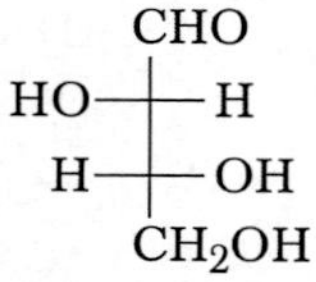

35. The configuration (R, S-notation) at C-1 and C-6 of the compound below are

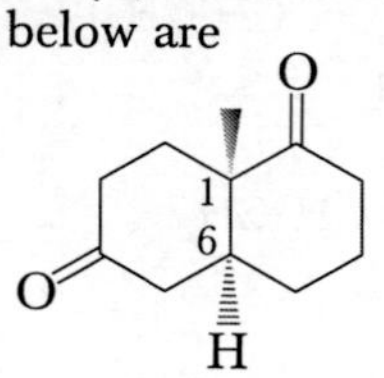

(a) 1S, 6S (b) 1S, 6R
(c) 1R, 6R (d) 1R, 6S

36. The most stable conformation of n-pentane is

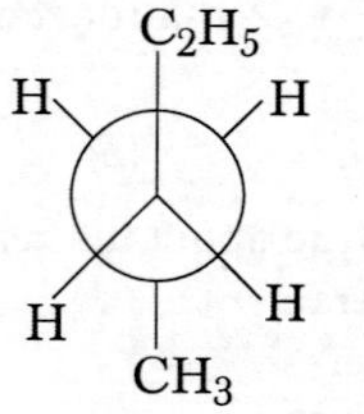
I
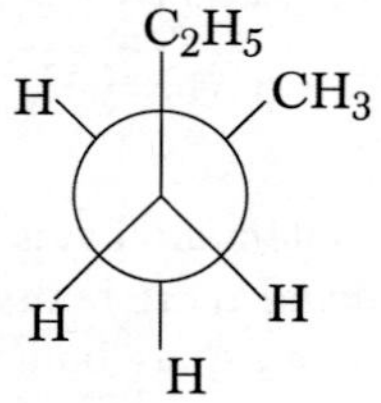
II
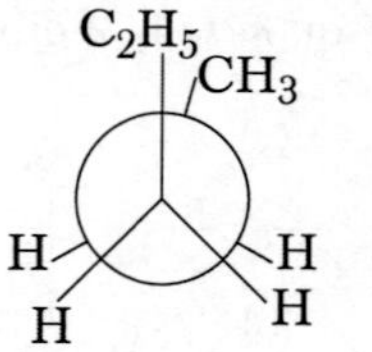
III
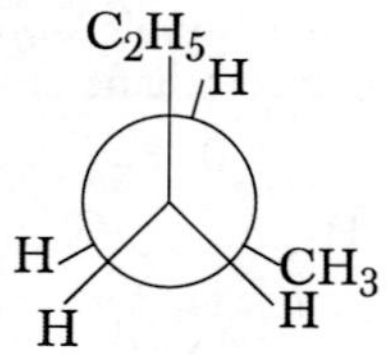
IV

(a) I (b) II
(c) III (d) IV

37. The following two compounds are

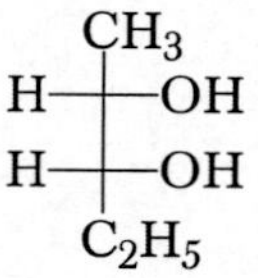
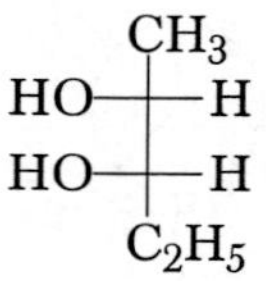

(a) epimers (b) diastereomers
(c) identical (d) enantiomers

38. Label the following pairs correctly

I. 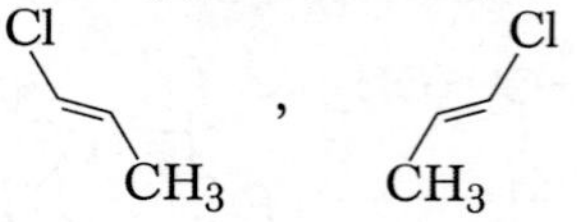

II. 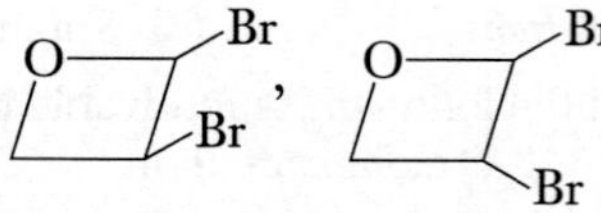

(a) Enantiomers, diastereoisomers
(b) Homomers, enantiomers
(c) Homomers, diastereoisomers
(d) Constitutional isomers,enantiomers

39. The number of stereoisomers that are possible for the following compound are

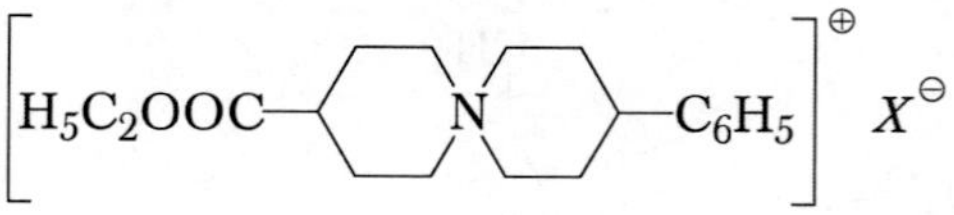

(a) 1 (b) 2
(c) 3 (d) 4

40. In the reaction given below, the orientation of two bromine substituents in the product is

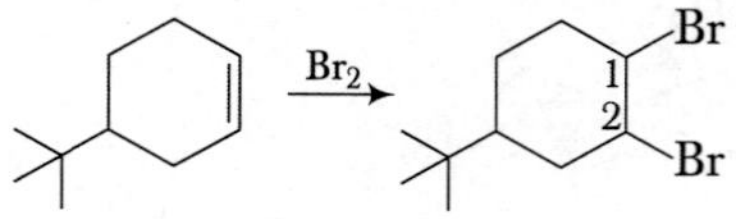

(a) equatorial at both C-1 and C-2
(b) equatorial at C-1 and axial at C-2
(c) axial at C-1 and equatorial at C-2
(d) axial at both C-1 and C-2

41. Which one of the following is the stablest conformation of butane-2, 3-diol?

(a)
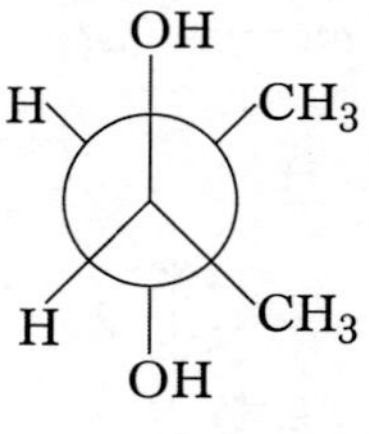
(b)
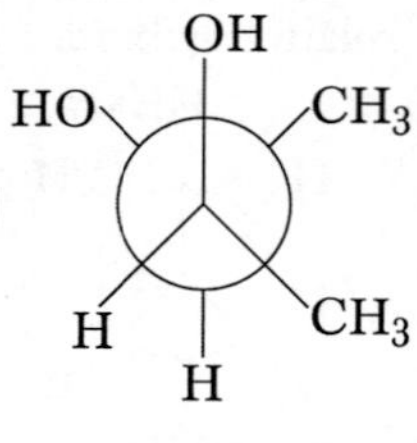

(c)
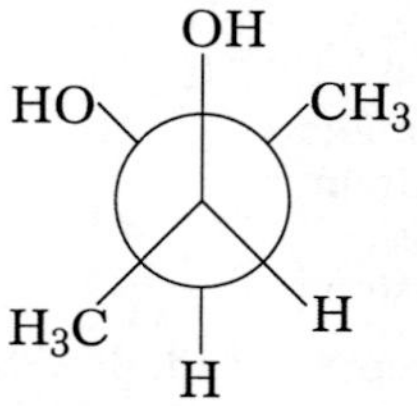
(d)
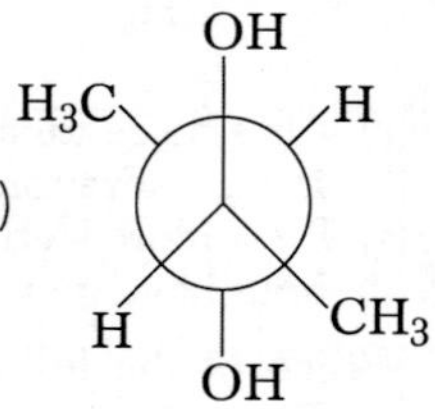

42. The preferred conformation of *cis*-1,3-dihydroxy cyclohexane is

(a) 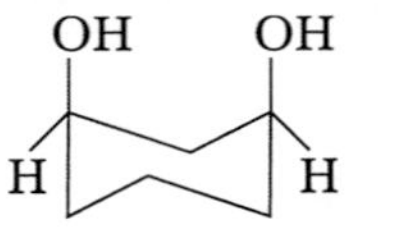 (b) 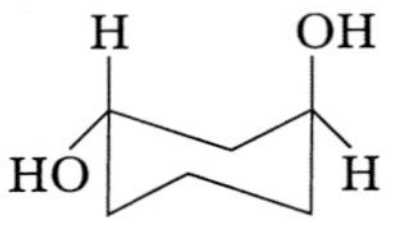

(c) 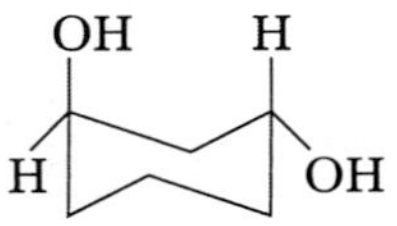 (d) 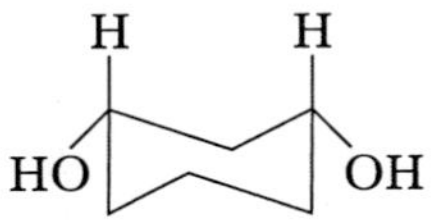

43. For 3-chloro butan-2-ol, which one of the following is true?

(a) 2*S*, 3*S* and 2*R*, 3*S* is a pair of diastereoisomers while 2*R*, 3*S* and 2*S*, 3*R* is a pair of enantiomers
(b) 2*S*, 3*S* and 2*R*, 3*S* is a pair of diastereoisomers while 2*R*, 3*R* and 2*S*, 3*S* is a pair of enantiomers
(c) 2*R*, 3*R* and 2*S*, 3*S* is a pair of diastereoisomers while 2*S*, 3*S* and 2*R*, 3*S* is a pair of enantiomers
(d) 2*R*, 3*R* and 2*S*, 3*S* is a pair of diastereoisomers while 2*R*, 3*R* and 2*S*, 3*S* is a pair of enantiomers

44. Which species exhibits a plane of symmetry?

(a) 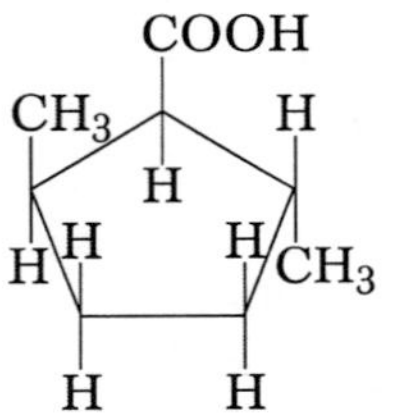 (b) 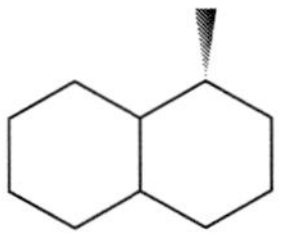

(c) 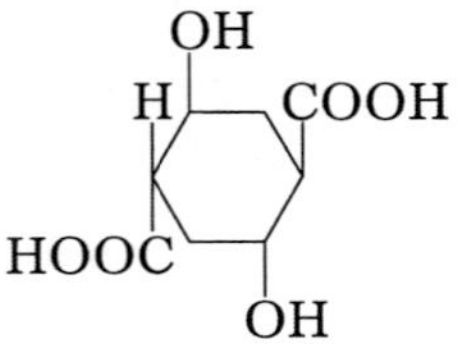 (d) 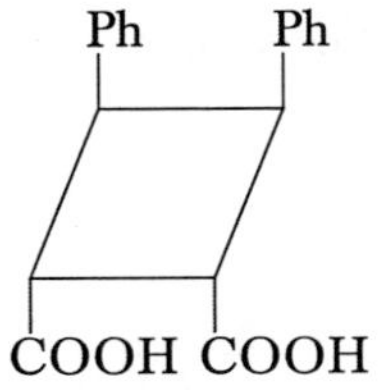

45. Choose the structure does not have the same absolute configuration as the structure given below :

 = ?

(a) 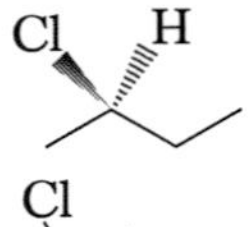 (b) 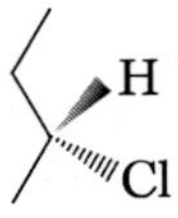

(c) 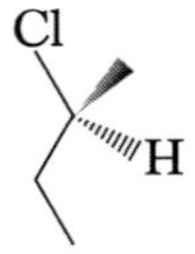 (d) 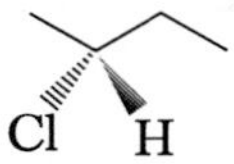

46. Which one of the following statements is true?

(a) Diastereomers are a pair of isomers related spatially as object and mirror image
(b) Diastereomers can often be separated by fractional crystallization
(c) Diastereomers have identical physical and chemical properties
(d) Diastereomers rotate the plane of polarization of plane-polarized light to an equal but opposite extent

47. Which of the following molecules have dipole moment?

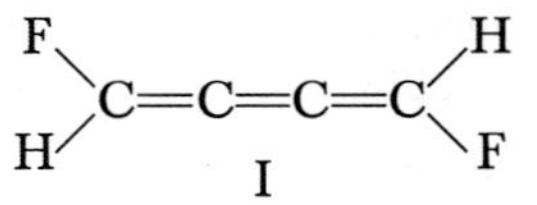
I

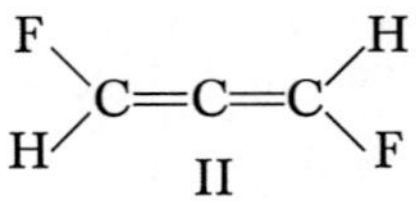
II

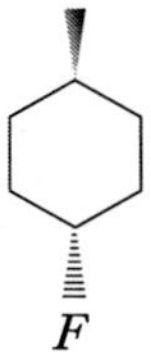
III

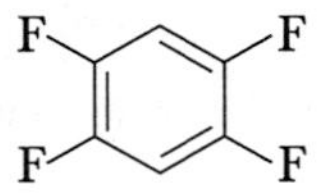
IV

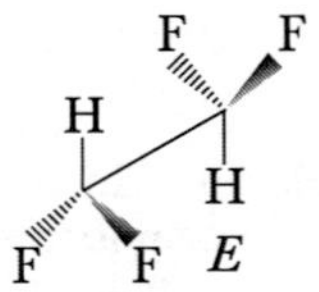
V

(a) I and IV (b) II and III
(c) III and V (d) II and V

48. The molecules are

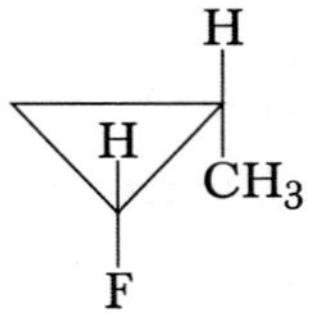 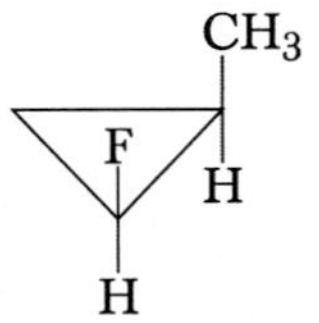

(a) enantiomers (b) diastereomers
(c) identical (d) constitutional isomers

49. On Pluto, where everything is frozen, astronauts discovered two forms of 1, 2-dibromoethane; *gauche* and *anti*. Assuming that there are no rotations around single bonds, which statement about the two forms is correct?

(a) They are enantiomers
(b) They are diastereomers
(c) They are *meso* compounds
(d) Both will show optical activity

50. Which type of conformation is shown by I and II?

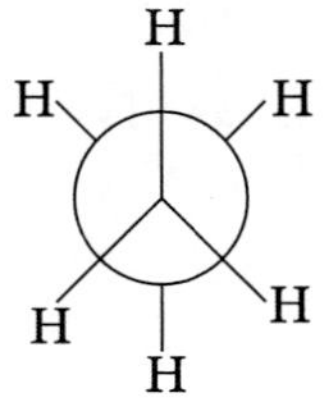
I

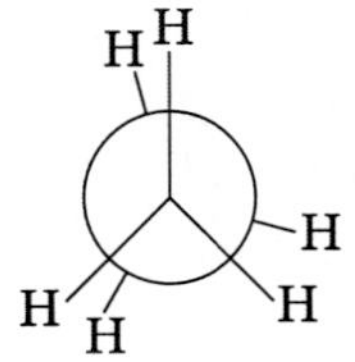
II

(a) I is eclipsed, II is staggered
(b) II is eclipsed, I is staggered
(c) both are eclipsed
(d) both are staggered

51. The most stable conformation of ethylene glycol is
(a) *anti* (b) *gauche*
(c) partially eclipsed (d) fully eclipsed

52. When methyl group is in the axial position in methyl cyclohexane, the molecule has
(a) one *n*-butane *gauche* interaction
(b) no *n*-butane *gauche* interaction
(c) two *n*-butane *gauche* interaction
(d) three *n*-butane *gauche* interaction

53. In the boat conformation of cyclohexane, the most destabilizing interaction is
(a) eclipsing (b) 1,3-diaxial
(c) 1,3-diequatorial (d) flagpole-flagpole

54. For which of the following compounds enantiomer is not possible?
(a) Phenyl ethane
(b) α-hydroxy propionic acid
(c) 2-amino pentane
(d) 1-chloro-1-phenyl thane

55. In Sawhorse projection, a fully eclipsed form can be transformed to *anti*-staggered form by a rotation of
(a) 60° (b) 90°
(c) 180° (d) 360°

56. Which of the compounds below are enantiomers?

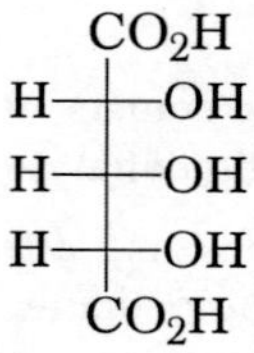
I

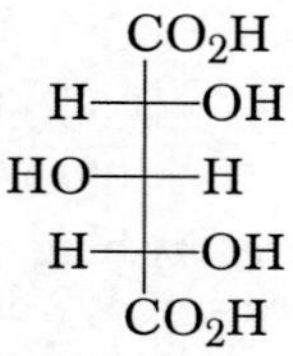
II

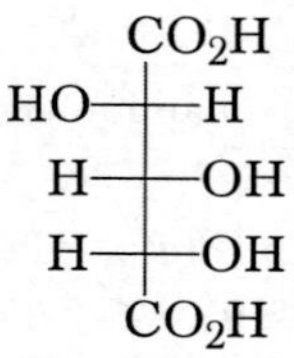
III

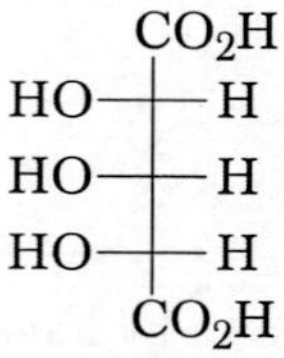
IV

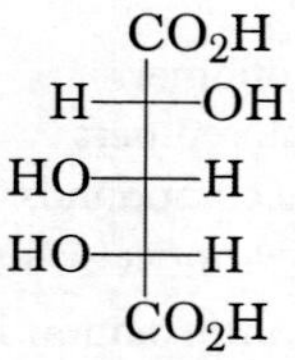
V

(a) II and III (b) III and IV
(c) III and IV (d) I and V

57. Which of the following Fischer projection is the enantiomer of the following molecule?

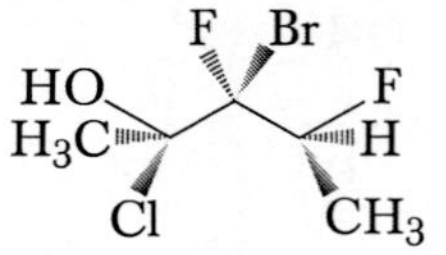

(a)
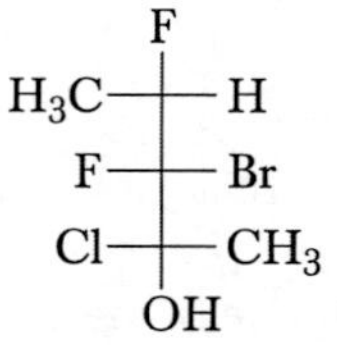

(b)
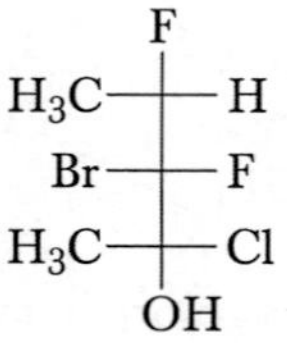

(c)
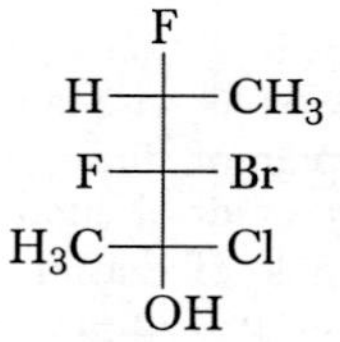

(d)
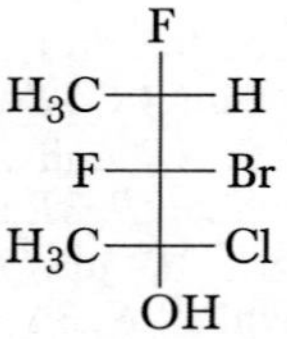

58. The configurations at the two stereocentres in the compound given below are

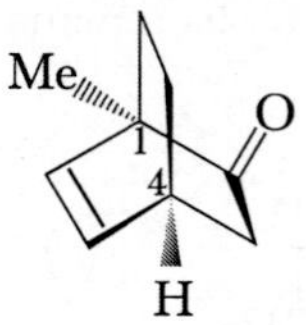

(a) 1*R*, 4*R* (b) 1*R*, 4*S*
(c) 1*S*, 4*R* (d) 1*S*, 4*S*

59. The two compounds given below are

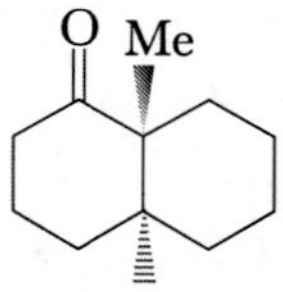
and
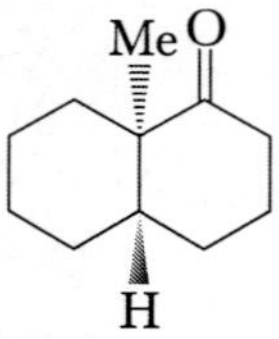

(a) enantiomers (b) identical
(c) diastereomers (d) regioisomers

60. In the most stable conformation of *trans*-1-*t*-butyl-3-methylcyclohexane, the substituents at C-1 and C-3, respectively, are
(a) axial and equatorial
(b) equatorial and equatorial
(c) equatorial and axial
(d) axial and axial

Exercise 2

(For Part 'C')

1. Which of the following regarding the structure of (E)-4-methyl-3-heptene are not correct?

I. The n-propyl and H are on the same side of the double bond.

II. The n-propyl and ethyl are on the same side of the C=C bond.

III. The methyl and H are on the same side of the double bond.

IV. The ethyl and methyl are on the same side of the double bond.

(a) I and II (b) II and IV
(c) III and IV (d) II and III

2. Which of the following compounds can be obtained in an optically active form? Select the correct answer using the codes given below

I. 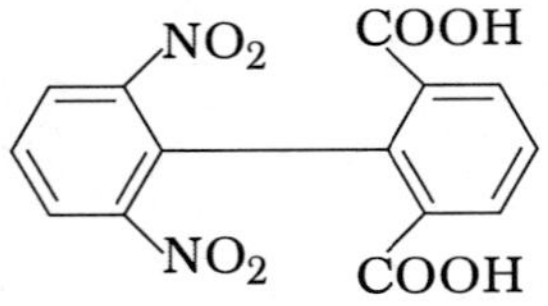

II. 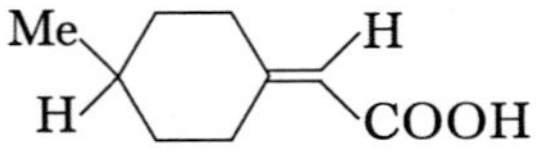

III. 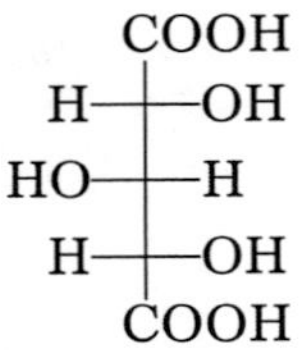

IV. 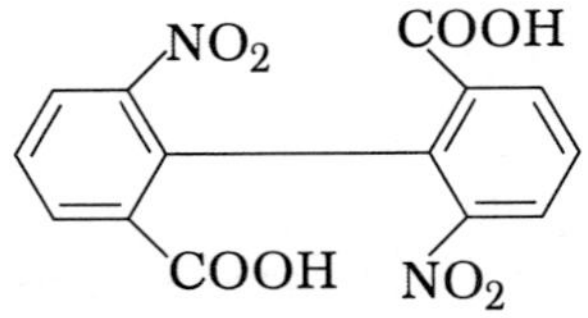

(a) I, II and III (b) II, III and IV
(c) II and IV (d) Only IV

3. Which of the following has 1E, 3Z configuration?

(a) 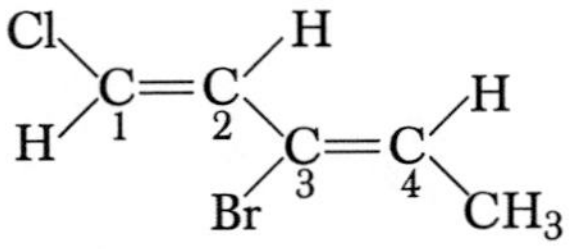

(b) 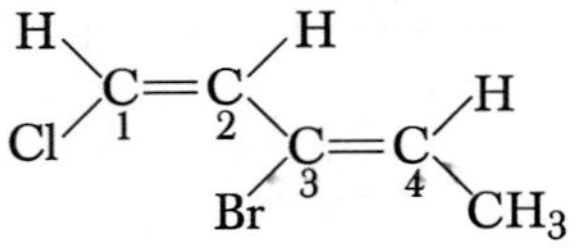

(c) 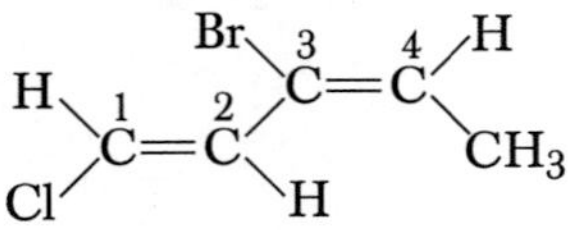

(d) 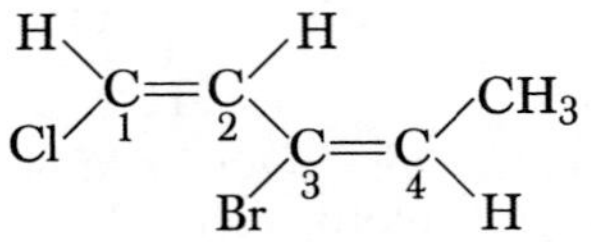

4. Which is the most stable conformation of 1-chloro-4-methylcyclohexane?

(a) 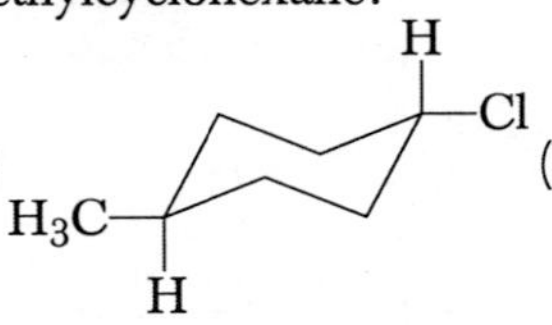

(b) 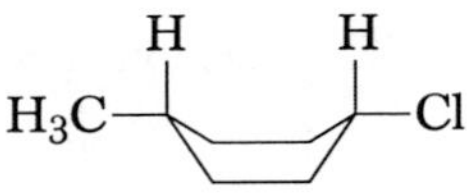

(c) 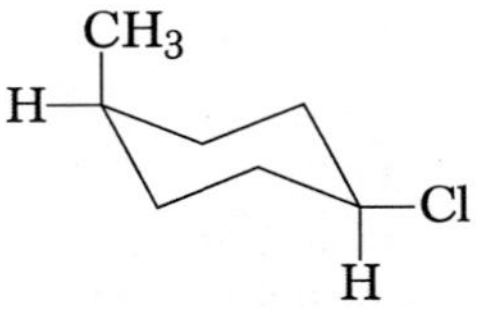

(d) 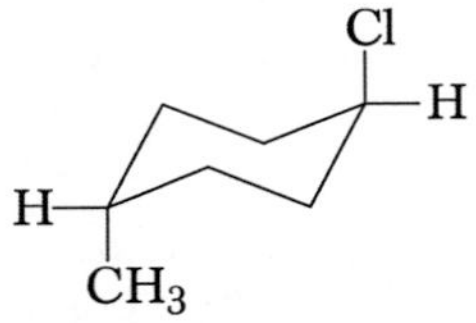

5. Chiral molecules are represented by

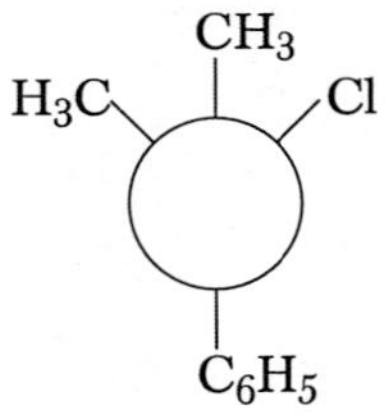

I

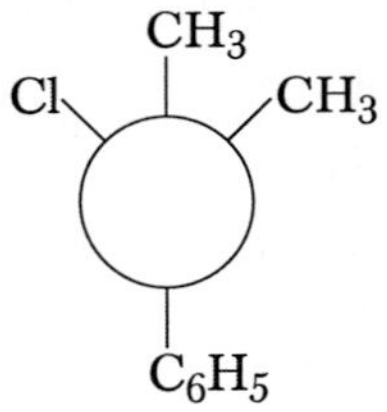

II

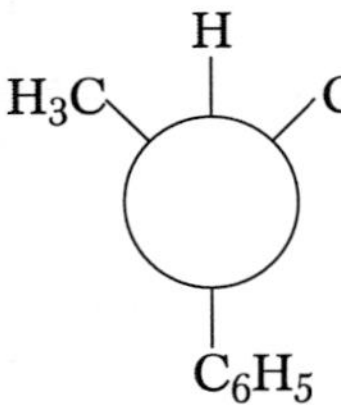

III

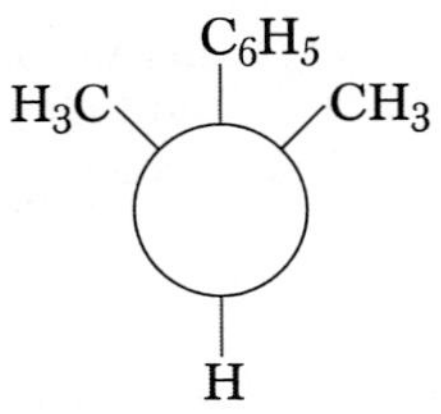

IV

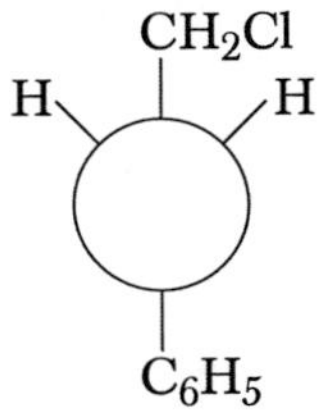

V

(a) III and IV (b) I, II, IV and V
(c) I, II, III and IV (d) I, II and IV

6. Which of the following pairs of structures are two drawings of the same enantiomer?

(a) 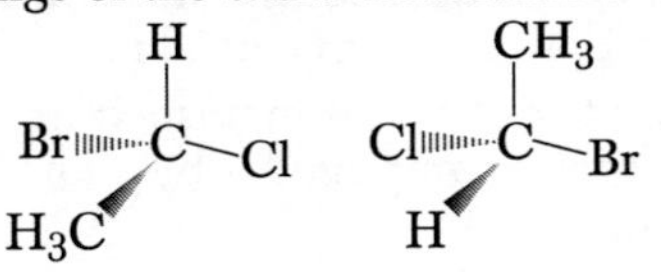

(b) 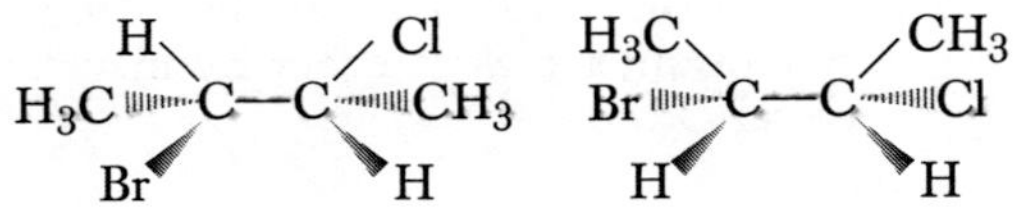

(c) 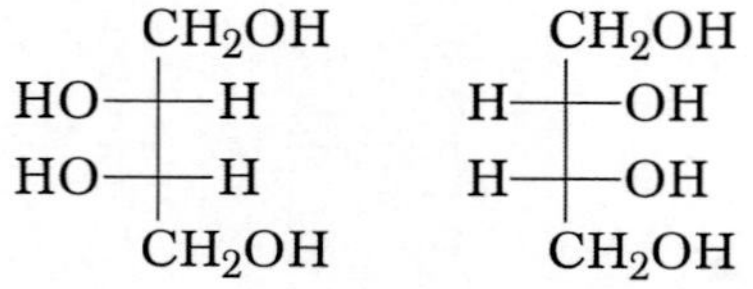

(d) 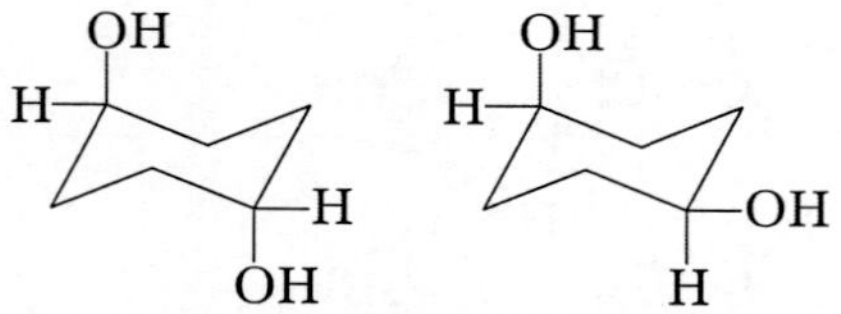

7. The favoured conformation (*gauche*, *anti* or eclipsed) for the molecules 1,2-dichloro ethene; 1, 2-ethanediol and propanaldehyde will be respectively
(a) *gauche, anti, eclipsed* (b) *eclipsed, gauche, anti*
(c) *anti, gauche, eclipsed* (d) *anti, eclipsed, gauche*

8. The reaction sequence of

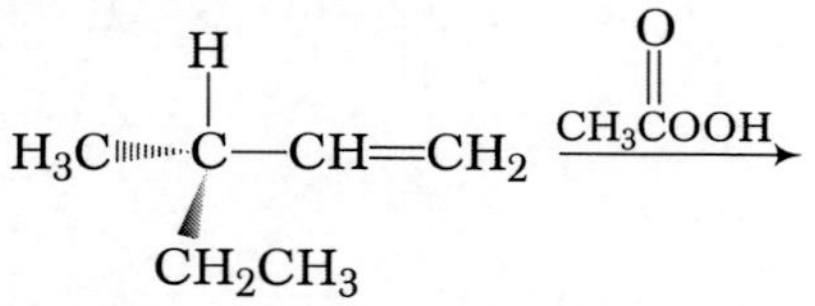

will yield
(a) a pair of products that are enantiomers
(b) a single product that is optically active
(c) a pair of products that are diastereomers
(d) a pair of products one of which is *meso*

9. Match the Column I with Column II.

	Column I		Column II
A.	1, 2-disubstituted cyclohexane	1.	*Meso* compound.
B.	*Cis*-1, 3-dimethyl cyclohexane	2.	Axially chiral molecules.
C.	Allenes, spiranes	3.	Identical representation of the same compound
D.	Homomers	4.	Four stereoisomers.

Codes

	A	B	C	D
(a)	4	3	2	1
(b)	3	1	4	2
(c)	4	1	2	3
(d)	2	3	4	1

10. Consider the following statements.
I. A reaction catalyzed by an enzyme always gives an optically active product.
II. A racemate can be distinguished from a *meso* or an achiral compound by an attempted resolution.
III. Conversion of an erythro to a threo stereoisomer always occur by inversion at one chiral C.
IV. A *D* enantiomer rotates the plane of polarized light to the right and *L* enantiomer to the left.
V. All stereospecific reactions are necessarily stereoselective, but the converse is not true.

Select the correct statements.
(a) II, III, V (b) I, II, IV
(c) III, IV, V (d) III, IV

11. Molecules in sample *A* are diastereomeric of molecules in sample *B*. Sample *A* show optical activity, while sample *B* does not. Which of the following statements must be incorrect?
(a) Sample *A* contains unequal amount of enantiomers while *B* is a racemic mixture
(b) Molecules in *A* have stereocentre while molecules in *B* have no stereocentre
(c) Molecules in *A* are chiral while molecules in *B* are *meso* compounds
(d) Molecules in *A* and *B* are geometrical isomers

12. Assign the correct *R*—*S* notation to the following structures.

	Column I (Structures)		Column I (Notation)
A.	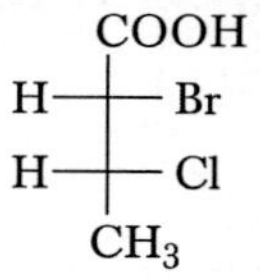	1.	2*S*, 3*S*
B.	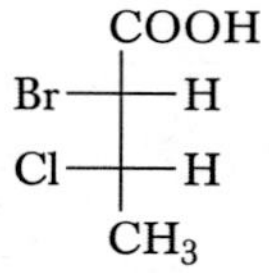	2.	2*R*, 3*R*
C.	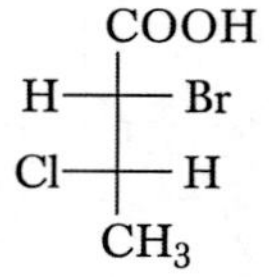	3.	2*S*, 3*R*
D.	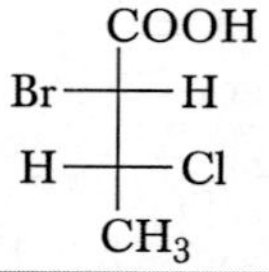	4.	2*R*, 3*S*

Codes

	A	B	C	D
(a)	1	2	3	4
(b)	2	1	4	3
(c)	3	4	1	2
(d)	4	1	4	3

13. How many conformations are possible for *trans*-decal- 2-ol?
(a) 3 (b) 4
(c) 5 (d) 2

14. Which of the following statements regarding the conformers of butane is correct?

(a) The *anti* and the two *gauche* staggered forms have the same energies.
(b) The *anti* has a greater energy than the two *gauche* forms.
(c) The *anti* has a lesser energy than the two *gauche* forms.
(d) The two *gauche* staggered forms have different energies.

15. What is the relationship between the molecules in the following pairs?

I. 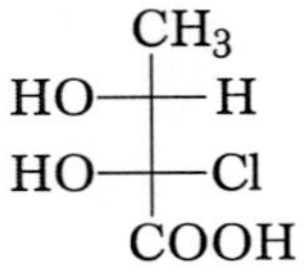 and 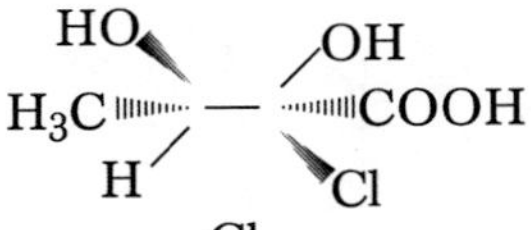

II. 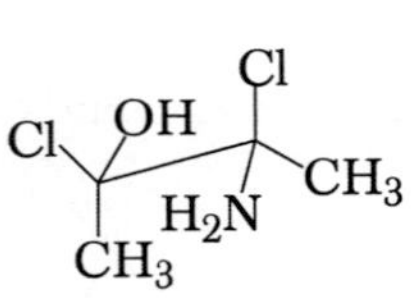 and 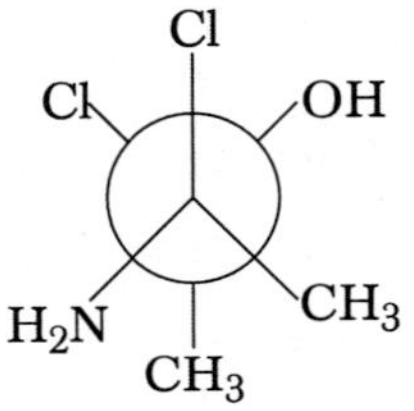

(a) Enantiomer-enantiomer
(b) Diastereomers-enantiomer
(c) Enantiomer-diastereomers
(d) Diastereomers-diastereomers

16. Which of the following structures below represents pair of enantiomers?

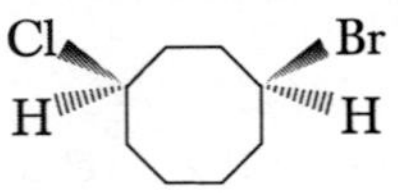
I

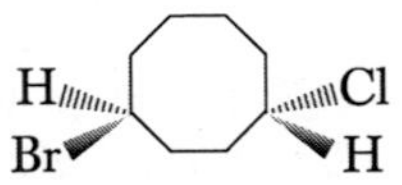
II

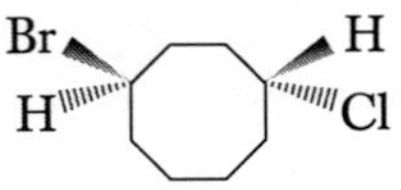
III

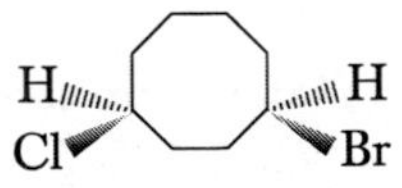
IV

(a) I + II and III + IV (b) I + IV and II + III
(c) I + III and II + IV (d) Only I + IV

17. The staggered-Sawhorse projection for

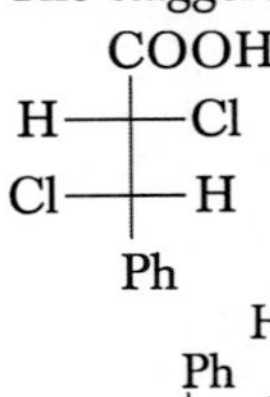 is

(a) 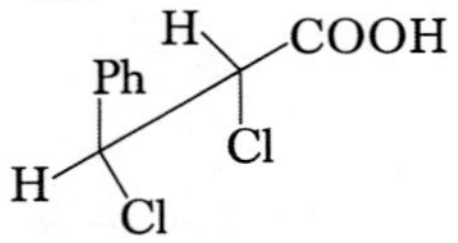
(b) 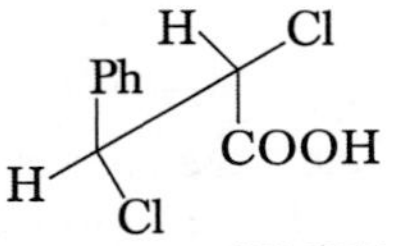
(c) 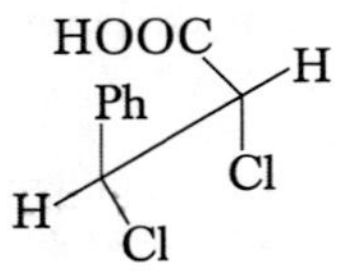
(d) 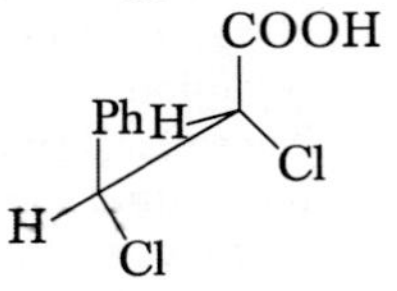

18. Among the following, the most stable conformation is

(a) 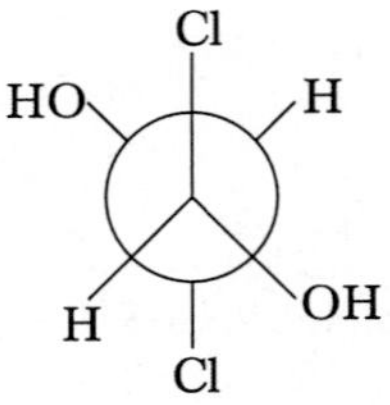
(b) 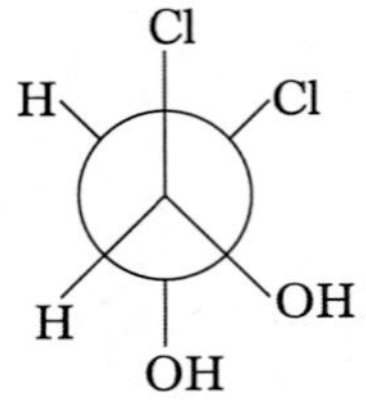
(c) 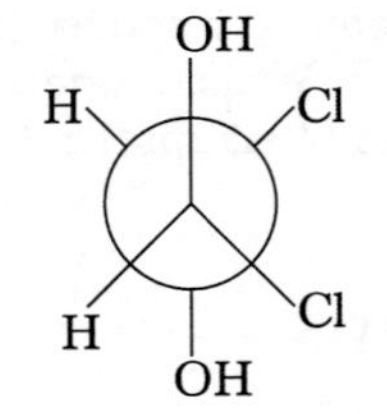
(d) 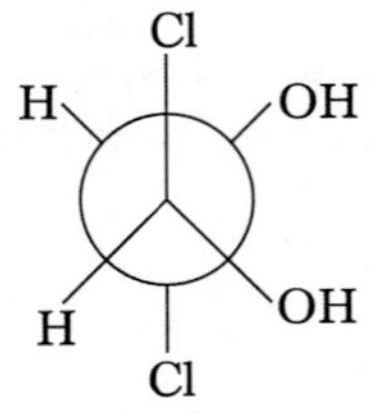

19. Enantiomer of 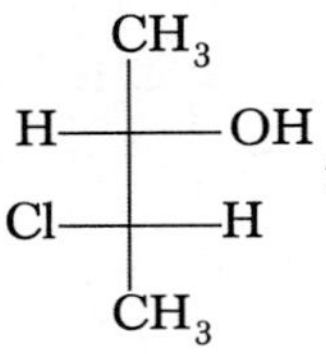 is

(a) 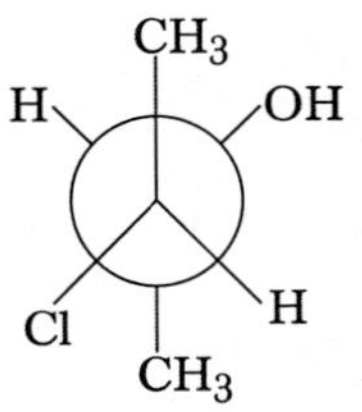
(b) 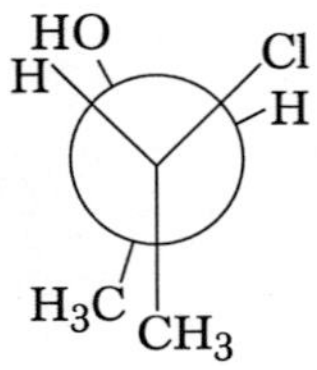
(c) 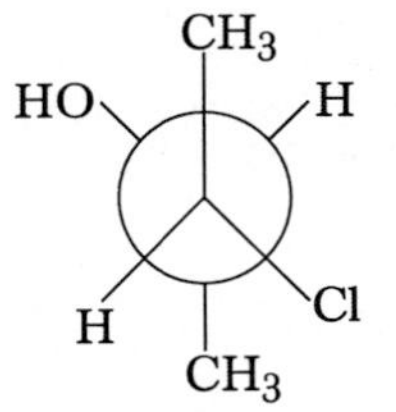
(d) 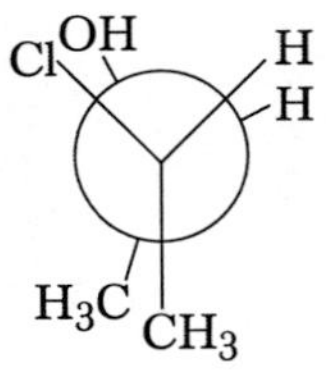

20. The correct representation of the eclipsed form of butane is

(a) 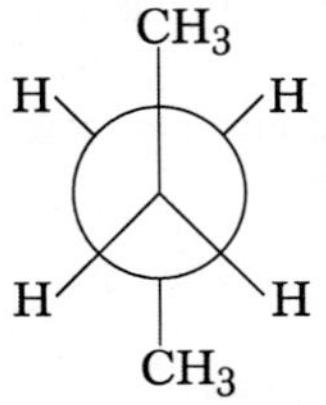
(b) 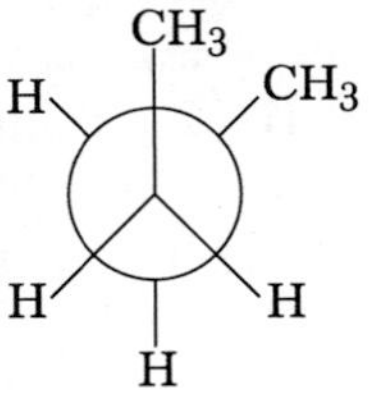
(c) 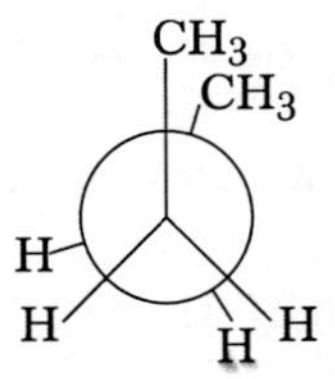
(d) 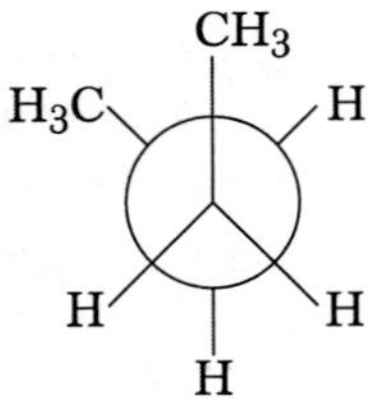

21. The configurations at the three chiral centres in the bicyclodecanol given below, are

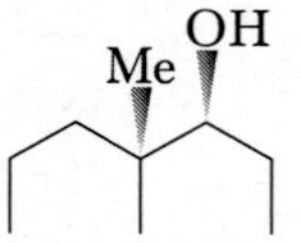

(a) 1*S*, 2*S*, 6*R* (b) 1*S*, 2*S*, 6*S*
(c) 1*R*, 2*S*, 6*R* (d) 1*R*, 2*S*, 6*R*

22. The *S* enantiomer of ibuprofen is responsible for its pain -relieving properties. Which one of the following structures shown in (*S*)-ibuprofen?

(a)

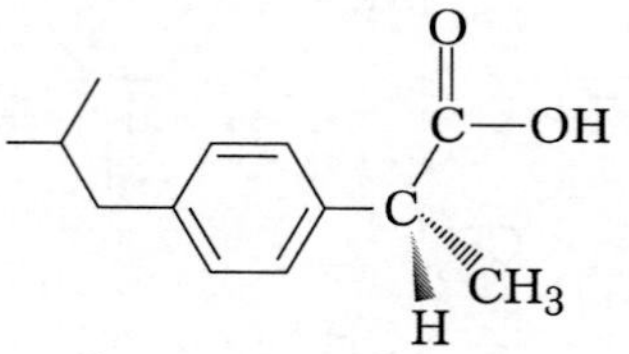

(b)

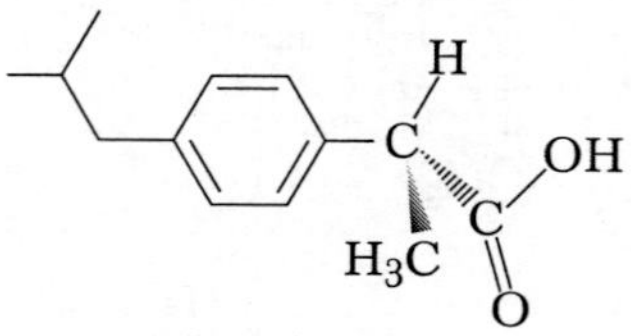

(c)

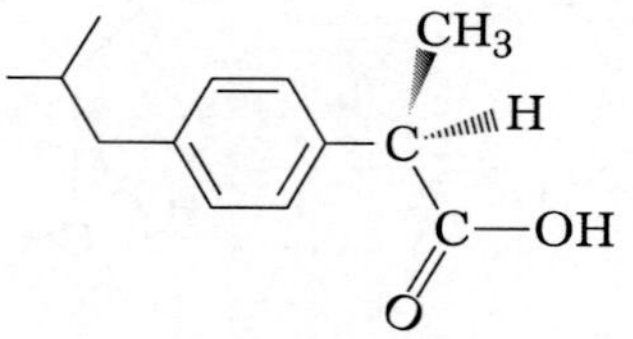

(d)

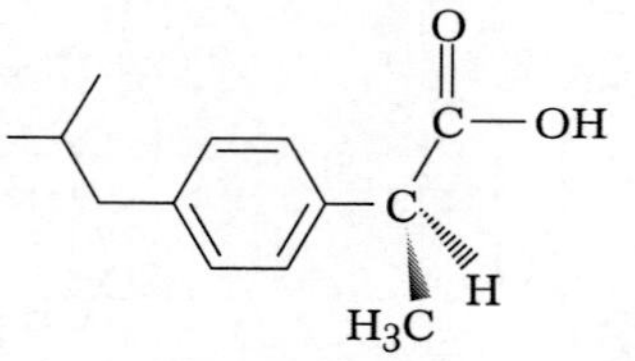

23. Consider the following statements.

I. Enantiomers in which there is restricted rotation about (C—C) single bond are called astropisomers.

II. 2, 3-pentadiene is chiral and can exist as pair of enantiomers.

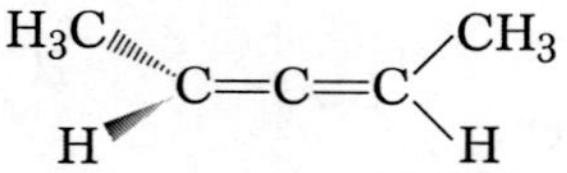

III. 2, 3-pentadiene can exist as CTS and *trans*-isomers.

IV. 2, 3-pentadiene is achiral and *meso* compound.

Select the correct statements.

(a) I, II, IV (b) II, III
(c) I, IV (d) I, II

24. Assign a configuration, *R* or *S* to each of these compounds

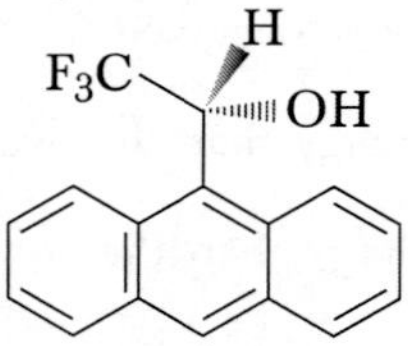

A

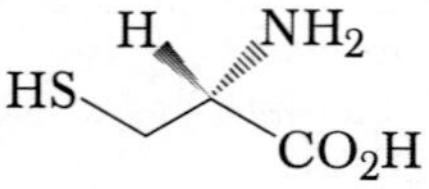

B

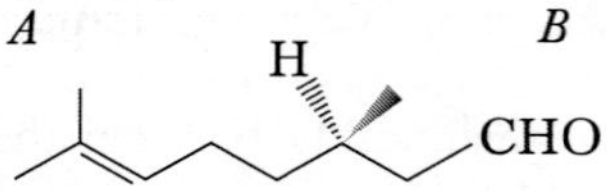

C

	A	*B*	*C*
(a)	*R*	*R*	*S*
(b)	*R*	*S*	*R*
(c)	*S*	*R*	*R*
(d)	*R*	*R*	*R*

25. Consider the following epoxides *A*, *B* and *C*.

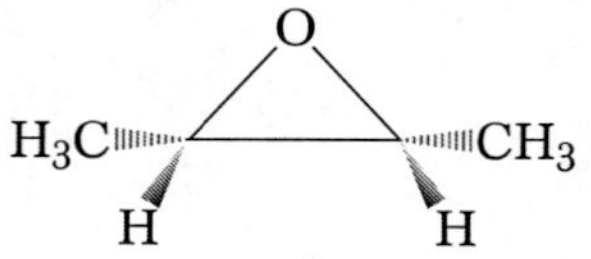

A

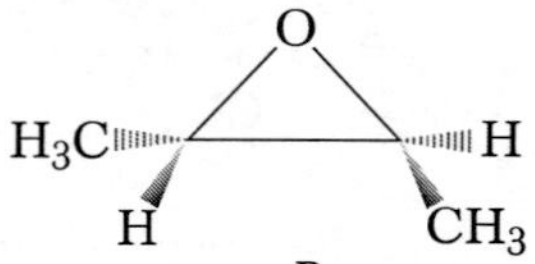

B

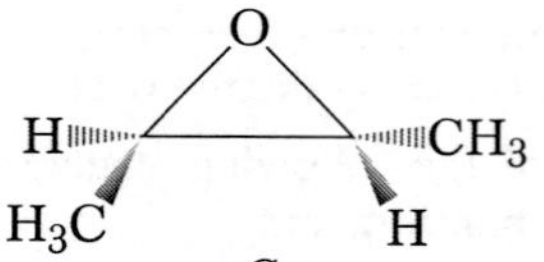

C

I. *A* is *cis*-isomer and is achiral.

II. *B* and *C* are *trans*-isomer and are achiral.

III. *B* and *C* are non-superimposable enantiomeric forms.

IV. *B* and *C* are *trans*-isomer and are chiral.

Select the correct statements about these epoxides.

(a) I, III, IV (b) I, II, III
(c) II, III (d) III, IV

26. Following compound (*P*) is subjected to reaction with C_6H_5COCl (*X*).

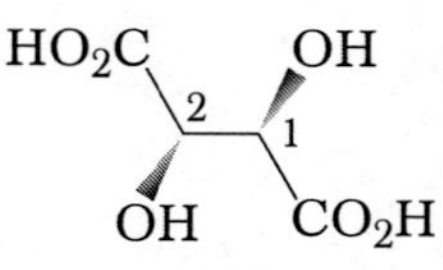

(*P*)

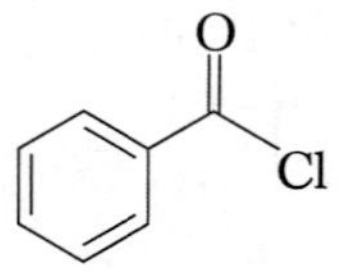

(*Q*)

Select the correct statement(s).

(a) There is no cleavage or formation of bonds at the chiral centres and thus, both acylation go with retention.

(b) There is cleavage and formation of bond at (1) at the chiral centre and thus, configuration at (1) inverted, but at (2) there is no change.

(c) There is cleavage and formation of bond at (2) at the chiral centre and thus, configuration at (2) is inverted but at (1) there is no change.
(d) There is cleavage and formation of bonds at both chiral centres and thus, configuration at both chiral centres are inverted.

Assertion & Reason

Codes
(a) Both A and R are true and R is the correct explanation of A.
(b) Both A and R are true but R is not the correct explanation of A.
(c) A is true but R is false.
(d) A is false but R is true.

27. Assertion (A) *Cis*-1, 3-dihydroxycyclohexane exists in boat conformation.

Reason (R) In the chair form, there will not be hydrogen bonding between the two hydroxyl groups.

28. Assertion (A) Twist boat conformation of cyclohexane is more stable than boat conformation.

Reason (R) Flagpole-flagpole interactions are less severe in boat conformation than in twist boat conformation.

29. Assertion (A) Molecules that are not superimposable on their mirror images are chiral.

Reason (R) All chiral molecules have chiral centres.

30. Assertion (A) Conformers are impractical to separate.

Reason (R) Conformers have negligibly small difference in their potential energy.

31. Match the following.

	Column I		Column II
A.	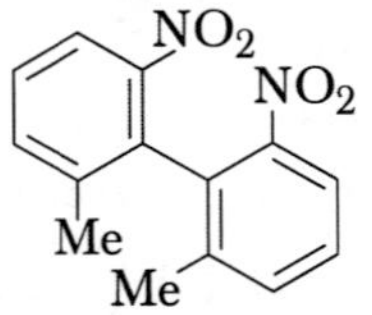	1.	Chiral centre
B.		2.	Chiral axis
C.	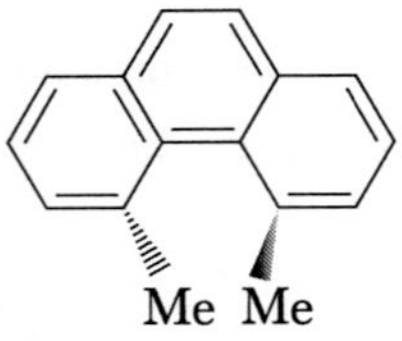	3.	Chiral plane
		4.	Helical chirality

Codes

	A	B	C
(a)	3	2	4
(b)	4	3	2
(c)	2	4	3
(d)	2	3	4

32. The *gauche* interaction values for Me/Me, Me/Br and Br/Br are 3.3, 0.8 and 3.0 kJ/mol, respectively. Among the following, the most stable conformation of 2, 3-dibromobutane is

(a) 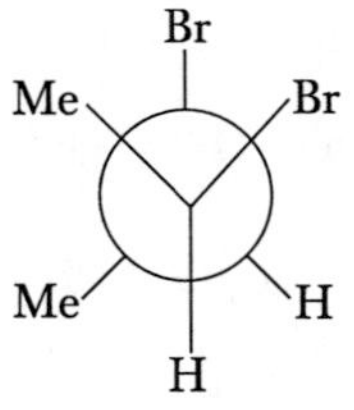

(b) 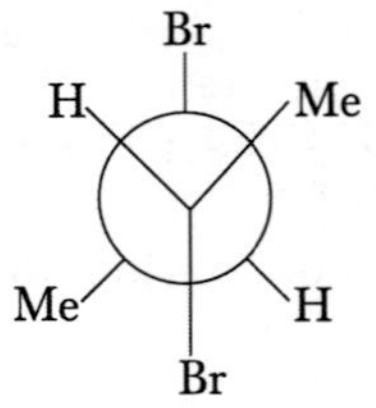

(c) 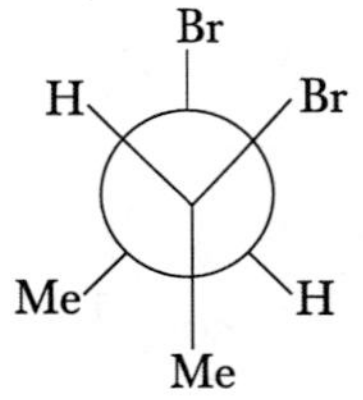

(d) 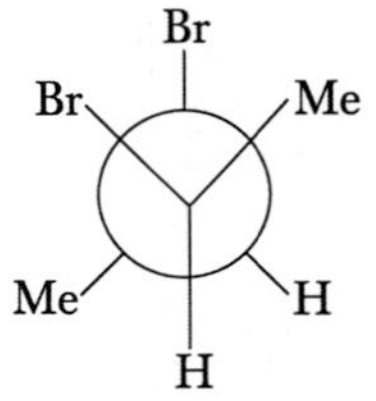

33. Which will show geometrical isomerism?

(a) $CH_2CH{=}NOH$
(b) 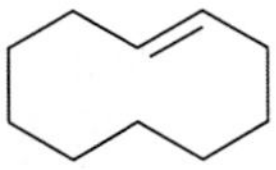
(c) $\begin{matrix}H_3C\\H_3C\end{matrix}\!>\!C{=}NOH$
(d) HO—N=N—OH

34. 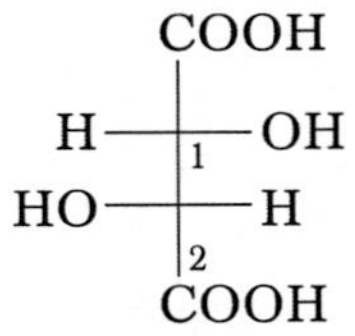

configuration at C_1 and C_2 atoms are

(a) *d* and *d*
(b) *l* and *l*
(c) *R* and *R*
(d) *R* and *S*

35. 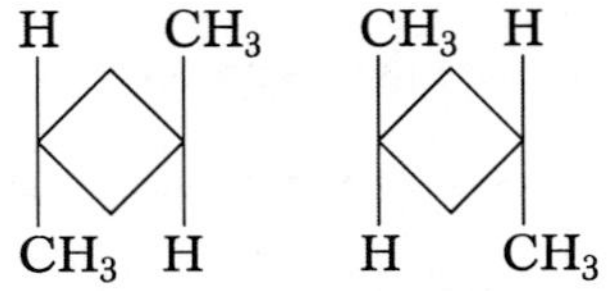

I II

I and II are

(a) achiral-idential mirror
(b) chiral-enantiomers
(c) geometrical isomer (each separately)
(d) racemic mixture

36. Which are correct statement.

(a) 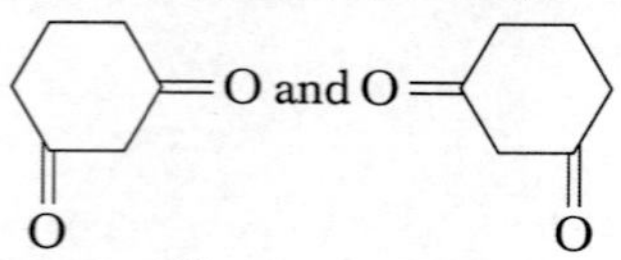 are enantiomers

(b) 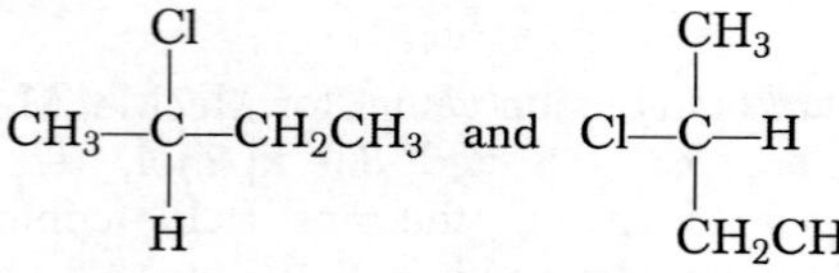 are same sructures

(c) Argol (sodium potassium tartarte) will show optical isomerism

(d) CH_3CHO on reaction with HCN gives racemic mixture

37. Which out the following are non-resolvable?

(a) 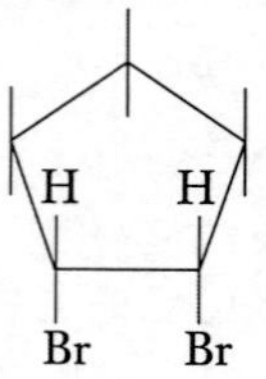

(b) 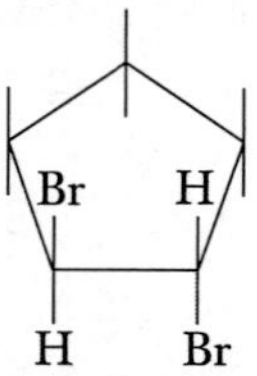

(c) 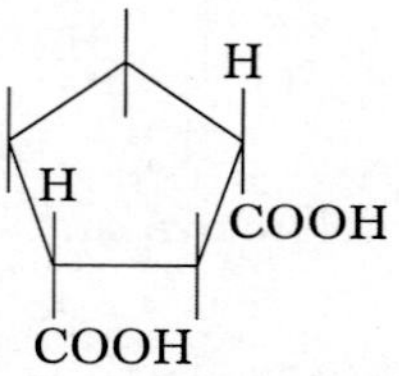

(d) 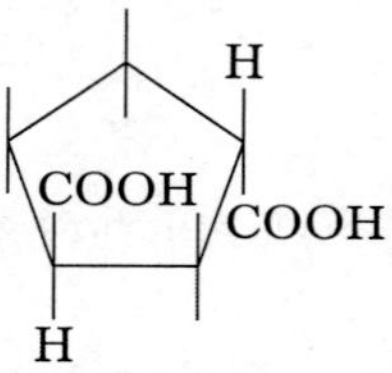

38. Which of the following will show optical isomerism as well as geometrical isomerism?

(a) 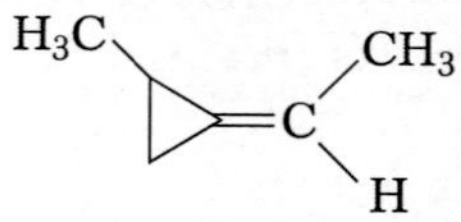

(b) 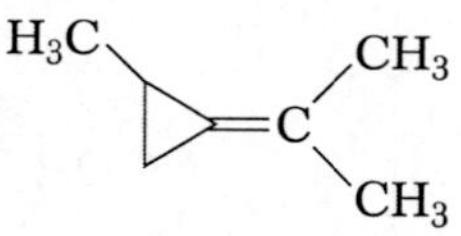

(c) 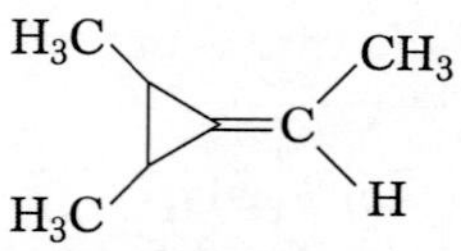

(d) 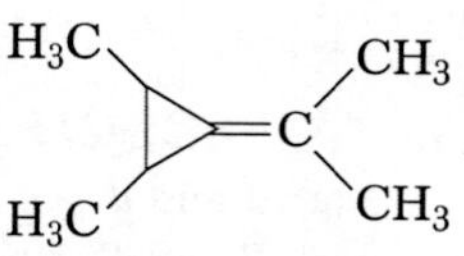

39. Which of the following statements is/are not correct for *D*-(+) glyceraldehyde?

(a) The symbol *D* indicates the dextrorotatory nature of the compounds

(b) The sign (+) indicates the dextrorotatory nature of the compounds

(c) The symbol *D* indicates that hydrogen atom lies left to the chiral centre in the Fischer projection diagram

(d) The symbol *D* indicates that hydrogen atom lies right to the chiral centre in the Fischer projection diagram

40. Which of the following is the correct representation of *L*-amino acids?

(a) 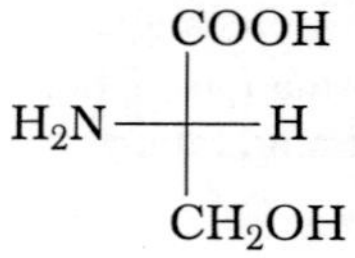

(b) 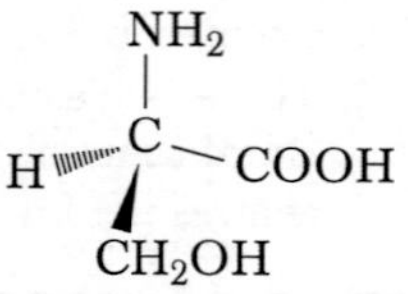

(c) 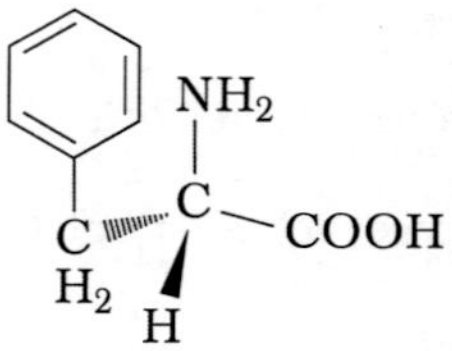

(d) 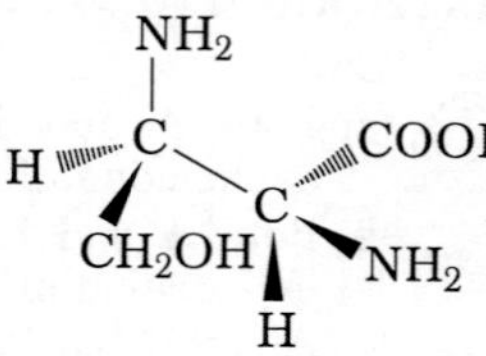

Directions (Q. Nos. 41 to 43)

Isomers are compounds that have the same chemical formula but different structures. There are two fundamental types of isomerism : constitutional isomerism and stereoisomerism.

Constitutional isomers are compounds whose atoms are connected differently. Stereoisomers are compounds whose atoms are connected in the same order but with a different geometry. Subtypes of stereoisomers include enantiomers (mirror-image stereoisomers) and diastereomers (non mirror-image stereoisomers). Further diastereomers can be classified as either *cis-trans* diastereomers or configurational diastereomers.

41. What kind of isomers are the two compounds below?

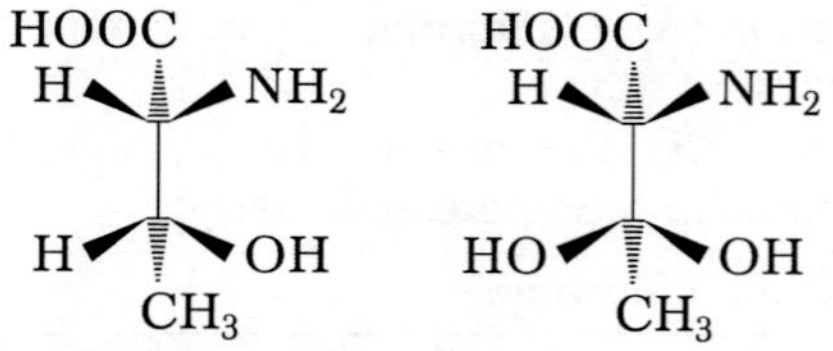

(a) Configurational diasteromers

(b) Enantiomers

(c) Constitutional isomers

(d) *Cis-trans* diastereomers

42. What kind of isomers are the two compounds below?

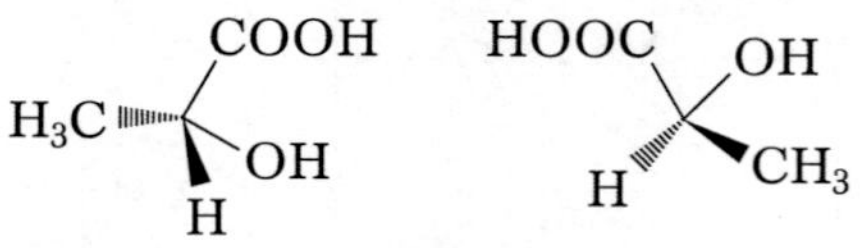

(a) Configurational diasteromers

(b) Enantiomers

(c) Constitutional isomers

(d) They are exactly the same compound

43. What kind of the isomers are the two compounds below?

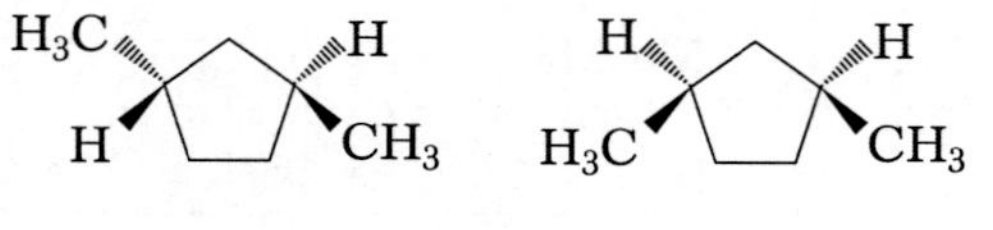

(a) Configurational diastereomers
(b) Enantiomers
(c) *Cis-trans* diastereomers
(d) They are exactly the same compound

Directions (Q. Nos. 44 and 45)
A racemic mixture containing following enantiomers are to be separated into pure enantiomers by reacting with a pure enantiomer.

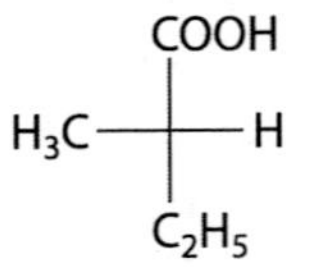

I

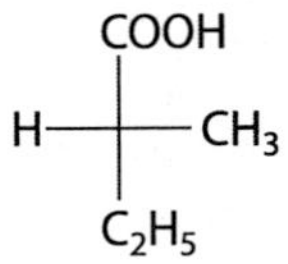

II

44. Which of the following amines can be used for the separation of the above-mentioned racemic mixture?

(a) 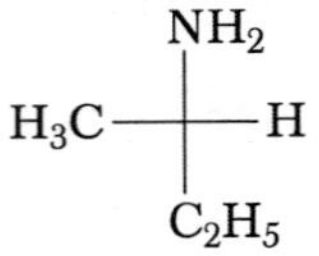

(b) 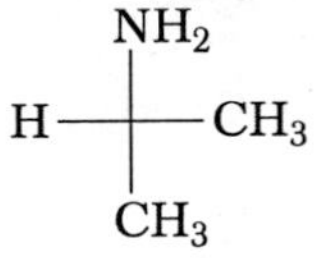

(c) 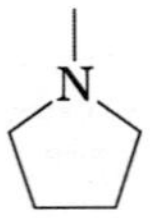

(d) 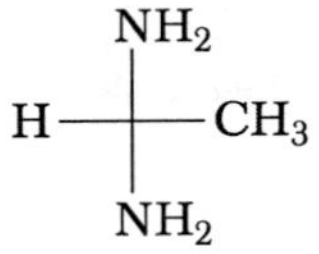

45. What would be the stereomeric relations between the products formed when the above-mentioned racemic mixture is allowed to react with desired amine of the previous question in order for the separation of racemic mixture?

(a) The products would be identical
(b) The products would be a pair of enantiomer
(c) The products would be a pair of diastereomers
(d) The products would not be stereoisomers

Directions (Q. Nos. 46 to 48)
A solution contain three stereoisomers of 2,3-dihydroxy butanedioic acid. On fractional crystallization of this solution, two fractions : **Fraction-I** and **Fraction-II** are separated. Fraction-I on reaction with (+)-2-butanamine gives a single salt while Fraction-II on reaction with the same (+)-2-butanamine gives a mixture of two salts. Answer the following three questions based on the above information.

46. What can be accurately predicted about the molecules of fraction-I?
(a) Molecules of fraction-I are enantiomers
(b) Molecules of fraction-I are *meso* compound
(c) Molecules of fraction-I are in racemic form
(d) Molecules of fraction-I has no chiral centre

47. What is the relationship between the molecules of fraction-I with the molecules of fraction-II?
(a) They are enantiomers
(b) They are identical
(c) They are diastereomers
(d) They are diastereomers as well as optically active

48. What is the relationship between the two different salts obtained from fraction-II?
(a) They are structural isomers
(b) They are enantiomers
(c) They are diastereomers
(d) They are conformers

Answers

Exercise 1

1. (c)	**2.** (b)	**3.** (b)	**4.** (a)	**5.** (b)	**6.** (b)	**7.** (c)	**8.** (d)	**9.** (b)	**10.** (b)
11. (b)	**12.** (d)	**13.** (c)	**14.** (a)	**15.** (b)	**16.** (b)	**17.** (c)	**18.** (c)	**19.** (a)	**20.** (d)
21. (d)	**22.** (a)	**23.** (a)	**24.** (b)	**25.** (a)	**26.** (d)	**27.** (a)	**28.** (a)	**29.** (b)	**30.** (b)
31. (c)	**32.** (a)	**33.** (c)	**34.** (b)	**35.** (b)	**36.** (a)	**37.** (d)	**38.** (c)	**39.** (b)	**40.** (a)
41. (a)	**42.** (a)	**43.** (b)	**44.** (d)	**45.** (c)	**46.** (b)	**47.** (d)	**48.** (a)	**49.** (b)	**50.** (b)
51. (a)	**52.** (c)	**53.** (c)	**54.** (a)	**55.** (c)	**56.** (c)	**57.** (a)	**58.** (a)	**59.** (c)	**60.** (c)

Exercise 2

1. (d)	**2.** (c)	**3.** (a)	**4.** (d)	**5.** (a)	**6.** (a)	**7.** (c)	**8.** (c)	**9.** (c)	**10.** (a)
11. (b)	**12.** (c)	**13.** (d)	**14.** (c)	**15.** (d)	**16.** (b)	**17.** (b)	**18.** (d)	**19.** (c)	**20.** (c)
21. (c)	**22.** (d)	**23.** (d)	**24.** (d)	**25.** (a)	**26.** (a)	**27.** (d)	**28.** (c)	**29.** (c)	**30.** (a)
31. (d)	**32.** (b)	**33.** (a,b,d)	**34.** (a,c)	**35.** (a,c)	**36.** (a,b,d)	**37.** (a,c)	**38.** (c,d)	**39.** (a,d)	**40.** (a,c,d)
41. (a)	**42.** (b)	**43.** (d)	**44.** (a)	**45.** (c)	**46.** (b)	**47.** (c)	**48.** (c)		

Hints & Solutions

Exercise 1

4. It has two chiral carbons as well as symmetrical. Hence, there will be a pair of enantiomers and a *meso*-form.

7. Compound(c) has two chiral carbons and no plane or centre of symmetry. Compound(d) also has two chiral carbons but it is the *meso* isomer of compound.

8. An optically active molecule has asymmetric carbon atom or chiral centre.

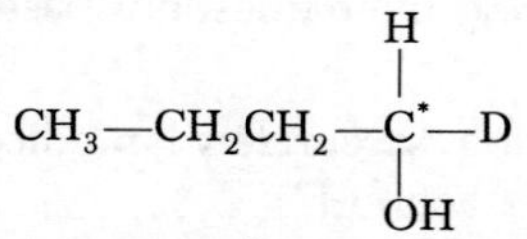

1-butanol-1-D (optically active)

14. It is a conformer of 2-methyl propane with dihedral angle 60°.

15. It has two chiral carbon and no elements of symmetry hence, four optical isomers.

18. 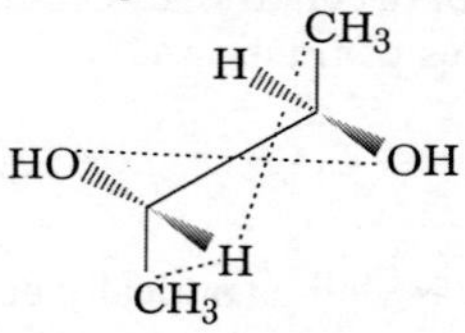

This compound has a centre of symmetry and hence, it is optically inactive.

23. 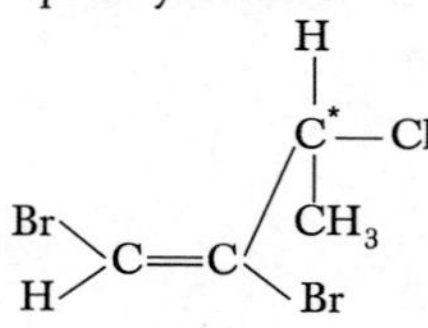
 contains a chiral carbon hence, it is optically active.

25. 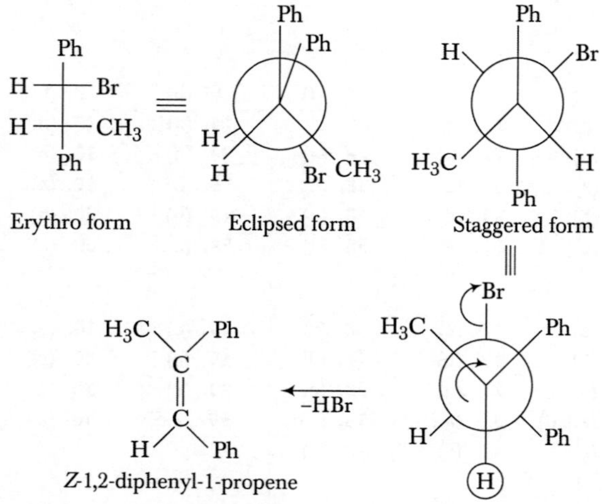

28. The structure or conformation (a) has the maximum number equatorial groups is the most stable and those with one axial group *i.e.*, (b and d) is less stable. The one with two axial groups (c) is the least stable.

29. Bromination is by *trans* (or *anti*) addition. So, addition of bromine to *cis*-2-butene yields a racemic mixture of 2, 3- dibromobutane.

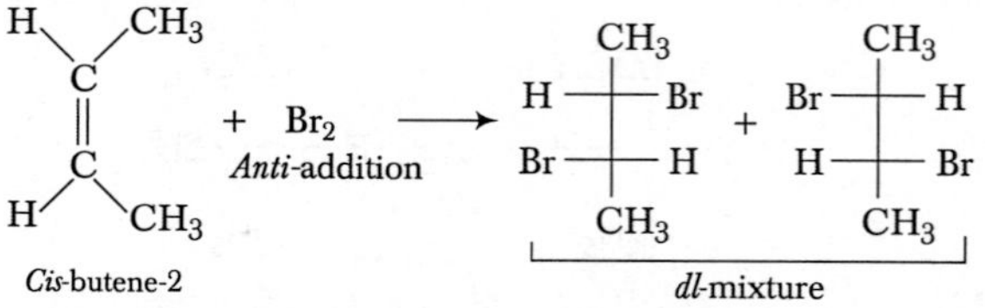

30. Structure II is eclipse hence, has more torsional strain. Also, it has more steric strain.

32. 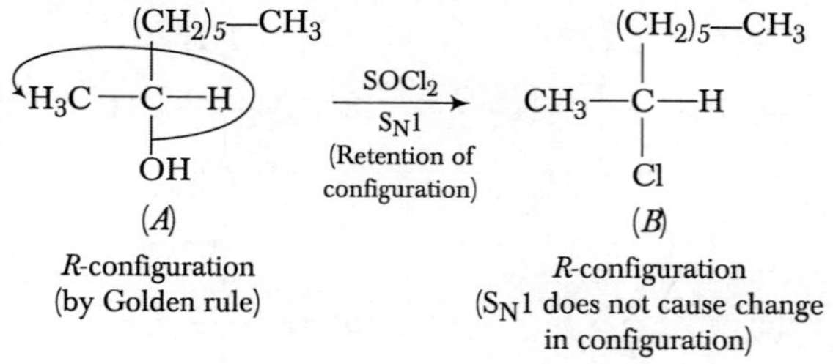

33. 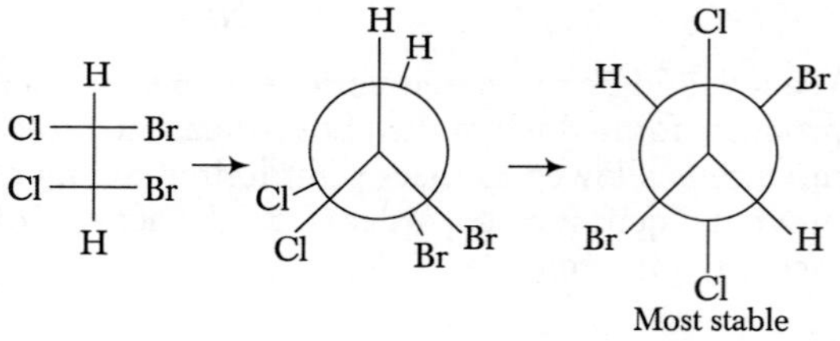

39. 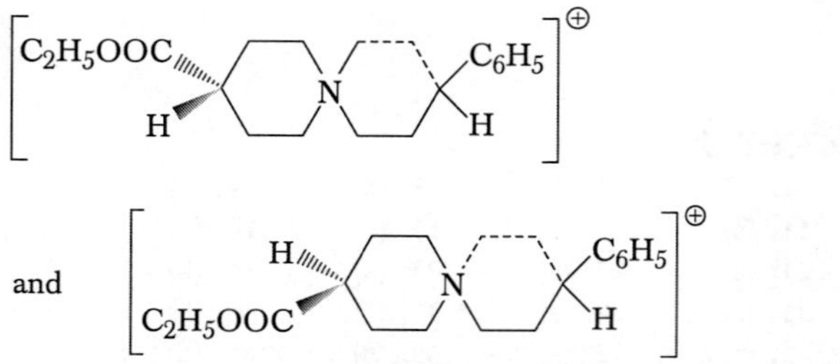

There are just two isomers which constitute a *dl*-pair.

40. The *t*-butyl group at C-4 is equatorial. Bromination is always *trans*, so 1, 2 must be *trans*. Since, 1, 2-diequatorial is *trans*, the substitutents at both C-1 and C-2 must be equatorial.

46. Diastereomers have different physical properties hence, different crystallization condition.

47. Compound *B* is polar because the two *F* are in different planes. Compound *E* is also polar.

49. *Gauche* and *anti*-conformers are stereoisomers, not related by mirror image relationship hence, diastereomers.

54. Phenylethane does not contain any asymmetric centre. All the other compounds have chiral centres and hence can show enantiomerism.

56. Compounds III and V are non-superimposable mirror images of one another.

57. The Fischer projection of the given compound is

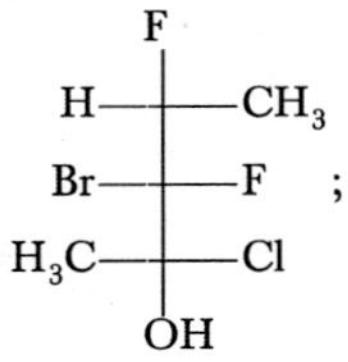

; It is enantiomer of (a).

Exercise 2

4. Both bulky groups are *trans* in the stable chair conformation of cyclohexane.

5. Both molecules III and IV have one chiral carbon each because four different groups are attached on the carbon atom.

10. I. The product could be *meso* or achiral.

   II. Unlike a racemate *meso* and achiral compounds cannot be resolved because they do not consists of enantiomers.

   III. Changing the configuration at one of the chiral C's converts one diastereomer to the other.

   IV. The term D and L do not refer to the sign of rotation. They refer to the configuration of a stereoisomer relative to that of D-glyceraldehyde.

   V. If a reaction is carried out on a compound which has no stereoisomers, it cannot be stereospecific but atmost it could be stereoselective.

13. If *trans*-decalin, the two cyclohexane rings are fused together by equatorial bonds. This cannot flip because the other form would require two axial bond of fusion, which would require the bonds pointing in opposite directions. Large rings could take up this strain, but not six-membered rings. Hence, two *trans*-decal-2-ols are possible and are not inter convertible.

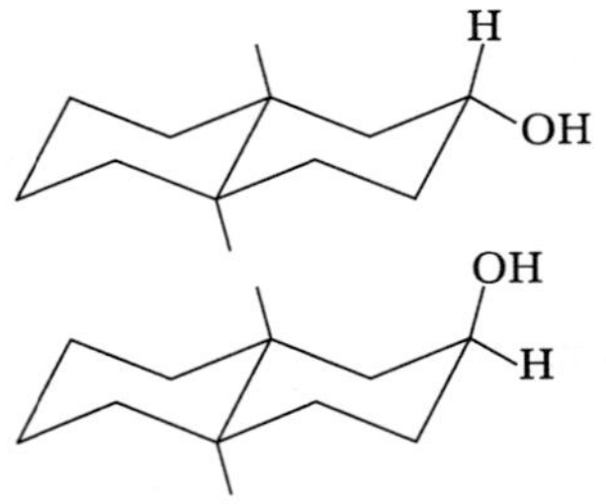

16. The pair of structures I, IV and II, III are non-superimposable mirror images hence these pair represents of pair of enantiomers.

18.

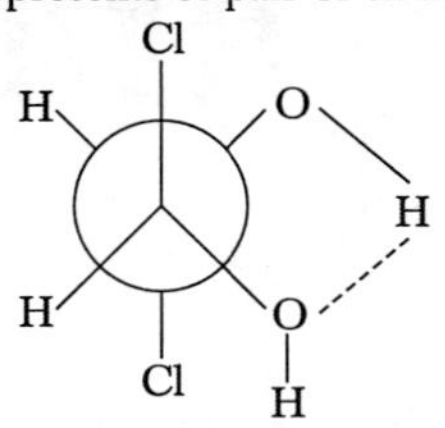

19.

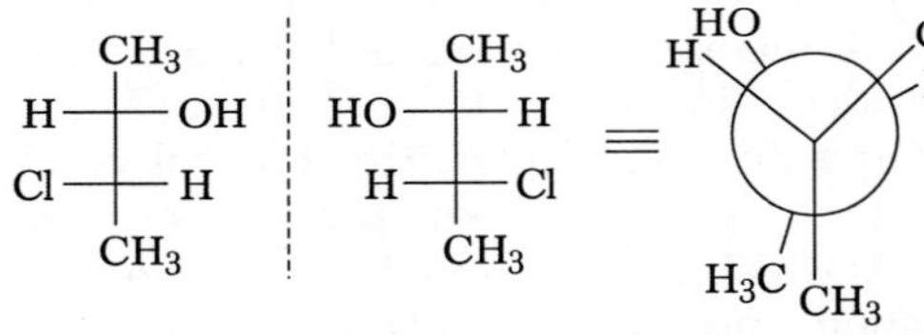

27. *Cis*-1, 3-dihydroxy cyclohexane exists in the chair form with the OH groups in the axial orientation. Presence of OH groups in the axial orientation favours H-bonding.

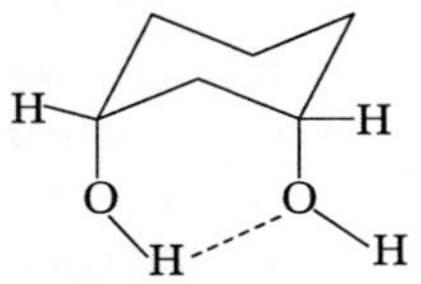

28. Flagpole-flagpole interactions are less severe in twist boat than in boat conformation.

36. Both (c, d) are capable of showing geometrical isomerism through the methyl substituents in the cyclopropyl ring. Simultaneously they are also chiral. "*a*" is chiral but does not show geometrical isomerism.

40. Conformers have very close potential energies practically impossible to resolve.

30

Aromaticity

Introduction

Originally the term aromaticity *i.e.,* aromatic characteristics was used to describe the unique properties of benzene and benzenoid compounds. These characteristics include the resistance to oxidation and addition (*e.g.,* hydrogenation), preference for substitution reactions over addition reaction etc. Later on such properties (aromaticity) were also seen in compounds which did not contain any benzene ring. The presence of alternate double bond and single bonds conferred aromaticity on the benzene ring owing to delocalization of the six π electrons over the carbon sextet.

Syllabus

- Aromaticity: Benzenoid and Non-benzenoid Compounds-Generation and Reactions

Aromaticity

Elwidge defined an aromatic compound as one which sustains an induced ring current. **Badger** defined an aromatic compound as those cyclic compound which possesses large resonance energy and where all the annular (periphery) atoms participate in single conjugated system. However, aromaticity is said to be present in compounds which have the following characteristics.

1. Presence of High Resonance Energy

Stability of a compound is explained by resonance. The greater is the number of resonating structures, the more stable is the molecule or compound. The resonating or Kekule structures of benzene are as :

I II Resonance hybrid

The increase in the number of resonating forms also increase the resonance energy and hence the stability increases *e.g.,* the resonance energy of benzene is 36 kcal/mol, pyridine is 25 kcal/mol while for the open chain conjugated dienes it is only 5 kcal/mol.

2. Planarity of Molecule

Since, the resonance involves only those atoms or π-electron which are coplanar hence another condition for the presence of aromaticity is the planarity of molecule.

3. Presence of Aromatic Sextet or Aromatic Loop

Compounds which possess aromatic sextet or loop are said to be aromatic compounds. This theory can be defined as follows in reference to benzene. There are six electrons more than required to link together the six carbon and six hydrogen atoms of the benzene ring. The six electrons, one being contributed by each carbon, unite to form a closed group or a sextet or a loop. This sextet or loop gives aromatic nature (aromaticity) to benzene and other compounds.

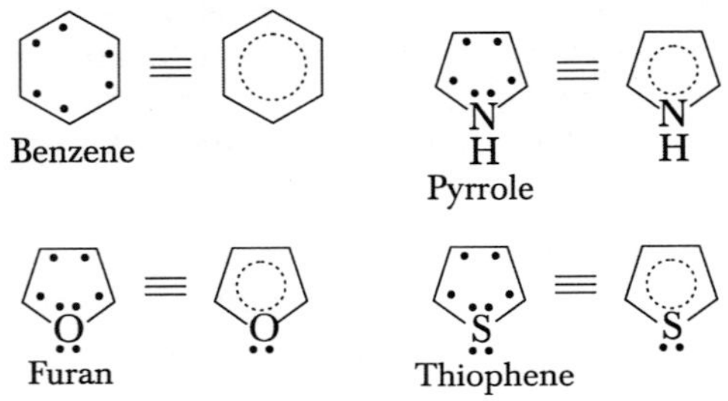

4. Presence of Delocalization of π-Electron

Benzene is a regular hexagon with all six carbon and six hydrogen atoms lying in the same plane and hence has a valency angle of 120°. All the C-atoms undergo sp^2-hybridised and hence each carbon is left with one $2p$-orbital unhydridised. All these six $2p$-orbital of the six C-atoms being parallel and equidistznt overlap each other to form a delocalised molecular orbital surrounding all these six C-atoms of benzene. The delocalization of π-electrons minimises the energy of benzene molecule leading to stabilization.

$H_2C{=}CH{-}CH_2{-}CH{=}CH_2$ less stable

$H_2C{=}CH{-}CH{=}CH{-}CH_3$ conjugate

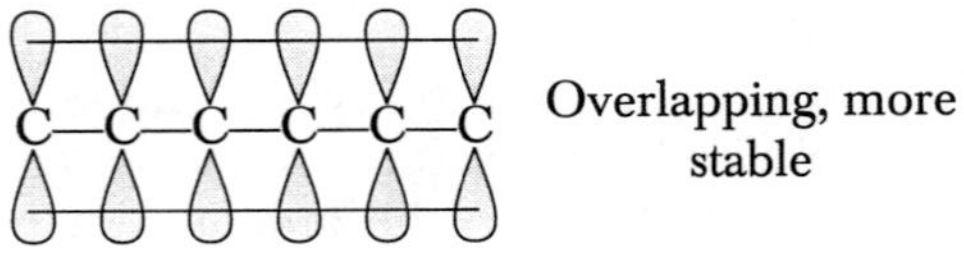

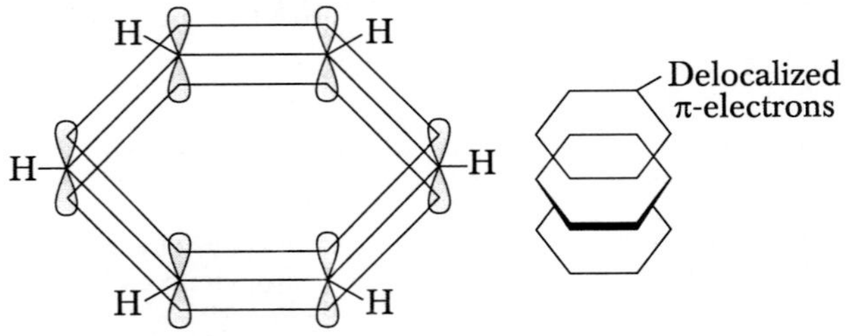

Sandwiched structure of benzene.

Note • A non-benzenoid aromatic compound does not have benzenoid ring but exhibits a degree of aromatic character.

• Aromaticity of non-benzenoid compounds can be known by Huckel's rule and Craig's rule. Huckel's rule is used in monocyclic polyenes while Craig's rule is used in bicyclic and polycyclic polyenes.

5. Presence of $(4n+2)\ \pi$ Electrons or Huckel Rule

Huckel carried out molecular orbital treatment of monocyclic conjugated system and connected aromaticity with the presence of $(4n + 2)$ π-electrons. According, to this rule, "Monocyclic conjugated polyenes possessing the symmetry of a regular polygon have a closed electron shell and consequently aromatic stability, if the number of π-electrons is in accordance with the formula $(4n + 2)\ \pi$ where, n is a integer (0, 1, 2, 3 ...). Thus, any molecule with 2, 6, 10, 14 π-electrons possess aromaticity.

Aromaticity of Compounds Containing Various Number of π-Electrons

System Containing 2π-Electrons

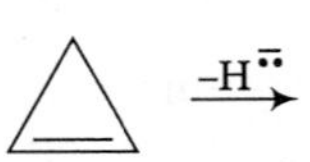

Cyclopropenyl cation

$(4 \times 0 + 2)\ \pi e^- = 2\pi e^-$

According to Huckel rule the simplest aromatic system $(n = 0)$ should have only 2π-electrons *e.g.,* cyclopropenyl cation. It is a non-benzenoid aromatic compound.

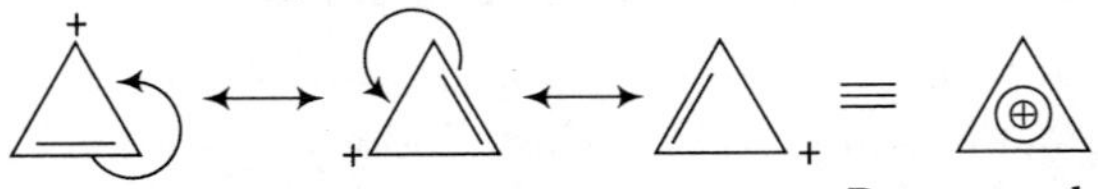

Resonance structure   Resonance hybrid

A cyclopropenyl cation with 2π-electrons corresponds to the Huckel's rule and is planar in configuration and hence shows resonance. It should show aromatic character and substituted cyclopropenyl cations have been prepared and were found to be stable despite the angle of only 60° (with a great strain).

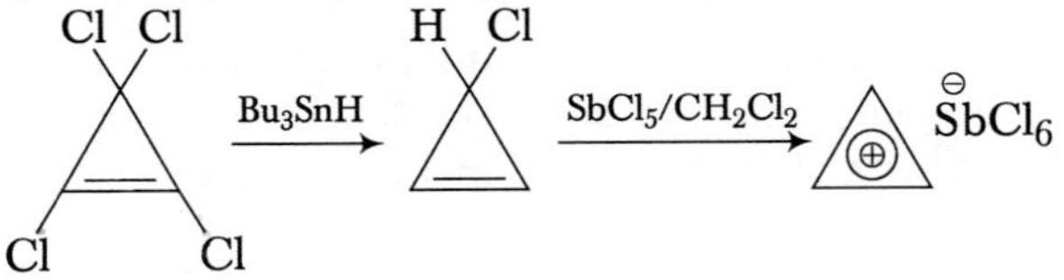

Cyclobutadienyl cations are also non-benzenoid aromatic compounds.

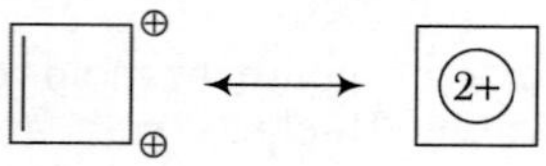

System Containing 4π-Electrons (Anti-aromaticity)

According to Huckel's rule a close system with π-electrons not in accordance with $(4n + 2)\ \pi$ should be non-aromatic. Such system like cyclopropenyl anion, cyclobutadiene, cyclopentadienyl cation and their derivatives were prepared and found not only non-aromatic but anti-aromatic.

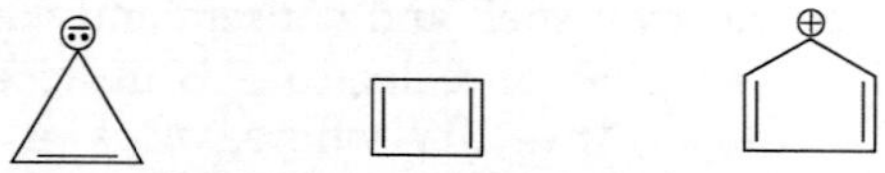

Cyclopropenyl anion $4\pi e^-$ Cyclobutadiene $4\pi e^-$ Cyclopentadienyl cation $4\pi e^-$

If these compounds simply lack aromaticity, they should be almost as stable as similar non-aromatic compounds. However, these have been found to be much less stable, *e.g.,* allyl carbanion ($CH_2{=}CH{-}\ddot{C}H_2$) is more stable than cyclopropenyl anion.

In cyclopropenyl anion the resonating structures do not give stability by conjugation but it actually losses the stability. The resonance in cyclopropenyl anion actually makes it less stable. Thus, when a closed loop of $4n$ π-electrons is taken the molecule destabilises due to resonance. Thus, any system in which cyclic delocalisation of electrons increases the energy (destabilisation), is defined as **anti-aromaticity.**

Cyclopentadienyl cation is also an example of anti-aromatic compound. When iodocyclopentane is treated with silver percolate, the molecule is readily solvalysed *i.e.,* the ion cyclopentanyl forms as an intermediate during the reaction.

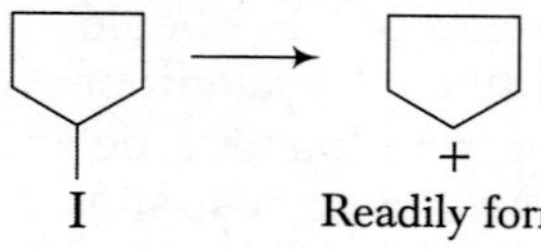

Readily form

However, under same condition iodocyclopentene does not undergo solvation *i.e.,* the cyclopentadienyl cation does not form as intermediate. It can be much less stable than ordinary ion. In other words cyclopentadienyl cation possesses anti-aromaticity.

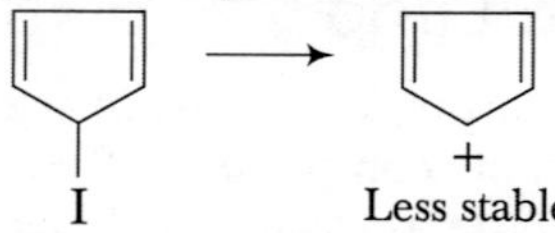

Less stable

Similarly, cyclobutadiene and its derivatives were prepared but found to be extremely unstable with a very short life period. They dimerize easily by Diels-Alder reaction.

System Containing 6π-Electrons

Those systems which are mono-cyclic planar molecules having 6π-electrons in accordance with Huckel's rule possess aromaticity, *e.g.,* benzene and its derivative along with heterocyclic compounds like pyridine, pyrrole, furan etc.

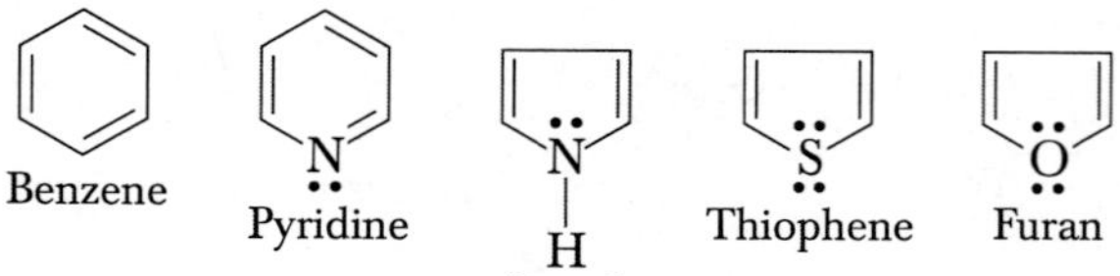

Benzene Pyridine Pyrrole Thiophene Furan

Pyrrole, thiophene and furan are known as π-excessive heteroaromatic compounds.

Apart from benzenoid and heterocyclic compounds some non-benzenoid compounds with 6π-electrons have been found to possess aromaticity.

Cyclopentadienyl anion Cyloheptatrienyl cation (Tropylium ion)

Cyclopentadienyl anion has a high resonance energy (42 kcal/mol). It can be prepared as :

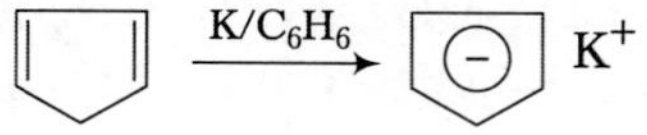

Cycloheptatrienyl cation or tropylium cation is planar, having delocalised 6π-electrons in accordance with Huckel's rule was found to be aromatic. It possesses high resonance energy 29 kcal/mol and equal distance of C—C (*i.e.,* 1.40 Å).

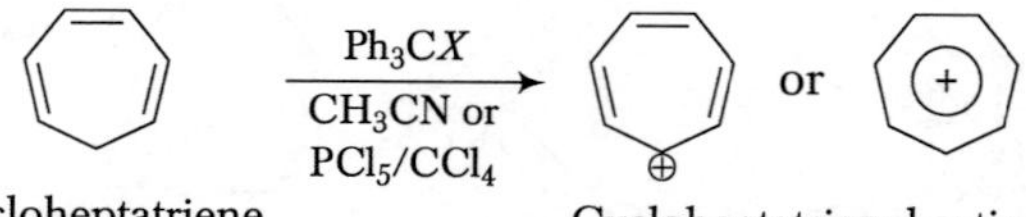

Cycloheptatriene R.E. = 6.7 kcal/mol

Cycloheptatrienyl cation or tropylium cation R.E. = 29 kcal/mol

Note • Tropone is a resonance hybrid of the following structures.

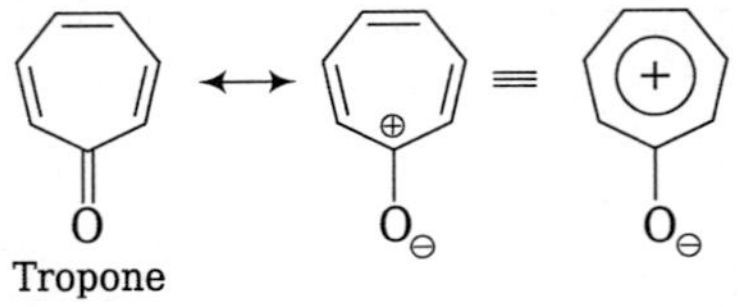

Tropone

• Chemically tropone behaves partially as an unsaturated compound and partially as aromatic compound.

The widely studied aromatic compound is tropolone having resonance energy 36kcal/mol and C—C distance of 1.39 Å. Tropolone possesses aromaticity owing to the presence of cycloheptatrienyl cation part.

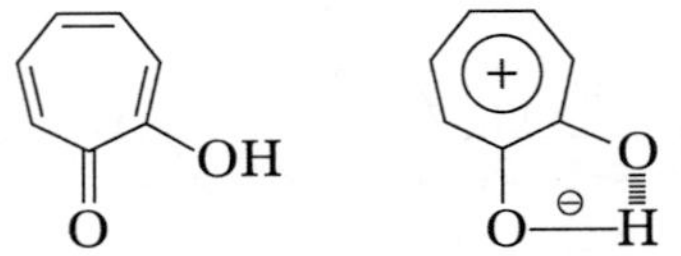

Tropolone Resonance hybrid

System Containing 8π-Electrons

Cyclooctatetraene is tub-shaped, being non-planar it should not possess aromaticity.

It would neither be an example of a aromatic compound nor an anti-aromatic compound. Since, both these conditions require resonance. It is not planar hence a regular octagon has an angle of 135° while sp^2 angles are more stable at 120°. To avoid steric strain the molecule assumes a non-planar shape in which orbital overlap is greatly diminished.

When cyclooctatetraene is dissolved in conc. H_2SO_4, a hydrogen proton adds to one of the double bond to form a **homotropylium ion.** In this species an aromatic sextet spreads over 7 C-atoms as in tropylium ion.

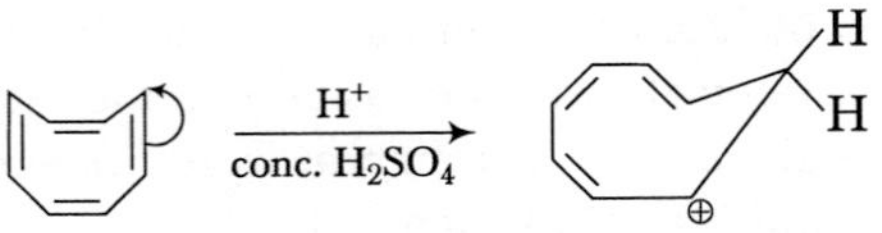

Homotropylium ion

The 8th carbon in this ion is sp^3-hybridied so cannot take part in aromaticity. NMR spectroscopy shows a presence of a diatropic ring current as in benzene. Homotropylium ion is an example of a **Homoaromatic compound** which may be defined as "A compound which contains one or more sp^3-hybridised carbon atom in an otherwise conjugated cycle *i.e.*, there is one C-atom which is sp^3 hybridised and rest is having conjugated state."

In order, for the orbitals to overlap most effectively so as to form a loop, the sp^3 atoms are forced to lie almost vertically above the plane of the aromatic atoms.

Annulenes (C_nH_n)

Annulenes are monocyclic conjugated polyenes (C_nH_n) containing six or more than six carbon atoms. They are commonly named as [*n*] annulenes. *e.g.*, benzene is [6] annulene because it has 6 C-atoms. Here, we will discuss aromaticity of various annulenes which come under $(4n + 2)$ system *i.e.*, Huckel's rule.

[10] Annulenes

An annulene with 10π-electrons or [10] annulene may also be named as cyclodecapentaene. [10] Annulene can exist in three isomeric forms : di-*trans* [10] annulene, all *cis*-[10] annulene, and mono-*trans* [10] annulene.

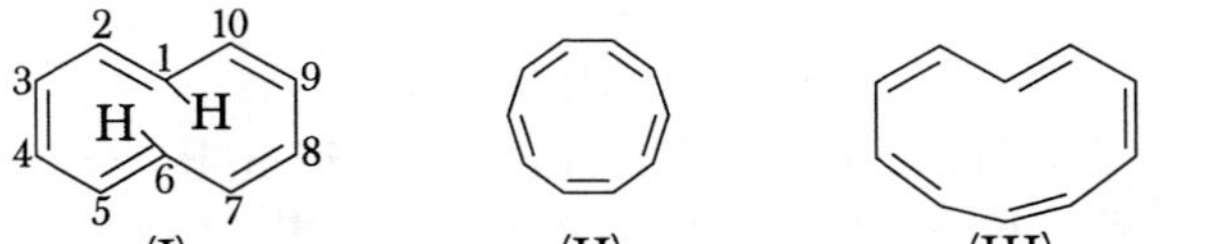

(I) *trans, cis, trans, cis, cis,* Cyclodecapentaene

(II) *cis, cis, cis, cis, cis* Cyclodecapentaene

(III) *trans, cis, cis, cis, cis* Cyclodecapentaene

Although these isomers have $(4n + 2)$ π-electrons, they are not aromatic. It has been found that it is not to be stable and thus non-aromatic. The low stability of [10] annulene(I) is due to its non-planar structure. The non-planarity is due to the steric repulsion produced between the two inner hydrogen atoms, present at C_1 and C_6. The compound behaves as olefinic compound and does not show magnetic properties required for aromaticity.

If the inner H-atoms were replaced by a methylene bridge, the molecule should become planar allowing delocalization of π-electrons and thus giving aromaticity to the compound.

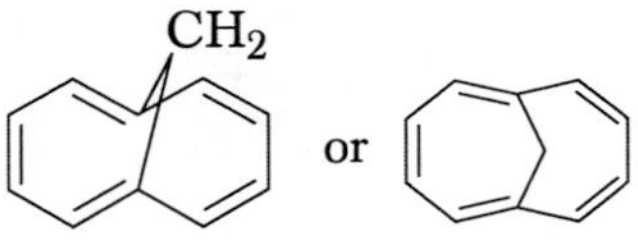

[14] Annulene

[14] annulene obeys Huckel's rule but models and scale drawings indicate that the four inner hydrogens overlap so that a planar molecule is unlikely. [14] annulene is a diatropic molecule. Although [14] annulene is aromatic, the overlapping of the van der Waals' radii of the four inner hydrogens reduces its aromaticity. Hence, [14] annulene is not very stable. It is completely destroyed by light and air in 24 hours. X-ray study shows that although alternating single or double bond, the molecule is non-planar due to steric repulsion.

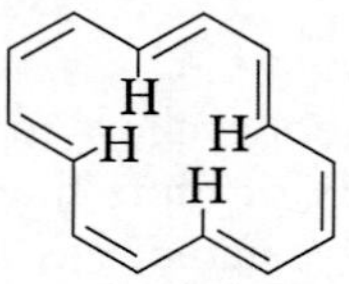

[14] annulene

However, the bridged compounds of [14] annulene are stable, planar and diatropic.

Another way of eliminating free hydrogen interferences of [14] annulene is to introduce one or more triple bonds into the system as in dehydro [14] annulene.

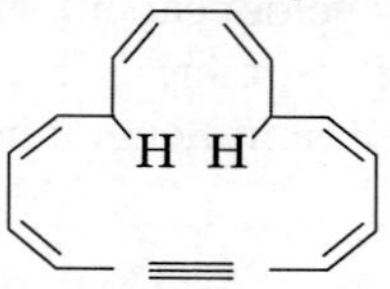

Dehydro [14] annulene

Dehydro [14] annulene is diatropic and can be nitrated and sulphonated. The extra electrons of the triple bond do not form part of the aromatic system but simply exist as localised bonds.

Azulene

Azulene is a deep blue compound. It is isomeric with naphthalene and less stable than naphthalene. It is a bicyclic non-benzenoid aromatic compound. Azulene on heating above 350°C isomerises to naphthalene. The dipolar structure azulene satisfies the Huckel rule, it shows considerable aromatic character.

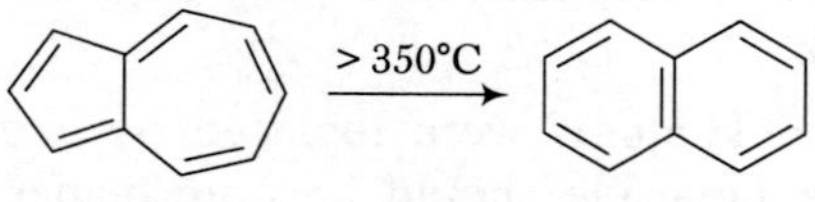

Azulene Naphthalene

Azulene is prepared from fulvene.

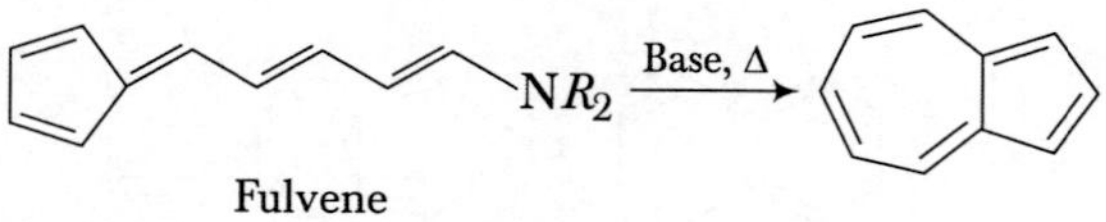

Fulvene

Azulene does not undergo autoxidation. It is capable of undergoing electrophilic substitution reactions in five membered ring. It forms azulenium cation with strong acid.

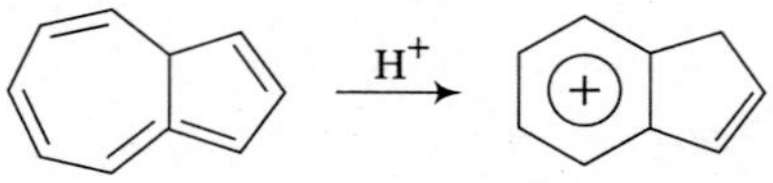

Azulenium cation

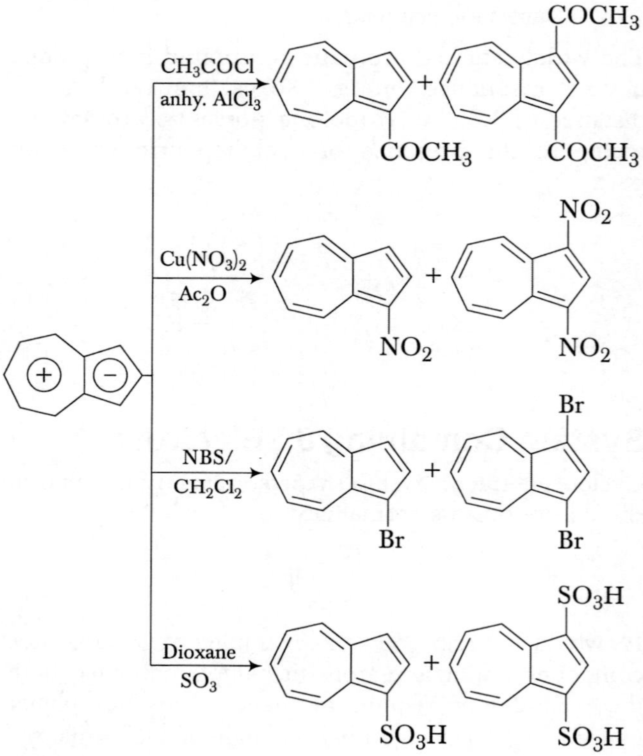

Polycyclic Aromatic Compounds

Aromatic compounds, such as naphthalene, anthracene, phenanthrene and pyrene in which the aromatic rings share at least one side are known as **polycyclic aromatic compounds** and are said to contain **fused ring system.**

In systems of fused six membered aromatic rings, the principal canonical forms are usually not all equivalent *e.g.*, in naphthalene (a) is different from (b) and (c), (b) and (c) are equivalent to each other.

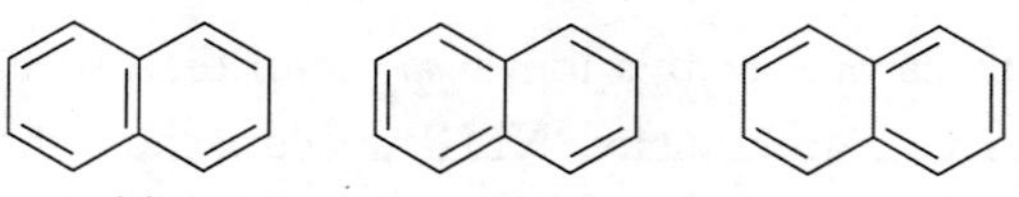

(a) (b) (c)

The 1-2 bond has more double bond character than the 2-3 bond. M.O. calculations shows bond order of 1.724 and 1.603 respectively (compare benzene 1.667). Ozone preferentially attacks the 1-2 bond. This non-equivalency on bonds is called **partial bond fixation** and is found in nearly all fused aromatic systems. In phenanthrene-9, 10 bonds have partial bond fixation. Anthracene undergoes many reactions across 9, 10 positions.

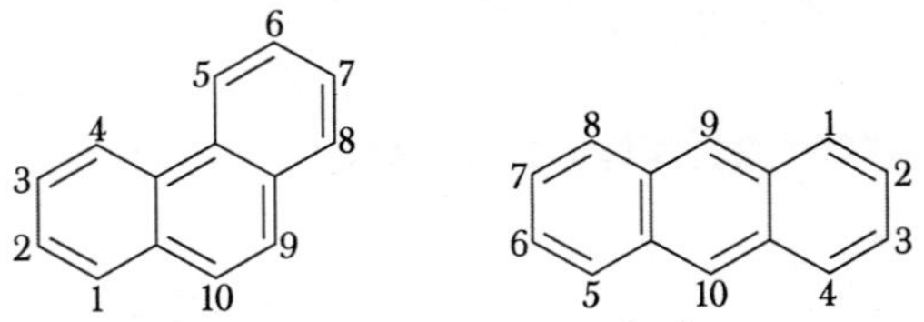

Phenanthrene Anthracene

Not all fused system can be fully aromatic, phenalene (I) is not aromatic but the corresponding anion (II) is aromatic.

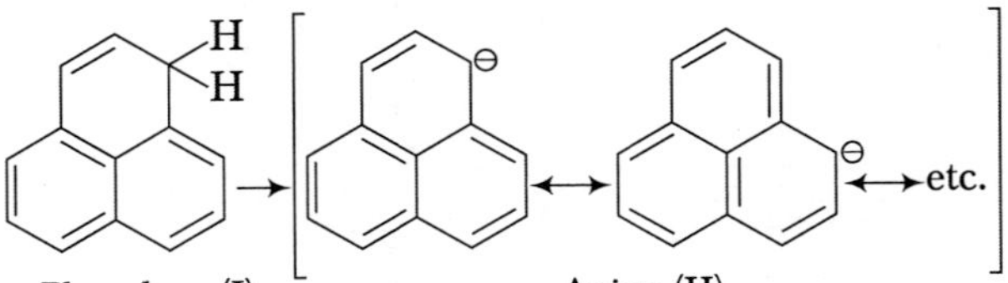

Phenalene (I) Anion (II)

In the case of triphenylene, there are eight canonical forms like (a) and only one like (b).

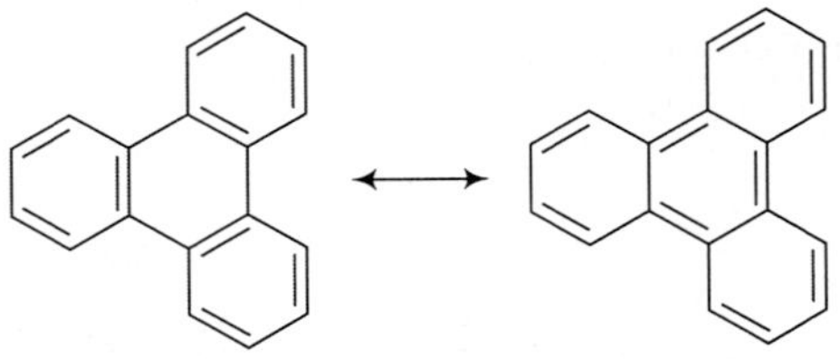

(a) (b)

Thus, the molecule behaves as if the 18π-electrons were distributed so as to give each of the outer rings a sextet; while the middle ring is "empty".

Since none of the outer rings need share their electrons with an adjacent ring, they are as stable as in benzene. It is unlike most fused aromatic hydrocarbons.

This phenomenon, whereby some rings in fused systems give up part of their aromaticity to adjacent rings called **annulation,** can be detected as low reactivity and changes in UV spectra.

Preparation of Polycyclic Aromatic Compounds

By Fittig reaction

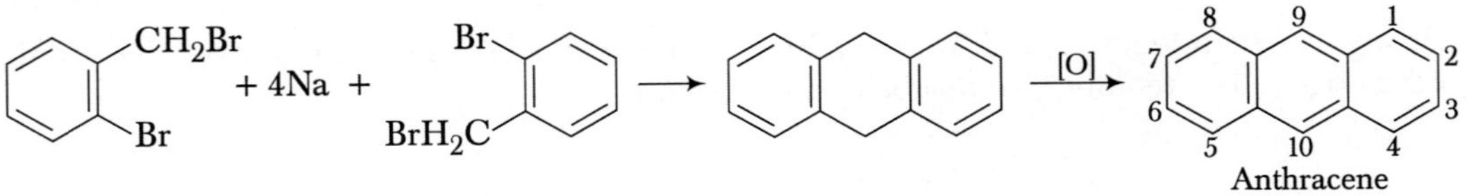

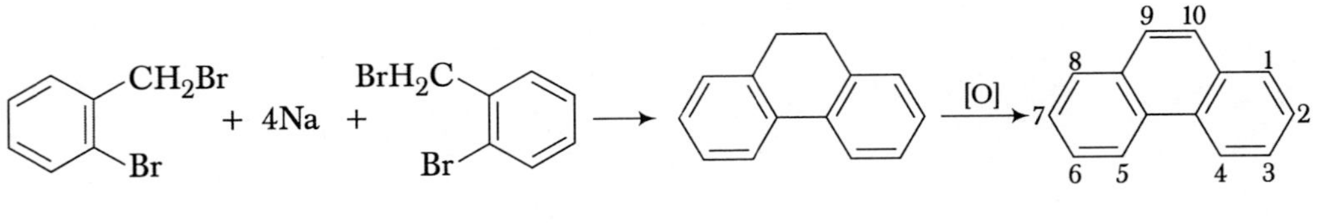

By Elbs reaction

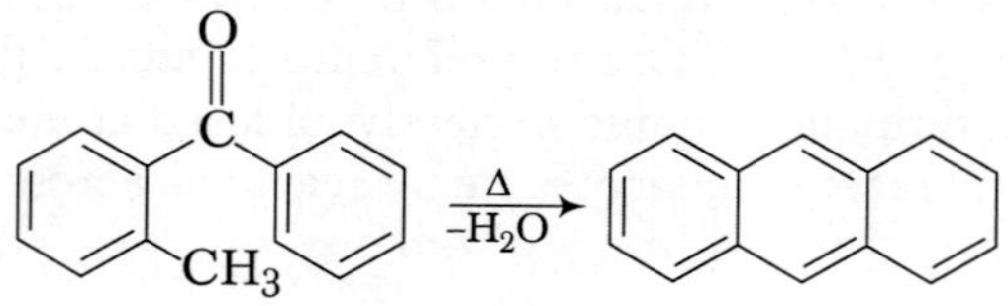

Reactions of Polycyclic Aromatic hydrocarbons

Electrophilic substitution reaction

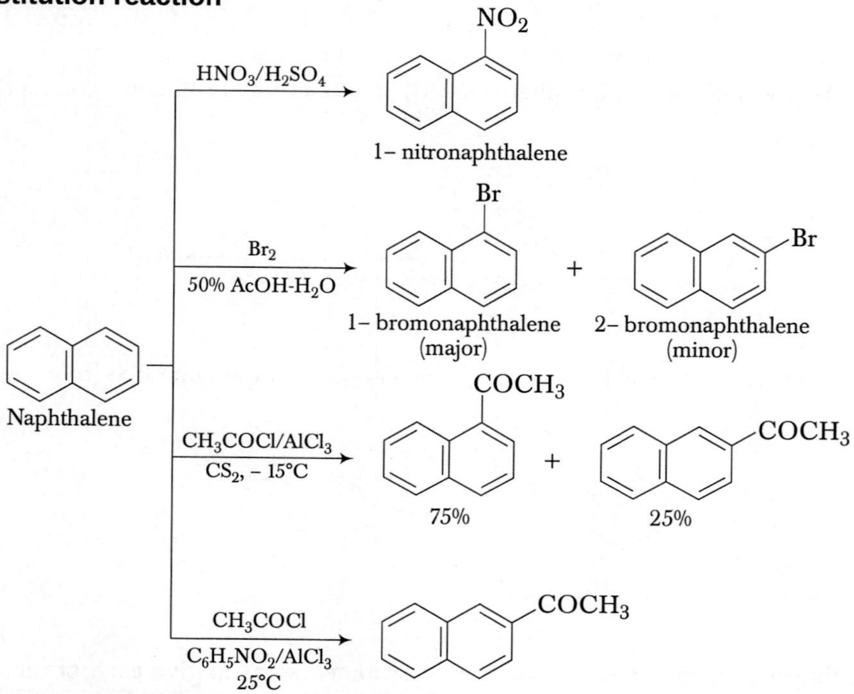

Note • Sulphonation of naphthalene is a reversible reaction.

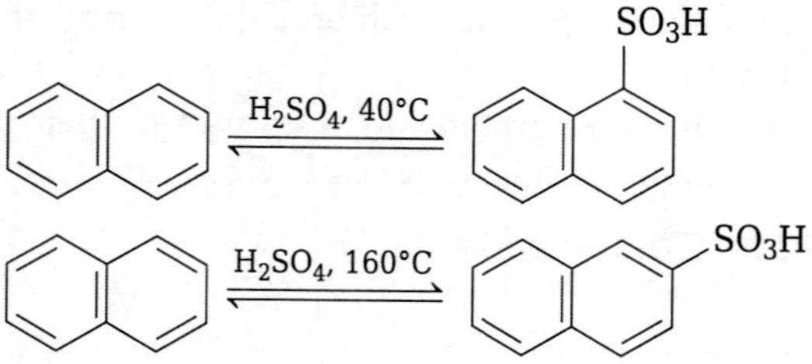

Anthracene has a greater tendency to add to the 9, 10 positions than to substitute. However the addition products of nitration and halogenation readily give 9-substitution products.

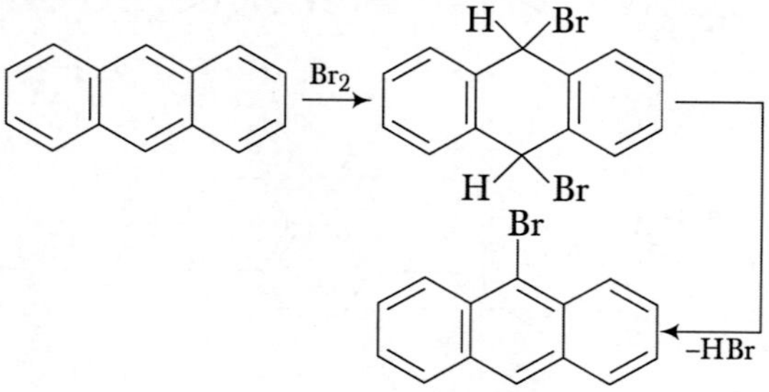

Oxidation reactions

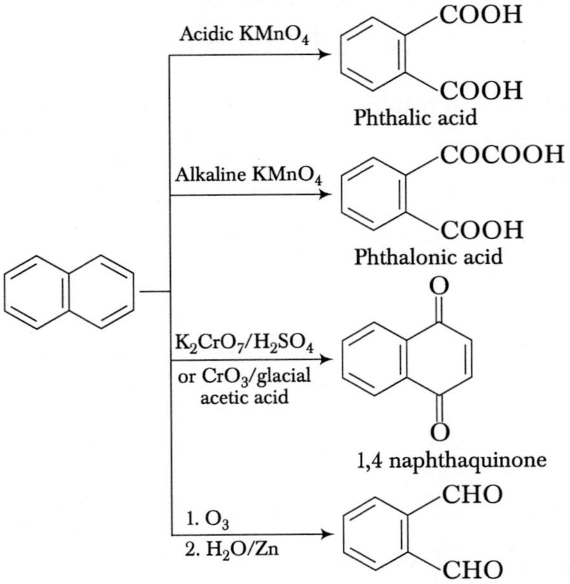

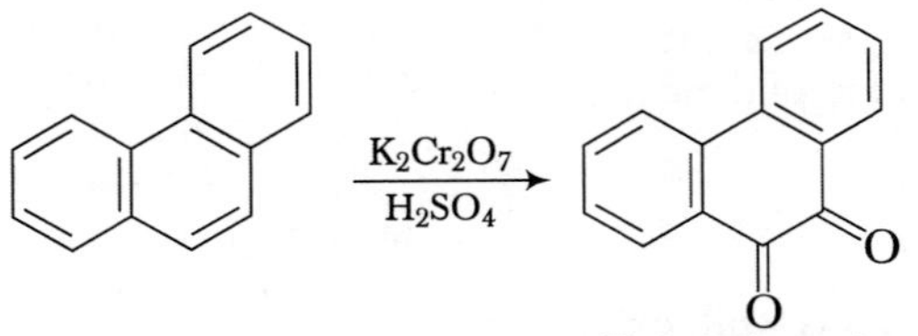

Phenanthraquinone

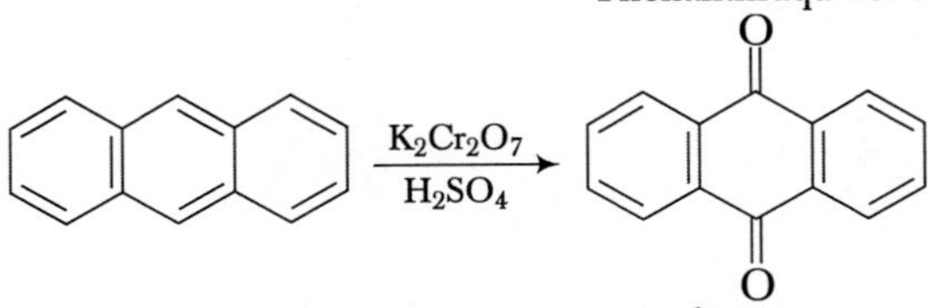

Anthraquinone

Note • The polycyclic hydrocarbons which produce cancer in the body are known as carcinogenic polycyclic hydrocarbons. They are mainly found in coal tar, tobacco tar, soot, shale oil etc. 20-methylcholanthrene is the most potent in producing skin cancer followed by 3, 4-benzpyrene and 1, 4-benzanthracene.

Exercise 1
(For Part 'B')

1. Among the following, the aromatic compound is

(a) 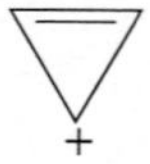 (b) 

(c) 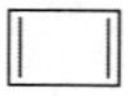 (d) 

2. Which of the following is not aromatic?

(a)  (b) 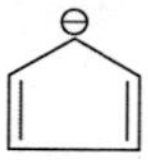

(c)  (d) 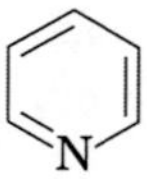

3. C_6H_6 consists of one ring, while naphthalene consists of two rings. Both of them are aromatic and obey the $(4n+2)\pi$ rule. Thus, the number of π-electrons inside rings of C_6H_6 and naphthalene are respectively

(a) 3, 5 (b) 5, 10
(c) 6, 10 (d) 6, 12

4. Which of the following hydrocarbons will exhibit aromatic stabilisation?

(a)  (b) 

(c)  (d) 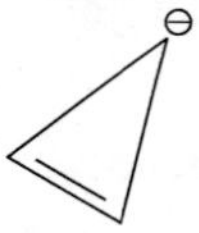

5. Which of the following are aromatic?

(a) 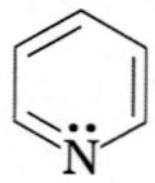 (b) 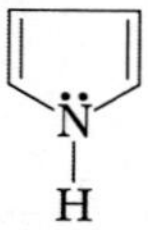

(c) 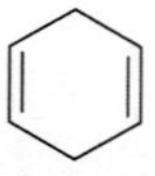 (d) Both (a) and (b)

6. Which, if any of the following structures represents an aromatic species?

(a) 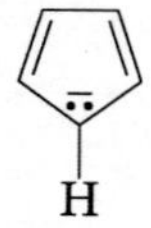 (b) 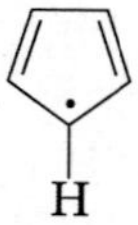

(c) 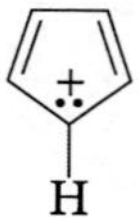 (d) None of these

7. Which of the following is best classified as heterocyclic aromatic compound?

(a) 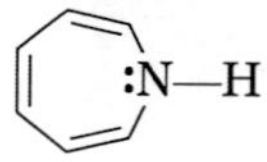 (b) 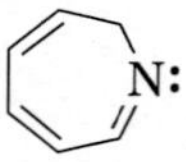

(c) 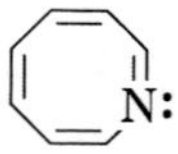 (d) 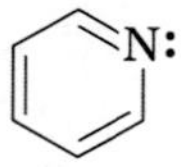

8. Cyclopentadiene is some 10^{30} times more acidic than cyclopentane. It is because

(a) cyclopentadiene is a conjugated olefin
(b) cyclopentadiene has both sp^2 and sp^3-hybridised carbon atoms
(c) loss of a proton from $-CH_2$ group of cyclopentadiene results in the formation of a stable anion
(d) cyclopentadiene is stable due to aromatic character

9. Nitration of benzene with conc. H_2SO_4 and HNO_3 at 333K gives

(a) nitrobenzene (b) 1, 3-dinitrobenzene
(c) 1, 3, 5-trinitrobenzene (d) nitrosobenzene

10. Which among the following is a better Diels Alder diene reacting with maleic anhydride?

(a)  (b) 

(c)  (d) 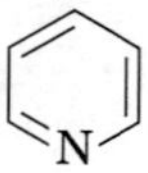

11. Which of the following is non-aromatic?

(a) 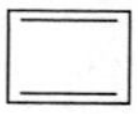 (b) 

(c) 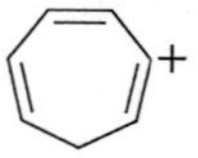 (d) 

12. Which of the following is anti-aromatic?

(a) 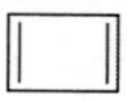 (b) 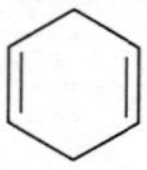

(c) 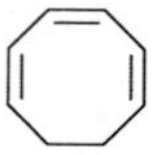 (d) 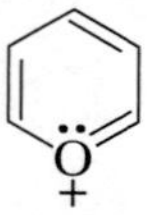

13. 1, 3, 5-cycloheptatriene can be converted to an aromatic substance by

(a) hydrogen atom abstractions
(b) hydride abstraction
(c) proton abstraction
(d) H_2 elimination

14. What is the product of the following acid-base reaction?

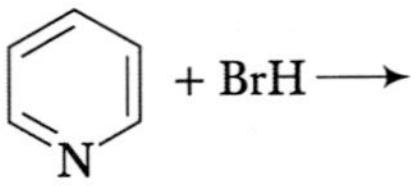

(a) 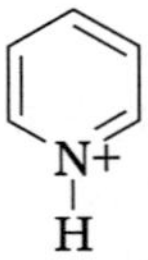

(b) 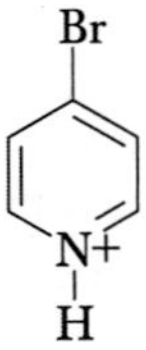

(c) 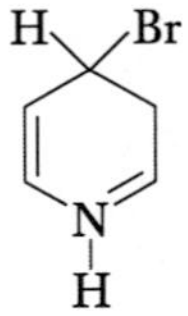

(d) 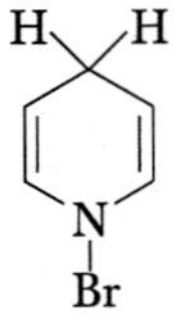

15. Which of the following resonance structure is not aromatic?

(a) 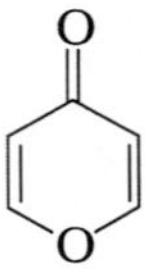

(b) 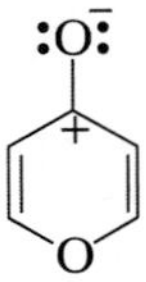

(c) 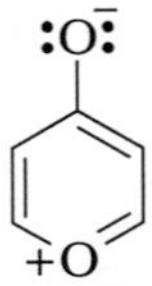

(d) 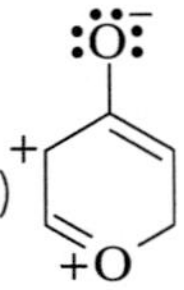

16. Which is the most likely to be protonated in the molecule below?

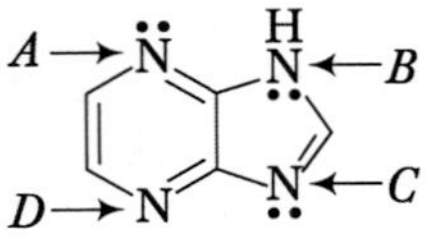

(a) *A*
(b) *B*
(c) *C*
(d) *D*

17. Which of these is anti-aromatic?

(a) 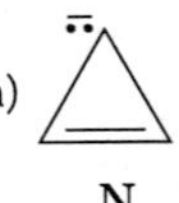

(b) 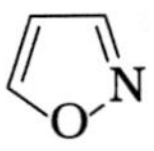

(c) 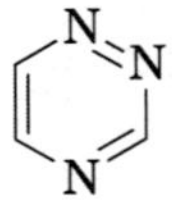

(d) 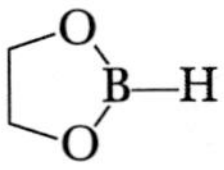

18. Which of the following compound(s) is/are aromatic?

(a) 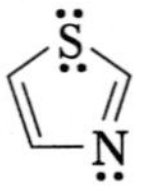

(b) 

(c) 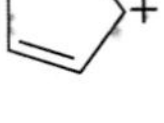

(d) All of these

19. Which of the following is aromatic?

(a) 

(b) 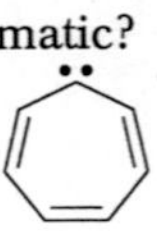

(c) 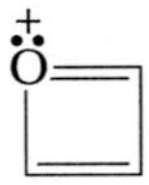

(d) None of these

20. The one among the compounds given below, with highest dipole moment is
(a) naphthalene
(b) phenanthrene
(c) anthracene
(d) azulene

21. C_{60} has
(a) 14 pentagons and 18 hexagons
(b) 12 pentagons and 20 hexagons
(c) 10 pentagons and 20 hexagons
(d) 12 pentagons and 18 hexagons

22. The following hydrocarbon has a dipole moment of 0.8 D because

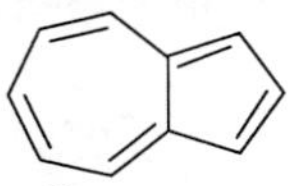

(a) it exists as 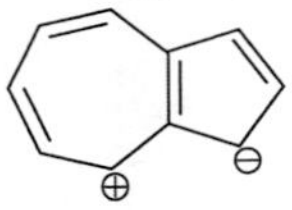 in which both the rings exhibit aromaticity
(b) charge separation permits conformational stability
(c) the two rings are of different size
(d) the molecule obeys $4n + 2$ Huckel rule

23. Among the resonance forms given below, the one which contributes most to the stability of azulene is

(a) 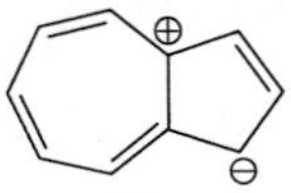

(b) 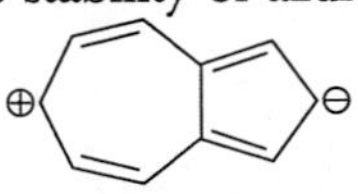

(c) 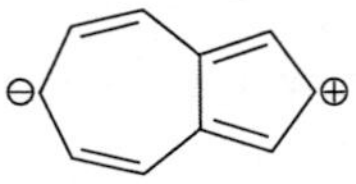

(d) 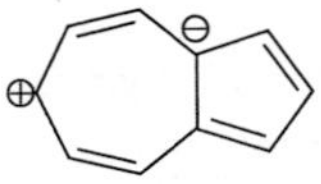

24. Which one of the following substances is not aromatic?

(a) 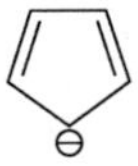

(b) 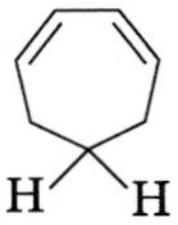

(c) 

(d) 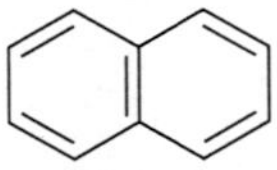

25. Which has maximum dipole moment?

(a) 

(b) 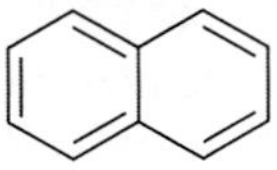

(c) 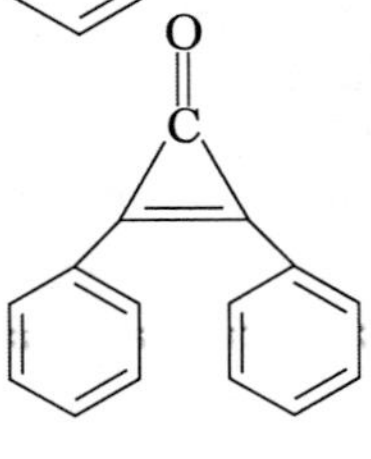

(d) 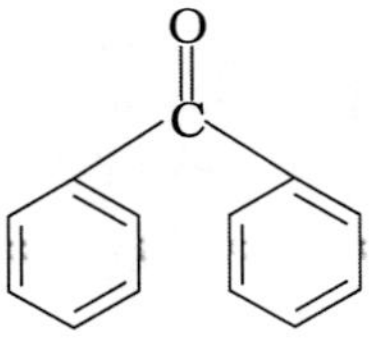

26. Which of the following carbocations would be the most stable?

(a) 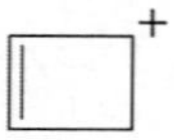
(b) 
(c) 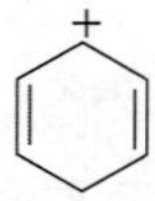
(d) 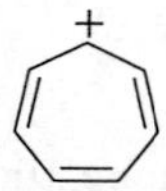

27. Which of the following would most readily react with a strong base, such as $NaNH_2$?

(a) 
(b) 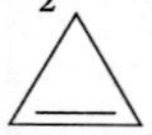
(c) 
(d) 

28. Which of the following compounds would not be considered aromatic in its behaviour?

(a) 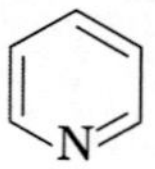

(b) 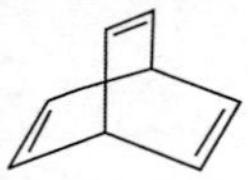
(c) 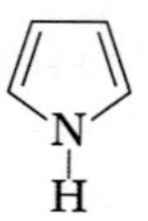

(d) 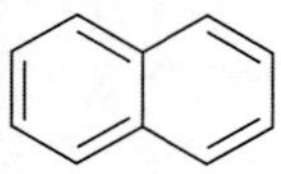

29. Which of the following heterocyclic compounds would have aromatic character?

(a) 

(b) 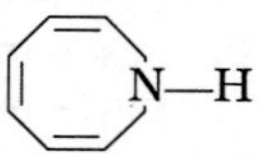

(c) 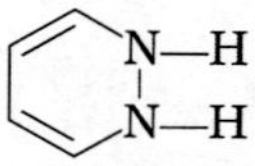

(d) 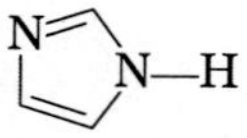

30. Assuming that all are planar, which structure would be aromatic?

(a) 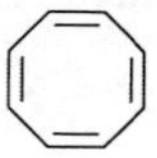
(b) 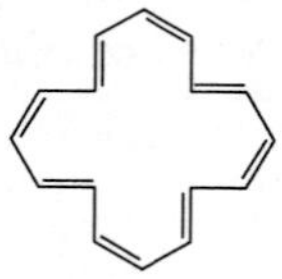
(c) 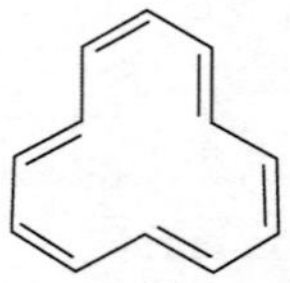
(d) 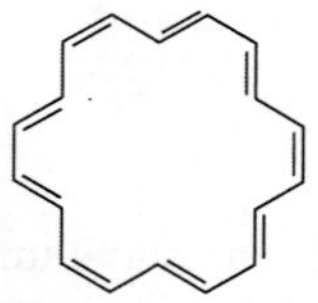

31. Which statement regarding Huckel's rule is false?
(a) There must be $(4n + 2)$ π-electrons
(b) The molecule must be planar
(c) The molecule must be cyclic
(d) Each of the π-electrons must be associated with a conjugated double bond

32. How many uncharged resonance structure are there for azulene?

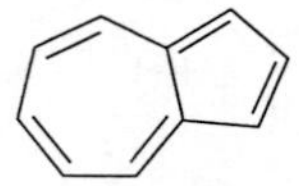

(a) 1 (b) 2
(c) 3 (d) 4

33. Which of the following structures is least likely to be a resonance form of the others in the group?

(a) 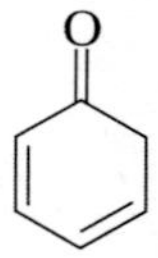

(b) 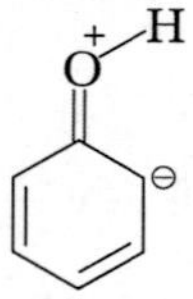

(c) 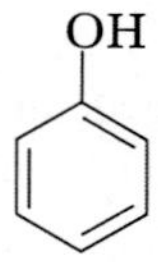

(d) 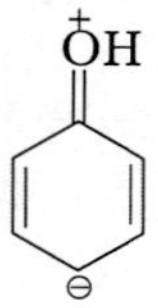

34. According to simple Huckel theory, which of the following rings should not be aromatic?

(a) 
(b) 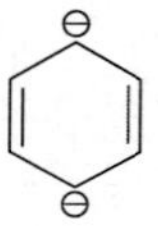
(c) 
(d) 

35. Which of the following compound would exhibit aromatic properties?

(a) 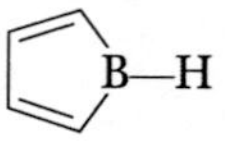

(b) 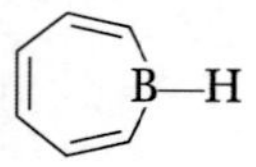

(c) 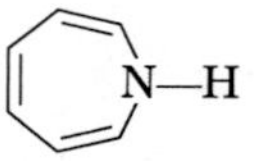

(d) 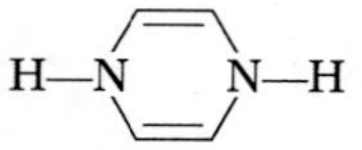

36. Which of the following compound is not aromatic?

(a) 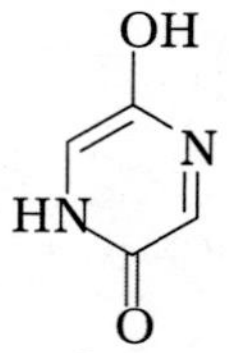

(b) 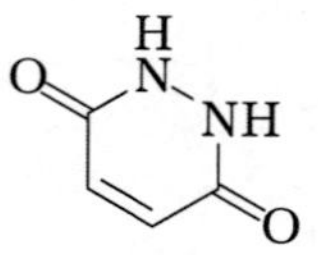

(c) 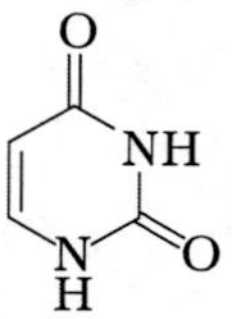

(d) 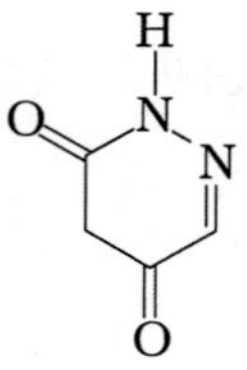

37. Which of the following compounds forms *ortho*-benzenedicarboxylic acid when oxidized by hot aqueous potassium permanganate?

(a) 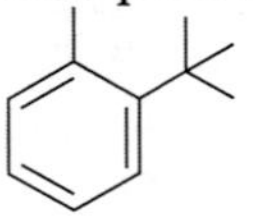 (b) 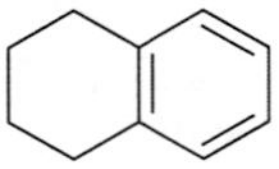

(c) 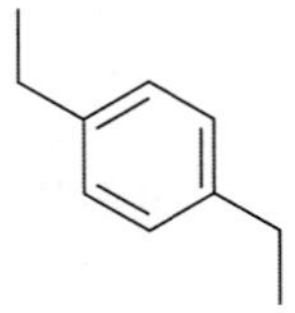 (d) 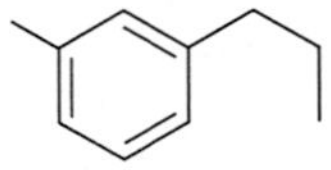

38. Which of the following is related to Huckel rule?
(a) $(4n + 4)$ π-electrons (b) $(4n + 1)$ π-electrons
(c) $4n\pi$-electrons (d) $(4n + 2)$ π-electrons

39.  + PhBr ⟶ Product.

Product is

(a) 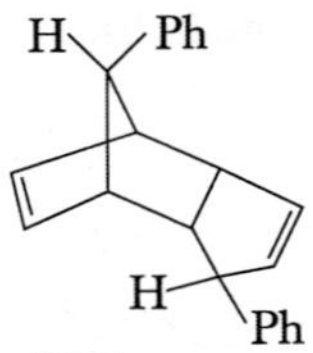 (b) 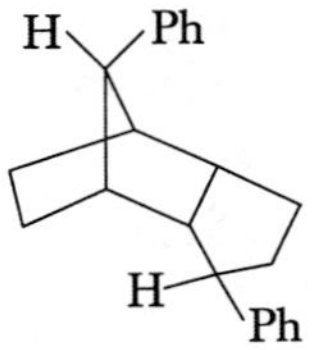

(c) 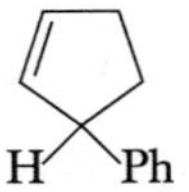 (d) None of these

40. Tropylium cation reacts with NH_3 to give

(a) 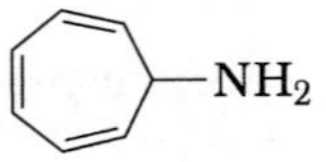 (b) 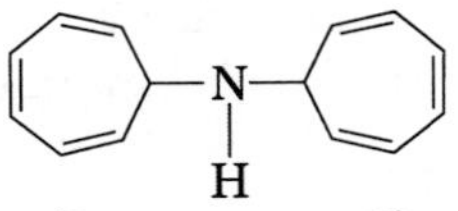

(c) 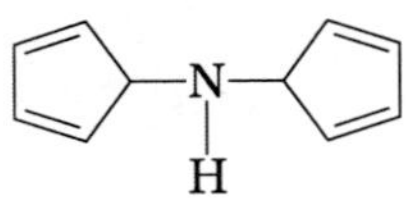 (d) 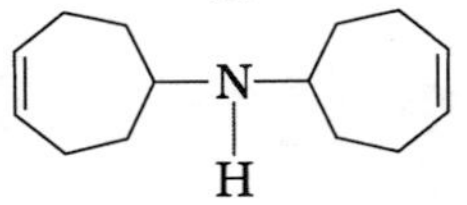

41. 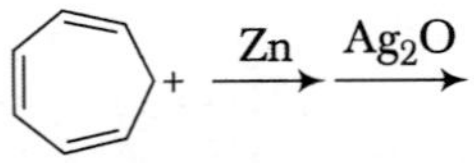

The end product of the reaction is
(a) C_6H_5COOH (b) C_6H_5CHO
(c) $C_6H_5COCOOH$ (d) $C_6H_5CH_2OH$

42. 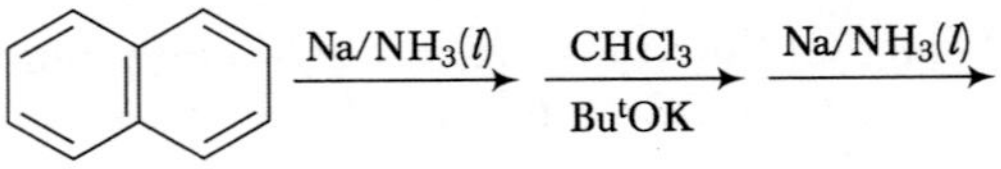

$\xrightarrow{\text{DDQ}}$ Product.

The product is
(a) 1, 6-methano [10] annulene
(b) [14] annulene
(c) dehydro [14] annulene
(d) [10] annulene

43. 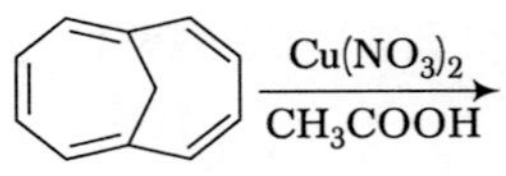 Product.

The product(s) is/are

(a) 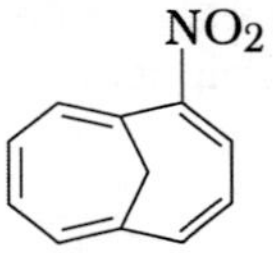 (b) 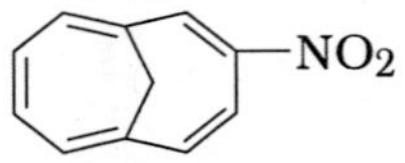

(c) Both (a) and (b) (d) None of these

44. Which of the following molecule(s) or ion(s) is/are aromatic?

(a) 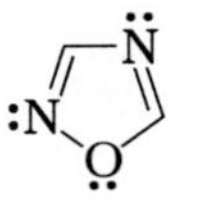 (b) 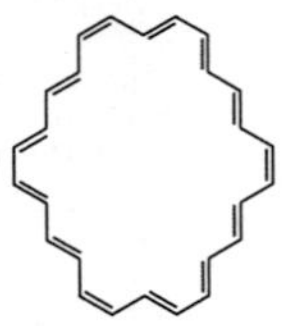

(c) 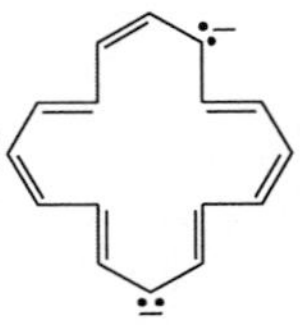 (d) All of these

45. In which of the following cases, reactants and products are correctly matched?

(a) 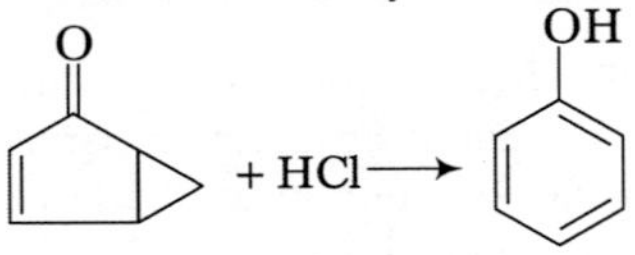

(b) 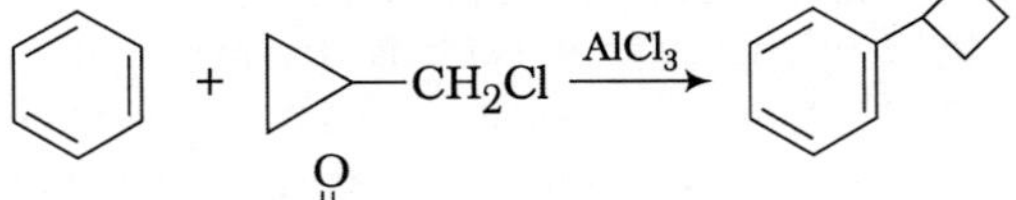

(c) 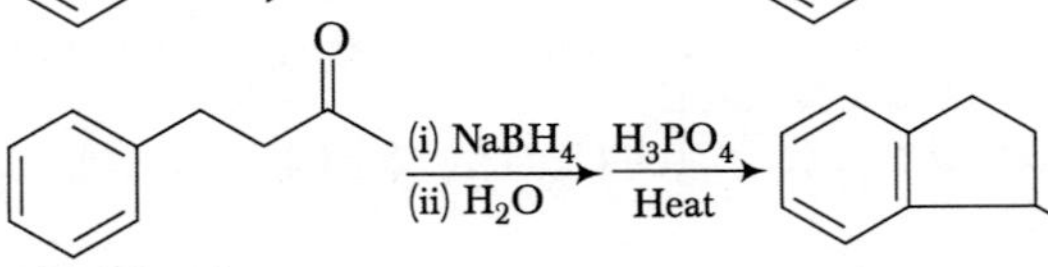

(d) All of the above

46. Compound *A* shows a large dipole moment. Which structure should be used to adequately explain the observation?

(a) 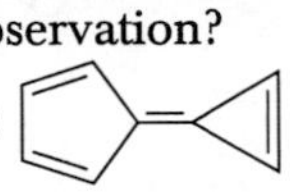 (b) 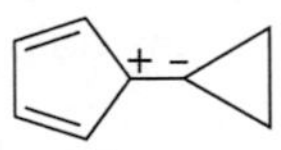

(c) 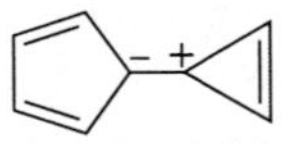 (d) 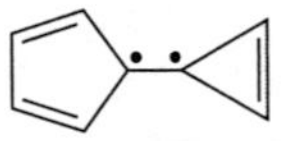

47. The major product of the following organic reaction is

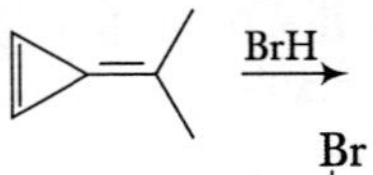

(a) 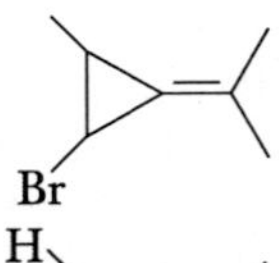 (b) 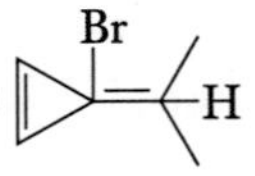

(c) 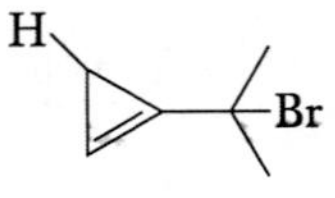 (d) 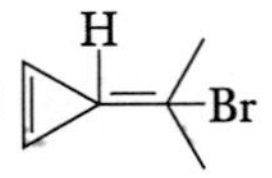

48. An aromatic hydrocarbon yielding single mononitro derivative is
(a) ethyl benzene (b) *o*-xylene
(c) *p*-xylene (d) naphthalene

49. 1-phenyl naphthalene can be prepared in 80% yield by one of the reaction below which one?

(a) 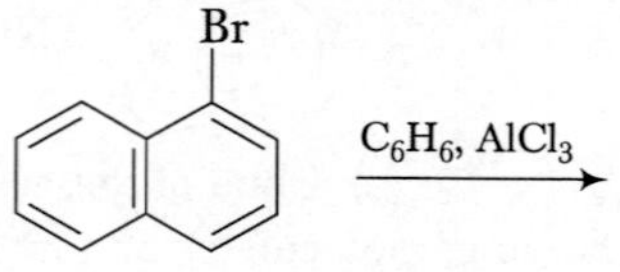

(b) 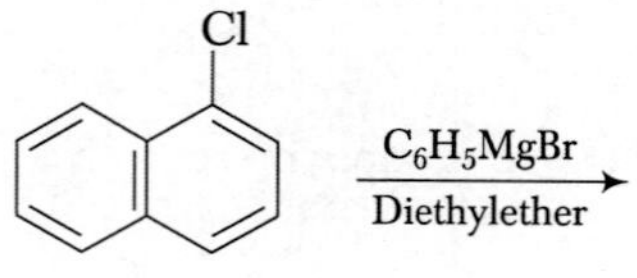

(c) 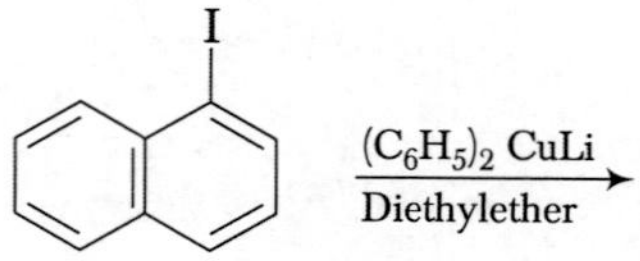

(d) 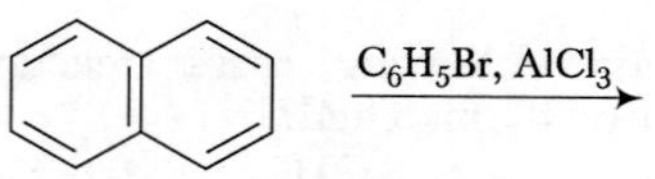

50. Which of the following is a incorrect statement?
(a) Cyclopropenyl cation is aromatic in nature
(b) According to Huckel rule an aromatic compound should have $(4n + 2)$ π electrons
(c) Tropylium cation is planar having eight π electrons
(d) Homotropylium ion is a homoaromatic compound

51. Which of the following ring compounds obey Huckel's rule?
(a) $C_{12}H_{12}^{2-}$ (b) $C_{20}H_{20}$ (c) $C_{20}H_{20}^{-}$ (d) $C_{20}H_{20}^{+}$

52. Which of the following statements is correct?
(a) $C_{12}H_{12}$ compound do not obey Huckel's rule
(b) Pyrrole does not follow Huckel's rule
(c) In fullerene each carbon is sp^3-hybridised
(d) In fullerene 12 pentagons and 16 hexagons are present

53. 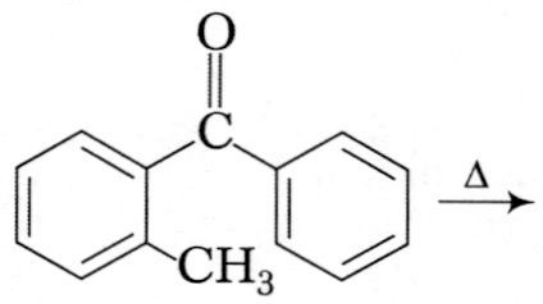 product. The product is

(a) 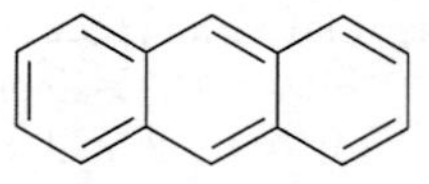 (b) 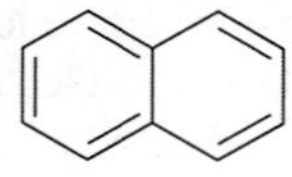

(c) 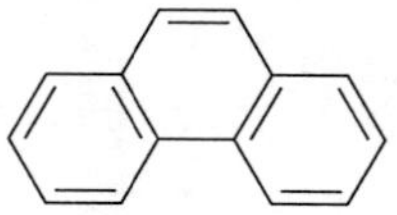 (d) None of these

54. Azulene reacts with acetyl chloride in the presence of anhy. $AlCl_3$ to give

(a) 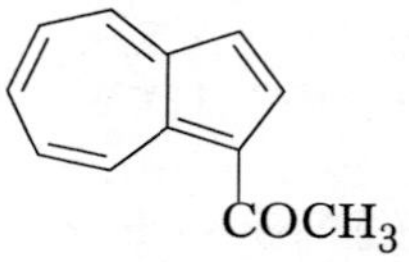 (b) 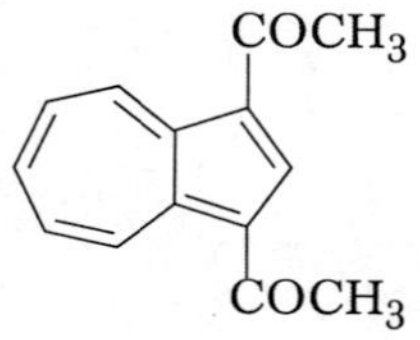

(c) Both (a) and (b) (d) None of these

55. Which of the following is a carcinogenic polycyclic hydrocarbon?
(a) 3, 4-benzpyrene (b) 1, 4-benzanthracene
(c) 20-methlycholanthrene (d) All of these

Exercise 2
(For Part 'C')

1. Which of the following are aromatic?

I.  II. 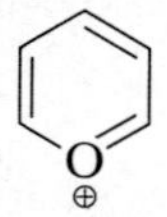 III. 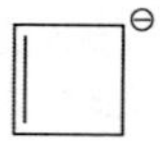

(a) I, II, III (b) I, II (c) II, III (d) II

2. Which of the following species should be aromatic by the Huckel's $(4n + 2)$ rule?

I. 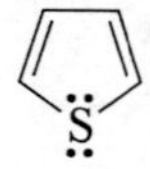 II. 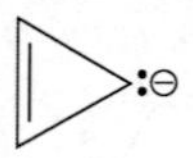

III. 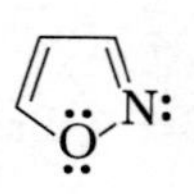 IV. 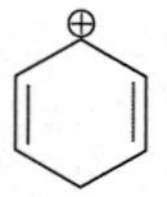 V. 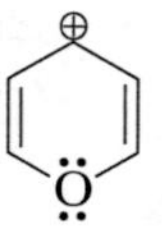

(a) I, III, V (b) I, II, IV, V
(c) II, III, V (d) II, III, IV, V

3. Protonation of a carbonyl group forms a cation with significant charge on the carbon atom.

$$>C{=}O + H^+ \longrightarrow >C{=}\overset{+}{O}H \longleftrightarrow >\overset{+}{C}{-}OH$$

Which of the following carbonyl compounds form an aromatic cation on protonation?

I. 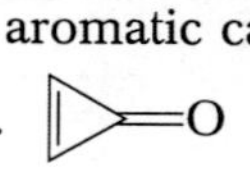 II. 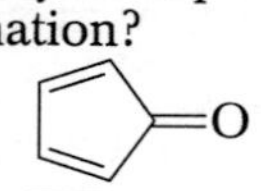

III. 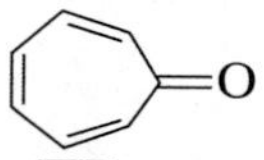 IV. 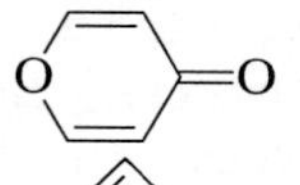

V. 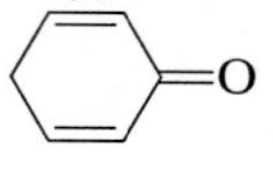 VI. 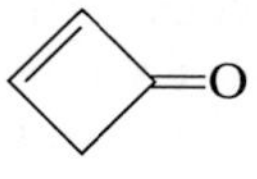

(a) I, II, IV (b) I, III, IV
(c) III, IV, V (d) I, III, V

4. Which of the compounds is aromatic?

(a) 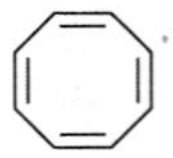 (b) 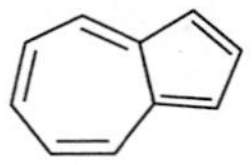

(c) 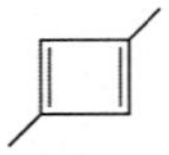 (d) 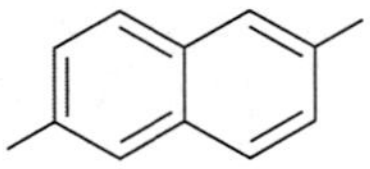

5. Which of these compounds is/are aromatic?

(a) 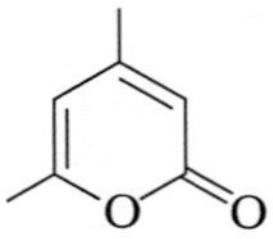 (b) 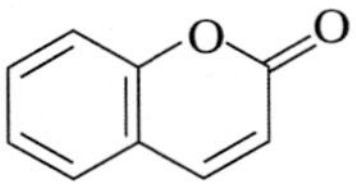

(c) 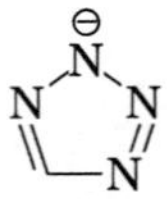 (d) All of these

6. What is the relationship between *A* and *B*?

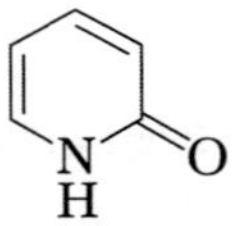
(*A*)

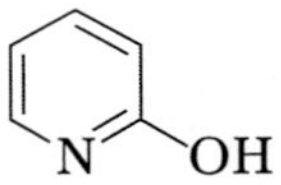
(*B*)

(a) They are tautomers (b) They are aromatic
(c) Both (a) and (b) (d) None of these

7. Select the correct statements from the given following statements.

I. 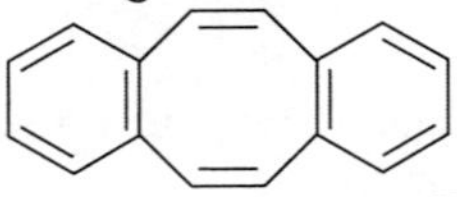 is more stable than

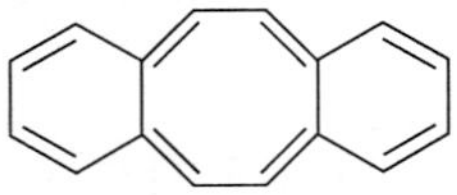

II. 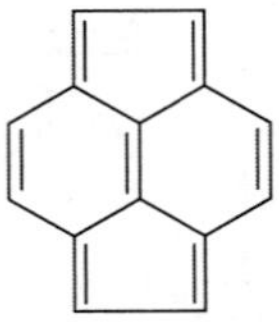 is more stable than 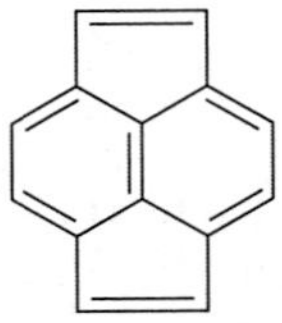

III. All these are aromatic compounds.

(a) I, III (b) II, III
(c) I, II, III (d) I

8. In structures I and II

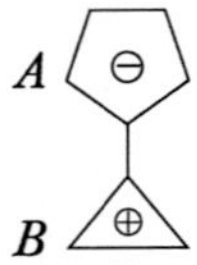
I

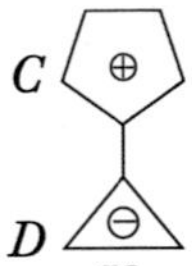
II

(a) rings *A* and *C* are aromatic while *B* and *D* are non-aromatic
(b) rings *A* and *C* are non-aromatic while *B* and *D* are aromatic
(c) rings *A* and *B* are aromatic while *C* and *D* are non-aromatic
(d) All rings *A* to *D* are aromatic

9. Consider the following statements.

I. Following structure can be stabilised by resonance involving a dipolar form.

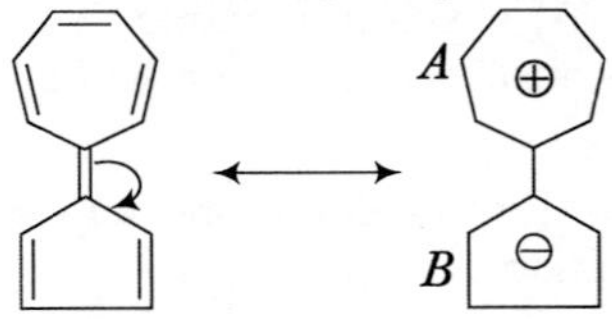

II. Rings *A* and *B* both are aromatic.
III. Rings *A* and *B* both are non-aromatic.
IV. Ring *A* is aromatic while ring *B* is non-aromtic.
V. Ring *A* is aromatic while ring *B* is anti-aromatic.

(a) I, III (b) I, II
(c) I, IV (d) I, V

Assertion & Reason

Codes

(a) Both A and R are true and R is the correct explanation of A.
(b) Both A and R are true and R is not the correct explanation of A.
(c) A is true and R is false.
(d) A is false and R is true.

10. Assertion (A) π-electron energy decreases for the hypothetical reaction.

$CH_2{=}CH{-}\overset{\oplus}{C}H_2 \longrightarrow$  $+ H_2$

Reason (R) Non-aromatic allyl carbocation is converted into more stable aromatic cyclopropenyl carbocation.

11. Assertion (A) Deprotonation of *A* produces aromaticity in the compound formed.

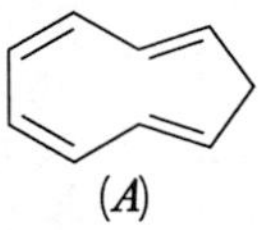
(*A*)

Reason (R) Product formed is carbanion with ten π-electrons.

12. Assertion (A) The following compound is not aromatic.

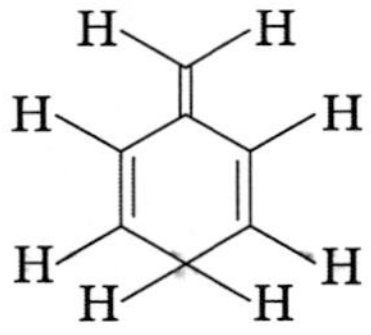

Reason (R) sp^3-hybridised carbon present in the ring acts as an insulator and prevents cyclic delocalisation of π-electrons (which are six in the compound).

13. **Assertion (A)** [10] annulene is non-aromatic which is shown below.

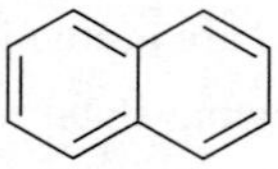

Reason (R) It has Huckel number of π-electrons.

14. **Assertion (A)** Cyclopropenone on reaction with HCl forms a salt which give a white precipitate with aqueous $AgNO_3$.

Reason (R) Protonation on oxygen forms an aromatic cation.

15. Which of the following carbanion is most stable?

(a) 
(b) 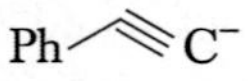

(c) 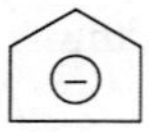
(d) 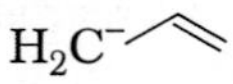

16. From the compounds shown below, choose the one that is aromatic.

(a) 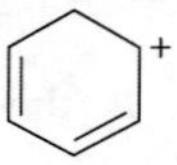
(b) 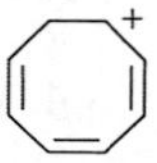
(c) 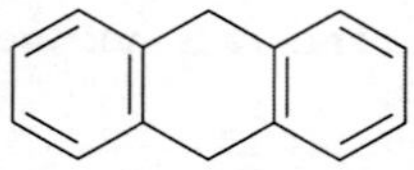
(d) 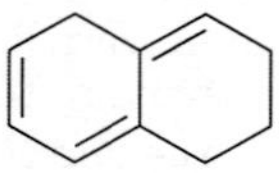

17. Which of the following C_6H_6 compounds has a single set of structurally equivalent hydrogen atoms?

I. 
II. 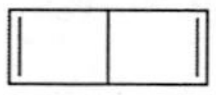
III. H—C≡C—CH_2CH_2—C≡C—H
IV. 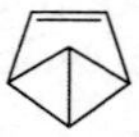
V. 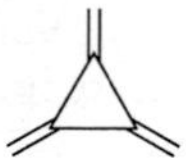
VI. 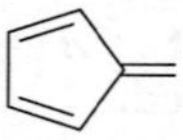

(a) I and II
(b) I, IV and VI
(c) I and V
(d) I, II and III

18. Which of the following are converted to an aromatic substance on loss of hydride ion?

I. 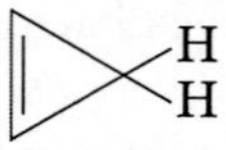
II. 
III. 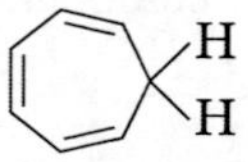
IV. 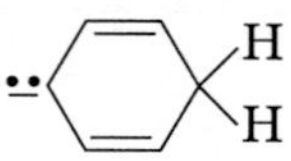
V. 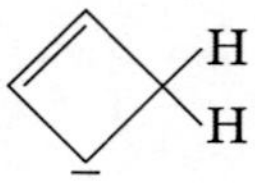

(a) I, II, III
(b) I, III, V
(c) III, IV, V
(d) I, III, IV

19. 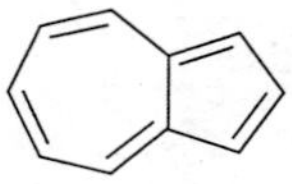 $\xrightarrow{NBS/CH_2Cl_2}$? Product is/are

(a) 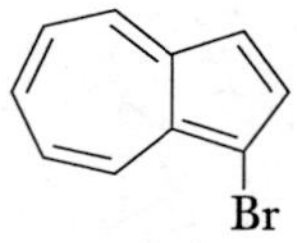

(b) 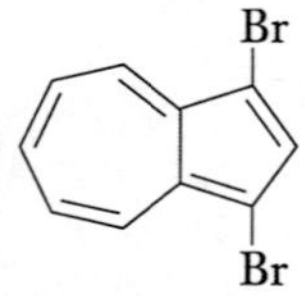

(c) Both (a) and (b)
(d) None of these

20. 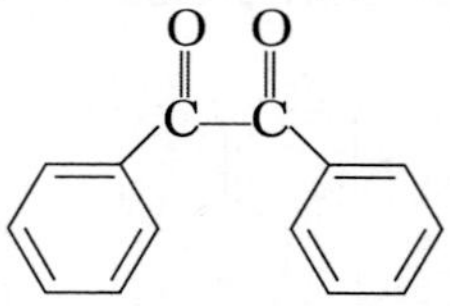

$\xrightarrow{AlCl_3}$

The product of the reaction is

(a) 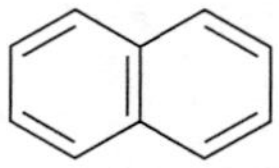
(b) 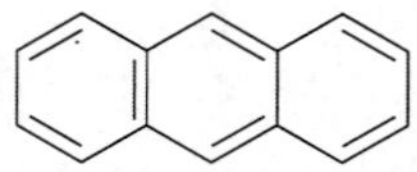
(c) 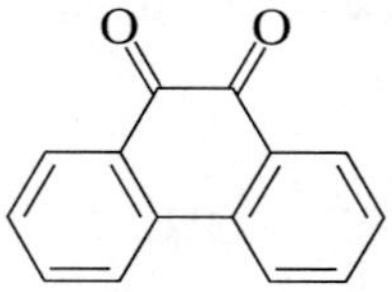

(d) None of these

21. Decalin on dehydrogenation with Pd-carbon, gives

(a) 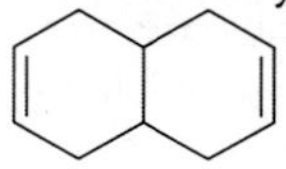
(b) 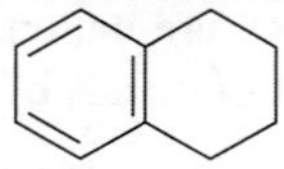
(c) 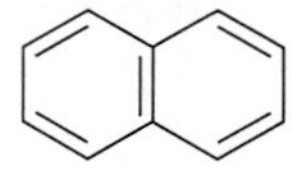
(d) 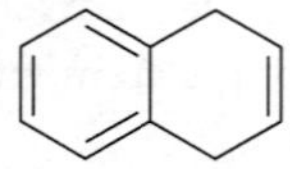

22. Which of the following has (have) fully delocalized π-electrons but is/are not aromatic?

I. 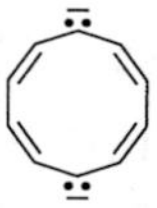
II. 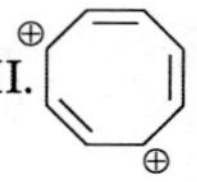
III. 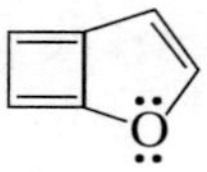

IV. 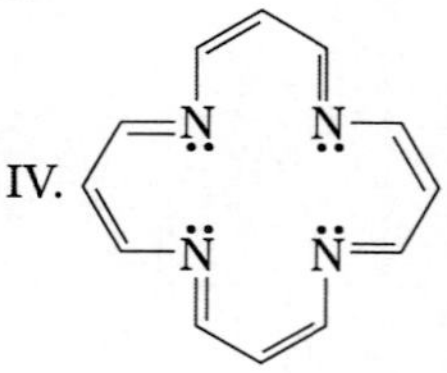

(a) I, III
(b) I, II
(c) II, III, IV
(d) I, III, IV

23. Consider the following molecular orbitals of benzene. Which of these molecular orbitals has the highest energy?

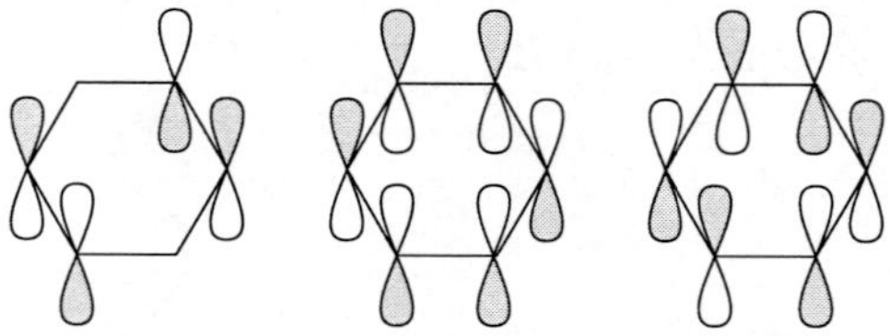

I II III

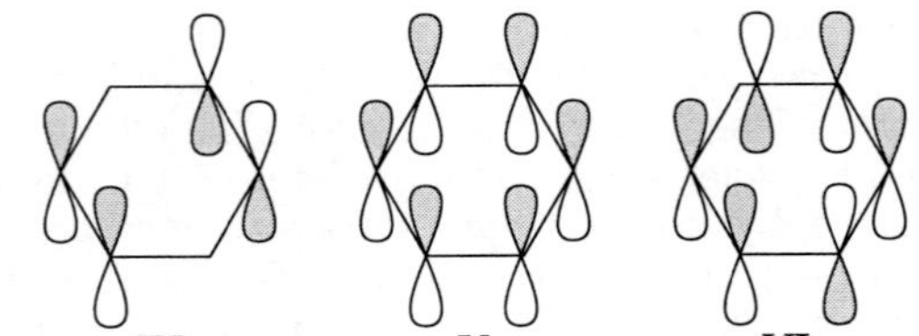

IV V VI

(a) Orbital I
(b) Orbital II
(c) Orbital III
(d) Orbital IV

24. Which of the followings has (have) $(4n+2)$ π-electrons but not aromatic?

(a) 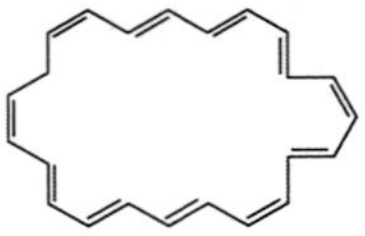
(b) 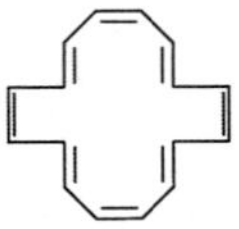
(c) 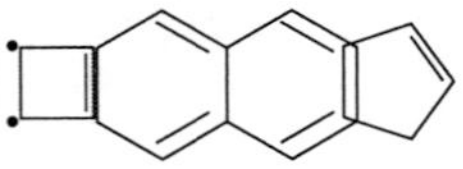
(d) 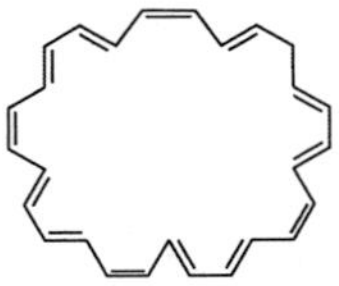

25. Match the Column I with Column II.

	Column I		Column II
A.	Football like molecule	1.	Ferrocene, azulene
B.	Bucky babies	2.	Fullerenes
C.	Buckite salt	3.	C_{32}, C_{44}, C_{50} and C_{58}
D.	Non-benzenoid aromatic compound	4.	K_3C_{60}

Codes

	A	B	C	D
(a)	4	3	2	1
(b)	2	3	4	1
(c)	2	1	4	3
(d)	2	4	3	1

26. Match the Column I with Column II.

	Column I		Column II
A.	Aromatic	1.	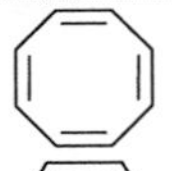
B.	Anti-aromatic	2.	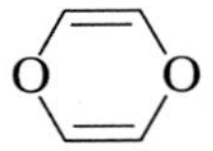
C.	Non-aromatic	3.	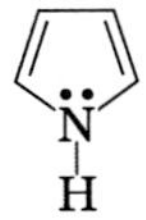

Codes

	A	B	C
(a)	3	1	2
(b)	2	3	1
(c)	1	3	2
(d)	3	2	1

27. On oxidation with alkaline $KMnO_4$, naphthalene gives

(a) 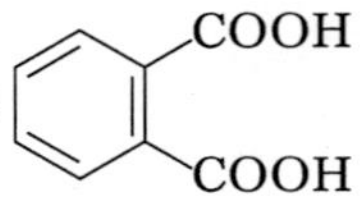
(b) 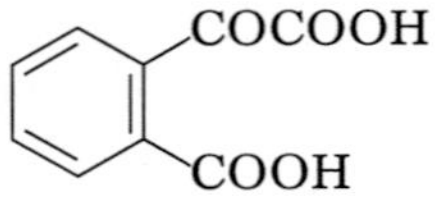
(c) 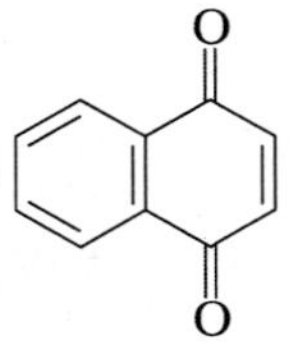
(d) 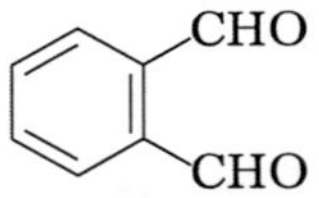

28. Select the correct statements from the following :
(a) Naphthalene on oxidation with acidic $KMnO_4$ gives phthalic acid
(b) Anthracene is less reactive than phenanthrene
(c) 20-methylcholanthrene is the most potent in producing skin cancer
(d) [10] annulene is aromatic in nature

29. Which of the following statements is incorrect?
(a) Phenalene is not aromatic but the corresponding anion is aromatic
(b) Azulene forms azulenium cation with strong acid
(c) Azulene on heating above 350°C gives anthracene
(d) [18] annulene is a diatropic molecule

30. A compound shows aromaticity when it have
(a) high resonance energy
(b) aromatic sextet
(c) $(4n+2)$ π-electrons
(d) planarity of molecule

31. Among the carbon cations given below

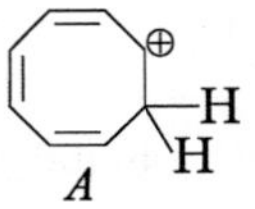
A

B

C

(a) *A* is homoaromatic, *B* is anti-aromatic and *C* is aromatic
(b) *A* is aromatic, *B* is antiaromatic and *C* is homoaromatic
(c) *A* is anti-aromatic, *B* is aromatic and *C* is homoaromatic
(d) *A* is homoaromatic, *B* is aromatic and *C* is anti-aromatic

32. Which of the following system is/are aromatic?

(a) 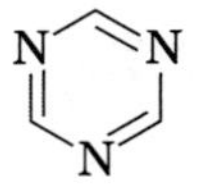
(b) 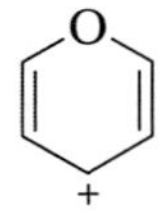
(c) 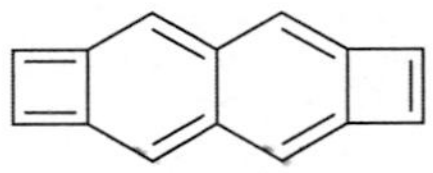
(d) 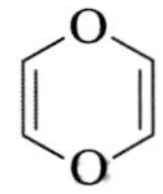

33. Select the compounds which is/are anti-aromatic?

(a) 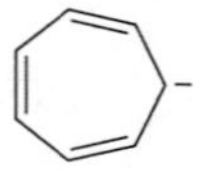
(b) 
(c) 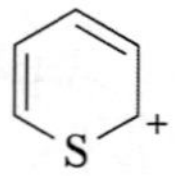
(d) 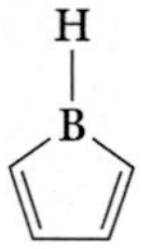

34. Which of the following compound is expected to undergo faster electrophilic aromatic substitution than unsubstituted benzene?

(a) 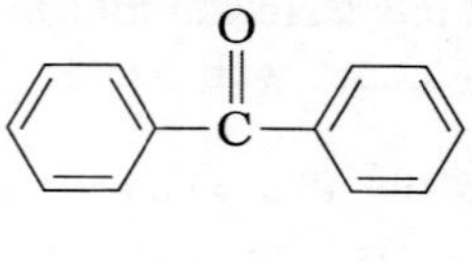
(b) 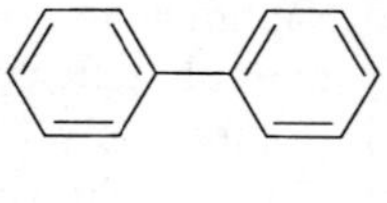
(c) 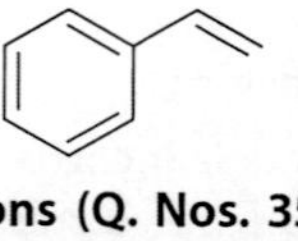
(d) 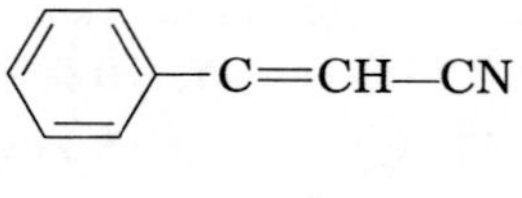

Directions (Q. Nos. 35 to 37)
Benzene and related compounds are aromatic possess high resonance stabilization energies and hence are very stable. Stability seems to be correlated with the overlap of its carbon 2*p*-orbitals to form π-molecular orbitals. Extra stability has been defined in terms of aromaticity. A molecule or ion which contain monocyclic planar ring and contain $(4n+2)\,\pi$ electrons delocalized in a cyclic loop of parallel overlapping *p*-orbitals is called aromatic. It has unusual stability.

35. Cyclopropenyl carbocation is aromatic because
(a) ring is planar
(b) it has two electrons
(c) π-electrons used in delocalization
(d) All of the above

36. According to Huckel rule, an aromatic compound should have
(a) $(4n+1)$ π-electrons
(b) $(4n+4)$ π-electrons
(c) $(4n)$ π-electrons
(d) $(4n+2)$ electrons

37. Which of the following compound is aromatic in nature?

(a) 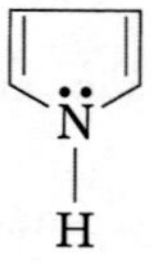
(b) 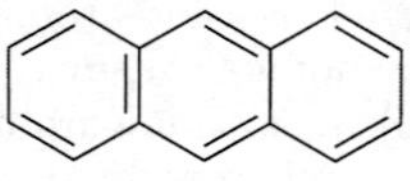
(c) 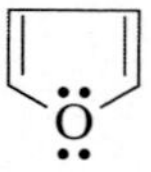
(d) All of these

Directions (Q. Nos. 38 to 40) Azulene is a deep blue compound. It is isomeric with naphthalene and less stable than naphthalene. It is a bicyclic non-benzenoid aromatic compound. Azulene on heating above 350°C to give naphthalene by isomerization. Azulene shows aromatic character because dipolar structure of azulene satisfies Huckel rule. Naphthalene is a polycyclic aroamatic compound. It has fused ring system. Azulene and naphthalene undergo electrophilic substitution reactions. Naphthalene also give addition and oxidation reactions.

38. 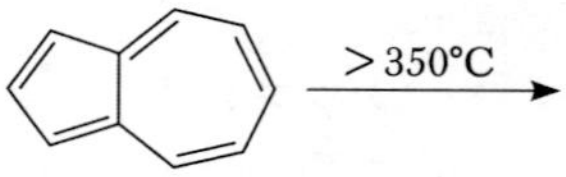

Product, the product is

(a) 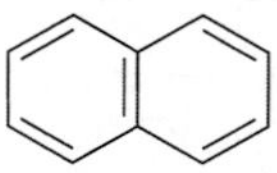
(b) 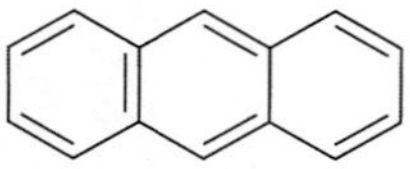
(c) 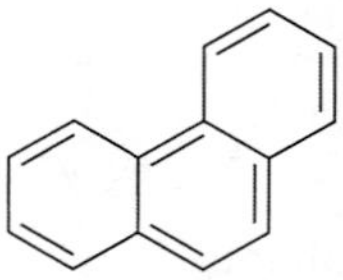
(d) None of these

39. Naphthalene on oxidation with acidified $K_2Cr_2O_7$ gives

(a) 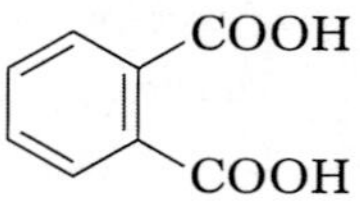

(b) 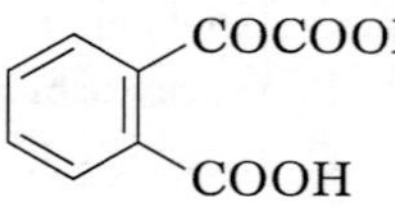

(c) 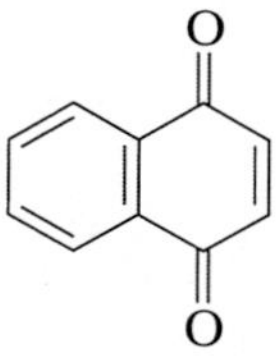
(d) 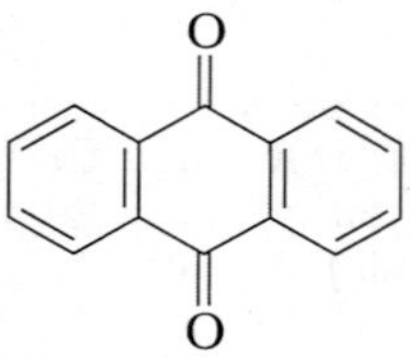

40. Identify the product in the given reaction.

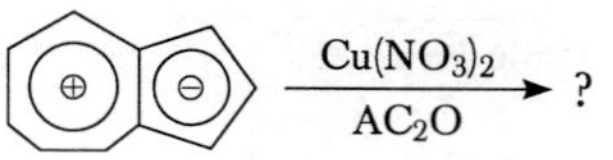

(a) 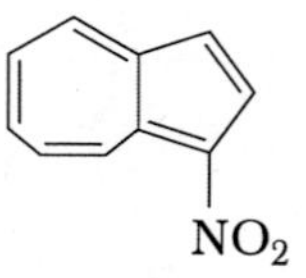

(b) 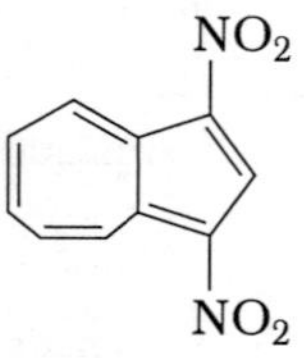

(c) Both (a) and (b)
(d) None of these

Answers

Exercise 1

1. (a)	**2.** (c)	**3.** (c)	**4.** (a)	**5.** (d)	**6.** (a)	**7.** (d)	**8.** (c)	**9.** (b)	**10.** (a)
11. (d)	**12.** (a)	**13.** (b)	**14.** (a)	**15.** (d)	**16.** (c)	**17.** (a)	**18.** (c)	**19.** (d)	**20.** (d)
21. (b)	**22.** (b)	**23.** (b)	**24.** (b)	**25.** (c)	**26.** (d)	**27.** (a)	**28.** (b)	**29.** (d)	**30.** (d)
31. (d)	**32.** (b)	**33.** (a)	**34.** (b)	**35.** (b)	**36.** (d)	**37.** (b)	**38.** (d)	**39.** (a)	**40.** (b)
41. (b)	**42.** (a)	**43.** (c)	**44.** (d)	**45.** (d)	**46.** (c)	**47.** (b)	**48.** (c)	**49.** (c)	**50.** (c)
51. (a)	**52.** (a)	**53.** (a)	**54.** (c)	**55.** (d)					

Exercise 2

1. (d)	**2.** (a)	**3.** (b)	**4.** (b,d)	**5.** (d)	**6.** (c)	**7.** (d)	**8.** (c)	**9.** (b)	**10.** (a)
11. (b)	**12.** (a)	**13.** (b)	**14.** (a)	**15.** (c)	**16.** (c)	**17.** (c)	**18.** (d)	**19.** (c)	**20.** (c)
21. (c)	**22.** (d)	**23.** (c)	**24.** (a,d)	**25.** (b)	**26.** (a)	**27.** (b)	**28.** (a,c)	**29.** (c)	**30.** (a,b,c,d)
31. (a)	**32.** (a,b,c)	**33.** (a,d)	**34.** (b,c)	**35.** (d)	**36.** (d)	**37.** (d)	**38.** (a)	**39.** (c)	**40.** (c)

Hints & Solutions

Exercise 1

4. Tropylium cation

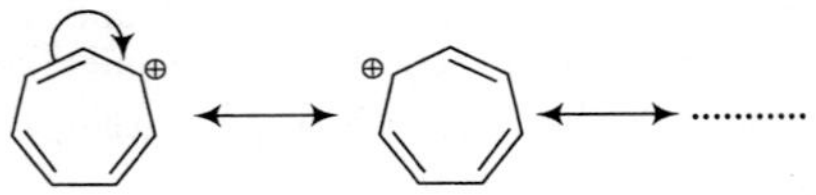

5. 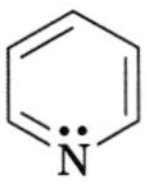 and 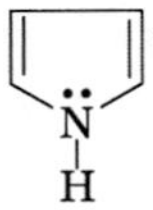 both are aromatic because in pyridine lone pair of nitrogen is not used in delocalization while in pyrrole lone pair on nitrogen is used in delocalization.

9. 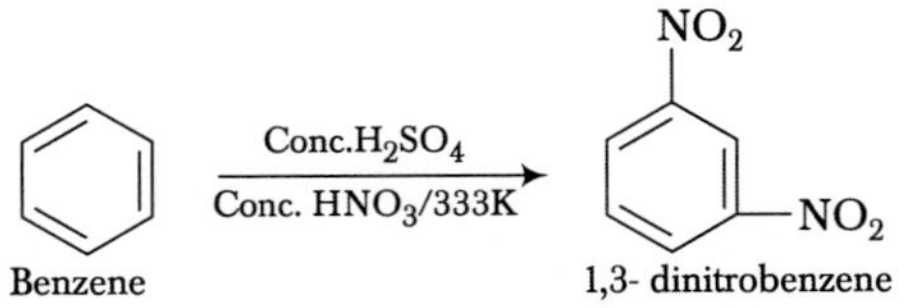

10. Among the dienes, furan is less aromatic than pyrrole and thiophene. So, it is more reactive.

17. 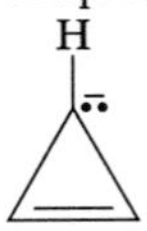 has $4n$ $(n = 1)$ delocalized π-electrons, hence it is anti-aromatic.

18.  has aromatic sextet and involve a lone pair of sulphur atom in aromaticity.

26. Tropylium ion is aromatic hence it is the most stable.

27. 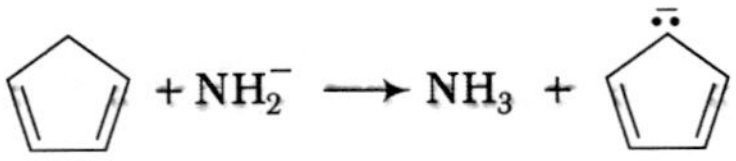

28. 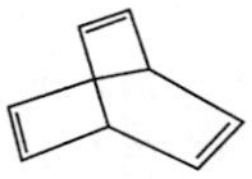 compound has lack of planarity which prevent it to be aromatic.

32. 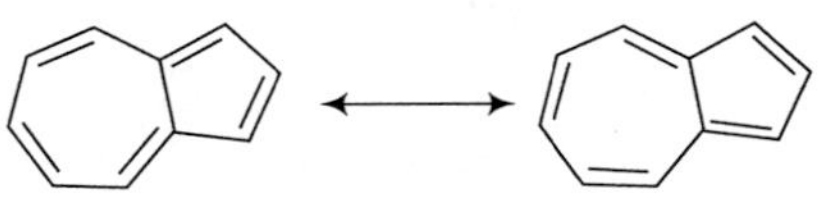

34. It has eight delocalized π-electrons, hence anti-aromatic in nature.

36. It has as sp^3 (uncharged) carbon in the ring, and lacks cyclic delocalization of π-electrons.

37. 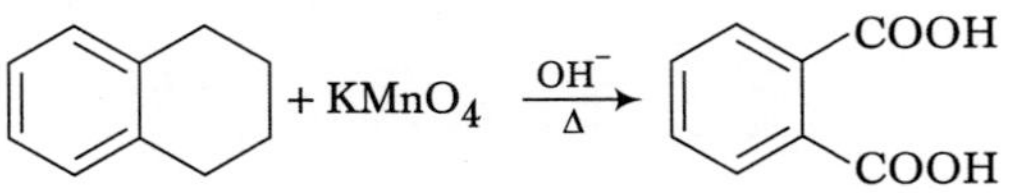

45. 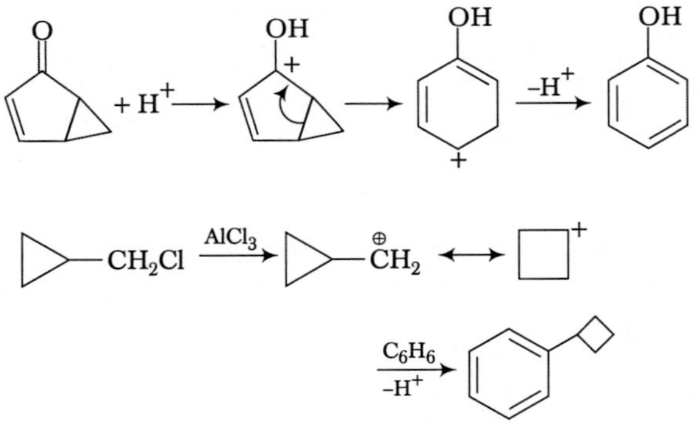

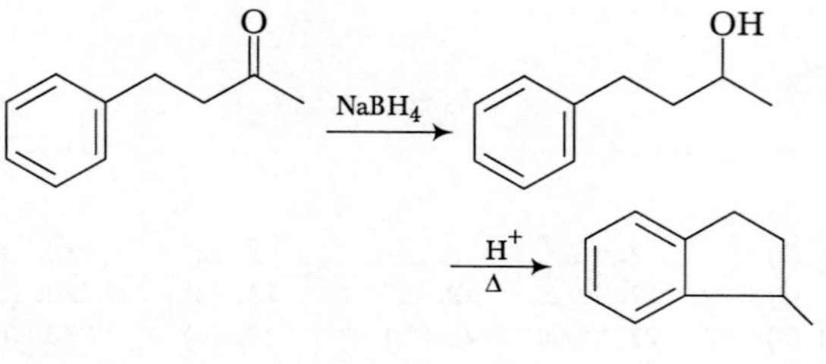

46. Both negatively and positively charged rings are independently aromatic.

51. $C_{12}H_{12}^{2-}$: 14π-electrons, $n = 3$.

Hence, $(4n + 2)$ molecule *i.e.,* it obeys Huckel rule.

Exercise 2

3. 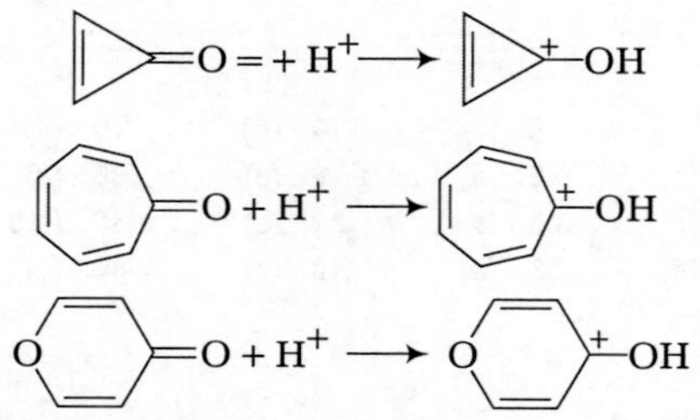

All these cations are aromatic.

4. 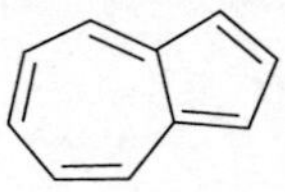 azulene is a bicyclic non-benzenoid aromatic compound.

Substituted naphthalene is also an aromatic hydrocarbon.

13. [10] anulene has Huckel number of π-electrons but it is non-aromatic due to 1,6-repulsions of *trans* hydrogens making the ring non-planar.

14. 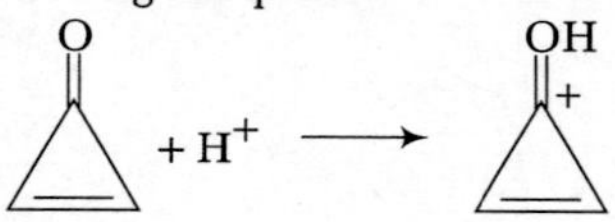

Aromatic

15. 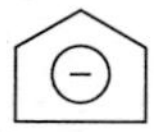 is an aromatic carbanion hence, it is the most stable.

16. The two benzene rings on the sides are independently aromatic.

17. 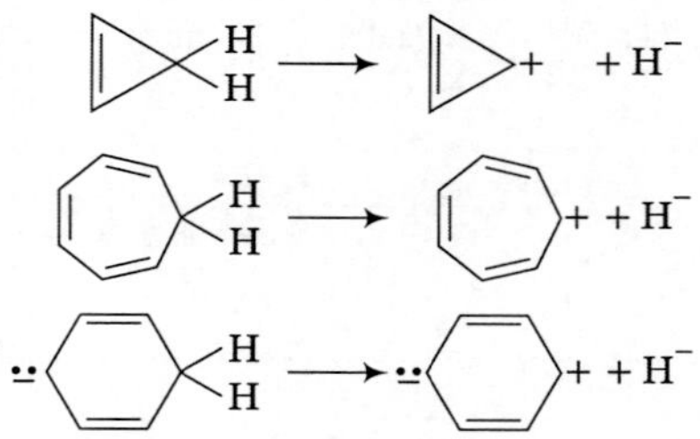

22. Compounds I, III and IV have 12, 8 and 16 delocalized π-electrons respectively. Hence, they are anti-aromatic.

24. Compound I and IV both have a sp^3 (uncharged) carbon in the ring hence not aromatic.

32. Compound (a), (b) and (c) have cyclic delocalization of $(4n + 2)$ n electrons while (d) is anti-aromatic.

33. Compound (a) and (d) have $4n$ delocalized π-electrons hence anti-aromatic.

31 Organic Reaction Mechanism and Reactive Intermediates

Introduction

In organic compounds, atoms are linked together through covalent bonds and during transformation to another organic compound, some old covalent bonds are broken, some new of them are formed. The breaking and making of bonds follow certain laws. Understanding of nature of covalent bonds, type of bond fission and direction of electronic movement during a chemical reaction helps to build up a theoretical generalization regarding this reaction, commonly known as **reaction mechanism.** The relative strength of acid and base, rate of reaction (kinetics) and energy change (thermodynamics) during reaction are the important area of emphasis in a chemical reaction.

Potential energy diagram of chemical reaction helps to understand both how fast is the reaction occurring and to what extent it goes before attaining equilibrium. In a chemical reaction, reactants on their way to product pass through a transition state or activated complex. In some cases a relatively less energetic but more stable chemical species than the activated complex may be first formed. This chemical species which is relatively less energetic but more stable than the activated complex is called the **reactive intermediates.** This reactive intermediate then gets converted into the product through another activated complex.

Syllabus

- Organic Reaction Mechanism Involving Addition, Elimination and Substitution Reactions with Electrophilic, Nucleophilic or Radial Species
- Determination of Reaction Pathways

Reaction Mechanism

A detailed step by step description of a chemical reaction showing as to how reactants are converted into products is called **mechanism of the reaction.**

Reaction mechanism are of two types :

Concerted Mechanism

The mechanism which involves the breaking and making of bond that takes place simultaneously on approach of reacting molecules without the formation of any intermediate is called **concerted mechanism.**

Non-concerted Mechanism

The mechanism in which a reaction occurs in two or more steps with the formation of a reactive intermediate is called **non-concerted mechanism.**

The activation energy diagram for concerted mechanism and non-concerted mechanism are given below in figure 31.1 and 31.2.

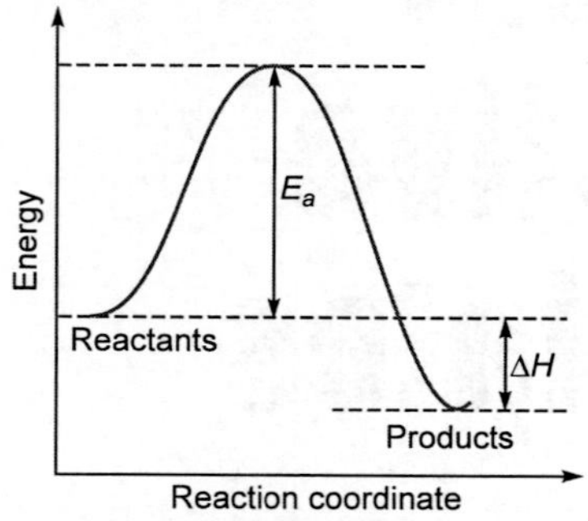

Fig. 31.1 For concerted mechanism.

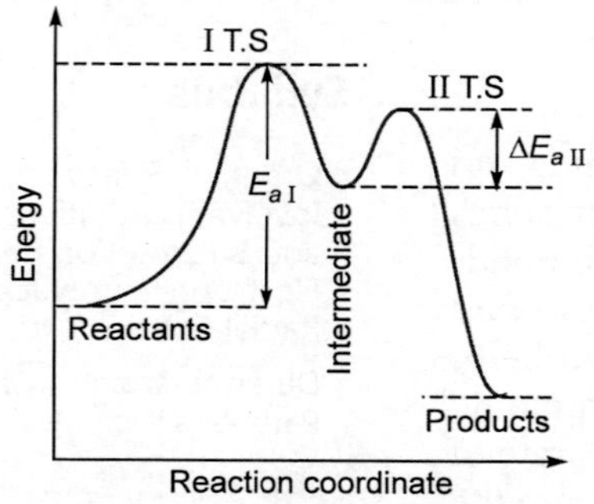

Fig. 31.2 For non-concerted mechanism.

Bond Fission

The reactions take place due to electron reorganization in the reactant molecule. One or more bonds are broken and a new bond or bonds are formed in the reaction. A bond may break in two different ways known as homolytic and heterolytic bond fission.

Homolytic Bond Fission

A bond cleavage in which the shared pair of electrons is distributed equally to bonded atoms after the cleavage of bond is known as homolytic bond fission. In homolytic bond fission odd electron species called free radicals are produced. This bond fission is invoked by the heat or radiation.

$$A{-}B \xrightarrow{\text{Light/Heat}} A^{\bullet} + B^{\bullet}$$

$$CH_3{-}CH_3 \xrightarrow{\text{Light/Heat}} \dot{C}H_3 + \dot{C}H_3$$

$$CH_3{-}NH_2 \xrightarrow{\text{Light/Heat}} \dot{C}H_3 + \dot{N}H_2$$

Heterolytic Bond Fission

When a covalent bond breaks in a fashion that both the bonding electrons are attracted by the more electronegative atoms, it is called heterolytic bond fission. It results in the formation of cation and anion.

$$CH_3{-}X \longrightarrow \overset{\oplus}{C}H_3 + \overset{\ominus}{X}$$

(X is more electronegative)

$$CH_3{-}X \longrightarrow \overset{\ominus}{C}H_3 + \overset{\oplus}{X}$$

(CH_3 is more electronegative)

Attacking Reagents

The species which attacks on reactant or intermediate and form product is known as attacking reagent. These are of following types

Electrophiles

Electrophilic reagents (electron loving) are those reagents that are positively charged (NO_2^+, Cl^+, etc.) or contain an electron deficient atom (SO_3, BF_3). They have incomplete octet or duplet and are also called Lewis acid, *i.e.,* electron-pair acceptor.

Nucleophiles

Nucleophilic reagents (nucleus loving) or electron repelling reagents are the species that are negatively charged (OH^-, CN^-, H^-, etc.) or have an electron rich atom (N in NH_3, O in H_2O, etc.). They are called Lewis base, *i.e.,* electron pair donor.

Ambiphiles

Ambiphilic reagents have electron-attracting (electrophile) and electron-repelling (nucleophile) sites hence, have dual (amphoteric) nature.

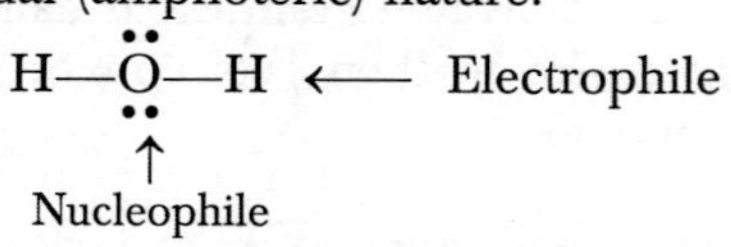

Nucleophiles attack electrophiles during the course of the reaction.

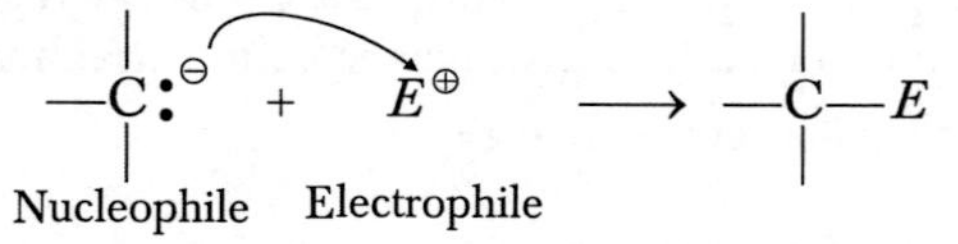

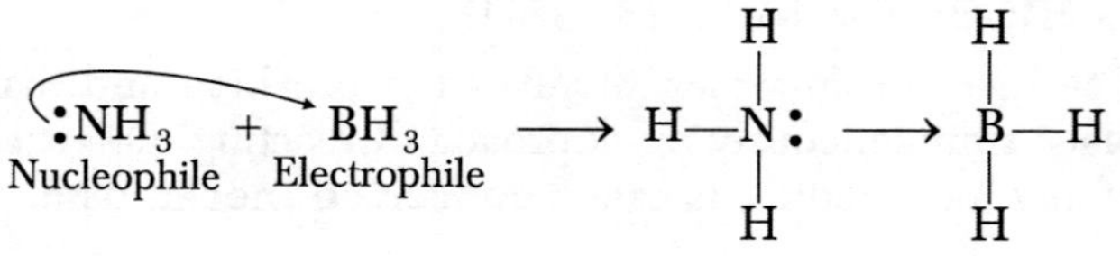

The reaction of an electrophile with a nucleophile is the same as the reaction of a Lewis acid with a Lewis base and is termed as **Lewis acid-base association reaction.**

Note • The nucleophiles which have more than one suitable atoms through which they can attack the substrate are known as ambident nucleophiles. **Example**, cyanide, isothiocyanate, nitrite ions, DMSO, etc. Methylation of DMSO with CH_3I gives two isomers, (*A*) and (*B*) from S-methylation and from O-methylation respectively. Since, S is a better nucleophilic site (because O is much more electronegative than S), hence, (*A*) is the major isomer

$$\underset{\text{DMSO}}{(CH_3)_2\ddot{\underset{..}{S}}{=}\ddot{O}\colon} + CH_3I \longrightarrow \underset{(A)}{[Me_3\overset{\oplus}{S}{=}O]\overset{\ominus}{I}} + \underset{(B)}{[Me_2\overset{\oplus}{S}{-}OMe]\overset{\ominus}{I}}$$

Table 31.1 **Electrophiles, Nucleophiles and Ambiphiles**

Reagents	Neutral	Charged
Electrophiles They are electron-deficients and accept electron pair from nucleophilies, (also called Lewis acid).	So_3, $BeCl_2$, BF_3, $AlCl_3$, FeCl, *R*COCl, $>C{=}O$, $\colon CCl_2$ (carbene) $\colon\ddot{N}{-}COOC_2H_5$ (nitrene)	$\overset{\oplus}{H}$, $\overset{\oplus}{X}$ ($\overset{\oplus}{Cl}$, $\overset{\oplus}{Br}$, $\overset{\oplus}{I}$, halonium), $H_3\overset{\oplus}{O}$ (hydronium), $\overset{\oplus}{N}O_2$ (nitronium), $\overset{\oplus}{N}O_2$ (nitrosonium), $C_6H_5\overset{\oplus}{N}_2$ (diazonium), $\overset{\oplus}{C}H_3$ (carbocation)
Nucleophiles They are electron rich and donate electrons to electrophiles (also called Lewis base).	NH_3, H_2O, *R*OH, RNH_2, R_2NH, R_3N, *ROR*, H_2S,	$\overset{\ominus}{N}H_2$, $\overset{\ominus}{H}$, $\overset{\ominus}{C}N$, $\overset{\ominus}{O}H$, $R\overset{\ominus}{N}H$, $R_2\overset{\ominus}{N}$, $\overset{\ominus}{N}_3$, $R\overset{\ominus}{O}$, $RCO\overset{\ominus}{O}$, $RCO\overset{\ominus}{C}H_2$, $S^{2\ominus}$, $HS^{\ominus}$,
Ambiphiles They behave like electrophilies and nucleophiles (amphoteric).	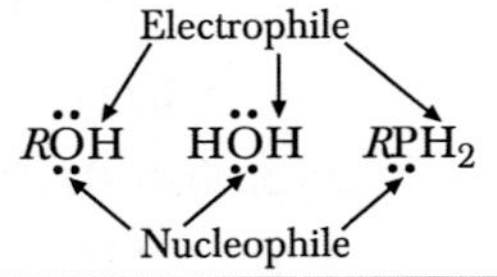	$H_3\overset{\oplus}{O}$ or $\left(H{-}\overset{\oplus}{\ddot{O}}{-}H \text{ with } H \text{ on O}\right)$

Nucleophilicity and Basicity

- Nucleophilicity is the ability to form bonds to carbon atom whereas basicity is the affinity for proton.
- Nucleophilicity is the kinetic property whereas basicity is thermodynamic property.
- Nucleophilicity increases with increase in electron density, hence a nucleophile with a negative charge is stronger than its conjugate acid.

$$^{\ominus}\colon\ddot{\underset{..}{O}}H > H_2\ddot{O}\colon,\quad {}^{\ominus}\colon\ddot{N}H_2 > \colon NH_3$$

- Within a period of the Periodic Table, nucleophilicity (parallel basicity) decreases with increasing atomic number of the atom having negative charge.

$$R_3C^{\ominus} > R_2N^{\ominus} > RO^{\ominus} > F^{\ominus}$$

- The nucleophilicity is also related to base strength when the nucleophilic atom is the same.

$$RO^{\ominus} > HO^{\ominus} > RCOO^{\ominus} > ROH > H_2O$$

- Within a group, in contrast, nucleophilicity increases with increasing atomic number (but basicity decreases as atomic number increases). Nucleophiles having large attacking atom, weakly solvated and having high polarizability are better nucleophiles. **Example** iodide ion being large, high polarizable and weakly solvated is a very strong nucleophile as compared to the small, less polarizable and strongly solvated fluoride ion.
  The nucleophilicity varies in the order

$$I^{\ominus} > Br^{\ominus} > Cl^{\ominus} > F^{\ominus}$$

$$RS^{\ominus} > RO^{\ominus}$$

$$R_3P\colon > R_3N\colon$$

- Steric bulk decreases nucleophilicity.

$$H_3C{-}C(CH_3)_2{-}O^{\ominus} < HO^{\ominus}$$

t-butoxide (hindered) stronger base yet weaker nucleophile

Hydroxide ion weaker base yet stronger nucleophile

Electron Displacement Effects

The effect occurring due to displacement of electron in organic compounds is called **electron displacement effect or electron delocalization effect**. These effects play a crucial role in the stabilization of the intermediate and the product of a reaction. Dispersal of a charge or electron density stabilizes a species. On the other hand, localization of a charge or electron density increases the reactivity of a species. The electron displacement effect is classified as

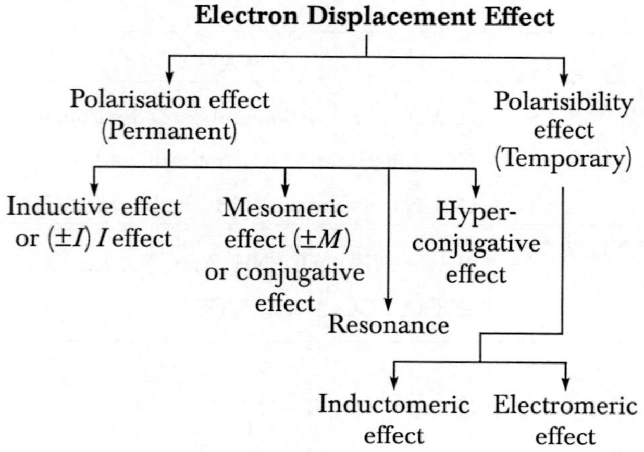

Inductive Effect

The polarization of one bond caused by the polarization of adjacent bond is called the **inductive effect.** In other words the phenomenon of withdrawing electrons through σ bonds to the more electronegative atom or group is called **inductive effect** or **I effect.**

The inductive effect depends on the electronegativity of the substituent. This effect is transmitted through sigma bonds and weakens as the distance between the substituent and the reactive centre increases. Hence, the effect is greatest for the adjacent bond and may be left weakly farther away. At C_4 carbon atom it becomes negligible.

$$\overset{\delta\delta\delta+}{C_4}—\overset{\delta\delta+}{C_3}—\overset{\delta\delta+}{C_2}—\overset{\delta+}{C_1}—\overset{\delta-}{Br}$$

Inductive effect is of two types :

(i) Negative inductive effect (–*I* effect)

(ii) Positive inductive effect (+*I* effect)

Negative inductive effect (–*I*) and positive inductive effect (+ *I*)

Inductive effect in which electrons are withdrawn away from carbon is known as –Inductive effect (–*I* effect) and the atoms or groups causing this effect is known as –*I* effect giving group. On the other hand, inductive effect in which electrons are pushed towards a carbon is known as +Inductive effect (+*I* effect) and the atoms or group causing this effect is known as + *I* effect giving group. Let us consider an example of nitro propane

Donate electrons to starred carbon, +*I* effect ⟶ $CH_3CH_2 \rightarrow \overset{*}{C}H_2 \rightarrow \overset{\oplus}{N}(=O)O^{\ominus}$

Withdraw electrons away from the starred carbon, –*I* effect.

–*I* effect is due to electron attracting group. The order of –*I* effect is as

$$—\overset{\oplus}{N}H_3 > —NO_2 > —CN > —COOH > —F >$$
$$—Cl > —Br > —I > —O—Ar > —COO—$$
$$R > —O—R > —\overset{O}{\overset{\|}{C}}—R > —OH > —C{\equiv}CH$$
$$> —C_6H_5 > —C{\equiv}CR > —CH{=}CH—R$$

+*I* effect is due to electron releasing groups. The order of +*I* effect is as :

$$—O^{\ominus} > —COO^{\ominus} > (CH_3)_3C— > (CH_3)_2CH—$$
$$> CH_3—CH_2 > CH_3— > —D > —H$$

Application of inductive effect

(a) **Dipole moment** Greater –*I* effect results greater dipole moment. **Example**

$$CH_3 \rightarrow I < CH_3 \rightarrow Br < CH_3 \rightarrow F < CH_3 \rightarrow Cl$$

The dipole moment of CH_3F is exceptionally less than CH_3Cl.

(b) **Acidic character of alcohols** Acidic character of alcohol is supported by – *I* effect, *i.e.,* greater –*I* effect results greater acidic character of alcohol. Similarly, +*I* effect decreases the acidic character of alcohol. **Example**

(i) $CH_3—CH_2—O—H < \overset{Cl}{\overset{\uparrow}{C}H_2} \leftarrow CH_2—OH < \overset{F}{\overset{\uparrow}{C}H_2} \leftarrow CH_2—O—H < \overset{NO_2}{\overset{\uparrow}{C}H_2} \leftarrow CH_2—OH$

(ii) $CH_3—OH > CH_3 \rightarrow CH_2—OH > (CH_3)_2C \rightarrow CH_2—OH > (CH_3)_3C—OH$

(c) **Acidic strength of carboxylic acids** Acidic strength of carboxylic acid increases with increasing

–*I* effect and decreases with increasing +*I* effect.

Example

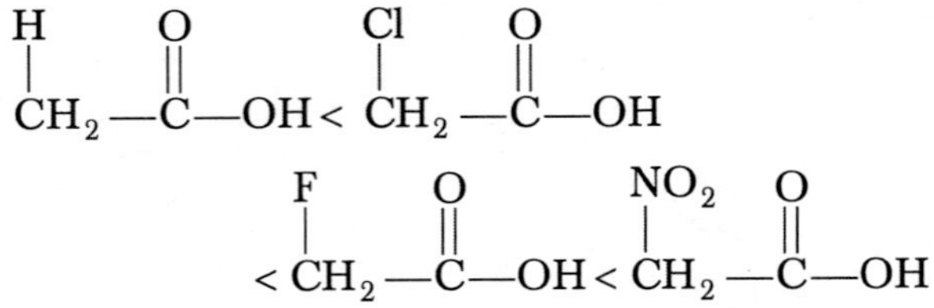

- On moving away from the source, electron withdrawing tendency decreases, hence, acidic nature also decreases.

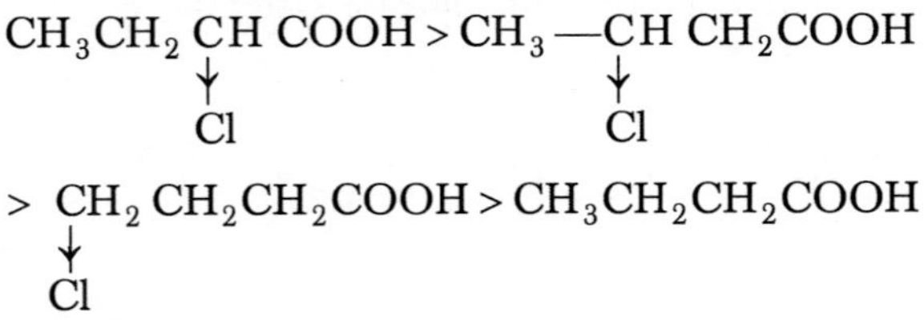

- Multiple halogen substitution increases the acidity.

$$Cl_3C—COOH > Cl_2CH—COOH > ClCH_2—COOH > CH_3COOH$$

(d) **Basic strength of amines** Ammonia and its alkyl derivatives amines, aryl derivatives anilines, are all Lewis-base because they have a lone-pair of non-bonded electrons on nitrogen atom that can be donated to a Lewis acid. An amine can also act as a Bronsted-Lowry base by accepting a proton from a proton acid.

Because amines are fairly strong base, their aqueous solutions are basic. An amine can abstract a proton from water giving an ammonia ion and a hydroxide ion as

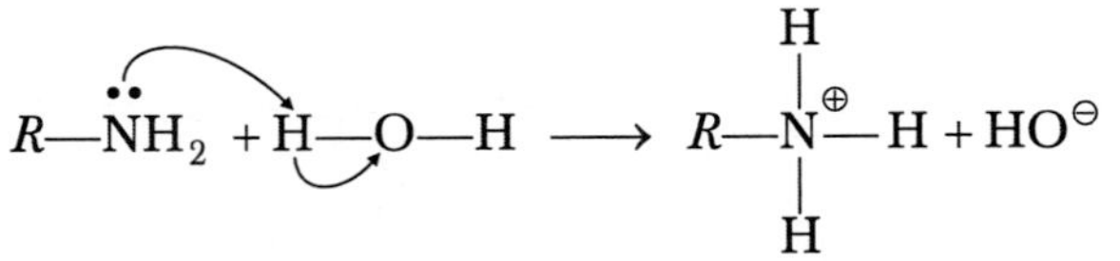

Alkyl groups are electron donating through induction, they stabilizes the charge on nitrogen in ammonium ion, therefore, increases the basic strength. Thus, methanamine, ($pK_b = 3.36$) is stronger base than ammonia ($pK_b = 4.47$).

"An electron donating group bonded to nitrogen increases basic strength of amines while, an electron withdrawing group decreases the basic strength".

On the basis of inductive effect, a secondary amine should be stronger base than a primary amine and tertiary amine further stronger than both primary and secondary amines. This in fact is true also so far as gas phase basicity is concerned but not true in aqueous solution.

In gas phase 1° < 2° < 3° Basicity of amines.

In aqueous solution situation is slightly different. Water solvate the conjugate acid of amine by means of H-bonding, and therefore, it should increase the strength of base.

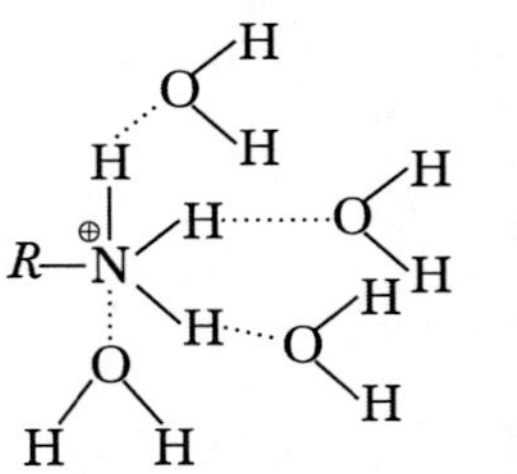

Solvated ammonium ion of 1°-amine

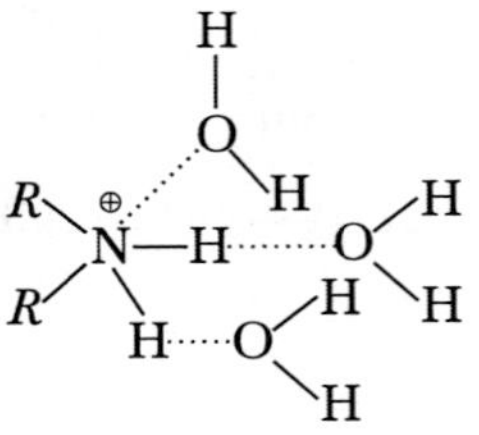

Solvated ammonium ion of 2°-amine

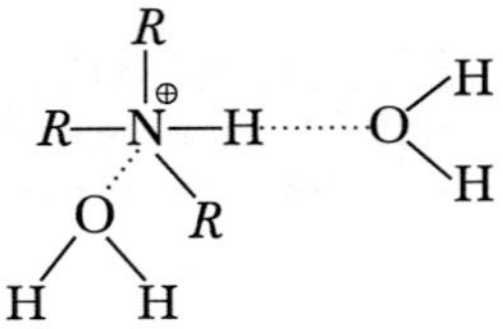

Solvated ammonium ion of 3°-amine

(Solvated ammonium ions of three different types of aliphatic amines)

As can be seen above, substitution of H by alkyl group increase the stabilization of positive charge on nitrogen by +*I* effect but decreases stabilization by solvation due to lesser number of water molecule attached with the ammonium ion of higher degree amines. Thus, the two factors are opposing each other. Up to secondary amine inductive effect is dominating but in tertiary amine solvation effect become more important as evidenced experimentally. The impact of decreased solvation on ammonium ion of tertiary amine goes to an extent that it becomes even weaker base than primary amine. Thus, in aqueous solution, strength of amines as base follows the order.

Further, the crowding of three bulkier alkyl group (steric effect) of tertiary amine make uneasy to attack the proton on lone pair. Thus, in aqueous solution, strength of amines as base follows the order.

$$\text{Secondary} > \text{Primary} > \text{Tertiary} > NH_3$$

Also if degree of amines are same, cyclic amine is stronger base than acyclic amine

$pK_b = 3$ $pK_b = 2.88$

Note • Due to –*I* effect of CF_3 group $CF_3—\ddot{N}(CF_3)—CF_3$ exhibit no any basic character.

(e) **Stability of carbocation** +*I* effect tends to decrease positive charge and thus stability increases. But –*I* effect tends to increase the positive charge and thus stability decreases. **Example**

$$\overset{\oplus}{C}H_3 < CH_3 \rightarrow \overset{\oplus}{C}H_2 < CH_3 \rightarrow \overset{\oplus}{C}H(\leftarrow CH_3) < CH_3 \rightarrow \overset{\oplus}{C}(\leftarrow CH_3) \leftarrow CH_3$$

(f) **Stability of free radical** Stability of carbon free radical increases with +*I* effect and decreases with –*I* effect. **Example**

$$\dot{C}H_3 < CH_3 \rightarrow \dot{C}H_2 < CH_3 \rightarrow \dot{C}H(\leftarrow CH_3) < CH_3 \rightarrow \dot{C}(\leftarrow CH_3)_2$$

(g) **Stability of carbanion** Stability of carbanion increases with increasing –*I* effect and decreases with increasing +*I* effect.

$$CH_3^{\ominus} > CH_3 \rightarrow \overset{\ominus}{C}H_2 > CH_3 \rightarrow \overset{\ominus}{C}H \leftarrow CH_3 > CH_3 \rightarrow \overset{\ominus}{C}(\leftarrow CH_3) \leftarrow CH_3$$

Mesomeric Effect

Mesomeric effect is defined as the permanent effect of π electron shifting from multiple bond to atom or from multiple bond to single bond or from lone pair to single bond.

$$:\ddot{\underset{..}{Cl}}—CH=CH_2 \leftrightarrow \overset{\oplus}{Cl}=CH_2—\overset{\ominus}{C}H_2$$

I II

I and II are resonating structures of $Cl—CH=CH_2$.

Similarly,

$$O_2N—CH=CH_2 \longleftrightarrow (O^{\ominus})(O)\overset{\oplus}{N}—CH=CH_2 \longleftrightarrow (O^{\ominus})(O)N=CH_2—\overset{\oplus}{C}H_2$$

This effect mainly operate in conjugated system of double bond.

Some conjugate system are as

$CH_2=CH—C(=O)—H$; Acrolein

$CH_2=CH—C(=O)—OH$ Acrylic acid

Benzene ; $CH_2=CH—\ddot{\underset{..}{Cl}}:$ Vinyl chloride

(lone pair of Cl behaves like a π-bond and thus, it also makes vinyl chloride a conjugate system).

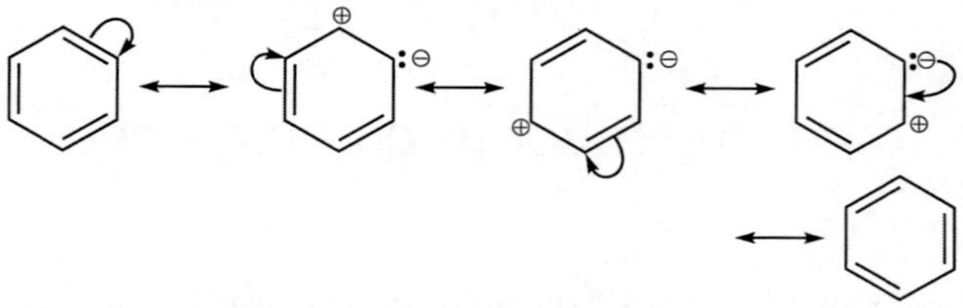

- The π-electrons get delocalised as a result of mesomeric effect giving a number of resonance structures.
- Mesomeric effect is of two types :

Positive mesomeric effect (+*M* effect)

In the +*M* effect the direction of electron displacement is away from the group. +*M* effect is shown by groups containing lone pairs of electron.

$$—\ddot{\underset{..}{O}}—H,\ —\ddot{\underset{..}{O}}—R,\ —\ddot{N}H_2,\ —\ddot{\underset{..}{S}}—R,\ —\ddot{\underset{..}{X}}:$$

$$H_2C=CH—CH=CH—\ddot{N}H_2 \longleftrightarrow H_2\overset{\ominus}{C}—CH=CH—CH=\overset{\oplus}{N}H_2$$

$$H_2C=CH—\ddot{\underset{..}{Cl}}: \longleftrightarrow H_2\overset{\ominus}{C}—CH=\overset{\oplus}{Cl}$$

- This effect extends the degree of delocalization and imparts stability to the molecule.
- +*M* effect activates benzene nucleus for electrophilic substitution (S_E) reaction at *o*- and *p*-positions hence +*M* effect groups are *o*- and *p*-directing.

Negative mesomeric effect (–*M* effect)

In the –*M* effect π-electron displacement takes place towards the electron withdrawing group (but away from conjugate system). Groups which can exhibit –*M* effect are

$$O=C<,\ —NO_2,\ —C\equiv N,\ —SO_3H,\ —COOH$$

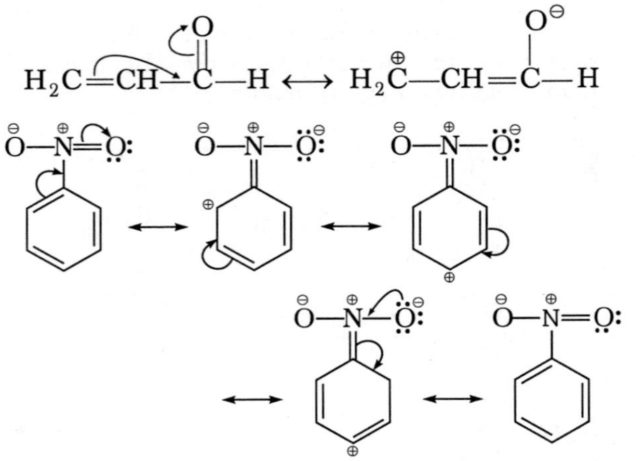

- $-M$ effect deactivates benzene nucleus for S_E but activates for S_N reaction. $-M$ effect groups are *m*-directing.

Application of mesomeric effect

(a) *M* effect does not diminish with increasing the length of carbon chain.

(b) *Ortho-para* directing character of the following groups can be explained by $+M$ effect.

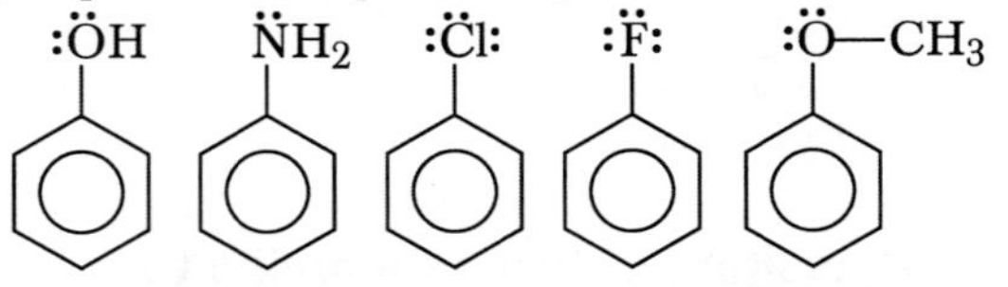

(c) *Meta* directing character of the following can be explained by $-M$ effect.

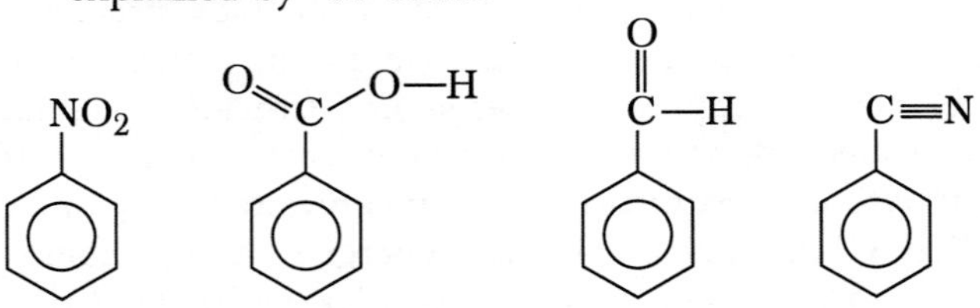

(d) $+M$ of Cl group can explain greater bond strength of Cl–C bond in

$$:\ddot{\underset{..}{Cl}}-CH=CH_2$$

(e) *M* effect also explains greater dipole moment of

$$\begin{array}{l} NO_2 \\ | \\ CH=CH_2 \end{array} \text{ type molecules.}$$

Resonance

If two or more structures are written for the true structure of a molecule or ion but no one can be said to be represent it uniquely, the phenomenon is called **resonance** or **mesomerism.** The true structure of the molecule is said to be a resonance hybrid of various possible alternative structures which are called **resonating** or **canonical structures.**

Example

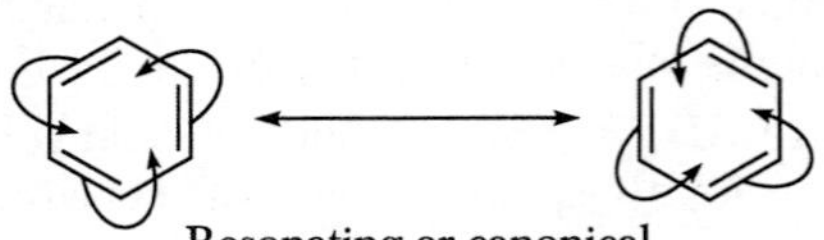

Resonating or canonical structure of benzene

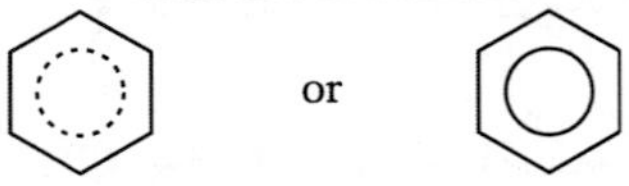

(Resonance hybrid of benzene)

Condition for resonance

One of the most basic conditions for resonance phenomena to exist is, the system must be "conjugated". A second condition is the, atoms involved in resonance must be coplanar or capable of adopting coplanar conformation. There are various types of conjugation possible in a system that allows delocalization of electrons to occur. They are :

(a) Case of alternate single-multiple bonds.

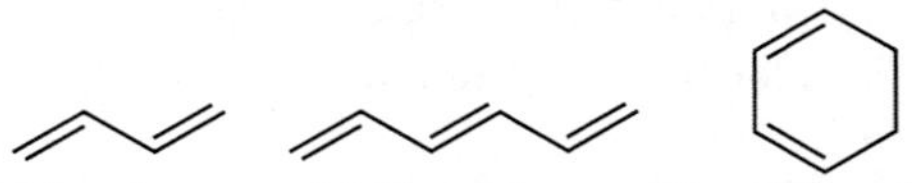

1,3-butadiene 1,3,5-hexatriene 1,3,-cyclohexadiene

$$H-C\equiv C-CH=CH_2$$

But-1-en-3-yne

(b) Case with a non-bonded electron pair bound to multiple bonds.

$$-\overset{|}{C}=\overset{|}{C}-\ddot{Z}$$

Z-must have an atom bonded to unsaturated carbon, with a lone pair of electrons, *e.g.,*

$$\underset{\text{I}}{H_2C=CH-\ddot{\underset{..}{Cl}}:} \quad \underset{\text{II}}{H_3C-\ddot{\underset{..}{O}}-CH=CH_2}$$

$$\underset{\text{III}}{H_2\ddot{N}-CH=CH_2}$$

(c) Case of molecule or ion that consist of a pair of bonded atoms in which one has a lone pair and other has deficiency of a lone pairs.

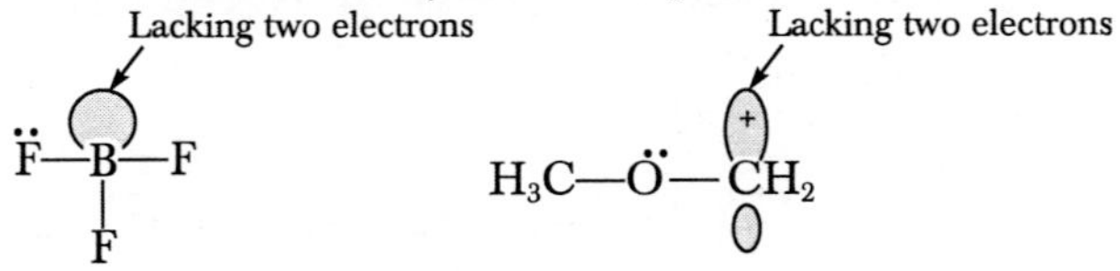

(d) A π bonded atoms bonded to an atom lacking a pair of electrons, *e.g.,*

$$H_2C{=}CH{-}BH_2 \quad H_2\overset{\oplus}{C}{-}CH{=}CH_2$$

Both lacking a pair of electron

Rules for writing resonance structure

(a) Resonance involves movement of electron, *i.e.*, movements of atoms is not allowed

Structure III is not a valid resonance structure since, it involves movement of H which is not allowed.

$$\underset{\text{I}}{CH_3{-}CH{=}CH{-}CH{=}CH_2} \longleftrightarrow \underset{\text{II}}{CH_3{-}\overset{\oplus}{C}H{-}CH{=}CH{-}\overset{\ominus}{C}H_2} \longleftrightarrow \underset{\text{III}}{\overset{\oplus}{C}H_2{-}CH_2{-}CH{=}CH{-}\overset{\ominus}{C}H_2}$$

(b) All the resonance structure must have valid Lewis dot formula, *i.e.*, octet should not be violated, *e.g.*,

$$H{-}\underset{H}{\overset{H}{C}}{-}\ddot{O}{-}H \longleftrightarrow H{-}\underset{H}{\overset{H}{\overset{\ominus}{C}}}{=}\overset{\oplus}{O}{-}H$$

Not a valid Lewis dot formula since, carbon has violated octet. Here, C is pentavalent which is not possible.

(c) If there are more than one possible ways of delocalization, electron prefer to move towards more electronegative atom as

$$\underset{\text{Not allowed}}{\overset{\ominus}{C}H_2{-}CH{=}\overset{O^{\oplus}}{C}{-}H} \longleftrightarrow H_2C{=}CH{-}\overset{O}{\overset{\|}{C}}{-}H \longleftrightarrow \underset{\text{Correct resonance structure}}{H_2\overset{\oplus}{C}{-}CH{=}\overset{O^{\ominus}}{C}{-}H}$$

$$\underset{\text{Not allowed}}{\overset{\ominus}{C}H_2{-}CH{=}C{=}\ddot{N}^{\oplus}} \longleftrightarrow H_2C{=}CH{-}C{\equiv}N \longleftrightarrow \underset{\text{Correct resonance structure}}{\overset{\oplus}{C}H_2{-}CH{=}C{=}\ddot{N}^{\ominus}}$$

However, if there is only one possible direction of delocalization, this restriction does not stands, *e.g.*,

$$\underset{\text{Oxygen is violating octet, not allowed}}{\overset{\oplus}{C}H_2{-}CH{=}\ddot{O}^{\ominus}{-}CH_3} \longleftrightarrow H_2C{=}CH$$

$$-\ddot{O}Me \longleftrightarrow \underset{\text{Electrons moved away from oxygen, still allowed}}{\overset{\ominus}{C}H_2{-}CH{=}\ddot{O}^{\oplus}{-}CH_3}$$

(d) Atoms involved in resonance must lies in same plane, *i.e.*, in order for electrons to be delocalized over more than two atoms, their *p*-orbitals must be parallel so that they can overlap.

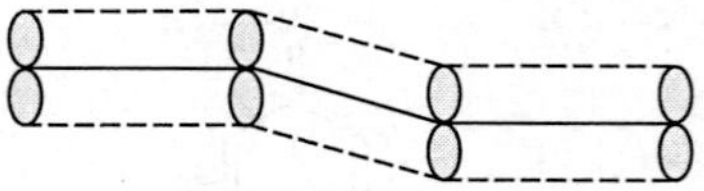

Parallel *p*-orbitals in 1,3-butadiene.

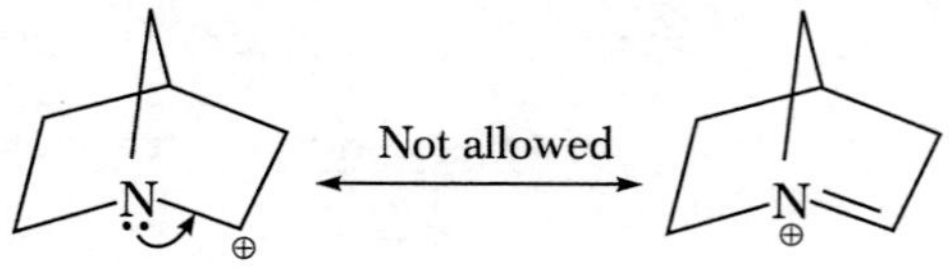

Since, the orbital holding lone pair and *p*-orbital carbon bearing positive charge are not in some plane, the above resonance is not allowed.

Another example of non-planar arrangement is a bicyclic amide where resonance is restricted due to non-planarity

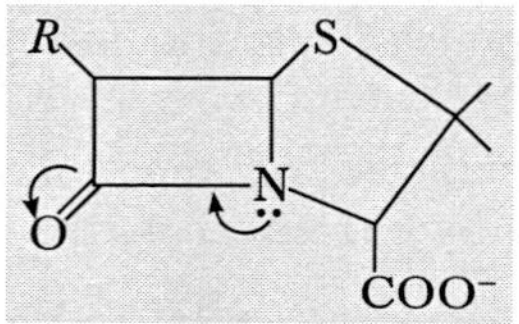

Non-planar arrangement (a β-lactamide)

Here, also delocalization is not possible

Rules for assigning relative stability to resonating structures

For a conjugated system all the resonance structures have either same potential energy or almost same potential energy. If the resonance structures are all equivalent, they have exactly same potential energy. If the resonance structures are non-equivalent, they differ slightly in their potential energies and stability. Therefore, resonating structures of a molecule or ion may or may not contribute equally to resonance hybrid. Following rules summarizes the relative stability of resonating structures. Moreover, these rules must be applied in the same order as described below.

Rule I Contributors with more covalent bonds are more stable than others with fewer covalent bonds, *e.g.*,

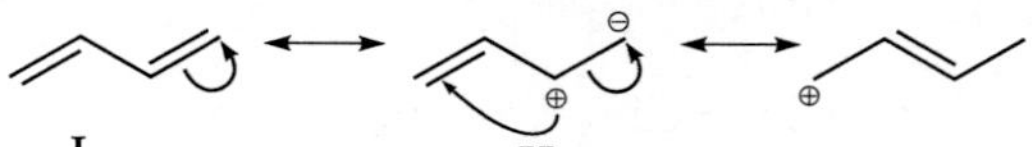

I II

In the above mentioned example, I has one extra covalent bond than both II and III and therefore, I is the most stable contributor of 1, 3-butadiene, contribute the most to resonance hybrid. Other examples are

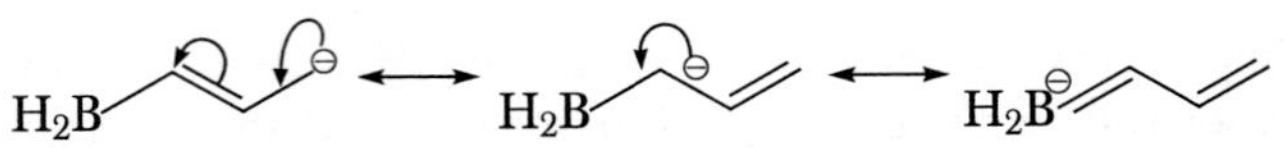

Rule II Contributor with complete octet of all the atoms have lower potential energy, more stable than those with an atom having complete octet, *e.g.,*

$$H_3C—\ddot{O}—\overset{\oplus}{C}H_2 \longleftrightarrow H_3C—\overset{\oplus}{O}=CH_2$$

Has incomplete octet of carbon — More stable, has complete octet of all the atoms

$$H_3C—\overset{\oplus}{C}=\ddot{O} \longleftrightarrow H_3C—C\equiv\overset{\oplus}{O}$$

Has incomplete octet of carbon — More stable, has complete octet of all the atoms

$$H_3C—\overset{\oplus}{C}H—\ddot{N}H_2 \longleftrightarrow H_3C—CH=\overset{\oplus}{N}H_2$$

Has incomplete octet of carbon — More stable, has complete octet of all the atoms

Rule III Resonating structure with negative charge on electronegative atom or positive charge on electropositive atom are more stable and contribute more to the resonance hybrid, *e.g.,*

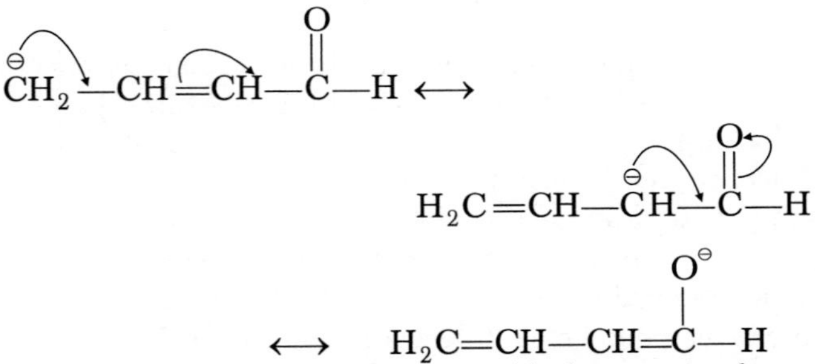

Most stable, has negative charge on more electronegative atom oxygen

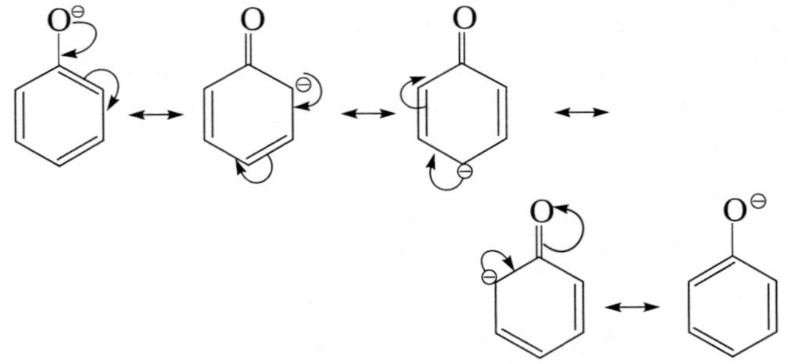

Resonance stabilization in phenoxide ion

I and V are equivalent resonance structures, and they are more stable than others because they have negative charge on electronegative oxygen atom.

Rule IV Equivalent resonance contributors have equal potentials energies, makes equal contribution to the resonance hybrid.

$$H_2C=CH—\overset{\oplus}{C}H_2 \longleftrightarrow \overset{\oplus}{C}H_2—CH=CH_2$$

Both are equivalent resonance structures; contribute equally to the resonance hybrid.

Greater the number of equivalent resonance contributors, more stable the molecule or ions. Some common examples where all the resonance structures are equivalent are shown below.

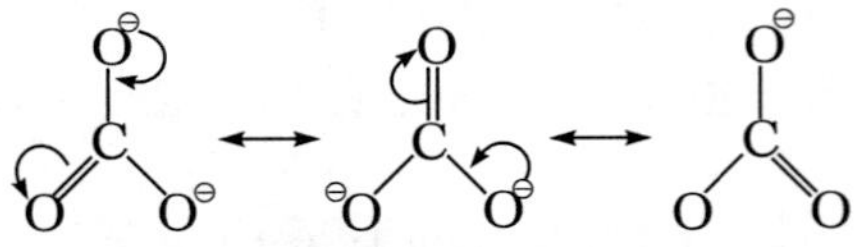

Equivalent resonance structures of carbonate ion

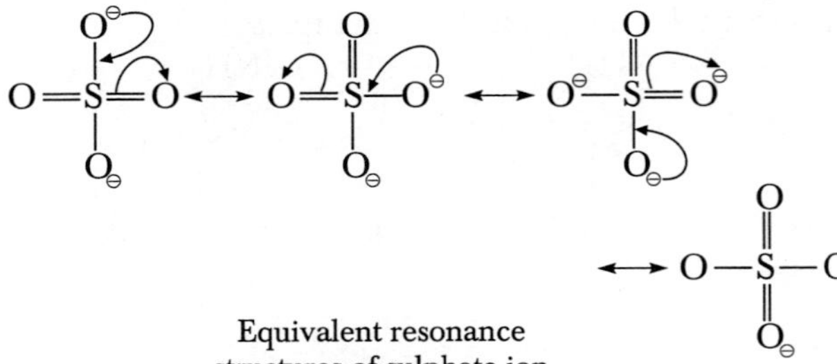

Equivalent resonance structures of sulphate ion

All of the above are equivalent resonance structures of sulphate ion. Due to such large number of equivalent resonance structures of sulphate ion, it is exclusively stable and its acid (H_2SO_4) is strongly acidic.

Rule V Charge separation decreases stability of resonating structure.

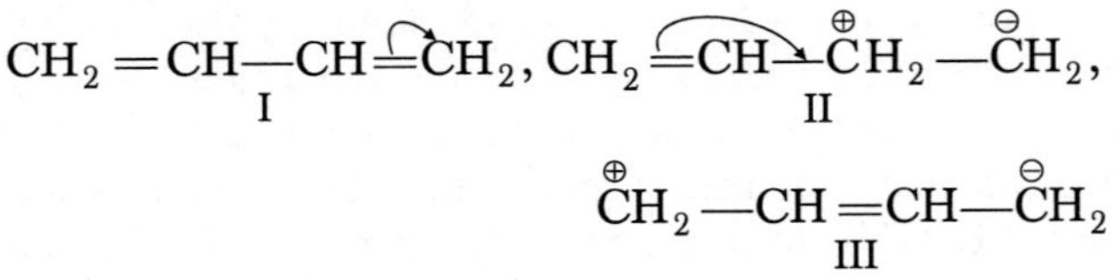

Between II and III, II is more stable due to smaller distance between opposite charges. Hence, the overall stability order is

$$III < II < I$$

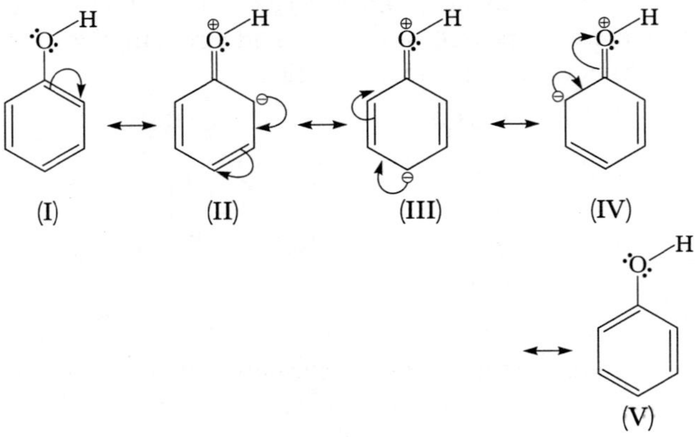

I and V are equivalent resonance structures and they are most stable because they are neutral. Also II and IV are equivalent resonance structure and they are not stable than III because there is smaller distance between opposite charges in II. Thus, the overall stability order is

$$\text{III} < \text{II} = \text{IV} < \text{I} = \text{V}$$

Steric inhibition to resonance and acid-base strength

Resonance ability of an atom is lost if it loses planarity with the other part of system due to steric crowding by bulky groups on adjacent positions. To illustrate it, let us consider the following two examples.

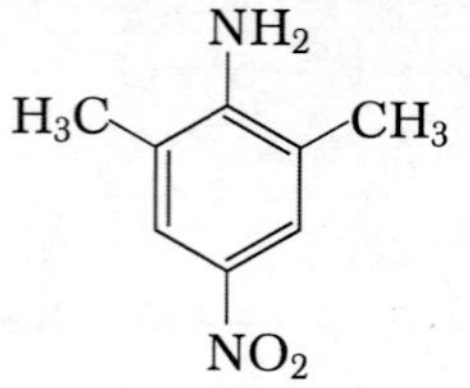

(*A*)

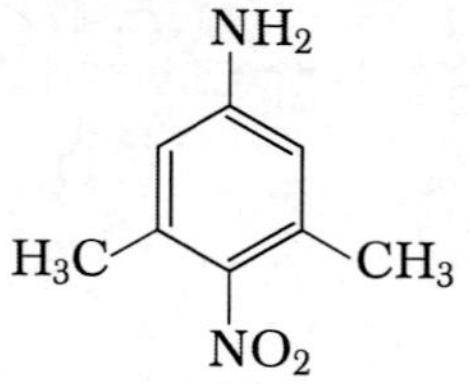

(*B*)

The above two compounds *A* and *B* have everything identical except positions of two methyl groups. It is expected that *A* should be stronger base than *B* due to closeness of two electron donating methyl groups to —NH_2. The fact is opposite to this. The significant factor affecting the basic strength of these two compounds is —*R* effect of —NO_2 group. In compound *B*, —NO_2 is surrounded by two bulky methyl group and they sterically repel the —NO_2 group. In order to minimize the steric repulsion by the two adjacent methyl group, the nitro group loses planarity with the benzene ring. So now —NO_2, due to lack of planarity weigh ring, not able to resonate. This is known as **steric inhibition to resonance.** Thus, in *B*, —NO_2 is not decreasing basic strength by resonance. In *A* —NO_2 lies in the plane of ring, it is in resonance with ring, decreases basic strength of —NH_2 by resonance, hence, weaker base. The above principle applies well in case of acid strength also. Let us consider the following two acids

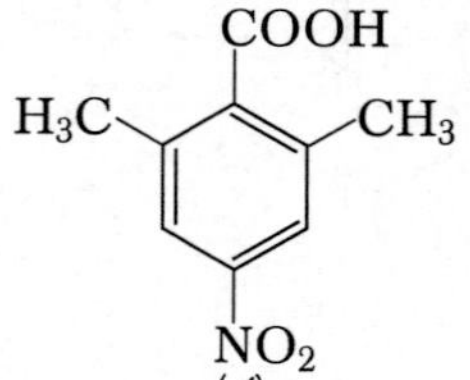

(*A*)

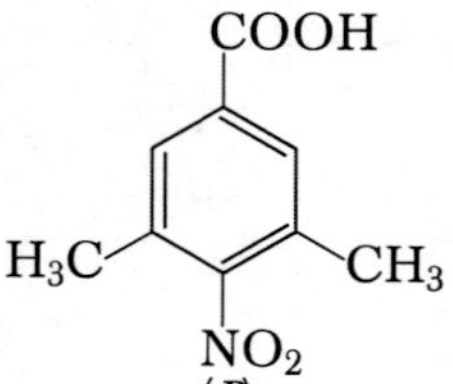

(*B*)

A is stronger acid inspite of closeness of two electron donating methyl group to —COOH. It is once again due to the same reason than in *A*, —NO_2 is in resonance with the ring, increases the acid strength. In *B*, there is steric inhibition to resonance to —NO_2 group, therefore, a weaker acid.

Hyperconjugative Effect

When a C—H σ-bond is separated from a π-system of C=C bond or a vacant *p*-AO by a σ-bond, that is when a C—H bond is conjugated with a C=C bondor a vacant *p*-AO, the bonded σ-electron pair of C—H is displaced toward the π-MO or the vacant *p*-AO. This increase the electron density at C=C bond or in the empty *p*-AO.

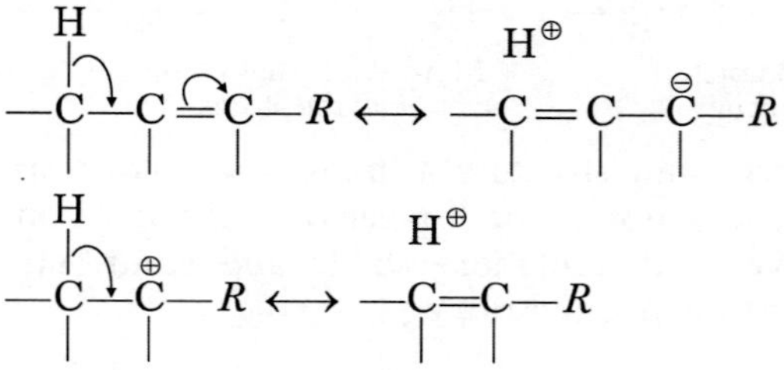

A hyperconjugation, therefore is a resonance effect where a C—H σ-bond snaps and the σ-electron pair is delocalized on to a C=C bond or a vacant *p*-AO. Since, in the resonating forms no bond exists between the C and H atoms this phenomenon is also termed as a **no bond resonance.** The concept of hyperconjugation was developed by Baker and Nathan and is also known as **Baker and Nathan effect.**

The hyperconjugative effect always releases the electron density to the reaction site. This effect plays an important role on the rate and regioselectivity of the electrophilic substitutions of alkyl benzenes and also on the stability of alkenes and reaction intermediates.

Example

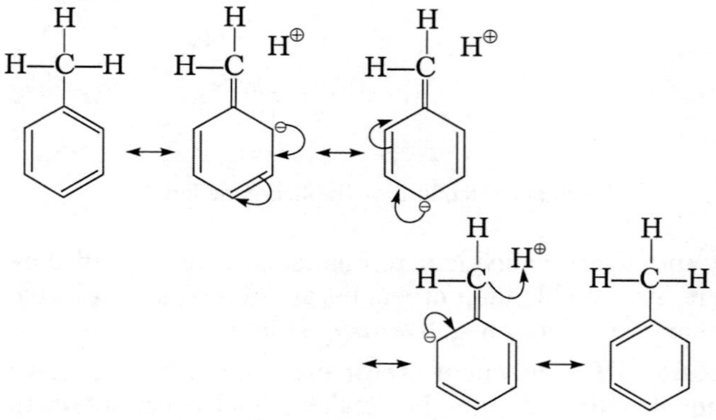

The hyperconjugative effect in toluene increases electron density on *o*- and *p*-positions.

Application of hyperconjugation

(a) **Heat of hydrogenation** Greater the number of α-hydrogen results greater stability and thus lower heat of hydrogenation.

$$CH_2{=}CH_2 < CH_3{-}CH{=}CH_2 < CH_3{-}\underset{\underset{CH_3}{|}}{C}{=}CH_2 <$$

$$CH_3{-}\underset{\underset{CH_3}{|}}{C}{=}CH{-}CH_3 < CH_3{-}\overset{\overset{CH_3}{|}}{C}{=}\overset{\overset{CH_3}{|}}{C}{-}CH_3$$

(b) **Stability of carbocation** Greater the number of α-hydrogen results greater stability of carbocation. **Example**

(i) $\overset{\oplus}{C}H_3 < CH_3{-}\overset{\oplus}{C}H_2 < CH_3{-}\underset{\underset{CH_3}{|}}{C}H^{\oplus} < CH_3{-}\underset{\underset{CH_3}{|}}{C^{\oplus}}{-}CH_3$

No. of α H → 0, 3, 6, 9

(ii) $CH_3{-}\overset{\oplus}{C}H_2 > CH_3{-}CH_2{-}\overset{\oplus}{C}H_2 > (H_3C)_2CH{-}\overset{\oplus}{C}H_2 > (H_3C)_3C{-}\overset{\oplus}{C}H_2$

No. of α H → 3, 2, 1, 0

(c) **Dipole moment** Hyperconjugation causes the development of charge hence, it also affects the dipole moment of the molecule. **Example**

$$CH_2{=}CH_2 < CH_3{-}CH{=}CH_2$$

Electromeric Effect

Electromeric effect may be defined as a temporary electron displacement effect in which a shared pair of electron (π-electrons pair) is completely transferred from a double or a triple bond to one of the atoms joined by the bond, at the requirement of attacking reagent.

$$H_2C{=}CH_2 \longrightarrow H_2\overset{\oplus}{C}{-}\overset{\ominus}{C}H_2$$

$$>C{=}O \longrightarrow >\overset{\oplus}{C}{-}\overset{\ominus}{O}$$

If electrophile is removed, charge disappears and substrate attains its original form. Thus, this effect is reversible and temporary.

Electromeric effect may be supported or opposed by other permanent effects in various conditions as follow.

Case I In the following two examples

(i) $CH_3{\rightarrow}CH{=}CH_2 \longrightarrow CH_3{-}\overset{\oplus}{C}H{-}\overset{\ominus}{C}H_2$

(ii) $CH_3{\rightarrow}CH{=}CH_2 \longrightarrow CH_3{-}\overset{\ominus}{C}H{-}\overset{\oplus}{C}H_2$

(i) is the condition in which *E*-effect is supported by +*I* effect while (ii) is the condition in which *E*-effect is opposed by +*I* effect, hence (i) is easily possible in the comparison of (ii).

Case II In the case of vinyl bromide,

(i) $CH_2{=}CH{-}Br \longrightarrow \overset{\ominus}{C}H_2{-}\overset{\oplus}{C}H{-}Br$

(ii) $CH_2{=}CH_2{-}Br \longrightarrow \overset{\oplus}{C}H_2{-}\overset{\ominus}{C}H_2{-}Br$

(i) is the condition of *E* effect supported by +*M* effect and opposed by −*I* effect therefore it is easier than (ii) because, in the condition of (ii) *E* effect is supported by −*I* effect and opposed by +*M* effect.

Note *M* effect is stronger than *I* effect.

Case III If the multiple bond is present between two different atoms, then electromeric shift will take place in the direction of the more electronegative atom.

$$>C{=}O \xrightarrow{E^+} >\overset{\oplus}{C}{-}\overset{\ominus}{O}$$

+*E* and −*E* Effect

The electromeric effect is denoted by *E* and it is of two **types** +*E* and−*E* depending upon the nature of the group or atom attached to the π-bonded carbon atom. When the displacement is away from the atom or group, it is known as +*E* and when the displacement is towards the atom or group, it is known as −*E*.

+***E* effect**

$$>C{=}C< + H^{\oplus} \longrightarrow >\overset{\oplus}{C}{-}\underset{\underset{H}{|}}{C}<$$

$$CH_3{-}CH{=}CH_2 + H^{\oplus} \longrightarrow CH_3{-}\overset{\oplus}{C}H{-}CH_3$$

−***E* effect**

$$>C{=}O + CN^{\ominus} \longrightarrow >\underset{\underset{CN}{|}}{C}{-}O^{\ominus}$$

Now, let us consider an example of vinyl cyanide undergoing nucleophilic attack by chloride ion

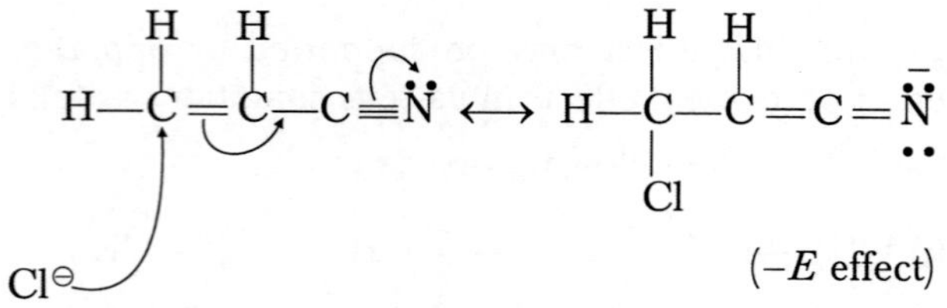

(−*E* effect)

It is the −*E* effect of cyano group which is directing the orientation of attack of chloride ion as shown. Other such groups which causes −*E* effect are —NO_2, —NO, —CHO, —COOH, etc.

Note
- The electromeric effect is polarisability effect and operates in the **excited state.**
- The combined mesomeric and electromeric effect of the atom or group is known as the **conjugative effect** or **tautomeric effect.**
- All permanent electron displacements in the molecule in ground state are described by **resonance.**

Reactive Intermediates

Reactive intermediates are short lived species that are present in low concentration because they react as quickly as they are formed. In most cases, reactive intermediates are fragments of molecules, often having atoms with unusual number bonds.. The formation of a reactive intermediate can be visualized by observing the following potential energy diagram (Figure 31.3)

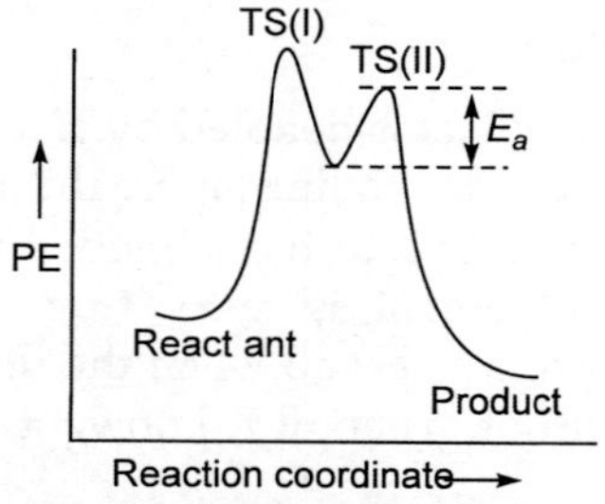

Fig. 31.3 Potential energy diagram showing formation

Some of the salient features of a reactive intermediate are as

(i) It is produced in the intermediate step of a chemical reaction, *i.e.,* it does not appear at the beginning or at the end of reaction.

(ii) Reactive intermediates, unlike transition states (shown at the peaks TS(I) and TS(II), in the above potential energy diagram, are real species, have very short but measurable lifetime.

(iii) Reactive intermediates are not usually preserved, *i.e.,* once formed it must be exhausted before end of the reaction.

(iv) The most stable reactive intermediate is formed in largest quantity that leads to formation of major product. Important types of reactive intermediates formed in organic reaction are : (i) Carbocation (also known as carbonium ion), (i) Free radical (iii) Carbanion, (iv) Carbene, (v) Benzyne and (vi) Nitrene.

Carbocations (Carbonium Ions or Carbenium Ions)

Carbocations are the reaction intermediate in which the carbon with the positive charge has only six electrons in the outermost orbit hence, they are highly electron deficient species. They are highly reactive and gets quickly converted into more stable molecule.

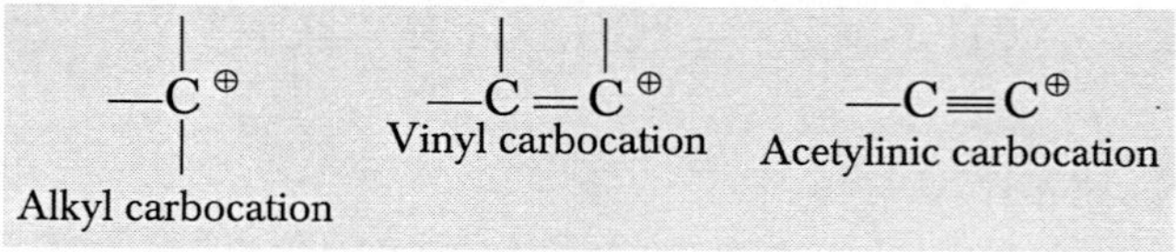

Carbocations are divided into two main classes

(a) **Classical carbocations** (carbenium ions) are trivalent C^+ ions containing sp^2-hybridized electron deficient carbon atom and tend to be planer.

(b) **Non-classical carbocations** (carbonium ions) are penta or tetra coordinated C^+ions.

Note
- According to modern nomenclature accepted by IUPAC $\overset{\oplus}{C}H_3$, $CH_3—\overset{\oplus}{C}H_2$, etc., are termed as **carbenium ion** (but not carbonium ion). Although some authors still refers to $CH_3^{\oplus}$, $CH_3—\overset{\oplus}{C}H_2$, etc. as **carbonium ion.**
- Pentavalent carbocations (*i.e.,* carbonium ions) are much rare than carbenium ion.

$$CH_4 + H^{\oplus} \xrightarrow{SbF_5} \overset{\oplus}{C}H_5$$

The methane on treatment with super acid gives pentavalent carbocation. This carbocation is prepared by George Olah (1963).

Stereochemistry

The carbon atom in a carbocation is sp^2 hybridized and it uses all its three hybridized orbitals for forming bonds with other atoms. The remaining p_z orbital is empty and is perpendicular to the plane of other three bonds. A carbocation has a triangular planar configuration with bond angle of 120°.

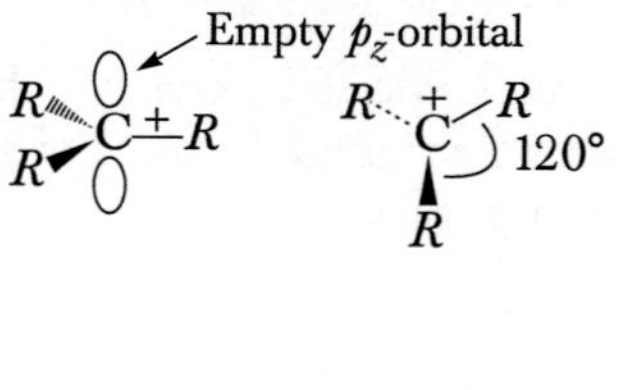

Generation of Carbocations

(a) **By the heterolytic fission of a C-hetero atom bond**

$$R\text{—}X \xrightarrow{\text{Solvolysis}} \underset{\text{Carbocation}}{R^{\oplus}} + X^{\ominus}$$

where, $X^{\ominus}$ = acetate, $^{\ominus}O\text{—}COCH_3$; *p*-nitrobenzoate,

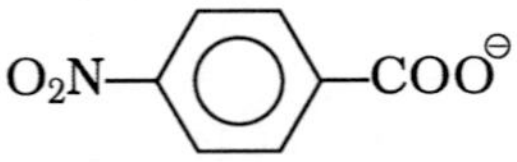
; trifluoroacetate, $CF_3COO^{\ominus}$

and tosylate, 

$$R\text{—}X \xrightarrow{Ag^{\oplus}} R^{\oplus} + AgX$$

where, X = Cl, Br and I.

By the heterolysis of onium salt

$$R\text{—}\ddot{O}H + H^{\oplus} \rightleftharpoons \underset{\text{Onium salt}}{R\text{—}\overset{\oplus}{O}H_2} \longrightarrow \underset{\text{Carbocation}}{R^{\oplus}} + H_2O$$

$$R\text{—}NH_2 + H^{\oplus} \rightleftharpoons R\text{—}\overset{\oplus}{N}H_3 \longrightarrow R^{\oplus} + NH_3$$

$$R\text{—}SH + H^{\oplus} \rightleftharpoons R\text{—}\overset{\oplus}{S}H_2 \longrightarrow R^{\oplus} + H_2S$$

By the heterolysis of diazonium salt

$$R\text{—}N_2^{\oplus} \longrightarrow R^{\oplus} + N_2$$

Stability of Carbocations

- Carbocations are electron deficient unstable and reactive species. They get quickly converted into more stable molecule. The groups bonded to positively charged carbon determine the relative stability of carbocations. Electron releasing group bonded to C^+ increases the stability of carbocation while electron withdrawing group bonded to C^+ lowers the stability.

  The carbocations may be stabilized by

  (1) Inductive effect

  (2) Hyperconjugation effect

  (3) Resonance

- **Alkyl carbocations** are stabilizes by both $+I$ **effect** and **hyperconjugative effect** because alkyl is an electron releasing group. So, the stability of carbocations falls in the order as :

$$\underset{\substack{\text{Tertiary}\\ \text{carbocation}}}{R_3C^{\oplus}} > \underset{\substack{\text{Secondary}\\ \text{carbocation}}}{R_2CH^{\oplus}} > \underset{\substack{\text{Primary}\\ \text{carbocation}}}{RCH_2^{\oplus}}$$

Two factors are deemed to play a role in this case : (i) electron-donating inductive effect of alkyl group, the more alkyl groups attached to the C, the greater is the stabilizing effect and (ii) by hyperconjugation some charge delocalization occurs between the *p*-orbital of positively charged carbon and σ bond of the β C–H. However, the presence of electron attracting groups (like nitro, carbonyl, etc.) adjacent to the carbon atom bearing positive charge makes the carbocation less stable. Thus, $O_2NCH_2CH_2^{\oplus}$ is less stable than $CH_3CH_2CH_2^{\oplus}$.

- A vinyl group stabilizes a carbocation more than does a methyl group because vinyl group is an extremely effective electron-releasing substituent. A resonance interaction of the type shown permits the π-electrons of the double bond to be delocalized and disperses the positive charge.

$$CH_2{=}\overset{\oplus}{C}H > \overset{\oplus}{C}H_3$$

- The stability of a carbocation can also be explained by **resonance.** By resonance the positive charge on the central carbon atom gets dispersed over other carbon atoms and this renders stability to the carbocation. The more the canonical structures for a carbocation, the more stable it will be.

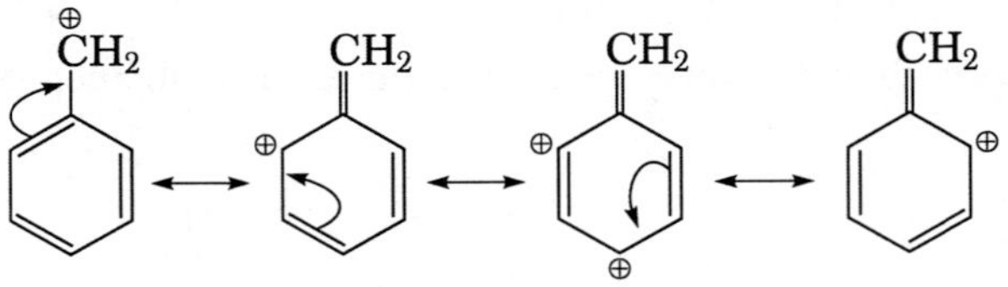

(Benzyl carbocation)
(Four canonical structures)

$$CH_2{=}CH\text{—}\overset{\oplus}{C}H_2 \longleftrightarrow \overset{\oplus}{C}H_2\text{—}CH{=}CH_2$$

Allyl carbocation
(Two canonical structures)

So, the order of reactivity of the three carbocations is :

$$C_6H_5\overset{\oplus}{C}H_2 > CH_2{=}CH\text{—}\overset{\oplus}{C}H_2 > CH_3CH_2\overset{\oplus}{C}H_2$$

- Cyclopropenyl cation is also stable due to aromatization.

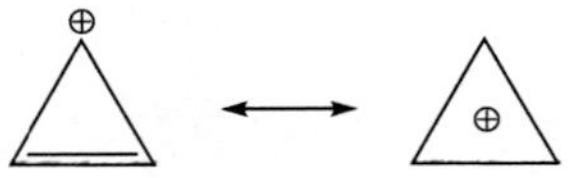

- The overall stability order of carbocation can be given as

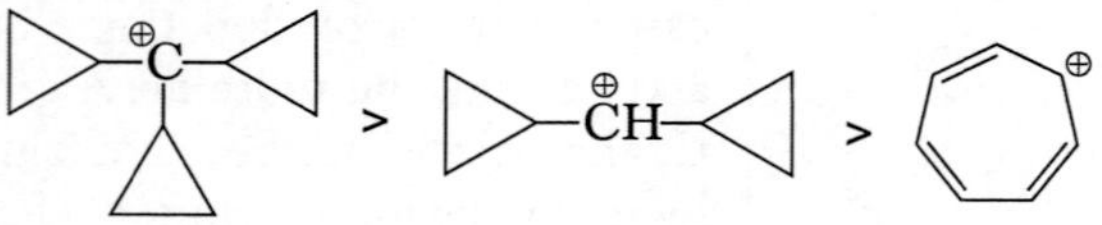

$$> (C_6H_5)_3\overset{\oplus}{C} > (C_6H_5)_2\overset{\oplus}{C}H >$$

$$C_6H_5-\overset{\oplus}{C}H_2 > CH_2{=}CH-\overset{\oplus}{C}H_2 \geq CH_3-\overset{\oplus}{C}(CH_3)-CH_3 > CH_3-\overset{\oplus}{C}H-CH_3 >$$

$$CH_3-\overset{\oplus}{C}H_2 > CH_2{=}\overset{\oplus}{C}H > \overset{\oplus}{C}H_3$$

Note • When the positive carbon is in conjugation with a double bond the stability of carbocation is greater due to increased delocalization of positive charge

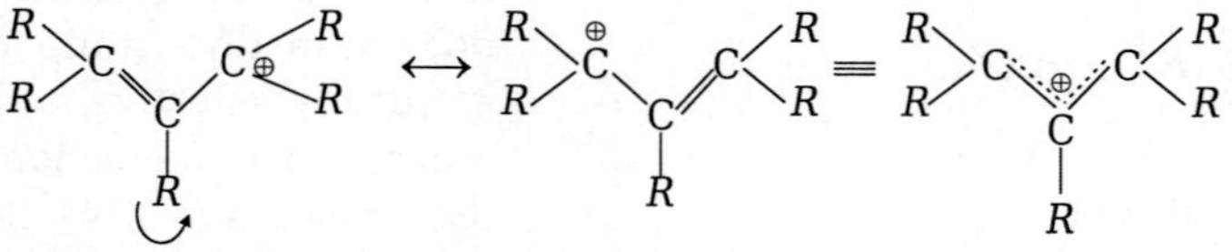

• The carbocation stability is also increased due to the presence of heteroatom having an unshared pair of electrons, *e.g.*, oxygen, nitrogen or halogen, adjacent to the cationic centre. Such carbocations are stabilized by resonance.

$$R-\overset{\oplus}{C}(R)-\ddot{O}-Me \longleftrightarrow R-C{=}\overset{\oplus}{\ddot{O}}-Me$$

The methoxymethyl cation is obtained as a stable solid, $MeOCH_2^+SbF_4^-$.

Reactions of Carbocations

Elimination of proton

A carbocation may lose a proton to form alkene, etc.

$$H-C(H)(H)-\overset{\oplus}{C}H_2 \xrightarrow{-H^\oplus} H-C(H){=}CH_2$$

$$CH_3-CH(H)-\overset{\oplus}{C}H-CH_2(H) \xrightarrow{-H^\oplus} CH_3-CH{=}CH-CH_3$$

Major product

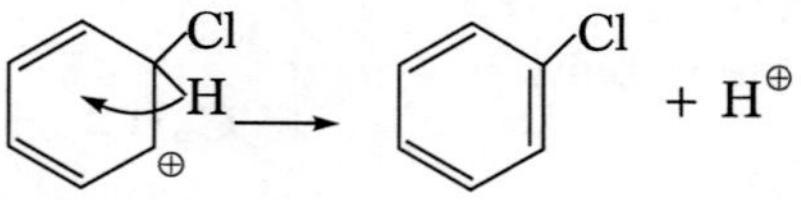

$$CH_3-\overset{\oplus}{C}H(O-H) \xrightarrow{-H^\oplus} CH_3-\overset{O}{\overset{\|}{C}}H$$

Molecular rearrangements

A carbocation undergoes molecular rearrangement to produce a more stable carbocation. A carbocation may undergo rearrangement to more stable carbocation by any of the following ways :

(a) **Hydride shift**

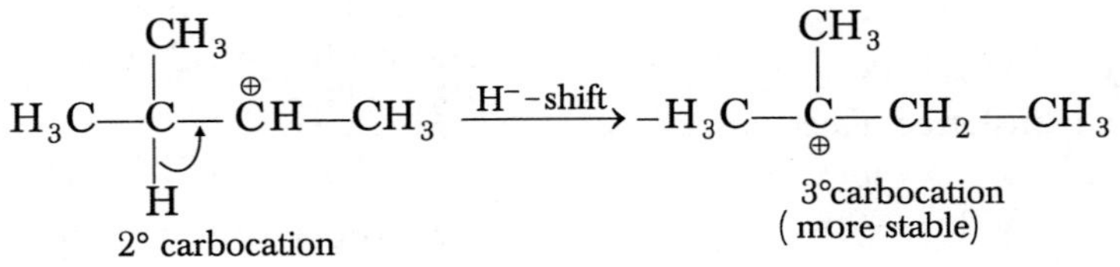

(b) **Alkyl shift**

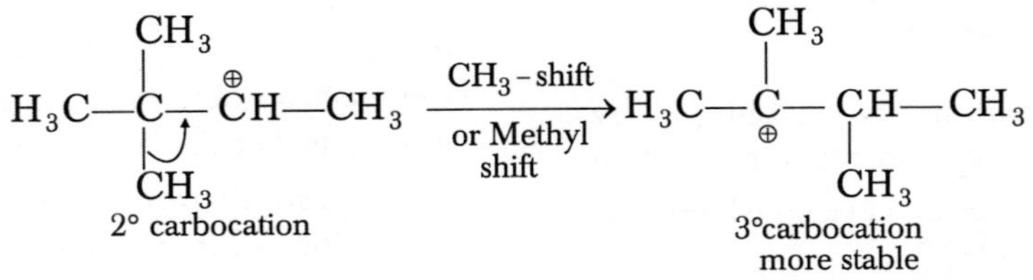

Hydride shift followed by alkyl shift. A carbocation may rearrange more than once. Rearrangement continues so long as the most stable carbocation is formed.

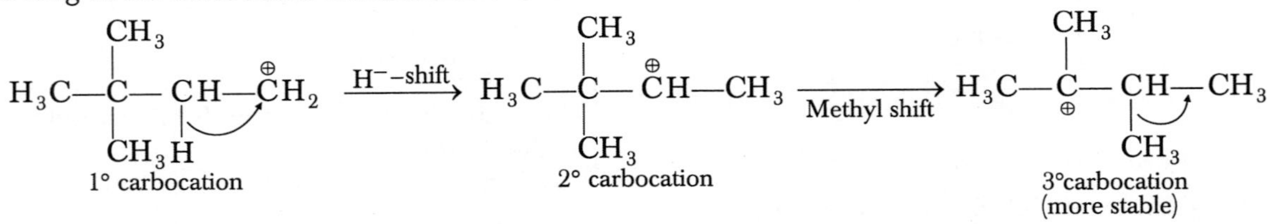

(c) **Ring expansion** Smaller rings like cyclopropyl and cyclobutyl rings are unstable due to angle strain. Hence, this type of rings may undergo stabilization by ring expansion.

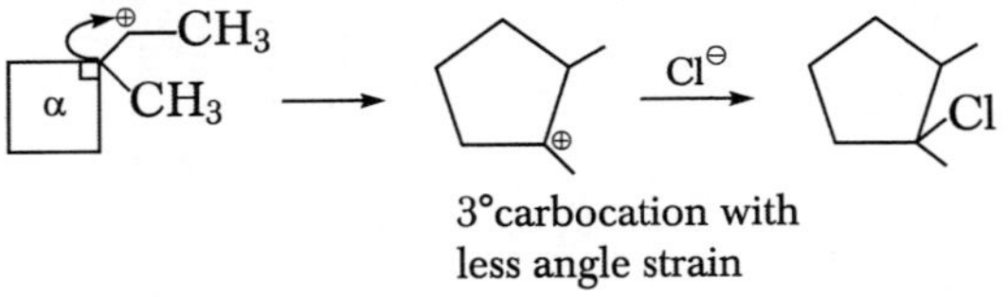

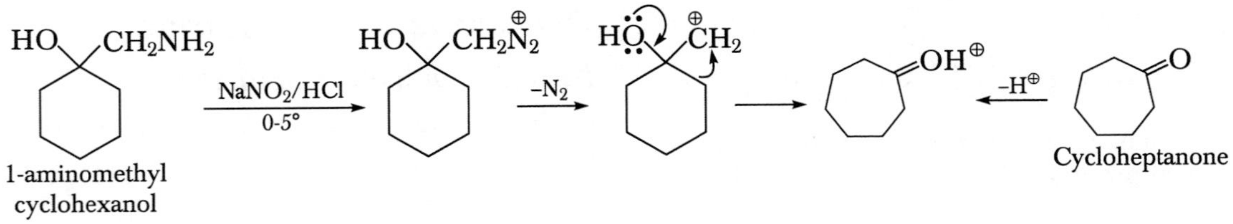

Other reactions

There are some other useful reactions involving carbocations, for example, **Friedel-Craft reaction, Baeyer-Villeger oxidation, Beckmann rearrangement, pinacol- pinacolone rearrangement and Wagner-Meerwein rearrangement.**

Carbanions

Carbanions are the intermediates which have a carbon atom with negative charge. Such carbon atoms have eight electrons in outer most orbit. Out of which six electrons are present in the form of three covalent bonds and two electrons are exclusively with the carbon atom acquiring the negative charge. These are all strong Lewis base and act as very strong nucleophile.

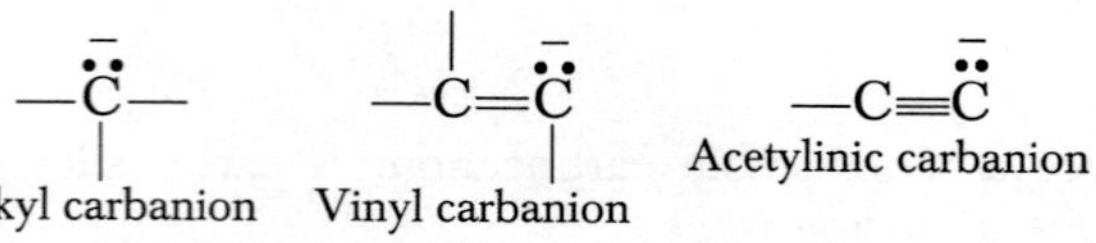

Stereochemistry

An alkyl carbanion has sp^3 hybridized negatively charged carbon possessing an unshared electron-pair. This gives pyramidal (non-planar) arrangements of bonds around the negatively charged carbon.

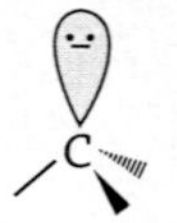

Pyramidal arrangements of bonds around negatively charged carbon with sp^3 hybridization.

However, when the carbanion is stabilized by delocalization, it assumes sp^2 hybridized for effective resonance. The lone pair of electrons are considered to be present in unhybridized $2p$-orbital.

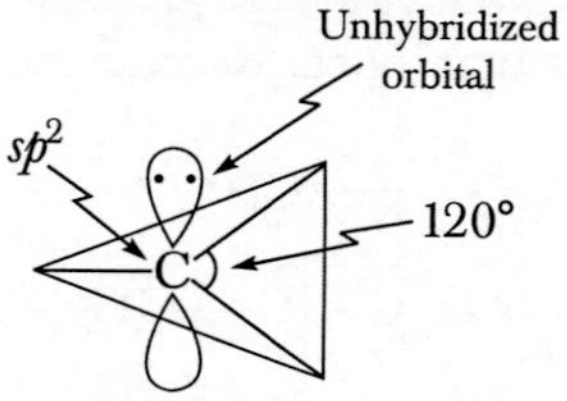

Planar sp^2 hybridized carbanion.

(a) **By the elimination of H^+ from certain organic compounds**

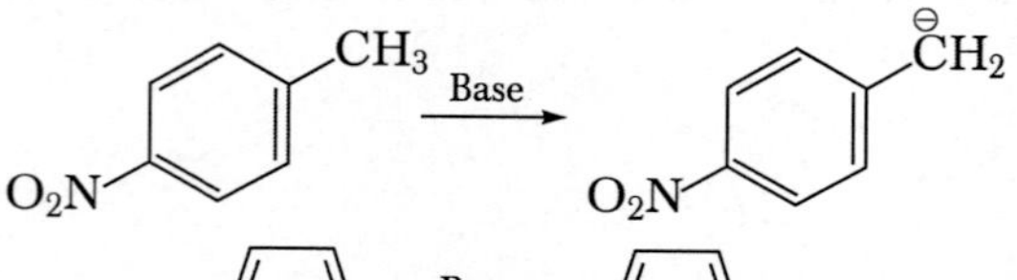

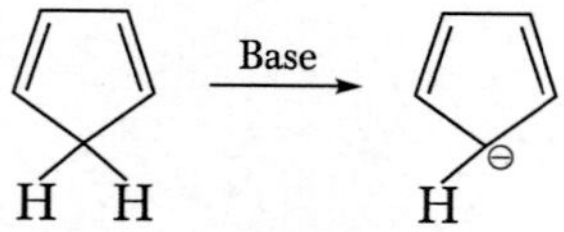

$$Ph_3C{-}H + \overset{+}{Na}\overset{-}{N}H_2 \xrightleftharpoons{\text{Liq. } NH_3} Ph_3\overset{-}{C}\overset{+}{Na} + NH_3$$

In general an acidic hydrogen can be abstracted using an appropriate base, such as NaOH/ether, aqueous NaOH, t-BuO$^-$/t-BuOH, RLi/DMF, HMPA or N-methylprrolidine (NMP) in ether.

(b) **By decomposition of anions**

$$R{-}\underset{\underset{O}{\|}}{C}{-}O^{\ominus} \xrightarrow{\Delta} R^{\ominus} + CO_2\uparrow$$

Stability of Carbanions

- The carbanions being electron rich are very reactive intermediates and are readily attacked by electrophiles (electrons-deficient reagents). The stability of carbanion is increased if an electron-attracting group (like —C≡N or carbonyl) is present in the molecule. However, the stability is decreased if an electron-releasing group is present in the molecule.

The stability of alkyl carbanions of different degree is as

$$CH_3^{\ominus} > RCH_2^{\ominus} > R_2CH^{\ominus} > R_3C^{\ominus}$$

The order of stability can be explained by inductive effect. In tertiary carbanions the stability is the least because the three alkyl groups have electron releasing tendency and therefore. Increase the electron density on negatively charged carbon atom and hence, make it unstable.

- Non-classical resonance also stabilizes some carbanions as in nor-bornenone anion.

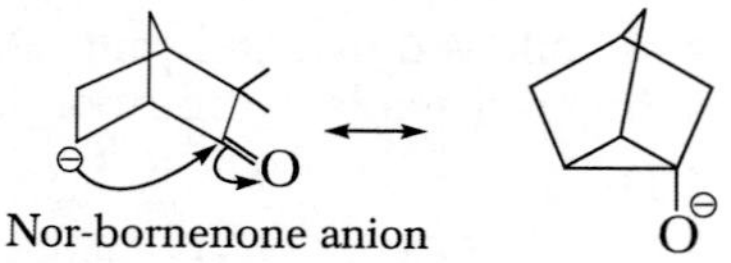

- **The stability of the carbanions is found to be in the order**

benzyl > vinyl > phenyl > cyclopropyl > ethyl > n-propyl > iso-butyl > neopentyl > cyclobutyl > cyclopentyl

The stability of the carbanion when a functional group (X) is present in the α-position, is of the order :

$$NO_2 > RCO > COOR > SO_2 > CN = CONH_2 > \text{halogens} > H > R$$

Reactions of Carbanions

Reaction with electrophiles

Carbanions often act as nucleophiles to react with electrophilic species.

$$R^{\ominus} + CH_3{-}Cl \longrightarrow R{-}CH_3 + Cl^{\ominus}$$

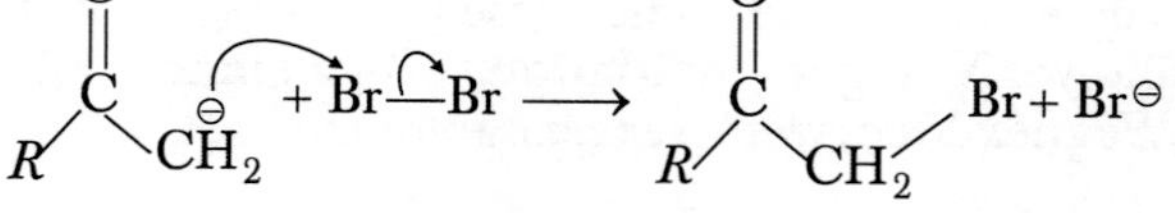

Addition reactions

The carbanions add to the carbonyl group of aldehydes (aldol condensation) or ketones.

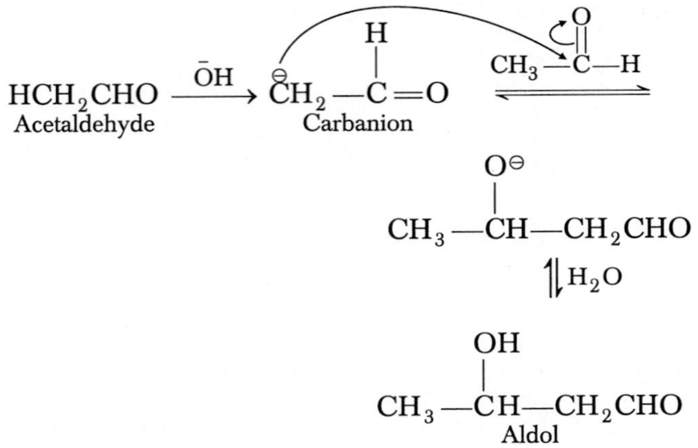

Other reactions which involve the addition of carbanions are reactions like **Perkin reaction, Claisen condensation, Dieckmann condensation, benzilic acid rearrangement** and **Michael addition** (for detail see chapter 32).

Free Radicals

Free radicals are the reactive intermediates that contain an unpaired electron on one of the atom. These are formed by homolysis of a covalent bond.

$$A:B \xrightarrow{\text{Homolytic fission}} A^{\bullet} + B^{\bullet}$$

Free radicals

In organic reactions most often are encountered a free radical with an unpaired electron on either carbon or on oxygen. Therefore, a free radical on a carbon atom consists of a carbon with three covalent bonds and an unpaired electron.

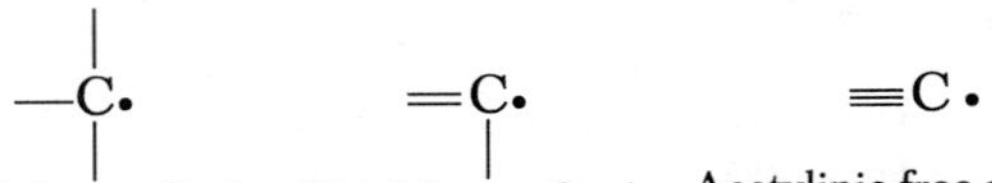

Alkyl free radical   Vinyl free radical   Acetylinic free radical

Likewise, an oxygen free radical contain an oxygen atom with one sigma bond and an unpaired electron in addition to two lone pair of electrons.

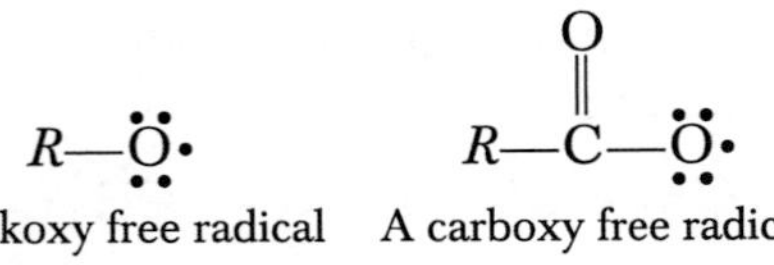

An alkoxy free radical   A carboxy free radical

Like carbocation, free radicals are also electron deficient, highly reactive species and act as strong electrophile in a chemical reaction.

Stereochemistry

A radical is paramagnetic and so can be observed by electron spin resonance (ESR) spectroscopy. For simple free radicals two possible structures have been postulated. The first is a planar sp^2 hybridized radical (*A*), similar to carbocation. The second is a pyramidal sp^3 hybridized radical (*B*), similar to a carbanion.

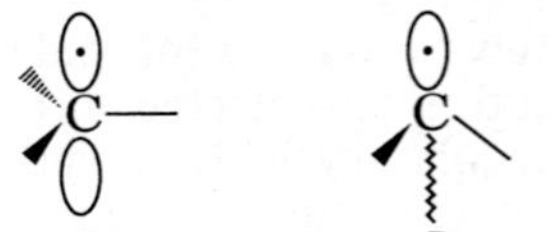

A (Planar)   *B* (Pyramidal)

There is no chemical evidence which supports either a planar structure (*A*) or pyramidal structure (*B*) for simple free radicals. However, using physical methods like ESR, UV and IR, it is believed that simple free radicals have the planar structure (*A*).

Generation of Free Radicals

(a) **By photolysis of compounds**

Acetone absorbs light in vapour phase and breaks to form free radicals.

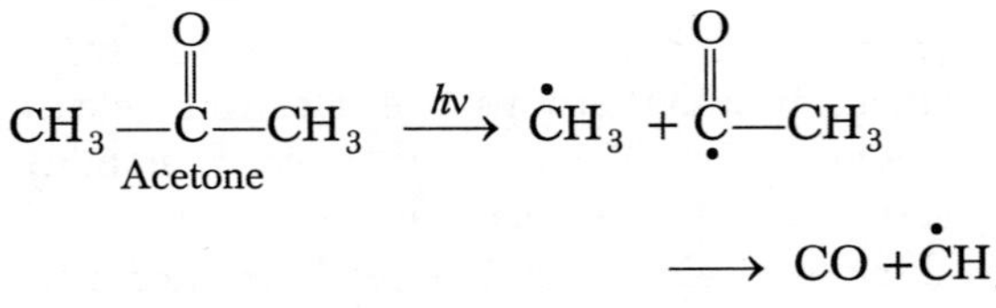

$$CH_3I \xrightarrow{h\nu} \dot{C}H_3 + I^{\bullet}$$

(b) **By thermolysis of organic compounds**

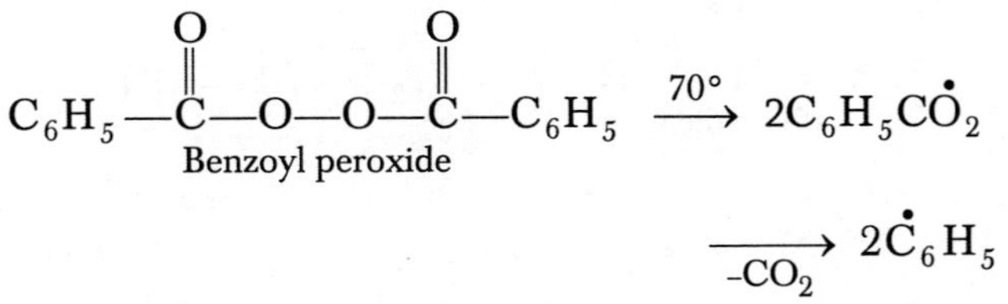

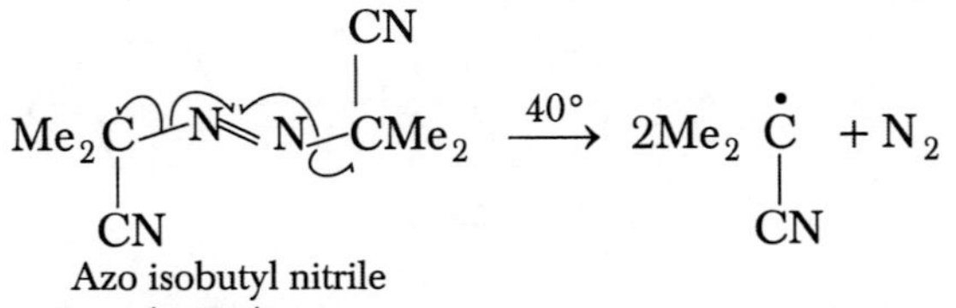

Peroxides and AIBN are generally used as free radical generators from other molecules, and often this triggers free radical chain reactions. **Example**

$$\dot{P}h + Cl{-}Cl \longrightarrow Ph{-}Cl + \dot{C}l$$

$$Me_2\dot{C}(CN) + H{-}R \longrightarrow Me_2CH(CN) + \dot{R}$$

Note • Photolysis can cleave strong bonds that are difficult to cleave by thermolysis.

$$\underset{\text{Azoalkanes}}{R{-}N{=}N{-}R} \xrightarrow{h\nu} \dot{R} + N_2 + \dot{R}$$

• In photolysis energy of only one particular wavelength is transferred to a molecule and in this way photolysis is a specific method for homolytic cleavage than pyrolysis. Thus, acyl peroxide on photolysis generates the free radicals.

$$R{-}\overset{O}{\overset{\|}{C}}{-}O{-}O{-}\overset{O}{\overset{\|}{C}}{-}R \xrightarrow{h\nu} 2R{-}\overset{O}{\overset{\|}{C}}{-}\dot{O} \longrightarrow 2\dot{R} + 2CO_2$$

However, in thermolysis besides the above a number of other by products are obtained.

Stability of Free Radicals

- The order of stability of alkyl free radicals is as :

$$^{\bullet}CH_3 < R\dot{C}H_2 < R_2\dot{C}H < R_3\dot{C}$$

The above order of stability is based on the fact that an alkyl groups are electron releasing by inductive effect, increases stability of electron-deficient free radicals.

Free radicals on carbon with greater *s*-character are less stable as :

$$CH_3CH_2^{\bullet} > CH_2{=}CH^{\bullet} > HC{\equiv}C^{\bullet}$$

- Resonance effect due to conjugation stabilizes the free radicals.

$$\underset{\text{Allyl radical}}{H_2C{=}CH{-}\dot{C}H_2} \longleftrightarrow H_2\dot{C}{-}CH{=}CH_2$$

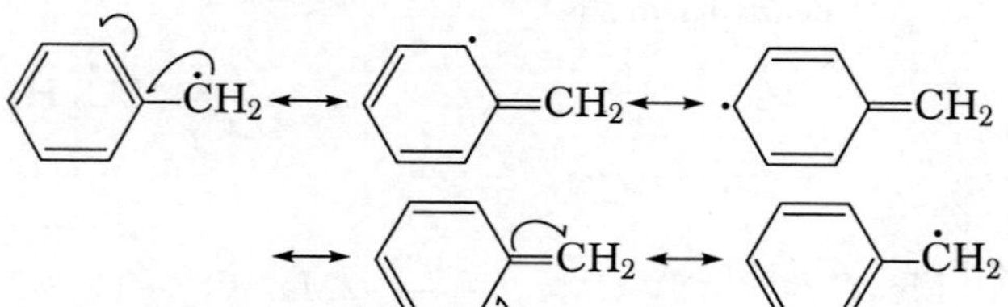

Benzyl radical

- Some cycohexyl free radicals are stabilized by non classical resonance forming bridged free radicals.

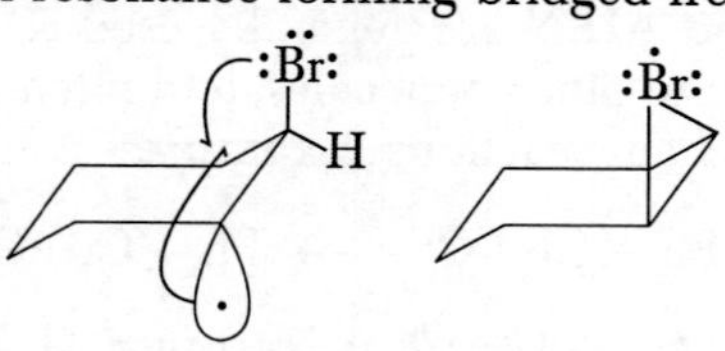

Free radical stablized by non-classical resonance

Some bridge head radicals are as

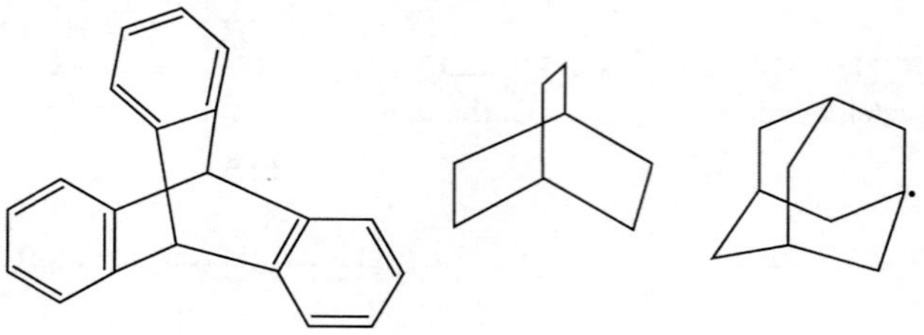

(Bridge head radicals)

Note Sometimes steric crowding prevents free radicals from acquiring an octet configuration and therefore these radicals are unusually stable. **Example** di-*ortho* substituted benzylic free radical is unusually stable.

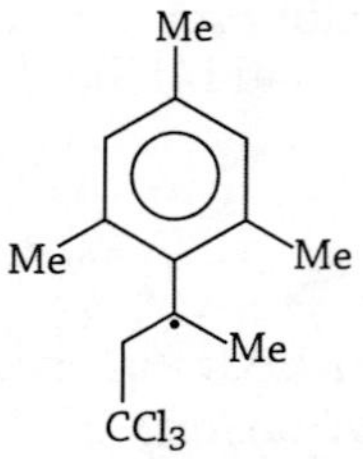

di-*o*-substituted benzylic free radical

Reaction of Free Radicals

Free radicals are very reactive reaction intermediates and have short half-life period. A free radical may couple with any free radical or attack an electrically neutral molecule and generate a new free radical.

Coupling reactions

$$\dot{C}H_3 + \dot{C}H_3 \longrightarrow CH_3{-}CH_3$$

$$CH_3\dot{C}H_2 + CH_3\dot{C}H_2 \longrightarrow CH_3{-}CH_2CH_2{-}CH_3$$

This reaction is used in the termination step.

Disproportionation reaction

At higher temperature the alkyl radical may undergo disproportionation.

$$CH_3\dot{C}H_2 + CH_3\dot{C}H_2 \longrightarrow CH_2{=}CH_2 + CH_3CH_3$$

It is found that coupling takes place with unbranched free radicals while disproportionation predominates with branched radicals.

Other reactions

Free radicals play an important role in a large number of reactions. It acts as intermediate in **Sandmeyer**

reaction, Gomberg reaction, Wurtz-Fittig reaction, Hunsdiecker reaction, Kolbe's electrolytic method, etc.

Carbenes

Carbene is an intermediate in which a carbon atom has two unpaired electrons and is linked to two atoms or groups through two single covalent bonds. Carbenes can be considered diradicals which are formed due to the homolytic fission of two bonds. Out of the four covalent bond of a carbon atom.

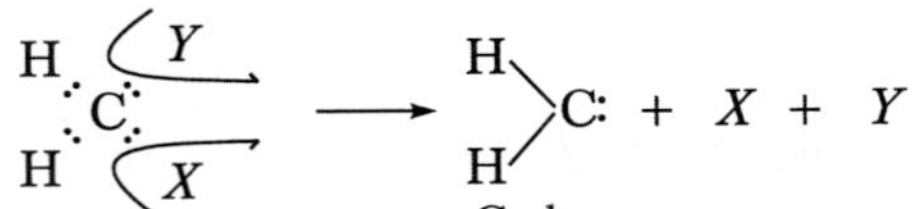

Carbene

Hence, carbenes are neutral, bivalent carbon intermediates. The carbon in carbene has six electrons and so it is electron deficient species analogous to carbocation. Thus, carbene normally reacts as a strong electrophile.

$:CH_2$	$:CCl_2$	$RCO\ddot{C}H$
Methylene	Dichloro carbene	Acyl carbene

Stereochemistry

A carbene is known to exist as a singlet or triplet. If both the eletrons go into one orbital (antiparallel spin), the carbene is in singlet state. There is no magnetic moment in this state. On the other hand, if the two electrons go into different orbitals, they will have parallel (unpaired) spins, such a carbene would have a magnetic moment and is called the triplet state.

The C-atom in singlet carbene is sp^2-hybridized in which the spin-paired electrons occupy an sp^2 orbital. The shape of such carbenes is, therefore, planar. On the other hand, the C-atom in many triplet carbenes is *sp*-hybridized with one electron each with parallel spin in the remaining two unhybridized *p*-AOs. These carbenes have a linear shape. However, bent triplet carbenes are also known where the C-atom is sp^2-hybridized, and two non bonding electrons occupy an sp^2-AO and an unhybridized *p*-AO with parallel spin.

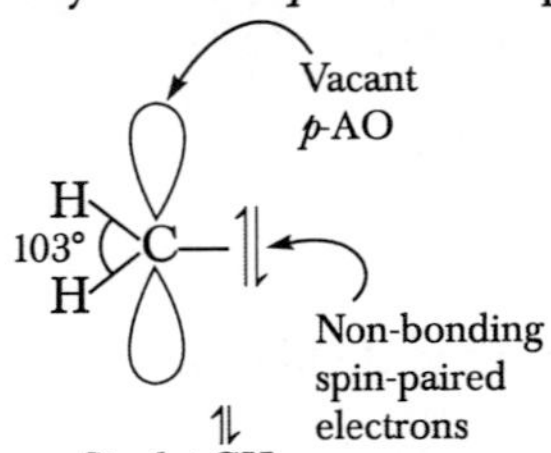

Singlet CH_2 carbene

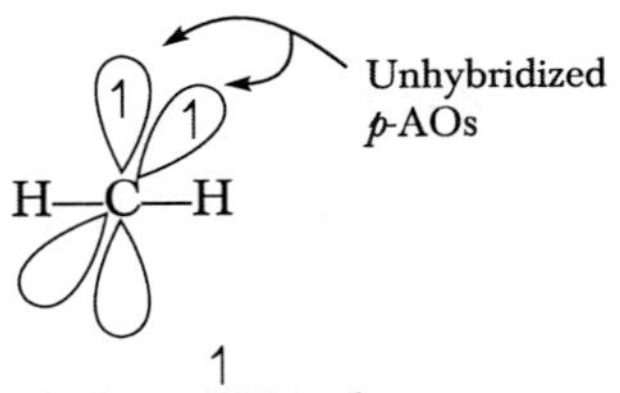

Tripler linear CH_2 carbene

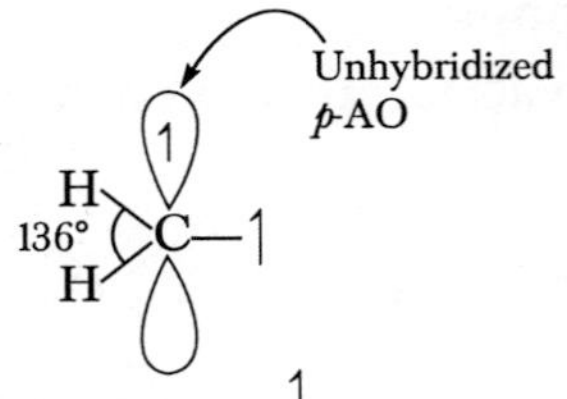

Tripler bent CH_2 carbene

Since, the triplet carbene is a diradical, it has been investigated by ESR measurements. However, ESR measurements cannot be made with singlet carbene.

Generation of Carbenes

(a) **By photolysis of diazo compounds**

$$R_2C{=}N_2 \xrightarrow{h\nu} R_2C\text{:} + N_2$$

$$[H_2C{=}\overset{\oplus}{N}{=}\overset{\ominus}{\ddot{N}}\text{:} \longleftrightarrow \text{:}\overset{\ominus}{C}H_2{-}\overset{\oplus}{N}{\equiv}N\text{:}] \xrightarrow[-N_2]{h\nu} H_2C\text{:}$$

$$\underset{\text{Diazomethane}}{CH_2N_2} \xrightarrow[\text{or } \Delta]{h\nu} \underset{\text{Carbene}}{\text{:}CH_2} + N_2$$

$$\underset{\text{Acyl diazo compound}}{RCOCHN_2} \longrightarrow \underset{\text{Acyl carbene}}{RCOCH\text{:}} + N_2$$

(b) **By thermolysis or photolysis of ketenes**

$$R_2C{=}C{=}O\text{:} \xrightarrow[\text{or } \Delta]{h\nu} R_2C\text{:} + CO$$

$$H_2C{=}C{=}O \xrightarrow[\text{or } \Delta]{h\nu} H_2C\text{:} + CO$$

Stability of Carbenes

- Carbenes in which the carbene carbon is attached to two atoms, each bearing a lone pair of electrons, are more stable due to resonance.

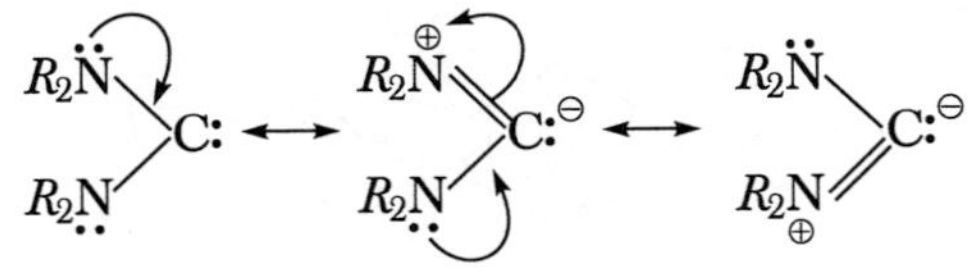

- Triplet carbenes are more stable than singlet carbenes.

Reactions of Carbenes

Carbenes are unstable but very reactive intermediates. Singlet carbenes are slightly more reactive than the triplet species. Their reactivity can be moderated by using copper powder in their reactions.

Addition reactions

Carbenes add to alkene to form cyclic compound.

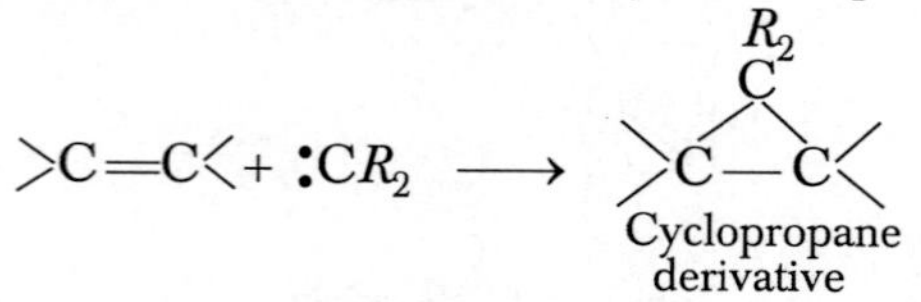

In the liquid medium singlet carbene is formed, which adds on in stereospecific way. Thus, *cis*-alkene gives *cis*-cyclopropane and *trans*-alkene gives *trans*-cyclopropane.

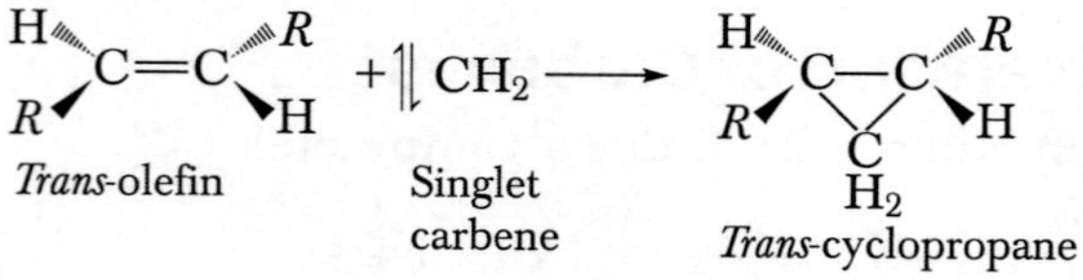

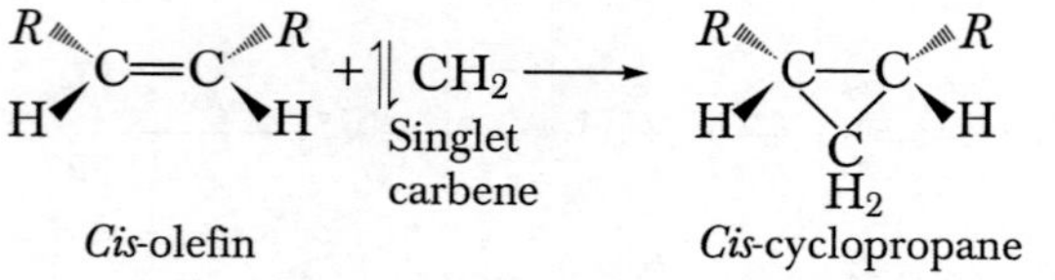

In gaseous medium, the attacking species is triplet carbene,which does not add stereospecifically.

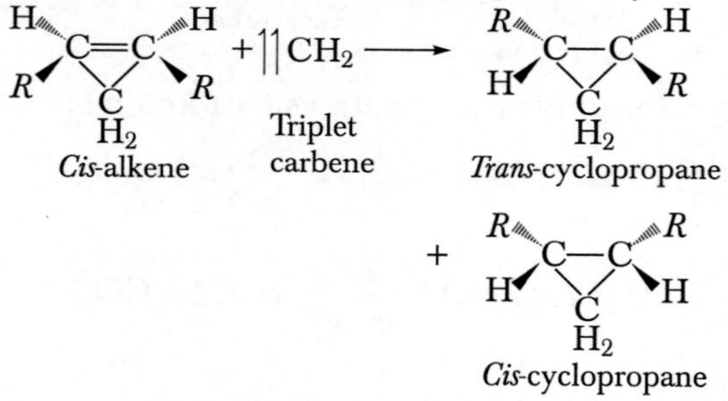

Ring expansion reactions

Ring expansion occurs by the addition of a halogenocarbene across a double bond followed by rearrangement.

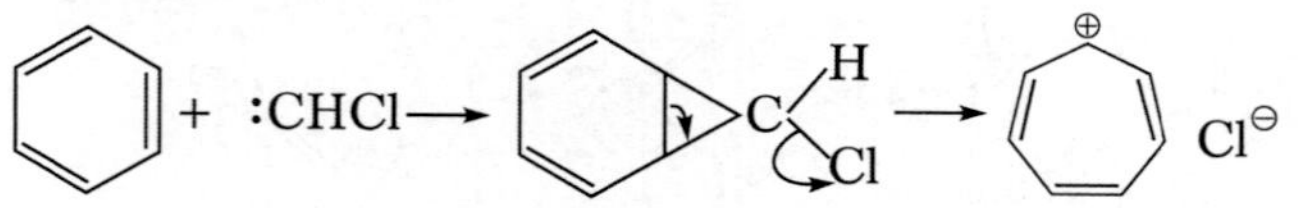

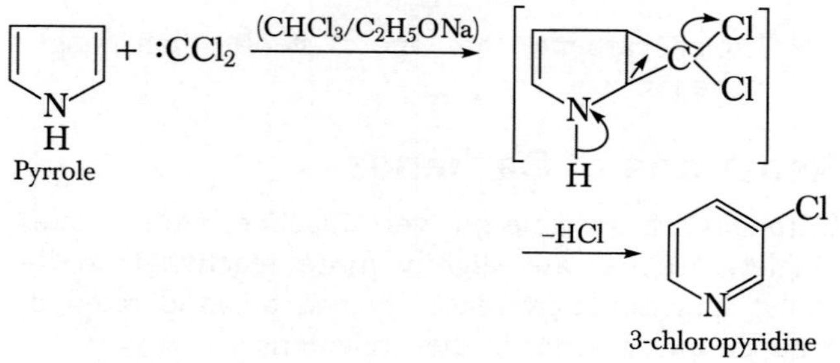

Other reactions

Carbene acts as intermediate in **carbylamine reaction, Wolff rearrangement, Reimer-Tiemann reaction,** etc.

Nitrenes

Nitrenes are highly reactive neutral reaction intermediates. These are electron deficient monovalent nitrogen species. The nitrogen atom in nitrenes has a sextet of electrons. These are also known as imidogen, azene or imene.

$$H—\ddot{N}:, \quad R—\ddot{N}:$$

Stereochemistry

Like carbene, nitrenes are also exist in two states, *i.e.,* singlet and triplet states. In singlet nitrene the two non-bonded electrons are antiparallel to each other and hence, does not show any magnetic moment. On the other hand, in triplet nitrene the two non-bonded electrons are parallel to each other and hence, it shows magnetic moment.

$$\underset{\text{Singlet}}{H—\overset{\uparrow\downarrow}{N}:} \qquad \underset{\text{Triplet}}{H—\overset{\uparrow\uparrow}{N}:}$$

In singlet nitrene the N-atom is sp^2-hybridized. Two of the three hybrid AOs accommodate two non-bonded electron pairs, and the third hybrid AO is engaged in a σ-bond formation. The unhybridized *p*-AO remains empty. The shape of such nitrenes is planar.

In triplet nitrene the N-atom is *sp*-hybridized. One of the two hybrid AOs accommodates a non-bonded electron pair and the other hybrid AO is involved in a σ-bond formation. Each unhybridized *p*-AO accommodates an electron of parallel spin. This imparts a diradical nature to triplet nitrenes that are linear in shape.

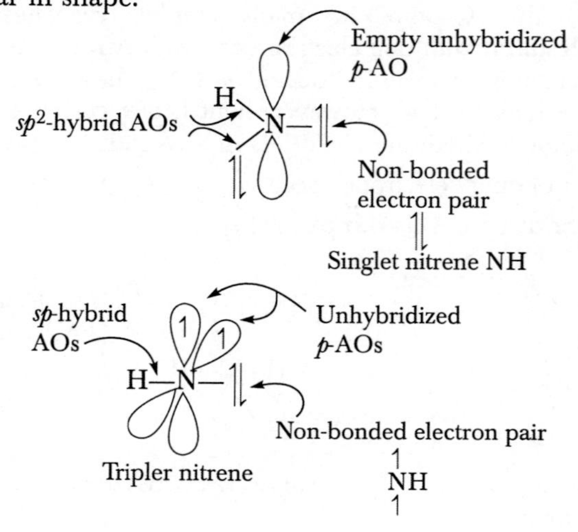

Generation of Nitrenes

(a) **By thermal or photolytic decomposition of azides**

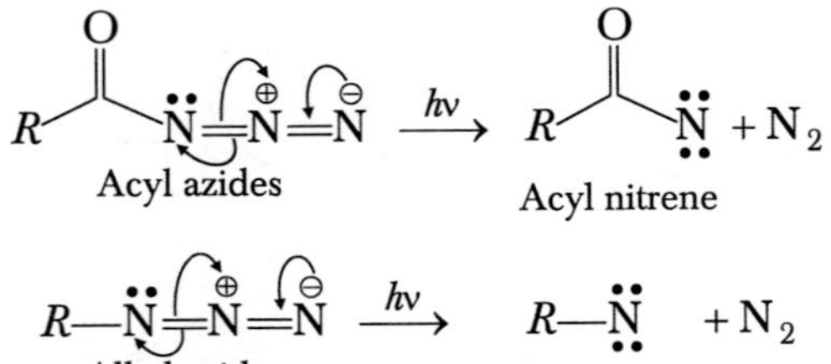

Acyl azides — Acyl nitrene

Alkyl azides — Alkyl nitrene

(b) **By photolysis of hydrazoic acid**

$$HN_3 \xrightarrow{h\nu} H\ddot{N}: + N_2$$

(c) **By photolysis of alkyl isocyanates**

$$R\text{—}N\text{=}C\text{=}O \xrightarrow{h\nu} R\ddot{N}: + CO$$

Stability of Nitrenes

Nitrenes are very reactive species and cannot be isolated. However, a nitrene has been trapped by its reaction with carbon monoxide to yield an isocyanate.

$$PhN_3 \xrightarrow{\Delta} Ph\ddot{N} \xrightarrow{CO} PhN\text{=}C\text{=}O$$

Phenyl isocyanate

Nitrenes can also be trapped in presence of ethylene.

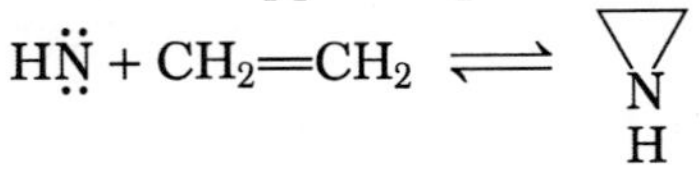

Reaction of Nitrenes

Insertion reactions

Singlet nitrene undergoes a σ-insertion to give 2°-amine.

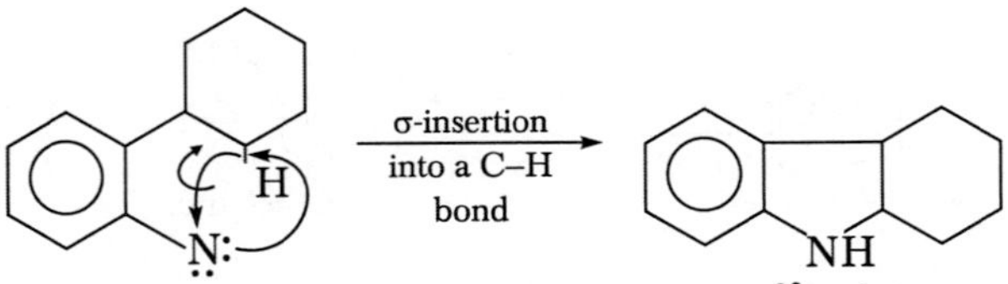

2°-amine

Nitrenes, particularly acyl nitrenes and sulfonyl nitrenes can insert into C–H bonds.

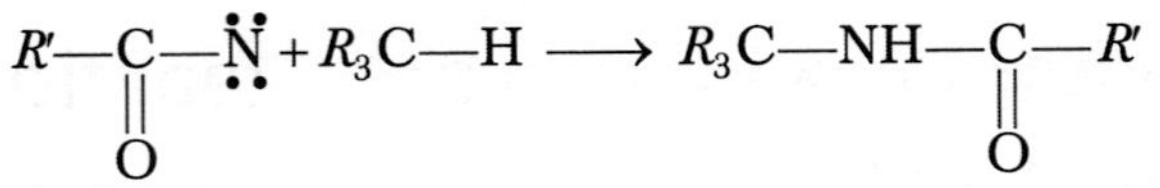

Acyl nitrene

Rearrangement reactions

Acyl nitrenes undergo skeletal rearrangement to give alkyl isocyanates. This rearrangement is involved in Curtius and Hofmann rearrangement.

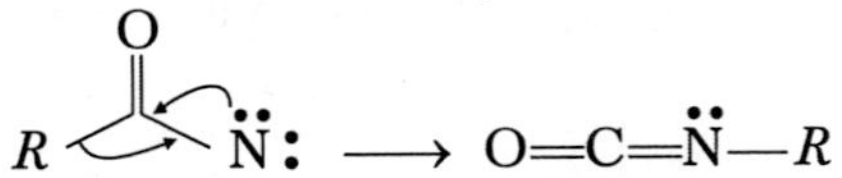

Acyl nitrene — Alkyl isocyanate

Nitrene also act as a intermediate in **Schmidt** and **Lossen** rearrangements.

Benzynes

Benzyne is a neutral, highly reactive intermediate in which the aromatic characters are not markedly disturbed. It has a formal C≡C bond and can be represented as

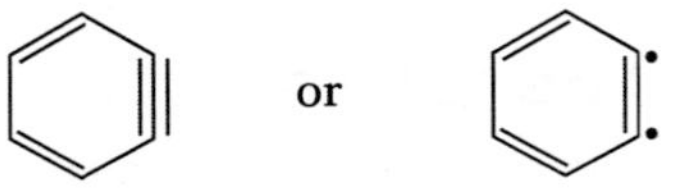

Benzynes are also known as didehydrobenzenes.

Stereochemistry

Except for the two carbon atoms which are linked through a ≡ bond, all the other remaining C-atoms are sp^2-hybridised. The C-atoms linked through the ≡ bond are *sp*-hybridized. Due to these two *sp* hybridized C-atom the intermediate is highly distorted or strained and hence, is highly reactive. However, the presence of *sp*-hybridization does not change its aromatic character. Hence, the intermediate still consist of aromatic sextet.

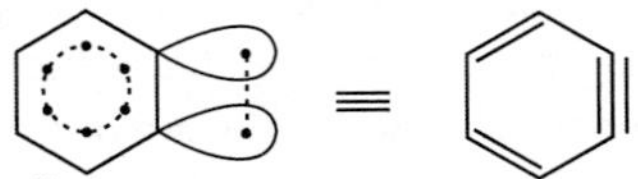

Benzyne

There are three possible ground states of benzyne. For example, a triplet state, a symmetric singlet state where the two half-filled *sp*-orbitals are symmetric with respect to a C_2-axis, and an anti symmetric singlet state.

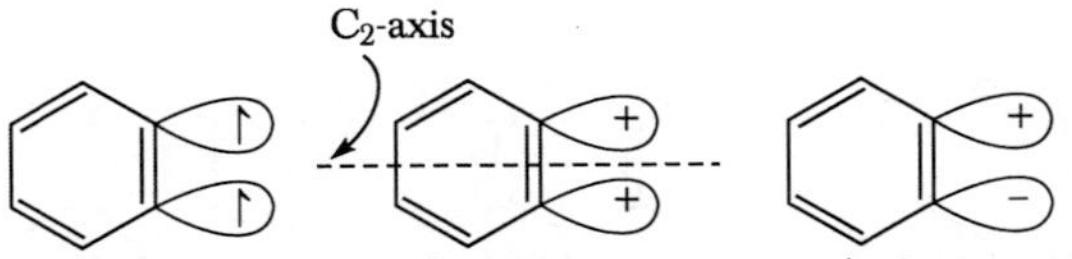

Triplet state of benzyne — Symmetric singlet — Anti-symmetric singlet state

Generation of Benzynes

(a) **By aryl halides**

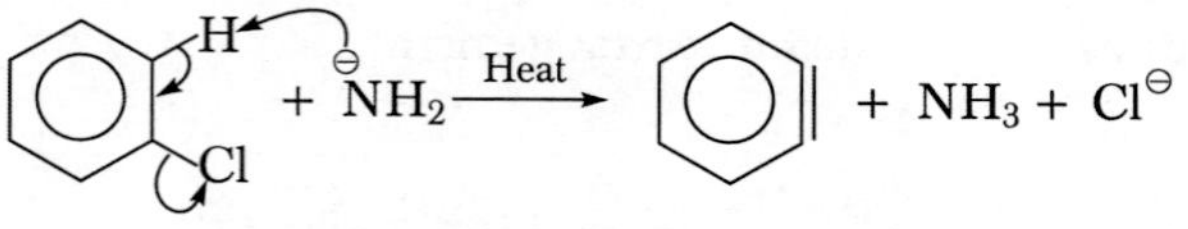

(b) **By *o*-aminobenzoic acid**

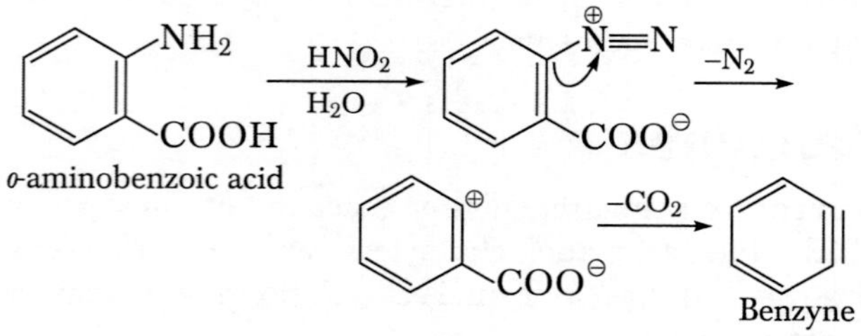

Stability of Benzynes

The structure of benzyne can be represented as

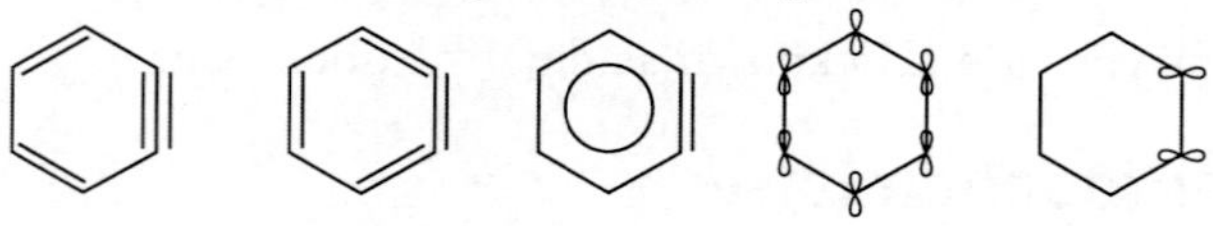

(i) (ii) (iii) (iv) (v)

Benzyne is like benzene stabilized by resonance between structure (i) and (ii) so like the case of benzene a better representation of the electronic structure would be (iii). The extra pi bond (iv) is localized and orthogonal to the other π-bonds making up the aromatic ring. Benzyne can also be drawn as diradical. The pi bond (v) splits homolytically leaving one electron on each of the two atoms that are formally part of that bond. It is an extremely reactive species due to the nature of its triple bond. In benzyne the *p*-orbitals are distorted to accommodate the ≡ bond with the ring system reducing their effect overlap. A suitable chemical trap for benzyne is a cyclopentadiene.

There are three possible diradical didehydrobenzenes as 1,2-didehydrobenzene, 1,3-didehydrobenzene and 1,4-didehydrobenzene. Their energies in silico are 106, 122 and 138 kcal/mol respectively.

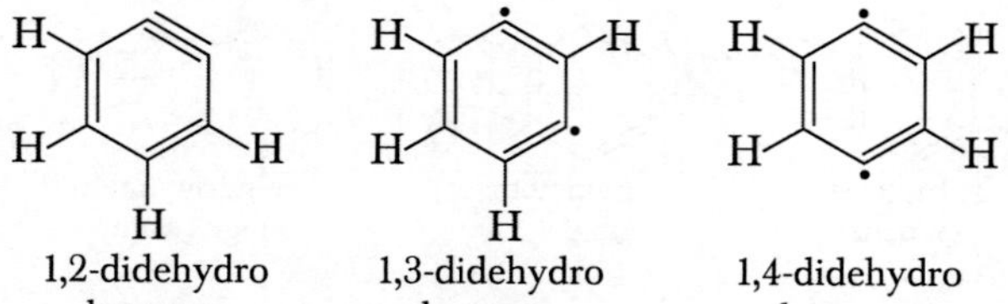

1,2-didehydro benzene   1,3-didehydro benzene   1,4-didehydro benzene

Reactions of Benzynes

Cycloaddition reactions

[2 + 2]-cycloaddition

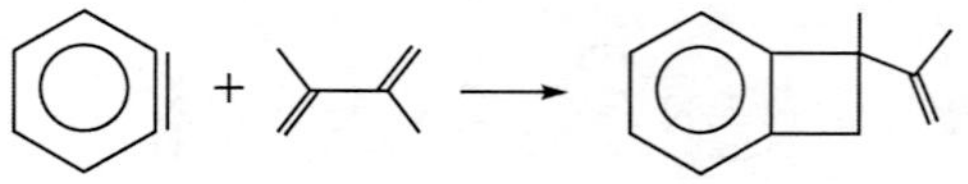

[2 + 3]-cycloaddition

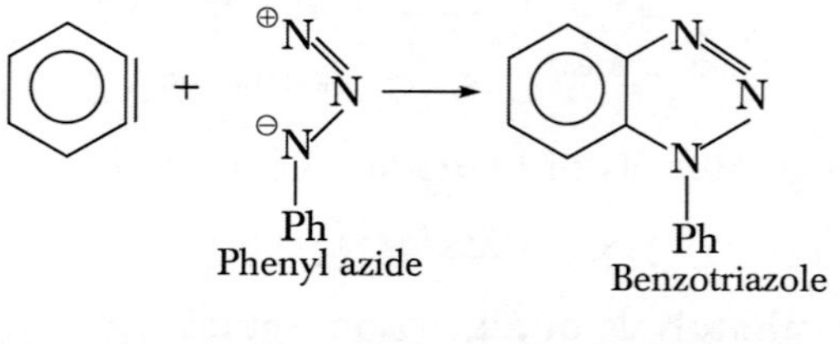

Demerization and trimerization reactions

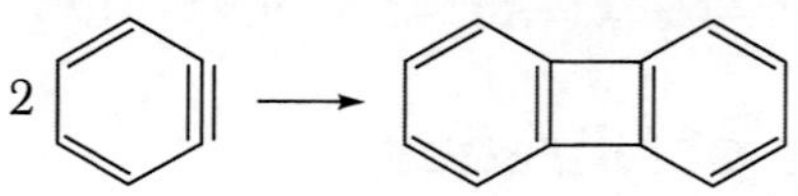

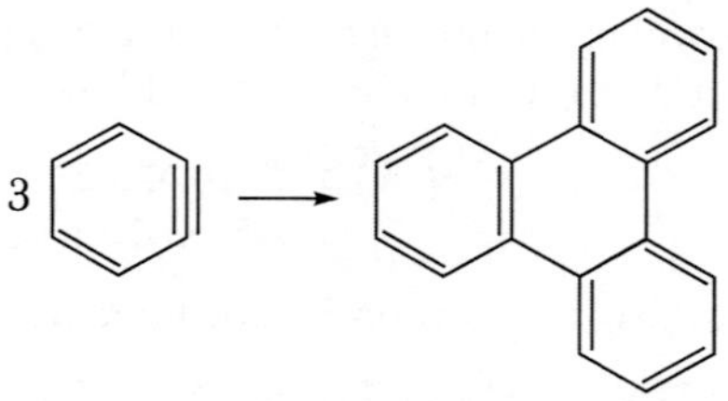

Reactions with nucleophiles

Benzyne reacts with many nucleophiles to form different classes of organic compounds. For example,

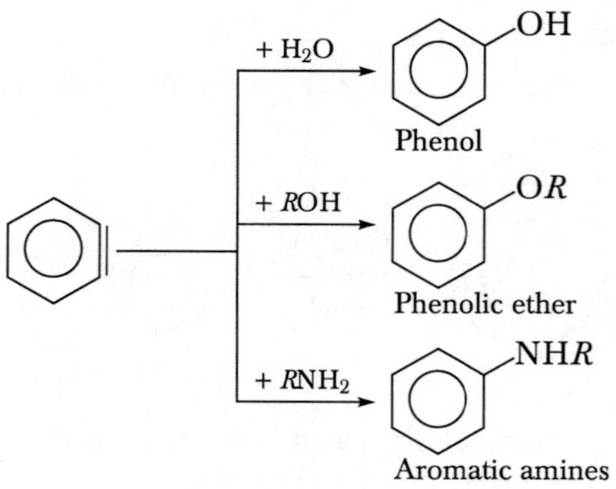

Chemical Kinetics and Reaction Pathways

Organic compounds can be transformed into product and the process. A detailed study of the sequence of steps which are involved in the conversion of reactant into product is known as **reaction mechanism.** Organic reactions proceed by the rupture of covalent bond and formation of new bonds. The bonds are broken by homolytic or heterolytic bond fission.

One necessary condition for a chemical reaction is that a molecule must be activated before it enters into a chemical reaction. A reaction occurs if the collision of reactant molecules is accompanied by a minimum amount of energy called **activation energy.** Moreover such a collision must occur with proper orientation of reactant molecules. The particular arrangement of reactant molecules at the peak of the energy mountain is called the **transition state.** Nearly all reactions must pass through an unstable high energy transition state in proceeding from reactants to products.

Figure 31.4, the reaction profile of the reaction between methyl chloride and hydroxide ion, shows the changes in energy as the reaction progresses. The point on the curve corresponding to the highest energy level represents the **transition state** of the reaction. The transition state is more unstable than either reactants or products, thus, it either continues on to form the products or returns to the reactants. The structure of the transition state is important because it shows how the molecules are interacting. In the reaction of hydroxide ion with methyl chloride, the transition state involves the formation of a bond between the OH and C, as the bond breaks between Cl and C. This structure, showing both bonds breaking and forming, is called an **activated complex.** An activated complex is generally written within brackets ([ ]) and with a double dagger (#) superscript.

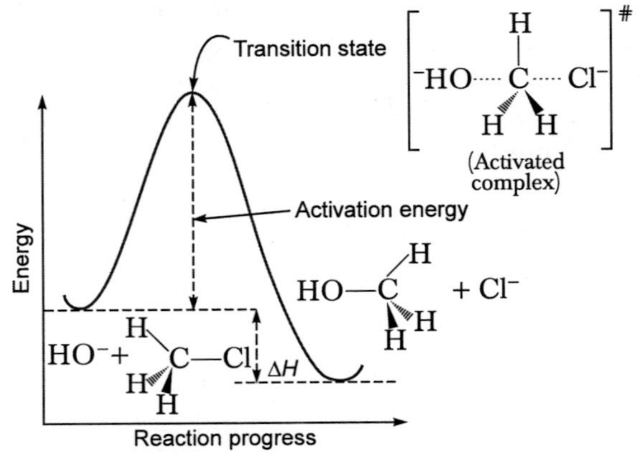

Fig. 31.4 A reaction profile for the reaction of CH_3Cl with ^-OH.

The transition state of a reaction is a molecular complex intermediate between the reactants and the products and is the result of the reactants colliding and reacting.

An activated complex is the chemical species present at the transition state of a reaction.

The rate of reaction is a function of the activation energy which represents the energy necessary to get reactants to the transition state. Let us consider the displacement reaction (S_N2) of methyl iodide with KCN. The activation energy is $\Delta G^{\#}$, which must be supplied to start the reaction (Fig.31.5)

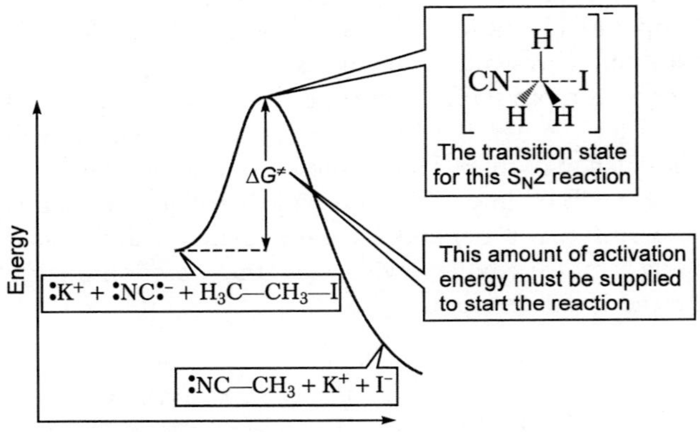

Fig. 31.5. The activation energy for the displacement of iodide by cyanide.

Consider the backward reaction, in which methyl iodide is formed from methyl cyanide and iodide ion. The transition state is exactly the same as that for the forward reaction. However activation energy is much higher than that for the forward reaction (Fig. 31.6).

$$\Delta G^{\#} \text{ (forward)} < \Delta G^{\#} \text{ (backward)}$$

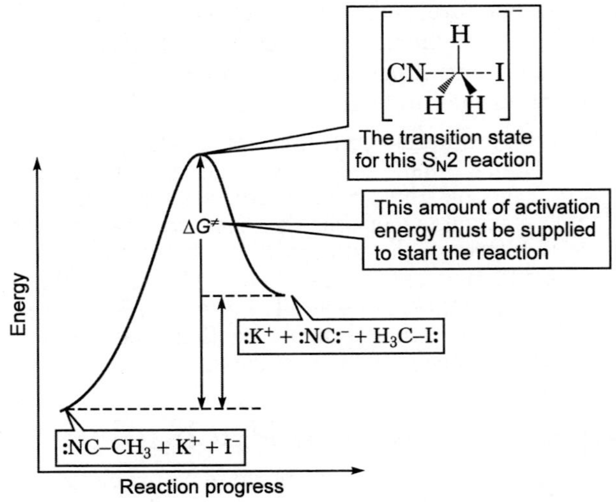

Fig. 31.6 The activation energy for displacement of cyanide by iodide.

Therefore, the backward reaction will not be very successful. Thus, the change in free energy $\Delta G^{\#}$ required to form transition states from reactant molecules is a direct measure of the ease of the reaction.

Kinetic *versus* Thermodynamic Control

Consider the energy diagrams of two reactions $A \rightarrow B$ and $A \rightarrow C$. Activation energy required for the conversion $A \rightarrow C$ being less, product C will form comparatively faster. Hence, *C* is known as **kinetic product.** However, *B*, being associated with less free energy, is more stable. Hence, if the reaction is proceed for a long time. *C* will revert back to *A* which will slowly change to *B*. Under these conditions, the three species will be in equilibrium and the relative amounts of *B* and *C* will depend on their relative stabilities. *B* being more stable will be the predominating thermodynamic product.

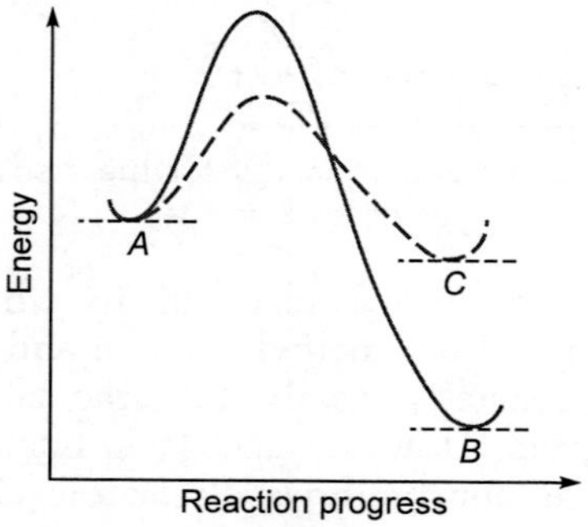

Fig. 31.7

Mild temperature and short reaction time favour the formation of kinetic product *C* whereas higher temperature and longer reaction time will favour the formation of thermodynamic product *B*.

Note • In exothermic reaction the products are more stable than reactants, and in endothermic reaction, the products are less stable than the reactants. For the exothermic reaction the difference in enthalpy ($\Delta H°$) between products and reactants is negative, and the equilibrium constant (*K*) is generally more than 1. Whereas, for an endothermic reaction the enthalpy difference ($\Delta H°$) is positive and *K* is less than 1.

Organic Reaction Mechanism

Based on the nature of reactants, products and by-products as well as the mechanism, organic reactions are classified into four major categories, **substitution, addition, elimination** and **rearrangement** reaction. Substitution, addition and elimination refer to whether atoms are changed, added, or removed from a molecule. Rearrangement changes the carbon skeleton of a molecule.

Addition Reaction

These are characteristic of compounds containing multiple bonds (*e.g.,* alkenes and alkynes). An unsaturated molecule is the only type of molecule that can accept additional atoms or groups of atoms from a reagent without exceeding the maximum number of groups allowed by carbon. Addition reactions take place very readily because σ-bonds are stronger than π-bonds. The following are some examples of addition reactions :

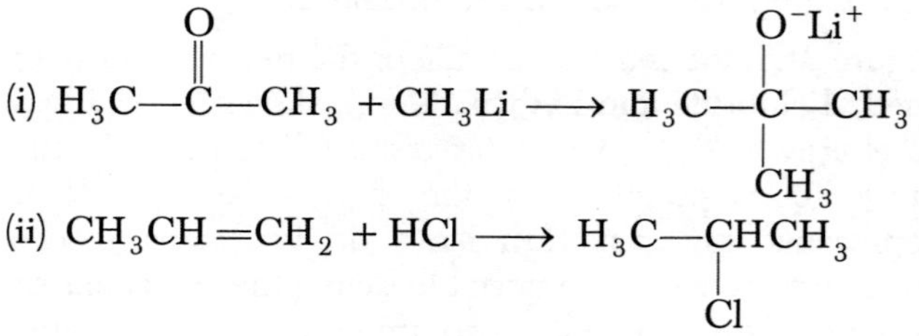

Electrophilic Addition

An electrophilic addition is the reaction of an electron deficient reagent with an electron-rich substrate. The above examples (ii and iii) are **electrophilic additions** to alkenes. Each of the two reactions proceeds through the addition of an electrophile to the double bond, followed by reaction with a nucleophile. In the (i) reaction, the electrophile is the hydrogen ion, H^+; in the (ii), it is the bromine ion, Br^+. Each of these reactions adds a positive electrophile to the electron-rich double bond. The electrophilic addition to carbon-carbon multiple bond proceeds through two step mechanism.

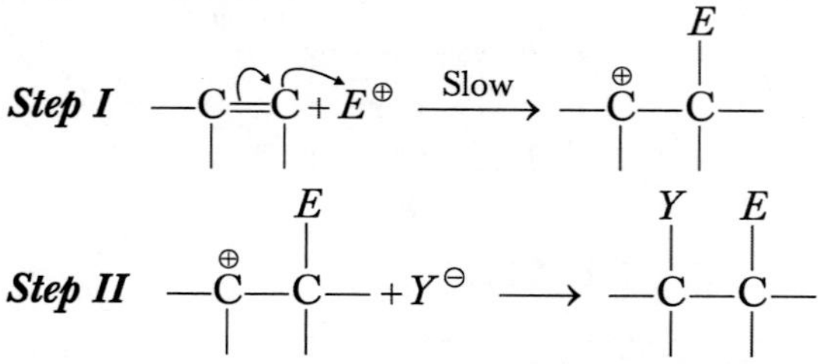

Fig. 31.8 Illustrates the mechanism of the addition of HCl to propene. The first step of the mechanism is an electron pair displacement operation; the second step is a heterogenic bond forming operation.

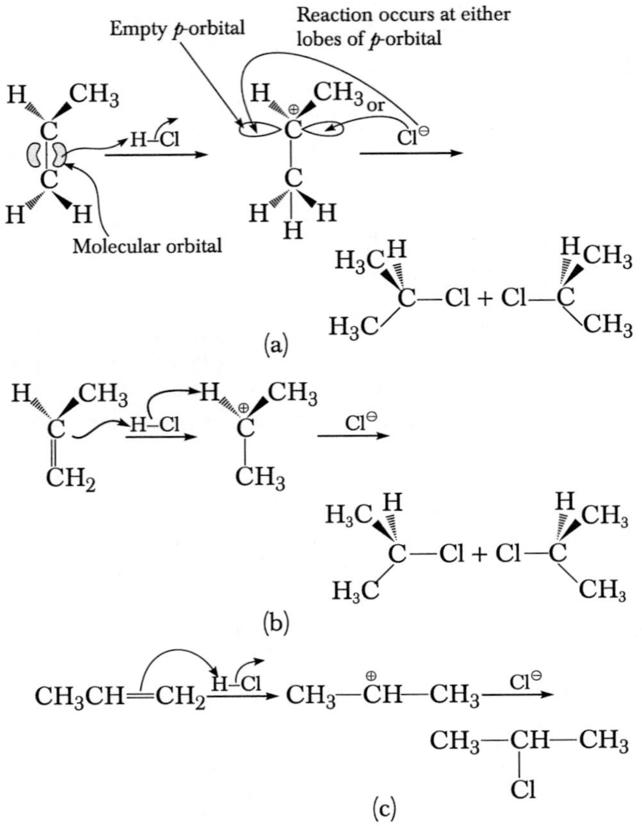

Fig. 31.8. The addition of HCl to a double bond
(a) A picture of the orbitals involved in the reaction.
(b) A three-dimensional drawing of the mechanism.
(c) A standard mechanistic representation.

The difference between the reaction of propene with HCl and the reaction of ethene with Br_2 is the bromine has non-bonding electrons that it donates to stabilize the intermediate cation, whereas, the hydrogen from HCl does not. As shown in the mechanism, a carbocation permits a reaction with a nucleophile from either side, but here the bromonium ion effectively blocks one side of the molecule. Thus, the nucleophile can only add *anti,* or opposite, to the bromine already present. This mechanism involves a 1,3-electron pair displacement operation followed by a heterogenic bond forming operations.

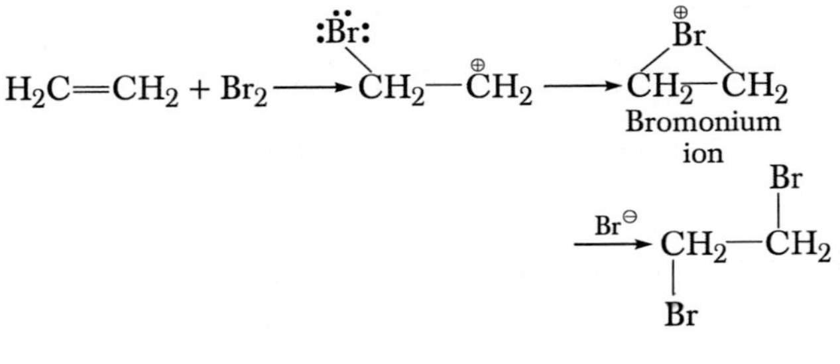

The bromination of *trans*-2-butene gives *meso*-dibromide and that bromination of *cis*-2-butene gives racemic modification (pair of enantiomers).This can also be explained by the addition of bromine on the cyclic intermediate bromonium ion. Hence, the reaction is stereoselective.

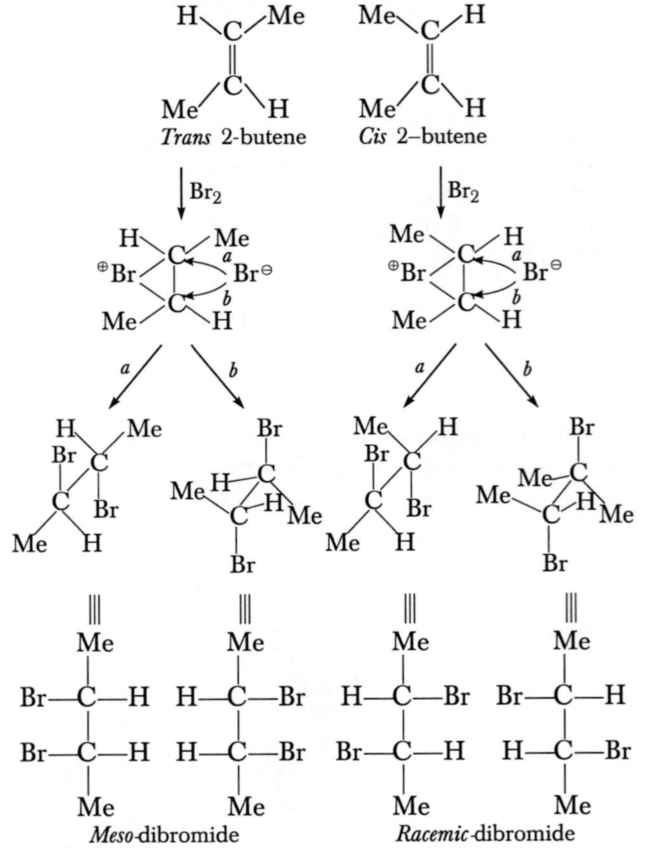

- The addition of unsymmetrical reagents to unsymmetrical alkenes and alkynes follows **Markownikoff's rule.** According to this rule "the negative end of the reagent goes to the carbon atom containing lesser number of hydrogen atoms." However, when both the carbon atoms forming the double bond have the same number of hydrogen atoms in an unsymmetrical alkene a mixture of two products are obtained.

$$\underset{\text{2-pentene}}{CH_3CH_2CH{=}CHCH_3} + HBr \longrightarrow$$

$$\underset{\text{2-bromopentane}}{CH_3CH_2CH_2\overset{\overset{\text{Br}}{|}}{C}HCH_3} \qquad \underset{\text{3-bromopentane}}{CH_3CH_2CH\overset{\overset{\text{Br}}{|}}{C}H_2CH_3}$$

Markownikoff's rule can be explained on the basis of relative stabilities of the intermediate carbocations.

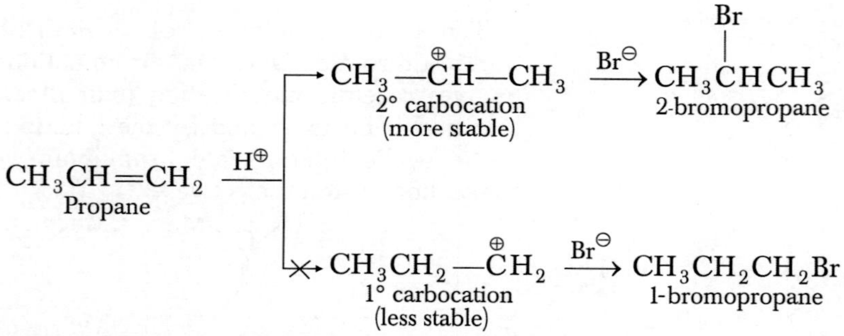

Markownikoff's rule can also be explained by a consideration of the electronic effect of the substituents on the double bond. In case of propene, due to $+I$ effect on the methyl group, the π-electrons are displaced towards the terminal carbon atom which in turn acquires a partial negative charge. So, the proton (H^+) adds on to the carbon atom which is farthest from the methyl group, followed by addition of halide ion to the formed secondary carbocation.

$$\underset{\text{Propene}}{CH_3-\overset{\delta^+}{C}H=\overset{\delta^-}{C}H_2} + HBr \xrightarrow{-Br^{\ominus}} \underset{2^\circ\text{ carbocation}}{CH_3\overset{\oplus}{C}H-CH_3} \xrightarrow{Br^{\ominus}} \underset{\text{2-bromopropane}}{CH_3\underset{Br}{\underset{|}{C}}HCH_3}$$

The Markownikoff's rule as stated above is not applicable in case of those alkenes which contain electron-withdrawing groups. **Example,**

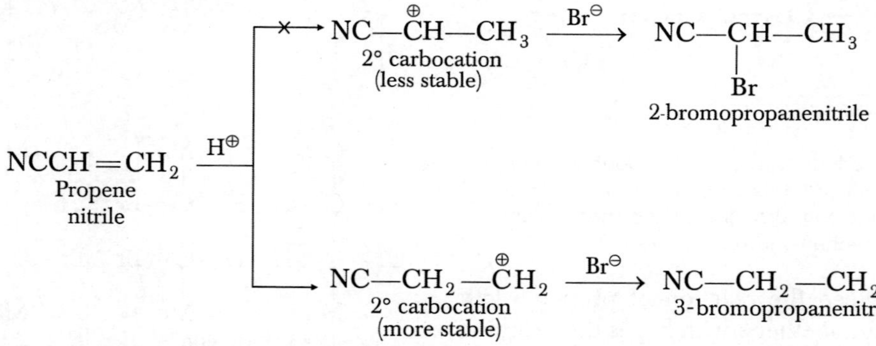

In the above case of propenenitrile, due to strong electron-withdrawing effect of CN-group, the secondary carbocation is less stable than the primary carbocation. In primary carbocation the carbon carrying positive charge is separated from the CN-group by two carbon atoms and the destabilisation by the inductive effect is less.

Hence, the Markownikoff's rule can be modified as "The addition of hydrogen halide to alkene leads to the formation of a more stable carbocation, which then adds the negative ion to for the product."

Addition to conjugated dienes

- A conjugated diene (1, 3-butadiene) gives two types of addition.

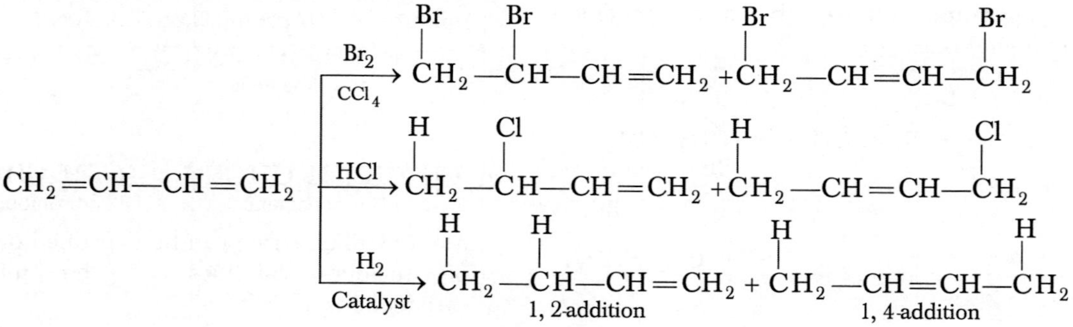

- The formation of 1, 2- and 1, 4-addition products in case of addition of bromine to 1, 3-butadiene can be explained as :

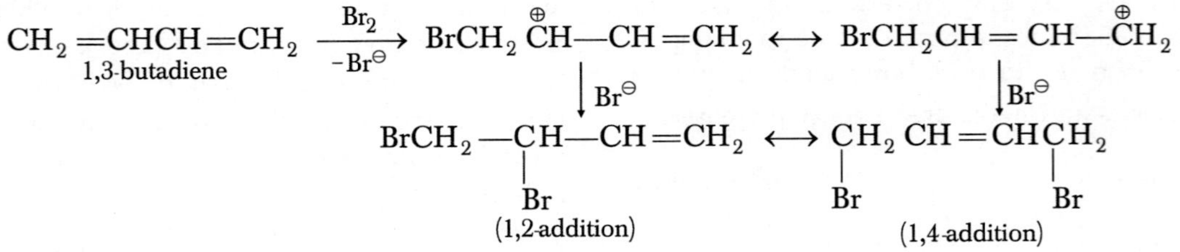

Now consider the addition of HBr to 1,3-butadiene.

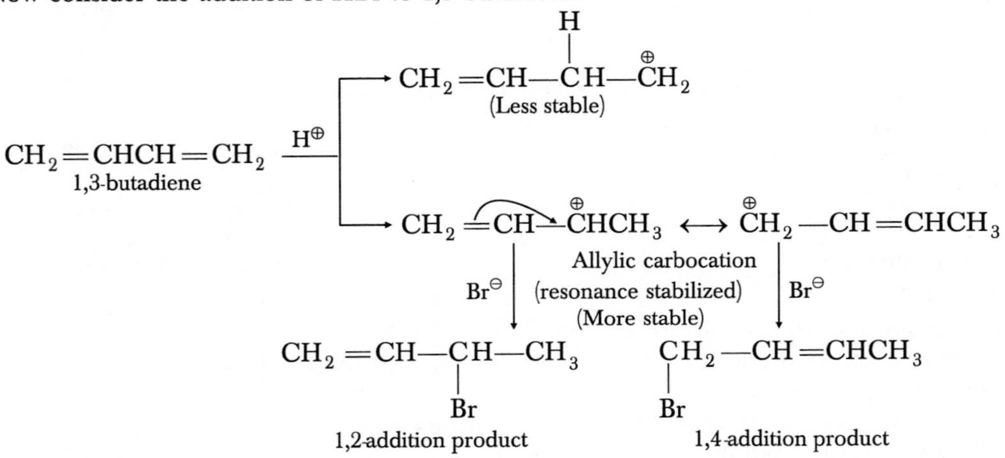

Nucleophilic Addition

These reactions are usually encountered in compounds containing polar functional groups. **Example** Carbonyl, —C≡N, C=S, etc. It is the reaction of an electron-rich reagent with an electron deficient substrate.

$$>C=O \longleftrightarrow >\overset{\oplus}{C}-O^{\ominus} \quad \text{or} \quad >\overset{\delta^+}{C}=\overset{\delta^-}{O}$$

The heteroatom, *i.e.,* oxygen in the case of aldehyde or ketone, reduces the π-electron density on the carbonyl carbon. Thus, attack of nucleophile takes place at carbonyl carbon.

$$\overset{\ominus}{Nu} + >C=O \longrightarrow Nu-\overset{|}{\underset{|}{C}}-\overset{\ominus}{O} \xrightarrow{\overset{\oplus}{E}} Nu-\overset{|}{\underset{|}{C}}-OE$$

Example (i) Addition of HCN to carbonyl group.

$$HCN + \overset{\ominus}{O}H \longrightarrow H_2O + \overset{\ominus}{C}N$$

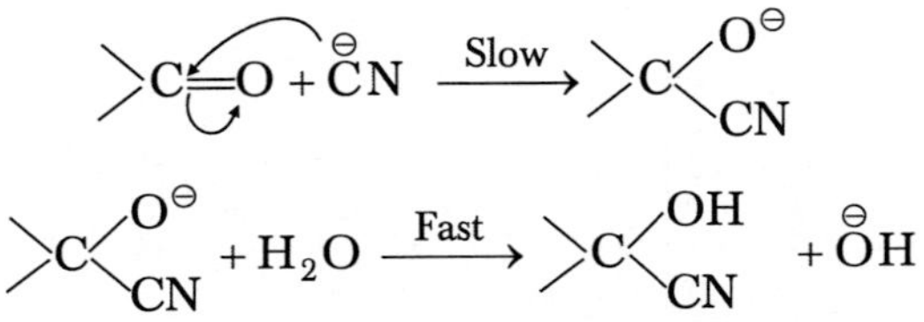

Cyanohydrin

Attack of the nucleophile occurs on the carbon of the carbonyl group rather than on the oxygen thus addition of HCN (or H_2O or nucleophile) to carbonyl group is regioselective–nucleophile always attacks the carbonyl carbon. As a result of this attack, the carbonyl carbon changes hybridisation from sp^2 to sp^3, and the oxygen accepts an electron pair. Also groups around the carbonyl carbon are brought closer together (Fig. 31.11). A **steric effect** also operates in carbonyl addition. As the size of the group attached to the carbonyl carbon increases, van der Waals' repulsions in the corresponding addition compounds become more important. Due to change in hybridisation (from sp^2 to sp^3), bond angle decreases, repulsion increases and hence free energy increases.

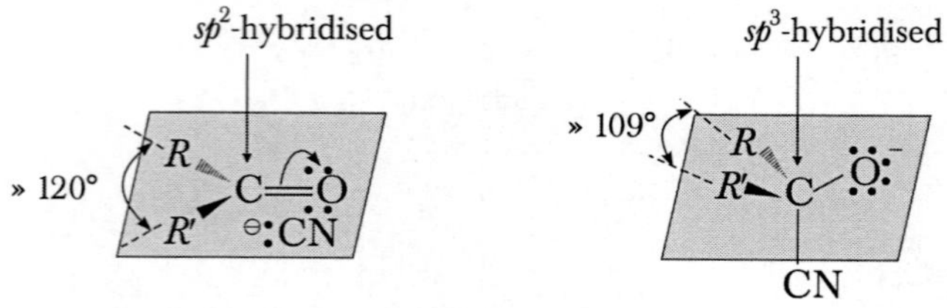

Fig. 31.11. The geometry of nucleophilic attack on a carbonyl carbon, with cyanide ion ($^-$CN) as the nucleophile.

Nucleophilic addition to activated carbon-carbon double bond

Due to the presence of negatively charged π-electron cloud on the carbon-carbon double bond nucleophilic attack is difficult. However, the presence of electron withdrawing group in the system decreases the π-electron density on the carbon-carbon double bond and thus facilitates the nucleophilic attack. The intermediate carbanion is stabilized by delocalization of the negative charge. Hence, compounds containing carbon-carbon double bonds conjugated with electron-withdrawing substituents (such double bonds are called activated carbon-carbon double bonds) undergo nucleophilic addition. The nucleophilic additions are observed in α, β-unsaturated aldehydes, ketones, esters, nitriles, etc. Such addition reactions are catalysed by base, which converts the nucleophile (HA) to a strong nucleophile (A^-).

Mechanism

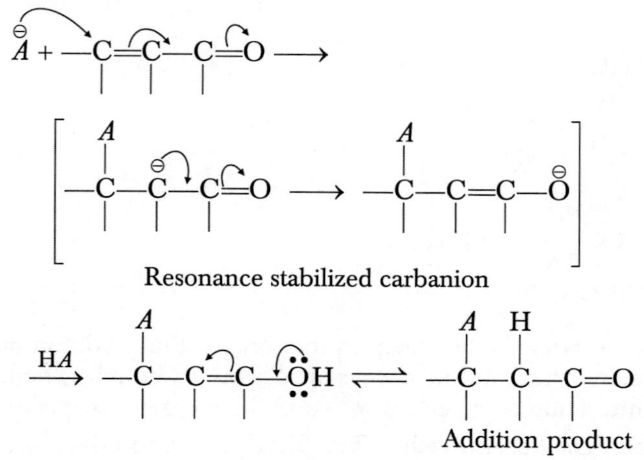

Free Radical Addition

Addition of HBr to unsymmetrical alkenes in the presence of organic peroxide (like benzoyl peroxide) takes place opposite to that of Markownikoff's rule. This is called **Kharash peroxide effect.** This is also known as **Peroxide effect.** It follows free radical addition.

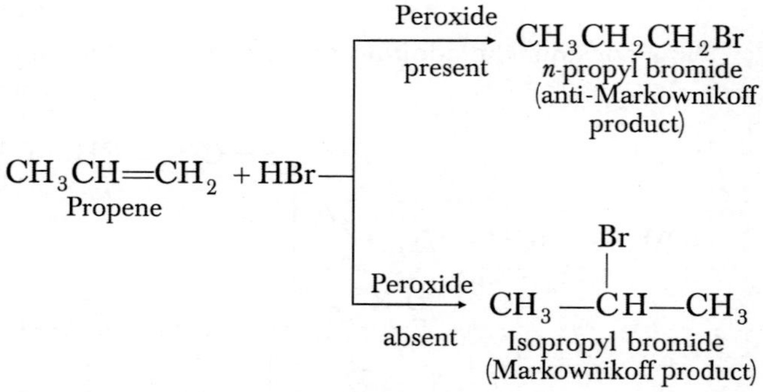

The mechanism of anti-Markownikoff's or Kharash peroxide effect is as

Step I **Chain-initiating step** (O—O) bond in peroxide is weak and is easily broken homolytically in presence of light or heat to form a radical ($R\dot{O}$) which in turn removes a hydrogen atom from HBr giving $Br^\bullet$ radical.

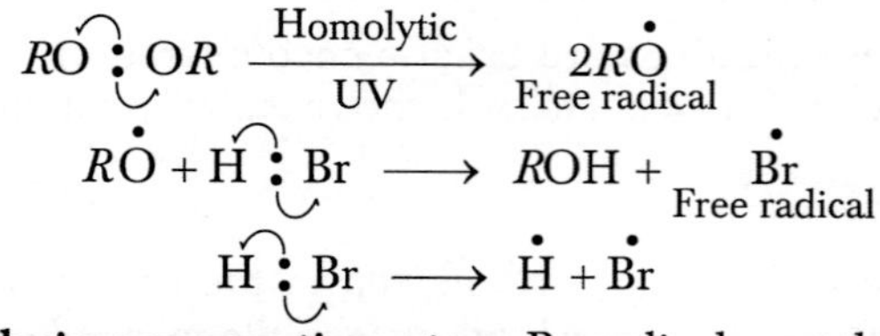

Step II **Chain-propagating step** By radical complete s its octet by combining with one of the electrons in the π-bond of the alkene to form a bromine–carbon bond. Bromine radical can join to any of the sp^2-hybridised carbons of the alkene to form primary or secondary free radicals.

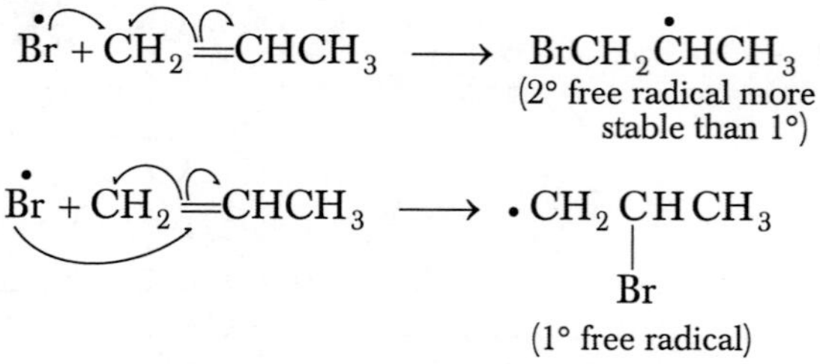

Since, secondary free radical is more stable than the primary free radical, only the secondary free radical is formed.

Step III Chain-terminating step The secondary free radical being more stable reacts with HBr forming anti-Markownikoff addition product and another bromine free radical is formed, which in turn propagates the chain.

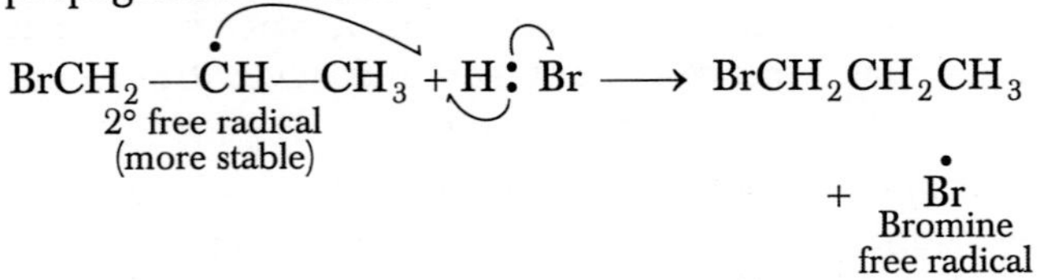

Note
- HCl and HF do not form free radical easily due to larger bond-energy, hence peroxide effect is not observed in such cases.
- HI with minimum bond energy is very reactive and instead forms I_2

$$HI \longrightarrow \dot{H} + \dot{I} \longrightarrow I_2$$

Example of free radical addition

(i) 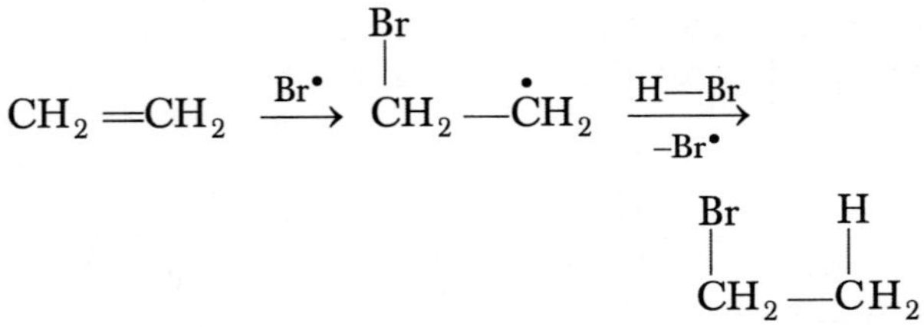

(ii) 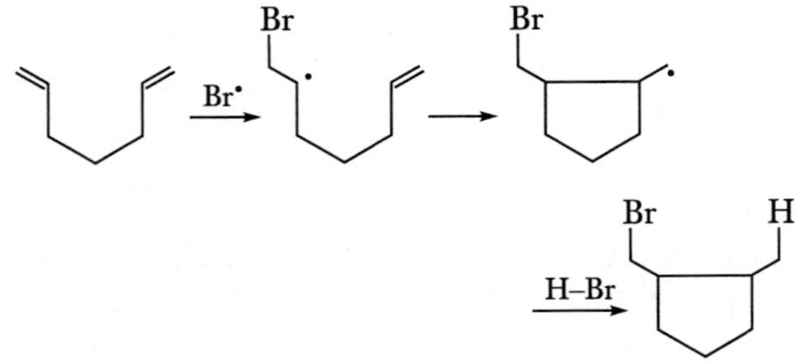

(iii) The polymerization of ethylene and propylene, **Sandmeyer reaction, Gomberg reaction,** etc., proceed by free radical mechanism.

Cis- and *Trans*-Addition

Cis-addition

If the group *AB* adds to —C=C< in such a way that both of *A* and *B* attack from same side the addition is called *cis* addition.

i.e.,

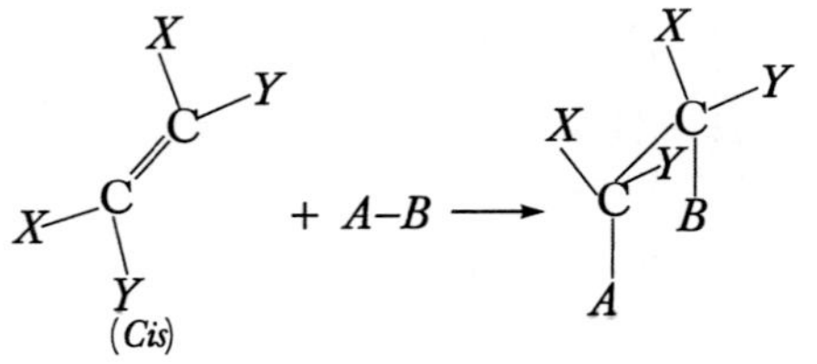

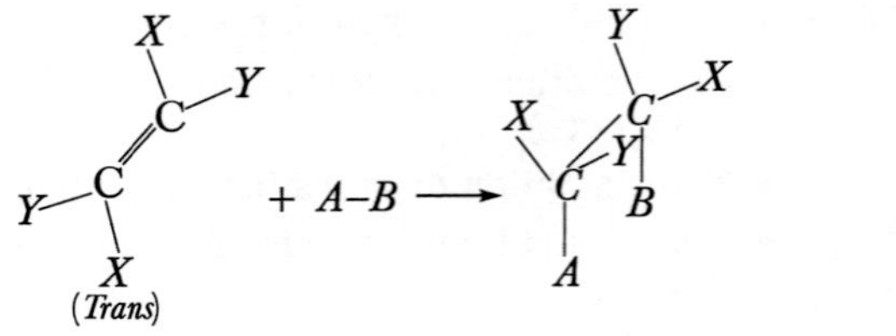

(a) **Addition *via* cyclic mechanism**

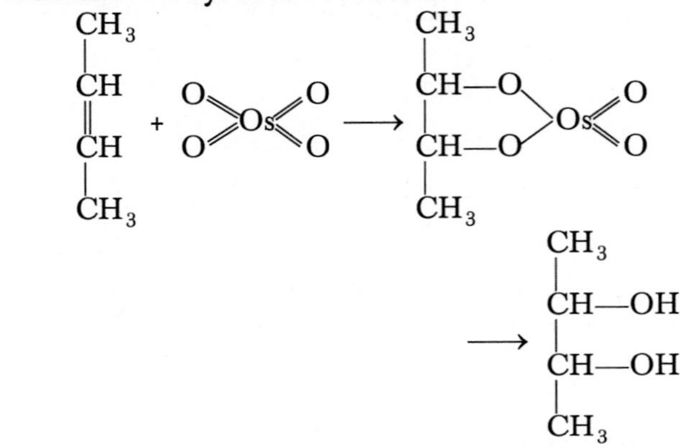

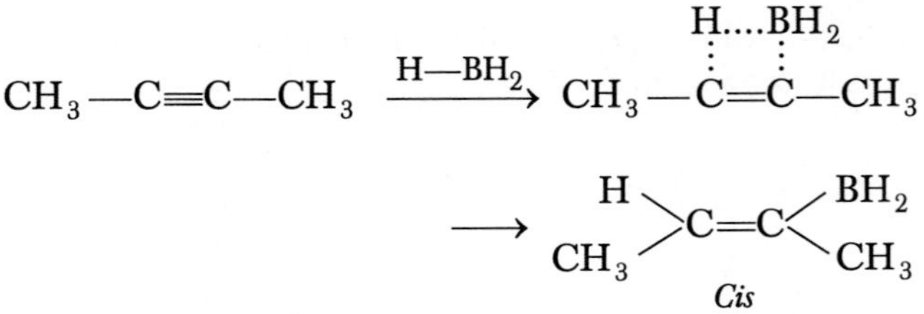

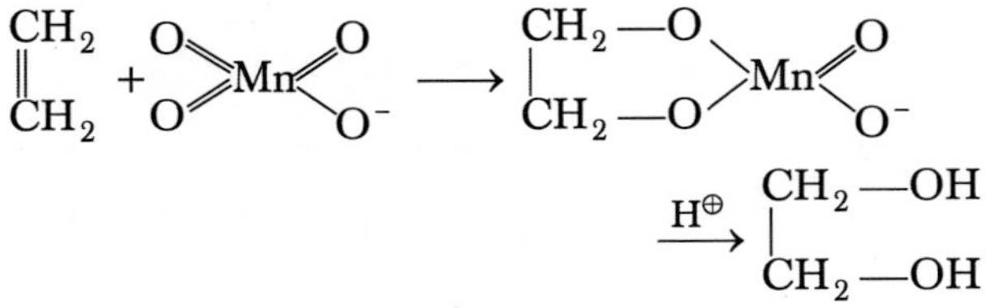

(b) **Addition on the surface of the catalyst**

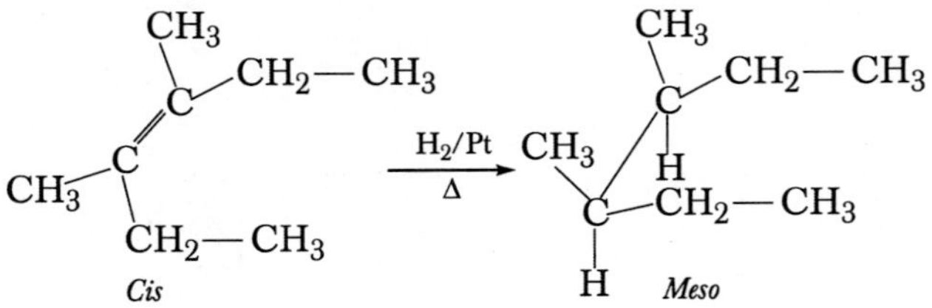

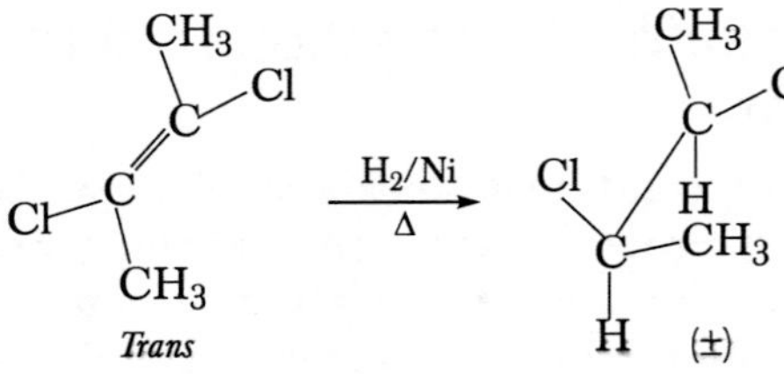

Note
- *Cis* addition on *cis* form results *meso.*
- *Cis* addition on *trans* form results racemic mixture (±).
- *Trans* addition on *trans* form results *meso.*
- *Trans* addition on *cis* for results raclmic mixture.

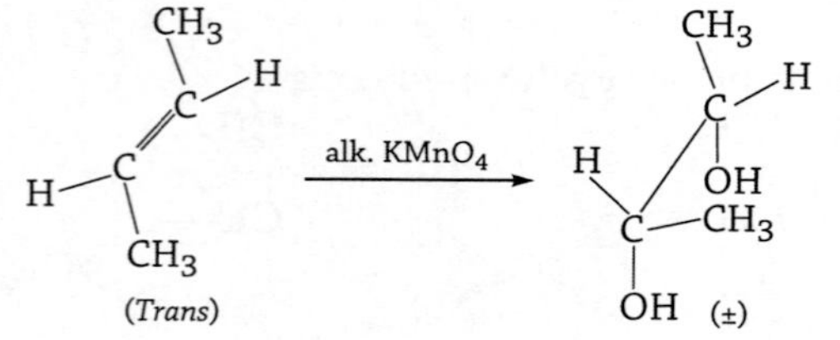

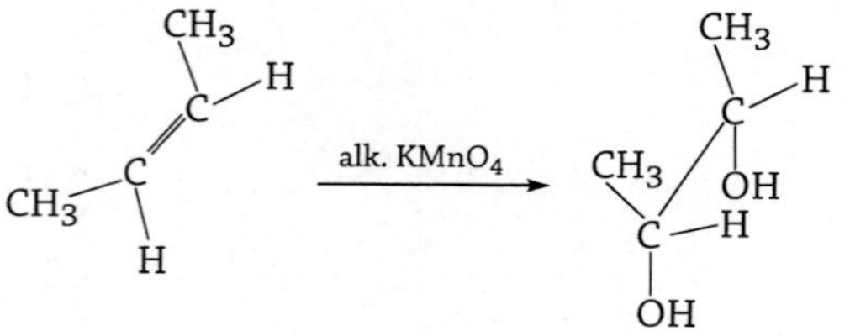

Trans-addition

In *trans*-addition groups of reagent add to a multiple bond in ***anti*** manner, *i.e.,*

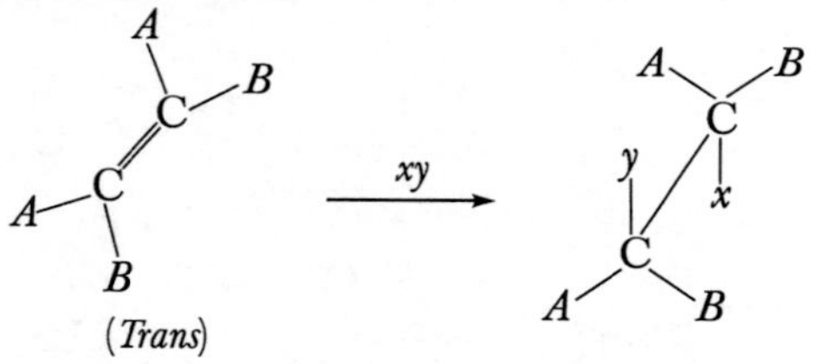

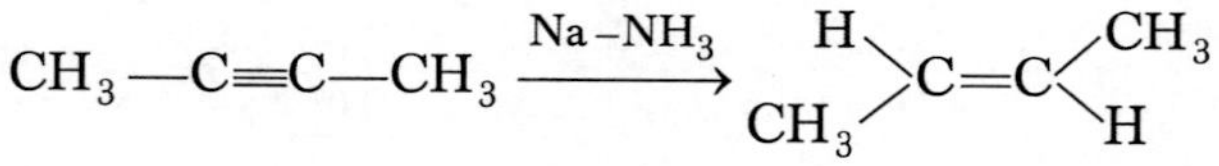

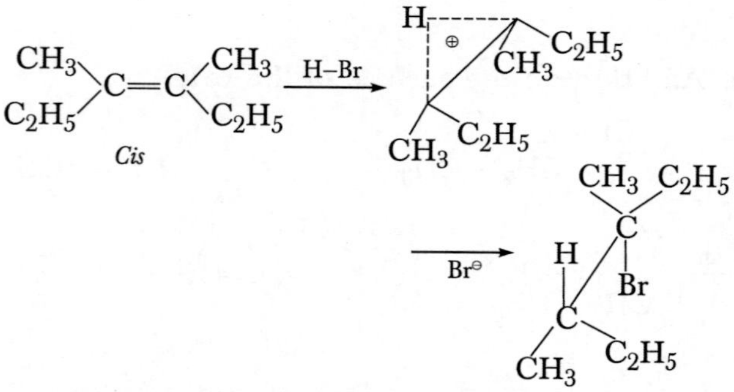

Stereochemistry of Alkene Addition Reactions

When a reactant that does not have a chirality centre undergoes an addition reaction that forms a product with one chirality centre, the product will be a *racemic* mixture. For example, the reaction of 1-butene with HBr forms equal amounts of (*R*)-2-bromobutane and (*S*)-2-bromobutane. In other words, an addition reaction that forms a compound with a single chirality centre from a reactant without any chirality centres is not stereoselective; it does not select for a particular stereoisomer.

We can understand why a *racemic* mixture is obtained, if we examine the structure of the carbocation formed in the first step of the reaction. The positively charged carbon is sp^2-hybridised and the three atoms to which it is bonded lie in a plane. When the bromide ion attacks the carbocation from above the plane, one enantiomer is formed, but when it attacks the carbocation from below the plane, the other enantiomer is formed. Because the bromide ion can attack the planar carbocation intermediate from the above just as well as it can attack it from below, equal amounts of the *R* and *S* enantiomers are obtained from the addition reaction.

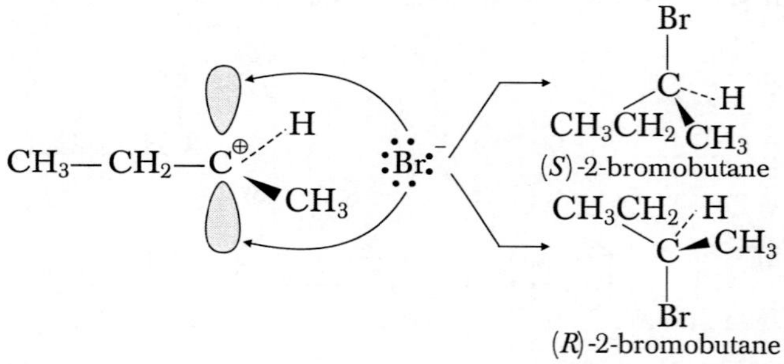

If an addition reaction creates a chirality centre in a compound that already has a chirality centre, a pair of diastereomers will be formed. Because none of the bonds to the chirality centre in (*R*)-3-chloro-1-butene is broken during the addition of HBr, the configuration of this chirality centre does not change. Because the bromide ion can attack the planar carbocation intermediate from either the top or the bottom in the process of creating the new chirality centre, two stereoisomers result. The stereoisomers are diastereomers because one of the chirality centres has the same configuration in both the isomers and the other has opposite configurations in the two isomers.

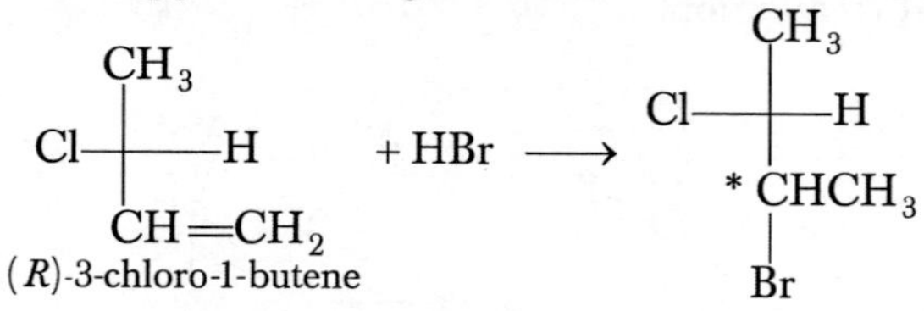

Stereochemistry of the product

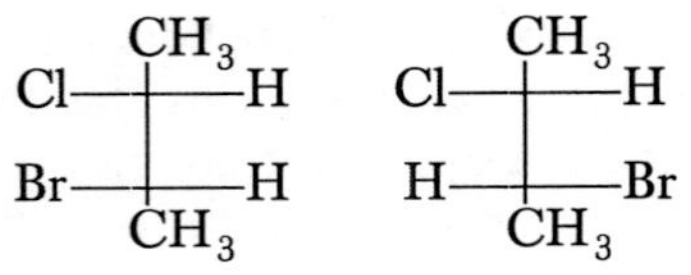

A pair of diastereomers

Because there is a chirality centre in the carbocation intermediate, it is a chiral ion and therefore, does not have a plane of symmetry. If the chirality centre is near the positively charged carbon, one face of the carbocation will be more sterically hindered than the other. The incoming bromide ion will have greater access to the less sterically hindered face. The diastereomers, therefore, will be formed in unequal amounts. **The reaction is stereoselective; more of one stereoisomer is formed than of the other.**

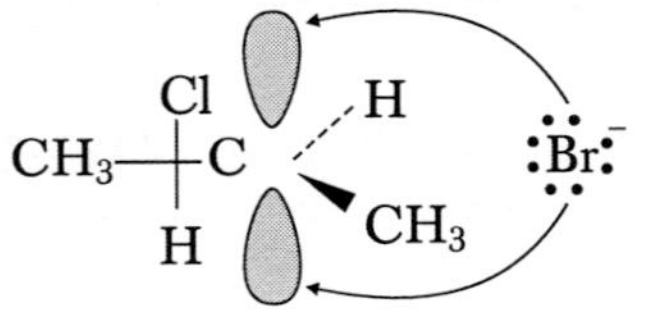

When a reactant that does not have a chirality centre undergoes an addition reaction that forms a product with two chirality centres the stereoisomers that are formed depend on the mechanism of the addition reaction.

(a) **Addition reactions that involve a carbocation intermediate or a radical intermediate**

If two chirality centres are created as the result of an addition reaction that forms a carbocation intermediate, four stereoisomers can be obtained as products.

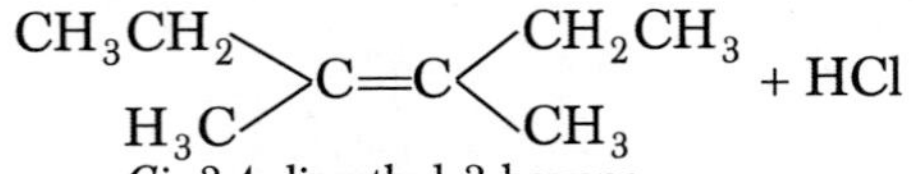

Cis-3,4-dimethyl-3-hexene

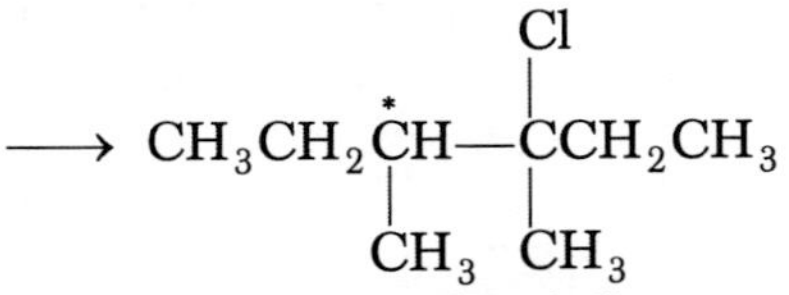

3-chloro-3,4-dimethylhexane

Stereochemistry of the product

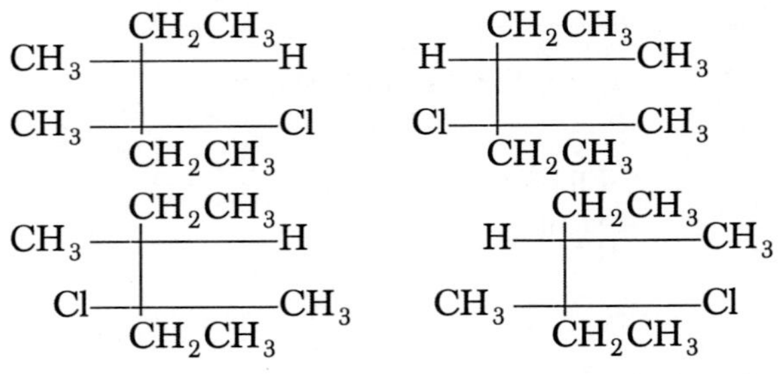

Fischer projections of the stereoisomers of the product

The proton can approach the plane containing the doubly-bonded carbons of the alkene from the above or below to form the carbocation in the first step of the reaction. Once, the carbocation is formed, the chloride ion can attack from the above or below. As a result, four stereoisomers are obtained as products. The two substituents can add from above-above, above-below, below-below or from below-above. When the two substituents add to the same side of the double bond, the **addition** is called ***syn*-addition**. When the two substituents add to opposite sides of the double bond, the **addition** is called ***anti*-addition**. Boty *syn* and *anti*-addition occur in alkene addition reactions that take place by the way of a carbocation intermediate. Because the four stereoisomers formed by the *cis*-alkene are identical to the four stereoisomers formed by the *trans*-alkene, the reaction is not stereospecific.

Similarly, if two chirality centres are created as the result of an addition reaction that forms a radical intermediate, four stereoisomers can be formed because both *syn* and *anti*-additions are possible. And since the stereoisomers formed by the *cis*-isomer are identical to those formed by the *trans*-isomer the reaction is not stereospecific.

(b) **Addition reaction that involve bromonium ion intermediate**

If two chirality centres are created as a result of an addition reaction that forms a bromonium ion intermediate, only one pair of enantiomers will be formed. In other words, the addition of Br_2 is a stereospecific reaction. Addition of Br_2 to the *cis*-alkene forms only the *threo* pair of enantiomers.

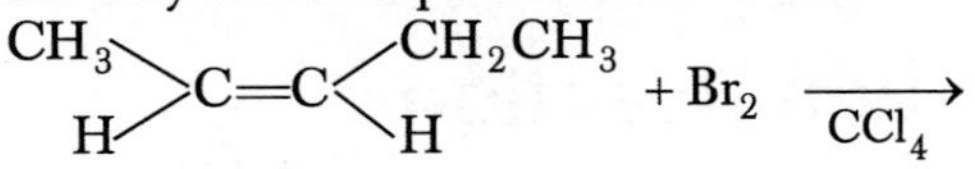

Cis-2-pentene

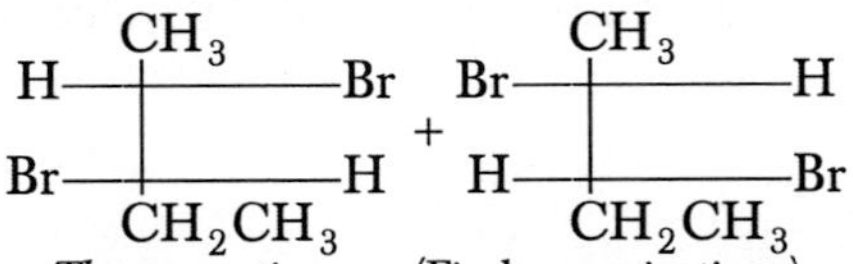

Threo enantiomers (Fischer projections)

Addition of Br_2 to the *trans*-alkene forms only the *erythro* pair of enantiomers.

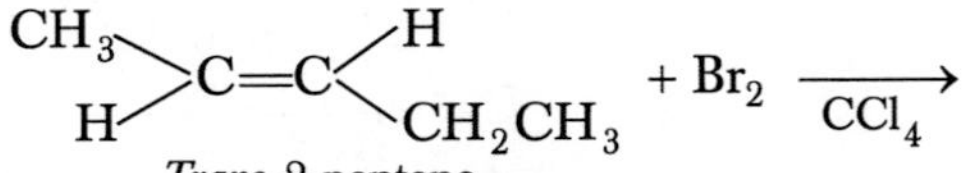

Trans-2-pentene

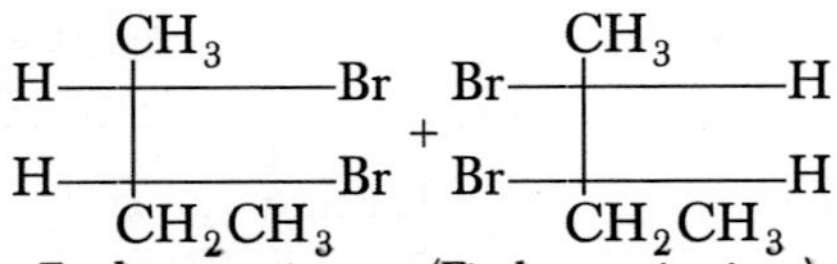

Erythro enantiomers (Fischer projections)

Since, addition of Br_2 to the *cis*-alkene forms the *threo* pair of enantiomers, we know that addition of Br_2 is an example of *anti*-addition because, as we have just seen, *syn*-addition to the *cis*-alkene forms the *erythro* pair of enantiomers. The addition of Br_2 is *anti* because the reaction intermediate is a cyclic bromonium ion. Once the cyclic bromonium ion forms, the bridged bromine atom blocks that side of the ion from further attack. So, the negatively charged bromide ion must attack from the opposite side of the ion.

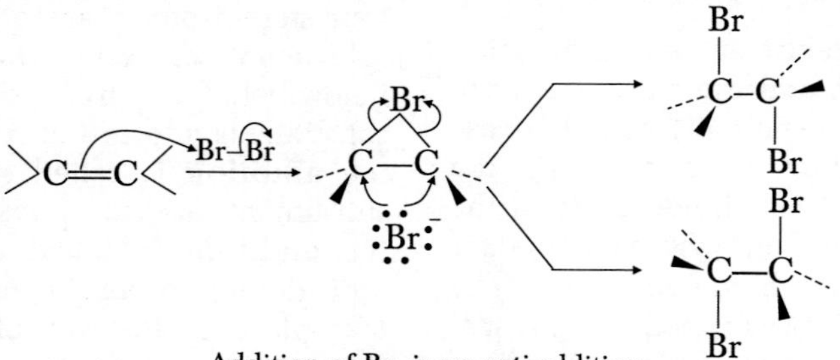

Addition of Br_2 is an *anti*-addition

Thus, the two bromine atoms add to opposite sides of the double bond. Because *syn*-addition of Br_2 cannot occur, only two of the four possible stereoisomers are obtained.

If the two chirality centres in the product each have the same four substituents, the *erythro* isomers are identical and constitute a *meso* compound. Therefore, addition of Br_2 to *trans*-2-butene forms a *meso* compound.

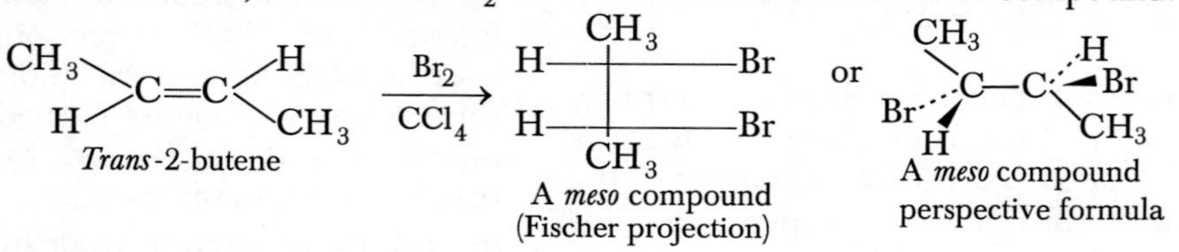

Because only *anti*-addition occurs, addition of Br_2 to a cyclic alkene results in the formation of only the pair of enantiomers that has the added bromine atoms on opposite sides of the ring.

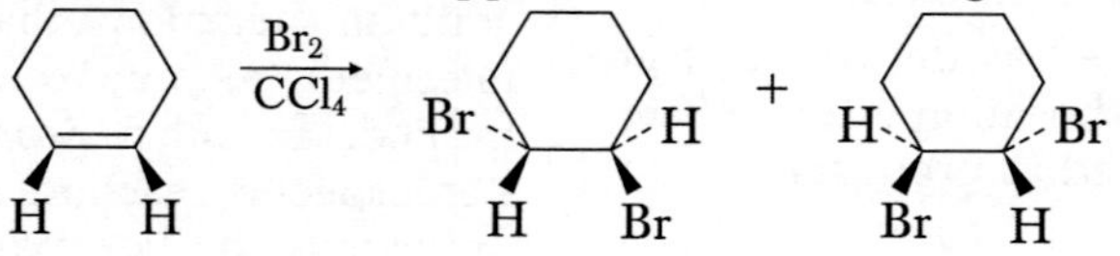

Elimination Reaction

The elimination reactions are reverse of addition reactions. In these reactions two atoms or groups attached to the adjacent carbon atoms of the substrate molecule are eliminated to form a multiple bond.

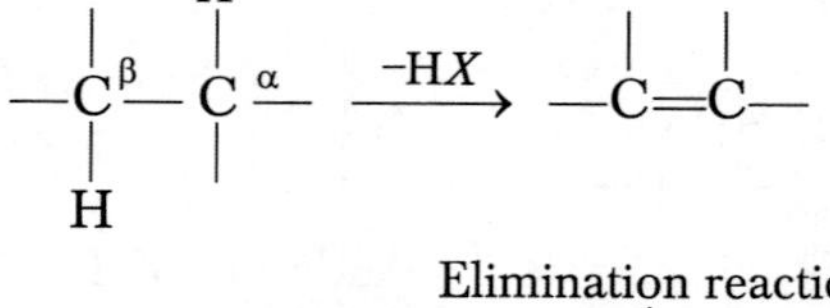

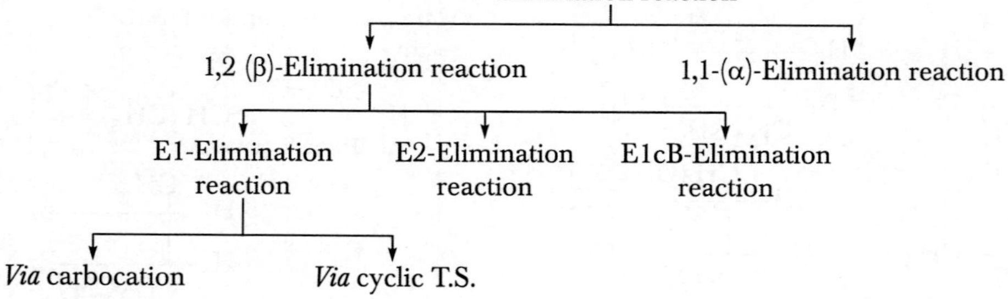

1,1-(α)-Elimination Reaction

When two group atoms are lost from the same carbon atom of the molecule, the elimination reaction is called 1,1-(α)-elimination.

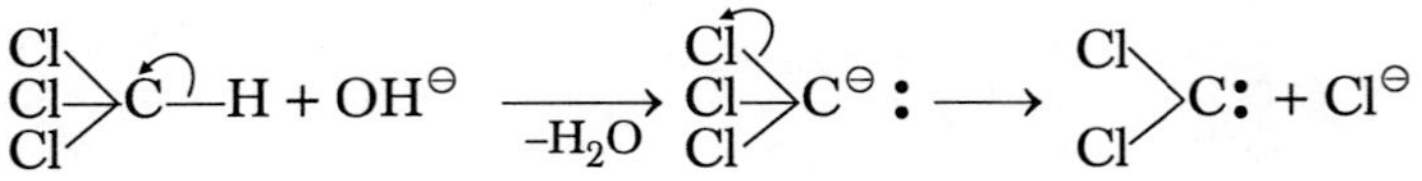

1,2-(β)-Elimination Reaction

When two groups or atoms are removed from the two adjacent carbon atoms, the process is known as β-elimination.

$$CH_3-\underset{\large Br}{CH}-\underset{\large Br}{CH_2} \xrightarrow{\text{Alc.NaOH}} CH_3-CH{=}CH_2$$

In most organic elimination reactions, one of the eliminated groups is hydrogen and the other is a leaving group ($L^\ominus$) and sp^3 hybridised carbon changes to sp^2.

$$H_3C\underset{L}{C}H\underset{H}{C}HCH_3 \longrightarrow H_3CCH{=}CHCH_3 + \overset{\oplus}{H} + \underset{\text{Leaving group}}{\overset{\ominus}{L}}$$

E1-Elimination Reaction

The mechanism of these reactions may explain by two ways

(a) **E1 mechanism *via* carbocation**

Step I The C–L bond is broken heterolytically to form a carbocation (as in S_N1 reaction).

Step II Carbocation loses a proton from an adjacent carbon atom to form a π-bond in presence of a nucleophile.

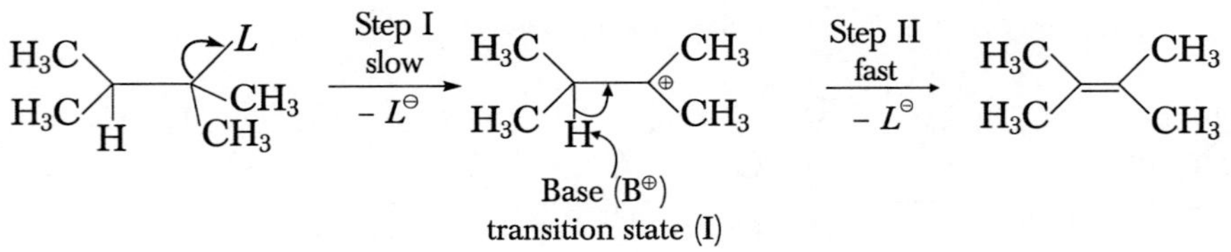

- Step I, in which L is lost, is rate determining step, hence, it is called E1 (unimolecular elimination) reaction.

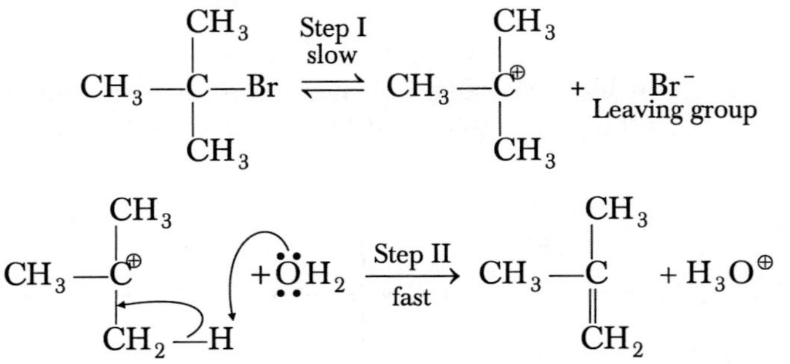

- In E1 reaction, the intermediate is carbocation and thus there can be rearrangement (leading to more stable carbocation) before proton is lost.

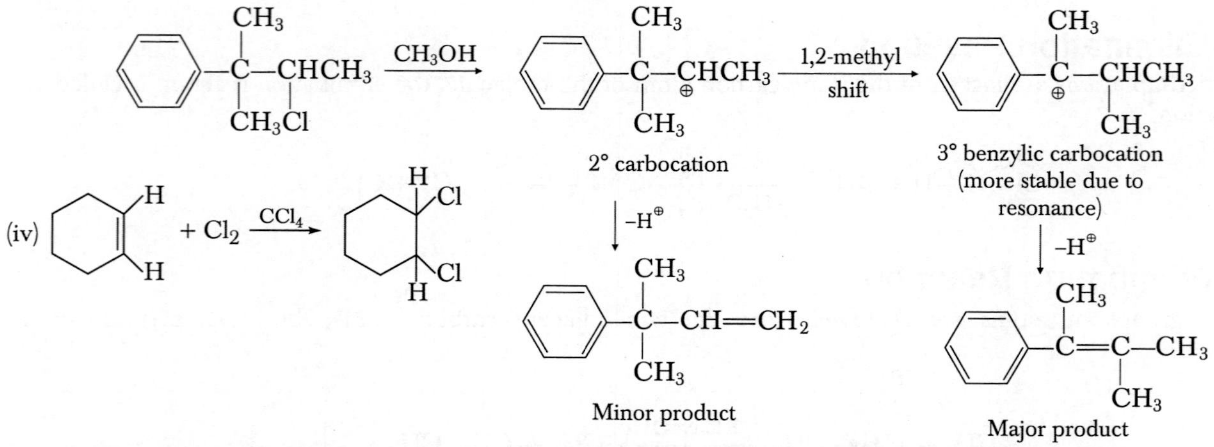

Note • When two elimination products can be formed, the major product is generally the one obtained by following Saytzeff's rule (the hydrogen is removed from the β-carbon bonded to the fewest hydrogens.)

$$CH_3CH_2C(CH_3)(Cl)CH_3 + H_2O \longrightarrow \underset{\text{2-methyl-2-butene (major)}}{CH_3CH{=}C(CH_3)CH_3} + \underset{\text{2-methyl-1-butene (minor)}}{CH_3CH_2C(CH_3){=}CH_2} + H_3O^{\oplus} + Cl^{\ominus}$$

(b) **E1 Mechanism** ***via*** **cyclic transition state**

It proceeds *via* ***cyclic*** **T.S.** and produce ***cis*** **product.**

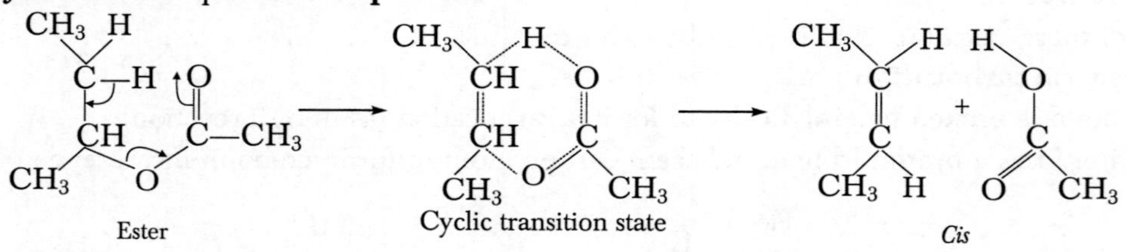

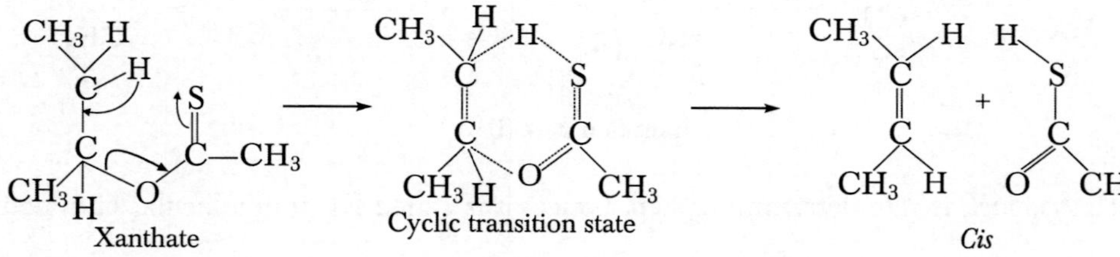

E2-Elimination reaction

In these bimolecular elimination reaction the two groups or atoms are lost simultaneously in a single concerted step. The rate of elimination depends on the concentration of the substrate and the nucleophile. The reaction is of second order.

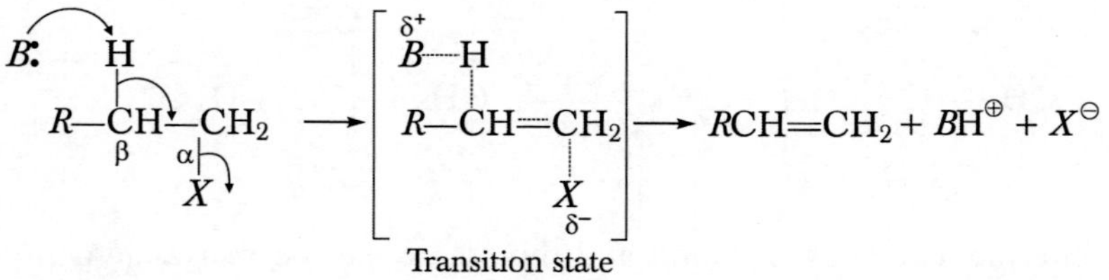

2-bromopropane has two β-carbons from which a proton can be removed in an E2 reaction. Being symmetrical, the proton can be removed from either one to form propene.

$$\underset{\underset{Br}{|}}{CH_3CHCH_3} + \underset{\text{Methoxide (base)}}{CH_3O^{\ominus}} \longrightarrow CH_3CH{=}CH_2 + CH_3OH + Br^-$$

But 2-bromobutane has two structurally different β-carbons from which a proton can be removed giving 1-butene and 2-butene. By Saytzeff's rule, substituted alkenes are more stable and thus 2-butene is predominant.

$$\overset{\beta}{C}H_3\underset{\underset{Br}{|}}{CH}\overset{\beta}{C}H_2CH_3 + CH_3O^- \xrightarrow[CH_3OH]{} \underset{\text{2-butene}}{CH_3CH{=}CHCH_3} + \underset{\text{1-butene}}{CH_3CH_2CH{=}CH_2}$$

Relative reactivities of alkyl halides in an E2 reaction is a tertiary alkyl halide > *a* secondary alkyl halide > *a* primary alkyl halide.

E-1cB-Elimination reaction

Step I It consists of the removal of a proton, H^+ by a base, generating a carbanion.

Step II Carbanion loses a leaving group to form an alkene. It is the slow and rate determining step.

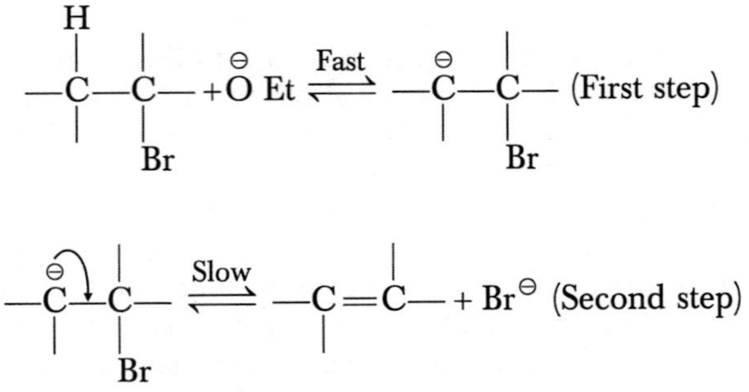

The rate of this reaction is dependent on the concentration of the carbanion (conjugate base of the substrate). So, this mechanism is called E1cB mechanism (Elimination, unimolecular from conjugate base).

E1cB mechanism is not common for the E2 reactions. The carbanion mechanism occurs only where the carbanion from the substrate is stabilized and where the leaving group is a poor leaving group. **Example** the formation of 1,1-dichloro-2,2-difluoroethene from 1,1-dichloro-2,2,2- trifluoroethane in presence of sodium ethoxide.

$$\underset{\text{1,1-dichloro-2,2,2-trifluoroethane}}{CHCl_2{-}CF_3} \overset{C_2H_5\overset{-}{O}\overset{+}{Na}}{\rightleftharpoons} \underset{\text{Carbanion}}{Cl_2\overset{\ominus}{C}{-}CF_3} \xrightarrow{-F^{\ominus}} \underset{\text{1,1-dichloro-2,2-difluoroethane}}{Cl_2C{=}CF_2}$$

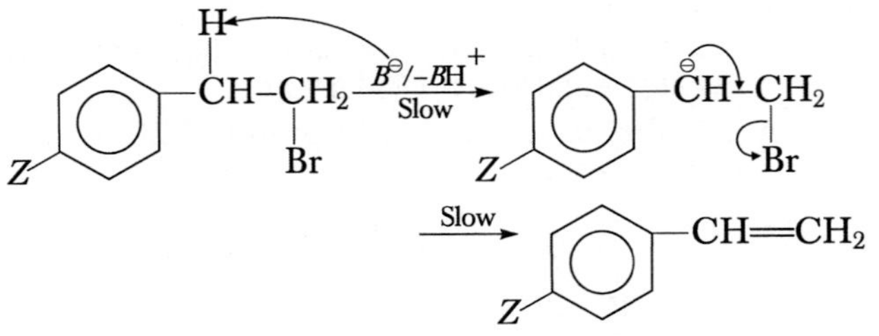

Where *Z* is a very strong electron withdrawing group.

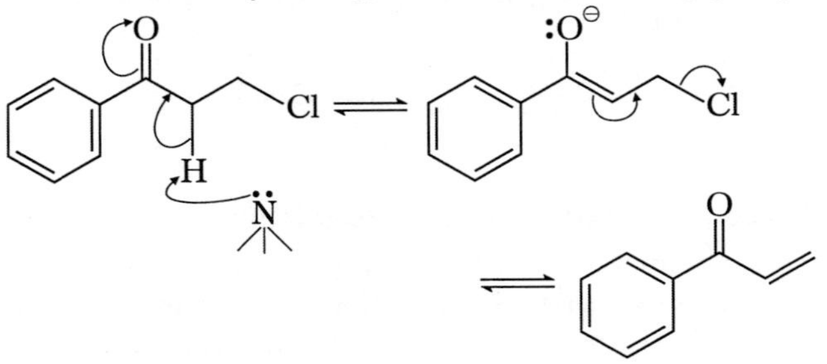

Orientation in elimination reaction

The orientation of the product formed in elimination reactions is governed by two rules, *i.e.*, Hofmann rule and Saytzeff rule.

(a) **Hofmann rule** This rule is applicable for those substrates in which α-carbon atom is attached to a positively charged atom. According to this rule, in the elimination reaction of positively charged species, the major product will be the alkene which is least substituted.

$$CH_3CH_2\overset{\oplus}{N}(CH_3)_2CH_2CH_2CH_3\ \overset{\ominus}{O}H \xrightarrow{\text{Heating}} CH_2{=}CH_2 + CH_3CH_2CH_2N(CH_3)_2$$

$$CH_3CH_2\overset{\oplus}{S}(CH_3)_2 \xrightarrow{C_2H_5\overset{\ominus}{O}} CH_2{=}CH_2 + S(CH_3)_2$$

(b) **Saytzeff rule** In case of unsymmetrical alkyl halides, the course of elimination is determined by Saytzeff rule. According to this rule, hydrogen is eliminated preferentially from the carbon atom which has less number of hydrogen atoms and so the highly substituted alkene is the major product.

$$\underset{\text{2-bromobutane}}{CH_3CH_2-\overset{\overset{Br}{|}}{C}H-CH_3} \xrightarrow{\text{Alc. KOH}} \underset{\substack{\text{2-butene}\\(80\%)}}{CH_3CH{=}CHCH_3} + \underset{\substack{\text{1-butene}\\(20\%)}}{CH_3CH_2CH{=}CH_2}$$

Note
- Dehydration of alcohols and dehydrohalogenation reactions are occurred through elimination mechanism.
- Dehydration of alcohol in presence of an acid gives alkene.

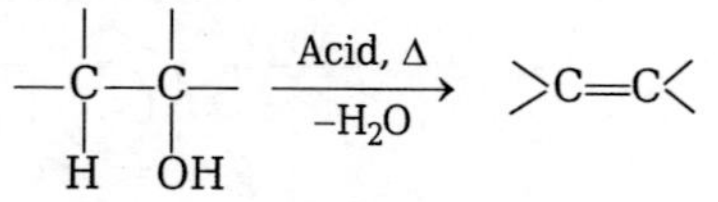

- Elimination of HX from alkyl halide called dehydrohalogenation. It takes place in presence of base

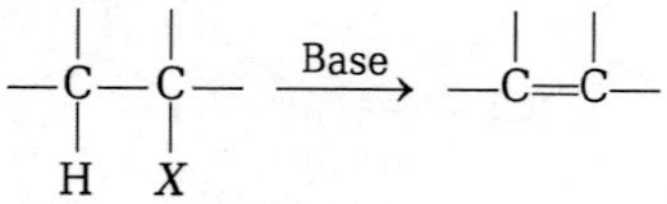

Stereochemistry of the E2 reaction

If an elimination reaction removes two substituents from the same side of the molecule, the reaction is a ***syn* elimination.** If the substituents are removed from opposite sides of the molecule, the reaction is an ***anti* elimination.** *Anti* elimination is favoured in an E2 reaction; *syn* elimination can occur, but it is a much slower reaction. There are several reasons for this. *Syn* elimination requires the molecule to be in an eclipsed conformation, while *anti* elimination requires it to be in a staggered conformation. Because the staggered conformer is more stable, the transition state leading to elimination from the staggered conformer is more stable than the transition state leading to elimination from the eclipsed conformer. Consequently, *anti* elimination occurs more rapidly.

In *anti* elimination, the electrons move to the back side of the carbon bonded to *X*. *Anti* elimination avoids the repulsion experienced by the electron-rich base when it is on the same side of the molecule as the electron-rich halogen.

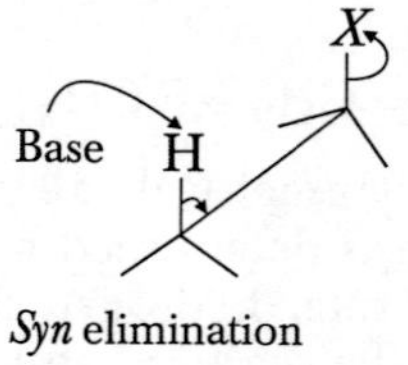

Syn elimination

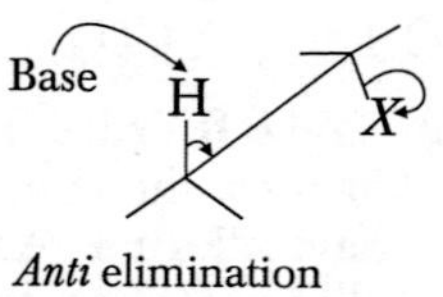

Anti elimination

An E2 reaction is regioselective *i.e.,* more of one constitutional isomer is formed than the other. For example, the major product formed from E2 elimination of 2-bromopentane is 2-pentene.

$$\underset{\text{2-bromopentane}}{CH_3CH_2CH_2\overset{\overset{Br}{|}}{C}HCH_3} \xrightarrow[CH_3CH_2OH]{CH_3CH_2O^-} \underset{\substack{\text{2-pentene}\\\text{(major)}}}{CH_3CH_2CH{=}CHCH_3} + \underset{\substack{\text{1-pentene}\\\text{(minor)}}}{CH_3CH_2CH_2CH{=}CH_2}$$

The E2 reaction is also stereoselective *i.e.,* more of one stereoisomer is formed than the other. For example, the 2-pentene obtained as the major product from the elimination reaction of 2-bromopentane can exist as a pair of stereoisomers, and more (*E*)-2-pentene is formed than (*Z*)-2-pentene.

We can make the following general statement about the stereoselectivity of E2 reactions : if the reactant has two (and only two) hydrogens on the carbon from which a hydrogen is to be removed, both *E* and *Z* products will be formed, but the one with the bulkiest group on opposite sides of the double bond will be formed in greater yield. More *E*-2-pentene is formed in the preceding reaction because the bulkiest groups (the methyl and ethyl groups) lie opposite each other.

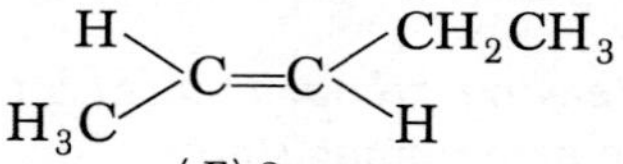

(*E*)-2-pentene
41%

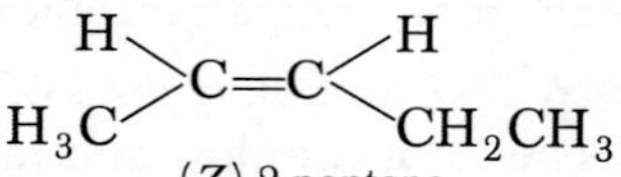

(*Z*)-2-pentene
14%

The reason that the alkene with the **bulkiest groups** on opposite sides of the **double bond** is formed in greater yield is because it is more stable than the alkene with the bulkiest groups on the same side of the double bond. We saw that the decreased stability of the alkene with the bulkiest groups on the same side of the double bond is due to the steric strain that isomer experiences as a result of the interacting electron clouds of the large substituents. Because the alkene with the largest groups on opposite sides of the double bond is more stable, it has the more stable transition state and therefore is formed more rapidly.

Elimination of HBr from 3-bromo-2,3, 4-trimethylpentane leads predominantly to the *E* isomer because this stereoisomer has the methyl group, the bulkiest group on one sp^2-carbon, opposite the *tert*-butyl group, the bulkiest group on the other sp^2-carbon.

Stereochemistry of the E1 reaction

An E1 elimination reaction takes place in two steps : the leaving group leaves in the first step, and a proton is lost from an adjacent carbon in the second step, following Saytzeff's rule in order to form the most stable alkene. If the β-carbon from which the proton is removed is bonded to two hydrogens, the products of an E1 reaction will be similar to those of an E2 reaction : the major product will be the one with the bulkiest groups on opposite sides of the double bond.

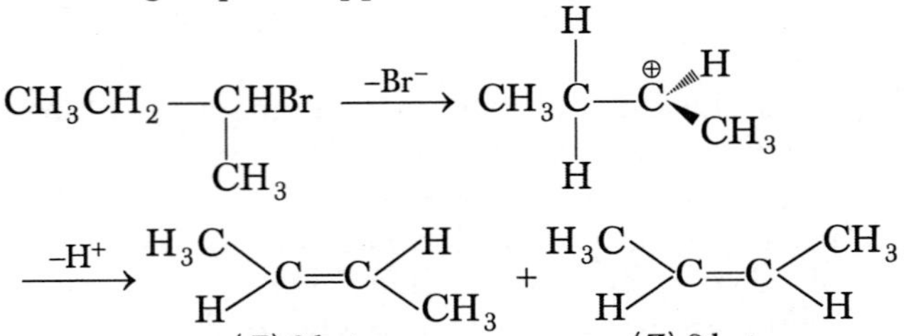

(*E*)-2-butene (major product) (*Z*)-2-butene (minor product)

The carbocation formed in the first step of an E1 reaction is planar. This means that the electrons from a departing hydrogen can move toward the positively charged carbon from either side. Therefore, both *syn* and *anti* elimination can occur.

Substitution Reaction

In a substitution reaction one atom or a group of atoms in a molecule is replaced by another. They are known to proceed by a free radical or ionic mechanism.

Ionic Substitution

Substitution reactions may be brought about by

(i) Replacement by nucleophiles called Nucleophilic Substitution reaction (S_N).
(ii) Replacement by electrophiles called Electrophilic Substitution reaction (S_E).

Nucleophilic Substitution Reaction (S_N)

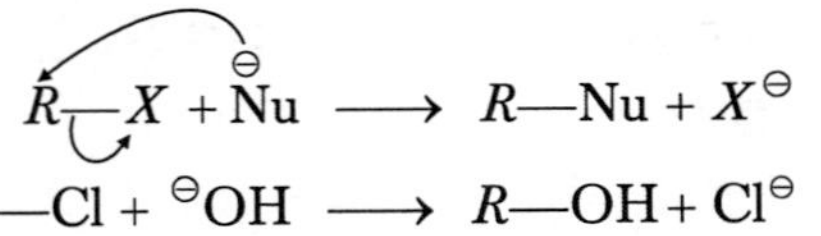

$$R—Cl + {}^{\ominus}OH \longrightarrow R—OH + Cl^{\ominus}$$

The compound on which substitution takes place is called the **substrate** and the group that becomes displaced from carbon, taking the electron pair with it, is called **leaving group.** The leaving group often leaves as an anion but may also be a neutral molecule.

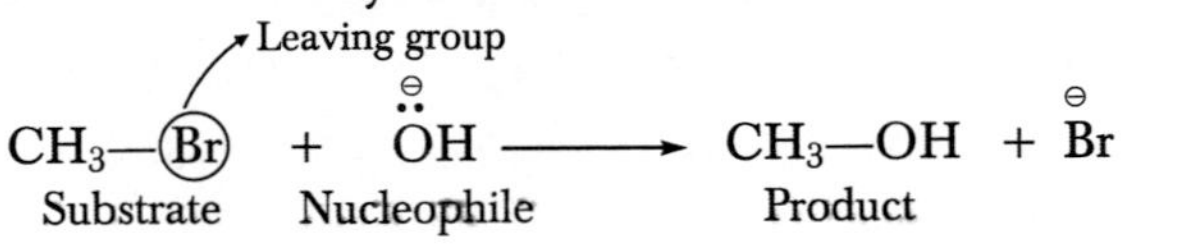

Nucleophilic substitution reaction can be mechanistically categorized as unimolecular (S_N1) or bimolecular (S_N2).

S_N1 (Substitution Nucleophilic Unimolecular)

A S_N1 reaction proceeds in two steps. The first step (slow step) is the rate determining step and involves the ionization of the reactant to form a carbocation intermediate.

Step I Formation of carbocation

$$R—X \xrightarrow{\text{Slow}} \underset{\text{Carbocation intermediate}}{\overset{\oplus}{R}} + \overset{\ominus}{\ddot{X}}$$

Step II Capture of the carbocation by the nucleophile

$$\overset{\oplus}{R} + \overset{-}{\ddot{N}u} \xrightarrow{\text{Fast}} R—Nu$$

S_N1 reaction shows first order kinetics because rate of the reaction depends only on the concentration of the substrate (RX).

$$\text{Rate} = k\,[RX]$$

where, k is rate constant

- In several reactions, nucleophile is a solvent molecule such as water, ammonia or alcohol. **(Solvolysis)**

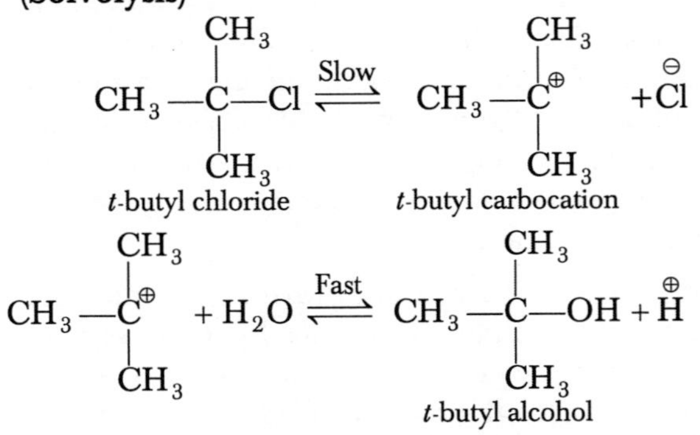

- Carbocation formed can undergo rearrangement to give more stable carbocation before attack of the nucleophile.

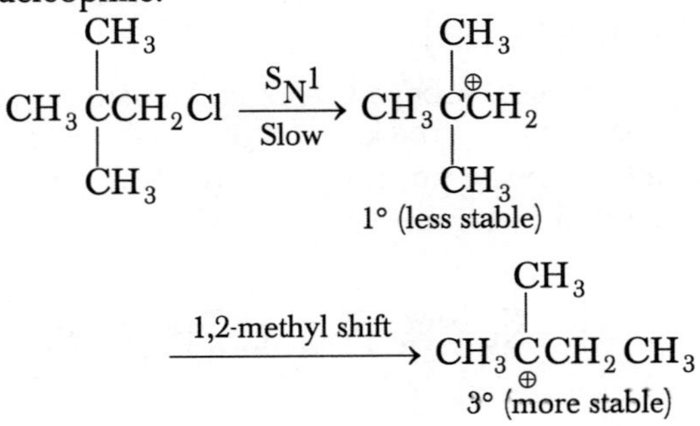

- As a result of S_N1 reaction, there can be **racemisation** and **inversion.** When (–) 2-bromo-butane having chiral centre is treated with low $[OH^-]$, S_N1 reaction is followed and (+) 2-butanol is obtained. There is also loss in optical activity. This loss in optical activity is due to formation of *d*- and *l*- isomers in equal amounts by S_N1 reaction.

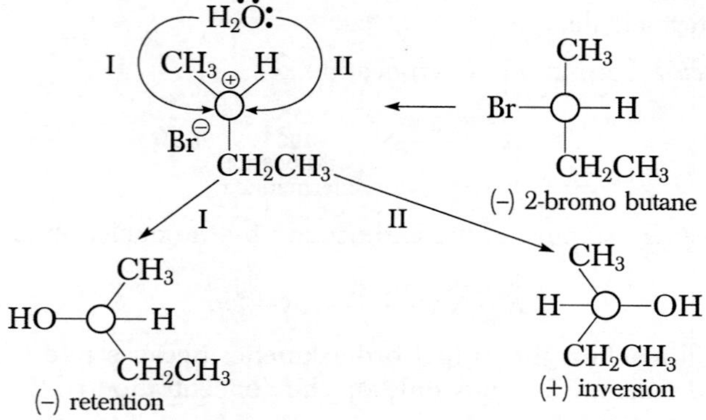

Nucleophilic reagent attacks both (I) backside and (II) front side of the carbocation. In back side attack (I), which is the side of the carbon from which the leaving group departed (in this case) configuration is retained but in front attack (II), inversion takes place. There can be racemisation if *d*- and *l*- are formed in equal amounts. Attack is preferred on the side opposite to where leaving group Br^- exists since, it shields the passage of nucleophile for attack. (In this case front attack is preferred, hence mixture is not purely *racemic* and some optical activity exists).

Thus, the reaction of an alkyl halide in which halogen is bonded to chirality centre leads to the formation of two stereoisomers: one with the same relative configuration as the reacting alkyl halide and the other with the inverted configuration.

S_N2 (<u>S</u>ubstitution <u>N</u>ucleophilic <u>Bi</u>molecular)

S_N2 process proceeds *via* a transition state. The nucleophile attacks the substrate carbon simultaneously pushing out the leaving group in a concerted fashion.

$$R{-}X + \ddot{N}u^{\ominus} \xrightarrow[\text{I}]{\text{Slow}} \underset{\text{T.S}}{[\overset{\delta-}{\ddot{N}u}\ldots R \ldots \overset{\delta-}{X}]} \xrightarrow[\text{II}]{\text{Fast}} Nu{-}R + X^{\ominus}$$

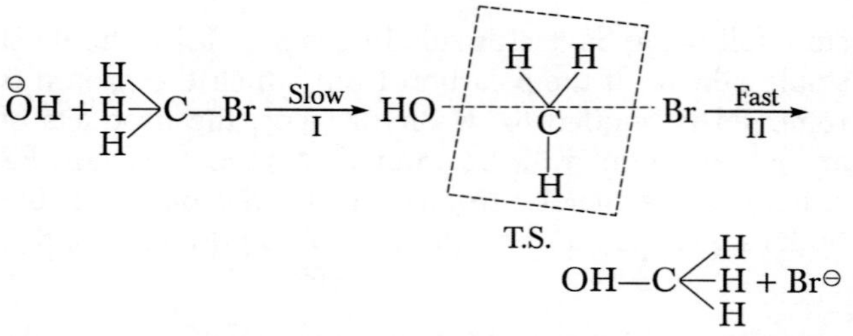

Step I is slowest and rate determining step. It has molecularity 2. Therefore, it is S_N2 mechanism.

- Kinetic evidence shows that the rate of this reaction is proportional to both the concentrations of substrate and nucleophile. Thus, S_N2 reactions follow second-order kinetics and is described by the rate expression :

$$\text{rate} = k\,[RX]\,[\ddot{N}u^{\ominus}]$$

where, k = rate constant

- When (+)-2-bromobutane (with one chiral carbon) is treated with conc. aq. KOH (OH^- being strong nucleophile). It gives (–)-2-butanol and no (+) isomer. There is thus complete **stereochemical inversion.**

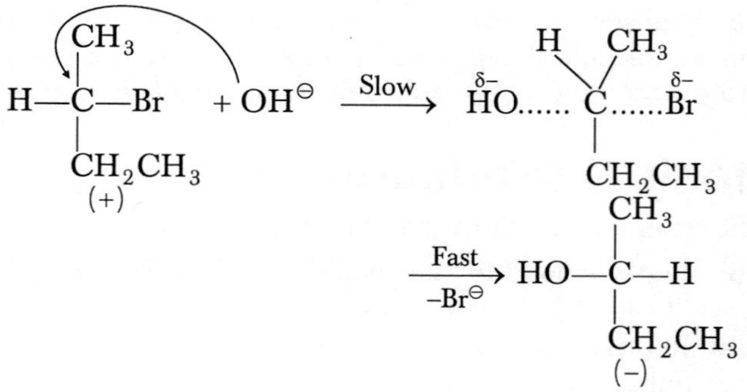

- Thus, in $\mathbf{S_N1}$ reaction, racemisation as well as inversion is observed, while is case of $\mathbf{S_N2}$ reaction, complete inversion takes place (where chiral carbon exists).

Factors Affecting S_N1 and S_N2 Mechanism

The following factors regulate the S_N1 and S_N2 mechanism.

(a) **Polar effect** *I*-effect, *M*-effect, *R*-effect, hyperconjugation etc., which can effect the stability of carbocation are collectively termed as polar effect. If polar effect stabilise the carbocation S_N1 will more probable than S_N2.

$>C{-}X$ (1°)	$>C{-}X$ (2°)	$>C{-}X$ (3°)
S_N2	S_N2 or S_N1	S_N1

(b) **Steric effect** More steric restriction opposes S_N2 mechanism. Simple alkyl halides show the order of reactivity in S_N2 reaction as

methyl > primary > secondary >> tertiary

- Even though the site of reaction in neopentyl derivatives is primary, the *t*-butyl group is large enough to slow down the bimolecular (S_N2) substitution **(steric effect).**

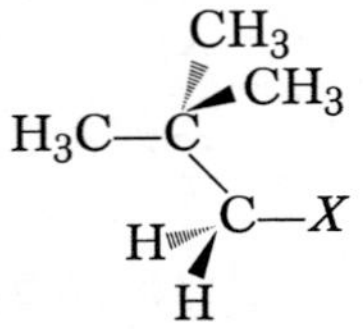

Neopentyl halide

(c) **The nature of leaving group**

- The rate of S_N1 reaction is largely influenced by the nature of the leaving group. The rate of ionization is affected by the stability of the leaving group, X^-. The more stable the leaving group, the more easily it will be lost S_N1 reactions therefore are favoured by the presence of good leaving group such as sulphonates (tosylate or mesylate).
- The ease of formation of carbocation supports S_N1.
- The decreasing order of leaving tendency of some group is as :

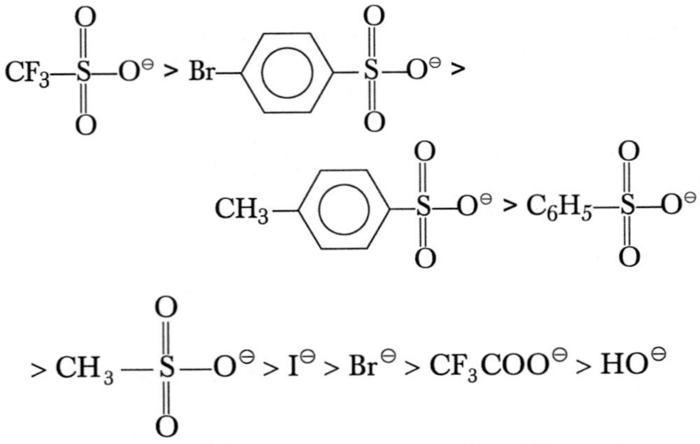

$> Cl^{\ominus} > F^{\ominus} > CH_3COO^{\ominus}$

(d) **Nature of nucleophile**

- Strong nucleophiles favour S_N2 mechanism while weak nucleophiles favour S_N1 mechanism.
- Strength of some nucleophiles is as :

$PhS^{\ominus} > CN^{\ominus} > I^{\ominus} > EtO^{\ominus} > OH^{\ominus} > Br^{\ominus} > PhO^{\ominus} > Cl^{\ominus} > Me_3N$

(e) **Neighbouring group participation**

Some neighbouring group such as $—COO^-$, $—X$, $—OH$, $—O—\overset{O}{\overset{\|}{C}}$, Ph^-, etc., can participate in nucleophilic substitution. **Example**

(i) Halogens as neighbouring groups.

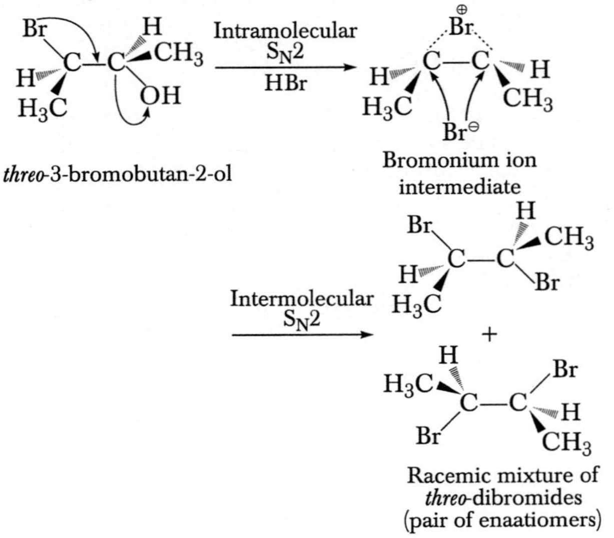

Bromine atom is acting as neighbouring group and the result is bromonium ion. opening of bromonium ion by bromide ion gives a pair of enantiomers.

(ii) Acetoxyl group as neighbouring group

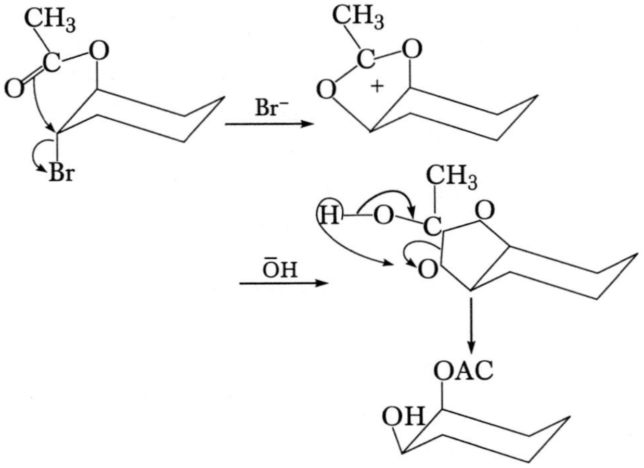

The rate of reaction is much faster due to the participation of acetoxyl group.

(f) **Nature of solvent** Polar solvents (*i.e.,* protic) favour S_N1 mechanism as they favour the ionisation of alkyl halide and therefore facilitate the formation of carbocation, *e.g.,* CF_3COOH, H_2O, CH_3OH,

CH_3COOH, etc. While S_N2 mechanism is favoured by aprotic solvents. These aprotic solvents are still relatively polar. They are especially favourable for S_N2 reaction because nucleophiles are more reactive in these solvents than protic one,

e.g., CH_3COCH_3, $CH_3—\overset{\overset{O}{\|}}{S}—CH_3$, $H—\overset{\overset{O}{\|}}{C}—N(CH_3)_2$.

Note • Benzylic and allylic halides under go S_N1 reaction because of the stability of their carbocations due to the resonance.

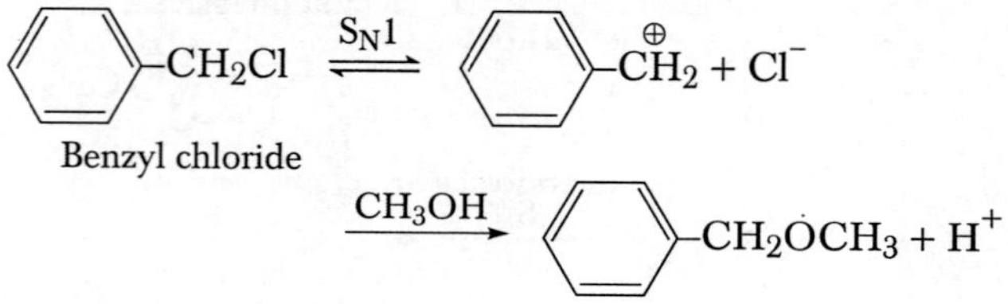

Benzyl chloride

$$\underset{\text{allyl bromide}}{CH_2{=}CHCH_2Br} \overset{S_N1}{\rightleftharpoons} CH_2{=}CH\overset{\oplus}{C}H_2 + Br^{\ominus}$$

$$\xrightarrow{H_2O} CH_2{=}CHCH_2OH + H^{\oplus}$$

• Vinyl halides ($CH_2{=}CHX$) and aryl halides

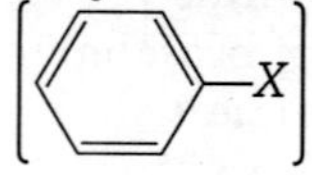

do not undergo S_N1 reaction due to instability of their carbocations.

$$RCH{=}CHCl \not\rightarrow \underset{\substack{\text{Vinyl cation}\\ \text{(too unstable to}\\ \text{be formed)}}}{RCH{=}\overset{\oplus}{C}H} + \underset{sp\text{-hybridised}}{Cl^{\ominus}}$$

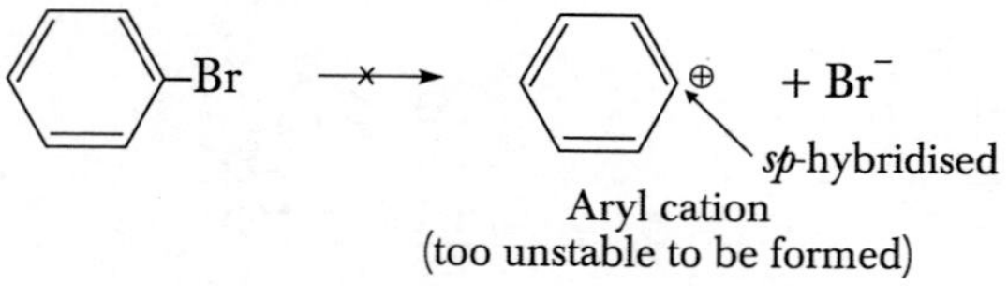

Table 31.2 **Summary of the S_N1 and S_N2 Reactions**

	S_N1	S_N2
Mechanism	two-step $R—L \rightarrow R^{\oplus} \rightarrow R—Nu$	one-step $R—L + Nu^{\ominus} \rightarrow R—Nu + L^{\ominus}$
Kinetics	first-order rate = $k\,[R—L]$	second-order rat = $k\,[R—L][Nu^{\ominus}]$
Effect of nucleophile	no effect on rate	stronger nucleophiles cause faster rate
Effect of carbon structure	tertiary > secondary resonance stabilisation of $R^{\oplus}$ important	methyl > primary > secondary
Stereochemistry	racemisation (possible excess inversion)	inversion
Effect of solvent	favoured by polar solvents	favoured by aprotic solvents
Competing reaction	elimination, rearrangement	elimination

$S_N i$ (Substitution Nucleophilic Internal)

In this process part of leaving group which attacks the substrate detaches itself from the rest of the leaving group. This is exemplified by the conversion of (*R*)-2-butanol to (*R*)-2-chlorobutane with $SOCl_2$ in non-polar solvent and absence of base. The product formed is with complete retention of configuration, *i.e.*, in which the starting material and product have the same configuration. The mechanism appears to involve the formation of intermediate chlorosulphite ester, *R*OSOCl (*R* = *sec*-butyl group), which dissociates into an intimate ion pair, $R^+ : {}^-OSOCl$ as in S_N1 mechanism. The Cl, with pair of electron, of the anion attacks the R^+ from the same side of the carbocation from which ${}^-OSOCl$ departed and the product (*R*Cl) is formed with complete retention of configuration.

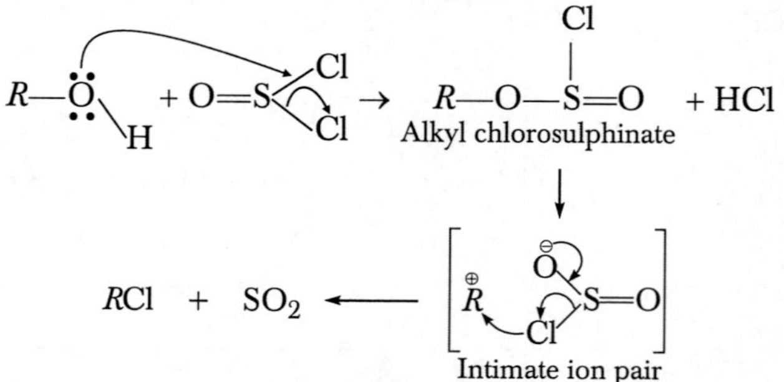

$S_N i$ mechanism

It is interesting that if a tertiary amine such as pyridine is added to the reaction mixture, the product *R*Cl is found now to have undergone inversion of configuration. The pyridine coordinates with the HCl, produced during the formation of intermediate chlorosulphite from *R*OH and $SOCl_2$, to form pyridine hydrochloride and the Cl^- is an effective nucleophile. The displacement of the chlorosulphinate ester by Cl^- *via* S_N2 mechanism gives product with complete inversion of configuration.

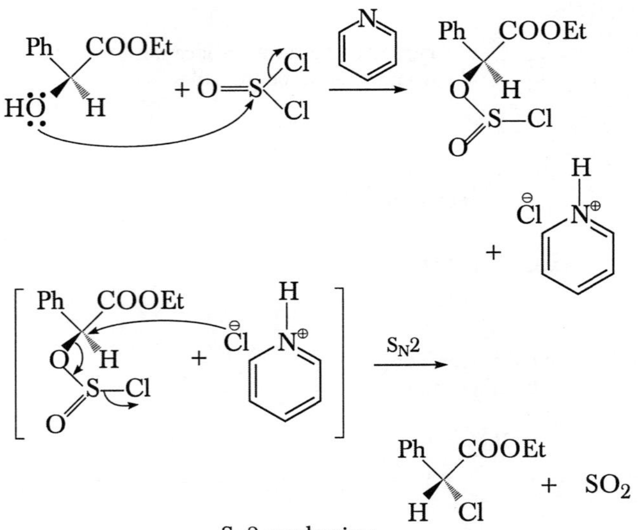

S_N2 mechanism

The Stereochemistry of S_N2 and S_N1 Reactions

Stereoisomers are not possible if the substitution products does not have chirality centre as in the following case :

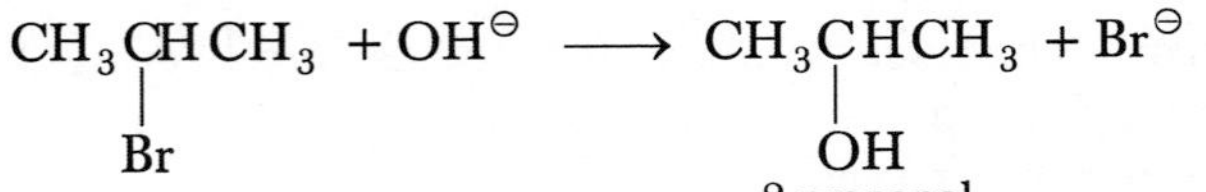

2-bromopropane 2-propanol

The substitution product obtained from the reaction of 2-bromobutane with $OH^{\ominus}$ ion has a chirality centre. Therefore, it can exist as a pair of enantiomers.

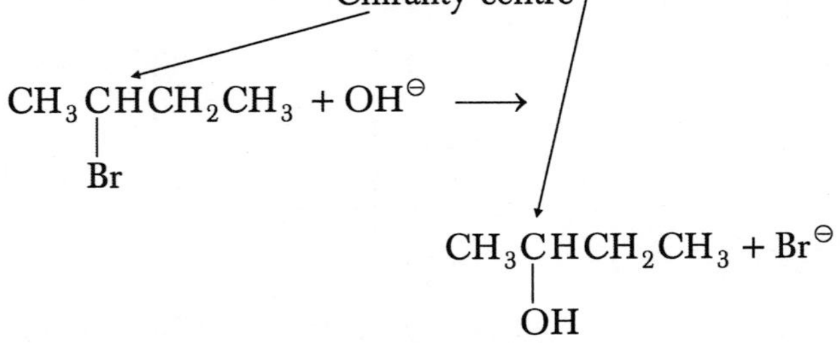

We cannot predict the configuration of the product formed for the given case, unless we know the configuration of the alkyl halide and we know whether the reaction is an S_N2 or S_N1 reaction. If the alkyl halide is (*S*)-2-bromobutane, the incoming nucleophile ($OH^{\ominus}$) attack the chirality centre on the side opposite to where the bromine is bonded. This results in the formation of the product whose configuration is inverted compared with the configuration of the reactant. Thus, an **S_N2 reaction takes place with the inversion of configuration.**

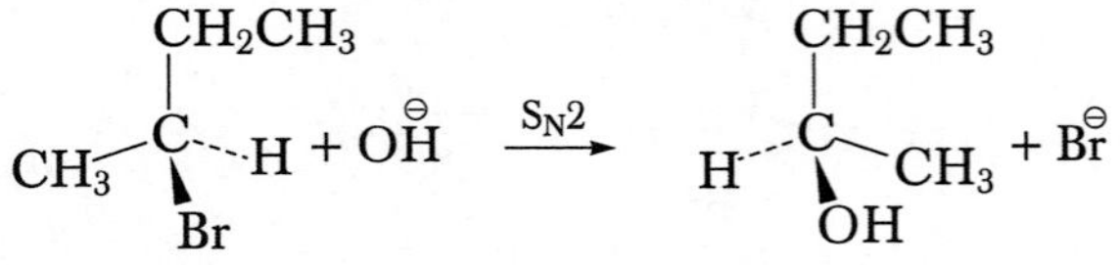

(*S*)-2-bromobutane (*R*)-2-butanol

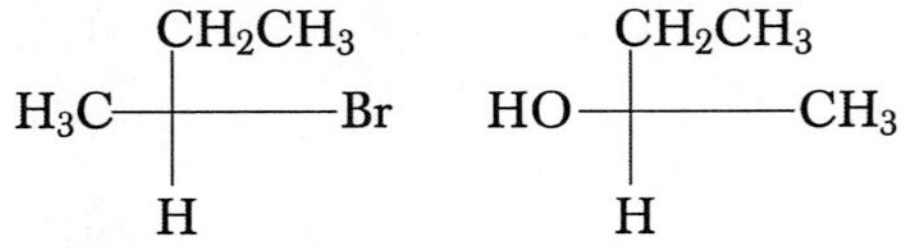

2-bromobutane 2-butanol

In the S_N1 reaction of (*S*)-2-bromobutane with H_2O, two substitution products formed, *i.e.,* one product has the same relative configuration as the reactant, and the other one has the inverted configuration. S_N1 reaction takes place through the formation of a carbocation. This means that the nucleophile is free to attack either side of the planar carbocation. If it attacks the side from which the bromide ion left, the product will have the same relative configuration as the reactant. If it attacks the opposite side, the product will have the inverted configuration.

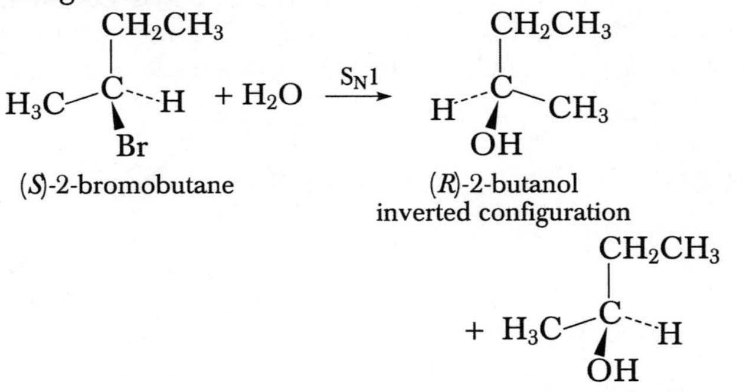

(*S*)-2-bromobutane

(*R*)-2-butanol
inverted configuration

(*S*)-2-butanol
retained configuration

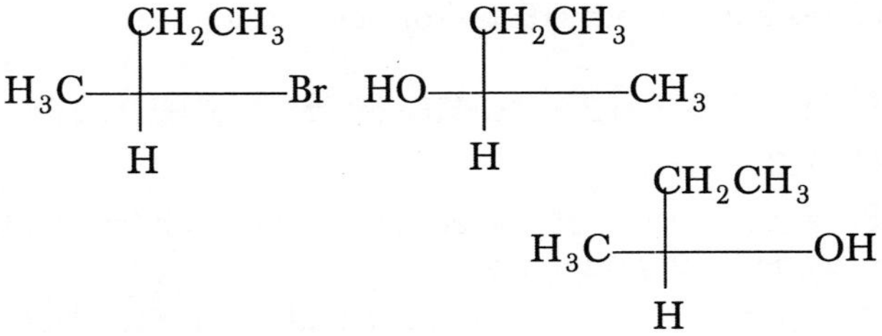

Although we might expect that equal amounts of both products should be formed in an S_N1 reaction, a greater amount of the product with the inverted configuration is obtained in most cases. In all, 50 to 70% of the product of an S_N1 reaction is the inverted product. If reaction leads to the equal amounts of the two stereoisomers, the reaction is said to take place with **complete racemisation.** When more the inverted product is formed, the reaction is said to take place with **partial racemisation.**

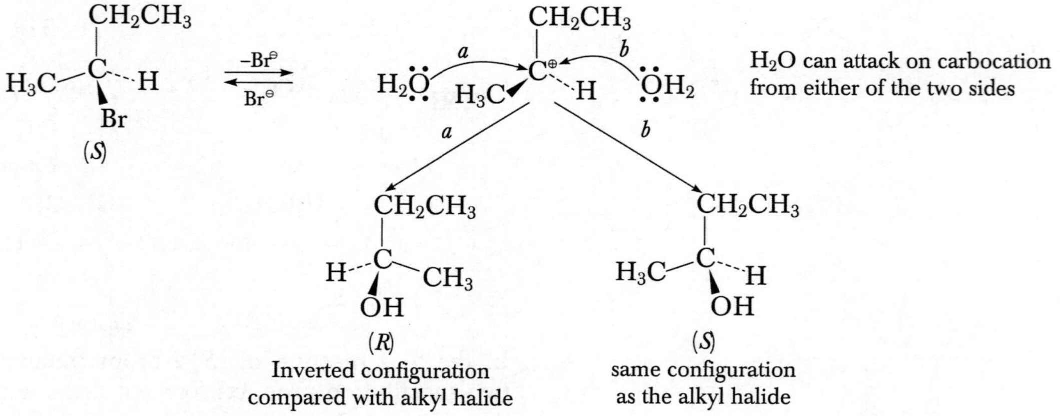

Consider the S_N reaction in cyclo compounds

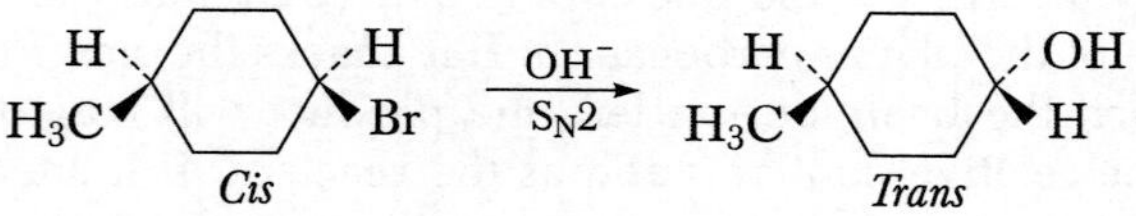

With S_N2 reaction, only the *trans*-product is obtained because the carbon bonded to the leaving group is attacked by the nucleophile only on its back side.

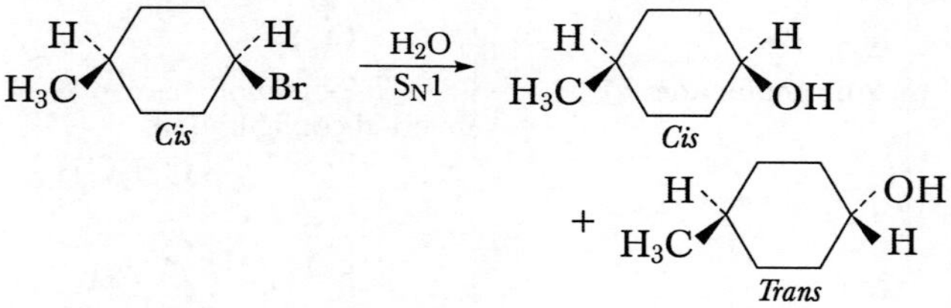

With S_N1 reaction, both the *cis* and *trans*-products are formed because the nucleophile can approach the carbocation intermediate from either side.

Nucleophilic Aromatic Substitution Reactions

Benzene does not react with nucleophiles under reaction conditions since :

(i) the π-electron clouds (above and below the plane of the ring) causes repulsion of the electrons of the nucleophile.

(ii) leaving group H^- (hydride) is a strong base (leaving group should be weak for a good result).

If the benzene ring has one or more electron-withdrawing substituents (such as nitro) in *ortho* or *para*-position *wrt* a good leaving group (such as halogen) then nucleophile aromatic substitution (S_NAr) can take place.

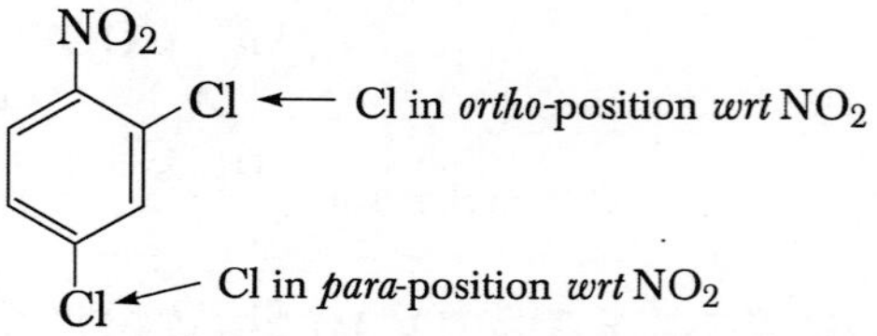

Strong electron-withdrawing substituents activate benzene ring towards S_N Ar reactions. Greater the number of such groups, easier the substitution. S_NAr reaction takes place in two steps :

Step I The nucleophile attacks the carbon bearing the leaving group and a carbanion is formed. Carbanion is resonancestabilised.

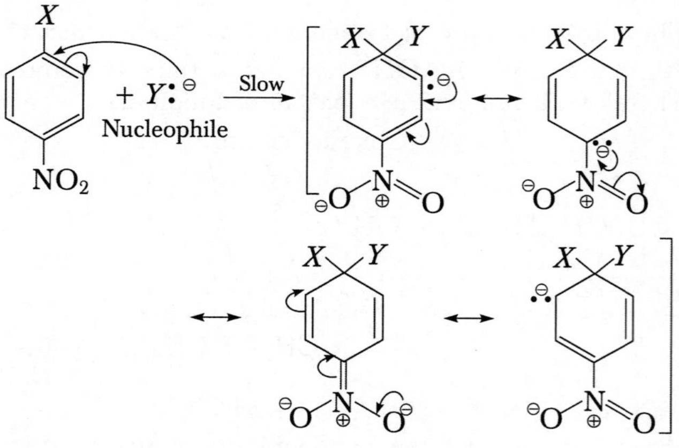

Step II Leaving group *X* departs from the carbanion giving the substitution product.

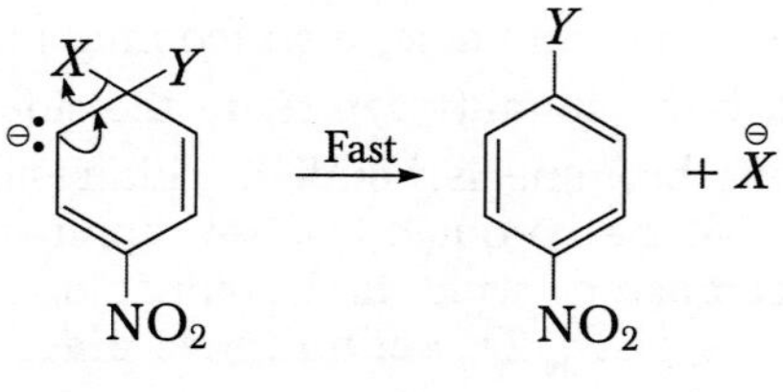

An aryl halide can undergo a nucleophilic substitution in the presence of a very strong base such as $NH_2^{\ominus}$. For this case

- the aryl halide does not have to contain an electron-withdrawing group.
- incoming group can occupy the vacated position or the adjacent position (in equal amounts)

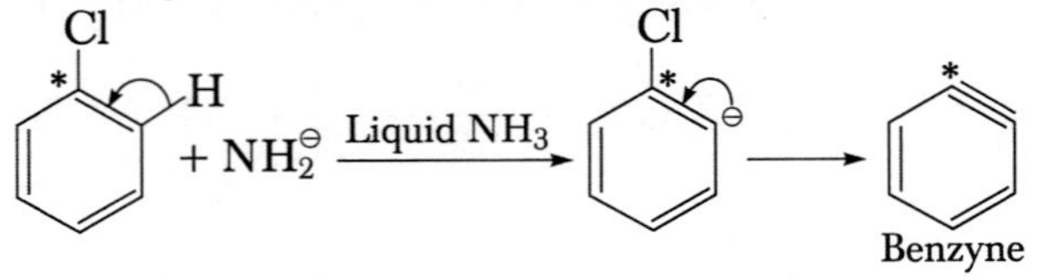

(C* is $\overset{14}{C}$–isotopically labelled)

This reaction takes place through the formation of **benzyne intermediate** which has an extra π-bond between two adjacent carbon atoms of benzene.

Step I Strong base ($NH_2^{\ominus}$) removes a proton from the proton the position *ortho* to halogen. The resulting anion eliminates halides ion and thus benzyne is formed.

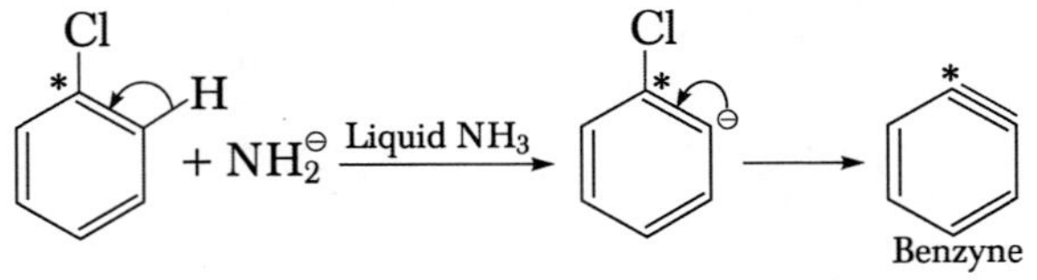

Step II Nucleophile ($NH_2^{\ominus}$) can attack either of the two carbons of the **"triple bond"** of benzyne which is extremely reactive species.

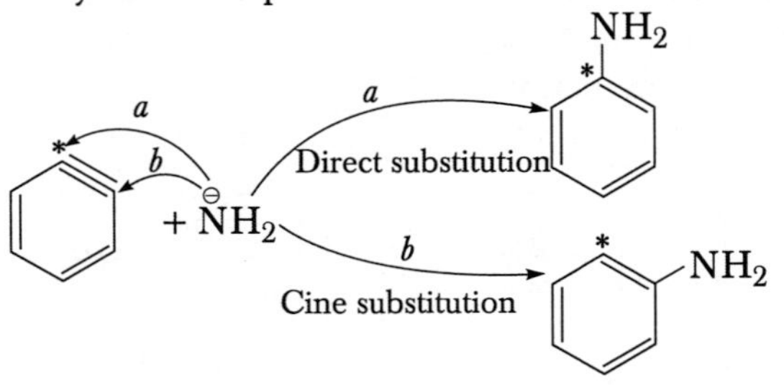

Substitution at the same carbon (from which leaving group departs) is called **direct substitution** while substitution at the adjacent carbon is called **cine substitution.**

Electrophilic Substitution Reaction (S_E)

Electrophilic substitution reaction takes place in benzene nucleus (aromatic compounds) in which π-electrons are highly delocalised and an electrophile can attack this region of high electron density.

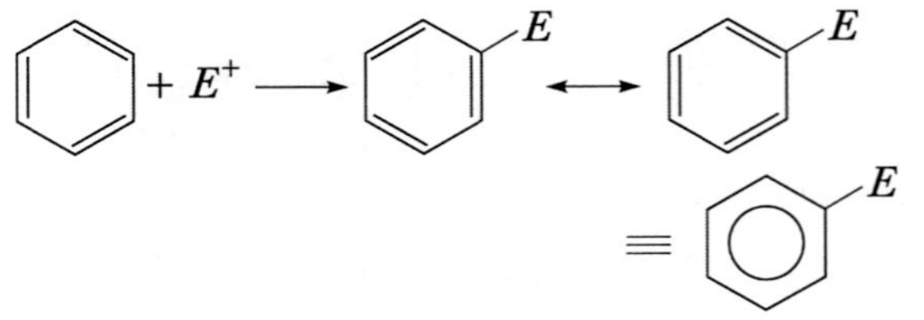

Mechanism

(a) **Generation of electrophile**

The substituting reagent is ionized in such a way as to generate an electrophile or polarized to create an electron-deficient species.

(b) **Attack of electrophile on π-electron system**

The electrophile attacks a benzene ring to give an intermediate, often called benzenonium ion intermediate, which is resonance stabilized. The carbocation intermediate (benzenonium ion) is too unstable to be isolated as salts except in special circumstances.

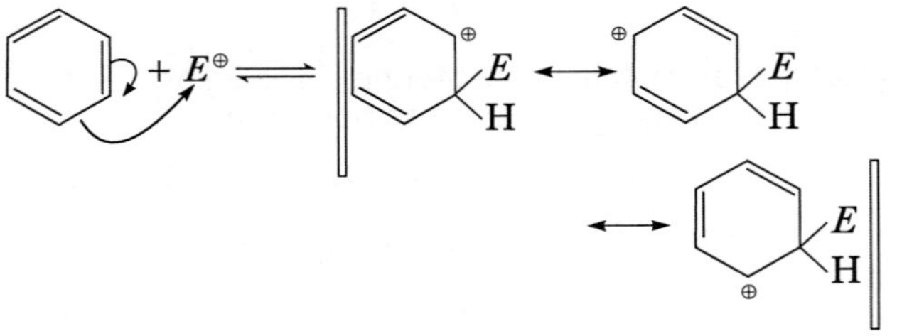

This step is rate-determining step in most electrophilic substitution reactions.

(c) **Removal of proton by base**

In the last step proton is removed from the intermediate benzenonium ion by a base to restore the aromatic ring. Thus, the aromatic system remains intact.

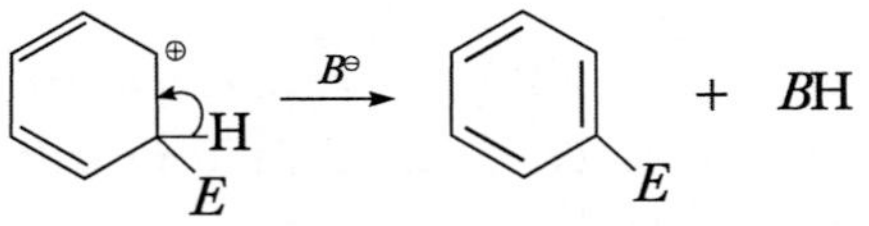

Example

(i) Nitration of benzene

$$H—O—NO_2 + H_2SO_4 \longrightarrow NO_2^{\oplus} + H_3O^{\oplus} + HSO_4^{\ominus}$$

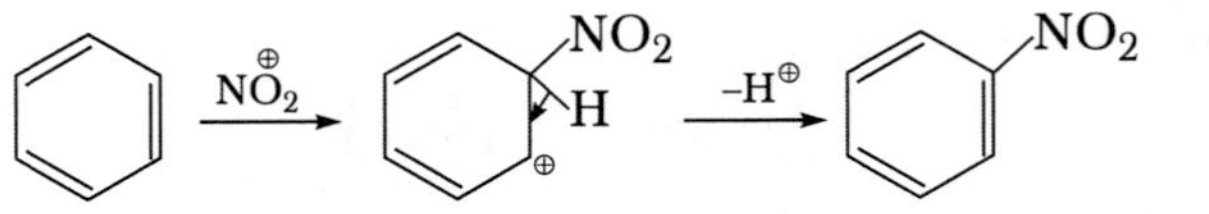

(ii) Chlorination of benzene

$$Cl—Cl + AlCl_3 \longrightarrow \overset{\oplus}{Cl} + AlCl_4^{\ominus}$$

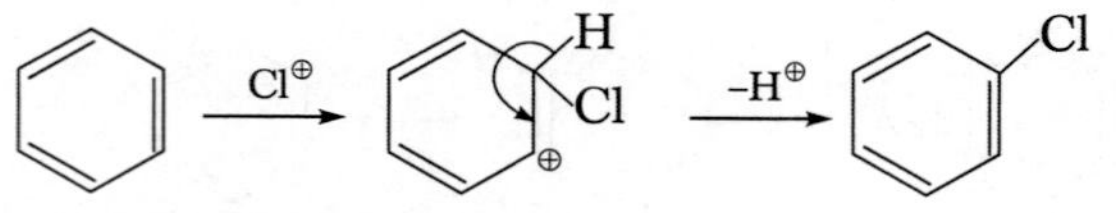

(iii) Friedel-Craft's alkylation

$$CH_3—Cl + AlCl_3 \longrightarrow \overset{\oplus}{C}H_3 + AlCl_4^{\ominus}$$

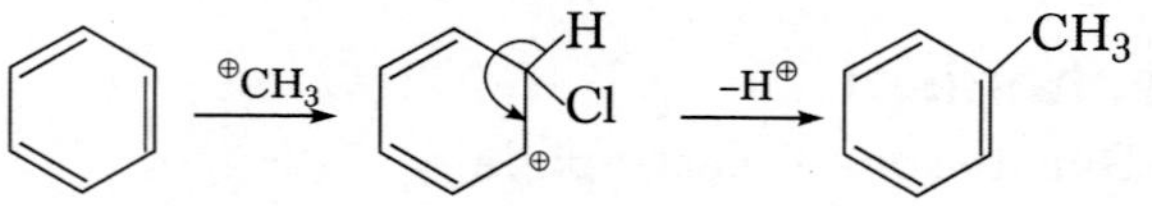

(iv) Friedel-Craft's acylation

$$CH_3—\overset{O}{\overset{\|}{C}}—Cl \xrightarrow{AlCl_3} CH_3—\overset{O}{\overset{\|}{\underset{\oplus}{C}}} + AlCl_4^{\ominus}$$

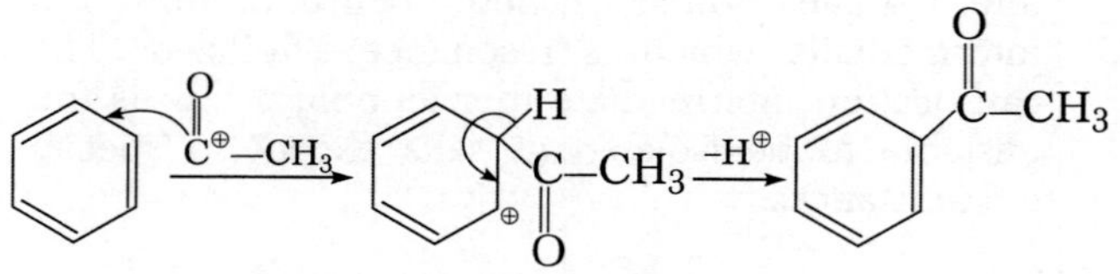

Note • Electrophilic substitution in aliphatic system are very rare. Some examples are

$$CH_3—\overset{-}{C}H_2\overset{+}{Mg}Br + HBr \longrightarrow CH_3—CH_3 + MgBr_2$$

$$CH_3—\overset{-}{C}H_2Na + H—C\equiv CH \longrightarrow CH_3—CH_3 + CH\equiv CNa$$

$$CH_3COOH + Na \longrightarrow CH_3COO^-Na^+ + \frac{1}{2}H_2$$

Free Radical Substitution

Alkanes react with Cl_2 or Br_2 to form alkyl chlorides or bromides. These reactions take place only at high temperatures or in presence of light.

$$CH_4 + Cl_2 \xrightarrow[\text{or } 670\text{ K}]{h\nu} CH_3Cl + HCl$$

$$CH_2{=}CHCH_3 + NBS \longrightarrow CH_2{=}CHCH_2Br$$

C—H bond is replaced by C–X bond in **free radical halogenation.** Reaction takes place through free radical intermediates and thus a **homolytic substitution** reaction.

$$CH_3CH_3 + Cl_2 \longrightarrow CH_3CH_2Cl + HCl$$

Mechanism

Step I **Initiation**

$$Cl—Cl \longrightarrow \dot{C}l + \dot{C}l$$

Step II **Propagation**

$$CH_3CH_2—H + \dot{C}l \longrightarrow CH_3\dot{C}H_2 + HCl$$

$$CH_3\dot{C}H_2 + Cl—Cl \longrightarrow CH_3CH_2Cl + \dot{C}l$$

Step III **Termination**

$$\dot{C}l + \dot{C}l \longrightarrow Cl_2$$

$$CH_3\dot{C}H_2 + \dot{C}l \longrightarrow CH_3CH_2Cl$$

$$CH_3\dot{C}H_2 + \dot{C}H_2CH_3 \xrightarrow{\text{Coupling}} CH_3CH_2CH_2CH_3$$

$$CH_3\dot{C}H_2 + CH_3\dot{C}H_2 \xrightarrow{\text{Disproportionation}} CH_2{=}CH_2 + CH_3—CH_3$$

- Reactivity of the halogens for free radical substitution is in order :
  The more reactive a species is, the less selective it will be $F_2 > Cl_2 > Br_2 > I_2$
- Abstraction of H from allylic carbon or benzylic carbon takes place using N-bromosuccinimide (NBS), in which weak nitrogen-bromine bond can be cleaved homolytically into radical upon warming or exposure to visible light.

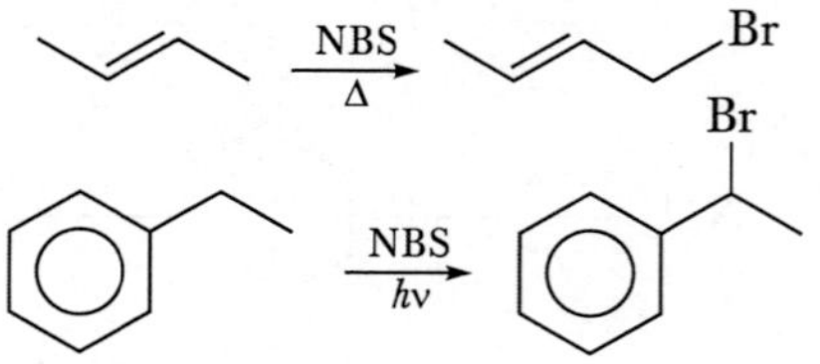

Free Radical Reaction in Cyclic Compounds

Cyclic compounds undergo the same reactions as the non-cyclic compounds.

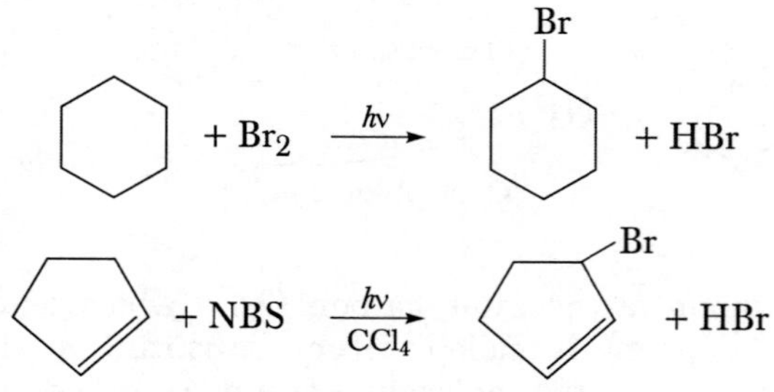

However cyclopropane or cyclobutane undergo electrophilic addition reactions as if it were an alkene. It is due to strain in small rings.

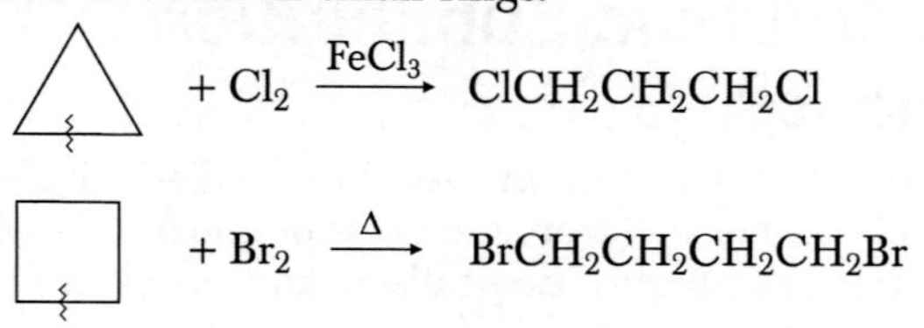

Bond angle in cyclopropane is 60° and in cyclobutane 90°. Each carbon atom is saturated and has sp^3-hybridised carbon and thus bond angle should be $109° 28'$. To minimise strain ring opening takes place.

Stereochemistry of Radical Substitution Reaction

If a radical substitution reaction creates a chirality centre in the product, both the *R* and *S* enantiomers will be formed.

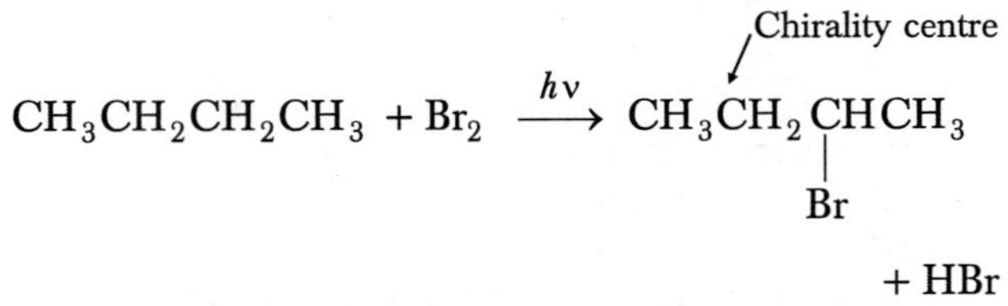

Configurations of the product are

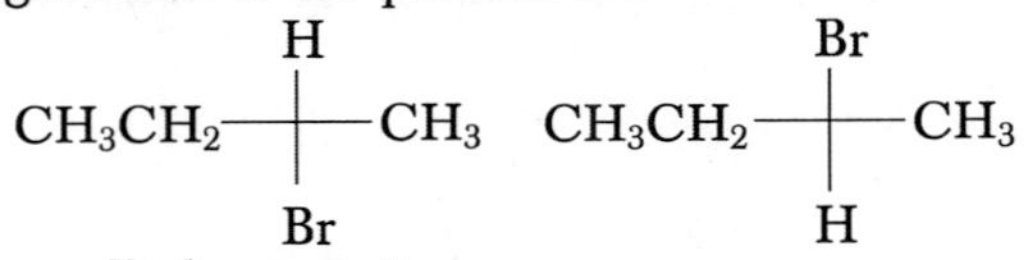

Fischer projections

(A pair of enantiomers)

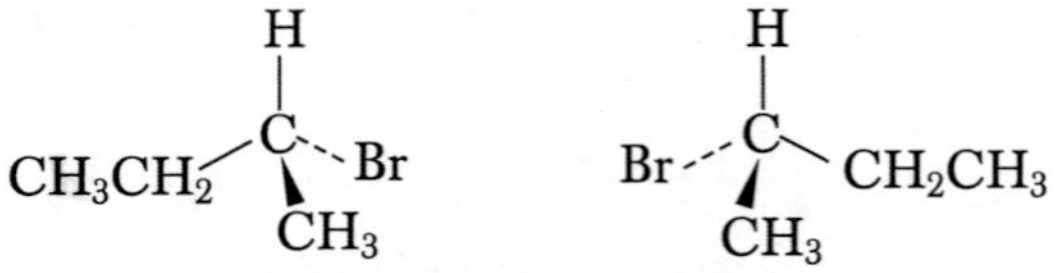

Perspective formulae

(A pair of enantiomers)

If the reactant already has chirality centre and the radical substitution reaction creates a second chirality centre a pair of diastereomers will be formed.

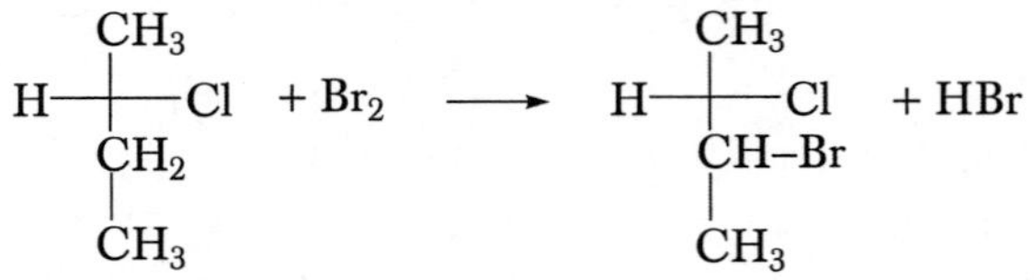

Fisher projections of this product can be represented as :

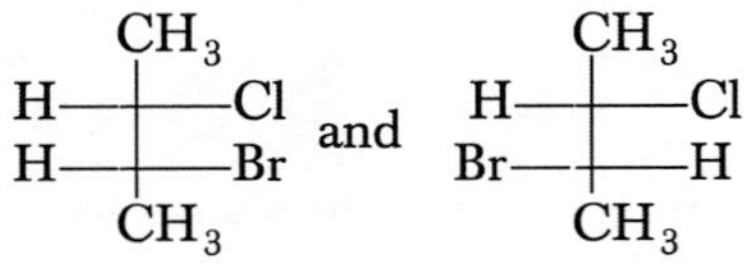

Exercise 1
(For Part 'B')

1. Which acid is the most highly ionized in water?
   (a) $(CH_3)_2CH \cdot COOH$ (b) $CH_3 \cdot CH_2 \cdot COOH$
   (c) $Cl_2CH \cdot CH_2 \cdot COOH$ (d) $CH_3 \cdot CCl_2 \cdot COOH$

2. Rank the following compounds in the order of decreasing basicity

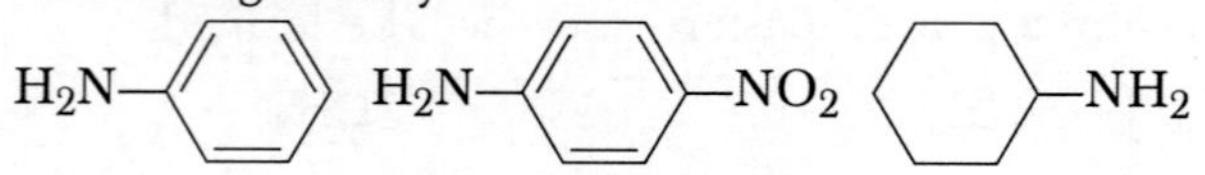

I II III

   (a) I, II, III (b) III, II, I
   (c) II, I, III (d) III, I, II

3. How many other major contributing resonance structures are possible for the following?

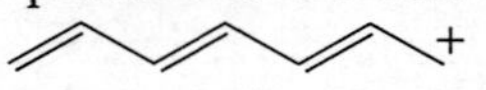

   (a) 1 (b) 2
   (c) 3 (d) 4

4. Given the reaction, fill in the blanks with appropriate resonance structure.

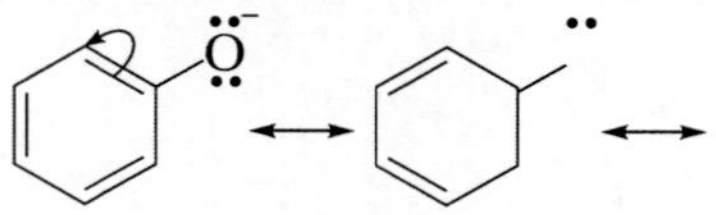

(a) 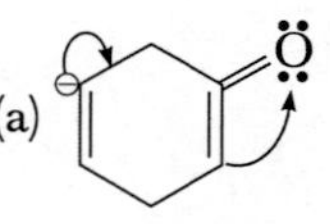 (b) 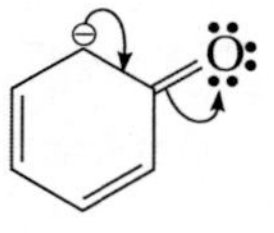

(c) 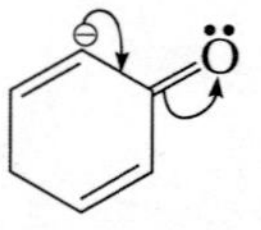 (d) 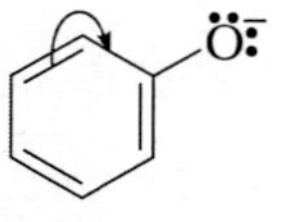

5. Which of the following is the strongest base?

(a) 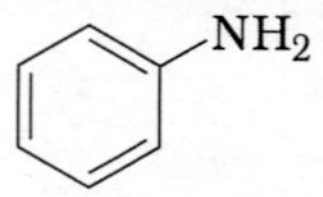 (b) 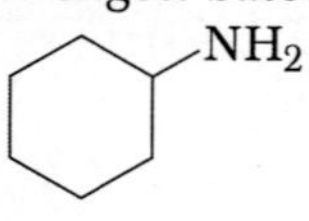

(c) 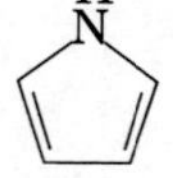 (d) 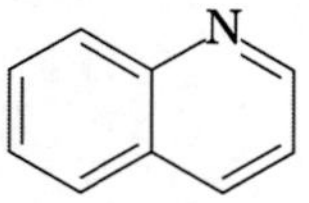

6. What is the approximate value of K for below at 25°C?

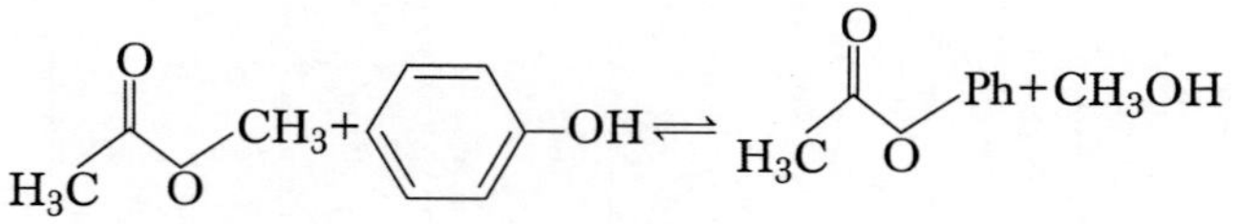

   (a) $K \approx I$ (b) $K > I$
   (c) $K < I$ (d) It is impossible

7. Select the statement that is not true about the following resonance structure

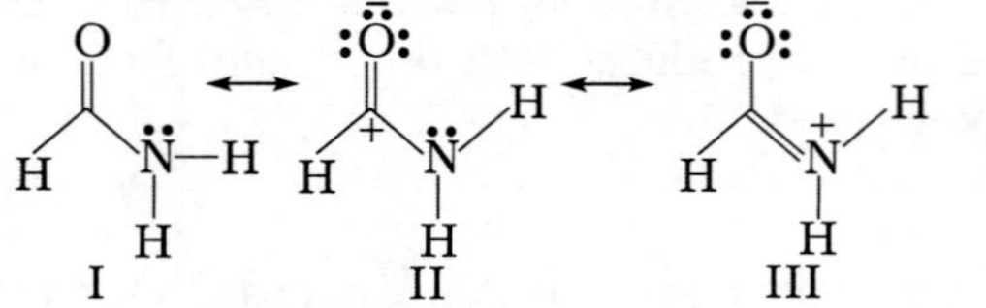

I II III

   (a) I is more stable than II
   (b) I is more stable than III
   (c) II is more stable than III
   (d) structure II has fewer bonds than I and III

8. Which of the following compound is conjugated?

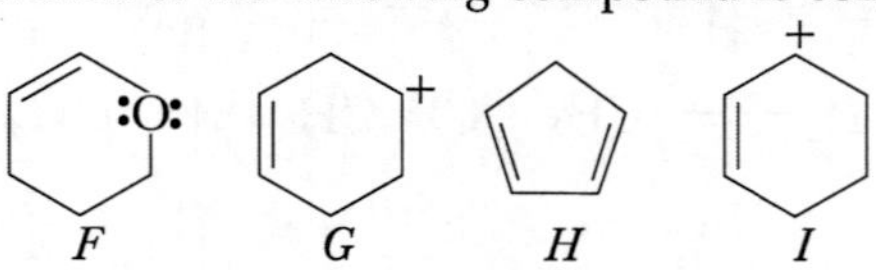

F *G* *H* *I*

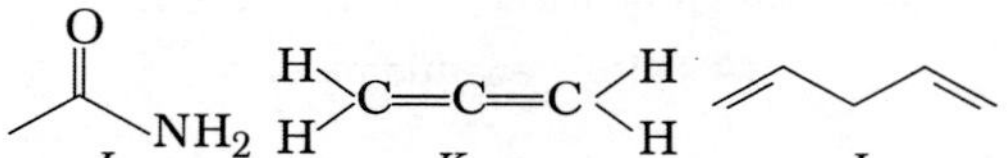

J *K* *L*

   (a) All are conjugated (b) *H, K, L*
   (c) *G* and *I* (d) *F, H, I* and *J*

9. What is the product of the reaction of one equivalent of imidazole with one equivalent of acid?

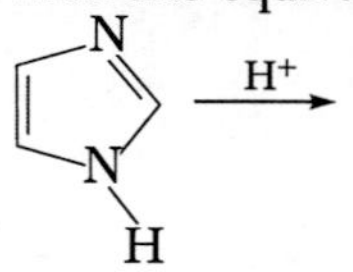

(a) 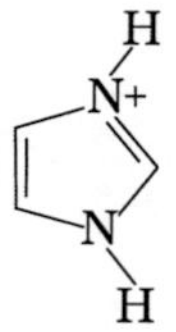 (b) 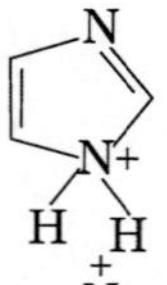

(c) 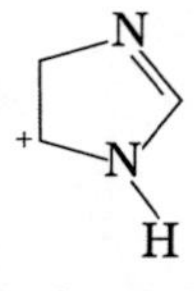 (d) 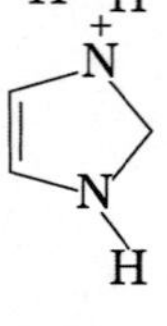

10. Which of the nitrogen compounds shown below is the strongest acid?

(a) 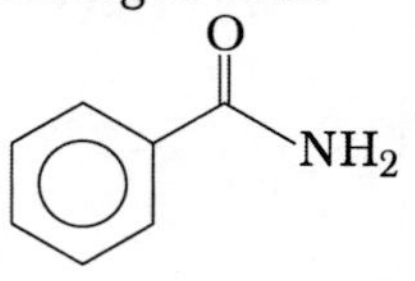 (b) 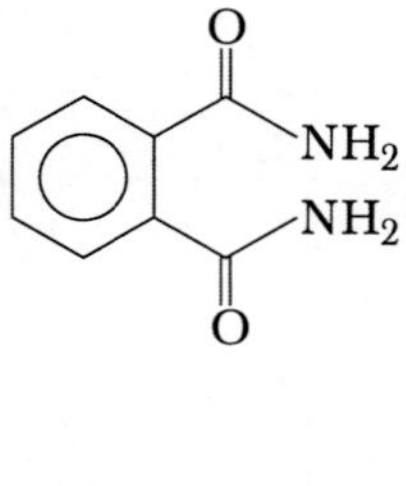

(c) 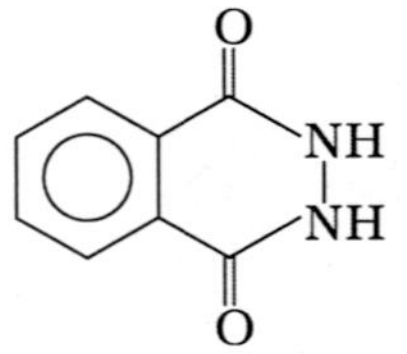 (d) 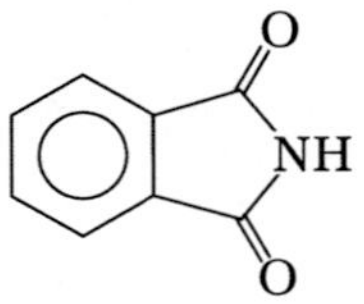

11. What is the decreasing order of strength of the bases?

$OH^-, NH_2^-, H—C{\equiv}C^-$ and $CH_3—CH_2^-$

(a) $CH_3—CH_2^- > NH_2^- > H—C{\equiv}C^- > OH^-$
(b) $H—C{\equiv}C^- > CH_3—CH_2^- > NH_2^- > OH^-$
(c) $OH^- > NH_2^- > H—C{\equiv}C^- > CH_3—CH_2^-$
(d) $NH_2^- > H—C{\equiv}C^- > OH^- > CH_3—CH_2^-$

12. The most unlikely representation of resonance structures of *p*-nitrophenoxide ion is

(a) 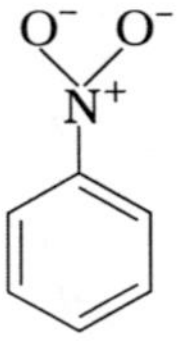 (b) 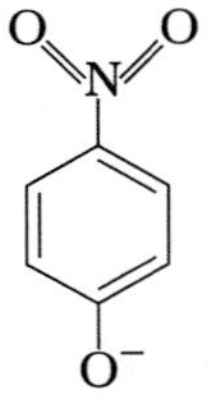

(c) 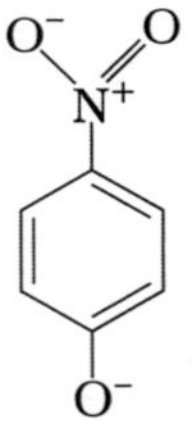 (d) 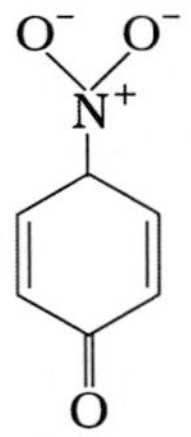

13. The correct order of basicities of the following compounds is

$H_3C—C(=NH)NH_2$ (I) $CH_3CH_2NH_2$ (II) $(CH_3)_2NH$ (III)

CH_3CONH_2 (IV)

(a) II > I > III > IV (b) I > III > II > IV
(c) III > I > II > IV (d) I > II > III > IV

14. For 1-methoxy-1,3-butadiene which of the following resonating structure is least stable?

(a) $\overset{\ominus}{C}H_2—\overset{\oplus}{C}H—CH{=}CH—O—CH_3$
(b) $\overset{\ominus}{C}H_2—CH{=}CH—CH{=}\overset{\oplus}{O}—CH_3$
(c) $CH_2{=}CH—\overset{\oplus}{C}H{=}\overset{\ominus}{C}H—O—CH_3$
(d) $CH_2{=}CH—\overset{\ominus}{C}H—CH{=}\overset{\oplus}{O}—CH_3$

15. Which of the following statements about the reactivity of 1-chloroapocamphane towards alcoholic $AgNO_3$ is true?

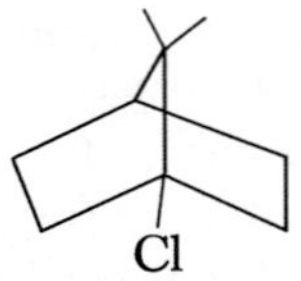

(a) Reacts by S_N1 mechanism
(b) Reacts by S_N2 mechanism
(c) Reacts by S_Ni mechanism
(d) Does not react

16. Most stable carbocation formed from $(CH_3)_3C—Br$, $(C_6H_5)_3C—Br$, $(C_6H_5)_2CHBr$ and $C_6H_5CH_2Br$ would be

(a) $C_6H_5\overset{+}{C}H_2$ (b) $(CH_3)_3\overset{+}{C}$
(c) $(C_6H_5)_3\overset{+}{C}$ (d) $(C_6H_5)_2\overset{+}{C}H$

17. Reaction of *R*-2-butanol with *p*-toluene sulphonyl chloride and pyridine by LiBr gives
(a) *R*-2-butyl tosylate (b) *S*-2-butyl tosylate
(c) *R*-2-butyl bromide (d) *S*-2-butyl bromide

18. Rearrange the following in the increasing order of acidity
I. benzoic acid
II. *p*-methoxy benzoic acid
III. *o*-methoxy benzoic acid
(a) I < II < III (b) III < I < II
(c) II < I < III (d) III < II < I

19. Which one of the following molecules exists as a monomer under ambient conditions?
(a) Trimethyl aluminium (b) Triethyl aluminium
(c) Triphenyl aluminium (d) Trimesityl aluminium

20. S_N1 reaction on optically active substrates mainly gives
(a) retention in configuration
(b) inversion of configuration
(c) racemic product
(d) no product

21. In E2 elimination, some compounds follow Hofmann's rule which means
(a) the double bond goes to the most substituted position
(b) the compound is resistant to elimination
(c) no double bond is formed
(d) the double bond goes mainly toward the least substituted carbon

22. One of the modern methods of studying free radicals is
(a) IR spectra (b) UV spectra
(c) CI DNP (d) microwave spectra

23. The number of unshared electrons on the carbene carbon is
(a) 1 (b) 2 (c) 3 (d) 4

24. In the singlet and the triplet states of methylene radical, the unshared electrons are respectively
(a) unpaired, unpaired (b) paired, paired
(c) unpaired, paired (d) paired, unpaired

25. For a reaction between an alkyl halide and OH^-, increase in solvent polarity generally
(a) increases the rate of S_N1 reaction
(b) decrease the rate of S_N1 reaction
(c) increase the rate of S_N2 reaction
(d) does not alter the rate of S_N1 and S_N2 reaction

26. Select the most easily cleaved by HBr

(a) 
(b) $H_2C—CH_2$ / O (epoxide)

(c) 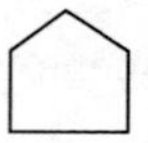
(d) 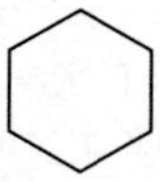

27. Which of the following is an example of non-classical carbocations?

I 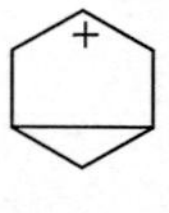 II 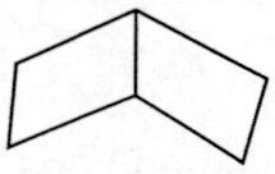 III 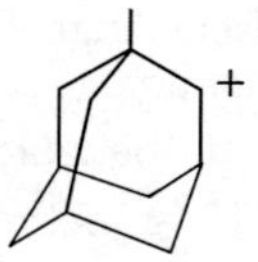

(a) I and II (b) II and II
(c) I and III (d) I, II and III

28. Which of the following reaction undergoes without formation of any intermediate?
(a) S_N1 reaction (b) S_Ni reaction
(c) Ar S_N1 reaction (d) S_N2 reaction

29. Which does not involve a carbocation?
(a) $(CH_3)_3CCl + AgNO_3 \longrightarrow$
(b) $(CH_3)_3COH + HCl \longrightarrow$
(c) $(CH_3)_3CH + Cl_2 + h\nu \longrightarrow$
(d) $CH_3CH{=}CHCH_2OH + H_3O^+ \longrightarrow$

30. Which pair will not form a stable carbocation?

I. 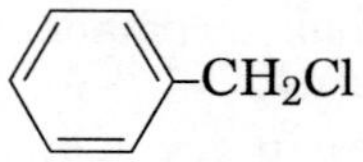 II. 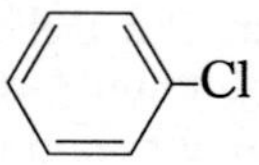

III.  IV. 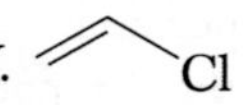

(a) I and II (b) II and III
(c) II and IV (d) III and IV

31. Which is not the intermediate of the transformation?

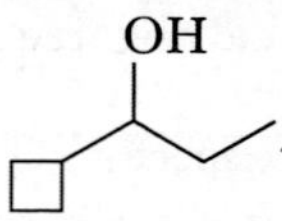 + HBr $\xrightarrow{\Delta}$ Major product

(a) 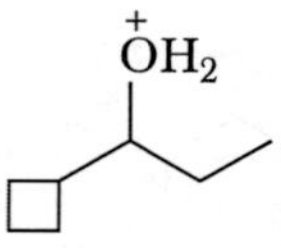 (b) 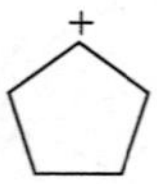

(c) 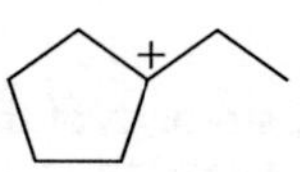 (d) 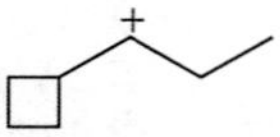

32. Which of the following reaction is the most exothermic?

(a) 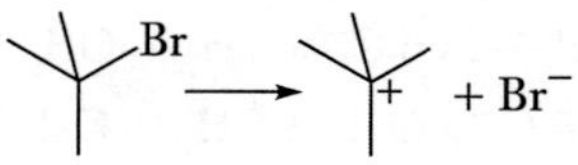

(b) 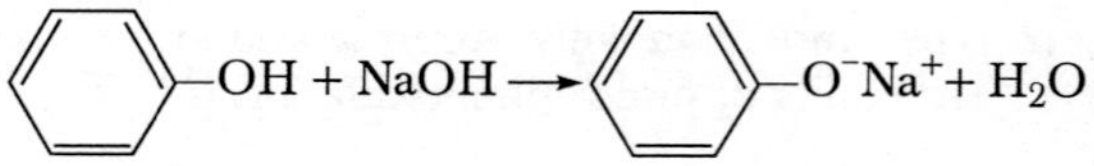

(c) 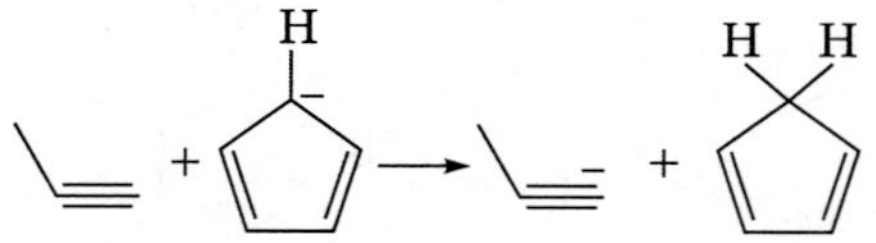

(d) $\dot{C}H_3 + CH_3CH_2CH_3 \longrightarrow \dot{C}H_4 + CH_3\dot{C}HCH_3$

33. Which of the following radical would be expected to be most selective?
(a) $HC{\equiv}C^{\bullet}$ (b) $H_3C^{\bullet}$
(c) $Ph^{\bullet}$ (d) $H_2C{=}CH—\dot{C}H_2$

34. Consider the following rearrangement reaction.

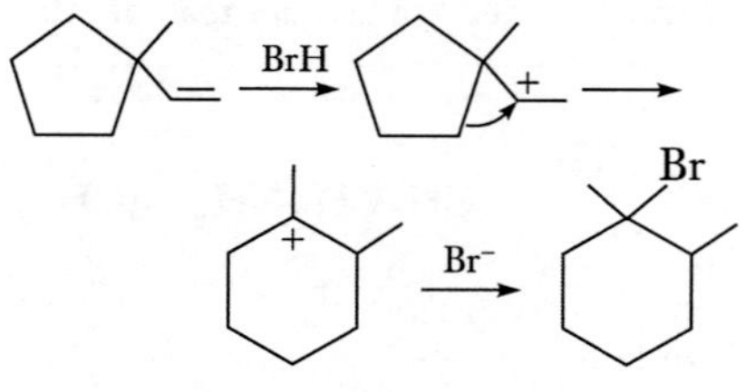

Which of the following reaction coordinate best represents the overall reaction?

(a) 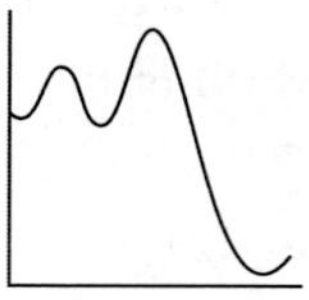 (b) 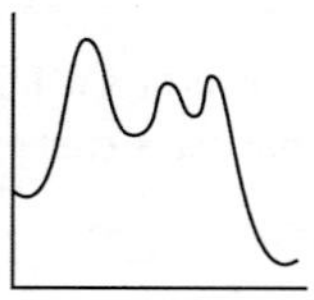

(c) 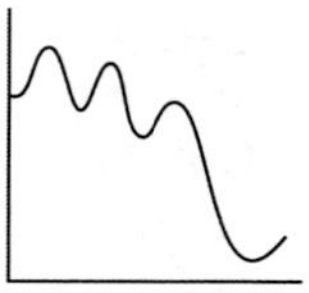 (d) 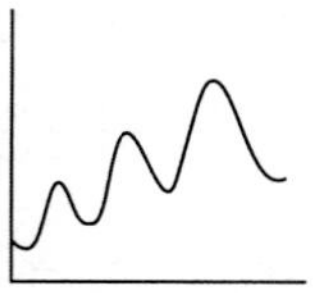

35. Which of the following is most likely to undergo a favourable hydride shift?

(a) 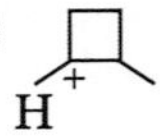
(b) 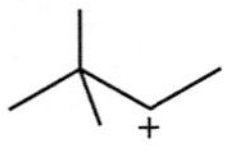
(c) 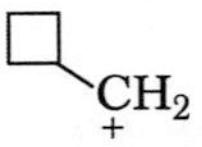
(d) 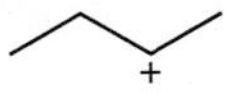

36. Which of the following is not a source of carbene?

(a) CH_2N_2 (b) $H_2C{=}C{=}O$
(c) $CHCl_3$ / KOH (d) CH_2I_2 / Zn

37. Select the reaction that would proceed as an exothermic reaction.

(a) $CH_3\dot{C}H_2 + CH_2{=}CH_2 \longrightarrow CH_3CH_3 + CH_2{=}\dot{C}H$

(b) $CH_4 + CH_3\dot{C}H_2 \longrightarrow \dot{C}H_3 + CH_3CH_3$

(c) $\dot{C}H_3 + CH_2{=}CH_2 \longrightarrow CH_4 + CH_2{=}\dot{C}H$

(d) $CH_3\dot{C}H_2 + CH_3{-}CH{=}CH_2 \longrightarrow CH_3CH_3 + \dot{C}H_2{-}CH{=}CH_2$

38. A resonance form of the allylic carbanion shown below is

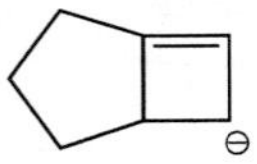

(a) 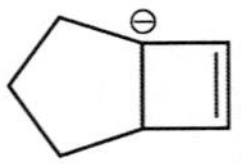
(b) 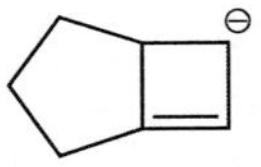
(c) 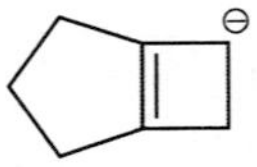
(d) All of these

39. Which of the following ions will be most effective in an S_N2 displacement on methyl bromide

(a) $C_2H_5O^-$ (b) HO^-
(c) $C_6H_5O^-$ (d) CH_3COO^-

40. Which of the following would react fastest with N-bromosuccinimide

(a) benzene (b) methane (c) pyridine (d) toluene

41. When 2-bromo-octane of specific rotation −34.6° is converted into the alcohol under low pH value where first-order kinetics are followed, there is obtained 2-octanol of specific rotation +3.6°. The conversion could be explained by

(a) free radical mechanism (b) carbonium mechanism
(c) carbanion mechanism (d) chain reaction

42. The reactive intermediate in the Reimer Tiemann reaction is

(a) formal anion
(b) formyl carbocation
(c) dichloromethyl carbocation
(d) dichlorocarbene

43. The nucleophilic attack on a carbon-carbon double bond generates

(a) carbanion (b) carbene
(c) carbocation (d) free radical

44. $CH_2{=}CH{-}CN + C_2H_5OH \xrightarrow{\text{Base}}$ Product,

product is

(a) $CH_2{=}CH{-}OH$
(b) $C_2H_5O{-}CH_2{-}CH_2CN$
(c) CH_3CH_2OH
(d) $C_2H_5OC_2H_5$

45. Which one of the following has all the effects namely inductive, mesomeric and hyperconjugative?

(a) CH_3Cl
(b) $CH_3CH{=}CH_2$
(c) $CH_3CH{=}CH{-}\underset{\underset{O}{\|}}{C}CH_3$
(d) $CH_2{=}CH{-}CH{=}CH_2$

46. 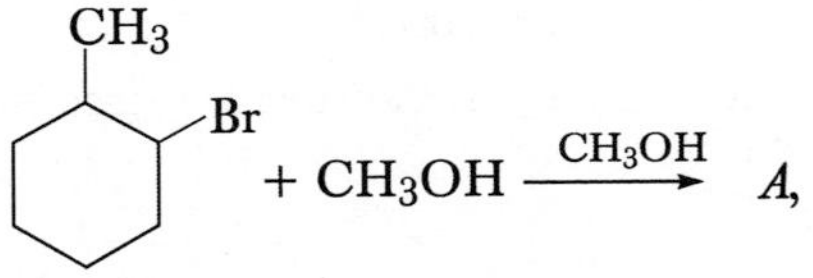

A (predominant *A*) is

(a) 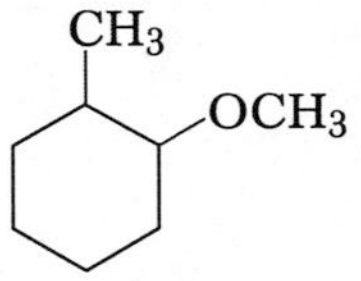
(b) 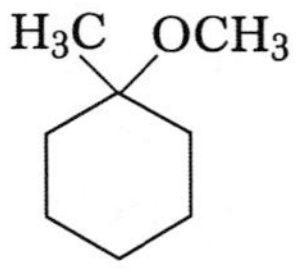
(c) 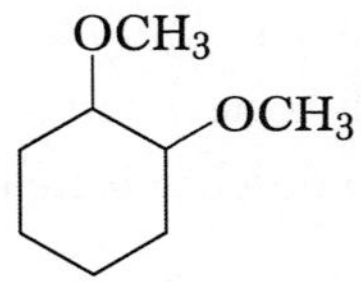
(d) 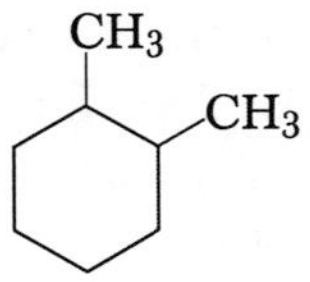

47. $CH_3\overset{CH_3}{\underset{CH_3}{C}}Br + CH_3CH_2OH \xrightarrow{CH_3CH_2OH} A$ (major)

$\xrightarrow[(CH_3CH_2OH)]{CH_3CH_2ONa} B$ (major)

Possible products can be

I. $CH_3\overset{CH_3}{\underset{CH_3}{C}}OCH_2CH_3$ II. $CH_3\overset{CH_3}{\underset{CH_2}{\overset{|}{\underset{\|}{C}}}}$

A and *B* can respectively

(a) I, II (b) II, I
(c) II in both cases (d) I in both cases

48. Most stable free radical is

(a) 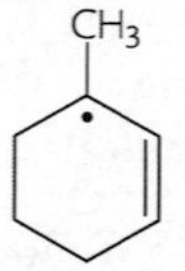 (b) 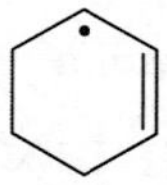

(c) 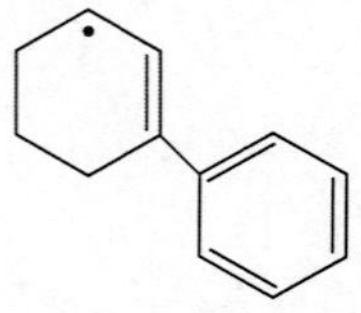 (d) 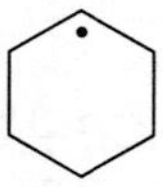

49. 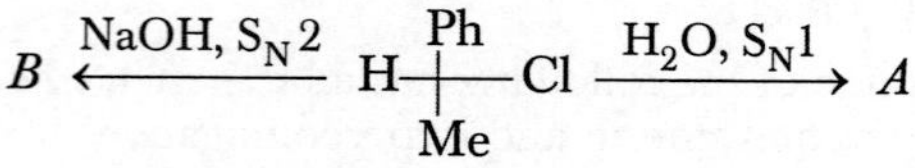

I. Formation of *A* has proceeded with racemisation.
II. Formation of *B* has proceeded with inversion.

Select the correct statements
(a) I and II both are correct
(b) only I is correct
(c) only II is correct
(d) None of the above is correct

50. Arrange these compounds in order of increasing S_N2 reaction rate

I. 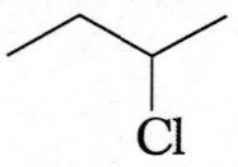 II. 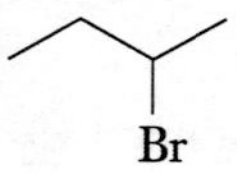

III. 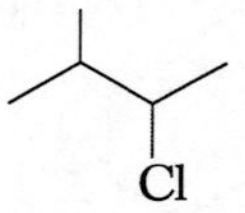 IV. 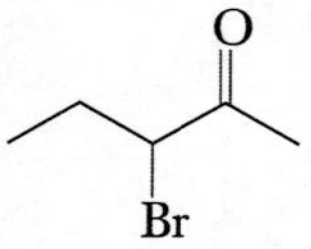

(a) III < I < II < IV (b) III < II < I < IV
(c) IV < III < I < II (d) none is correct

51. Arrange these compounds in order of increasing S_N1 reaction rate

I 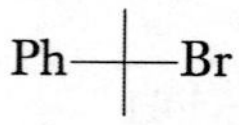 II 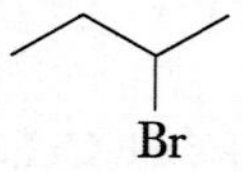

III 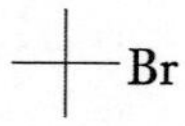 IV 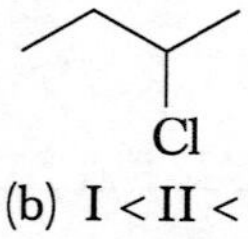

(a) IV < II < III < I (b) I < II < III < IV
(c) IV < I < III < II (d) IV < I < II < III

52. 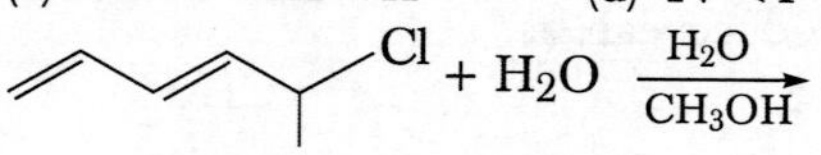

In this reaction we get ... types of substituted alcohols (stereoisomers not considered)
(a) one (b) two
(c) three (d) four

53. 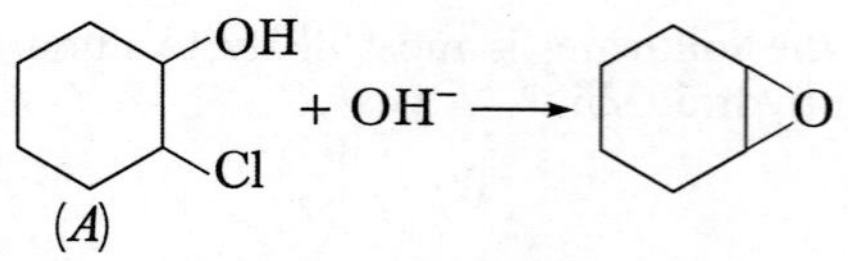

This reaction is possible when *A* is
(a) *cis* (b) *trans*
(c) Both (a) and (b) (d) None of these

54. Least reactive is
(a) CH_2N_2 (b) $CH_2{=}C{=}O$
(c) $:CH_2$ (d) $\cdot\dot{C}H_2$

55. 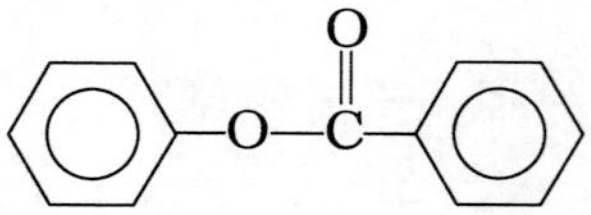 + NO_2^+ ⟶ Product of this reaction by single S_E reaction.

(a) 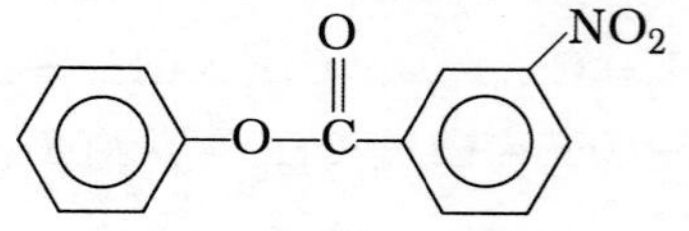

(b) 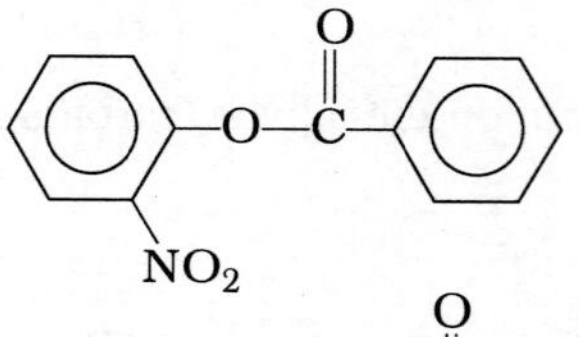

(c) 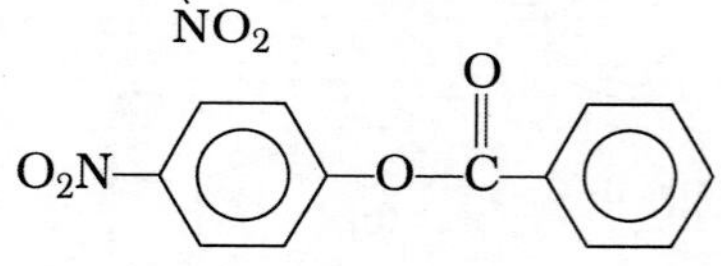

(d) 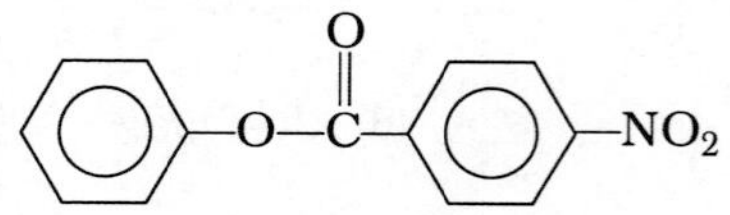

56. Electrophile $\overset{\oplus}{N}O_2$ attacks the following

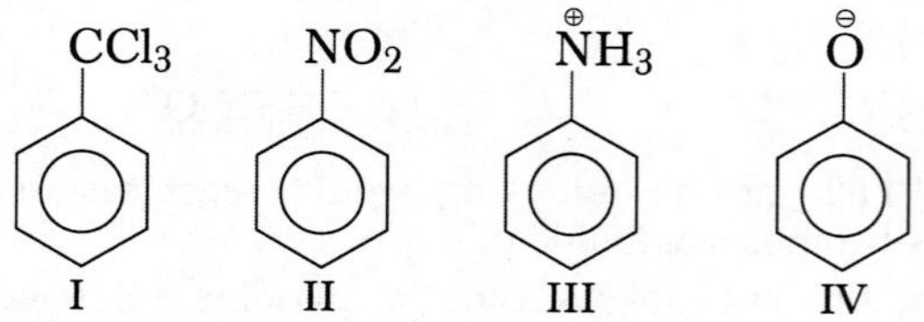

I II III IV

In which cases $\overset{\oplus}{N}O_2$ will be at *meta*-position
(a) II and IV (b) I, II and III
(c) II and III (d) I only

57. Dehydrobromination (—HBr) of the following in increasing order is

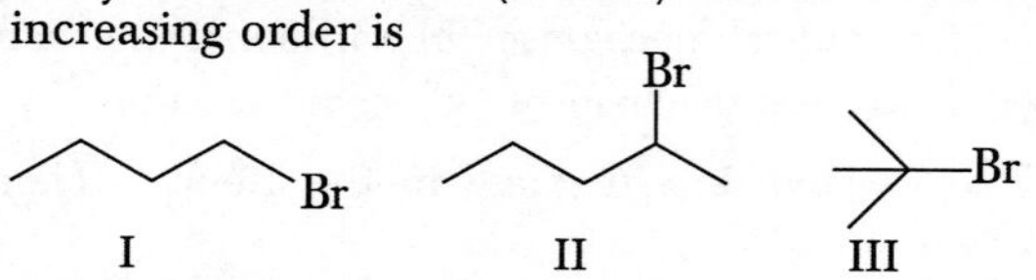

I II III

(a) I < II < III (b) III < II < I
(c) I = II < III (d) III < I = II

58. 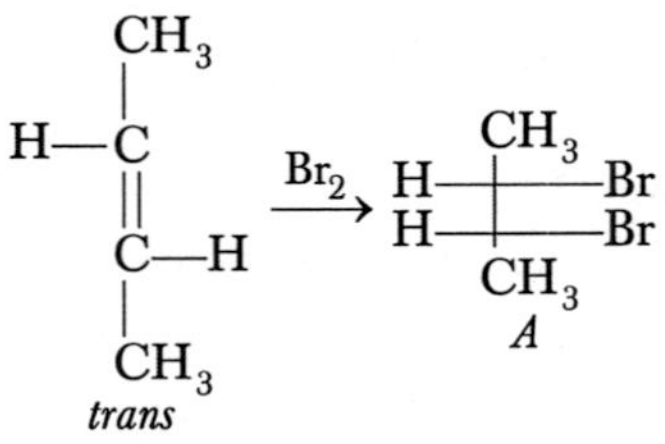

Which is true statement?

(a) *A* is formed by *anti*-addition and is *meso*
(b) *A* is formed by *syn*-addition and is *meso*
(c) *A* is formed by *anti*-addition and is racemic
(d) *A* is formed by *syn*-addition and is racemic

59. Most stable radical is

(a) $CH_2=\dot{C}H$
(b) $CH_2=CH\dot{C}H_2$
(c) 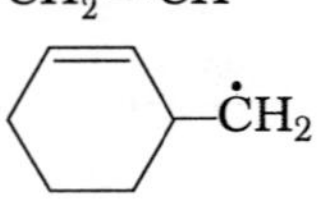
(d) 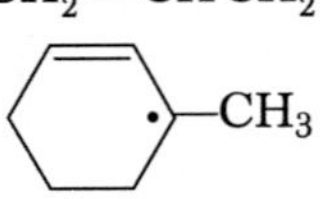

60. Carbanion (*A*) loses a leaving group to form alkene. Which is/are correct statement(s)?

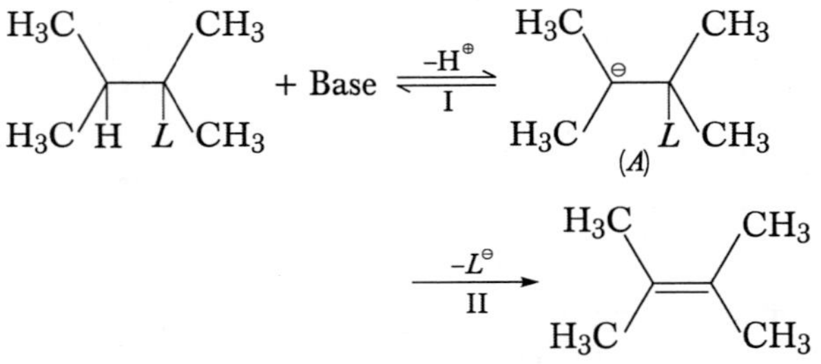

(a) it is E1-cB type
(b) it is E2 type
(c) it is E1 type
(d) None of these

61. The reactive intermediate in a typical Simmons-Smith reaction is a

(a) Carbonium ion
(b) Carbene
(c) Carbanion
(d) Free radical

62. The electrophilic aromatic substitution proceeds through a

(a) free radical
(b) sigma complex
(c) benzyne
(d) carbene

63. 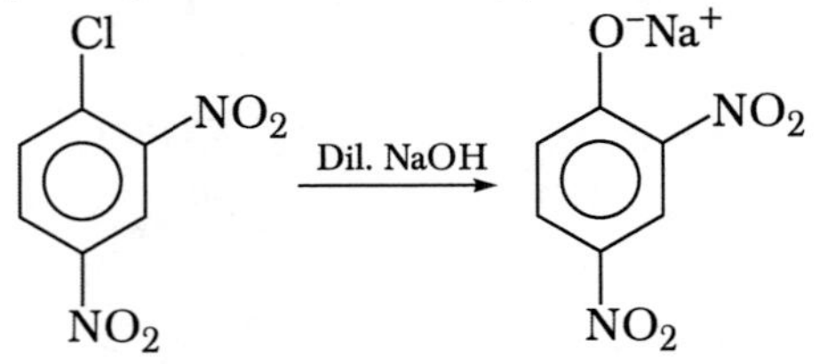

The above transformation proceeds through

(a) electrophilic addition
(b) benzyne intermediate
(c) activated nucleophilic substitution
(d) oxirane

64. The reaction of E2-butene with CH_2I_2 and zinc copper couple in ether medium leads to the formation of

(a) 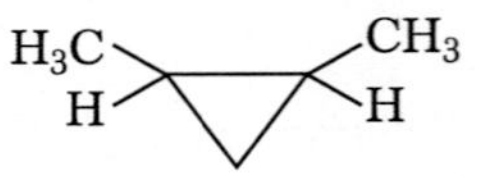
(b) 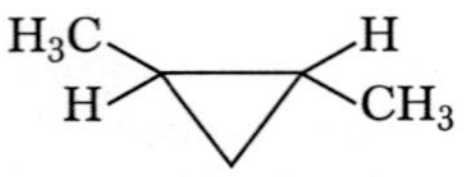
(c) 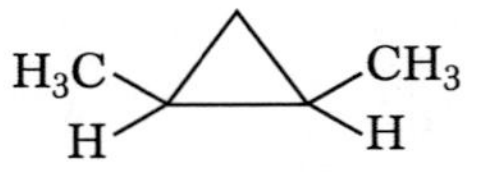
(d) 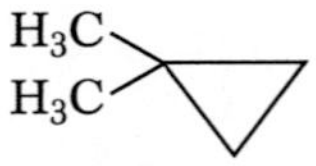

65. The reaction of erythro 1-bromo-1,2-diphenylpropane with alcoholic KOH gives

(a) (*Z*)-1,2-diphenyl-1-propene
(b) (*E*)-1,2-diphenyl-1-propene
(c) both (*Z*) and (*E*)-1,2-diphenyl-1-propene
(d) 1,2-diphenyl-1-propanol

66. The major product expected from the mono-bromination of phenyl benzoate is

(a) 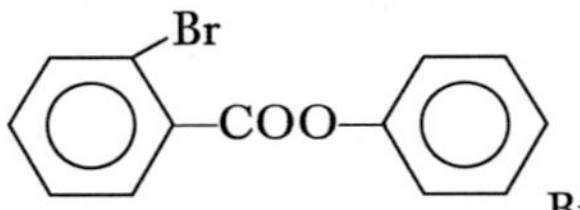
(b) 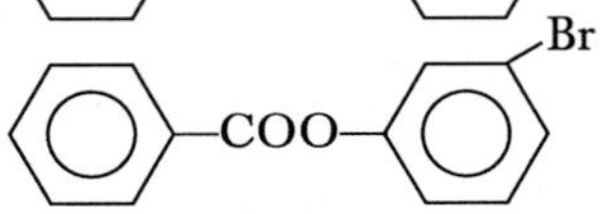
(c) 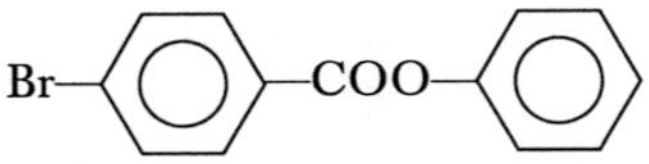
(d) 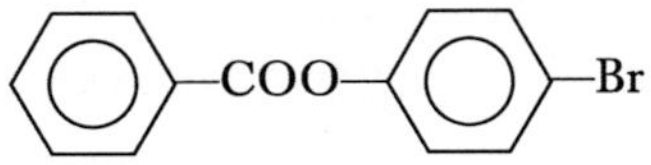

67. The following tetraene upon photolysis gives

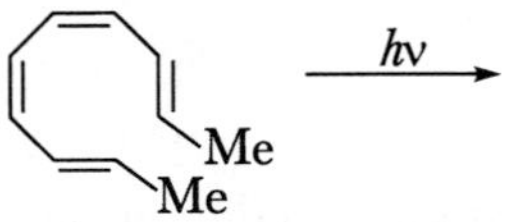

(a) 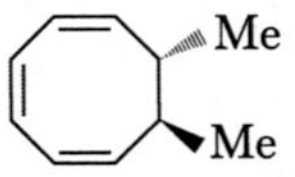
(b) 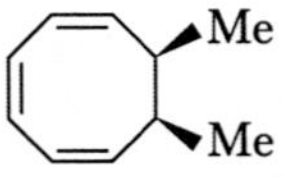
(c) 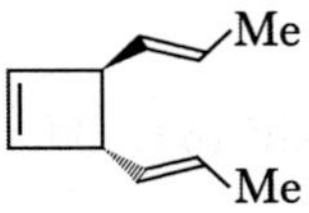
(d) 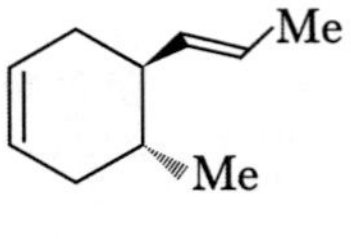

68. *o*-chlorotoluene reacts with sodamide in liquid ammonia to give *o*-toluidine and *m*-toluidine. This reaction proceeds through an intermediate

(a) 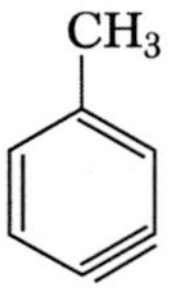
(b) 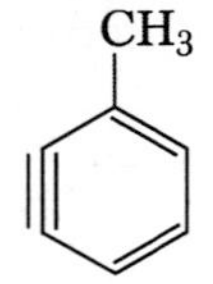

(c) 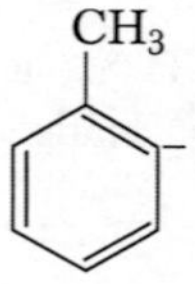 (d) 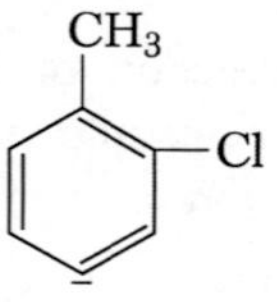

69. The reaction of 2-methylfuran with DMF-$POCl_3$ would give

(a) 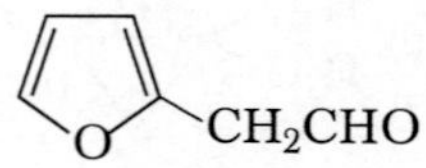 (b) 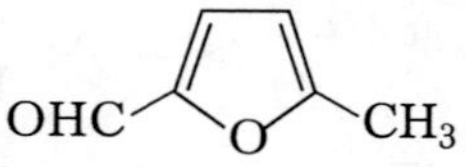

(c) 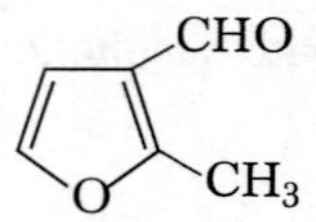 (d) 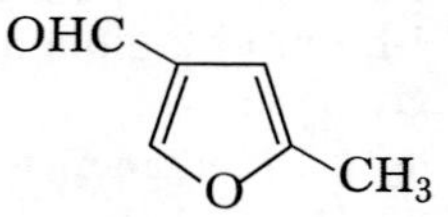

70.  + $CH_2{=}CHCN \longrightarrow$ Product. Product is

(a) 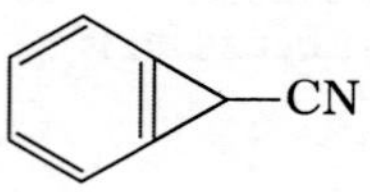 (b) 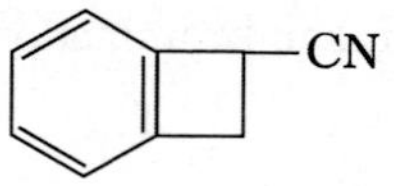

(c) 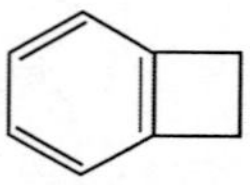 (d) 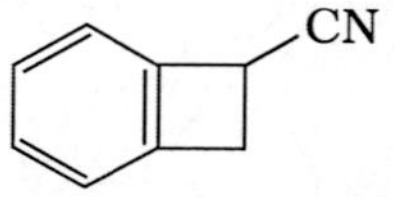

71. Thermal decomposition of tetrazoles give
(a) carbene (b) nitrene
(c) carbocation (d) free radical

72. In singlet state of carbene carbon atom is
(a) *sp* hybridised (b) sp^3 hybridised
(c) sp^2 hybridised (d) None of these

73. In S_N reactions the best leaving group among the following is
(a) chloride (b) fluoride
(c) tosylate (d) bromide

74. In E2 reaction the dihedral angle of anti periplanar conformation is
(a) 0° (b) 90°
(c) 120° (d) 180°

75. Benzyne is generated from
(a) chlorobenzene in presence of sodamide in liquid NH_3
(b) benzene with sodium in liquid NH_3
(c) benzene in liquid NH_3
(d) action of heat on benzoic acid

76. The major product in the following reaction is

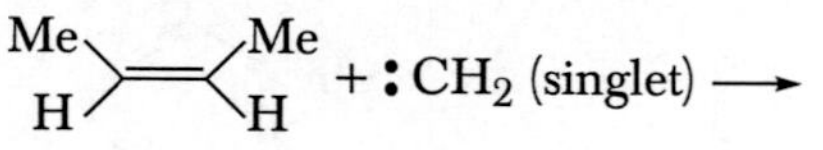

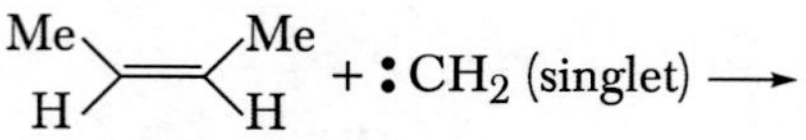

(a) 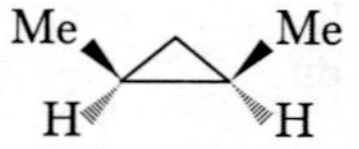

(b) 

(c) 50 : 50 mixture of above two compounds

(d) 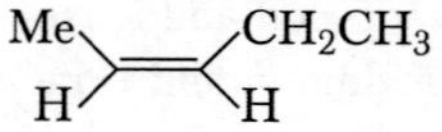

77. The major product formed in the thermal reaction given below is

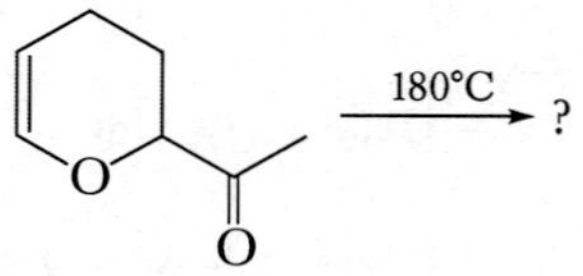

(a) 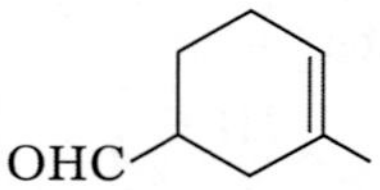 (b) 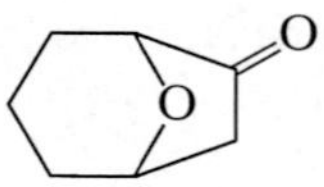

(c) 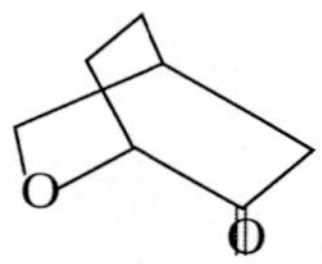 (d) None of these

78. With *cist*-alkene singlet carbenes give *cis*-product whereas triplet carbenes gives
(a) *cis*-product
(b) *trans*-product
(c) both *cis* and *trans*-product
(d) no product

79. Identify the major product *P* in the following reaction.

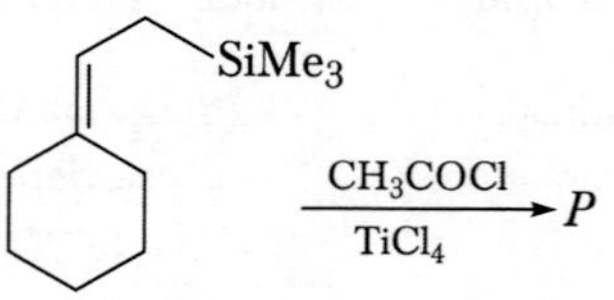

(a) 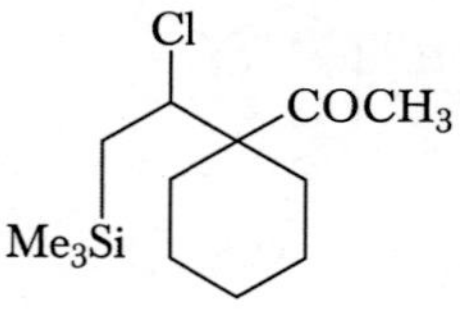 (b) 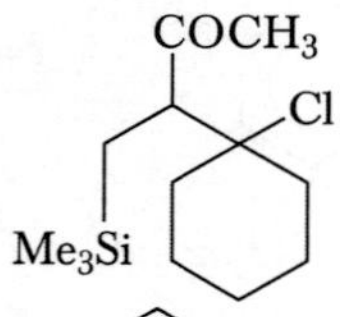

(c) 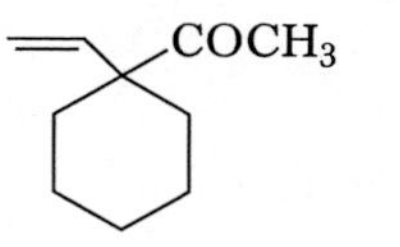 (d) 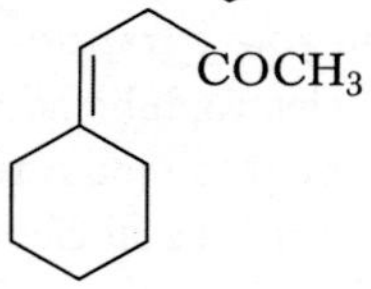

80. Identify the major product *P* in the following reaction.

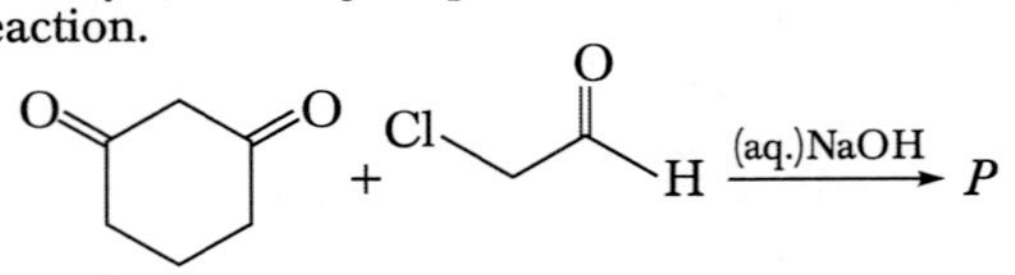

(a) 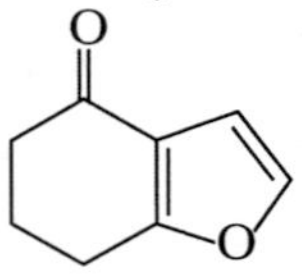 (b) 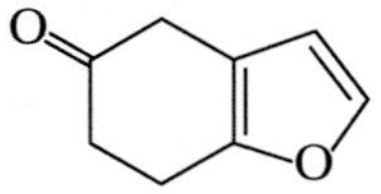

(c) 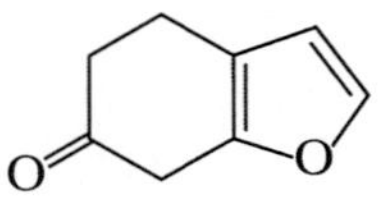 (d) 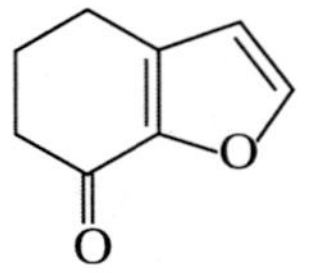

81. A solution of (+)-2-chloro-2-phenylethane in toluene racemises slowly in the presence of a small amount of $SbCl_5$ due to the formation of

(a) carbanion (b) carbene
(c) free radical (d) carbocation

82. A nitrene can be trapped by

(a) CO (b) CO_2 (c) SO_2 (d) SO_3

83. On reaction with HBr 3-bromopropenenitrile gives the major product of

(a) 2-bromopropane nitrile (b) 3-bromopropane nitrile
(c) cyanopropane (d) 3-bromobutane nitrile

84. 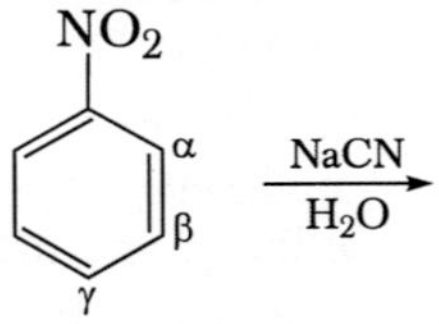

Product of this reaction is

(a) 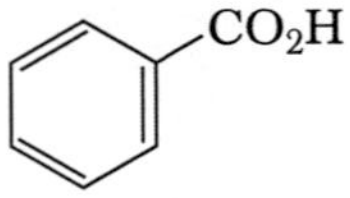 by cine substitution

(b) 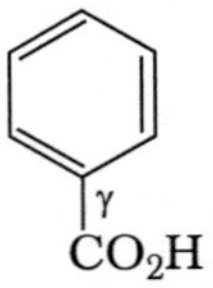 by tele substitution

(c) 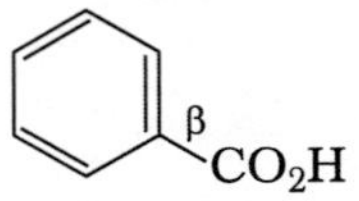 by *meta* substitution

(d) None of the above

85. The reaction,

$$(CH_3)_2C{=}CH_2 + Br^{\bullet} \longrightarrow (CH_3)_2\dot{C}CH_2Br$$

is an example of *A*(*n*)–step in a radical chain reaction

(a) initiation (b) termination
(c) propagation (d) heterolytic cleavage

86. Which one of the following compounds undergoes predominantly S_N2 reaction with aqueous NaOH in polar aprotic solvents?

(a)  (b) 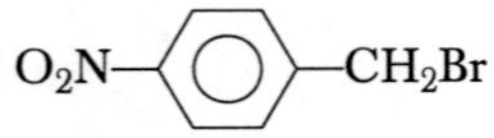

(c) 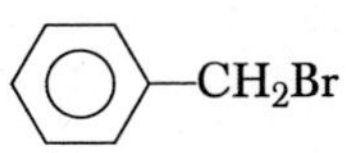 (d) 

87. Identify the end product in the following reaction

(a) 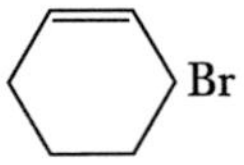 (b) 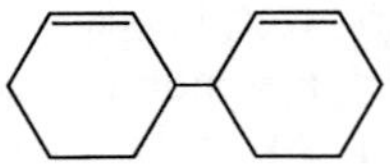

(c) Both (a) and (b) (d) None of these

88. 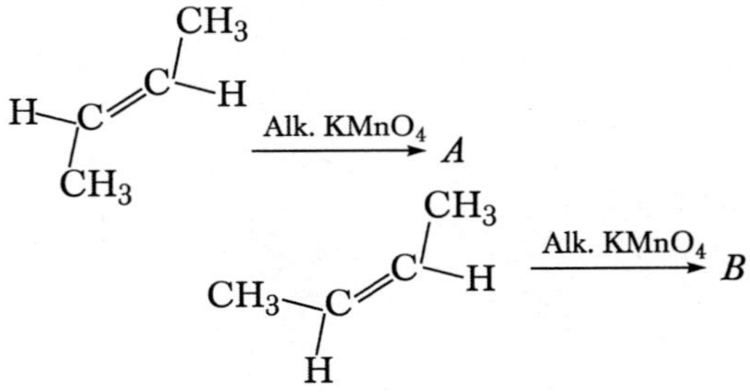

Product *A* and *B* are respectively

(a) racemic mixture, *meso*
(b) *meso*, racemic mixture
(c) *meso*, *meso*
(d) racemic mixture, racemic mixture

89. 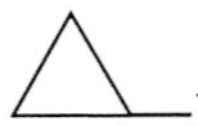—Bu + F_3C—COOH ⟶ Product. Product is

(a) CH_3CH_2CH—Bu (with COOH on CH)

(b) CH_3—CH_2—CH—Bu (with O—C(=O)—CF_3 on CH)

(c) CH_3CH—Br (with O—C(=O)—CF_3 on CH)

(d) $CH_3CH_2CH_2$—CH—C_2H_5 (with O—C(=O)—CF_3 on CH)

90. 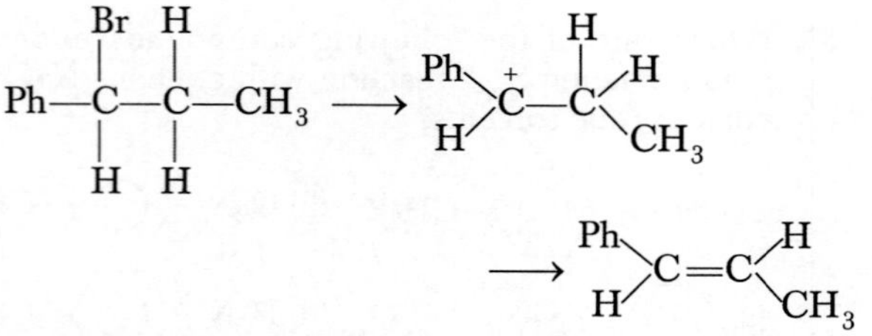

The product is formed by

(a) E2 mechanism (b) E1 mechanism
(c) E1cB mechanism (d) None of these

91. Nitrene is generated as a intermediate in

(a) Hofmann rearrangement
(b) Curtius rearrangement
(c) Insertion reaction
(d) All of the above

92. 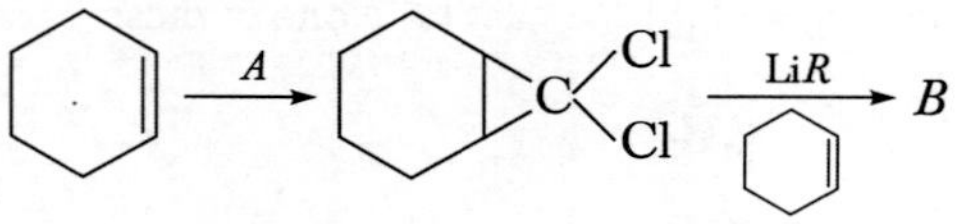

A and *B* are

(a) $:CCl_2$, 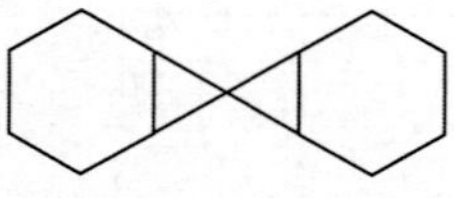

(b) $:CCl_2$, 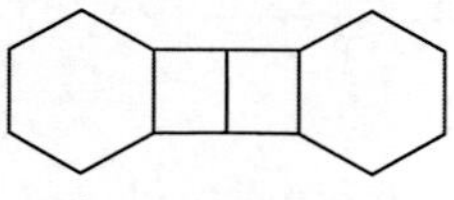

(c) $:CH_2$, 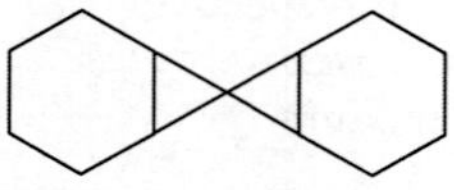

(d) $:CH_2$, 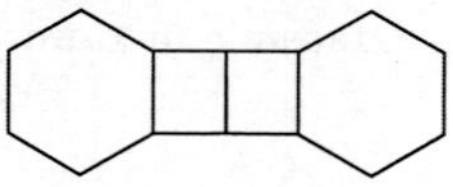

93. Arrangement the following in increasing order of acidic strength

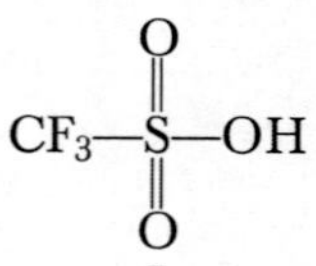
I

Cl_3CCOOH
II

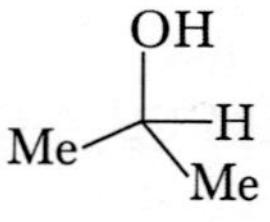
III

Cl_3COOH
IV

V

(a) I < II < III < IV < V (b) V < IV < III < II < I
(c) III < II < IV < I < V (d) III < V < IV < II < I

94. 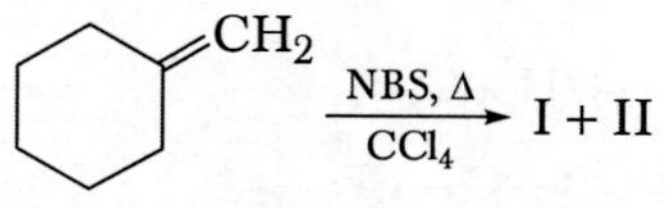

Product I and II are respectively

(a) 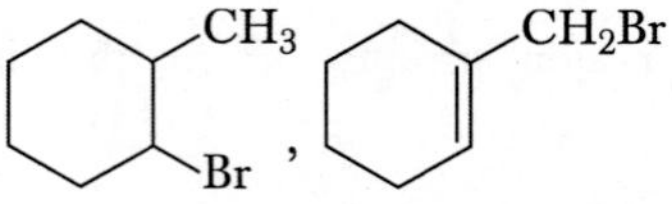

(b) 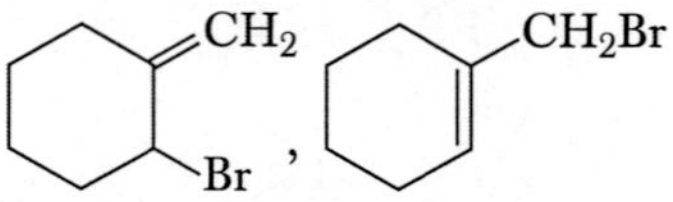

(c) 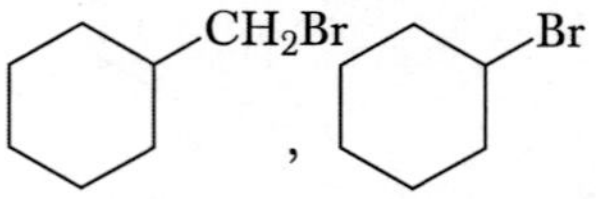

(d) 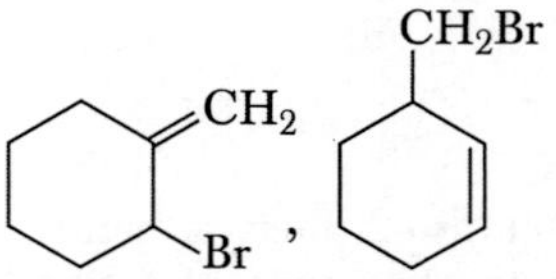

95. Consider the following reaction

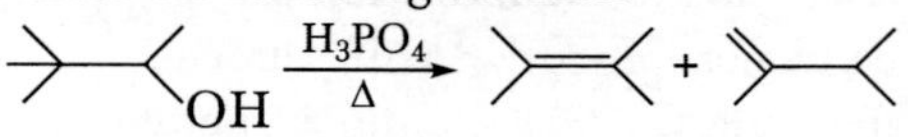

Which response contains all the corrects statements about this process?

I. Dehydration
II. Carbon skeleton migration
III. E2 mechanism
IV. Most stable carbocation is formed

(a) I, II (b) I, II, III
(c) I, II, IV (d) I, III, IV

96. Which of the following compounds will react by unimolecular nuceophilic substitution mechanism?

(A) 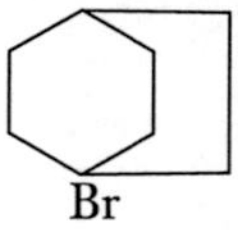

(B) 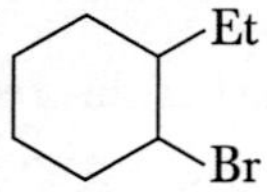

(C) 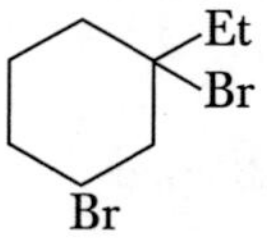

(D) Et_3CBr

(a) A, B, C (b) A, C, D
(c) B, C, D (d) A, B, D

97. 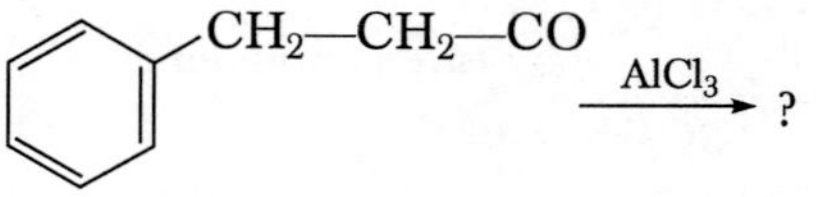

Identify the product

(a) 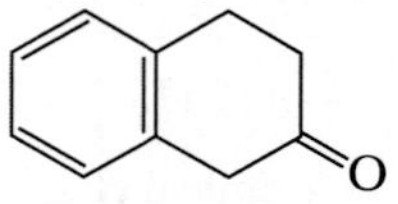

(b) 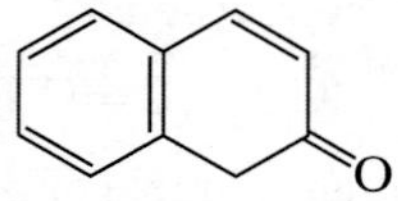

(c) 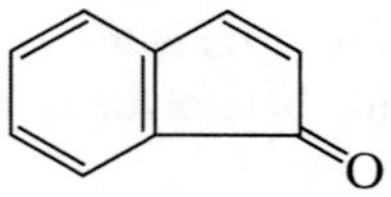

(d) 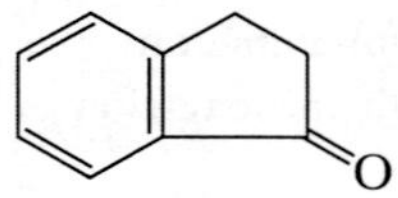

98. Which of the following reactions contains a carbene intermediate?

(a) Reformatsky reaction
(b) Reimer-Tiemann reaction
(c) Wittig reaction
(d) Perkin reaction

99. $C_6H_5—CH_2—CH_2Br + EtONa \longrightarrow$ Intermediate $\downarrow$ Product

The intermediate and product are

(a) carbene, $C_6H_5CH{=}CH_2$
(b) carbocation, $C_6H_5CH_2CH_3$
(c) carbanion, $C_6H_5CH{=}CH_2$
(d) carbanion, $C_6H_5CH_2OH$

100. Benzoyl peroxide when heated to about 80°C gives

(a) carbonium ion (b) carbanion
(c) carbene (d) free radical

Exercise 2

(For Part 'C')

1. Rank the compounds below in order of decreasing basicity.

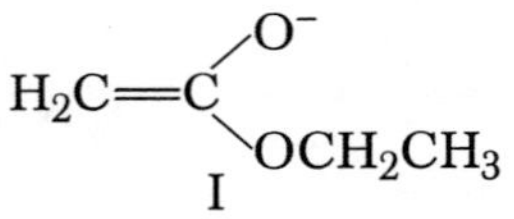
I

$[(CH_3)_2CH]_2\overset{-}{N}\overset{+}{Li}$
II

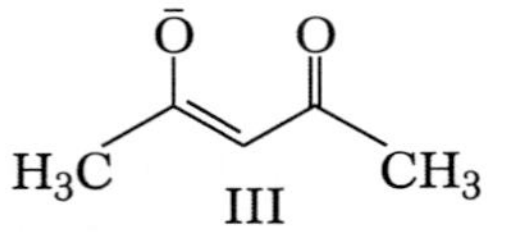
III

(a) I, II, III (b) III, II, I
(c) II, III, I (d) II, I, III

2. Identify the major species in solution for reaction.

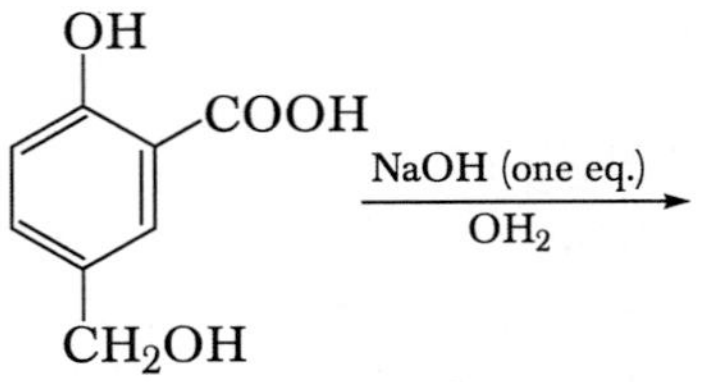

(a) 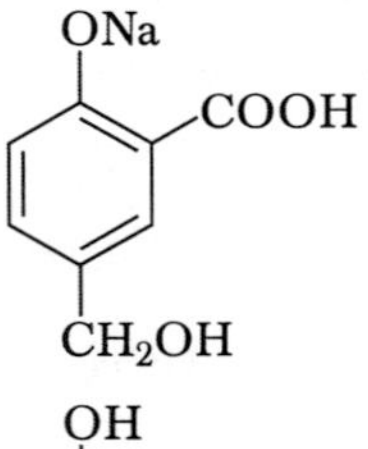

(b) 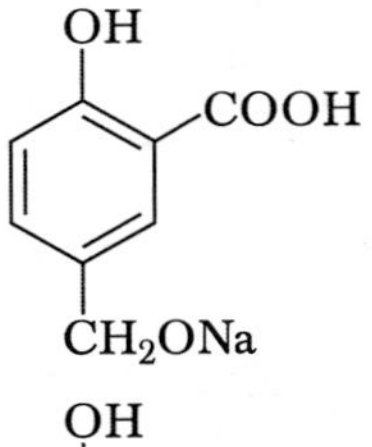

(c) 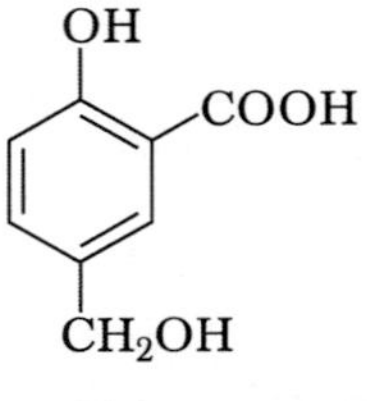

(d) 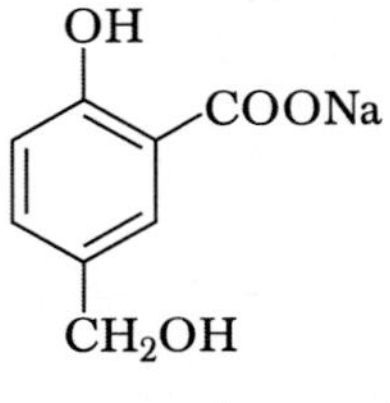

3. The chlorination of CH_4 may proceed according to one of the two alternative mechanism which statements about these mechanisms is correct?

Mechanism A: $Cl^{\bullet} + CH_4 \longrightarrow HCl + H_3C^{\bullet}$
$H_3C^{\bullet} + Cl_2 \longrightarrow CH_3Cl + Cl^{\bullet}$

Mechanism B: $Cl^{\bullet} + CH_4 \longrightarrow CH_3Cl + H^{\bullet}$
$H^{\bullet} + Cl_2 \longrightarrow HCl + Cl^{\bullet}$

(a) Mechanism A is preferred because none of the steps is strongly endothermic
(b) Mechanism A is preferred because II step is strongly exothermic
(c) Mechanism B is preferred because none of the steps is strongly endothermic
(d) Mechanism B is preferred because II step is strongly exothermic

4. Choose the statement that corresponds to structure of an allyl radical.

(a) The carbon atoms of an allyl radical is sp^3 hybridized. p-orbitals are involved in the delocalization of electrons
(b) The carbon atoms of an allyl radical is sp^2 hybridized. Hybrid orbitals are involved in the delocalization of π-electrons
(c) The carbon atom of an allyl radical is sp hybridized. p-orbitals are involved in the delocalization of electrons
(d) The carbon atoms of an allyl radical is sp^2 hybridized. p-orbitals are involved in the delocalization of electrons

5. The major resonance contributor of allyl radical

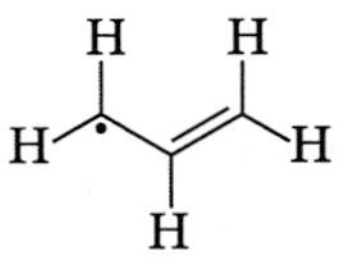
I

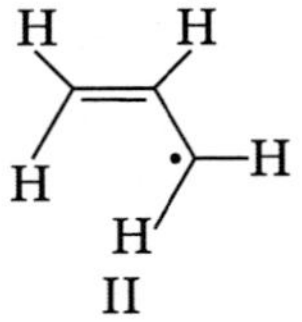
II

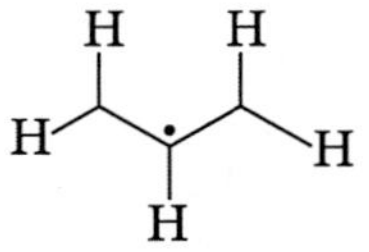
III

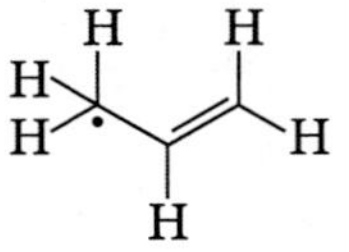
IV

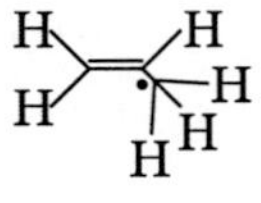
V

(a) I and II (b) IV and V
(c) II and III (d) I and V

6. Which of the following would produce the least stable radical upon abstraction of indicated H atom?

(a) 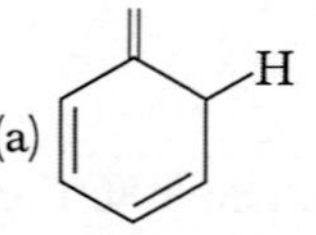

(b) 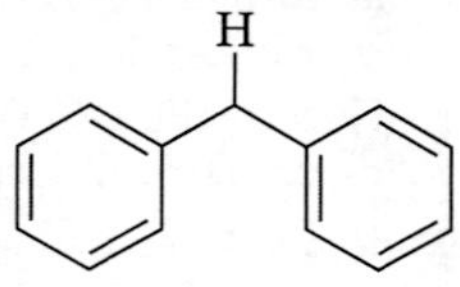

(c) 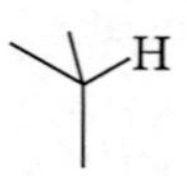

(d) 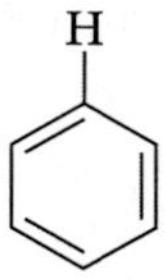

7. Which of the following statements is true about carbocations given below?

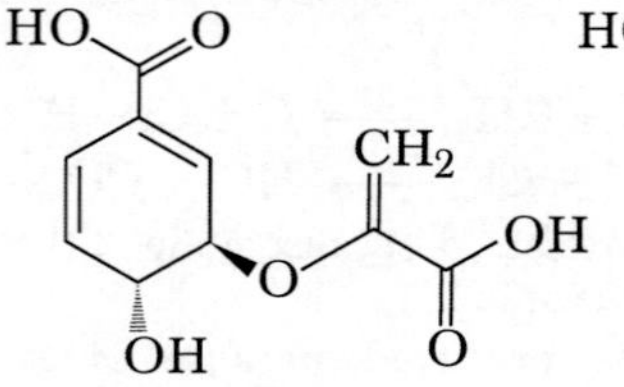

Chorismic acid

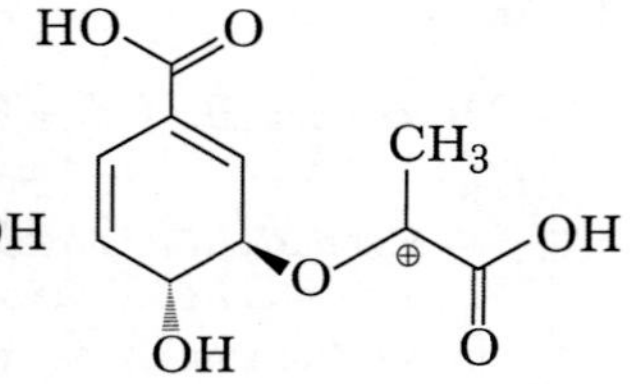

I

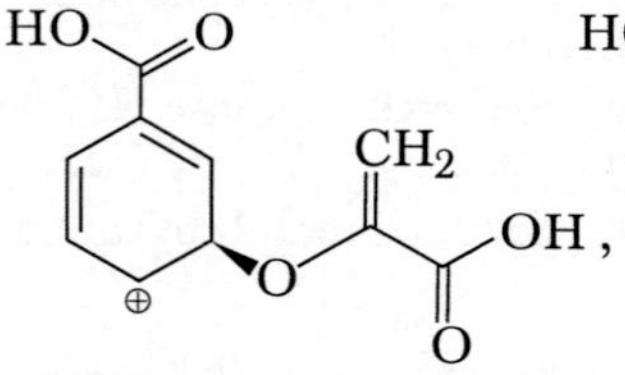

II

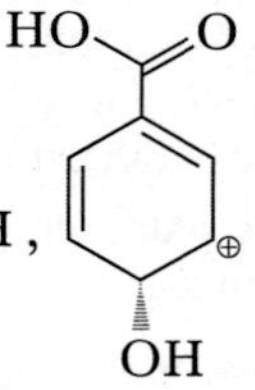

III

(a) All three carbocations could be generated from chorismic acid with strong acid under thermodynamic conditions

(b) An aromatic ring could be generated from carbocation (I) and (III) *via* E1 reaction

(c) Reaction of carbocation (II) with Cl-will give a racemic mixture

(d) Both (a) and (b)

8. A resonance form of pentazocine is

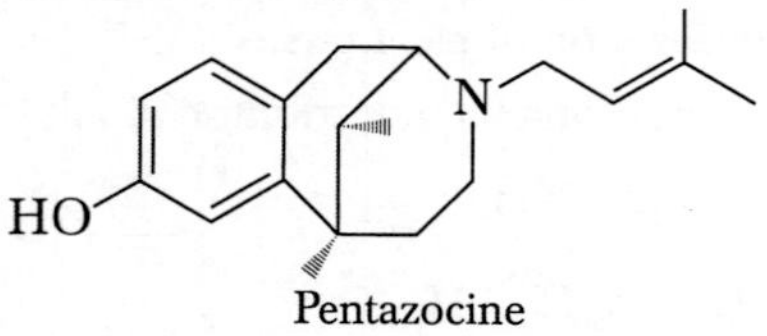

Pentazocine

(a) 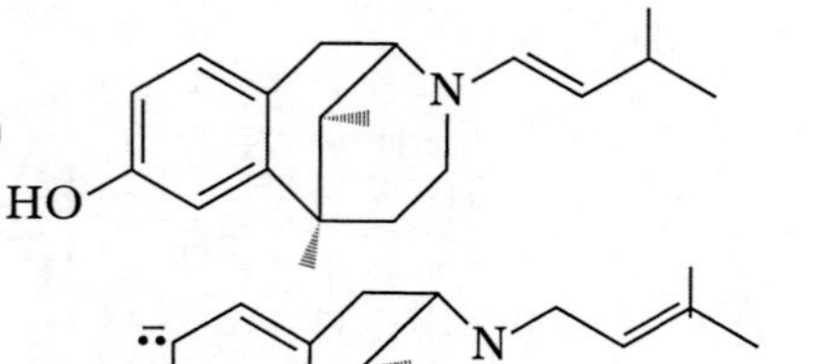

(b) 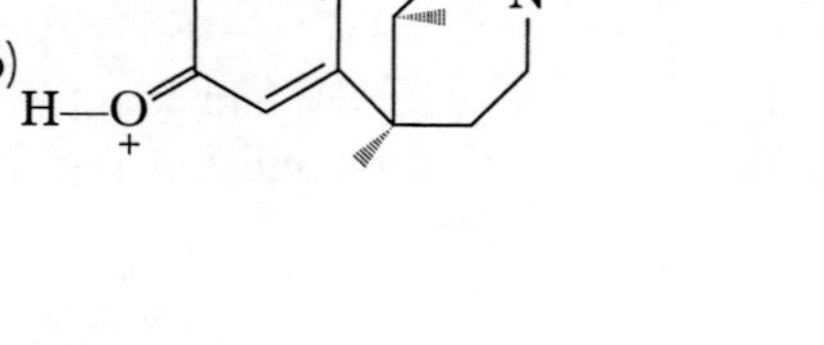

(c) 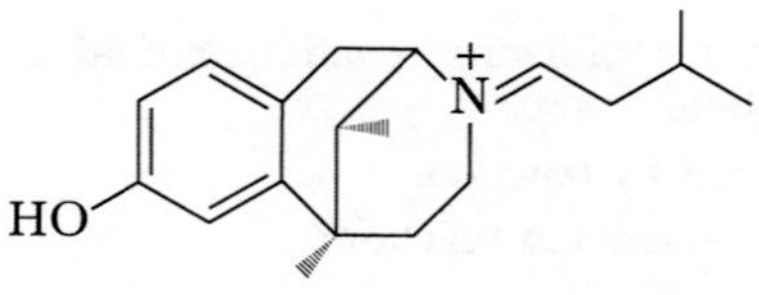

(d) 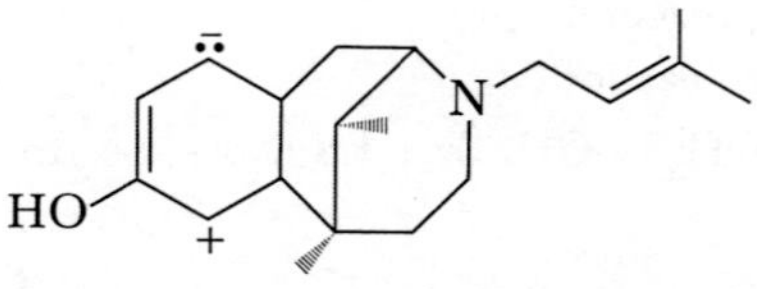

9. Hypoglycine *A* can be reacted with strong acid to generate a carbocation, which then react to generate a new cyclopropene. Which of the following statement is true concerning to the following transformation?

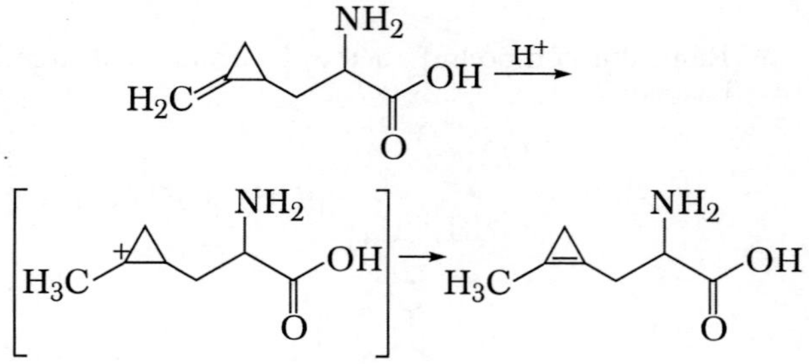

(a) The reaction is endothermic

(b) The product has more angle strain than reactant

(c) Both reactant and products are α-amino acids

(d) All of the above statements are true

10. In which of the following processes, carbene ($:CH_2$) is formed?

I. $CH_2N_2 + \text{Heat} \longrightarrow$

II. $CH_2I_2 + Zn \longrightarrow$

III. $CHBr_3 + NaOH \longrightarrow$

IV. $CH_3HC{=}C{=}O + \text{Heat} \longrightarrow$

(a) I and III (b) I, II and IV

(c) I and II (d) II and III

11. Which of the following reaction is wrong?

(a) $CH_3CH_2CHO \xrightarrow{\overset{\ominus}{O}H} CH_3-\overset{\ominus}{C}H-CHO$

(b) 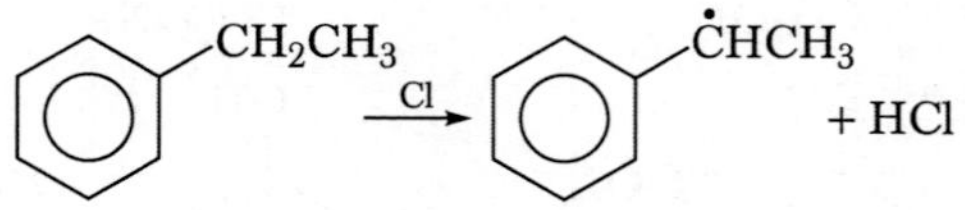

(c) 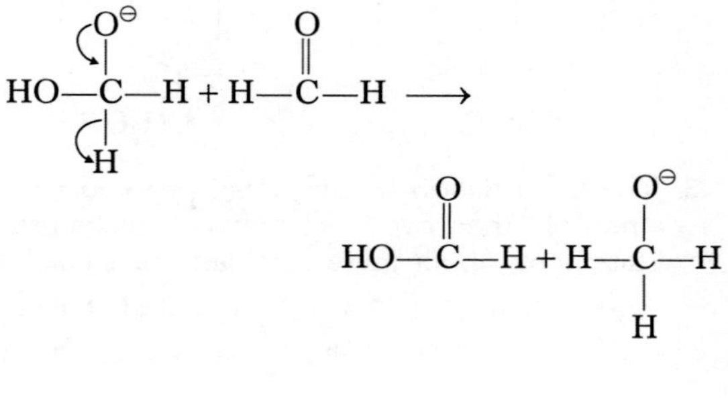

(d) 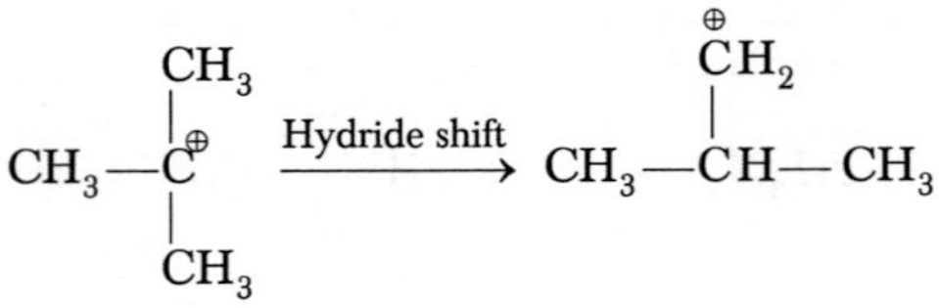

12. Addition of HCl to 3,3-dimethyl-1-butene gives the major product

(a) 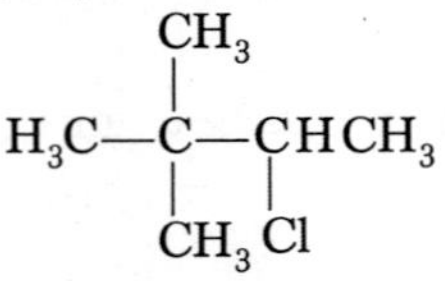
(b) 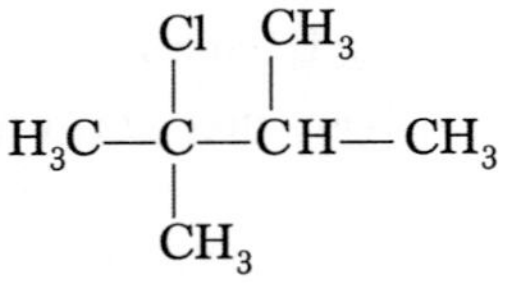
(c) 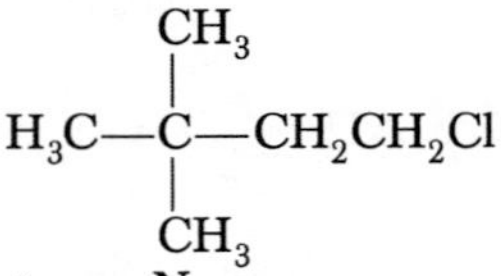
(d) 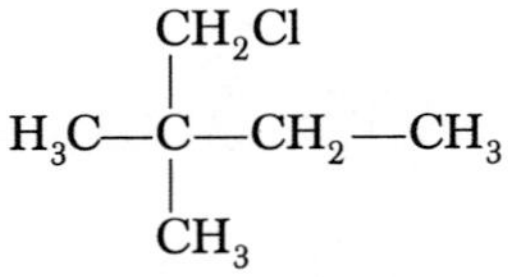

13. 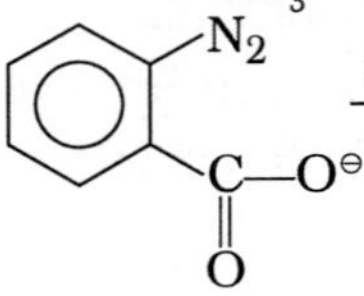 $\xrightarrow{\text{Decompose}}$ Intermediate + gaseous product

The intermediate in the above reaction is

(a) free radical
(b) nitrene
(c) benzyne
(d) carbene

14. $Ph_2C{=}O \xrightarrow{Na} A \xrightarrow{ROH} B \longrightarrow C$

A, *B* and *C* are respectively

(a) 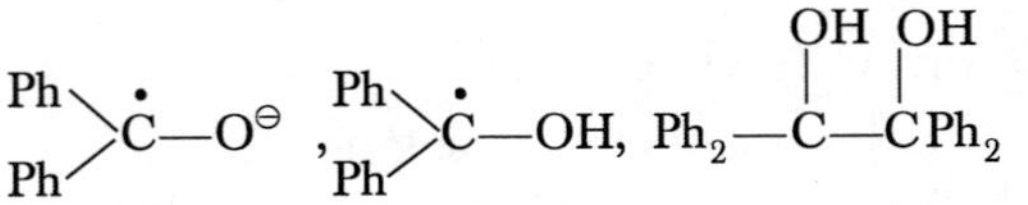
(b) 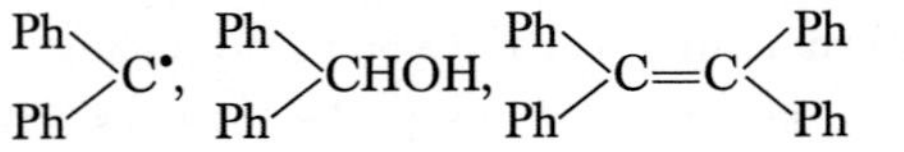
(c) 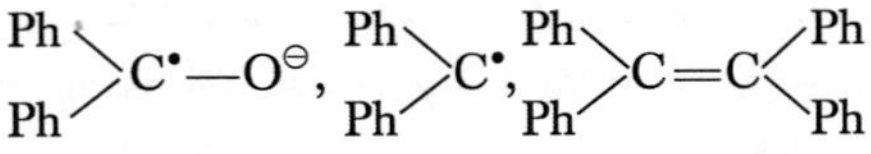
(d) 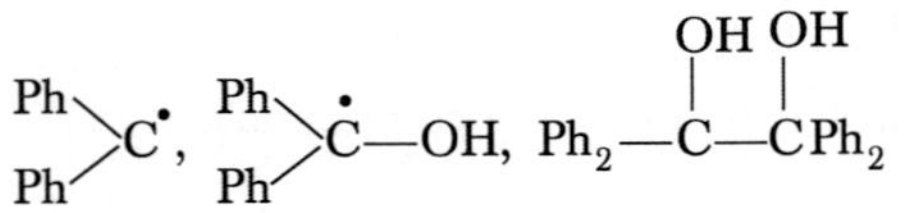

15. 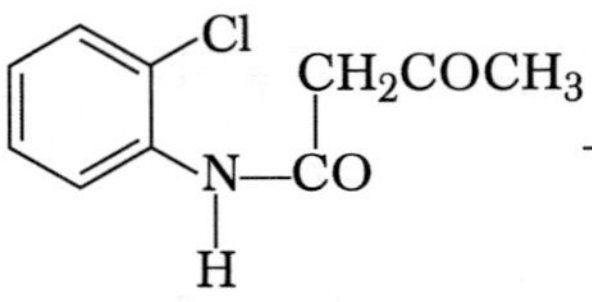 $\xrightarrow{\text{Base}}$ Product;

Identify the product

(a) 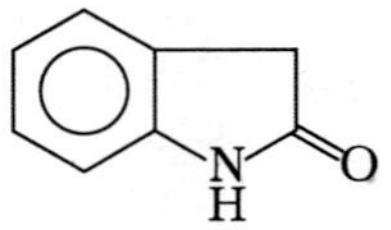
(b) 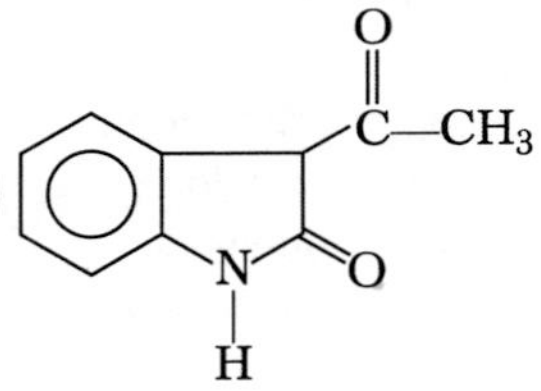
(c) 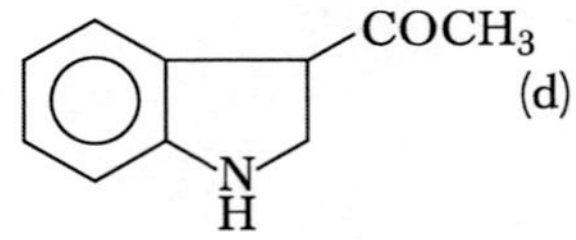
(d) 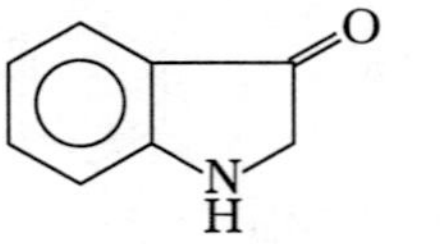

16. 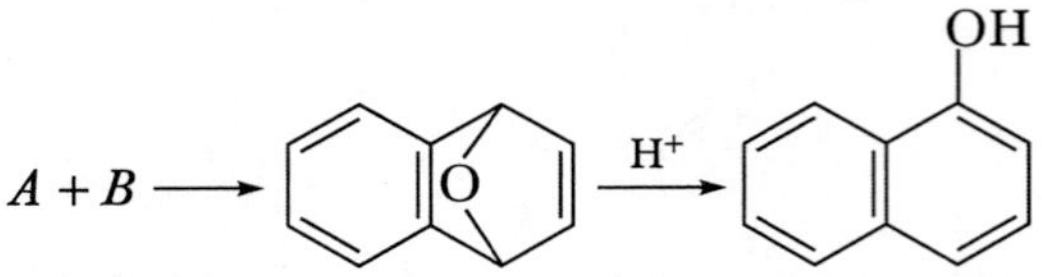

A and *B* are respectively

(a) 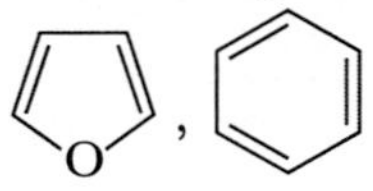
(b) 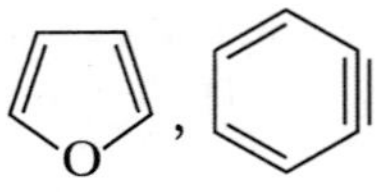
(c) 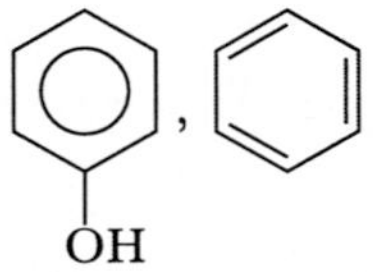
(d) 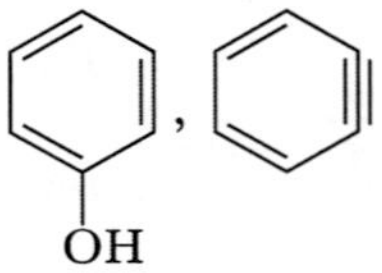

17. Match the Column I with Column II.

	Column I		Column II
A.	Phthaloyl peroxide	1.	Free radical
B.	Tetrazole	2.	Benzyne
C.	Benzoyl peroxide	3.	Carbene
D.	Alkyl halide	4.	Carbocation

	A	B	C	D
(a)	2	3	4	1
(b)	3	2	1	4
(c)	2	3	1	4
(d)	2	4	1	3

18. 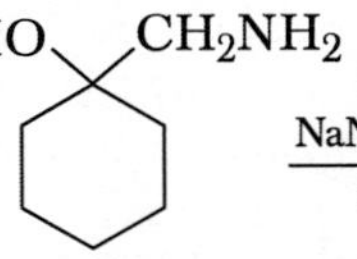 $\xrightarrow[0\text{-}5°C]{NaNO_2/HCl} A \longrightarrow B \longrightarrow C \longrightarrow D$

The end product of the above reaction

(a) cyclohexanone
(b) cyclopentanone
(c) cycloheptanone
(d) cyclohexanol

19. 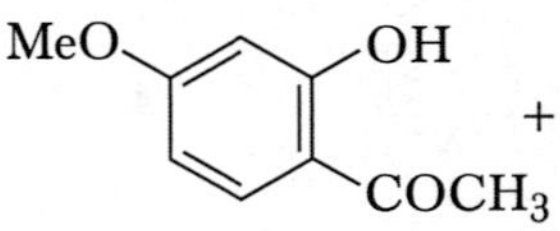 $+ C_6H_5COOCH_3 \xrightarrow{Na} \xrightarrow{H^+}$ Product.

Identify the product

(a) 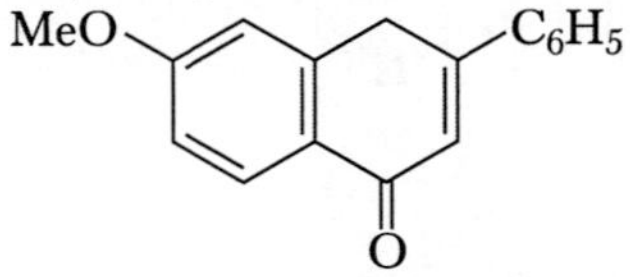
(b) 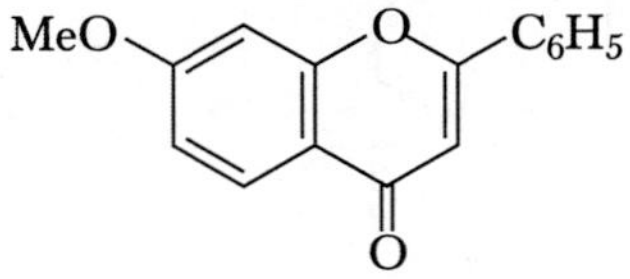

(c) 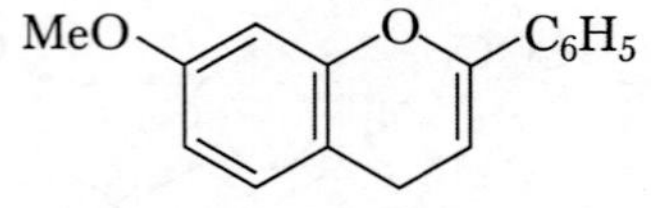

(d) 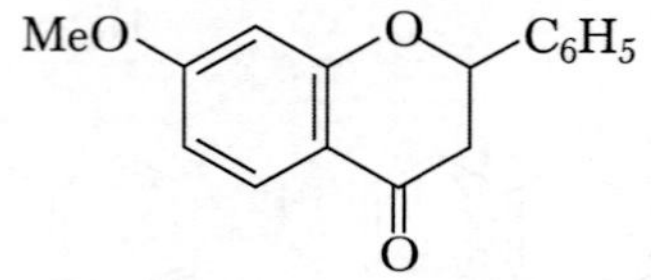

20. *Trans*-butene reacts with diazomethane gives insertion reaction. The insertion products is/are from the following

I. 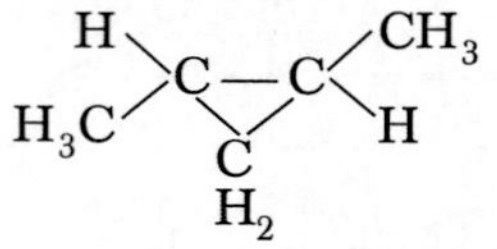

II. 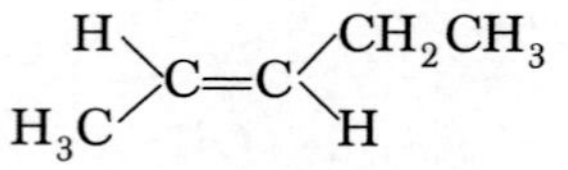

III. 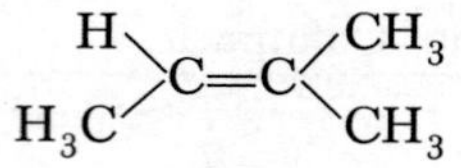

(a) I and II (b) I and III
(c) II and III (d) I, II and III

21. 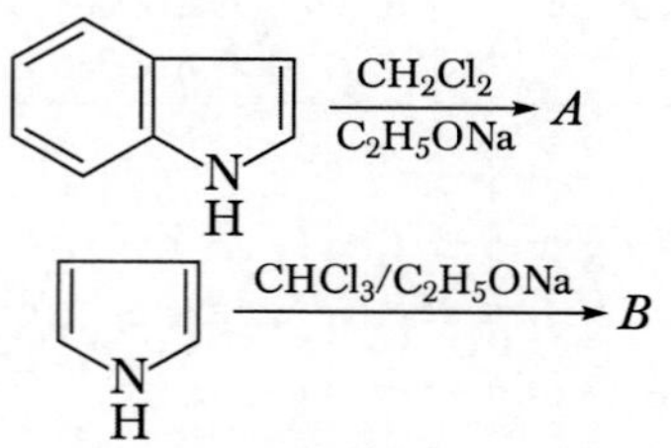

Product (*A*) and (*B*) are

(a) 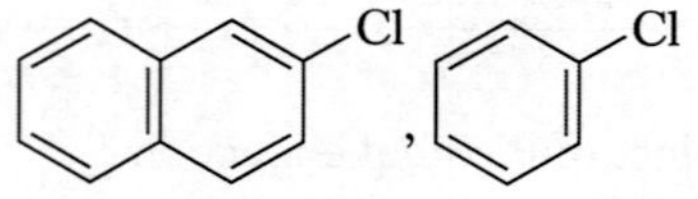

(b) 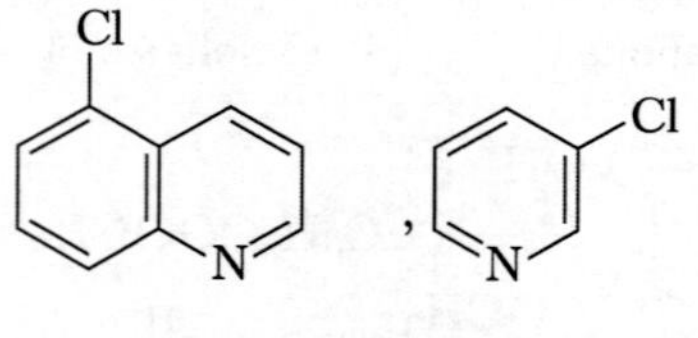

(c) 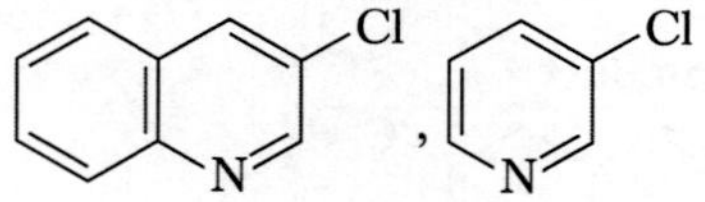

(d) 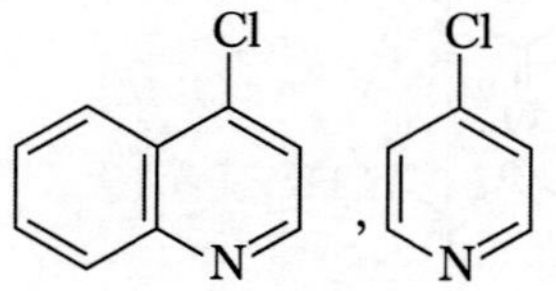

22. Which of the following reaction gives carbene as intermediate?

I. $CH_2N_2 \xrightarrow{h\nu}$ II. $R_2C{=}C{=}O \xrightarrow{h\nu}$

III. $RCON_3 \xrightarrow{h\nu}$ IV. $R{-}N{=}C{=}O \xrightarrow{h\nu}$

(a) I and II (b) I, II and III
(c) III and IV (d) I and II

23. Benzene reacts with 1-chlorobutane to give

(a) 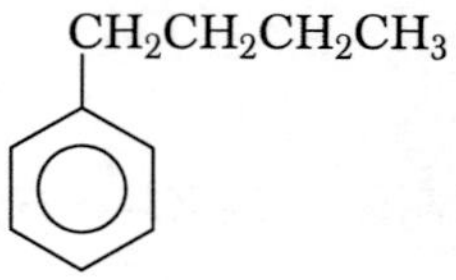 (b) 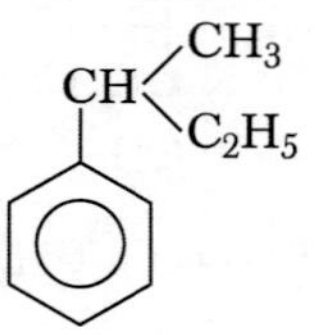

(c) Both (a) and (b) (d) None of these

24. The solvolysis reaction of diastereomeric exo- and endo-2-norbornyl tosylate in acetic acid gives
(a) exo-2-norbornyl acetate
(b) endo-2-norbornyl acetate
(c) Both exo- and endo-2-norbornyl acetate
(d) None of the above

25. Consider the following statement :

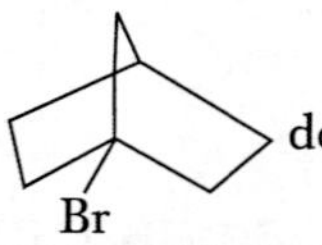 does not undergo S_N reaction when treated with $C_2H_5O^-$ because

I. Br^- is a poor leaving group
II. the geometry of the molecule does not permit formation of carbocation of bridgehead
III. the geometry of the molecule does not permit backside attack by $C_2H_5O^-$ are bridgehead

Which of the statements given above is/are correct?
(a) I and II (b) II and III
(c) II only (d) III only

26. Consider the following compounds.

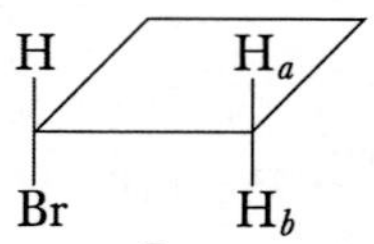 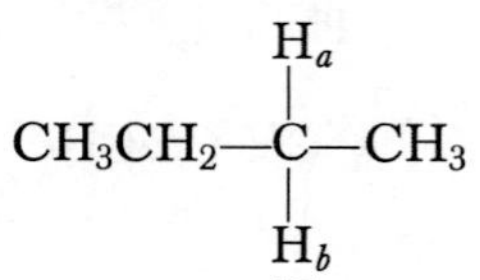 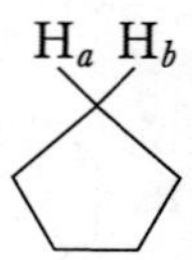

I II III

Identify H_a and H_b hydrogens in the above compounds.

	I	II	III
(a)	Diastereotopic	Enantiotopic	Homotopic
(b)	Enantiotopic	Diastereotopic	Homotopic
(c)	Homotopic	Diastereotopic	Diastereotopic
(d)	Diastereotopic	Enantiotopic	Diastereotopic

27. Major product of the following reaction is

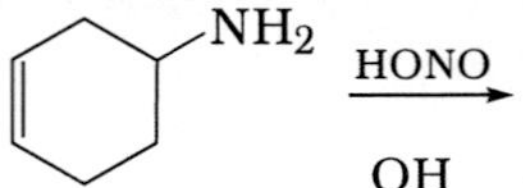

(a) 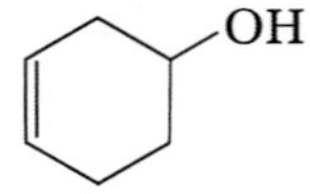 (b) 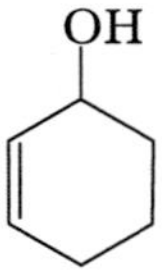

(c) 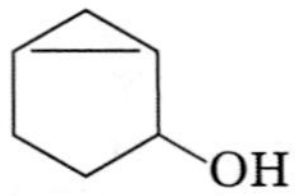 (d) None of these

28. Optically pure 2(*s*)-butanol is subjected to the following reaction,

$$2(s)\text{-BuOH} \xrightarrow{\text{Na}} ? \xrightarrow{\text{MeI}}$$

Which of the following statements is correct for stereochemical outcome of the reaction?

(a) The reaction proceeds with inversion
(b) The reaction proceeds with racemisation
(c) The reaction proceeds with complete retention of configuration
(d) The reaction leads to destruction of chirality in the molecule

29. Which alkyl halide undergoes E2 elimination at the fastest rate?

(a) 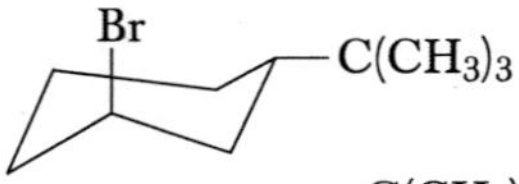

(b) 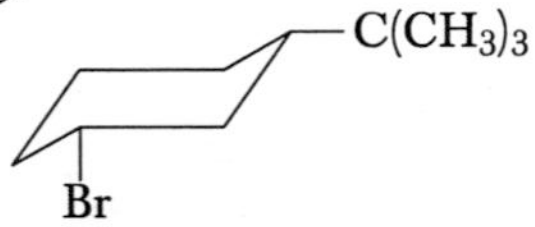

(c) 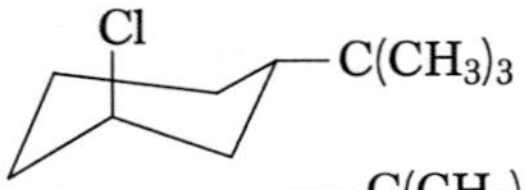

(d) 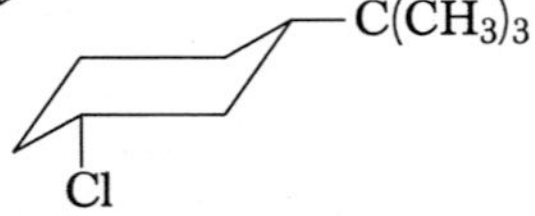

30. Provide a sequence of reaction to carryout the following change

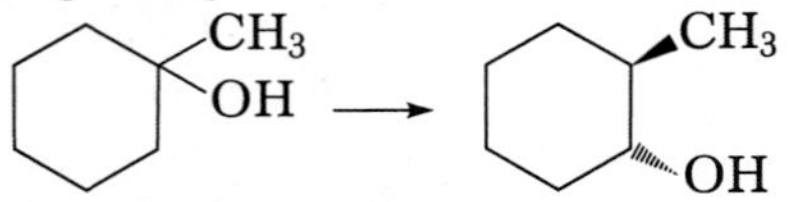

(a) $\xrightarrow[\Delta]{\text{Conc. } H_2SO_4} \xrightarrow[OH^-]{B_2H_6,\ H_2O_2}$

(b) $\xrightarrow[\Delta]{\text{Conc. } H_2SO_4} \xrightarrow{H_3O^+}$

(c) $\xrightarrow[\Delta]{\text{Conc. } H_2SO_4} \xrightarrow{Hg(OOCCH_3)_2}$

(d) $\xrightarrow[\Delta]{\text{Conc. } H_2SO_4} \xrightarrow{MnO_4^-,\ OH^-}$

31. Which one of the following alkyl halides would be expected to give the highest substitution to elimination ratio (most substitution, least elimination) on treatment with sodium ethoxide in ethanol?

(a) 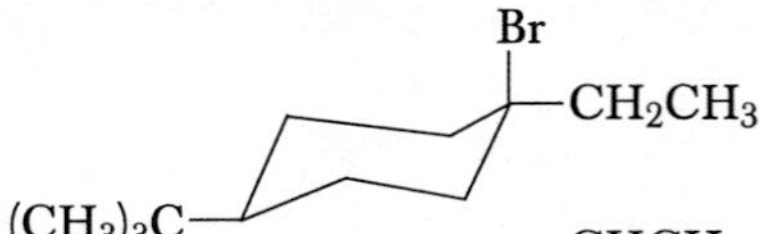

(b) 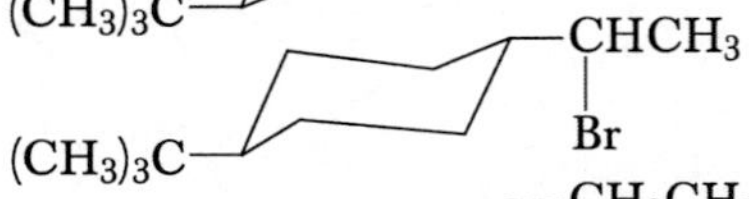

(c) 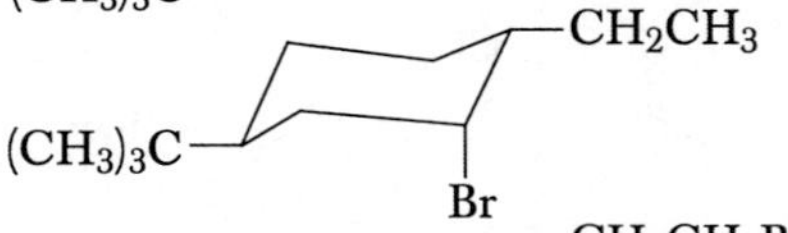

(d) 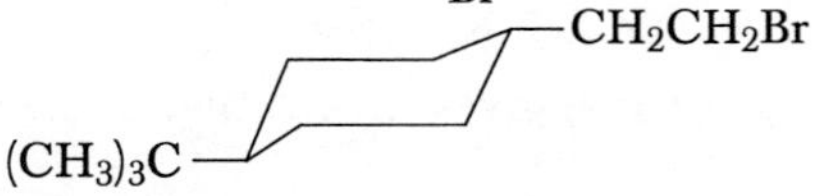

32. Predominant product in the following addition reaction is

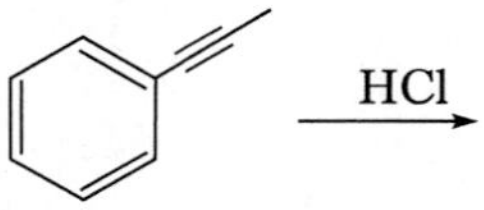

(a) 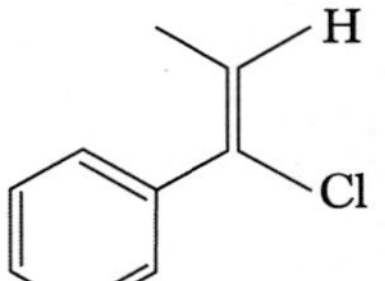 (b) 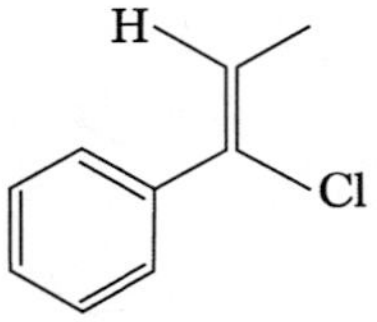

(c) 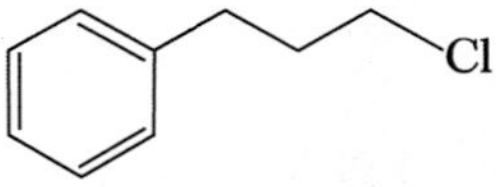 (d) 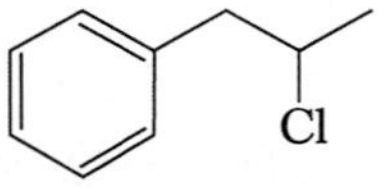

33. Rank the following in order of decreasing rate of solvolysis with aqueous ethanol (fastest → slowest)

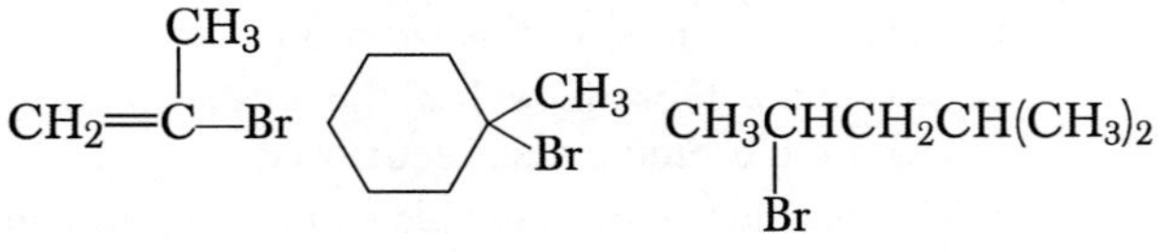

I II III

(a) II > I > III (b) I > II > III
(c) II > III > I (d) I > III > II

34. Find the intermediate and product in the following reaction.

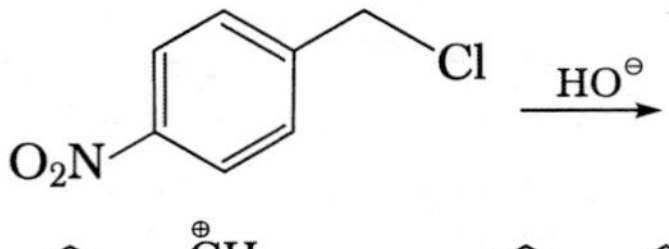

(a) 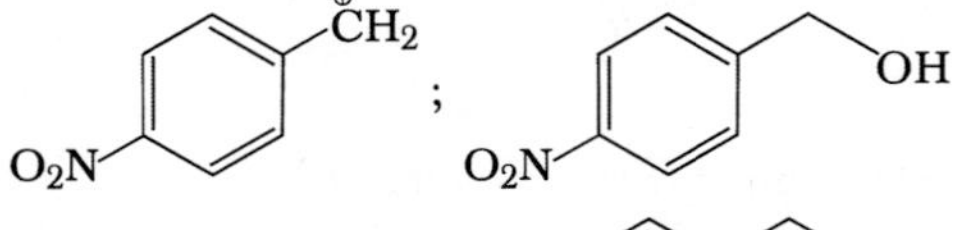

(b) 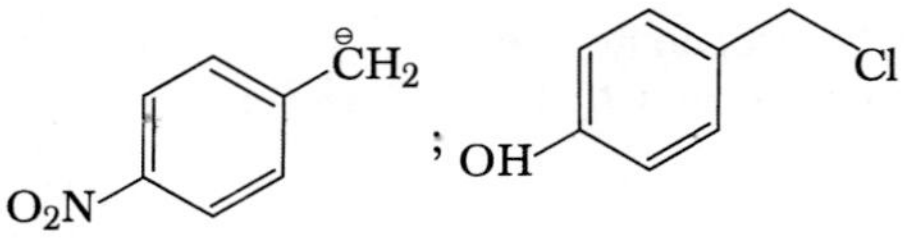

(c) 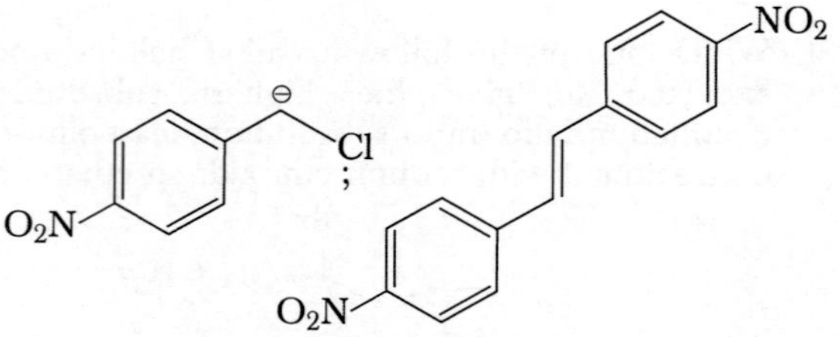

(d) 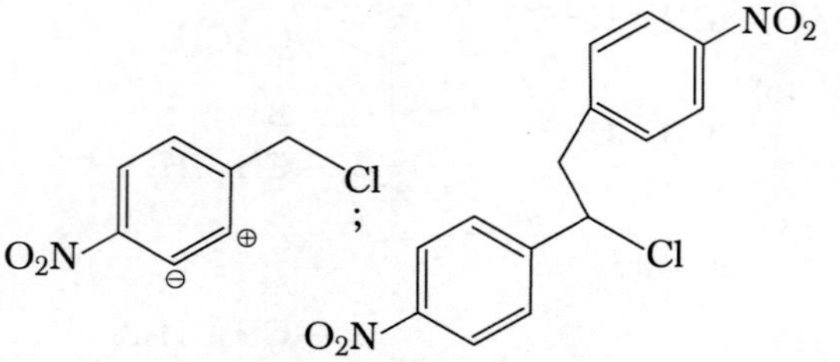

35. Following reaction gives .... by .... reaction

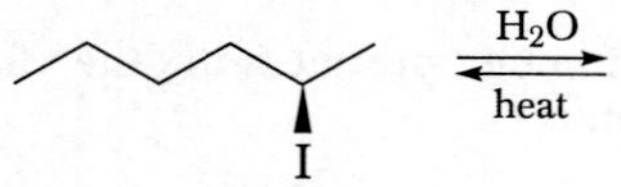

(a) 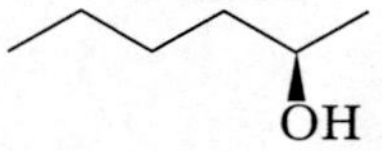

S_N2

(b) 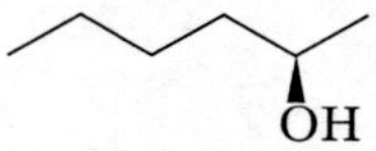

S_N1

(c) 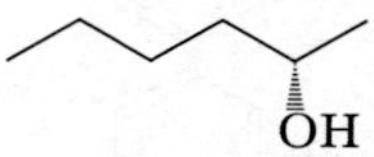

S_N1

(d) products in (b) and (c) by S_N1

36. When cyclohexyl bromide is treated with a base, it does undergo E2 reaction to give cyclohexene. Select correct statement(s) in this reaction

(a) Cyclohexyl bromide has the chair conformation with the bromine atom equatorial

(b) E2 reaction is not possible in this conformation as E2 reaction requires the reacting C—H and C—Br bonds to be antiperiplanar

(c) There is changing of conformation of an unfavourable

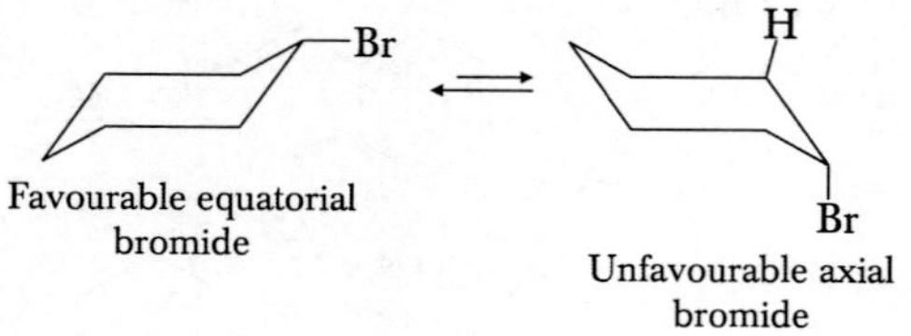

37. Select the correct statement (s).

I. Hydrogenaton of (A) or (B) gives a mixture *cis*-1,4- and *trans*-1, 4-cyclohexane

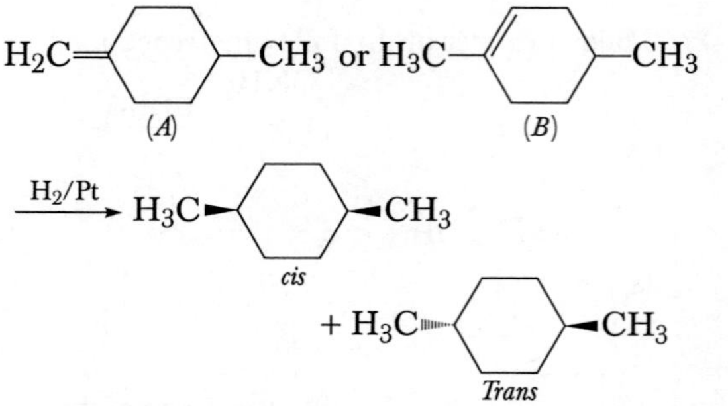

II. Hydrogenation of (*C*) forms *cis*-isomer

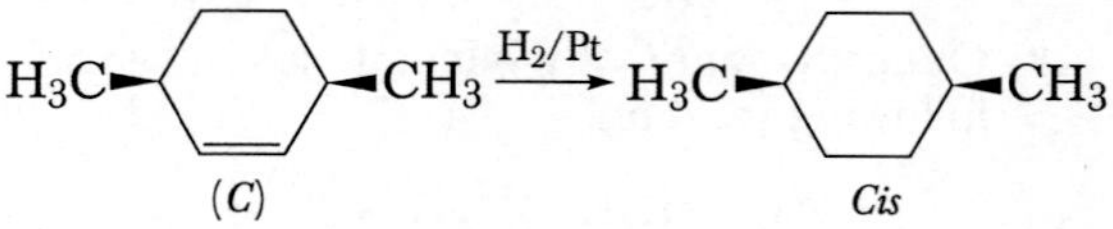

III. Hydroboration-oxidation of (D) occurs from the axial direction to give major product

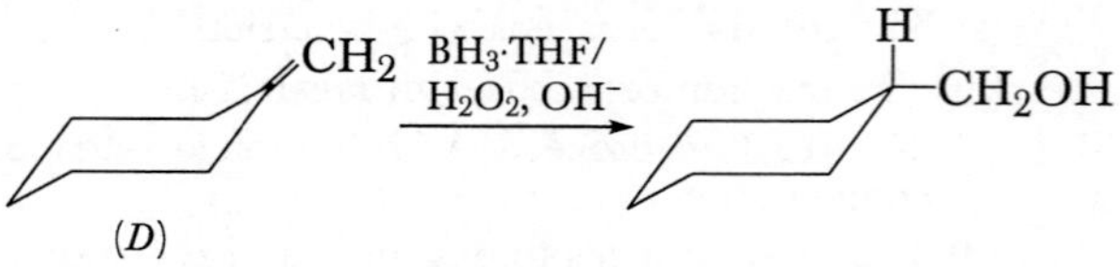

IV. Hydroboration-oxidation of (*D*) occurs from the equatorial direction to give major product

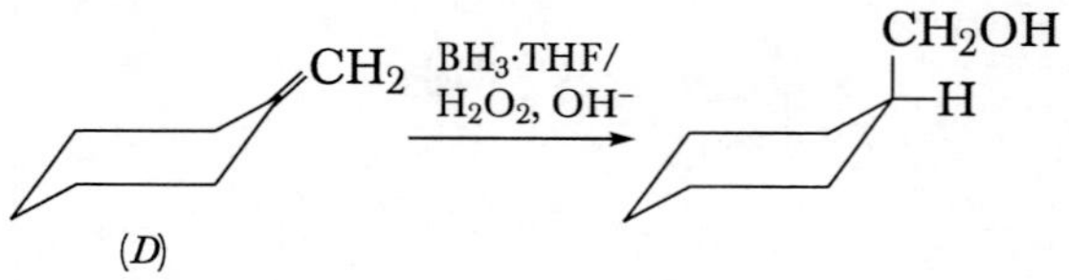

(a) I and III (b) I and II
(c) III and IV (d) II and III

38. End product of the following reaction is

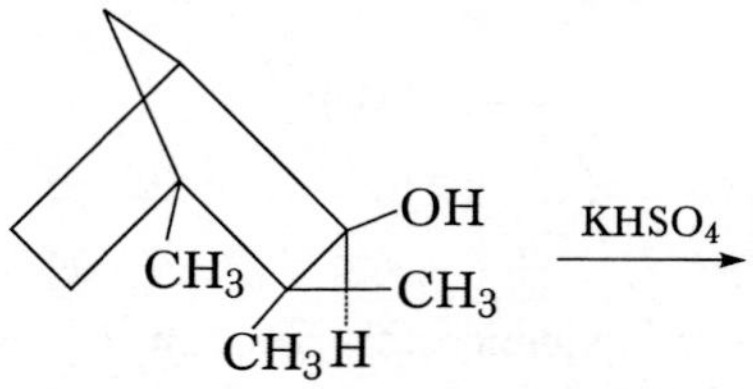

(a) 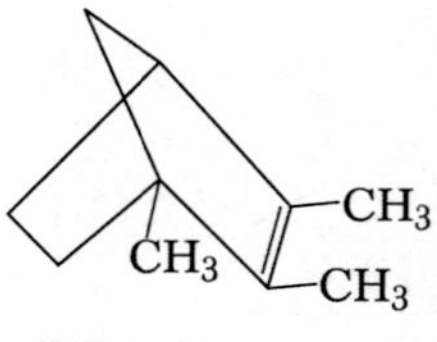

(b) 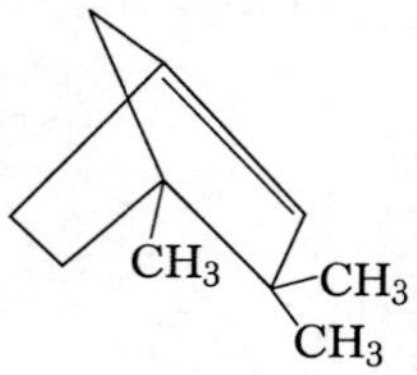

(c) 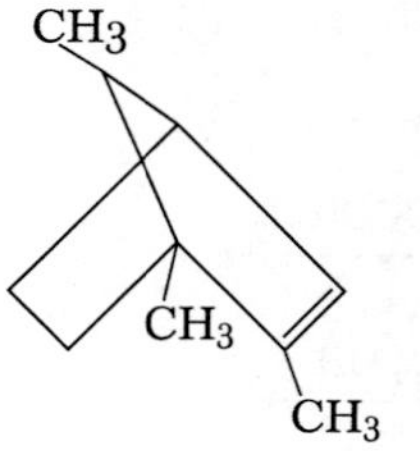

(d) 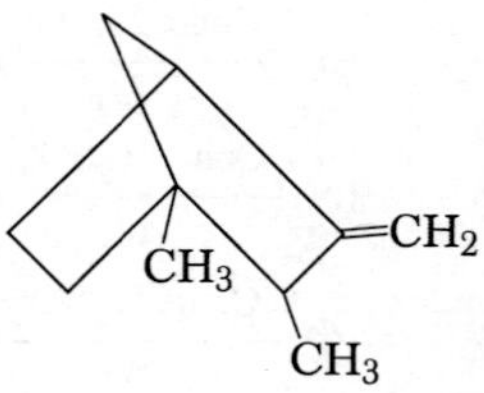

39. Consider reaction *A* and *B*

A :

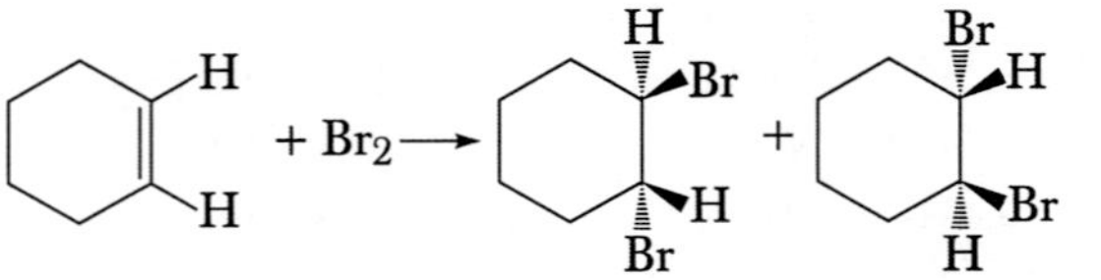

B :

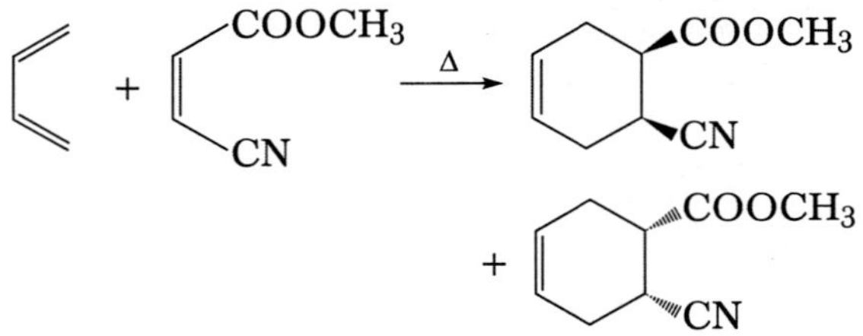

Select the correct statement(s) about *A* and *B*.

	A	*B*
(a)	Stereospecific *trans*	Stereoselective *cis*
(b)	Stereoselective *trans*	Stereoselective *cis*
(c)	Stereospecific *cis*	Stereoselective *trans*
(d)	enantiospecific *trans*	enantiospecific *cis*

40. 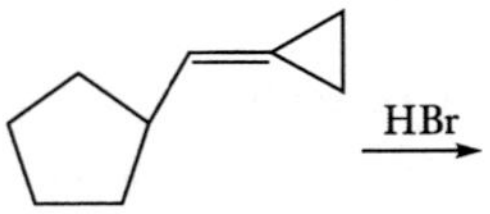 Product, product is

(a) 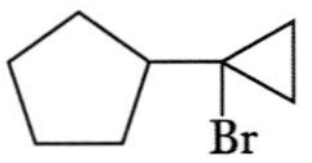

(b) 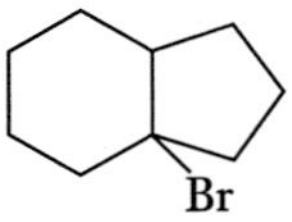

(c) 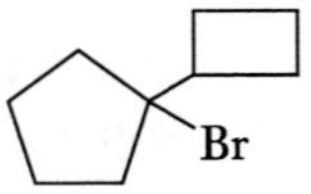

(d) 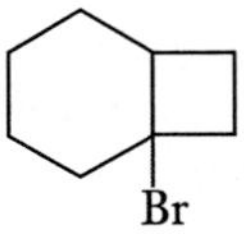

41. The main reason for the rearrangement are

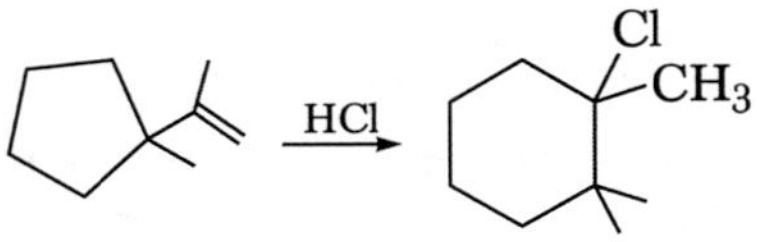

(a) The initially formed carbocation is secondary and it rearranges to the more stable tertiary one by shift of alkyl group
(b) The reaction converts one tertiary carbocation into another to relieve torsional strain
(c) The tertiary chloride is much more stable than a secondary one, because of hyperconjugation
(d) This is a radical chain reaction, controlled by relative bonds strengths

42. Two products formed by addition of HBr to 1,2-dimethylcyclohexene

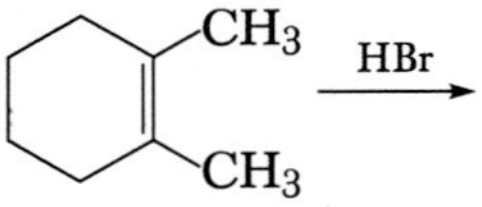

I. are *cis*- and *trans*-1,2-dimethylcyclohexyl bromide

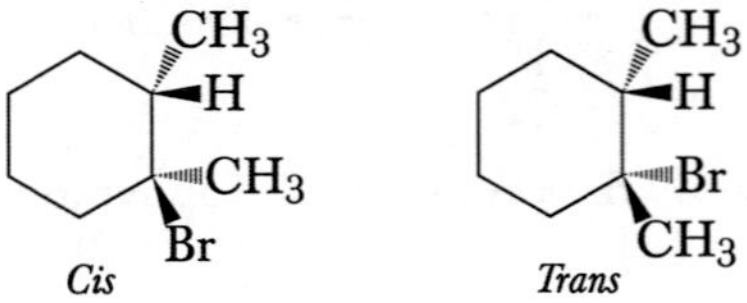

Cis *Trans*

II. cannot be regioisomers
III. can also be formed by addition of HBr to 1,6-dimethylcyclohexene

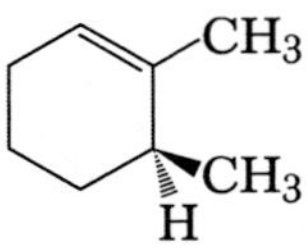

Select the correct answer.

(a) I and II (b) I and III
(c) I, II and III (d) only I

43. Alkene + Cl_2 ⟶ 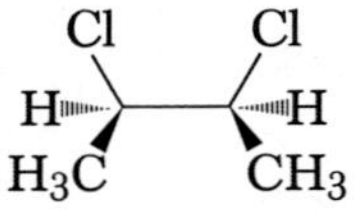

In the above reaction alkene is

(a) *Z*-but-2-ene (b) *E*-but-2-ene
(c) *Z*-but-1-ene (d) *E*-but-1-ene

44. Addition of HCl to 3,3-dimethyl-1-butene yields two products, one of which has a rearranged carbon skeleton. Which of the following cations are intermediates in that reaction?

$(CH_3)_3C\overset{\oplus}{C}HCH_2Cl$ (I) $(CH_3)_3C\overset{\oplus}{C}HCH_3$ (II)

$(CH_3)_2\overset{\oplus}{C}C(CH_3)_2$ with Cl on the second carbon (III) $(CH_3)_2\overset{\oplus}{C}CH(CH_3)_2$ (IV)

(a) I, II (b) I, III (c) II, III (d) II, IV

45. What is/are the products in the following reaction?

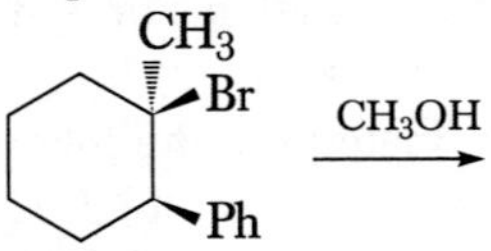

I. 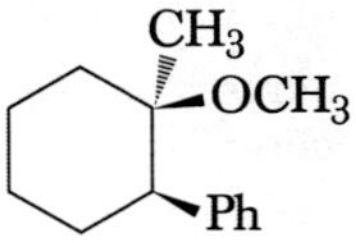

II. 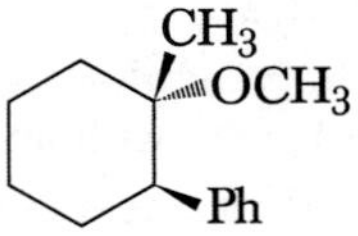

III. 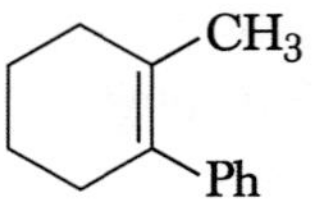

(a) I and III (b) II and III
(c) I and II (d) I, II and III

46. 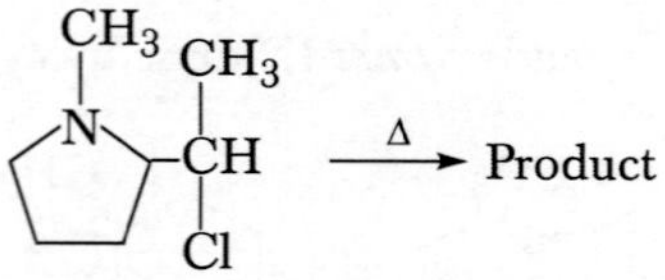

Identify the product in the above reaction

(a) 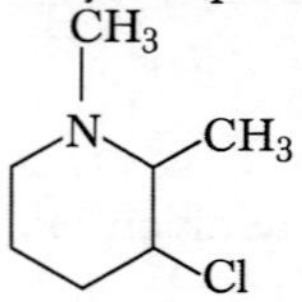
(b) 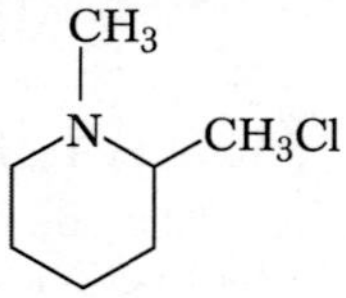
(c) 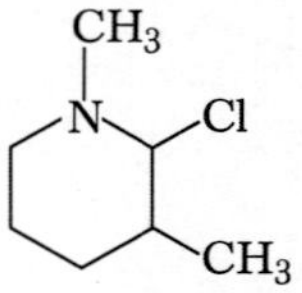
(d) 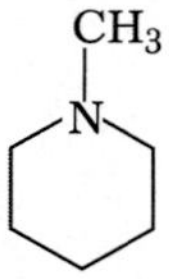

47. Identify the final organic product of the following reaction.

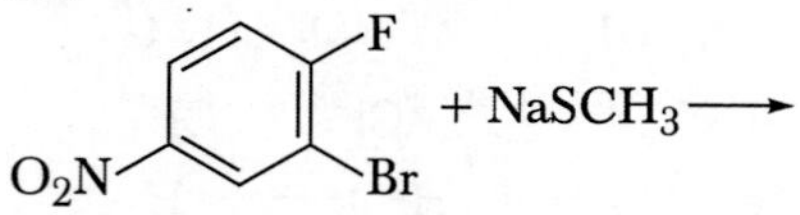

(a) 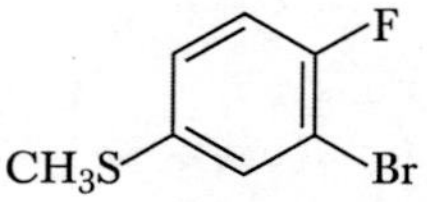
(b) 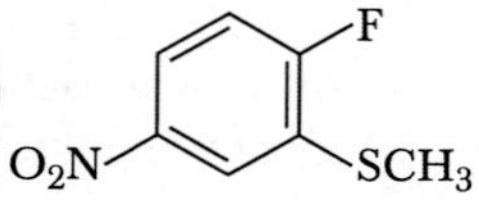
(c) 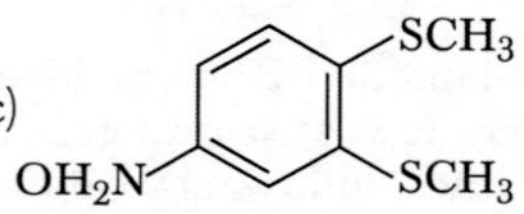
(d) 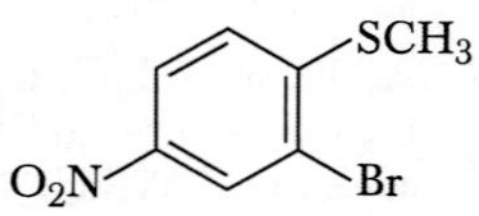

48. Which of the following statements pertaining to an S_N2 reaction are true?

I. The rate of reaction is independent of the concentration of the nucleophile

II. The nucleophile attacks carbon on the side of the molecule opposite the group being displaced

III. The reaction proceeds with simultaneous bond formation and bond rupture

IV. Partial racemisation of an optically active substrate results

Select the alternate from the following

(a) I, IV
(b) I, III, IV
(c) II, III
(d) All of these

49. Which of the following phrases are not correctly associated with an S_N1 reaction?

I. Rearrangement is possible

II. Rate is affected by solvent polarity

III. The strength of the nucleophile is important in determining rate

IV. The reactivity series is : tertiary > secondary > primary

V. Proceeds with complete inversion of configuration

Select the correct alternate from the following

(a) III, V
(b) II, III, V
(c) V only
(d) III only

50. Which of the following resonance structures is not a contributor to the cyclohexadienyl cation (carbocation σ-complex) intermediate in the nitration of benzene?

(a) 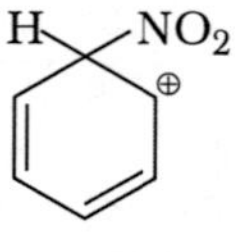
(b) 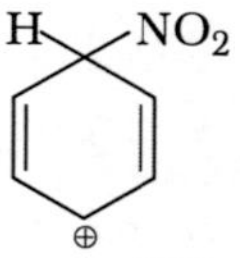
(c) 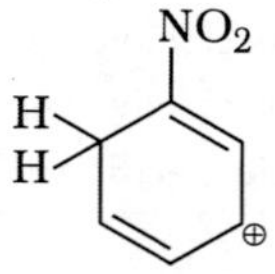
(d) None of the above (all are contributors)

51. Select correct statement(s) about following

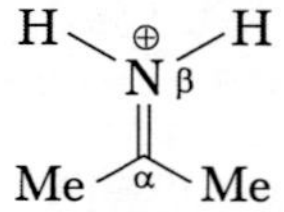

(a) It is an electrophile at two atoms at α and β

(b) It is converted into...when nucleophile attacks at α-position

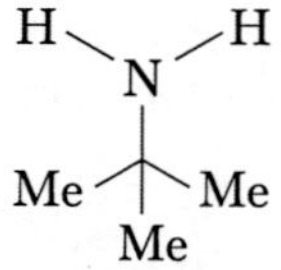

(c) It is converted into...when nucleophile attacks at β-position

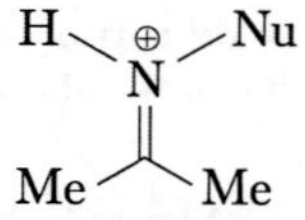

(d) It is converted into...when nucleophile attacks at β-position

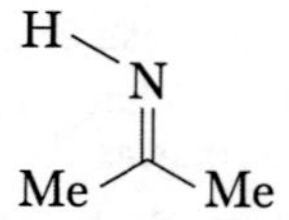

52. End product(s) of the following reaction is/are

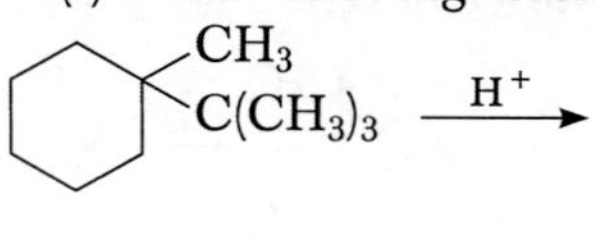

(a) 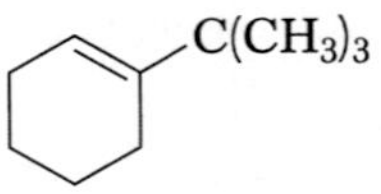

(b) 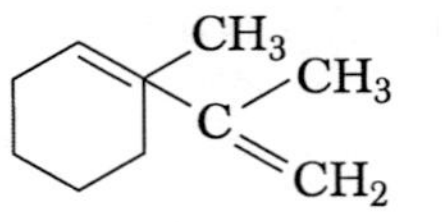

(c) 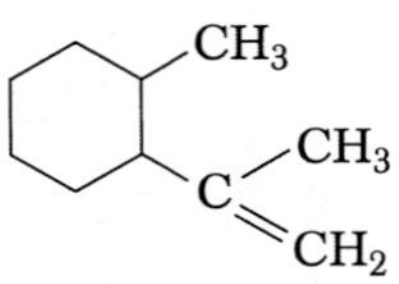

(d) 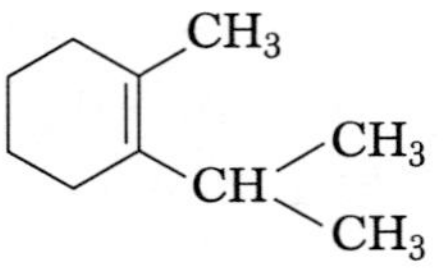

53. In the following reaction :

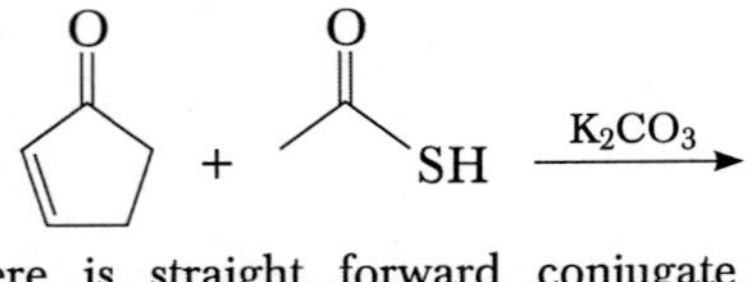

(a) there is straight forward conjugate addition of sulphur nucleophile and product is

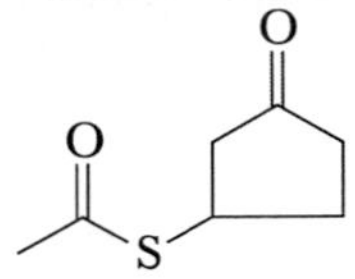

(b) one stereogenic centre is formed
(c) product is *racemic* mixture
(d) product is *meso* compound

54. 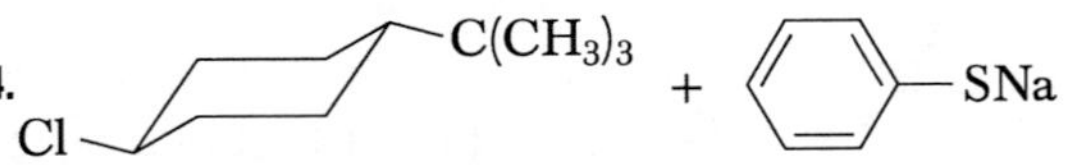

Trans-4-*tert*-butylcyclohexyl chloride

Select correct statement(s).

(a) Product is 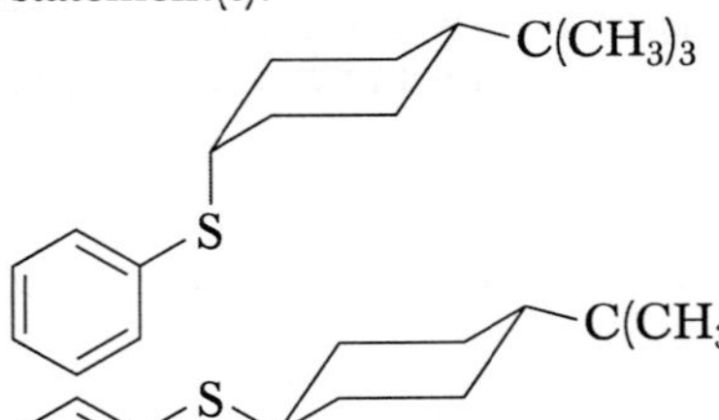

(b) Product is 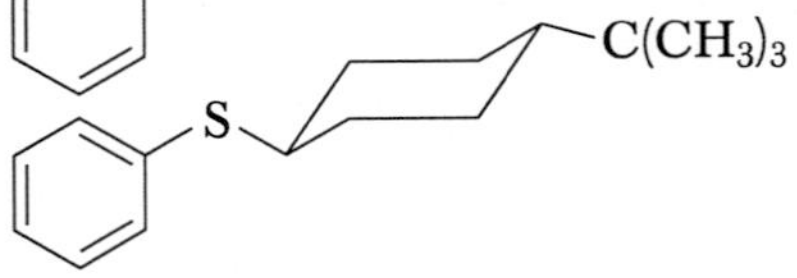

(c) S_N2 mechanism is followed
(d) There is inversion of configuration

55. Which of the following is/are true for a free radical?
(a) It is always formed by homolytic cleavage of bond.
(b) It is always electron deficient, act as a Lewis acid.
(c) It is always paramagnetic.
(d) It always disproportionate to some extent.

56. Which of the following statements applies appropriately to acid strength of carbonic acid and acetic acid?
(a) Carbonic acid is stronger acid, due to $-I$ effect by —OH on —COOH.
(b) Carbonic acid is weaker due to electron donating resonance effect of —OH group on —COOH group.
(c) $NaHCO_3$ is a stronger base than CH_3COONa.
(d) CH_3COONa reacts with carbonic acid to form CH_3COOH and $NaHCO_3$.

57. Which of the following on protonation will roduce a carbocation that will rearrange to a further more stable carbocation?

(a) 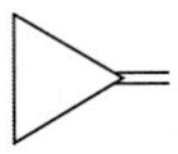

(b) 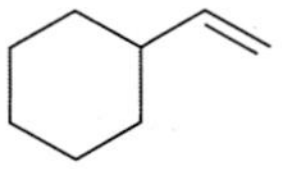

(c) 

(d) 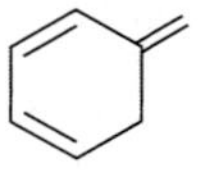

Assertion & Reason

Codes
(a) Both A and R are true and R is the correct explanation of A.
(b) Both A and R are true and R is not the correct explanation of A.
(c) A is true and R is false.
(d) A is false and R is true.

58. Assertion (A) Bromobenzene, upon reaction with Br_2/Fe gives 1, 4-dibromobenzene as the major product.

Reason (R) In bromobenzene, the inductive effect of the bromo group is more dominant than the mesomeric effect in directing the incoming electrophile.

59. Assertion (A) S_N1 reaction at the chiral carbon results in the formation of *racemic* mixture and S_N2 reaction at the chiral carbon results in the change in configuration.

Reason (R) For a given alkyl group R, S_N1 and S_N2 reaction follows :

$$R\text{—Cl} < R\text{—Br} < R\text{—I}$$

60. Assertion (A) 1-propenamine exist as an equilibrium mixture of its *cis* and *trans*-forms.

Reason (R) 1-propenamine is a conjugated system and a resonance form has all C—C single bonds.

61. Assertion (A) A carbocation with oxygen bonded to positively charged carbon is exceptionally stable.

Reason (R) Such carbocations have resonance stabiliztion.

62. Match the Column I compound with Column II elimination product.

Column I (Compound)		Column II (Elimination product)	
A.	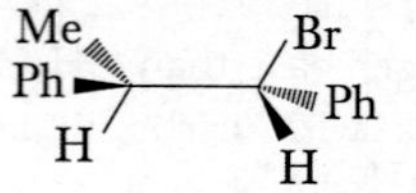 (1*S*, 2*R*)	1.	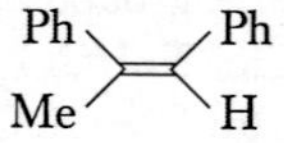
B.	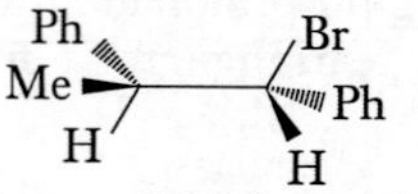 (1*S*, 2*S*)	2.	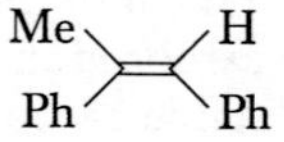
C.	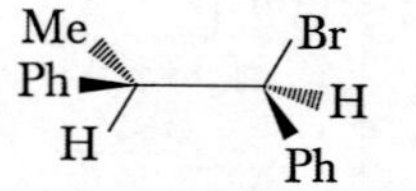 (1*R*, 2*R*)	3.	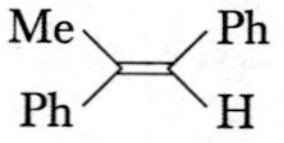
		4.	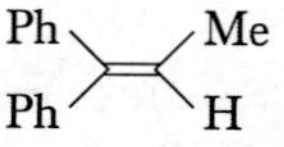

Codes

	A	B	C
(a)	4	3	2
(b)	3	4	1
(c)	3	1	2
(d)	2	1	4

Directions (Q. Nos. 63 to 65)

Alkenes are characterized by C=C bonds. As such, they are subjected to electrophilic addition reactions. Most electrophilic additions obey Markownikoff's rule. However, there are some exceptions. Examples of alkenes are given below.

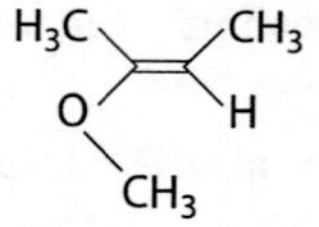
I

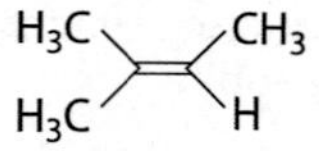
II

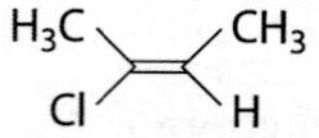
III

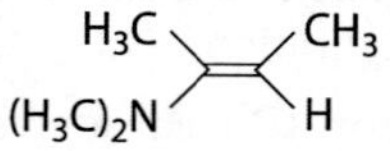
IV

63. When HBr adds to compound 2 above, the main product is

(a) 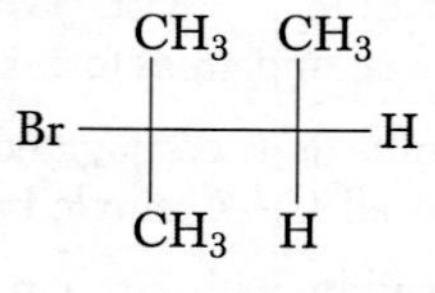

(b) 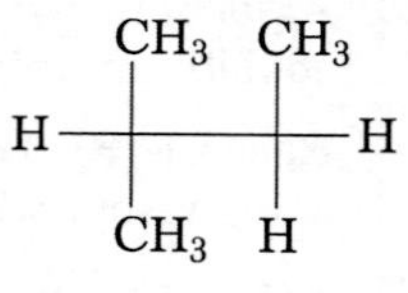

(c) 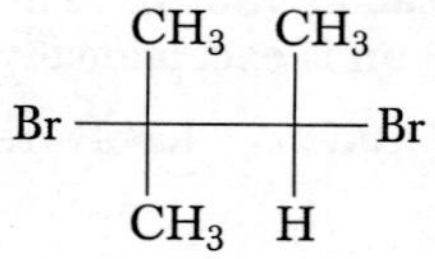

(d) 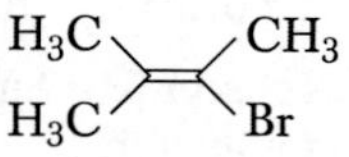

64. What is the major product of the following reaction?

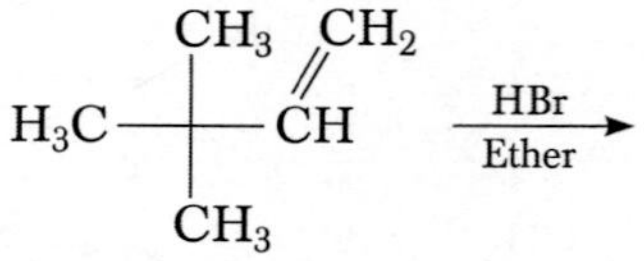

(a) 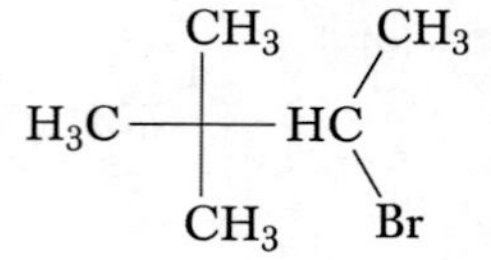

(b) 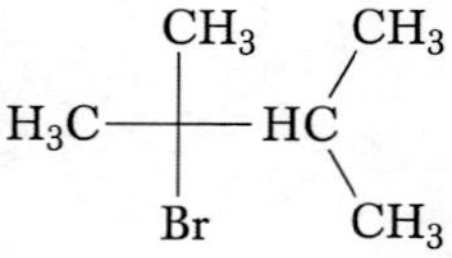

(c) 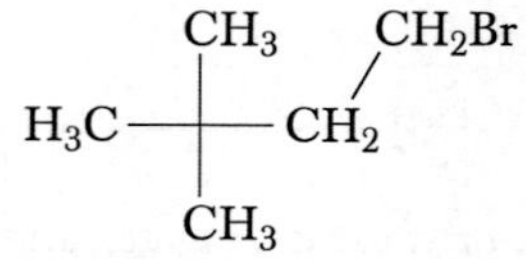

(d) 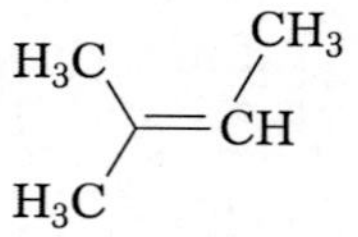

65. What is the major product of the following reaction?

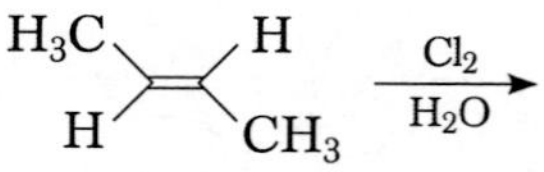

(a) 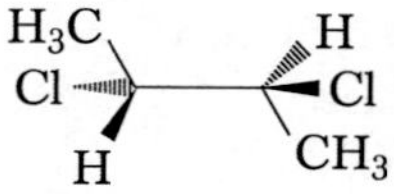

(b) 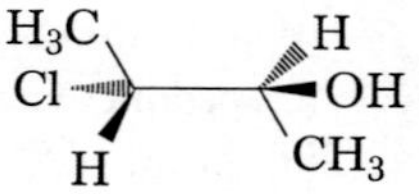

(c) 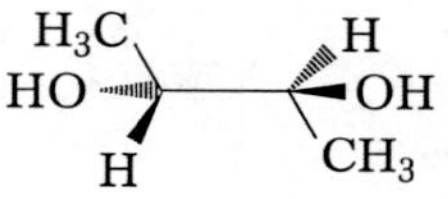

(d) 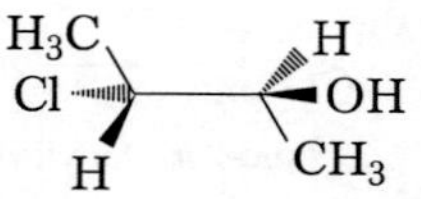

Directions (Q. Nos. 66 to 87)

Consider the following system to answer the next three questions

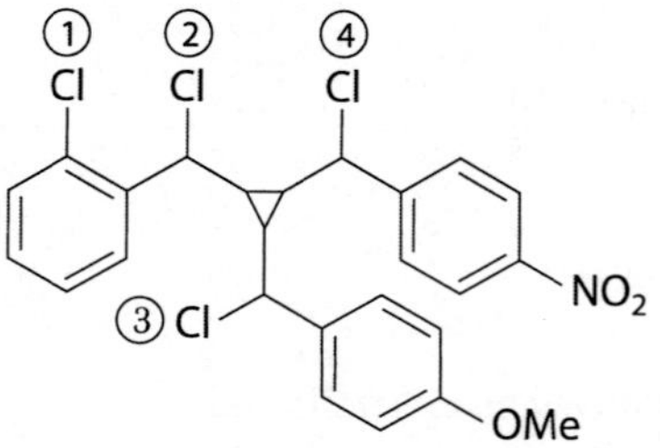

66. If the above compound is treated with boiling water, S_N1 reaction takes place through a carbocation intermediate. The chlorine which will be lost in the first step of reaction is

(a) 1
(b) 2
(c) 3
(d) 4

67. If only one chlorine is substituted by hydroxyl group in the given experimental condition in the previous question, the major product would be

(a) 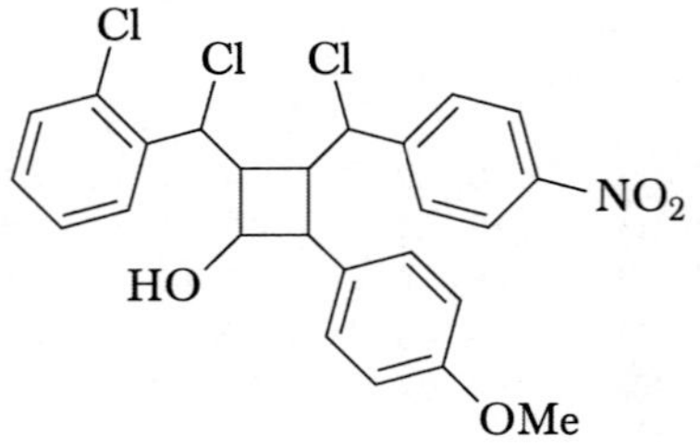

(b) 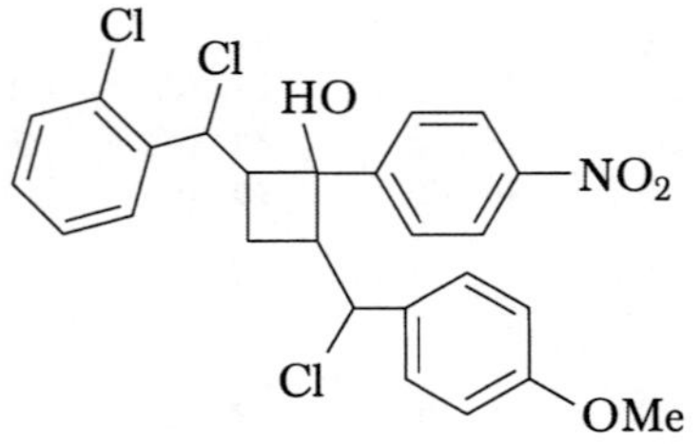

(c) 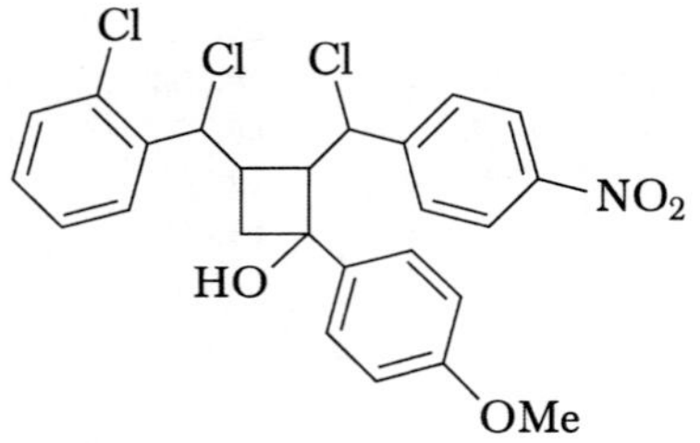

(d) 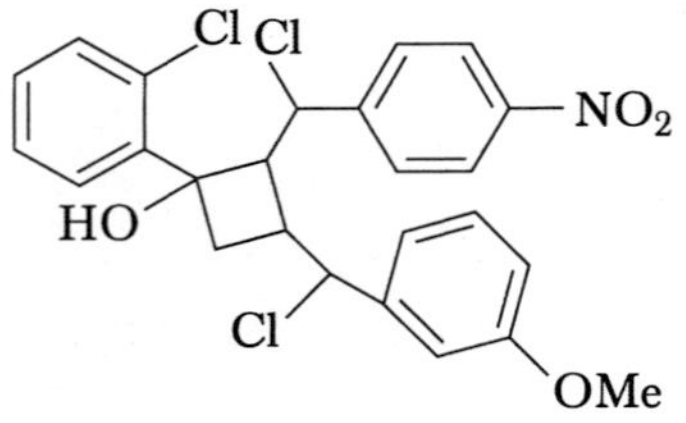

68. If the given starting compound is to lose a Cl^+, forming a carbanion, the chlorine that will be lost first is

(a) 1 (b) 2
(c) 3 (d) 4

69. The intermediate involved in the react given below is

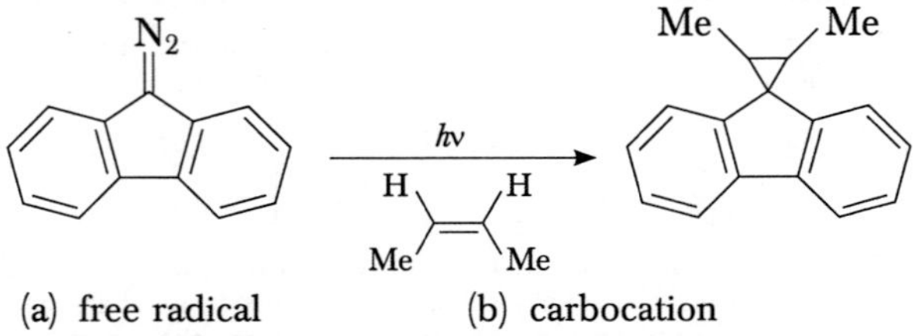

(a) free radical (b) carbocation
(c) carbanion (d) carbene

70. The reaction given below is an example of

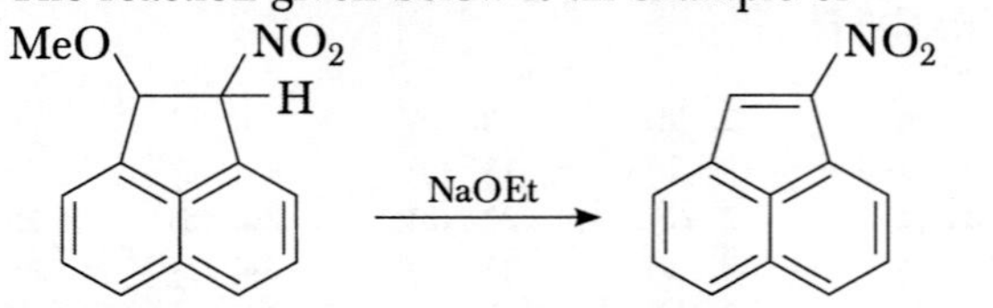

(a) E2-elimination (b) E1-elimination
(c) *syn*-elimination (d) E1cB-elimination

71. The relative rates of solvolysis of iodides *A*-*C* are

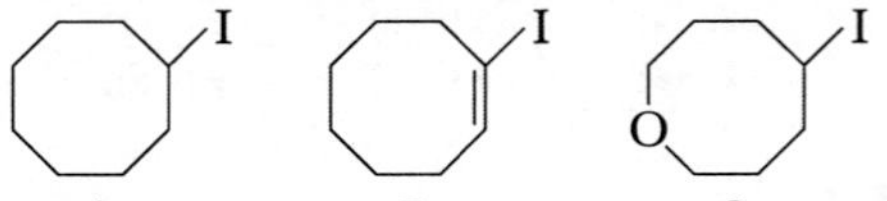

A *B* *C*

(a) $C > A > B$ (b) $C > B > A$
(c) $B > C > A$ (d) $B > A > C$

72. The correct order of acidity of the following compounds *A*-*C*, is

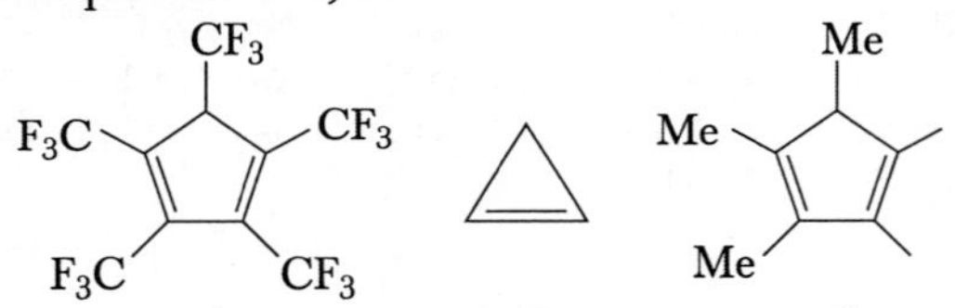

A *B* *C*

(a) $B > C > A$ (b) $C > B > A$
(c) $A > C > B$ (d) $A > B > C$

73. Consider the following reaction

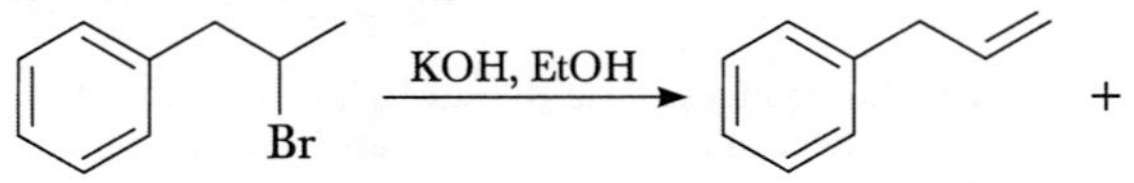

A *B*

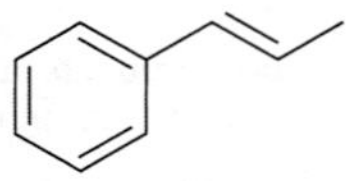

C

In an experiment, 1.99 g of bromide *A* on reaction with ethanolic potassium hydroxide gave 1.062 g of a mixture of the olefins *B* and *C*. If the ratio of olefins *B* : *C* formed is 2 : 1, the yields for their formation, respectively, are

(a) 60 and 30% (b) 50 and 25.5%
(c) 66 and 33% (d) 54 and 27%

Answers

Exercise 1

1. (d)	2. (d)	3. (c)	4. (b)	5. (b)	6. (c)	7. (c)	8. (d)	9. (a)	10. (d)
11. (a)	12. (b)	13. (b)	14. (c)	15. (b)	16. (c)	17. (b)	18. (c)	19. (d)	20. (c)
21. (d)	22. (c)	23. (b)	24. (d)	25. (a)	26. (b)	27. (d)	28. (d)	29. (c)	30. (c)
31. (b)	32. (b)	33. (d)	34. (c)	35. (a)	36. (c)	37. (d)	38. (a)	39. (a)	40. (d)
41. (b)	42. (d)	43. (a)	44. (b)	45. (c)	46. (b)	47. (a)	48. (c)	49. (a)	50. (a)
51. (a)	52. (c)	53. (b)	54. (c)	55. (c)	56. (b)	57. (a)	58. (a)	59. (d)	60. (a)
61. (b)	62. (b)	63. (c)	64. (c)	65. (c)	66. (d)	67. (b)	68. (b)	69. (a)	70. (b)
71. (a)	72. (c)	73. (c)	74. (d)	75. (a)	76. (a)	77. (c)	78. (c)	79. (c)	80. (a)
81. (d)	82. (a)	83. (b)	84. (a)	85. (c)	86. (a)	87. (c)	88. (a)	89. (b)	90. (b)
91. (d)	92. (a)	93. (d)	94. (b)	95. (d)	96. (b)	97. (d)	98. (b)	99. (c)	100. (d)

Exercise 2

1. (d)	2. (d)	3. (a)	4. (d)	5. (a)	6. (d)	7. (d)	8. (b)	9. (d)	10. (c)
11. (d)	12. (b)	13. (c)	14. (a)	15. (b)	16. (b)	17. (c)	18. (c)	19. (b)	20. (d)
21. (c)	22. (d)	23. (c)	24. (a)	25. (a)	26. (a)	27. (b)	28. (c)	29. (a)	30. (a)
31. (d)	32. (a)	33. (c)	34. (c)	35. (d)	36. (d)	37. (b)	38. (a)	39. (a)	40. (b)
41. (b)	42. (c)	43. (b)	44. (d)	45. (d)	46. (a)	47. (c)	48. (c)	49. (a)	50. (c)
51. (a,b,c)	52. (a,b)	53. (a,b,c)	54. (a,c,d)	55. (a,c)	56. (b,c)	57. (a,b)	58. (a)	59. (b)	60. (a)
61. (a)	62. (c)	63. (a)	64. (b)	65. (c)	66. (c)	67. (c)	68. (d)	69. (d)	70. (d)
71. (a)	72. (c)	73. (a)							

Hints & Solutions

Exercise 1

2. III is the strongest base due to lack of delocalisation of lone pair of electron. II is weaker base than I due to electron withdrawing resonance effect of $—NO_2$.

7. III is more stable than II because III has an extra covalent bond.

9. The conjugate acid is highly stable as it has two equivalent resonance structures.

13. I is most basic due to formation of resonance stabilised conjugate acid.

$$H_3C—C(=NH)NH_2 \xrightarrow{H^+} H_3C—C(=\overset{+}{N}H_2)\ddot{N}H_2 \longleftrightarrow H_3C—C(\ddot{N}H_2)=\overset{+}{N}H_2$$

IV is amide and it is the least basic.

$$CH_3—\overset{O}{\overset{\|}{C}}—\ddot{N}H_2 \longleftrightarrow CH_3—\overset{O^-}{\overset{|}{C}}=\overset{+}{N}H_2$$

lone pair is part of delocalisation

Also, among alkyl amines, 2° is more basic than 1° amine.

Hence, the order of basic strength is

I > III > II > IV

14. $H_2C=CH—\overset{\oplus}{C}H—\overset{\ominus}{C}H—O—CH_3$

Lone pair of oxygen is not the part of this mode of delocalisation.

17. 2-butanol (R) + *p*-toluene sulphonyl chloride + pyridine $\xrightarrow{LiBr}$ *S*-2-butyl tosylate

19. Due to steric hinderence, trimesityl aluminium does not dimerize hence, it exists as a monomer under ambient conditions.

22. CIDNP is Chemically Induced Dynamic Nuclear Polarization.

26. Epoxides are very reactive due to the great strain in the three membered ring which is relieved by cleavage.

31.

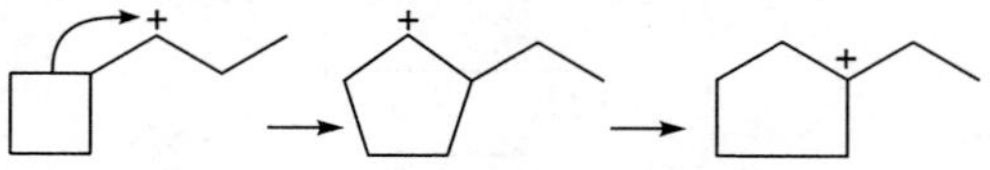

34. Reaction involve two reactive intermediates and three transition states. Every subsequent step is easier than previous step and product is more stable (exothermic) than reactant.

35.

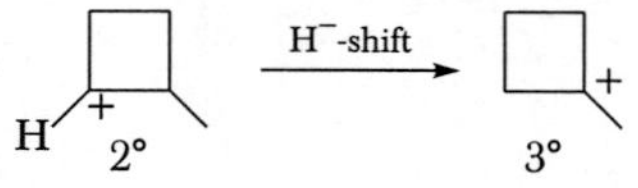

The carbocation 'b' will undergo methyl shift while 'c' will undergo ring expansion to produce more stable carbocation.

36. 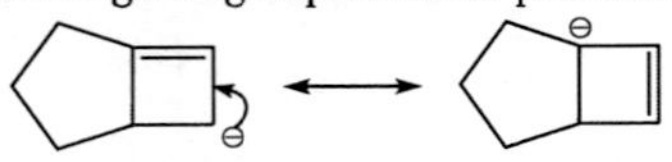

39. $C_2H_5O^-$ is the most basic anion and hence it would be the best nuceophile for S_N2 displacement.

40. NBS is used for allylic brominations by a free radical chain mechanism. The compound which give themost stable free radical would react fastest with NBS. Hence, toluene react fastest with NBS.

41. 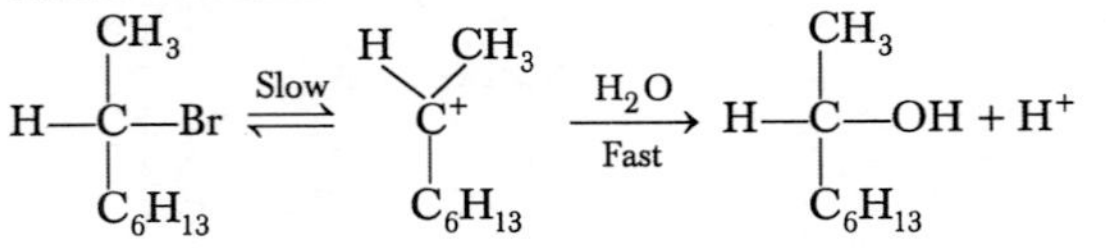

46. 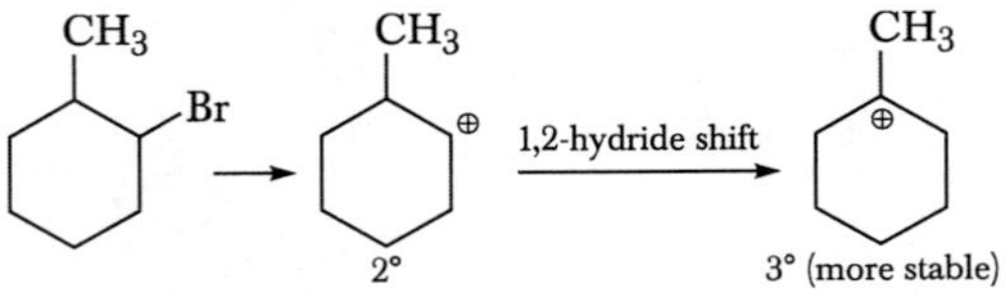

50. BE of C—Cl > C—Br

BE of C—Br in (IV) is decreased due to electron withdrawing group (>C=O). Thus, S_N2 is favoured most.

52. 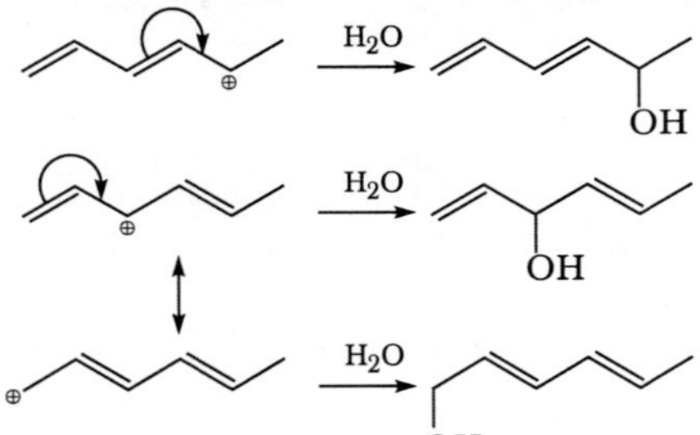

56. CCl_3, NO_2 and NH_3 are electron withdrawing group. They are

deactivating and *m*-directing group. In 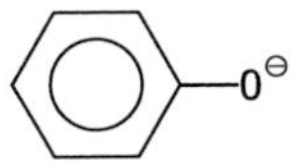 negative

charge on O is delocalised and increases elctron density at *o*- and *p*-position.

61. 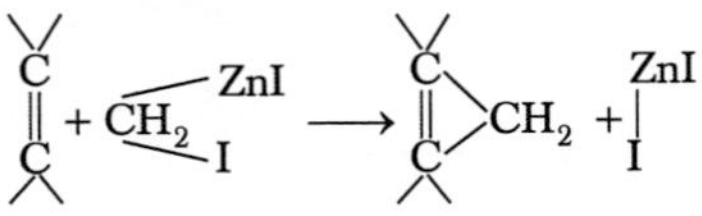

68. 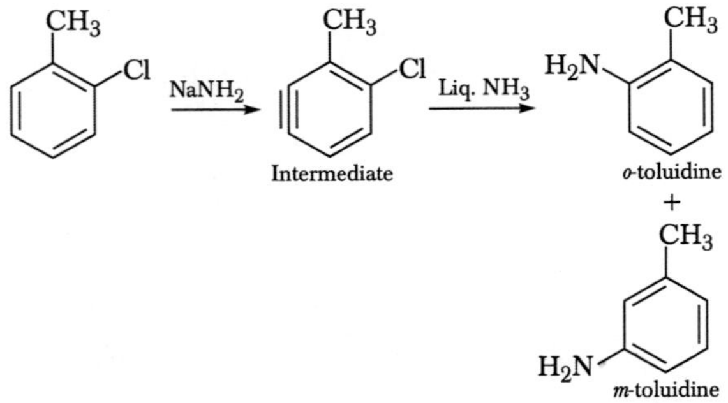

70. Benzyne reacts with olefins to give four-membered rings.

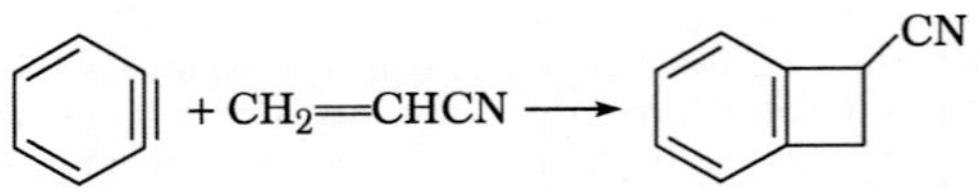

76. Singlet carbene adds in stereospecific way. Hence, *cis*-alkene gives *cis*-product.

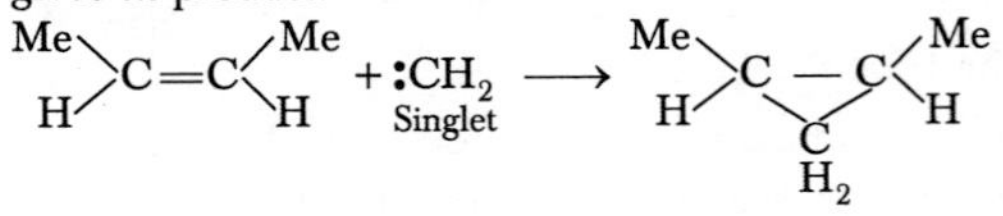

81. In presence of $SbCl_5$, 2-chloro-2-phenylethane forms a carbocation as shown below

CH_3—CHCl—C_6H_5 + $SbCl_5$ ⟶

$[CH_3—\overset{+}{C}H—C_6H_5]\ SbCl_6^-$

87. 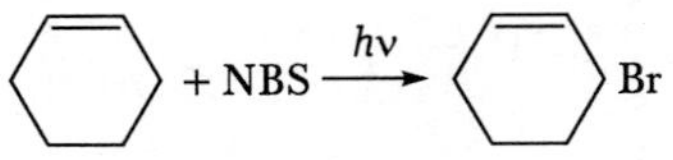

Intermediate is 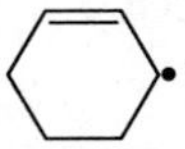 which can also combine with other molecule in termination step.

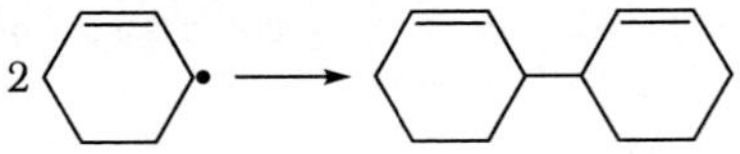

92. 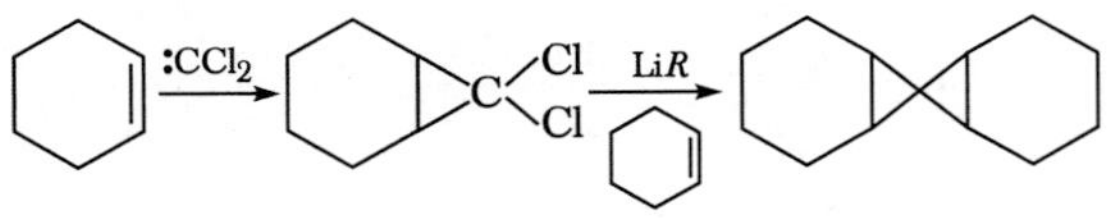

95. 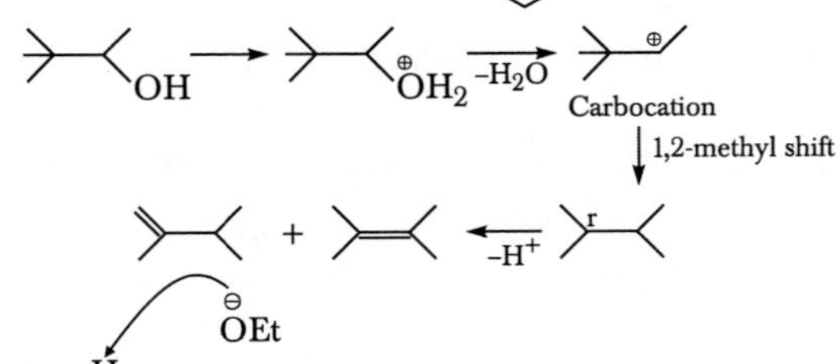

99. 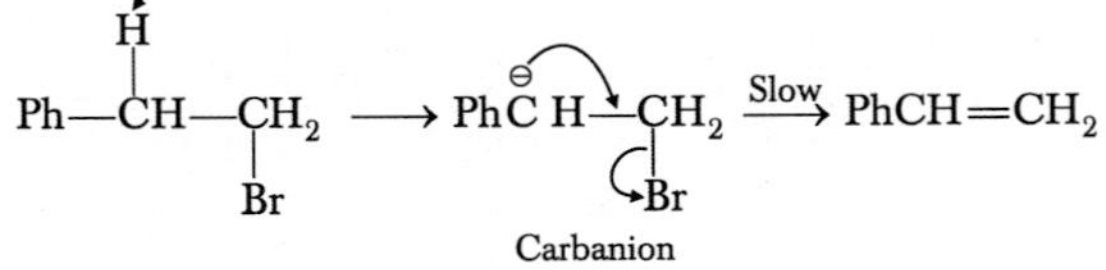

100. $C_6H_5—\overset{O}{\overset{\|}{C}}—O—O—\overset{O}{\overset{\|}{C}}—C_6H_5 \xrightarrow{80°C} 2C_6H_5CO_2^{\bullet}$

Benzoyl peroxide

$\xrightarrow[-CO_2]{} 2\dot{C}_6H_5$

Exercise 2

1. III is the weakest base since, it has resonance stability and both resonance structures have negative charge on more electronegative (oxygen) atom. I is weaker base than II since, former has resonance stability.

4. 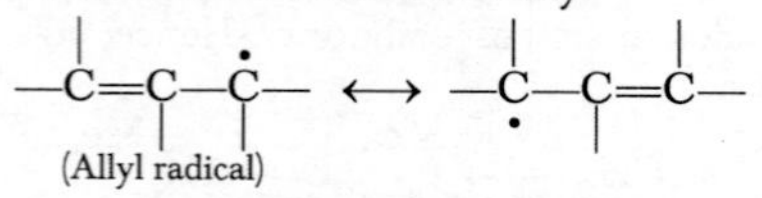

The carbon bearing odd electron is sp^2 hybridized and this electron is present in *p*-orbital of carbon.

7. Protonation at carbon gives I. Protonation at hydroxyl group followed by loss of H_2O gives II. I rearranges to give III as–

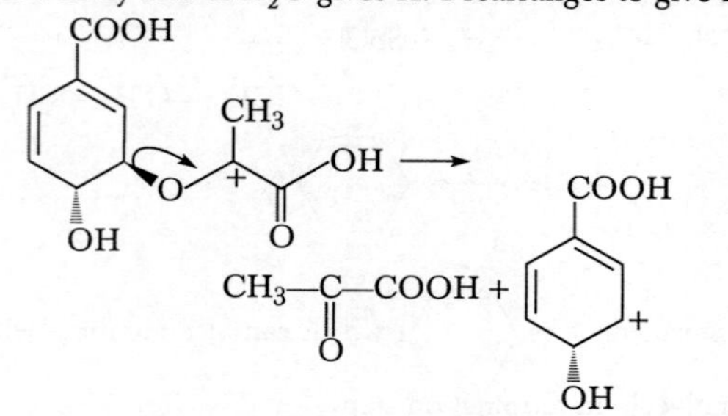

11. More stable carbocation does not change into less stable carbocation by hydride shift.

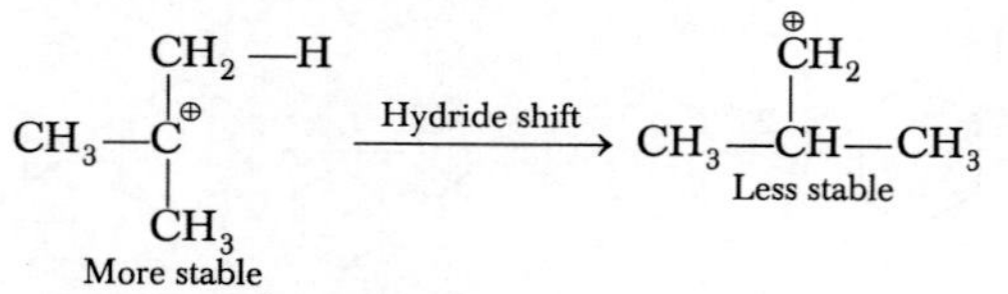

Hence, this reaction is wrong.

12. 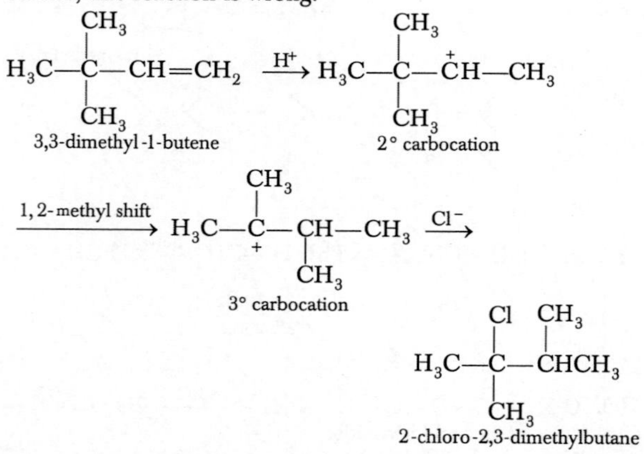

14. 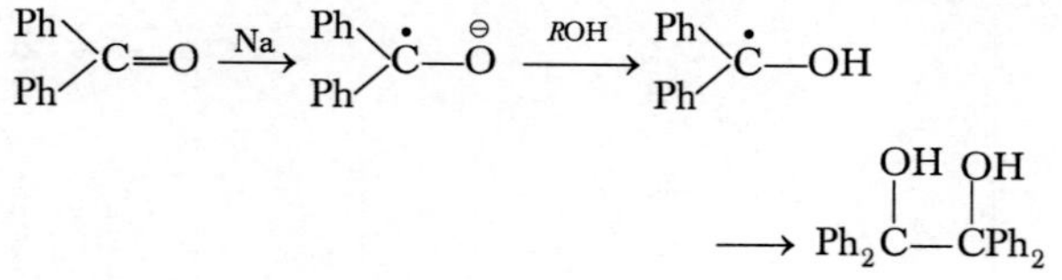

18. 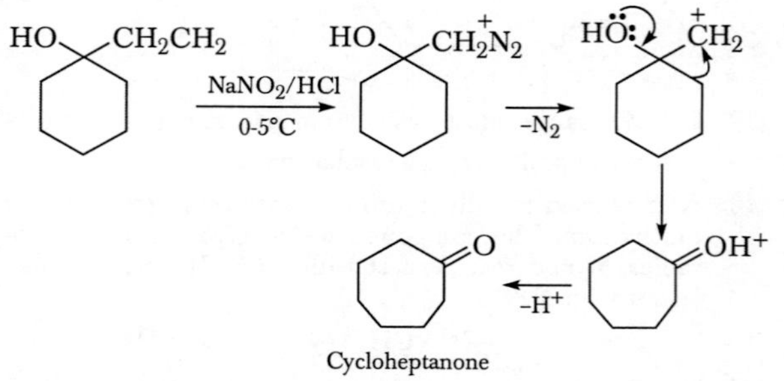

21. 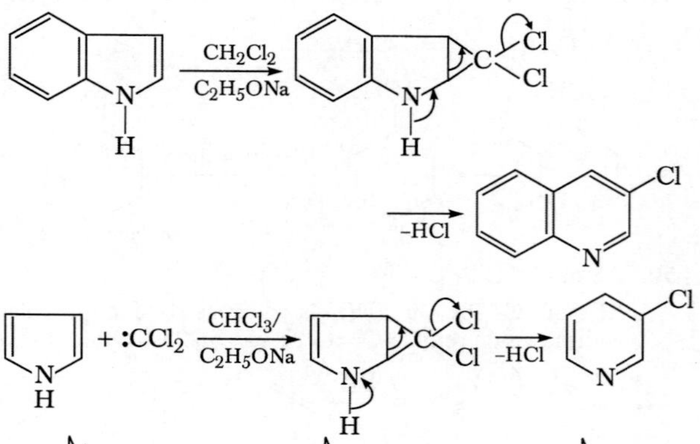

24. 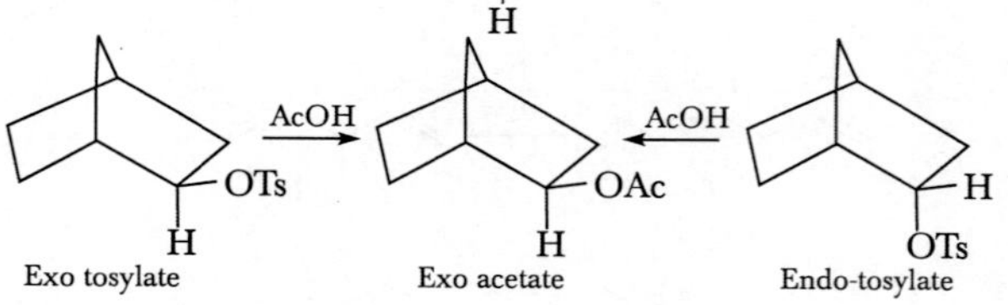

27. 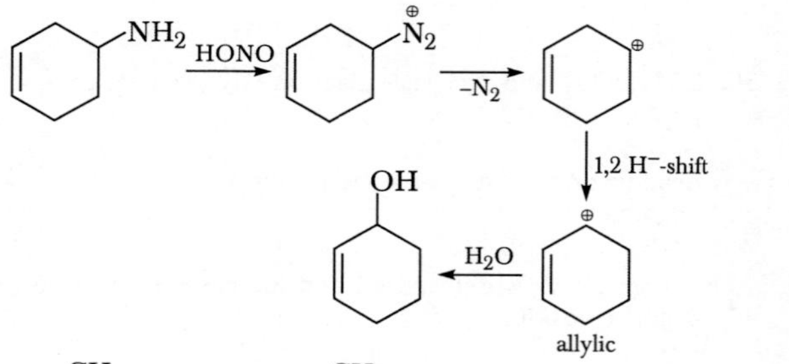

28. 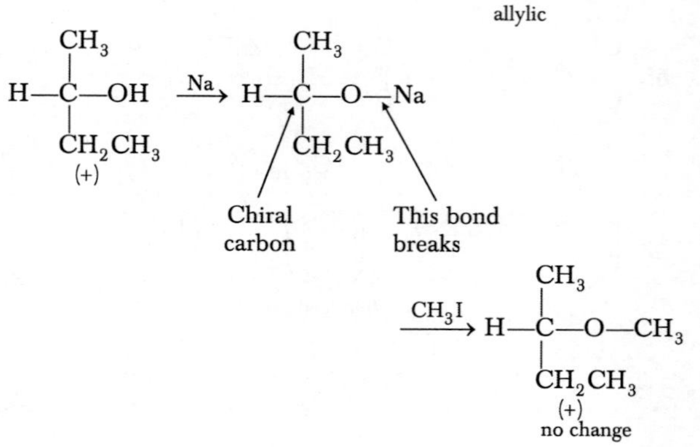

34.

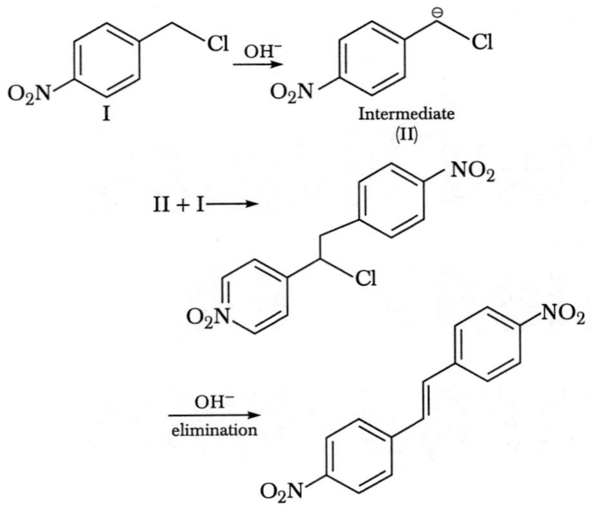

40.

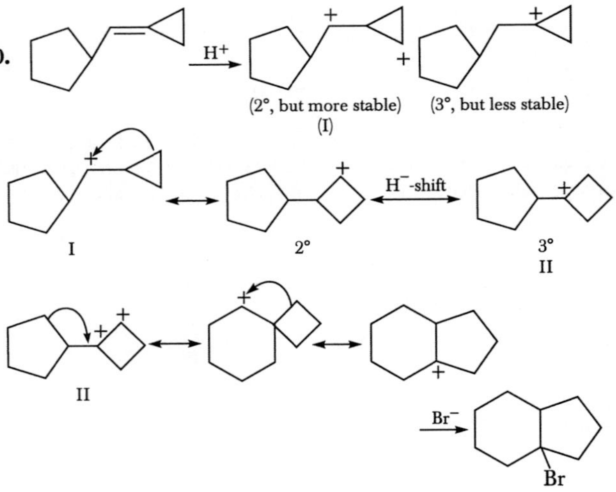

43. Addition of Cl_2 is *anti*. Thus *E*-but-2-ene forms *cis*-isomer.

44.

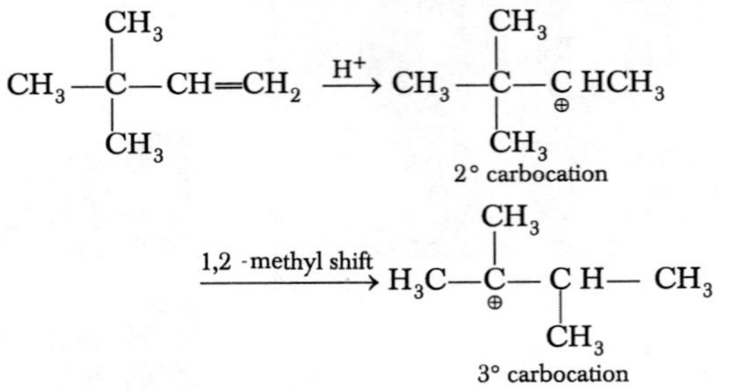

55. Homolytic bond fission produces free radicals. A free radical contains an unpaired electron hence it is paramagnetic in nature.

56.

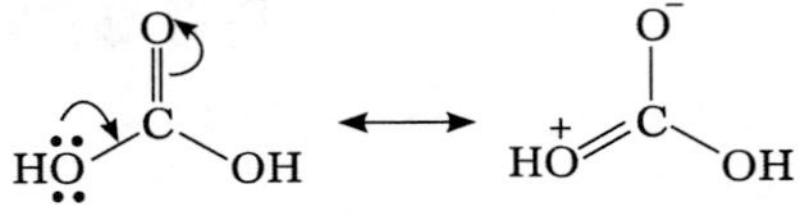

The resonance lowers the acidity of H-attached to other —OH group. Hence, carbonic acid is weaker acid than acetic acid and HCO_3^- is stronger base than CH_3COO^-.

57.

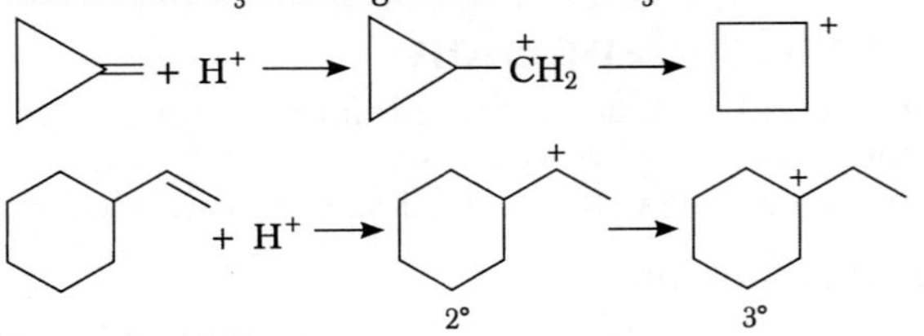

60.

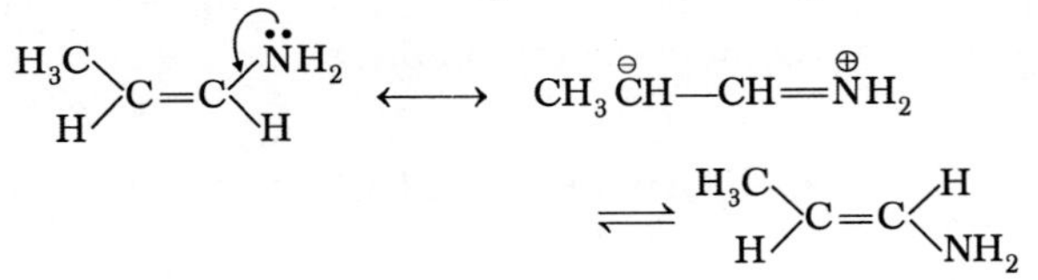

Resonance remove the double bond character and allows rotation to take place.

32 Common Named Reactions and Rearrangements

Syllabus

- Common Named Reactions and Rearrangements, Applications in Organic Synthesis

Common Named Reactions

Aldol Condensation

Aldol condensation is the addition of an α-carbon atom of an aldehyde or ketone to the carbonyl carbon of another molecule of aldehyde or ketone. It may be acid catalysed as well as base catalysed reaction.

Base catalysed

Base catalysed aldol condensation generally generates aldols of the type β-hydroxy carbonyl compounds.

$$CH_3CHO + CH_3CHO \overset{OH^{\ominus}}{\rightleftharpoons} CH_3-\underset{}{\overset{OH}{\overset{|}{C}}}H-CH_2-CHO$$

3-hydroxy butanal

Mechanism

Step I

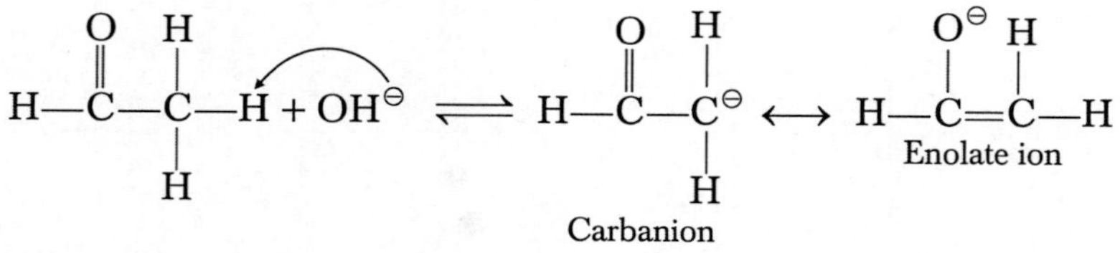

Step II

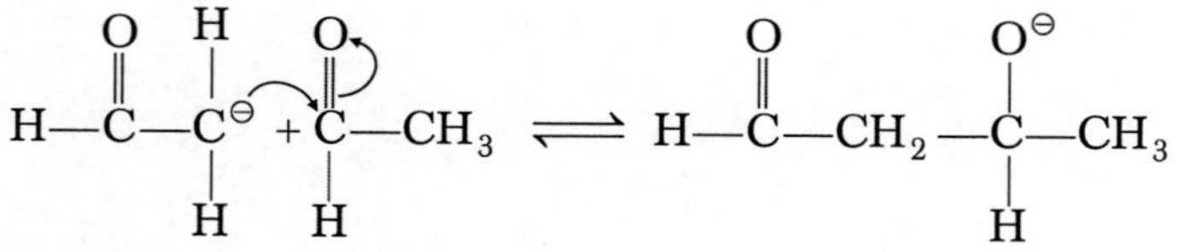

Step III

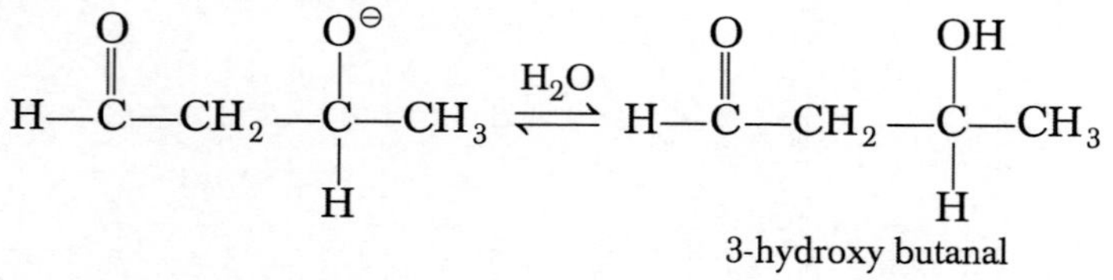

Sometimes α, β-unsaturated carbonyl compounds are also formed by dehydration of β-hydroxy carbonyl compounds.

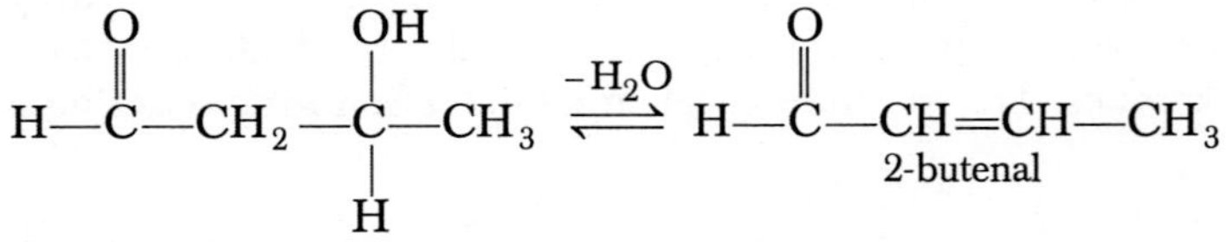

Acid catalysed

The acid catalysed aldol condensation generally generates aldols of the type α, β-unsaturated carbonyl compounds.

Mechanism

Step I

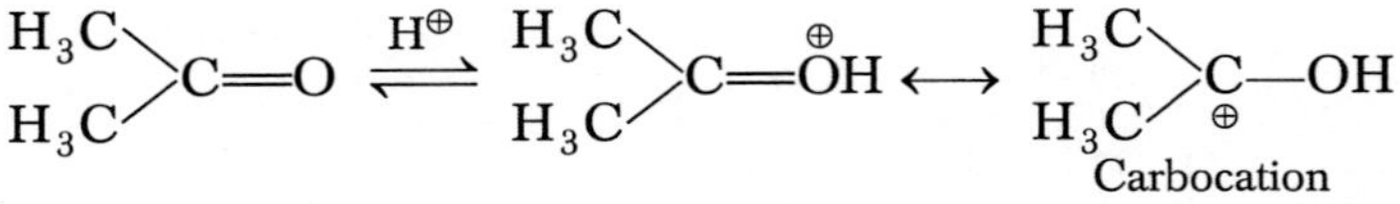

Step II

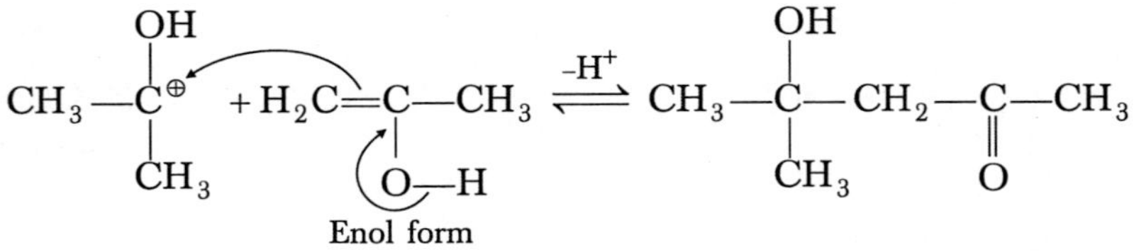

Step III

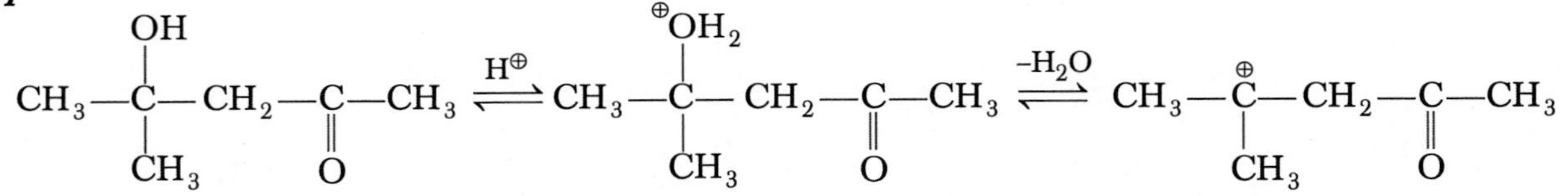

Step IV

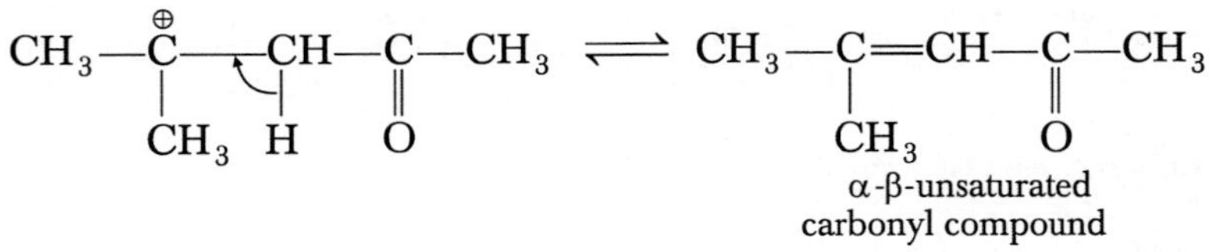

Retro aldol condensation

The entire reaction of aldol condensation is an equilibrium including dehydration and hence, α, β-unsaturated and β-hydroxy carbonyl compounds may be cleaved in presence of hydroxyl anion to give back the carbonyl compounds. This reverse reaction is known as **Retro aldol condensation.**

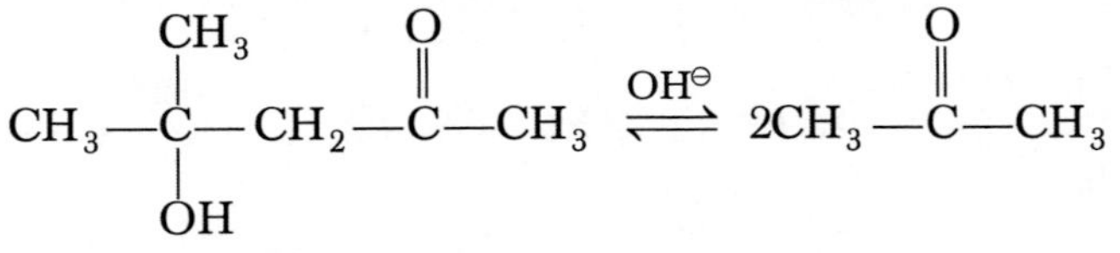

Note
- When a mixture of two aldehyde both possessing α-H-atom, is treated with a base, four different aldol products are formed.
- Cross aldol condensation between an excess of an aldehyde that has no α-hydrogen atom (such as C_6H_5CHO or HCHO) and a second enolisable aldehydes gives mainly one crossed aldol condensation product.

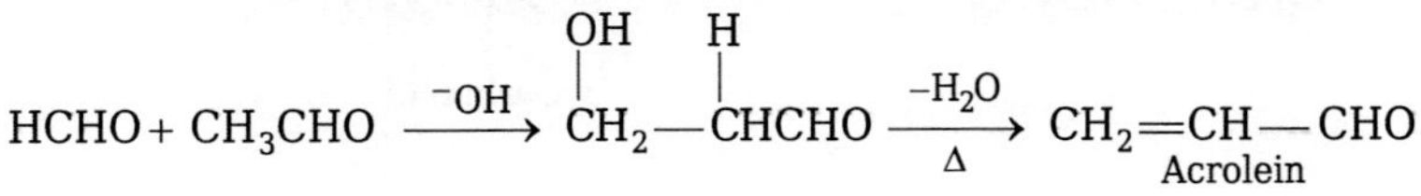

Claisen-Schmidt Reaction

Aromatic aldehydes or ketones react with aliphatic aldehydes or ketones having α-hydrogen in presence of mild alkaline medium (10% NaOH) at low temperature to give cross aldol product, followed by dehydration to give α, β-unsaturated aldehydes or ketones. This reaction is called **Claisen-Schmidt reaction.**

$$C_6H_5CHO + CH_3CHO \xrightarrow[\text{8-10 days}]{\text{10\% NaOH, room temp.}} \underset{\text{Cinnamaldehyde}}{C_6H_5CH{=}CH{-}CHO}$$

$$C_6H_5CHO + CH_3COCH_3 \xrightarrow[\text{2-3 days}]{\text{10\% NaOH, 30°C}} \underset{\text{Benzal acetone}}{C_6H_5CH{=}CHCOCH_3}$$

Mechanism

$$H{-}CH_2CHO \underset{}{\overset{^-OH}{\rightleftharpoons}} \overset{\ominus}{C}H_2CHO \xrightleftharpoons{H{-}C(=O){-}C_6H_5} C_6H_5{-}\underset{H}{\overset{O^{\ominus}}{C}}{-}CH_2CHO \overset{H_2O}{\rightleftharpoons} C_6H_5{-}\underset{H}{\overset{OH}{C}}{-}CH_2CHO$$

$$\xrightarrow{-H_2O} \underset{\text{Cinnamaldehyde}}{C_6H_5CH{=}CH{-}CHO}$$

Applications

(a) $C_6H_5COCH_3 + C_6H_5CHO \xrightarrow[C_2H_5OH]{NaOH} \underset{\text{Benzal acetophenone (chalcone)}}{C_6H_5COCH{=}CHC_6H_5}$

(b)

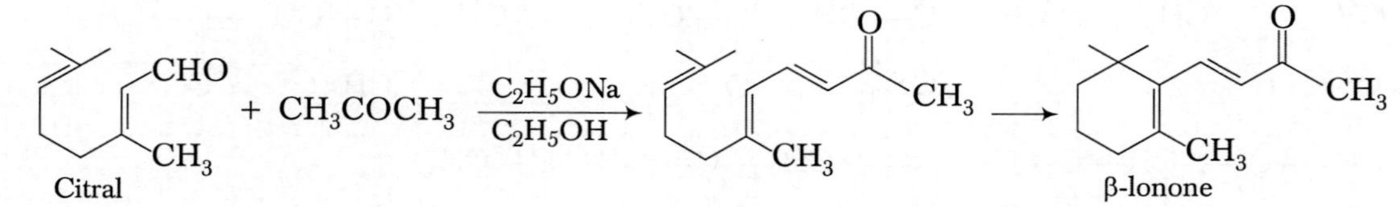

Citral β-Ionone

β-Ionone is the intermediate in the synthesis of vitamin A.

Stobbe Condensation

The condensation between dialkyl succinate or its derivative and aldehydes or ketones in presence of a strong base like sodium hydride, sodium ethoxide, etc., to form salts of α, β-unsaturated half esters is known as **Stobbe condensation.**

$$R_2C{=}O + \underset{\text{Diethyl succinate}}{\begin{matrix} CH_2COOC_2H_5 \\ | \\ CH_2COOC_2H_5 \end{matrix}} \xrightarrow{C_2H_5ONa} R{-}\underset{OH}{\overset{R}{C}}{-}\overset{CH_2COONa}{CH}{-}COOC_2H_5 \xrightarrow{-H_2O} R{-}\overset{R}{C}{=}\overset{CH_2COONa}{C}{-}COOC_2H_5$$

Mechanism

$$\begin{matrix} CH_2COOC_2H_5 \\ | \\ CH_2COOC_2H_5 \end{matrix} \xrightarrow{C_2H_5ONa} \underset{\text{Carbanion}}{\begin{matrix} CH_2COOC_2H_5 \\ | \\ \overset{\ominus}{C}HCOOC_2H_5 \end{matrix}}$$

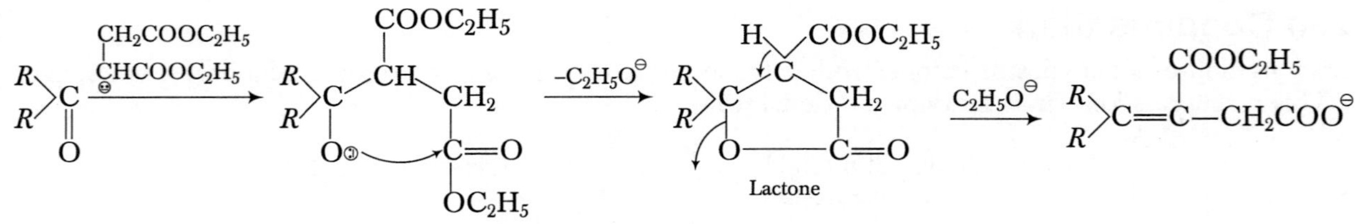

Claisen Condensation

The base catalysed condensation of an ester containing an α-hydrogen atom with a molecule of the same ester or a different ester to give β-keto ester is known as **Claisen condensation.**

$$\underset{\text{Ethyl acetate}}{CH_3COOC_2H_5} + CH_3COOC_2H_5 \xrightarrow{C_2H_5O^{\ominus}} \underset{\text{Ethyl acetoacetate}}{CH_3COCH_2COOC_2H_5} + C_2H_5OH$$

Mechanism

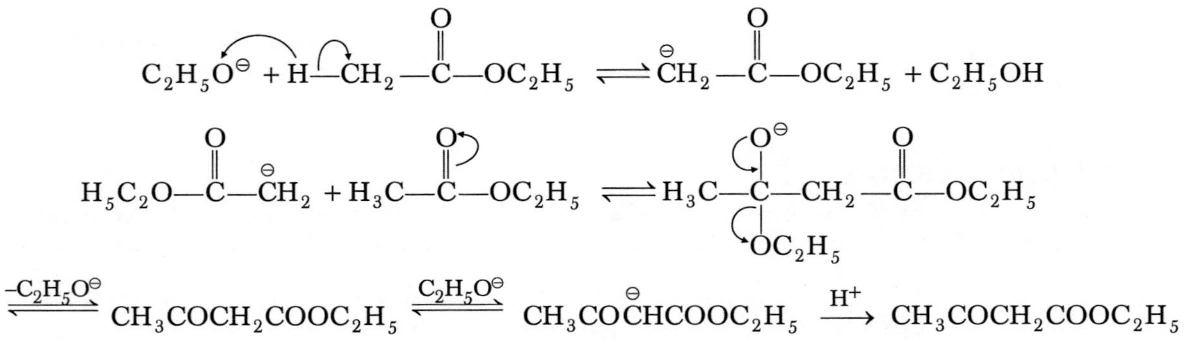

Knoevenagel Reaction

The condensation of reactive methylene compound like malonic ester with aldehydes or ketones in presence of base is known as **Knoevenagel reaction.** The base catalyst used are aniline, alkyl amines, pyridine, piperidine, etc.

$$C_6H_5CHO + \underset{\text{Malonic ester}}{H_2C(COOR)_2} \xrightarrow[\text{Piperidine}]{\text{Pyridine}} C_6H_5CH{=}C(COOR)_2 \xrightarrow[\text{(ii) }\Delta,\ -CO_2]{\text{(i) }H_2O/H^+} \underset{\text{Cinnamic acid}}{C_6H_5{-}CH{=}CH{-}COOH}$$

Mechanism

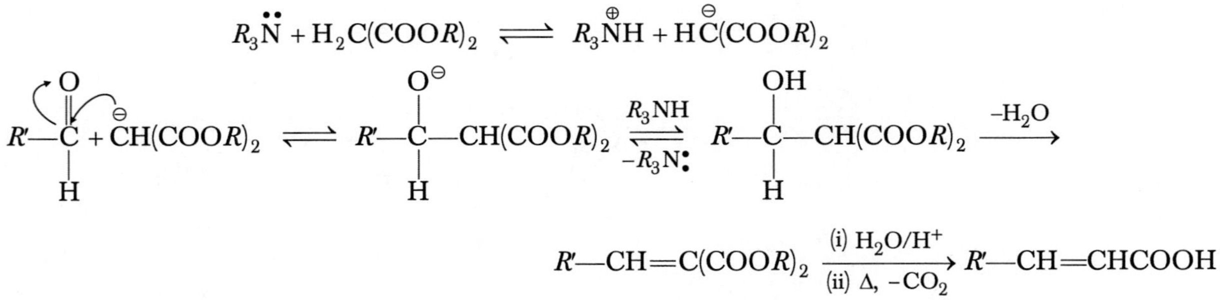

Note Due to steric hindrance ketone is less reactive hence, more active methylene group is used.

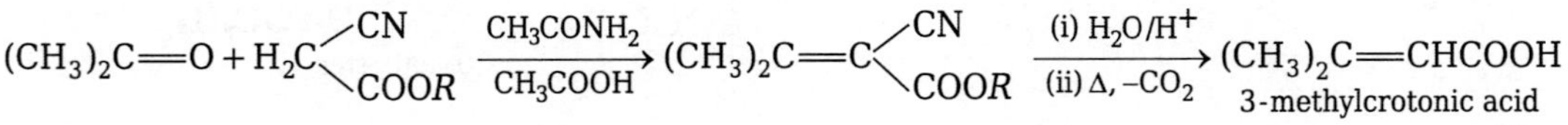

The Knoevenagel reaction is more useful with aromatic aldehydes.

Darzen Condensation

The condensation of aldehydes or ketones with α-haloester takes place in the presence of a base gives α, β-epoxy esters. This reaction is known as **Darzen condensation.**

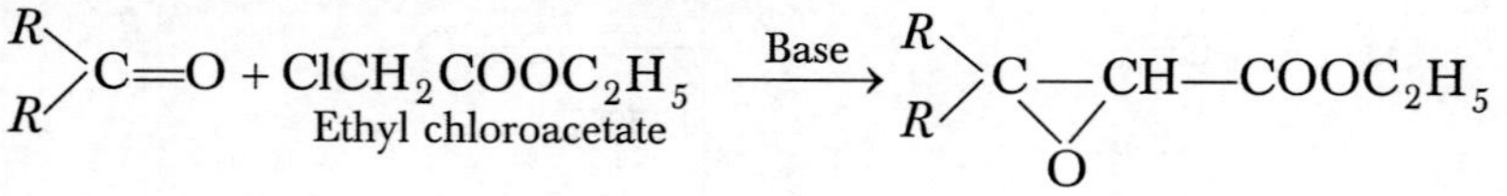

Mechanism

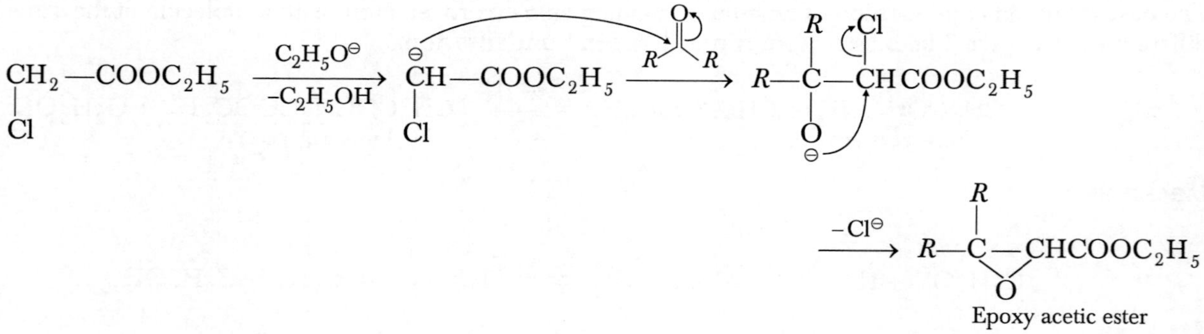

Dieckmann Condensation

The intermolecular condensation of dibasic esters (like Claisen condensation) is called **Dieckmann condensation.** The product will be cyclic β-ketone derivative. The bases used are sodium ethoxide, sodium hydride, potassium *t*-butoxide, etc.

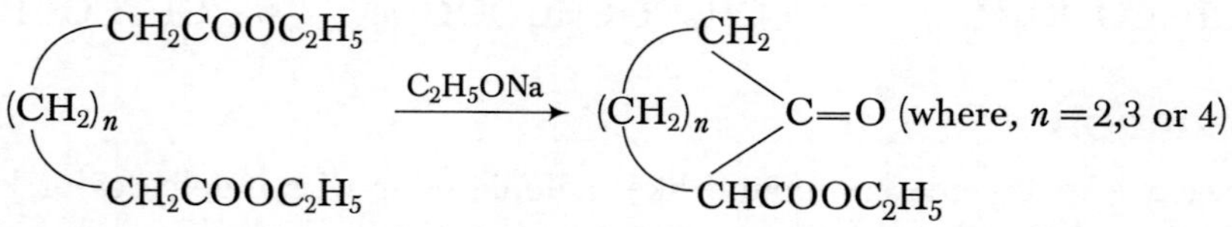

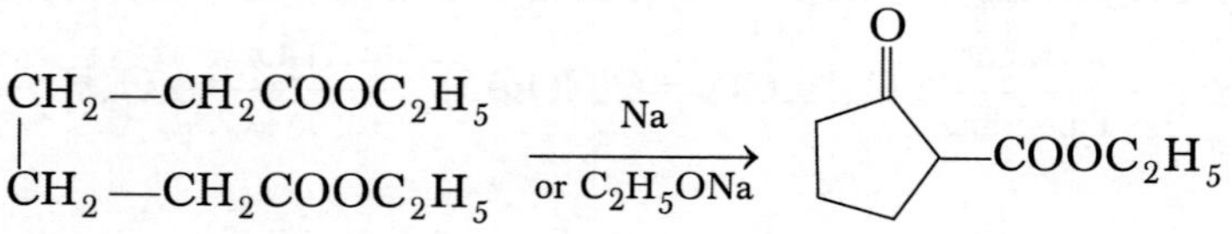

Mechanism

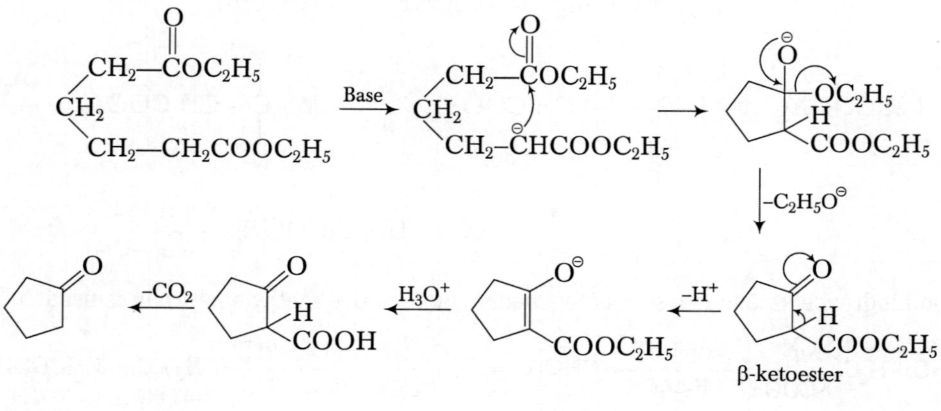

Other example

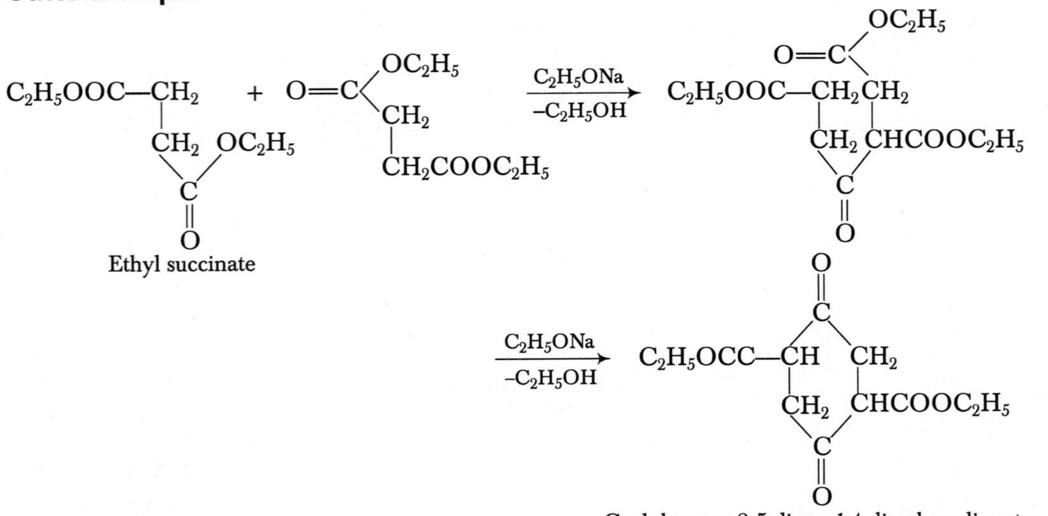

Ethyl succinate

Cyclohexane-2,5-dione-1,4-dicarboxylic ester

Perkin Reaction

The reaction of aromatic aldehyde with an aliphatic acid anhydride in presence of sodium or potassium salt of the acid corresponding to anhydride to give α, β-unsaturated acid is called **Perkin reaction.**

$$C_6H_5CHO + (CH_3CO)_2O \xrightarrow[\Delta]{CH_3COONa} C_6H_5CH{=}CH{-}COOH + CH_3COOH$$

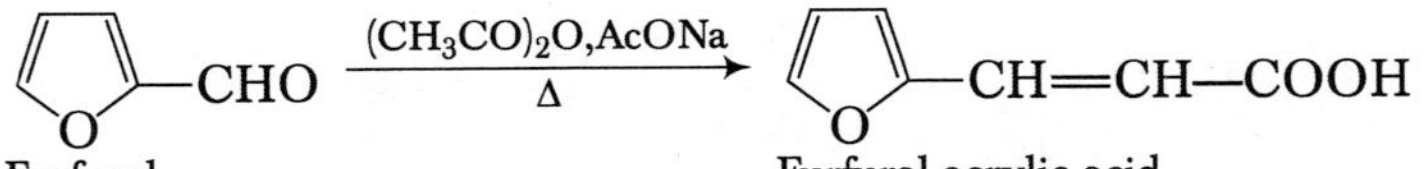

Furfural → Furfural acrylic acid

Mechanism

$$CH_3COONa \rightleftharpoons CH_3CO\bar{O} + \overset{+}{Na}$$

$$CH_3CO\bar{O} + H{-}CH_2{-}CO{-}O{-}CO{-}CH_3 \rightleftharpoons CH_3COOH + \bar{C}H_2{-}CO{-}O{-}CO{-}CH_3$$

Acetic anhydride

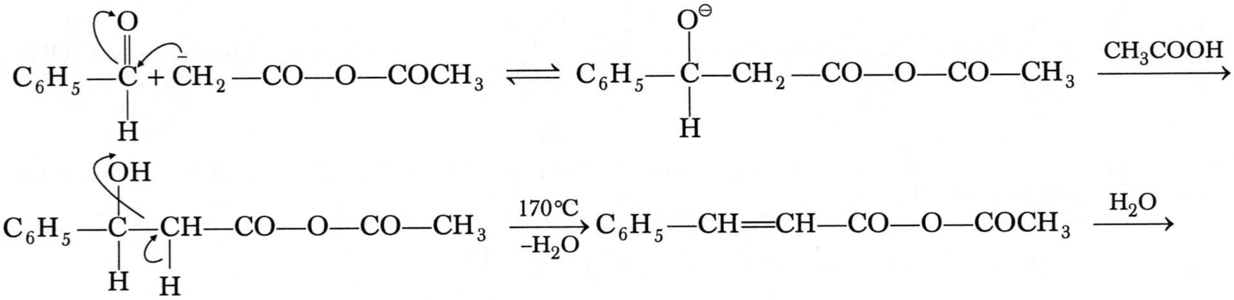

$$C_6H_5CH{=}CH{-}COOH + CH_3{-}COOH$$

Reimer-Tiemann Reaction

Reaction of phenol with chloroform in presence of alkali (NaOH or KOH solution) to give *ortho* and *para* formyl phenol is known as **Reimer-Tiemann reaction.**

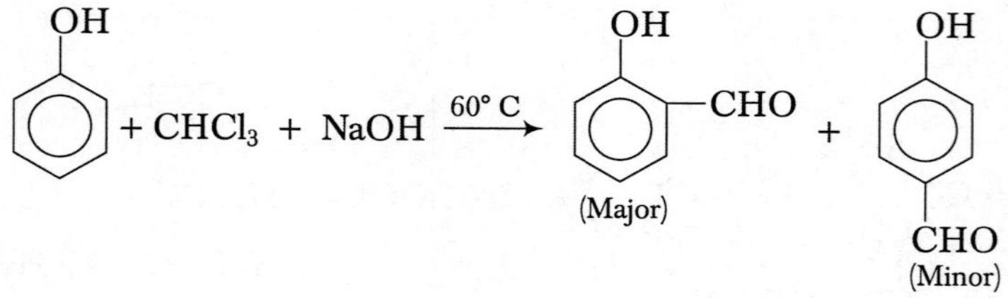

Mechanism

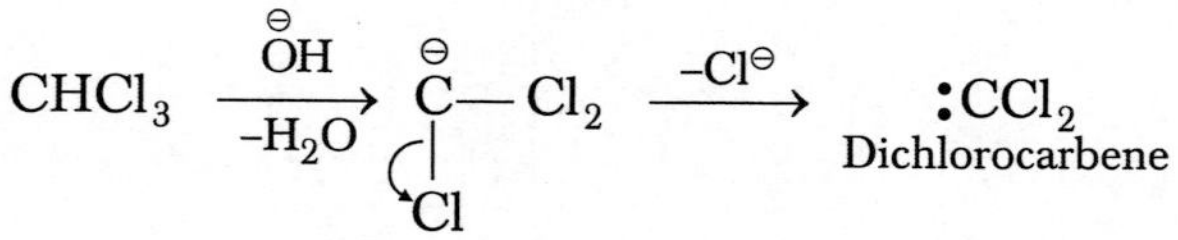

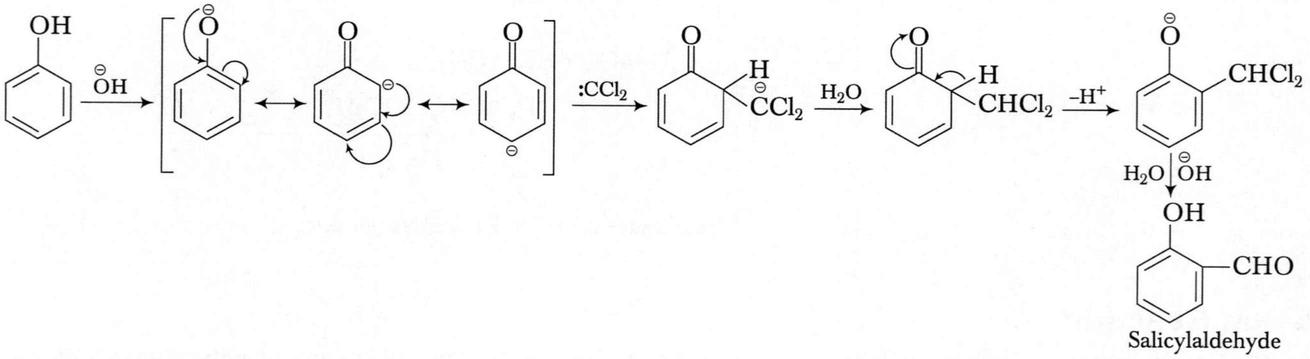

Reformatsky Reaction

The reaction of α-haloester (usually α-bromoesters) with carbonyl compounds in presence of zinc metal in an inert solvent, followed by hydrolysis to give β-hydroxyester is known as **Reformatsky reaction.**

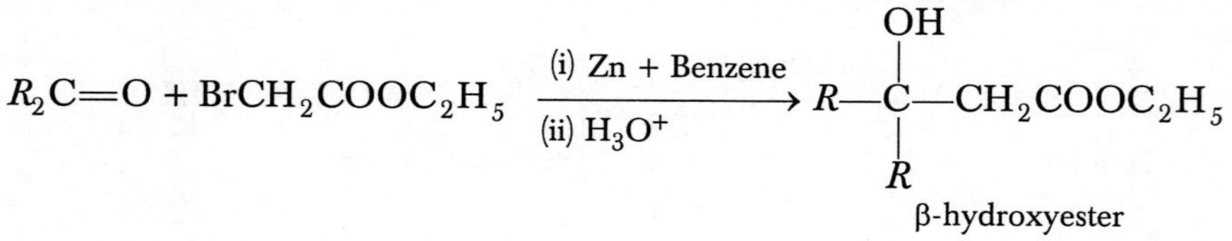

Mechanism

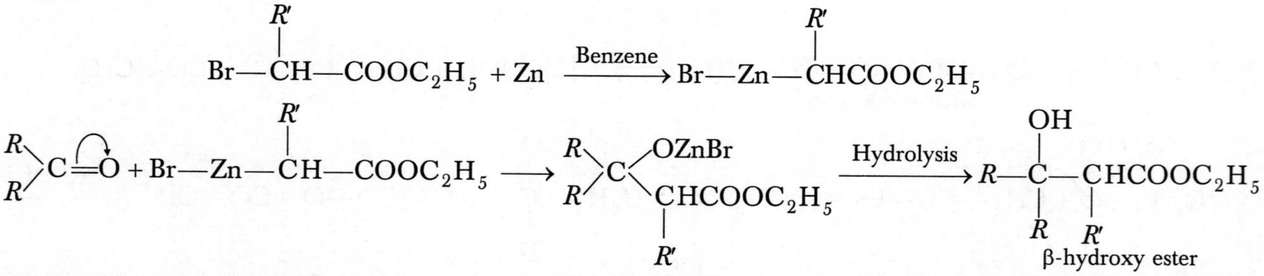

Note In case of sterically hindered carbonyl compounds (ketones), the reaction is not possible. Hence, same ester reacts to give β-ketoester.

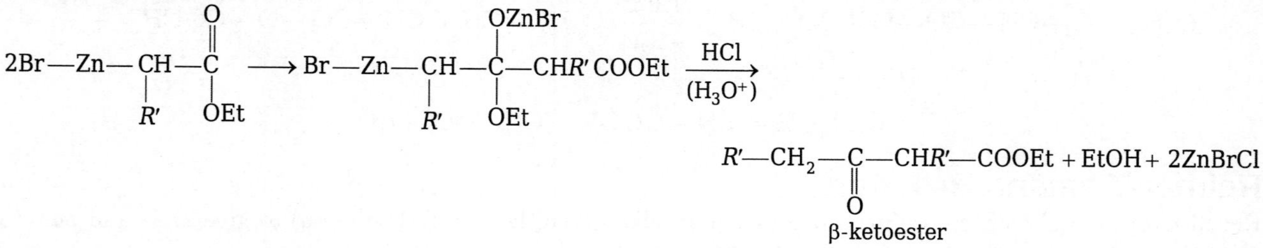

Diels-Alder Reaction

The 1, 4-addition of unsaturated molecule (dienophile) with a conjugated diene (diene) to give a six membered cyclic product. This reaction is called **Diels-Alder reaction**. Such reaction is also known as pericyclic reaction. It is a *syn* addition.

Examples

(i) 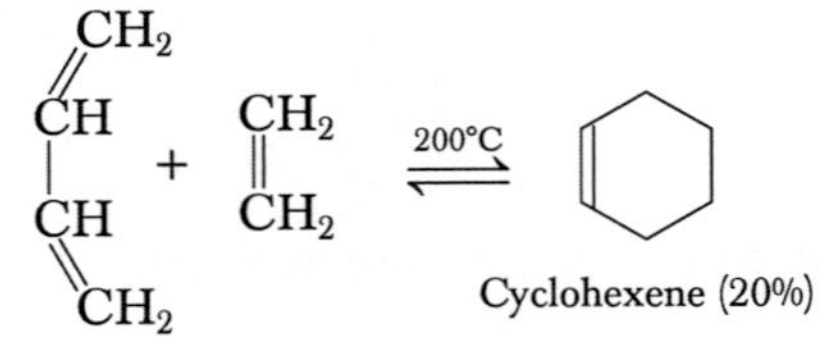

Cyclohexene (20%)

(ii) 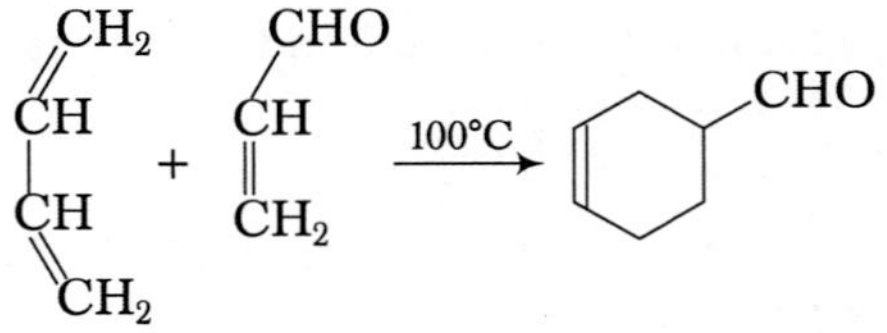

Dienophiles

The simplest unsubstituted alkene, *i.e.,* ethene makes a poor dienophile. Most reactive dienophile are those which possess 1 or 2 electronegative groups α to unsaturation.

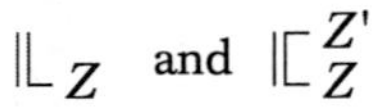

Z and *Z'* may be —CHO, —CO*R*, —COOH, —COO*R*, —COCl, —CN, $—NO_2$, —*X*, C═C, etc. Most reactive dienophile is tetracyano ethene.

Dienes

It may be conjugated diene or polyene or enyne or diynes. **Example**

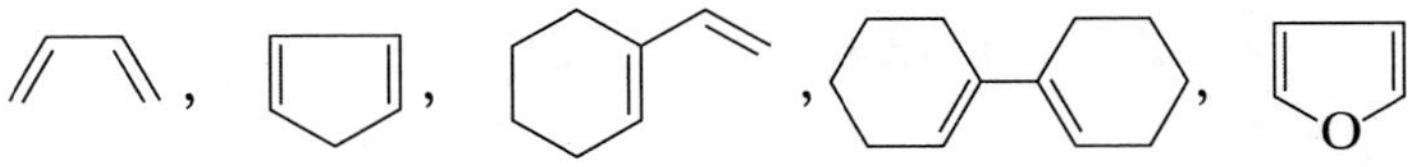

Note • When the electronegative group in a dienophile is C═C the dienophile can also act as a diene.

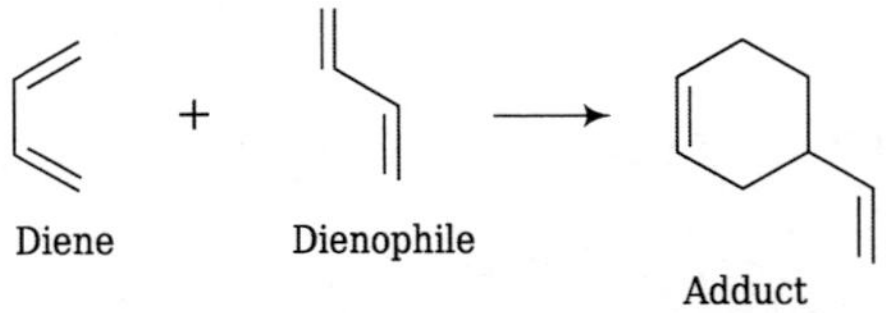

• An aromatic compound can act as a diene only when it has at least three benzene rings fused linearly. *e.g.,*

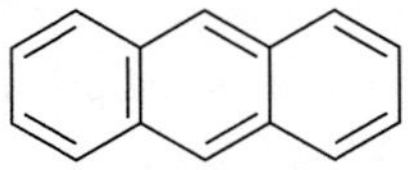

• Maleic anhydride and quinones are the most widely used dienophiles.

Mechanism

Browdly suggested three types of mechanism.

(a) Ionic mechanism

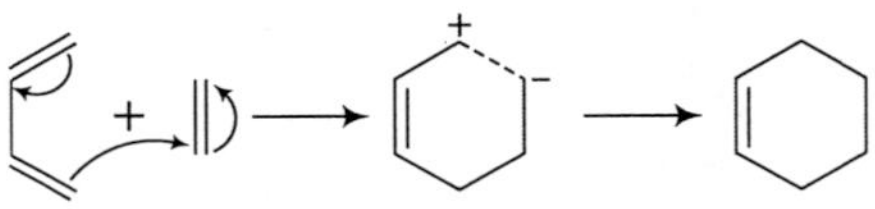

(b) Free radical mechanism

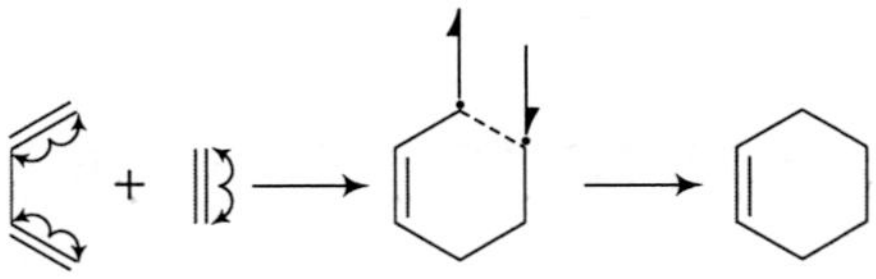

(c) Concerted mechanism

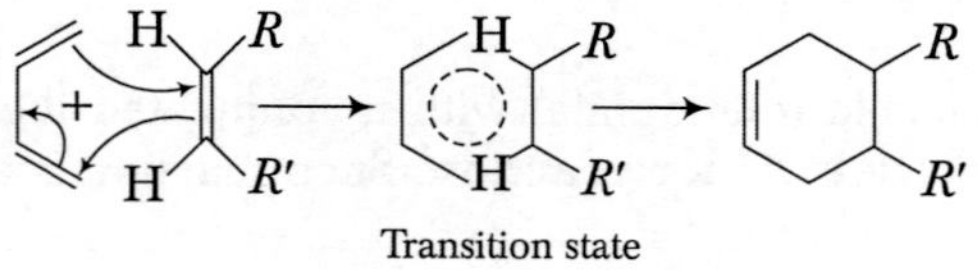

cis-addition occurs in this case.

In case of cyclic dienes two *cis*-addition, *i.e.*, exo and endo are possible.

Friedel-Crafts Reaction

The Friedel-Crafts reaction involves the introduction of an alkyl or an aryl or an acyl group into an aromatic ring in presence of a Lewis acid or a protonic acids as catalyst.

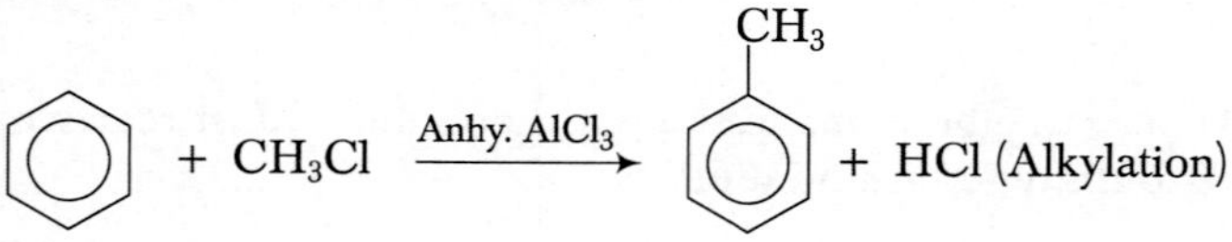

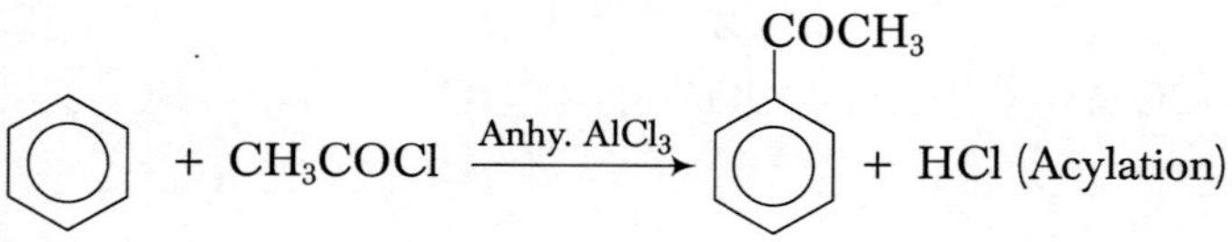

Mechanism

(a) **Alkylation**

$$R\text{—Cl} + AlCl_3 \rightleftharpoons AlCl_4^- + R^+$$

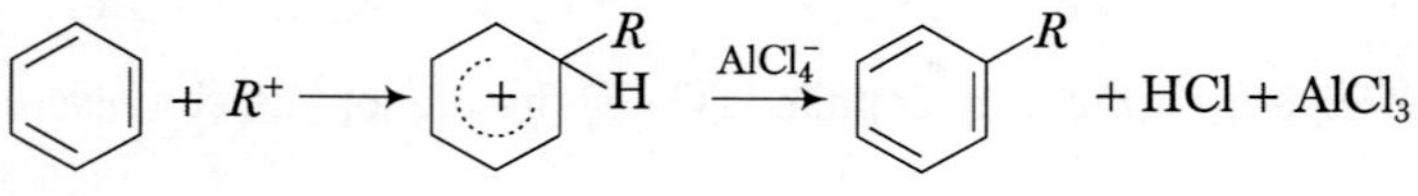

(b) **Acylation**

$$CH_3COCl + AlCl_3 \rightleftharpoons CH_3CO^+ + AlCl_4^-$$

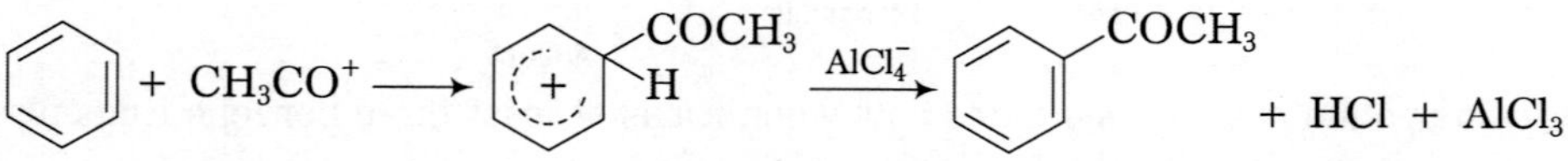

- In case of *n*-propyl chloride the major product will be isopropyl benzene (rearrangement).

$$CH_3CH_2CH_2Cl \overset{AlCl_3}{\rightleftharpoons} \underset{1^\circ\text{ carbocation}}{CH_3CH_2\overset{+}{C}H_2} + AlCl_4^-$$

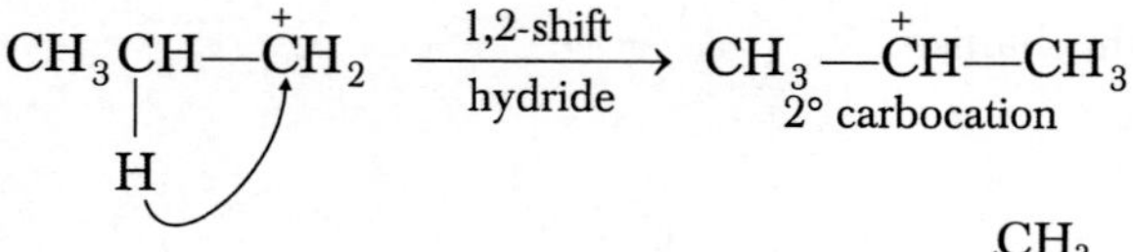

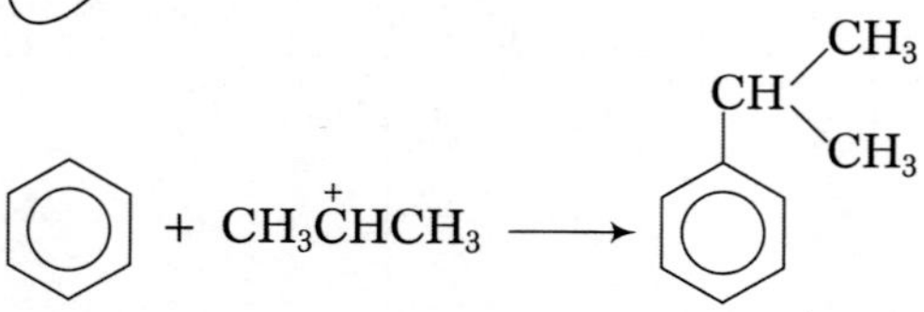

However, at low temperature *n*-propyl benzene is predominant and the proportion of isopropyl benzene increases with increase in temperature.

Wittig Reaction

It is a general method for the synthesis of alkenes. The reaction consists of the interaction of an aldehyde or ketone with triphenyl phosphene alkylidene $Ph_3P{=}CH_2$ or alkylidene triphenyl phosphorane (ylide) in which the carbonyl oxygen is replaced by an alkylidene.

$$Ph_3P{=}CH_2 + Ph_2C{=}O \longrightarrow Ph_2C{=}CH_2 + Ph_3P{=}O$$

$$Ph_3{=}CHR' + R_2C{=}O \longrightarrow R_2C{=}CHR' + Ph_3P{=}O$$

Mechanism

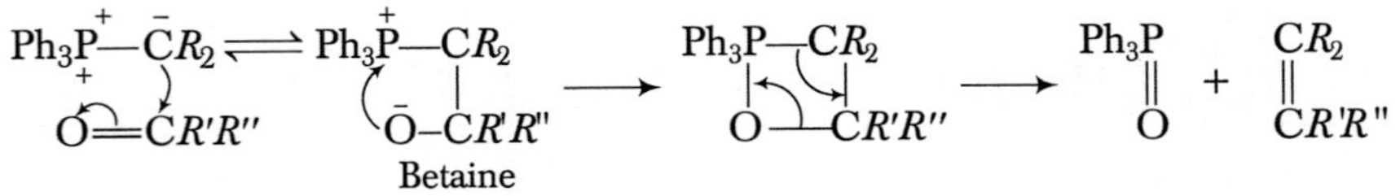

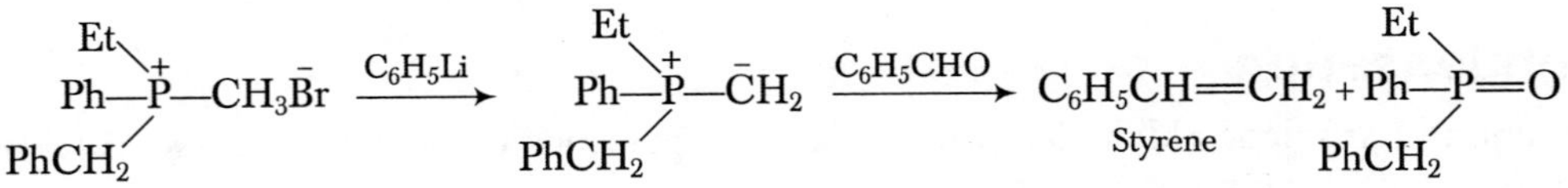

Note

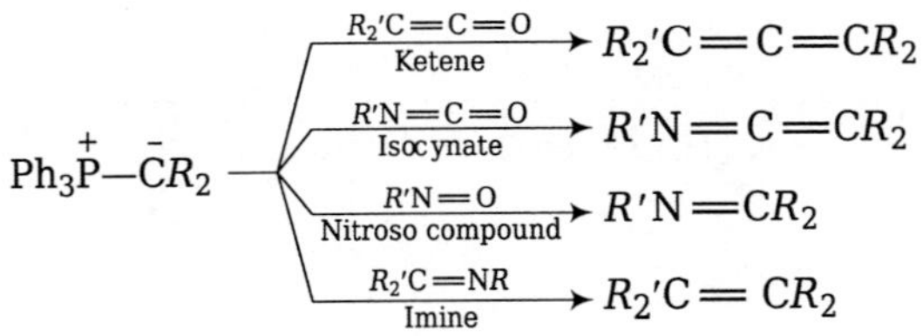

Robinson Annulations (Cyclization)

When a cyclic ketone is converted to another cyclic ketone with an additional six membered ring containing a double bond is known as **Robinson annulation**. It is often used for the synthesis of steroids and terpenes.

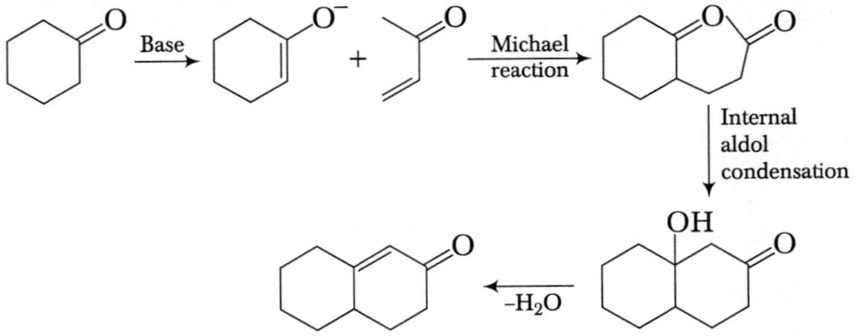

Ene Reaction

Ene reaction involves the addition of an olefin having an allylic hydrogen (ene) to a compound having a double bond (C=C, C=O, N=N, called the enophile) with the formation of a new σ-bond to the terminal carbon of the allyl group. This is followed by the 1,5-migration of the allylic hydrogen and subsequent change in the position of allylic double bond.

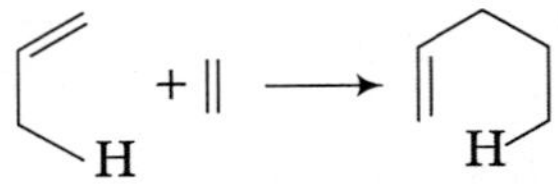

Mechanism

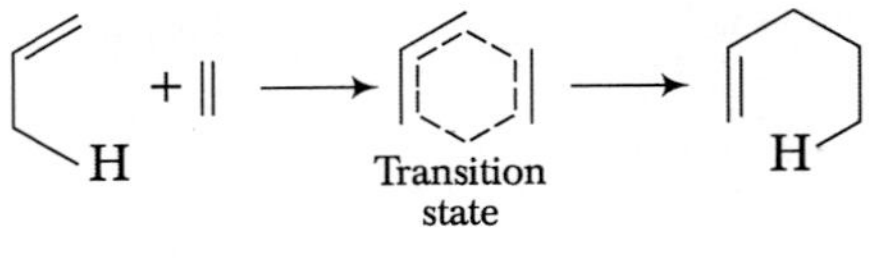

The reaction is reversible.

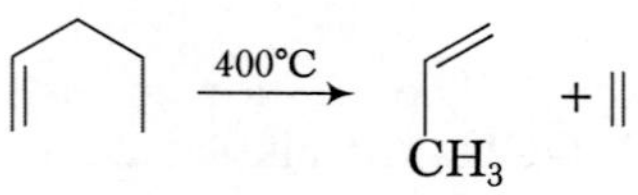

Intramolecular ene reaction is also possible.

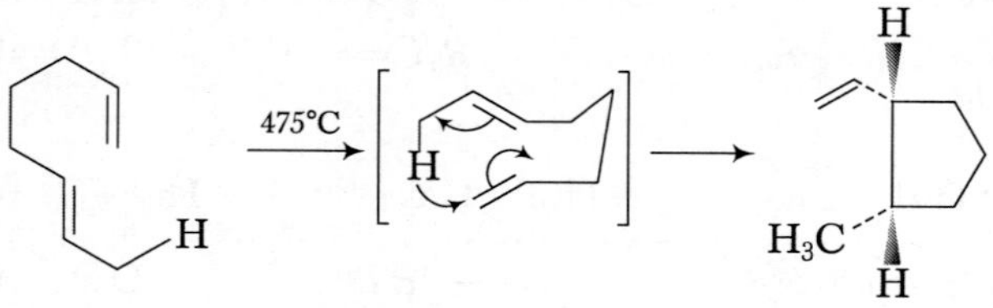

Benzoin Condensation

The self condensation of aromatic aldehydes (with no α-H) in presence of cyanide ions as a catalyst to α-hydroxy ketone (benzoin) is called benzoin condensation.

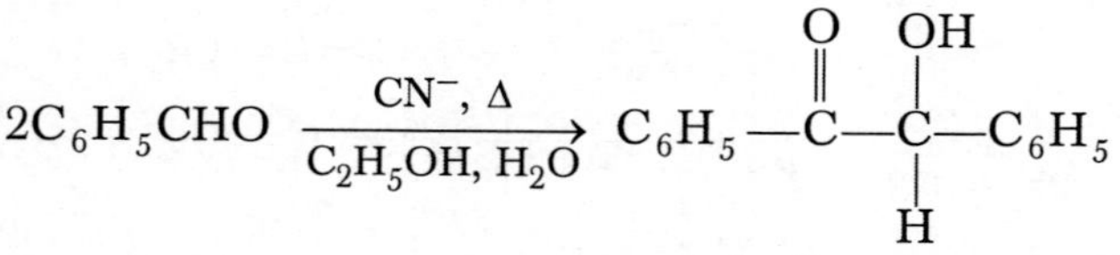

Benzoin

Mechanism

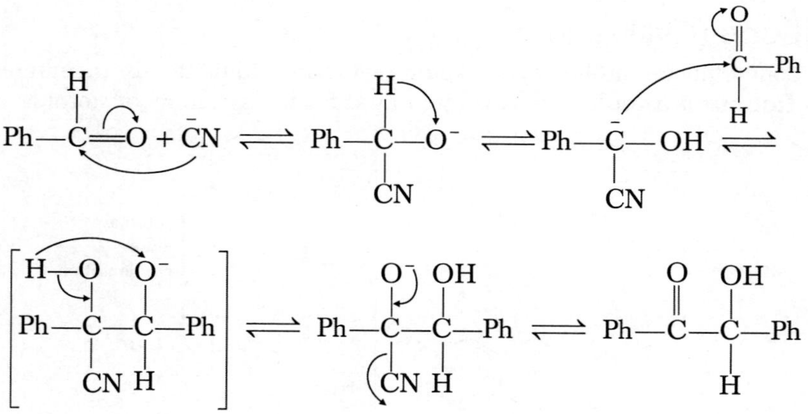

Clemmensen Reduction

The reduction in which carbonyl group of aldehyde and ketone convert into methylene group in the presence of conc. HCl and zinc amalgam is called **Clemmensen reduction.**

$$\underset{\text{Acetophenone}}{C_6H_5COCH_3} \xrightarrow[\text{Reflux}]{\text{Zn–Hg, HCl}} \underset{\text{Ethyl benzene}}{C_6H_5CH_2CH_3}$$

$$\underset{\text{Acetone}}{CH_3COCH_3} \xrightarrow[\text{Reflux}]{\text{Zn–Hg, HCl}} \underset{\text{Propane}}{CH_3CH_2CH_3}$$

Mechanism

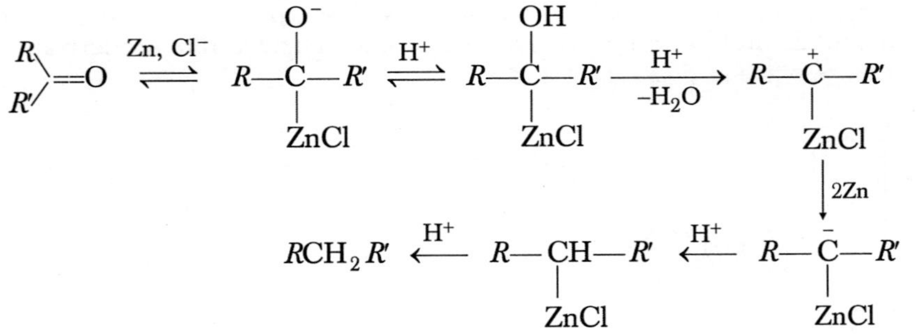

Wolff-Kishner Reduction

The reduction of carbonyl compound (aldehyde or ketone) to give alkane in presence of hydrazones semicarbazones or azines in presence of strong base like NaOH or C_2H_5ONa, is called **Wolff-Kishner reduction.**

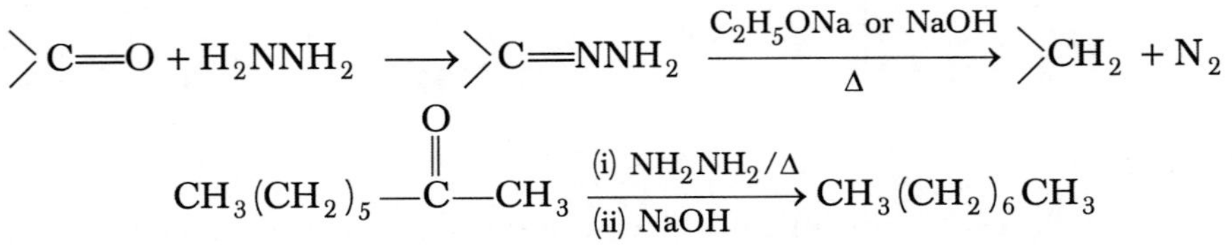

Mechanism

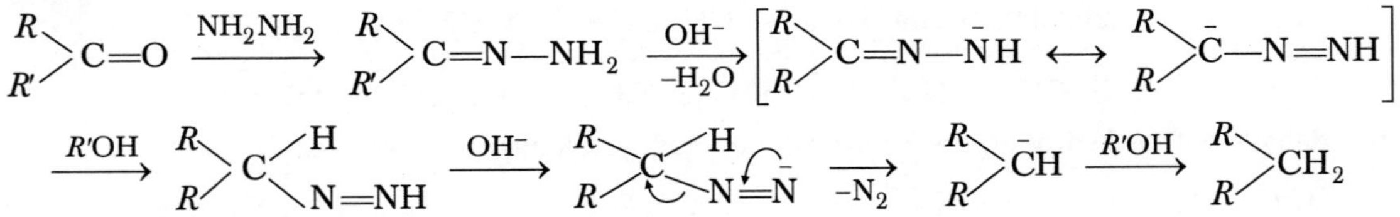

Meerwein Ponndorf-Verley Reduction

The reduction of aldehydes or ketones to the corresponding alcohols with aluminium alkoxides (aluminium isopropoxide) in isopropyl alcohol is known as Meerwein Ponndorf-Verley reduction. This is the revese of Oppenauer oxidation.

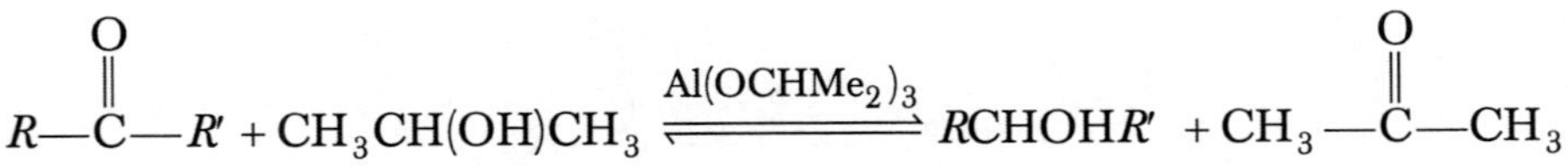

Mechanism

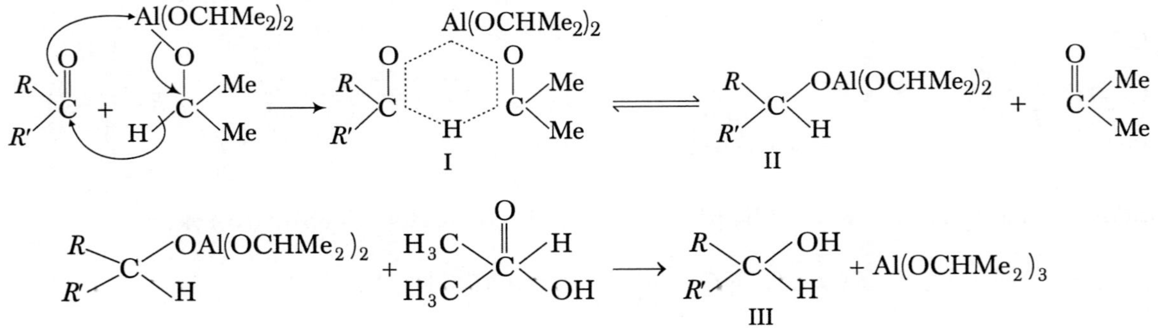

Birch Reduction

Reduction of aromatic rings by means of alkali metals such as sodium, potassium or lithium in liquid ammonia or amine in presence of ethanol as proton donor, to give mainly unconjugated dihydroderivatives is known as Birch reduction. The addition takes place at positions 1 and 4.

Example

(i) 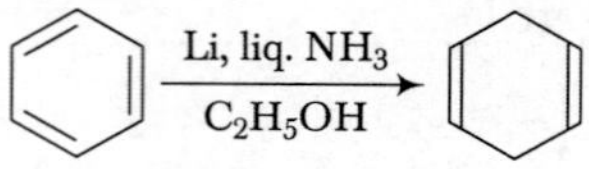

(ii) 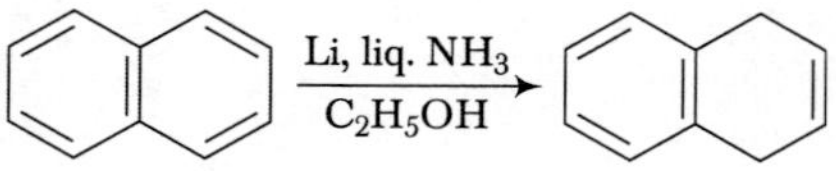

(iii) 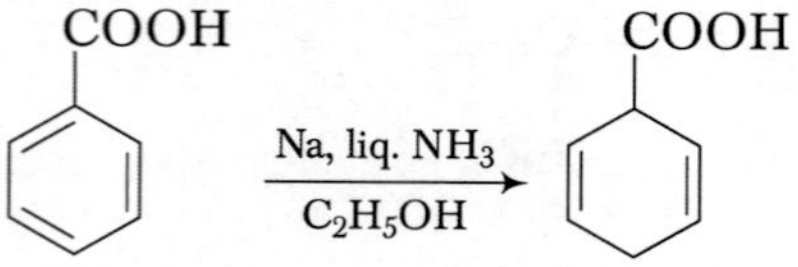

Mechanism

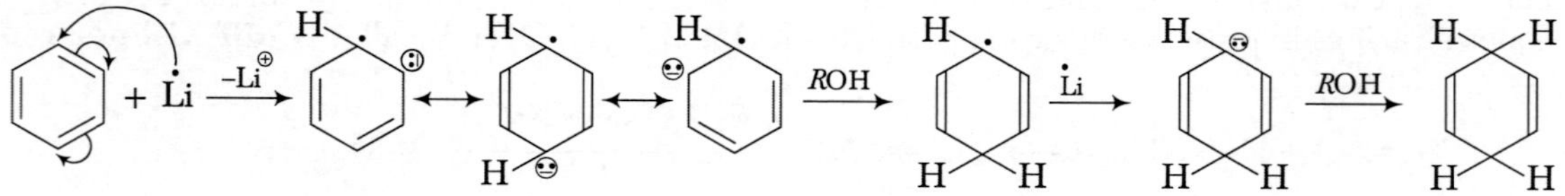

Cannizzaro Reaction

Aldehydes that do not have α-hydrogen, on treatment with concentrated aqueous alkali undergo self oxidation and reduction to give alcohol and the salt of the corresponding acid.

$$2HCHO + NaOH \xrightarrow{\Delta} CH_3OH + HCOONa$$

$$2C_6H_5CHO + NaOH \xrightarrow{\Delta} C_6H_5CH_2OH + C_6H_5COONa$$

Note • A few aldehyde with α-hydrogen are known which undergo Cannizzaro reaction.

$$\underset{\text{Dimethyl acetaldehyde}}{2(CH_3)_2CHCHO} + NaOH \xrightarrow{200°C} \underset{\text{2-methylpropanol-1}}{(CH_3)_2CHCH_2OH} + \underset{\text{Sodium-2-methyl propanoate}}{(CH_3)_2CHCOONa}$$

• If an alkoxide is used in the Cannizzaro reaction the product is an ester.

$$C_6H_5CHO \xrightarrow[C_6H_5CH_2OH]{C_6H_5CH_2ONa} C_6H_5COOCH_2C_6H_5$$

Mechanism

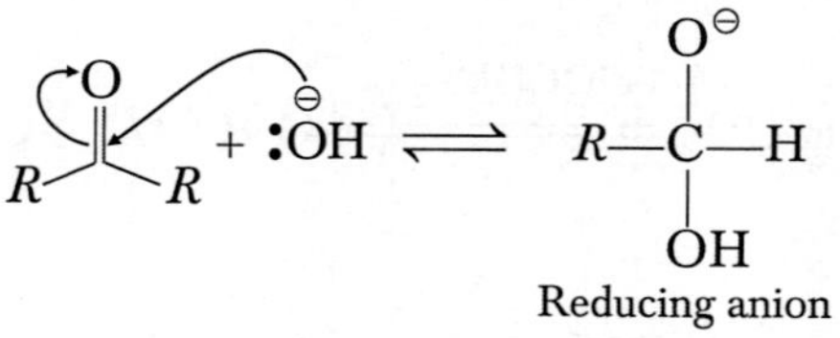

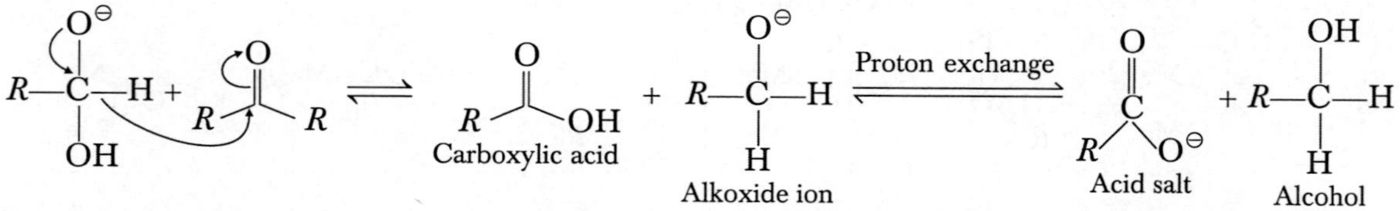

A mixture of two aldehydes having no α-hydrogen atom undergo **crossed Cannizzaro reaction.**

$$C_6H_5CHO + HCHO \xrightarrow[\Delta]{NaOH} C_6H_5CH_2OH + HCOONa$$

Glyoxal gives intramolecular Cannizzaro reaction.

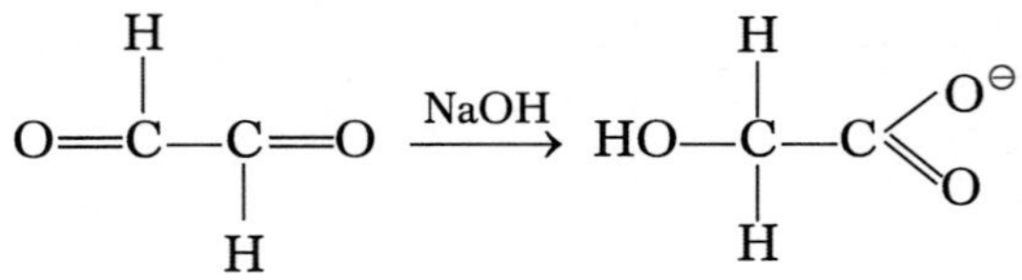

Oppenauer Oxidation

Oxidation of a secondary alcohol to give ketone by interchange of alkyl groups of acetone and 2° alcohol in presence of aluminium isopropoxide or aluminium *t*-butoxide and acetone is called **Oppenauer oxidation**.

$$\underset{2^\circ\text{ alcohol}}{R_2CHOH} + \underset{\text{Acetone}}{(CH_3)_2CO} \underset{}{\overset{Al(OCMe_3)_3}{\rightleftharpoons}} \underset{\text{Ketone}}{R_2CO} + \underset{2^\circ\text{ alcohol}}{CH_3CHOHCH_3}$$

Cyclohexanone Cyclohexanol

Mechanism

$$3R_2CHOH + Al(OCMe_3)_3 \rightleftharpoons (R_2CHO)_3Al + 3Me_3C(OH)$$

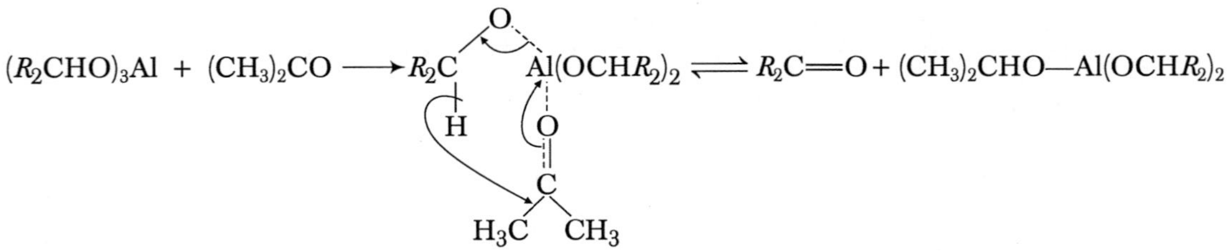

Mannich Reaction

The reactions involves the condensation of a compound containing at least one active hydrogen atom, formaldehyde and NH_3 or 1° or 2° amine in the form of its salt like NH_4Cl. The compound formed in this reaction is known as Mannich base. The catalyst is an acid or base.

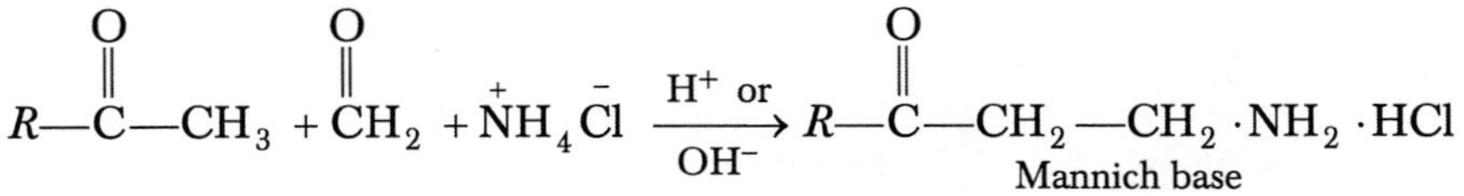

Mannich base

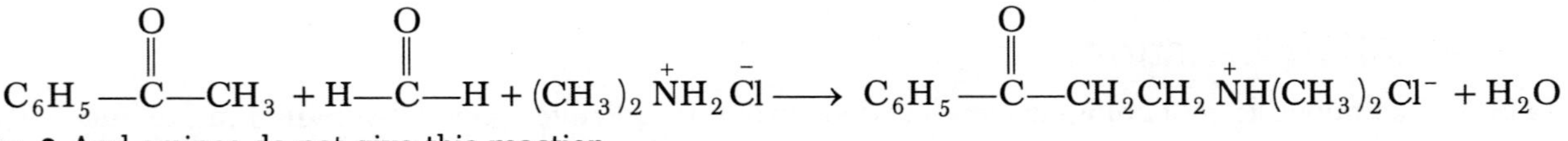

Note
- Aryl amines do not give this reaction.
- The amines may be primary or secondary but the most convenient are 2° amines since, they possess only one replaceable H-atom.
- The product with 1° amine is 2° amine (Mannich base) which further reacts to give a 3° amine.

Mechanism

Acid catalysed mechanism

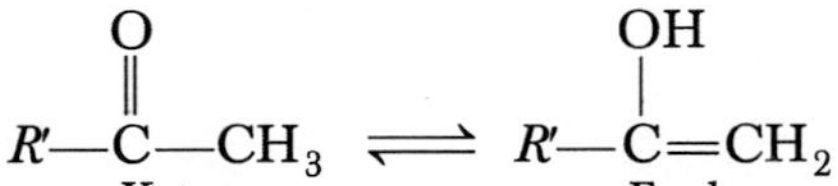

Keto Enol

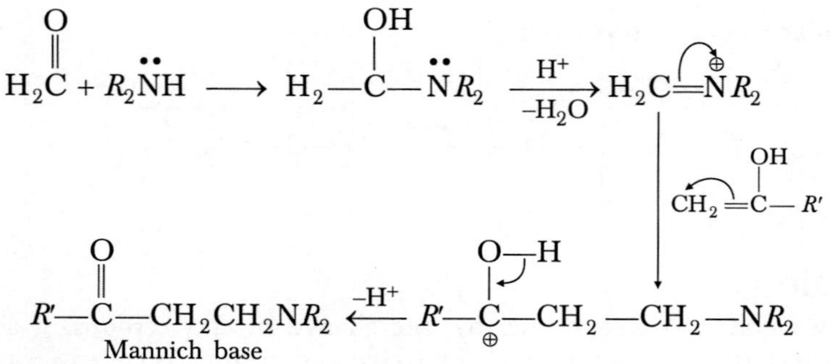

Base catalysed mechanism

$$RCOCH_3 \text{ or } RCOCH_2\text{—H} \xrightarrow[\text{or :B}]{EtO^-Na^+} RCO\ddot{C}H_2^- + EtOH$$

Carbanion   or H : B

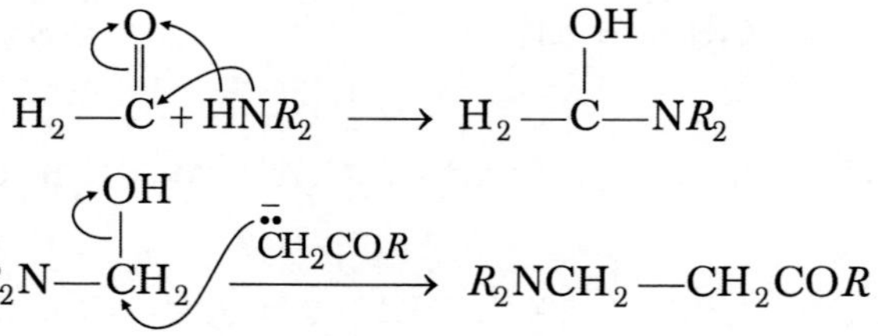

Most favourable mechanism is acid catalysed.

Note • With unsymmetrical ketone more highly alkylated α-carbon is substituted by the amino methyl group.

$$CH_3\text{—}\overset{O}{\overset{\|}{C}}\text{—}CH(CH_3)_2 + HCHO + R_2NH \longrightarrow CH_3COC(CH_3)_2CH_2NR_2$$

• 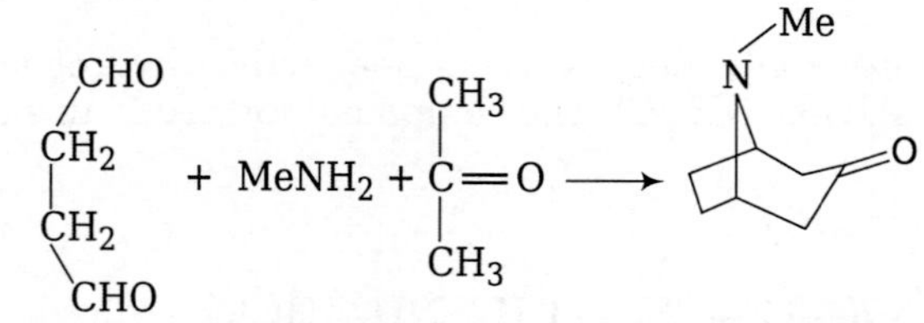

Succindialdehyde   Tropinone

Michael Addition Reaction

The addition of compounds containing active methylene group (or relatively acidic hydrogen) in presence of base catalyst to an activated oliphinic bond of the type $\text{—}\overset{|}{C}\text{=}\overset{|}{C}\text{—}X$ (X = electron withdrawing group) is called **Michael reaction**.

$$\underset{\text{Ethyl cinnamate}}{C_6H_5\text{—}CH\text{=}CH\text{—}COOC_2H_5} + \underset{\text{Malonic ester}}{H_2C(COOC_2H_5)_2} \xrightarrow{C_2H_5ONa} C_6H_5\text{—}\underset{CH(COOC_2H_5)_2}{\underset{|}{CH}}\text{—}CH_2\text{—}COOC_2H_5$$

Mechanism

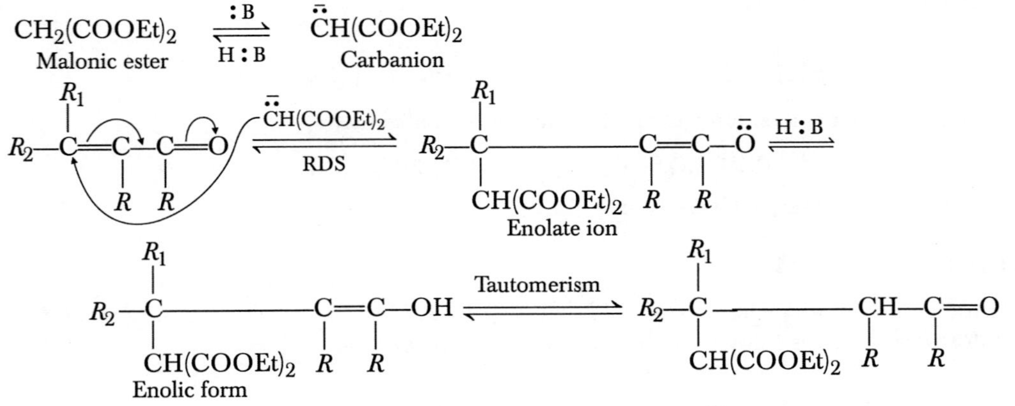

Note • The alkenes compounds (acceptor) may be $RCH{=}CH{-}\overset{O}{\overset{\|}{C}}H$, $RCH{=}CHCOR'$, $RC{=}CHCOOR'$, $R{-}CH{=}CHCN$, etc.

- The methylene compound (addendum) may be malonic ester, cyanoacetic ester, acetoacetic ester.
- Generally basic catalysts sodium ethoxide, or secondary amine (usually piperidine) are used in Michael reaction.

- Compounds containing two double bonds conjugated with a carbonyl group react with active methylene compounds to give 1,6-addition products. Thus, methyl vinylacrylate condenses with dimethyl malonate as follows

$$CH_2{=}CH{-}CH{=}CH{-}\overset{O}{\overset{\|}{C}}{-}OCH_3 + CH_2(COOCH_3)_2$$

$$\xrightarrow{NaOC_2H_5} (CH_3OOC)_2CHCH_2CH_2CH{=}CH{-}\overset{O}{\overset{\|}{C}}{-}OCH_3$$

Rearrangement Reactions

Hofmann Rearrangement

The conversion of an amide to an amine with one carbon atom less by the action of alkaline hypohalite or bromine in alkali is known as **Hofmann rearrangement**.

$$RCONH_2 + Br_2 + 4KOH \longrightarrow RNH_2 + 2KBr + K_2CO_3 + 2H_2O$$

Mechanism

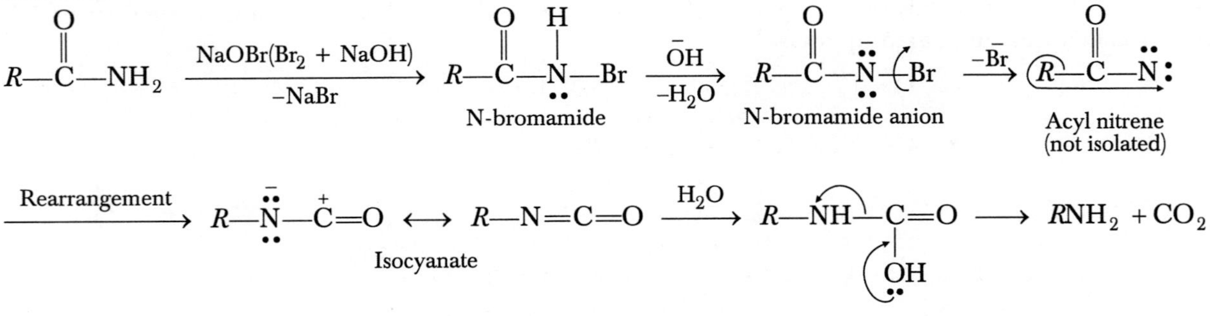

$$CO_2 + 2NaOH \longrightarrow Na_2CO_3 + H_2O$$

Note • The possibility of the formation of acyl nitrine has been rejected because it would react with water to give hydroxmic acid which has not be detected.

$$R\text{—}\overset{\overset{\displaystyle O}{\|}}{C}\text{—}\ddot{N}\colon + H_2O \longrightarrow R\text{—}\overset{\overset{\displaystyle O}{\|}}{C}\text{—NHOH (Hydroxmic acid)}$$

• If R is chiral asymmetric, then it migrates with unchanged configuration.

$$CH_3\overset{*}{C}H(C_6H_5)CONH_2 \longrightarrow CH_3\overset{*}{C}H(C_6H_5)NH_2$$

• The rearrangement is sterospecific in nature.

Curtius Rearrangement

Thermal or photochemical rearrangement of acid azides (acyl azides) to isocyanates in presence of inert solvents like benzene, chloroform, etc., is known as **Curtius rearrangement.**

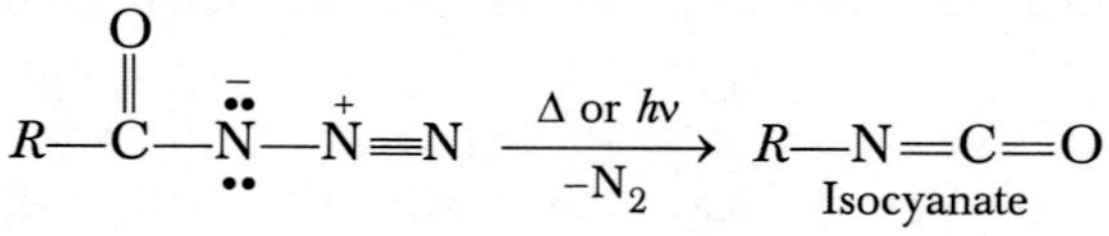

$$R\text{—N=C=O} \xrightarrow{H_3O^+} RNH_2 + CO_2$$

But, if the reaction is carried out in alcoholic or aqueous medium, the isocyanate reacts further to give urethane, substituted urea or amine.

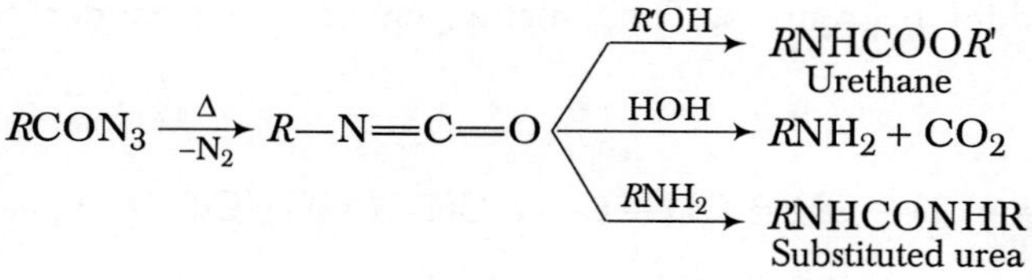

Mechanism

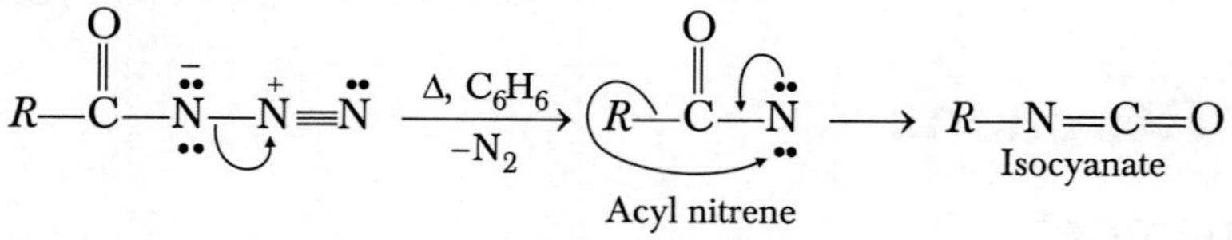

Note The essential difference between the Curtius and Hofmann rearrangement is that isocyanate can be isolable in Curtius but not in Hofmann. In Hofmann rearrangement, base is present and the isocyanate cannot survive.

Lossen Rearrangement

The thermal, acid or base catalysed conversion of hydroxamic acids and their *o*-acyl and *o*-aroyl derivatives to isocyanate is called **Lossen rearrangement.**

$$R\text{—}\overset{\overset{\displaystyle O}{\|}}{C}\text{—NHOH} \xrightarrow[\text{or } \Delta]{^{\ominus}OH \text{ or } H^{\oplus}} R\text{—N=C=O} \xrightarrow{H_2O/\Delta} R\text{—}NH_2$$

$$R\text{—}\overset{\overset{\displaystyle O}{\|}}{C}\text{—NH—O—}\overset{\overset{\displaystyle O}{\|}}{C}\text{—}R' \xrightarrow[\text{or } \Delta]{^{\ominus}OH \text{ or } H^{\oplus}} R\text{—N=C=O} \xrightarrow{H_2O} R\text{—}NH_2$$

Mechanism

Base-catalysed mechanism

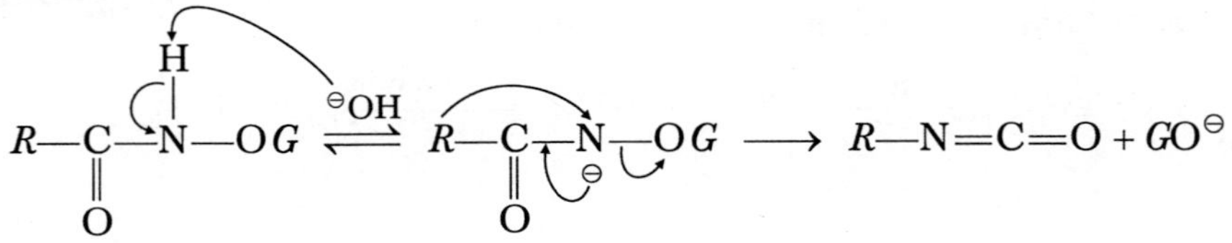

(where, G = H, COR, COAr)

Acid-catalysed mechanism

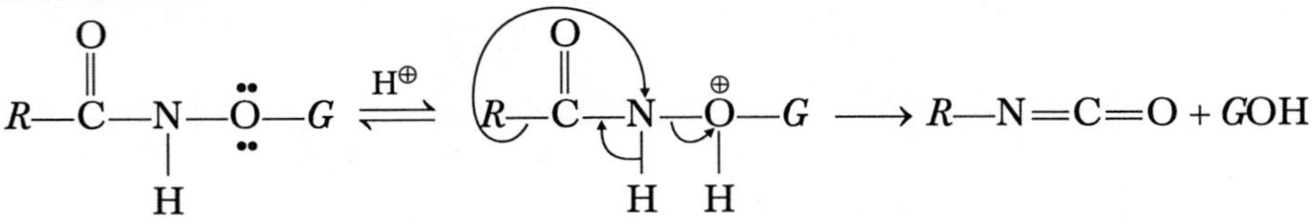

Schmidt Rearrangement

The addition of hydrazoic acid to carboxylic acids, aldehydes and ketones in presence of H_2SO_4 gives primary amine cyanide and amide respectively is known as **Schmidt rearrangement**.

$$\underset{\text{Carboxylic acids}}{RCOOH} + N_3H \xrightarrow{H^{\oplus}} \underset{\text{Isocyanate}}{R—N{=}C{=}O} \xrightarrow{H_2O} \underset{\text{Amine}}{RNH_2} + CO_2$$

$$\underset{\text{Aldehyde}}{RCHO} + N_3H \xrightarrow{H^{\oplus}} RNHCHO + \underset{\text{Cyanide}}{RCN} + N_2\uparrow$$

$$\underset{\text{Ketone}}{R—\underset{\underset{O}{\|}}{C}—R'} + N_3H \xrightarrow{H^{\oplus}} \underset{\text{Amide}}{R—\underset{\underset{O}{\|}}{C}—NH—R'}$$

The most common is the reaction with carboxylic acids. Sulphuric acid is the most common catalyst but Lewis acids have also been used.

Mechanism

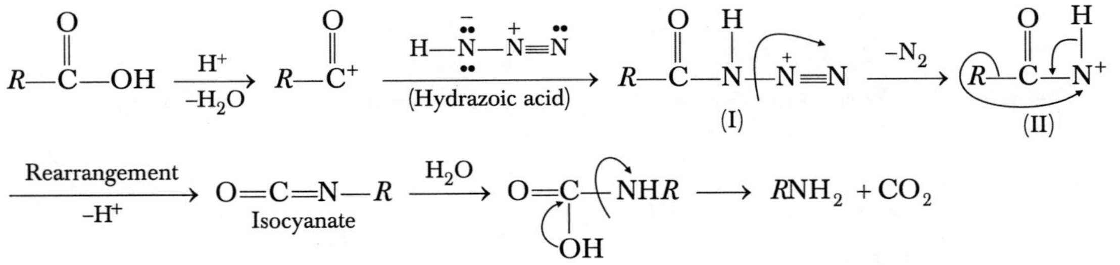

The acid which do not form acyl cation react to the protonated acid on heating. The mechanism in that case is given as,

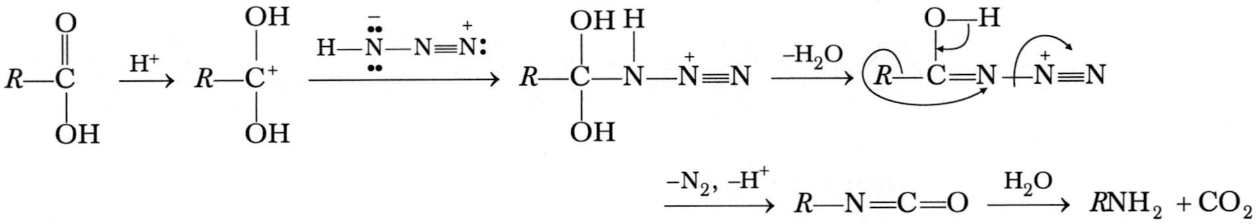

Beckmann Rearrangement

The acid-catalysed conversion of ketoximes to N-substituted amides in which the alkyl or aryl group attached to carbon migrates to nitrogen is known as **Beckmann rearrangement**.

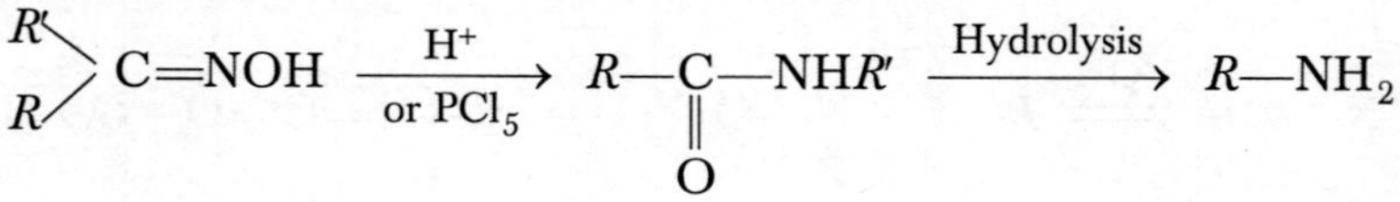

Mechanism

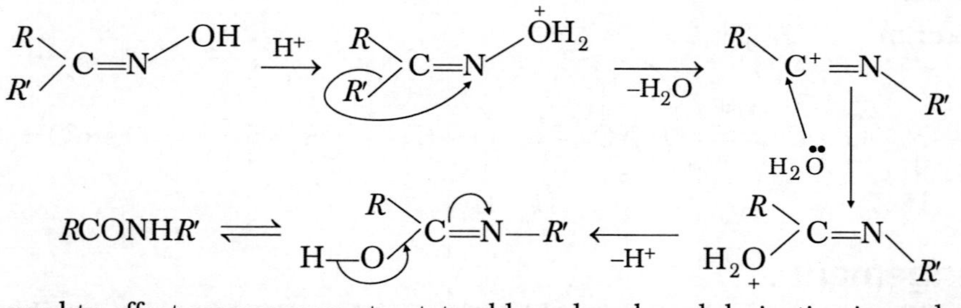

- When PCl_5 is used to effect rearrangement, a tetrachlorophosphonyl derivative is produced first.

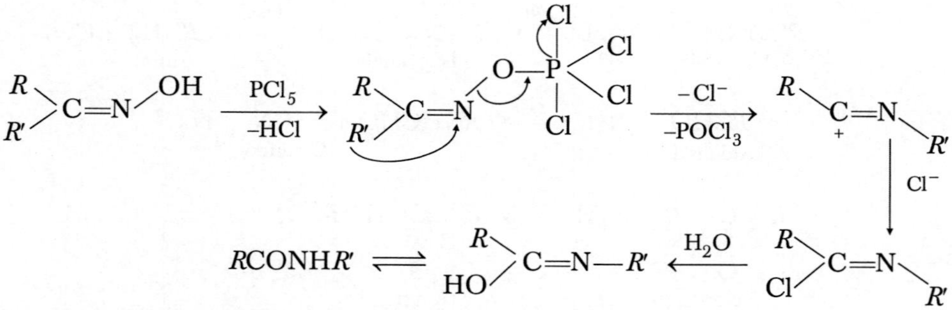

- The chiral groups migrate intramolecularly with retention of configuration.

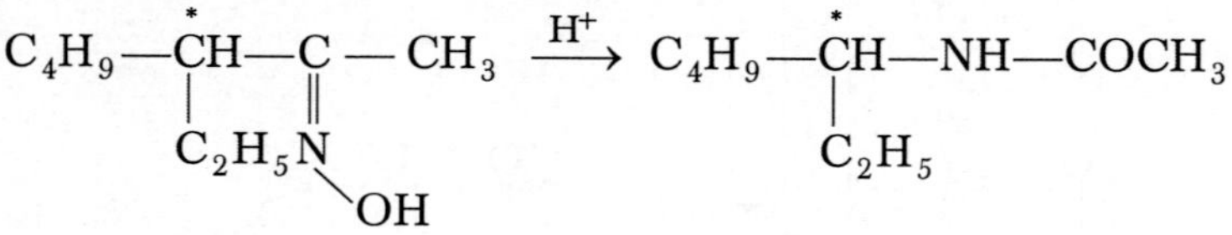

- The rearrangement is highly stereospecific, *i.e.*, the group anti to the oxime hydroxyl group always migrates regardless of relative migratory aptitude of the two groups.

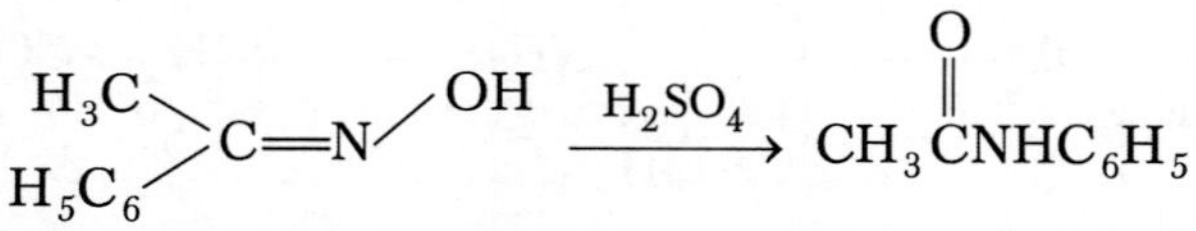

- Not only the oximes but also some of their esters and ethers undergo Beckmann rearrangement.

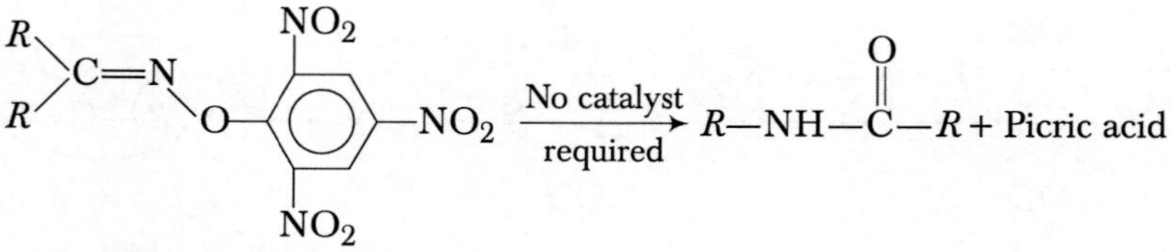

Ketoxime of picryl ether

Fries Rearrangement

The rearrangement in which phenolic esters on heating with aluminium chloride (Lewis acid) give *ortho* and *para* acyl phenol, is called **Fries rearrangement**.

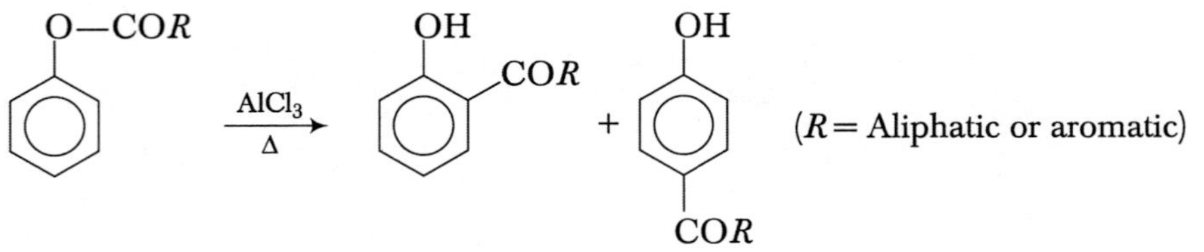

In general low temperature favours *para* product whereas high temperature *ortho* product.

Mechanism

Intermolecular mechanism

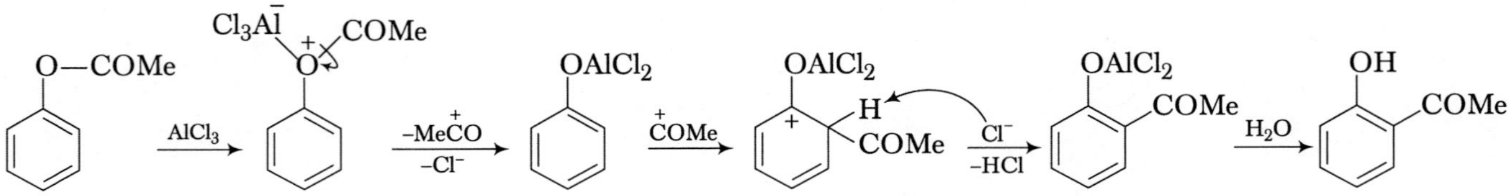

Similar attack on *para* position gives *para* isomer.

Intramolecular mechanism or concerted mechanism

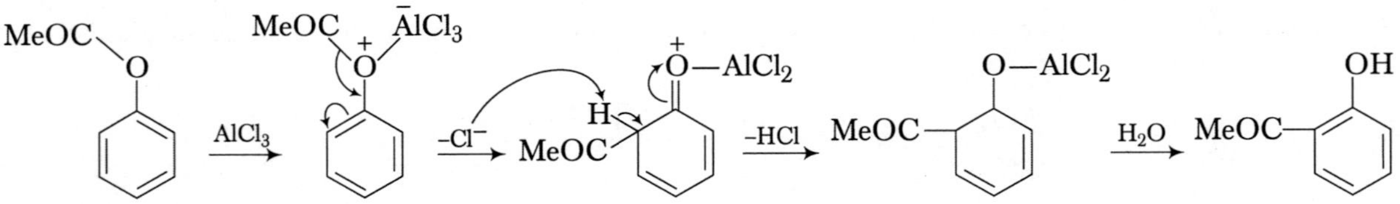

Claisen Rearrangement

Rearrangement of allyl aryl ethers to *o*- or *p*- allyl phenols is an example of sigmatropic rearrangement and known as **Claisen rearrangement**. The allyl group migrates from oxygen to the ring preferably at *o*-position.

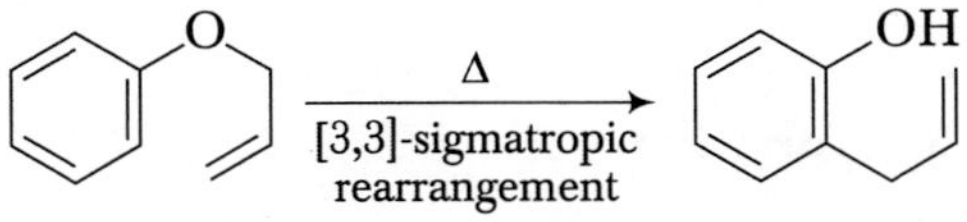

If the *o*-positions are already occupied the migration occurs at *p*-position.

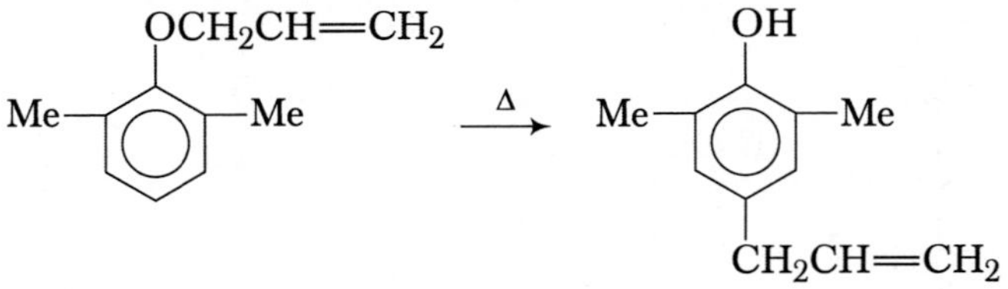

Mechanism

The Claisen rearrangement mechanism is believed to be intramolecular concerted pericyclic [3, 3] sigmatropic rearrangement *via* a six membered cyclic transition state.

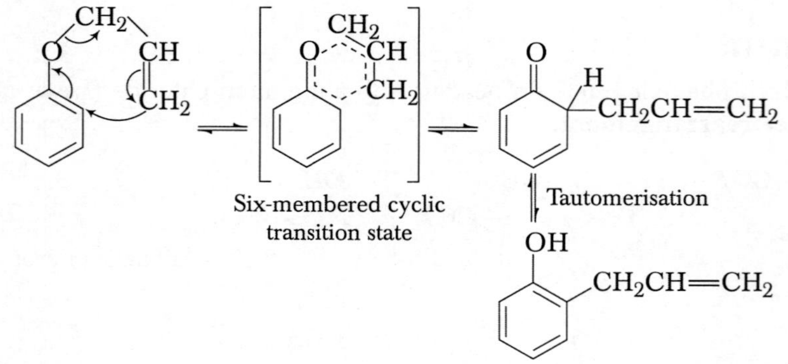

- ^{14}C labelling experiments shows that the position of the ^{14}C atom in the allyl group is inverted during migration to *o*-position.

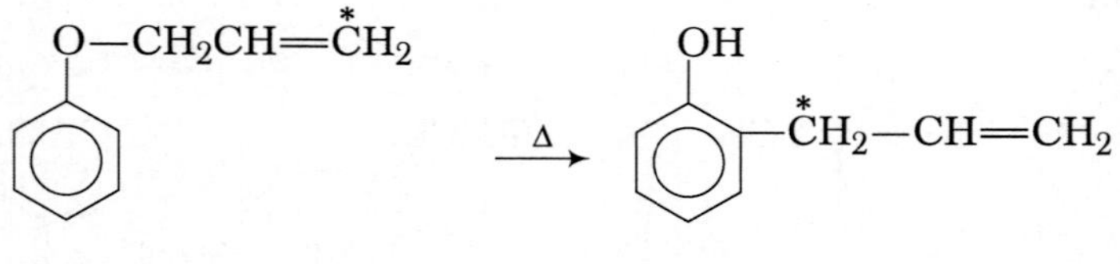

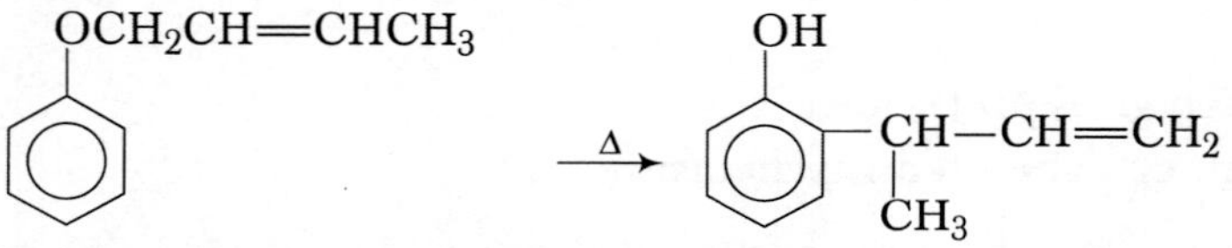

- Claisen rearrangement is sterospecific with respect to the = bond present in the initial allylic alcohol.

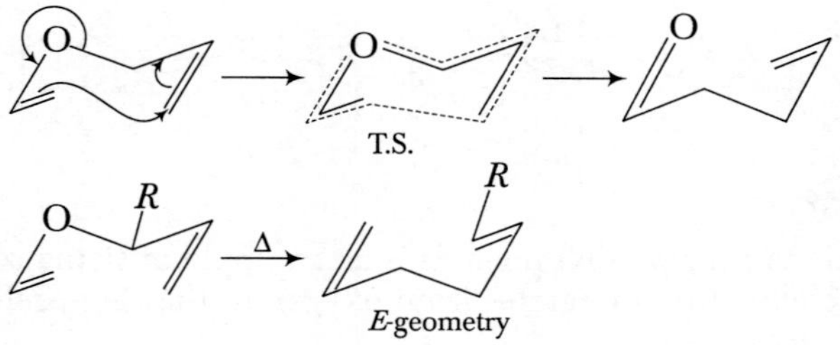

Pinacol-Pinacolone Rearrangement

The acid catalysed rearrangement in which *vicinal* 1,2-diol is converted into ketone or aldehyde with elimination of water is called **Pinacol-Pinacolone rearrangement**. One of the step of this reaction is rearrangement.

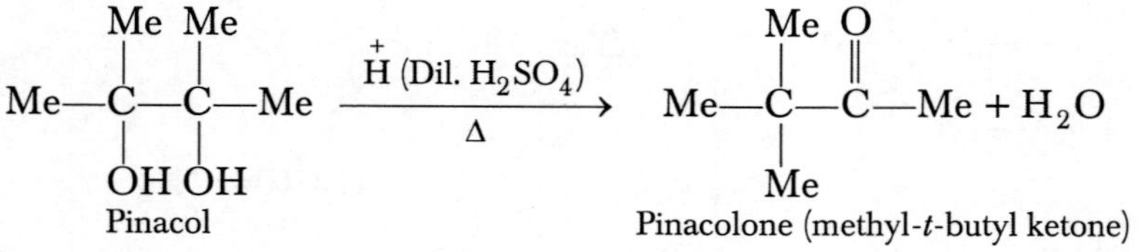

Mechanism

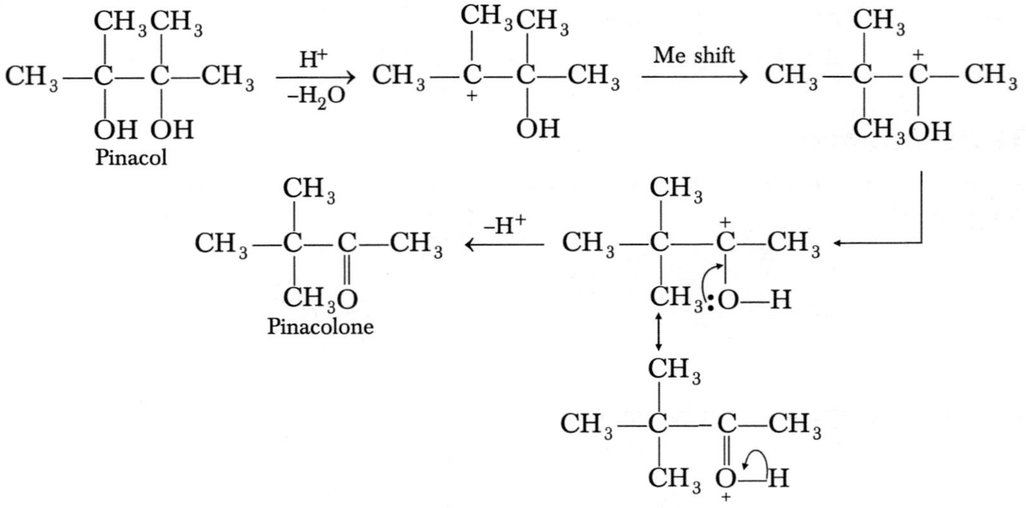

Features of pinacol-pinacolone rearrangement

(a) When two OH groups are different then OH group will be removed which produces more stable carbocation.

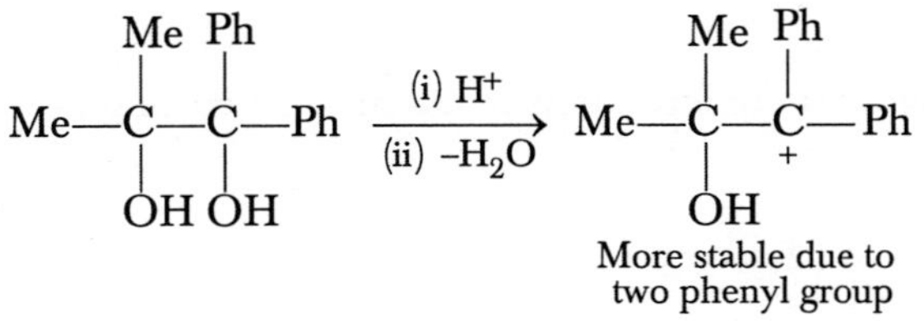

(b) The migrating group in the pinacols may be alkyl, aryl or even H-atom. H-atom may migrate in preference to *R* or Ar.

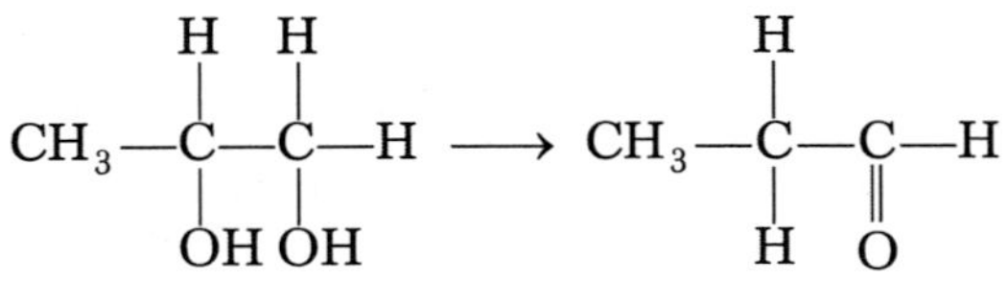

However, H-atom does not always preferentially migrate.

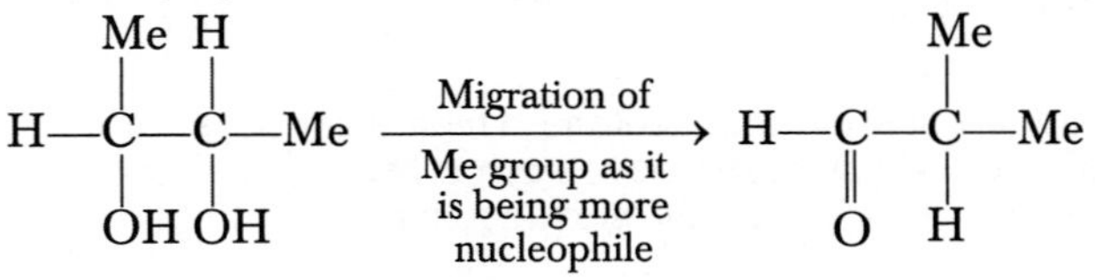

(c) When each C-atom of glycol has an aryl and alkyl group, then more nucleophilic aryl group migrates.

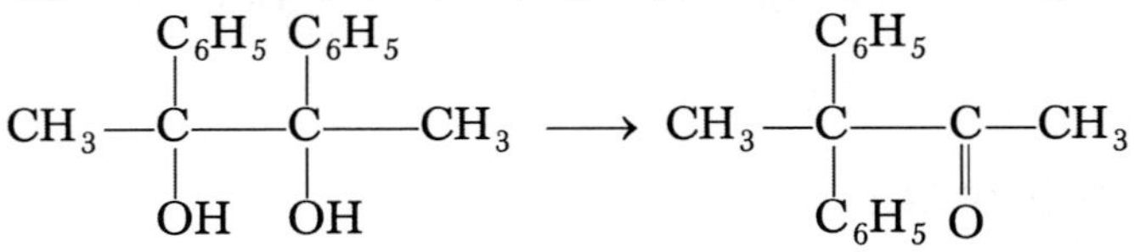

(d) When one C-atom of glycol has two aryl groups and the other two alkyl groups, then the alkyl group migrates to the greater stability of its carbonium ion.

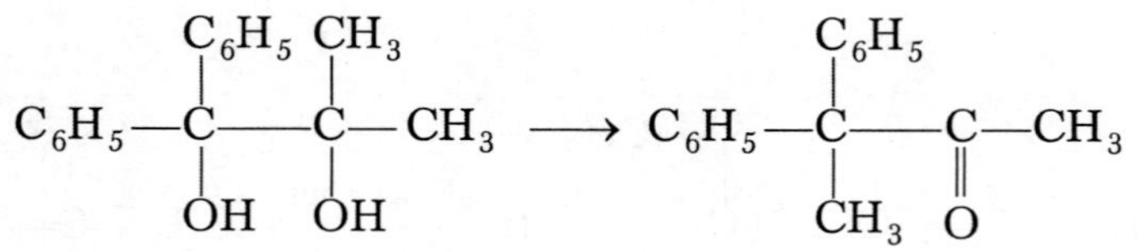

Favorskii Rearrangement

The reaction of α-haloketones (chloro and bromo) with alkoxide ion to give a rearranged esters is known as **Favorskii rearrangement.**

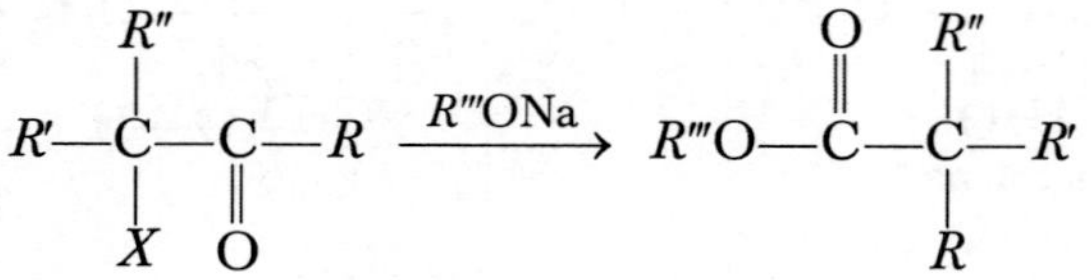

Cyclo α-haloketone gives an ester with contraction of ring.

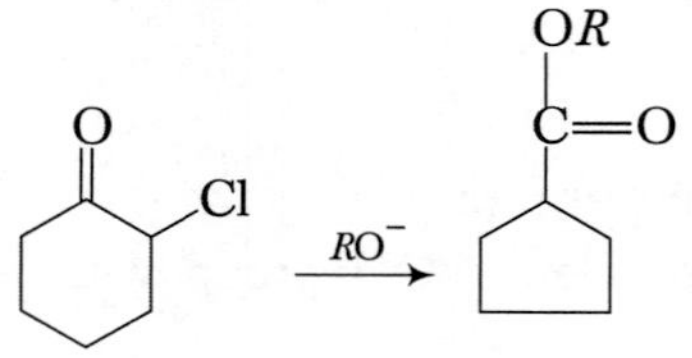

Mechanism

The most acceptable mechanism involves the formation of a 3-membered ring as an intermediate.

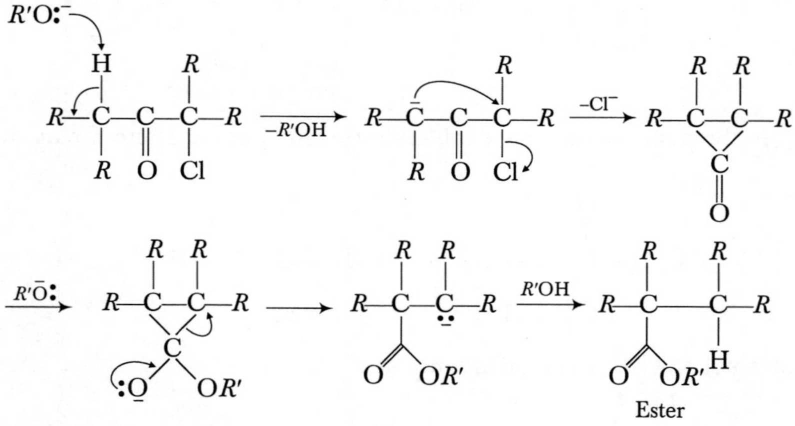

Note Favorskii rearrangement is undergone by a haloketone which must have an α-H-atom on the other side of the carbonyl group. However, ketones which do not have such a hydrogen also undergoes rearrangement to give a similar product. This is called the quasi Favorskii rearrangement.

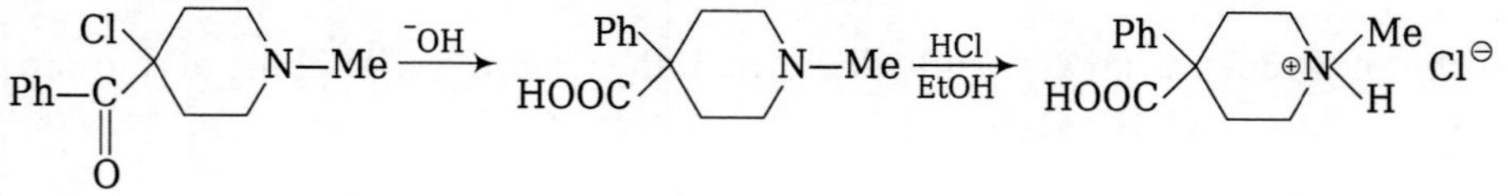

Baeyer-Villiger Rearrangement

It is a carbon to oxygen rearrangement. The treatment of ketones with peracids (RCO_3H) or hydrogen peroxide gives esters by insertion of oxygen. The reaction is called **Baeyer Villiger rearrangement** or **Baeyer Villiger oxidation.**

It is an example of nucleophilic rearrangement in which an alkyl or aryl group migrates along with its bond pair of electrons to an electron deficient oxygen atom.

The reaction is a method of conversion of a cyclic ketone into a lactone or an open chain ketone into an ester in presence of peracids such as perbenzoic acid, peracetic acid, peroxytrifluoro acetic acid, permonosulphuric acid, performic acid, *m*-chloroperbenzoic acid (*m*-CPBA).

$$R'-\overset{\overset{\displaystyle O}{\|}}{C}-R \xrightarrow{CF_3COOOH} R'-\overset{\overset{\displaystyle O}{\|}}{C}-OR + CF_3COOH$$

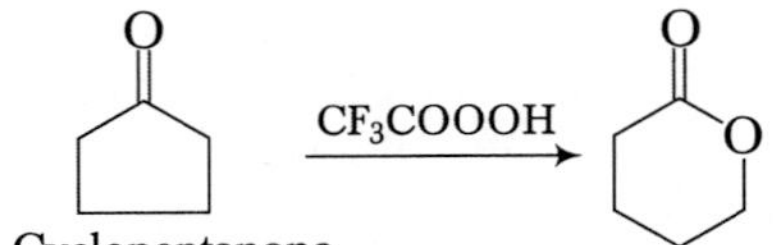

Cyclopentanone Lactone

Note Peroxytrifluoro acetic acid is the most reactive per acid because trifluoro acetate ion is a good leaving group.

Mechanism

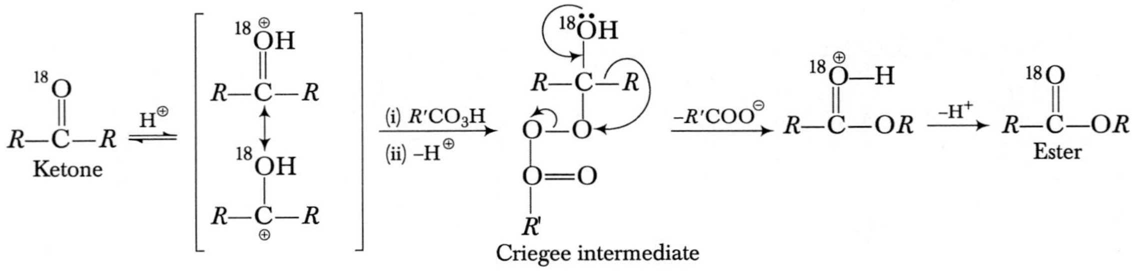

- During the mechanism an alkyl group migrates from carbon to oxygen.
- During the oxidation of an unsymmetrical ketone the migrating group will always be that which is more nucleophilic. Thus, the migrating aptitude among the alkyl group is $T > S > P >$ methyl.
- Aryl group migrates in preference to methyl and primary alkyl group. In aryl series migration is facilitated by electron releasing *para* substituents, *i.e.*,

$$p\text{-}CH_3OC_6H_4 > C_6H_5 > p\text{-}O_2NC_6H_4$$

Example Phenyl-*p*-nitrophenyl ketone gives only phenyl-*p*-nitrobenzoate by migration of phenyl group.

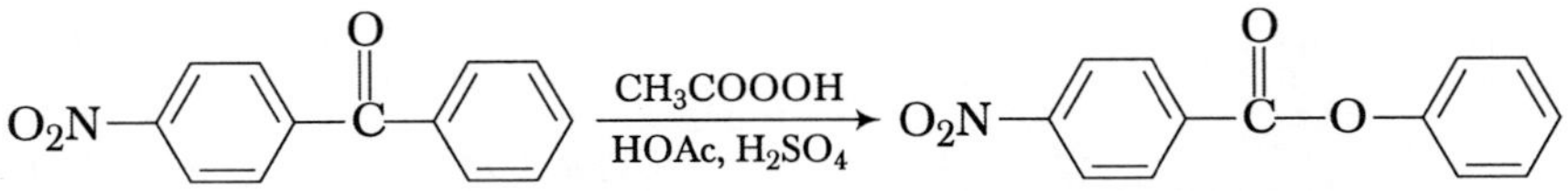

Like other rearrangement involving electron deficient species the Baeyer-Villiger reaction also takes place with the retention of configuration in migrating group.

$$C_6H_5-\overset{*}{C}H(CH_3)-COCH_3 \xrightarrow{RCOOOH} C_6H_5-\overset{*}{C}H(CH_3)-O-COCH_3$$

Optically active Optically active

Exercise 1

(For Part 'B')

1. 1-bromo-3-chlorocyclobutane when treated with two equivalents of Na, in the presence of ether which of the following will be formed?

(a) 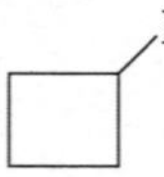 (b) 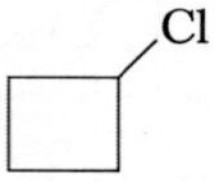 (c) 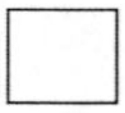 (d) 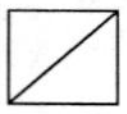

2 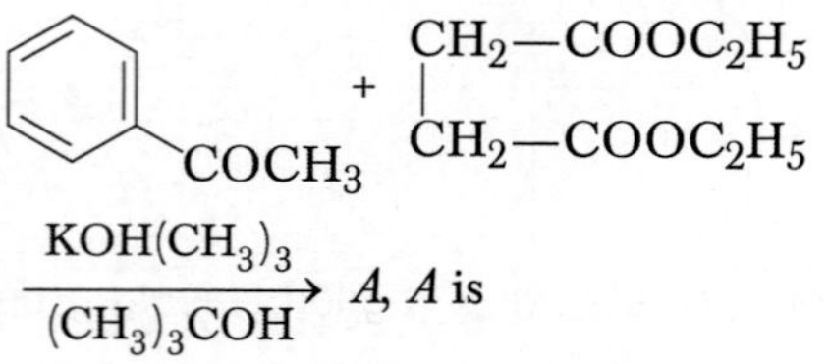

(a) 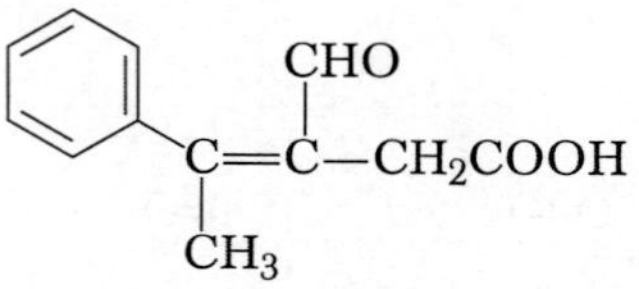

(b) 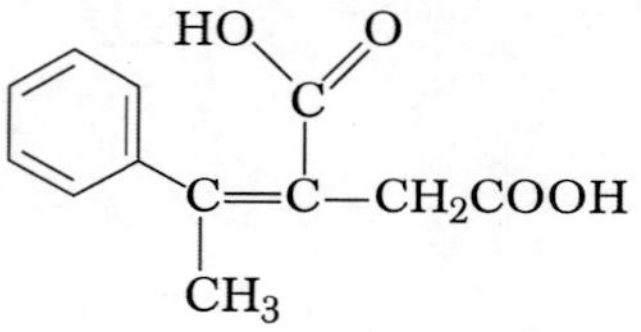

(c) 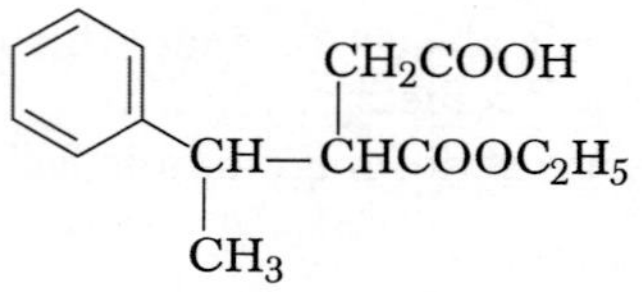

(d) 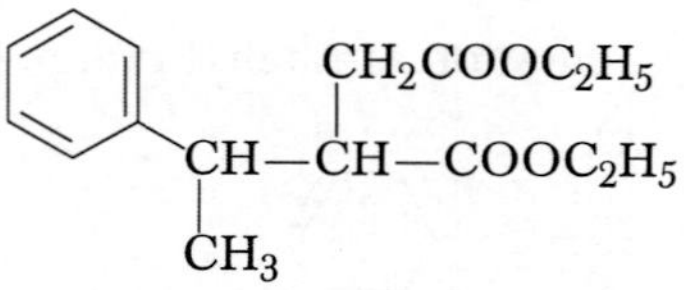

3. The appropriate reagent for the following transformation

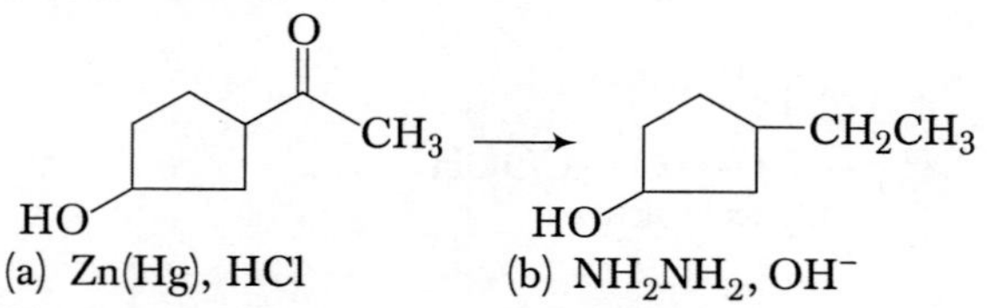

(a) Zn(Hg), HCl (b) NH_2NH_2, OH^-

(c) H_2/Ni (d) $NaBH_4$

4. A mixture of benzaldehyde and formaldehyde on heating with aqueous NaOH solution gives

(a) benzyl alcohol and sodium formate
(b) sodium benzoate and methyl alcohol
(c) sodium benzoate and sodium formate
(d) benzyl alcohol and methyl alcohol

5. What are the reactants in the following incomplete reaction?

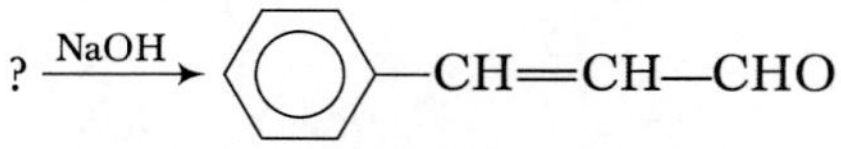

(a) Benzaldehyde and formaldehyde
(b) Benzaphenone and acetaldehyde
(c) Benzaldehyde and acetaldehyde
(d) Acetophenone and acetone

6. 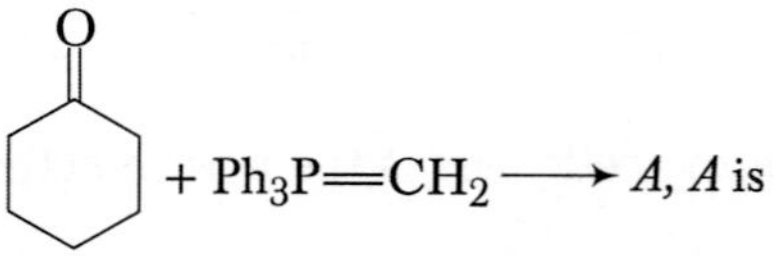

(a) 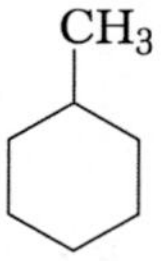 (b) 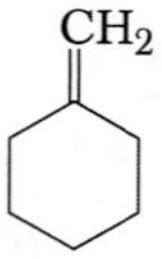

(c) 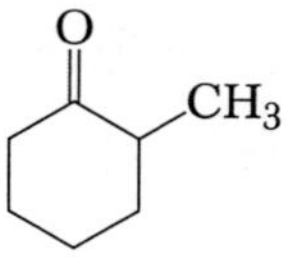 (d) 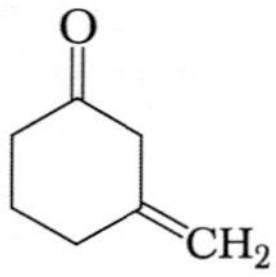

7. Cyclohexene on ozonolysis followed by reaction with zinc dust and water gives compound *E*. Compound *E* on further treatment with aqueous KOH yields compound *F*. Compound *F* is

(a) 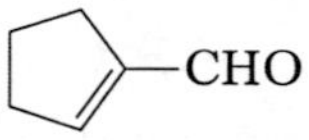 (b) 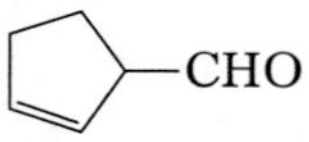

(c) 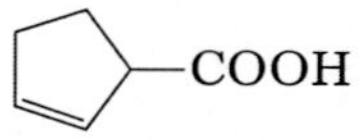 (d) 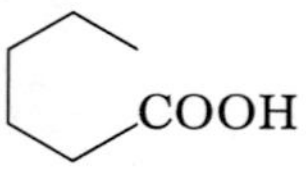

8. The Hofmann rearrangement has an intermediate that is electronically similar to that in the

(a) Claisen rearrangement
(b) Cope rearrangement
(c) Beckmann rearrangement
(d) Pinacol rearrangement

9. α, β-unsaturated carbonyl compounds undergo a ring closure reaction with conjugated dienes. This is known as the

(a) Perkin reaction (b) Sandmeyer reaction
(c) Wittig reaction (d) Diels-Alder reaction

10. The Claisen condensation is used in the preparation of

(a) δ-keto ester (b) γ-keto ester
(c) β-keto ester (d) β-hydroxyl ester

11. The conversion of $-\overset{\overset{\displaystyle O}{\|}}{C}-CH_2-$ to $-CH_2-CH_2-$ by using Zn-Hg/HCl is known as Clemmensen reduction. The other alternative method for the same conversion is
(a) Rosenmund reduction
(b) Birch reduction
(c) Meerwein-Ponndorf-Verley reduction
(d) Wolff-Kishner reduction

12. 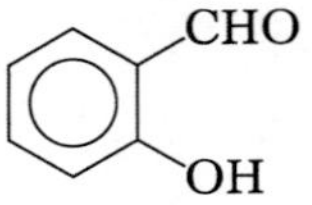 $\xrightarrow[\Delta]{Ac_2O,\ AcONa}$ Product ; Product is

(a) 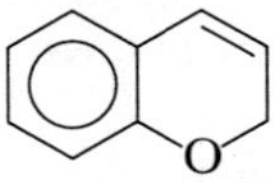
(b) 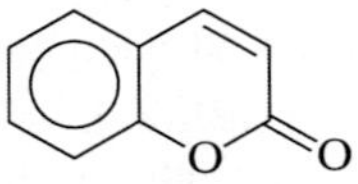
(c) 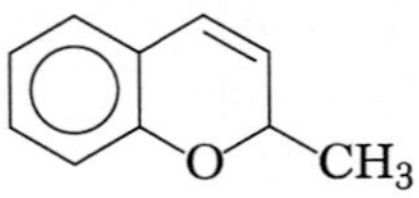
(d) 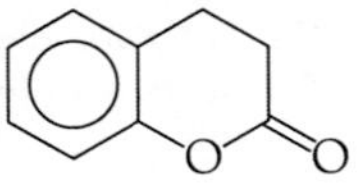

13. 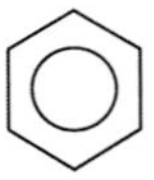 $+ CH_3\underset{\underset{\displaystyle Cl}{|}}{CH}-CH_2-CH_2-\underset{\underset{\displaystyle Cl}{|}}{CH}CH_3 \xrightarrow[\Delta]{AlCl_3}$ Product

Name the product and reaction
(a) Tetralin, Friedel-Craft reaction
(b) Tetralin, Favorskii reaction
(c) 1,4-dimethyl tetralin, Friedel-Craft reaction
(d) 1,4-dimethyl tetralin, Perkin reaction

14. The reaction, $R-CO-N_3 \xrightarrow[H_2O]{\Delta} R-NH_2$ is an example of
(a) Hofmann rearrangement
(b) Lossen rearrangement
(c) Curtius rearrangement
(d) Cope rearrangement

15. Which of the following compounds under basic conditions undergoes self addition to give aldol?
(a) Acetaldehyde
(b) Benzaldehyde
(c) Formaldehyde
(d) All of the above

16. Which one of the following can be easily synthesised by Diels-Alder reaction?

(a) 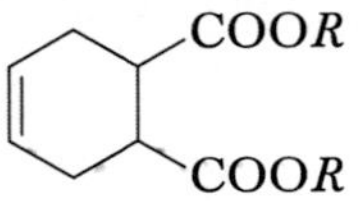
(b) 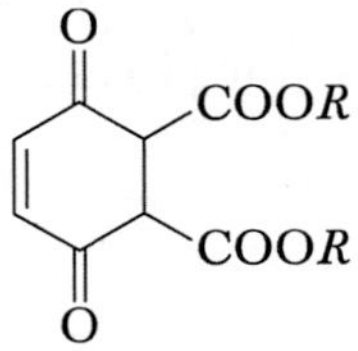
(c) 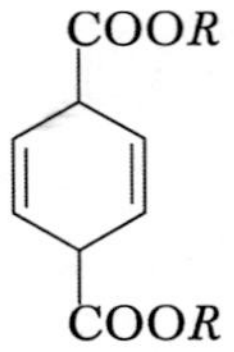
(d) 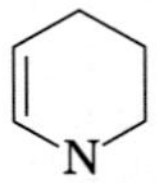

17. 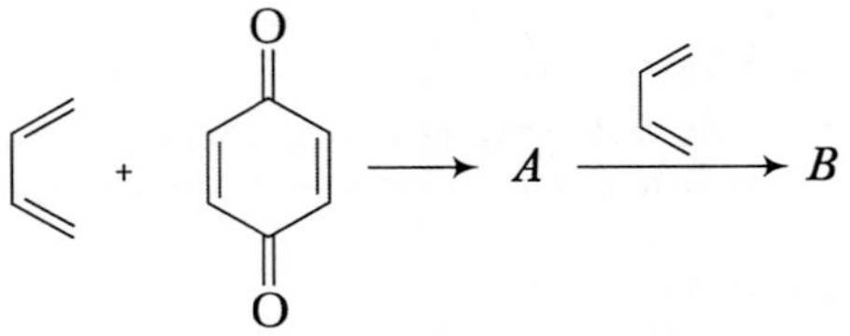

The compound A and B in the above reaction series

(a) 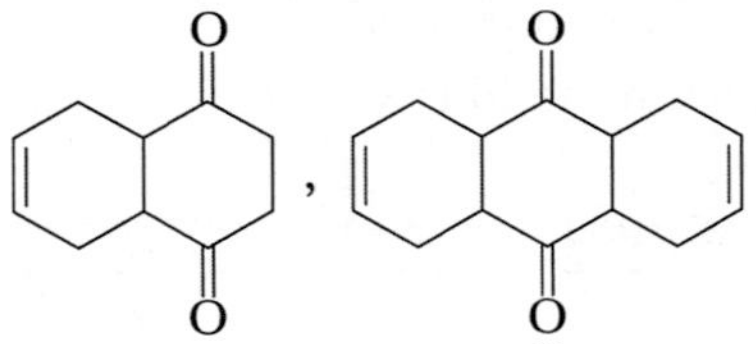
(b) 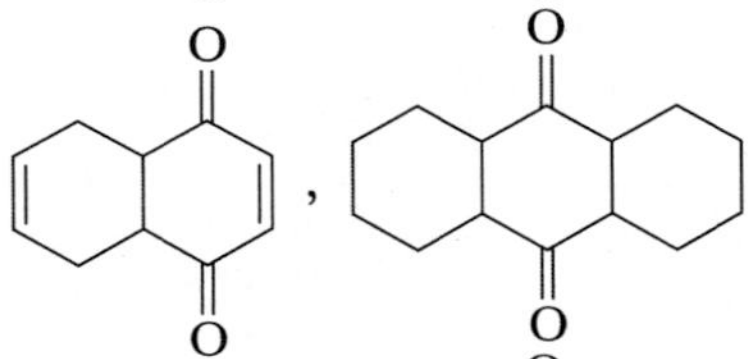
(c) 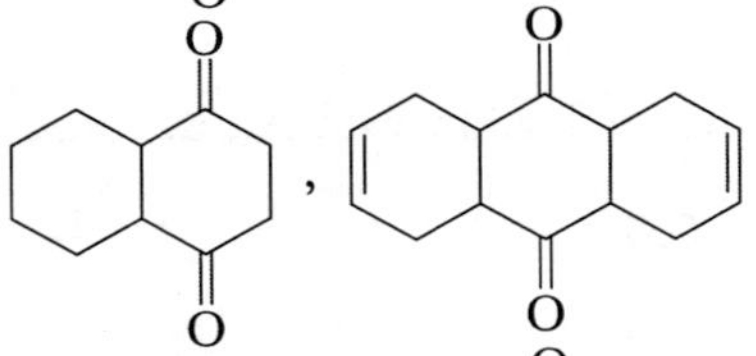
(d) 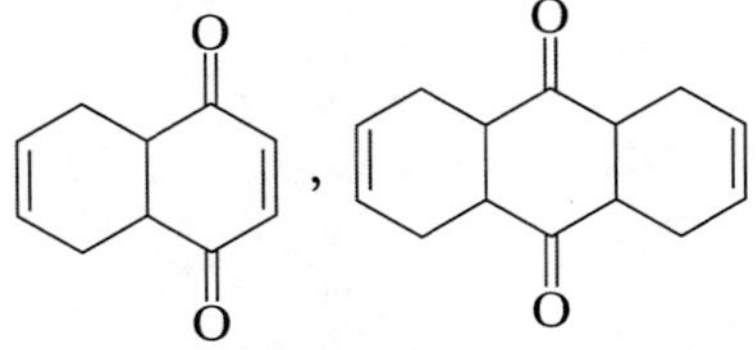

18. Which of the following reaction does not proceeds *via* a six membered transition state?
(a) Claisen rearrangement
(b) MPV reduction
(c) Hofmann rearrangement
(d) Oppenauer oxidation

19. 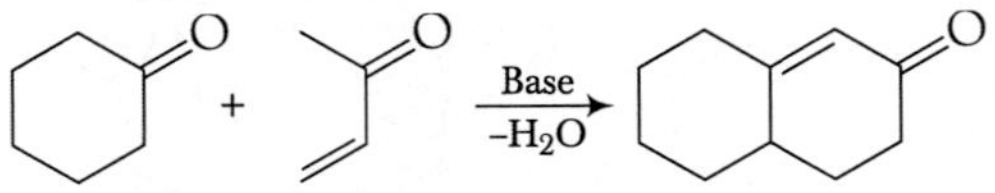

The above reaction is an example of
(a) Robinson annulation
(b) Dieckmann condensation
(c) Stobbe condensation
(d) Aldol condensation

20. Oppenauer oxidation is a reverse reaction of
(a) Birch reduction
(b) Clemmensen reduction
(c) MPV reduction
(d) Rosenmund reduction

21. The reagent used in Stobbe condensation is
(a) $KOC(CH_3)_3$ (b) Anhy. $AlCl_3$
(c) HCl, $SnCl_2$ (d) Zn/HCl

22. Betaine is an intermediate of
(a) Robinson annulation
(b) Wittig reaction
(c) Stobbe reaction
(d) Reformatsky reaction

23. In which of the following reaction amide is reduced to amine which has one carbon less than the starting material?
(a) Lossen rearrangement
(b) Beckmann rearrangement
(c) Dieckmann rearrangement
(d) Hofmann rearrangement

24. End product in the following sequence of reaction is

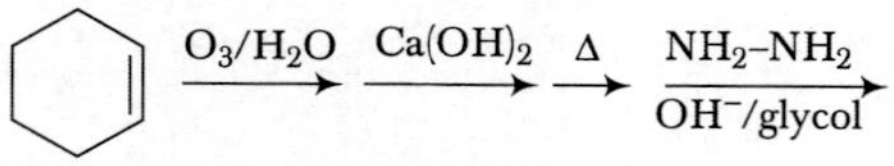

(a) 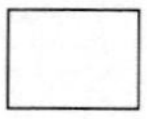 (b) 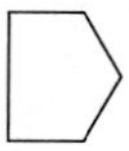

(c) 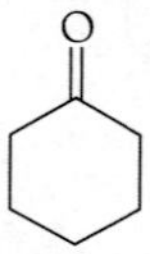 (d) 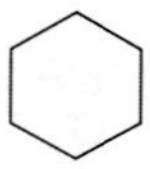

25. 1-naphthol on reduction with Na/liq. ammonia will give

(a) 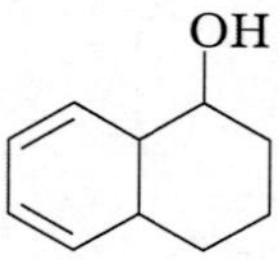 (b) 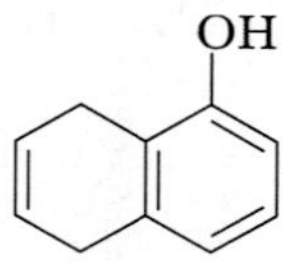

(c) 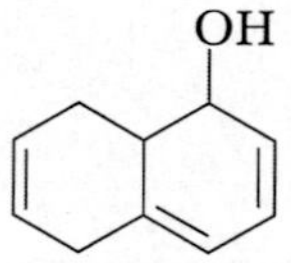 (d) 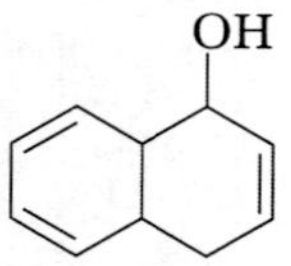

26. 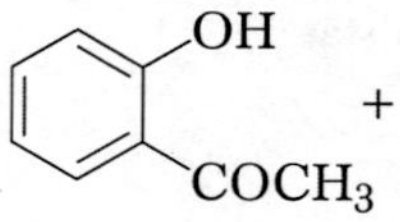 $+ CH_3COOEt \xrightarrow{Na} \xrightarrow{H^+}$ Product;

Product is

(a) 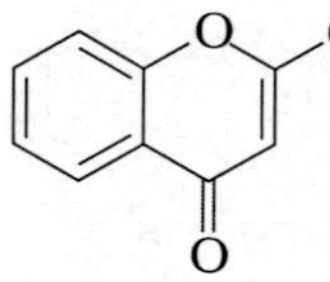 (b) 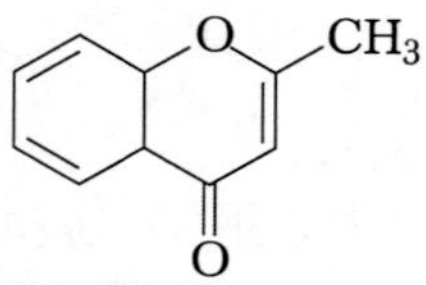

(c) 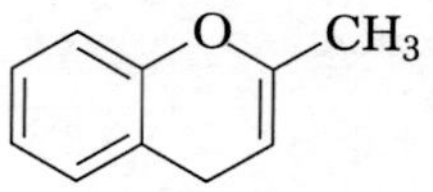 (d) 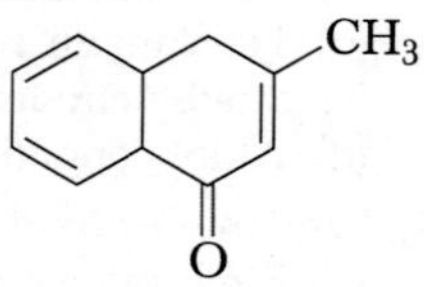

27. 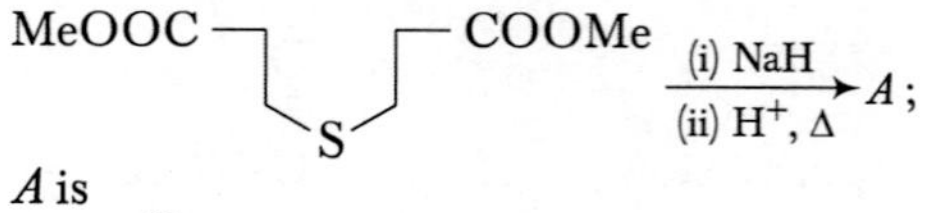

A is

(a) 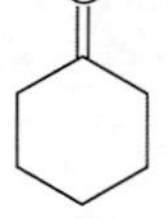 (b) 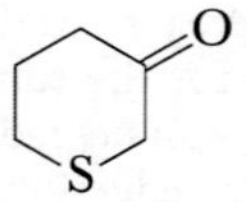

(c) 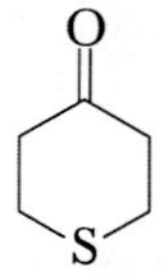 (d) 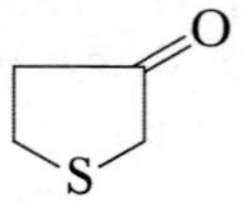

28. Diels-Alder reaction is a
(a) [4 + 2] cyclo addition (b) [4 + 4] cyclo addition
(c) [2 + 2] cyclo addition (d) None of these

29. Ene reaction involves
(a) 4π electrons electrocyclic reaction
(b) 8π electrons electrocyclic reaction
(c) 5π electrons electrocyclic reaction
(d) 6π electrons electrocyclic reaction

30. 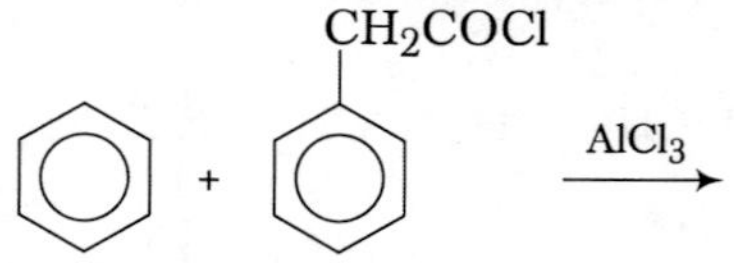

The product of the above reaction is

(a) 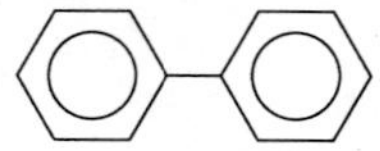

(b) 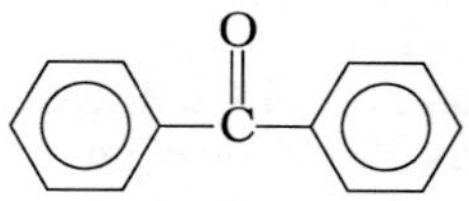

(c) 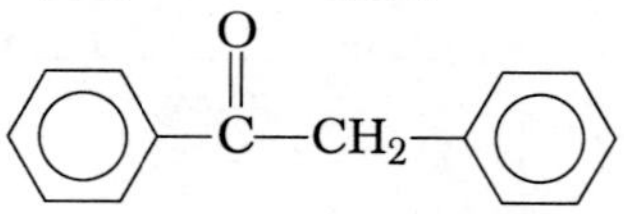

(d) 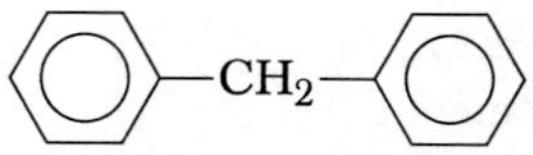

31. The addition reaction between an α, β-unsaturated carbonyl compound with an active methylene group compound in presence of piperidine is known as
(a) Mannich reaction (b) Michael reaction
(c) Aldol reaction (d) Mukaiyama reaction

32. The product obtains in Reformatsky reaction
(a) β-hydroxy ester (b) β-keto ester
(c) γ-hydroxy ester (d) γ-keto ester

33. Which of the following reactants on reaction with conc. NaOH followed by acidification gives following lactone as the main product?

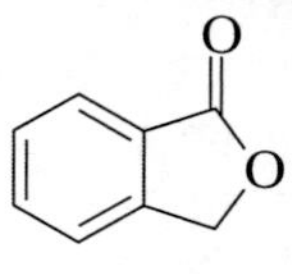

(a) 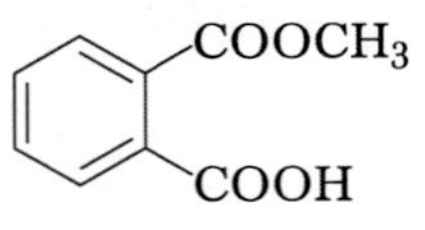
(b) 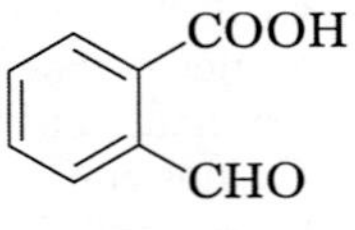

(c) 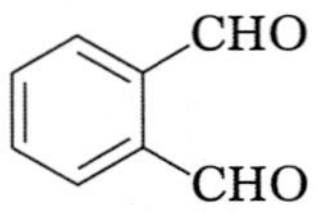
(d) 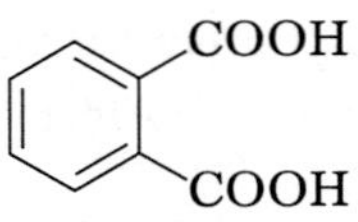

34. In Beckmann rearrangement migrating group is chiral. Select the correct statement for it.
(a) It will change its configuration while in migration
(b) It will retain its configuration while in migration
(c) It can change as well as it can retain its configuration
(d) There is nothing to do with configuration

35. Which of the following reactions are involved in the Robinson annulation?
(a) Perkin reaction and Mannich reaction
(b) Oppenauer oxidation and aldol condensation
(c) Mannich reaction and aldol condensation
(d) Michael reaction and aldol condensation

36. The product of the following Michael addition is

$$\text{Acrylonitrile} + \text{allyl cyanide} \longrightarrow A \xrightarrow{H_2O,\,H^+} B + 2NH_4^+$$

(a) CH_2CH_2COOH | CH—$COOH$ | CH_3

(b) CH_2COOH | CH—$COOH$ | $CH{=}CH_2$

(c) CH_2CH_2COOH | H—C—COOH | $CH{=}CH_2$

(d) CH_2CH_2COOH | CH—CH_2—$COOH$ | $CH{=}CH_2$

37. 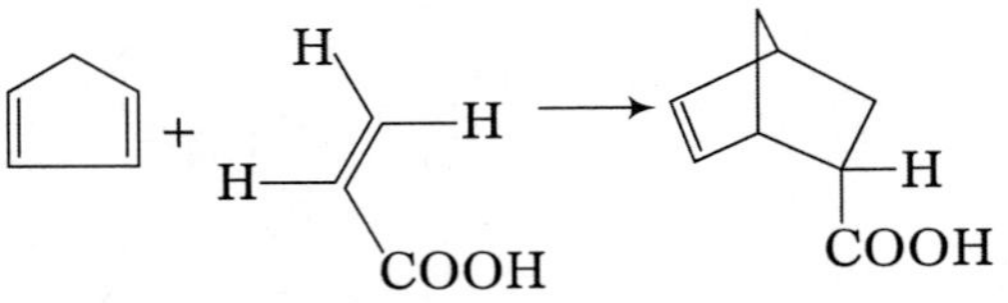

is an example of
(a) exo addition
(b) endo addition
(c) retro Diels-Alder reaction
(d) ring inversion

38. The base in Perkin reaction is
(a) extra base like alkoxide, hydroxide, etc.
(b) generally the salt of the acid corresponding to the anhydride
(c) the anhydride itself
(d) the anion of the starting material

39. 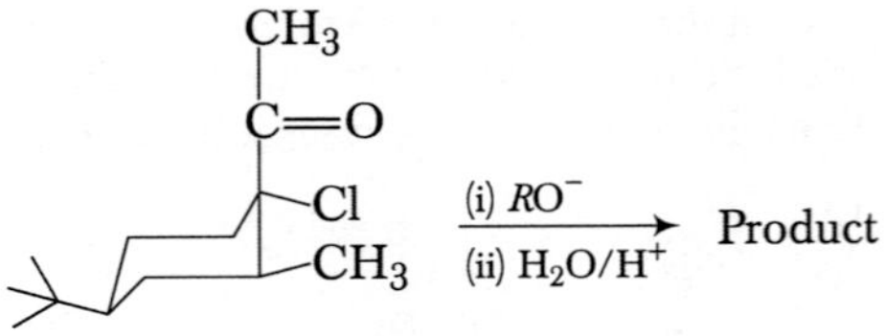

Product is

(a) 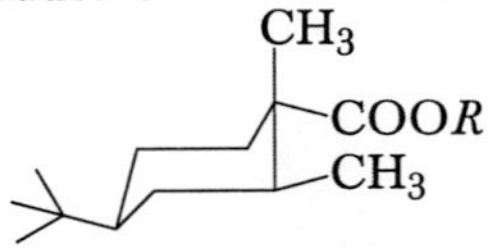

(b) 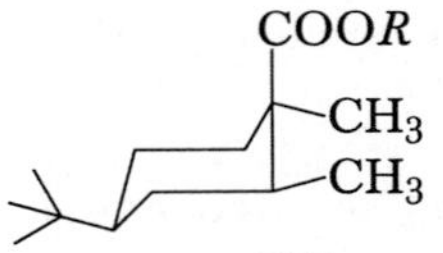

(c) 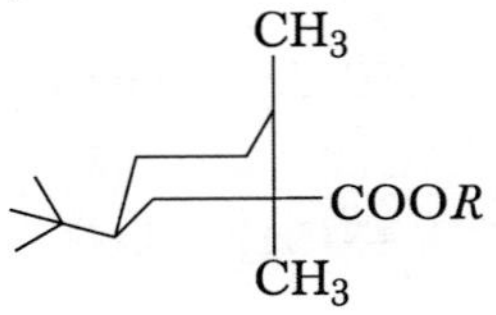

(d) 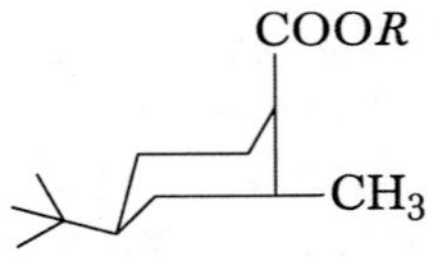

40. Which of the following statements about Birch reduction is false?
(a) It is a dissolving metal reduction
(b) The reduction does not affect the non-conjugated double bonds in the side chain
(c) The metal is the source of electrons
(d) It follows an ionic mechanism

41. In Reformatsky reaction
(a) the components are more active than Grignard reagents
(b) organo zinc compounds are involved
(c) an α-hydroxy ester is obtained
(d) Mg metal is treated with a halo ester

42. 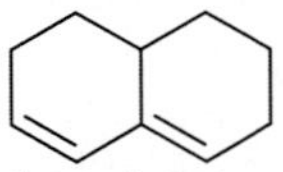 fails to undergo a Diels-Alder reaction, though it is a conjugated diene, because
(a) it has a rigid geometry
(b) the double bonds are *trans* to each other
(c) the two double bonds are in two rings
(d) the compound is unstable

43. The reaction/rearrangement that involves carbene intermediate is
(a) Beckmann rearrangement
(b) Reimer-Tiemann reaction
(c) Curtius rearrangement
(d) Lossen rearrangement

44. Name the other reactant with which compound '*A*' is converted into product '*B*' under the set of conditions given. Give the name of the reaction also

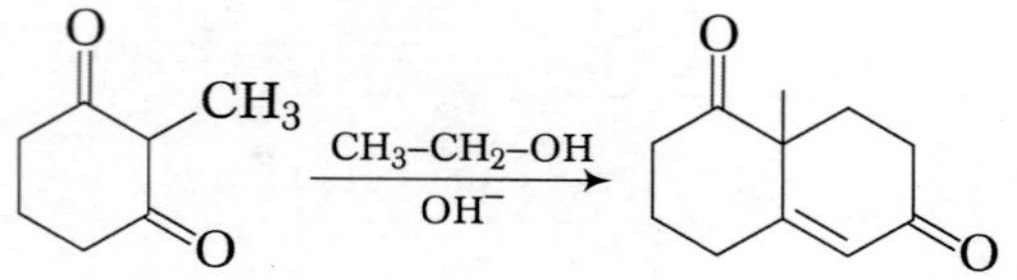

(*A*) (*B*)

(a) $CH_2{=}CH{-}\overset{O}{\overset{\|}{C}}{-}CH_3$ by Reformatsky reaction

(b) $CH_2{=}CH{-}\overset{O}{\overset{\|}{C}}{-}CH_3$ by Robinson annulation reaction

(c) $CH_2{=}CH{-}CH_2{-}CHO$ by Perkins reaction

(d) $CH_2{=}CH{-}\overset{O}{\overset{\|}{C}}{-}CH_2{-}CH_3$ by Favorskii reaction

45. Which one of the following reactions involves a hydride shift in its reaction mechanism?
(a) Claisen condensation
(b) Beckmann rearrangement
(c) Cannizzaro reaction
(d) Benzylic acid rearrangement

46. 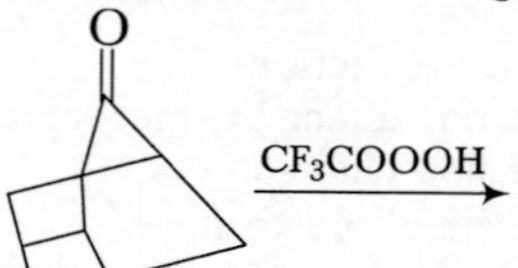

Product

Product is

(a) 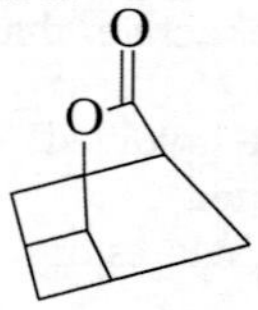
(b) 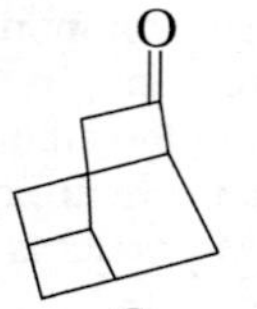
(c) 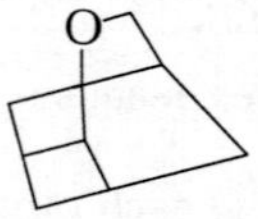
(d) 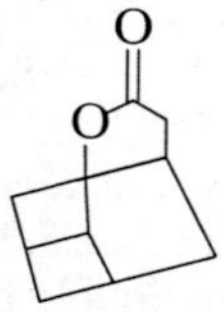

47. Acetophenone reacts with hydrazoic acid in the presence of concentrated sulphuric acid to give
(a) aniline (b) benzamide
(c) ethyl benzene (d) acetanilide

48. $ArCOOH \xrightarrow[(H_3PO_4)_n/\Delta]{CH_3NO_2} \xrightarrow{^{\ominus}OH} ?$

The final product of the above reaction series
(a) Ar NO_2 (b) Ar NH_2
(c) Ar CN (d) Ar NC

49. In which of the following rearrangements, acyl azide is an intermediate?
(a) Hofmann and Curtius
(b) Curtius and Lossen
(c) Lossen and Schmidt
(d) Curtius and Schmidt

50. In a Diels-Alder reaction, rate of reaction is increased by
(a) electron donating substituents in the diene
(b) electron donating substituents in the dienophile
(c) electron withdrawing substituents in the dienophile
(d) electron withdrawing substituents in either of the reactants

51. The reaction,

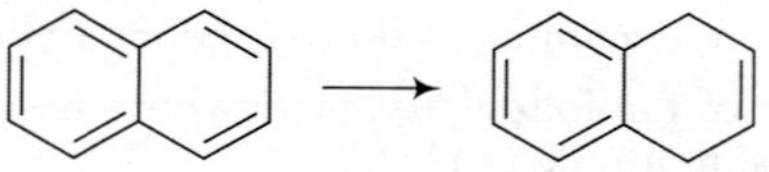

is brought about by
(a) Na/EtOH
(b) Na, liquid NH_3, ethanol
(c) H_2/Ni
(d) $NH_2{-}NH_2/NaOEt$

52. Reduction of α,β-unsaturated aldehyde to the corresponding α,β-unsaturated alcohol is brought about by
(a) aluminium isopropoxide/isopropanol
(b) Na-ethanol
(c) H_2/Ni
(d) electrolytic reduction

53. The product of the following reaction is

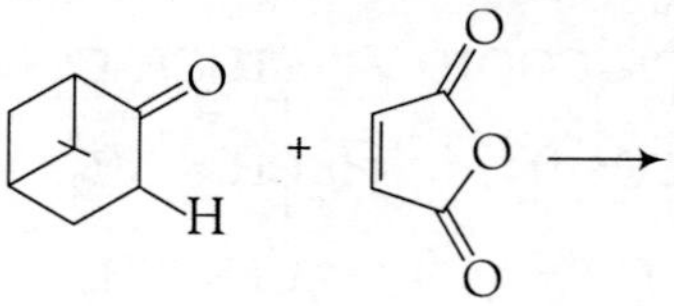

Product

(a) 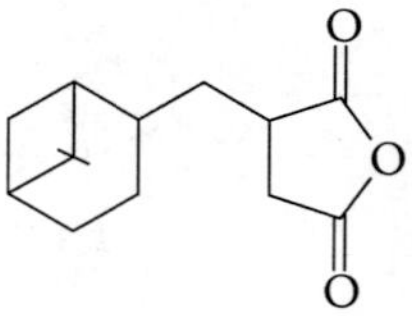
(b) 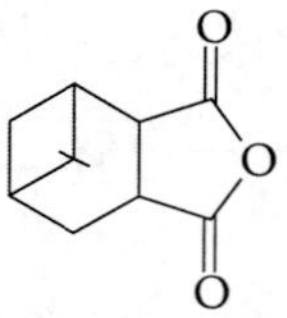
(c) 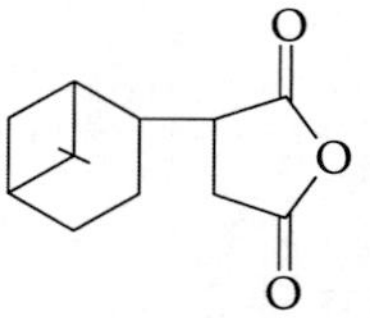
(d) 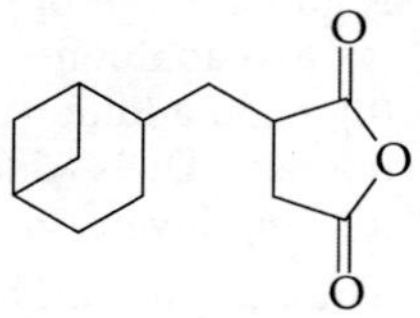

54. The product and reaction name of the following reaction is

$$\begin{matrix} CH_2{-}CHO \\ | \\ CH_2{-}CHO \end{matrix} + CH_3NH_2 + CH_3{-}\overset{O}{\overset{\|}{C}}{-}CH_3 \xrightarrow{:B} ?$$

(a) Michael reaction 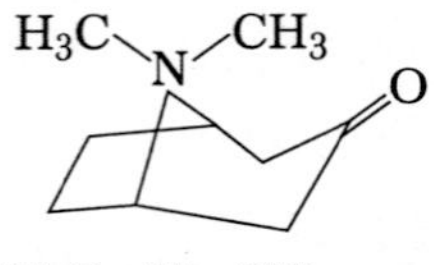

(b) Mannich reaction 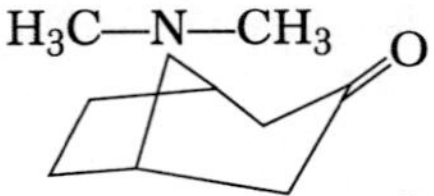

(a) Shapiro reaction 

(a) Stork enamine reaction 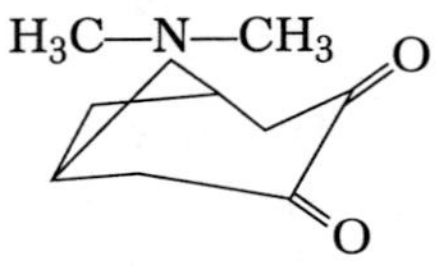

55. 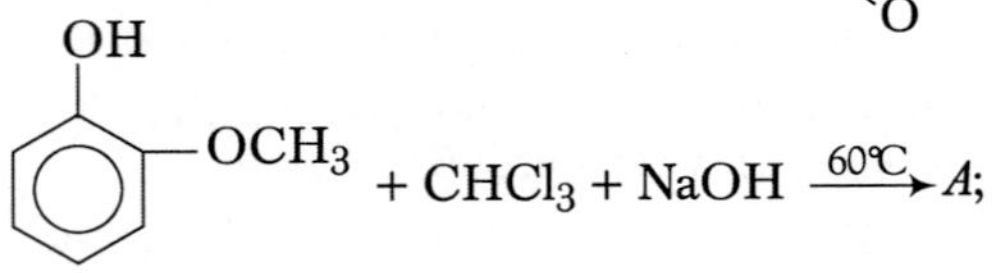

A is

(a) 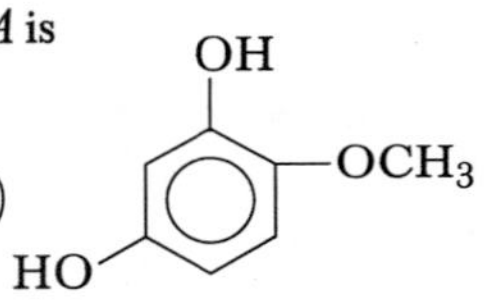 (b) 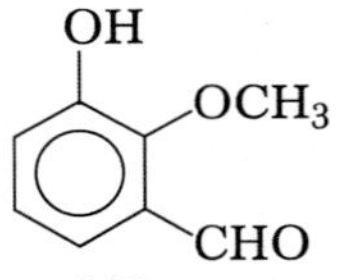

(c) 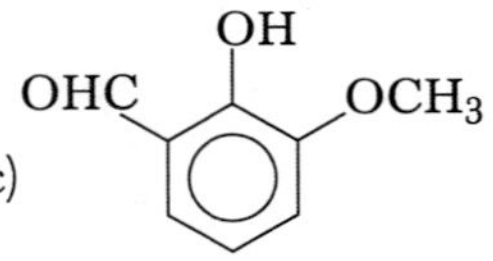 (d) 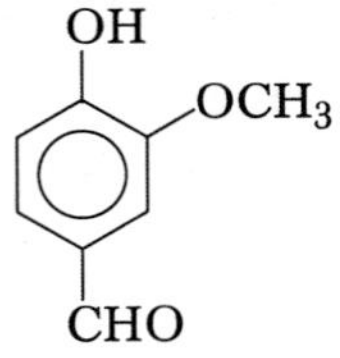

56. 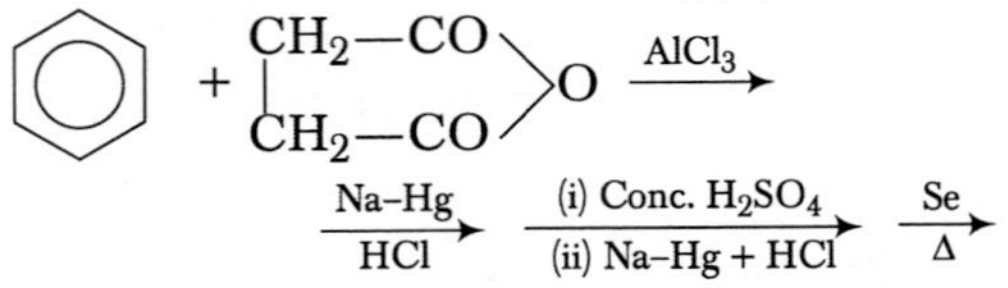

The end product of the above reaction series is

(a) anthracene (b) naphthalene
(c) anthraquinone (d) tetralin

57. 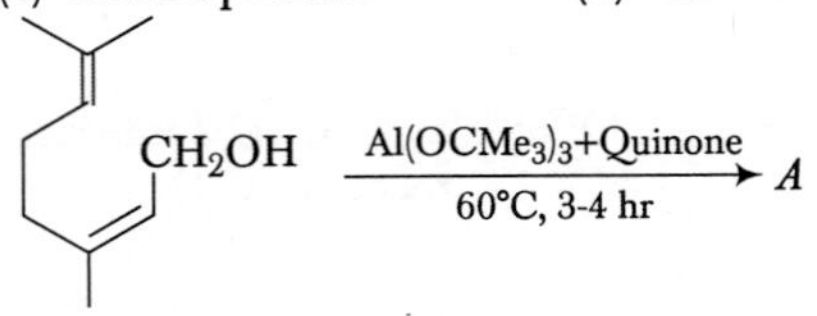

Identify the product *A*.

(a) 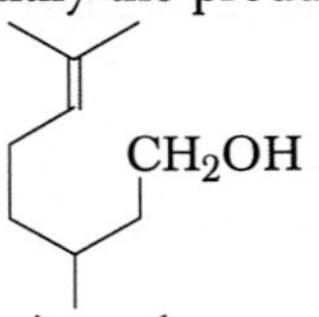 (b) 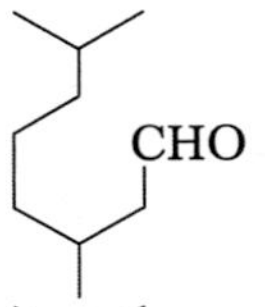

(c) 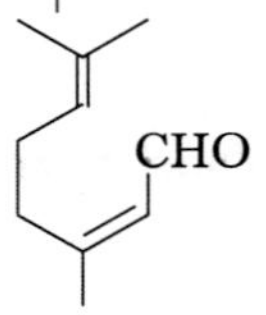 (d) 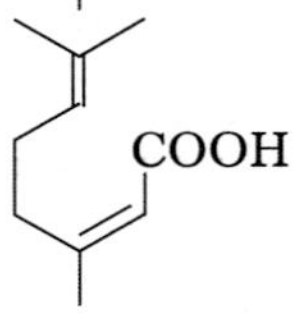

58. Beckmann transformation of (*A*) followed by hydrolysis will yield

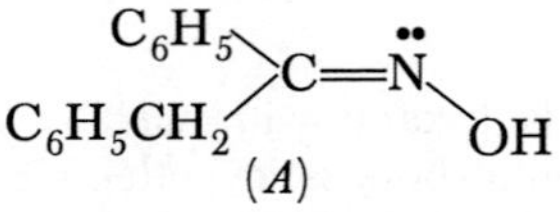

(a) benzoic acid + benzylamine
(b) phenyl acetic acid + benzylamine
(c) aniline + phenyl acetic acid
(d) benzoic acid + aniline

59. 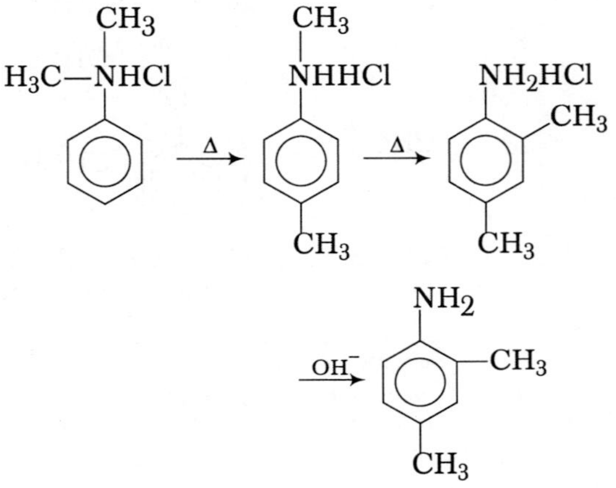

This is called

(a) Hofmann-Martius rearrangement
(b) Hofmann-degradation reaction
(c) Fries migration
(d) Reformatsky reaction

60. *p*-cresol reacts with chloroform in alkaline medium to give the compound *A* which adds hydrogen cyanide to form the compound *B*. The latter on acidic hydrolysis gives chiral carboxylic acid *C* which is

(a) 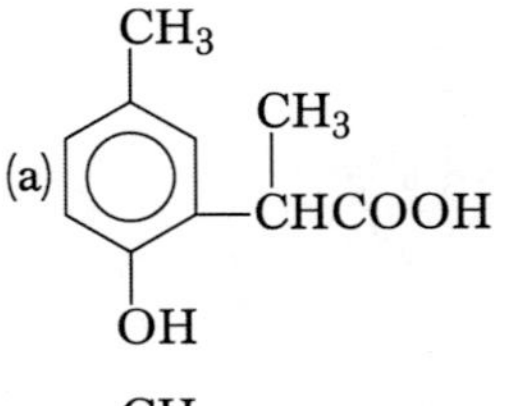 (b) 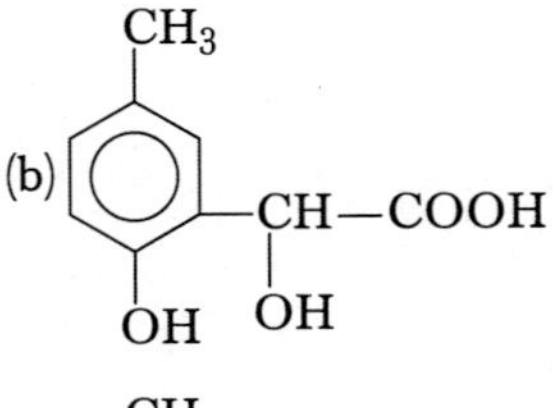

(c) 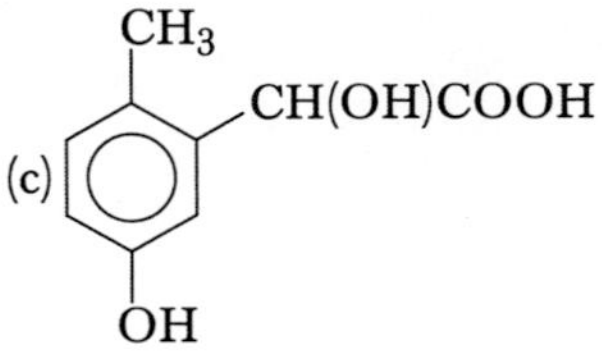 (d) 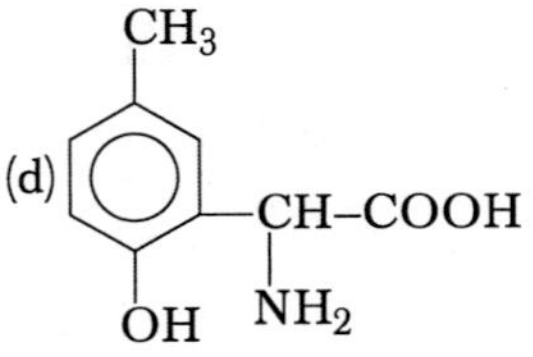

Exercise 2

(For Part 'C')

1. When phenol is treated with $CHCl_3$ and NaOH followed by acidification, salicylaldehyde is obtained. Which of the following species are involved in the above mentioned reaction as intermediates?

(a) 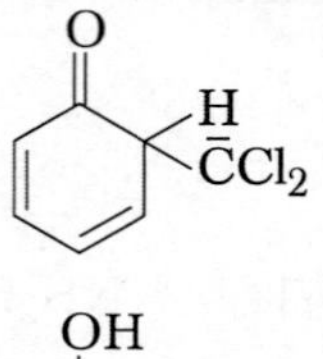

(b) 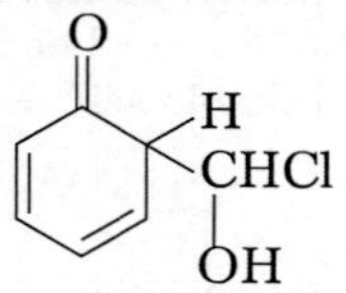

(c) 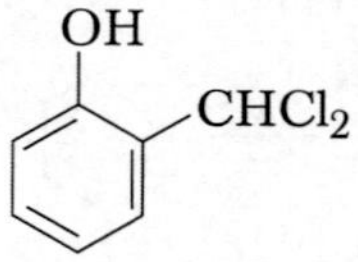

(d) 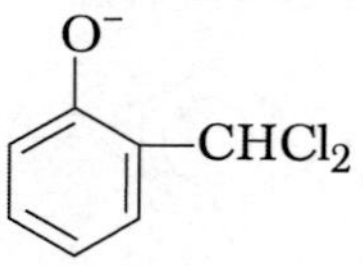

2. Match the Column I with Column II and select the correct answer using the code given below the Columns.

Column I	Column II
A. Aldol condensation	1. Hydride ion transfer
B. Cannizzaro reaction	2. Organozinc compound
C. Reformatsky reaction	3. CN^- as catalyst
D. Benzoin condensation	4. Enolate ion

	A	B	C	D
(a)	4	1	2	3
(b)	2	3	4	1
(c)	4	3	2	1
(d)	2	1	4	3

3. What is the product obtained by heating the following allylic ether of phenol?

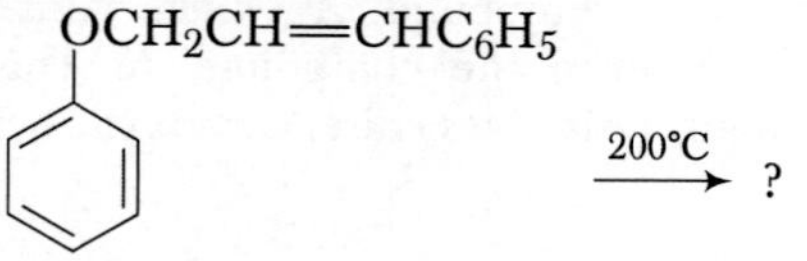

(a) 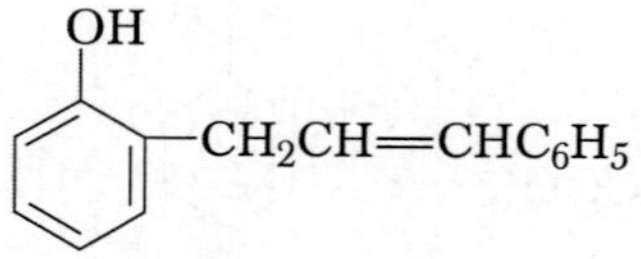

(b) 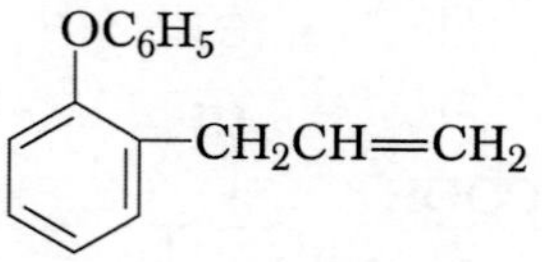

(c) 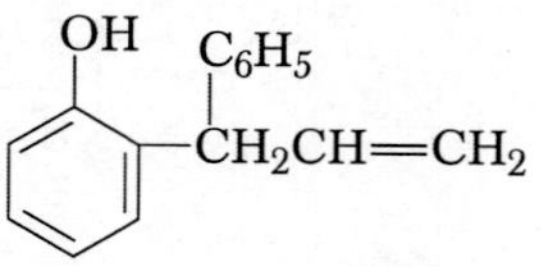

(d) 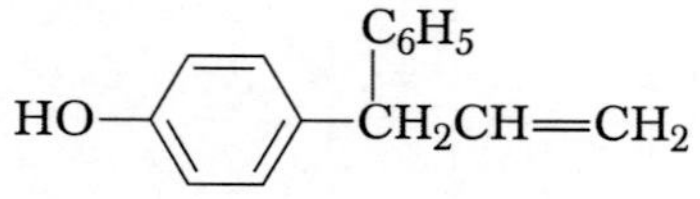

4. There is intramolecular Friedel-Crafts acylation reaction on

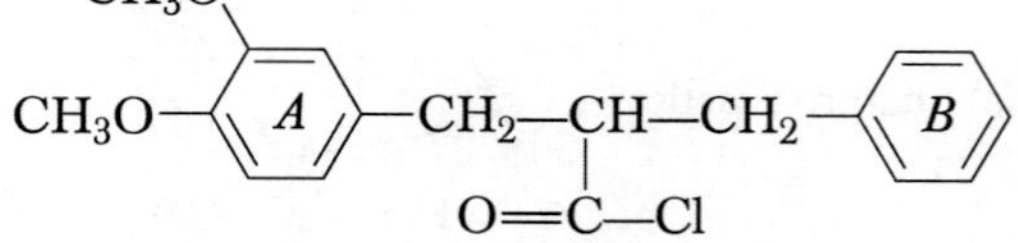

Select the correct statements from the following.

I. Acylation is on the more active ring *A* since, it contains two activating methoxy groups.

II. Acylation is on the more active ring *B* since, it lacks deactivating groups.

III. Acylation product formed at the faster rate is

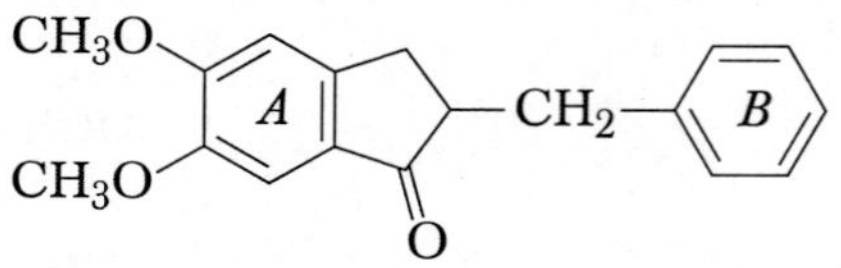

IV. Acylation product formed at the faster rate is

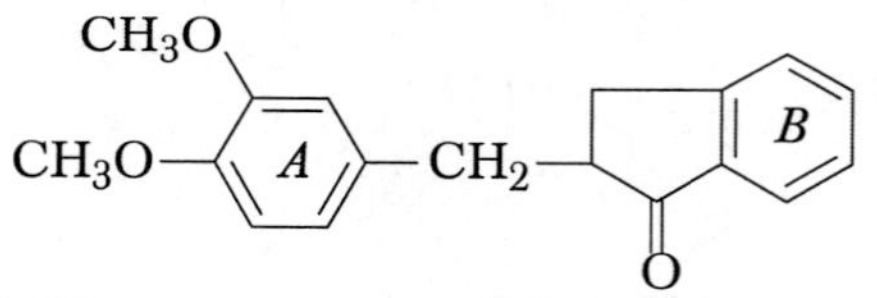

(a) I, III
(b) I, IV
(c) II, III
(d) II, IV

5. 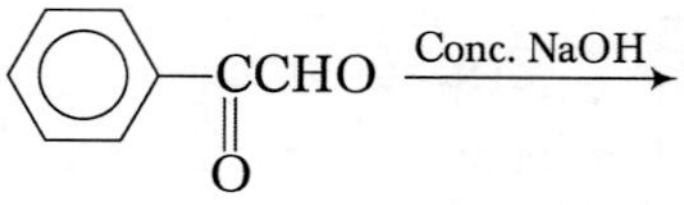

A by reaction *R*; *A* and *R* can be

(a) 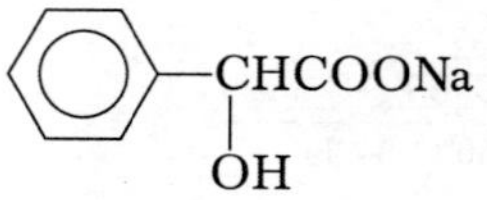

by crossed Cannizzaro reaction (CR)

(b) 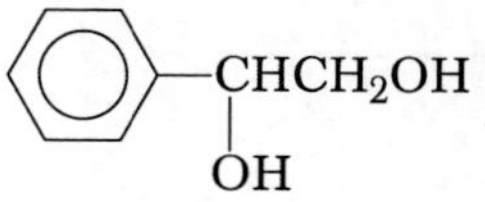

by intramolecular CR

(c) 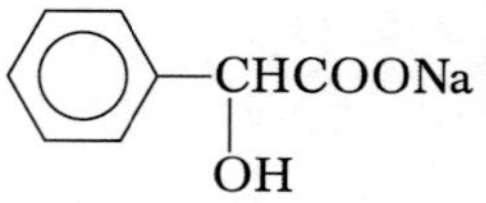

by intermolecular CR

(d) 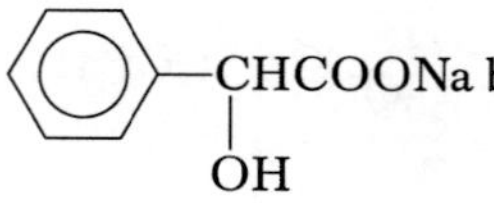

by intramolecular CR

6. 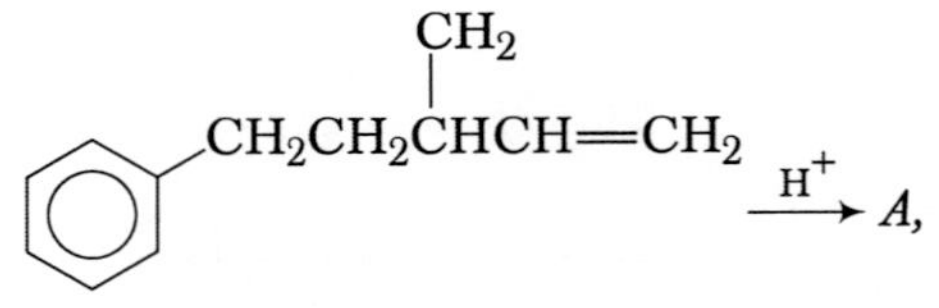

A is

(a) 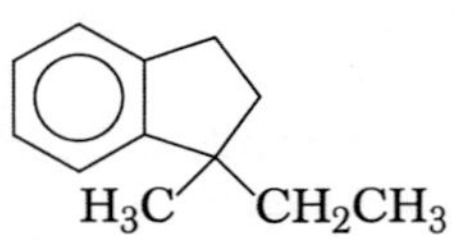 (b) 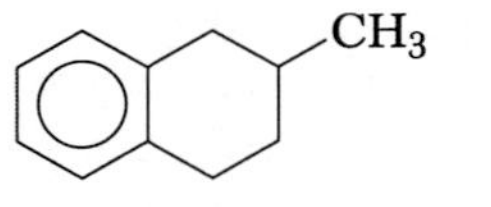

(c) 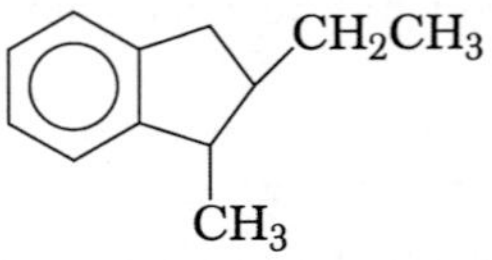 (d) 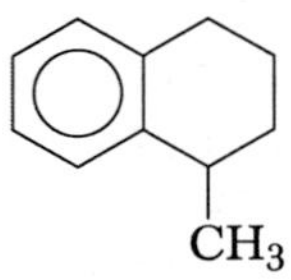

7. Consider the following statements regarding the reactions given below.

$$C_6H_5CHO \xrightarrow[CH_3COONa,\ \Delta]{(CH_3CO)_2O} \xrightarrow{H_2O} C_6H_5CH{=}CHCOOH + CH_3COOH$$

I. The reaction is a representative example of Perkin reaction.

II. The anhydride having at least one α-H, provides an enolate ion for the reaction.

III. The acetate deprotonates the anhydride to form the nucleophile needed for the reaction.

Which of the above statements are correct?

(a) I, II, III (b) I, II

(c) II, III (d) I, III

8. $2C_6H_5CHO \xrightarrow{NaOH} C_6H_5CH_2OH + C_6H_5COONa$

The same reaction takes place with which one of the following aldehydes?

(a) CH_3CHO (b) CH_3CH_2CHO

(c) $(CH_3)_3CCHO$ (d) $(CH_3)_2CHCHO$

9. Consider the following reactions

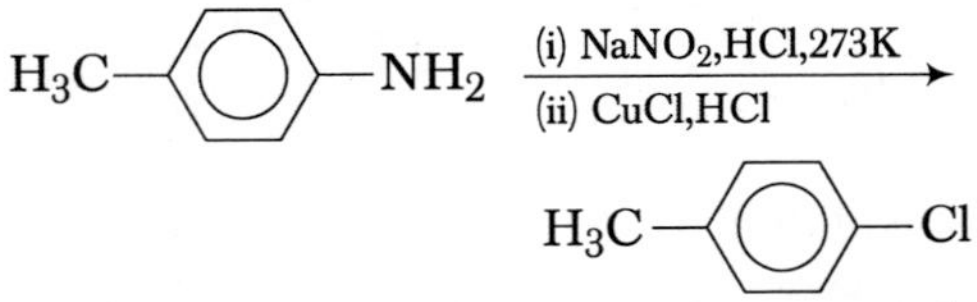

The name of the reaction and the intermediate *via.* which it is known to proceed, are respectively

(a) Hunsdiecker and benzyne

(b) Sandmeyer and a free radical

(c) Meerwein and a free radical

(d) Sandmeyer and a carbanion

10. When cyclohexanone oxime is treated with H_2SO_4, the ring expansion take place which is due to

(a) Curtius reaction

(b) Beckmann rearrangement

(c) Favorskii rearrangement

(d) Claisen rearrangement

11. Which one of the following name reactions is an example of **atom economy reaction?**

(a) Wittig reaction (b) Grignard reaction

(c) Dieckmann condensation (d) Diels-Alder reaction

12. Match the items in Column I with the appropriate in Column II and choose the correct answer from the codes given.

	Column I		Column II
A.	Perkin reaction	1.	β-hydroxy ester
B.	Beckmann rearrangement	2.	$RCOO^-$ as base
C.	Reformatsky reaction	3.	Reversal of allylic chain
D.	Claisen rearrangement	4.	Caprolactum

	A	B	C	D
(a)	3	2	1	4
(b)	2	1	4	3
(c)	2	4	1	3
(d)	4	3	2	1

13. Match each of the reactions given in Column I with the appropriate reagent from Column II.

	Column I		Column II
A.	Vilsmeir-Haack reaction	1.	Amino alcohol + HNO_2
B.	Wolff rearrangement	2.	$POCl_3$ + dialkyl formamide
C.	Demjanov rearrangement	3.	Pyrolysis of xanthate
		4.	Diazoketone + Ag_2O

	A	B	C
(a)	3	4	1
(b)	2	4	3
(c)	3	4	2
(d)	2	4	1

14. 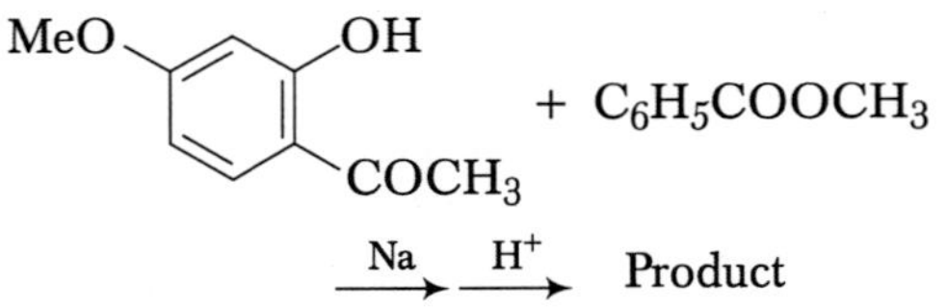

The product of the above reaction is

(a) 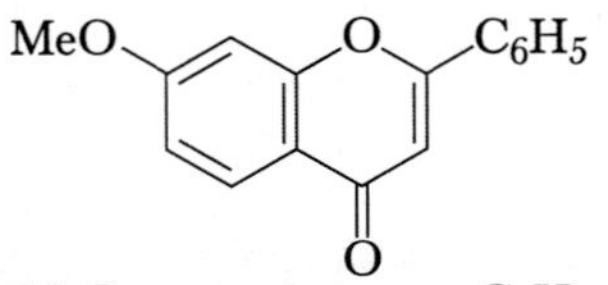

(b) 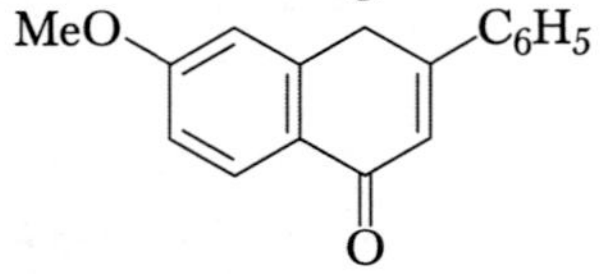

(c) 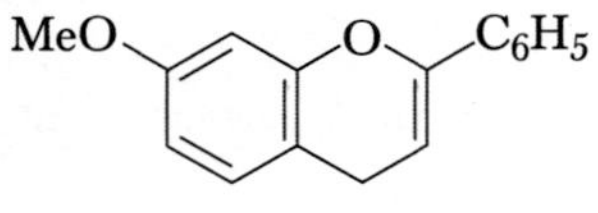

(d) 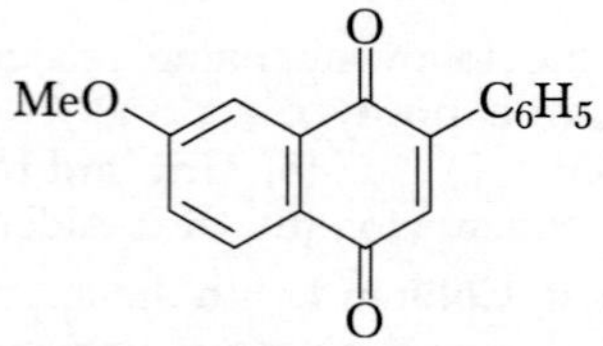

15. Oppenauer oxidation
(a) is used to prepare ketone
(b) uses aluminium *t*-butoxide as catalyst
(c) is the reverse reaction of MPV reduction
(d) All of the above are correct

16. $2CH_3—\overset{\displaystyle O}{\overset{\|}{C}}OC_2H_5 \xrightarrow{C_2H_5ONa} A$; *A* is formed by Claisen condensation. The correct statements about *A* is/are

I. *A* forms oxime I. *A* shows tautomerism
III. *A* shows iodoform test
(a) I, III (b) I, II, III (c) I, II (d) Only III

17. 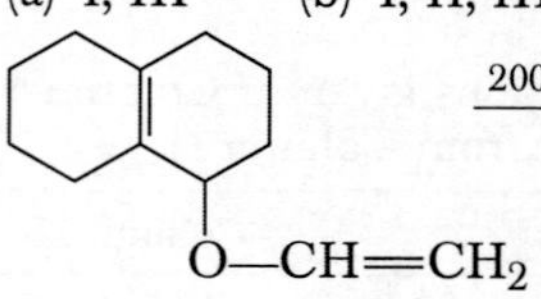 $\xrightarrow{200°C}$ *A*; *A* is

(a) 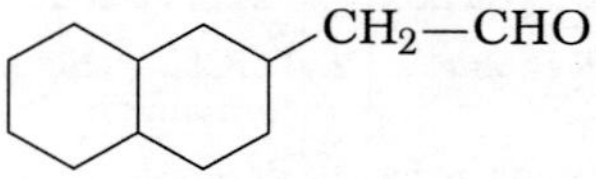

(b) 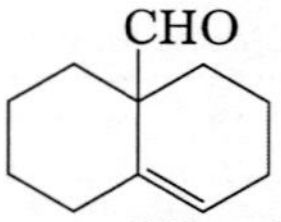

(c) 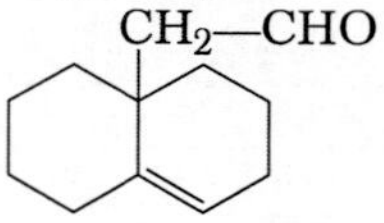

(d) 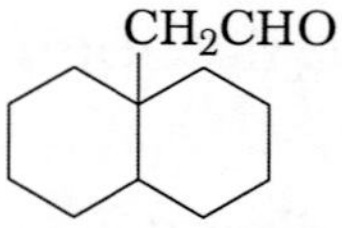

18. 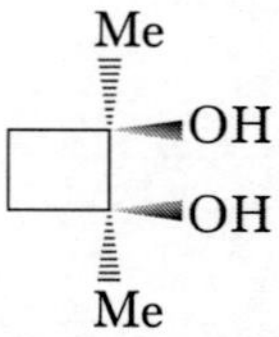 $\xrightarrow{TsOH}$?

Give the name of the rearrangement and identify the product.

(a) 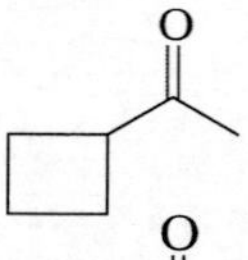 Beckmann rearrangement

(b) 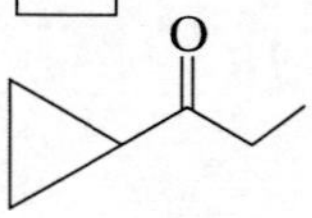 Pinacol rearrangement

(c) 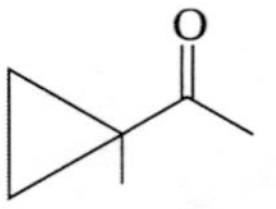 Pinacol rearrangement

(d) 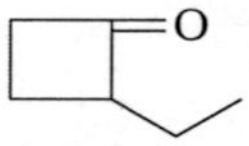 Beckmann rearrangement

19. Select the correct statements from the following given statements.

I. Baeyer-Villiger oxidation involves 1,2-migrations to an electron deficient oxygen.
II. In Lossen rearrangement isocyanate intermediate is formed.
III. In Curtius rearrangement conversion of acyl azide to an isocyanate takes place.
IV. In Curtius rearrangement isocyanate cannot be isolable.

(a) I, II (b) III, IV
(c) II, III, IV (d) I, II, III

20. 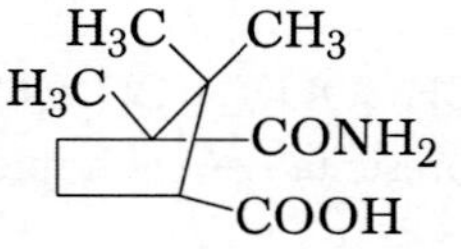 $\xrightarrow{KOBr} \xrightarrow{\Delta} A$

The compound *A* is

(a) 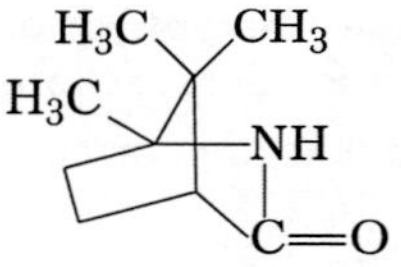 (b) 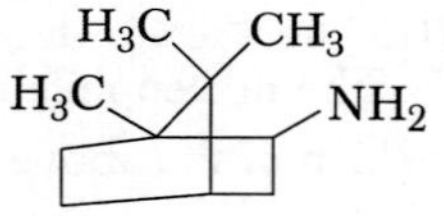

(c) 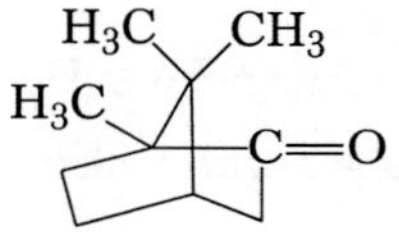 (d) 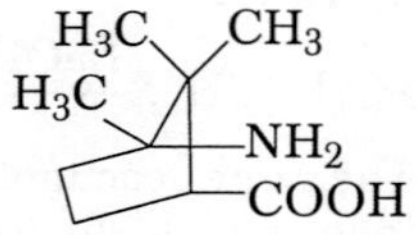

21. 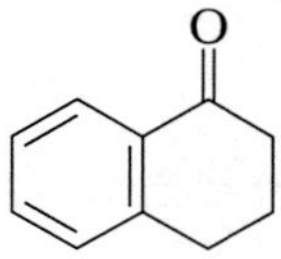 $\xrightarrow[\text{(ii) Zn (iii) } H_3O^+]{\text{(i) Br } CH_2COOCH_3}$ $\xrightarrow{H_2SO_4/\Delta}$ $\xrightarrow[\text{(ii) } H_2O]{\text{(i) Se}/\Delta}$

The end product of the reaction is

(a) 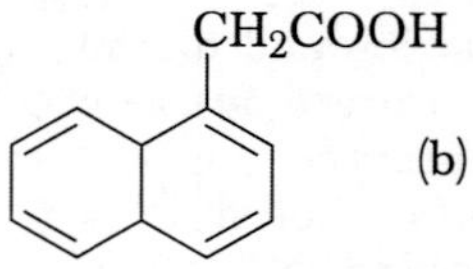 (b) 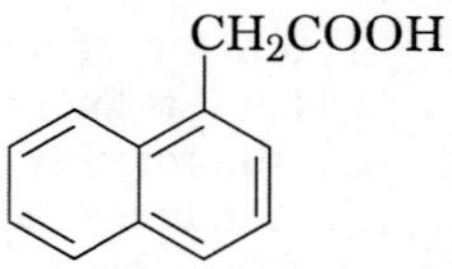

(c) 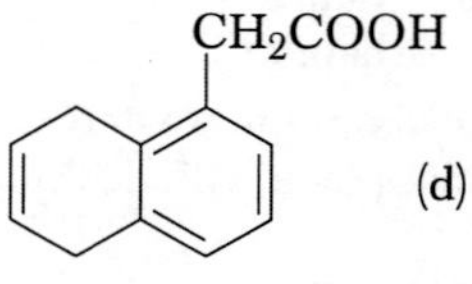 (d) 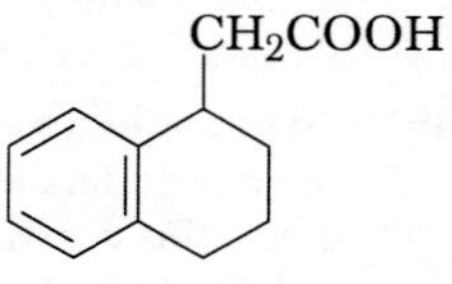

22. Match the Column I with Column II.

	Column I	Column II
A.	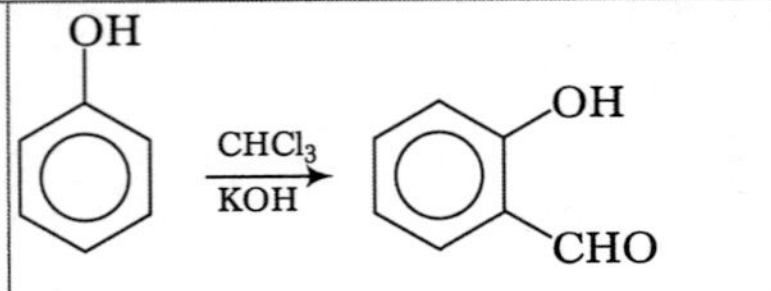	1. Diels-Alder reaction
B.	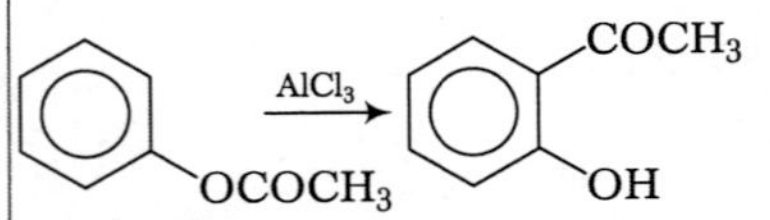	2. Friedel-Crafts reaction
C.	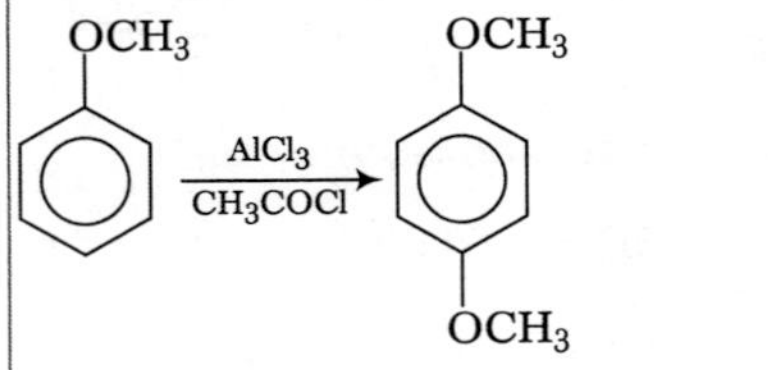	3. Reimer-Tiemann reaction
D.	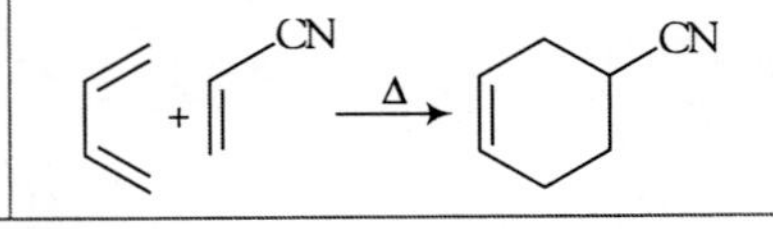	4. Fries rearrangement

Codes

	A	B	C	D
(a)	2	3	4	1
(b)	2	4	1	3
(c)	3	4	2	1
(d)	3	4	1	2

23. The reaction,

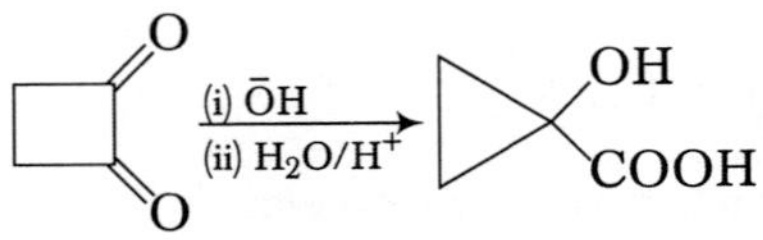

is an example of

(a) Wolff rearrangement
(b) Benzylic acid rearrangement
(c) Steven's rearrangement
(d) Wagner-Meerwein rearrangement

24. 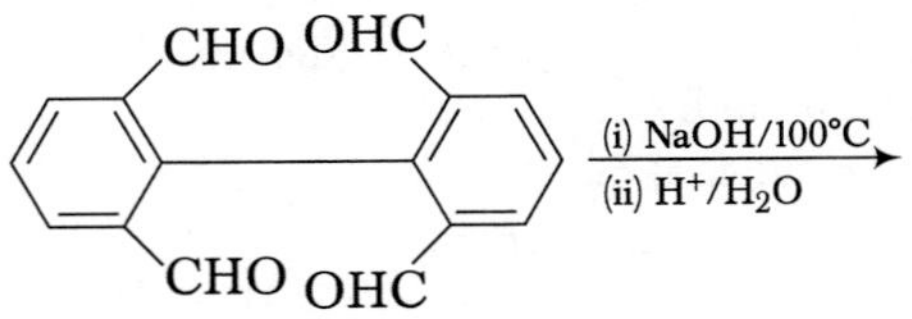

Major product is

(a) 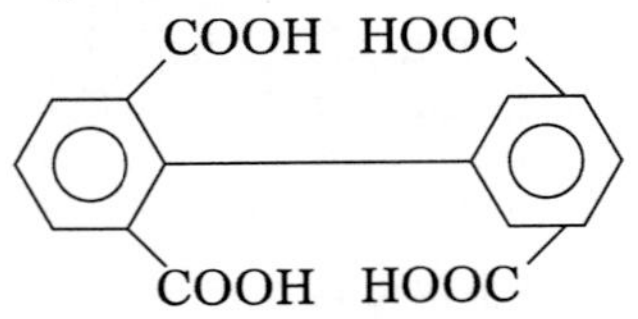

(b) 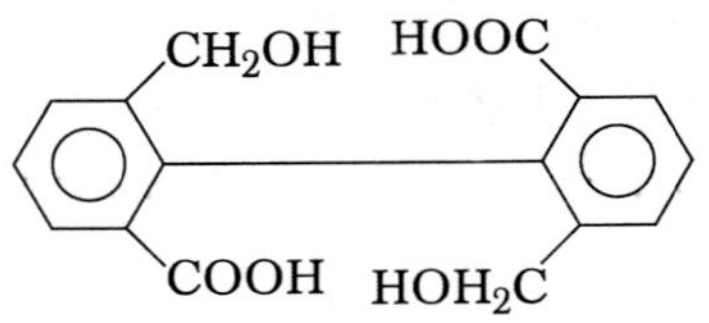

(c) 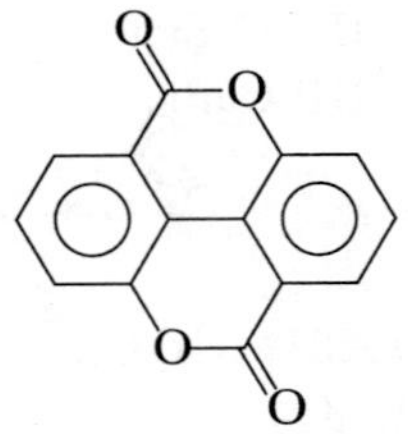

(d) 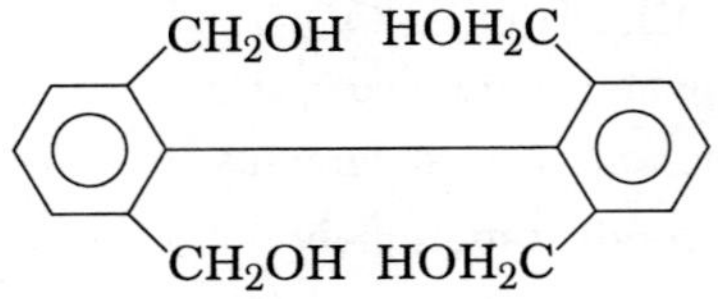

25. 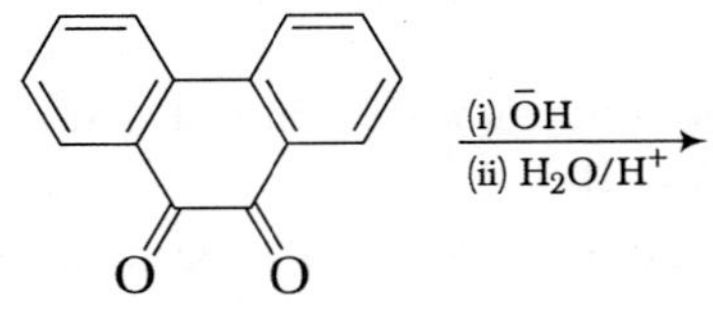 Product.

Product is

(a) 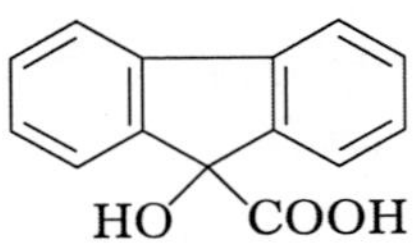

(b) 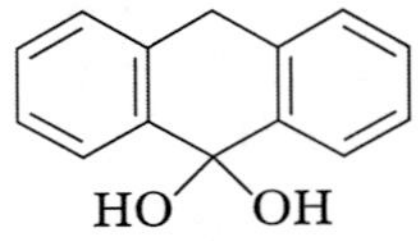

(c) 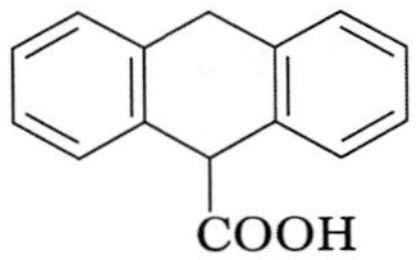

(d) 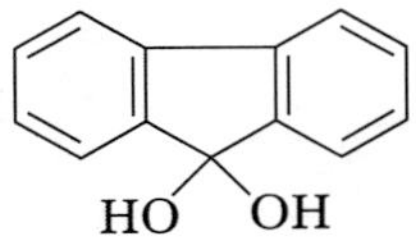

26. In the preparation of acetophenone ($PhCOCH_3$) from benzene, acetyl chloride and aluminium chloride, a considerable excess of aluminium chloride is used. This is because aluminium chloride

(a) is a poor Friedel-Crafts reaction catalyst
(b) deactivates benzene
(c) complexes with acetophenone
(d) deactivates acetyl chloride due to common ion-effect

27. The following group of reaction very closely related to Hofmann involve the formation of an isocyanate, name them

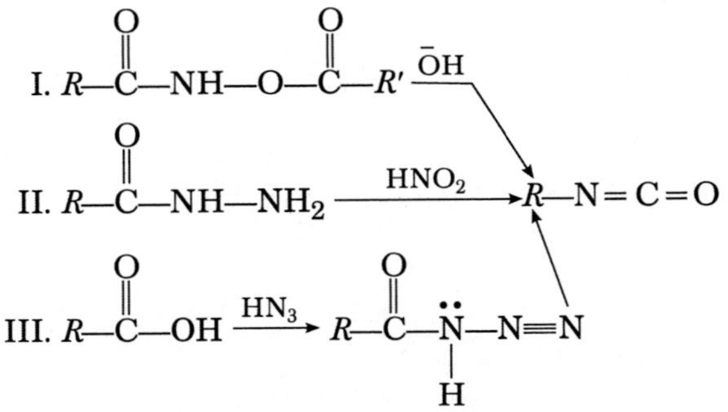

(a) (I) Schmidt (II) Curtius (III) Lossen
(b) (I) Lossen (II) Curtius (III) Schmidt

(c) (I) Curtius (II) Lossen (III) Schmidt
(d) (I) Schmidt (II) Lossen (III) Curtius

28. $CH_3CHO \xrightarrow{Al(OC_2H_5)_3} A \xrightarrow{C_2H_5ONa} B$, A and B are
(a) $CH_3COOC_2H_5$; $CH_3COCH_2COOC_2H_5$
(b) CH_3COOH; $CH_3COOC_2H_5$
(c) CH_3COOH; $CH_3CH_2COOC_2H_5$
(d) All of the above are incorrect

29. Consider the following statements.
I. Claisen condensation gives a β-keto ester.
II. Diels-Alder reaction is a [2 + 2] cyclo addition reaction.
III. Wolff-Kishner reduction is carried with zinc amalgam and HCl.
IV. Beckmann rearrangement is the acid-catalysed conversion of ketoximes to amides.
Select the correct statement.
(a) I, III (b) I, IV
(c) I, II (d) III, IV

30. 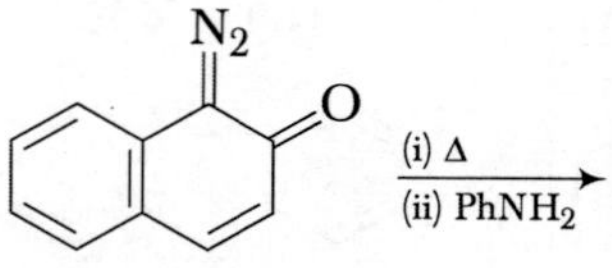 Product;

Product is

(a) 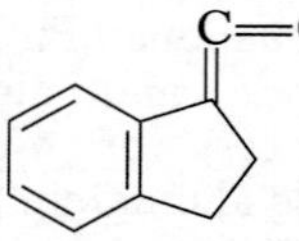 (b) 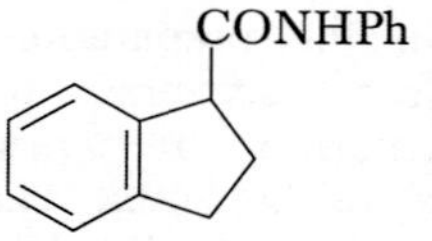

(c) 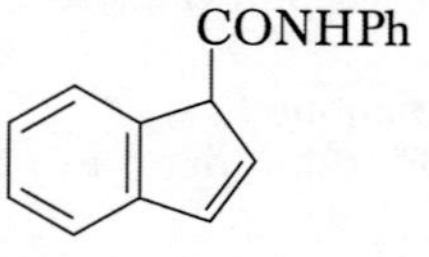 (d) 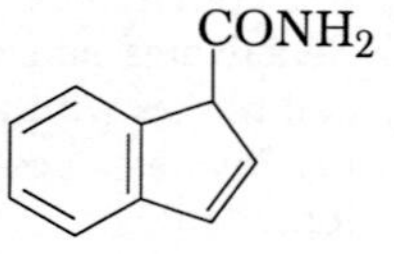

31. 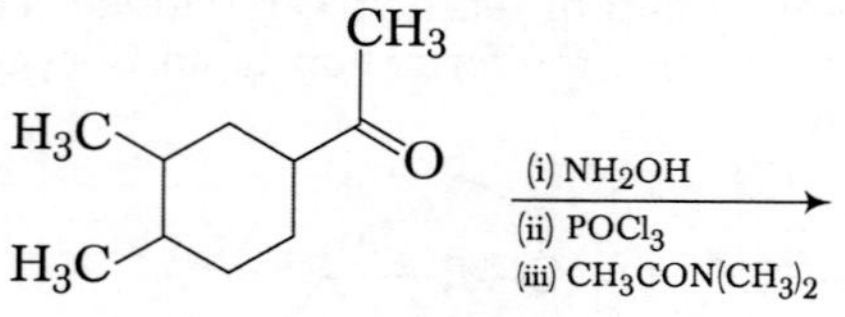

A is

(a) 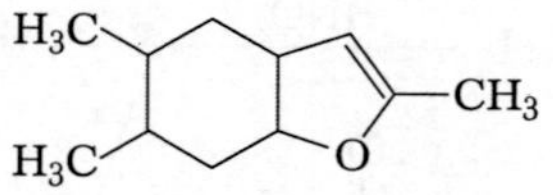

(b) 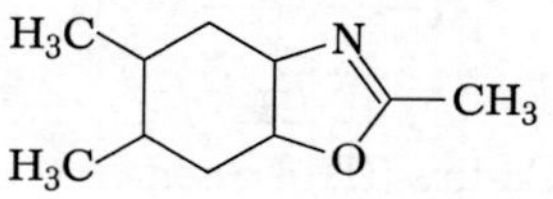

(c) 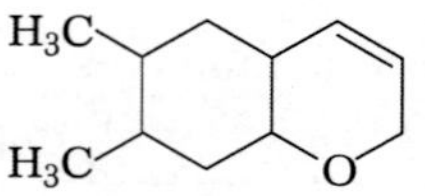

(d) 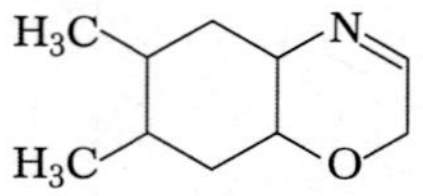

32. 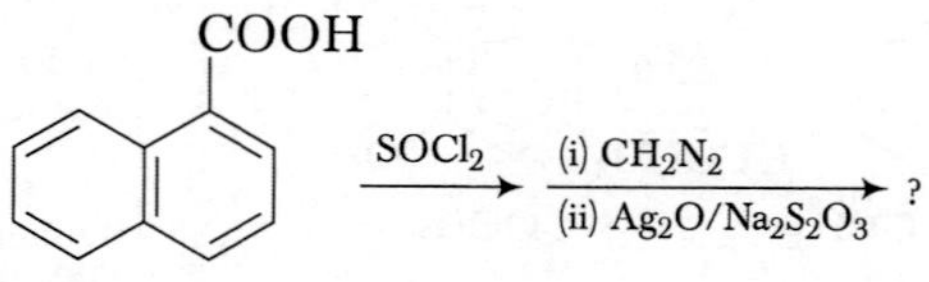

The product of the above synthesis is

(a) 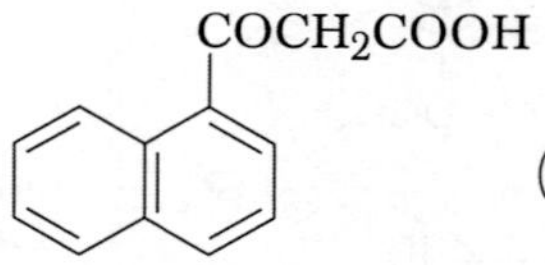 (b) 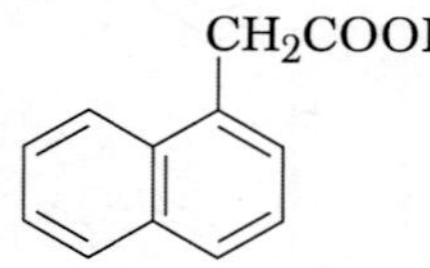

(c) 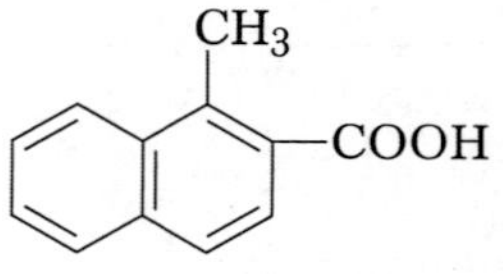 (d) 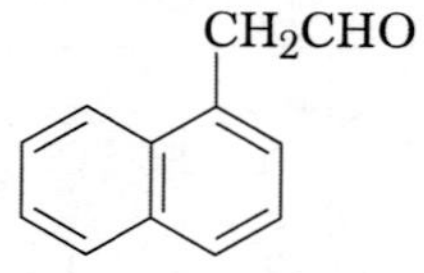

33. 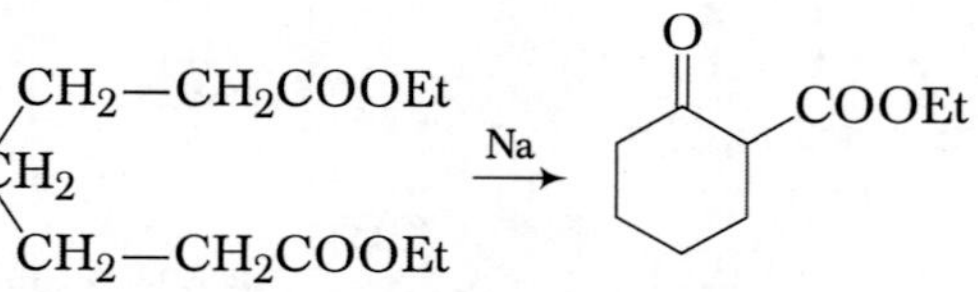

This transformation is an example of
(a) Dieckmann condensation
(b) Stobbe condensation
(c) Claisen condensation
(d) Darzen condensation

34. Coumafin is prepared industrially from salicylaldehyde by
(a) aldol condensation
(b) Dieckmann condensation
(c) Perkin reaction
(d) Stobbe condensation

35. The oxidation of aromatic methyl groups to aldehydes with chromyl chloride (CrO_2Cl_2) is known as
(a) Etard reaction
(b) Elbs persulphate oxidation
(c) Jones oxidation
(d) Oppenauer oxidation

36. Match the Column I with Column II.

	Column I		Column II
A.	Hofmann rearrangement	1.	Phenolic ketone
B.	Benzyl-benzylic acid rearrangement	2.	α-diazoketone
C.	Wolff rearrangement	3.	Isocyanate
D.	Fries rearrangement	4.	α-diketone

Codes

	A	B	C	D
(a)	3	4	1	2
(b)	3	4	2	1
(c)	4	3	2	1
(d)	3	1	4	2

37. Consider the following statements.

I. Claisen rearrangement is a [2,2]-sigmatropic rearrangement.

II. Claisen rearrangement proceeds *via* cyclic transition state.

III. Claisen rearrangement is concerted intramolecular rearrangement.

Select the correct statements.

(a) I, II (b) I, III
(c) II, III (d) Only I

38. Predict the product in the following reaction

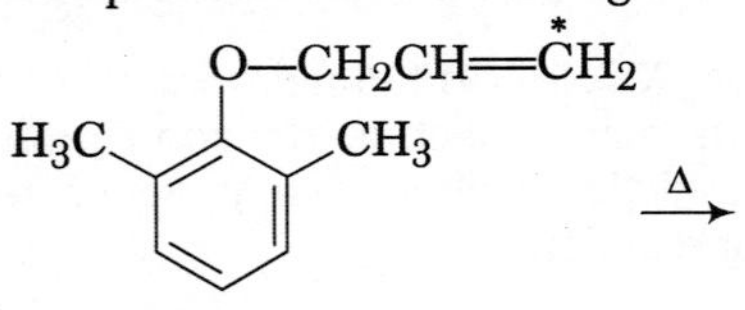

(a) 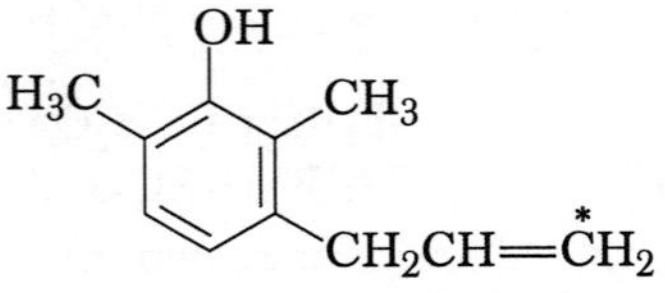

(b) 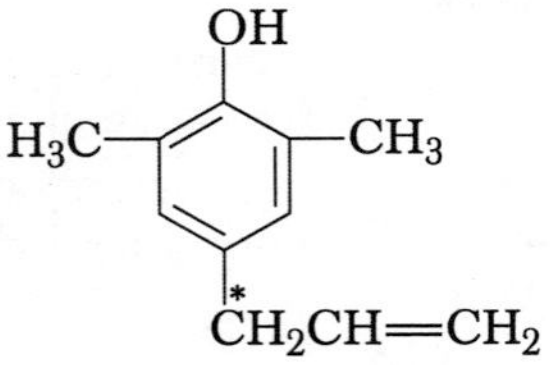

(c) 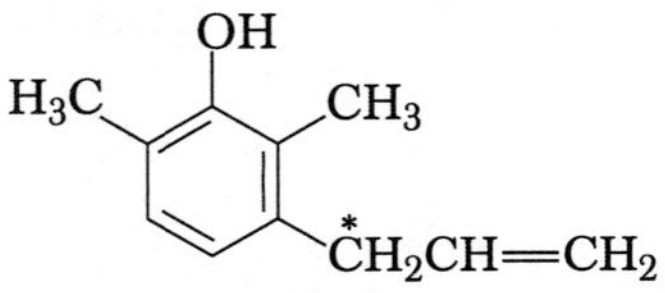

(d) 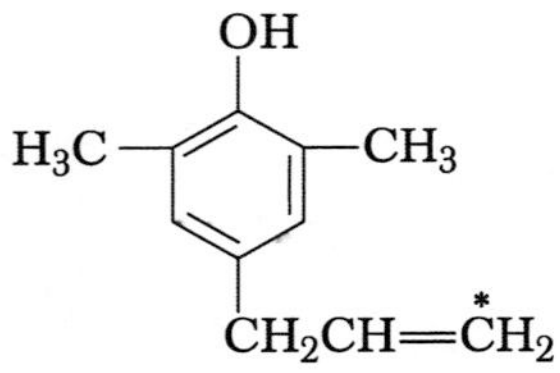

39. 2-chlorocyclobutanone on treatment with sodium methoxide followed by hydrolysis to give

(a) 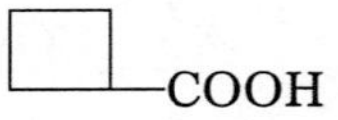 (b) 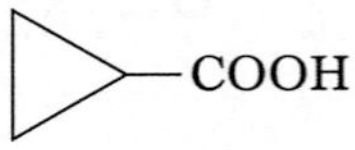

(c) 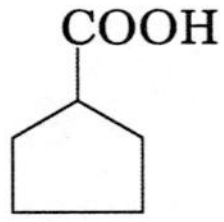 (d) None of these

40. Consider the following statements.

I. In Baeyer Villiger oxidation migration of alkyl group is 3° > 2° > 1° > methyl.

II. In Reimer-Tiemann reaction the electrophile is dichlorocarbene.

III. Organomagnesium compound is intermediate in Reformatsky reaction.

IV. The product of Perkin reaction is α, β-unsaturated acid.

Select the correct statements.

(a) I, II (b) I, III, IV
(c) I, II, IV (d) II, III, IV

41. Write the correct statements about the following reaction

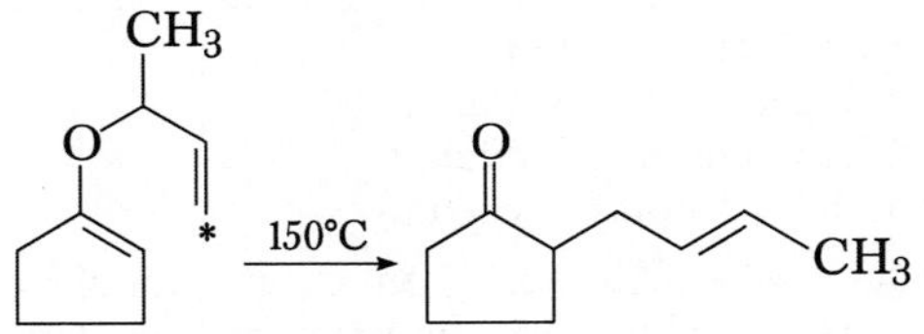

(a) It is a case of Claisen rearrangement
(b) There is thermal shift in allyl vinyl ether
(c) Isotopic C* retains its position
(d) Isotopic C* is in side chain —CH_3

42. What is/are the product(s) of the following Friedel-Crafts acylation of benzene?

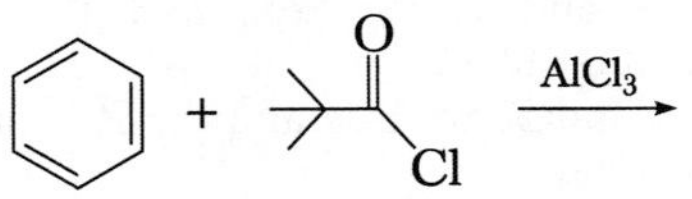

(a) 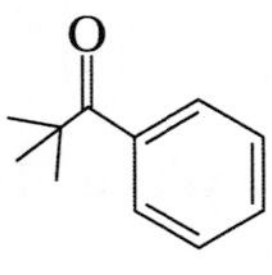 (b) 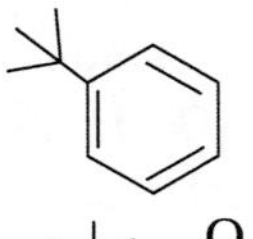

(c) 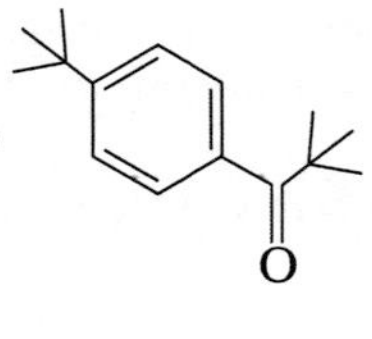 (d) 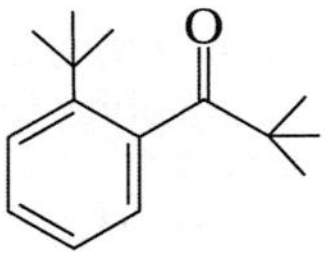

43. In the following reaction,

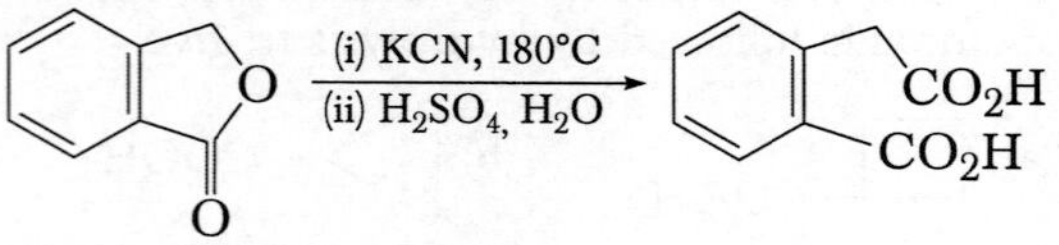

intermediates can be

(a) 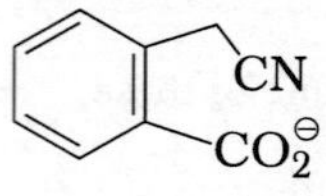 (b) 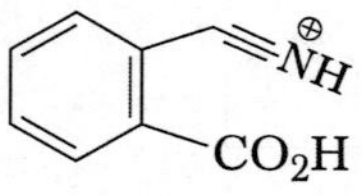

(c) 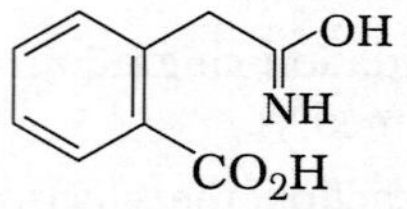 (d) 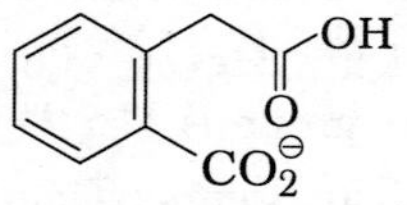

44. Friedel-Crafts acylation can be accomplished on

(a) 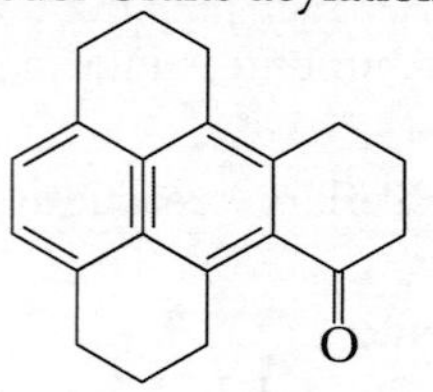 (b) 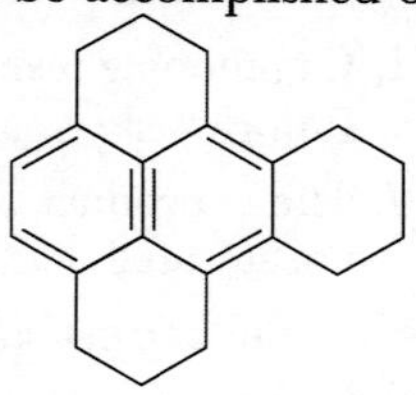

(c) 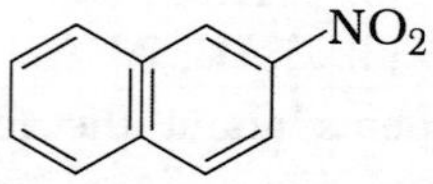 (d) 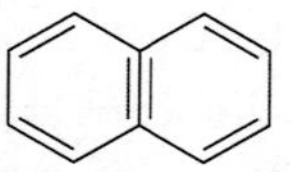

45. A new carbon-carbon bond formation is possible in
(a) Cannizzaro reaction
(b) Friedel-Crafts reaction
(c) Clemmensen reduction
(d) Reimer-Tiemann reaction

46. Under Wolff-Kishner reduction conditions the conversions which may be brought about are
(a) benzophenone into diphenylmethane
(b) benzaldehyde into benzyl alcohol
(c) cyclohexanone into cyclohexane
(d) cyclohexanone into cyclohexanol

Assertion & Reason

Codes
(a) Both A and R are true and R is the correct explanation of A.
(b) Both A and R are true and the R is not the correct explanation of A.
(c) A is true and R is false.
(d) R is true and A is false.

47. Assertion (A) Cannizzaro reaction is a disproportionation reaction.

Reason (II) It is a proton hydride ($H^+—H^-$) transfer reaction.

48. Assertion (A) Hofmann bromamide degradation reaction involves intramolecular migration of aryl or alkyl group.

Reason (R) Acid amide is converted to primary amine.

49. Assertion (A) Hofmann degradation and Curtius degradation methods are used to prepare 1° amines.

Reason (R) Both involve intramolecular alkyl shift.

50. Assertion (A) Crossed Cannizzaro reaction between formaldehyde and benzaldehyde gives benzyl alcohol and formate ion.

Reason (R) Formaldehyde is a better hydride donor than benzaldehyde.

Directions (Q. Nos. 51 to 53)

*R*eONH$_2$ is converted into *R*NH$_2$ by means of Hofmann bromamide degradation.

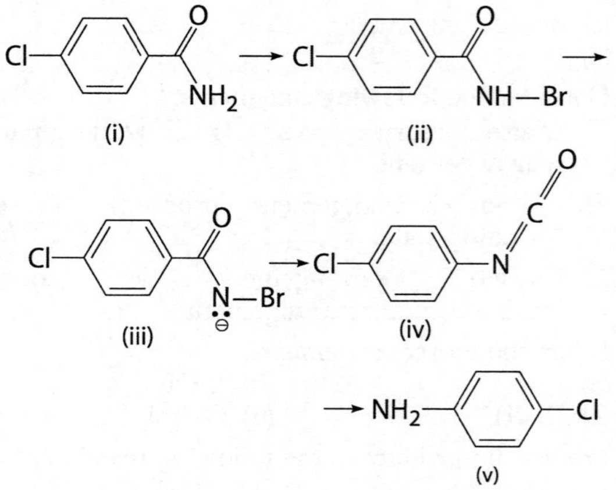

In this reaction, *R*CONHBr is formed from which this reaction has derived its name. Electron donating group at phenyl activates the reaction; Hofmann degradation reaction is an intramolecular reaction.

51. How can the conversion of (i) to (ii) be brought about?
(a) KBr (b) KBr + CH_3ONa
(c) KBr + KOH (d) Br_2 + KOH

52. Which is the rate determining step in Hofmann bromamide degradation?
(a) Formation of (i) (b) Formation of (ii)
(c) Formation of (iii) (d) Formation of (iv)

53. What are the constituent amines formed when the mixture of (i) and (ii) undergoes Hofmann bromamide degradation?

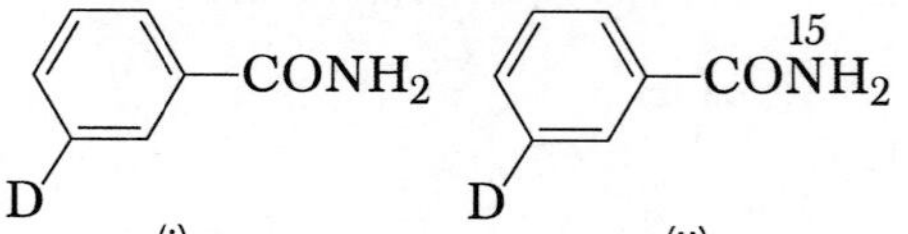

(i) (ii)

(a) 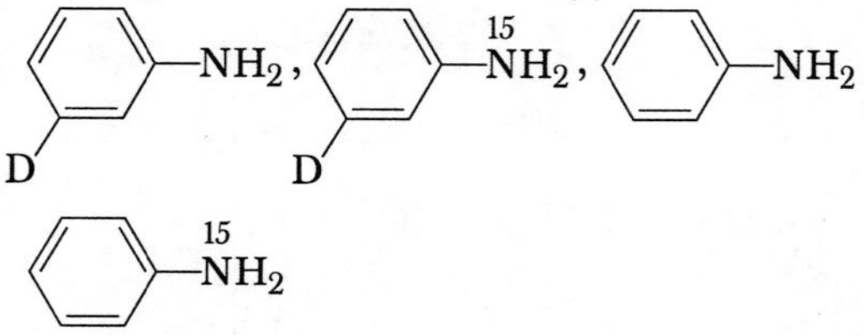

(b) 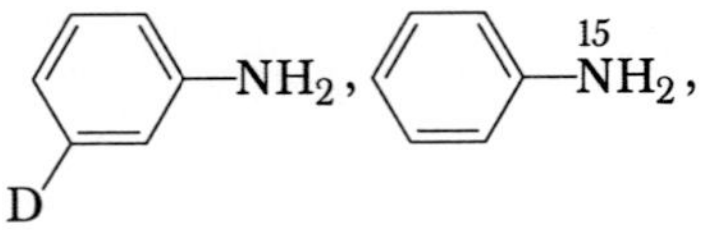

(c) 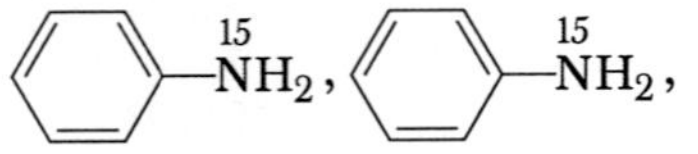

(d) 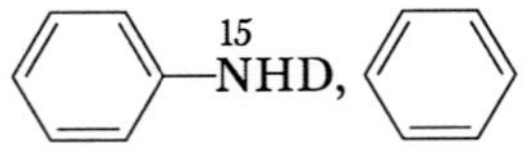

Directions (Q. Nos. 54 to 56)

Reimer-Tiemann reaction introduces an aldehyde group, on to the aromatic ring of phenol, *ortho* to the hydroxyl group. This reaction involves electrophilic aromatic substitution. This is a general method for the synthesis of substituted salicyladehydes as depicted below.

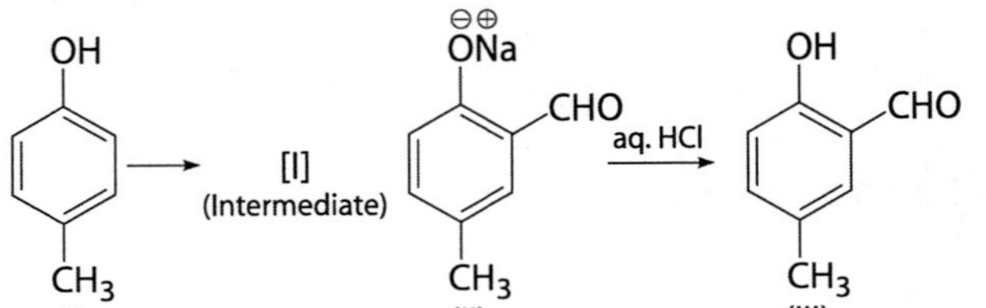

(I) (II) (III)

54. Which one of the following reagents is used in the above reaction?
(a) Aq. $NaOH + CH_3Cl$ (b) Aq. $NaOH + CH_2Cl_2$
(c) Aq. $NaOH + CHCl_3$ (d) Aq. $NaOH + CCl_4$

55. The electrophile in this reaction is
(a) $:CHCl$ (b) $^{\oplus}CHCl_2$
(c) $:CCl_2$ (d) $\bullet CCl_3$

56. The structure of the intermediate I is

(a) 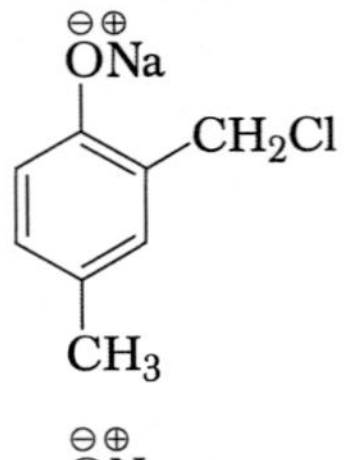

(b) 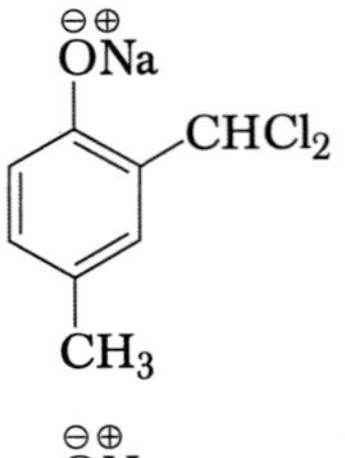

(c) 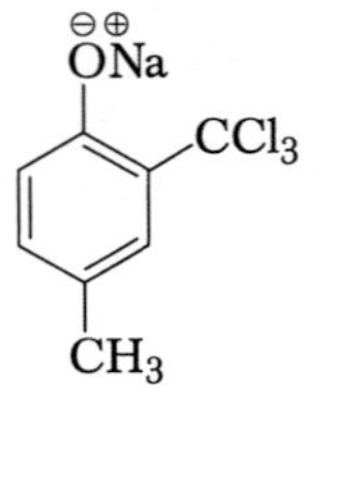

(d) 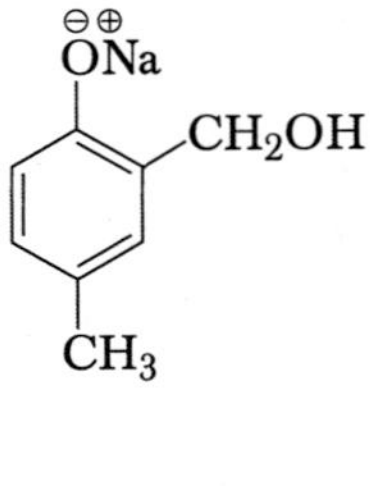

Directions (Q. Nos. 57 to 60)

Carboxylic acid derivatives can be converted into primary amines with loss of one carbon atom by both the Hofmann rearrangement and the Curtius rearrangement. Both proceed through similar mechanism. Based on the above paragraph, answer the following questions.

57. Select the correct statement(s).
(a) Hofmann rearrangement involves a primary amide
(b) Hofmann rearrangement involves an acyl azide
(c) Curtius rearrangement involes an acyl azide
(d) Curtius rearragement involves primary amide

58. Similar mechanism is
(a) intramolecular alkyl shift
(b) intramolecular hydride shift
(c) intermolecular acyl shift
(d) intramolecular acyl shift

59. The appetite-supporting drug **phentermine** (*A*)

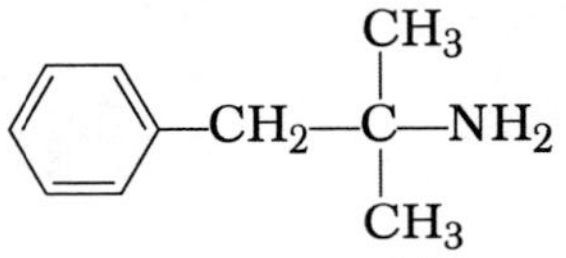

(*A*)

is prepared commercially by
(a) Hofmann rearrangement
(b) Curtius rearrangement
(c) Both (a) and (b)
(d) None of the above

60. Following antidepressant drug tranylcypromine (*A*) is made by

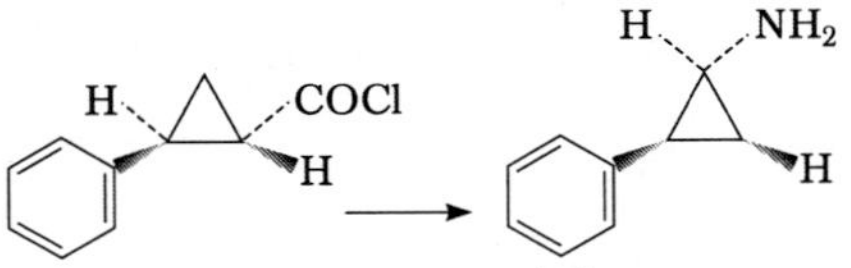

(*A*)

(a) (i) NH_3 (ii) $KBrO/\Delta$
(b) (i) H_2O (ii) N_3H, Δ
(c) (i) NaN_3 (ii) Δ (iii) H_2O
(d) (i) H_2O (ii) Δ (iii) NH_3

Answers

Exercise 1

1. (d)	**2.** (b)	**3.** (b)	**4.** (a)	**5.** (c)	**6.** (b)	**7.** (b)	**8.** (c)	**9.** (d)	**10.** (c)
11. (d)	**12.** (b)	**13.** (c)	**14.** (c)	**15.** (a)	**16.** (a)	**17.** (d)	**18.** (c)	**19.** (a)	**20.** (c)
21. (a)	**22.** (b)	**23.** (d)	**24.** (b)	**25.** (b)	**26.** (a)	**27.** (c)	**28.** (a)	**29.** (d)	**30.** (c)
31. (b)	**32.** (a)	**33.** (c)	**34.** (b)	**35.** (d)	**36.** (c)	**37.** (b)	**38.** (b)	**39.** (a)	**40.** (d)
41. (b)	**42.** (a)	**43.** (b)	**44.** (b)	**45.** (c)	**46.** (a)	**47.** (d)	**48.** (b)	**49.** (d)	**50.** (a)
51. (b)	**52.** (a)	**53.** (a)	**54.** (b)	**55.** (d)	**56.** (b)	**57.** (c)	**58.** (c)	**59.** (a)	**60.** (b)

Exercise 2

1. (b)	**2.** (a)	**3.** (c)	**4.** (a)	**5.** (d)	**6.** (a)	**7.** (d)	**8.** (c)	**9.** (b)	**10.** (b)
11. (d)	**12.** (c)	**13.** (d)	**14.** (a)	**15.** (d)	**16.** (b)	**17.** (c)	**18.** (c)	**19.** (d)	**20.** (a)
21. (b)	**22.** (c)	**23.** (b)	**24.** (b)	**25.** (a)	**26.** (c)	**27.** (b)	**28.** (a)	**29.** (b)	**30.** (c)
31. (b)	**32.** (b)	**33.** (a)	**34.** (c)	**35.** (a)	**36.** (b)	**37.** (c)	**38.** (d)	**39.** (b)	**40.** (c)
41. (a,b,d)	**42.** (a,b,c)	**43.** (a,b,c)	**44.** (b,d)	**45.** (b,d)	**46.** (a,c)	**47.** (a)	**48.** (b)	**49.** (a)	**50.** (a)
51. (d)	**52.** (d)	**53.** (b)	**54.** (c)	**55.** (c)	**56.** (b)	**57.** (a,c)	**58.** (a)	**59.** (a)	**60.** (c)

Hints & Solutions

Exercise 1

1.
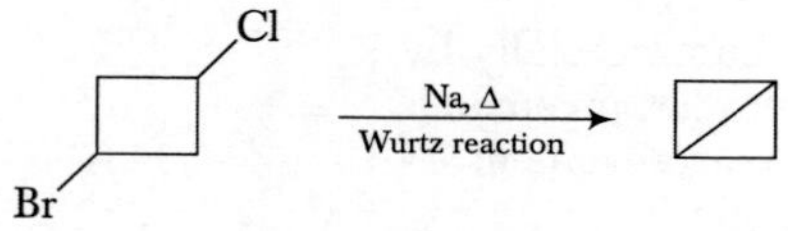

1-bromo-3-chlorocyclobutane

2.
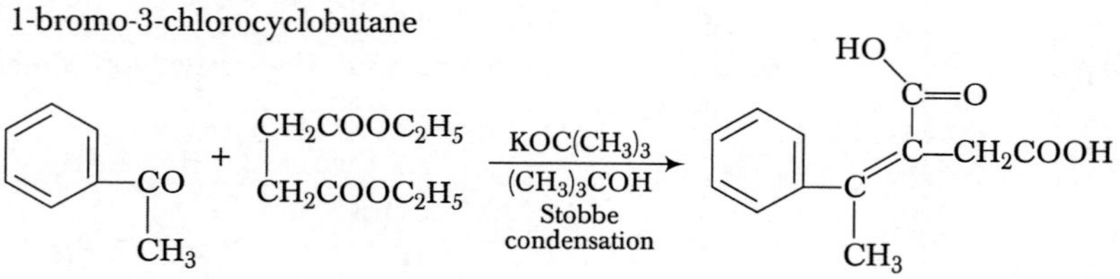

3.
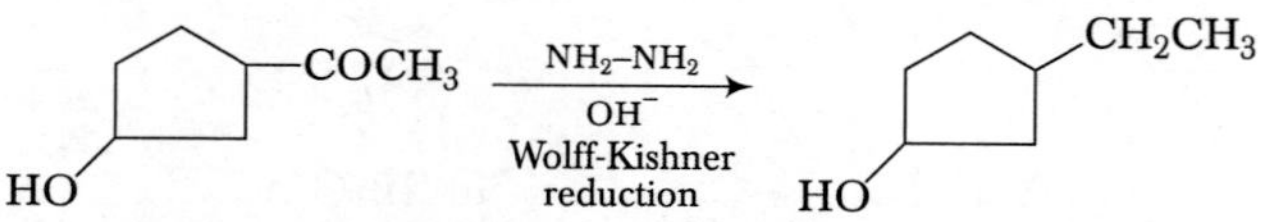

With Zn(Hg)/HCl the —OH group will also react.

7.
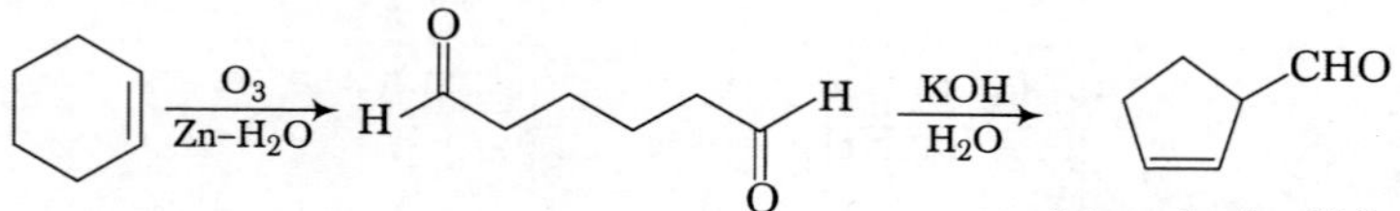

Intramolecular aldol condensation reaction

12.
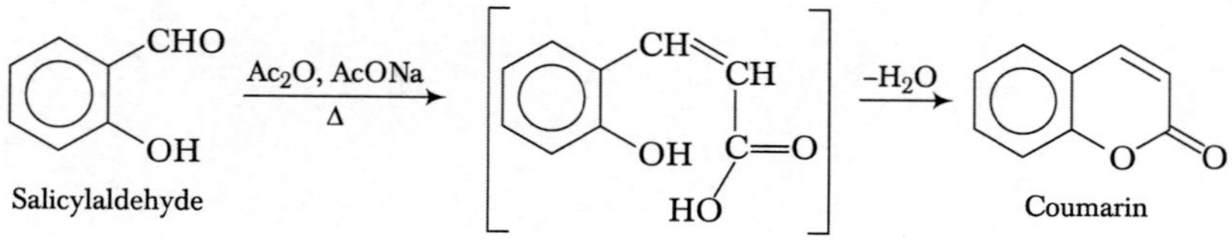

17. 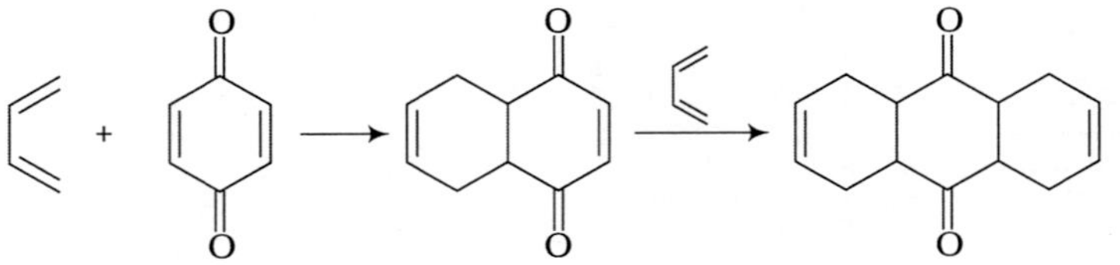

24. 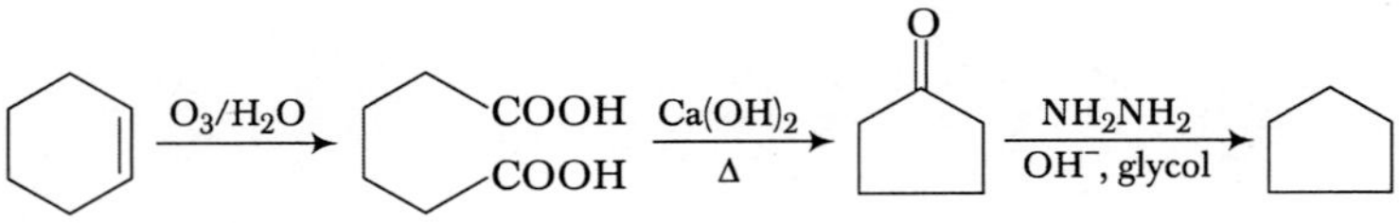

26. 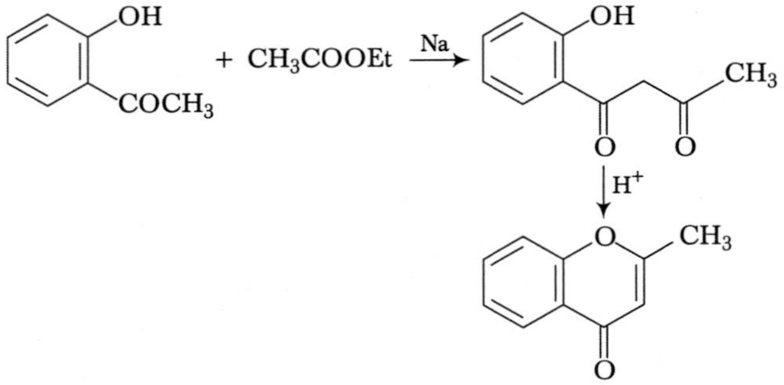

2-methylchromone

29. Ene reaction involves 6π-electron electrocyclic reaction.

30. 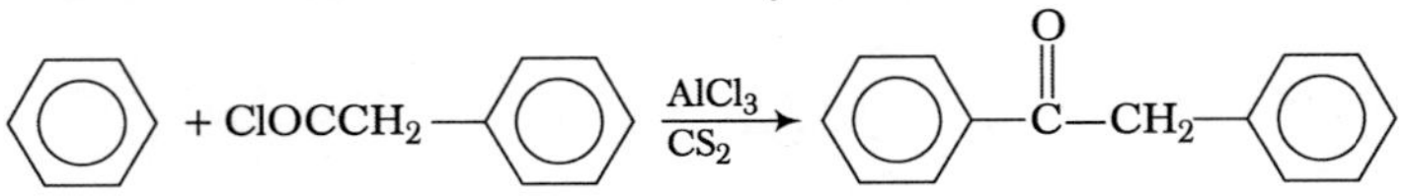

33. 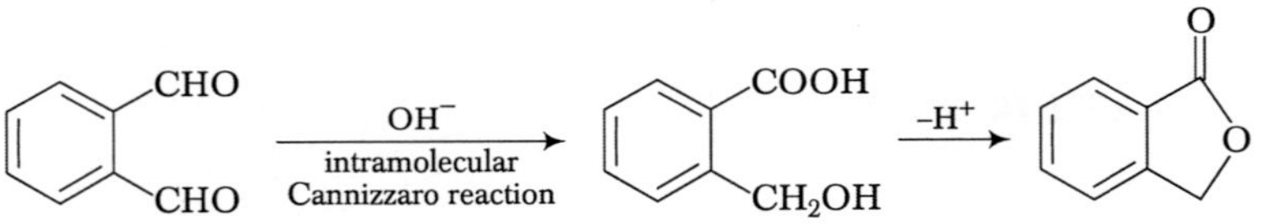

36. 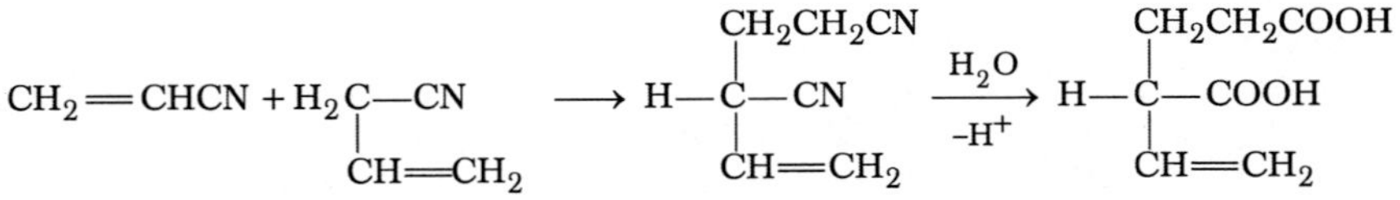

39. 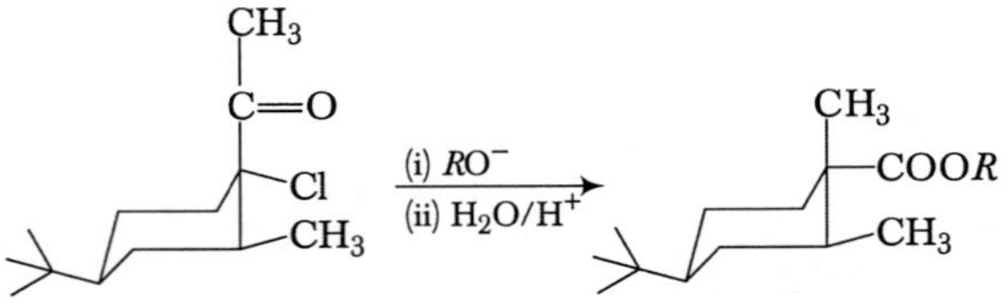

47. 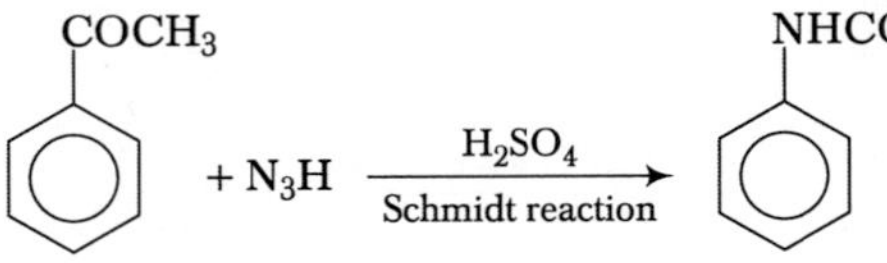

48. $\text{ArCOOH} \xrightarrow[(H_3PO_4)_n/\Delta]{CH_3NO_2} \left[\text{Ar—}\overset{\overset{\text{O}}{\|}}{\text{C}}\text{—NHOH}\right] \longrightarrow \text{Ar}\overset{\oplus}{\text{N}}\text{H}_3 \xrightarrow{^{\ominus}OH} \text{Ar—NH}_2$

52. $CH_3—CH═CH—CHO \xrightarrow[(CH_3)_2CHOH]{Al(OCHMe_2)_3} CH_3—CH═CH—CH_2OH$

Crotonaldehyde — MPV reduction — Crotyl alcohol

54. 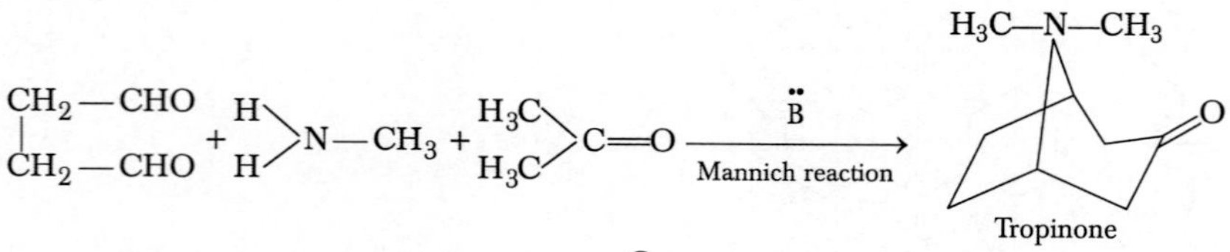

56. 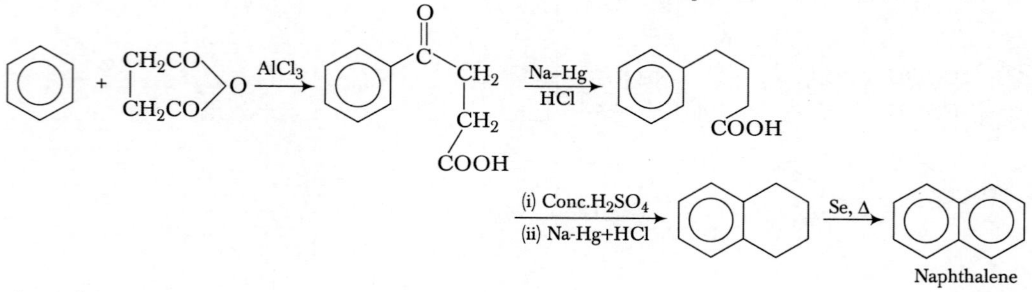

57. 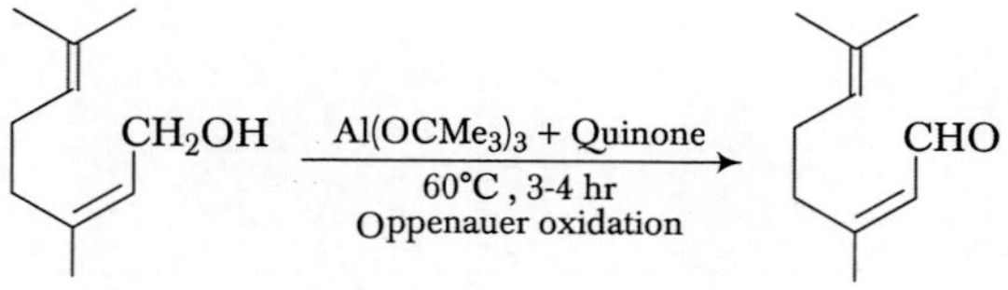

60. 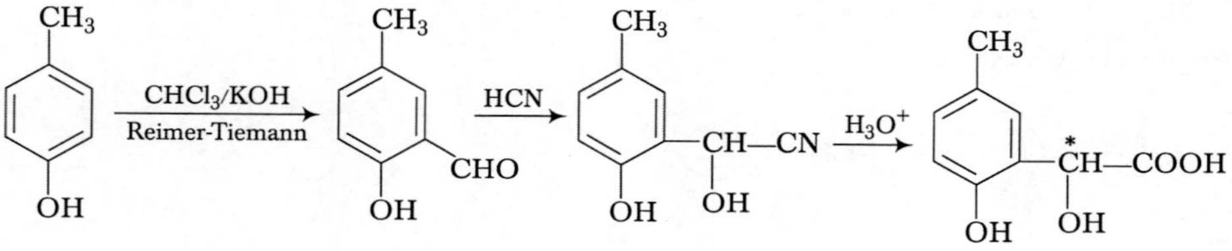

Exercise 2

1. $CHCl_3 \xrightarrow{\bar{O}H} \bar{C}Cl_3 \xrightarrow{-Cl^-} :CCl_2$

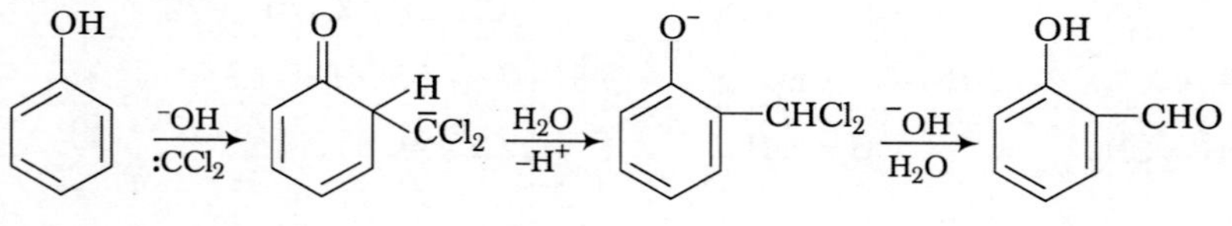

3. 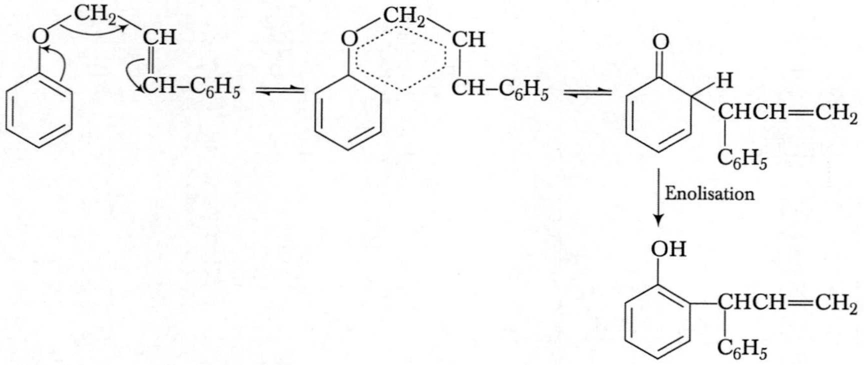

6.

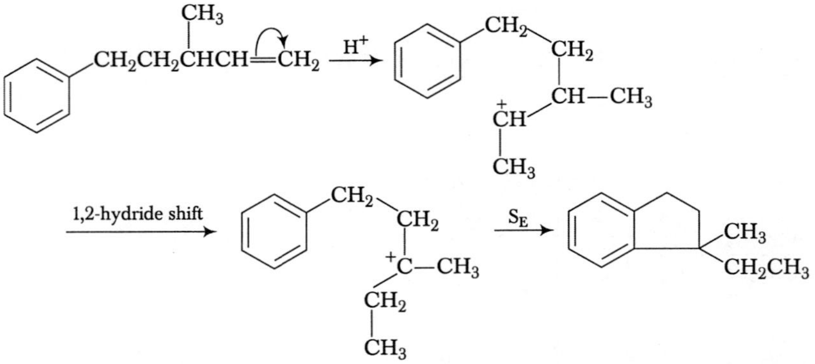

11. Diels-Alder reaction involves only addition without elimination. Hence, it is an **"atom economy reaction."**

14.

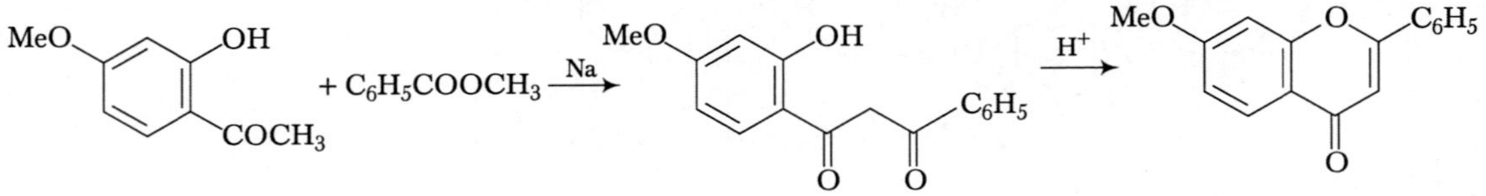

17.

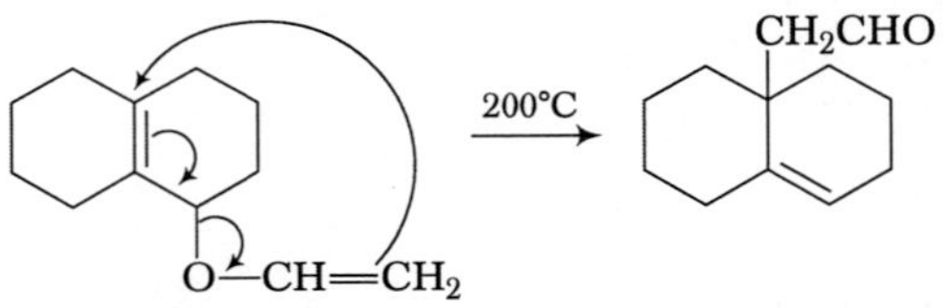

18. This reaction is a pinacol rearrangement.

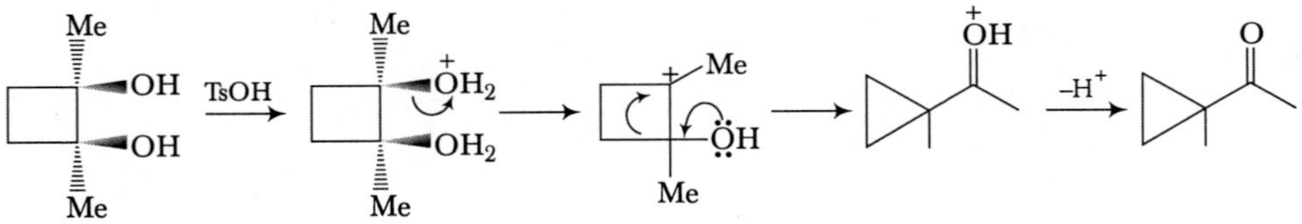

20.

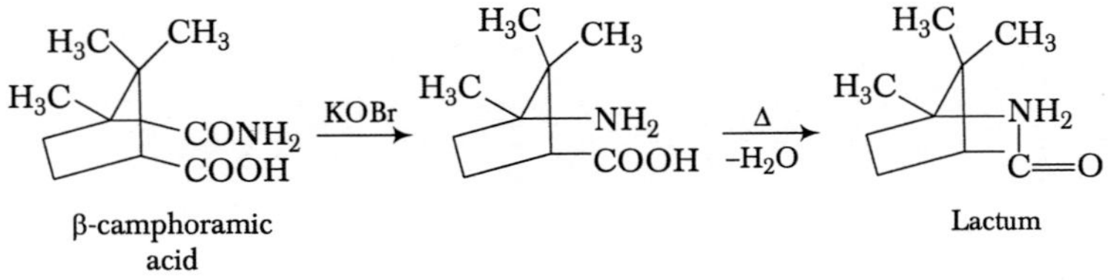

24.

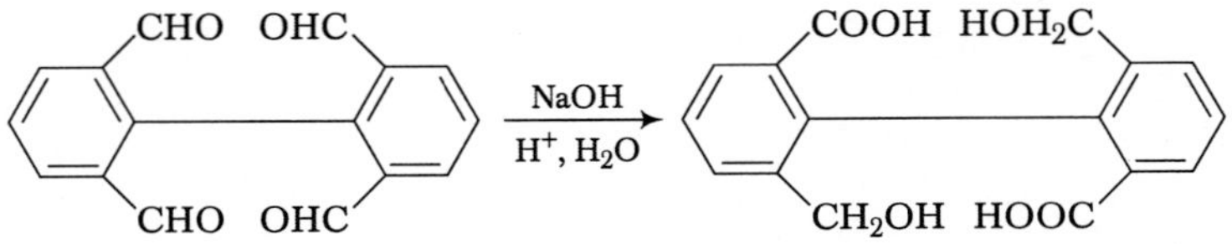

It is an example of intramolecular Cannizzaro reaction.

28. $CH_3CHO \xrightarrow[\text{Tischenko reaction}]{Al(OC_2H_5)_3} CH_3COOC_2H_5 \xrightarrow[\text{Claisen reaction}]{C_2H_5ONa} CH_3COCH_2COOC_2H_5$

30. 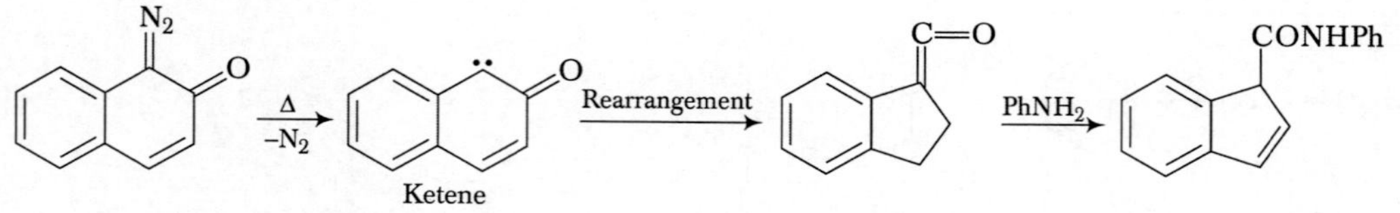

N2
O
Δ
–N2
Ketene
Rearrangement
C=O
PhNH2
CONHPh

32. 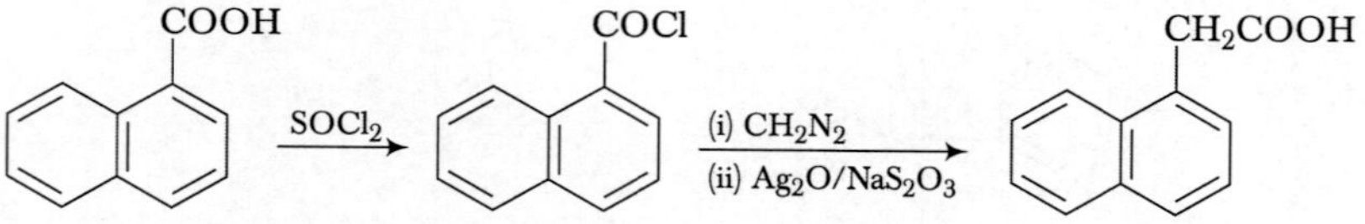

COOH
SOCl2
COCl
(i) CH2N2
(ii) Ag2O/NaS2O3
CH2COOH

38. 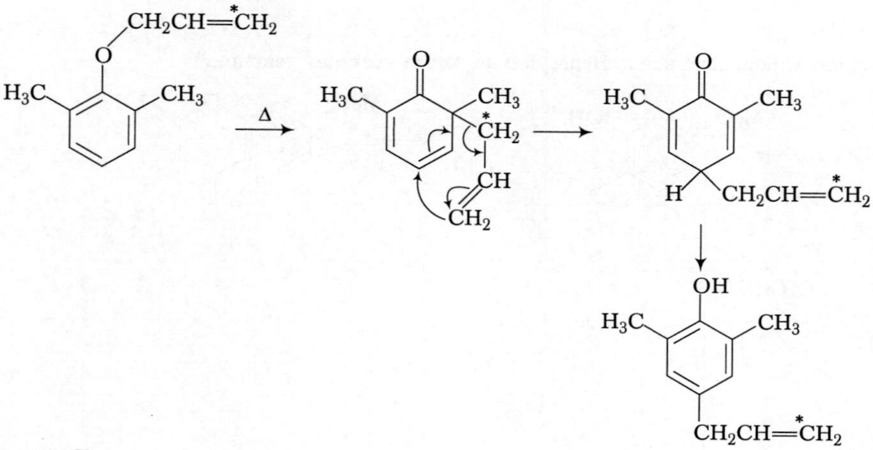

CH2CH=*CH2
O
H3C
CH3
Δ
*CH2
CH
CH2
H
OH

39. 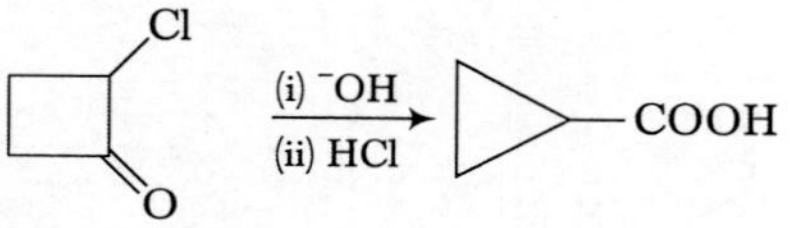

Cl
O
(i) ⁻OH
(ii) HCl
COOH

33 Organic Transformations and Reagents

Oxidation

Oxidation of an organic compound is defined as addition of oxygen, removal of hydrogen or removal of electrons from that compound.

$$RCHO \xrightarrow{[O]} R\text{—}COOH$$

$$R\text{—}CH_2OH \xrightarrow{-[2H]} R\text{—}CHO$$

$$C_6H_5O^{\ominus} \xrightarrow{Ce^{4+}} C_6H_5O^{\bullet}$$

Oxidation of Hydrocarbons

Oxidation of alkenes

(a) **Epoxidation** Olefinic double bonds react with per acids to give epoxides. *Meta*-chloroperbenzoic acid (*m*-CPBA) is the most useful reagent for effecting alkene-epoxidation oxidation.

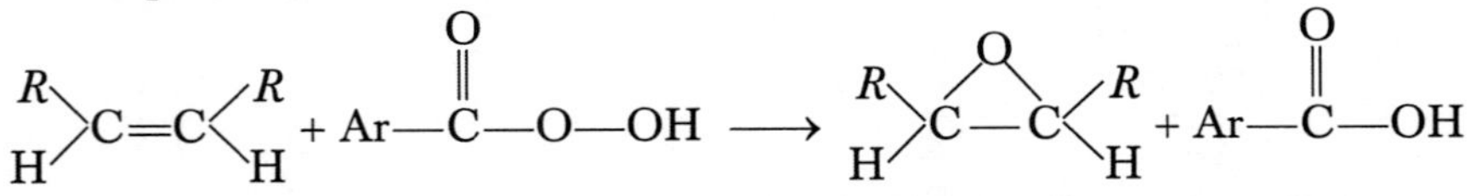

The epoxidation with per acids is stereospecific and take place by *syn*-addition to the double bond.

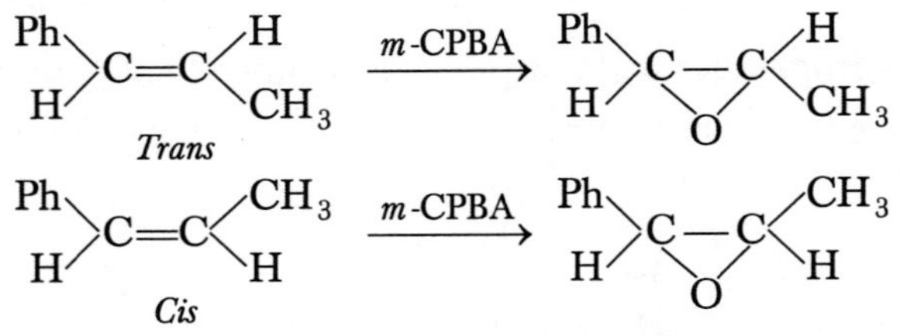

In case of cyclic alkenes, the reagent approaches from less hindered side of the double bond.

Syllabus

- Functional Group Interconversion Including Oxidations and Reductions
- Common Catalysts and Reagents (Organic, Inorganic, Organometallic and Enzymatic).
- Chemo, Regio and Stereoselective Transformations

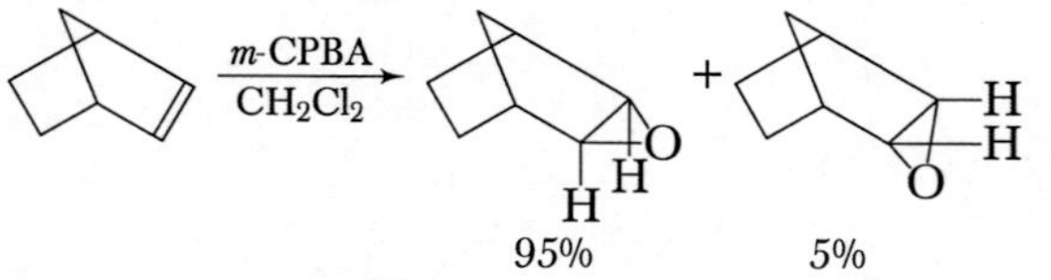

Dimethyldioxirane is also used for epoxidation.

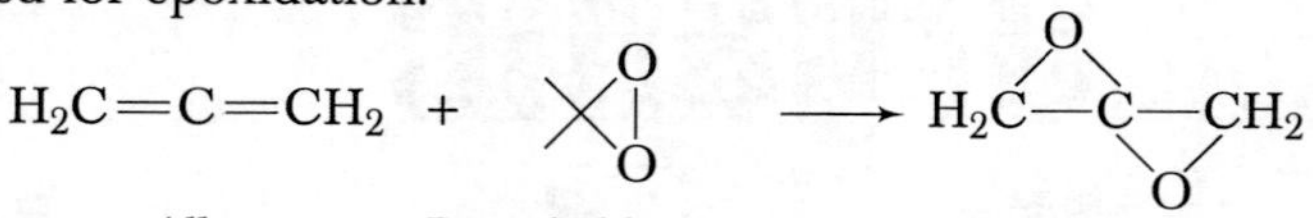

Allene Dimethyldioxirane Spirodioxide

(b) **Hydroxylation *i.e.*, diol or glycol formation** There are many reagents which add two OH groups to C=C but potassium permanganate, osmium tetroxide and iodine/silver acetate are most important reagents for this purpose.

- Alkaline $KMnO_4$ and osmium tetroxide (OsO_4) give *syn*-addition from the less hindered side of the double bond. The reaction is stereospecific *cis*-2-butene gives *meso* form whereas *trans*-2-butene gives (*dl*) mixture.

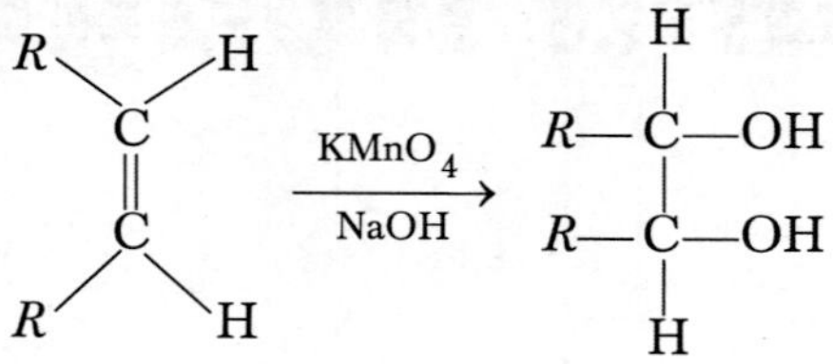

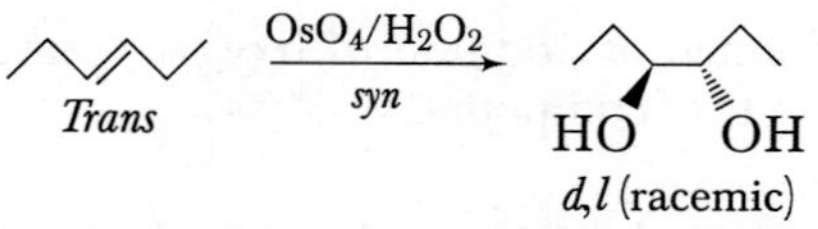

Note Oxidation of norbornene with $KMnO_4$ in basic medium gives 1,2-glycol while in neutral medium a dialdehyde is obtained.

(c) **Oxidative cleavage of alkenes by ozone**

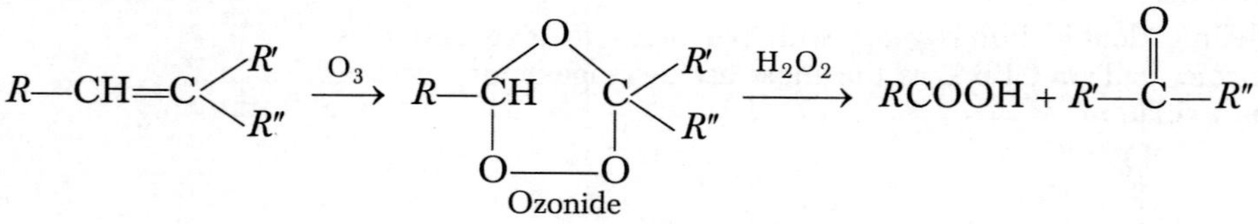

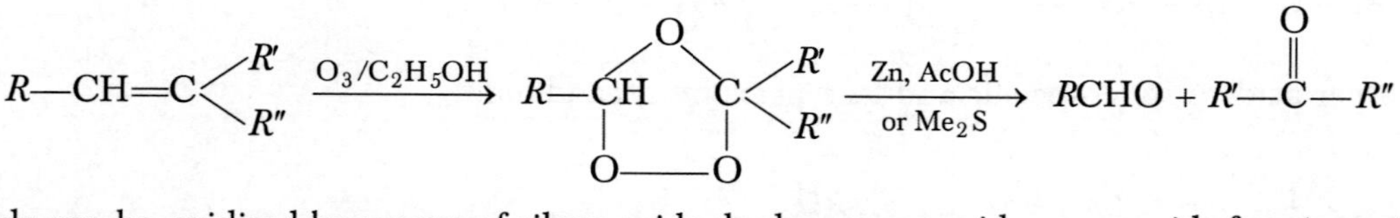

Ozonide can be oxidised by means of silver oxide, hydrogen peroxide or peracids forming acid and/or ketones. Ozonide can be reduced with zinc-acid, triphenyl phosphine and dimethyl sulphide, etc., giving aldehydes and/or ketones while $LiAlH_4$ or $NaBH_4$ to form alcohols.

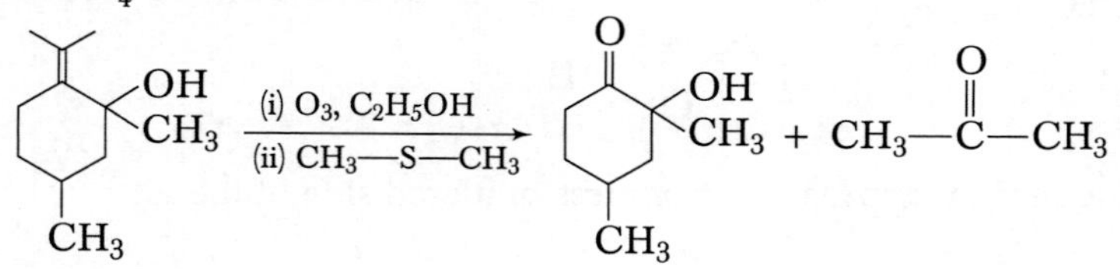

Oxidation of activated saturated C—H groups

Saturated C—H groups adjacent to a carbon-carbon multiple bonds or carbon-hetero atom multiple bonds are the example of activated C—H groups. Allylic system, benzylic systems and —CH_2—CO systems are the example of such groups.

(a) **Oxidation of benzylic systems**

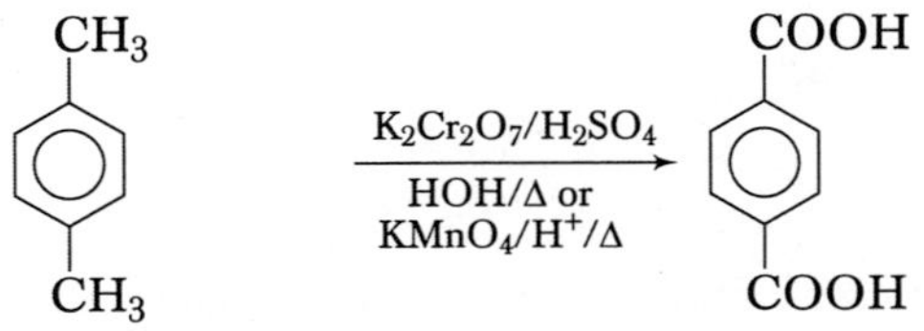

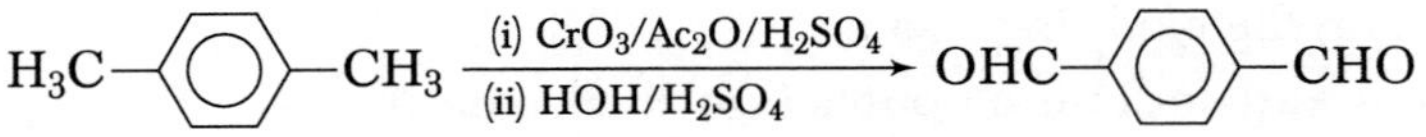

(b) **Oxidation at allylic positions**

$$CH_3CH_2CH_2CH_2CH{=}CH{-}Bu \xrightarrow[\text{Pyridine}/CH_2Cl_2]{SeO_2} CH_3CH_2CH_2{-}\underset{}{\overset{OH}{\overset{|}{C}}}H\,CH{=}CHBu$$

The oxidation occurs at the more substituted end of the double bond.

(c) **Oxidation at —CH_2—CO— system**

Activated C—H group adjacent to carbonyl group can be oxidised by the following reagents :

(i) **SeO_2**

$$C_6H_5{-}\overset{O}{\overset{\|}{C}}{-}CH_3 \xrightarrow[\text{Dioxane/HOH}]{SeO_2} C_6H_5{-}\overset{O}{\overset{\|}{C}}{-}CHO$$

The reactivity of methylene group is more than methyl group for SeO_2.

Oxidation of unactivated C—H group

(a) The oxidation of tertiary C—H to C—OH group can be achieved by alkaline $KMnO_4$.

$$CH_3{-}\underset{C_3H_7}{\underset{|}{\overset{C_2H_5}{\overset{|}{C}}}}{-}H \xrightarrow[^{\ominus}OH]{KMnO_4} CH_3{-}\underset{C_3H_7}{\underset{|}{\overset{C_2H_5}{\overset{|}{C}}}}{-}OH$$

(b) **Hofmann-Loeffler-Freytag reaction**

N-haloamines having hydrogen on δ-carbon give this reaction. Oxidation takes place at unactivated δ-carbon having hydrogen. The N-halogenated amine converts into N-containing heterocycles.

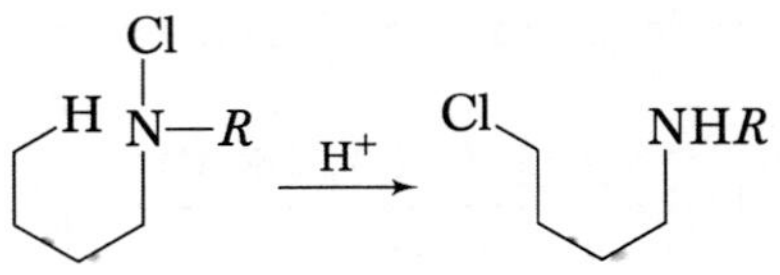

$$R\text{—}CH_2\text{—}CH_2\text{—}CH_2\text{—}CH_2\text{—}\underset{\substack{|\\ Cl}}{N}\text{—}R' \xrightarrow[H_2SO_4/\Delta]{H^+} R\text{—}\underset{\substack{|\\ Cl}}{C}H\text{—}CH_2CH_2CH_2NHR'$$

$$\downarrow -HCl$$

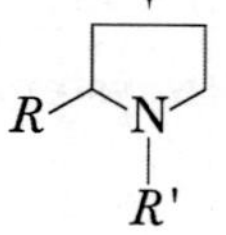

Pyrrolidine

Oxidation of Alcohols

This is the most useful and wide spread area of oxidation as it encompasses the alcohol → carbonyl compound → carboxylic acid sequence. Whether the resulting carbonyl compound is an aldehyde, a ketone or a carboxylic acid depends on the alcohol and on the oxidizing agent.

Oxidation by chromic acid and sodium or potassium dichromate

Primary alcohol on oxidation with sodium or potassium dichromate in H_2SO_4 gives aldehyde which are further oxidized to carboxylic acid.

$$3RCH_2OH + Cr_2O_7^{2-} + 4H_2SO_4 \longrightarrow 3RCHO + 7H_2O + 2Cr^{3+} + 4SO_4^{2-}$$

$$3RCHO + Cr_2O_7^{2-} + 4H_2SO_4 \longrightarrow 3RCOOH + 2Cr^{3+} + 4SO_4^{2-} + 4H_2O$$

Secondary alcohols on the other hand give ketones which usually do not undergo further oxidation.

$$CH_3\text{—}\overset{\substack{OH\\ |}}{C}H\text{—}(CH_2)_5\text{—}CH_3 \xrightarrow[H_2SO_4,\ HOH]{Na_2Cr_2O_7} CH_3\text{—}\overset{\substack{O\\ \|}}{C}\text{—}(CH_2)_5\text{—}CH_3$$

- **Jones reagent** (combination of CrO_3, H_2SO_4 and acetone solvent) is useful for the oxidation of alcohols which contain C—C double or triple bonds, allylic or benzylic C—H bonds and other sensitive groups. It is carried out at 0–20°C.

$$HC{\equiv}C\text{—}CH{=}CHCH_2OH \xrightarrow[\text{Jones reagent}]{[O]} HC{\equiv}C\text{—}CH{=}CH\text{—}COOH$$

$$C_4H_9\text{—}C{\equiv}C\text{—}\overset{\substack{OH\\ |}}{C}H\text{—}CH_3 \xrightarrow[\text{Jones reagent}]{[O]} C_4H_9\text{—}C{\equiv}C\text{—}\overset{\substack{O\\ \|}}{C}\text{—}CH_3$$

- Chromium trioxide-pyridine complex, $CrO_3 \cdot 2C_5H_5N$ is known as **Collins reagent** and is useful for the oxidation of alcohols containing acid-sensitive groups. Oxidations are generally carried out in CH_2Cl_2 solution under anhydrous conditions.

$$\underset{\text{Cinnamyl alcohol}}{C_6H_5{=}CH\text{—}CH_2OH} \xrightarrow{CrO_3,\ \text{Pyridine}} \underset{\text{Cinnamaldehyde}}{C_6H_5CH{=}CH\text{—}CHO}$$

Oxidation by dimethyl sulphoxide (DMSO)

- The most important reagent for the oxidation of primary alcohols into aldehydes is the mixture of triethylamine, DMSO and oxalyl chloride (**Swern reaction**). The reaction is done in dichloromethane at low temperature (below –30°C).

$$C_6H_5CH{=}CH\text{—}CH_2\text{—}\underset{\substack{|\\ CH_3}}{C}H\text{—}CH_2OH \xrightarrow[Et_3N,\ CH_2Cl_2]{(COCl_2)_2,\ DMSO} C_6H_5CH{=}CH\text{—}CH_2\underset{\substack{|\\ CH_3}}{C}HCHO$$

- Alcohol can also be oxidised by DMSO by converting it into tosylate ester. The formation of tosylate is achieved *in situ* by the reaction of primary alcohol with TsCl in presence of dicyclohexyl carbodiamide (DCC) followed by the treatment with DMSO.

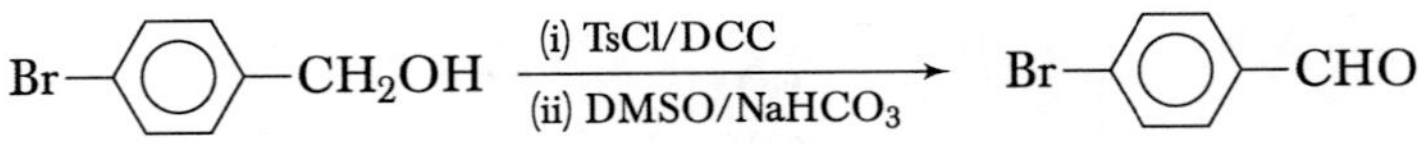

Note DMSO is also used to convert alkyl halides into aldehydes.

$$RCH_2I \xrightarrow[\text{DMSO}]{\text{NaHCO}_3} RCHO$$

$$\left.\begin{array}{l} RCOCH_2X \\ ROOCCH_2X \\ C_6H_5CH_2X \end{array}\right] \xrightarrow[\text{DMSO}]{\text{NaHCO}_3} \begin{array}{l} RCOCHO \\ ROOCCHO \\ C_6H_5CHO \end{array}$$

Oxidation of Aldehydes

$$C_6H_{13}CHO \xrightarrow{KMnO_4/H_2SO_4} C_6H_{13}\text{—}COOH$$

$$R\text{—}CHO \xrightarrow{K_2Cr_2O_7/H_2SO_4} R\text{—}COOH$$

Silver oxide (Ag_2O) is used for selective oxidation since it has no effect on other oxidisable functional groups.

$$R\text{—}CH\text{=}CH\text{—}CHO \xrightarrow[\text{NaOH}]{Ag_2O} R\text{—}CH\text{=}CH\text{—}COOH$$

$$2CH_3CHO \xrightarrow[\text{Tischenko reaction}]{Al(OC_2H_5)_3} CH_3\text{—}\overset{O}{\overset{\|}{C}}\text{—}O\text{—}CH_2\text{—}CH_3$$

Oxidation of Ketones

$$R\text{—}\overset{O}{\overset{\|}{C}}\text{—}CH_2R' \xrightarrow{\text{Alk. }KMnO_4} R\text{—}COOH + R'COOH$$

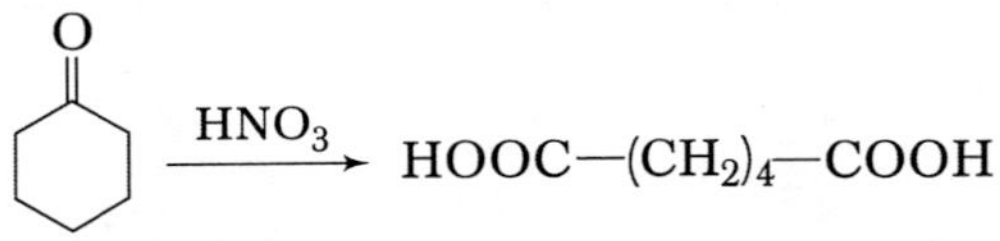

Ketones having α-methyl group give haloform reaction with X_2/OH^-.

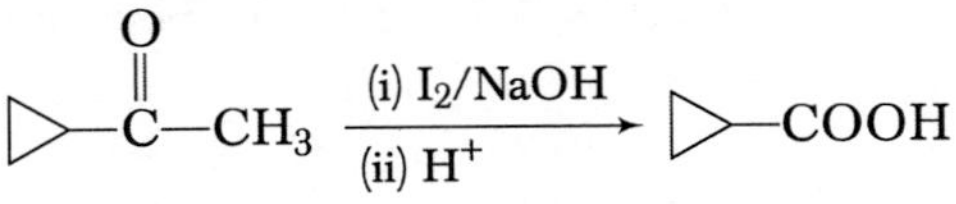

Oxidation of ketones to esters and cyclic ketones to lactones by treatment with peracids is known as **Baeyer-Villiger oxidation.**

$$CH_3\text{—}\underset{CH_3}{\overset{CH_3}{\overset{|}{\underset{|}{C}}}}\text{—}\overset{O}{\overset{\|}{C}}\text{—}CH_3 \xrightarrow{CF_3COOOH} CH_3\text{—}\overset{O}{\overset{\|}{C}}\text{—}O\text{—}\underset{CH_3}{\overset{CH_3}{\overset{|}{\underset{|}{C}}}}\text{—}CH_3$$

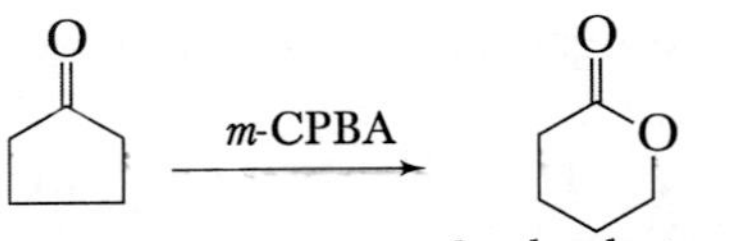

δ-valerolactone

Oxidation of Carboxylic Acids

The carboxylic acids on oxidation will always give CO_2 hence the oxidation of carboxylic acids is known as oxidative decarboxylation.

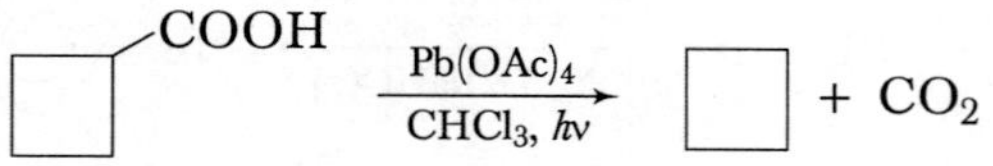

1,2-dicarboxylic acids give alkene with lead tetraacetate.

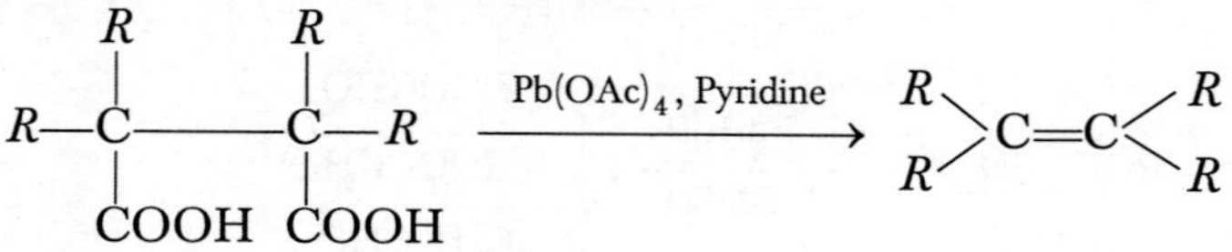

Oxidation of Amines

- The most common reagents for the oxidation of aliphatic primary amines are H_2O_2 and peracids.

$$CH_3CH_2CH_2NH_2 \xrightarrow{H_2O_2} \underset{\text{Aldoxime}}{CH_3CH_2CH{=}NOH}$$

$$CH_3-(CH_2)_3-CH_2NO_2 \xrightarrow{CH_3COOOH} CH_3-(CH_2)_3CH_2NO_2$$

$$R_2NH \xrightarrow{H_2O_2} \underset{\text{Hydroxyl amine}}{R_2N-OH}$$

$$R_2\ddot{N}-R \xrightarrow[\text{or peracid}]{H_2O_2/CH_3OH} (R)_3-\overset{+}{N}-O^-$$

- The usual reagent for the oxidation of primary amines into aldehydes and ketones is N-bromosuccinimide providing imine derivatives.

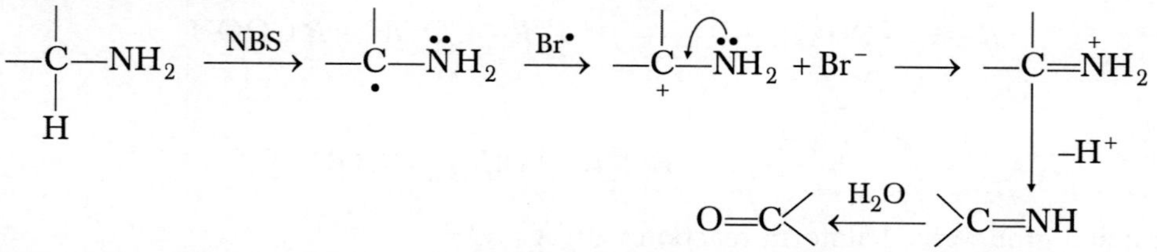

- Aliphatic primary amines can also be oxidised by 4,5-di-*t*-butyl-*o*-benzoquinone.

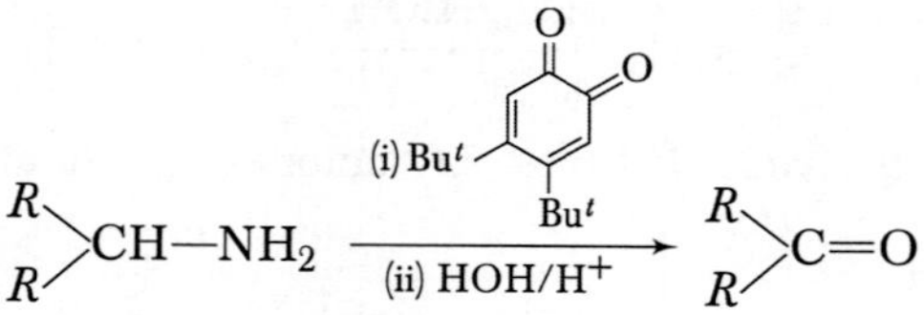

This reagent oxidises only those aliphatic primary amines whose α-carbon is only secondary.

Reduction

The removal of oxygen or the addition of hydrogen or the addition of electrons to an organic substrate is known as reduction.

$$RCH{=}CH_2 + H_2 \xrightarrow{Pt} R-CH_2-CH_3$$

Reduction of Hydrocarbons

Reduction of alkenes

(a) **Catalytic hydrogenation** This is the most convenient methods for the reduction of alkenes.

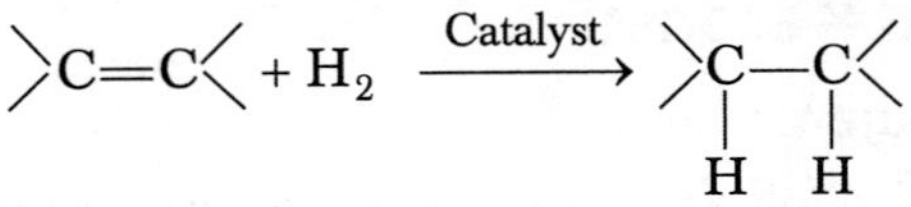

The addition of hydrogen is *syn*. Hence, reaction is stereospecific.

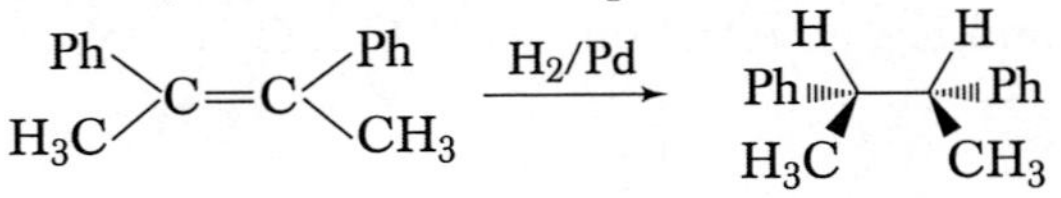

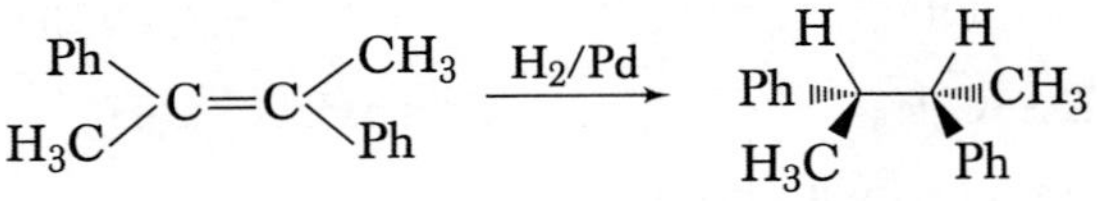

Wilkinson's catalyst ($[Ph_3P]_3RhCl$) is a most useful homogeneous catalyst for hydrogenation of alkenes.

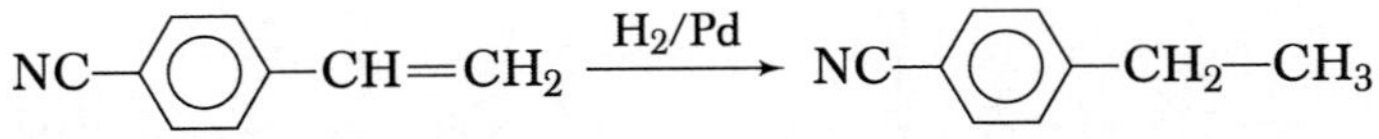

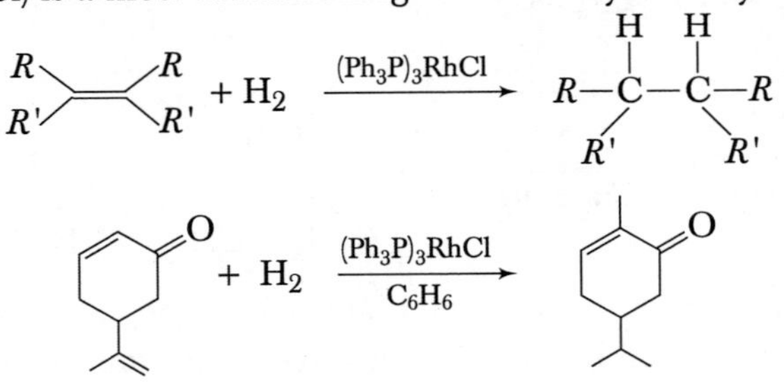

Reduction of alkynes

(a) **Catalytic hydrogenation**

$$RC\equiv CR \xrightarrow[\text{Catalyst}]{H_2} RCH{=}CHR \xrightarrow[\text{Catalyst}]{H_2} RCH_2CH_2R$$

The reduction can be stopped at the alkene stage by using Pd poisoned with $BaSO_4$ (Lindlar's catalyst) or nickel boride (P-2 catalyst or Brown's catalyst)

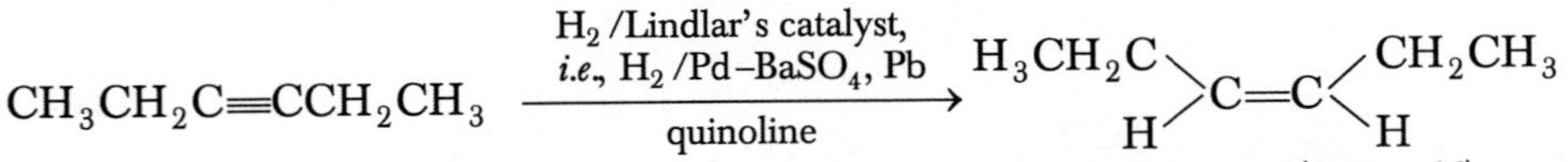

Cis-2-hexene (95% yield)

Hence, reduction of alkyne in presence of Lindlar's catalyst is stereoselective reaction.

(b) **Reduction with boranes** The reaction is stereoselective and the addition is *syn.*

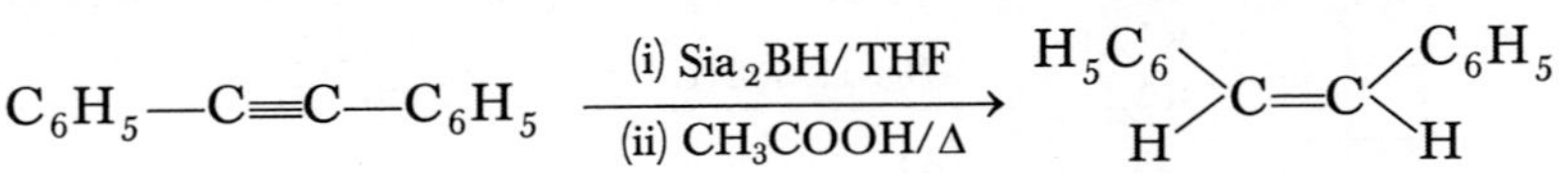

Cis-alkene

Sia_2BH is disiamyl borane. It is sterically hindered dialkyl borane.

(c) **Reduction with IA metals in liquid ammonia**

Non-terminal alkyne reacts with a solution of IA group metals (Li, Na, K) in liquid ammonia to give *trans*-alkene.

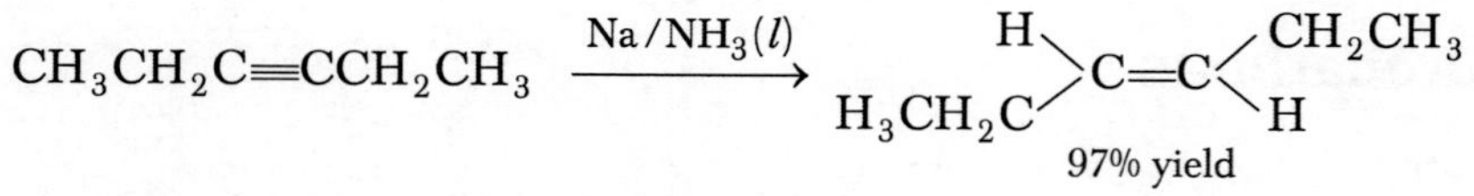

Reduction of Aldehydes and Ketones

Reduction with hydride-transfer reagents

The reduction of aldehydes to primary alcohols and ketones to secondary alcohols by using sodium borohydride or lithium aluminium hydride. $LiAlH_4$ is commonly used in ether solutions. $NaBH_4$ is a mild reducing agent. It reduces only aldehydes and ketones and has no effect on C=C, C≡C, N=N, ester, nitriles, etc.

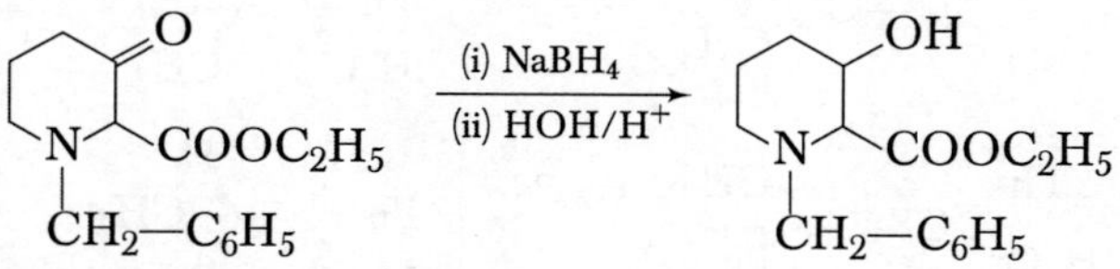

Aldehydes and ketones can also be reduced with borane.

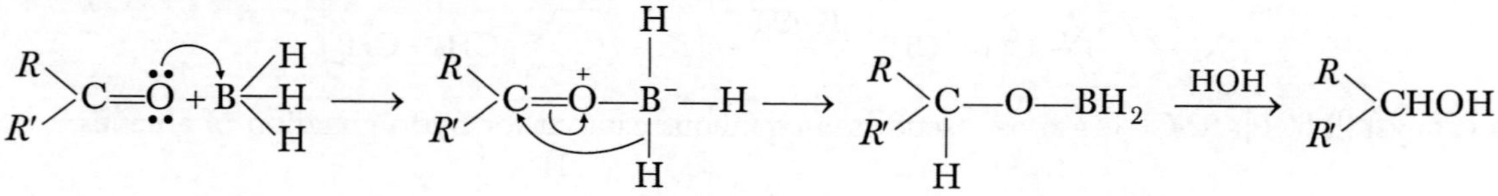

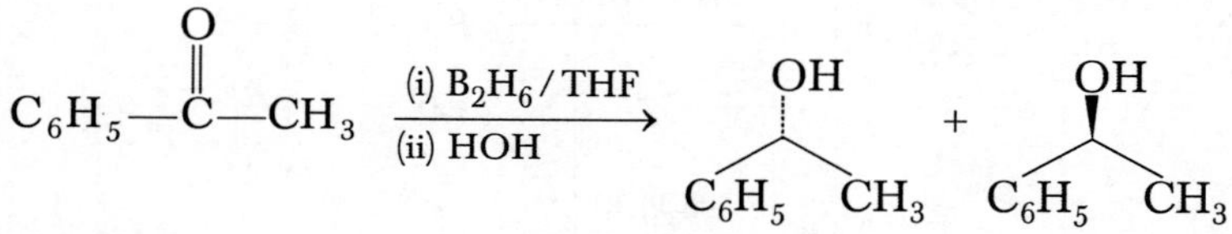

Aluminium isopropoxide reagent is highly specific for aldehydes and ketones. The other groups which are susceptible to reduction do not get reduced by this reagent (**Meerwein-Ponndrof-Verley reduction**).

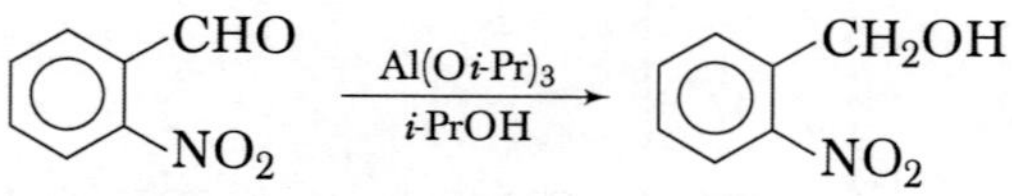

Reductive cleavage of a carbon-oxygen double bond

CO group of aldehydes and ketones can be reduced to CH_2 group by Wolff-Kishner reduction, Clemmensen reduction.

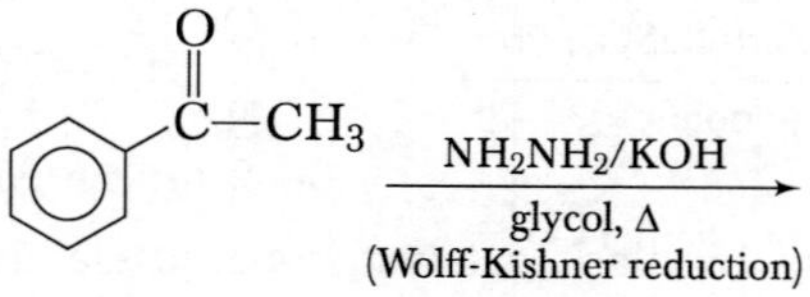

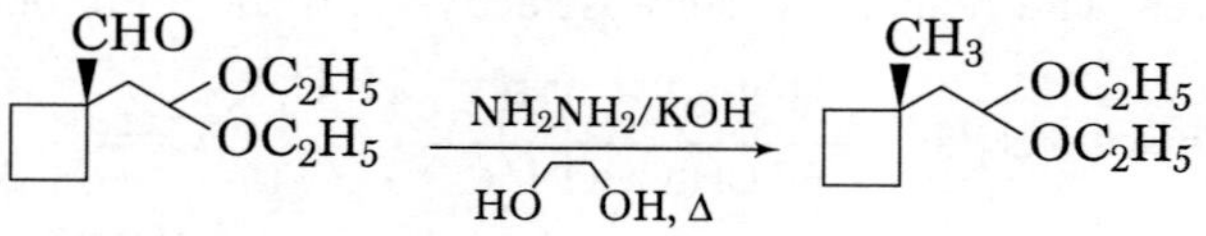

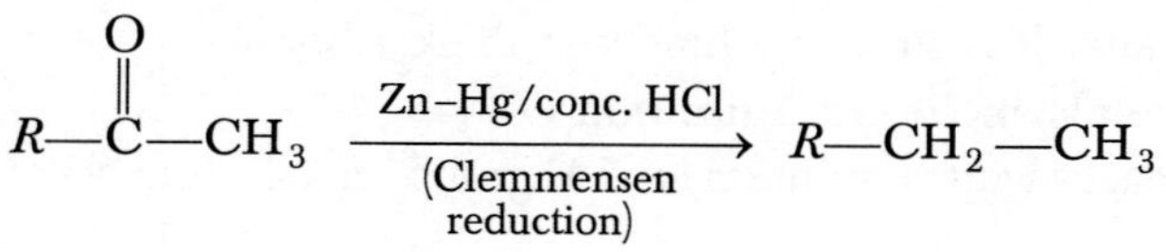

Reduction of Carboxylic Acids and Their Derivatives

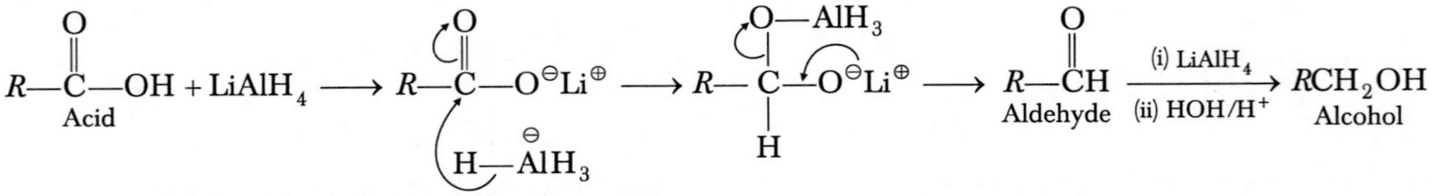

The order of reactivity of acid and their derivative is as :

$$RCOCl > RCOOCOR > RCOOR > RCONH_2 > RCOOH$$

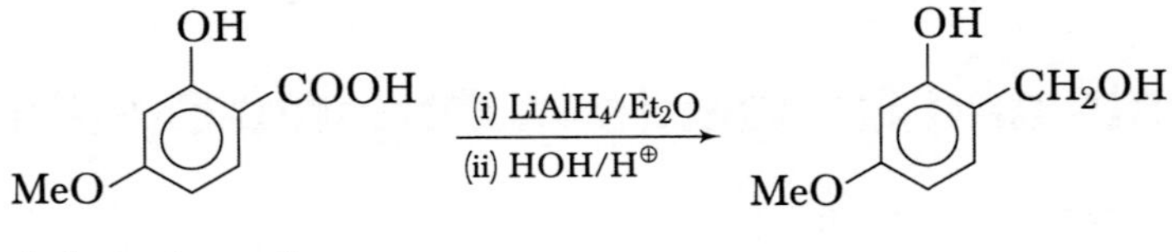

Alanes also reduce acid and their derivatives.

The order of reactivity is as

$$RCOOH > RCONH_2 > RCOOR > RCOCl$$

Diisobutyl aluminium hydride (DIBAL) is the most important alane.

$$CH_3—CH_2—CH_2COOH \xrightarrow[\text{Benzene, 25°C}]{\text{DIBAL}} CH_3—CH_2—CH_2—CH_2OH$$

$LiAlH_4$ is a powerful reducing agent and reduces most of the organic functional groups.

$$C_6H_5CH{=}CH—COOC_2H_5 \xrightarrow[\text{(ii) HOH/H}^+]{\text{(i) LiAlH}_4} C_6H_5CH_2CH_2OH + C_2H_5OH$$

$$\underset{\displaystyle CH_2}{\overset{Br}{|}}—CH_2COCl \xrightarrow[C_2H_5OH]{LiAlH_4/AlCl_3} \underset{\displaystyle CH_2}{\overset{Br}{|}}—CH_2—CH_2OH$$

Note Tertiary amides on reduction with $LiAlH_4$, lithium triethoxy aluminium hydride, etc., give aldehydes. Primary and secondary amides do not give aldehydes. Tertiary amide can reduced to alcohols generally by $LiAlH_4$.

$$CH_3(CH_2)_2COOC_2H_5 \xrightarrow[\text{Bouveault–Blanc method}]{Na,\ C_2H_5OH} CH_3(CH_2)_2CH_2OH + C_2H_5OH$$

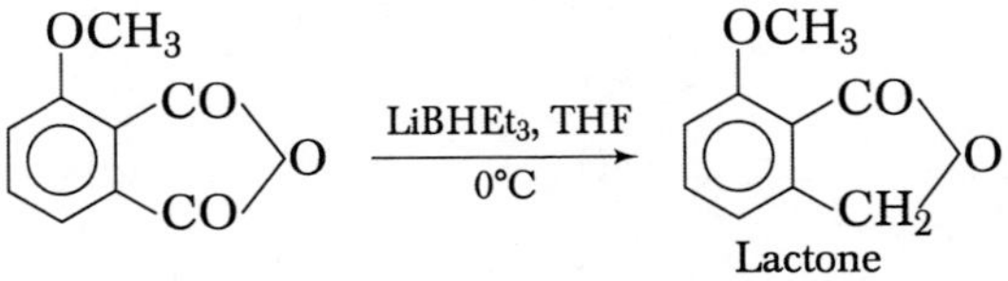

Lactone

Note Lithium *tris* (*sec*-butyl) borohydride (*i.e.*, L-selectride) is the most stereoselective in the reduction of 3-substituted phthalic anhydride. The reagent reduces the less sterically hindered carbonyl group.

Reduction of Nitriles

$$RC{\equiv}N + HCl \longrightarrow R—\overset{\overset{\displaystyle Cl}{|}}{C}{=}NH \xrightarrow[20°C]{SnCl_2/HCl} RCH{=}NH \xrightarrow{HOH/\Delta} R—CHO$$

This is known as Stephen reduction.

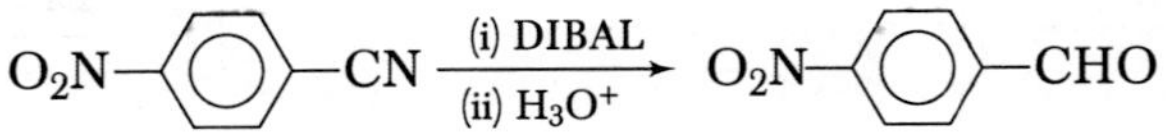

$$RCN + H_2 \longrightarrow RCH{=}NH \xrightarrow{H_2} R{-}CH_2NH_2$$

$$R{-}CH_2CN \xrightarrow[120°C,\ 120\ atm]{H_2-Ni/NH_3} R{-}CH_2{-}CH_2NH_2$$

$$R{-}CN + 4H \xrightarrow{LiAlH_4,\ ether} R{-}CH_2NH_2$$

Note Isocyanides are reduced to secondary amines either by $Na-C_2H_5OH$ or by catalytic hydrogenation

$$RNC + 2H_2 \xrightarrow{Na,\ C_2H_5OH} \underset{2°\ amine}{R{-}NH{-}CH_3}$$

Common Catalysts and Reagents in Organic Synthesis

Lithium Dimethyl Cuprate [$LiCu(CH_3)_2$]

It is an organometallic reagent. It is a source of carbanion and hence, widely used for alkylation by nucleophilic mechanism. It is prepared starting from alkyl halide. It is less reactive than Gilman reagent.

$$CH_3{-}X \xrightarrow{Li} CH_3{-}Li$$

$$2CH_3Li + CuI \longrightarrow \underset{\text{Lithium dimethyl cuprate}}{(CH_3)_2CuLi} + LiI$$

Note The organocopper reagents are also called as Gilman reagents.

Applications

It is used in nucleophilic substitution, nucleophilic addition and conjugate addition.

$$RCOCH_2CH_2I + (CH_3)_2CuLi \longrightarrow RCOCH_2CH_2CH_3$$

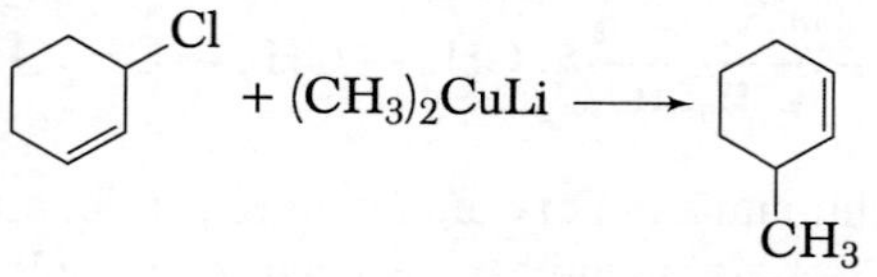

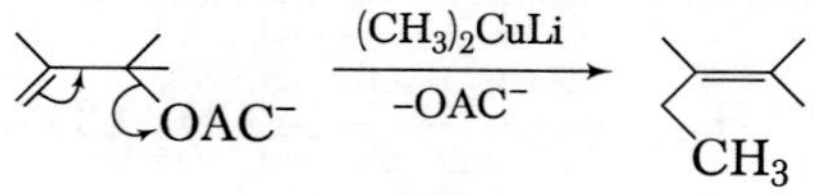

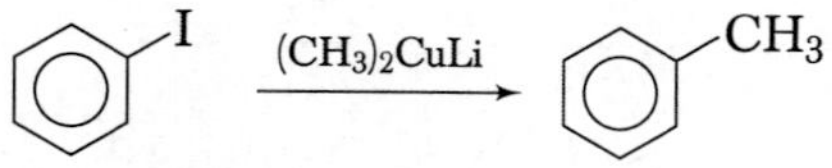

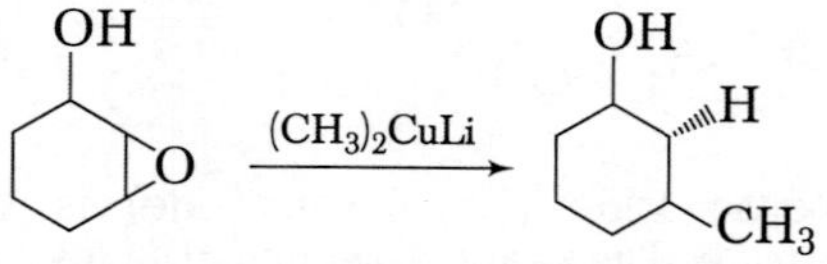

The lithium organocuprates react with α,β-unsaturated carbonyl compounds to give the 1,4-addition product.

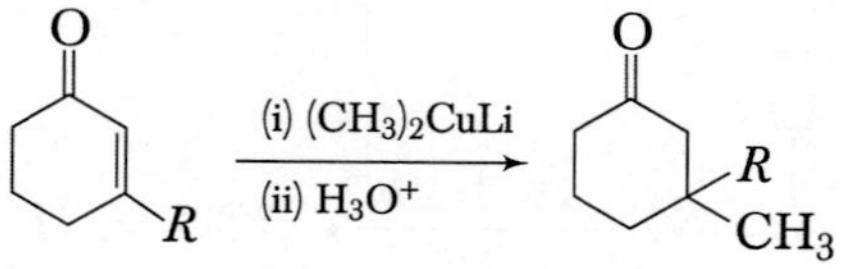

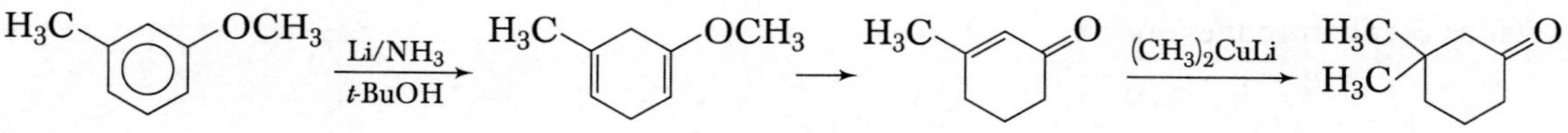

They bring about nucleophilic substitution reaction with tosylates.

$$RO\text{—}SO_2\text{—}OR \xrightarrow{(CH_3)_2CuLi} R\text{—}CH_3$$

N,N-Dicyclohexyl Carbodiimide (DCC)

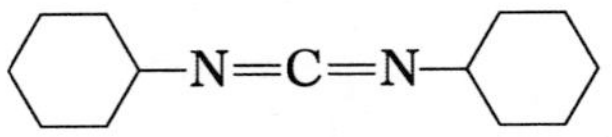

or $C_6H_{11}\text{—}N{=}C{=}N\text{—}C_6H_{11}$

DCC is a powerful dehydrating agent and stored under anydrous conditions.
It is prepared by oxidation of dicyclohexylurea with *p*-toluene sulphonyl chloride in hot pyridine.

$$C_6H_{11}NHCONHC_6H_{11} \xrightarrow[\text{Hot pyridine}]{p\text{-}CH_3C_6H_4SO_2Cl} C_6H_{11}N{=}C{=}NC_6H_{11} + H_2O$$

Applications

It is a versatile reagent that brings about condensation reaction very smoothly, practically bringing the two reacting groups together. Hence, etherification, esterification, lactonization, formation of amide, lactam, etc., can be carried out.

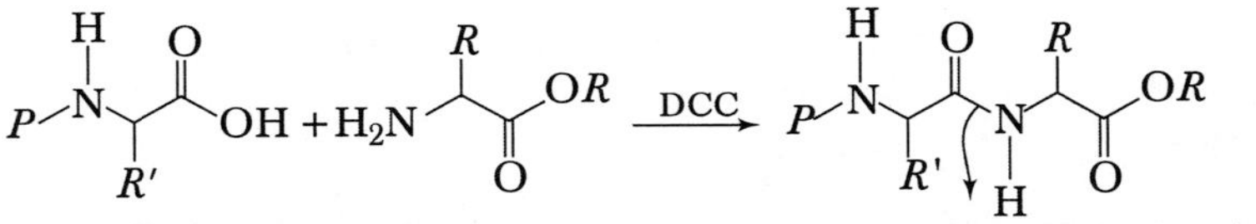

P = protecting group   New peptide bond

$$PhOH + HOC_2H_5 \xrightarrow[100°C]{DCC} Ph\text{—}O\text{—}C_2H_5 + H_2O$$

Alcohols can be reduced to hydrocarbons.

$$R\text{—}OH \xrightarrow{DCC} [o\text{-acyl urea}] \xrightarrow[Pd/C]{H_2} R\text{—}H$$

$$RCOOH + CH_2N_2 \xrightarrow{DCC} \underset{\alpha\text{-diazoketones}}{R\text{—}\overset{\overset{O}{\|}}{C}\text{—}CHN_2}$$

Lithium Diisopropylamide (LDA)

LDA is prepared from diisopropylamine and butyl lithium in presence of THF at 0°C.

$$\left(CH_3\text{—}\underset{\underset{CH_3}{|}}{CH}\text{—}\right)_2 NH + BuLi \xrightarrow[0°C]{THF} \left(CH_3\text{—}\underset{\underset{CH_3}{|}}{CH}\text{—}\right)_2 \overset{\ominus}{N}\overset{\oplus}{Li} + BuH$$

Applications

It is such a strong base that it abstracts hydrogen from active carbon.

$$CH_2{=}C{=}CH_2 + LDA \longrightarrow CH_2{=}C{=}\overset{\ominus}{CH}\overset{\oplus}{Li}$$

Normally it is used in the generation of carbanion.

$$RCH_2COR' \xrightarrow{LDA} R\bar{C}HCOR' \xrightarrow{R''X} R\text{—}\underset{\underset{R''}{|}}{CH}\text{—}COR'$$

Sulphones and sulphinic esters can be alkylated in α-position.

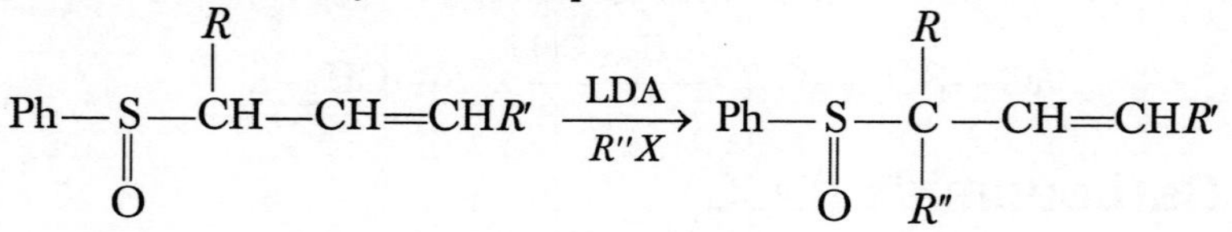

Alkylation at benzylic carbon takes palce by LDA.

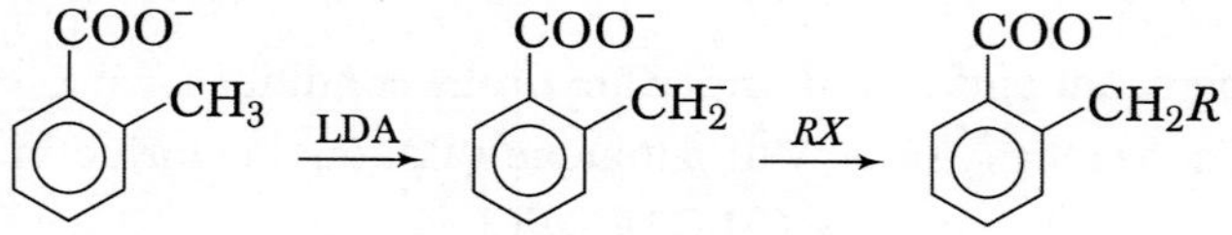

Alkylation and acylation of carboxylate anions

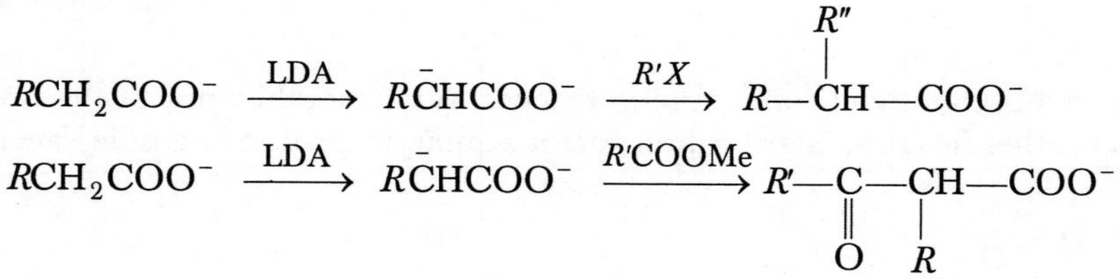

Tri-*n*-Butyl Tin in Hydride [(*n*-Bu)$_3$ SnH]

This reagent is specific for the reduction of carbon-halogen bond to C—H bond. It can be prepared by the reduction of tri-*n*-butyl tin chloride or *tri-n*-butyl trioxide with $LiAlH_4$.

$$(n\text{-}C_4H_9)_3SnCl + LiAlH_4 \xrightarrow[\text{reflux}]{\text{Ether}} \xrightarrow{H_2O} (n\text{-}C_4H_9)_3SnH$$

Applications

This reagent can be used for alkyl halides, acyl halides, diazonium salts, aromatic halides, etc.

$$ClCH_2CH_2OCOCH_3 + (n\text{-}C_4H_9)_3SnH \longrightarrow CH_3CH_2OCOCH_3 + n\text{-}Bu_3SnCl$$

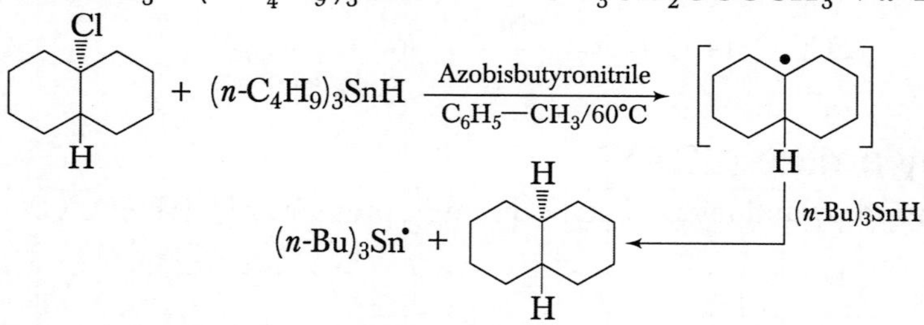

Unsaturated acids can be converted into saturated lactones.

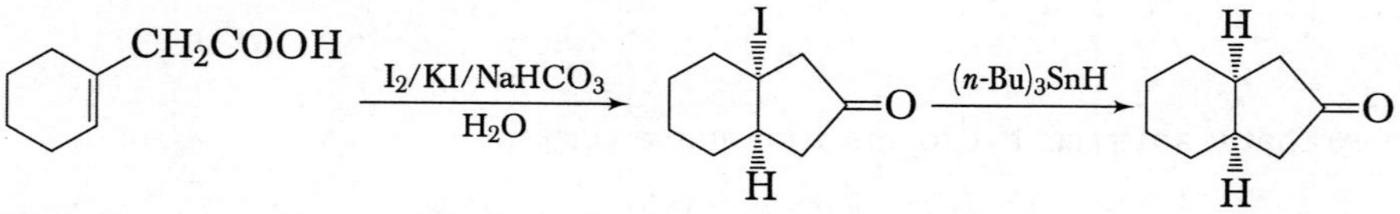

Aryl diazonium salts can be reduced in non-aqueous media with tri-*n*-butyl tin hydride to aromatic hydrocarbons.

Osmium Tetroxide (*Cis*-Hydroxylating Agent)

Osmium tetroxide is commonly known as osmic acid. It is used for *syn*-hydroxylation of alkenes. It is expensive and toxic in nature.

Applications

Hydroxylation of alkenes with OsO_4 is proceed with the formation of cyclic ester which then cleave to give diols.

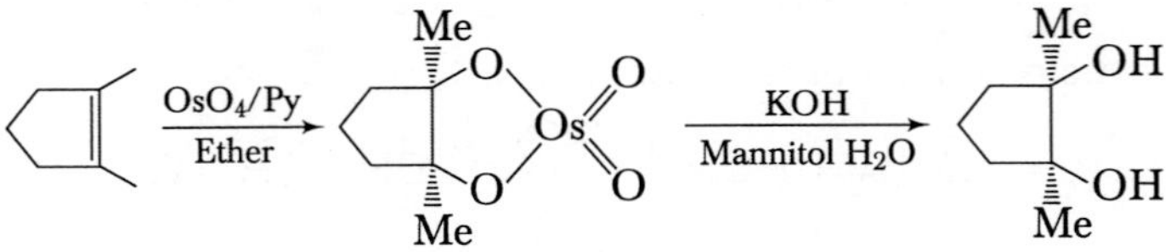

OsO_4 reagent is stereoselective.

Strained, unhindered olefins react rapidly with OsO_4. The attack of the reagent is from the less hindered side of olefinic bond.

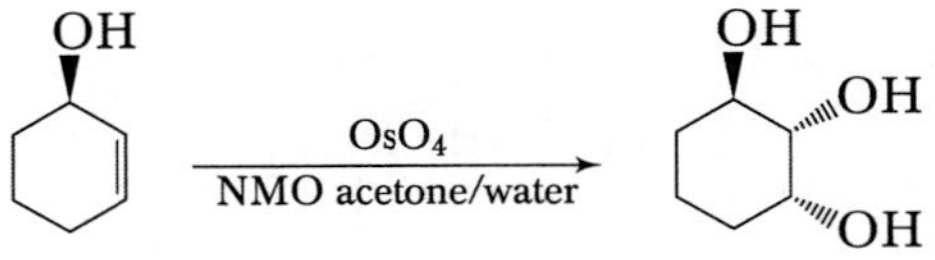

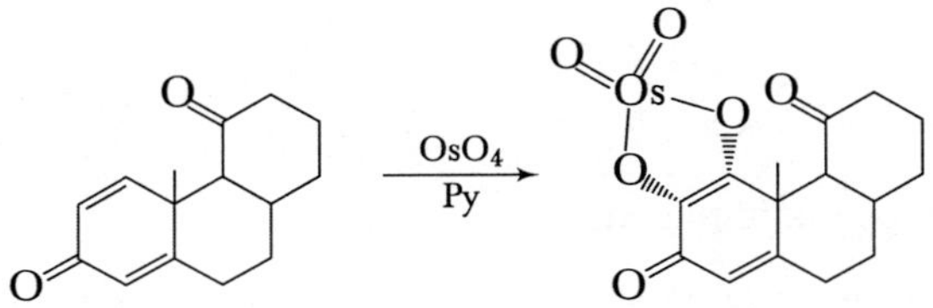

The same result (*syn*-addition) can be accomplished more economically by the use of H_2O_2, with catalytic amount OsO_4.

When more than one double bonds are present, hydroxylation occurs at the most electron rich double bond. Thus, the reagent can be used regioselectivity.

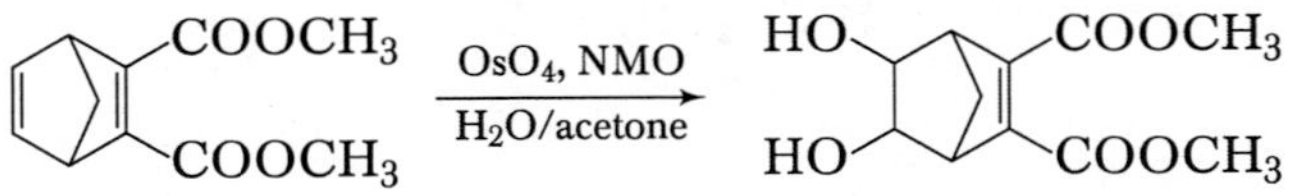

Selenium Dioxide (SeO_2)

It is an important oxidising agent and is specific in bringing about α-oxidation and allylic oxidation. It is toxic substance used as a solution in dioxan, acetic acid, acetic anhydride, water and ethanol. It is very useful in the oxidatioin of ketones and aldehydes to 1,2-dicarbonyl compounds. During oxidation, selenium dioxide is reduced to metallic Se.

Applications

SeO_2 oxidises α-carbon of carbonyl group. The oxidation is possible when α-carbon has at least two hydrogens. If α-carbon is methylene then it is oxidised into —CO group and if α-carbon is —CH_3 group then it is oxidised into —CHO group. The reactivity of CH_2 group is more than CH_3 group hence reaction is regioselective.

$$CH_3CH_2—\overset{O}{\overset{\|}{C}}—CH_2CH_3 \xrightarrow{SeO_2} CH_3CH_2—\overset{O}{\overset{\|}{C}}—\overset{O}{\overset{\|}{C}}—CH_3$$

$$CH_3—CH_2—\overset{O}{\overset{\|}{C}}—CH_3 \xrightarrow{SeO_2} CH_3—\overset{O}{\overset{\|}{C}}—\overset{O}{\overset{\|}{C}}—CH_3$$

$$CH_3CHO \xrightarrow{SeO_2} \begin{array}{c} CHO \\ | \\ CHO \end{array}$$

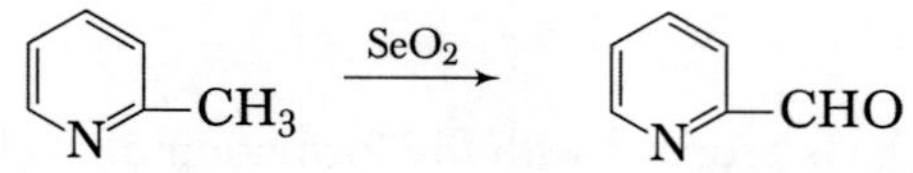

α-picoline α-picolinic aldehyde

It is also useful reagent for allylic oxidation of alkenes.

$$RCH{=}CHCH_3 \xrightarrow{SeO_2} RCH{=}CH{-}CH_2OH$$

$$RCH{=}CHCH_2OH \xrightarrow{SeO_2} RCH{=}CH{-}CHO$$

Selenium dioxide exhibits a useful stereoselectivity in reaction with trisubstituted *gem*-dimethyl alkenes. The products are always predominantly the *E*-allylic alcohol or unsaturated aldehyde.

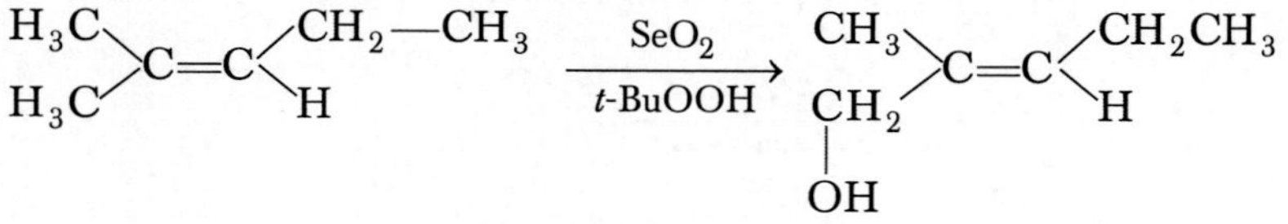

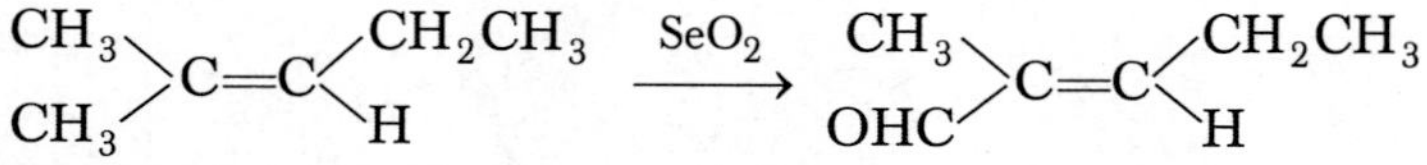

SeO_2 can also be used as a dehydrogenating agent.

$$R{-}COCH_2CH_2CO{-}R \xrightarrow{SeO_2} RCOCH{=}CHCOR$$

1,3-Dithianes

1,3-dithianes can be prepared by the reaction of an aldehyde or its acetal with 1,3-propanedithiol.

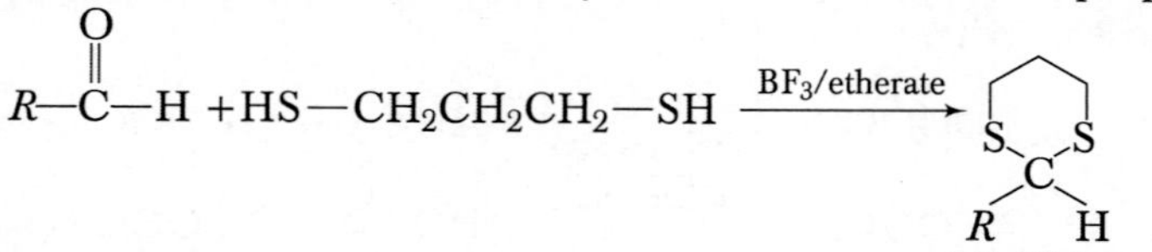

1, 3-dithiane

Applications

The reaction of 1,3-dithiane, with *n*-butyl lithium form a carbanion which can be alkylated.

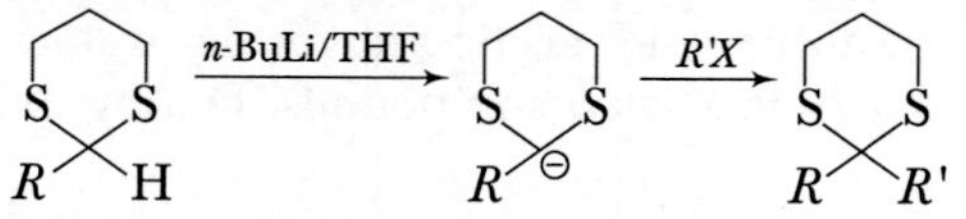

The 1,3-dithiane obtained is a thio ketal and hence can be hydrolysed to aldehydes or ketones by treatment with $HgCl_2$ or $HgO\text{-}BF_3$. Thus, in this sequence of reaction the normal mode of reaction is reversed. Normally, electrophilic carbon by conversion to 1,3-dithiane is made to behave as a nucleophile. This is known as **'reversal of polarity'** and is otherwise called **'Umpolung'**.

From the 1,3-dithiane derivative of formaldehyde a wide variety of aldehydes and ketones can be prepared

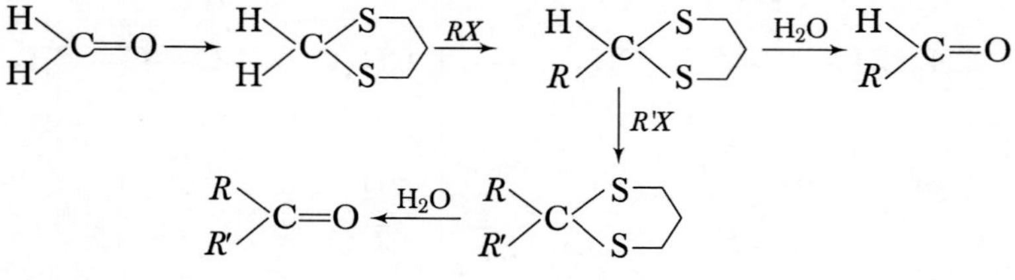

R = alkyl, benzylic
X = iodide

With epoxides, the anion of 1,3-dithiane gives β-hydroxy aldehydes or ketones.

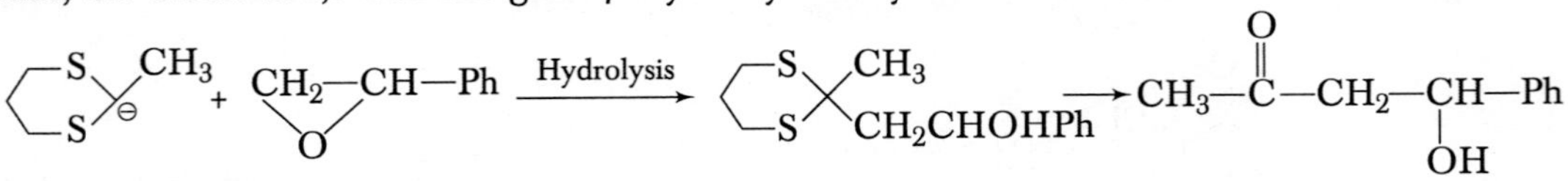

α-hydroxy carbonyl compounds can also be prepared.

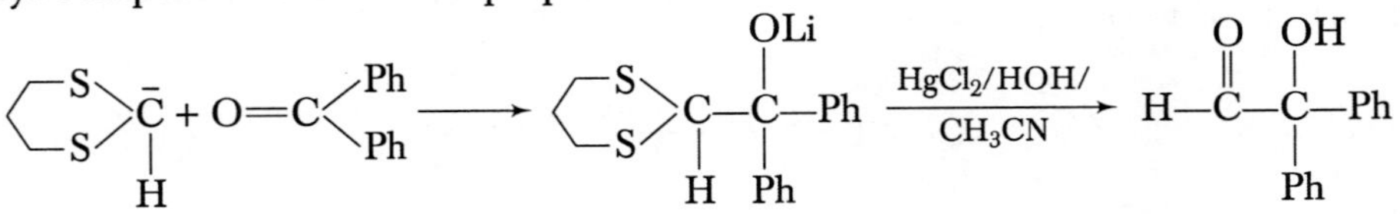

Anion of 1,3-dithiane reacts with solid CO_2 to give addition product which on hydrolysis give α-keto acid.

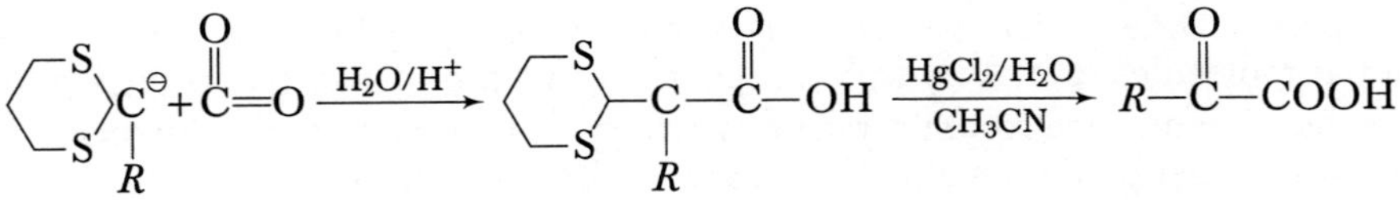

Acyl halides give the dicarbonyl compounds

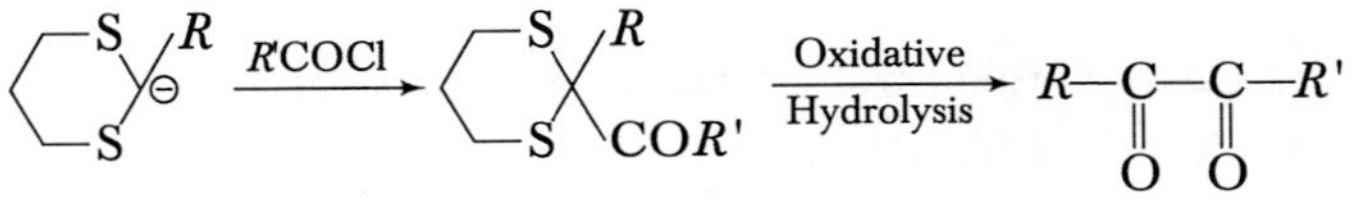

Crown Ethers

These are large ring compounds containing several oxygen atoms, usually in a large cyclic structure. Example :

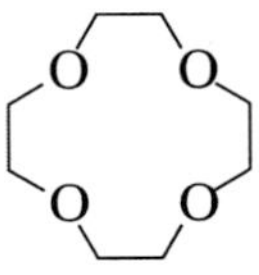

12-crown-4

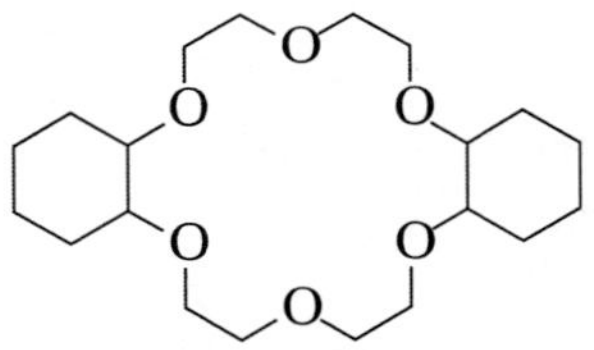

Dicyclohexyl-18-crown-6

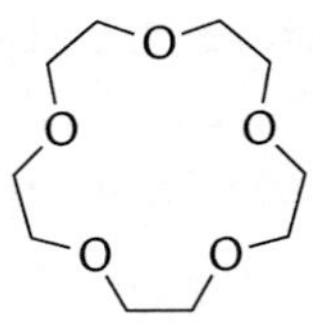

15-crown-5

Applications

Dicyclohexyl-18-crown-6 complex with $KMnO_4$ (II) is an efficient oxidant soluble in benzene. This complex containing free permanganate ion is a powerful oxidising agent and used in oxidising olefins, alcohols, aldehydes and alkyl benzenes.

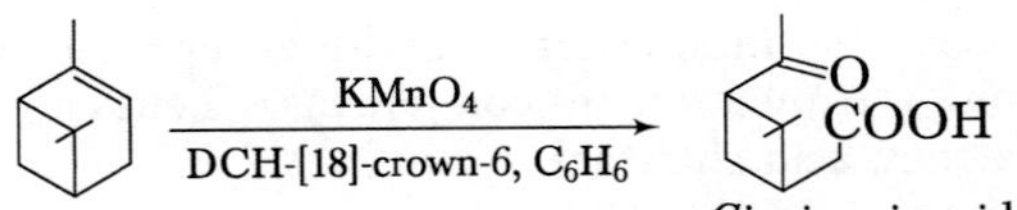

Cis-pinonic acid

Coordination of cation of salts (*e.g.,* KF in acetonitrile) with 18-crown-6-ethers enhances the reactivity of its anion(s) for nucleophilic substitution and elimination reactions.

$$C_6H_5CH_2Br \xrightarrow[\text{in acetonitrile - crown ether}]{K^{\oplus}F^{\ominus}} C_6H_5CH_2F + KBr \qquad \text{(Substitution)}$$

$$CH_3COCl \xrightarrow[\text{Crown ether}]{K^{\oplus}F^{\ominus}} CH_3COF + KCl \qquad \text{(Substitution)}$$

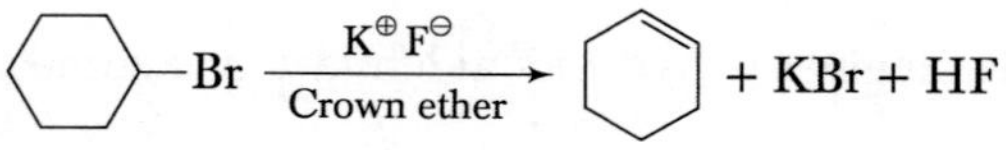

(Elimination)

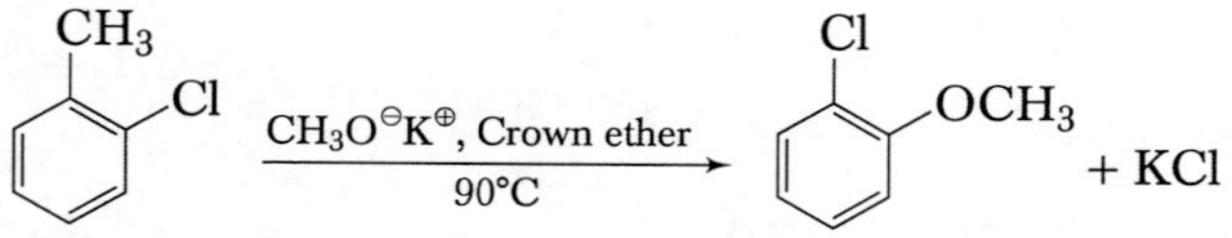

(Nucleophilic substitution)

Crown ethers have been used for esterifications.

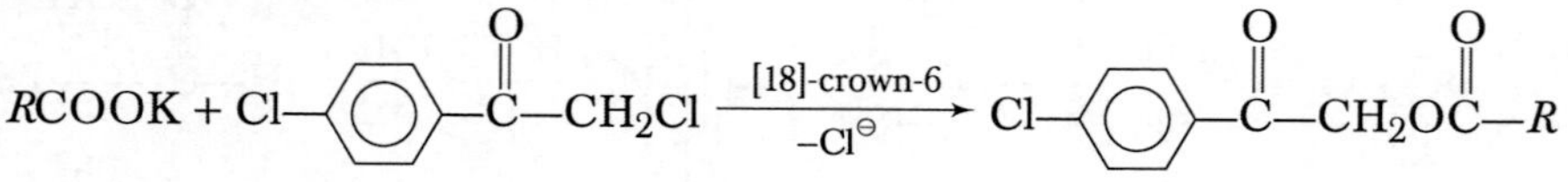

Complex Metal Hydrides

Metal hydrides encompass a wide variety of reducing agents which may be used for the selective reduction of groups in polyfunctional molecules. Metal hydride reducing agents are of two types–nucleophilic reagents which reduce polar multiple bonds and electrophilic reagents which can readily react with non-polar C—C multiple bonds. The most common nucleophilic metal hydrides are $LiAlH_4$ and $NaBH_4$.

$$LiAlH_4 \longrightarrow Li^+[AlH_4]^-$$

$LiAlH_4$ is denoted by LAH.

Some other reagents that can be easily derived from metal hydrides are as :

Lithium tri tertiary butoxy aluminium hydride denoted as LTBA.

$$LiAlH_4 + 3Me_3COH \xrightarrow{\text{Ether}} LiAlH[—OCMe_3]_3 + 3H_2$$

Lithium trimethoxy aluminium hydride

$$LiAlH_4 + 3MeOH \longrightarrow LiAlH(OCH_3)_3 + 3H_2$$

Diisobutylaluminium hydride

$[(CH_3)_2CHCH_2]_2AlH$ denoted as DIBAL-H

$NaAlH_2[—O—CH_2CH_2—O—CH_3]_2$ denoted ad RED-AL

These reagents have varying capacity for reduction.

Applications

These metal hydrides are hydride donors.

(Elimination)

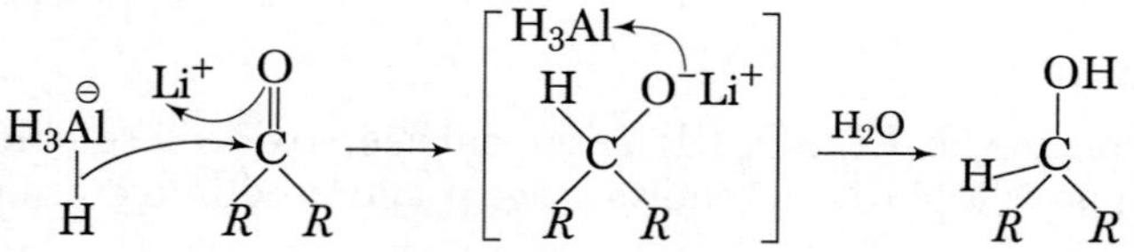

(Nucleophilic substitution)

(a) **LAH** reduces aldehydes, ketones, acid chlorides, esters, anhydrides, epoxides and acids to alcohols. Nitroalkanes, amides, cyanides are reduced to amines. Aromatic intro compounds, alkenes are not reduced.

(b) **$NaBH_4$** reduces only aldehydes, ketones, acid chlorides.
$NaBH_4$/LiCl reduces aldehydes, ketones, acid chlorides, epoxides and esters.
$NaBH_4/AlCl_3$ reduces all except nitroalkanes and carboxylate anions.

(c) **Diborane (B_2H_6)** and its derivatives are electrophilic reagents. They reduce carboxylic acids, ketones and epoxides to alcohols, cyanides to amines. Alkenes are converted to trialkyl boranes.

$$RCH{=}CHR + B_2H_6 \longrightarrow (RCH_2—CHR)_3B$$

Diborane is inert towards acid chlorides and nitroalkanes.

LiR_3BH is more powerful than $LiBH_4$ because of $+I$ effect of R and reduction in solvation of anion. $LiBH_4$ and $Mg(BH_4)_2$ are more powerful reducing agents than $NaBH_4$ because Li^+, Mg^{2+} ions are more powerful complexing ions than Na^+ ion.

Lithium tri isobutyl borohydride and LTBA give predominantly axial cyclohexanols. The former is thermodynamically controlled and the latter kinetically controlled.

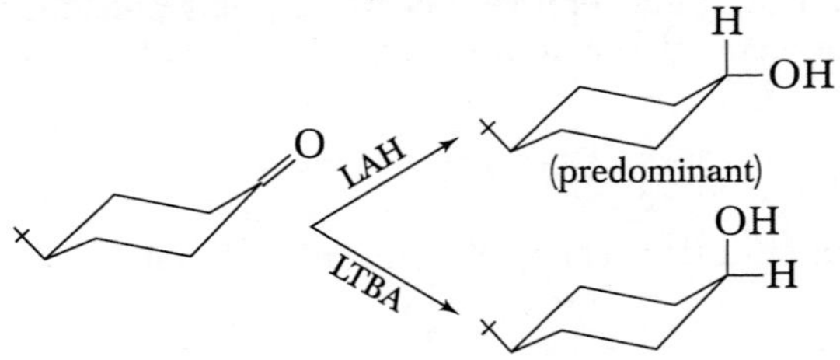

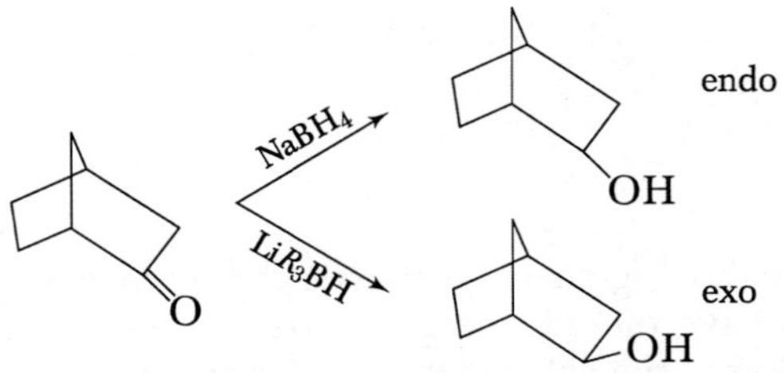

Borane (BH_3) is capable of reducing a variety of functional groups. The most useful applications of the reagent have involved addition to carbon-carbon multiple bonds called hydroboration.

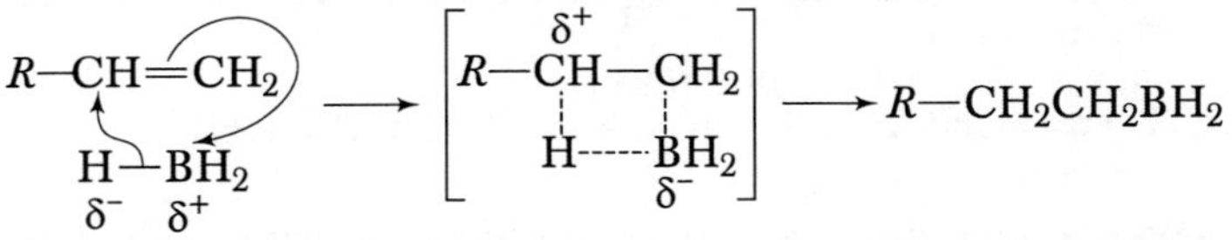

Two dialkylboranes 9BBN and Sia_2BH are common in use. These two reagents are used in those cases where one hydroboration is required. Dialkyl boranes though less reactive, are more selective reagents than borane itself.

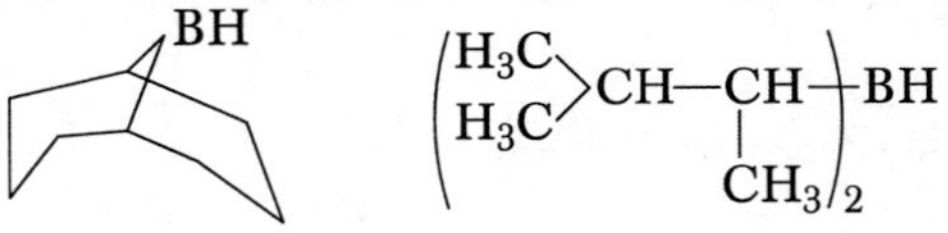

9-BBN　　Disiamyl borane or Sia_2BH

Further, by increasing the bulk of the alkyl substituents, the dialkylboranes can be made sensitive to steric control in order to give stereospecific reduction. Thus, *bis*-isopinocamphenylborane obtained from α-pinene and diborane,

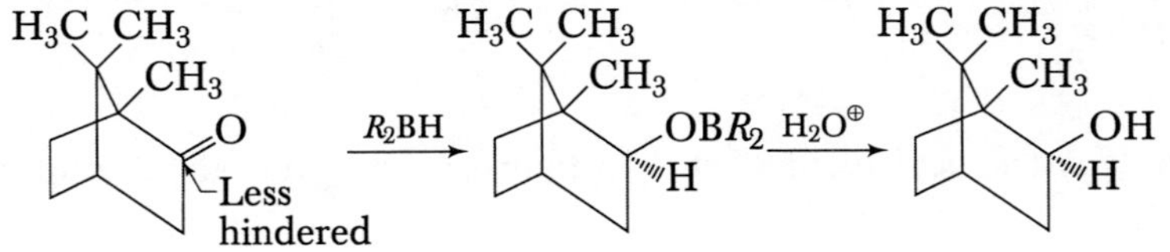

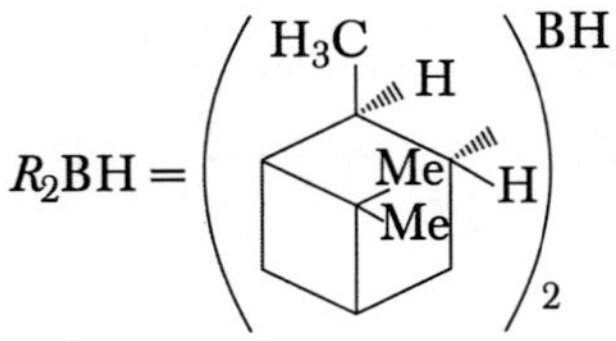

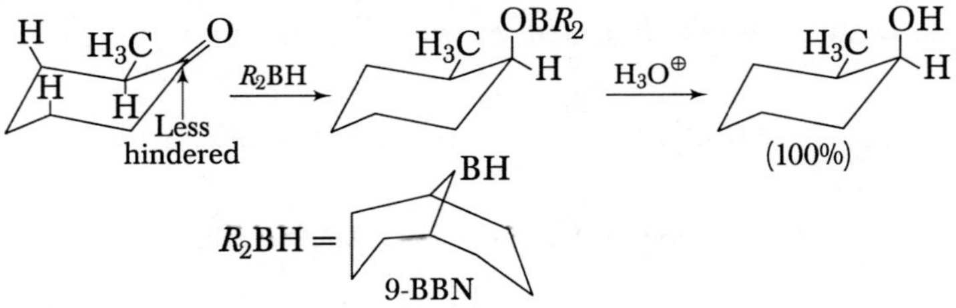

reduces camphor exclusively to the thermodynamically less stable isoborneol, by an approach from the less hindered endo side (steric approach control). Similarly, 2-methylcyclohexanone can be reduced 100 per cent to the *cis* alcohol, which is less stable than the other epimer, by using bulky substituted boranes, whereas borane itself gives a mixture containing 75 per cent of the more stable *trans* alcohol and 25 per cent of the *cis* (product development control).

Wilkinson's Catalyst

Chloro *tris* (triphenyl phospine) rhodium (I) is called Wilkinson's catalyst.

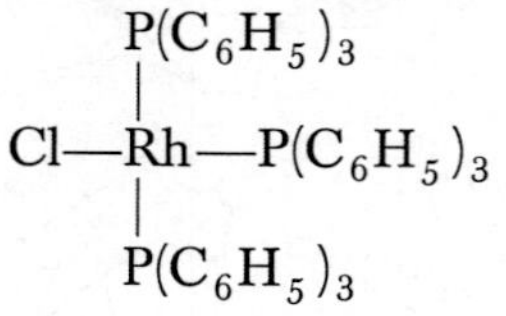

Applications

This reagent is used bring about homogeneous catalytic hydrogenation, hydrogenolysis, decarbonylation desulphonation, etc. These catalysts have the advantages of better catalyst reproducibility and better selectivity. The disadvantage is that the separation of the catalyst from the reaction mixture may not be easy.

$$\underset{\text{Cinnamic acid}}{Ph—CH{=}CH—COOH} \xrightarrow[H_2]{RhCl(PPh_3)_3} Ph—CH_2CH_2COOH$$

$$\underset{\text{Allene}}{CH_3CH{=}C{=}CHCH_3} \xrightarrow[H_2]{RhCl(PPh_3)_3} CH_3CH{=}CHCH_2CH_3$$

The mechanism of hydrogenation involves reaction of the catalyst with hydrogen to form a metal hydride $(PPh_3)_2RhH_2Cl$ which rapidly transfers two hydrogen atoms to the alkene. The intermediate can be isolated. The addition of hydrogen is molecular and no scission of H—H bond occurs.

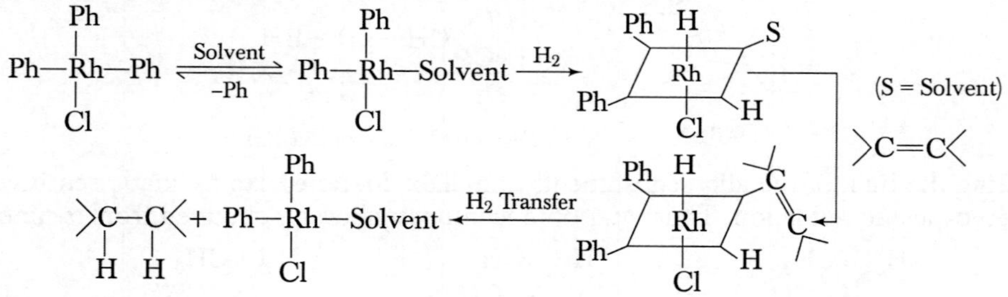

The addition is '*syn*'.

The decarbonylation of aldehydes, acyl halides, etc., to hydrocarbons and alkyl halides respectively follows the following mechanism :

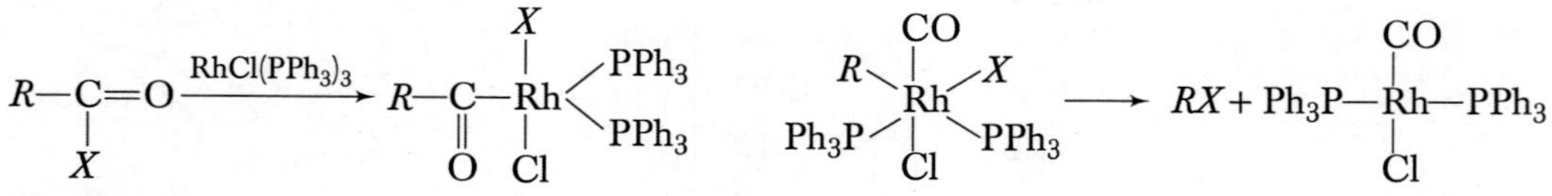

Both the intermediates have been isolated. When $X = H$, the reaction has been shown to give retention of configuration at a chiral *R*. Deuterium labelling demonstrates that the reaction is intramolecular. *R*—CO—D give *R*—D.

$$ArSO_2Br \xrightarrow[H_2]{RhCl(PPh_3)_3} ArBr + SO_2$$

$$ArCOCN \xrightarrow[H_2]{W.C.} ArCN + CO$$

Note Hydrogenation by Wilkinson catalyst takes place readily at the least hindered double bond, *i.e.*, terminal multiple bonds are easily reduced. Bulky portion is not hydrogenated by this bulky catalyst.

Baker's Yeast

Enzymatic reductions are highly stereoselective. Enzymes are an important tool in organic synthesis. The most common enzyme is the Baker's yeast. It consists of an oxidoreductase called alcohol dehydrogenase which catalyses the reduction of ketones into alcohols stereoselectively. Baker's yeast is obtained from fungus *Saccharomyces cerevisiae.* It consists two types of alcohol dehydrogenases. Hence, stereoselctivity of reduction by Baker's yeast depends on the amount of *R*-enzyme and *S*-enzyme, the presence of some additive and solvent.

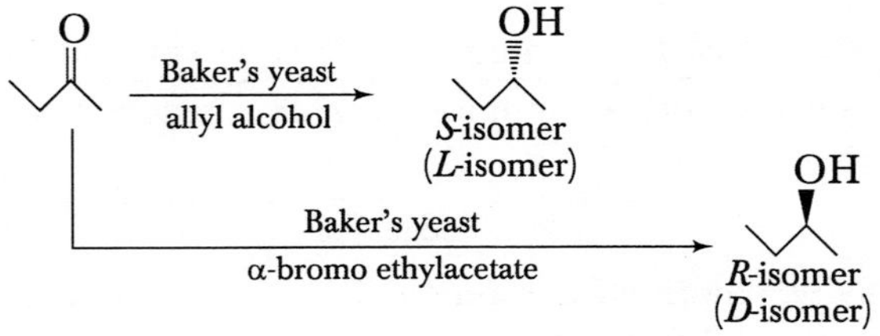

Applications

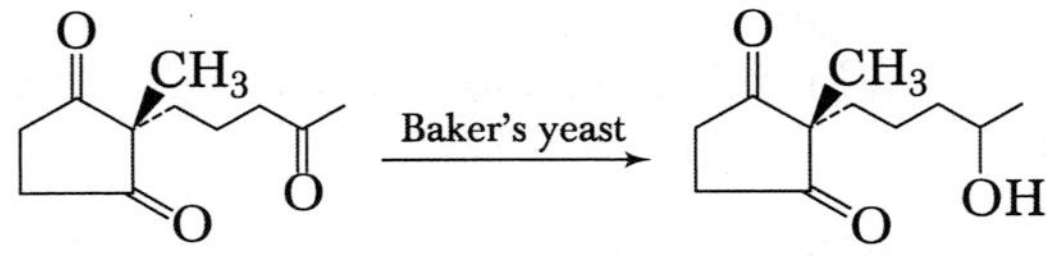

Selective Organic Transformations

Chemioselective Reaction

A reaction in which one functional group within a molecule reacts leaving other potentially reactive functional groups unaltered is called a chemoselective reaction. Such a reaction is said to display chemioselectivity. In organic reactions, reactivity of the attacking species and the selectivity of the place of attack are related. If the attacking species is more reactive, it will be less selective and the yields will be determined by the probability factor as well as reactivity of hydrogen atoms while if the attacking species is less reactive and more selective, the yield of the product is governed exclusively by reactivity of hydrogen atoms.

$$CH_3CH_2CH_2CH_3 \xrightarrow[298K]{Cl_2/h\nu} \underset{28\%}{CH_3CH_2CH_2CH_2Cl} + \underset{72\%}{CH_3CH_2CH(Cl)CH_3}$$

$$(CH_3)_2CHCH_3 \xrightarrow[298K]{Cl_2/h\nu} \underset{64\%}{(CH_3)_2CHCH_2Cl} + \underset{36\%}{(CH_3)_3C\text{—}Cl}$$

$$CH_3CH_2CH_2CH_3 \xrightarrow[400K]{Br_2/h\nu} \underset{2\%}{CH_3CH_2CH_2CH_2Br} + \underset{98\%}{CH_3CH_2CH(Br)CH_3}$$

$$(CH_3)_2CHCH_3 \xrightarrow[400K]{Br_2/h\nu} \underset{\text{Traces}}{(CH_3)_2CHCH_2Br} + \underset{\text{Over } 99\%}{(CH_3)_3C\text{—}Br}$$

In the chlorination of *iso*-butane, abstraction of one of the nine primary hydrogens leads to the formation of *iso*-butyl chlorides, whereas abstraction of a single tertiary hydrogen leads to the formation of *tert*-butyl chloride.

The probability favours formation of *iso*-butyl chloride by the ratio of 9 : 1. But the experimental results show the ratio roughly to be 2 : 1 or 9 : 4.5. Evidently, about 4.5 times as many collisions with the tertiary hydrogen are successful as collisions with the primary hydrogens. The E_{act} is less for abstraction of a tertiary hydrogen than for the abstraction of a primary hydrogen.

The rate of abstraction of hydrogen atoms is always found to follow the sequence 3° > 2° > 1°. At room temperature 298 K the relative rates in chlorination are 5.0 : 3.8 : 1.0 respectively for 3°, 2° and 1° hydrogen atoms. Using these values, we can predict quite well the ratio of isomeric chlorination products from a given alkane. For example,

$$CH_3CH_2CH_2CH_3 \xrightarrow[298\ K]{Cl_2/h\nu} CH_3CH_2CH_2CH_2Cl + CH_3CH_2CH(Cl)CH_3$$

$$\frac{n\text{-butyl chloride}}{sec\text{-butyl chloride}} = \frac{\text{number of 1° H}}{\text{number of 2° H}} \times \frac{\text{reactivity of 1° H}}{\text{reactivity of 2° H}}$$

$$= \frac{6}{4} \times \frac{1.0}{3.8} = \frac{3}{7.6} \text{ equivalent to } \frac{28\%}{72\%}$$

Inspite of these difference in reactivity, chlorination rarely yields a great excess of any single isomer. In most cases, both the products are formed in considerable amounts.

The same reactivity sequence is found in bromination (*i.e.,* 3° > 2° > 1°), but with enormously larger reactivity ratios. At 400 K, the relative rates per H-atom in bromination are 1600 : 82 : 1 respectively for 3°, 2° and 1° H-atoms. The differences in reactivity are so large hence, bromination almost exclusively gives selective product.

In bromination of *iso*-butane at 400 K,

$$\frac{Iso\text{-butyl bromide}}{Tert\text{-butyl bromide}} = \frac{\text{number of 1° H}}{\text{number of 3° H}} \times \frac{\text{reactivity of 1° H}}{\text{reactivity of 3° H}}$$

$$= \frac{9}{1} \times \frac{1}{1600} = \frac{9}{1600} \text{ equivalent to } \frac{0.5\%}{99.5\%}$$

Hence, *tert*-butyl bromide is the exclusive product (over 99%) with traces of *iso*-butyl bromide. The higher selectivity in bromination as compared to chlorination is due to the following reason :

Some other reactions of chemoselectivity are as

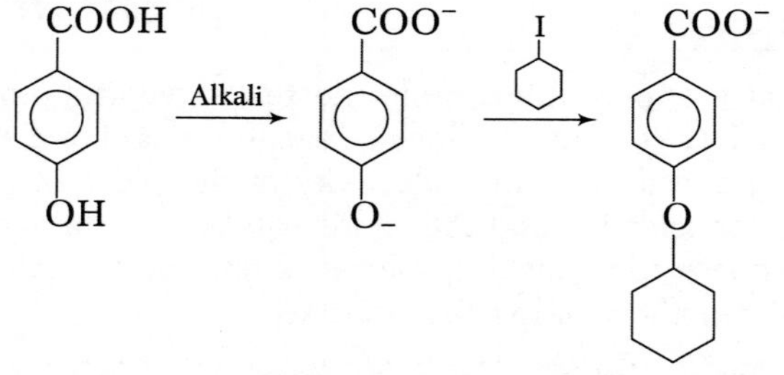

The phenolate ion is more reactive than carboxylate ion hence only phenol is alkylated.

$NaBH_4$ reduces only aldehydes, ketones, acid chlorides and imines. It has no effect on C=C, C≡C, N=N, esters, nitriles, etc., groups.

$$CH_3-CH=CH-CH_2-\overset{\overset{O}{\|}}{C}-CH_3 \xrightarrow{NaBH_4} CH_3CH=CH-CH_2-\overset{\overset{OH}{|}}{CH}-CH_3$$

Regioselective Reaction

A regioselective reaction is one in which two constitutional isomers can be obtained as products but some of one is obtained than of the other. A regioselective reaction selects for a particular constitutional isomer.

A regioselective reaction : $X \longrightarrow Y + M$

more Y is formed than M where Y and M are constitutional isomers.

Ambident nucleophiles have two attacking site. In most cases, a nucleophile with two potentially attacking atoms can attack with either of them, depending on conditions, and mixtures are often obtained, though this is not always the case. For example, the nucleophile NCO^- usually gives only isocyanates *R*NCO and not the isomeric cyanates *R*OCN. When a reaction can potentially give rise to two or more structural isomers (*e.g.*, *R*OCN or *R*NCO) but actually produces only one, the reaction is said to be **regioselective.** Some important ambident nucleophiles are :

(i) Ions of the type $—CO—\overset{\ominus}{\ddot{C}}R—CO—$. These ions, which are derived by removal of a proton from malonic esters, β-keto esters, β-diketones, etc., are resonance hybrids.

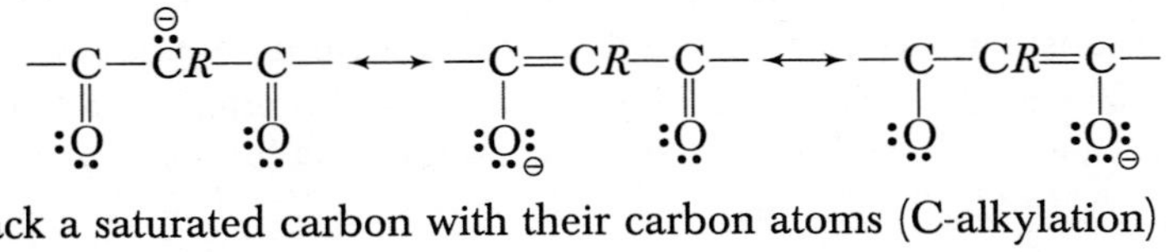

They can thus attack a saturated carbon with their carbon atoms (C-alkylation) or with their oxygen atoms (O-alkylation).

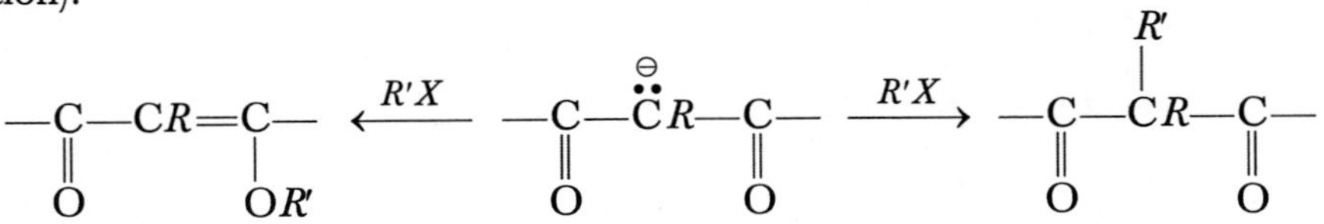

With unsymmetrical ions, three products are possible, since either oxygen can attack. With a carbonyl substrate the ion can analogously undergo C-acylation or O-acylation.

(ii) Compounds of the type $CH_3CO—CH_2—CO—$ can give up two protons, if treated with 2 moles of a strong enough base, to give dicarbanions :

$$\underset{\text{(I)}}{CH_3—COCH_2—CO—} \xrightarrow[\text{of base}]{\text{2 moles}} \underset{\text{(II)}}{\overset{\ominus}{\ddot{C}}H_2—CO—\overset{\ominus}{\ddot{C}}H—CO—}$$

Such ions are ambident nucleophiles, since they have two possible attacking carbon atoms, aside from the possibility of attack by oxygen. In such cases, the attack is virtually always by the more basic carbon. Since, the hydrogen of a carbon bonded to two carbonyl groups is more acidic than that of a carbon bonded to just one, the —CH group of (II) is less basic than the $—CH_2$ group, so the latter attacks the substrate. This gives rise to a useful general principle : whenever we desire to remove a proton at a given position for use as a nucleophile but there is a stronger acidic group in the molecule, it may be possible to take off both protons; if it is, then attack is always by the desired position since it is the ion of the weaker acid. On the other hand, if it is desired to attack with the more acidic position, all that is necessary to remove just one proton. For example, ethyl acetoacetate can be alkylated at either the methyl or the methylene group.

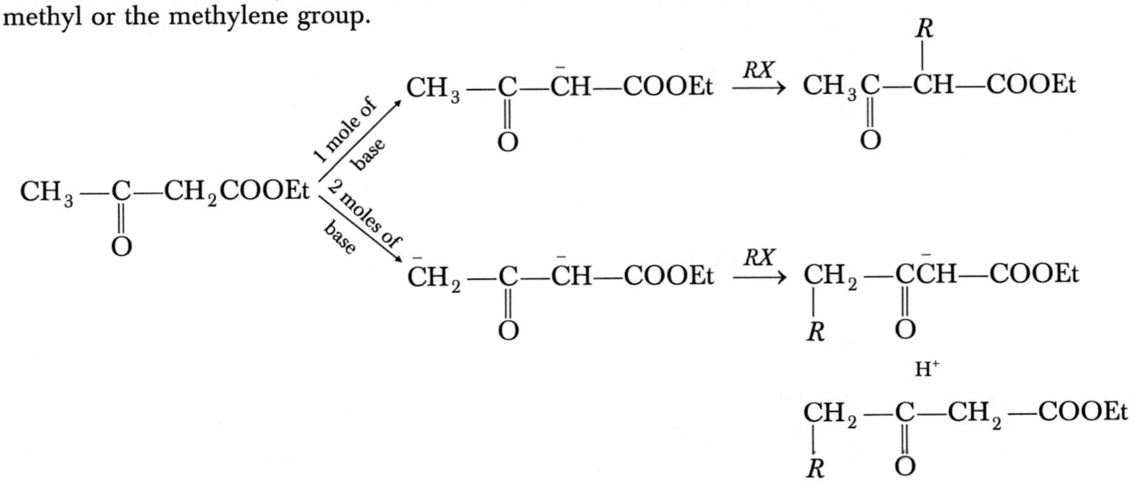

Regioselectivity of Mannich reaction

With unsymmetrical ketone as the active hydrogen component it is possible to get two products when performed minium ions are used.

(a) Unsymmetrical ketone $+ Me_2\overset{\oplus}{N}{=}CH_2$, CF_3COO^- in CF_3COOH gives substitution at the more highly substituted position.

(b) Unsymmetrical ketone + *Iso* $Pr_2\overset{\oplus}{N}{=}CH_2$, ClO_4^- the reaction takes place at a less highly substituted position.

Regioselectivity of Diels-Alder reaction

Diels-Alder reactions between unsymmetrical dienes and unsymmetrical dienophiles are regioselective.

Example 1-substituted butadienes give *'ortho'* products and 2-substituted butadienes give *'para'* products, particularly under Lewis acid catalysis. The *'meta'* products cannot be made this way.

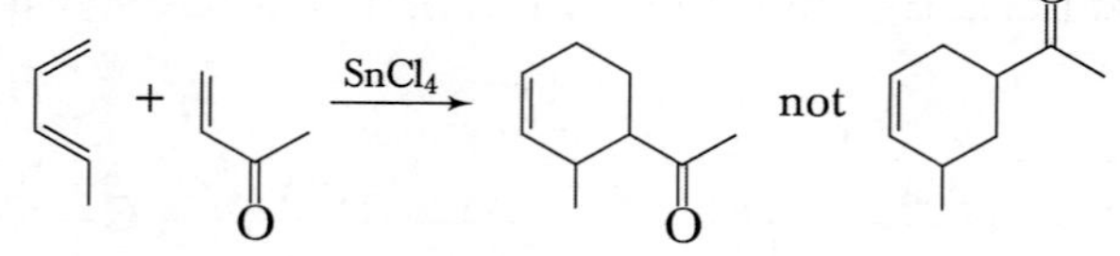

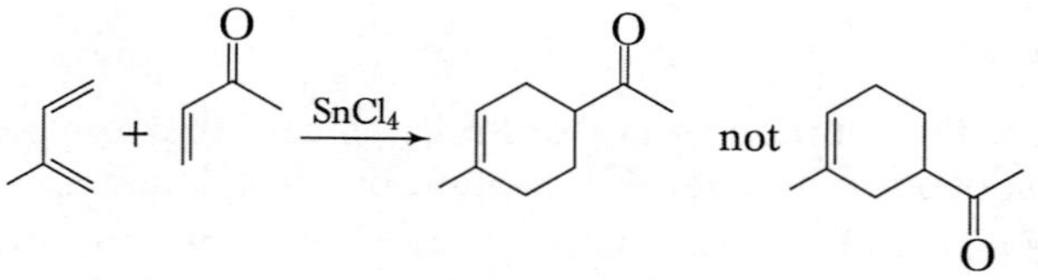

Stereoselective Reaction

Like regioselective reaction, stereoselective is a similar term but in this case preferentially formation of a stereoisomer occurs rather than a constitutional isomer. If a reaction that generates a carbon-carbon double bond or a chirality centre in a product leads to the preferential formation of one stereoisomer over another, it is called a stereoselective reaction. In other words, it selects for a particular stereoisomer.

A stereoselective reaction : $X \longrightarrow Y + M$

more Y is formed than M where Y and M are stereoisomer.

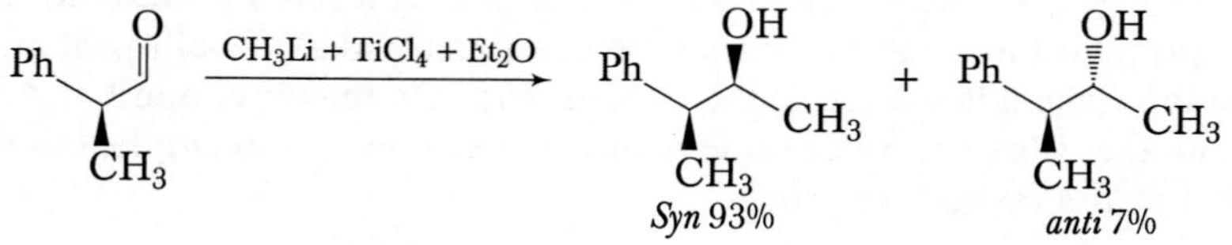

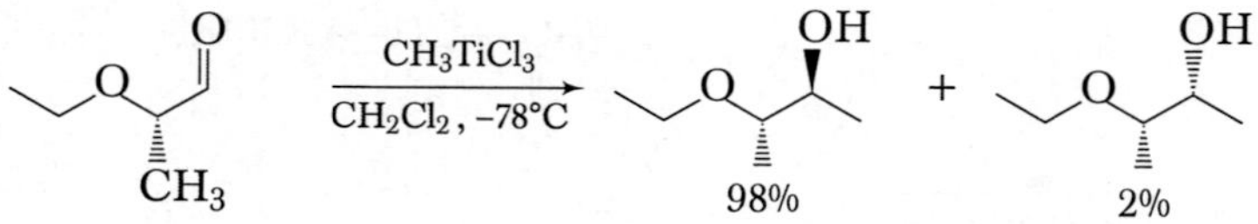

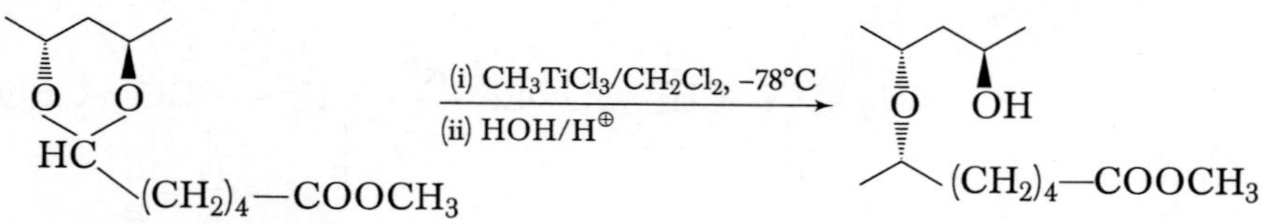

Note A reaction is stereospecific if the reactant can exist as stereoisomers and each stereoisomeric reactant leads to a different stereoisomeric product or a different set of stereoisomeric products. All stereospecific reactions are also stereoselective but all stereoselective reactions are not stereospecific.

Some Important Reaction

Stork-Enamine Reaction

The enamine usually refers to α,β-unsaturated amines. It can be prepared by reaction of an aldehyde or ketone atom and a secondary amine under acid catalysis.

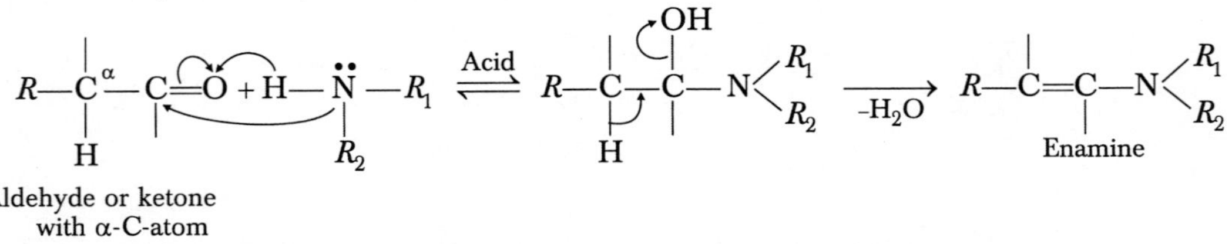

- More stable enamine are those derived from ketones rather than aldehyde.
- A cyclic secondary amines can be used for the preparation of enamine. **Example**

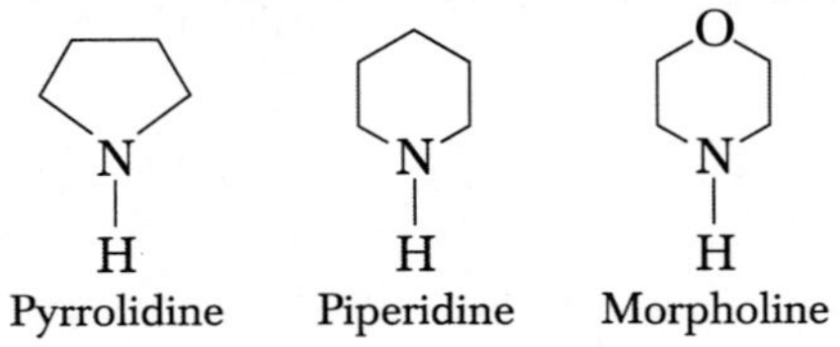

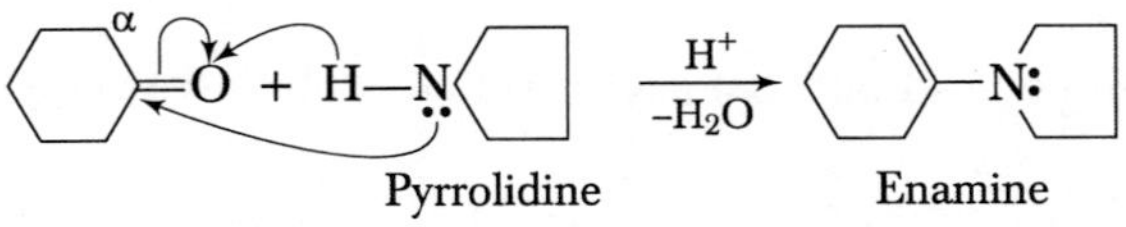

- Primary amines also form enamine, however in their case enamine-imine tautomerism is possible. The equilibrium lies on the imine side, it being more stable than enamine. Thus, an enamine from a *p*-amine can not be isolated

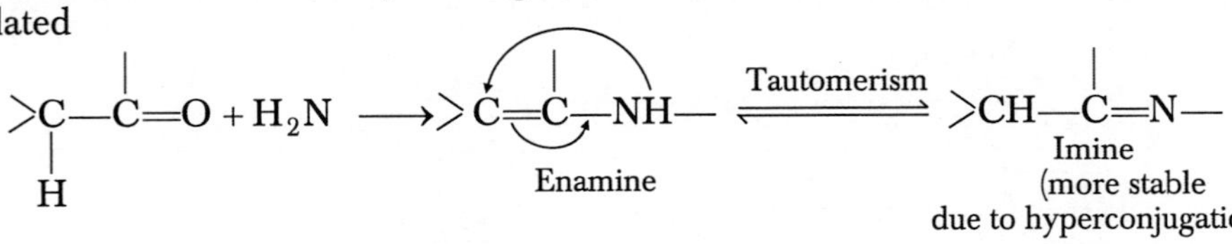

- When enamine is treated with alkyl halide a imine salt is formed. Hydrolysis of imine salt formed gives alkylated aldehyde or ketone. Thus, the net result of this reaction is the alkylation of ketone at α-carbon atom.

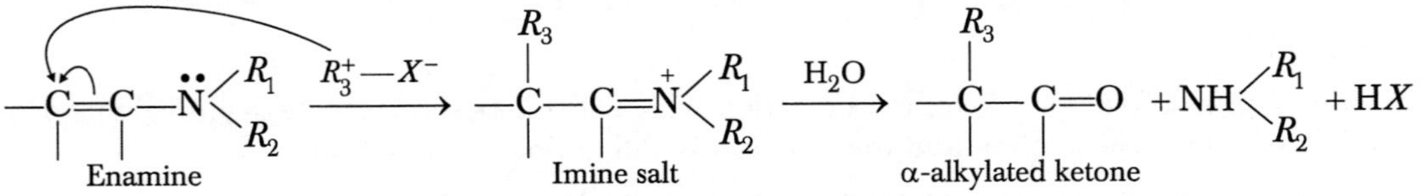

Mechanism

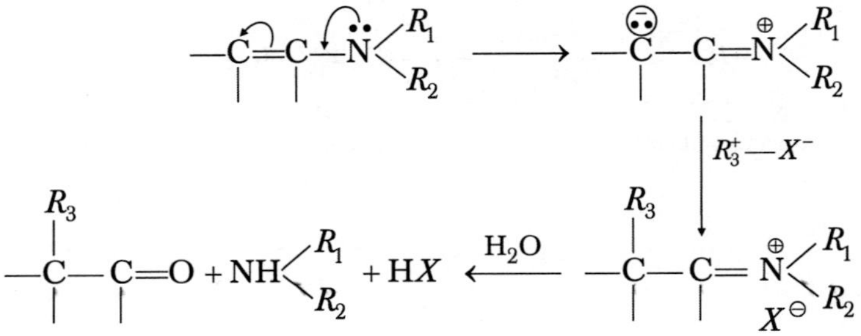

Chichibabin Reaction

Chichiabin amination reaction is the amination of pyridines, quinolines and other N-heterocycles with alkali-metal amides ($NaNH_2$) in a solvent. The nucleophilic attack at C-2 or C-6 takes place. If both *ortho* positions are blocked than amination takes place at 4-position.

Amination of pyridine takes place at the 2-position on heating it with sodamide in dry toluene at 110°C.

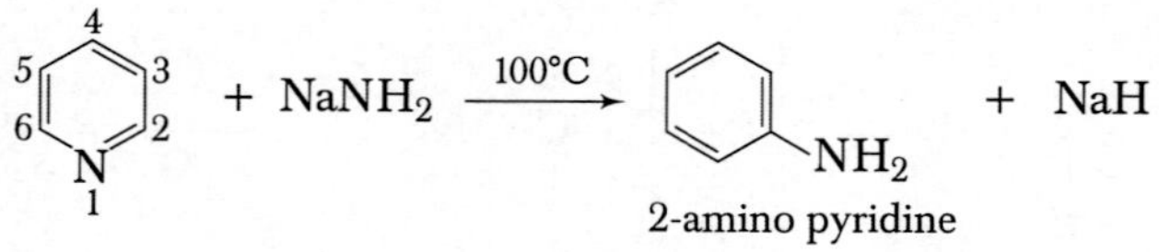

Mechanism

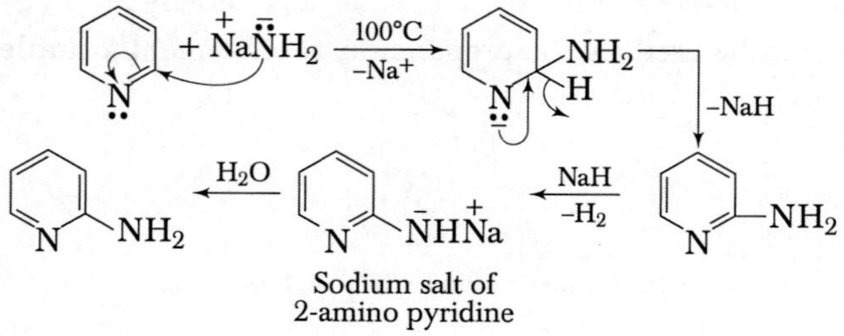

Note Organolithium compound can be used but 2-phenyl pyridine is obtained. This is known as Ziegler alkylation.

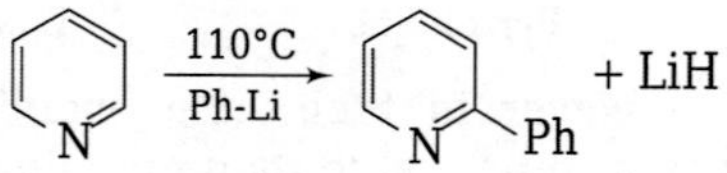

If KOH is used. 2-pyridone is obtained.

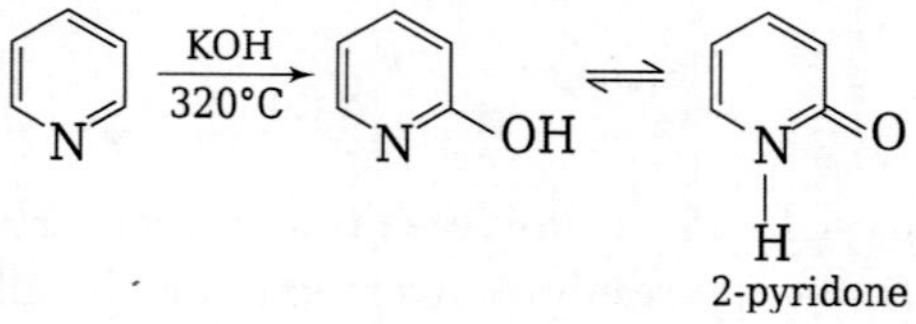

Shapiro Reaction

The tosyl hydrazone of an aldehyde or a ketone on reaction with a strong base at least two equivalents of an organo lithium compound (MeLi) gives an olefine and the reaction is called Shapiro reaction.

Note The reaction can also be carried out using other base like NaOMe, LiH, Na in ethylene glycol.

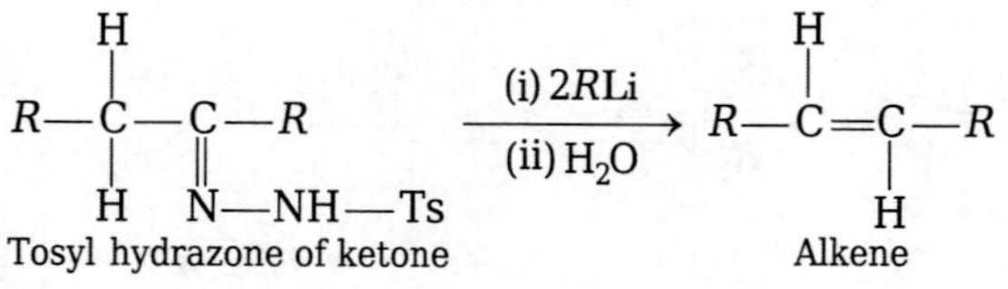

Mechanism

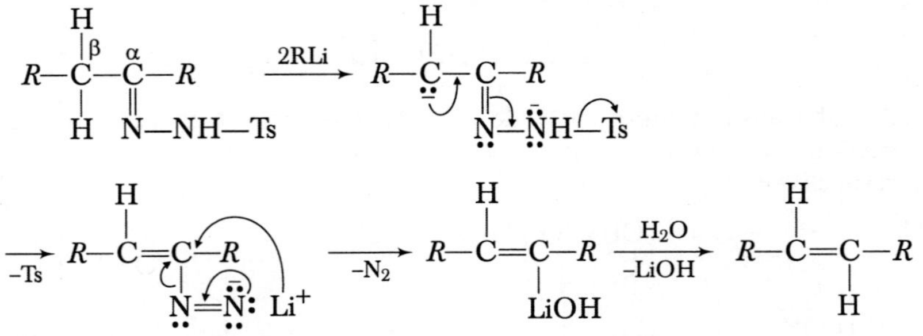

Note The reaction with Na in ethylene glycol is called **Bamford Stevens** reaction. In these cases two mechanism are possible.

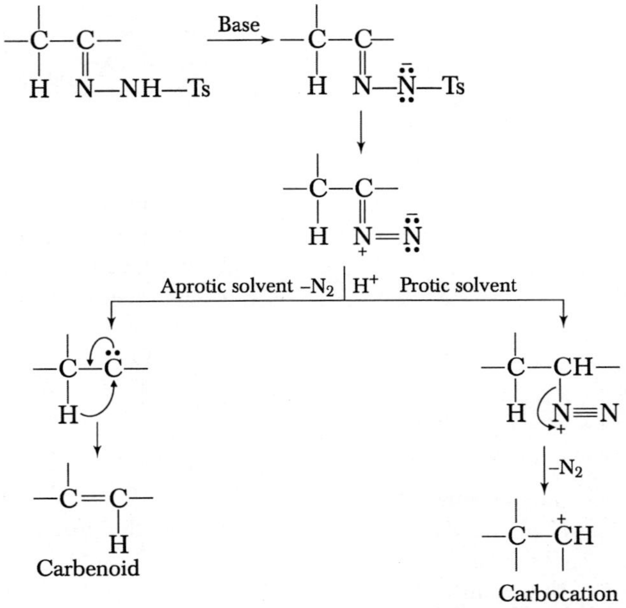

The carbocation mechanism is operative in protic solvents and carbenoid mechanism in aprotic solvents.

Exercise 1
(For Part 'B')

1. In the following series of transformations, provide the required information wherever a question mark(?) is indicated respectively.

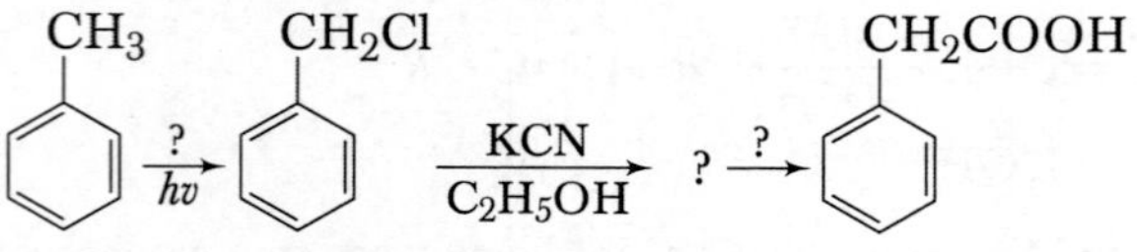

(a) H_3O^+, 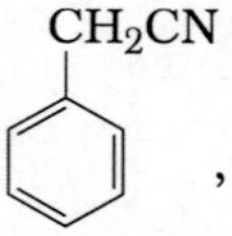, Cl_2

(b) Cl_2, 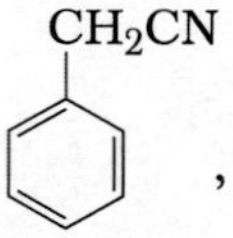, H_3O^+

(c) HCl, 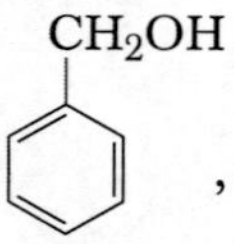, H_3O^+

(d) Cl_2, 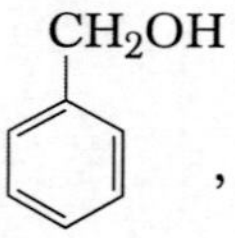, HCl

2. Pick out the correct match.

Reduction	Reducing agent
(a) Clemmensen reduction	Na/C_2H_5OH
(b) Wolff-Kishner reduction	Zn/HCl
(c) Meerwein-Pondorf-Verley reduction	Aluminium isopropoxide
(d) Rosenmund's reduction	H_2/Ni

3. Aldehydes and ketones react with α-bromo esters and metallic zinc to yield

(a) δ-keto esters
(b) β-keto alcohols
(c) β-hydroxyl esters
(d) γ-keto acids

4. Conversion of cyclohexene to cyclohexanol can be conveniently achieved by

(a) $NaOH\text{-}H_2O$
(b) $Br_2\text{-}H_2O$
(c) Hydroboration, oxidation
(d) Hydroboration, hydrolysis

5. A suitable catalyst for bringing out the transformation given below is

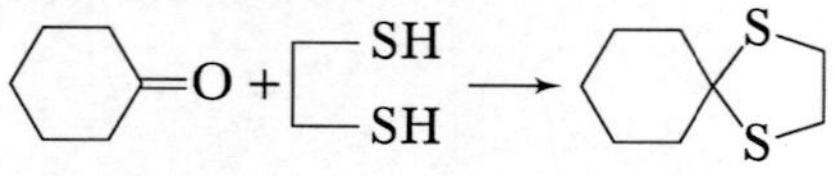

(a) $BF_3 \cdot Et_2O$
(b) NaOEt
(c) tungsten lamp
(d) dibenzoyl peroxide

6. The most suitable reagent for the following transformation is

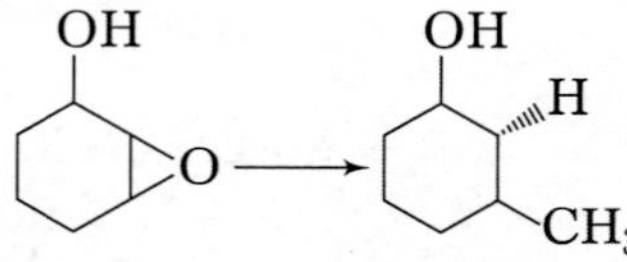

(a) Li/liq. NH_3
(b) $(CH_3)_2CuLi$
(c) NH_2NH_2 /KOH
(d) $LiAlH_4$

7. 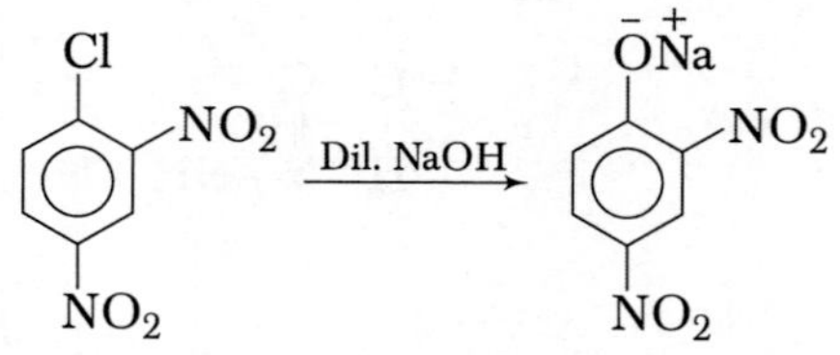

The above transformation proceeds through

(a) electrophilic addition
(b) benzyne intermediate
(c) activated nucleophilic substitution
(d) oxirane

8. 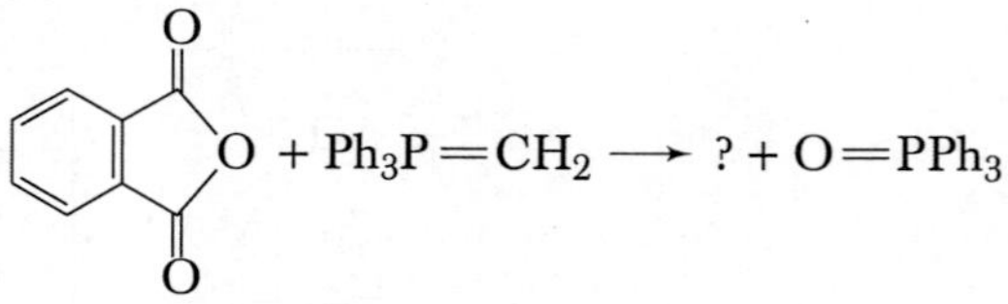

Identify the product

(a) 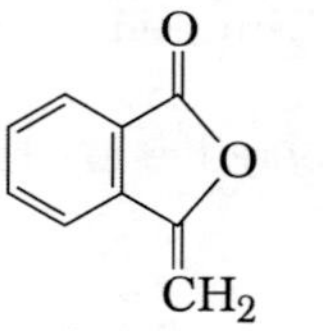
(b) 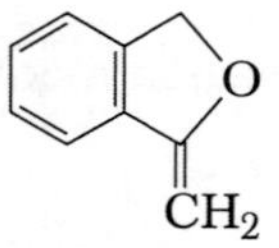
(c) 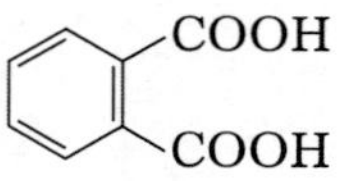
(d) 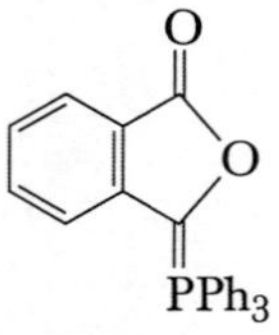

9 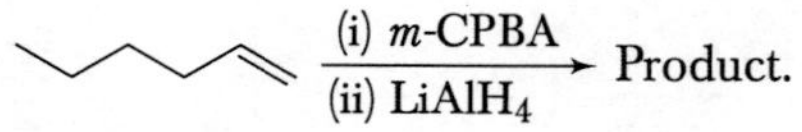

The product is

(a) racemic mixture
(b) hexan-2-ol
(c) hexan-1-ol
(d) hexane

10. The product of the reaction

$$C_6H_5CH_2SH + H\text{—}\overset{\overset{\displaystyle O}{\|}}{C}\text{—}H \xrightarrow[ZnCl_2]{HCl}, \text{ is}$$

(a) $C_6H_5CH_2SCH_2Cl$ (b) $C_6H_5CH_2Cl$

(c) 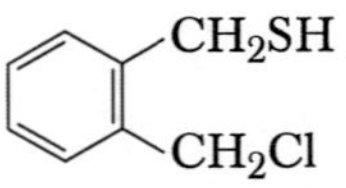 (d) 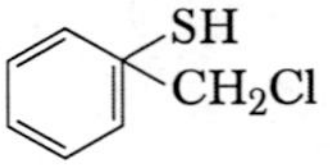

11. The structure of 9-BBN is

(a) 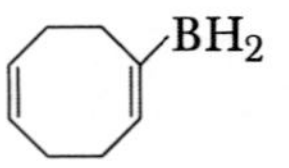 (b) 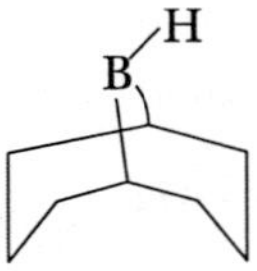

(c) 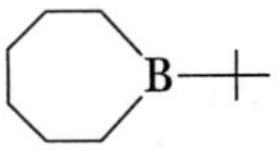 (d) 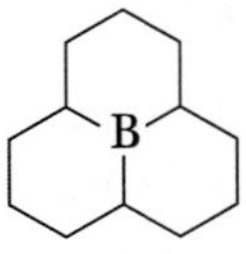

12. The product of the following transformation is

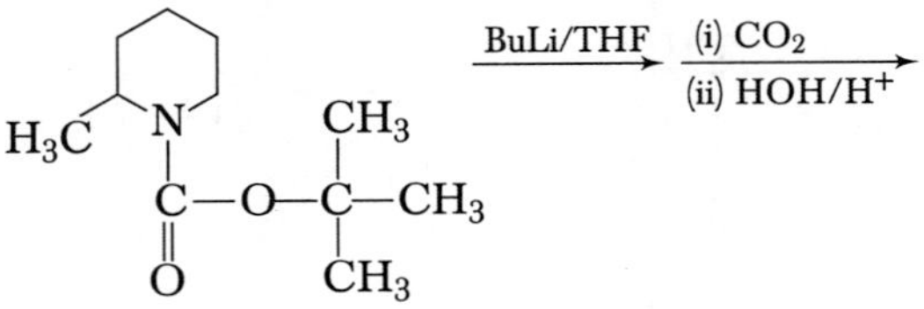

(a) 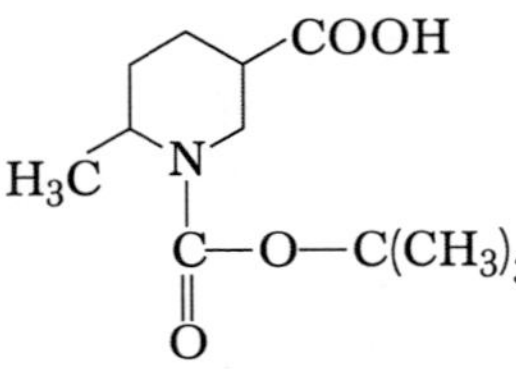

(b) 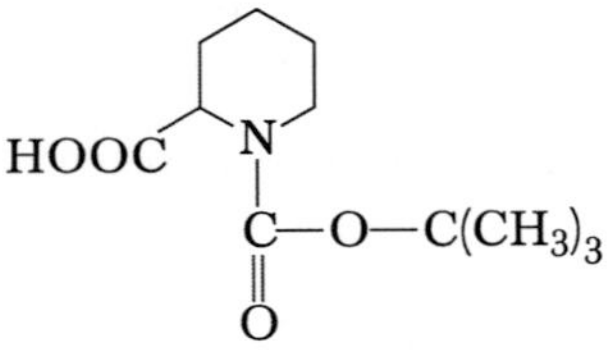

(c) 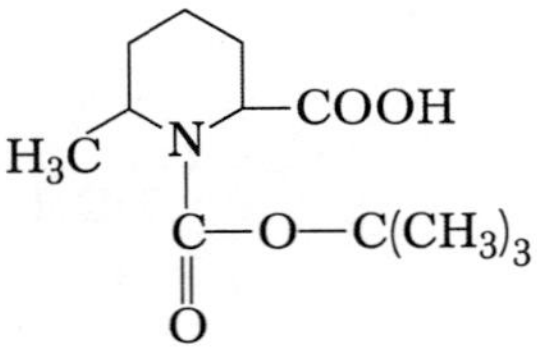

(d) 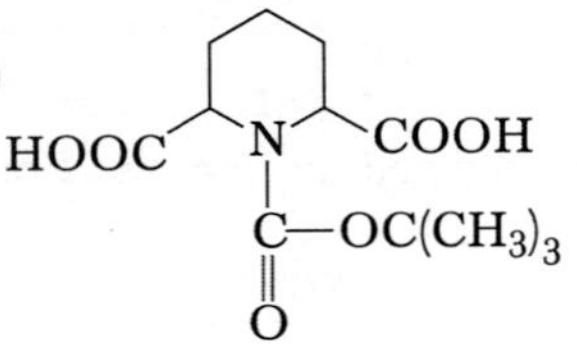

13. The major product in the following reaction

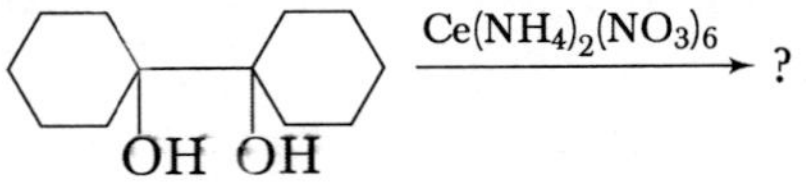

(a) 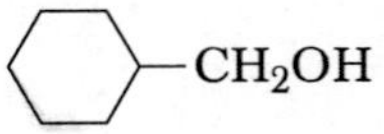 (b) 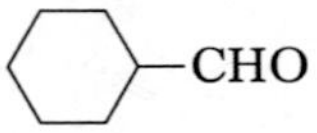

(c) 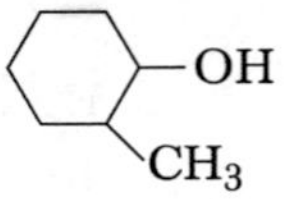 (d) 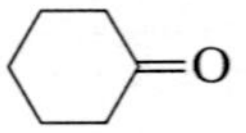

14. The product of the transformation

$$C_6H_5-\overset{O}{\overset{\|}{C}}-\underset{CH_3}{\underset{|}{\overset{OH}{\overset{|}{C}}}}-CHOH-CHO \xrightarrow{Pb(OAc)_4} ?$$ is

(a) C_6H_5COOH (b) CH_3COOH
(c) HCOOH (d) All of these

15. Which one of the following statements is correct with the following Diels-Alder addition to give exo and endo products?

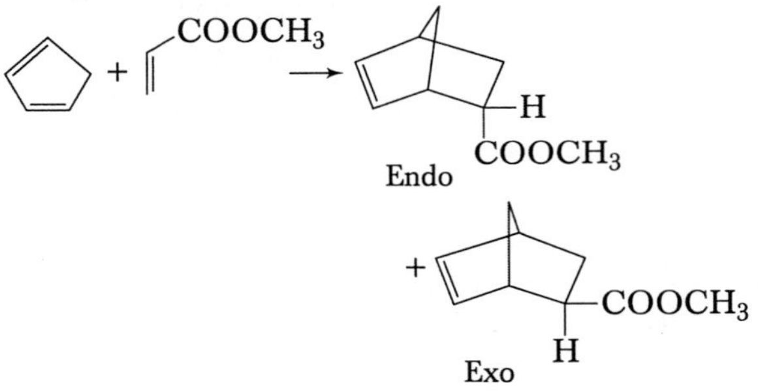

(a) The endo product is formed faster than exo product.
(b) The endo product is thermodynamically more stable than the exo product.
(c) The exo product is formed faster than endo product.
(d) The exo product is thermodynamically more stable than the endo product.

16. Addition of Br_2 to methyl acetylene yielding *trans*-1,2-dibromopropene is
(a) a stereoselective reaction
(b) a stereospecific reaction
(c) a stereoselective as well as a stereospecific reaction
(d) neither stereoselective nor stereospecific reaction

17. Reduction of 3-hexyne to *trans*-3-hexene can be effected by
(a) H_2/Lindlar's catalyst (b) Na/liq. NH_3
(c) Fe/NaCl (d) DIBAL

18. Identify the major product in the transformation given below.

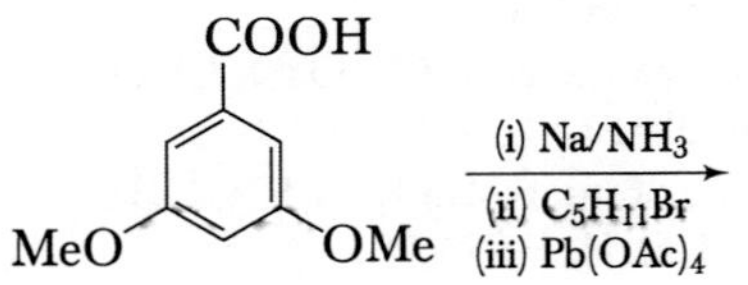

(a) 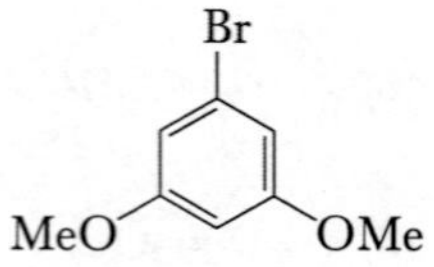

(b) 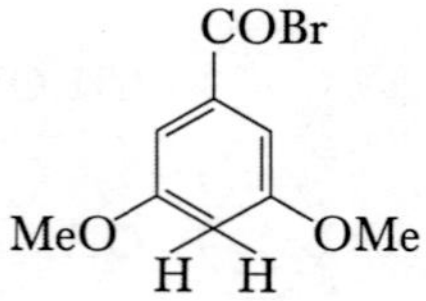

(c) 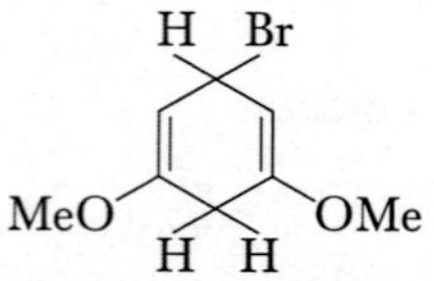

(d) 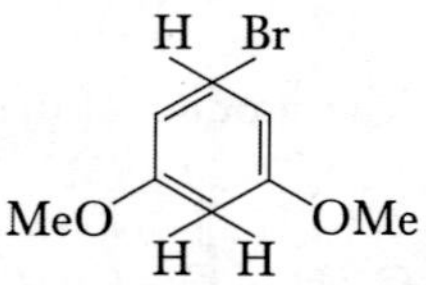

19. The reagent suitable for effecting the following transformation is

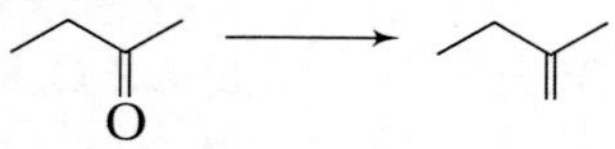

(a) CH_2N_2 (b) CH_3Li
(c) $(CH_3)_2CuLi$ (d) $Ph_3P{=}CH_2$

20. Among the following, the reagent not suitable for effecting the following transformation is

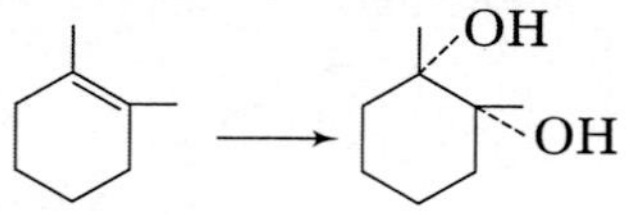

(a) alkaline $KMnO_4$
(b) OsO_4; N-methylmorpholine oxide
(c) $Pb(OAc)_4/HOH$
(d) I_2; AgOAc

21. $RR'R''OH$ can be prepared by the action of excess of a suitable Grignard reagent on a/an
(a) nitrile or an aldehyde (b) ester or an alcohol
(c) aldehyde or a ketone (d) ketone or an ester

22. Addition of BH_3 to a carbon-carbon double bond is
(a) anti-Markownikoff *syn*-addition
(b) anti-Markownikoff *anti*-addition
(c) Markownikoff *syn*-addition
(d) Markownikoff *anti*-addition

23. 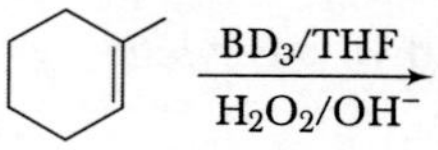 Product *A*, *A* is

(a) 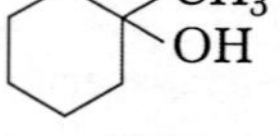

(b) 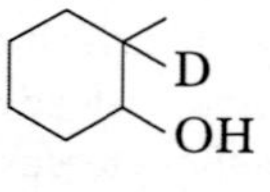

(c) 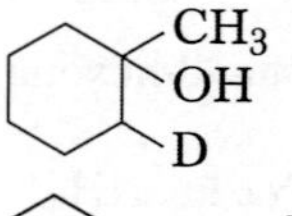

(d) 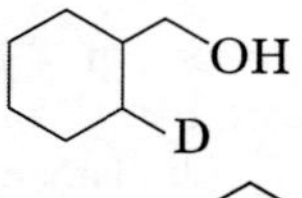

24. 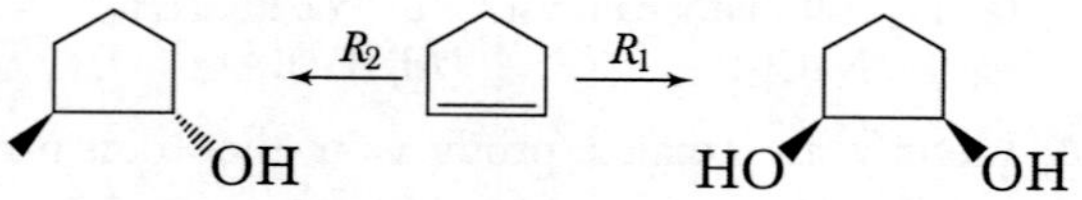

Reagent R_1 and R_2 are
(a) cold alkaline $KMnO_4$, OsO_4/H_2O_2
(b) cold alkaline $KMnO_4$, HCO_3H
(c) cold alkaline $KMnO_4$, $C_6H_5CO_3H$
(d) $C_6H_5CO_3H$, HCO_3H

25. 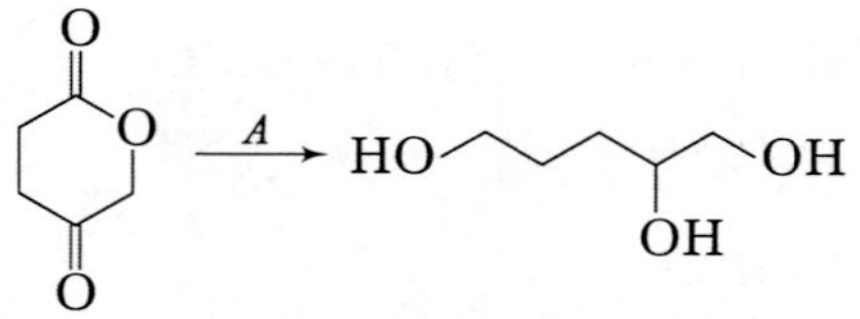

Reagent *A* used in this change is
(a) B_2H_6 (b) $LiAlH_4$
(c) Sn/HCl (d) CH_3OH/Na

26. 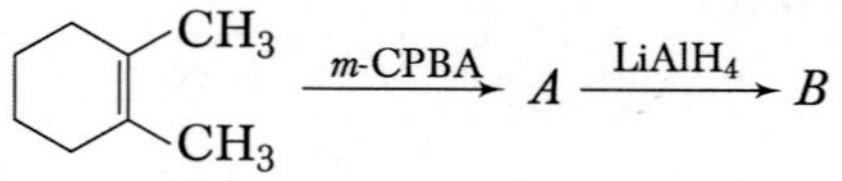

A and *B* respectively are

(a) 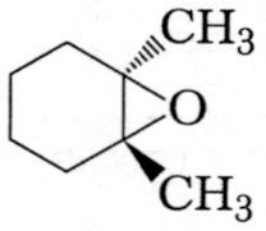 ; 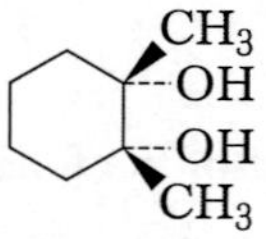

(b) 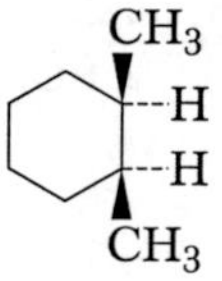 ; 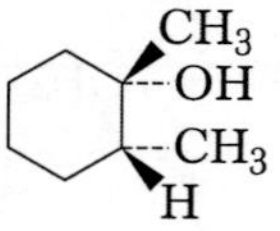

(c) 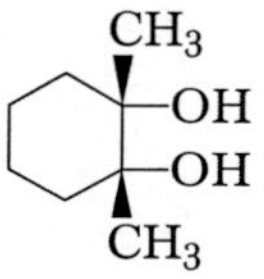 ; 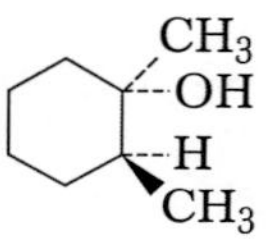

(d) 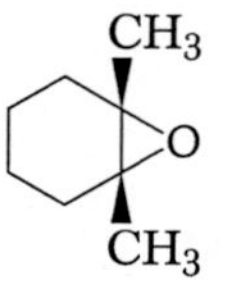 ; 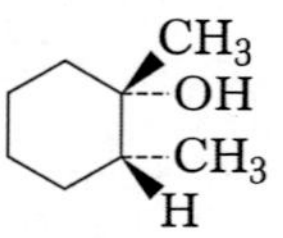

27. The product of the following reaction is

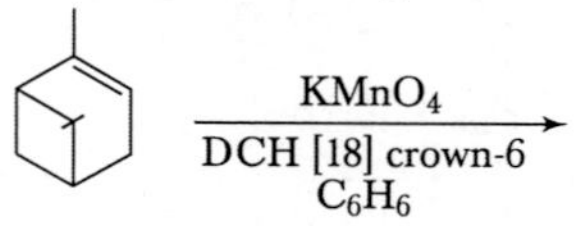

(a) 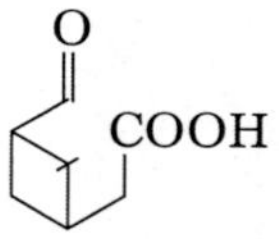

(b) 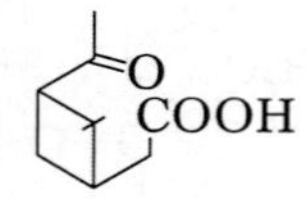

(c) 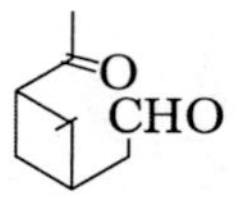

(d) 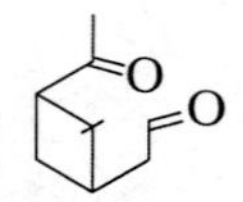

28. The major product formed in the reaction given below is

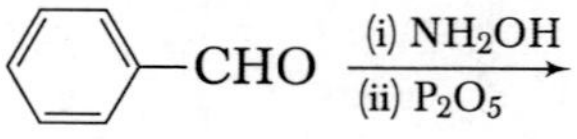

(a) 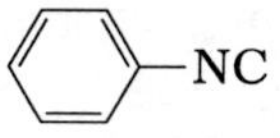

(b) 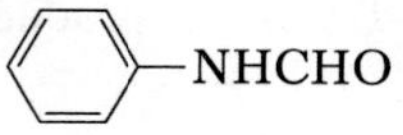

(c) 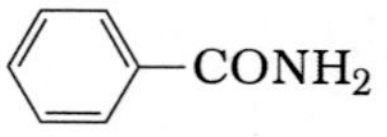

(d) 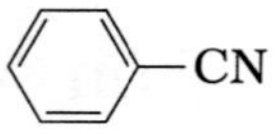

29. The transformation given below can be achieved by using

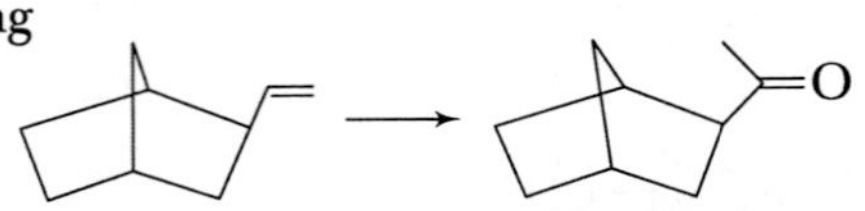

(a) BH_3, THF followed by H_2O_2/NaOH
(b) alkaline $KMnO_4$/$NaIO_4$
(c) pyridinium chlorochromate
(d) $PdCl_2$/$CuCl_2$/O_2/H_2O

30. Cyclohexyl benzyl ether is converted to cyclohexanol using
(a) 5% aq. KOH
(b) hydrazine hydrate
(c) H_2-Pd/C
(d) tetrabutylammonium fluoride

31. The mildest reducing agent which reduces only carbonyl group in presence of nitro, carboxyl, double bond and ester groups is
(a) $LiAlH_4$ (b) Na–NH_3
(c) $NaBH_4$ (d) H_2–Ni

32. The product in the reaction

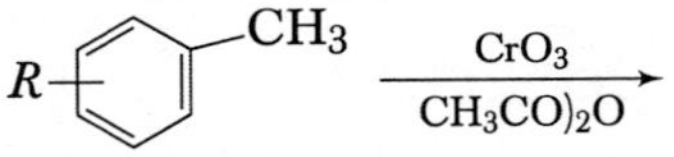

, is

(a) 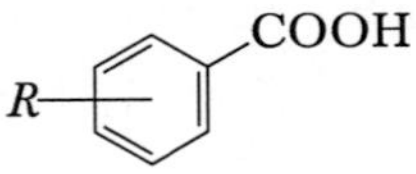 (b) 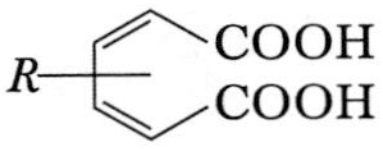

(c) 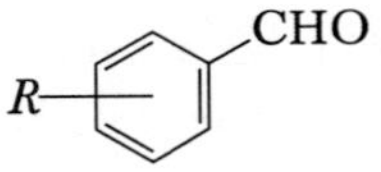 (d) 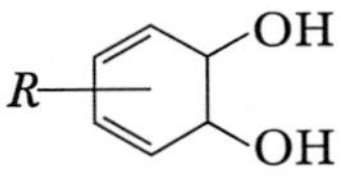

33. 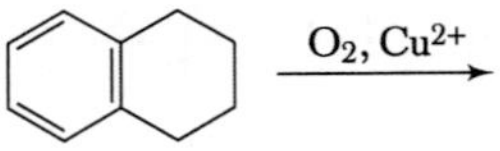 A ; compound A is

(a) 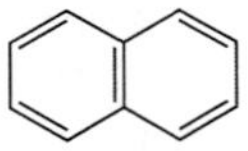 (b) 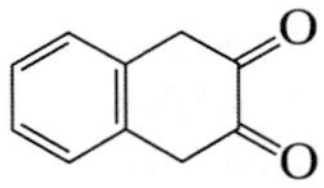

(c) 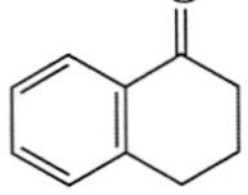 (d) 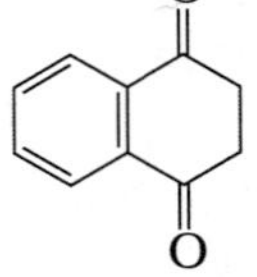

34. The product in the following transformation is

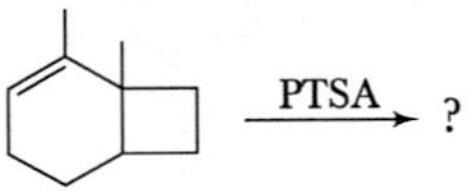

(a) 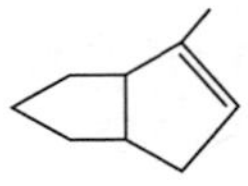 (b) 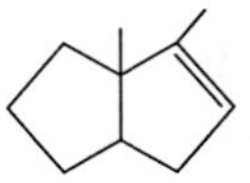

(c) 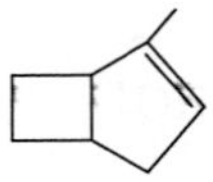 (d) 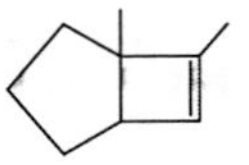

35. 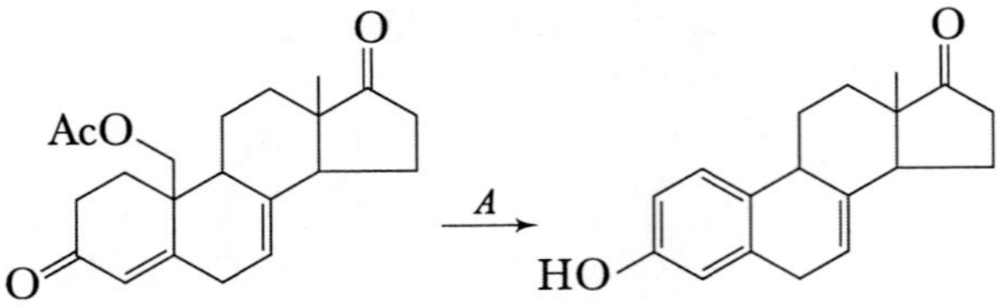

The reagent A is
(a) DDQ/Dioxan (b) CH_2N_2
(c) NBS (d) DCC

36. The end product of this transformation is

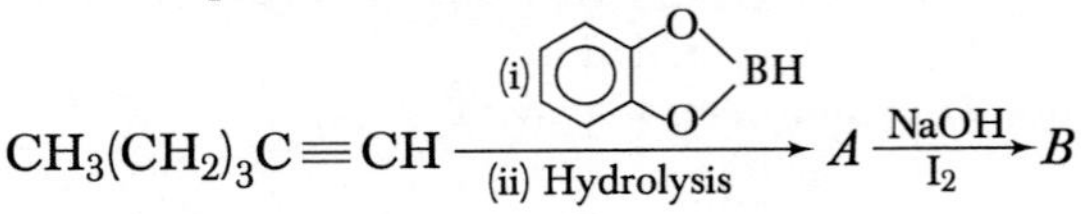

(a) 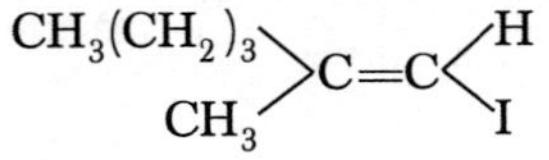

(b) 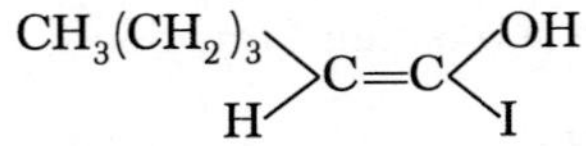

(c) 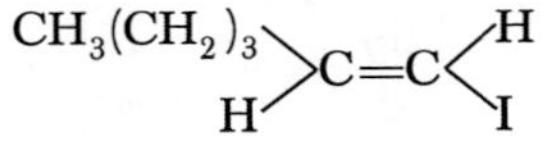

(d) 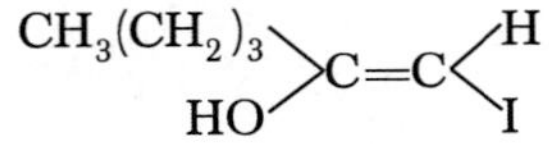

37. $CH_3C(=O)CH_2CH_2CH_2Cl \xrightarrow{CH_3MgBr} A$: A is

(a) $CH_3—CH(OH)CH_2CH_2CH_2Cl$

(b) 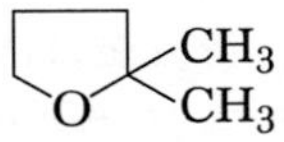

(c) 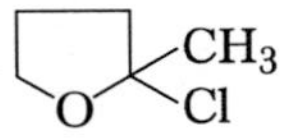

(d) 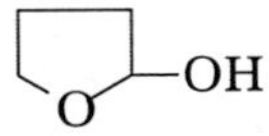

38. The end product of the following transformation is

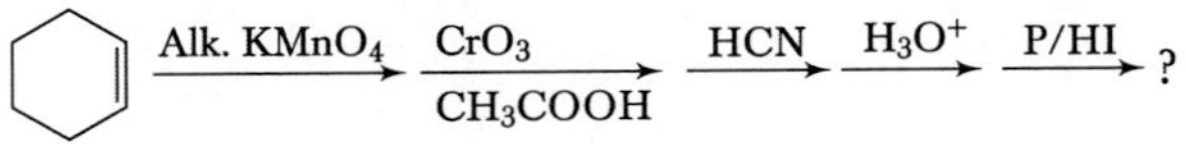

(a)  (b) 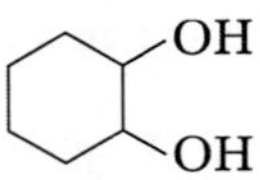

(c) 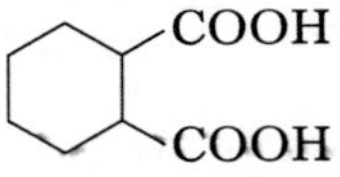 (d) 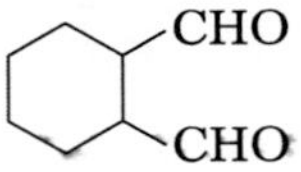

39. The reagent for effecting the following transformation is

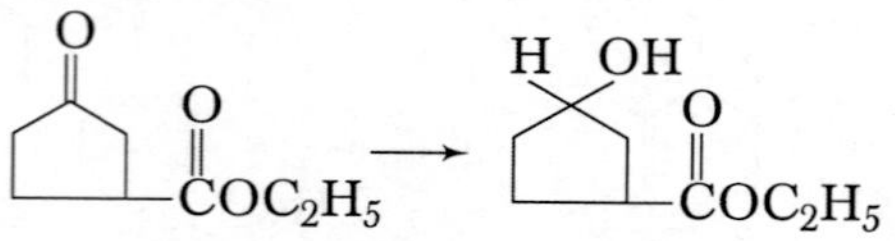

(a) $LiAlH_4$ (b) $NaBH_4$ (c) B_2H_6 (d) $NaNH_2$

40. The catalyst used in Fries rearrangement is the same as that used in
(a) Friedel-Crafts alkylation
(b) Cannizzaro reaction
(c) Oppenauer oxidation
(d) Hofmann rearrangement

41. 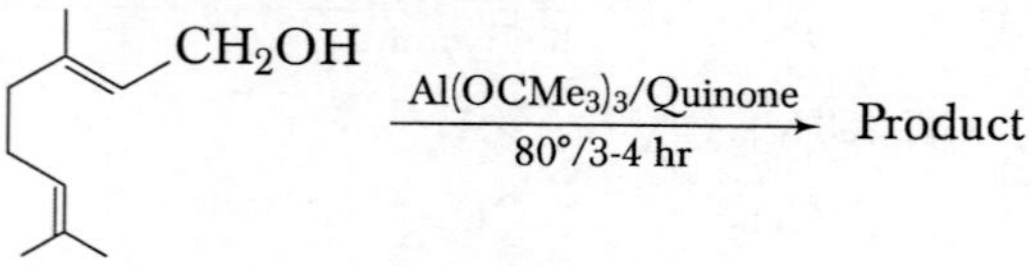

The product of the above transformation is

(a) 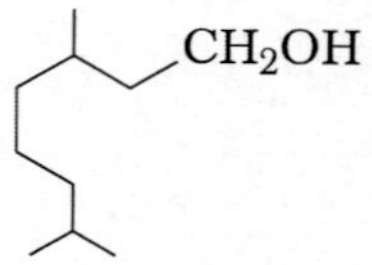

(b) 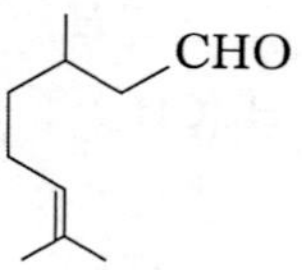

(c) 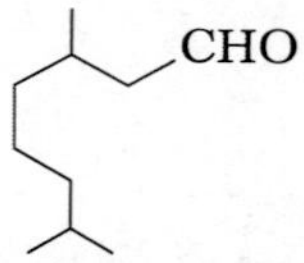

(d) 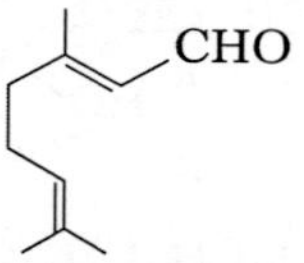

42. The false statement for osmium tetroxide reagent is
(a) OsO_4 is commonly known as osmic acid
(b) OsO_4 reagent always attacks on the less hindered side of the olefinic bond
(c) OsO_4 is most often used for anti-hydroxylation of alkenes
(d) OsO_4 reagent can be used for regioselectively

43. The major product for the following transformation is

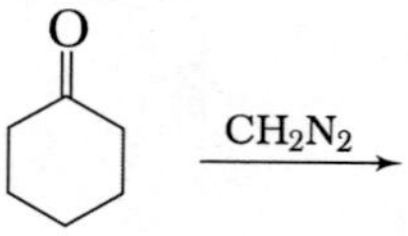

(a) 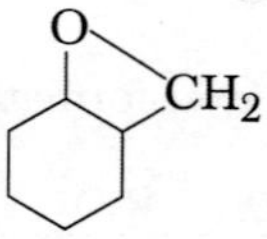

(b) 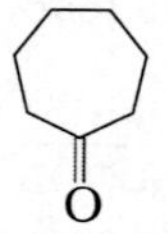

(c) 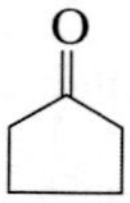

(d) 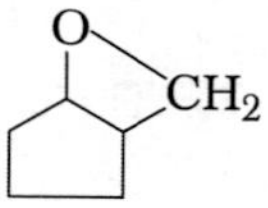

44. The end product of the following transformation is

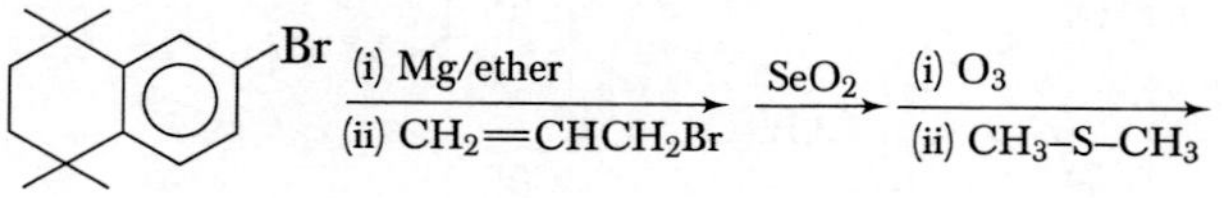

(a) 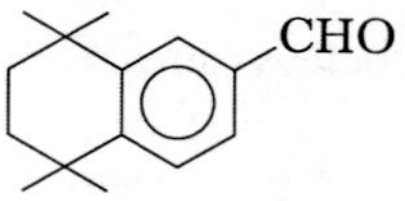

(b) 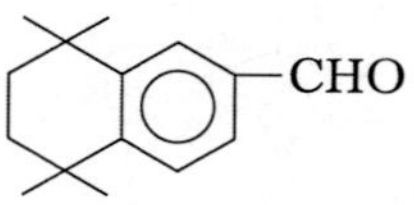

(c) 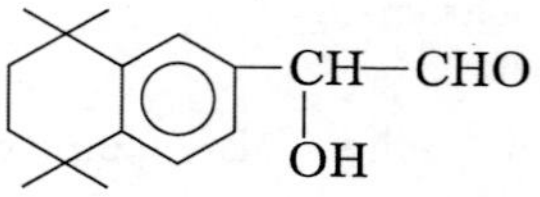

(d) 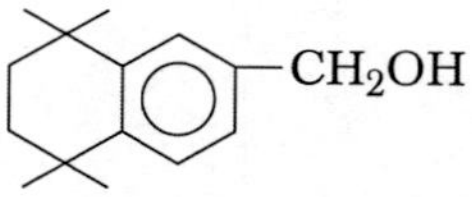

45. Buta-1,3-diene on heating with maleic anhydride would be

(a) 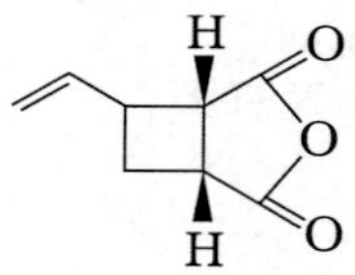
(b) 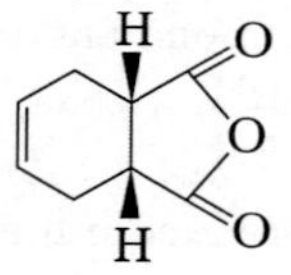
(c) 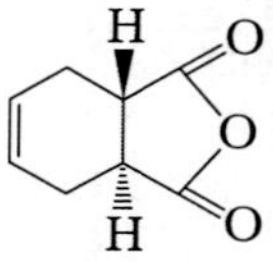
(d) 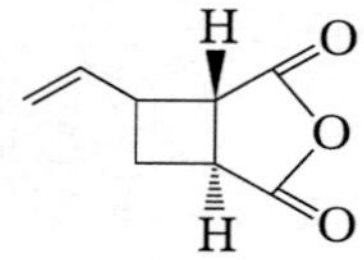

46. The incorrect statement about Baker's yeast is
(a) Baker's yeast consists only one type of alcohol dehydrogenases
(b) Baker's yeast is obtained by Saccharomyces cerevisiae fungus
(c) Stereoselectivity reduction by Baker's yeast depends on the amount of *R*-enzyme and *S*-enzyme
(d) β-keto esters on reduction with Baker's yeast give β-hydroxy esters

47. 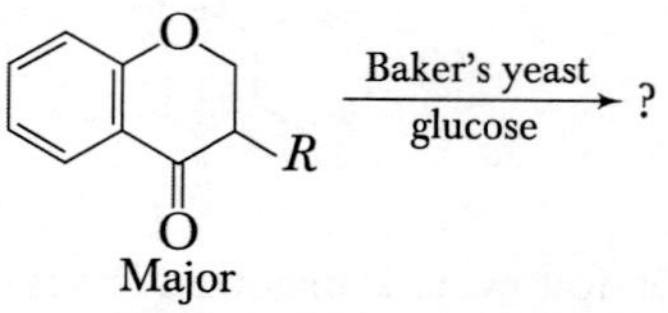

The major product of the above transformation is

(a) 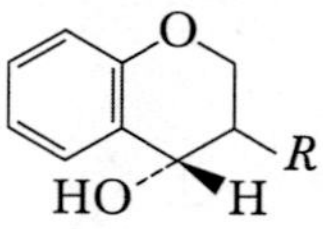
(b) 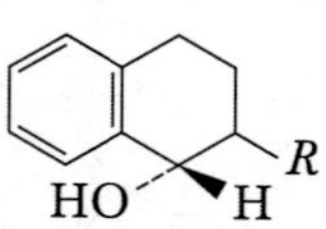
(c) 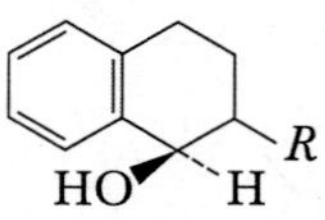
(d) 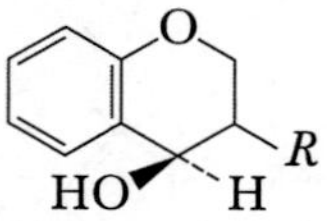

48. The reagent for the following transformation is

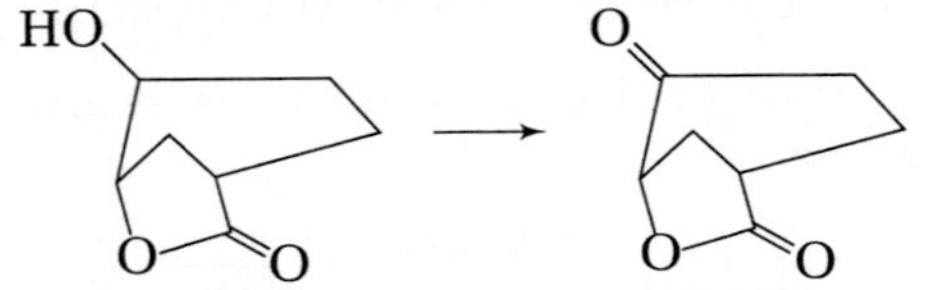

(a) SeO_2 (b) $RuO_4/NaIO_4$
(c) OsO_4 (d) DDQ

49. The oxidation of primary and secondary alcohols to aldehydes and ketones respectively can be carried out by reaction with DMSO activated by DCC. This oxidation is known as

(a) Swern oxidation
(b) Oppenauer oxidation
(c) Baeyer-Villiger oxidation
(d) Moffatt oxidation

50. Quinoline on oxidation with alkaline $KMnO_4$ gives

(a) 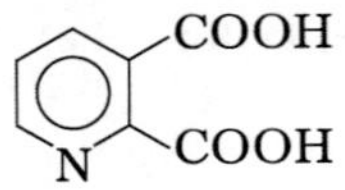

(b) 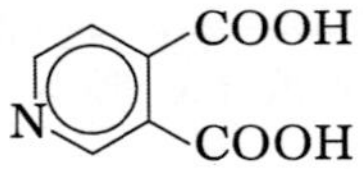

(c) 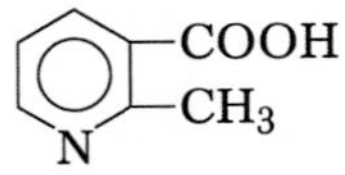

(d) 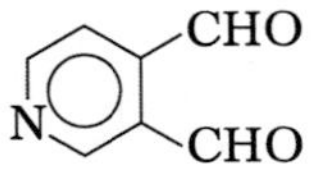

51. 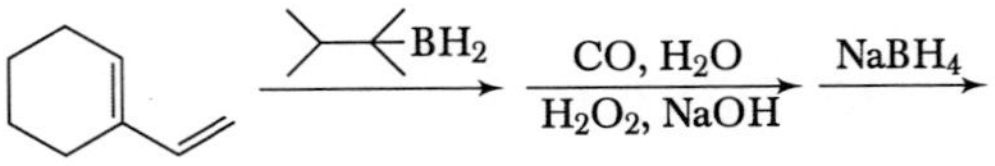

The end product of the above transformation is

(a) 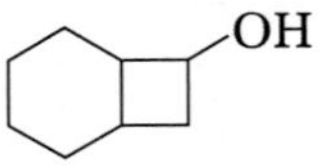

(b) 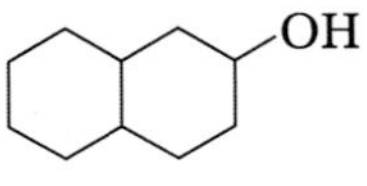

(c) 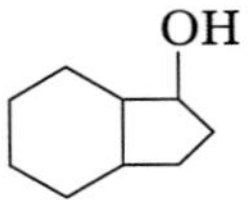

(d) 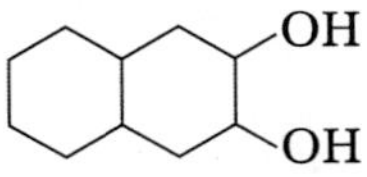

52. 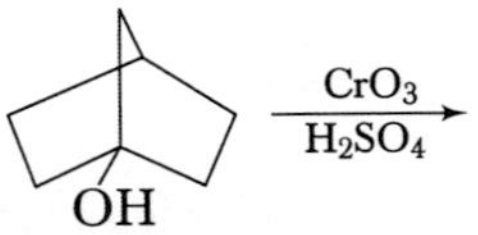

Product ; product is

(a) 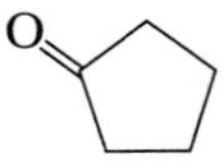

(b) 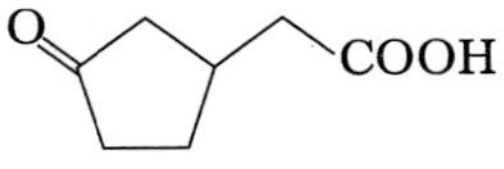

(c) 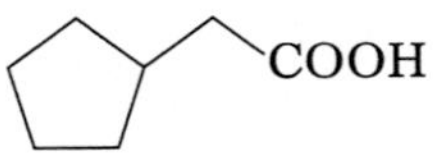

(d) 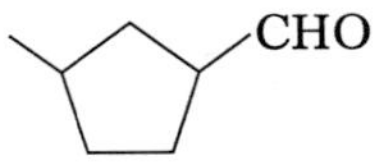

53. The major product in the following transformation is

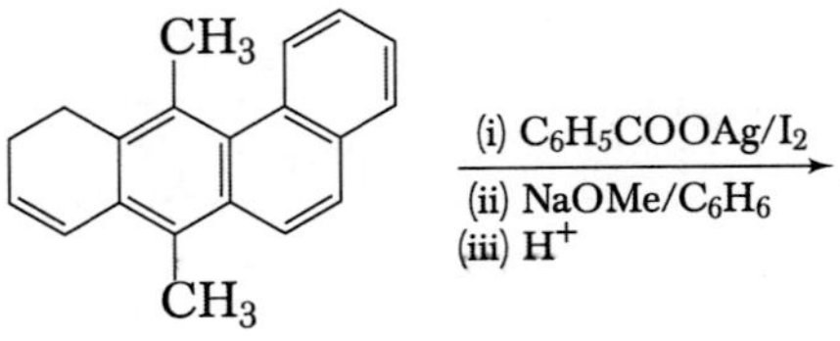

(a) 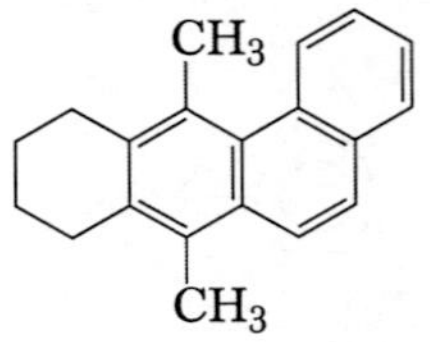

(b) 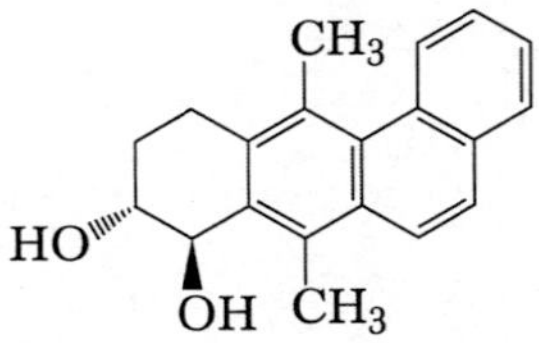

(c) 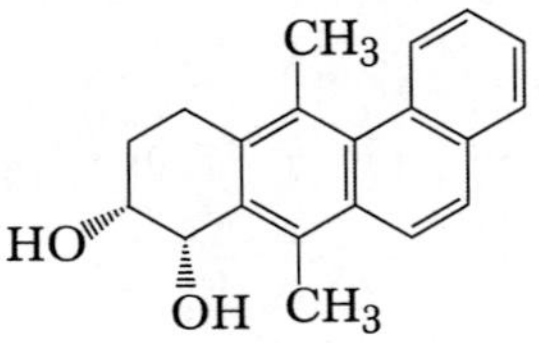

(d) 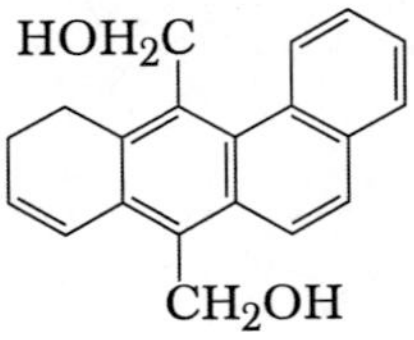

54. 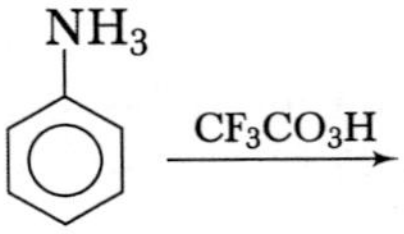

A; A is

(a) 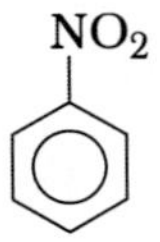

(b) 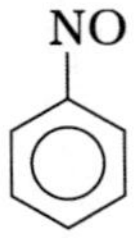

(c) 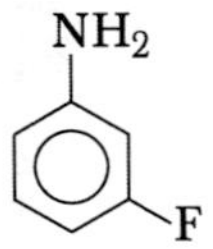

(d) 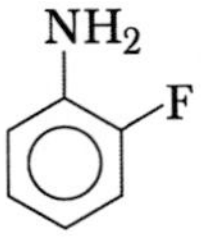

55. 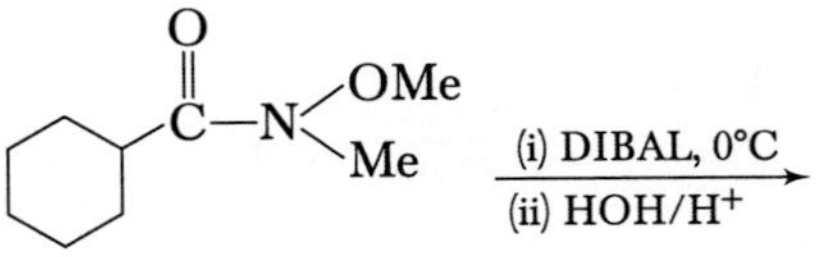

The major product of the above transformation is

(a) 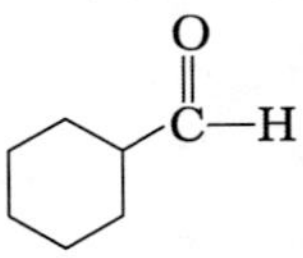

(b) 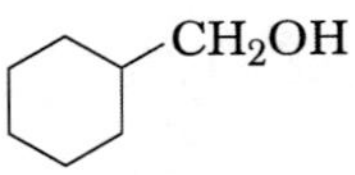

(c) 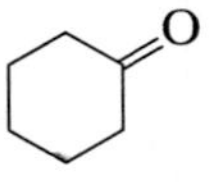

(d) 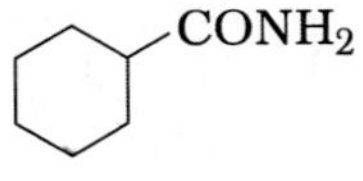

56. 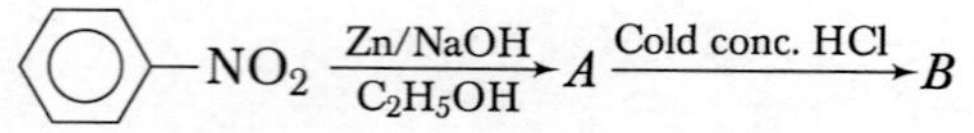

A and *B* are

(a) 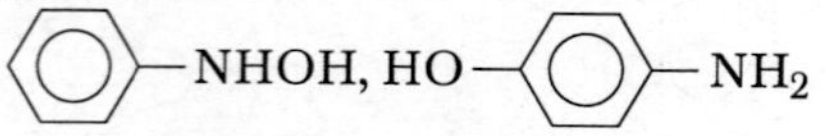

(b) 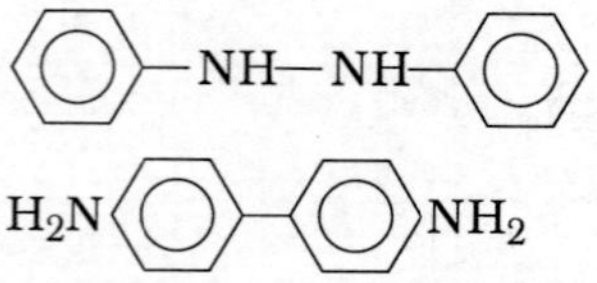

(c) 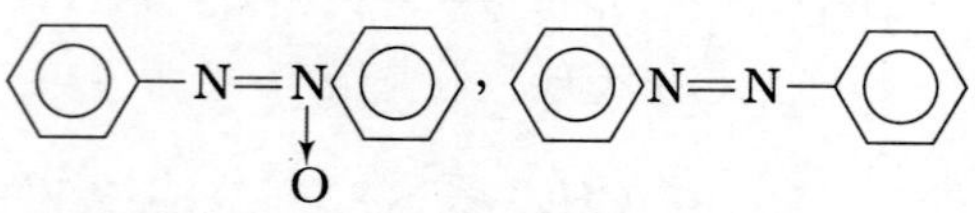

(d) None of the above is correct

57. Camphor on oxidation with SeO_2 in CH_3COOH gives

(a) 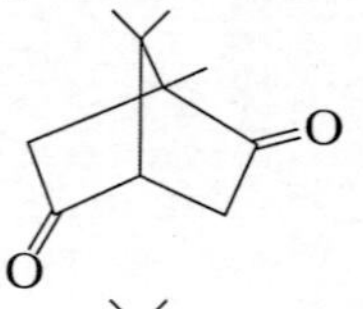

(b) 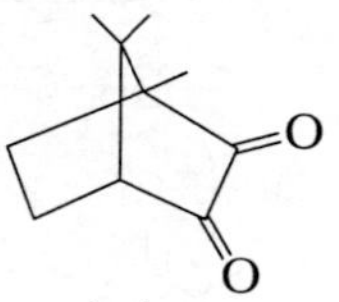

(c) 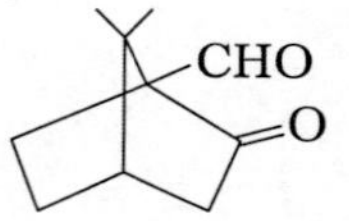

(d) 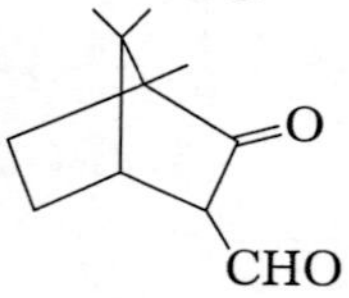

58. The suitable reagent for the following conversion is

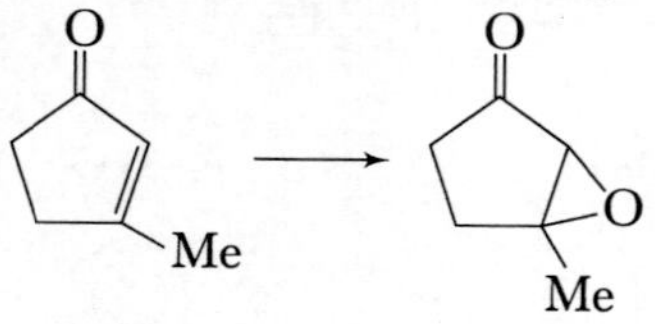

(a) *m*-CPBA
(b) H_2O_2/AcOH
(c) ^{t}BuOOH/HCl
(d) H_2O_2/NaOH

59. The major product formed in the reaction given below is

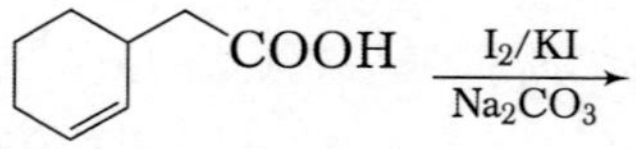

(a) 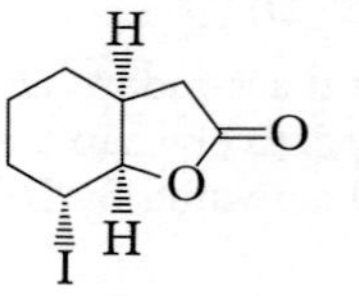

(b) 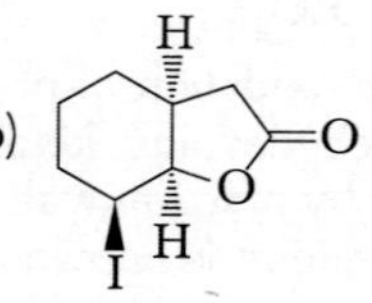

(c) 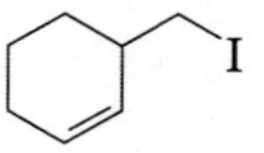

(d) 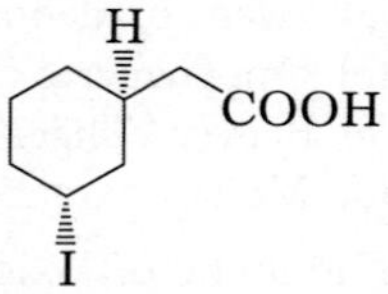

60. The most suitable reagent for the following transformation is

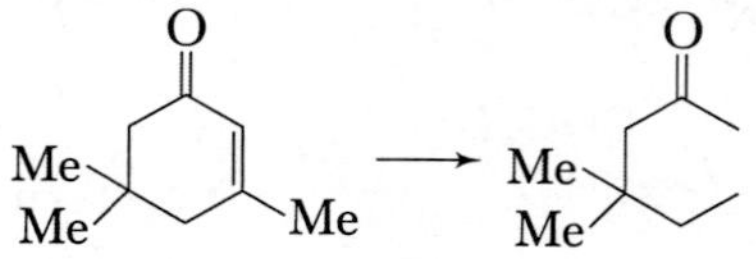

(a) $LiAlH_4$
(b) NH_2NH_2/KOH
(c) $NaBH_4/CeCl_3$
(d) Li/liq. NH_3

Exercise 2
(For Part 'C')

1. Give the major product of the following reaction

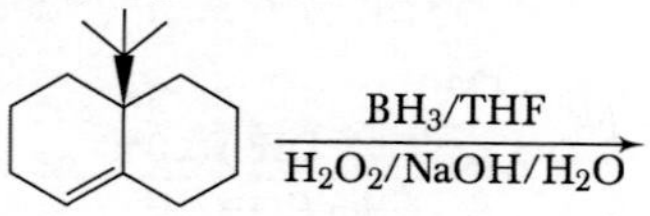

(a) 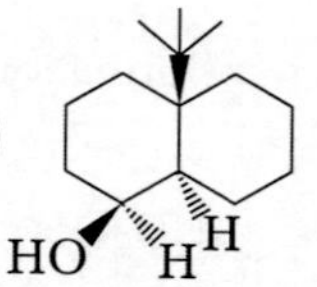

(b) 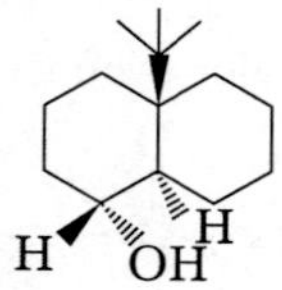

(c) 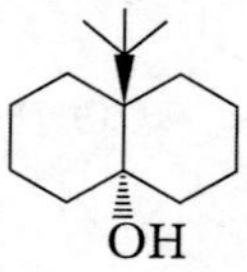

(d) 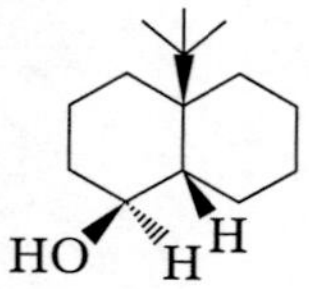

2. What is the major product of the following reaction

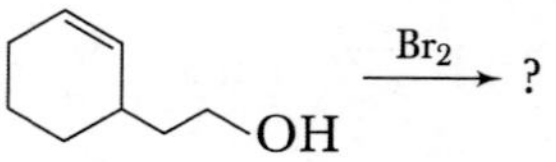

(a) 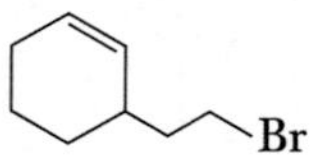

(b) 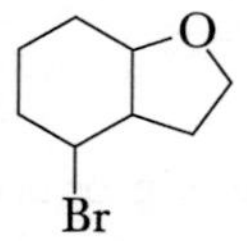

(c) 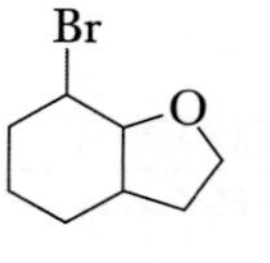

(d) 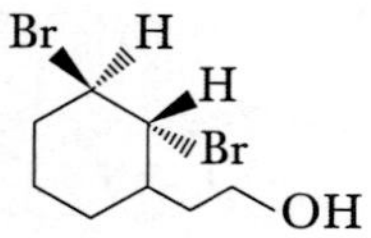

3. The major product of the following transformation is

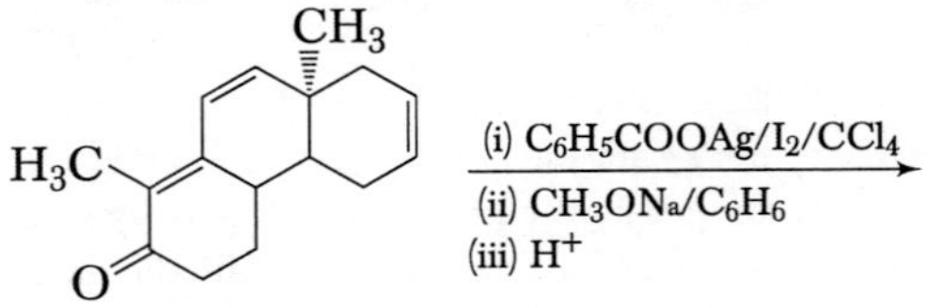

(a) 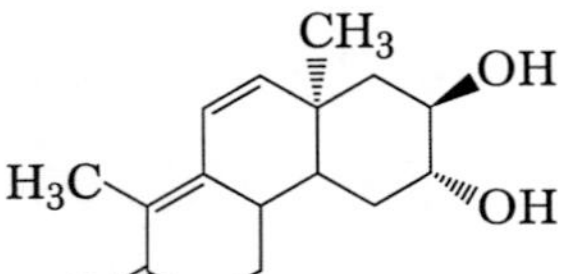

(b) 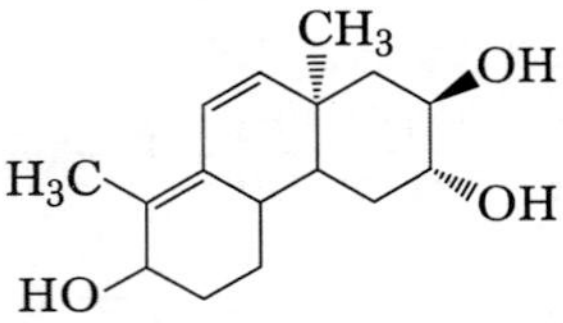

(c) 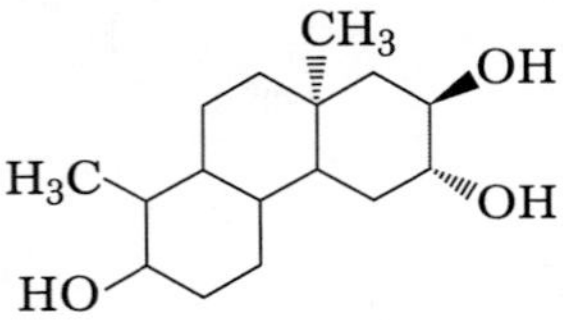

(d) 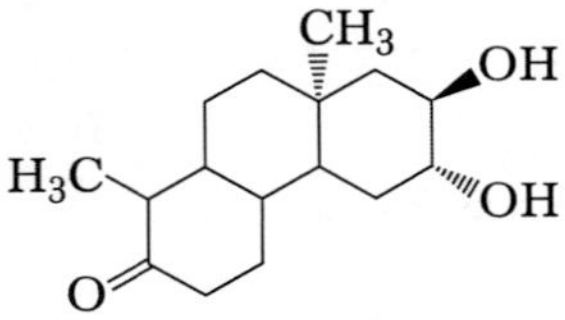

4. Consider the following statements.
   I. A solution of iodine and silver acetate in moist acetic acid is known as Woodward reagent.
   II. OsO_4 is known as Lemieux-Johnson reagent.
   III. DDQ is a powerful dehydrogenating agent.

   Select the correct statement.
   (a) I, II (b) II, III
   (c) I, III (d) Only I

5. The major product of the following sequence of reaction is

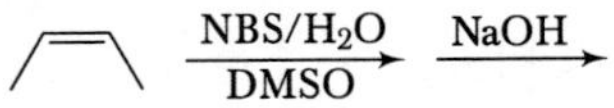

(a) 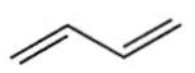 (b) 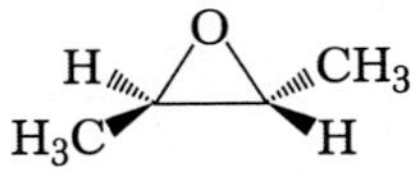

(c) 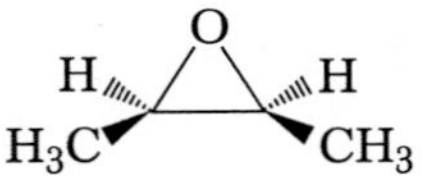 (d) 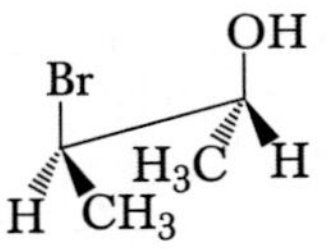

6. Consider the reaction sequence below

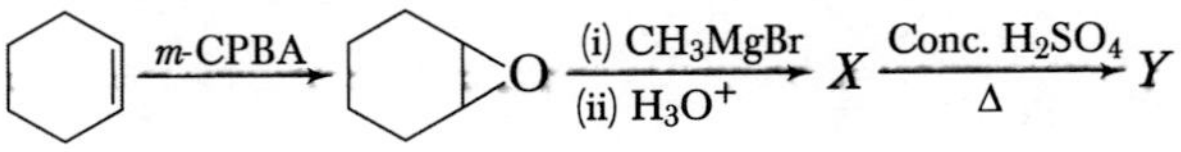

The correct statement is/are
   I. The major product Y is1-methylcyclohexene
   II. X is a racemic mixture
   III. X is a single pure enantiomer
   IV. Y is 2-methylcyclohexene
   (a) I, III (b) I, II
   (c) II, IV (d) II, III, IV

7. What is the product of the following reaction sequence?

$$CH_3CH_2CH_2Br \xrightarrow[CH_3Li]{P(C_6H_5)_3} \xrightarrow{\text{Cyclopentanone}}$$

(a) 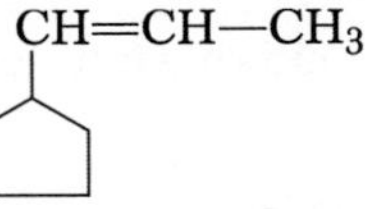 (b) 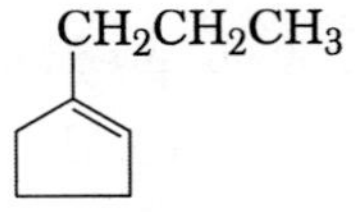

(c) 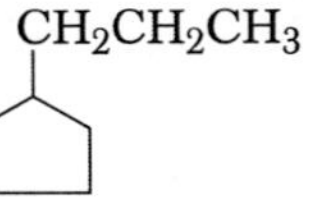 (d) 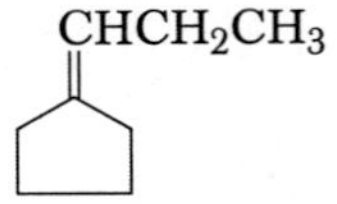

8. Select the reaction which is not correctly shown.

(a) 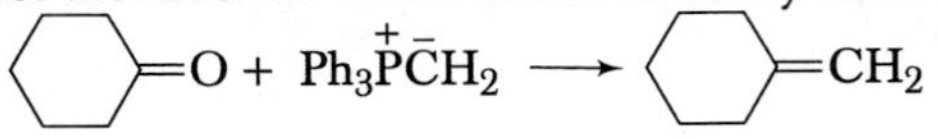

(b) 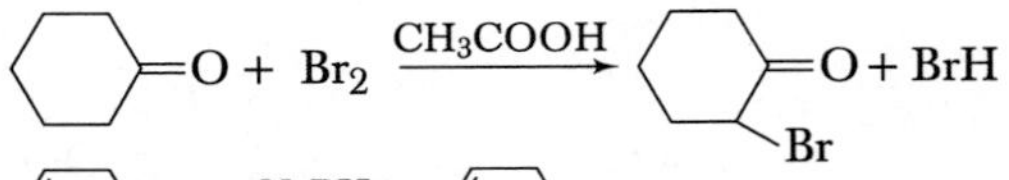

(c) 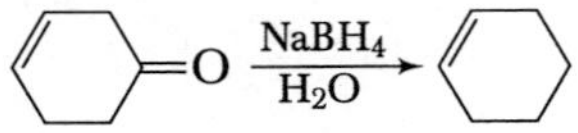

(d) 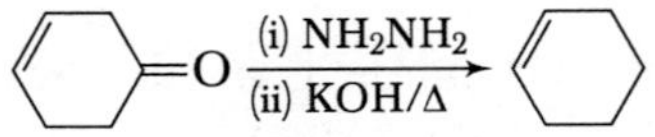

9. Consider the following reaction and select the correct option.

I. 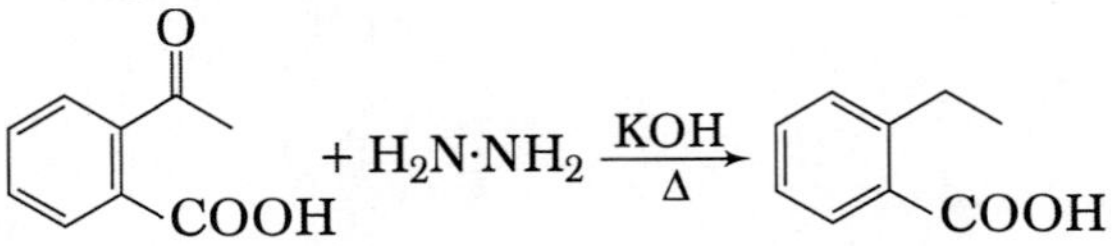

II. 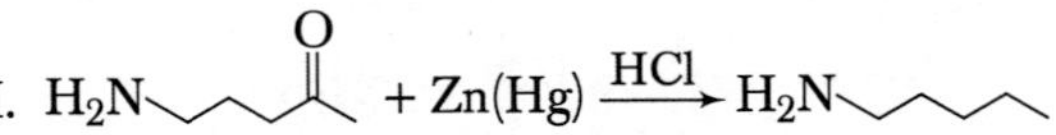

III. 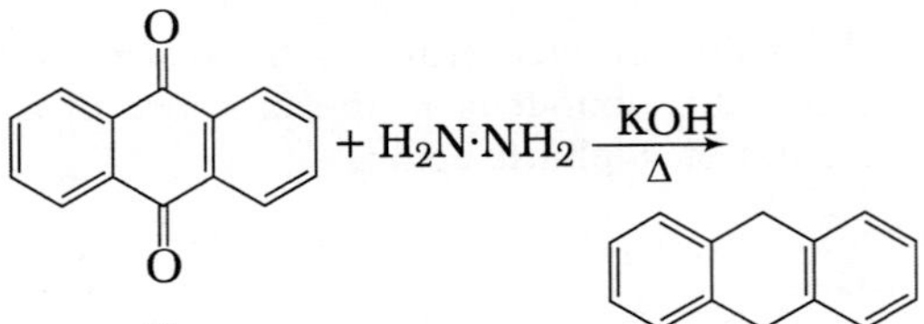

IV. 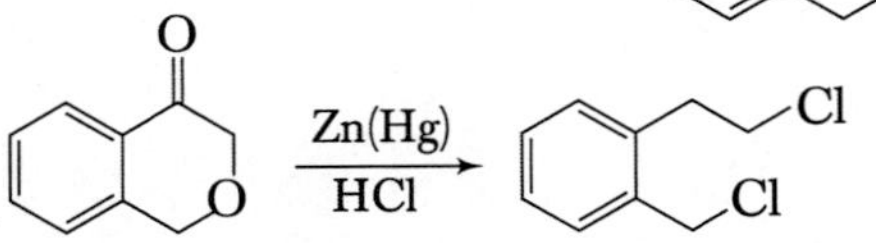

(a) I, III (b) III, IV
(c) II, III, IV (d) I, IV

10. The product of the following reaction is/are

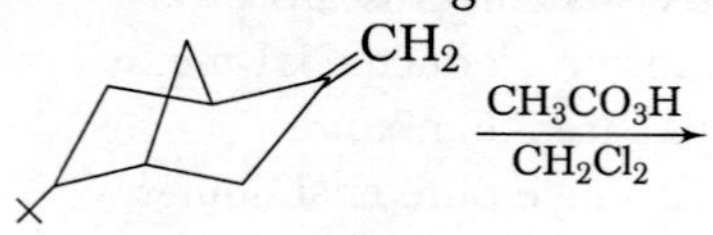

(a) 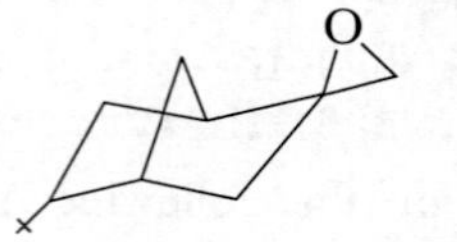 (b) 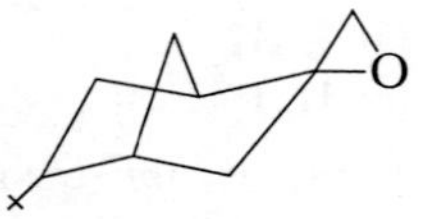

(c) 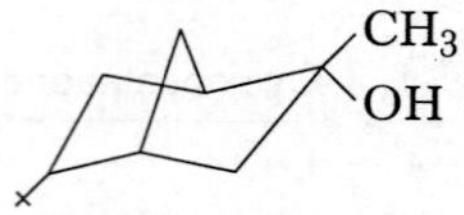 (d) 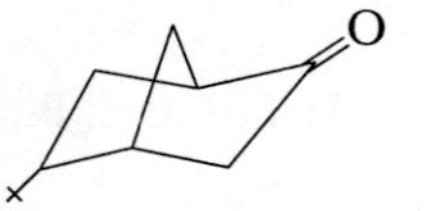

11. The major product of the following transformation is

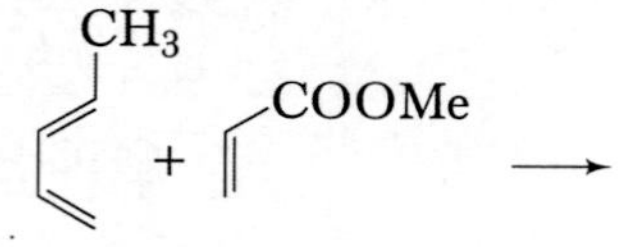

(a) 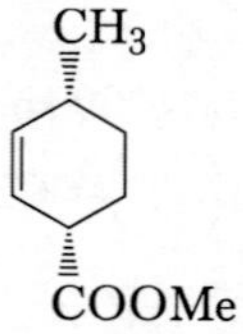 (b) 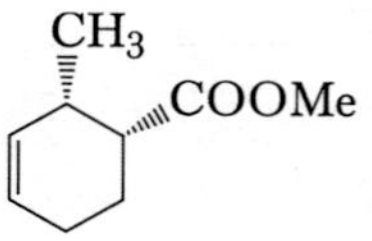

(c) 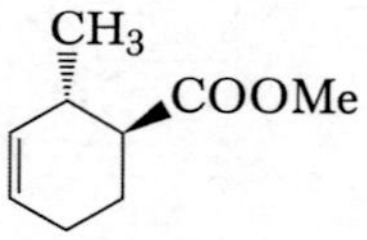 (d) 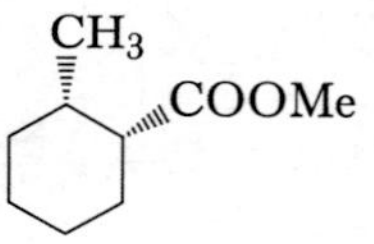

12. The major product formed in the reaction of 1,5-cyclooctadiene with 0.5 equivalent of diborane is

(a) 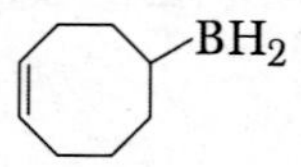 (b) 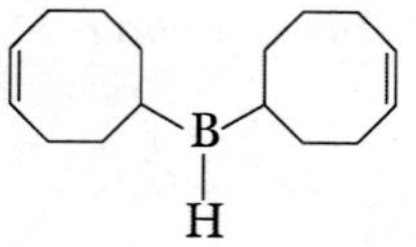

(c) 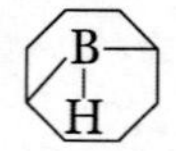 (d) 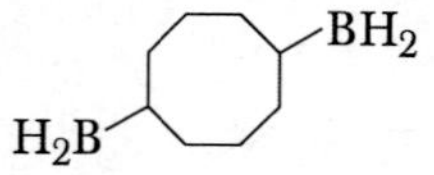

13. The major product formed in the reaction of benzoic acid with isobutylene in the presence of a catalytic amount of sulphuric acid is

(a) 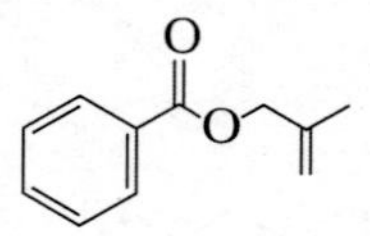 (b) 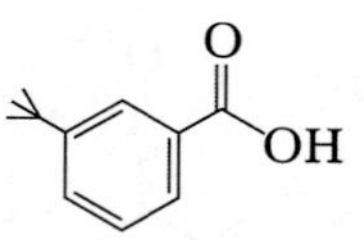

(c) 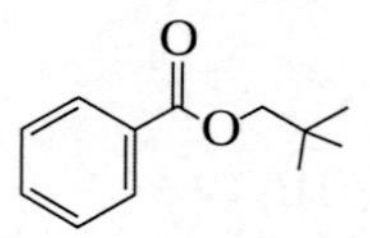 (d) 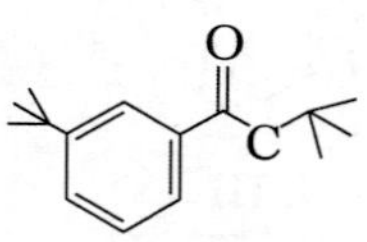

14. Match the Column I and Column II.

	Column I		Column II
A.	Wilkinson's catalyst	1.	Hydrosilation
B.	Speier's catalyst	2.	$RhCl(PPh_3)_3$
C.	Water gas shift catalyst	3.	Zinc-copper oxide
D.	Zeolite ZSM-5-catalyst	4.	Synthetic gasoline

Codes

	A	B	C	D
(a)	2	3	4	1
(b)	3	2	4	1
(c)	2	1	4	3
(d)	2	4	1	3

15. 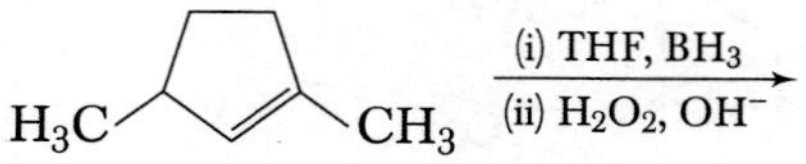 Product *A*, *A* is

(a) 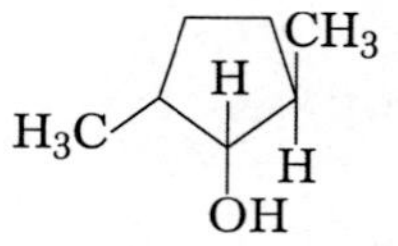 (b) 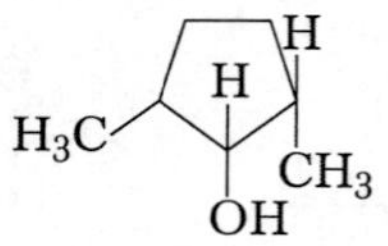

(c) 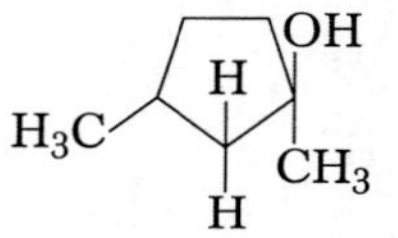 (d) 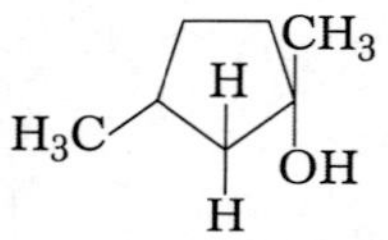

16. The product of the reaction is

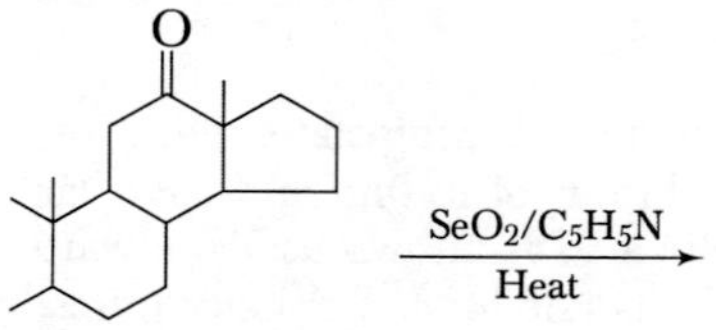

(a) 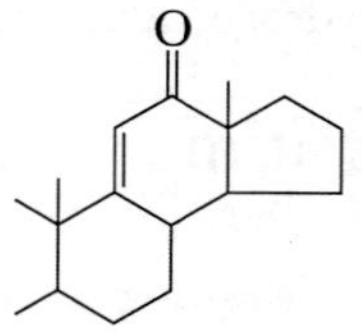 (b) 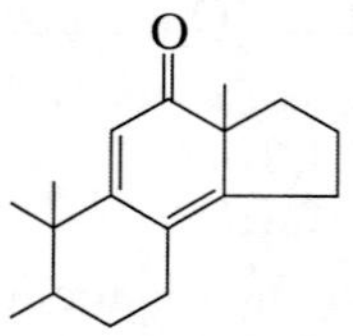

(c) 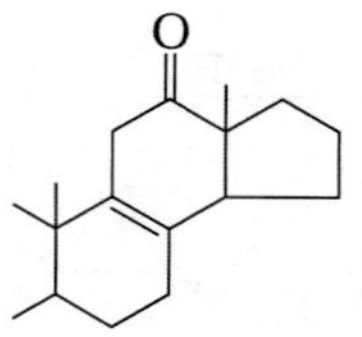 (d) 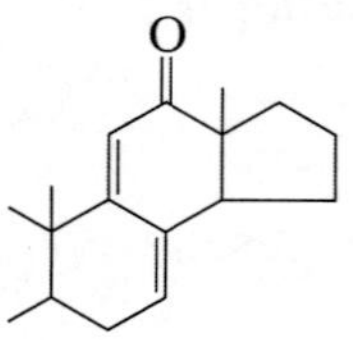

17. The product of the reduction

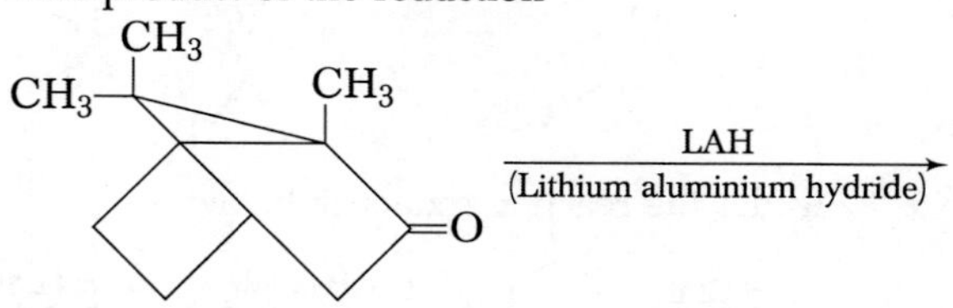

Product, is

(a) A 50-50 mixture is *iso*borneol and borneol
(b) Predominantly *iso*borneol with a little quantity of borneol
(c) Predominantly borneol with a little *iso*borneol
(d) No reduction is possible

18. 1,3-butadiene adds to allene $H_2C{=}C{=}CH_2$ to give

(a) 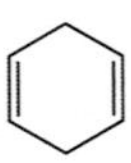
(b) 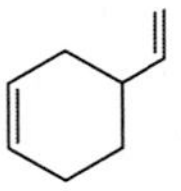
(c) 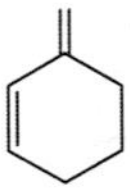
(d) 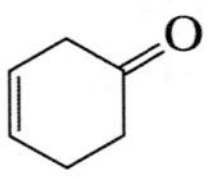

19. Match the reactions given under Column I with the reagents given under Column II and select the correct answer.

Column I	Column II
A. $PhCOOC_2H_5 + CH_3COOC_2H_5 \rightarrow PhCOCH_2COOC_2H_5 + EtOH$	1. anhydrous $ZnCl_2$
B. $CH_3COOH + Cl_2 \rightarrow ClCH_2COOH$	2. $C_2H_5O^-$
C. $C_6H_6 + (Ac)_2O \rightarrow C_6H_5COCH_3$	3. P
D. Cyclohexene → *Cis*-1, 2-cyclohexanediol	4. OsO_4

Codes

	A	B	C	D
(a)	2	3	1	4
(b)	3	4	1	2
(c)	4	1	2	3
(d)	3	2	4	1

20. The major product formed in the reaction given below is

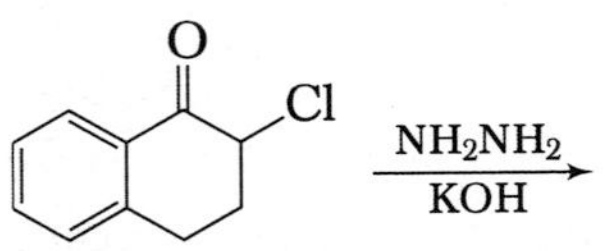

(a) 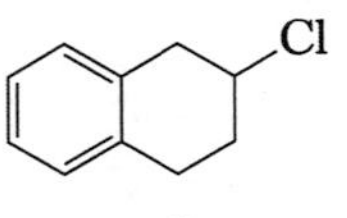

(b) 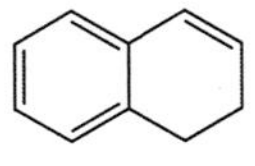
(c) 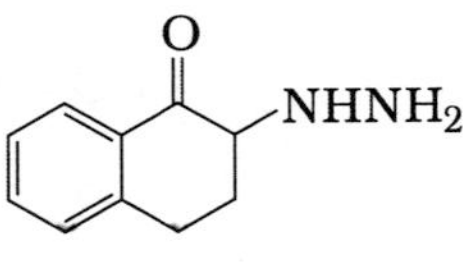

(d) 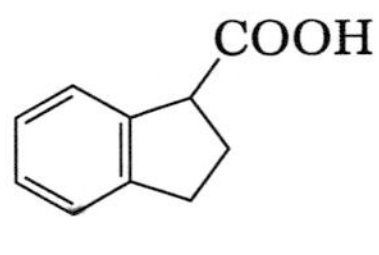

21. Match Column I with Column II and select the correct answer.

Column I	Column II
A. Acetophenone ⇌ Phenylethane	1. Zinc-Hg and HCl
B. Acetophenone ⇌ 1-phenylethanol	2. $SnCl_2$
C. Nitrobenzene ⇌ phenylhydroxylamine	3. $NaBH_4$
D. Benzyl tosylate ⇌ Toluene	4. Zinc and NH_4Cl

Codes

	A	B	C	D
(a)	1	3	4	2
(b)	1	3	2	4
(c)	2	4	1	3
(d)	3	2	1	4

22. The most suitable reagent for carrying out the transformation given below is

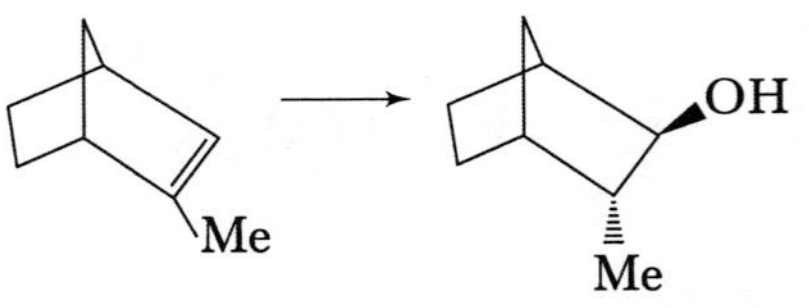

(a) aq. H_2SO_4
(b) $Hg(OAc)_2$ followed by reaction with $NaBH_4/NaOH$
(c) B_2H_6 followed by reaction with $H_2O_2/NaOH$
(d) *m*-CPBA followed by reaction with dil. H_2SO_4

23. The major product formed in the reaction, given below, is

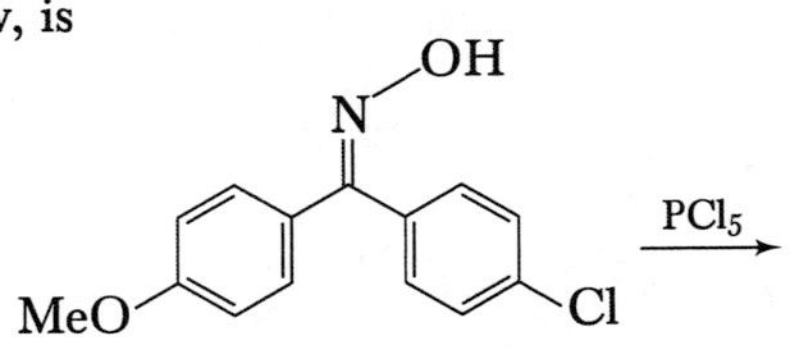

(a) 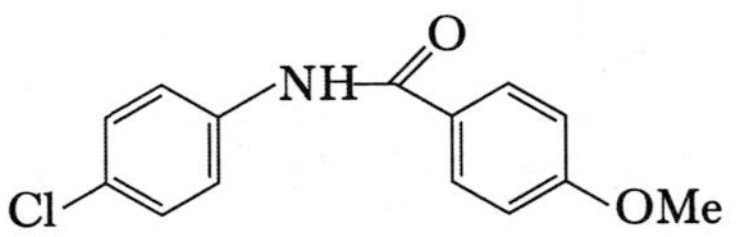

(b) 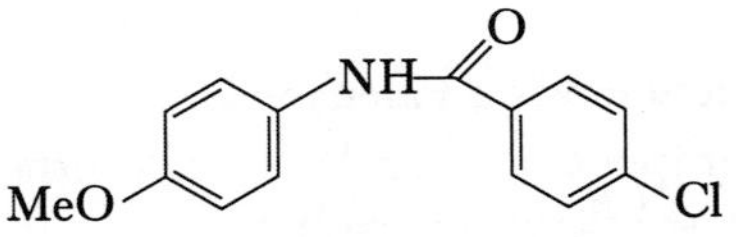

(c) 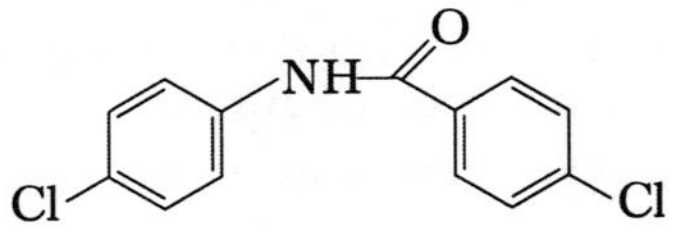

(d) 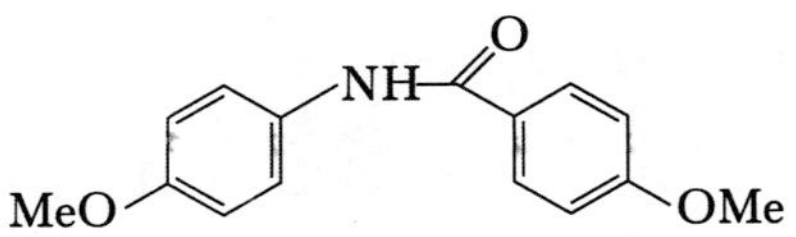

24. The major product formed in the reaction of ethyl acetoacetate with sodium hydride (1 equivalent) and methyl iodide (1 equivalent) is

(a) 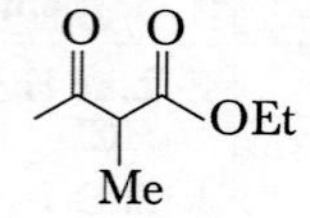
(b) 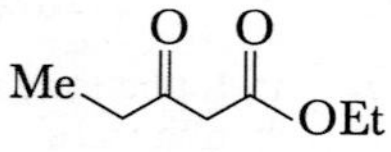
(c) 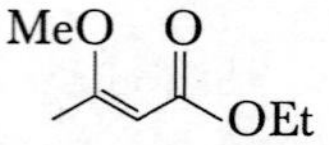
(d) 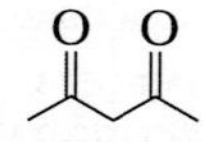

25. The reaction of phenyl acetylene with one equivalent of methyl magnesium bromide followed by reaction with benzaldehyde provides

(a) 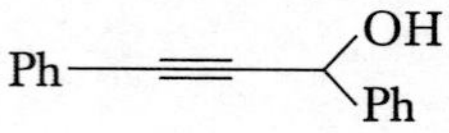
(b) 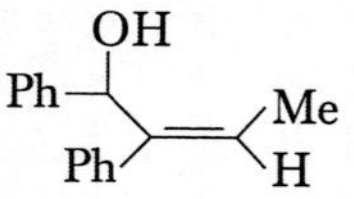
(c) 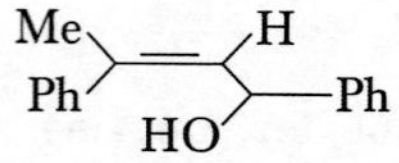
(d) 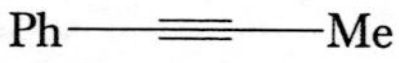

26. The major product in the following reaction is

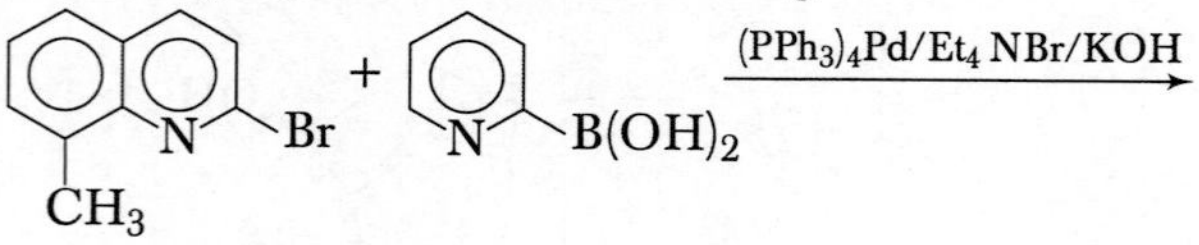

(a) 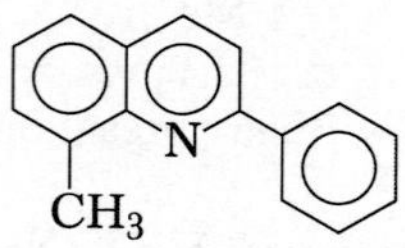
(b) 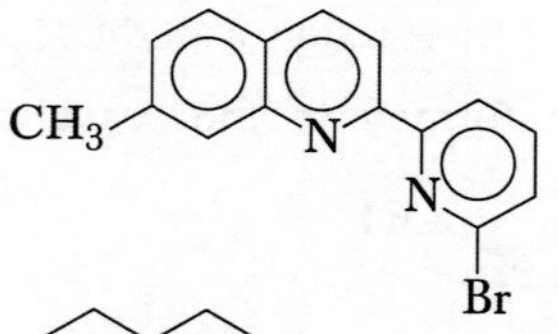
(c) 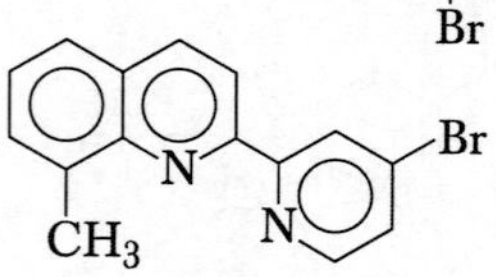
(d) 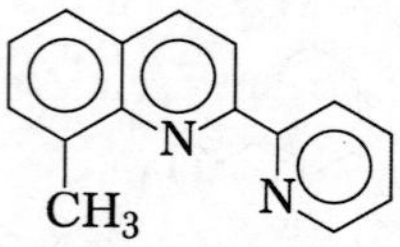

27. Consider the following statements.

I. Tetra (triphenyl phosphine) chlororhodium is known as Wilkinson catalyst.

II. Umpolung refers to the reversal of the normal polarity of a functional group.

III. Lithium dialkyl cuprates are also called Gilman reagent.

Select the correct statement.

(a) I, II
(b) II, III
(c) I, III
(d) Only III

28. The major product of the following transformation is

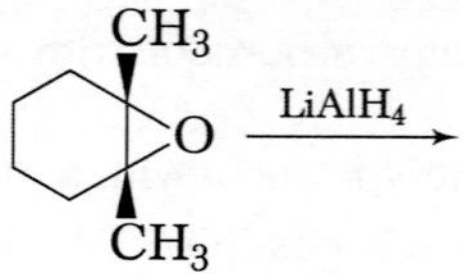

(a) 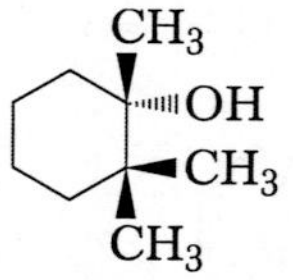
(b) 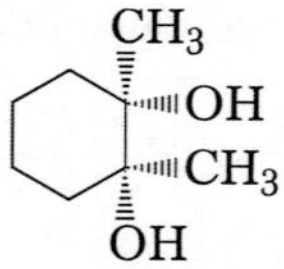
(c) 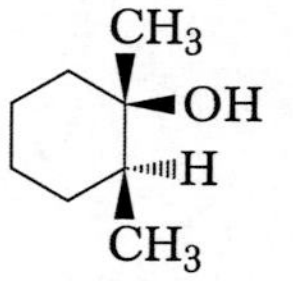
(d) 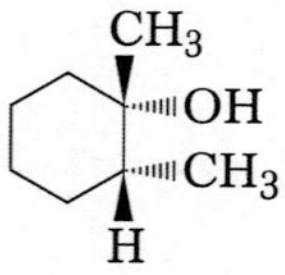

29. The most suitable reagent of the following transformation is

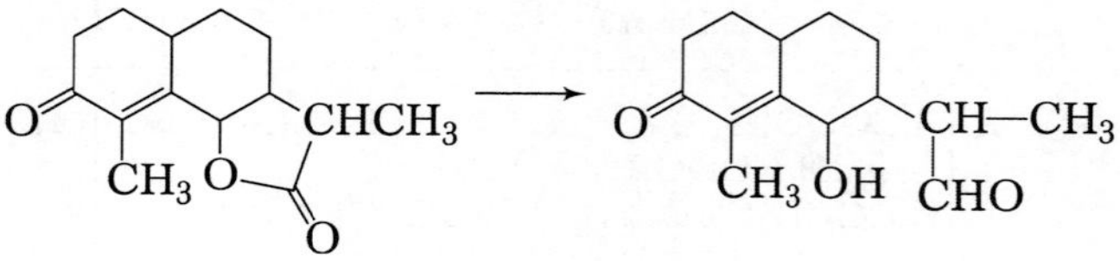

(a) $LiAlH_4$
(b) H_2/Ni
(c) DIBAL
(d) $NaBH_4$

30. The major product of the following reaction is

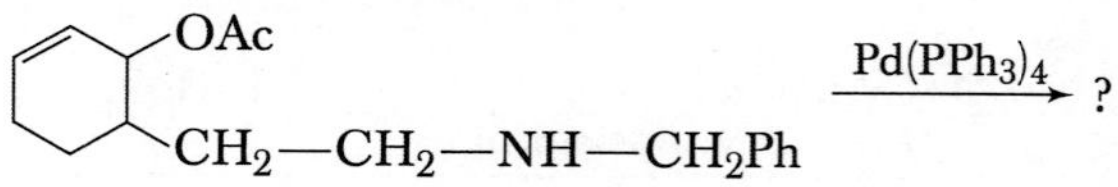

(a) 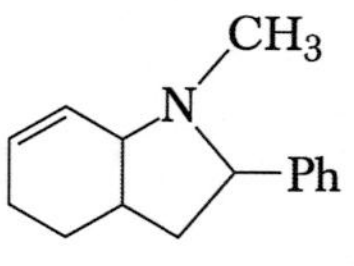
(b) 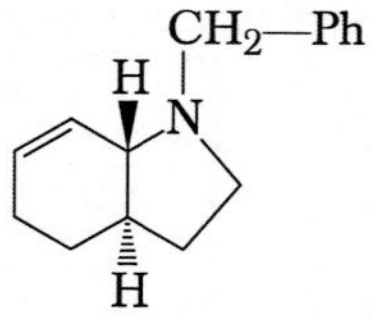
(c) 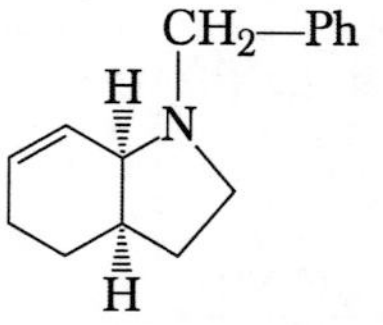
(d) 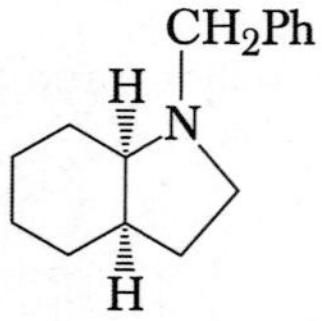

31. Quinoline reacts with chromic acid to give quinolic acid which on being heated give

(a) 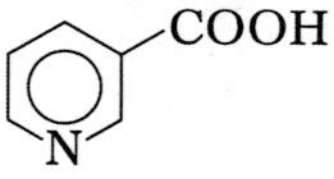
(b) 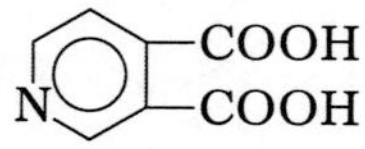
(c) 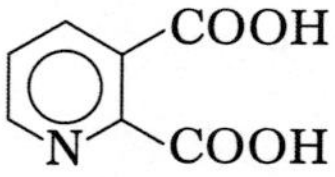
(d) 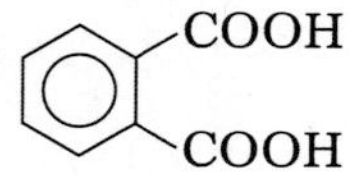

Assertion & Reason

Codes

(a) Both A and R are true and R is the correct explanation of A.
(b) Both A and R are true but R is not the correct explanation of A.
(c) A is true but R is false.
(d) A is false but R is true.

32. Assertion (A) Alkaline $KMnO_4$ cannot be used for oxidation of allyl alcohol to acrylic acid.

Assertion (R) Hydroxylation and in some cases cleavage of (C=C bond also takes place.

33. Assertion (A) Baker's yeast is a good reducing enzyme.

Reason (R) Baker's yeast is a stereoselective enzyme.

34. Assertion (A) H_2 reduces *R*COCl to *R*CHO using Pd/$BaSO_4$ catalyst.

Reason (B) *R*CHO is further reduced to RCH_2OH.

35. Assertion (A) Expoxidation followed by acid catalysed hydrolysis results in *anti*-addition of hydroxyl groups to the double bond.

Reason (R) *Trans*-2-butene is converted to *meso*-2, 3-butanediol.

36. Ethyl benzene is treated with the reagents listed, in the order shown

1. NBS, peroxides, heat
2. $CH_3CH_2O^-$
3. B_2H_6
4. H_2O_2, HO^-

The structure of the final product is

(a) $C_6H_5CH_2CH_2OH$

(b) $C_6H_5CH(Br)CH_2OH$

(c) $C_6H_5CH(OH)CH_3$

(d) $C_6H_5CH(OH)CH_2OH$

37. In the following reaction major product is

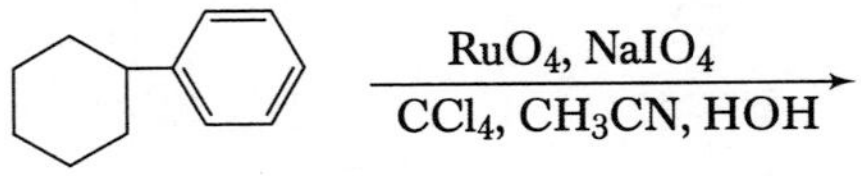

(a) 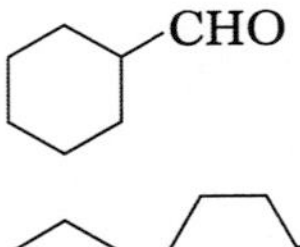

(b) 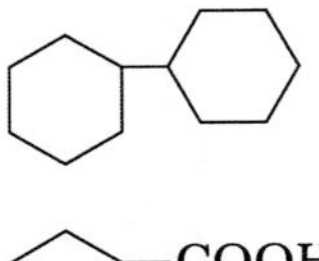

(c) 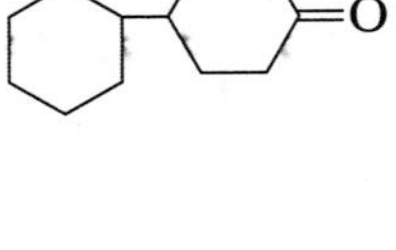

(d) 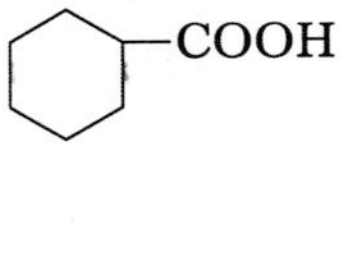

38. The end product of following reaction sequence is

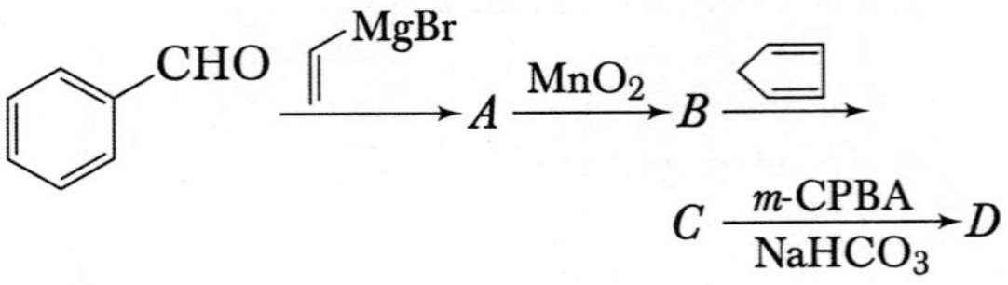

(a) 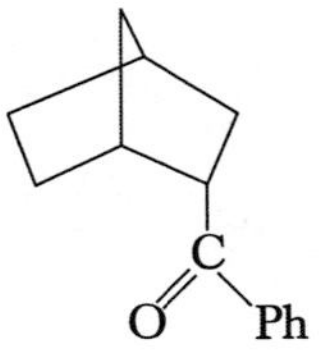

(b) 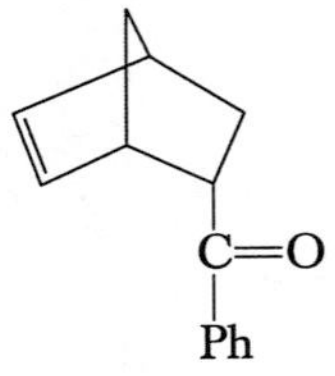

(c) 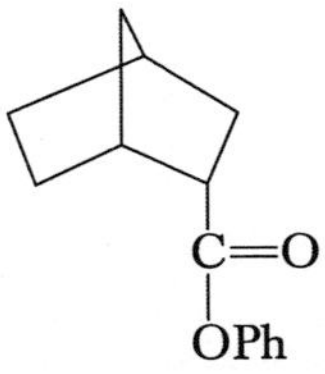

(d) 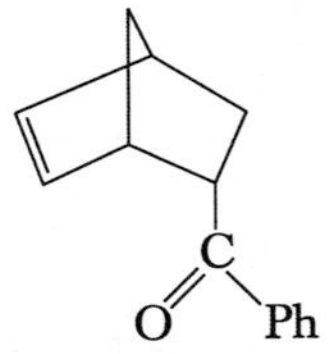

39. $(H_3C)(H_5C_2)C{=}O + BrCH_2COOC_2H_5 \xrightarrow[\text{2. } H_3O^+]{\text{1. Zn/Ether}} A;$

Product *A* is

(a) $(CH_3)(C_2H_5)C(H)—CH(OH)—COOC_2H_5$

(b) $(HOH_2C)(C_2H_5)CH—CH_2COOC_2H_5$

(c) $(CH_3)(C_2H_5)C(OH)—CH_2COOC_2H_5$

(d) $(CH_3)(C_2H_5)C(OH)—CH(OH)—COOC_2H_5$

40. The intermediate *A* and the major product *B* in the following conversion are

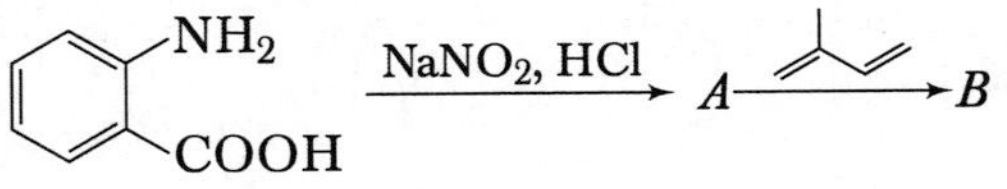

(a) *A* is a carbocation and *B* is 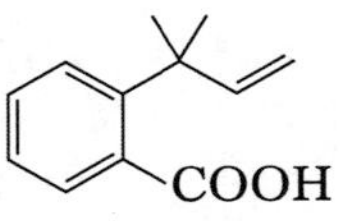

(b) *A* is a carbocation and *B* is 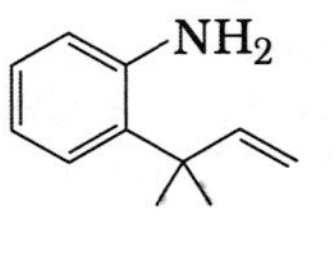

(c) A is a free radical and B is 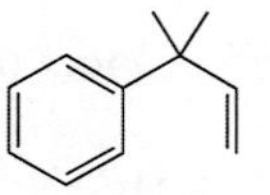

(d) A is a benzyne and B is 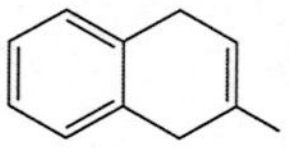

41. The major product formed in the following reaction is

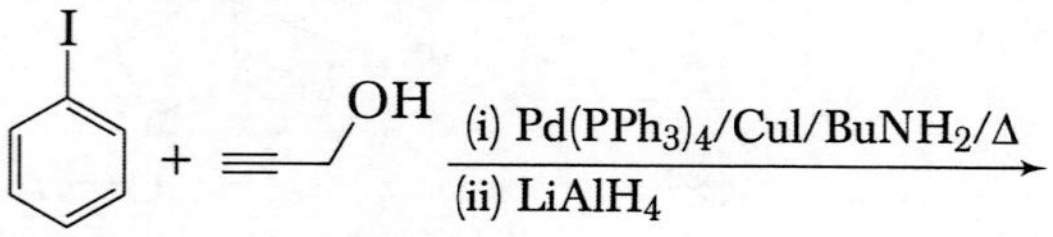

(a) 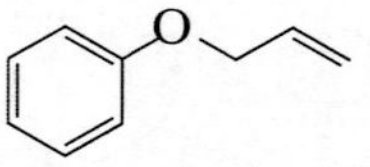 (b) 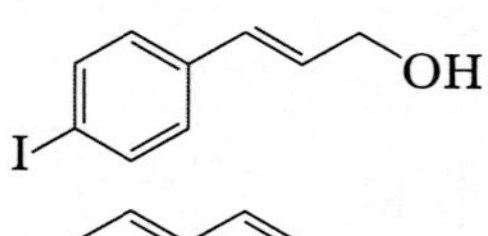

(c) 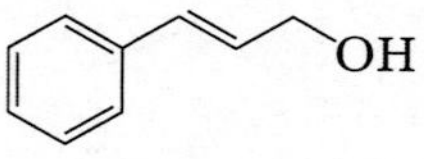 (d) 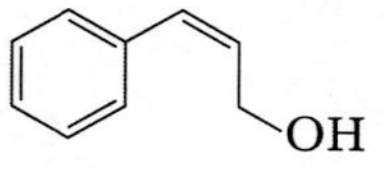

42. For the following allylic oxidation reaction, the appropriate statement, among the choices given below is

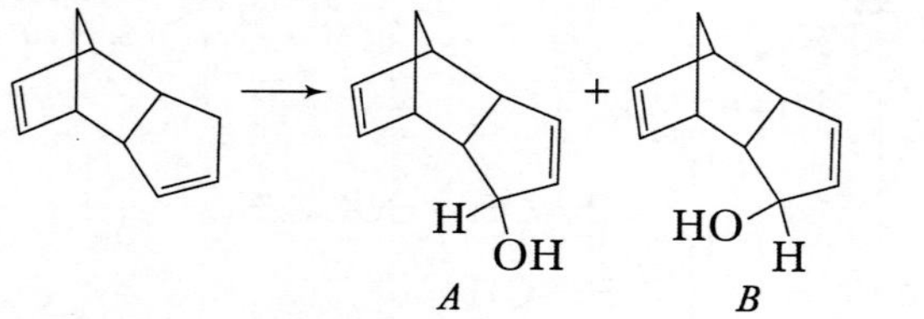

(a) suitable reagent is $KMnO_4$ and the major product is A

(b) suitable reagent is $KMnO_4$ and the major product is B

(c) suitable reagent is SeO_2 and the major product is A

(d) suitable reagent is SeO_2 and the major product is B

43. The major product formed in the following reaction is

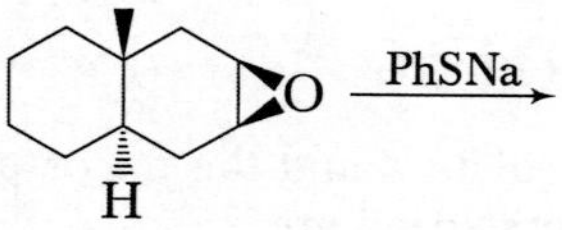

(a) 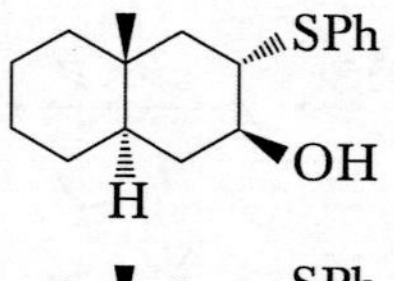 (b) 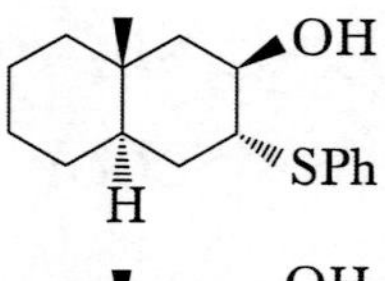

(c) 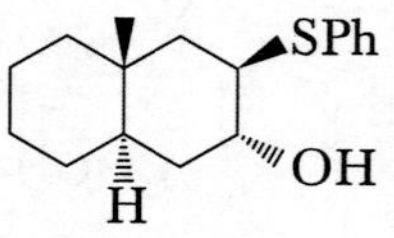 (d) 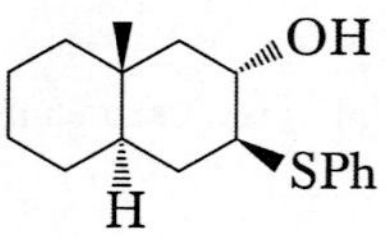

44. Papaverine on oxidation with potassium permanganate gives a ketone, which on fusion with potassium hydroxide gives

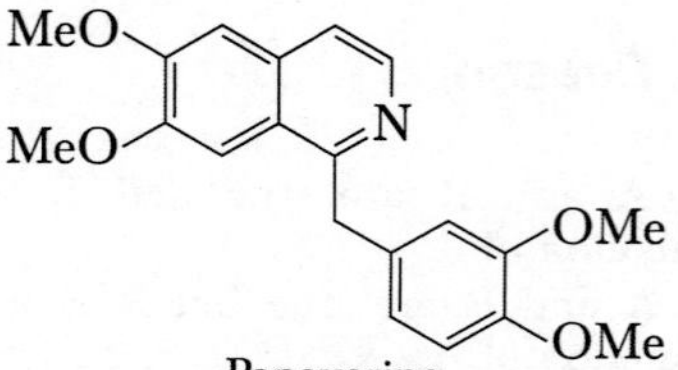

Papaverine

(a) 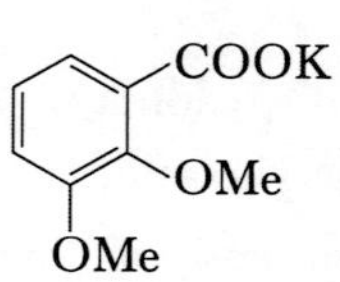 (b) 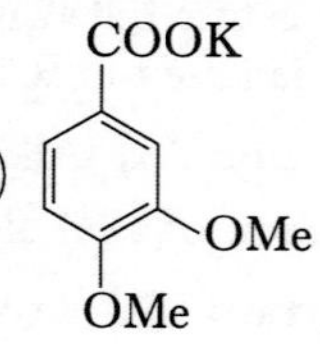

(c) 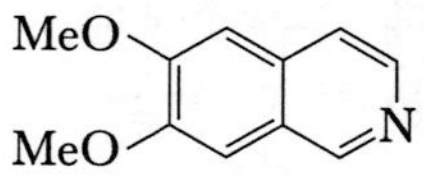 (d) 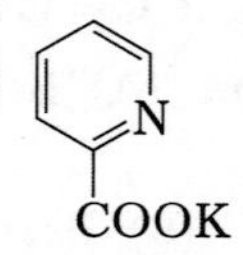

45. The major product formed on nitration (HNO_3/H_2SO_4) of uridine followed by reduction with tin and HCl is

(a) 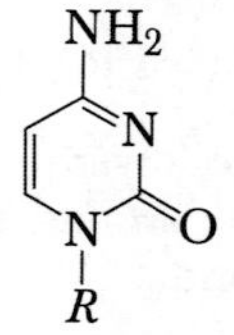 (b) 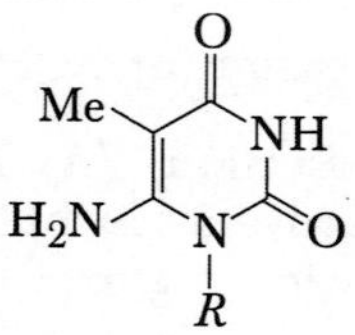

(c) 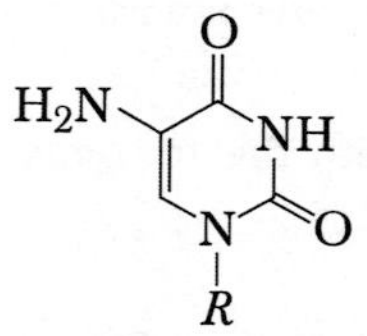 (d) 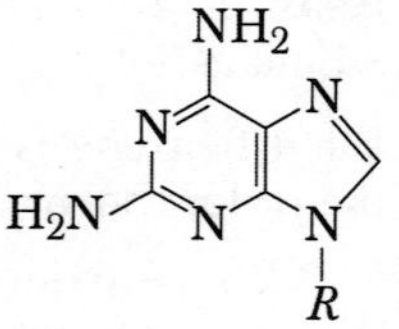

46. In the following reaction sequence, the correct structures for the major products X and Y are

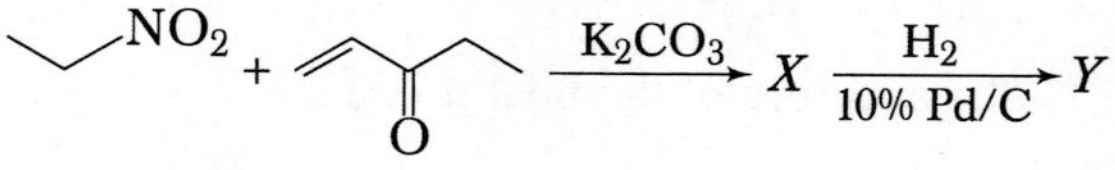

(a) $X =$ 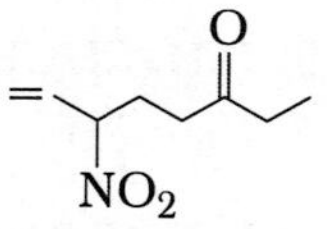 $Y =$ 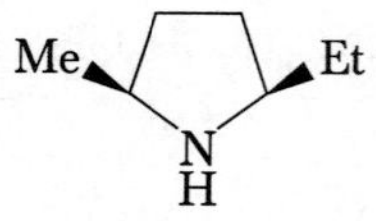

(b) $X =$ 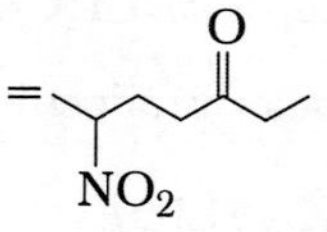 $Y =$ 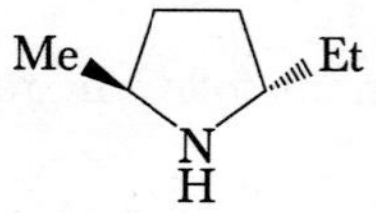

(c) $X =$ 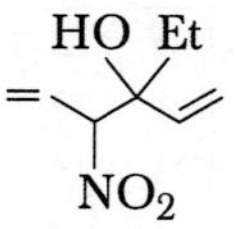 $Y =$ 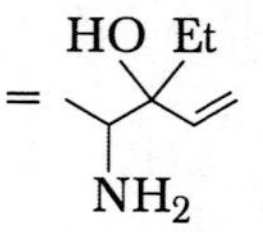

(d) $X =$ 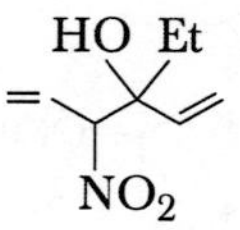 $Y =$ 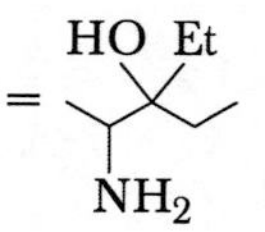

47. The major product formed in the following reaction is

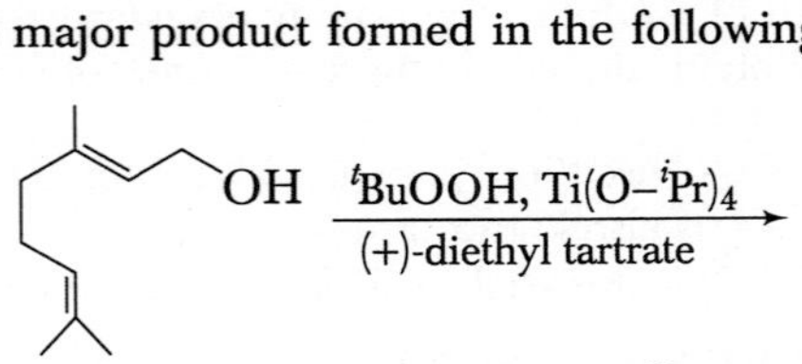

(a) 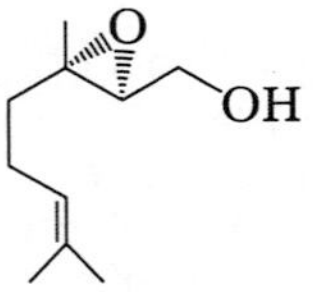

(b) 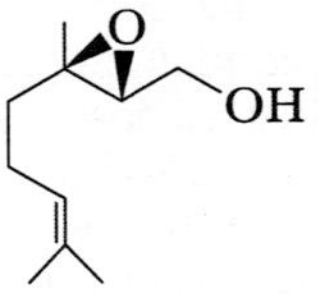

(c) 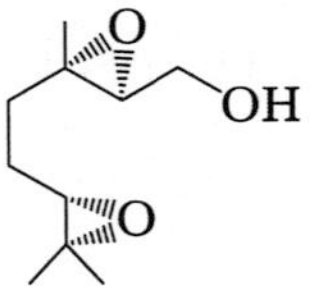

(d) 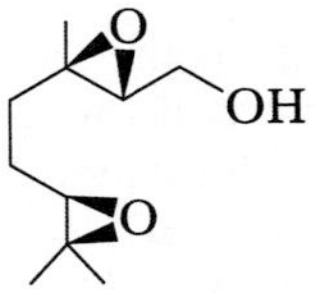

48. The major product formed in the reaction of (*S*)-1,2,4-butanetriol with 3-pentanone in the presence of a catalytic amount of *p*-TSA is

(a) 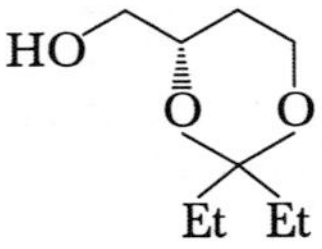

(b) 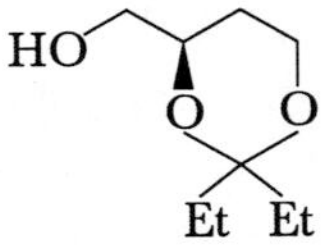

(c) 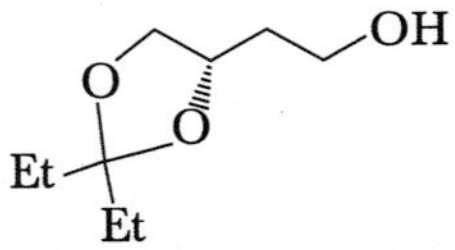

(d) 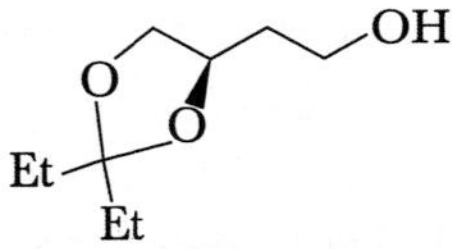

49. The major product formed in the following reaction is

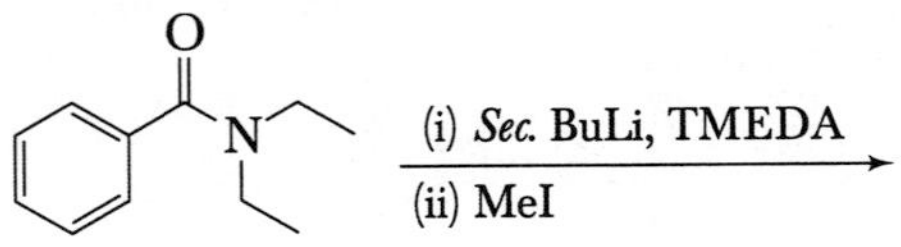

(a) 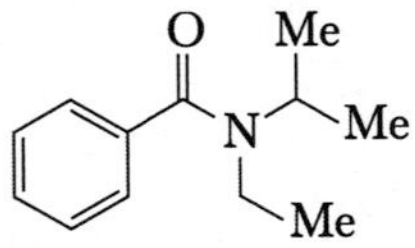

(b) 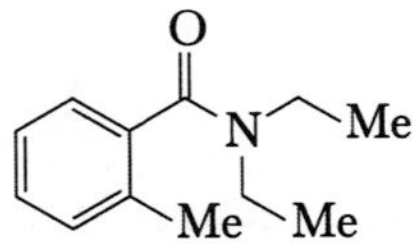

(c) 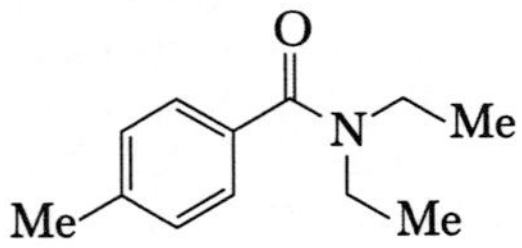

(d) 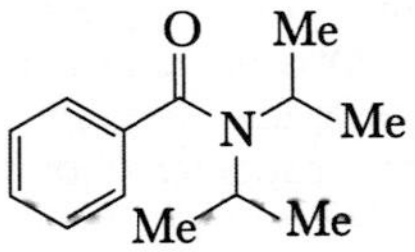

50. The major product formed in the following transformation is

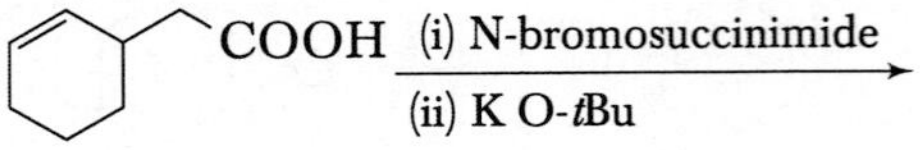

(a) 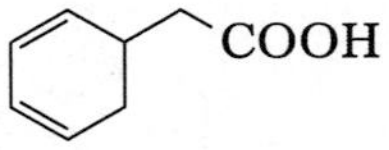

(b) 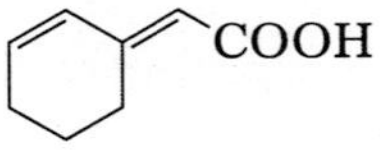

(c) 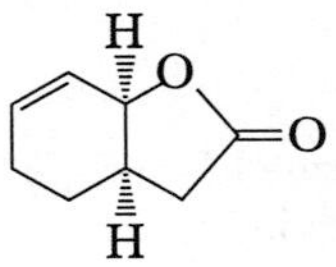

(d) 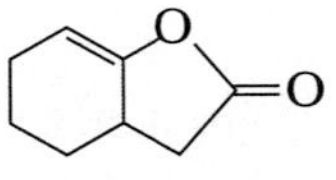

51. The major product formed in the following transformation is

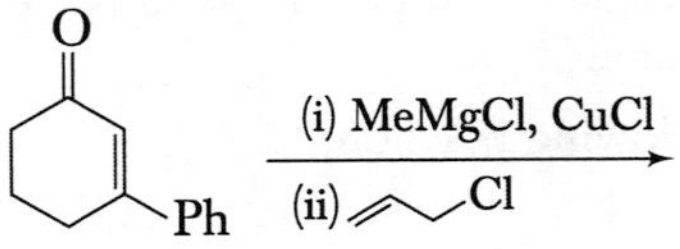

(a) 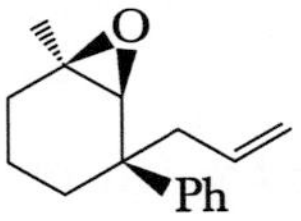

(b) 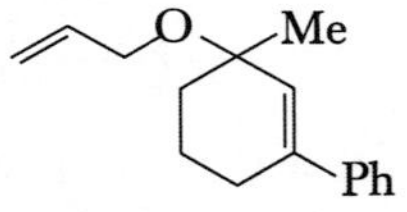

(c) 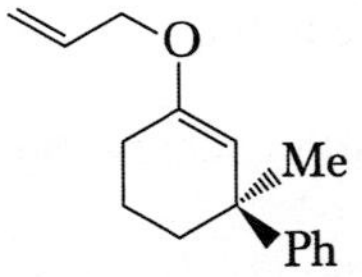

(d) 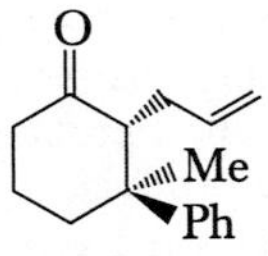

52. The structures of the major products *X* and *Y* in the following transformation are

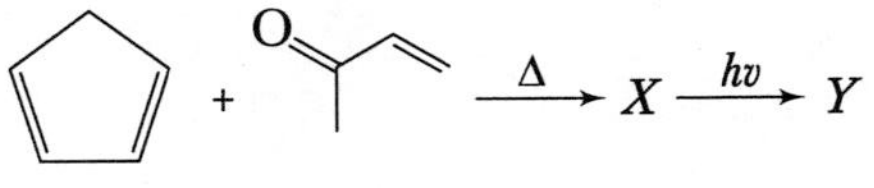

(a) $X=$ 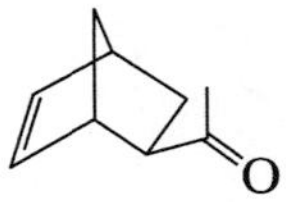 $Y=$ 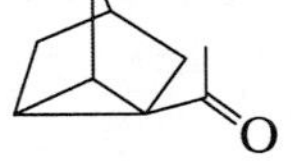

(b) $X=$ 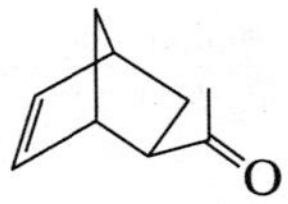 $Y=$ 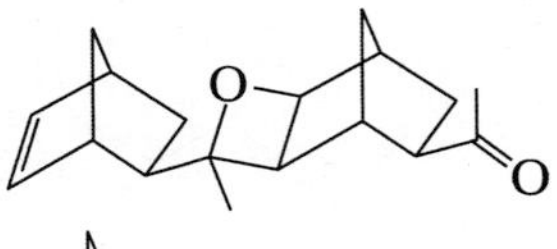

(c) $X=$ 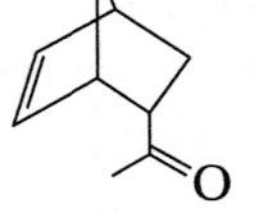 $Y=$ 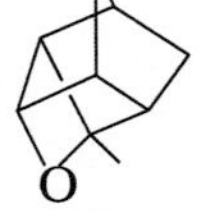

(d) $X=$ 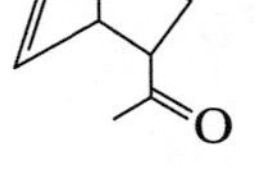 $Y=$ 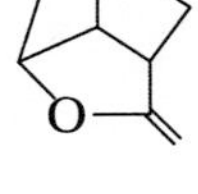

53. In the following reaction, what is/are the true statement(s)?

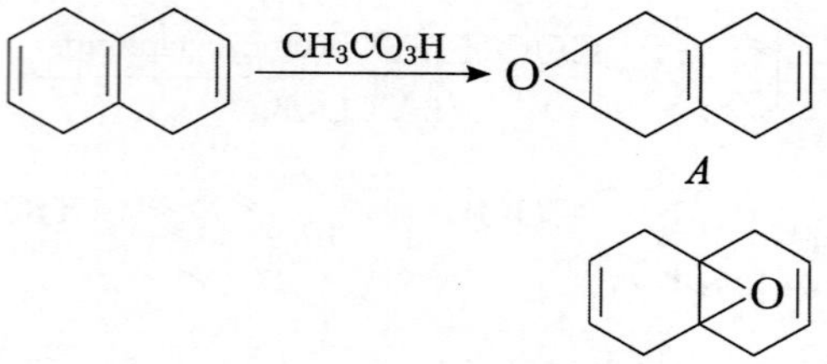

A

B

(a) Major product is *A* and formed faster
(b) Major product is *B* and formed faster
(c) Expoxidation is an electrophilic addition, oxygen is transferred to the more electron-rich, more highly substituted double bond
(d) A tetrasubstituted double bond reacts faster than a disubstituted one

54. In the following reaction,

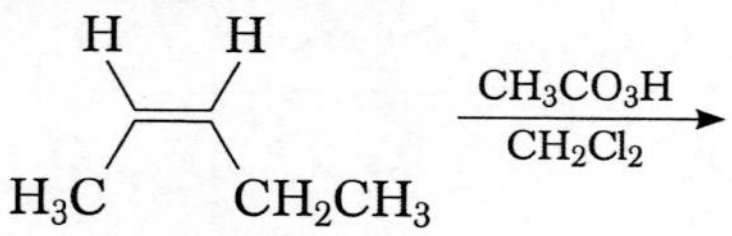

(a) two enantiomeric epoxides are formed in equal amounts
(b) there is stereospecific *syn*-addition
(c) product is *meso*-isomer
(d) *cis* alkyl groups in the starting alkene remain *cis* in the product

55. Which of the following reactions is/are correct?

(a) 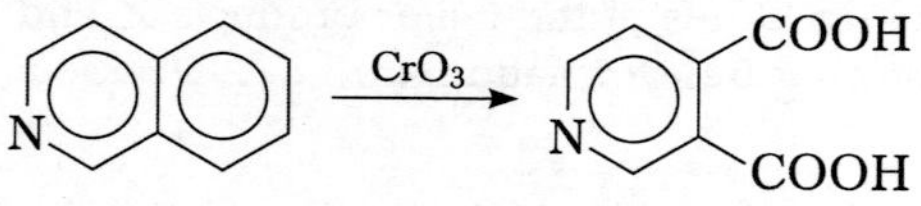

(b) 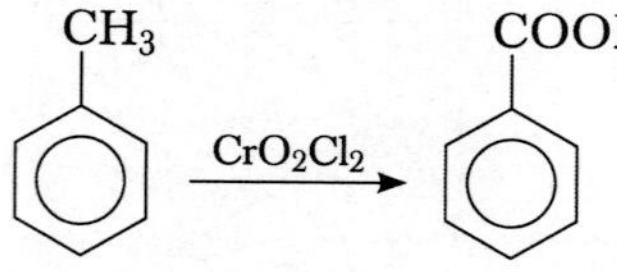

(c) 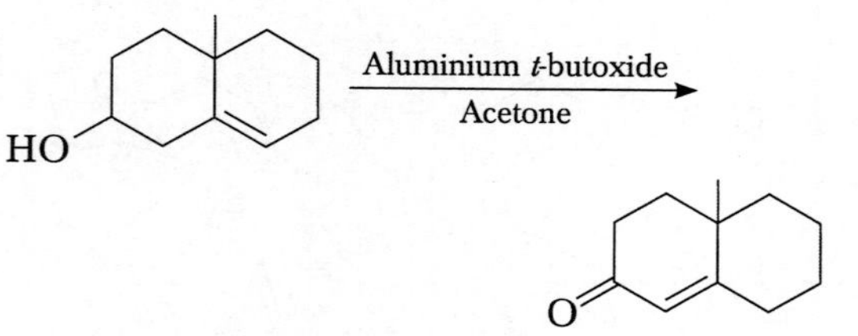

(d) 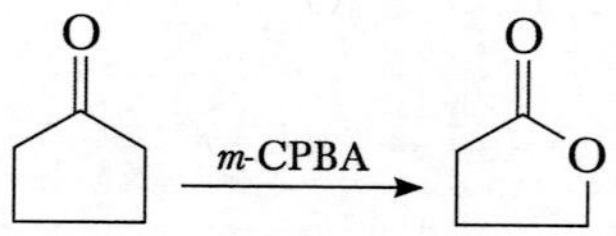

56. Which of the following statements is/are correct?
(a) Lithium dimethyl cuprate is an organometallic reagent
(b) OsO_4 is used for *syn*-hydroxylation of alkenes
(c) OsO_4 is also known as osmic acid
(d) DDQ is prepared by Thiele and Ganther method

Directions (Q. Nos. 57 to 59)
Alkynes normally react with two equivalents of hydrogen to produce alkanes. However, it is possible to react an alkyne with only one equivalent of hydrogen and stop the reaction at the alkene stage. Choice of the catalyst enables to synthesize alkene of desired configuration.

57. Some of the catalysts given below can be used to convert alkyne to alkene.
I. P-2 catalyst (Ni_2B)
II. Pd/$CaCO_3$/quinoline
III. Li/NH_3 (liquid)
IV. $LiAlH_4$
Choice can be
(a) I, II
(b) I, II, IV
(c) I, II, III
(d) I, II, III, IV

58. Li/NH_3 (liquid) reduces 2-butyne to *trans*-2-butene and solution turns blue. This blue colour is due to
(a) solvated Li^+ as $[Li(NH_3)]^+$
(b) solvated electrons as $[e\,(NH_3)]^-$
(c) vinyl anion
(d) completion of reaction

59. The *anti*-stereochemistry of sodium-ammonia reduction appears a a result of
(a) greater stability of vinyl radical in the *trans*-configuration

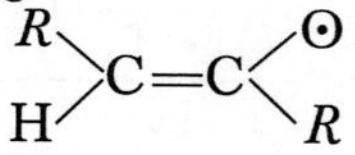

(b) greater stability of vinyl radical in the *cis*-configuration

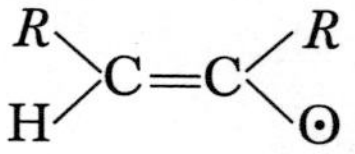

(c) greater stability of *cis*-alkene
(d) greater stability of *trans*-alkene

Directions (Q. Nos. 60 to 62)
Chromium in the +6 oxidation state, Cr(VI), is a very important and effective oxidant in the organic laboratory. The major drawback to the use of reagents based on this species is that the product, Cr(III), is toxic. Chromium is just one example of a toxic heavy metal that requires quite expensive disposal procedures.

The development of environmentally safe reagents that can be used to replace more toxic materials in organic reactions in an area that deserves and is receiving considerable research attention, especially in industrial laboratories.

60. Cr(VI) is reduced to Cr(III) and oxidise
(a) a secondary alcohol to a ketone
(b) a primary alcohol to an aldehyde
(c) a tertiary alcohol to an alkene
(d) SO_3 to SO_4^{2-}

61. Cyclohexanol is oxidised to cyclohexanone by $Cr_2O_7^{2-}/H^+$ and Cr^{3+} being toxic heavy metals, its use is causing environmental problem. Recently a new oxidant has been suggested that is environment friendly and can affect the following oxidation.

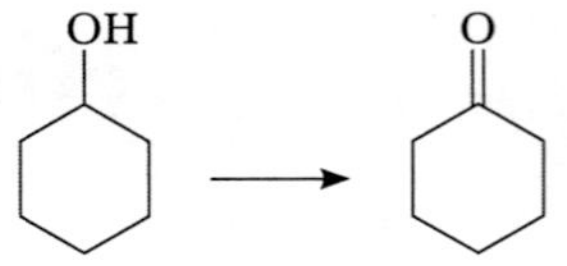

This is
(a) $KMnO_4/H^+$
(b) Ag_2O
(c) $NaOCl/CH_3COOH$
(d) PCC

62. Cr(VI) oxidant used in organic chemistry is in the form of
(a) CrO_2Cl_2
(b) CrO_3/H_2SO_4
(c) PCC
(d) $Cr_2O_7^{2-}/H^+$

Answers

Exercise 1

1. (b)	2. (c)	3. (c)	4. (c)	5. (a)	6. (b)	7. (c)	8. (a)	9. (b)	10. (a)
11. (b)	12. (c)	13. (d)	14. (d)	15. (a)	16. (a)	17. (b)	18. (c)	19. (d)	20. (d)
21. (d)	22. (c)	23. (b)	24. (b)	25. (b)	26. (d)	27. (b)	28. (c)	29. (d)	30. (d)
31. (c)	32. (c)	33. (c)	34. (b)	35. (a)	36. (c)	37. (b)	38. (c)	39. (b)	40. (a)
41. (d)	42. (c)	43. (b)	44. (c)	45. (a)	46. (a)	47. (a)	48. (b)	49. (d)	50. (a)
51. (c)	52. (b)	53. (b)	54. (a)	55. (a)	56. (b)	57. (b)	58. (b)	59. (a)	60. (d)

Exercise 2

1. (b)	2. (c)	3. (a)	4. (c)	5. (c)	6. (b)	7. (d)	8. (c)	9. (b)	10. (a,b)
11. (b)	12. (c)	13. (d)	14. (a)	15. (a)	16. (a)	17. (b)	18. (d)	19. (a)	20. (a)
21. (a)	22. (c)	23. (b)	24. (a)	25. (a)	26. (d)	27. (b)	28. (d)	29. (c)	30. (c)
31. (a)	32. (a)	33. (b)	34. (c)	35. (b)	36. (a)	37. (d)	38. (b)	39. (c)	40. (d)
41. (c)	42. (c)	43. (b)	44. (b)	45. (c)	46. (b)	47. (a)	48. (c)	49. (b)	50. (c)
51. (d)	52. (c)	53. (b,c)	54. (a,b,c,d)	55. (a,c)	56. (a,b,c,d)	57. (d)	58. (b)	59. (a)	60. (a)
61. (c)	62. (b,c,d)								

Hints & Solutions

Exercise 1

1. 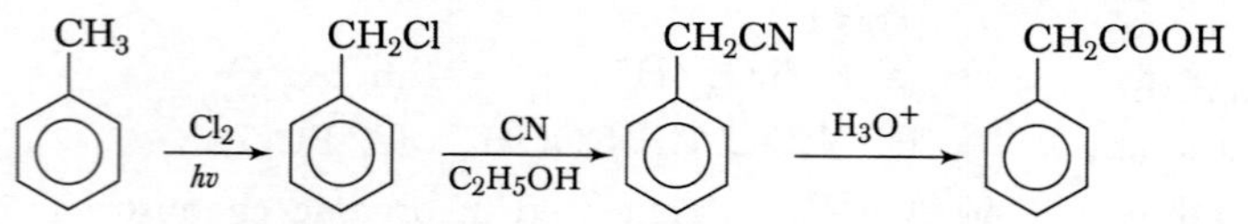

6. 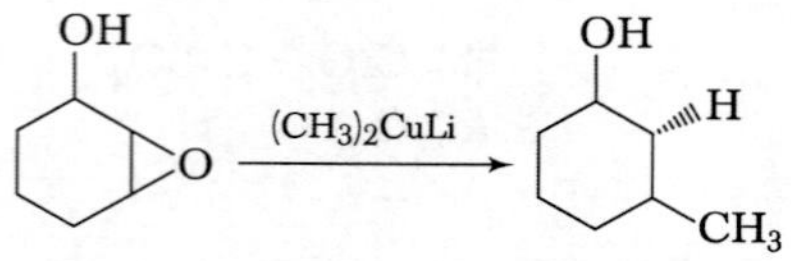

9. 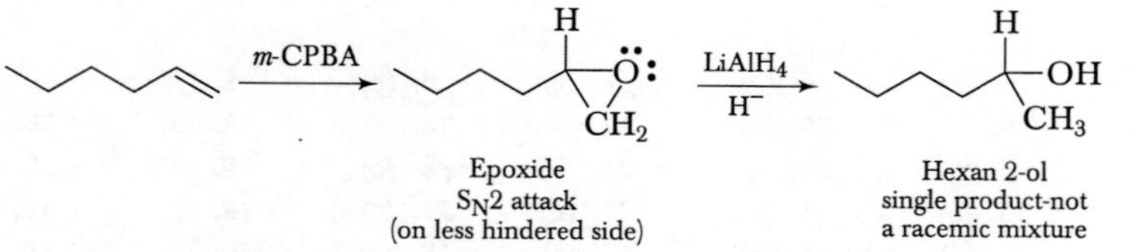

10. 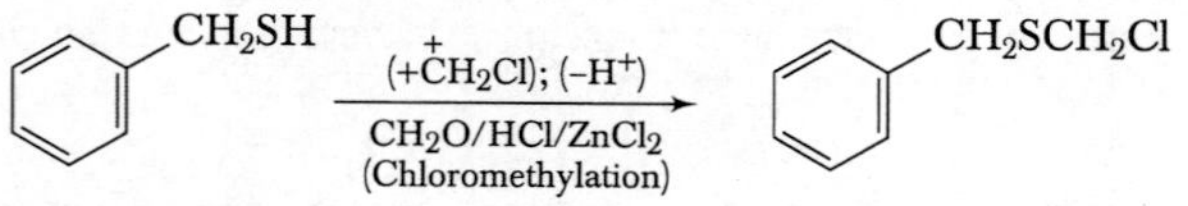

12. 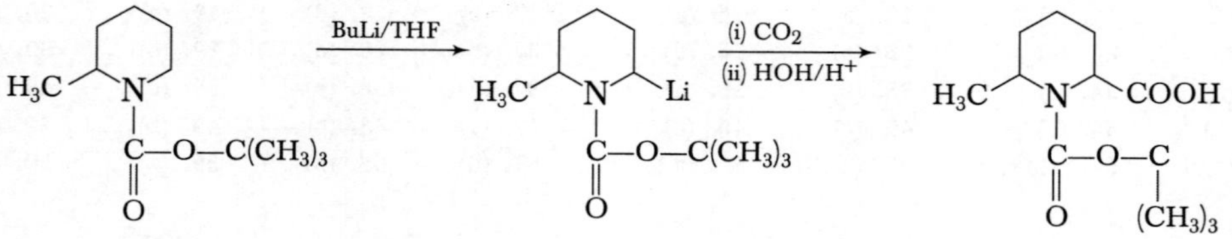

18. 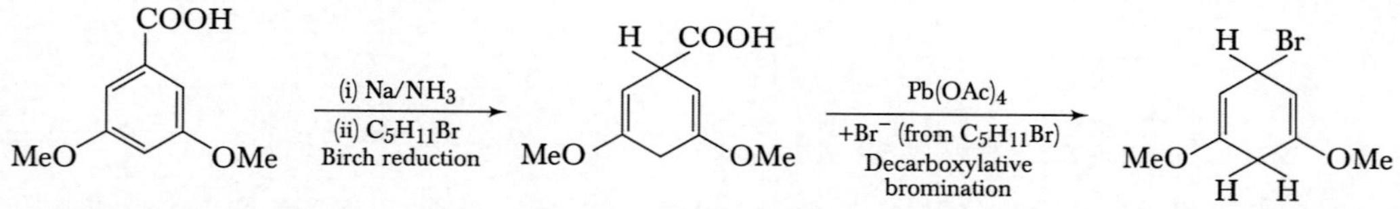

22. Hydroboration is regioselective and it will be *syn*-addition across carbon-carbon double bond. The addition of H—B to alkene follows Markownikoff's addition rule. Since, boron is more electropositive than hydrogen hence, attachment of boron takes place readily to the less substituted carbon of double bond.

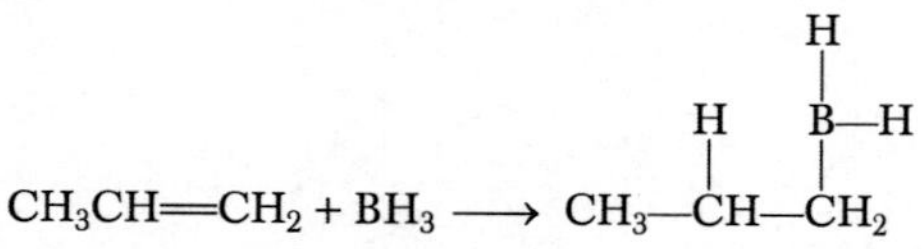

23. 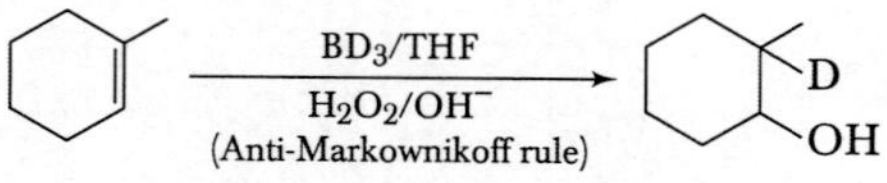

26. 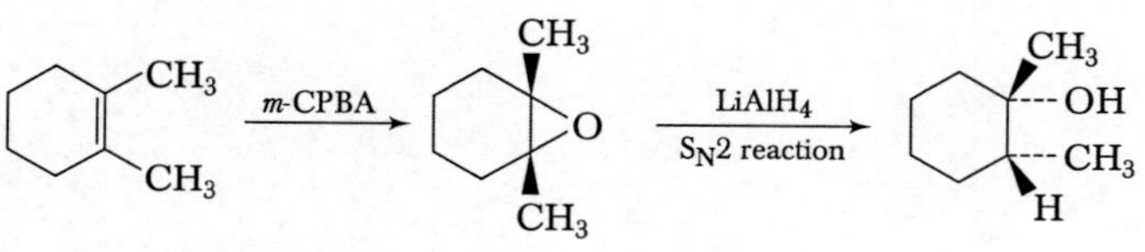

28. 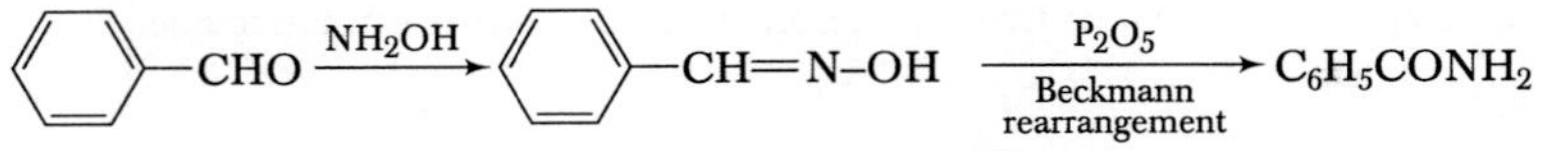

29. 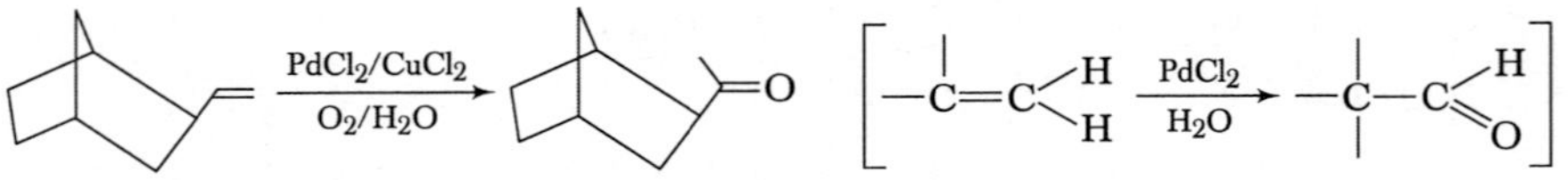

33. Tetralin on oxidation by O_2 in presence of Cu^{2+} salt as catalyst forms 1-tetralone.

34. 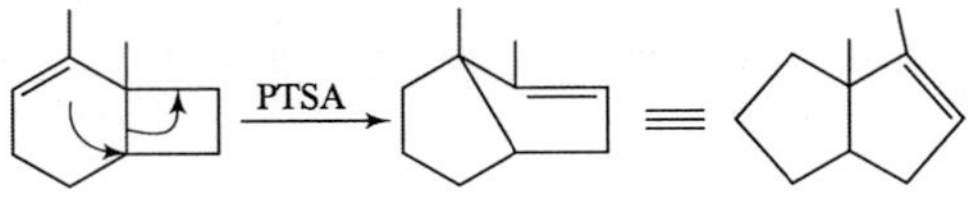

36. 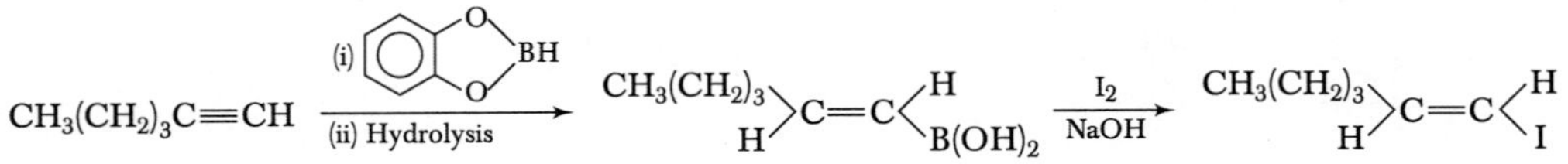

37. 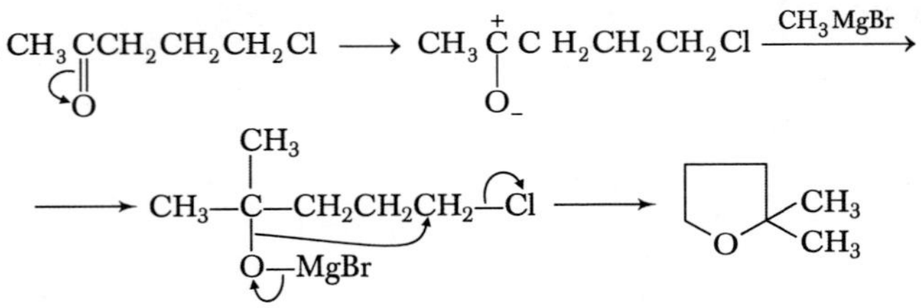

38. 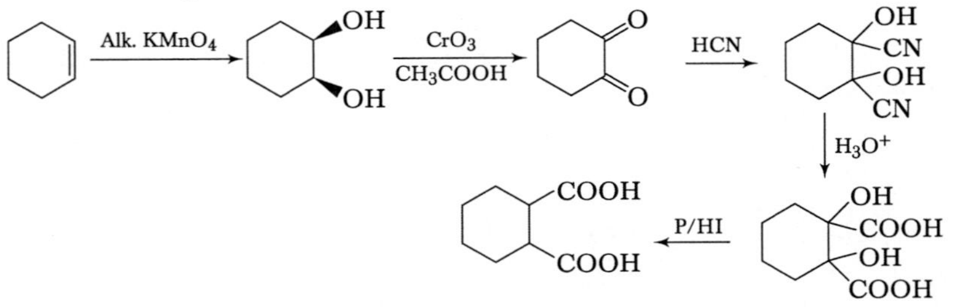

(P/HI reduces OH only).

43. 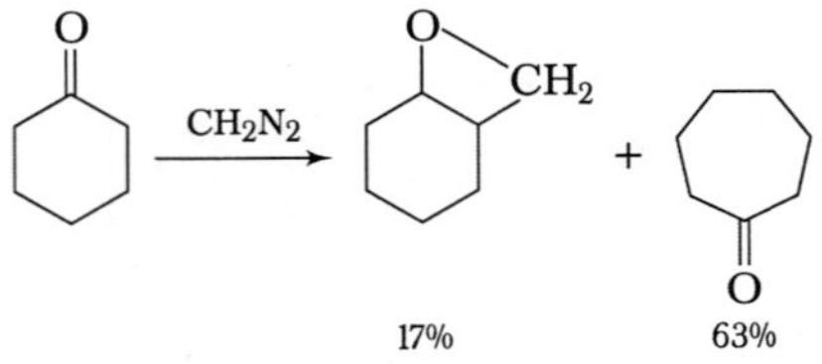

44. 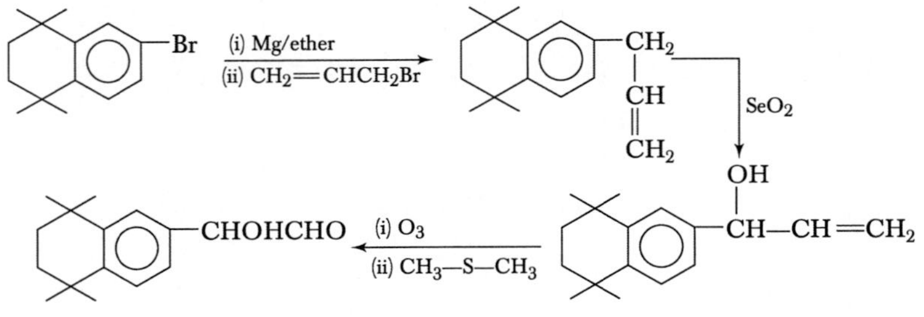

48. Ruthenium tetraoxide sodium periodate is the only reagent that converts hydroxy lectone into acid sensitive keto lactone.

51.

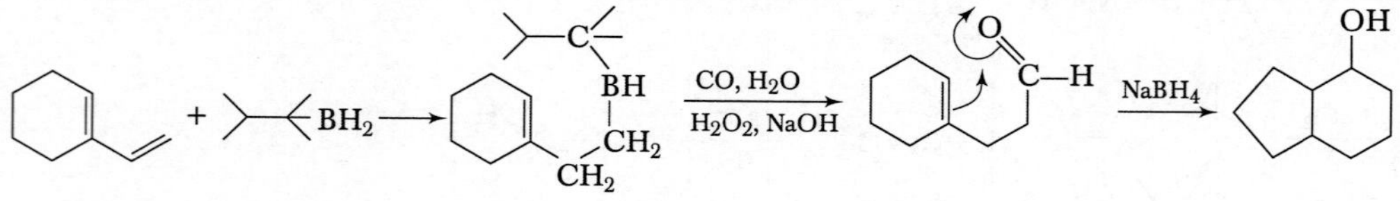

55.

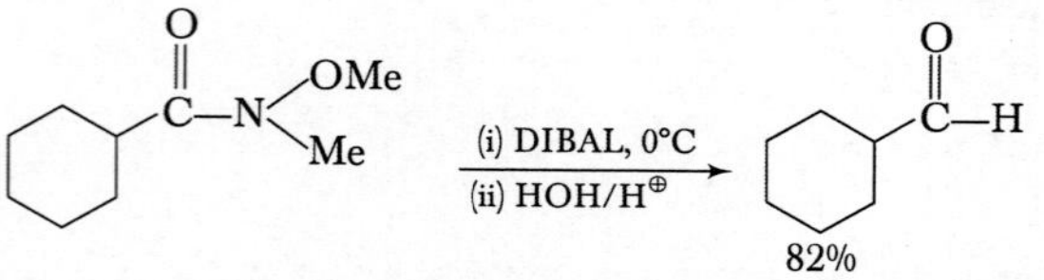

58. Epoxidation of α, β-unsaturated aldehydes and ketones is best performed by the action of nucleophilic reagents such as H_2O_2 or *t*-butyl hydroperoxide in alkaline solution.

59.

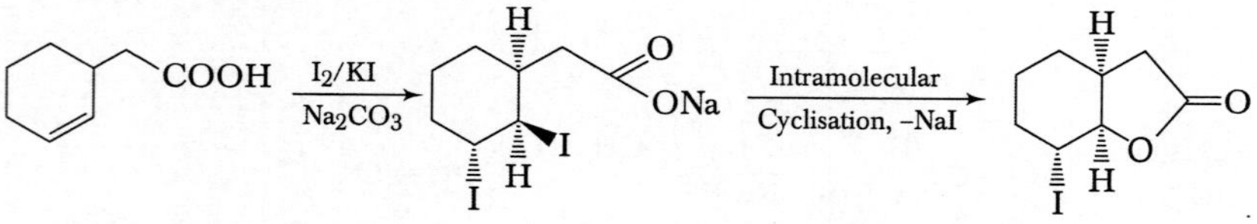

Exercise 2

3.

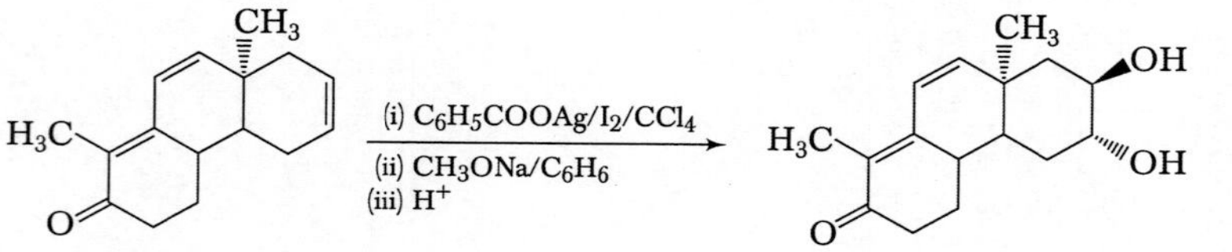

5.

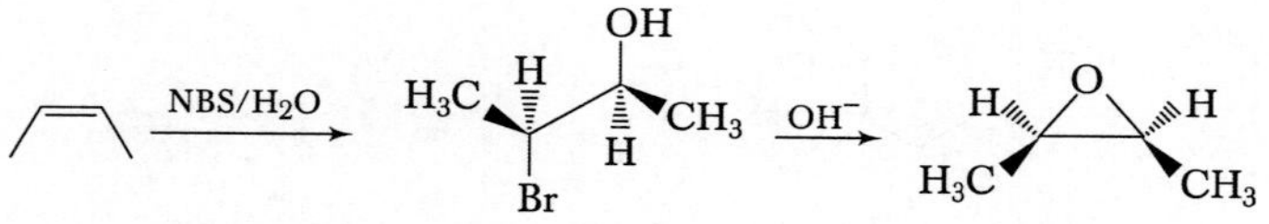

10.

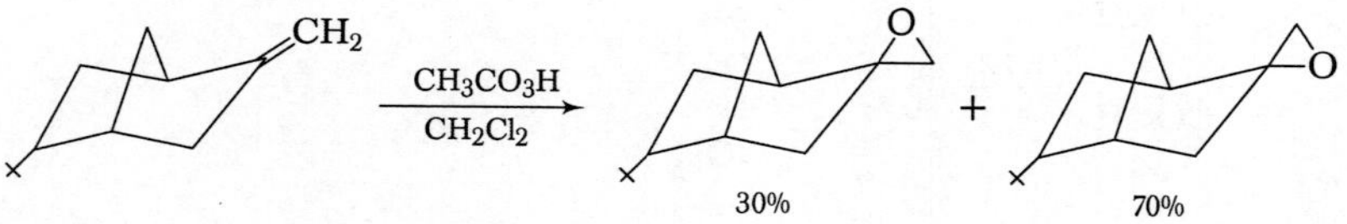

11.

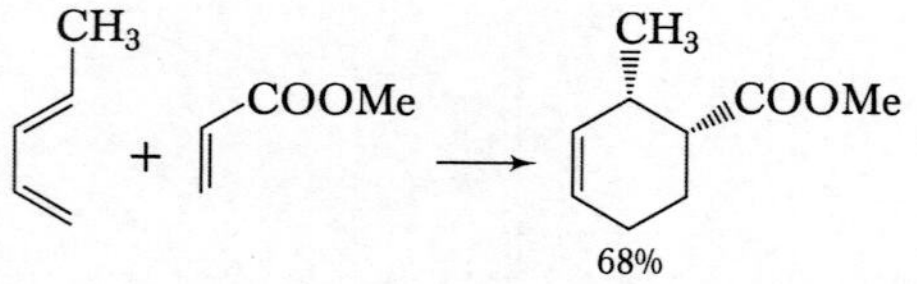

16. SeO_2 in acidic or alkaline medium dehydrogenates ketones introducing α, β-unsaturation.

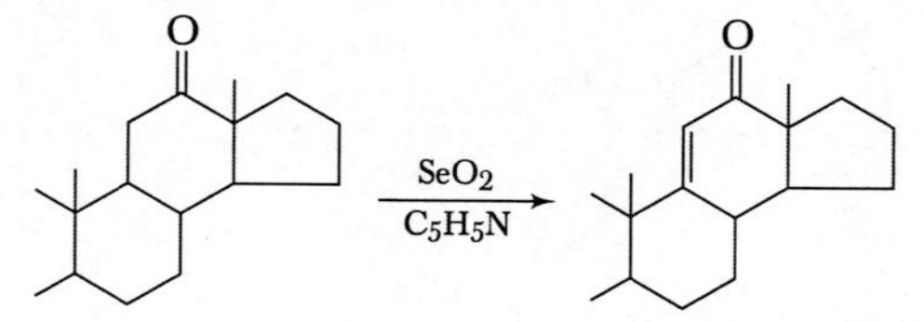

α, β-unsaturated ketone

17. 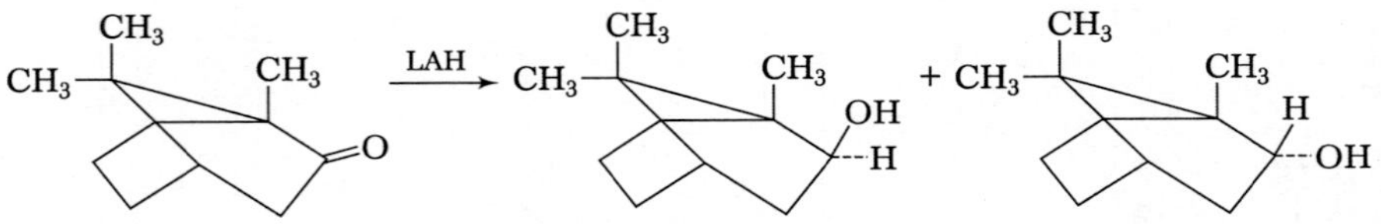

Iso-borneol 90% Borneol 10%

In the reduction of camphor, due to steric hindrance to the approach of the reagent to the hindered exo side of carbonyl group, the product is predominantly *iso*-borneol.

23. 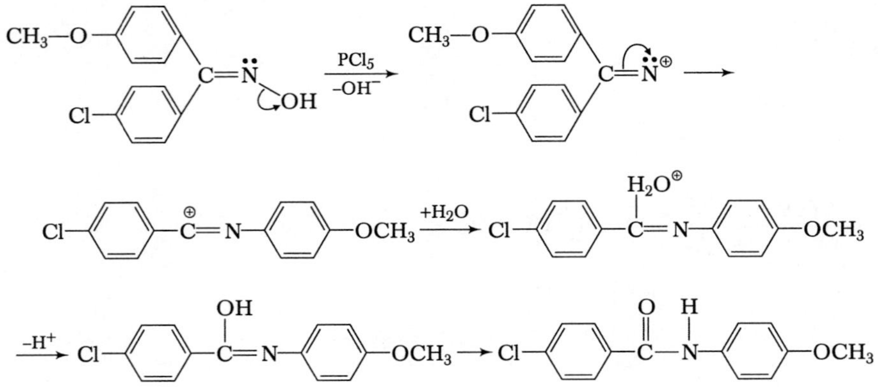

24. 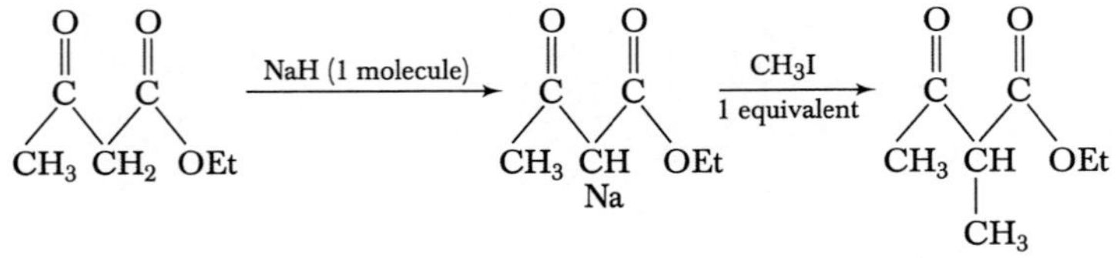

25. 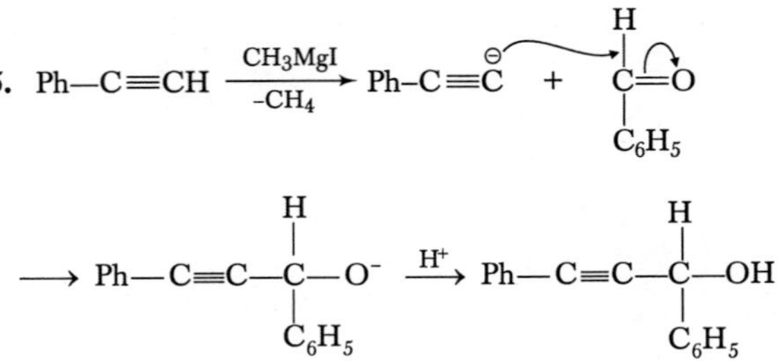

31. 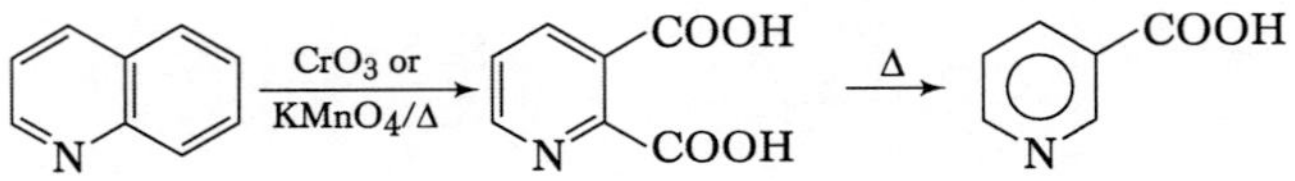

36. 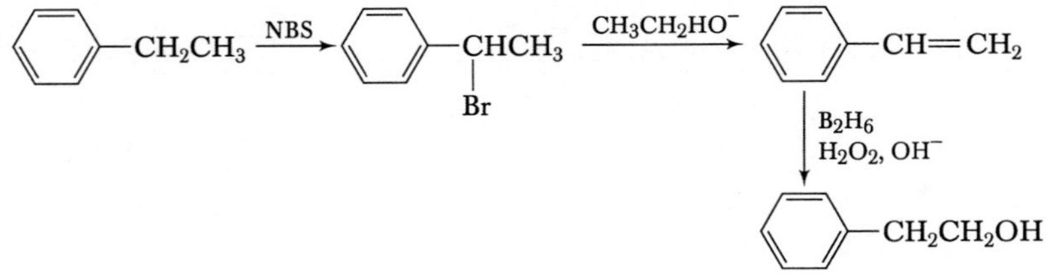

37. 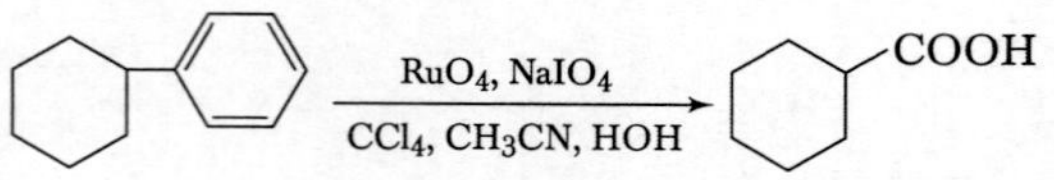
RuO4, NaIO4
CCl4, CH3CN, HOH
COOH

38. 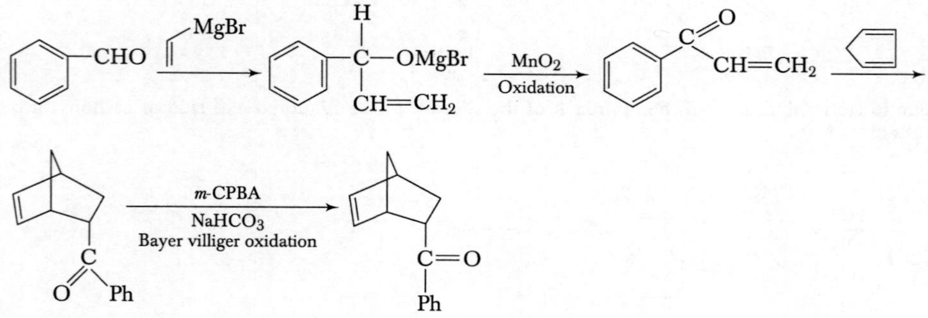
CHO
MgBr
H
C—OMgBr
CH=CH2
MnO2
Oxidation
C=O
CH=CH2
m-CPBA
NaHCO3
Bayer villiger oxidation
C
O
Ph
C=O
Ph

37. 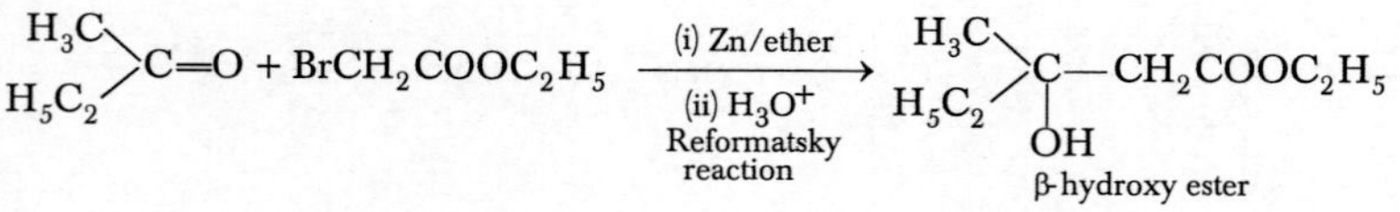
H3C
H5C2
C=O + BrCH2COOC2H5
(i) Zn/ether
(ii) H3O+
Reformatsky
reaction
C—CH2COOC2H5
OH
β-hydroxy ester

34 Concept in Organic Synthesis and Asymmetric Synthesis

Concept in Organic Synthesis

Disconnection Approach or Retrosynthesis

A logical approach for designing organic synthesis which involves breaking down of the target molecule into available starting materials by imaginary breaking of bonds and by functional group interconversions (FGI) is known as disconnection approach or retrosynthesis or synthesis backwards.

A double line arrow (⇒) called a retrosynthetic arrow is used to indicate a reaction written backwards.

$$Z \xRightarrow{\text{Retrosynthetic arrow}} X + Y$$

This reaction with a retrosynthetic arrow shows that Z could be prepared from X and Y. Similarly, the following ester can be prepared by benzyl alcohol and benzoyl chloride.

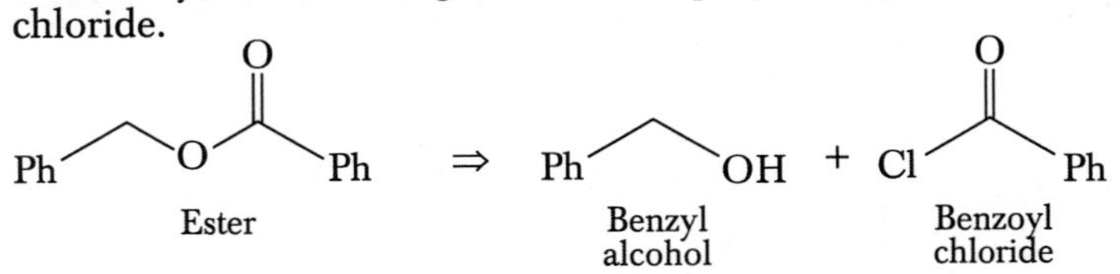

The site of disconnection is indicated by a wiggly line.

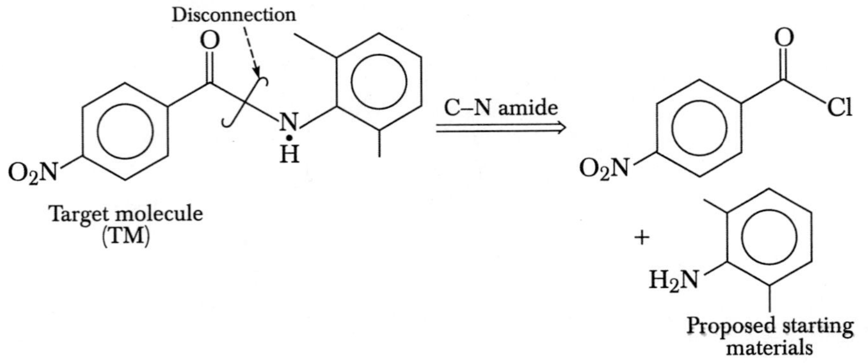

Syllabus

- Retrosynthesis, Disconnection, Synthons, Linear and Convergent Synthesis, Umpolung of Reactivity and Protecting Groups
- Asymmetric Synthesis Chiral Auxiliaries, Methods of Asymmetric Induction-Substrate, Reagent and Catalyst Controlled Reactions; Determination of Enantiomeric and Diastereomeric Excess; Enantio-Discrimination
- Resolution-Optical and Kinetic

Synthons

Synthons are idealised fragments (reagents) usually cations or anions resulting from a disconnection.

e.g., paracetamol is an amide and it can be disconnected either to amine + acyl chloride or amine + anhydride.

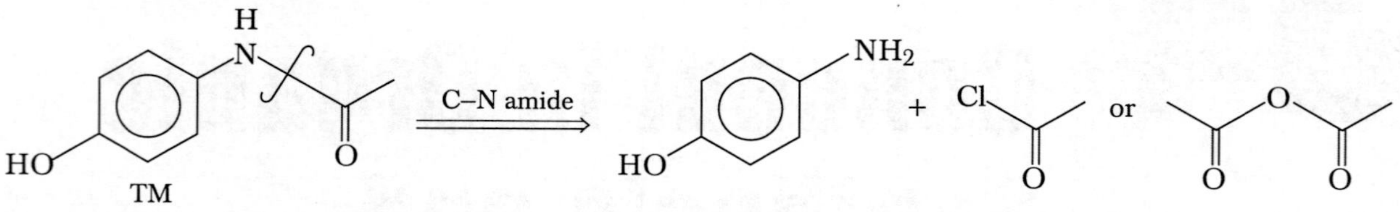

Which reagent is best can only be determined by experiment. Commercially, paracetamol is made by *p*-aminophenol and acetic anhydride largely because by product CH_3COOH is easier to handle than HCl. In a retrosynthesis one should not bother for this sort of decision, which is best made later. Hence, it is useful to have a single way of representing key characteristics of alternative reagents. For example, we can depict both acyl chloride and anhydride in the above scheme as a single idealised reagent (fragment), *viz.* the cation of electrophilic acetyl group ($CH_3\overset{+}{C}{=}O$). Such idealised reagent or fragments are known as synthons. Synthons stand for reagents which are used in the forward synthesis. They are not themselves reagents. However, they may occasionally be intermediates in the reaction pathway. Synthons need to be replaced by reagents (synthetic equivalents) in a suggested synthesis.

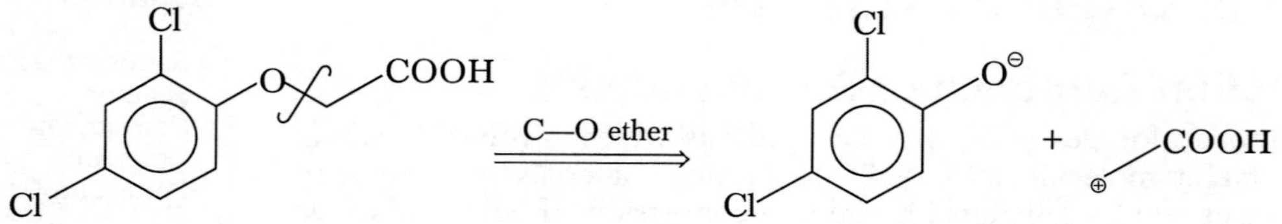

Target molecule (TM) : 2,4-D
(2,4-dichlorophenoxy acetic acid)

Synthons

Some synthons and their synthetic equivalents (reagents) are given in Table 34.1.

Table 34.1

Synthons	**Synthetic equivalent** (Reagent)
$R^{\oplus}$	*R*Br, *R*I, *R*OMs, *R*OTs
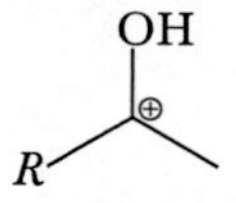	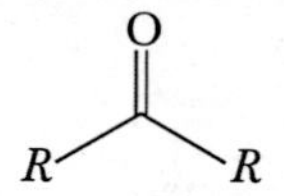
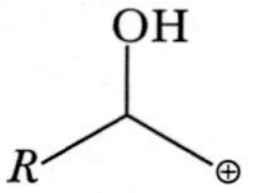	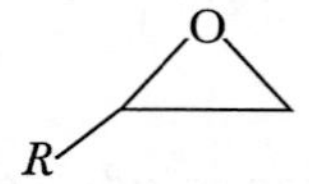
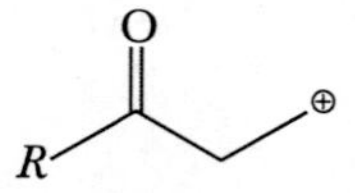	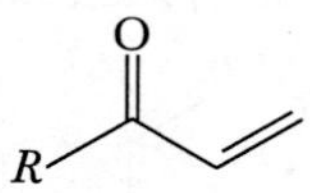
$R^{\ominus}$	*R*MgBr, *R*Li
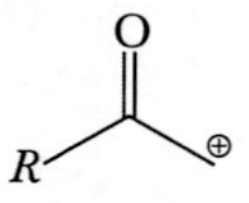	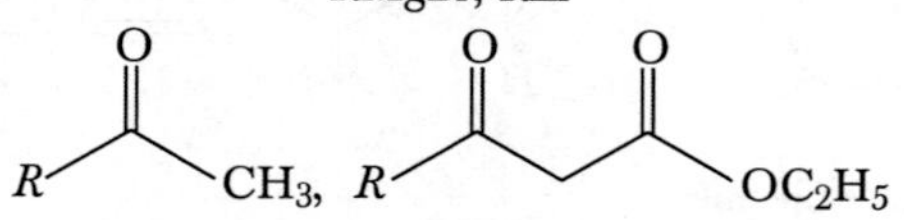
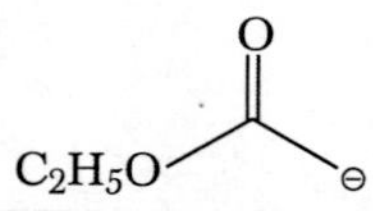	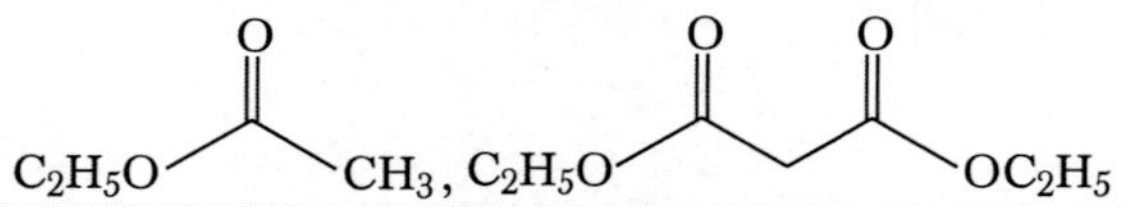

Linear and Convergent Synthesis

In chemistry a **convergent synthesis** is a strategy that aims to improve the efficiency of multi step chemical synthesis, most often in organic synthesis. In **linear synthesis** the overall yield quickly drops with each reaction step :

$$A \longrightarrow B \longrightarrow C \longrightarrow D$$

Suppose the yield is 50% for each reaction, the overall yield of *D* is only 12.5% from *A*.

In a convergent synthesis

$$A \longrightarrow B\ (50\%)$$
$$C \longrightarrow D\ (50\%)$$
$$B + D \longrightarrow E\ (25\%)$$

the overall yield of *E* (25%) looks much better. Convergent synthesis is applied in the synthesis of complex molecules and involve **fragment coupling** and **independent synthesis.**

Examples

- Convergent synthesis is encountered in dendrimer synthesis where branches (with the number of generations preset) are connected to the central core.
- Proteins of up to 300 amino acids are produced by a convergent approach using chemial ligation.

An example of its use in total synthesis is the final step (photochemical [2+2] cycloaddition) towards the compound *Biyouyanagin A.*

For Eq. (i)

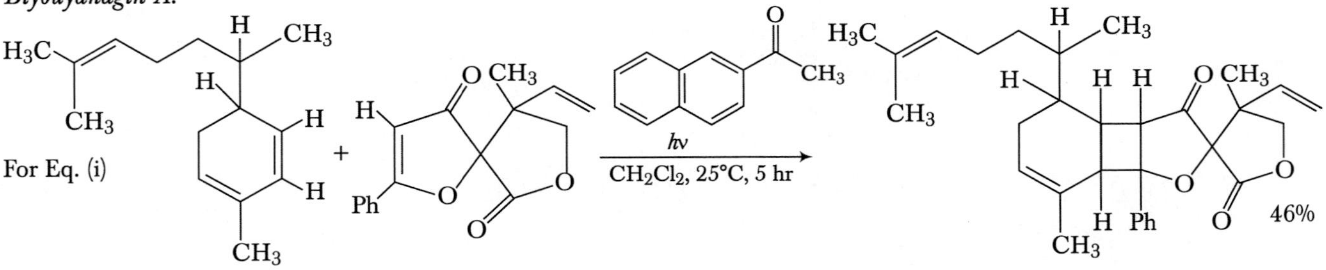

Umpolung

The situation in which a synthon of polarity opposite to that normally associated with the required functional group must be used is called reversal of polarity or umpolung. (Umpolung, a German word meaning reverse polarity). Thus, the term umpolung refers to the reversal of the normal polarity of a functional group (*i.e.,* electrophilic into nucleophilic and nucleophilic into electrophilic transformation).

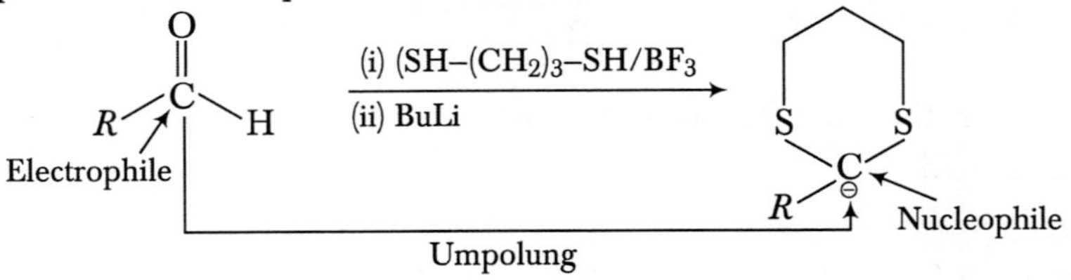

The retrosynthetic analysis of (1) may lead to synthons (2) and (3). Synthon (2) corresponds to the enolate of acetone whereas the charge in (3) does not correspond to the polarity normally associated with α-carbon of a carbonyl groups or its derivatives. Hence, synthon (3) is an umpolung synthon.

Reterosynthetic analysis

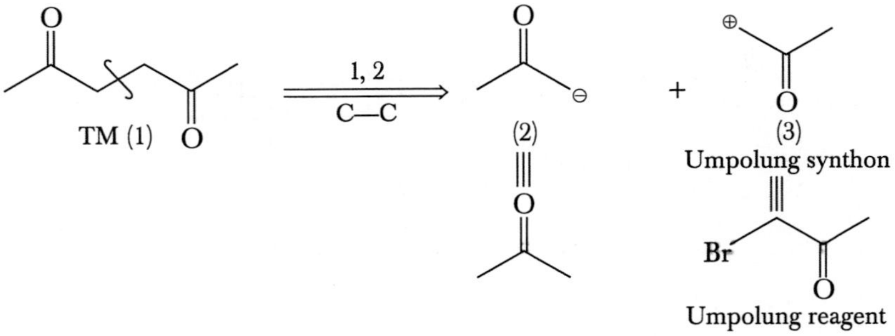

Synthesis

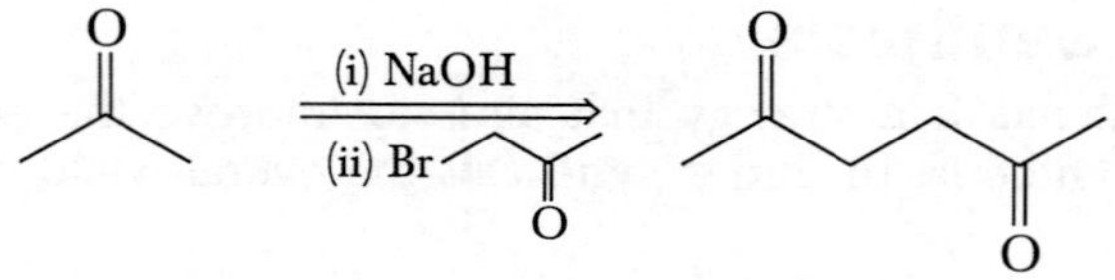

Protecting Groups

When there are two functional groups of unequal reactivity within a molecule, the more reactive group can be made to react alone, but it may not be possible to react the less reactive functional group selectively. "A group whose use makes possible to react a less reactive functional group selectively in the presence of a more reactive group is known as a protecting group." A protecting group blocks the reactivity of a functional group by converting it into a different group which is inert to the conditions of some reactions that is to be carried out as part of a synthetic route.

e.g., A tertiary alcohol (*A*) can be prepared from a keto ester (acetoacetic ester), when phenylmagnesium bromide reacts with the less reactive ester group rather than with the more reactive keto group. Hence, one way of preparing the desired alcohol, is to protect the ketone as a ketal *i.e.,* a ketal protecting group (dioxolane)is used in this case.

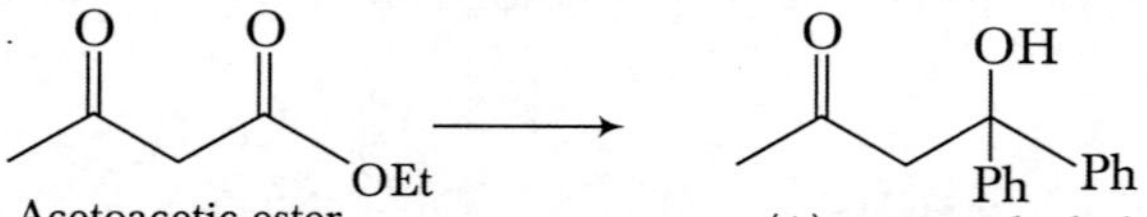

Acetoacetic ester

(A) tertiary alcohol

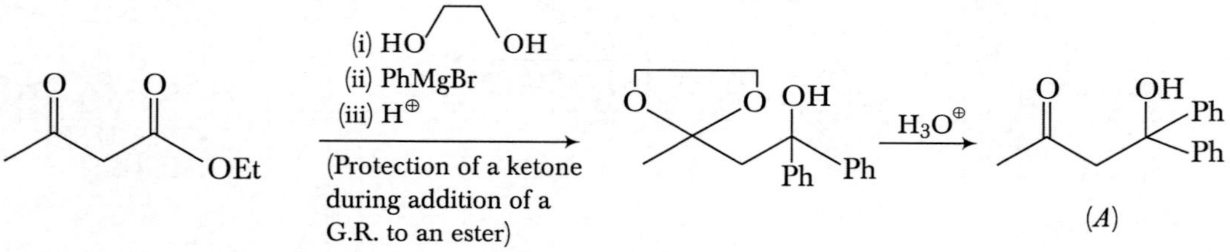

By simple addition of phenyl magnesium bromide to acetoacetic ester, addition to the more electrophilic ketone mainly takes place.

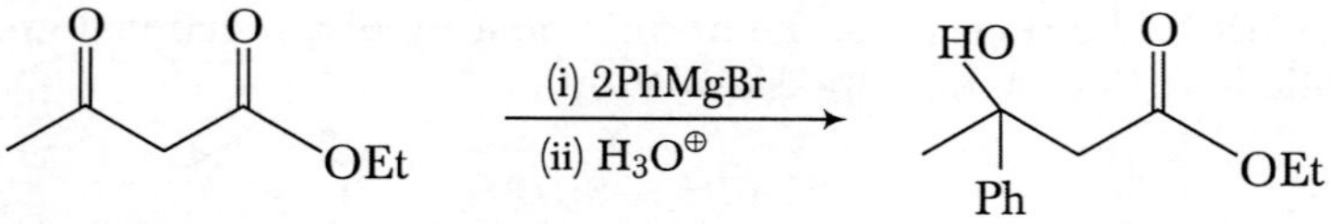

- The protecting groups must have the following features :

1. Simple to put on, in high yield.
2. Easy to remove, in high yield.
3. Stable to reaction conditions.

Protecting groups for alcohols

(a) **Acetals or ketals as protecting groups for alcohols** Acetals or ketals not only serve as useful protecting groups for aldehydes and ketones but they also find widespread use in the protection of alcohols.

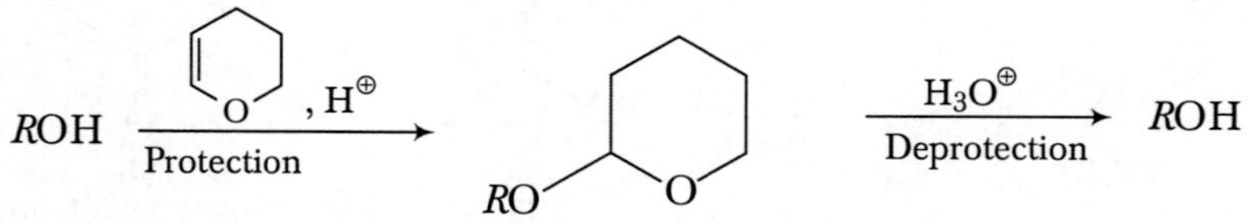

Tetrahydropyranyl
(THP), ether stable to
oxidation, reduction and base

(b) **Ethers as protecting groups for alcohols**

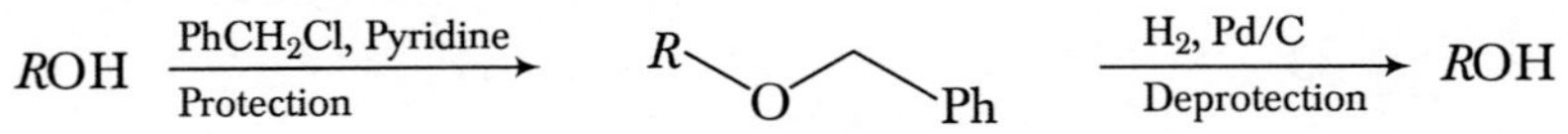

Benzyl ether (*R*O—Ph)
stable to base, mild
acid, oxidation and reduction

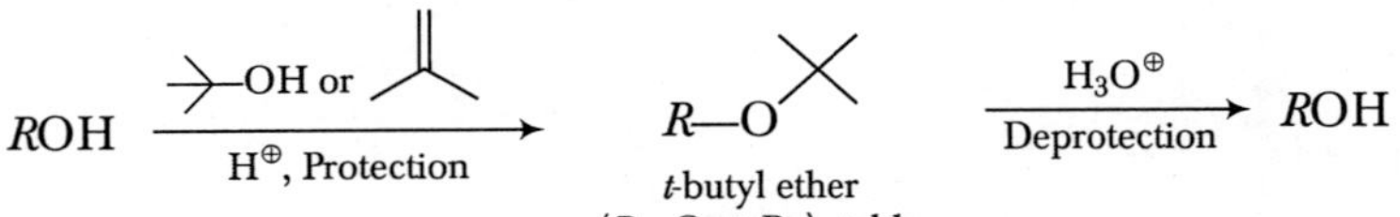

t-butyl ether
(*R*—O–*t*–Bu) stable
to base, mild acid,
oxidation and reduction

Protecting groups for carboxylic acids

(a) **Esters as protecting groups for carboxylic acids**

$$RCOOH + CH_3OH \xrightarrow[-H_2O]{H^{\oplus}} RCOOCH_3 \xrightarrow[\text{(ii) NaI, MeCN}]{\text{(i) } Me_3SiCl} RCOOH$$

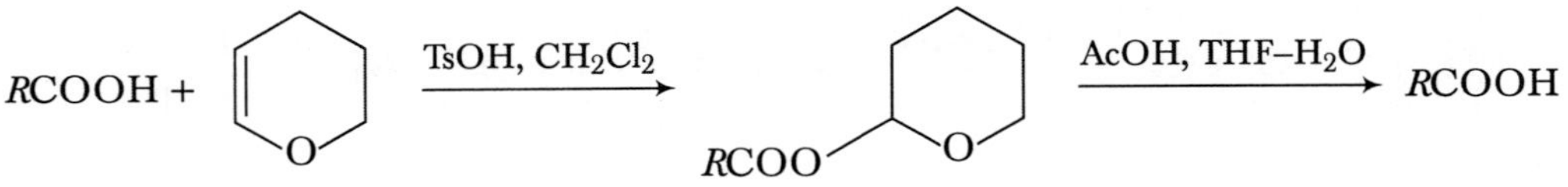

$$RCOOH + t\text{-}BuOH \xrightarrow{R'NC} RCOO\text{-}t\text{-}Bu \xrightarrow[NaI/MeCN]{Me_3SiCl} RCOOH$$

(b) **Amides as protecting groups for carboxylic acids**

$$RCOOH + R'R''NH \xrightarrow{Ph_3P} RCONR'R'' \xrightarrow[\text{or } HNO_2]{KOH,\ HO(CH_2)_2OH} RCOOH$$

Protecting groups for amines

(a) **Carbamates as protecting groups for amines**

$$RR'NH \xrightarrow[\text{(ii) NaOH/MeOH}]{\text{(i) } ClCOOCH_3/K_2CO_3} RR'NCOOMe \xrightarrow{Me_3SiI \text{ or } HBr/AcOH} RR'NH$$

$$RR'NH + Me_3COCOCl \xrightarrow{Base} RR'NCOOCMe_3 \xrightarrow{F_3C\cdot COOH/PhSH} RR'NH$$

Asymmetric Synthesis

The direct synthesis of an optically active compound from an optically inactive compound with or without the use of an optically active reagent is known as asymmeteric synthesis. Or asymmetric synthesis is a reaction in which an achiral unit in a substrate molecule (having either enantiotropic or diastereotropic groups or faces) is converted into a chiral unit in such a manner than unequal amounts of stereo isomers are produced.

Example Reduction of 2-butanone with a chiral reagent gives either (+) or (–)-2-butanol depending upon the chiral reagent used.

$$\underset{\text{2-butanone}}{CH_3-\overset{\overset{\displaystyle O}{\|}}{C}-CH_2CH_3} \xrightarrow[\text{(chiral reagent)}]{\text{Reduction}} \underset{\text{(+) or (–)-2-butanol}}{CH_3-\overset{\overset{\displaystyle OH}{|}}{C}H-CH_2CH_3}$$

The actual configuration of the optically active compound, however depends upon the nature of chiral reagent used.

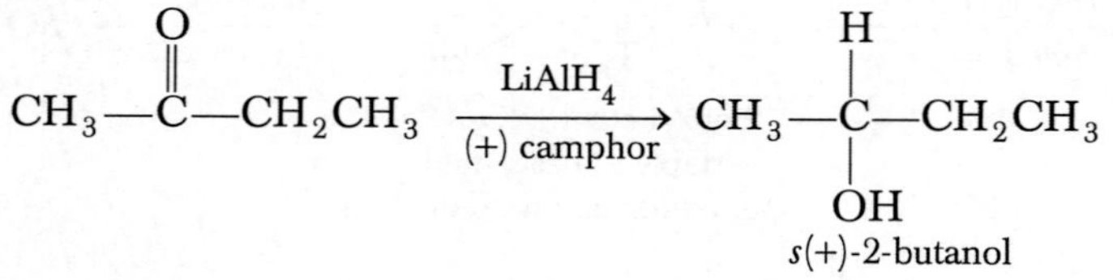

It may be of two types

1. Partial asymmetric synthesis
2. Absolute asymmetric synthesis.

Partial Asymmetric Synthesis

It is the synthesis of an optically active compound from an optically inactive compound by the intermediate use of some optically active reagent. Various methods have been used for the partial asymmetric synthesis.

1. Optically active lactic acid mixture can be prepared by the reduction of pyruvic acid in presence of optically active alcohols like *l*-menthol.

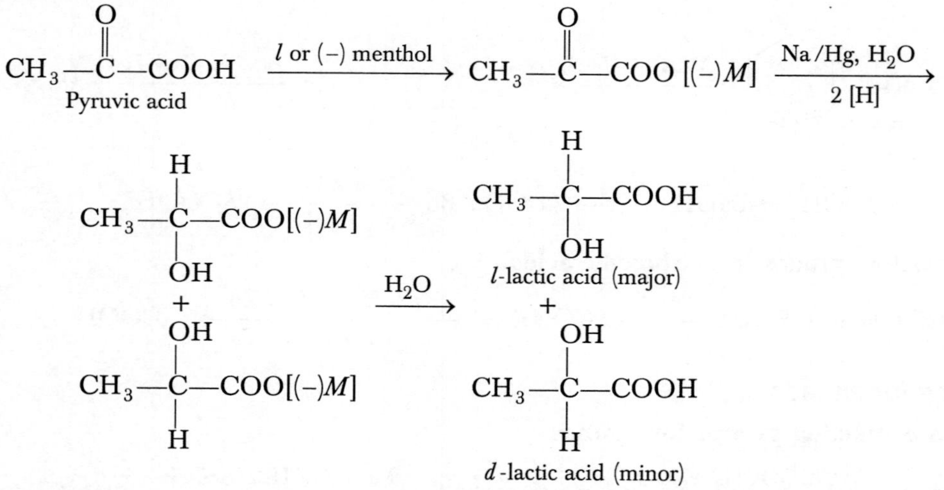

2. The *laevo* isovaleric acid was prepared by heating the half brucine salt of ethylmethylmalonic acid at 440 K. (Brucine is a naturally occurring optically active base)

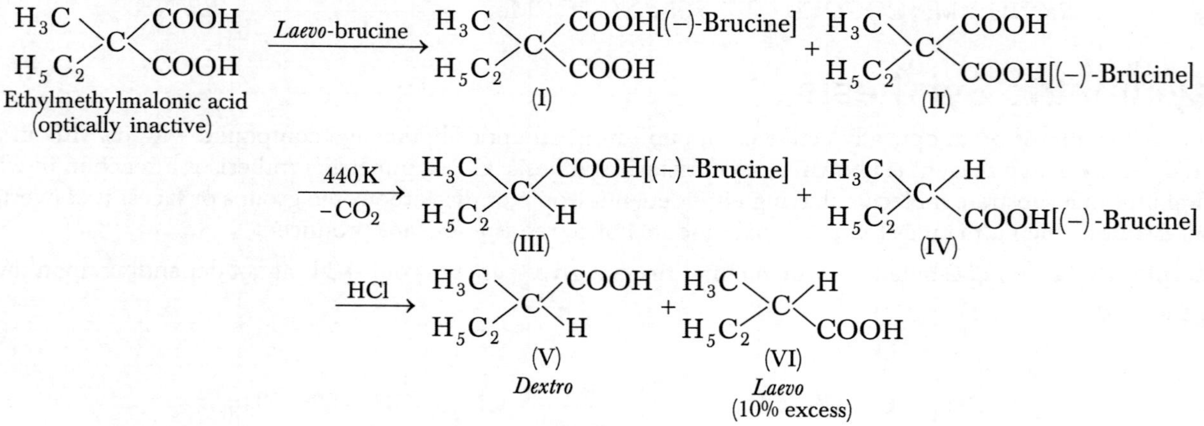

As the resulting product was laevorotatory hence, the *laevo* isomer was produced in excess to the extent of about 10%. The reason for unequal formation of two enantiomers was the difference in the rate of formation of diastereoisomers (III + IV) from the same anion.

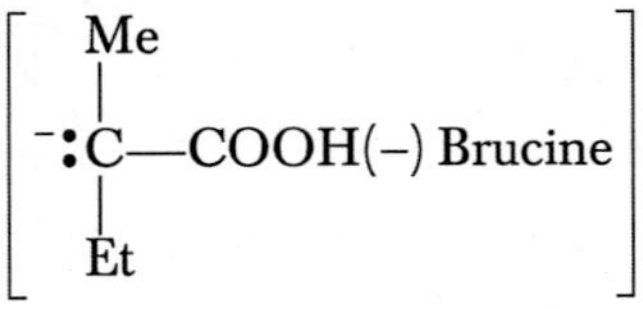

Hence, the resulting product will be an optically active mixture.

Absolute Asymmetric Synthesis

The formation of an optically active compound from inactive compound, without the intermediate use of optically active reagent is known as absolute aymmetric synthesis.

Many absolute asymmetric synthesis have been done under the influence of circularly polarized light. A few example of absolute asymmetric synthesis include :

1. When racemic mixture of ethyl α-bromopropionate (CH_3—$\overset{*}{C}HBr$—COOEt) was irradiated with right and left circularly polarised light, the compound obtained with rotation of *dextro* (+) 0.05 or *laevo* (–) 0.05 respectively.
2. Irradiation of racemic *N,N* -dimethyl α-azido- propionamide with right circularly polarised light gave the product with a rotation of + 0.78 and with left circularly polarised light gave the product with the rotation of – 1.04. From above example it is clear that one of the enantiomers is decomposed by these circularly polarised light hence absolute asymmetric synthesis is also known as **absolute asymmetric decomposition.**

Note One form of the enantiomer either (–) or (+) is decomposed by right or left circularly polarised light and hence, the phenomenon is known as absolute asymmetric decomposition.

$$(-)\text{- Form} \xleftarrow[\text{polarised light}]{\textit{Laevo}\text{ circularly}} CH_3 \cdot CHN_3 \cdot CONMe_2 \xrightarrow[\text{polarised light}]{\textit{Dextro}\text{ circularly}} (+)\text{-Form}$$

3. Preparation of tartaric acid, having a very small positive rotation from ethyl fumarate and H_2O_2 under the influence of *dextro*-circularly polarised light.

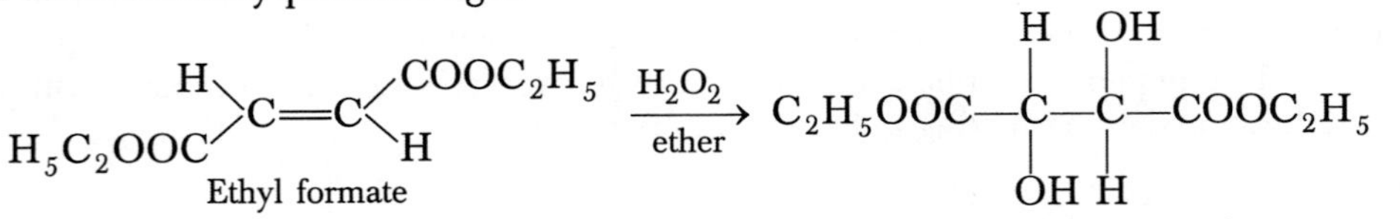

Ethyl formate

d-diethyl tartaric acid

Asymmetric Induction

Asymmetric induction is the use of a chiral reagent or catalyst to convert an achiral reactant to a chiral product having only one of the enantiomers or an excess of one enantiomer. In biochemistry the chiral catalyst is often an enzyme.

$$CH_3COCOOH + \text{Co - enzyme} \xrightarrow{\text{Reductase enzyme}} \underset{(S)\ (+)\ \text{Lactic acid}}{CH_3CH(OH)COOH} + \text{Oxidized enzyme}$$

Presence of a prochiral unit in the substrate asymmetric induction brought about by the presence of a chiral reagent, chiral solvent, chiral catalyst, circularly polarised light, chirality in a portion of the substrate molecule, chirality due to the mechanism of reaction.

Homotopic atoms or groups are those which can be interconverted by rotation about an axis of symmetry. *e.g.,* all the H-atoms in CH_4, methyl group of any compound and methylene group of methylene dichloride.

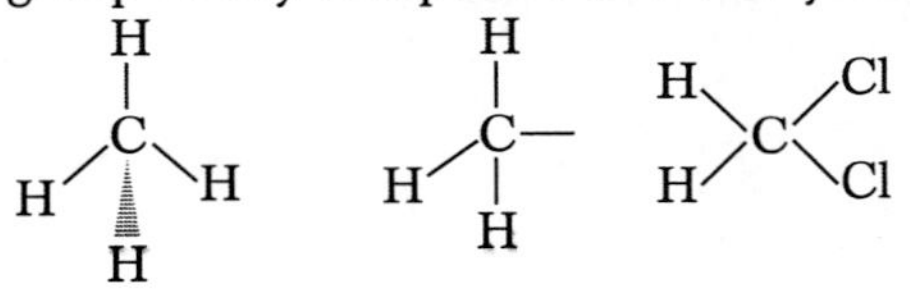

Enantiotropic atoms or groups are those which can be interchanged by a rotation-reflection operation. The two H-atom of chlorobromomethane are enantiotropic because replacement of one H by X gives one enantiomer and replacement of the other H by X gives the other enantiomer.

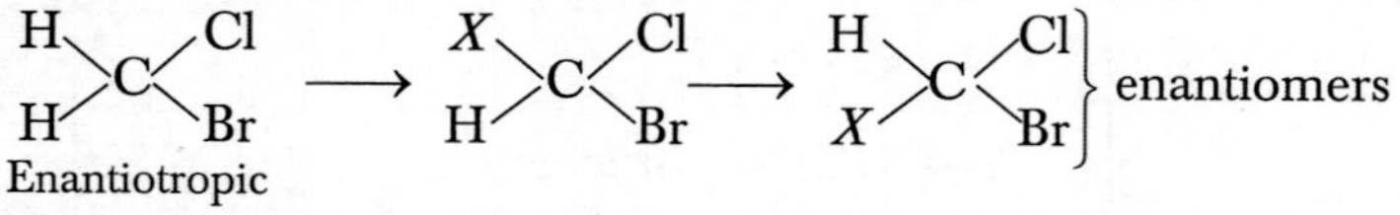

The compound chlorobromomethane is said to have a prochiral centre. Ethanol has a prochiral centre because it has the two enantiotropic H-atoms in the methylene groups.

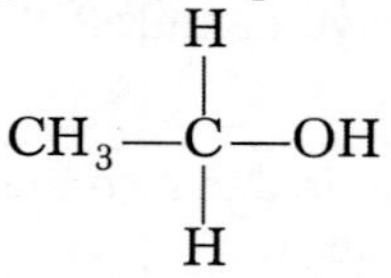

Enantiotropic face of a molecule generates chirality by a suitable reaction.

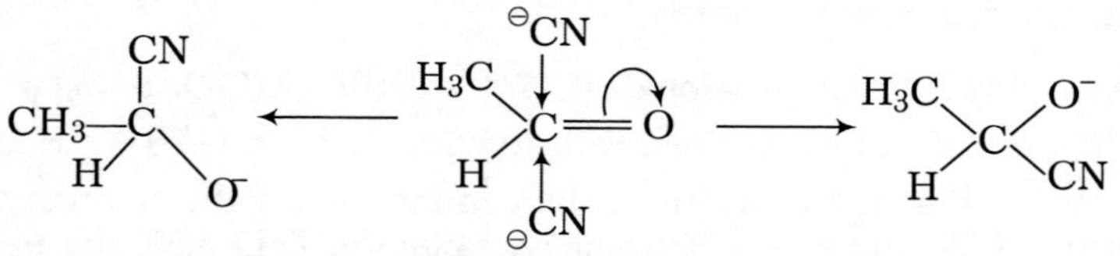

Diastereomeric atoms or groups cannot be interchanged by any symmetry operation. Replacement of them by any other atom or group gives a diastereomer. A molecule is said to have a diastereotropic face, if addition to each face results in a diastereomer.

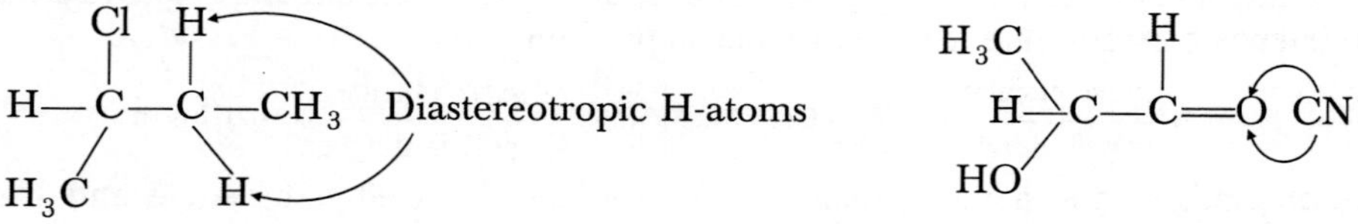

Diastereotropic face

Cram's rule When a new chiral centre is created in a molecule which already contains one or more, two diastereomers are formed in unequal amounts. Thus, rule helps to predict which diastereomer will predominate in a reaction when an aldehyde or ketone having a chiral α-carbon reacts.

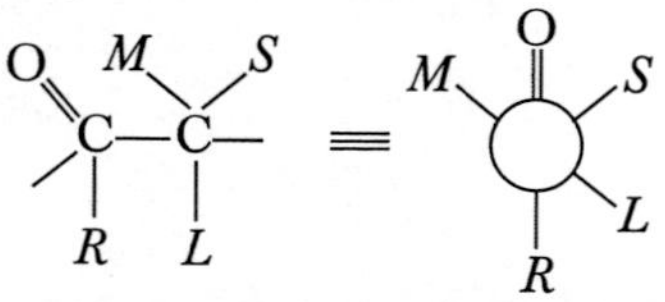

The carbonyl group orients itself in between medium M and small S groups such that the approaching nucleophile prefers the least hindered side is from the side of small *S-group i.e.,* that product which results predominates.

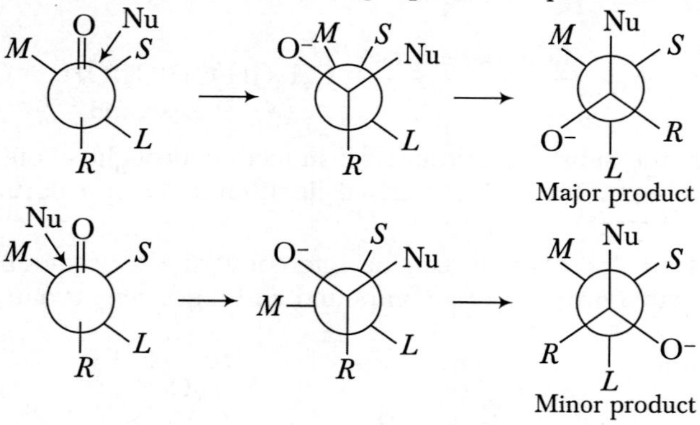

$M = CH_3$, $L = \text{Ph}$, $S = \text{H}$, $R = CH_3$

Since, the reaction is controlled by steric factors, the size of M, S, L and the nucleophile (Nu) play an important role. Larger the 'Nu' higher is the selectivity.

The example given below as illustration of Cram's rule.

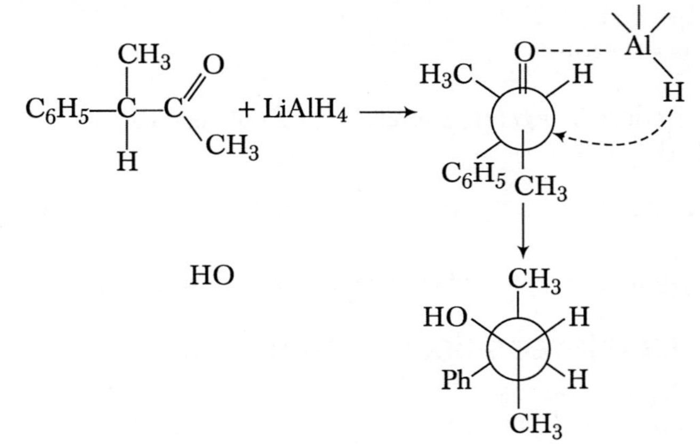

Threo (70%)

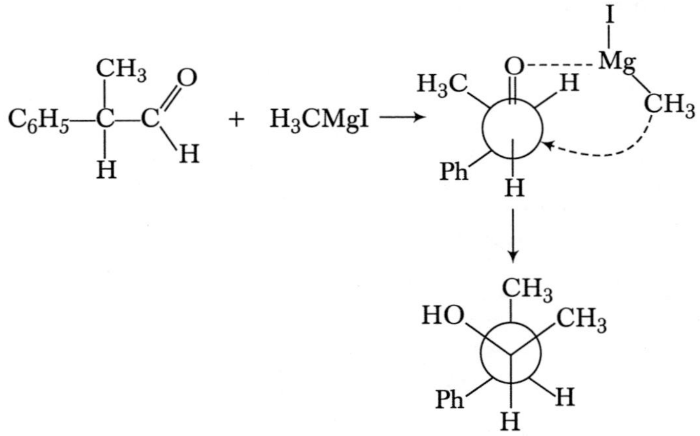

Prelog's rule It is applicable to the nucleophilic addition to the keto group of a keto ester. The keto ester is derived from a keto acid and an optially active alcohol.

The molecule is oriented in such a way as to keep the two carbonyl groups in antiparallel relationship and the smallest group in the alcohol portion is eclipsed by the ketone carbonyl. The incoming group prefers the side of smaller group.

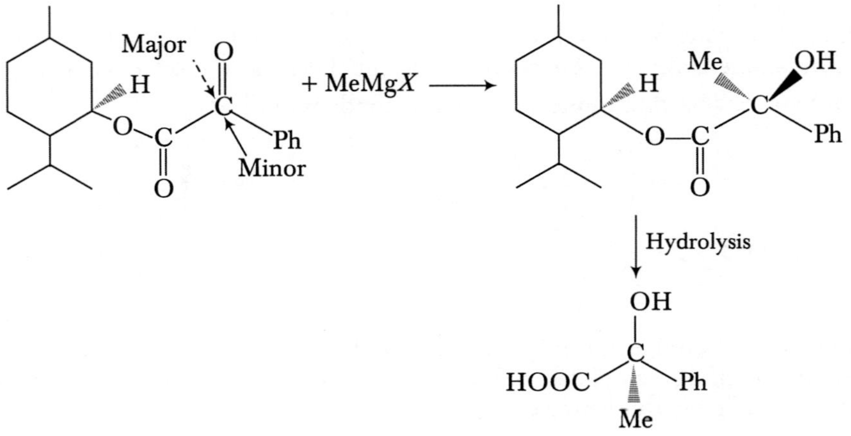

Chiral synthesis catalysed by optically active substances

Addition of HCN to cinnamaldehyde is catalysed by the alkaloids like quinine, cinchonine to predominantly one enantiomer.

$$\underset{\text{Cinnamaldehyde}}{\phi\,CH{=}CH{-}CHO} \xrightarrow[\text{Quinine}]{HCN} \underset{60\%\text{ optical pure}}{\phi{-}CH{=}CH{-}CH\begin{matrix}OH\\CN\end{matrix}}$$

Olefins can be reduced by reducing agents containing chiral ligands. *i.e.,* Rhodium complex containing (–) Ph—CH—(Me)—NH—CHO as ligands.

$$PhC(Me){=}CHCO_2Me \xrightarrow[H_2]{(-)\text{ cat}} \underset{(-)}{PhCH(Me)CH_2CO_2H}$$

Similarly, alcohols can be dehydrated to yield optically active olefin using chiral acids.

Enantioselective and Diastereoselective Synthesis

Many natural products contain highly strained expoxide ring. Starting from allyl alcohols using a titanium complex in which tartaric ester is the chiral ligand, the stereo selection was achieved by them. The allyl alcohol is treated with *t*-butyl hydroperoxide in presence of titanium (IV) isopropoxide and optically active diisopropyl tartrate. First, a ten membered intermediate is formed.

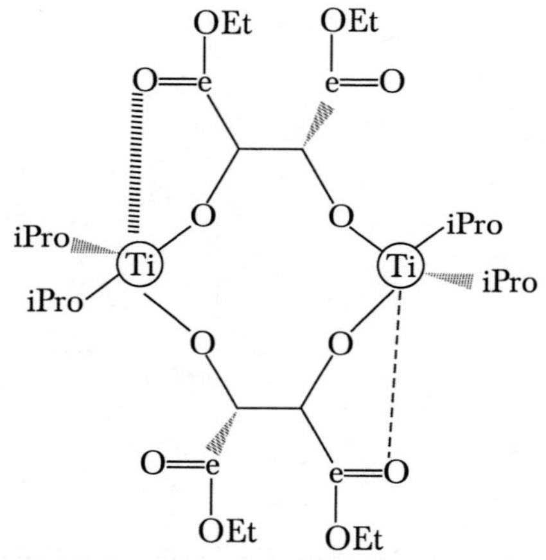

The allyl alcohol and hydroperoxide form a rigid chiral matrix with Ti replacing the isopropoxide units. The approach of oxygen towards the double bond of allyl alcohol is selectively from one side or face of the intermediate leading to predominantly one enantiomeric epoxide.

Enantioselective alkylation can be achieved using chiral phase transfer catalyst. Thus, the alkylation of 2-phenyl indanone using benzylcinchoninium cation as phase transfer catalyst leads to a high degree of enantioselectivity, π-interaction and hydrogen bonding by the phase transfer catalyst with indanone molecule effectively prevents the back side attack of the indanone carbon by the alkylating agent. This leads to selective attack from the front side.

Enantioselective, chiral base catalysed, intramolecular aldol condensation.

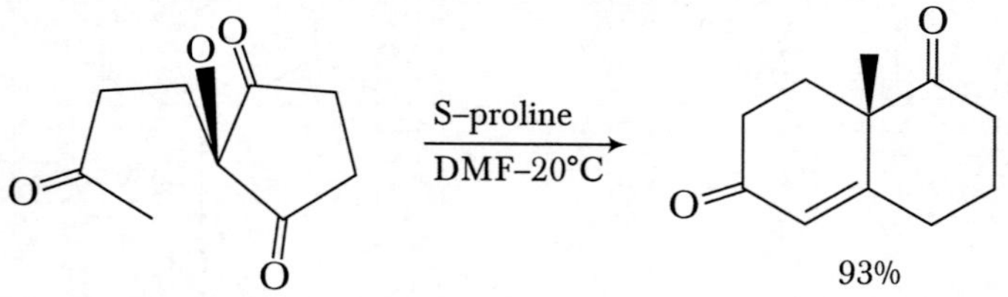

A polymer bound chiral base or chiral acid can be used efficiently to catalyse some enantioselective reactions *e.g.,* if chiral amino acids bound to chloromethylated polystyrene has been used to effect enantioselective addition of organometallic reagents to aldehyde and ketones.

When a single reactant is capable of giving two enantiomeric products during a reaction, but one is formed predominantly, then the reaction is **'enantioselective'.**

When a single reactant is capable of giving two diastereomeric products during a reaction, but one is formed predominantly, then the reaction is **'diastereoselective'**.

Cram's rule and Prelog's rule require the presence of a chiral centre already in the reactant molecule. Thus, these rules are applicable to diastereoselective synthesis.

Creation of a chiral centre in a molecule not having one, resulting in the formation of predominantly one enantiomer is known as enantioselective reaction.

In addition to the enantioselective reactions seen above, enantioselectivity has also been achieved under photochemical conditions.

Photochemical reactions in presence of optically active sensitizers lead to predominantly one enantiomeric product.

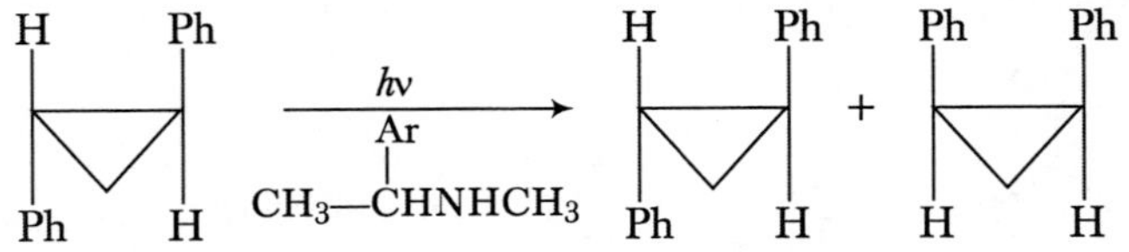

(*d*l) (Active)

Similarly, the presence of right or left circularly polarised light during some photo reactions result in predominantly one enantiomer. For example, the light induced cyclisation of 1, 2-di aryl ethylenes to dihydrophenanthrenes followed by oxidation with iodine and oxygen resulted in active octahelicene.

The dehydrogenation of a dihydropyridyl benzene in presence of circularly polarised light lead to a chiral product. The product similar to biphenyl derivatives *i.e.,* optically active because of atropisomerism.

Chiral Auxiliaries

A **chiral auxiliary** is a chemical compound or unit that is temporarily incorporated into an organic synthesis so that it can be carried out asymmetrically with the selective formation of one of two enantiomers. Chiral auxiliaries are optically active compounds and introduce chirality in otherwise racemic compounds. The temporary stereocentre then forces the asymmetric formation of a second stereocentre using steric hindrance or directing groups to determine chirality. After the creation of the second stereocentre the original auxiliary can be removed in a third step and recycled.

Chiral auxiliaries were introduced by **E.J. Corey** in 1978 with chiral 8-phenylmenthol and by **B.M. Trost** in 1980 with chiral mandelic acid. The menthol compound is difficult to prepare and an alternative is *trans*-2-phenyl-1-cyclohexanol introduced by **J. K. Whitesell** in 1985.

Oxazolidone Auxiliaries

A good example of chiral auxiliaries are the class of Evans auxiliaries comprising oxazolidinones substituted at the 4 and 5 positions. Through steric hindrance, the substitutents direct the direction of substitution of various groups. The auxiliary is subsequently removed *e.g.,* through hydrolysis.

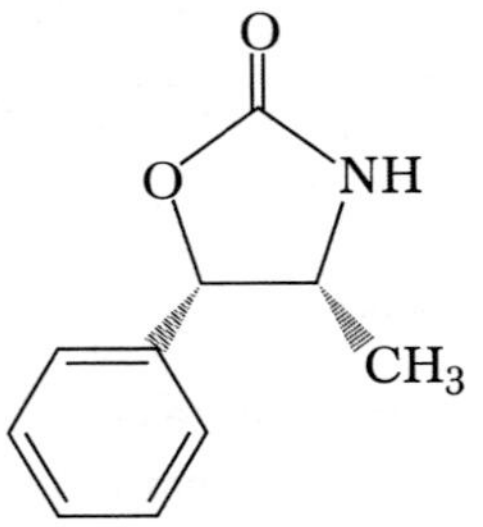

1

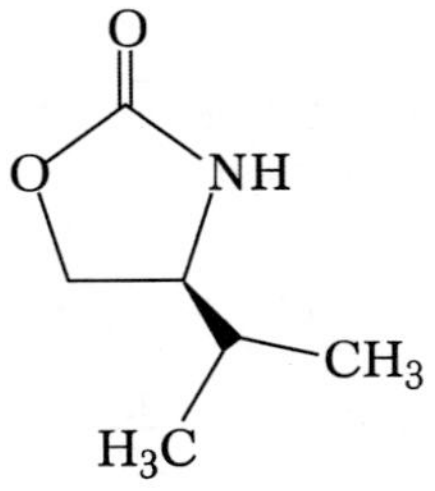

2

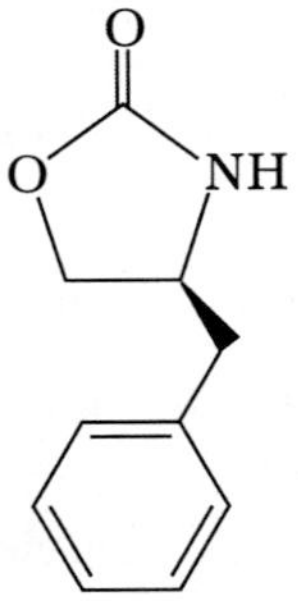

3

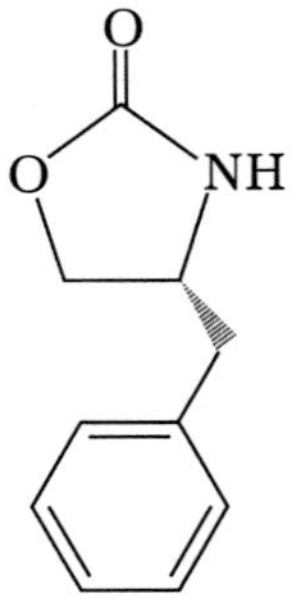

4

Pseudoephedrine Auxiliaries

Both (*R, R*)- and (*S, S*)-pseudoephedrine are used as a chiral auxiliary. Pseudoephedrine is reacted with a carboxylic acid, acid anhydride, or acyl chloride to give a pseudoephedrine amide. The α-proton of the carbonyl compound is easily deprotonated by a non-nucleophilic base to give the enolate, which can further react. The configuration of the addition compound, such as with an alkyl halide, is directed by the methyl group. Thus, any addition product will be *anti* to the methyl and *syn* with the hydroxyl group. The pseudoephedrine chiral auxiliary is subsequently removed by cleaving the amine bond with an appropriate nucleophile.

The amide not only can be hydrolysed but also reduced to the aldehyde (Lithium aluminium hydride alkoxide) or to the alcohol (borane complex with pyrrolidine).

In one study the chiral auxiliary is (–)-ephedrine :

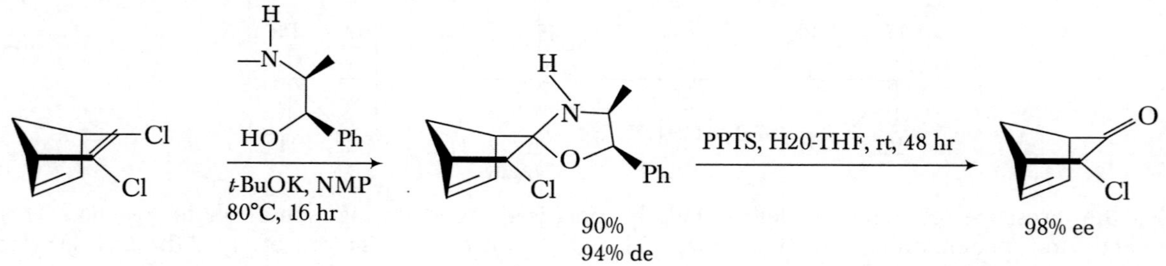

The use of chiral auxiliaries in the synthesis of enantiomerically pure compounds has found wide application for a variety of reactions over the last three decades. Despite the extensive developments in this area by many academic and industrial research groups, new auxiliary controlled reactions continue to evolve frequently. First objectives in this area have been to develop chiral enolate-derived reactions, wherein the chiral auxiliary (X_c) is both readily available and easily recovered after the desired bond construction has been achieved (Fig. 34.1).

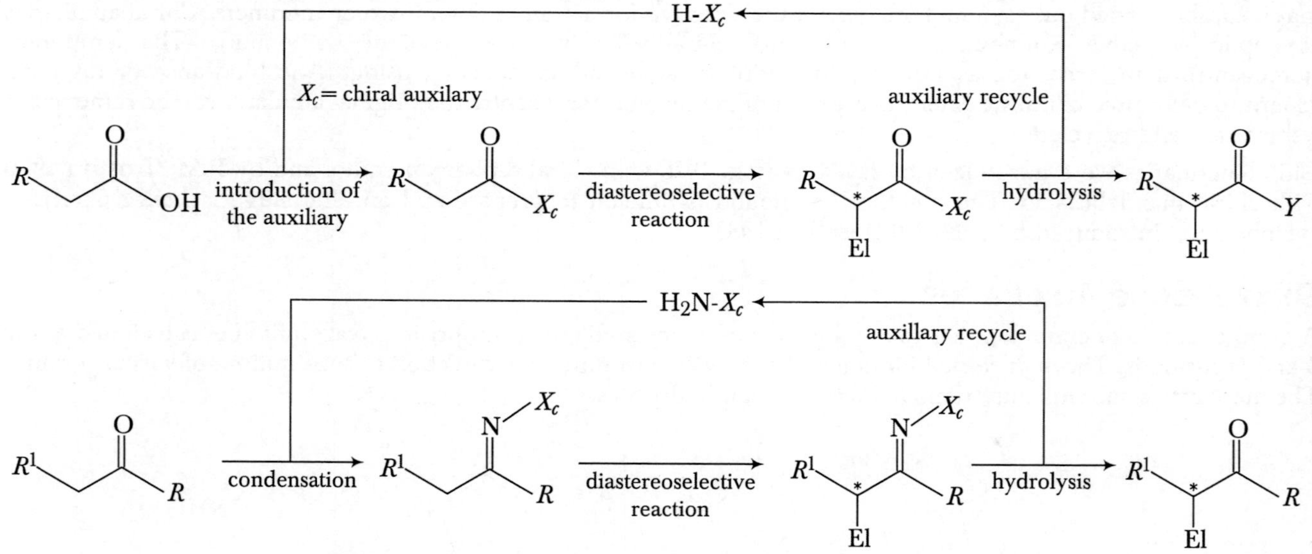

Fig. 34.1 Diasteroselective synthesis with chiral auxiliaries.

Generally, the major issues which have to be addressed in the development of diastereoselective transformations using chiral auxiliaries are threefold in nature. Subsequent to a facile introduction, the chiral auxiliary X_c must provide a strong predisposition for a highly selective enolization process; it must provide a strong bias for enolate diastereoface selection in the new bond construction; and its non-desctrutive and mild cleavage must occur without racemization of the desired products. Today an arsenal of chiral auxiliaries is available meeting the above criteria in full or in part. Of the numerous chiral auxiliaries that have been developed over the past years some of the effectively applied auxiliaries are shown in Fig. 34.1. The majority of chiral auxiliaries are derived from inexpensive, chiral natural sources and most of the diastereoselective reactions reported proceed with high levels of diastereoselection. The most widely employed auxiliary controlled reactions are the asymmetric alkylations, aldol and Diels-Alder reactions.

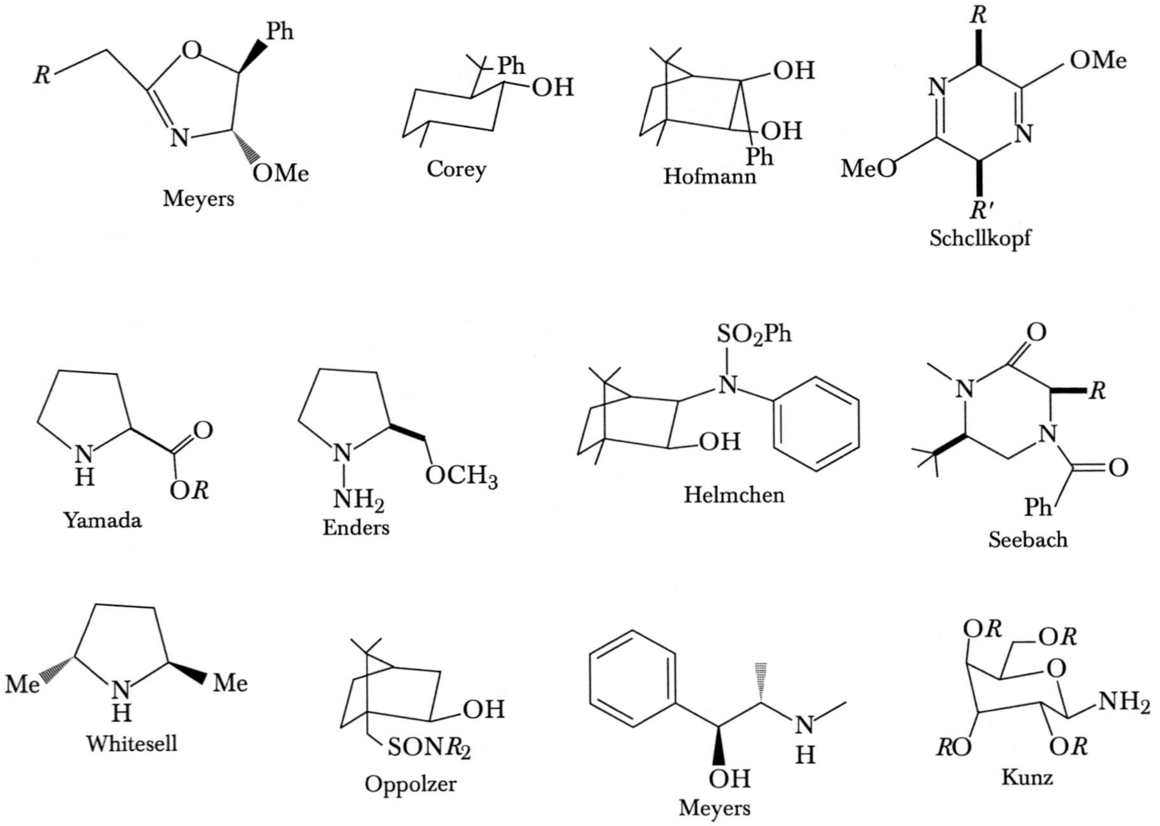

Fig. 34.2 Selected chiral auxiliaries which have been successfully applied in asymmetric synthesis.

Resolution

Whenever an optically active compound is synthesised in the laboratory, the *dextro-* and the *laevo* varieties are obtained in equal amounts and a racemic mixture results. The two components called enantiomorphs can, however, be obtained from the racemic mixture. The separation of racemic mixture into its enantiomorphs (*dextro* and *laevo* components) is called **resolution**. Since, the pair of enantiomers exhibit the same chemical and physical properties, they cannot be separated by ordinary physical or chemical methods. One of the most common methods is to allow a racemic mixture to react with an enantiomer of some other compound. This changes a racemic form into a mixture of diastereomers which have different melting and boiling points and solubilities. Then these can be separated from one another by usual methods of separation of compounds. The separated diastereoisomer is then broken down to give purse enantiomers.

Chemical Resolution of a Racemic Mixture

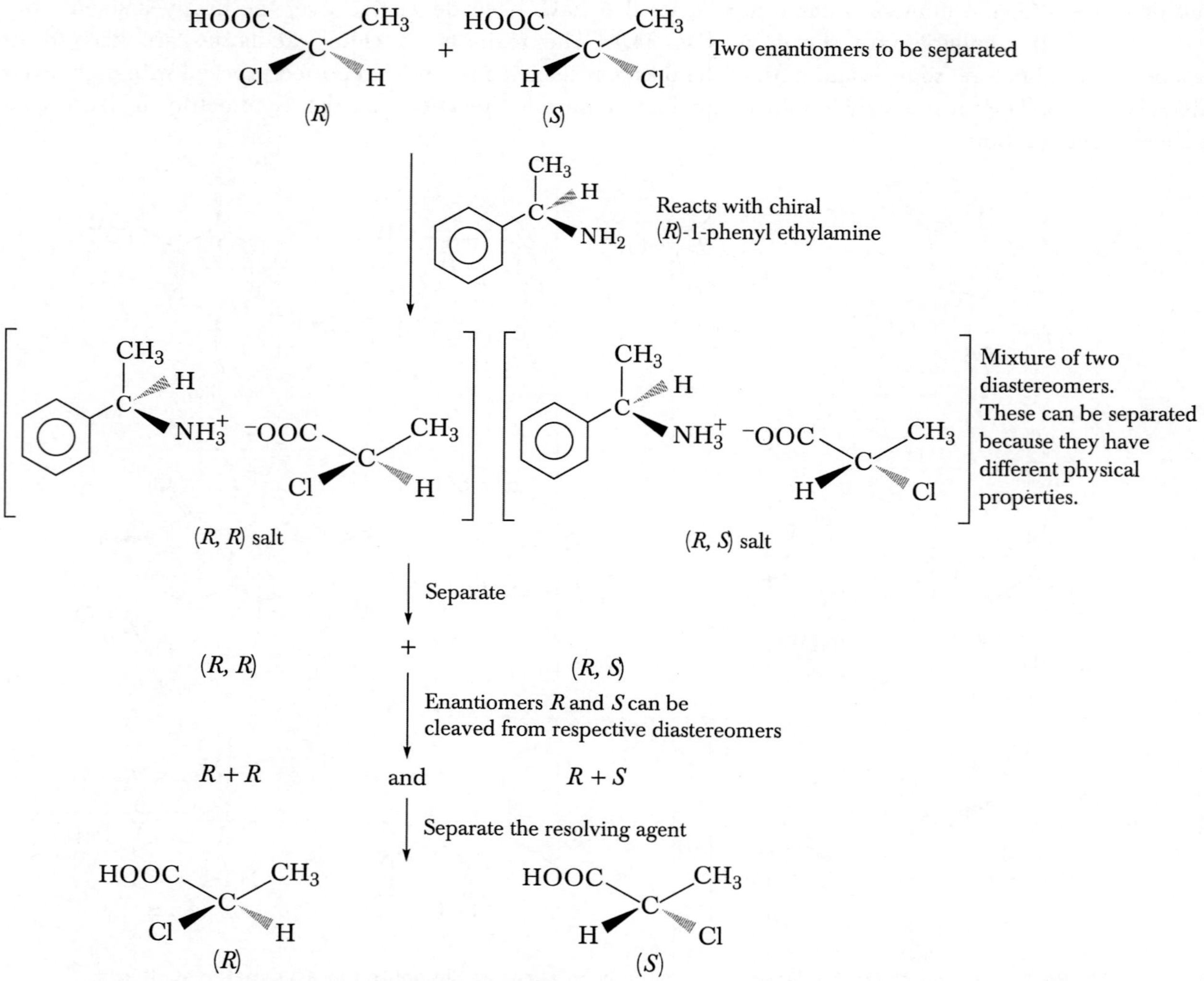

Pure enantiomers are obtained

Some other methods for resolution

(a) **Mechanical method** is applicable rarely to those organic compounds which differ in their crystal shapes.

(b) **Bio-chemical method** using enzymes or microorganism. In this method one of the isomer is completely destroyed and only one isomer is recovered.

(c) **Chemical method** (salt formation) Racemic acid can be resolved by using an optically active base by salt formation and similarly racemic base can be resolved by using optically active acid. The salts thus, obtained usually differ in their solubilities in particular solvents. The salts are separated and followed by hydrolysis to produce the two isomers.

$$\underset{\text{Racemic acid}}{AA'} + \underset{\text{Optically active base}}{B} \longrightarrow \underset{\text{Salt}}{AB} + \underset{\text{Salt}}{A'B}$$

$$\underset{\text{Racemic base}}{BB'} + \underset{\text{Optically active acid}}{A} \longrightarrow \underset{\text{Salt}}{BA} + \underset{\text{Salt}}{B'A}$$

Exercise 1

(For Part 'B')

1. The herbicide 2, 4 *D* (2, 4-dichlorophenoxy acetic acid) can be prepared by the reaction of

(a) 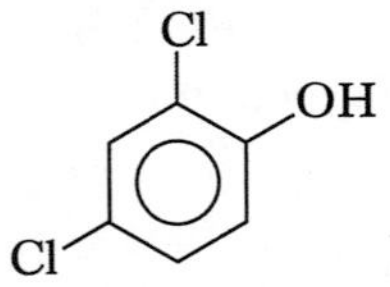 and 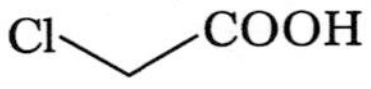

(b) 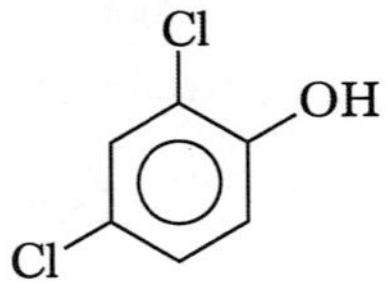 and CH_3COOH

(c) 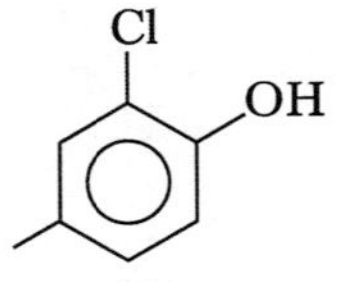 and 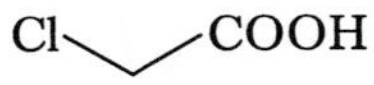

(d) 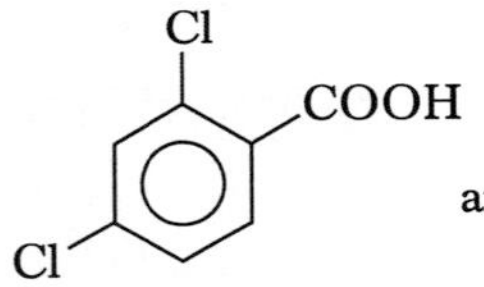 and 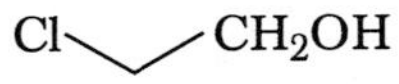

2. The synthons of chlorbenside is

(a) 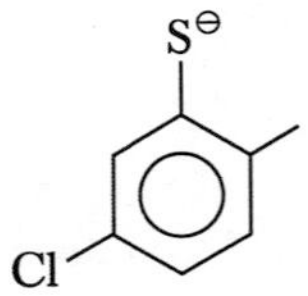 and 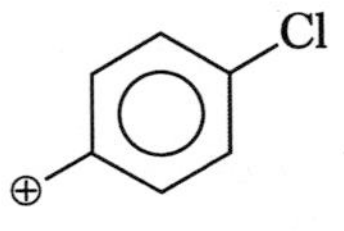

(b) 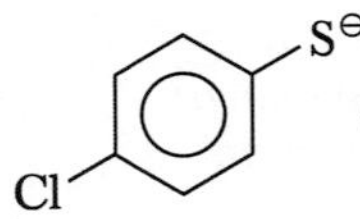 and 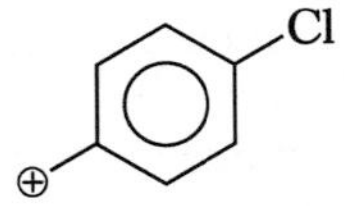

(c) 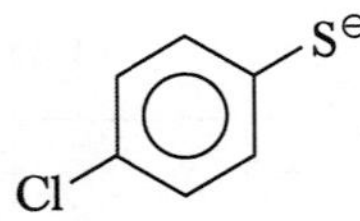 and 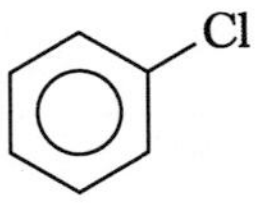

(d) 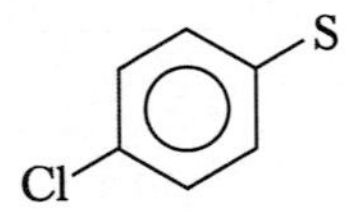 and 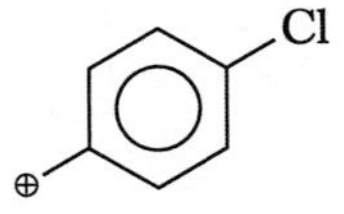

3. Consider the following retrosynthetic analysis.

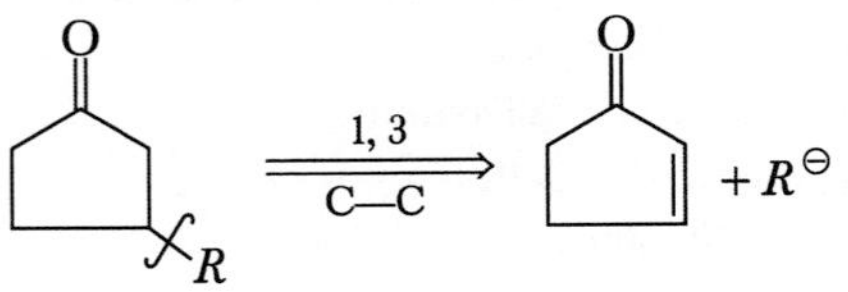

Select the reagent for target molecule synthesis.

(a) 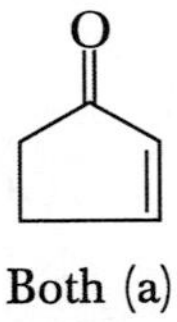

(b) *R*Li

(c) Both (a) and (b)

(d) None of these

4. The situation in which a synthon of polarity opposite to that normally associated with the required functional group must be used is called

(a) resolution

(b) asymmetric induction

(c) umpolung

(d) protection

5. The product of the following reaction

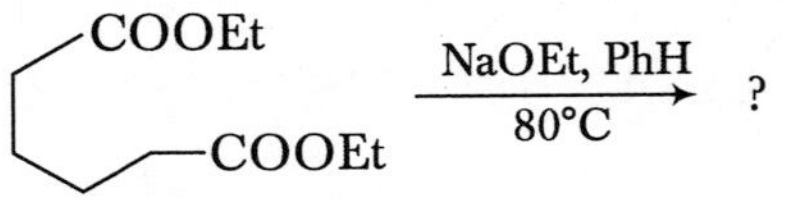

(a) 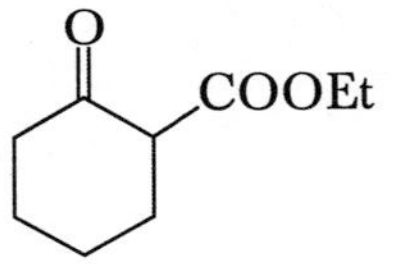

(b) 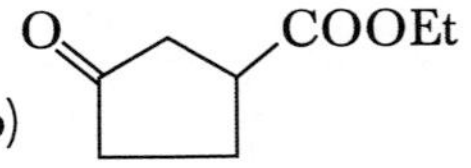

(c) 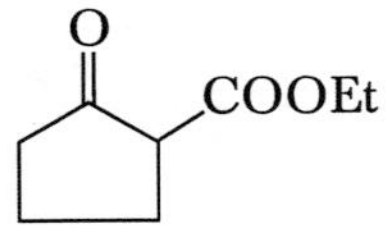

(d) 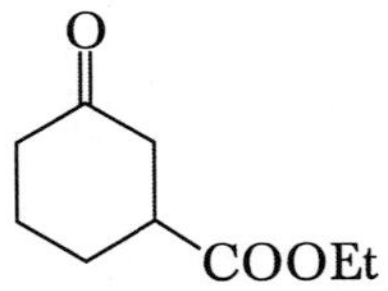

6. A group whose use makes possible to react a less reactive functional group selectively in the presence of a more reactive group is known as

(a) umpolung

(b) synthon

(c) synthetic equivalent

(d) protecting group

7. Which of the following compounds act as protecting group for alcohols?

(a) Ethers

(b) Acetals

(c) Ketals

(d) All of these

8. What is the product of the following reaction?

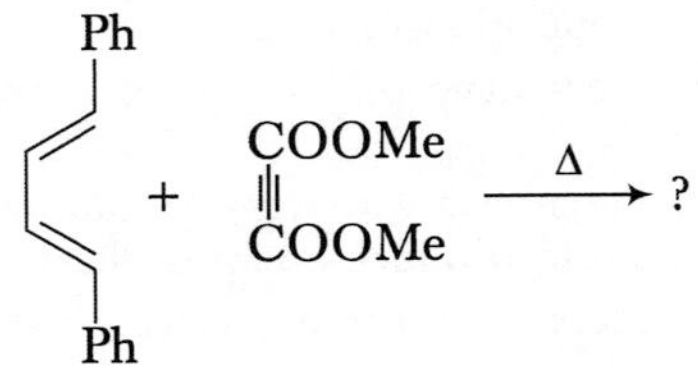

(a) 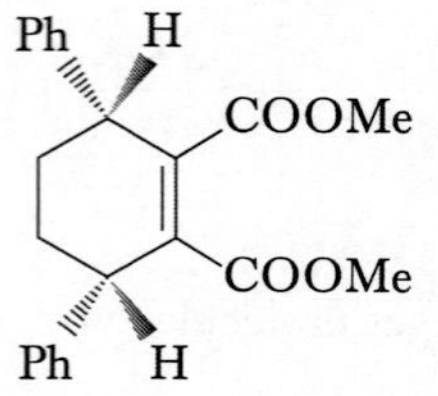

(b) 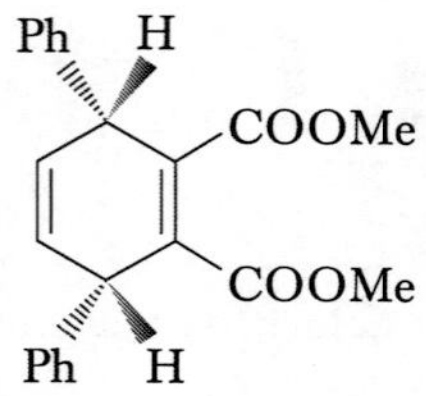

(c) 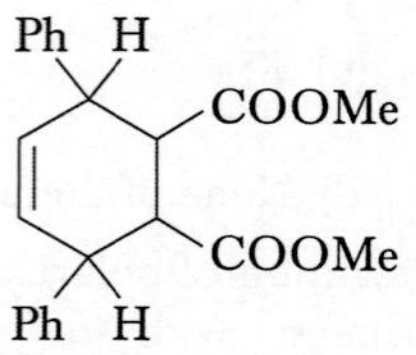

(d) 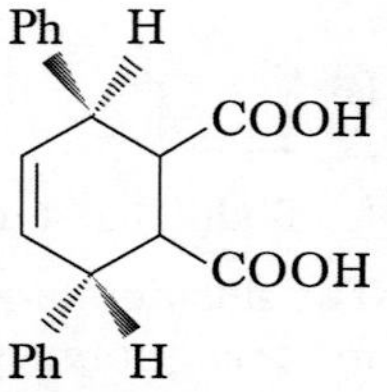

9. The end product (B) of the following reaction

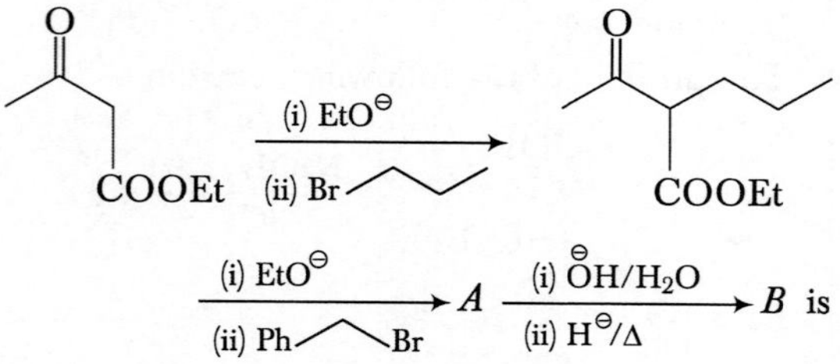

(a) 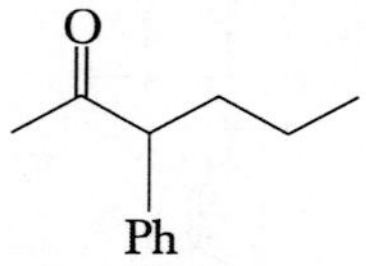

(b) 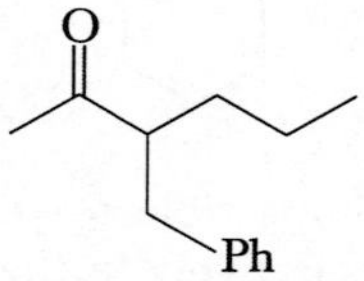

(c) 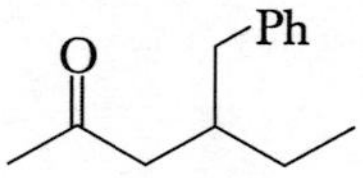

(d) 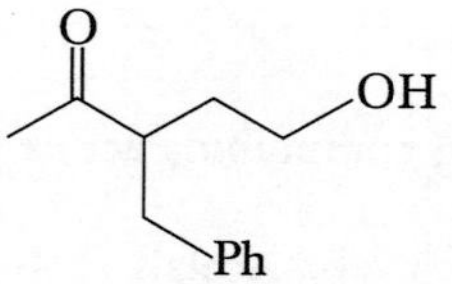

10. Which of the following statements regarding a pair of enantiomers is incorrect?

(a) Enantiomers have same magnitude of optical rotations but opposite sign

(b) Enantiomers have different configuration at chiral centres

(c) Enantiomers react with a pure enantiomers of other compound to produce a pair of diastereomers

(d) Enantiomers have same surface tensions in liquid state

11. Which of the following does not possess any element of symmetry?

(a) Ethane (b) (+) tartaric acid

(c) Carbon tetrachloride (d) Mesotartaric acid

12. A molecule is divided into two halves which are mirror images of each other by

(a) a centre of symmetry (b) a plane of symmetry

(c) an axis of symmetry (d) None of these

13. The product of the following reaction

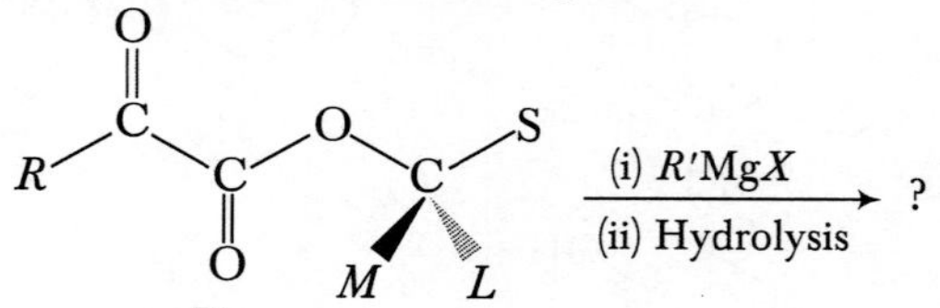

(a) 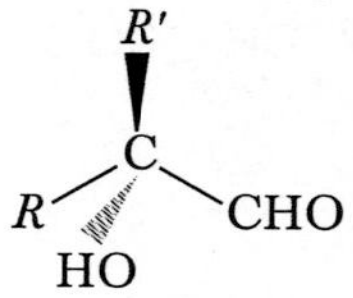

(b) 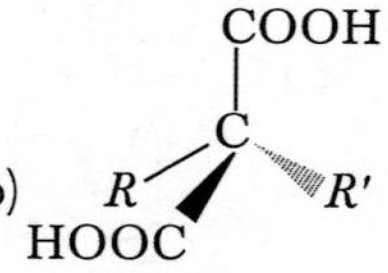

(c) 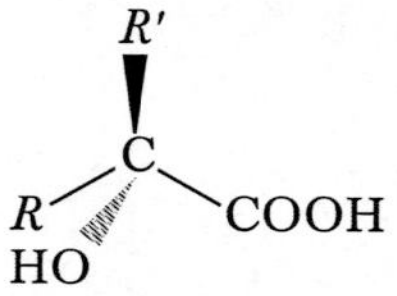

(d) None of these

14. The following compound

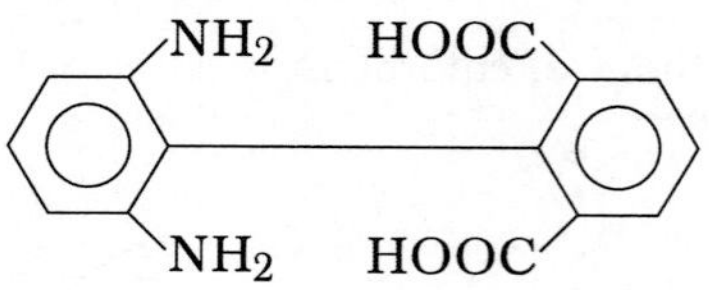

is

(a) chiral due to the presence of asymmetric carbon atom

(b) achiral due to plane of symmetry

(c) achiral due to centre of symmetry

(d) chiral due to restricted rotation

15. The following pair is

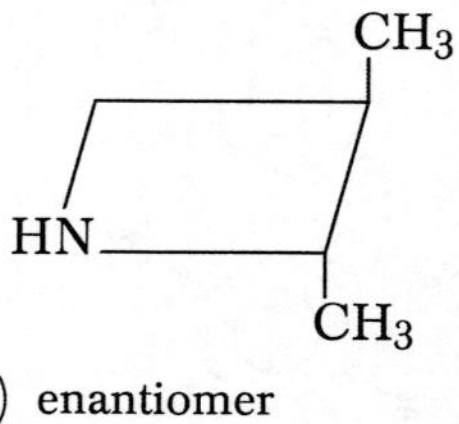

and

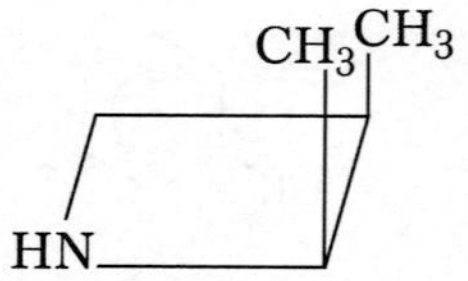

(a) enantiomer (b) homomer

(c) diastereomer (d) None of these

16. Racemic modification can be resolved by

(a) the use of enzymes

(b) fractional crystallisation

(c) fractional distillation

(d) All of the above

17. The production of an optically active compound from a symmetrical molecule without resolution is known as
(a) symmetric synthesis
(b) asymmetric synthesis
(c) linear synthesis
(d) retrosynthesis

18. The compound I and II are respectively

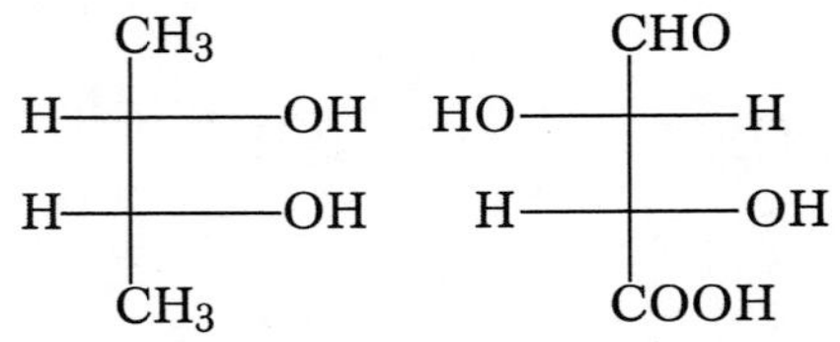

(I) (II)

(a) erythro, erythro
(b) threo, erythro
(c) erythro, threo
(d) threo, thero

19. In the compound given below, the hydrogens H_A and H_B are

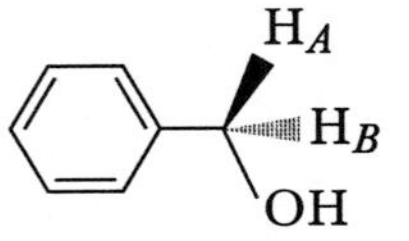

(a) homotropic
(b) enantiotropic
(c) diastereotropic
(d) isotropic

20. In the following transformation, identify the structure of end product.

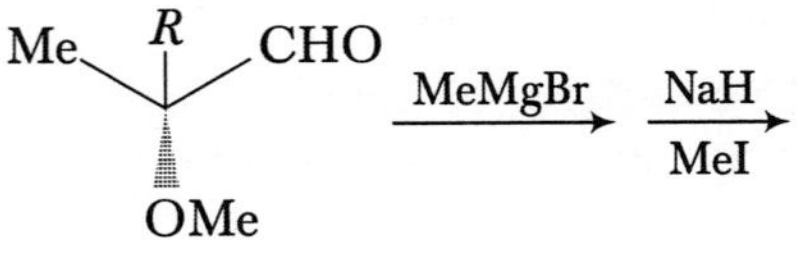

(a) $R—C(OCH_3)(C_2H_5)—CH(OH)CH_3$

(b) $R—C(OCH_3)(CH_3)—CH(OCH_3)—CH_3$

(c) $R—C(OCH_3)(CH_3)—CH(OH)CH_3$

(d) $R—C(CH_2OH)(OCH_3)—CH_3$

21. The priority sequence for assigning *R*, *S* configuration to lactic acid is
(a) $—CH_3$, —COOH, —OH, —H
(b) —COOH, —OH, $—CH_3$, —H
(c) —OH, $—CH_3$, —COOH, —H
(d) —OH, —COOH, $—CH_3$, —H

22. Absolute asymmetric synthesis can be carried out by
(a) using optically active solvent
(b) reacting an optically active reactant with a non-optically active one
(c) using irradiation with circularly polarised light
(d) using quartz vessel as the reaction container

23. Which of the following can be used for the resolution of a racemic base?
(a) Mesotartaric acid
(b) *dl*-tartaric acid
(c) Acetic acid
(d) (–) mandelic acid

24. Optically pure 2-methyl-1-butanol on treatment with HCl gas gives 1-chloro-2-methylbutane which is
(a) also optically pure
(b) a racemic mixture
(c) 20% optically pure
(d) 80% optically pure

25. Which of the following compounds might you use to resolve a racemic mixture of carboxylic acid?

(a) 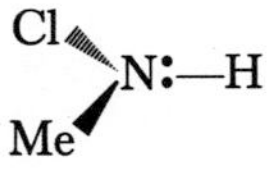

(b) 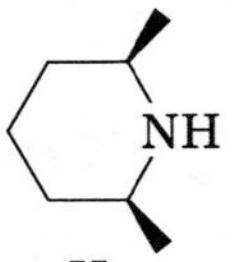

(c) 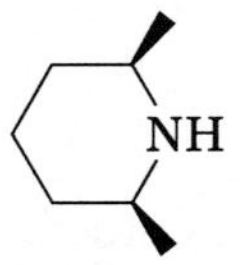

(d) 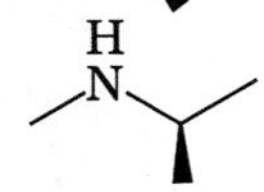

26. Addition of Br_2 to *trans*-2-butene produces
(a) a pair of enantiomers
(b) a *meso* compound
(c) a compound with a single chiral centre
(d) a pair of diastereomers

Exercise 2
(For Part 'C')

1. The separation of a racemic mixture into the pure enantiomers is termed as
(a) racemization (b) resolution
(c) isomerization (d) equilibrium

2. The reaction sequence of

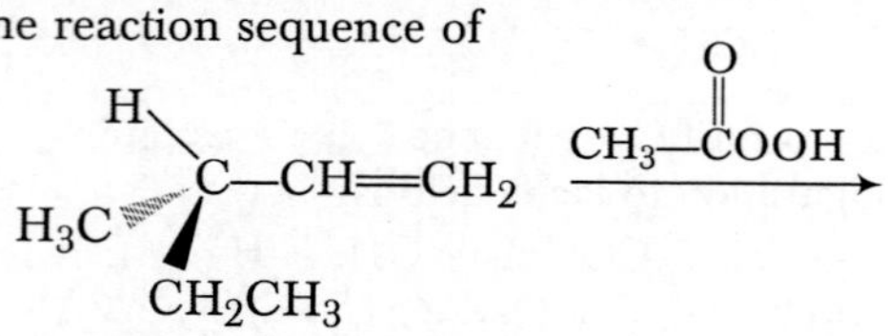

will yield
(a) a pair of products that are enantiomers
(b) a single product that is optically active
(c) a pair of product that are diastereomers
(d) a pair of products one of which is *meso*

3. The major product(s) from the reaction of Br_2 with (Z)-3-hexene is (are)
(a) optically pure
(b) a racemic mixture of enantiomers
(c) the *meso* form
(d) both the racemic mixture and the *meso* form

4. $A(C_4H_6) \xrightarrow{H_2/Pt} B(C_4H_8) \xrightarrow{O_3/H_2O/Zn} C \xrightarrow{HCN} D$

D has chiral carbon and can be hydrolysed to lactic acid. Hence, *A* is
(I) $CH_3C{\equiv}CCH_3$
(II) $CH_2{=}CH{-}CH{=}CH_2$
(III) 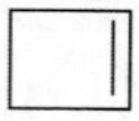
(IV) 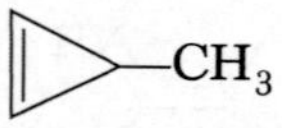

(a) I, II (b) II, III (c) I, IV (d) Only I

5. 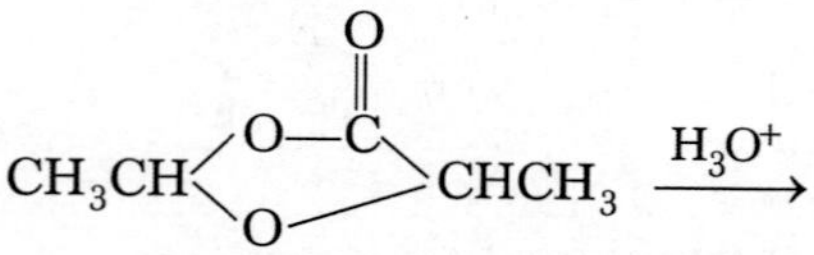 product can be
(a) $CH_3CH(OH)_2$, $CH_3CH(OH)COOH$
(b) CH_3CHO, $CH_3CH(OH)COOH$
(c) CH_3CH_2COOH, CH_3CH_2OH
(d) $CH_3CH(OH)COOH$, CH_3CH_2OH

6. Select the correct stereochemistry (chiral/achiral) of the reactants and products.

I. 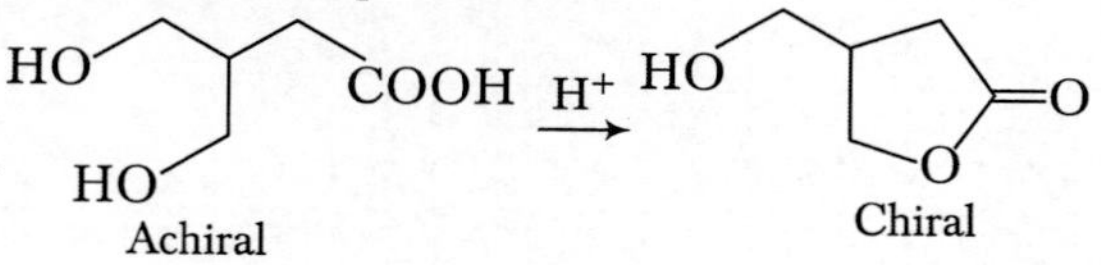

II. 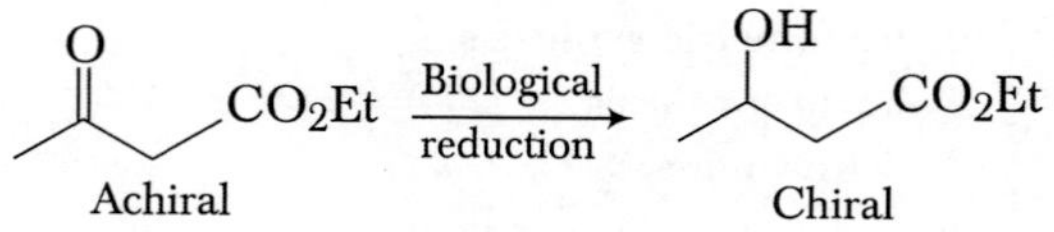

III. 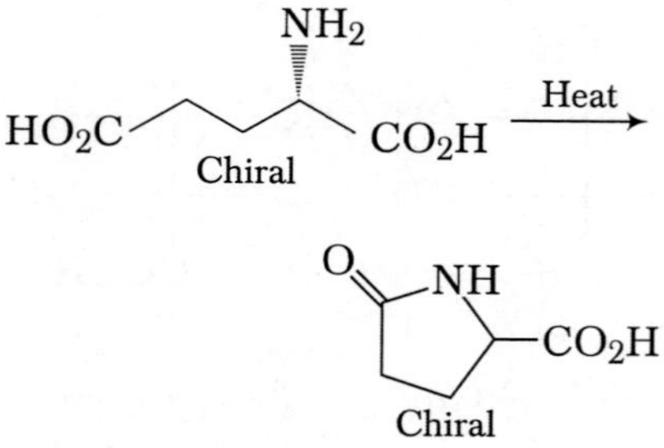

IV. 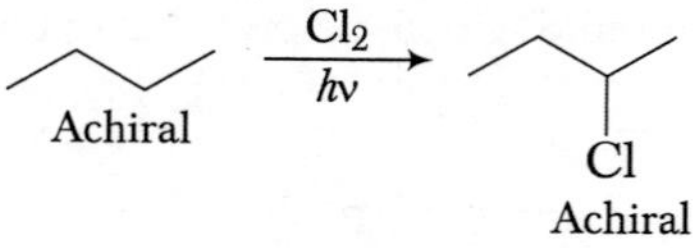

(a) I, II (b) II, IV
(c) II, III, IV (d) I, II, III

7. An S_N2 reaction of an asymmetric carbon of a compound always gives
(a) an enantiomer of the substrate
(b) a product with opposite optical rotation
(c) a mixture of diastereomers
(d) a single stereoisomer

8. The best reagent to resolve racemic mixture of 2-hydroxy butanoic acid would be

(a) 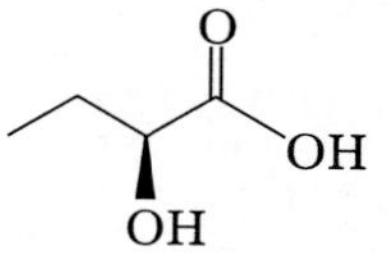

(b) 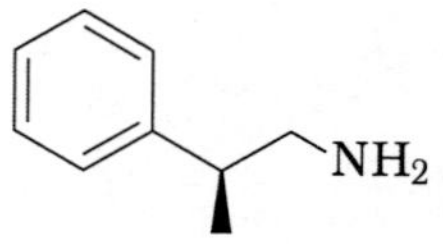

(c) 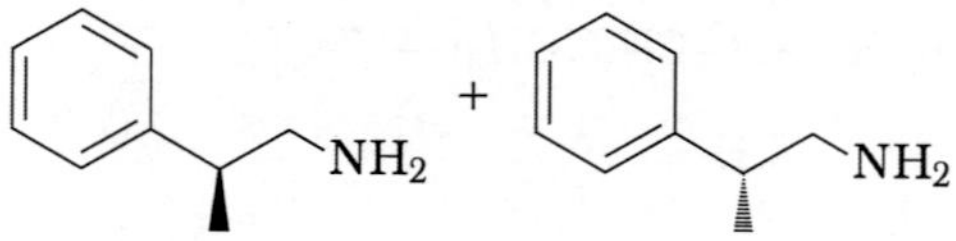

(d) 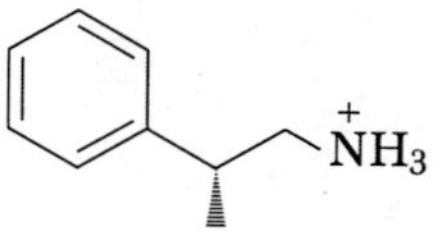

9. Methylethylamine cannot be resolved into enantiomers because
(a) it is planar
(b) it undergoes rapid inversion
(c) it has a plane of symmetry
(d) a tricovalent atom cannot be a centre of chirality

10. Which of the following amines can be resolved into enantiomers?
(a) $CH_3CH_2NHCH_3$
(b) $CH_3CH_2\underset{}{\overset{CH_3}{\overset{|}{C}}}HNHCH_3$
(c) 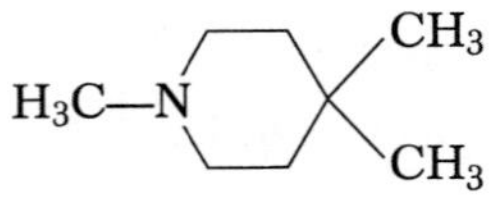
(d) 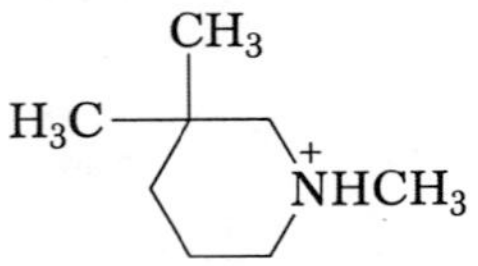

11. Which one of the nitrogen compounds below can be resolved into enantiomers at room temperature?

(a) 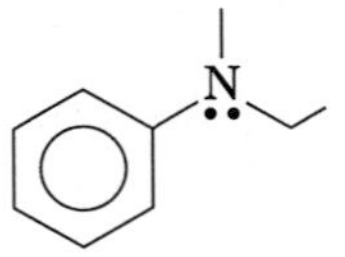
(b) 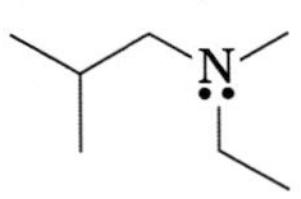
(c) 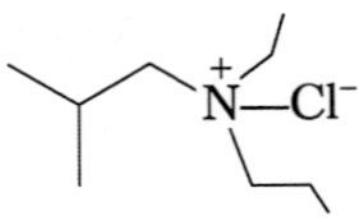
(d) 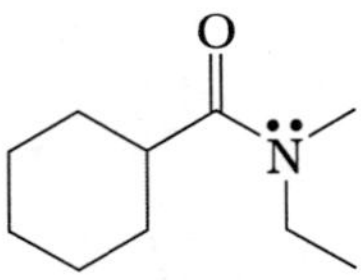

12. Which of the following below would be a reasonable reagent to try in the resolution of *cis*-3-methoxycyclohexanecarboxylic acid (*A*) into its enantiomeric forms?

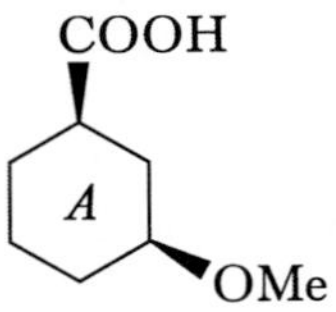

(a) 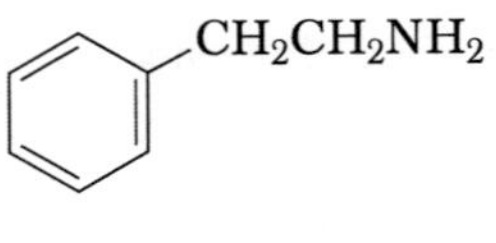
(b) 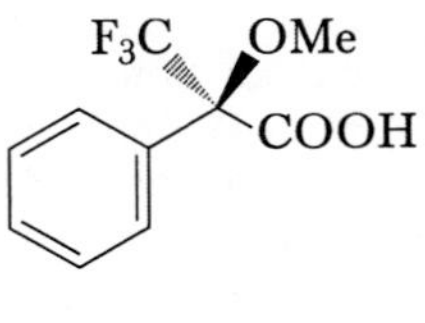
(c) 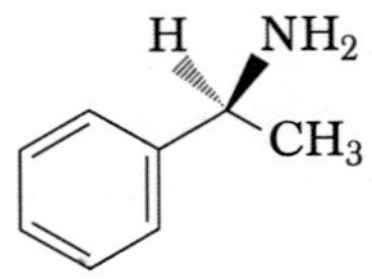
(d) 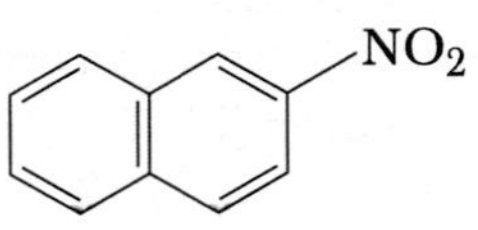

13. Select the correct statements from the given below :
I. A single line arrow (⟶) is known as retrosynthetic arrow.
II. Synthons are idealised fragments usually cations or anions resulting from a disconnection.
III. The term umpolung refers to the reversal of the normal polarity of a functional group.
IV. The protecting groups should be unstable to reaction conditions.
(a) I, III (b) II, IV
(c) III, IV (d) II, III

14. The product of the following reaction

$$RCOCOOH \xrightarrow[\text{liver extract}]{NH_3} \text{is}$$

(a) $R—\underset{}{\overset{NH_2}{\overset{|}{C}}}H—COOH$
(b) $R—CH_2CONH_2$
(c) $R—\overset{NH_2}{\overset{|}{C}}H—CONH_2$
(d) $R—\underset{OH}{\underset{|}{C}}H—CONH_2$

15. The product of the given reaction is

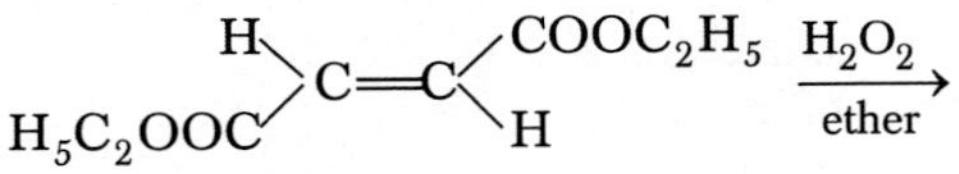

(a) $C_2H_5OOC—CH_2—CH_2—COOC_2H_5$
(b) $C_2H_5OO—\overset{H}{\overset{|}{\underset{OH}{\underset{|}{C}}}}—CH_2COOC_2H_5$
(c) $C_2H_5OOC—\overset{H}{\overset{|}{\underset{OH}{\underset{|}{C}}}}—\overset{OH}{\overset{|}{\underset{H}{\underset{|}{C}}}}—COOC_2H_5$
(d) $HOOC—\overset{H}{\overset{|}{\underset{OH}{\underset{|}{C}}}}—\overset{OH}{\overset{|}{\underset{H}{\underset{|}{C}}}}—COOH$

16. Resolution can be done by
I. Mechanical method
II. Bio-chemical method
III. Chemical method
(a) I, II (b) II, III
(c) I, III (d) I, II, III

Directions (Q. Nos. 17 to 19) The following compounds have keto as well as aldehyde group if one group is to be changed into desired alcohol, then other will have to be protected (shield) carrying the necessary reactions and finally removing the protecting group. *A* can be converted into *B* by protection of —CHO.

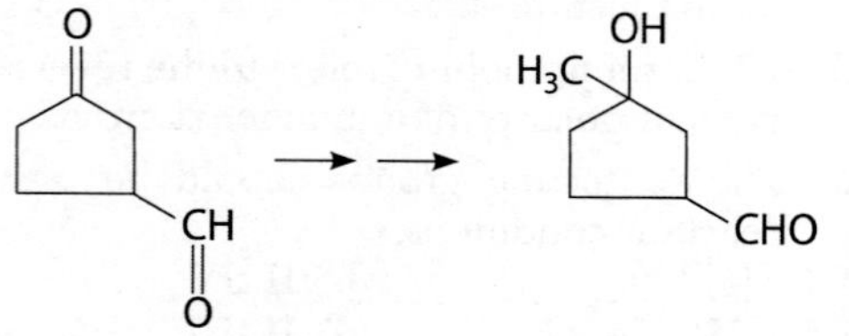

A *B*

17. Group can be protected by .... due to the formation of ....

(a) diol, acetal
(b) thiol, mercaptal
(c) Both (a) and (b)
(d) None of these

18.

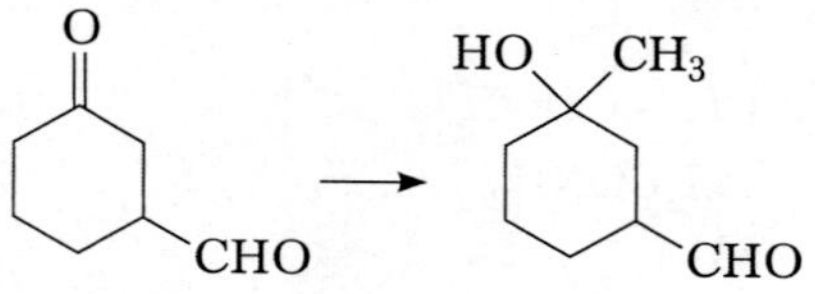

A *B*

A can be converted to *B* by

(a) $A \xrightarrow{\substack{CH_2OH \\ | \\ CH_2OH}} \xrightarrow{CH_3MgBr} \xrightarrow{H_3O} B$

(b) $\xrightarrow{CH_3MgBr} \xrightarrow{H_3O} B$

(c) Both (a) and (b)
(d) None of the above

19.

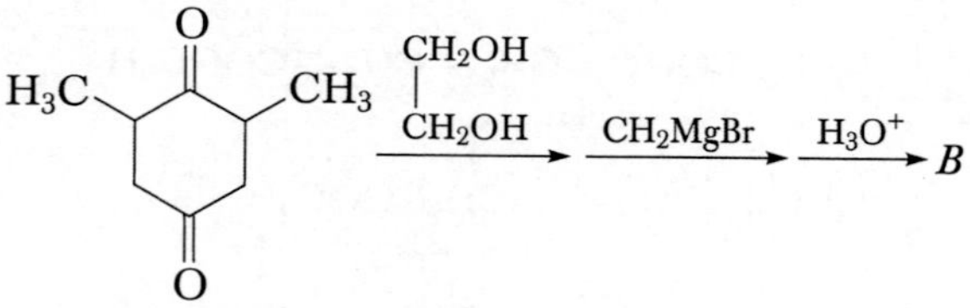

A

B is identified as

(a)

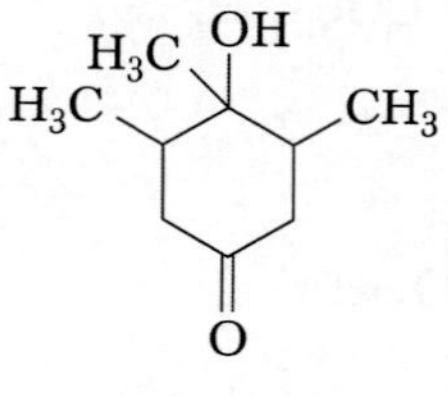

(b)

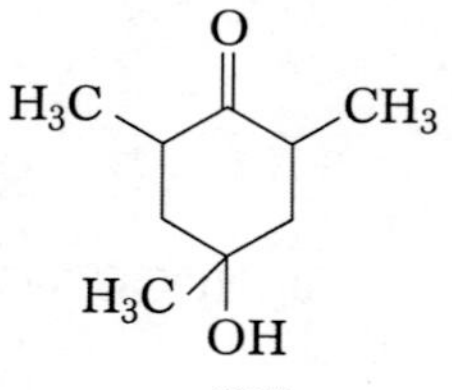

(c)

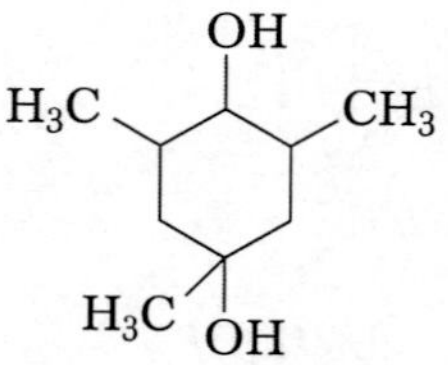

(d)

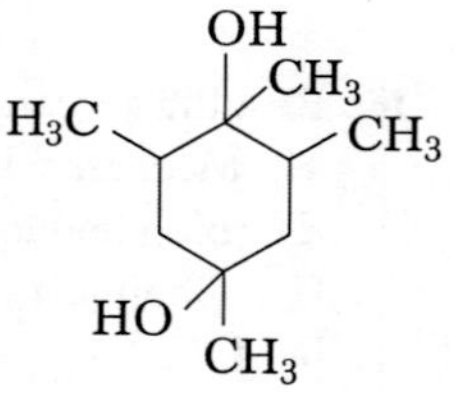

20. In which case chiral cabon is generated?

(a) $CH_3COCH_3 + HCN \xrightarrow{H_3O^+}$

(b) $CH_3CHO + HCN \xrightarrow{H_3O^+}$

(c) $CH_3COCOOH + HCN \xrightarrow{H_3O^+}$

(d) 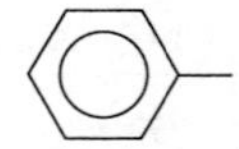 —CHO + HCN $\xrightarrow{H_3O^+}$

21. Enantiomorphs cannot be separated by

(a) fractional crystallization
(b) fractional distillation
(c) use of enzymes
(d) chromatography over alumina

22. Match the Column I with Column II.

Column I		Column II	
A.	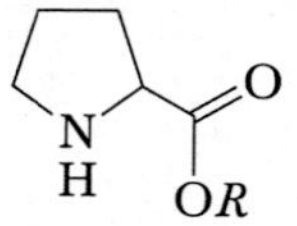	1.	Enders
B.	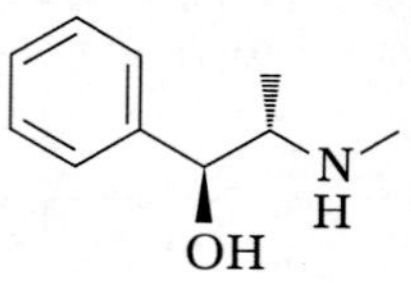	2.	Yamada
C.	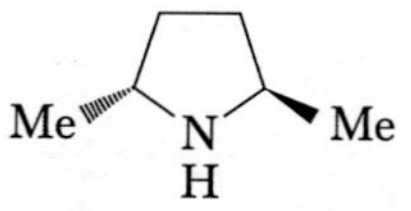	3.	Meyers
D.	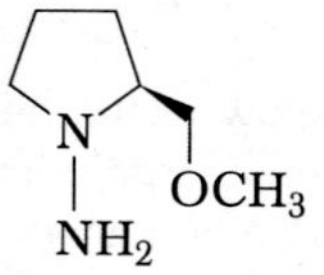	4.	Whitesell

Codes

(a) A-2, B-3, C-4, D-1
(b) A-3, B-2, C-1, D-4
(c) A-3, B-2, C-4, D-1
(d) A-2, B-3, C-1, D-4

Assertion & Reason

Codes

(a) Both A and R are true and R is the correct explanation of A.
(b) Both A and R are true but R is not the correct explanation of A.
(c) A is true but R is false.
(d) A is false but R is true.

23. Assertion (A) The separation of racemic mixture into its enantiomorphs is called resolution.

Reason (R) The racemic mixture can resolved byfractional distillation.

24. **Assertion (A)** Synthons are idealised fragments usually cations or anions resulting from a disconnection.

Reason (R) Umpolung refers to the reversal of the normal polarity of a functional group.

25. Which of the following is/are protecting group for carboxylic acids?
(a) Esters (b) Amides
(c) Hydrazides (d) Carbamates

Answers

Exercise 1

1. (a)	2. (b)	3. (c)	4. (c)	5. (c)	6. (d)	7. (d)	8. (b)	9. (b)	10. (a)
11. (b)	12. (b)	13. (c)	14. (b)	15. (c)	16. (a)	17. (b)	18. (c)	19. (a)	20. (b)
21. (d)	22. (c)	23. (d)	24. (a)	25. (c)	26. (b)				

Exercise 2

1. (b)	2. (c)	3. (b)	4. (a)	5. (b)	6. (d)	7. (b)	8. (c)	9. (b)	10. (b,d)
11. (c)	12. (c)	13. (d)	14. (a)	15. (c)	16. (d)	17. (c)	18. (a)	19. (a)	20. (b,c,d)
21. (a,b,d)	22. (a)	23. (c)	24. (b)	25. (a,b,c)					

Hints & Solutions

Exercise 1

1. 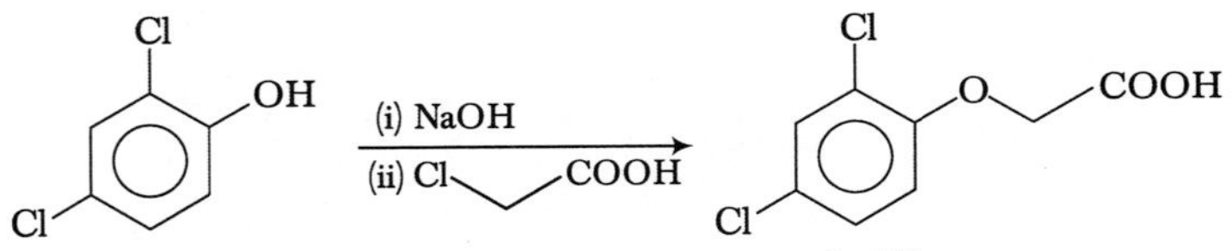

2, 4-D

2. 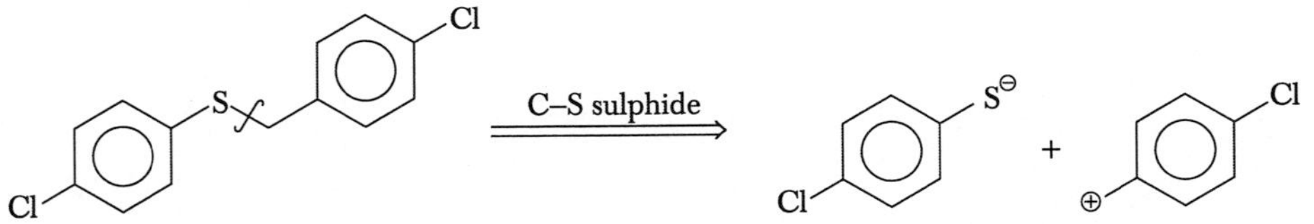

Chlorbenside Synthons

5. 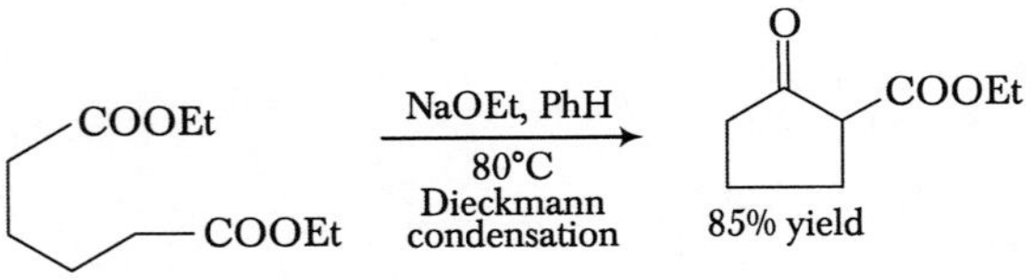

9. 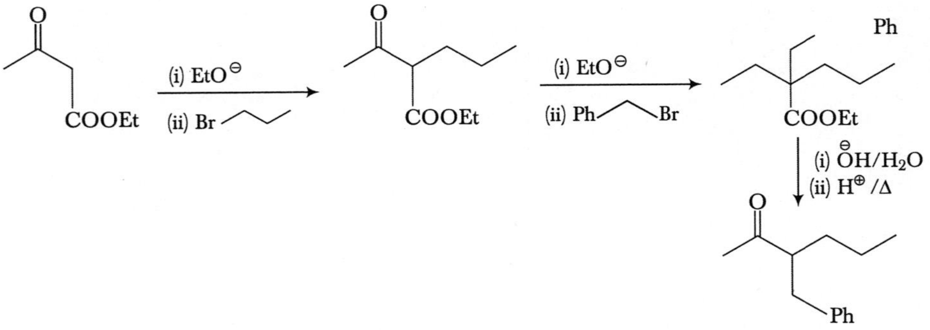

20. 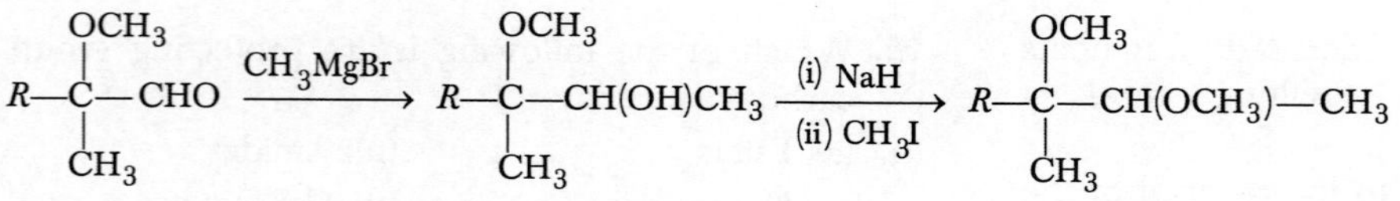

26. 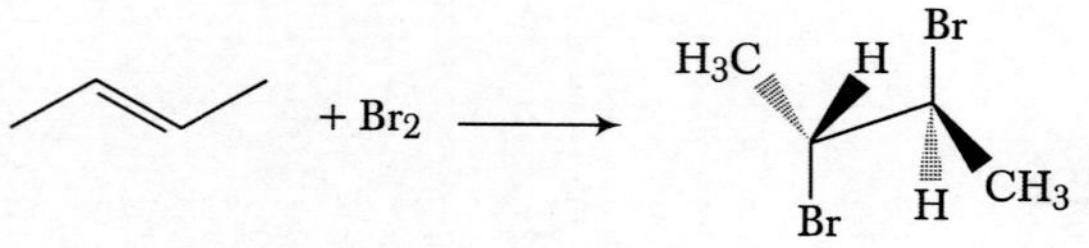

meso

Exercise 2

9. Methylethylamine cannot be resolved into enantiomers because it undergoes rapid inversion.

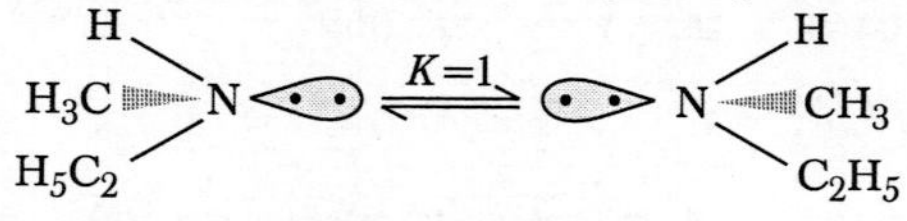

10. Compound II has α-carbon chiral while in compound IV, N is stereocentre.

12. The amine is chiral and its pure enantiomer, when treated with racemic acids, will produce a pair of diastereomers of salt.

35

Pericyclic Reactions

Syllabus

- Electrocyclisation, Cycloaddition, Sigmatropic Rearrangements and Other Related Concerted Reactions
- Principles and Applications of Photochemical Reactions in Organic Chemistry

Introduction

In organic reactions usually a covalent bond break either homolytically or heterolytically followed by the formation of new bond. The mechanism of such reaction may either be free radical or ionic involving the reaction intermediate

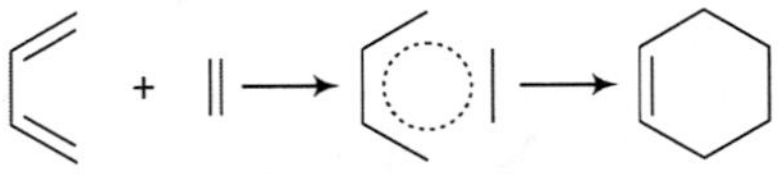

Cyclic transition state

in the form of free radicals or ions. However there is another type of mechanism in which electrons (usually 6 sometimes 4 or some other number) move in a closed ring. There are no intermediates (ions or free radicals) formed and it is impossible to say whether the electrons are paired or unpaired. Such reactions are cyclic concerted (*i.e.,* complete in one step), have a cyclic transition state, attended by a high degree of stereo selectivity and may, be then are reversible also. All such concerted reactions which proceed *via* cyclic transition state are known as **pericyclic reactions.**

Pericyclic reactions are divided into five categories :

1. Cycloaddition reaction
2. Electrocyclic reaction
3. Sigmatropic reaction
4. Cheletropic reaction
5. Group transfer and elimination reactions.

Principle of Conservation of Orbital Symmetry or Woodword Hoffman Rules

The theory of pericyclic reactions was developed by Woodward and Hoffman. Woodward Hoffman selection rules are based on the principal of conservation of orbital symmetry. Some reactions are symmetry allowed while other are symmetry forbidden or dissolved. Hoffman rule apply only to concerted mechanisms. The best way to follow these rules is by Frontier orbitals and orbital symmetry. According to this for a molecule, it is HOMO (Highest

Occupied Molecular Orbital) which is key to determine reactivity and hence it is called **Frontier Orbital.** The theory is based on the following points :

1. The ground state of all molecules has a pair of electrons in HOMO. The HOMO of one molecule interact with the LUMO (Lowest Unoccupied Molecular Orbital) of the other molecule.

   $$\text{HOMO} + \text{LUMO} \longrightarrow \text{Product}$$

2. The positive lobes of one orbital overlap with the positive lobes of another orbitals and likewise the negative lobes of one orbital can overlap with the negative lobes of another orbital. The positive lobe of an orbital can't overlap with the negative lobe of another molecule or *vice-versa.*

3. The way in which this mode of overlap achieve however depends on the number of II electron involved in the reaction and also whether the reaction is either thermal or photochemical.

   For thermally controlled intramolecular cyclization the reactant molecule assumed to be in a vibrationally excited ground state and that the $2\pi e^-$ in the highest occupied molecule orbital (HOMO) are involve in the formation of the new σ bond.

   For photochemically control intramolecular cyclisation the reactant molecules is in its first electronic excited state *i.e.,* π, $\overset{*}{\pi}$ and the $2e^-$ (one in the highest occupied bonding molecular orbital and the other in the lowest unoccupied antibonding molecular orbital) are involved in the formation of new σ bond.

4. Orbitals of same symmetry interact *i.e.,* a symmetric orbital will interact only with a symmetric orbital and an antisymmetric orbital will interact only with an antisymmetric orbital.

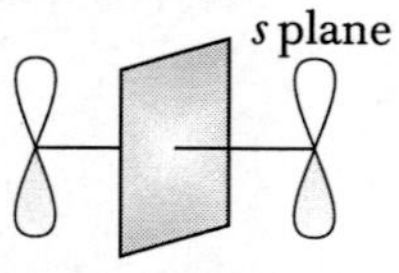

(Bonding M.O.)

The bonding M.O. of ethylene is symmetric with respect to a vertical plane (σ). That is one half of the M.O. is a reflection of the other half.

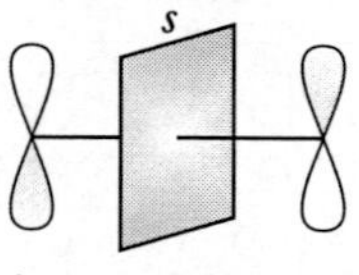

(Anti-bonding M.O.)

The anti-bonding M.O. is anti-symmetric with respect to σ plane, that is one half is not a mirror image of the other.

Similarly we can find out symmetric (S) or anti-symmetric (A) property of M.O.'s of butadiene. Two MO's of butadiene are shown on the left and the M.O.'s of ethylene on the right in the Figure 35.1.

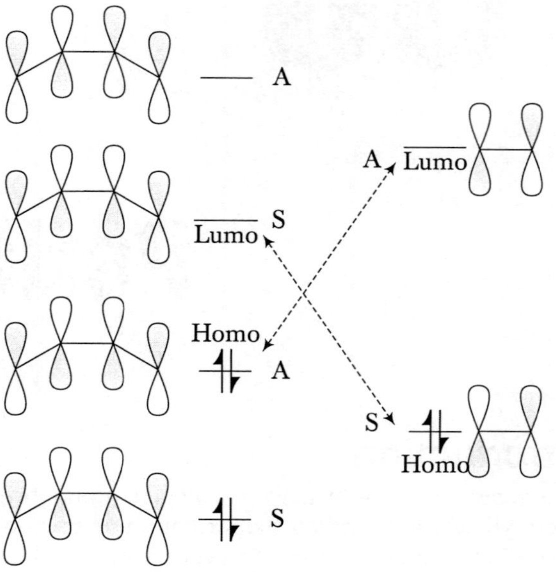

Fig. 35.1

According to Woodward Hoffman theory, the HOMO of butadiene can interact with the LUMO of ethylene in a cyclo addition reaction provided there is a symmetry match.

Note The orbital symmetry rule predicts that [2 + 2] cycloaddition is thermally forbidden and photochemically allowed.
[2 + 4] cyclo addition is thermally allowed and photochemically forbidden.
[4 + 4] cyclo addition is thermally forbidden and photochemically allowed.
[4 + 6] cylco addition is thermally allowed and photochemically forbidden.

5. Cyclo addition reaction can be classified according to facility of the interacting orbital *i.e.,* the classification is based on whether the addition is 'suprafacial' or 'antarafacial' with respect to a particular reactant.

Table 35.1 **Woodward Hoffman Rule for $(i + j)$ Cycloadditions**

$i + j$	Thermal	Photochemical
$4n(2 + 2m, 4 + 4, \ldots)$	Supra, antara Antara, supra	Supra, supra Antara, antara
$4n + 2(4 + 2, 6 + 4 \ldots)$	Supra, supra	Supra, antara
(n is an integer)	Antara, antara	Antara, supra

Table 35.2 **Woodward Hoffman Rules for Electrocyclic Reactions**

Number of π electrons	Reaction	Motion
$4n$	Thermal	Conrotatory
$4n$	Photochemical	Disrotatory
$4n + 2$	Thermal	Disrotatory
$4n + 2$	Photochemical	Conrotatory

Electrocyclic Reactions

Under the influence of heat or light, a conjugated polyene can undergo isomerization to form a cyclic compound with a single bond between the terminal carbons of the original conjugated system; one double bond disappears and the remaining double bond shift their positions.

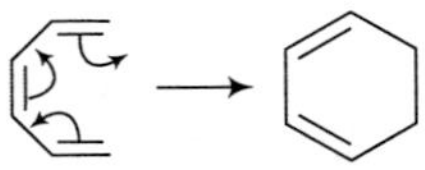

The reverse process can also take place. A single bond is broken and a cyclic compound yields an open-chain polyene,

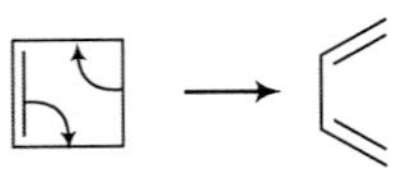

Such interconversions are called **electrocyclic reactions.** These reaction are completely stereospecific and stereoselective.

The stereochemistry depends upon the number of double bond in the polyene and whether the reaction is thermal or photochemical.

Note A stereospecific reaction is one where a given isomer gives one product while another stereoisomer gives the opposite product.

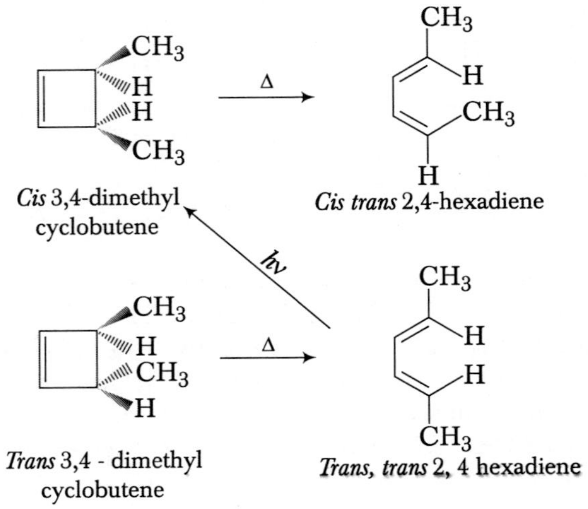

Similarly, the interconversions of dimethyl cyclohexadienes and 2, 4-octatrienes are also stereospecific.

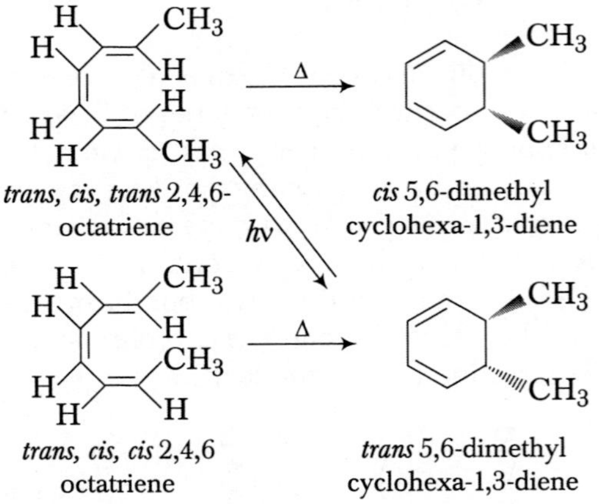

Let us examine these reactions more closely. The formation of the stereopecific products can be visualized in terms of overlap of orbitals on the terminal carbon atoms of the polyene. To maintain this stereospecificity, there must be rotation about the two bonds C_1-C_2 and C_3-C_4 in the case of conjugated butadiene (or C_1-C_2 and C_5-C_6 in the case of conjugated hexadiene). These can be represented as follows :

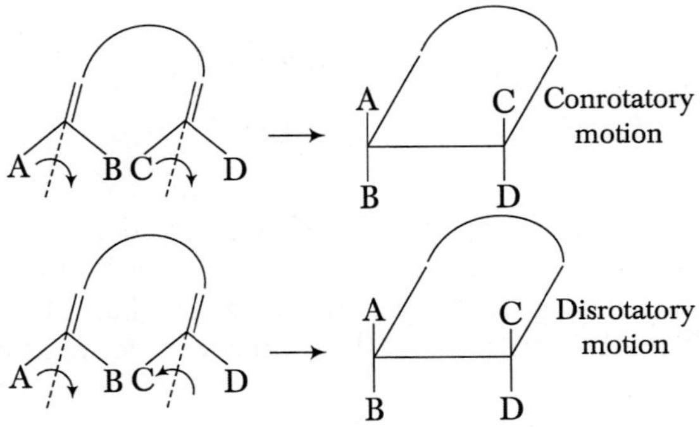

In conrotatory motion, bonds rotate in the same direction and in disrotatory motion, bonds rotate in the opposite directions. Conotatory motion brings together lobes of the same phase, thus, overlap occurs and a bond forms. On the other hand disrotatory motion brings together lobes of opposite phase and interaction is antibonding and repulsive. Hence, it is conrotatory motion that produces the stereochemisty actually observed.

Thermal Cyclisation of Conjugated Butadiene

The HOMO of a conjugated diene involved in cyclisation is ψ_2.

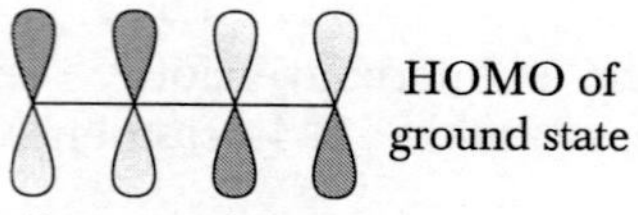

Conjugated diene

Bond formation between C_1 and C_4 required for cyclisation can occur only if the lobes of C_1 and C_4 are in overlapping position. The lobes as clear from the diagram can be in overlapping position (*i.e.,* positive with positive or negative with negative) only when there is a rotation about two bond *i.e.,* C_1-C_2 and C_3-C_4. Rotation about these two bond can take place either in the same direction (*i.e.,* conrotatory or in opposite direction (*i.e.,* disrotatory).

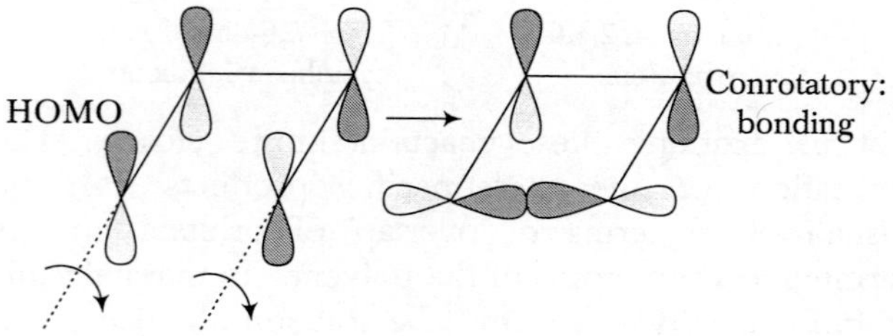

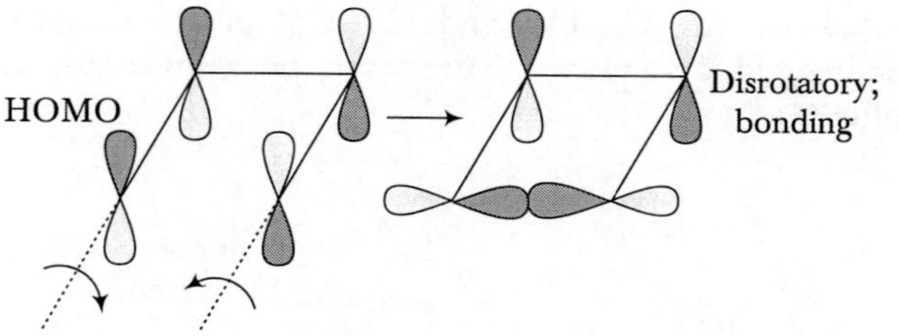

Thus, in thermal cyclisation of conjugated butadiene, conrotatory motion takes place and hence observed stereochemistry of the product must be that which is produced by this motion. The same will be in case of opening of ring.

The example given below show that it is conrotatory motion that produces the stereochemistry actually observed.

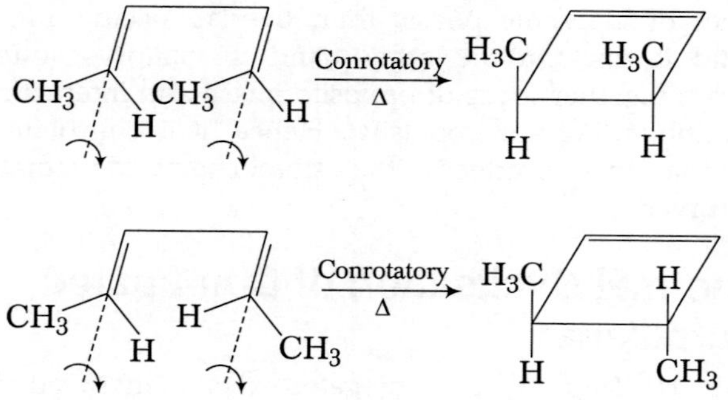

Photochemical Cyclisation of Conjugated Butadiene

On absorption of light, butadiene is converted into the excited state *i.e.,* one electron from ψ_2 has been raised to ψ_3. Now the highest occupied molecular orbital (HOMO) is ψ_3 *i.e.,* frontier lobe.

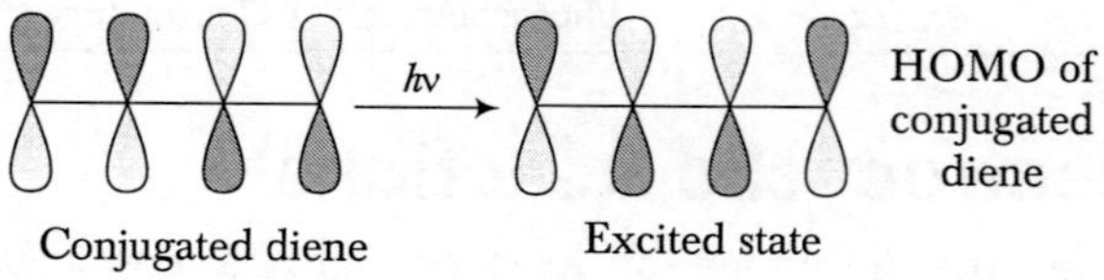

Hence, in the photochemical cyclisation of a 1, 3-butadiene to a cyclobutene, disrotatory motion leads to bonding while conrotatory motion leads to anti-bonding.

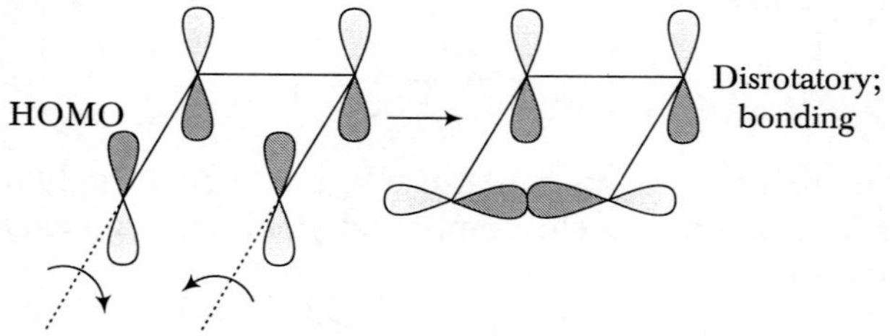

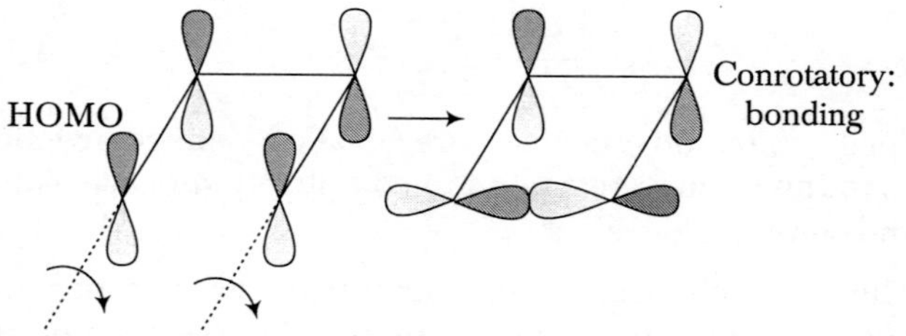

These generalisations have been found to be true by the experimental observations.

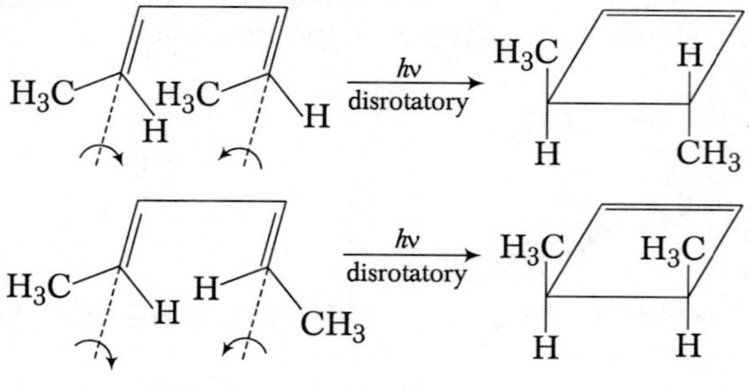

To consider the electrocyclic reactions of disubstituted hexatriene, *R*CH=CH—CH=CH—CH=CH*R* whose electronic configuration is given in figure 35.2, the HOMO for the ground state of the hexatriene is ψ_3. On comparing this with the HOMO for the ground state of butadiene (ψ_2), we see that the relative symmetry about the terminal carbons is opposite in the two cases.

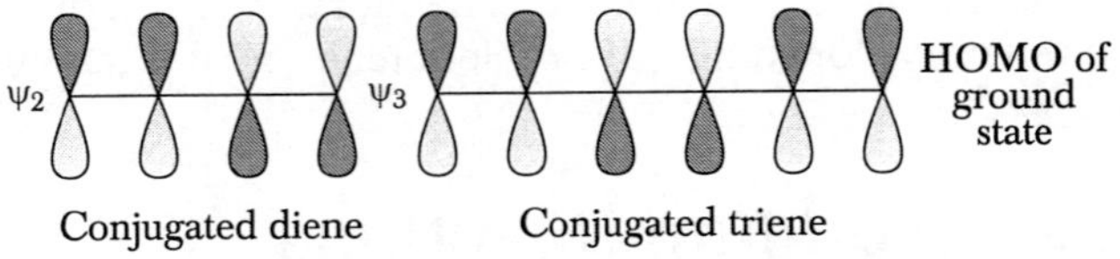

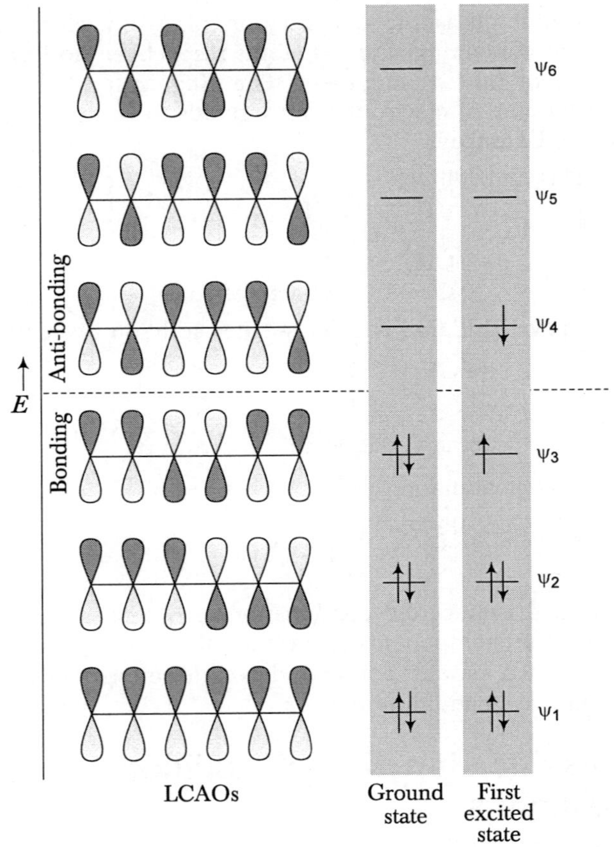

Fig. 35.2 A 1,3,5-hexatriene. Configuration of π electrons in the ground state and the first excited state.

For ground-state hexatriene, it is disrotatory motion that leads to bonding and give rise to be observed

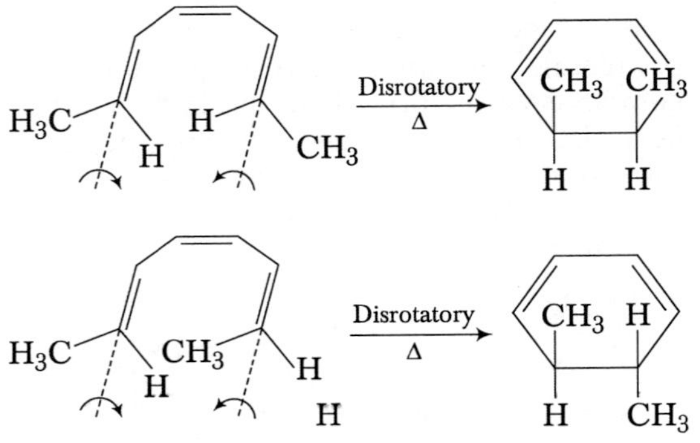

stereochemistry while in the excited state (*i.e.,* in the photochemical conditions) of hexatriene, ψ_4 is HOMO and here conrotatory motion leads to bonding.

In the thermal cyclisation of substituted hexatrienes, observed stereochemistry indicates disrotatory motion.

Hence, the following generalisation is given for electrocyclic reactions. (Woodward Hoffman rules)

No. of π electrons	Reaction	Motion
$4n$	Thermal	Conrotatory
$4n$	Photochemical	Disrotatory
$4n + 2$	Thermal	Disrotatory
$4n + 2$	Photochemical	Conrotatory

Symmetry Control of Electrocyclic Reactions

The two important symmetry operations to be considered are mirror plane (σ) symmetry and C_2 axis of symmetry. Let us apply this to the interconversion of butadiene and cyclobutene.

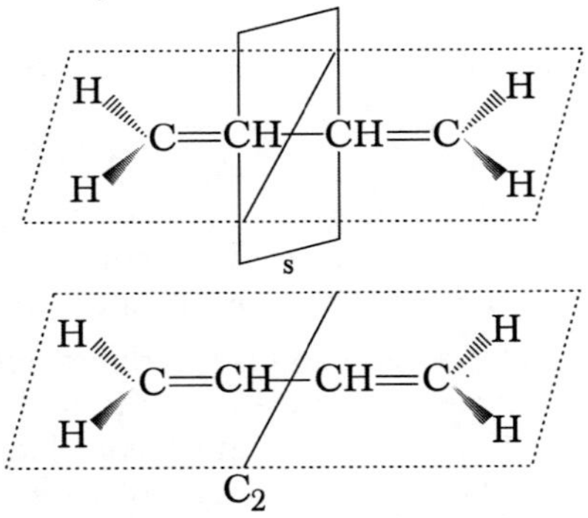

The symmetry and antisymmetric properties of the four molecular orbitals (ψ_1, ψ_2, ψ_3 and ψ_4) are given as :

	σ	C_2
ψ_4	A	S
ψ_3	S	A
ψ_2	A	S
ψ_1	S	A

Similarly for the molecular orbitals of the product cyclobutene *viz* σ, π, $\overset{*}{\pi}$ and $\overset{*}{\sigma}$, the symmetric and antisymmetric properties are given as

	σ	C_2
$\overset{*}{\sigma}$	A	A
$\overset{*}{\pi}$	A	S
π	S	A
σ	S	S

Here the letters S and A refer to the symmetric and antisymmetric character of the orbitals with respect to the two symmetry operations σ and C_2.

According to Woodward and Hoffman, orbital symmetry should be conserved in a concerted reaction. According to this, a symmetric orbital in the reactant transforms to a symmetric orbital in the product and an antisymmetric orbital of reactant transforms to an antisymmetric product orbital.

Let us consider the disrotatory conversion of cyclobutene to butadiene in which plane of symmetry is maintained.

The following correlation diagram can be obtained for the disrotatory conversion of cyclobutene to butadiene.

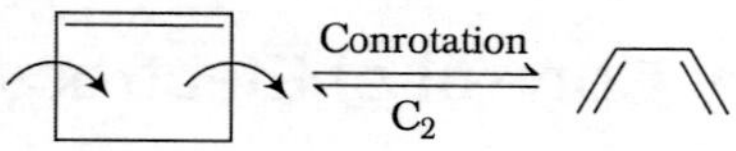

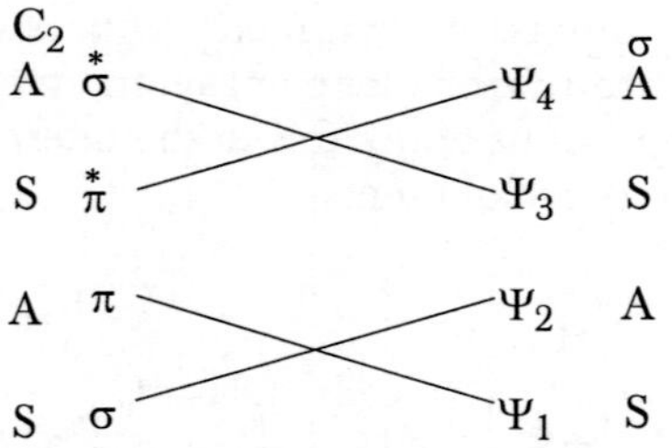

From the correlation diagram, we see that the ground state configuration $\sigma^2\pi^2$ of cyclobutene correlates with $\psi_1^2\psi_3^2$ of butadiene which corresponds to a doubly excited state of butadiene and is clearly an energetically unfavourable process. Since in thermal reactions ground state of the reactant must correlate with the ground state of the product, the disrotatory conversion is symmetry forbidden.

The same reaction under photochemical conditions becomes symmetry allowed as the first excited state configuration of cyclobutene (σ^2 $\pi\pi^*$) correlates with the first excited state $\psi_1^2\psi_2\psi_3$ of butadiene.

Let us now consider the conrotatory conversion of cyclobutane to butadiene. In this reaction, the C_2 axis of symmetry is maintained.

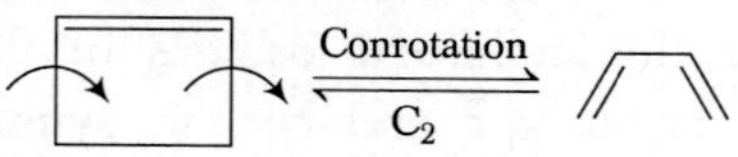

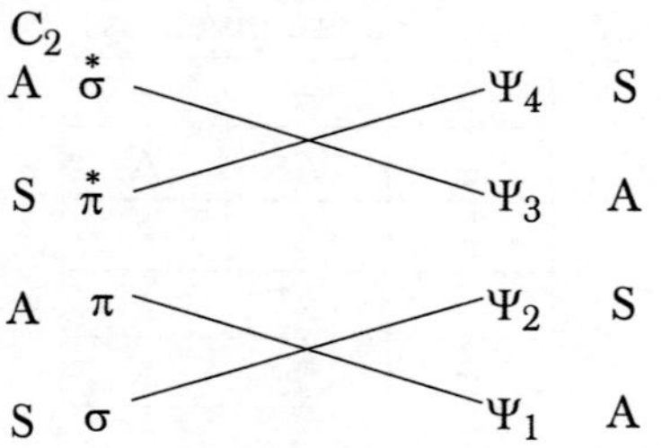

Now the correlation is like this : $\sigma^2\pi^2$ correlates with $\psi_1^2\psi_2^2$ which incidentally is the ground state configuration of butadiene. Therefore, the thermal conrotatory opening of cyclobutene is thermally allowed.

Cycloaddition Reactions

Cycloaddition is the combination of two π electron systems containing m and n atoms respectively to form a ring of $(m + n)$ members. The ring is formed by transference of electrons from π bonds to form new σ bonds. **Examples**

[2 + 2] cycloaddition

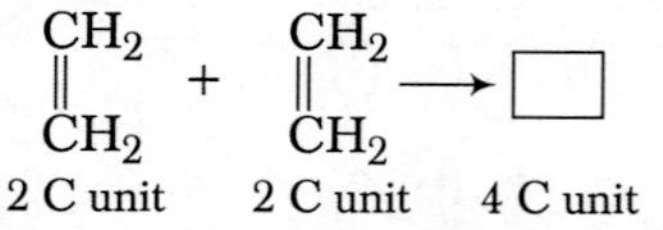

[4 + 2] cycloaddition is a Diels-Alder addition reaction.

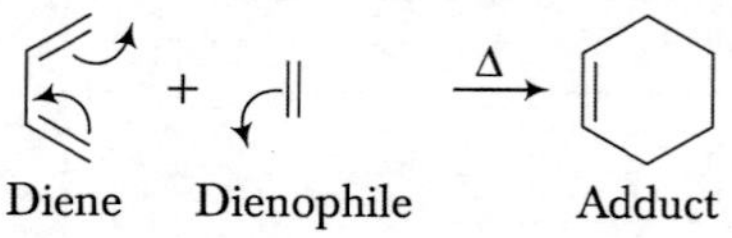

[4 + 4] cycloaddition.

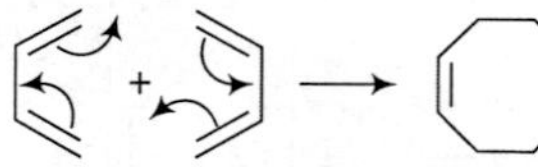

Hence, the concerted combination of two unsaturated (π electron) components to form a stable cyclic product having two new σ bonds and two fewer π bonds is called a cycloaddition reaction.

Classification of Cycloaddition Reactions

They are classified with respect to three aspects of the reaction.

1. The number of electrons in each unit participating in the reaction.
2. The nature of the orbitals (π or σ) undergoing reaction.
3. The stereochemical mode of cycloaddition (supra or antara). In a suprafacial reaction, both bonds to a component are formed (or broken) on the some face. In an antarafacial reaction, the bond are formed on the opposite face of the component. 'Supra' and 'antara' are represented by the symbols '*S*' and '*A*' respectively.

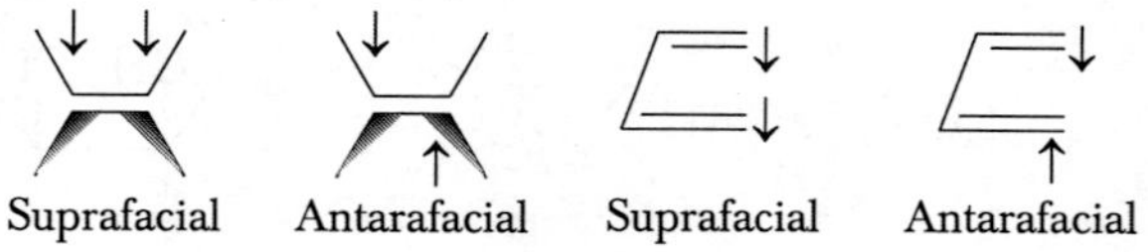

Note The thermal cycloaddition of [4 + 1] is easy and [2 + 2] is difficult. Of [2 + 2] cycloadditions, the thermal reaction is difficult and photochemical reaction is easy.

[4 + 2] Cycloaddition (Diels' Alder reaction)

The [4 + 2] cycloaddition of 1, 3-butadiene and ethylene is the simplest example of the Diels' Alder reaction.

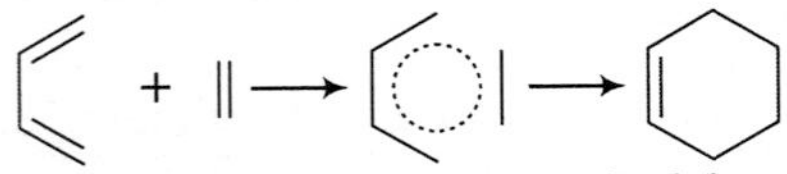

Diene Dienophile Cyclohexane

The electronic configuration of 1, 3-butadiene is given in (Fig. 35.3). For 1, 3-butadiene, with four component *P* orbitals, there are four molecular orbitals for π electrons. The ground state has the configuration ψ_1^2, ψ_2^2; that is, there are two electrons in each of the bonding orbitals, ψ_1 and ψ_2.

Orbital ψ_1 has delocalization of electrons and hence, it is the most stable. The ψ_2 is somewhat less stable owing to isolated orbitals but is more stable than ψ_3 and ψ_4. Absorption of light of the right frequency raises one electron from ψ_2 (HOMO) to ψ_3 (LUMO). It is the first excited state.

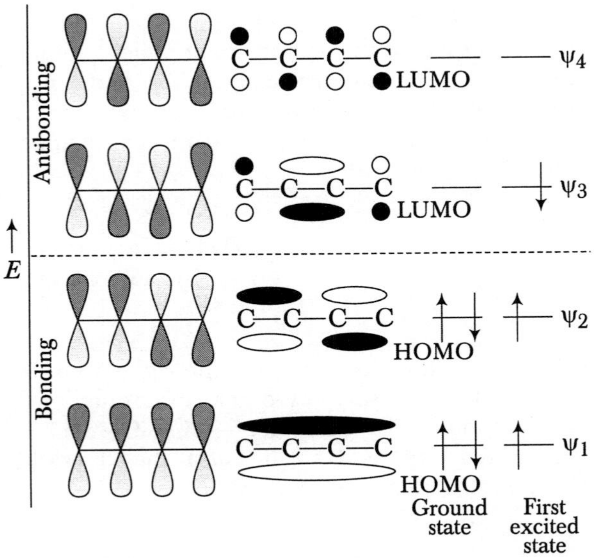

Fig. 35.3 1,3-butadiene, configuration of π electrons in the ground state and the first excited state.

$$\underset{\text{Ground state}}{\psi_1^2\psi_2^2} \longrightarrow \underset{\text{Lowest excited state}}{\psi_1^2\psi_2\psi_3}$$

The electronic configuration of ethylene is given in (Fig. 35.4). With $2p$ orbitals ethene has one bonding and one antibonding molecular orbital.

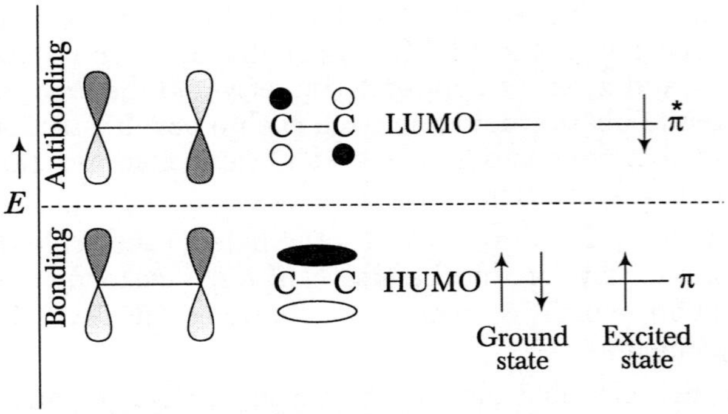

Fig. 35.4 Ethylene configuration of π-electrons in the ground state and the excited state.

From the symmetry of butadiene and ethylene, it is apparent that there are two combination : overlap of the HOMO of butadiene (ψ_2) with the LUMO of ethylene ($\overset{*}{\pi}$); and overlap of the HOMO of ethylene (π) with the LUMO of butadiene (ψ_3). In either case, as Fig. 35.5 shows, overlap brings together lobes of the same phase. There is a flow of electrons from HOMO to LUMO, and bonding occurs.

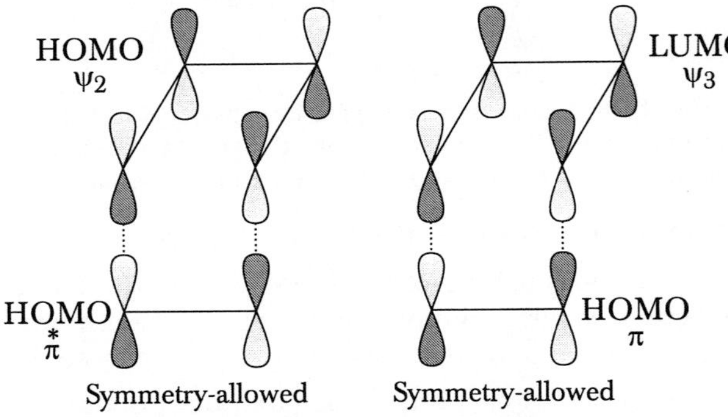

Fig. 35.5 Symmetry-allowed thermal [4 + 2] cycloaddition : 1,3-butadiene and ethylene. Overlap of (a) the HOMO of 1,3-butadiene and the LUMO of ethylene, and (b) the HOMO of ethylene and the LUMO of 1,3-butadiene.

[2 + 2] Cycloaddition

In the presence of heat, [2 + 2] cycloaddition *i.e.,* thermal [2 + 2] cyclization, dimerization of ethylene

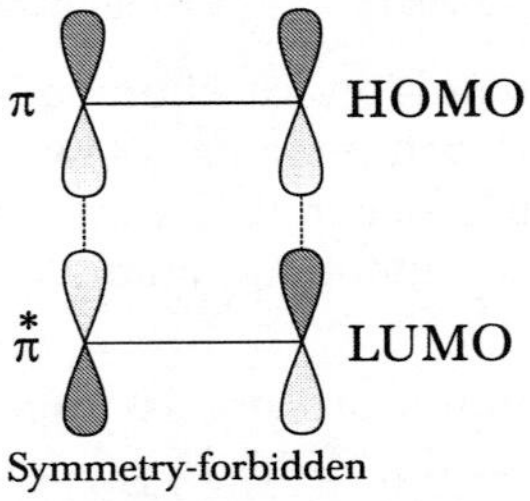

Fig. 35.6 Symmetry-forbidden thermal [2 + 2] cycloaddition : two molecules of ethylene. Interaction is antibonding.

would involve overlap of the HOMO (π) of one molecule with the LUMO ($\overset{*}{\pi}$) of the other molecule. But π and $\overset{*}{\pi}$ are of opposite symmetry and the lobes of opposite phase would approach each other. Interaction is antibonding and repulsive and concerted reaction does not occur. (Fig. 35.6)

However, the dimerisation of ethylene molecule is possible by photochemical [2 + 2] cycloaddition reaction which is symmetry allowed. This can be explained as :

As ethylene molecule absorbs a quantum of light, an e^- jump from HOMO to LUMO resulting in the formation of two singly occupied molecular orbital (SOMO). The excited HOMO [SOMO] hence has the symmetry of LUMO ($\overset{*}{\pi}$) of another molecule and hence the two can interact (Fig. 35.7).

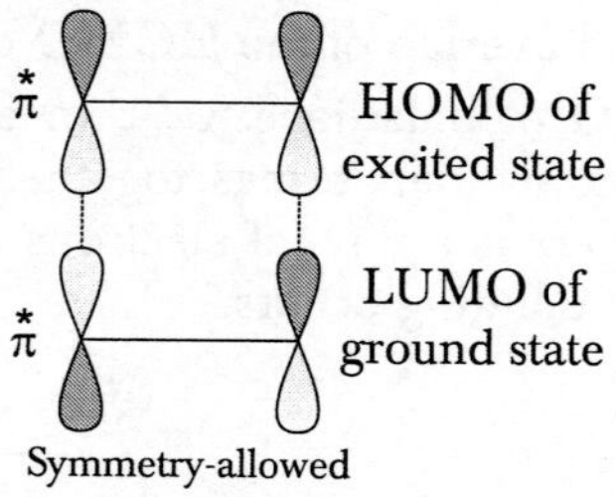

Fig. 35.7 Symmetry-allowed photochemical [2 + 2] cycloaddition : two molecules of ethylene, one excited and one in the ground state. Interaction is bonding.

Suprafacial and Antarafacial Migration

As in cycloaddition reaction, there occur addition of two system having double bond This addition may occur on the same or the opposite side of the system.

If, in a concerted reaction of this kind, both bonds to a component are being formed (or broken) on the same face, the process is said to be *suprafacial.* If the bonds are being formed (or broken) on opposite faces, the process is *antarafacial.*

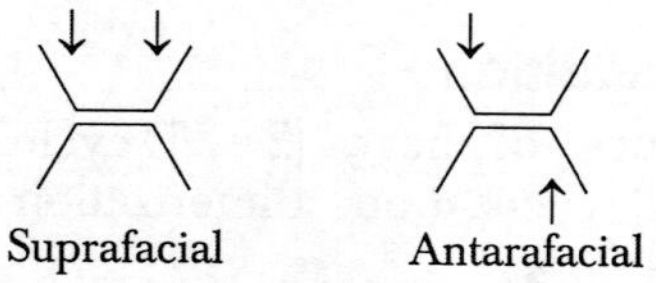

The [2 + 2] cycloaddition reaction is suprafacial with respect to both components. The thermal [2 + 2] cycloaddition could occur if it were suparafacial with respect to one component and antarafacial with respect to the other.

Such a supra, antara process is impossible here on geometric grounds. But if the ring being formed is big enough, both supra, supra and supra, antara processes are geometrically possible.

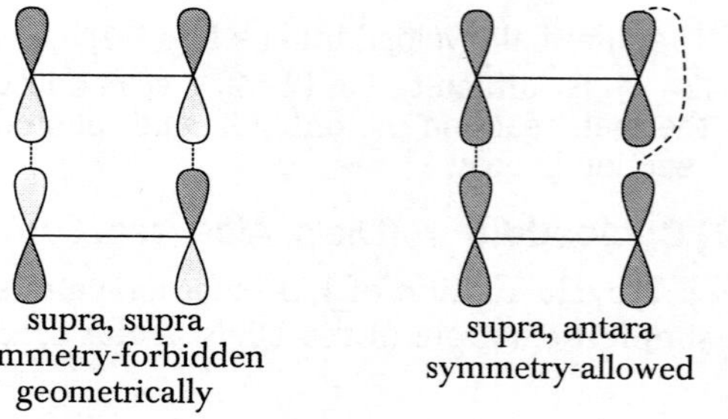

Woodward-Hoffman rules for [*i* + *j*] cycloadditions are as

i + *j*	Thermal	Photochemical
4*n*	supra, antara antara, supra	supra, supra antara, antara
4*n* + 2	supra, supra antara, antara	supra, antara antara, supra

Note There are several aspects to the stereochemistry of Diels, Alder reaction.

The diene must be in the conformation s (s-*cis*) that permits the ends of the conjugated system to reach the doubly bonded carbons of the dienophile.

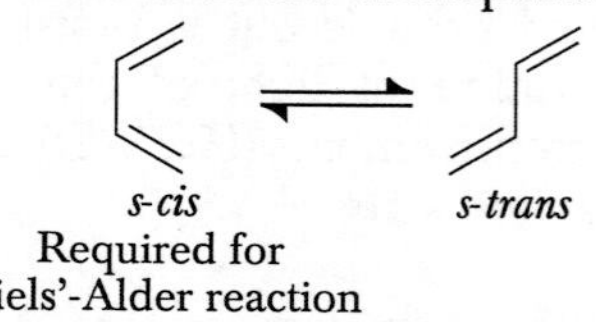

Next, with respect to the alkene (dienophile) addition is clear-cut *syn,* this stereoselectivity is part of the evidence that the Diels-Alder reaction is, indeed, a concerted one, that is both new bonds are formed in the same transition state.

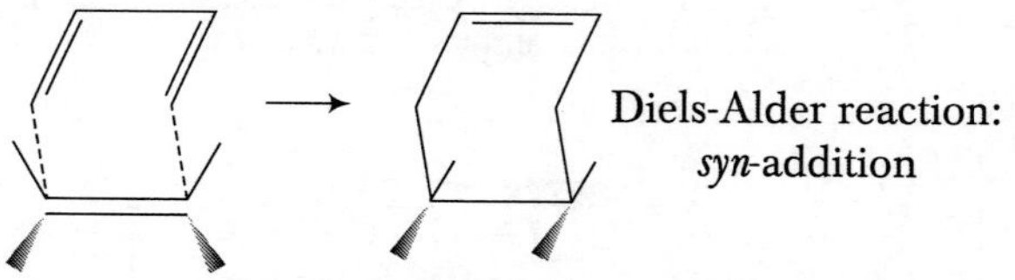

Diels-Alder reaction takes place in the *endo,* rather than *exo,* sense. That is to say, any other unsaturated groups in the dienophile (for example, —CO—O—CO— in maleic anhydride) tend to lie *near* the developing double bond in the diene moiety.

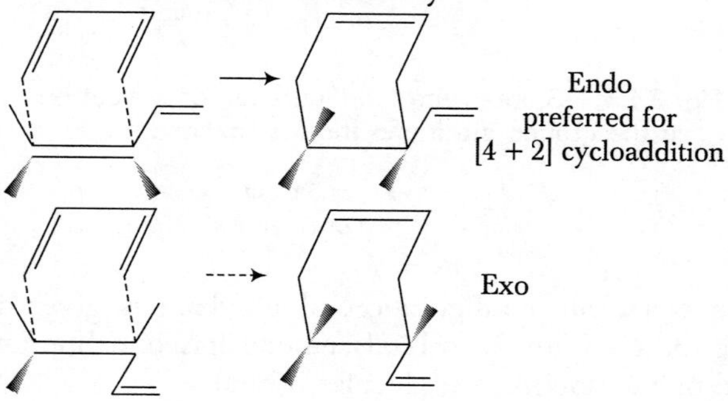

Sigmatropic Rearrangements

Sigmatropy means migration of a sigma (σ) bond. A concerted reaction in which a σ bond migrates along with the group attached to it, to a new position within a π framework (an ene or a polyene) is refered to as sigmatropic rearrangement. This rearrangement is also accompanied by a shift in π bonds. These reactions are classified as [*i*, *j*] order where *i* and *j* refer to the number of atom to which each end of the migrating bond joins.

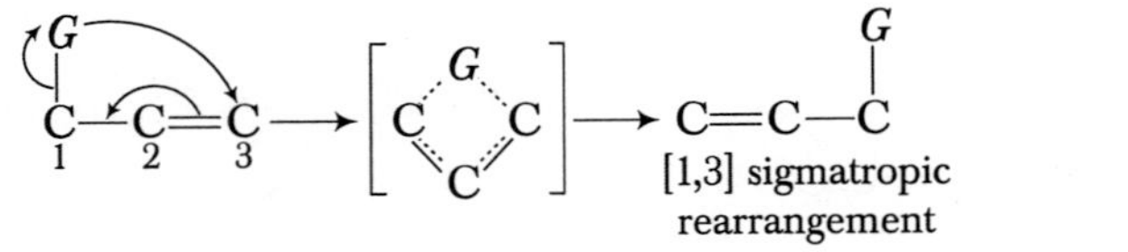

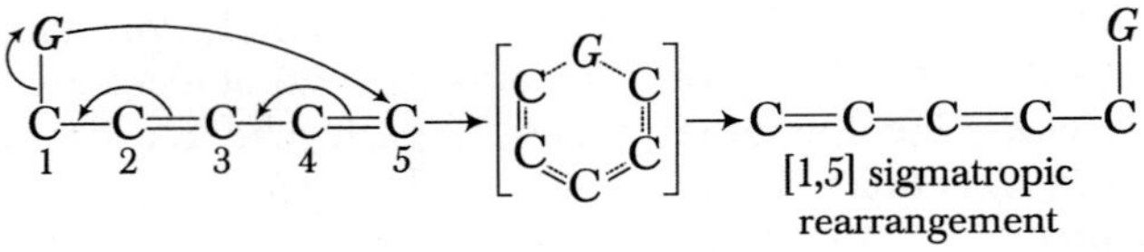

If a sigma bond moves across two parts of a polyene system, the numbers of both the termini are indicated.

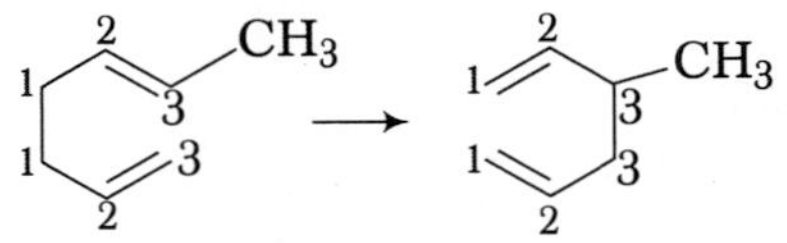
[3, 3] sigmatropic rearrangement

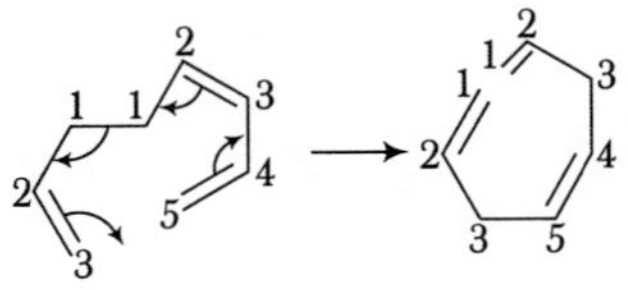
[3, 5] sigmatropic rearrangement

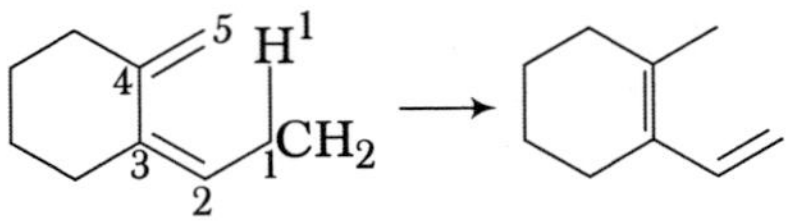
[1, 5] sigmatropic reaction

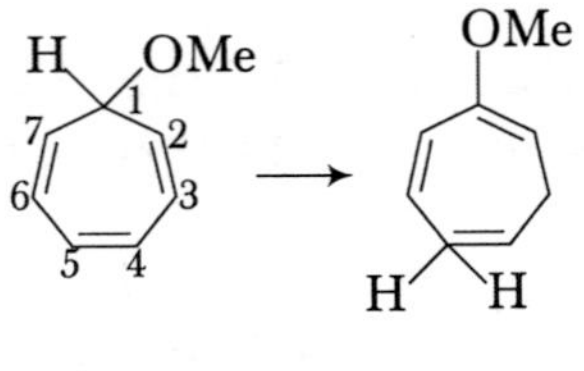
[1, 7] sigmatropic reaction

Note Claisen and cope rearrangement are the examples of order [3, 3]

Sigmatropic Migration of Hydrogen

Stereochemically in a sigmatropic reaction, the migration of hydrogen can be suprafacial or antarafacial.

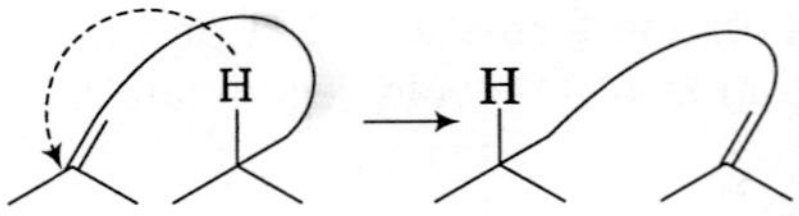
Suprafacial Sigmatropic shift

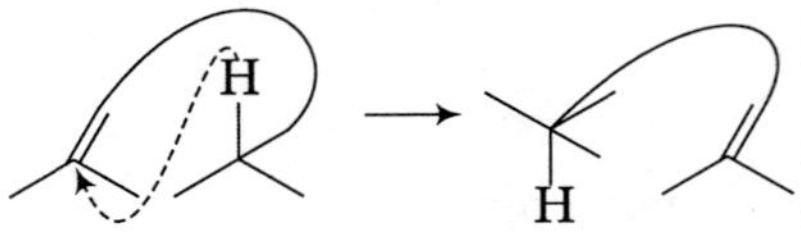
Antarafacial Sigmatropic shift

In the transition state, a *three-center bond* is required, and this must involved overlap between the *s* orbital of the hydrogen and lobes of *p* orbitals of the two terminal carbons. Whether a suprafacial or antarafacial shift is allowed depends upon the symmetry of these terminal orbitals as well as on the geometry of system.

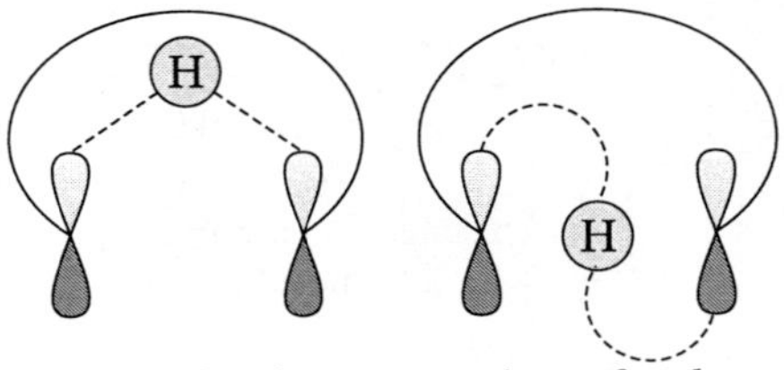
Symmetry-allowed migration of H

Suprafacial

Antarafacial Difficult for [1, 3] or [1, 5] shift

Geometry makes it difficult for the [1, 3] and [1, 5] antarafacial hydrogen shift.

In actual experimental conditions between [1, 3] and [1, 5] hydrogen shift, [1, 3] shift in suprafacial manner is symmetry forbidden whereas [1, 5] suprashift is symmetry allowed.

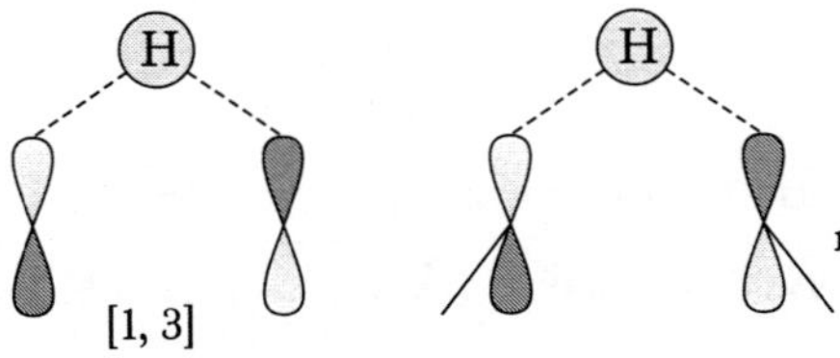
Suprafacial migration of H

[1, 3] Symmetry forbidden

[1, 5] Symmetry allowed

The preference for [1, 5]-H shifts over [1, 3]-H shifts is been demonstrated many times. For example, the heating of 3-deuterioindene (I) scrambling of the label to all three non-aromatic positions. Let us examine this reaction.

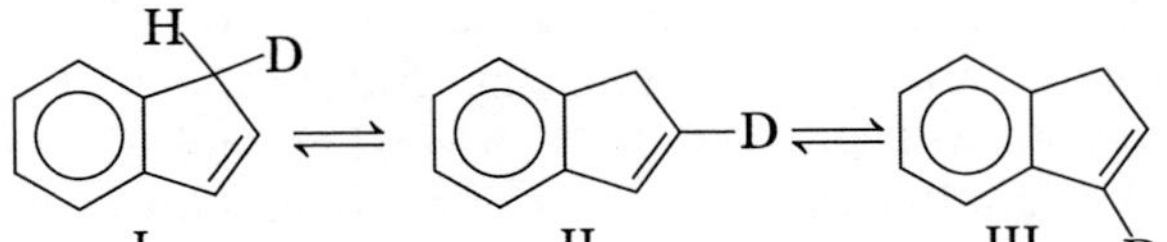
I II III

We cannot account for the formation of II on the basis of [1, 3] shifts. Migration of D would regenerate I.

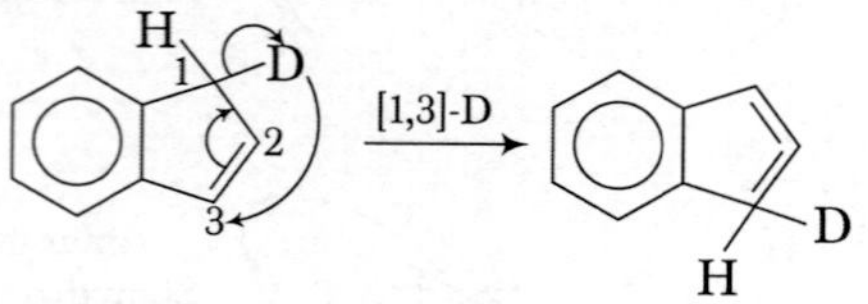

migration of H would yield only III.

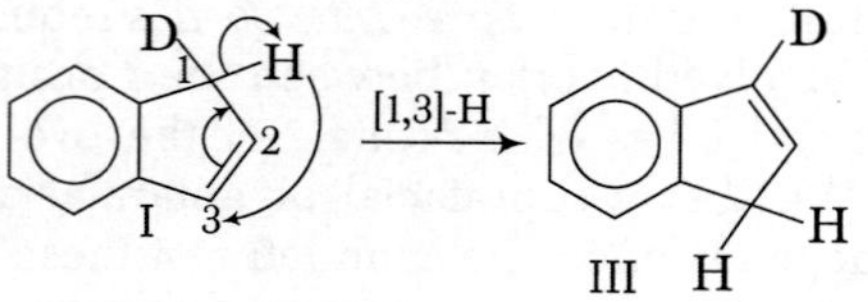

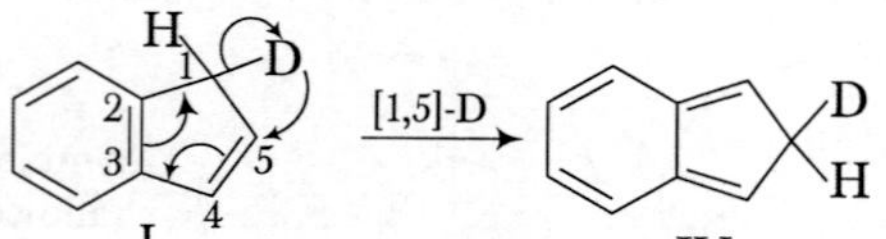

Unstable non-aromatic intermediate

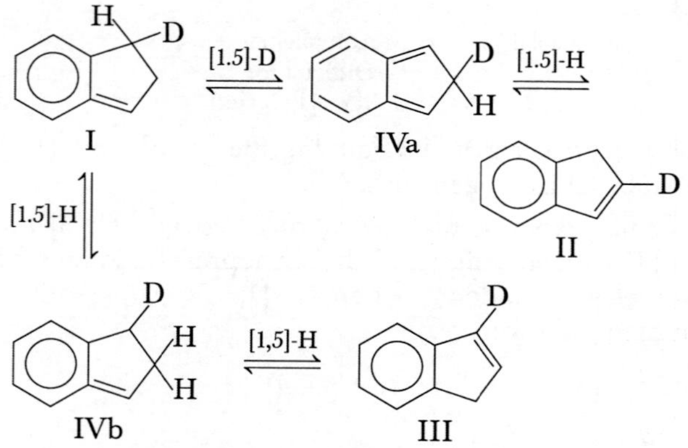

The predicted course for sigmatropic reactions is as :

i, j	Thermal reaction	Photochemical reaction
1, 3	Antarafacial	Suprafacial
1, 5	Suprafacial	Antarafacial
1, 7	Antarafacial	Suprafacial
3, 3	Suprafacial	Antarafacial

Sigmatropic Migration of Carbon

Suprafacial sigmatropic rearrangement in which carbon is the migrating group are always allowed both thermally and photochemically. But thermal [1, 3] migration will proceed with inversion and thermal [1, 5] migration with retention of configuration with in the migrating group.

Generally we can say that suprafacial migration of electron in system where $J = 4n - 1$ proceed with inversion thermally and retention photochemically while in system where $J = 4n + 1$ show that opposite behaviour where antrafacial migration take place all these predications are of course reversed.

Cheletropic Reactions

These are reactions in which two sigma bonds that terminates at a single atom are made or broken in a concerted manner.

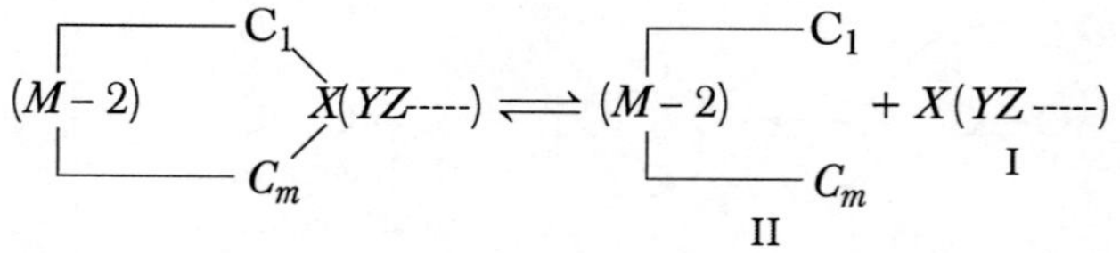

The products of the reaction are (I) a small molecule, $X(YZ\ ...)$ and (II) a polyene containing an m electron π system. Like the other types of pericyclic reactions, these reactions have geometrical aspects and the principle of conservation of orbital symmetry may be used in predicting the detailed course of the reaction.

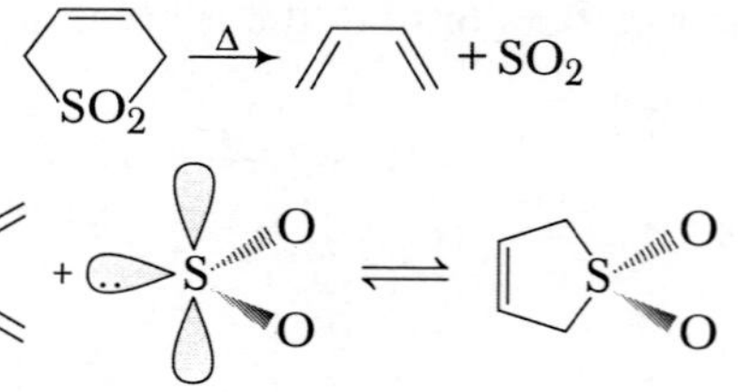

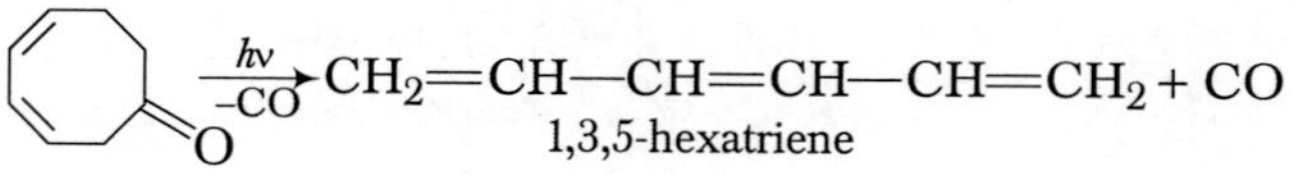

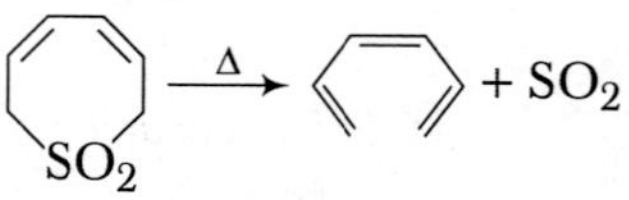

Cope Rearrangement

The thermal isomerisation of 1, 5-dienes by a 3, 3-sigmatropic shift is known as cope rearrangement.

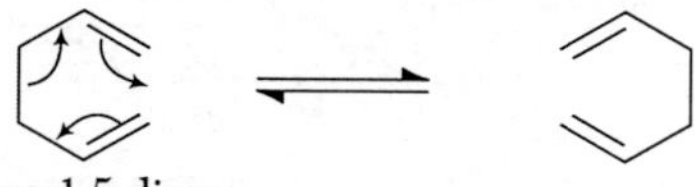

Hexa 1,5-diene

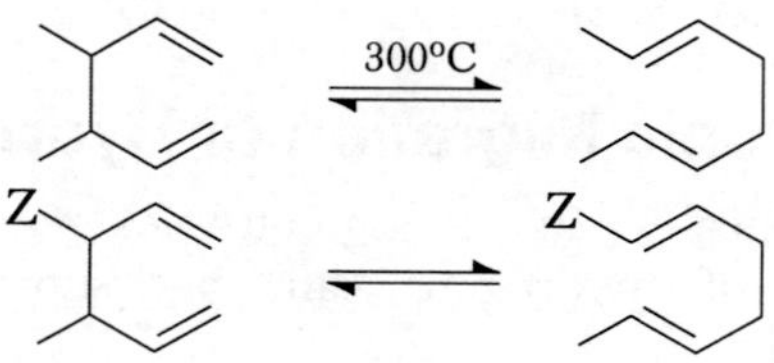

Z may be any substituent such as an alkyl, acyl, aryl group etc.

Groups like acyl, aryl etc., capable of forming conjugation with the πe^- of the product if present at 3 or 4 C-atom, helps the rearrangement to occur comparatively at lower temperature. The rearrangement is reversible *i.e.,* the substrate and the product are present in almost equimolar amount except for when the groups which do not form conjugation with πe^- may be present, the equilibrium is towards the product and rearrangement is not reversible.

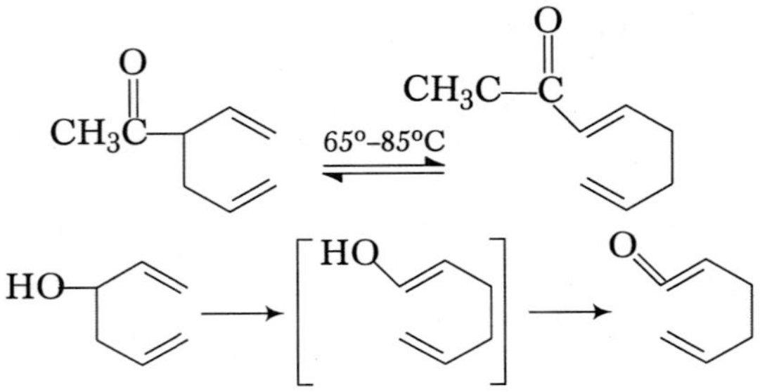

Rearrangement is not reversible due to ketonisation of the product. Hence, thermal rearrangement of 1,5-hexadienes with a hydroxyl substituent at C-3 provides a convenient and useful route for the synthesis of unsaturated aldehydes and ketones. If there are hydroxyl substituents at C-3 and C-4 of dienes, 1,6-dicarbonyl compounds are obtained. Such rearrangement are called **oxy-cope rearrangement.**

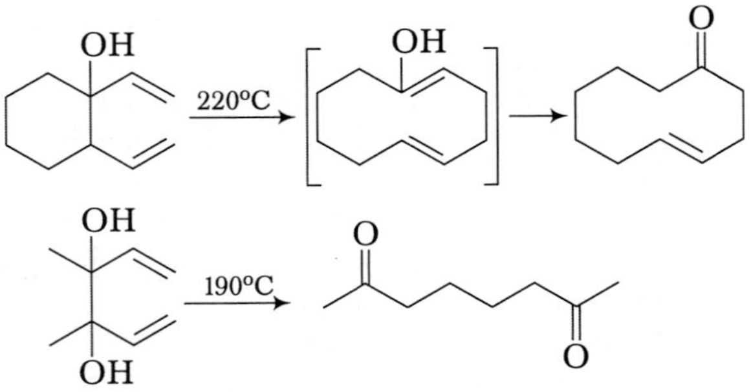

Another type of cope rearrangement is known as **aza-cope rearrangement.**

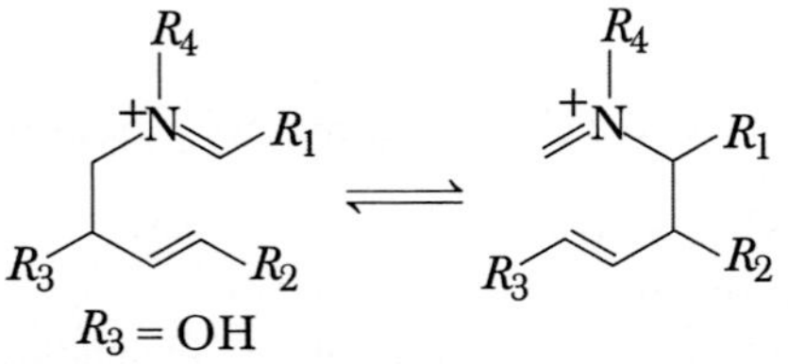

Cyclic 1, 5-diene also undergoes cope rearrangement.

Cyclodeca 1, 2, 6, 7-diene Divinyl cyclohexadiene

Note If one of the = bonds of 1, 5 diene is a part of an aromatic system, the rearrangement does not take place.

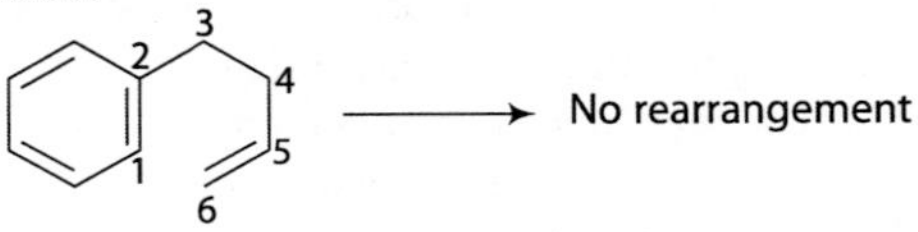

Mechanism

Cope rearrangement proceeds *via* a chair like transition state which is energetically preferred over the boat like transition state by 5.7 kcal/mol. However if the chair transition state is inaccessible than the rearrangement proceeds *via* the boat like transition state.

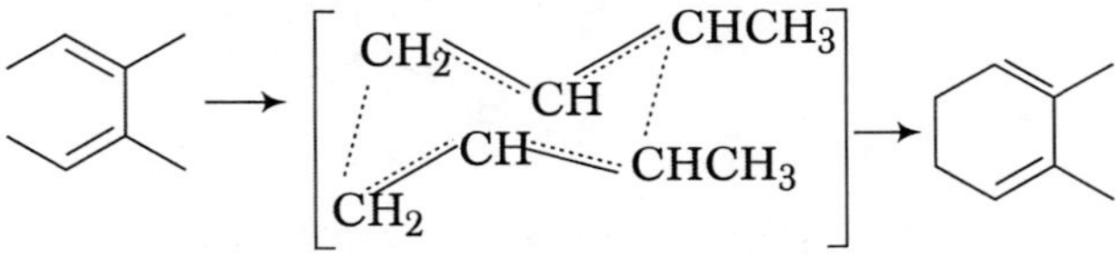

Note Sommelet-Hauser rearrangement is an example of 2, 3-sigmatropic rearrangement.

Claisen rearrangement is a [3, 3] sigmatropic rearrangement.

Ene reaction is a 6π-electrons electrocyclic reaction.

Exercise 1
(For Part 'B')

1. The electrocyclic reaction for ground state of hexatrienes
(a) conrotatory
(b) disrotatory
(c) conrotatory or disrotatory depending on the temperature at which reaction is carried out
(d) Cannot be predicted

2. The thermal ring opening reactions of cyclobutenes are
(a) conrotatory
(b) disrotatory
(c) conrotatory or disrotatory depending on the temperature at which reaction is carried
(d) Cannot be predicted

3. Claisen rearrangement is an example of
(a) [2, 3] sigmatropic rearrangement
(b) [2, 4] sigmatropic rearrangement
(c) [1, 5] sigmatropic rearrangement
(d) [3, 3] sigmatropic rearrangement

4. The product of the following reaction is

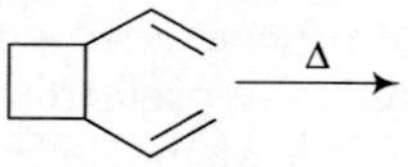

(a) 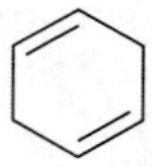 (b) 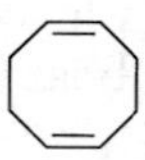

(c) 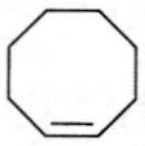 (d) 

5. In sigmatropic thermal expansion of 1, 1-dicyclopropyl ethene, the final product

(a) 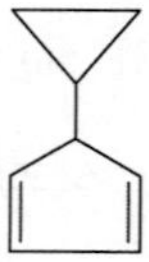 (b) 

(c) 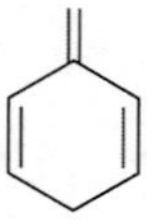 (d) 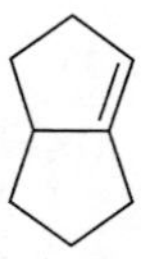

6. Give the structure of the product in the following reaction

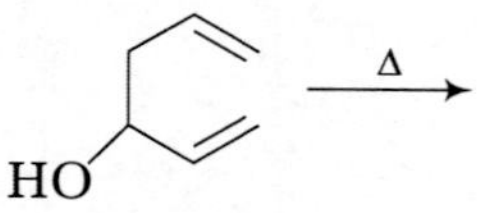

(a) 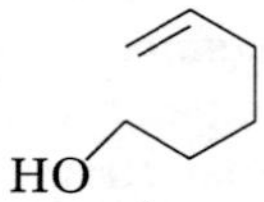 (b) 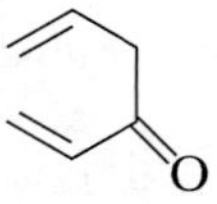

(c) 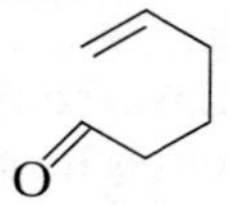 (d) 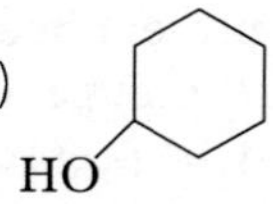

7. The major product of the following electrocyclic addition reaction is

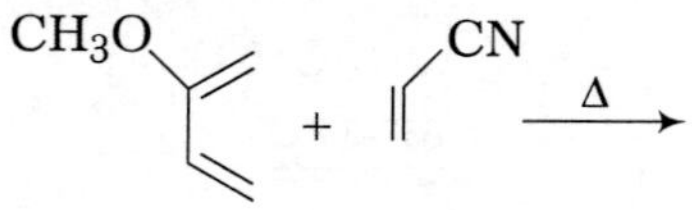

(a) 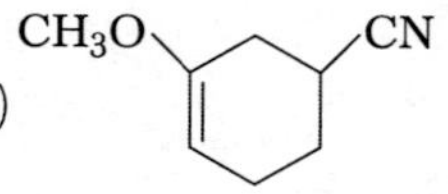 (b) 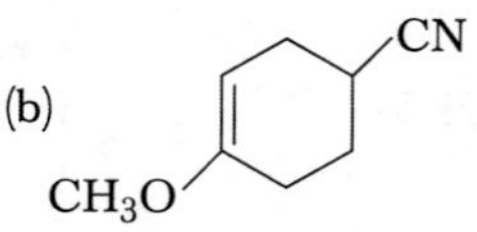

(c) 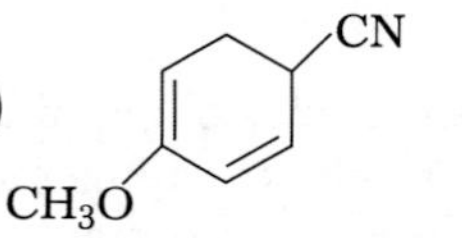 (d) 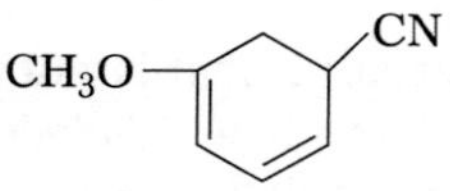

8. In a cycloaddition reaction, if both the bonds to a component are formed on the same face, the process is termed as :
(a) suprafacial (b) antarafacial
(c) suprafacial-suprafacial (d) antarafacial-antarafacial

9. In the reaction of cyclopentadiene with acrylate ester giving Diels-Alder reaction products, the interacting frontier orbitals are
(a) HOMO of a diene and LUMO of a dienophile
(b) HOMO of a dienophile and LUMO of a diene
(c) HOMO of a diene and HOMO of a dienophile
(d) LUMO of a diene and LUMO of a dienophile

10. Diels-alder reaction normally yields endo-adduct as a major product. This is due to
(a) higher stability of the product
(b) faster rate of formation of the endo product
(c) steric hindrance
(d) secondary orbital interactions between a diene and a dienophile

11. Transformation

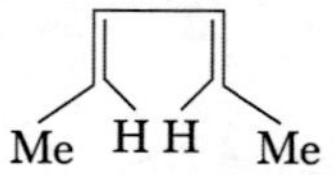 to 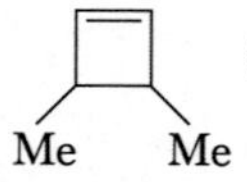 is feasible by a

(a) Thermal disrotatory process
(b) Photochemical disrotatory process
(c) Thermal conrotatory process
(d) Photochemical conrotatory process

12. On heating 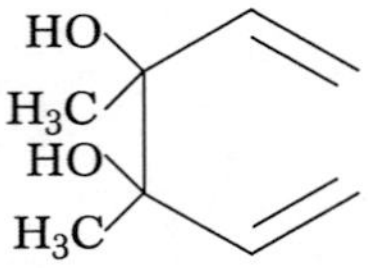

undergoes oxy-cope rearrangement to give

(a) 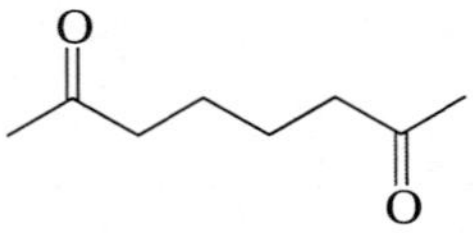

(b) 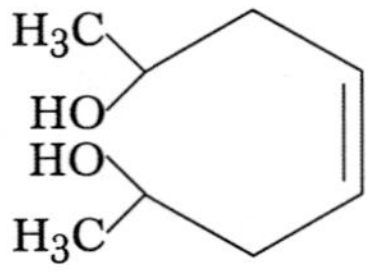

(c) 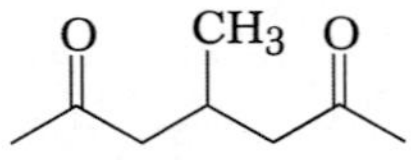

(d) 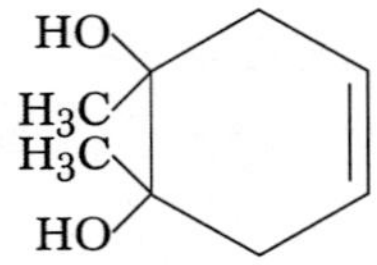

13. The conversion of vinylcyclopropane to cyclopentene upon heating is an example of which of the following sigmatropic rearrangement?

(a) [3, 3] (b) [1, 3]
(c) [1, 5] (d) [1, 2]

14. The following tetraene upon photolysis gives

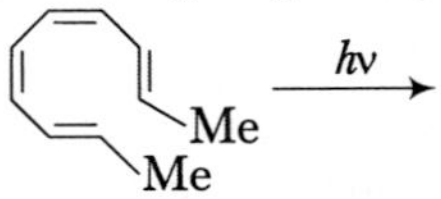

(a) 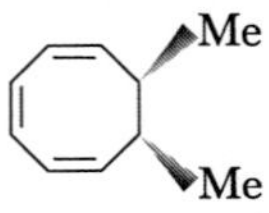

(b) 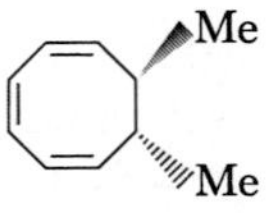

(c) 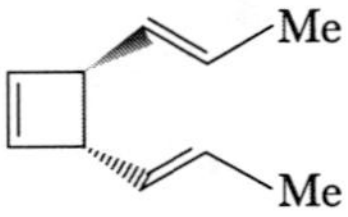

(d) 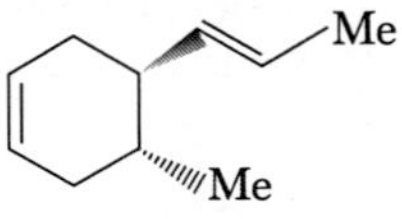

15. The two pericyclic reactions successively involved in the thermal transformation given below

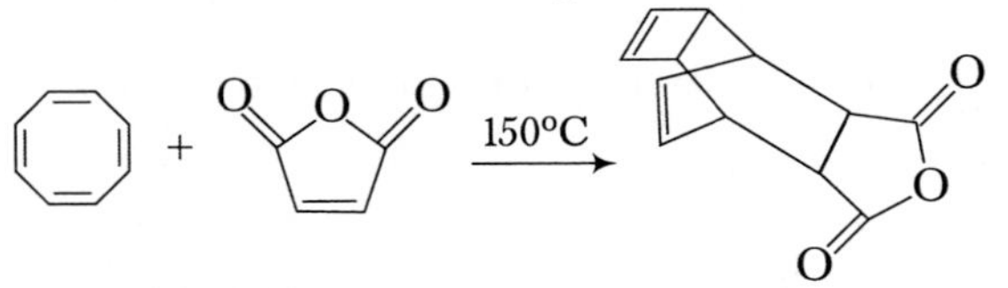

(a) 6π-electrocyclization followed by [4 + 2] π cycloaddition
(b) 8π-cycloaddition followed by [2 + 2] π-electrocylization
(c) 6π-cycloaddition followed by [2 + 2] π-electrocyclization
(d) 4 π-electrocyclization followed by [4 + 2] π-cycloaddition

16. 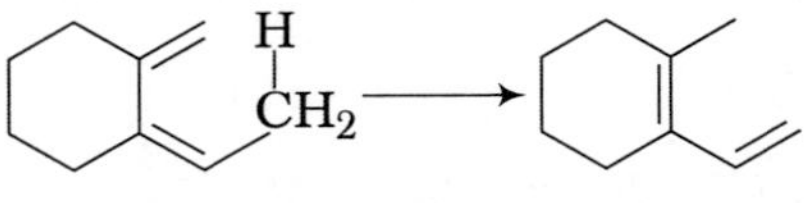

The above sigmatropic reaction is example of
(a) [1, 5] sigmatropic reaction
(b) [1, 4] sigmatropic reaction
(c) [2, 3] sigmatropic reaction
(d) [2, 5] sigmatropic reaction

17. Which one among the dienes A-D will undergo [3, 3] sigmatropic shift upon heating

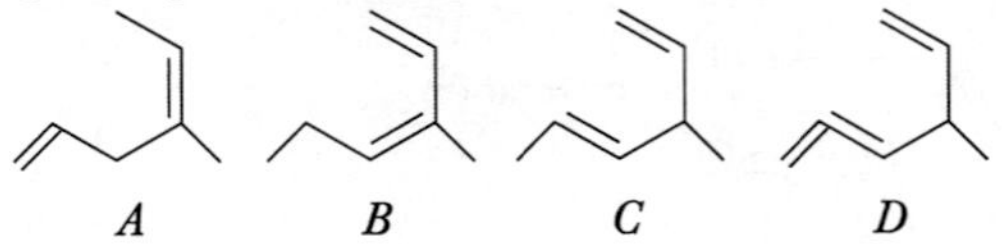

(a) A (b) C
(c) D (d) B

18. The LUMO of the ground state buta-1, 3-diene is

(a) 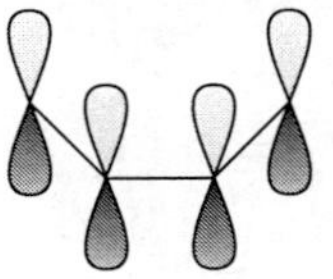

(b) 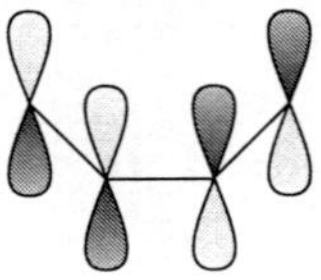

(c) 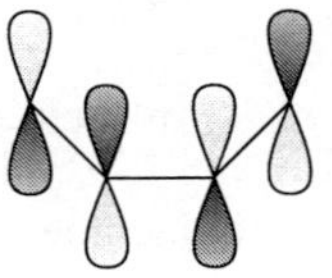

(d) 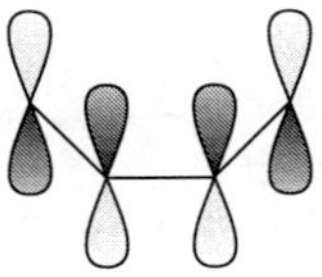

19. 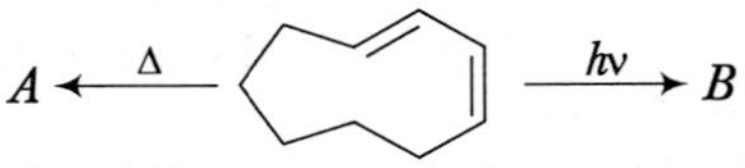

A and *B* are respectively

(a) 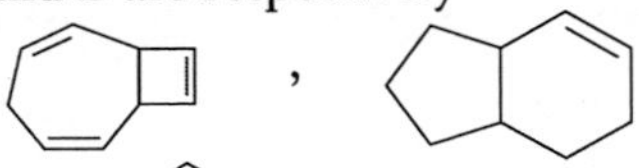

(b) 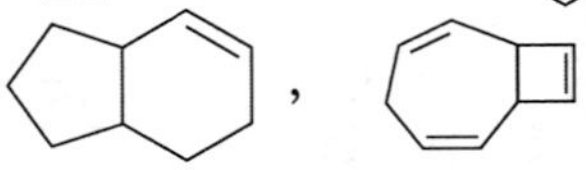

(c) 

(d) 

20. Diels-alder reaction is a
(a) [2 + 2] thermal cyclization
(b) [4 + 2] photoaddition
(c) [4 + 2] cycloaddition
(d) [3 + 3] cycloaddition

21. The products *Y* and *Z* are formed, respectively, from *via*

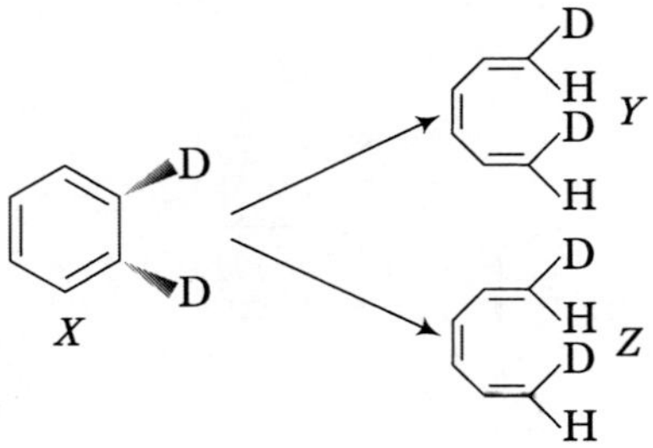

(a) *hv*, conrotatory opening and Δ, disrotatory opening
(b) *hv* disrotatory opening and Δ conrotatory opening
(c) Δ conrotatory opening and *hv* disrotatory opening
(d) Δ disrotatory opening and *hv* conrotatory opening

22. 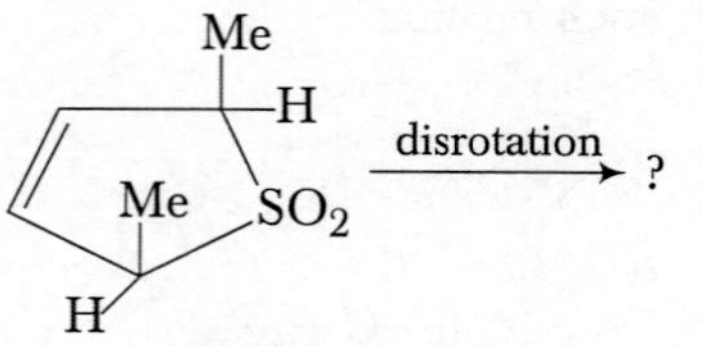

(a) 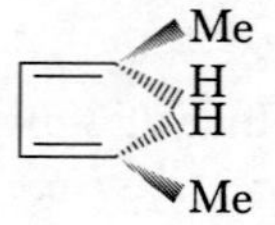 (b) 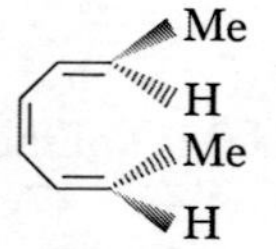

(c) 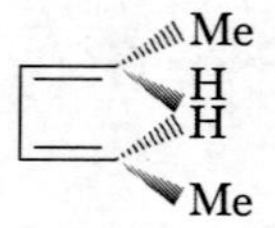 (d) 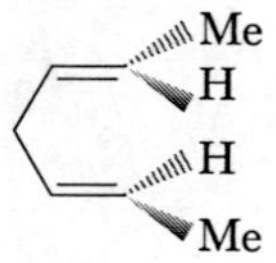

23. In the [4 + 2] cycloaddition of 1, 3-butadiene and ethylene
(a) Overlap of the HOMO of butadiene with the LUMO of ethylene
(b) Overlap of the HOMO of ethylene with the LUMO of butadiene
(c) Both (a) and (b)
(d) None of these

24. 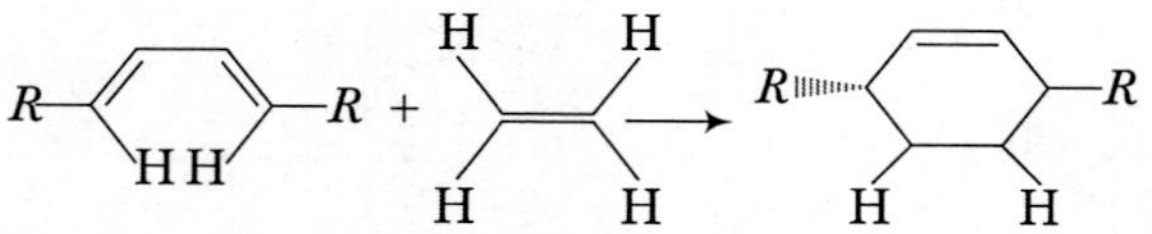

This reaction is an example of
(a) $\pi_s^2 + \pi_a^4$ cycloaddition (b) $\pi_a^2 + \pi_s^4$ cycloaddition
(c) $\pi_a^2 + \pi_a^4$ cycloaddition (d) $\pi_s^2 + \pi_s^4$ cycloaddition

25. The product of the following reaction

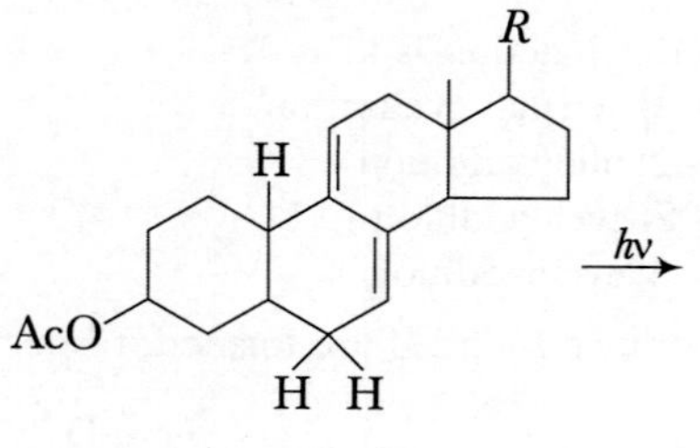

(a) 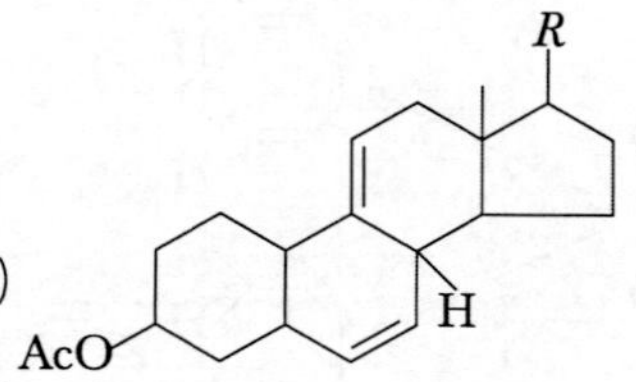

(b) 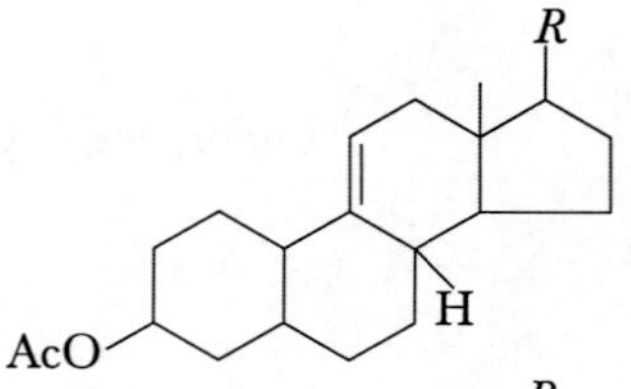

(c) 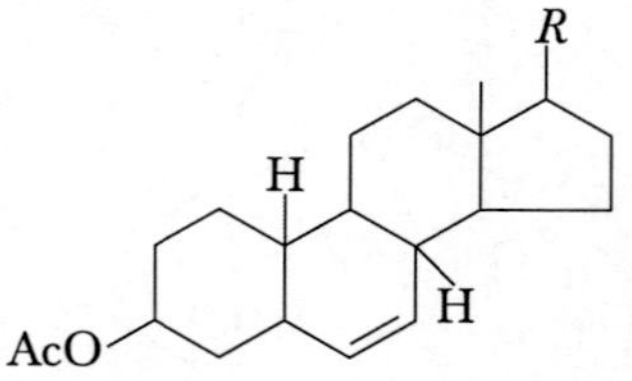

(d) 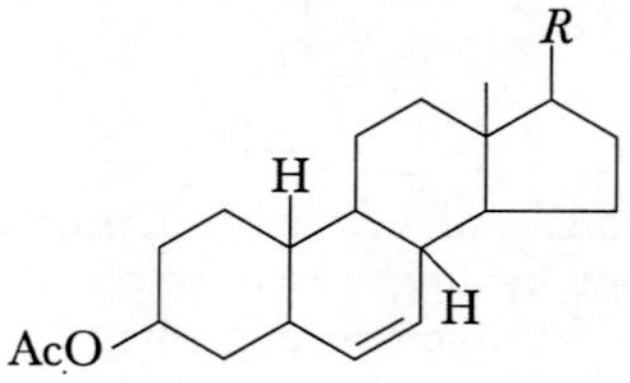

26. 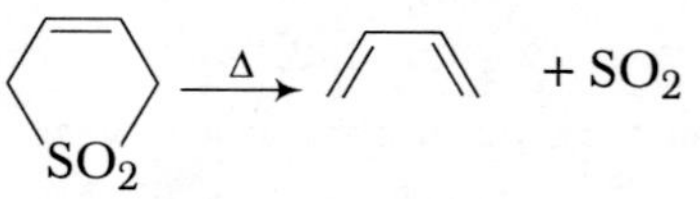

This reaction is an example of
(a) Electrocyclic reaction (b) Cycloaddition reaction
(c) Cheleotropoic reaction (d) Sigmatropic reaction

27. Ene reaction is a
(a) 2π electron electrocyclic reaction
(b) 4π electron electrocyclic reaction
(c) 6π electron electrocyclic reaction
(d) None of the above

28. 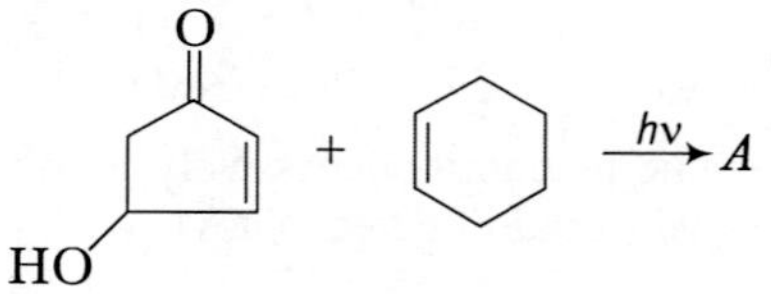

Identify the structure of *A* in the above reaction.

(a) 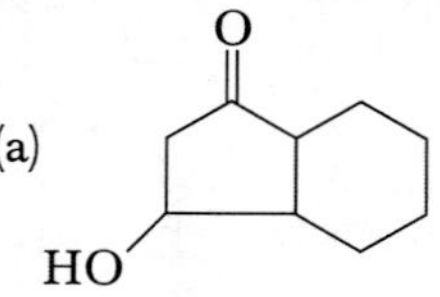 (b) 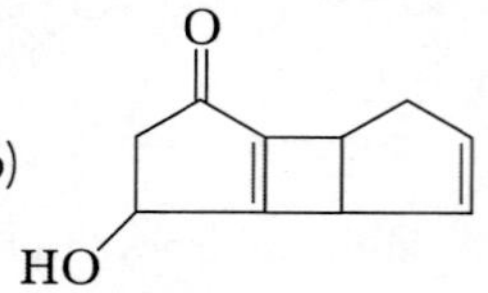

(c) 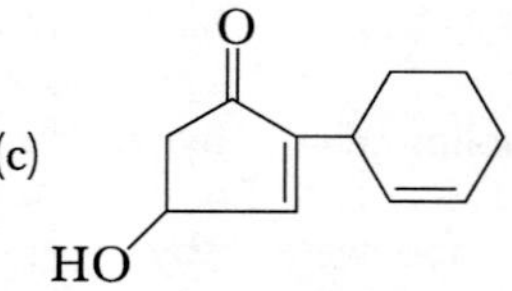 (d) 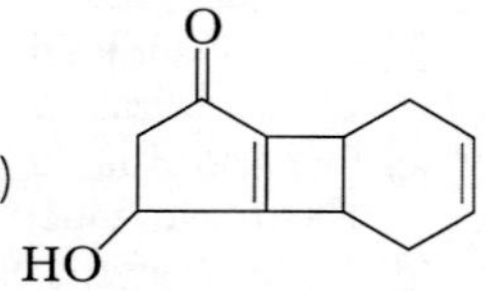

29. What are products *A* and *B* in the following thermal reactions?

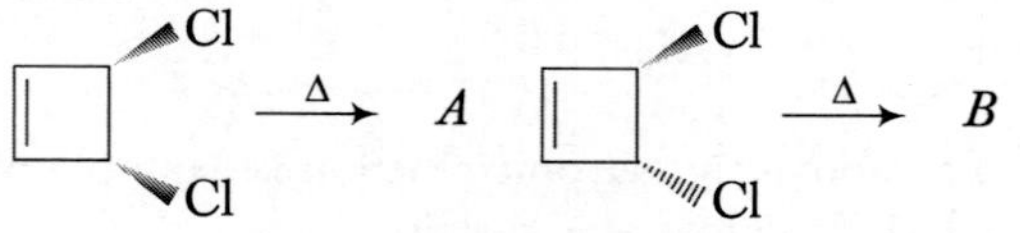

(a) 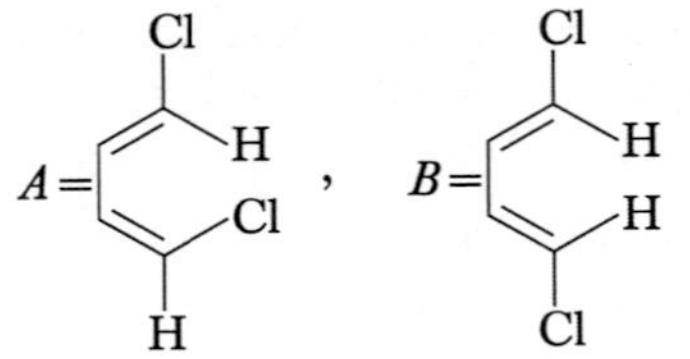

(b) 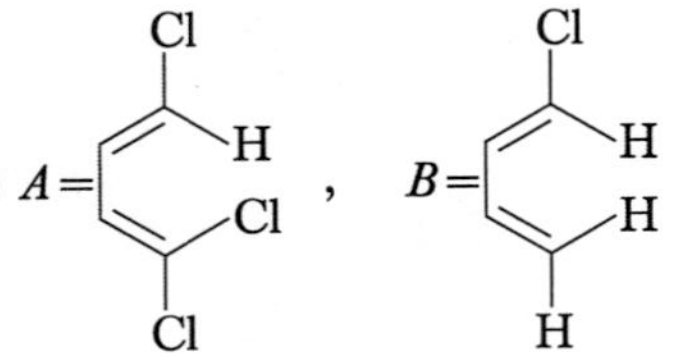

(c) 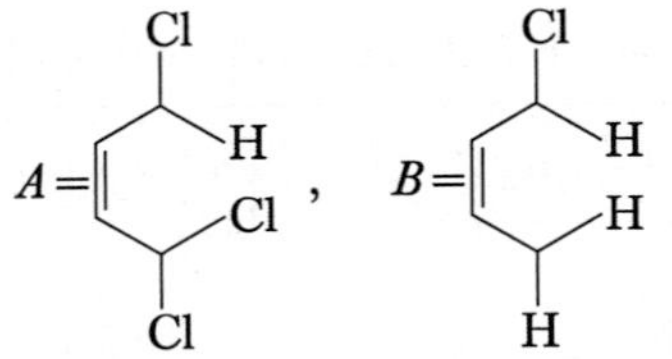

(d) 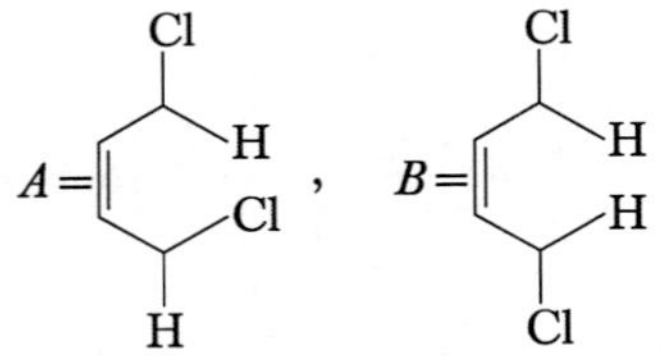

30. The following transformation proceeds by the sequence indicated. Give the structure of product

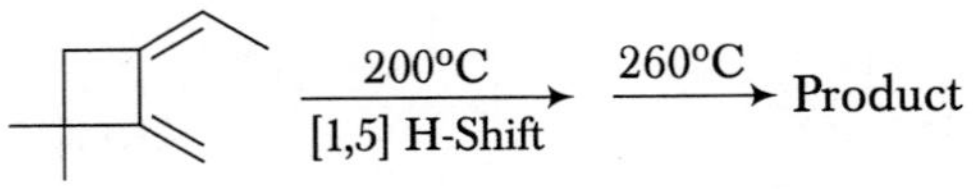

(a) 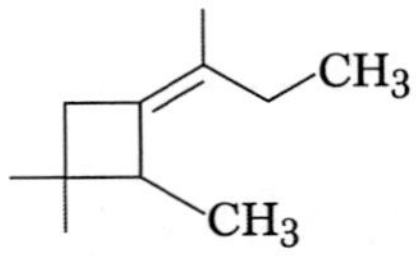
(b) 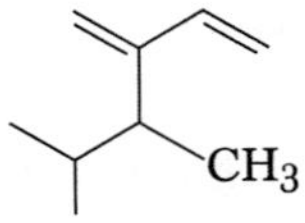
(c) 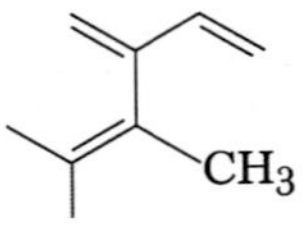
(d) 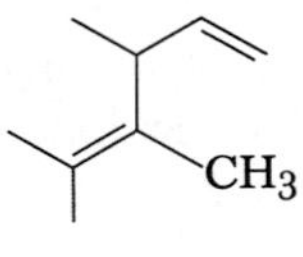

31. 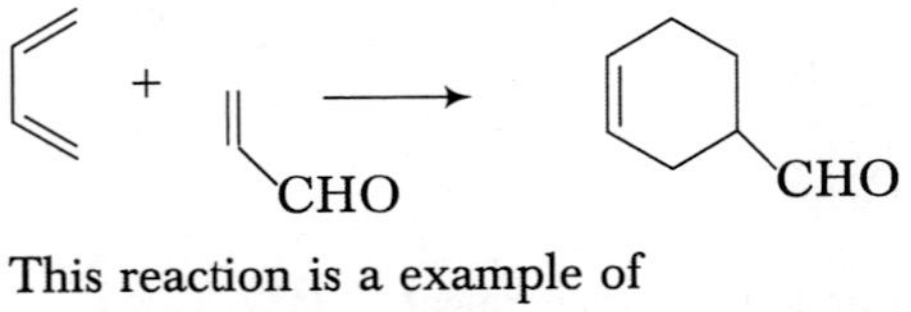

This reaction is a example of
(a) [2 + 2] cycloaddition
(b) [4 + 2] cycloaddition
(c) [2 + 1] cycloaddition
(d) None of the above

32. Allyl aryl ether on heating at 200°C give the major product

(a) 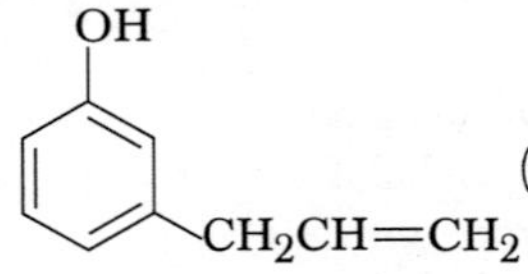
(b) 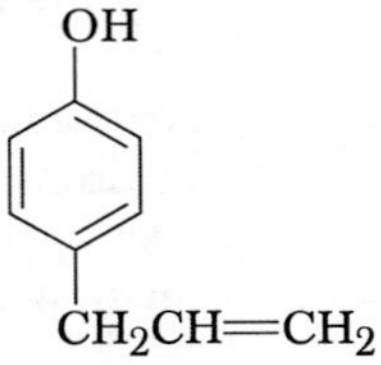
(c) 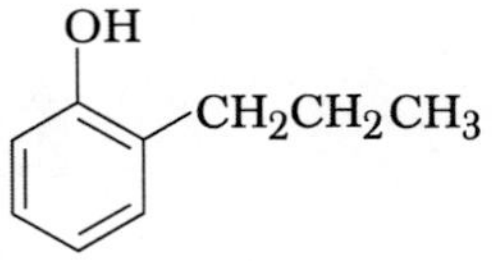
(d) 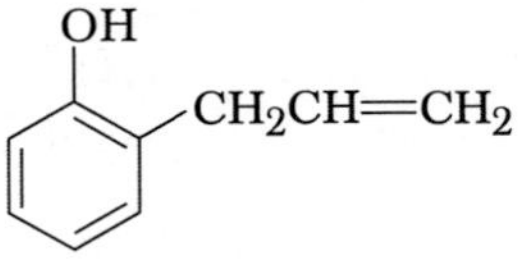

33. 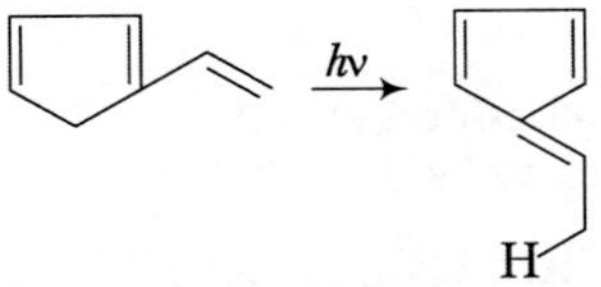

In the above transformation which shift takes place?
(a) [1, 5] (b) [1, 7] (c) [3, 5] (d) [3,. 7]

34. 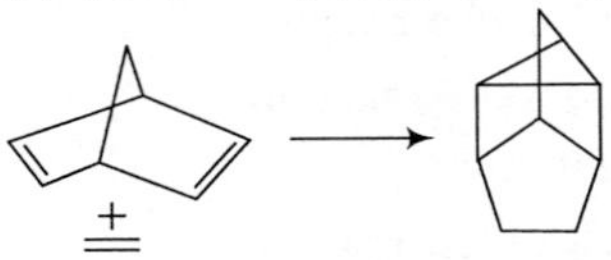

This cycloaddition reaction is a type of
(a) [4 + 2] cycloaddition
(b) [2 + 2] cycloaddition
(c) [2 + 2 + 2] cycloaddition
(d) None of the above

35. Select the incorrect statement from the given statements.
(a) HOMO is the highest occupied molecular orbital
(b) In conrotatory motion bonds rotate in the same direction
(c) Diels-Alder reaction is a [4 + 2] cycloaddition
(d) In the suprafacial reaction both bonds are formed on the opposite face of the component

36. What is the major product from the thermal cycloaddition of $F_2C{=}CCl_2$?

(a) 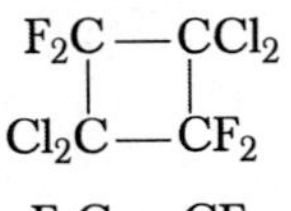
(b) 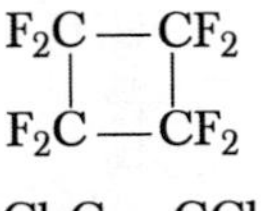
(c) 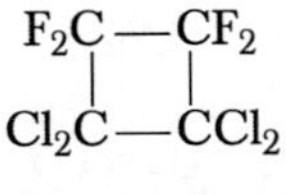
(d) 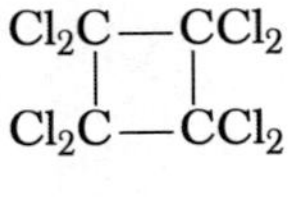

37. Cope rearrangement is
(a) [2, 3] sigmatropic rearrangement
(b) [3, 2] sigmatropic rearrangement
(c) [3, 3] sigmatropic rearrangement
(d) [1, 3] sigmatropic rearrangement

38. Thermolysis of allyl phenyl ether generate
(a) *o*-allylphenol only (b) *o*- and *p*-allylphenols
(c) *o*-, *m*-and *p*-allylphenols (d) *m*-allylphenol only

39. The reaction given below is an example

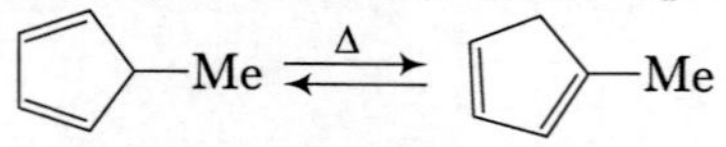

(a) 1, 3-sigmatropic hydrogen shift
(b) 1, 3-sigmatropic methyl shift
(c) 1, 5-sigmatropic hydrogen shift
(d) 1, 5-sigmatropic methyl shift

40. The concerted photochemical reaction between two olefins leading to a cyclobutane ring is
(a) $\pi 2_s + \pi 2_a$ cycloaddition
(b) $\pi 2_s + \pi 2_s$ cycloaddition
(c) $\sigma 2_s + \sigma 2_s$ cycloaddition
(d) $\pi 2_s + \sigma 2_a$ cycloaddition

Exercise 2
(For Part 'C')

1. Select the correct classification of the following reaction from option I to IV gives below

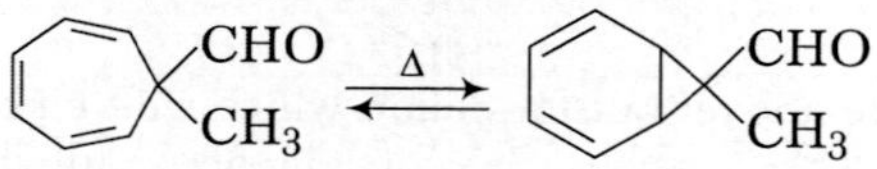

I. Conrotatory electrocyclic reaction
II. Disrotatory electrocyclic reaction
III. Valence isomerization
IV. $[\pi^4 s + \pi^2 a]$ cycloaddition reaction
(a) I and III (b) II and IV
(c) II and III (d) I and IV

2. The reaction given below in an example of

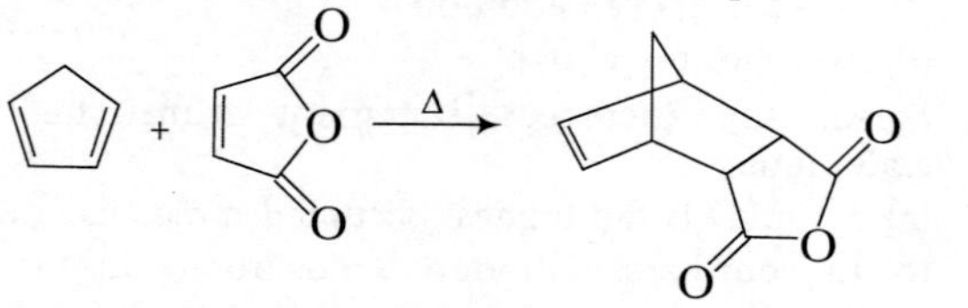

(a) $\pi^4 s + \pi^2 s$ cycloaddition (b) $\pi^4 s + \pi^2 a$ cycloaddition
(c) $\pi^4 a + \pi^2 s$ cycloaddition (d) $\pi^4 a + \pi^2 a$ cycloaddition

3. The direction of rotation of the following thermal electroclic reaction

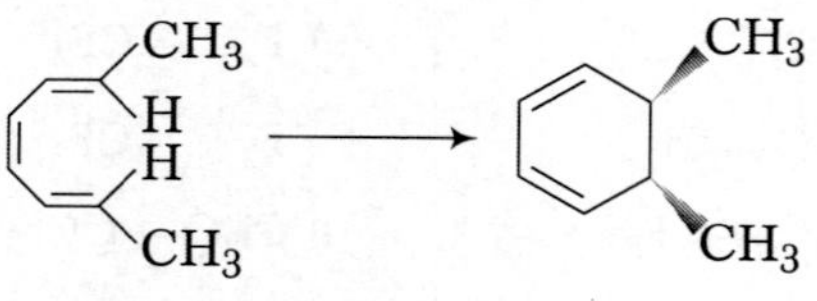

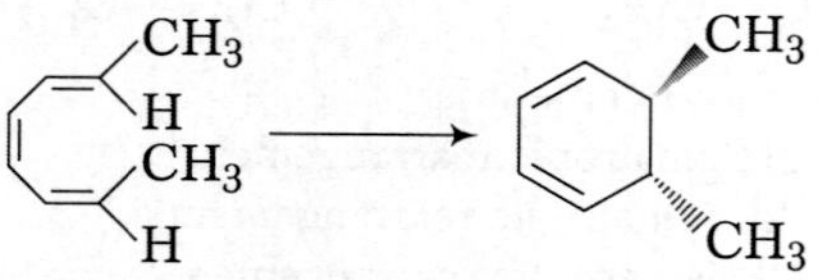

(a) conrotatory, conrotatory
(b) conrotatory, disrotatory
(c) disrotatory, disrotatory
(d) disrotatory, conrotatory

4. Match the following Column I and with Column II.

	Column I	Column II
A.	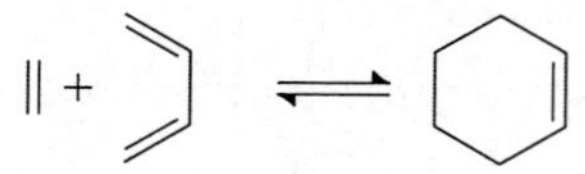	1. Cheleotropic
B.	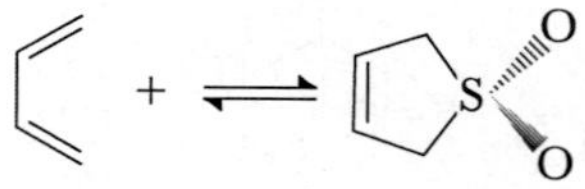	2. Group transfer
C.		3. Cycloaddition
D.	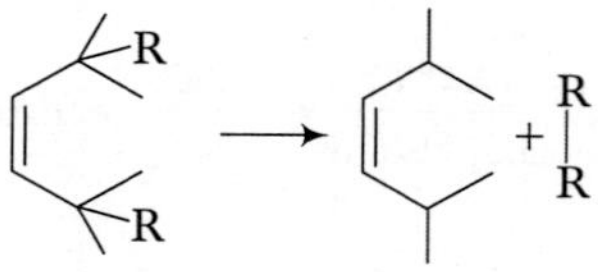	4. Sigmatropioc

Codes
(a) A-1, B-3, C-4, D-2 (b) A-3, B-4, C-1, D-2
(c) A-4, B-3, C-2, D-1 (d) A-3, B-1, C-4, D-2

5. For the following concerted reaction specify the condition and mode of rotation

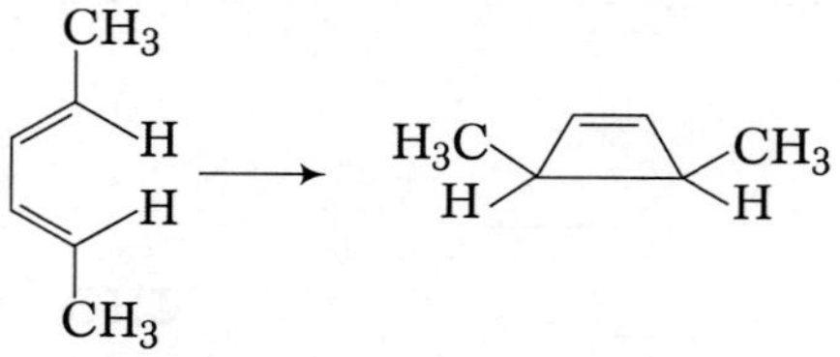

(a) Disrotation, photochemical
(b) Conrotation, photochemical
(c) Both (a) and (b)
(d) None of the above

6. 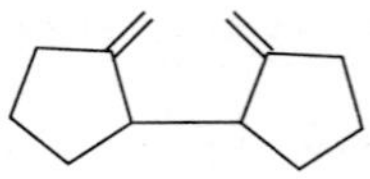 $\xrightarrow{\Delta}$ *A* ; *A* is

(a) 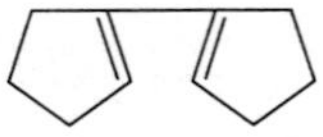
(b) 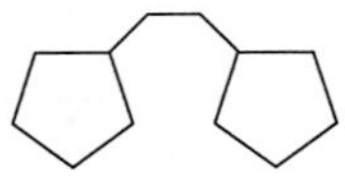
(c) 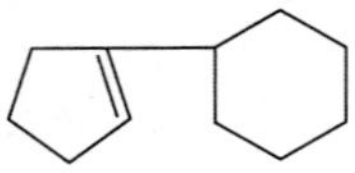
(d) 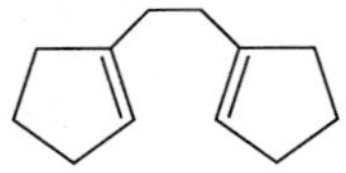

7. 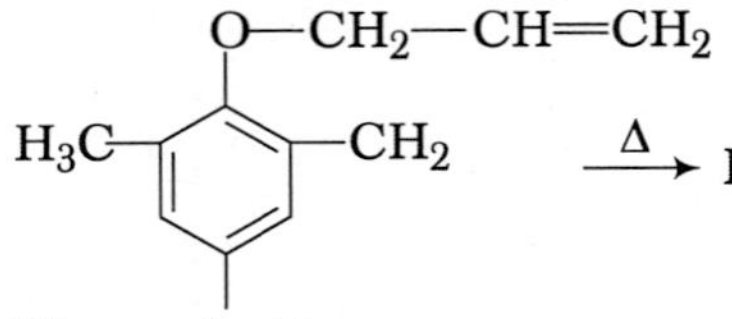 $\xrightarrow{\Delta}$ Product

The product is

(a) 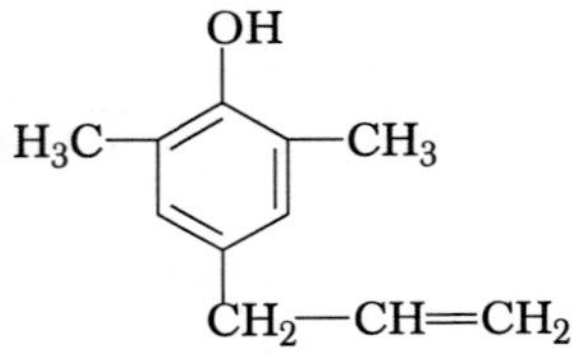

(b) 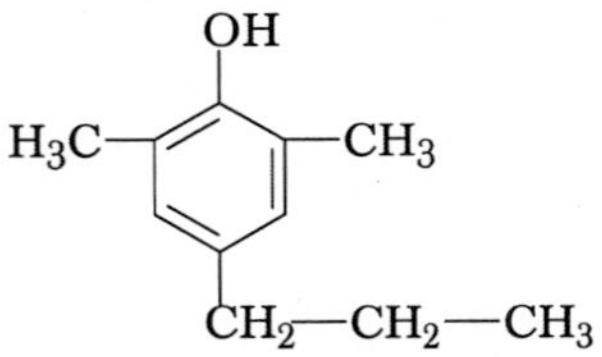

(c) Both (a) and (b)
(d) None of the above

8. Match the Column I and with Column II

	Column I	Column II
A.	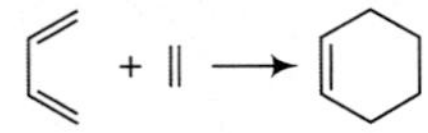	1. 4 + 4
B.	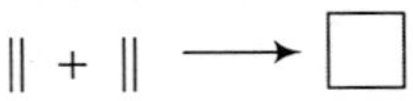	2. 2 + 2
C.	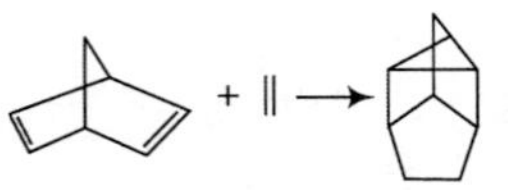	3. 4 + 2
D.	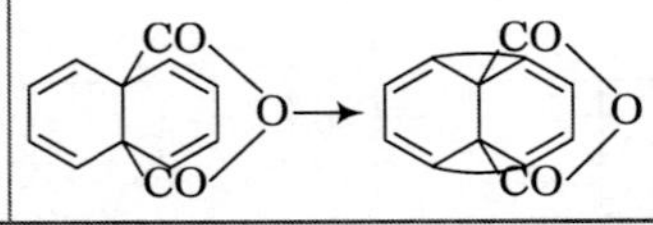	4. 2 + 2 + 2

(a) A-3, B-1, C-4, D-2 (b) A-3, B-2, C-4, D-1
(c) A-2, B-3, D-4, D-1 (d) A-3, B-2, C-1, D-4

9. The product of the following thermal reaction is

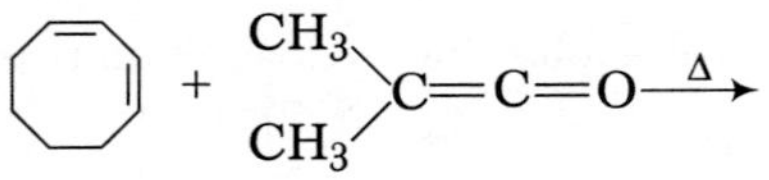

(a) 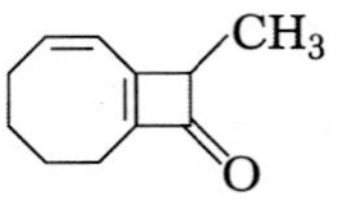
(b) 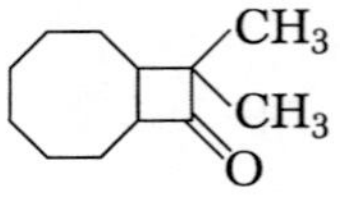
(c) 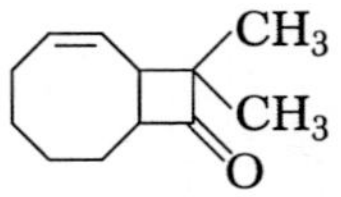
(d) 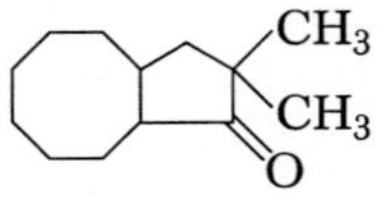

10. $C_6H_5—C{\equiv}N + {>}C{=}C{<} \xrightarrow{h\nu}$?

The product is

(a) 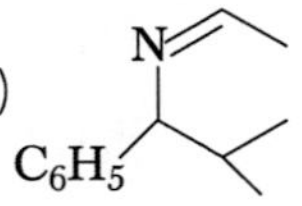
(b) 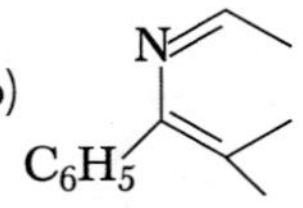
(c) 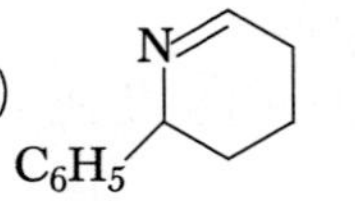
(d) 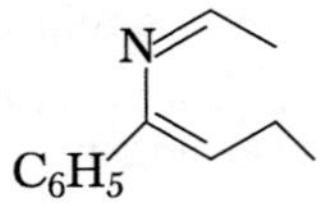

11. 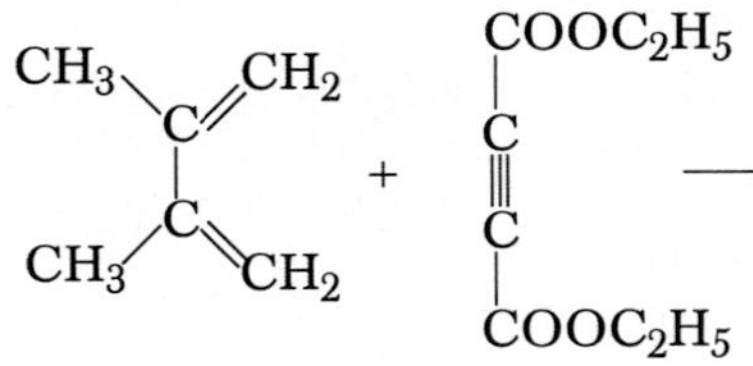 $\longrightarrow A \xrightarrow{\text{Pt/Heat}} B$

(a) 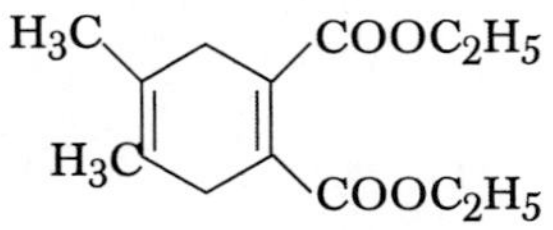

(b) 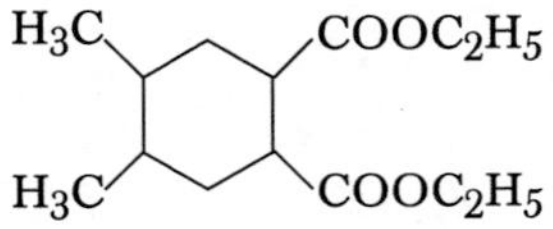

(c) 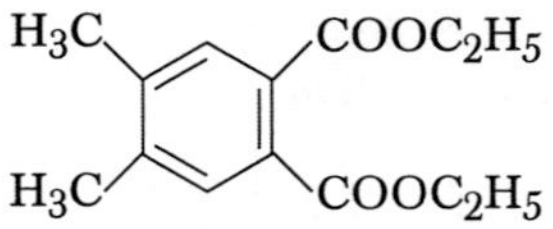

(d) None of the above

12. 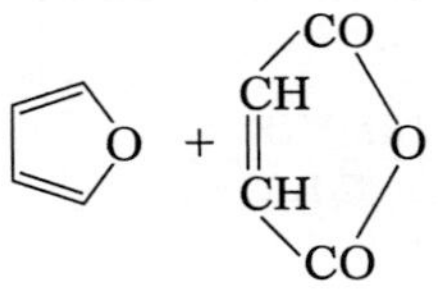 $\xrightarrow{\text{heat}}$ *A* ; Product *A* is

(a) 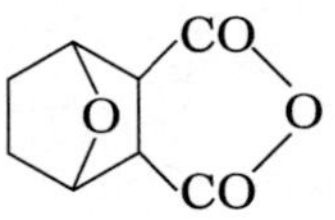
(b) 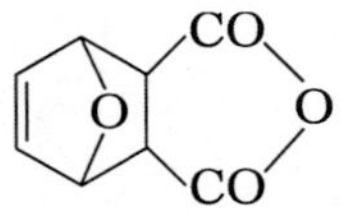
(c) 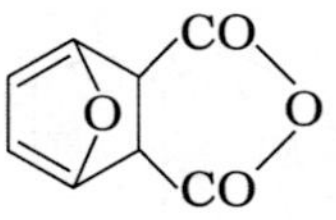
(d) 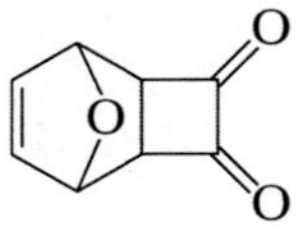

13. 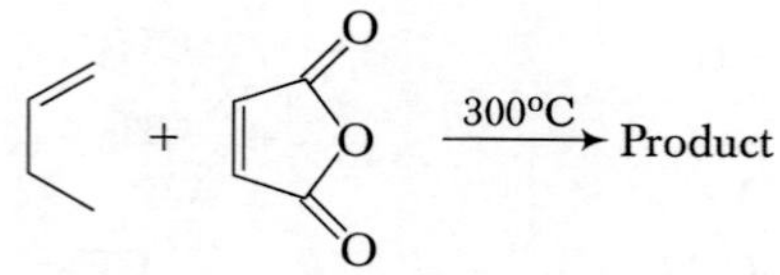

(a) 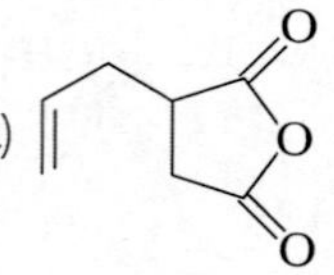 (b) 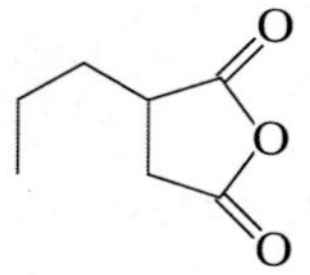

(c) 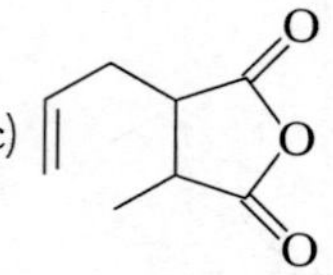 (d) 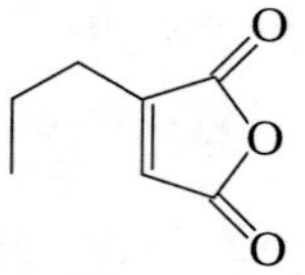

14. Consider the following statements

I. Clasisen rearrangement is a [3, 3] sigmatropic rearrangement.

II. Cope rearrangement proceeds *via* is chair like transition state.

III. In the photochemical [2 + 2] cycloaddition of ethylene overlapping of HOMO of one molecule with LUMO of the other molecular takes place.

Select the correct statements.

(a) I and III (b) II and III
(c) Only II (d) I and II

15. 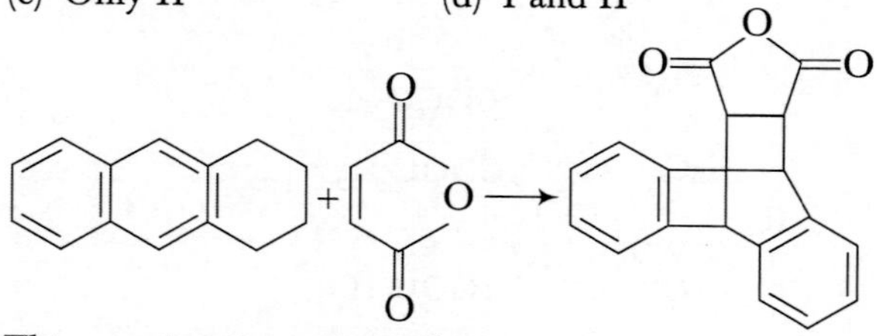

This reaction is an example is
(a) Diels-alder addition reaction
(b) Ene reaction
(c) Sigmatropic reaction
(d) None of the above

16. The major product of the following transformation is

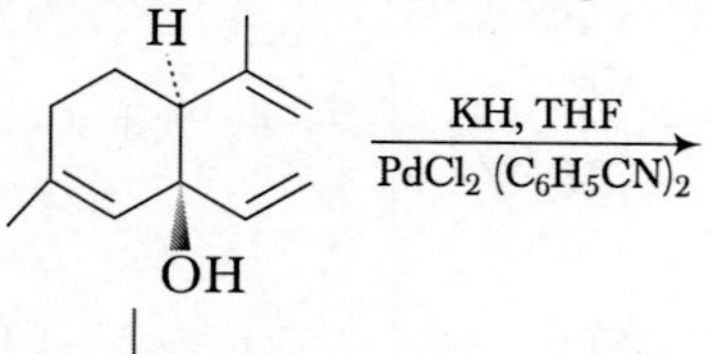

(a) 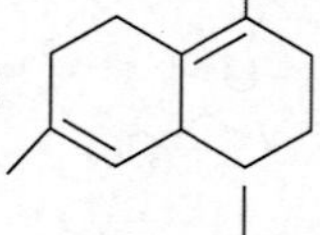 (b) 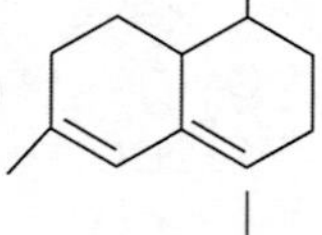

(c) 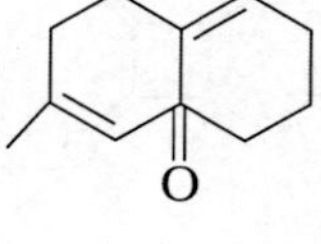 (d) 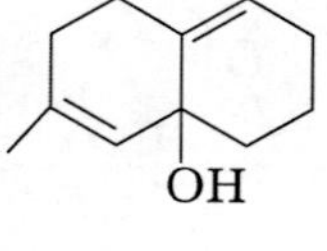

17. The end product of the following reaction series is

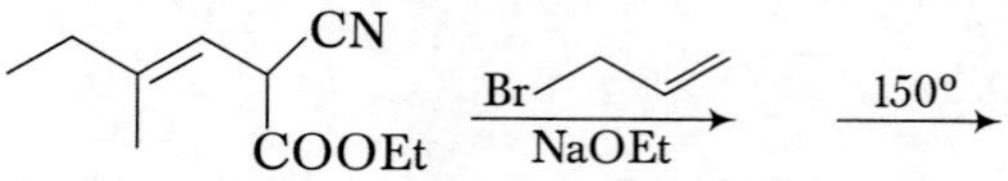

(a) 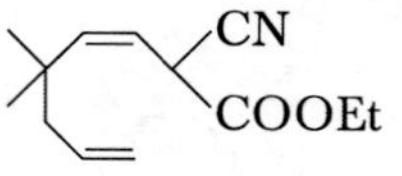 (b) 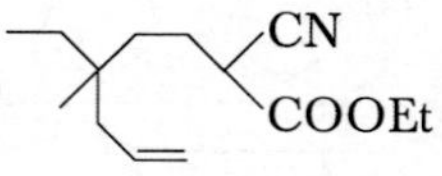

(c) 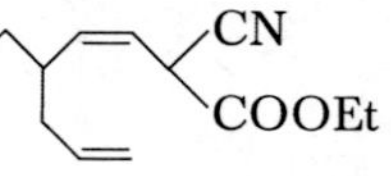 (d) 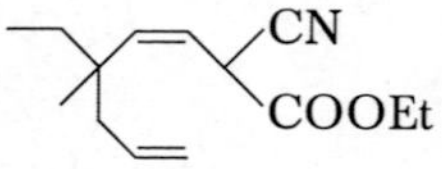

18. 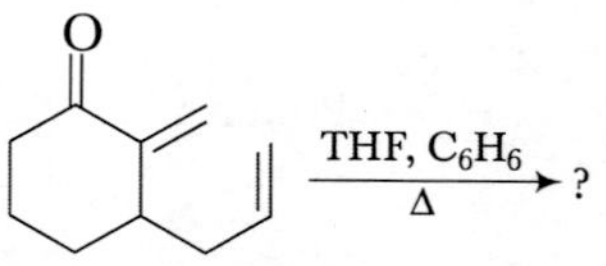

The product of above thermal rearrangement is

(a) 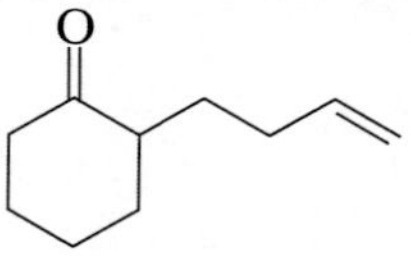 (b) 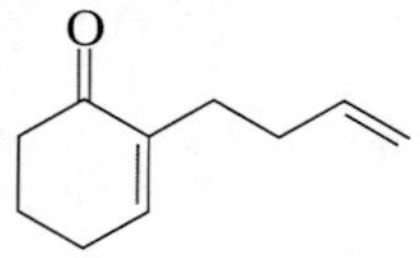

(c) 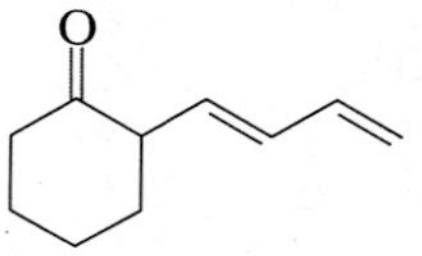 (d) 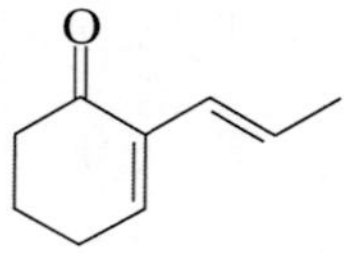

19. Which diene and dienophile is employed to synthesize norbornadiene?

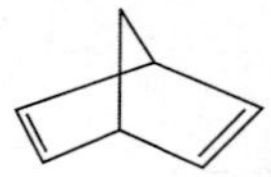

(a) 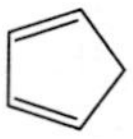 and ≡ (b) 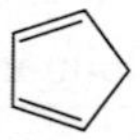 and =

(c)  and = (d) None of these

20. Give the product expected from heating following compound

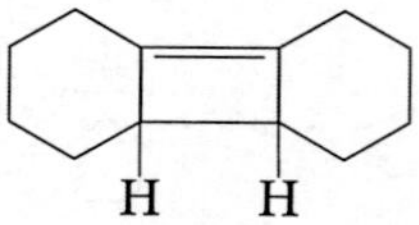

(a) 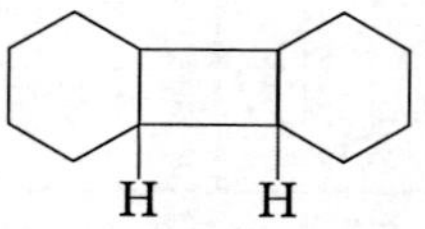 (b) 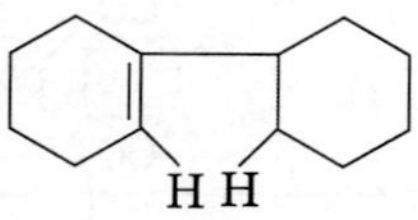

(c) 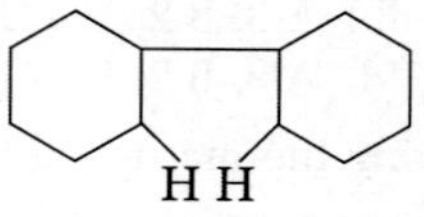 (d) 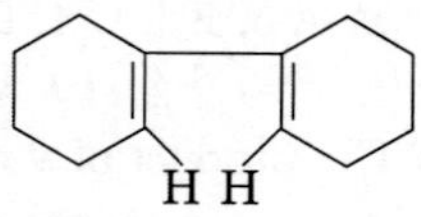

21. Consider the following cycloaddition reaction

(I) $\parallel + \parallel \longrightarrow \square$

(II) 

(III) 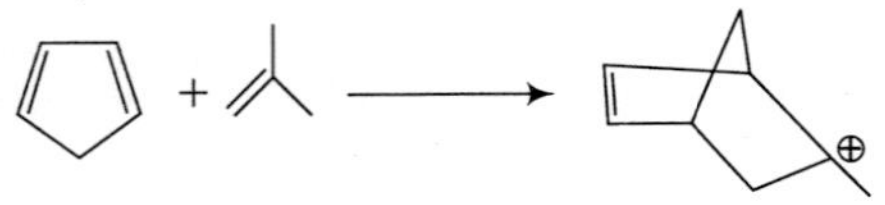

(IV) 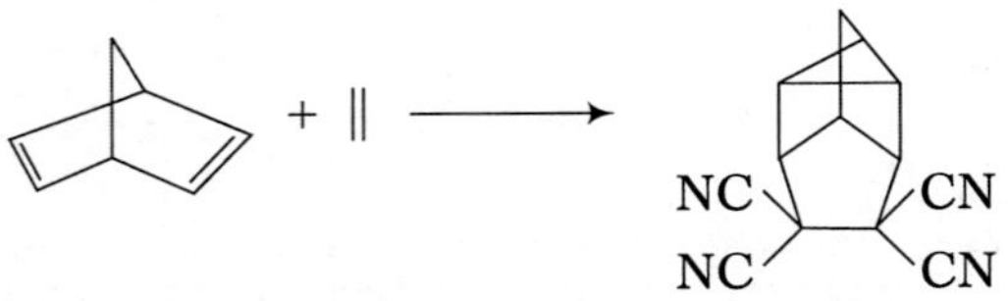

Select the [4 + 2] cycloaddition reaction

(a) I and III (b) II and III
(c) II, III and IV (d) II and IV

22. The product of the following cycloaddition reaction is

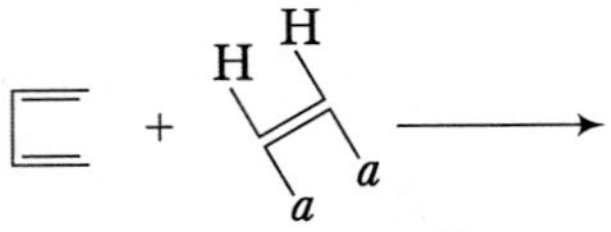

(a) 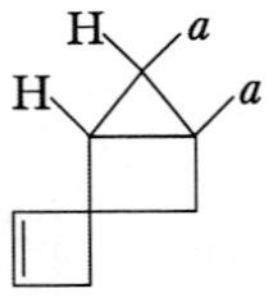

(b) 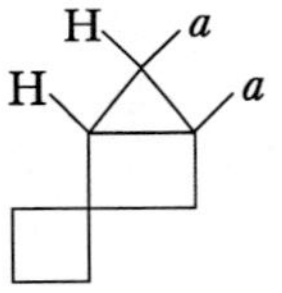

(c) 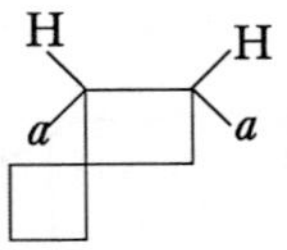

(d) 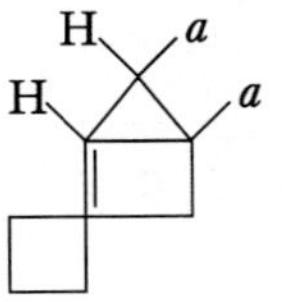

Assertion & Reason

Codes

(a) Both A and R are true and R is the correct explanation of A.
(b) Both A and R are true but R is not the correct explanation of A.
(c) A is true but R is false.
(d) A is false but R is true.

23. **Assertion (A)** The thermal isomerisation of 3, 4-dimethyl-1, 5-hexadiene to 2, 6-octadiene takes place by cope rearrangement,

Reason (R) The thermal isomerisation of 1, 5 diene by a 3, 3-sigmatropic shift is known as cope rearrangement.

24. **Assertion (A)** *cis,* 3,4 dimethyl cyclobutene gives *trans, trans*-2, 40-hexadiene on heating.

Reason (R) *trans* 5, 6-dimethyl cyclohexa 1,3-diene gives *trans, cis, cis 2, 4, 6-octatriene by photochemically.*

Answers

Exercise 1

1. (b)	**2.** (a)	**3.** (d)	**4.** (b)	**5.** (d)	**6.** (c)	**7.** (b)	**8.** (a)	**9.** (a)	**10.** (d)
11. (c)	**12.** (a)	**13.** (c)	**14.** (a)	**15.** (d)	**16.** (a)	**17.** (c)	**18.** (d)	**19.** (b)	**20.** (c)
21. (a)	**22.** (c)	**23.** (c)	**24.** (a)	**25.** (a)	**26.** (c)	**27.** (c)	**28.** (d)	**29.** (a)	**30.** (d)
31. (b)	**32.** (d)	**33.** (b)	**34.** (c)	**35.** (d)	**36.** (c)	**37.** (c)	**38.** (a)	**39.** (a)	**40.** (b)

Exercise 2

1. (c)	**2.** (a)	**3.** (c)	**4.** (d)	**5.** (a)	**6.** (d)	**7.** (a)	**8.** (b)	**9.** (c)	**10.** (b)
11. (c)	**12.** (b)	**13.** (a)	**14.** (d)	**15.** (a)	**16.** (c)	**17.** (d)	**18.** (b)	**19.** (a)	**20.** (d)
21. (b)	**22.** (a)	**23.** (a)	**24.** (d)						

Hints & Solutions

Exercise 1

4. 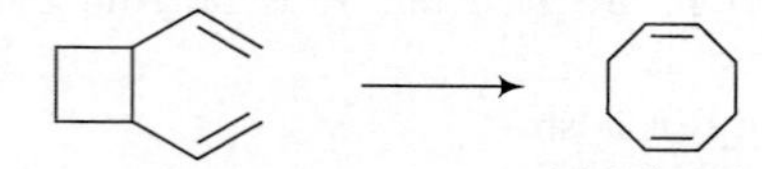

7. In diels-alder reaction, 2-substituted dienes give a mixture in which 1, 4-product predominates.

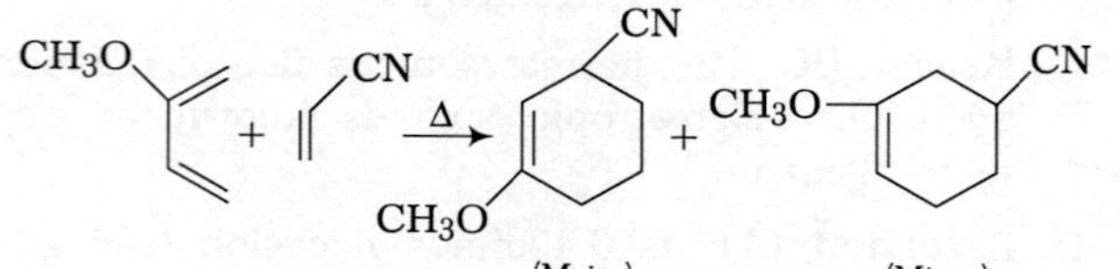

10. The secondary interaction of orbitals in the transition state is not sterically possible for the exo product.

11. *trans* 2, 4-hexadiene $\xrightarrow[\text{Conrotation}]{\text{Thermal}}$ *cis* 3, 4-dimethyl cyclobutene.

13. 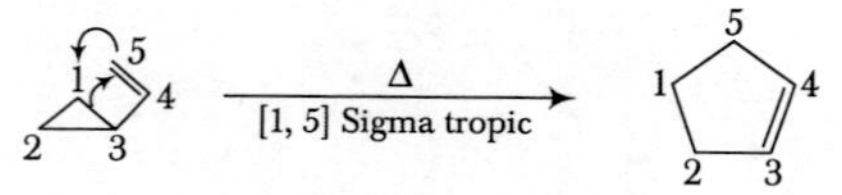

It is given by *cis*-vinyl cyclopropanes. *Trans*-vinylcyclo propanes do not give this rearrangement.

19. 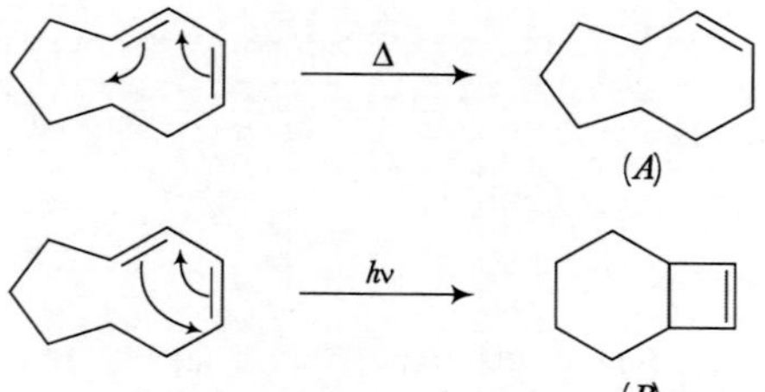

22. 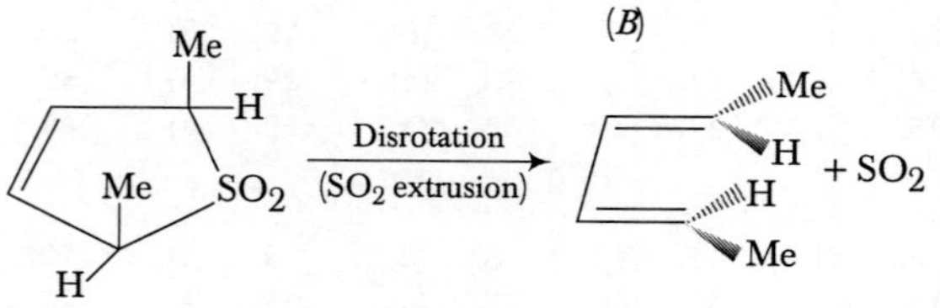

28. 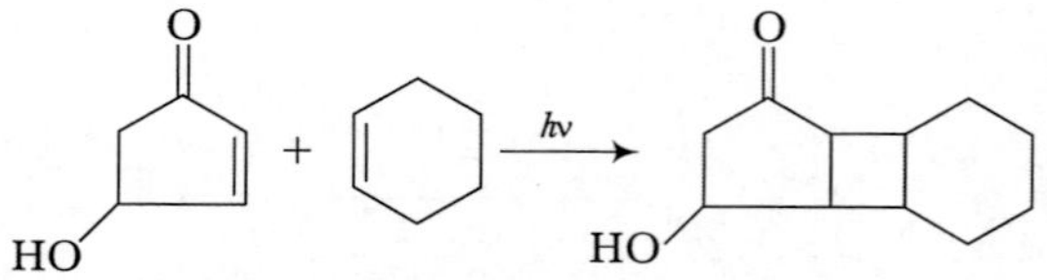

29. Conrotatory movement must convert a *cis*-3, 4-disubstituted cyclobutene into *cis, trans* diene and *trans* into a *trans, trans* diene.

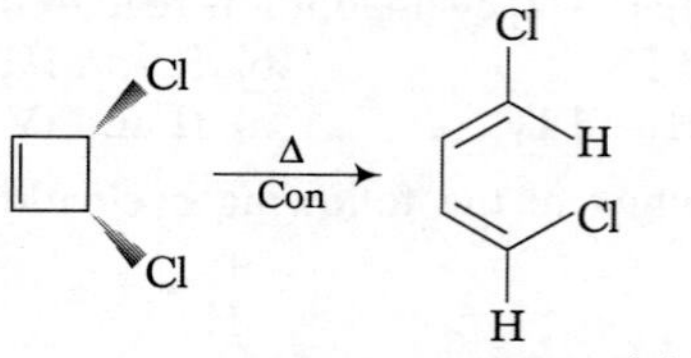

cis, trans-Diene (A)

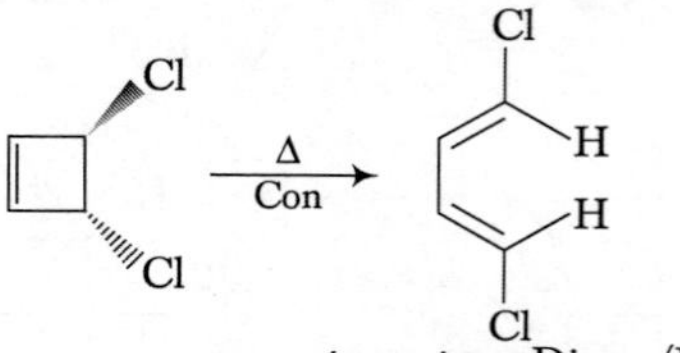

trans, trans-Diene (B)

30. 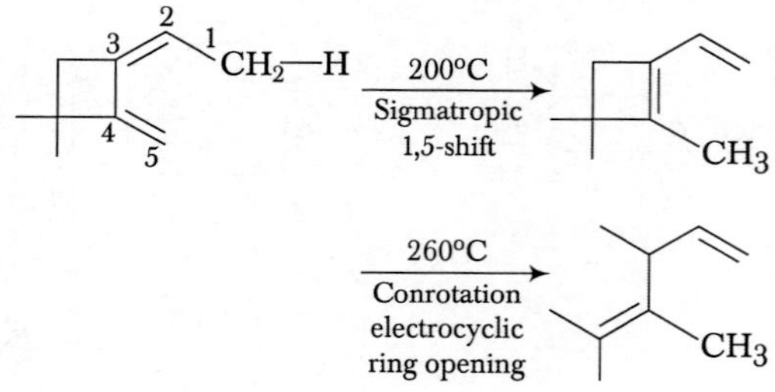

33. 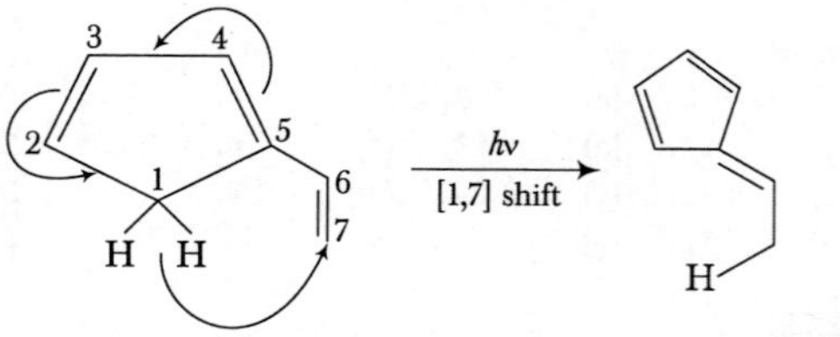

36. 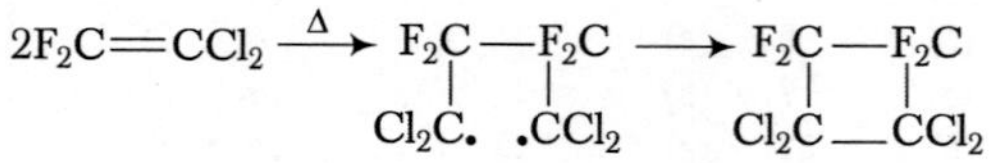

Exercise 2

2. 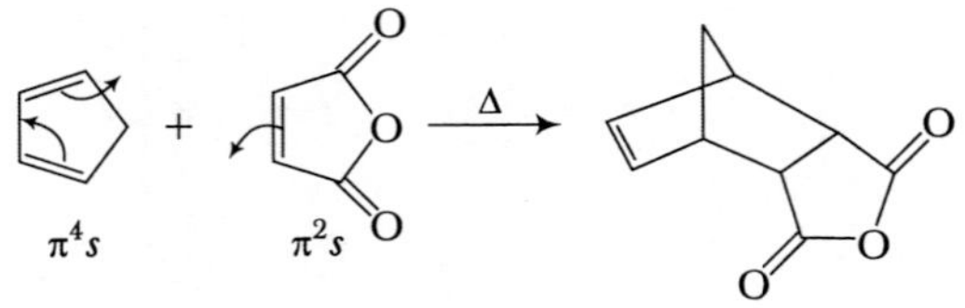

Hence, $\pi_s^4 + \pi_s^2$ cycloaddition.

5. 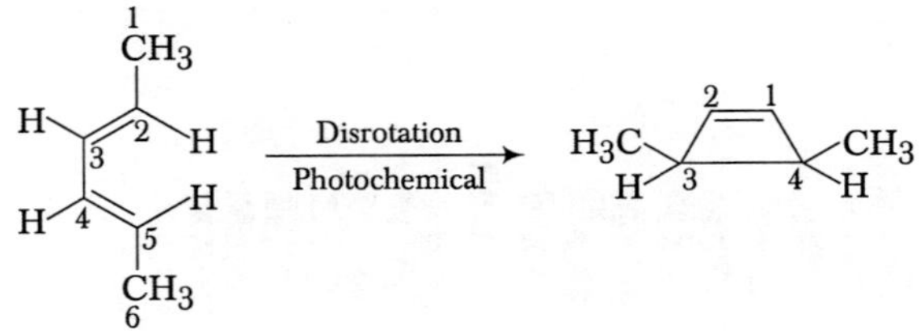

10. 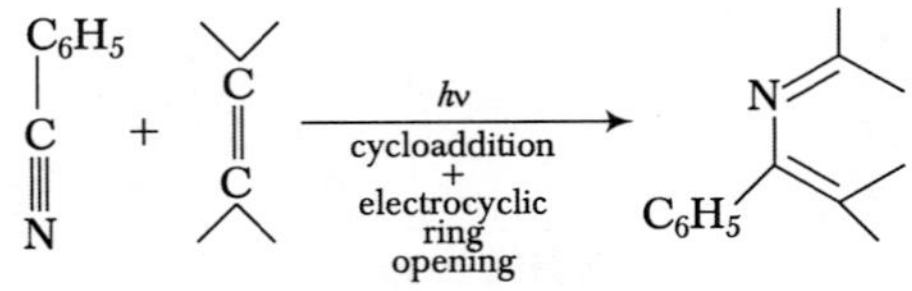

16. 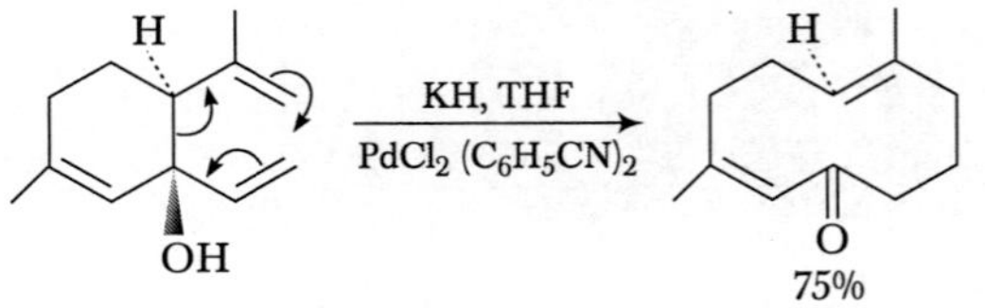

17. 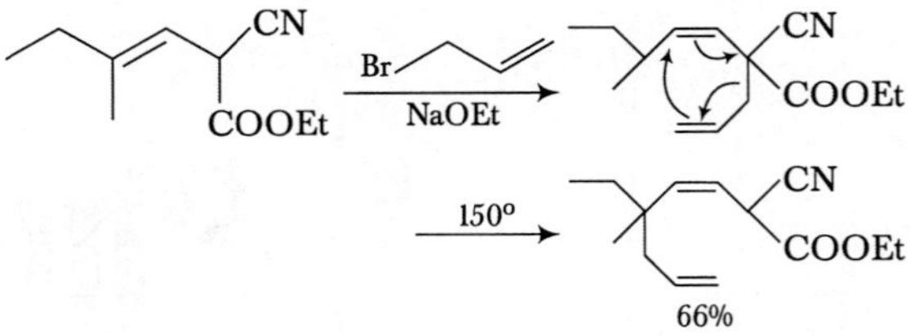

18. 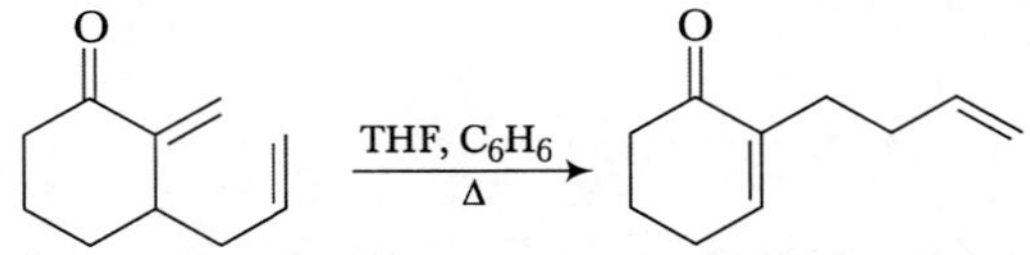

This is an example of cope rearrangement.

36

Photochemistry

Syllabus

- Principles and Applications of Photochemical Reactions in Organic Chemistry

Introduction

Photochemistry is the study of reaction that are brought about by the action of visible or ultraviolet light. When a molecule absorbs electromagnetic radiation, it is excited. The amount of energy that such a radiation contains depends upon its wavelength.

$$E = h\nu = \frac{hc}{\lambda}$$

where, h = Planck's constant.

When the absorption of light brings about a chemical reaction, it is referred to as a photochemical reaction. Most organic molecules have an even number of electrons with all the electrons paired which state is called a **singlet** state. When electromagnetic radiation is absorbed in the visible or UV region, the molecule is excited to higher electronic state. This involves the promotion of an electron from bonding molecular orbital to anti-bonding molecular orbital.

Electronic Excitation

The absorption of light energy of molecules in the visible and ultraviolet region involves the promotion of an electron from the bonding orbital (σ or π) to the corresponding anti-bonding orbital ($\overset{*}{\sigma}$ or $\overset{*}{\pi}$). The non-bonding electrons (n) are generally not involved in bond formation.

There are four types of excitation found in most of the organic molecules which are as :

1. $\sigma \longrightarrow \overset{*}{\sigma}$ Alkanes contain only σ-bonds. They do not have π or n-electrons in their molecules. Hence, they can be excited by $\sigma \longrightarrow \overset{*}{\sigma}$ excitation.
2. $n \longrightarrow \overset{*}{\sigma}$ Oxygen and nitrogen atoms of alcohols, amines, ethers etc., contain unused long pair of electrons (n). Hence, they can be excited by $n \longrightarrow \overset{*}{\sigma}$ excitation.
3. $\pi \longrightarrow \overset{*}{\sigma}$ Compounds of alkenes, ketones, aldehydes and esters etc., having unsaturated π-bonds, consist of π-electrons. Hence, they can be excited by $\pi \longrightarrow \overset{*}{\pi}$ excitation.

4. $n \longrightarrow \overset{*}{\pi}$ Aldehydes, ketones, esters etc., have π-electrons as well as unused lone pair of n-electrons. They can undergo $n \longrightarrow \overset{*}{\pi}$ excitation as well as above three promotions.

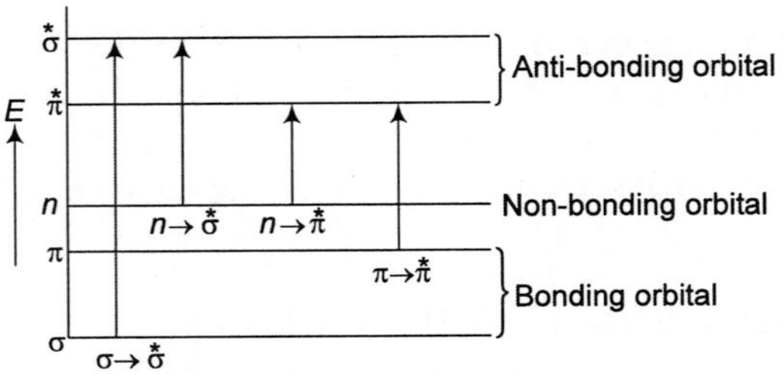

Fig. 36.1 Different types of electronic excitations.

The order of energy required for various electronic transition is as :

$$\sigma \longrightarrow \overset{*}{\sigma} > n \longrightarrow \overset{*}{\sigma} > \pi \longrightarrow \overset{*}{\pi} > n \longrightarrow \overset{*}{\pi}$$

Fate of Photoexcited Molecules (Photophysical Processes)

There are an even number of electrons in a typical organic molecule, and these electrons are usually paired in the ground state (S_0). Absorption of light of the correct energy occurs without spin inversion and so the electron spins remain paired in the excited state. This state is commonly called excited **singlet state** (S_1). However, in many cases electronic excitation is followed by spin inversion thus giving rise to a new excited state with two unpaired electrons. This state is called an excited **triplet state** (T_1). Direct excitation of the ground state (S_0) to a triplet state is not possible and hence T_1 is populated *via* S_1.

Note
- The singlet states do not split in a magnetic field while triplet states have three possible energy states in an applied magnetic field.
- A triplet state is more stable than the corresponding excited singlet state.

Fate of the excited molecule can be explained by **Jablonski diagram** which is a pictorial illustration of different energy states which are absorbed by a molecule. When the molecule absorbs UV light radiations, it gets excited and promotes to excited singlet electronic state S_1 or S_2 or S_3. In the above state, the molecule collides with neighbouring molecules and after 10^{-13} to 10^{-11} second it comes back rapidly to the S_1 state and releases energy to the environment. This entire process is called **energy cascade.**

The life time of singlet excited state S_1 is relatively long, hence this state can undergo different physical and chemical processes. A molecule returns to its ground state, S_0 from its excited singlet state, S_1 or S_2 by giving up its energy as heat. This process is called **internal conversion** (IC). If the molecule returns to its ground state S_0 from excited singlet state S_1 or S_2 by emitting energy in the form of light radiation within 10^{-9} seconds, then the process is known as **fluorescence.** This process is generally slow and not very common. Smaller molecules and the rigid molecules (*e.g.*, aromatic compounds) are the example of this process. The emitted fluorescent light is of slightly lower energy than absorbed light, hence, has longer wavelength.

Most molecules in S_1 state can undergo an inter system crossing to the lowest triplet state, T_1. The first excited triplet state, T_1 is more stable, because it has lower energy than the first excited singlet state. Hence, inter system crossing process is an energetically down hill process. After sometime (10^{-4} to several minutes) the triplet state also drops to the ground state, S_0 by emitting a photon of light by the process of **phosphorescence**. As the triplet state is more stable than singlet state, hence triplet state can undergo chemical reaction more rapidly than singlet state and therefore photochemistry is largely the chemistry of triplet state.

Note • If phosphorescene and fluorescence both takes place in the same molecule, the phosphorescene is found at lower frequency than fluorescence.

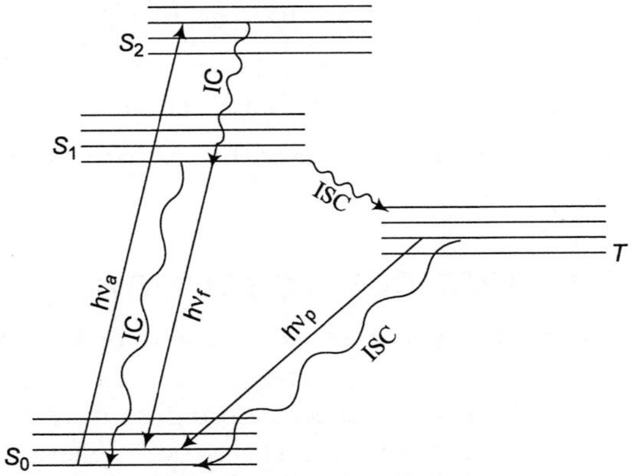

Fig. 36.2 Jablonski diagram.

Here, S_0 = Singlet ground state
S_1 and S_2 = Excited singlet state
T = Triplet state
IC = Internal conversion
ISC = Intersystem crossing
$h\nu_a$ = Energy absorbed
$h\nu_f$ = Energy lost as fluorescent light
$h\nu_p$ = Energy lost as phosphorescent light

Some physical processes which occur by the excited molecules are as :

States	Physical process
$S_0 + h\nu \longrightarrow S_1$	Excitation singlet state
$S_1 \longrightarrow S_1 + \text{heat}$	Vibrational cascade
$S_1 \longrightarrow S_0 + h\nu$	Fluorescence
$S_1 \longrightarrow S_0 + \text{heat}$	Internal conversion (IC)
$S_1 \longrightarrow T$	Intersystem crossing (ISC)
$T \longrightarrow T + \text{heat}$	Vibrational cascade
$T \longrightarrow S_0 + \text{heat}$	ISC
$T \longrightarrow S_0 + h\nu$	Phosphorescence

Quantum Yield (ϕ)

The efficiency of a photochemical reaction is expressed in terms of quantum efficiency or quantum yield (ϕ). It is defined as the number of molecules reacting per quantum of light absorbed.

$$\phi = \frac{\text{Number of molecules reacting in given time}}{\text{Number of quantum of radiation absorbed in the same time}}$$

The energy absorbed per molecule of the reacting substance is called one Einstein.

$$\phi = \frac{\text{Number of mole reacting or produced}}{\text{Number of Einstein absorbed}}$$

The value of ϕ is rarely a unity in actual practice. Its value varies from 10^{-2} to 10^4 or more. If $\phi > 1$, it indicates a chain reaction whereas $\phi < 1$ shows either a non-chain process or a reversible reaction.

The quantum yield is measured by the process called actinometry.

Photochemical Reactions

The chemical behaviour of molecules depends on the most weakly bound electrons in the molecules. A molecule in the photoexcited state differs from that in the ground state with respect to both energy and electron wave function and hence, differs in its chemical behaviour. Irradiation of light photons on a molecule produce an excited electronic state, which alters the reactivity of molecules in number of ways which decide the nature of photochemical reaction.

Photolysis of Carbonyl Compounds

Aldehyde and ketone absorb light in the region of 230-330 nm which results in $n \longrightarrow \overset{*}{\pi}$ transition. Each of primary reaction occur from the $n \longrightarrow \overset{*}{\pi}$ triplet state (T_1). The final reaction product can be formed after the secondary process of reaction.

Norrish type I reaction or α-cleavage

When the cleavage of C—C bond α to the carbonyl group takes place, it is called Norrish type I reaction or α-cleavage. In this type of excited molecule of an aldehyde or ketone undergo following change.

$$R\text{—}CH_2CH_2\text{—}\overset{\overset{\displaystyle O}{\|}}{C}\text{—}CH_2\text{—}CH_2\text{—}R'$$

$$\xrightarrow[\text{Homolysis of C—C}]{h\nu} R\text{—}CH_2CH_2\overset{\overset{\displaystyle O}{\|}}{C}\bullet + R'CH_2\dot{C}H_2$$

The acyl free radical can further undergo the following three process.

(a) Disproportionation to give a ketene

$$RCH_2CH_2\text{—}\overset{\overset{\displaystyle O}{\|}}{C}\bullet + H_2\dot{C}\text{—}CH_2\text{—}R' \longrightarrow \underset{\text{Ketene}}{RCH_2CH{=}C{=}O} + \underset{\text{Alkane}}{R'CH_2CH_3}$$

(b) Intermolecular hydrogen atom abstraction by the acyl radical.

$$RCH_2CH_2\text{—}\overset{\overset{\displaystyle O}{\|}}{C}\bullet + H_2C^\bullet\text{—}CH_2\text{—}R' \longrightarrow \underset{\text{Aldehyde}}{RCH_2CH_2CHO} + \underset{\text{Alkene}}{R'CH{=}CH_2}$$

(c) Decarbonylation followed by disproportionation or dimerisation.

$$2RCH_2CH_2\text{—}\overset{\overset{\displaystyle O}{\|}}{C}\bullet \longrightarrow 2RCH_2\dot{C}H_2 + 2CO$$

$$2RCH_2\dot{C}H_2 \xrightarrow{\text{Disproportionation}} RCH{=}CH_2 + RCH_2CH_3$$

$$2RCH_2\dot{C}H_2 \xrightarrow{\text{Dimerisation}} RCH_2CH_2\text{—}CH_2CH_2R$$

Norrish type II reaction or β-cleavage

If the carbonyl compound contains at least one H-atom at γ-carbon atom, intramolecular abstraction of the γ-hydrogen atom occurs followed by cleavage or cyclisation of diradical to form an aldehyde or ketone or cyclobutanol derivative respectively.

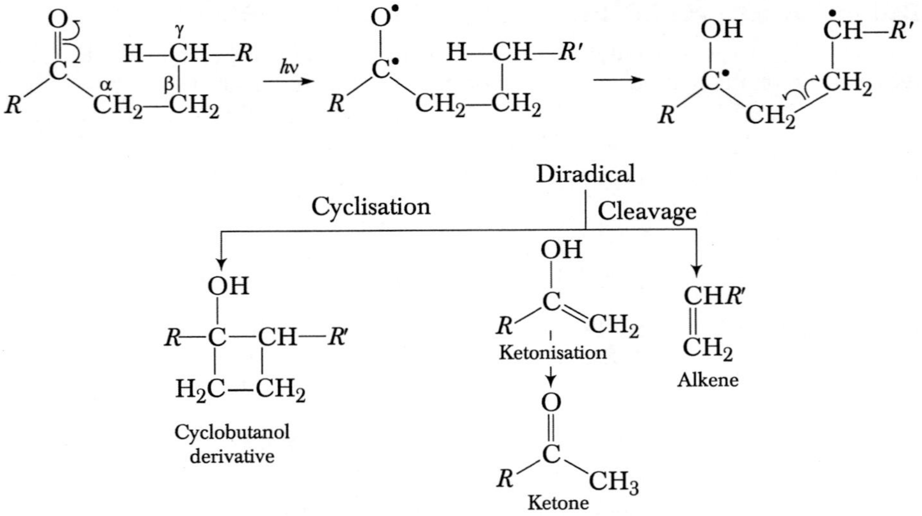

Note • If the α-carbon has only H-atom on it, the major product is the carbonyl compound but if it has alkyl substituent the major product would be cyclobutanol derivative.

• Norrish type II reaction is possible if bond between α and β carbon is weak.

Photochemical cleavage of cyclic ketones

Photochemical cleavage of smaller cyclic ketones is dominated by Norrish type I reaction to form a diradical by breaking of acyl carbon bond which may undergo following different intramolecular reaction.

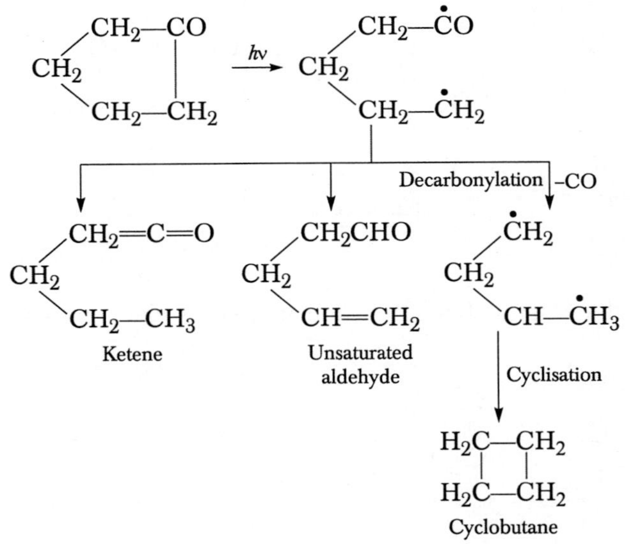

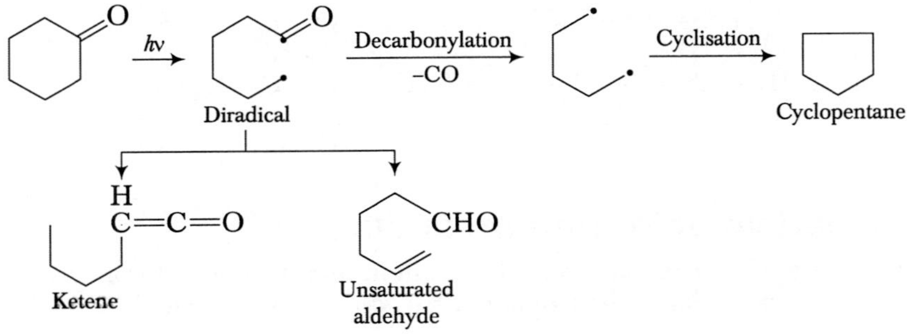

Photochemical Addition Reaction (Paterno Buchi Reaction)

Photoaddition of alkenes (olefins) to carbonyl compound is an example of Paterno Buchi reaction. The reaction occurs normally between the triplet state of carbonyl compound and the ground state of olefin.

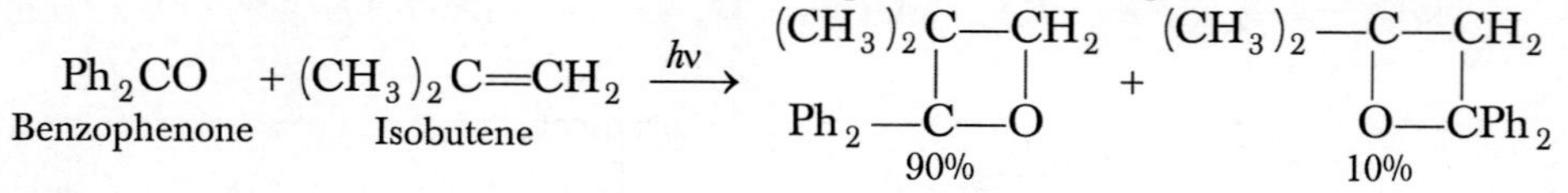

The reaction completes in two steps :

1. The excited carbonyl compound in triplet state add through its oxygen to the olefin and form two diradicals.

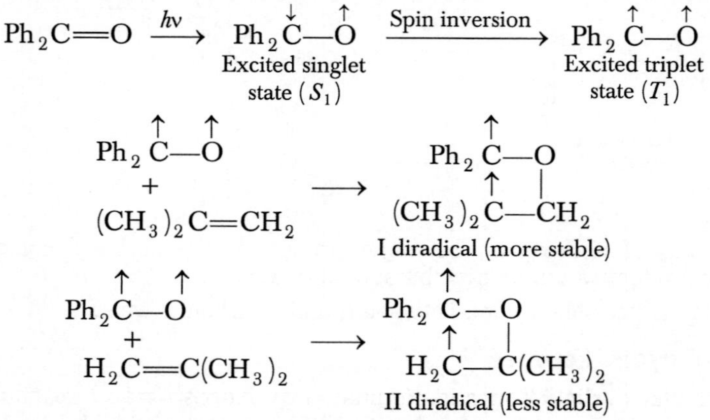

2. In the second step, spin inversion takes place and the second bond is form.

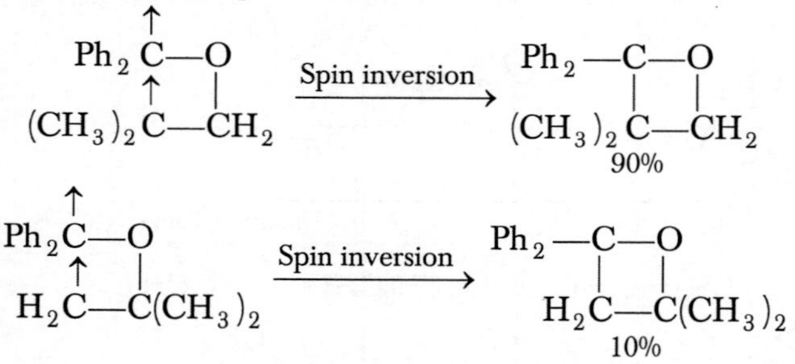

Acetylenes also participate in the Paterno Buchi reaction to give products which probably arise *via* an unstable oxetene.

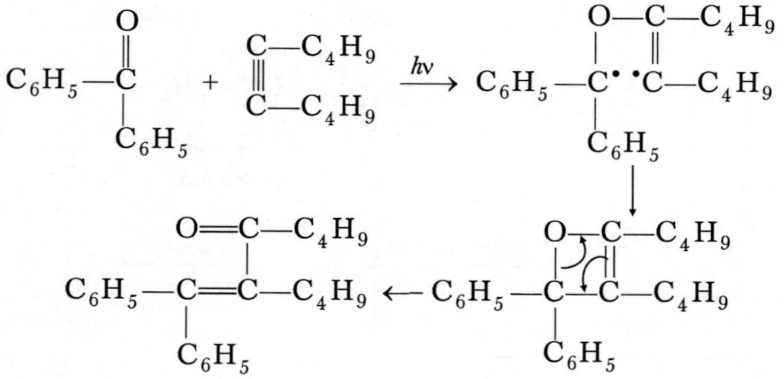

Photochemical Dimerisation or Photoreduction

A diaryl or an aryl alkyl ketone when irradiated with UV light in presence of a H-donor such as isopropyl alcohol, dimerises to pinacol. The photoreduction of benzophenone leading to benzpinacol.

$$\underset{\text{Benzophenone}}{2Ph_2C{=}O} \xrightarrow[(CH_3)_2CHOH]{\text{UV light}} \underset{\text{Benzpinacol}}{\begin{array}{c} Ph_2{-}C{-}OH \\ | \\ Ph_2{-}C{-}OH \end{array}}$$

Benzophenone when irradiated in the presence of isopropyl alcohol, undergoes $n \longrightarrow \overset{*}{\pi}$ excitation. The signlet (S_1) species formed crosses to triplet state (T_1) with a very high efficiency. The T_1 species abstract H from the alcohol to form a ketyl radical which then dimerises to pinacol. The isopropyl free radical formed by this process donates the remaining hydrogen as free radical to another molecule of benzophenone producing acetone and another molecule of ketyl radical.

$$Ph_2C{=}O \xrightarrow[n \to \overset{*}{\pi}]{h\nu} \underset{\text{Excited singlet state }(S_1)}{Ph_2\overset{\uparrow}{C}{-}\overset{\downarrow}{O}} \xrightarrow{\text{ISC}} \underset{\text{Excited triplet state }(T_1)}{Ph_2{-}\overset{\uparrow}{C}{-}\overset{\uparrow}{O}}$$

$$Ph_2{-}\overset{\uparrow}{C}{-}\overset{\uparrow}{\ddot{O}}{:} + H{-}C(CH_3)_2OH \longrightarrow \underset{\text{Ketyl F.R.}}{Ph_2{-}\overset{\uparrow}{C}{-}OH} + \underset{\text{2-hydroxypropyl radical}}{(CH_3)_2{-}\overset{\uparrow}{C}{-}OH}$$

$$2Ph_2\dot{C}{-}OH \longrightarrow \underset{\text{Benzpinacol}}{\begin{array}{c} Ph_2{-}C{-}OH \\ | \\ Ph_2{-}C{-}OH \end{array}}$$

$$Ph_2C{=}O + (CH_3)_2\dot{C}{-}OH \longrightarrow \underset{\text{Ketyl F.R.}}{Ph_2\dot{C}{-}OH} + \underset{\text{Acetone}}{(CH_3)_2C{=}O}$$

Note • Benzpinacol formation can also take place by irradiating benzophenone and benzhydrol in benzene solution.

$$(C_6H_5)_2CO + (C_6H_5)_2CHOH \xrightarrow{h\nu} \begin{array}{c} (C_6H_5)_2{-}C{-}OH \\ | \\ (C_6H_5)_2{-}C{-}OH \end{array}$$

In this reaction simultaneous formation of two radicals which subsequently dimerize.

$$\underset{\text{Triplet excited state }(T_1)}{{}^3[(C_6H_5)_2CO]} + (C_6H_5)_2CHOH \longrightarrow 2(C_6H_5)_2\overset{\overset{OH}{|}}{C^{\bullet}} \longrightarrow \begin{array}{c} (C_6H_5)_2{-}C{-}OH \\ | \\ (C_6H_5)_2{-}C{-}OH \end{array}$$

Photochemistry of Olefins or Alkenes

In the photo excitation of a C═C in alkenes only $(\pi, \overset{*}{\pi})$ state is involved. But since ISC of $S_1 \longrightarrow T_1$ is inefficient, the $^3(\pi, \overset{*}{\pi})$ state can only be populated *via* photosensitization. The products formed in the photoreaction of alkenes depends on the following factors.

1. Nature of olefin
2. Number of C═C present in molecule
3. Excited state

Cis-trans isomerisation of alkenes

Alkenes can be irradiated in solution when it undergoes *cis-trans* isomerisation. The same reaction can be carried out in the presence of a sensitizer. Direct irradiation of solutions of either *cis* or *trans* stilbene yields a constant mixture consisting of 93% *cis*-stilbene and 7% *trans*-stilbene

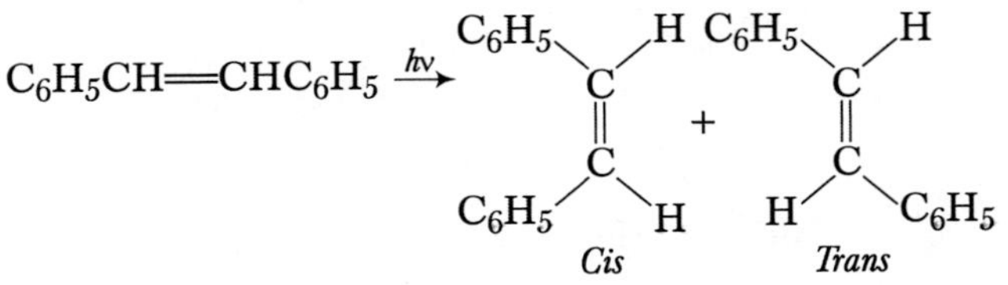

Initial absorption of light either of these isomers is rapidly followed by ISC to the respective triplet states. Photoisomerization then occurs *via* interconversion or *via* a common triplet intermediate.

$$\left.\begin{array}{l} \textit{Cis}\text{ - stilbene} \\ \textit{Trans}\text{ - stilbene} \end{array}\right] \xrightarrow{h\nu} \begin{array}{l} ^{1}[\textit{cis}\text{ - stilbene}] \\ ^{1}[\textit{trans}\text{ - stilbene}] \end{array} \longrightarrow \begin{array}{c} ^{3}[\textit{cis}\text{- stilbene}] \\ \rightleftharpoons \\ ^{3}[\textit{trans}\text{-stilbene}] \end{array}$$

$$\equiv {}^{3}[C_6H_5CH{=}CHC_6H_5] \longrightarrow \underset{93\%}{\textit{cis}\text{-stilbene}} + \underset{7\%}{\textit{trans}\text{- stilbene}}$$

Photoisomerisation can also be carried out in presence of sensitizers. Benzophenone sensitized process may be depicted in the following steps :

$$(C_6H_5)_2CO \xrightarrow{h\nu} {}^{1}[(C_6H_5)_2CO] \longrightarrow {}^{3}[(C_6H_5)_2CO]$$

$$\left.\begin{array}{l} \textit{Cis}\text{-stilbene} \\ \textit{Trans}\text{-stilbene} \end{array}\right] + {}^{3}[(C_6H_5)_2CO] \longrightarrow {}^{3}[C_6H_5CH{=}CHC_6H_5] + (C_6H_5)_2CO$$

$${}^{3}[C_6H_5CH{=}CHC_6H_5] \longrightarrow \underset{93\%}{\textit{cis}\text{-stilbene}} + \underset{7\%}{\textit{trans}\text{-stilbene}}$$

Photodimerisation of olefines

This reaction involves the interaction of an excited triplet with a ground state olefin. The reaction can be inter or intra molecular.

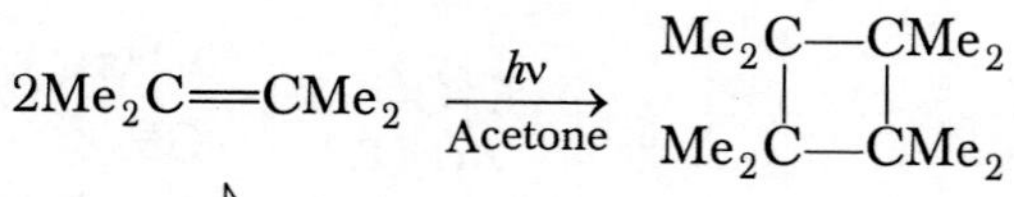

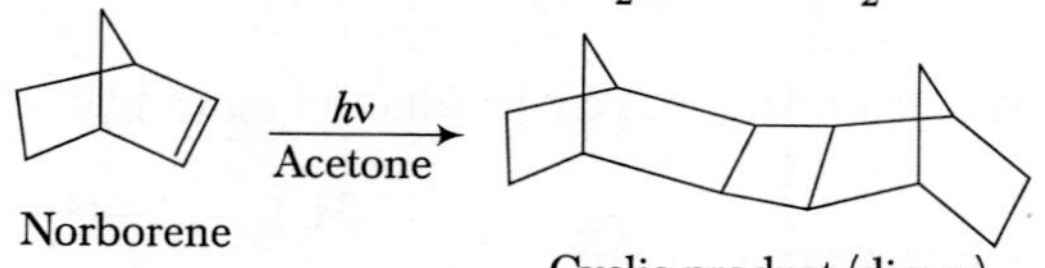

Norborene

Cyclic product (dimer)

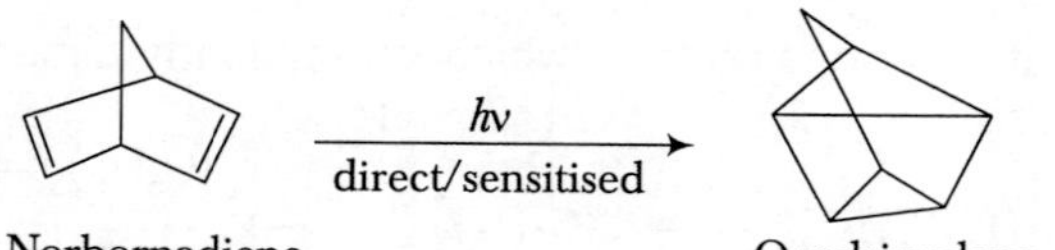

Norbornadiene

Quadricyclane

Certain non-conjugated dienes in mercury sensitised reactions give products derived from cross addition of double bonds.

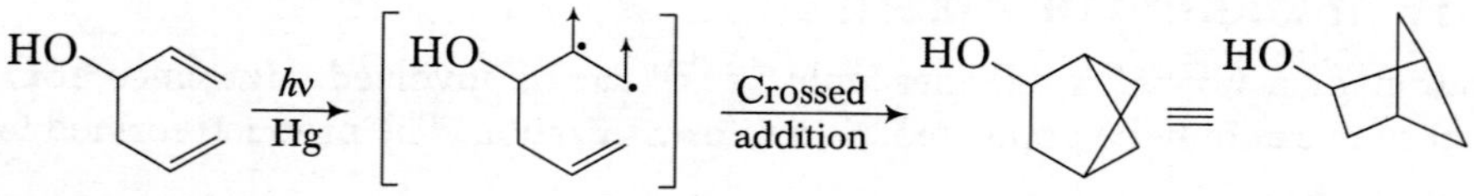

Rearrangement of 1, 4-dienes

1,4-dienes carrying alkyl or aryl substituents on C-3 can be photochemically rearranged to vinyl cyclopropanes. This reaction is called di-π methane rearrangement.

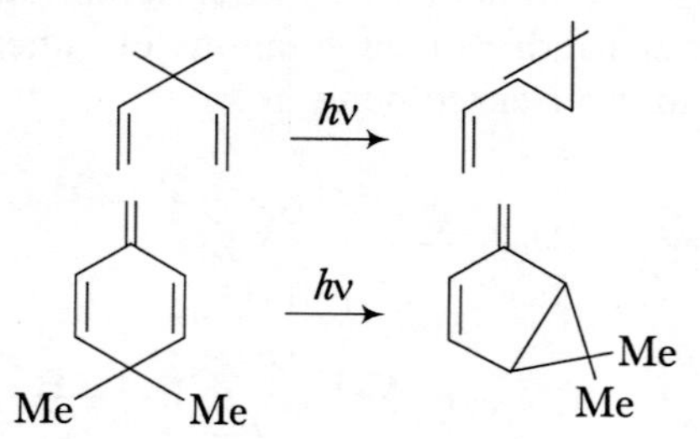

The efficiency and mechanism of the reaction depends on the nature of substrate. For acyclic and monocyclic compounds the singlet state is the reactive species and reaction is stereospecific at all centres with retension at C-1 and C-5 and inversion at C-3 and reaction is concerted reaction.

For unsymmetrical dienes the reaction is regioselective. *e.g.*, compound I gives II not III.

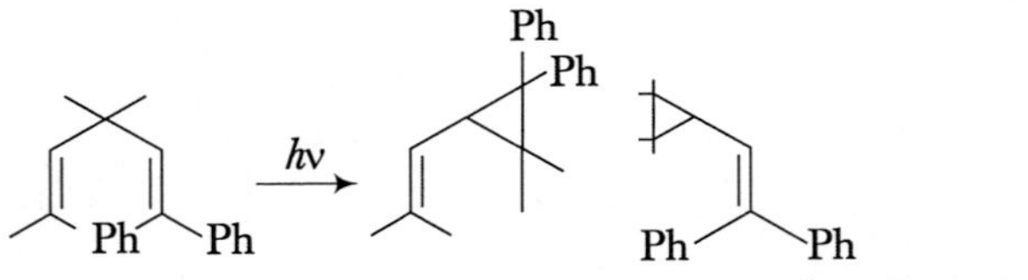

I II III (Not formed)

Mechanism It can be described by the diradical pathway (the C-3 substituents act to stabilize the radical).

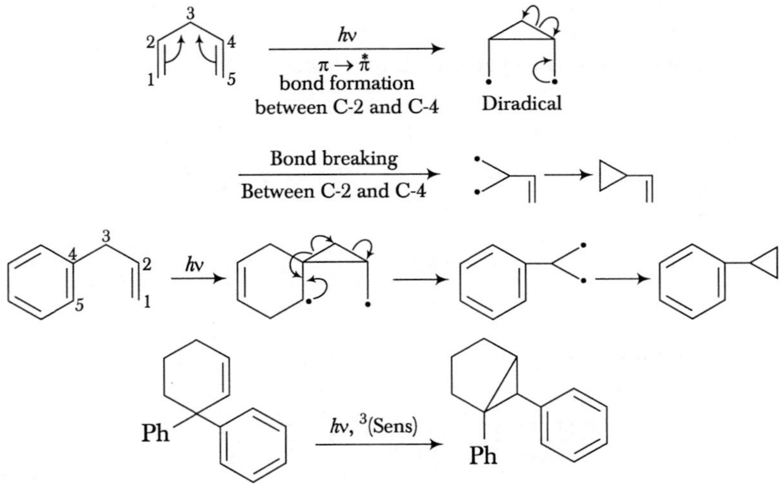

Note • When 1,5-dienes are heated they isomerize in a 3,3-sigmatropic rearrangement known as Cope rearrangement.

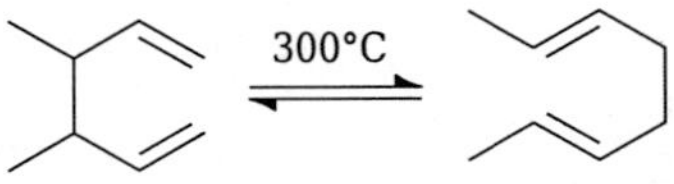

Photo-oxygenation

Photo-oxygenation is also known as photo-peroxidation. The molecular O_2 participates as an oxidizing agent in the reaction. For the addition of molecular O_2, aromatic hydrocarbons and olefins are good substrates because these compounds consist of double bond in their structure. The unsaturated cyclic hydrocarbons also give endoperoxides.

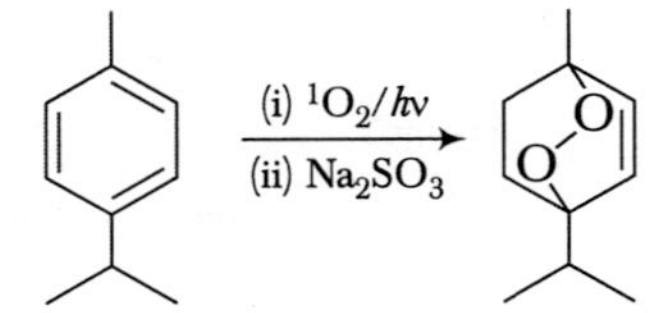

α-terpene α-terpineol

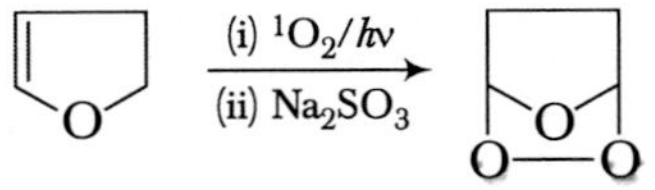

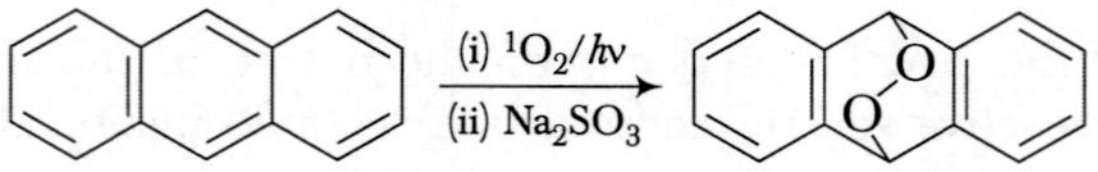

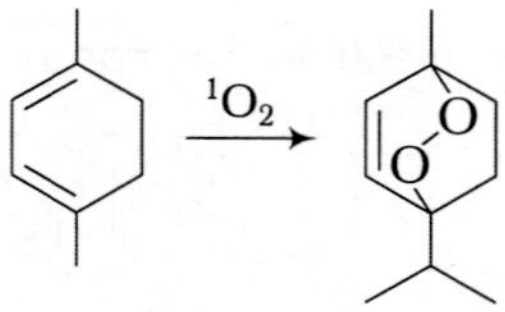

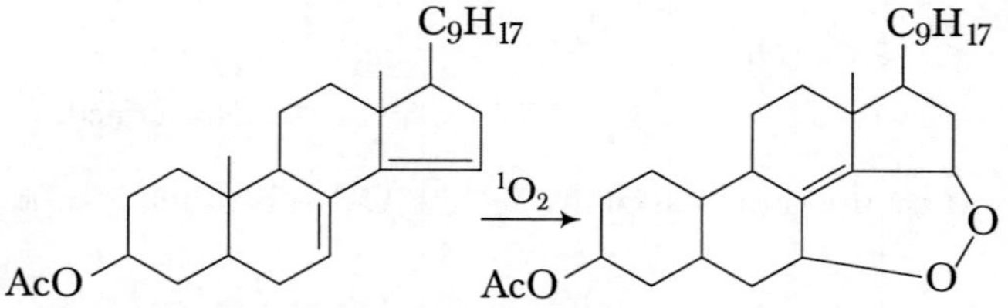

α,β-unsaturated ketones also undergo photo-oxygenation reaction.

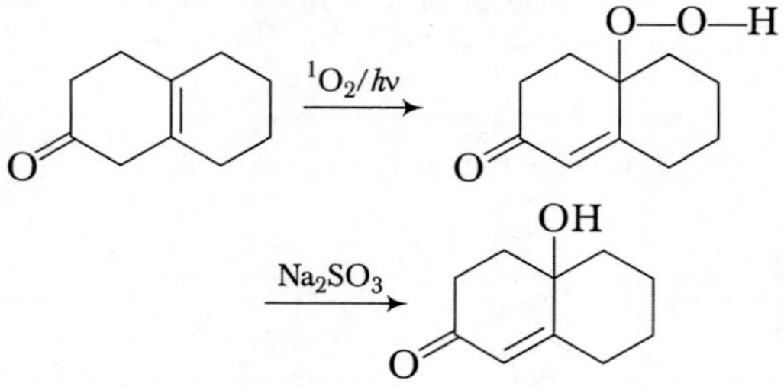

Synthetic utility of this reaction is due to the reduction of peroxides to diols.

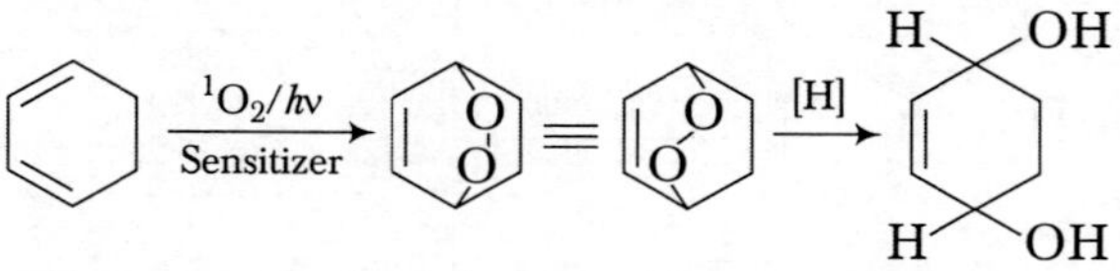

Another *e.g.*, of singlet oxygen reaction is combination of singlet oxygen with a reactive = bond to give 1, 2-dioxetane as intermediate for fragmentation products.

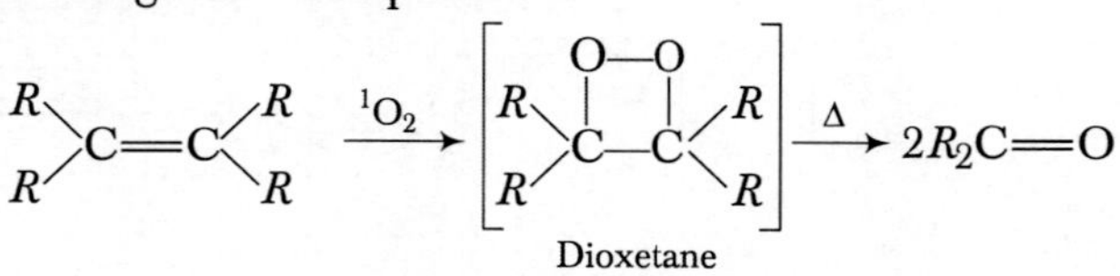

Note • Photolytic conversion of organic nitrites into nitroso alcohols is known as Barton reaction.

• Aliphatic diazo compounds are photoexcited to the $^1(n\pi^*)$ state with visible light.

$$CH_2N_2 \xrightarrow{h\nu} \underset{^1(n\pi^*)}{CH_2N_2^*} \longrightarrow N_2 + \underset{\text{Singlet carbene}}{\overset{\uparrow\downarrow}{CH_2}}$$

$$R_2CN_2 \xrightarrow{h\nu^3(\text{sens.})} \underset{\text{Triplet carbene}}{R_2\overset{\uparrow\downarrow}{C}} + N_2$$

Exercise 1
(For Part 'B')

1. Which type of electronic transition can be seen in saturated aldehydes and ketones?
(a) $\sigma \longrightarrow \sigma^*$
(b) $n \longrightarrow \sigma^*$
(c) $n \longrightarrow \pi^*$ and $\pi \longrightarrow \pi^*$
(d) Only $\pi \longrightarrow \pi^*$

2. Which of the following decay with change in multiplicity is known as ISC?
(a) $S_1 \longrightarrow S_0$ (b) $S_2 \longrightarrow S_1$
(c) $T_2 \longrightarrow T_1$ (d) $S_1 \longrightarrow T_1$

3. In fluorescence which one of the following decay of excited state takes place?
(a) $S_1 \longrightarrow S_0$ (b) $T_1 \longrightarrow S_0$
(c) $T_2 \longrightarrow T_1$ (d) $T_1 \longrightarrow S_0$

4. Which one of the following excited state has a long life?
(a) S_1 (b) S_2 (c) T_1 (d) T_2

5. Dimerisation of cyclopentadiene yields a stable compound represented by

(a) 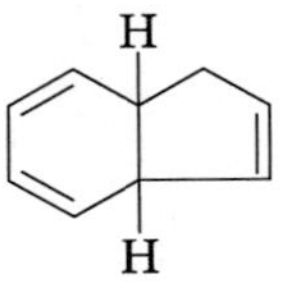

(b) 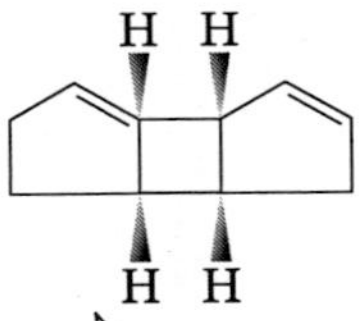

(c) 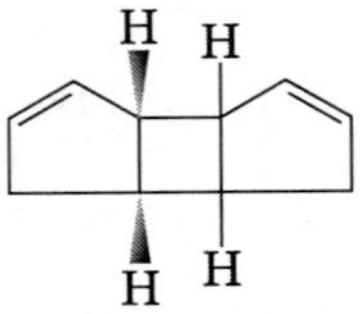

(d) 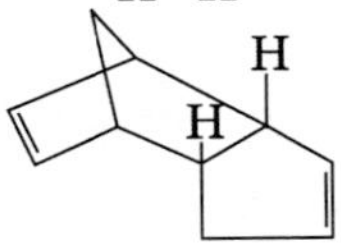

6. Photochemical cyclisation of $2E, 4Z, 6E$ octatriene gives

(a) 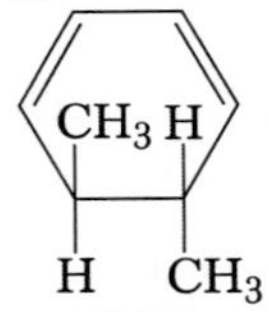

(b) 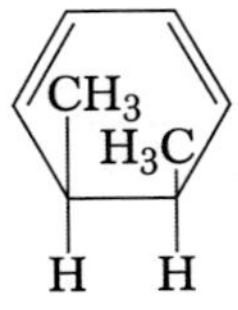

(c) 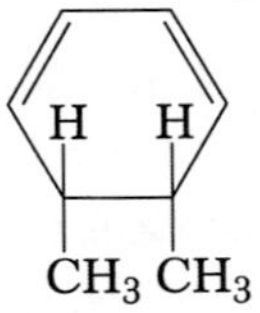

(d) 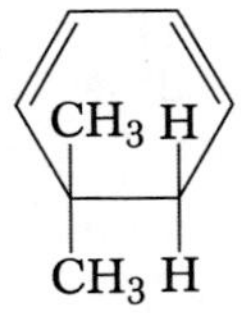

7. Photochemical cyclisation of 1, 6-diene to give

(a) 
(b) 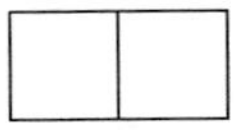
(c) 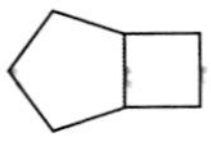
(d) 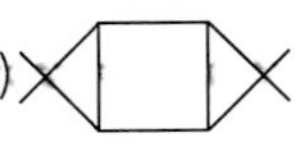

8. Which of the following electronic transitions is disallowed?
(a) $\pi \longrightarrow \pi^*$ (b) $\sigma \longrightarrow \sigma^*$
(c) $n \longrightarrow n^*$ (d) $\delta \longrightarrow \delta^*$

9. Photochemical Paterno Buchi reaction is a cycloaddition between
(a) two >C=C< groups
(b) a >C=O and >C=C< groups
(c) a >C=N—R and >C=C< groups
(d) a >C=S and >C=C< groups

10. The end product of the following reaction is

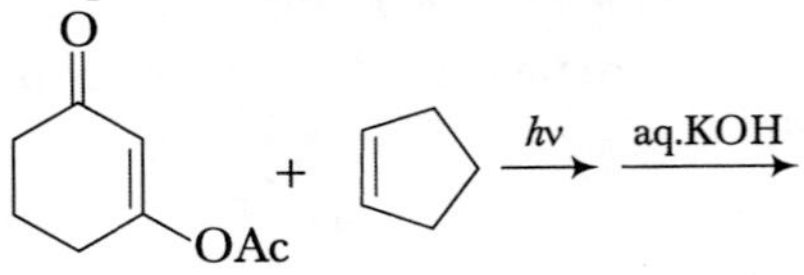

(a) 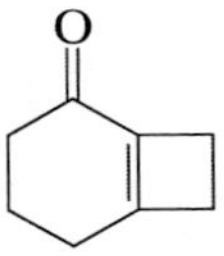

(b) 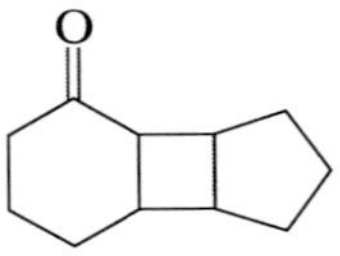

(c) 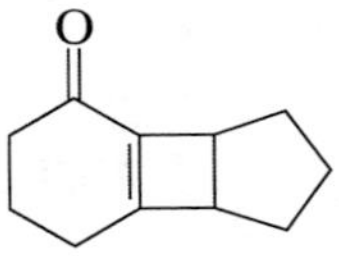

(d) 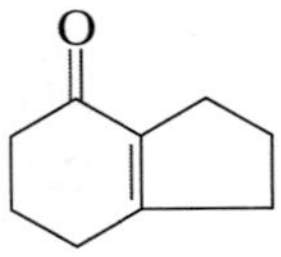

11. 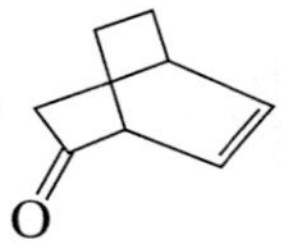

$\xrightarrow[\text{Sensitizer}]{hv}$ A; A is

(a) 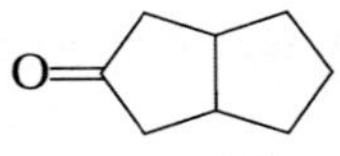

(b) 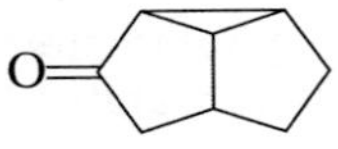

(c) 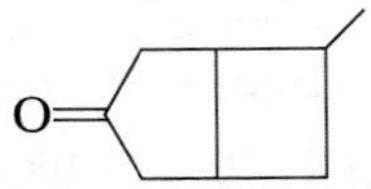

(d) 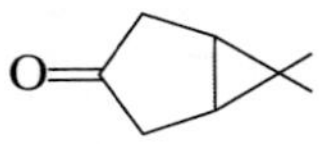

12. The product of the following transformation is

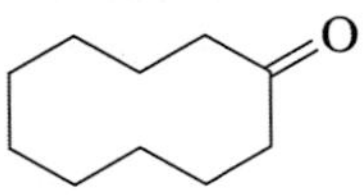

(a) 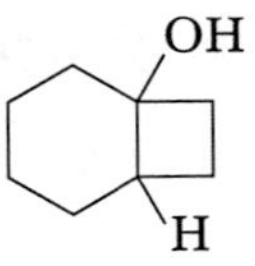

(b) 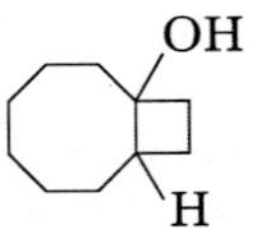

(c) 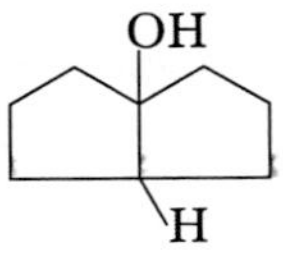

(d) 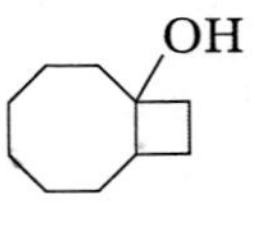

13. Which one of the following decay takes place in phosphorescence?
(a) $S_1 \longrightarrow S_0$ (b) $T_1 \longrightarrow S_0$
(c) $T_2 \longrightarrow T_1$ (d) $T_2 \longrightarrow S_1$

14. Which one of the following statement is false for a photosensitizer as a donor?
(a) It must have sufficient life time
(b) Able to transfer its energy to acceptor molecule
(c) Transfer of energy reaction has higher energy than acceptor
(d) Acceptor has higher energy than donor

15. The free energy change in a photochemical reaction is
(a) always zero
(b) always negative
(c) always positive
(d) may be positive or negative

16. The major product of the following photo cyclo addition is

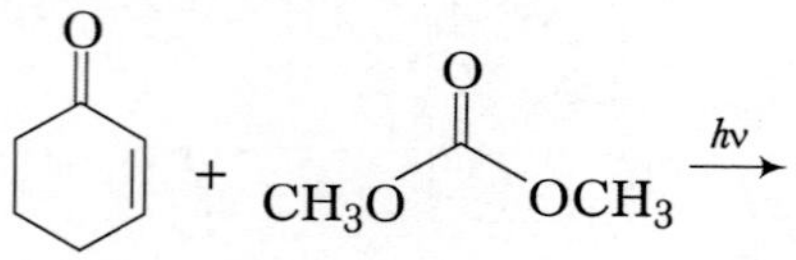

(a)
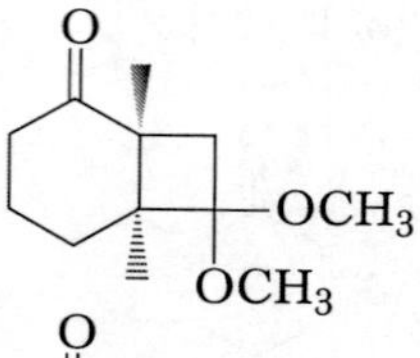

(b)
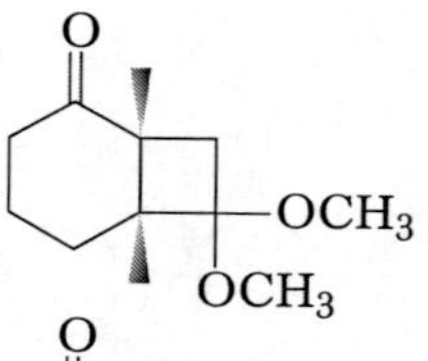

(c)
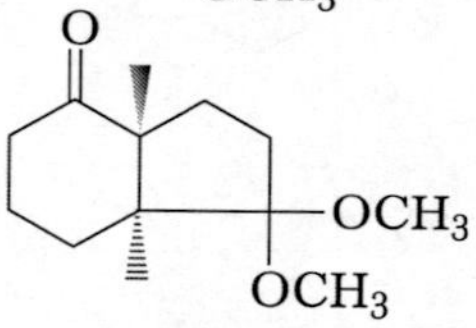

(d)
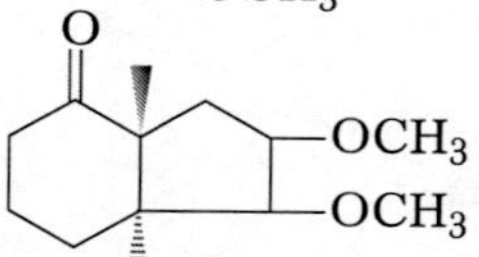

17. If a photochemical reaction has higher quantum yield than unity, it indicates
(a) reversible reaction (b) elementary reaction
(c) chain reaction (d) None of these

18. Oxetanes can be prepared by photochemical reaction between
(a) carbonyl compounds and olefins
(b) carbonyl compounds and alkanes
(c) alcohols and olefins
(d) alcohols and alkanes

19. During the photolysis of ketones in Norrish type II cleavage
(a) a homolytic scisson leads to the formation of a radical intermediate
(b) CO is produced
(c) photoexcited carbonyl group abstracts a gamma hydrogen in primary step
(d) radicals formed dimerize

20. Toluene when refluxed with Br_2 in the presence of light mainly gives
(a) *o*-bromotoluene
(b) *p*-bromotoluene
(c) mixture of *o*- and *p* -bromotoluene
(d) benzylbromide

21. Which one of the following molecules will have $n \longrightarrow \pi^*$ transition at the longest wavelength?
(a) HCHO (b) $CH_3CO\,C_2H_5$
(c) $C_6H_5COC_6H_5$ (d) $CH_3COC_6H_5$

22. The major product *P* formed in the following photochemical reaction is

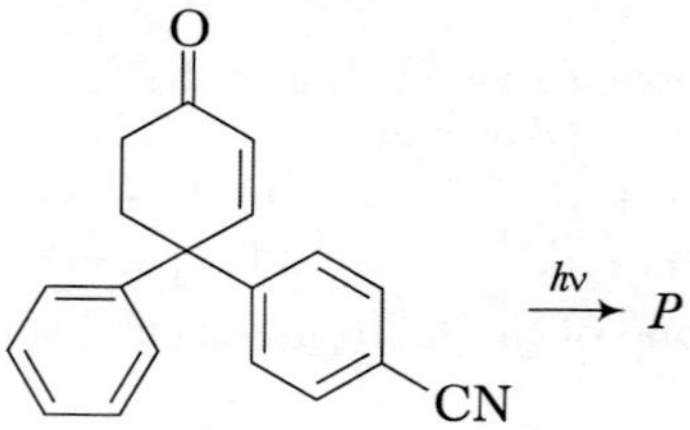

(a)
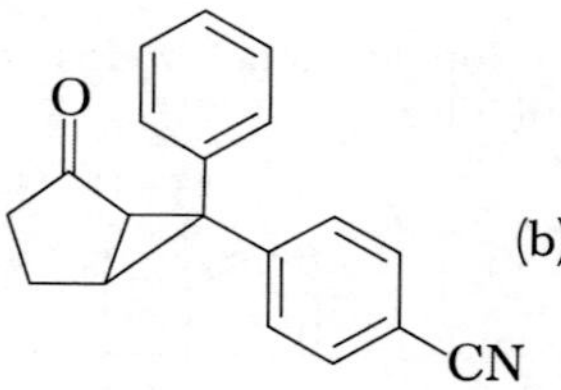

(b)
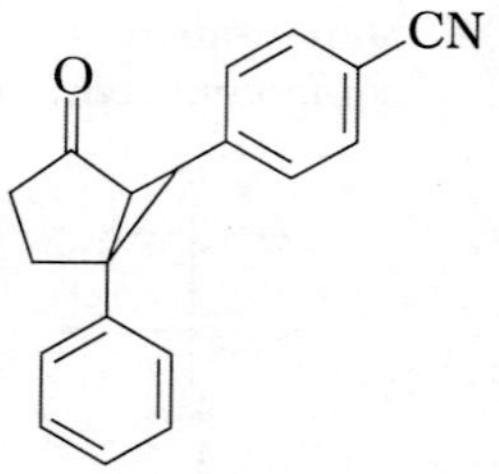

(c)
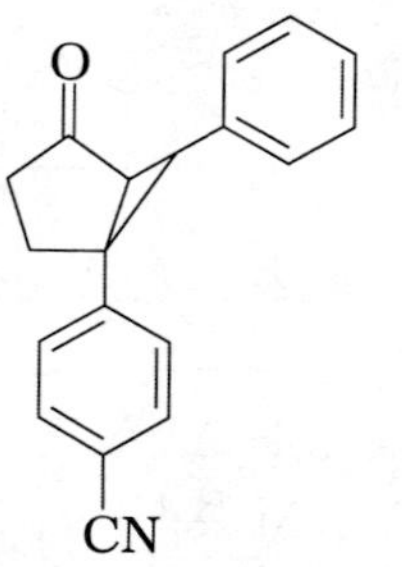

(d)
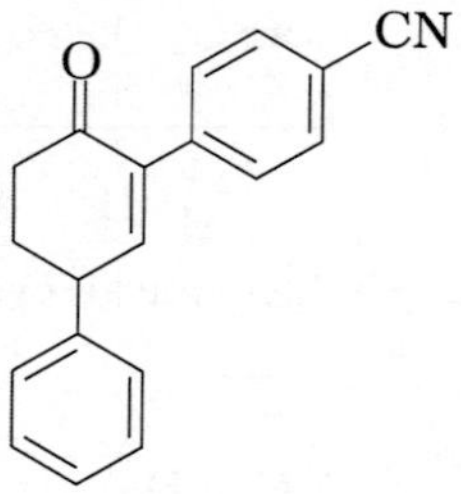

23. Irradiation of benzene in liquid phase at 166 nm–200 nm gives
(a) benzvalene (b) Dewar benzene
(c) fulvene (d) All of these

24. The product of the given photochemical reaction is

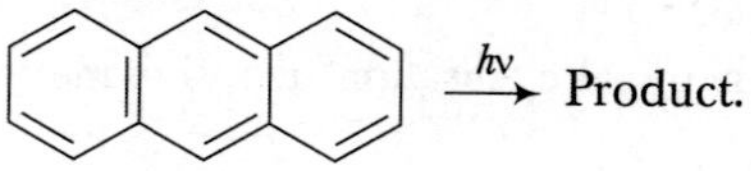

(a)

and
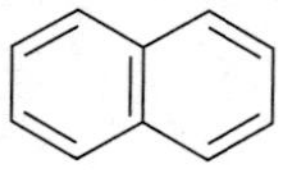

(b) 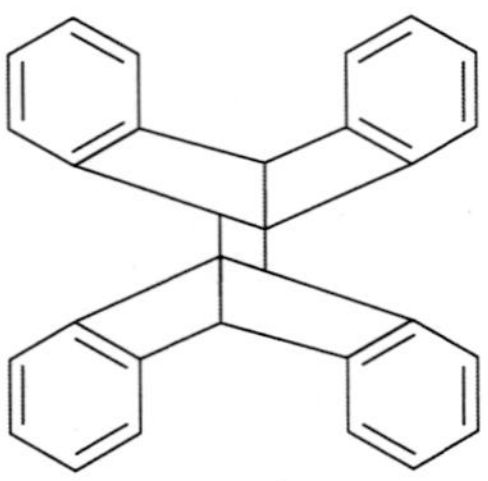

(c) 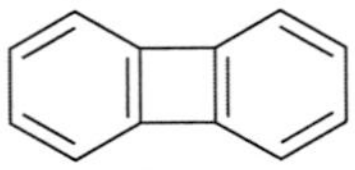

(d) None of the above

25. Addition of oxygen to anthracene in presence of light is known as
(a) Norrish type I reaction
(b) Photochemical addition
(c) Photochemical oxidation
(d) Photochemical reduction

26. Which of the following reactions is an example of photochemical reduction?
(a) Benzophenone into benzpinacol
(b) Ketone into oxetane
(c) Norborene into its dimer
(d) All of the above

27. Photolytic conversion of organic nitrites into nitroso alcohols is known as
(a) Ritter reaction (b) Birch reduction
(c) Barton reaction (d) Paterno-Buchi reaction

28. The product P of the reaction is

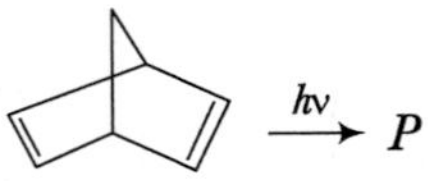

(a) 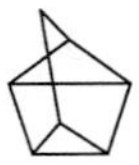 (b) 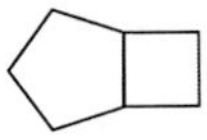

(c) 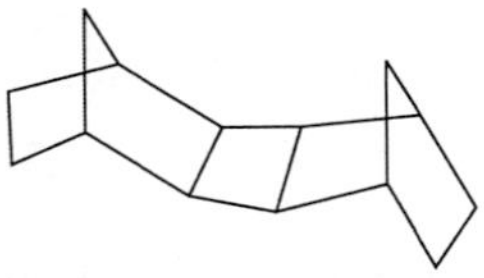 (d) None of these

29. The product of the following photochemical transformation is

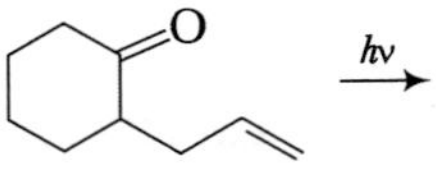

(a) 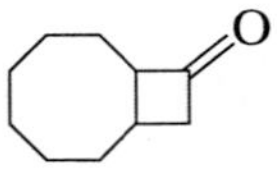 (b) 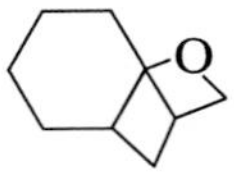

(c) 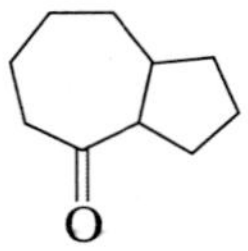 (d) 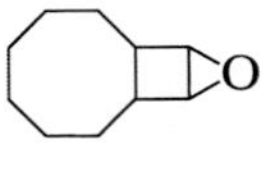

30. The product P is

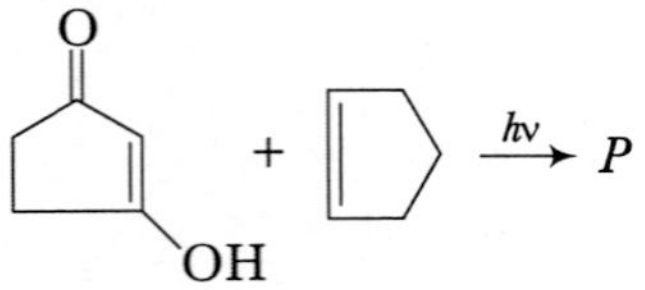

(a) 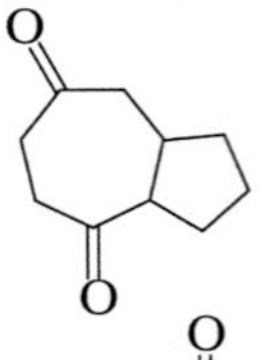 (b) 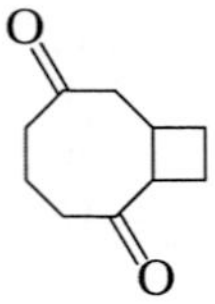

(c) 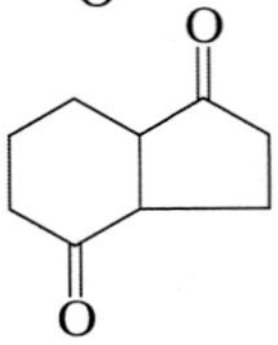 (d) 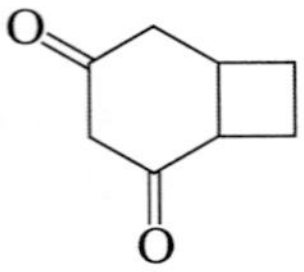

31. Photolysis of carbonyl compound, in which intramolecular abstraction of γ-H-atom, followed by cleavage takes place, is known as
(a) Norrish type III process
(b) Norrish type I process
(c) Norrish type II process
(d) None of the above

32. How many types of electronic transitions are taking place in visible and UV regions?
(a) Two types (b) Three types
(c) Five types (d) Four types

33. Which of the following compounds is found in the photochemical smog?
(a) Formaldehyde (b) Acrolein
(c) Peroxyacetyl nitrate (d) All of these

34. 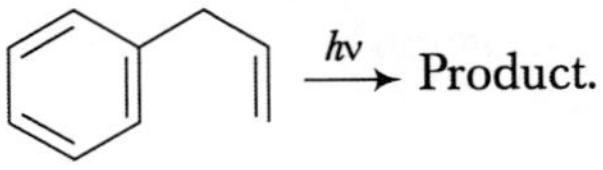

Product is

(a) 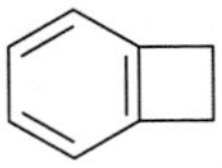 (b) 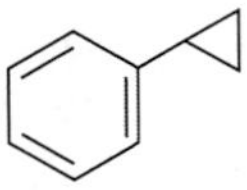

(c) 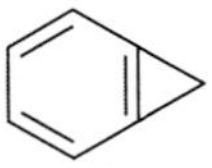 (d) 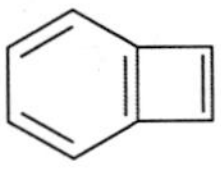

35. Benzene reacts with but-2-ene in presence of light to give

(a) 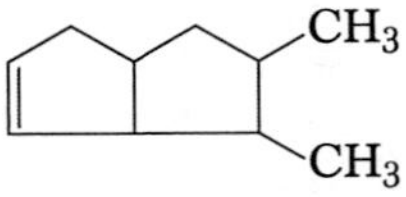 (b) 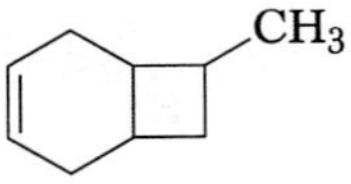

(c) 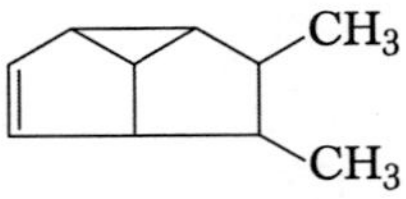 (d) 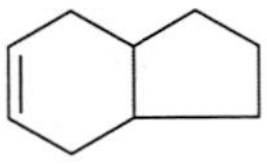

36. Benzophenone reacts with benzhydrol in presence of light to give

(a) $(C_6H_5)_2C(OH)—C(OH)(C_6H_5)_2$

(b) $(C_6H_5)_2—C(=O)—C(OH)(C_6H_5)_2$

(c) $(C_6H_5)_2—C(=O)—C(=O)(C_6H_5)_2$

(d) $C_6H_5—C(=O)—CH(OH)—C_6H_5$

37. The product of the transformation is

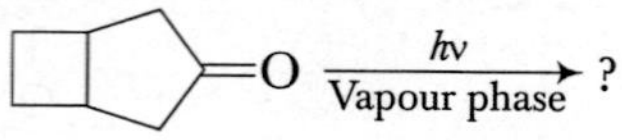

(a) 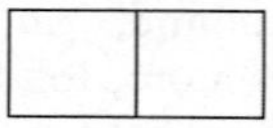 (b) 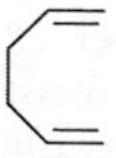

(c) Both (a) and (b) (d) None of these

38. On irradiation with ultraviolet light cyclohexanone gives

(a) 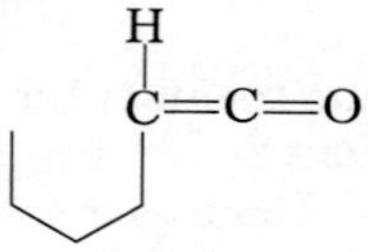 (b) 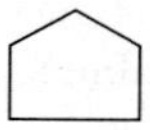

(c) 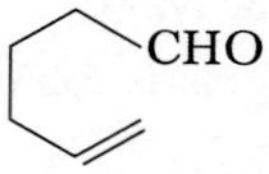 (d) All of these

39. Acetone has been photolyzed in the vapour phase as well as in the liquid phase. The main product of this photochemical transformation is

(a) $CH_3—C(=O)—C(=O)—CH_3$ (b) $CH_3—CH_3$

(c) Both (a) and (b) (d) None of these

40. 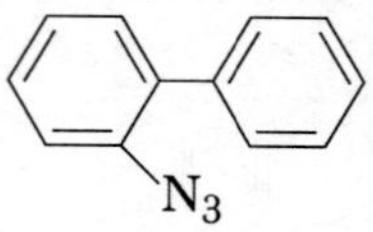 $\xrightarrow{h\nu}$ Product

The product is

(a) 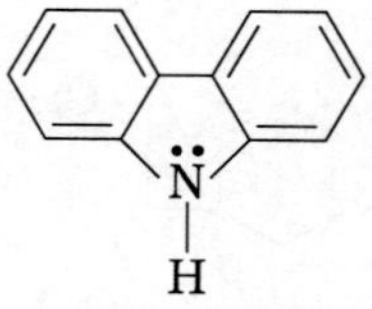

(b) 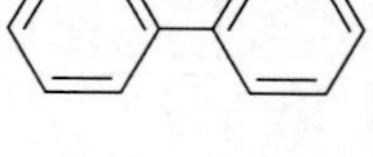

(c) 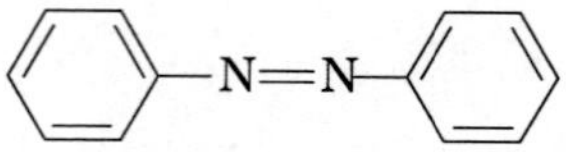

(d) All of the above

41. The product of the following photochemical reaction is

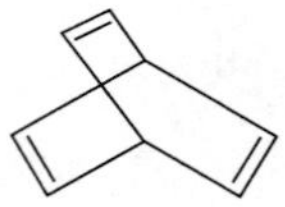

(a) 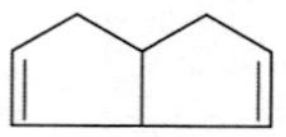 (b) 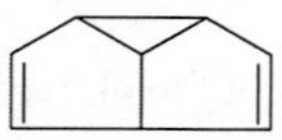

(c) 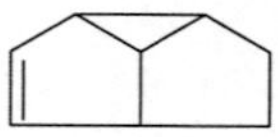 (d) 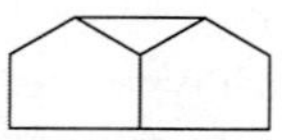

42. Identify the product

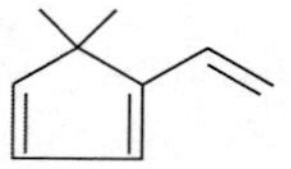 $\xrightarrow{h\nu}$ Product

(a) 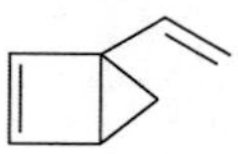 (b) 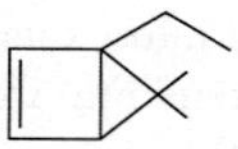

(c) 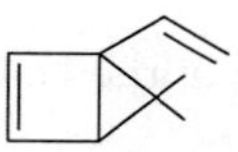 (d) None of these

43. 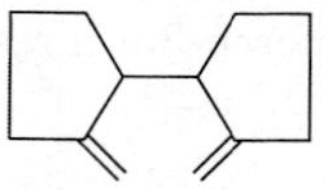 $\xrightarrow{380°C}$ A ; A is

(a) 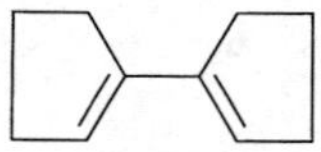 (b) 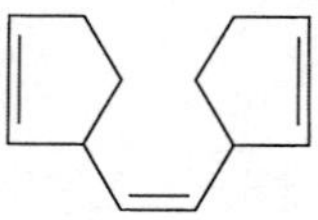

(c) 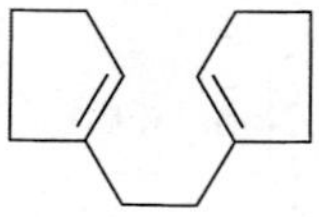 (d) 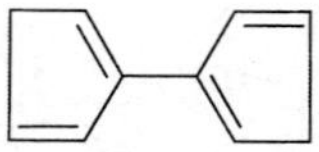

44. The quantum yield of the following reaction is

$$2HBr \longrightarrow H_2 + Br_2$$

(a) 1.5 (b) 1.0

(c) 0.01 (d) 2.0

45. The wavelength of light absorbed for the following reaction is

$$SO_2 + Cl_2 \longrightarrow SO_2Cl_2$$

(a) 4000-4360

(b) 2000-2800

(c) 4200

(d) 1710-1720

Exercise 2
(For Part 'C')

1. Identify the major products P and Q in the following reactions from the list of compounds I to IV.

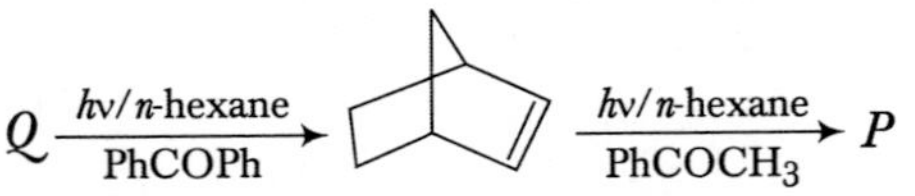

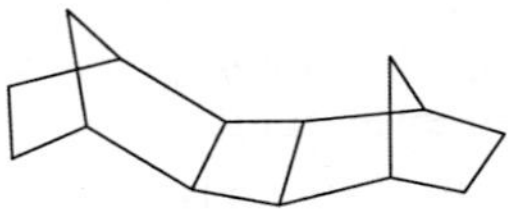

I

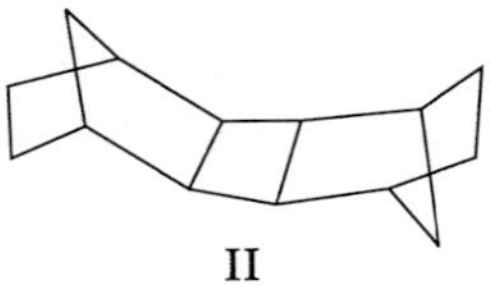

II

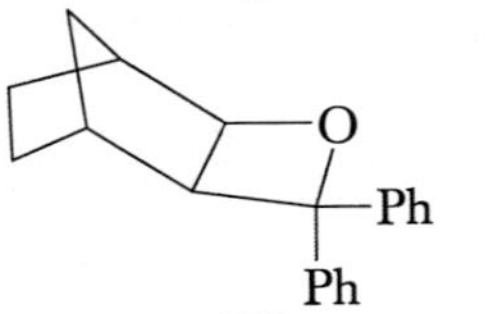

III

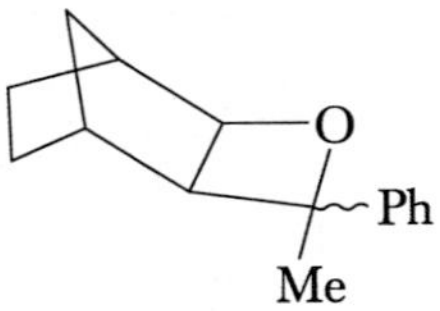

IV

(a) P : I and Q : II
(b) P : II and Q : III
(c) P : IV and Q : II
(d) P : IV and Q : III

2. 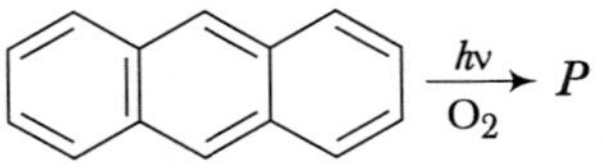

Product P is

(a) 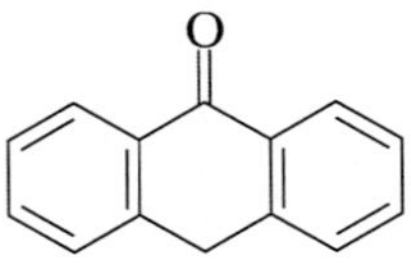

(b) 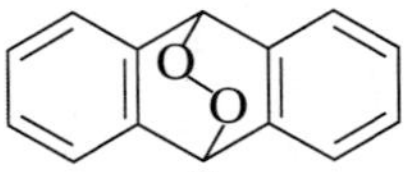

(c) 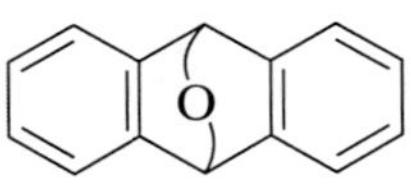

(d) 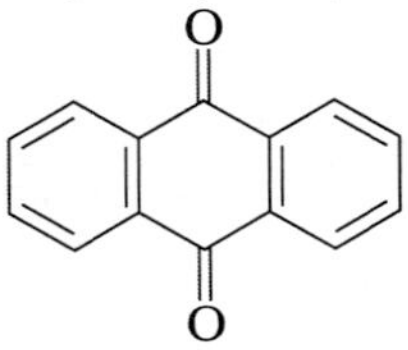

3. The product of the following photochemical reaction is/are

$$\text{2-hexanone} \xrightarrow[\text{Vapour phase}]{h\nu}$$

(a) $CH_3—\underset{H_2C—CH_2}{\overset{OH}{C}}—CH—CH_3$ (cyclobutanol ring: C and CH joined through $H_2C—CH_2$)

(b) $CH_3—\overset{O}{\overset{\|}{C}}—CH_3$

(c) $CH_3CH{=}CH_2$

(d) All of the above

4. Match the Column I with Column II

	Column I (Reaction)		Column II (Type of Photoisomerization reaction)
A.	*cis* $ML_nX_m \xrightarrow{h\nu}$ *trans* ML_nX_m; $n = 2$ or 4; $m = 2$; $n = 3$; $m = 3$	1.	Optical
B.	$(d)\ M(L—L)_3 \xrightarrow{h\nu} (l)M(L—L)_3$	2.	Linkage
C.	$L_nM—XY \xrightarrow{h\nu} L_nM—Y—X$	3.	Geometrical

Codes

	A	B	C
(a)	3	1	2
(b)	2	3	1
(c)	3	2	1
(d)	2	1	3

5. 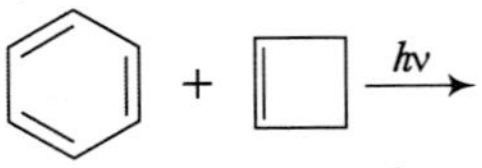 $\xrightarrow{h\nu}$ A; A is

(a) 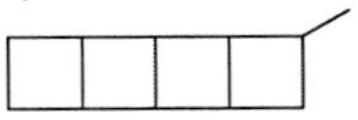

(b) 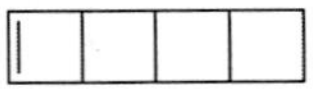

(c) 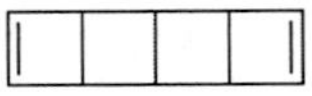

(d) 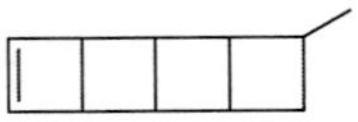

6. 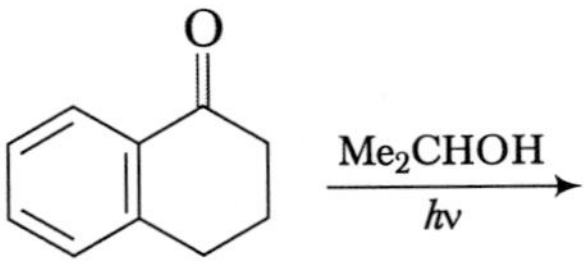

The product of the above transformation is

(a) 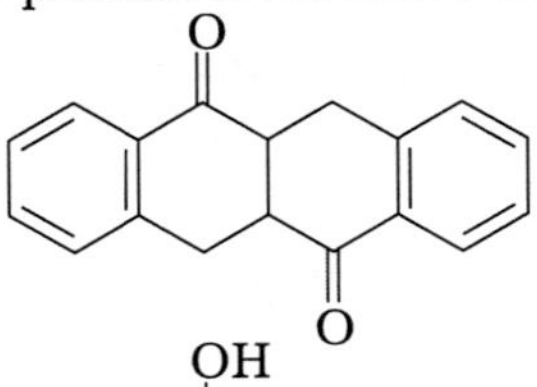

(b) 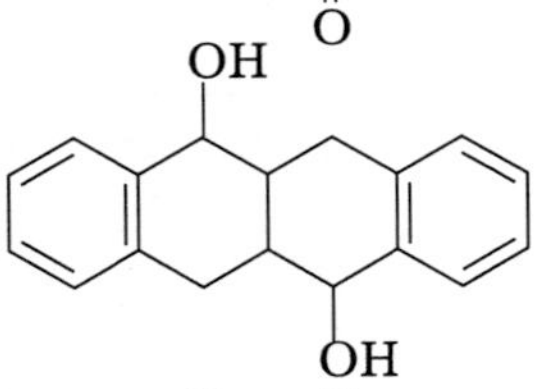

(c) 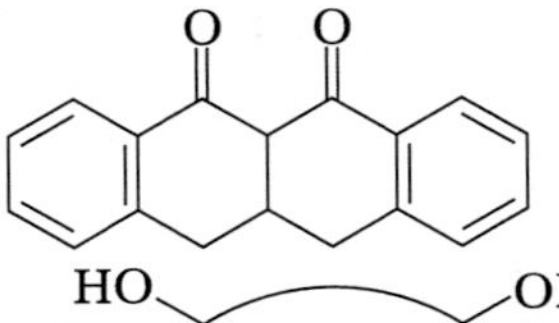

(d) 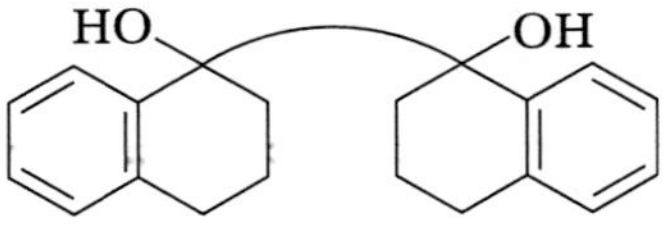

7. The product of the following transformation is

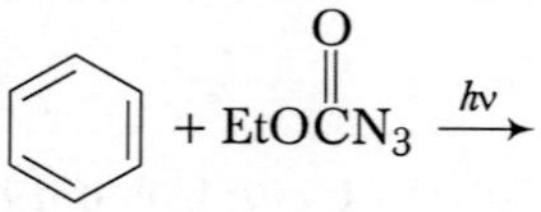

(a) 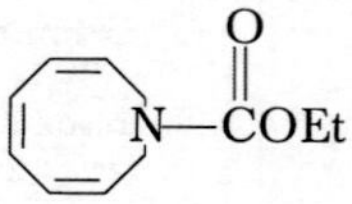 (b) 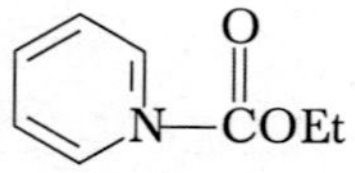

(c) Both (a) and (b) (d) None of these

8. Consider the following statements.

I. In aldehyde both $\pi \longrightarrow \pi^*$ and $n \longrightarrow \pi^*$ transition can be possible.

II. The order of energy required for various electronic transition is $\sigma \longrightarrow \sigma^* > n \longrightarrow \pi^* > \pi \longrightarrow \pi^* > n \longrightarrow \sigma^*$.

III. In fluorescence $S_1 \longrightarrow S_0$ decay of excited state takes place.

Select the correct statement.

(a) I, II (b) I, II, III
(c) I, III (d) II, III

9. 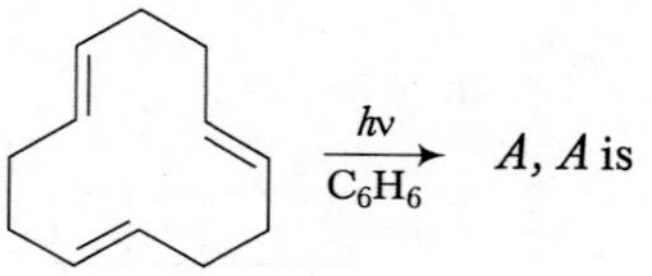

(a) 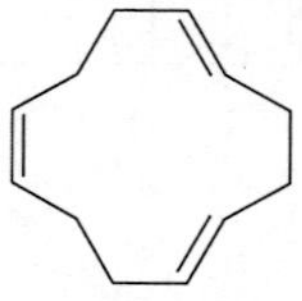 (b) 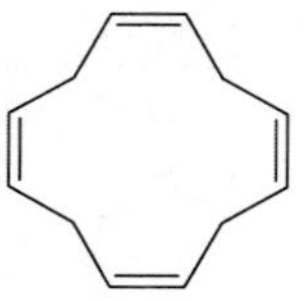

(c) 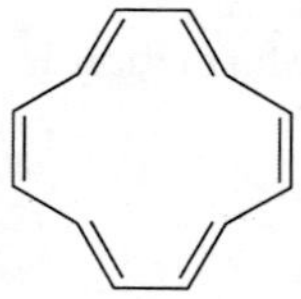 (d) None of these

10. Match the Column I with Column II.

Column I	Column II
A. $S_1 \longrightarrow S_0 + h\nu$	1. Heat internal conversion
B. $S_1 \longrightarrow S_0$	2. Phosphorescence
C. $S_1 \longrightarrow T_1$	3. Fluorescene
D. $T_1 \longrightarrow S_0 + h\nu$	4. Intersystem crossing

Codes

	A	B	C	D
(a)	2	1	4	3
(b)	3	1	4	2
(c)	2	4	1	3
(d)	3	4	1	2

11. The product is/are

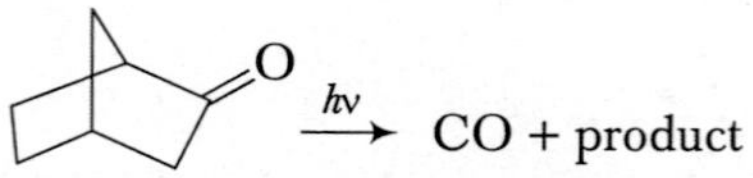

(a) 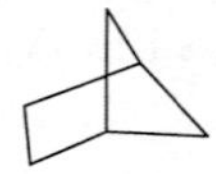 (b) 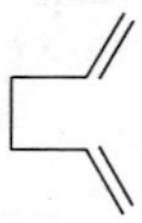

(c) Both (a) and (b) (d) None of these

12. The major product forms, when benzophenone and isobutene reacts in the presence of light

(a) 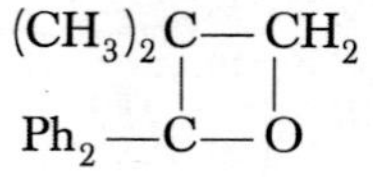 (b) 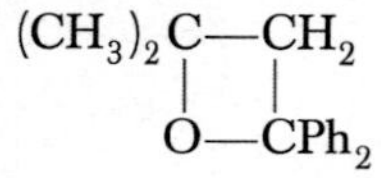

(c) 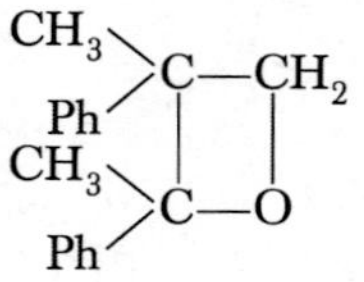 (d) 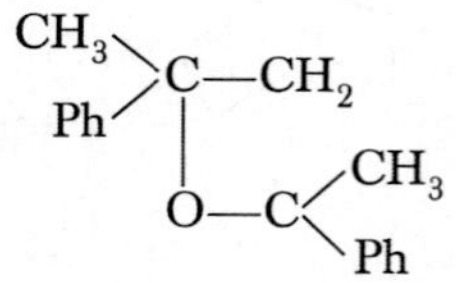

13. 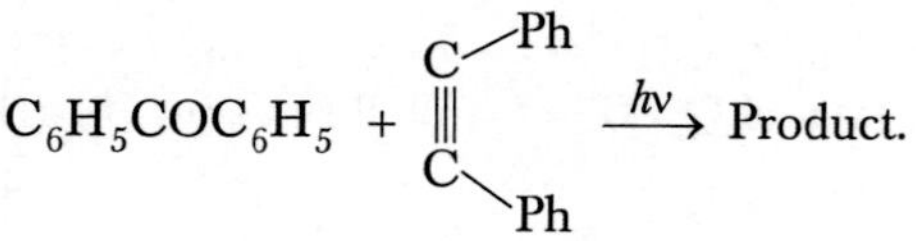

Identify the product.

(a) 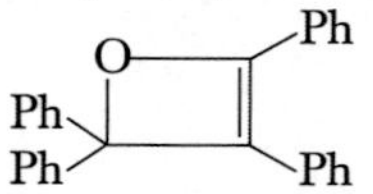 (b) 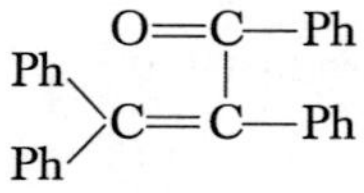

(c) 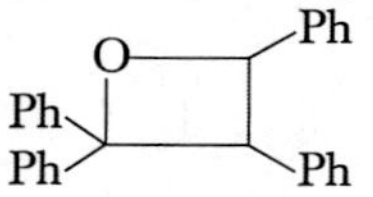 (d) 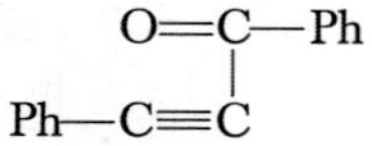

14. 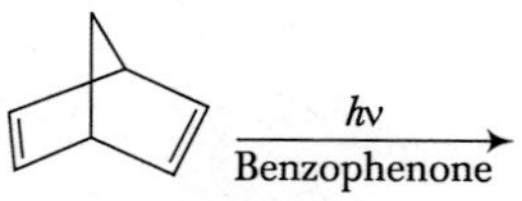

The product of the above photochemical transformation is

(a) 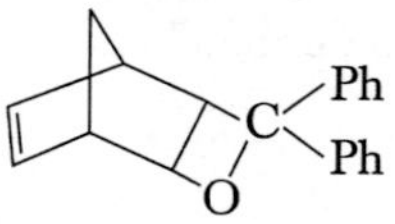 (b) 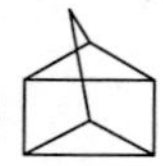

(c) Both (a) and (b) (d) None of these

15. Consider the following statements.

I. Photosensitization is a important route for the production of triplet excited state in organic molecules.

II. The transition from excited singlet to excited triplet state takes place *via* intersystem crossing.

III. Ultraviolet and visible radiations are useful to bipolymers.

IV. Mercury atoms can be used as photosensitizers in vapour phase reactions.

Select the incorrect statements.

(a) II, III (b) I, III, IV
(c) II, III, IV (d) Only III

16. The products form in the following photochemical reaction

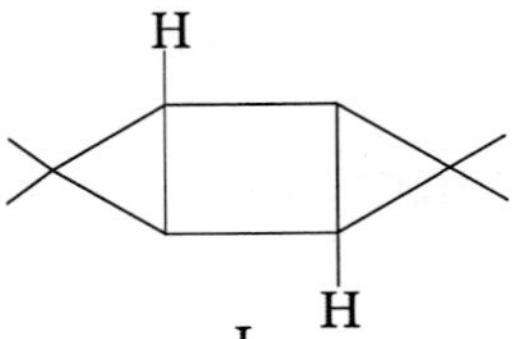

I

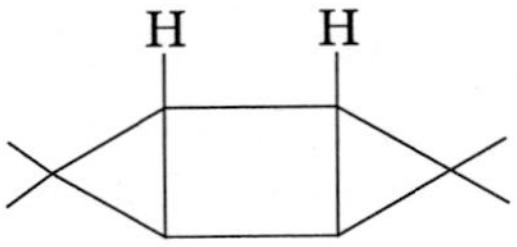

II

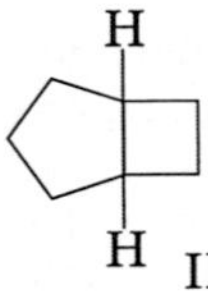

III

(a) I, III (b) I, II
(c) II, III (d) I, II, III

17. The product '*P*' in the following transformation is

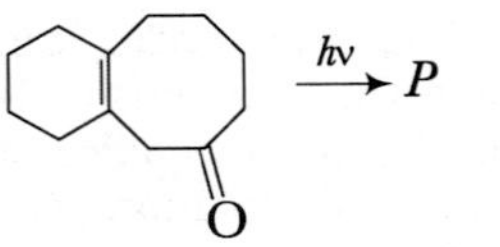

(a) 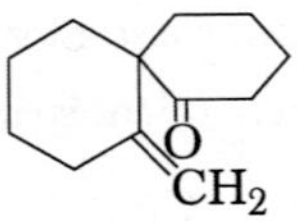
(b) 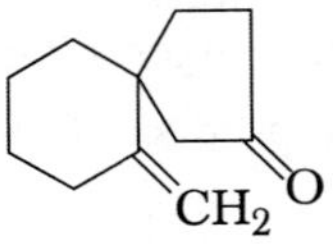
(c) 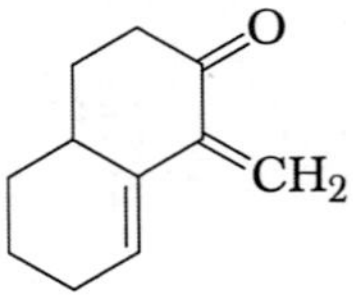
(d) None of these

18. 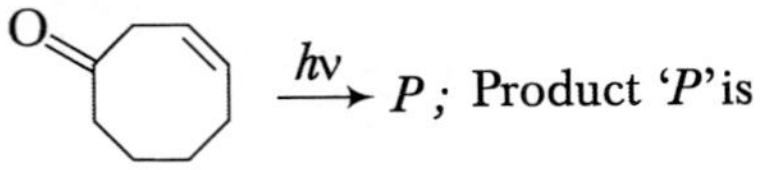 Product '*P*' is

(a) 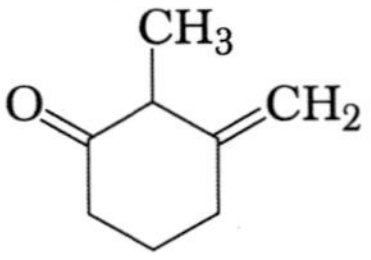
(b) 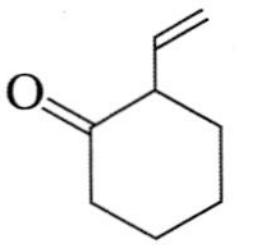
(c) 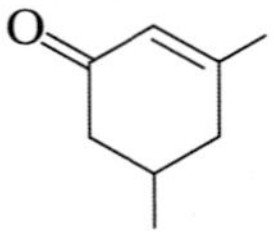
(d) 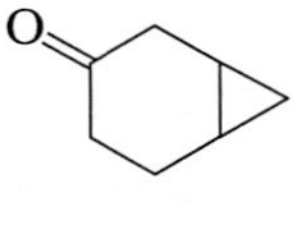

19. 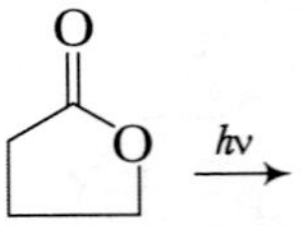 Product

What is/are the product in the above reaction?

(a) 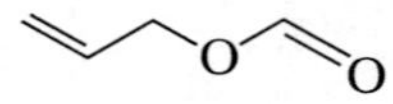
(b) $CHOCH_2CH_2CHO$
(c) Both (a) and (b) (d) None of these

20. Match the Column I with Column II.

	Column I		Column II
A.	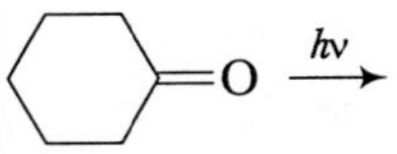	1.	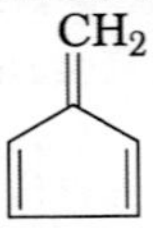
B.	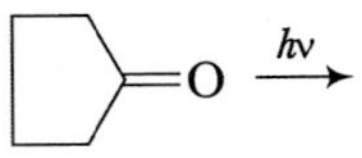	2.	
C.	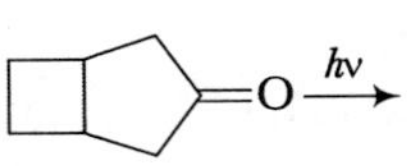	3.	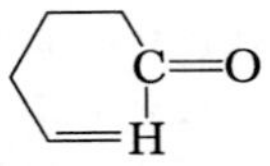
D.	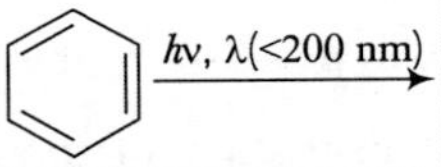	4.	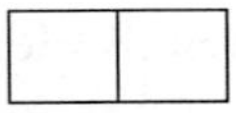

Codes

	A	B	C	D
(a)	3	2	4	1
(b)	2	3	4	1
(c)	3	4	1	2
(d)	4	2	1	3

21. 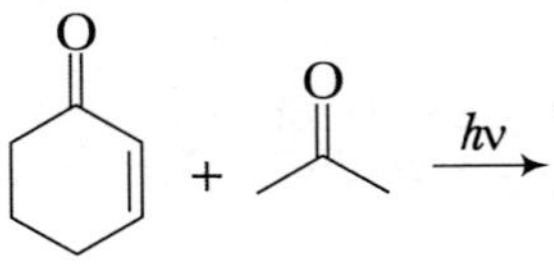 Product

Select the product from the given compounds

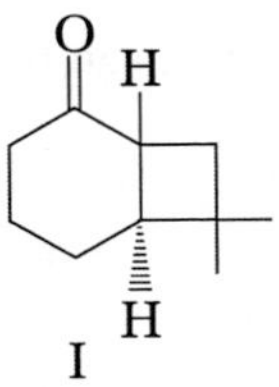

I

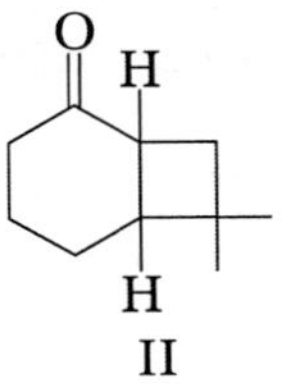

II

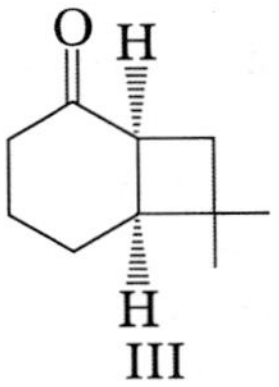

III

(a) I, II (b) II, III
(c) I, II, III (d) Only III

22. The major product in the following transformation is

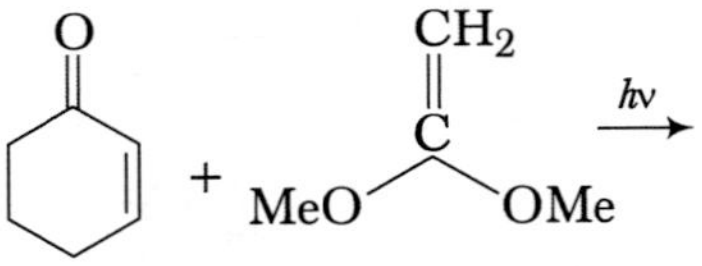

(a) 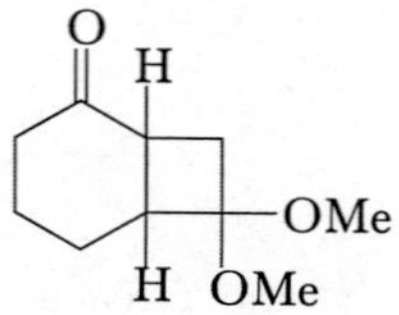

(b) 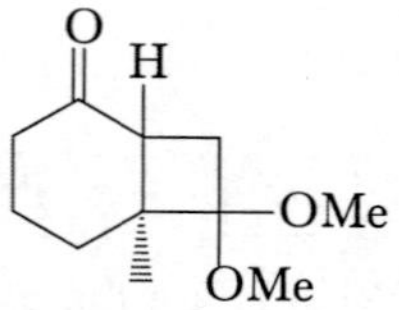

(c) 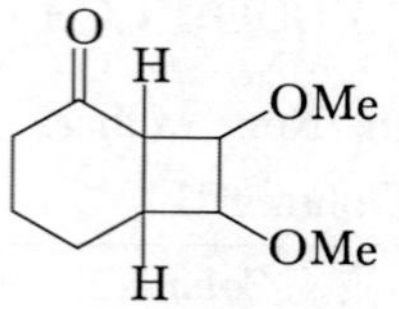

(d) 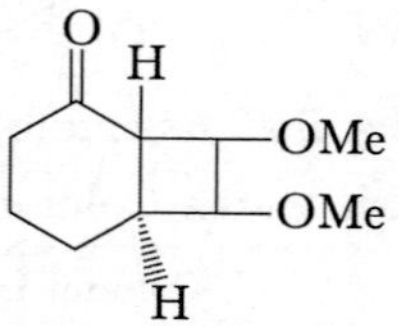

Assertion & Reason

Codes

(a) Both A and R are true and R is the correct explanation of A.
(b) Both A and R are true but R is not the correct explanation of A.
(c) A is true but R is false.
(d) A is false but R is true.

23. **Assertion (A)** Aldehyde and ketone absorb light in the 230-330 nm region.

Reason (R) It results in $n \longrightarrow \overset{*}{\pi}$ transition.

24. **Assertion (A)** Direct excitation of the S_0 to T_1 is not possible.

Reason (R) Triplet state is populated *via* excited singlet state (S_1).

25. **Assertion (A)** The singlet excited state S_1 can undergo different physical and chemical process.

Reason (R) The life time of singlet excited state S_1 is relatively long.

26. **Assertion (A)** In presence of oxygen and a photosensitizing dye, cotton, fibres undergo photodegradation.

Reason (R) Ultraviolet light and visible radiations are harmful to bipolymers.

27. Which type of the electronic transition can be seenin esters?

(a) $\sigma \rightarrow \overset{*}{\sigma}$ (b) $n \rightarrow \overset{*}{\sigma}$ (c) $\pi \rightarrow \overset{*}{\pi}$ (d) $n \rightarrow \overset{*}{\pi}$

28. In photophysical process of a organic molecule, which of the following process is occured?

(a) Fluorescence (b) Phosphorescence
(c) Intersystem crossing (d) Internal conversion

29. The product/s of the following photochemical reaction is/are

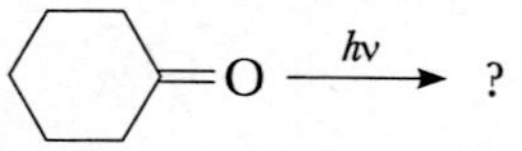

(a) 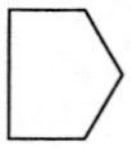 (b) 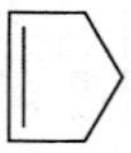

(c) 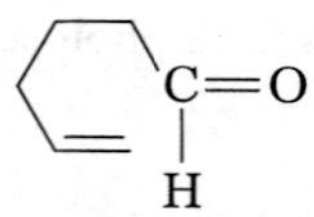 (d) 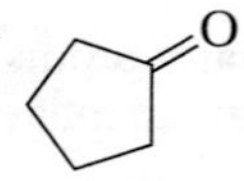

30. In the Norrish type I reaction of the following compound which of the products are obtained?

$$CH_3CH_2CH_2-\overset{\overset{\displaystyle O}{\|}}{C}-CH_2CH_2CH_3 \xrightarrow{h\nu}$$

(a) $CH_3CH_2CH{=}C{=}O$
(b) $CH_3CH_2CH_2CHO$
(c) $CH_3CH{=}CH_2$
(d) $CH_3-\underset{\displaystyle CH_3}{\underset{|}{CH}}-CH_2CHO$

31. Select the correct statements from the following.

(a) PAN is a important compound of photochemical smog
(b) Photolytic conversion of organic nitrites into nitroso alcohols is known as Baton reaction
(c) In alkanes $\sigma \rightarrow \overset{*}{\pi}$ transitions occur.
(d) A triplet state is more stable than corresponding excited singlet state.

Directions (Q. Nos. 32 to 34)

Intramolecular reaction in cyclic carbonyl compounds occurs by α-cleavage. On photolysis cyclic ketones, lactones, lactams and anhydrides give a biradical species. These photo reactions take place in solution or gas phase. After formation of a biradical, a hydrogen atom is abstracted from α-carbon. Ultimately it gives hydrocarbons and olefins.

32. The product of following photochemical reaction is

(a) 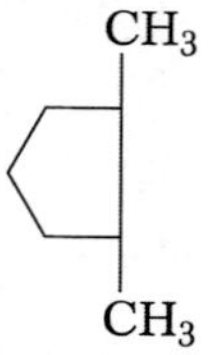 (b) 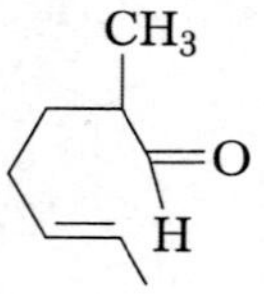

(c) Both (a) and (b) (d) None of these

33. 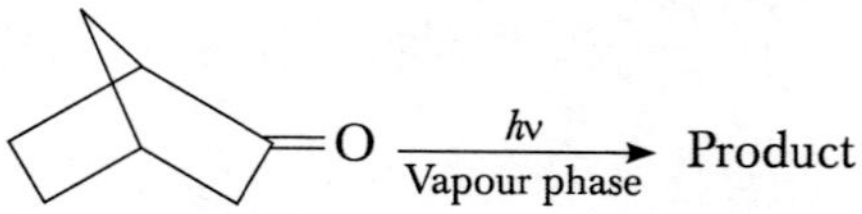

Product is

(a) 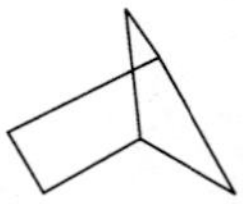 (b) 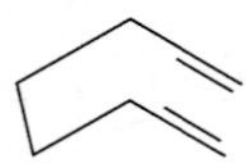

(c) Both (a) and (b) (d) 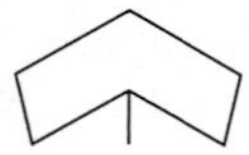

34. 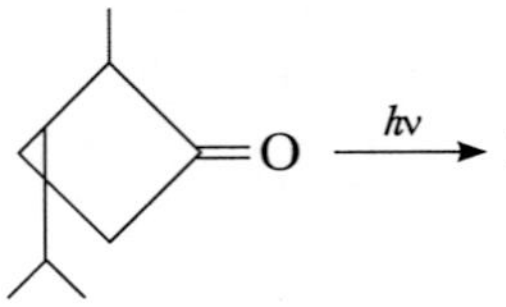 Product ; Product is

(a) 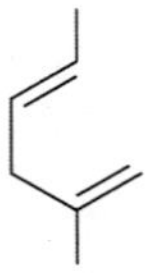
(b) 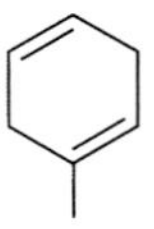

(c) 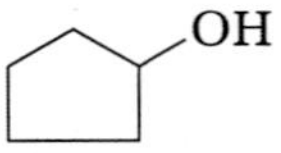
(d) 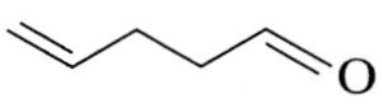

Directions (Q. No. 35 to 37)

It has been observed that automobiles contribute a large number of hydrocarbons emitted to the atmosphere. Among those hydrocarbons, methane, ethane, propane, ethene, *iso*-pentane, *iso*-butane, toluene, *m*-xylene etc., are found in the atmosphere. Hydrocarbons are removed from the atmosphere by several chemical and photochemical reactions. By oxidation process they give CO_2, acids and aldehydes as end products which are washed away by rain. An important property of atmosphere is that it is trapped by an inversion layer of automobile pollutants and at the same time is exposed to intense sunlight and forms photochemical oxidants in the atmosphere. This gives rise to the phenomenon of photochemical smog.

35. Which of the following is the major, naturally occurring compound emitted into the earth?
(a) Methane (b) Ethane
(c) Ethene (d) *Iso*-pentane

36. Sometimes, a specific smell is found during the smog. It is due to the
(a) higher concentration level of hydrogen
(b) higher concentration level of ozone
(c) higher concentration level of oxygen
(d) higher concentration of chlorine

37. The compound which is/are found in the photochemical smog
(a) peroxyacetyl nitrate (b) acrolein
(c) ethyl alcohol (d) Both (a) and (b)

Answers

Exercise 1

1. (c)	**2.** (d)	**3.** (a)	**4.** (c)	**5.** (d)	**6.** (a)	**7.** (c)	**8.** (d)	**9.** (b)	**10.** (c)
11. (b)	**12.** (b)	**13.** (b)	**14.** (d)	**15.** (d)	**16.** (a)	**17.** (c)	**18.** (a)	**19.** (c)	**20.** (d)
21. (c)	**22.** (b)	**23.** (d)	**24.** (b)	**25.** (c)	**26.** (a)	**27.** (c)	**28.** (a)	**29.** (b)	**30.** (a)
31. (c)	**32.** (d)	**33.** (d)	**34.** (b)	**35.** (c)	**36.** (a)	**37.** (c)	**38.** (d)	**39.** (c)	**40.** (a)
41. (b)	**42.** (c)	**43.** (c)	**44.** (d)	**45.** (c)					

Exercise 2

1. (b)	**2.** (b)	**3.** (d)	**4.** (a)	**5.** (b)	**6.** (d)	**7.** (a)	**8.** (c)	**9.** (a)	**10.** (b)
11. (c)	**12.** (a)	**13.** (b)	**14.** (c)	**15.** (d)	**16.** (b)	**17.** (a)	**18.** (b)	**19.** (c)	**20.** (a)
21. (c)	**22.** (b)	**23.** (a)	**24.** (a)	**25.** (a)	**26.** (b)	**27.** (b,d)	**28.** (a,b,c,d)	**29.** (a,c)	**30.** (a,b,c)
31. (a,b,d)	**32.** (c)	**33.** (c)	**34.** (a)	**35.** (a)	**36.** (b)	**37.** (d)			

Hints & Solutions

Exercise 1

7. 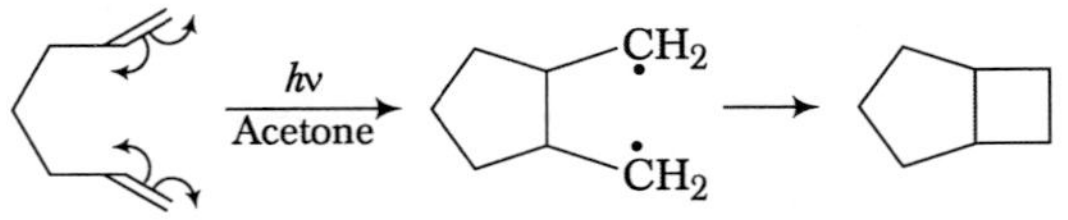

1,6-diene

9. Paterno Buchi reaction is the cycloaddition of an excited ketone to an olefin to give oxetane.

10. 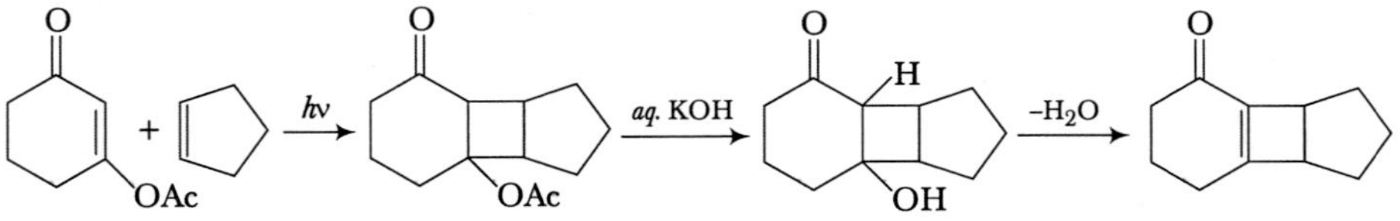

12.

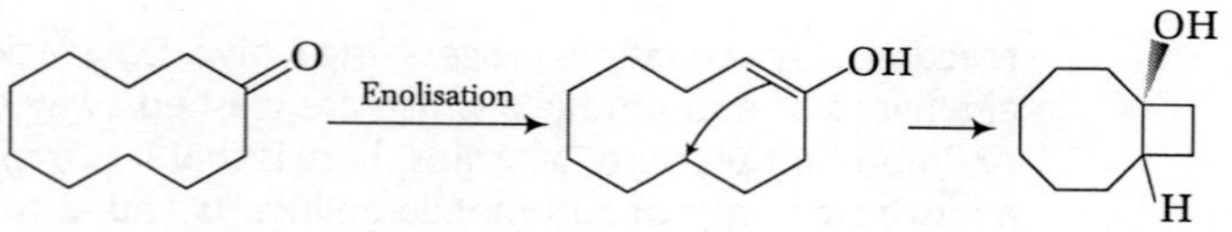

16.

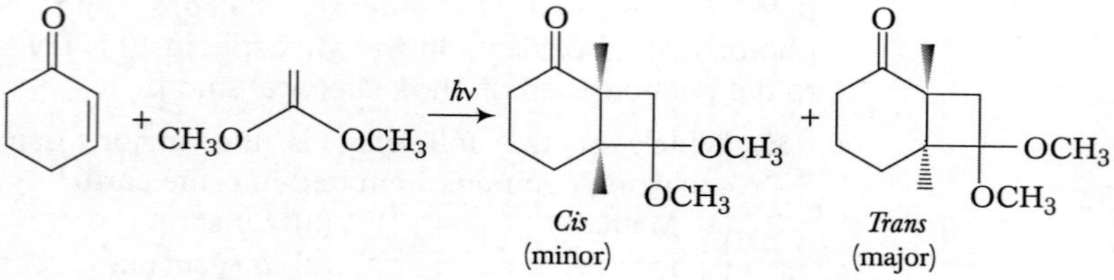

23.

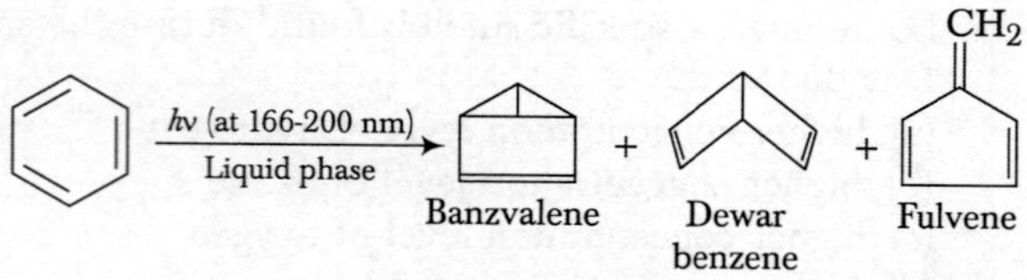

24.

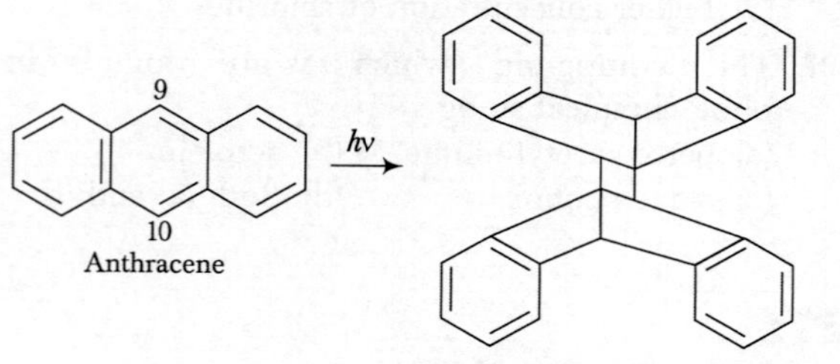

(Dimerisation) join at 9, 10 position

30.

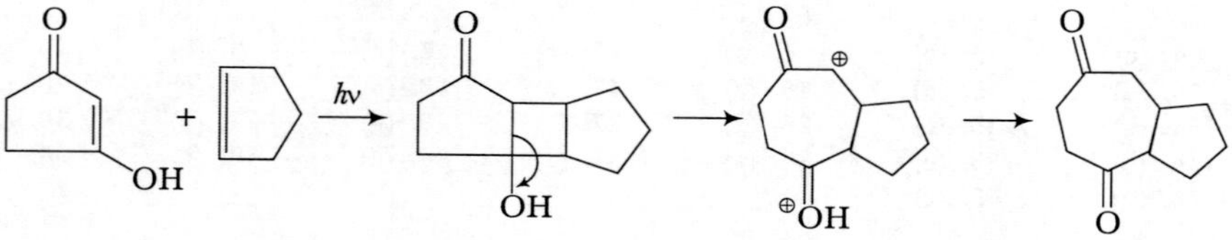

35.

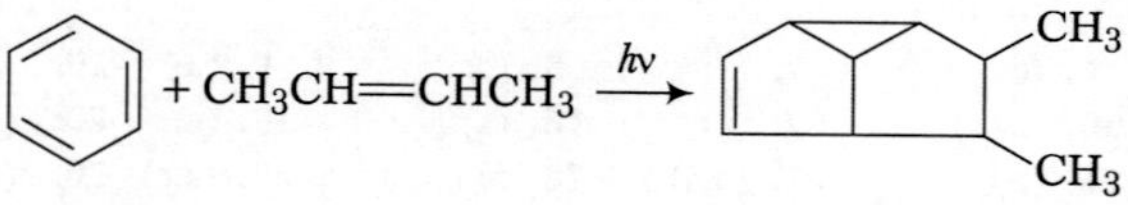

37.

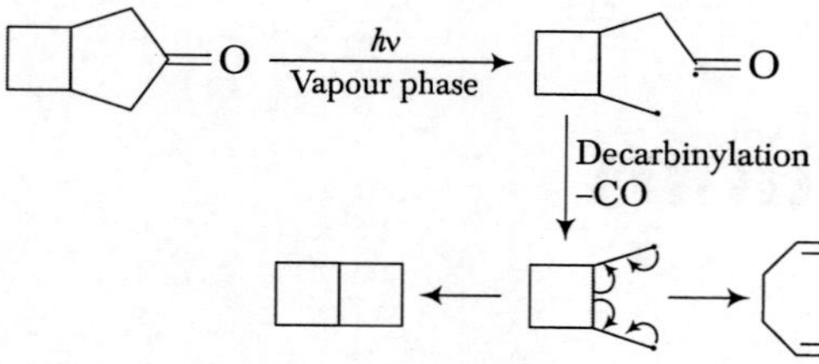

39.

$$CH_3-\overset{O}{\overset{\|}{C}}-CH_3 \xrightarrow{h\nu} \dot{C}H_3 + CH_3\overset{O}{\overset{\|}{C}}\bullet$$

$$2CH_3\overset{O}{\overset{\|}{C}}\bullet \longrightarrow CH_3\overset{O}{\overset{\|}{C}}-\overset{O}{\overset{\|}{C}}CH_3$$

$$CH_3-\overset{O}{\overset{\|}{C}}\bullet \longrightarrow {}^{\bullet}CH_3 + CO$$

$$2CH_3^{\bullet} \longrightarrow CH_3-CH_3$$

40. 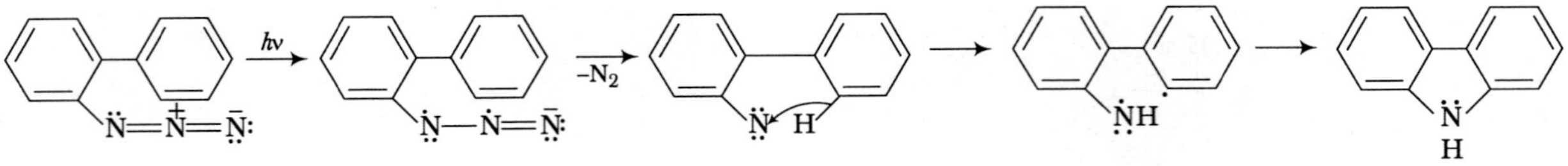

Exercise 2

3. 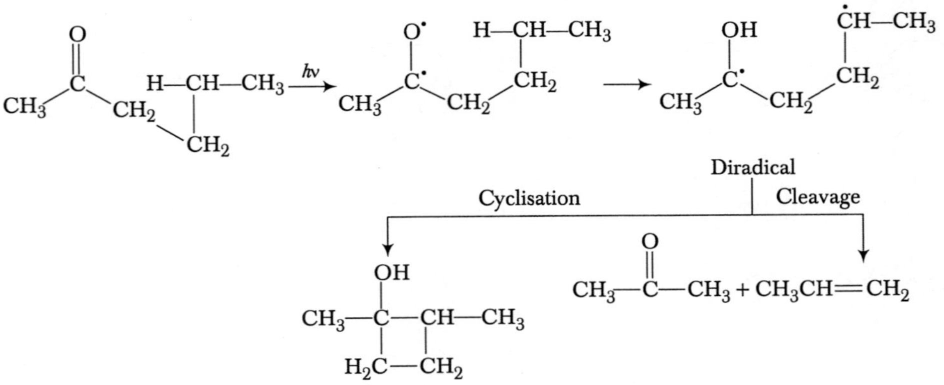

5. 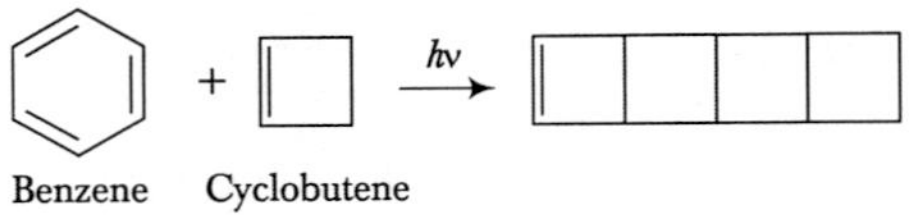

6. 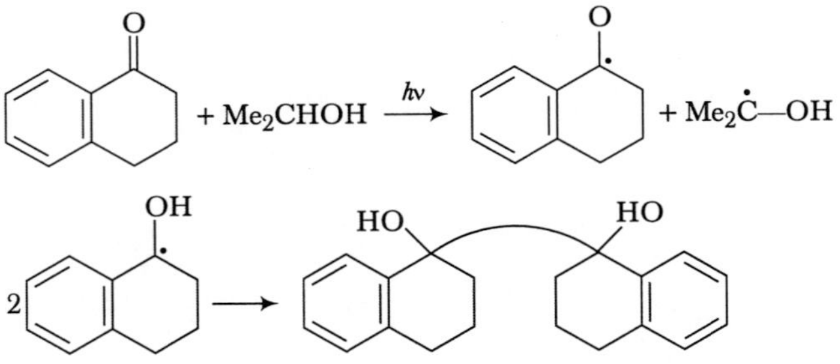

11. 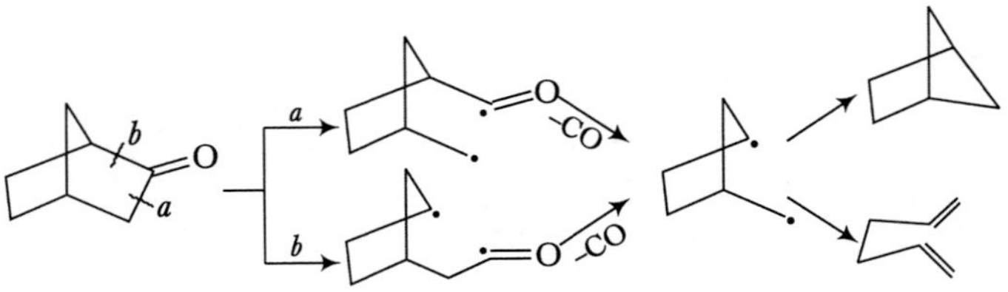

13. 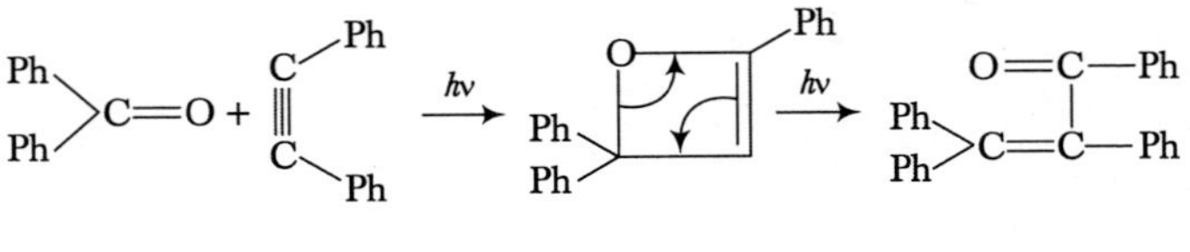

14. 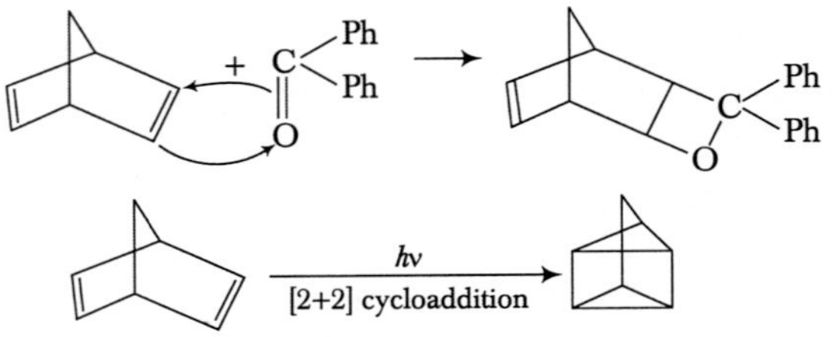

16. 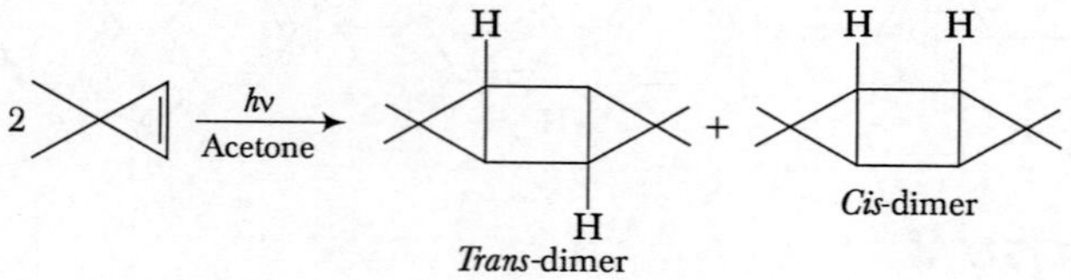
2
hν
Acetone
H
H
H H
Trans-dimer
Cis-dimer

17. 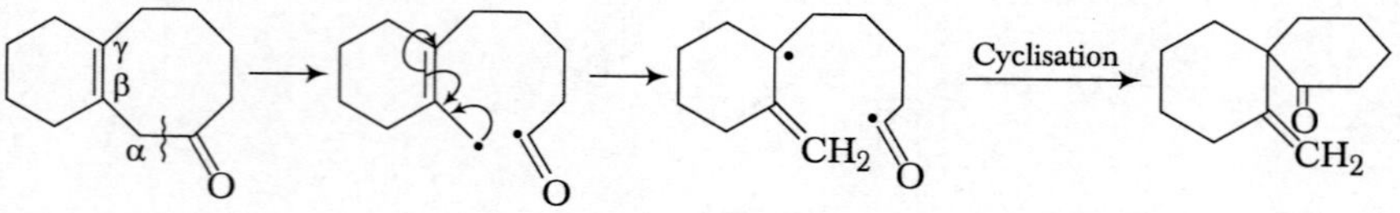
γ
β
α
Cyclisation
CH2
O
CH2

19. 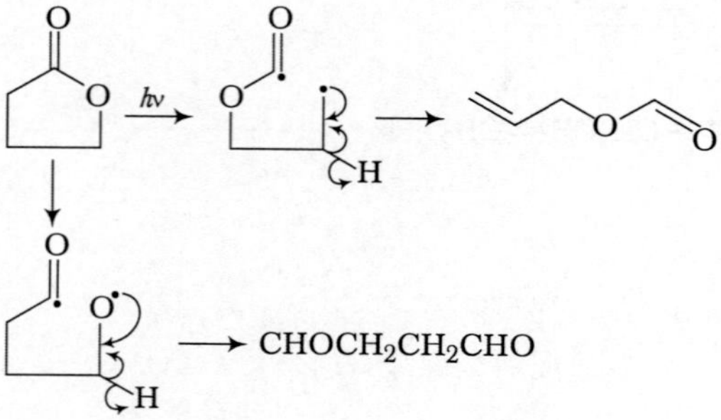
hν
O
H
CHOCH2CH2CHO

37 Heterocyclic Compounds

Introduction

Heterocyclic compounds are those where one or more atoms of the ring are heteroatoms for, *e.g.*, N, O, S, P, As, Se and so on. Depending on their structures heterocyclic compounds are classified as non-aromatic and aromatic.

Non-aromatic heterocyclic compounds are as

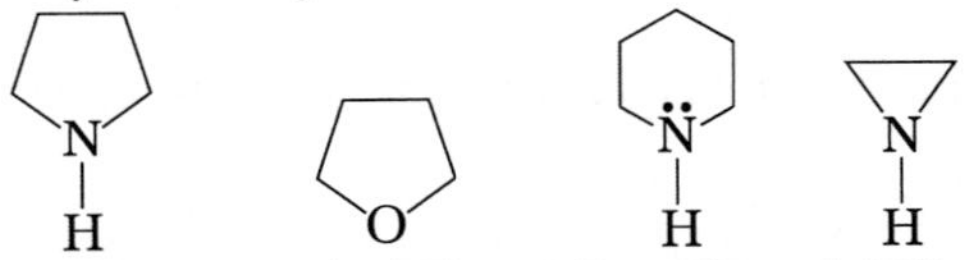

Pyrrolidine Tetrahydrofuran Piperidine Aziridine

Aromatic heterocyclic compounds are as

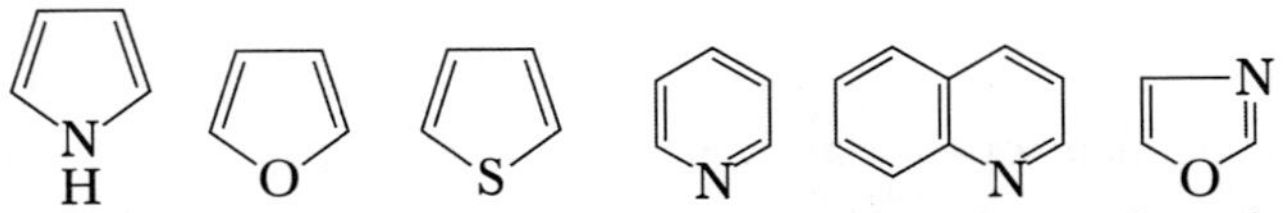

Pyrrole Furan Thiophene Pyridine Quinoline Oxazole

Note Some partially saturated non-aromatic heterocycles are as

Dihydropyrrole Azirine Oxetene

Syllabus

- Synthesis and Reactivity of Common Heterocyclic Compounds Containing One or Two Heteroatoms (O, N, S)

Furan

Furan is a five membered heterocyclic compound with oxygen atom as the hetero atom. The structure of furan is as follows

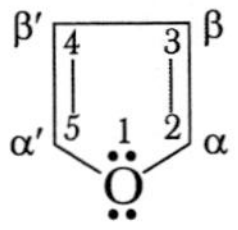

Synthesis of Furan

(1) Furan is available from furfural which is obtained by the acid hydrolysis of polysaccharides of naturally occurring substances such as corn cobs and starch which contain pentose fragments.

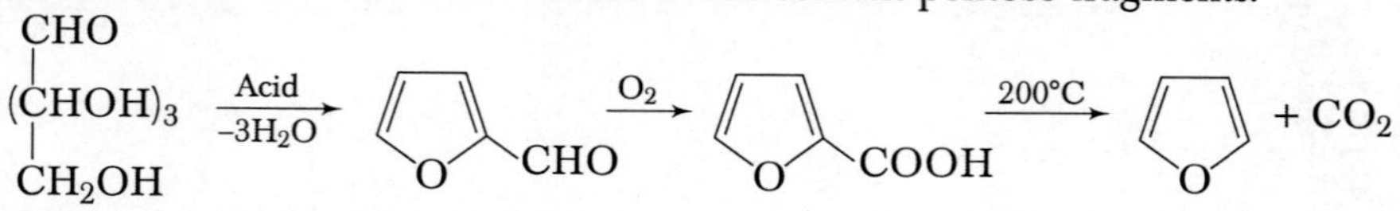

Pentose Furfural Furan

(2) It can also be manufactured by the catalytic decomposition of furfural in steam in the presence of an oxide catalyst.

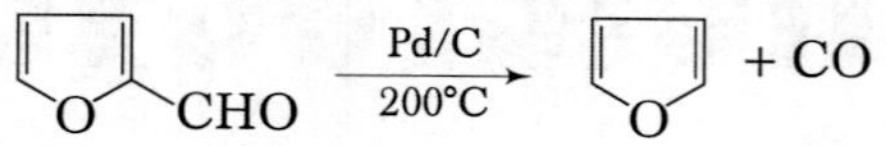

Synthesis of furan derivatives

By dehydrating 1,4-diketones or aldehydes with P_2O_5 or conc. H_2SO_4 (**Paal-Knorr synthesis**)

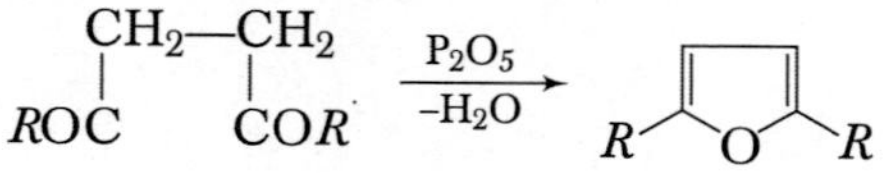

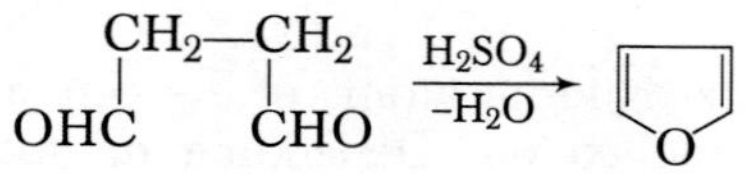

Structure of Furan

It is a π excessive aromatic $(4n + 2)$ π system. It is a monocyclic planar molecule and resonance hybrid.

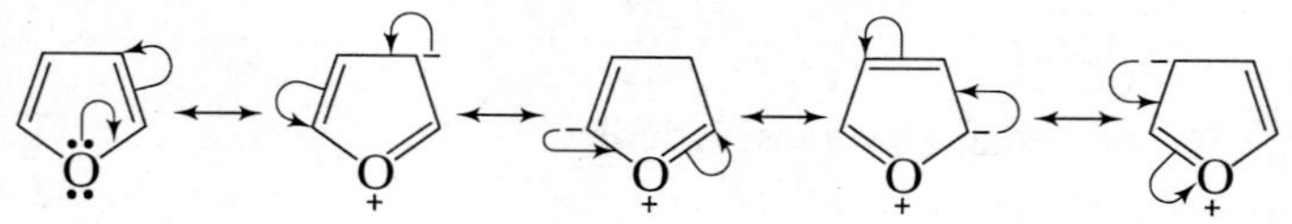

Reactivity of Furan

Chemically furan resembles benzene but tends to break open readily at the oxygen link ages. Some important reactions of furan are as

Diels-Alder reaction

Furan undergoes **Diels-Alder** reaction with maleic anhydride.

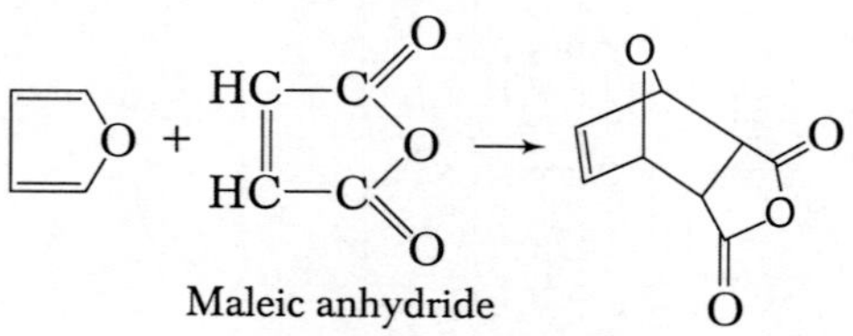

Maleic anhydride Cycloadduct

Reduction

Furan is catalytically reduced to tetrahydrofuran

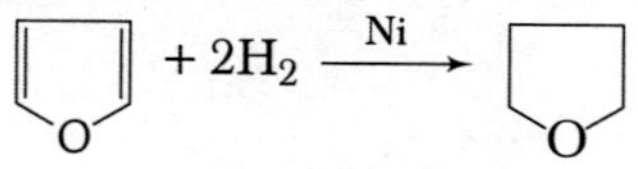

Oxidation

Oxidation of furan gives succinaldehyde

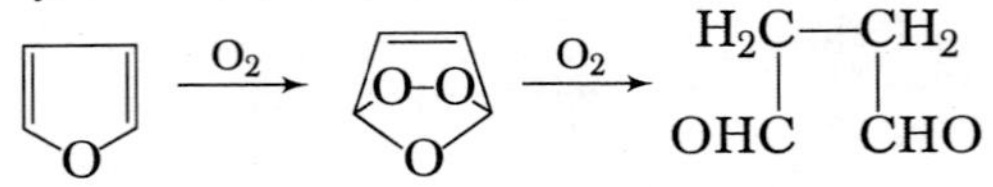

Electrophilic substitution reactions

Furan undergoes electrophilic substitution at the 2-position. The furan ring is labile to the action of acids.

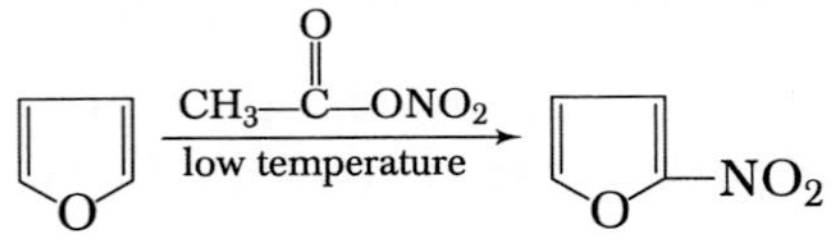

2-nitrofuran

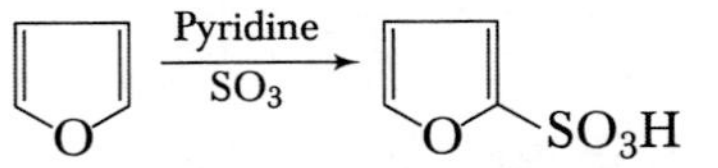

2-furan sulphonic acid

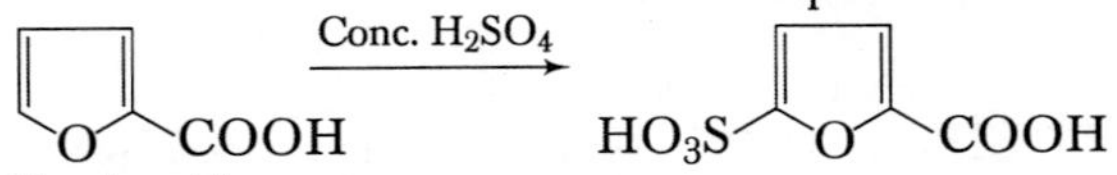

Furoic acid

Furan cannot be halogenated directly since furan is prone to polymerisation.

2-bromofuran

Chlorination of furan at –40°C gives a mixture of 2-chloro and 2,5-dichlorofuran.

By **Gattermann reaction** furan gives furfural

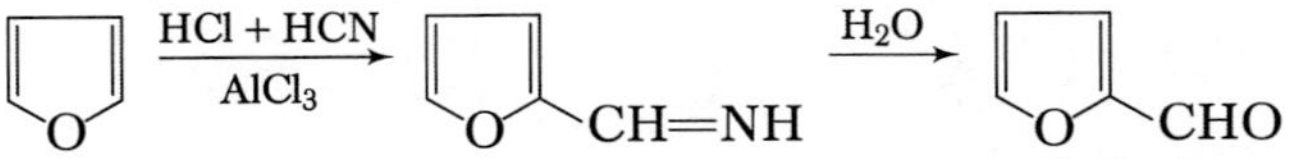

Furfural

Furan undergoes **Friedel-Crafts reaction** in presence of $SnCl_4$ (since $AlCl_3$ attacks the ring, $SnCl_4$ is used).

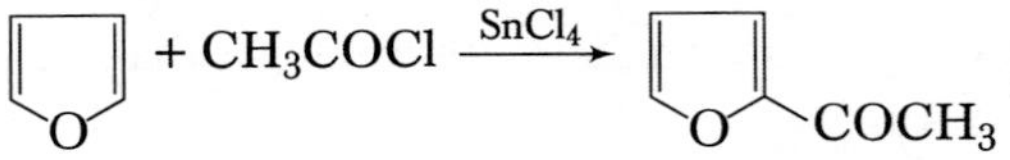

2-acetylfuran

For acylation using anhydrides, boron trifluoride in ether is used as the catalyst.

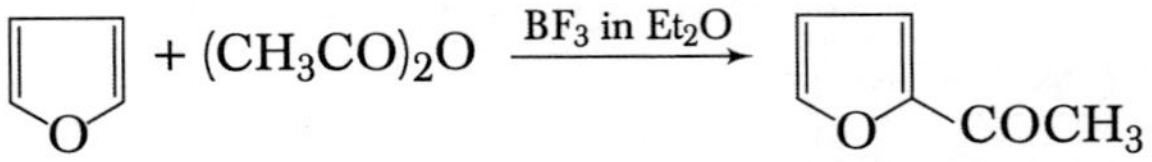

2-acetylfuran

Note Alkylation is not possible because of the formation of polymer products.

The furan ring opens up when treated with acids as follows resulting in the formation of a 1,4-dimethoxy compound. 2,5-dimethylfuran on treatment with dil. H_2SO_4 gives a 1,4-diketone.

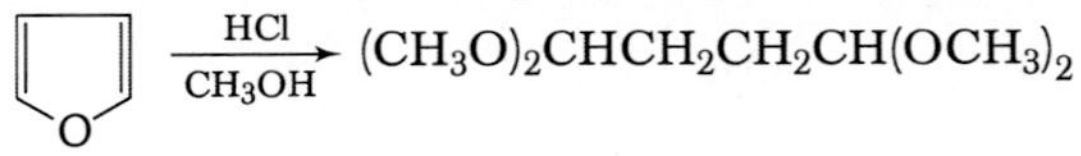

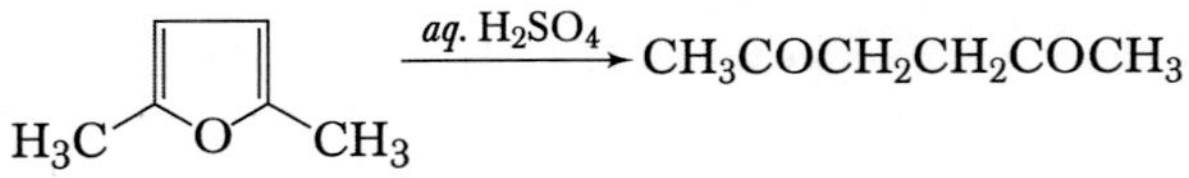

Thiophene

Thiophene is a five membered heterocyclic compound with sulphur atom as the hetero atom (sulphur analogue of furan). The structure of thiophene is as follows

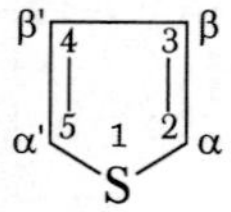

It occurs in coal tar and crude petroleum. The thiophene ring occurs in the vitamin B_1 (thiamine) molecule.

Synthesis of Thiophene

(1) Commercially thiophene is prepared by passing a mixture of acetylene and H_2S through a tube containing alumina at 400°C.

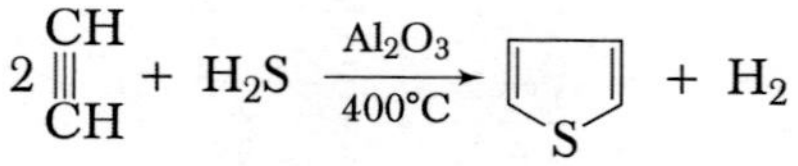

(2) An enolizable 1,4-diketone on heating with P_2S_5 to give thiophene **(Paul-Knorr synthesis)**

Structure of Thiophene

Thiophene has more number of resonating structures than furan since sulphur atom has vacant *d*-orbitals. Sulphur can donate the lone pair of electrons as well as accept electrons using empty *d*-orbitals. By donating electrons it attains aromaticity [$(4n + 2)$ π-electron system]. Two sets of resonating structures (I) and (II) are possible. (I) is attained by donating electrons whereas (II) is attained by accepting electrons.

I.

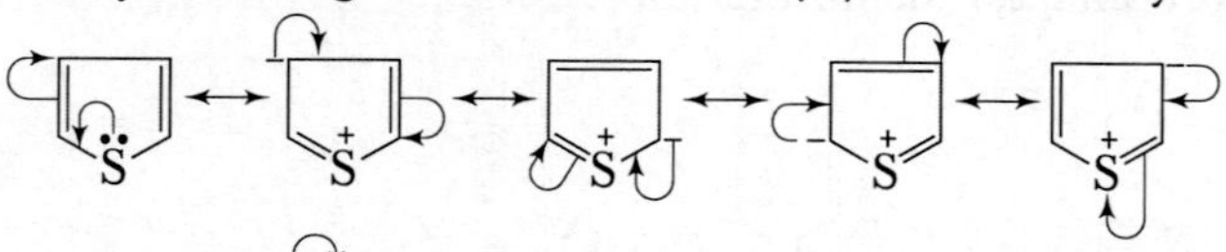

II.

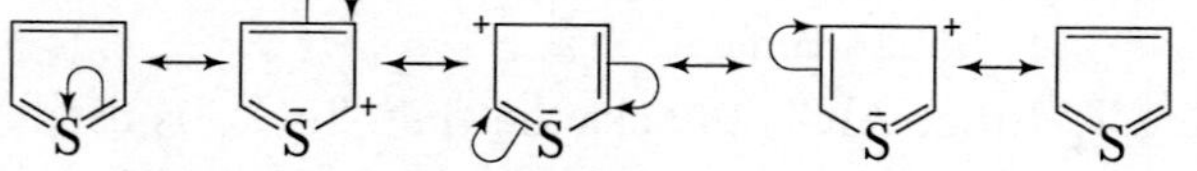

The estimation of ring current shows that thiophene is more aromatic than furan.

Reactivity of Thiophene

Reduction

Reduction of thiophene can be done by Na/liq. NH_3, H_2/Pd and H_2/Raney nickel.

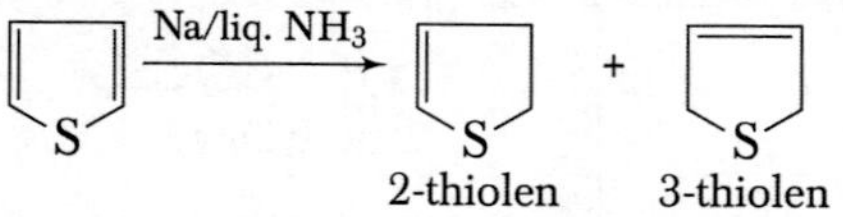

2-thiolen 3-thiolen

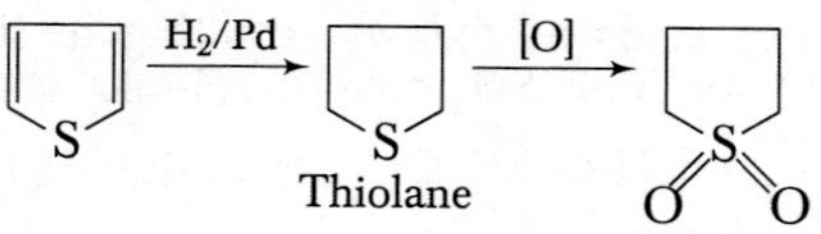

Thiolane

Sulphone

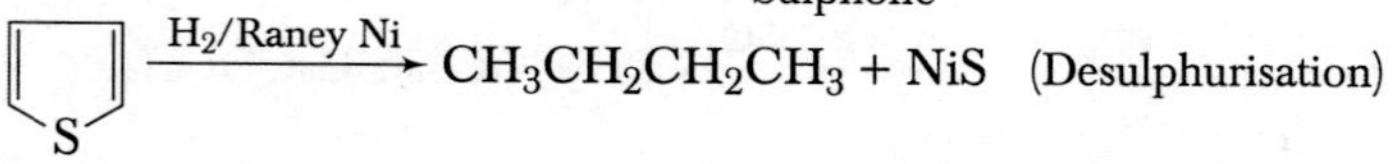

Note Desulphurisation of thiophene derivatives can be brought about by Raney-Ni. During this reaction mono or dicarboxylic acids are formed.

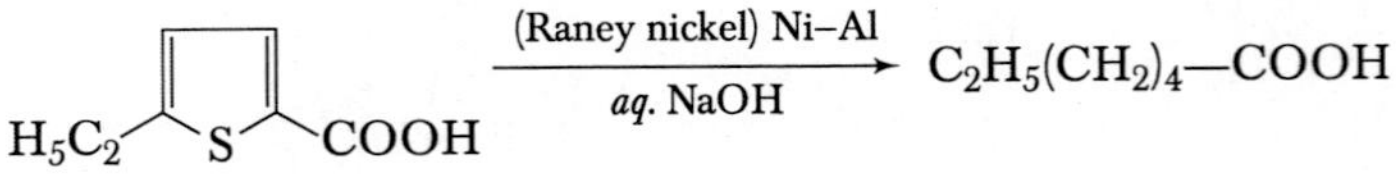

Electrophilic substitution reaction

Like furan, thiophene undergoes electrophilic substitution. On the basis of charge distribution and stabilities of the carbocations the electrophilic substitution takes place at position 2 (or 5).

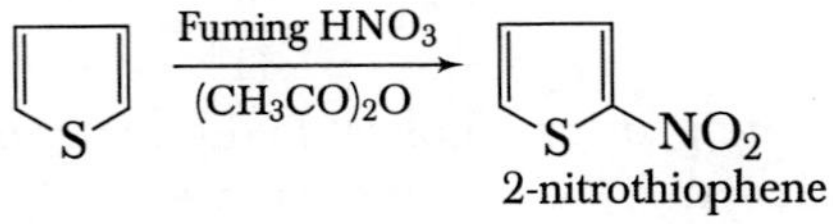

Thiophene is acylated by acid chlorides in presence of stannic chloride or by acid anhydrides in presence of phosphoric acid.

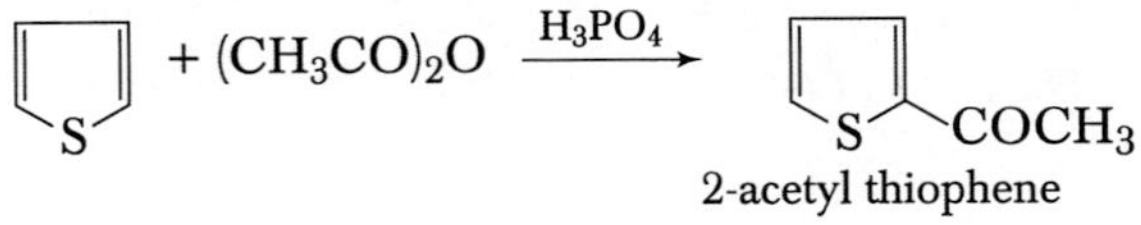

Other reactions

Thiophene can be formylated at 2-position by using dimethyl formamide and phosphorus oxychloride **(Vilsmier-Haack reaction)**

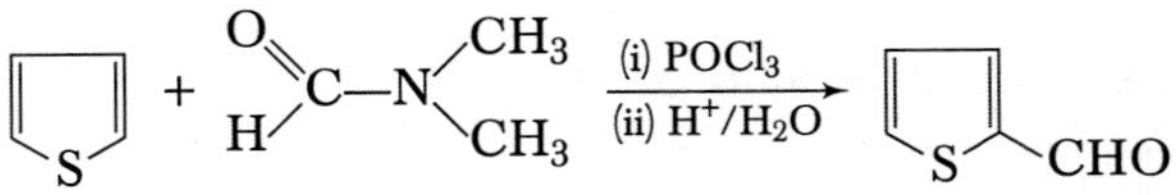

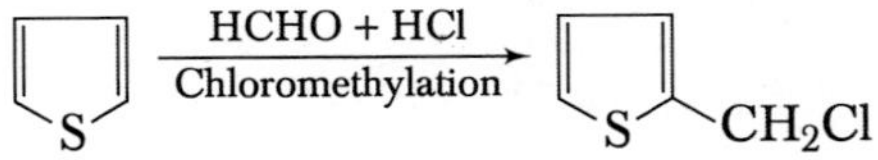

Note • Mercury, lithio and bromo derivatives of thiophene are used as the intermediate for the preparation of various 2-substituted thiophene derivatives, *e.g.*,

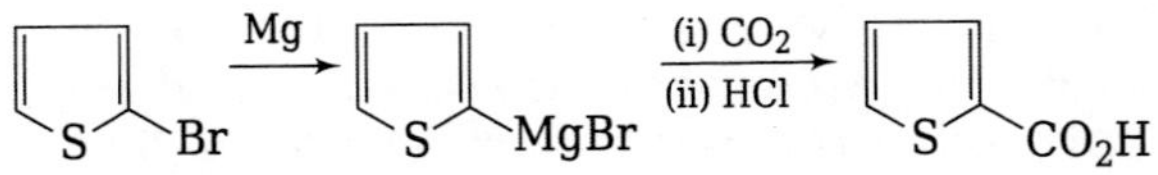

Pyrrole

Pyrrole is a five membered heterocyclic compound with nitrogen as hetero atom. The structure of pyrrole is as follows

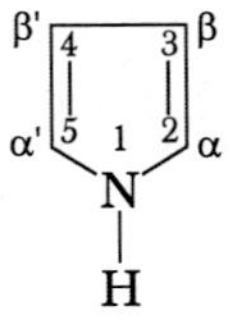

Synthesis of Pyrrole

(1) Commercially, pyrrole is obtained by passing a mixture of furan, ammonia and steam over heated Al_2O_3 as catalyst.

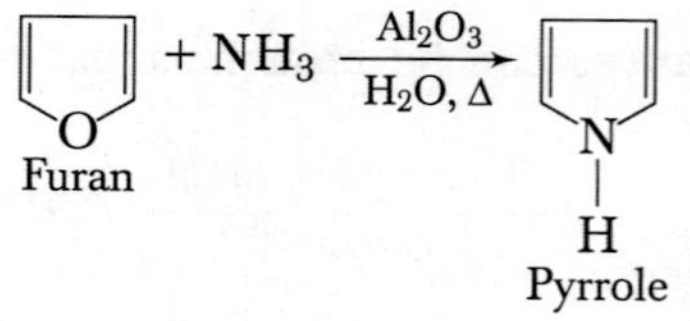

(2) Heating ammonium mucate in glycerol at 200°C yields pyrrole **(Laboratory method)**

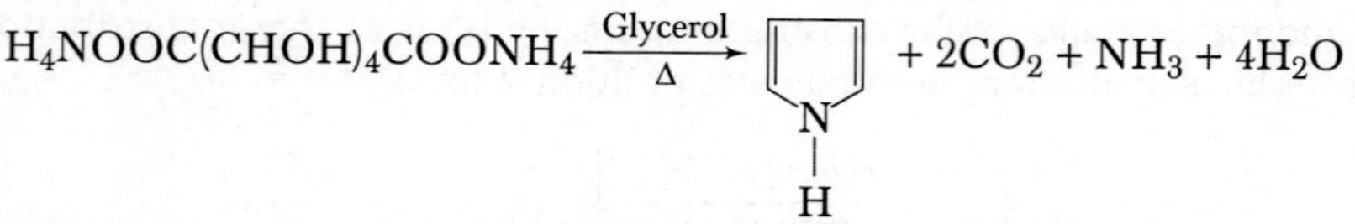

(3) Paul-Knorr synthesis involves the heating of an enolizable 1,4-diketone with ammonia or a primary amine. Pyrrole is formed from succinaldehyde and ammonia while 2,5-dimethyl pyrrole is obtained from acetonylacetone and ammonia.

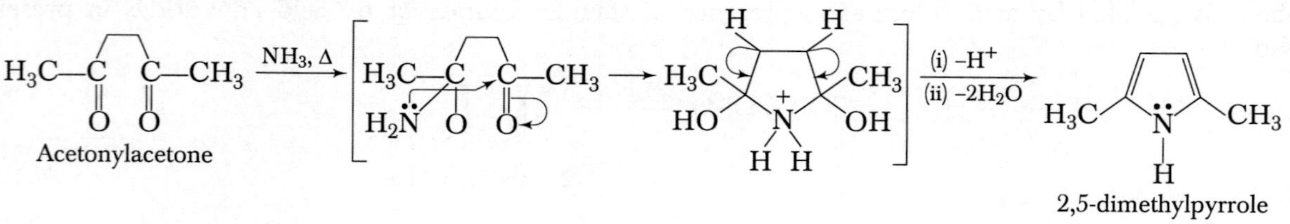

Structure of Pyrrole

Pyrrole is a resonance hybrid of the following resonating structures. It is less aromatic than thiophene and more aromatic than furan.

The order of aromaticity is thiophene > pyrrole > furan

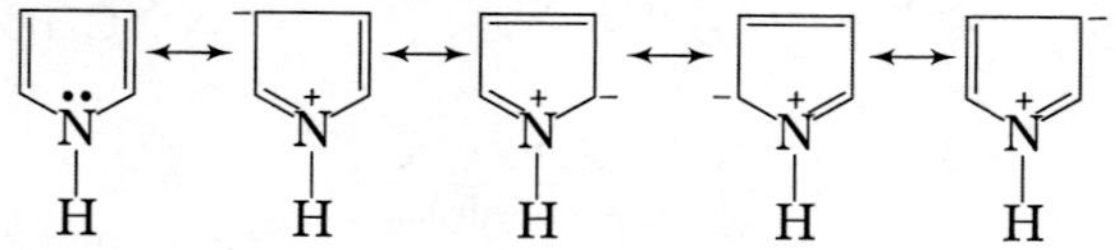

Reactivity of Pyrrole

Basic nature

Pyrrole is a weaker base. It is less basic since the lone pair of electrons on nitrogen are involved in the formation of a $(4n + 2)$ π-electron, and not available for protonation. However, in acid solution, protonation occurs more at carbon. In concentrated solution, pyrrole polymerises to form pyrrole-red. On contact with dilute acid for a brief period, pyrrole forms the trimer.

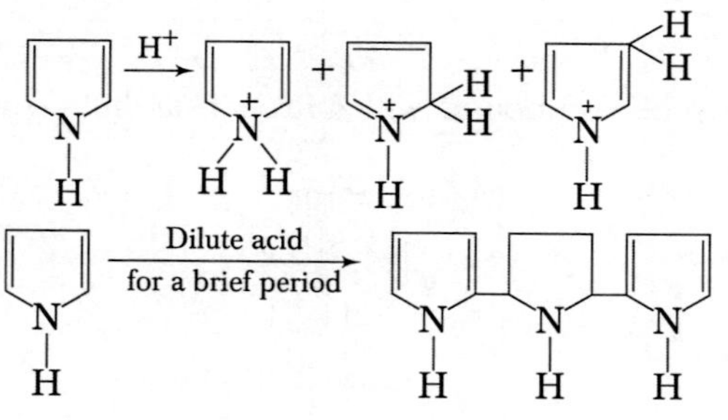

Replacement of imino-hydrogen

The imino-hydrogen of pyrrole is replaceable by potassium, alkyl or acyl groups. When pyrrole is heated with solid potassium hydroxide, potassiopyrrole is formed.

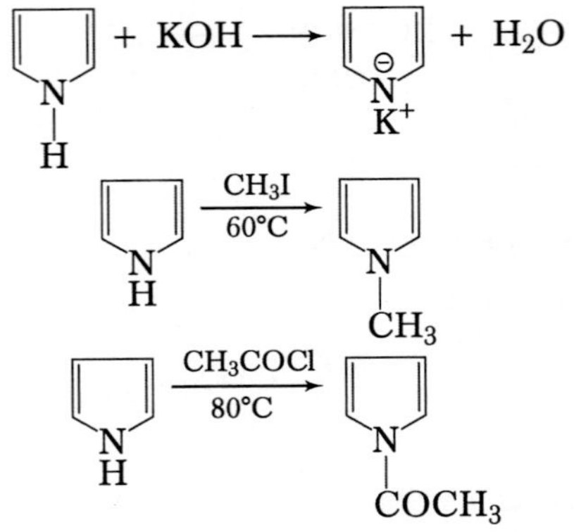

Reduction

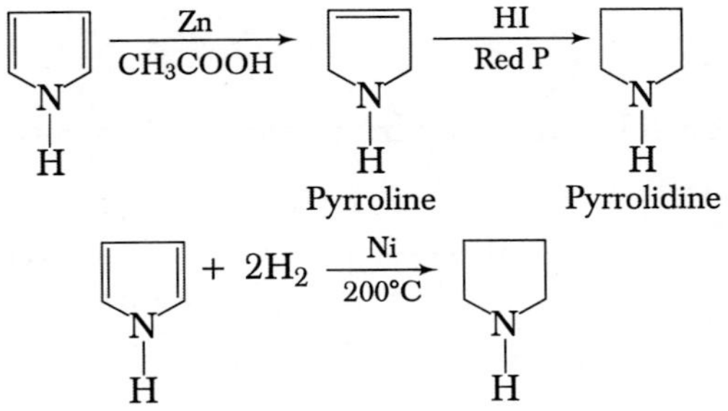

Oxidation

Pyrrole is oxidised by chromium trioxide in sulphuric acid to maleic imide.

•

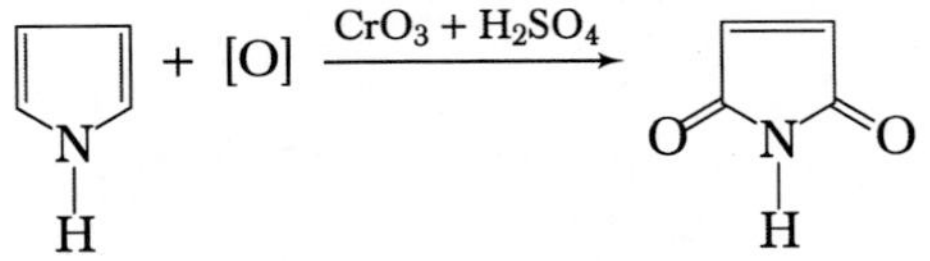

Electrophilic substitution reactions

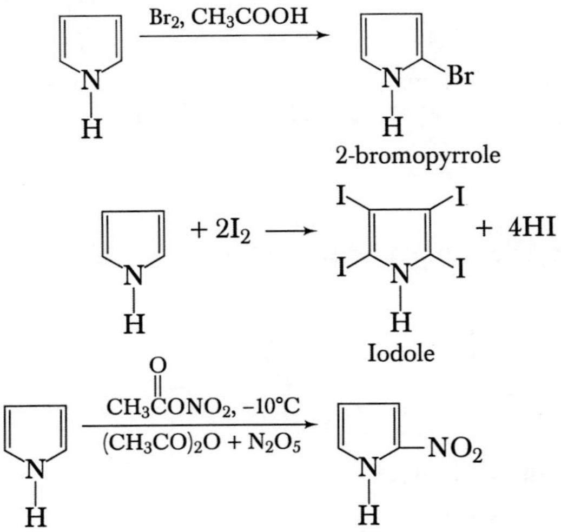

Other reactions

Pyrrole can be formylated at 2-position with dimethylformamide and phosphorus oxy chloride **(Vilsmier-Haack reaction)**

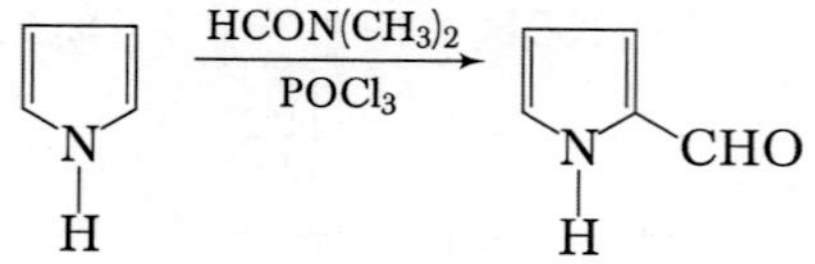

Pyrrole undergoes **Houben-Hoesch reaction** to give 2-ketones

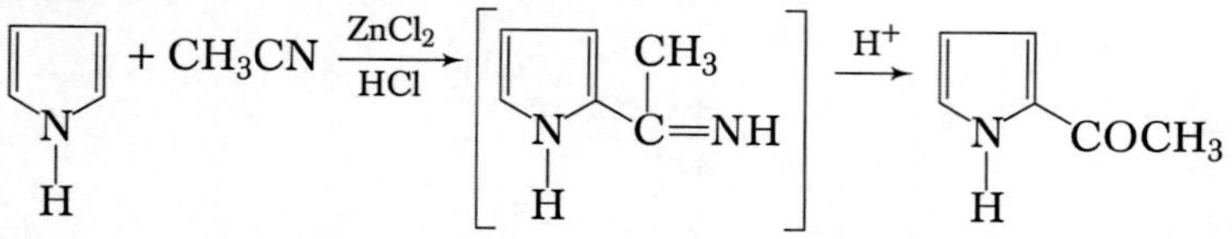

Pyrrole reacts with sodium methoxide and methylene iodide to give pyridine by ring expansion.

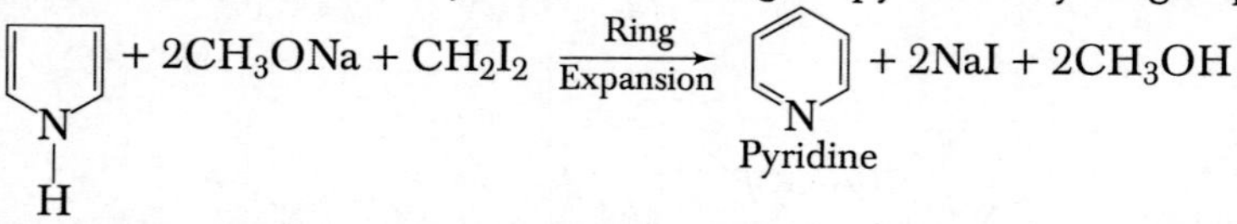

Pyrrole **on refluxing with ethanolic solution of hydroxylamine** gives succinaldehyde dioxime through a **ring opening reaction.**

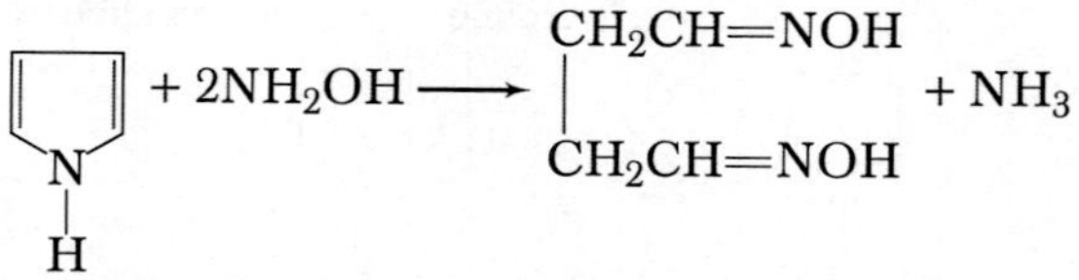

Pyrrole reacts with Grignard reagent to give a salt with the evolution of methane.

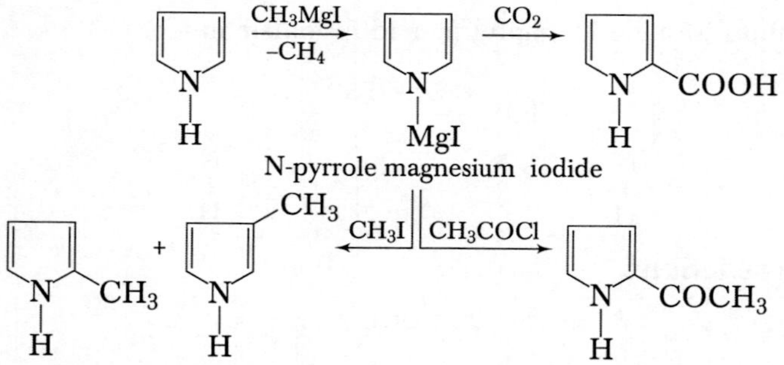

Note Pyrrole-2-aldehyde does not give the usual reactions such as the Perkin reaction, benzoin condensation, Cannizzaro reaction, etc., expected of aromatic aldehydes. This is so because of the resonance of the —CHO group with the pyrrole ring.

Pyridine

Pyridine is a six membered heterocyclic compound with nitrogen as the hetero atom. The structure of pyridine is as follows

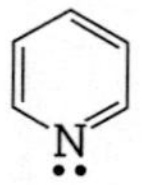

Synthesis of Pyridine

(1) By distillation of nicotinic acid with soda lime.

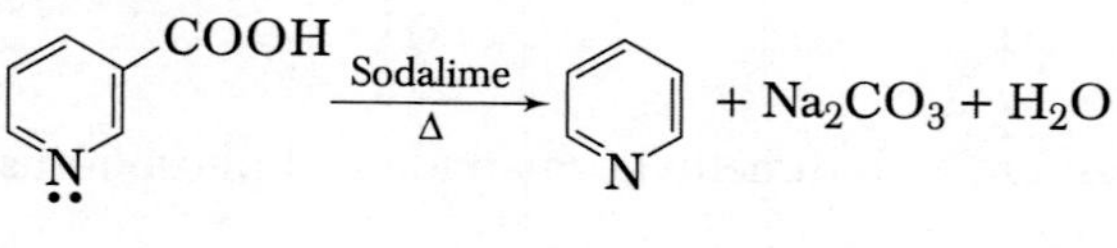

(2) 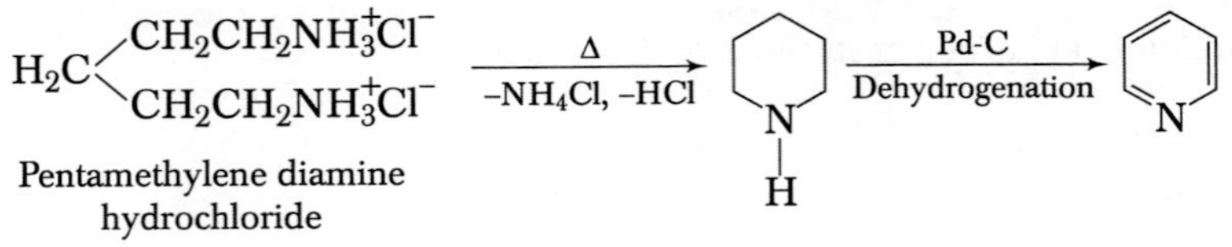

Pentamethylene diamine hydrochloride

(3) Pyridine derivatives can be synthesized from 2-furyl ketones by ring expansion process.

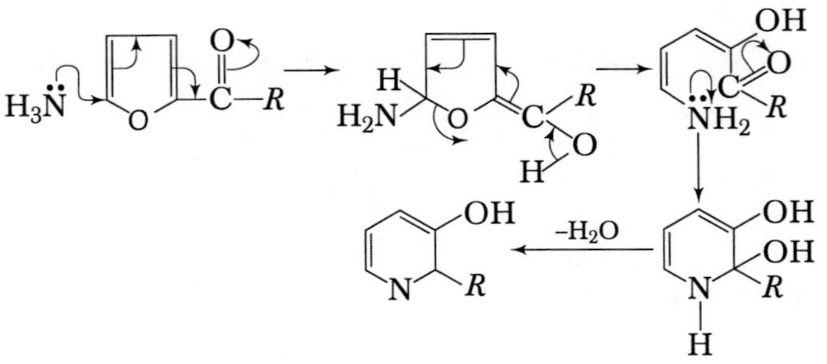

Structure of Pyridine

The structure of pyridine is a resonance hybrid of the following canonical structure.

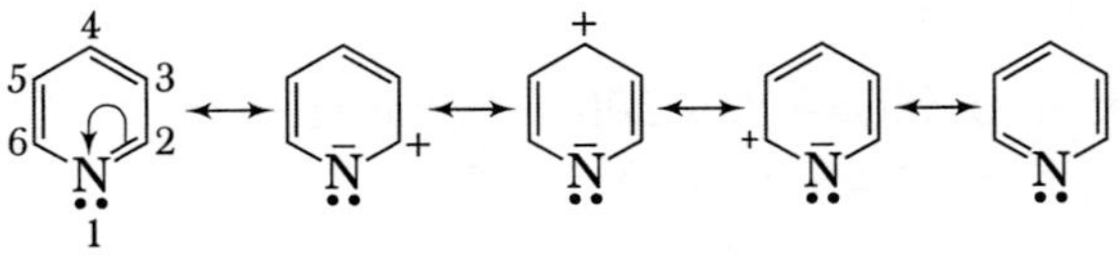

Reactivity of Pyridine

The lone pair of electrons are not involved in resonance. Hence, pyridine is basic. The positions 3 and 5 are the sites for electrophilic attack and positions 2, 4 and 6 are sites for nucleophilic attack. Due to electron withdrawing nature of nitrogen, the ring is highly deactivated. Hence, nitration and sulphonation are difficult. Presence of $+I$ group accelerates the electrophilic substitutions. If the $+I$ group is present at the 3-position the substitution takes place at 2 or 6-position. If the $+I$ group is present at the 2 or 4-position, the substitution takes place at 3 or 5-position.

Basic nature

It is a strong tertiary base which gives salts with inorganic acids and forms quaternary salts when heated with alkyl halides.

$$C_5H_5N + HCl \longrightarrow \underset{\text{Pyridine hydrochloride}}{C_5H_5\overset{+}{N}HCl^-}$$

$$C_5H_5N + CH_3I \xrightarrow{\Delta} \underset{\substack{\text{Pyridine methiodide} \\ \text{or N-methyl pyridinium iodide}}}{C_5H_5\overset{+}{N}\cdot CH_3I^-}$$

The quaternary halides of pyridine undergo **Hofmann-Martius rearrangement** to form 2 and 4-methylpyridines.

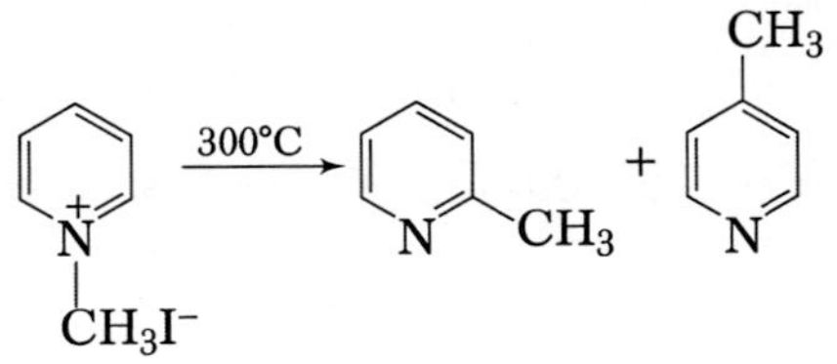

Note The quaternary hydroxides of pyridine on heating give **anhydro-bases** with the removal of a molecule of water. However, this is possible only when a suitable alkyl group is in the 2 or 4-position.

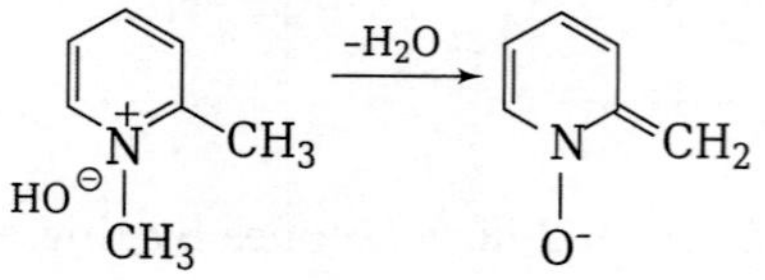

Oxidation

Pyridine is easily oxidized with H_2O_2 or perbenzoic acid to give pyridine N-oxide.

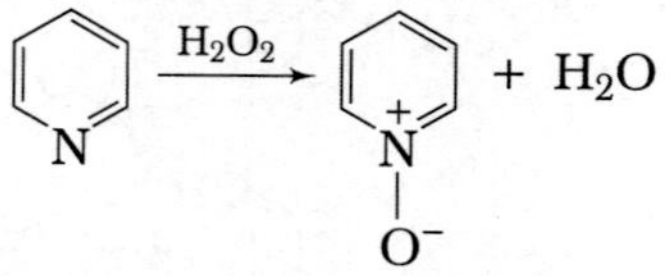

Note Pyridazine also gives N-oxides with peracids.

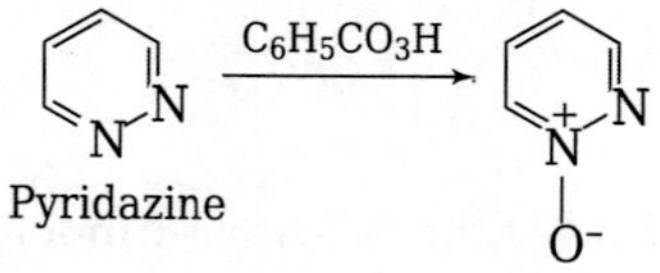

Reduction

On reduction pyridine gives different products, depending on the method.

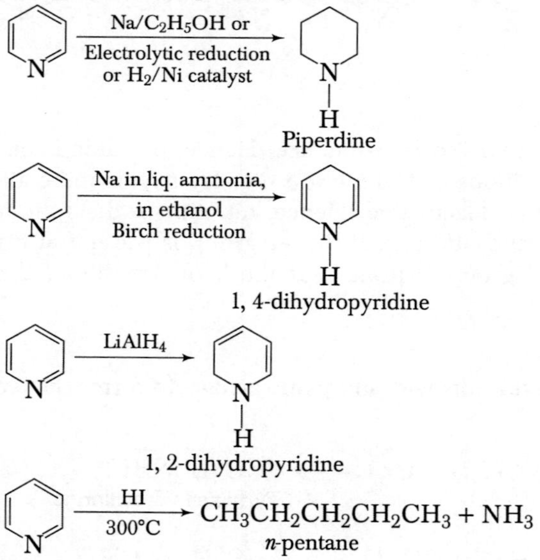

Electrophilic substitution reactions

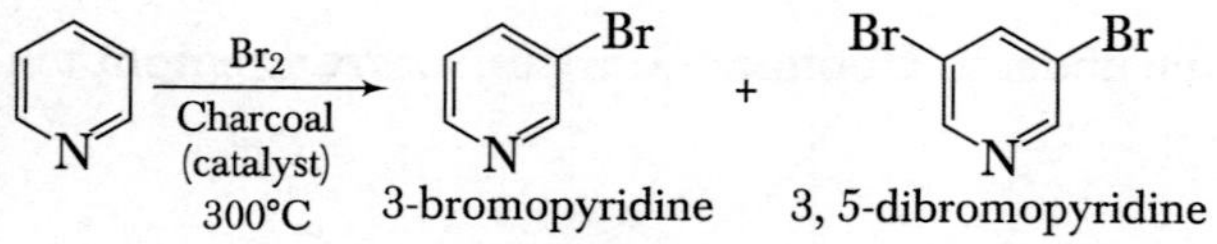

However, at 500°C a mixture of 2-bromo and 2,6-dibromo derivatives are obtained. The reaction is considered to proceed by radial mechanism.

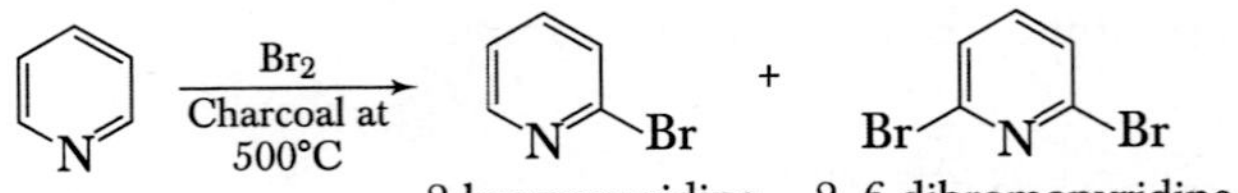

2-bromopyridine 2, 6-dibromopyridine

Note 2-chloropyridine is obtained by the following process.

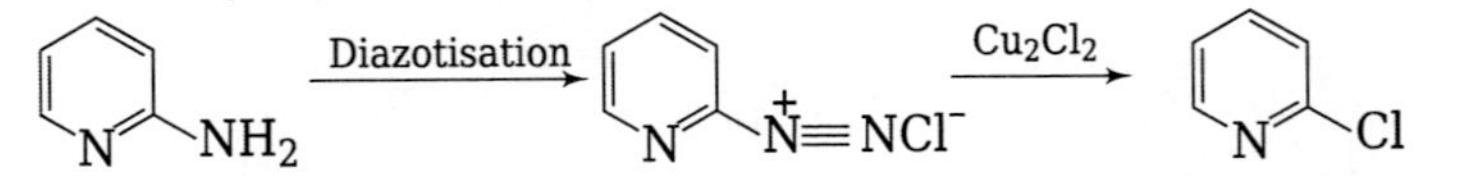

2-aminopyridine 2-chloropyridine

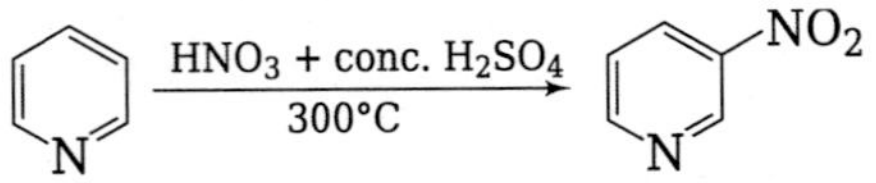

3-nitropyridine

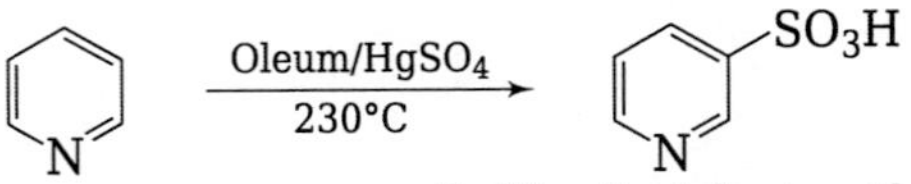

Pyridine 3-sulphonic acid

- Pyridine does not undergo Friedel-Crafts reaction. Since, it is having a complex forming tendency.

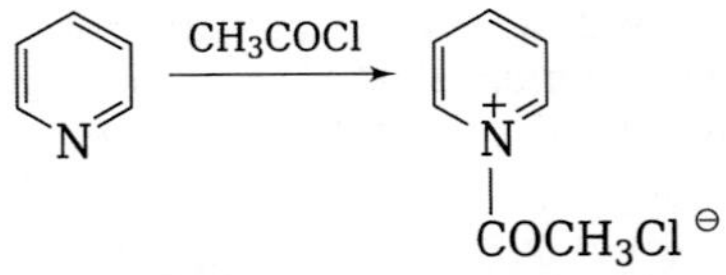

- 2 and 4-pyridine sulphonic acids are obtained by oxidising corresponding thiols.

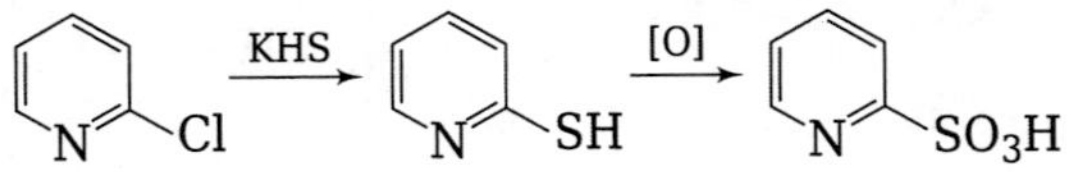

Nucleophilic substitution reactions

On heating with sodamide, pyridine gives 2-aminopyridine **(Chichibabin reaction)**

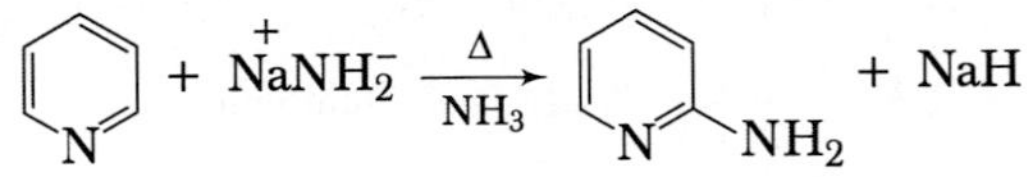

If sodamide is in excess 2,6-diaminopyridine is obtained.

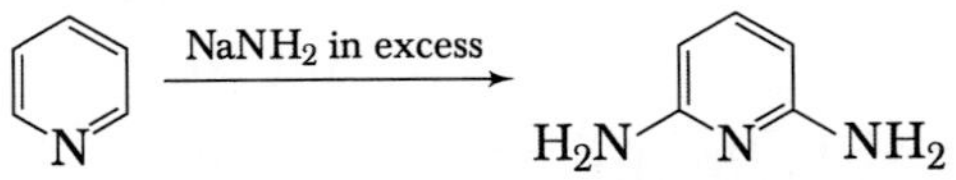

2, 6-diaminopyridine

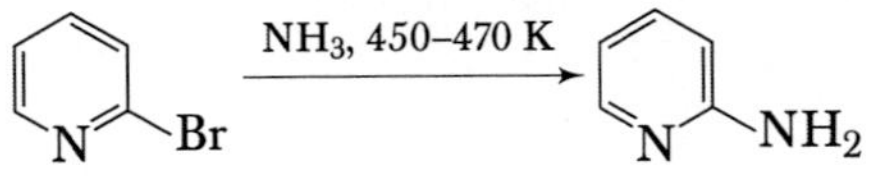

Other reactions

Pyridine forms 2-hydroxypyridine when heated with potassium hydroxide at 320°C which can tautomerize to pyridone.

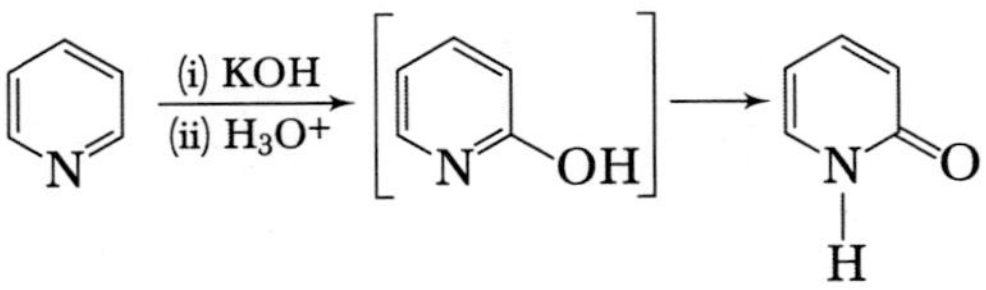

On heating with *n*-butyllithium, pyridine forms 2-*n*-butylpyridine.

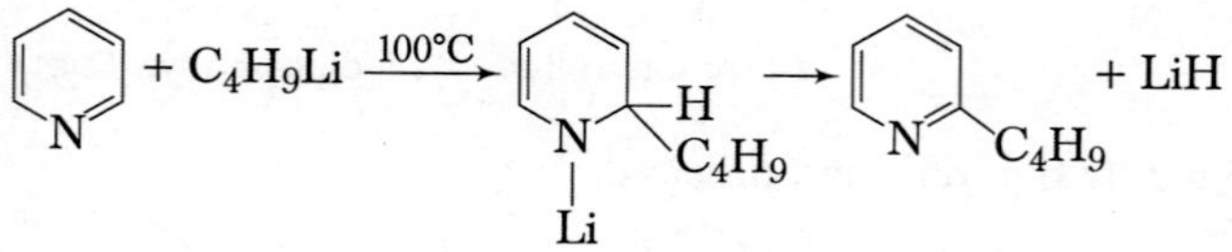

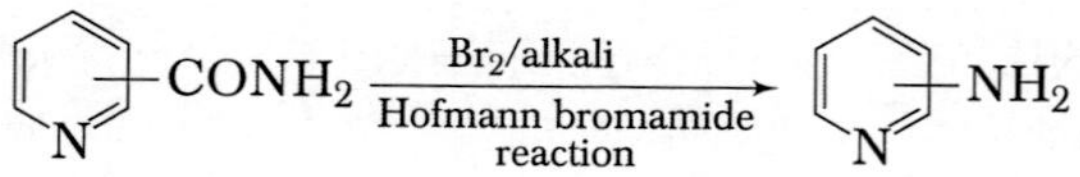

Quinoline

Quinoline is 2,3-benzopyridine in which one benzene and one pyridine ring are fused together at α, β-positions.

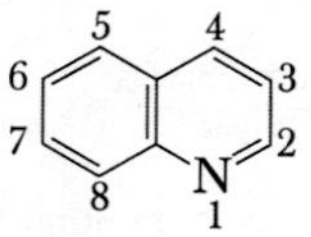

Synthesis of Quinoline

(1) **Skraup synthesis** It is the commercial method for the preparation of quinoline. It is carried out by heating a mixture of aniline, nitrobenzene, glycerol, conc. H_2SO_4 and $FeSO_4$. Nitrobenzene acts as an oxidizing agent and ferrous sulphate makes the reaction less violent. Glycerol loses water to give acrolein.

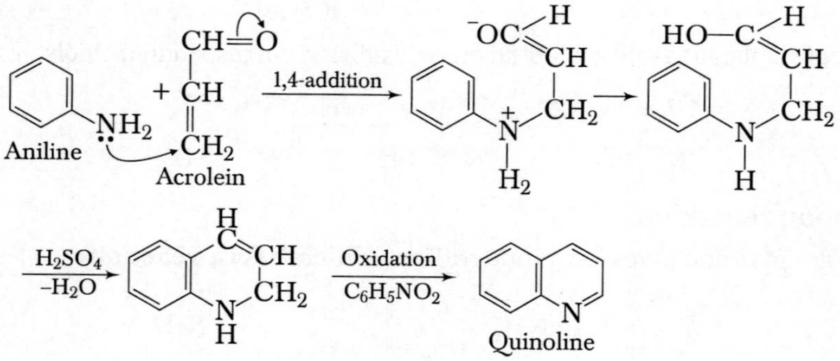

(2) **Friedlander's synthesis** It involves the alkaline condensation of *o*-aminobenzaldehyde with a carbonyl compound containing —CH_2CO group, *i.e.*, having a reactive methylene group adjacent to the carbonyl group.

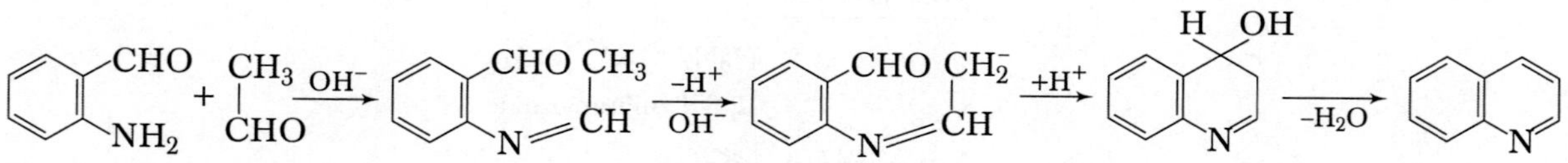

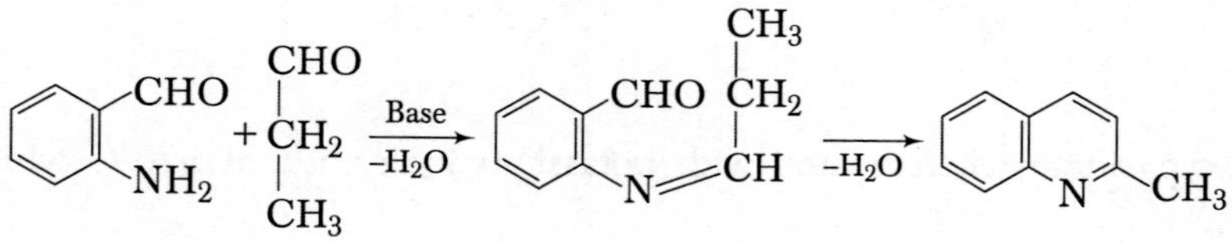

(3) **Knorr-quinoline synthesis**

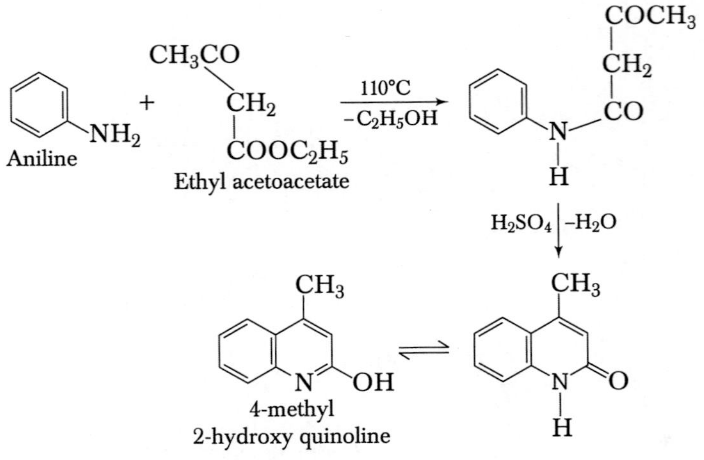

Reactivity of Quinoline

Basic nature

Quinoline is a tertiary base and forms quaternary salts with alkyl halides.

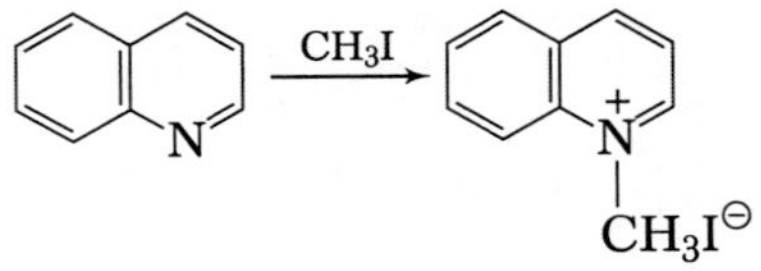

Similarly, it forms 1-methyl quinolinium methyl sulphate with dimethyl sulphate.

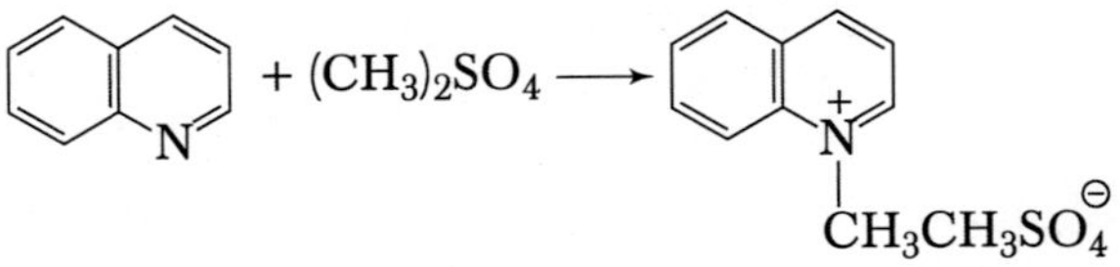

Oxidation

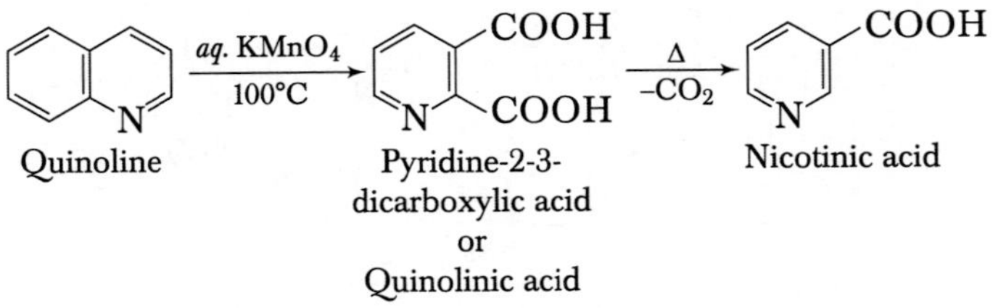

With perbenzoic acid quinoline is oxidised to quinoline N-oxide.

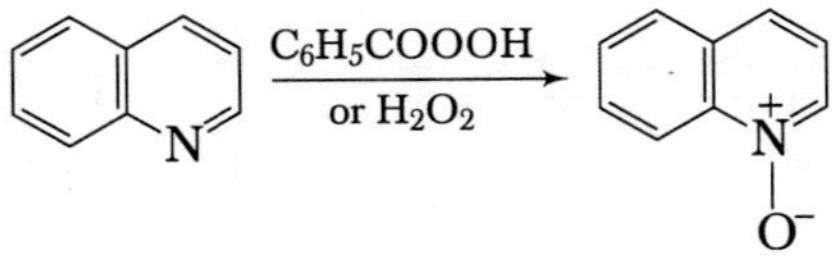

Reduction

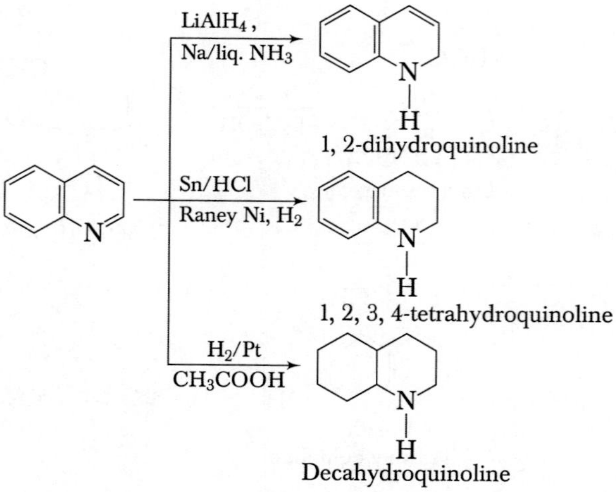

Electrophilic substitution reactions

Vapour phase bromination of quinoline gives 3-bromoquinoline. At 500°C, the product is 2-bromoquinoline. Under high acidic conditions bromination occurs at 5 and 8-positions hence, 5 and 8-bromoquinolines are formed.

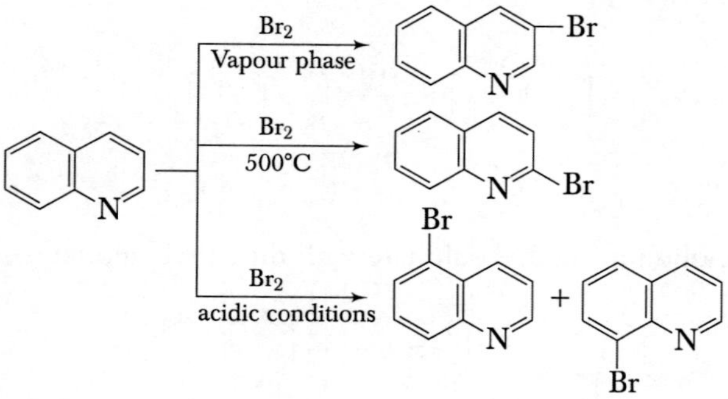

On nitration with acid mixture (conc. HNO_3 + conc. H_2SO_4) quinoline gives 5 and 8-nitroquinolines. However, nitration with nitric acid and acetic anhydride gives 3-nitroquinoline.

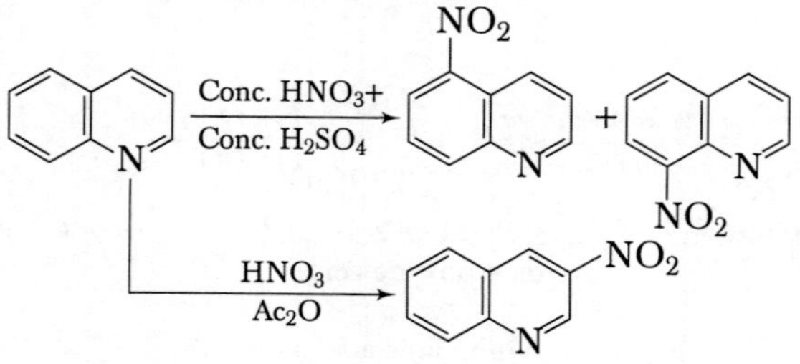

Fuming sulphuric acid at 200°C gives 8-quinoline sulphonic acid with a small amount of 5-quinoline sulphonic acid.

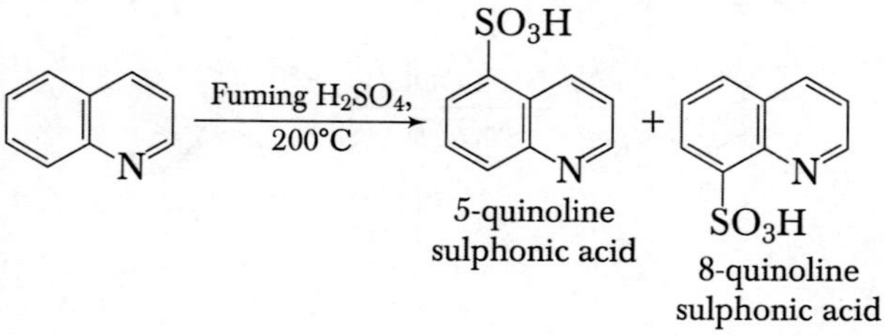

Other reactions

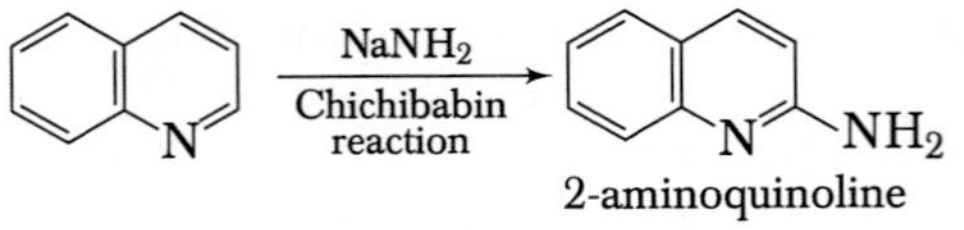

2-aminoquinoline

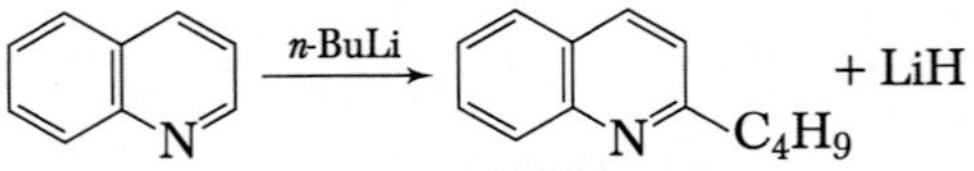

2-butylquinoline

Isoquinoline

Isoquinoline is a bicyclic heterocyclic compound with nitrogen as the hetero atom and isomeric with quinoline.

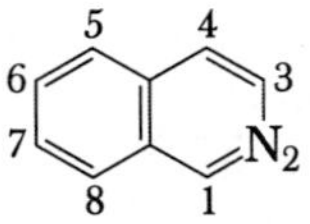

Synthesis of Isoquinoline

(1) **Bischler-Napieralski synthesis**
It involves the cyclodehydration of an acyl derivative of β-phenylethylamine.

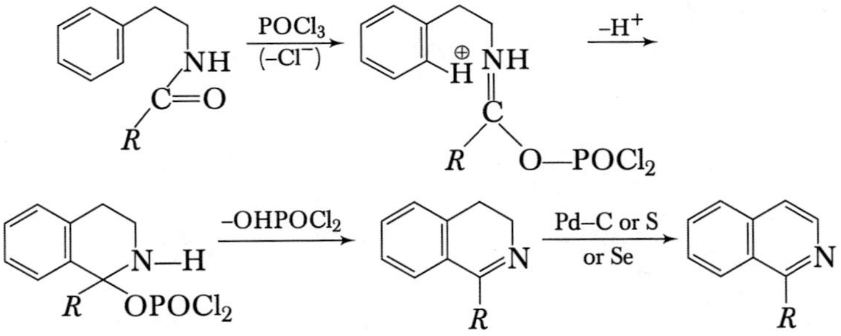

(2) **Pomeranz-Fritsch synthesis** A Schiff's base is first obtained between the reaction of an aromatic aldehyde and an aminoacetal. Cyclization is then accomplished in the presence of a catalytic amount of an acid to give isoquinoline.

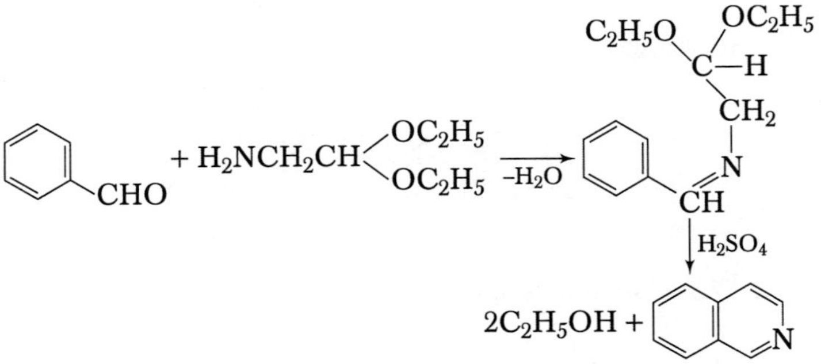

Reactivity of Isoquinoline

Basic nature

It is a stronger base as compared with quinoline and gives quaternary salts with alkyl halides.

Oxidation

Isoquinoline is oxidised by alkaline permanganate to a mixture of phthalic acid and cinchomeronic acid by ring opening.

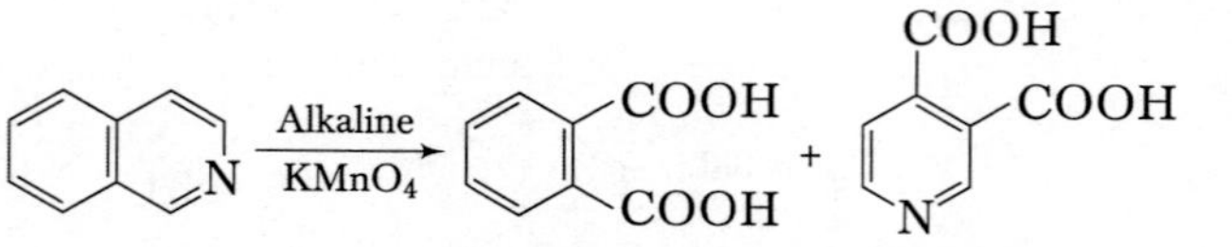

Phthalic acid   Cinchomeronic acid

With perbenzoic acid isoquinoline is oxidised to its N-oxide.

Reduction

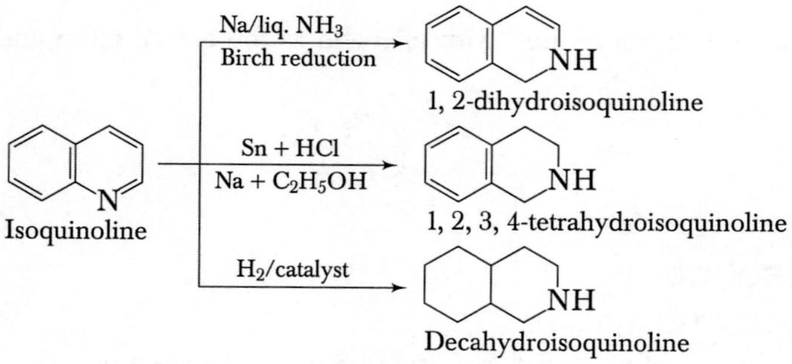

Electrophilic substitution reactaons

Electrophilic attack occurs predominantly at 5 and 8 positions.

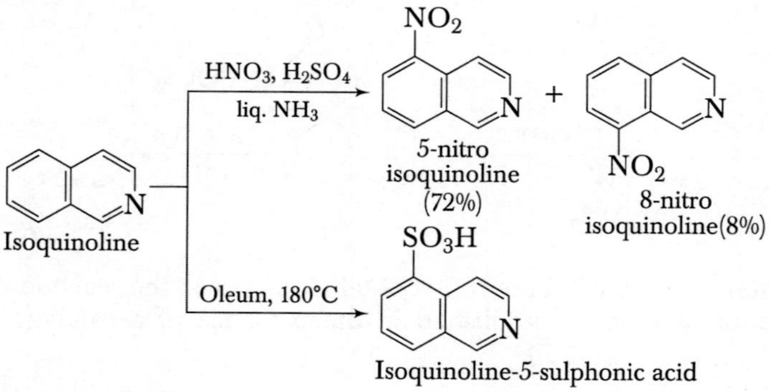

Bromination mainly occurs at 4-position.

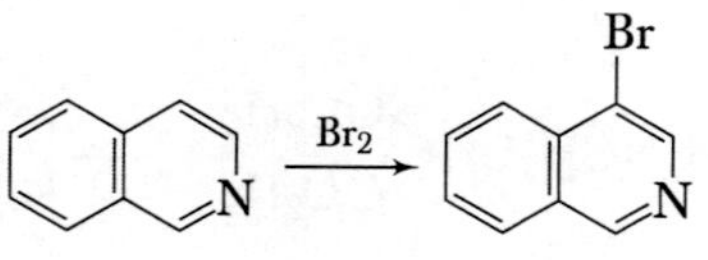

Other reactions

Isoquinoline undergoes the usual Chichibabin reaction with sodamide in liq. NH_3.

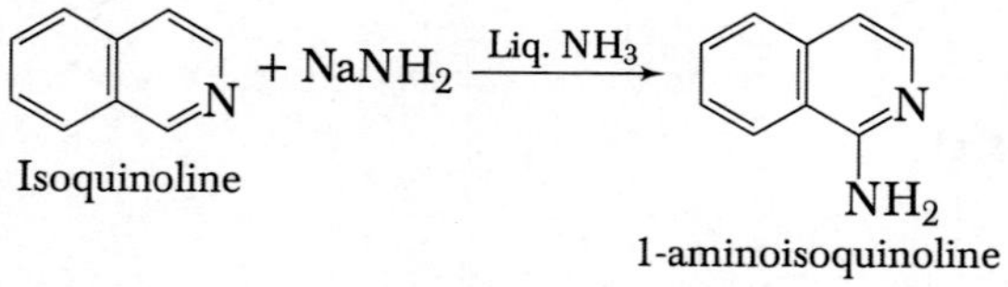

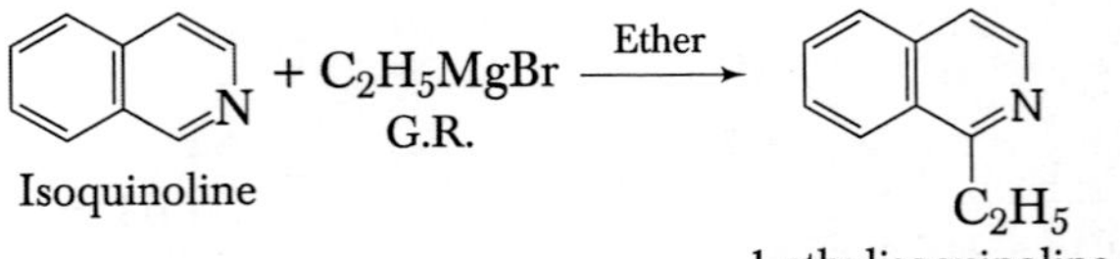

Isoquinoline 1-ethylisoquinoline

Note Nucleophilic substitution occurs at 1-position.

Indole

Indole is benzopyrrole, a bicyclic heterocyclic compound with nitrogen as hetero atom. The structure of indole is as

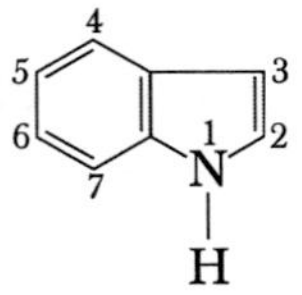

Synthesis of Indole

(1) Fischer's indole synthesis

Phenylhydrazones having an α-methylene group on treatment with a mineral acid undergoes ring closure through a [3, 3] sigmatropic shift with the loss of ammonia.

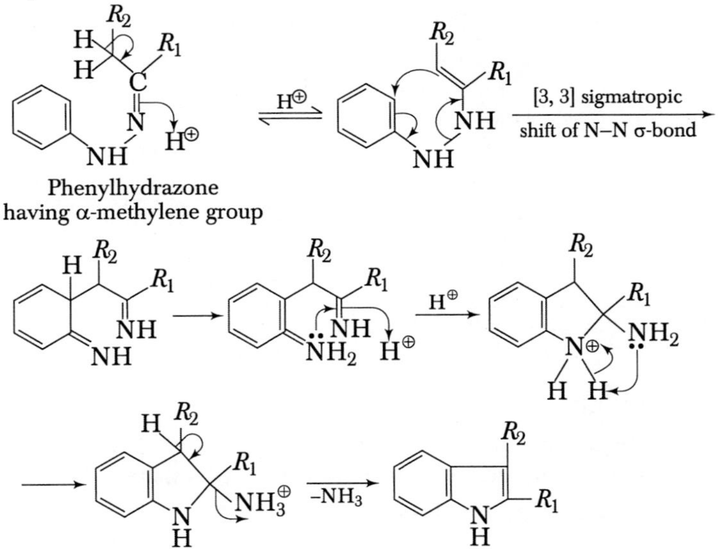

(2) Madelung synthesis

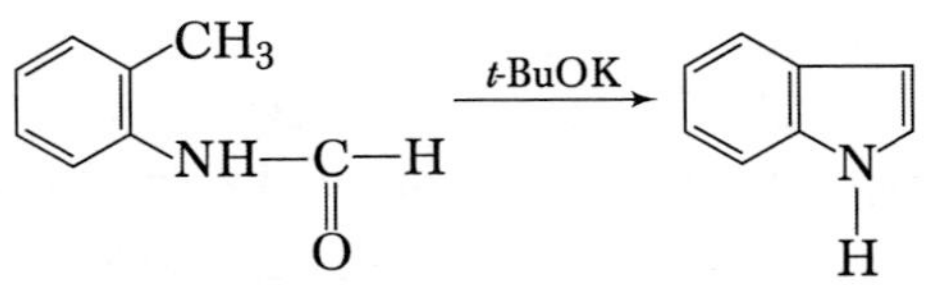

o-formamidotoluene Indole

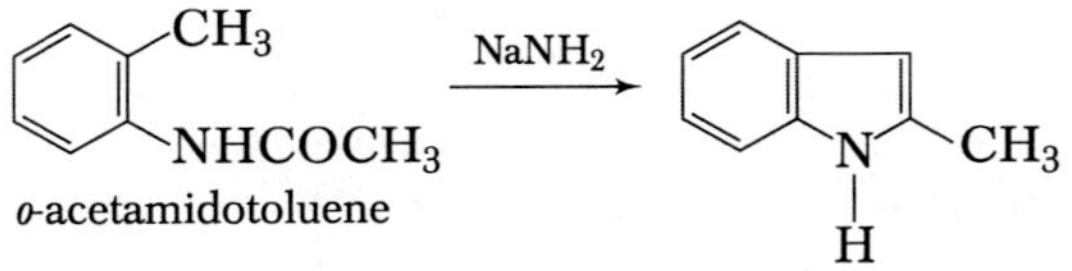

o-acetamidotoluene 2-methylindole

Mechanism

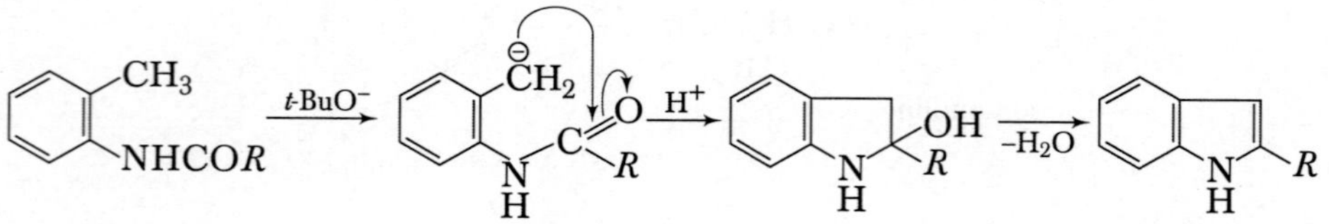

Reactivity of Indole

Oxidation

Indole is oxidised by ozone to indigotin.

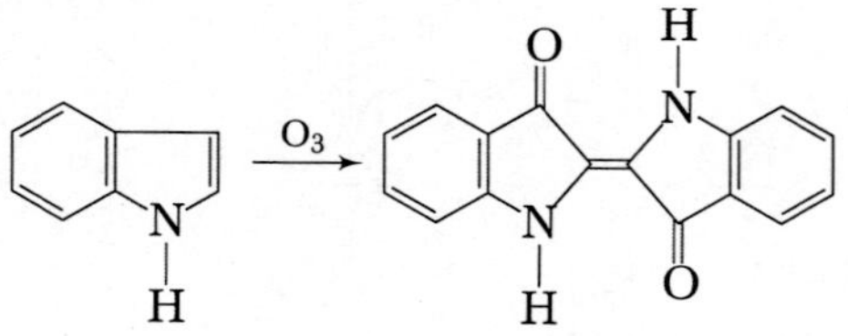

Reduction

Indole is reduced electrolytically, by Sn and HCl, by Zn and phosphoric acid and by copper chromite to 2,3-dihydroindole (indoline).

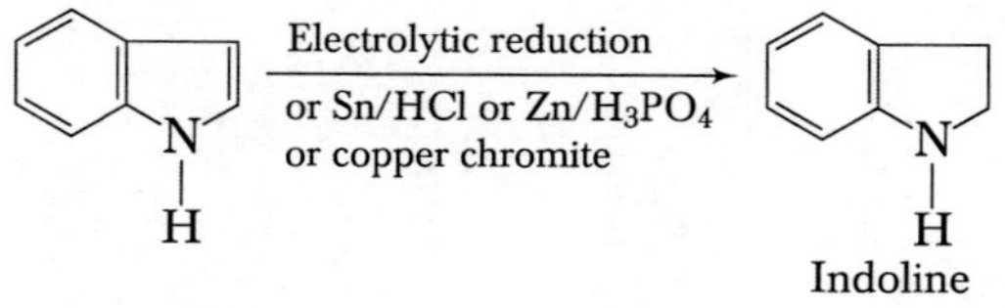

Raney nickel reduces indole to octahydroindole.

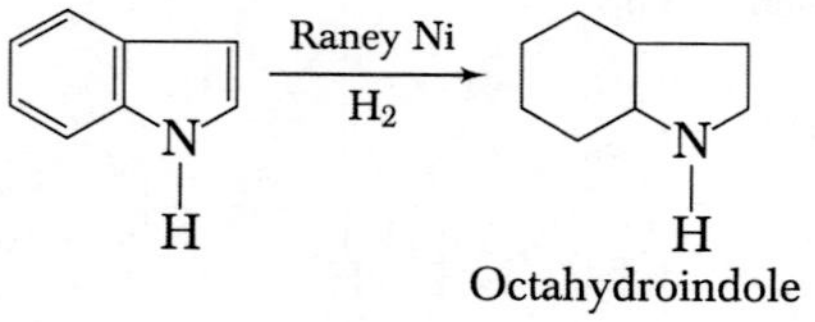

Electrophilic substitution reaction

Electrophilic substitution normally occurs in the 3-position. If 3-position is occupied, substitution in 2-position occurs. If both 3- and 2-positions are occupied, substitution occurs at 6-position.

Indole is chlorinated at 3-position by sulphuryl chloride.

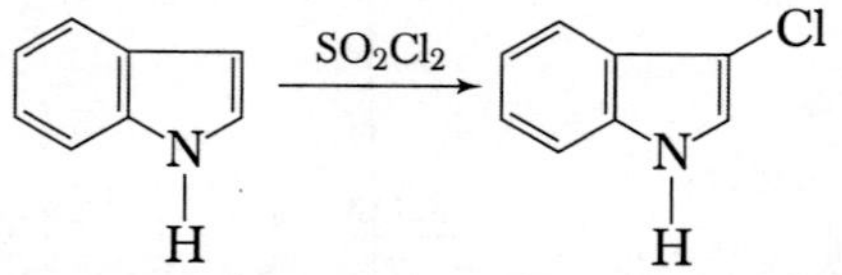

On treating indole with sodium ethoxide and ethyl nitrate, 3-nitroindole is obtained.

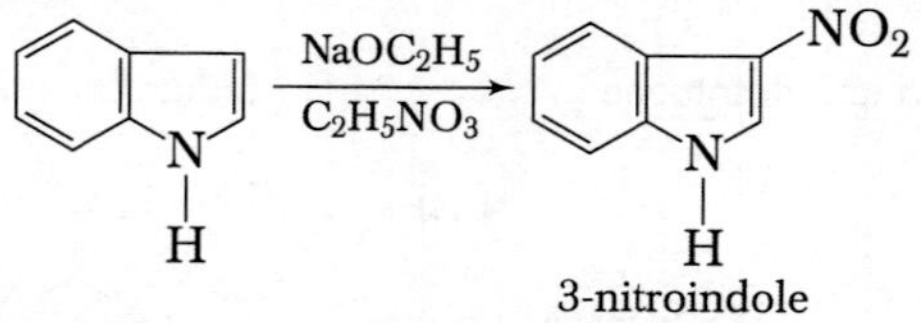

Mixed acids convert 2,3-dimethylindole into 6-nitro derivative.

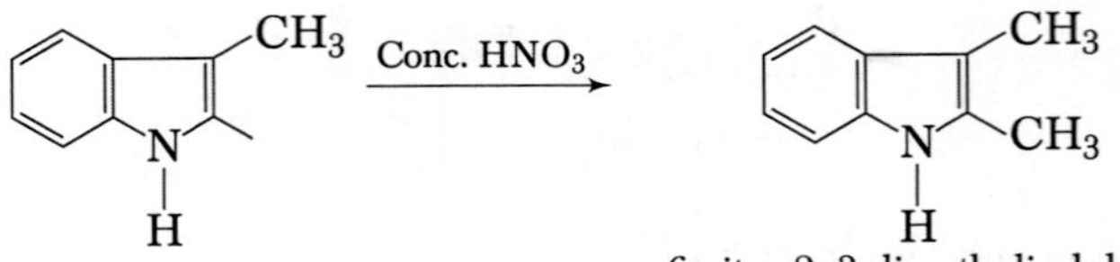

6-nitro-2, 3-dimethylindole

Other reactions

By **Reimer-Tiemann reaction** indole-3-aldehyde can be prepared. However, a small amount of 3-chloroquinoline is also formed.

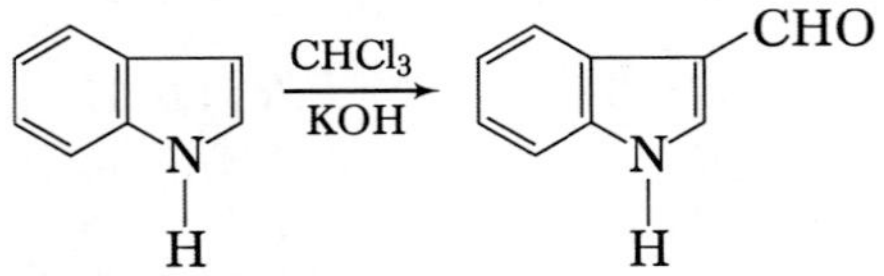

Indole-3-aldehyde is also formed by the **Gattermann reaction** or by the action of dimethyl formamide and phosphoryl chloride. **(Vilsmier-Haack reaction)**

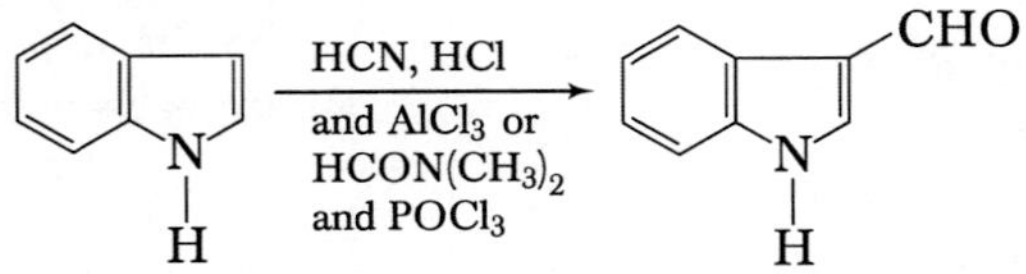

N-acetylindole undergoes rearrangement to give 3-acetylindole.

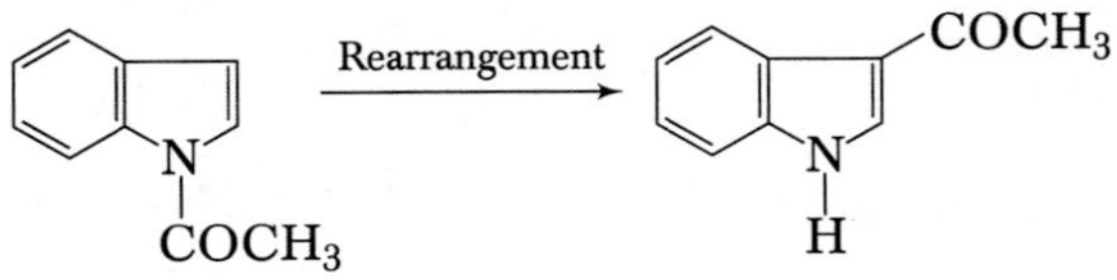

Exercise 1
(For Part 'B')

1. Which of the following is not a heterocyclic compound?

(a) 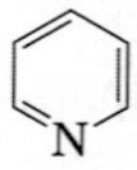 (b) 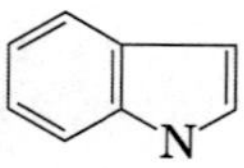

(c) 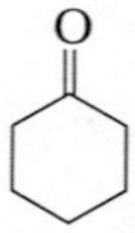 (d) 

2. Which of the following heterocyclic compounds is not aromatic?
(a) Pyridine (b) Pyrrole
(c) Furan (d) Piperidine

3. The nitrogen atom in pyridine is
(a) sp^2 hybridized (b) sp^3 hybridized
(c) sp hybridized (d) Cannot be predicted

4. Pyridine has a delocalized π-molecular orbital containing
(a) $4\pi e^-$ (b) $6\pi e^-$
(c) $8\pi e^-$ (d) $12\pi e^-$

5. Pentose $\xrightarrow{\text{Acid}}$ $\xrightarrow{O_2}$ $\xrightarrow{\Delta}$ product, the product is

(a)  (b) 

(c) 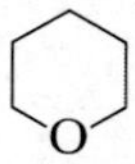 (d) 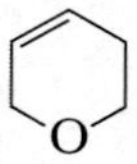

6. $\underset{CH_2Cl}{\overset{COCH_3}{|}}$ + $\underset{COCH_3}{\overset{CH_2COOC_2H_5}{|}}$ $\longrightarrow A$;

A is

(a) 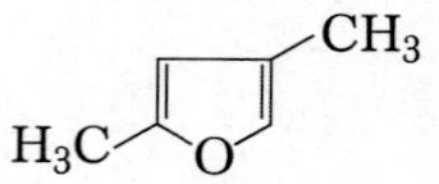

(b) 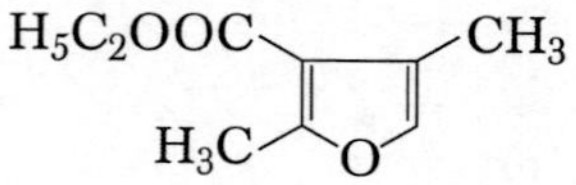

(c) 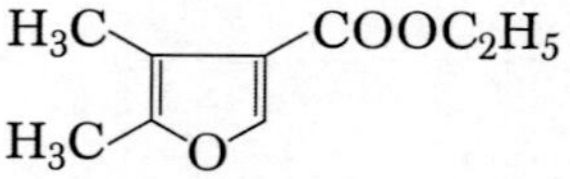

(d) 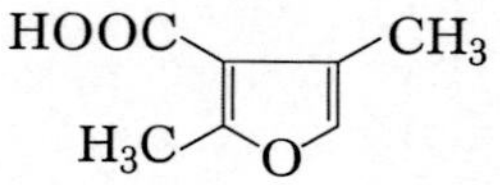

7. 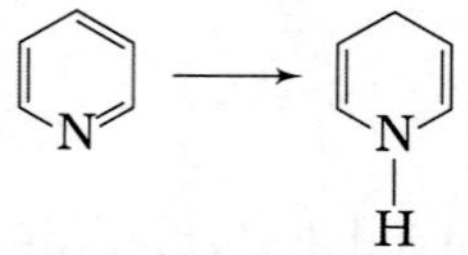

The above reaction is brought about by
(a) Na/liq. NH_3 (b) Na/C_2H_5OH
(c) $LiAlH_4$ (d) HI/Δ

8. Pyrrole is less basic than pyridine because the lone pair of electrons of N-atom in pyrrole
(a) is part of the delocalized π-molecular orbital
(b) is not part of the delocalized π-molecular orbital
(c) resides in sp^2 hybrid orbital
(d) resides in sp hybrid orbital

9. Furan reacts with maleic anhydride to give

(a) 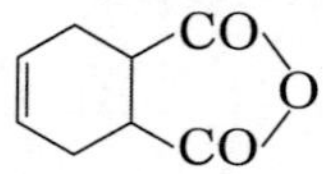 (b) 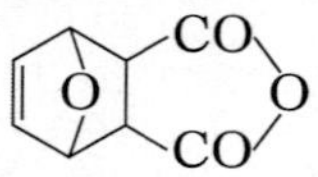

(c) 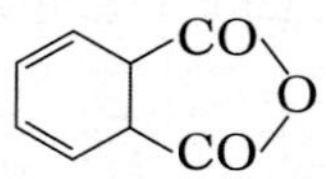 (d) 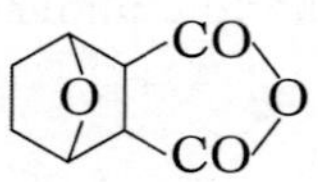

10. The major product of the reaction is

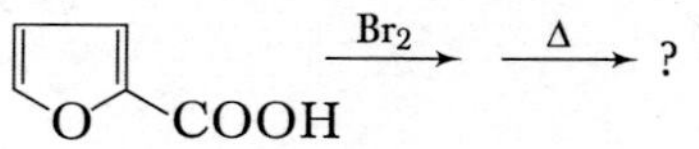

(a) 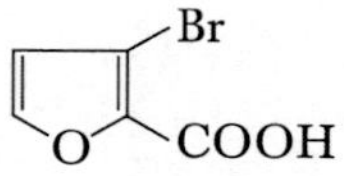 (b) 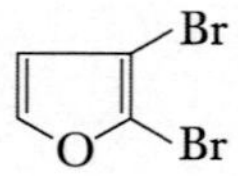

(c) 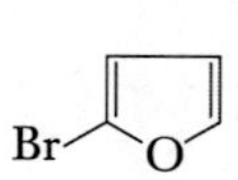 (d) 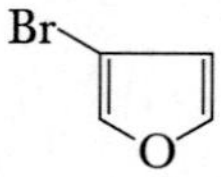

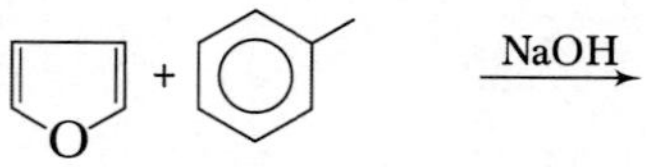

The above reaction is known as
(a) Gattermann reaction (b) Schmidt reaction
(c) Vilsmier-Haack reaction (d) Gomberg reaction

12. Which of the following product is formed, on passing a mixture of furan, ammonia and steam over heated alumina?

(a) 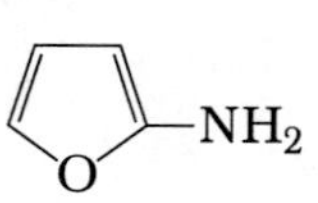 (b) 

(c) 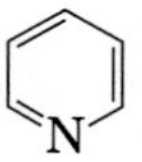 (d) 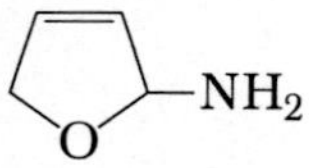

13. An enolizable 1,4-diketone on heating with P_2S_5 to give

(a) 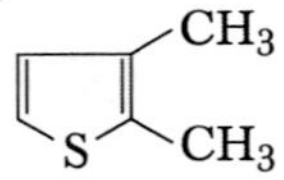

(b) 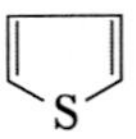

(c) 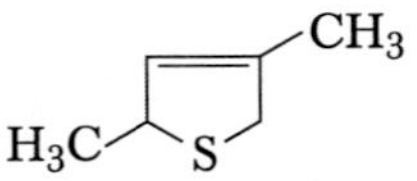

(d) 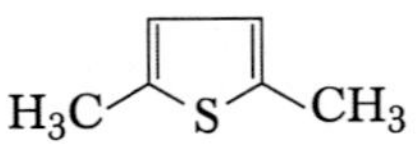

14. Pyridine is less basic than aliphatic amine because the lone pair of electrons on N-atom in pyridine resides in

(a) sp^2 hybrid orbital
(b) sp hybrid orbital
(c) sp^3 hybrid orbital
(d) sp^2d hybrid orbital

15. The end product of the following reaction series

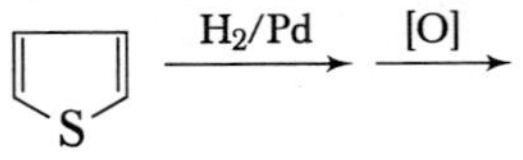

(a) 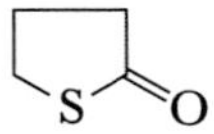

(b) 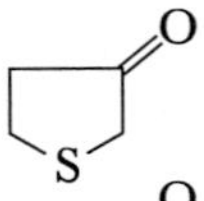

(c) 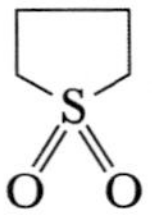

(d) 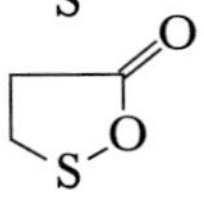

16. Thiophene reacts with dimethyl formamide and phosphorus oxychloride to give

(a) 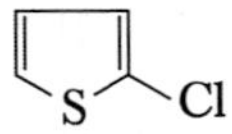

(b) 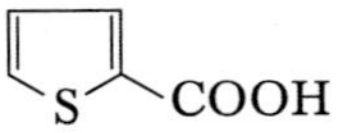

(c) 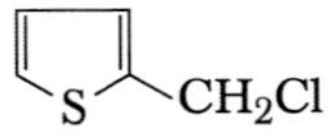

(d) 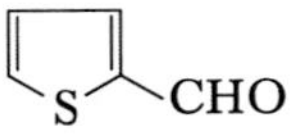

17. The product '*A*' in the given reaction is

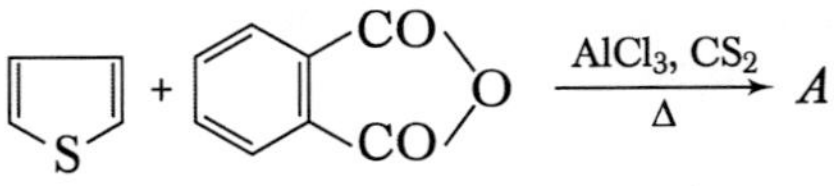

(a) 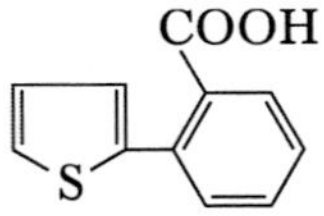

(b) 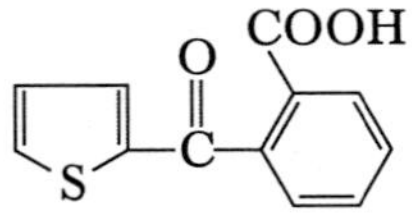

(c) 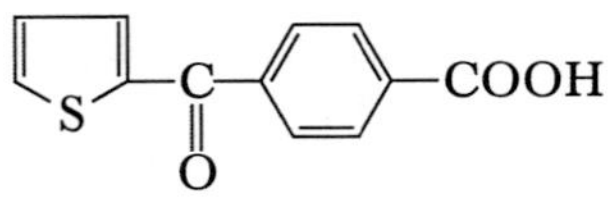

(d) 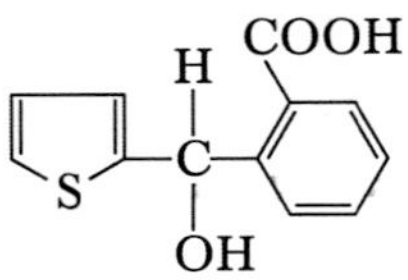

18. The order of aromaticity of furan, thiophene and pyrrole is as

(a) thiophene > furan > pyrrole
(b) furan > pyrrole > thiophene
(c) thiophene > pyrrole > furan
(d) pyrrole > thiophene > furan

19. On oxidation by chromium trioxide in sulphuric acid, pyrrole gives

(a) 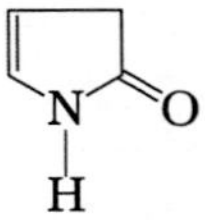

(b) 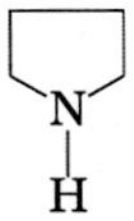

(c) 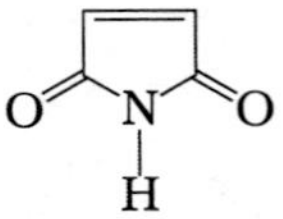

(d) 

20. Pyrrole reacts with chloroform in presence of base to give pyrrole-2-carboxyaldehyde. This reaction is an example of

(a) Reimer-Tiemann reaction
(b) Gomberg reaction
(c) Houben-Hoesch reaction
(d) Cannizzaro reaction

21. Nicotinic acid reacts with soda lime to give

(a) pyrrole
(b) piperidine
(c) pyrrolidine
(d) pyridine

22. Pyridine undergoes electrophilic substitution with fuming H_2SO_4 at 350°C to give

(a) 2-pyridinesulphonic acid
(b) 4-pyridinesulphonic acid
(c) 3-pyridinesulphonic acid
(d) None of the above

23. Pyridine reacts with a mixture of KNO_3 and H_2SO_4 at 300°C to give

(a) 1-nitropyridine
(b) 2-nitropyridine
(c) 3-nitropyridine
(d) 4-nitropyridine

24. Which of the following reagents will react with pyrrole to form 2-formylpyrrole?

(a) HCOOH
(b) $CHCl_3$/KOH
(c) H_2O_2
(d) $(CH_3CO)_2O/SnCl_4$

25. 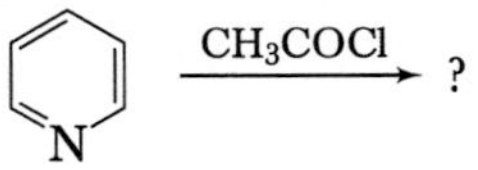

The product of the above reaction is

(a) 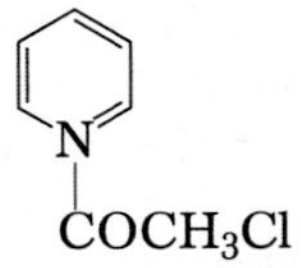

(b) 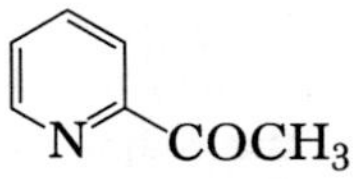

(c) 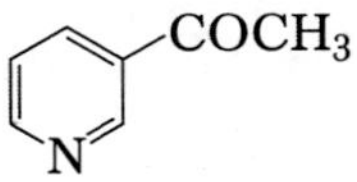

(d) 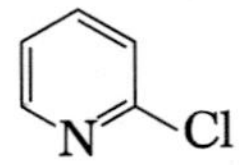

26. When aniline is heated with glycerol in the presence of H_2SO_4 and nitrobenzene, it gives quinoline. This reaction is called
(a) Fischer synthesis (b) Skraup synthesis
(c) Corey-House synthesis (d) Friedlander's synthesis

27. 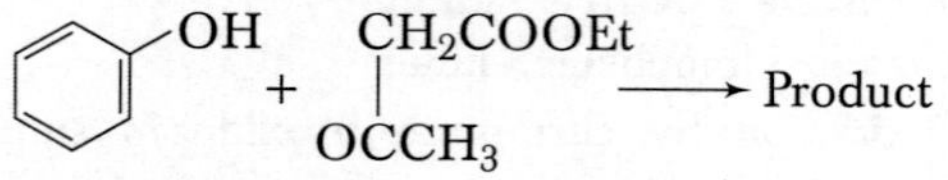

The product is

(a) 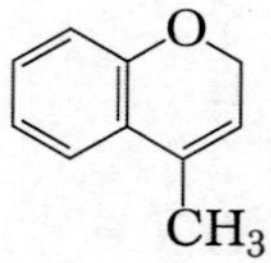 (b) 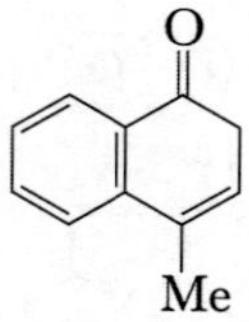

(c) 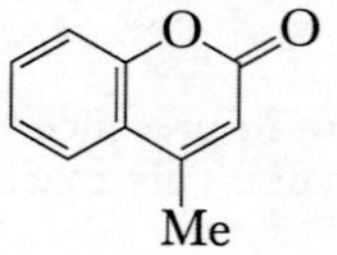 (d) 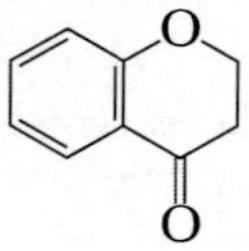

28. 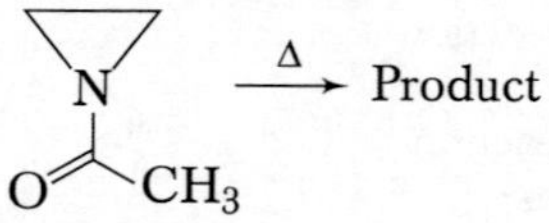

The product is

(a) 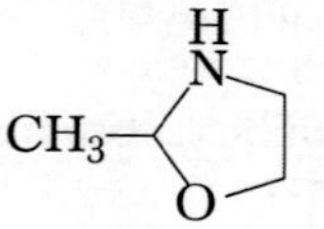 (b) 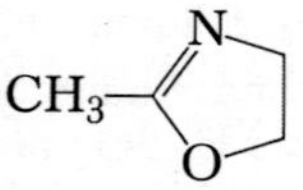

(c) 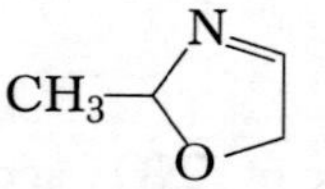 (d) 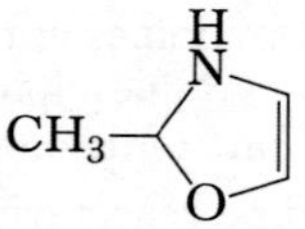

29. Quinoline undergoes nucleophilic substitution on heating with $NaNH_2$ to give
(a) 2-aminoquinoline (b) 4-aminoquinoline
(c) 3-aminoquinoline (d) 8-aminoquinoline

30. Which of the following reagents will react with furan to form 2-furansulphonic acid?
(a) Dilute H_2SO_4 at 200°C
(b) SO_2 at 100°C
(c) Dilute H_2SO_4 at 100°C
(d) SO_3 in pyridine at 100°C

31. Pyridine undergoes nucleophilic substitution with $NaNH_2$ at 100°C to give
(a) 3-aminopyridine (b) 2-aminopyridine
(c) 3,5-diaminopyridine (d) 2,5-diaminopyridine

32. Identify the major product, *P* in the following two step reaction.

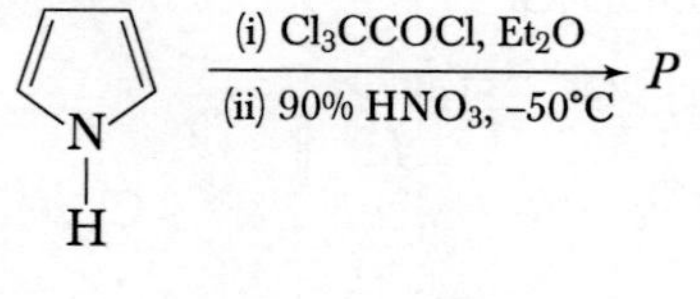

(a) 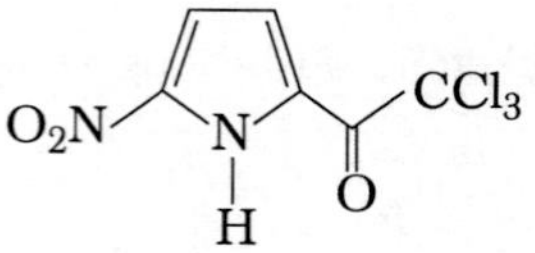

(b) 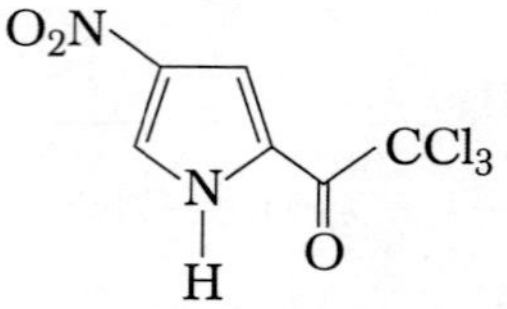

(c) 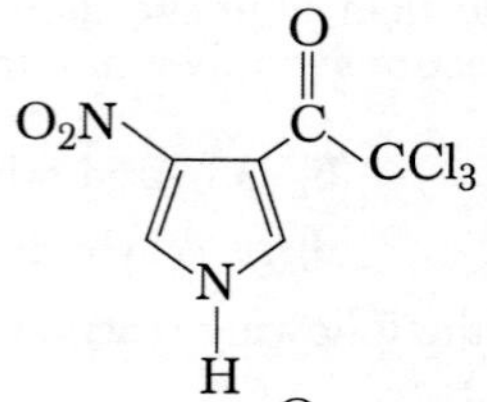

(d) 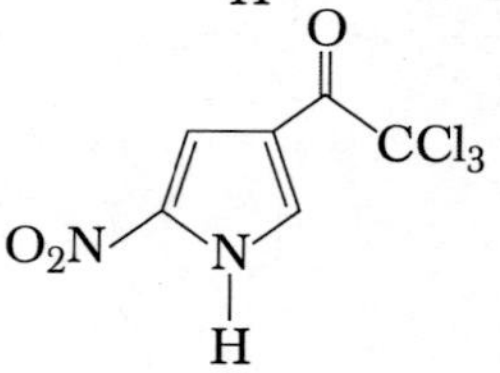

33. The correct order of the basicity of the following compounds is

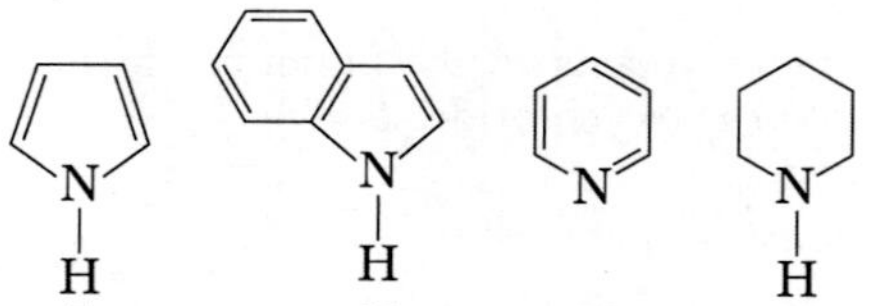

I II III IV

(a) III > IV > I > II (b) III > IV > II > I
(c) IV > III > I > II (d) IV > III > II > I

34. Among the following compounds, the most basic compound is

(a) 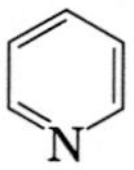 (b) 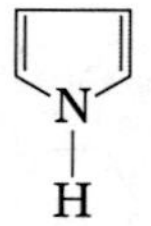

(c) 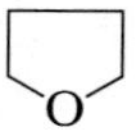 (d) 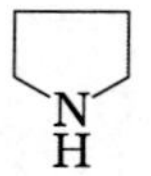

35. Thiophene reacts with HCHO in presence of aqueous HCl to give

(a) 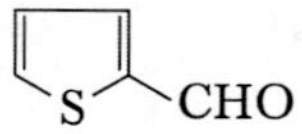 (b) 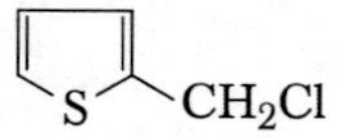

(c) 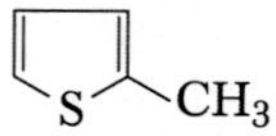 (d) 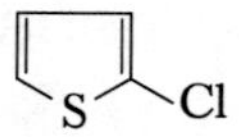

36. Reaction of furfural with NaOH gives
(a) Furoin
(b) Furoic acid
(c) Furfuryl alcohol and sodium salt of furane-2-carboxylic acid
(d) No reaction

37. 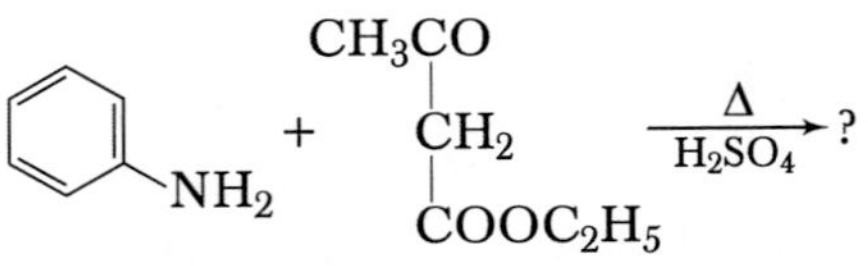

The product of the above reaction is

(a) 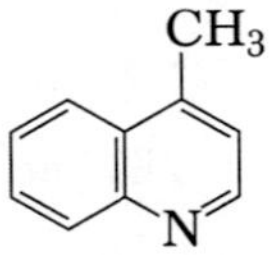 (b) 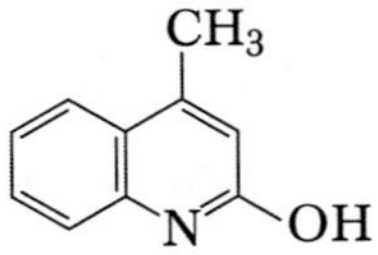

(c) 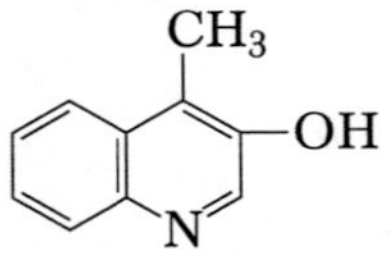 (d) 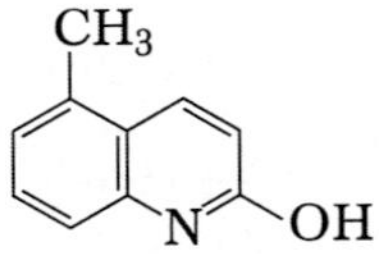

38. 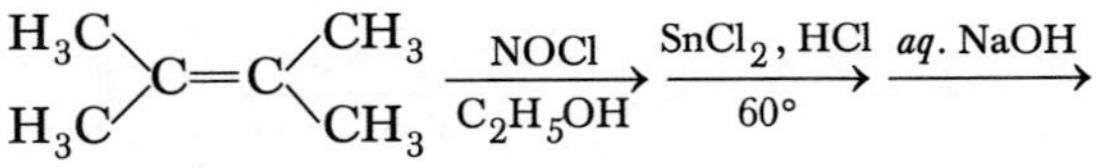

product. The product of the above reaction series

(a) 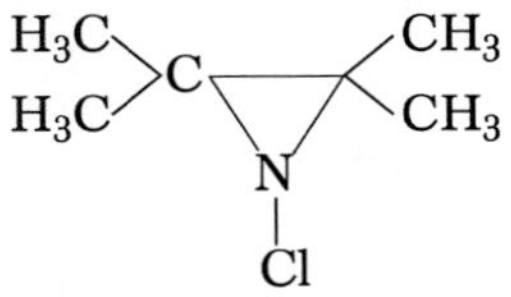

(b) 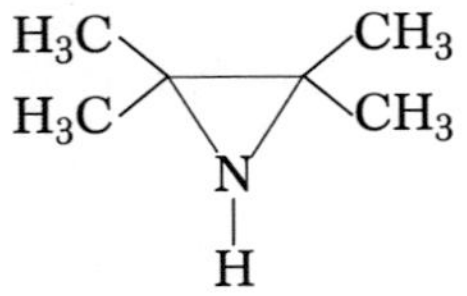

(c) 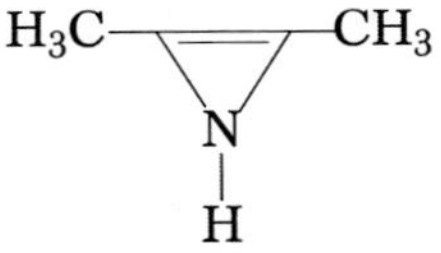

(d) 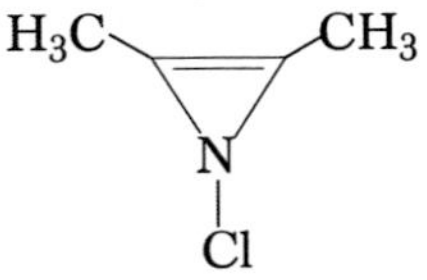

39. Azetidine reacs with H_2O_2 to give
(a) $CH_3CH{=}CH_2 + NH_3$
(b) $CH_3CH{=}CH_2 + N_2$
(c) $CH_3CH_2CH_3 + N_2$
(d) $CH_3CH_2CH_3 + NH_3$

40. 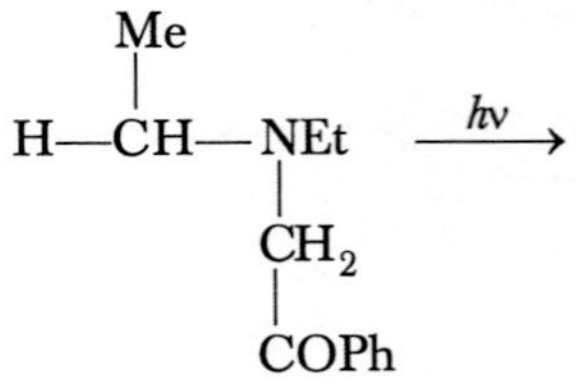 A; Identify the A

(a) 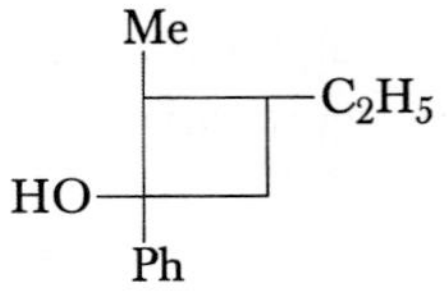

(b) 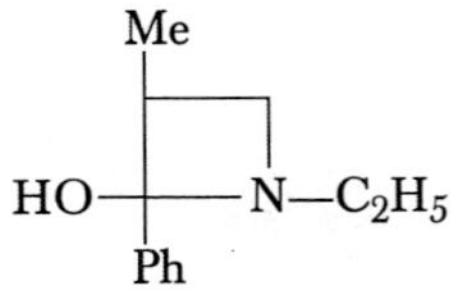

(c) 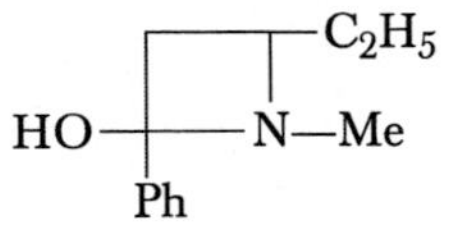

(d) 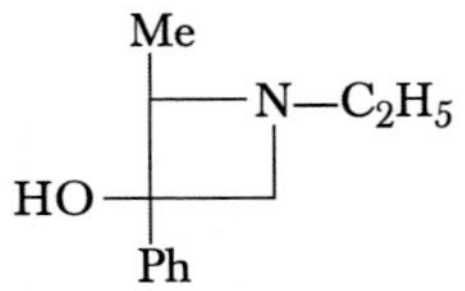

41. Prophin consists the
(a) 3 pyrrole ring (b) 4 pyrrole ring
(c) 5 pyrrole ring (d) 6 pyrrole ring

42. The structure of coumarone is as

(a) 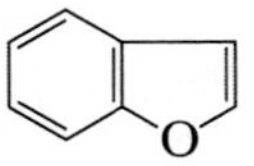 (b) 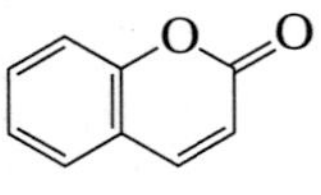

(c) 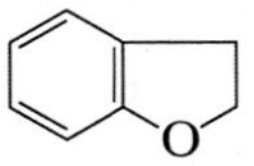 (d) 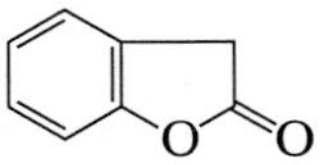

43. The reduction of 2-nitrobenzofuran with Sn/HCl to gives

(a) 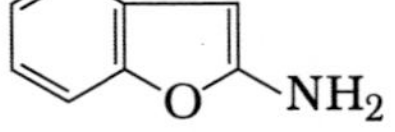 (b) 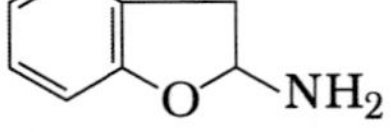

(c) 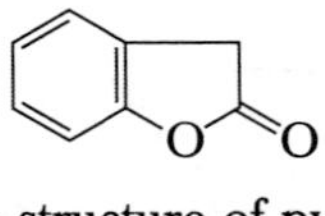 (d) 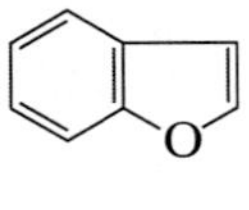

44. The structure of pyrazine is

(a) 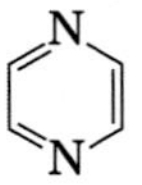 (b) 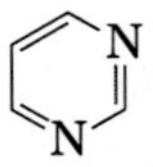

(c) 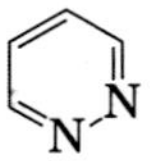 (d) 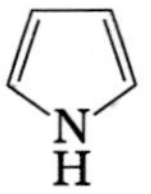

45. The suitable reagent for the following transformation is

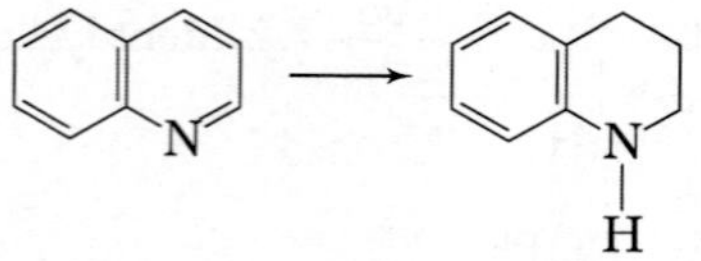

(a) Na/liq. NH_3 (b) H_2/Pt
(c) Sn/HCl (d) All of these

46. The product of the following reaction is
Indole + CH_2O + $(C_2H_5)_2NH \longrightarrow$

(a) 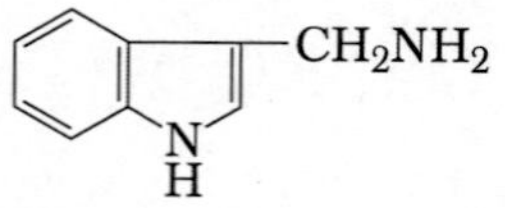

(b) 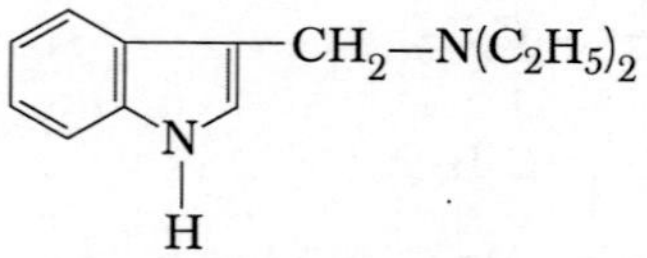

(c) 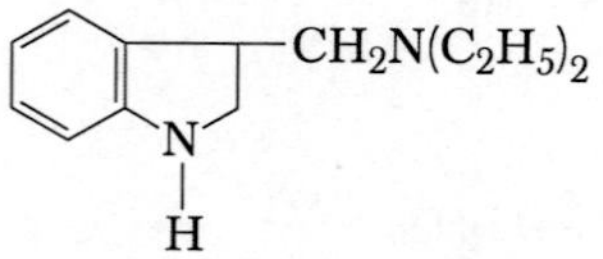

(d) 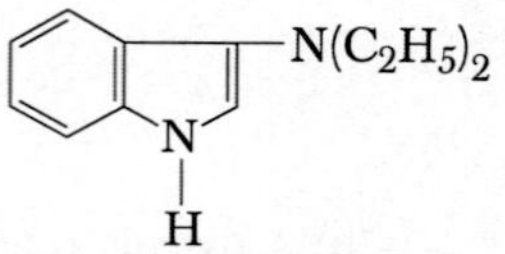

47. Which of the following compounds is formed, when α-naphthylamine is used in the Skraup synthesis?

(a) 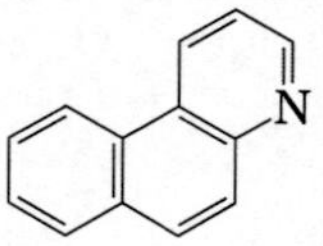 (b) 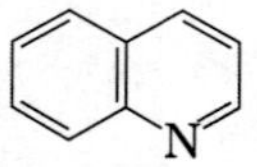

(c) 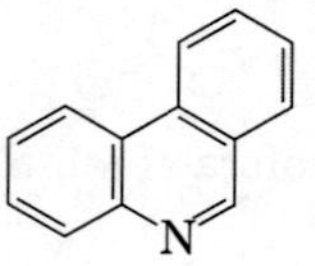 (d) 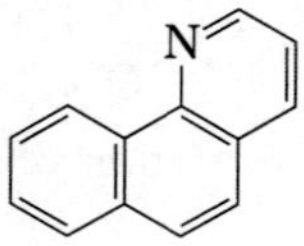

48. On nitration with nitric acid and acetic anhydride quinoline gives the major product of
(a) 5-nitroquinoline (b) 8-nitroquinoline
(c) 3-nitroquinoline (d) 2-nitroquinoline

49. 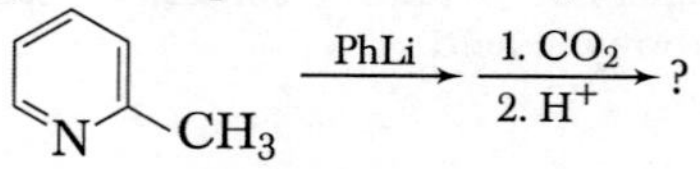

The product is

(a) 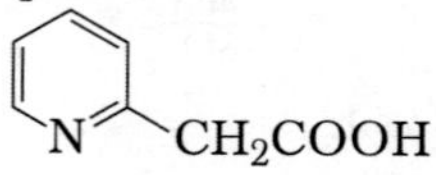 (b) 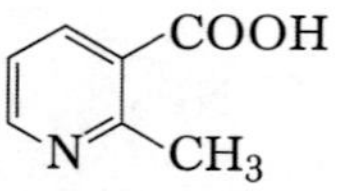

(c) 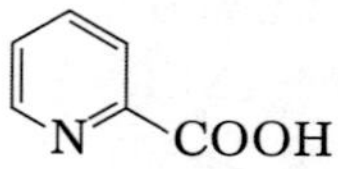 (d) 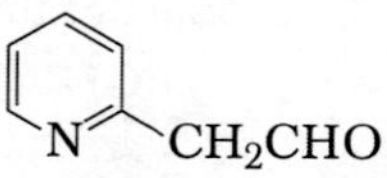

50. Isoquinoline on oxidation with alkaline $KMnO_4$ gives

(a) 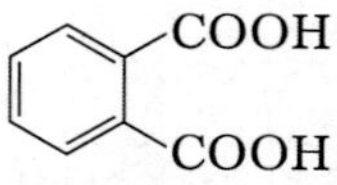 (b) 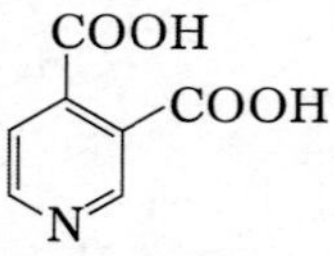

(c) Both of these (d) None of these

51. 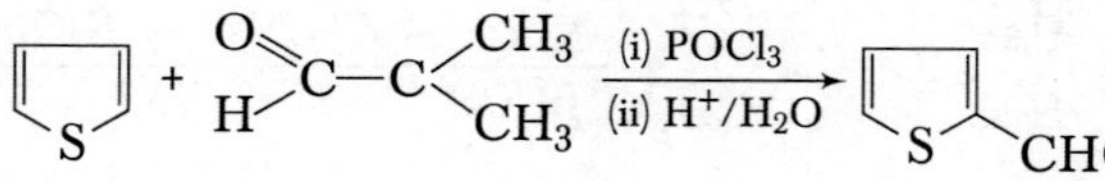

This reaction is known as
(a) Vilsmier-Haack reaction
(b) Friedlander reaction
(c) Pfitzinger reaction
(d) Dobereiner's-Miller reaction

52. Pyrrole reacts with iodine to give

(a) 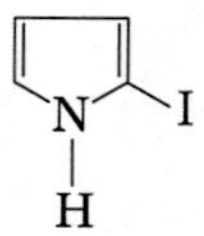 (b) 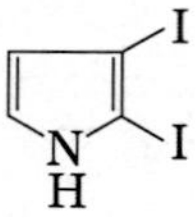

(c) 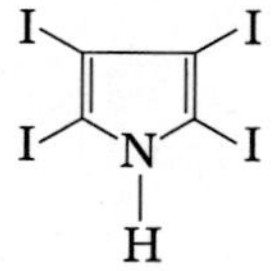 (d) 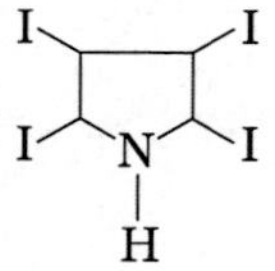

Exercise 2

1. 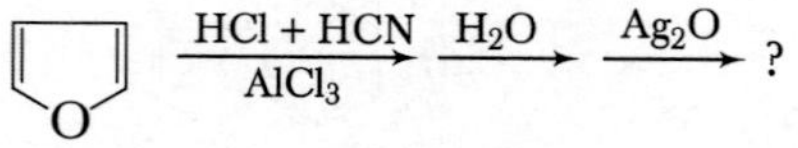

The product of the above reaction series is

(a) 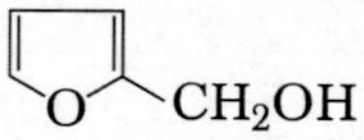

(b) 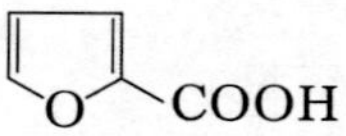

(c) 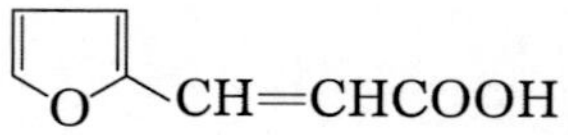

(d) 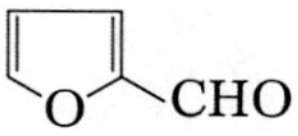

2. Reduction of thiophene by Na/liq. NH_3 gives

(a)  (b) 

(c) 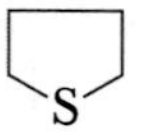 (d) $CH_3CH_2CH_2CH_3$

3. In alkaline medium pyrrole reacts with benzene diazonium chloride to give

(a) 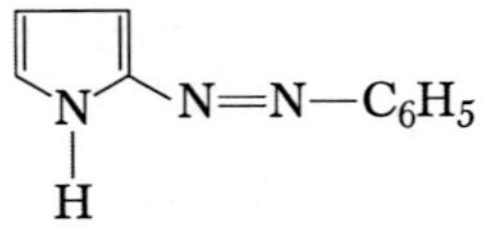

(b) 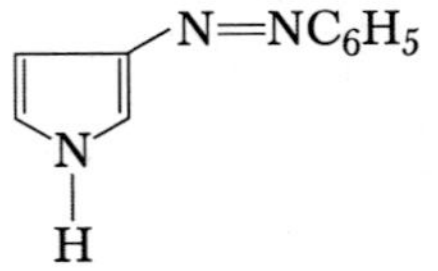

(c) 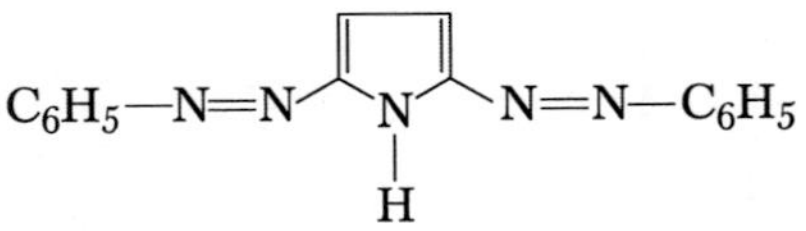

(b) 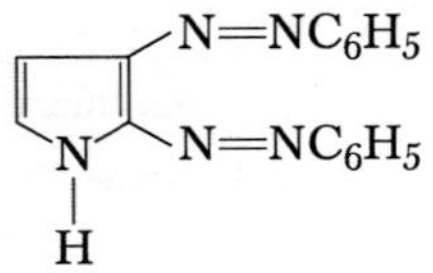

4. 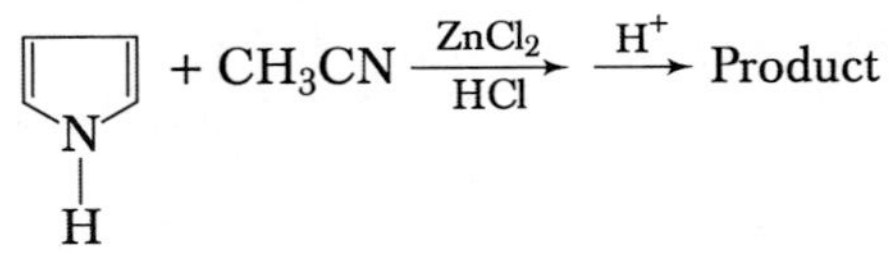

The product is

(a) 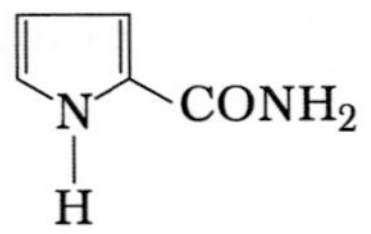 (b) 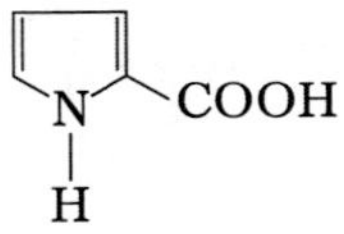

(c) 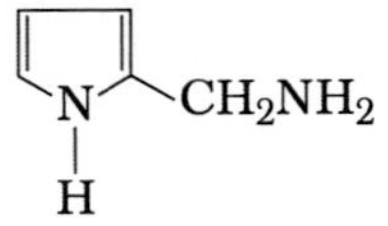 (d) 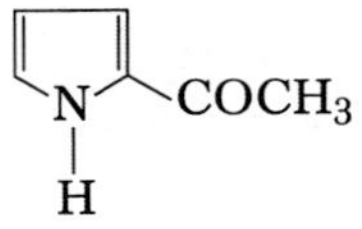

5. Consider the following statements.

I. Furan undergoes electrophilic substitution at the 2-position.

II. Thiophene ring occurs in the vitamin C molecule.

III. Thiophene is more aromatic than furan.

IV. Pyrrole is more basic than pyridine.

Select the correct statements.

(a) I, III (b) I, III, IV
(c) I, II, III (d) III, IV

6. The major product of the following transformation is

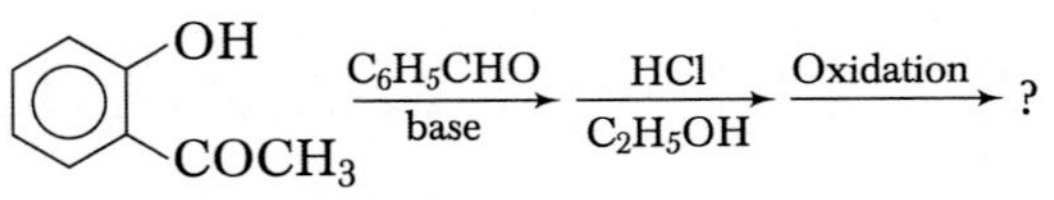

(a) 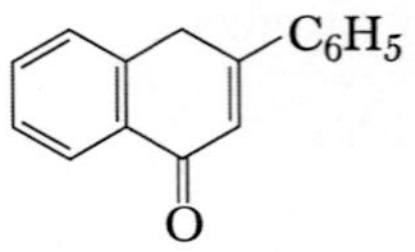 (b) 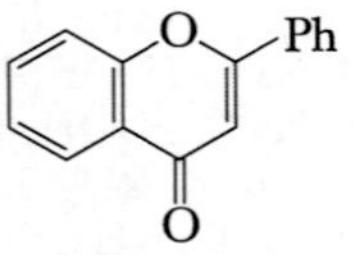

(c) 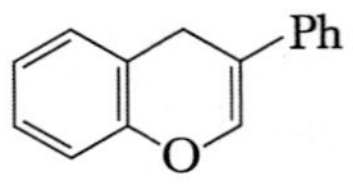 (d) 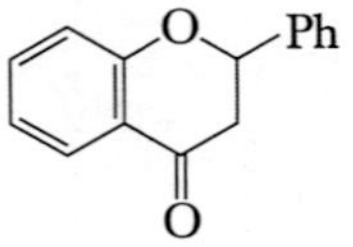

7. Select the correct statements.

(a) Indole (I) is more stable than isoindole (II)

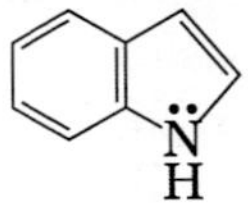 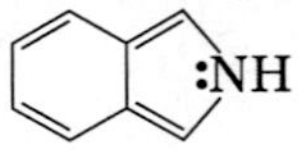

(I) (II)

(b) Imidazole (III) is a much stronger base than pyrrole (IV).

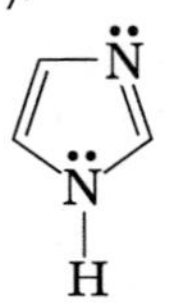 

(III) (IV)

(c) In (III), N attached to double bond is protonated

(d) Furan is more aromatic than thiophene

8. 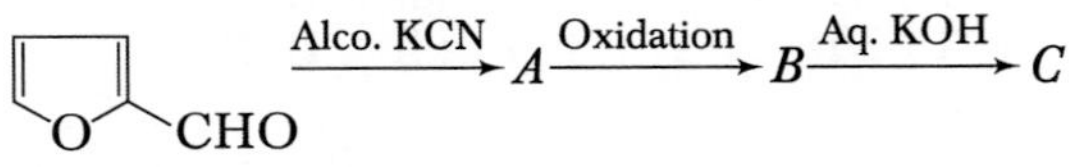

The structure of *B* and *C* are respectively

(a) 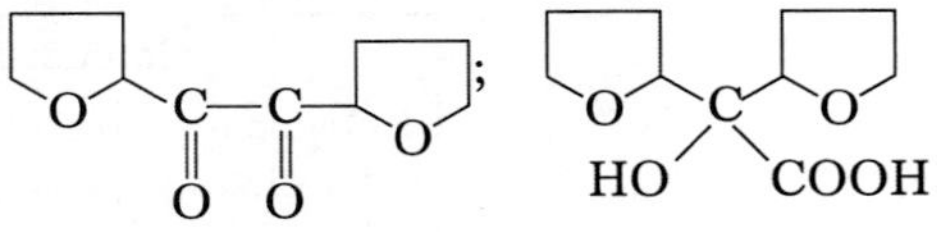

(b) 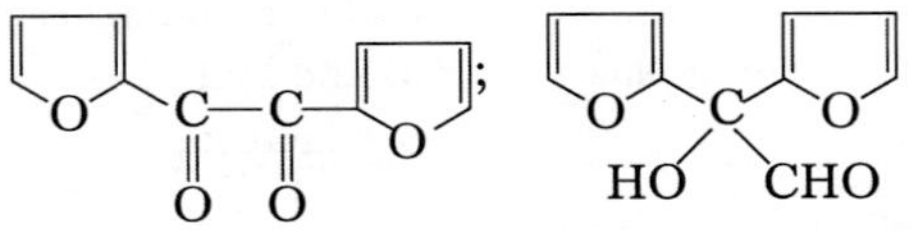

(c) 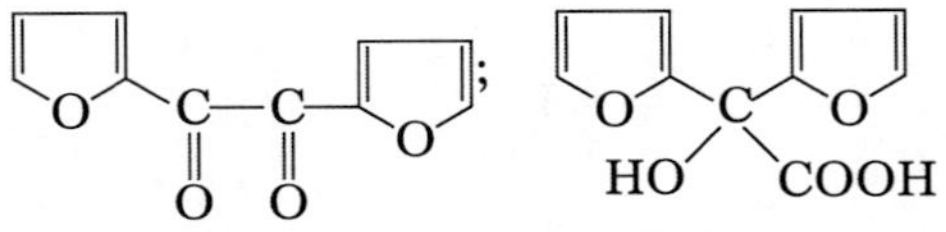

(d) 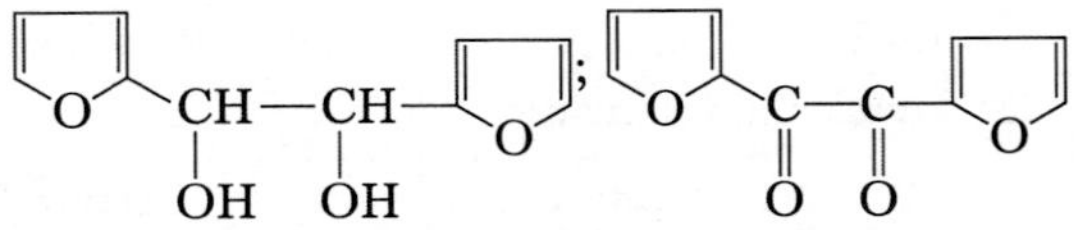

9. 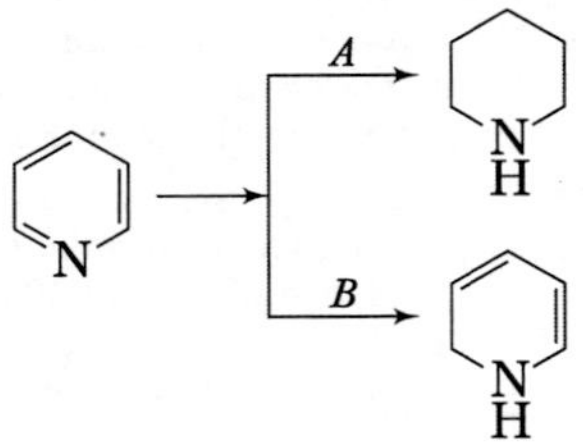

Reagent A and B are respectively
(a) Na/C_2H_5OH; $LiAlH_4$
(b) Na/C_2H_5OH; $Na/liq.\ NH_3$
(c) $Na/liq.\ NH_3$; $LiAlH_4$
(d) $Na/liq.NH_3$; HI/Δ

10. 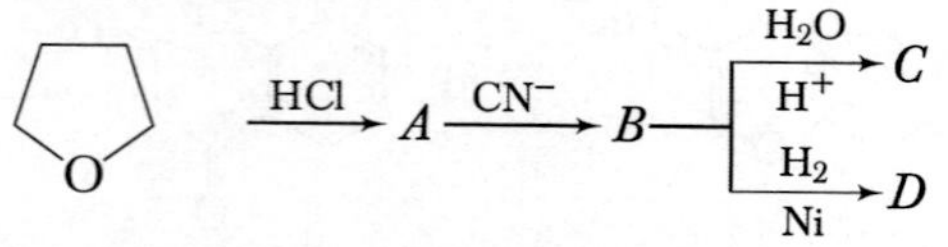

In the above reaction series the product C and D are
(a) $HOOC(CH_2)_3COOH$; $H_2N(CH_2)_4NH_2$
(b) $HOOC(CH_2)_4COOH$; $H_2NCH_2(CH_2)_4CH_2NH_2$
(c) $HOOC(CH_2)_4CH_2NH_2$; $H_2N(CH_2)_4NH_2$
(d) $HOOC(CH_2)_4COOH$; $H_2N\overset{\overset{O}{\|}}{C}(CH_2)_4—\overset{\overset{O}{\|}}{C}NH_2$

11. Consider the following statements.
I. Quinoline is a secondary base.
II. Quinoline on oxidation with aqueous $KMnO_4$ gives quinolinic acid.
III. Isoquinoline is a stronger base as compared with quinoline.
IV. In isoquinoline nucleophilic substitution occurs at 5-position.

Select the correct statements.
(a) II, III, IV
(b) I, II
(c) II, III
(d) I, II, IV

Matching Type

12. Match the Column I with Column II.

	Column I		Column II
A.	Pyrrole	1.	Indophenin reaction
B.	Pyridine	2.	Dippels oil (bone oil)
C.	Indole	3.	In denaturing rectified spirit
D.	Quinoline	4.	Indigotin
		5.	Antiseptic

Codes

	A	B	C	D
(a)	2	3	4	5
(b)	2	5	1	5
(c)	3	2	4	5
(d)	3	4	1	5

13. Match the following.

	Column I		Column II
A.	Hantzsch synthesis	1.	Aniline on heating with paraldehyde and H_2SO_4 gives 2-methylquinoline.
B.	Houben Hoesch reaction	2.	β-arylethylamine is condensed with aldehyde in presence of HCl at 100°C to get 1, 2, 3, 4-tetrahydroisoquinoline.
C.	Fried Lander's synthesis	3.	Condensation between chloroacetone, a ketoester and a primary amine to form a substituted pyrrole.
D.	Dobeiner's Miller synthesis	4.	Quinoline is synthesised by condensing *o*-amino benzaldehyde with acetaldehyde in aqueous NaOH.
		5.	Pyrrole gives 2-ketones.

Codes

	A	B	C	D
(a)	2	5	4	1
(b)	5	3	4	1
(c)	3	5	2	1
(d)	3	5	4	1

14. Match the Column I with Column II.

	Column I		Column II
A.	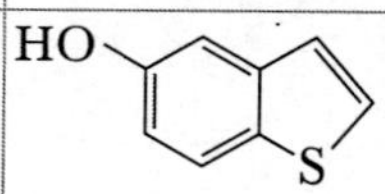	1.	Indigotin
B.	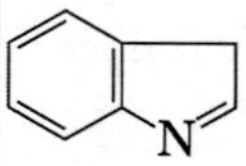	2.	5-hydroxybenzothiazole
C.	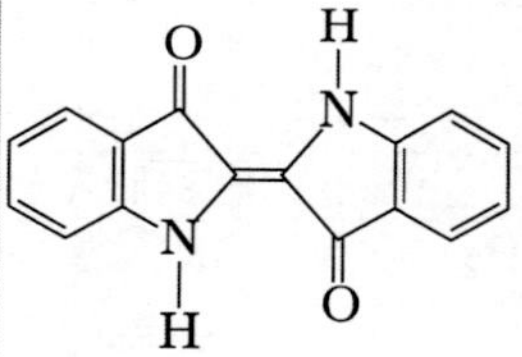	3.	Furfuryl alcohol
D.		4.	Indolenine

Codes

	A	B	C	D
(a)	2	4	1	3
(b)	3	4	1	2
(c)	2	1	4	3
(d)	2	4	3	1

15. Match the following.

	Column I		Column II
A.	Pyrrole	1.	Pictet-Spengler
B.	1,4-dihydropyridine	2.	Chichibabin
C.	Isoquinoline	3.	Paal-Knorr
		4.	Hantzsch

Codes

	A	B	C
(a)	1	2	3
(b)	2	3	4
(c)	4	1	2
(d)	3	4	1

16. 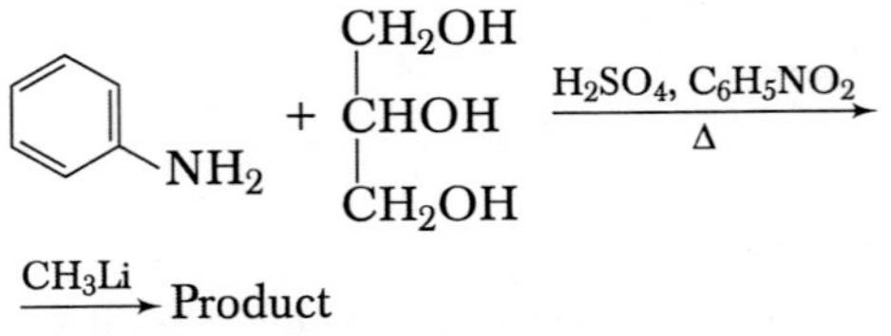

The product is

(a) 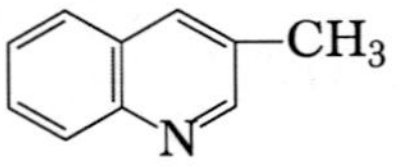 (b) 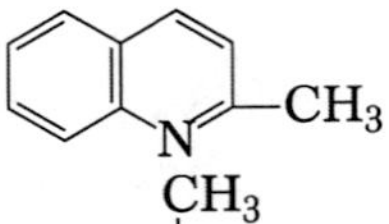

(c) 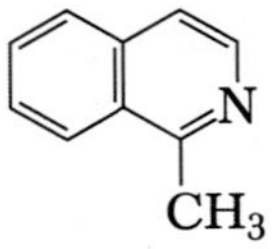 (d) 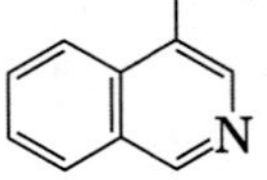

17. 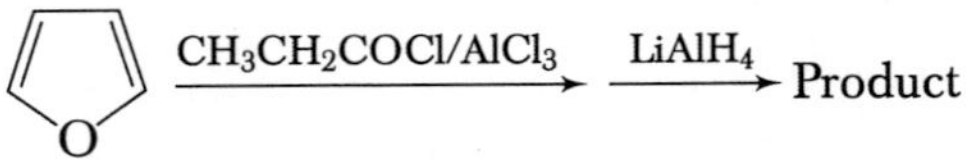

The product of the above reaction series is

(a) 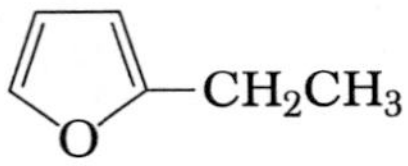

(b) 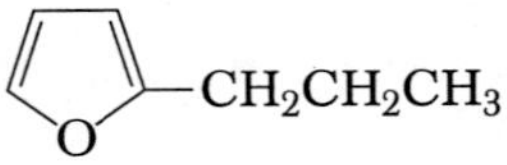

(c) 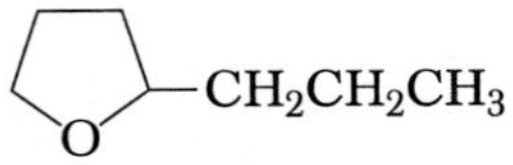

(d) 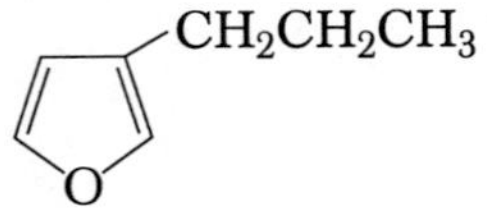

18. The product of the following transformation is

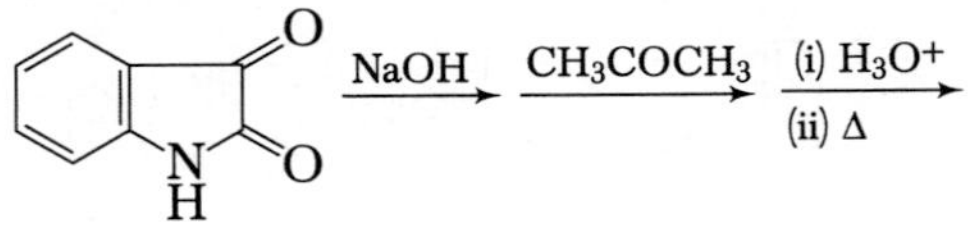

(a) 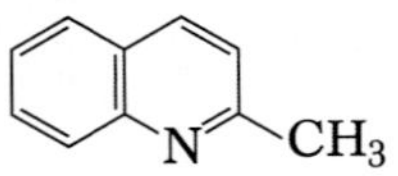 (b) 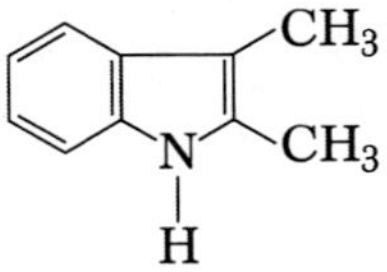

(c) 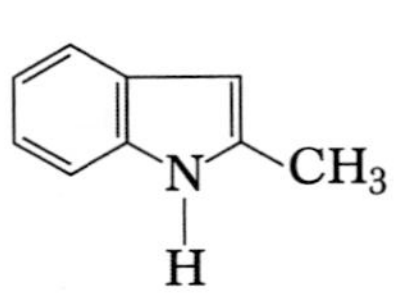 (d) 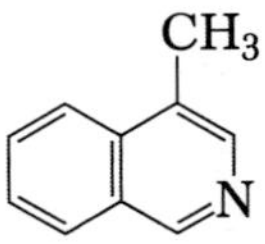

19. On nitration with conc. HNO_3 and conc. H_2SO_4, isoquinoline gives the major product of
(a) 8-nitroisoquinoline (b) 3-nitroisoquinoline
(c) 5-nitroisoquinoline (d) 1-nitroisoquinoline

20. Fischer's indole synthesis involves
(a) [2, 3] sigmatropic shift (b) [3, 3] sigmatropic shift
(c) [3, 2] sigmatropic shift (d) [2, 2] sigmatropic shift

21. 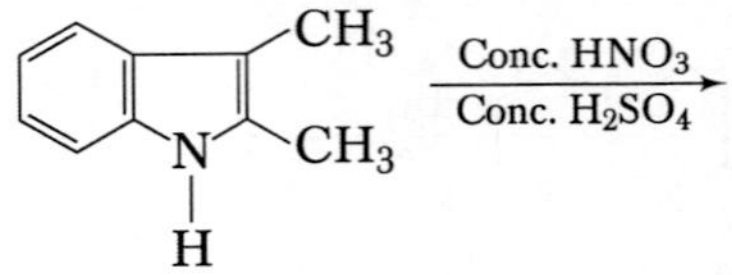

The major product of the above nitration reaction is

(a) 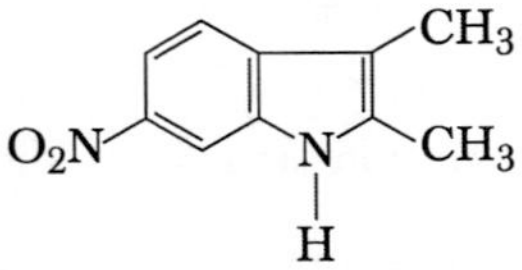

(b) 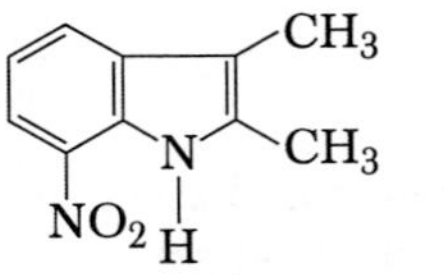

(c) 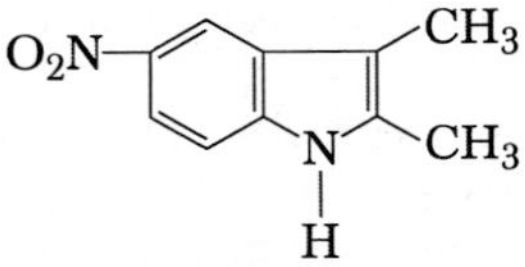

(d) 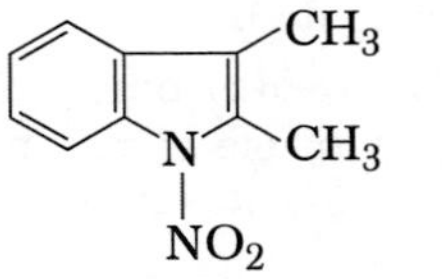

22. Benzofuran reacts with peracid to give

(a) 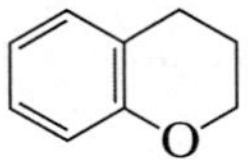 (b) 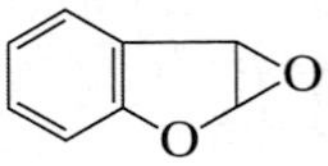

(c) 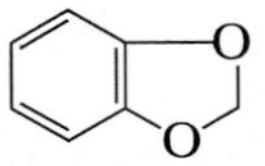 (d) 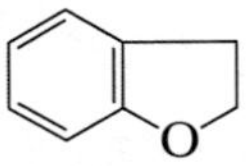

23. 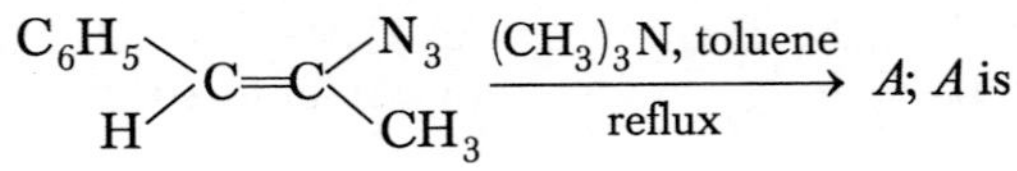

(a) 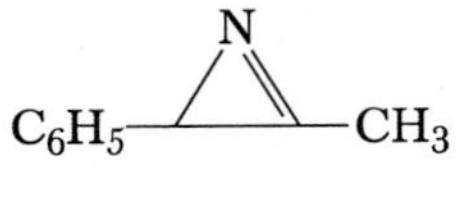

(b) 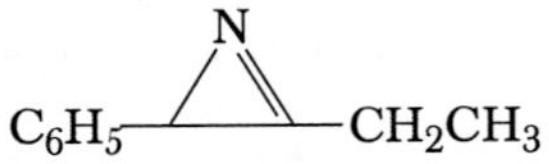

(c) 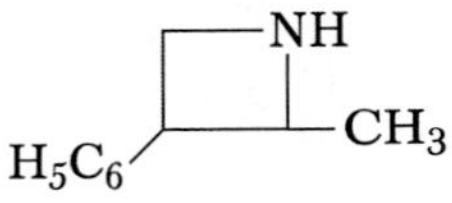

(d) 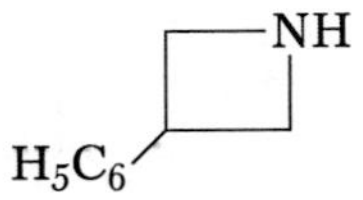

24. Bromination of acridine gives

(a) 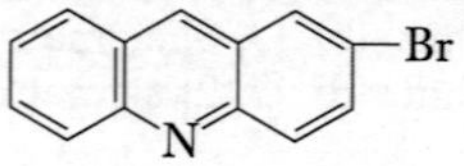

(b) 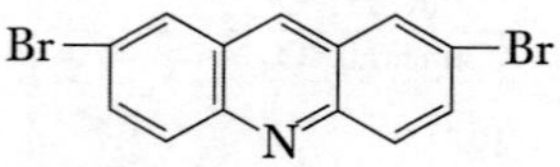

(c) Both (a) and (b)
(d) None of the above

Assertion & Reason

Codes
(a) Both A and R are true and R is the correct explanation of A.
(b) Both A and R are true but R is not the correct explanation of A.
(c) A is true but R is false.
(d) A is false but R is true.

25. **Assertion (A)** Pyridine is more basic than pyrrole.
Reason (R) Nitrogen in trigonal geometry is generally more basic than the nitrogen in tetrahedral geometry.

26. **Assertion (A)** Pyrrole reacts with chloroform in the presence of base to give pyrrole carbaldehyde.
Reason (R) Pyrrole couples with diazonium salt in the 3-position in alkaline medium.

27. **Assertion (A)** Pyrrole is a weaker base.
Reason (R) The lone pair of electrons on nitrogen atom are involved in the formation of a $(4n+2)\pi$ -electron.

28. **Assertion (A)** Pyridine does not undergo Fiedel-Crafts reaction.
Reason (R) Pyridine has a complex forming tendency

29. 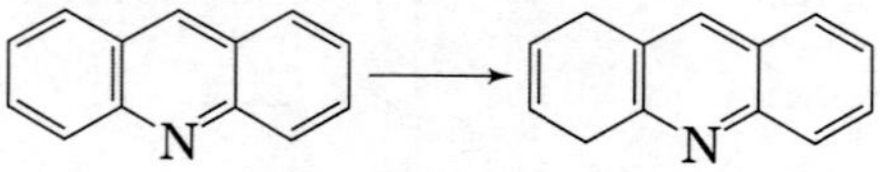

The reagent for the above transformation is
(a) H_2/Raney Ni (b) H_2/PtO_2 in CF_3COOH
(c) Li/liq. NH_3 (d) All of these

30. 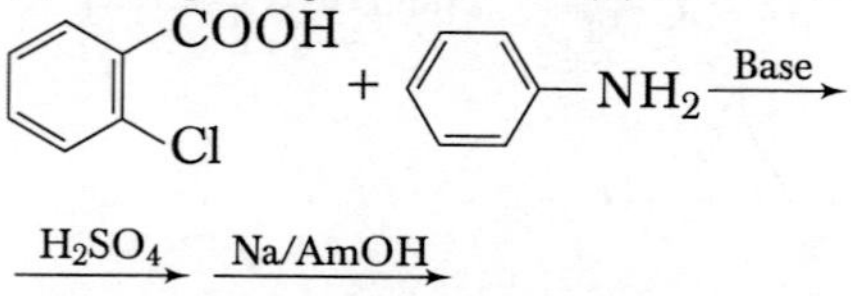

The end product of the above reaction series is

(a) 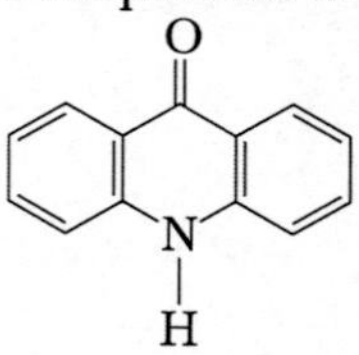

(b) 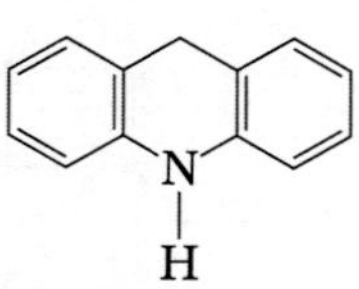

(c) 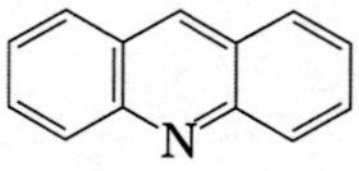

(d) 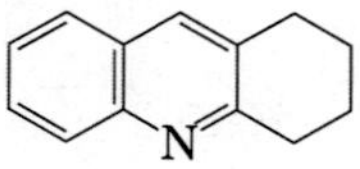

31. 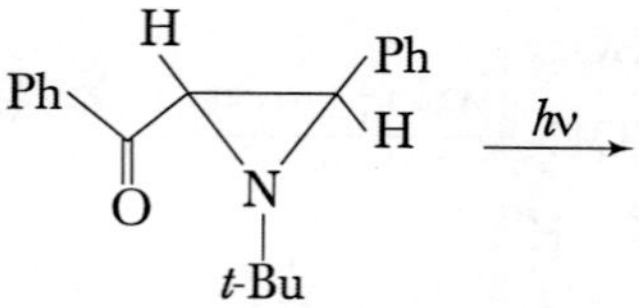

The product of the above photochemical reaction is

(a) 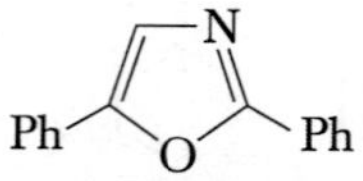

(b) 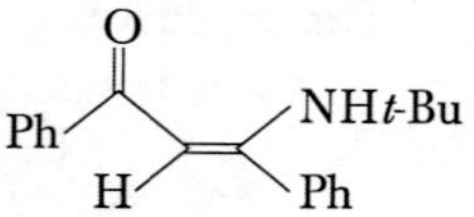

(c) Both (a) and (b) (d) None of these

32. 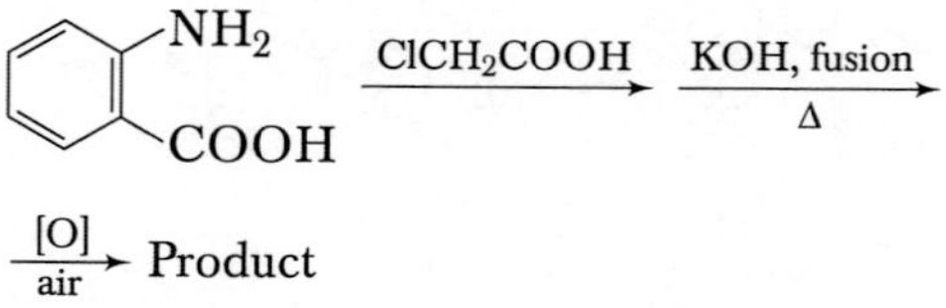

The product is

(a) 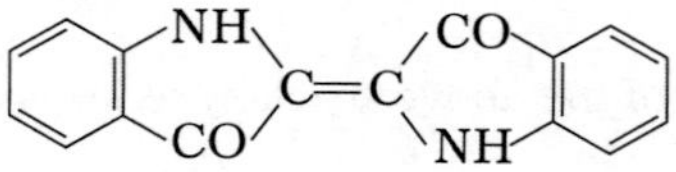

(b) 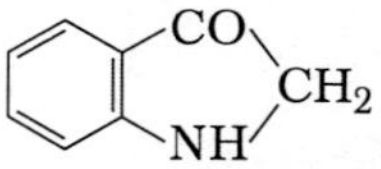

(c) 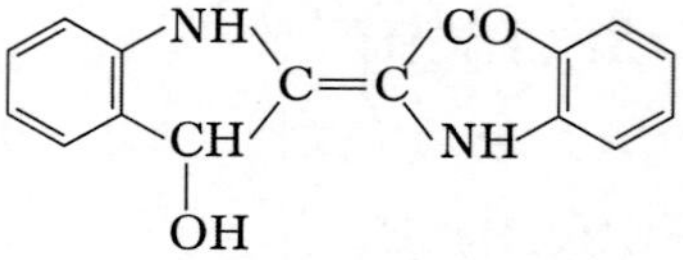

(d) 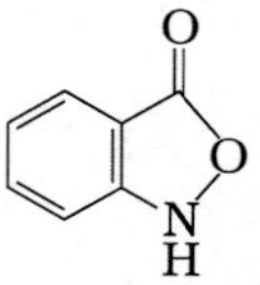

33. Select the correct reaction from the following.

(a) 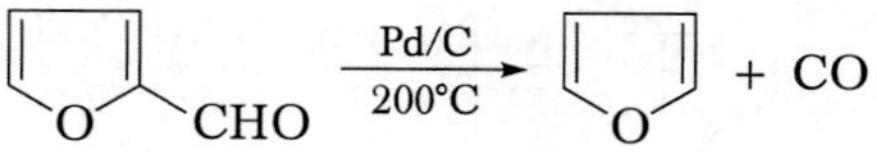

(b) 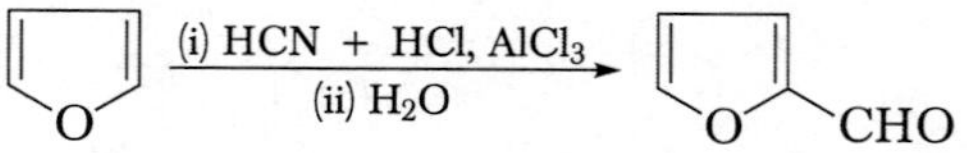

(c) 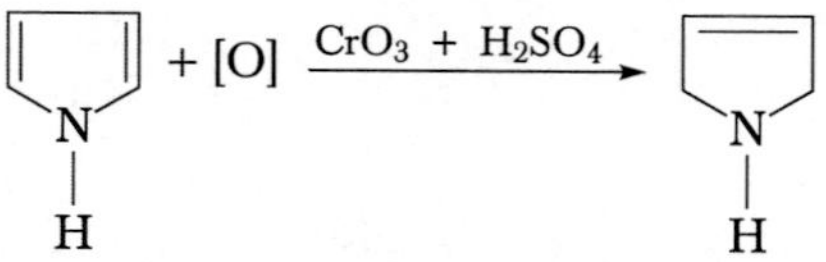

(d) 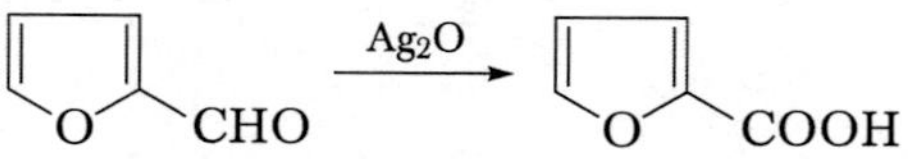

34. Which of the following compounds are aromatic heterocyclic compound?
(a) Aniline (b) Pyridine
(c) Piperidine (d) Pyrrole

Directions (Q. Nos. 35 to 37)

Following reaction sequence is used to prepare compound 'C'. Compound 'C' is also be prepared by the catalytic decomposition of 'A'. On oxidation with silver oxide compound 'A' give furoic acid.

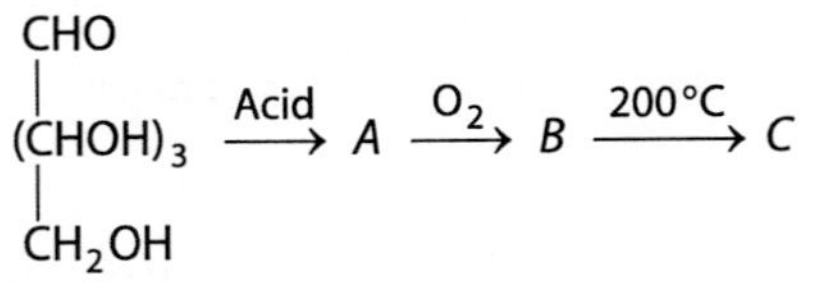

35. The structure of the compound C is

(a) 

(b) 

(c) 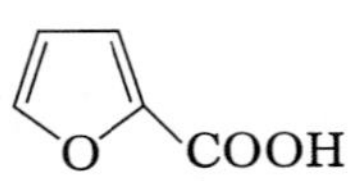

(d) 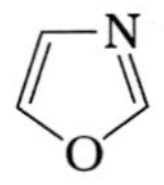

36. Compound A is

(a) 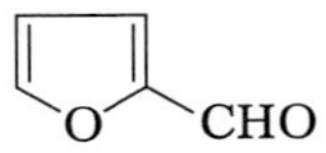

(b) 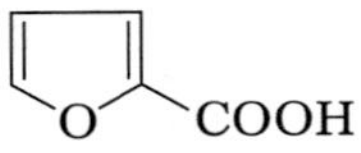

(c) 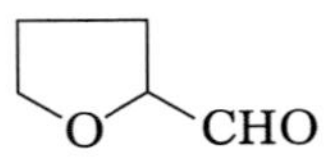

(d) 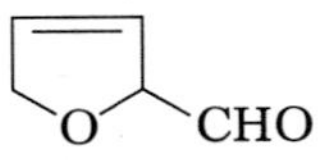

37. Compound A and C respectively are called

(a) furan, furfural (b) pyrrole, furan
(c) furfural, furan (d) furfural, oxazole

Directions (Q. Nos. 38 to 40)

Furfural is formed by the action of dilute mineral acids on pentoses. It closely resemblance with benzaldehyde in its reaction. It gives Cannizzaro reaction, benzoin condensation, Perkin reaction etc. In the electrophilic substitution reaction electrophile attacks at the 4-position.

38. 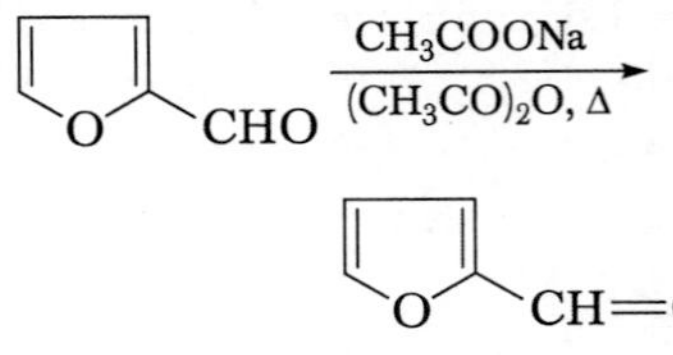

The above reaction is called

(a) Cannizzaro reaction (b) Perkin reaction
(c) Benzoin reaction (d) Chichibabin reaction

39. 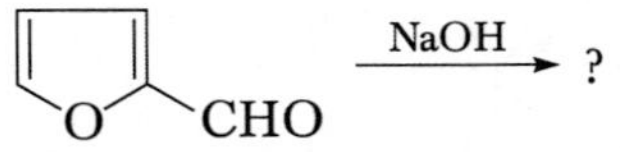

The product of the above reaction is/are

(a) 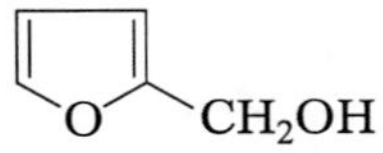

(b) 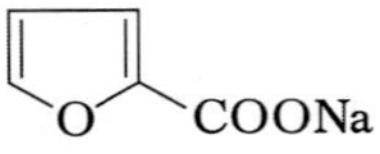

(c) Both (a) and (b) (d) None of these

40. On reaction with base *via* benzylic acid rearrangement, furfural gives

(a) Furoic acid (b) Furylacrylic acid
(c) Furoin (d) Furilic acid

Answers

Exercise 1

1. (c)	2. (d)	3. (a)	4. (b)	5. (b)	6. (b)	7. (a)	8. (a)	9. (b)	10. (c)
11. (d)	12. (b)	13. (d)	14. (a)	15. (c)	16. (d)	17. (b)	18. (c)	19. (c)	20. (a)
21. (d)	22. (c)	23. (c)	24. (b)	25. (a)	26. (b)	27. (c)	28. (b)	29. (a)	30. (d)
31. (b)	32. (a)	33. (d)	34. (a)	35. (b)	36. (c)	37. (b)	38. (b)	39. (a)	40. (d)
41. (b)	42. (a)	43. (c)	44. (a)	45. (c)	46. (b)	47. (d)	48. (c)	49. (a)	50. (c)
51. (a)	52. (c)								

Exercise 2

1. (b)	2. (a,b)	3. (c)	4. (d)	5. (a)	6. (b)	7. (a,b,c)	8. (c)	9. (a)	10. (b)
11. (c)	12. (a)	13. (d)	14. (a)	15. (d)	16. (b)	17. (b)	18. (a)	19. (c)	20. (b)
21. (a)	22. (b)	23. (a)	24. (c)	25. (c)	26. (c)	27. (a)	28. (a)	29. (a)	30. (b)
31. (c)	32. (a)	33. (a,b,d)	34. (b,d)	35. (a)	36. (a)	37. (c)	38. (b)	39. (c)	40. (d)

Hints & Solutions

Exercise 1

3. In pyridine the N-atom, like each of the carbon atoms is bonded to other members of the ring by the use of sp^2 orbitals.

7. 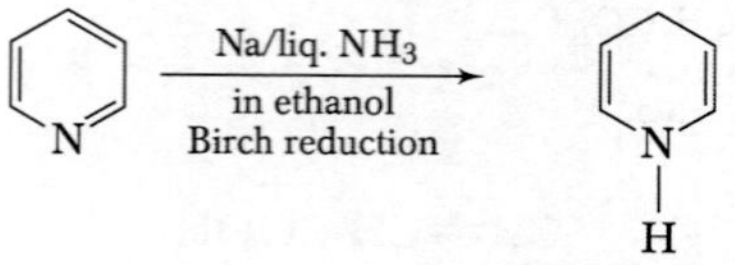

1, 4-dihydropyridine

8. Pyrrole is an extremely weak base because the lone pair of electrons on N-atom involved in the π-cloud and is not available for sharing with acids.

12. 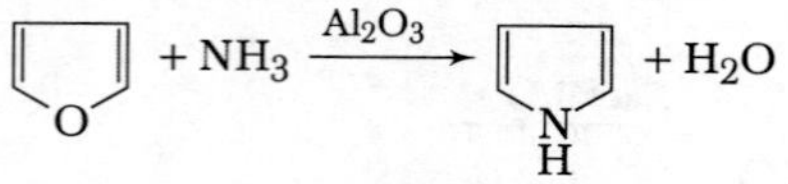

14. The lone pair of electrons that gives pyridine its basicity occupies an sp^2 orbital. It is held more tightly and is less available for sharing with acids than the pair of electrons of an aliphatic amine which occupies an sp^3-orbital.

27. 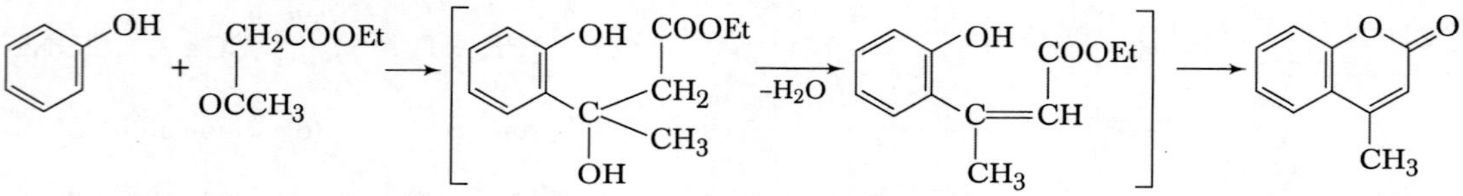

28. 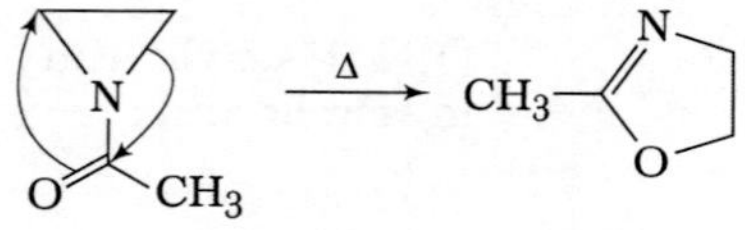

31. 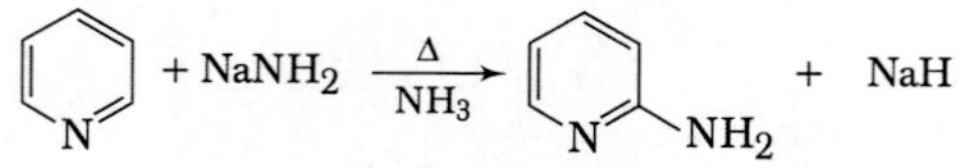

2-aminopyridine

If sodamide is in excess 2,6-diaminopyridine is obtained.

35. 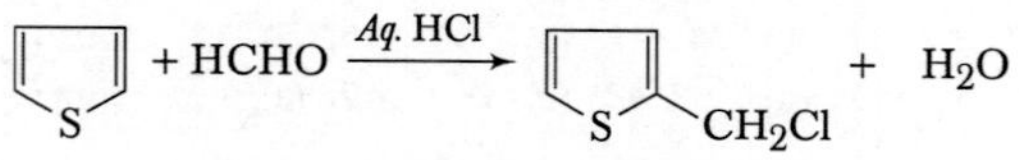

38. 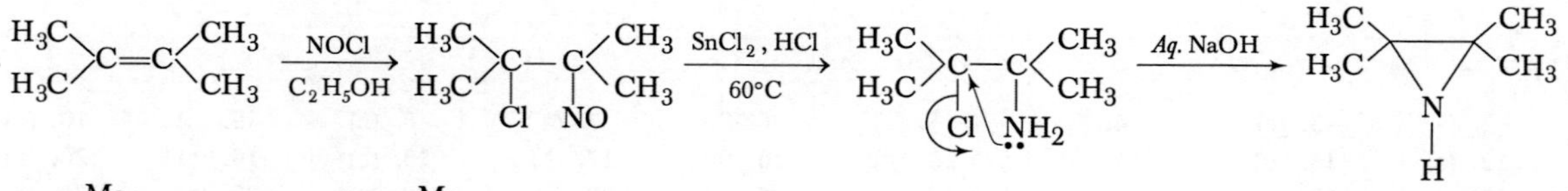

40. 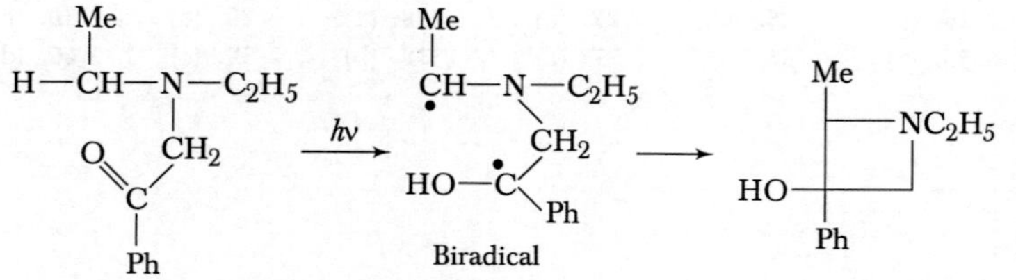

43. The reduction of 2-nitrobenzofuran with Sn/HCl gives benzofuranone and not the expected 2-amino benzofuran.

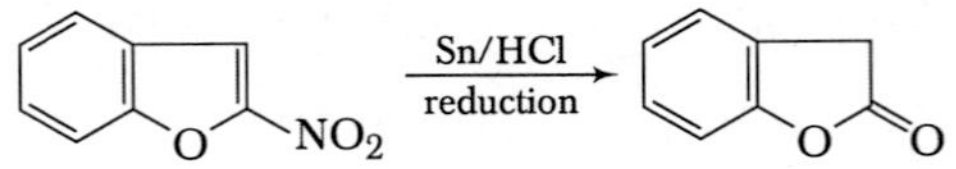

46. 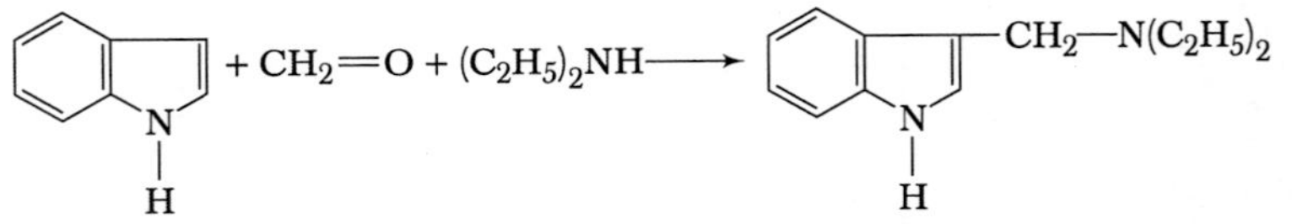

3-N, N-diethylaminomethyl indole
(Mannich reaction)

47. 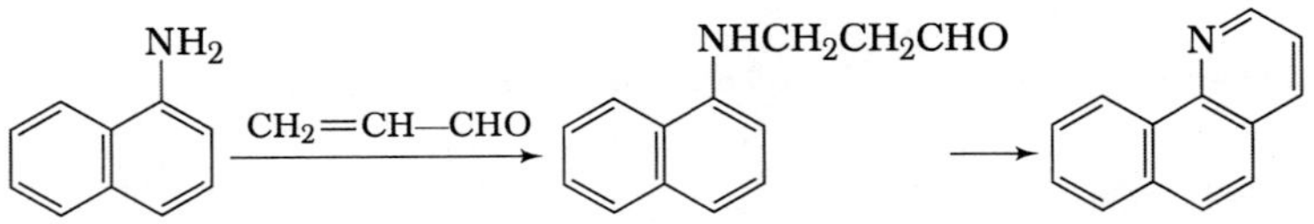

49. 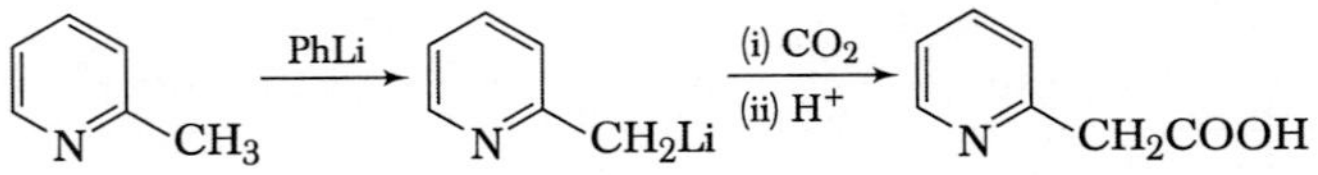

Exercise 2

1. 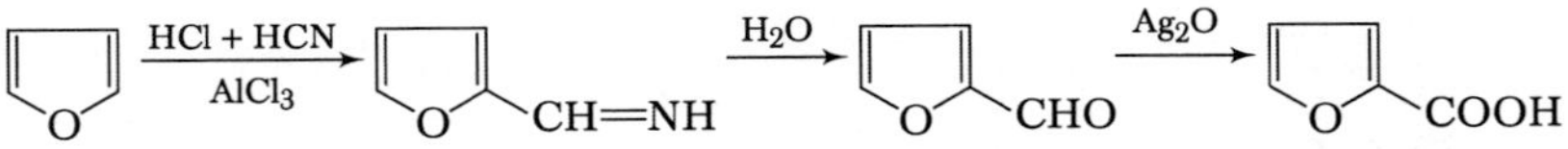

Furoic acid

6. 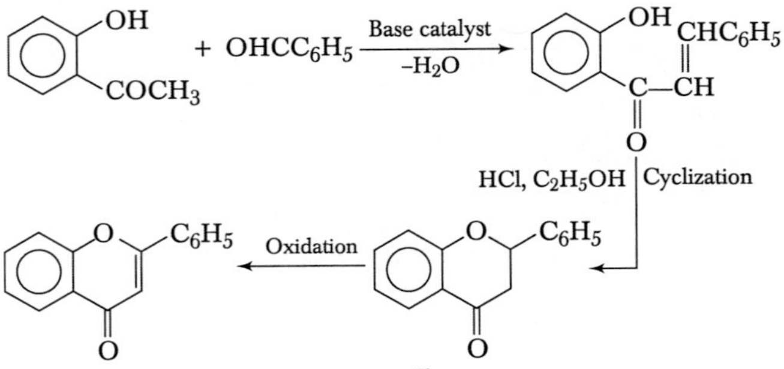

Flavone　　Flavanone

10. 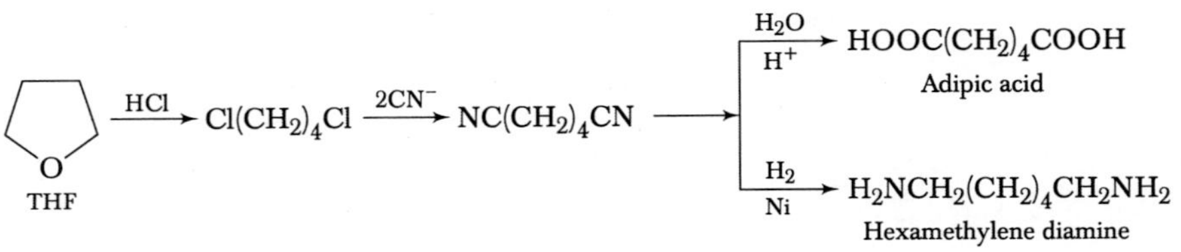

16. 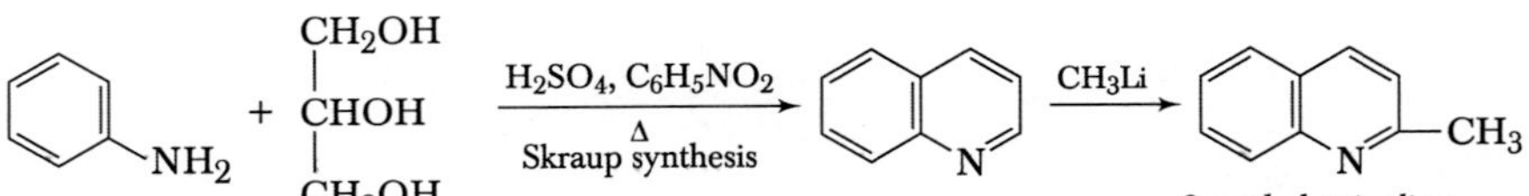

2-methyl quinoline

17.

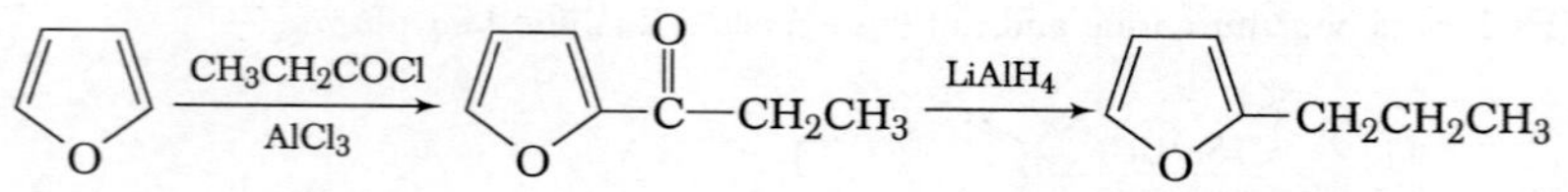

2-propylfuran

23.

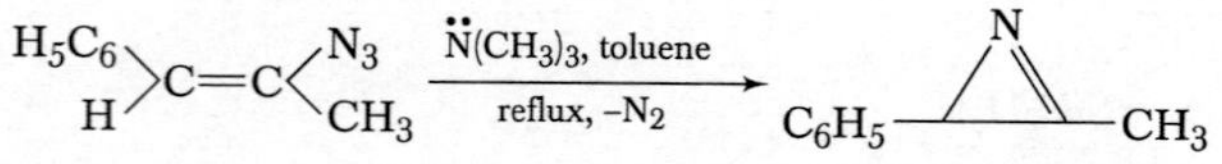

2-methyl-3 phenyl
1-azirine

24. Bromination of acridine gives 2 and 2,7-dibromoproducts.

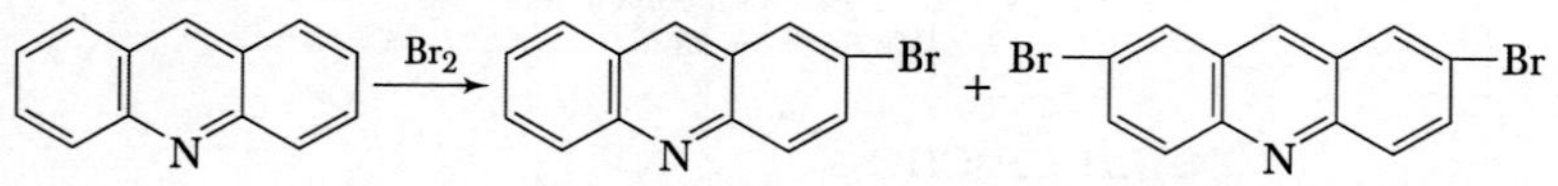

2-bromoacridine

2, 7-dibromoacridine

30.

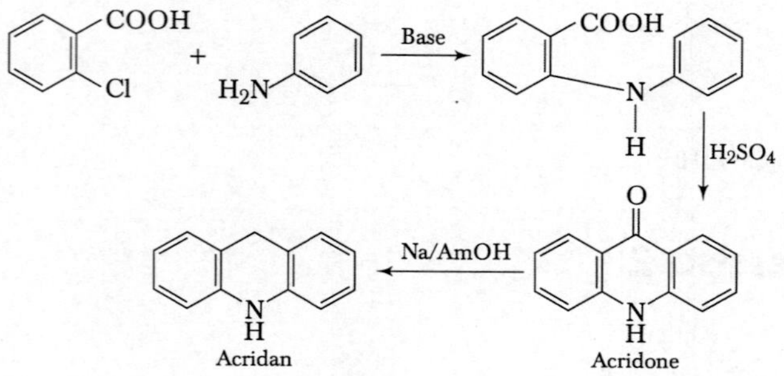

32.

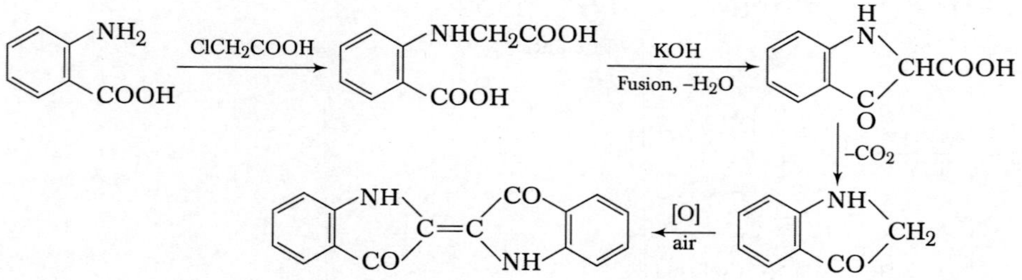

38

Chemistry of Natural Products

Syllabus

- Chemistry of Natural Products
- Carbohydrates, Proteins and Peptides
- Fatty Acids, Nucleic Acids, Terpenes
- Steroids and Alkaloids
- Bigenesis of Terpenoids and Alkaloids

Carbohydrates

Carbohydrates (saccharides) occur naturally in the animal and vegetable kingdom. Sugars, starch and cellulose are the best known members of this class. Chemical analysis of sugar and other carbohydrates show that they are composed of only the carbon, hydrogen and oxygen and they appear to be the **hydrates of carbon.**

Glucose $(C_6H_{12}O_6) : C_6{\cdot}6H_2O$

Sucrose $(C_{12}H_{22}O_{11}) : C_{12}{\cdot}11H_2O$

Carbohydrates usually contain carbonyl, hydroxyl and ether groups. Hence, carbohydrates are polyhydroxy aldehydes or ketones or substances which yield such products on hydrolysis. The names of the individual sugars are characterised by the ending-*ose*. Carbohydrates are stored as glycogen in the body.

Classification

Carbohydrates are classified as

Monosaccharides

These are the simplest carbohydrates and also called **simple sugars.** They cannot be hydrolysed further to simpler sugars.

(a) Aldose is polyhydroxy aldehyde (glucose, galactose)

(b) Ketose is polyhydroxy ketone (fructose).

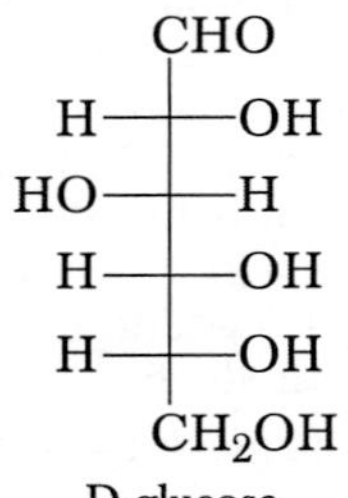

D-glucose
(aldohexose)

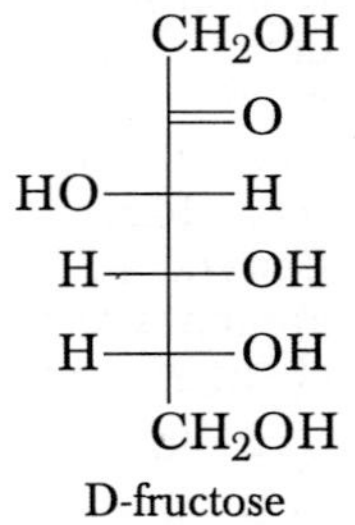

D-fructose
(ketohexose)

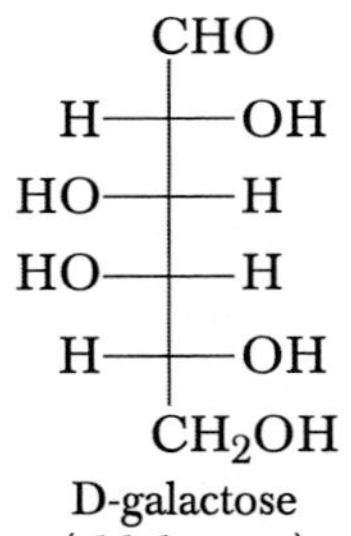

D-galactose
(aldohexose)

Glucose is also called grape sugar or blood sugar; fructose is also called fruit sugar.

Oligosaccharides

The oligosaccharides are the carbohydrates which yield a definite number (2-9) of monosaccharides on hydrolysis (by cleavage of ether linkage which links two or more monosaccharides).

(a) **Disaccharides** yield two monosaccharide molecules on hydrolysis *e.g.,* sucrose and maltose.

(b) **Trisaccharides** yield three monosaccharide molecules on hydrolysis. *e.g.,* raffinose.

(c) **Tetrasaccharides** yield four monosaccharide on hydrolysis.

Polysaccharides

These are the carbohydrates of high molecular weight which yield many (> 10) monosaccharide molecules on hydrolysis, *e.g.,* starch and cellulose.

Note The carbohydrates are also classified as either **reducing sugar** or **non-reducing sugars**. Carbohydrates which can reduce Fehling's solution and Tollen's reagent are called **reducing sugars** while others are non-reducing sugars. All the monosaccharides are reducing sugars. The disaccharides may be reducing or non-reducing depending upon the position of linkages between the two monosaccharides units. If the glycosidic linkage involves the carbonyl functions of both the monosaccharides units, the resulting disaccharide would be non-reducing (as in sucrose). If one of the carbonyl functions in anyone of the monosaccharide unit is free, the resulting disaccharide would be a reducing sugar (as in maltose and lactose). All polysaccharides like starch, cellulose are non-reducing carbohydrates.

Monosaccharides

Monosaccharides are straight chain aldehydes or ketones with hydroxyl groups on all or nearly all the other carbons. The common monosaccharides are glucose, an aldohexose (dextrose), fructose, a ketohexose (levulose) and ribose an aldopentose.

Glucose : An aldohexose (Dextrose, grape sugar)

It has the molecular formula $C_6H_{12}O_6$ and many of its chemical reactions indicate that glucose is a six carbon straight chain pentahydroxy aldehyde *i.e.,* an aldohexose.

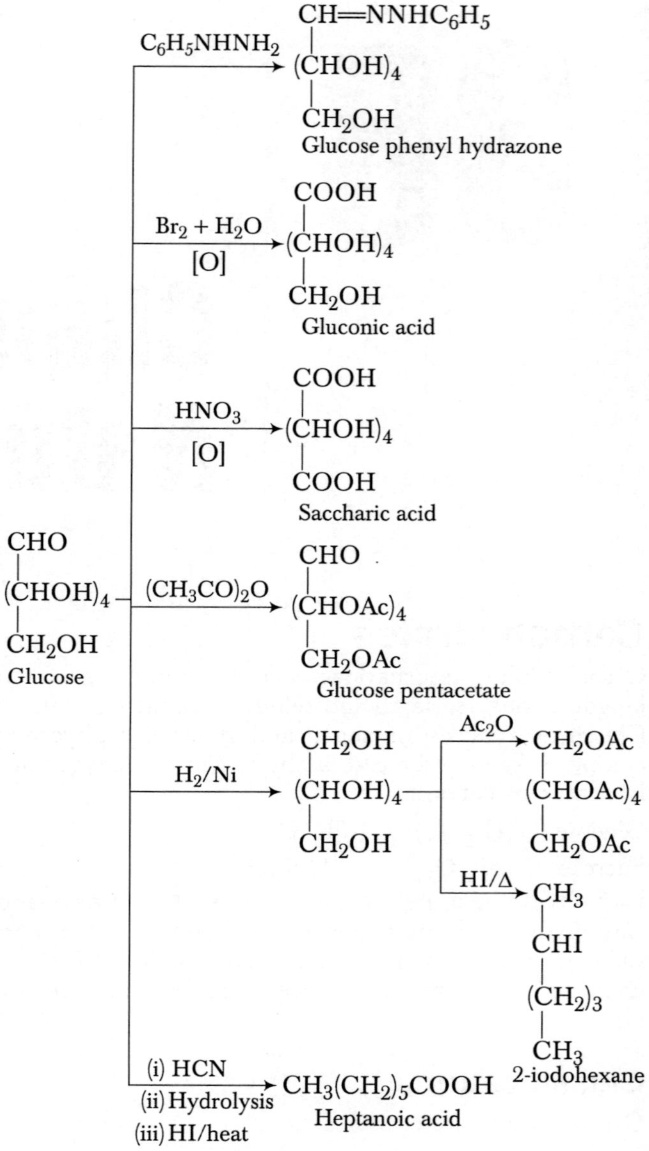

Note
- Glucose and fructose both reduce Tollen's reagent and Fehling's solution (a test of reducing sugars).
- On heating with concentrated solution of sodium hydroxide, glucose first turns yellow, then brown and finally resinifies. However, with dilute sodium hydroxide glucose undergoes a reversible isomerization and is converted into a mixture of D-glucose, D-mannose and D-fructose. This reaction is known as **Lobry de Bruyn-van Ekenstein** rearrangement. Mannose or fructose also undergoes this type of change on reaction with alkali.

$$\text{D-glucose} \rightleftharpoons \text{D-mannose} \rightleftharpoons \text{D-fructose}$$

- It is due to the fact (isomerization) that fructose also reduces Tollen's reagent and Fehling's solution in alkaline medium although it does not contain a —CHO group.

Configuration of monosaccharides

(a) **Open chain** (Fischer projections)

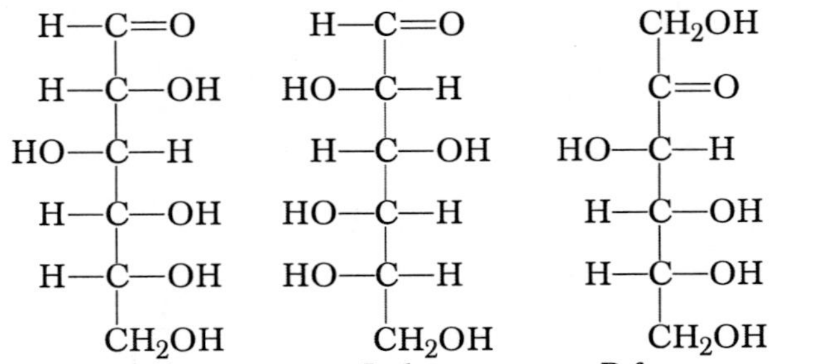

D-glucose (specific rotation = 53°) L-glucose D-fructose (specific rotation = –92°)

The aldohexoses have four asymmetric carbons and therefore exists as 2^4 (=16) possible stereoisomers. These can be divided into two enantiomeric sets of eight diastereomers.

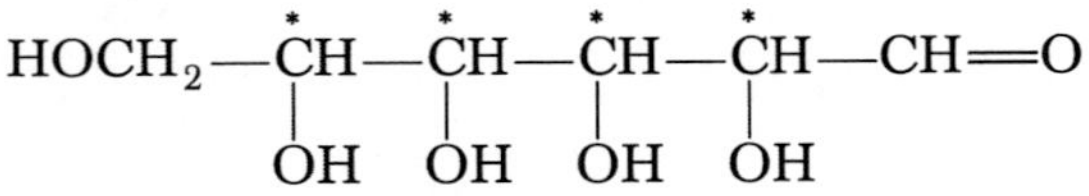

Aldohexoses
four asymmetric carbons (*)
2^4 = 16 stereoisomers

The configuration of a carbohydrate is specified by applying in the following conventions :

I. The naturally occurring stereoisomers of the aldotriose glyceraldehyde (the *R*-enantiomer) is arbitrarily said to have the D-configuration, its enantiomer is then said to have the L-configuration.

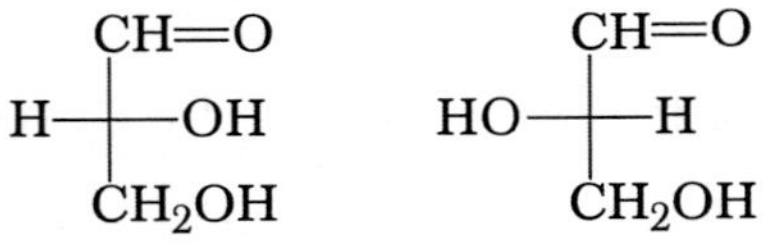

D-glyceraldehyde L-glyceraldehyde

II. The other aldoses or ketoses are written in a Fischer projection with their carbon atoms in a straight vertical line and carbons are numbered in such a way that the carbonyl carbon receives the lower possible number.

III. The aymmetric carbon of highest number is designated as a reference carbon. If this carbon has the H, OH and CH_2OH groups in the same relative configuration as the same groups of D-glyceraldehyde, the carbohydrate is said to have the D-configuration. If this is identical to L-glyceraldehyde then it is also called L-configuration.

- Open structure of glucose, fructose, etc., was proposed by **Baeyer**. Although, it explained most of the properties but could not explain the following properties of the aldehydic group of glucose.
  I. It does not form addition compounds with $NaHSO_3$, NH_3 and Grignard's reagent.
  II. It does not give Schiff's test.
  III. Glucose pentaacetate does not react with hydroxyl amine.
  IV. It shows mutarotation.
  V. Two isomeric monomethyl derivatives known as α-D-glucoside and β-D-glucoside are formed, on reaction of glucose with methanol in presence of dry HCl gas.

The above facts discard open structure of glucose and thus ring (cyclic) structure was proposed.

(b) **Cyclic hemiacetal forms of glucose**

When two cyclic forms of a carbohydrate differ in configuration only at hemiacetal carbons, they are said to be **anomers**. Thus, anomers are cyclic forms of carbohydrates that are epimeric at hemiacetal carbon and hemiacetal carbon (carbon-1 of aldose) is called **anomeric carbon.**

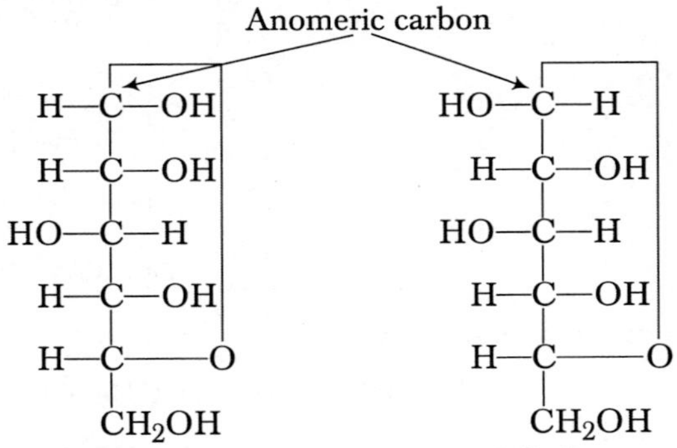

α-D-glucose (specific rotation = 113°) β-D-glucose (specific rotation = 19°)

(c) **Cyclic hemiketal forms of fructose**

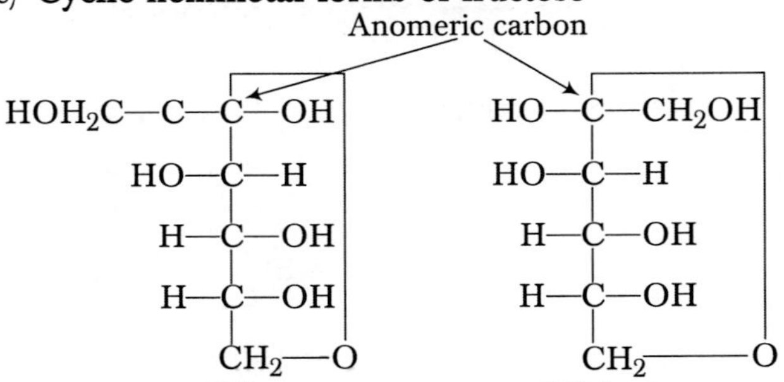

α-D-fructose (not isolated) β-D-fructose (specific rotation = –113°)

- A spontaneous change in the specific rotation of a solution of an optically active compound is called **mutarotation**. The hemiacetal forms of α-D-glucose and hemiketal forms of D-fructose are stable in solid state but in aqueous solution, there is opening of the cyclic structure which gives solution of constant specific rotation.

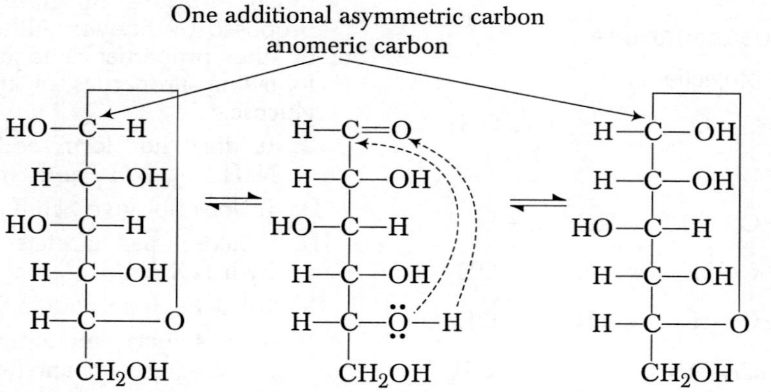

β-D
[α] = +18.7°
m.p. = 423 K

D-glucose
[α] = + 152.6°

α-D
[α] = +112.2°
m.p. = 419 K

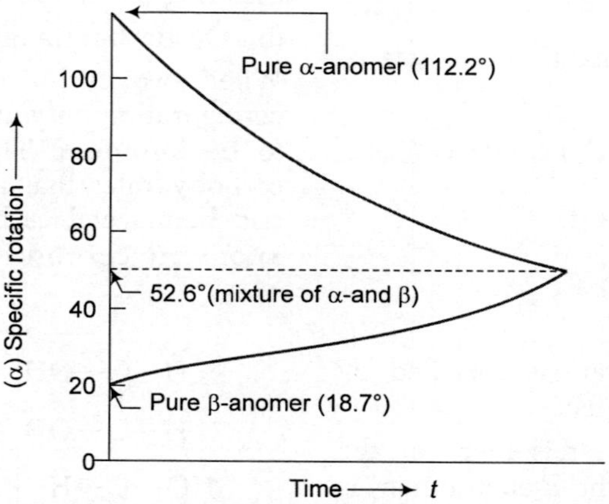

Fig. 38.1 Mutarotation of D-glucose.

(d) **Haworth projections**

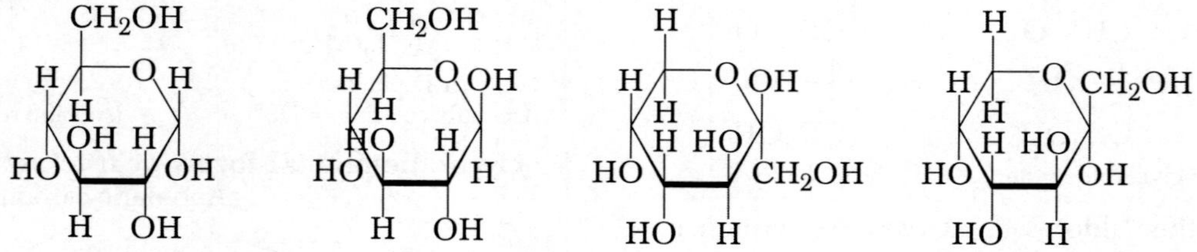

α-D-glucopyranose β-D-glucopyranose β-D-fructopyranose α-D-fructopyranose

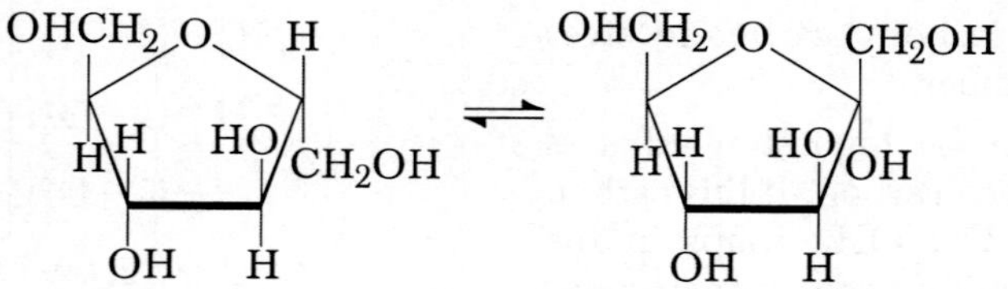

β-fructofuranose α-D-fructofuranose

Disaccharides

Disaccharides are carbohydrates that are made up of two monosaccharide units. On hydrolysis a molecule of disaccharide gives two molecules of monosaccharide. *e.g.,* maltose (malt sugar), cellobiose, lactose (milk sugar) and sucrose (cane or beet sugar).

Maltose ($C_{12}H_{22}O_{11}$)

It is found mainly in malt liquors. On hydrolysis one mole of maltose gives two moles of D-glucose units. It is a reducing sugar and composed to two α-D-glucose units which are condensed together through C_1 of one unit and C_4 of the other unit. The following structure for maltose is proposed.

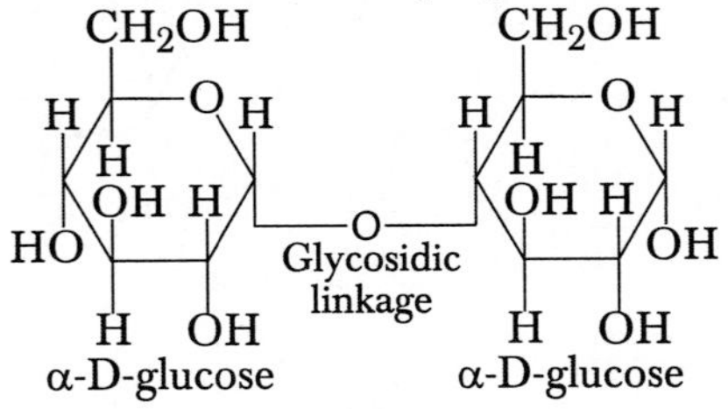

Maltose

Sucrose ($C_{12}H_{22}O_{11}$)

It is obtained from sugarcane and sugar beets. It does not reduce Tollen's reagent or Fehling's solution hence, it is a non-reducing sugar.

$$\underset{\substack{\text{Sucrose}\\ [\alpha]_D = +66.5^\circ}}{C_{12}H_{22}O_{11}} + H_2O \xrightarrow{HCl} \underset{\substack{\text{D-glucose}\\ [\alpha]_D = +52.5^\circ}}{C_6H_{12}O_6} + \underset{\substack{\text{D-fructose}\\ [\alpha]_D = -92.4^\circ}}{C_6H_{12}O_6}$$

Sucrose is dextrorotatory but after hydrolysis give dextrorotatory glucose and laevorotatory fructose. D(–) fructose has greater specific rotation than D(+) glucose. Hence, the resultant solution upon hydrolysis is laevorotatory in nature. The reaction is called inversion reaction and the mixture (glucose + fructose) is called invert sugar.

Sucrose is composed of α-D-glucose and β-D-fructose which are held together by α, β-glycosidic linkage between C_1 of glucose unit and C_2 of the fructose unit. The following structure for sucrose was proposed by Haworth.

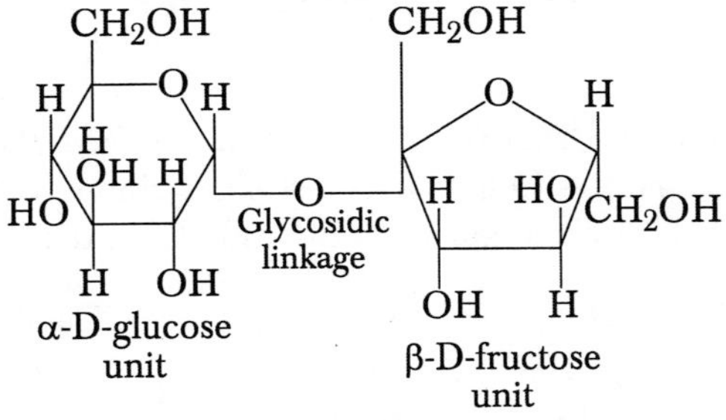

Sucrose

Polysaccharides

These are neutral polymeric compounds in which hundreds or even thousands of monosaccharide units are joined by glycosidic linkages. They are colourless, tasteless and are insoluble in water.

Starch ($C_6H_{10}O_5$)$_n$

It is the main storage polysaccharide of plants. It is a white powder and insoluble in cold water. Starch does not reduce Fehling's solution or Tollen's reagent. It also does not form an osazone indicating that all hemiacetal hydroxyl groups of glucose units (C_1) are not free but are linked with glycosidic linkages. Starch is a polymer of D-glucose and consists of two components, 10-20% amylose and 80-90% amylopectin.

Amylose is water soluble fraction and is a linear polymer of α-D-glucose. The glucose units are linked to one another through α-linkage involving C_1 of one glucose and C_4 of other glucose.

Amylopectin is water insoluble fraction. It consists branched chains of α-D-glucose. The main chain involves α-linkages between C_1 of one α-D-glucose unit and C_4 of the other. The C_1 of terminal glucose in each chain is further linked to C_6 of other glucose unit in the next chain through C_1–C_6 α-linkage.

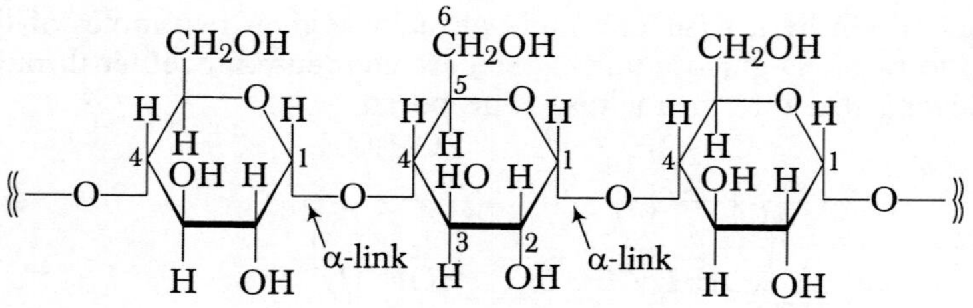

Amylose

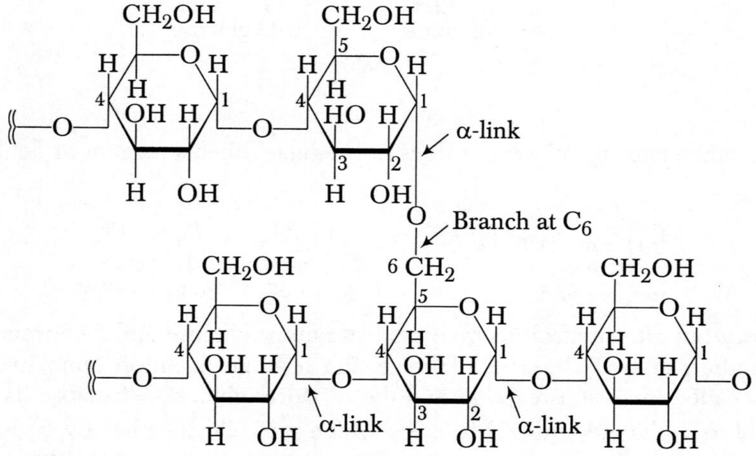

Amylopectin

Cellulose $(C_6H_{10}O_5)_n$

It is the major structural polysaccharide in higher plants. It constitutes the bulk of cell wall. It is probably the most abundant organic compound found in nature. Cellulose is a straight chain polysaccharide, composed of D-glucose units by β-glycosidic linkages between C_1 of one glucose unit and C_4 of the other glucose unit.

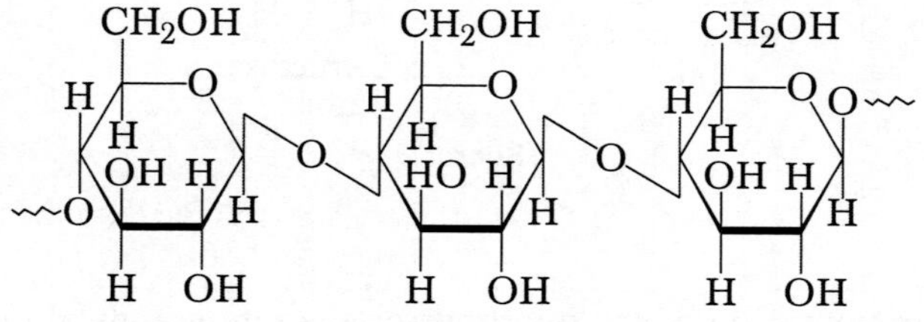

Cellulose

Glycogen

Glycogen is a polysaccharide that is structurally similar to starch. It is the form in which animals store glucose for further use. It is found in most tissues, but the best source is liver or muscle. Glycogen has a structure similar to that of amylopectin but is more highly branched.

Proteins

Proteins are long-chain polyamides formed from α-amino acids, alkanoic acids carrying an amine group on the carbon alpha to the carboxyl carbon. The amide bond of a protein is formed when the amine group of one α-amino acid connects to the carboxyl group of another α-amino acid. The amide bond between two α-amino acids is called a peptide bond. Thus, the amino acids are the hydrolysis products of proteins by the cleavage of peptide bond.

Classification

Proteins are large biomolecules that occur in every living organism. They are of many different types and have several biological functions. The keratin of skin and fingernails, the fibroin of silk and spider web, and DNA polymerase that catalyses the synthesis of DNA in cells are proteins. Regardless of their appearance or function, all proteins are made up of many **amino acid units** linked together into a long chain, through the peptide bonds.

Proteins have an amazing range of structural and catalytic properties as a result of their varying amino acid composition. Some of the functions of the major classes of proteins are given in Table 38.1.

Table 38.1 **Examples of Protein Functions**

S.No.	Classification of proteins	Example	Function of example
1.	Structural proteins	Collagen, keratin	Tendons, skin, hair, nails
2.	Enzymes	DNA polymerase	Replicate and repair DNA
3.	Transport proteins	Haemoglobin	Transport O_2 to the cells
4.	Contractile proteins	Actin, myosin	Cause contraction of muscles
5.	Protective proteins	Antibodies	Complex with foreign proteins
6.	Hormones	Insulin	Regulate glucose metabolism
7.	Toxins	Snake venoms	Incapacitate prey.

Amino Acids

Amino acids are organic acids having an acidic carboxyl group (—COOH) and a basic amino group ($—NH_2$).

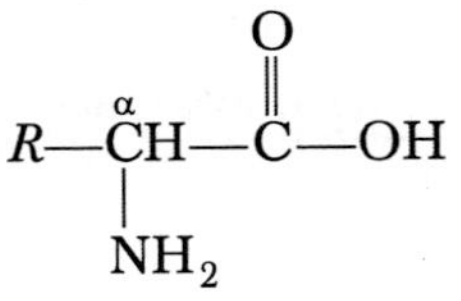

Classification of amino acids

Amino acids are classified as neutral, acidic, or basic according to the relative number of amino and carboxyl groups in the molecule. Neutral amino acids contain one amino group and one carboxyl group. Acidic amino acids contain one amino group and two carboxyl groups. Basic amino acids contain two amino groups and one carboxyl group.

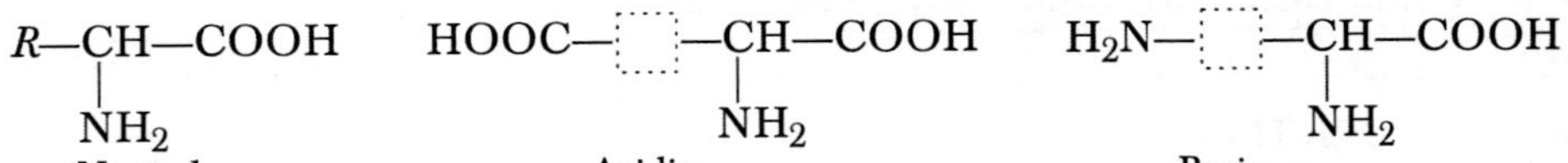

Neutral amino acids   Acidic amino acids   Basic amino acids

There are about 20 amino acids commonly found in proteins.(Table -38.2)

Table 38.2 **Name, Structures, Abbreviations and Properties of Amino Acids**

General structure $H_3\overset{+}{N}-\underset{R}{\underset{|}{CH}}-\overset{O}{\overset{\|}{C}}-O^-$

Name and abbreviations	R	Optical rotation of *L* enantiomer in H_2O sign of $[\alpha]_D$	pK_{a_1}	pK_{a_2}	pK_{a_3}	Isoelectric point PI	Water solubility % at 25°C
Amino acids with simple aliphatic side chains							
Glycine, Gly (G)	—H		2.34	9.60	–	5.97	20
Aanine, Ala (A)	$-CH_3$	(+)	2.35	9.69	–	6.02	14
Valine, Val (V)	$-CH(CH_3)_2$	(+)	2.32	9.62	–	5.97	6.5
Leucine, Leu (L)	$-CH_2CH(CH_3)_2$	(–)	2.36	9.60	–	5.98	2.2
Isoleucine, Ile (I)	$-\underset{CH_3}{\underset{|}{CH}}-C_2H_5$ [*S*-configuration]	(+)	2.36	9.68	–	6.02	3.9
Amino acids with aromatic side chains							
Phenylalanine, Phe (F)	$-CH_2Ph$	(–)	1.83	9.13	–	5.48	2.9
Tryptophan, Trp (W)	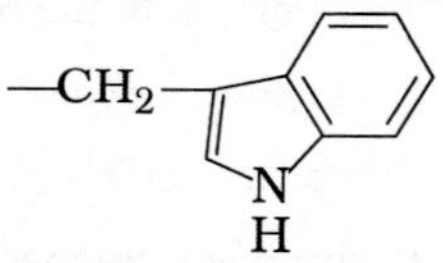	(–)	2.38	9.39	–	5.88	1.1
Tyrosine, Tyr (Y)	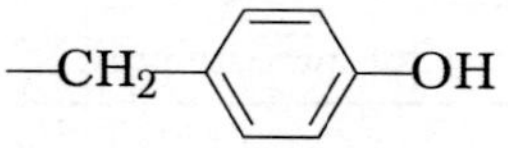	(–)	2.20	9.11	10.07	5.65	0.05
Histidine, His (H)	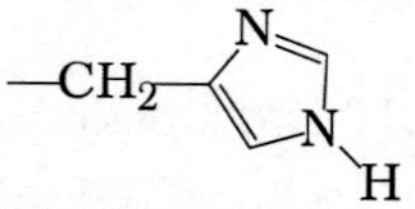	(–)	1.82	6.00	9.17	7.58	7.1
Amino acids with aliphatic side chains containing —OH, —SH and —SCH_3 groups							
Serine, Ser (S)	$-CH_2-OH$	(–)	2.21	9.15	–	5.68	4.8
Threonine, Thr (T)	$-\underset{CH_3}{\underset{|}{CH}}-OH$ (*R* configuration)	(–)	2.71	9.62	–	5.16	17
Methionine, Met (M)	$-CH_2CH_2-SCH_3$	(–)	2.28	9.21	–	5.75	3.4
Cystenine, Cys (C)	$-CH_2-SH$	(–)	1.71	8.18	10.28	5.02	very sol.
Amino acids with side chains containing carboxylic acid or amide groups							
Aspartic acid, Asp (D)	$-CH_2-CO_2H$	(+)	1.88	3.65	9.60	2.76	0.50
Glutamic acid, Glue (E)	$-CH_2CH_2CO_2H$	(+)	2.16	4.32	9.67	3.24	0.84
Asparagine, Asn (N)	$-CH_2-CO-NH_2$	(–)	2.02	8.80	–	5.41	3.0
Glutamine, Gln (Q)	$-CH_2CH_2-CO-NH_2$	(+)	2.17	9.13	–	5.65	3.5

Amino acids with side chains containing strongly basic groups							
Lysine, Lys (K)	$—(CH_2)_4—NH_2$	(+)	2.18	9.12	10.53	9.82	very sol.
Arginine, Arg (R)	$—(CH_2)_3NH—C(=NH)NH_2$	(+)	2.17	9.04	12.48	10.76	13
Cyclic (secondary) amino acid							
Proline, Pro (P)	–	(-)	1.99	10.60	–	6.30	63

Note

- Most of amino acids have primary amino group $—NH_2$. However, proline is a secondary amine. The structure of proline is as

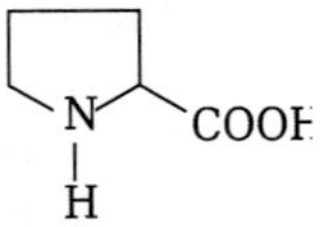

- Human beings can synthesised about half of the amino acids needed to make protein. These are called non-essential amino acids. Other amino acids, called the essential amino acids, must be provided in the diet.

Amino acids as dipolar ions

Amino acids have both basic $—NH_2$ group and acidic $—COOH$ group hence they are amphoteric. In dry solid state, they exist as dipolar ions, when COO^- and $\overset{+}{N}H_3$ groups are present in a molecule.

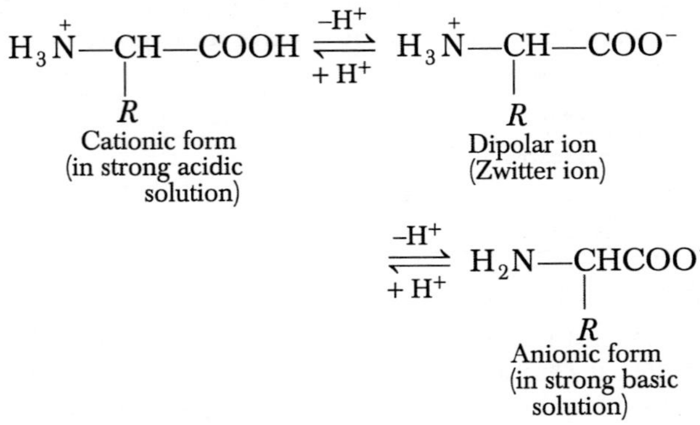

The isoelectric point (PI) of the amino acids is the pH at which it has no net charge. It is the pH at which the amount of negative charge on an amino acid exactly balances the amount of the positive charge.

PI (isoelectric point) = pH at which there is no net charge.

Peptides

Peptides are amino acids polymers in which the individual amino acid units, called residues, are linked together by amide bonds. An amino group from one residue forms an amide bond with the carboxyl of a second residue; the amino group of the second forms an amide bond with the carboxyl of a third, and so on. For example, alanylserine is the **dipeptide** that results when an amide bond is formed between the alanine carboxyl and the serine amino group :

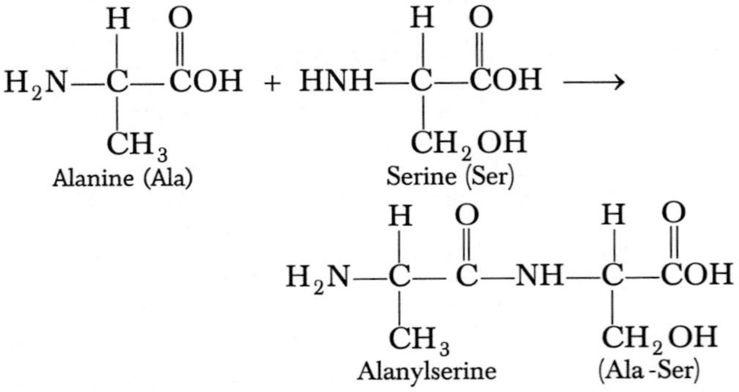

If the alanine amino group reacts with the serine carboxyl, serylalanine results.

Each amino acid unit in a peptide is called a **residue.** The term **oligopeptide** is generally used for the peptides containing about four to ten amino acid residues.

By convention, peptides are always written with the **N-terminal amino acid** (with free $—NH_2$ group) on the left and the **C-terminal amino acid** (with free $—COOH$ group) on the right. The name of the peptide is usually indicated by using three-letter names for each amino acid.

Thus, alanylserine is abbreviated **Ala-Ser** and serylalanine is abbreviated as **Ser-Ala.**

A peptide bond has about 40% double-bond character because of resonance. Steric hindrance causes the *trans* configuration to be more stable than the *cis* configuration, so the α-carbons of adjacent amino acids are *trans* to each other.

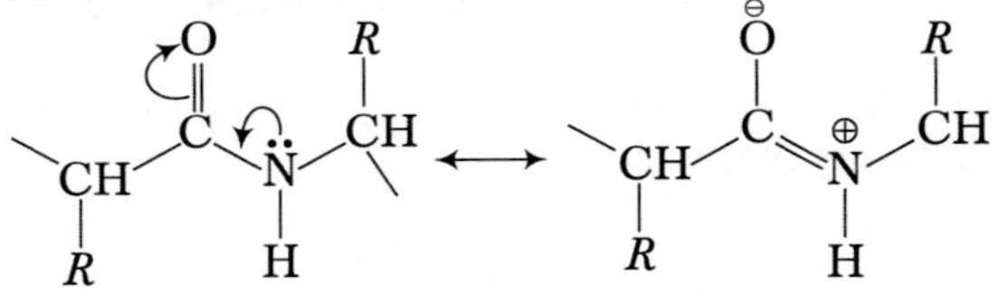

As a consequence of the partial double-bond character of the peptide bond, free rotation is not possible about this bond.

Note
- Sanger reagent (2,4-dinitrofluorobenzene) is used to identify N-terminal amino acids.
- A newer and more efficient approach makes use of dansyl chloride, 5-N-dimethylaminonaphthalene-1-sulphonyl chloride, as the reagent.

Structure of Proteins

The structure of proteins is much more complex than that of any of the families of organic compounds studied. This structural complexity arises from the fact that the proteins are such large molecules, often referred to as **macromolecules**. A protein may consist of just a single strand, or it may include several strands. A protein may have just a few α-amino acids, or it may have thousands.

S.No.	Protein	Structure-type	Number of amino acids
1.	Oxytocin	Single-stranded protein	9α-amino acids
2.	Insulin	Two-chain protein	51α-amino acids
3.	Myoglobin	Single-chain protein	153 α-amino acids
4.	Gamma globulin	Four-chain protein	1320 α-amino acids.

There are four levels of protein structure that are important in understanding the proteins function. The simplest two-dimensional description of connectivity is called the **primary structure.** The three-dimensional gross structure-specifically, the secondary, tertiary and quaternary structure–describes how protein molecules are aggregated in order to carryout their specific functions.

Primary structure

The most basic aspect of protein structure is the primary structure–a specific sequence in which the α-amino acids are joined together by peptide bonds. The primary structure is represented using the three-letter abbreviations for the α-amino acids. For example, insulin has two chains of insulin held together by two **disulphide (–S–S–) linkages.**

Secondary structure

The arrangement or orientation of a protein chain in three-dimensional space is described by the secondary structure. Resonance delocalisation within the amide (peptide) group causes restricted rotation about the nitrogen-carbon bond because it acquires partial double bond character.

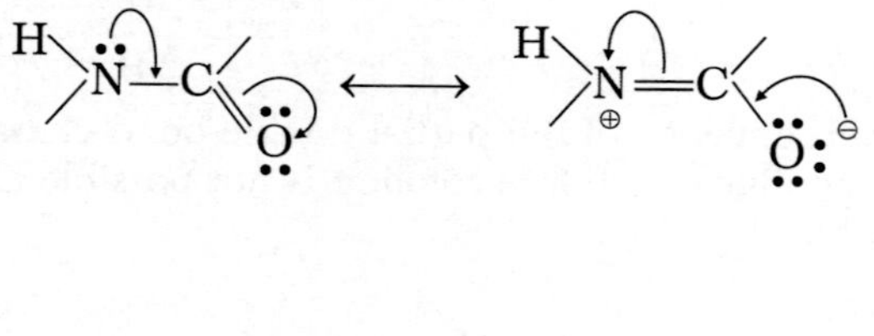

There is free rotation about the single bonds in a peptide. The secondary structure of a protein is generally held in place by H-bonding between the –NH group of one amide and the C=O group of another amide.

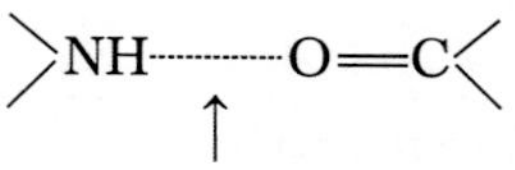

H-bonding

Because, a protein chain contains a large number of peptide bonds, there is extensive hydrogen bonding between the peptide linkages of two separate chains or between the peptide linkages within a single chain.

Secondary structure can be in the form of α-helix and pleated sheet In **α-helix,** a protein chain is coiled about a central axis. It is held by hydrogen bonding that occurs between the hydrogens of –NH groups and oxygens of C=O groups that are oriented toward each other on the inside of the helix. It takes 3.6 amino acids to complete one turn of the helix to enable such hydrogen bonding and a 13-member ring is formed by H-bonding. An α-helix is also known as 3.6_{13} helix.

In pleated sheet two protein chains are lined up parallel to each other but running in opposite directions–that is, the N-terminus of one chain is near the C-terminus of the other. This puts the —NH group of one chain opposite to the C=O group of the other chain, permitting hydrogen bonding that holds the sheet together. Examples of α-helix and pleated sheet are given below :

α-helix	Pleated sheet
α-keratin	Fibroin
Myosin	Protein of silk
Actin	Dragline of silk (spider wave)

Tertiary structure

The overall shape of a protein molecule is defined by the tertiary structure. For example, how the protein chains, whether pleated or helical are folded. The tertiary structure determines whether a protein is elongated (and thus, **fibrous**) or folded (thus, globular).

Type	Characteristic	Examples
Fibrous	Elongated, insoluble in water because of hydrophobic *R* group.	Keratin, collagen
Globular	Spherical, water soluble because of hydrophilic amino acids with polar *R* group.	Enzymes, antibodies myoglobin.

The tertiary structure of a protein brings into close proximity of α-amino acids that are very far apart in the primary structure, thereby creating chemical sites. The tertiary structure is held together through a number of chemical interactions such as :

- Hydrogen bonding, disulphide linkages (–S–S–), electrostatic attraction.

Quaternary structure

Certain proteins, usually globular proteins further organise into aggregate, or assemblies. The spatial orientation of these aggretages is described as the **quaternary structure** of the protein. Haemoglobin (the substance in red blood cells responsible for transporting oxygen from the lungs and carbon dioxide to the lungs) consists of four individual protein chains, two α-chains of 141 α-amino acids each, and two β-chains of 146 α-amino acids each. Each protein chain is bonded to haeme molecule containing an iron atom in the centre of a porphyrin ring structure. It is an iron atom that binds to the oxygen or carbon dioxide during transport in the blood stream. It is also the iron atom that will complex even more strongly and irreversibly with carbon monoxide or cyanide ion, making exposure to these substances so deadly.

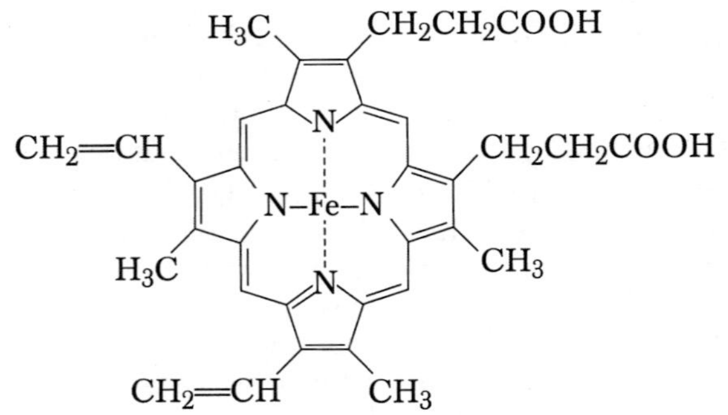

Heme molecule

Denaturation of Proteins

A protein must be in its proper shape (tertiary structure) to fulfill its designated biological function. When a protein is **denatured,** such as by the treatment with acid or alcohol or by heating, it unfolds and becomes biologically inactive– its tertiary structure has been destroyed. In most cases, protein denaturation is irreversible, as when an egg is cooked. However, with some proteins (such as some enzymes), **renaturation** may occur, with the protein folding itself back into its tertiary structure. **After refolding, a process that has recently been observed using high speed laser techniques, a protein's biological function is reactivated.**

Biological Functions of Proteins and Polypeptides

One important function of the proteins is structural. α-keratin is an important structural component of skin, hair, feathers and nails. Collagen is the material that forms the basis of the connective tissues - tendon, bone and cartilage. Fibroin is the silk of spider webs and of cocoons. The hard exoskeleton of insects are composed of sclerotin. Muscle tissue contains two important structural proteins-myosin is the stationary component and actin is the contractile component.

Regulatory proteins serve an immense variety of purposes. Certain enzymes like trypsin catalyse the hydrolysis of polypeptide chains. Haemoglobin and myoglobin are transport substances to carry oxygen, former in blood stream and latter in muscle tissue. Cytochrome and cytochrome P-450 carry electrons in phosphorylation cycle. Some proteins are used for storage. Ovalbumin is used by nature as a food reservoir in egg white. Casein plays a similar role in mammalian milk. The body manufactures antibodies as defensive substances-these materials form insoluble complexes with foreign substances that invade the blood stream. Finally, some polypeptides are hormones. Examples are insulin, which regulate the metabolism of glucose and β-endorphin, a polypeptide with morphine like activity that appears to be a pain reliever.

Lipids

Chemically, lipids are esters of long chain fatty acids and alcohols. They can be divided into three main classes.

Simple Lipids

They constitute long chain fatty acids and all their acid derivatives. Oils and fats are simple lipids. These are esters of glycerol and three fatty acids hence these are also called triglycerides. The fatty acids may be saturated or unsaturated. *e.g.,*

Saturated fatty acids

Lauric acid : $CH_3(CH_2)_{10}COOH$
Palmitic acid : $CH_3(CH_2)_{14}COOH$
Stearic acid : $CH_3(CH_2)_{16}COOH$

Unsaturated fatty acids

Oleic acids : $C_{17}H_{33}COOH$
Linoleic acid : $C_{17}H_{31}COOH$
Linolenic acid : $C_{17}H_{29}COOH$

Note
- The higher members of carboxylic acid are known as fatty acids.
- Fats contain large proportion of saturated acids while oils contain large proportion of unsaturated acids.
- Oil can be converted into fats by hydrogenation.
- Waxes are esters of fatty acids with long chain monohydroxy alcohols. They are simple lipids.

Compound Lipids

These give fatty acids, alcohols and other compounds on hydrolysis. These include phospholipids and glycolipids.

Phospholipids are mixed glycerides of higher fatty acids and phosphoric acid. *e.g.,* lecithins and cephalins.

Glycolipids are esters of fatty acids with carbohydrates and may contain nitrogen but no phosphorus.

Derived Lipids

These are the substances derived from simple and compound lipids. These include fatty acids, fatty alcohols, mono and diglycerides steroids, terpenes etc.

Fats and Oils

Fats and oils are triesters of glycerol and are called triglycerides. They undergo hydrolysis to give one molecule of glycerol and three molecules of fatty acids.

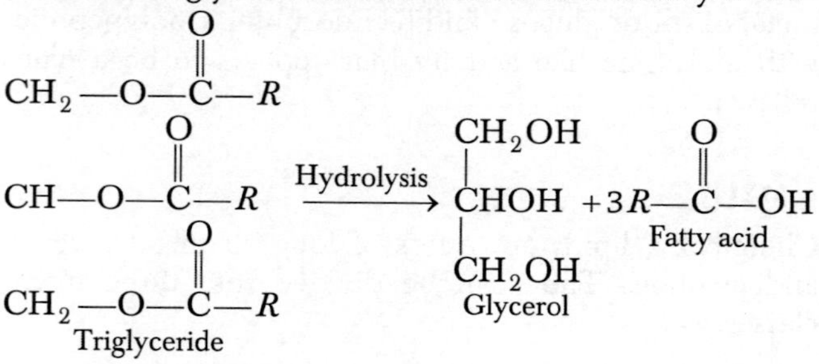

- The alkaline hydrolysis of fat or oil is known as saponification.

Acid value

It is the number of milligrams of potassium hydroxide required to neutralize the free carboxylic acids present in one gram of fat or oil. It gives an idea about the amount of free acids present in a particular oil or fat. A high acid value indicates a stale or rancid fat or oil stored under improper conditions.

Saponification value

The hydrolysis provides a method for the determination of a constant called saponification number or value, which is defined as the number of milligrams of potassium hydroxide required to saponify 1 g of the fat or oil, *i.e.,* to neutralize the fatty acids resulting from the complete hydrolysis of 1 g of the fat or oil.

The higher the molecular weight of the fat, the smaller is its saponification value.

Iodine value or number

The degree of absorption of halogen by a fat or oil is proportional to the number of double bonds present in carbon chain of fatty acid moieties. Thus, this addition reaction is used as an index of the degree of unsaturation in fat or oil. The index value is called iodine value/number and is defined as "the number of grams of iodine (or its equivalent like ICl) that will add to 100 g of fat or oil."

Greater the number of double bonds (unsaturation) in an oil or fat, the greater is its iodine value.

Mineral oils

They are mainly made up of saturated and unsaturated hydrocarbons and not esters/glycerides. They cannot be saponified. They are oils only in the their physical appearance. They resemble oils in being insoluble in water. They are non-edible and are mainly used as domestic fuels and in automobiles. Paraffin oil is a typical mineral oil.

Drying oils

Oils, such as linseed oil and tung oil (China wood oil) form hard, elastic and water insoluble coatings, when exposed to air in thin layers. This phenomenon is known as drying and such oils are called drying oils.

Drying oils are highly unsaturated oils, as indicated by their high iodine values. Oils (*e.g.,* olive oil) having iodine values less than 100 are non-drying oils, whereas drying oils have iodine values above 150 [*e.g.,* linseed oil has value 170-185]. Oils having intermediate iodine iodine values are often known as semidrying oils (*e.g.,* cotton-seed oil has iodine value 105-114).

Functions of Lipids in Biosystems

1. Simple lipids acts as important sources of energy.
2. Phospholipids acts as structural materials of cells and tissues such as cell membrane.
3. Lipids are essential for the absorption of fat soluble vitamins such as A, D, E and K.
4. Simple lipids act as heat insulators and shock absorbers for living organisms.

Nucleic Acids

Nucleic acids are biologically important polymers which are present in all living cells. Nucleic acids are also regarded as polynucleotides.

There are two types of nucleic acids :

1. DNA (deoxyribonucleic acid)
2. RNA (ribonucleic acid).

A nucleotide consists of three chemical components :

1. **Nitrogen containing heterocyclic base** *e.g.,* adenine (A), guanine (G), thymine (T), cytosine (C) and uracil (U).

Adenine and guanine belong to the class of heterocyclic bases known as **purines.**

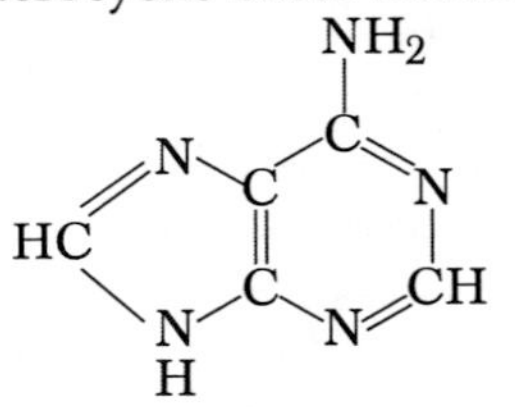

Adenine (A)

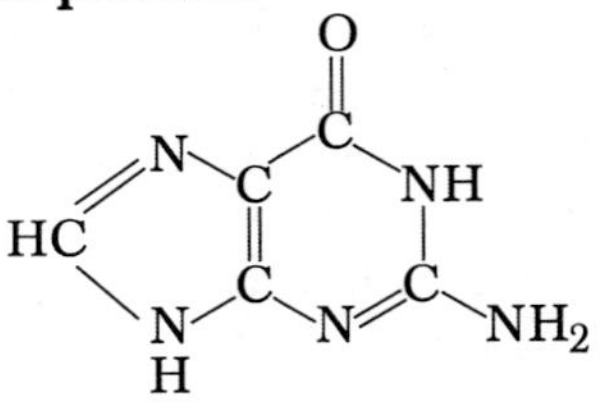

Guanine(G)

Cytosine, thymine and uracil belong to the family of **pyrimidines.**

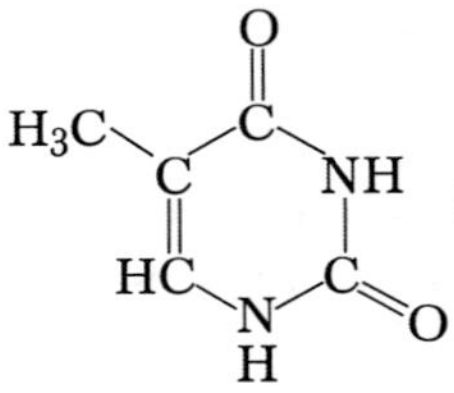

Thymine (T)

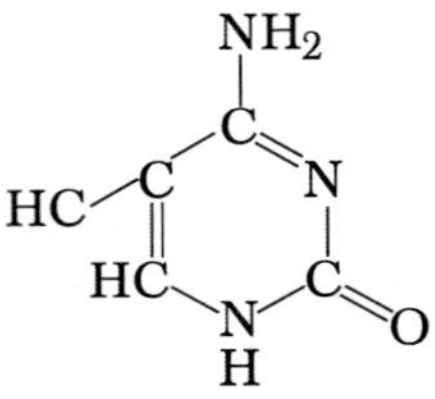

Cytosine (C)

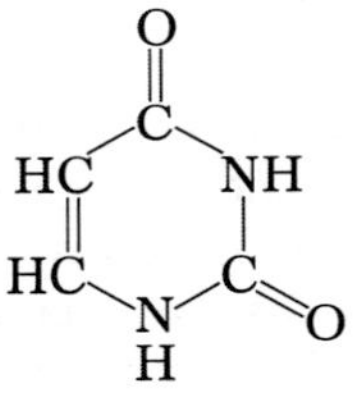

Uracil (U)

Note DNA contains adenine, guanine, cytosine and thymine while RNA contains adenine, guanine, cytosine and uracil.

2. **Sugars** There are two types of sugars present in nucleic acids. Sugar present in RNA is D-ribose and in DNA is D-2-deoxyribose.

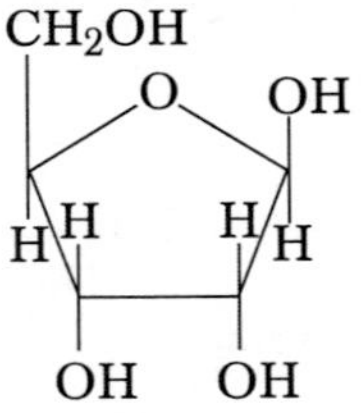

β-D-ribose

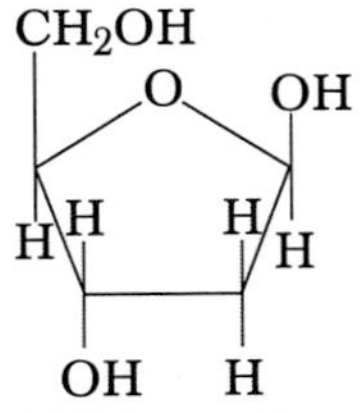

β-D-2-deoxyribose

Note The suffix 2-deoxy in the name of 2-deoxyribose means that it lacks an oxygen at position-2.

3. **Phosphate group** These are responsible for the linkage in nucleic acid polymers. The phosphate group is bonded to a hydroxyl group of sugar. The phosphate group in nuclei acid is :

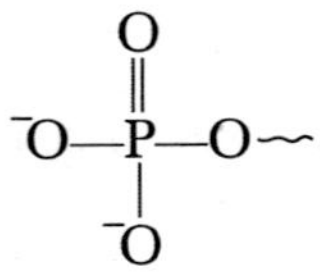

Nucleosides and Nucleotides

Nucleoside

A base-sugar unit formed by the combination of a sugar (ribose or deoxyribose) and a nitrogenous base is known as a nucleoside.

Nucleoside = base + sugar

Adenine riboside (commonly known as adenosine) is a simple example of a nucleoside formed by the combination of adenine (base) and D-ribose (sugar).

Nucleotide

Esterification of one of the hydroxyl groups of the sugar part of the nucleoside with phosphoric acid converts a nucleoside into a nucleotide.

Nucleotide = base + sugar + phosphate

Adenosine phosphate furnishes a simple example of a nucleotide.

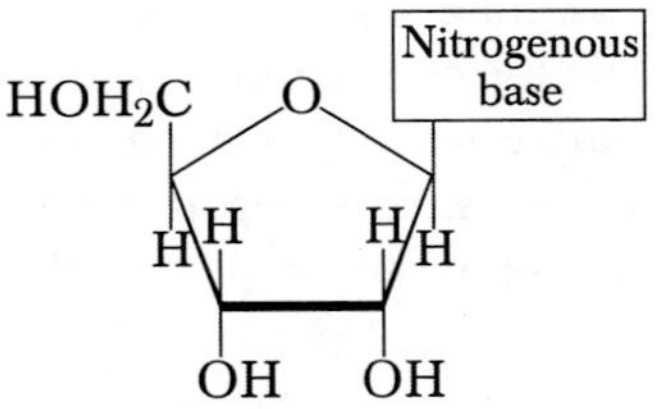

Nucleoside

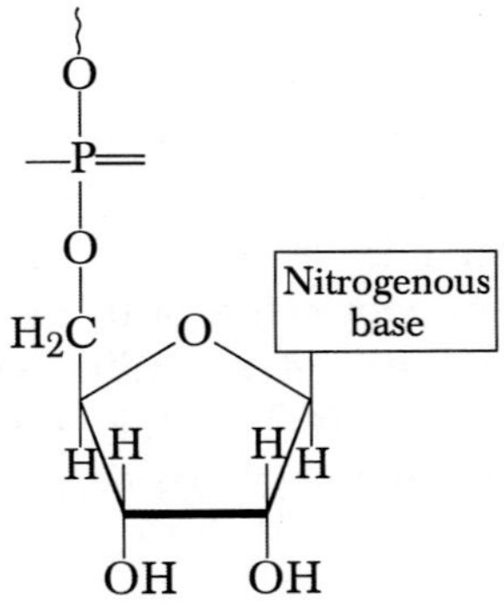

Nucleotide

Nucleotides are joined together by phosphodiester linkages between 5′ and 3′ carbon atoms of pentose sugar.

Polynucleotides are the nucleic acids consist of long chains of nucleotide units joined together by phosphate bridges.

Structure of DNA

The three dimensional structure of DNA was given by James Watson and Francis Crick in 1953. DNA polymers form a duplex structure consisting of two strands of polynucleotide chains coiled around each other in the form of a double helix. Hence, it is called double helical structure for DNA. The two strands are antiparallel *i.e.,* their 5′ ⟶ 3′ phosphodiester linkages run in opposite directions. The bases of one strand of DNA are paired with bases on the other strand by means of hydrogen bonding. Thymine and adenine can be joined by two hydrogen bonds while cytosine and guanine can be jonied by three hydrogen bonds. The diameter of double helix is 2 nm and the double helical structure repeats at interval of 3.4 nm when it completes one turn. This one turn corresponds to ten base pairs. The two strands of DNA are said to be complementary to each other.

Structure of RNA

The structure of RNA is similar to that of DNA except that it is a single strand structure. In the secondary structure of RNA helices are involved but they are always single stranded helices. These molecules vary a good deal in size, some are very large like DNA molecule, others are much smaller and containing fewer than a hundred residues. RNA are of three types : *m*-RNA, *r*-RNA and *t*-RNA.

Biological Functions of Nucleic Acids

Replication

The concept of complementary pairing of nucleoside bases is again coming as a tool for this process. Somewhere along the polynucleotide chain, the two strands of double helix separate. Each separated segment acts as a template for the formation of a new daughter strand with the complementary sequence of base pairs. When the process is complete, a parent and its complementary daughter strand are a new DNA helix.

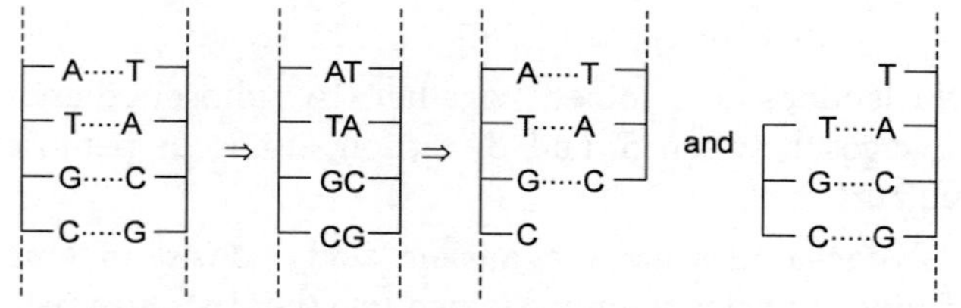

Parent DNA separated strands   Formation of daughter strands

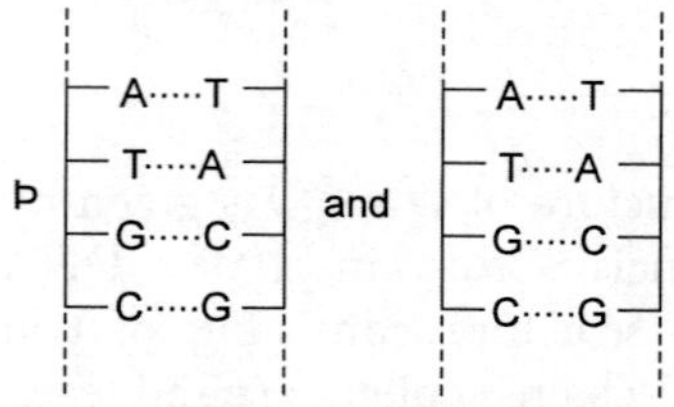

Two identical DNA molecules

Mechanics of duplication process is complex. Parent DNA is reproduced before cell division. The DNA becomes part of the genes of two identical sets of chromosomes which subsequently determine the biochemical capabilities of the two new cells.

Synthesis of proteins

DNA is not directly involved in protein synthesis. Most protein synthesis takes place at ribosomes in the cytoplasm and away from the DNA in the cell nucleus. Genetic information is carried to the cytoplasm by messenger RNA (*m*RNA). There the genetic message is related to transfer RNA (*t*RNA) which actually provides the specific amino acid for the growing peptide chain.

RNA is synthesised by DNA in the same way it duplicates itself. RNA has uracil instead of thymine of DNA, however uracil pairs with adenine. Three types of RNA are synthesised each performing one type of function. One acts as messenger, *viz*, *m*RNA. Second type is transfer RNA (*t*RNA) and third type ribosomal RNA (*r*RNA). RNA molecules are very much smaller than DNA molecules and so a number of RNA*s* can be synthesised on one DNA each particular RNA being synthesised on a specified part of the DNA molecule.

The four bases in *m*RNA, A, C, G and U, act in the form of triplets, each triplet has a code for a particular amino acid. Since, there are 4 bases, 64 triplet combinations are possible. There are only 20 amino acids. So, each amino acid is associated with a number of particular triplets or **codons**.

*m*RNA would migrate to the ribosome, where it would relay the message to *t*-RNA through pairing with its complementary base sequence at the anticodon.

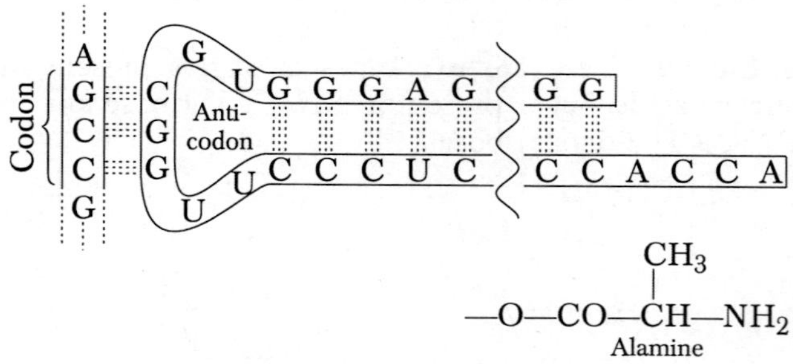

Alanine transfer RNA

The *m*RNA complexes with the ribosome (length of *m*RNA is known as cistron. Since, proteins of different lengths are known, there are also different cistrons *i.e.*, *m*RNAs of different lengths). Complementary *t*RNA carrying a particular amino acid pairs at the appropriate *m*RNA site. Peptide bonds are formed with the help of enzyme between amino acids carried by *t*RNAs. Then *t*RNA is released. The growing peptide chain is attached to the most recently added *t*RNA amino acid fragment and released only when the protein synthesis is complete.

The step involving synthesis of *m*RNA is called **transcription**. The two steps, namely, the combination of each amino acid to its specific *t*RNA and the attachment of each *t*RNA to a specific site on *m*RNA are called **translation**. There are three codons-UAA, UAG and UGA which do not code for any of the amino acids. These are known as **nonsense** or **release** codons and their function is assumed to terminate protein synthesis.

Absence of a single base in the DNA molecule or a single error in the reading of the code can cause a change in the amio acid sequence. The tiny defect in the haemoglobin molecule results in sickle cell anemia (codon GUG appear instead of GAG).

Note Mutation is a chemical change in a DNA molecule that could lead to synthesis of proteins with different amino acid sequence.

Chemistry and heredity

Nucleic acid stores heredity in a molecular level. The information is stored as sequence of bases along the nucleotide chain-message carried by the four bases, adenine, guanine, thymine and cytosine. DNA preserve the information and use if by

1. Duplicating themselves, *i.e.,* by synthesising another DNA molecule identical to it.
2. Controlling the synthesis, in exact and specific way, proteins that are characteristic of each kind of organism. Every activity of DNA requires catalysis by an enzyme. All these enzymes are proteins and exist only because they were originally made with enzyme catalysis at the direction of DNA.

Terpenes or Terpenoids

Terpenoids form a group of compounds the majority of which occur in plants. A few terpenoids have been obtained from other sources. Terpenoids are volatile substances, which give plants and flowers their fragrance. They occur widely in the leaves and fruits of higher plants, conifers, citrus and eucalyptus. The odour in a conifer forest on a hot summer day is partially due to the terpenes originating from pine trees. The name **'terpene'** is derived from the compounds isolated from terpentine, a volatile liquid obtained from pine trees. They are used as medicines and fragrance. The simpler terpenoids (mono and sesqui terpenoids) are the chief constituents of essential oils (oily water-insoluble compounds obtained by steam distillation of plant source). Di and tri terpenoids, which are not steam volatile, are obtained from plant and tree gums. Tetra terpenoids form a group of compounds called carotenoids. Rubber is the most important polyterpenoid.

The term terpenoid is used for terpene like compounds, like hydrocarbons or related oxygenated derivatives. Most natural terpenoids have molecular formula $(C_5H_8)_n$.

The reason for rejecting the term terpene is that since the suffix 'ene' signifies unsaturated hydrocarbons, the term 'terpene' is inappropriate to include compounds such as alcohols, aldehydes, ketones etc. The term terpene is restricted to hydrocarbons of molecular formula $C_{10}H_6$.

Isoprene Rule

Thermal decomposition of terpenoids give isoprene as one of the products. **Otto Wallach** pointed out that, "The skeleton structure of all naturally occurring terpenoids are built up of isoprene units". Further **Ingold** (1925) pointed out that the isoprene units in terpenoids are linked in head to tail fashion.

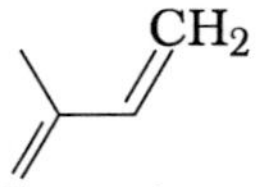

Isoprene
(2-methyl-1,3-butadiene)

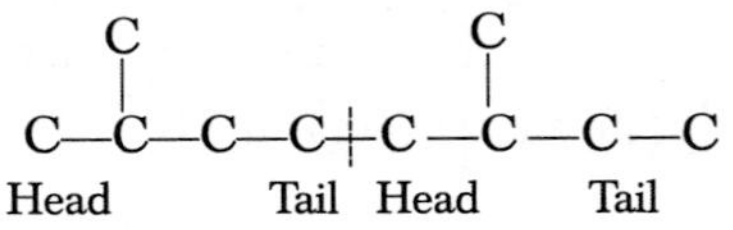

Isoprene rule states that the terpenoid molecules are constructed from two or more isoprene units. Special isoprene rule states that the terpenoid molecules are constructed of two or more isoprene units joined in a 'head to tail' fashion. This rule which has proved very useful, can only be used as a guiding principle and not a fixed rule. *e.g.,* carotenoids are joined 'tail to tail' at centre. Certain terpenoids are known whose carbon content is not a multiple of five.

In applying isoprene rule, look only for skeletal unit of carbon, neglecting the number and position of double bonds.

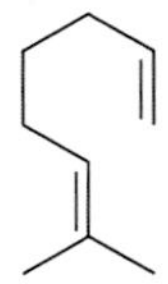

Myrcene

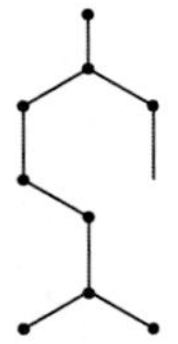

Carbon skeleton head to tail rearrangement

Classification of Terpenoids

Terpenoids have been classified on the basis of the number of C_5 (or isoprene) units present in them. Thus, terpenoids are classified as :

Class	Number of carbon atoms	Number of C_5 (Isoprene units)	Example
Monoterpenes	10	2	Limonene, α-pinene, citral etc.
Sesquiterpenes	15	3	Farnesol, Eudesmol, Zingiberene
Diterpenes	20	4	Vitamin A
Triterpenes	30	6	Squalene, Lanosterol, etc.
Tetraterpenes	40	8	Lycopene, β-carotene, etc.
Polyterpenes	$5n$	$n > 8$	Rubber

The terpenoids are further sub-divided into acyclic (open chain) and cyclic terpenoids, depending upon their open chain or cyclic structures.

Alyclic monoterpenoids

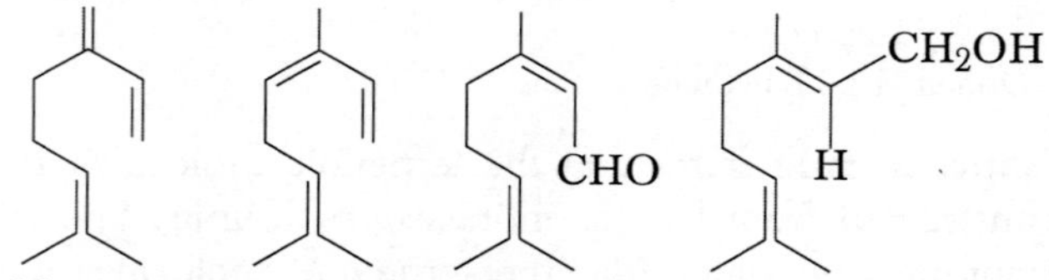

Myrcene Ocimene Citral Geraniol

Monocyclic monoterpenoids

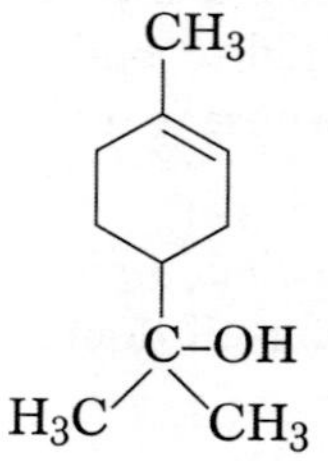

α-terpineol

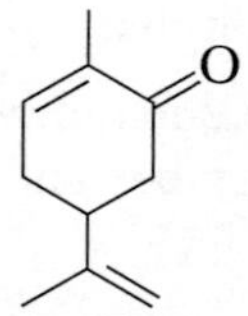

Carvone

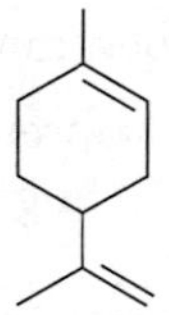
Limonene

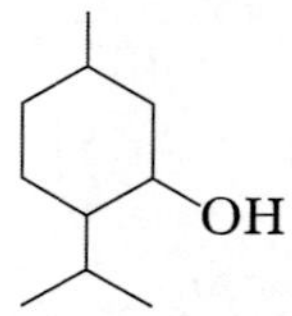

Menthol

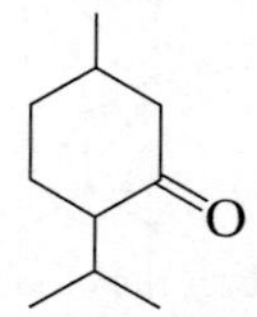

Menthone

Bicyclic monoterpenoids

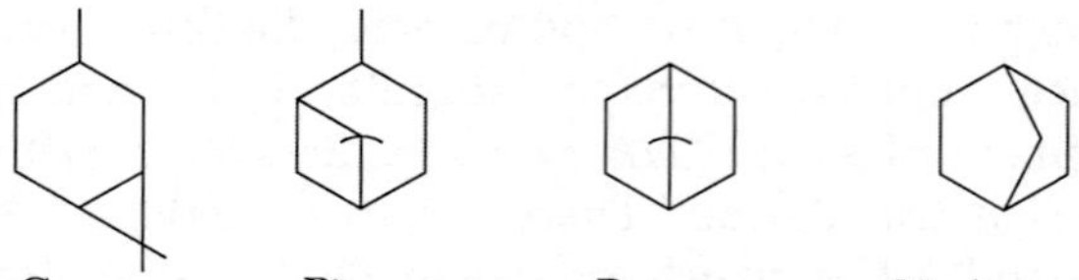
Carane Pinane Bornane (Camphane) Norbornane

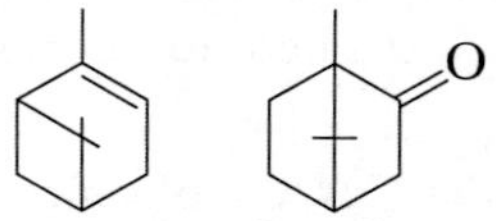

α-pinene Camphor

Isolation of Terpenoids

Concentration of terpenoid is maximum at a particular time in plants, containing essential oils. *e.g.,* jasmine at sunset. The extraction of essential oils (terpenoids) from plant source is mainly by three methods.

1. Steam distillation
2. Extraction with solvent
3. Fat adsorption method

General Properties of Terpenoids

1. They are generally colourless pleasant smelling liquids, lighter than water and possessing high indices of refraction. Solid terpenoids (*e.g.,* camphor) are also known.
2. They are steam volatile and are generally optically active.
3. Chemically, they show the properties of double bond and functional groups present in them. Unsaturated hydrocarbon terpenoids like myrcene or limonene undergo addition reactions with bromine, hydrogen chloride, nitrosyl chloride and ozone.

   Hydroxylic terpenoids like geraniol and menthol exhibit the properties of alcohols.

   Terpenoids containing —CHO group (*e.g.,* geranial), keto group (*e.g.,* menthone, carvone), would show a behaviour characteristic to these functional groups.
4. Soluble in organic solvents, usually insoluble in water.

Citral

It is considered to be the most important member of the acyclic monoterpenoids. It is the main constituent of lemon grass oil. It is also present in oil of citrus fruits. It is a pale yellow liquid having a strong lemon like odour.

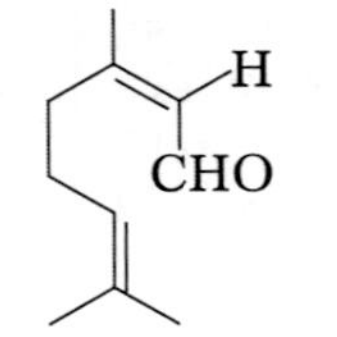

Cis-citral; citral-b
neral; *Z*-form

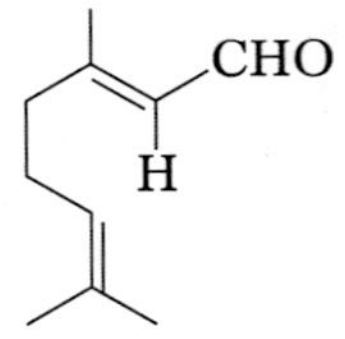

Trans-citral; citral-a
geranial; *E*-form

Citral is obtained from lemon grass oil by treating with sodium bisulphite solution. Crystalline bisulphite derivative separates and this on hydrolysis with sodium carbonate gives pure citral.

It is used extensively in perfume and flavour industry to stimulate lemon like odour and for the manufacture of vitamin A. It is also used for reducing the blood pressure.

Structure of citral

It is confirmed by the ozonolysis.

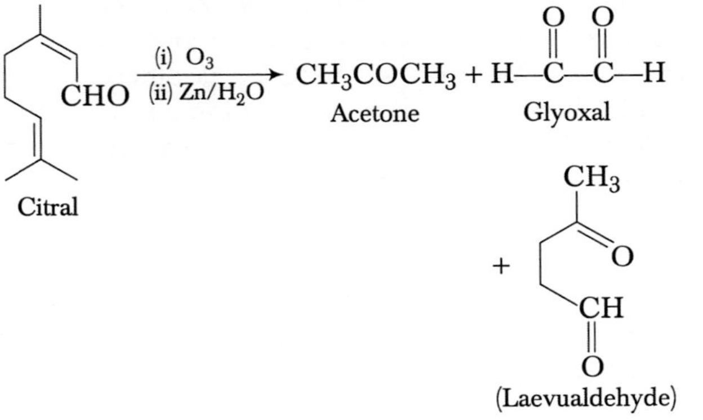

Further, the structure for citral has been confirmed on the basis of synthesis.

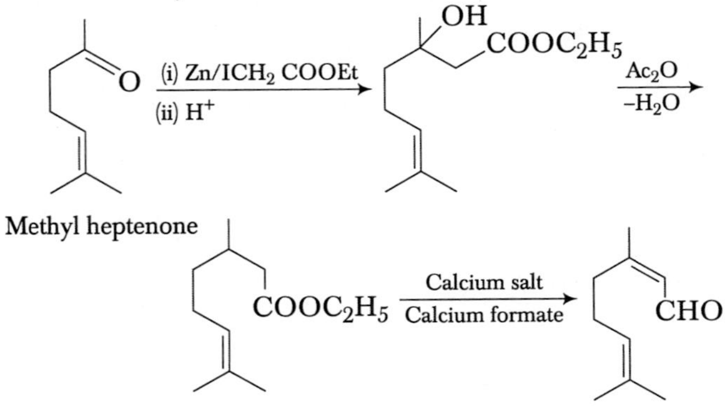

Camphor

Camphor occurs in camphor tree of Formosa and Japan. It is optically active; (+) and (–) forms occur naturally whereas racemic camphor is the usual form of synthetic camphor. It is obtained by the steam distillation of wood, leaves or bark of camphor tree.

Camphor has characteristic odour and sublimes at room temperature. It is used as plastisizer for cellulose nitrate and as an insect repellents embalming fluids, preservative in cosmetics.

Due to its analgesic, stimulant, antiseptic, and carminative effects, it is used in pharmaceutical preparations.

The structure of camphor is as

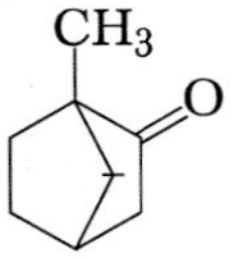

Commerically, camphor is prepared from α-pinene.

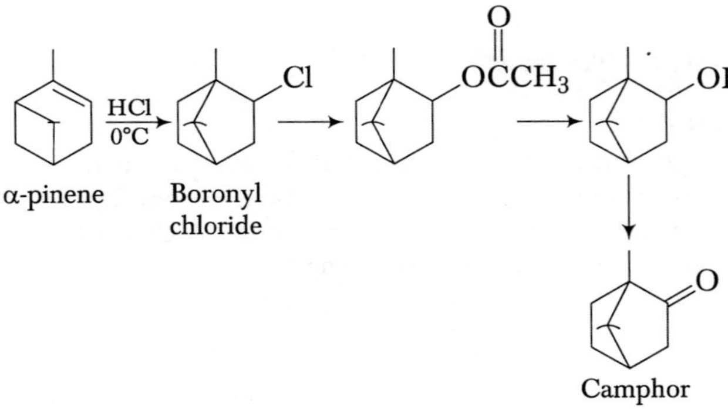

Structure of camphor

Camphor contains —CH_2CO group, because it forms an oxime with nitrous acid. Hence, two structures are possible for camphor.

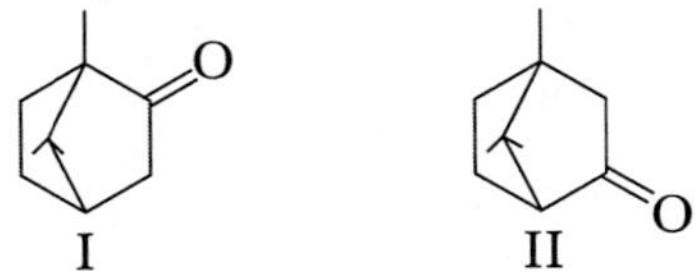

Structure I is confirmed for camphor since camphor gives carvarol when distilled with iodine.

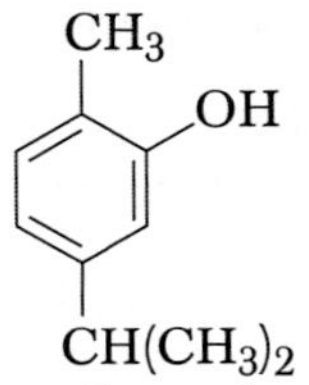

Carvarol

Money et al have synthesised camphor from dihydrocarvone in two steps.

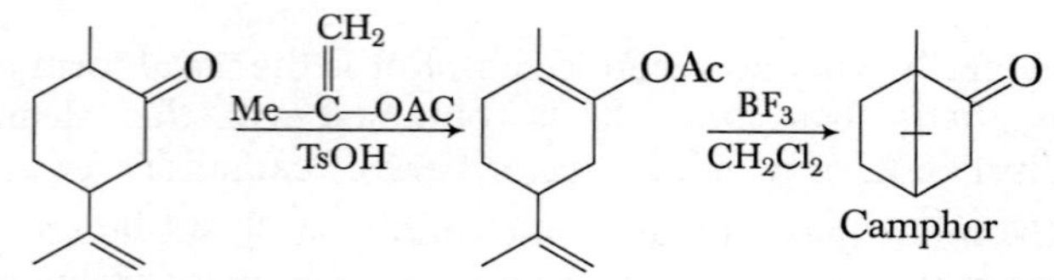

Dihydrocarvone Camphor

Stereochemistry of camphor

Though camphor has two dissimilar chiral centres only one pair of enantiomers is possible, since only *cis* fusion of the *gem* dimethylmethylene to cyclohexane ring is possible. Boat conformation with *cis* fusion of *gem* dimethylmethylene is shown below.

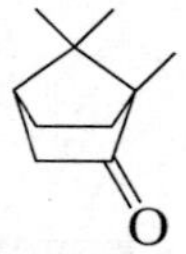

Camphor

Polyterpenoid

Rubber

Is made up of isoprene units which are joined in head to tail fashion. Double bonds have *cis*-configuration hence, rubber is *cis*-1, 4-polyisoprene. With no highly polar substituents intermolecular attraction is limited to van der Waals' forces. These are weak due to *cis* configuration of double bond.

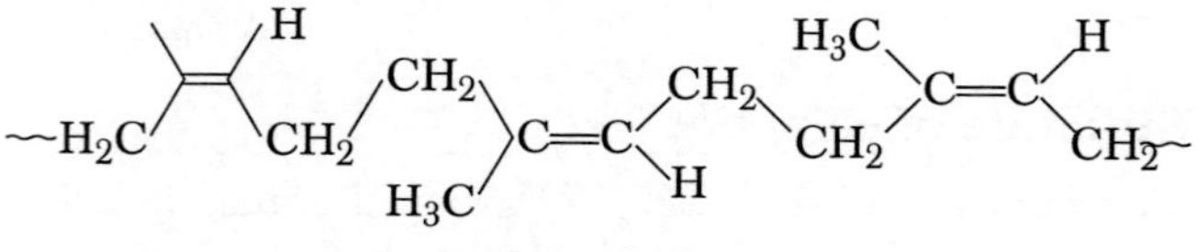

Natural rubber (Polyisoprene)

Trans-configuration permits highly regular *zig-zag* rearrangement that fix together very well whereas *cis*-configuration does not. *Gutta purcha* is obtained from the bark of trees. It is hard and has very little elasticity.

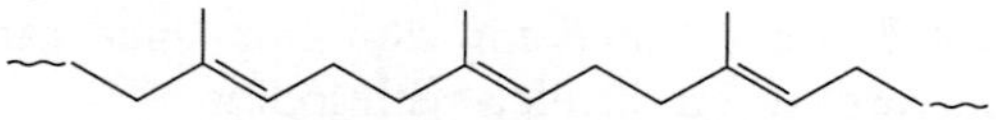

Gutta purcha-trans 1,4-polyisoprene

Cross-linking is brought about by vulcanisation.

In this process rubber is heated with sulphur. Hence, sulphur bridges are introduced between different chains. These cross links make rubber harder and stronger.

Carotenoids

These are yellow or red pigments found mainly in plants. Carotenoids are also known as lipochromes or chromolipids because they are fat soluble pigments. Chemically carotenoids are polyenes. Their parent hydrocarbons have molecular formula $C_{40}H_{56}$ and have eight isoprene units. Hence, they are called **tetraterpenes**.

Some carotenoids are hydrocarbons and they are called **carotenes.** Other carotenoids which are oxygenated derivatives of carotenes are called **xanthophylls.** They give deep blue colour with concentrated sulphuric acid and with a chloroform solution of antimony trichloride (Carr-Price reaction). Carr-Price reaction is the basis of quantitative estimation of carotenoids.

There are some natural polyenes, which have less than 40 carbons atoms, but structurally related to carotenoids. They are classified as **'apocarotenoids'**. Structures of most of the carotenoids can be broken into two halves. Each half comprises of four isoprene units, joined 'head to tail' fashion. Two parts are joined at the centre of the molecule in 'tail to tail' fashion. Each of chain may be two open chain structures, one open chain structure and one ring or two rings. Majority of natural carotenoids have double bonds in all-*trans* position, a few have *cis-trans*. Representing ends of chain by *R*, all-*trans* carotenes may be shown as

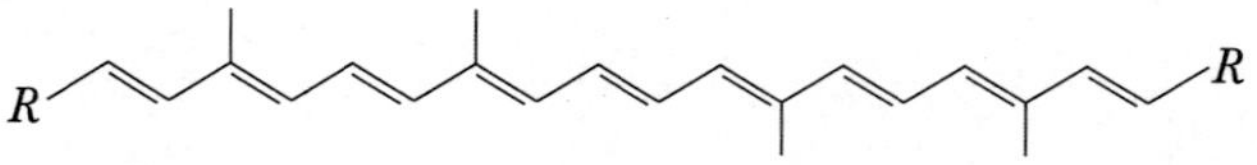

Carotenoids are separated by chromatographic techniques.

Steroids

Steroids are members of a large class of organic compounds occurring widely in plants and animals. They are characterised by the presence of a 1, 2-cyclopentenophenanthrene ring system. The steroids include a wide variety of naturally occurring and synthetic substances such as sterols, bile acids, sex hormone, contraceptive drugs etc. On selenium dehydrogenation at 360°C, all the steroids give Diel's hydrocarbon.

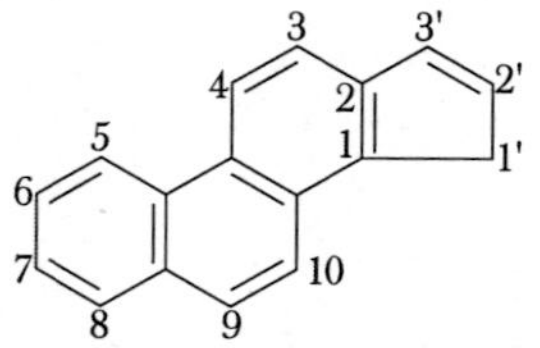

1,2-cyclopentenophenanthrene

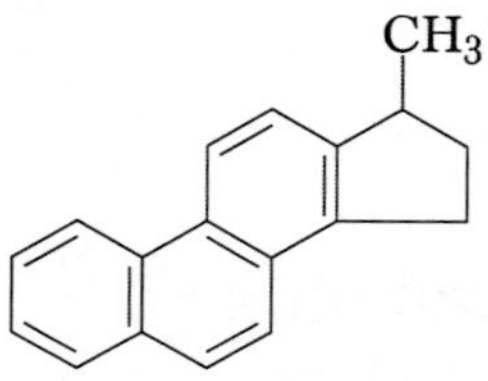

Diel's hydrocarbon

Nomenclature of Steroids

Steroid can be represented by the general formula.

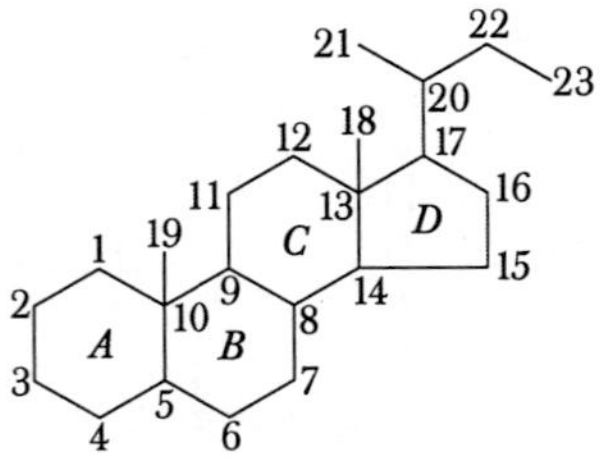

Substituents attached to the ring system from above are designated β (preferably thickened), those attached from below are designated α (dotted or broken line). If the configuration of substituent is not known, its bond to the nucleus is represented by a wavy line.

The methyl groups that are attached at points of ring junction (*i.e.,* 18 and 19) are called angular methyl groups.

Stereochemistry is indicated by solid lines (β-bonds, coming out of the plane of the paper) and broken lines (α-bonds, going behind the plane of the paper).

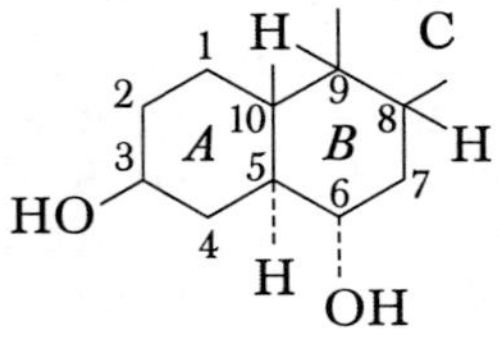

A 3β, 6α-diol

Thus, in above structure the —H and —OH at the 5- and 6-position are *cis* to each other, but *trans* to the 3-OH and to the angular methyl at the 10-position. Fusion of the rings to each other can be *cis* or *trans*, thus increasing the complication of the stereochemistry.

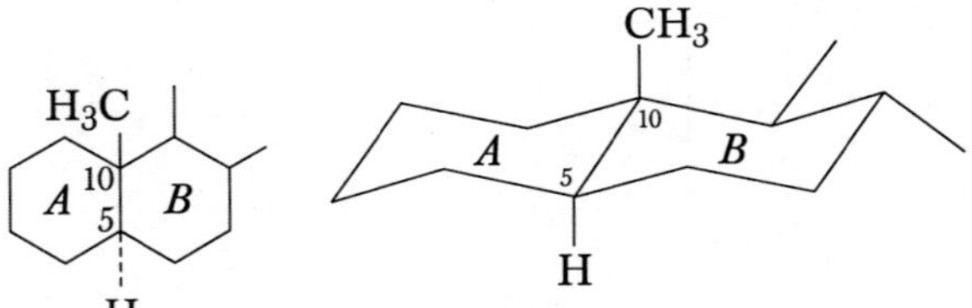

Trans fusion

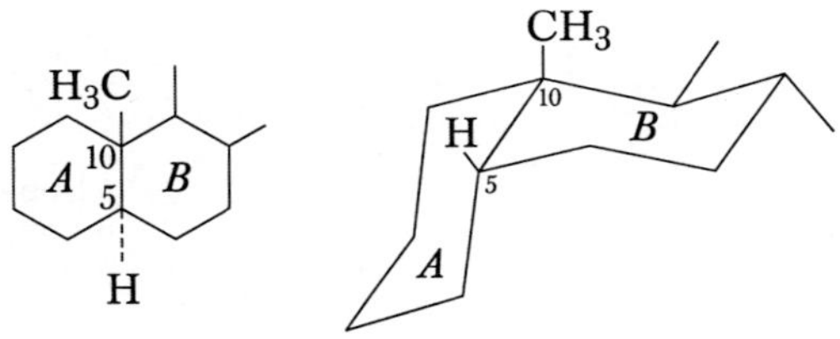

Cis fusion

Structure of Some Important Steroids

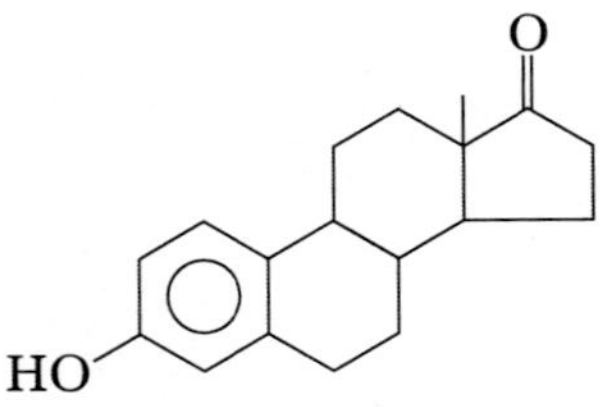

Oestrone
(Female sex hormone)

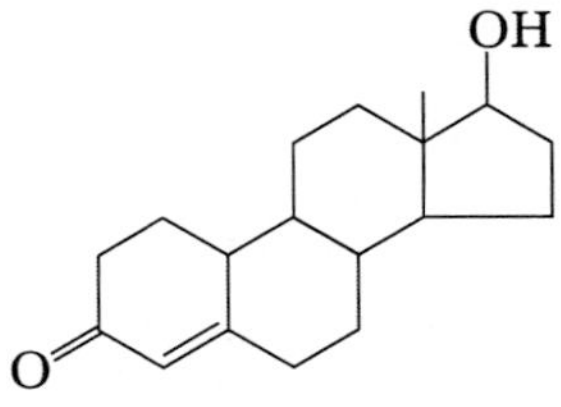

Testosterone
(Male sex hormone)

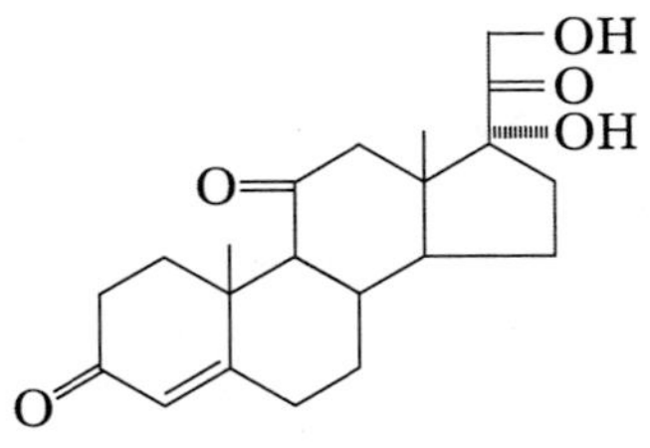

Cortisone

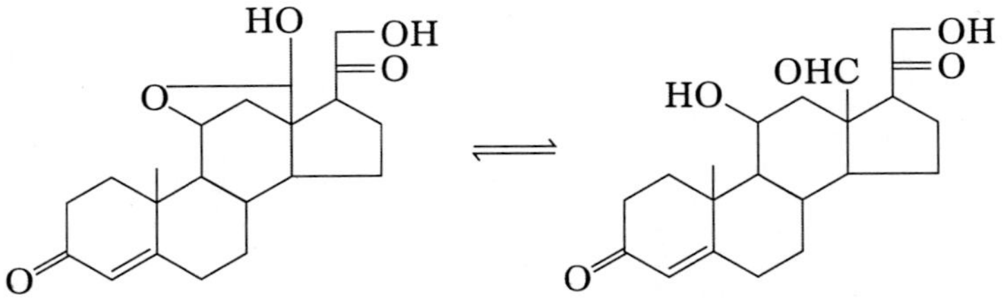

Aldosterone

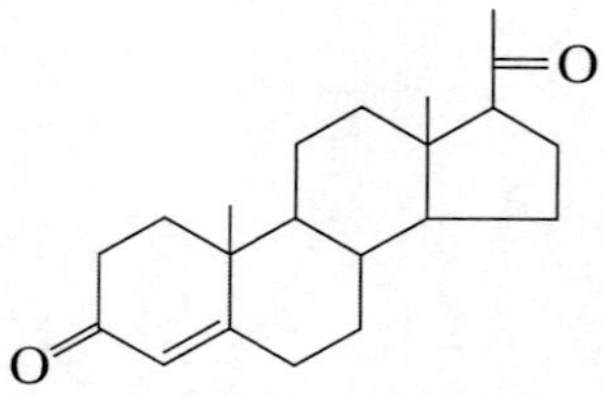

Progesterone

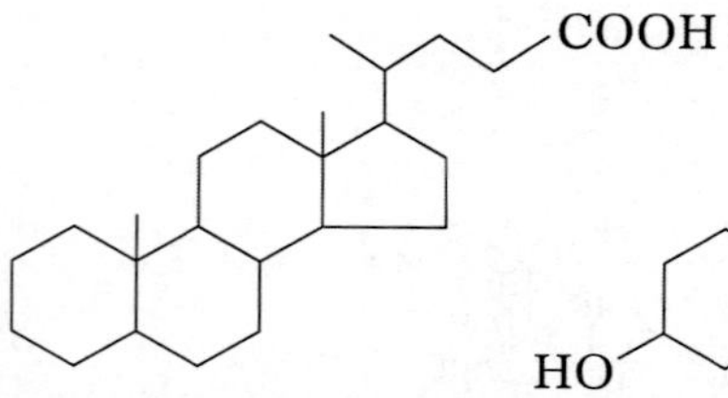

Allo-Cholanic acid
(bile acid)

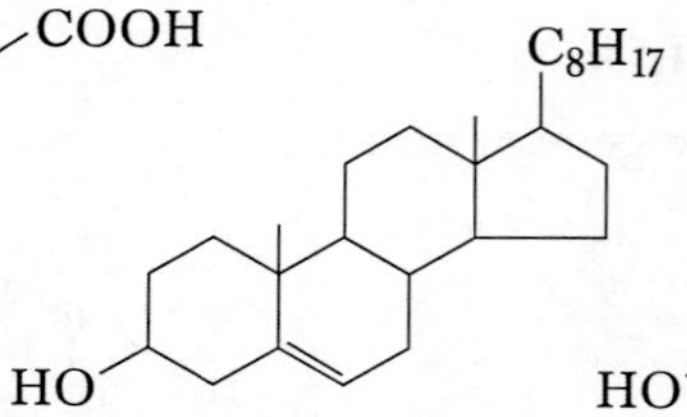

Cholesterol

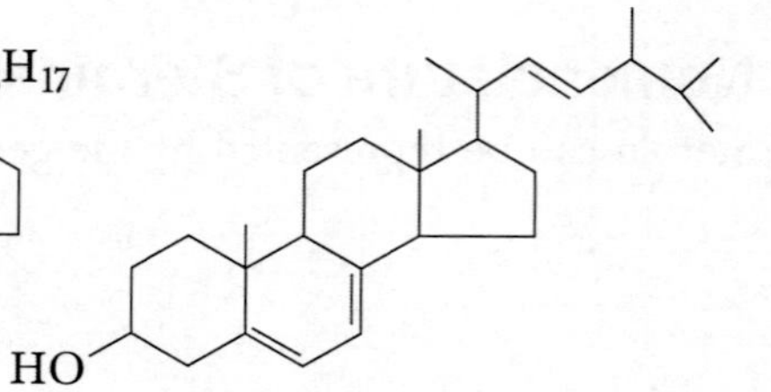

Ergosterol
(A precursor of vitamin D)

Steroids includes sex hormones and adrenal cortical hormones (*e.g.*, cartisone) and bile acids. Because of their biological importance the study of steroids has been one of the most active areas of organic chemial research.

Cholesterol

Cholesterol, notorious as the substance deposited on the walls of arteries and as the chief constituent of gallstones, is the kind of alcohol called a sterol. The cholesterol level in the blood generally rises with a person's age and body weight. Main source of cholesterol are fish, liver oils and brain and spinal cord of cattle. Lanoline, the fat from wool is a mixture of cholesterol, palmitate, stearate and oleate.

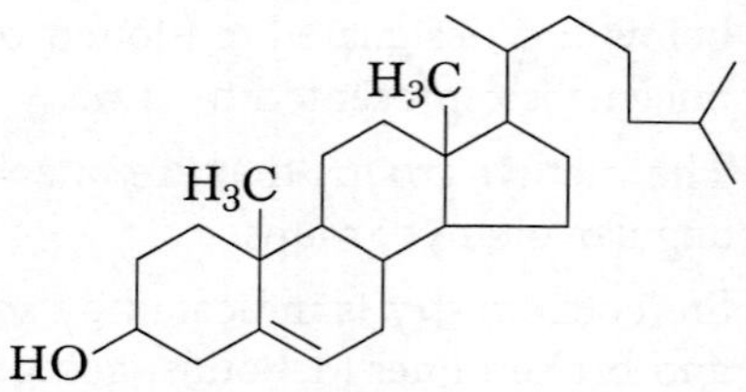

Cholesterol

Cholesterol, despite its bad popular image is an essential constituent of all cells. Like the terpenes, cholesterol is built up step by step from isoprene units. These like all isoprene units in nature, appear to originate from isopentenyl pyrophosphate.

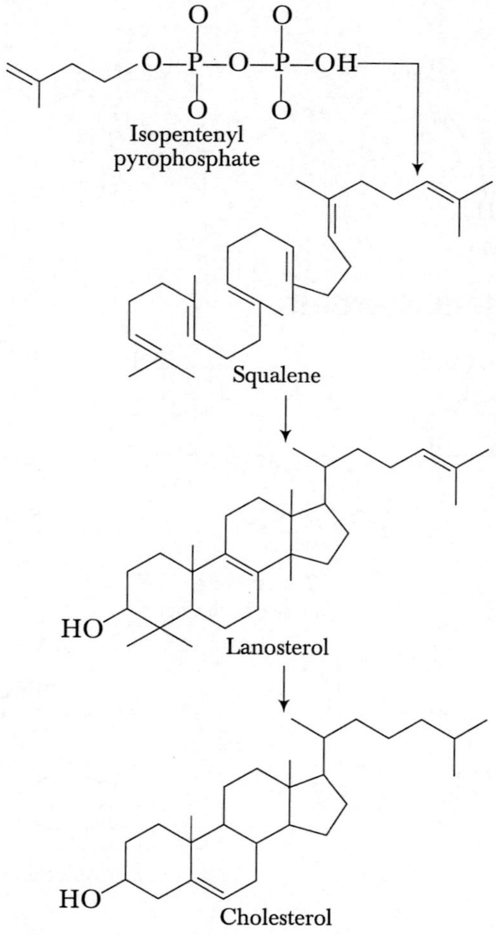

Phytosterols

Plants provide a variety of sterols (*e.g.*, stigmasterol from soyabeans, *ergosterol* from yeast, *sitosterol* from several plants etc.), which are closely related to cholesterol. These plants sterols are known as phytosterols.

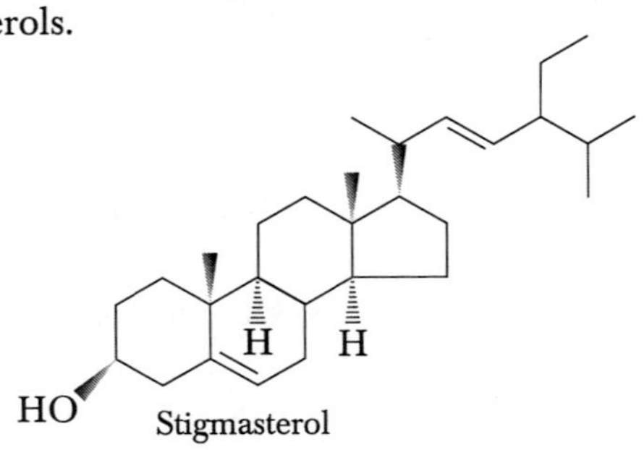

Stigmasterol

Biological Importance

The metabolic processes of higher animals require the participation of numerous steroids. Sex hormones, regulate the sexual processes in animals, bile acids are important in the assimilation of fatty materials in the intestinal tract of animals, and hormones of the adrenal cortex, regulate a variety of physiological processes in animals are mostly steroidal in character.

Plants also have a variety of steroids, which are similar to animal steroids in structure, but are not utilized by animal organisms. Thus, steroids are organic compounds of great applied interest.

Note *Homo* and *nor steroids* are mainly synthetic steroids which have been obtained by modification of carbon skeleton of natural steroids. When any ring is increased in size, the compound is called *homosteroid* and when decreased or an angular methyl group has been removed the compound is called *nor steroid*.

Alkaloids

Alkaloids are an important class of basic organic compounds that occur in higher plants. They are known to contain one or more nitrogen heterocyclic rings as an integral part of their structure. They can induce pronounced physiological activity in animals and human systems.

Extraction of Alkaloids

The plant material is macerated. If the material is rich in fat, it is first extracted with petroleum ether to remove the fats. The plant residue is then extracted with methanol and the cellulosic material separated by filtration. The filtrate is evaporated to give crude plant extract. This is dissolved in diluted acid and extracted with ether. The acid solution, basified and extracted with ether to obtain the mixture of alkaloids.

General Properties of Alkaloids

1. Most of the alkaloids are crystalline solids which cannot be distilled. Some alkaloids are liquids and can volatilize without decomposition *e.g.*, coniine and nicotine.
2. Most alkaloids have bitter taste and are optically active (laevorotatory).
3. Generally, tertiary nitrogen compounds contain one or two nitrogen atoms usually in the tertiary state in a ring system.
4. They possess physiological activity on administering orally. Coniine is a poison, quinine is an anti-malarial, cocaine is local anaesthetic, morphine relieves pain etc.
5. Alkaloids are precipitated from their aqueous or acid solution by a number of substances such as picric acid, tannic acid, perchloric acid, potassium mercuric iodide, phosphotungstic acid.

Classification

Various groups of alkaloids, based on the nucleus present and structures of some of the alkaloids of each group are as :

Phenylethylamine group

$C_6H_5CH_2CH_2NH_2$

β-phenyl ethylamine

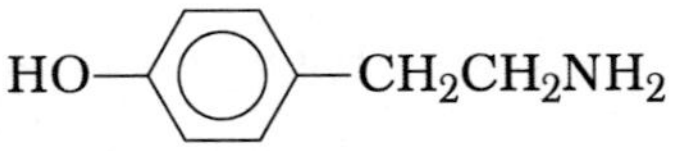

β-*p*-hydroxy phenylethylamine (tyramine)

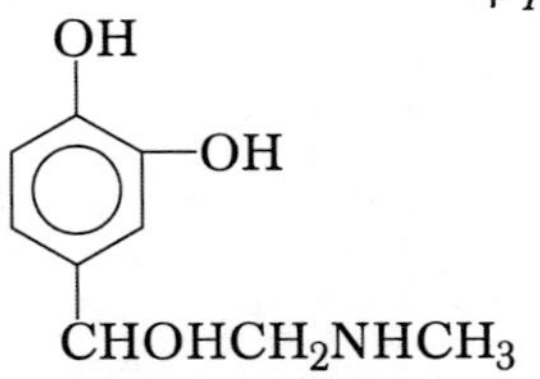

Adrenaline

Pyrrolidine group

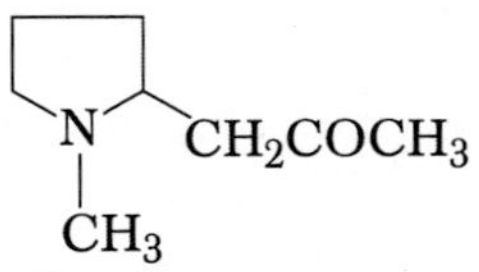

Hygrine

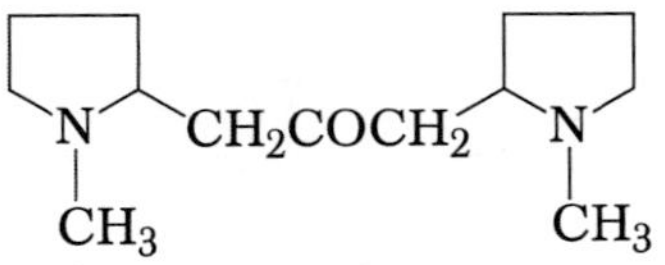

Cusohygrine

Pyridine and piperidine group

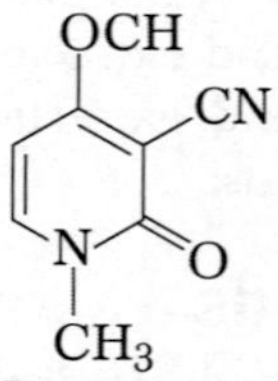

Ricinine

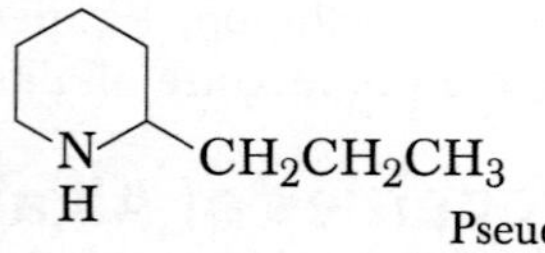

Coniine

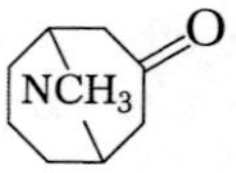

Pseudopelletierine
(Pomegranate alkaloid)

Pyrrolidine-pyridine group

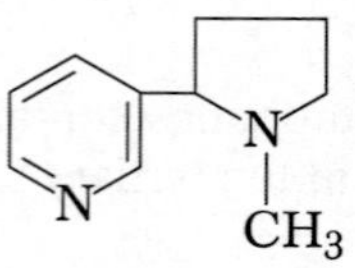

Nicotine
(Tobacco alkaloid)

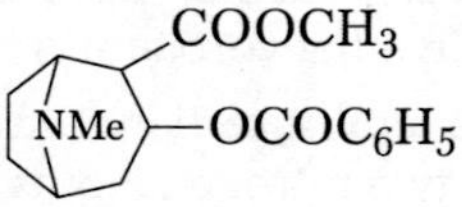

Cocaine
(Coca alkaloid)

Quinoline group

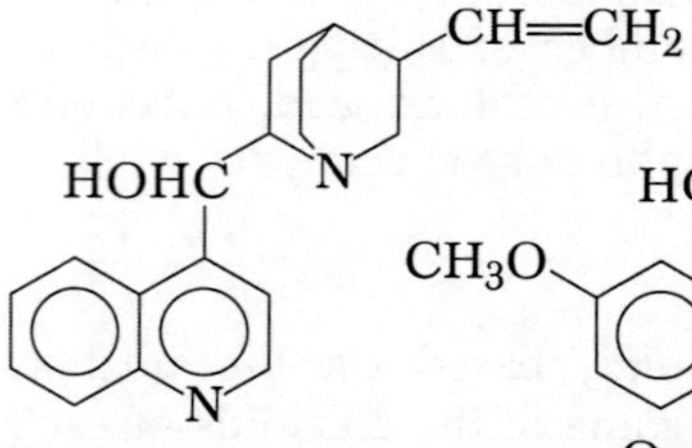

Cinchonine

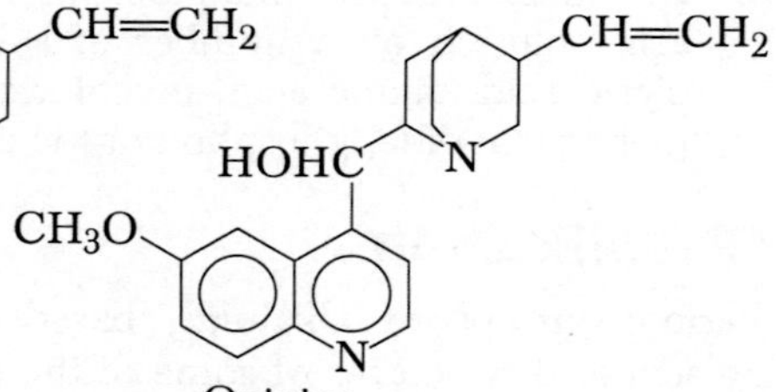

Quinine

Isoquinoline group

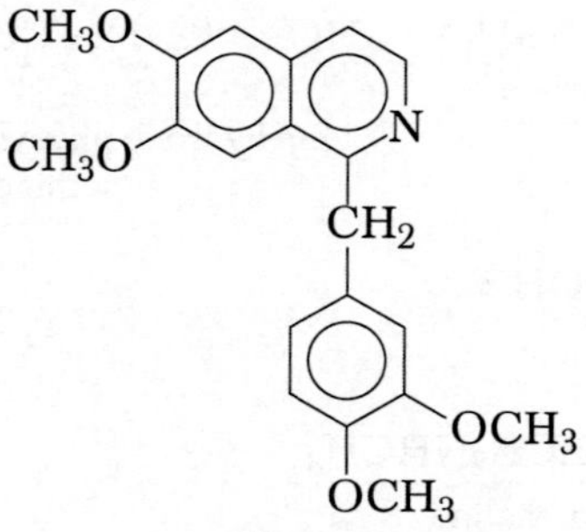

Papaverine

Phenanthrene group

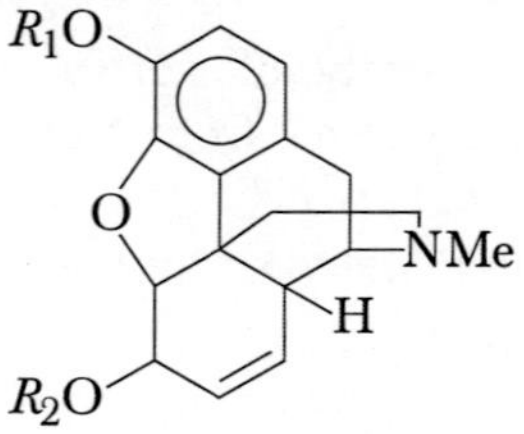

$R_1 = R_2 = $ H, morphine
$R_1 = $ Me, $R_2 = $ H, codeine
$R_1 = R_2 = CH_3$, thebaine
$R_1 = R_2 = COCH_3$, heroin

Coniine, $C_8H_{17}N$

Spotted cowbane or hemlock contains five structurally related alkaloids, of which coniine is a major component. The other four are conhydrine, coniceine, psudoconhydrine and N-methyl coniine. Mixture of these five alkaloids is highly toxic and was used by the Greek's as an official poison to executre criminals. (Socrates was executed with this mixture).

Naturally occurring coniine is a dextrorotatary compound, but synthetic compound is racemic which can be resolved into D-and L-coniine. It is a liquid having high boiling point and an unpleasant taste and odour (b.p. 166-167°C).

The structure of coniine was confirmed by Ladenberg's synthesis.

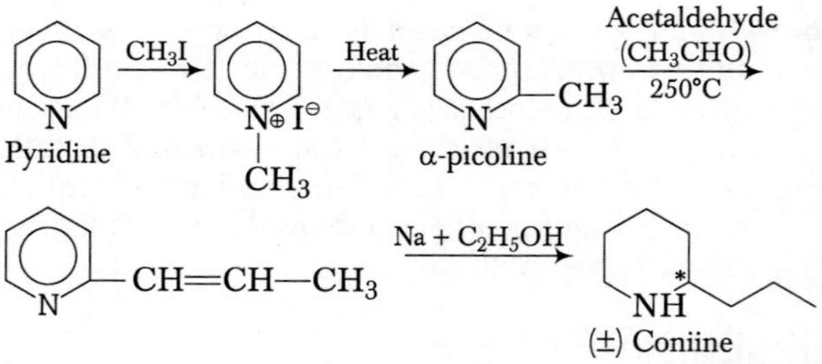

(Such an aldol-type condensation between an α-methyl and the —CHO group takes place because $—CH_3$ group is activated by the strongly-I α-N-atom.)

The important reactions of coniine are as :

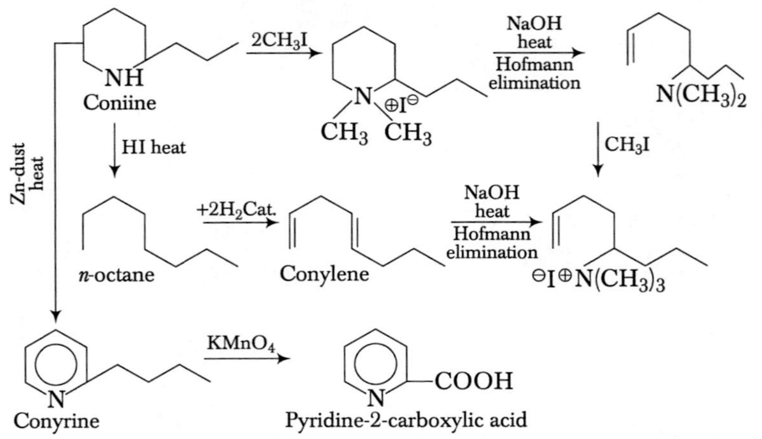

Nicotine, $C_{10}H_{14}N_2$

It is the chief alkaloid of the tobacco plant wherein it is present as a salt of malic or citric acid. It is an optically active, levorotatory liquid having a very high boiling point. In small quantities it stimulates the nervous system for a while, followed by depression. The structure of nicotine was confirmed by Craig's synthesis.

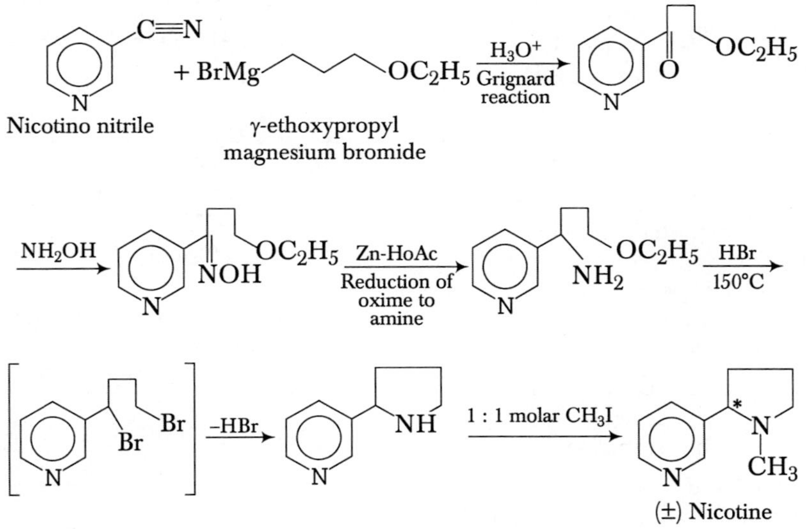

Nicotine on oxidation followed by heating at 460 K yields nicotinic acid.

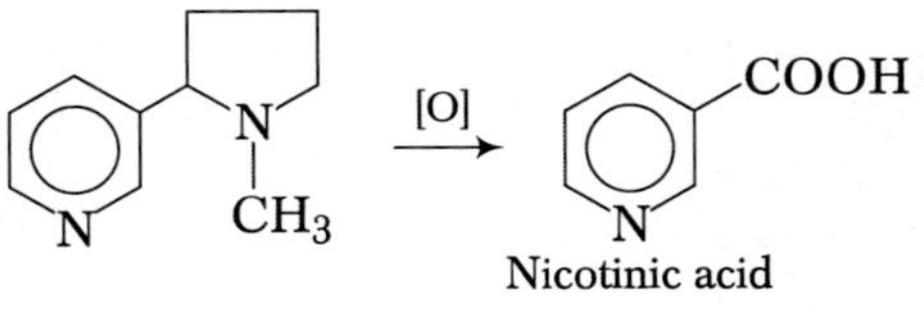

Exercise 1
(For Part 'B')

1. α-D (+) glucose and β-D (+) glucose are
   (a) enantiomers (b) geometrical isomers
   (c) epimers (d) anomers

2. The product of the following reaction is

   Glucose ($C_6H_{12}O_6$) $\xrightarrow{HCN} \xrightarrow{H_3O^+} \xrightarrow{P/HI}$
   (a) *n*-heptanoic acid
   (b) 2-methyl heptanoic acid
   (c) tartaric acid
   (d) D-sorbitol

3. Which polysaccharide has α-glucoside linkage?
   (a) Amylose (b) Amylopectin
   (c) Cellulose (d) All of these

4. Haworth's projection of α-D glucose is :

   (a) 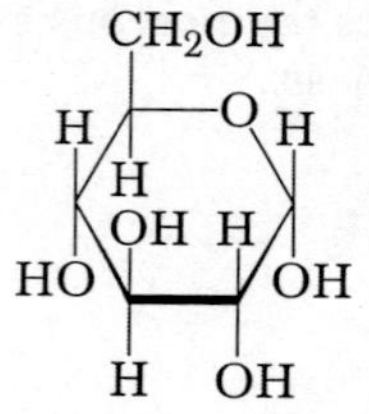 (b) 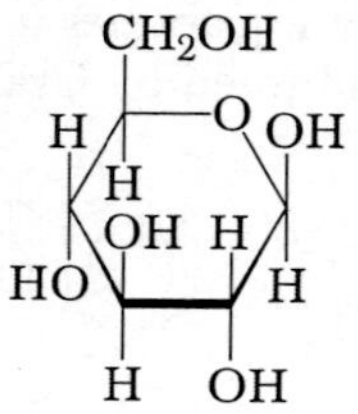

   (c) Both (a) and (b) (d) None of these

5. Glucose is said to have —CHO group. Which of the following reaction is not expected with glucose?
   (a) It does not form oxime
   (b) It does not react with CH_3MgBr
   (c) It does not reduce Tollen's reagent
   (d) It does not form osazones

6. Which substance is not present in nucleic acid?
   (a) Cytosine (b) Adenine
   (c) Thymine (d) Guanidine

7. Cellulose upon acetylation with excess acetic anhydride-H_2SO_4 (catalytic) gives cellulose triacetate whose structure is

   (a) 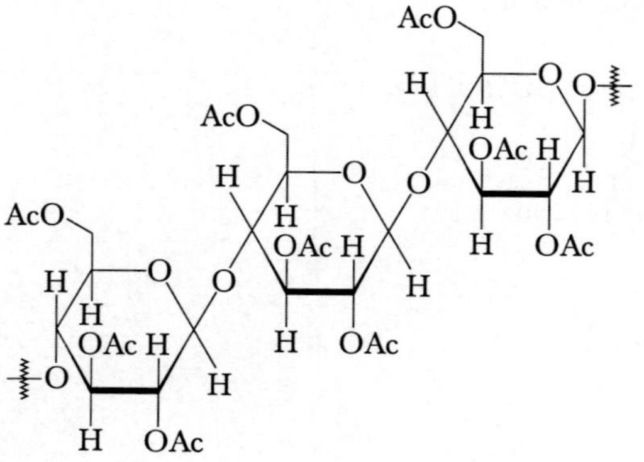

   (b) 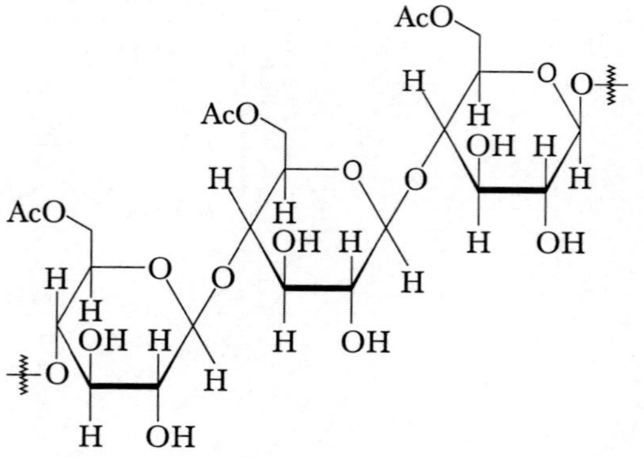

   (c) 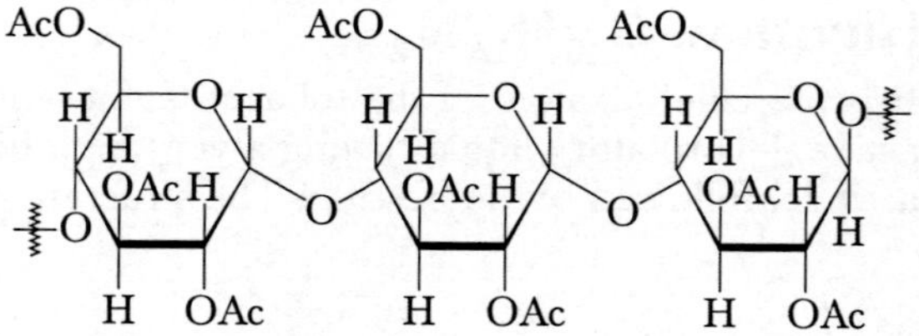

   (d) 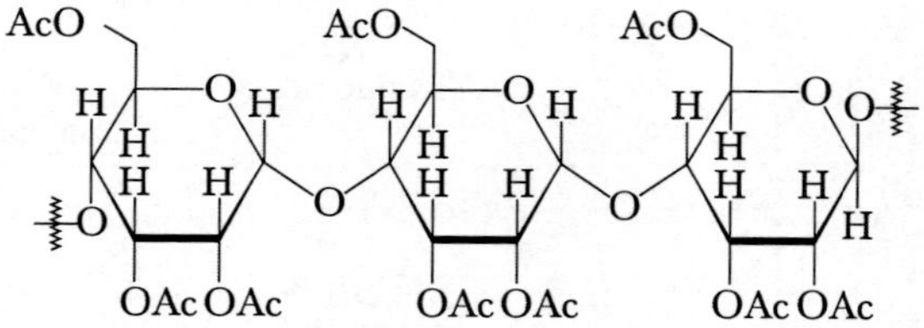

8. Which of the following represents the anomer of the compound shown?

   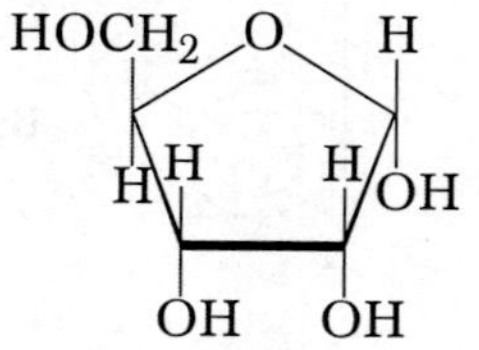

   (a) 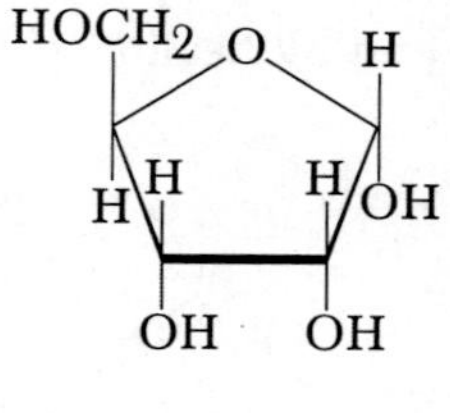 (b) 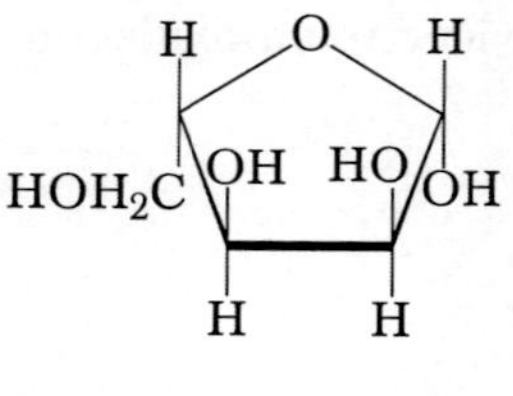

   (c) 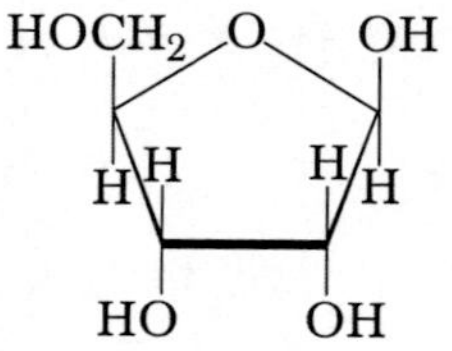 (d) None of these

9. Which description fit the following sugar best?

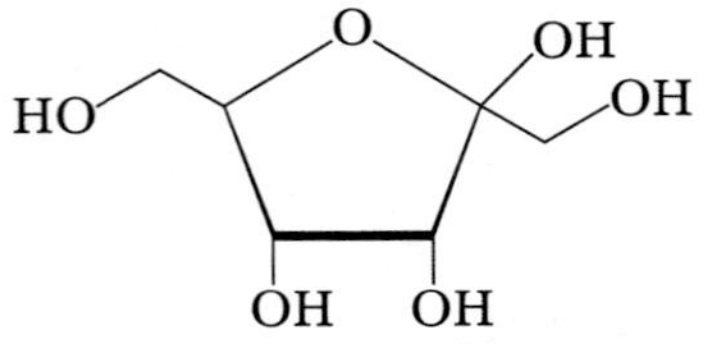

(a) Ketose, furanose, α (b) Ketose, furanose, β
(c) Aldose, pyranose, β (d) Aldose, pyranose, α

10. Which of the following structures is a D-aldotetrose that gives a *meso* diacid upon oxidation with dilute aq. HNO_3?

(a)
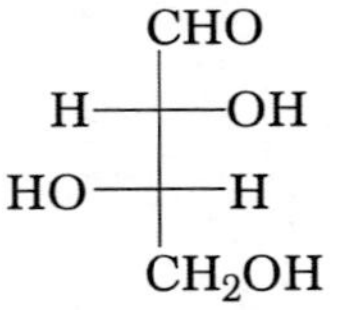

(b)
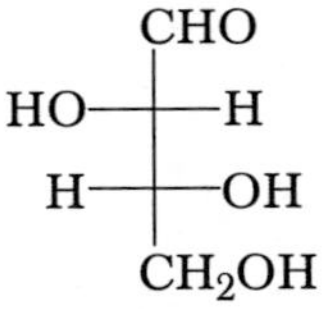

(c)
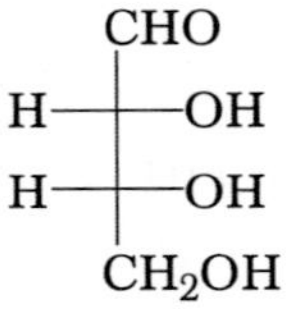

(d)
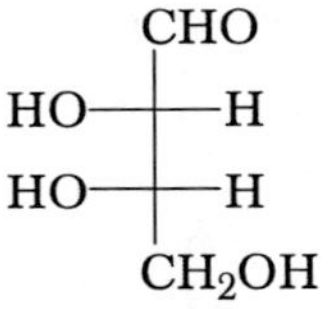

11. Which of the structures is methyl α-D-galactopyranoside?

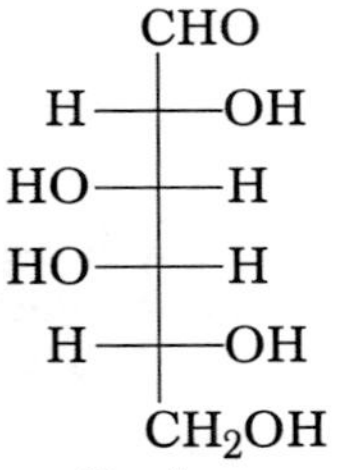

D-galactose

(a)
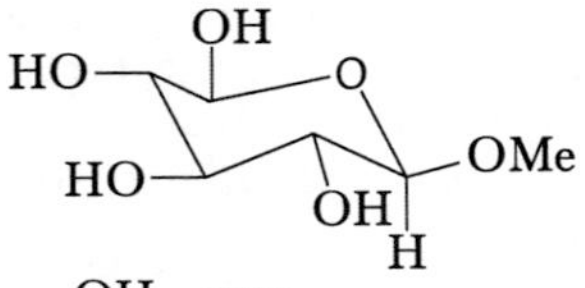

(b)
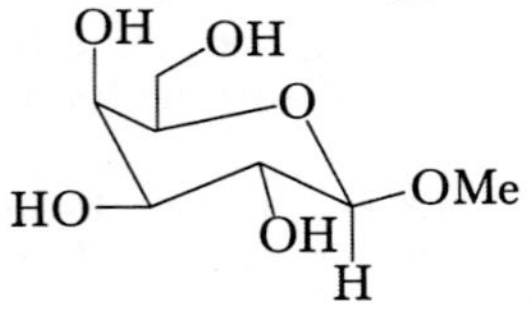

(c)
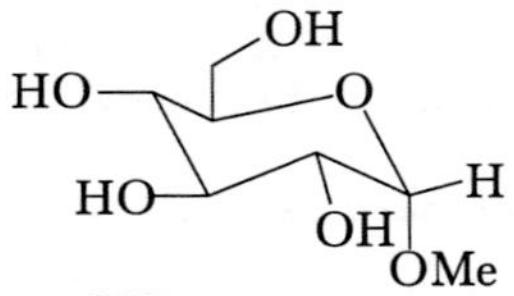

(d)
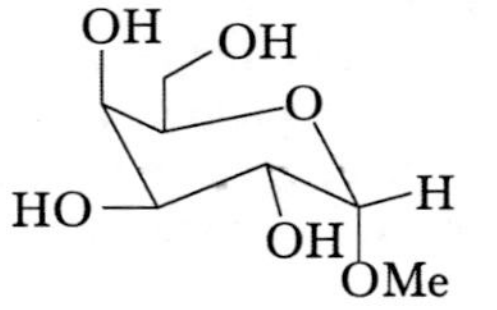

12. To identify the N-terminal amino acid of peptide 1-fluoro-2, 4-dinitrobenzene (DNFB) is used. This is called
(a) van-Slyke reagent (b) Sorenson reagent
(c) Sanger reagent (d) None of these

13. $\underset{\underset{NH_2}{|}}{CH_2}\overset{O}{\overset{\|}{C}}OH\,[pK_a = 2.34]$; $NH_2 \longleftarrow [pK_b = 4.40]$ Hence, isoelectric point is
(a) 3.37 (b) 10.63
(c) 5.97 (d) 8.03

14. A protein is said to have following groups
I. $-NH_2$; II. $-\overset{O}{\overset{\|}{C}}OH$; III. $-\overset{O}{\overset{\|}{C}}NH-$
(a) I, II (b) I, III
(c) II, III (d) I, II, III

15. By adding SDS (sodium dodecyl sulphate) during the electrophoresis of proteins, it is possible to
(a) determine a proteins's isoelectric point
(b) determine an enzyme's specific activity
(c) determine the amino acid composition of the protein
(d) preserve a protein's native structure and biological activity

16. Pepetide bond formation from protected amino acid reactants is often carried out with which reagent?
(a) *p*-toluene sulphonyl chloride
(b) Di-*t*-butyl dicarbonate
(c) Dicyclohexylcarbodiimide
(d) Benzyl chloroformate

17. (Gly-Ala) has structures
(a) $H_3\overset{\oplus}{N}CH_2\overset{O}{\overset{\|}{C}}NH\underset{\underset{CH_3}{|}}{C}HCO_2^{\ominus}$
(b) $H_3\overset{\oplus}{N}\underset{\underset{CH_3}{|}}{C}H\overset{O}{\overset{\|}{C}}-NHCH_2CO_2^{\ominus}$
(c) $\overset{\ominus}{O}_2C\underset{\underset{CH_3}{|}}{C}HNH-\overset{O}{\overset{\|}{C}}CH_2\overset{\oplus}{N}H_3$
(d) $\overset{\ominus}{O}_2CCH_2NH-\overset{O}{\overset{\|}{C}}\underset{\underset{CH_3}{|}}{C}H\overset{\oplus}{N}H_3$

18. In DNA, adenosine pairs with thymine, and guanine pairs with cytosine. If adenosine constitutes 18% and guanine constitutes 24% of all nucleotides in a DNA preparation, it must be
(a) single stranded DNA
(b) double stranded DNA
(c) very short stretch of double stranded DNA
(d) multi-chromosomal DNA

19. Sucrose is a disaccharide consisting of
(a) glucose and glucose (b) glucose and galactose
(c) glucose and fructose (d) glucose and mannose

20. When methyl glucopyranoside reacts with periodic acid, how many moles of the oxidising agent are consumed per mole of the sugar?
(a) 2 (b) 1
(c) 3 (d) 4

21. Table sugar is
(a) a disaccharide consisting of D-glucose and D-fructose
(b) a monosaccharide
(c) a disaccharide consisting of two D-glucose units
(d) D-glucose

22. Rapid interconversion of α-D-glucose and β-D-glucose in solution is known as
(a) asymmetric induction (b) mutarotation
(c) racemization (d) fluxional isomerization

23. Lactose on hydrolysis with dil. HCl gives
(a) glucose and fructose
(b) glucose and mannose
(c) fructose and mannose
(d) glucose and galactose

24. Which reagent is used in the Edman degradation for N-terminal group analysis of peptides?
(a) Phenyl isothiocyanate
(b) Di-*t*-butyl dicarbonate
(c) Dicyclohexyl carbodiimide
(d) Benzyl chloroformate

25. Which of the following structures is not a dipeptide?

(a) 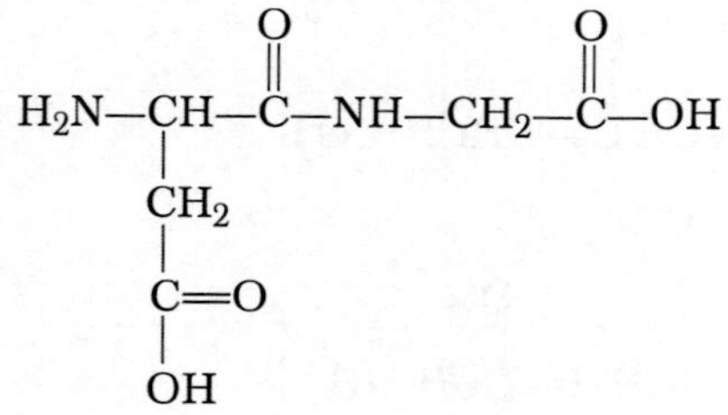

(b) 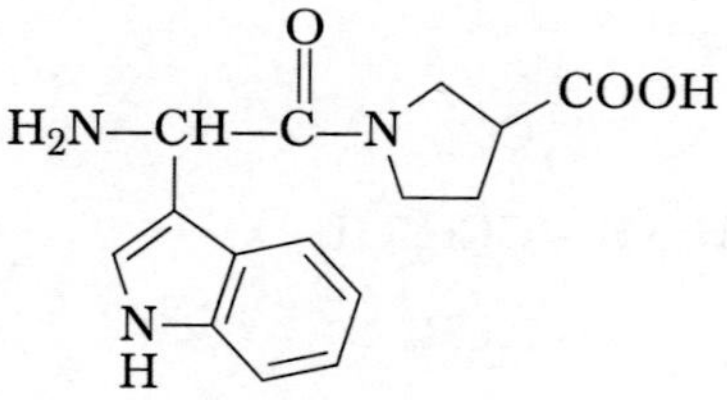

(c) 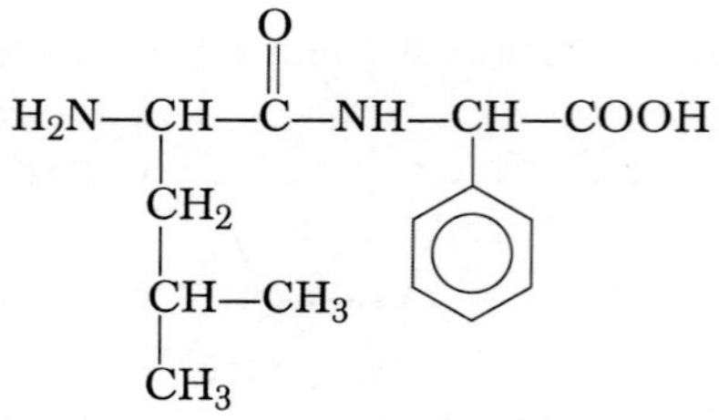

(d) 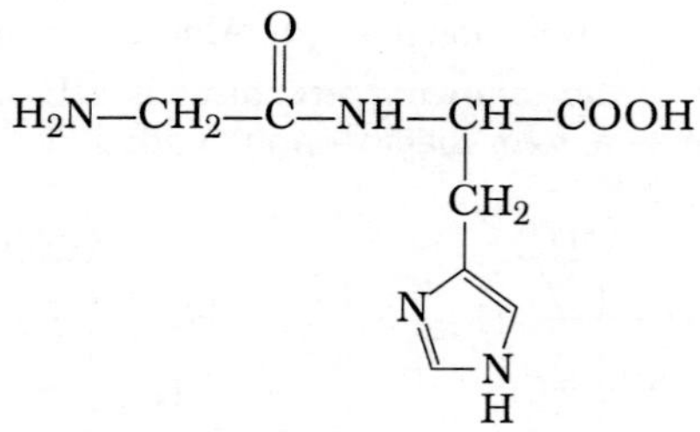

26. The correct statement about the following disaccharide is

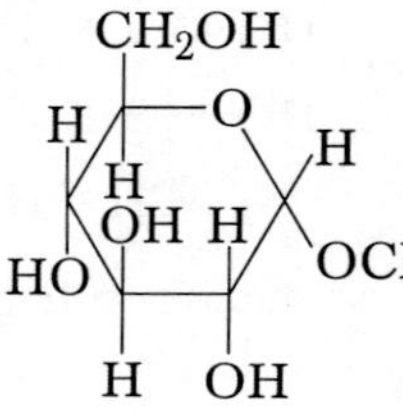
(*A*)

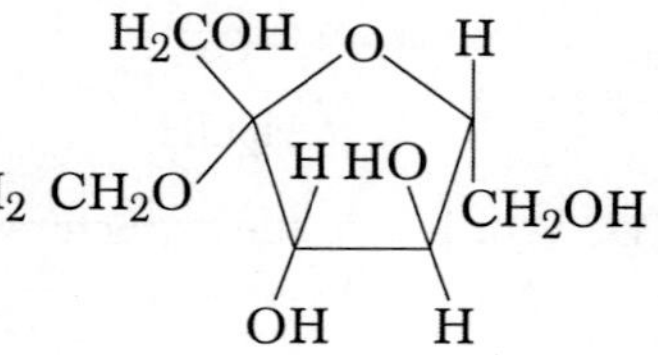
(*B*)

(a) Ring (*A*) is pyranose with α-glycosidic link
(b) Ring (*A*) is furanose with α-glucosidic link
(c) Ring (*B*) is furanose with α-glycosidic link
(d) Ring (*B*) is pyranose with β-glycosidic link

27. A nucleoside on hydrolysis gives
(a) an aldopentose and orthophosphoric acid
(b) an aldopentose and a heterocyclic base
(c) an aldopentose, a heterocyclic base and orthophosphoric acid
(d) a heterocyclic base and orthophosphoric acid

28. Chargaff's rule states that in an organism.
(a) Amount of adenine (A) is equal to that of thymine (T) and the amount of guanine (G) is equal to that of cytosine (C)
(b) Amont of adenine (A) is equal to that of guanine (G) and the amount of thymine (T) is equal to that of cytosine (C)
(c) Amount of adenine (A) is equal to that of cytosine (C) and the amount of thymine (T) is equal to that of guanine (G)
(d) Amounts of all bases are equal

29. In DNA, the complementary bases are
(a) Uracil and adenine; cytosine and guanine
(b) Adenine and thymine; guanine and cytosine
(c) Adenine and thymine; guanine and uracil
(d) Adenine and guanine; thymine and cytosine

30. The process by which synthesis of protein takes place based on the genetic information present in *m*-RNA is called
(a) messenger hypothesis (b) replication
(c) transcription (d) translation

31. Which one of the following is a steroid hormone?
(a) Adrenaline (b) Thyroxine
(c) Cholic acid (d) Roboflavin

32. The fundamental unit in terpenes/terpenoids is
(a) 1, 3-butadiene
(b) 2-methyl-1, 3-butadiene
(c) allene
(d) 1, 2-butadiene

33. Which one of the following is a sesquiterpene?
(a) Limonene (b) Rubber
(c) Zingiberene (d) Squalene

34. Which one of the following is a bicyclic monoterpene?
(a) α-pinene (b) Zingiberene
(c) Menthol (d) Limonene

35. Which is the following methods is/are used for isolation of terpenoids?
(a) Steam distillation (b) Solvent extraction
(c) Enfleurange process (d) All of these

36. Myrcene on hydration followed by oxidation gives
(a) myrcenol (b) citral
(c) 2, 6-dimethyloctane (d) 2-oxopentanedial

37. Which one of the following on ring closure with H_2SO_4 gives α-terpineol?
(a) Geraniol (b) Menthol
(c) Limonene (d) Camphor

38. Which one of the following terpenoid occur in peppermint oil?
(a) Citral (b) Pulegone
(c) Menthol (d) Camphor

39. Which one of the following is the constituent of indigenous medicine Amrit Dhara?
(a) Neral (b) Zingiberene
(c) Camphor (d) Menthol

40. Which of the following terpene is a provitamin A ?
(a) Camphor (b) β-carotene
(c) Squalene (d) Zingiberene

41. Which of the following compound on oxidation gives β-ionone?
(a) Camphor (b) α-terpineol
(c) Borneol (d) β-carotene

42. A terpenoid which is used in the manufacture of celluloid and also as a moth repellent is
(a) menthol (b) α-pinene
(c) camphor (d) zingiberene

43. Which of the following is used as a local anaesthetic?
(a) Qunine (b) Cocaine
(c) Morphine (d) Reserpine

44. Oxidation of conyrine with $KMnO_4$ gives
(a) α-picolinic acid (b) β-picolinic acid
(c) γ-picolinic acid (d) None of these

45. Nicotine methiodide on oxidation gives
(a) hygrinic acid (b) nicotinic acid
(c) atropic acid (d) tropic acid

46. On fusion with conc. KOH quinine gives
(a) 6-methoxy quinoline + lipidine
(b) quininic acid
(c) meroquinene
(d) 6-hydroxyquinoline

47. Atropine when moistened with fuming HNO_3 followed by evaporation to dryness develops a .... stain.
(a) Violet (b) Yellow (c) Red (d) Green

48. Quinine on oxidation with chromic acid gives quininic acid and
(a) lutidine
(b) meroquinene
(c) formic acid
(d) pyridine-3-carboxylic acid

49. Meroquinene on reduction with Zn and HI gives
(a) γ-picoline (b) cincholoipon
(c) cincholoiponic acid (d) loipoic acid

50. Cocaine hydrolysed under controlled condition to give
(a) benzoylecgonine (b) ecgonine
(c) tropinone (d) None of these

51. Poisonous shrub hemlock contains an alkaloid that was given to socrates before sentenced to death was
(a) Cocaine (b) Coniine (c) Nicotine (d) Morphine

52. Quinine contains a 6-methoxy quinoline nucleus linked to position-8 of quinuclidine *via*
(a) CH_2 group at 4-position
(b) —CHOH group at 4-position
(c) $—CH{=}CH_2$ group at 4-position
(d) Two $—CH_2$ groups at 4-position

53. 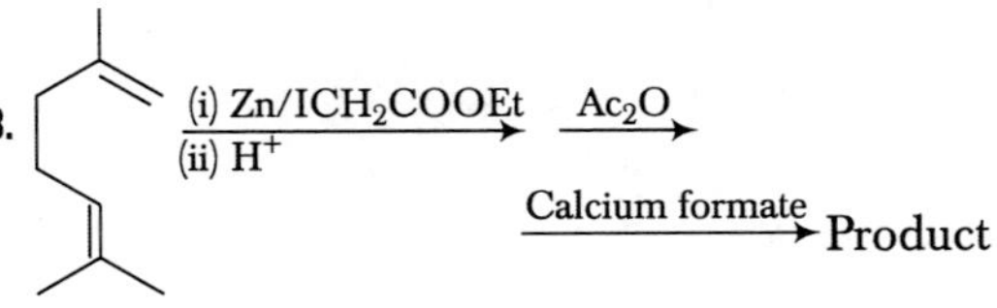

The product is

(a) 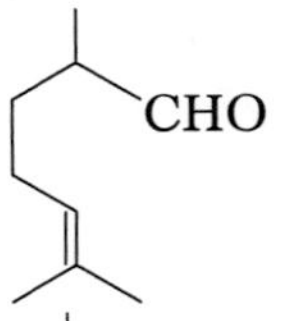

(b) 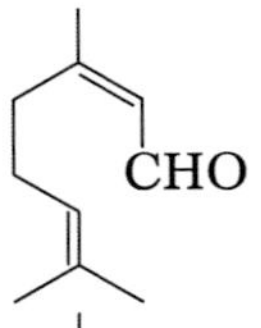

(c) 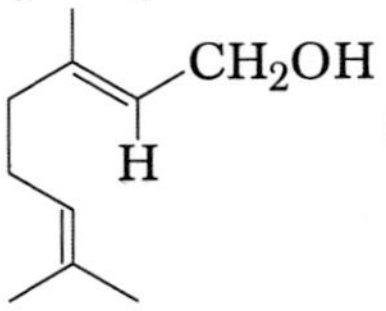

(d) 

54. 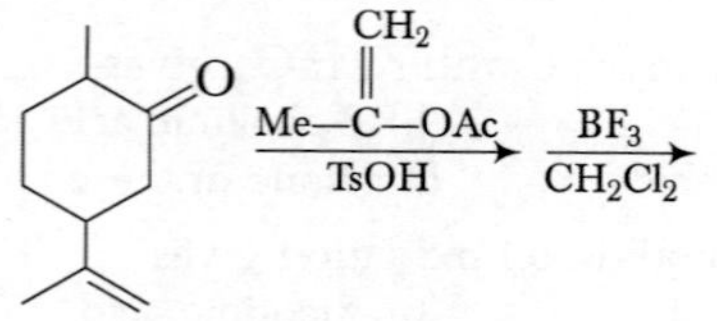 A; A is

(a) 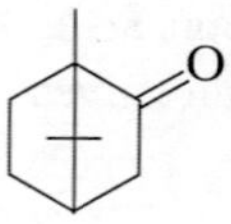
(b) 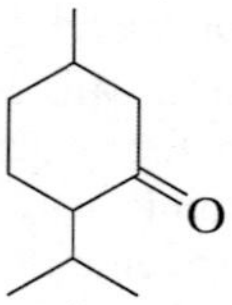
(c) 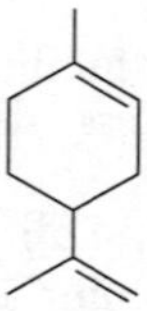
(d) 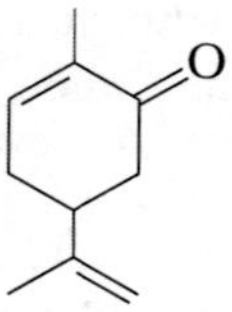

55. 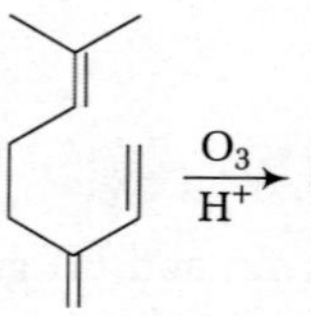 Products are

(a) 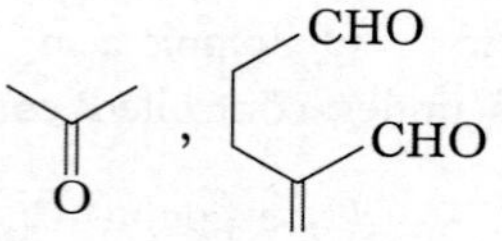 , HCOOH
(b) 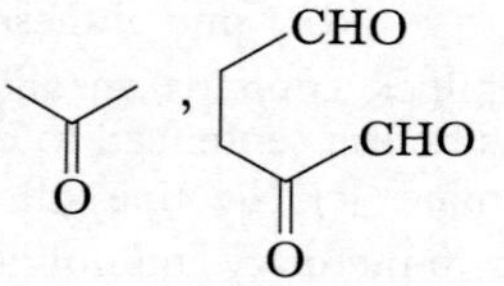 , HCHO
(c) CH_3CHO, 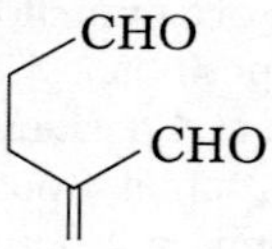 , HCHO
(d) CH_3CHO, 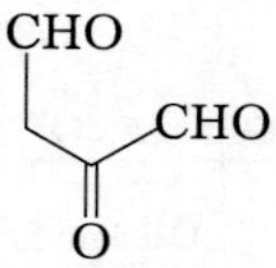 , HCHO

56. 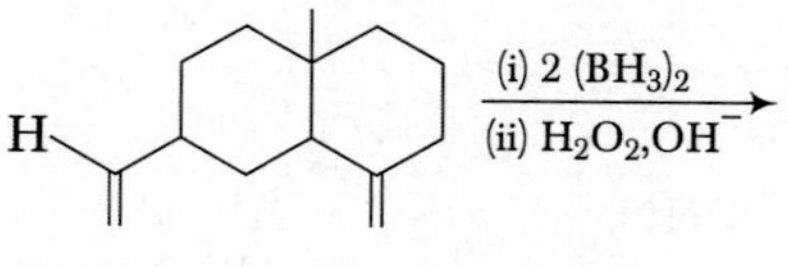 A; A is

(a) 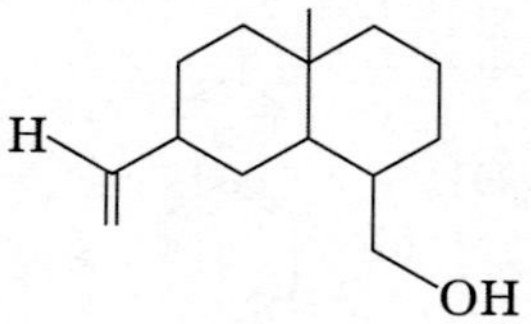
(b) 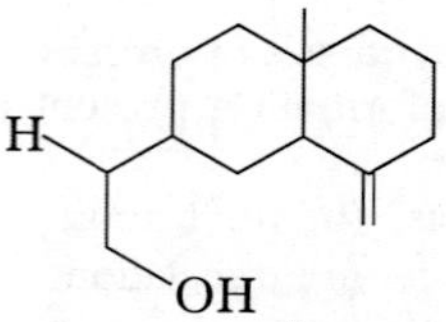
(c) 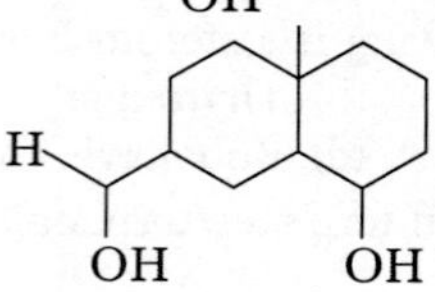
(d) 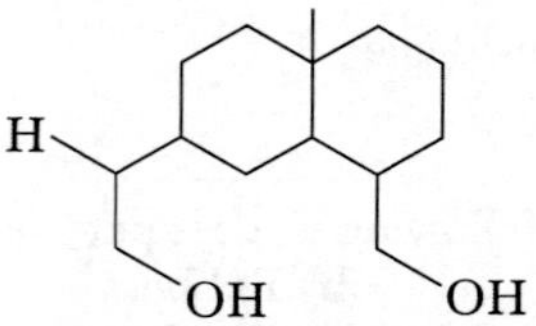

57. Phospholipids are esters of glycerol with
(a) three carboxylic acid residues
(b) two carboxylic acid residues and one phosphate group
(c) one carboxylic acid residue and two phosphate groups
(d) three phosphate groups

58. The dipeptide glycylalanine contains
(a) glycine as C-terminal residue
(b) glycine as N-terminal residue
(c) alanine as N-terminal residue
(d) either (a) or (b)

59. Ninhydrin reagent reacts with α-amino acids to give purple colour. When ninhydrin reacts with phenyl alanine, which of the following is responsible for purple colour?

(a) 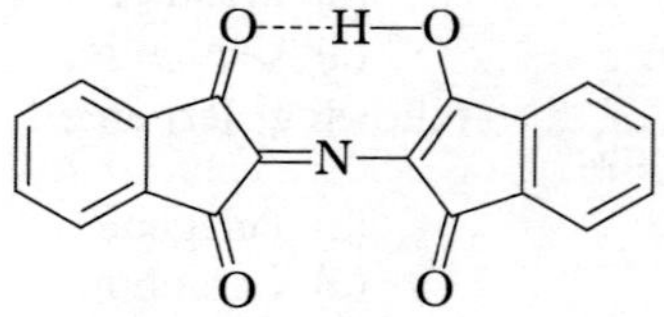
(b) 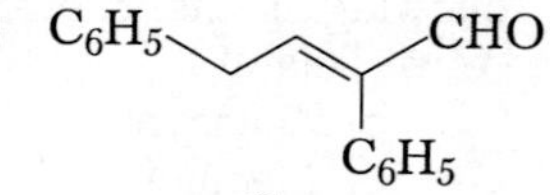
(c) 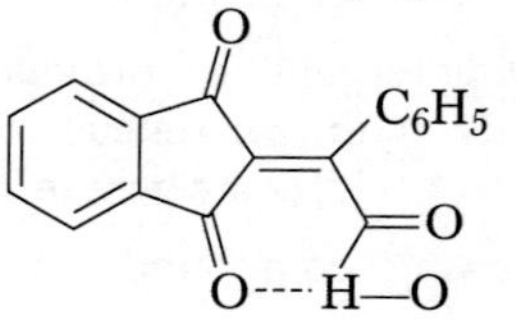
(d) 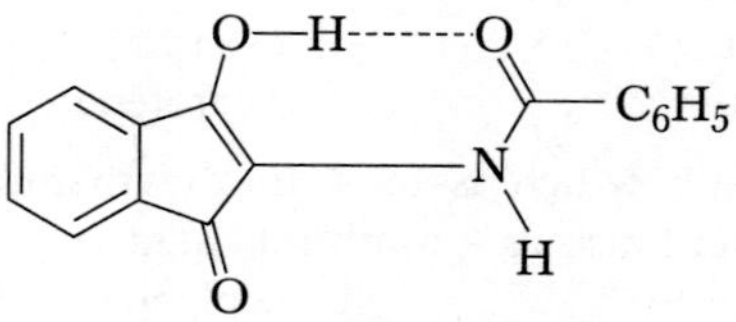

60. Which of the following alkaloid contains phenanthrene group?
(a) Cinchonine
(b) Papaverine
(c) Cocaine
(d) Morphine

Exercise 2
(For Part 'C')

1. Consider the following reagents.
I. Br_2 water
II. Tollens' reagent
III. Fehling's solution
Which can be used to make distinction between an aldose and a ketose?
(a) I, II, III (b) II, III
(c) I only (d) II only

2. Consider the following synthetic compounds :

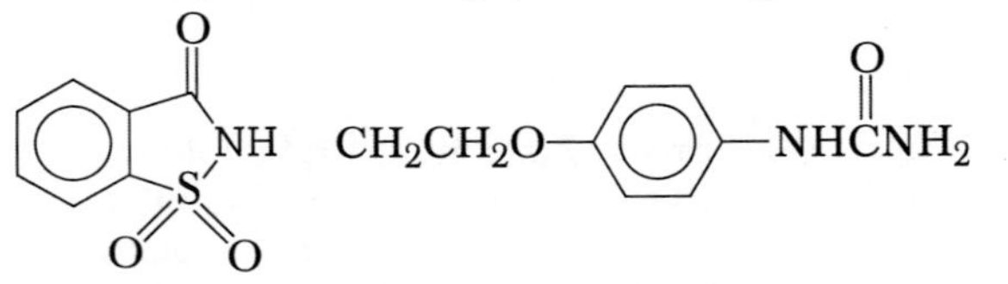

I (Saccharin) II (Dulcin)

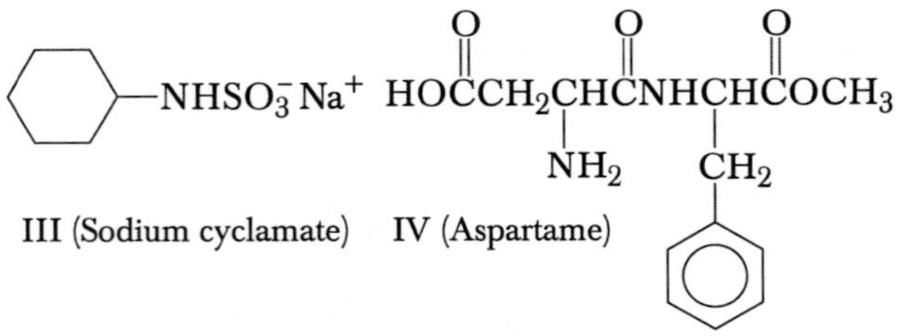

III (Sodium cyclamate) IV (Aspartame)

Which of the above examples are used as sweetening agents?
(a) All I, II, III, IV (b) II, III, IV
(c) I, II, IV (d) I, III, IV

3. Consider the following compounds :
I. Glycine; II. Sulphanilic acid;
III. Anthranilic acid.
Which can form dipolar (Zwitter ion)?
(a) I, II, III (b) I, II (c) II, III (d) I, III

4. What is the D-monosaccharide used in the following reaction?

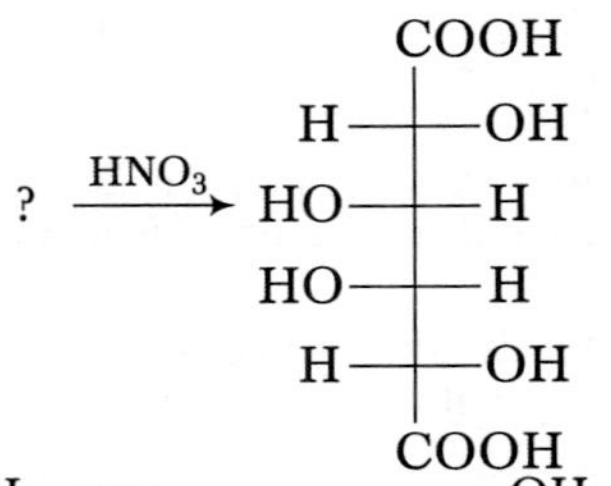

(a) 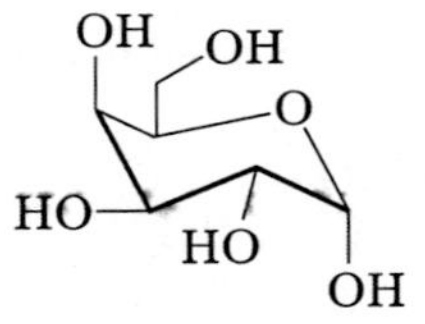

(b) 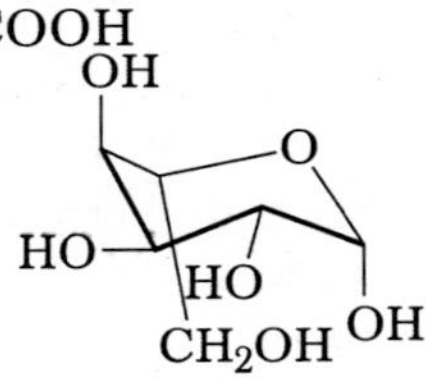

(c) 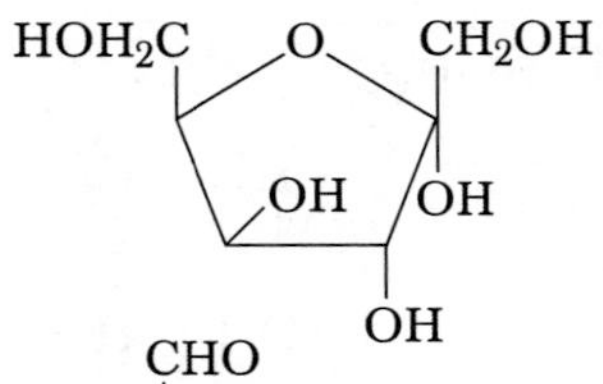

(d) 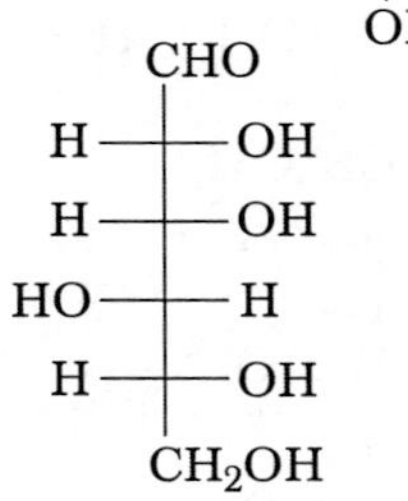

5. Choose the response that provides the best match between the terms given and the structures shown.

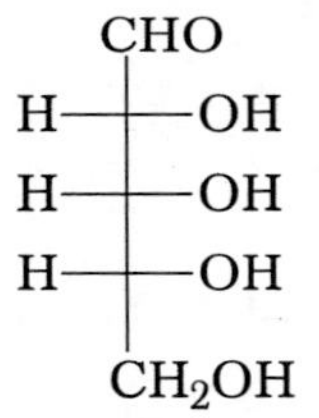

I.

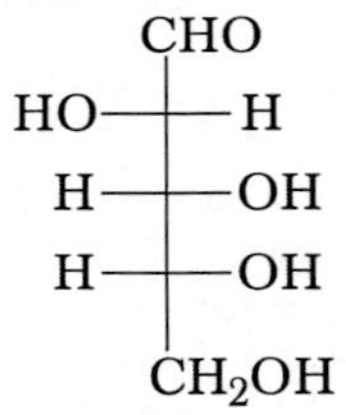

II.

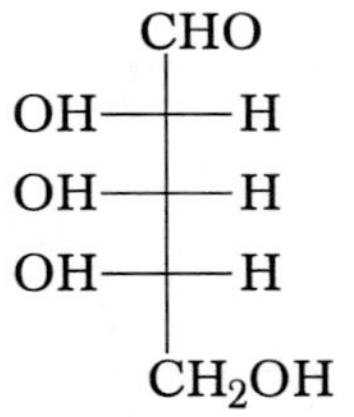

III.

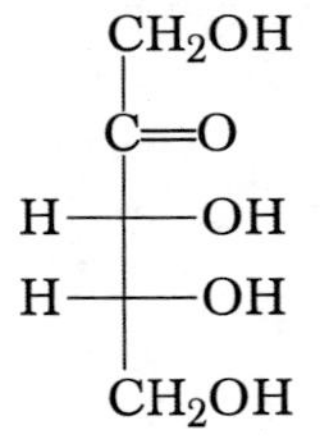

IV.

	Diastereomers	Enantiomers
(a)	I, III and IV	I and III
(b)	I and II	I and III
(c)	I, II and III	I and III
(d)	I and IV	I and II

6. Select the correct statements for the following structure of lactose (carbohydrate).

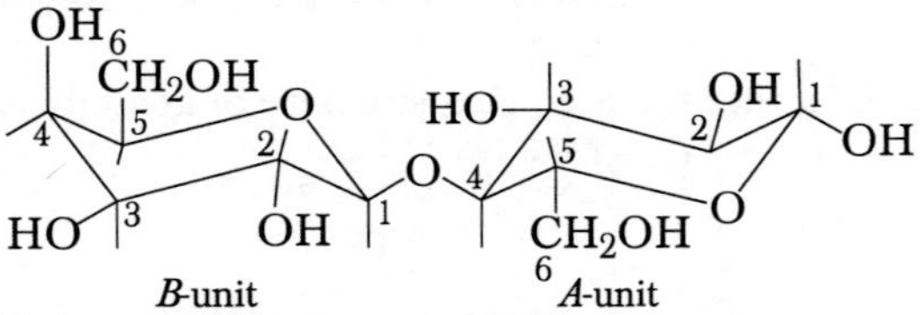

B-unit *A*-unit

(a) there is a free anomeric OH
(b) β-galactoside linkage is used
(c) *A* and *B* units are respectively D-glucose and D-galactose

(d) *A* and *B* are pyranoses joined through the C^4 OH of the *A*-unit

7. The correct statement(s) about the following sugars *X* and *Y* is (are)

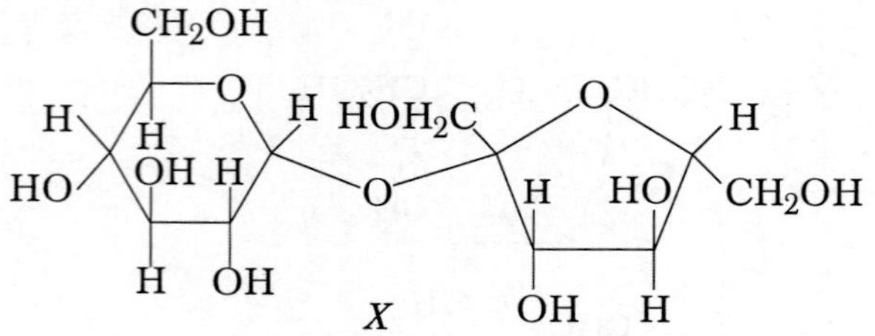

X

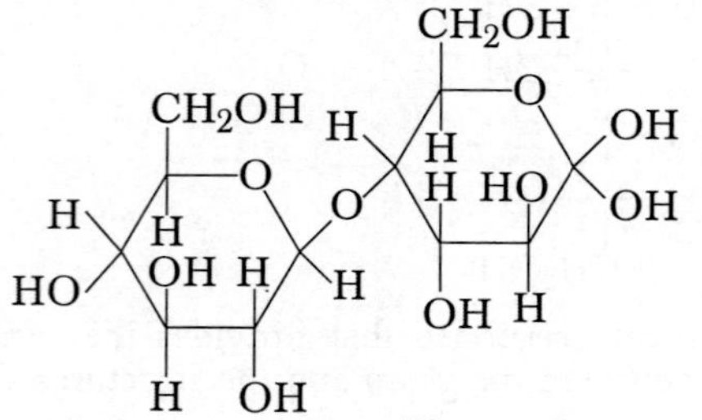

Y

(a) *X* is a reducing sugar and *Y* is a non-reducing sugar.
(b) *X* is a non-reducing sugar and *Y* is a reducing sugar.
(c) The glucosidic linkages in *X* and *Y* are α and β, respectively.
(d) The glucosidic linkages in *X* and *Y* are β and α respectively.

8. Consider the following structure of sucrose.

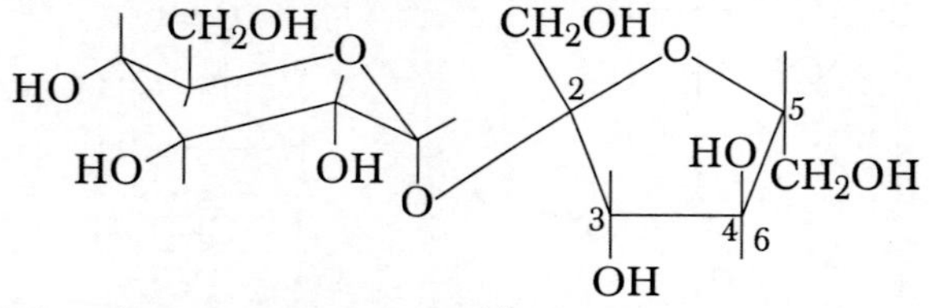

Select the correct statement(s) about this structure.
(a) There are two free anomeric OH.
(b) *D*-glucose and D-fructose are linked by their anomeric OH.
(c) the glucose unit and fructose unit both are pyranosides.
(d) structure can be named as α-D-glucopyranosyl-β-D-fructofuranoside or β-D-fructofuranosyl-α-D-glucopyranoside

9. Consider the following structure of gentiobiose

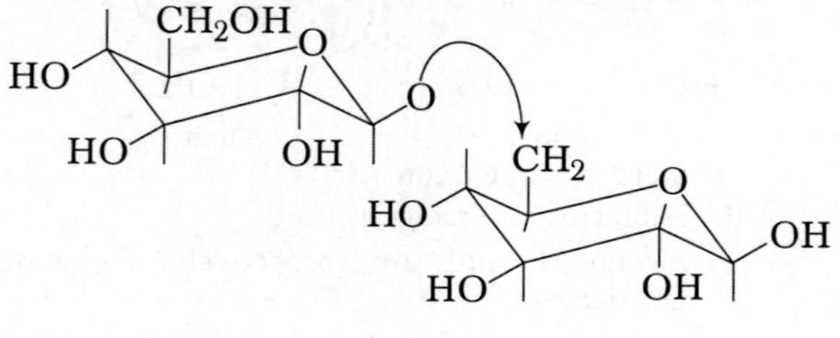

Select the correct statement(s).
(a) It is a β-disaccharide composed of two glucose units
(b) It undergoes mutarotation
(c) It is hydrolysed by emulsion to D-glucose
(d) All of the above

10. Consider the following structure of a nucleosides

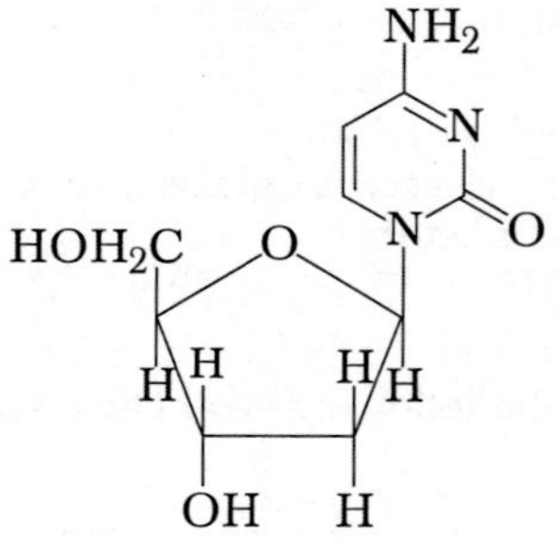

Select the correct statement from the following.
(a) It represents an amino acid joined to sucrose
(b) It represents β-glycosides of D-ribofuranose
(c) It represents β-glycosides of D-deoxyribofuranose
(d) It represents α-glycosides of D-ribofuranose

11. Consider the following structure and select the correct statements.

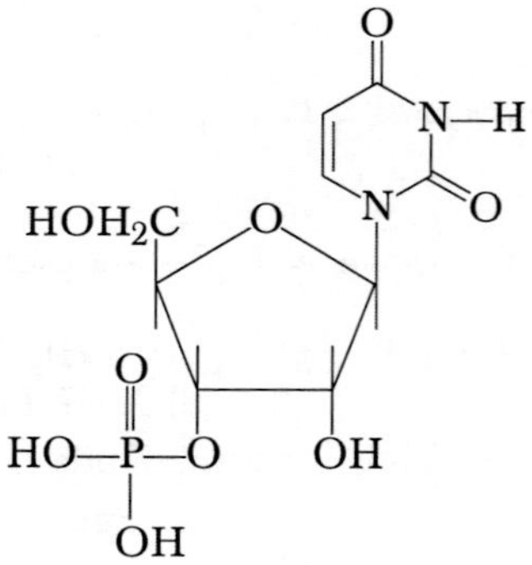

(a) represents a nucleotide
(b) represents a nucleoside
(c) has a base, a sugar and a phosphate group
(d) has an acid, a sugar and a phosphate group

12. Consider the following statements about haemoglobin.

I. It has four separate peptide subunits : two identical α-chains and two identical β-chains each bonded to heme.
II. In CO poisoning, since much of the haemoglobin is tied up with CO, O_2 transport to the tissues is inhibited.
III. Normal haemoglobin found is red blood cells has a glutamic acid residue.

Select the correct statements.
(a) I, II (b) II, III
(c) I, III (d) I, II, III

13. 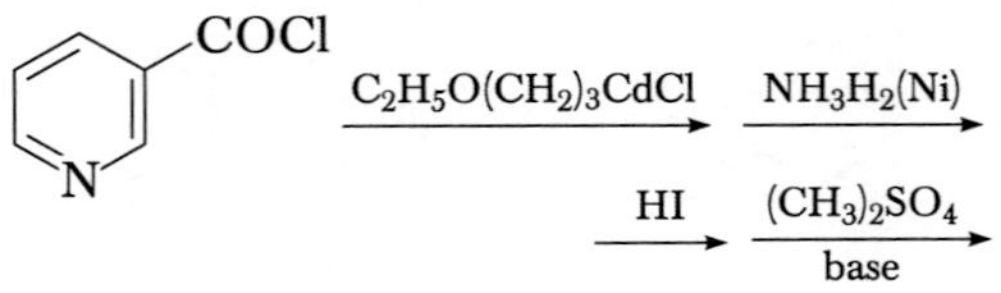

The end product of the reaction is

(a) nicotine (b) quinine

(c) ephedrine (d) piperine

14. 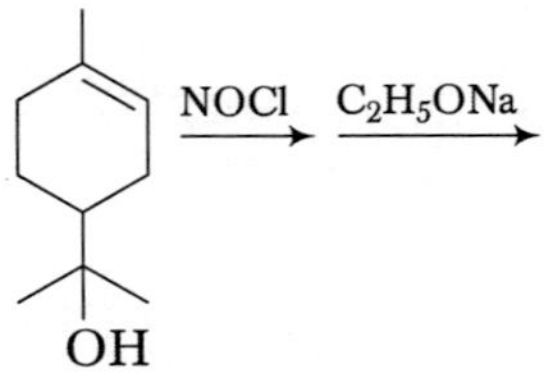

The product of the above reaction is

(a) 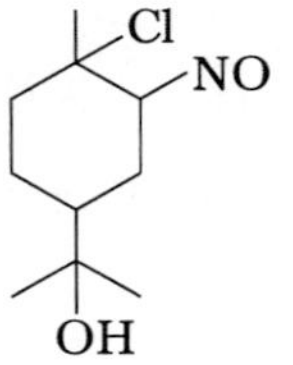

(b) 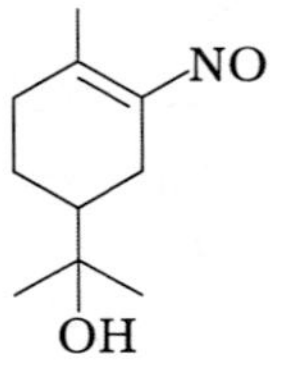

(c) 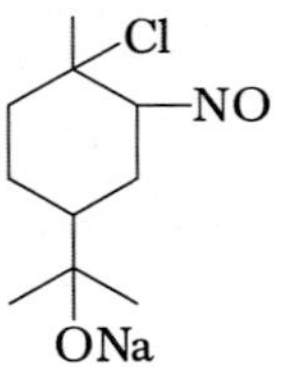

(d) 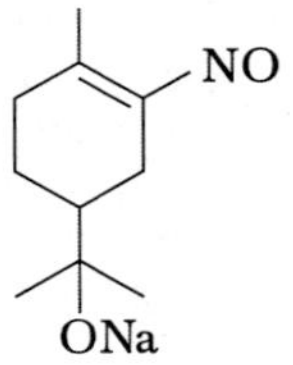

15. Match the following compounds with their respective classes.

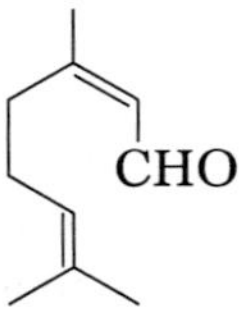

I

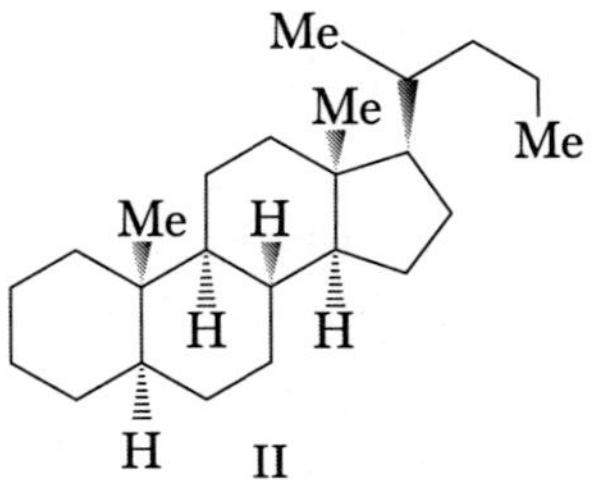

II

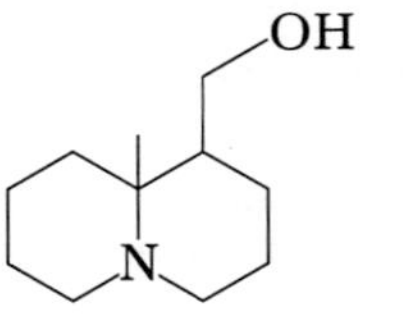

III

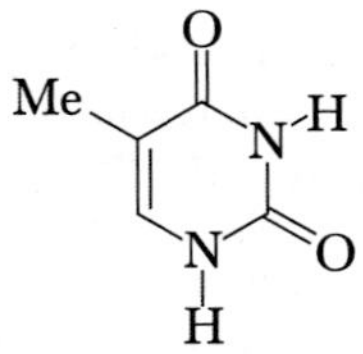

IV

(a) I steroid; II terpenoid; III alkaloid; IV DNA base

(b) I terpenoid; II steroid; III alkaloid; IV DNA base

(c) I terpenoid; II steroid; III DNA base; IV alkaloid

(d) I steroid; II terpenoid; III DNA base; IV alkaloid

16. Identify the correct set of stereochemical relationships amongst the following monosaccharides I-IV.

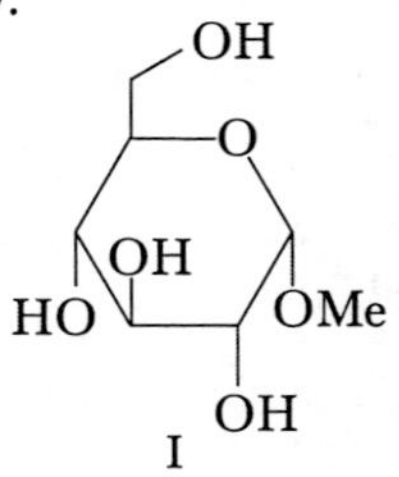

I

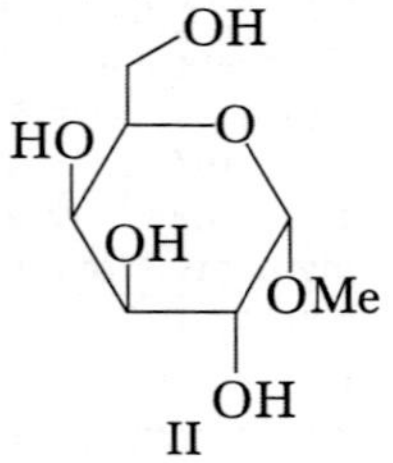

II

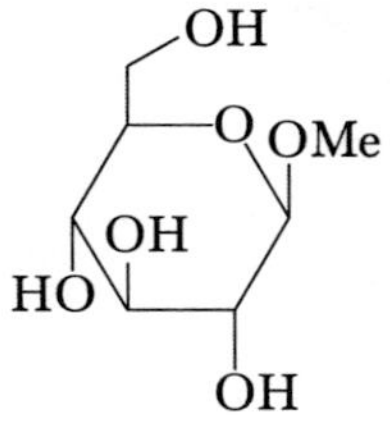

III

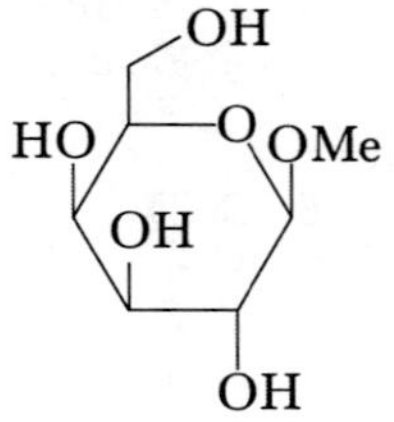

IV

(a) I and II are anomers; III and IV are epimers

(b) I and III are epimers; II and IV are anomers

(c) I and II are epimers; III and IV are anomers

(d) I and III are anomers; I and II are epimers

17. Select the correct pair of statements.

I. Complementary strands run antiparallel in a double stranded DNA.

II. The triplet codons, represented by the genetic code, are expressed by ribonucleic acid.

III. *t*-RNA carries the genetic information to the site of DNA replication.

IV. A nucleoside contains a ribose or deoxyribose and phosphate constituents only.

(a) I, II (b) II, III

(c) III, IV (d) I, IV

Matching Type

18. Match the following precursors (Column I) with alkaloids (Column II) which are biosynthesised by them.

	Column I		Column II
A.	Lysine	1.	Nicotinic acid
B.	Glycerol and aspartic acid	2.	Pepaverine
C.	Tyrosine	3.	Indole alkaloids
D.	Tryptophan	4.	Pelletierines

Codes

	A	B	C	D
(a)	4	1	2	3
(b)	3	2	4	1
(c)	4	1	3	2
(d)	2	3	4	1

19. Match the following Column I with Column II.

	Column I (Statements)		Column II (Natural products)
A.	It is an important acyclic monoterpenoid, occurs up to 80% in lemon grass oil.	1.	Carotenoids
B.	It is used as moth repellent and as preservative in cosmetics.	2.	Citral
C.	They are yellow or red pigments found mainly in plants.	3.	Camphor
D.	It is a straight chain alkaloid that is produced by animal glands and has physiological activity.	4.	Ephedrine

Codes

	A	B	C	D
(a)	3	2	4	1
(b)	2	4	1	3
(c)	2	3	1	4
(d)	2	3	4	1

20. Match the Column I with Column II.

	Column I		Column II
A.	D-fructose	1.	Trisaccharide
B.	D-galactose	2.	Disaccharide
C.	Maltose	3.	Ketohexose
D.	Raffinose	4.	Aldohexose

Codes

	A	B	C	D
(a)	3	4	2	1
(b)	3	4	1	2
(c)	4	3	2	1
(d)	4	3	1	2

21. Consider the following statements.

I. α-pinene contains an exocyclic double bond.
II. Dipentene is (±) limonene.
III. Camphor is a bicyclic compound.
IV. Stigmasterol is commercially obtained from soyabean oil.

Select the correct statements.

(a) I, II, IV (b) II, III
(c) II, III, IV (d) I, III

22. Identify the end product of the following reaction.

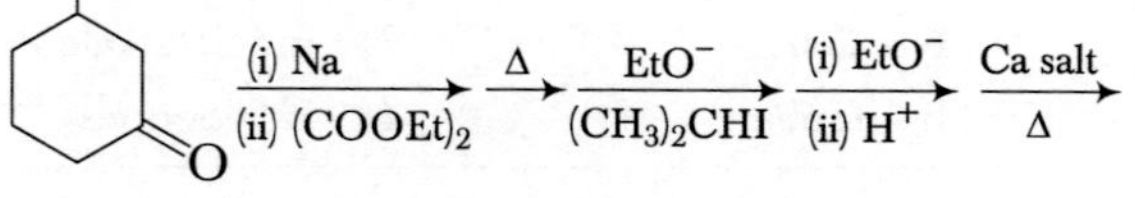

(a) 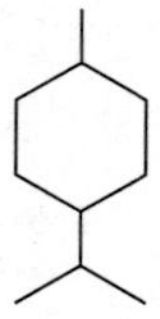

(b) 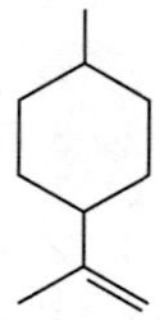

(c) 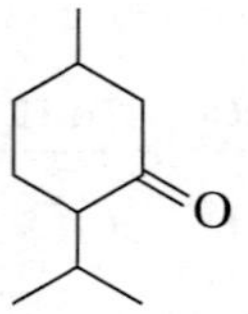

(d) 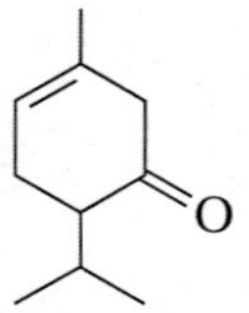

23. Which of the following alkaloid is obtained by heating tropine and atropic acid in presence of HCl?

(a) Atropine (b) Nicotine
(c) Codeine (d) Coniine

24. 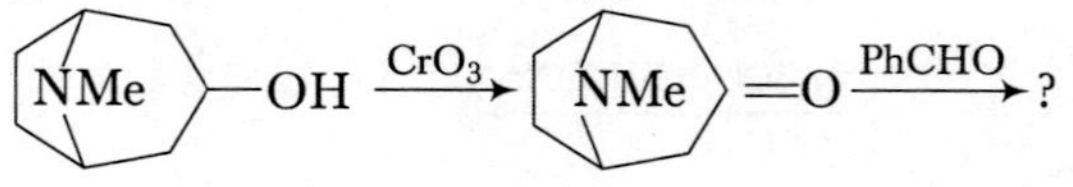

The product is

(a) 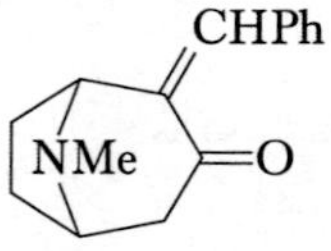

(b) 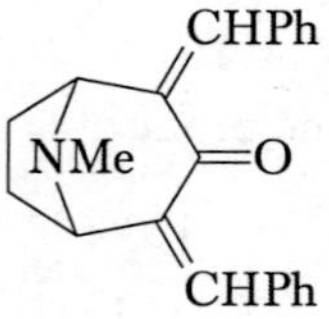

(c) 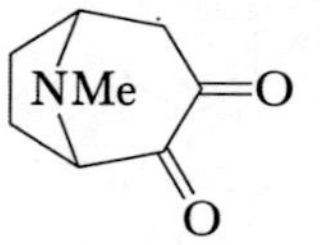

(d) None of these

25. Which of the following statements is incorrect?

(a) Ergosterol is a steroid.
(b) Steroids are characterised by the presence of a 1,2-cyclopentenophenanthrene ring system
(c) Testosterone contains a α, β-unsaturated ketonic group
(d) Progesterone does not give haloform reaction.

Assertion & Reason

Codes

(a) Both A and R are true and R is the correct explanation of A.
(b) Both A and R are true but R is not the correct explanation of A.
(c) A is true but R is false.
(d) A is false but R is true.

26. Assertion (A) Reduction of fructose with $NaBH_4$ forms two products differing in configuration.

Reason (R) A chiral carbon is formed due to reduction of keto group at C_2.

27. Assertion (A) A peptide bond has about 40% double bond character.

Reason (R) Steric hindrance causes the *trans* configuration to be more stable than the *cis* configuration.

28. Assertion (A) Cellulose on treatment with excess of CH_3I in presence of Ag_2O followed by hydrolysis yields 2, 3, 6-tri-O-methyl-D-glucose.

Reason (R) Cellulose is a polymer of D-glucose.

29. Assertion (A) Cortisone reduces alkaline solution of silver nitrate and Fehling's solution.

Reason (R) Cortisone contains α-ketol group.

30. Isoprene + Methyl vinyl ketone $\xrightarrow{\text{Diel's Alder reaction}}$ $\xrightarrow[\text{(ii) } H^+]{\text{(i) } CH_3MgBr}$ Product

Identify the product.

(a) α-pinene (b) α-terpineol
(c) Citral (d) Menthol

31. Identify the end product of the following reaction

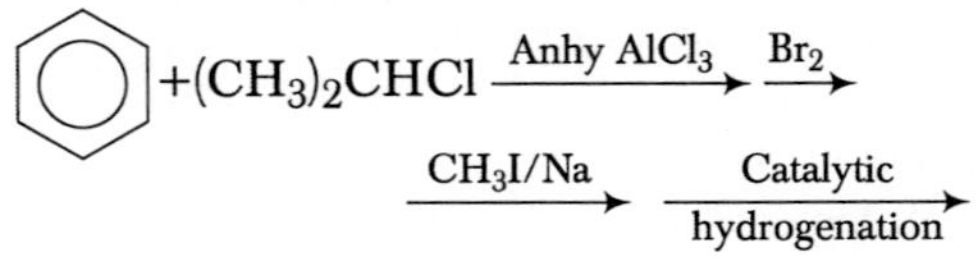

(a) 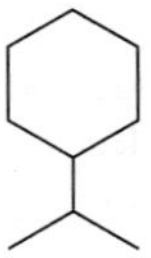 (b) 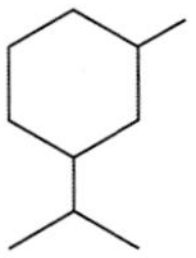

(c) 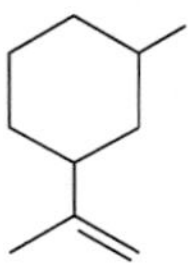 (d) 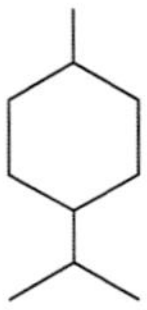

32. α-terpineol on dehydration with oxalic acid to give

(a) terpinolene (b) dipentene
(c) Both (a) and (b) (d) None of these

33. Exposing an organism to a certain chemical can change nucleotide bases in a gene, causing mutation. In one such mutated organism if a protein had only 70% of the primary amino acid sequence, which of the following is likely?

(a) Mutation broke the protein
(b) The organism could not make amino acids
(c) Mutation created a terminator codon
(d) The gene was not transcribed

34. The major product formed in the reaction sequence is

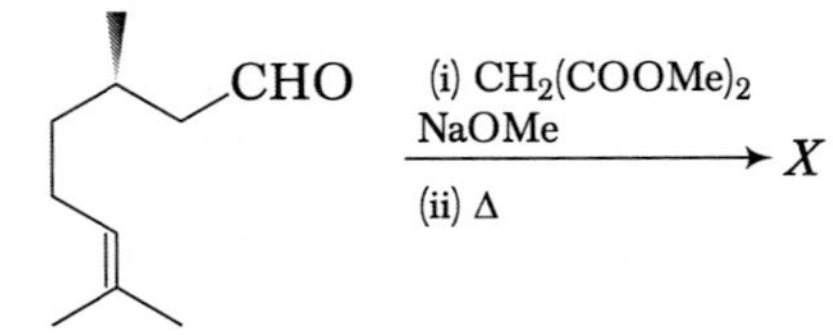

(Citronellal)

(a) 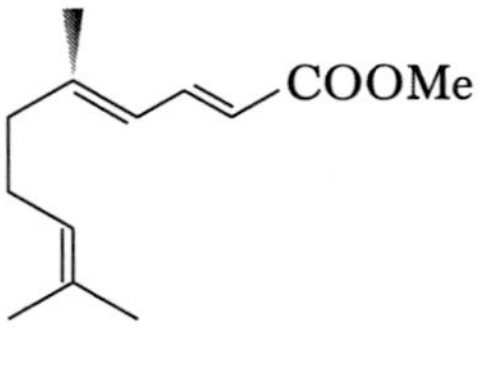

(b) 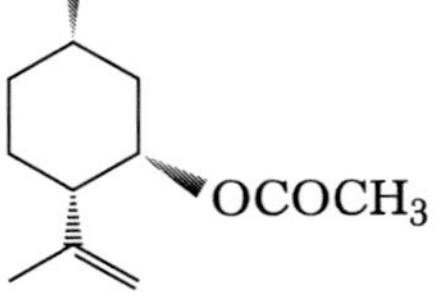

(c) 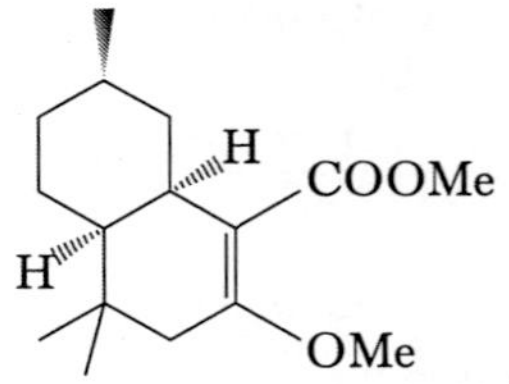

(d) 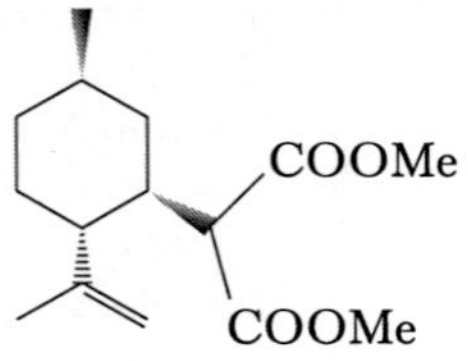

35. The major product formed in the reaction of glucose with benzaldehyde and *p*-TSA is

(a) 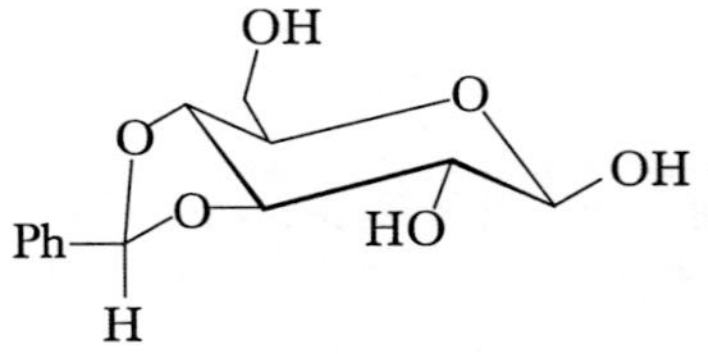

(b) 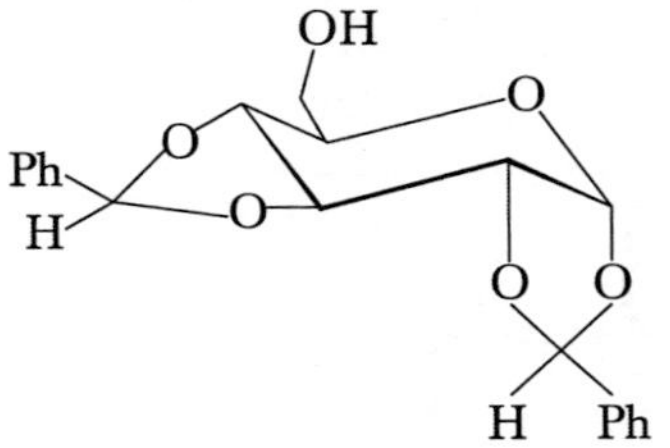

(c) 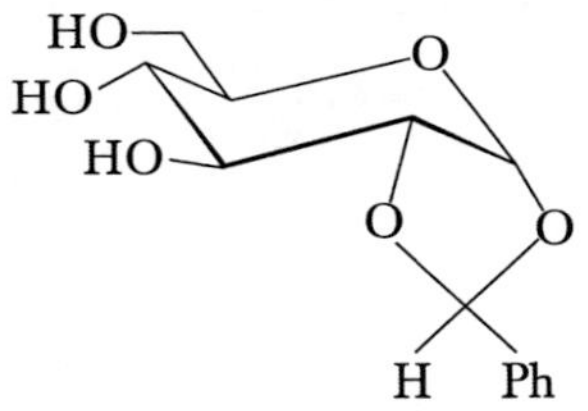

(d) 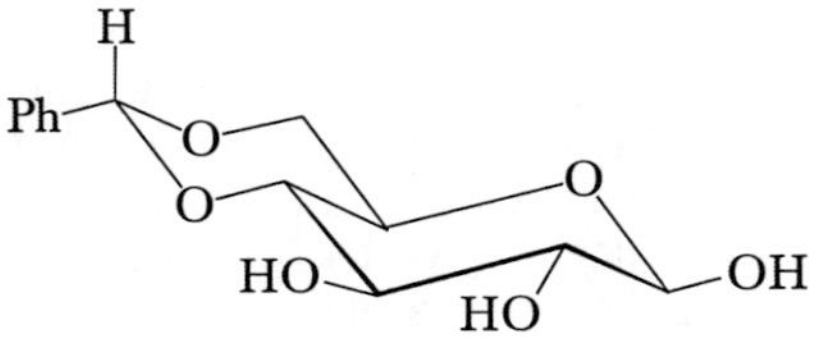

36. Which of the following group/s is/are present in testosterone hormone?

(a) Alcoholic (b) Ketonic
(c) Aldehydic (d) Carboxylic

Directions (Q.Nos. 37 and 38)

Say the word sugar and most people immediately think of sweet tasting candies, desserts and suck. With sucrose as a reference point, fructose is heavily twice as sweet, but lactose is only about one-sixth as sweet. The desire of many people to cut caloric intake has led to the development of synthetic sweetners.

37. Which is not the synthetic sweetener?

(a) Aspartame (b) Saccharin
(c) Cyclamate (d) Fructose

38. Which is incorrect grading of sugars?

Sugar	Sweetness
(a) Sucrose	1.00
(b) Fructose	1.75
(c) Lactose	6.00
(d) Saccharin	3500

Directions (Q. Nos. 39 and 40)

You have been given a mixture of alanine, lysine and aspartic acid in a buffer at pH 6. The isoelectric point of

alanine : 6

lysine : 9.7

aspartic acid : 2.8

A voltage is applied to this mixture. Answer the following questions based on the above experimental facts.

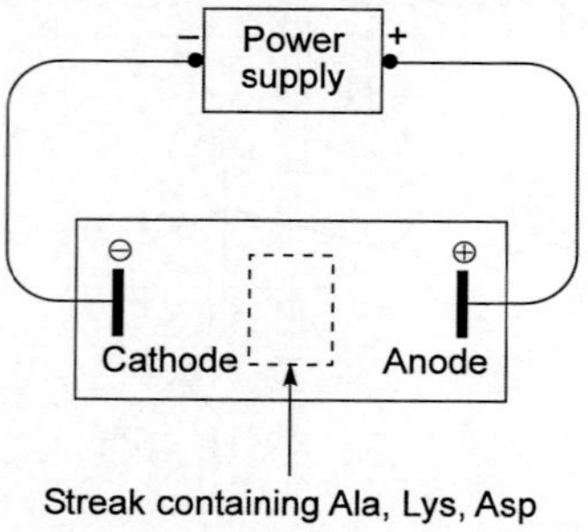

39. Consider the following statements.
Under the influence of an electric field

I. Ala does not move.

II. Aspartic acid is in anionic form and moves towards the anode.

III. Lysine is in cationic form and moves towards cathode.

IV. Above method is based on electrodialysis.

Select the correct statements.

(a) all but IV
(b) all but III
(c) all but I
(d) all but I and IV

40. Difference in isoelectric points can be used to separate the mixture of amino acids by

(a) electrodialysis (b) electrophoresis
(c) potentiometry (d) polarography

Answers

Exercise 1

1. (d)	**2.** (a)	**3.** (a)	**4.** (a)	**5.** (b)	**6.** (d)	**7.** (a)	**8.** (c)	**9.** (b)	**10.** (c)
11. (d)	**12.** (c)	**13.** (c)	**14.** (d)	**15.** (d)	**16.** (c)	**17.** (a)	**18.** (c)	**19.** (c)	**20.** (d)
21. (a)	**22.** (b)	**23.** (d)	**24.** (a)	**25.** (b)	**26.** (a)	**27.** (b)	**28.** (a)	**29.** (b)	**30.** (d)
31. (c)	**32.** (b)	**33.** (c)	**34.** (a)	**35.** (d)	**36.** (b)	**37.** (a)	**38.** (c)	**39.** (d)	**40.** (b)
41. (d)	**42.** (c)	**43.** (b)	**44.** (a)	**45.** (a)	**46.** (a)	**47.** (b)	**48.** (b)	**49.** (b)	**50.** (a)
51. (b)	**52.** (b)	**53.** (b)	**54.** (a)	**55.** (b)	**56.** (d)	**57.** (b)	**58.** (b)	**59.** (a)	**60.** (d)

Exercise 2

1. (c)	**2.** (a)	**3.** (a)	**4.** (a)	**5.** (b)	**6.** (a,b,c,d)	**7.** (b,c)	**8.** (b,d)	**9.** (d)	**10.** (b)
11. (a,c)	**12.** (d)	**13.** (a)	**14.** (b)	**15.** (b)	**16.** (d)	**17.** (d)	**18.** (a)	**19.** (c)	**20.** (a)
21. (c)	**22.** (c)	**23.** (a)	**24.** (b)	**25.** (d)	**26.** (a)	**27.** (b)	**28.** (b)	**29.** (a)	**30.** (b)
31. (d)	**32.** (a)	**33.** (c)	**34.** (d)	**35.** (d)	**36.** (a,b)	**37.** (d)	**38.** (c)	**39.** (a)	**40.** (b)

Hints & Solutions

Exercise 1

2. $$\underset{\text{CH}_2\text{OH}}{\overset{\text{CHO}}{(\text{CHOH})_4}} \xrightarrow{\text{HCN}} \underset{\text{CH}_2\text{OH}}{\overset{\text{CN}}{(\text{CHOH})(\text{CHOH})_4}} \xrightarrow{\text{H}_3\text{O}^+} \underset{\text{CH}_2\text{OH}}{\overset{\text{COOH}}{(\text{CHOH})(\text{CHOH})_4}} \xrightarrow{\text{P/HI}} \underset{\text{CH}_3}{\overset{\text{COOH}}{(\text{CH}_2)_5}}$$

n-heptanoic acid

Due to —CHO group C-chain is increased.

9. It is a cyclic hemiacetal of ketose. Since, two —CH_2OH groups are on opposite side of ring, it is a β-furanose.

10. 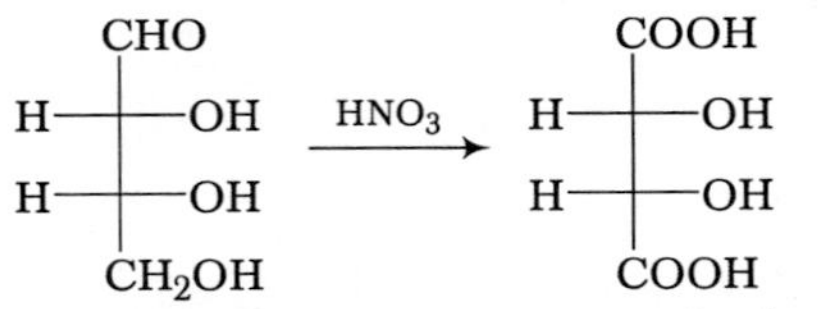

D-tetrose → *meso*-diacid

11. 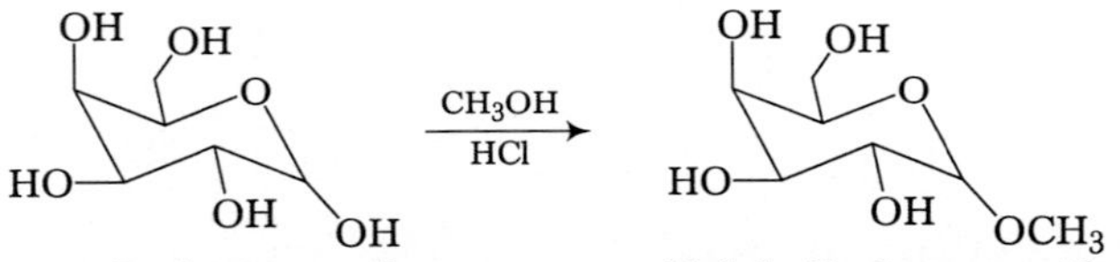

α-D-galactopyranoside → Methyl-α-D-galactopyranoside

15. Adding SDS during electrophoresis of amino acids preserve the proteins native and biological activity.

24. Phenyl isothiocyanate is known as Edman degradation.

25. 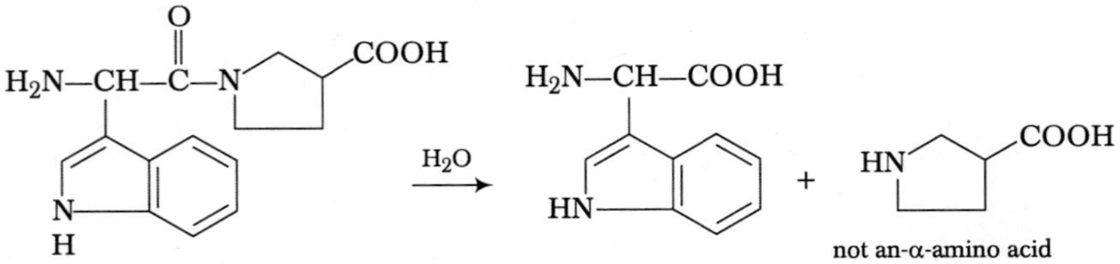

not an-α-amino acid

(Dipeptide is formed by joining up of two α-amino acids.)

26. The six-membered cyclic ether is known as pyranose while the five membered cyclic ether is known as furanose. Hence, ring (A) is a pyranose and it has ether linkage at α-position that is known as α-glycosidic linkage in carbohydrate chemistry.

33. Zingiberene is a monocyclic sesquiterpenoid. It occurs in the (–) form in ginger oil. Its structure is as :

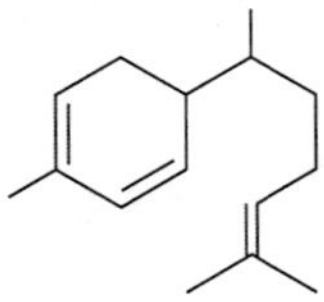

36. On hydration with H_2SO_4, myrcene yields an alcohol which on oxidation gives citral.

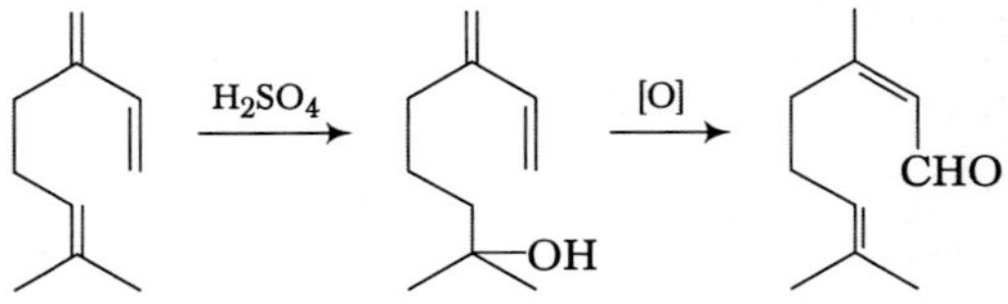

Myrcene → Myrcenol → Citral

37. Geraniol reacts with dilute sulphuric acid to give α-terpineol which is a cyclic terpene.

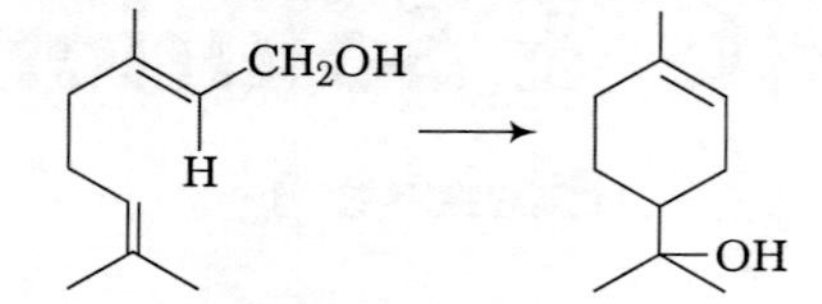

41. β-carotene on oxidation with aqueous $KMnO_4$ to give β-ionone.

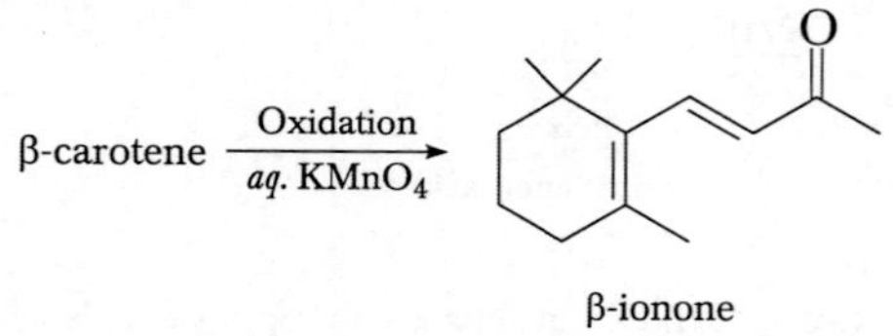

45.

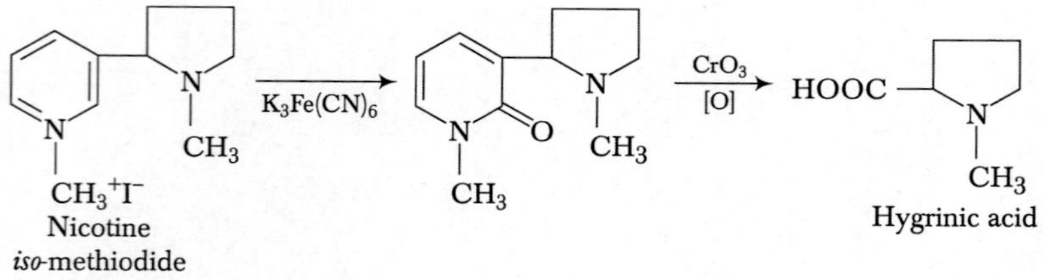

55.

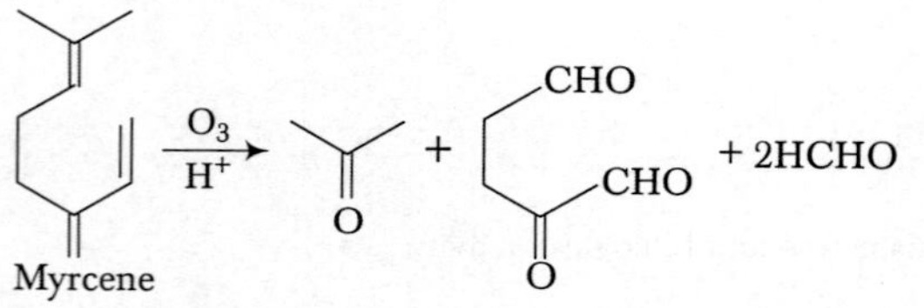

56.

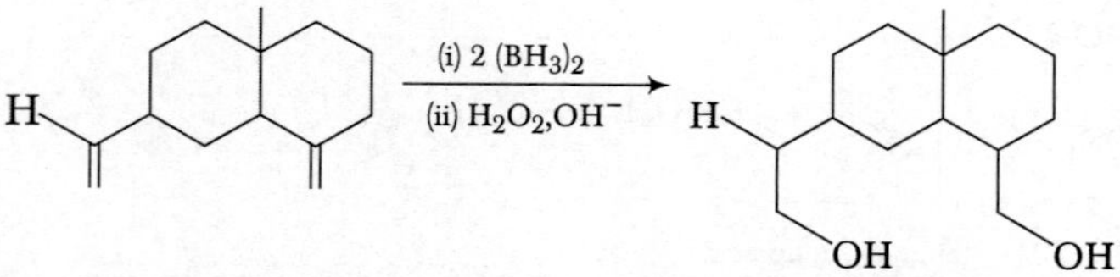

It is the hydroboration-oxidation reaction of alkene hence addition of water to double bond is according to anti-Markownikoff's rule.

59.

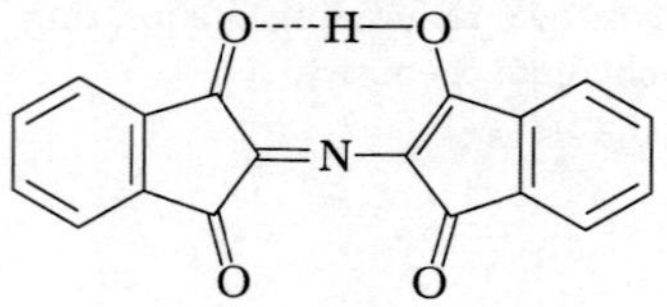

is responsible for purpule colour in ninhydrin test irrespective of α-amino acids.

Exercise 2

4.

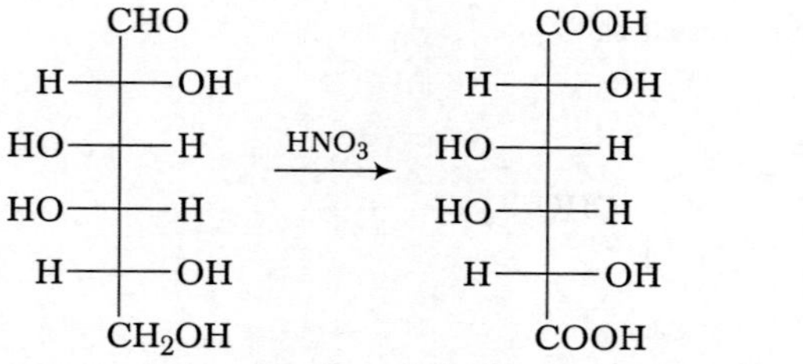

Hence, cyclic hemiacetal form of D-monosaccharide is

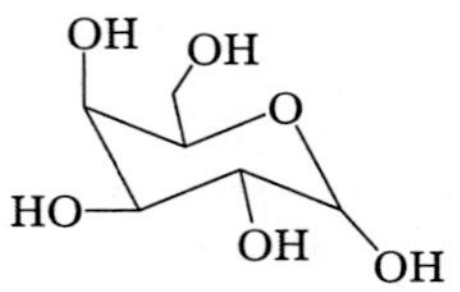

2,3 —OH are *trans* and 3, 4 —OH are *cis*.

7. *X* is acetal, has no free hemiacetal, hence a non-reducing sugar while *Y* has a free hemiacetal group, it is reducing sugar. Also, glucosidic linkage of *X* is 'α' while that of *Y* is β-linkage.

13.

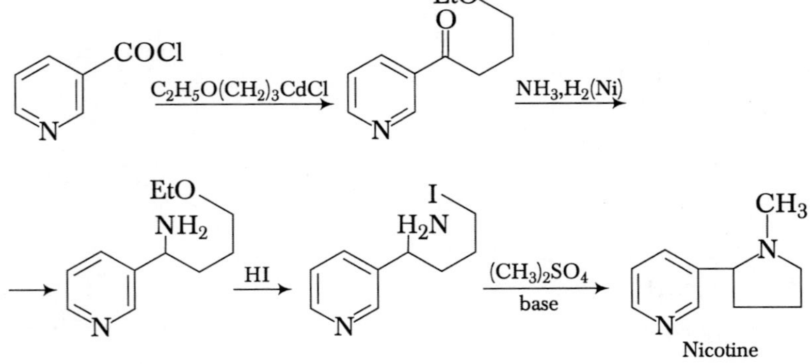

14.

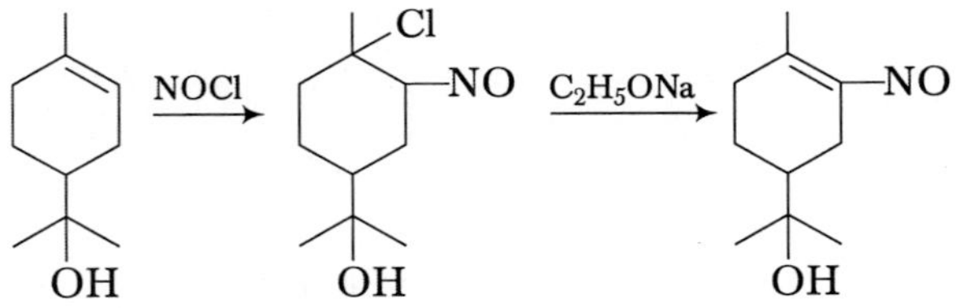

21.

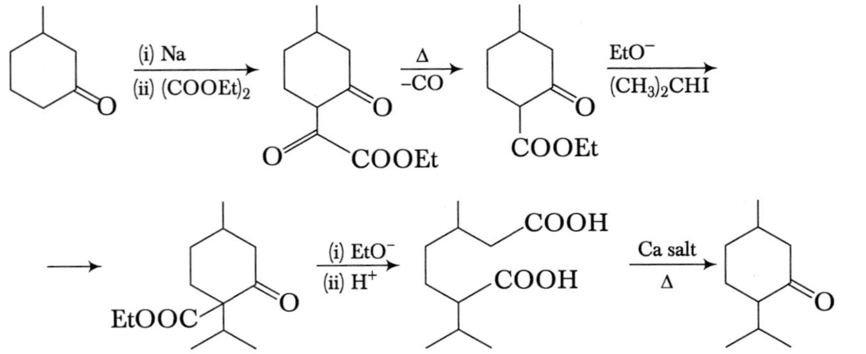

22.

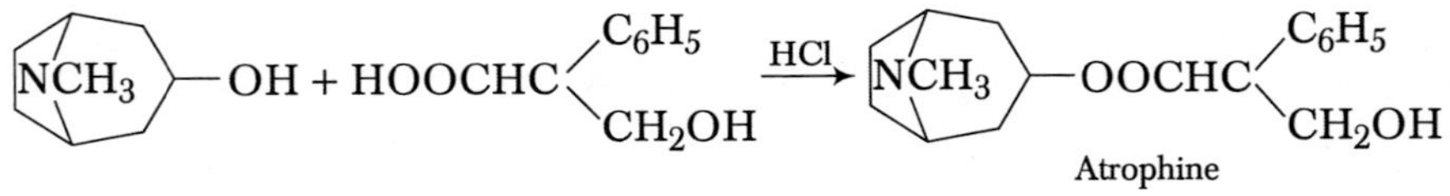

23. Tropine gives tropinone on oxidation which forms of dibenzylidene derivative with benzaldehyde.

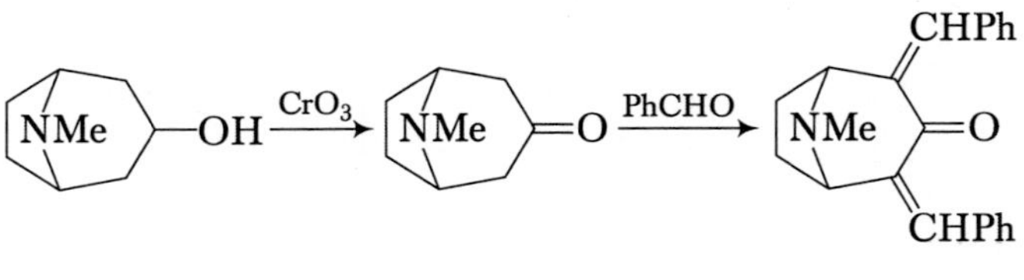

24. When progesterone is heated with halogens and NaOH, it gives haloform due to the presence of $CH_3—\overset{O}{\overset{\|}{C}}—$ group.

27. Cellulose has three free —OH groups per repeating unit hence, trimethylation takes place.

28. Cortisone contains α-ketol (—$COCH_2OH$) group hence, it reduces alkaline solution of silver nitrate and Fehling's solution.

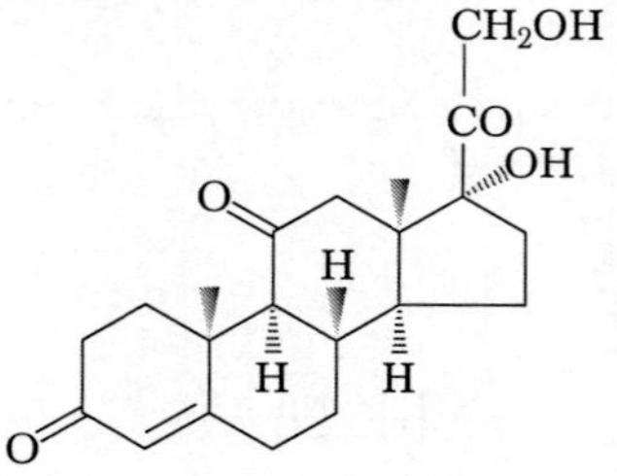

29.

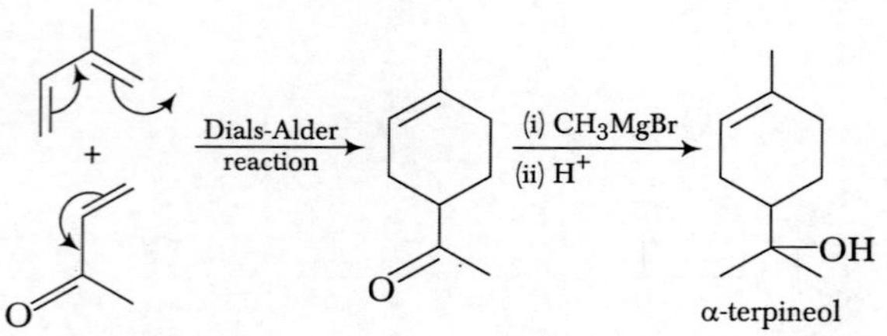

30.

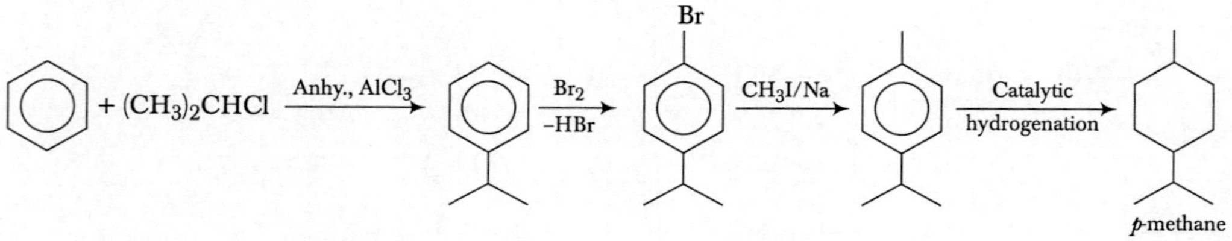

32.

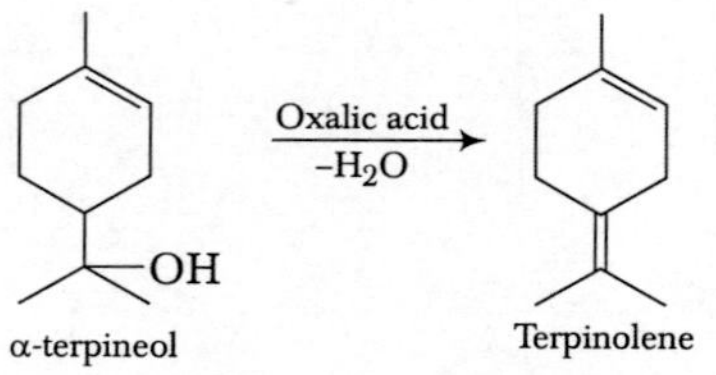

On dehydration with $KHSO_4$, α-terpineol gives dipentene.

39 Interdisciplinary Topics

Syllabus

- Chemistry of Nanoscience and Technology
- Catalysis and Green Chemistry
- Medicinal Chemistry
- Supramolecular Chemistry
- Environmental Chemistry

Chemistry in Nanoscience and Technology

Engineers and scientists concerted with development and practical applications of advanced materials need to understand the microstructure and macrostructure of various materials and the ways of controlling them. Microstructure is the structure of material at a length-scale of ~ 10 to 1000 nm. Length-scale is a characteristic length or range of dimensions over which we are describing the properties of a material or the phenomena occurring in materials. Microstructure typically includes such features as average grain size, grain size distribution, grain orientation, and other features related to defects in materials (A grain is a portion of the material within which the arrangement of atoms is nearly identical). Macrostructure is the structure of a material at a macroscopic level where the length-scale is ~ > 1000 nm. Features that constitute macrostructure include porosity, surface coatings, the such features as internal or external micro-cracks.

It is also important to understand atomic structure and how the atomic bonds lead to different atomic or ionic arrangements in materials. The atomic structure includes all atoms and their arrangements, which constitute the building blocks that all the nano, micro, and macrolevels of structures emerge.

Properties and behaviour of materials at these "micro" levels can vary greatly when compared to those in their "macro" or bulk state. As a result, understanding the structure at nanoscale or nanostructure (*i.e.,* the structure and properties of materials at a nanoscale or length scale 1-100 nm) and microstructure are areas that have received considerable attention. The term "nanotechnology" is used to describe a set of technologies that are based on physical, chemical, and biological phenomena occurring at nanoscale.

Fullerenes and nanotubes, recently discovered, are the building blocks of a new class of ordered materials spherical fullerene C_{60} molecules can assemble in fcc crystal called fullerites and single-wall nanotubes can gather in ropes, the cross section of which makes an hexagonal lattice. These structures, called nanocrystals differ from ordinary crystals in many points. In particular, they have spatial periods of the order of 1 nm, which is much larger than those of ordinary crystals (typically 0.2 nm).

According to the operative definition, nanotechnology relate presently to nano structured objects with crucial dimensions below 100 nm. The objects could be 0-(particles), 1-(rods, tubes) or 2-dimensional (layers, films).

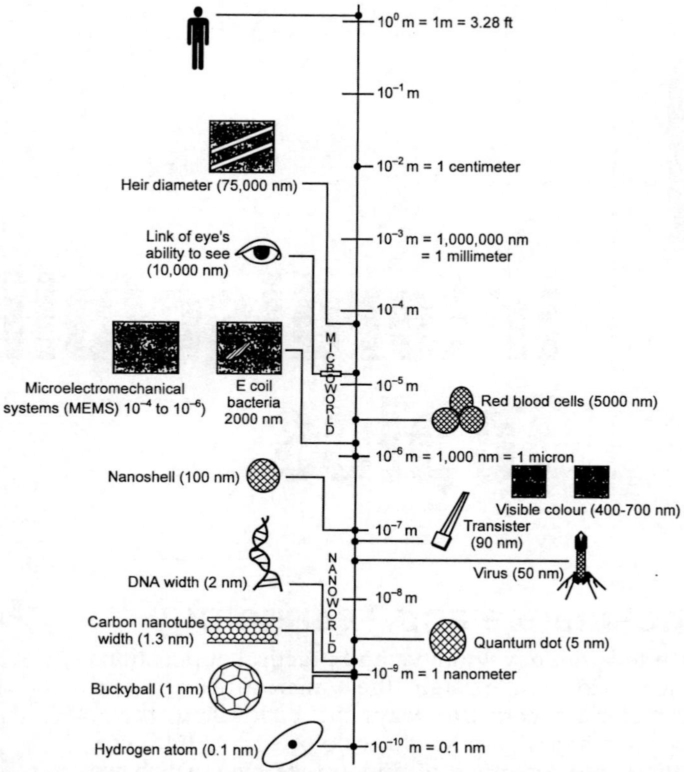

Fig. 39.1 Size comparisons, from person (1.75 m, or approximately 5 ft. 7 in.) all the way down to the hydrogen atom. (0.1 nm)

Table 39.1

Level of structure	Example of technologies	Approximate length-scale
Nanostructure	Nano-sized particles (– 5-10 nm) of iron oxide are used in ferrofluids or liquid magnets	$\sim 10^{-9}$ to 10^{-7} m (1 to 100 nm)
Microstructure	The mechanical strength of many metals and alloys depends very strongly on the grain size. The grains and grain boundaries in this accompanying micrograph of steel are part of the microstructural features of this crystalline material. In general, at room temperature a finer grain size leads to higher strength.	$\sim >10^{-8}$ to 10^{-6} m (10 nm to 1000 nm)
Macrostructure	In automobiles to provide corrosion resistance.	$\sim 10^{-4}$ m (1000 nm)
Atomic structure	**Diamond** is based on carbon-carbon (C–C) covalent bonds. Materials with this type of bonding are expected to be relatively hard. Thin films of diamonds are used for providing a wear-resistant edge in cutting tools.	~ Up to 10^{-10} m or 1 Å
Atomic Arrangements Long-Range Order (LRO)	Lead-zirconium-titanate [$Pb(Zr_x\ Ti_{1-x})$] or PZT When ions in this material are arranged such that they exhibit tetragonal and/or rhombohedral crystal structures, the material is piezoelectric (*i.e.*, it develops a voltage when subjected to pressure or stress). PZT ceramics are used widely for many applications including gas igniters, ultrasound generation, and vibration control.	$\sim 10^{-10}$ to 10^{-9} m (1 to 10 Å), ordering can exist up to a few cm in larger crystals
Atomic Arrangements Short-Range Order (SRO)	Ions in silica (SiO_2) glass exhibit only a short-range order in which Si^{4+} and O^{2-} ions are arranged in a particular way (each Si^{4+} is bonded with $4O^{2-}$ ions in a tetrahedral coordination). This order, however, is not maintained over long distances, thus make silica glass amorphous. Amorphous silica glasses based on silica and certain other form the basis for the entire fiber optical communications industry.	$\sim 10^{-10}$ to 10^{-9} m (1 to 10 Å)

Carbon Nanotubles (CNT's)

There are many allotropes of carbon like cubic diamond, hexagonal dimaond, graphite, fullerenes C_{60} and C_{70}. In 1991, Ijima discovered single wall carbon nanotubes (SWCNT's). In recent years, world wide as well as India, the focus in condensed matter research is on nanomaterials of these, carbon nanotubes (CNT's) are the most studied. Carbon nanotubes have unique and fascinating structural, mechanical, electronic and chemical properties. They have novel applications such as pressure-flow sensors nanoscale electronic devices, high strength composites, catalyst, light weight batteries and hydrogen-storage devices.

A carbon nanotube can be regarded as one gigantic carbon molecule (fullerene) which is obtained by folding graphite planes into a cylinder whose diameter is measured in nanometers and whose length can reach macroscopic dimensions. This linear structure determines the extremely high mechanical strength of nanotubes whereas their electrical conductivity depends strongly on the diameter and the helicity which is the angle between the most highly packed chains of atoms and the axis of the cylinder. There exist nanotubes whose walls contain a single layer of atoms (single wall nanotubes or SWNT) and nanotubes with walls consisting of several concentric or onion-like layers (multi-wall nanotubes, or MWNT).

Geometrical Structure of Nanotubes

A single wall carbon nanotube can be thought of as a graphene sheet rolled up into a cylinder with caps made up of C hemispheres. In general, SWNT can be specified in terms of the diameter, *d* and chiral angle, θ as shown in the following Fig. 39.2.

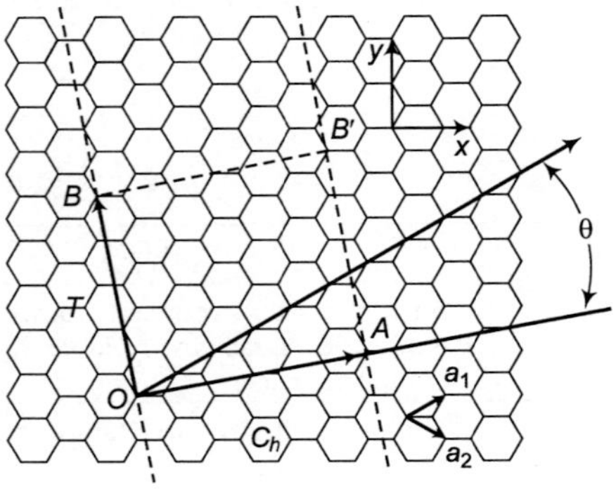

Fig. 39.2 The chiral vector $C_h = na_1 + ma_2$ is defined on the honeycomb lattice of carbon atoms by unit vectors a_1 and a_2 and the chiral angle θ with respect to the *zig-zag* axis. Also the lattice vector $OB = T$ of 1 D tubule unit cell is shown. The diagram is constructed for $(n, m) = (4, 2)$.

A carbon nanotube is a cylinder of carbon atoms covalently bonded together sort of like a sheet of graphite rolled into a cylinder. Some of these cylinders are closed at the ends and some are open. Each carbon atom is bonded to three other carbon atoms and forms a lattice in the shape of hexagons (six-sided rings of carbon atoms), except near the end. For nanotubes with closed ends, where the ends start to curve to form a cap the lattice forms pentagons (five-sided rings of carbon atoms).

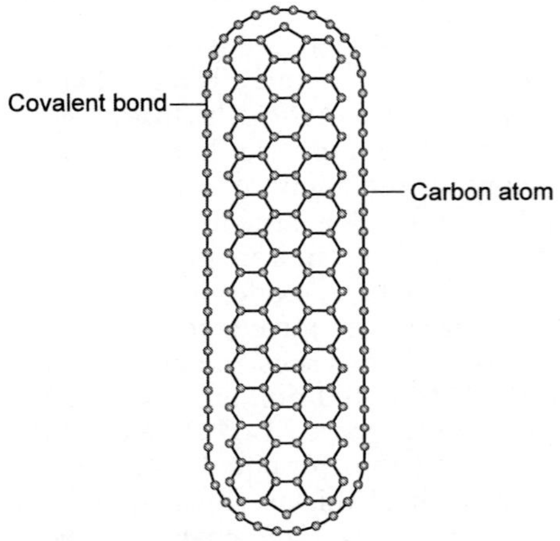

Fig. 39.3 Illustration of a carbon nanotube.

The chiral vector is defined as

$$C_h = na_1 + ma_2$$

which connects two crystallographically equivalent sites *O* and *A* on a two dimensional graphene sheet a_1 and a_2 are the unit vectors of the honeycomb lattice connecting two inequivalent sites; *n* and *m* are integers.

The chiral angle θ is given by

$$\theta = \tan^{-1}\left[\frac{\sqrt{3}m}{(m+2n)}\right]$$

Depending on the θ value SWNT's can be classified into three categories, armchair tube (θ = 30°), *zig-zag* tube (θ = 0°) and chiral tube (0°< θ < 30°). Each SWNT can be specified by the pair of integers (n, m).

Armchair tube (n, n) : $n \neq m$

Zig-zag tube $(n, 0)$: $m \neq 0$

Chiral tube (n, m) : $n \neq m \neq 0$

The lattice can be oriented differently, which makes for three different kinds of nanotubes. As shown in the Fig. 39.4 in armchair nanotubes, there is a line of hexagones parallel to the axis of the nanotube. In *zig-zag* nanotubes, there's a line of carbon bonds down the centre. Chiral nanotubes exhibit a twist or spiral (called chirality) around the nanotube.

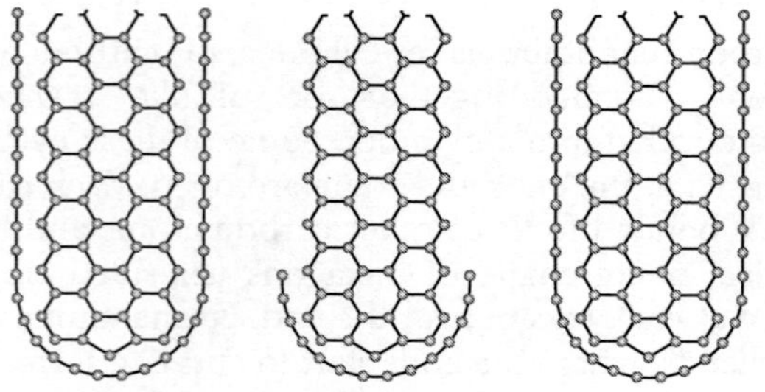

Fig. 39.4 Armchair, *zig-zag*, and chiral nanotubes.

Thin film (2-dimensional) are grown by sol-gel with spin-coating or by atomic layer chemical layer deposition (ALCLD). Whereas the former gives films in the range 50 – 1000 nm, the latter provides a real means to control and monitor chemical composition, microstructure and crystal structure at the atomic level. By means of ALCLD, tailored superlattices are made by combining 2D-slabs of oxides with different physical properties. These multilayered materials, with individual layer thicknesses tunable from 0.5 nm (monolayer) to 50 or 100 nm, are expected to exhibit novel physical properties. ALCLD can furthermore be used to providing thin, oriented, substrate layers for subsequent growth of thicker films by MOCLD (MO for metal oyenic) or spin-coating. The ALCLD technique may provide ultrathin films that are dense pinhole-free, and coat conformally. This is highly beneficial for coatings in relation to semiconductor for physics and semiconductors for power electronics. ALCLD/MOCLD as well as spin coating can furthermore be used for ferroelectric and piezoelectric thin films.

Properties of Nanomaterials

1. Nanotubes are really strong. Tensile strength is measure of the amount of force an object can withstand without tearing apart. The tensile strength of carbon nanotubes is 100 times greater than that of steel of the same diameter. The materials have super hardness.
2. Thermal properties such as melting point depend on size as shown for gold in the graph given below.

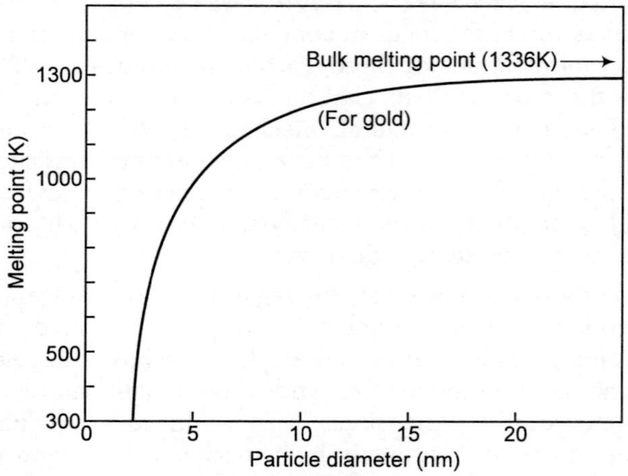

Fig. 39.5

Quantum Dot

A quantum dot is defined as :

A crystal of semiconductor compound (*e.g.*, CdSe, PdS) with a diameter on the order of the compounds Exciton Bohr Radius. Quantum dots have a range of useful electrical and optical properties that diverge in character from these of bulk material. Quantum dots are between 2 and 10 nanometers wide (10 and 50 atoms). [1 million QD's lined up end to end is of 1/5 of inch].

Quantum dots are a new form of matter that can be considered as artificial atoms. They have linear discrete absorption spectra and photoluminescence that is tunable over a wide range from far infrared to deep ultraviolet.

Applications of Nanomaterials

Table 39.2 **Applications of Nanophase Materials**

S.No.	Field/Product	Applications	Examples	Features
1.	Electrical devices	Ceramic capacitors	$BaTiO_3$	Smaller size, reduced power losses, enhanced capacitance values for a given component size.
2.	Thermostats	Devices for thermal protection, current controlling devices	ZnO	High sensitivity to temperature, low lossess, smaller size.
3.	Magnetic devices	RAM, READ/WRITE heads, sensors	Cu-Fe alloys	High performance, improve sensitivity.
4.	Inks, pastes, slurries	Screen printing, ink-jet printing, powder impregnating, spin coating	$BaTiO_3$ $SiCSnO_2$ $ZnOZrO_2$ ferrites	Dispersion is easily controlled, wide variation in viscosity can be accommodated.
5.	Additives	Additions for powder coating of ceramic devices.	$BaTiO_3$ ZnO	Reduction in processing time, cost and higher productivity.

Quantum dot LEDs (QLED)

Traditional LEDs suffer large application restrictions due to limitations in traditional semiconductors, including difficult to alter bandgaps and inflexible structure. QLEDs, made of quantum dots, can emit at any visible or infrared wavelength, and can be fabricated into plastic, coatings, paint, filters and other forms, allowing them to be used almost anywhere.

Optoelectronics

Desirable properties include broad photoluminescence (PL) tunability, high PL quantum efficiency, and enhanced non-linear optical properties. Applications include tunable IR-UV lasers and LEDs, display luminophores, optical electro-modulation, switches, memory storage, optical limiting, DNA sites markers, and efficient sensors of explosives and toxic materials.

Quantum dots are also possible materials for making ultrafast, all-optical switches and logic gates. For comparison, the Ethernet generally can handle only 10 megabits.

Quantum information processing

Desirable properties include enhanced spin level splitting, single electron-spin manipulation, and very long spin-coherence times. Applications include spin-transistors, nanosize magnets, quantum computing and electron spin-based memory.

Tougher and harder cutting tools

Cutting tools made of nanocrystalline materials, such as tungsten carbide, tantalum carbide, and titanium carbide are much harder, much more wear-resistant, erosion-resistant, and last longer than their conventional (large-grained) counterparts. They also enable the manufacturer to machine various materials much faster, thereby increasing productivity and significantly reducing manufacturing costs and hence useful for the miniaturization of microelectronic circuits, as microdrills.

High-power magnets

The strength of a magnet is measured in terms of coercivity and saturation magnetization values. These values increase with decrease in the grain size and an increase in the specific surface area (surface area per unit volume of the grains) of the grains. It has been shown that magnets made of nanocrystalline yttrium-samarium cobalt grains possess very unusual magnetic properties due to their extremely large surface area. Typical applications for these high-power rare-earth magnets include quieter submarines, automobile alternators, land-based power generators, motors for ships, ultra-sensitive analytical instruments, and magnetic resonance imaging (MRI) in medical diagnostics.

High-sensitivity sensors

Sensors employ their sensitivity to the changes in various parameters they are designed to measure. The measured parameters include electrical resistivity, chemical activity, magnetic permeability, thermal conductivity, and capacitance. All of these parameters depend greatly on the microstructure (grain size) of the materials employed in the sensors. A change in the sensor's environment is menifested by the sensor material's chemical, physical, or mechanical characteristics, which is exploited for detection. For instance, a carbon monoxide sensor made of zirconium oxide (zirconia) uses its chemical stability to detect the presence of carbon monoxide. In the event of carbon monoxide's presence, the oxygen atoms in zirconium oxide react with the carbon in carbon monoxide to partially reduce zirconium oxide. This reaction triggers a change in the sensor's characteristics, such as conductivity (or resistivity) and capacitance. The rare and the extent of this reaction are greatly increased by a decrease in the grain size. Hence, sensors made nanocrystalline materials are extremely sensitive to the change in their environment. Typical applications for sensors made out of nanocrystalline materials are smoke detectors, ice detectors on aircraft wings, automobile engine performance sensor.

Next-generation computer chips

Nanomaterials help the modern electronic industry break these barriers down by providing the manufacturers with nanocrystalline starting materials, ultra-high purity materials, materials with better thermal conductivity, and longer-lasting, durable interconnections (connections between various components in the microprocessors).

Nano-solar cells

When light hits an atom in a semiconductors, those photons of light with lots of energy can push an electron out of its nice stable orbital around the atom. The electron is then free to move from atom to atom, like the electrons in a piece of metal when it conducts electricity.

Using nanosize bits of semiconductors embedded in a conductive plastic maximizes the chance that an electron can escape the nanoparticle and reach the conductive plastic before it is trapped by another atom that has also been stripped of an electron. Once in the plastic, the electron can travel nappily through wire connecting the solar cell to the gadget like cellphone, laptop etc. It can than wander back to the nanocrystal to join an atom that has positive charge.

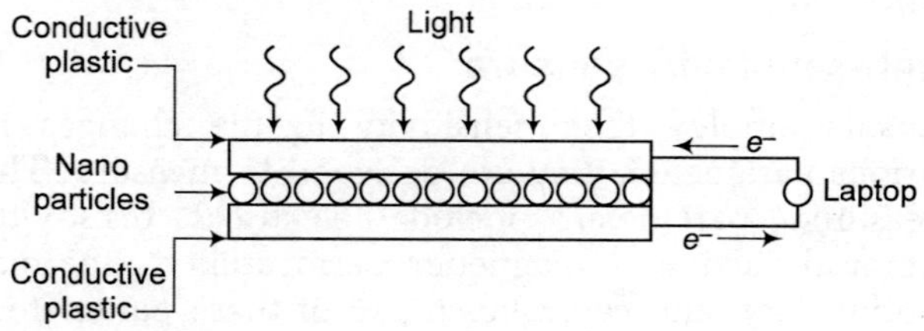

Fig. 39.6 Solar cell working nanotechnology.

Catalysis for Green Chemistry

Catalysis which has played such a vital role in the success of the industry in 20th century, will also play an important role in the new greener industry of the new century. Catalysis cannot only help to green chemical processes but the demonstration of their value to reduce the environmental impact of processes and reduce the costs of the processes will catalyze the greening of chemistry.

Note Green chemistry is a way of thinking and is about utilising the existing knowledge and principle of chemistry and other sciences to reduce the adverse impact on environment. Green chemistry is a production process that would bring about minimum pollution or deterioration to the environment.

The concept of atom efficiency has proven to be a popular tool in the evaluation of the 'greenness' of a chemical process. It is also revealing to compare sectors of chemical manufacturing. Most people would associate oil refining more than pharmaceutical manufacturing with dirty processes and waste, yet, while the sheer scale of the former leads to the largest volume of waste, the ratio of waste to the product is greater for the latter by a factor of 10^2-10^3. In pharmaceutical and fine chemicals manufacturing, the high value of the product has been a particularly significant feature in the establishment of many highly (atom) inefficient processes. Stoichiometric reagents (*e.g.*, chromate oxidants), catalysts that cannot easily be recovered and reused, and large volumes of volatile organic solvents are routinely used with all the consequential waste at the end of the reaction when the organic products need to be separated from the inorganic reagents, catalysts and solvents.

Step changes that move toward the ideal synthesis can be achieved with the application of several technologies including catalysis, process intensification alternative energy sources and supercritical fluids. Since, the major source of waste from a chemical process is the separation stage, it would seem sensible to focus heavily on that. The heterogenization of catalysts (and, where appropriate reagents) so that they can easily be separated (and reused) at the end of a process, is a logical and versatile approach to simplifying the process, removing the need for an aqueous quench (or other destructive separation step) and reducing the demand for raw materials.

Note An ideal synthesis would be atom efficient, safe, one step, involving no wasted reagents and enviromentally acceptable.

Catalyst heterogenization

It is possible to prepare heterogeneous analogs of most, if not all, of the most commonly used soluble and homogeneous catalysts. Heterogenization through chemical surface modification is most conveniently carried out using a silica (or silica-rich) backbone.

There are essentially two methods for preparing organically modified materials grafting and in situ sol-gel. The latter found to be preferable in terms of thermal stability and in particular in terms of loading.

Reactions catalyzed by solid acids

Acid catalysis is by far the most important area of catalysis. It is employed by industries in all sectors of chemical manufacturing, but suffers from the use of traditional Bronsted and Lewis acids that are hazardous to use and give rise to enormous volumes of dangerous effluent. We have studied the use of mesoporous solid acids based on silica and zirconia and many important organic reactions.

A particularly interesting challenge in this context is to try to design purely Lewis and purely Bronsted solid acids as well as those that show both characteristics. Variable strength of acidity is also important. There are some important organic reactions where careful control of the type of strength of acidity is very important if high, reaction selectivity is to be achieved. In this context, we have been working for several years on developing controlled acidity.

Early research at York, and in collaboration with a UK specialty chemical manufacturer, led to the discovery of clay-supported zinc chloride ("clayzic"). Clayzic became the basis of commercial "Envirocat" catalyst which has proven to be useful for typically Lewis acid-catalyzed reactions, including benzylations, olefinations, and some cyclizations. More recently, we have extended this concept to a new solid Lewis acid, HMS-supported zinc triflate which shows resonable selectivity in the rearrangement of α-pinene oxide to campholenic aldehyde (a reaction that rapidly loses selectivity with any Bronsted acidity in the system) and excellent reusability compared to conventional homogeneous processes.

Solid Bronsted acids based on mesoporous inorganic solids have only become available quite recently. HMS-sulphonic acid is a particularly interesting material and can be prepared at high (ca 3 mmole g^{-1}) loadings and with very high surface areas ($> 1000\ m^2\ g^{-1}$). The material behaves like a solid form of methanesulphonic acid, yet it is safe to handle, recoverable, and reusable in reactions including transesterifications. A simplified one-step procedure for making some mesoporous solid sulphonic acids has recently been reported and lends weight to the belief that materials of this type have a very promising future as environmentally friendly replacements for traditional acids such as sulphuric acid and its organic derivatives. The main restriction to the widespread use of these solid acids is cost.

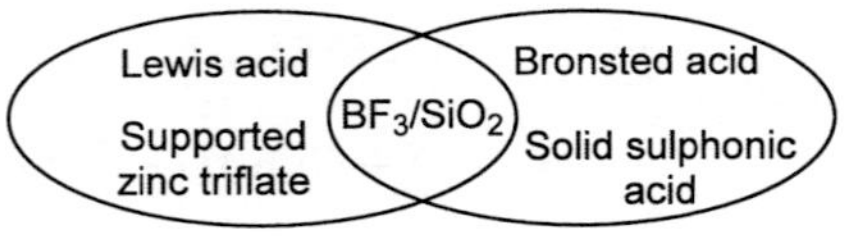

Controlled acidity in solid acids

Partial oxidation

The partial oxidation of hydrocarbons and the selective oxidation of functionalized organic compounds are reactions of diverse importance. Traditional synthetic methods employ a variety of reagents and catalyst systems including stoichiometric high oxidation state metals (highly toxic and leading to large volumes of waste), catalytic metal-acid-bromide system (leading to emissions due to solvent burning and corrosion problems for reactions vessels) and harmful organic peroxides which give organic waste by-products.

Hydrogen peroxide is safe alternative to its organic derivatives and has only water as a by product. The solid reagents offer significant advantages over their soluble counterparts they have good shelf-life, reasonable thermal and shock stability and can be easily recycled at very high oxygen efficiencies. Chemically modified mesoporous materials based on silicas, alumino silicates, and many other environmentally compatible materials have enormously diverse potential as benign replacements for the many hazardous and enviromentally threatening chemicals.

Palladium, a highly versatile metal for organic synthesis, can be effectively immobilized on chemically modified mesoporous materials that provide the right ligand geometry.

It is also possible to build quite complex organic structures on the surfaces of mesoporous materials, including those active in typically phase-transfer-catalyzed processes where a membrane version could be used in an interfacial reaction system that keeps the organic and inorganic component of an organic process separate, hence alleviating separation difficulties and reducing waste.

Medicinal Chemistry

Medicinal chemistry and pharamaceutical chemistry are disciplines at the intersection of chemistry, especially synthetic organic chemistry and pharmacology and various other biological specialities where it is involved with design, chemical synthesis and development for market of pharmaceutical agents (drugs). Compound used as medicines are most often organic compounds which are often divided into the broad classes of small organic molecules (*e.g.,* atorvastatin, erythropoietin, insulin). Inorganic and organometallic compounds are also useful as drugs (*e.g.,* lithium and platinum based agents as lithium carbonate and *cis*-platin).

Medicinal chemistry is a highly interdisciplinary science combining organic chemistry with biochemistry, computational chemistry, pharmacology, molecular biology etc.

Pharmacophore group is responsible for the activity of drug. On removing pharmacophore groups, the drug loses its activity.

Unsaturated compounds are more toxic than saturated compounds. Activity of the drug decreases with increase in length of carbon chain, because the solubility of substances lowers and they are unable to get into blood and thus do not cause required effect.

Factors Effecting the Nature of Drug

1. **Effect of isomerism** *m* and *p*-hydroxy benzoic acids are inactive while *o*-hydroxy benzoic acid is active in aspirin, salol etc. (–) laevorotatory compounds are highly active than (+) dextrorotatory compound *e.g.,* (–) nicotine is twice as active as (+) nicotine.
2. **Effect of halogens** Substituted compounds are generally toxic than parent hydrocarbon.

   Negative halogens Halogen substituted in non-conjugated positions usually increases the activity of the compounds (increases toxic properties also.)

Positive halogens Introduction of positive halogens as in (α-halogen carbonyl compounds), acid chlorides etc., decreases their toxicity. Increase in atomic weight dereases the hyponotic activity, but increases the antiseptic property.

Hypnotic property
←
$CHCl_3$ $CHBr_3$ CHI_3
→
Antiseptic property (Increases)

e.g., C_6H_5OH is highly toxic and a stronger antiseptic than C_6H_6. Salicylic acid is a strong antifungal and antirheumatic agent than the parent compound, benzoic acid. Caffeine is physiological active but hydroxyl caffeine is inactive.

3. **Effect of alkyl group** Alkylation generally decreases the biological activity. Alkylated or acylated carboxyl, hydroxyl and amino groups are highly active. *e.g.*, cocaine is anaesthetic.

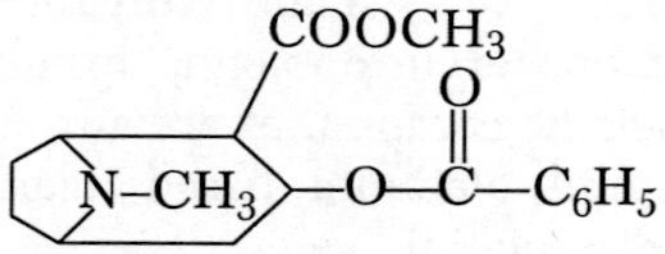

Active (cocaine)

Different Classes of Drugs

Neurologically active drugs

Tranquilizers and analgesics and neurologically active drugs. These affect the message transfer mechanism from nerve to receptor.

Tranquilizers are used for the treatment of stress and mild or even severe mental diseases. Chlordiazepoxide and meprobamate are mild tranquilizer suitable for relieving tension. Equanil is used in controlling depression and hypertension.

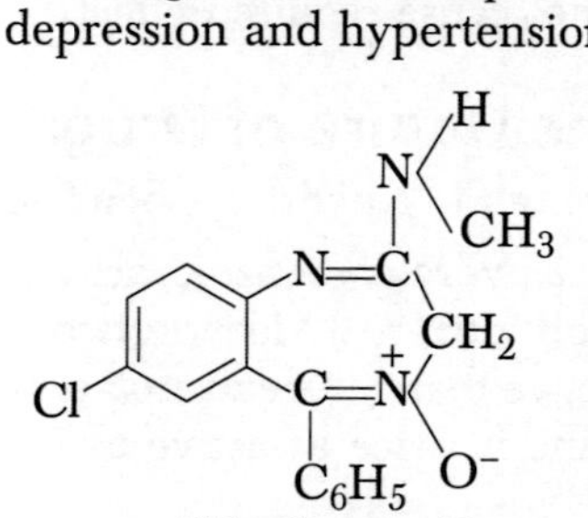

Chlordiazepoxide

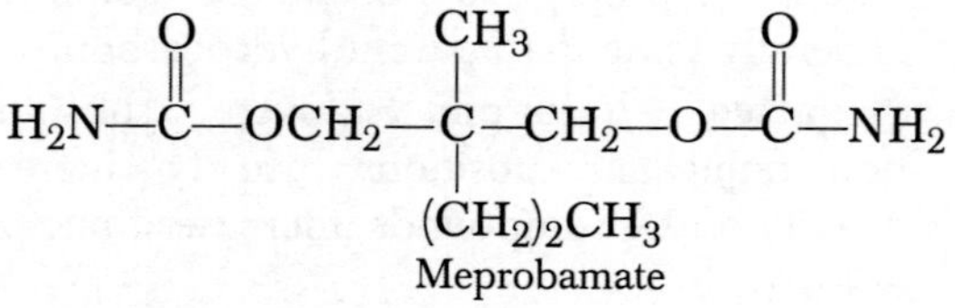

Meprobamate

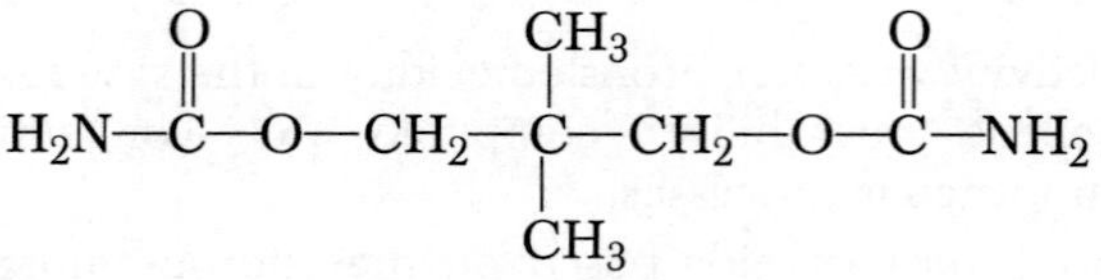

Equanil

Derivative of barbituric acid *viz.*, veronal, amytal, nembutal constitute an important class of tranquilizers. These derivatives are called barbiturates. These are hypnotic *i.e.*, sleep producing agents.

Analgesics reduce or abolish pain without causing impairment of consciousness, mental confusion, incoordination or paralysis or some other disturbances of nervous system. These are classified into non-narcotic (non-addictive) analgesics and narcotic analgesics.

Non-narcotic analgesics

(a) Salicylic acid derivatives

(i) Aspirin (acetyl salicylic acid)

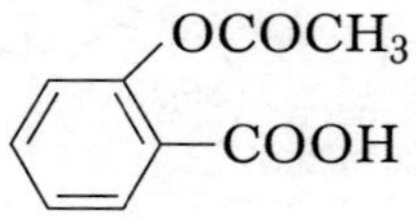

Anti-rheumatic, antipyretic

(ii) Methyl salicylate (oil of winter green)

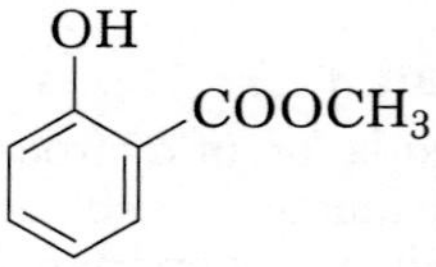

Flavouring agent

(iii) Sodium salicylate

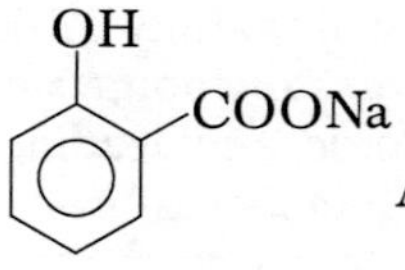

Anti-rheumatic

(iv) Salicilin

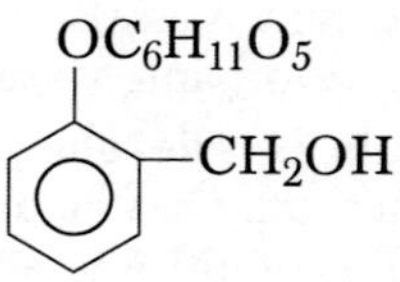

Anti-rheumatic

The main disadvantage of salicylic acid derivatives is that these distrub in gastrointenstinal tract.

(b) Para-amino phenol derivative

(i) Paracetamol

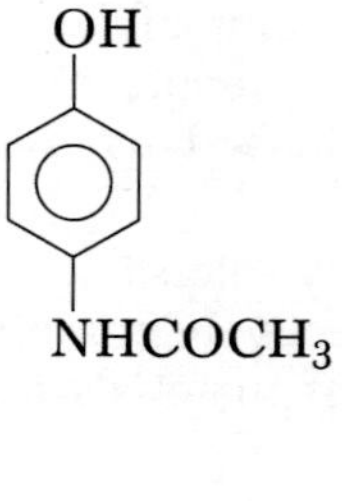

(ii) Phenacetin (more toxic than aspirin)

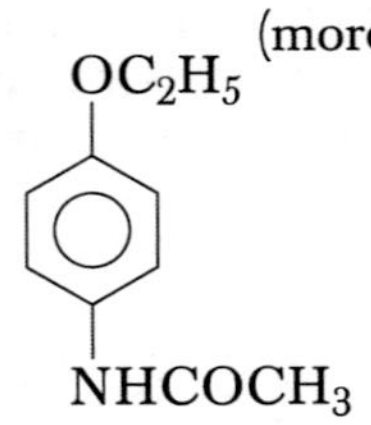

Narcotic analgesics Morphine and many of its homologues when administered in medicinal does, relieve pain and produce sleep. Morphine is used before surgery during operations. Excess use causes addiction, dryness to mouth, vomiting, headache and constipation. Heroin and apomorphine are derivative of morphine.

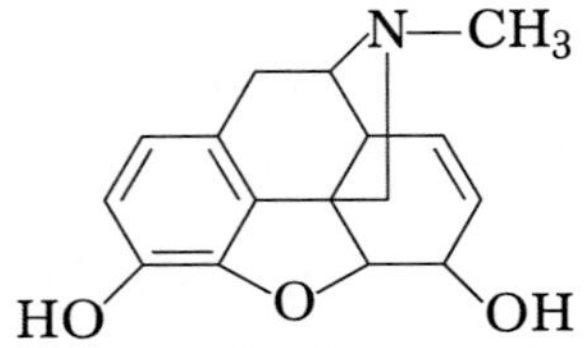

Morphine

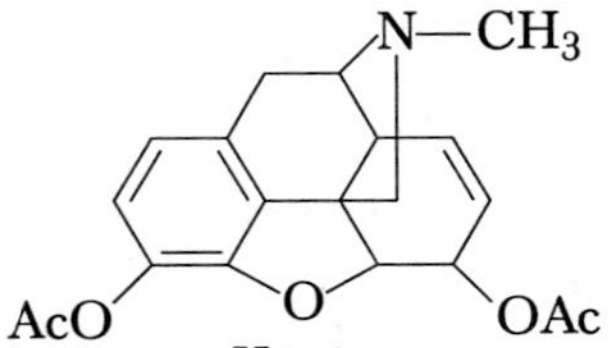

Heroin

Antiseptics and disinfectants

These are the chemicals which either kill or prevent the growth of microorganisms. **Antiseptics** are applied to the living tissues such as wounds, cuts, ulcers etc. Dettol is a commonly used antiseptic. It is a mixture of chloroxylenol and terpineol. Bithionol is added to soaps to impart antiseptic properties. Iodine, iodoform and chlorocresol are also used as antiseptic.

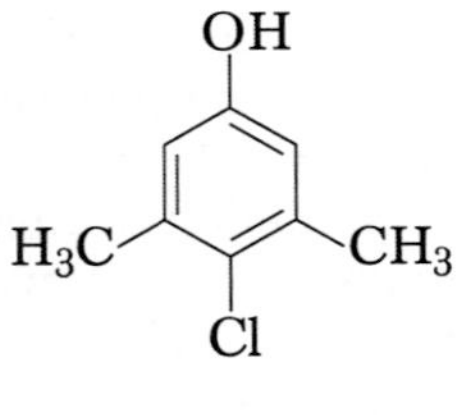

Chloroxylenol

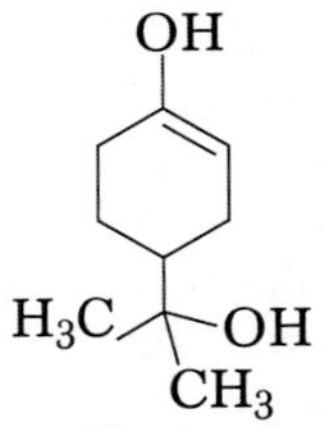

Terpineol

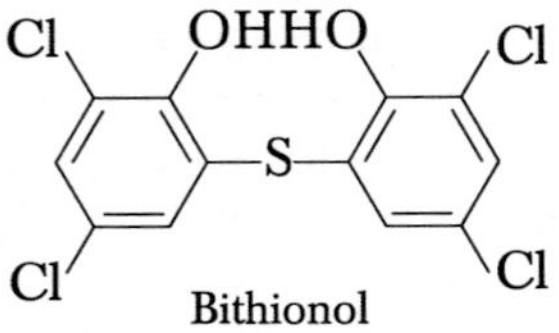

Bithionol

Disinfectants are applied to inanimate objects such as floors, drainge system, instruments etc. Dichloramine-T is used for dressing wounds, halozone is used for purification of drinking water.

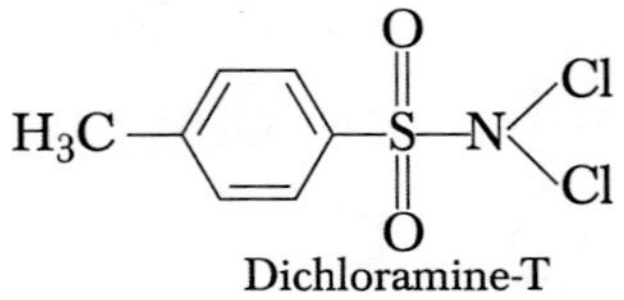

Dichloramine-T

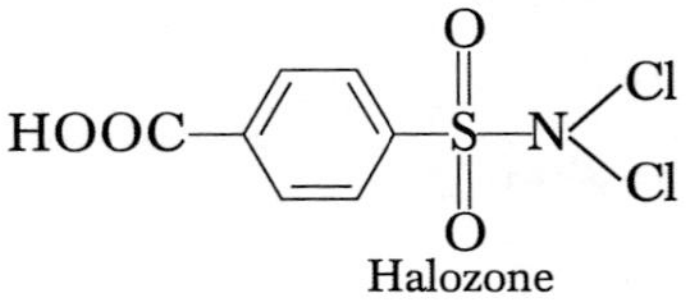

Halozone

Antifertility drugs

These drugs are used to control birth and population hence, also called as birth control pills. These contain a mixture of synthetic estrogen and progesterone derivatives. *e.g.*, norethindrone and ethynylestradiol are widely used as antifertility drugs.

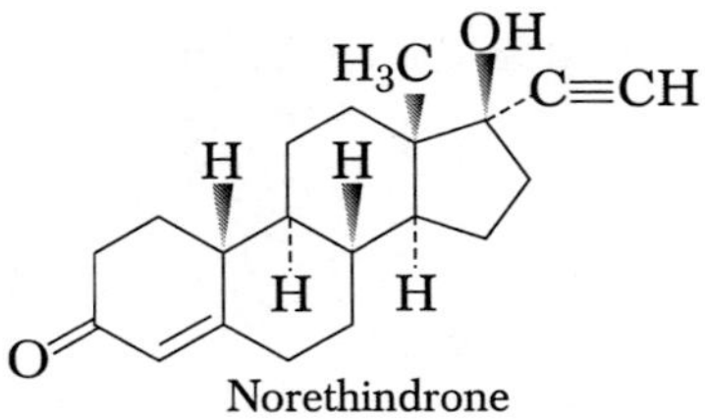

Norethindrone

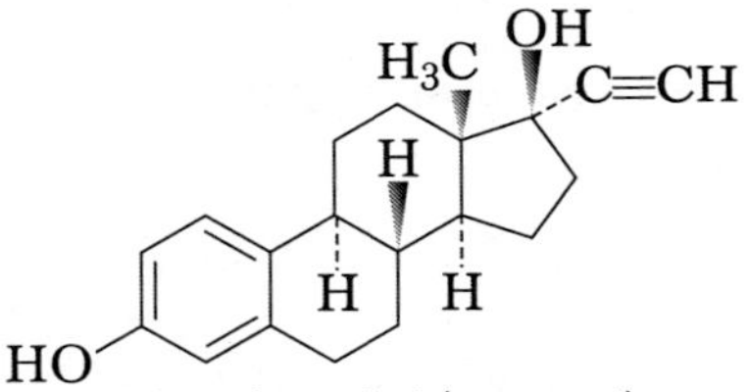

Ethynylestradiol (novestrol)

Anaesthetics

These are the chemical substances which produce general or local insensibility to pains and other sensations.

(a) **General anaesthetics**
- (i) Ether (Volatile) and its derivatives
- (ii) Chloroform
- (iii) Trichloroethylene

} Muscular relaxant, Maintains blood pressure.

- (iv) Ethyl chloride ⟶ Local anaesthetic for minor surgeries.

(b) **Gaseous anaesthetics**
- (i) Nitrous oxide
- (ii) Cyclopropane

(c) **Non-volatile anaesthetics**

Thiopental sodium

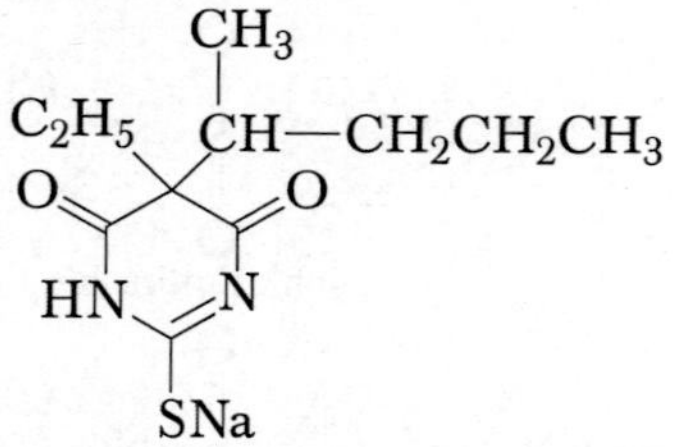

(d) **Local anaesthetics**

Cocaine

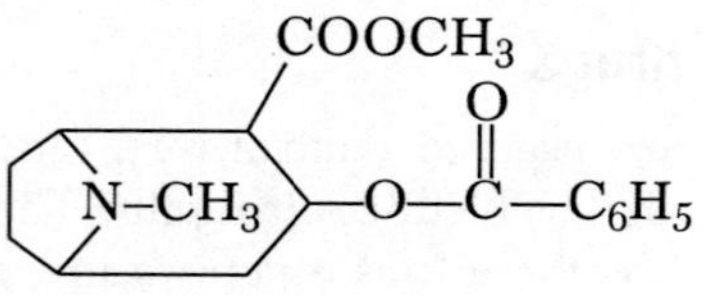

Cardiovascular drugs

(a) **Antiarrhythmic drugs**

Quinidine used in the treatment of hypertension.

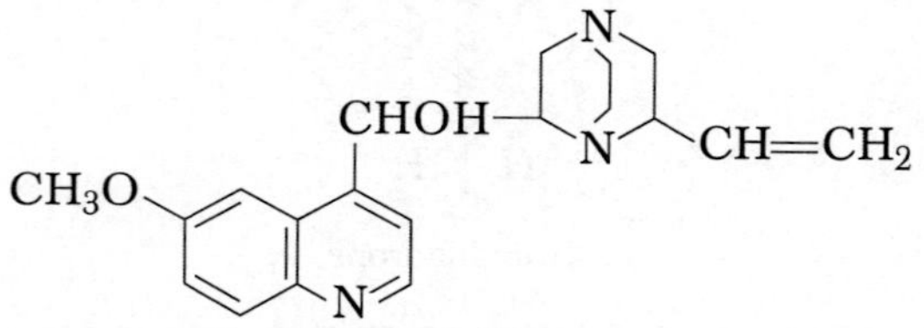

(b) **Anti-hypertensive or hypotensive drug**

Reserpine

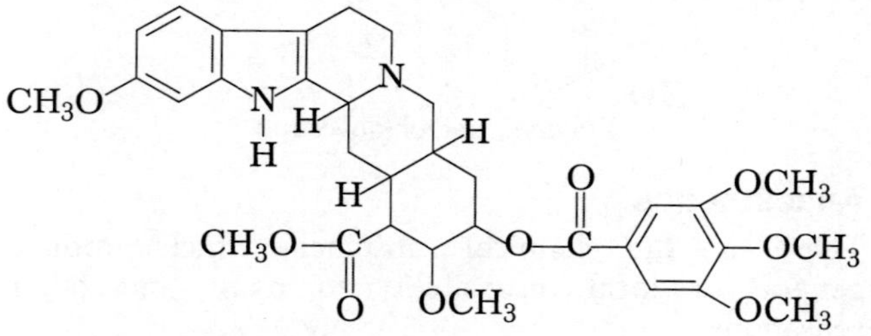

(c) **Antianginal agents**

Glyceryl trinitrate

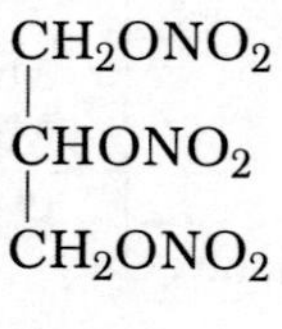

Antibiotics

These are used as drugs to treat infections because of their low toxicity for humans and animals. Now, an antibiotic refers to a substance produced wholly or partly by chemical synthesis, which in low concentrations inhibits the growth or destroys microorganisms by intervening in their metabolic processes. Salvarsan is used in the treatment of syphilis.

Sulphonamides

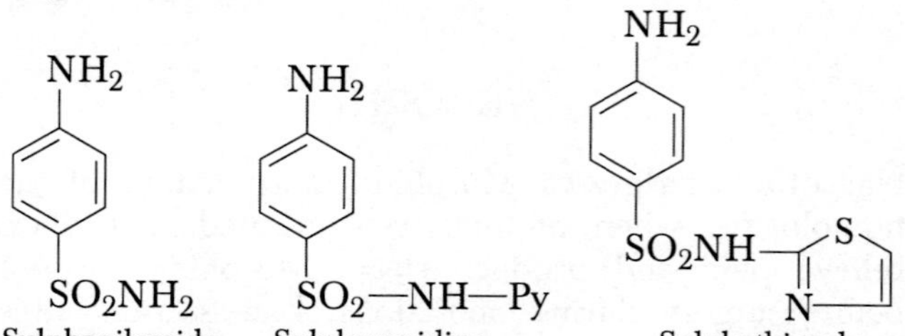

Sulphanilamide Sulphapyridine Sulphathiazole

Antibiotics have ether cidal effect or a static effect on microbes.

Bactericidal Penicillin, ofloxacin.

Bacteriostatic Erythromycin, tetracycline chloramphenicol.

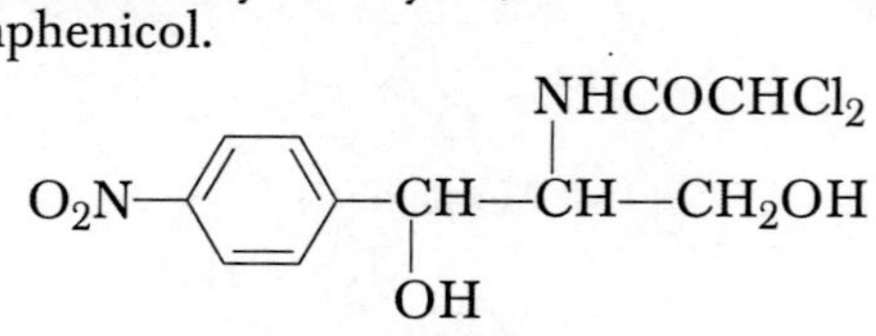

Chloramphenicol

Note Chlorambucil is used in the treatment of leukemia.

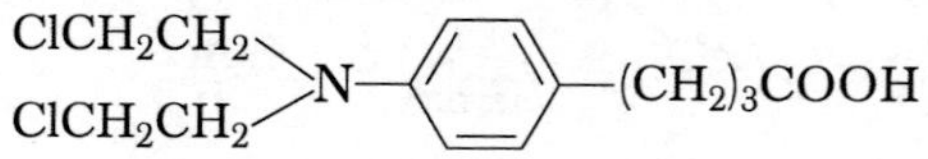

Supramolecular Chemistry

Supramolecular chemistry focuses on the noncovalent bonding interactions of molecules. These forces include hydrogen bonding, metal coordination, hydrophobic forces, π - π interactions etc. The concepts that have been demonstrated by supramolecular chemistry include molecular self assembly, folding, molecular recognition, dynamic covalent chemistry. Supramolecular chemistry deals with the chemistry and collective behaviour of organized ensembles of molecules. As one of the modern frontiers in chemistry, supramolecular chemistry heralds many promises that range from bicompatible materials and biomimetic catalysts to sensors and nanoscale fabrication of electronic devices.

Broadly speaking, supramolecular chemistry is the study of interactions between, rather than within, molecules—in other words, chemistry using molecules rather than atoms as building blocks. Whereas traditional chemistry deals with the construction of individual molecules (1 – 100 Å length scale) from atoms, supramolecular chemistry deals with the constrution of organized molecular "arrays" with much larger length scales (1 – 100 nm). In molecular chemistry, strong association forces such as covalent and ionic bonds are used to assemble atoms into discrete molecules and hold them together. In contrast, the forces used to organize and hold together supramolecular assemblies are weaker non-covalent interactions, such as hydrogen bonding, polar attractions, van der Waals' forces, and hydrophilic-hydrophobic interactions.

First and foremost among the motivations for exploring supramolecular chemistry is the desire to synthesize new robust, functional and technologically important materials by mimicking nature. A second impetus is the desire to design, using functional small molecule building blocks, new synthetic materials that feature even more useful ensemble properties emanating directly from nanoscale and microscale ordering.

Lastly, the need for improved miniaturization and device performance in the microelectronics industry has inspired many investigations into supramolecular chemistry. It is conceivable that "bottom up" materials fabrication approaches based on supramolecular chemistry will provide a solution to the anticipated size limitations of "top down" approaches, such as photolithography, thereby providing the means to fabricate ultra-small electronic components. Perhaps more likely is that hybrid devices will become increasingly ubiquitous and important. These devices integrate the outstanding electronic and photonic properties of non-molecular hard materials such as silicon to the excellent bio-recognition, chemical sensing, and related properties of designed, soft molecular materials to yield structures capable of performing disease diagnosis, environmental monitoring, controlled drug delivery, and so on.

Synthetic approaches to supramolecular chemistry can be categorized based on the nature, of the molecular building blocks, *i.e.,* whether they are organic or inorganic in nature, or whether they are small molecules or macromolecules. Small-molecule organic building blocks include molecular liquid crystals, hydrogen bonding molecules, catenanes, and rotaxanes. These have been used to create supramolecular ensembles ranging from nanostructured catalytic reactors to electrochemically switched molecular shuttles. Macromolecular organic building blocks include phase-separated block copolymers and more recently dendrimers. These have been used to generate sophisticated ordered composites and to allow nanopatterning on surfaces. "Self-assembling" coordination compounds featuring ligand-functionalized porphyrins and related components have been a mainstay of inorganic supramolecular chemistry. More recently, semiconductor or metal nanoparticles have been used as "macromolecular inorganic components for supramolecular arrays with interesting electronic properties.

The principles of supramolecular chemistry can be applied to the facile synthesis of new mesostructured assemblies featuring long-range order and displaying useful functional behaviour (molecular recognition and sensing, biomimetic catalysis, size and shape selective molecular transport, etc.).

Environmental Chemistry

Environmental chemistry is the scientific study of the chemical and biochemical phenomena that occur in natural places. Environmental chemistry is an interdisciplinary science that includes atmospheric, aquatic and soil chemistry as well as heavily relying on analytical chemistry and being related to environmental and other areas of science. Environmental chemistry involves first understanding how the uncontaminated environment works, which chemicals in what concentrations are present naturally and with what effects.

Environmental Pollution

Environmental pollution may be described as the contamination of the environment with harmful wastes arising mainly from certain human activities. These activities release into the environment certain materials which pollute the atmosphere, water and soil. Any substance, which causes pollution, is known as a **pollutant.** A substance becomes a pollutant when it is present in concentrations harmful to the natural environment.

In an environmental pollution process a pollutant originates from a source and gets transported by air or water or is dumped on land by man. Some of the **pollutants** may be absorbed (assimilated) or chemically changed by the environment; the rest build up to concentrations which are harmful to the environment.

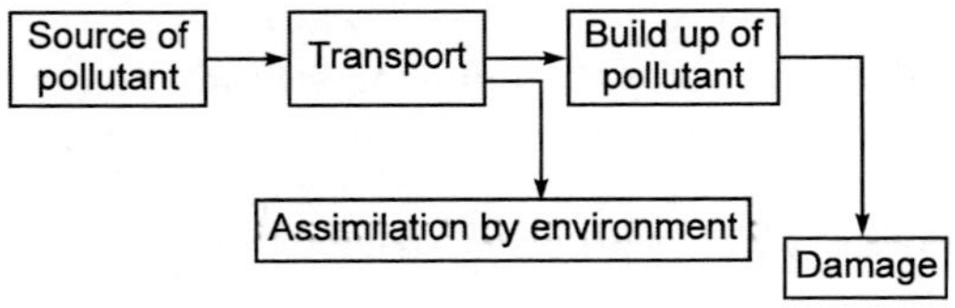

Atmospheric Pollution

The atmosphere that surrounds the earth is not of the same thickness at all heights. There are concentric layers of air or regions and each layer has different density. The lowest region of atmosphere in which the human beings along with other organisms live is called **troposphere**. It extends up to the height of ~ 10 km from sea level. Above the troposphere, between 10 and 50 km above sea level lies **stratosphere**. Troposphere is a turbulent, dusty zone containing air, much water vapour and clouds. This is the region of strong air movement and cloud formation. The stratosphere, on the other hand, contains dinitrogen, dioxygen, ozone and little water vapour.

Atmospheric pollution is generally studied as tropospheric and stratospheric pollution. The presence of ozone in the stratosphere prevents about 99.5 per run's of the Sun's harmful ultraviolet (UV) radiations from reaching the earth's surface and thereby protecting humans and other animals from its effect.

Tropospheric Pollution

It occurs due to the presence of undesirable solid on gaseous particles in the air. The following are the major gaseous and particulate pollutants present in troposphere.

Gaseous air pollutants

(a) **Oxides of sulphur** are produced when sulphur containing fossil fuel is burnt. Sulphur dioxide is the most widespread and serious air pollutant. It has been reported that even a low concentration of sulphur dioxide causes respiratory diseases *e.g.,* asthma, bronchitis, emphysema in human beings. Sulphur dioxide causes irritation to the eyes, resulting in tears and redness. High concentration of SO_2 leads to stiffiness of flower buds which eventually fall off from plants. However, the presence of particulate matter in polluted air catalyses the oxidation of sulphur dioxide to sulphur trioxide.

$$2SO_2(g) + O_2(g) \longrightarrow 2SO_3(g)$$

The reaction can also be promoted by ozone and hydrogen peroxide.

$$SO_2(g) + O_3(g) \longrightarrow SO_3(g) + O_2(g)$$

$$SO_2(g) + H_2O_2(l) \longrightarrow H_2SO_4(aq)$$

(b) **Oxides of nitrogen** Dinitrogen and dioxygen are the main constituents of air. These gases do not react with each other at a normal temperature. At high altitudes when lightning strikes, they combine to form oxides of nitrogen. NO_2 is oxidised to nitrate ion, NO_3^- which is washed into soil, where it serves as a fertilizer. In an automobile engine, (at high temperature) when fossil fuel is burnt, dinitrogen and dioxygen combine to yield significant quantities of nitric oxide (NO) and nitrogen dioxide (NO_2) as given below :

$$N_2(g) + O_2(g) \xrightarrow{1483\ K} 2NO(g)$$

NO reacts instantly with oxygen to give NO_2

$$2NO(g) + O_2(g) \longrightarrow 2NO_2(g)$$

Rate of production of NO_2 is faster when nitric oxide reacts with ozone in the stratosphere.

$$NO(g) + O_3(g) \longrightarrow NO_2(g) + O_2(g)$$

The irritant red haze in the traffic and congested places is due to oxides of nitrogen. Higher concentrations of NO_2 damage the leaves of plants and retard the rate of photosynthesis. Nitrogen dioxide is a lung irritant that can lead to an acute respiratory disease in children. It is toxic to living tissues also. Nitrogen dioxide is also harmful to various textile fibres and metals.

(c) **Oxides of carbon** Carbon monoxide (CO) is one of the most serious air pollutants. It is a colourless and odourless gas, highly poisonous to living beings because of its ability to block the delivery of oxygen to the organs and tissues. It is produced as a result of incomplete combustion of carbon. Carbon monoxide is mainly released into the air by automobile exhaust. Other sources, which produce CO, involve incomplete combustion of coal, firewood, petrol etc.

Carbon monoxide binds the haemoglobin to form carboxyhaemoglobin, which is about 300 times more stable than the oxygen-haemoglobin complex. In blood, when the concentration of carboxy haemoglobin reaches about 3-4 per cent, the oxygen carrying capacity of blood is greatly reduced. This oxygen deficiency, results into headache, weak eyesight, nervousness and cardiovascular disorder.

Carbon dioxide (CO_2) is released into the atmosphere by respiration, burning of fossil fuels for energy, and by decomposition of limestone during the manufacture of cement. It is also emitted during volcanic erruptions. **Carbon dioxide** gas is confined to troposphere only. Normally, it forms about 0.03 per cent by volume of the atmosphere. With the increased use of fossil fuels, a large amount of carbon dioxide gas released into the atmosphere.

Deforestation and burning of fossil fuel increases the CO_2 level and disturb the balance in the atmosphere.

The increased amount of CO_2 in the air is mainly responsible for global warming.

Global Warming and Greenhouse Effect About 75% of the solar energy reaching the earth is absorbed by the earth's surface, which increases its temperature. The rest of the heat radiates back to the atmosphere. Some of the heat is trapped by gases such as carbon dioxide, methane, ozone, chlorofluorocarbon compounds (CFCs) and water vapour in the atmosphere. Thus, they add to the heating of the atmosphere. This causes **global warming.**

Greenhouse effect is the phenomenon in which earth's atmosphere traps the heat from the sun and prevents it from escaping into the outer space. The carbon dioxide molecules trap heat as they are transparent to sunlight but not to the heat radiation. If the amount of carbon dioxide crosses the delicate proportion of 0.03 per cent, the natural greenhouse balance may get disturbed. Carbon dioxide is the major contributor to global warming.

Besides carbon dioxide, other greenhouse gases are methane, water vapour, nitrous oxide, CFCs and ozone. Methane is produced naturally when vegetation is burnt, digested or rotted in the absence of oxygen. Large amounts of methane are released in paddy fields, coal mines, from rotting garbage dumps and by fossil fuels. Chlorofluorocarbons (CFCs) are man-made industrial chemicals used in air conditioning etc. CFCs are also damaging the ozone layer. Nitrous oxide occurs naturally in the environment. In recent years, their quantities have increased significantly due to the use of chemical fertilizers and the burning of fossil fuels. If these trends continue the average global temperature will increase to a level which may lead to melting of polar ice caps and flooding of low laying areas all over the earth. Increase in the global temperature increases the incidence of infectious diseases like dengue, malaria, yellow fever, sleeping sickness etc.

Acid rain Normally rain water has a pH of 5.6 due to the presence of H^+ ions formed by the reaction of rain water with carbon dioxide present in the atmosphere.

$$H_2O(l) + CO_2(g) \rightleftharpoons H_2CO_3(aq)$$
$$H_2CO_3(aq) \rightleftharpoons H^+(aq) + HCO_3^-(aq)$$

When the pH of the rain water drops below 5.6, it is called acid rain.

Acid rain is a byproduct of a variety of human activities that emit the oxides of sulphur and nitrogen in the atmosphere. As mentioned earlier, burning of fossil fuels (which contain sulphur and nitrogenous matter) such as coal and oil in power stations and furnaces or petrol and diesel in motor engines produce sulphur dioxide and nitrogen oxides. SO_2 and NO_2 after oxidation and reaction with water are major contributors to acid rain, because polluted air usually contains particulate matter that catalyse the oxidation.

$$2SO_2(g) + O_2(g) + 2H_2O(l) \longrightarrow 2H_2SO_4(aq)$$
$$4NO_2(g) + O_2(g) + 2H_2O(l) \longrightarrow 4HNO_3(aq)$$

Acid rain is harmful for agriculture, trees and plants as it dissolves and washes away nutrients needed for their growth. It causes respiratory ailments in human beings and animals. When acid rain falls and flows as ground water to reach rivers, lakes etc., it affects plants and animal life in aquatic ecosystem. It corrodes water pipes resulting in the leaching of heavy metals such as iron, lead and copper into the drinking water. Acid rain damages buildings and other structures made of stone or metal. The Taj Mahal in India has been affected by acid rain.

Particulate pollutants

Particulates pollutants are the minute solid particles or liquid droplets in air. These are present in vehicle emissions, smoke particles from fires, dust particles and ash from industries. Particulates in the atmosphere may be viable or non-viable. The viable particulates *e.g.*, bacteria, fungi, moulds, algae etc. are minute living organisms that are dispersed in the atmosphere.

Non-viable particulates may be classified according to their nature and size as follows :

(a) Smoke particulates consist of soid or mixture of solid and liquid particles formed during combustion of organic matter. Examples are cigarette smoke, smoke from burning of fossil fuel, garbage and dry leaves, oil smoke etc.

(b) Dust is composed of fine solid particles (over 1 μm in diameter), produced during crushing, grinding and attribution of solid materials. Sand from sand blasting, saw dust from wood works, pulverized coal, cement and fly ash from factories, dust storms etc., are some typical examples of this type of particulate emission.

(c) Mists are produced by particles of spray liquids and by condensation of vapours in air. Examples are sulphuric acid mist and herbicides and insecticides that miss their targets and travel through air and form mists.

(d) Fumes are generally obtained by condensation of vapours during sublimation, distillation, boiling and several other chemical reactions. Generally, organic solvents, metals and metallic oxides form fume particles.

Note Lead used to be a major air pollutant emitted by vechicles. Leaded petrol used to be the primary source of air-borne lead emission in Indian cities. This problem has now been overcome by using unleaded petrol in most of the cities in India. Lead interferes with the development and maturation of red blood cells.

Smog

The word smog is derived from smoke and fog. This is the most common example of air pollution that occurs in many cities throughout the world. There are two types of smog

(a) **Classical smog** occurs in cool humid climate. It is a mixture of smoke, fog and sulphur dioxide. Chemically it is a reducing mixture and so it is also called as reducing smog.

(b) **Photochemical smog** occurs in warm, dry and sunny climate. The main components of the photochemical smog result from the action of sunlight on unsaturated hydrocarbons and nitrogen oxides produced by automobiles and factories. Photochemical smog has high concentration of oxidising agents and is, therefore, called as oxidising smog.

Formation of photochemical smog

When fossil fuels are burnt, a variety of pollutants are emitted into earth's troposphere. Two of the pollutants that are emitted are hydrocarbons (unburnt fuels) and nitric oxide (NO). When these pollutants build up to sufficiently high levels, a chain reaction occurs from their interaction with sunlight in which NO is converted into nitrogen dioxide (NO_2). This NO_2 in turn absorbs energy from sunlight and breaks up into nitric oxide and free oxygen atom.

$$NO_2(g) \xrightarrow{h\nu} NO(g) + O(g) \quad \text{...(i)}$$

Oxygen atoms are very reactive and combine with the O_2 in air to produce ozone.

$$O(g) + O_2(g) \rightleftharpoons O_3(g) \quad \text{...(ii)}$$

The ozone formed in the above reaction (ii) reacts rapidly with the NO(g) formed in the reaction (i) to regenerate NO_2. NO_2 is a brown gas and at sufficiently high levels can contribute to haze.

$$NO(g) + O_3(g) \longrightarrow NO_2(g) + O_2(g) \quad \text{...(iii)}$$

Ozone is a toxic gas and both NO_2 and O_3 are strong oxidising agents and can react with the unburnt hydrocarbons in the polluted air to produce chemicals such as formaldehyde, acrolein and peroxyacetyl nitrate (PAN).

$$3CH_4 + 2O_3 \longrightarrow \underset{\text{Formaldehyde}}{3CH_2{=}O} + 3H_2O$$

$$\underset{\text{Acrolein}}{CH_2{=}CHCH{=}O} \qquad \underset{\text{Peroxyacetyl nitrate (PAN)}}{CH_3\overset{}{\underset{\| \atop O}{C}}OONO_2}$$

Effects of photochemical smog

The common components of photochemical smog are ozone, nitric oxide, acrolein, formaldehyde and peroxyacetyl nitrate (PAN). Photochemical smog causes serious health problems. Both ozone and PAN act as powerful eye irritants. Ozone and nitric oxide irritate the nose and throat and their high concentration causes headache, chest pain, dryness of the throat, cough and difficulty in breathing. Photochemical smog leads to cracking of rubber and extensive damage to plant life. It also causes corrosion of metals, stones, building materials, rubber and painted surfaces.

Stratospheric Pollution

The upper stratosphere consists of considerable amount of ozone (O_3), which protects us from the harmful ultraviolet (UV) radiations. These radiations cause skin cancer (melanoma) in humans.

Ozone in the stratosphere is a product of UV radiations on dioxygen (O_2) molecules.

$$O_2(g) \xrightarrow{UV} O(g) + O(g)$$

$$O(g) + O_2(g) \overset{UV}{\rightleftharpoons} O_3(g)$$

Ozone is thermodynamically unstable and decomposes to molecular oxygen. Thus, a dynamic equilibrium exists between the production and decomposition of ozone molecules. In recent years, there have been reports of the depletion of this protective ozone layer because of the presence of certain chemicals in the stratosphere. The main reason of ozone layer depletion is believed to be the release of chlorofluorocarbon compounds (CFCs). also known as freons. These compounds are non-reactive, non-flammable, non-toxic organic molecules and therefore, used in refrigerators, air conditioners.

Once CFCs are released in the atmosphere, they mix with the normal atmospheric gases and eventually reach the stratosphere. In stratosphere, they get broken down by powerful UV radiations, releasing chlorine free radical.

$$CF_2Cl_2(g) \xrightarrow{UV} \dot{C}l(g) + \dot{C}F_2Cl(g) \quad \text{...(i)}$$

The chlorine radical then react with stratospheric ozone to form chlorine monoxide radicals and molecular oxygen.

$$\dot{C}l(g) + O_3(g) \longrightarrow Cl\dot{O}(g) + O_2(g) \quad \ldots(ii)$$

Reaction of chlorine monoxide radical with atomic oxygen produces more chlorine radicals.

$$Cl\dot{O}(g) + O(g) \longrightarrow \dot{C}l(g) + O_2(g) \quad \ldots(iii)$$

The chlorine radicals are continuously regenerated and cause the breakdown of ozone. Thus, CFCs are transporting agents for continuously generating chlorine radicals into the stratosphere and damaging the ozone layer.

Ozone depletion over Antarctica

In 1980s atmospheric scientists working in Antarctica reported about depletion of ozone layer commonly known as ozone hole over the South Pole. In summer season, nitrogen dioxide and methane react with chlorine monoxide and chlorine atoms forming chlorine sinks, preventing much ozone depletion, whereas (in winter, special type of clouds called polar stratospheric clouds are formed over Antarctica. These polar stratospheric clouds provide surface on which chlorine nitrate formed gets hydrolysed to form hypochlorous acid. It also reacts with hydrogen chloride to give molecular chlorine.

$$Cl\dot{O}(g) + NO_2(g) \longrightarrow ClONO_2(g)$$

$$\dot{C}l(g) + CH_4(g) \longrightarrow \dot{C}H_3(g) + HCl(g)$$

$$ClONO_2(g) + H_2O(g) \longrightarrow HOCl(g) + HNO_3(g)$$

$$ClONO_2(g) + HCl(g) \longrightarrow Cl_2(g) + HNO_3(g)$$

When sunlight returns to the Antarctica in the spring, the sun's warmth breaks up the clouds and HOCl and Cl_2 are photolysed by sunlight.

$$HOCl(g) \xrightarrow{h\nu} \dot{O}H(g) + \dot{C}l(g)$$

$$Cl_2(g) \xrightarrow{h\nu} 2\dot{C}l(g)$$

The chlorine radicals thus formed, initiate the chain reaction for ozone depletion as described earlier.

Effects of depletion of the ozone layer

With the depletion of ozone layer, more UV radiation filters into troposphere. UV radiations lead to ageing of skin, cataract, sunburn, skin cancer, killing of many phytoplanktons, damage to fish productivity etc. It has also been reported that plant proteins get easily affected by UV radiation which leads to the harmful mutation of cells. It also increases evaporation of surface water through the stomata of the leaves and decreases the moisture content of the soil. Increase in UV radiations damage paints and fibres, causing them to fade faster.

Water Pollution

The quality of drinking water is very important for human welfare. Pollution of water originates from human activities. The list of major water pollutants and their sources are given in the Table 39.3.

Table 39.3 **Major Water Pollutants**

Pollutant	Source
Microorganisms	Domestic sewage.
Organic wastes	Domestic sewage, animal excreta and waste, decaying animals and plants, discharge from food processing factories.
Plant nutrients	Chemical fertilizers.
Toxic heavy metals	Industries and chemical factories.
Sediments	Erosion of soil by agriculture and strip mining.
Pesticides	Chemicals used for killing insects, fungi and weeds.
Radioactive substances	Mining of uranium containing minerals.
Heat	Water used for cooling in industries.

Causes of Water Pollution

Pathogens

The most serious water pollutants are the disease causing agents called pathogens. Pathogens include bacteria and other organisms that enter water from domestic sewage and animal excreta. Human excreta contain bacteria such as *Escherichia coli* and Streptococcus faecalils which cause gastrointestinal diseases.

Organic wastes

The other major water pollutant is organic matter such as leaves, grass, trash etc., They pollute water as a consequence of run off. Excessive phytoplankton growth within water is also a cause of water pollution. These wastes are biodegradable.

Chemical pollutants

Water is an excellent solvent, water soluble inorganic chemicals that include heavy metals such as cadmium, mercury, nickel etc., constitute and important class of pollutants. All these metals are dangerous to humans because our body cannot excrete them. These metals then can damage kidneys, central nervous system, liver etc. Acids (like sulphuric acid) from mine drainage and salts from many different sources including raw salt used to melt snow and ice in the colder climates (sodium and calcium chloride) are water soluble chemical pollutants.

Petroleum products, pesticides, polychlorinated biphenyl (PCBs), detergent and fertilizers etc., are important water pollutants. Now a days most of the detergents available are biodegradable. However, their use can create other problems. The bacteria responsible for degrading biodegradable detergent feed on it and grow rapidly. While growing, they may use up all the oxygen dissolved in water. The lack of oxygen kills all other forms of aquatic life such as fish and plants. Fertilizers contain phosphates as additives. The addition of phosphates in water enhances algae growth. Such profuse growth of algae, covers the water surface and reduces the oxygen concentration in water. This leads to anaerobic conditions, commonly with accumulation of abnoxious decay and animal death. Thus, bloom-infested water inhibits the growth of other living organisms in the water body. This process in which nutrient enriched water bodies support a dense plant population, which kills animal life by depriving it of oxygen and results in subsequent loss of biodiversity is known as ***Eutrophication***.

Note The amount of oxygen required by bacteria to break down the organic matter present in a certain volume of a sample of water, is called **Biochemical Oxygen Demand (BOD).** The amount of BOD in the water is a measure of the amount of organic material in water, in terms of how much oxygen will be required to break it down biologically. Clean water would have BOD value of less than 5ppm whereas highly polluted water could have a BOD value of 17 pp or more.

International Standards for Drinking Water

The international standards for drinking water are given below :

Table 39.4 **Maximum Prescribed Concentration of Some Metals in Drinking Water**

Metal	Maximum concentration (ppm or mg dm^{-3})
Fe	0.2
Mn	0.05
Al	0.2
Cu	3.0
Zn	5.0
Cd	0.005

Land Pollution

Most of the land pollution is caused by pesticides and other chemicals which are added to the soil to grow better crops. Some of these poisons pass through food chains and reach to harmful proportions. Solid wastes are another cause of land pollution.

Pesticides

Pesticides are basically synthetic toxic chemicals with ecological repercussions. They are used to kill or block the reproductive processes of unwanted organisms. They include insecticides herbicides, fungicides. Control of insects by insecticides helps to curb disease and protect crops. DDT (dichlorodiphenyl trichloroethane) is used in agriculture to control the damages caused by insects, rodents etc. However, due to adverse effects its use has been banned in various countries. Organochlorines are used as insecticide since the 1950. These are stable in the environment, toxic to insects but much less to humans. Most of them are water insoluble and non-biodegradable. These high persistant toxins and transferred from lower trophic level to higher trophic level through food chain. Over the time the concentration of toxins in higher animals reach a level which causes serious metabolic and pysiological disorders.

Herbicides are used to kill weeds. Sodium chlorate ($NaClO_3$) and sodium arsinite (Na_3AsO_3) were used as weed killers in the first half of the last century. Most herbicides are toxic to animals. Organic herbicides such as triazines are presently widely used to kill weeds in cornfields.

Fungicides are used to check the growth of fungi. Organic compounds of mercury have been used as fungicides. These compounds break down in soil and this has disastrous consequences, many human deaths in Iraq (1971-1972) resulted from the people eating bread made from grain that had been treated with the fungicide methylmercury.

Strategy for Control of Environmental Pollution

The management of waste

The production and improper disposal of waste are causes for a great deal of environmental pollution. In addition to the household waste, which includes sewage and municipal garbage, many toxic industrial wastes from manufacturing processes require treatment and/or safe disposal.

Recycling

When materials are recycled, there are several benefits, apart from saving on the cost of raw materials, waste disposal costs are reduced. Examples of recycling by industry are :

(a) the collection and recycling of glass (in bottle banks);

(b) the use of scrap metal in the manufacture of steel;

(c) the recovery of energy from burning combustible waste.

Thus, recycling converts waste into wealth.

Sewage treatment

The main stages in the treatment of sewage are as follows :

(a) The removal of large solids that get into the system by filtering the waste water through screens. The solids that are removed are disposed of in landfill sites.

(b) Settlement in tanks to allow the removal of solids that settle out (called sludge). This process also allows removal of grease, which floats to the surface and can be skimmed off.

(c) The degradation of the organic content of waste water by microbial oxidation.

(d) Application of various physical and chemical processes for improving the quality of waste water. The processes include chemical removal of phosphate, coagulation, filtration and disinfection using chlorine.

The safe disposal of the sludge produced during water treatment is a problem.

The sludge is dried and then may be (i) incinerated, (ii) digested or (iii) dumped.

(a) **Incineration** Incinertion converts organic materials to CO_2 and H_2O. It may serve to destroy household waste, chemical waste and biological waste (*e.g.,* from hospitals). A high temperature is required, usually in excess of 1000°C, and a plentiful supply of oxygen. Exhaust gases must be filtered. the process greatly reduces the volume of waste an inorganic ash is left behind, which is disposed of as landfill. The chief disadvantage of incineration is that it leads to air pollution. Further the ash from municipal incinerators is very finely divided and can be ingested into the lungs.

(b) **Digestion** Anaerobic digestion occurs when microorganisms degrade wastes in the absence of oxygen. It may be used to treat sewage sludge, but process can also be used to degrade a variety of toxic organic wastes. Carbon dioxide and methane, which may be used as a fuel, are the products. The overall process is the conversion of the organic material into carbon dioxide and methane *i.e.,*

$$2(CH_2O) \longrightarrow CO_2(g) + CH_4(g)$$

(c) **Dumping** Ocean dumping of sewage sludge has been widely practiced in the seas around the world. However, the practice of application of sludge to the land is increasing. The sludge contains nitrogen and phosphorus which make it useful as a fertilizer. Urban areas produce sludge with high toxic metal content, so the amount of such sludge dumped in this way must be carefully controlled.

Exercise 1
(For Part 'B')

1. Pixels in the high definition T.V. monitors are made of
(a) CsCl (b) LiF
(c) ZnS (d) BaS

2. The high tensile strength of nano materials is due to
(a) the high density of the nanotubes
(b) efficient interlocking of the particles
(c) each nanotube is one large molecule
(d) Both (b) and (c)

3. Yttrium-Samarium-Cobalt grains have unusual magnetic properties due to the
(a) very high paramagnetism
(b) large specific surface area
(c) high melting point
(d) very strong intermetallic forces

4. Material in nanophase employed in the manufacture of ceramic capacitors is
(a) $BaTiO_3$ (b) $ZnOZrO_2$
(c) ZnO (d) Cu-Fe alloy

5. Nanoscale refers to the length of
(a) 1-100 nm (b) 10-1000 nm
(c) > 1000 nm (d) 1-10 Å

6. Supramolecular chemistry is the study of
(a) strong bonds like covalent bonds
(b) hydrogen bonding and van der Waals' forces
(c) π-π interactions
(d) Both (b) and (d)

7. Supramolecular chemistry deals with molecules of length scales
(a) 1 – 100 Å (b) 1 – 100 nm
(c) 1 – 100 cm (d) 1 – 100 pm

8. Green chemistry aims to
(a) grow trees around chemical factories
(b) reduce environmental degradation
(c) reduce costs of chemical process
(d) Both (b) and (c)

9. Catalyst heterogenisation involves
(a) solidification of liquid catalyst
(b) surrface modification using silica base
(c) performing catalytic reaction at freezing conditions
(d) using liquid catalytic for gaseous reactants

10. Which of the following is a hypnotic drug?
(a) Salol (b) Luminal
(c) Piperazine (d) Novalgin

11. A sulpha drug which is used in the treatment of bacillary dysentery is
(a) sulphathiazole (b) sulphadiazine
(c) sulphaguanidine (d) sulphamezathine

12. The drug used against AIDS is
(a) Enovid E (b) AZT
(c) BHA (d) LSD

13. Hypnotic property is maximum in
(a) $CHCl_3$ (b) $CHBr_3$
(c) CHI_3 (d) CH_2Cl_2

14. An example of non-narcotic analgesic is
(a) ketoprofen (b) cocaine
(c) morphine (d) pethidine

15. Which of the following is not an antiseptic drug?
(a) Iodoform (b) Dettol
(c) Gentian violet (d) Gammexane

16. Which of the following is used as a local anaesthetic agent?
(a) Diazepam (b) Procaine
(c) Mescaline (d) Seconal

17. Antiseptics and disinfectants generally contain
(a) acetamide group (b) chlorophenolic groups
(c) ether function (d) nitro group

18. An anticonvulsant drug is
(a) reserpine (b) nicotinic acid
(c) barbiturate (d) prontosil

19. Arsenic drugs are mainly used in the treatment of
(a) jaundice (b) malaria
(c) syphilis (d) cholera

20. Which of the following can possibly be used as analgesic without causing addiction and modification?
(a) Morphine
(b) N-Acetyl *para*-aminophenol
(c) Diazepam
(d) Tetrahydrocatenol

21. Tranquilisers are substances used for the treatment of
(a) AIDS (b) cancer
(c) blood infection (d) mental diseases

22. Photochemical smog is formed in
(a) summer during morning time
(b) summer during day time
(c) winter during morning time
(d) winter during day time

23. Ozone layer of stratosphere requires protection from indiscriminate use of
(a) pesticides
(b) balloons
(c) atomic explosions
(d) aerosols and high flying jets

24. During Bhopal tragedy the gas released was
(a) potassium isothiocyanate
(b) phosgene
(c) methyl isocyanate
(d) ammonia

25. Which of the following gas reacts with haemoglobin blood and produce toxic effect?
(a) CO_2 (b) SO_2
(c) NO_2 (d) CO

26. A drug that is antipyretic as well as analgesic is
(a) chloropromazine hydrochloride
(b) *para*-acetamidophenol
(c) chloroquin
(d) penicillin

27. The structure given below is known as

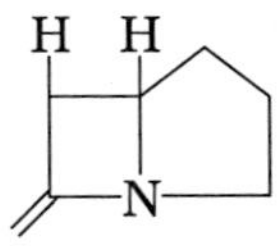

(a) penicillin F (b) ampicillin
(c) sulphadiazine (d) penicillin G

28. Barbituric acid and its derivatives are well known as
(a) tranquillizers (b) antiseptics
(c) analgesics (d) antipyretics

29. Which of the following is not an example of green chemistry?
(a) Catalytic dehydrogenation of the diethanol amine without using cyanide and formaldehyde
(b) Replacement of CFC by CO_2 as blowing agent in the manufacture of polystyrene foam sheets
(c) Reacting methyl amine and phosgene to produce methyl isocyanate
(d) Replacement of organotins by sea nine as antifouling compounds in sea marines

30. Which one of the following is mainly responsible for depletion of ozone layer?
(a) Methane (b) Carbon dioxide
(c) Water (d) Chlorofluorocarbons

31. Disease caused by eating fish containing industrial mercury waste is
(a) minamata disease (b) parkinson disease
(c) hashimoto disease (d) osteoschlerosis

32. Which of the following is not a herbicide?
(a) Sodium chlorate (b) Sodium arsenite
(c) Polyphosphate (d) Triazines

33. Which of the following statements is false?
(a) The main reason for river water pollution is industrial and domestic sewage discharge
(b) Surface water contains a lot of organic matter, mineral nutrients and radioactive materials
(c) Oil slick in sea water increases D.O. value
(d) Oil spill in sea water causes heavy damage to fishery

34. Addition of phosphate fertilizers into water leads to
(a) increased growth of decomposers
(b) increased algal growth
(c) nutrient enrichment
(d) None of the above

35. Organomercury compounds are
(a) herbicides (b) fungicides
(c) fumigants (d) insecticides

36. The brown, hazy fumes of photochemical smog are due to
(a) nitrogen dioxide (b) aldehydes
(c) SO_2 (d) CO_2

Exercise 2
(For Part 'B')

1. The compound 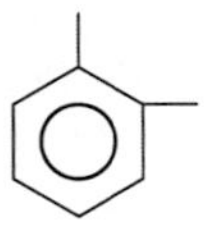 is used as
(a) antiseptic (b) antibiotic
(c) analgesic (d) pesticide

2. Which of the following is/are B-lactam antibiotic?
(a) Terramycin (b) Cephalosporin
(c) Penicillin (d) Both (b) and (c)

3. Drugs which prevent the formation of acid in the stomach is/are
I. Omepyrazole II. Lansopyrazole
III. Phenylbutazone IV. Magnesium trisilicate
(a) I, II (b) I, III
(c) II, III (d) III, IV

4. Which of the following drugs are used for the treatment of tuberculosis?
I. PAS II. I NH
III. Streptomycin IV. Chloromycetin
(a) I, II (b) II, III, IV
(c) I, II, III (d) I, IV

5. Non-narcotic analgesics are
I. Heroin II. Morphine
III. Phenylbutazone IV. Ibuprofen
(a) I, II (b) I, III
(c) II, IV (d) III, IV

Assertion & Reason

Codes

(a) Both A and R are true and R is the correct explanation of A.
(b) Both A and R are true but R is not the correct explanation of A.
(c) A is true but R is false.
(d) A is false but R is true.

6. **Assertion (A)** Aspirin can cause ulcer in the stomach.

Reason (R) The ester group in aspirin gets hydrolysed to acid group in the stomach where the pH is 2.

7. **Assertion (A)** Heroin is morphine diacetate.

Reason (R) Heroin is non-narcotic analgesics.

8. **Assertion (A)** Rain water normally has pH of 5.6.

Reason (R) It is due to the presence of H_2SO_4 and HNO_3 produced from oxides of sulphur and nitrogen.

9. **Assertion (A)** The lower of concentration of D.O., the more polluted is the water sample.

Reason (R) Oxygen is consumed by microbes for the decomposition of organic matter present in water.

10. When rain is accompanied by a thunderstorm the collected rain water will have a pH value
(a) slightly higher than that when the thunderstorm is not there
(b) uninfluenced by occurrence of thunderstorm
(c) which depends upon the amount of dust in air
(d) slightly lower than that of rain water without thunderstorm

11. The green house effect is caused by
(a) NO_2 (b) NO
(c) CO (d) CO_2

12. Peeling of ozone umbrella is due to
I. PAN II. Freons
III. CO_2 IV. NO
(a) I, IV (b) II, IV
(c) I, III (d) II, III

Matching Type

13. Match Column I with Column II and select the correct answer.

Column I		Column II	
A.	Microorganisms	1.	Chemical fertilizers
B.	Plant nutrients	2.	Abandoned coal mines
C.	Sediments	3.	Domestic sewage
D.	Mineral acids	4.	Erosion of soil by strip mining
		5.	Detergents

Codes

	A	B	C	D
(a)	3	1	4	2
(b)	2	5	3	1
(c)	1	3	2	4
(d)	4	2	1	5

14. Match Column with Column and select the correct answer.

Column I		Column II	
A.	Iodoform	1.	Anaesthetic
B.	Methyl salicylate	2.	Antiseptic
C.	Diethyl ether	3.	Insecticide
D.	Hexachlorocyclohexane	4.	Pain balm

Codes

	A	B	C	D
(a)	2	4	3	4
(b)	4	2	1	3
(c)	2	4	1	3
(d)	3	1	4	2

15. Which of the following statements about polar stratospheric clouds (PSCs) is not correct?
(a) Type I clouds are formed at about −77°C and contain solid $HNO_3 \cdot 3H_2O$
(b) Type II clouds are formed at about −85°C and contain some ice
(c) A tight whirlpool of wind called polar vortex is formed which surrounds Antarctica
(d) PSCs do not react with chlorine nitrate and HCl

16. Ozone is an important constituent of stratosphere because it
(a) prevents the formation of smog over large cities
(b) removes poisonous gases of the atmosphere by reacting with them
(c) destroys bacteria which are harmful to human life
(d) absorbs ultraviolet radiation which is harmful to human life

17. Select the correct statement about green chemistry from the following given statements.
(a) Green chemistry produces chemicals of our daily life by the use of green house gases.
(b) Green chemistry performs chemical processes which use green plants.
(c) Green chemistry performs only those reactions which are of biological origin.
(d) In green chemistry the use of non-toxic reagents and solvents to produce environmental friendly products.

18. White lung cancer is caused by
(a) asbestos (b) silica (c) paper (d) textiles

19. Eutrophication causes reduction in
(a) nutrients (b) dissolved salts
(c) dissolved oxygen (d) All of these

20. Which of the following statements about sewage treatment is false?
    (a) In primary treatment, large sized particles are filtered through screens and residual water is subjected to sedimentation
    (b) Secondary treatment involves aerobic digestion of the organic waste
    (c) In tertiary treatment, the waste water is treated with lime to remove phosphate followed by coagulation
    (d) Coagulation can be carried out by passing ozone through waste water

21. Which of the following is not a part of green chemistry?
    (a) Biochemistry (b) Sonochemistry
    (c) Photochemistry (d) Nuclear chemistry

22. Which of the following statements is not correct for nanomaterials?
    (a) Nanotubes are really, really strong
    (b) Thermal properties of nanotubes depend on size
    (c) Nanotubes do not used as cathodes for electron emitting devices
    (d) Cutting tools made of nanocrystalline materials

23. The structure of coacine is

(a)
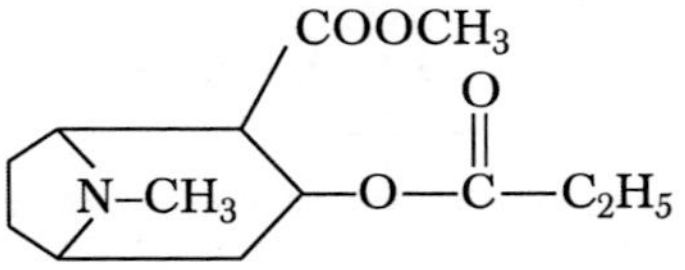

(b)
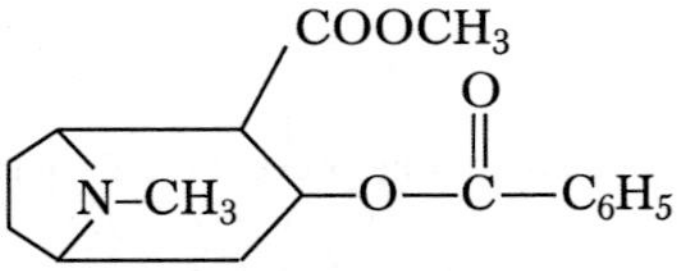

(c)
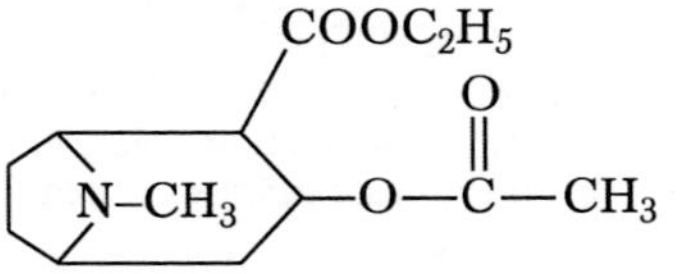

(d)
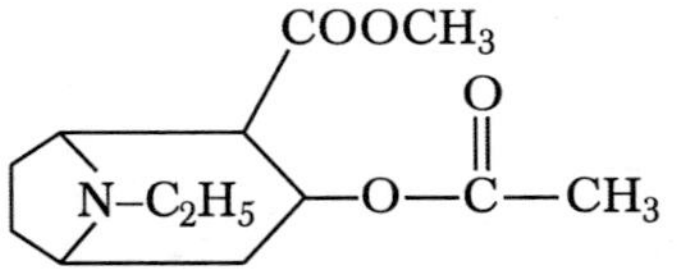

24. The acidity of normal rain water is due to
    (a) SO_2 (b) CO_2
    (c) NO_2 (d) NO

Answers

Exercise 1

1. (c)	**2.** (d)	**3.** (b)	**4.** (a)	**5.** (a)	**6.** (d)	**7.** (b)	**8.** (d)	**9.** (b)	**10.** (b)
11. (c)	**12.** (b)	**13.** (a)	**14.** (a)	**15.** (d)	**16.** (b)	**17.** (b)	**18.** (c)	**19.** (c)	**20.** (b)
21. (d)	**22.** (b)	**23.** (d)	**24.** (c)	**25.** (d)	**26.** (b)	**27.** (d)	**28.** (a)	**29.** (c)	**30.** (d)
31. (a)	**32.** (c)	**33.** (c)	**34.** (c)	**35.** (b)	**36.** (a)				

Exercise 2

1. (c)	**2.** (d)	**3.** (a)	**4.** (c)	**5.** (d)	**6.** (a)	**7.** (c)	**8.** (c)	**9.** (a)	**10.** (d)
11. (d)	**12.** (b)	**13.** (a)	**14.** (c)	**15.** (d)	**16.** (d)	**17.** (d)	**18.** (d)	**19.** (c)	**20.** (d)
21. (d)	**22.** (c)	**23.** (b)	**24.** (b)						

Hints & Solutions

Exercise 1

4. In the manufacture of ceramic capacitors $BaTiO_3$ materials in nanophase are employed.

6. Supramolecular chemistry is the study of weaker and reversible non-covalent interactions between molecules such as hydrogen bonding, metal coordination, hydrophobic forces, van der Waals' forces, pi-pi interactions etc.

10. Luminal is a hypnotic drug since it produces sleep.

11. Sulphaguanidine is used for bacillary dysentery.

19. Arsenic drugs such as salvarsan is used for the treatment of syphilis.

20. The chemical name of paracetamol is N-acetyl-*para*-aminophenol.

23. Aerosols use CFC and high flying jets release NO. Both are responsible for depletion of ozone layer.

24. The poisonous gas methyl isocyanate (MIC) is released during Bhopal gas tragedy.

30. Chlorofluorocarbons react with O_3 and cause depletion of ozone layer in the upper atmosphere.

31. Due to mercury poisoning in fishing water minamata disease is caused.

34. Addition of phosphate fertilizers into water leads to nutrient enrichment *i.e.,* eutrophication.

36. Photochemical smog is characterized by brown hazy fumes due to NO_2 which irritate the eyes and lungs, lead to the cracking of rubber etc.

Exercise 2

3. Omepyrazole and lansopyrazole prevent the formation of acid in the stomach.

8. Rain water normally has pH of 5.6. It is due to the dissolution of CO_2 present in the atmosphere.

10. The pH value of normal rain water is 5.6. Thunderstorm forms NO which gives HNO_3 on oxidation. Hence, rain water accompanying thunderstorm has a pH lower than 5.6.

12. Peeling of ozone umbrella is due to freons (*i.e.,* chlorofluorocarbons) and NO.

14. Iodoform – Antiseptic
Methyl salicylate – Pain balm
Diethyl ether – Anaesthetic
Hexachlorocyclohexane – Insecticide.

15. PSC reacts with chlorine nitrate and HCl to give HOCl and Cl_2 respectively.

18. White lung cancer is caused by textiles.

Solutions of Sample Questions as Provided on CSIR Website

Part 'B'

21. $[CoCl_4]^{2-}$ shows a deep blue colour because of

(a) metal to ligand charge transfer transition
(b) ligand to metal charge transfer transition
(c) spin allowed and Laporte forbidden *d-d* transition
(d) spin allowed and Laporte allowed *d-d* transition

Sol. (*d*) The electronic configuration of Co metal is

$$Co_{27} = [Ar]\,3d^7\,4s^2$$
$$Co^{2+} = [Ar]\,3d^7$$

The degenerate *d*-orbitals get splitted into two sets of orbitals in the presence of tetrahedral field as

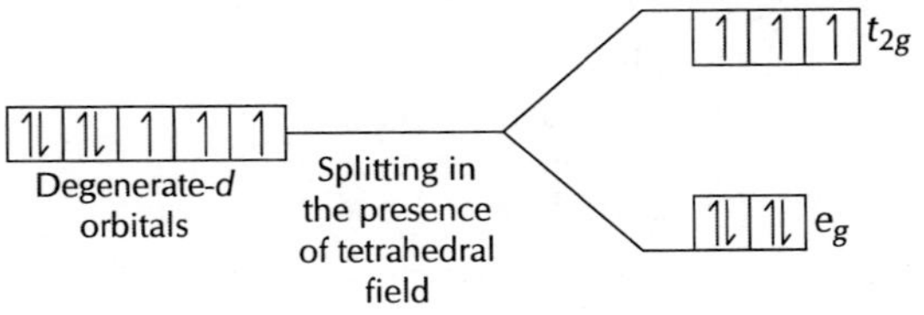

Tetrahedron has no centre of symmetry, and hence, the orbital in such a symmetry cannot be gerade. This largely overcomes the Laporte selection rules ($\Delta l \neq 0$, it is $= 1$) so that $[CoCl_4]^{2-}$ is very intense in colour.

Moreover, during the transition (e_g to t_{2g}), the number of unpaired electron remains the same, *i.e.*, $\Delta s = 0$, so it is also spin allowed.

22. The violet colour of iodine vapour is due to

(a) n-$\overset{*}{\pi}$ transition (b) n-$\overset{*}{\pi}$ transition
(c) n-$\overset{*}{\sigma}$ transition (d) $\overset{*}{\pi}$ - $\overset{*}{\sigma}$ transition

Sol. (*d*) The violet colour of iodine vapours is due to the absorption of certain wavelength, when an electronic transition takes place from the highest occupied $\overset{*}{\pi}$ molecular orbital to the lowest unoccupied $\overset{*}{\sigma}$ Mo. (*i.e.*, $\overset{*}{\pi}$ – $\overset{*}{\sigma}$ transition).

23. Choose the correct statement among the following.

(a) Diamond has lower thermal and electrical conductivities compared to graphite
(b) Diamond has similar thermal and electrical conductivities compared to graphite
(c) Diamond has higher thermal conductivity but lower electrical conductivity compared to graphite
(d) Diamond has the same thermal but lower electrical conductivity compared to graphite

Sol. (*c*) Diamond has three-dimensional network structure, in which each carbon atom is bonded covalently to each of the four other carbon atoms situated around it tetrahedrally. Since, no free electrons are present in it, so it is a bad conductor of electricity but the fixed atom can vibrate at their mean position and thus, make is thermally conducting.

Graphite, on the other hand, is composed of flat two-dimensional sheets of carbon atoms and contains free electrons, which make it conductor of electricity.

Thus, diamond has higher thermal conductivity but lower electrical conductivity as compared to graphite.

24. Which of the following is a nido-borane?

(a) B_4H_{10} (b) B_5H_9
(c) $[B_6H_6]^{2-}$ (d) B_5H_{11}

Sol. (*b*) The general formula of nidoborane is B_nH_{n+4}.

If $n = 5$, $B_5\,H_{5+4} = B_5H_9$

Thus, B_5H_9 is a ninoborane.

25. The oxidation number of sulphur in dithionite $[S_2O_4]^{2-}$ and dithionate $[S_2O_6]^{2-}$ are, respectively,

(a) + 3 and + 4 (b) + 3 and + 5
(c) + 4 and + 5 (d) + 4 and + 6

Sol. (*b*) Let the oxidation state of S in dithionite $[S_2O_4^{2-}]$ ion is *x*.

$S_2O_4^{2-}$

$$2x + (-2)\,4 = -2$$
$$2x = -2 + 8$$
$$x = \frac{6}{2} = +3$$

Let the oxidatioin of S in $[S_2O_6^{2-}]$ is *y*.

$S_2O_6^{2-}$

$$2y + (-2)\,6 = -2$$
$$2y = -2 + 12$$
$$y = \frac{10}{2} = +5$$

26. Among the three types of orbitals *p*, *d* and *f*

(a) both *p* and *f* orbitals have centre of symmetry
(b) both *p* and *d* orbitals have centre of symmetry
(c) only *d* orbitals have centre of symmetry
(d) *f* orbitals alone have centre of symmetry

Sol. (*c*) Only *s* and *d*-orbitals have centre of symmetry.

27. The absorbance of solution having 20% transmittance is

(a) 0.301 (b) 0.699
(c) 1.301 (d) 1.699

Sol. (*b*) Absorbance, $A = \log \frac{1}{T}$

$$= \log \frac{100}{20} = \log 5$$

$$= 0.699$$

28. The active site of enzyme nitrogenase contains

(a) Mo (b) Mn
(c) Fe (d) Cu

Sol. (*a*) Mo is present in the catalysts of dinitrogen fixing bacteria. The best known example is rhizobium which contains the metalloenzyme nitrogenase.

Nitrogenase, indeed, contains two proteins, molybdoferredoxin and azoferredoxin. The former one is brown, air sensitive and contain two Mo atoms.

29. Which one of the following is a free radical?

(a) CO (b) CN^-
(c) NO (d) CS

Sol. (*c*) Free radicals are the species having unshared pair of electrons or an open shell configuration. *e.g.,* NO (nitric oxide), Cl^-, CH_3 etc.

30. Choose the $16e^-$ complex from the following.

(a) $Ni(CO)_4$ (b) $Rh(PPh_3)_3Cl$
(c) $Fe(CO)_5$ (d) $(\eta^6\text{-}C_6H_6)_2Cr$

Sol. (*b*)

$$Ni(CO)_4 = 10 + 2 \times 4 = 18\ e^-$$
$$Rh(PPh_3)_3Cl = 9 + 3 \times 2 + 1 = 16\ e^-$$
$$(Fe(CO)_5 = 8 + 5 \times 2 = 18\ e^-$$
$$(\eta^6 - C_6H_6)_2Cr = 6 + 6 \times 2 = 18\ e^-$$

31. The species having metal-metal bond is

(a) $Mn_2(CO)_{10}$ (b) $Al_2(CH_3)_6$
(c) $V_2(O)_{12}$ (d) $Al_2(OPr^i)_{12}$

Sol. (*a*) Number of *M*-*M* bonds are calculated as

$$2 \times m + An + 2Z = Z \times n$$

(where, *m* = number of *M*-*M* bond

A = Atomic number of metal atom

n = number of metals in the formula

L = number of CO ligands

and *Z* = atomic number of nearest inert gas)

For $Mn_2(CO)_{10}$,

$$2x + 25 \times 2 + 2 \times 10 = 36 \times 2$$
$$2x + 70 = 72$$
$$2x = 2$$
$$x = 1$$

Thus, it contains only *M*-*M* bond.

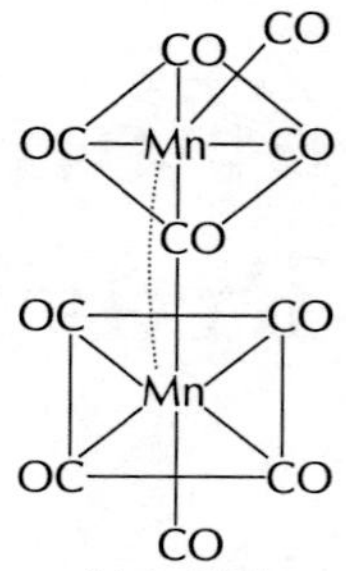

$(Mn)_2\ (CO)_{10}$

32. Choose the incorrect statement from the following.

(a) Fluorine has higher electronegativity than chlorine
(b) Fluorine molecule (F_2) has lower bond energy than chlorine molecule (Cl_2)
(c) Fluorine has higher electron affinity than chlorine
(d) Fluorine has a lesser tendency to form cation than chlorine

Sol. (*c*) The electron affinity of fluorine is lower than that of chlorine due to its smaller size as the incoming electron experience greater force of repulsion from the existing electrons.

33. The only molecule having bridging oxygen is

(a) phosphorus trioxide
(b) phosphorus pentoxide
(c) cyclic tetraphosphate
(d) pyrophosphate

Sol. (*c*) Cyclic tetraphosphate is the only such molecule among the given.

34. The coordination number of phosphorus in $[PMo_{12}O_{40}]^{3-}$ is

(a) 2 (b) 4 (c) 5 (d) 6

Sol. (*b*) In $[PMo_{12}O_{40}]^{3-}$, the central P atom is located at the centre of a PO_4 tetrahedra, which is surrounded by 12 MoO_6 octahedron, which share corners so that correct number of O atoms is utilised. Thus, the coordination number of P is 4.

35. Using phenolphthalein as the indicator, which of the following titration is possible?

(a) Acetic acid with pyridine
(b) Oxalic acid with sodium hydroxide
(c) Hydrochloric acid with aniline
(d) Sulphuric acid with aqueous ammonia

Sol. (*b*) For the titrations of weak acids and strong bases or strong acids and strong bases, phenolphthalein is used as a indicator.

Among the given pairs, oxalic acid is a weak acid and sodium hydroxide is a strong base, thus, for their titration,the indicator used is phenolphthalein.

36. Which of the following species is ESR-active?

(a) $VOSO_4$ (b) $K_2Cr_2O_7$
(c) $KMnO_4$ (d) $[Co(NH_3)_6]Cl_3$

Sol. (*a*) Only those species are ESR-active in which central atom contains unpaired electrons.

In $VOSO_4$, V is present as V^{4+}.

$$V^{4+} = [Ar]\,3d^1$$

One unpaired electron, so it is ESR-active.

In $K_2Cr_2O_7$, Cr is present as Cr^{6+}.

Thus, $$Cr^{6+} = [Ar]\,3d^0 4s^0$$

No unpaired electron is present, so it in not ESR-active.

In $KMnO_4$, Mn is present as Mn^{7+}.

Thus, $$Mn^{7+} = [Ar]\,3d^0 4s^0$$

No unpaired electron is presnet, so it is not ESR-active.

In $[Co(NH_3)_6]Cl_3$, Co is present as Co^{3+}.

$$Co^{3+} = [Ar]\,3d^6$$

NH_3 being a strong field ligand, pair up the unpaired electrons of Co, thus, $[Co(NH_3)_6]Cl_3$ contains no unpaired electron and hence, is ESR-inactive.

37. Ozone (O_3) absorbs UV radiation in the atmosphere and is decomposed mainly into

(a) O_2, O (b) O^{2-}, O^{2+}
(c) O_2^{2-}, O^+ (d) atomic oxygen

Sol. (*a*) $O_3 \xrightarrow{UV} O_2 + O^{\bullet}$

38. Large derivation from Trouton's rule is observed for systems which are

(a) having more ordered structure
(b) having more disordered structure
(c) having low melting points
(d) having low boiling points

Sol. (*a*) Liquids having strong molecular interaction, resist molecular motion and hence show a significant deviation from Trouton's rule.

39. The concentration of a reactant decreases linearly with time. What is the order of the reaction?

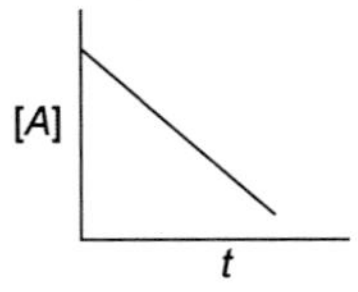

(a) First order (b) Fractional order
(c) Second order (d) Zero order

Sol. (*d*) For a zero order reaction, the concentration of a reactant decreases linearly with time.

40. The point group symmetry of the molecule *cis*-ML_4X_2 is

(a) C_{4v} (b) D_{4h} (c) C_{2h} (d) C_{2v}

Sol. (*d*) The symmetry element of *cis*-$[ML_4X_2]$ are

$$E, 2C_{2(x)}, C_{xz}, \sigma_{yz}$$

So, the point group is C_{2v}.

41. The point group symmetries of a square and a rectangle respectively, are

(a) D_{4h} and D_{2h} (b) C_{4h} and C_{2h}
(c) D_{4h} and C_{2h} (d) C_{4h} and D_{2h}

Sol. (*c*)

42. The number of rotational degrees of freedom of CO_2 is

(a) one (b) two (c) three (d) four

Sol. (*b*) For linear molecule like CO_2, the number of rotational degree of freedom is 2.

43. The magnitude of the nuclear spin angular momentum of a nuclei is $\sqrt{15}/2\hbar$ unit. The value of I is

(a) 5/2 (b) 1/2 (c) 1 (d) 3/2

Sol. (*d*)

44. Identify the molecule whose rotational constant cannot be determined by spectroscopic methods.

(a) CH_4 (b) H_2 (c) CO_2 (d) HCl

Sol. (*b*)

45. Which of the following transitions in the electronic spectrum of a homonuclear diatomic molecule is forbidden?

(a) $\Sigma_u^+ \to \Sigma_g^+$ (b) $\Sigma_g^+ \longrightarrow \Pi_u$
(c) $\Sigma_u^+ \to \Pi_g$ (d) $\Sigma_g^+ \to \Delta_u$

Sol. (*d*) For $\Sigma_g^+ \longrightarrow \Delta_u$ transition,

$$\Delta\wedge = 2 - 0 = 2$$

but for the allowed transition selection rule is $\Delta\wedge = 0, \pm 1$.

So, the above transition is forbidden.

46. The diffraction pattern of a cubic solid has an intense 110 Bragg reflection, but the 100 and 111 Bragg reflections are absent. The structure of the solid is

(a) body-centred cubic (b) primitive cubic
(c) face-centred cubic (d) edge-centred cubic

Sol. (*a*)

47. The logarithmic conductivity of a crystalline solid shows a linear variation with inverse temperature ($1/T$). The band gap may be obtained from

(a) slope of the plot
(b) intercept on the conductivity axis
(c) intercept on the temperature axis
(d) inverse slope

Sol. (*a*)

48. The molar masses of monodisperse and polydisperse polymers obey respectively the conditions ($\overline{M}_n$ = Number average molecular weight and $\overline{M}_w$ = Weight average molecular weight).

(a) $\overline{M}_n > \overline{M}_w$ and $\overline{M}_n < \overline{M}_w$ (b) $\overline{M}_n = \overline{M}_w$ and $\overline{M}_n < \overline{M}_w$
(c) $\overline{M}_n < \overline{M}_w$ and $\overline{M}_n < \overline{M}_w$ (d) $\overline{M}_n = \overline{M}_w$ and $\overline{M}_n = \overline{M}_w$

Sol. (*b*)

49. Curding from milk, an enzyme-catalysed reaction, is most efficient around

(a) 0°C and pH ≥10 (b) 0° C and pH ≤ 4
(c) 0° C and 4 ≤ pH ≤10 (d) 25° C and 4 ≤ pH ≤10

Sol. (*d*)

50. The spatial part of hydrogen molecular wave function in the simplest molecular orbital theory is given by σ_g^2 where, σ_g is normalized linear combination of two hydrogen 1*s* orbitals. Which of the following is true about the above wavefunction?

(a) It contains only covalent terms
(b) It includes only a small amount of ionic terms
(c) It contains only ionic terms
(d) it overstimates the ionic terms

Sol. (*b*)

51. A $2p_z$ orbital of hydrogen atom is an eigen function of

(a) H only (b) H and L^2 only
(c) H, L^2 and L_z only (d) H, L^2, L_z and L_x

Sol. (*c*)

52. By a reversible process, we mean one that always

(a) takes infinite time for completion
(b) satisfies ΔS (universe) = 0
(c) satisfies $\Delta G = 0$
(d) gives maximum work

Sol. (*a*)

53. A hydrogenic 3*p* orbital has the following form of the radial wave function (α_j = constant).

(a) $r(\alpha_1 - r)\, e^{-\alpha_2 r}$ (b) $r^2 e^{-\alpha_3 r}$
(c) $r(\alpha_4 - r)(\alpha_5 - r)\, e^{-\alpha_6 r}$ (d) $r^3 e^{-\alpha_7 r}$

Sol. (*a*)

54. The wave function $\sin^{-1} x$ is not acceptable because it is

(a) not continuous
(b) not differentiable
(c) not an eigen function of kinetic energy operator
(d) not a single-valued function

Sol. (*c*)

55. IUPAC name for the compound given below is

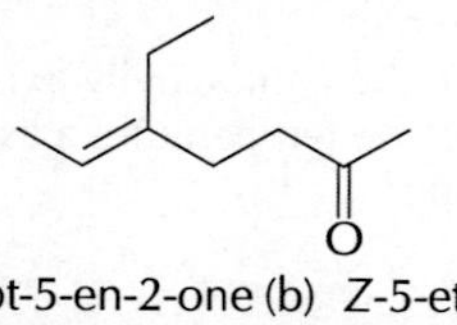

(a) *E*-5-ethylhept-5-en-2-one (b) *Z*-5-ethylhept-5-en-2-one
(c) *E*-3-ethylhept-2-en-6-one (d) *Z*-3-ethylhept-2-en-6-one

Sol. (*a*)

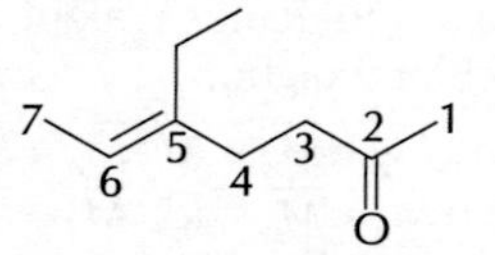

E-5-ethylhept-5-en-2-one

56. The most suitable reagent for the following transformation is

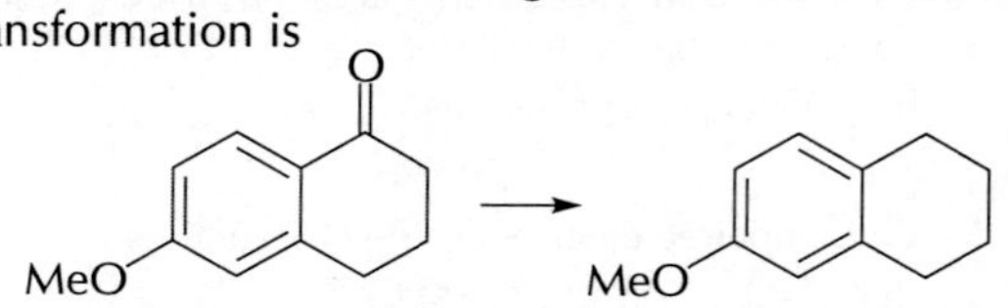

(a) $NaBH_4$ (b) B_2H_6
(c) Zn-Hg/HCl (d) NH_2NH_2/HCl

Sol. (*d*)

57. Acetophenone can be converted to phenol by reaction with

(a) *m*-CPBA followed by base catalysed hydrolysis
(b) conc. HNO_3
(c) iodine and NaOH
(d) singlet oxygen followed by base catalysed hydrolysis

Sol. (*a*) Baeyer-Villiger oxidation of ketones with peracids (like *m*-CPBA) results in ester which on base catalysed hydrolysis gives alcohol and salts of acid.

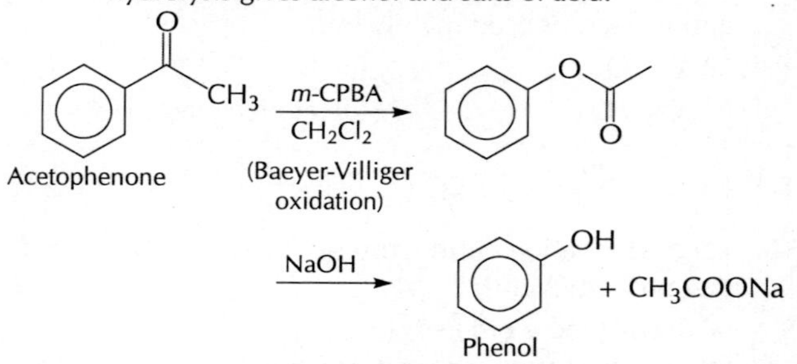

58. Reaction of phenyl benzoate with an excess of methylmagnesium bromide gives a mixture of

(a) triphenylmethanol and phenol
(b) 2-phenylpropan-2-ol and phenol
(c) acetophenone and toluene
(d) 2-phenylbenzoic acid and toulene

Sol. (*b*)

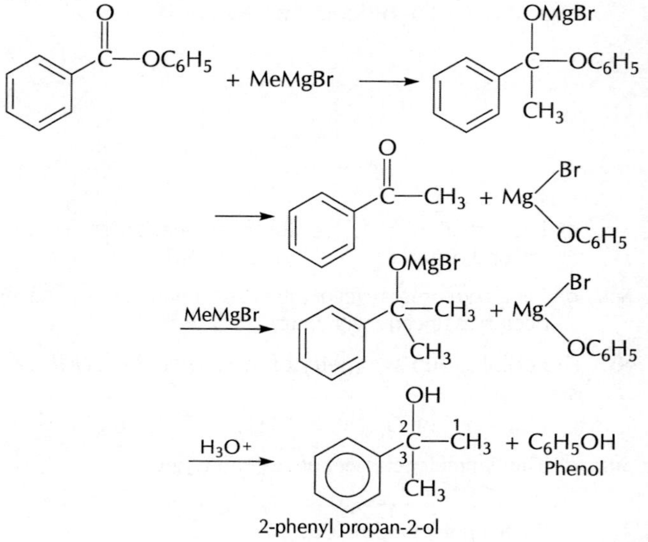

59. The major product formed in the reaction of 2-methylbut-3-en-2-ol with HBr is

(a) 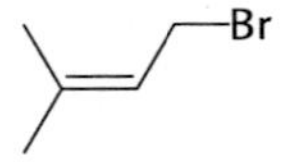

(b) 

(c) 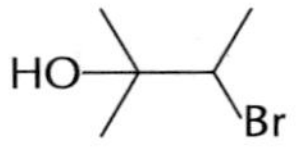

(d) 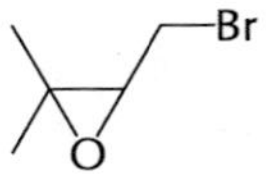

Sol. (*a*)

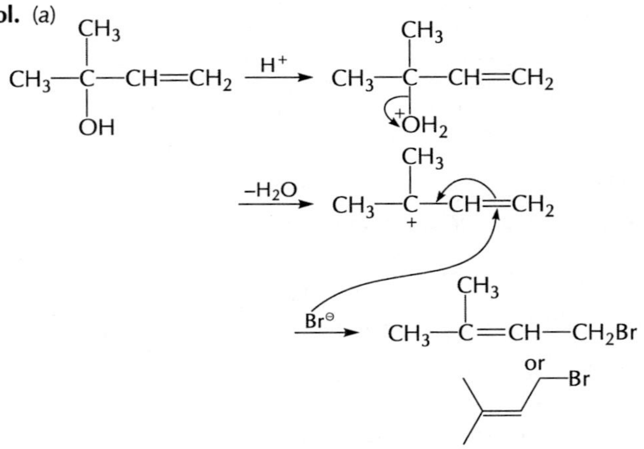

60. Among dimethylcyclobutanes, which one can exhibit optical activity?

(a) *Cis*-1,2-dimethylcyclobutane
(b) *Trans*-1,2-dimethylcyclobutane
(c) *Cis*-1,3-dimethylcyclobutane
(d) *Trans*-1,3-dimethylcyclobutane

Sol. (*b*) The structures of the given dimethylcyclobutanes are as

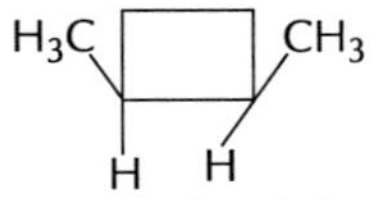

Cis-1,2-dimethyl cyclobutane

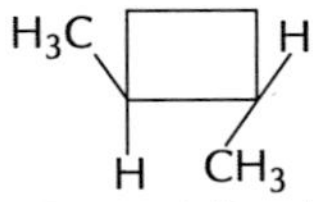

Trans-1,2-dimethyl cyclobutane

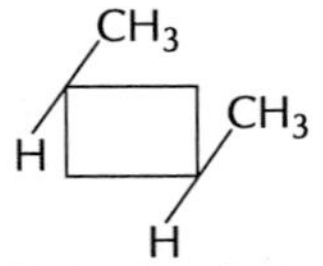

Cis-1,2-dimethyl cyclobutane

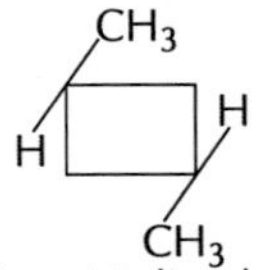

Trans-1,2-dimethyl cyclobutane

Thus, only *trans*-1,-2-dimethylcyclobutane exhibits optical activity due to the absence of symmetry elements.

61. The monomer of biopolymer DNA is a

(a) nucleotide (b) amino acid
(c) disaccharide (d) fatty acid

Sol. (*a*) Nucleotides are the monomer units of polymer DNA.

62. The order of chemical shifts (δ value) in the ^{1}H NMR spectrum of crotonaldehyde is

(a) olefinic > CHO > Me (b) CHO > Me > olefinic
(c) CHO > olefinic > Me (d) olefinic > Me > CHO

Sol. (*c*)

63. Natural sugars and amino acids are predominantly

(a) D-sugars and L-amino acids
(b) D-sugars and D-amino acids
(c) L-sugars and D-amino acids
(d) L-sugars and L-amino acids

Sol. (*a*) Natural sugars are predominantly D-sugars and natural amino acids are predominantly *L*-amino acids.

64. The product formed in the reaction given below is

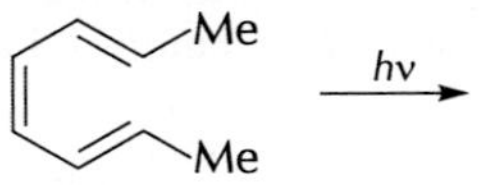

(a) 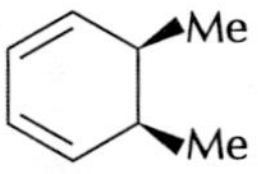

(b) 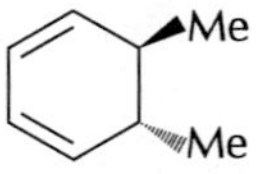

(c) 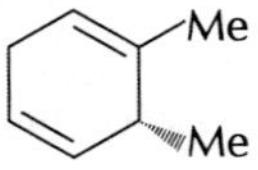

(d) 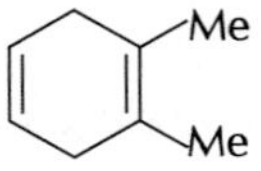

Sol. (*b*)

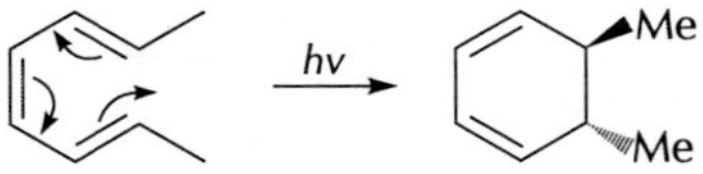

65. The major product formed in the reaction given below is

(a) 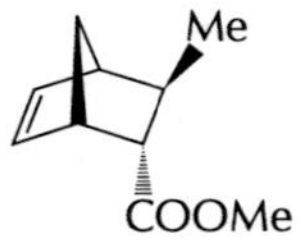

(b) 

(c) 

(d) 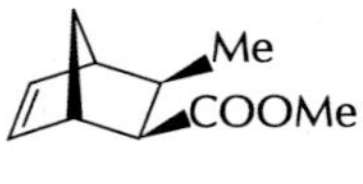

Sol. (*b*) The given reaction is a (2 + 4) cyclo addition reaction. It is an example of Diels' Alder reaction.

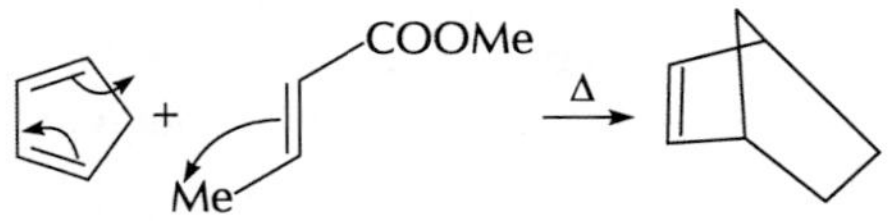

66. The conversion of excited singlet state (S_1) of a molecule to triplet state (T_1) is known as

(a) fluorescence
(b) phosphorescence
(c) intersystem crossing
(d) internal conversion

Sol. (*c*) Inter system crossing involves the conversion of excited singlet state (S_1) of a molecule to triplet state (T_1). This is because, the triplet state has a higher multiplicity and invertitably has a lower energy state than the excited singlet state.

67. The decreasing order of stability of the free radicals *A, B* and *C* is

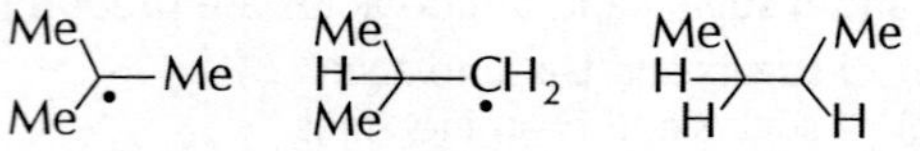

A *B* *C*

(a) $A > B > C$ (b) $C > A > B$
(c) $B > A > C$ (d) $A > C > B$

Sol. (*d*) Stability of free radicals depends upon the number of hyperconjugative structures. More the number of hyperconjugative structure (or more the number of α-H atoms to unsaturation), more will be the stability of free radical.

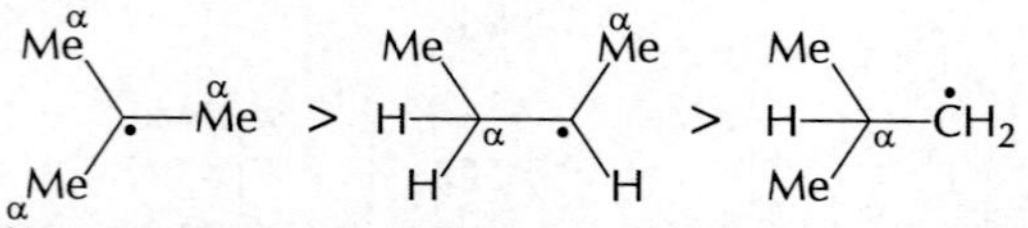

(9 hyperconjugative structure) (*A*) > (5 hyperconjugative structure) (*C*) > (1 hyperconjugative structure)

68. The major product formed in the reaction given below is

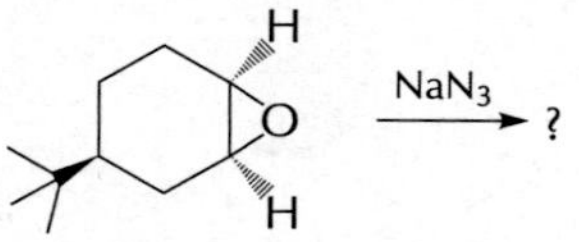

(a) 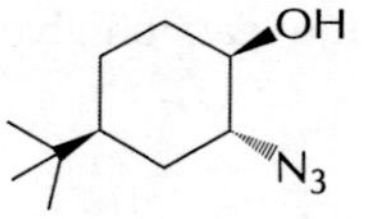 (b) 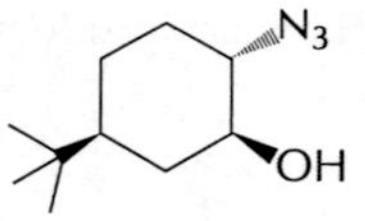

(c) 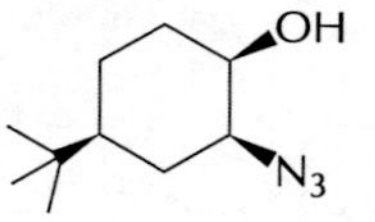 (d) 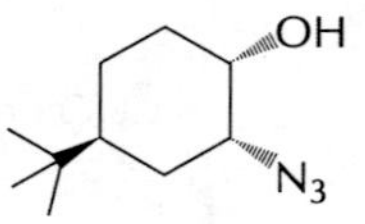

Sol. (a)

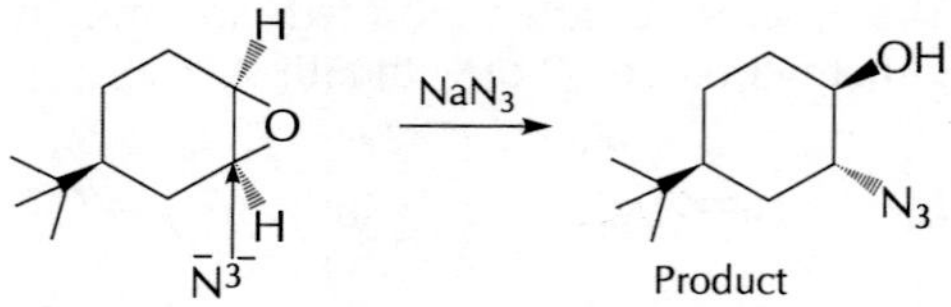

Product

69. The rate of keto-enol tautomerism in the ketones *A*-*C*, given below, are in the order

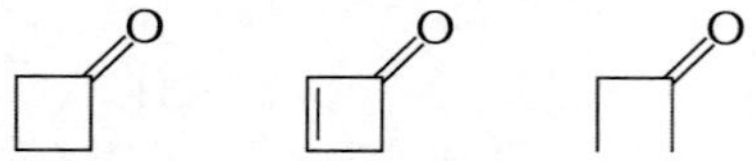

A *B* C

(a) $A > B > C$ (b) $A > C > B$
(c) $C > A > B$ (d) $C > B > A$

Sol. (c)

70. The reaction given below is an example of

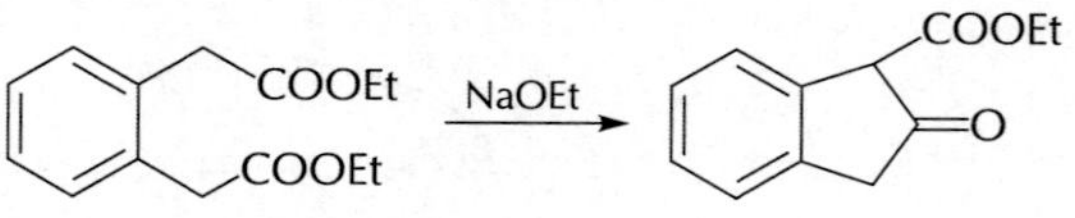

(a) aldol condensation
(b) Knoevenagel condensation
(c) Dieckmann condensation
(d) acyloin condensation

Sol. (*c*) The base catalysed intramolecular condensation of diester is called Dickmann condensation. It give five or six-membered keto cyclic ester, *e.g.*,

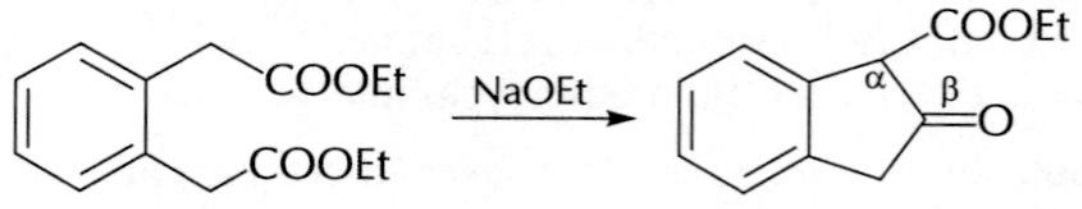

Diester β-keto ester

Part-C

71. The covalent radii vary gradually in the Periodic Table. From the orders given below for such radii, the correct ones are

(i) Ce > Lu (ii) Co > Ti
(iii) Sr > Ca (iv) I > Se
(a) (i) and (ii) only (b) (i) and (iii) only
(c) (i), (iii) and (iv) only (d) (ii), (iii) and (iv) only

Sol. (*c*) Covalent radii increases on moving down a group due to increase in the number of shells and decreases along a period due to increase in effective nuclear charge.

Thus, the correct orders of radii are

(a) Ce > Lu (due to lanthanoid contraction)

(b) Ti (1.32) > Co (1.16)

(c) Sr (1.92Å) > Ca (1.74 Å)

(d) I (1.33 Å) > Se (1.16 Å)

72. The first ionisation energy for the elements Si, P, S and Cl, follows the order

(a) Si < P < S < Cl (b) Si < S < P < Cl
(c) S < Si < P < Cl (d) S < Si < Cl < P

Sol. (*b*) The electronic configuration of the given elements is

$$_{14}Si = [Ne]3s^2\,3p^2$$
$$_{15}P = [Ne]\,3s^2\,3p^3$$
$$_{16}S = [Ne]\,3s^2\,3p^4$$
$$_{17}Cl = [Ne]\,3s^2\,3p^5$$

Generally along a period from left to right ionisation energy increases due to increased effective nuclear charge thus, the order should be

$$Si < P < S < Cl$$

But the ionisation energy of P is higher than that of S because of the presence of exactly half filled *p*-orbitals in P. Thus, the actual order of ionisation energy is

$$Si < S < P > Cl$$

73. The pair of gaseous molecules/ions having tetrahedral structure is

(a) $SnCl_4, PH_4^+$ (b) $SeCl_4, XeF_4$
(c) ICl_4^-, PH_4^+ (d) $SnCl_4, ICl_4^-$

Sol. (a) $SnCl_4 \Rightarrow$ 4 *bp* $\Rightarrow$ tetrahedral geometry

$PH_4^+ \Rightarrow$ 4 *bp* + 0 *lp* $\Rightarrow$ tetrahedral geometry
$SeCl_4 \Rightarrow$ 4 *bp* + 1*lp* $\Rightarrow$ distorted tetrahedral geometry
$XeF_4 \Rightarrow$ 4 *bp* + 2*lp* $\Rightarrow$ square planar geometry
$ICl_4^- \Rightarrow$ 4 *bp* + 2 *lp* $\Rightarrow$ square planar geometry

Thus, the geometry of only $SnCl_4$ and PH_4^+ is tetrahedral.

74. Consider the following.

	Volumetric method for Ag(I)	Indicator used
(i)	Fajan method	Chromate
(ii)	Mohr's method	Fluorescein
(iii)	Vohlard method	Ferric salt

The method and indicator matches correctly in

(a) (i) and (ii) only (b) (ii) and (iii) only
(c) (iii) only (d) (ii) only

Sol. (*c*) (i) In **Kazimeirz Fajans method** indicator used is dichlorofluorescein. The end point of this titration is marked by green suspension turning to pink.

(ii) In **Mohr's method** potassium chromate is used as a indicator.

(iii) **Vohlard method**, an example of back titration, involves the addition of exces of $AgNO_3$ to the analyte, the AgCl formed is filtered and the remaining $AgNO_3$ is titrated against NH_4SCN, with ferric ammonium sulphate as indicator.

75. An unknown lead solution has diffusion current of 1.0 μA. To a 10 mL of this solution 0.5 mL of 0.04 M lead is added. The diffusion current of the spiked solution is 1.50 μA. The concentration of the unknown lead solution is

(a) 0.0020 M (b) 0.0050 M
(c) 0.0035 M (d) 0.0010 M

Sol. (*d*)

76. The ^{32}P radioisotope, used in leukemia therapy, has $t_{1/2} = 14.26$ days. What % of ^{32}P remains after 35 days?

(a) 30% (b) 8%
(c) 81.7% (d) 18.3%

Sol. (*d*)

$$T = n \times t^{1/2}$$
$$35 = n \times 14.26$$
$$n = \frac{35}{14.26} = 2.45$$
$$N = N_0 \times \left(\frac{1}{2}\right)^n$$
$$N = 100 \times \left(\frac{1}{2}\right)$$
$$= 100 \times 0.1824$$
$$= 18.24\,\%$$

77. On a 30 cm column, the t_R of *A* and *B* respectively are 16.40 and 17.63 minutes. The t_0 of the column is 1.30 minute. The peak width at base lines for *A* and *B* are 1.11 and 1.21 minutes respectively. The column resolution R_S is

(a) 1.06 (b) 1.23 (c) 2.12 (d) 2.23

Sol. (*a*) Column resolution, $Rs = \dfrac{2\,\Delta Z}{w_A + w_B}$

where, w_A and w_B are the widths at the base for *A* and *B* respectively and ΔZ is the difference in time of their arrival at the electron.

$\therefore$
$$\Delta Z = 17.63 - 16.40 = 1.23$$
$$w_A + w_B = 1.11 + 1.21 = 2.32$$
$$Rs = \frac{2 \times 1.23}{2.32}$$
$$= 1.06$$

78. Which one of the following pairs of electronic configurations of high-spin transition metal ions (3*d*) in an octahedral field undergoes a substantial Jahn-Teller distortion?

(a) d^3, d^9 (b) d^4, d^9 (c) d^5, d^9 (d) d^6, d^9

Sol. (*b*) d^4 and d^9 configuration.

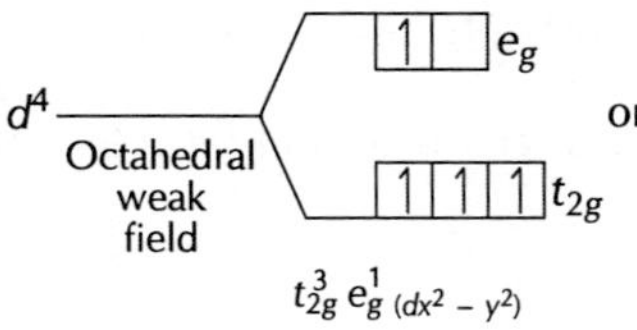

or

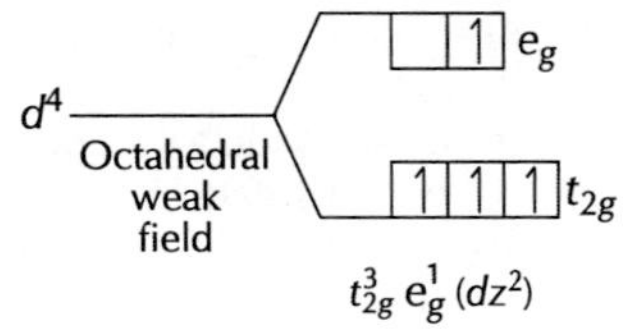

Similarly

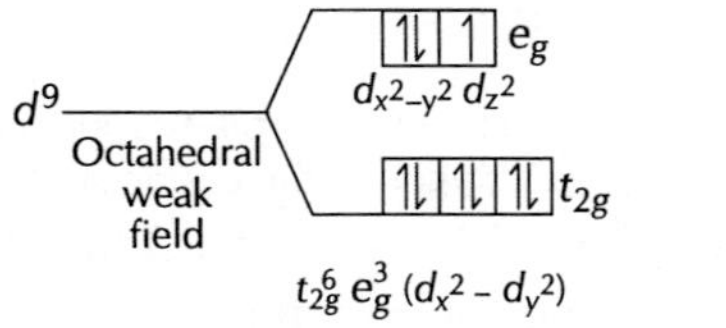

or

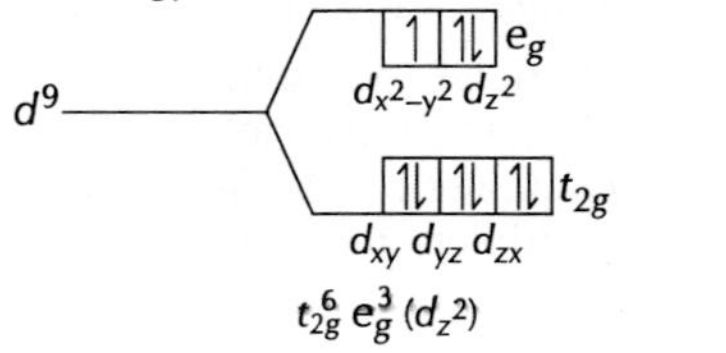

Thus, only d^4 and d^9 configuratiion show Jahn-Teller distortion due to unequal number of electrons in e_g orbital.

79. Which one of the following pairs consists of a good oxidising and a good reducing agent respectively?

(a) Ce(IV), Ln(III) (b) Ln(III), Eu(II)
(c) Ce(IV), Eu(II) (d) Ln(III), Ce(III)

Sol. (*c*)

$$Ce^{4+} = 4p^0\,6s^0$$
$$Ln^{3+} = 5d^0\,6s^0$$
$$Eu^{2+} = 4f^7\,6s^0$$

Ce^{4+} in aqueous solution have a strong tendency to change into Ce^{3+} ions and thus,it behaves as a good oxidising agent. (It is as strong as MnO_4^-).
Eu(II) is a good reducing agent.

80. Which one of the pairs of the following statements about reduction of $[CoCl(NH_3)_5]^{2+}$ by Cr(II) is correct?

(a) Reactant $[CoCl(NH_3)_5]^{2+}$ has non-labile coordination sphere
(b) Reaction proceeds by outer-sphere mechanism
(c) Reactant $[CoCl(NH_3)_5]^{2+}$ has labile coordination sphere
(d) Reaction proceeds by inner-sphere mechanism

Sol. (*b*) $[Co(NH_3)_5Cl]^{2+}$ is a inert oxidant. The Cl^- attached to it gets transferred to the reductant. The intermediate or the transition state must have X^- associated with both the oxidant and reductant. This suggests that the reaction proceeds by inner-sphere mechanism.

$$[Cr(H_2O)_6]^{2+} + [Co(NH_3)_5Cl]^{2+} \xrightarrow{\text{Slow}} [(H_2O)_5Cr{-}Cl{-}Co(NH_3)_5]^{4+} + H_2O$$

$$[(H_2O)_5Cr{-}Cl{-}Co(NH_3)_5]^{4+} \xrightarrow[\text{fast}]{\text{Hydrolysis}} [Cr(H_2O)_5Cl]^{2+} + [Co(NH_3)_5(H_2O)]^{2+}$$

81. Hemocyanin contains

(a) a dinuclear copper core and binds dioxygen in the cuprous state
(b) a dinuclear copper core and binds dioxygen in the cupric state
(c) a mononuclear copper core and binds dioxygen in the cuprous state
(d) a mononuclear coppper core and binds dioxygen in the cupric state

Sol. (*b*) Each subunit of homocyanin contains a pair of Cu atom and they can bind one O_2 molecule per pair of Cu atoms. It generally, display cooperativity of O_2 binding and binds dioxygen in the cupric state.

82. The ^{31}P NMR spectrum of $PF_4N(CH_3)_2$ at room temperature and low temperature (173 K) respectively shows (assume that N and H do not couple)

(a) triplet and quintet
(b) quintet and triplet
(c) quintet and triplet of triplets
(d) triplets and triplet of triplets

Sol. (*d*)

83. The number of hyperfine lines in the EPR spectrum of a one electron reduced produced of $[Co_3(CO)_9Se]$ (I = 7/2 for Co nucleus) is

(a) 8 (b) 15 (c) 22 (d) 1

Sol. (*a*)

84. The highest oxidation state of a metal in the following compounds is $(\eta^6\text{-}C_6H_6)_2Cr$, $Mn(CO)_5Cl$, $Na_2[Fe(CO)_4]$, $K[Mn(CO)_5]$ and $K[Mo(CO)_5Br]$

(a) 1 (b) 2 (c) −1 (d) −2

Sol. (*b*) $(\eta^6-C_6H_6)_2Cr$

$$-2 + x = 0$$
$$x = +2$$

$Mn(CO)_5Cl$

$$x + 0 \times 5 + (-1) = 0$$
$$x = +1$$

$Na_2[Fe(CO)_4]$

$$+2 + x + (0 \times 4) = 0$$
$$x = -2$$

$K[Mn(CO)_5]$

$$+1 + x + 0 \times 5 = 0$$
$$x = -1$$

$K[Mo(CO)_5Br]$

$$+1 + x + (0 \times 5) + (-1) = 0$$
$$x + 0 = 0$$
$$\therefore \quad x = 0$$

85. The maximum number of valence electrons of a metal in these complexes are :
$Mn_2(CO)_{10}$, $(\eta^5\text{-}C_5H_5)Mo(CO)_3Cl$, $(\eta^5\text{-}C_5N_5)_2Ni$, and $(\eta^5\text{-}C_5H_5)_2TiCl_2$

(a) 16 (b) 18 (c) 20 (d) 22

Sol. (*c*) $Mn_2(CO)_{10}$

⇒	2Mn	$14e^-$
	10 CO	$20e^-$
		$34e^-$ or $17e^-$

$(\eta^5-C_5H_5)Mo(CO)_3Cl$

⇒	$\eta^5\ C_5H_5$	$5e^-$
	Mo	$6e^-$
	3Co	$6e^-$
	Cl	$1e^-$
		$18e^-$

$(\eta^5-C_5H_5)_2Ni$

⇒	$\eta^5-C_5H_5$	$10e^-$
	Ni	$10e^-$
		$20e^-$

$(\eta^5-C_5H_5)_2TiCl_2$

⇒	$\eta^5C_5H_5$	$10e^-$
	Ti	$4e^-$
	2Cl	$2e^-$
		$16e^-$

86. The number of bridging and terminal carbonyls present in $Co_4(CO)_{12}$ at low temperature are respectively

(a) 3 and 9 (b) 4 and 8
(c) 6 and 6 (d) 0 and 12

Sol. (a) The structure of $Co_4(CO)_{12}$ is as

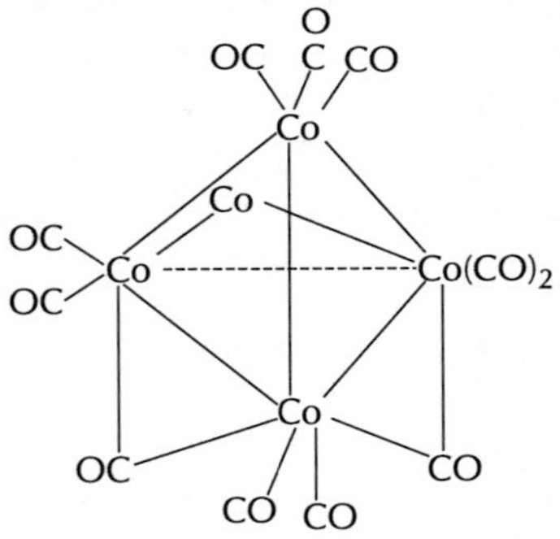

Thus, it contains 3 bridging and 9 terminal carbonyl groups.

87. Olefin hydrogenation using Wilkinson's catalyst initiates with

(a) olefin addition to $Rh(PPh_3)_2Cl$
(b) olefin addition to $Rh(PPh_3)_3Cl$
(c) a phosphine dissociation from $Rh(PPh_3)_3Cl$
(d) a phosphine addition to $Rh(PPh_3)_2Cl$

Sol. (c) Wilkinson's catalyst catalyses the hydrogenation of olefins. The mechanism of this reactions involves the initial dissociation of one or two triphenyl phosphine ligands to give 14 or 12-electron complexes, respectively followed by oxidative addition of H_2 to the metal.

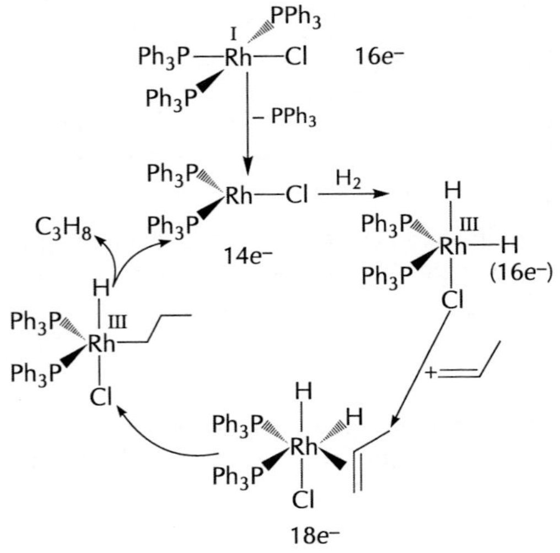

88. Although Fe(III) is a better Lewis acid compared to Zn(II), most hydrolytic enzymes contain Zn(II) at the active site because

(a) Fe(III) is a redox active ion
(b) Fe(III) has less abundance compared to Zn(II)
(c) Fe(III) generally makes octahedral complexes while Zn(II) makes tetrahedral complexes
(d) Zn(II) makes kinetically labile complexes

Sol. (c) Because Zn(II) makes generally tetrahedral complexes.

89. Considering the two complexes (*A*) $[Ni(H_2O)_6]^{2+}$ and (*B*) $[Ni(NH_3)_6]^{2+}$, the right statement is

(a) Complex (*A*) is diamagnetic and complex (*B*) is paramagnetic
(b) Complex (*A*) is paramagnetic and complex (*B*) is diamagnetic
(c) Both (*A*) and (*B*) are paramagnetic
(d) Both (*A*) and (*B*) are diamagnetic

Sol. (c) $[Ni(H_2O)_6]^{2+}$ contains Ni as Ni^{2+}

$Ni^{2+} = [Ar]\,3d^8\,4s^0$

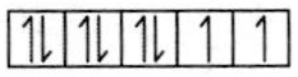

$[Ni(H_2O)_6]^{2+}$ =

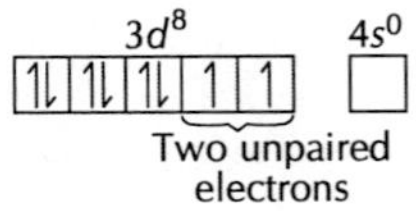

H_2O being weak field ligand cannot pair up the unpaired electron, thus it is paramagnetic

$[Ni(NH_3)_6]^{2+}$ = [Ar]

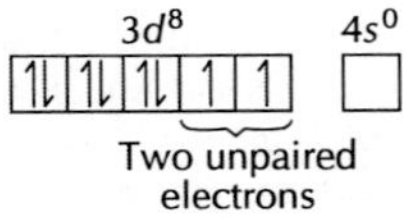

Because of the presence of two unpaired electrons, it is also paramagnetic.

90. Unlike *d*-*d* transitions, the *f*-*f* transitions

(a) do not change much with change in the ligand
(b) change significantly with change in ligand
(c) appear at low energies *i.e.*, at the near-IR region
(d) appear as broad bands

Sol. (a)

91. The solvent that will enhance electrical conductivity of N_2O_4 considerably is

(a) hexane (b) benzene
(c) nitromethane (d) carbon tetrachloride

Sol. (c)

92. The major product obtained by the reaction of PCl_5 with NH_3, NH_4Cl and $(NH_4)_2SO_4$ respectively are

(a) $(PNCl_2)_n$, $P(NH_2)_4Cl$ and $Cl_3P{=}NPOCl_2$
(b) $P(NH_2)_4Cl$, $(PNCl_2)_n$ and $Cl_3P{=}NPOCl_2$
(c) $Cl_3P{=}NPOCl_2$, $(PNCl_2)_n$ and $P(NH_2)_4Cl$
(d) $[PNCl_2)_n$ only

Sol. (a) $nPCl_5 + nNH_4Cl \xrightarrow{150°C} (NPCl_2)_n + 4nHCl$

93. Strongest superacid among the following is a

(a) solution of HNO_3 in H_2SO_4
(b) solution of $HClO_4$ in H_2SO_4
(c) solution of SbF_5 in HF
(d) solution of $SbCl_5$ in HCl

Sol. (c)

94. Consider the following statements regarding borazine

(i) It is isoelectronic with benzene.

(ii) Each nitrogen receives more σ-electron density from neighbouring boron than it given away as a π-donor.

(iii) It does not undergo addition reactions.

(iv) Nitrogen retains its basicity and boron its acidity.

The true statements among the above are

(a) (i), (iii) and (iv) (b) (i), (ii) and (iv)

(c) (i) and (iii) only (d) (ii), (iii) and (iv)

Sol. (*b*) The structure of borazine ($B_3N_3H_6$) is as

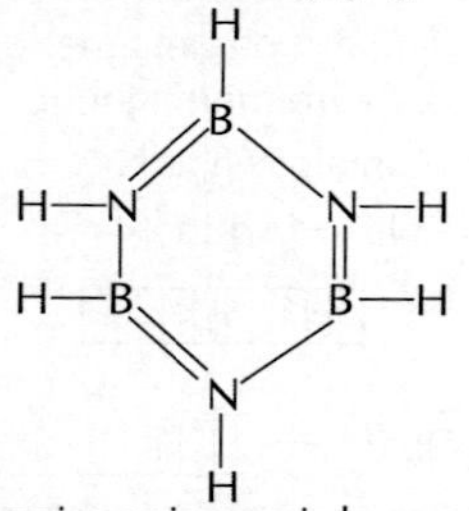

(Borazine or inorganic benzene)

It is isoelectronic with benzene. Molecular orbital calculations indicate that the π-electrons in borazine are only partially delocalised unlike benzene. In fact complete delocalisation in B_3N_3 ring is not expected either since N π-orbitals are of lower energy than the Bπ-orbitals, MO calculations indicate that the π-electron drift from N to B is less than the σ electron-drift from B to N due to greater electronegativity of N. These are thus the N-atoms which are relatively more negative than B-atoms in borazine.

The retention of negative charge by nitrogen implies that chemically borazine would be different from benzene. It is more reactive than benzene and readily undergoes addition reaction.

$$B_3N_3H_6 + 3HX \longrightarrow (H_2N - BHX)_3 \quad (X = Cl, OH)$$

95. Which of the following has linear shape?

(a) $H_3C—N=C=S$ (b) $H_3Si—N=C=S$

(c) $H_3C—N=C=O$ (d) $H_3C—O—CH_3$

Sol. (*b*) Because of the presence of empty orbitals in Si, $H_3Si—N=C=S$ has linear shape.

96. For a diffusion-controlled bimolecular reaction, the rate constant (k_D) is proportional to (T = temperature; η = coefficient of viscosity of medium).

(a) ηT (b) $\frac{1}{\eta T}$ (c) $\frac{T}{\sqrt{\eta}}$ (d) $\frac{T}{\eta}$

Sol. (*d*)

97. Consider the unimolecular reaction

$$A(g) \longrightarrow \text{products}$$

for which the following remarks were made.

(i) The reaction is second order at low pressure and becomes first order at high pressure

(ii) The reaction is first order at low pressure and becomes second order at high pressure

(iii) The reaction is zero order

Which of these is correct?

(a) (i) and (ii) (b) (ii) and (iii)

(c) Only (iii) (d) Only (i)

Sol. (*a*) Pseudo unimolecular reactions behave in this manner.

98. A random distribution of errors obeys the Gaussian form $\sqrt{A/\pi}\ \exp\ [-Ax^2]$. The mean and standard deviation of this distribution obeys

(a) $<x>=0$ and $\sigma_x = 1/\sqrt{A}$ (b) $<x>\neq 0$ and $\sigma_x = 1/\sqrt{A}$

(c) $<x>=0$ and $\sigma_x = \sqrt{A}$ (d) $<x>=0$ and $\sigma_x = A$

Sol. (*b*)

99. The function $\sin^{-1} x$ is not an acceptable wave function because

(a) it is not differentiable

(b) its first derivative is not continuous

(c) It does not cover the entire space

(d) it is not a single-valued function

Sol. (*b*) Because its derivative is not continuous in entire space.

100. The following is true of $2p_x, 2p_y$ and $2p_z$ orbitals of a H atom.

(a) All are eigen functions of L_z

(b) Only $2p_x$ and $2p_z$ orbitals are eigen functions of L_z

(c) Only $2p_y$ orbital is an eigen function of L_z

(d) Only $2p_z$ orbital is an eigen function of L_z

Sol. (*a*)

101. Given two Hermitian operators A and B, we construct the followng four additional operators

$$AB, ABA, i[A, B], A^2B.$$

Choose the correct option from below.

(a) All these 4 operators are Hermitian

(b) Only 3 of these operators are Hermitian

(c) Only 2 of these operators are Hermitian

(d) Only 1 of these operators is Hermitian

Sol. (*c*)

102. The first-order correction to energy for the ground state of a particle-in-a-box due to a perturbation λx would be

(a) $\lambda L/2$ (b) λL

(c) $2\lambda L$ (d) 2

Sol. (*c*)

103. Characters of a few symmetry operations are given below. Identify the character of the irreducible representation A'_{2g}

	E	C_n	C_2	i	σ_h
(a)	1	1	1	−1	−1
(b)	1	1	−1	1	1
(c)	1	−1	−1	1	1
(d)	1	1	−1	−1	1

Sol. (*b*)

104. The character of the irreducible representation A_1 in C_{3v} point group is given below

	E	$2C_3$	$3\sigma_v$
A_1	1	1	1

Identify one irreducible repreentation orthogonal to A_1 among the following.

	E	$2C_3$	$3\sigma_v$
Γ_1	1	-1	1
Γ_2	2	-1	0
Γ_3	2	0	-1
Γ_4	1	-1	-1

(a) Γ_1 (b) Γ_2 (c) Γ_3 (d) Γ_4

Sol. (a)

105. The energy levels of cyclopropene are $\alpha + 2\beta$, $\alpha - \beta$ and $\alpha - \beta$. The delocalisation energy in $C_3H_3^-$ is

(a) 2β (b) 0 (c) β (d) 3β

Sol. (a)

106. The rotational constant (B) of $H^{35}Cl$, $H^{37}Cl$ and $D^{35}Cl$ follow the order

(a) $H^{35}Cl > D^{35}Cl > H^{37}Cl$ (b) $H^{35}Cl > H^{37}Cl > D^{35}Cl$
(c) $D^{35}Cl > H^{35}Cl > H^{37}Cl$ (d) $H^{37}Cl > H^{35}Cl > D^{35}Cl$

Sol. (c)

107. Observe the following statements.

(i) Atomic mass of isotopes can be obtained from rotational spectra.
(ii) The separation between two successive rotational spectra lines of gaseons NO is $2B$ cm^{-1}.
(iii) The nmr spectrum of a compound gave a singlet at 300 Hz away from TMS using a nmr spectrometer operating at 60 Mhz. Its chemical shift is 3 ppm.

Which of the following is correct?

(a) (i), (ii) and (iii) (b) Only (iii)
(c) (i) and (ii) (d) Only (i)

Sol. (c)

108. In a crystal, atom A is at the corners of the unit cell, B is at the centre of the cell and the oxygen atoms are at the face-centred positions. What is the formula per unit cell?

(a) A_8BO_6 (b) ABO_6 (c) A_8BO_3 (d) ABO_3

Sol. (*d*) In the given a unit cell,

the number of A atoms per unit cell $= 8 \times \frac{1}{8} = 1$ atom

(because each corner atom is shared with 7 other unit cells.),
the number of B atoms per unit cell = 1 atom
and the number of O-atoms $= 6 \times \frac{1}{2} = 3$ atoms

$\therefore \quad A : B : O = 1 : 1 : 3$

Thus this formula per unit cell is ABO_3.

109. On mixing 100 ML of 0.1 M CH_3COOH and 50 mL of 0.1 M NaOH, the pH of the solution will be

(a) $pK_a + 0.301$ (b) pK_a
(c) $pK_a - 0.301$ (d) $pK_a + 0.477$

Sol. (*b*) $CH_3COOH + NaOH \rightleftharpoons CH_3COONa + H_2O$

CH_3COOH	$NaOH$	CH_3COONa	
100×0.1 mmol	50×0.1 m mol	0	0 Initially
$(100 \times 0.1 - 50 \times 0.1)$		50×0.1 mmol	At equilibrium
= 5 mmol		5 mmol	

Since, the solution contains a weak acid (CH_3COOH), and its conjugate base (CH_3COO^-), so acts as an acidic buffer and for acidic buffer,

$$pH = pK_a + \log \frac{[\text{salt}]}{[\text{acid}]}$$

$$= pK_a + \log \frac{(5)}{(5)} = pK_a$$

110. Using the fundamental equation $dA = -SdT - pdV$, the Maxwell relation is

(a) $\left(\frac{\partial S}{\partial p}\right)_T = \left(\frac{\partial V}{\partial S}\right)_V$ (b) $\left(\frac{\partial S}{\partial V}\right)_p = \left(\frac{\partial p}{\partial T}\right)_V$

(c) $\left(\frac{\partial T}{\partial V}\right)_S = \left(\frac{\partial p}{\partial S}\right)_T$ (d) $\left(\frac{\partial S}{\partial V}\right)_T = \left(\frac{\partial p}{\partial T}\right)_V$

Sol. (*d*) $dA = -SdT - pdV$ gives

$$\left(\frac{\partial S}{\partial v}\right)_T = \left(\frac{\partial p}{\partial T}\right)_V$$

111. The relationship between mean ionic activity coefficient of $Ca_3(PO_4)_2$ and its ions is given by

(a) $\gamma_\pm = \gamma_+^3 \gamma_-^2$ (b) $\gamma_\pm = \gamma_+^2 \gamma_-^3$
(c) $\gamma_\pm^5 = \gamma_+^3 \gamma_-^2$ (d) $\gamma_\pm^5 = \gamma_+^2 \gamma_-^3$

Sol. (a)

112. Assuming that C—H and C—X bond lengths

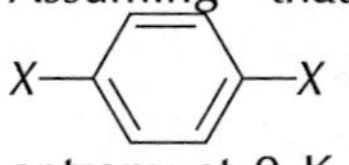

are nearly equal, the molar residual entropy at 0 K is

(a) 0 (b) $R\ln 2$ (c) $R\ln 3$ (d) $R\ln 6$

Sol. (a)

113. The contributions to the molar entropy by translational (tr), rotational (rot), vibrational (vib) and electronic (ele) degrees of freedom is in order

(a) tr > rot > vib > ele (b) rot > vib > tr > ele
(c) ele > vib > rot > tr (d) vib > rot > tr > ele

Sol. (a)

114. A binary mixture of A_2 and B_2 will show negative deviation from Raoult's law when

(a) A-B and B-B interactions are stronger than A-B
(b) A-A and B-B interactions are weaker than A-B
(c) Both A-A and B-B interactions are equal to A-B
(d) Either A-A or B-B interactions is equal to A-B

Sol. (*b*) For the solutions showing negative deviation from Raoult's law, the A-A (solute-solute) and B-B

(solvent-solvent) interactions are weaker than *A-B* (solute-solvent) interactions. For such solutions,

$$P_T^\circ < P_A{}^\circ x_A + P_B{}^\circ x_B$$

115. In the presence of external magnetic field the transition $^3D_1 \rightarrow {}^3P_1$ splits into

(a) 3 (b) 5 (c) 7 (d) 9

Sol. (a)

116. The term symbol for the ground state of rhodium (Rh, atomic number 45) is ^4F. The electronic configuration for this term symbol is

(a) [Kr] $4d^7\ 5s^2$ (b) [Kr] $4d^8\ 5s^1$
(c) [Kr] $4d^9\ 5s^0$ (d) [Kr] $4d^7\ 5s^1\ 5p^1$

Sol. (a) ^4F shows that

$$\Sigma L = 3 \qquad (\because \text{Orbital is } F)$$

and $$2S + 1 = 4$$

$$S = \frac{3}{2} \quad \text{so three unpaired electron}$$

Thus, configuration in [Kr] $4d^7 5s^2$.

117. Ionic equivalent conductance value for Ca^{2+} is 0.0119 ($Sm^2\ mol^{-1}$) and for Cl^- is 0.0076 ($Sm^2\ mol^{-1}$). The correct expected molar conductivity at infinite dilution for $CaCl_2$ is

(a) 0.0195 $Sm^2\ mol^{-1}$ (b) 0.0271 $Sm^2\ mol^{-1}$
(c) 0.0542 $Sm^2\ mol^{-1}$ (d) 0.01355 $Sm^2\ mol^{-1}$

Sol. (b)
$$\Lambda_m{}^\circ = \lambda^\circ_{Ca^{2+}} + 2 \times \lambda^\circ_{Cl^-}$$
$$= 0.0119 + 2 \times 0.0076$$
$$= 0.0271\ S\ m^2\ mol^{-1}$$

118. Find correct pair for ionic strengths of (i) a 0.02 molal solution of KCl and (ii) a 0.02 molal solution of K_2SO_4.

(a) (i) 0.020 $mol\,kg^{-1}$ (ii) 0.020 $mol\,kg^{-1}$
(b) (i) 0.20 $mol\,kg^{-1}$ (ii) 0.060 $mol\,kg^{-1}$
(c) (i) 0.020 $mol\,kg^{-1}$ (ii) 0.050 $mol\,kg^{-1}$
(d) 0.020 $mol\,kg^{-1}$ (ii) 0.030 $mol\,kg^{-1}$

(b) For 0.02 m KCl solution,

$$Z_+ = 1, Z_- = 1, m_+ = 0.02, m_- = 0.02$$
$$\mu = \frac{1}{2}(m_+z_+^2 + m_-z_-^2)$$
$$= \frac{1}{2}[0.02 \times (1)^2 + 0.02 \times (1)^2]$$
$$= \frac{1}{2}(0.04) = 0.020\ mol\,kg^{-1}$$

For 0.02 m K_2SO_4 solution,

$$Z_+ = 1, Z_- = 2, m_+ = 2 \times 0.02, m_- = 0.02$$
$$\mu = \frac{1}{2}[0.04 \times (1)^2 + 0.02 \times (2)^2]$$
$$= \frac{1}{2}[0.04 + 0.08]$$
$$= \frac{1}{2}[0.12] = 0.060\ mol\ kg^{-1}$$

119. The term symbol for the ground state configuration of NO is

(a) $^2\Pi_u$ (b) $^2\Pi_g$ (c) $^1\Pi_u$ (d) $^1\Pi_g$

Sol. (b) The MO electronic configuration of NO (7 + 8 = 15) is as

$$1\sigma_g^2, 1\sigma_u^{*2}, 2\sigma_g^2, 2\sigma_u^{*2}, 2\sigma_g^2, 2\pi_{4(x)}^2 \approx 2\pi_{4(y)}^2, 2\pi_{g(x)}^{*1}$$

120. The kinetic chain length (ν) is a measure of chain propagation. If the rates of consumption are denoted by R_c and rates production by R_p ; M and $M^\bullet$ denote the monomer and the active center, respectively. The correct definition of ν is

(a) $R_c(M) / R_p(M^\bullet)$ (b) $R_p(M^\bullet)/R_c(M)$
(c) $R_c\ (M^\bullet)/R_p(M)$ (d) $R_c(M)/R_c(M^\bullet)$

Sol. (a)

121. Amongst the following the correct statement for the compounds *A*, *B* and *C* is

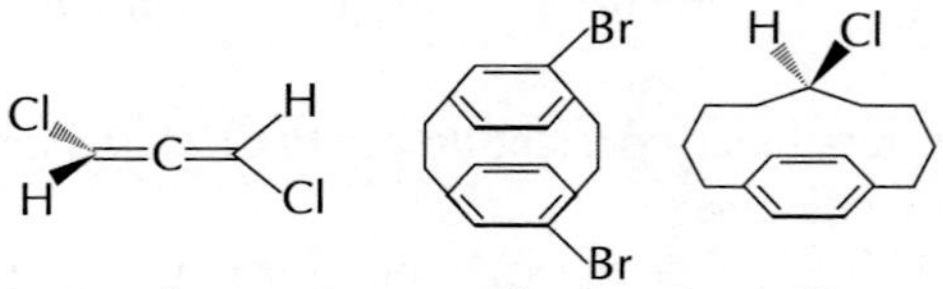

A *B* *C*

(a) *A* and *B* are achiral and *C* is chiral
(b) *A* is chiral and *B* and *C* are achiral
(c) *A* and *B* are chiral and *C* is achiral
(d) *A* is achiral and *B* and *C* are chiral

Sol. (c) *A* is a chiral allene, *B* is also chiral but *C* is achiral.

122. 4-*tert*-butylcyclohexanone on reduction gives two isomeric alcohols which are

(a) enantiomers (b) diasteromers
(c) rotamers (d) homomers

Sol. (a)

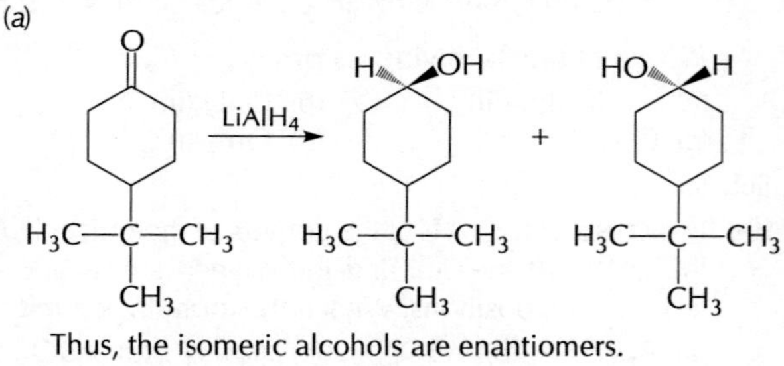

Thus, the isomeric alcohols are enantiomers.

123. For the following compounds *A* and *B* the correct statement is

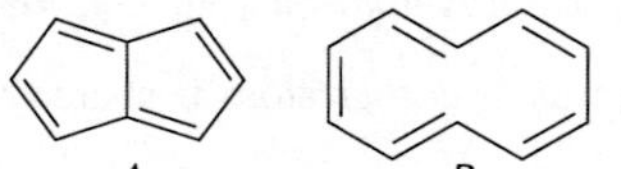

A *B*

(a) *A* is aromatic and *B* is anti-aromatic
(b) *A* is anti-aromatic and *B* is non-aromatic
(c) *A* and *B* are both aromatic
(d) *A* and *B* are both non-aromatic

Sol. (*b*)

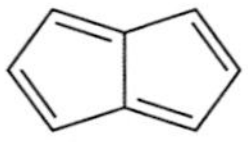

Because of the presence of $8\pi e^-$ ($4n\pi e^-$), it is an anti-aromatic compound.

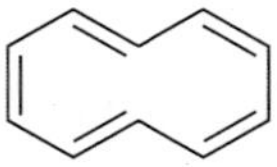

Number of $\pi e^- = 10\ e^-$ which are in accordance to Huckel's rule, but it is non-aromatic due to its non-planar structure.

124. Identify the product formed in the following transformations

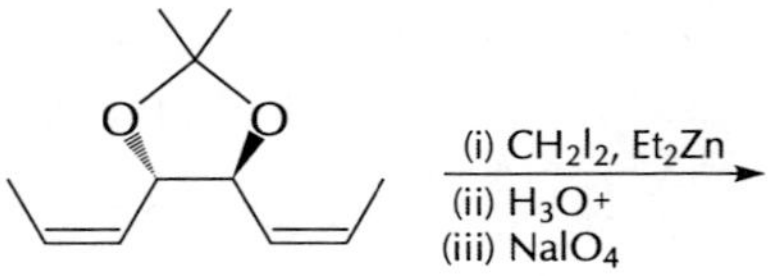

(a) 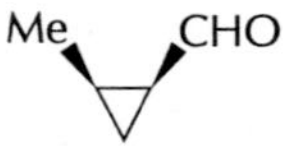

(b) 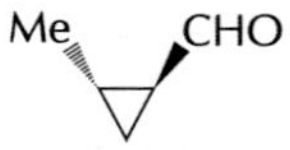

(c) 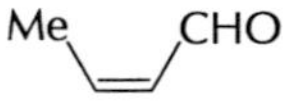

(d) 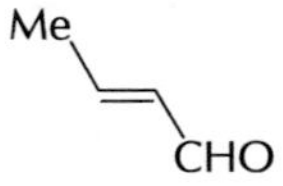

Sol. (*b*)

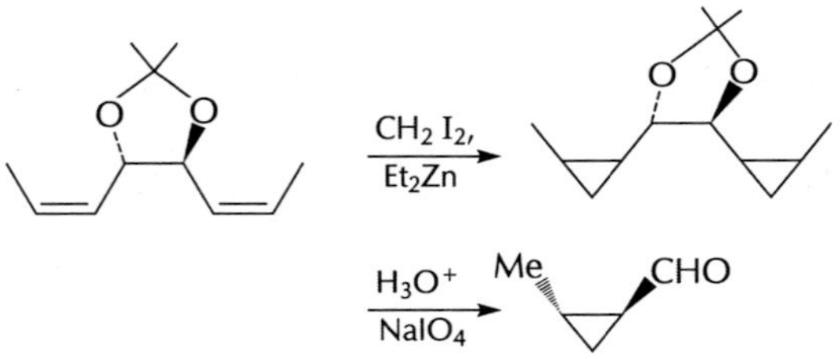

125. Identify the product formed in the following sequence of reactions

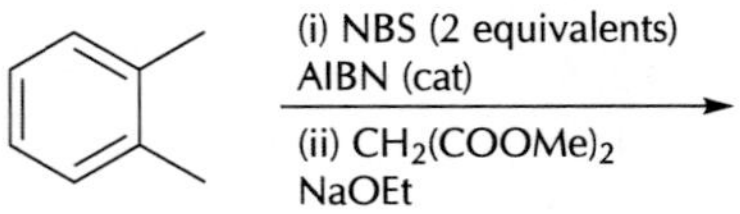

(a) 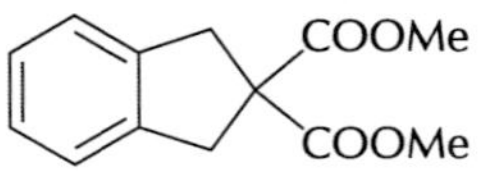

(b) 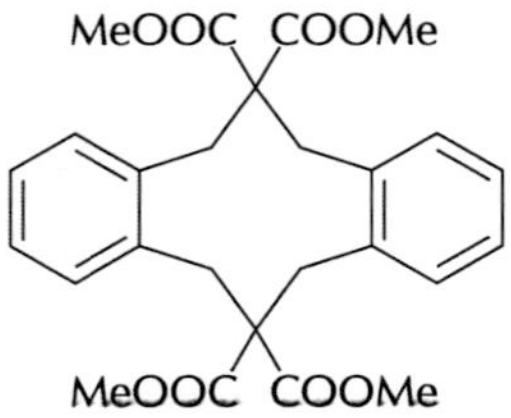

(c) 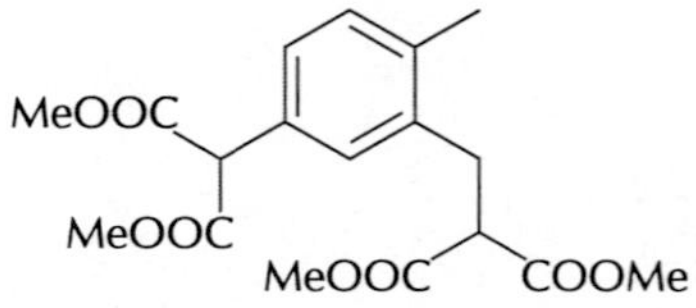

(d) 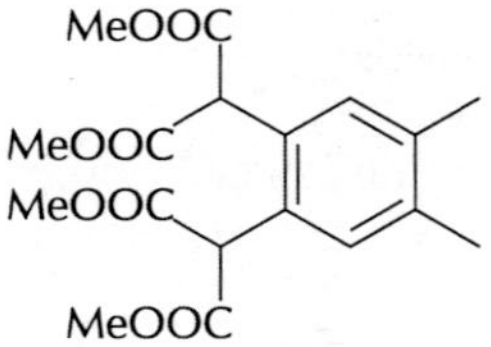

Sol. (*a*)

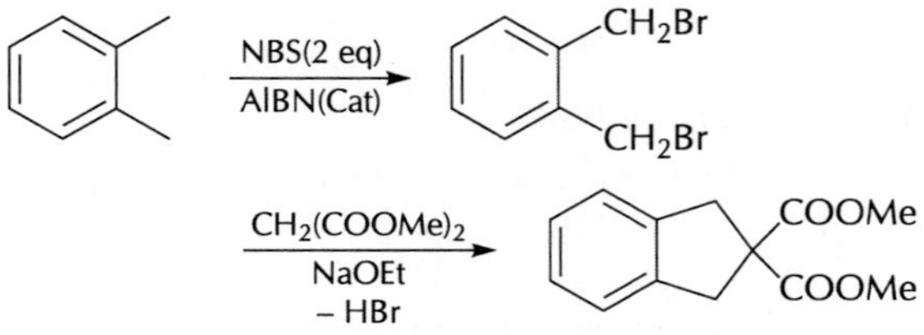

126. Identify the products *A* and *B* in the following reaction sequence

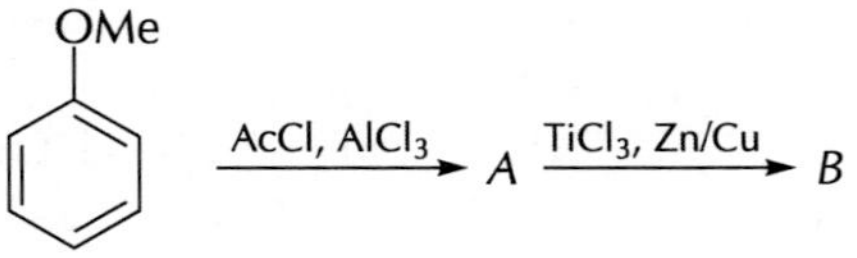

(a) *A* is 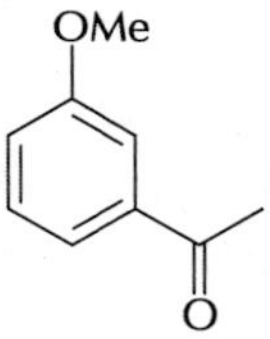 and *B* is 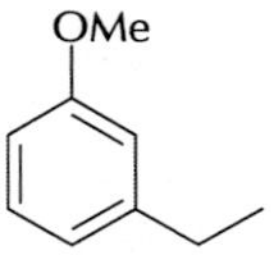

(b) *A* is 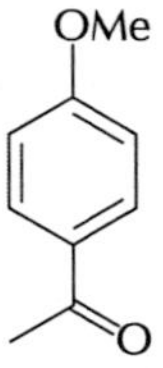 and *B* is 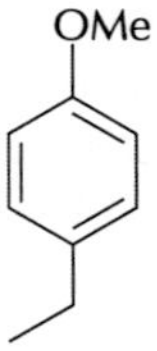

(c) *A* is 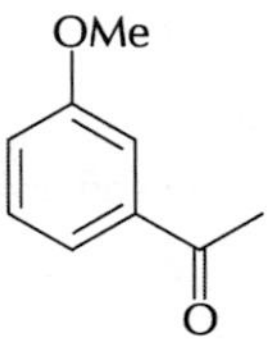 and *B* is 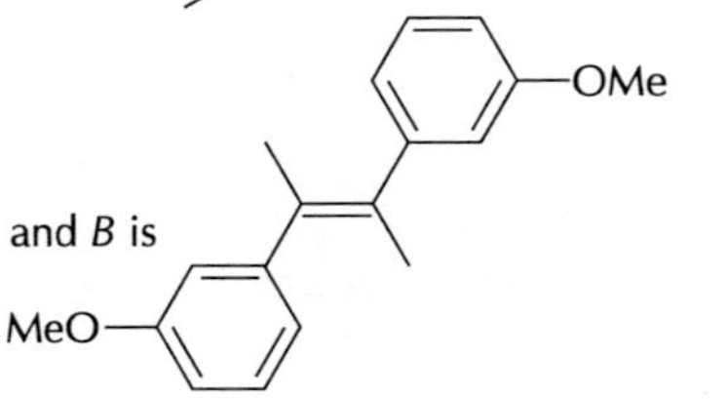

(d) *A* is 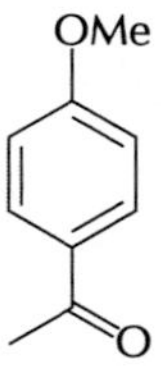 and *B* is 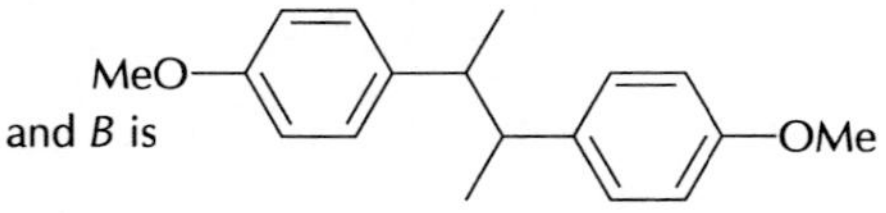

Sol. *(d)*

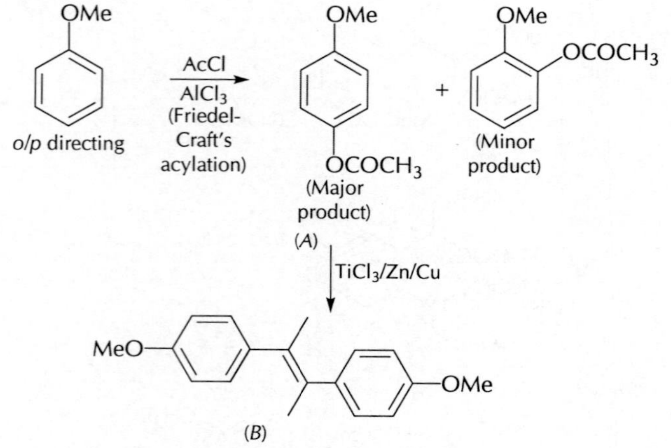

127. Match the following.

A. Conversion of 1,7-octadiene to cyclohexene — (i) Wacker oxidation

B. Conversion of bromobenzene to ethyl cinnamate — (ii) McMurry coupling

C. Conversion of 1-hexene to 2-hexanone — (iii) Heck reaction

(iv) Olefin Metathesis

(a) A : iv; B : ii; C : iii (b) A : ii; B : iv; C : i

(c) A : iv; B : iii; C : i (d) A : i; B : iii; C : iv

Sol. *(c)* (i) Wacker oxidation allow the synthesis of 2-hexan one from 1-hexene by $PdCl_2$ catalyst/$CuCl_2$ (cat) and O_2.

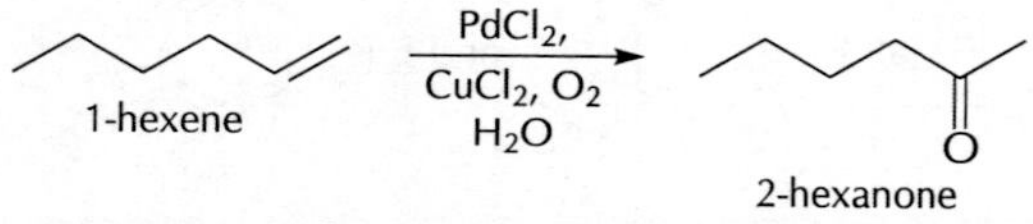

(ii) McMurry coupling is induced by single electron transfer to the >C=O from alkali metal followed by deoxygenation of the 1, 2-diol with low valent Ti.

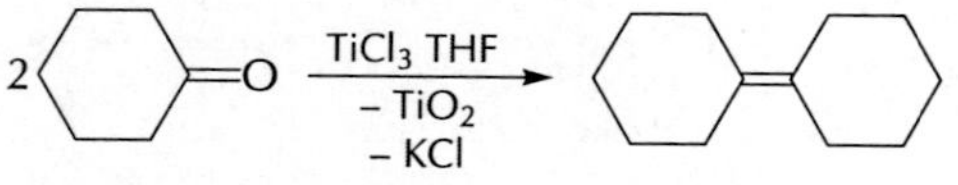

Heck reaction is a Pd-catalysed C—C coupling reaction between aryl halide or vinyl halide and activated alkene in the presence of a base.

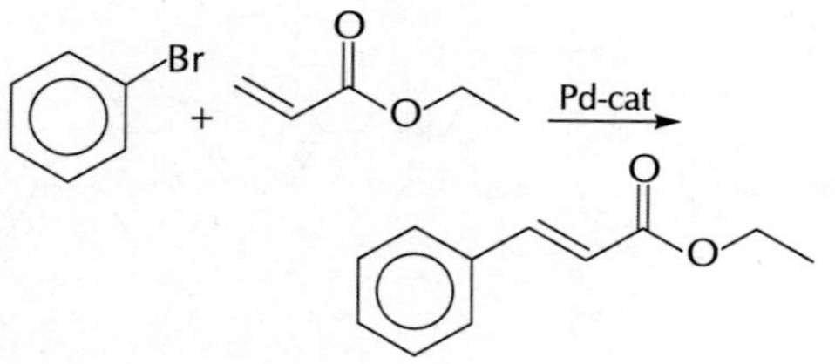

Olefin metathesis

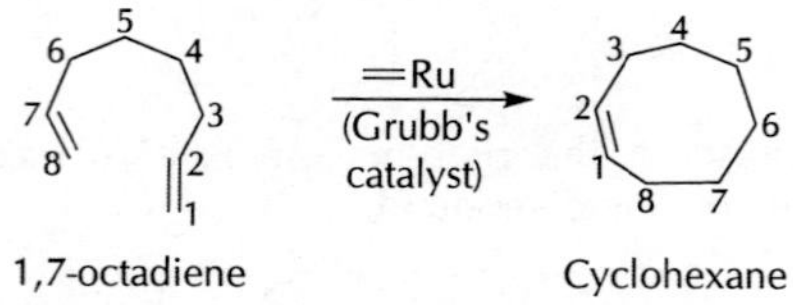

128. Reagents that can be used in the following conversion are

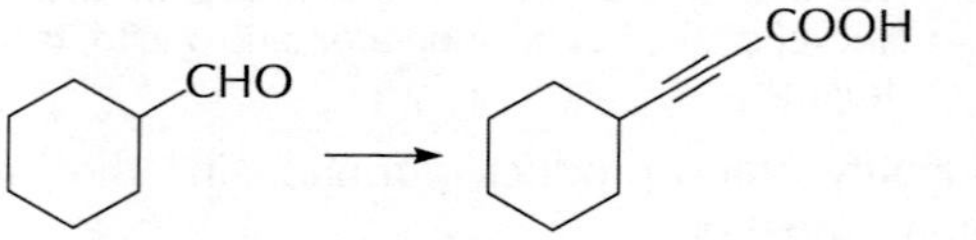

(a) (i) $Ph_3P{=}CH_2$, (ii) HCN, (iii) H_3O^+

(b) (i) $HS(CH_2)_2SH$, (ii) *n*-BuLi, (iii) $BrCH_2COOH$

(c) (i) EtMgI, (ii) $KMnO_4$

(d) (i) Ph_3P, CBr_4, (ii) *n*-BuLi, (iii) CO_2

Sol. *(d)*

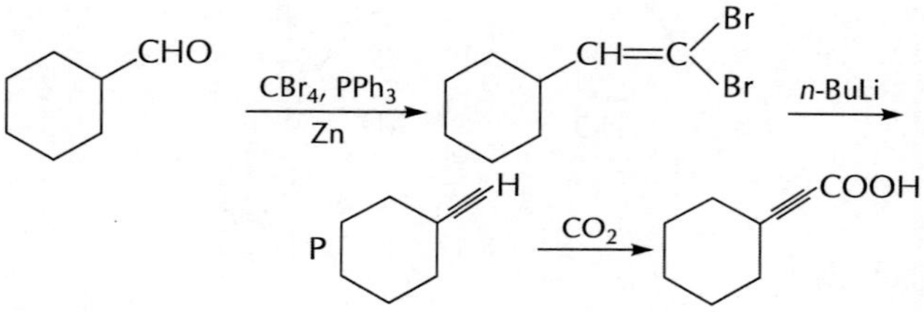

129. The major product formed in the following reaction is

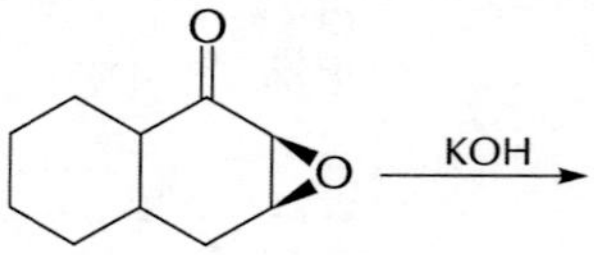

(a) 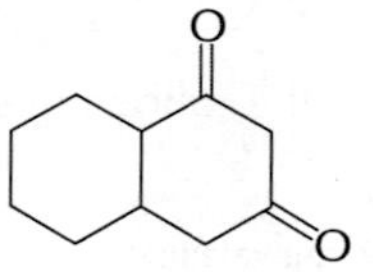 (b) 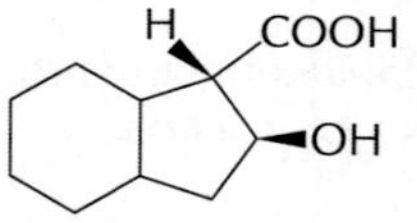

(c) 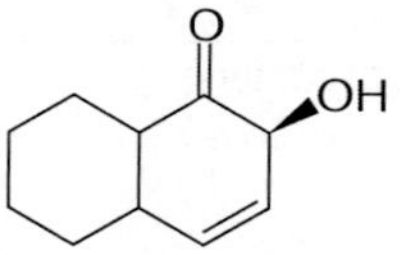 (d) 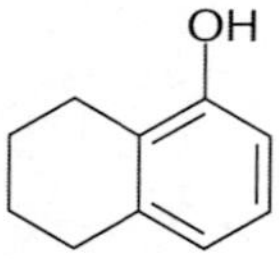

Sol. *(b)*

130. In the following reaction, the structure of the major product is

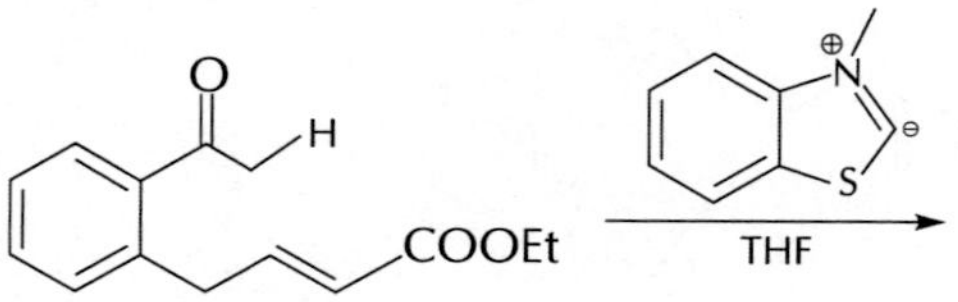

(a) 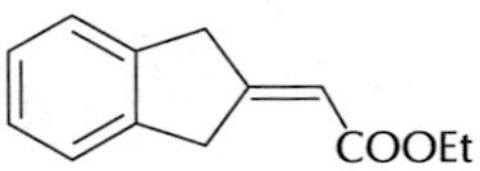

(b) 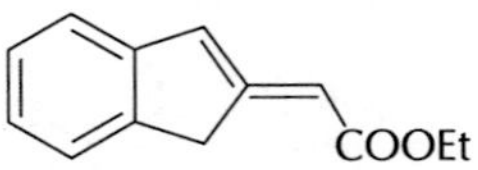

(c) 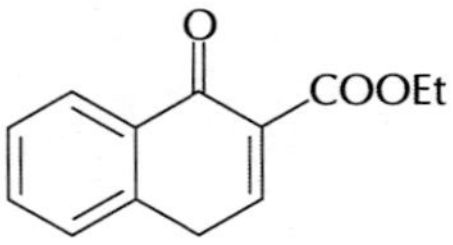

(d) 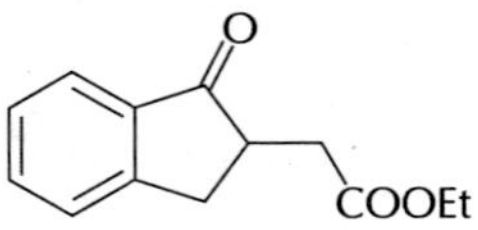

Sol. (*a*)

131. For the following reaction, the structure of the major product is

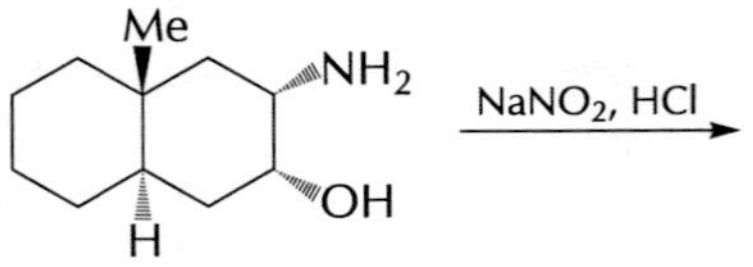

(a) 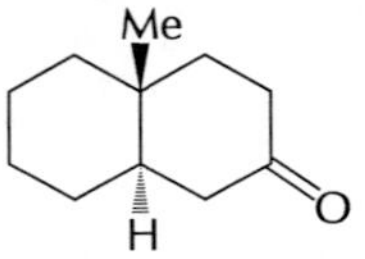

(b) 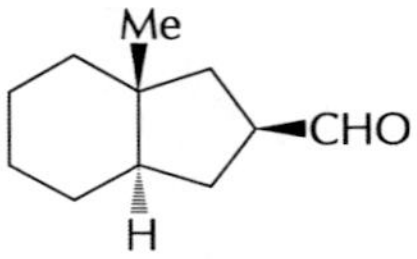

(c) 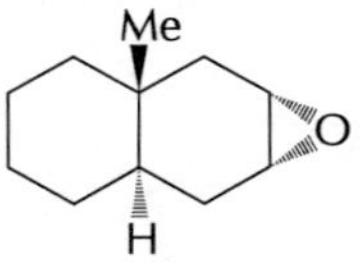

(d) 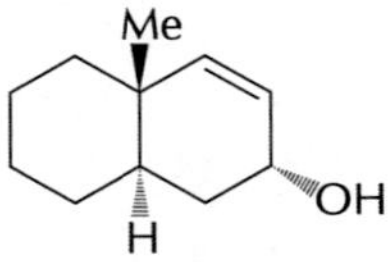

Sol. (*a*)

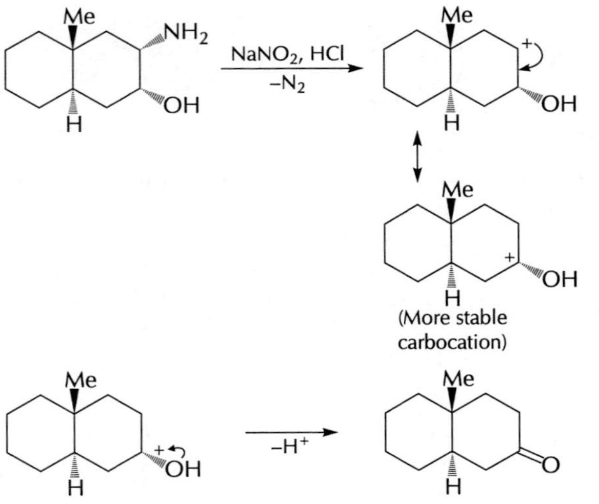

132. Identify the products *A* and *B* in the following reaction sequence.

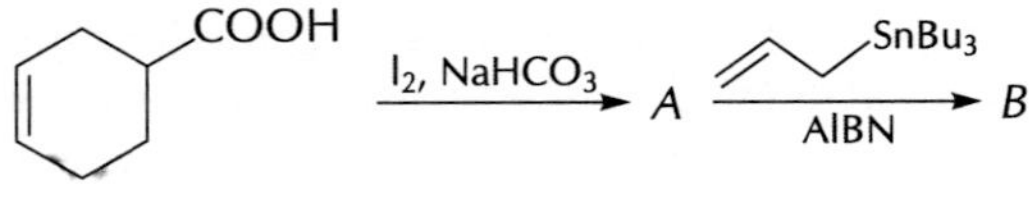

(a) *A* is 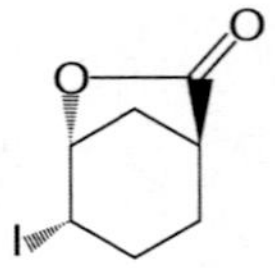 *B* is 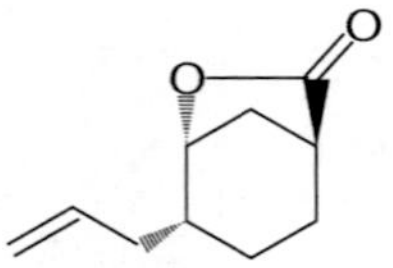

(b) *A* is 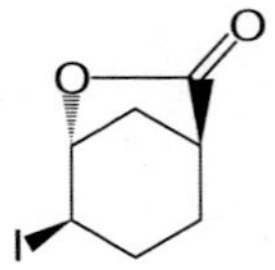 *B* is 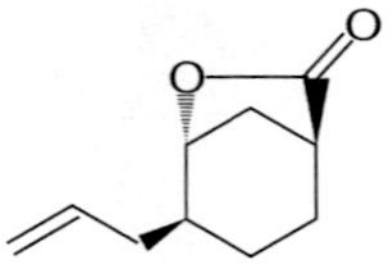

(c) *A* is 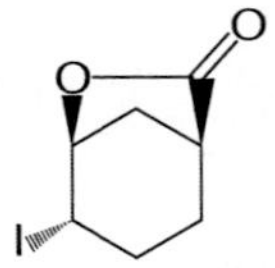 *B* is 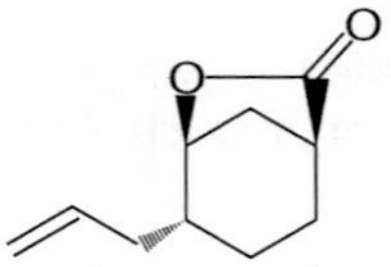

(d) *A* is 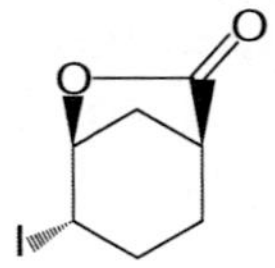 *B* is 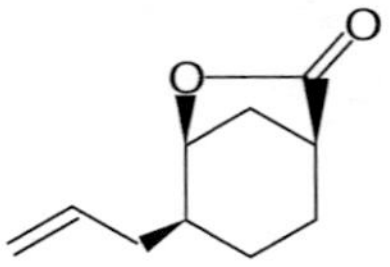

Sol. (*b*)

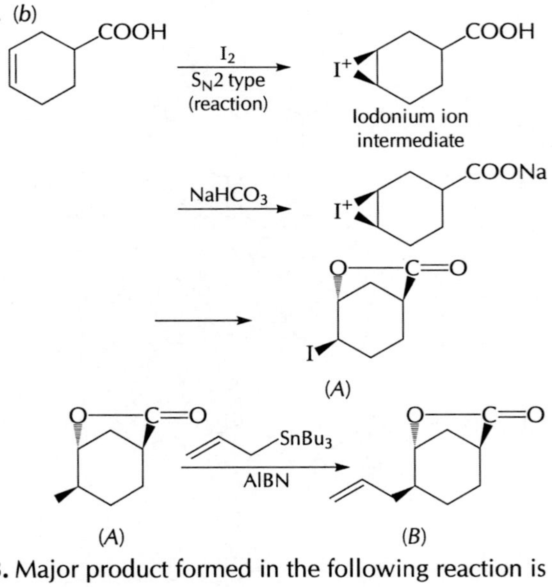

133. Major product formed in the following reaction is

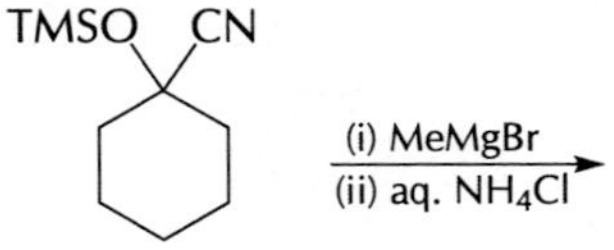

(a) 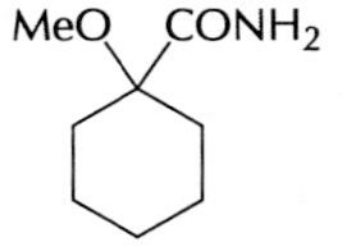

(b) 

(c) 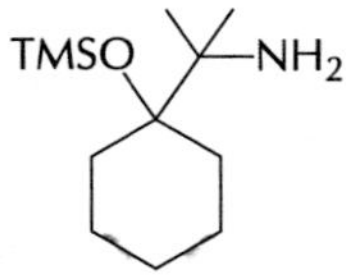

(d) 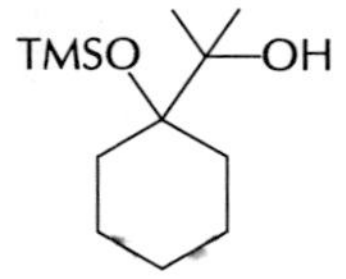

Sol. (*a*)

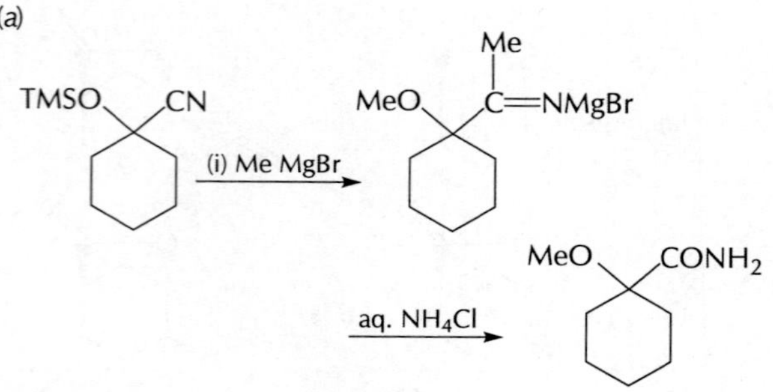

134. In the following reaction sequence the structure of the major products *X* and *Y* are

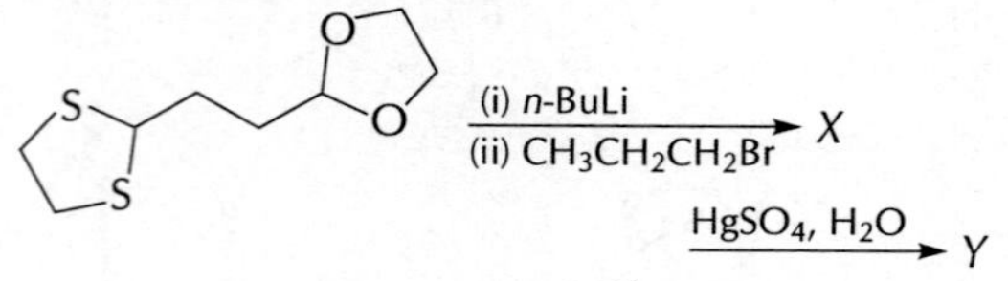

(a) *X* is 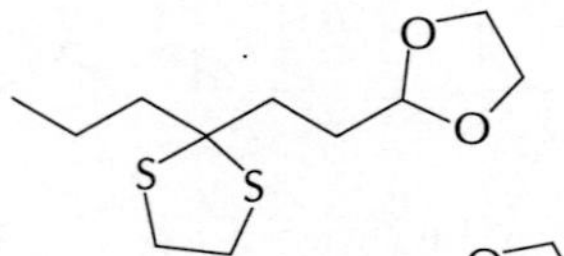

and *Y* is 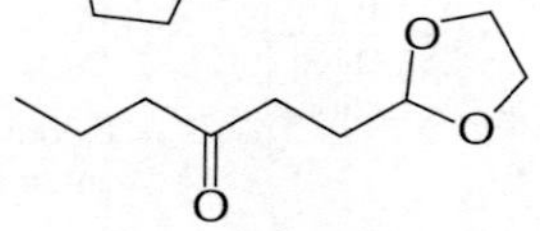

(b) *X* is 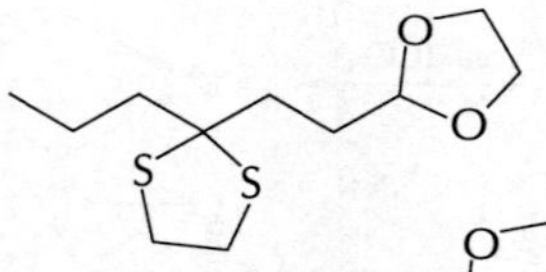

and *Y* is 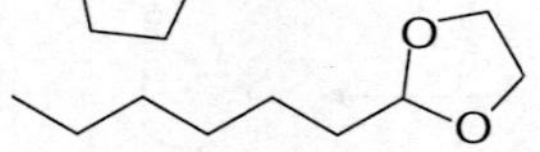

(c) *X* is 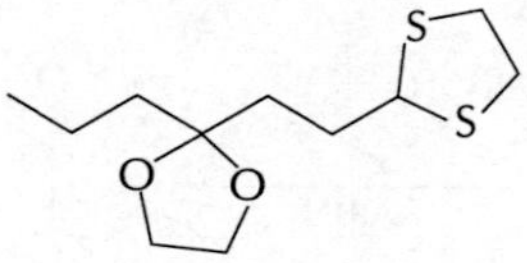

and *Y* is 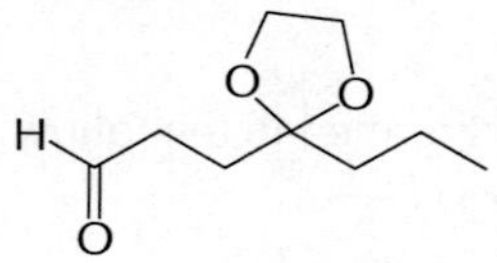

(d) *X* is 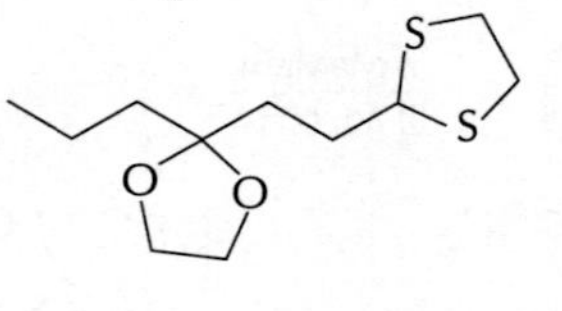

Sol. (*b*)

135. Product of sharpless kinetic resolution of the following alcohol with (–)-diethyl tartrate is

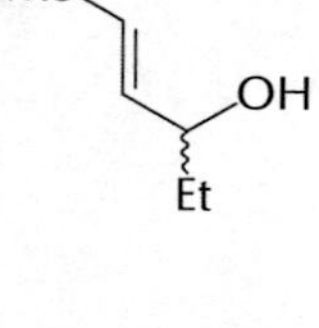

(a) 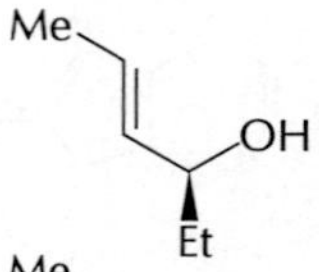 (b) 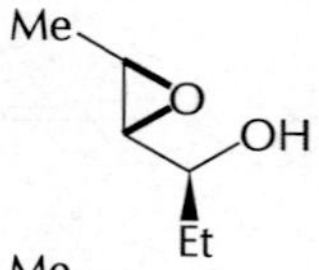

(c) 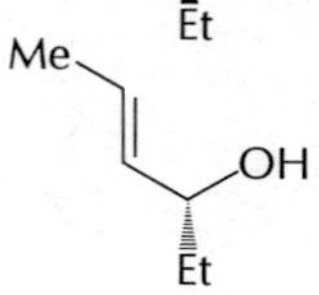 (d) 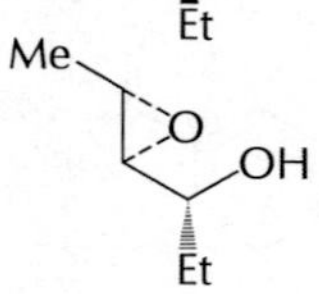

Sol. (*b*)

136. Select the product of the reaction of (*Z*)-(2-methoxyvinyl) benzene with dichloroacetyl chloride in presence of triethyl amine.

(a) 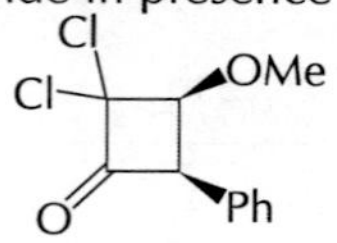 (b) 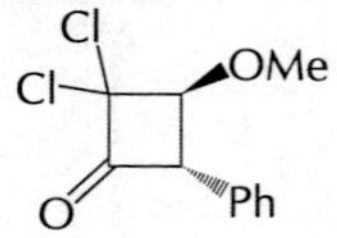

(c) 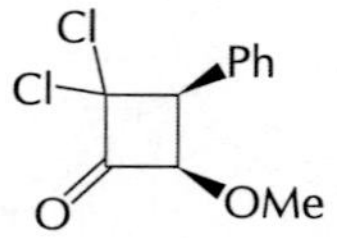 (d) 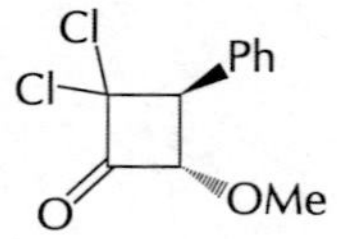

Sol. (*c*)

137. Identify the product formed in the following reaction

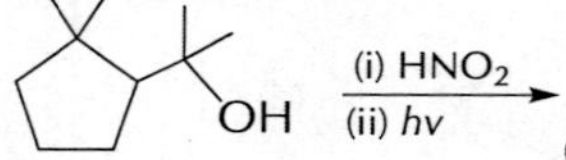

(a) 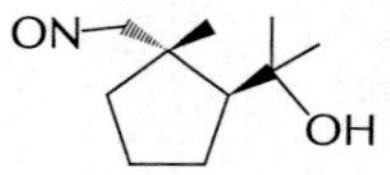 (b) 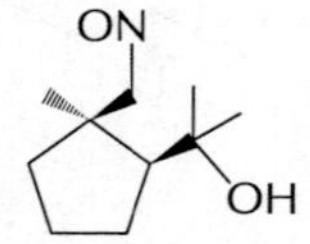

(c) 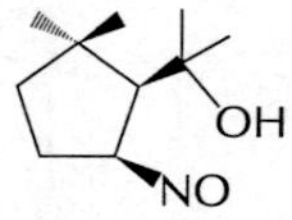 (d) 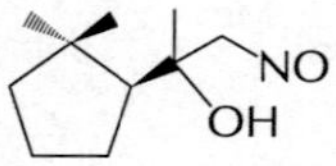

Sol. (*a*)

138. The compound formed in the following reaction sequence is

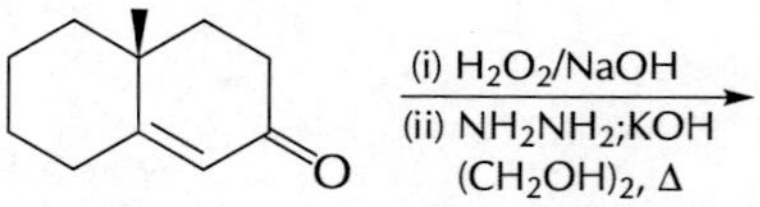

(a) 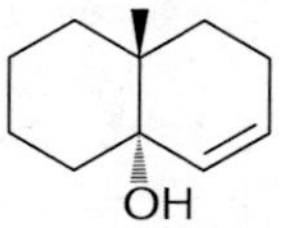 (b) 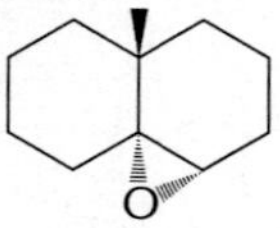

(c) 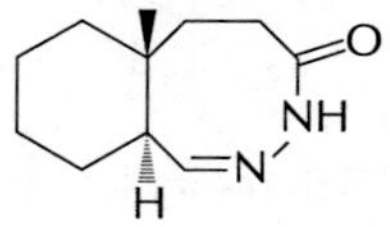 (d) 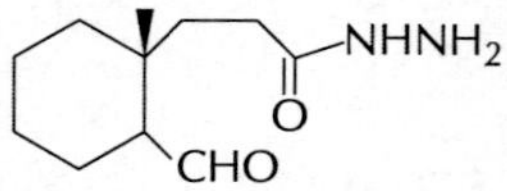

Sol. (*b*)

139. Cholestanol on oxidation with chromium trioxide in acetic acid/pyridine gives a dicarboxylic acid, which on pyrolysis in the presence of a catalytic amount of barium hydroxide gives compound *A* as the major product. The structure of *A* is

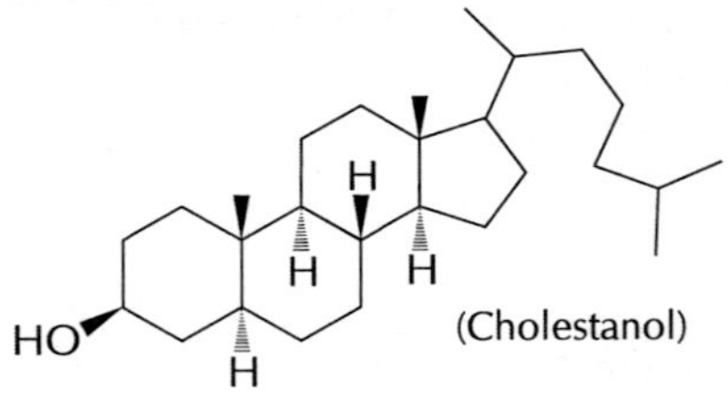

(a) 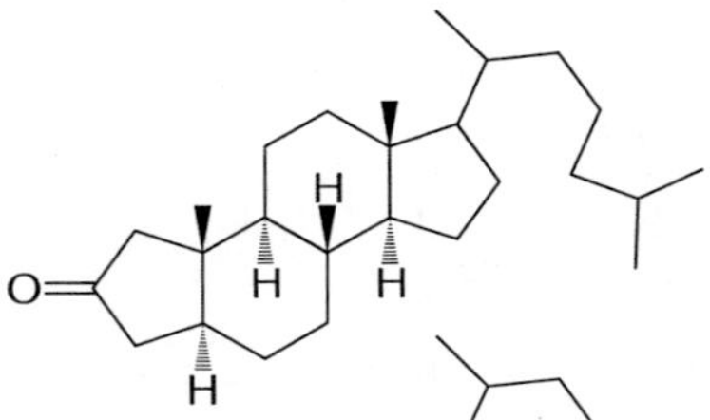

(b) 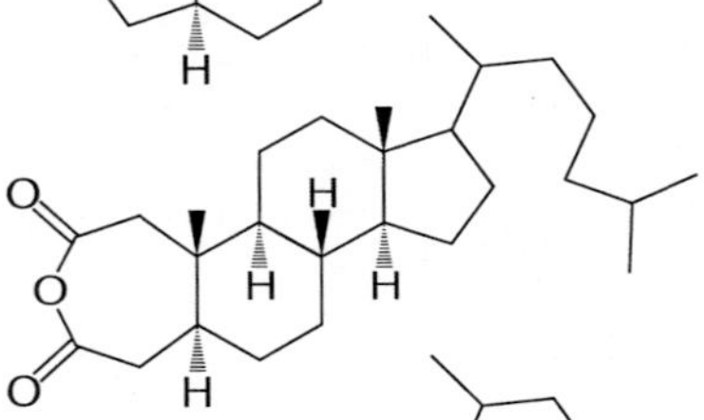

(c) 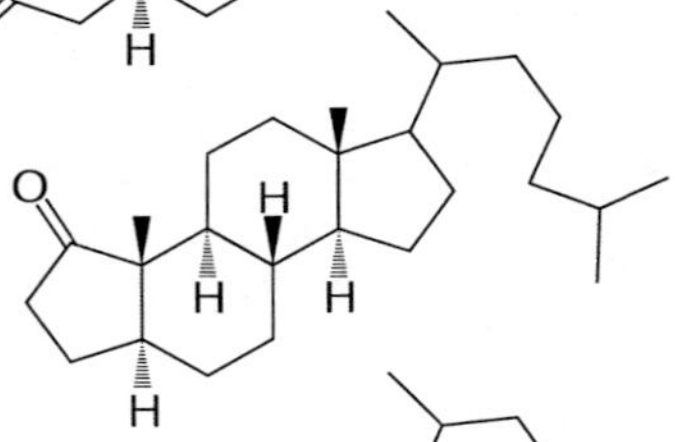

(d) 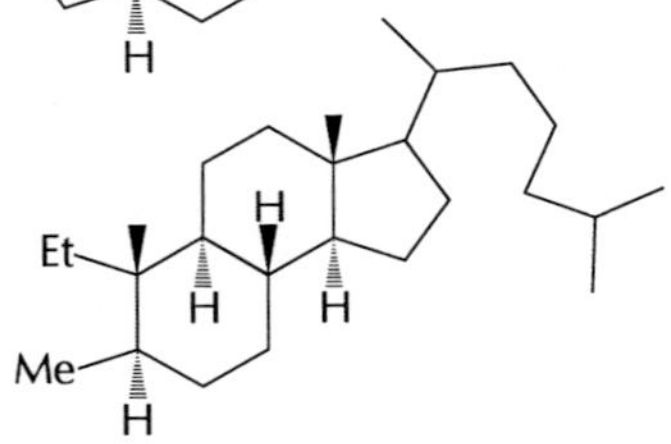

Sol. (*c*)

140. Photolysis of 1,4-dimethyl-1,3-cyclohexadiene in presence of excess oxygen and catalytic amount of Rose Bengal followed by reduction with H_2/Pt provides

(a) 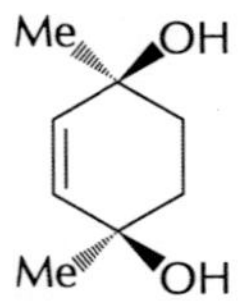

(b) 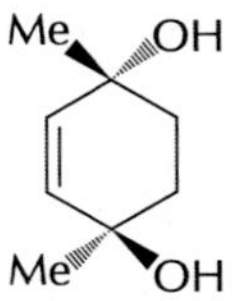

(c) 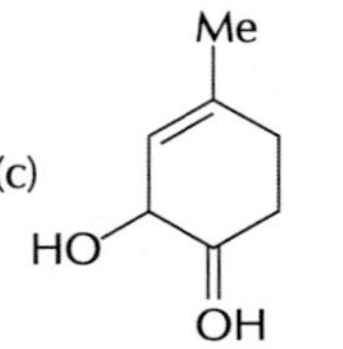

(d) 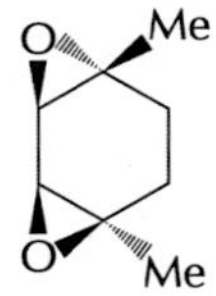

Sol. (*b*)

141. In the following reaction sequence, the correct structures of the major products *X* and *Y* are

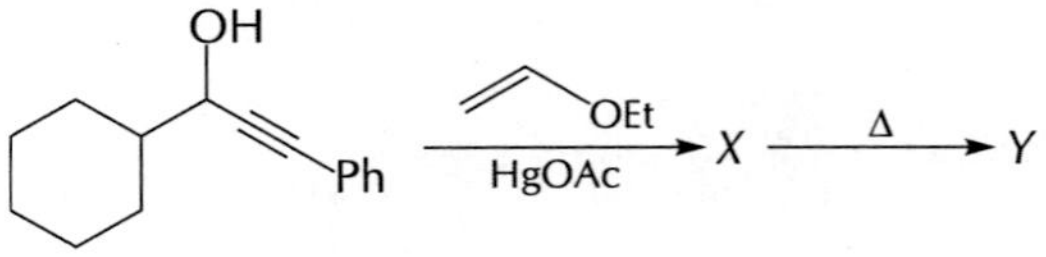

(a) *X* is 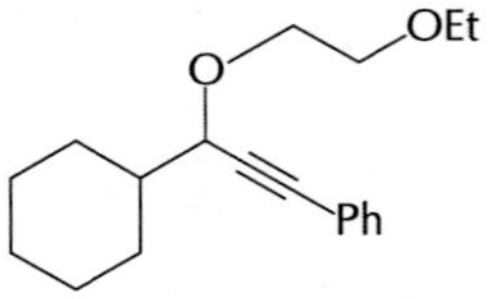

and *Y* is 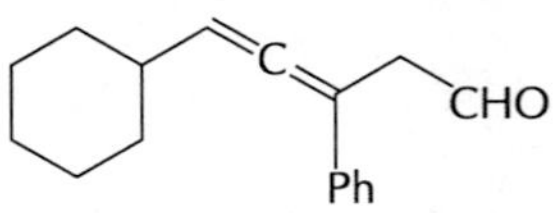

(b) *X* is 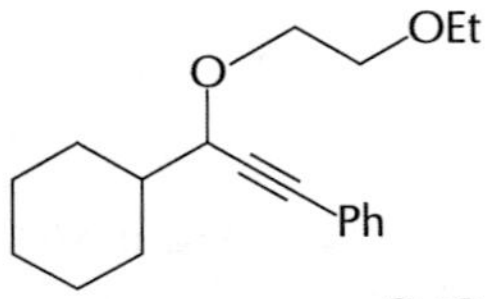

and *Y* is 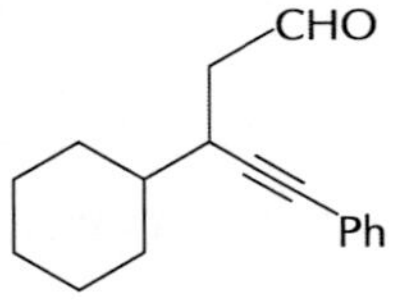

(c) *X* is 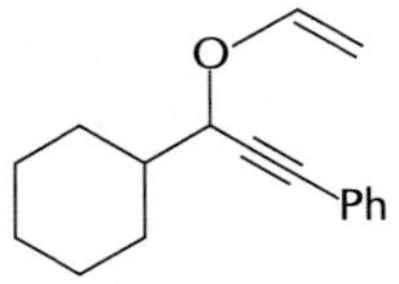

and *Y* is 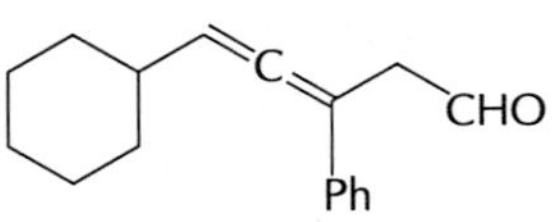

(d) *X* is 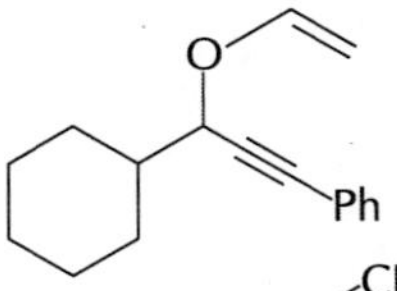

and *Y* is 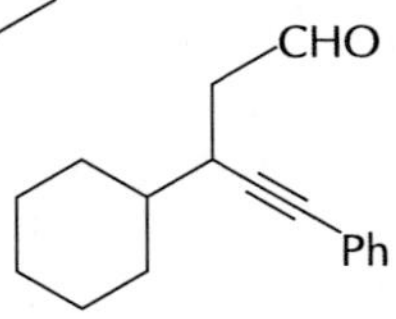

Sol. (*d*)

142. Structure of the *X* and *Y* in the reaction sequence of thiophene given below are

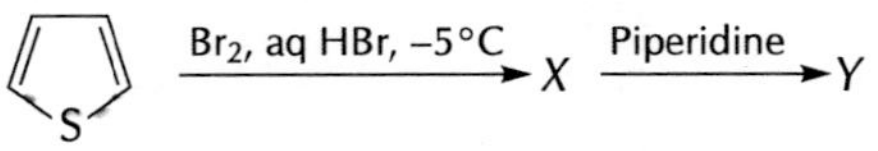

(a) *X* is 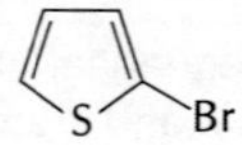 and *Y* is 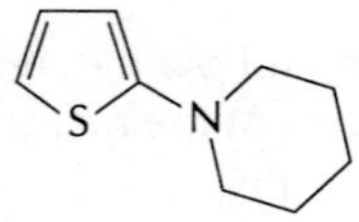

(b) *X* is 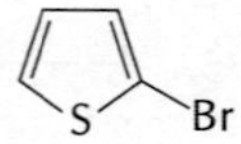 and *Y* is 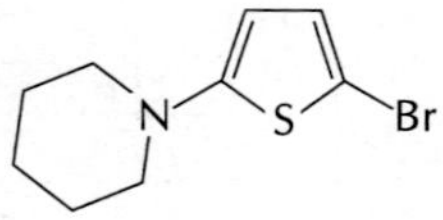

(c) *X* is 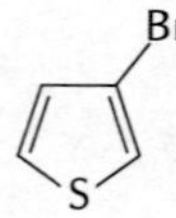 and *Y* is 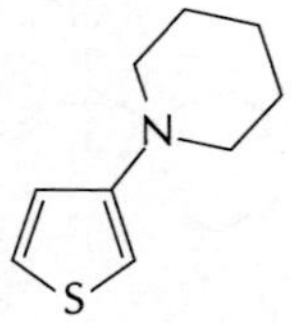

(d) *X* is 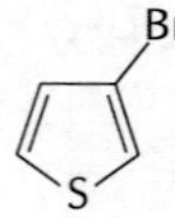 and *Y* is 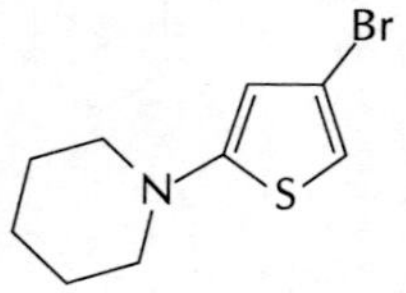

Sol. (*b*)

143. Identify the product of hydrogenation (H_2, Pd/C) of the protected amino acid given below.3

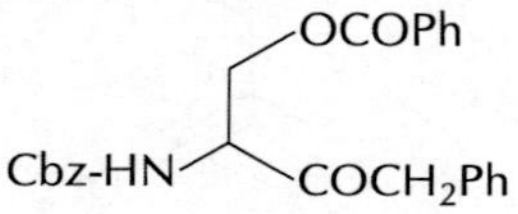

(a) 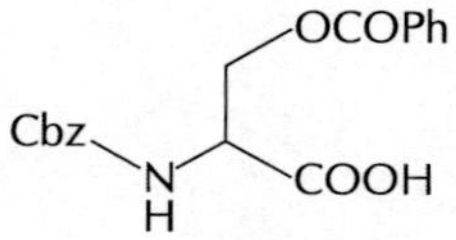

(b) 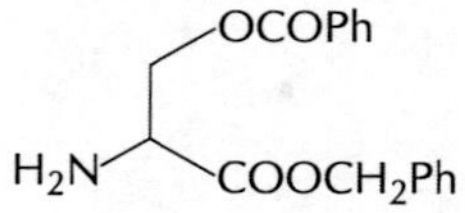

(c) 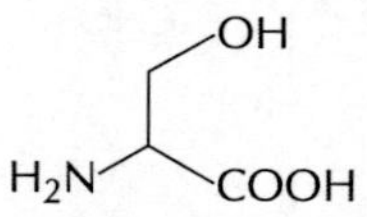

(d) 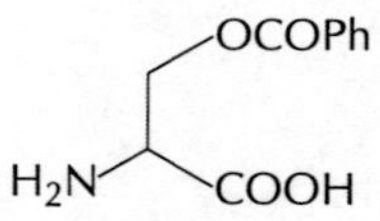

Sol. (*a*)

144. In the broad band decoupled ^{13}C NMR spectrum, the number of signals appear for (i) catechol, (ii) resorcinol and (iii) hydroquinone, respectively, are

(a) six, four and two
(b) six, six and four
(c) three, four and four
(d) three, four and two

Sol. (*d*)

145. In the proton NMR spectrum, an organic compound exhibited the following spectral data

δ 7.2 (1H, dd, $J = 8$ and 1.5 Hz), 6.8 (1H, *d*, $J = 1.5$ Hz), 6.7 (1H, *d*, $J = 8$ Hz),

4.9 (2H, *s*), 3.9 (3H, *s*), 3.85 (3H, s) 3.5 (1H, br *s*, exchangeable with D_2O).

The compound among the choices given below is

(a) 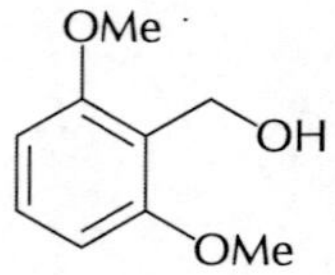

(b) 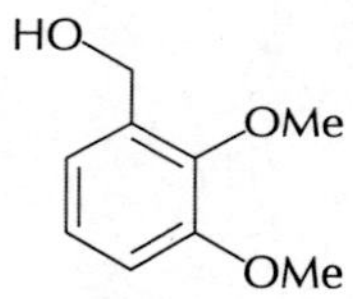

(c) 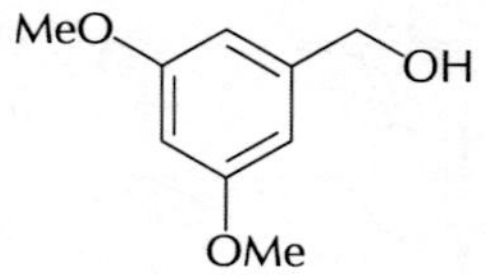

(d) 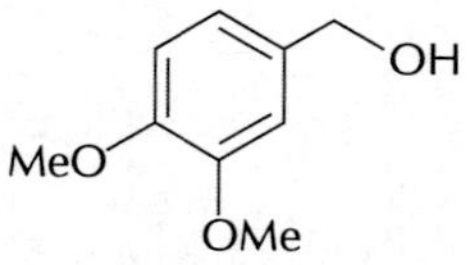

Sol. (*d*)

Solved Paper

UGC CSIR

NET Chemical Sciences*

Solved Paper 2024

PART B

21 Choose the correct statements for oxymyoglobin and cytochrome P_{450} (resting state) from the following:

A. Both contain dianion of protoporphyrin-IX.
B. They have same fifth-ligand bonded to metal centre from the protein backbone.
C. They contain single active site.
D. They contain metal ion in + 3 oxidation state.

1 A, B and C
2 A, C and D
3 A, B and D
4 B and C only

22 The hydrogen atomic orbital given by $Nr^2e^{-r/3a_0}(3\cos^2\theta-1)$ represents

1 2*p*-orbital
2 3*p*-orbital
3 3*d*-orbital
4 4*d*-orbital

23 The major product formed in the following reaction is

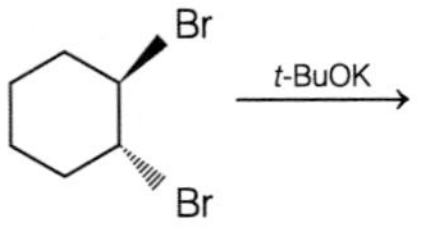

1 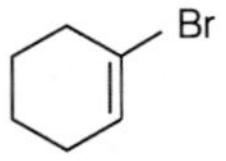

2 

3 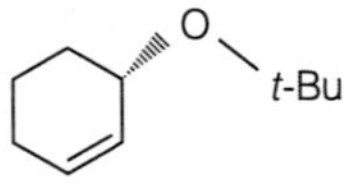

4 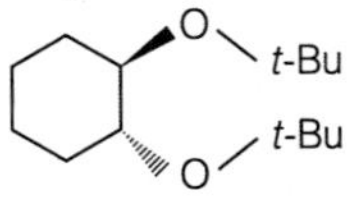

24 The major product formed in the following reaction is

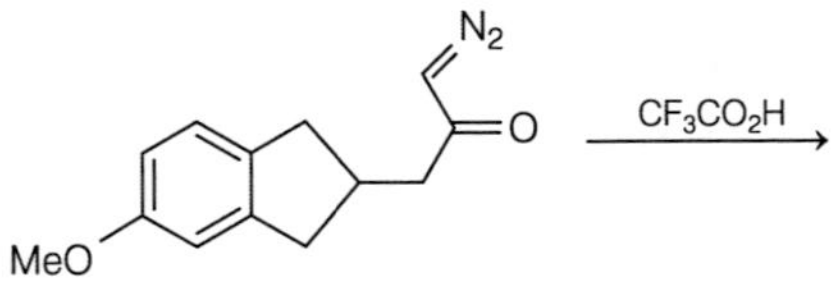

1 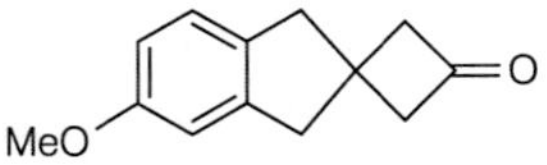

2 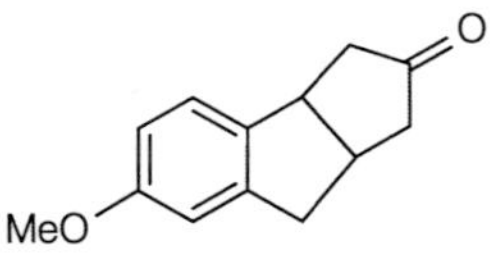

3 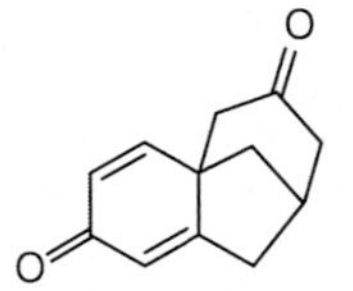

4 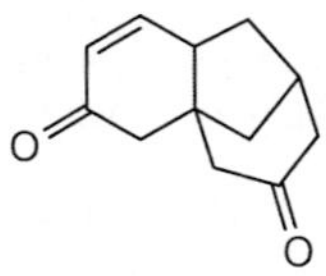

25 The correct match of ^{13}C NMR chemical shift values (δ ppm) for pyridine is

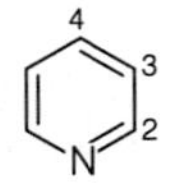

1 C2: 136; C3: 124; C4: 150
2 C2: 124; C3: 150; C4: 136
3 C2: 150; C3: 124; C4: 136
4 C2: 150; C3: 136; C4: 124

26 The value of a physical variable was found to be 196, 198, 194, 199 and 198 in a set of five independent measurements. The average value and the standard deviation would be closest respectively, to

1 198 and 2
2 197 and 4
3 197 and 2
4 198 and 4

27 The ion having the highest bond order is

1 NO^+ 2 O_2^+ 3 N_2^+ 4 C_2^+

28 The major product formed in the following reaction is

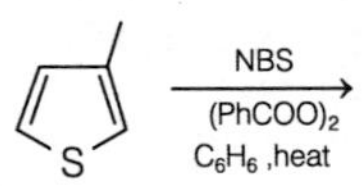

1 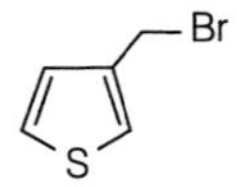

2 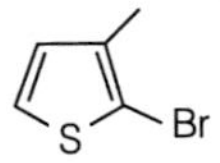

3 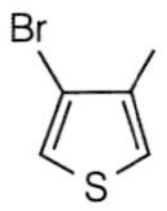

4 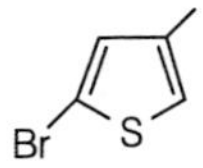

* ***Based on memory***

29 The expected number of V_{CO} bands in the IR spectra of *fac*-$[Mo(PPh_3)_3(CO)_3]$ and *trans*-$[Mo(PPh_3)_2(CO)_4]$ are respectively

1 one and one
2 two and two
3 two and one
4 three and one

30

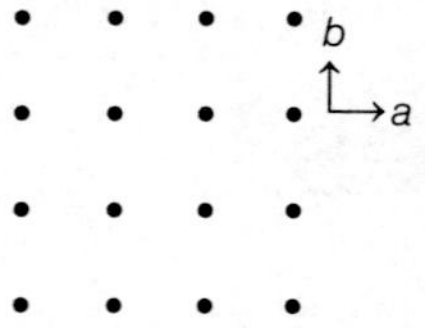

The Miller index for the plane as shown in the figure and parallel to the *c*-axis, is

1 110
2 120
3 210
4 220

31 In IR spectrum, recorded neat, a compound shows a strong and broad band at 3300 cm^{-1}. The band becomes sharp and shifts to 3600 cm^{-1} when the spectrum is recorded in CCl_4 at high dilution. This proves that the compound has

1 OH group, which is involved in intra molecular H–bonding
2 OH group, which is involved in intermolecular H–bonding
3 a terminal alkyne group
4 OH group, present in severely sterically hindered environment

32 Correct order of molar extinction coefficient values of the visible absorption bands for the following species is

1 $[Cr(H_2O)_6]^{2+} > [Mn(H_2O)_6]^{2+} >$ Chlorophyll $> [NiCl_4]^{2-}$
2 Chlorophyll $> [NiCl_4]^{2-} > [Cr(H_2O)_6]^{2+} > [Mn(H_2O)_6]^{2+}$
3 $[NiCl_4]^{2-} >$ Chlorophyll $> [Cr(H_2O)_6]^{2+} > [Mn(H_2O)_6]^{2+}$
4 Chlorophyll $> [Cr(H_2O)_6]^{2+} > [NiCl_4]^{2-} > [Mn(H_2O)_6]^{2+}$

33 The cell potential (in V) of a Ag / AgCl / KCl electrode connected to the standard hydrogen electrode at 298 K is closest to
(Given; $E^\circ_{(AgCl/Ag\cdot Cl^-)} = 0.222$ V and assume that the activity of KCl is 0.01)

1 0.197
2 0.297
3 0.340
4 0.440

34 Consider the entropy changes in a system undergoing transformation, as depicted in the diagram, below

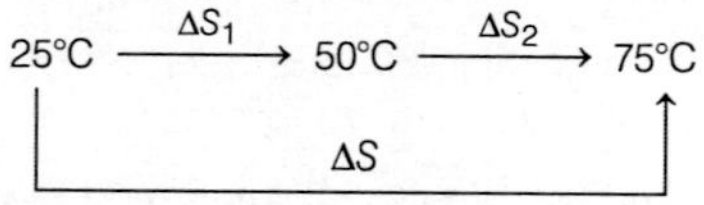

The correct statement among the following is

1 $\Delta S_1 = \Delta S_2$ and $\Delta S \neq \Delta S_1 + \Delta S_2$
2 $\Delta S_1 > \Delta S_2$ and $\Delta S \neq \Delta S_1 + \Delta S_2$
3 $\Delta S_1 = \Delta S_2$ and $\Delta S = \Delta S_1 + \Delta S_2$
4 $\Delta S_1 > \Delta S_2$ and $\Delta S = \Delta S_1 + \Delta S_2$

35 Consider four species *A*, *B*, *C* and *D*. $A + B \xrightarrow{KI, H^+} C$
Oxidation of *A* with *C* in an acidic medium gives *D*, *A*, *B*, *C* and *D* are respectively

1 $S_4O_6^{2-}$, I_2, KIO_3 and SO_4^{2-}
2 $S_4O_6^{2-}$, KIO_3, I_2 and SO_4^{2-}
3 $S_2O_3^{2-}$, KIO_3, I_2 and $S_4O_6^{2-}$
4 $S_2O_3^{2-}$, KIO_3, I_2 and SO_4^{2-}

36 The common heptacity observed for coordination of C_{60} to a metal center is

1 2
2 4
3 5
4 6

37 For an octahedral Cu^{2+} complex depicting axial EPR spectrum (g $g_{\perp}$), the geometry of Cu^{2+} and the orbital containing the unpaired electron are respectively

1 tetragonally elongated, $d_{x^2-y^2}$
2 tetragonally compressed, d_{z^2}
3 tetragonally elongated, d_{z^2}
4 tetragonally compressed, $d_{x^2-y^2}$

38 A liquid of density 1.1 g cm^{-3} climbs to a height of 5.0 cm when a capillary with internal radius of 0.2 mm is dipped into it. The surface tension (in Nm^{-1}) of the liquid is closest to

1 0.05
2 0.108
3 0.018
4 0.005

39 Identify from following, the products of *K*-electron capture by the nucleus

A. neutron
B. neutrino
C. positron

Choose the correct option.

1 A only
2 A and B
3 C only
4 B and C

40 The correct order for the rate of thermal decarboxylation of the following compounds is

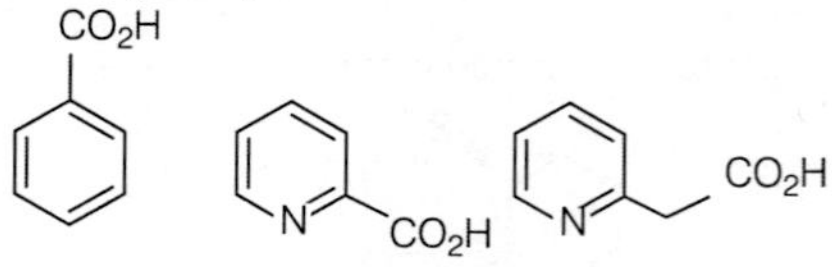

A *B* *C*

1 *C*>*B*>*A*
2 *C*>*A*>*B*
3 *A*>*C*>*B*
4 *B*>*C*>*A*

41 True statement for the following transformation is

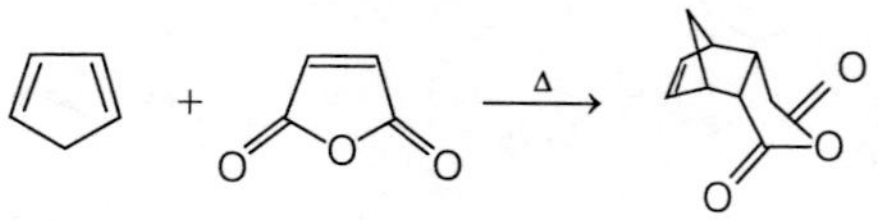

1 ΔH° and ΔS° are positive
2 ΔH° and ΔS° are negative
3 ΔH° is positive and ΔS° is negative
4 ΔH° is negative and ΔS° is positive

42 The most stable vanadium species in aqueous medium is

1 $[V(H_2O)_5(OH)]^{2+}$
2 $[VO(H_2O)_5]^{2+}$
3 $[VO(H_2O)_5]^{+}$
4 $[V(H_2O)_4(OH)_2]^{2+}$

43 The correct match for the bond dissociation energies (BDE) of the C—H bonds of compounds in Column I, with the values in Column II is (as an example, the BDE for Me-H is 105.0 kcal/mol)

Column-I	Column-II BDE (kcal/mol)
A. 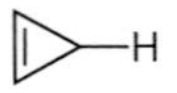	1. 110.9
B. 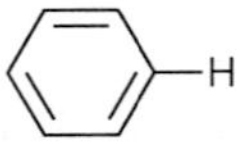	2. 71.1
C. 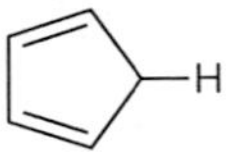	3. 132.0
D. HC≡C—H	4. 90.6

Codes

	A	B	C	D
1	3	4	1	2
2	1	3	2	4
3	3	1	4	2
4	4	1	2	3

44 The ozonolysis of a hydrocarbon in the presence of water produced pentanoic acid and carbonic acid. The hydrocarbon is

1 1-hexene 2 1-hyxyne 3 5-decene 4 5-decyne

45 The correct order of C=O stretching frequency in IR spectrum for the following compounds is

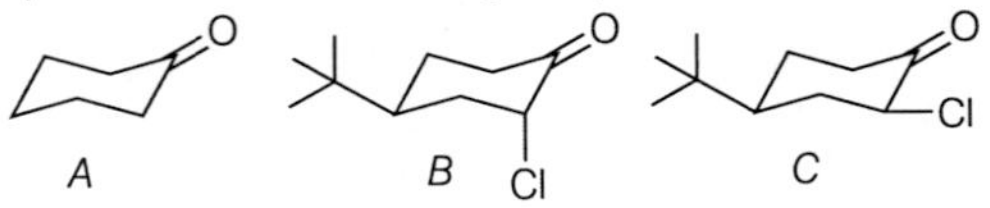

A B C

1 $A > C > B$
2 $B > C > A$
3 $C > B > A$
4 $B > A > C$

46 Which of the following compound has the ^{1}H NMR Spectrum
^{1}H NMR: δ 2.4 (s, 3H), 3.9 (s, 3H), 7.25 (d, J = 7 Hz, 2H), 7.95 (d, J = 7 Hz, 2H) ppm

1 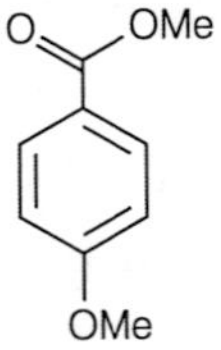

2 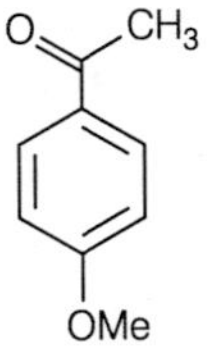

3 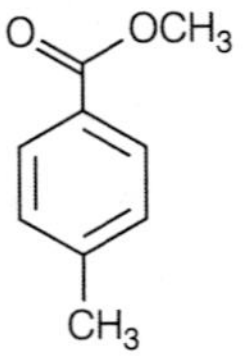

4 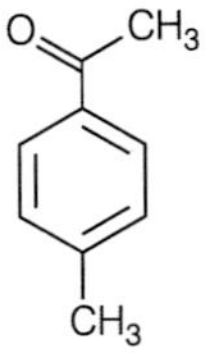

47 The combination of two reflections, $\sigma_v^* \sigma_v^*$, about an intersecting mirror plane is equivalent to

1 S_n
2 C_n
3 σ_h
4 i_t

48 Molar composition of a mixture of P and Q at equilibrium is 3 : 1 ($P : Q$). A small disturbance in composition results in change of chemical potential of P by 10 J mol^{-1}. The chemical potential of Q will change (in J mol^{-1}) by

1 30
2 3.3
3 −30
4 −3.3

49 The magnitude of bond angles in gaseous NF_3, SbF_3 and $SbCl_3$ follow the order

1 $NF_3 > SbF_3 > SbCl_3$
2 $SbCl_3 > SbF_3 > NF_3$
3 $SbF_3 > SbCl_3 > NF_3$
4 $NF_3 > SbCl_3 > SbF_3$

50 The major product formed in the following reaction is

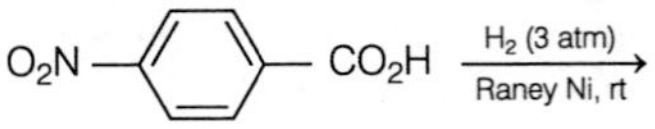

1 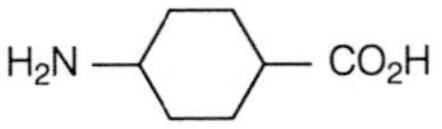

2 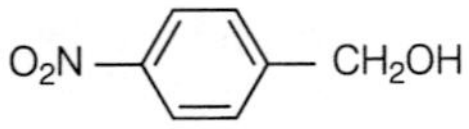

3 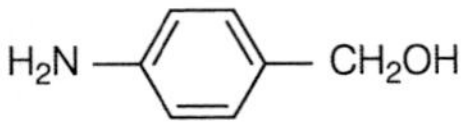

4 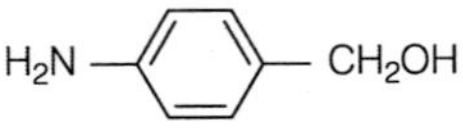

51 A cube does not have the symmetry element

1 C_2
2 C_3
3 C_4
4 C_6

52 The pair of light source and atomiser resulting highest sensitivity to atomic absorption spectrometric measurement is

1 Hg lamp, nitric oxide flame
2 Hg lamp, graphite furnace
3 hollow cathode lamp; graphite furnace
4 hollow cathode lamp; acetylene-nitric oxide flame

53 In common glass electrode, alkaline error caused at pH > 10 is least for

1 0.01 M NaCl
2 1.0 M NaCl
3 1.0 M LiCl
4 1.0 M KCl

54 Pair of lanthanide ions which show significant deviation between the experimental and calculated magnetic moments, considering contribution from the ground state only (given $\mu_{eff} = g[J(J+1)]^{1/2}$, is

1 Gd^{3+} and Lu^{3+}
2 Sm^{3+} and Tb^{3+}
3 Eu^{3+} and Tb^{3+}
4 Sm^{3+} and Eu^{3+}

55 The major product formed in the following reaction is

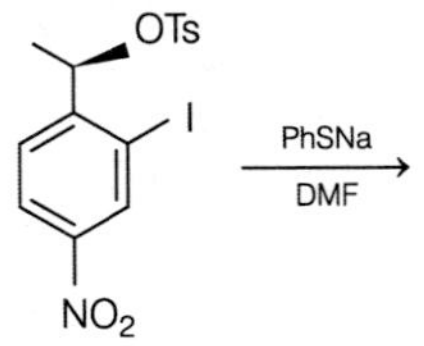

1 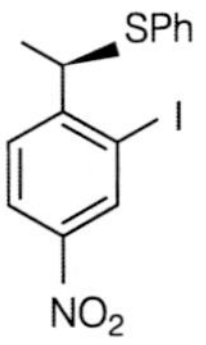

2 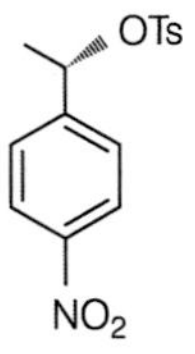

3 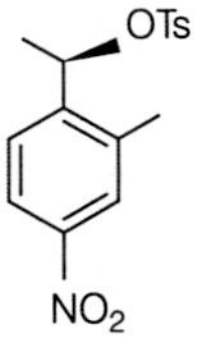

4 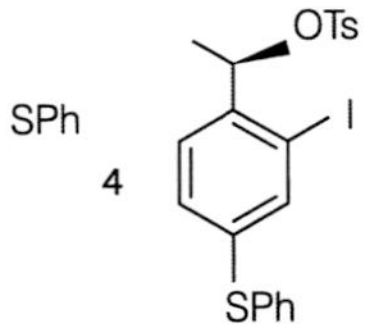

56 The major product formed in the following reaction is

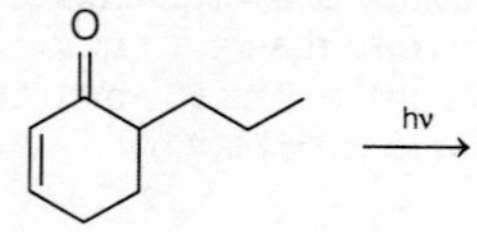

1 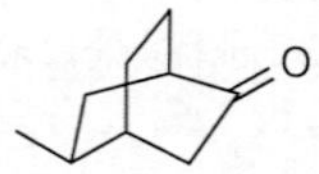

2 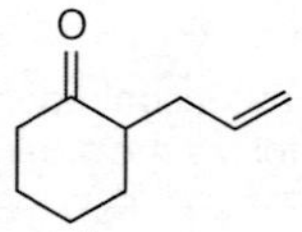

3 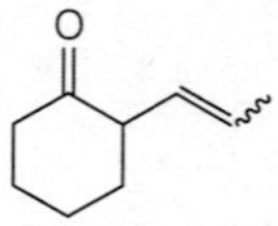

4 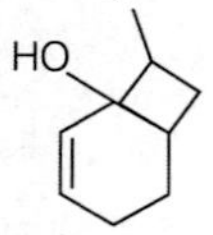

57 E1cb mechanism is followed in the reaction of

1 2-bromopentane with *t*-BuOK to give pent-2-ene
2 nitromethane with benzaldehyde in the presence of KOH to give β-nitrostyrene
3 bromobenzene with $NaNH_2$ to give aniline
4 *p*-chloronitrobenzene with NaOMe to give *p*-nitroanisole

58 Consider a two-level system in which the excited state, separated from the ground state by energy ε, is doubly degenerate. The fraction of the molecules in the excited state, as $T \to \infty$, is

1 $\frac{1}{3}$ 2 $\frac{1}{2}$
3 $\frac{2}{3}$ 4 1

59 The rate of decomposition of a gas is 10 mM s^{-1} when 10% is reacted and it is 5 mM s^{-1} when 40% is reacted. The order of the reaction is

1 2 2 1.71
3 0 4 2.15

60 For a person weighing 70 kg the minimal volume (in mL) of a fatal dose of a compound with $LD_{50} = 80$ mg. kg^{-1}, and density $= 1.45$ g. mL^{-1} is

1 5.6 2 3.9
3 0.8 4 0.4

PART C

61 Identify the thermodynamically stable structure of $[(\eta^5 - C_5H_5)Fe(\mu_2 - CO)(NO)]_2$

1 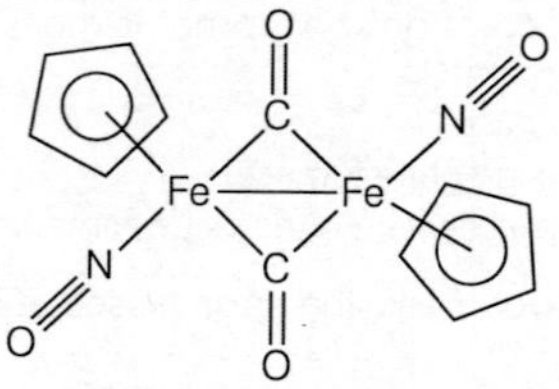

2 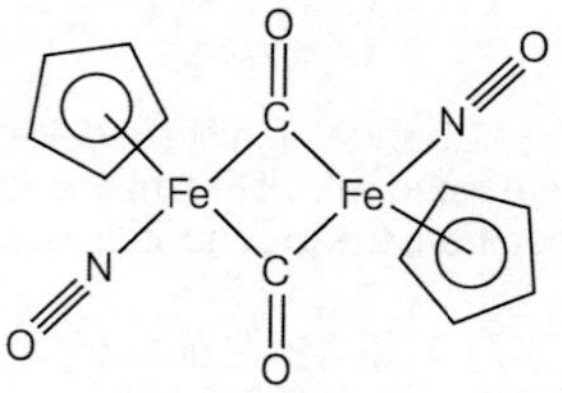

3 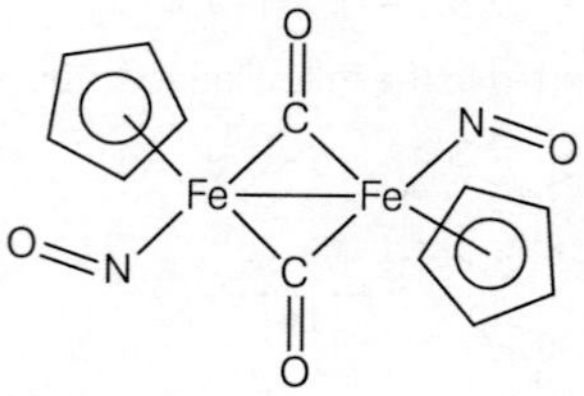

4 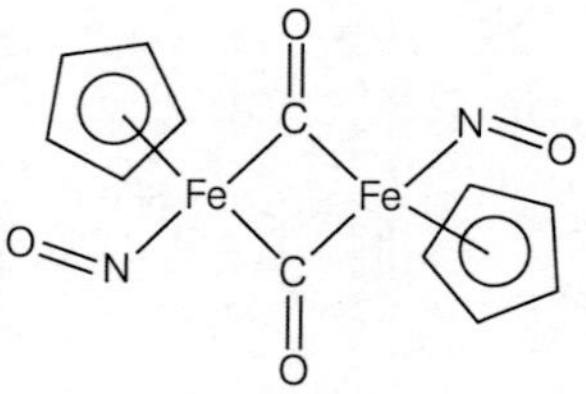

62 The rate constant of a second order reaction $2A \to Z$ is k_2. If the initial concentration of the reactant is a_0 and the concentration of the product at time *t* is *x*, then a linear function of *t* with the slope k_2a_0 is

1 $\ln\left(\frac{x}{a_0 - x}\right)$ 2 $\frac{x}{a_0(a_0 - x)}$
3 $\frac{x}{a_0 - x}$ 4 $\ln\left(\frac{x}{a_0(a_0 - x)}\right)$

63 The major product *A* and the byproducts *B* formed in the following reaction are

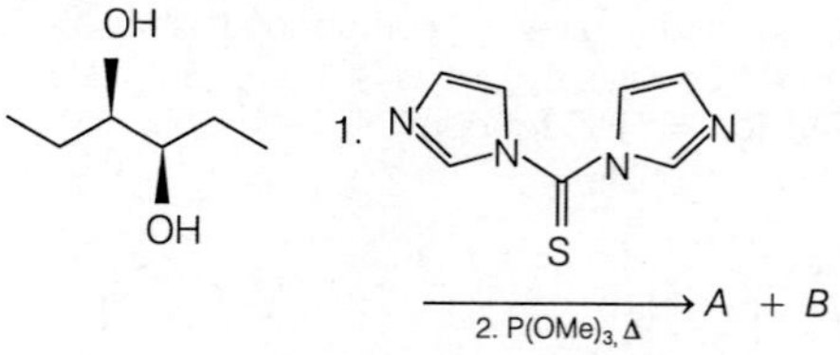

1 *A* = 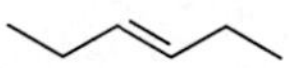 $B = CO_2$, S=P(OMe)$_3$
2 *A* = 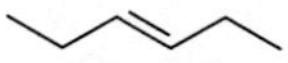 *B* =O=C=S,O=P(OMe)$_3$
3 *A* =  *B* =CO2, S=P(OMe)$_3$
4 *A* =  *B* =O=C=S,O=P(OMe)$_3$

64 Choose the equilibria from the following that are not favoured to go to right :

A. $As_2S_5 + 5HgO \rightleftharpoons As_2O_5 + 5HgS$
B. $La_2(CO_3)_3 + Bi_2S_3 \rightleftharpoons La_2S_3 + Bi_2(CO_3)_3$
C. $CdSO_4 + CaS \rightleftharpoons CdS + CaSO_4$
D. $BeF_2 + HgI_2 \rightleftharpoons BeI_2 + HgF_2$

1 *A* and *B* 2 *A* and *C* 3 *B* and *C* 4 *B* and *D*

65 The correct absolute configuration of the following compounds is

I

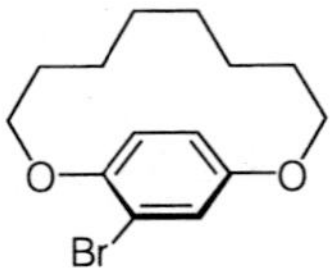

II

1 I : *M*; II : *R*
2 I : *M*; II : *S*
3 I : *P*; II : *R*
4 I : *P*; II : *S*

66 The compound that shows peaks in the EI mass spectrum at *m/z* 121, 105, 77, 44 is

1 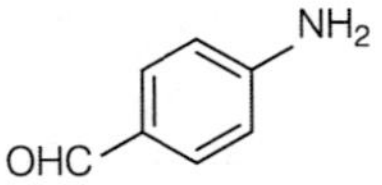

2 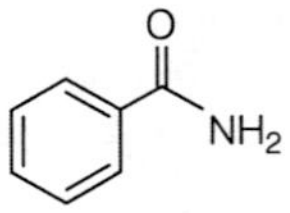

3 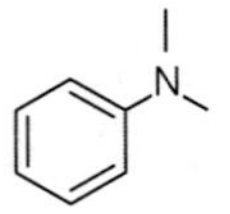

4 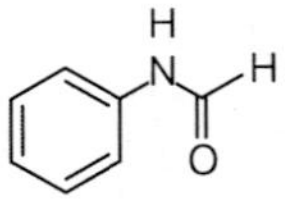

67 The major product formed in the following reaction is

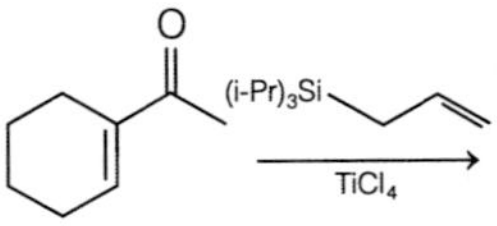

1 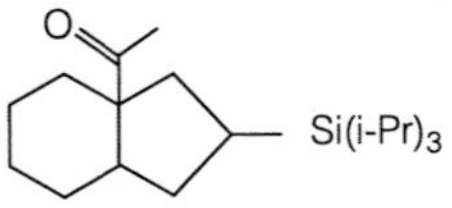

2 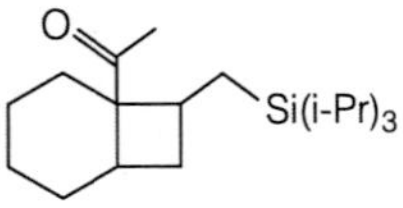

3 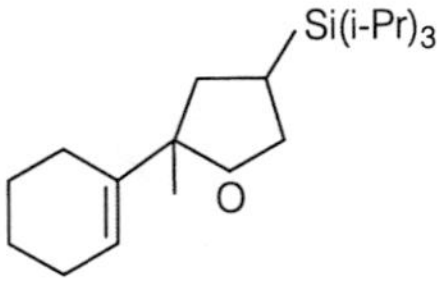

4 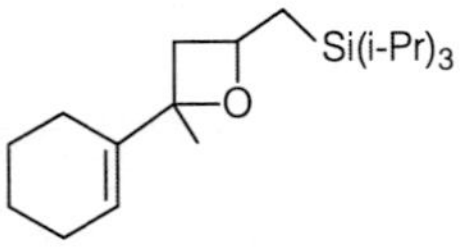

68 The major products *A* and *B* in the following reaction sequence are

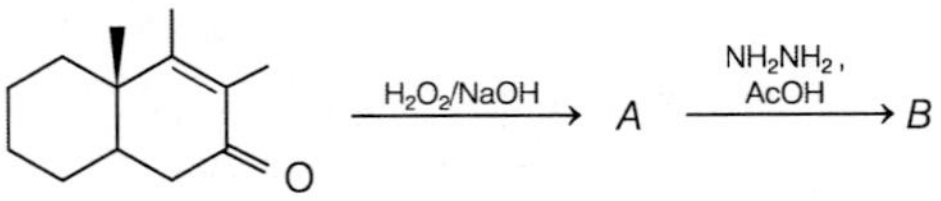

1 *A* = 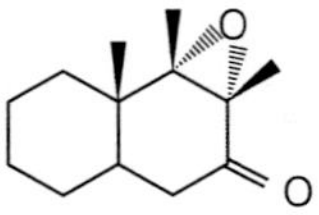 *B* = 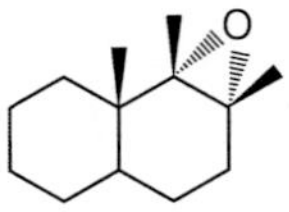

2 *A* = 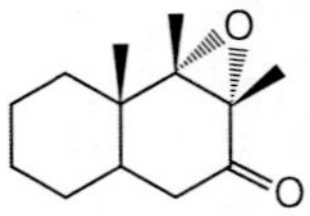 *B* = 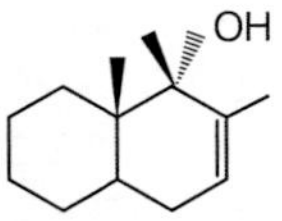

3 *A* = 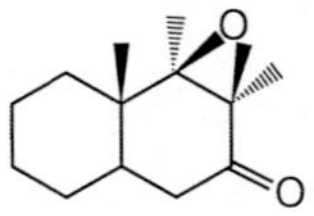 *B* = 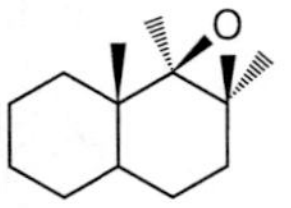

4 *A* = 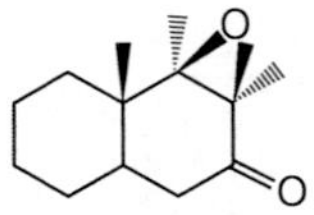 *B* = 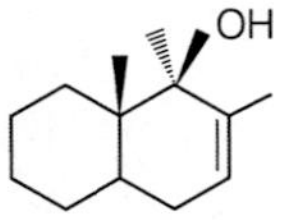

69 Match the items in Column I with those of Column II.

Column I (species)		**Column II** (structure/properties)
A. NaH	(i)	Polymeric chain
B. BeH_2	(ii)	Interstitial hydride
C. $HfH_{2.10}$	(iii)	Tricapped trigonal prismatic
D. $[TcH_9]^{2-}$	(iv)	Saline hydride

The correct match is
1 A-(iv), B-(ii), C-(iii), D-(i)
2 A-(i), B-(iv), C-(ii), D-(iii)
3 A-(iv), B-(i), C-(ii), D-(iii)
4 A-(iv), B-(i), C-(iii), D-(ii)

70 In 3-iron ferredoxins, the number of sulphide bridges and cysteinyl ligands, respectively, are:
1 3, 3
2 4, 3
3 3, 4
4 4, 4

71 The absorption spectrum of $[Cr(NH_3)_6]^{3+}$ in water shows two bands around 475 and 365 nm. The ground term and the spin-allowed transitions, respectively, are
1 ^4F; $^4T_{1g}(F) \rightarrow {}^4T_{2g}$ and $^4T_{1g} \rightarrow {}^4A_{2g}$
2 ^4F; $^4A_{2g} \rightarrow {}^4T_{2g}$ and $^4A_{2g} \rightarrow {}^4A_{1g}(F)$
3 ^2G; $^2E_g \rightarrow {}^2T_{1g}$ and $^2E_g \rightarrow {}^2T_{2g}$
4 ^2F; $^2A_{2g} \rightarrow {}^2T_{2g}$ and $^2A_{2g} \rightarrow {}^2T_{1g}(F)$

72 Choose the correct statement(s) from the following :
(i) The trend in Lewis acidity among silicon halides is $SiI_4 < SiBr_4 < SiCl_4 < SiF_4$.
(ii) Tin (II) chloride can act as a Lewis acid and not as a Lewis base.
(iii) Aluminosilicates can display Bronsted acidity.
1 (i) and (ii)
2 (i) and (iii)
3 (ii) and (iii)
4 (ii) only

73 Consider the following statements.
A. $PbCl_2$ has low solubility in water.
B. Sulphides of As (III) and Sb(III) are soluble in ammonium sulphide.
C. SnS is soluble in yellow ammonium sulphide.
D. MnS is precipitated by passing H_2S through acidic $MnCl_2$.
Correct statements are
1 A, B and C
2 B, C and D
3 A, C and D
4 A and C only

74 The cluster types of $[Fe_5(CO)_{14}N]^-$ and $[Co_6(CO)_{13}N]^-$ are respectively
1 *nido-, nido-*
2 *nido-, closo-*
3 *closo-, nido-*
4 *closo-, closo-*

75 The structure of the compound, which displays the following spectral data is IR = 1690, 1100 cm^{-1}

^{1}H NMR : δ 2.8 (*s*, 3H), 3.8 (*s*, 3H), 6.9 (*d*, *J* = 8 Hz, 2H), 7.8 (*d*, *J* = 8 Hz, 2H)

^{13}C NMR : δ 197, 165, 130, 129, 114, 56, 26

1 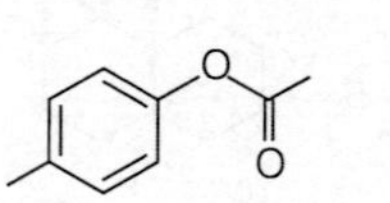

2 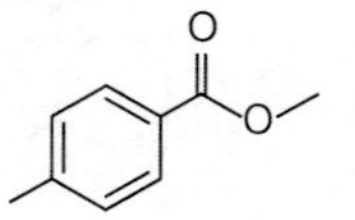

3 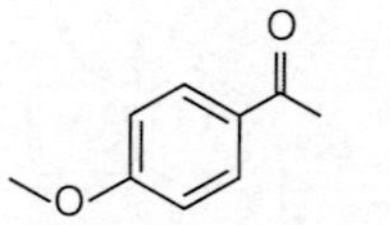

4 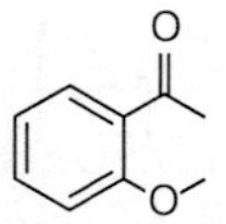

76 The species for which the shapes (geometry) can be predicted by VSEPR theory is/are

A. $[PtCl_4]^{2-}$ B. $[TeCl_6]^{2-}$

C. PF_3 and SF_6

Choose the correct option.

1 *A* and *C* 2 *B* and *C* 3 *C* only 4 *A* and *B*

77 The correct statement about base hydrolysis of $[Co(py)_4Cl_2]^+$ (py= pyridine) is

1 rate expression is, rate = $k[Co(py)_4Cl_2]^+[OH]^-$

2 reaction does not depend on hydroxide ion concentration

3 reaction proceeds through S_N1CB mechanism

4 intermediate involved in this reaction is $[Co(py)_4Cl_2(OH)]$

78 Complex(es) which has/have unpaired electron(s) that is equal to that of iron center in oxymyoglobin is/are

A. $[Fe(ox)_3]^{3-}$ B. $[Fe(CN)_6]^{3-}$

C. $[NiCl_4]^{2-}$ D. $[Cu(NH_3)_4]^{2+}$

(Given, *ox* = oxalato)

Choose the correct option.

1 *A* and *B* 2 *B* and *D* 3 *C* only 4 *C* and *D*

79 The main product of nucleophilic attack of H^- on the complex ion given below is

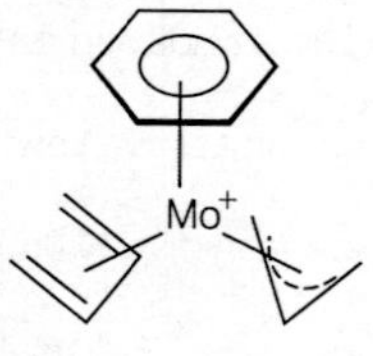

1 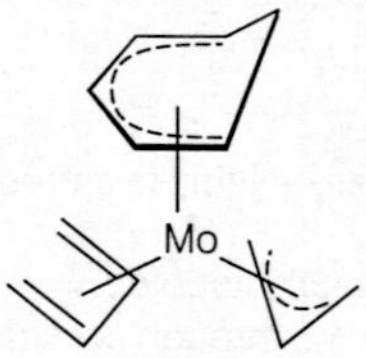

2 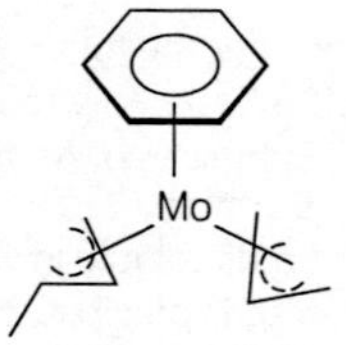

3 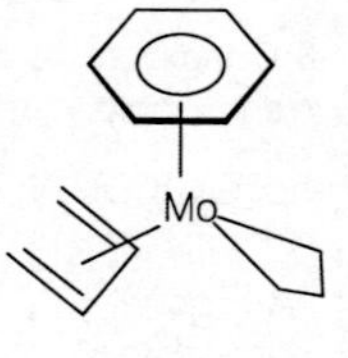

4 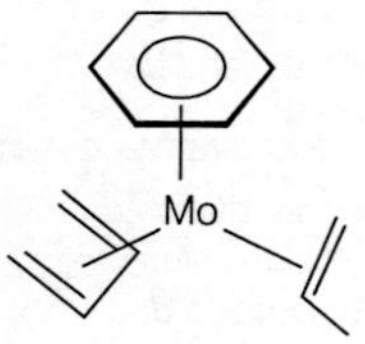

80 The major product formed in the following reaction is

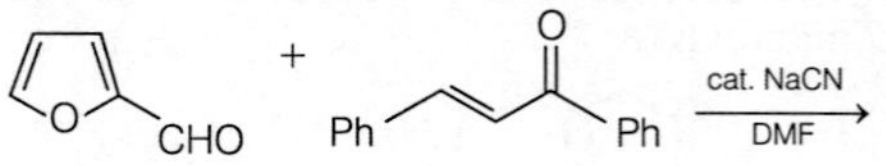

1 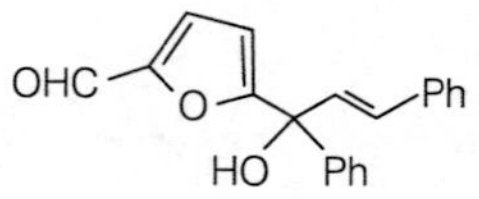

2 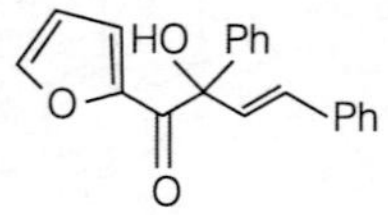

3 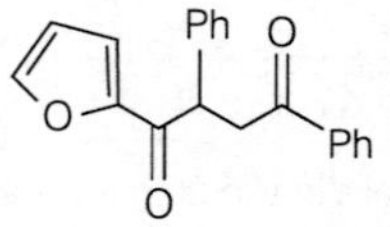

4 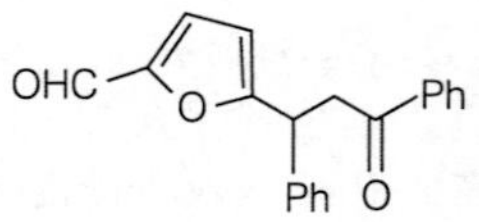

81 The intermediate *A* and the major product *B* formed in the following reaction are

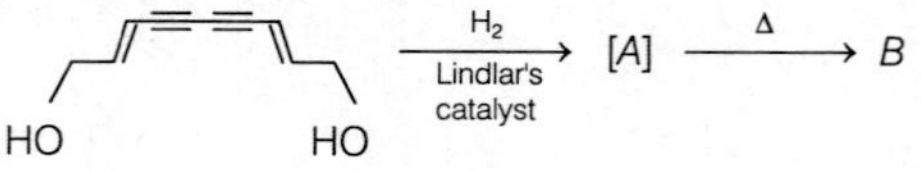

1 [*A*] = 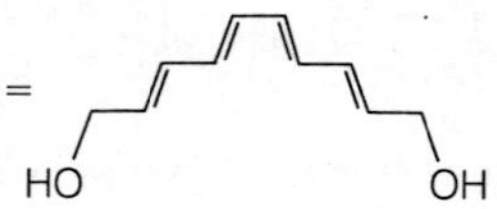 *B* = 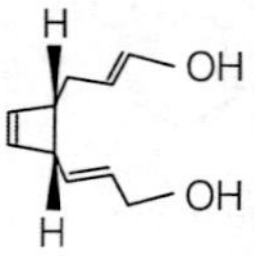

2 [*A*] = 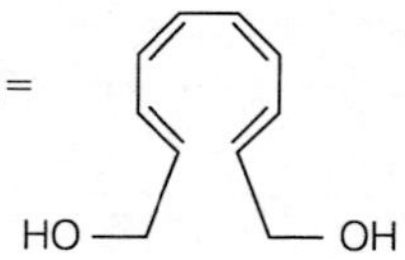 *B* = 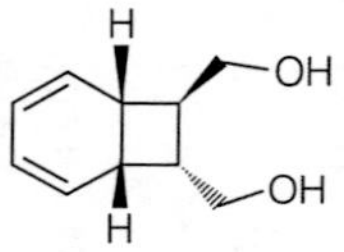

3 [*A*] = 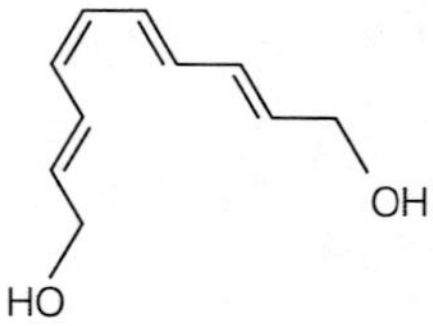 *B* = 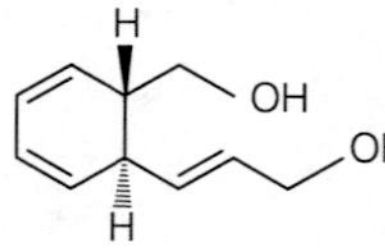

4 [*A*] = 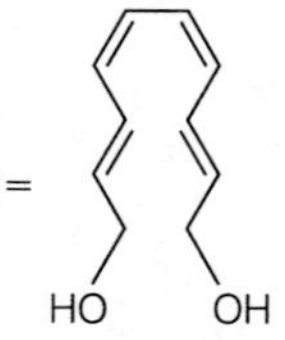 *B* = 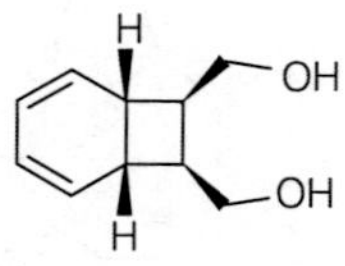

82 Consider the gas phase reaction $2A(g) + 3B(g) \rightleftharpoons 2C(g)$ at a given temperature. When 2.0 moles of *A*(*g*) are reacted with 2.0 moles of *B*(*g*), 0.8 moles of *C*(*g*) are formed at equilibrium at a total pressure of 2.0 bar. The value of the equilibrium constant, K_p of this reaction at the given temperature is closest to

1 0.3 2 0.9 3 2.4 4 19.1

83 In a polymer of *N* monomer units, the root mean square separation between the two ends is proportional to

1 $N^{\frac{1}{2}}$ 2 N

3 $N^{\frac{3}{2}}$ 4 N^2

84 For the electrochemical cell Ag|AgCl | *M*Cl (0.01 M) | *M*Cl (0.02 M) | AgCl| Ag, the junction potential is the highest when M^+ is

1 H^+ 2 Li^+
3 Na^+ 4 K^+

85 The function, which is not an eigenfunction of the indicated operator, is

	Operator	**Function**
1	$\frac{d^2}{dx^2} - x^2$	$e^{-x^2/2}$
2	$\frac{d^2}{dx^2} + x^2$	$e^{-x^2/2}$
3	$\frac{d^2}{dx^2}$	$\cos\frac{\pi x}{4}$
4	$\frac{d^2}{dx^2}$	e^{4ix}

86 The oxidation of NO to NO_2 occurs *via* the mechanism given below.

$$2NO \underset{K_{-1}}{\overset{K_1}{\rightleftharpoons}} N_2O_2$$

$$N_2O_2 + O_2 \xrightarrow{K_2} 2NO_2$$

$\frac{d[NO_2]}{dt}$ in the presence of large excess of O_2 can be written as

1 $2k_1\,(NO)^2$ 2 $2k_1\,k_2\,(NO)^2\,(O_2)$
3 $\frac{k_1}{k_2}(NO)^2$ 4 $2k_2\,(NO)^2$

87 Among $SO_2(OH)F$, CH_3CO_2H, LiF and H_2O, the compound(s) which behave(s) as a base in liquid HF is/are

1 CH_3CO_2H and LiF only 2 LiF only
3 $SO_2(OH)F$ and LiF only 4 CH_3CO_2H, LiF and H_2O

88 The reducible representation Γ, in the table is equal to the following superposition of the irreducible representations of C_{2v} point group.

C_{2v}	E	C_2	σ_v	σ_v'
A_1	1	1	1	1
A_2	1	1	−1	−1
B_1	1	−1	1	−1
B_2	1	−1	−1	1
Γ	8	−2	−6	4

1 $A_1 \oplus 2A_2 \oplus 5B_1$ 2 $A_1 \oplus 2A_2 \oplus 5B_2$
3 $5A_1 \oplus A_2 \oplus 2B_1$ 4 $A_1 \oplus 5A_2 \oplus 2B_2$

89 The major product formed in the following reaction is

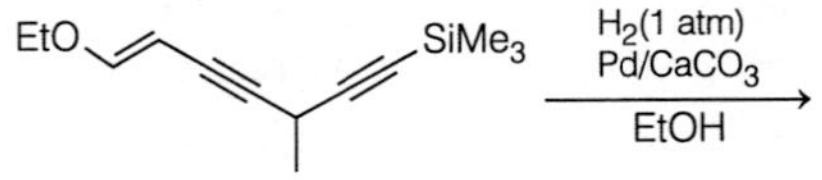

1 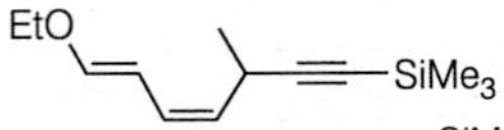

2 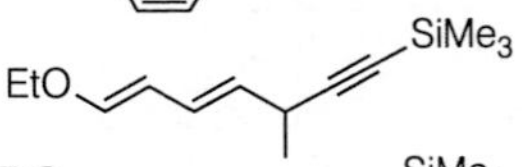

3 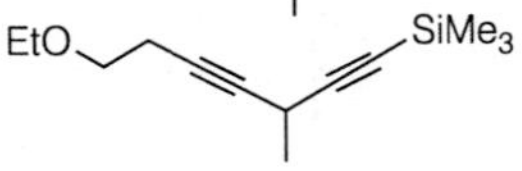

4 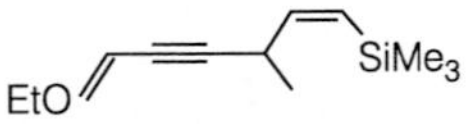

90 The reagent that will effect the following selective conversion is

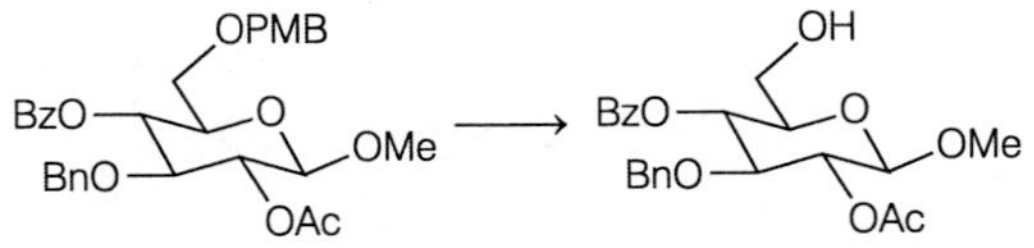

1 NaOMe, MeOH 2 TBAF, THF
3 DDQ, CH_2Cl_2 4 Et_3N,MeOH

91 The major product formed in the following reaction is

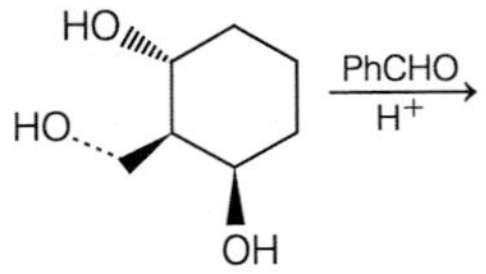

1 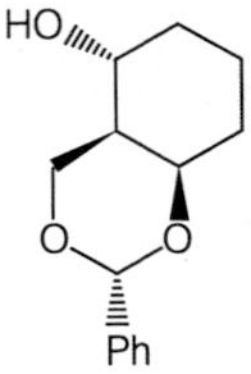

2 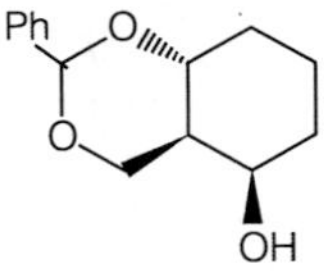

3 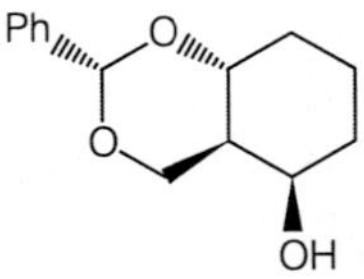

4 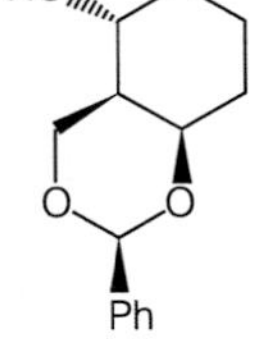

92 The major product formed in the following reaction is

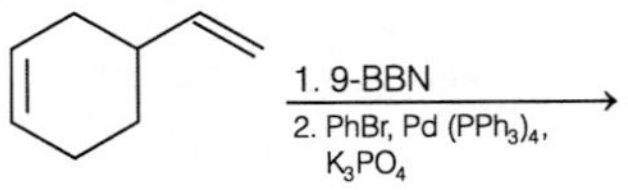

1 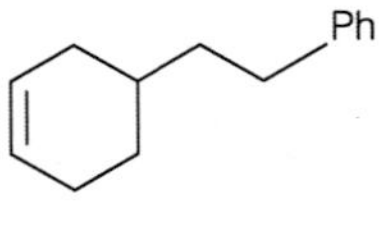

2 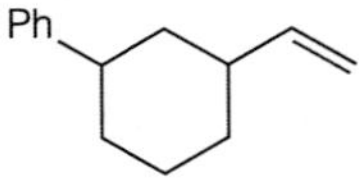

3 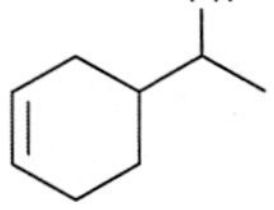

4 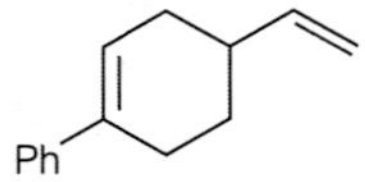

93 Match the items in Column I with those of Column II.

Column I	Column II
A. Conductometric titration	(i) Voltage
B. Amperometric titrations	(ii) Resistance
C. pH metric tritration	(iii) ΔI
D. Differential pulse polarography	(iv) I_d

Correct match is

1 A-ii, B-iv, C-i, D-iii
2 A-iii, B-i, C-ii, D-iv
3 A-iii, B-ii, C-iv, D-i
4 A-i, B-iii, C-iv, D-ii

94 The major product formed in the following reaction is

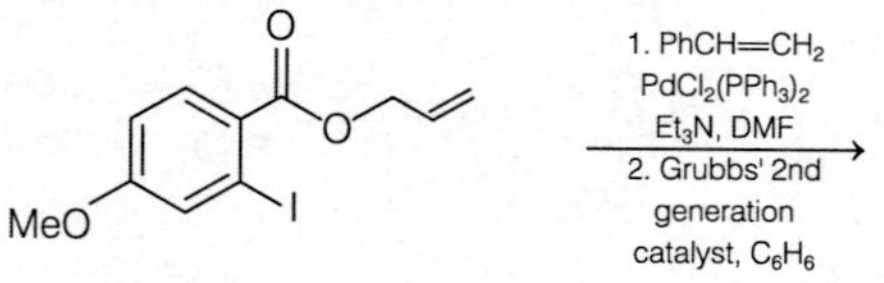

1 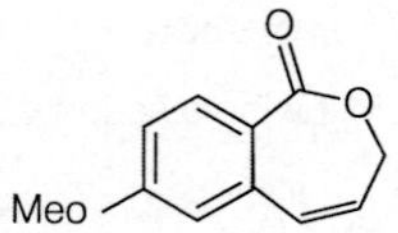

2 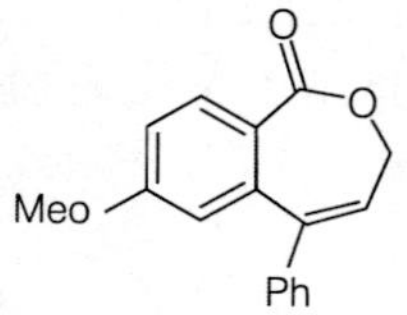

3 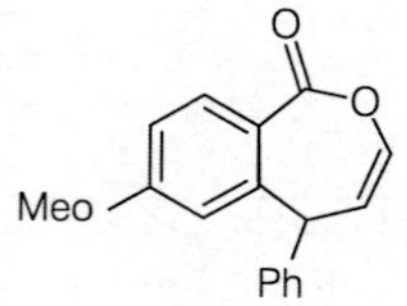

4 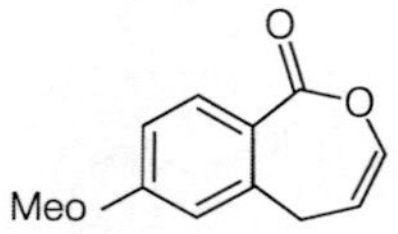

95 X-rays of 173 pm wavelength are reflected by the (111) plane of a cubic primitive crystal at $\theta = 30°$. The unit cell length (in pm) is closest to

1 173
2 300
3 346
4 600

96 The molar residual entropy (in JK^{-1}) of solid OCS would be closest to

1 0
2 2.9
3 5.8
4 8.7

97 The major product formed in the following reaction is

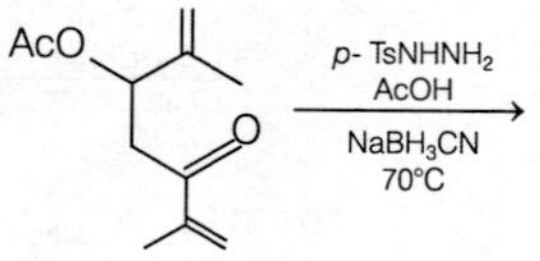

1 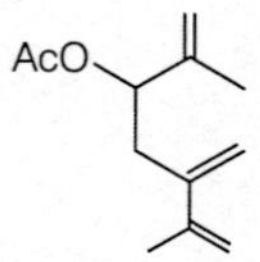

2 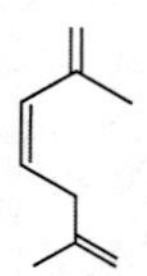

3 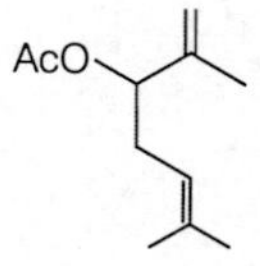

4 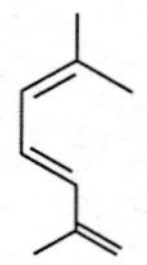

98 True statement regarding Hammett reaction constant (ρ) for the following transformations given in equations *A* and *B* is

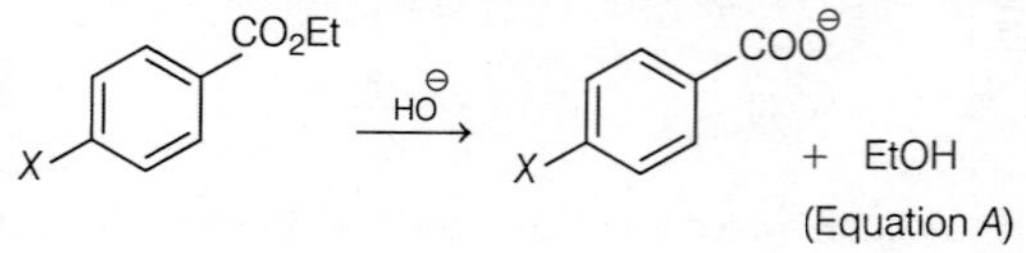

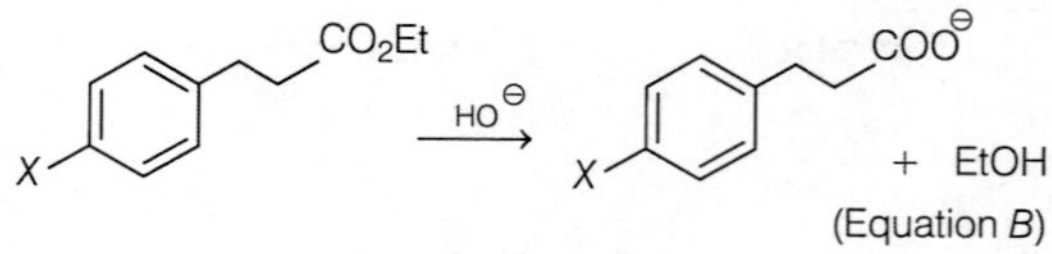

1 ρ for *A* and *B* is same and positive
2 ρ for *A* and *B* is same and negative
3 ρ for *A* is larger positive value than for *B*
4 ρ for *A* is negative and for *B* is positive

99 1.0 mol of a perfect monatomic gas is put through the cycle shown in the figure. The total work (in J) done during the cycle is

(use 1 L-bar $= 100$ J, $R = 8.3\ \text{J K}^{-1}\ \text{mol}^{-1} = 0.083$ L-bar $\text{K}^{-1}\ \text{mol}^{-1}$, $\ln 2 = 0.7$)

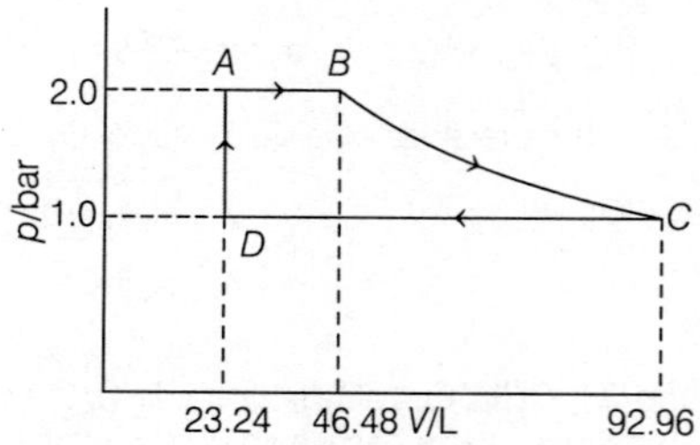

1 930
2 −4183
3 8831
4 −5113

100 The correct relationship between the two faces of the C=O group in compounds *A* and *B* is

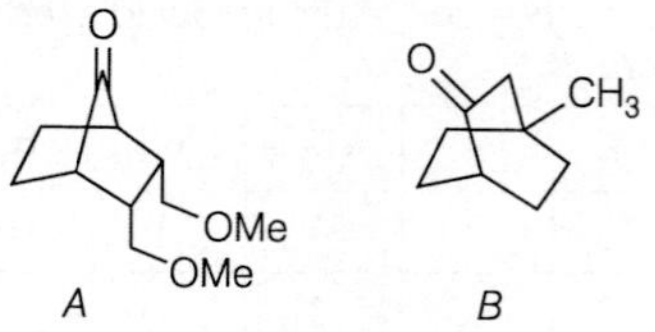

1 *A* = diastereotopic; *B* = enantiotopic
2 *A* = *B* = enantiotopic
3 *A* = enantiotopic; *B* = diastereotopic
4 *A* = *B* = diastereotopic

101 For every atom that is not shifted under C_4 and σ symmetry operations, the characters are, respectively,

1 −1, −1
2 0, 0
3 1, 1
4 −1, 1

102 The equivalent symmetry operations for S_6^3 and S_3^6 are, respectively,

1 C_3 and C_2
2 σ_h and *i*
3 σ_h and *E*
4 *i* and *E*

103 A system consists of *N* identical distinguishable non-interacting particles, each having only two energy levels 0 and ε. The expression of the heat capacity at constant volume (C_V) is given by ($\beta = 1/k_BT$)

1 Nk_B

2 $Nk_B\left(\frac{\varepsilon\beta}{1+e^{\varepsilon\beta}}\right)^2$

3 $Nk_B\left(\frac{\varepsilon\beta e^{\frac{\varepsilon\beta}{2}}}{1+e^{\varepsilon\beta}}\right)^2$

4 $Nk_B\left(\frac{\varepsilon\beta e^{-2\varepsilon\beta}}{1+e^{-\varepsilon\beta}}\right)^2$

104 The correct match of spin-only magnetic moment for the complexes *cis*-[Fe(phen)$_2$(NCS - *N*)$_2$] (A) and [Fe(phen)$_3$]Cl$_2$ (B) at 300 K is (phen = 1, 10-phenanthroline)

1 4.89 BM for both *A* and *B*
2 0 BM for both *A* and *B*
3 4.89 BM for *A* and 0 BM for *B*
4 0 BM for *A* and 4.89 BM for *B*

105 In spectrofluorimetric determination in solution
A. absorbance of analyte solution is kept near to 0.05
B. oxygen is eradicated from solution
C. pH of solution is controlled
D. wavelength of incident light is always above 400 nm
Correct from the above is

1 A, B and D 2 B, C and D 3 A, B and C 4 A, C and D

106 The electrolyte solution that has the smallest Debye-length at 298 K is

1 0.01 M NaCl 2 0.01 M Na_2SO_4
3 0.01M $CuCl_2$ 4 0.01 M $LaCl_3$

107 Consider the following statements :
A. The highest oxidation state of group 8 elements is more readily shown in their oxides than in fluorides.
B. Fe can exist in −2 formal oxidation state also.
C. Mn, Tc and Re easily form *M*(II) compounds.
The correct statement(s) is/are

1 A and B 2 A and C 3 B and C 4 C only

108 $(C_p - C_V)$ for a non-ideal gas differs from $(C_p - C_V)$ for a perfect gas by the expression

1 $\left(\frac{\partial p}{\partial T}\right)_V\left(\frac{\partial U}{\partial p}\right)_S$

2 $\left(\frac{\partial V}{\partial T}\right)_p\left(\frac{\partial U}{\partial V}\right)_T$

3 $-\frac{1}{T}\left(\frac{\partial V}{\partial T}\right)_p\left(\frac{\partial U}{\partial V}\right)_T$

4 $\left(\frac{\partial p}{\partial T}\right)_V\left(\frac{\partial U}{\partial p}\right)_p$

109 In *trans*-1, 2-dichloroethylene, the IR inactive mode is

1 C — Cl symmetric stretch
2 C — Cl asymmetric stretch
3 C — H asymmetric stretch
4 In phase out of plane C — Cl bend

110 The reaction that gives (*E*)-2-methylhex-3-ene as the major product is

1 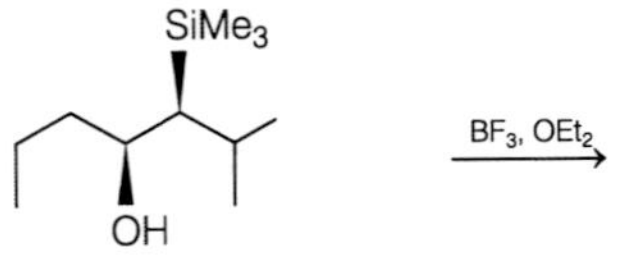

2 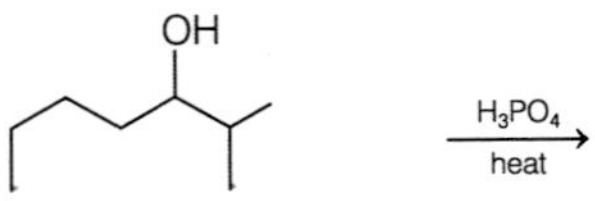

3 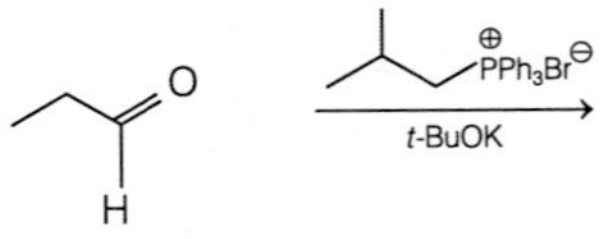

4 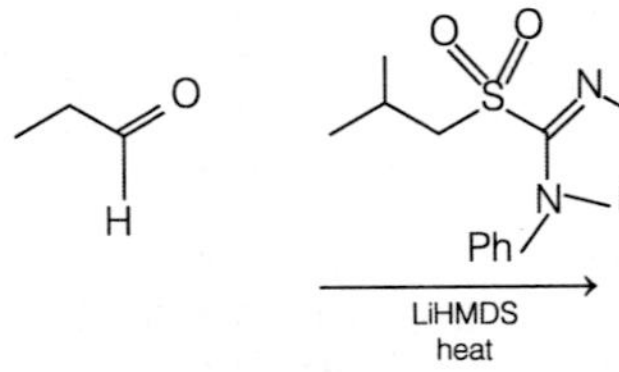

111 The correct order of metal-carbon distance is

1 $Fe(\eta^5 - Cp)_2 > Co(\eta^5 - Cp)_2 > Ni(\eta^5 - Cp)_2$
2 $Fe(\eta^5 - Cp)_2 > Ni(\eta^5 - Cp)_2 > Co(\eta^5 - Cp)_2$
3 $Ni(\eta^5 - Cp)_2 > Fe(\eta^5 - Cp)_2 > Co(\eta^5 - Cp)_2$
4 $Ni(\eta^5 - Cp)_2 > Co(\eta^5 - Cp)_2 > Fe(\eta^5 - Cp)_2$

112 The major product formed in the following reaction is

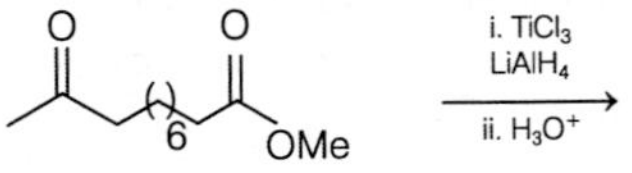

1 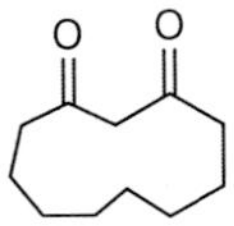

2 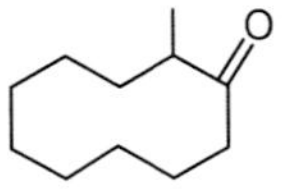

3 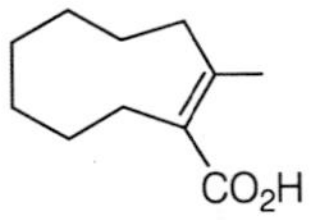

4 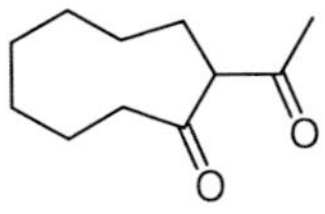

113 The major product formed in the following reaction is

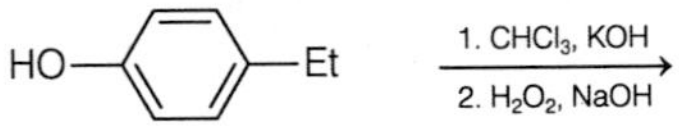

1 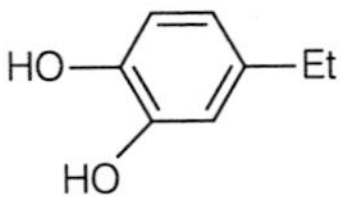

2 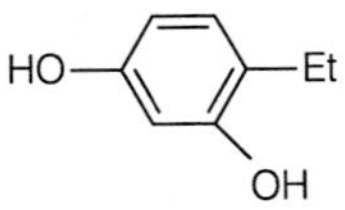

3 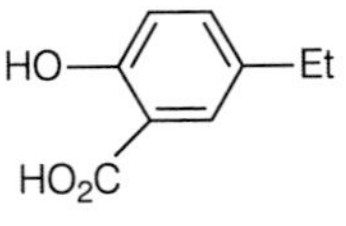

4 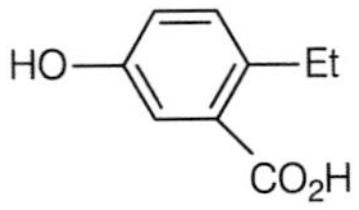

114 The order of a surface catalysed unimolecular reaction, at very low and very high pressures of the reactant, would be respectively

1 0, 0 2 1, 0 3 0, 1 4 1, 1

115 The major product formed in the following reaction is

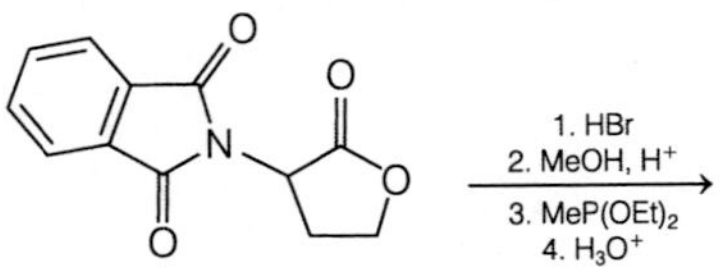

1 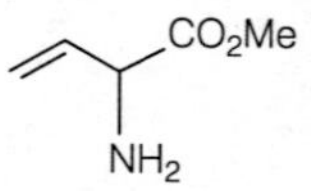

2 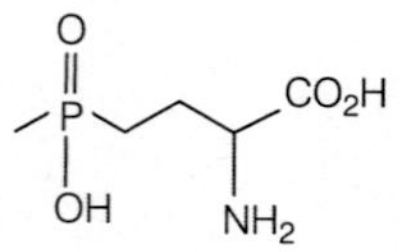

3 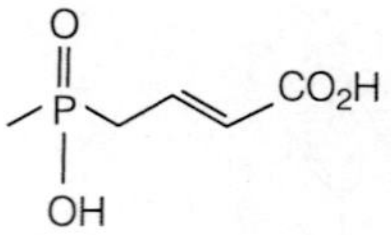

4 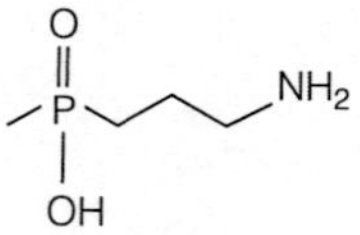

116 In the electronic spectrum of $[IrBr_6]^{2-}$, the number of charge transfer band(s) and their origin are respectively

1 two, ligand $\rightarrow$ metal ($\sigma \rightarrow t_{2g}$ and $\sigma \rightarrow a_{1g}$*)
2 one, ligand $\rightarrow$ metal $\sigma \rightarrow e_g$)
3 two, ligand $\rightarrow$ metal ($\sigma \rightarrow t_{2g}$ and $\sigma \rightarrow e_g$)
4 one, ligand $\rightarrow$ metal ($\sigma \rightarrow t_{2g}$)

117 The correct statements for dithionite and dithionate anions from the following are

A. Both have S—S bond
B. Both are dianionic
C. Oxidation state of sulphur is +3 and +5, respectively
D. Sulphur in dithionate has lone pair of electrons

1 A, B and C 2 A, B and D
3 B, C and D 4 A and B only

118 The major product formed in the following reaction is

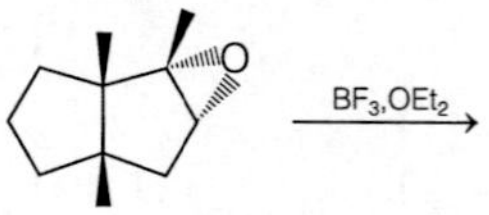

1 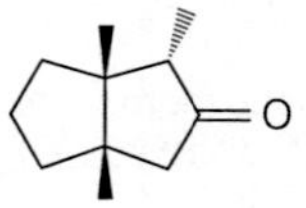

2 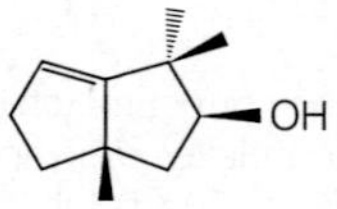

3 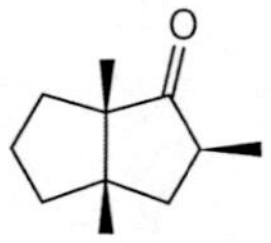

4 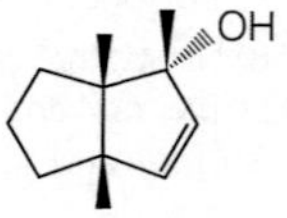

119 Quantum number corresponding to the z-component of the total electronic orbital momentum in the nitric oxide molecules is/are

1 0 2 1 3 2 4 3

120 When a hydrogen atom is exposed to a perturbation $V = E \cdot z$, the first order correction to the wave function comes only from the orbital

1 $2s$ 2 $2p_z$
3 $3p_y$ 4 $3d_{z^2}$

ANSWERS

PART B

21. 2	22. 3	23. 2	24. 3	25. 3	26. 3	27. 1	28. 1	29. 3	30. 2
31. 2	32. 2	33. 3	34. 4	35. 3	36. 1	37. 1	38. 1	39. 2	40. 1
41. 2	42. 2	43. 4	44. 2	45. 3	46. 3	47. 2	48. 3	49. 4	50. 3
51. 4	52. 3	53. 4	54. 4	55. 1	56. 4	57. 2	58. 3	59. 2	60. 2

PART C

61. 2	62. 3	63. 1	64. 4	65. 1	66. 2	67. 1	68. 2	69. 3	70. 2
71. 2	72. 2	73. 4	74. 2	75. 3	76. 3	77. 2	78. 2	79. 2	80. 3
81. 2	82. 3	83. 1	84. 1	85. 2	86. 1	87. 4	88. 2	89. 1	90. 3
91. 3	92. 1	93. 1	94. 1	95. 2	96. 3	97. 3	98. 3	99. 2	100. 1
101. 3	102. 4	103. 3	104. 3	105. 3	106. 4	107. 1	108. 2	109. 1	110. 4
111. 4	112. 2	113. 1	114. 2	115. 2	116. 3	117. 1	118. 1	119. 2	120. 2